BUTTERWORTHS

STONE'S
JUSTICES' MANUAL
2006

One Hundred and Thirty-Eighth Edition

edited by

A P CARR

District Judge (Magistrates' Courts)

and

A J TURNER

Barrister, Chambers of Adrian Turner, Eastbourne

Human Rights contributor

Keir Starmer QC

Doughty Street Chambers, visiting lecturer at King's College, London

Licensing contributor

Ian Seeley

Principal Solicitor, Ipswich Borough Council

VOLUME 2

LexisNexis®
Butterworths

Members of the LexisNexis Group worldwide

United Kingdom	LexisNexis Butterworths, a Division of Reed Elsevier (UK) Ltd, Halsbury House, 35 Chancery Lane, London, WC2A 1EL, and RSH, 1–3 Baxter's Place, Leith Walk Edinburgh EH1 3AF
United Kingdom	LexisNexis Butterworths, a Division of Reed Elsevier (UK) Ltd, RSH, 1–3 Baxter's Place, Leith Walk, EDINBURGH EH1 3AF and Halsbury House, 35 Chancery Lane, LONDON WC2A 1EL
Argentina	LexisNexis Argentina, Buenos Aires
Australia	LexisNexis Butterworths, Chatswood, New South Wales
Austria	LexisNexis Verlag ARD Orac GmbH & Co KG, Vienna
Benelux	LexisNexis Benelux, Amsterdam
Canada	LexisNexis Canada, Markham, Ontario
Chile	LexisNexis Chile Ltda, Santiago
China	LexisNexis China, Beijing and Shanghai
France	LexisNexis SA, Paris
Germany	LexisNexis Deutschland GmbH, Munster
Hong Kong	LexisNexis Hong Kong, Hong Kong
India	LexisNexis India, New Delhi
Italy	Giuffrè Editore, Milan
Japan	LexisNexis Japan, Tokyo
Malaysia	Malayan Law Journal Sdn Bhd, Kuala Lumpur
Mexico	LexisNexis Mexico, Mexico
New Zealand	LexisNexis NZ Ltd, Wellington
Poland	Wydawnictwo Prawnicze LexisNexis Sp, Warsaw
Singapore	LexisNexis Singapore, Singapore
South Africa	LexisNexis Butterworths, Durban
USA	LexisNexis, Dayton, Ohio

© Reed Elsevier (UK) Ltd 2006
Published by LexisNexis Butterworths

A CIP Catalogue record for this book is available from the British Library.

ISBN for this volume

ISBN 10: 1405712538
ISBN 13: 9781405712538

ISBN 1-4057-1253-8

9 781405 712538

ISBN for the complete set of volumes

ISBN 10: 1405711000
ISBN 13: 9781405711005

ISBN 1-4057-1100-0

9 781405 711005

Typeset by David Lewis XML Associates Limited
Printed and bound in Great Britain by William Clowes Limited, Beccles, Suffolk

Visit LexisNexis Butterworths at www.lexisnexis.co.uk

CONTENTS

(WITH REFERENCE TO PARAS)

VOLUME 1

VOLUME 2

VOLUME 3

PART VIII—OFFENCES, MATTERS OF COMPLAINT, ETC

Ready Reference

	Statutory provision		Narrative
Bail	Bail Act 1976	1–1560	1–464
Exceptions to right to bail	Bail Act 1976, Sch 1	1–1570	1–469
Prosecution appeal	Bail (Amend) Act 1993, s 1	1–3447	1–488
Remand	MCA 1980, ss 128–131	1–2211	1–464
Custody time limits	PO (CTL) Regs 1987	1–6220	
Disclosure			
Advance	CrimPR Pt 21	1–7441	1–425
Public interest immunity			1–605
Primary	CPIA 1996, s 3	1–3583	1–602
Code of Practice	CPIA 1996, s 23	1–6539	
A-G Guidelines		1–7750	
Representation order			
Criteria for grant	AJ A 1999, Sch 3 para 5	1–3983	1–884
Application for	CDS (Gen) (No 2) R 2001	1–5691	1–885
Appeal	CDS (Rep Ord App) Regs 2001	1–5681	1–889
Disqualification and Bias			1–119
Abuse of process			1–447
Information			1–386
Time limit	MCA 1980, s 127	1–2210	1–387
Statement of offence	CrimPR Pt 7 r 7.2	1–7427	1–388
Several offences			1–444

Contents

PART VI
FAMILY LAW

INTRODUCTION AND CONTENTS

6–1 PART VI of this manual deals with the constitution and jurisdiction of the family proceedings court and examines the practice and procedure of these courts when hearing applications under the Domestic Proceedings and Magistrates' Courts Act 1978, the Children Act 1989 and the Family Law Act 1996.

Our approach is first to provide a basic statement of principle or authority, followed by a commentary, in smaller type, of secondary principles, exceptions and other considerations. Finally, we set out the text of statutes and statutory instruments, including rules of court, relating to family proceedings before magistrates, arranged chronologically and annotated.

Family Proceedings Courts: constitution and jurisdiction

Family Proceedings Courts: procedure and general principles

Marriage

Proceedings under section 2 of the Domestic Proceedings and Magistrates' Courts Act 1978

Proceedings under the Children Act 1989: general principles

Proceedings on an application for an order under section 8 of the Children Act 1989

Financial provision

Care and supervision orders; child assessment and emergency protection orders

Reciprocal enforcement

Statutes on Family Law

Statutory Instruments and Practice Directions on Family Law

Adoption and Parental Orders

Scientific Tests

Children

Family Proceedings Courts

Guardianship and Custody

Registration and Enforcement

Family Proceedings Courts: constitution and jurisdiction

6–2   Family proceedings courts.   A family proceedings court is a magistrates' court which is constituted in accordance with s 67 of the Magistrates' Courts Act 1980[1] to sit for the purpose of hearing family proceedings. So far as is consistent with the due dispatch of business of magistrates' courts, family proceedings shall be arranged in such manner as may be requisite for separating the hearing of family proceedings from other business[2]. In practice, family proceedings courts sit at pre-arranged times when only family business will be listed for hearing. Most family proceedings courts sit at frequent intervals; however, when an expedited or emergency hearing is required special arrangements may need to be made by the justices' chief executive.

  The circumstances in which information may disclosed about proceedings involving children which are heard in private either with the permission of the court or without the need for such permission, are prescribed in rules of court[3].

---

1. See PART I: MAGISTRATES' COURTS, PROCEDURE, ante.
2. Magistrates' Courts Act 1980, s 69, in PART I: MAGISTRATES' COURTS, PROCEDURE, ante.
3. See the Family Proceedings Courts (Children Act 1989) Rules 1991, rr 23 and 23A, in this PART, post.

6–2A   Privacy of proceedings .   No person shall be present during the hearing and determination by the court of family proceedings except—

(a)   officers of the court;

(b)   parties to the case before the court, their solicitors and counsel, witnesses and other persons directly concerned in the case;

(c)   representatives of newspapers or news agencies; and

(d)   any other person whom the court may in its discretion permit to be present, save that permission shall not be withheld from a person who appears to the court to have adequate grounds for attendance[1].

When hearing family proceedings under the Adoption Act 1976, only those persons referred to in paragraphs (a) and (b) above are permitted to be present[2].

When hearing family proceedings, a court may, if it thinks it is necessary in the interest of the administration of justice or of public decency, direct that any persons, not being officers of the court or parties to the case, the parties' solicitors or counsel, or other persons directly concerned in the case, be excluded during the taking of any indecent evidence[3]. This power is in addition and without prejudice to any other powers of the court to hear proceedings in camera[3].

When hearing proceedings involving children, the court may, where it considers it expedient to do so, hear the proceeding in private when only the officers of the court, the parties, their legal representatives and such other persons as specified by the court may attend[4].

---

1. Magistrates' Courts Act 1980, s 69(2) in PART I: MAGISTRATES' COURTS, PROCEDURE, ante.
2. Magistrates' Courts Act 1980, s 69(3), in PART I: MAGISTRATES' COURTS, PROCEDURE, ante.
3. Magistrates' Courts Act 1980, s 69(4), (5) in PART I: MAGISTRATES' COURTS, PROCEDURE, ante.
4. Family Proceedings Courts (Children Act 1989) Rules 1991, r 16(7), in this PART, STATUTORY INSTRUMENTS AND PRACTICE DIRECTIONS ON FAMILY LAW, post.

6–2B Publication of information.   It is a contempt of court to publish "information relating to proceedings before any court sitting in private where the proceedings . . . are brought under the Children Act 1989 or the Adoption and Children Act 2002; or otherwise relate wholly or mainly to the . . . upbringing of a minor."[1] Most forms of dissemination, whether oral or written, will constitute a publication. There is not a "publication" however, where there is a communication of information by someone to a professional, each acting in furtherance of the protection of children[2]. Any contempt under this provision is not punishable by the magistrates' court and proceedings would have to be brought in the High Court. Furthermore, it is provided that nothing is to be construed as implying that any publication is punishable as contempt of court which would not be so punishable apart from s 12 of the Administration of Justice Act 1960[3] and in particular publication is not punishable as a contempt by reason of being authorised by rules of court[4]. Accordingly, as regards magistrates' courts, publication is restricted by the following statutory provisions and disclosure of documents is regulated by rules of court[5].

It is unlawful for the proprietor, editor or publisher of a newspaper or periodical to print or publish, or cause or procure to be printed or published, in it any particulars of the proceedings other than—

(a)   the names, addresses and occupations of the parties and witnesses;
(b)   the grounds of the application, and a concise statement of the charges, defences and counter-charges in support of which evidence has been given;
(c)   submissions on any point of law arising in the course of the proceedings and the decision of the court on the submissions; and
(d)   the decision of the court, and any observations made by the court in giving it[6].

Privacy is also afforded to a child who may be involved in proceedings in which any power under the Children Act 1989 may be exercised by the court with respect to that or any other child. Accordingly, no person shall publish any material which is intended, or likely, to identify any such child or an address or school as being that of a child involved in any such proceedings[7]. Contravention of these provisions is punishable on summary conviction[8]. However such publication is only prohibited in relation to publication of information to the public or any section of the public[9]. This means that passing on information identifying, or likely to identify, a child (his school or his address) as being involved in court proceedings to an individual or a number of individuals will not generally be a criminal offence. There is no requirement for leave of the court to disclose documents to a court approved McKenzie friend provided that an appropriate assurance is given by the litigant in person and the McKenzie friend about the use of court documents nor to a public authority with a proper interest in the subject matter of the disclosure, such as the local government ombudsman or the police[10].

Whilst article 6(1) of the European Convention on Human Rights provides a general rule that requires civil proceedings to be held in public, a state may designate a class of proceedings as an exception to the general rule. Exclusion of press and public can be justified in order to protect the privacy of a child and parties and to avoid prejudicing the interests of justice[11]. Furthermore the publishing of such judgments was not required to be made available to the public[11].

---

1. Administration of Justice Act 1960, s 12(1)(a), in this PART I: MAGISTRATES' COURTS, PROCEDURE, ante.
2. See the summary of the effect of s 12 of the Administration of Justice Act 1960, by Munby J in *Re B (A Child) (Disclosure)* [2004] EWHC 411 (Fam), [2004] 2 FLR 142.
3. For the difficulties in connexion with the concept of "publication" and defining the scope of contempt, see *Re G (Litigants in Person)* [2003] EWCA Civ 1055, [2003] 2 FLR 963, and *Re B (A Child) (Disclosure)* [2004] EWHC 411 (Fam), [2004] FLR 142, (decided before amendments introduced by the Children Act 2002, s 62).
4. Administration of Justice Act 1960, s 12(4), in this PART I: MAGISTRATES' COURTS, PROCEDURE, ante.
5. See the Family Proceedings Court (Matrimonial Proceedings Rules 1991, r 14 and the Family Proceedings Rules 1991, rr 23 and 23A in this PART, STATUTORY INSTRUMENTS AND PRACTICE DIRECTIONS ON FAMILY LAW, post and para **6–29 Disclosure**, post.
6. Magistrates' Courts Act 1980, s 71(1) in PART I: MAGISTRATES' COURTS, PROCEDURE, ante. As to the confidentiality generally of family proceedings, when publication of information relating to a court sitting in private amounts to a contempt of court under s 12 of the Administration of Justice Act 1960 and the appropriateness of the use of

s 11 of the Contempt of Court Act 1981 to prevent disclosure of any or all the information given in a private hearing, see *Clibbery v Allan* [2002] EWCA 45, [2002] Fam 261, [2002] 1 All ER 865, [2002] 2 WLR 1511, [2002] 1 FCR 385.

7. Children Act 1989, s 97, this PART, post. However, s 97 does not impose an absolute prohibition on publicity and the court can be asked to exercise its discretion to allow the identity of the child to be published; if the court is not so asked or refuses to give its permission s 97(2) bites and no material that is intended or is likely to identity the child can be published: *P v BW (children cases: hearings in public)* [2003] EWHC 1541 (Fam), [2003] 3 FCR 523, [2004] 1 FLR 171.

8. For penalty, see Magistrates' Courts Act 1980, s 71(3), and as to consent of the Attorney General before a prosecution is begun, see Magistrates' Courts Act 1980, s 71(4), in PART I: MAGISTRATES' COURTS, PROCEDURE, ante.

9. Children Act 1989, s 97(2) in this PART: STATUTES ON FAMILY LAW, post.

10. *Re O (children) (representation: McKenzie friend)* [2005] EWCA Civ 759, [2005] 2 FCR 563.

11. *B v United Kingdom* [2001] 2 FCR 221, [2001] 2 FLR 261, ECtHR. See also *P v BW (children cases: hearings in public)*, supra.

6–3 Family proceedings. Family proceedings for the purposes of the Magistrates' Courts Act 1980 means proceedings under any of the following enactments[1]—

(a) Maintenance Orders (Facilities for Enforcement) Act 1920[2];
(b) National Assistance Act 1948, s 43[3];
(c) Marriage Act 1949, s 3[2];
(d) Matrimonial Causes Act 1973, s 35[2];
(e) Part I of the Maintenance Orders (Reciprocal Enforcement) Act 1972[2];
(f) Adoption and Children Act 2002[2];
(g) Supplementary Benefits Act 1976, s 18[3];
(h) Part I of the Domestic Proceedings and Magistrates' Courts Act 1978[2];
(i) Magistrates' Courts Act 1980, s 60[4];
(j) Part I of the Civil Jurisdiction and Judgments Act 1982, so far as that Part relates to the recognition or enforcement of maintenance orders[2];
(k) Children Act 1989[2];
(l) Social Security Administration Act 1992, s 106[3];
(m) Child Support Act 1991, s 20 (so far as it provides, by virtue of an order under s 45, for appeals to be made to a court) or s 27[2];
(n) Part IV of the Family Law Act 1996[2];
(o) sections 11 and 12 of the Crime and Disorder Act 1998[4].

Proceedings for the variation of any provision for the making of periodical payments contained in an order made, confirmed or registered, and proceedings for the enforcement of a magistrates' court maintenance order may be treated as family proceedings[1].

The meaning of "family proceedings" set out above must be distinguished from a separate definition of the expression which is contained in the Children Act 1989[5]. For the purposes of the 1989 Act "family proceedings" means any proceedings—

(a) under the inherent jurisdiction of the High Court in relation to children; and
(b) under the enactments mentioned in section 8(4) of the Act[5]; and
(c) in relation to magistrates' courts, any proceedings under the 1989 Act[6].

1. Magistrates' Courts Act 1980, s 65, in PART I: MAGISTRATES' COURTS, PROCEDURE, ante.
2. See this PART, post.
3. See PART VIII, title SOCIAL SECURITY, post.
4. See PART I: MAGISTRATES' COURTS, PROCEDURE, ante.
5. Children Act 1989, s 8(3), (4), this PART, post.
6. Children Act 1989, s 92(2), this PART, post. See also *R (J) v Oxfordshire County Council* [1992] 3 All ER 660 (proceedings for a secure accommodation order "family proceedings" for purposes of the Children Act 1989).

6–4 Family panels[1]. Outside Greater London, there is a family panel of magistrates for each petty sessions area save where there has been a direction for combination of two or more panels in the same commission area by the magistrates' courts committee or by the Lord Chancellor[2]. Appointments to family panels are made by the justices for each petty sessions area. Justices must be eligible[3] for appointment and must undertake to comply with the requirements of the Lord Chancellor to receive instruction in the work of the family proceedings court. The Lord Chancellor may remove from a family panel any justice who, in his opinion, is unsuitable to serve in a family proceedings court[4].

In Greater London there is one family panel which consists of justices nominated for the purpose by the Lord Chancellor, and in such number as he thinks fit[5].

A District Judge (Magistrates' Courts) who has been nominated by the Lord Chancellor to hear family proceedings shall be a member of the panel for the petty sessions area or areas in which he exercises jurisdiction by virtue of his appointment[6]. A District Judge (Magistrates' Courts) may be similarly nominated to hear family proceedings[7] in Greater London.

1. See note to title of para **1–20**, in PART I: MAGISTRATES' COURTS, PROCEDURE, ante. The Courts Act 2003 prospectively abolishes family panels.
2. Magistrates' Courts Act 1980, ss 67 and 68, in PART I: MAGISTRATES' COURTS, PROCEDURE, ante.
3. The criteria for eligibility are prescribed by the Family Proceedings Courts (Constitution) Rules 1991, r 5, and the Family Proceedings Courts (Constitution) (Greater London) Rules 2003, r 5, this PART, post.
4. Family Proceedings Courts (Constitution) Rules 1991, r 5, this PART, post.
5. Family Proceedings Courts (Constitution) (Greater London) Rules 2003, r 4 this PART, post.

6. Magistrates' Courts Act 1980, s 67(7), in PART I: MAGISTRATES' COURTS, PROCEDURE, ante, and the Family Proceedings Courts (Constitution) Rules 1991, r 5(3), this PART, post.
7. Family Proceedings Courts (Constitution) (Greater London) Rules 2003, r 4, this PART, post.

6–5   Composition of court. A family proceedings court shall be composed of not less than two and not more than three justices, including so far as practicable a man and woman[1]. Each sitting of a family proceedings court shall take place under the chairmanship of the chairman of the panel or a deputy chairman elected (or, in Greater London, nominated) in accordance with the Rules[2]. If the chairman or a deputy chairman is not available because of circumstances unforeseen when the justices to sit were chosen or because the chairman or deputy chairman cannot properly sit, the members of the court shall choose one of their number to preside[3].

For limited purposes which are prescribed by Rules a family proceedings court may be constituted by a single justice[4]. A justice who is a member of a family panel may be transferred temporarily to sit as a member of another family panel within the same commission area to hear a particular case, provided the justices' chief executive to the first mentioned panel consents in writing to the transfer. The transfer of a justice to another panel outside the commission area in which he serves requires the approval of the Lord Chancellor[5].

Where a District Judge (Magistrates' Courts) is a member of the family panel he may sit as a member of the family proceedings court with one or two lay justices who are also members of the panel, but he may also sit alone[6].

In London, a family proceedings court may be composed of a District Judge (Magistrates' Courts) as chairman and one or two lay justices who are members of the panel[7]. If it is not practicable for a court to be so composed, a District Judge (Magistrates' Courts) may sit alone[8].

Generally, once justices have begun to hear an application or complaint the hearing of which is adjourned, the same justices, or at least two of them, must resume the hearing. However, where the hearing of an application under s 1 of the Domestic Proceedings and Magistrates' Courts Act 1978 is adjourned after the court has decided that it is satisfied of any ground mentioned in that section, the court which resumes the hearing of that application may include justices who were not sitting when the hearing began if—

    (*a*)   the parties to the proceedings agree; and
    (*b*)   at least one of the justices composing the court which resumes the hearing was sitting when the hearing of the application began.

Where by virtue of this provision a court is composed of justices who were not sitting when the hearing began, the court which resumes the hearing shall make inquiry into the facts and circumstances of the case so that the justices who were not sitting at the earlier hearing may be fully acquainted with those facts and circumstances[9]. In children's cases the practice is to be commended of the same bench hearing the case throughout[10], indeed in the High Court steps are taken to ensure the same judge will manage the case up to and including the final hearing where practicable[11].

---

1. Magistrates' Courts Act 1980, s 66(1), in PART I: MAGISTRATES' COURTS, PROCEDURE, ante.
2. Family Proceedings Courts (Constitution) Rules 1991, r 10; Family Proceedings Courts (Constitution) (Constitution) (Greater London) Rules 2003, r 8, (and r 8(4) for sitting by a non-chairman under supervision), this PART, post.
3. Family Proceedings Courts (Constitution) Rules 1991, r 10(4), this PART, post.
4. Family Proceedings Courts (Children Act 1989) Rules 1991, r 2(5), this PART, post.
5. Family Proceedings Courts (Constitution) Rules 1991, r 7, this PART, post.
6. Family Proceedings Courts (Constitution) Rules 1991, r 10(3), this PART, post; Magistrates' Courts Act 1980, s 66(7) in PART I: MAGISTRATES' COURTS, PROCEDURE, ante.
7. Magistrates' Courts Act 1980, s 66(2)(*a*) in PART I: MAGISTRATES' COURTS, PROCEDURE, ante; Family Proceedings Courts (Constitution) (Greater London) Rules 2003, r 8, this PART, post.
8. Magistrates' Courts Act 1980, s 66(2), in PART I: MAGISTRATES' COURTS, PROCEDURE, ante.
9. Domestic Proceedings and Magistrates' Courts Act 1978, s 31, this PART, post.
10. *F v R (Contact: Justices' Reasons)* [1995] 1 FLR 227.
11. See *Practice Direction (family division: judicial continuity)* [2002] 3 All ER 603, [2002] 1 WLR 2183, [2002] 2 FCR 667.

6–6   Jurisdiction. The jurisdiction of a family proceedings court to hear an application or complaint is governed by the enactment under which it is made, or, in the case of a complaint, where no express provision is made, in accordance with the Magistrates' Courts Act 1980[1]. If the latter applies, a family proceedings court shall have jurisdiction if the complaint relates to anything done within the commission area for which the court is appointed or anything left undone that ought to have been done there or elsewhere, or relates to any other matter arising within the area[1].

Jurisdiction in relation to an application under Part I of the Domestic Proceedings and Magistrates' Courts Act 1978, subject to certain qualifications, is determined by the place of residence of the applicant or respondent. Accordingly, a family proceedings court shall have jurisdiction to hear an application under the Act if at the date of the making of the application either the applicant or the respondent ordinarily resides within the commission area for which the court is appointed[2].

Any family proceedings court has jurisdiction to hear an application under Part IV of the Family Law Act 1996 (family homes and domestic violence) subject to the qualification that it is not competent to entertain any application, or make any order, involving any disputed question as to a party's entitlement to occupy any property by virtue of a beneficial estate or interest or contract or by virtue of any enactment giving him the right to remain in occupation unless it is unnecessary to determine the question in order to deal with the application or make the order[3].

With respect to proceedings under the Children Act 1989, application may be made to any family proceedings court, and jurisdiction is not governed by reference to the residence of the applicant or child, or restricted to a particular commission area. The jurisdiction of a family proceedings court in such a case will be terminated on transfer to another family proceedings court or to the county court. Where there are indications that a place to which a person has moved is intended as his home for an indefinite period, he is ordinarily resident there[4]. The jurisdiction conferred on a court by Part I of the Domestic Proceedings and Magistrates' Courts Act 1978 is exercisable notwithstanding that any party to the proceedings is not domiciled in England[5].

Jurisdiction under the 1978 Act may be exercised in inner London and the City of London subject to specific provisions contained in the Magistrates' Courts Act 1980[6] and any determination of the committee of magistrates thereunder[7].

A family proceedings court does not have jurisdiction to make an order under s 8 of the Children Act 1989, in connection with matrimonial proceedings or on an application under the Children Act 1989, with respect to a child unless either of the conditions referred to in s 2 of the Family Law Act 1986 is satisfied[8].

---

1. Magistrates' Courts Act 1980, s 52, in PART I: MAGISTRATES' COURTS, PROCEDURE, ante.
2. Domestic Proceedings and Magistrates' Courts Act 1978, s 30, this PART, post.
3. Family Law Act 1996, ss 57 and 59, this PART, post.
4. *Macrae v Macrae* [1949] P 397, [1949] 2 All ER 34, 113 JP 342; applied in *Hopkins v Hopkins* [1951] P 116, [1950] 2 All ER 1035; *Stransky v Stransky* [1954] P 428, [1954] 2 All ER 536; *Lewis v Lewis* [1956] 1 All ER 375.
5. Domestic Proceedings and Magistrates' Courts Act 1978, s 30(5), this PART, post.
6. See Magistrates' Courts Act 1980, s 70, in PART I: MAGISTRATES' COURTS, PROCEDURE, ante.
7. See Magistrates' Courts Act 1980, s 70; and see Domestic Proceedings and Magistrates' Courts Act 1978, s 30(1), this PART, post.
8. See this PART, post.

Family Proceedings Courts: procedure and general principles

6–11   European Convention on Human Rights.   Most family proceedings in the magistrates' court will engage Article 6(1) and Article 8 of the European Convention on Human Rights. Article 6(1) provides that "In the determination of his civil rights and obligations ... everyone is entitled to a fair and public hearing within a reasonable time by an independent and impartial tribunal established by law". Article 8(1) provides that "Everyone has the right to respect for his private and family life, his home and his correspondence". Article 8(2) prohibits public authorities from interfering with this right except where:

1.   the grounds for interference are 'in accordance with law;
2.   the grounds for interference are legitimate; and
3.   the interference is both necessary and proportionate.

Other Convention rights may also be engaged in family proceedings in the magistrates' court.

Under the Human Rights Act 1998, so far as it is possible to do so, all legislation (primary and subordinate, and whenever enacted) must be read and given effect in a way which is compatible with Convention rights, including Article 6(1) and Article 8[1]. In addition, it is unlawful for a public authority, including any court or tribunal, to act in a way which is incompatible with Convention rights[2].

Applications for relief under the Human Rights Act 1998. Where proceedings have come to an end a freestanding application may be made for relief under the Human Rights Act 1998 but where proceedings are still on foot any complaint should normally be dealt with within the existing proceedings and should not be dealt with separately in proceedings before the Family Division[3]. Any claim in public law proceedings that involves a breach of a party's rights under arts 6 or 8 can and should be dealt with by the court which is hearing the care proceedings and is neither necessary nor desirable to transfer proceedings to a superior level of court merely because a breach of Convention rights is alleged[4].

Hearing in private. The ECommHR has declared admissible an application alleging that a child case heard in private and judgement not publicly pronounced, is in breach of art 6(1) and that an order prohibiting identification of child is contrary to the father's rights under art 10[5].

Rights of unmarried father. The refusal of an application under the Hague Convention on Civil Aspects of International Child Abduction as set out in Sch 1 to the Child Abduction and Custody Act 1985 by an unmarried father on the basis that the father did not have parental responsibility when the child was taken abroad by the mother, did not breach articles 8 and 14. The different responsibilities borne by fathers who have a child in their care and those who do not provide an objective and reasonable justification for the difference in treatment between married and unmarried fathers with regard to the automatic acquisition of parental rights under the Children Act 1989[6].

Paramountcy of child's interests. It has been held that '[t]here is nothing in the European Human Rights Convention which requires the Courts of this country to act otherwise than in accordance with the interests of the child'[7], so that a local authority was refused leave to withdraw care proceedings in respect of a child in whose case an emergency protection order had been made at birth where the guardian ad litem had advanced solid and cogent reasons and there was a pressing social need for state intervention to protect a child from a real risk of harm in the future[8]. In judicial decisions where the rights under art 8 of parents and those of a child are at stake, the European Court of Human Rights has affirmed that the child's right must be of paramount consideration and if any balancing exercise needs to be done the interests of the child must prevail[9].

---

1. Human Rights Act 1998, s 3(1) in PART VIII, title HUMAN RIGHTS, post.
2. Human Rights Act 1998, s 6(1) in PART VIII, title HUMAN RIGHTS, post.
3. *Re L (care proceedings: human rights claims)* [2003] EWHC 665 (Fam), [2004] 1 FCR 289, [2003] 2 FLR 160 (attempt

to compel the local authority to change the care plan); *affd Re V (a child) (care proceedings: human rights claims)* [2004] EWCA Civ 54, [2004] 1 All ER 997, [2004] 1 WLR 1433, [2004] 1 FCR 338.
    4. *Re V (a child) (care proceedings: human rights claims)* [2004] EWCA Civ 54, [2004] 1 All ER 997, [2004] 1 WLR 1433, [2004] 1 FCR 338.
    5. *B v United Kingdom* [2000] 2 FCR 97, ECommHR.
    6. *B v United Kingdom* [2000] 1 FCR 289, [2000] 1 FLR 1, ECtHR.
    7. *Dawson v Wearmouth* [1999] 2 AC 308.
    8. *Re N (leave to withdraw care proceedings)* [2000] 1 FCR 258, [2000] 1 FLR 134, FD.
    9. *Elsholz v Germany* (2002) 34 EHRR 58, [2000] 2 FLR 486, ECtHR, *TP and KM v United Kingdom* (2002) 34 EHRR 2, [2001] 2 FLR 549, ECtHR, *Yousef v Netherlands* (2002) 36 EHRR 345, [2003] 1 FLR 210, ECtHR.

6–12   Commencement of proceedings.   Proceedings for an order in the family proceedings court are generally commenced by making application in accordance with the appropriate Rules, and not by making a complaint. The application procedure must be adopted when making an application under the Domestic Proceedings and Magistrates' Courts Act 1978, Part IV of the Family Law Act 1996, the Children Act 1989, the Maintenance Orders (Facilities for Enforcement) Act 1920 and the Maintenance Orders (Reciprocal Enforcement) Act 1972, and may be applied to an application to vary an order made under the Guardianship of Minors Acts 1971 and 1973[1].

Proceedings by way of complaint apply to the variation of a maintenance order registered in a magistrates' court under Part I of the Maintenance Orders Act 1958[2], to an application for an order against a liable relative[3], to an application for consent to marriage[4], and on the enforcement of a magistrates' court maintenance order[5]. An application to vary or revoke an order made under earlier repealed legislation, eg the Affiliation Proceedings Act 1957, will continue to attract the complaint procedure.

    1. See s 15 of the Children Act 1989, post, by virtue of which the Guardianship of Minors Acts 1971 and 1973 have been re-enacted in Sch 1 to the Children Act 1989.
    2. See this PART, post.
    3. See the National Assistance Act 1948, s 43, and the Social Security Administration Act 1992, s 106, in PART VIII: title SOCIAL SECURITY, post.
    4. See the Magistrates' Courts (Guardianship of Minors) Rules 1974, r 5, this PART, post.
    5. See the Magistrates' Courts Act 1980, s 93, PART I: MAGISTRATES' COURTS, PROCEDURE, ante.

6–13   Filing the application.   To commence proceedings where the application procedure must be followed, the applicant must file with the justices' chief executive the application in the prescribed form, or where there is no such form, in writing, together with sufficient copies for one to be served on each respondent[1]. On receipt of the documents the justices' clerk shall fix the date, time and place for a hearing or a directions appointment, allowing the applicant sufficient time to comply with the requirements for service, and endorse the date, time and place so fixed upon the copies of the application filed by the applicant. The justices' chief executive shall then return copies of the application to the applicant forthwith. The applicant must serve a copy of the application, endorsed by the justices' chief executive, on the respondent(s) allowing the period of time fixed by the relevant Rules prior to the date fixed for the hearing or a directions appointment. Written notice of the proceedings must also be given by the applicant to such persons who may be specified in the Rules[2].

    1. See the Family Proceedings Courts (Children Act 1989) Rules 1991, r 4, post; the Family Proceedings Courts (Matrimonial Proceedings etc) Rules 1991, rr 3 and 3A, post. The procedure described above is somewhat modified in relation to reciprocal enforcement of maintenance orders and claims for maintenance: see for example the Maintenance Orders (Facilities for Enforcement) Rules 1922, this PART, post, or the Magistrates' Courts (Reciprocal Enforcement of Maintenance Orders) Rules 1974, rr 6–4C, this PART, post.
    2. See the Family Proceedings Courts (Children Act 1989) Rules 1991, r 4(3), this PART, post.

6–14   Making a complaint[1].   Where a complaint is required, this must be made to a justice of the peace acting for the petty sessions area upon which a magistrates' court acting for that area has power to make the order sought[2]. Alternatively, complaint may be made to the justices' clerk, or duly authorised assistant, who has the powers of a single justice for this purpose[3]. A complaint may be made orally or in writing[4]. The justice or justices' clerk to whom a complaint is made must apply his mind to the complaint and go through the judicial exercise of deciding whether or not a summons should be issued[5].

Save where the complainant prefers to prepare both the complaint and summons, the justices' clerk will normally draw up a summons based on the complaint. In family proceedings, invariably, the complainant will be expected to take responsibility for service of the summons where service by post does not prove successful.

    1. See Note to title of para **1–20**, in PART 1 MAGISTRATES' COURTS, PROCEDURE, ante. The Courts Act 2003 prospectively empowers magistrates' courts to hear any complaint regardless of where the subject matter arose.
    2. Magistrates' Courts Act 1980, s 51, in PART I: MAGISTRATES' COURTS, PROCEDURE, ante.
    3. Justices' Clerks Rules 1999, Schedule, in PART I: MAGISTRATES' COURTS, PROCEDURE, ante.
    4. Magistrates' Courts Rules 1981, r 4(2), in PART I: MAGISTRATES' COURTS, PROCEDURE, ante.
    5. See *R v Brentford Justices, ex p Catlin* [1975] QB 455, [1975] 2 All ER 201; *R v Manchester Stipendiary Magistrate, ex p Hill* [1983] 1 AC 328, [1982] 2 All ER 963, HL.

6–15   Applications for leave to commence proceedings.   Where the leave of the court is required to bring any relevant proceedings under the Children Act 1989[1], the person seeking leave shall file a written request for leave setting out the reasons for the application, and a draft of the application for the making of which leave is sought[2]. On considering the request, the court shall grant the request or direct that a date be fixed for a hearing of the request. The justices' chief executive shall then inform the person of the grant or fix such date and give such notice as the court directs to the person making the request and to such other persons as the court requires to be notified of the date so fixed[3].

The request for leave must be considered judicially, and, if for leave to make an application under s 8 of the Children Act 1989, must be considered having regard to s 10(9) of the Act. Normally, save in cases of urgency, or where there are other circumstances which make it right to grant leave without giving the other parties an opportunity to adduce evidence or make representations, the court will decline the request for leave and direct an *inter partes* hearing of the request[4].

---

1. As to "relevant proceedings", see the Family Proceedings Courts (Children Act 1989) Rules 1991, r 1, and the Children Act 1989, s 93, this PART, post.
2. Family Proceedings Courts (Children Act 1989) Rules 1991, r 3(1), this PART, post.
3. Family Proceedings Courts (Children Act 1989) Rules 1991, r 3(2), this PART, post.
4. *Re M (prohibited steps order: application for leave)* [1993] 1 FCR 78, [1993] 1 FLR 275.

6–16   Ex parte applications[1].   An application for any of the following orders under the Children Act 1989 may, with leave of the justices' clerk, be made *ex parte*—

   (*a*) a s 8 order;
   (*b*) an emergency protection order[2];
   (*c*) a warrant under s 48(9) of the Act;
   (*d*) a recovery order, or
   (*e*) a warrant under s 102(1) of the Act.

On making such an application, the applicant shall file with the justices' chief executive or the court the application in respect of each child, in the appropriate form, unless directed otherwise by the justices' chief executive. In the case of an application for a prohibited steps order or a specific issue order under s 8 of the Act, or an emergency protection order, or for an order under s 75(1) of the Act where the application is *ex parte*, the applicant shall serve a copy of the application on each respondent within 48 hours after the making of the order[3].

Where the court refuses to make an order on an *ex parte* application, it may direct that the application be made *inter partes*[4].

An application for an occupation order or a non-molestation order under Part IV of the Family Law Act 1996 may, with leave of the justices' chief executive or of the court, be made ex parte, in which case—

   (*a*) the applicant must file with the justices' chief executive or the court the application at the time when the application is made or as directed by the justices' chief executive; and
   (*b*) the evidence in support of the application must state the reasons why the application is made *ex parte*[5].

Ex parte applications in children's cases should rarely be made, and should rarely be granted, except in the most compelling of circumstances. Where the circumstances justify the making of an order *ex parte*, the order should provide for an early return date before the court, not a date two months ahead[6]. It is possible that there may be a breach of the right to a fair trial under Art 6(1) of the European Convention for the Protection of Human Rights if no opportunity is provided to challenge an *ex parte* order[7].

On an application for an order for the cancellation of the registration of a child minder under s 75(1) of the Act, the gravity of the application requires that the party affected is given, in accordance with general principles and fairness, a right to an *inter partes* hearing and an opportunity to challenge its correctness[8].

---

1. Ex parte applications may raise issues under art 6(1) (fair trial) and art 8 (right to respect for private and family life) of the European Convention on Human Rights, particularly in proceedings involving children.
2. For detailed guidance in respect of applications for EPOs see para 4–2153, post.
3. Family Proceedings Courts (Children Act 1989) Rules 1991, r 4(4), this PART, post.
4. Family Proceedings Courts (Children Act 1989) Rules 1991, r 4(5), this PART, post.
5. Family Proceedings Courts (Matrimonial Proceedings etc) Rules 1991, r 3A(4), this PART, post.
6. *M v C (children orders: reasons)* [1993] 1 FCR 264.
7. *Re J (abduction: wrongful removal)* [2000] 1 FCR 160, [2000] 1 FLR 78, CA.
8. *R v St Albans Magistrates' Court, ex p Read* [1994] 1 FCR 50.

6–17   Service.   Service of a document, including an application, with respect to proceedings under the Domestic Proceedings and Magistrates' Courts Act 1978 or the Children Act 1989 shall be effected in accordance with the Rules[1]. If the person to be served is not known by the person serving to be acting by solicitor, service may be effected by delivering the document to him personally, or by delivering at, or by sending it by first-class post to, his residence or his last known residence. If the person to be served is known by the person serving to be acting by solicitor, service may be effected by delivering the document at, or by sending it by first-class post to, the solicitor's address for service. Where the solicitor's address for service includes a numbered box at a document exchange, service may be effected by leaving the document at that document exchange or at a document exchange which transmits documents on every business day to that document exchange. Service may also be effected by sending a legible copy of the document by facsimile transmission to the solicitor's office[2].

Service of an application on notice for an occupation order or a non-molestation order under Part IV of the Family Law Act 1996 (together with any statement supporting it and notice of proceedings) must be effected by the applicant on the respondent personally not less than 2 business days prior to the date on which the application will be heard[3]. The period of 2 days may be abridged by the court or the justices' clerk[4]. Where the applicant is acting in person, service of the application, may with the leave of the justices' clerk, be effected in accordance with the procedure described above for an application under the 1978 Act[5].

Service of a document in connection with proceedings under the 1978 Act and the 1989 Act shall, unless the contrary is proved, be deemed to have been served (*a*) in the case of service by first-class post[6], on the second business day after posting, and (*b*) in the case of service on a solicitor at a document exchange on the second business day after the day on which it is left at the document exchange[7]. In all proceedings the applicant must file with the justices' chief executive at or before the first directions appointment or hearing date, whichever occurs first, a statement that service of a copy of the application has been effected on each respondent and the statement shall indicate the manner, date, time and place of service, or where service was effected by post, the date, time and place of posting[8]. In any proceedings under the 1978 Act, the justices' clerk or the court may direct that a requirement in the Rules as to service shall not apply or shall be effected in such manner as the justices' clerk or the court directs[9].

Where proceedings are commenced by complaint, the summons must be served on the respondent in accordance with the Magistrates' Courts Rules 1981, and service must be proved in the manner prescribed by the Rules[10].

In proceedings under the Children Act 1989, where a child who is a party to any relevant proceedings is required by the rules to serve a document, service shall be effected by the solicitor acting for the child, or where there is no such solicitor, by the children's guardian, or where there is neither a solicitor nor a children's guardian, by the justices' chief executive[11]. Service of any document on a child, subject to any direction of the justices' chief executive or the court, shall be effected by service on the solicitor acting for the child; where there is no such solicitor, the guardian ad litem, or where there is neither such a solicitor nor a children's guardian, with leave of the justices' chief executive or the court, on the child[12].

Where an application has been sent to a respondent in accordance with the Rules and, after an order has been made on the application, it appears to the court that the application did not come to the knowledge of the respondent in due time, the court may of its own motion set aside the order and may give such directions as it thinks fit for the rehearing of the application[13].

---

1. Family Proceedings Courts (Children Act 1989) Rules 1991, r 8; Family Proceedings Courts (Matrimonial Proceedings etc) Rules 1991, r 4, this PART, post.
2. Family Proceedings Courts (Children Act 1989) Rules 1991, r 8(1)(*b*); Family Proceedings Courts (Matrimonial Proceedings etc) Rules 1991, r 4(1)(*b*).
3. Family Proceedings Courts (Matrimonial Proceedings etc) Rules 1991, r 3A(5), this PART, post.
4. Family Proceedings Courts (Matrimonial Proceedings etc) Rules 1991 r 3A(6), this PART, post.
5. Family Proceedings Courts (Matrimonial Proceedings etc) Rules 1991, r 3A(7), this PART, post.
6. "First-class post" means first-class post which has been pre-paid or in respect of which pre-payment is not required (Family Proceedings Courts (Children Act 1989) Rules 1991, r 8(2); Family Proceedings Courts (Matrimonial Proceedings etc) Rules 1991, r 4(2)).
7. Family Proceedings Courts (Children Act 1989) Rules 1991, r 8(6) and Family Proceedings Courts (Matrimonial Proceedings etc) Rules 1991, r 4(3), this PART, post.
8. Family Proceedings Courts (Children Act 1989) Rules 1991, r 8(7); Family Proceedings Courts (Matrimonial Proceedings etc) Rules 1991, r 4(4).
9. Family Proceedings Courts (Children Act 1989) Rules 1991, r 8(8); Family Proceedings Courts (Matrimonial Proceedings etc) Rules 1991, r 4(5).
10. Magistrates' Courts Act 1981, r 99, in PART I: MAGISTRATES' COURTS, PROCEDURE, ante.
11. Family Proceedings Courts (Children Act 1989) Rules 1991, r 8(3), this PART, post.
12. Family Proceedings Courts (Children Act 1989) Rules 1991, r 8(4), this PART, post.
13. Family Proceedings Courts (Children Act 1989) Rules 1991, r 33B; Family Proceedings Courts (Matrimonial Proceedings etc) Rules 1991, r 24, this PART, post.

6–18 Answer to application. Within 14 days of the service of an application for an order under the Domestic Proceedings and Magistrates' Courts Act 1978 or an order under s 8 of or Sch 1 to the Children Act 1989, each respondent shall file and serve on the parties an answer to the application in the prescribed form[1].

---

1. Family Proceedings Courts (Children Act 1989) Rules 1991, r 9; Family Proceedings Courts (Matrimonial Proceedings etc) Rules 1991, r 5, this PART, post.

6–19 Appointment of children's guardian. As soon as practicable after the commencement of specified proceedings[1] under the Children Act 1989 or the transfer of such proceedings to the court, the justices' clerk or the court shall appoint a children's guardian[2] unless—

(*a*) such an appointment has already been made by the court which made the transfer and is subsisting, or

(*b*) the justices' clerk or the court considers that such an appointment is not necessary to safeguard the interests of the child[3].

At any stage in specified proceedings the justices' clerk or the court may appoint a children's guardian even though no application is made for such an appointment[4]. It is open to a party at any stage to apply to the justices' clerk or the court for such an appointment to be made[5]. The justices' clerk or the court must grant such an application unless it is considered that such an appointment is not necessary to safeguard the interests of the child, in which case reasons shall be given, and a note of such reasons shall be taken by the justices' clerk[6]. The Justices' Chief Executive or the Court may, in specified proceedings, appoint more than one children's guardian in respect of the same child[7].

Upon appointment of a children's guardian the justices' chief executive must, as soon as practicable, notify him of the appointment and serve on him copies of the application and documentary evidence filed with the court[8]. When appointing a children's guardian the justices' clerk or the court must consider the appointment of anyone who has previously acted as children's guardian of the same child[9].

The appointment of a children's guardian continues for such time as is specified in the appointment or until terminated by the court[10]. When terminating an appointment, the court must give reasons in writing for so doing, a note of which shall be taken by the justices' clerk[11].

Where an order is made under s 37(1) of the Children Act 1989 directing a local authority to undertake an investigation of a child's circumstances and the court has made or is considering whether to make an interim care order, the proceedings become "specified proceedings" by virtue of s 41(6)(b) of the Act and a children's guardian may be appointed under s 41(1). However, if, as a result of their investigation, the local authority decides not to apply for a care or supervision order and so informs the court, the proceedings cease to be "specified proceedings" and any appointment of a children's guardian under s 41(6)(b) will cease to be an appointment under s 41(1) and should be terminated by an order of the court[12]. The role of a guardian generally ceases when the specified proceedings are at an end. However a children's guardian was permitted to act for a child in proceedings subsequently brought by the police for disclosure of documents in care proceedings even though the care proceedings had been concluded[13].

The children's guardian is under a duty to safeguard the interests of the child and is required to act in accordance with the powers and duties as laid down in the Rules[14]. In carrying out his duties, the childrens' guardian must have regard to a number of factors, including how capable any person, in relation to whom the children's guardian considers the question to be relevant, is of meeting the child's needs. This will include the likely effect on the child of living with proposed adopters[15] and how capable they would be of meeting the child's needs. For this purpose, the guardian has the right, under s 42 of the Children Act 1989, to see and take copies of the case record relating to the prospective adopters and to include relevant information derived from it in his report for the court[16]. The children's guardian must be alert from the outset to the possibility either that the child wishes to instruct his solicitor direct or that there is likely to be a conflict between the guardian's recommendations and the views of the child. When either situation arises the guardian should take an early opportunity to discuss the likely difficulties with the solicitor instructed on behalf of the child and bring the matter to the attention of the court at a directions hearing[17].

A children's guardian is not entitled in law to disclose documents of a local authority in breach of public interest immunity – as to disclosure and application for the court's direction, see para **6–29 Disclosure**.

A children's guardian who is faced in the course of his or her duties with allegations of sexual abuse, (a) should limit any report to factual observations and assessments which are within his or her professional expertise as a social worker, and (b) should always seek expert advice on the interpretation of controversial material relating to allegations of sexual abuse[18]. A statement made to a children's guardian in the course of an investigation is as confidential as the report itself and, eg, an admission to causing injuries to the child, should not be disclosed without the leave of the court[19].

---

1. "Specified proceedings" has the meaning assigned to it by s 41(6) of the Children Act 1989, and r 2(2) of the Family Proceedings Courts (Children Act 1989) Rules 1991, this PART, post; (Family Proceedings Courts (Children Act 1989) Rules 1991, r 1(1)).

2. However, CAFCASS is not under a duty to make provision to enable it, immediately on request by the court, to make available an officer of the service for appointment as a guardian; the relevant statutory provisions imply that, while CAFCASS should respond as soon as practicable after a request is made, there can be a gap between the request made by the court and CAFCASS making an officer available for appointment (*R v Children and Family Court Advisory and Support Service* [2003] EWHC 235 (Admin), [2003] 1 FLR 953).

3. Family Proceedings Courts (Children Act 1989) Rules 1991, r 10(1), this PART, post.

4. Family Proceedings Courts (Children Act 1989) Rules 1991, r 10(4).

5. Family Proceedings Courts (Children Act 1989) Rules 1991, r 10(2).

6. Family Proceedings Courts (Children Act 1989) Rules 1991, r 10(3).

7. Family Proceedings Courts (Children Act 1989) Rules 1991, r 10 (4A), this PART, post.

8. Family Proceedings Courts (Children Act 1989) Rules 1991, r 10(6).

9. Family Proceedings Courts (Children Act 1989) Rules 1991, r 10(8).

10. Family Proceedings Courts (Children Act 1989) Rules 1991, r 10(9).

11. Family Proceedings Courts (Children Act 1989) Rules 1991, r 10(10).

12. *Re CE (Section 37 Direction)* [1995] 1 FCR 387, [1995] 1 FLR 26 and see *Re S (contact: grandparents)* [1996] 3 FCR 30, [1996] 1 FLR 158, CA.

13. *Oxfordshire County Council v L and F* [1997] 3 FCR 124.

15. Children Act 1989, s 41(2); Family Proceedings Courts (Children Act 1989) Rules 1991, rr 11 and 11A, this PART, post.

15. Where the guardian objects on behalf of the child to the proposed adopters (on the ground that the child is of mixed heritage and the adopters are "too Jewish") the proper forum for the challenge to that aspect of the care plan is in the care proceedings, rather than by way of judicial review (*Re C (adoption: religious observance)* [2002] 1 FLR 1119).

16. *Re T (a minor) (guardian Ad litem: case ecord)* [1994] 2 All ER 526, [1994] 2 WLR 594, [1994] 1 FLR 632.

17. *Re M (minors) (care proceedings: child's wishes)* [1994] 1 FLR 749.

18. *B v B (procedure: alleged sexual abuse)* [1994] 1 FCR 809.

19. *Oxfordshire County Council v P* [1995] Fam 161 [1995] 2 All ER 225, [1995] 2 WLR 543.

6–20   Solicitor for the child.   In specified proceedings[1] a solicitor must be appointed by the children's guardian[2] or, where no children's guardian has been appointed, may be appointed by the court[3]. A solicitor so appointed shall represent the child in accordance with instructions received from the children's guardian unless the solicitor considers, having taken into account the views of the children's guardian and any direction of the court, that the child wishes to give instructions which conflict with those of the children's guardian and that he is able, having regard to his understanding, to give such instructions on his own behalf in which case the solicitor shall conduct the proceedings in accordance with instructions received from the child[4]. Where no children's guardian has been appointed for the child, the solicitor must represent the child in accordance with instructions received from the child[5]. In default of instructions, whether or not a children's guardian has been appointed, the solicitor must represent the child in furtherance of the best interests of the child[6].

The conditions under which the court may appoint a solicitor are that:

(a)   no children's guardian has been appointed for the child;
(b)   the child has sufficient understanding to instruct a solicitor and wishes to do so;
(c)   it appears to the court that it would be in the best interests of the child for him to be represented by a solicitor[7].

A solicitor appointed in such proceedings shall serve and accept service of documents on behalf of the child in accordance with the Rules, and, where the child has not himself been served and has sufficient understanding, advise the child of the contents of any document so served[8].

The child or the children's guardian may apply to the court for the appointment of a solicitor to be terminated, and when terminating an appointment the court must give reasons for so doing, a note of which must be taken by the justices' chief executive[9].

Where an advocate represents several children in care proceedings and advances the position of the local authority in respect of some of the children, it is impossible for him to represent the interests of a child who is opposed to the care plan[10].

---

1. "Specified proceedings" has the meaning assigned to it by s 41(6) of the Children Act 1989, and r 2(2) of the Family Proceedings Courts (Children Act 1989) Rules 1991, this PART, post.
2. Family Proceedings Courts (Children Act 1989) Rules 1991, r 11(2), this PART, post.
3. Children Act 1989, s 41(3), this PART, post.
4. Family Proceedings Courts (Children Act 1989) Rules 1991, r 12(1)(a), this PART, post.
5. Family Proceedings Courts (Children Act 1989) Rules 1991, r 12(1)(b).
6. Family Proceedings Courts (Children Act 1989) Rules 1991, r 12(1)(c).
7. Children Act 1989, s 41(4), this PART, post.
8. Family Proceedings Courts (Children Act 1989) Rules 1991, r 12(2), this PART, post.
9. Family Proceedings Courts (Children Act 1989) Rules 1991, r 12(3)–(5).
10. *Re P (representation)* [1996] 1 FCR 457, [1996] 1 FLR 486, CA.

6–21   Children and family reporter and welfare officer.   A court which is considering any question with respect to a child under the Children Act 1989 may (a) ask an officer of the Children and Family Court Advisory and Support Service; or (b) ask a local authority to arrange for an officer of the authority or such other person (other than an officer of the Service) as the authority considers appropriate, to report to the court on such matters relating to the welfare of the child as are required to be dealt with in the report[1]. The report may be made in writing, or orally, as the court requires[2].

It is the duty of the local authority or officer of the Service to comply with any request for a report. Officers of the Service who undertake such reports are 'children and family reporters' and a 'welfare officer' is a person who has been asked to prepare a report on behalf of a local authority[3]. The children and family reporter or welfare officer is required to act in accordance with the powers and duties as laid down in rules[4]. The discretion to arrange for a person other than an officer of the local authority to report to the court is that of the authority and the court cannot compel the instruction of an independent psychiatrist[5].

Where a children's guardian has been appointed, in the absence of special circumstances, the court should be discouraged from seeking a welfare report in addition to the report of the children's guardian[6]. However, where the court has a report of a social worker before it, the serious implications of the application may make it appropriate also to request a report of a children and family reporter who will have specialist expertise in the court process[7].

Where the court has directed that a written report be made by a children and family reporter or welfare officer, the report shall be filed at or by such time as the court directs or, in the absence of such direction, at least 14 days before the relevant hearing. The justices' chief executive must, as soon as practicable, serve a copy of the report on the parties and any children's guardian[8]. After the filing of a written report by a children and family reporter or the welfare officer, the court or the justices' clerk may direct that the children and family reporter or the welfare officer attend any hearing at which the report is to be considered, and unless the children and family reporter or the welfare officer is present at the hearing at which such a direction is given, the justices' chief executive must inform the children and family reporter or the welfare officer of the direction[9]. There is no hard-and-fast rule which requires attendance of the children and family reporter or the welfare officer[10]. However, it is wrong for a court to reject the evidence or recommendation of a children and family reporter or the welfare officer without hearing from the officer[11]. Where the justices are contemplating rejecting the recommendation of the children and family reporter or the welfare officer, it is important that the court should afford the children and family reporter or the welfare officer an opportunity to consider the justices' misgivings or anxieties, particularly if the children and family reporter or the welfare officer is the last to enter the witness box having heard all the oral evidence. Equally, if there is a consideration which in the minds of the justices is of particular significance, and if that consideration has not appeared in the children and family reporter or the children and family reporter's or the welfare officer's report, it is important that the court should disclose its direction of thought so that the children and family reporter or the children and family reporter or the welfare officer can have an opportunity of commenting on this further consideration[12].

At the hearing at which a welfare report is considered any party may question the children and family reporter or the welfare officer about his report[12]. The court may limit the issues on which an officer of CAFCASS may be cross-examined[13]. The parties are entitled to see the contents of a welfare report, and the court may only depart from the fundamental principle that the administration of justice must be open in the most exceptional circumstances. The test as to whether all the evidence contained in a welfare report must be disclosed to the parties falls into three parts. First, the court has to be well satisfied that the confidential information was in truth reliable. Secondly, the court must be well satisfied that real harm to the child will ensue from the disclosure of the information. Thirdly, the discretion of the court is only to be exercised in rare and exceptional circumstances[14]. It is not open to a children and family reporter or the welfare officer to give assurances of confidentiality to an informant[14].

1. Children Act 1989, s 7(1), this PART, post.
2. Children Act 1989, s 7(3), this PART, post.
3. Family Proceedings Courts (Children Act 1989) Rules 1991, r 1(2), this PART, post.
4. Family Proceedings Courts (Children Act 1989) Rules 1991, r 11 and 11B (children and family reporter), r 13 (welfare officer)
5. *Re K (contact: psychiatric report)* [1995] 2 FLR 432.
6. *Re S (a minor) (care proceedings: reports)* [1992] 2 FCR 554, [1993] 1 FLR 110.
7. *Re W (welfare reports)* [1995] 3 FCR 793, [1995] 2 FLR 142, CA.
8. Family Proceedings Courts (Children Act 1989) Rules 1991, r 13(1), this PART, post.
9. Family Proceedings Courts (Children Act 1989) Rules 1991, r 13(3)(a).
10. *Re C (Section 8 Order: welfare officer)* [1995] 1 FLR 617.
11. *Re CB (access: attendance of court welfare officer)* [1995] 1 FLR 622.
12. See *Re A (a minor) (residence order)* [1998] 2 FCR 633.
13. Family Proceedings Courts (Children Act 1989) Rules 1991, r 22A, this PART, post.
14. Family Proceedings Courts (Children Act 1989) Rules 1991, r 13(3)(b).

6–22   Conciliation.   Conciliation does not form part of the legal process, but as a matter of good practice most courts offer, either through the probation service or other agency, some form of conciliation service. Conciliation has been described as "assisting the parties to deal with the consequences of the established breakdown of their marriage, whether resulting in a divorce or separation, by reaching agreements or giving consents or reducing area of conflict upon custody, support, access to and education of the children, financial provision, the disposition of the matrimonial home, lawyers' fees, and every other matter arising from the breakdown which calls for a decision on future arrangements"[1].

The facilities of a local conciliation scheme will generally be available to parties contemplating proceedings, or on the commencement of proceedings. Where a scheme does exist, the court will wish to consider whether the case is a suitable one for referral to a conciliator with a view to settling any of the issues by the conciliation process, before requesting a welfare report from a welfare officer. A distinction is to be made between conciliation and a welfare investigation, and if conciliation fails, any welfare report which is requested must be made by an officer who did not act as conciliator[2].

Statements made in the course of conciliation are *prima facie* entitled to privilege unless both parties choose to waive it. Accordingly, evidence may not be given of statements made by one or other of the parties in the course of meetings held or communications made for the purpose of conciliation save in the very unusual case where a statement is made clearly indicating that the maker has in the past caused or is likely in the future to cause serious harm to the well-being of the child. In such exceptional case, it will be for the court to exercise a discretion and only admit the evidence where the public interest in protecting the child's interests outweighs the public interest in preserving the confidentiality of attempted conciliation[3].

1. Report of the Committee on One-Parent Families (1974) Cmnd 5629, para 4.288.
2. See *Re H (conciliation: welfare reports)* [1986] 1 FLR 476; *Clarkson v Winkley* [1987] FCR 33; *Merriman v Hardy* [1987] FCR 44, and commentary thereto at FCR 49.
3. In *Re D (minors) (conciliation: disclosure of information)* [1993] 2 All ER 693.

6–23   Reconciliation.   Where an application is made for an order under s 2 of the Domestic Proceedings and Magistrates' Courts Act 1978, the family proceedings court, before deciding whether to exercise its powers under that section, must consider whether there is any possibility of reconciliation between the parties to the marriage in question[1]. If at any stage of the proceedings on such an application it appears to the court that there is a reasonable possibility of a reconciliation, the court may adjourn the case for such period as it thinks fit to enable attempts to be made to effect a reconciliation[1].

Where the court adjourns any proceedings for the purposes of an attempted reconciliation, it may request a probation officer or other person to attempt to effect a reconciliation between the parties to the marriage, and where any such request is made, the probation officer or other person must report in writing to the court whether the attempt has been successful or not. The report shall not, however, include any other information[2].

1. Domestic Proceedings and Magistrates' Courts Act 1978, s 26(1), this PART, post.
2. Domestic Proceedings and Magistrates' Courts Act 1978, s 26(2), this PART, post.

6–24   Directions.   The justices' clerk or the court may give, vary or revoke directions for the conduct of the proceedings. Directions may be given in any family proceedings commenced by application[1] (but excluding proceedings under Part IV of the Family Law Act 1996), and in all such proceedings directions may include the following:

(a) the timetable for the proceedings[2];
(b) varying the time within which or by which an act is required by Rules to be done[3];
(c) the service of documents[4];
(d) the submission of evidence[5].

In relevant proceedings[6] for the purposes of the Children Act 1989 further directions may be given to include the following:

(*e*)   the attendance of the child[7];
(*f*)   the appointment of a children's guardian or a solicitor for the child[8];
(*g*)   the submission of experts' reports[9];
(*h*)   the preparation of welfare reports[10];
(*i*)   the transfer of the proceedings to another court[11];
(*j*)   consolidation with other proceedings[12].

Directions appointments are not formalities but are important, especially where time estimates are discussed. Further, the counsel who would have the conduct of the substantive hearing should attend if possible[13].

In *public law proceedings* a standard form of directions has been specified[14].

Solicitors for the parties have a duty in children's cases to ensure that a case does not drift and is either brought to a hearing or resolved in some way with the minimum of delay[15].

Section 11 of the Children Act 1989 imposes on the court a duty to be proactive in children's cases in drawing up a timetable to ensure that the issues in the case are resolved without delay[16].

It is the duty of the court to be precise and to direct its mind to the most speedy and effective means of ensuring that a case is brought into court in a fully prepared state at the earliest opportunity. If there is any risk of drift or delay, the court should not give leave to apply for further directions, but should fix a date at which further directions will be given[15].

Where a pre-hearing review is held, the justices' clerk or the court should adopt a pro-active and rigorous approach to the issues in the case with a view to ensuring that all the issues have been appropriately defined and addressed[17]. Counsel and solicitors must talk to each other freely about case preparation and when advocates attend a pre-hearing review, it is their *collective* responsibility to ensure:

(1)   that the issues in the case to be addressed at the final hearing are clearly identified:
(2)   that the evidence to address those issues is either already available or that directions are sought from the court to ensure that it is available in good time for the hearing;
(3)   that all the expert witnesses in the case have been sent – or will prior to giving evidence be sent – all relevant material which has emerged since their reports were written; or where the material required by an expert witness has not been seen by that witness, that the material will be sent and a further report, if necessary, commissioned;
(4)   that the witnesses required to give evidence at the hearing have been identified;
(5)   that the length of time required for the evidence of each witness has been appropriately estimated;
(6)   that the witnesses have been time-tabled;
(7)   that expert witnesses, in particular, have been allotted specific dates and times for their evidence; and that the length of time allotted for their evidence has been carefully assessed to ensure that it can be given without the witnesses being inconvenienced by having to return to court on a second occasion to complete their evidence;
(8)   that the documents required for the case are in good order and bundled appropriately; that there is a chronology and, where required, a short statement of case from each party;
(9)   that the guardian's report will be available in proper time for the hearing;
(10) that appropriate reading time and time for the recording of reasons has been allowed to the justices[17].

A failure to comply with the above guidelines may give rise to consideration being given to the making of a wasted costs order[17].

The justices' clerk or the court must, on receipt of an application for hearing before a family proceedings court consider whether any directions need to be given[18]. If the justices' clerk or a single justice who is holding a directions appointment considers, for whatever reason, that it is inappropriate to give a direction on a particular matter, he must refer the matter to the court which may give any appropriate direction[19].

Directions may be given, varied or revoked either of the justices' chief executive's or the court's own motion or on the written request of a party. Where the justices' chief executive or the courts acts of his or its own motion, notice of the intention to do so and an opportunity to attend and be heard or to make written representations must be given to the parties[20].

A written request for directions by a party must specify the direction which is sought. It must be filed with the justices' chief executive and served on the other parties or if the other parties consent to the direction sought be signed by them or their representatives[20].

When considering a request for a direction to which the other parties consent, the justices' clerk or the court shall either grant the request, whereupon the justices' chief executive shall inform the parties of the decision, or direct that a date be fixed for the hearing of the request, whereupon the justices' clerk shall fix such a date and give not less than two days' notice to the parties of the date which has been fixed[21]. The justices' clerk must fix a hearing date and give similar notice to the parties on receipt of any other written request for a direction[22]. In an urgent case, a request by a party for a direction may, with the leave of the justices' clerk or the court, be made orally or without notice to the parties, or both orally and without such notice[23].

In relevant proceedings for the purposes of the Children Act 1989, a party may request that an order be made under s 11(3)[24] or, if he is entitled to apply for such an order, under s 38(1)[25] of that Act. Where a direction is given for the transfer of relevant proceedings to another court, the justices' chief executive shall issue a certificate in the appropriate form and send a copy of the certificate to the parties, to any children's guardian, and to the family proceedings court or the county court to which the proceedings are to be transferred[26].

In all directions hearings, the justices' clerk or the court shall take a note of the giving, variation or revocation of a direction and serve, as soon as practicable, a copy of the note on any party who was not present at the directions appointment[27]. A party shall attend a directions appointment of which he has been given notice unless the justices' clerk or the court otherwise directs[28].

Not every order for directions requires reasons to be given, but where an issue is contentious and requires a ruling from the court after full argument, it is good practice as well as obedience to the rules for succinct reasons to be given for the course which is being taken. A few, short, simple sentences explaining the decision should be sufficient[29].

When giving directions for case preparation, the court will be mindful of the importance of reducing costs and delay of litigation. Especially in public law cases, the court will direct parties to prepare case bundles and define the issues to facilitate the reception of evidence[30].

---

1. See the Family Proceedings Courts (Children Act 1989) Rules 1991, r 14; Family Proceedings Courts (Matrimonial Proceedings etc) Rules 1991, r 6; Maintenance Orders (Facilities for Enforcement) Rules 1922, Sch 1, para 4; Magistrates' Courts (Reciprocal Enforcement of Maintenance Orders) Rules 1974, Sch A1, para 4; Magistrates' Courts (Reciprocal Enforcement of Maintenance Orders) (Republic of Ireland) Rules 1975, Sch A1, para 4; Magistrates' Courts (Recovery Abroad of Maintenance) Rules 1975, Sch 2, para 4, and Magistrates' Courts (Reciprocal Enforcement of Maintenance Orders) (Hague Convention Countries) Rules 1980, Sch 2A, para 4, this PART, post.
2. See in particular the Family Proceedings Courts (Children Act 1989) Rules 1991, r 14(2)(*a*), and the Family Proceedings Courts (Matrimonial Proceedings etc) Rules 1991, r 6(1)(*a*), this PART, post.
3. See in particular Family Proceedings Courts (Children Act 1989) Rules 1991, rr 14(2)(*b*), and 6(1)(*b*), respectively, this PART, post.
4. See in particular Family Proceedings Courts (Children Act 1989) Rules 1991, rr 14(2)(*e*) and 6(1)(*c*), respectively, this PART, post.
5. See in particular Family Proceedings Courts (Children Act 1989) Rules 1991, rr 14(2)(*f*) and 6(1)(*d*), respectively, this PART, post.
6. "Relevant proceedings" has the meaning assigned to it by s 93(3) of the Children Act 1989, this PART, post (Family Proceedings Courts (Children Act 1989) Rules 1991, r 1(2), this PART, post).
7. Family Proceedings Courts (Children Act 1989) Rules 1991, r 14(2)(*c*), this PART, post.
8. Family Proceedings Courts (Children Act 1989) Rules 1991, r 14(2)(*d*), this PART, post.
9. Family Proceedings Courts (Children Act 1989) Rules 1991, r 14(2)(*f*), this PART, post.
10. Family Proceedings Courts (Children Act 1989) Rules 1991, r 14(2)(*g*), this PART, post.
11. Family Proceedings Courts (Children Act 1989) Rules 1991, r 14(2)(*h*), this PART, post.
12. Family Proceedings Courts (Children Act 1989) Rules 1991, r 14(2)(*i*), this PART, post.
13. See *Re MD and TD (children's cases: times estimates)* [1994] 2 FCR 94 (time estimates in the Family Division).
14. See the *Protocol for Judicial Case Management in Public Law Children Act Cases* Appendix A/1 at para 6–5103, post.
15. *B v B (child abuse: contact)* [1994] 2 FLR 713.
16. *Re A and B (minors) (No 2)* [1995] 1 FLR 351. This is reinforced by art 6(1) of the European Convention on Human Rights which requires that proceedings which determine civil rights and obligations be heard within a reasonable time.
17. *Re G (children) (care proceedings: wasted costs)* [1999] 4 All ER 371, [2000] 2 WLR 1007, [1999] 3 FCR 303, [2000] 1 FLR 52.
18. Family Proceedings Courts (Children Act 1989) Rules 1991, r 14(2); Family Proceedings Courts (Matrimonial Proceedings etc) Rules 1991, r 6(1), this PART, post.
19. Family Proceedings Courts (Children Act 1989) Rules 1991, r 14(3); Family Proceedings Courts (Children Act 1989) Rules 1991, r 6(2), this PART, post.
20. Family Proceedings Courts (Children Act 1989) Rules 1991, r 14(5); Family Proceedings Courts (Children Act 1989) Rules 1991, r 6(3), this PART, post.
21. Family Proceedings Courts (Children Act 1989) Rules 1991, r 14(8); Family Proceedings Courts (Children Act 1989) Rules 1991, r 6(6), this PART, post.
22. Family Proceedings Courts (Children Act 1989) Rules 1991, r 14(7); Family Proceedings Courts (Children Act 1989) Rules 1991, r 6(5), this PART, post.
23. Family Proceedings Courts (Children Act 1989) Rules 1991, r 14(6); Family Proceedings Courts (Children Act 1989) Rules 1991, r 6(4), this PART, post.
24. A s 8 order made otherwise than on disposal of the proceedings.
25. An interim care or interim supervision order.
26. Family Proceedings Courts (Children Act 1989) Rules 1991, rr 6(2) and 14(4), this PART, post.
27. See in particular the Family Proceedings Courts (Children Act 1989) Rules 1991, r 14(12); Family Proceedings Courts (Matrimonial Proceedings etc) Rules 1991, r 6(7), this PART, post.
28. See in particular the Family Proceedings Courts (Children Act 1989) Rules 1991, r 16(1); the Family Proceedings Courts (Matrimonial Proceedings etc) Rules 1991, r 8(1), this PART, post.
29. See *London Borough of Croydon v R* [1997] 2 FLR 675, sub nom *Re R (a minor) (child care: procedure)* [1997] 3 FCR 705, per Wall J.
30. See *Practice Note (Civil Litigation: Case Management)*, [1995] and *Practice Direction (Family Proceedings: Court Bundles)* [2000] 1 WLR 737, [2000] 1 FCR 521, [2000] 1 FLR 536, both in this PART, post.

6–25 Allocation of proceedings.

Children's proceedings: There is a common jurisdiction in proceedings under the Children Act 1989 between the High Court, county court and family proceedings court. In private law cases the applicant may choose the level of court in which it is thought appropriate for the proceedings to be determined, although this decision may be influenced by the existence of other proceedings, perhaps in a divorce county court.

In the case of public law applications, such as application for care or supervision orders or emergency protection orders, the proceedings must be commenced in a family proceedings court[1]. There are, however, exceptions to this rule. First, proceedings which arise from an investigation directed under s 37 of the Children Act 1989 shall be commenced in the court which directs the investigation, where that court is the High Court or a care centre, or in such care centre as the court which directs the investigation may order[2]. Secondly, where there are other proceedings pending in respect of the same child, any further application concerning that child must be made to the same court[3].

Proceedings under Part IV of the Family Law Act 1996: A similar jurisdiction between the High Court, county court and the family proceedings court exists with respect to proceedings under Part IV of the Family Law Act 1996[4]. Subject to the provisions of the Family Law Act 1996[5], proceedings under Part IV, generally, may be commenced in a county court or a family proceedings court[6]. Where proceedings are pending in a county court or a family proceedings court, an application under Part IV may be made in those proceedings[7]. However, there are exceptions to this rule, and an application under Part IV brought by an applicant who is under the age of 18, and an application for the grant of leave under s 43 of the 1996 Act (leave of court required for application by child under age of 16) must be commenced in the High Court[8].

---

1. Children (Allocation of Proceedings) Order 1991, art 3(1), this PART, post.
2. Children (Allocation of Proceedings) Order 1991, art 3(2), this PART, post.
3. Children (Allocation of Proceedings) Order 1991, art 3(3), this PART, post.
4. Family Law Act 1996, s 57, this PART, post.
5. Section 59 of and para 1 of Sch 7 to the Family Law Act 1996, this PART, post.
6. Family Law Act 1996 (Part IV) (Allocation of Proceedings) Order 1997, art 4(1), this PART, post.
7. Family Law Act 1996 (Part IV) (Allocation of Proceedings) Order 1997, art 4(3), this PART, post.
8. Family Law Act 1996 (Part IV) (Allocation of Proceedings) Order 1997, art 4(2), this PART, post.

6–26   Transfer of children's proceedings.   Provision is made for proceedings under the Children Act 1989 to be transferred from one court to another. Proceedings may be transferred from one family proceedings court to another, from a family proceedings court to a county court and from a county court to a family proceedings court[1].

Before transferring proceedings under the Children Act 1989 the court must have regard to the principle set out in s 1(2) of the Act, namely that delay in determining any question with respect to the upbringing of a child is likely to prejudice the welfare of the child[2]. When transferring from one family proceedings court to another, the transferring court must also consider that the transfer is in the interests of the child—

(1)   because it is likely significantly to accelerate the determination of the proceedings;
(2)   because it would be appropriate for those proceedings to be heard together with other family proceedings which are pending in the receiving court; or
(3)   for some other reason; and

be satisfied that the receiving court, by the justices' clerk, consent to the transfer[3].

A family proceedings court may, upon application by a party or of its own motion, transfer to a county court *public law proceedings* of any of the kinds mentioned in art 3(1) of the Children (Allocation of Proceedings) Order 1991[4] where it considers it in the interests of the child to do so having regard, first, to the principle set out in s 1(2) of the Act and, secondly, to the following questions:

(*a*)   whether the proceedings are exceptionally grave, important or complex, in particular—

(i)   because of complicated or conflicting evidence about the risks involved to the child's physical or moral well-being or about other matters relating to the welfare of the child;
(ii)   because of the number of parties;
(iii)   because of a conflict with the law of another jurisdiction;
(iv)   because of some novel and difficult point of law; or
(v)   because of some question of general public interest;

(*b*)   whether it would be appropriate for those proceedings to be heard together with other family proceedings which are pending in another court; and
(*c*)   whether transfer is likely significantly to accelerate the determination of the proceedings, where—

(i)   no other method of doing so, including transfer to another family proceedings court, is appropriate, and
(ii)   delay would seriously prejudice the interests of the child who is the subject of the proceedings[5].

Where a family proceedings court refuses to transfer *public law proceedings* to a county court, a party to those proceedings may apply to the care centre[6] for the petty sessions area or London commission area in which the family proceedings court is situated. On hearing such an application, the care centre may transfer the proceedings to itself where, having regard to the principle set out in s 1(2) of the Act and the criteria set out above, it considers it in the interests of the child to do so[7]. On hearing an application for transfer from the family proceedings court, the care centre may transfer the proceedings to the High Court where it considers that the proceedings are appropriate for determination in the High Court, and that such determination would be in the interests of the child[8].

A family proceedings court may transfer to a county court *private law proceedings* under the Children Act 1989 or the Adoption and Children Act 2002 (being proceedings to which art 7 of the Children (Allocation of Proceedings) Order 1991 does not apply) where, having regard to the principle set out in s 1(2) of the Children Act 1989, the court considers that in the interests of the child the proceedings can be dealt with more appropriately in that county court[9].

Any directions of the justices' clerk or the court which are still in force immediately before a transfer of proceedings to another court shall continue to apply following the transfer, subject to any changes of terminology which are required to apply to those directions[10].

Where the estimate of the length of hearing is in excess of two or three days, justices should consider transferring a case to the district judge for consideration whether it should be heard by a circuit judge or a High Court judge[11]. Similarly, justices should consider transfer where they are unable to offer consecutive hearing dates when the case is likely to take two or three days[12]. Care proceedings involving a mother who is very young should be transferred to the High Court without delay and a separate children's guardian appointed for the mother and the child immediately[13].

A case which seems to bristle with complexity at the outset should be transferred upwards, even if it simplifies as it progresses so as to justify a transfer back to the family proceedings court[14]. Whether or not to return a battered baby to its parents involves a balancing of risk which cannot be anything but exceptionally grave and important, with conflicting if not complex evidence. Such cases are often better heard by a judge and not justices[15]. Cases which require a decision as to whether a child should be removed from the jurisdiction are not suitable for justices[16].

For the purpose of considering the question of transfer, it may be relevant to remember that a county court has no inherent jurisdiction to grant an injunction to protect children. Accordingly, in care proceedings a county court has no inherent jurisdiction to accept undertakings from the parent of a child who is the subject of an application for a care or supervision order[17].

When considering an application for the transfer of a *private law case*, although the court must have regard to the question of delay, its main function is to consider the interests of the child and to decide whether the proceedings can be more appropriately dealt with in a county court[18]. Such cases include those where there is an issue of international child abduction where it is sensible for them to be transferred to the county court and in cases of difficulty to be transferred from there to the High Court[19].

Wherever possible, proceedings relating to siblings should be heard together and where separate proceedings have been instituted in different jurisdictions, every effort should be made at the earliest possible stage for the proceedings to be consolidated[20].

---

1. Children (Allocation of Proceedings) Order 1991, arts 6, 7 and 11, this PART, post.
2. Children (Allocation of Proceedings) Order 1991, arts 6(1), 7(1), 8 and 11, this PART, post.
3. Children (Allocation of Proceedings) Order 1991, art 6(1), this PART, post.
4. See this PART, post.
5. Children (Allocation of Proceedings) Order 1991, art 7(1), this PART, post.
6. See Children (Allocation of Proceedings) Order 1991, art 2 and Sch 2, this PART, post.
7. Children (Allocation of Proceedings) Order 1991, art 9(1) and (2), this PART, post.
8. Children (Allocation of Proceedings) Order 1991, art 9(3), this PART, post.
9. Children (Allocation of Proceedings) Order 1991, art 8, this PART, post.
10. Family Proceedings Courts (Children Act 1989) Rules 1991, r 14(11), this PART, post.
11. *Re H (a minor) (care proceedings)* [1992] 2 FCR 330; *Re L (care proceedings: transfer)* [1993] 1 FCR 689.
12. *Re L (care proceedings: transfer)* [1993] 1 FCR 689.
13. *Re R (a child) (care proceedings: teenage pregnancy)* [2000] 2 FCR 556, [2000] 2 FLR 660, FD.
14. *Re H (a minor) (care proceedings)* [1992] 2 FCR 330.
15. *Re C (a minor) (care proceedings)* [1992] 2 FCR 341.
16. *Re L (a minor) (removal from jurisdiction)* [1993] 1 FCR 325.
17. *In re B (a minor) (supervision order: parental undertaking)* [1996] 1 WLR 716, [1996] 3 FCR 446, [1996] 1 FLR 676, CA.
18. *R v South East Hampshire Family Proceedings Court, ex p D* [1994] 2 All ER 445, [1994] 1 WLR 611, [1994] 1 FCR 620, [1994] 2 FLR 190.
19. *R v R (residence order)* [1996] 1 FCR 480, [1995] 2 FLR 625.
20. *W v Wakefield City Council* [1995] 1 FLR 170.

6–27 Transfer of matrimonial proceedings. *Proceedings under the Domestic Proceedings and Magistrates' Courts Act 1978:* There is no power for proceedings under the Domestic Proceedings and Magistrates' Courts Act 1978 to be transferred from one family proceedings court to another.

On hearing an application under s 2 of the 1978 Act, if the family proceedings court is of the opinion that any of the matters in question between the parties would be more conveniently dealt with by the High Court, the family proceedings court shall refuse to make any order on the application, and no appeal lies from that refusal[1].

The matters in question must be ones in which the High Court has concurrent jurisdiction[2]. It is not proper for the justices to hear evidence on the application and then refer to the High Court the question whether or not an order should be made[3].

Proceedings under Part IV of the Family Law Act 1996: A family proceedings court *may*, on application or of its own motion, transfer proceedings under Part IV to a county court where it considers that—

(a) it would be appropriate for those proceedings to be heard together with other family proceedings which are pending in that court; or

(b) the proceedings involve—

    (i) a conflict with the law of another jurisdiction;

    (ii) some novel and difficult point of law;

    (iii) some question of general public interest; or

(c) the proceedings are exceptionally complex[4].

A family proceedings court *must* transfer proceedings under Part IV to a county court where—

(a) a child under the age of 18 is the respondent to the application or wishes to become a party to the proceedings; or

(b) a party to the proceedings is a person who, by reason of mental disorder within the meaning of the Mental Health Act 1983 is incapable of managing and administering his property and affairs[5].

A family proceedings court may, on application or of its own motion, transfer proceedings under Part IV to the High Court where it considers that it would be appropriate for those proceedings to be heard together with other family proceedings which are pending in that court[6].

There is also power for a family proceedings court, (the transferring court) to transfer proceedings under Part IV to another family proceedings court (the receiving court) where the transferring court considers that it would be appropriate for those proceedings to be heard together with other family proceedings which are pending in the receiving court and the receiving court, by its justices' clerk consents to the transfer[7].

The High Court or a county court have power in certain circumstances to transfer proceedings under Part IV to a family proceedings court[8].

Where a person is brought before—

(a) a relevant judicial authority in accordance with s 47(7)(a) (arrest under power of arrest) of the 1996 Act, or

(b) a court by virtue of a warrant issued under s 47(9) of the 1996 Act (arrest under warrant where no power of arrest attached),

and the matter is not disposed of forthwith, the matter may be transferred to be disposed of by the relevant judicial authority or court which issued the warrant, or as the case may be, which attached the power of arrest under s 47(2) or (3) of the 1996 Act if different[9].

1. Domestic Proceedings and Magistrates' Courts Act 1978, s 27, this PART, post.
2. *Perks v Perks* [1946] P 1, [1945] 2 All ER 580, 110 JP 94; *Smyth v Smyth* [1956] P 427, [1956] 2 All ER 476, 120 JP 307.
3. *Davies v Davies* [1957] P 357, [1957] 2 All ER 444, 121 JP 369.
4. Family Law Act 1996 (Part IV) (Allocation of Proceedings) Order 1997, art 8(1), this PART, post.
5. Family Law Act 1996 (Part IV) (Allocation of Proceedings) Order 1997, art 8(2), this PART, post.
6. Family Law Act 1996 (Part IV) (Allocation of Proceedings) Order 1997, art 9, this PART, post.
7. Family Law Act 1996 (Part IV) (Allocation of Proceedings) Order 1997, art 7, this PART, post.
8. Family Law Act 1996 (Part IV) (Allocation of Proceedings) Order 1997, arts 11 and 13, this PART, post.
9. Family Law Act 1996 (Part IV) (Allocation of Proceedings) Order 1997, art 15, this PART, post.

6–28   Timing of proceedings.   At the transfer, postponement or adjournment of any hearing or directions appointment in the course of family proceedings, or the conclusion of any such hearing or directions appointment other than one at which the proceedings are determined, or as soon thereafter as practicable, the justices' clerk or the court must fix a date when the proceedings shall come before the justices' clerk or the court again for such purpose as may be directed, and the justices' chief executive must give notice to the parties of the date so fixed[1].

It is important that advocates give a realistic time estimate for hearing a children's case which should include judicial reading time and time for preparing the judgment. The estimate should be arrived at by a co-operative planning process between the lawyers for the parties[2]. In order to reduce the time spent on trying a case, the lawyers should think well in advance of trial about the documentation required for the proper conduct of the proceedings[3]. Pre-trial discovery is an essential part of this process[3].

In *public law proceedings* a detailed six step process with targets has been specified[4].

Any period of time fixed by the Rules, or by any order or direction, for doing any act shall be reckoned in accordance with the Rules[5].

1. Family Proceedings Courts (Children Act 1989) Rules 1991, r 15(5); Family Proceedings Courts (Matrimonial Proceedings etc) Rules 1991, r 7(5), this PART, post.
2. See *Re MD and TD (children's cases: time estimates)* [1994] 2 FCR 94 (time estimates in the Family Division).
3. *Re JC (care proceedings: procedure)* [1996] 1 FCR 434, [1995] 2 FLR 77.
4. See the *Protocol for Judicial Case Management in Public Law Children Act Cases* at para **4–5103**, post.
5. Family Proceedings Courts (Children Act 1989) Rules 1991, r 15; Family Proceedings Courts (Matrimonial Proceedings etc) Rules 1991, r 7, this PART, post.

6–29   Disclosure.   No document, other than a record of an order, held by a family proceedings court and relating to proceedings under the Children Act 1989 (except proceedings in private[1]), Part IV of the Family Law Act 1996 or the Domestic Proceedings and Magistrates' Courts Act 1978 shall be disclosed, other than to—

(a) a party,
(b) the legal representative of a party,
(c) the children's guardian,
(d) the Legal Aid Board, or
(e) a children and family reporter or a welfare officer,

without leave of the officer of the court or the court[2]. In addition, there is no requirement for leave of the court to disclose documents to a court approved McKenzie friend provided that an appropriate assurance is given by the litigant in person and the McKenzie friend about the use of court documents

nor to a public authority with a proper interest in the subject matter of the disclosure, such as the local government ombudsman or the police[3].

Where proceedings are in private under the Children Act 1989, the categories of persons to whom disclosure may be made without the leave for prescribed purposes are much more extensive[4].

Application for disclosure is not limited to the parties to the proceedings and may be made by a non-party such as the police for the purpose of investigating alleged abuse[5]. Disclosure may not be ordered against a non-party to the proceedings, the appropriate procedure is to issue a witness summons. Where the police are required to make available video recordings of interviews made in the course of a criminal investigation for use in care proceedings, the court may impose conditions on the copying of the tapes in order to protect confidentiality and the integrity of the tapes[6].

On an application for disclosure the court must conduct a balancing exercise, balancing the importance of confidentiality against the public interest in seeing that justice is properly served, while treating as a priority the interests of the child[7]. The proper approach to disclosure in adoption proceedings is a three stage test: would disclosure of the material involve a real possibility of significant harm to the child; (if it would) would the overall interests of the child benefit from non-disclosure, weighing on the one hand the interest of the child in having the material properly tested, and on the other both the magnitude of the risk that harm would occur, and the gravity of the harm if it did occur; and (if the court is satisfied that the interests of the child point toward non-disclosure) weigh that consideration, and its strength in the circumstances of the case, against the interest of the parent or other party in having an opportunity to see and respond to the material, taking into account the importance of the material to the issues in the case. Non disclosure is the exception rather than the rule[8]. The same principles apply in other cases involving children[9].

The entitlement to a fair trial under art 6 is absolute, but that does not mean an absolute and unqualified right to see all the documents. Since the Human Rights Act 1998 came into force, it is not only the interests of a child involved in litigation, but also the interests of anyone else who is involved as a victim, party or witness, who can demonstrate that his or her art 8 rights are engaged, that may be capable of denying a litigant access to documents. Non-disclosure must be limited to what the situation imperatively demands and is justified only when the case is compelling or strictly necessary; but where the litigant's right to a fair trial will not be impeded by denial of access to certain documents, proper respect for the art 8 rights of other persons requires non-disclosure, and the harm suffered by disclosure will be disproportionate to any legitimate forensic purpose served, it will be appropriate to authorise non-disclosure[10].

Where leave for disclosure of a document in family proceedings is sought for the purpose of criminal proceedings, the court should not seek to erect a barrier which would prejudice the operation of another court. Accordingly, disclosure may be made where appropriate to the Crown Prosecution Service. Similar considerations will apply to defendants because it is in the interests of justice that a defendant in a criminal trial should have available all relevant and necessary material for the proper conduct of his or her defence[7]. Moreover, the use by a party or a legal adviser in other proceedings of *information* acquired in family proceedings bound by confidentiality, requires the leave of the family court[11].

Guidance has been given by the High Court as to the propositions which should govern the grant of leave and the directions which should be given on disclosure of reports to experts; see para **6–35A**, post.

A local authority who bring care proceedings have a duty to disclose all relevant information in their possession or power, excluding that protected by public interest immunity[12]. This duty includes, in particular, disclosure of attendance notes of meetings and conversations and minutes of case conferences, core group meetings and the like; social workers should at all times keep clear, accurate, full and balanced notes of all relevant conversations and meetings between themselves, parents, and others involved with the case, and where meetings are held, there should be a written agenda circulated in advance to all concerned, full, balanced, clear and accurate minutes should be taken, and once agreed, these should be disclosed to all parties[13]. This duty requires the local authority to produce not only documents which support their case but also, in the interests of the child and of justice, documents which may modify or cast doubt on their case: in particular, documents which actually help the case of an opposing party. If the documents are apparently relevant but appear to be protected from disclosure by public interest immunity, the local authority should draw the attention of the other parties' legal advisers and the children's guardian to the existence of the documents and invite application to the court if disclosure is required[14].

If the children's guardian, in the course of inspecting the social services files, comes upon records which he believes to be relevant but which are not likely to be disclosed by the local authority, he should invite the local authority to disclose the documents and if they refuse he should seek the court's directions. The children's guardian is not entitled in law to disclose documents in breach of public interest immunity[14]. Moreover, the confidentiality enjoyed by a report of a children's guardian extends to information collected by the children's guardian for the purpose of preparing the report. The confidentiality is that of the court and it is therefore wrong for a children's guardian to make a witness statement without the prior leave of the court for the disclosure to be made[15].

Since the children's guardian has the limited function of being guardian for the purpose of the proceedings, it will never be proper for a guardian to promise a child that information disclosed by the child will not be communicated to the court[16].

Communications between solicitor and client are subject to legal professional privilege which cannot be overridden[17]. This must be contrasted with litigation privilege which attaches to documents or other written communications prepared with a view to litigation and is an essential component of adversarial proceedings. Proceedings where the welfare of a child is under consideration are non-adversarial[18] and such privilege does not therefore have a role to play[19]. Accordingly, litigation privilege does not arise in respect of reports obtained by a party thereto which could not have been prepared without the leave of the court to disclose documents already filed or to examine the child[19]. Moreover, legal representatives in possession of material adverse to their client's case are under a positive duty to disclose it to the other parties and to the court and not to resist disclosure by relying on legal professional privilege[20].

Notwithstanding the fact that in Children Act proceedings the welfare of the child is the court's paramount consideration, and that there is a high duty of disclosure in such proceedings, a party to Children Act proceedings retains the right to claim legal professional privilege which arises in, or in connection with, other proceedings. Accordingly, a parent may claim legal professional privilege in care proceedings in respect of his direct, or indirect, communications with medical experts who had been instructed solely for the purposes of criminal proceedings, and in respect of their reports[21].

The need to protect the integrity of the criminal process and to ensure that the respective party has a fair trial are factors of the greatest weight in concluding that there should be no disclosure of prosecution papers until the criminal proceedings have ended[22].

The power of the court to control disclosure does not arise until documents created for the purpose of court proceedings have actually been filed with the court[23]. Accordingly, there is no requirement in the Rules for the court's leave to be obtained for an exchange of information between a social worker and the police as part of their joint investigation[23] nor in respect of documents held by social workers which have not been filed with the court such as notes and drafts[24]. Similarly, a Child and Family Reporter does not need the leave of the court to disclose material to Social Services raising concerns about a child's welfare. However, the CAFCASS officer should consider whether the information is a discovery or direct report as opposed to an account of someone else's discovery or a secondhand report for which different considerations may apply[25].

Once proceedings are at an end the principle of confidentiality must be strictly observed and further distribution of the children's guardian's report must be controlled by the court[26].

Notice of an application for leave not to disclose to another party information which may be relevant to that party's case in contested care proceedings should be given to that party[16]. Proceeedings in which such applications are made should be heard by the High Court[9]. In adoption proceedings however there is an emphasis on confidentiality, especially in serial number applications, and the file is not open to inspection by other parties to the application and the court may exercise a discretion to entertain an application for non disclosure without notice to another party[27].

When considering whether to issue a summons to the police to produce video evidence arising from a joint investigation with social services for use in private law proceedings similar principles will apply. Whilst it is not always wrong to consider the proportionality of the cost of the resources in making such an order for disclosure and the benefits to the welfare of the child, it should be borne in mind that the court is actively seeking the best solution for the child[28].

An order for disclosure, compliance with which is likely to involve the danger of self incrimination by the party, should not be made[19]. Where at the time an order is made granting leave for an expert to prepare a report coupled with an order for disclosure to all parties and only later does its possible incriminating effect become known, the party must claim privilege against incrimination at that stage or risk being deemed to have waived privilege[19].

The prohibition against the admissibility in criminal proceedings of a statement or admission does not extend to a police investigation since s 98 of the Children Act 1989 refers only to court proceedings and evidence given therein[29]. In exercising the discretion whether to order disclosure for a police investigation the following are amongst the matters to which the court will have regard:—

(1) The welfare and the interests of the child or children concerned.
(2) The welfare and interests of other children generally.
(3) The maintenance of confidentiality in children's cases.
(4) The importance of encouraging frankness in children's cases.
(5) The public interest in the administration of justice.
(6) The public interest in the prosecution of serious crime and the punishment of offenders, including the public interest in convicting those who have been guilty of violent or sexual offences against children.
(7) The gravity of the alleged offence and the relevance of the evidence to it.
(8) The desirability of co-operation between various agencies concerned with the welfare of children, including the social services departments, the police service, medical practitioners, health visitors, schools etc.
(9) In a case to which s 98(2) of the Act applies, the terms of the section itself, namely that the witness was not excused from answering incriminating questions, and that any statement of admission would not be admissible against him in criminal proceedings. Fairness to the person who has incriminated himself and any others affected by the incriminating statement and any danger of oppression will also be relevant considerations.
(10) Any other material disclosure which has already taken place[29].

Section 98(2) of the Children Act 1989 does not apply to private law proceedings, in deciding whether or not to grant leave to disclose the need to encourage candour has to be balanced against other factors, such as the gravity of the offence concerned, any risk to children, and issues of public policy, and the court should also have regard to the welfare of the children concerned and to the factors set out in *Re C (a minor) (care proceedings: disclosure)* (infra), but in carrying out this balancing exercise the court should bear in mind that the need to encourage frankness ought to be given greater weight in private law proceedings than in public law proceedings[30].

Unless the application for disclosure comes within these broad principles, it is inappropriate to direct disclosure of information about findings of abuse in Children Act 1989 cases[31].

A child protection conference relies on the contribution to be made by the relevant medical and mental health professionals. Accordingly where a local authority seeks leave to disclose litigation material to a child protection conference, the court should not restrict disclosure to the police and exclude the health authority[32]. Leave may be granted to persons not the subject of care proceedings but who have been sexually abused by one of the parties to disclose the findings of the court[33].

The court will view with gravity a breach of the terms of an order for disclosure such as in a case where the disclosure of confidential material was restricted to medical and legal advisers only and a solicitor inadvertently forwarded a copy to the client[34].

In considering whether to permit disclosure of material and to what extent to one of the parties for the purpose of other proceedings to be brought by him relevant factors to consider and balance include:

(i)   the interests of the children concerned;
(ii) the interests of the good conduct of children cases generally in preserving the confidence of those who gave evidence or information to or for the purpose of those proceedings;
(iii) the interests of the administration of justice; and
(iv) the interests of children generally.

Furthermore, seeking disclosure simply to pursue litigation or complaints which would clearly be frivolous, vexatious or an abuse of process would not weigh heavily in the balancing exercise. However, seeking disclosure in order to pursue a proper appeal, to make a proper complaint to a professional body, or to persuade the medical authorities of the need for a further medical examination would weigh much more heavily. Much would depend on how relevant the material in question was likely to be, which depended on the particular complaint or litigation in issue and the particular content of the material[35].

---

1. In accordance with the Family Proceedings (Children Act 1989) Rules 1991, r 16(7), in this PART, STATUTORY INSTRUMENTS AND PRACTICE DIRECTIONS ON FAMILY LAW, post.

2. Family Proceedings Courts (Children Act 1989) Rules 1991, r 23(1); Family Proceedings Courts (Matrimonial Proceedings etc) Rules 1991, r 14, this PART, post.

3. *Re O (children) (representation: McKenzie friend)* [2005] EWCA Civ 759, [2006] Fam 1, [2005] 2 FCR 563.

4. See the Family Proceedings (Children Act 1989) Rules 1991, r 23A, in this PART, STATUTORY INSTRUMENTS AND PRACTICE DIRECTIONS ON FAMILY LAW, post.

5. *Re L (police investigation: privilege)* [1995] 2 FCR 12, [1995] 1 FLR 999 at 1008, [1995] 2 FCR 12 (sub nom *Re L (minors) (document: non-party disclosure)*, and see *A County Council v W (disclosure)* [1997] 1 FLR 574 (application for disclosure by the General Medical Council) and *Re L (care proceedings: disclosure to third party)* [2000] 1 FLR 913, FC (disclosure to UK Central Council for Nursing, Midwifery and Health Visiting). Cases that involve disclosure to the police of confidential material generated by care proceedings will be decided by carrying out the discretionary balancing exercise identified in *Re C (a minor) (care proceedings: disclosure)* [1997] Fam 76, [1997] 2 WLR 322, [1996] 3 FCR 521. There is no presumption in favour of disclosure to the police in 1989 Act cases; each case will be judged on its own merits according to the relevant guidelines, but where very serious crimes may have been committed and an expert's report is of direct relevance to the police inquiry the public interest in the prosecution of serious crime and the punishment of offenders is particularly strong (*A Chief Constable v A County Council* [2002] EWHC 2198 (Fam), [2003] 2 FCR 385, [2003] 1 FLR 579(sub nom *Re AB (care proceedings: disclosure of medical evidence to police)*).

6. *Re M (child abuse: video evidence)* [1996] 1 FCR 261, [1995] 2 FLR 571.

7. *Re K (minors) (disclosure of privileged material)* [1994] 3 All ER 230, [1994] 1 WLR 912 (sub nom *Kent County Council v K*) and see *Oxfordshire County Council v L and F* [1997] 1 FLR 235. See also *Re Z (children) (disclosure: criminal proceedings)* [2003] EWHC 61 (Fam), [2003] 1 FLR 1194.

8. *Re D (minors) (adoption reports: confidentiality)* [1996] AC 593, [1995] 4 All ER 385, [1995] 3 WLR 483, HL. See also *Re X (children) (adoption: confidentiality)* [2002] EWCA Civ 828, [2002] 3 FCR 648, [2002] 2 FLR 476.

9. *Re M (disclosure)* [1999] 1 FCR 492, CA. See also *Re W* [2003] EWHC 1624 (Fam), [2004] 1 All ER 787, [2004] 1 WLR 1494, [2003] 2 FLR 1023 (disclosure of material obtained by police informant).

10. *Re B (disclosure to other parties)* [2001] 2 FLR 1017, [2002] 2 FCR 32, approved and applied in *Re B (children) (care proceedings: disclosure)* [2002] All ER (D) 167 (Nov), [2002] JPN 903..

11. *Re A (aare proceedings: disclosure of information)* [1996] 1 FCR 533, [1996] 1 FLR 221.

12. If the document the guardian wishes to examine and take copies of falls within s 42 of the Children Act 1989, pubic interest immunity simply does not arise so far as the guardian's inspection is concerned (*Re J (care proceedings: disclosure)* [2003] EWHC 976 (Fam), [2003] 2 FLR 522).

13. *Re G (care: challenge to local authority's decision)* [2003] EWHC 551 (Fam), [2003] 2 FLR 42.

14. *Re C (expert evidence: disclosure: practice)* [1995] 2 FCR 97, [1995] 1 FLR 204.

15. *Oxfordshire County Council v P* [1995] Fam 161, [1995] 2 All ER 225, [1995] 2 WLR 543; followed in *Cleveland County Council v F* [1995] 1 WLR 785, [1995] 3 FCR 174, [1995] 1 FLR 797.

16. *Re C (disclosure)* [1996] 3 FCR 765, [1996] 1 FLR 797.

17. *R v Derby Magistrates' Court, ex p B* [1995] 4 All ER 526, [1995] 3 WLR 681, 159 JP 785, HL.

18. *Oxfordshire County Council v M* [1994] Fam 151, [1994] 2 All ER 269, [1994] 2 WLR 393, CA.

19. *Re L (minors)* [1996] 2 All ER 78, [1996] 2 WLR 395, [1996] 1 FLR 731, HL (and see *L v United Kingdom* [2000] 2 FCR 145, [2000] 2 FLR 322, ECtHR: applicant not deprived of her right to a fair trial under the European Convention on Human Rights art 6(1) nor did the production of the expert's report breach the applicant's right not to incriminate herself; the interference with her rights under art 8(1) was compatible with art 8(2) in particular "the protection of health and morals" and "the protection of the rights and freedoms of others" in relation to the child).

20. *Essex County Council v R* [1994] Fam 167n [1993] 4 All ER 702, [1994] 2 WLR 407n (sub nom *Re R (a minor) (disclosure of privileged material)*, *Oxfordshire County Council v P* [1995] Fam 161, [1995] 2 All ER 225 [1995] 2 WLR 543. (However, the issue was left open by the House of Lords in *Re L (minors)* [1996] 2 All ER 78, [1996] 2 WLR 395, [1996] 1 FLR 731, HL).

21. *S County Council v B* [2000] Fam 76, [2000] 3 WLR 53, [2000] 1 FCR 536, [2000] 2 FLR 161.

22. See *Re P (Disclosure: Criminal Proceedings)* [2003] EWHC 1713 (Fam), [2004] 1 FLR 407.

23. *Re G (a minor) (social worker: disclosure)* [1996] 2 All ER 65, [1996] 3 FCR 77, [1996] 1 FLR 276, CA.

24. *Re W (minors) (social worker: disclosure)* [1998] 2 All ER 801, [1999] 1 WLR 205, [1998] 2 FCR 405, CA.

25. See *In re M (A Child) (Children and Family Reporter: Disclosure)* [2002] EWCA Civ 1199, [2003] Fam 26, [2002] 4 All ER 401, [2002] 3 FCR 208, [2002] 2 FLR 893.

26. *Re C (guardian ad litem: disclosure of report)* [1996] 1 FLR 61.

27. *Re K (adoption: disclosure of information)* [1998] 2 FCR 388, [1997] 2 FLR 74.

28. *Re S (a minor) (contact: evidence)* [1998] 3 FCR 70, [1998] 1 FLR 798, CA.

29. *In Re C (a minor) (care proceedings: disclosure)* [1997] Fam 76, [1997] 2 WLR 322, [1996] 3 FCR 521, and see *Oxfordshire County Council v L and F* [1997] 3 FCR 124 and *Re R (disclosure)* [1998] 1 FLR 433 (public interest justified disclosure of psychiatrist's report on father, a court welfare officer, to his probation officer contrast *Re M (disclosure: police investigation)* [2002] 1 FCR 655, [2001] 2 FLR 1316 (disclosure of subsequent admission in care proceedings refused where it would affect chances of successfully reuniting child with his parents).

30. *Re D and M (disclosure: private law)* [2002] EWHC 2820 (Fam), [2003] 1 FLR 647.

31. *Re L (sexual abuse: disclosure)* [1999] 1 WLR 299, [1999] 1 FCR 308, [1999] 1 FLR 267, CA (inappropriate for local authority to disclose findings against men in care proceedings to, in one case, another local authority and, in another, to an area football league). For disclosure by local authorities other than in court proceedings, see also the European Convention on Human Rights, article 8 in PART VIII, title HUMAN RIGHTS, post. For an example of a case where, applying the above tests, there was held to be "real and cogent evidence of a pressing need" for disclosure (to identified officers of a housing association of findings of serious sexual abuse made against one of its tenants in care proceedings), see: *Re C (sexual abuse: disclosure to landlords)* [2002] EWHC 234 (Fam), [2002] 2 FLR 375, [2002] 2 FCR 385.

32. *Re M (disclosure)* [1998] 1 FLR 734.

33. *Re X (disclosure of information)* [2001] 2 FLR 440, FD.

34. *Re A Solicitor (disclosure of confidential records)* [1997] 2 FCR 316, [1997] 1 FLR 101.

35. *Re R (children: disclosure)* [2003] EWCA Civ 19, [2003] 1 FCR 193.

6–35 Documentary evidence. In any family proceedings which are commenced by application, a party shall file with the justices' chief executive and serve on other parties, as well as on any children and family reporter or welfare officer or children's guardian whose appointment has been notified to him—

    (*a*)   written statements of the substance of the oral evidence which the party intends to adduce at a hearing of, or a directions appointment in, those proceedings, which shall—

        (i)   be dated,

        (ii)   be signed by the person making the statement,

        (iii)   contain a declaration that the maker of the statement believes it to be true and understands that it may be placed before the court, and

    (*b*)   copies of any documents, including experts' reports, upon which the party intends to rely, at a hearing of, or a directions appointment in, those proceedings[1].

Service of such written statement or copy document shall be undertaken at or by such time as the justices' clerk or the court directs, or in the absence of a direction, before the hearing or appointment[1].

Where a party has failed to comply with the above requirements he may not without leave of the justices' clerk, in the case of a directions appointment, or the court, adduce evidence or seek to rely on a document at a hearing or directions appointment[2]. A party may, subject to any direction of the justices' clerk or the court about the timing of statements, file with the justices' chief executive and serve on the parties a statement which is supplementary to a statement which has already been served[3].

A document which has been filed with the justices' chief executive or served may not be amended without leave of the justices' clerk or the court and a request for leave must be made in writing, unless the justices' clerk or the court directs otherwise[4]. A person amending a document shall file it with the justices' chief executive and serve it on those persons on whom it was served prior to amendment, and the amendment shall be identified[5].

In *public law proceedings* particular requirements have been specified[6].

Until the maker of the written statement which has been filed attests to or affirms the truth of what is set out in the statement, the statement is not oral evidence at all, and for the purposes of its evidential value it is merely a hybrid class of documentary evidence which is capable of being admitted in the discretion of the court[6,7].

There is a presumption that every witness statement will stand as the evidence in chief of the witness concerned. The evidence should be sufficiently detailed but not prolix and (except for the evidence of professional witnesses) confined to matters of fact not opinion. The source of any hearsay evidence must be declared or good reason given for not doing so[8].

In proceedings under the Children Act 1989, any written statement which is filed shall also show in the top right-hand corner of the first page—

    (*a*)   the initials and surname of the person making the statement,

    (*b*)   the number of the statement in relation to the maker,

    (*c*)   the date on which the statement was made, and

    (*d*)   the party on whose behalf it is filed[9].

In children's cases, when the court gives leave to the parties to obtain experts' reports, it has power to override legal professional privilege and direct disclosure of such reports. This will ensure that relevant information is made available to the court in order that it can arrive at a conclusion which is in the paramount interests of the child[10].

If an adjournment is brought about by the late service of important statements or documents, the court should consider applying the sanction of costs against the party responsible. Generally, in such cases the exclusion of the evidence would not be realistic[11].

---

1. Family Proceedings Courts (Children Act 1989) Rules 1991, r 17(1); Family Proceedings Courts (Matrimonial Proceedings etc) Rules 1991, r 9(1), this PART, post.

2. Family Proceedings Courts (Children Act 1989) Rules 1991, r 17(3); Family Proceedings Courts (Matrimonial Proceedings etc) Rules 1991, r 9(3), this PART, post.

3. Family Proceedings Courts (Children Act 1989) Rules 1991, r 17(2); Family Proceedings Courts (Matrimonial Proceedings etc) Rules 1991, r 9(2), this PART, post.

4. Family Proceedings Courts (Children Act 1989) Rules 1991, r 19(1); Family Proceedings Courts (Matrimonial Proceedings etc) Rules 1991, r 10(1), this PART, post.
5. Family Proceedings Courts (Children Act 1989) Rules 1991, r 19(3); Family Proceedings Courts (Matrimonial Proceedings etc) Rules 1991, r 10(3), this PART, post.
6. See the *Protocol for Judicial Case Management in Public Law Children Act Cases* at para 4–5103, post.
7. *S v Merton London Borough* [1994] 1 FCR 186.
8. See *Practice Note (civil litigation: case management)*, this PART, post.
9. Family Proceedings Courts (Children Act 1989) Rules 1991, r 17(1)(*a*)(iv), this PART, post.
10. *Oxfordshire County Council v M* [1994] 2 All ER 269, [1994] 1 FCR 753, [1994] 1 FLR 175.
11. *R v Nottinghamshire County Council* [1993] 1 FCR 576.

6–35A   Expert evidence.   No person may, without the leave of the family proceedings court, cause a child to be medically or psychiatrically examined, or otherwise assessed, for the purpose of the preparation of expert evidence for use in the proceedings[1]. Where the leave of the court is not given, no evidence arising out of such an examination or assessment may be adduced without the leave of the court[2]. An application for leave must, unless the court otherwise directs, be served on all the parties to the proceedings and on the children's guardian[3].

Detailed provision for the use of experts in family proceedings is made by *Code of Practice for Expert Witnesses in Family Proceedings* which includes in particular: the duties of experts; procedural steps for instructing experts; obtaining the leave of the court; letters of instruction; content of the expert's report; arrangements for discussions between experts instructed by the parties; professionals' meetings between the local authority and professionals and arrangements for the expert to attend court[4].

Where there is a genuine disagreement on a scientific or medical issue, or where it is necessary for a party to advance a particular hypothesis to explain a given set of factors, the expert advancing such a hypothesis owes a very heavy duty to explain to the court that what he is advancing is a hypothesis, whether it is controversial, and to place before the court all the material which is contradicted by the hypothesis. Furthermore, the expert must make all his material available to the other experts in the case[5]. Where the evidence of an expert may become pivotal, such as in a case of non-accidental injuries, parents may be entitled to a second opinion[6].

Cases concerning children often involve expert medical and psychiatric evidence which may relate to the presence and interpretation of mental, behavioural and emotional signs which may include a conclusion as to the veracity of the child. Section 3 of the Civil Evidence Act 1972 provides that the opinion of a witness in civil proceedings or any relevant matter on which he is qualified to give expert evidence is admissible in evidence. 'Relevant matter' includes an issue in the proceedings. Therefore expert evidence as to the accuracy or truthfulness of a person's testimony may be received in evidence even though it may relate to the ultimate issue in the case. However, the opinion of the expert must be on a matter on which he is qualified to give expert evidence and often such evidence would be inadmissible because he had no expertise as to the final question such as whether one witness' evidence was to be preferred to that of another. The modern view is to regulate the reception of such evidence by way of weight rather than admissibility[7].

Courts should be cautious in receiving supportive testimony from adult psychiatrists who are called on behalf of a parent who is a vulnerable patient, especially if the psychiatrist is not an expert in child care or child placement[8]. See also any future diagnosis of "Temporary Brittle Bone Disease" by a Dr Patterson should be given rigorous scrutiny by a High Court judge before he was given leave to report[9].

Where there has been a jointly instructed expert report, apportionment of the costs should be resolved by agreement in a collaborative way; ultimately any order will be a matter for the discretion of the court having regard to such considerations as to whether the information ought to have formed part of the local authority's core assessment and preparation or whether the information gathering was a putting together of evidence for the forensic process[10].

The following approach for experts is suggested:

(i)   identify possible causes of the relevant death, injuries or harm setting out in respect of each the reasons why it might be a cause and thus why it should be considered;

(ii) state their views as to the likelihood of each possibility being the cause of the relevant death, injuries or harm and the reasons why they include or reject it as a reasonable (as opposed to a fanciful or merely theoretical) possible cause;

(iii) compare the likelihood of the cause (or causes) identified as reasonable possibilities being the actual cause of the relevant death, injuries or harm;

(iv) state whether they consider that a cause (or causes) is (are) the most likely cause (or causes) of the relevant death, injuries or harm and their reasons for that view; and

(v)   to state whether they consider that a cause (or causes) is (are) more likely than not to be the cause (or causes) of the relevant death, injuries or harm and their reasons for that view[11].

1. Family Proceedings Courts (Children Act 1989) Rules 1991, r 18(1), this PART, post.
2. Family Proceedings Courts (Children Act 1989) Rules 1991, r 18(3), this PART, post.
3. Family Proceedings Courts (Children Act 1989) Rules 1991, r 18(2), this PART, post.
4. See the *Protocol for Judicial Case Management in Public Law Children Act Cases* Appendix C at para 6–5103, post.
5. *Re AB (child abuse: expert witnesses)* [1995] 1 FCR 280, [1995] 1 FLR 181.
6. *W v Oldham Metropolitan Borough Council* [2005] TLR 510, CA.
7. *Re M and R (minors) (sexual abuse: expert evidence)* [1996] 4 All ER 239, [1996] 2 FCR 617, [1996] 2 FLR 195, CA.
8. See *Re D (simultaneous applications for care and freeing orders)* [1999] 3 FCR 65, [1999] 2 FLR 49, CA.
9. *Re X (non accidental injury: expert evidence)* [2001] 2 FLR 90, FD.

10. See the guidance given by Bodey J in *Calderdale Metropolitan Council v S* [2004] EWHC 2529 (Fam), [2005] 1 FLR 236.

11. *A County Council v K, D and L* [2005] EWHC 144 (Fam), [2005] 1 FLR 851 per Charles J at para [89].

6–36   Attendance at directions appointment and at hearing.   A party shall attend a directions appointment of which he has been given notice unless the justices' clerk or the court otherwise directs[1]. Where at the time and place appointed for a hearing or directions appointment the applicant appears but one or more of the respondents do not, the justices' clerk or the court may proceed with the hearing or the appointment[2]. However, the court shall not begin to hear an application in the absence of a respondent unless—

(a)   it is proved to the satisfaction of the court that he received reasonable notice of the date of the hearing; or

(b)   the court is satisfied that the circumstances of the case justify proceeding with the hearing[3].

Where the respondent appears, but the applicant does not, the court may refuse the application or, if sufficient evidence has previously been received, proceed in the absence of the applicant[4]. Where neither the applicant nor the respondent appears, the court may refuse the application[5].

Relevant proceedings[6] under the Children Act 1989 shall take place in the absence of any party including the child if—

(a)   the court considers it in the interests of the child, having regard to the matters to be discussed or the evidence likely to be given, and

(b)   the party is represented by a children's guardian or solicitor;

provided when considering the interest of the child under (a) above, the court must give the children's guardian, solicitor for the child and, if he is of sufficient understanding, the child, an opportunity to make representations[7].

In *matrimonial proceedings* it is undesirable for the court to proceed to hear the application in the absence of one of the parties who has indicated that he has a case on which he wishes to be heard[8]. Where the respondent does not appear but sends written details of his finances, which the applicant cannot agree, the court should adjourn so that the respondent can be required to attend and deal with those matters[9]. Where through inadvertence a respondent fails to appear and an order is made in his absence, and he later wishes to be heard on quantum of maintenance alone he should apply for a variation of the order rather than appeal to the Family Division[10].

Where an application is made for an occupation order or a non-molestation order under Part IV of the Family Law Act 1996, the court may in any case where it considers it is just and convenient to do so, make an order even though the respondent has not been given such notice of the proceedings as would otherwise be required by the Rules[11].

---

1. Family Proceedings Courts (Children Act 1989) Rules 1991, r 16(1); Family Proceedings Courts (Matrimonial Proceedings etc) Rules 1991, r 8(1), this PART, post.
2. Family Proceedings Courts (Children Act 1989) Rules 1991, r 16(3), this PART, post.
3. Family Proceedings Courts (Children Act 1989) Rules 1991, r 16(4); Family Proceedings Courts (Matrimonial Proceedings etc) Rules 1991, r 8(2), this PART, post.
4. Family Proceedings Courts (Children Act 1989) Rules 1991, r 16(5); Family Proceedings Courts (Matrimonial Proceedings etc), r 8(3), this PART, post.
5. Family Proceedings Courts (Children Act 1989) Rules 1991, r 16(6); Family Proceedings Courts (Matrimonial Proceedings etc), r 8(4), this PART, post.
6. "Relevant proceedings" has the meaning assigned to it by Children Act 1989, s 93(3), post (Family Proceedings Courts (Children Act 1989) Rules 1991, r 1(2), this PART, post).
7. Family Proceedings Courts (Children Act 1989) Rules 1991, r 16(2), this PART, post.
8. See *Smith v Smith* [1957] 2 All ER 397; *Kaye v Kaye* [1964] 1 All ER 620; *Walker v Walker* [1967] 1 All ER 412.
9. *Whittingstall v Whittingstall* [1989] FCR 759, [1990] 2 FLR 368.
10. *Kaye v Kaye* [1964] 1 All ER 620.
11. Family Law Act 1996, s 45, this PART, post; see also the Family Proceedings Courts (Matrimonial Proceedings etc) Rules 1991, r 3A(4) this PART, post.

6–36A   Protocol for Judicial Case Management in Public Law Children Act Cases.   Detailed provision is made for the procedure to be followed in *public law proceedings* by the *Protocol for Judicial Case Management in Public Law Children Act Cases*[1] which envisages the following six steps:

Step 1   *The Application* (by Day 3)
Step 2   *The First Hearing in the Family Proceedings Court* (by Day 6)
Step 3   *The Allocation Hearing and Directions* (by Day 11)
Step 4   *The Case Management Conference* (between days 15 and 60)
Step 5   *The Pre-hearing Review* (by week 37)
Step 6   *The Final Hearing* (by week 40)

---

1. Reproduced at para **6–5103**, post. See *Route Map* on following page.

6–37   Conduct of proceedings.   Before the hearing, the justice or justices who will be dealing with the case shall read any documents which have been filed with the justices' chief executive in respect of the hearing[1].

In *children's proceedings*, subject to any directions which may have been given by the justices' clerk or the court, the parties and the children's guardian shall adduce their evidence in the following order—

(a)   the applicant,

(b)   any party with parental responsibility for the child,

(c)   other respondents,

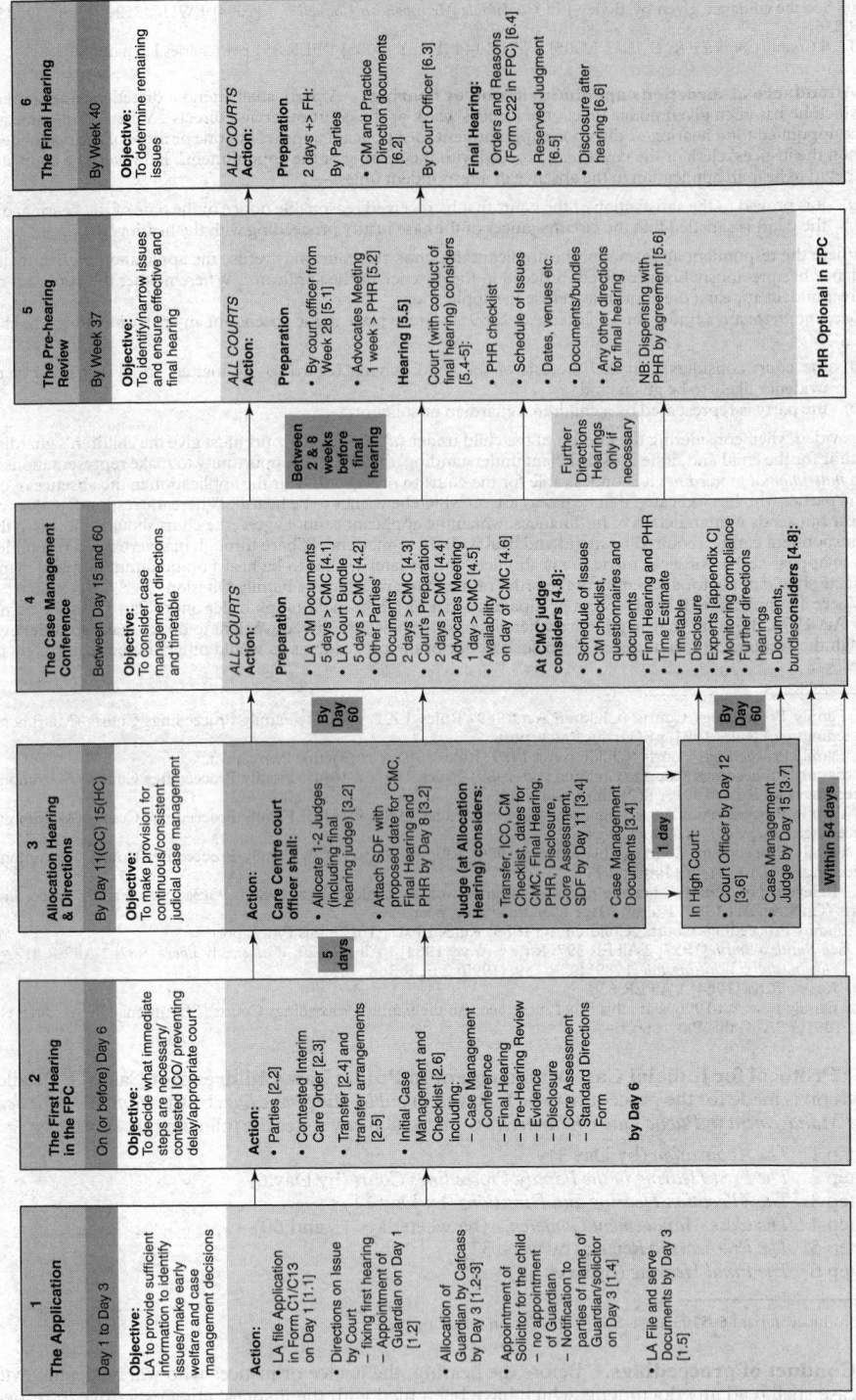

1 — The Application

Day 1 to Day 3

Objective:
LA to provide sufficient information to identify issues/make early welfare and case management decisions

Action:
- LA file Application in Form C1/C13 on Day 1 [1.1]
- Directions on Issue by Court
  – fixing first hearing
  – Appointment of Guardian on Day 1 [1.2]
- Allocation of Guardian by Cafcass by Day 3 [1.2-3]
- Appointment of Solicitor for the child
  – no appointment of Guardian
  – Notification to parties of name of Guardian/solicitor on Day 3 [1.4]
- LA File and serve Documents by Day 3 [1.5]

2 — The First Hearing in the FPC

On (or before) Day 6

Objective:
To decide what immediate steps are necessary/ contested ICO/ preventing delay/appropriate court

Action:
- Parties [2.2]
- Contested Interim Care Order [2.3]
- Transfer [2.4] and transfer arrangements [2.5]
- Initial Case Management and Checklist [2.6] including:
  – Case Management Conference
  – Final Hearing
  – Pre-Hearing Review
  – Evidence
  – Disclosure
  – Core Assessment
  – Standard Directions Form

by Day 6

3 — Allocation Hearing & Directions

By Day 11(CC) 15(HC)

Objective:
To make provision for continuous/consistent judicial case management

Action:
Care Centre court officer shall:
- Allocate 1-2 Judges (including final hearing judge) [3.2]
- Attach SDF with proposed date for CMC, Final Hearing and PHR by Day 8 [3.2]

Judge (at Allocation Hearing) considers:
- Transfer, ICO, CM Checklist, dates for CMC, Final Hearing, PHR, Disclosure, Core Assessment, SDF by Day 11 [3.4]
- Case Management Documents [3.4]

In High Court:
- Court Officer by Day 12 [3.6]
- Case Management Judge by Day 15 [3.7]

1 day

Within 54 days

5 days

4 — The Case Management Conference

Between Day 15 and 60

Objective:
To consider case management directions and timetable

ALL COURTS
Action:
Preparation
- LA CM Documents 5 days > CMC [4.1]
- LA Court Bundle 5 days > CMC [4.2]
- Other Parties' Documents 2 days > CMC [4.3]
- Court's Preparation 2 days > CMC [4.4]
- Advocates Meeting 1 day > CMC [4.5]
- Availability on day of CMC [4.6]

At CMC Judge considers [4.8]:
- Schedule of issues
- CM checklist, questionnaires and documents
- Final Hearing and PHR
- Time Estimate
- Timetable
- Disclosure
- Experts [appendix C]
- Monitoring compliance
- Further directions hearings
- Documents, bundlesonsiders [4.8]:

By Day 60

Between 2 & 8 weeks before final hearing

Further Directions Hearings only if necessary

5 — The Pre-hearing Review

By Week 37

Objective:
To identify/narrow issues and ensure effective and final hearing

ALL COURTS
Action:
Preparation
- By court officer from Week 28 [5.1]
- Advocates Meeting 1 week > PHR [5.2]

Hearing [5.5]
Court (with conduct of final hearing) considers [5.4-5]:
- PHR checklist
- Schedule of Issues
- Dates, venues etc.
- Documents/bundles
- Any other directions for final hearing

NB: Dispensing with PHR by agreement [5.6]

PHR Optional in FPC

6 — The Final Hearing

By Week 40

Objective:
To determine remaining issues

ALL COURTS
Action:
Preparation
2 days +> FH:
By Parties
- CM and Practice Direction documents [6.2]

By Court Officer [6.3]

Final Hearing:
- Orders and Reasons (Form C22 in FPC) [6.4]
- Reserved Judgment [6.5]
- Disclosure after hearing [6.6]

    (*d*) the children's guardian,
    (*e*) the child if he is a party to the proceedings and there is no children's guardian[2].

In *matrimonial proceedings*, subject to any directions which may have been given by the justices' clerk or the court, the parties shall adduce their evidence in the following order—

    (*a*) the applicant,
    (*b*) the respondent other than the child, and
    (*c*) the child if he is a respondent[3].

Where in any family proceedings, or in any proceedings for the enforcement or variation of an order made in family proceedings, it appears to a magistrates' court that any party to the proceedings who is not legally represented is unable effectively to examine or cross-examine a witness, the court must ascertain from that party what are the matters about which the witness may be able to depose or on which the witness ought to be cross-examined, as the case may be, and must put, or cause to be put, to the witness such questions in the interests of that party as may appear to the court to be proper[4].

Proceedings in public law cases involving children are intended to be non-adversarial. Accordingly, if the justices are in the process of making or appear likely to make a decision which is procedurally plainly wrong, it is the duty of all advocates—notably, of those acting for the children's guardian and the local authority—to advise the justices that they are about to make a fundamental error[5].

A family court must be prepared to assert greater control over preparation for and conduct of proceedings and may exercise its discretion to limit (*a*) discovery; (*b*) the length of opening and closing oral submissions; (*c*) the time allowed for the examination and cross-examination of witnesses; (*d*) the issues on which it wishes to be addressed; (*e*) reading aloud from documents and authorities.

The parties and their legal advisers must use their best endeavours: (*a*) to confine issues and the evidence called to what is reasonably considered to be essential for the proper presentation of their case; (*b*) to reduce or eliminate issues for expert evidence; (*c*) in advance of the hearing to agree which are the issues or the main issues.

Justices should, where possible, be given the papers in advance so they may read them at their leisure, rather than under the pressure of the knowledge that the parties, their witnesses and the advocates in the case are waiting outside[6]. The requirement to file written statements before the hearing is mandatory, and the justices are under a duty to read the written evidence[7].

The court should afford assistance in the examination of a witness in a case where the respondent writes a letter to the court setting out his answers to the application[8]. In split hearings the danger must be avoided of the impression that the fact-finding stage is akin to a criminal trial[9]. In care proceedings a parent is a competent and compellable witness[9] who is privileged against incrimination[10]. In cases concerning children there is no room for 'no comment' interviews found in criminal cases and generally, where a parent declines to answer questions or give evidence in care proceedings the court ought usually to draw the inference that any allegations against the parent are true[11].

The fact that a witness in family proceedings is found to have committed perjury is no reason for the justices discontinuing the hearing and ordering a re-hearing before a different bench[12]. Justices, who have read the written evidence, are not entitled, save in the most hopeless of cases, to dismiss the application out of hand without first hearing all the oral evidence of the parties[13].

The applicant in a family case is entitled to a fair hearing but this must be consistent with other considerations. First and foremost is the welfare of any children and also factors such as: pressure on court time; expense of litigation; finite resources and that a line has to be drawn somewhere between practicality and perfection in the forensic process[14].

In Children Act proceedings the court is there in a quasi-inquisitorial role; child protection is one of its principal responsibilities and serious allegations against a party must either be withdrawn or adjudicated upon[15].

The extent of the evidence permitted to be adduced at the hearing will be in the discretion of the court having regard to the issues involved and the evidence available[16].

The principles for exercising the court's discretion were set out by Butler-Sloss LJ in *Re B (minors) (Contact)*[17]:

"There is a spectrum of procedure for family cases from the ex parte application on minimal evidence to the full and detailed investigations on oral evidence which may be prolonged. Where on that spectrum a judge decides a particular application should be placed is a matter for his discretion. Applications for residence orders or for committal to the care of a local authority or revocation of a care order are likely to be decided on full oral evidence, but not invariably. Such is not the case on contact applications which may be and are heard sometimes with and sometimes without oral evidence or with a limited amount of oral evidence."

Considerations which should weigh with the court are:

  (1) whether there is sufficient evidence on which to make the relevant decision;
  (2) whether the proposed evidence (which should be available at least in outline) which the applicant for a full trial wishes to adduce is likely to affect the outcome of the proceedings;
  (3) whether the opportunity to cross examine witnesses for the local authority, in particular the expert witnesses, is likely to affect the outcome of the proceedings;
  (4) the welfare of the child and the effect of further litigation–whether the delay in itself will be so detrimental to the child's well-being that exceptionally there should not be a full hearing. This may be because of the urgent need to place the child, or the emotional stress suffered by the child;
  (5) the prospects of success of the applicant for a full trial;
  (6) does the justice of the case require a full investigation with oral evidence?

A court is entitled to take an independent line, particularly so when sitting in the family jurisdiction and when considering issues of child protection and child welfare; but as a generalisation it is for the court to support and encourage any communications between the parties, particularly when represented by experienced advocates, that might lead to a consent order. There is a particular value in orders achieved by consent rather than orders imposed by the court[18].

The concept of "no case to answer" has no place in family proceedings and in particular proceedings under the Children Act 1989[12].

Accordingly magistrates were right in what was clearly a hopeless case to stop an application to discharge care proceedings after the applicant's mother had given oral evidence for more than a day where they were of the view that she had no reasonable prospects of success. However such a step may only be adopted in exceptional circumstances[14].

The court has a discretion to permit a witness to give evidence anonymously, but the need for protection must be balanced against unfairness or prejudice; it is accepted in the criminal justice system that even where counterbalancing procedures can compensate any handicap to a defendant a conviction shall not be based on anonymous statements and the same principle applies in public law family proceedings where the consequences to the parents of accepting anonymous evidence are as dire as a conviction[19].

In some contested cases where stark factual issues need to be determined, such as an allegation of physical or sexual abuse, and the early resolution of those issues will enable the substantive hearing to proceed more speedily and to focus on the child's welfare with greater clarity, it may be appropriate to conduct the hearing in two stages: to determine the factual issues and then determine the outcome after an assessment on those findings[20]. Where a factual issue is critical to the establishment of the threshold criteria and a split hearing is ordered, the parties and the court should concentrate their energies on assembling evidence relevant to that issue to the exclusion of other evidence, such as an assessment of the parents, which will only be relevant if and when the threshold criteria are established[21]. Where there are subsequent admissions which contradict the earlier finding of fact, the proper approach, rather than reopening issues of fact or excluding subsequent developments from consideration, is to make such adjustments as are necessary after they have been tested in cross-examination and re-examination[22].

The Children (Admissibility of Hearsay Evidence) Order[21] is designed to provide a way for the evidence of children to be placed before the court without the requirement for them to come to court[23]. Accordingly a local authority in care proceedings may adduce in evidence the written and videotaped record of a child's interview and decline to call him to give oral evidence. The only means by which another party can procure the attendance of the child to give oral evidence is to issue a witness summons. In considering such an application the principle that the welfare of the child is the paramount consideration in section 1(1) of the Children Act 1989 does not apply but the court will not require the attendance of a witness in circumstances that would be oppressive[24]. The court will be very cautious in requiring the attendance of a child witness in that the philosophy of the Children Act would be thwarted by the ability of an alleged abuser himself being able to require the attendance of the child at court[25]. Even where a witness summons has been issued, the person at whose instigation it has been issued would only be able to examine the witness in chief, although where fairness requires that an advocate should be able to cross-examine, the court is able to call the witness itself[26]. While a good audio or video tape will sometimes be accepted by the court in lieu of a child giving evidence, courts will normally expect *adults* to give evidence, and at least give a statement; only exceptionally will an adult be in such need of protection as to make a statement an acceptable alternative to giving evidence, and no court in the land should accept a social worker's account of an interview without a careful transcript of how the interview took place[27].

---

1. Family Proceedings Courts (Children Act 1989) Rules 1991, r 21(1); Family Proceedings Courts (Matrimonial Proceedings etc) Rules 1991, r 12(1), this PART, post.
2. Family Proceedings Courts (Children Act 1989) Rules 1991, r 21(3), this PART, post.
3. Family Proceedings Courts (Matrimonial Proceedings etc) Rules 1991, r 12(3), this PART, post.
4. Magistrates' Courts Act 1980, s 73, in PART I: MAGISTRATES' COURTS, PROCEDURE, ante.
5. See *Re F (a minor) (care order: procedure)* [1994] 1 FCR 729, [1994] 1 FLR 240.
6. *M v C (children orders: reasons)* [1993] 1 FCR 264.
7. *S v Merton London Borough* [1994] 1 FCR 186.
8. *Marjoram v Marjoram* [1955] 2 All ER 1, 119 JP 291.
9. *Re Y (children) (care proceedings: split hearing)* [2003] EWCA Civ 669, [2003] 3 FCR 240 [2003] 2 FLR 273 also reported at a later stage of the proceedings as *Re Y (evidence of abuse: use of photographs)* [2003] EWHC 3090 (Fam), [2004] 1 FLR 855.
10. Children Act 1989, s 98, in this PART, post.
11. *In re O (children: care proceedings evidence)* [2003] EWHC 2011 (Fam), [2004] 1 FLR 161.
12. *R v Plymouth Justices, ex p W* [1994] 1 FCR 80.
13. *Re M (a minor) (contact)* [1994] 2 FCR 968, [1995] 1 FLR 1029.
14. *Re S and P (discharge of care order)* [1995] 2 FLR 782, sub nom *P v Bradford Metropolitan Borough Council* [1996] 2 FCR 227.
15. *Re H (a child: residence)* [2002] 3 FCR 277, CA (allegations of sexual and physical abuse).
16. *Re B (minors) (contact)* [1994] 2 FCR 812, [1994] 2 FLR 1.
17. [1994] 2 FCR 812, [1994] 2 FLR 1.
18. *Re B (children) (residence: interim care order)* [2002] EWCA Civ 1225, [2002] 3 FCR 562 (where it was held that the judge had wrongly refused to make the interim care order to which all parties had agreed, and had further erred, inter alia, in failing, without giving reasons, to follow expert opinion and in declining, twice, to permit the guardian to give evidence).
19. *Re W (care proceedings: anonymity)* [2003] 1 FLR 329, CA.
20. *In re S (minor) (care order: split hearing)* [1996] 2 FLR 773.
21. *Re CB and JB (minors) (care proceedings: case conduct)* [1998] 2 FCR 313, [1998] 2 FLR 211.
22. *Re M (children: determination of responsibility for injuries)* [2002] EWCA Civ 499, [2002] 2 FCR 377, [2003] 1 FLR 461.
23. In this PART, post.
24. *C v C (minors) (contempt proceedings)* [1993] 4 All ER 690, [1993] 1 FLR 220, CA.
25. *Re P (witness summons)* [1997] 3 FCR 322, [1997] 2 FLR 447, CA.
26. *R v B County Council, ex p P* [1991] 2 All ER 65, [1991] 1 WLR 221, [1991] 1 FLR 470, CA.
27. *Re D (sexual abuse allegations: evidence of adult victim)* [2002] 1 FLR 723.

6–39 Role of the justices' clerk. In family proceedings the justices' clerk or the court shall keep a note of the substance of the oral evidence given at a hearing or at a directions appointment[1].

The justices' clerk may grant an authorisation whereby anything authorised to be done by, to or before a justices' clerk under the Rules may be done instead by, to or before a person employed as a clerk in court where that person is appointed by the magistrates' courts committee to assist him and where that person has been specifically authorised by the justices' clerk for that purpose[2].

It is quite wrong for the justices' clerk to refer the justices to an authority without giving the advocates appearing before the court the opportunity of dealing with and commenting on that authority[3].

---

1. Family Proceedings Courts (Children Act 1989) Rules 1991, r 20; Family Proceedings Courts (Matrimonial Proceedings etc) Rules 1991, r 11, this PART, post.
2. Family Proceedings Courts (Children Act 1989) Rules 1991, r 32; Family Proceedings Courts (Matrimonial Proceedings etc), r 15, this PART, post.
3. *Re U (T) (a minor) (care order contact)* [1993] 2 FCR 565.

6–40   Reasons for decision.   After the final hearing of family proceedings, the court must make its decision as soon as is practicable[1]. Before the court makes an order or refuses an application, the justices' clerk must record in writing the names of the justices constituting the court by which the decision is made, and in consultation with the justices, the reasons for the court's decision and any findings of fact[2]. When making an order or when refusing an application, the court, or one of the justices constituting the court by which the decision is made, shall state any findings of fact and the reasons for the court's decision[3]. It is fundamental that the justices should formulate their reasons *before* making their order, and unless this can clearly be seen to have been done the High Court will regard the decision as unsafe and one which cannot be relied upon[4].

After the court announces its decision, the justices' clerk must as soon as practicable (*a*) make a record of any order made in the appropriate form, or where no form is prescribed, in writing, and (*b*) the justices' chief executive must serve, in accordance with the Rules, a copy of any order made on the parties to the proceedings[5]. However, in the case of proceedings under Part IV of the Family Law Act 1996, service of the order will normally be the responsibility of the applicant[6].

The justices' clerk must supply a copy of the record of the reasons for a decision made to any person on request, if he is satisfied that it is required in connection with an appeal or possible appeal[7].

The requirement to record in writing the reasons for a decision applies on the hearing of an application for an interim order as it does on the hearing of an application for a substantive order[8]; when hearing a request for leave[9]; or for withdrawal of an application[10]; on an application for an education supervision order under s 36 of the Children Act 1989[11], on the refusal of an application for an adjournment[12], a decision on an interim application as to disclosure of a medical report[13], or on the imposition of a leave restriction under s 91(14) of the Children Act 1989[14]. Although an application under s 4 of the Maintenance Orders Act 1958 for the variation of a registered maintenance order is not automatically family proceedings within the meaning of s 65(1) of the Magistrates' Courts Act 1980, and thereby there is no statutory requirement to record reasons in writing before announcing the decision, as a matter of good practice, reasons in such cases should be recorded at the time of the decision[15]. The court should give succinct reasons for making or refusing to make directions on a contentious matter after hearing full argument[16].

It is not permissible for the justices to announce their decision immediately after the hearing and then defer stating their reasons and findings of fact to a later date, even though the parties may purport to agree to such a course being followed[17].

The reasons must record the facts which the justices judged to be significant in the making of their decision and also the salient considerations which have led them to their conclusion[18]. Justices should also take care to state their assessment of the credibility and reliability at least of the most important witnesses[19]. It is precisely because justices are not lawyers that they are able and under a duty to set out in plain layman's language their assessment of the parties and what they have found the facts to be[20]. The consequences of a failure fully to articulate findings of fact and assessment of witnesses will frequently be that an appeal against an order made will succeed[20]. Nevertheless, the concern of the High Court is with substance and not semantics. Justices' reasons are to be read as a whole and in a common sense way. Justices are not required to spell out a detailed analysis of the documents they have read, the evidence they have heard and submissions that have been made. Their duty is to give reasons for the decision reached, not to give reasons for every individual conclusion arrived at in the course of the decision. Although the findings of fact and the reasons stated orally in court must be the same as those previously recorded in writing, there is no legal obligation on justices to read out verbatim the whole of the document in which the clerk has previously recorded in writing their reasons and findings of fact including those parts of the document which record their reasons and findings of fact provided there is no material or significant (as opposed to merely verbal) departure or deviation from the corresponding parts of the written document. Any litigant who seeks to demonstrate that justices in the course of their oral statement have departed or deviated in some material or significant way from their previously recorded written reasons bears a heavy evidential burden[21].

It is not acceptable for a court to make a bland statement that it has "considered all aspects of the welfare check-list" without further particularisation unless, elsewhere in the course of its judgment or reasons it has, in considering the evidence or in making findings, dealt in detail with the relevant aspects of the checklist[22].

The Divisional Court has given guidance as to how the requirement to record reasons for a decision in *children's cases* should be complied with[23]:

1.   The statutory criteria in s 1 of the Children Act 1989 and in the particular section under which the application is being made (eg s 25 in a secure accommodation application) give a checklist round which the findings of fact and reasons can be built.
2.   The record of reasons should comprise the following headings—

(*a*)   facts not in dispute;
(*b*)   disputed facts;
(*c*)   facts found proved;

(d) the extent to which the parties and witnesses were believed or disbelieved and the information on which the court relied in reaching its decision;
(e) authorities cited by the parties;
(f) whether a welfare report has been considered;
(g) the judgment or findings of fact in relation to each of the heads under the appropriate "checklist" section (eg s 1(3), s 25(1)).

Moreover, if the recommendations of the children's guardian[24] or children and family reporter or welfare officer[25] are not followed, it is important for the justices to state their reasons for following a different course. Justices' reasons must clearly address the important issue of race where this is a feature of the case[26]. An absence of findings in the reasons on issues which are agreed by the parties is unhelpful and contrary to current practice in Children Act cases. In such circumstances, at the very minimum, the parties should be invited by the court to agree the bases of facts on which the court is invited to proceed and to acknowledge it either by a signature of the parties or their legal representatives[27].

On appeal to the High Court, the only findings of fact and the only reasons that may be relied on to support the decision of the justices under appeal, are those announced by the justices at the time the decision is delivered[28]. It is not open to justices, therefore, to further reason their conclusion in response to the knowledge that there is to be an appeal; anything that supports the order of the court must be contained within the stated reasons[29]. However, where magistrates have given inadequate reasons, the court may fill in the gaps if there is sufficient evidence to do so[30].

1. Family Proceedings Courts (Children Act 1989) Rules 1991, r 21(4); Family Proceedings Courts (Matrimonial Proceedings etc) Rules 1991, r 12(4), this PART, post.
2. Family Proceedings Courts (Children Act 1989) Rules 1991, r 21(5); Family Proceedings Courts (Matrimonial Proceedings etc) Rules 1991, r 12(5), this PART, post. Moreover, under art 6(1) of the European Convention on Human Rights it is a requirement of a fair trial in both criminal and civil matters that a court should give reasons for its judgment. The extent of the duty to give reasons may, however, vary according to the nature of the decision. See para 1–34, ante.
3. Family Proceedings Courts (Children Act 1989) Rules 1991, r 21(6); Family Proceedings Courts (Matrimonial Proceedings etc) Rules 1991, r 12(6), this PART, post.
4. *Hertfordshire County Council v W* [1992] 2 FCR 885, [1993] 1 FLR 118; *Re W (child: contact)* [1993] 2 FCR 731.
5. Family Proceedings Courts (Children Act 1989) Rules 1991, r 21(7); Family Proceedings Courts (Matrimonial Proceedings etc) Rules 1991, r 12(7), this PART, post.
6. See the Family Proceedings Courts (Matrimonial Proceedings etc) Rules 1991, r 12A, this PART, post.
7. Family Proceedings Courts (Matrimonial Proceedings etc) Rules 1991, r 12(8); see also the Family Proceedings Rules 1991, r 4.22, this PART, post.
8. *Hertfordshire County Council v W* [1992] 2 FCR 885, [1993] 1 FLR 118, *D v R (Interim Contact Order)* [1995] 1 FCR 501, and *F v R (Contact: Justices' Reasons)* [1995] 1 FLR 227.
9. *Re M (Prohibited Steps Order: Application for Leave)* [1993] 1 FCR 78, [1993] 1 FLR 275 and *T v W (Contact: Reasons for Refusing Leave)* [1997] 1 FCR 118, [1996] 2 FLR 473.
10. *Re F (a minor) (Care Proceedings: Withdrawal)* [1993] 1 FCR 389.
11. *Essex County Council v B* [1993] 1 FCR 145.
12. *Essex County Council v F* [1993] 1 FLR 847.
13. *Re NW (a minor) (Medical Reports)* [1994] 1 FCR 121, [1993] 2 FLR 591.
14. *Re C (Contact : No order for contact)* [2000] 2 FLR 723, FD.
15. See *Hackshaw v Hackshaw* [1999] 3 FCR 451, [1999] 2 FLR 876.
16. *London Borough of Croydon v R* [1997] 2 FLR 675 sub nom *Re R (A Minor) (Child Care: Procedure)* [1997] 3 FCR 705, per Wall J.
17. *Re K (minors) (Justices Reasons)* [1994] 1 FCR 616.
18. *Hillingdon London Borough Council v H* [1993] 1 All ER 198, [1992] 2 FCR 299.
19. *Re H (a minor) (Care Proceedings)* [1992] 2 FCR 330.
20. *Re M (a minor) (Contact: Conditions)* [1994] 1 FCR 678, [1994] 1 FLR 272, (overruled on another aspect by *Re O (Contact: Imposition of Conditions)* [1995] 2 FLR 124, sub nom *Re O (a minor) (Contact: Indirect Contact)* [1996] 1 FCR 317, CA).
21. *Oxfordshire County Council v S* [2003] EWHC 2174 (Fam), [2004] 1 FLR 426.
22. See *D v R (Interim Contact Order)* [1995] 1 FCR 501.
23. *R (J) v Oxfordshire County Council* [1992] 3 All ER 660. See also *Re O (a minor)* [1992] 4 All ER 905, [1992] 1 WLR 912.
24. *S v Oxfordshire County Council* [1993] 1 FLR 452; *Leicestershire County Council v G* [1995] 1 FCR 205, [1994] 2 FLR 329.
25. *Re L (Residence: Justices' Reasons)* [1995] 3 FCR 684, [1995] 2 FLR 445. See also: *Re J (children)(residence: expert evidence)* [2001 2 FCR 43, CA; and *Re E (children)(residence order)* [2001] EWCA Civ 567, [2001] 2 FCR 662.
26. *Re M (Section 94 Appeals)* [1995] 1 FLR 546, [1995] 2 FCR 435.
27. *Re C (a minor) (Care Order: Appeal)* [1996] 1 FCR 332.
28. *Hillingdon London Borough Council v H* [1993] 1 All ER 198, [1992] 2 FCR 229.
29. *N v B (Children: Orders as to Residence)* [1993] 1 FCR 231 and see *Re W B (Residence Orders)* [1995] 2 FLR 1023.
30. *Oxfordshire County Council v R* [1999] 1 FCR 514, FD.

6–41   Costs. In any relevant proceedings[1] under the Children Act 1989 or in proceedings under the Domestic Proceedings and Magistrates' Courts Act 1978, the court may at any time during the proceedings in that court, make an order that a party pay the whole or any part of the costs of any other party. A party against whom the court is considering making a costs order must be given an opportunity to make representations as to why the order should not be made[2]. Failure to conduct cases economically will be visited by appropriate orders for costs, including wasted costs orders[3].

Where the proceedings are commenced by way of complaint, the power to award costs is governed by the Magistrates' Courts Act 1980, s 64[4].

As a general proposition, it is unusual to order costs in children cases, except where, for example, the conduct of a party has been reprehensible or the party's stance has been beyond the band of what is reasonable[5]. Therefore where the court found that a mother who had been obstructing contact had no reason for her concerns the court could make an order for costs where the mother's unreasonableness related to the conduct of litigation rather than her approach to the child. Although irrational behaviour is commonplace in contact disputes there is a limit to what allowance made for a parent who deliberately and unreasonably obstructs contact by the other parent where contact is in the interests of the child[6].

However, where an applicant successfully appeals to justices to be registered as a childminder under s 71 of the Children Act 1989, the proceedings are adversarial and the principle that costs should follow the event should apply[7].

It is the duty of solicitors making a claim for a substantial amount to provide the court with a detailed statement of the costs and to make that statement available to the other parties well in advance of the hearing[8]. Where there is ample material available to the justices to determine the amount of costs they may proceed to assess the costs to be ordered. Otherwise, they should adjourn the case pending assessment. Where the successful party is legally aided and where the costs are large, the court should consider adjourning the case pending assessment by the Legal Services Commission or, where s 64(2) of the Magistrates' Courts Act 1980 does *not* apply, making an order in the amount of the future assessment of the Legal Services Commission, rather than proceeding to specify the amount in advance of assessment[7].

---

1. "Relevant proceedings" has the meaning assigned to it by s 93(3) of the Children Act 1989, this PART, post (Family Proceedings Courts (Children Act 1989) Rules 1991, r 1(2), this PART, post).
2. Family Proceedings Courts (Children Act 1989) Rules 1991, r 22; Family Proceedings Courts (Matrimonial Proceedings etc) Rules 1991, r 13, this PART, post.
3. See *Practice Note (Civil Litigation: Case Management)*, this PART, post.
4. See PART I: MAGISTRATES' COURTS, PROCEDURE, ante.
5. *Havering London Borough Council v S* [1986] 1 FLR 489; *Gojkovic v Gojkovic (No 2)* [1992] 1 All ER 267, [1991] 3 WLR 621; *Re M (Child Case: Costs)* [1995] 1 FCR 649, [1995] 1 FLR 533; *K v K (Legal Aid: Costs)* [1995] 2 FCR 189, [1995] 1 FLR 259, CA; *Re R (A Minor) (Legal Aid: Costs)* [1997] 1 FCR 613, CA; *R v R (Costs: Child Case)* [1997] 2 FLR 95, CA (father unreasonable in relation to conduct of litigation about residence of a child); *Re G (Costs: Child case)* [1999] 2 FLR 250 (a finding that the father's case was hopeless did not justify a costs order being made against him).
6. *Re T (a child) (order for costs)* [2005] EWCA Civ 311, [2005] 1 FCR 624, [2005] 2 FCR 681.
7. *Sutton London Borough Council v Davis (No 2)* [1995] 1 All ER 65, [1994] 1 WLR 1317, [1994] 2 FLR 569.
8. *Hillingdon London Borough Council v H* [1993] 1 All ER 198, [1992] 2 FCR 299.

6–43 Appeals to the High Court in family proceedings. A right of appeal to the High Court exists where a magistrates' court makes or refuses to make, or to vary or revoke, an order other than an interim maintenance order under Part I of the Domestic Proceedings and Magistrates' Courts Act 1978[1]; where a magistrates' court makes or refuses to make any order under the Children Act 1989 or under the Adoption and Children Act 2002[2]; under Part IV of the Family Law Act 1996[3] or where it varies or refuses to vary a High Court or County Court maintenance order registered with it[4]; or where a magistrates' court deals with a person for disobedience to an order other than for payment of money[5].

For procedure in respect of appeals to the High Court see the Civil Procedure Rules 1998, Part 52[6].

---

1. Domestic Proceedings and Magistrates' Courts Act 1978, s 29, this PART, post.
2. Children Act 1989, s 94, this PART, post.
3. Family Law Act 1996, s 61, this PART, post.
4. Maintenance Orders Act 1958, s 4(7), this PART, post.
5. Magistrates' Courts Act 1980, s 63(3), Administration of Justice Act 1960, s 13; Supreme Court Act 1981, Sch 1, para 3(d) and see *B(B) v B(M)* [1969] P 103, [1969] 1 All ER 891, 133 JP 245.
6. In PART I: MAGISTRATES' COURTS, PROCEDURE, ante. See also Family Proceedings Rules 1991, rr 4.22 and 8.2, this PART, post.

Marriage

6–50 Nature of marriage. Where there is no personal incapacity attaching upon either party, marriage according to the law of the place of its celebration is good everywhere, and its validity does not depend upon whether under that law it could be dissolved subsequently more or less easily[1]. A "proxy" marriage may be valid when celebrated in a foreign country between a person domiciled in England and a person domiciled in that country, if it is valid in that country and is performed strictly in accordance with the laws of that country and contains nothing abhorrent to Christian ideas[2]. There is authority as to the validity of Jewish marriages[3] and the formality of an Akan customary marriage[4]. Matrimonial relief may be granted in respect of polygamous marriages: see the Matrimonial Causes Act 1973, s 47. As to the situation with regard to a Muslim second marriage reference should be made to a decision of the Court of Appeal[5].

The Matrimonial Causes Act 1973 contains provisions relating to void and voidable marriages. Section 11 provides that a marriage which takes place after 31st July 1971 shall be void on the following grounds only—

(a) that it is not a valid marriage under the provisions of the Marriage Acts 1949 to 1986 (that is to say where—

    (i) the parties are within the prohibited degrees of relationship;

    (ii) either party is under 16;

    (iii) the parties have intermarried in disregard of certain requirements as to the formation of marriage);

(b) that at the time of the marriage either party was already lawfully married[1];

(c) that the parties are not respectively male and female;

(*d*) in the case of a polygamous marriage entered into outside England and Wales, that either party was at the time of the marriage domiciled in England and Wales.

It is provided by s 11 that for the purposes of para (*d*) above a marriage is not polygamous if at its inception neither party has any spouse in addition to the other.

Section 12 of the 1973 Act states the grounds upon which a marriage is voidable, and s 16 provides that where a marriage has been annulled as voidable, the marriage shall be treated as if it existed up to the time of annulment.

For recognition of the validity of a divorce or legal separation granted outside England and Wales see the Recognition of Divorces and Legal Separations Act 1971[6].

1. *Nachimson v Nachimson* [1930] P 217, 94 JP 211; *Mehta (otherwise Kohn) v Mehta* [1945] 2 All ER 690.
2. *Apt v Apt* [1947] P 127, [1947] 1 All ER 620; affd [1948] P 38, [1947] 2 All ER 677, CA.
3. See *Spivack v Spivack* (1930) 94 JP 91.
4. *McCabe v McCabe* [1994] 1 FCR 257, [1994] 1 FLR 410.
5. See *Quoraishi v Quoraishi* [1985] FLR 780, CA.
6. The Muslim *khula* and *talaq* divorces were considered in *Quazi v Quazi* [1980] AC 744, [1979] 3 All ER 897 and *R v Secretary of State for the Home Department, ex p Fatima, ex p Bi* [1985] QB 190, [1984] 2 All ER 458, [1984] FLR 928, CA.

6–51 Proof of marriage. If the marriage is disputed, a marriage certificate or other evidence should be produced before the order is made. In civil cases, where there is evidence of a ceremony of marriage having been gone through, followed by cohabitation of the parties, everything necessary for the validity of the marriage will be presumed, in the absence of decisive evidence to the contrary, even though it may be necessary to presume a special licence[1].

In a suit for nullity on the ground that the marriage (after banns) was void because, at the time, the parties were not resident in the parish where the banns had been published, evidence of such non-residence cannot be given[2]. A marriage after the publication of banns in a false name fraudulently and to the knowledge of both parties is void under (what is now) s 25 of the Marriage Act 1949[3], if used with the intention of concealment of identity for the purpose of avoiding inquiries[4]; but not otherwise[5]. As to presuming death of a former spouse after many years' absence reference should be made to the relevant authorities[6]. The Matrimonial Causes Act 1973, s 19, empowers the Divorce Court to make a decree of presumption of death and dissolution of marriage, and in those proceedings the fact of continual absence for seven years or more, the petitioner having no reason to believe that the other party has been living within that period, shall be evidence of death until the contrary is proved and procedure as to decree nisi, decree absolute, and the intervention of the Queen's Proctor, applies as if it were a decree of divorce. The interpretation of a previous corresponding section was considered in *Thompson v Thompson* [1956][7].

Unless there is a presumption of death on proof of seven years' absence, the onus is on the wife to prove that at the date of her second marriage her former husband was dead[8]. The justices are entitled to look at all the facts at the date of the application and not that of the subsequent marriage[9]. Foreign law is a question of fact for the tribunal in England to determine. So where a magistrate in an application by a married woman for a separation found as a fact that there had been a marriage in Russia, and that absence of proof of its registration did not invalidate the marriage, the court refused to review the magistrate's decision[10].

By Orders in Council made under the Evidence (Foreign, Dominion and Colonial Documents) Act 1933 (amended by the Oaths and Evidence (Overseas Authorities and Countries) Act 1963, s 5), duly authenticated certificates of entries in public registers in Belgium, France and Australia may be admitted in evidence[11]; similar Orders in respect of other parts of the Commonwealth are listed in *Halsbury's Statutory Instruments*, Vol 7, Evidence, and the current Supplement thereto. As to proof of certificate of Jewish marriage, see *Prager v Prager and Goodison* (1913) 108 LT 734. It is not necessary to produce the written contract[12]. An "irregular" Scottish marriage afterwards duly registered pursuant to warrant of the sheriff-substitute is proved in an English court by production of a copy of the entry in the register, duly signed by the registrar, pursuant to s 2 of the Marriage (Scotland) Act 1856[13]. The register of a marriage contracted in a British Colony, according to the rites of the Church of England, is sufficient evidence of the marriage and its validity[14], and of marriage contracted in a part of China, where no building was registered for its solemnisation[15]; and the production of an entry in an ecclesiastical register is proof of such marriage without expert evidence of its validity according to local law[16]. A certified copy of the entry of the marriage in the marriage register-book is evidence of a marriage in Ireland before 1922[17]; a marriage in Eire after 1922 must be proved as a foreign marriage, unless it was celebrated according to the rites of the Church of England[18]. A decree of restitution of conjugal rights estop the parties[19], from subsequently denying the validity of the marriage[20], but not so as to override the law of the land; thus, there is no estoppel to avoid asserting that the marriage was bigamous[21]. As to a common law marriage in China which was not performed by an episcopally ordained priest, see *Wolfenden v Wolfenden* [1946][22].

1. *Morris v Davies* (1837) 5 Cl & Fin 163; *Piers v Piers* (1849) 2 HL Cas 331; *Re Shephard, George v Thyer* [1904] 1 Ch 456; *Carlin v Carlin* (1906) 70 JP 143; *Spivack v Spivack* (1930) 94 JP 91; *Re Taylor, Taylor v Taylor* [1961] 1 All ER 55.
2. *Bodman v Bodman (otherwise Perry)* (1913) 108 LT 383.
3. *Small v Small and Furber* (1923) 67 Sol Jo 277.
4. *Chipchase v Chipchase* [1942] P 37, [1941] 2 All ER 560, *Chipchase v Chipchase* [1939] P 391, [1939] 3 All ER 895.
5. *Dancer v Dancer* [1949] P 147, [1948] 2 All ER 731.

6. See *Spurgeon v Spurgeon* (1930) 46 TLR 396, followed by *Tweney v Tweney* [1946] P 180, [1946] 1 All ER 564; *Bullock v Bullock* [1960] 2 All ER 307.

7. *Thompson v Thompson* [1956] P 414, [1956] 1 All ER 603.

8. *Ivett v Ivett* (1930) 94 JP 237; cf *R v Twyning (Gloucestershire) Inhabitants* (1819) 2 B & Ald 386.

9. *Hogton v Hogton* (1933) 97 JP 303; *Deakin v Deakin* (1869) 33 JP 805, followed; *Ivett v Ivett*, supra, explained; see also *Bradshaw v Bradshaw* [1956] P 274n.

10. *Carlin v Carlin* (1906) 70 JP 143.

11. See *Practice Direction* [1955] 2 All ER 465; *Motture v Motture* [1955] 3 All ER 242n.

12. *R v Hammer* [1923] 2 KB 786, 87 JP 194.

13. *Drew v Drew* [1912] P 175.

14. *Browning v Browning* (1918) 35 TLR 159.

15. *Phillips v Phillips* (1921) 38 TLR 150.

16. *Perry v Perry* [1920] P 361. See also *Bonhote v Bonhote* (1920) 89 LJP 140, and *Winmill v Winmill* (1934) 78 Sol Jo 536.

17. *Bury v Bury* (1919) 35 TLR 220; see also *Lemon v Lemon* (1920) 123 LT 585.

18. *Todd v Todd* [1961] 2 All ER 881.

19. At the trial, *H v H* [1928] P 206.

20. *Woodland v Woodland (otherwise Belin or Barton)* [1928] P 139.

21. *Hayward v Hayward* [1961] P 152, [1961] 1 All ER 236.

22. *Wolfenden v Wolfenden* [1946] P 61, [1945] 2 All ER 539.

6–52   Civil partnership. A civil partnership is a relation between two people of the same sex which is formed when they register as civil partners of each other[1]. There are absolute and prohibited degrees of relationship[2]. Eligibility is otherwise subject only to the same age/consent requirements as marriage except that the parties must, of course, be of the same sex[3].

The law relating to acquiring parental responsibility, adoption, applications for residence and contact orders and financial provision for children has been updated to accommodate civil partners[4]. The interpretation of terms such as "brother-in-law" has similarly been updated[5]. There are provisions for financial relief in magistrates' courts which mirror those under the Domestic Proceedings Magistrates' Courts 1978[6]. Various amendments have also been made to the Family Law Act 1996 to bring civil partners within that legislation.

1. Civil Partnership Act 2004, s 1. See this PART, post.
2. Civil Partnership Act 2004, Sch 1.
3. Civil Partnership Act 2004, ss 3, 4.
4. See Civil Partnership Act 2004, ss 75–79.
5. Civil Partnership Act 2004, s 246 et seq.
6. Civil Partnership Act 2004, Sch 6.

Proceedings under section 2 of the Domestic Proceedings and Magistrates' Courts Act 1978[1]

6–60   Application for order for financial provision under section 2 of the 1978 Act. Either party to a marriage may apply to a family proceedings court for an order for financial provision under section 2 of the Domestic Proceedings and Magistrates' Courts Act 1978 on the ground that the other party to the marriage—

(a)   has failed to provide reasonable maintenance for the applicant; or

(b)   has failed to provide, or to make a proper contribution towards, reasonable maintenance for any child of the family; or

(c)   has behaved in such a way that the applicant cannot reasonably be expected to live with the respondent; or

(d)   has deserted the applicant[2].

For Proof of Marriage, see para **6–51**, ante.

"Child of the family", in relation to the parties to a marriage, means—

(a)   a child of both of those parties; and

(b)   any other child, not being a child who is placed with those parties as foster parents by a local authority or voluntary organisation, who has been treated by both of those parties as a child of their family[3].

The grounds of application and the law relating to those grounds are considered in the ensuing paragraphs.

1. For proceedings by one civil partner against the other in the magistrates' court for financial provision, see Civil Partnership Act 2004, Sch, this PART, post.
2. Domestic Proceedings and Magistrates' Courts Act 1978, s 1, this PART, post.
3. Domestic Proceedings and Magistrates' Courts Act 1978, s 88(1), this PART, post.

6–61   Failure to maintain: failure to provide reasonable maintenance for the applicant. Either party to a marriage has an equal right to apply for financial provision. It is not necessary for the applicant to establish that the failure to maintain was "wilful", and accordingly the court does not need to be satisfied that the respondent knew what he was doing and intended what he was doing[1].

Adultery on the part of the applicant is no longer an absolute bar to the award of financial relief, but is to be treated in the same way as other forms of misconduct. Before making an order under section 2 for periodical payments or for payment of a lump sum in favour of the applicant the court shall have regard to the matters contained in section 3 of the Domestic Proceedings and Magistrates' Courts Act 1978.

---

1. But see *Santa Cruz Ruiz v United Kingdom* [1998] EHRLR 208, European Court of Human Rights (proceedings to enforce maintenance payments criminal in nature under art 6 of the European Convention on Human Rights).

6–62   Failure to provide, or contribute towards, reasonable maintenance for a child of the family.   Either party to a marriage has an equal right to apply for financial provision on this ground. An order may require payments in favour of the applicant, as well as the child, notwithstanding that the failure to provide reasonable maintenance is established with respect only to a child of the family. It is not necessary for the applicant to establish that the failure to provide reasonable maintenance was "wilful". The phrase "child of the family", in relation to the parties to a marriage, is defined by section 88(1) of the Domestic Proceedings and Magistrates' Courts Act 1978 to mean "(*a*) a child of both of those parties; and (*b*) any other child, not being a child who is being boarded-out with those parties by a local authority or voluntary organisation, who has been treated by both of those parties as a child of their family", thereby bringing the definition of this term into line with that contained in section 52(1) of the Matrimonial Causes Act 1973.

6–63   Behaviour.   This ground, namely that the respondent has behaved in such a way that the applicant cannot reasonably be expected to live with the respondent, follows section 1(2)(*b*) of the Matrimonial Causes Act 1973[1]. It replaces the ground of "persistent cruelty" and provides a wider basis on which financial relief may be obtained in a magistrates' court. This ground must be interpreted in the same way as s 1(2)(b) of the 1973 Act, and justices must apply the same test as that laid down by the High Court in the cases referred to below[2].

In *Livingstone-Stallard v Livingstone-Stallard*[3] DUNN J, said that the evidence in a case under section 1(2)(*b*) of the 1973 Act should be approached in the following terms; ". . . Coming back to my analogy of a direction to a jury, I ask myself the question; would any right-thinking person come to the conclusion that this husband has behaved in such a way that this wife cannot reasonably be expected to live with him, taking into account the whole of the circumstances and the characters and personalities of the parties?" That passage was approved in *O'Neill v O'Neill*[4], where the Court of Appeal held that although the words "reasonably be expected" *prima facie* suggest an objective test, it is necessary in considering what is reasonable for the court to have regard to the history of the marriage and to the individual spouses before it, and from this point of view to have regard to *this* petitioner and *this* respondent in assessing what is reasonable. Where the respondent is subject to mental illness the correct test to apply is whether, after making all allowances for his disabilities and for the temperaments of both parties, it must be held that the character and gravity of his behaviour is such that the petitioner cannot reasonably be expected to live with him (*Katz v Katz*[5]). The word "reasonably" qualifies "expect" and not "behaviour" (*Carew-Hunt v Carew-Hunt*[6]), and it is inaccurate to refer to the ground as one of "unreasonable behaviour" (*Bannister v Bannister*[7]).

"Behaviour is something more than a mere state of affairs or a state of mind, such as for example, a repugnance to sexual intercourse, or a feeling that the wife is not reciprocating his love, or not being as demonstrative as he thinks she should be. Behaviour in this context is action or conduct by the one which affects the other. Such conduct may take either acts or the form of an act or omission or may be a course of conduct and, in my view, it must have some reference to the marriage": per Sir George BAKER P, in *Katz v Katz*[5]. In *Thurlow v Thurlow*[8], where the wife suffered from epilepsy, eventually becoming a permanent in-patient unable to look after herself, REES J, held that behaviour may be either positive or negative in character, or both, and may include cases where the behaviour is caused by mental or physical illness or injury, and may be involuntary. It will be for the judge to decide whether behaviour is sufficiently grave to make it unreasonable to expect the petitioner to endure it. In reaching the decision the judge will have regard to all the circumstances including the disabilities and temperaments of both parties the causes of the behaviour and whether the causes were or were not known to the petitioner, the presence or absence of intention, the impact of it on the petitioner and the family unit, its duration, and the prospects of cure or improvement in the future. Desertion or behaviour leading up to desertion does not constitute "behaviour" (*Stringfellow v Stringfellow*[9]). In *Bradley v Bradley*[10] it was held that the fact that the wife was living with the husband because she had nowhere else to live did not prevent her relying on s 1(2)(*b*) of the 1973 Act.

---

1. Section 1(2)(*b*) of the Matrimonial Causes Act 1973 provides that irretrievable breakdown may be proved by satisfying the court "that the respondent has behaved in such a way that the petitioner cannot reasonably be expected to live with the respondent".
2. *Bergin v Bergin* [1983] 1 All ER 905, 147 JP 118.
3. [1974] Fam 47, [1974] 2 All ER 766.
4. [1975] 3 All ER 289.
5. [1972] 3 All ER 219.
6. (1972) Times, 28 June.
7. (1980) 10 Fam Law 240.

8. [1976] Fam 32, [1975] 2 All ER 979.
9. [1976] 2 All ER 539.
10. [1973] 3 All ER 750.

6–64 **Desertion.** *To prove desertion, it is necessary to establish a termination of cohabitation brought about by the intention of the defendant and the absence of consent thereto of the complainant.* Desertion involves an intention[1]; plus a course of conduct[2]. It has never been exhaustively defined[3], but in *Lane v Lane* [1951] P 284, Lord MERRIMAN P, formulated the general principles of the law on the subject. The effect of separation must be qualified by the subsequent history of the spouses[4]. Desertion is a matter of inference. It can exist independently of its duration[5].

The question whether a deserting spouse has reasonable cause for not trying to bring the desertion to an end, and the corresponding question whether desertion without cause has continued to exist, must always be questions of fact, and the determination must depend upon the circumstances of the particular case[6]. The decision in *Stevenson v Stevenson* [1911] P 191, which laid down a general principle that the presentation of a petition for divorce or judicial separation puts an end to desertion, was overruled[7]. Where the intention of the husband to desert his wife has been established, the intention is presumed to continue, unless he proves genuine repentance and sincere and reasonable attempts to get her back[8]. The court should never discourage friendly attempts at reconciliation[9]. A husband may not be expected to take his wife back if she recklessly makes gross charges against him which are unfounded[10]. Where one spouse deserts the other and later becomes insane, there is no irrebuttable presumption of inability to form or retain an *animus deserendi*; it is for the deserted spouse to prove that the deserter was capable of retaining such *animus* and did in fact retain it[11]. Similarly where the spouse is a patient in a mental hospital, it is a question of fact whether the spouse can form the intention to desert or to continue to desert[12]. Desertion of a wife may take place although she is a patient in a mental hospital[13].

1. *Clark v Clark (No 2)* [1939] P 257, [1939] 2 All ER 392.
2. *Wilkinson v Wilkinson* (1894) 58 JP 415, approved by CA in *Thomas v Thomas* [1924] P 194.
3. *Pulford v Pulford* [1923] P 18.
4. *Bradshaw v Bradshaw* [1897] P 24, 61 JP 8; *Pulford v Pulford*, supra; *Papadopoulos v Papadopoulos* [1930] P 55, 94 JP 39; *Joseph v Joseph* [1953] 2 All ER 710.
5. *Jordan v Jordan* [1939] P 239, [1939] 2 All ER 29; *Higgins v Higgins and Bannister* [1943] P 58, [1943] 2 All ER 86.
6. See *Pratt v Pratt* [1939] AC 417, [1939] 3 All ER 437.
7. *Cohen v Cohen* [1940] AC 631, [1940] 2 All ER 331; *Tickler v Tickler* [1943] 1 All ER 57.
8. *Bowron v Bowron* [1925] P 187, 89 JP 43.
9. *Cohen v Cohen*, supra.
10. *Kay v Kay* [1904] P 382.
11. *Crowther v Crowther* [1951] AC 723, [1951] 1 All ER 1131.
12. *Monckton v Monckton* [1942] P 28, [1941] 3 All ER 133; *Brown v Brown* [1947] P 95, [1947] 2 All ER 160, 111 JP 426.
13. *Sotherden v Sotherden* [1940] P 73, [1940] 1 All ER 252, CA.

6–65 **Cohabitation.** *The legal relationship known as "cohabitation" exists immediately upon marriage.* Where the parties separated at the church door immediately after the marriage ceremony and never lived together as man and wife, but it appeared that it was the husband who refused to cohabit, the wife having been always willing to do so, desertion was held to have taken place[1].

Cohabitation does not necessarily imply that a husband and wife are living together physically under the same roof. Desertion is not a withdrawal from a place but from a state of things. What the law seeks to enforce is recognition and discharge of the obligations of the conjugal state[2]. Parties had not lived together, the appellant being a domestic servant employed elsewhere and being only occasionally visited by the respondent but had had two children by him. The respondent refused to help the appellant and said that if she sent her boxes to his house they would be returned. The President (Sir F JEUNE) said that a person cannot complain of desertion after *voluntarily* leaving his or her consort; and also that when parties are living apart by mutual consent—as under a separation deed—there cannot be desertion. It was clear that cohabitation exists without the parties living under the same roof as in the case of married persons living in domestic service. The court held that the deliberate cessation of all intercourse by the husband and his wilful refusal to see his wife or to receive her at the house where he was staying, or to contribute anything towards the expenses of the burial of either of their children, constituted an act of desertion, and he was also guilty of wilful neglect to maintain[3]. A man who enlisted and went with his regiment to India was held to be still cohabiting with his wife in this country, and to have subsequently deserted her when after a time he ceased to correspond with her or to contribute towards her support, and committed adultery[4].

Cohabitation may also exist while a spouse is absent from home, working or seeking work elsewhere, or while absent for the benefit of his or her health. Where a husband left his wife with her knowledge and consent to go to the gold diggings in Australia and wrote affectionate letters to her, cohabitation was held to exist, and desertion to take place when the correspondence ceased at the end of four years and he had formed an adulterous connection[5]. A wife, with her husband's consent, went to her mother's house for her approaching confinement. For six months the husband sent her money, and then refused to allow her to return to cohabitation, or to contribute towards her maintenance. The Court of Appeal held that the husband deserted his wife when he refused to receive or maintain her, and the justice had jurisdiction to make an order[6]. A (non exhaustive) list of criteria for determining the existence of cohabitation, including factors derived from the Social Security Contributions and Benefits Act 1992 were set out in *Kimber v Kimber*[7].

When special circumstances prevent the establishment of a matrimonial home, cohabitation may consist of meetings and acts of intercourse[8].

Cohabitation can also exist, or be treated as merely suspended, while a spouse is compulsorily detained in a mental hospital by the act of the public authorities[9]. The absence of a spouse owing to imprisonment, not being a voluntary abandonment of the other spouse, does not constitute desertion[10].

1. *De Laubenque v De Laubenque* [1899] P 42; see also *Buckmaster v Buckmaster* (1869) LR 1 P & D 713; *Lee Shires v Lee Shires* (1910) 54 Sol Jo 874; and *Fassbender v Fassbender* [1938] 3 All ER 389.
2. *Pulford v Pulford* [1923] P 18.
3. *Bradshaw v Bradshaw*, [1897] P 24, 61 JP 8; approved and followed in *Kay v Kay* [1904] P 382.
4. *Henty v Henty* (1875) 33 LT 263.
5. *Stickland v Stickland* (1876) 35 LT 767.
6. *Chudley v Chudley* (1893) 69 LT 617.
7. [2000] 1 FLR 383.
8. *Abercrombie v Abercrombie* [1943] 2 All ER 465, 107 JP 200.
9. *Pulford v Pulford*, supra.
10. *Townsend v Townsend* (1873) LR 3 P & D 129.

6–66 Determination of cohabitation. *Desertion may take place even if the wife continues to live under the same roof, if the husband has completely withdrawn from cohabitation*[1]; but not if it is still one household[2]. The common home must be put an end to by the husband[3]. Where for a long period the husband did not speak to his wife and abstained from conjugal intercourse the parties sleeping separately in the same house and having their meals together, it was held that there was no desertion[4]. The wilful and unjustifiable refusal of one spouse to continue sexual relations, coupled with an intimation to the other spouse that he or she is at liberty to seek sexual gratification elsewhere, is not by itself desertion[5], but it will be if the refusing spouse can be taken to realise that the refusal will probably bring the marriage to an end[6]. The conduct of the defendant, taken as a whole, including the refusal of sexual intercourse, may amount to such a total disregard of the fundamental obligations of matrimony as to afford evidence of an intention to desert[7]. The case of *Weatherley v Weatherley*, supra, should be contrasted with *Smith v Smith*, and the later cases referred to supra, and with *Angel v Angel* [1946] 2 All ER 635, 111 JP 14.

1. *Powell v Powell* [1992] P 278; *Tobin v Tobin* (1930) 94 JP Jo 303; *Smith v Smith* [1940] P 49, [1939] 1 All ER 533, 109 LJP 100.
2. *Littlewood v Littlewood* [1943] P 11, [1942] 2 All ER 515; *Hopes v Hopes* [1949] P 277, [1948] 2 All ER 920, 113 JP 10); see also *Walker v Walker* [1952] 2 All ER 138, 116 JP 346, and *Baker v Baker* [1952] 2 All ER 248, 116 JP 447.
3. *Wilkes v Wilkes* [1943] P 41, [1943] 1 All ER 433.
4. *Jackson v Jackson* [1924] P 19; *Stevens v Stevens* (1929) 93 JP 120.
5. *Weatherley v Weatherley* [1947] AC 628, [1947] 1 All ER 563, 111 JP 220.
6. *Slon v Slon* [1969] P 122, [1969] 1 All ER 759.
7. *Scotcher v Scotcher* [1947] P 1, 110 JP 342.

6–67 Constructive desertion. *It is not necessary that the husband should have turned his wife out of doors; it is sufficient if by his conduct*[1] *he has compelled her to leave the house, the question being whether it was his intention to break off matrimonial relations*[2].
Proof of persistent cruelty (or seemingly neglect to maintain), coupled with proof of a purpose and intention by the husband to force his wife to leave him, constitute desertion, and such intention may be presumed to continue unless the husband satisfies the justices that his acts and declarations from the time of his wife's leaving him should have convinced her that she might safely return to him. Difficulty arises where the conduct complained of is of the nature of cruelty, especially having regard to more recent decisions in cases of cruelty. It has long been an established principle that conduct of the nature of, but not amounting to, cruelty may be just cause for a wife to leave her husband.[3]. The proposition that an unproved case of cruelty cannot be made the basis of a case of constructive desertion[4] must be considered in the light of the particular circumstances, and other decisions in which conduct akin to cruelty has been held to amount to constructive desertion[5].
Decisions made before 1963 must be read having regard to the case of *Gollins v Gollins* (infra).
In *Edwards v Edwards* [1948] P 268, [1948] 1 All ER 157, 112 JP 109, it was held that there may be "constructive" desertion if it is a natural consequence of the behaviour of the husband that the wife leaves the matrimonial home. In *Lang v Lang*[6] the decision in *Edwards v Edwards*, supra, was approved and it was held that the desire of one spouse that cohabitation should continue does not, in itself, rebut an inference that he intended the other to leave, where he may normally be expected to know that his conduct would have that result. This decision was explained in *Gollins v Gollins* [1964] AC 644, [1963] 2 All ER 966, per Lord REID, in the terms ". . . if without just cause or excuse you persist in doing things which you know your wife will probably not tolerate, and which no ordinary woman would tolerate, and then she leaves, you have wilfully deserted her, whatever your desire or intention may have been". In *Lewis v Lewis* [1956] P 205n, [1955] 3 All ER 598, 120 JP 21, where a husband had committed an isolated offence of indecent assault upon another woman, it was held that his wife was not justified in leaving him and claiming that she had constructively been deserted. The issue is whether it is reasonable for the complainant to put up with the behaviour of the respondent bearing in mind the character of each, trying to be fair to both and expecting neither heroic virtue nor selfless abnegation from either[7].

1. In *Devi v Gaddu* (1974) 4 Fam Law 159 the wife alleged persistent cruelty, desertion and wilful neglect and complained of assaults by her husband and his mother; the Divisional Court held that justices should not disregard the conduct of other members of the husband's family when considering whether the wife was justified in leaving the husband and that a husband was not entitled to say that his family had driven the wife out of the house and that he was not involved.
2. Per JEUNE P; *Charter v Charter* (1901) 65 JP 246.
3. See *Mackenzie v Mackenzie* [1895] AC 384, a Scottish case, quoted with approval in *Oldroyd v Oldroyd* [1896] P 175, and *Timmins v Timmins* [1953] 2 All ER 187.
4. See *Pike v Pike* [1954] P 81n, [1953] 1 All ER 232.
5. See *Timmins v Timmins* (supra); *Hall v Hall* [1962] 3 All ER 518; and a consideration of earlier authorities by DAVIS J, in *Dixon v Dixon* [1953] P 103, [1953] 1 All ER 910, see also *Slon v Slon* [1969] P 122, [1969] 1 All ER 759, but cf *Ogden v Ogden* [1969] 3 All ER 1055, 1 WLR 1425 and 1436.
In addition to the above cases reference may be made to the following: *Powell v Powell* [1922] P 278; *Sayers v Sayers*

(1929) 93 JP 72; *Knowles v Knowles* (1936) 100 JP Jo 736; *Leng v Leng* [1946] 2 All ER 590, 110 JP 395; *Foster v Foster* [1954] P 67, [1953] 2 All ER 518, 117 JP 377; *Cooper v Cooper* [1954] 3 All ER 358; *Hill v Hill* [1954] P 291, [1954] 1 All ER 491, 119 JP 163; *Fisher v Fisher* [1960] P 36, [1959] 3 All ER 131; *Young v Young* [1964] P 182, [1962] 3 All ER 120, 126 JP 406; *Thoday v Thoday* [1964] P 181, [1964] 1 All ER 341.

    6. [1955] AC 402, [1954] 3 All ER 571, 119 JP 368. A decision of the Privy Council commended by the President of the Divorce Division in *Marjoram v Marjoram* [1955] 2 All ER 1 at 8, 119 JP 291 at 296.

    7. *Pheasant v Pheasant* [1972] Fam 202, [1972] 1 All ER 587.

6–68   *Adulterous association.*—A wife, whose husband is carrying on an adulterous intercourse with another woman, is not bound to remain in cohabitation with him, whether the adulterous intercourse is carried on in the matrimonial residence or elsewhere. She may withdraw from cohabitation, whereby her husband is guilty of constructive desertion[1]. It need not be shown that the adulterous association is still subsisting or that there is an intention on the part of the husband to persist in it: discovery of a past adultery, even though not persisted in, may be held to justify a wife in leaving him and establishing constructive desertion[2]. A husband brought to his house a woman with whom he had immoral intercourse. The wife refused to stay in the house with the woman, and the husband said she might do as she pleased, but the woman would remain. The wife left the house, and no further cohabitation took place. The Divorce Division held the husband had been guilty of desertion[3]. Where the husband clearly intended not to live with his wife, and before and after marriage was carrying on an adulterous intercourse, it was held to be desertion, though the wife actually left the matrimonial home, and after she was aware of the adulterous connection refused to return unless she was satisfied that such connection was at an end[4]. A wife whose husband has, by his conduct, induced belief that he has committed adultery, may, on leaving him, claim that she has been constructively deserted[5], but it must be a suspicion reasonably existing, not a suspicion unsupported by evidence of opportunity[6]. Furthermore, in such a case, the suspected spouse must be given an opportunity of explaining his conduct, unless the evidence points to adultery beyond reasonable doubt[7].

    1. *Sickert v Sickert* [1899] P 278.
    2. *Teall v Teall* [1938] P 250, [1938] 3 All ER 349, 102 JP 428, explained in *Kemp v Kemp* [1961] 2 All ER 764.
    3. *Dickinson v Dickinson* (1889) 62 LT 330; see also *Koch v Koch* [1899] P 221.
    4. *Graves v Graves* (1864) 3 Sw & Tr 350; followed in *Pizzala v Pizzala* (1896) 68 LJP 91n.
    5. *Kemp v Kemp* [1953] 2 All ER 553, 117 JP 409; *Baker v Baker* [1954] P 33, [1953] 2 All ER 1199, 117 JP 556; cf *Glenister v Glenister* [1945] P 30, [1945] 1 All ER 513, 109 JP 194; *Forbes v Forbes* [1954] 3 All ER 461, 119 JP 30; *Kemp v Kemp* [1961] 2 All ER 764.
    6. Cf *Wood v Wood* [1947] P 103, [1947] 2 All ER 95, 111 JP 428; *Cox v Cox* [1958] 1 All ER 569, 122 JP 173.
    7. *Marsden v Marsden* [1968] P 544, [1967] 1 All ER 967.

6–69   **Other causes of non-cohabitation.**   *Disagreement regarding matrimonial home.* There is no proposition of law that the husband has the right to say where the matrimonial home shall be. The decision affects both the parties and their children and is to be decided not by the imposition of the will of one over the other. If an arrangement is frustrated by unreasonableness on either side, and a separation results, then the party causing the separation by his or her unreasonable behaviour is guilty of desertion[1]. But where a husband agreed before marriage that the matrimonial home should be at the house of his wife, and he afterwards went back on the agreement without any valid reason, it was held that the wife was entitled to refuse to live in the house that he chose and was not guilty of desertion[2]. Under certain circumstances, a wife's refusal to live with her husband at her mother-in-law's house is justifiable[3]. The withdrawal by the husband from the matrimonial home to the headquarters of the Tramp Preachers movement, coupled with the refusal of sexual intercourse, is desertion[4].

    1. Per DENNING LJ, in *Dunn v Dunn* [1949] P 98, [1948] 2 All ER 822, 112 JP 436, explaining *Mansey v Mansey* [1940] P 139, [1940] 2 All ER 424.
    2. *King v King* [1942] P 1, [1941] 2 All ER 103.
    3. *Millichamp v Millichamp* (1931) 95 JP 207; cf *Jackson v Jackson* (1932) 96 JP 97.
    4. *Fletcher v Fletcher* [1945] 1 All ER 582.

6–70   *Separation by arrangement is not desertion*[1]. The mere refusal of a husband to continue the payment of alimony under a separation agreement does not constitute desertion[2]. If the agreement is to separate for a limited time, there may be desertion on the expiration of that period[3]. A separation agreement or deed constitutes in the first instance *prima facie* evidence against desertion[4]. By putting the deed in suit, the wife makes a conclusive election to treat it as subsisting, and cannot afterwards say it was a sham. She cannot approbate and reprobate it[5]. Where the deed itself contains an admission that the husband had previously deserted his wife, and where the husband has repudiated it and scarcely complied with it at all[6], or the agreement has not operated in any way or to any material extent[7], or has not been acted upon[8], the deed or agreement may be treated as a mere incident in the desertion already commenced[9]. A maintenance agreement which does not bind the parties to live apart does not terminate a prior desertion[10]. The mere fact that a man has not kept up his payments due under the agreement is not sufficient to enable the court to say that the agreement is thereby repudiated[11], because, unless the withholding payment is wilful, it has no significance[12]. In *Pardy v Pardy* [1939] P 288, [1939] 3 All ER 779, the Court of Appeal held that "desertion" may describe an act or a state. For the sake of desertion, both the factum of separation and the *animus deserendi* are required. A *de facto* separation may take place without there being an *animus deserendi*, but if that *animus* supervenes, desertion will begin from that moment unless, of course, there is consent by the other spouse. In order that a separation which began by being consensual may be changed into desertion it must lose its consensual element on both sides. Suing on a separation deed is evidence of continuing consent to the separation. Repudiation may be established by proof that a spouse regards himself as free to resume cohabitation, which the deed prohibits, but that he does not propose to resume cohabitation. The conduct of the other party cannot affect his intention to desert, it is only important as affecting the question of the intention of the other spouse. Consent by the other spouse can come to an end without notifying the repudiating spouse that the repudiation has been accepted or a reassertion of conjugal rights. The Court of Appeal in *Pardy v Pardy*, supra, summarised its opinion as follows: (1) where the original separation was by mutual consent, desertion may supervene without a resumption of cohabitation; (2) this can happen where (*a*) on the part of the spouse alleged to be in desertion there is repudiation of the agreement under which separation took place, no step taken towards the resumption of cohabitation in fact, and in addition to repudiation, the *animus deserendi*, and (*b*) on the part of the spouse alleging desertion there is not only no insistence on the terms of the separation agreement, but a *bona fide* willingness to resume cohabitation without regard to its terms—in short, if it can be said that both parties are during the relevant period in truth regarding the agreement as a dead letter which no longer regulates their matrimonial relations; (3) whether or not these conditions exist during the relevant period is a question of fact in each case, the answer to which depends upon the true inference to be drawn from the words and conduct of the parties; (4) once these conditions are fulfilled, all the elements necessary to constitute a state of desertion are present, namely, *de facto* separation, *animus deserendi*, and absence of consent on the part of the spouse alleging desertion. But in *Lord Long of Wraxall v Lady Long of Wraxall* [1940] 4 All ER 230, where the separation deed, in which desertion by the wife was admitted, had remained in effective operation, it was held that the deed was a bar to the husband asserting that the wife was continuing in a state of separation without his consent. A separation agreement is no bar to proceedings for desertion where it is the desire only of one spouse to live separate and apart[13].

1. *Parkinson v Parkinson* (1869) LR 2 P & D 25; *Crabb v Crabb* (1868) LR 1 P & D 601.
2. *Pape v Pape* (1887) 20 QBD 76, 52 JP 181, approved by CA in *R v Leresche* [1891] 2 QB 418, 56 JP 37.
3. *Shaw v Shaw* [1939] P 269, [1939] 2 All ER 381.
4. *Ratcliffe v Ratcliffe* [1938] 3 All ER 41.
5. *Clark v Clark (No 2)* [1939] P 257, [1939] 2 All ER 392.
6. *Watson v Watson* [1938] P 258, [1938] 3 All ER 770; see also *Lord Long of Wraxall v Lady Long of Wraxall* [1940] 4 All ER 230.
7. *Starkey v Starkey* [1938] 3 All ER 773.
8. *Tate v Tate* [1938] 4 All ER 264.
9. *Watson v Watson* [1938] P 258, [1938] 3 All ER 770.
10. *Crabtree v Crabtree* [1953] 2 All ER 56, 117 JP 334.
11. *Ratcliffe v Ratcliffe* [1938] 3 All ER 41.
12. *Clark v Clark (No 2)* [1939] P 257, [1939] 2 All ER 392.
13. *Smith v Smith* [1945] 2 All ER 452; *Bosley v Bosley* [1958] 2 All ER 167; *Hall v Hall* [1960] 1 All ER 91; *Gallagher v Gallagher* [1965] 2 All ER 967.

6–71   *An agreement between husband and wife to live apart may be evidenced by conduct*[1]. Where in the case of a separation under a deed it was found that the wife was not in fact a consenting party, being forced into signing the deed by the circumstances of her position, BUCKNILL J, held that she was not prevented from relying on desertion[2]. Desertion is not in abeyance by the existence of a separation deed that has not operated in any way or to any material extent[3], nor a separation agreement that the wife has never attempted to enforce, and under which the husband has never paid any substantial sum[4].

1. *Bowen v Bowen* (1908) 73 JP 87; *Spence v Spence* [1939] 1 All ER 52.
2. *Adamson v Adamson* (1907) 23 TLR 434; followed in *Holroyd v Holroyd* (1920) 36 TLR 479; cf *Matthews v Matthews* [1932] P 103, 96 JP 290.
3. *Starkey v Starkey* [1938] 3 All ER 773.
4. *Watson v Watson* [1938] P 258, [1938] 3 All ER 770.

6–72   *The repudiation may be by agreement or by conduct*[1]. Mere casual acts of marital intercourse may not put an end to covenants in a deed of separation[2], but they do put an end to "the separation" as it is understood in the Divorce Court[3]. In certain circumstances these acts will be evidence of resumption of cohabitation, sufficient to put an end to the deed[4]. In *Thurston v Thurston* (1910) 26 TLR 388, EVANS, P, held that intermittent visits to the wife without the intention of remaining or of resuming marital intercourse did not constitute a return to cohabitation, the wife being entitled to the permanent protection of her husband[5]. In *Graeff v Graeff* (1928) 93 JP 48, it was held that a tacit consent of the parties to live apart prevents desertion, and mere casual acts of marital intercourse do not avoid such agreement. A written agreement between the parties is not admissible to prove the separation was by agreement unless it is stamped[6]. A covenant by the wife not to sue cannot fetter the Divorce Court's discretion when a decree for divorce or nullity of marriage has been pronounced[7].

1. *Hussey v Hussey* (1913) 109 LT 192.
2. *Rowell v Rowell* [1900] 1 QB 9; cf *Mummery v Mummery* [1942] 1 All ER 553, [1942] P 107.
3. *Edwards v Edwards* (1905) 69 JP 344.
4. *Eaves v Eaves* [1939] P 361, [1939] 2 All ER 789.
5. See also *Bevan v Bevan* (1923) 87 JP Jo 452.
6. *Fengl v Fengl* [1914] P 274.

7. *Hyman v Hyman* [1929] AC 601, 93 JP 209; *Hughes v Hughes* [1929] P 1, 93 JP 3; this principle is now enacted in the Matrimonial Causes Act 1973, ss 36–36.

6–73 *Maintenance not inconsistent with desertion.* A man may be guilty of desertion even though he is making his wife an allowance[1]; or his wife is making him one[2]. A wife is entitled to her husband's society and to protection of his name and home in cohabitation. The permanent denial of these rights may be aggravated by leaving her destitute or mitigated by a liberal allowance for her support[3].

1. *Macdonald v Macdonald* (1859) 4 Sw & Tr 242.
2. *Nott v Nott* (1866) LR 1 P & D 251.
3. *Yeatman v Yeatman* (1868) LR 1 P & D 489.

6–74 **Effect of offer to resume cohabitation after desertion.** *Offer by husband.* Desertion is presumed to continue[1], but it may be terminated, if the husband makes a *bona fide* offer to resume cohabitation, and the wife refuses to accept it: but the offer must be made under such circumstances that she could be reasonably expected to accept it. The question whether the offer is made *bona fide* is a question of fact[2]. The wife is entitled to refuse to resume cohabitation if the husband has frequently ill-treated her. When a husband, after compelling the wife to leave his home, repented the next day but failed after repeated offers to induce her to return, and the justices found that he had frequently ill-treated her before she left; it was held that past ill-usage was a factor in the case which the justices were bound to consider. In a considered judgment the President said, "They (the justices) came to the conclusion that a wife who had been ill-used in the past was in a different position from the victim of a sudden outburst of temper, immediately repented of. They were entitled to take those facts into consideration to determine, first, whether there had been any desertion, and, secondly, whether there having been desertion, it continued, not through the misconduct of the husband, but because of the capricious refusal of the wife to return to cohabitation. They came to the conclusion that this wife could not reasonably be expected to go back. Her refusal to return was not unreasonable or unjustifiable, and they found that the husband had deserted the wife, and that the desertion had not been put an end to within the law which they administered. I consider that they were entitled so to find"[3].

1. *Sifton v Sifton* [1939] P 221, [1939] 1 All ER 109.
2. *Kershaw v Kershaw* (1887) 51 JP 646; *Fleming v Fleming* [1942] 2 All ER 337; *Ellis v Ellis and Wilby* [1962] 1 All ER 797.
3. *Thomas v Thomas* (1923) 129 LT 575; affd by CA [1924] P 194. See also *Bowron v Bowron* [1925] P 187; 89 JP 43; *Pratt v Pratt* [1939] AC 417, [1939] 3 All ER 437; *Bevan v Bevan* [1955] 3 All ER 332, 119 JP 576; *Brewer v Brewer* [1962] P 69, [1961] 3 All ER 957; *Pheasant v Pheasant* [1972] Fam 202, [1972] 1 All ER 587.

6–75 *Offer by wife.* A withdrawal from cohabitation by the wife, unaccompanied by any other matrimonial misconduct, does not disentitle her to an order for maintenance if she repents and shows a genuine desire to resume married life, even if the separation had been brought about by her act and had been unjustified in the first instance; a refusal by the husband to accept such a genuine offer to resume cohabitation turns him into a deserter[1]. There may be circumstances in which an offer to resume cohabitation may be *bona fide* even where not accompanied with a suggestion of repentance, where, eg there has been no violent conduct by the deserting spouse[2]; applied in a case where the wife's adultery had been condoned[3]. Cf *Dunn v Dunn* [1967] P 217, [1965] 1 All ER 1043.

1. *Thomas v Thomas* [1946] 1 All ER 170, 110 JP 203.
2. *Price v Price* [1951] 1 All ER 877, 115 JP 273; affd [1951] P 413, [1951] 2 All ER 580n, 115 JP 468n, CA.
3. *Wells v Wells* [1954] 3 All ER 491.

6–76 *Offer to be bona fide.* The offer to return must be distinct and *bona fide*[1]; and the husband must intend what he offers[2]. The offer must be definite and not a mere suggestion to return[3]. As to an offer of alternative accommodation, see *Dunn v Dunn* [1949] P 98, [1948] 2 All ER 822, 112 JP 436. In a case of "constructive desertion" the onus of proving that the intention to desert continues may be much lighter than in a case of withdrawal from cohabitation[4]. Cf *Boyd v Boyd* [1938] 4 All ER 181, 102 JP 525. If the husband fails to comply with a reasonable requirement, insisted upon by his wife as a condition of her return to cohabitation, desertion will continue[5]. But if the condition is unreasonable, the desertion will not continue[6]. An offer to live under the same roof, each party to be free from molestation by the other, is not an offer to resume cohabitation[7].

1. *Cudlipp v Cudlipp* (1858) 1 Sw & Tr 229; *French-Brewster v French-Brewster* (1889) 62 LT 609.
2. *Harris v Harris* (1866) 15 LT 448.
3. *Ware v Ware* [1942] P 49, [1942] 1 All ER 50.
4. *Herod v Herod*, infra.
5. *Gibson v Gibson* (1859) 23 JP 535; *Pizzala v Pizzala* (1896) 68 LJP 91n. See also *Slawson v Slawson* [1942] 2 All ER 527.
6. *Dallas v Dallas* (1874) 43 LJP & M 87; *Dickinson v Dickinson* (1889) 62 LT 330; *Fletcher v Fletcher* [1945] 1 All ER 582.
7. *Wily v Wily* [1918] P 1; *Casey v Casey* [1952] 1 All ER 453, 116 JP 111.

6-77   *Grounds for refusal of offer.*   A wife is not bound to return, if her husband has frequently ill-treated her[1], or has not fully withdrawn unfounded charges of immorality against her[2], or has been guilty of adultery which is uncondoned, or the wife has an amply justified belief that the husband has committed adultery[3]. The wilful abstention by the wife from cohabitation desired *bona fide* by her husband suspends her right to maintenance for desertion or neglect to maintain, but the dismissal is not *res judicata* for all time. Where during the subsequent twelve months the wife took no step but the husband offered to take her back but not her children, she was not bound to entertain this offer[4].

---

1. *Thomas v Thomas* (1923) 129 LT 575.
2. *Sayers v Sayers* (1929) 93 JP 72.
3. *Everitt v Everitt* [1949] P 374, [1949] 1 All ER 908, 113 JP 279.
4. *Balchin v Balchin* [1937] 3 All ER 733.

6-78   Just and reasonable cause for separation.   It is necessary to enquire whether there is reasonable cause for the separation, and the husband may show that there is reasonable cause or excuse on his part[1]. In *Herod v Herod* [1939] P 11, [1938] 3 All ER 722; it was held that "cause" must be that which operates to produce an effect, and that the wife's desertion continued without cause as the husband's adultery had no influence on the wife's intention[2]. Such cause is not necessarily a distinct matrimonial offence, but it must be grave and weighty. Mere frailty of temper or distasteful habits are not sufficient[3]. Examples of conduct which is sufficiently "grave and weighty" are contained in the judgment of DENNING LJ, in *Timmins v Timmins* [1953] 2 All ER 187 at 191. As to misbehaviour jeopardising husband's employment, see *Lynch v Lynch* (1933) 97 JP Jo 745. Adultery by the wife whereby she did not know who was the father of an expectant child is a just and reasonable cause[4]. The test as laid down in *Oldroyd v Oldroyd* [1896] P 175, is whether the petitioner has been guilty of conduct which renders it practically impossible for the spouses to live properly together[5]. Conduct falling short of legal cruelty may justify one spouse in leaving the other, if it is of a grave and convincing character[6]. The husband is justified in withdrawing from cohabitation where the wife has so conducted herself as to give him reasonable ground for supposing that she had committed adultery[7]. But it must be a suspicion reasonably existing at the time of withdrawing from cohabitation and not a suspicion, not capable of proof, formed after withdrawal[8], or unfounded by reason of an absence of evidence of opportunity[9]. The considerations to be applied to such a claim by the husband are discussed in *Jones v Jones* [1953] 2 All ER 345, 117 JP 348. If the alleged adultery has been the ground of a divorce petition which has failed, a husband is no longer entitled to resist a wife's claim for maintenance on the ground that he believes her to have committed adultery[10]; but the failure of the petition would not have retrospective effect if the belief had been reasonable and *bona fide*[11]. Similarly, acts relied upon on an unsuccessful petition for cruelty cannot be pleaded as "just cause" in reply to a subsequent petition for desertion[12]; at least when the wife's allegations have been rejected in the previous suit[13].

Mental or physical illness may amount to just cause for a refusal of cohabitation[14].

Where a wife refused full marital rights to her husband without reasonable excuse, and he declined to live with her, it was held that he was not guilty of desertion[15]; and where, being separated, a spouse offers to return to living together on the unjustified condition that there shall be no sexual intercourse, there may be constructive desertion[16]. In such a case, there would be no constructive desertion where, the spouses continuing to live together, one refused to continue sexual relations[17]; but these cases should be compared with *Slon v Slon* [1969] P 122, [1969] 1 All ER 759, in which the unreasonable refusal of sexual intercourse was held to be a sufficiently grave and weighty matter, even though it did not cause injury to health, as to amount to constructive desertion since it drove the other party from the home. If, however, a wife's refusal is due to an invincible repugnance, just as though she had been rendered structurally incapable of intercourse by some accident or disease, the husband has no excuse for leaving her[18]. The innocent contraction of a venereal disease by a wife before marriage, even though communicated to her husband, does not justify the husband leaving her, and is therefore no defence to summary proceedings instituted by her for desertion[19].

---

1. *Frowd v Frowd* [1904] P 177, 68 JP 436.
2. Applied in *Richards v Richards* [1952] P 307, [1952] 1 All ER 1384, 116 JP 358; *Church v Church* [1952] P 313, [1952] 2 All ER 441; *Dryden v Dryden* [1953] 2 All ER 553n, 117 JP 397n, and in *Day v Day* [1957] P 202, [1957] 1 All ER 848, where the adultery was before the date of desertion.
3. *Yeatman v Yeatman* (1868) LR 1 P & D 489.
4. *Roast v Roast* [1938] P 8, [1937] 4 All ER 423, 102 JP 25.
5. Cf *Jackson v Jackson* [1924] P 19; *Jones v Jones* (1941) 105 JP 353; *Buchler v Buchler* [1947] P 25, [1947] 1 All ER 319, 111 JP 179; *Bartholomew v Bartholomew* [1952] 2 All ER 1035, 117 JP 35.
6. *Edwards v Edwards* [1950] P 8, [1949] 2 All ER 145, 113 JP 383; *Young v Young* [1964] P 152, [1962] 3 All ER 120, 126 JP 406.
7. *Glenister v Glenister* [1945] P 30, [1945] 1 All ER 513, 109 JP 194.
8. *Wood v Wood* [1947] P 103, [1947] 2 All ER 95, 111 JP 428.
9. *Cox v Cox* [1958] 1 All ER 569, 122 JP 173.
10. *Allen v Allen* [1951] 1 All ER 724, 115 JP 229.
11. *West v West* [1954] P 444, [1954] 2 All ER 505.
12. *Hill v Hill* [1954] P 291, [1954] 1 All ER 491, 181 JP 163.
13. *Fisher v Fisher* [1960] P 36, [1959] 3 All ER 131, discussed (1960) 110 LJ 201.

14. *Keeley v Keeley* [1952] 2 TLR 756), and see *Tickle v Tickle* [1968] 2 All ER 154.
15. *Synge v Synge* [1900] P 180, 64 JP 454; affd by Court of Appeal [1901] P 317.
16. *Hutchinson v Hutchinson* [1963] 1 All ER 1.
17. See *Weatherley v Weatherley* [1946] 2 All ER 1, 110 JP 255; *Scotcher v Scotcher* [1947] P 1, 110 JP 342.
18. *Beevor v Beevor* [1945] 2 All ER 200, 109 JP 241.
19. *Butler v Butler* [1917] P 244.

6–79 Resumption of cohabitation. *Voluntary resumption of cohabitation* puts an end to desertion and is an absolute bar to pending proceedings[1]. But not where a wife returns to the matrimonial home as a housekeeper without being reinstated as a wife[2], or where she merely lives in the house without intention to resume a matrimonial home[3], or permits acts of intercourse during efforts to effect a reconciliation[4]. Where a husband has intercourse with his wife, without fraud on her part, after a previous maintenance order has been discharged on the ground of her adultery, this is sufficient resumption of cohabitation to render his subsequent turning her from the home desertion[5]. Similarly, condonation of conduct upon which constructive desertion was based will bring that desertion to an end[6].

1. *Williams v Williams* [1904] P 145, 68 JP 188; *Mummery v Mummery* [1942] P 107, [1942] 1 All ER 553.
2. *Cook v Cook* [1949] 1 All ER 384, 113 JP 164.
3. *Bartram v Bartram* [1950] P 1, [1949] 2 All ER 270, 113 JP 422, but cf *Bull v Bull* [1953] 2 All ER 601, 117 JP 415.
4. *Whitney v Whitney* [1951] P 250, [1951] 1 All ER 301, 115 JP 71, approved and applied in *Perry v Perry* [1952] P 203, [1952] 1 All ER 1076, 116 JP 258, where it was held that the doctrine of condonation did not apply.
5. *Viney v Viney* [1951] P 457, [1951] 2 All ER 204, 115 JP 397.
6. *Pizey v Pizey* [1961] P 101, [1961] 2 All ER 658.

6–80 Notice of allegations. Whenever adultery is alleged in a matrimonial matter, proper and particular notice of the substance of the allegation should be given, in writing, to the party against whom it is alleged[1]. Similarly, such notice must be given whenever a party's case is based on a reasonable belief in the adultery of the other party[2]; or when a party's case is based on an allegation of conduct by the other party in relation to members of the opposite sex, albeit not giving rise to a reasonable belief in adultery, but nevertheless so inconsistent with the married relationship as to amount to expulsion[3].

In *Broadbent v Broadbent*, supra, it was stated that proper notice of adultery was particulars of the time and place of adultery and the name of the alleged adulterer, and this was re-affirmed in *Duffield v Duffield*, supra. In *Jones v Jones*, supra, it was stated that similar particulars must be given in relation to reasonable suspicion of adultery, and in *Hind v Hind*, supra, this was extended to "improper association".

If adultery is alleged to have taken place more than six months prior to the complaint, the particulars must include the date (within six months) when it is alleged the adultery first became known to the complainant[4].

It is apprehended that if any of these particulars are not known (eg, where an allegation of adultery is based on the birth of a child to a wife living apart from her husband or where any allegation is based on a confession) the hearing may proceed so long as the adultery, suspicion or association is specified as fully as possible[5].

In *Frith v Frith*[6], the Divisional Court stated, as a rule of practice, that a party may apply for particulars of a matrimonial offence alleged other than adultery and that if no, or no sufficient particulars are given, or a new matter arises in the course of the proceedings, an adjournment may be granted and an interim order made.

The general effect of the decisions is that whilst the parties to summary proceedings should not be subject to the detailed pleadings appropriate to the High Court, proper notice of an allegation should be given so that a party may develop his case in an atmosphere in which he is not taken by surprise.

1. *Broadbent v Broadbent* (1927) 43 TLR 186; *Duffield v Duffield* [1949] 1 All ER 1105, 113 JP 308; *Boston v Boston* (1928) 92 JP 44; *Hind v Hind* [1969] 1 All ER 1083, 133 JP 293.
2. *Frampton v Frampton* [1951] WN 250; *Jones v Jones* [1954] 3 All ER 476n, 118 JP 563; *Sullivan v Sullivan* [1956] 1 All ER 611n, 120 JP 161.
3. *Hind v Hind*, supra.
4. *Hind v Hind*, supra.
5. See *Boston v Boston*, and *Hind v Hind*, supra.
6. [1963] 1 All ER 43, 127 JP 74.

6–81 Powers of court to make order for financial provision under section 2 of the 1978 Act. Where on an application for an order for financial provision under section 2 of the Domestic Proceedings and Magistrates' Courts Act 1978, the applicant satisfies the court of any of the grounds set out in section 1 of the Act, the court may make any one or more of the following orders—

(*a*) an order that the respondent shall make to the applicant such periodical payments, and for such term, as may be specified in the order;

(*b*) an order that the respondent shall pay to the applicant such lump sum as may be so specified;

(c) an order that the respondent shall make to the applicant for the benefit of a child of the family to whom the application relates, or to such a child, such periodical payments, and for such term, as may be so specified;

(d) an order that the respondent shall pay to the applicant for the benefit of a child of the family to whom the application relates, or to such a child, such lump sum as may be so specified[1].

Without prejudice to the generality of the power to order payment of a lump sum under paragraphs (b) and (d) above, a lump sum may be ordered for the purpose of enabling any liability or expenses reasonably incurred in maintaining the applicant, or any child of the family to whom the application relates, before the making of the order to be met[2]. The amount of any lump sum ordered under either of those paragraphs shall not exceed £1,000[3].

The family proceedings court may not exercise its powers to order financial provision for a child otherwise than in accordance with the Child Support Act 1991[4].

The order may be made in the respondent's absence if it is proved to the satisfaction of the court that he received reasonable notice of the hearing, or the circumstances justify proceeding with the hearing in his absence[5].

Any order should include a statement that the ground of the application is found to be true[6], and in a case of desertion the date upon which desertion is found to have commenced should appear in the order[7].

Guidance on the making of an order against a member of Her Majesty's forces is given in Home Office Circular No 251/1970 and Home Office Circular No 25/1986, dated 4 April 1986. For orders against members of the Royal Navy and the Royal Marines, see Home Office Circular No 12/1982, dated 10 February 1982. See also the Army Act 1955, sections 144 and 150 to 152, the Air Force Act 1955, sections 144 and 150 to 152[8].

---

1. Domestic Proceedings and Magistrates' Courts Act 1978, s 2(1), this PART, post.
2. Domestic Proceedings and Magistrates' Courts Act 1978, s 2(2), this PART, post.
3. Domestic Proceedings and Magistrates' Courts Act 1978, s 2(3), this PART, post.
4. See in particular s 8 of the Child Support Act 1991, this PART, post.
5. Family Proceedings Courts (Matrimonial Proceedings etc) Rules 1991, r 8, this PART, post.
6. *Brown v Brown* (1898) 62 JP 568, 711; *Wilcox v Wilcox* (1902) 66 JP 166; *Bullivant v Bullivant* (1902) 18 TLR 317; *Dodd v Dodd* [1906] P 189, 70 JP 163.
7. *Fengl v Fengl* [1914] P 274.
8. See post, in PART VIII: title ARMED FORCES. See also *Barnish v Barnish* (1976) 6 Fam Law 174, 120 Sol Jo 450.

6–82   Evidence as to means on an application under section 2.   Before the court makes an order for financial provision under section 2 of the 1978 Act, the court must receive evidence of the means of the parties. Such evidence may be received through written statements which have been filed with the court and served on the parties[1], or by way of oral evidence at the hearing.

A statement in writing to the effect that wages of any amount have been paid to a person during any period, purporting to be signed by or on behalf of his or her employer, is evidence of the facts therein stated[2].

The court also has power in any proceedings where it has power to make an attachment of earnings order to order the debtor to give to the court a statement of earnings[3].

Where the husband does not appear but sends written details of his finances, which his wife cannot agree, the court should adjourn the hearing so that he can be required to attend and deal with those matters[4].

---

1. See Family Proceedings Courts (Matrimonial Proceedings etc) Rules 1991, r 9, this PART, post; see also para **6–35 Documentary evidence**, ante.
2. Magistrates' Courts Act 1980, s 100, in PART I: MAGISTRATES' COURTS, PROCEDURE, ante.
3. Attachment of Earnings Act 1971, s 14(1), in PART I: MAGISTRATES' COURTS, PROCEDURE, ante.
4. *Whittingstall v Whittingstall* [1989] FCR 759.

6–83   Assessment of maintenance.   The approach of the family proceedings court to the assessment of maintenance under section 3 of the Domestic Proceedings and Magistrates' Courts Act 1978 should follow that of the divorce courts in the assessment of maintenance under section 25 of the Matrimonial Causes Act 1973[1].

Section 3 of the 1978 Act sets out the matters to which the court is to have regard in exercising its power to make an order for financial provision. The section states that it shall be the duty of the court, in deciding whether to exercise its powers under section 2 and, if so, in what manner, to have regard to all the circumstances of the case, first consideration being given to the welfare while a minor of any child of the family who has not attained the age of 18[2].

As regards its power to order financial provision for the *applicant* (whether by way of periodical payments or a lump sum), the court must in particular have regard to the following matters—

(a) the income, earning capacity, property and other financial resources which each of the parties to the marriage has or is likely to have in the foreseeable future, including in the case of earning capacity any increase in that capacity which it would in the opinion of the court be reasonable to expect a party to the marriage to take steps to acquire;

(b) the financial needs, obligations and responsibilities which each of the parties to the marriage has or is likely to have in the foreseeable future;

(c) the standard of living enjoyed by the parties to the marriage before the occurrence of the conduct which is alleged as the ground of the application;

(d) the age of each party to the marriage and the duration of the marriage;

(e) any physical or mental disability of either of the parties to the marriage;

(*f*)   the contributions which each of the parties has made or is likely in the foreseeable future to make to the welfare of the family, including any contribution by looking after the home or caring for the family;

(*g*)   the conduct of each of the parties, if that conduct is such that it would in the opinion of the court be inequitable to disregard it[3].

As regards its power to order financial provision for the benefit of a *child of the family* (whether by way of periodical payments or a lump sum), the court must in particular have regard to the following matters—

(*h*)   the financial needs of the child;

(*i*)   the income, earning capacity (if any), property and other financial resources of the child;

(*j*)   any physical or mental disability of the child;

(*k*)   the standard of living enjoyed by the family before the occurrence of the conduct which is alleged as the ground of the application;

(*l*)   the manner in which the child was being and in which the parties to the marriage expected him to be educated or trained;

(*m*)   the matters mentioned in relation to the parties to the marriage in paragraphs (*a*) and (*b*) above[4].

As regards the exercise of its powers under section 2 of the Act in favour of a child of the family who is not the child of the respondent, the court must also have regard—

(*a*)   to whether the respondent had assumed any responsibility for the child's maintenance and, if he did, to the extent to which, and the basis on which, he assumed that responsibility and to the length of time during which, he discharged that responsibility;

(*b*)   to whether in assuming and discharging that responsibility the respondent did so knowing that the child was not his own child;

(*c*)   to the liability of any other person to maintain the child[5].

The court is required to make findings *seriatim* upon each of the matters set out above and then balance the factors one against another so as to arrive at an order which is just and reasonable[6].

It should be noted that when determining the question of financial provision the court must give "first consideration" to the welfare, while a minor, of a child, whereas when deciding questions relating to the upbringing of a child, the child's welfare shall be the court's paramount consideration[7].

"Earnings capacity" includes the ability to earn higher wages by working overtime[8]. Although the court must have regard to all the resources of the wife, it does not follow that the husband is entitled to have the whole of her income or capacity to earn taken into account in assessing her maintenance. Each case depends on its own facts[9]. A husband who, on application to vary a maintenance order, alleges that the wife should be working must make that allegation in his written application so that the wife has notice[10].

Where a wife is in receipt of state benefits, the amount she so receives is not to be regarded as "financial resources". It is, therefore, an irrelevant factor in assessing the amount the husband should pay that the wife would receive no benefit from the order as her state benefits would be reduced by that amount. But where the available resources of the husband are so modest that an order making adequate contribution for the wife would leave him with a sum quite inadequate to enable him to meet his own financial requirements, then the court can have regard to the fact that state benefits will be available to the wife[11]. Courts must bear in mind that principle, and the "clean break" objective, and strike whatever balance, or make whatever choice, between them that the requirements of justice in the particular circumstances appear to dictate[12].

The fact that the husband has undertaken the responsibility of maintaining a new wife must be fully borne in mind and be given the same degree and weight as his responsibilities in any other financial respect[11].

In deciding whether to take the conduct of the parties into account the court is not restricted to conduct contributing to the breakdown of the marriage, nor to the conduct of one party where the other was blameless. The court is entitled to look at the whole of the picture, including the conduct during the marriage and after the marriage which may or may not have contributed to the breakdown of the marriage or which in some other way makes it inequitable to ignore the conduct of each of the parties[13].

Further guidelines on the assessment of maintenance are contained in the notes to section 3 of the Domestic Proceedings and Magistrates' Courts Act 1978, in para **6–1493**.

---

1. *Macey v Macey* (1981) 3 FLR 7.
2. Domestic Proceedings and Magistrates' Courts Act 1978, s 3(1), this PART, post.
3. Domestic Proceedings and Magistrates' Courts Act 1978, s 3(2), this PART, post.
4. Domestic Proceedings and Magistrates' Courts Act 1978, s 3(3), this PART, post.
5. Domestic Proceedings and Magistrates' Courts Act 1978, s 3(4), this PART, post.
6. *Vasey v Vasey* (1984) 149 JP 219, [1985] FLR 596, CA.
7. See s 1 of the Children Act 1989, this PART, post.
8. *Klucinski v Klucinski* [1953] 1 All ER 683, 117 JP 187.
9. *Attwood v Attwood* [1968] P 591, [1968] 3 All ER 385.
10. *Adams v Adams* (1978) 8 Fam Law 141.
11. *Barnes v Barnes* [1972] 3 All ER 872, [1972] 1 WLR 1381.
12. See *Ashley v Blackman* [1988] Fam 85, [1988] 3 WLR 222, [1988] FCR 699.
13. *Kyte v Kyte* [1988] Fam 145, [1987] 3 All ER 1041, [1988] FCR 325.

6–84   Duration of order under section 2.   In an order for financial provision for a *party to a marriage*, the term to be specified must be such term as the court thinks fit except that the term shall not begin earlier than the date of the making of the application for the order and shall not extend beyond the death of either of the parties to the marriage. If the marriage of the parties affected by the order is subsequently dissolved or annulled but the order continues in force, the order shall cease to have effect on the remarriage of the party in whose favour it was made, except in relation to any arrears due under the order on the date of the remarriage[1].

The term to be specified in an order for periodical payments to be made for the benefit of a child may begin with the date of the making of an application for the order in question or any later date. Such an order must not in the first instance extend beyond the date of the birthday of the child next following his attaining the upper limit of the compulsory school age, unless the court considers that in the circumstances of the case that the welfare of the child requires that it should extend to a later date, and shall not, in any event, extend beyond the date of the child's eighteenth birthday[2].

An order for periodical payments or the payment of a lump sum shall not be made in favour of a child who has attained the age of eighteen unless it appears to the court—

   (a) that the child is, or will be, or if such an order or provision were made would be, receiving instruction at an educational establishment or undergoing training for a trade, profession or vocation, whether or not he is also, or will also be, in gainful employment; or

   (b) that there are special circumstances which justify the making of the order or provision[3].

---

1. Domestic Proceedings and Magistrates' Courts Act 1978, s 4, this PART, post.
2. Domestic Proceedings and Magistrates' Courts Act 1978, s 5(2), this PART, post.
3. Domestic Proceedings and Magistrates' Courts Act 1978, s 5(1) and (3), this PART, post.

6–85 Refusal of order in case more suitable for the High Court. Where on the hearing of an application for an order under section 2 of the 1978 Act, a family proceedings court is of the opinion that any of the matters in question between the parties would be more conveniently dealt with by the High Court, the justices shall refuse to make any order on the application, and no appeal shall lie from that refusal. However, if in any proceedings in the High Court relating to or comprising the same subject matter as that application the High Court so orders, the application shall be reheard and determined by a family proceedings court acting for the same area as the first mentioned court[1].

This provision applies only in matters in which the High Court has concurrent jurisdiction with the justices, but not in cases where the High Court has no jurisdiction to grant relief[2]. There is power to make an interim order where an order is refused under this provision[3].

---

1. Domestic Proceedings and Magistrates' Courts Act 1978, s 27, this PART, post.
2. *Perks v Perks* [1946] P 1, [1945] 2 All ER 580, 110 JP 94; *Smyth v Smyth* [1956] 2 All ER 476, 120 JP 307; *Davies v Davies* [1957] P 357, [1957] 2 All ER 444, 121 JP 369.
3. Domestic Proceedings and Magistrates' Courts Act 1978, s 19, this PART, post.

6–86 Application and service: section 2 order. Proceedings for an order under s 2 of the 1978 Act are commenced by filing with the justices' chief executive an application in writing in the prescribed form. The application must include a statement of means of the applicant which is also prescribed, and sufficient copies of the application must be filed for one to be served on the respondent[1]. On receipt of the application, the justices' clerk shall fix the date, time and place for a hearing or a directions appointment and the justices' chief executive must endorse the date, time and place so fixed upon the copies of the application filed by the applicant. The justices' chief executive must then return the copies to the applicant[1].

The applicant must serve a copy of the application, endorsed by the justices' chief executive, on the respondent at least 21 days prior to the date fixed for the hearing or a directions appointment. Service must be effected in accordance with the Rules[2]. Within 14 days of service of an application, the respondent must file with the justices' chief executive and serve on the parties an answer to the application in the appropriate form which is prescribed[3].

---

1. Family Proceedings Courts (Matrimonial Proceedings etc) Rules 1991, r 3, this PART, post.
2. As to service of documents generally, see para **6–17**, ante.
3. Family Proceedings Courts (Matrimonial Proceedings etc) Rules 1991, r 5, this PART, post.

Proceedings under section 6 of the Domestic Proceedings and Magistrates' Courts Act 1978

6–95 Application for agreed order for financial provision under section 6 of the 1978 Act.
Under s 6 of the Domestic Proceedings and Magistrates' Courts Act 1978 either party to a marriage may apply to a family proceedings court for an order for financial provision on the ground that either the party making the application or the other party to the marriage has *agreed* to make such financial provision as may be specified in the application[1].

A party to a marriage who has applied for an order under s 2 of the Act is not precluded at any time before the determination of that application, from applying for an order under s 6 of the Act. However, if an order is made under s 6 on the application of either party and either of them has also made an application for an order under s 2 of the Act, the application for the order under s 2 shall be treated as if it had been withdrawn[2].

1. Domestic Proceedings and Magistrates' Courts Act 1978, s 6(1), this PART, post.
2. Domestic Proceedings and Magistrates' Courts Act 1978, s 6(4), this PART, post.

6–96 **Powers of the court to make order for financial provision under section 6 of the 1978 Act.** On an application for an order under s 6 the court may, if—

(a) it is satisfied that the applicant or the respondent, as the case may be, has agreed to make that provision, and

(b) it has no reason to think that it would be contrary to the interests of justice to exercise its powers,

order that the applicant or the respondent, as the case may be, shall make the financial provision specified in the application[1].

Where the financial provision specified in an application includes or consists of provision in respect of a child of the family, the court shall not make an order unless it considers that the provision which the applicant or the respondent, as the case may be, has agreed to make in respect of that child provides for, or makes a proper contribution towards, the financial needs of the child[2].

Where the court decides—

(a) that it would be contrary to the interests of justice to make an order for the making of the financial provision specified in the application, or

(b) that any financial provision which the applicant or the respondent, as the case may be, has agreed to make in respect of a child of the family does not provide for, or make a proper contribution towards, the financial needs of that child,

but is of the opinion—

(i) that it would not be contrary to the interests of justice to make an order for the making of some other financial provision specified by the court, and

(ii) that, in so far as that other financial provision contains any provision for a child of the family, it provides for, or makes a proper contribution towards, the financial needs of that child,

then, if both the parties agree, the court may order that the applicant or the respondent, as the case may be, shall make that other financial provision[3].

The family proceedings court may not exercise its powers to order financial provision in respect of a child otherwise than in accordance with the Child Support Act 1991[4].

The reference to "financial provision" means the provision mentioned in any one or more of the following—

(a) the making of periodical payments by one party to the other;

(b) the payment of a lump sum by one party to the other;

(c) the making of periodical payments by one party to a child of the family or to the other party for the benefit of such a child;

(d) the payment by one party of a lump sum to a child of the family or to the other party for the benefit of such a child[5].

1. Domestic Proceedings and Magistrates' Courts Act 1978, s 6(1), this PART, post.
2. Domestic Proceedings and Magistrates' Courts Act 1978, s 6(3), this PART, post.
3. Domestic Proceedings and Magistrates' Courts Act 1978, s 6(5), this PART, post.
4. See in particular s 8 of the Child Support Act 1991, this PART, post.
5. Child Support Act 1991, s 6(2), this PART, post.

6–97 **Evidence as to means on an application under section 6.** Where the respondent is not present or represented at the hearing of an application for an order under s 6, the court must not make an order unless there is produced to it evidence of—

(a) the consent of the respondent to the making of the order,

(b) the financial resources of the respondent, and

(c) in a case where the financial provision specified in the application includes or consists of provision in respect of a child of the family to be made by the applicant to the respondent for the benefit of the child or to the child, the financial resources of the child[1].

Evidence of the matters in (a) to (c) above shall be given by way of written statement in the prescribed form signed by the respondent or, where the application is in respect of financial provision for a child and the child has completed the appropriate form, the child[2].

1. Domestic Proceedings and Magistrates' Courts Act 1978, s 6(9), this PART, post.
2. Family Proceedings Courts (Matrimonial Proceedings etc) Rules 1991, r 17, this PART, post.

6–98 **Duration of order under section 6.** The provisions under ss 4 and 5 of the 1978 Act apply to an order under s 6 as they apply to an order under s 2: see para **6–84**.

Where the court makes an order under s 6 which contains provision for the making of periodical payments and an application under s 2 of the Act is treated as if it had been withdrawn, the term which may be specified as the term for which the payments are to be made may begin with the date of the making of the application for the order under s 2 or any later date[1].

1. Domestic Proceedings and Magistrates' Courts Act 1978, s 6(8), this PART, post.

6–99 Application and service: section 6 order. Proceedings for an order under s 6 of the 1978 Act are commenced by filing with the justices' chief executive an application in writing in the prescribed form. The application must include a statement of means of the applicant which is also prescribed, and sufficient copies of the application must be filed for one to be served on the respondent[1]. On receipt of the application the justices' clerk shall fix the date, time and place for a hearing or a directions appointment and the justices' chief executive must endorse the date, time and place so fixed upon the copies of the application filed by the applicant. The justices' chief executive must then return copies to the applicant forthwith[1].

The requirements as to service of the application and the respondent's answer are the same as those on an application for an order under s 2 of the Act; see para **6–86**.

Where either party has made an application for an order under s 2 of the 1978 Act, and the court is asked to proceed to consider making an order under s 6 of the 1978 Act by virtue of s 6(4), the application for the order under s 6 may be made orally and the court may dispense with the requirements as to service[2].

1. Family Proceedings Courts (Matrimonial Proceedings etc) Rules 1991, r 3, this PART, post.
2. Family Proceedings Courts (Matrimonial Proceedings etc) Rules 1991, r 3(3), this PART, post.

Maintenance agreements and proceedings under section 7 of the Domestic Proceedings and Magistrates' Courts Act 1978

6–105 Maintenance agreement: application for order under section 7 of the 1978 Act. Where the parties to a marriage have been living apart for a continuous period exceeding three months, neither party having deserted the other, and one of the parties has been making periodical payments for the benefit of the other party or of a child of the family, that other party may apply to a family proceedings court for an order under s 7 of the Act. The application must specify the aggregate amount of the payments so made during the period of three months immediately preceding the date of the application[1].

1. Domestic Proceedings and Magistrates' Courts Act 1978, s 7(1), this PART, post.

6–106 Maintenance agreement: powers of the court to make order under section 7 of the 1978 Act. Where on an application for an order under s 7 the court is satisfied that the respondent has made the payments specified in the application, the court may make one or both of the following orders—

(*a*) an order that the respondent shall make to the applicant such periodical payments, and for such term, as may be specified in the order;

(*b*) an order that the respondent shall make to the applicant for the benefit of a child of the family to whom the application relates, or to such a child, such periodical payments, and for such term, as may be so specified[1].

In exercising its powers, the court—

(i) shall not require the respondent to make payments which exceed in aggregate during any period of three months the aggregate amount paid by him for the benefit of the applicant or a child of the family during the period of three months immediately preceding the date of the making of the application;

(ii) shall not require the respondent to make payments to or for the benefit of any person which exceed in amount the payments which the court considers that it would have required the respondent to make to or for the benefit of that person on an application under s 1 of the Act;

(iii) shall not require payments to be made to or for the benefit of a child of the family who is not a child of the respondent unless the court considers that it would have made an order in favour of that child on an application under s 1 of the Act[2].

Where on an application for an order under s 7 the court considers that the orders which it has power to make under the section (*a*) would not provide reasonable maintenance for the applicant, or (*b*) if the application relates to a child of the family, would not provide, or make a proper contribution towards reasonable maintenance for that child, the court shall refuse to make an order, but may treat the application as if it were an application for an order under s 2 of the Act[3].

1. Domestic Proceedings and Magistrates' Courts Act 1978, s 7(2), this PART, post.
2. Domestic Proceedings and Magistrates' Courts Act 1978, s 7(3), this PART, post.
3. Domestic Proceedings and Magistrates' Courts Act 1978, s 7(4), this PART, post.

6–107 Evidence as to means on application under section 7. If there is agreement between the parties as to the terms of the proposed order and the court is satisfied that an order on those terms would provide reasonable maintenance for the applicant and make a proper contribution towards reasonable maintenance for a child of the family, the court may proceed on the basis of formal oral evidence which supports the written statements of the parties as to their means and resources. Fuller oral evidence will be required if the court is not so satisfied or where issues in dispute as to the means of the parties remain to be resolved.

The prescribed form of application includes a statement of means which the applicant must complete[1].

---

1. As to Application and Service, see para **6–109**.

6–108   Duration of order under section 7.   The provisions of ss 4 and 5 of the 1978 Act apply to an order under s 7 as they apply in relation to orders under section 2(1)(*a*) and section 2(1)(*c*) of the Act[1].

---

1. Domestic Proceedings and Magistrates' Courts Act 1978, ss 4 and 5, this PART, post. As to duration of order under s 2, see para **6–84**.

6–109   Application and service: section 7 order.   Proceedings for an order for periodical payments under s 7 of the 1978 Act must be commenced by filing with the justices' chief executive an application in writing in the prescribed form. The application must include a statement of means of the applicant which is also prescribed, and sufficient copies of the application must be filed for one to be served on the respondent[1]. The application must specify the aggregate amount of the payments which have been made during the period of three months immediately preceding the date of the making of the application.

On receipt of the application the justices' clerk must fix the date, time and place for a hearing or a directions appointment and the justices' chief executive must endorse the date, time and place so fixed upon the copies of the application filed by the applicant. The justices' chief executive must then return copies of the application to the applicant forthwith[1].

The requirements as to service of the application and the respondent's answer are the same as those on an application for an order under s 2 of the Act; see para **6–86**.

---

1. Family Proceedings Courts (Matrimonial Proceedings etc) Rules 1991, r 3, this PART, post.

6–110   Alteration of maintenance agreement.   Where a maintenance agreement is for the time being subsisting and each of the parties to the agreement is for the time being either domiciled or resident in England and Wales, either party may apply to a family proceedings court[1] for an order under s 35 of the Matrimonial Causes Act 1973[2].

If the court to which the application is made is satisfied either—

(*a*) that *by reason of a change in the circumstances* in the light of which any financial arrangements contained in the agreement were made or, as the case may be, financial arrangements were omitted from it (including a change foreseen by the parties when making the agreement), the agreement should be altered so as to make different, or, as the case may be, so as to contain, financial arrangements, or

(*b*) that the agreement does not contain proper financial arrangements with respect to any child of the family,

the court may by order make such alterations in the agreement[3]. Those alterations may vary or revoke any financial arrangements contained in the agreement, or insert in the agreement financial arrangements for the benefit of one of the parties to the agreement or of a child of the family, as appear to the court to be just having regard to all the circumstances[3].

A family proceedings court shall not entertain an application unless both the parties to the agreement are resident in England and Wales and at least one of the parties is resident within the commission area for which the court is appointed and shall not have power to make an order on the application except—

(*a*) in a case where the agreement includes no provision for periodical payments by either of the parties, an order inserting provision for the making by one of the parties of periodical payments for the maintenance of the other party or for the maintenance of any child of the family;

(*b*) in a case where the agreement includes provision for the making by one of the parties of periodical payments, an order increasing or reducing the rate of, or terminating, any of those payments[4].

Where a court decides to alter by order an agreement, the provisions of s 35 of the Matrimonial Causes Act 1973 regulate the term for which the payments or the additional payments are to be made[5]. A variation may be back-dated[6].

An application under s 35 is to be made by way of complaint and summons[7].

For what constitutes a maintenance agreement, reference should be made to the Matrimonial Causes Act 1973, s 34(2)[8].

The expression "by reason of a change in the circumstances" has received judicial consideration in two reported cases. In the first[9], it was decided that the occurrence of an event during the currency of the agreement, contemplated by the parties when the agreement was made, is not within the intent of the section. In the second case, it was held that although there was a change in the circumstances it was not just that by reason of the change there should be an alteration in the financial arrangements (change brought about by husband's voluntary and unilateral action)[10]. In another case, it was held that an application for altering an agreement was not made out because, *inter alia*, a wife for whose maintenance no provision had been made was not debarred from instituting proceedings against her husband for his wilful neglect to provide reasonable maintenance for her[11].

---

1. The application shall be treated as family proceedings by virtue of the Magistrates' Courts Act 1980, s 65, in PART I: MAGISTRATES' COURTS, PROCEDURE, ante.
2. See this PART, post.
3. Matrimonial Causes Act 1973, s 35(2), this PART, post.
4. Matrimonial Causes Act 1973, s 35(3), this PART, post.
5. Matrimonial Causes Act 1973, s 35(4), (5), this PART, post.
6. *Warden v Warden* [1982] Fam 10, [1981] 3 All ER 193.
7. See the Magistrates' Courts Rules 1981, r 105, in PART I: MAGISTRATES' COURTS, PROCEDURE, ante. See also Commencement of proceedings, paras **6–12** and **6–14**.
8. See this PART, post.
9. *K v K* [1961] 2 All ER 266.
10. *Ratcliffe v Ratcliffe* [1962] 3 All ER 993.
11. *Gorman v Gorman* [1964] 3 All ER 739.

Welfare of children in proceedings under the Domestic Proceedings and Magistrates' Courts Act 1978

6–112   Welfare of children: restriction on making of orders under the 1978 Act.   Where an application is made by a party to a marriage for an order under ss 2, 6 or 7 of the Domestic Proceedings and Magistrates' Courts Act 1978 and there is a child of the family who is under the age of 18, the court must not dismiss or make a final order on the application until it has decided whether to exercise any of its powers under the Children Act 1989[1] with respect to the child[2]. Proceedings under the 1978 Act are "family proceedings" within the meaning of the Children Act 1989[3], and the court may, for example, make a s 8 order under that Act[4].

---

1. See this PART, post.
2. Domestic Proceedings and Magistrates' Courts Act 1978, s 8, this PART, post.
3. Children Act 1989, s 8(3), (4), this PART, post.
4. As to s 8 orders, see paras **6–150** to **6–157**.

Interim maintenance orders; variation or revocation of order for financial provision

6–115   Interim maintenance order.   Where an application is made to a family proceedings court for an order under ss 2, 6 or 7[1] of the Domestic Proceedings and Magistrates' Courts Act 1978, the court may, at any time before making a final order on or dismissing the application, make an interim maintenance order[2]. The justices may also make an interim order if they refuse to make an order on the ground that the case would be more conveniently dealt with by the High Court[3].

An interim maintenance order may require the respondent to make to the applicant or to any child of the family who is under the age of 18, or to the applicant for the benefit of such a child, such periodical payments as the court thinks reasonable[4]. Where an application is made for an agreed order for financial provision under s 6 of the Domestic Proceedings and Magistrates' Courts Act 1978, by the party to the marriage who has agreed to make the financial provision specified in the application, the interim maintenance order may require the applicant to make payments to the respondent or to any child of the family[5].

Section 3 of the Domestic Proceedings and Magistrates' Courts Act 1978[6] (matters to which the court shall have regard in deciding whether to make an order for financial provision under s 2 of the Act) does not apply to the making of an interim maintenance order, but the court will wish to be satisfied that the terms of any interim order which have been agreed between the parties are appropriate having regard to the circumstances and the financial position of the parties. The justices may require oral evidence to be given as to such matters before approving the terms of an agreed interim maintenance order, and such evidence will be required if the court is required to determine the quantum of interim maintenance.

On the making of an interim maintenance order the court must give consideration to the means of payment under the order. If the interim order is a qualifying order within the meaning of the Magistrates' Courts Act 1980, s 59(2)[7], the court shall exercise its powers under that section by determining the method by which payments under the order shall be made[7].

No appeal shall lie from the making of or refusal to make an interim maintenance order, or from the making of or refusal of a variation or revocation of an interim maintenance order[8]. An interim maintenance order is enforceable as a magistrates' court maintenance order[9].

1. See this PART, post.
2. Domestic Proceedings and Magistrates' Courts Act 1978, s 19(1)(*a*), this PART, post.
3. Domestic Proceedings and Magistrates' Courts Act 1978, s 19(1)(*b*), this PART, post. As to the power of the family proceedings court to make an order on such ground, see paras **6–27** and **6–85**.
4. Domestic Proceedings and Magistrates' Courts Act 1978, s 19(1)(i), this PART, post.
5. Domestic Proceedings and Magistrates' Courts Act 1978 s 19(3A), this PART, post.
6. See this PART, post.
7. See PART I: MAGISTRATES' COURTS, PROCEDURE, ante.
8. Domestic Proceedings and Magistrates' Courts Act 1978, s 19(8), this PART, post.
9. Domestic Proceedings and Magistrates' Courts Act 1978, s 32.

6–116 Interim maintenance order: duration. Only one interim maintenance order may be made with respect to any application and payments shall commence from such date as may be specified in the order, not being earlier than the date on which the original application for an order under s 2, 6 or 7 of the 1978 Act was made[1].

An interim maintenance order shall cease to have effect on whichever of the following dates occurs first: (*a*) the date of cessation, if any, specified in the order; (*b*) the date of expiration of a period of three months beginning with the making of the interim order; or (*c*) the date on which the court either makes a final order on or dismisses the application[2].

The court may direct that an interim order shall continue in force for a further period which may be specified, but the order shall not have effect for more than three months from the date of the extension of the order. The total period, therefore, for which an interim order could run is six months if the extension is ordered on the last day of an initial six-month order[3]. An interim maintenance order shall continue to have effect and remain enforceable notwithstanding that the parties to the marriage are living with each other at the date of the making of the order, or that they subsequently resume living with each other[4].

1. Domestic Proceedings and Magistrates' Courts Act 1978, s 19(5) and (7), this PART, post.
2. Domestic Proceedings and Magistrates' Courts Act 1978, s 19(5), this PART, post.
3. Domestic Proceedings and Magistrates' Courts Act 1978, s 19(6), this PART, post.
4. Domestic Proceedings and Magistrates' Courts Act 1978, s 25, this PART, post.

6–117 Variation or revocation of a periodical payments order. An application under s 20 of the Domestic Proceedings and Magistrates' Courts Act 1978 for the variation or revocation of an order for periodical payments may be made where a magistrates' court has made an order under ss 2(1)(*a*), 2(1)(*c*), 6, 7 or 19 of the 1978 Act. Moreover, the court may also make an order for the payment of a lump sum under s 2(1)(*b*) or 2(1)(*d*), or 6 of the Act[1].

An order made under s 20 which varies an order for the making of periodical payments may provide that the payments as so varied shall be made from such date as the court may specify, but the date shall not be earlier than the date of the making of the application under the section. However, where the application is made before the end of the period of six months beginning with the date on which a maintenance assessment took place, the court may direct that the variation or revocation shall take effect from the date on which the assessment took effect or any later date. Similarly, if the application is made before the end of the period of six months beginning with the date on which a child order is affected by a maintenance assessment, the court may direct that the variation or revocation of a spousal order shall take effect from the date on which the child order became affected by the assessment or any later date[2].

In exercising the powers conferred by s 20 the court must, so far as it appears to the court just to do so, give effect to any agreement which has been reached between the parties in relation to the application and, if there is no such agreement or if the court decides not to give effect to the agreement, the court must have regard to all the circumstances of the case, first consideration being given to the welfare while a minor of any child of the family who has not attained the age of 18. The circumstances of the case shall include any change in any of the matters to which the court was required to have regard when making the order to which the application relates or (in the case of an application for the variation or revocation of an order made under s 6) to which the court would have been required to have regard if that order had been made under s 2 of the Act[3].

The court, therefore, must have regard not only to all the circumstances of the case, but also any changes in the matters referred to in s 3 of the Act. This means that the court must consider all appropriate circumstances under s 3 *de novo*[4]. The proper approach for the court is to make findings *seriatim* upon each of the matters set out in s 3(1) and then to balance the factors against one another so as to arrive at an order which is just and reasonable[5].

Provided there is no question of injustice to the parties, the court must give effect to any agreement which has been reached. A solicitor's letter saying that his client did not oppose an application to reduce the amount of periodical payments and remission of arrears and consented to the order being reduced to a nominal order was held to amount to an agreement to such reduction and remission within the meaning of s 20[6].

The power of the court to vary or revoke an interim maintenance order does not permit the court to extend the period for which the order is in force[7].

The court's power under s 20 also extends temporarily to suspending any provision of a periodical payments order and reviving any provision so suspended[8].

1. Domestic Proceedings and Magistrates' Courts Act 1978, s 20(1)–(3), this PART, post.
2. Domestic Proceedings and Magistrates' Courts Act 1978, s 20(9), (9A) and (9B), this PART, post.

3. Domestic Proceedings and Magistrates' Courts Act 1978, s 20(11), this PART, post.
4. *Riley v Riley* (1986) 151 JP 650.
5. *Vasey v Vasey* (1984) 149 JP 219, [1985] FLR 596, CA.
6. *Whitton v Devizes Magistrates' Court* (1984) 150 JP 330.
7. Domestic Proceedings and Magistrates' Courts Act 1978, s 20(5), this PART, post.
8. Domestic Proceedings and Magistrates' Courts Act 1978, s 20(6), this PART, post.

6-118 Variation of order for periodical payments: method of payment. The power of the court under s 20 of the 1978 Act also includes, if the court is satisfied that payment has not been made in accordance with the order, to exercise one of its powers under paragraphs (*a*) to (*d*) of s 59(3) of the Magistrates' Courts Act 1980[1]. In any case where a magistrates' court has made an order under Part I of the Domestic Proceedings and Magistrates' Courts Act 1978 for the making of periodical payments, and payments under the order are required to be made by any method of payment falling within s 59(6) of the 1980 Act, an application may be made to the clerk to the justices for the order to be varied[2].

Where such an application is made, the justices' clerk, after giving written notice of the application to the respondent and allowing the respondent, within the period of 14 days beginning with the date of the giving of that notice, an opportunity to make written representations, may vary the order to provide that payments under the order shall be made to the justices' chief executive. If the justices' clerk considers that it is inappropriate for him to exercise his power under s 20ZA(3) of the 1978 Act, he may refer the matter to the court[3].

The court's power is governed by s 20ZA(3) and the court must have regard to any representations made by the parties to the application[4].

1. See PART I: MAGISTRATES' COURTS, PROCEDURE, ante.
2. Domestic Proceedings and Magistrates' Courts Act 1978, s 20ZA(2), this PART, post.
3. Domestic Proceedings and Magistrates' Courts Act 1978, s 20ZA(3)–(5), this PART, post.
4. Domestic Proceedings and Magistrates' Courts Act 1978, s 20ZA(7), this PART, post.

6-119 Revival of orders for periodical payments. Where an order made by a magistrates' court under Part I of the Domestic Proceedings and Magistrates' Courts Act 1978 for the making of periodical payments to or in respect of a child ceases to have effect on the date on which the child attains the age of 16, or at any time after that date but before or on the date on which he attains the age of 18, the child may apply to the court which made the order for an order for its revival[1].

If on such an application it appears to the court that (*a*) the child is, will be or would be receiving instruction at an education establishment or undergoing training for a trade, profession or vocation, whether or not while in gainful employment, or (*b*) there are special circumstances which justify the making of an order, the court may revive the order from such date as the court may specify, not being earlier than the date of the application. Any order revived under this provision may be varied or revoked under s 20 in the same way as it could have been varied or revoked had it continued in force[2].

1. Domestic Proceedings and Magistrates' Courts Act 1978, s 20A(1), this PART, post.
2. Domestic Proceedings and Magistrates' Courts Act 1978, s 20A(2), (3), this PART, post.

6-120 Variation of instalments of lump sum. Where the court has ordered that a lump sum shall be paid by instalments, the court, on an application made by either the person liable to pay or the person entitled to receive that sum, shall have power to vary that order by varying the number of instalments payable, the amount of any instalment payable and the date on which any instalment becomes payable[1].

1. Domestic Proceedings and Magistrates' Courts Act 1978, s 22, this PART, post.

6-121 Proceedings for variation or revocation against a person outside England and Wales. The jurisdiction conferred on a family proceedings court by virtue of s 20 of the 1978 Act is exercisable notwithstanding that the proceedings are brought by or against a person residing outside England and Wales[1].

If the court is satisfied that the respondent has been living outside England and Wales for the whole of the period beginning one month before the making of the application and ending with the date of hearing, it may proceed with an application made under s 20, provided that—

(*a*) the applicant has taken steps to notify the respondent of the making of the application and of the time and place appointed for the hearing by—

    (i) causing a notice in writing to that effect to be delivered to the respondent;

    (ii) causing a notice in writing to that effect to be sent by post addressed to the respondent at his last known or usual place of abode or at his place of business or at such other address at which there is ground for believing that it will reach the respondent, in accordance with directions given for the purpose by a justice acting for the same petty sessions area as that of the court; or

(iii) causing a notice to that effect to be inserted in one or more newspapers, in accordance with directions given by a justice; and

(*b*) it is reasonable in all the circumstances to proceed in the absence of the respondent[2].

For other conditions governing proceedings in these circumstances, reference should be made to the Rules[3].

---

1. Family Proceedings Courts (Matrimonial Proceedings etc) Rules 1991, r 22(1), this PART, post.
2. Family Proceedings Courts (Matrimonial Proceedings etc) Rules 1991, r 22(2), this PART, post.
3. Family Proceedings Courts (Matrimonial Proceedings etc) Rules 1991, r 22, this PART, post.

6–122   Application and service: proceedings under section 20 of the 1978 Act.   Proceedings under s 20 of the 1978 Act for the variation or revocation of a periodical payments order shall be commenced by filing with the justices' chief executive an application in writing in the prescribed form. The application must include a statement of means of the applicant which is also prescribed, and sufficient copies of the application must be filed for one to be served on the respondent. On receipt of the application the justices' clerk shall fix the date, time and place for a hearing or a directions appointment and the justices' chief executive must endorse the date, time and place so fixed upon copies of the application filed by the applicant and return the copies to the applicant forthwith[1].

The requirements as to service of the application and the respondent's answer are the same as those on an application for an order under s 2 of the Act; see para **6–86**. It should be noted that the above provisions under s 20 do not apply to an application for the variation of the rate of payments specified by a registered maintenance order; such application must be commenced by complaint[2].

---

1. Family Proceedings Courts (Matrimonial Proceedings etc) Rules 1991, r 3, this PART, post.
2. See for example, the Maintenance Orders Act 1958, ss 4(2) and 20(2), this PART, post, as respects orders registered in magistrates' courts under Pt I of that Act. As to commencement of proceedings by complaint, see para **6–14 Making a complaint**.

6–123   Resumption of cohabitation: effect on order.   Section 25 of the Domestic Proceedings and Magistrates' Courts Act 1978 provides that where periodical payments are required to be made to one of the parties to a marriage (whether for his own benefit or for the benefit of a child of the family) by an order made under s 2 or 6 of the Act or by an interim maintenance order made under s 19 (otherwise than on an application under s 7), the order shall be enforceable notwithstanding that the parties to the marriage are living with each other at the date of the making of the order or that, although they are not living with each other at that date, they subsequently resume living with each other. However, the order shall cease to have effect if after that date the parties continue to live with each other, or resume living with each other, for a continuous period exceeding six months[1].

Where an order under s 2 or 6 of the Act, or an interim maintenance order under s 19 of the Act (otherwise than on an application under s 7), requires periodical payments to be made to a child of the family, then, unless the court otherwise directs, the order shall continue to have effect and be enforceable notwithstanding that the parties to the marriage are living with each other at the date of the making of the order or that, although they are not living with each other at that date, they subsequently resume living with each other[2].

References to the parties to a marriage "living with each other" are to be construed as references to their living with each other in the same household[3].

Any order made under s 7 of the Act, and any interim maintenance order made on an application for an order under that section, shall cease to have effect if the parties to the marriage resume living with each other[4].

Where an order ceases to have effect by virtue of s 25, the court may on the application of either party to the marriage, make an order declaring that the first mentioned order ceased to have effect from such date as the court may specify[5].

---

1. Domestic Proceedings and Magistrates' Courts Act 1978, s 25(1), this PART, post.
2. Domestic Proceedings and Magistrates' Courts Act 1978, s 25(2), this PART, post.
3. Domestic Proceedings and Magistrates' Courts Act 1978, s 88(2), this PART, post.
4. Domestic Proceedings and Magistrates' Courts Act 1978, s 25(3), this PART, post.
5. Domestic Proceedings and Magistrates' Courts Act 1978, s 25(4), this PART, post.

Proceedings under Part IV of the Family Law Act 1996

6–125   Proceedings under Part IV of the Act.   A family proceedings court has jurisdiction, together with the High Court and a county court, to hear applications under Part IV of the Family Law Act 1996[1]. This jurisdiction is subject to any order made by the Lord Chancellor specifying proceedings or specifying circumstances in which proceedings may be commenced in (a) a specified level of court; (b) a court which falls within a specified class of court; or (c) a particular court determined in accordance with, or specified in, the order[2]. Such order may also provide for the transfer of proceedings between the High Court, a county court or a family proceedings court[3].

The jurisdiction of a family proceedings court is subject to the further qualification that it shall not be competent to entertain any application, or make any order, involving any disputed question as to a party's entitlement to occupy any property by virtue of a beneficial estate or interest or contract or by virtue of any enactment giving him the right to remain in occupation, unless it is unnecessary to determine the question in order to deal with the application or make the order[4].

In addition to the power to transfer proceedings, a family proceedings court may decline jurisdiction in any proceedings under Part IV if it considers that the case can more conveniently be dealt with by another court[5].

The orders which may be made under Part IV of the Act are an "occupation order", which means an order under s 33, 35, 36, 37 or 38 of the Act, and a "non-molestation order" which means an order under s 42 of the Act[6].

An application for an occupation order may be made in other family proceedings or without any other family proceedings being instituted[7]. If an application for an occupation order is made under ss 33, 35, 36, 37 or 38 of the Act, and the court considers that it has no power to make the order under the section concerned, but that it has power to make an order under one of the other sections, the court may make an order under that other section[8].

The fact that a person has applied for an occupation order under ss 35 to 38 of the Act, or that an occupation order has been made, does not affect the right of any person to claim a legal or equitable interest in any property in any subsequent proceedings[9].

A child under the age of 16 may not apply for an occupation order or a non-molestation order except with the leave of the court, and the court may grant leave only if it is satisfied that the child has sufficient understanding to make the proposed application for the order[10].

An application for an occupation order or a non-molestation order under Part IV must be made in the prescribed form[11]. An application must be supported (a) by a statement which is signed and declared to be true, or (b) with the leave of the court, by oral evidence[12]. An application may, with leave of the justices' clerk or of the court, be made *ex parte*[13]. An application made on notice, together with any statement supporting it and a notice of proceedings, must be served by the applicant on the respondent personally not less than 2 business days prior to the date on which the application is to be heard; the court or the justices' clerk may abridge the period of 2 days[14]. After service the applicant must file a statement of service[15].

Where an application for an occupation order or a non-molestation order is pending, the court must consider (on the application of either party or of its own motion) whether to exercise its powers to transfer the hearing of that application to another court and the justices' clerk or the court must make an order for transfer if it seems necessary or expedient to do so. Where an order for transfer is made, the justices' clerk must send a copy of the order (a) to the parties, and (b) to the family proceedings court or to the county court to which the proceedings are to be transferred[16].

On hearing an application under Part IV a record of hearing and any order made on the hearing must be drawn up in accordance with the prescribed forms[17]. Where an order is made on an application made *ex parte*, a copy of the order together with a copy of the application and of any statement supporting it must be served by the applicant on the respondent personally[18]. Where the applicant is acting in person, service of a copy of an order made on an application made *ex parte* shall be effected by the justices' clerk if the applicant so requests[19].

A copy of an order made on an application heard *inter partes* must be served by the applicant on the respondent personally, and where, in such applications, the applicant is acting in person, service of a copy of the order made may, with the leave of the justices' clerk be effected in accordance with the Rules[20].

A copy of an application for an occupation order under s 33, 35 or 36 of the Family Law Act 1996 must be served by the applicant by first-class post on the mortgagee or, as the case may be, the landlord of the dwelling-house in question, with a notice in the prescribed form informing him of his right to make representations in writing or at any hearing[21]. Similarly, where on such an application an order is made, a copy of the order must be served by the applicant by first-class post on the mortgagee or, as the case may be, the landlord of the dwelling-house in question[22]. The court may direct that a further hearing be held in order to consider any representations made by a mortgagee or a landlord[23].

---

1. Family Law Act 1996, s 57(1), this PART, post.
2. Family Law Act 1996, s 57(3)–(4) this PART, post. See also the Family Law Act 1996 (Part IV) (Allocation of Proceedings) Order 1997, this PART, post.
3. Family Law Act 1996, s 57(5), this PART, post. See for example arts 7 and 8 of the Family Law Act 1996 (Part IV) (Allocation of Proceedings) Order 1997, this PART, post.
4. Family Law Act 1996, s 59(1), this PART, post.
5. Family Law Act 1996, s 59(2), this PART, post.
6. Family Law Act 1996, s 39(1) and s 42, this PART, post.
7. Family Law Act 1996, s 39(2), this PART, post.
8. Family Law Act 1996, s 39(3), this PART, post.
9. Family Law Act 1996, s 39(4), this PART, post.
10. Ibid, s 43, this PART, post.
11. Family Proceedings Courts (Matrimonial Proceedings etc) Rules 1991, r 3A(1), this PART, post.
12. Family Law Act 1996, r 3A(3), this PART, post.
13. Family Law Act 1996, r 3A(4), this PART, post. As to applications made *ex parte*, see also paras **6–16** and **6–133**.
14. Family Law Act 1996, r 3A(5), this PART, post.
15. Family Law Act 1996, r 3A(11), this PART, post.
16. Family Law Act 1996, r 3A(8)–(9), this PART, post.

17. Family Law Act 1996, r 12A(1), this PART, post.
18. Family Law Act 1996, r 12A(2), this PART, post.
19. Family Law Act 1996 r 12A(3), this PART, post.
20. Family Law Act 1996, r 12A(5), (6), this PART, post.
21. Family Law Act 1996, r 3A(10), this PART, post.
22. Family Law Act 1996, r 12A(4), this PART, post.
23. Family Law Act 1996, r 12A(7), this PART, post.

6–126   Matrimonial home rights.   An occupation order may be applied for by a person who (*a*) is entitled to occupy a dwelling-house by virtue of a beneficial estate, interest, contract or other statutory right to remain in occupation, or (*b*) has matrimonial home rights in relation to a dwelling-house. If one spouse is entitled to occupy a dwelling-house by virtue of—

1.   a beneficial estate or interest or contract; or
2.   any enactment giving that spouse the right to remain in occupation; and

the other spouse is not so entitled, the spouse not so entitled has the matrimonial home rights as follows:

(*a*)   if in occupation, a right not to be evicted or excluded from the dwelling-house or any part of it by the other spouse except with the leave of the court given by order under s 33 of the Act;
(*b*)   if not in occupation, a right with the leave of the court so given to enter into and occupy the dwelling-house[1].

----

1. Family Law Act 1996, s 30, this PART, post.

6–127   Occupation orders.   If a person ("the person entitled")—

1.   is entitled to occupy a dwelling-house by virtue of a beneficial estate or interest or contract or by virtue of any enactment giving him the right to remain in occupation, or
2.   has matrimonial home rights in relation to a dwelling-house, and

the dwelling-house—

(i)   is or at any time has been the home of the person entitled and of another person with whom he is associated[1], or
(ii)   was at any time intended by the person entitled and any such other person to be their home,

the person entitled may apply to the court for an occupation order under s 33 of the Family Law Act 1996 containing the provisions described below.

Such an order may—

(*a*)   enforce the applicant's entitlement to remain in occupation as against the other person ("the respondent");
(*b*)   require the respondent to permit the applicant to enter and remain in the dwelling-house or part of the dwelling-house;
(*c*)   regulate the occupation of the dwelling-house by either or both parties;
(*d*)   if the respondent is entitled to occupy the dwelling-house by virtue of a beneficial estate or interest or contract or by virtue of any enactment giving him the right to remain in occupation, prohibit, suspend or restrict the exercise by him of his right to occupy the dwelling-house;
(*e*)   if the respondent has matrimonial home rights in relation to the dwelling-house and the applicant is the other spouse, restrict or terminate those rights;
(*f*)   require the respondent to leave the dwelling-house or part of the dwelling-house; or
(*g*)   exclude the respondent from a defined area in which the dwelling-house is included[2].

An occupation order under s 33 of the Act may also declare that the applicant is entitled to occupy a dwelling-house by virtue of a beneficial estate or interest or contract or by virtue of any enactment giving him the right to remain in occupation, or that he has matrimonial home rights in relation to a dwelling-house[3]. If the applicant has matrimonial home rights and the respondent is the other spouse, an order under s 33 made during the marriage may provide that those rights are not brought to an end by — (*a*) the death of the other spouse; or (*b*) the termination (otherwise than by death) of the marriage[4]; and such power may be exercised in any case where the court considers that in all the circumstances it is just and reasonable to do so[5].

In deciding whether to exercise its powers under paragraphs (*a*) to (*g*) above, and, if so, in what manner, the court shall have regard to all the circumstances including—

(*a*)   the housing needs and housing resources of each of the parties and of any relevant child[1];
(*b*)   the financial resources of each of the parties;
(*c*)   the likely effect of any order, or of any decision by the court not to exercise its powers under subsection (3), on the health, safety or well-being of the parties and of any relevant child[1]; and
(*d*)   the conduct of the parties in relation to each other and otherwise[6].

If it appears to the court that the applicant or any relevant child[1] is likely to suffer significant harm attributable to conduct of the respondent if an order under s 33 of the Act containing one or more of the provisions mentioned in paragraphs (*a*) to (*g*) above is not made, the court shall make the order unless it appears to it that—

(*a*)   the respondent or any relevant child is likely to suffer significant harm if the order is made; and

(*b*)   the harm likely to be suffered by the respondent or child in that event is as great as, or greater than, the harm attributable to conduct of the respondent which is likely to be suffered by the applicant or child if the order is not made[7].

An occupation order under s 33 of the Act may not be made after the death of either of the parties; and, save where an order has been made that the matrimonial home rights are not to be brought to an end by the death of the other spouse, an order under s 33 shall cease to have effect on the death of either party[8]. An order under s 33 may, in so far as it has continuing effect, be made for a specified period, until the occurrence of a specified event or until further order[9].

If a spouse's matrimonial home rights are a charge on the estate or interest of the other spouse or of trustees for the other spouse—

(*a*)   an order under s 33 against the other spouse has, except so far as a contrary intention appears, the same effect against persons deriving title under the other spouse or under the trustees and affected by the charge, and

(*b*)   certain provisions of s 33[10] apply in relation to any person deriving title under the other spouse or under the trustees and affected by the charge as they apply in relation to the other spouse[11].

The court may make an order under s 33 by virtue of this provision if it considers that in all the circumstances it is just and reasonable to do so[12].

In approaching its functions under s 33, the court has first to consider whether the evidence establishes that the applicant or any relevant child is likely to suffer significant harm attributable to the conduct of the respondent if an order is not made. If the court answers the question in the affirmative, then it knows that it must make the order unless balancing one harm against the other, the harm to the respondent or the child is likely to be as great. If, however, the court answers the question in the negative, then it enters the discretionary regime provided by s 33(6) and must exercise a broad discretion having regard to all the circumstances of the case, particularly those factors set out in the statutory checklist within paragraphs (*a*)–(*d*) inclusive[13]. In considering for the purposes of s 33(7) whether any harm likely to be suffered by the applicant or any relevant child is attributable to the conduct of the respondent, the court's concentration must be upon the effect of conduct rather than on the intention of the doer. Lack of intent may be a relevant consideration, but of itself it does not mean that any such harm cannot be attributed to the respondent's conduct[14].

The exercise of the discretion to evict a co-owner of a matrimonial home is a Draconian remedy; it is a last resort and is not an order lightly to be made. Its purpose is not to break a matrimonial deadlock by evicting one of the parties; it is to afford necessary protection which can be afforded in no better way[15].

---

1. For the meaning of "associated", see ss 62 and 63 of the Family Law Act 1996, this PART, post; for the meaning of "relevant child", see Family Law Act 1996, s 62(2).
2. Family Law Act 1996, s 33(3), this PART, post.
3. Family Law Act 1996, s 33(4), this PART, post.
4. Family Law Act 1996, s 33(5), this PART, post.
5. Family Law Act 1996, s 33(8), this PART, post.
6. Family Law Act 1996, s 33(6), this PART, post.
7. Family Law Act 1996, s 33(7), this PART, post.
8. Family Law Act 1996, s 33(9), this PART, post.
9. Family Law Act 1996, s 33(10), this PART, post.
10. The provisions applied are ss 33(1), (3), (4) and (10) and 30(3)–(6).
11. Family Law Act 1996, s 34(1), this PART, post.
12. Family Law Act 1996, s 34(2), this PART, post.
13. *Chalmers v Johns* [1999] 2 FCR 110, [1999] 1 FLR 392, CA.
14. *G v G (occupation order: conduct)* [2000] 3 FCR 53, [2000] 2 FLR 36, CA.
15. *Re Y (children) (occupation order)* [2000] 2 FCR 470, CA.

6–128   Occupation orders: one former spouse or former civil partner with no existing right to occupy.   If—

1. one former spouse or former civil partner is entitled to occupy a dwelling-house by virtue of a beneficial estate or interest or contract, or by virtue of any enactment giving him the right to remain in occupation;

2. the other former spouse or former civil partner is not so entitled; and

3. the dwelling-house was at any time their matrimonial home or was at any time intended by them to be their matrimonial home,

the former spouse or former civil partner not so entitled may apply to the court for an occupation order under s 35 of the Family Law Act 1996.

If the applicant *is* in occupation, an order under s 35 of the Act must contain provision—

(*a*)   giving the applicant the right not to be evicted or excluded from the dwelling-house or any part of it by the respondent for the period specified in the order; and

(*b*)   prohibiting the respondent from evicting or excluding the applicant during that period[1].

If the applicant *is not* in occupation, an order under section 35 must contain provision—

(*a*) giving the applicant the right to enter into and occupy the dwelling-house for the period specified in the order; and

(*b*) requiring the respondent to permit the exercise of that right[2].

An order under s 35 may also—

(*a*) regulate the occupation of the dwelling-house by either or both of the parties:

(*b*) prohibit, suspend or restrict the exercise by the respondent of his right to occupy the dwelling-house;

(*c*) require the respondent to leave the dwelling-house or part of the dwelling-house; or

(*d*) exclude the respondent from a defined area in which the dwelling-house is included[3].

Circumstances to which the court must have regard in deciding whether to make an order containing provision of the kind referred to above are set out in s 35 of the Act[4].

An order under s 35—

(*a*) may not be made after the death of either of the former spouses or former civil partners; and

(*b*) ceases to have effect on the death of either of them[5].

Moreover, an order must be limited so as to have effect for a specified period not exceeding six months, but may be extended on one or more occasions for a further specified period not exceeding six months[6].

---

1. Family Law Act 1996, s 35(3), this PART, post.
2. Family Law Act 1996, s 35(4), this PART, post.
3. Family Law Act 1996, s 35(5), this PART, post.
4. Family Law Act 1996, s 35(6)–(8), this PART, post.
5. Family Law Act 1996, s 35(9), this PART, post.
6. Family Law Act 1996, s 35(10), this PART, post.

6–129   Occupation orders: one cohabitant or former cohabitant[1] with no existing right to occupy. If—

1. one cohabitant or former cohabitant is entitled to occupy a dwelling-house by virtue of a beneficial estate or interest or contract or by virtue of any enactment giving him the right to remain in occupation;

2. the other cohabitant or former cohabitant is not so entitled; and

3. that dwelling-house is the home in which they live together as husband and wife or a home in which they at any time so lived together or intended so to live together,

the cohabitant or former cohabitant not so entitled may apply to the court for an order under s 36 of the Act against the other cohabitant or former cohabitant ("the respondent").

If the applicant *is* in occupation, an order under section 36 must contain provision—

(*a*) giving the applicant the right not to be evicted or excluded from the dwelling-house or any part of it by the respondent for the period specified in the order; and

(*b*) prohibiting the respondent from evicting or excluding the applicant during that period[2].

If the applicant *is not* in occupation, an order under s 36 must contain provision—

(*a*) giving the applicant the right to enter into and occupy the dwelling-house for the period specified in the order; and

(*b*) requiring the respondent to permit the exercise of that right[3].

An order under s 36 of the Act may also—

(*a*) regulate the occupation of the dwelling-house by either or both of the parties;

(*b*) prohibit, suspend or restrict the exercise by the respondent of his right to occupy the dwelling-house;

(*c*) require the respondent to leave the dwelling-house or part of the dwelling-house; or

(*d*) exclude the respondent from a defined area in which the dwelling-house is included[4].

Circumstances to which the court must have regard in deciding whether to make an order containing provision of the kind referred to above are set out in s 36 of the Act[5].

An order under s 36—

(*a*) may not be made after the death of either of the parties; and

(*b*) ceases to have effect on the death of either of them[6].

Moreover, an order under s 36 must be limited so as to have effect for a specified period not exceeding six months, but may be extended on one occasion for a further specified period not exceeding six months[7].

In any case where the parties are cohabitants or former cohabitants and the court is required to consider the nature of the parties' relationship, it is to have regard to the fact that they have not given each other the commitment involved in marriage[8].

1. Section 3 of the Domestic Violence, Crime and Victims Act 2004 (see this PART, post) extended "cohabitants" to include same-sex couples and extended Part 4 of the Family Law Reform Act 1996 to certain non-cohabiting couples.
2. Family Law Act 1996, s 36(3), this PART, post.
3. Family Law Act 1996, s 36(4), this PART, post.
4. Family Law Act 1996, s 36(5), this PART, post.
5. Family Law Act 1996, s 36(6)–(8), this PART, post.
6. Family Law Act 1996, s 36(9), this PART, post.
7. Family Law Act 1996, s 36(10), this PART, post.
8. Family Law Act 1996, s 41, this PART, post. (However, this is prospectively repealed by s 2 of the Domestic Violence, Crime and Victims Act 2004: see this PART, post.)

6–129A Occupation orders: neither spouse/civil partner entitled to occupy. If—

1. one spouse or former spouse and the other spouse or former spouse/one civil partner or former civil partner and the other civil partner or former civil partner occupy a dwelling-house which is or was the matrimonial home; but
2. neither of them is entitled to remain in occupation—

(i) by virtue of a beneficial estate or interest or contract; or
(ii) by virtue of any enactment giving him the right to remain in occupation;

either of the parties may apply to the court for an occupation order against the other under s 37 of the Family Law Act 1996.
An order under s 37 of the Act may—

(a) require the respondent to permit the applicant to enter and remain in the dwelling-house or part of the dwelling-house;
(b) regulate the occupation of the dwelling-house by either or both of the spouses;
(c) require the respondent to leave the dwelling-house or part of the dwelling-house; or
(d) exclude the respondent from a defined area in which the dwelling-house is included[1].

Sections 33(6) and (7)[2] apply to the exercise by the court of its powers under s 37 as they apply to the exercise by the court of its powers under s 33(3) of the Act[3]. An order under s 37 must be limited so as to have effect for a specified period not exceeding 6 months, but may be extended on one or more occasions for a further specified period not exceeding six months[4].

1. Family Law Act 1996, s 37(3), this PART, post.
2. See para **6–127**, ante.
3. Family Law Act 1996, s 37(4), this PART, post.
4. Family Law Act 1996, s 37(5), this PART, post.

6–129B Occupation orders: neither cohabitant or former cohabitant entitled to occupy. If—

1. one cohabitant or former cohabitant and the other cohabitant or former cohabitant occupy a dwelling-house which is the home in which they live or lived together as husband and wife; but
2. neither of them is entitled to remain in occupation—

(i) by virtue of a beneficial estate or interest or contract; or
(ii) by virtue of any enactment giving him the right to remain in occupation;

either of the parties may apply to the court for an order against the other under section 38 of the Family Law Act 1996.
An order under s 38 of the Act may—

(a) require the respondent to permit the applicant to enter and remain in the dwelling-house or part of the dwelling-house;
(b) regulate the occupation of the dwelling-house by either or both of the parties;
(c) require the respondent to leave the dwelling-house or part of the dwelling-house; or
(d) exclude the respondent from a defined area in which the dwelling-house is included[1].

In deciding whether to exercise its powers to include one or more of the provisions referred to in paragraphs (a) to (d) above in an order, the court must have regard to all the circumstances including—

(i) the housing needs and housing resources of each of the parties and of any relevant child;
(ii) the financial resources of each of the parties;
(iii) the likely effect of any order, or of any decision by the court not to exercise its powers, on the health, safety or well-being of the parties and of any relevant child;
(iv) the conduct of the parties in relation to each other and otherwise; and
(v) the following questions:-

(a) whether the applicant or any relevant child is likely to suffer significant harm attributable to conduct of the respondent if the provision under s 38(3) of the Act is not included in the order; and

(b)   whether the harm likely to be suffered by the respondent or child if the provision is included is as great as or greater than the harm attributable to conduct of the respondent which is likely to be suffered by the applicant or child if the provision is not included[2].

An order under s 38 of the Act must be limited so as to have effect for a specified period not exceeding 6 months, but may be extended on one occasion for a further specified period not exceeding 6 months[3].

In any case where the parties are cohabitants or former cohabitants and the court is required to consider the nature of the parties' relationship, it is to have regard to the fact that they have not given each other the commitment involved in marriage[4].

---

1. Family Law Act 1996, s 38(3), this PART, post.
2. Ibid, s 38(4), (5), this PART, post.
3. Ibid, s 38(6), this PART, post.
4. Ibid, s 41, this PART, post.

6–129C   Occupation orders: additional provisions in orders.

At the time of making an occupation order under section 33, 35 or 36, or at any time thereafter, the court may:

1.   impose on either party obligations as to—

   (a)   the repair and maintenance of the dwelling-house; or
   (b)   the discharge of rent, mortgage payments or other outgoings affecting the dwelling-house;

2.   order a party occupying the dwelling-house or any part of it (including a party who is entitled to do so by virtue of a beneficial estate or interest or contract or by virtue of any enactment giving him the right to remain in occupation) to make periodical payments to the other party in respect of the accommodation, if the other party would (but for the order) be entitled to occupy the dwelling-house by virtue of a beneficial estate or interest or contract or by virtue of any such enactment;

3.   grant either party possession or use of furniture or other contents of the dwelling-house;
4.   order either party to take reasonable care of any furniture or other contents of the dwelling-house;
5.   order either party to take reasonable steps to keep the dwelling-house and any furniture or other contents secure[1].

In deciding whether and, if so, how to exercise its powers under the above provision, the court shall have regard to all the circumstances of the case including—

(a)   the financial needs and financial resources of the parties; and
(b)   the financial obligations which they have, or are likely to have in the foreseeable future, including financial obligations to each other and to any relevant child[2].

An order made under these additional provisions ceases to have effect when the occupation order to which it relates ceases to have effect[3].

---

1. Family Law Act 1996, s 40(1), this PART, post.
2. Family Law Act 1996, s 40(2), this PART, post. For the meaning of "relevant child", see s 62(2) of the Family Law Act 1996, this PART, post.
3. Family Law Act 1996, s 40(3), this PART, post.

6–130   Non-molestation orders.

The family proceedings court may make a non-molestation order under section 42 of the Family Law Act 1996—

1.   if an application for the order has been made (whether in other family proceedings or without any other family proceedings being instituted) by a person who is associated with the respondent; or
2.   if in any family proceedings to which the respondent is a party the court considers that the order should be made for the benefit of any other party to the proceedings or any relevant child even though no such application has been made[2].

A "non-molestation order" means an order containing either or both of the following provisions—

(a)   provision prohibiting a person ("the respondent") from molesting another person who is associated with the respondent;
(b)   provision prohibiting the respondent from molesting a relevant child[3].

In deciding whether to exercise its powers to make a non-molestation order, and, if so, in what manner, the court shall have regard to all the circumstances including the need to secure the health, safety and well-being—

(a)   of the applicant or, in a case falling within paragraph 2 above, the person for whose benefit the order would be made; and
(b)   of any relevant child[4].

A non-molestation order may be expressed so as to refer to molestation in general, to particular acts of molestation, or to both[5]. A non-molestation order may be made for a specified period or until further order[6]. A non-molestation order which is made in other family proceedings ceases to have effect if those proceedings are withdrawn or dismissed[7].

Remedies to protect those subject to domestic violence may also be provided by prosecutions and civil proceedings under the Protection from Harassment Act 1997[8].

The reference to "family proceedings" in paragraphs 1 and 2 above includes proceedings in which the court has made an emergency protection order under section 44 of the Children Act 1989[9] which includes an exclusion requirement[10].

Where an agreement to marry is terminated, no application under paragraph 1 above may be made by reference to that agreement after the end of the period of 3 years beginning with the day on which it is terminated[11].

Non-molestation orders should be for a specified period of time unless there are exceptional or unusual circumstances[12].

There is no definition of "molestation", but it has been held that the word implies some quite deliberate conduct which is aimed at a high degree of harassment of the other party so as to justify the intervention of the court. Accordingly, s 42 of the 1996 Act could not be used to enforce an invasion of privacy *per se*[13]. Section 42 provides a discretionary remedy and even if the facts amounting to molestation by the respondent and the association between the respondent and the applicant are proved, the court is not bound to make an order[14]. If further civil proceedings between the parties are likely, this may justify the court refusing to make an order in family proceedings[14]. If the court does make a non-molestation order, it is clear from the wording of s 47(2) of the Family Law Act 1996 (see para **6–3095**, post) that it will, in all but exceptional circumstances, be obliged to include a power of arrest where the respondent had used or threatened violence[14].

---

1. For the meaning of "associated", see ss 62 and 63 of the Family Law Act 1996, this PART, post.
2. Family Law Act 1996, s 42(2), this PART, post.
3. Family Law Act 1996, s 42(1), this PART, post.
4. Family Law Act 1996, s 42(5), this PART, post. For the meaning of "relevant child", see Family Law Act 1996, s 62(2), this PART, post.
5. Family Law Act 1996, s 42(6), this PART, post.
6. Family Law Act 1996, s 42(7), this PART, post.
7. Family Law Act 1996, s 42(8), this PART, post.
8. In PART VIII title PERSONS, OFFENCES AGAINST, post.
9. See this PART, post.
10. Family Law Act 1996, s 42(3), this PART, post.
11. Family Law Act 1996, s 42(4), this PART, post.
12. *M v W (Non-molestation order: duration)* [2000] 1 FLR 107, FD.
13. *C v C (application for non-molestation order)* [1998] 2 WLR 599, [1998] 1 FCR 11 (giving information to newspaper reporters resulting in the publication of offensive articles in newspapers held not to amount to conduct which would justify the application of s 42).
14. *Chechi v Bashier* [1999] 2 FCR 241, [1999] 2 FLR 489, CA.

6–131 Evidence of agreement to marry. The court shall not make an occupation order under section 33 of the Act or a non-molestation order with respect to parties who have agreed to marry one another (whether or not that agreement has been terminated) unless there is produced to it evidence in writing of the existence of the agreement to marry. However, this requirement for evidence in writing does not apply if the court is satisfied that the agreement to marry was evidenced by—

(a) the gift of an engagement ring by one party to the agreement to the other in contemplation of their marriage, or

(b) a ceremony entered into by the parties in the presence of one or more other persons assembled for the purpose of witnessing the ceremony[1].

---

1. Family Law Act 1996, s 44, this PART, post.

6–132 Undertakings. In any case where the court has power to make an occupation order or a non-molestation order, the court may accept an undertaking from any party to the proceedings[1]. However, no power of arrest may be attached to such an undertaking[2], and the court shall not accept an undertaking in any case where apart from this provision a power of arrest would be attached to the order[3].

An undertaking given to a court is enforceable as if it were an order of the court[4].

---

1. Family Law Act 1996, s 46(1), this PART, post.
2. Family Law Act 1996, s 46(2), this PART, post.
3. Family Law Act 1996, s 46(3), this PART, post.
4. Family Law Act 1996, s 46(4), this PART, post.

6–133 Occupation order and non-molestation order: ex parte orders. The court may, in any case where it considers that it is just and convenient to do so, make an occupation order or a non-molestation order even though the respondent has not been given such notice of the proceedings as would otherwise be required by rules of court. In determining whether to exercise its powers to make an order *ex parte*, the court shall have regard to all the circumstances including—

1. any risk of significant harm to the applicant or a relevant child[1], attributable to conduct of the respondent, if the order is not made immediately;

2. whether it is likely that the applicant will be deterred or prevented from pursuing the application if an order is not made immediately; and

3. whether there is reason to believe that the respondent is aware of the proceedings but is deliberately evading service and that the applicant or a relevant child will be seriously prejudiced by the delay involved—

 (i) where the court is a magistrates' court, in effecting service of proceedings; or

 (ii) in any other case, in effecting substituted service[2].

If the court makes an order *ex parte* it must afford the respondent an opportunity to make representations relating to the order as soon as is just and convenient at a full hearing[3]. If, at a full hearing, the court makes an occupation order ("the full order"), the maximum period for which the full order may be made to have effect is to be calculated in accordance with the Act[4].

---

1. For the meaning of "relevant child", see the Family Law Act 1996, s 62(2), this Part, post.
2. Family Law Act 1996, s 45(1), (2), this Part, post.
3. Family Law Act 1996, s 45(3), this Part, post.
4. See the Family Law Act 1996, s 45(4), this Part, post.

6–134 Arrest for breach of order made under Part IV[1]. If the family proceedings court makes an occupation order or a non-molestation order (referred to as "a relevant order"), and it appears to the court that the respondent has used or threatened violence against the applicant or a relevant child[2], the court shall attach a power of arrest to one or more provisions of the order unless satisfied that in all the circumstances of the case the applicant or child will be adequately protected without such a power of arrest[3].

The court may attach a power of arrest to one or more provisions of a relevant order which is made *ex parte* only if it appears to the court—

1. that the respondent has used or threatened violence against the applicant or a relevant child[1]; and

2. that there is a risk of significant harm to the applicant or child, attributable to conduct of the respondent, if the power of arrest is not attached to those provisions immediately[4].

If, by virtue of this provision, the court attaches a power of arrest to any provisions of a relevant order, it may provide, where the order has been made ex parte, that the power of arrest is to have effect for a shorter period than the other provisions of the order[5] otherwise the power of arrest made on an inter parties hearing must be for the same period as the non-molestation order[6]. Any period so specified may be extended by the court on an application to vary or discharge the order[7].

If a power of arrest is attached to certain provisions of an order, a constable may arrest without warrant a person whom he has reasonable cause for suspecting to be in breach of any such provision[8]. Where the respondent is arrested under a power of arrest—

(*a*) he must be brought before a magistrates' court within the period of 24 hours beginning at the time of his arrest; and

(*b*) if the matter is not then disposed of forthwith, the court before which he is brought may remand him.

In reckoning for this purpose any period of 24 hours, no account shall be taken of Christmas Day, Good Friday or any Sunday[9].

If the court has made a relevant order but has not attached a power of arrest to any provisions of the order, or has attached that power only to certain provisions of the order, then, if at any time the applicant considers that the respondent has failed to comply with the order, he may apply to a magistrates' court for the issue of a warrant for the arrest of the respondent[10]. A warrant shall not be issued unless the application is substantiated on oath, and the magistrates' court has reasonable grounds for believing that the respondent has failed to comply with the order[11]. If a person is brought before a court by virtue of a warrant issued on such an application and the court does not dispose of the matter forthwith, the court may remand him[12].

Although it will usually be preferable to attach the power of arrest for the same period as the non-molestation order, the power of arrest may be made for a shorter period, including orders made at a with-notice hearing[13].

Where a power of arrest is attached to one or more provisions of an order made under Part IV of the Act, the relevant provisions must be set out in the prescribed form and a copy of the form must be delivered to the officer for the time being in charge of any police station for the applicant's address or of such other police station as the court may specify. The copy of the form so delivered must be accompanied by a statement showing that the respondent has been served with the order or informed of its terms[14].

An application for the issue of a warrant for the arrest of the respondent must be made on the prescribed form and the warrant shall be delivered by the justices' chief executive to the officer for the time being in charge of any police station for the respondent's address or of such other police station as the court may specify[15].

The court before whom a person is brought following his arrest may—

(*a*) determine whether the facts, and the circumstances which led to the arrest, amounted to disobedience of the order, or

(*b*) adjourn the proceedings and, where such an order is made, the arrested person may be released, and

 (i) be dealt with within 14 days of the day on which he was arrested; and (ii)　be given not less than 2 business days' notice of the adjourned hearing[16].

　　When an arrested person is brought before the relevant judicial authority the attendance of the arresting officer will not be necessary, unless the arrest itself is in issue. A written statement from the arresting officer as to the circumstances of the arrest should normally be sufficient. In those cases where the arresting officer was also a witness to the events leading to the arrest and his evidence regarding those events is required, arrangements should be made for him to attend at a subsequent hearing to give evidence[17].

　　If a person is remanded following arrest he may be required by the magistrates' court to comply, before release on bail or later, with such requirements as appear to the court to be necessary to secure that he does not interfere with witnesses or otherwise obstruct the course of justice[18]. An application for bail made by a person arrested under a power of arrest or a warrant of arrest may be made either orally or in writing; a written application must be made in accordance with the Rules[19].

　　1.　Section 1 of the Domestic Violence, Crime and Victims Act 2004 (see this PART, post) prospectively inserts a new s 42A in the Family Law Act 1996 under which breach of a non-molestation order will be an either way offence carrying a maximum of 5 years imprisonment and a fine on conviction on indictment.
　　2.　For the meaning of "relevant child", see the Family Law Act 1996, s 62(2), this PART, post.
　　3.　Family Law Act 1996, s 47(1), (2), this PART, post.
　　4.　Family Law Act 1996, s 47(3), this PART, post.
　　5.　Family Law Act 1996, s 47(4), this PART, post.
　　6.　*M v W (non-molestation order: duration)* [2000] 1 FLR 107, FD.
　　7.　Family Law Act 1996, s 47(5), this PART, post.
　　8.　Family Law Act 1996, s 47(6), this PART, post.
　　9.　Family Law Act 1996, s 47(7), this PART, post.
　　10.　Family Law Act 1996, s 47(8), this PART, post.
　　11.　Family Law Act 1996, s 47(9), this PART, post.
　　12.　Family Law Act 1996, s 47(10), this PART, post. Sections 128 and 129 of the Magistrates' Courts Act 1980, in PART I: MAGISTRATES' COURTS, PROCEDURE, ante, will have effect in relation to such a remand by a magistrates' court.
　　13.　*Re B – J (a child) (non-molestation order: power of arrest)* [2001] Fam 415, [2000] 2 FCR 599, [2000] 2 FLR 443, CA.
　　14.　Family Proceedings Courts (Matrimonial Proceedings etc) Rules 1991, r 20(1), this PART, post.
　　15.　Family Proceedings Courts (Matrimonial Proceedings etc) Rules 1991, r 20(3), this PART, post.
　　16.　Family Proceedings Courts (Matrimonial Proceedings etc) Rules 1991, r 20(4), this PART, post.
　　17.　*President's Direction (Family Law Act 1996 – attendance of arresting officer)* [2000] 1 WLR 83, [2000] 1 FCR 86, [2000] 1 FLR 270, FD.
　　18.　Family Law Act 1996, s 47(12), this PART, post.
　　19.　Family Proceedings Courts (Matrimonial Proceedings etc) Rules 1991, r 21, this PART, post.

6–135　Remand for medical examination and report.　If a court has reason to consider that a medical report will be required with respect to a person who has been arrested under a power of arrest or a warrant of arrest, the power to remand that person may be exercised for the purpose of enabling a medical examination and report to be made[1].

　　If such power is so exercised, the adjournment must not be for more than 4 weeks at a time unless the court remands the person in custody, in which case the adjournment must not be for more than 3 weeks at a time[2].

　　If there is reason to suspect that the person arrested is suffering from mental illness or severe mental impairment, the court has the same power to make an order under s 35 of the Mental Health Act 1983[3] (remand for report on accused's mental condition) as the Crown Court has under s 35 of the Act of 1983 in the case of an accused person within the meaning of that section[4].

　　1.　Family Law Act 1996, s 48(1), this PART, post.
　　2.　Family Law Act 1996, s 48(2), (3), this PART, post.
　　3.　See PART VIII, title MENTAL HEALTH, post.
　　4.　Family Law Act 1996, s 48(4), this PART, post.

6–136　Variation and discharge of orders.　An occupation order or non-molestation order may be varied or discharged by the court on an application by—

　　1.　the respondent, or
　　2.　the person on whose application the order was made[1].

　　Where a non-molestation order has been made by virtue of section 42(2)(b) of the Act, the order may be varied or discharged by the court even though no such application has been made[2].

　　If a spouse's matrimonial home rights are a charge on the estate or interest of the other spouse or of trustees for the other spouse, an order under section 33 of the Act against the other spouse may also be varied or discharged by the court on an application by any person deriving title under the other spouse or under the trustees and affected by the charge[3].

　　If a power of arrest has been attached to certain provisions of an occupation order or a non-molestation order, the court may vary or discharge the order in so far as it confers a power of arrest (whether or not any application has been made to vary or discharge any other provision of the order)[4].

　　An application to vary, extend or discharge an order made under Part IV of the Act must be made on the prescribed form and the Rules apply to the hearing of such an application[5].

　　Where an order is made varying or discharging the relevant provisions for the purposes of a power of arrest attached to an order made under Part IV of the Act, the justices' chief executive shall—

(a) immediately inform the police officer who received a copy of the form containing the relevant provisions to which the power of arrest was attached, and, if the applicant's address has changed, the officer for the time being in charge of the police station for the new address; and

(b) deliver a copy of the order to any officer so informed[6].

---

1. Family Law Act 1996, s 49(1), this PART, post.
2. Family Law Act 1996, s 49(2), this PART, post.
3. Family Law Act 1996, s 49(3), this PART, post.
4. Family Law Act 1996, s 49(4), this PART, post.
5. Family Proceedings Courts (Matrimonial Proceedings etc) Rules 1991, r 12B, this PART, post; rr 12 and 12A are applied to the hearing of such an application.
6. Family Proceedings Courts (Matrimonial Proceedings etc) Rules 1991, r 20(2), this PART, post.

6–137 Enforcement of orders made under Part IV—application for committal. Where any person disobeys an order made by a family proceedings court to do anything other than the payment of money or to abstain from doing anything the order may be enforced in accordance with section 63(3) of the Magistrates' Courts Act 1980[1]. The powers available to the court are—

1. to order the person who has disobeyed the order to pay a sum not exceeding £50 for every day during which he is in default or a sum not exceeding £5,000; or

2. commit him to custody until he has remedied his default or for a period not exceeding 2 months;

but a person who is ordered to pay a sum for every day during which he is in default or who is committed to custody until he has remedied his default shall not be ordered to pay more than £1,000 or be committed for more than 2 months in all for doing or abstaining from doing the same thing contrary to the order[2].

Where a magistrates' court has power to commit a person to custody for breach of a relevant requirement, the court may by order direct that the execution of the order of committal be suspended for such period or on such terms and conditions as it may specify[3]. For this purpose "a relevant requirement" means—

(i) an occupation order or a non-molestation order;

(ii) an exclusion requirement included by virtue of s 38A of the Children Act 1989[4] in an interim care order; or

(iii) an exclusion requirement included by virtue of s 44A of the Children Act 1989[4] in an emergency protection order[5].

Save where the court dispenses with the requirement for service of a copy of the order, an order under Part IV of the 1996 Act shall not be enforced by committal order unless—

(a) a copy of the order in Form FL 404 has been served personally on the respondent; and

(b) where the order requires the respondent to do an act, the copy has been so served before the expiration of the time within which he was required to do the act and was accompanied by a copy of any order, made between the date of the order and the date of service, fixing that time[6].

At the time when the order is drawn up, the justices' clerk shall—

(a) where the order made is (or includes) a non-molestation order, and

(b) where the order made is an occupation order and the court so directs,

issue a copy of the order, indorsed with or incorporating a notice as to the consequences of disobedience, for service in accordance with the above requirement[7].

If the respondent fails to obey the order, the justices' chief executive must, at the request of the applicant, issue a notice in the prescribed form warning the respondent that an application will be made for him to be committed, and unless the court dispenses with the requirement, the notice must be served on him personally[8]. The request for issue of such notice shall be treated as a complaint and shall—

(a) identify the provisions of the order or undertaking which it is alleged have been disobeyed or broken;

(b) list the ways in which it is alleged that the order or undertaking has been disobeyed or broken;

(c) be supported by a statement which is signed and is declared to be true and which states the grounds on which the application is made,

and unless the service is dispensed with, a copy of the statement shall be served with the notice[9].

On hearing an application for committal, the court may adjourn consideration of the penalty to be imposed for contempts found proved and such consideration may be restored if the respondent does not comply with any conditions specified by the court[10].

For the Guidance on the interrelationship of the remedies in the Family Law Act 1996 and the Protection From Harassment Act 1997, see *Lomas v Parle*[11].

If a committal order is made, the form of order shall include provision for the issue of a committal warrant in the prescribed form[12] and, unless the court otherwise orders—

(a) a copy of the order shall be served personally on the person to be committed either before or at the time of the execution of the warrant; or

(b) the order for the issue of the warrant may be served on the person to be committed at any time within 36 hours after the execution of the warrant[13].

The provisions in the Rules which are referred to above are modified in so far as they apply to the enforcement of undertakings[14].

Where a person in custody under a warrant or order, desires to apply to the court for his discharge, he shall make his application in writing attested by the governor of the prison showing that he has purged or is desirous of purging his contempt and the justices' chief executive shall, not less than one day before the application is heard, serve notice of it on the party (if any) at whose instance the warrant or order was issued[15].

---

1. See PART I: MAGISTRATES' COURTS, PROCEDURE, ante.
2. Magistrates' Courts Act 1980, s 63(3), in PART I: MAGISTRATES' COURTS, PROCEDURE, ante.
3. Family Law Act 1996, s 50(1), this PART, post. See also the Family Proceedings Courts (Matrimonial Proceedings etc) Rules 1991, r 20(16) and (17), this PART, post.
4. See this PART, post.
5. Family Law Act 1996, s 50(2), this PART, post. For consideration of an exclusion requirement included in an interim care order, see para **6–170A Interim care order: exclusion requirement**, and in an emergency protection order, see para **6–175A Emergency protection order: exclusion requirement**.
6. Family Proceedings Courts (Matrimonial Proceedings etc) Rules 1991, r 20(6) this PART, post. For power to dispense with requirement for service, see Family Proceedings Courts (Matrimonial Proceedings etc) Rules 1991 r 20(11) and (12), this PART, post.
7. Family Proceedings Courts (Matrimonial Proceedings etc) Rules 1991, r 20(7) this PART, post.
8. Family Proceedings Courts (Matrimonial Proceedings etc) Rules 1991, r 20(8), this PART, post.
9. Family Proceedings Courts (Matrimonial Proceedings etc) Rules 1991, r 20(9), this PART, post.
10. Family Proceedings Courts (Matrimonial Proceedings etc) Rules 1991, r 20(18), this PART, post.
11. [2003] EWCA Civ 1804, [2004] 1 All ER 1173, [2004] 1 WLR 1642, [2004] 1 FCR 97, [2004] 1 FLR 812. See also the Magistrates' Courts Act 1980, s 63 and notes thereto.
12. For the prescribed form of committal order, see Form FL419, and for the prescribed form of committal warrant, see Form FL420.
13. Family Proceedings Courts (Matrimonial Proceedings etc) Rules 1991, r 20(10) this PART, post.
14. Family Proceedings Courts (Matrimonial Proceedings etc) Rules 1991, r 20(14), this PART, post.
15. Family Proceedings Courts (Matrimonial Proceedings etc) Rules 1991, r 20(15), this PART, post.

6–138 Power to order hospital admission or guardianship. A magistrates' court has the same power to make a hospital order or guardianship order under section 37 of the Mental Health Act 1983[1] or an interim hospital order under section 38 of that Act[1] in the case of a person suffering from mental illness or severe mental impairment who could otherwise be committed to custody for breach of a relevant requirement as a magistrates' court has under those sections in the case of a person convicted of an offence punishable on summary conviction with imprisonment. For this purpose "a relevant requirement" has the meaning given by s 50(2) of the Family Law Act 1996; see para **6–137** ante[2].

Where the court makes a hospital order or a guardianship order, the justices' chief executive shall—

(a) send to the hospital any information which will be of assistance in dealing with the patient;
(b) inform the applicant when the respondent is being transferred to hospital[3].

Where a transfer direction given by the Secretary of State under s 48 of the Mental Health Act 1983 is in force in respect of a person remanded in custody by the court, the justices' clerk shall notify—

(a) the governor of the prison to which that person was remanded; and
(b) the hospital where he is detained,

of any committal hearing which that person is required to attend and the justices' chief executive shall give notice in writing to the hospital where that person is detained of any further remand[4].

---

1. See PART VIII: title MENTAL HEALTH, post.
2. Family Law Act 1996, s 51, this PART, post.
3. Family Proceedings Courts (Matrimonial Proceedings etc) Rules 1991, r 20(19), this PART, post.
4. Family Proceedings Courts (Matrimonial Proceedings etc) Rules 1991, r 20(20), this PART, post.

Proceedings under the Children Act 1989: general principles

6–140 Welfare of the child. Section 1 of the Children Act 1989[1] establishes the general principle that when a court determines any question with respect to the upbringing of a child[2], or the administration of a child's property or the application of any income arising from it, the child's welfare shall be the court's paramount consideration[3]. The welfare of the child is also the paramount consideration whenever a court or an adoption agency is coming to a decision in relation to the adoption of a child, and here it is expressed to 'the child's welfare throughout his life'[4].

It should be noted that the welfare of the child is only to be regarded as the court's paramount consideration when the court determines a question with respect to the child's upbringing or an issue relating to property or income. The principle does not apply where such issues are not directly raised[5].

On an application by a local authority under s 34(4) of the Children Act 1989 for termination of contact between a mother and her child, where both are minors, the principle that the child's welfare shall be the court's paramount consideration should be applied only to the mother's child and not to the mother herself[6]. Where the interests of two children are each paramount, the court has to perform a balancing exercise[7]. As to cases involving challenges to decisions of public authorities – whether proceedings should be brought by way of judicial review or wardship, the principles by reference to which such cases should be decided and whether public or private law is involved – see *A (A Patient) v A Health Authority; Re J: R (on the application of S) v Secretary of State for the Home Department* [2002] EWHC 18 (Fam/Admin), [2002] Fam 213, [2002] 1 FCR 481, [2002] 1 FLR 845, where it was held that the crucial issue was what test was to be a applied as a matter of substantive law. If the task of the court is to come to a decision for and on behalf of a child (or an incompetent adult), then the welfare of that person must be the paramount consideration. If, however, the task is to review the decision of a public authority taken in the exercise of some statutory power, then the governing principles are those of public law.

The application of the welfare principle may be specifically excluded by statute; one example of is the Child Abduction and Custody Act 1985[8]. Where, however, the application is to return the child to a non-Hague Convention country, the courts have consistently held that they must act in accordance with the welfare of the individual child[9].

---

1. See this PART, post. There is also a requirement for trial within a reasonable period under art 6(1) of the European Convention on Human Rights. In cases involving children the European Court has emphasised that the authorities are under a duty to exercise "exceptional diligence" in this regard: see *H v United Kingdom* (1988) 10 EHRR 95 and *Hokkanen v Finland* (1995) EHRR 139.
2. A choice between international jurisdictions is not a question with respect to the upbringing of a child; therefore the welfare of the child is not the paramount consideration, though it is a very important factor (*Re D (stay of Children Act proceedings)* [2003] EWHC 565 (Fam), [2003] 2 FLR 1159.
3. For the position under art 8 of the European Convention on Human Rights, see para **6–11 European Convention on Human Rights**, ante.
4.
5. *Richards v Richards* [1984] AC 174, [1983] 2 All ER 807, 147 JP 481, HL.
6. *Birmingham City Council v H (a minor)* [1994] 1 All ER 12, [1994] 2 WLR 31, [1993] 1 FCR 896, [1994] 1 FLR 224, HL.
7. *Re H (minors) (parental contact)* [1993] 1 FCR 904.
8. See this PART, post.
9. See *Re J (a child) (return to foreign jurisdiction: convention rights)* [2005] UKHL 40, [2005] 3 All ER 291 and the authorities referred to therein.

6–141　Delay: prejudicial to welfare of child.　In any proceedings in which any question with respect to the upbringing of a child arises, the court shall have regard to the general principle that any delay in determining the question is likely to prejudice the welfare of the child[1].

While delay is ordinarily inimical to the welfare of the child, a planned and purposeful delay to enable an assessment to be undertaken may well be beneficial; in such cases a delay of the final decision for the purpose of ascertaining the result of an assessment is proper delay and is to be encouraged[2].

Unnecessary delay which is detrimental to the welfare of the child will justify the court in refusing an adjournment to enable a psychological assessment to be completed where the court already has sufficient information contained in the statements, reports and plans already before it to make a final decision[3].

The no delay principle does not, however, place CAFCASS under a duty to make provision to enable it, immediately on request by the court, to make available an officer of the service for appointment as a guardian; the relevant statutory provisions imply that, while CAFCASS should respond as soon as practicable after a request is made, there can be a gap between the request made by the court and CAFCASS making an officer available for appointment[4].

---

1. Children Act 1989, s 1(2), this PART, post.
2. *Re C (a minor) (care proceedings)* [1992] 2 FCR 341; *C v Solihull Metropolitan Borough Council* [1993] 1 FLR 290; *Hounslow London Borough Council v A* [1993] 1 WLR 291, [1993] 1 FLR 702.
3. *Re S (minors) (care order: delay principle)* [1997] 1 FCR 490.
4. *R v Children and Family Court Advisory and Support Service* [2003] EWHC 235 Admin, [2003] 1 FLR 953.

6–142　Welfare checklist.　When the court is considering:

(i)　whether to make, vary or discharge an order under s 8 of the Children Act 1989, and the making, variation or discharge of the order is opposed by any party to the proceedings; or
(ii)　whether to make, vary or discharge an order under Part IV of the 1989 Act,

the court shall have regard in particular to—

(a)　the ascertainable wishes and feelings of the child concerned (considered in the light of his age and understanding);
(b)　his physical, emotional and educational needs;
(c)　the likely effect on him of any change in his circumstances;
(d)　his age, sex, background and any characteristics of his which the court considers relevant;
(e)　any harm which he has suffered or is at risk of suffering;
(f)　how capable each of his parents, and any other person in relation to whom the court considers the question to be relevant, is of meeting his needs;

(g)   the range of powers available to the court under this Act in the proceedings in question[1].

The checklist is there to remind the court of important pointers, and in a finely balanced case the court will need to use it in order to steer it towards a conclusion[2]. The child's ascertainable wishes and feelings should not be elevated as a factor of paramount consideration[2]. It is not the court's function to judge religious beliefs, tenets, doctrines or rules, but the impact of these factors upon a child must be a relevant consideration. The child's religious beliefs are a feature which the court must consider, but the child's wishes are not the paramount consideration[3]. But children of mixed heritage who have sufficient age and understanding should be allowed to decide for themselves which, if any, religion they wish to follow[4]. In considering whether to remove a child under a care order the court should balance the risk of the child remaining with the parents against the risk of emotional harm arising from his removal[5].

While there is a strong supposition that, other things being equal, it is in the interests of the child that it shall remain with its natural parents, that has to give way to particular needs in particular situations[6].

Where a children's guardian has been appointed to act on behalf of the child or a welfare officer has been requested to supply a report dealing, *inter alia*, with the child's wishes, it should not be necessary or desirable for the justices to see the child privately. Any questions the justices may have as to the child's strength of feeling, or as to the reasons which he has for the wishes he expresses, should properly be put by the court, or by the parties, to the guardian ad litem or to the welfare officer concerned. It should only be in rare and exceptional cases, where a children's guardian or a children and family reporter or a welfare officer is so involved, that the justices should themselves see a child in private. But where the justices do see a child in private, it is crucial that they should make known to the parties in the proceedings any matter that the child has told them which may affect their own views or which may influence the decision that they are likely to reach[7]. If a child is seen by the justices, this should preferably be after the evidence has been completed, but before the speeches[2].

1. Children Act 1989, s 1(3), this PART, post.
2. *B v B (minors) (Interviewing and Listing Arrangements)* [1994] 2 FCR 667, [1994] 2 FLR 489, CA.
3. *Re R (a minor) (Residence: Religion)* [1993] 2 FLR 163, CA (a case concerning the Exclusive Brethren sect).
4. *Re S (Specific Issue Order: Religion: Circumcision)* [2004] EWHC 1282 (Fam), [2005] 1 FLR 236.
5. *In re M (Children) (Care Order: Removal)* [2005] TLR 517, CA.
6. See *Re W (a minor) (residence order)* [1993] 2 FCR 589, [1993] 2 FLR 625, CA; *Re D (care: natural parent presumption)* [1999] 2 FCR 118, [1999] 1 FLR 134, CA; *Re D (a child) (residence: natural parent)* [2000] 1 FCR 97. See also *Re H (a child: residence)* [2002] 3 FCR 277, CA, where it was held that there was no presumption in favour of the natural parent to be found anywhere in the Children Act 1989 and any judicial overlay of the words of the statute had to be treated with caution. In any event, the biological parent might not always be the natural parent in the eyes of the child (the child had been living with the maternal grandmother for some years under a residence order).
7. *Re M (a minor) (Justices' Discretion)* [1993] 2 FCR 721, [1993] 2 FLR 706; see also *Re W (Child: Contact)* [1993] 2 FCR 731.

6–143   Principle of no order.   Where a court is considering whether or not to make one or more orders under the Children Act 1989 with respect to a child, it must not make the order or any of the orders unless it considers that doing so would be better for the child than making no order at all[1].

Where the making of "no order" on an application for contact, is likely to result in a termination of contact, it will be appropriate for the court to go on to consider the future and what steps might be taken in the future to ensure that any subsequent application is heard both timeously and at the appropriate level[2].

1. Children Act 1989, s 1(5), this PART, post.
2. *D v D (Application for Contact)* [1994] 1 FCR 694.

6–144   Parental responsibility: meaning.   For the purposes of the Children Act 1989, "parental responsibility" means all the rights, duties, powers, responsibilities and authority which by law a parent of a child has in relation to the child and his property[1]. It also includes the rights, powers and duties which a guardian of the child's estate would have had in relation to the child and his property[2].

The rights referred to above include, in particular, the right of the guardian to receive or recover in his own name, for the benefit of the child, property of whatever description and wherever situated which the child is entitled to receive or recover[3].

The fact that a person has, or does not have, parental responsibility for a child shall not affect:

(a)   any obligation which he may have in relation to the child (such as a statutory duty to maintain the child); or
(b)   any rights which, in the event of the child's death, he (or any other person) may have in relation to the child's property[4].

A person who does not have parental responsibility for a particular child, but has care of the child, may, subject to the provisions of the Act, do what is reasonable in all the circumstances of the case for the purpose of safeguarding or promoting the child's welfare[5].

1. Children Act 1989, s 3(1), this PART, post.
2. Children Act 1989, s 3(2), this PART, post.
3. Children Act 1989, s 1(3), this PART, post.
4. Children Act 1989, s 1(4), this PART, post.
5. Children Act 1989, s 1(5), this PART, post.

6–145   Parental responsibility for children.   Where a child's father and mother were married to each other at the time of his birth, they shall each have parental responsibility for the child[1]. Where the parents were not married to each at the time of the birth, the mother will have parental responsibility for the child but the father will not have parental responsibility unless he acquires it in one of the ways specified in para **6–146**, post.

The rule of law that a father is the natural guardian of his legitimate child has been abolished[2]. Accordingly, where the father and mother were married at the time of the child's birth they are in a position of equality.

More than one person may have parental responsibility for the same child at the same time[3]. A person who has parental responsibility for a child at any time shall not cease to have that responsibility solely because some other person subsequently acquires parental responsibility for the child[4]. Where more than one person has parental responsibility for a child, each of them may act alone and without the other (or others) in meeting that responsibility[5].

The fact that a person has parental responsibility for a child does not entitle him to act in any way which would be incompatible with any order made with respect to the child under the Children Act 1989[6]. A person who has parental responsibility for a child may not surrender or transfer any part of that responsibility to another but may arrange for some or all of it to be met by one or more persons acting on his behalf[7].

---

1. Children Act 1989, s 2(1), this PART, post.
2. Children Act 1989, s 2(4), this PART, post.
3. Children Act 1989, s 2(5), this PART, post.
4. Children Act 1989, s 2(6), this PART, post.
5. Children Act 1989, s 2(7), this PART, post.
6. Children Act 1989, s 2(8), this PART, post.
7. Children Act 1989, s 2(9), this PART, post.

6–146   Parental responsibility: acquisition by (*a*) father; (*b*) step-parent; (*c*) civil partner

Father

Where a child's father and mother were not married to each other at the time of his birth, the father may acquire parental responsibility in one of the following ways:

(*a*) by an order of the court, on the father's application, that he shall have parental responsibility for the child[1];

(*b*) by a parental responsibility agreement made between the father and the mother whereby the father shall have parental responsibility for the child[2];

(*c*) by an order of the court when making a residence order in favour of the child[3].

(*d*) by being registered as the child's father under any of the Births and Deaths legislation applicable to England, Wales, Scotland or Northern Ireland (however, since an unmarried father is not a qualified informant this will require the mother's agreement and co-operation)[4].

On an application for a parental responsibility order the court must consider, amongst other things, the degree of commitment which the father has shown to the child, the degree of attachment between the father and the child, and the reasons for the father applying for the order[5]. These three requirements are the starting point for the making of an order and are not intended to be the only factors in considering an application for parental responsibility. Section 1 of the Children Act 1989 applies to parental responsibility orders and the welfare of the child is therefore paramount. Accordingly, the court has a duty in each case to take into account all the relevant circumstances and to decide whether the order proposed is in the best interests of the child[6]. Applications for contact and parental responsibility orders are to be treated as wholly separate applications. Accordingly, a refusal to grant contact does not mean that a parental responsibility order should also be refused since a parental responsibility order does no more than confer on the natural father the status he would have when married to the mother[7]. However, where the child expresses serious reluctance to have contact with and fear and anxiety about the father it is inappropriate to grant a parental responsibility order[8].

Accordingly, where the court is dealing with an application for a parental responsibility order by a father who has shown a degree of commitment towards the child, it being established that there is a degree of attachment between the father and the child, and that his reasons for applying for the order are not demonstrably improper or wrong, then prima facie it will be for the welfare of the child that such an order should be made[9]. The father's failure to provide financially for his children does not disentitle him to a parental responsibility order. It is not right for the court to use the weapon of withholding a parental responsibility order for the purpose of extracting from the father what may be regarded as his financial dues[10]. A cardinal circumstance of importance to an understanding of the father's motivation is whether the issue of the application for parental responsibility was preceded by a request that the mother sign a parental responsibility agreement[11]. In considering an application for a parental responsibility order, the court is determining the grant of status and it is wrong for the court to place undue emphasis on the rights and duties and the powers comprised in parental responsibility. The wide exercise of s 8 orders can control the abuse, if any, of the exercise of parental responsibility which is adverse to the welfare of the child. Interferences with the day-to-day management of the child's life have nothing to do with whether or not a parental responsibility order should be allowed[12].

A person who has been given parental responsibility by a family proceedings court may apply to the

Central Office, Filing Department, for the enrolment of a deed poll to change the surname (family name) of a child who is under 18 years of age, unless in the case of a female she is married below that age[13].

In considering an application to terminate a parental responsibility agreement the court will have regard to the same principles that are applicable to the making of a parental responsibility order. Since the desire to have and to exercise parental responsibility is laudable and is to be encouraged, it should not be terminated in the case of a non-marital father on less than solid grounds, with a presumption for continuance rather than termination. It should not be allowed to become a weapon in the hands of a dissatisfied mother[14].

Step-parent

Where a child's parent who has parental responsibility for the child is married to a person who is not the child's parent, the latter may acquire parental responsibility in any of the following ways:

    (*a*) by agreement with the parent or, if the child's other parent also has parental responsibility, by agreement with both parents;

    (*b*) by an order of the court on the application of the step-parent to have parental responsibility[15].

An agreement or parental responsibility order may only be brought to an end by an order of the court on the application of any person who has parental responsibility for the child or, with the leave of the court, of the application of the child himself[16]. As to the latter, the court may only grant leave if it is satisfied that the child has sufficient understanding to make the proposed application[17].

Civil Partner

The law relating to acquiring parental responsibility, adoption, applications for residence and contact orders and financial provision for children has been updated to accomodate civil partners by ss 75–79 of the Civil Partnership Act 2004. In relation, however, to same-sex couples that have not registered as civil partners, the only means for the non-parent to acquire parental responsibility is through obtaining a residence order[18].

---

  1. Children Act 1989, s 4(1)(*a*), this PART, post.
  2. Children Act 1989, s 4(1)(*b*), this PART, post. For procedure and prescribed form, see the Parental Responsibility Agreement Regulations 1991, SI 1991/1478 amended by SI 1994/3157 and SI 2001/2262.
  3. Children Act 1989, s 12(1), this PART, post.
  4. Section 4 of the Children Act 1989, as amended by s 11 of the Adoption and Children Act 2002.
  5. *Re H (a minor) (Contact and Parental Responsibility)* [1993] 1 FCR 85, [1993] 1 FLR 484. See also *Re CB (a minor) (Parental Responsibility Order)* [1993] 1 FLR 920.
  6. *Re H (parental responsibility)* [1998] 1 FLR 855.
  7. *Re C and V (minors) (parental responsibility and contact)* [1998] 1 FCR 52, [1998] 1 FLR 392.
  8. *Re G (a child) (domestic violence: direct contact)* [2001] 2 FCR 134.
  9. *Re G (a minor) (Parental Responsibility)* [1993] 2 FCR 1037, CA. See also *Re J-S (a child) (contact: parental responsibility)* [2002] EWCA Civ 1028, [2002] 3 FCR 433, [2003] 1 FLR 399.
  10. *Re H (a minor) (Parental Responsibility Order)* [1996] 3 FCR 49, [1996] 1 FLR 867, CA.
  11. *Re A (a minor) (Parental Responsibility)* [1996] 1 FCR 562.
  12. *Re S (a minor) (Parental Responsibility)* [1995] 3 FCR 225, [1995] 2 FLR 648, CA.
  13. *Practice Direction (Child: Change of Surname)* [1995] 1 All ER 832, [1995] 1 WLR 365, [1995] 2 FCR 136, [1995] 1 FLR 458
  14. *Re P (Terminating Parental Responsibility)* [1995] 3 FCR 753, [1995] 1 FLR 1048.
  15. Children Act 1989, s 4A (inserted by the Adoption and Children Act 2002, s 112). See note 2 infra for procedure and prescribed form for the acquisition of parental responsibility by agreement.
  16. Children Act 1989, s 4A(3).
  17. Children Act 1989, s 4A(4).
  18. As to this, see *Re G (residence: same-sex partner)* [2005] EWCA Civ 462, [2005] 2 FLR 957. See also *Ghaidan v Godin-Mendoza* [2004] UKHL 30, [2004] 3 WLR 113, [2004] 2 FLR 600, in which Baroness Hale said: "...the presence of children is a relevant factor in deciding whether a relationship is marriage-like but if the couple are bringing up children together, it is unlikely to matter whether or not they are the biological children of both parties. Both married and unmarried couples, both homosexual and heterosexual, may bring up children together. One or both may have children from another relationship: this is not at all uncommon in lesbian relationships and the court may grant them a shared residence order so that they may share parental responsibility. The lesbian couple may have children by donor insemination who are brought up as the children of them both: it is not uncommon for each of them to bear a child in this way...[143] It follows that a homosexual couple whose relationship is marriage-like in the same ways that an unmarried heterosexual couple's relationship is marriage-like are indeed in an analogous situation. Any difference in treatment is based upon their sexual orientation".

Proceedings on an application for an order under section 8 of the Children Act 1989

6–150   Section 8 orders.   In family proceedings[1], the court may make one or more of the following orders:

    (*a*) a contact order;
    (*b*) a prohibited steps order;
    (*c*) a residence order;

(*d*)   a specific issue order.

A "section 8 order" means any of the above orders and any order varying or discharging such an order. The powers of the court to make a section 8 order are governed and restricted by detailed provisions in the Children Act 1989[2].

In this context, for the purposes of the Children Act 1989, "family proceedings" means any proceedings under the inherent jurisdiction of the High Court in relation to children, and under the enactments mentioned in s 8(4) of the Act[3]. This meaning must be contrasted with that under s 65 of the Magistrates' Courts Act 1980 which is explained in para **6–3**.

In any family proceedings in which a question arises with respect to the welfare of any child, the court may make a s 8 order with respect to the child if—

(*a*)   an application for the order has been made by a person who—

(i)   is entitled to apply for a s 8 order with respect to the child; or
(ii)   has obtained the leave of the court to make the application; or

(*b*)   the court considers that the order should be made even though no such application has been made[4].

The court may also make a s 8 order with respect to any child on the application of a person who—

(*a*)   is entitled to apply for a s 8 order with respect to the child; or
(*b*)   has obtained the leave of the court to make the application[5].

Any parent or guardian of the child, or any person in whose favour a residence order is in force with respect to the child, may apply to the court for a s 8 order to be made with respect to the child[6]. The following persons are entitled to apply for a residence or contact order with respect to a child—

(*a*)   any party to a marriage (whether or not subsisting) in relation to whom the child is a child of the family;
(*b*)   any person with whom the child has lived for a period of at least three years;
(*c*)   any person who—

(i)   in any case where a residence order is in force with respect to the child, has the consent of each of the persons in whose favour the order was made;
(ii)   in any case where the child is in the care of a local authority, has the consent of that authority; or
(iii)   in any other case, has the consent of each of those (if any) who have parental responsibility for the child[7].

Any person who falls within a category of person prescribed by rules of court is entitled to apply for any such s 8 order as may be prescribed in relation to that category of person[8].

Where the person applying for leave to make an application for a s 8 order is the child concerned, the court may only grant leave if it is satisfied that he has sufficient understanding to make the proposed application for the s 8 order[9]. The broad principles to be applied are that the best interests of the child are of importance, but are not paramount[10]. Moreover, when considering such an application for leave, it is right for the court to have regard to the likelihood of success of the proposed application[11]. Such an application is likely to raise issues which are more appropriate for determination in the High Court and should be transferred there for the hearing of the application[12].

No application may be made by a local authority for a residence order or contact order and no court shall make such an order in favour of a local authority[13]. A local authority may not by leave be allowed to become a party to proceedings on an application for a residence or contact order[14]. A local authority may, however, apply for a specific issue order or a prohibited steps order, but neither of those orders shall be made with a view to achieving a result which could be achieved by a residence or contact order[15]. The means by which a local authority generally can seek to intervene are the public law remedies of care and supervision orders provided by Part IV of the Children Act 1989[16].

---

1. Proceedings under the Children Act 1989 shall be treated as family proceedings in relation to magistrates' courts (Children Act 1989, s 92(2), this PART, post).
2. Children Act 1989, s 8(2), this PART, post.
3. Children Act 1989, s 8(3), this PART, post.
4. Children Act 1989, s 10(1), this PART, post.
5. Children Act 1989, s 10(2), this PART, post.
6. Children Act 1989, s 10(4), this PART, post.
7. Children Act 1989, s 10(5), this PART, post.
8. Children Act 1989, s 10(7), this PART, post.
9. Children Act 1989, s 10(8), this PART, post.
10. *Re C (Residence: Child's Application for Leave)* [1996] 1 FCR 461, [1995] 1 FLR 927.
11. *Re SC (a minor) (Leave to Seek Residence Order)* [1994] 1 FCR 609, [1994] 1 FLR 96.
12. *Practice Direction (Family Proceedings Orders: Applications by Children)* [1993] 1 All ER 820, [1993] 1 FCR 584, [1993] 1 FLR 668. See also *Re AD (a minor)* [1993] 1 FCR 573.
13. Children Act 1989, s 9(2), this PART, post.
14. *F v Cambridgeshire County Council* [1995] 2 FCR 804, [1995] 1 FLR 516.
15. Children Act 1989, s 9(5), this PART, post.
16. See *Nottinghamshire County Council v P* [1993] 3 All ER 815, [1993] 2 FLR 134.

6–151   Contact order.   A contact order is an order requiring the person with whom a child lives, or is to live, to allow the child to visit or stay with the person named in the order, or for that person and the child otherwise to have contact with each other[1].

A contact order which requires the parent with whom a child lives to allow the child to visit, or otherwise have contact with, his other parent shall cease to have effect if the parents live together for a continuous period of more than six months[2].

The approach to "contact" should be on the same principles as were applied in relation to access, and the authorities which pre-dated the coming into force of the Children Act 1989 are still relevant[3].

The court should start with the premise that the child's right is to know both its parents, but recognise that there may be cases where there are cogent reasons why the child should be denied that opportunity[3]. In cases in which, for whatever reason, direct contact cannot for the time being be ordered, it is ordinarily highly desirable that there should be indirect contact so that the child grows up knowing of the love and interest of the absent parent with whom, in due course, direct contact should be established[4]. However, while this is the correct approach to a significant number of contact cases, there will be the exceptional case where it will not be in the best interests of the child at that time to make an order for indirect contact[5]. The right to contact extends to a father within the meaning of s 28 of the Human Fertilisation and Embryology Act 1990[6] and the right cannot be disregarded by reason of the absence of a biological link[7]. However, there is no presumption that a grandparent who has obtained leave is entitled to contact unless there are cogent reasons for denying it to the grandparent[8].

On the general issue of contact, the overwhelming weight of current authority is that:

(*a*)   wherever possible a child should get to know his estranged parent;

(*aa*)   any civil partner in a civil partnership (whether or not subsisting) in relation to whom the child is a child of the family;

(*b*)   no court should deprive a child of contact with a natural parent unless it is wholly satisfied that it is in the interests of the child that contact should cease; and

(*c*)   it is a normal assumption that a child will benefit from continued contact with a natural parent[9].

In the past, caution has been urged about making interim orders where the principle of contact is in dispute[10]. There has also been reluctance to use penalties, especially committal, to enforce contact orders[11]. However, art 6 and art 8 considerations must now govern the courts' approach to these matters[12].

No court should deprive a child of contact with either parent unless it is wholly satisfied that it is in the interests of the child that contact should cease, and that is a conclusion at which the court should be extremely slow to arrive. Where parents have separated, and one has the care of the child, contact with the other often results in some upsets to the child, but those upsets are usually minor and superficial and are heavily outweighed by the long-term advantages to the child of keeping in touch with the parent concerned. Save in exceptional cases, to deprive a parent of contact is to deprive a child of an important contribution to his emotional and material growing up in the long-term[13]. It is not a ground for denying contact with a father that the child is very young and has no knowledge of his biological father. It is more appropriate and better to enable the child, in ways appropriate to his age, to gently assimilate the truth about his parentage and in such circumstances it may be appropriate to make an order for indirect contact[14]. In cases where it is alleged that a parent has alienated a child against the other parent, the jurisprudence of the European Court of Human Rights requires the court to investigate the issue thoroughly and make sufficient findings on the issue[15].

The court should take into account, as one of the factors in its decision-making, whether the father has had some contact with the child since the child's birth[3]. The implacable hostility of the mother towards contact is a factor which is capable, according to the circumstances of each case, of supplying a cogent reason for departing from the general principle that a child should grow up in the knowledge of both his parents[3]. However, the court should be very reluctant to allow the implacable hostility of one parent (usually the parent who has a residence order in his or her favour) to deter it from making a contact order where the court believes the child's welfare requires it[16]. Where there are no rational grounds for a parent's hostility to contact, an order will only be refused if it would create a serious risk of emotional harm to the child. Where the hostility is based on rational but not decisive grounds, the hostility may be an important, and occasionally determinative factor, provided what is measured is the effect of the hostility on the child[17]. Where the physical risks to the children (their father had previously planned to kill himself and them) could be prevented by proper supervision, there was mutual love between the children and their father and a particular need, in view of his degenerative illness, for contact to take place, but the mother suffered from acute post traumatic stress disorder because of the suicide attempt and took a 'zero risk position', nothing could reassure her about direct contact and there was a likelihood that that would cause her to suffer a nervous breakdown, the children's need for a competent and confident primary carer outweighed their need to have direct contact with their father[18]. In some cases where the residential parent's distorted and false beliefs about the other parent are causing significant harm to the children, an option for the court may be to make an interim care order under the s 37 procedure but such a course of action requires considerable thought and is not a panacea[19]. In some circumstances, where the party with a residence order is implacably opposed to contact such as to amount to emotional abuse of the children and the other party can meet their needs, the court may consider that the interests of the children require there to be a change of residence[20]. (Because of this complexity we would submit that such matters should be allocated to the higher courts.) In considering an application by a parent for contact with a child of mixed race, the court should have regard to the child's origins and deal with any concerns about the child's confusion over racial identity[21].

Issues arising out of contact applications where allegations of domestic violence have been made were considered by the Court of Appeal in *Re L (a child) (contact: domestic violence)*[22] where the President stated that:

'[F]amily judges and magistrates need to have a heightened awareness of the existence of and consequences (some long term), on children of exposure to domestic violence between their parents or other partners. There has, perhaps, been a tendency in the past for courts not to tackle allegations of violence and to leave them in the background on the premise that they were matters affecting the adults and not relevant to issues regarding the children. The general principle that contact with the non-resident parent is in the interests of the child may sometimes have discouraged sufficient attention being paid to the adverse effects on children living in the household where violence has occurred. It may not necessarily be widely appreciated that violence to a partner involves a significant failure in parenting - failure to protect the child's care and failure to protect the child emotionally.

In a contact or other s 8 application, where allegations of domestic violence are made which might have an effect on the outcome, those allegations must be adjudicated upon and found proved or not proved. It will be necessary to scrutinise such allegations which may not always be true or may be grossly exaggerated, however there is a firm basis for finding that violence has occurred, the psychiatric advice becomes very important. There is not, however, nor should there be, any presumption that, on proof of domestic violence, t offending parent has to surmount a prima facie barrier of no contact. As a matter of principle, domestic violence of itself cannot constitute a bar to contact. It is one factor in the difficult and delicate balancing exercise of discretion. The court deals with the facts of a specific case in which the degree of violence and the seriousness of the impact on the child and on the resident parent have to be taken into account. In cases of proved domestic violence, as in cases of other proved harm or risk of harm to the child, the court has the task of weighing in the balance the seriousness of the domestic violence, the risks involved and the impact on the child against the positive factors (if any), of contact between the parent found to have been violent and the child. In this context, the ability of the offending parent to recognise his past conduct, be aware of the need for change and make genuine efforts to do so, will be likely to be an important consideration. Wall J in *Re M (Contact: Violent Parent)* [1999] 2 FLR 321 suggested at 333 that often in cases where domestic violence had been found, too little weight had been given to the need for the father to change. He suggested that the father should demonstrate that he was a fit person to exercise contact and should show a track record of proper behaviour. Assertions, without evidence to back it up, may well not be sufficient.

In expressing these views I recognise the danger of the pendulum swinging too far against contact where domestic violence has been proved. It is trite but true to say that no two child cases are exactly the same. The court always has the duty to apply s 1 of the Children Act 1989 that the welfare of the child is paramount and, in considering that welfare, to take into account all the relevant circumstances including the advice of the medical experts as far as it is relevant and proportionate to the decision in that case. It will also be relevant in due course to take into account the impart of Art 8 of the European Convention for the Protection of Human Rights and Fundamental Freedoms 1950 on a decision to refuse direct contact.

In cases of serious domestic violence the reluctance of a child to see a parent is a matter that must be examined with care[23].

Where it is in the interests of a child that there should be a monitored programme reintroducing contact with a parent, it is wrong for the court to refuse to adjourn the case for such a programme to take place on the ground that delay is likely to be prejudicial to the child[24].

A court, when declaring a child free for adoption, may also make an order for contact between the child and the natural family pending adoption. However, where both such orders are made, the court should give appropriate directions to ensure continuity of judicial approach in the subsequent proceedings[25].

Where a family proceedings court makes "no order" on an application for contact, which effectively terminates contact, the court should consider the practical effect of its order and if it is of the view that contact in the future will be in the interests of the child, indicate what steps might be taken to ensure that any subsequent application is heard both timeously and at the appropriate level[26].

Sections 26 and 27 of the Adoption and Children Act 2002 make provision for applications for contact in respect of children placed for adoption and where an adoption agency is authorised to place a child for adoption under s 19 of the Act or under a placement order[27]. Section 26 does not prevent an application for a contact order under s 8 of the Children Act 1989 being made where the application is to be heard together with an application for an adoption order[28]. Section 46(5) provides that before making an adoption order the court must consider whether there should be arrangements for allowing any person contact with the child; and for that purpose the court must consider any existing or proposed arrangements and obtain any views of the parties to the proceedings.

A contact order is only capable of founding a complaint to enforce the order under s 63 of the Magistrates' Courts Act 1980[9] if the terms of the order are precise. Committal under s 63 applies only to non-compliance of an order of the court, not for non-performance of an agreement between the parties[10]. Although the ordering of committal of a mother is a last resort, there does come a limit to the tolerance of the court to see its orders flouted by mothers even if they have to care for their young children. The court has a duty to the child and has to decide whether contact will promote the child's welfare. The court is not concerned to preserve its own dignity but to maintain the due administration of justice and to do what is best for the child in the long term[29].

---

1. Children Act 1989, s 8(1), this PART, post.
2. Children Act 1989, s 11(6), this PART, post.
3. *Re D (a minor) (contact: mother's hostility)* [1993] 2 FLR 1, CA.
4. *Re P (contact supervision)* [1996] 2 FLR 314, CA.
5. *Re C (contact: no order for contact)* [2000] 2 FLR 723, FD.
6. See this PART, post.
7. *Re CH (contact)* [1996] 1 FCR 768, [1996] 1 FLR 569.
8. *Re A (Section 8 Order: grandparent application)* [1995] 2 FLR 153, [1996] 1 FCR 467, CA
9. *Re O (contact: imposition of conditions)* [1995] 2 FLR 124, sub nom *Re O (a minor) (contact: indirect contact)* [1996] 1 FCR 317, CA.
10. See, for example, *Re D (a minor) (contact: interim order)* [1995] 1 FLR 495; and *Re D (a child)* [2001] EWCA Civ 1827 (which concerned staying contact).
11. *Re H (Contact: Enforcement)* [1996] 2 FCR 784, [1996] 1 FLR 531.
12. See *Re D (a child) (intractable contact dispute: publicity)* [2004] EWHC 727 (Fam), [2004] 3 FCR 234. The case involved 43 hearings over 5 years, culminating in the father giving up his attempt to obtain contact. Munby J held that, from a judicial perspective, there were two disturbing features: (i) the court's frequent response to problematic contact matters was, inter alia, to reduce contact and obtain expert reports which produced further delay and exacerbated matters, and (ii) the court's failure to recognise the case as intractable until it was too late for any effective intervention. His lordship held that from European jurisprudence a number of principles could be drawn: (i) art 8 protected both the parent's and the child's right to contact with each other; (ii) it was essential that matters should be dealt with speedily, as relations between parent and child should not be determined by the passing of time; (iii) a non-custodial parent had a right to have measures taken to facilitate contact with the child and the national authorities were obliged to take action; (iv) the right to a court guaranteed by art 6 also protected the implementation of final, binding decisions which could not remain inoperative to the detriment of one party. Those positive obligations extended in principle to the taking of coercive measures, against both the recalcitrant parent and even the child. His lordship added that courts must also resist the temptation to put contact 'on hold', or to direct that it is to be supervised, pending investigation of allegations by the other parent; and such

allegations should be speedily resolved and the findings should determine the approach made to the case thereafter. See also *Re M (intractable contact dispute: interim care order)* [2003] EWHC 1024 (Fam), and *Re O (a child) (contact: withdrawal of application)* [2003] EWHC 3031 (Fam), [2004] 1 FCR 687.

13. *Re H (minors) (Access)* [1992] 1 FLR 148; applied in *Re H (a minor) (Contact)* [1994] 2 FCR 249, CA. See also *Re J-S (a child: contact: parental responsibility)* [2002] EWCA Civ 1028, [2002] 3 FCR 433, [2003] 1 FLR 399.

14. *A v A (contact)* [1998] 2 FCR 204, [1998] 1 FLR 361.

15. *Re L, a child: contact)* [2002] EWCA Civ 1736, [2003] 1 FCR 302, [2003] 1 FLR 531.

16. *Re J (minor) (contact)* [1994] 2 FCR 741, [1994] 1 FLR 729, and see also *Re P (minors) (contact: parental hostility)* [1997] 1 FCR 459, CA.

17. *Re P (minors) (contact: discretion)* [1999] 1 FCR 566, [1998] 2 FLR 696, FD.

18. *Re H (children) (contact order) (No 2)* [2001] 3 FCR 385 (see also *Re H (children) (contact order)* [2001] 1 FCR 49, CA, [2002] 1 FLR 2, CA).

19. *Re M (intractable contact dispute: interim care order)* [2003] EWHC 1024 (Fam), [2003] 2 FLR 636.

20. *V v V (Contact: Implacable Hostility)* [2004] EWHC 1215 (Fam), [2004] 2 FLR 851.

21. *Re M (a minor)* (1994) Independent, 14 December.

22. *[2001] 2 FLR 339, [2000] 2 FCR 404, [2000] 2 FLR 334, CA. See also *A Report to the Lord Chancellor on the Question of Parental Content in Cases where there is Domestic Violence* The Advisory Board on Family Law Children Act Sub-Committee (1 April 2000).

23. *Re G (a child) (domestic violence: direct contact)* [2001] 2 FCR 134, CA.

24. *Re B (a minor) (contact: Interim Order)* [1994] 2 FLR 269.

25. *Re R (a minor) (Adoption: Contact Order)* [1994] 1 FCR 105.

26. *D v D (Application: Contact)* [1994] 1 FCR 694.

27. See this PART, post.

28. Adoption and Children Act 2002, s 26(5).

29. *A v N (Committal; Refusal of Contact)* [1997] 2 FCR 475, [1997] 1 FLR 533, CA.

6-152 Prohibited steps order. A prohibited steps order is an order that no step which could be taken by a parent in meeting his parental responsibility for a child, and which is of a kind specified in the order, shall be taken by any person without the consent of the court[1].

The court must not exercise its power to make a prohibited steps order with a view to achieving a result which could be achieved by making a residence or contact order[2]. Consequently, a prohibited steps order under which it was stated that there should be no contact except as the local authority approved was held to be prohibited by s 9(5) of the Act[3].

A prohibited steps order does not allow a court to make an order prohibiting the parents from having contact with each other because such contact is not a step which can be taken by a parent in meeting his parental responsibility towards his child[4]. There is no jurisdiction to make a prohibited steps order to prevent a father staying overnight in the matrimonial home while having contact with his children[5].

A prohibited steps order may be made against a person who is not a party to the proceedings[6]. Where an order is made in such circumstances a requirement that the person to whom it is directed shall not have or seek contact with a child will not contravene s 9(5) of the Act[6].

---

1. Children Act 1989, s 8(1), this PART, post.

2. Children Act 1989, s 9(5), this PART, post.

3. *Nottingham County Council v P* [1993] 3 All ER 815, [1993] 2 FLR 134, CA.

4. *Croydon London Borough Council v A* [1992] 3 All ER 788, [1992] 3 WLR 267.

5. *D v D (Ouster Order)* [1996] 2 FCR 496, CA.

6. *Re H (minors) (Prohibited Steps Order)* [1995] 4 All ER 110, [1995] 1 WLR 667, [1995] 2 FCR 547, [1995] 1 FLR 638, CA.

6-153 Residence order. A residence order is an order settling the arrangements to be made as to the person with whom a child is to live[1].

The power of the court to make a residence order in favour of any person who is not the parent or guardian of the child concerned includes power to direct, at that person's request, that the order shall continue in force until the child attains 18 years, and any power to vary a residence order is exercisable accordingly; where a residence order includes such a direction an application to vary or discharge the order can only be made with the leave of the court[2].

Where a residence order is made in favour of two or more persons who do not themselves all live together, the order may specify the periods during which the child is to live in the different households concerned[3].

Where a residence order has been made with respect to a child; and as a result of the order the child lives, or is to live, with one of two parents who each have parental responsibility for him, the residence order shall cease to have effect if the parents live together for a continuous period of more than six months[4].

There is no presumption of law that a child of any given age is better off with one parent or another, but no court can be ignorant of the natural position if other things are equal; a baby of under four weeks old will normally be with his or her mother[5]. Nevertheless, it is wrong for the court to start with the proposition that little girls naturally go with their mothers; the overriding factor is that the child's welfare is the paramount consideration[6]. On an application for a residence order, it is the welfare of the child which is the test. However, there is a strong supposition that, other things being equal, it is in the interests of the child that it shall remain with its natural parents, but that has to give way to particular needs in particular situations. Accordingly, the court is not permitted to conduct a balancing exercise between two households, but should consider on the totality of the evidence whether there are good grounds for rejecting the natural parent as a potential carer[7].

Where the court is considering cross-applications for residence orders, the correct approach is to look at the issue of where the child will live as one of the relevant factors. If the case is finely balanced between the respective advantages and disadvantages of the parents, the proposals put forward by each parent will assume considerable importance. If one parent's plan is to remove the child against his wishes to another part of the country less suitable for him, it is an important factor to be taken into account by the court and might persuade the court in some cases to make a residence order in favour of the other parent. Save for exceptional cases, it will not be appropriate to impose a condition of residence specifying where the child shall live since that would be an unwarranted imposition upon the right of the parent to choose where he/she will live or with whom[8].

While a shared residence order may be made under the provisions of s 11(4) of the Children Act 1989, the usual order will be a sole residence order, and there must be positive benefit to the child in making an order which is not the conventional order. The child's welfare requires that he should have a settled home, and giving him two competing homes may only lead to confusion and stress. Nevertheless, the decision whether or not to make a shared residence order is in the discretion of the court, in the light of the principles set out in s 1 of the Children Act 1989[9], and where there is a proximity of homes and a relatively fluid passage of the children between those homes, the judicial convention that the welfare of the children demands a choice between one parent or the other as a guardian of the residence order in order to promote the welfare of the children no longer runs as it used to[10]. Moreover, if it was planned or had turned out that children were spending substantial amounts of time with each of their parents then a shared residence order was an appropriate order to make; there was no need to show exceptional circumstances or a positive benefit to the children[11]. However, a residence order is an order that settles the arrangements to be made as to the person with whom a child is to live, and the order has to be designed to reflect the real position on the ground[12]. An order granting shared residence of children, but with care and control to one parent only, does not conform to the Children Act 1989, which does not deal with the concept of care and control[12]. The fact that the parents' homes are separated by a considerable distance does not preclude the possibility that the children's year can be divided between the homes of two separated parents in such a way as to validate the making of a shared residence order; nor does the fact that one of the parties lives in another legal jurisdiction (Scotland) preclude the making of a shared residence order[13].

The court may make a residence order *ex parte* under s 10(1)(*b*) of the Act, but such power should be exercised only occasionally where there are exceptional circumstances[14]. Directions contained in a residence order, including an interim residence order made *ex parte*, may require a child who has been removed or abducted to be restored to his home[14].

---

1. Children Act 1989, s 8(1), this PART, post.
2. Children Act 1989, s 12(5) and (6).
3. Children Act 1989, s 11(4), this PART, post.
4. Children Act 1989, s 11(5), this PART, post.
5. *Re W (Residence Order: Baby)* [1992] 2 FCR 603.
6. *Re A (a minor) (residence order)* [1998] 2 FCR 633.
7. *Re W (a minor) (residence order)* [1993] 2 FCR 589, [1993] 2 FLR 625, CA; *Re D (care: natural parent presumption)* [1999] 2 FCR 118, [1999] 1 FLR 134, CA; *Re D (a child) (residence: natural parent)* [2000] 1 FCR 97. See also *Re H (a child: residence)* [2002] 3 FCR 277, CA, where it was held that there was no presumption in favour of the natural parent to be found anywhere in the Children Act 1989 and any judicial overlay of the words of the statute had to be treated with caution. In any event, the biological parent might not always be the natural parent in the eyes of the child (the child had been living with the maternal grandmother for some years under a residence order).
8. *Re E (Minors) (Residence Conditions)* [1997] 3 FCR 245, [1997] 2 FLR 638, CA; *Re S (a child) (residence order: condition)* [2001] EWCA Civ 847, [2001] 3 FCR 154 (where there were exceptional circumstances justifying such a restriction: *Re S (a child) (residence order: condition) (No 2)* [2002] EWCA Civ 1795, [2003] 1 FCR 138).
9. *A v A (minors) (Shared Residence Order)* [1995] 1 FCR 91, [1994] 1 FLR 669, CA; applied in *Re AB (a minor) (Adoption: Parental Consent)* [1996] 1 FLR 27, [1996] 1 FCR 633 (joint residence order made in favour of foster parents, the foster mother being unable to join in adoption application as not married to foster father); see also *Re H (Shared Residence: Parental Responsibility)* [1996] 3 FCR 321 [1995] 2 FLR 883, CA (shared residence order made for purpose of conferring parental responsibility on stepfather).
10. *Re A (children) (shared residence)* [2002] EWCA Civ 1343, [2003] 3 FCR 656.
11. *Re A (children) (shared residence)* [2001] EWCA Civ 1795, [2002] 1 FCR 177, [2002] 1 FLR 495.
12. *Re A (children) (shared residence)*, supra. See also *A v A (children) (shared residence order)* [2004] EWHC 142 (Fam), [2004] 3 FCR 201, wherein it was stated: "Where children are living with one parent and are either not seeing the other parents or the amount of time to be spent with the other parent is limited or undecided, there cannot be a shared residence order. However, where children are spending a substantial amount of time with both their parents, a shared residence order reflects the reality of the children's lives. It is not necessarily to be considered an exceptional order and should be made if it is in the best interests of the children concerned" (para 119).
13. *Re F (shared residence order)* [2003] EWCA Civ 592, [2003] 2 FCR 164, [2003] 2 FLR 397.
14. *Re B (minors)* [1992] 3 All ER 867, [1992] 3 WLR 113, [1992] 1 FCR 555.

6–154 Specific issue order. A specific issue order is an order giving directions for the purpose of determining a specific question which has arisen, or which may arise, in connection with any aspect of parental responsibility for a child[1].

The court must not exercise its power to make a specific issue order with a view to achieving a result which could be achieved by making a residence or contact order[2].

The phrase "any aspect of parental responsibility" means any aspect of the manner in which parental responsibility falls to be exercised, but it does not include whether or not the child is a child in need[3]. Although a specific issue order may be suitable for determining where a child should live, it is inappropriate to make such an order where a right of occupation is involved since in these circumstances the specific issue order would have the effect of an ouster order which was not what Parliament intended[4]. Courts should use their power and influence to steer parents from unnecessary discord whenever they can e.g. through use of adjournments but ultimately the parties have a right to a judicial determination and the court may not delegate that to one of the parties[5].

An application for a s 8 order by an area health authority in respect of a child in care who needs medical treatment is unnecessary, since consent can be given by a competent child, or by a person having parental responsibility or, if this is not possible, by the High Court[6]. Nevertheless, a specific issue order on the application of a local authority has been held to be appropriate to secure a blood transfusion. Such application should be made to a High Court judge to allow for the proceedings to be transferred to the inherent jurisdiction should this become necessary[7]. A specific issue order has also been granted by the High Court to enable a child, whose mother was infected with HIV and who rejected advice not to breastfeed, to be tested for HIV[8]; and for the immunisation of a child whose custodial mother was radically opposed to it[9].

Section 2(7) of the Children Act 1989 does not enable a parent to arrange male circumcision on a child without the consent of the other parent sharing parental responsibility. Where applications for specific issue orders are made by the father of a male child that his son be brought up in the Muslim religion and that the son be circumcised, both applications are to be approached applying the paramountcy of welfare test under s 1 of the 1989 Act. In such cases, a relevant factor will be each parent's religious beliefs and practices[10].

It would appear that an interview with a child by the solicitor of a parent charged with a criminal offence is an exercise of parental responsibility[11]. The court may make a specific issue order to determine the conditions on which such an interview may be conducted except where the child is subject to a care order in which case it will be necessary to invoke the inherent jurisdiction of the High Court[12].

1. Children Act 1989, s 8(1), this PART, post.
2. Children Act 1989, s 9(5), this PART, post.
3. *Re J (a minor) (Specific Issue Order)* [1995] 3 FCR 799.
4. *Pearson v Franklin* [1994] 2 All ER 137, [1994] 1 WLR 370, [1994] 1 FLR 246.
5. *Re P (parental dispute: judicial determination)* [2002] EWCA Civ 1627, [2003] 1 FLR 286 ("future questions about children's schooling to be determined by mother after consultation with father").
6. *Re K, W and H (minors) (consent to treatment)* [1993] 1 FCR 240, [1993] 1 FLR 854.
7. *Re R (a minor) (blood transfusion)* 2 FCR 544, [1993] 2 FLR 757.
8. *In re C (a child) (HIV testing)* [2000] Fam 48, [2000] 2 WLR 270, FD.
9. *Re B (a child) (immunisation)* [2003] EWCA Civ 1148, [2003] 3 FCR 156, [2003] 2 FLR 1095 (sub nom *Re C (welfare of child: immunisation)*; *Re C (welfare of child: immunisation)* [2003] EWHC 1376 (Fam), [2003] 2 FLR 1054
10. *Re J (child's religious upbringing and circumcision)* [2000] 1 FCR 307, [2000] 1 FLR 571, CA.
11. *Re F (minors) (solicitors' interviews)* [1995] 2 FCR 200, [1995] 1 FLR 819, CA.
12. *Re M (minors) (solicitor's interviews)* [1995] 2 FCR 643, [1995] 1 FLR 825.

6–154A   Interim orders.   Whilst there is no provision for an *interim* section 8 order in contrast to that for an interim care or supervision order in public law proceedings[1], the same effect may be obtained by the making of a section 8 order limited in extent during the course of the substantive proceedings. In determining whether to make an interim order the guidance to justices on hearing applications for interim care orders[2] is relevant to private law applications[3].

In cases involving contact in private family law proceedings where the principle of contact is not in issue but only the quantum, interim contact is likely to be in the interests of the child. An interim order may often be made without detailed investigation or oral evidence either by seeking the lowest common denominator acceptable to the parties or imposing an interim regime which in no way prejudices the final outcome.

Where the principle of contact is in issue, the test remains the welfare test under section 1 of the Act applied to the facts of the case with the fact that contact is in issue as a factor to be considered in the welfare equation. Interim orders for contact can be made in such cases on the papers and without oral evidence but the greatest care must be taken to ensure (*a*) that on the facts as they currently present themselves it is truly in the interests of the child, and (*b*) (where this consideration is relevant) that the order does not prejudge the issue[3].

In disputed cases of contact, an interim order is likely to be made either as part of the overall adjudication process, eg where on the recommendation of a welfare officer there is a monitored trial of contact. Secondly, where the court has sufficient information to conclude that contact is in the child's interests even though there is the possibility that the court at the final hearing may come to a different conclusion such as, for example, where previous satisfactory contact had been arbitrarily terminated by the residential parent. Otherwise where the principle of contact is genuinely in dispute and substantial factual issues are unresolved it is unlikely the court could properly make an interim order for contact without hearing oral evidence and/or having the advice of a welfare officer or other expert as to the likely effect of contact on the child. Justices should be cautious about making interim orders where the issue of contact is in dispute and should only do so if, on the material before them, they are satisfied that it is in the interests of the child for an order for contact to be made pending a full inquiry[3].

1. See *Re S (Residence Order: Jurisdiction)* [1995] 1 FCR 497, per BRACEWELL J.
2. See para **6–170**, post.
3. *Re D (a minor) (Contact: Interim Order)* [1995] 1 FCR 501, [1995] 1 FLR 495. See also *Re D (a child)* [2001] EWCA Civ 1827 in which it was held that, at a directions hearing, the court should not increase contact to include staying contact where the custodial mother objects, she has not had a chance to place her concerns before the court and the issue of staying contact is to be decided at a subsequent, full hearing.

6–155   Section 8 orders: general principles on hearing application.   In proceedings in which any question of making a s 8 order, or any other question with respect to such an order, arises, the court shall, in accordance with the Rules[1]—

(*a*)   draw up a timetable with a view to determining the question without delay; and
(*b*)   give such directions as it considers appropriate for the purpose of ensuring, so far as is reasonably practicable, that that timetable is adhered to[2].

Where a court has power to make a s 8 order, it may do so at any time during the course of the proceedings in question even though it is not in a position to dispose finally of those proceedings[3].

A s 8 order may—

(a) contain directions about how it is to be carried into effect;

(b) impose conditions which must be complied with by any person—

    (i) in whose favour the order is made;

    (ii) who is a parent of the child concerned;

    (iii) who is not a parent of his but who has parental responsibility for him; or

    (iv) with whom the child is living,

    and to whom the conditions are expressed to apply;

(c) be made to have effect for a specified period, or contain provisions which are to have effect for a specified period;

(d) make such incidental, supplemental or consequential provision as the court thinks fit[4].

No court shall make a s 8 order which is to have effect for a period which will end after the child has reached the age of 16 unless it is satisfied that the circumstances of the case are exceptional. Similarly, no court shall make a s 8 order, other than one varying or discharging an existing order, with respect to a child who has reached the age of 16 unless it is satisfied that the circumstances of the case are exceptional[5]. This, however, is subject to the following qualification. The power of the court to make a residence order in favour of any person who is not the parent or guardian of the child concerned includes power to direct, at that person's request, that the order shall continue in force until the child attains 18 years, and any power to vary a residence order is exercisable accordingly; where a residence order includes such a direction an application to vary or discharge the order can only be made with the leave of the court[6].

It is a sound rule of practice that where a court has decided in one year that certain arrangements for the future care of a child were most likely to promote welfare, then the court will not arrive at a different conclusion in a subsequent application made in a subsequent year without some fairly fundamental change of circumstance in the interim; but this is not a rule of law, merely one of practice[7].

A court which is considering an application for an order under ss 8 and 10 of the Children Act 1989 has the power, in its discretion, to receive and act on evidence adduced by one party, or emanating from a welfare officer, which is not disclosed to the other party. Such power, however, should be exercised only in most exceptional circumstances, and where the court is satisfied that disclosure of the evidence would be so detrimental to the welfare of the child as to outweigh the normal requirements for a fair trial that all evidence must be disclosed[8].

The power in s 11(7) of the Act to make directions or impose conditions is ancillary to the making of a s 8 order and does not allow the importation by the back door of matters laid down in the Matrimonial Homes Act or the making of ouster orders[9]. It is inappropriate to make injunctive orders dressed up as conditions of a contact order[10]. Moreover, the court is not able by means of a condition attached to a s 8 order to overrule the mother's right to allow her cohabitee back into her life if she so wishes[11].

The court has wide and comprehensive powers to ensure contact between the child and the non-custodial parent including ample power to compel a mother to send photographs, medical reports and school reports in order to promote meaningful contact with the father. The court has jurisdiction to order the mother to write progress reports on the child to the father[12].

---

1. See the Family Proceedings Courts (Children Act 1989) Rules 1991, r 14, this PART, post.
2. Children Act 1989, s 11(1), this PART, post.
3. Children Act 1989, s 11(3), this PART, post.
4. Children Act 1989, s 11(7), this PART, post.
5. Children Act 1989, s 9(6), (7), this PART, post.
6. Children Act 1989, s 12(5) and (6).
7. *Re H (a child: residence)* [2002] 3 FCR 277, CA.
8. *Re B (a minor)* [1993] 1 All ER 931, [1992] 2 FCR 617, [1993] 1 FLR 191.
9. *Re D (Prohibited Steps Order)* [1996] 2 FLR 273; *D v D (Ouster Order)* [1996] 2 FCR 496.
10. *Re D (a minor) (Contact: Conditions)* [1997] 3 FCR 721; sub nom *D v N (Contact Order: Conditions)* [1997] 2 FLR 797.
11. See *Re D (minors) (Residence Conditions)* [1996] 2 FCR 820, [1996] 2 FLR 281.
12. *Re O (Contact: Imposition of Conditions)* [1995] 2 FLR 124 sub nom *Re O (a minor) (Contact: Indirect Contact)* [1996] 1 FCR 317.

6–156 Change of child's name or removal from jurisdiction. Where a residence order is in force with respect to a child, no person may—

(a) cause the child to be known by a new surname; or

(b) remove him from the United Kingdom[1];

without either the written consent of every person who has parental responsibility for the child or the leave of the court[2]. The removal of a child from the United Kingdom, for a period of less than one month, by the person in whose favour the residence order has been made is, however, permissible[3].

The surname of a child who is under the age of 16 may be changed in the following circumstances—

(a) where only one person has parental responsibility for a child (eg a surviving parent after the death of the other; or the mother of a non-marital child where there has been no order or agreement for parental responsibility) that person has the right and power lawfully to cause a change of surname without any other permission or consent;

(b) where two or more people have parental responsibility for a child then one of those people can only cause a change of surname if all other people having parental responsibility consent or agree;

(c) where two or more people have parental responsibility for a child and either a residence order or a care order is in force, then one of those people can only lawfully cause a change of surname if all other people having parental responsibility consent in writing;

(d) in any other situation an appropriate order of the court is required[4].

The change of a child's surname is an important matter not to be undertaken lightly. It is for the discretion of the justices hearing the case, seeing the witnesses, seeing the parents, possibly seeing the children, to decide whether or not it is in the interests of the child in the particular circumstances of the case that his surname should or should not be changed. The court must take into account all the circumstances of the case, including where appropriate, any embarrassment which may be caused to the child by not changing his name and, on the other hand, the long-term interests of the child, the importance of maintaining the child's links with his paternal family, and the probable stability or otherwise of the mother's remarriage[5]. Where no residence order is in force it is inapt to make an application under section 13 of the Children Act 1989; the court may determine any question relating to a surname by a specific issue order. In determining an order for change of name under section 8, the court must have regard to the criteria in section 1 and not make an order for the change of name unless there is some evidence that this would lead to an improvement from the point of view of the child. The fact that a child has been registered with a name is a relevant and maybe important factor in assessing where the balance of advantage for the child's welfare lies. But it is not all-important[6]. However whilst registration is always a relevant and important consideration, it is not in itself decisive. Relevant considerations will include factors which may arise in the future; reasons based on the fact that the child's name is or is not the same as the parent making the application do not generally carry much weight; the reasons for an earlier unilateral decision to change a child's name; changes in the child's circumstances; where the parents were not married, the mother has control over registration so that the degree of commitment of the father to the child, the quality of content, if it occurs, between father and child; and the existence or absence of parental responsibility are all relevant factors to take into account[7]. In appropriate cases, parents and courts should be more prepared to contemplate the use of both surnames to recognise the importance of both parents[8]. Particular considerations may apply where parents are of different cultures[9].

On a parent's application for a specific issue order to change back a child's surname, lawfully, changed by the other parent, to the one entered on the birth register, the correct approach is to question whether the original change had been in the best interests of the child as registration of a child's name is a profound issue and the welfare of the child is paramount[10].

None of the authorities in relation to surnames has any application to a dispute about a child's first name, which a judge must look at in a worldly, commonsense manner in deciding what is best for the child; a given name has a much less concrete nature than a surname and a number of different names may be used over the course of a child's life[11].

The Enrolment of Deeds (Change of Name) Regulations 1994[12] prescribes the procedure to be followed by a person who wishes to enrol a deed poll evidencing change of name in the Central Office of the Supreme Court. In the case of a child under the age of 16, the deed poll must be executed by a person having parental responsibility for him. The application for enrolment must be supported by an affidavit showing that the change of name is for the benefit of the child and indicating whether it is submitted by or with the consent of all persons having parental responsibility[13].

When making a residence order the court may grant leave for the removal of the child from the United Kingdom, either generally or for specified purposes[14]. Since welfare of the child is the paramount consideration, leave should not be withheld unless the interests of the child and those of the parent with whom the child is living are shown to be incompatible[15]. Regard may be had to the reasonableness of the parent's plans and the effect of a refusal of leave[16]. There is no presumption that once a proposal to move abroad has been shown to be reasonable permission to leave the jurisdiction will be granted, but this is the first hurdle to cross to trigger the next stage, at which the court has to assess whether the grant of the application will best promote the welfare of the child, considering the manner in which the competing welfare factors apply in the specific case[17].

In determining whether to grant leave for a child to be taken permanently out of the jurisdiction, the court must have regard to whether the decision was reasonable in all the circumstances[18], following the principles set out in *Re F (a ward) (Leave to Remove a Ward out of the Jurisdiction*[19]). The court must, therefore, consider:

(i) to what extent a refusal of permission would cause the parent making the application unhappiness, distress, or bitterness in having their reasonable desire to leave the jurisdiction with the child frustrated;

(ii) how such a refusal and the unhappiness which it would cause the parent would react on the child;

(iii) if the decision in itself was reasonable;

(iv) if a refusal to allow the parent with whom the child was residing to move out of the jurisdiction would have those consequences; and

(v) whether the child's well being and future happiness would be incompatible with allowing the parent to carry out his or her wish of taking the child out of the jurisdiction[20].

Where a custodial mother has entered into a new and committed relationship with a man who is rooted in another jurisdiction, the impact on the relationship of refusing an application to relocate must be carefully evaluated, especially if the stepfather is a foreign national; if the stepfather's employment requires him to live in another jurisdiction that may well be a decisive consideration[21].

Where the choice lies between deciding the question of what is best for any individual child here or deciding it in a foreign country, differences between the legal systems cannot be irrelevant. If there is a genuine issue between the parents as to whether it is in the best interests of the child to live in this country or elsewhere it must be relevant whether that issue is capable of being tried in the courts of the country to which he is to be returned, and if those courts have no choice but to do as one parent wishes, so that the other cannot ask them to decide, with an open mind, whether the child will be better off living here or there, then the domestic courts must ask themselves whether it is in the interests of the child to enable that dispute to be heard. The absence of a relocation jurisdiction may be a decisive factor, but if it appears that the mother will be unable to make a good cause for relocation, that factor may not be decisive; there are also bound to be many cases where the connection of the child and all the family with the other country is so strong that any difference between the legal systems here and there should carry little weight[22].

The considerations relevant to an application for permission to relocate permanently were not automatically applicable to applications for temporary removal[23].

In relocation cases there is an acute dissension between parents, usually expressed in the form of cross applications, and to make no order is simply not an option[24].

Applications to remove a child to a country which is not a signatory to the Hague Convention on the Civil Aspects of International Child Abduction should be heard before a judge of the Family Division of the High Court[25].

For the effect of orders restricting removal of a child from the United Kingdom, and the surrender of passports, see the Family Law Act 1986, ss 36 and 37[26]; as to the offence of abduction of a child by the child's parent, see the Child Abduction Act 1984[26].

---

1. "United Kingdom", in this context, includes Northern Ireland; however, whilst a primary carer may not need to apply under s 13(1)(*b*) where he/she seeks to remove a child to Northern Ireland, he/she may still have to meet the challenge of an application for a prohibited steps order or for the imposition, under s 11(7), of a condition to the residence order to prevent such a removal: *Re H (children) (residence order: condition)* [2001] EWCA Civ 1338, [2001] 3 FCR 182.

2. Children Act 1989, s 13(1), this PART, post.

3. Children Act 1989, s 13(2), this PART, post.

4. *Re C (Minors) (Change of Surname)* [1997] 3 FCR 310; sub nom *Re PC (Change of Surname)* [1997] 2 FLR 730 and see *Re T (minors) (change of surname)* [1999] 1 FCR 476, [1998] 2 FLR 620, CA. For application by local authority to change name of children in care proceedings, see *Re M (Care: change of name* [2000] 2 FLR 645, FD).

5. *W v A (Child: Surname)* [1981] 1 All ER 100, [1981] 2 WLR 124; followed in *Re F (Children: Surname)* [1994] 1 FCR 110. For a case involving consideration of Muslim law and Somali law and practice, see *Re A (a child) (change of name)* [2003] EWCA Civ 56, [2003] 1 FCR 493, [2003] 2 FLR 1.

6. *Dawson v Wearmouth* [1999] 2 All ER 353, [1999] 2 WLR 960, [1999] 1 FCR 625, HL.

7. *Re W (A Child) (Illegitimate Child: Change of Surname)* [2000] 2 WLR 258, [1999] 3 FCR 337, [1999] 2 FLR 930, CA per BUTLER-SLOSS LJ.

8. *Re R (a child)* [2001] EWCA Civ 1344, [2002] 1 FCR 170 *per* HALE LJ at para [15].

9. *Re S (change of name: cultural factors)* [2001] 3 FCR 648, [2001] 2 FLR 1005, FD.

10. *Re C (a minor) (change of surname)* [1999] 1 FCR 318.

11. *Re H (Child's Name: First Name)* [2002] EWCA Civ 190, [2002] 1 FLR 973.

12. SI 1994/604.

13. See reg 8 of the Enrolment of Deeds (Change of Name) Regulations 1994, SI 1994/604.

14. Children Act 1989, s 13(3), this PART, post.

15. *K v K (Removal of Child from Jurisdiction)* [1992] 2 FCR 161.

16. *M v A (Removal of Children from Jurisdiction)* [1994] 2 FCR 57.

17. *Re C (permission to remove from jurisdiction)* [2003] EWHC 596 (Fam). [2003] 1 FLR 1066.

18. *Re B (minors) (Removal from Jurisdiction)* [1994] 2 FCR 309, CA.

19. [1988] 2 FLR 116. See also *Payne v Payne* [2001] EWCA Civ 166, [2001] 2 WLR 1826, [2001] 1 FLR 1052, [2001] UKHRR 484.

20. *Re F (A Ward) (Leave to Remove a Ward out of the Jurisdiction)* [1988] 2 FLR 116. See also *Re H (application to remove from jurisdiction)* [1999] 2 FCR 34, CA and *Re G-A (a child) (removal from jurisdiction: human rights)* [2001] 1 FCR 43, CA. See also *Re B (children) (termination of contact)* [2004] EWCA Civ 956, [2005] 1 FCR 480, [2005] 2 FLR 239 (*sub nom Re B (leave to remove: impact of refusal)*, in which it was held, inter alia, that there was no difference in principle between a "lifestyle" case—one in which the desire to relocate was inspired by a desire to improve general living conditions—and the more familiar relocation caases in which a foreign national sought to return to their native country with their own or their step-children, or where a speific employment opportunity had arisen for a member of the family. The principles were to be applied no matter what the facts. As to assessment of the relocation plans and the impact of refusal of relocation, see *Re G (removal from jurisdiction)* [2005] EWCA Civ 170, [2005] 2 FLR 166.

21. *Re B (children) (removal from jurisdiction), Re S (a child) (removal from jurisdiction)* [2003] EWCA Civ 1149, [2003] 2 FCR 673, [2003] 2 FLR 1043.

22. *Re J (a child) (return to foreign jurisdiction: convention rights)* [2005] UKHL 40, [2005] 3 All ER 291 (which concerned an application to remove a child to a non-Hague Convention country).

23. *Re A (temporary removal from jurisdiction)* [2004] EWCA Civ 1587, [2005] 1 FLR 639.

24. *Re H (children) (residence order: condition)* [2001] EWCA Civ 1338, [2001] 3 FCR 182 (in which the Court declined to follow *Re X and Y (leave to remove from jurisdiction: no order principle)* [2001] 2 FCR 398).

25. *Re K (removal from jurisdiction: practice)* [1999] 3 FCR 673, [1999] 2 FLR 1084, CA.

26. See this PART, post.

6–157 Enforcement of residence order.

Where a residence order is in force with respect to a child in favour of any person, and any other person is in breach of the arrangements settled by the order, provided the order has been served on that other person, it may be enforced under s 63(3) of the Magistrates' Courts Act 1980[1] as if it were an order requiring the other person to produce the child to him[2].

---

1. See PART I, ante.

2. Children Act 1989, s 14, this PART, post.

6–158 Family assistance order.

Where in any family proceedings the court has power to make an order under Part II of the Children Act 1989 (ss 8–16) with respect to any child, it may (whether or not it makes such an order) make an order requiring an officer of CAFCASS to be made available; or a local authority to make an officer of the authority available, to advise, assist and (where appropriate) befriend any person named in the order[1].

The persons who may be named in a family assistance order are—

(a) any parent or guardian of the child;

(b) any person with whom the child is living or in whose favour a contact order is in force with respect to the child;

(c) the child himself[2].

No court may make a family assistance order unless it is satisfied that the circumstances of the case are exceptional, and it has obtained the consent of every person to be named in the order other than the child[3]. A family assistance order may direct the person named in the order, or such of the persons named in the order as may be specified, to take such steps as may be so specified with a view to enabling the officer concerned to be kept informed of the address of any person named in the order and to be allowed to visit any such person[4]. Unless the court specifies a shorter period, a family assistance order shall have effect for a period of six months beginning with the day on which it is made[5].

Where a family assistance order is in force with respect to a child and a s 8 order is also in force with respect to that child, the officer concerned may refer to the court the question whether the s 8 order should be varied or discharged[6].

A family assistance order must not be made so as to require a local authority to make an officer of theirs available unless the authority agree or the child concerned lives or will live within their area[7]. Nor should the court order a local authority in the guise of a family assistance order to escort children to a prison to have face to face contact with their father unless the local authority consent to use their powers on this basis[8]. If the local authority is of opinion that it does not have the resources with which to carry out the family assistance order, there is no appropriate order which the court can make to enforce the order[9].

1. Children Act 1989, s 16(1), this PART, post.
2. Children Act 1989, s 16(2), this PART, post.
3. Children Act 1989, s 16(3), this PART, post.
4. Children Act 1989, s 16(4), this PART, post.
5. Children Act 1989, s 16(5), this PART, post.
6. Children Act 1989, s 16(6), this PART, post.
7. Children Act 1989, s 16(7), this PART, post.
8. *S v P (Contact Application)* [1997] 2 FCR 185, [1997] 2 FLR 277.
9. *Re C (a minor) (Family Assistance Order)* [1996] 3 FCR 514, [1996] 1 FLR 424.

Financial provision

6–160 Financial provision for children. On an application made by a parent or guardian of a child, or by any person in whose favour a residence order is in force with respect to a child, a family proceedings court may make one or both of the following orders—

(a) an order requiring either or both parents of a child—

(i) to make to the applicant for the benefit of the child; or
(ii) to make to the child himself,

such periodical payments, for such term, as may be specified in the order;

(b) an order requiring either or both parents of a child—

(i) to pay to the applicant for the benefit of the child; or
(ii) to pay to the child himself,

such lump sum as may be so specified[1].

Further provision is made with respect to financial relief for persons over 18 years of age[2]. The Act lays down the matters to which the court is to have regard in making orders for financial relief[3], provides for the variation or discharge of an order for periodical payments[4], and the making of interim orders[5].

The family proceedings court may not exercise its powers to order financial provision for children otherwise than in accordance with the Child Support Act 1991[6].

Where, under the Child Support Act 1991, the absent parent is possessed of capital assets but no income so that a nil assessment is made, the court may not make an order for a lump sum under Sch 1 to the Children Act 1989 to provide for regular support of the child which would ordinarily have been provided by way of periodic payments. A lump sum may only be ordered to meet a particular item of capital expenditure[7].

1. Children Act 1989, Sch 1, para 1, this PART, post.
2. Children Act 1989, Sch 1, para 2, this PART, post.
3. Children Act 1989, Sch 1, para 4, this PART, post.
4. Children Act 1989, Sch 1, para 6, this PART, post.
5. Children Act 1989, Sch 1, para 9, this PART, post.
6. See in particular s 8 of the Child Support Act 1991, this PART, post.
7. *Phillips v Peace* [1996] 2 FLR 230, [1996] 2 FCR 237.

Care and supervision orders; child assessment and emergency protection orders

6–164   Care and supervision orders.   A court may make a care or supervision order on the application of a local authority or authorised person only if it is satisfied—

    (*a*) that the child concerned is suffering, or is likely to suffer, significant harm; and

    (*b*) that the harm, or likelihood of harm, is attributable to—

        (i) the care given to the child, or likely to be given to him if the order were not made, not being what it would be reasonable to expect a parent to give him; or

        (ii) the child's being beyond parental control[1].

The Children Act 1989, for these purposes, defines certain of the expressions used above as follows:

Harm means ill-treatment or the impairment of health or development including, for example, impairment suffered from seeing or hearing the ill-treatment of another;

Development means physical, intellectual, emotional, social or behavioural development;

Health means physical or mental health;

Ill-treatment includes sexual abuse and forms of ill-treatment which are not physical[2].

No care order can be made until the court has considered a care plan[3]. Where an application is made on which a care order might be made with respect to a child the appropriate local authority (ie the local authority proposed to be designated in the order) must, within such time as the court may direct, prepare a care plan for the future of the child; and while the application is pending the authority must keep its care plan under review and, if they are of the opinion that some change is required, revise the plan, or make a new plan, accordingly[4]. References in the foregoing to a "car order" do not include an interim care order[5].

The Act further provides that where the question of whether harm suffered by a child is significant turns on the child's health or development, his health or development shall be compared with that which could reasonably be expected of a similar child[6].

In cases where a child is found to be at risk of suffering significant harm, the local authority has a clear duty to take steps to protect the child by invoking the specific powers under the public law provisions of Part IV of the Children Act 1989[7]. Part IV of the Act specifically provides the local authority with wide powers and a wide discretion; it will rarely be appropriate for a local authority instead to seek leave to apply for a prohibited steps order since such an order is no substitute for an order under Part IV of the Act[8].

Where Children Act proceedings relate to a child who is liable to removal or deportation the jurisdiction should be exercised very sparingly; in particular, it will be an abuse of process to use care proceedings to influence the decision of the Secretary of State as to removal[9].

It has been said that there is an important partnership to be played between the court and the local authority in considering applications under Part IV of the Children Act 1989 which deal with care and supervision. The part played by the court is to consider all the facts that are presented to it by the local authority and to make a decision finally disposing of the case when all of those facts are as clearly known to the court as can be hoped. A delay of a final decision for the purpose of ascertaining the result of a programme of assessment is proper delay and is to be encouraged. It is for the local authority to put all material facts before the court, including the results of an assessment, before inviting the court to pass to them the responsibility of the management of a full care order. The court must be slow to abdicate its responsibility until all the facts are known[10]. The local authority should produce to the court a care plan which should accord so far as is practicable with para 2.62 of Vol 3 of the D of H *Guide to the Children Act 1989*[11]. The court cannot direct a particular type of placement or direct that particular services be provided for a child.

Parliament has entrusted to local authorities, not the courts, the responsibility for looking after children who are the subject of care orders. The Human Rights Act 1998 does not justify empowering the courts to intervene in the way local authorities discharge their parental responsibilities under final care orders eg by such devices as 'starred care plans' where failure to meet essential 'starred' milestones in the care plan would require the local authority to reactivate the inter-disciplinary process that contributed to the creation of the care plan and inform the children's guardian who might apply to the court for directions where the court might also require a report on progress. The process for making a care order complies with art 6(1) and where there is a failure to implement the care plan any failure of the 1989 Act to make provision for the protection of the art 8 rights of a child and his parents is not in itself a breach of art 8. In substitution for art 13 (right to provide effective remedy for breach of Convention rights) the remedy for a violation of the art 8 rights of a child or its parents is provided by ss 7 and 8 of the 1998 Act, although there may be a lacuna where a child has no parents to act on his behalf and is too young to initiate proceedings himself[12]. However, there is a continuing obligation of a local authority to comply with art 8 after a care order has been made and breaches can be remedied by an application under ss 7 and 8 of the Human Rights Act 1998[13]. Thus, before a local authority can properly arrive at a decision to remove children from their parents, contrary to the original care plan, which was for rehabilitation, it must tell the parents precisely what it is proposing to do, it must spell out the reasons and, in precise terms, the factual matters it is relying on, and then provide the parents with proper opportunities to respond to the allegations and to make representations as to why the local authority should not take the threatened step; in particular, the parents (together with their representatives if they wish to be assisted) should normally be given the opportunity to attend at, and address, any critical meeting at which crucial decisions are to be made[14]. In the same way, applications for habeas corpus are to be deprecated where care proceedings are on foot and where the purpose of the application is to challenge the exercise by the local authority of its powers[15].

The proper forum for a challenge to the care plan is in the care proceedings, rather than by way of judicial review; only in the event of a failure by a local authority to amend its proposals for the child so as to accord with the court's determination of the child's interests is it proper for the guardian to consider taking proceedings for judicial review[16]. Save in a wholly exceptional case, judicial review is not the appropriate procedure to prevent a local authority commencing emergency protection or care proceedings as it is a remedy of last resort as it is a blunt and unsatisfactory tool to deal with the sensitive issues involved. A family proceedings court should be protected from the embarrassment it is likely to feel if told, just as it is about to embark upon the hearing of an urgent application for an emergency protection or interim care order, that judicial review proceeding are pending in the Administrative Court which seek to restrain the bringing of the proceedings by the local authority[17]. Where proceedings are still on foot any human rights issue should be dealt with within the existing proceedings and should not be dealt with separately in proceedings before the Family Division[18].

Where it is necessary to prove primary facts in issue in order to form a basis for assessing future risk, the burden is on the local authority to prove those facts. The standard of proof is on the balance of probabilities but the more serious the allegation, the more convincing must be the evidence to tip the balance[19]. Care proceedings are civil proceedings and all competent witnesses are compellable. Parents can be compelled to give evidence in care proceedings: they have no right to refuse to do so and cannot refuse to answer questions which might incriminate them. If they do not wish to give evidence themselves, they can be called by another party and the most appropriate person normally to do this would be the guardian acting on behalf of the child[20].

Where the parties are agreed that a care order should be made, but are not agreed on a factual substratum for it, the court has a duty to investigate. However, the nature and scope of the investigation will depend on the facts of the particular case[21]. Where a care plan proposes that a child should be placed under a care order with his father rather than with his grandparents, the court should first consider the parent as a potential carer for the child and then ask itself whether there are any compelling factors which require it to override the *prima facie* right of a child to an upbringing by that parent[22].

A county court hearing care proceedings does not have jurisdiction to accept undertakings from the parent of a child who is the subject of an application for a care or supervision order[23].

Where there are concurrent criminal proceedings pending against the parents that is not of itself a reason for adjourning the care proceedings. The welfare of the child has to take precedence over the detriment to the family who are coming up for trial. The issue of delay is all important and while there will be cases where it is right in the interests of the children that the care proceedings are delayed for the outcome of the criminal proceedings, it is a relevant but not a determining factor in considering the welfare of children that they should have parents whose case has been properly tried at their criminal trial[24].

The doctrine of issue estoppel does not apply when a family proceedings court hears an application for a care order, where the father has been acquitted by a jury of a criminal charge of abuse. Accordingly, the court must be free to investigate and make findings on the underlying facts relating to the alleged abuse of a child, even though an investigation of the same facts in criminal proceedings has led to an acquittal[21].

As to the child of a parent who enjoys diplomatic immunity through being a member of the administrative and technical staff of a foreign mission, by virtue of the exception contained in article 37(2) of the Vienna Convention such members are not immune from civil proceedings in respect of acts performed outside the course of their duties, there is no bar to the making of an interim care order as against such a person in public law proceedings, and the immunity conferred on the private residence of a diplomatic agent by article 30(1) relates to the premises themselves and not to the consequences of acts done by individuals in those premises[25].

1. Children Act 1989, s 31(2), this PART, post.
2. Children Act 1989, s 31(9), this PART, post.
3. Children Act 1989, s 31(3A).
4. Children Act 1989, s 31A.
5. Children Act 1989, s 31A(5).
6. Children Act 1989, s 31(10), this PART, post.
8. Part IV of the Children Act 1989 contains ss 31–42; see this PART, post.
8. *Nottinghamshire County Council v P* [1993] 3 All ER 815, CA.
9. *Re A (care proceedings: asylum seekers)* [2003] EWHC 1086 (Fam), [2003] 2 FLR 921.
10. *Hounslow London Borough Council v A* [1993] 1 WLR 291, [1993] 1 FLR 702.
11. *Re R (minors) (Care Proceedings: Care Plan)* [1994] 2 FCR 136.
12. *S (Minors) (Care Order: Implementation of Care Plan)* [2002] UKHL 10, [2002] 2 AC 291, [2002] 2 All ER 192, [2002] 2 WLR 720 overruling *Re W and B (children: care plan)* [2001] EWCA Civ 757, [2001] 2 FCR 450, [2001] 2 FLR 582.
13. *Re G (care: challenge to local authority's decision)* [2003] EWHC 551 (Fam), [2003] 2 FLR 42.
4. *Re G (care: challenge to local authority's decision),* supra.
15. *R (on the application of S) v Haringey London Borough Council* [2003] EWHC 2734 (Admin), [2004] 1 FLR 590.
16. *Re C (adoption: religious observance)* [2002] 1 FLR 1119.
17. *Re M (care proceedings: judicial review)* [2003] EWHC 850 (Admin), [2004] 1 FCR 302, [2003] 2 FLR 171.
18. *Re L (care proceedings: human rights claims)* [2003] EWHC 665 (Fam), [2004] 1 FCR 289, [2003] 2 FLR 160; *affd Re V (a child) (care proceedings: human rights claims)* [2004] EWCA Civ 54, [2004] 1 All ER 997, [2004] 1 WLR 1433, [2004] 1 FCR 338, [2004] 1 FLR 944.
19. *Re M (a minor) (No 2) (care proceedings: appeal)* [1995] 1 FCR 417; *Re P (a minor) (Care Proceedings: Evidence)* [1995] 1 FCR 583.
20. *Re Y (children) (care proceedings: split hearing)* [2003] EWCA Civ 669, [2003] 3 FCR 240 [2003] 2 FLR 273 and see the Children Act 1989, s 98, in this PART, post.
21. *Re G (a minor) (care proceedings)* [1994] 2 FLR 69, [1994] 2 FCR 216 (sub nom *Hackney London Borough Council v G*).
22. *Re D (a minor) (natural parent: presumption of care)* [1999] 2 FCR 118.
23. *In Re B (a minor) (supervison order: parental undertaking)* [1996] 1 WLR 716, [1996] 1 FLR 767, CA.
24. *Re T B (care proceedings: criminal trial)* [1995] 2 FLR 801, [1996] 1 FCR 101.
25. *In re B (a child) (care proceedings: diplomatic immunity)* [2002] EWHC 1751 (Fam), [2003] Fam 16, [2003] 2 WLR 168, [2003] 1 FLR 242.

6–164A   Care and supervision orders: European Convention on Human Rights. An application for a care order will engage, in particular, Articles 6 and 8[1] of the European Convention on Human Rights. Article 6 – right to a fair trial – applies to care proceedings and an oral hearing should be held at some stage in the proceedings[2]. Article 8 – right to respect for private and family life – reads as follows: —

"1. Everyone has the right to respect for his private and family life, his home and his correspondence.

2. There shall be no interference by a public authority with the exercise of this right except such as is in accordance with the law and is necessary in a democratic society in the interests of national security, public safety or the economic well-being of the country, for the prevention of disorder or crime, for the protection of health or morals, or for the protection of the rights and freedoms of others".

The European Court of Human Rights has held that the mutual enjoyment by parent and child of each other's company constitutes a fundamental element of family life, and domestic measures hindering such enjoyment amount to an interference with the right protected by Article 8[3].

The state has positive and negative obligations under art 8, the boundaries of which cannot be precisely drawn; balances must be struck where the interests of the community and of the individual may be conflict, and in this area of judgment the state enjoys a margin of appreciation, but it must give sufficient consideration to additional measures of support as an alternative to the most extreme measure of separating the children from their parents[4].

For the purposes of art 8(2) any order relating to the public care of a child must be capable of convincing an objective observer that the measure was based on a careful and unprejudiced assessment of all the evidence on file; the decision-making authorities and courts must provide such detailed reasons as to enable any parent participating in the proceedings to have adequate opportunities to appeal; and it is essential that a parent is placed in a position where he or she may obtain access to information which is relied on by the authorities in taking measures of protective care, such as being informed of the nature and extent of the allegations of abuse made by their child, provided that careful consideration does not show that disclosure would place the child at risk[5].

Article 8 affords parents involved in care proceedings not merely substantive protection against any inappropriate interference with their private and family life, but also procedural safeguards that are not confined to the trial process but extend to all stages of the decision-making process in child protection cases; art 8 further requires that parents are properly involved in the decision-making process, not merely before and during care proceedings, but also after those proceedings have come to an end and whilst the local authority is implementing the care order[6]. Where a local authority seeks to make significant changes to the care plan it is under a duty to inform the parents of the proposed changes, setting out precisely the factual matters being relied upon; to give the parents an opportunity to answer the allegations being made against them and to make representations as to why the authority should not take the threatened steps; and, normally, to give the parents and their representatives the opportunity to attend and address any critical meeting at which crucial decisions are being taken[7].

Article 6 requires the entire proceedings to be conducted on a fair basis, with the need to maintain a balance between the rights of adults to fair justice and the rights of children to an early determination of their future. Therefore, where parents had changed solicitors five times during the course of the proceedings and had had plenty of time to put their case together, and it was essential for the court to reach a conclusion about the future of the children as a matter of urgency, the court was entitled to refuse to break the fixture even though that put the parents in the position of having to conduct their own case[8]. However, in general having regard to the crucial consequences for the parents' relationship with their child, the assistance of a lawyer is an indispensable requirement and the importance of proceeding with expedition does not necessitate the draconian action of proceeding to a full and complex hearing without legal representation where the delay in reaching a final conclusion is not so prejudicial to the child's interests[9].

It was held in *Re C (care proceedings: disclosure of local authority's decision-making process)* [2002] EWHC 1379 (Fam), [2002] 2 FCR 673: (1) that the right to a fair trial guaranteed by art 6 of the Convention was not confined to the 'purely judicial' part of the proceedings and, whereas rights under art 8 were inherently qualified, a parent's right to a fair trial under art 6 was absolute and could not be qualified by reference to, or balanced against, the child's or anyone else's rights under art 8. (2) Where a jointly instructed or other sole expert's report, though not binding on the court, was likely to have a preponderant influence on the assessment of fact by the court there might be a breach of art 6 if a litigant was denied the opportunity, before the expert report was produced to (a) examine and comment on the documents being considered by the expert, and (b) cross-examine witnesses interviewed by the expert and on whose evidence the report was based. (3) It could not be proper for a single jointly instructed expert to have a conference with the applicant in the absence of the respondent. (However, the Court found that by the end of the final hearing the earlier unfairness in the decision-making process had been overcome and, overall, the mother had received the fair hearing to which she had been entitled under arts 6 and 8.)

In principle a care order should be regarded as a temporary measure, to be discontinued as soon as circumstances permit, and any measures that implement temporary care should be consistent with the ultimate aim of reuniting the natural parents and the child[10].

---

1. See PART VIII, title HUMAN RIGHTS, post.
2. *L v Finland* [2000] 3 FCR 219, [2000] 2 FLR 118, ECtHR.
3. *Johansen v Norway* (1996) 23 EHRR 33, ECtHR.
4. *Kutzner v Germany* (App no 46544/99), [2003] FCR 249, EctHR.
5. *KA v Finland* (App no 27751/95) [2003] 1 FCR 201, [2003] 1 FLR , ECtHR.

6. *Re G (care: challenge to local authority's decision)* [2003] EWHC 551 (Fam), [2003] 2 FLR 42.
7. *Re G (care: challenge to local authority's decision)*, supra.
8. *Re B and T (care proceedings: legal representation)* [2001] 1 FCR 512, [2001] 1 FLR 485, CA. For a case where the balance pointed the other way and the court should have adjourned to enable fresh legal representation, see *Re G (adoption proceedings: representation of parents)* [2001] 1 FCR 353.
9. *P, C and S v United Kingdom* [2002] 3 FCR 1, [2002] 2 FLR 631, ECtHR.
10. *Kutzner v Germany*, supra (see also *KA v Finland*, supra).

6–165   Care and supervision orders: test to be applied.   When considering an application for a care or supervision order to be made, the first stage is to determine whether or not the significant harm test in s 31(2) of the Act is satisfied. If the court accepts that as a matter of factual proof, and the criteria are satisfied, then the court must go on to the second stage when it must consider whether or not make an order, and at that stage it must apply the welfare principles contained in s 1 of the Act[1].

If these two stages of the test are satisfied, it is not wrong in law to make a care order where the local authority intend to leave the child in the day-to-day care of the parents. Such an arrangement will enable the local authority to plan an alternative placement without delay in the event of the parents failing to sustain an adequate level of parenting[2]. However, where the risks are not significant, or are very low, and the mother will sufficiently protect the child and co-operate without having to share parental responsibility with the local authority, a care order is not warranted[3]. Moreover, the action taken must be proportionate and where there are no long-standing problems of the sort that interfere with the capacity to provide adequate parenting, though there is a real possibility of future harm, the local authority should take time to explore other options than care and removal. The principle of proportionality requires the local authority to support and eventually reunite the family unless the risks are so high that the child's welfare requires alternative care[4].

The burden of proof in establishing the existence of the relevant conditions lies on the applicant and the standard of proof is that of the balance of probability. There is no different standard in cases involving allegations of sexual abuse of children; however, the more serious the allegation the more cogent is the evidence required to overcome the unlikelihood of what is alleged and thus to prove it[5]. Notwithstanding dicta in cases[6] relating to civil proceedings before magistrates for a sex offender order or an anti-social behaviour order, the standard of proof is the balance of probabilities[7] and it is wrong to describe the difference between this and the standard in criminal proceeding as "largely illusory"[8]. In child abuse cases, there may be clear evidence of abuse, but difficulty in identifying which of the child's parents was the perpetrator or whether both were the perpetrators. The same, balance of probabilities standard applies to the identification issue as to the proof of abuse. If there is not sufficient evidence to make such a finding, the court has to apply the test as to whether there is a real possibility or likelihood that one or more of a number of people with access to the child might have caused the injury to the child. For this purpose, real possibility and likelihood can be treated as the same test[9].

Where medical expert evidence is all one way the court is entitled not to accept it if it has contrary evidence on which it can rely, but the court must give reasons for setting the medical evidence aside[10].

Courts must be careful not to jump to conclusions or to accept too readily the diagnosis of non-accidental injury in 'brain injury' cases; courts must, however, continue to deal with medical evidence on the basis of generally recognised medical opinion, giving due weight in individual cases to any advances in medical knowledge[11].

Where, during the course of care proceedings, specific allegations of child sexual abuse are made against a non-party to the proceedings and are brought for trial as a preliminary issue, it is vital that that person's evidence is before the court. Accordingly, a local authority making such allegations against a named individual must, at the very least, apply to the court to consider whether he should be joined in the proceedings, even if he is unlikely to have party status at the substantive hearing when welfare considerations will predominate and the long term decisions will be taken as to the future of the child[12].

The significant harm threshold must be crossed by the date on which the local authority first intervened to protect the child, but in establishing that the threshold was crossed on that date the local authority may rely on information acquired after that date and even on later events if those are capable of proving the state of affairs at the date of intervention[13].

The parents' admissions are sufficient to cross the "threshold" under s 31. If there is a concession by the parents, it is contrary to the public interest that the proceedings should be prolonged simply to resolve differences as to the expression of the essential concessions. Once formal admissions have been made that pass the "threshold" and extend to a recognition that the parents cannot safely be entrusted with the care of any child, the court should accept the terminology used by those making the admissions rather than the terminology used by the local authority[14]. The same principle will apply even where the mother, although conceding grounds for the threshold criteria to be met, denies the major allegation against her since there is no need in such circumstances to try that allegation simply to provide the necessary protection for the child[15], though where forensic experts require a clear determination as to whether a mother was a deliberate abuser or a thoroughly careless parent, that core issue should be tried and determined even if the court has previously ruled that the threshold criteria were proved on the mother's admission only as to carelessness[16]. Where however, there is an issue between the local authority and the parent on the one hand and the guardian ad litem on the other over whether the threshold criteria are met, the court may have to resolve the issue as the guardian may inevitably form an opinion as to whether they are met which may be critical to his recommendations on behalf of the child[17].

Before the final hearing in care proceedings it should be routine for the local authority to make a clear statement of the facts which they wish the court to find, and the basis on which it is alleged that the case crosses the threshold[18].

The same principles and approach apply to the making of an interim care or supervision order as they apply to the making of a full care or supervision order, save that, under s 38(1) of the Act, the threshold criteria are modified and the court is required to be satisfied only that there are reasonable grounds for believing that the circumstances with respect to the child are as mentioned in s 31(2) of the Act[1]. The threshold criteria do not apply to an application to extend a supervision order under paragraph 6 on Part of Sch 3[19].

To obtain care orders the local authority must surmount the restriction contained in s 31(2) which is designed to protect families from invasive care orders unless there is a manifest need evidenced by a perceptible risk of significant harm[20].

For the purposes of the expression "is suffering" in s 31(2)(a) of the Act, the relevant date is the date on which the local authority initiated the protective arrangements which have since been continuously in place. This means the court must consider the position before the making of an emergency protection order or an interim order, if there was one, or when the child went into voluntary care[21]. If after a local authority has initiated protective arrangements the need for these has terminated, because the child's welfare has been satisfactorily provided for otherwise, in any subsequent proceedings, it is not possible to found jurisdiction on the situation at the time of initiation of these arrangements. It is permissible only to look back from the date of disposal to the date of initiation of protection as a result of which local authority arrangements have been continuously in place thereafter to the date of disposal[21]. The House of Lords' decision in *Re M (a minor) (care order: threshold conditions)* applies to both limbs of the threshold criteria, and the relevant date in respect of both actual harm and the likelihood of harm is the date upon which the local authority initiated protective arrangements for the relevant child, so long as such protective arrangements have been continuously in place from the time of such intervention and initiation until disposal of the case by the court[20]. Under the two-stage process whereby the court has first to satisfy itself that the making of the care order is better for the child than making no order, the court is able to consider any subsequent developments at the second stage[22].

The phrase "*likely to suffer*" should not be equated with "on the balance of probabilities". In considering the phrase "likely to suffer" the court is looking to the future and has to assess the future risk to the child in the light of the evidence[23].

In order to establish that a child is *likely to suffer significant harm* in the future there has to be a real possibility of risk based on actual facts rather than mere suspicions. For this purpose, the possibility must be one that cannot sensibly be ignored having regard to the nature and gravity of the feared harm in the particular case[5].

The "*care*" given to a child goes beyond the physical care and includes the emotional care which a reasonable parent would give the child[24]. "Care" refers to the care provided by the person whose lack of care has caused the significant harm; the care which others might give is not relevant to the threshold test but only to the discretion regarding disposal once the threshold test is met.

In a case of truancy from school it is open to the court to conclude that the child's social, intellectual and educational development did suffer harm likely to be sufficiently significant to warrant a care order being made. In such a case, the reference to "*a similar child*" in s 31(10) of the Act means a child of equivalent intellectual and social development, who has gone to school, and not merely an average child who may or may not be at school[25].

The condition "*that the harm, or likelihood of harm, is attributable to—(i) the care given to the child ...*" does not require the harm to be proved due to a failure of care by one or more identified individuals before the court can make a care order: it is sufficient that the harm was attributable to an absence of proper care to the objective standard laid down in s 31(2)(b)(i)[26]. Accordingly, the condition in s 31(2)(b)(i) was met, where the court was satisfied that a child, whose care was shared between the parents and a child minder whilst the parents were at work, had suffered significant harm, even though the court was unable to identify which of the carers had inflicted the injuries on the child and there was no more than a possibility that the parents were responsible for inflicting those injuries[27]. Where the threshold criteria have been satisfied, the court will proceed to the "welfare stage" to decide whether it is in the interests of the child to make a care order. In so doing the court must have regard to all the circumstances. Where the court has found it proved that a child has suffered significant physical harm at the hands of his parents but is unable to say which, where the facts leave open the possibility that a parent or other carer was a perpetrator of proved harm, the circumstances will include this possibility which should not be excluded at the disposal stage. The importance of the possibility depends on the facts of each case. However, the court must not proceed at the welfare stage on possibilities arising from unproven allegations e.g. where the threshold criteria are satisfied on the basis of neglect or failure to protect the court must not proceed on the basis that an unproved allegation of physical harm might be true. In a split hearing the court must express such views as it can at the preliminary hearing to assist social workers and psychiatrists in making their assessments and preparing the draft care plan[28]. In referring to likelihood of future risk and the likelihood that carers were possible perpetrators of past injuries to children the test to be applied is "real possibility"[29].

1. *Humberside County Council v B* [1993] 1 FCR 613, [1993] 1 FLR 257. Until the court had determined the facts and evaluated whether or not the threshold test is satisfied it is not appropriate to say that there will, in fact, be no public law order; all that can be said before that stage is that no party will be positively seeking such an order, but it remains lawful and within the discretion of the court to carry out a fact-finding exercise even though the parties have adopted that position. Before deciding whether or not to conduct such a fact-finding exercise the factors to consider are: the interests of the child (relevant, but not paramount); the time the investigation will take; the likely cost to public funds; the evidential result; the necessity of the investigation; the relevance of the potential result to the future care plans for the child; the impact of any fact-finding process upon the other parties; the prospects of a fair trial on the issue; and the justice of the case: *A County Council v DP, RS, BS (by the Children's Guardian)* [2005] EWHC 1593 (Fam), [2005] 2 FLR 1031.
2. *Re T (a minor) (Care or Supervision Order)* [1994] 1 FCR 663, [1994] 1 FLR 103.
3. *Re C (care order or supervision order)* [2001] 2 FLR 466.

4. *Re C and B (care order: future harm)* [2001] 1 FLR 611, CA.

5. *In Re H (minors) (Sexual Abuse: Standard of Proof)* [1996] 1 All ER 1, [1996] 2 WLR 8, [1996] 1 FCR 509, [1996] 1 FLR 80,. Justices had no right to make findings of sexual abuse where the alleged victim, though by then an adult, did not give evidence or provide a statement and the allegations, which were denied by the alleged perpetrator, were raised before the justices by a social worker who gave an account of an informal, unrecorded interview in a generalised way (*Re D (Sexual Abuse Allegations: Evidence of Adult Victim)* [2002] 1 FLR 723).

6. *B v Chief Constable of the Avon and Somerset Constabulary* [2001] 1 All ER 562, [2001] 1 WLR 340; *R (on the application of McCann) v Crown Court at Manchester and Clingham v Kensington and Chelsea Royal London Borough Council* [2002] UKHL 39, [2003] 1 AC 787, [2002] 4 All ER 593, [2002] 3 WLR 1313.

7. *Re H (minors) (Sexual Abuse: Standard of Proof)*, supra.

8. *Re U (Serious Injury: Standard of Proof); Re B (a child)* [2004] EWCA Civ 567, [2005] Fam 134, [2004] 3 WLR 753, [2004] 2 FCR 257, *Re T (Abuse: Standard of Proof)* [2004] EWCA Civ 558, [2004] 2 FLR 838 disapproving dicta of Bodey J in *Re ET (Serious Injuries: Standard of Proof)* [2003] 2 FLR 1205.

9. *North Yorkshire County Council v SA* [2003] EWCA Civ 839, [2003] 3 FCR 118, [2003] 2 FLR 849; *Re G (a child) (care order: threshold criteria)* [2001] 1 FCR 165, CA. See also *Re A (a child) (care proceedings: non-accidental injury)* [2003] EWCA Civ 839, (2003) 167 JPN 542.

10. *Re B (a child) (split hearings: jurisdiction)* [2000] 1 WLR 790, [2001] 1 FCR 297, [2000] 1 FLR 334, CA. See also *Re B (children: non-accidental injury)* [2002] EWCA Civ 902, [2002] 2 FCR 654, [2002] 2 FLR 599, where findings that a bruise was fresh and that the child had an unusually high pain threshold where unsustainable in the light of medical evidence to the contrary.

11. *Re A and D (Non-Accidental Injury: Subdural Haematomas)* [2002] 1 FLR 337, CA.

12. *Re H (children) (care proceedings: sexual abuse)* [2000] 2 FCR 499.

13. *Re G (care proceedings: theshold conditions)* [2001] EWCA Civ 968, [2001] 1 WLR 2100, [2001] 2 FCR 757, [2001] 2 FLR 1111.

14. *Stockport Metropolitan Borough Council v D* [1995] 1 FLR 873.

15. *Re B (threshold criteria: agreed facts)* [1999] 2 FCR 328.

16. *Re D (child: threshold criteria)* [2001] 1 FLR 274, CA.

17. *Re K (supervision order)* [1999] 2 FLR 303, RF.

18. *Re G (care proceedings: threshold conditions)*, supra.

19. *Re A (a minor) (supervision order: extension)* [1995] 3 All ER 401, [1995] 1 WLR 482, [1995] 1 FLR 335, CA. See also *Re K (supervision order)* [1999] 2 FLR 303.

20. *Birmingham City Council v D* [1994] 2 FLR 502 and see *Re M (care order: parental responsibility)* [1996] 2 FLR 84.

21. *Re M (a minor) (care order: threshold conditions)* [1994] 3 All ER 298, [1994] 3 WLR 558, HL.

22. *Southwark London Borough Council v B* [1999] 1 FCR 550, [1998] 2 FLR 1095.

23. *Newham Borough Council v AG* [1992] 2 FCR 119, [1993] 1 FLR 281; *Re A (a minor) (care proceedings)* [1993] 1 FCR 824.

24. *Re B (child: interim care order)* [1993] 1 FCR 565.

25. *Re O (a minor) (care order: education: procedure)* [1992] 4 All ER 905, [1992] 1 WLR 912.

26. *Lancashire County Council v A* [1999] 3 FCR 241; sub nom *Re B and W (Threshold Criteria)* [1999] 2 FLR 833, CA.

27. *Lancashire County Council v A* [2000] 2 All ER 97, [2000] 1 FCR 509, [2000] 1 FLR 583, HL.See also *Re K (children) (adoption: freeing order)* [2004] EWCA Civ 1181, [2004] 3 FCR 123 (freeing order set aside when mother subsequently volunteered information as to the identity of the perpetrator). See also *Re K (Non-accidental injuries: Perpetrator: New Evidence)* [2004] EWCA Civ 1181, [2005] 1 FLR 285, for the circumstances in which the perpetrator issue could be revisited and a care order reopened.

28. *Re O (children) (non-accidental injury)* [2003] UKHL 18, [2004] 1 AC 523, [2003] 2 All ER 305, [2003] 2 WLR 1075, [2003] 1 FCR 673.

29. *North Yorkshire County Council v SA*, supra.

6–166 Care and supervision orders: procedure on application. An application for a care or supervision order may be made on its own or in any other family proceedings[1]. No care order or supervision order may be made with respect to a child who has reached the age of 17, or 16 in the case of a child who is married[2]. The court may on an application for a care order make a supervision order, and on an application for a supervision order make a care order[3].

An "authorised person" may apply for a care order or supervision order. This means the National Society for the Prevention of Cruelty to Children and any of its officers, and any person authorised by order of the Secretary of State to bring proceedings under s 31 of the Act and any officer of a body which is so authorised[4]. The Children Act 1989 contains special provisions relating to applications by an authorised person, and requires that person, where practicable, to consult with the local authority in whose area the child lives before making the application[5].

Courts in England and Wales have jurisdiction to make orders under Part IV of the Children Act 1989 in relation to children who are present in the jurisdiction when the application is made, irrespective of whether or not they are habitually resident either abroad or in another part of the United Kingdom[6].

A court hearing an application for a care or supervision order must, in accordance with the Rules[7], draw up a timetable with a view to disposing of the application without delay, and give such directions as it considers appropriate for the purpose of ensuring, so far as is reasonably practicable, that the timetable is adhered to[8].

Where a court is considering an application for a care order together with an application for a freeing order for adoption, the application for a care order is the primary consideration and should be determined first[9].

For case management and procedure at the hearing, see **6–5103 Protocol for Judicial Case Management in Public Law Children Act Cases** and **6–37 Conduct of proceedings**, ante.

1. Children Act 1989, s 31(4), this PART, post.
2. Children Act 1989, s 31(3), this PART, post.
3. Children Act 1989, s 31(5), this PART, post.
4. Children Act 1989, s 31(9), this PART, post.
5. Children Act 1989, s 31(6), (7), this PART, post.
6. *Re M (a minor) (care orders: jurisdiction)* [1997] 1 All ER 263, [1997] 2 WLR 314 [1997] 1 FLR 456.
7. Family Proceedings Courts (Children Act 1989) Rules 1991, r 14, this PART, post.
8. Children Act 1989, s 32(1), this PART, post.
9. *Re D (Simultaneous applications for care and freeing orders)* [1999] 3 FCR 65, [1999] 2 FLR 49, CA; *Re M (a child) (adoption)* [2003] EWCA Civ 1874, [2004] 1 FCR 157.

6–167   Care order: meaning and effect.   A care order means an order placing the child with respect to whom the application is made in the care of a designated local authority, and except where express provision is made to the contrary, includes an interim care order[1]. While a care order gives parental responsibility for the child to the local authority, the relationship between the child and his parents remains within the court's jurisdiction, especially in relation to the contact that there is to be between the child, his parents and other people[2].

The local authority designated in a care order must be—

(a). the authority within whose area the child is ordinarily resident; or

(b). where the child does not reside in the area of a local authority, the authority within whose area any circumstances arose in consequence of which the order is being made[3].

Where a care order is made with respect to a child it shall be the duty of the local authority designated by the order to receive the child into their care and to keep him in their care while the order remains in force[4]. While a care order is in force, the local authority designated by the order shall have parental responsibility for the child, and have the power to determine the extent to which a parent or guardian of the child may meet his parental responsibility for him. However, the local authority may not exercise the latter power unless they are satisfied that it is necessary to do so in order to safeguard or promote the child's welfare[5]. A court does not have power to impose conditions on a care order, nor may a court require the local authority, whether as a condition of the making of the care order or otherwise, to place a child in a given setting[6].

The Children Act 1989 contains specific provision with respect to the following in relation to a child who is subject to a care order, namely, religious persuasion[7], adoption[8], change of surname[9] and removal from the United Kingdom[9].

A care order, other than an interim care order, continues in force until the child reaches the age of 18 unless it is brought to an end earlier[10]. It may be discharged by the court on the application of any person who has parental responsibility for the child, the child himself and the local authority designated in the order[11].

When during the pendency of care proceedings, the child concerned becomes ordinarily resident in the area of another local authority, consideration should be given to that local authority becoming a party to or taking over conduct of the proceedings. Where it is clear that the court will designate another local authority under s 31(8)(b) other than the applicant authority there must be full and early liaison. The care plan needs to be prepared in cooperation between the two local authorities, put forward as a joint document and any points of disagreement should be clearly identified in the plan[12].

In cases where a permanent substitute family may need to be found, the plan should assess the potential for an adoptive placement and balance that option with that of rehabilitation. In such cases, it should be made abundantly clear to the natural family at the earliest date that the local authority are considering two options, namely, rehabilitation within a strictly time-limited framework, or adoption outside the family and that inquiries are proceeding on a twin track so that the court can be presented with well-researched options in order to prevent delay[13].

The proper forum for a challenge to the care plan is in the care proceedings, rather than by way of judicial review; only in the event of a failure by a local authority to amend its proposals for the child so as to accord with the court's determination of the child's interests is it proper for the guardian to consider taking proceedings for judicial review[14]. Judicial review is a remedy of last resort as it is a blunt and unsatisfactory tool to deal with the sensitive issues involved[15]. Where proceedings are still on foot any human rights issue should be dealt with within the existing proceedings and should not be dealt with separately in proceedings before the Family Division[16].

When making a care order, or in any family proceedings in connection with a child who is in the care of the local authority, the court may make an order under s 34 of the Act with respect to contact if the court considers that such an order should be made[17]. See para **6–173 Parental contact with children in care**.

Under the Foster Placement (Children) Regulations 1991, reg 3, a local authority may not place a child unless the foster parent is approved under that regulation, and, by virtue of reg 3(4A), a person is not suitable to be regarded as a foster parent if he has been convicted of a specified offence. However, when making a care order with a planned placement, the court has power under reg 2(3) to waive the effect of reg 3(4A) if it is in the interests of the child not to do so[18].

---

1. Children Act 1989, s 31(1) and (11), this PART, post.

2. *Berkshire County Council v B* [1997] 3 FCR 88. See in particular *Northamptonshire County Council v Islington London Borough Council* [1999] 3 FCR 385, [1999] 2 FLR 881, noted to s 31(8), post.

3. Children Act 1989, s 31(8), this PART, post.

4. Children Act 1989, s 33(1), this PART, post.

5. Children Act 1989, s 33(3), (4), this PART, post.

6. *Re T (a minor) (Care Order: Conditions)* [1994] 2 FLR 423, sub nom *Re KDT (a minor) (Care Order: Conditions)* [1994] 2 FCR 721. See also *S and D (Children: Powers of Court)* [1995] 1 FCR 626, [1995] 2 FLR 456.

7. Children Act 1989, s 33(6)(a), this PART, post.

8. Children Act 1989, s 33(6)(b), this PART, post.

9. Children Act 1989, s 33(7), this PART, post.

10. Children Act 1989, s 91(12), this PART, post.

11. Children Act 1989, s 39(1), this PART, post.

12. *L v London Borough of Bexley* [1997] 1 FCR 277, [1996] 2 FLR 595.

13. *Re D and K (Minors) (Care plan: twin-track planning)* [1999] 3 FCR 109, [1999] 2 FLR 872.

14. *Re C (adoption: religious observance)* [2002] 1 FLR 1119.

15. *Re M (care proceedings: judicial review)* [2003] EWHC 850 (Admin), [2004] 1 FCR 302, [2003] 2 FLR 171.

16. *Re L (care proceedings: human rights claims)* [2003] EWHC 665 (Fam), [2004] 1 FCR 289, [2003] 2 FLR 160; *affd Re V (a child) (care proceedings: human rights claims)* [2004] EWCA Civ 54, [2004] 1 All ER 997, [2004] 1 WLR 1433, [2004] 1 FCR 338, [2004] 1 FLR 944.

17. Children Act 1989, s 34(5), this PART, post.

18. *Re A (a child) (protection from offenders)* [1999] 3 FCR 620.

6–168   Supervision order: meaning and effect.   A supervision order means an order putting the child with respect to whom the application is made under the supervision of a designated local authority or of a probation officer[1].

While a supervision order is in force it is the duty of the supervisor—

(a) to advise, assist and befriend the supervised child;
(b) to take such steps as are reasonably necessary to give effect to the order; and
(c) where—

     (i) the order is not wholly complied with; or
     (ii) the supervisor considers that the order may no longer be necessary, to consider whether or not to apply to the court for its variation or discharge[2].

Detailed provisions relating to supervision orders including the giving of directions to the supervised child, imposing obligations on responsible persons, requiring psychiatric and medical examinations or treatment, are contained in Sch 3, Pts I and II, to the Children Act 1989[3].

A supervision order does not grant parental responsibility to the local authority and it is not capable of achieving the same ends as a care order. The court may not impose conditions on a supervision order which may only contain a requirement to comply with the directions of the supervisor specified in Sch 3 and with requirements which have the consent of a responsible person. Nor can any of the requirements be directly enforced by the court; the only remedy for any breach is for the supervisor to make fresh application for a care order[4]. Once an application is made under s 31(1) the court is free to make a different order from that which is asked for by the local authority. Nevertheless if the court is to impose an order other than that which is asked for by the local authority there must be very cogent reasons to do so. The court should approach the question of the child's interests from the point of view exemplified by s 1(5) of the Act, with a preference for a less interventionist approach[5]. Even where children are to remain at home there may be need for a care order such as where there is a need for extreme vigilance and where the likelihood of harm to the child is such that the local authority should be in a position to remove a child immediately[6]. One consideration may be the court's assessment of how best to achieve the parents' cooperation in working with them to understand and meet the child's needs[5]. It is inappropriate to make a care order in preference to a supervision order in circumstances where there is no evidence that the circumstances are serious enough to warrant the local authority having the power to remove a child without judicial sanction; where the parents have shown a willingness to meet their responsibilities in a way advised by the local authority even though they might need considerable help and advice over a long period; and where the care order is made not in the best interests of the child but to encourage the local authority to perform it statutory duties towards children in need[7]. The action taken must be proportionate and where there are no long-standing problems of the sort that interfere with the capacity to provide adequate parenting, though there is a real possibility of future harm, the local authority should take time to explore other options than care and removal. The principle of proportionality requires the local authority to support and eventually reunite the family unless the risks are so high that the child's welfare requires alternative care[8].

A supervision order ceases to have effect at the end of the period of one year beginning with the date on which it was made[9]. This is a maximum period and does not preclude the making of an initial order for a period of less than 12 months[10]. On the application of the supervisor the court may extend, or further extend, the order for such period as it may specify, but the order may not be extended so as to remain in force for more than three years beginning with the date on which it was made[11]. On an application to extend a supervision order the threshold criteria in s 31(2) do not apply and therefore there is no jurisdiction to make a care order on an extension application[12].

---

1. Children Act 1989, s 31(1) and (11), this PART, post.
2. Children Act 1989, s 35(1), this PART, post.
3. See this PART, post.
4. *Re V (Care or Supervision Order)* [1996] 2 FCR 555, [1996] 1 FLR 776, CA.
5. *Re O (Minors) (Care or Supervision Order)* [1997] 2 FCR 17.
6. See for example *Re T (A Minor) (Care Order)* [1994] 1 FCR 663.
7. See *Oxfordshire County Council v L (Care or Supervision Order)* [1998] 1 FLR 70.
8. *Re C and B (care order: future harm)* [2001] 1 FLR 611, CA. See also *Re C (care order or supervision order)* [2001] 2 FLR 466.
9. Children Act 1989, Sch 3, para 6(1), this PART, post.
10. *M v Warwickshire County Council* [1994] 2 FCR 121, [1994] 2 FLR 593.
11. Children Act 1989, Sch 3, para 6(3), (4), this PART, post.
12. *In re A (a minor) (Supervision Order: Extension)* [1995] 3 All ER 401, [1995] 1 WLR 482, [1995] 1 FLR 335, CA.

6-169   **Education supervision order.**   On the application of any local education authority, the court may make an education supervision order putting the child with respect to whom the application is made under the supervision of a designated local education authority[1]. A court may only make an education supervision order if it is satisfied that the child concerned is of compulsory school age and is not being properly educated[2]. For this purpose a child is being properly educated only if he is receiving efficient full-time education suitable to his age, ability and aptitude and any special educational needs he may have[3].

An education supervision order may not be made with respect to a child who is in the care of a local authority[4].

The local education authority designated in an education supervision order must be—

(a) the authority within whose area the child concerned is living or will live; or
(b) where—

     (i) the child is a registered pupil at a school; and
     (ii) the authority mentioned in paragraph (a) above and the authority within whose area the school is situated agree,

the latter authority[5].

Where an education supervision order is in force with respect to a child, it is the duty of the supervisor to advise, assist and befriend, and give directions to the supervised person and his parents, in such a way as will, in the opinion of the supervisor, secure that he is properly educated[6].

An education supervision order shall have effect for a period of one year, beginning with the date on which it is made. The order may be extended, but no one extension may be for a period of more than three years. An education supervision order shall cease to have effect on the child's ceasing to be of compulsory school age, or on the making of a care order with respect to the child[7].

Detailed provisions as to the giving of directions by the supervisor, discharge of orders, and power of local education authority on the persistent failure of a child to comply with any direction given under an education supervision order are contained in Pt III of Sch 3 to the Children Act 1989[8].

---

1. Children Act 1989, s 36(1), this PART, post.
2. Children Act 1989, s 36(3), this PART, post.
3. Children Act 1989, s 36(4), this PART, post.
4. Children Act 1989, s 36(6), this PART, post.
5. Children Act 1989, s 36(7), this PART, post.
6. Children Act 1989, Sch 3, para 12, this PART, post.
7. Children Act 1989, Sch 3, para 15, this PART, post.
8. See this PART, post.

6–170 Interim care and supervision orders: principles. Where in any proceedings on an application for a care or supervision order, the proceedings are adjourned the court may make an interim care order or an interim supervision order with respect to the child concerned. This power is also available when the court gives a direction under s 37(1) of the Children Act 1989 for an investigation of the child's circumstances[1]. A local authority is not obliged to prepare and file a care plan before or with an application for an interim care order[2].

The use of interim orders has come under scrutiny in the context of the preparation and approval of care plans. Guidance on the correct approach has been given by Lord Nicholls in the leading judgement in *Re S (children: care plan)*[3]:

[90] 'From a reading of s 38 as a whole it is abundantly clear that the purpose of an interim care order, so far as presently material, is to enable the court to safeguard the welfare of a child until such time as the court is in a position to decide whether or not it is in the best interests of the child to make a care order. When that time arrives depends on the circumstances of the case and is a matter for the judgment of the trial judge. That is the general, guiding principle. The corollary to this principle is that an interim care order is not intended to be used as a means by which the court may continue to exercise a supervisory role over the local authority in cases where it is in the best interests of a child that a care order should be made.

[91] An interim care order, thus, is a temporary 'holding' measure. Inevitably, time is needed before an application for a care order is ready for decision. Several parties are usually involved: parents, the child's guardian, the local authority, perhaps others. Evidence has to be prepared, parents and other people interviewed, investigations may be required, assessments made, and the local authority must produce its care plan for the child in accordance with the guidance contained in Local Authority Circular LAC (99) 29 *Care Plans and Care Proceedings Under the Children Act 1989*. Although the 1989 Act itself makes no mention of a care plan, in practice this is a document of key importance. It enables the court and everyone else to know, and consider, the local authority's plans for the future of the child if a care order is made.

[92] When a local authority formulates a care plan in connection with an application for a care order, there are bound to be uncertainties. Even the basic shape of the future life of the child may be far from clear. Over the last ten years problems have arisen about how far courts should go in attempting to resolve these uncertainties before making a care order and passing responsibility to the local authority. Once a final care order is made, the resolution of the uncertainties will be a matter for the authority, not the court.

[93] In terms of legal principle one type of uncertainty is straightforward. This is the case where the uncertainty needs to be resolved before the court can decide whether it is in the best interests of the child to make a care order at all. In *C v Solihull Metropolitan Borough Council* [1992] 2 FCR 341 the court could not decide whether a care order was in the best interests of a child, there a 'battered baby', without knowing the result of a parental assessment. Ward J made an appropriate interim order. In such a case the court should finally dispose of the matter only when the material facts are as clearly known as can be hoped. Booth J adopted a similar approach, for a similar reason, in *Re A (a minor) (care proceedings)* [1993] 1 WLR 291, [1993] 1 FCR 164.

[94] More difficult, as a matter of legal principle, are cases where it is obvious that a care order is in the best interests of the child but the immediate way ahead thereafter is unsatisfactorily obscure. These cases exemplify a problem, or a 'tension', inherent in the scheme of the 1989 Act. What should the judge do when a care order is clearly in the best interests of the child but the judge does not approve of the care plan? This judicial dilemma was described by Balcombe LJ in *Re S and D (child case: powers of court)* [1995] 1 FCR 626 at 635 perhaps rather too bleakly, as the judge having to choose between 'the lesser of two evils'.

[95] In this context there are sometimes uncertainties whose nature is such that they are suitable for immediate resolution, in whole or in part, by the court in the course of disposing of the care order application. The uncertainty may be of such a character that it can, and should, be resolved so far as possible before the court proceeds to make the care order. Then, a limited period of 'planned and purposeful' delay can readily be justified as the sensible and practical way to deal with an existing problem.

[96] An instance of this occurred in *Re CH (a minor) (care or interim order)* [1998] 2 FCR 347. In that case the mother had pleaded guilty to causing grievous bodily harm to the child. The judge was intensely worried by the sharp divergence of professional view on placement. The local authority cautiously favoured rehabilitation. The child's guardian ad litem believed adoption was the realistic way to promote the child's future welfare. The judge made the care order without hearing any expert evidence on the disputed issue. The local authority would itself obtain expert advice, and then reconsider the question of placement. The Court of Appeal (Kennedy and Thorpe LJJ) held that the fact that a care order was the inevitable outcome should not have deflected the judge from hearing expert evidence on this issue. Even if the issue could not be finally

resolved before a care order was made, it was obviously sensible and desirable that, in the circumstances of the case, the local authority should have the benefit of the judge's observations on the point.

[97] Frequently the case is on the other side of this somewhat imprecise line. Frequently the uncertainties involved in a care plan will have to be worked out after a care order has been made and while the plan is being implemented. This was so in the case which is the locus classicus on this subject: *Re R (minors) (care proceedings: care plan)* [1994] 2 FCR 136. There the care plan envisaged placing the children in short-term foster placements for up to a year. Then a final decision would be made on whether to place the children permanently away from the mother. Rehabilitation was not ruled out if the mother showed herself amenable to treatment. Wall J said (at 149):

'there are cases (of which this is one) in which the action which requires to be taken in the interests of children necessarily involves steps into the unknown provided the court is satisfied that the local authority is alert to the difficulties which may arise in the execution of the care plan, the function of the court is not to seek to oversee the plan but to entrust its execution to the local authority.'

In that case the uncertain outcome of the treatment was a matter to be worked out after a care order was made, not before. The Court of Appeal decision in *Re L (minors) (care proceedings: appeal)* [1996] 2 FCR 352 was another case of this type: see Butler-Sloss LJ (at 362). So also was the decision of the Court of Appeal in *Re R (care proceedings: adjournment)* [1998] 3 FCR 654.

[98] These are all instances of cases where important issues of uncertainty were known to exist before a care order was made. Quite apart from known uncertainties, an element of future uncertainty is necessarily inherent in the very nature of a care plan. The best laid plans 'gang aft a-gley'. These are matters for decision by the local authority, if and when they arise. A local authority must always respond appropriately to changes, of varying degrees of predictability, which from time to time are bound to occur after a care order has been made and while the care plan is being implemented. No care plan can ever be regarded as set in stone.

[99] Despite all the inevitable uncertainties, when deciding whether to make a care order the court should normally have before it a care plan which is sufficiently firm and particularised for all concerned to have a reasonably clear picture of the likely way ahead for the child for the foreseeable future. The degree of firmness to be expected, as well as the amount of detail in the plan, will vary from case to case depending on how far the local authority can foresee what will be best for the child at that time. This is necessarily so. But making a care order is always a serious interference in the lives of the child and his parents. Although art 8 contains no explicit procedural requirements, the decision making process leading to a care order must be fair and such as to afford due respect to the interests safeguarded by art 8: see *TP v United Kingdom* [2001] 2 FCR 289 at 311 (para 72). If the parents and the child's guardian are to have a fair and adequate opportunity to make representations to the court on whether a care order should be made, the care plan must be appropriately specific.

[100] Cases vary so widely that it is impossible to be more precise about the test to be applied by a court when deciding whether to continue interim relief rather than proceed to make a care order. It would be foolish to attempt to be more precise. One further general point may be noted. When postponing a decision on whether to make a care order a court will need to have in mind the general statutory principle that any delay in determining issues relating to a child's upbringing is likely to prejudice the child's welfare: s 1(2) of the 1989 Act.'

Where there is a finding that the threshold criteria for the making of an order have been crossed, the next stage is to consider all the options that are open; the court must weigh the relevant factors balancing one against an other and must deliver a reasoned decision to explain its choice[3]. Where the application is for a care order empowering the local authority to remove a child or children from the family, the court may not make such an order without considering the art 8 rights of the adult members of the family and of the children of the family; accordingly it must not sanction such an interference with family life unless it is satisfied that that is both necessary and proportionate and that no other less radical form of order would achieve the essential end of promoting the welfare of the children[4].

---

1. Children Act 1989, s 38(1), this PART, post. As to an investigation of a child's circumstances, see para **6–172**, post.
2. *Westminster City Council v RA* [2005] TLR 321, FD.
3. [2002] UKHL 10, [2002] 2 All ER 192, [2002] 2 WLR 720, [2002] 1 FCR 577 overruling *Re W and B (children: care plan)* [2001] EWCA Civ 757, [2001] 2 FCR 450, [2001] 2 FLR 582.
4. *Re B (children) (care: interference with family life)* [2003] EWCA Civ 786, [2004] 1 FCR 463.

6–170A Interim care and supervision orders: procedure. Where interim orders are involved, the justices are masters of their own procedure and are entitled within proper limits to exercise their discretion to hear or refuse to hear evidence. That is not to say that after the first interim order has been made no later application can be tested absent a change in circumstances, but the court, having the discretion to control its procedure, can exercise that discretion in appropriate cases by focusing upon changes in circumstances[1].

However, if the justices hear oral evidence from one side, they must also hear evidence from the other[2].

A court shall not make an interim care order or interim supervision order unless it is satisfied that there are reasonable grounds for believing that the circumstances with respect to the child are as mentioned in s 31(2) of the Act[3].

Where, in any proceedings on an application for a care or supervision order, a court makes a residence order with respect to the child concerned, it shall also make an interim supervision order with respect to him unless satisfied that his welfare will be satisfactorily safeguarded without an interim order being made[4].

An interim order shall have effect for such period as may be specified in the order, but shall cease to have effect as provided by s 38(4) of the Act[5]; normally the expiry will be after eight weeks beginning with the date of the making of the order or the date of the disposal of the application if earlier[6].

On the making of an interim care order the court is entitled to make such directions as it considers appropriate for assessments of the child, including a direction as to a residential placement that involves such assessment[7].

Where the court makes an interim care order, or interim supervision order, it may give such directions as it considers appropriate with regard to the medical or psychiatric examination or other assessment of the child. However, if the child is of sufficient understanding to make an informed decision he may refuse to submit to the examination or other assessment[8]. In this event, the High Court, under its inherent jurisdiction, may override in a proper case the wishes of a child and give consent for medical assessment[9].

When granting an interim care order at one sitting it is inappropriate for the court to attempt to lay down a policy which will or may fetter the discretion of any future court in regard to the grant or refusal of a further interim order[10]. It does not follow that when the statutory conditions under s 38(2) are satisfied an interim care order automatically ensues; the court has to address the further question of whether an interim care order should now be made for the welfare of the children[11].

The following guidelines to justices on hearing applications for *interim care orders* have been given, with the approval of the President of the Family Division, by CAZALET J:

1. Justices should bear in mind that they are not, at an interim hearing, required to make a final conclusion; indeed it is because they are unable to reach a final conclusion that they are empowered to make an interim order. An interim order or decision will usually be required so as to establish a holding position, after weighing all the relevant risks, pending the final hearing. Nevertheless justices must always ensure that the substantive issue is tried and determined at the earliest appropriate date. Any delay in determining the question before the court is likely to prejudice the welfare of the child (see s 1(2) of the 1989 Act).
2. If justices find that they are unable to provide the appropriate hearing time, be it through pressure of work or for some other reason, they must, when an urgent interim order may have to be made, consider taking steps pursuant to r 14(2)(*h*) to transfer the proceedings laterally to an adjacent family proceedings court.
3. At the start of a hearing which is concerned with interim relief, justices will usually be called upon to exercise their discretion under r 21(2) as to the order of speeches and evidence. The circumstances prevailing will almost certainly not permit full evidence to be heard. Accordingly, in such proceedings, justices should rarely make findings as to disputed facts. These will have to be left over to the final hearing.
4. Justices must bear in mind that the greater the extent to which an interim order deviates from a previous order or the status quo the more acute the need is likely to be for an early final hearing date. Any disruption in a child's life almost invariably requires early resolution. Justices should be cautious about changing a child's residence under an interim order. The preferred course should be to leave the child where it is with a direction for safeguards and the earliest possible hearing date.
5. When an interim order may be made which will lead to a substantial change in a child's position, justices should consider permitting limited oral evidence to be led and challenged by way of cross-examination. However, it will necessarily follow that, in cross-examination, the evidence will have to be restricted to the issues which are essential at the interim stage. To this end the court may well have to intervene to ensure that this course is followed and that there is not a "dress rehearsal" of the full hearing.
6. Justices should, if possible, ensure that they have before them written advice from the guardian ad litem. When there are substantial issues between the parties the guardian should, if possible, be at court to give oral advice. A party who is opposed to a recommendation made by the guardian should normally be given an opportunity to put questions to him/her in regard to advice given to the court.
7. Justices must always comply with the mandatory requirements of the 1991 rules. These include compliance with: (*a*) r 21(1), which requires the justices to read, before the hearing, any documents which have been filed under r 17; (*b*) r 21(5), which requires the justices' clerk to make the appropriate written record of the hearing and in consultation with the justices to record the reasons for the court's decision and any findings of fact; and (*c*) r 21(6), which requires the court, when making its order, or giving its decision, to state any findings of fact and the reasons for the court's decision.
8. If shortage of time or some other circumstance delays the court in the preparation of its written findings of fact and reasons, justices should adjourn the making of their order or the giving of their decision until the following court day or the earliest possible date. At that further hearing it is permissible for one of their number to return to court and state the decision, findings of fact and reasons (see r 21(6)). When the length of a hearing lasts beyond normal hours it will often be sensible for the court to take this course so that it is not formulating its reasons and making perhaps a difficult decision under the sort of pressure which can arise when a sitting runs late into the day.
9. When justices grant interim relief, they should state their findings and reasons concisely. Although it will not normally be open to them to make findings on disputed facts (because the court will not have heard the full evidence) it may assist if justices summarise briefly the essential factual issues between the parties[12].

The Court of Appeal, when approving of the guidance set out above, has said that a party intending to seek a change in the nature of the interim order applied for should, except in an urgent case, give notice of at least two days to the other party. Where an application is made for a change in the nature of the interim care order sought, the court should, as a general proposition, permit some oral evidence to be called and allow cross-examination. In such a case the court must satisfy itself about the change of circumstances which it is said will justify a different order[13].

As regards the power to make directions for an assessment of the child, ss 38(6) and (7) of the Act confer jurisdiction on the court to order or prohibit any assessment. This involves the participation of the child and is directed to providing the court with the material which, in the view of the court, is required to enable it to reach a proper decision at the final hearing of the application for a full order. In exercising its discretion whether to order any particular assessment or assessment, the court will take into account the cost of the proposed assessment and the fact that local authorities' resources are limited[14].

The House of Lords in *In re G (A Minor) (Interim Care Order: Residential Assessment)*[15] considered the use of the power under s 38(6) to order residential assessments. It was held that since the assessment of the child was intended to provide the court with the information necessary to make a final decision regarding the child's future with the minimum of delay, any assessment had to take place within a relatively short period and should not be prolonged by repeated interim orders. The court's jurisdiction was confined to obtaining information about the current state of affairs and did not extend to a continuing survey of the effects of treatment over a long period. The purpose of s 38(6) was to enable the court to control, and therefore be able to limit, the number and type of examinations or assessments that a child who had become the subject of care proceedings would be required to undergo. The assessment of the child could include, where appropriate, an assessment of the child's relationship with her parents, the risk that her parents might present to her and the ways in which those risks could be avoided or managed, so long as the focus was always on the child. Where, however, the main purpose of the proposed programme was to provide therapy for the child's mother in order to give her the opportunity to change and thereby become a safe and acceptable carer for the child, those proposals focused on the treatment and improvement of the mother and her parenting skills and could not be regarded as an assessment of the child for the purposes of s 38(6). The right to respect for family life under art 8 of the European Convention for the Protection of Human Rights and Fundamental Freedoms did not include the right to be made a better parent at public expense to give the family the optimum chance of being able to live together.

Although the court may include a particular named social worker in a direction the practice is not encouraged as the court must take into account the views and resources of the local authority who employs that social worker. A better direction may be that the assessment should be carried out by a "suitably qualified worker"[16]. In addition the court will only make such a direction if (i) what is proposed is truly an assessment and not treatment, (ii) the assessment is not contrary to the child's best interests, (iii) the assessment is necessary to enable the court to discharge its functions and (iv) it is not unreasonable for the local authority to be involved in and fund the assessment[17]. Where an order is made for an assessment, the court may direct an apportionment of the costs between the parties, including the Legal Services Commission, in accordance with the principles applicable to the provision of expert reports[18].

There is a distinction between obtaining/controlling the obtaining of information, on the one hand, and the provision of services, on the other. Section 38(6) and (7) are concerned with the former: "[64] The purpose of these provisions is, therefore, not only to enable the court to obtain the information it needs, but also to enable the court to control the information-gathering activities of others. But the emphasis is always on obtaining information. This is clear from the use of the words 'examination' and 'other assessment'. If the framers of the Act had meant the court to be in charge, not only of the examination and assessment of the child, but also of the medical or psychiatric treatment to be provided for her, let alone for her parents, it would have said so. Instead, it deliberately left that in the hands of the local authority. [65] A fortiori, the purpose of s 38(6) cannot be to ensure the provision of services either for the child or his family. There is nothing in the 1989 Act which empowers the court hearing care proceedings to order the provision of specific services for anyone. To imply such a power into s 38(6) would be quite contrary to the division of responsibility which was the 'cardinal principle' of the 1989 Act... [69] In short, what is directed under s 38(6) must clearly be an examination or assessment of the child, including where appropriate her relationship with her parents, the risk that her parents may present to her, and the ways in which those risks may be avoided or managed, all with a view to enabling the court to make the decisions which it has to make under the Act with the minimum of delay. Any services which are provided for the child and her family must be ancillary to that end"[19].

1. *Re B (interim care orders: renewal)* [2001] 2 FLR 1217.
2. *Re F (a minor) (Care Order: Procedure)* [1994] 1 FCR 729, [1994] 1 FLR 240.
3. Children Act 1989, s 38(2), this PART, post. For commentary on s 31(2), see paras **6–164** and **6–165**, ante.
4. Children Act 1989, s 38(3), this PART, post.
5. See this PART, post.
6. Children Act 1989, s 38(4), this PART, post.
7. Children Act 1989, s 38(6), this PART, post.
8. *Re B (Interim Care Order: Directions)* [2002] EWCA 25, [2002] 2 FCR 367, [2002] 1 FLR 545.
9. *South Glamorgan County Council v B* [1993] 1 FCR 626.
10. *Re P (minors) (Interim Order)* [1993] 2 FLR 742. See also *Re H (a child)(Adoption: Parental Consent)* (2001) 165 JPN 734, where it was held that a change in the mother's circumstances, whatever it potential, had simply come too late to benefit the child and any delay in moving the child to a permanent family would be to his detriment. Where, however, there is still too much flux within the scene to enable the court to make a final care order an interim order should be made: *Re C (a child)* [2001] EWCA Civ 810, [2001] 3 FCR 381.
11. *Re A (children) (interim care order)* [2001] 3 FCR 402.
12. *Hampshire County Council v S* [1993] 1 FLR 559, [1993] 1 All ER 944.
13. *Re W (a minor) (Care Proceedings: Interim Orders)* [1994] 3 FCR 102, CA.
14. *In re C (a minor) (Interim Care Order: Residential Assessment)* [1996] 4 All ER 871, [1997] 1 FCR 149, [1997] 1 FLR 1, HL. Where, however, local authorities want to persuade a court that a direction under s 38(6) for residential assessment will involve disproportionate expenditure on a single family they must present a case that has been properly prepared in accordance with the ordinary rules and practices regarding the filing of statements and the conduct of trials: *Re C (children) (residential assessment)* [2001] EWCA Civ 1305, [2001] 3 FCR 164, CA.
15. [2005] UKHL 68, [2005] 3 WLR 1196.
16. *Re W (a minor) (Care Proceedings: Assessment)* [1998] 1 FCR 287.
17. *Re M (residential assessment directions)* [1998] 2 FLR 371. See also *Re D (Jurisdiction: programme of assessment or therapy)* [2000] 1 FCR 436, [1999] 2 FLR 632, CA.
18. *Lambeth London Borough Council v S, C, V and J* [2005] EWHC 776 (Fam), [2005] 2 FLR 1171. See *Calderdale Metropolitan Council v S* [2004] EWHC 2529 (Fam), [2005] 1 FLR 236 and para **6–35A Expert evidence**, post.
19. Per Baroness Hale in *Re G (a child) (interim care order: residential assessment)* [2005] UKHL 68, [2005] 3 FCR 521.

6–170B   Interim care order: exclusion requirement.   Where, on being satisfied that there are reasonable grounds for believing—

   (*a*) that the child concerned is suffering, or is likely to suffer, significant harm; and
   (*b*) that the harm, or likelihood of harm, is attributable to the care given to the child, or likely to be given to him if the order were not made, not being what it would be reasonable to expect a parent to give to him,

the court makes an interim care order with respect to the child, the court may include an exclusion requirement in the interim care order if the following conditions are satisfied[1].

The conditions are—

(a)   that there is reasonable cause to believe that, if a person ("the relevant person") is excluded from a dwelling-house in which the child lives, the child will cease to suffer, or cease to be likely to suffer, significant harm, and

(b)   that another person living in the dwelling-house (whether a parent of the child or some other person)—

     (i)   is able and willing to give to the child the care which it would be reasonable to expect a parent to give him, and

     (ii)   consents to the inclusion of the exclusion requirement[2].

An exclusion requirement is any one or more of the following—

(a)   a provision requiring the relevant person to leave a dwelling-house in which he is living with the child,

(b)   a provision prohibiting the relevant person from entering a dwelling-house in which the child lives, and

(c)   a provision excluding the relevant person from a defined area in which a dwelling-house in which the child lives is situated[3].

The court may provide that the exclusion requirement is to have effect for a shorter period than the other provisions of the interim care order[4].

Where the court makes an interim care order containing an exclusion requirement, the court may attach a power of arrest to the requirement[5] and where it does so it may provide that the power of arrest is to have effect for a shorter period than the exclusion requirement[6]. Such a power of arrest enables a constable to arrest without warrant any person whom he has reasonable cause to believe to be in breach of the requirement[7]. Provisions of the Family Law Act 1996[8] are applied and have effect in relation to a person arrested under a power of arrest to an exclusion requirement as they have effect in relation to a person arrested under s 47(6) of that Act[9].

The applicant for the interim care order must —

(a)   prepare a separate statement of the evidence in support of the application for an exclusion requirement;

(b)   serve the statement personally on the relevant person with a copy of the order containing the exclusion requirement (and of any power of arrest which is attached to it); and

(c)   inform the relevant person of his right to apply to vary or discharge the exclusion requirement[10].

Best practice guidelines with respect to an application for an exclusion requirement in connection with either an interim care order or an emergency protection order have been given by Cazalet J[11] and are summarised as follows—

1   The statement of evidence must be separate and self-standing, and set out in concise form the factual material on which the applicant is to rely for the purposes of obtaining the exclusion requirement.

2   The requirements for obtaining an exclusion order, as set out in s 38A(2) (for an interim care order) or s 44A(2) (for an emergency protection order) of the Children Act 1989 must be stated. In particular, the statement should set out — to the extent that it meets a particular case — the relevant subsections, namely (a) that there is reasonable cause to believe that, if the relevant person is excluded from a dwelling-house in which the child lives the child will cease to suffer, or cease to be likely to suffer, significant harm, and (b) that another person living in the dwelling-house (whether a parent of the child or some other person) — (i) is able and willing to give the child the care which it would be reasonable to expect a parent to give it, and (ii) consents to the inclusion of the exclusion requirement. The evidence in support of these contentions must also be summarised in the statement.

3   The statement should make clear that an exclusion requirement is one requiring (as may be appropriate in the particular case) that the relevant person is to leave the dwelling-house in which he is living with the child and/or that provision is sought prohibiting the relevant person from entering a dwelling-house in which the child is living and/or excluding the relevant person from a defined area in which the dwelling-house in which the child lives is situated.

4(i)   Quite frequently it happens that, although the original application has been for an interim care order or emergency protection order only, the court of its own motion will impose an exclusion requirement. In this event there will have been no separate statement of evidence prepared by the applicant prior to the hearing directed towards the requirements and evidence necessary for the obtaining of this. Rule 25A(7) provides that in such circumstances r 25A(2)(a) shall apply with the omission of any reference to the statement of evidence as set out therein. Accordingly, if at a hearing at which the relevant person against whom the exclusion requirement is ordered is not present and the court of its own motion has made such an order, then in order to ensure that the relevant person will have received the appropriate information to enable him to determine whether to apply to vary or discharge the exclusion requirement, it will usually be appropriate for the court to direct that a concise statement be prepared of the evidence led at that hearing, and the other matters set out in paras 2 and 3 above, such to be served personally on the relevant person in like manner as to service of the statement of evidence had one been in existence.

4(ii)   If the hearing has been before the justices then it may be that the best way of dealing with this is to serve the justices' findings on the evidence and their reasons which led them to making the exclusion order. If the matter is before a higher court then it may be that a summary of the relevant evidence leading to the exclusion order can be concisely stated, alternatively the judge may direct the content of such summary should be prepared and served so that the relevant person is aware of the nature of the evidence found against him. The other necessary requirements set out in paras 1, 2 and 3 above should also be set out.

4(iii)   On the other hand, when the relevant person has been present in court and has heard the evidence led against him for the purpose of obtaining an exclusion requirement the court may, in appropriate circumstances, disapply any requirements as to service of the separate statement or notice of the evidence led before it.

5   Sections 38A and 44A and r 25A do not require that a specific application for an exclusion requirement is necessary. The application will be for an interim care order or emergency protection order and the question of an exclusion requirement is simply ancillary to this. Accordingly, no separate application form under the rules is required.

6   It is to be noted that the consent of the other person living in the dwelling-house (whether parent or some other person), who is able and willing to give the child the care which it is reasonable to expect that parent to give him, can give the consent in question either orally in court or in writing signed by him to the justices' clerk (where the hearing is before the magistrates) or to the higher court (as appropriate) (see r 25 of the Family Proceedings Courts (Children Act 1989) Rules 1991 and its counterpart, r 4.24 of the Family Proceedings Rules 1991). The written consent must be given for the purpose of sub-s (2) of s 38A or s 44A and should provide the necessary details of the person who is able and willing to give the child the care which it would be reasonable to expect a parent to give it; also it should be stated that that person understands that the giving of consent could lead to the exclusion of the relevant person from the dwelling-house in which the child lives.

7   Once the appropriate separate statement in compliance with r 25A has been served, then it will not be necessary at subsequent renewals of the order in question again to serve a separate statement, unless of course there has been a further hearing and the grounds have changed.

If, while an interim care order containing an exclusion requirement is in force, the local authority have removed the child from the dwelling-house from which the relevant person is excluded to other accommodation for a continuous period of more than 24 hours, the interim care order shall cease to have effect in so far as it imposes the exclusion requirement[10].

In any case where the court has power to include an exclusion requirement in an interim care order, the court may accept an undertaking from the relevant person, but no power of arrest may be attached to any undertaking. Such an undertaking given to a court shall be enforceable as if it were an order of the court, and shall cease to have effect if, while it is in force, the local authority have removed the child from the dwelling-house from which the relevant person is excluded to other accommodation for a continuous period of more than 24 hours[11].

---

1. Children Act 1989, s 38A(1), this PART, post.
2. Children Act 1989, s 38A(2), this PART, post.
3. Children Act 1989, s 38A(3), this PART, post.
4. Children Act 1989, s 38A(4), this PART, post.
5. Children Act 1989, s 38A(5), this PART, post.
6. Children Act 1989, s 38A(6), this PART, post.
7. Children Act 1989, s 38A(8), this PART, post.
8. Sections 47(7), (11) and (12) and 48 of, and Sch 5 to, the Family Law Act 1996, this PART, post, are applied.
9. Children Act 1989, s 38A(9), this PART, post.
10. Family Proceedings Courts (Children Act 1989) Rules 1991, r 25A, this PART, post.
11. *W v A local authority (exclusion requirement)* [2000] 2 FCR 662.
12. Children Act 1989, s 38A(10), this PART, post.
13. Children Act 1989, s 38B(1), (2), this PART, post.

6–171   Care and supervision orders: discharge, variation, etc.   A care order may be discharged by the court on the application of—

(*a*)   any person who has parental responsibility for the child;
(*b*)   the child himself; or
(*c*)   the local authority designated by the order[1].

A supervision order may be varied or discharged by the court on the application of—

(*a*)   any person who has parental responsibility for the child;
(*b*)   the child himself; or
(*c*)   the supervisor[2].

A supervision order may also be varied on the application of the person with whom the child is living, in so far as it imposes a requirement which affects that person[3].

Where a care order is in force with respect to a child the court may, on the application of any person entitled to apply for the order to be discharged, substitute a supervision order for the care order[4].

On the application of a person who is not entitled to apply for the order to be discharged, but who is a person to whom an exclusion requirement contained in the order applies, an interim care order may be varied or discharged by the court in so far as it imposes the exclusion requirement[5]. Where a power of arrest has been attached to an exclusion requirement of an interim order, the court may on the application of any person entitled to apply for the discharge of the exclusion requirement, vary or discharge the order in so far as it confers a power of arrest[6].

A court hearing an application under s 39 of the Children Act 1989 to discharge an order under s 31 of the Act must have regard to the provisions of s 1. In particular, the court is bound by s 1(3)(*e*) to have regard to any harm which the child has suffered or is at risk of suffering. The "risk" is that current at the date of the hearing. Although in the great majority of cases the court is likely to be concerned with evidence of recent harm and appraisal of current risk, there will be instances where it may be relevant in the light of evidence before it, for the court, exceptionally, to question the relevance and soundness of an antecedent decision reached by an earlier tribunal[7].

---

1. Children Act 1989, s 39(1), this PART, post.
2. Children Act 1989, s 39(2), this PART, post.

3. Children Act 1989, s 39(3), this PART, post.
4. Children Act 1989, s 39(4), this PART, post.
5. Children Act 1989, s 39(3A), this PART, post.
6. Children Act 1989, s 39(3B), this PART, post.
7. *Re S (Discharge of Care Order)* [1995] 2 FLR 639.

6–172 Investigation of child's circumstances. Where, in any family proceedings in which a question arises with respect to the welfare of any child, it appears to the court that it may be appropriate for a care or supervision order to be made with respect to him, the court may direct the appropriate authority to undertake an investigation of the child's circumstances[1].

Where the court gives such a direction, the local authority concerned shall, when undertaking the investigation, consider whether they should—

(a)   apply for a care order or for a supervision order with respect to the child;
(b)   provide services or assistance for the child or his family; or
(c)   take any other action with respect to the child[2].

If after a local authority has undertaken such an investigation, they decide not to apply for a care order or supervision order with respect to the child concerned, they shall inform the court of—

(a)   their reasons for so deciding;
(b)   any service or assistance which they have provided, or intend to provide, for the child and his family; and
(c)   any other action which they have taken, or propose to take, with respect to the child[3].

This information must be given to the court before the end of the period of eight weeks beginning with the date of the direction, unless the court otherwise directs[4]. Where the local authority decide not to apply for a care or supervision order, they shall consider whether it would be appropriate to review the case at a later date, and if so, determine the date when the further review is to begin[5].

The local authority named in a direction to investigate a child's circumstances must be the authority in whose area the child is ordinarily resident; or where the child is not ordinarily resident in the area of a local authority, the authority within whose area any circumstances arose in consequence of which the direction is being given[6].

Where the local authority decides not to apply for a care or supervision order, its duty to inform the court should be performed at a directions appointment. Accordingly, when ordering an investigation under s 37 it is recommended that the court should fix a date by which the report is to be provided and also fix a directions appointment shortly thereafter at which the report can be considered[7]. It is good practice to disclose the report to parties in private law proceedings[7].

If the court actually makes an interim care order the circumstances of the case are likely to be serious and it may be appropriate to appoint a children's guardian immediately[7].

---

1. Children Act 1989, s 37(1), this PART, post. See also *Re H (Child's Circumstances: Direction to Investigate)* [1993] 2 FCR 277.
2. Children Act 1989, s 37(2), this PART, post.
3. Children Act 1989, s 37(3), this PART, post.
4. Children Act 1989, s 37(4), this PART, post.
5. Children Act 1989, s 37(6), this PART, post.
6. Children Act 1989, s 37(5), this PART, post.
7. See *Re CE (Section 37 Direction)* [1995] 1 FCR 387, [1995] 1 FLR 26.

6–173 Parental contact with children in care[1]. Where a child is in the care of a local authority, the authority shall, subject to the provisions of s 34 of the Children Act 1989, allow the child reasonable contact with—

(a)   his parents;
(b)   any guardian of his;
(c)   where there was a residence order in force with respect to the child immediately before the care order was made, the person in whose favour the order was made; and
(d)   where, immediately before the care order was made, a person had care of the child by virtue of an order made in the exercise of the High Court's inherent jurisdiction with respect to children, that person[2].

An authority may refuse to allow the contact required as set out above if—

(i)   they are satisfied that it is necessary to do so in order to safeguard or promote the child's welfare; and
(ii)   the refusal is decided upon as a matter of urgency, and does not last for more than seven days[3].

Application may be made to the court for such order as the court considers appropriate with respect to the contact which is to be allowed between the child and any named person. Such application may be made by the authority or the child. Moreover, application may also be made by any person referred to in paragraphs (a) to (d) above, or by any person who has obtained the leave of the court to make the application[4]. When the application is made by the authority or the child, the court may make an order authorising the authority to refuse to allow contact between the child and any person mentioned in paragraphs (a) to (d) above[5]. An order as to contact may also be made by the court when making a care order with respect to a child, or in any family proceedings in connection with a child who is in the care of a local authority[6]. Any such order as to contact may impose such conditions as the court considers appropriate[7].

There is nothing in s 34 of the Children Act 1989 which is not "Human Rights compliant" when used in appropriate cases as an inherent part of a care plan approved by the court, and as a means of avoiding drift or delay in the interests of the child concerned[8].

Contact applications generally fall into two main categories—those which ask for contact as such, and those which are attempts to set aside the care order itself. In the first category, while the proposals of the local authority must command the respect and consideration of the court, the court has a duty to decide on contact between the child and those mentioned in paragraphs (*a*) to (*d*) above. Consequently, the court may need to require the local authority to justify their long-term plans to the extent only that those plans exclude contact between parent and child. In the second category, s 1 of the Children Act 1989 has to be considered and the local authority has the task of justifying the cessation of contact. The local authority's long-term plans for the child must be considered and it is only in unusual cases that a parent will be able to show that there has been such a change of circumstances as to require further investigation and consideration of the local authority's plan[9].

The question of contact becomes one of balancing the respective factors in the welfare of the child. At one end of the spectrum there are cases where the child clearly needs a new family for life and contact with his family of birth will bring little or no benefit and is likely to impede this. At the other end of the spectrum are cases where the child is likely to return home in the short to medium term and contact is essential to enable this to take place. There are also many cases in the middle where the child is unlikely to return home in the short to medium term and so needs a long-term stable placement but where relationships with his family of origin are so important to him that they must be maintained[10]. Even in cases of babies removed from their mothers, an order for daily contact would be exceptionally unusual; regard must be had to the extent to which the quantum of contact may impose unreasonable burdens on foster carers and on the resources of the local authority (substantiated by some basic information as to costs)[11].

It is wrong for the court to assume that it is unable to exercise its jurisdiction over contact in a manner which is inconsistent with the local authority's long term plans for the child. However, the court must balance the various advantages against the difficulties that contact is likely to cause in finding and sustaining an appropriate placement for the child. Contact, however important, must not be pursued to a level which makes a successful placement impossible to find because the child needs a home and to be properly looked after and that must be a first priority[10].

The effect of The Children Act 1989 is to remove from the court any continuing control over children after the making of a care order unless and until a further application to the court. The future arrangements for the child are handed over to the local authority. The 1989 Act also imposes a duty to promote contact between children in care and parents and others who have a significant place in their lives. The power of the court to supervise and control is the power to require the local authority to go further in the promotion of contact than the local authority themselves consider appropriate and the other power is to monitor the local authority's proposal to refuse contact in order to ensure that their proposal is not excessive. However, the jurisdiction under s 34 is not to be deployed so as to inhibit the local authority in the performance of their statutory duty by preventing contact which the local authority considers advantageous to welfare[12]. A court should not make an order which in effect gave the local authority power and responsibility to implement the court's programme of contact by making an order in terms that a local authority could terminate contact without further application to a court if any agreement for contact were not kept by the parent in future. The court should make the order in positive terms and if a decision was required whether to reduce or terminate contact, there would then be a judicial umpire to rule on any disputed areas between a parent and the local authority[13].

Where an application under s 34(2) is appropriate, namely where the named children and their parents are content with the proposed contact and the resistance thereto emanates from the local authority, it will be the interests of the applicant child which are paramount[14].

The function of the judge in upholding the Parliamentary intention of s 34 and in granting s 34(4) orders restrictively and stringently is an important one; the practical convenience of the local authority matters, but only to the extent that to impede it would be contrary to the best interests of the children[15]. Where on an application under s 34(4) by a local authority to terminate contact between a mother and her child, both the mother and the child are minors, the principle that the child's welfare shall be the court's paramount consideration should be applied only to the mother's child and not to the mother even though she is herself a child for the purposes of the 1989 Act[16].

The order made by the court may be for as short or as long a period as is considered to be for the child's welfare[17]. The provisions of s 34 are sufficiently wide to enable the court to make what is, in effect, an interim contact order with a specific provision for a further hearing with a view to making some more enduring provision for contact at the later hearing[18].

It should be noted that under the Contact with Children Regulations 1991, reg 3, the local authority may depart from the terms of any order made under s 34 of the Act by agreement between the local authority and the person in relation to whom the order is made, and where the child is of sufficient understanding, subject to agreement also with him; and subject also to appropriate written notice being given in accordance with the Regulations[19].

In exercising its discretion whether to grant leave to make an application under s 34 (3)(*b*), the criteria in s 10(9) of the Act are apposite. The court must at least have regard to the following factors:

(*a*) the nature of the contact sought, whether frequent, direct or indirect;

(*b*) the applicant's connection to the child—the more important and meaningful the connection, the greater weight to be given to the application;

(*c*) any disruption—the need for stability and security is vital. The court must consider the risk that there might be of the proposed application disrupting the child's life to such an extent that he would be harmed by it;

(*d*)   the wishes of the parents and the local authority are very material though not determinative.

In weighing up the factors the following test should be applied:

(*a*)   if the application is frivolous, vexatious or an abuse of process it must fail;

(*b*)   if the applicant fails to disclose that there is any eventual real prospect of success, or the prospect is so remote as to make the application unsustainable, then the application for leave should be dismissed;

(*c*)   the applicant must satisfy the court that there is a serious issue to try and must present a good arguable case[20].

Where an order has been made under sub-s (4) granting leave for the local authority to refuse contact with the mother on the basis of a care plan which envisages placement with a view to adoption, the court will only make an order under sub-s (9) where there has been some material change in circumstances since the making of the order and, bearing those changes in mind, the extent to which it would be appropriate to reinvestigate the central question of whether contact should be terminated[21].

---

1. For the position under the European Convention on Human Rights see *B v United Kingdom* (1988) 10 EHRR 87, *Eriksson v Sweden* (1990) 12 EHRR 183 and *Johansen v Norway* (1996) 23 EHRR 33. See also the observations of Wall J in *Re F (care: termination of contact)* [2000] 2 FCR 481.
2. Children Act 1989, s 34(1), this Part, post.
3. Children Act 1989, s 34(6), this Part, post.
4. Children Act 1989, s 34(2), (3), this Part, post.
5. Children Act 1989, s 34(4), this Part, post.
6. Children Act 1989, s 34(5), this Part, post.
7. Children Act 1989, s 34(7), this Part, post.
8. *Re F (care: termination of contact)* [2000] 2 FCR 481.
9. *Re B (minors) (Care: Contact: Local Authority's Plans)* [1993] 1 FLR 543; applied in *Re E (a minor) (Care Order: Contact)* [1994] 1 FCR 584, [1994] 1 FLR 146, CA.
10. *Berkshire County Council v B* [1997] 3 FCR 88.
11. *Kirklees Metropolitan Borough Council v S (Contact: Newborn Babies)* [2006] 1 FLR 333.
12. *Re W (a child) (parental contact: prohibition)* [2000] Fam 130, [2000] 2 WLR 1276, [2000] 1 FCR 752, [2000] 1 FLR 502 CA.
13. *In Re S (termination of contact)* [2004] EWCA Civ 1397, [2005] 1 FCR 488, [2005] 1 FLR 469.
14. *Re F (Contact: Child in Care)* [1995] 1 FLR 510.
15. *Re H (children) (termination of contact)* [2005] EWCA Civ 318, [2005] 1 FCR 658, [2005] 2 FLR 408.
16. *Birmingham City Council v H (a minor)* [1994] 1 All ER 12, [1994] 2 WLR 31, [1993] 1 FCR 896, [1994] 1 FLR 224, HL.
17. *West Glamorgan County Council v P* [1992] 2 FCR 378.
18. *Cheshire County Council v B* [1992] 2 FCR 572.
19. Contact with Children Regulations 1991, SI 1991/891.
20. *Re M (Care: Contact: Grandmother's Application for Leave)* [1995] 2 FLR 86, [1995] 3 FCR 550, CA.
21. *Re T (minors) (termination of contact: discharge of order)* [1997] 1 All ER 65, [1997] 1WLR 393, [1997] 1 FLR 517, CA.

6–174   Child assessment order.   On the application of a local authority or authorised person, the court may make a child assessment order with respect to a child if it is satisfied that—

(*a*)   the applicant has reasonable cause to suspect that the child is suffering, or is likely to suffer, significant harm;

(*b*)   an assessment of the state of the child's health or development, or of the way in which he has been treated, is required to enable the applicant to determine whether or not the child is suffering, or is likely to suffer, significant harm; and

(*c*)   it is unlikely that such an assessment will be made, or be satisfactory, in the absence of an order[1].

A child assessment order shall not be made if the court is satisfied that there are grounds for making an emergency protection order with respect to the child and that it ought to make such an order rather than a child assessment order[2].

A child assessment order must specify the date by which the assessment is to begin and shall have effect for such period, not exceeding seven days beginning with that date, as may be specified in the order[3].

Where a child assessment order is in force with respect to a child it shall be the duty of any person who is in a position to produce the child—

(*a*)   to produce him to such person as may be named in the order; and

(*b*)   to comply with such directions relating to the assessment of the child as the court thinks fit to specify in the order[4].

If the child is of sufficient understanding to make an informed decision, he may refuse to submit to a medical or psychiatric examination or other assessment[5]. The child may only be kept away from home—

(*a*)   in accordance with directions specified in the order;

(*b*)   if it is necessary for the purposes of assessment; and

(*c*)   for such period or periods as may be specified in the order[6].

An "authorised person" means a person who is an authorised person for the purposes of s 31 of the Children Act 1989[7].

Any person making an application for a child assessment order must take such steps as are reasonably practicable to ensure that notice of the application is given to—

(i) the child's parents;
(ii) any person who is not a parent of his but who has parental responsibility for him;
(iii) any other person caring for the child;
(iv) any person in whose favour a contact order is in force with respect to the child;
(v) any person who is allowed to have contact with the child by virtue of an order under s 34 of the Children Act 1989; and
(vi) the child[8].

The court may treat an application for a child assessment order as an application for an emergency protection order[9].

---

1. Children Act 1989, s 43(1), this PART, post.
2. Children Act 1989, s 43(4), this PART, post.
3. Children Act 1989, s 43(5), this PART, post.
4. Children Act 1989, s 43(6), this PART, post.
5. Children Act 1989, s 43(8), this PART, post.
6. Children Act 1989, s 43(9), this PART, post.
7. Children Act 1989, s 43(13), this PART, post.
8. Children Act 1989, s 43(11), this PART, post.
9. Children Act 1989, s 43(3), this PART, post.

6–175 Emergency protection order. A court may make an emergency protection order with respect to a child if it is satisfied that—

(*a*) there is reasonable cause to believe that the child is likely to suffer significant harm if—

(i) he is not removed to accommodation provided by or on behalf of the applicant; or
(ii) he does not remain in the place in which he is then being accommodated;

(*b*) in the case of an application made by a local authority—

(i) enquiries are being made with respect to the child under s 47(1)(*b*) of the Children Act 1989; and
(ii) those enquiries are being frustrated by access to the child being unreasonably refused to a person authorised to seek access and that the applicant has reasonable cause to believe that access to the child is required as a matter of urgency; or

(*c*) in the case of an application made by an authorised person—

(i) the applicant has reasonable cause to suspect that a child is suffering, or is likely to suffer, significant harm;
(ii) the applicant is making enquiries with respect to the child's welfare; and
(iii) those enquiries are being frustrated by access to the child being unreasonably refused to a person authorised to seek access and the applicant has reasonable cause to believe that access to the child is required as a matter of urgency[1].

While it is in force an emergency protection order operates as a direction to any person who is in a position to do so to comply with any request to produce the child to the applicant; it also authorises the removal of the child at any time to accommodation provided by the applicant or the prevention of the removal of the child from any hospital or other place in which he is being accommodated immediately before the making of the order. An emergency protection order gives the applicant parental responsibility for the child[2].

Detailed provisions are contained in s 44 of the Children Act 1989 as to the directions which may be given in an emergency protection order, including directions with respect to contact between the child and any named person, and the medical, psychiatric or other assessment of the child[3].

The Grand Chamber of the European Court of Human Rights has held that the taking of a new born baby into public care at the moment of its birth is an extremely harsh measure and there must be extraordinarily compelling reasons before a baby can be physically removed from its mother's care against her will immediately after birth as a consequence of a procedure in which neither she nor her partner has been involved[4].

An emergency protection order shall have effect for such period, not exceeding eight days, as may be specified in the order. Special provision is made if the order would otherwise expire on a public holiday. The order may be extended once, and an application may be made for its discharge but no application for discharge shall be heard by the court before the expiry of the period of 72 hours beginning with the making of the order[5].

An "authorised person" means a person who is an authorised person for the purposes of s 31 of the Children Act 1989[6].

Where a grave emergency, such as the need for a blood transfusion in respect of a child whose parents oppose such a course on religious grounds, occurs the inherent jurisdiction of the High Court should be invoked. If proceedings in such a case are commenced under the Children Act 1989, they should be transferred to the Family Division as a matter of urgency[7].

In circumstances prescribed by s 46 of the Children Act 1989, a constable may use powers to take a child into police protection without the requirement for a court hearing. The removal of children should usually be effected pursuant to an emergency protection order, police protection should be invoked only where it is not practicable to execute an emergency protection order. In deciding whether it is practicable to execute an emergency protection order, the police must always have regard to the paramount need to protect children from significant harm[8]. Home Office Circular 44/2003 provides that police protection powers should only be used when necessary, the principle being that wherever possible the decision to remove a child from a parent or carer should be made by a court. All local authorities should have in place arrangements (through their local administration and Clerks to the Justices) whereby out of hours applications for emergency protection orders may be made speedily and without an excess of bureaucracy. Police protection powers should only be used when this is not possible[9].

1. Children Act 1989, s 44(1), this PART, post.
2. Children Act 1989, s 44(4), this PART, post.
3. Children Act 1989, s 44(6)–(9), this PART, post.
4. *K and T v Finland* [2001] 2 FCR 673, [2001] 2 FLR 707.
5. Children Act 1989, s 45, this PART, post.
6. Children Act 1989, s 44(2), this PART, post.
7. *Re O (a minor) (Medical Treatment)* [1993] 1 FCR 925. See also *Camden London Borough Council v R (a minor) (Blood Transfusion)* (1993) 137 Sol Jo LB 151.
8. *Langley v Liverpool City Council* [2005] EWCA Civ 1173, [2006] 1 WLR 375, [2005] 3 FCR 303.
9. Approved by Dyson LJ in *Langley v Liverpool City Council*, supra.

6–175A   Emergency protection order: exclusion requirement.   Where, on being satisfied as to sub-paragraphs (*a*), (*b*) or (*c*) in para **6–175** above, the court makes an emergency protection order with respect to a child, the court may include an exclusion requirement in the emergency protection order if the conditions set out below are satisfied[1].
The conditions are—

(*a*)   that there is reasonable cause to believe that, if a person ("the relevant person") is excluded from a dwelling-house in which the child lives, then—

    (i)   in the case of an order made on the ground mentioned in section 44(1)(*a*), the child will not be likely to suffer significant harm, even though the child is not removed as mentioned in section 44(1)(*a*)(i) or does not remain as mentioned in section 44(1)(*a*)(ii), or

    (ii)   in the case of an order made on the ground mentioned in paragraph (*b*) or (*c*) of section 44(1), the enquiries referred to in that paragraph will cease to be frustrated, and

(*b*)   that another person living in the dwelling-house (whether a parent of the child or some other person)—

    (i)   is able and willing to give to the child the care which it would be reasonable to expect a parent to give him, and

    (ii)   consents to the inclusion of the exclusion requirement[2]

An exclusion requirement is any one or more of the following—

(*a*)   a provision requiring the relevant person to leave a dwelling-house in which he is living with the child,

(*b*)   a provision prohibiting the relevant person from entering a dwelling-house in which the child lives, and

(*c*)   a provision excluding the relevant person from a defined area in which a dwelling-house in which the child lives is situated[3].

The court may provide that the exclusion requirement is to have effect for a shorter period than the other provisions of the order[4].
Where the court makes an emergency protection order containing an exclusion requirement, the court may attach a power of arrest to the exclusion requirement[5], and where it does so it may provide that the power of arrest is to have effect for a shorter period than the exclusion requirement[6]. Such a power of arrest enables a constable to arrest without warrant any person whom he has reasonable cause to believe to be in breach of the requirement[7]. Provisions of the Family Law Act 1996[8] are applied and have effect in relation to a person arrested under a power of arrest to an exclusion requirement as they have effect in relation to a person arrested under s 47(6) of that Act[9].
On the application of a person who is not entitled to apply for the emergency protection order to be discharged, but who is a person to whom an exclusion requirement contained in the order applies, the emergency protection order may be varied or discharged by the court in so far as it imposes the exclusion requirement[10]. Where a power of arrest has been attached to an exclusion requirement of an emergency protection order, the court may, on the application of any person entitled to apply for the discharge of the order so far as it imposes the exclusion requirement, vary or discharge the order in so far as it confers a power of arrest[11].
The applicant for the emergency protection order must—

(a)   prepare a separate statement of the evidence in support of the application for an exclusion requirement;

(b) serve the statement personally on the relevant person with a copy of the order containing the exclusion requirement (and of any power of arrest which is attached to it); and

(c) inform the relevant person of his right to apply to vary or discharge the exclusion requirement[12].

Best practice guidelines with respect to an application for an exclusion requirement in connection with either an emergency protection order or an interim care order have been given by Cazalet J[13] and are summarised in paragraph **6–170A** Interim care order: exclusion requirement.

If, while an emergency protection order containing an exclusion requirement is in force, the applicant has removed the child from the dwelling-house from which the relevant person is excluded to other accommodation for a continuous period of more than 24 hours, the order will cease to have effect in so far as it imposes the exclusion requirement[14].

Where in any case the court has power to include an exclusion requirement in an emergency protection order, the court may accept an undertaking from the relevant person, but no power of arrest may be attached to any undertaking. Such an undertaking given to a court shall be enforceable as if it were an order of the court, and shall cease to have effect if, while it is in force, the applicant has removed the child from the dwelling-house from which the relevant person is excluded to other accommodation for a continuous period of more than 24 hours[15].

---

1. Children Act 1989, s 44A(1), this PART, post.
2. Children Act 1989, s 44A(2), this PART, post.
3. Children Act 1989, s 44A(3), this PART, post.
4. Children Act 1989, s 44A(4), this PART, post.
5. Children Act 1989, s 44A(5), this PART, post.
6. Children Act 1989, s 44A(6), this PART, post.
7. Children Act 1989, s 44A(8), this PART, post.
8. Sections 47(7), (11) and (12) and 48 of, and Sch 5 to the Family Law Act 1996, this PART, post, are applied.
9. Children Act 1989, s 44A(9), this PART, post.
10. Children Act 1989, s 45(8A), this PART, post.
11. Children Act 1989, s 45(8B), this PART, post.
12. Family Proceedings Courts (Children Act 1989) Rules 1991, 25A, this PART, post.
13. *W v A local authority (exclusion requirement)* [2000] 2 FCR 662.
14. Children Act 1989, s 44A(10), this PART, post.
15. Children Act 1989, s 44B, this PART, post.

6–175B　Child safety order.

If a family proceedings court, on the application of a local authority, is satisfied that one or more of the conditions referred to below are fulfilled with respect to a child under the age of 10, it may make a child safety order which places the child for a specified period under the supervision of a responsible officer and which requires the child to comply with such requirements as are so specified[1].

Before a child safety order may be made, one or more of the following conditions must be satisfied—

(a) that the child has committed an act which, if he had been aged 10 or over, would have constituted an offence;

(b) that a child safety order is necessary for the purpose of preventing the commission by the child of such an act as is mentioned in paragraph (a) above;

(c) that the child has contravened a ban imposed by a curfew notice; and

(d) that the child has acted in a manner that caused or was likely to cause harassment, alarm or distress to one or more persons not of the same household as himself[2].

The standard of proof in civil proceedings applies[3].

The maximum period permitted for the duration of a child safety order is 3 months or, where the court is satisfied that the circumstances of the case are exceptional, 12 months[4].

The requirements that may be specified in a child safety order are those which the court considers desirable in the interests of—

(i) securing that the child receives appropriate care, protection and support and is subject to proper control; or

(ii) preventing any repetition of the kind of behaviour which led to the child safety order being made[5].

Requirements included in a child safety order must, as far as practicable, be such as to avoid any conflict with the parent's religious beliefs, and any interference with the times, if any, at which the child normally attends school[6].

A court shall not make a child safety order unless it has been notified[7] by the Secretary of State that arrangements for implementing such orders are available in the area in which it appears that the child resides or will reside and the notice has not been withdrawn[8].

Before making a child safety order, a family proceedings court shall obtain and consider information about the child's family circumstances and the likely effect of the order on those circumstances[9]. Moreover, before making such an order the court must also explain to the parent or guardian of the child in ordinary language—

(i) the effect of the order and of the requirements proposed to be included in it;

(ii) the consequences which may follow if the child fails to comply with any of those requirements; and

(iii) that the court has power to review the order on the application either of the parent or guardian or of the responsible officer[10].

If while a child safety order is in force it appears to the court which made it, on the application of the responsible officer or a parent or guardian of the child, that it is appropriate to do so, the court may make an order discharging the child safety order or varying it by cancelling any provision included in it or by inserting in it any provision that could have been included in the order if the court had then had power to make it and were exercising that power[11]. Where an application for the discharge of a child safety order is dismissed, no further application for its discharge shall be made by any person except with the consent of the court which made the order[12].

Where a child safety order is in force and it is proved to the satisfaction of the court which made it or another family proceedings court for the same petty sessions area, on the application of the responsible officer, that the child has failed to comply with any requirement included in the order, the court—

(a) may discharge the order and make in respect of him a care order under s 31(1)(a) of the Children Act 1989[13]; or

(b) make an order varying the order—

(i) by cancelling any provision included in it; or

(ii) by inserting in it any provision that could have been included in the order if the court had then had power to make it and were exercising the power[14].

A care order may be made under paragraph (a) above whether or not the court is satisfied that the conditions mentioned in s 31(2) of the 1989 Act are fulfilled[15].

References above to a "responsible officer", in relation to a child safety order, mean one of the following who is specified in the order, namely: a social worker of a local authority social services department, and a member of a youth offending team[16]. References to "local authority" with respect to child safety orders have the same meaning as in the Children Act 1989[17].

An appeal shall lie to the High Court against the making of a child safety order, and on such an appeal the High Court may make such orders as may be necessary to give effect to its determination of the appeal, and may also make such incidental or consequential orders as appear to it to be just[18].

---

1. Crime and Disorder Act 1998, s 11(1), in PART I: MAGISTRATES' COURT, PROCEDURE, ante.
2. Crime and Disorder Act 1998, s 11(3), in PART I: MAGISTRATES' COURT, PROCEDURE, ante.
3. Crime and Disorder Act 1998, s 11(6), in PART I: MAGISTRATES' COURT, PROCEDURE, ante.
4. Crime and Disorder Act 1998, s 11(4), in PART I: MAGISTRATES' COURT, PROCEDURE, ante.
5. Crime and Disorder Act 1998, s 11(5), in PART I: MAGISTRATES' COURT, PROCEDURE, ante.
6. Crime and Disorder Act 1998, s 12(3), in PART I: MAGISTRATES' COURT, PROCEDURE, ante.
7. All courts in England and Wales were notified by Home Office letter dated 27 April 2000 that arrangements for implementing the child safety order would be available in their area with effect from 1 June 2000.
8. Crime and Disorder Act 1998, s 11(2), in PART I: MAGISTRATES' COURT, PROCEDURE, ante.
9. Crime and Disorder Act 1998, s 12(1), in PART I: MAGISTRATES' COURT, PROCEDURE, ante.
10. Crime and Disorder Act 1998, s 12(2), in PART I: MAGISTRATES' COURT, PROCEDURE, ante.
11. Crime and Disorder Act 1998, s 12(4), in PART I: MAGISTRATES' COURT, PROCEDURE, ante.
12. Crime and Disorder Act 1998, s 12(5), in PART I: MAGISTRATES' COURT, PROCEDURE, ante.
13. See this PART, post.
14. Crime and Disorder Act 1998, s 12(6), in PART I: MAGISTRATES' COURT, PROCEDURE, ante.
15. Crime and Disorder Act 1998, s 12(7), in PART I: MAGISTRATES' COURT, PROCEDURE, ante.
16. Crime and Disorder Act 1998, s 11(8), in PART I: MAGISTRATES' COURT, PROCEDURE, ante.
17. Crime and Disorder Act 1998, s 11(7), in PART I: MAGISTRATES' COURT, PROCEDURE, ante.
18. Crime and Disorder Act 1998, s 13, in PART I: MAGISTRATES' COURT, PROCEDURE, ante.

Reciprocal enforcement

6–176 Scope and general principles. Provision for the enforcement of maintenance orders between countries within the United Kingdom is made by the Maintenance Orders Act 1950 and the Domestic Proceedings and Magistrates' Courts Act 1978 and the Children Act 1989 to which reference should be made. Enforcement of maintenance orders with Foreign and Commonwealth countries and countries in the European Union is provided for by three statutes: the Maintenance Orders (Facilities for Enforcement) Act 1920, the Maintenance Orders (Reciprocal Enforcement) Act 1972 and the Civil Jurisdiction and Judgments Act 1982.

The Maintenance Orders (Facilities for Enforcement) Act 1920 applies to some Commonwealth countries but has been superseded in respect of those countries which have subsequently been designated as reciprocating countries for the purposes of Part I of the 1972 Act[1]. In such cases transitional provisions have been made by the Reciprocal Enforcement of Maintenance Orders (Designation of Reciprocating Countries) Order 1974 as amended[2] which applies the provisions of Part I of the 1972 Act to such orders.

The Maintenance Orders (Reciprocal Enforcement) Act 1972 Part I applies to countries designated by Order in Council made under s 1 of the Act where the law in the foreign state applies similar benefits in respect of maintenance orders made by courts in the United Kingdom as will be applied under the Act to maintenance orders made in that country[3]. Part II applies to those countries which are signatories to the United Nations Convention of the Recovery Abroad of Maintenance done at New York on 20th June 1956[4]. In addition the provisions of the Act may be extended to other countries by Order made under s 40. Orders have been made applying the provisions of

Part I of the Act (with modifications) to the Republic of Ireland[5], countries which are signatories to the Convention on the Recognition and Enforcement of Decisions Relating to Maintenance Obligations concluded at The Hague on 2nd October 1973[6] and certain States of the United States of America[7]. Part II of the Act is applied (with modifications) to certain States of the United States of America by the Recovery of Maintenance (United States of America) Order 1993[8].

The Civil Jurisdiction and Judgments Act 1982 gives effect to the Brussels Convention 1968 and the Lugano Convention 1988 which, with their attendant Protocols and additional Conventions on the accession of further states to the 1968 and 1988 Conventions, make provision for jurisdiction and enforcement of judgments in civil and commercial matters which include the recognition and enforcement of maintenance orders[9]. The Conventions have the force of law in the United Kingdom and judicial notice is to be taken of them[10]. The Brussels Convention was concluded to further implement the provisions of Article 220 of the Treaty establishing the European Economic Community by securing the simplification of formalities governing the reciprocal recognition and enforcement of judgments by courts and tribunals. The Lugano Convention was concluded to achieve a similar effect but including members of the European Free Trade Association.

---

1. Maintenance Orders (Reciprocal Enforcement) Act 1972, s 24, this PART, post.
2. This PART, post.
3. Maintenance Orders (Reciprocal Enforcement) Act 1972, s 1, this PART, post. The Reciprocal Enforcement of Maintenance Orders (Designation of Reciprocating Countries) Orders 1974 to 2001, this PART, post, have been made.
4. Maintenance Orders (Reciprocal Enforcement) Act 1972, s 25, this PART, post.
5. Reciprocal Enforcement of Maintenance Orders (Republic of Ireland) Order 1993, this PART, post.
6. Reciprocal Enforcement of Maintenance Orders (Hague Convention Countries) Order 1993, this PART, post.
7. Reciprocal Enforcement of Maintenance Orders (United States of America) Order 1995, this PART, post.
8. This PART, post.
9. See the Preamble to the Brussels and Lugano Conventions in Sch 1 to the Civil Jurisdiction and Judgments Act 1982, this PART, post.
10. Civil Jurisdiction and Judgements Act 1982, ss 2 and 3A, this PART, post.

6-177   In proceedings under the Maintenance Orders (Facilities for Enforcement Act 1920 and Part I of the Maintenance Orders (Reciprocal Enforcement) Act 1972, the law applicable to the proceedings before the court is that of England and Wales. Where there is already an order in existence between the parties, for example where both parties were at one time habitually resident in England and Wales and one party has subsequently left the jurisdiction, the order may be transmitted to the reciprocating country for registration and enforcement. However, the making of a new order under Part I is a two stage process. The court in the country where the applicant resides may determine to make a provisional order. This is transmitted to the reciprocating country where the court there may determine whether to confirm the order.

Orders made under s 40 of the 1972 Act apply the provisions of Part I of the Act with such exceptions, adaptations and modifications as may be specified in the order[1].

In respect of the Republic of Ireland, Part I of the 1972 Act as amended by the Reciprocal Enforcement (Republic of Ireland) Order 1993 Sch 1[2] applies a modified procedure in that the court which makes the provisional order transmits the prescribed documentation by way of the Lord Chancellor's Department to the responsible authority in Ireland for service on the respondent. The respondent may make representations and adduce evidence to the court which made the provisional order before it determines whether or not to confirm the provisional order.

For Hague Convention countries the procedure is modified by Sch 2 to the Reciprocal Enforcement of Maintenance (Hague Convention Countries) Order 1993[3]. The court to which application is made will adjourn the proceedings so that notice of the proceedings and prescribed documentation may be sent by way of the Lord Chancellor's Department to the responsible authority in the country in which the respondent is habitually resident. No provisional order is made. The respondent is enabled to submit a defence and accompanying documentation to the court in which proceedings were commenced and the court will consider the whole case before determining whether to make an order.

In the case of American States which are designated by the Reciprocal Enforcement of Maintenance Orders (United States of America) Order 1995 for the purposes of Part I of the 1972 Act, applications may be made under the provisions of Part I as modified by Sch 2 to transmit maintenance orders for enforcement. Such orders when registered may also be varied or revoked. However, no provision is made for the making of new orders where one of the parties is outside the jurisdiction of the court. In such cases a claim for recovery of maintenance must be made under Part II of the 1972 Act which is available only in respect of those States specified in the Reciprocal Enforcement of Maintenance Orders (United States of America) Order 1993[4].

In the case of countries to which the provisions of Part II of the Act apply, procedure is by way of transmission of a written form of claim to the relevant United Nations country or American State. The applicable law is that of the Convention country. The procedure and appropriate forms of claim are set out in the Magistrates' Courts (Recovery Abroad of Maintenance) Rules 1975 and Home Office Circular 54/1975[4].

---

1. Maintenance Orders (Reciprocal Enforcement) Act 1972, s 40, this PART, post.
2. Part I of the 1972 Act as modified, is set out in Sch 2 to the Order, in this PART, post.
3. Part I of the 1972 Act as modified, is set out in Sch 3 to the Order, in this PART, post.
4. In this PART, post.

6-178   **Choice of procedure.**   More than one statutory scheme may be applicable to a country. Australia, Cyprus and New Zealand, which are reciprocating countries under Part I of the 1972 Act, are also designated for formal reasons as Convention countries under Part II. Courts are advised strongly in these cases to use the procedure under Part I[1].

The Hague Convention countries are also signatories to the United Nations Convention on the Recovery Abroad of Maintenance. Therefore, the reciprocal enforcement of maintenance with these countries will be possible under either Part I or Part II of the 1972 Act. Home Office Circular 15/ 1980 gives the following guidance:

"So far as proceedings initiated by a complainant in a Hague Convention country are concerned, the documents received from the authorities in that country will indicate which procedure is being followed and will govern the manner in which the case is dealt with in this country. However, where a complainant in this country wishes to proceed against a defendant in a Hague Convention country, a choice will exist. Normally, courts will probably find it quicker and more straightforward to proceed under the new Hague Convention arrangements (that is, by making an order and transmitting it to the other country concerned for recognition and enforcement) than to rely on the earlier United Nations Convention arrangements (which entail the transmission of a claim for determination by a foreign court). There may, however, be some circumstances in which it could be to the complainant's advantage still to use the United Nations Convention, where, for example, leaving the order to be made in a country with a higher standard of living could lead to its being made for a higher amount than would be ordered in this country."

There is also an overlap between the provisions of the Maintenance Orders (Reciprocal Enforcement) Act 1972 and the Civil Judgments and Jurisdiction Act 1982. In deciding which procedure to adopt, it may be borne in mind that the 1972 Act only applies in respect of orders for maintenance whereas the 1982 Act additionally encompasses orders in respect of any assets so that, for example, lump sum orders may be made. Furthermore, the 1982 Act makes no provision for the variation of orders.

---

1. Lord Chancellor's Department Letter dated 20 August 1996.

6–179   Obtaining and the admissibility of evidence.   In proceedings for reciprocal enforcement and claims for the recovery of maintenance provision is made for statements which have been duly authenticated and which purport to set out or summarise evidence given in proceedings in a foreign country to be admissible in a court in the United Kingdom to the same extent as oral evidence of the facts contained therein is admissible[1].

---

1. Maintenance Orders (Facilities for Enforcement) Act 1920, s 9 (depositions); Maintenance Orders (Reciprocal Enforcement) Act 1972, s 13 (proceedings under Part I), s 36 (proceedings under Part II); Reciprocal Enforcement (Hague Convention Countries Order) 1993, Sch 2; Reciprocal Enforcement (Republic of Ireland) Order 1993, Sch 1; Reciprocal Enforcement (United States of America) Order 1995, Sch 2, all this PART, post.

6–180   Legal Aid.   Representation under the Community Legal Service may only be granted in respect of proceedings under Part I of the Maintenance Orders (Reciprocal Enforcement) Act 1972[1].

Representation before a court is only relevant to reciprocal enforcement proceedings, nevertheless representation is not available for proceedings under the Maintenance Orders (Facilities for Enforcement) Act 1920.

Claims for the recovery of maintenance under the United Nations Convention are by way of written application and justices' chief executives are required to assist the applicant in completing an application to ensure that the application will comply with the law as applied by the convention country and that the required documentation is completed[2]. Justices' chief executives have been provided with specimen forms of application[3].

---

1. Access to Justice Act 1999, Sch 2 para 2 (3)(b), in PART I : MAGITRATES' COURTS, PROCEDURE, ante.
2. Maintenance Orders (Reciprocal Enforcement) Act 1972, s 26(3), in this PART, post.
3. HOC 54/1975, appended to the Magistrates' Courts (Recovery Abroad of Maintenance) Rules 1975, in this PART, post.

6–182   Maintenance Orders (Facilities for Enforcement) Act 1920[1].   The provisions of the Act extend to the following countries[2]:

Antigua;	Jamaica;
Bahamas;	*Jersey;
Belize;	Montserrat;
Botswana;	Nigeria;
British Solomon Islands Protectorate;	Seychelles;
Canada *Newfoundland and Prince Edward Island;	Sri Lanka;
*Yukon Territory	
Cayman Islands;	Sierra Leone;
*Christmas Island (Indian Ocean);	St Christopher and Nevis;
*Cocos (Keeling) Islands;	St. Lucia;
Cyprus;	St Vincent;
Dominica;	Swaziland Protectorate;
Gambia;	Trinidad and Tobago;
Gilbert and Ellis Islands;	Uganda;
Grenada;	Virgin Islands;
*Guernsey;	Zambia;
Guyana;	Zanzibar.

In respect of places marked with an asterisk, money when collected shall be paid to the court from which the order originally issued; where not so marked money collected shall be paid to the Crown Agents for Overseas

Governments and Administrations for transmission to the person to whom it is due (see r 6 of the Maintenance Orders (Facilities for Enforcement) Rules 1922).

---

1. This Act will remain in force for, and only for, the Commonwealth countries which are not designated as a reciprocating country under Pt I of the Maintenance Orders (Reciprocal Enforcement) Act 1972.
2. Maintenance Orders (Facilities for Enforcement) Act 1920, s 12, in this PART, post.

6–183   Enforcement of order made in Commonwealth country.   Where the Lord Chancellor[1] has received a certified copy of a maintenance order made in a Commonwealth country to which the Act extends[2] he shall send a copy of the order to the prescribed officer of a court for registration. Thereafter, proceedings may be taken on such order as if it had been an order originally obtained in the court in which it is registered[3].

A maintenance order is an order other than an affiliation order for the periodical payment of sums of money for the maintenance of a wife or other dependants of the defendant ie persons whom he is liable to maintain[4]. An adopter is liable to maintain adopted children[5]. An order made in a court of superior jurisdiction will be registered in the Family Division of the High Court[6], an order of an inferior court will be registered in a magistrates' court for the division in which the defendant is living[7].

The justices' chief executive must enter it in his court register on the date when he receives it, showing that it is entered in pursuance of the Act[8]. The court shall, unless satisfied that it is undesirable to do so, direct that all payments due thereunder shall be made through an officer of the court, or such other person as it may specify for the purpose. No application is required[9]. The court may direct that payments are to be made by a particular means which shall be recorded on the order[10]. An order registered under s 1 of the Act has full retrospective effect from the date specified in the original order, or, if no such date is specified, from the date of the order[11].

Registration is an administrative act, against which the defendant cannot show cause; neither can the defendant appeal against the registration, nor, by reason thereof, against the order itself[12].

---

1. References in the Act to the Secretary of State are to be construed as references to the Lord Chancellor: SI 1992/709, art 4(1).
2. For countries to which the Act extends, see para **6–182**.
3. Maintenance Orders (Facilities for Enforcement) Act 1920, s 1(1), this PART, post.
4. Maintenance Orders (Facilities for Enforcement) Act 1920, s 10, this PART, post.
5. *Coventry Corpn v Surrey County Council* [1935] AC 199, 98 JP 401.
6. Maintenance Orders (Facilities for Enforcement) Act 1920, s 1(2), this PART, post.
7. Maintenance Orders (Facilities for Enforcement) Act 1920, s 1(2), this PART, post and the Maintenance Orders (Facilities for Enforcement) Rules 1922, r 1, this PART, post.
8. Maintenance Orders (Facilities for Enforcement) Rules 1922, r 3, this PART, post.
9. Maintenance Orders (Facilities for Enforcement) Rules 1922, r 5, this PART, post.
10. Maintenance Orders (Facilities for Enforcement) Rules 1922, r 5A, this PART, post.
11. Home Office Circular, 469, 726/4, dated 15th June 1925.
12. *Pilcher v Pilcher* [1955] P 318, [1955] 2 All ER 644, [1955] 3 WLR 231.

6–184   Transmission of an order made in England and Wales for enforcement in a Commonwealth Country.   Where a maintenance order has been made against a person and it is proved to that court that the person against whom the order has been made is resident in a Commonwealth Country to which the Act extends[1], the court shall send to the Lord Chancellor[2] a certified copy[3] of the order for transmission to the governor of the relevant country[4]. Information sufficient for ascertaining the whereabouts of the defendant and for his identification, including his last known address, a personal description and a photograph if one is available, should be annexed to the depositions, together with a certificate of marriage and, where provision is made for the maintenance of a child, a certificate of birth of the child. The name and address of the justices' chief executive should be notified and there should also be sent a sworn statement of arrears due under the order[5].

---

1. For the countries to which the Act extends see para **6–182**.
2. References in the Act to the Secretary of State are to be construed as references to the Lord Chancellor: SI 1992/709, art 4(1).
3. "Certified copy" means a copy of the order certified by the proper officer of the court to be a true copy: Maintenance Orders (Facilities for Enforcement) Act 1920, s 10, this PART, post.
4. Maintenance Orders (Facilities for Enforcement) Act 1920, s 2, this PART, post.
5. Home Office Circular, 469, 726/4, dated 15 June 1925.

6–185   Proceedings for a provisional maintenance order.   Where application is made to a magistrates' court for a maintenance order against a person who is proved to be resident in a Commonwealth country to which the Act extends[1], the court may, if after hearing the evidence it is satisfied of the justice of the application, make such order as it might have made if the person had been resident in England and Wales. Such order will be provisional and of no effect until confirmed by a competent court in the relevant Commonwealth country[2].

No form of application under the Maintenance Orders (Facilities for Enforcement) Act 1920 is prescribed. We would suggest that the form of application in the Family Proceedings Courts (Matrimonial Proceedings etc) Rules 1991[3] (maintenance for a spouse) or the Family Proceedings Courts (Children Act 1989) Rules 1991[4] (maintenance for a child) are used as appropriate. Application is to a family proceedings court[5].

Application must be made to a family proceedings court with jurisdiction; in a matrimonial case the jurisdiction is as stated in s 30(1) of the Domestic Proceedings and Magistrates' Courts Act 1978[6]. A family proceedings court would have jurisdiction where the applicant resided within the commission area for which the court acts even if the cause of application arose wholly outside the area of that court and even outside England and Wales altogether[7].

Rules of procedure are prescribed by the Schedule to the Maintenance Orders (Facilities for Enforcement) Rules 1922[8] which make provision analogous to that in the Family Proceedings Courts (Matrimonial Proceedings etc) Rules 1991[9] and the Family Proceedings Courts (Children Act 1989) Rules 1991[10] and include the power to transfer proceedings to another magistrates' court[11], service of documents[12], the making of directions for the conduct of proceedings[13], filing of documentary evidence[14] and the reading of documents that have been filed by the justices in advance of the hearing[15]. The evidence of any witness who is examined on any application shall be put into writing and such deposition shall be read over to and signed by him[16]. We would suggest that any statements filed with the court should be exhibited to the deposition. Before the court makes a provisional order or refuses an application, the clerk, in consultation with the justices, shall record the reasons for the court's decision and any findings of fact[15]. The justices' chief executive may delegate his functions under the Act to any person appointed by the Magistrates' Courts Committee to assist him[17].

1. For the countries to which the Act extends see para **6–182**.
2. Maintenance Orders (Facilities for Enforcement) Act 1920, s 3(1), this PART, post.
3. This PART, post.
4. This PART, post.
5. Magistrates' Courts Act 1980, s 65, in PART I; MAGISTRATES' COURTS, PROCEDURE, ante.
6. This PART, post.
7. See *Collister v Collister* [1972] 1 All ER 334, [1972] 1 WLR 54, 136 JP 163.
8. This PART, post.
9. This PART, post.
10. This PART, post.
11. Maintenance Orders (Facilities for Enforcement) Rules 1922, Schedule, para 2, this PART, post.
12. Maintenance Orders (Facilities for Enforcement) Rules 1922, Schedule, para 3, this PART, post.
13. Maintenance Orders (Facilities for Enforcement) Rules 1922, Schedule, para 4, this PART, post.
14. Maintenance Orders (Facilities for Enforcement) Rules 1922, Schedule, para 7, this PART, post.
15. Maintenance Orders (Facilities for Enforcement) Rules 1922, Schedule, para 10 this PART, post.
16. Maintenance Orders (Facilities for Enforcement) Act 1920, s 3(2), this PART, post.
17. Maintenance Orders (Facilities for Enforcement) Rules 1922, Schedule, para 12, this PART, post.

6–186 Where a provisional order has been made, the court shall send to the Lord Chancellor the depositions and any exhibited statements, a certified copy of the order and a statement of the grounds on which the making of the order might have been opposed and such information as the court possesses for facilitating the identification of that person and ascertaining his whereabouts[1].

A form of statement of the grounds on which an application may have been opposed is advised in Home Office Circular 469, 726/4, dated 15th June 1925, and 86 JP 225. If a dependant is an adopted child one of the grounds will be that no valid adoption order exists. It should be signed by one of the adjudicating justices.

Information sufficient for ascertaining the whereabouts of the defendant and for his identification, including his last known address, a personal description, and a photograph if one is available, should be annexed to the depositions, together with a certificate of marriage, and, where provision is made for the maintenance of a child, a certificate of birth of the child. The name and address of the justices' chief executive should be notified[2].

1. Maintenance Orders (Facilities for Enforcement) Act 1920, s 3(3), this PART, post.
2. Home Office Circular, 469, 726/4, dated 15th June 1925.

6–187 Taking further evidence. A Commonwealth country to which the Act extends[1], may, on receipt of a provisional order, remit the proceedings to the court which made the order for the purpose of taking further evidence. Any family proceedings court for the commission area of the court which made the provisional order may, after giving proper notice to the applicant, proceed to take such evidence in like manner as the evidence in support of the original application[2].

If it appears to the court that the order should not have been made, it may revoke the order[2]. Otherwise any deposition should be transmitted to the Lord Chancellor[3].

1. For countries to which the Act extends, see para **6–182**.
2. Maintenance Orders (Facilities for Enforcement) Act 1920, s 3(4), this PART, post.
3. References in the Act to the Secretary of State are to be construed as reference to the Lord Chancellor: SI 1992/709, art 4(1).

6–188 Application for provisional order: procedural steps

Procedure	Statutory Provision[1]
Application for maintenance order	(FPC (CA 1989), R 1991 Forms 1 and 10 (amended as appropriate) FPC (MP) R 1991 Form 1 (amended as appropriate)
File with the court	s 3(1)
Justices' clerk to fix directions appointment and the justices' chief executive to notify applicant of date, time and place so fixed	r 6A(3)
(Before the hearing or appointment)	
Applicant to file:	Rules Sch, para 7(1)
—written statements of the substance of the oral evidence which he intends to adduce at a hearing or directions appointment, which shall:	

Procedure	Statutory Provision[1]
(i) be dated;	
(ii) be signed by the person making the statement;	
(iii) contain a declaration that the maker of the statement believes it to be true and understands that it may be placed before the court, and	
(iv) show in the top right hand corner of the first page	
(*a*) the initials and surname of the person making the statement,	
(*b*) the number of the statement in relation to the maker,	
(*c*) the date on which the statement was made, and	
(*d*) the party on whose behalf it is filed.	
—copies of any documents upon which he intends to rely at a hearing or directions appointment	Rules Sch, para 10(1)
Justices to read any statements filed before the hearing	
(At the hearing)	
Applicant to prove respondent resident in commonwealth country to which the Act extends	
—evidence of applicant to be taken in form of deposition, read over to, and signed by him.	s 3(2)
Court determines whether to	
—make provisional order	
—refuse the application	
Justices' clerk or court to keep note of any oral evidence given at the hearing	Rules Sch, para 9
(Before the court makes an order or refuses an application)	
Justices' clerk in consultation with the justices to record names of justices and their reasons in writing	
(After the hearing)	
Justices' clerk to make a written record of any order	Rules Sch, para 10(5)
Justices' chief executive to send to the Lord Chancellor's Department:	s 3(3)
—depositions that have been taken	HOC 469, 726/4 1925
—certified copy of the order	
—statement of grounds on which the making of the order might have been opposed	
—information as to the whereabouts of respondent including last known address	
—description and photograph of respondent	
—certificate of marriage —certificate of birth of child } as appropriate	

---

1. Unless otherwise stated, references are to the Maintenance Orders (Facilities for Enforcement) Act 1920 and the Maintenance Orders (Facilities for Enforcement) Rules 1922, this Part, post.

6–189 Confirming a provisional order made out of the United Kingdom. The Lord Chancellor[1] may by notice served by post[2] require the prescribed officer of a court for the area in which a person is living against whom a provisional order for maintenance has been made in a Commonwealth country to which the Act extends[3] to serve notice that he may attend a hearing to show cause why the order should not be confirmed[4].

At the hearing the respondent may oppose the confirmation of the order on any grounds on which he might have opposed the making of the order in the original proceedings but on no other grounds[5].

The court may, as a result of the hearing, confirm the order without modification or with such modifications as to the court may seem just[6]. Where the respondent appears at the hearing and satisfies the court that it is necessary for the purpose of establishing any ground on which he opposes the confirmation of the order, the case may be remitted to the court which made the provisional order for the taking of any further evidence[7].

Unless the order was made by a court of superior jurisdiction, a certified copy of the provisional order, together with the deposition of witnesses and a statement of the grounds on which the order might have been opposed will be sent to the justices' chief executive for the court for the area in which the respondent is living[8]. On receipt of the order the justices' chief executive will send to the respondent a certified copy of the order and copies of the accompanying documents and a notice of hearing[9]. The justices' chief executive shall also enter the order in the court register on the date on which it is received and such entry shall show that it was received in pursuance of the Act[10].

Where a provisional order has been confirmed, with or without modification, or the court has decided not to confirm it, the court shall send notice to the court from which it issued and to the Lord Chancellor[11].

Although confirmation of a provisional order can only be opposed on grounds on which the respondent might have opposed the making of the order in the original proceedings had he been a party to them, the certificate from the court which made the provisional order of the grounds on which the order might have been opposed is conclusive evidence of those grounds[12] but not exclusive of any other grounds[13]. Accordingly the certificate does not prevent the person to whom notice has been given from raising any defence not included in those grounds[13], for example, that the court had no jurisdiction to make the order[14].

---

1. References in the Act to the Secretary of State are to be construed as references to the Lord Chancellor: SI 1992/709, art 4(1).

2. Maintenance Orders (Facilities for Enforcement) Act 1920, s 4(2), this PART, post.
3. For countries to which the Act extends, see para **6–182**.
4. Maintenance Orders (Facilities for Enforcement) Act 1920, s 4(1), this PART, post.
5. Maintenance Orders (Facilities for Enforcement) Act 1920, s 4(3), this PART, post.
6. Maintenance Orders (Facilities for Enforcement) Act 1920, s 4(4), this PART, post.
7. Maintenance Orders (Facilities for Enforcement) Act 1920, s 4(5), this PART, post.
8. Maintenance Orders (Facilities for Enforcement) Act 1920, s 4(1); Maintenance Orders (Facilities for Enforcement) Rules 1922, r 1, this PART, post.
9. Maintenance Orders (Facilities for Enforcement) Rules 1922, r 2A, this PART, post.
10. Maintenance Orders (Facilities for Enforcement) Rules 1922, r 3, this PART, post.
11. Maintenance Orders (Facilities for Enforcement) Rules 1922, r 4, this PART, post.
12. Maintenance Orders (Facilities for Enforcement) Act 1920, s 4(3), this PART, post.
13. *Re Wheat* [1932] 2 KB 716, [1932] All ER Rep 48, 96 JP 399.
14. *Harris v Harris* [1949] 2 All ER 318, 113 JP 495, 64 TLR 519.

6–190 Procedure. Rules of procedure are prescribed by the Schedule to the Maintenance Orders (Facilities for Enforcement) Rules 1922[1] which make provision analogous to that in the Family Proceedings Courts (Matrimonial Proceedings etc) Rules 1991[1] and the Family Proceedings Courts (Children Act 1989) Rules 1991[1] and include the power to transfer proceedings to another magistrates' court[2], service of documents[3], the making of directions for the conduct of proceedings[4], filing of documentary evidence[5] and the reading of documents that have been filed by the justices in advance of the hearing[6]. The evidence of any witness who is examined on any application shall be put into writing and such deposition shall be read over to and signed by him[7]. We would suggest that any statements filed with the court should be exhibited to the deposition. Before the court makes a provisional order or refuses an application, the clerk, in consultation with the justices, shall record the reasons for the court's decision and any findings of fact[8]. The justices' chief executive may delegate his functions under the Act to any person appointed by the Magistrates' Courts Committee to assist him[9].

1. This PART, post.
2. Maintenance Orders (Facilities for Enforcement) Rules 1922, Schedule para 2, this PART, post.
3. Maintenance Orders (Facilities for Enforcement) Rules 1922, Schedule para 3, this PART, post.
4. Maintenance Orders (Facilities for Enforcement) Rules 1922, Schedule para 4, this PART, post.
5. Maintenance Orders (Facilities for Enforcement) Rules 1922, Schedule para 7, this PART, post.
6. Maintenance Orders (Facilities for Enforcement) Rules 1922, Schedule para 10, this PART, post.
7. Maintenance Orders (Facilities for Enforcement) Act 1920, s 3(2), this PART, post.
8. Maintenance Orders (Facilities for Enforcement) Rules 1922, Schedule para 10, this PART, post.
9. Maintenance Orders (Facilities for Enforcement) Rules 1922, Schedule para 12, this PART, post.

6–191 Confirming a provisional order: procedural steps[1]

Procedure	Statutory Provision (1)
Certified copy of order, depositions of witnesses, grounds on which order might have been opposed and requisition for notice of hearing received by justices' chief executive	s 4(1)
	r 2
Justices' chief executive records receipt of provisional order in court register on date it is received	r 3
Justices' clerk fixes time and place of hearing	s 4 (1)
	s 4 (1)(2)
Notice if hearing served by post on person against whom provisional order made together with certified copies of the order and accompanying documents	r 2A
Justices' chief executive or the court gives consideration to the need to give directions for the conduct of the proceedings	Rules Sch, para 4
(Before the hearing or appointment)	
Payer to file before the hearing or appointment:	Rules Sch, para 7(1)
—written statements of the substance of the oral evidence which he intends to adduce at a hearing or directions appointment, which shall:	
(i) be dated;	
(ii) be signed by the person making the statement;	
(iii) contain a declaration that the maker of the statement believes it to be true and understands that it may be placed before the court, and	
(iv) show in the top right hand corner of the first page	
(*a*) the initials and surname of the person making the statement,	
(*b*) the number of the statement in relation to the maker,	
(*c*) the date on which the statement was made, and	
(*d*) the party on whose behalf it is filed.	
—copies of any documents upon which he intends to rely at a hearing or directions appointment	
Justices to read any statements filed before the hearing	Rules Sch, Para 10(1)
(At the hearing)	
Court determines whether to confirm the order either without modification or with such modification as appears just; or	s 4(4)
—remit the case to the original court for further evidence	s 4(5)

Procedure	Statutory Provision (1)
—refuse to confirm the order	
Justices' clerk or court to keep note of any oral evidence given at the hearing	Rules Sch, para 9
Court specifies method of payment which is recorded on the order and notice sent to payer	s 4(5A)–(5C)
	r 5A
Order for payment modified so as to make the amount payable in sterling	HOC 469, 726/4, 1925
(Before the court makes an order or refuses an application)	
Justices' clerk in consultation with the justices to record names of justices and their reasons in writing	Rules Sch, para 10(4)
(After the hearing)	
Justices' clerk to make a written record of any order	Rules Sch, para 10(5)
Justices' chief executive to send notification of confirmation, modification or non-confirmation to court from which it issued and to Lord Chancellor	r 4

1. Unless otherwise stated, references are to the Maintenance Orders (Facilities for Enforcement) Act 1920 and the Maintenance Orders (Facilities for Enforcement) Rules 1922, this PART, post.

6–192   Terms of payment. Where a court registers an order[1] or confirms a provisional order[2] it shall make one of the following orders as to payment having regard to any representations made by the person liable to make payments:

— order that payments be made directly to the justices' chief executive of that or any other magistrates' court;
— order that payments be made to the justices' chief executive by such method falling within section 59(6) of the Magistrates' Courts Act 1980 (standing order, etc)[3] as may be specified;
— make an attachment of earnings order.

An order for payment in currency other than sterling should be modified so as to make the amount payable in sterling[4].

1. Maintenance Orders (Facilities for Enforcement) Act 1920, s 1(1), and the Maintenance Orders (Facilities for Enforcement) Rules 1922, r 5, this PART, ante.
2. Maintenance Orders (Facilities for Enforcement) Act 1920, s 4(5A)–(5C), this PART, post.
3. In PART I: MAGISTRATES' COURTS, PROCEDURE, ante.
4. Home Office Circular 469, 726/4, dated 15 June 1925.

6–193   Appeal against the making of a provisional order. Where a provisional order has been confirmed, the person bound by the order has the same right of appeal against the confirmation of the order as he would have had against the making of the order had the order been an order made by the confirming court[1].

On appeal, the court may reverse the confirmation on the basis that the ground for making a matrimonial order according to the law of the Commonwealth country in question was not established. Appeal lies to a Divisional Court of the Family Division in accordance with the rules of the Supreme Court[2], appeal by case stated against a determination of justices regarding the enforcement of an order confirmed or registered under this Act lies to the same court[1].

1. Maintenance Orders (Facilities for Enforcement) Act 1920, s 4(7), this PART, post.
2. In PART I: MAGISTRATES' COURTS PROCEDURE, ante.

6–193A   Enforcement. A maintenance order which has been registered or a provisional maintenance order which has been confirmed under the Act where it is of such a nature that, if it were made by the court in which it is registered or by which it were confirmed, would be enforceable as a magistrates' court maintenance order, shall be so enforceable[1].

The person through whom the payments are directed to be made shall collect the moneys due under the order in the same manner as though it were a magistrates' court maintenance order, and may take proceedings in his own name for enforcing payment and shall send the moneys, when so collected, to the court from which the order originally issued or otherwise as that court or the Lord Chancellor may direct[2]. Provided that if the court from which the order originally issued is in Malta or in a colony not possessing responsible government, or in a British Protectorate, the moneys so collected shall be paid to the Crown Agents for Overseas Governments and Administrations for transmission to the person to whom they are due. Where Crown Agents do not act for the countries concerned, remittances cannot be made through them and must be sent to the court from which the order originally issued.

1. Maintenance Orders (Facilities for Enforcement) Act 1920, s 6(2), this PART, post.
2. Maintenance Orders (Facilities for Enforcement) Rules 1922, r 6, this PART, post.

6–194   Variation and revocation of maintenance orders. Although in the case of an order made in a Commonwealth country and *registered* under the Act in the United Kingdom, all proceedings may be taken on such order as if it had been an order originally obtained in the court in which it is registered[1], this does not enable an application to be maintained in a court in the United Kingdom for the variation or discharge of such an order[2].

In the case of a *provisional* order which has been confirmed against a person either resident in England or Wales, or in favour of a person living in England or Wales, the party living in England and Wales may apply to a family proceedings court to vary or revoke the order if the court would have had jurisdiction had the respondent been living in England and Wales[3].

No form of application is prescribed but we would suggest that the appropriate forms in the Family Proceedings Courts (Matrimonial Proceedings) Rules 1991[4] and the Family Proceedings Courts (Children Act 1989) Rules 1991[5] are used.

---

1. Maintenance Orders (Facilities for Enforcement) Act 1920, s 1(1), this PART, post.
2. *Pilcher v Pilcher* [1955] P 318, [1955] 2 All ER 644, 119 JP 458; *R v Rose, ex p McGibbon* (1959) 123 JP 374.
3. Maintenance Orders (Facilities for Enforcement) Act 1920, ss 3(5) and 4A (UK order confirmed in Commonwealth country); ss 4(6) and 4A (Commonwealth order confirmed in UK), this PART, post.
4. This PART, post.
5. This PART, post.

6–195 Maintenance Orders (Reciprocal Enforcement) Act 1972, Part I: Reciprocating Countries. The provisions of Part I of the Act[1] extend to the following countries designated by Order under s 1[2].

‡Anguilla	‡Falkland Islands and Dependencies
Australia	‡Fiji
Australian Capital Territory	*‡Ghana
New South Wales	‡Gibraltar
Queensland	‡Hong Kong
South Australia	Isle of Man
Tasmania	*India
Victoria	*‡Kenya
Western Australia	Malta
‡Barbados	Nauru
‡Bermuda	New Zealand
Brunei Darussalam	Norfolk Island
Canada	*Papua New Guinea
*Alberta	‡St. Helena
*British Columbia	*South Africa
†Manitoba	‡Singapore
*New Brunswick	*‡Turks and Caicos Islands
Newfoundland and Labrador	*‡Tanzania (except Zanzibar)
*Northwest Territories	*Zimbabwe
*Nova Scotia	
Nunavut	
*Ontario	
*Sasketchewan	

*   Reciprocating countries to which documents are transmitted via the Secretary of State.
†   Courts in Manitoba and Ontario require a photocopy of the relevant domestic legislation with the provisional maintenance order; the certificate referred to at s 3(5)(c) of the 1972 Act is no longer sufficient.
‡   Countries and territories in which sums are payable through Crown Agents for Overseas Governments and Administrations.

Reciprocating countries are designated by Orders in Council made under s 1 of the Maintenance Orders (Reciprocal Enforcement) Act, s 1[2]. These should be referred to because, in some instances, they effect substantial modifications to the Act in relation to its operation for the particular countries.

¥   As a consequence of the centralisation of child support cases under the Australian Child Support Agency, Australia became a party to the Hague Convention which is regarded as more versatile than its agreements with the United Kingdom and other European countries. As a result of the changes, Australia can no longer deal with applications from the United Kingdom for confirmation of provisional orders[3].

---

1. This PART, post.
2. See the Reciprocal Enforcement of Maintenance Orders (Designation of Reciprocating Countries) Orders 1974, SI 1974/556, SI 1975/2187, SI 1979/115, SI 1983/1125, SI 2001/3501 and SI 2002/788, this PART, post.
3. See LCD Letter 209/2002, 16 December 2002.

6–196 Reciprocating countries designated by Orders under s 40. Three orders have been made which apply the provisions of Part I of the Act (with modifications contained in the respective Orders) to:

—   countries which are signatories to the Hague Convention on the Recognition and Enforcement of Decisions Relating to Maintenance Obligations concluded at The Hague on the 2nd October 1973[1];

—   certain states of the United States of America[2];
—   the Republic of Ireland[3]

---

1. Reciprocal Enforcement of Maintenance Orders (Hague Convention Countries) Order 1993, in this PART, post.
2. The Recovery of Maintenance (United States of America) Order 1993 and the Reciprocal Enforcement (United States of America) Order 1995, both in this PART, post.
3. The Reciprocal Enforcement of Maintenance Orders (Republic of Ireland) Order 1993, in this PART, post.

6–197   Hague Convention countries.   These are:

Australia	Portugal
Denmark	Republic of Estonia
Finland	Republic of Poland
France	Slovakia
Germany	Spain
Italy	Sweden
Luxembourg	Switzerland
Netherlands (incl N Antilles)	Czech Republic
Norway	Turkey

The provisions of the 1972 Act are amended by Sch 2 to the Reciprocal Enforcement of Maintenance Orders (Hague Convention Countries) Order 1993 and the Act as amended is set out in Sch 3 to the Order[1]. Procedure is regulated by the Magistrates' Courts (Reciprocal Enforcement of Maintenance Orders) (Hague Convention Countries) Rules 1980[1].

---

1. In this PART, post.

6–198   United States of America.   The provisions of Part I of the Act have been extended to those States listed below by the Reciprocal Enforcement (United States of America) Order 1995[1]. In relation to these States the procedure in Part I of the Act is modified by Sch 2 to the Order and Part I of the Act as modified is set out in Sch 3 to the Order. Part I as so modified, does not make provision for the making of originating claims for maintenance which will continue to be governed by Part II of the Act. Accordingly, these States (with the exception of West Virginia) are also designated by the Recovery of Maintenance (United States of America) Order 1993[1] for the purpose of applications for recovery of maintenance under the provisions of Part II of the Act[2].

The following Table lists those States to which the provisions of Part I of the 1972 Act (reciprocal enforcement) applies.

Alaska	Montana
Arizona	Nebraska
Arkansas	Nevada
California	New Jersey
Colorado	New Mexico
Connecticut	North Carolina
Delaware	North Dakota
Florida	Ohio
Georgia	Oklahoma
Idaho	Oregon
Illinois	Pennsylvania
Indiana	South Dakota
Iowa	Tennessee
Kansas	Texas
Kentucky	Utah
Louisiana	Vermont
Maine	Virginia
Maryland	Washington
Massachusetts	West Virginia
Michigan	Wisconsin
Minnesota	Wyoming
Missouri	

---

1. In this PART, post
2. See para **6–220**, post.

6–199   Republic of Ireland.   The Reciprocal Enforcement of Maintenance Orders (Republic of Ireland) Order 1993[1] applies the provisions of Part I of the Reciprocal Enforcement Act 1972 (reciprocal enforcement) in relation to the Republic of Ireland but with modifications. The Act as modified is set out in Sch 2 to the Order. The procedure in respect of such applications is prescribed in the Magistrates' Courts (Reciprocal Enforcement of Maintenance Orders) Republic of Ireland Rules 1975[1].

---

1. In this PART, post.

Countries designated by Order under s 1 of the Act to which Part I of the Act applies

6–200 Transmission of maintenance order made in the United Kingdom. Where the payer under a maintenance order, resides, or has assets in a reciprocating country, the payee may apply to the prescribed officer of the court which made the order for the order to be sent to that country for enforcement[1].

In the case of a magistrates' court, the prescribed officer is the justices' chief executive[2] and the justices' chief executive may delegate any of his functions under the Act to any person appointed by the Magistrates' Courts Committee to assist him[3].

Application may be made in writing by or on behalf of the payee and should

— specify the date on which the order was made;
— contain such particulars as are known to the applicant of the whereabouts of the payer and the nature and location of his assets;
— specify any matters likely to assist in the identification of the payer;
— where possible, be accompanied by a recent photograph of the payer[4].

Where the justices' chief executive is satisfied that the payer is residing or has assets in a reciprocating country, he will send the following documents to the Lord Chancellor[5] for transmission to the responsible authority in the reciprocating country:

— a certified copy of the maintenance order;
— a certificate signed by the justices' chief executive certifying that the order is enforceable in the United Kingdom;
— a certificate of arrears so signed;
— a statement giving such information as the justices' chief executive possesses for facilitating the identification of the payer; and
— where available, a photograph of the payer[6].

---

1. Maintenance Orders (Reciprocal Enforcement) Act 1972 s 2(1), this PART, post.
2. Magistrates' Courts (Reciprocal Enforcement of Maintenance Orders) Rules 1974, r 3, this PART, post.
3. Magistrates' Courts (Reciprocal Enforcement of Maintenance Orders) Rules 1974, Sch A1, r 12, this PART, post.
4. Magistrates' Courts (Reciprocal Enforcement of Maintenance Orders) Rules 1974, r 4, this PART, post.
5. References in the Act to the Secretary of State are to be construed as references to the Lord Chancellor: SI 1992/709, art 4(5).
6. Maintenance Orders (Reciprocal Enforcement) Act 1972, s 2(1), this PART, post..

6–201 Proceedings for a provisional maintenance order (defendant resident in a reciprocating country). Where application is made to a magistrates' court for a maintenance order which the court would have had power to make under the Domestic Proceedings and Magistrates' Court Act 1978 or the Children Act 1989 if the person against whom the order is sought were residing in England and Wales and not in a reciprocating country, the court has power to make a provisional order for maintenance[1].

The power to allocate such proceedings under the Children (Allocation of Proceedings) Rules 1991 to a county court or the High Court does not apply, neither may the court refuse to make an order on an application on the ground that any matter in question is one that would be more conveniently dealt with by the High Court[2].

Application shall be filed in an appropriate form. No form of application is prescribed but we would suggest that the form of application in the Family Proceedings Courts (Matrimonial Proceedings etc) Rules 1991[3] (maintenance for a spouse) or the Family Proceedings Courts (Children Act 1989) Rules 1991[3] (maintenance for a child) are used as appropriate. Application is to a family proceedings court[4]. On receipt of an application the clerk shall fix the time, date and place for the hearing of the application on a directions appointment and the justices' chief executive must notify the applicant accordingly[5].

Rules of procedure are prescribed by Sch A1 to the Magistrates' Courts (Reciprocal Enforcement of Maintenance) Rules 1974[3] which make provision analogous to that in the Family Proceedings Courts (Matrimonial Proceedings etc) Rules 1991[3] and the Family Proceedings Courts (Children Act 1989) Rules 1991[3] and include the power to transfer proceedings to another magistrates' court[6], service of documents[7], the making of directions for the conduct of proceedings[8], filing of documentary evidence[9] and the reading of documents that have been filed by the justices in advance of the hearing[10]. Before the court makes a provisional order, or refuses an application, the clerk, in consultation with the justices, shall record the reasons for the court's decision and any findings of fact[11].

---

1. Maintenance Orders (Reciprocal Enforcement) Act 1972, s 3(1), (2), this PART, post
2. Maintenance Orders (Reciprocal Enforcement) Act 1972, s 3(4), this PART, post.
3. This PART, post.
4. Magistrates' Courts Act 1980, s 65(1), in PART I: MAGISTRATES' COURTS PROCEDURE, ante.
5. Magistrates' Courts (Reciprocal Enforcement of Maintenance) Rules 1974, r 4A, this PART, post.
6. Magistrates' Courts (Reciprocal Enforcement of Maintenance Orders) Rules 1974, Sch A1, para 2, this PART, post.
7. Magistrates' Courts (Reciprocal Enforcement of Maintenance Orders) Rules 1974, Sch A1, para 3, this PART, post.
8. Magistrates' Courts (Reciprocal Enforcement of Maintenance Orders) Rules 1974, Sch A1, para 4, this PART, post.

9. Magistrates' Courts (Reciprocal Enforcement of Maintenance Orders) Rules 1974, Sch A1, para 7, this PART, post.
10. Magistrates' Courts (Reciprocal Enforcement of Maintenance Orders) Rules 1974, Sch A1, para 10(1), this PART, post.
11. Magistrates' Courts (Reciprocal Enforcement of Maintenance Orders) Rules 1974, Sch A1, para 10(4), this PART, post.

6–202 Where the court has made a provisional order the justices' chief executive shall send to the Lord Chancellor[1] with a view to their being transmitted to the responsible authority in the reciprocating country in which the payer is residing the following documents:

— a certified copy of the maintenance order;
— a document setting out or summarising the evidence given in the proceedings;
— a certificate signed by the justices' clerk certifying that the grounds stated in the certificate are the grounds on which the making of the order might have been opposed by the payer under the order;
— a statement giving such information as was available to the court as to the whereabouts of the payer; and
— where available, a photograph of the payer[2].

A document setting out or summarising any evidence shall be authenticated by a certificate signed by one of the justices before whom that evidence was given, that the document is the original document containing that evidence or a true copy thereof[3]. In view of the requirement for the justices' clerk to keep a note of the substance of any oral evidence and for the applicant to file written statements of the substance of the oral evidence and copies of any documents upon which he intends to rely at the hearing, we suggest that such a certificate is appended to such record and documentary evidence that has been filed.

---

1. References to Secretary of State in the Act are to be construed as references to the Lord Chancellor: SI 1992/709, art 4(5).
2. Maintenance Orders (Reciprocal Enforcement) Act 1972, s 3(5), this PART, ante.
3. Magistrates' Courts (Reciprocal Enforcement of Maintenance) Rules 1974, r 5, this PART, post.

6–203 Application for provisional order: procedural steps

Procedure	Statutory Provision[1]
Application for maintenance order	(FPC (CA 1989), R 1991 Forms 1 and 10 (amended as appropriate) FPC (MP) R 1991 Form 1 (amended as appropriate)
Applicant to file with court	s 3(5)
—information as to the whereabouts of respondent;	
—respondent's last known address;	
—personal description;	
—photograph of respondent;	
—(certificate of marriage);	
—(certificate of birth of child).	
Justices' clerk to fix directions appointment	r 4(A)(3)
(Before the hearing or appointment)	
Applicant to file:	Rules Sch, para 7(1)
—written statements of the substance of the oral evidence which he intends to adduce at a hearing or directions appointment, which shall:	
(i) be dated;	
(ii) be signed by the person making the statement;	
(iii) contain a declaration that the maker of the statement believes it to be true and understands that it may be placed before the court, and	
(iv) show in the top right hand corner of the first page	
(a) the initials and surname of the person making the statement,	
(b) the number of the statement in relation to the maker,	
(c) the date on which the statement was made, and	
(d) the party on whose behalf it is filed.	
—copies of any documents upon which he intends to rely at a hearing or directions appointment	
Justices to read any statements filed before the hearing	Rules Sch A1, para 10(1)
(At the hearing)	
Court determines whether to make provisional order or refuse application	
Justices' clerk or court to keep note of any oral evidence given at the hearing	Rules Sch, para 9
(Before the court makes an order or refuses an application)	Rules Sch A1, para 10(4)
Justices' clerk in consultation with the justices to record names of justices and their reasons in writing	
(After the hearing)	Rules Sch A1, para 10(5)
Justices' clerk to make a written record of any order	
Justices' chief executive to send to Lord Chancellor—	s 3(5)
—certified copy of the maintenance order;	r 5
—duly authenticated document setting out or summarising the evidence;	

Procedure	Statutory Provision[1]

 —certificate signed by the justices' clerk certifying the grounds on which
  the making of an order might have been opposed by the payer;
—statement giving such information as is available as to the whereabouts f
 the payer;
 —statement giving such information as is available for facilitating the
  identification of the payer;
 —where available, photograph of the payer.
—certificate of marriage
—certificate of birth of child   } as appropriate

---

1. Unless otherwise stated, references are to the Maintenance Orders (Reciprocal Enforcement) Act 1972 and the Magistrates' Courts (Reciprocal Enforcement of Maintenance Orders) Rules 1974, this PART, post.

6–204   Taking further evidence.

A court in a reciprocating country may, for the purpose of proceedings before that court, request a court in the United Kingdom to take evidence on the matters specified in the request[1].

The court which is to take the evidence is prescribed by the rule 10 of the Magistrates' Courts (Reciprocal Enforcement of Maintenance Orders) Rules 1974 but the power to take evidence may with agreement be exercised by another magistrates' court[2]. Any oral evidence shall be put into writing and read over to the witness who shall be required to sign the document[3]. A witness summons may be issued[4] and the expenses of a witness who is neither the payer or payee may be paid out of central funds[5].

---

1. Maintenance Orders (Reciprocal Enforcement) Act 1972, s 14(1), this PART, post.
2. Maintenance Orders (Reciprocal Enforcement of Maintenance Orders) Rules 1974, r 10(2), this PART, post.
3. Maintenance Orders (Reciprocal Enforcement of Maintenance Orders) Rules 1974, r 10(3), this PART, post.
4. Maintenance Orders (Reciprocal Enforcement) Act 1972, s 14(3), this PART, post.
5. Maintenance Orders (Reciprocal Enforcement) Act 1972, s 14(2), this PART, post.

6–205   Appeal.

No appeal lies from a provisional order made under these provisions by a court in the United Kingdom[1].

---

1. Maintenance Orders (Reciprocal Enforcement) Act 1972, s 12(1), this PART, post.

6–206   Variation and revocation of maintenance order made in the United Kingdom.

A court in the United Kingdom has power to vary:

 —an order originally made in the United Kingdom and transmitted to a reciprocating country for
  registration;
 —a provisional order made in the United Kingdom which has been confirmed in a reciprocating
  country[1]

and where a provisional order made in a reciprocating country has varied or revoked a maintenance order made in the United Kingdom which has been sent to the reciprocating country for registration or is a provisional order, the court may in proceedings for confirming the order vary the order as it sees fit as if an application had been made for a variation[2].

The procedural rules are set out in Sch A1 to the Maintenance Orders (Reciprocal Enforcement of Maintenance Orders) Rules 1974[3].

Where the court makes a provisional order varying a maintenance order the justices chief executive[4] shall send by post to the court or to the Lord Chancellor for transmission to the court[5] a certified copy of the provisional order and a duly authenticated document setting out or summarising the evidence[6].

---

1. Maintenance Orders (Reciprocal Enforcement) Act 1972, s 5, this PART, post.
2. Maintenance Orders (Reciprocal Enforcement) Act 1972, s 5(5), (6), this PART, post.
3. This PART, post.
4. Magistrates' Courts (Reciprocal Enforcement of Maintenance Orders) Rules 1974, r 3, this PART, post.
5. Maintenance Orders (Reciprocal Enforcement) Act 1972, s 5(4) and the Magistrates' Courts (Reciprocal Enforcement of Maintenance Orders) Rules 1974, r 6, this PART, post.
6. Magistrates' Courts (Reciprocal Enforcement of Maintenance Orders) Rules 1974, r 5, this PART, post.

6–207   Registration in United Kingdom Court of maintenance order made in reciprocating country.

Where the Lord Chancellor[1] has received a certified copy of a maintenance order made in a reciprocating country[2] he shall send a copy of the order to the prescribed officer of the appropriate court for registration[3].

The appropriate court in England and Wales within the jurisdiction of which the payer is residing or has assets[4] is a magistrates' court, the prescribed officer is the justices' chief executive[5]. Before registering the order the justices' chief executive shall satisfy himself that the payer is residing within the jurisdiction of the court and if he is not so satisfied he shall return the certified copy of the order to the Lord Chancellor with such information as he possesses as to the whereabouts of the payer and the nature and location of his assets[6]. In any other case, the justices' chief executive shall register the order[7] by means of a minute or memorandum entered and signed by him in the court register which specifies the section of the Act under which the order is registered[8]. Legal representation may be granted under the Access to Justice Act 1999 for proceedings under Part I of this Act relating to a maintenance order made by a court of a country outside the United Kingdom[9].

1. References to the Secretary of State in the legislation should be construed as references to the Lord Chancellor: SI 1992/709, art 4(1).
2. For reciprocating countries see paras **6–195** to **6–199**.
3. Maintenance Orders (Reciprocal Enforcement) Act 1973 s 6(2), this PART, post.
4. Maintenance Orders (Reciprocal Enforcement) Act 1972, s 21(1), this PART, post.
5. Magistrates' Courts (Reciprocal Enforcement of Maintenance Orders) Rules 1974 r 3, this PART, post.
6. Maintenance Orders (Reciprocal Enforcement) Act 1972, s 6(4), this PART, post.
7. Maintenance Orders (Reciprocal Enforcement) Act 1972, s 6(3), this PART, post.
8. Magistrates' Courts (Reciprocal Enforcement of Maintenance Orders) Rules 1974, r 8, this PART, post.
9. Access to Justice Act 1999, Sch 2, para 2(3)(*b*), in PART I, MAGISTRATES' COURTS, PROCEDURE, ante.

6–208 Terms of payment. Where an order is registered in a magistrates' court the court shall order that payments shall be made to the justices' chief executive of the registering court[1], and may specify the particular means by which it should be paid and where appropriate should notify the payer of the number and location of the account into which the payments are to be made[2]. Where the sums required to be paid under a registered order are expressed in a currency other than sterling that sum shall be deemed to be the equivalent sum in the currency of the United Kingdom[3].

The sum in the order shall be converted into the equivalent sum in sterling at the rate of exchange prevailing at the time the order is first registered or if earlier, the date on which it is confirmed by a court in the United Kingdom, or the date of registration or confirmation after the order has been varied. The prevailing exchange rate may be proved by certificate[4].

The justices' chief executive shall send any payments received by post to the court which made the order or such other court as the Lord Chancellor may direct, or in respect of countries specified in Sch 2 to the Rules[5], the Crown Agents for Overseas Governments and Administrations[6].

1. Magistrates' Courts (Reciprocal Enforcement of Maintenance Orders) Rules 1974, r 9(1), this PART, post.
2. Magistrates' Courts (Reciprocal Enforcement of Maintenance Orders) Rules 1974, rr 9(1), 9B, this PART, post and see the Maintenance Orders (Reciprocal Enforcement) Act 1972, s 8(1) (registered order to be enforced as if made by the registering court), this PART, post, and the Magistrates' Courts Act 1980 ss 59–59A, in PART I, MAGISTRATES' COURTS, PROCEDURE, ante
3. Maintenance Orders (Reciprocal Enforcement) Act 1972, s 16(2), (3), this PART, post.
4. Maintenance Orders (Reciprocal Enforcement) Act 1972, s 16(4), this PART, post.
5. For the countries specified in Sch 2 see para **6–195**.
6. Magistrates' Courts (Reciprocal Enforcement of Maintenance Orders) Rules 1974, r 9(1A), this PART, post.

6–209 Enforcement of maintenance order registered in United Kingdom court. An order registered in a magistrates' court may be enforced as if it had been made by the registering court[1]. The person obliged to make payment under the order is under a duty to inform the justices' chief executive of the registering court of any change of address[2]. The justices' chief executive must take reasonable steps to inform the payee of the means of enforcement available to the court including the possibility of registration of the whole or part of the order in the High Court under Part I of the Maintenance Order Act 1958[3]. Where the order is in arrear to an amount equal to four times the weekly sum payable, the justices' chief executive must proceed in his own name and whether requested by the payee or not, for the recovery of the sums owing unless he considers it unreasonable in the circumstances to do so[4]. The provisions of Part III of the Magistrates' Courts Act 1980[5] with necessary modifications[6] will then apply.

1. Maintenance Orders (Reciprocal Enforcement) Act 1972, s 8(1), this PART, post.
2. Maintenance Orders (Reciprocal Enforcement) Act 1972, s 8(3), this PART, post.
3. Magistrates' Courts (Reciprocal Enforcement of Maintenance Orders) Rules 1974, r 9A, this PART, post.
4. Magistrates' Courts (Reciprocal Enforcement of Maintenance Orders) Rules 1974, r 9(2), this PART, post.
5. In PART I, MAGISTRATES' COURTS, PROCEDURE, ante.
6. See the Maintenance Orders (Reciprocal Enforcement) Act 1972, s 8(4)–(8), this PART, post.

6–210 Confirmation by United Kingdom court of provisional maintenance order made in reciprocating country. Where the court has received from the Lord Chancellor[1]

—a certified copy of a maintenance order made in a reciprocating country;
—a duly authenticated document setting out or summarising the evidence given in proceedings in which the order was made;
—a statement of grounds on which the order might have been opposed;

the court may either refuse to confirm the order or confirm the order either without alteration or with such alterations as it thinks reasonable[2].

The "appropriate court" in England and Wales is a magistrates' court within the jurisdiction of which the payer resides or has assets[3] and the prescribed officer in relation to a magistrates' court is the justices' chief executive[4].

On receipt of the application the justices' clerk shall fix the date, time and place for a directions appointment allowing at least 21 days for service and the justices' chief executive must serve a notice of hearing and copies of the order and documents on the resident party[5]. The resident party shall file an answer in 14 days[6].

Confirmation of a provisional order can only be opposed on grounds on which the making of the order might have been opposed[7]. The certificate from the court which made the provisional order of the grounds on which the making of the order might have been opposed is conclusive evidence of those grounds[8] but not exclusive of any other grounds[9]. Accordingly, the certificate does not prevent the person to whom notice has been given from raising any defence not included in those grounds, for example, that the court had no jurisdiction to make the order[10].

---

1. References in the legislation to the Secretary of State are to be construed as references to the Lord Chancellor: SI 1992/709, art 4(1).
2. Maintenance Orders (Reciprocal Enforcement) Act 1972, s 7(2), this PART, post.
3. Maintenance Orders (Reciprocal Enforcement) Act 1972, s 21(1), this PART, post.
4. Magistrates' Courts (Reciprocal Enforcement of Maintenance Orders) Rules 1974, r 3, this PART, post.
5. Magistrates' Courts (Reciprocal Enforcement of Maintenance Orders) Rules 1974, r 4(2), this PART, post.
6. Magistrates' Courts (Reciprocal Enforcement of Maintenance Orders) Rules 1974, r 4(3), this PART, post.
7. Maintenance Orders (Reciprocal Enforcement) Act 1972, s 7(2), this PART, post.
8. Maintenance Orders (Reciprocal Enforcement) Act 1972, s 7(3), this PART, post.
9. *Re Wheat* [1932] 2 KB 716, [1932] All ER Rep 48, 96 JP 399.
10. *Harris v Harris* [1949] 2 All ER 318, 113 JP 495, 65 TLR 519.

6–211   Variation and revocation of maintenance order registered in United Kingdom court (applicant resident in United Kingdom).   The registering court has the like power to vary or revoke a registered order as if it had been made by the registering court[1] except in respect of a lump sum[2]. However a registered order may only be varied by a provisional order unless:

—both the payer and payee are for the time being resident in the United Kingdom; or
—application to vary is made by the payee; or
—the variation is to reduce the rate of payments on the ground that there has been a change of circumstances and the court in the reciprocating country which made the order has no power to confirm a provisional order of variation[3].

The registering court may not revoke a registered order otherwise than by a provisional order unless both the parties are for the time being resident in the United Kingdom[4]. No form of application has been prescribed and we suggest that the appropriate forms in the Family Proceedings Courts (Matrimonial Proceedings) Rules 1991[5] and the Family Proceedings Courts (Children Act 1989) Rules are used[5]. On receipt of the application the justices' clerk shall fix the date, time and place for a hearing or directions appointment and the justices' chief executive must notify the applicant[6].

---

1. Maintenance Orders (Reciprocal Enforcement) Act 1972, s 9(1), this PART, post.
2. Maintenance Orders (Reciprocal Enforcement) Act 1972, s 9(1A), this PART, post.
3. Maintenance Orders (Reciprocal Enforcement) Act 1972, s 9(2), this PART, post.
4. Maintenance Orders (Reciprocal Enforcement) Act 1972, s 9(3), this PART, post.
5. This PART, post.
6. Magistrates' Courts (Reciprocal Enforcement of Maintenance Orders) Rules 1974, r 4B, this PART, post.

6–212   Variation and revocation of maintenance order made by court in United Kingdom (applicant resident in reciprocating country).   Where a magistrates' court receives a certified copy of a provisional order varying or revoking a maintenance order together with a duly authenticated document setting out or summarising the evidence given in the proceedings, it may refuse to confirm the order, or confirm it either without alteration or with such alteration as it thinks reasonable[1].

On receipt of the documents the justices' clerk shall fix the date, time and place for a hearing or directions appointment allowing at least 21 days for the justices' chief executive to serve a notice on the resident party and copies of the order and the documents. The resident party shall file an answer to the provisional order within 14 days[2]. The order as varied shall have effect from the date it was varied by the provisional order[3]. A revocation of the order does not affect any arrears due under the maintenance order at that date[4].

---

1. Maintenance Orders (Reciprocal Enforcement) Act 1972, s 5(5), this PART, post.
2. Magistrates' Courts (Reciprocal Enforcement of Maintenance Orders) Rules 1974, r 4B, this PART, post.
3. Maintenance Orders (Reciprocal Enforcement) Act 1972, s 5(7), this PART, post.
4. Maintenance Orders (Reciprocal Enforcement) Act 1972, s 5(8), this PART, post.

Countries designated by the Reciprocal Enforcement of Maintenance (Hague Convention Countries) Order 1974 to which Part I of the Act applies with modifications

6–213   Transmission of maintenance order made in the United Kingdom.   Where the payer under a maintenance order resides in a Hague Convention country, the payee may apply to the prescribed officer of the court which made the order for the order to be sent to that country for enforcement[1].

The prescribed officer of a magistrates' court is the justices' chief executive[2]. An application in respect of a maintenance order made by a magistrates' court shall be made in writing and shall specify

—the date of which the order was made;
—contain such particulars as are known to the applicant of the whereabouts of the payer and the nature and location of his assets;
—specify any matters likely to assist in the identification of the payer;
—where possible, be accompanied by a recent photograph of the payer[3].

If the justices' chief executive is satisfied that the payer resides in a Hague-Convention country, he will send to the Lord Chancellor:

—a certified copy of the maintenance order;

—a certificate signed by that officer certifying that the order is enforceable and that it is no longer subject to the ordinary form of review;

—a certificate of arrears so signed;

—a statement giving such information as the officer possesses as to the whereabouts of the payer;

—a statement giving such information as the officer possesses for facilitating the identification of the payer;

—where available, a photograph of the payer;

—a written statement signed by that officer as to whether or not the payer appeared in the proceedings in which the maintenance order was made and, if he did not appear, the original or a certified copy of a document which establishes that notice of the institution of proceedings, including notice of the substance of the claim, was served on the payer;

—a document which establishes that notice of the order was sent to the payer; and

—a written statement signed by that officer as to whether or not the payer received legal aid either in the said proceedings or in connection with the said application[1].

---

1. Maintenance Orders (Reciprocal Enforcement) Act 1972, s 2 as adapted and modified by the Reciprocal Enforcement of Maintenance Orders (Hague Convention Countries) Order 1993 Sch 2, in this PART, post, and see Sch 3 thereto.

2. Magistrates' Courts (Reciprocal Enforcement of Maintenance Orders) (Hague Convention Countries) Rules 1980, r 3, in this PART, post.

3. Magistrates' Courts (Reciprocal Enforcement of Maintenance Orders) (Hague Convention Countries) Rules 1980, r 4, this PART, post.

6–214 Application for maintenance order against person residing in Hague Convention country. Application may be made to a magistrates' court by a person habitually resident in the United Kingdom for a maintenance order against a person residing in a Hague Convention country[1]. On making the application the court will send to the Lord Chancellor for transmission to the appropriate authority in the Hague Convention country for service on the respondent the following documents—

—notice of the institution of the proceedings, including notice of the substance of the application;

—a statement signed by the justices' chief executive giving such information as he possesses as to the whereabouts of the respondent;

—a statement giving such information as the officer possesses for facilitating the identification of the respondent; and

—where available, a photograph of the respondent[2].

The justices' chief executive will fix the date, time and place for a hearing or a directions appointment[3], six weeks should be allowed for service of the notice of institution of the proceedings on the respondent by the Lord Chancellor[4], and notify the applicant[5] and the respondent[6]. At the hearing, the court in considering whether or not to make a maintenance order shall take into account any representations made and any evidence adduced by the respondent which should have been served on the applicant before the hearing[7].

Where a maintenance order has been made the justices' chief executive shall send to the Lord Chancellor the following documents:

—a certified copy of the order;

—a certificate signed by the justices' chief executive that the order is enforceable and that it is no longer subject to the ordinary forms of review;

—a written statement, signed by the justices' chief executive as to whether or not the respondent appeared in the proceedings in which the order was made, and, if he did not appear, the original or a certified copy of a document which establishes that the notice of institution of proceedings has been served on the payer not less than six weeks before the hearing;

—a document that established that notice of the order was sent to the respondent; and

—a written statement signed by the justices' clerk as to whether or not the applicant received legal aid in the proceedings[8].

---

1. Maintenance Orders (Reciprocal Enforcement) Act 1972, s 3(1) as adapted and modified by the Reciprocal Enforcement of Maintenance Orders (Hague Convention Countries) Order 1993, Sch 2, in this PART, post, and see Sch 3 thereto.

2. Maintenance Orders (Reciprocal Enforcement) Act 1972, s 3(5) as adapted and modified by the Reciprocal Enforcement of Maintenance Orders (Hague Convention Countries) Order 1993, Sch 2, in this PART, post, and see Sch 3 thereto.

3. Magistrates' Courts (Reciprocal Enforcement of Maintenance Orders) (Hague Convention Countries) Rules 1980, r 4A(3)(*a*), this PART, post.

4. Maintenance Orders (Reciprocal Enforcement) Act 1972, s 3(6C) as adapted and modified by the Reciprocal Enforcement of Maintenance Orders (Hague Convention Countries) Order 1993, Sch 2, in this PART, post, and see Sch 3 thereto.

5. Magistrates' Courts (Reciprocal Enforcement of Maintenance Orders) (Hague Convention Countries) Rules, 1980, r 4A(3)(*b*) this PART, post.

6. Maintenance Orders (Reciprocal Enforcement) Act 1972, s 3(6B) as adapted and modified by the Reciprocal Enforcement of Maintenance Orders (Hague Convention Countries) Order 1993, Sch 2, in this PART, post, and see Sch 3 thereto.

7. Maintenance Orders (Reciprocal Enforcement) Act 1972, s 3(6A) as adapted and modified by the Reciprocal Enforcement of Maintenance Orders (Hague Convention Countries) Order 1993, Sch 2, in this PART, post, and see Sch 3 thereto.

8. Maintenance Orders (Reciprocal Enforcement) Act 1972, s 3(6D) as adapted and modified by the Reciprocal Enforcement of Maintenance Orders (Hague Convention Countries) Order 1993, Sch 2, in this PART, post, and see Sch 3 thereto.

6–215 Variation and revocation. In proceedings under the Hague Convention proceedings for variation (except to vary method of payment) or revocation may only be conducted in the country which made the original order. An order sent to a Hague Convention country for recognition and enforcement may be varied by a United Kingdom court on the application of the payer or the payee[1]. Where application is made by the payee, the procedure is analogous to that for the making of the original order[2]. On application by the payer to a court in the United Kingdom, the justices' chief executive shall serve on the payee notice of the institution of the proceedings including notice of the substance of the application[3], the proceedings will then follow the same course as outlined above. A maintenance order which has been varied by a competent court in the United Kingdom, shall, as from the date on which the order of variation took effect, have effect as varied by the order[4]. Where an order is revoked, the revocation is deemed to have had effect from that date except as respects any arrears due[5].

---

1. Maintenance Orders (Reciprocal Enforcement) Act 1972, s 5 as adapted and modified by the Reciprocal Enforcement of Maintenance Orders (Hague Convention Countries) Order 1993, Sch 2, in this PART, post, and see Sch 3 thereto.
2. See para **6–214**.
3. Maintenance Orders (Reciprocal Enforcement) Act 1972, s 5(7) as adapted and modified by the Reciprocal Enforcement of Maintenance Orders (Hague Convention Countries) Order 1993, Sch 2, in this PART, post, and see Sch 3 thereto.
4. Maintenance Orders (Reciprocal Enforcement) Act 1972, s 5(9) as adapted and modified by the Reciprocal Enforcement of Maintenance Orders (Hague Convention Countries) Order 1993, Sch 2, in this PART, post, and see Sch 3 thereto.
5. Maintenance Orders (Reciprocal Enforcement) Act 1972, s 5(10) as adapted and modified by the Reciprocal Enforcement of Maintenance Orders (Hague Convention Countries) Order 1993, Sch 2, in this PART, post, and see Sch 3 thereto.

6–216 Registration of maintenance order made in Hague Convention country. Where a justices' chief executive receives a certified copy of a maintenance order made by a competent court in a Hague Convention country from the Lord Chancellor, he shall register the order in that court[1]. Before doing so the justices' chief executive shall take such steps as he thinks fit to ascertain whether the payer under the order resides in the jurisdiction of the court and if he is not, the certified copy of the order and the accompanying documents shall be returned to the Lord Chancellor with a statement giving such information as he possesses as to the whereabouts of the payer[2].

The justices' chief executive may refuse to register the order where:

—the court in the Hague Convention country did not have jurisdiction;
—registration is manifestly contrary to public policy;
—the order was obtained by fraud in connection with procedure;
—proceedings were already pending before a United Kingdom court;
—the order is incompatible with another order made between the parties which is enforceable under the Act;
—notice of the proceedings and notice of the substance of the claim was not served on the payer in accordance
    with the law in the Hague Convention country and he did not have sufficient time to defend the proceedings[3].

The justices' chief executive shall serve notice on the payer and the payee that the order has been registered[4]. The payer has a calendar month to appeal to the court to set aside the registration[5]. The payee has two calendar months to appeal to the court against the refusal to register the order[6].

The justices' chief executive shall register the order by means of a minute or memorandum signed by him in the court register specifying the section of the Act under which it is registered[7]. Notice of the registration shall be sent to the Lord Chancellor[8]. In deciding whether a court in a Hague Convention country had jurisdiction to make the order, the court is bound by any finding of fact on which the court based its jurisdiction[9]. Notice of registration is prescribed in Part I and notice of appeal by the payee on refusal to register an order is prescribed in Part II of Schedule 2 to the Magistrates' Courts (Reciprocal Enforcement of Maintenance Orders) (Hague Convention Countries) Rules 1980[10].

---

1. Maintenance Orders (Reciprocal Enforcement) Act 1972, s 6(2) as adapted and modified by the Reciprocal Enforcement of Maintenance Orders (Hague Convention Countries) Order 1993, Sch 2 this PART, post, and see Sch 3 thereto.
2. Maintenance Orders (Reciprocal Enforcement) Act 1972, s 6(4) as adapted and modified by the Reciprocal Enforcement of Maintenance Orders (Hague Convention Countries) Order 1993, Sch 2 this PART, post, and see Sch 3 thereto.
3. Maintenance Orders (Reciprocal Enforcement) Act 1972, s 6(5), (6), (7) as adapted and modified by the Reciprocal Enforcement of Maintenance Orders (Hague Convention Countries) Order 1993, Sch 2 this PART, post, and see Sch 3 thereto.
4. Maintenance Orders (Reciprocal Enforcement) Act 1972, s 6(8) as adapted and modified by the Reciprocal Enforcement of Maintenance Orders (Hague Convention Countries) Order 1993, Sch 2 this PART, post, and see Sch 3 thereto.
5. Maintenance Orders (Reciprocal Enforcement) Act 1972, s 6(9) as adapted and modified by the Reciprocal Enforcement of Maintenance Orders (Hague Convention Countries) Order 1993, Sch 2 this PART, post, and see Sch 3 thereto.
6. Maintenance Orders (Reciprocal Enforcement) Act 1972, S 6(12) as adapted and modified by the Reciprocal Enforcement of Maintenance Orders (Hague Convention Countries) Order 1993, Sch 2 this PART, post, and see Sch 3 thereto.
7. Magistrates' Courts (Reciprocal Enforcement of Maintenance Orders) (Hague Convention Countries) Rules 1980, r 5(1), (2), this PART, post.
8. Magistrates' Courts (Reciprocal Enforcement of Maintenance Orders) (Hague Convention Countries) Rules 1980, r 5(3), this PART, post.

9. Maintenance Orders (Reciprocal Enforcement) Act 1972, s 6(5)(b) as adapted and modified by the Reciprocal Enforcement of Maintenance Orders (Hague Convention Countries) Order 1993, Sch 2 this PART, post, and see Sch 3 thereto.

10. This PART, post.

6–217 Enforcement of maintenance order registered in United Kingdom court. Except where a registered order is for the time being registered in the High Court under Part I of the Maintenance Orders Act 1958[1], a registered order shall be enforceable as a magistrates' courts maintenance order as if it had been made by the registering court[2], and the provisions of Part III of the Magistrates' Courts Act 1980 (satisfaction and enforcement)[3] apply with necessary modifications[4]. The payer is required to notify the justices' chief executive of any change of address[5].

---

1. This PART, post.

2. Maintenance Orders (Reciprocal Enforcement) Act 1972, s 8(1), (2), as adapted and modified by the Reciprocal Enforcement of Maintenance Orders (Hague Convention Countries) Order 1993, Sch 2, this PART, post, and see Sch 3 thereto.

3. In PART I, MAGISTRATES' COURTS, PROCEDURE, ante.

4. Maintenance Orders (Reciprocal Enforcement) Act 1972, s 8(4A), (4B), as adapted and modified by the Reciprocal Enforcement of Maintenance Orders (Hague Convention Countries) Order 1993, Sch 2, this PART, post, and see Sch 3 thereto.

5. Maintenance Orders (Reciprocal Enforcement) Act 1972, s 8(3) as adapted and modified by the Reciprocal Enforcement of Maintenance Orders (Hague Convention Countries) Order 1993, Sch 2, this PART, post, and see Sch 3 thereto.

6–218 Variation of the method of payment of maintenance order registered in United Kingdom court. The court in which the order is registered has power on application by the payee or payer to vary the method of payment of the order; application may not be made to the court in which the order is registered, to vary the amount of the order[1]. The provisions of s 60 of the Magistrates' Courts Act 1980[2] apply with necessary modifications[3]. The registering court shall not vary the method of payment of a registered order unless at the time when the proceedings to vary the order were instituted, the payer had his habitual residence in the United Kingdom or the respondent has submitted to the jurisdiction of the court[4].

The order as varied shall be registered in the registering court[5] and has effect from the date the variation order took effect[6].

---

1. Maintenance Orders (Reciprocal Enforcement) Act 1972, s 9(1) as adapted and modified by the Reciprocal Enforcement of Maintenance Orders (Hague Convention Countries) Order 1993, Sch 2, this PART, post, and see Sch 3 thereto.

2. PART I, MAGISTRATES' COURTS, PROCEDURE, ante.

3. Maintenance Orders (Reciprocal Enforcement) Act 1972, s 9(1ZA) as adapted and modified by the Reciprocal Enforcement of Maintenance Orders (Hague Convention Countries) Order 1993, Sch 2, this PART, post, and see Sch 3 thereto.

4. Maintenance Orders (Reciprocal Enforcement) Act 1972, s 9(2) as adapted and modified by the Reciprocal Enforcement of Maintenance Orders (Hague Convention Countries) Order 1993, Sch 2, this PART, post, and see Sch 3 thereto.

5. Maintenance Orders (Reciprocal Enforcement) Act 1972, s 9(8) as adapted and modified by the Reciprocal Enforcement of Maintenance Orders (Hague Convention Countries) Order 1993, Sch 2, this PART, post, and see Sch 3 thereto.

6. Maintenance Orders (Reciprocal Enforcement) Act 1972, s 9(9) as adapted and modified by the Reciprocal Enforcement of Maintenance Orders (Hague Convention Countries) Order 1993, Sch 2, this PART, post, and see Sch 3 thereto.

6–219 Cancellation of registration and transfer of order. Registration will be cancelled where a notice of revocation has been received from a court in a Hague Convention Country, except that arrears due before the revocation shall continue to be recoverable[1].

Where the justices' chief executive is of the opinion that the payer under a registered order is residing within the jurisdiction of another magistrates' court, he may transfer the order by means of sending a certified copy of the order, a certificate of arrears, information as to the payer's whereabouts and any relevant documents for registration in that court, or where the payer is believed to reside elsewhere in the United Kingdom the justices' chief executive shall send a certified copy of the order to the Lord Chancellor[2].

---

1. Maintenance Orders (Reciprocal Enforcement) Act 1972, s 10(1) as adapted and modified by the Reciprocal Enforcement of Maintenance Orders (Hague Convention Countries) Order 1993, Sch 2, this PART, post, and see Sch 3 thereto.

2. Maintenance Orders (Reciprocal Enforcement) Act 1972, s 10(2)–(7) as adapted and modified by the Reciprocal Enforcement of Maintenance Orders (Hague Convention Countries) Order 1993, Sch 2, this PART, post, and see Sch 3 thereto.

Maintenance Orders Reciprocal Enforcement Act 1972, Part II: Enforcement of claims for the recovery of maintenance

6–220 United Nations Convention countries. Claims for the recovery of maintenance in respect of the following countries may be made under the provisions of Part II of the Maintenance Orders (Reciprocal Enforcement) Act 1972[1]:

Algeria	Hungary
†Australia	Ireland
Austria	Israel
Barbados	Italy
Belgium	Luxembourg
Bosnia and Herzegovina	Macedonia (Ex Yugoslavian Rep)
Brazil	Mexico
Burkina Faso	Monaco
Cape Verde	Morocco
Central African republic	Netherlands (& N Antilles & Aruba)
Chile	†New Zealand
Croatia	Niger
†Cyprus	Norway
Czech Republic	Pakistan
Denmark	Philippines
Ecuador	Poland
Finland	Portugal
France (including—Guadeloupe, Guiana, Martinique	Romania
and Reunion, Comoro Archipelago; French Polynesia,	Slovakia
St. Pierre and Miquelon)	Spain
Germany	Sri Lanka
Haiti	Suriname
Holy See	Sweden
	Uruguay

†   Australia, New Zealand and Cyprus have been added to the list of United Nations Convention countries for formal reasons and it is strongly recommended that courts continue to use the arrangements under Part I of the Maintenance Orders (Reciprocal Enforcement) Act 1972, in the case of Australia and New Zealand; and the Maintenance Orders (Facilities for Enforcement) Act 1920 in respect of Cyprus[2].

1. Maintenance Orders (Reciprocal Enforcement) Act 1972, s 25, and the Recovery Abroad of Maintenance (Convention Countries) Order 1975 and the Recovery of Maintenance (United States of America) Order 1979, this PART, post.
2. Lord Chancellor's Department Letter 20 August 1996.

6–221 Application for recovery etc of maintenance in a Convention country. A person in the United Kingdom may apply to the Lord Chancellor[1] to have his claim for the recovery of maintenance, or the variation of provision of maintenance, transmitted to the convention country in which the payer resides[2]. In England and Wales such application is made through a magistrates' court[3] and the justices' chief executive [4] must assist the claimant to complete the application[5] in the prescribed form[6].

1. References in the legislation to the Secretary of State are to be construed as references to the Lord Chancellor: SI 1992/709, art 4(1).
2. Maintenance Orders (Reciprocal Enforcement) Act 1972, s 26(1), (2), this PART, post.
3. Maintenance Orders (Reciprocal Enforcement) Act 1972, s 26(6), this PART, post.
4. Maintenance Orders (Reciprocal Enforcement) Act 1972, s 26(6) and the Magistrates' Courts (Recovery Abroad of Maintenance) Rules 1975, r 3, this PART, post.
5. Maintenance Orders (Reciprocal Enforcement) Act 1972, s 26(3), this PART, post.
6. Recommended forms of application and evidence are set out immediately following the Schedule to the Magistrates' Courts (Recovery Abroad of Maintenance) Rules 1975, this PART, post.

6–222 Extension of Part II of the Act to other countries. The provisions of Part II of the Act may be extended to other countries by Orders made under s 40 of the Act. The only order currently having effect in respect of Part II of the Act is the Recovery of Maintenance (United States of America) Order 1993, made in respect of certain States of the United States of America[1].

1. Recovery of Maintenance (United States of America) Order 1993, this PART, post.

6–223 Where the claim is in relation to the United States of America, the claim must be registered in the magistrates' court and be accompanied by a certificate signed by a justice of the peace to the effect that the claim sets forth facts from which it may be determined that the respondent owes a duty to maintain the applicant and any other person named in the application and that a court in the specified state has jurisdiction[1]. The following States have been designated[2] under these provisions:

Alaska	Illinois
Arizona	Indiana
Arkansas	Iowa
California	Kansas
Colorado	Kentucky
Connecticut	Louisiana
Delaware	Maine
Florida	Maryland
Georgia	Massachusetts
Hawaii	Michegan
Idaho	Minnesota
Missouri	Oregon
Montana	Pennsylvania
Nebraska	Rhode Island
Nevada	South Dakota
New Hampshire	Tennesee
New Jersey	Texas
New Mexico	Utah
New York	Vermont
North Carolina	Virginia
North Dakota	Washington
Ohio	Wisconsin
Oklahoma	Wyoming

Part I of the Maintenance Orders (Reciprocal Enforcement) Act 1972 applies to those States which are designated by the Reciprocal Enforcement (United States of America) Order 1995[3] but only in respect of the registration of maintenance orders which have been made by a court having jurisdiction over both of the parties at the time it was made ie where the parties were resident in the jurisdiction. An originating application for maintenance where one of the parties resides in the United States must be made by way of an application for the recovery of maintenance under Part II of the Act as modified by the Recovery of Maintenance (United States of America) Order 1993[4].

---

1. Maintenance Orders (Reciprocal Enforcement) Act 1972, s 26(3), this PART, post and see the Magistrates' Courts (Recovery Abroad of Maintenance) Rules 1975, r 5A, this PART, post.
2. Reciprocal Enforcement of Maintenance Orders (United States of America) Order 1995, in this PART, post. Other States are designated by this Order but are also now designated for the purposes of Pt I of the Act by the Reciprocal Enforcement (United States of America) Order 1995, this PART, post. See further para **6–198**, ante.
3. This PART, post.
4. This PART, post, and see para **6–198**, ante.

6–224   Application by person in Convention country for recovery of maintenance in England and Wales.   An application for maintenance of a spouse is treated as an application under the Domestic Proceedings and Magistrates' Courts Act 1978, or where the claim is for a child alone, Sch 1 to the Children Act 1989[1]. The claim is sent by the Lord Chancellor to the justices' chief executive for the magistrates' court in whose area the respondent is residing[2].

On receipt of an application sent from the Lord Chancellor, the justices' clerk shall fix a date, time and place for a hearing or directions appointment allowing at least 21 days for the justices' chief executive to serve a notice of hearing and copies of any documents accompanying the application. Within 14 days the respondent shall file an answer to the application[3]. Procedure with respect to the hearing is prescribed by Sch 2 to the Magistrates' Courts (Recovery of Maintenance Abroad) Rules 1975[4].

---

1. Maintenance Orders (Reciprocal Enforcement) Act 1972, s 27A this PART, post.
2. Maintenance Orders (Reciprocal Enforcement) Act 1972, s 27B this PART, post.
3. Magistrates' Courts (Recovery Abroad of Maintenance) Rules 1975, r 3A, this PART, post.
4. This PART, post.

6–225   Modifications of the Domestic Proceedings and Magistrates' Courts Act 1978 and the Children Act 1989.   Where the application is treated as if it were made under the Domestic Proceedings and Magistrates' Courts Act 1978, the provisions of that Act are deemed to extend to parties who were formerly married and whose marriage has been dissolved by a divorce or annulment recognized as valid by the law in England and Wales where by reason of the divorce or annulment, a maintenance order has been made in a convention country[1]. The court may only make an order for periodical payments or a lump sum, and only in favour of a spouse or a child, where such order or person is provided for in the order made in the convention country[2].

Apart from consequential amendments, those provisions of the 1978 Act relating to orders made by agreement between the parties, the duty to consider whether to exercise powers under the Children Act 1989, powers to make protection orders against domestic violence and provisions to vary orders for periodical payments, effect of the parties living together, reconciliation and provisions relating to the High Court, are excluded[3]. Procedures requiring or permitting the allocation of children's cases to the county court or High Court are disapplied[4].

---

1. Maintenance Orders (Reciprocal Enforcement) Act 1972, s 28A, this PART, post.
2. Maintenance Orders (Reciprocal Enforcement) Act 1972, s 28A(4), (5), this PART, post.

3. Maintenance Orders (Reciprocal Enforcement) Act 1972, ss 28(2), 28A (6), this PART, post.
4. Maintenance Orders (Reciprocal Enforcement) Act 1972, s 28B, this PART, post.

6-226 Making or refusing an order. Where the court has made an order the court shall exercise one of the following powers—

—the power to order that payments under the order be made directly to the justices' chief executive for the court or the justices' chief executive for any other magistrates' court in England and Wales;

—the power to order that payments under the order be made to the justices' chief executive for the court or to the justices' chief executive for any other magistrates' court in England and Wales, by such method of payment falling within s 59(6) of the Magistrates' Courts Act 1980 (standing order, etc) as may be specified;

—the power to make an attachment of earnings order under the Attachment of Earnings Act 1971 to secure payments under the order[1].

The debtor may make representations as to the method of payment[2] and may be required to open an account[3]. The order will be registered in the court[4]. The means of payment shall be recorded on the order and the payer should be notified in writing including the number and location of the account into which payments are to be made[5]. Where the court has registered[6] or dismissed an application[7] notice shall be sent by the justices' chief executive to the Lord Chancellor[8].

1. Maintenance Orders (Reciprocal Enforcement) Act 1972, s 27C(4), this PART, post.
2. Maintenance Orders (Reciprocal Enforcement) Act 1972, s 27C(5), this PART, post.
3. Maintenance Orders (Reciprocal Enforcement) Act 1972, s 27C(6), this PART, post.
4. Maintenance Orders (Reciprocal Enforcement) Act 1972, s 27C(7), Magistrates' Courts (Recovery Abroad of Maintenance) Rules 1975, r 5, this PART, post.
5. Maintenance Orders (Reciprocal Enforcement) Act 1972, s 27C(7), Magistrates' Courts (Recovery Abroad of Maintenance) Rules 1975, r 7A, this PART, post.
6. Maintenance Orders (Reciprocal Enforcement) Act 1972, s 27C(7), Magistrates' Courts (Recovery Abroad of Maintenance) Rules 1975, r 6, this PART, post.
7. Maintenance Orders (Reciprocal Enforcement) Act 1972, s 27C(7), Magistrates' Courts (Recovery Abroad of Maintenance) Rules 1975, r 4, this PART, post.
8. References in the legislation to the Secretary of State are to be construed as reference to the Lord Chancellor: SI 1992/709, art 4(1).

6-227 Transfer of orders. Where the justices' chief executive is satisfied that the payer has ceased to reside within the jurisdiction of that court ie outside England and Wales he shall send a certified copy of the order and the related documents to the Lord Chancellor, and also if the justices' chief executive is of the opinion that he has ceased to reside in the United Kingdom, a notice to that effect[1], otherwise he may send a certified copy of the order and the related documents to the justices' chief executive for another magistrates' court in whose area the payer is believed to reside. Where the order is re-registered, the court shall give notice of the registration to the court in which the order had been registered[2]. If the Lord Chancellor is satisfied that the payer has ceased to reside in the United Kingdom, the order and the relevant documents will be returned to the court in which the order was registered and the registration will be cancelled[3].

	Action
Payer's whereabouts in area of another magistrates' court	(i) Certified copy of order and relevant documents tp clerk of that area; (ii) order registered in that court.
Outside jurisdiction of any magistrates' court but in United Kingdom	(i) order registered in that court to Lord Chancellor and then to court in U.K. with jurisdiction; (ii) order registered in court in United Kingdom.
Outside United Kingdom	(i) order registered in court in United Kingdom to Lord Chancellor and notice to that effect; (ii) enquiries by Lord Chancellor; (iii) order and relevant documents returned to court in which order registered; (iv) registration cancelled.

1. Maintenance Orders (Reciprocal Enforcement) Act 1972, s 32(1), this PART, post.
2. Maintenance Orders (Reciprocal Enforcement) Act 1972, s 32(2), (6), this PART, post.
3. Maintenance Orders (Reciprocal Enforcement) Act 1972, s 32(5), (7), this PART, post.

6-228 Enforcement of registered orders. A registered order is enforced as if it were a magistrates' court maintenance order[1] made by the registering court[2] and the provisions of Part III of the Magistrates' Courts Act 1980[3] apply with minor modifications. Where payments are four weeks in arrears the justices' chief executive may proceed in his own name for recovery of the sums owing[4].

1. Maintenance Orders (Reciprocal Enforcement) Act 1972, s 33(3), this PART, post.
2. Maintenance Orders (Reciprocal Enforcement) Act 1972, s 33(1), this PART, post.

3. In PART I, MAGISTRATES' COURTS, PROCEDURE, ante.
4. Magistrates' Courts (Recovery Abroad of Maintenance) Rules 1975, r 7(2).

6–229 Variation and revocation of orders. The court in which an order is registered has the like power to vary or revoke a registered order as if it had been made by the registering court and no other court has the power to vary or revoke the order. Application may be made by the payer or the person residing in a convention country[1]. The power to vary an order is provided in s 60(1)–(2) of the Magistrates' Courts Act 1980[2] supplemented by ss 34A and 35 of the Maintenance Orders (Reciprocal Enforcement) Act 1972[3] and includes the power to vary the method of payment[4]. On receipt of an application to vary an order the justices' clerk shall fix the date, time and place for a hearing or directions appointment and the justices' chief executive must notify the applicant of the date, time and place so fixed[5]. The procedure in respect of the hearing is as set out in Sch 2 to the Magistrates' Courts (Recovery Abroad of Maintenance) Rules 1975[6].

1. Maintenance Orders (Reciprocal Enforcement) Act 1972, s 34(1), (3), this PART, post.
2. In PART I, MAGISTRATES' COURTS, PROCEDURE, ante.
3. This PART, post.
4. Maintenance Orders (Reciprocal Enforcement) Act 1972, s 34A(3), this PART, post.
5. Magistrates' Courts (Recovery Abroad of Maintenance) Rules 1975, r 7B, this PART, post.
6. This PART, post.

6–230 Civil Jurisdiction and Judgments Act 1982. The United Kingdom became a party to the 1968 Brussels Convention on jurisdiction and enforcement of judgments in civil and commercial matters by an Accession Convention signed in 1978. The 1988 Lugano Convention made similar arrangements with a number of non-Member States. The Civil Jurisdiction and Judgments Act 1982 (as amended by the Civil Jurisdiction and Judgments Act 1991) gives domestic legislative effect to these two Conventions. In respect of Member States (except Denmark) however, the Brussels Convention has been superseded by the coming into force on 1st March 2002 of Council Regulation (EC) No. 44/2001 of 22nd December 2000 on jurisdiction and the recognition and enforcement of judgments in civil and commercial matters. Regulation 44/2001 is directly applicable to Member States. The Civil Jurisdiction and Judgments Order 2001 amends the 1982 Act so as to preserve the current position in respect of the Brussels Convention, so far as it relates to Denmark, and the Lugano Convention, and in Schedule 1 to the Order makes new but analogous provision in respect of the Regulation[1]. The Civil Jurisdiction and Judgments (Authentic Instruments and Court Settlements) Order 2001[2] makes provision for authentic instruments and court settlements which are enforceable under Chapter IV of the Regulations as if they were judgments. A person domiciled in a state to which the Regulation or the Conventions apply may as a general rule be sued in the courts of that State[3] except that in matters relating to maintenance, the creditor may sue in the court of the State in which he is domiciled. where that court would have jurisdiction according to its own law[4]. An application made by a person who is domiciled or habitually resident in the United Kingdom shall be by way of complaint[5].

The procedures under the 1982 Act do not apply to orders relating to property rights arising under a marriage[6]. Where a spouse is awarded a lump sum, the enforcing court is required to distinguish between those rights which relate to property only and those which relate to maintenance. Therefore where a decision relates to the division of property between spouses it is not enforceable under the Brussels convention, but a decision designed to enable a spouse to provide for herself or where the needs or resources of each party were taken into account is enforceable under the convention. Therefore, a lump sum by way of capitalised maintenance on a clean break basis is enforceable[7].

"Maintenance creditor" for the purpose of bringing proceedings under the Brussels Convention covers any person applying for maintenance including a person bringing a maintenance action for the first time[8].

On making of the complaint the justices' chief executive shall send to the Lord Chancellor—

— a notice of the institution of the proceedings, including a statement of the grounds of the complaint;
— a statement signed by the justices' chief executive, giving such information as he possesses as to the whereabouts of the defendant;
— a statement giving such information as the justices' chief executive possess for facilitating the identification of the defendant, and
— where available, a photograph of the defendant[9].

The justices' chief executive shall give the defendant notice of the hearing by notice in writing addressed to his last known or usual place of abode[10].

Any representations made by the defendant in response shall be considered by the court[11].

Where an order is made notice shall be given to the defendant by post[12] and the following documents shall be given on request to the complainant with a view to an application being made by the complainant for registration and enforcement under Articles 38 and 39 of Council Regulation (EC) No 44/2001 (Articles 31 and 32 of the Brussels Convention)—

— a certified copy of the order;
— a written statement signed by the justices' chief executive as to whether or not the defendant appeared and if not whether a notice of the institution of the proceedings was served on him;
— a document establishing that a notice of the order was sent to the defendant;
— a written statement signed by the justices' chief executive as to whether the complainant received legal aid[12].

1. For the (Civil Jurisdiction and Judgments) Rules 1986, r 10, in this PART, post.
relationship between Council Regulation (EC) No. 44/2001, the Brussels Convention and the Lugarno Convention, see the Civil Jurisdiction and Judgments Order Act 1982, s 1(4), in the PART, post.

2. In this PART, post.
3. Council Regulation (EC) No. 44/2001 art 2.1, Brussels Convention, art 2, this PART, post.
4. Council Regulation (EC) No. 44/2001 art 5.2, Brussels Convention, art 5, this PART, post.
5. Magistrates' Courts
6. Brussels Convention, art 1, this PART, post.
7. *Van Den Boogaard v Laumen* [1997] 3 FCR 493, [197] 2 FLR 399, ECJ.
8. C-295/95: *Farrell v Long* [1997] QB 842, [1997] 3 WLR 613, [1997] 3 FCR 460, ECJ.
9. Magistrates' Courts (Civil Jurisdiction and Judgments Act 1982) Rules 1986, r 10(2), this PART, post.
10. Magistrates' Courts (Civil Jurisdiction and Judgments Act 1982) Rules 1986, r 10(3), this PART, post.
11. Magistrates' Courts (Civil Jurisdiction and Judgments Act 1982) Rules 1986, r 10(4), this PART, post.
12. Magistrates' Courts (Civil Jurisdiction and Judgments Act 1982) Rules 1986, r 10(6), this PART, post.

6–231   Recognition and Enforcement of Judgments made in Member and Contracting States.   A judgment in a Contracting State may be recognised without special procedure[1] except where the circumstances set out in Article 34 or 35 (EC Regulation 44/2000) or 27 or 28 (Brussels Convention) apply (contrary to public policy, judgment impugned for want of notice to the party etc). A judgment is enforceable in a Contracting State where on the application of an interested party it has been declared enforceable there[2]. In England and Wales, the order must be registered for enforcement[3].

Where the justices' chief executive receives an application under Article 33 (EC Regulation 44/2000) or 31 (Brussels Convention), then unless the application is refused under Articles 27 or 28, he shall cause it to be registered by means of a signed minute or memorandum in the court register. Before doing so such steps as are appropriate should be taken to ascertain the whereabouts of the payer and to consider on the available information, the nature and extent of the assets. If the justices' chief executive is satisfied that the payer is not residing within the jurisdiction of the court but there are assets which may be recovered by registration in the High Court, he shall refuse the application and return the documents to the Lord Chancellor with information as to his whereabouts. The justices' chief executive may also return the documents to the Lord Chancellor where he is of the opinion that the payer is residing in the area of another magistrates' court.

On registering the order, notice to be given by the justices' chief executive to the Lord Chancellor, the payer and the payee.

1. Council Regulation (EC) No 44/2001, art 33, Brussels Convention, art 26, this PART, post.
2. Council Regulation (EC) No 44/2001, art 38, Brussels Convention, art 31.
3. Magistrates' Courts (Civil Jurisdiction and Judgments Act 1982) Rules 1986, r 4(1), this PART, post.

6–232   Terms of payment.   Payment shall be ordered to be made to the justices' chief executive who shall remit payments to the court which made the order or as the Lord Chancellor directs[1]. The court may order payment by a particular means[2] and where it does so this shall be notified to the payer in writing[3].

1. Magistrates' Courts (Civil Jurisdiction and Judgments Act 1982) Rules 1986, r 6(1), this PART, post.
2. Magistrates' Courts Act 1980, s 59, PART I, MAGISTRATES' COURTS, PROCEDURE, ante.
3. Magistrates' Courts (Civil Jurisdiction and Judgments Act 1982) Rules 1986 r 6A, this PART, post.

6–233   Enforcement.   The justices' chief executive shall notify the payee of the means available to enforce a registered order including in an appropriate case, registration of the whole or part of the order in the High Court under Part I of the Maintenance Orders Act 1958[1]. The justices' chief executive may proceed in his own name for recovery of sums owing where payments are the equivalent of four weeks in arrears[2].

1. Magistrates' Courts (Civil Jurisdiction and Judgments Act 1982) Rules 1986, r 6(3), this PART, ante.
2. Magistrates' Courts (Civil Jurisdiction and Judgments Act 1982) Rules 1986, r 6(2), this PART, ante.

Statutes on Family Law

Maintenance Orders (Facilities for Enforcement) Act 1920
(10 & 11 Geo 5 c 33)
This Act will remain in force for, and only for, the Commonwealth countries which are not designated as a reciprocating country under Part I of the Maintenance Orders (Reciprocal Enforcement) Act 1972.

6–235   1. Enforcement in England and Ireland of maintenance orders made in Her Majesty's dominions outside the United Kingdom.   (1) Where a[1] maintenance order has, whether before or after the passing of this Act, been made against any person by any court in any part of Her Majesty's dominions outside the United Kingdom to which this Act extends[2], and a certified copy of the order has been transmitted by the governor of that part of Her Majesty's dominions to the Secretary of State[3], the Secretary of State[3] shall send a copy of the order to the prescribed officer[4] of a court in England or Ireland for registration; and on receipt thereof the order shall be registered in the prescribed manner[5], and shall, from the date of such registration, be of the same force and effect, and, subject to the provisions of this Act, all proceedings may be taken on such order as if it had been an order originally obtained in the court in which it is so registered[6], and that court shall have power to enforce the order accordingly.

(2) The court in which an order is to be so registered as aforesaid shall, if the court by which the order was made was a court of superior jurisdiction, be the Probate, Divorce, and Admiralty Division of the High Court, or in Ireland the Queen's Bench Division (Matrimonial) of the High Court of Justice on Ireland, and, if the court was not a court of superior jurisdiction, be a court of summary jurisdiction.

[Maintenance Orders (Facilities for Enforcement) Act 1920, s 1.]

---

1. For definition of "maintenance order", "certified copy", and "prescribed" see s 10, post.
2. See note 1 to s 12, post.
3. Reference to the Secretary of State is to be construed as reference to the Lord Chancellor: SI 1992/709, art 4(1).
4. See Maintenance Orders (Facilities for Enforcement) Rules 1922, r 1, this PART, post.
5. The clerk must enter it in his court register on the date when he receives it, showing that it is entered in pursuance of this Act (r 3). The court shall, unless satisfied that it is undesirable to do so, direct that all payments due thereunder shall be made through an officer of the court, or such other person as it may specify for the purpose. No application is required (r 5). The Home Secretary is advised that a provisional order made by an overseas court takes effect (subject to any modifications made in it) from the date on which it is confirmed in this country under s 4, but an order registered under s 1 has full retrospective effect from the date specified in the original order, or, if no such date is specified, from the date of the order (Home Office Circular, 469, 726/4, dated 15 June 1925). Registration is an administrative act, against which the husband cannot show cause; neither can he appeal against the registration, nor, by reason thereof, against the order itself (*Pilcher v Pilcher* [1955] P 318, [1955] 2 All ER 644, 119 JP 458).
6. This does not enable an application to be maintained for the variation or discharge of an order registered under this subsection (*Pilcher v Pilcher* [1955] P 318, [1955] 2 All ER 644, 119 JP 458; *R v Rose, ex p McGibbon* (1959) 123 JP 374).

6–236   2. Transmission of maintenance orders made in England or Ireland   Where a court in England or Ireland has, whether before or after the commencement of this Act, made a maintenance order against any person, and it is proved to that court that the person against whom the order was made is resident in some part of Her Majesty's dominions outside the United Kingdom to which this Act extends, the court shall send to the Secretary of State[1] for transmission to the governor of that part of Her Majesty's dominions a certified copy of the order[2]. [Maintenance Orders (Facilities for Enforcement) Act 1920, s 2.]

---

1. Reference to the Secretary of State is to be construed as reference to the Lord Chancellor: SI 1992/709, art 4(1).
2. See note 3 to s 3, infra. In transmitting an order under this section there should also be sent a sworn statement of arrears due under the order.

6–237   3. Power to make provisional orders of maintenance against persons resident in Her Majesty's dominions outside the United Kingdom.   (1) Where an application is made to a court of summary jurisdiction in England or Ireland for a maintenance order[1] against any person, and it is proved that that person is resident in a part of Her Majesty's dominions outside the United Kingdom to which this Act extends, the court may, in the absence of that person, if after hearing the evidence it is satisfied of the justice of the application, make any such order as it might have made if that person had been resident in England and Wales, had received reasonable notice of the date of the hearing of the application and had failed to appear at the hearing, but in such case the order shall be provisional[2] only, and shall have no effect unless and until confirmed by a competent court in such part of Her Majesty's dominions as aforesaid.

(2) The evidence of any witness who is examined on any such application shall be put into writing, and such deposition[3] shall be read over to and signed by him.

(3) Where such an order is made, the court shall send to the Secretary of State[4] for transmission to the governor of the part of Her Majesty's dominions in which the person against whom the order is made is alleged to reside the depositions so taken and a certified copy of the order, together with a statement[5] of the grounds on which the making of the order might have been opposed if the person against whom the order is made had been resident in England and Wales, had received reasonable notice of the date of the hearing and had appeared at the hearing, and such information as the court possesses for facilitating the identification[3] of that person, and ascertaining his whereabouts.

(4) Where any such provisional order has come before a court in a part of Her Majesty's dominions outside the United Kingdom to which this Act extends for confirmation, and the order has by that court been remitted to the court of summary jurisdiction which made the order for the purpose of taking further evidence, that court or any other court of summary jurisdiction shall, after giving the prescribed notice[6], proceed to take the evidence in like manner and subject to the like conditions as the evidence in support of the original application.

If upon the hearing of such evidence it appears to the court that the order ought not to have been made, the court may revoke the order, but in any other case the depositions shall be sent to the Secretary of State[4] and dealt with in like manner as the original depositions.

(5) The confirmation of an order made under this section shall not affect any power of a court of summary jurisdiction to vary or revoke that order: Provided that on the making of a varying or

revoking order the court shall send a certified copy thereof to the Secretary of State[4] for transmission to the governor of the part of Her Majesty's dominions in which the original order was confirmed, and that in the case of an order varying the original order the order shall not have any effect unless and until confirmed in like manner as the original order.

(6)   The applicant shall have the same right of appeal[7], if any, against a refusal to make a provisional order as he would have had against a refusal to make the order had the person against whom the order is sought to be made been resident in England and Wales and received reasonable notice of the date of the hearing of the application.

(7)   Where subsection (1) of section 60 of the Magistrates' Courts Act 1980 (revocation, variation etc of orders for periodical payment) applies in relation to an order made under this section which has been confirmed, that subsection shall have effect as if for the words "by order on complaint," there were substituted "on an application being made, by order".

(8)   In this section "revoke" includes discharge.★

[Maintenance Orders (Facilities for Enforcement) Act 1920, s 3, as amended by the Domestic Proceedings and Magistrates' Courts Act 1978, Sch 2, the Justices of the Peace Act 1979, Sch 2, the Maintenance Orders (Reciprocal Enforcement) Act 1992, Sch 1, the Justices of the Peace Act 1997, Sch 5, the Access to Justice Act 1999, Sch 15 and the Courts Act 2003, Sch 8.]

★Repealed by the Maintenance Orders (Reciprocal Enforcement) Act 1972, s 22, when in force.
   1.   Although the section does not refer to jurisdiction, the application must be made to a magistrates' court with jurisdiction; in a matrimonial case the jurisdiction is as stated in s 30(1) of the Domestic Proceedings and Magistrates' Courts Act 1978 (*Collister v Collister* [1972] 1 All ER 334, 136 JP 163). The court expressed the view that a magistrates' court would have jurisdiction where the applicant resided within the petty sessions area for which the court acts even if the cause of application arose wholly outside the area of that court and even outside England and Wales altogether. This Act confers no power to make a contact order; it is uncertain whether a court can make a provisional maintenance order in favour of a child (compare the Maintenance Orders (Reciprocal Enforcement) Act 1972, s 3(3), post, which specifically gives such a power). In this situation an applicant would have to have recourse to the wider powers of the High Court.
   2.   Therefore the order should not be for the payment of money "henceforth".
   3.   For a form of deposition, see 86 JP Jo 225. Information sufficient for ascertaining the whereabouts of the defendant and for his identification, including his last known address, a personal description, and a photograph if one is available, should be annexed to the depositions, together with a certificate of marriage, and, where provision is made for the maintenance of a child, a certificate of birth of the child. The name and address of the clerk should be notified (Home Office Circular).
   4.   Reference to the Secretary of State is to be construed as reference to the Lord Chancellor: SI 1992/709, art 4(1).
   5.   For a form, see Home Office Circular 469, 726/4, dated June 15, 1925, and 86 JP Jo 225. If a dependant is an adopted child one of the grounds will be that no valid adoption order exists. It should be signed by one of the adjudicating justices.
   6.   The notice specifying the further evidence required and the time and place fixed for taking it should be sent by the clerk to the person on whose application the provisional order was made (r 7).
   7.   See the Domestic Proceedings and Magistrates' Courts Act 1978, s 29, post. As to appeals relating to the enforcement of orders, see note 5 to s 4, infra.

6–238   4. Power of court of summary jurisdiction to confirm maintenance order made out of the United Kingdom. (1)   Where a maintenance[1] order has been made by a court in a part of Her Majesty's dominions outside the United Kingdom to which this Act extends, and the order is provisional only and has no effect unless and until confirmed by a court of summary jurisdiction in England or Ireland, and a certified copy of the order, together with the depositions of witnesses and a statement of the grounds on which the order might have been opposed has been transmitted to the Secretary of State[2], and it appears to the Secretary of State[2] that the person against whom the order was made is resident in England or Ireland, the Secretary of State[2] may send the said documents to the prescribed officer[3] of a court of summary jurisdiction, with a requisition that a notice be served on the person informing him that he may attend a hearing at the time and place specified in the notice to show cause why that order should not be confirmed, and upon receipt of such documents and requisition the court shall cause such a notice to be served upon such person.

(2)   A notice required to be served under this section may be served by post.

(3)   At the hearing it shall be open to the person on whom the notice was served to oppose the confirmation of the order on any grounds on which he might have opposed the making of the order in the original proceedings had he been a party to them, but on no other grounds, and the certificate from the court which made the provisional order stating the grounds on which the making of the order might have been opposed if the person against whom the order was made had been a party to the proceedings shall be conclusive[4] evidence that those grounds are grounds on which objection may be taken.

(4)   If at the hearing the person served with the notice does not appear or, on appearing, fails to satisfy the court that the order ought not to be confirmed, the court may confirm the order either without modification or with such modifications[5] as to the court after hearing the evidence may seem just.

(5)   If the person served with the notice appears at the hearing and satisfies the court that for the purpose of establishing any grounds on which he opposes the confirmation of the order it is necessary to remit the case to the court which made the provisional order for the taking of any further evidence, the court may so remit the case and adjourn the proceedings for the purpose.

(5A)   Where a magistrates' court confirms a provisional order under this section, it shall at the same time exercise one of its powers under subsection (5B).

(5B) The powers of the court are—

(*a*) the power to order that payments under the order be made directly to the designated officer for the court or for any other magistrates' court;

(*b*) the power to order that payments under the order be made to the designated officer for the court or for any other magistrates' court by such method of payment falling within section 59(6) of the Magistrates' Courts Act 1980 (standing order, etc) as may be specified;

(*c*) the power to make an attachment of earnings order under the Attachment of Earnings Act 1971 to secure payments under the order.

(5C) In deciding which of the powers under subsection (5B) it is to exercise, the court shall have regard to any representations made by the person liable to make payments under the order.

(5D) Subsection (4) of section 59 of the Magistrates' Courts Act 1980 (power of court to require debtor to open account) shall apply for the purposes of subsection (5B) as it applies for the purposes of that section but as if for paragraph (*a*) there were substituted—

"(*a*) the court proposes to exercise its power under paragraph (*b*) of section 4(5B) of the Maintenance Orders (Facilities for Enforcement) Act 1920, and"

(6) Subject to subsection (6A), where a provisional order has been confirmed under this section, it may be varied or revoked in like manner as if it had originally been made by the confirming court.

(6A) Where the confirming court is a magistrates' court, section 60 of the Magistrates' Courts Act 1980 (revocation, variation etc of orders for periodical payment) shall have effect in relation to a provisional order confirmed under this section—

(*za*) as if in subsection (1) for the words "by order on complaint" there were substituted "on an application being made, by order";

(*a*) as if in subsection (3) for the words "paragraphs (*a*) to (*d*) of section 59(3) above" there were substituted "section 4(5B) of the Maintenance Orders (Facilities for Enforcement) Act 1920";

(*b*) as if in subsection (4) for paragraph (*b*) there were substituted—

"(*b*) payments under the order are required to be made to the designated officer for the court or for any other magistrates' court by any method of payment falling within section 59(6) above (standing order, etc.)",
and as if after the words "the court" there were inserted "which made the order";

(*c*) as if in subsection (5) for the words "to the designated officer for the court" there were substituted "in accordance with paragraph (*a*) of section 4(5B) of the Maintenance Orders (Facilities for Enforcement) Act 1920";

(*d*) as if in subsection (7), paragraph (*c*) and the word "and" immediately preceding it were omitted;

(*e*) as if in subsection (8) for the words "paragraphs (*a*) to (*d*) of section 59(3) above" there were substituted "section 4(5B) of the Maintenance Orders (Facilities for Enforcement) Act 1920";

(*f*) as if for subsections (9) and (10) there were substituted the following subsections—

"(9) In deciding, for the purposes of subsections (3) and (8) above, which of the powers under section 4(5B) of the Maintenance Orders (Facilities for Enforcement) Act 1920 it is to exercise, the court shall have regard to any representations made by the debtor.

(10) Subsection (4) of section 59 above (power of court to require debtor to open account) shall apply for the purposes of subsections (3) and (8) above as it applies for the purposes of that section but as if for paragraph (*a*) there were substituted—

'(*a*) the court proposes to exercise its power under paragraph (*b*) of section 4(5B) of the Maintenance Orders (Facilities for Enforcement) Act 1920, and'."

(7) Where an order has been so confirmed, the person bound thereby shall have the same right of appeal[6], if any, against the confirmation of the order as he would have had against the making of the order had the order been an order made by the court confirming the order.★

[Maintenance Orders (Facilities for Enforcement) Act 1920, s 4 amended by the Maintenance Enforcement Act 1991, Sch 1, the Maintenance Orders (Reciprocal Enforcement) Act 1992, Sch 1, the Access to Justice Act 1999, Sch 13 and the Courts Act 2003, Sch 8.]

★Section 4 is prospectively repealed by the Maintenance Orders (Reciprocal Enforcement) Act 1972, s 22(2)(*a*) from a date to be appointed.

1. Where the relevant dominion statute gives jurisdiction to make an order for custody and maintenance of children, such an order made provisionally may be confirmed in the United Kingdom, even if it is for an amount greater than the maximum which an English court could award (*Harris v Harris* [1949] 2 All ER 318, 113 JP 495).

2. Reference to the Secretary of State is to be construed as reference to the Lord Chancellor; SI 1992/709, art 4(1).

3. See r 1. The clerk shall enter the order in his court register on the date on which he receives it, and such entry shall show that it was entered in pursuance of this Act (r 3).

4. This does not prevent the person to whom notice has been given from raising any defence not included in these grounds (*Re Wheat* [1932] 2 KB 716, 96 JP 399). As for instance, that the court had no jurisdiction to make the order (*Harris v Harris* [1949] 2 All ER 318, 113 JP 495).

5. The order is made in accordance with the laws of the outside dominion (*Peagram v Peagram* [1926] 2 KB 165, 90 JP 136; *Harris v Harris*, supra). The Home Secretary advises that an order for payment in currency other than sterling should be modified so as to make the amount payable in sterling (Home Office Circular 469, 726/4, dated June 15th, 1925). The

clerk shall send notice of the confirmation, and modification (if any), or non-confirmation to the court from which it was issued, and also to the Lord Chancellor (r 4).

6. On appeal, the court may reverse the confirmation on the ground that the matrimonial offence according to the Dominion Law in question has not been committed. Appeal lies to a Divisional Court of the Family Division in accordance with the Rules of the Supreme Court, in PART I: MAGISTRATES' COURTS, PROCEDURE, ante; appeal by case stated against a determination of justices regarding the enforcement of an order confirmed or registered under this Act lies to the same court (Rules of the Supreme Court, Ord 56, r 5(2)).

6–239   4A. Variation and revocation of maintenance orders.   (1) This section applies to—

    (*a*)   any maintenance order made by virtue of section 3 of this Act which has been confirmed as mentioned in that section; and

    (*b*)   any maintenance order which has been confirmed under section 4 of this Act.

(2) Where the respondent to an application for the variation or revocation of a maintenance order to which this section applies is residing in a part of Her Majesty's dominions outside the United Kingdom to which this Act extends, a magistrates' court in England and Wales shall have jurisdiction to hear the application (where it would not have such jurisdiction apart from this subsection) if that court would have had jurisdiction to hear it had the respondent been residing in England and Wales.

(3) Where the respondent to an application for the variation or revocation of a maintenance order to which this section applies is residing in a part of Her Majesty's dominions outside the United Kingdom to which this Act extends, a court of summary jurisdiction in Northern Ireland shall have jurisdiction to hear the application (where it would not have such jurisdiction apart from this subsection) if that court would have had jurisdiction to hear it had the respondent been residing in Northern Ireland.

(4) Where—

    (*a*)   the respondent to an application for the variation or revocation of a maintenance order to which this section applies does not appear at the time and place appointed for the hearing of the application by a magistrates' court in England and Wales, and

    (*b*)   the court is satisfied that the respondent is residing in a part of Her Majesty's dominions outside the United Kingdom to which this Act extends,

the court may proceed to hear and determine the application at the time and place appointed for the hearing or for any adjourned hearing in like manner as if the respondent had appeared at that time and place.

(5) Subsection (4) shall apply to Northern Ireland with the following modifications—

    (*a*)–(*b*)   (*Repealed*);

    (*c*)   for the words "a magistrates' court in England and Wales" there shall be substituted "a court of summary jurisdiction in Northern Ireland".

(6) In this section "revocation" includes discharge.

[Maintenance Orders (Facilities for Enforcement) Act 1920, s 4A, as inserted by the Maintenance Orders (Reciprocal Enforcement) Act 1992, Sch 1 and amended by SI 1995/755.]

6–240   5. Power of Secretary of State[1] to make regulations for facilitating communications between courts.   The Secretary of State[1] may make[2] regulations as to the manner in which a case can be remitted by a court authorised to confirm a provisional order to the court which made the provisional order, and generally for facilitating communications between such courts.

[Maintenance Orders (Facilities for Enforcement) Act 1920, s 5.]

---

1.   Reference to the Secretary of State is to be construed as reference to the Lord Chancellor: SI 1992/709, art 4(1).
2.   No regulations have been made.

6–241   6. Mode of enforcing orders.   (1) A court of summary jurisdiction in which an order has been registered under this Act or by which an order has been confirmed under this Act, and the officers of such court, shall take all such steps for enforcing the order as may be[1] prescribed.

(2) Every such order shall be enforceable in like manner as if the order were for the payment of a civil debt[2] recoverable summarily:

Provided that, if the order is of such a nature that if made by the court in which it is so registered, or by which it is so confirmed, it would be enforceable[3] as a magistrates' court maintenance order, the order shall, subject to the modifications of sections 76 and 93 of the Magistrates' Courts Act 1980 (enforcement of sums adjudged to be paid and complaint for arrears) specified in subsections (2ZA) and (2ZB) of section 18 of the Maintenance Orders Act 1950 (enforcement of registered orders), be so enforceable.

In this subsection "magistrates' court maintenance order" has the same meaning as in section 150(1) of the Magistrates' Courts Act 1980.

(3) A warrant of distress or commitment issued by a court of summary jurisdiction for the purpose of enforcing any order so registered or confirmed may be executed in any part of the United Kingdom in the same manner as if the warrant had been originally issued or subsequently endorsed by a court of summary jurisdiction having jurisdiction in the place where the warrant is executed.

[Maintenance Orders (Facilities for Enforcement) Act 1920, s 6 as amended by the Family Law Reform Act 1987, Sch 2 and the Maintenance Enforcement Act 1991 Sch 1.]

1. The person through whom the payments are directed to be made shall collect the moneys due under the order in the same manner as though it were a magistrates' court maintenance order, and may take proceedings in his own name for enforcing payment, and shall send the moneys, when so collected, to the court from which the order originally issued or otherwise as that court of the Secretary of State may direct (see r 6 of the Maintenance Orders (Facilities for Enforcement) Rules 1922, as amended, this Part, post). Provided that if the court from which the order originally issued is in Malta or in a colony not possessing responsible government, or in a British Protectorate, the moneys so collected shall be paid to the Crown Agents for the Colonies for transmission to the person to whom they are due (r 6). Such Crown Agents do not act for the places marked *in note 1 to s 12, infra, and remittances there cannot be made through them (Home Office Circular No 469, 726/4, dated June 15, 1925).
2. See Magistrates' Courts Act 1980, s 58, in Part I, Magistrates' Courts, Procedure, ante.
3. See the Magistrates' Courts Act 1980, ss 93–95, in Part I, Magistrates' Courts, Procedure, ante.

6–242 7. Application of Summary Jurisdiction Acts. (1) The Magistrates' Courts Act 1952[1] shall apply to proceedings before courts of summary jurisdiction under this Act in like manner as they apply to proceedings under those Acts[2].

(2) For the purpose of giving effect to this Act rules of court may make, in relation to any proceedings brought under or by virtue of this Act, any provision which—

(a) falls within subsection (2) of section 93 of the Children Act 1989, and
(b) may be made in relation to relevant proceedings under that section.

[Maintenance Orders (Facilities for Enforcement) Act 1920, s 7 as amended by the Maintenance Orders (Reciprocal Enforcement) Act 1992, Sch 1 and the Courts Act 2003, Sch 8.]

1. Now the Magistrates' Courts Act 1980.
2. See now the Magistrates' Courts Act 1980 in Part I: Magistrates' Courts, Procedure; s 145(5) preserves Rules made under repealed enactments. See the Maintenance Orders (Facilities for Enforcement) Rules 1922, this Part, post.

6–243 8. Proof of documents signed by officers of court. Any document purporting to be signed by a judge or officer of a court outside the United Kingdom shall, until the contrary is proved, be deemed to have been so signed without proof of the signature or judicial or official character of the person appearing to have signed it, and the officer of a court by whom a document is signed, until the contrary is proved, be deemed to have been the proper officer of the court to sign the document.
[Maintenance Orders (Facilities for Enforcement) Act 1920, s 8.]

6–244 9. Depositions to be evidence. Depositions taken in a court in a part of Her Majesty's dominions outside the United Kingdom to which this Act extends for the purposes of this Act, may be received in evidence in proceedings before courts of summary jurisdiction under this Act.
[Maintenance Orders (Facilities for Enforcement) Act 1920, s 9.]

6–245 10. Interpretation. For the purposes of this Act, the expression "maintenance order" means an order other than an order of affiliation for the periodical payment of sums of money towards the maintenance of the wife or other dependants of the person against whom the order is made, and the expression "dependants" means such persons as that person is, according to the law in force in the part of Her Majesty's dominions in which the maintenance order was made, liable to maintain[1]; the expression "certified copy" in relation to an order of a court means a copy of the order certified by the proper officer of the court to be a true copy, and the expression "prescribed" means prescribed by rules of court.
[Maintenance Orders (Facilities for Enforcement) Act 1920, s 10.]

1. An adopter is liable to maintain adopted children (*Coventry Corpn v Surrey County Council* [1935] AC 199, 98 JP 401).

6–246 12. Extent of Act. (1) Where Her Majesty is satisfied that reciprocal provisions have been made by the legislature of any part of Her Majesty's dominions outside the United Kingdom for the enforcement within that part of maintenance orders made by courts within England and Ireland, Her Majesty may by[1] Order in Council extend this Act to that part, and thereupon that part shall become a part of Her Majesty's dominions to which this Act extends.

(2) Her Majesty may by[1] Order in Council extend this Act to any British protectorate, and where so extended this Act shall apply as if any such protectorate was a part of Her Majesty's dominions to which this Act extends.
[Maintenance Orders (Facilities for Enforcement) Act 1920, s 12.]

1. The parts to which the Act has been so extended are:—**Africa:** The Gambia; Malawi; Mauritius; Nigeria; Zambia; Seychelles; Sierra Leone; Botswana; Lesotho; Swaziland Protectorate; Uganda; Zanzibar. **America:** Bahamas; Guyana; Belize; *in Canada:* *Yukon Territory; Cayman Islands; Dominica; Grenada; Jamaica; *Leeward Islands:* Antigua, Montserrat, St. Christopher and Nevis, and Virgin Islands; St. Lucia; St. Vincent; Trinidad and Tobago. **Asia:** Ceylon; Cyprus; Malaysia. **Australasia:** British Solomon Islands Protectorate; in *Australia:* *Territory of Cocos (Keeling) Islands,

*Territory of Christmas Island (Indian Ocean), and Gilbert and Ellice Islands. **Europe:** *Guernsey, Bailiwick of; *Jersey (Home Office Circular No 90/1959, dated July 7th, 1959 amended to take account of subsequent constitutional changes.)

In respect of places marked with an asterisk, money when collected shall be paid to the court from which the order originally issued; where not so marked money collected shall be paid to the Crown Agents for overseas governments and administrations (at 4, Millbank, London, SW1) for transmission to the person to whom it is due (see r 6 of the Maintenance Orders (Facilities for Enforcement) rules 1922).

An Order in Council made under this section may be revoked or varied by Order in Council (Maintenance Orders Act 1958, s 19).

Marriage Act 1949

(12, 13 & 14 Geo 6 c 76)

6-247　This Act (amended by the Marriage Act 1949 (Amendment) Act 1954, the Marriage Acts Amendment Act 1958, the Marriage (Secretaries of Synagogues) Act 1959, the Marriage (Enabling) Act 1960, the Marriage (Wales and Monmouthshire) Act 1962, the Marriage Act 1983, the Marriage (Prohibited Degrees of Relationship) Act 1986 and the Marriage Act 1994) consolidates previous enactments relating to the solemnisation and registration of marriages in England. It sets out the law as to restrictions on marriages, marriages according to the rites of the Church of England, marriages under a Superintendent Registrar's certificate, and marriages in Naval, Military and Air Force Chapels, and the registration of all such marriages. Schedules to the Act contain tables of kindred and affinity with prohibited degrees of relationship and statutory exemptions therefrom, and modifications of the general law in certain cases. The Act should be consulted where any question is raised as to the validity of any marriage. The Registration of Births, Deaths and Marriages Regulations 1968 (SI 1968/2049 as amended) have been made.

Consent to Marriage of Infant

6-248　**3. Marriages of persons under eighteen.**　(1) Where the marriage of a child, not being a widower or widow, is intended to be solemnized on the authority of a certificates issued by a superintendent registrar under Part III[1] of this Act, the consent of the appropriate persons shall be required. Provided that—

(a)　if the superintendent registrar is satisfied that the consent of any person whose consent is so required cannot be obtained by reason of absence or inaccessibility or by reason of his being under any disability, the necessity for the consent of that person shall be dispensed with, if there is any other person whose consent is also required; and if the consent of no other person is required, the Registrar-General may dispense with the necessity of obtaining any consent, or the court may, on application being made, consent to the marriage, and the consent of the court so given shall have the same effect as if it had been given by the person whose consent cannot be so obtained[1];

(b)　if any person whose consent is required refuses his consent, the court may, on application being made, consent to the marriage, and the consent of the court so given shall have the same effect as if it had been given by the person whose consent is refused.

(1A)　The appropriate persons are—

(a)　if none of paragraphs (b) to (h) apply, each of the following—

(i)　any parent of the child who has parental responsibility for him; and

(ii)　any guardian of the child;

(b)　where a special guardianship order is in force with respect to a child, each of the child's special guardians, unless any of paragraphs (c) to (g) applies;

(c)　where a care order has effect with respect to the child, the local authority designated in the order, and each parent, guardian or special guardian (in so far as their parental responsibility has not been restricted under section 33(3) of the Children Act 1989), unless paragraph (e) applies;

(d)　where a residence order has effect with respect to the child, the persons with whom the child lives, or is to live, as a result of the order, unless paragraph (e) applies;

(e)　where an adoption agency is authorised to place the child for adoption under section 19 of the Adoption and Children Act 2002, that agency or, where a care order has effect with respect to the child, the local authority designated in the order;

(f)　where a placement order is in force with respect to the child, the appropriate local authority;

(g)　where a child has been placed for adoption with prospective adopters, the prospective adopters (in so far as their parental responsibility has not been restricted under section 25(4) of the Adoption and Children Act 2002), in addition to those persons specified in paragraph (e) or (f);

(h)　where none of paragraphs (b) to (g) apply but a residence order was in force with respect to the child immediately before he reached the age of sixteen, the persons with whom he lived, or was to live, as a result of the order.

(1B) In this section—

"guardian of a child", "parental responsibility", "residence order", "special guardian", "special guardianship order" and "care order" have the same meaning as in the Children Act 1989;

"adoption agency", "placed for adoption", "placement order" and "local authority" have the same meaning as in the Adoption and Children Act 2002;

"appropriate local authority" means the local authority authorised by the placement order to place the child for adoption.

(2) Subsection (1) shall apply to marriages intended to be solemnized on the authority of a common licence, with the substitution of references to the ecclesiastical authority by whom the licence was granted for references to the superintendent registrar, and with the substitution of a reference to the Master of the Faculties for the reference to the Registrar-General.

(3) Where the marriage of a child, not being a widower or widow, is intended to be solemnised after the publication of banns of matrimony then, if any person whose consent to the marriage would have been required under this section in the case of a marriage intended to be solemnized otherwise than after the publication of the banns, openly and publicly declares or causes to be declared, in the church or chapel in which the banns are published, at the time of the publication, his dissent from the intended marriage, the publication of banns shall be void.

(4) A clergyman shall not be liable to ecclesiastical censure for solemnising the marriage of a child after the publication of banns without the consent of the parents or guardians of the child unless he had notice of the dissent of any person who is entitled to give notice of dissent under the last foregoing subsection.

(5) For the purposes of this section, "the court" means the High Court, the county court of the district in which any applicant or respondent resides, or a court of summary jurisdiction appointed for the commission area in which any applicant or respondent resides, and rules[2] of court may be made for enabling applications under this section—

(a) if made to the High Court, to be heard in chambers;

(b) if made to the county court, to be heard and determined by the registrar subject to appeal to the judge;

(c) if made to a court of summary jurisdiction, to be heard and determined otherwise than in open court,

and shall provide that, where an application is made in consequence of a refusal to give consent, notice of the application shall be served on the person who has refused consent.

(6) Nothing in this section shall dispense with the necessity of obtaining the consent of the High Court to the marriage of a ward of court.

[Marriage Act 1949, s 3, as amended by the Family Law Reform Act 1969, the Children Act 1975, Sch 3, the Domestic Proceedings and Magistrates' Courts Act 1978, Sch 2, the Justices of the Peace Act 1979, Sch 2, the Family Law Reform Act 1987, Sch 2, the Children Act 1989, Schs 12 and 15, the Justices of the Peace Act 1997, Sch 5, the Immigration and Asylum Act 1999, Schs 14 and 16, the Access to Justice Act 1999, Sch 15 and the Adoption and Children Act 2002, Sch 3.]

---

1. There is no right of appeal against the court's decision (*Re Queskey* [1946] Ch 250, [1946] 1 All ER 717, 110 JP 272). It is doubtful whether a court, after once giving its consent, may afterwards retract it, as a parent or guardian would be entitled to do (see *Hodgkinson v Wilkie* (1795) 1 Hag Con 262; *Yonge v Furse* (1856) 26 LJ Ch 117; on appeal (1857) 26 LJ Ch 352; *Re Brown, Ingall v Brown* [1904] 1 Ch 120); on the authority of the cases cited it is probable that a court would be upheld if it assumed power, after a re-hearing, to retract a consent previously given. A person whose consent is required, where the court has not consented to the marriage, may forbid the issue of a superintendent registrar's certificate by taking the steps prescribed in s 30 of the Act.

2. For procedure, see the Magistrates' Courts (Guardianship of Minors) Rules 1974 this PART, post. Applications under this Act are "family proceedings" (Magistrates' Courts Act 1980, s 65).

General

6–249   75. Offences relating to solemnization of marriages[1]. (1) Any person who knowingly and wilfully—

(a) solemnizes a marriage at any other time[2] than between the hours of eight in the forenoon and six in the afternoon (not being a marriage by special licence, a marriage according to the usages of the Society of Friends or a marriage between two persons professing the Jewish religion according to the usages of the Jews);

(b) solemnizes a marriage according to the rites of the Church of England without banns of matrimony having been duly published (not being a marriage solemnized on the authority of a special licence, a common licence or certificates of a superintendent registrar);

(c) solemnizes a marriage according to the said rites (not being a marriage by special licence or a marriage in pursuance of s 26(1)(*dd*) of this Act) in any place other than a church or other building in which banns may be published;

(d) solemnizes a marriage according to the said rites falsely pretending to be in Holy Orders;

shall be guilty of an offence[3] and shall be liable to imprisonment for a term not exceeding fourteen years.

(2) Any person who knowingly and wilfully—

(*a*) solemnizes a marriage (not being a marriage by special licence, a marriage according to the usages of the Society of Friends or a marriage between two persons professing the Jewish religion according to the usages of the Jews) in any place[4] other than

(i) a church or other building[5] in which marriage may be solemnised according to the rites of the Church of England, or

(ii) the registered building[6] office, approved premises or person's residence specified as the place where the marriage was to be solemnized in the notices of marriage and certificates required under Part III of this Act;

(*aa*) solemnizes a marriage purporting to be in pursuance of section 26(1)(*bb*) of this Act on premises that are not approved premises;

(*b*) solemnizes a marriage in any such registered building as aforesaid (not being a marriage in the presence of an authorised person[7]) in the absence of a registrar of the district in which the registered building is situated; (*bb*) solemnizes a marriage in pursuance of s 26(1)(*dd*) of this Act, otherwise than according to the rites of the Church of England, in the absence of a registrar of the registration district in which the place where the marriage is solemnized is situated;

(*c*) solemnizes a marriage in the office of a superintendent registrar in the absence of a registrar of the district in which the office is situated;

(*cc*) solemnizes a marriage on approved premises in pursuance of section 26(1)(*bb*) of this Act in the absence of a registrar of the district in which the premises are situated;

(*d*) solemnizes a marriage on the authority of certificates of a superintendent registrar before the expiry of the waiting period in relation to each notice of marriage; or

(*e*) solemnizes a marriage on the authority of certificates of a superintendent registrar after the expiration of the period which is, in relation to that marriage, the applicable period for the purposes of section 33 of this Act;

shall be guilty of an offence[8] and shall be liable to imprisonment for a term not exceeding **five years**.

(2A) In subsection (2)(*d*) "the waiting period" has the same meaning as in section 31(94A).

(3) A superintendent registrar who knowingly and wilfully—

(*a*) issues any certificate for marriage

(*b*) issues any certificate for marriage before the expiry of 15 days from the day on which the notice of marriage was entered in the marriage notice book;

(*c*) issues any certificate the issue of which has been forbidden under s 30[9] of this Act by any person entitled to forbid the issue of such a certificate; or

(*d*) solemnizes or permits to be solemnized in his office or, in the case of a marriage in pursuance of section 26(1)(*bb*) or (*dd*) of this Act, in any other place any marriage which is void by virtue of any of the provisions of Part III[10] of this Act;

shall be guilty of an offence[8] and shall be liable to imprisonment for a term not exceeding **five years**.
[Marriage Act 1949, s 75 as amended by the Marriage Act 1983, Sch 1, the Marriage Act 1994, Sch and the Immigration and Asylum Act 1999, Sch 14 and SI 1997/986.]

1. No prosecution under this section shall be commenced after the expiration of three years from the commission of the offence (sub-s (4)). The state of mind of the accused is a relevant factor. A mere charade or a ceremony not intended to deceive anyone is not an offence against this section (*R v Kemp, R v Else* [1964] 2 QB 341, [1964] 1 All ER 649).
2. The provisions of this part of this section do not apply to a marriage solemnised on the authority of the Registrar General's licence. [Marriage (Registrar General's licence) Act 1970, s 16(4), post.]
3. "Offence" is substituted for "felony" to accord with Criminal Law Act 1967, s 12(5).
4. The provisions of this part of this section do not apply to a marriage solemnised on the authority of the Registrar General's licence. [Marriage (Registrar General's licence) Act 1970, s 16(4), post.]
5. For provisions as to the sharing and using of church buildings by different churches, see Sharing of Church Buildings Act 1969.
6. "Registered building" means a building registered under Pt III of the Act (s 78) and the reference to such a building in this subsection includes any chapel registered under s 70 of the Act (s 75(4)).
7. "Authorised person" has the meaning assigned by s 43 of the Act (s 78).
8. "Offence" is substituted for "felony" to accord with Criminal Law Act 1967, s 12(5).
9. Section 30 relates to the forbidding of a marriage of a person under twenty-one years by a person whose consent to such a marriage is required by s 3 of the Act, ante.
10. Part III includes ss 26–52; see in particular s 49 as to void marriages.

6–249A 76. Offences relating to registration of marriages. (1) Any person who refuses or without reasonable cause omits to register any marriage which he is required by this Act to register, and any person on having the custody of a marriage register book or a certified copy of a marriage register book or part thereof who carelessly loses or injures the said book or copy or carelessly allows the said book or copy to be injured while in his keeping, shall be liable on summary conviction to a fine not exceeding **level 3** on the standard scale[1].

(2) Where any person who is required under Part IV of this Act to make and deliver to a superintendent registrar a certified copy of entries made in the marriage register book kept by him,

or a certificate that no entries have been made therein since the date of the last certified copy, refuses to deliver any such copy or certificate, or fails to deliver any such copy or certificate during any month in which he is required to do so, he shall be liable on summary conviction to a fine not exceeding **level 1** on the standard scale[2].

(3) Any registrar who knowingly and wilfully registers any marriage which is void by virtue of any of the provisions of Part III[3] of this Act shall be guilty of an offence[4] and shall be liable[5] to imprisonment for a term not exceeding **five years**.

[Marriage Act 1949, s 76 amended by Criminal Justice Act 1967, 3rd Sch and the Criminal Justice Act 1982, ss 38 and 46.]

---

1. A superintendent registrar may prosecute for offences committed in his district (sub-s (5)). Any fine imposed under this subsection is payable to the Exchequer (sub-s (4)).

2. A superintendent registrar may prosecute for offences committed in his district (sub-s (5)). Any fine imposed under this subsection is payable to the Registrar-General or such other person as may be appointed by the Treasury (sub-s (4)).

3. Part III includes ss 26–52; see in particular s 49 as to void marriages.

4. "Offence" is substituted for "felony" to accord with the Criminal Law Act 1967, s 12(5).

5. See note 1 to s 75, supra. No prosecution shall be commenced after the expiration of three years from the commission of the offence (sub-s (6)).

6–249B   77. Offences by authorised persons[1]. Any authorised person who refuses or fails to comply with the provisions of this Act or any regulations made under s 74[2] thereof shall be guilty of an offence against this Act, and, unless the offence is one for which a specific penalty is provided under the foregoing provisions of this Part of this Act, shall be liable[3], on summary conviction, to a fine not exceeding **the statutory maximum** or, on conviction on indictment, to imprisonment for a term not exceeding **two years** or to a fine, and shall on conviction cease to be an authorised person. [Marriage Act 1949, s 77, as amended by the Criminal Law Act 1977, ss 28 and 32.]

---

1. "Authorised person" has the meaning assigned by s 43 of the Act (s 78).

2. See, eg, the Registration of Births, Deaths and Marriages Regulations 1968, SI 1968/2049.

3. For procedure in respect of this offence triable either way, see the Magistrates' Courts Act 1980, ss 18–21, in PART I, ante.

6–249C   78. Interpretation. (1) In this Act, except where the context otherwise requires, the following expressions have the meanings hereby respectively assigned to them, that is to say—

"approved premises" means premises approved in accordance with regulations under section 46A of this Act as premises on which marriages may be solemnized in pursuance of section 26(1)(*bb*) of this Act;

"authorised chapel" means—

    (*a*) in relation to a chapelry, a chapel of the chapelry in which banns of matrimony could lawfully be published immediately before the passing of the Marriage Act 1823, or in which banns may be published and marriages may be solemnised by virtue of section two of the Marriages Confirmation Act 1825, or of an authorisation given under section three of the Marriage Act 1823;

    (*b*) in relation to an extra-parochial place, a church or chapel of that place in which banns may be published and marriages may be solemnized by virtue of section two of the Marriages Confirmation Act 1825, or of an authorisation given under section three of the Marriage Act 1823, or section twenty-one of this Act;

    (*c*) in relation to a district specified in a licence granted under section twenty of this Act, the chapel in which banns may be published and marriages may be solemnized by virtue of that licence;

"authorised person" has the meaning assigned to it by section forty-three of this Act;

"brother" includes a brother of the half blood;

"child" means a person under the age of eighteen;

"child of the family", in relation to any person, means a child who has lived in the same household as that person and been treated by that person as a child of his family;

"clergyman" means a clerk in Holy Orders of the Church of England;

"common licence" has the meaning assigned to it by section five of this Act;

"ecclesiastical district" in relation to a district other than a parish, means a district specified in a licence granted under section twenty of this Act, a chapelry or an extra-parochial place;

"marriage notice book" has the meaning assigned to it by section twenty-seven of this Act;

"parish" means an ecclesiastical parish and includes a district constituted under the Church Building Acts 1818 to 1884 notwithstanding that the district has not become a new parish by virtue of section fourteen of the New Parishes Act 1856, or section five of the New Parishes Measure 1943, being a district to which Acts of Parliament relating to the publication of banns of matrimony and the solemnization of marriages were applied by the said Church Building Acts as if the district had been an ancient parish, and the expression "parish church" shall be construed accordingly;

"prescribed" means prescribed by regulations made under section seventy-four of this Act;

"registered building" means a building registered under Part III of this Act;

"registrar" means a registrar of marriages;

"Registrar General" means the Registrar General of Births, Deaths and Marriages in England;

"registration district" means the district of a superintendent registrar;

"sister" includes a sister of the half blood.

"special licence" has the meaning assigned to it by section five of this Act;

"superintendent registrar" means a superintendent registrar of births, deaths and marriages;

"trustees or governing body", in relation to Roman Catholic registered buildings, includes a bishop or vicar general of the diocese.

(1A) (*Repealed*).

(2) Any reference in this Act of the Church of England shall, unless the context otherwise requires, be construed as including a reference to the Church in Wales.

(3) For the purposes of this Act a person is house-bound if—

(*a*) each notice of his or her marriage given in accordance with section 27 of this Act is accompanied by a medical statement (within the meaning of section 27A(7) of this Act) made, not more than fourteen days before the date on which that notice was given, in relation to that person; and

(*b*) he or she is not a detained person.

(4) For the purposes of this Act a person is a detained person if he or she is for the time being detained—

(*a*) otherwise than by virtue of section 2, 4, 5, 35, 36 or 136 of the Mental Health Act 1983 (short term detentions), as a patient in a hospital; or

(*b*) in a prison or other place to which the Prison Act 1952 applies,

and in paragraph (*a*) above "patient" and "hospital" have the same meanings as in Part II of the Mental Health Act 1983.

(5) For the purposes of this Act a person who is house-bound or is a detained person shall be taken, if he or she would not otherwise be, to be resident and usually resident at the place where he or she is for the time being.

[Marriage Act 1949, s 78, as amended by the Family Law Reform Act 1969 s 2(1), the Marriage Act 1983, s 1 and Sch 1, the Marriage (Prohibited Degrees of Relationship) Act 1986, s 1 and Sch 1, the Family Law Reform Act 1987, Sch 2, the Children Act 1989, Sch 15 and the Marriage Act 1994, Sch.]

Maintenance Orders Act 1950

(14 Geo 6 c 37)

PART I

JURISDICTION

Jurisdiction of English Courts

6–250 4. Contributions under Children and Young Persons Act 1933 and National Assistance Act 1948.   (1) A court of summary jurisdiction in England shall have jurisdiction in proceedings against a person residing in Scotland or Northern Ireland—

(*a*) Repealed.

(*b*) for an order under section forty-three of the National Assistance Act 1948 (which provides for the recovery from spouses or parents of sums in respect of assistance given under that Act)[1];

(*c*) for an order under section 18 of the Supplementary Benefits Act 1976 (which provides for the recovery of expenditure on supplementary benefits from persons liable for maintenance);

(*d*) for an order under section 106 of the Social Security Administration Act 1992 (which provides for the recovery of expenditure on income support from such persons).

(2) A court in England by which an order has been made under the said section forty-three[2] or the said section eighteen or the said section 106 shall have jurisdiction in proceedings by or against a person residing in Scotland or Northern Ireland for the revocation, revival or variation of that order.

[Maintenance Orders Act 1950, s 4, as amended by the Supplementary Benefits Act 1976, Sch 7, the Child Care Act 1980, Sch 6, the Social Security Act 1986 Sch 10 and the Social Security (Consequential Provisions) Act 1992, Sch 2.]

---

1. See PART VIII, title SOCIAL SECURITY, post.
2. Section 60 of the Magistrates' Courts Act 1980, in PART I: MAGISTRATES' COURTS, PROCEDURE, ante, will apply.

Supplemental

6–251 **15. Service of process.** (1) Where—

   (*a*) proceedings are begun in a court having jurisdiction under or by virtue of the following, namely—

      (i) this Part of this Act; or

      (ii) section 24(1) and 30(3) of the Domestic Proceedings and Magistrates' Courts Act 1978; or

      (iii) section 92 of and Schedule 11 to the Children Act 1989; or

      (iv) section 93(2)(*g*) of that Act (including that provision as applied in relation to Northern Ireland by section 116(3) of the Courts and Legal Services Act 1990); or

      (v) Article 164 of and Schedule 7 to the Children (Northern Ireland) Order 1995 or Article 165(2)(*g*) of that Order; or

      (vi) Article 5(2) of Schedule 4 to the Civil Jurisdiction and Judgments Act 1982; or

   (*b*) an action which contains a conclusion for aliment not falling within the scope of paragraph (*a*)(i) above is commenced in a sheriff court in Scotland,

and the person against whom the action or other proceedings is or are brought resides in another part of the United Kingdom, any summons or initial writ addressed to him in the proceedings may, if endorsed in accordance with the provisions of this section in that part of the United Kingdom[2], be served within that part of the United Kingdom as if it had been issued or authorised to be served, as the case may be, by the endorsing authority.

(2) A summons or writ may be endorsed under this section, in England by a justice of the peace, in Scotland by a sheriff, and in Northern Ireland by a resident magistrate; and the endorsement shall be made in the form numbered 1 in the Second Schedule to this Act, or any form to the like effect.

(3) In any proceedings in which a summons or writ is served under this section, the service may be proved by means of a declaration[3] made in the form numbered 2 in the Second Schedule to this Act, or any form to the like effect, before a justice of the peace, sheriff, or resident magistrate, as the case may be.

(4) Nothing in this section shall be construed as authorising the service of a summons or writ otherwise than personally[4].

(5) Section four of the Summary Jurisdiction (Process) Act 1881[5], shall not apply to any process which may be served under this section; and nothing in this section or in any other enactment shall be construed as authorising the execution in one part of the United Kingdom of a warrant for the arrest of a person who fails to appear in answer to any such process issued in another part of the United Kingdom.

[Maintenance Orders Act 1950, s 15, as amended by the Guardianship of Minors Act 1971, Sch 1, the Maintenance Orders (Reciprocal Enforcement) Act 1972, s 41, the Children Act 1975, Sch 3, the Administration of Justice Act 1977, Sch 3, the Domestic Proceedings and Magistrates' Courts Act 1978, Sch 2, the Child Care Act 1980, Sch 5, the Maintenance Orders (Northern Ireland Consequential Amendments) Order 1980, SI 1980/564, the Civil Jurisdiction and Judgments Act 1982, s 16 and Sch 12, the Courts and Legal Services Act 1990, Sch 16 and SI 1995/756.]

---

   2. England, Scotland and Northern Ireland (England includes Wales) (s 28). References to parts of the United Kingdom are references to England, Scotland, and Northern Ireland (s 28(2)). The Act cannot therefore be misused so as to transfer proceedings to another court in the same part of the Kingdom.

   3. See s 26(1), post.

   4. In England, Scotland and Northern Ireland process will normally be served by the police. In Scotland and Northern Ireland process is served by a court official to whom a fee is payable. Arrangements for the service of process sent to Northern Ireland for endorsement will be made by the clerk of the court there. Advice regarding the service of process in Scotland may be obtained from the Sheriff Clerk or Deputy to whom it is sent for endorsement.

   5. See PART I: MAGISTRATES' COURTS, PROCEDURE—STATUTES ON PROCEDURE, ante.

PART II

ENFORCEMENT

6–252 **16. Application of Part II.** (1) Any order to which this section applies (in this Part of this Act referred to as a maintenance order) made by a court in any part of the United Kingdom[1] may, if registered in accordance with the provisions of this Part of this Act in a court in another part of the United Kingdom[1], be enforced in accordance with those provisions in that other part of the United Kingdom.

(2) This section applies to the following orders, that is to say—

   (*a*) an order for alimony, maintenance or other payments made or deemed to be made by a court in England under any of the following enactments—

      (i) sections 15 to 17, 19 to 22, 30, 34 and 35 of the Matrimonial Causes Act 1965 and sections 22, 23(1), (2) and (4) and 27 of the Matrimonial Causes Act 1973 and section 14 or 17 of the Matrimonial and Family Proceedings Act 1984;*

      (ii) Part I of the Domestic Proceedings and Magistrates' Courts Act 1978;

      (iii) Schedule 1 to the Children Act 1989;

(iv) *(Repealed).*

(v) paragraph 23 of Schedule 2 to the Children Act 1989, or section 43 of the National Assistance Act 1948;

(vi) section 18 of the Supplementary Benefits Act 1976;

(vii) *(Repealed);*

(viii) section 106 of the Social Security Administration Act 1992;

(b) a decree for payment of aliment granted by a court in Scotland, including—

(i) an order for the payment of an annual or periodical allowance under section two of the Divorce (Scotland) Act 1938 or an order for the payment of a periodical allowance or a capital sum under section 26 of the Succession (Scotland) Act 1964 or section 5 of the Divorce (Scotland) Act 1976 or section 29 of the Matrimonial and Family Proceedings Act 1984 or an order for financial provision in the form of a monetary payment under s 8 of the Family Law (Scotland) Act 1985;

(ii) an order for the payment of weekly or periodical sums under subsection (2) of section three or subsection (4) of section five of the Guardianship of Infants Act 1925;

(iii) an order for the payment of sums in respect of aliment under subsection (3) of section one of the Illegitimate Children (Scotland) Act 1930;

(iv) a decree for payment of aliment under section forty-four of the National Assistance Act 1948, or under section twenty-six of the Children Act 1948; and

(v) an order under section forty-three of the National Assistance Act 1948;

(vi) a contribution order under section 80 of, or a decree or an order made under section 81 of, the Social Work (Scotland) Act 1968;

(vii) an order for the payment of weekly or other periodical sums under subsection (3) of section 11 of the Guardianship Act 1973;

(viii) an order made on an application under section 18 or 19(8) of the Supplementary Benefits Act 1976;

(ix) an order made on an application under section 106 of the Social Security Administration Act 1992;

(c) an order for alimony, maintenance or other payments made by a court in Northern Ireland under or by virtue of any of the following enactments—

(i) subsection (2) of section seventeen, subsections (2) to (7) of section nineteen, subsection (2) of section twenty, section twenty-two or subsection (1) of section twenty-eight of the Matrimonial Causes Act (Northern Ireland) 1939;

(ii) Schedule 1 to the Children (Northern Ireland) Order 1995;

(iii) *Repealed.*

(iv) Article 41 of the Children (Northern Ireland) Order 1995 or Article 101 of the Health and Personal Social Services (Northern Ireland) Order 1972;

(v) any enactment of the Parliament of Northern Ireland containing provisions corresponding with section 22(1), 34 or 35 of the Matrimonial Causes Act 1965, with section 22, 23(1), (2) or (4) or 27 of the Matrimonial Causes Act 1973;*

(vi) Article 23 or 24 of the Supplementary Benefits (Northern Ireland) Order 1977;

(vii) the Domestic Proceedings (Northern Ireland) Order 1980;

(viii) any enactment applying in Northern Ireland and corresponding to section 106 of the Social Security Administration Act 1992.

(ix) Articles 18 or 21 of the Matrimonial and Family Proceedings (Northern Ireland) Order 1989.

[Maintenance Orders Act 1950, s 16(1), (2), as amended by the Social Work (Scotland) Act 1968, s 95 and Sch 8, the Guardianship of Minors Acts 1971, Sch 1, and 1973, s 9 and Sch 5, the Matrimonial Causes Act 1973, Sch 2; the Children Act 1975, Sch 3, the Divorce (Scotland) Act 1976, s 12 and Sch 1, the Supplementary Benefits Act 1976, Sch 7, the Administration of Justice Act 1977, Sch 3, SI 1977/2158, the Domestic Proceedings and Magistrates' Courts Act 1978, Sch 2, the Child Care Act 1980, Sch 5; the Maintenance Orders (Northern Ireland Consequential Amendments) Order 1980, SI 1980/564; the Social Security and Housing Benefits Act 1982, Sch 4, the Civil Jurisdiction and Judgments Act 1982, Sch 14, the Matrimonial and Family Proceedings Act 1984, Sch 1, the Family Law (Scotland) Act 1985, Sch 1, the Social Security Act 1986, Sch 10, the Family Law Reform Act 1987, Schs 2 and 4, the Matrimonial and Family Proceedings (Northern Ireland Consequential Amendment) Order 1989, SI 1989/678, the Courts and Legal Services Act 1990, Schs 16 and 20, the Social Security (Consequential Provisions) Act 1992, Sch 2 and SI 1995/756.]

---

*Amended by the Family Law Act 1996, Sch 8, this PART, POST, WHEN IN FORCE.

1. England, Scotland and Northern Ireland (England includes Wales) (s 28). References to parts of the United Kingdom are references to England, Scotland, and Northern Ireland (s 28(2)). The Act cannot therefore be misused so as to transfer proceedings to another court in the same part of the kingdom.

6–253 **17. Procedure for registration of maintenance orders[1].** (1) An application for the registration of a maintenance order under this Part of this Act shall be made in the prescribed manner[2] to the appropriate authority, that is to say—

(a) where the maintenance order was made by a court of summary jurisdiction in England, a justice or justices acting in the same local justice area as the court which made the order;

(b) where the maintenance order was made by a court of summary jurisdiction in Northern Ireland, a resident magistrate acting for the same petty sessions district as the court which made the order;

(c) in every other case, the prescribed officer of the court which made the order.

(2) If upon application made as aforesaid by or on behalf of the person entitled to payments under a maintenance order it appears that the person liable to make those payments resides in another part of the United Kingdom[3], and that it is convenient that the order should be enforced there, the appropriate authority shall cause a certified copy[4] of the order[5] to be sent to the prescribed officer of a court in that part of the United Kingdom in accordance with the provisions of the next following subsection.

(3) The Court to whose officer the certified copy[4] of a maintenance order is sent under this section shall be—

(a) where the maintenance order was made by a superior court, the Supreme Court of Judicature in England, the Court of Session or the Supreme Court of Judicature of Northern Ireland, as the case may be;*

(b) in any other case, a court of summary jurisdiction acting for the place in England or Northern Ireland in which the defendant appears to be, or, as the case may be, the sheriff court in Scotland within the jurisdiction of which he appears to be.

(4) Where the prescribed officer of any court receives a certified copy[4] of a maintenance order sent to him under this section, he shall cause the order to be registered in that court in the prescribed manner, and shall give notice of the registration in the prescribed manner to the prescribed officer of the court which made the order[6].

(5) The officer to whom any notice is given under the last foregoing subsection shall cause particulars of the notice to be registered in his court in the prescribed manner[2].

(6) Where the sums payable under a maintenance order, being an order made by a court of summary jurisdiction in England or Northern Ireland, are payable to or through an officer of any court, that officer shall, if the person entitled to the payments so requests, make an application on behalf of that person for the registration of the order under this Part of this Act; but the person at whose request the application is made shall have the same liability for costs properly incurred in or about the application as if the application had been made by him.

(7) An order which is for the time being registered under this Part of this Act in any court shall not be registered thereunder in any other court.

[Maintenance Orders Act 1950, s 17 as amended by the Courts Act 2003, Sch 8.]

---

*Amended by the Constitutional Reform Act 2005, Sch 11 from a date to be appointed.

1. Maintenance orders made by the Court of Session or the High Court in Northern Ireland which were registered in the High Court and purportedly thereafter registered in a magistrates' court before the coming into force of Schedule 3 to the Administration of Justice Act 1977 shall be deemed to be and always to have been validly registered in the magistrates' court, and accordingly the provisions of Part I of the Maintenance Orders Act 1958 shall apply to them (Administration of Justice Act 1977, Sch 3, para 10).

2. See the Maintenance Orders Act 1950 (Summary Jurisdiction) Rules 1950 (SI 1950/2035), this PART, post.

3. See note 1 to s 16, ante.

4. Ie a copy certified by the proper officer of the court to be a true copy of the order or of the official record thereof (s 28(1)).

5. See *Practice Direction (maintenance: registration of orders)* [1980] 1 All ER 1007, [1980] 1 WLR 354 which discourages orders for payment direct to a child where no benefit would accrue to the parties, and registration of nominal orders and orders for maintenance pending suit and interim orders.

6. The Magistrates' Courts Rules 1981, rr 68, 69, in PART I: MAGISTRATES' COURTS, PROCEDURE, ante, are applied by s 26(2).

6-254　18. Enforcement of registered orders.　(1) Subject to the provisions of this section, a maintenance order registered under this Part of this Act in a court in any part of the United Kingdom[1] may be enforced in that part of the United Kingdom in all respects as if it had been made by that court and as if that court had had jurisdiction to make it; and proceedings for or with respect to the enforcement of any such order may be taken accordingly[2].

(1A) A maintenance order registered under this Part of this Act in a court of summary jurisdiction in England or Northern Ireland shall not carry interest; but where a maintenance order so registered is registered in the High Court under Part I of the Maintenance Orders 1958 or section 36 of the Civil Jurisdiction and Judgments Act 1982, this subsection shall not prevent any sum for whose payment the order provides from carrying interest in accordance with section 2A of the said Act of 1958 or section 11A of the Maintenance and Affiliation Orders Act (Northern Ireland) 1966.

(1B) A maintenance order made in Scotland which is registered under this Part of this Act in the Supreme Court in England or Northern Ireland shall, if interest is by the law of Scotland recoverable under the order, carry the like interest in accordance with subsection (1) of this section.*

(2) Every maintenance order registered under this Part of this Act in a magistrates' court in England and Wales shall, subject to the modifications of sections 76 and 93 of the Magistrates' Courts Act 1980 specified in subsections (2ZA) and (2ZB) of this section, be enforceable as a

magistrates' court maintenance order within the meaning of section 150(1) of the Magistrates' Courts Act 1980[3].

(2ZA) Section 76 (enforcement of sums adjudged to be paid) shall have effect as if for subsections (4) to (6) there were substituted the following subsections—

"(4) Where proceedings are brought for the enforcement of a magistrates' court maintenance order under this section, the court may vary the order by exercising one of its powers under subsection (5) below.

(5) The powers of the court are—

(a) the power to order that payments under the order be made directly to the designated officer for the court or for any other magistrates' court;

(b) the power to order that payments under the order be made to a the designated officer for the court or for any other magistrates' court, by such method of payment falling within section 59(6) above (standing order, etc.) as may be specified;

(c) the power to make an attachment of earnings order under the Attachment of Earnings Act 1971 to secure payments under the order.

(6) In deciding which of the powers under subsection (5) above it is to exercise, the court shall have regard to any representations made by the debtor (within the meaning of section 59 above).

(7) Subsection (4) of section 59 above (power of court to require debtor to open account) shall apply for the purposes of subsection (5) above as it applies for the purposes of that section but as if for paragraph (a) there were substituted—

"(a) the court proposes to exercise its power under paragraph (b) of section 76(5) below, and"."

(2ZB) In section 93 (complaint for arrears), subsection (6) (court not to impose imprisonment in certain circumstances) shall have effect as if for paragraph (b) there were substituted—

"(b) if the court is of the opinion that it is appropriate—

(i) to make an attachment of earnings order; or

(ii) to exercise its power under paragraph (b) of section 76(5) above."

(2A) Any person under an obligation to make payments under a maintenance order registered under this Part of this Act in a court of summary jurisdiction in England or Northern Ireland shall give notice of any change of address to the proper officer of the court; and any person who without reasonable excuse fails to give such a notice shall be liable on summary conviction to a fine not exceeding **level 2** on the standard scale.

(2B) In subsection (2A) of this section "proper officer" means—

(a) in relation to a court of summary jurisdiction in England and Wales, the designated officer for the court; and

(b) in relation to a court of summary jurisdiction in Northern Ireland, the clerk of the court.

(3) Every maintenance order registered under this Part of this Act in a court of summary jurisdiction in Northern Ireland shall be enforceable as an order made by that court to which Article 98 of the Magistrates' Courts (Northern Ireland) Order 1981 applies, subject to the modifications of that Article specified in subsection (3ZA) of this section.

(3ZA) Article 98 (enforcement of sums adjudged to be paid) shall have effect—

(a) as if for paragraph (7)(a) there were substituted the following sub-paragraph—

"(a) if the court is of the opinion that it is appropriate—

(i) to make an attachment of earnings order; or

(ii) to exercise its power under paragraph (8C)(b)";

(b) as if for paragraphs (8B) to (8D) there were substituted the following paragraphs—

"(8B) Upon the appearance of a person or proof of service of the summons on him as mentioned in paragraph (4) for the enforcement of an order to which this Article applies, the court or resident magistrate may vary the order by exercising one of the powers under paragraph (8C).

(8C) The powers mentioned in paragraph (8B) are—

(a) the power to order that payments under the order may be made directly to the collecting officer;

(b) the power to order that payments under the order be made to the collecting officer by such method of payment falling within Article 85(7) (standing order, etc) as may be specified;

(c) the power to make an attachment of earnings order under Part IX to secure payments under the order.

(8D) In deciding which of the powers under paragraph (8C) is to be exercised, the court or, as the case may be, a resident magistrate shall have regard to any representations made by the debtor (within the meaning of Article 85).

(8E) Paragraph (5) of Article 85 (power of court to require debtor to open account) shall apply for the purposes of paragraph (8C) as it applies for the purposes of that Article but as if for sub-paragraph (*a*) there were substituted—

"(*a*) the court proposes to exercise its power under sub-paragraph (*b*) of Article 98(8C), and".

(3A) Notwithstanding subsection (1) above, no court in England in which a maintenance order is registered under this Part of this Act shall enforce that order to the extent that it is for the time being registered in another court in England under Part I of the Maintenance Orders Act 1958.

(3B) Notwithstanding subsection (1) above, no court in Northern Ireland in which a maintenance order is registered under this Part of this Act shall enforce that order to the extent that it is for the time being registered in another court in Northern Ireland under section 36 of the Civil Jurisdiction and Judgments Act 1982.

(4) *Repealed.*

(5) *Repealed.*

(6) Except as provided by this section, no proceedings shall be taken for or with respect to the enforcement of a maintenance order which is for the time being registered in any court under this Part of this Act.

[Maintenance Orders Act 1950, s 18, amended by Ministry of Social Security Act 1966, 8th Sch, the Administration of Justice Act 1977, Sch 3, the Civil Jurisdiction and Judgments Act 1982, Schs 11 and 12, the Matrimonial and Family Proceedings Act 1984, Sch 1, the Family Law Reform Act 1987, Sch 2, the Matrimonial and Family Proceedings (Northern Ireland) Order 1989, SI 1989/677, the Maintenance Enforcement Act 1991, Sch 1, the Statute Law (Repeals) Act 1993, Sch 1, SI 1993/1577, SI 1995/756, the Access to Justice Act 1999, Sch 13 and the Ocurts Act 2003, Sch 8.]

---

*Amended by the Constitutional Reform Act 2005, Sch 11 from a date to be appointed.

1. See note 2 to s 15, ante.

2. The method of enforcement in Northern Ireland is similar to that prevailing in England. In Scotland, however, the court does not normally itself enforce the order and persons seeking enforcement are advised to instruct a legal representative in Scotland to act on their behalf. The recovery of arrears due prior to the passing of the Act is restricted by s 20(3).

3. See PART I: MAGISTRATES' COURTS, PROCEDURE, ante.

6–255   19. Functions of collecting officer, etc.   (1) Where a maintenance order made in England or Northern Ireland by a court of summary jurisdiction is registered in any court under this Part of this Act, any provision of the order by virtue of which sums payable thereunder are required to be paid through or to any officer or person on behalf of the person entitled thereto shall be of no effect so long as the order is so registered[1].

(2) Where a maintenance order is registered under this Part of this Act in a court of summary jurisdiction in England or Northern Ireland, the court shall, order that all payments to be made under the maintenance order (including any arrears accrued before the date of the registration) shall be made through the collecting officer of the court or the collecting officer of some other court of summary jurisdiction in England or Northern Ireland, as the case may be[2].

(3) An order made under subsection (2) of this section—

(*a*) by a court of summary jurisdiction in England may be varied or revoked[3] by an exercise of the powers conferred by virtue of section 18(2ZA) or section 22(1A) or (1E) of this Act;

(*b*) by a court of summary jurisdiction in Northern Ireland may be varied or revoked by an exercise of the powers conferred by virtue of section 18(3ZA) or section 22(1F) or (1J) of this Act.

(4) Where by virtue of the provisions of this section or any order made thereunder payments under a maintenance order cease to be or become payable through or to any officer or person, the person liable to make the payments shall, until he is given the prescribed notice to that effect, be deemed to comply with the maintenance order if he makes payments in accordance with the maintenance order and any order under this section of which he has received such notice.

(5) *(Repealed).*

[Maintenance Orders Act 1950, s 19(1)–(4) amended by the Maintenance Enforcement Act 1991, Sch 1 and the Family Law (Northern Ireland Consequential Amendments) Order 1993, SI 1993/1577.]

---

1. There are collecting officers in England and Northern Ireland, but not in Scotland. When an order has been registered elsewhere, an English collecting officer cannot assent to enforce the order by taking proceedings in his own name; see note 2 to s 18, ante.

2. The justices' chief executive will be obliged to notify the person entitled to payments if these payments fall into arrear and to take steps to enforce the order; see Magistrates' Courts Act 1980, s 59A, in PART I: MAGISTRATES' COURTS, PROCEDURE, ante. The Maintenance Orders Act 1950 (Summary Jurisdiction) Rules 1950 (SI 1950/2035), this PART, post, prescribe the notices to be given to the defendant in respect of sub-s (2) and sub-s (4).

3. An application would for example be appropriate where despite the order the parties have persisted in making and receiving payment direct. Rule 50 of the Magistrates' Courts Rules 1981 will apply.

4. These subsections also have effect for the purposes of orders registered under Pt I of the Maintenance Orders Act 1958 (Maintenance Orders Act 1958, s 2(6), post).

6–256   20. Arrears under registered maintenance orders.   (1) Where application is made for the registration of a maintenance order under this Part of this Act[1], the applicant may lodge with the appropriate authority[2]—

(*a*)   if the payments under the order are required to be made to or through an officer of any court, a certificate in the prescribed form[3], signed by that officer, as to the amount of any arrears due under the order;

(*b*)   in any other case, a statutory declaration or affidavit[4] as to the amount of those arrears;

and if a certified copy[5] of the maintenance order is sent to the prescribed officer of any court in pursuance of the application, the certificate, declaration or affidavit shall also be sent to that officer.

(2)   In any proceedings for or with respect to the enforcement of a maintenance order which is for the time being registered in any court under this Part of this Act, a certificate, declaration or affidavit sent under this section to the appropriate officer of that court shall be evidence, and in Scotland sufficient evidence, of the facts stated therein.

(3)   Where a maintenance order made by a court in England or Northern Ireland is registered in a court in Scotland, a person shall not be entitled, except with the leave of the last-mentioned court, to enforce, whether by diligence or otherwise, the payment of any arrears accrued and due under the order before the commencement of this Act; and on any application for leave to enforce the payment of any such arrears, the court may refuse leave, or may grant leave subject to such restrictions and conditions (including conditions as to the allowing of time for payment or the making of payment by instalments) as the court thinks proper, or may remit the payment of such arrears or of any part thereof.

[Maintenance Orders Act 1950, s 20.]

1.   Under s 17, ante.
2.   See s 17, ante.
3.   Maintenance Orders Act 1950 (Summary Jurisdiction) Rules 1950, Form 3, this PART, post.
4.   See precedents in PART IX: PRECEDENTS AND FORMS, title FAMILY LAW, post.
5.   See note 4, to s 17, ante.

6–257   22. Discharge and variation of maintenance orders registered in summary or sheriff courts.   (1)   Where a maintenance order is for the time being registered under this Part of this Act[1] in a court of summary jurisdiction or sheriff court, that court may, upon application[2] made in the prescribed manner[3] by or on behalf of the person liable to make periodical payments under the order or the person entitled to those payments, by order make such variation as the court thinks fit in the rate of the payments under the maintenance order but no such variation shall impose on the person liable to make payments under the maintenance order a liability to make payments in excess of the maximum rate (if any) authorised by the law for the time being in force in the part of the United Kingdom in which the maintenance order was made.

(1A)   The power of a magistrates' court in England and Wales to vary a maintenance order under subsection (1) of this section shall include power, if the court is satisfied that payment has not been made in accordance with the order, to vary the order by exercising one of its powers under subsection (1B) of this section.

(1B)   The powers of the court are—

(*a*)   the power to order that payments under the order be made directly to the designated officer for the court or for any other magistrates' court in England and Wales;

(*b*)   the power to order that payments under the order be made to the designated officer for the court or for any other magistrates' court in England and Wales, by such method of payment falling within section 59(6) of the Magistrates' Courts Act 1980 (standing order, etc) as may be specified;

(*c*)   the power to make an attachment of earnings order under the Attachment of Earnings Act 1971 to secure payments under the order.

(1C)   In deciding which of the powers under subsection (1B) of this section it is to exercise, the court shall have regard to any representations made by the person liable to make payments under the order.

(1D)   Subsection (4) of section 59 of the Magistrates' Courts Act 1980 (power of court to require debtor to open account) shall apply for the purposes of subsection (1B) of this section as it applies for the purposes of that section but as if for paragraph (*a*) there were substituted—

"(*a*) the court proposes to exercise its power under paragraph (*b*) of section 22(1B) of the Maintenance Orders Act 1950, and".

(1E)   Subsections (4) to (11) of section 60 of the Magistrates' Courts Act 1980 (power of clerk and court to vary maintenance order) shall apply in relation to a maintenance order for the time being registered under this Part of this Act in a magistrates' court in England and Wales as they apply in relation to a maintenance order made by a magistrates' court in England and Wales but—

(*a*)   as if in subsection (4) for paragraph (*b*) there were substituted—

"(*b*) payments under the order are required to be made to the designated officer for the court or for any other magistrates' court, by any method of payment falling within section 59(6) above (standing order, etc)";

(b) as if in subsection (5) for the words "to the the designated officer for the court" there were substituted "in accordance with paragraph (a) of section 22(1B) of the Maintenance Orders Act 1950";

(c) as if in subsection (7), paragraph (c) and the word "and" immediately preceding it were omitted;

(d) as if in subsection (8) for the words "paragraphs (a) to (d) of section 59(3) above" there were substituted "section 22(1B) of the Maintenance Orders Act 1950";

(e) as if for subsections (9) and (10) there were substituted the following subsections—

"(9) In deciding which of the powers under section 22(1B) of the Maintenance Orders Act 1950 it is to exercise, the court shall have regard to any representations made by the debtor.

(10) Subsection (4) of section 59 above (power of court to require debtor to open account) shall apply for the purposes of subsection (8) above as it applies for the purposes of that section but as if for paragraph (a) there were substituted—

'(a) the court proposes to exercise its power under paragraph (b) of section 22(1B) of the Maintenance Orders Act 1950, and'."

(1F) The power of a court of summary jurisdiction in Northern Ireland to vary a maintenance order under subsection (1) of this section shall include power, if the court is satisfied that payment has not been made in accordance with the order, to vary the order by exercising one of its powers under subsection (1G) of this section.

(1G) The powers of the court are—

(a) the power to order that payments under the order be made directly to the collecting officer;

(b) the power to order that payments under the order be made to the collecting officer by such method of payment falling within Article 85(7) of the Magistrates' Courts (Northern Ireland) Order 1981 (standing order, etc) as may be specified;

(c) the power to make an attachment of earnings order under Part IX of the Order of 1981 to secure payments under the order;

and in this subsection "collecting officer" means the officer mentioned in Article 85(4) of the Order of 1981.

(1H) In deciding which of the powers under subsection (1G) of this section it is to exercise, the court shall have regard to any representations made by the person liable to make payments under the order.

(1I) Paragraph (5) of Article 85 of the Magistrates' Courts (Northern Ireland) Order 1981 (power of court to require debtor to open account) shall apply for the purposes of subsection (1G) of this section as it applies for the purposes of that Article but as if for sub-paragraph (a) there were substituted—

"(a) the court proposes to exercise its power under paragraph (b) of section 22(1G) of the Maintenance Orders Act 1950, and".

(1J) Paragraphs (4) to (11) of Article 86 of the Magistrates' Courts (Northern Ireland) Order 1981 (power of clerk and court to vary maintenance order) shall apply in relation to a maintenance order for the time being registered under this Part of this Act in a court of summary jurisdiction in Northern Ireland as they apply in relation to a maintenance order made by a court of summary jurisdiction in Northern Ireland but—

(a) as if in paragraph (4) for sub-paragraph (b) there were substituted—

"(b) payments under the order are required to be made to the collecting officer by any method of payment falling within Article 85(7) (standing order, etc)";

and as if after the words "petty sessions" there were inserted "for the petty sessions district for which the court which made the order acts";

(b) as if in paragraph (5) for the words "to the collecting officer" there were substituted "in accordance with paragraph (a) of section 22(1G) of the Maintenance Orders Act 1950";

(c) as if in paragraph (7), sub-paragraph (c) and the word "and" immediately preceding it were omitted;

(d) as if in paragraph (8) for the words "sub-paragraphs (a) to (d) of Article 85(3)" there were substituted "section 22(1G) of the Maintenance Orders Act 1950";

(e) as if for paragraphs (9) and (10) there were substituted the following paragraphs—

"(9) In deciding which of the powers under section 22(1G) of the Maintenance Orders Act 1950 it is to exercise, the court shall have regard to any representations made by the debtor.

(10) Paragraph (5) of Article 85 (power of court to require debtor to open account) shall apply for the purposes of paragraph (8) as it applies for the purposes of that Article but as if for sub-paragraph (a) there were substituted—

'(a) the court proposes to exercise its power under paragraph (b) of section 22(1G) of the Maintenance Orders Act 1950, and'."

(2) For the purposes of subsection (1) of this section, a court in any part of the United Kingdom may take notice of the law in force in any other part of the United Kingdom[4].

(3) Section fifteen of this Act shall apply to the service of process for the purposes of this section as it applies to the service of process in proceedings begun in a court having jurisdiction by virtue of Part I of this Act.

(4) Except as provided by subsection (1) of this section, no variation shall be made in the rate of the payments under a maintenance order which is for the time being registered under this Part of this Act in a court of summary jurisdiction or sheriff court, but without prejudice to any power of the court which made the order to discharge it or vary it otherwise than in respect of the rate of the payments thereunder.

(5) Where a maintenance order is for the time being registered under this Part of this Act in a court of summary jurisdiction or sheriff court—

(a) the person entitled to payments under the order or the person liable to make payments under the order may, upon application made in the prescribed manner to the court by which the order was made, or in which the order is registered, as the case may be, adduce in the prescribed manner[3] before the court in which the application is made any evidence on which he would be entitled to rely in proceedings for the variation or discharge of the order;

(b) the court in which the application is made shall cause a transcript or summary of that evidence, signed by the deponent, to be sent to the prescribed officer of the court in which the order is registered or of the court by which the order was made, as the case may be; and in any proceedings for the variation or discharge of the order the transcript or summary shall be evidence[5] of the facts stated therein.

[Maintenance Orders Act 1950, s 22, as amended by the Domestic Proceedings and Magistrates' Courts Act 1978, Sch 2, the Maintenance Enforcement Act 1991, Sch 1, the Access to Justice Act 1999, Sch 13, SI 1999/1577 and the Courts Act 2003, Sch 8.]

1. Under s 17, ante.
2. Representation may be granted in proceedings under this section; see Sch 2 to the Legal Aid Act 1988, ante.
3. See the Maintenance Orders Act 1950 (Summary Jurisdiction) Rules 1950, rr 3, 8 and 9, this PART, post.
4. Enquiry regarding this matter should be made of the clerk of the court which made the order.
5. But not *conclusive* evidence.

6–258 **23. Notice of variation, etc.** (1) Where a maintenance order registered under this Part of this Act is discharged or varied by any court, the prescribed officer of that court shall give notice of the discharge or variation in the prescribed manner[1]—

(a) to the prescribed officer of any court in which the order is registered; and
(b) if the order was made by another court, to the prescribed officer of that court.

(2) Any officer to whom a notice is given under this section shall cause particulars of the notice to be registered in his court in the prescribed manner.

[Maintenance Orders Act 1950, s 23, as substituted by the Administration of Justice Act 1977, Sch 3.]

1. See note 3 to s 22, supra, and rr 4 and 10 of the Rules there noted.

6–259 **24. Cancellation of registration.** (1) At any time while a maintenance order is registered under this Part of this Act in any court, an application for the cancellation of the registration may be made in the prescribed manner[1] to the prescribed officer of that court by or on behalf of the person entitled to payments under the order; and upon any such application that officer shall (unless proceedings for the variation of the order are pending in that court), cancel the registration, and thereupon the order shall cease to be registered in that court.

(2) Where after a maintenance order has been registered under this Part of this Act in a court of summary jurisdiction in England or Northern Ireland or a sheriff court in Scotland, it appears to the appropriate authority (as defined by section seventeen of this Act), upon application made in the prescribed manner by or on behalf of the person liable to make payments under the order, that that person has ceased to reside in England, Northern Ireland or Scotland, as the case may be, the appropriate authority may cause a notice to that effect to be sent to the prescribed officer of any court in which the order is registered; and where such a notice is sent the prescribed officer shall cancel the registration of the maintenance order, and thereupon the order shall cease to be registered in that court.

(3) Where the prescribed officer of any court cancels the registration of a maintenance order under this section, he shall give notice of the cancellation in the prescribed manner[1]—

(a) to the prescribed officer of the court by which the order was made; and
(b) to the prescribed officer of any court in which it is registered under Part I of the Maintenance Orders Act 1958 or section 36 of the Civil Jurisdiction and Judgments Act 1982.

(3A) On receipt of a notice under subsection (3) above—

(a) any such officer as is mentioned in paragraph (a) of that subsection shall cause particulars of the notice to be registered in his court in the prescribed manner: and

(b) any such officer as is mentioned in paragraph (b) of that subsection shall cause particulars of the notice to be registered in his court in the prescribed manner and shall cancel the registration of the order.

(4) Except as provided by subsection (5) of this section, the cancellation of the registration of a maintenance order shall not affect anything done in relation to the maintenance order while it was registered.

(5) On the cancellation of the registration of a maintenance order, any order made in relation thereto under subsection (2) of section nineteen of this Act shall cease to have effect; but until the person liable to make payments under the maintenance order receives the prescribed notice[1] of the cancellation, he shall be deemed to comply with the maintenance order if he makes payments in accordance with any order under the said subsection (2) which was in force immediately before the cancellation.

(5A) On the cancellation of the registration of a maintenance order registered in a magistrates' court in England and Wales, any order—

(a) made in relation thereto by virtue of the powers conferred by section 18(2ZA) or section 22(1A) or (1E) of this Act, and

(b) requiring payment to the designated officer for a magistrates' court in England and Wales (whether or not by any method of payment falling within section 59(6) of the Magistrates' Courts Act 1980),

shall cease to have effect; but until the person liable to make payments under the maintenance order receives the prescribed notice of the cancellation, he shall be deemed to comply with the maintenance order if he makes payments in accordance with any such order which was in force immediately before the cancellation.

(5B) On the cancellation of the registration of a maintenance order registered in a court of summary jurisdiction in Northern Ireland, any order—

(a) made in relation thereto by virtue of the powers conferred by section 18(3ZA) or section 22(1F) or (1J) of this Act, and

(b) requiring payment to the collecting officer in Northern Ireland (whether or not by any method of payment falling within Article 85(7) of the Magistrates' Courts (Northern Ireland) Order 1981),

shall cease to have effect; but until the person liable to make payments under the maintenance order receives the prescribed notice of the cancellation, he shall be deemed to comply with the maintenance order if he makes payments in accordance with any such order which was in force immediately before the cancellation.

(6) Where, by virtue of an order made under subsection (2) of section nineteen of this Act, sums payable under a maintenance order registered in a court of summary jurisdiction in England or Northern Ireland are payable through the collecting officer of any court, that officer shall, if the person entitled to the payments so requests, make an application on behalf of that person for the cancellation of the registration.

[Maintenance Orders Act 1950, s 24, as amended by the Administration of Justice Act 1977, Sch 3, the Civil Jurisdiction and Judgments Act 1982, Sch 12, the Maintenance Enforcement Act 1991, Sch 1, SI 1993/1577, the Access to Justice Act 1999, Sch 13 and the Courts Act 2003, Sch 8.]

---

1. See the Maintenance Orders Act 1950 (Summary Jurisdiction) Rules 1950, this Part, post, rr 5, 6, 11, 12 and 15, and Form 4.

6–260   25. Rules as to procedure of courts of summary jurisdiction.   (1) The power of the Lord Chancellor to make rules under section 144 of the Magistrates' Courts Act 1980, shall include power to make rules for regulating the practice to be followed in courts of summary jurisdiction in England under this Part of this Act.*

(3) Rules of court made for the purposes of this Part of this Act may require that any order or other matter required under this Part of this Act to be registered in a court of summary jurisdiction in England or Northern Ireland shall be registered—

(a) in England, in accordance with the rules.

[Maintenance Orders Act 1950, s 25, as amended by the Magistrates' Courts Act 1980, Sch 7, SI 1995/756 and the Courts Act 2003, Sch 8—summarised.]

Part III
General

6–261   26. Proof of declarations, etc.   (1) Any document purporting to be a declaration made under section fifteen of this Act, or to be a certified copy, statutory declaration, affidavit, certificate, transcript or summary made for the purposes of this Act or of any rules made thereunder shall, unless the contrary is shown, be deemed without further proof to be the document which it purports to be, and to have been duly certified made or signed by or before the person or persons by or before whom it purports to have been certified, made or signed.

(2) Paragraph 7 of the Second Schedule to the Emergency Laws (Miscellaneous Provisions) Act

1947[1] (which relates to the proof of affiliation orders and maintenance orders and of orders for the discharge or variation of such orders), shall apply to the registration of orders under Part II of this Act, and to the cancellation of such registration, as it applies to the variation of orders; and for the purposes of that paragraph—

(a) a maintenance order registered under the said Part II in a court of summary jurisdiction; and

(b) any proceedings under the said Part II relating to a maintenance order made by or registered in such a court, being a proceeding of which a memorandum is required to be entered in the register kept by the clerk of that court pursuant to section twenty-two of the Summary Jurisdiction Act 1879[2],

shall be deemed to be an order made by that court.
[Maintenance Orders Act 1950, s 26.]

---

1. Repealed and replaced by Magistrates' Courts Rules 1981, rr 68, 69, in PART I: MAGISTRATES' COURTS, PROCEDURE, ante.
2. Repealed and replaced by Magistrates' Courts Rules 1981, r 66, in PART I: MAGISTRATES' COURTS, PROCEDURE, ante.

6–262   27. General provisions as to jurisdiction.   (1) Nothing in this Act shall be construed as derogating from any jurisdiction exercisable, apart from the provisions of this Act, by any court in any part of the United Kingdom.

(2) It is hereby declared that any jurisdiction conferred by Part I of this Act, or any enactment therein referred to, upon a court in any part of the United Kingdom is exercisable notwithstanding that any party to the proceedings is not domiciled in that part of the United Kingdom; and any jurisdiction so conferred in affiliation proceedings shall be exercisable notwithstanding that the child to whom the proceedings relate was not born in that part of the United Kingdom.
[Maintenance Orders Act 1950, s 27(1), (2).]

SECOND SCHEDULE
FORMS

6–370

FORM NO 1: ENDORSEMENT OF SUMMONS

6–371

FORM NO 2: DECLARATION AS TO SERVICE

Maintenance Orders Act 1958[1]
(6 & 7 Eliz 2 c 39)

PART I

REGISTRATION, ENFORCEMENT AND VARIATION OF CERTAIN MAINTENANCE ORDERS

6–372   1. Application of Part I.   (1) The provisions of this Part of this Act shall have effect for the purpose of enabling maintenance orders to which this Part of this Act applies to be registered[2]—

(a) in the case of an order made by the High Court or a county court, in a magistrates' court; and

(b) in the case of an order made by a magistrates' court, in the High Court,

and, subject to these provisions, while so registered—

(i) to be enforced[3] in like manner as an order made by the court of registration; and

(ii) in the case of an order registered in a magistrates' court, to be varied[4] by a magistrates' court.

(1A) In the following provisions of this Act "maintenance order" means any order specified in Schedule 8 to the Administration of Justice Act 1970.

(2) For the purposes of subsection (1) above, a maintenance order made by a court in Scotland or Northern Ireland and registered in England under Part II of the Maintenance Orders Act 1950 shall be deemed to have been made by the court in England in which it is so registered.

(2A) This Part of this Act applies—

(a) to maintenance orders made by the High Court or a county court, or a magistrates' court, other than orders registered in Scotland or Northern Ireland under Part II of the Maintenance Orders Act 1950, and

(b) to maintenance orders made by a court in Scotland or Northern Ireland and registered in England under Part II of the Maintenance Orders Act 1950.

(3) Without prejudice to the provisions of s 21 of this Act, in this Part of this Act, unless the context otherwise requires, the following expressions have the following meanings—

"High Court order", "county court order" and "magistrates' court order" mean an order made by the High Court, a county court or a magistrates' court, as the case may be;

"order" means a maintenance order to which this Part of this Act applies;

"original court" and "court of registration" in relation to an order, mean the court by which the order was made or, as the case may be, the court in which the order is registered;

"registered" means registered in accordance with the provisions of this Part of this Act, and "registration" shall be construed accordingly;

and for the purposes of this Part of this Act an order for the payment by the defendant[5] of any costs[6] incurred in proceedings relating to a maintenance order, being an order for the payment of costs made while the maintenance order is not registered, shall be deemed to form part of that maintenance order.

(4) For the purposes of this section a maintenance order which is registered in a magistrates' court under Part I of the Maintenance Orders (Reciprocal Enforcement) Act 1972 or Council Regulation (EC) No 44/2001 of 22nd December 2000 on jurisdiction and the recognition and enforcement of judgments in civil and commercial matters or Part I of the Civil Jurisdiction and Judgments Act 1982 shall be deemed to be a maintenance order made by that court.

[Maintenance Orders Act 1958, s 1, as amended by the Administration of Justice Act 1970, Sch 11, the Maintenance Orders (Reciprocal Enforcement) Act 1972, Schedule, the Administration of Justice Act 1977, Sch 3, the Civil Jurisdiction and Judgments Act 1982, Sch 12 and SI 2001/3929.]

---

1. For rules prescribing procedure in magistrates' courts under this Act, see Magistrates' Courts (Maintenance Orders Act 1958) Rules 1959, this PART, post.

2. For meaning of "registered", "registration", see sub-s (3), infra; for registration of an order, s 3, post; for cancellation of registration, s 5, post.

3. An order registered in a magistrates' court is enforceable as a magistrates' court maintenance order, see s 3, post, for procedure for enforcement, see Magistrates' Courts Act 1980, s 93, and notes thereto, ante. The magistrates' court should proceed to enforce such an order even when an appeal is contemplated, unless the payer applies for and obtains a stay from the High Court or county court; see *Smith v Smith* (1976) 6 Fam Law 245.

4. For special provisions relating to the variation of an order registered in a magistrates' court, see s 4, post. Note that there is no power in a magistrates' court to revoke or revive a registered order such as is contained in the Magistrates' Courts Act 1980, s 60, in relation to an order made by a magistrates' court as the original court.

5. "Defendant" means the person liable to make payments (see s 21(1), post).

6. Where these costs were incurred in the High Court the reference is to costs relating solely to the maintenance order (see s 21(4), post).

6–373   2. Registration of orders[1]. (1) A person entitled to receive payments under a High Court or county court order[2] may apply for the registration of the order to the original court[2], and the court may, if it thinks fit,[3] grant the application.

(2) Where an application for the registration of such an order is granted—

(a) no proceedings shall be begun, and no writ, warrant or other process shall be issued, for the enforcement of the order before the registration of the order or the expiration of the prescribed[4] period from the grant of the application, whichever first occurs; and

(b) the original court[2] shall, on being satisfied within the period aforesaid by the person who made the application[5] that no such proceedings or process begun or issued before the grant of the application remain pending or in force, cause a certified copy of the order to be sent to the designated officer for the magistrates' court[6] acting in the local justice area in which the defendant[7] appears to be;

but if at the expiration of the period aforesaid[4] the original court[2] has not been so satisfied, the grant of the application shall become void.

(3) A person entitled to receive payments[8] under a magistrates' court order[2] who considers that the order could be more effectively enforced if it were registered may apply for the registration of the order to the original court, and the court may, if it thinks fit, grant the application.

(3A) Without prejudice to subsection (3) of this section, where a magistrates' court order provides both for the payment of a lump sum and for the making of periodical payments, a person entitled to receive a lump sum under the order who considers that, so far as it relates to that sum, the order could be more effectively enforced if it were registered may apply to the original court for the registration of the order so far as it so relates, and the court may, if it thinks fit, grant the application.

(3B) Where an application under subsection (3A) of this section is granted in the case of a magistrates' court order, the provisions of this Part of this Act shall have effect in relation to that order as if so far as it relates to the payment of a lump sum it were a separate order.

(4) Where an application for the registration of a magistrates' court order[9] is granted—

(a) no proceedings for the enforcement of the order shall be begun before the registration takes place and no warrant or other process for the enforcement thereof shall be issued in consequence of any such proceedings begun before the grant of the application;

(b) ... and

(c) the original court[10] shall, on being satisfied in the prescribed[11] manner that no process for the enforcement of the order issued before the grant of the application remains in force, cause a certified copy[12] of the order to be sent to the prescribed[11] officer of the High Court.

(5) The officer of, or for, a court who receives a certified copy of an order sent to him under this section shall cause the order to be registered in that court.

4143 Maintenance Orders Act 1958 6-374

(6) Where a magistrates' court order is registered under this Part of this Act in the High Court, then—

(a) if payments under the magistrates' court order are required to be made (otherwise than to the designated officer for a magistrates' court) by any method of payment falling within section 59(6) of the Magistrates' Courts Act 1980 (standing order, etc), any order requiring payment by that method shall continue to have effect after registration;

(b) any order by virtue of which sums payable under the magistrates' court order are required to be paid to the designated officer for a magistrates' court (whether or not by any method of payment falling within section 59(6) of that Act) on behalf of the person entitled thereto shall cease to have effect.

(6ZA) Where a High Court or county court order is registered under this Part of this Act in a magistrates' court, then—

(a) if a means of payment order (within the meaning of section 1(7) of the Maintenance Enforcement Act 1991) has effect in relation to the order in question, it shall continue to have effect after registration; and

(b) in any other case, the magistrates' court shall order that all payments to be made under the order in question (including any arrears accrued before registration) shall be made to the designated officer for the court or for any other magistrates' court.

(6ZB) Any such order as to payment—

(a) as is referred to in paragraph (a) of subsection (6) of this section may be revoked, suspended, revived or varied by an exercise of the powers conferred by section 4A of this Act; and

(b) as if referred to in paragraph (a) or (b) of subsection (6ZA) of this section may be varied or revoked by an exercise of the powers conferred by section 3(2A) or (2B) or section 4(2A), (5A) or (5B) of this Act.

(6ZC) Where by virtue of the provisions of this section or any order under subsection (6ZA)(b) of this section payments under an order cease to be or become payable to the designated officer for a magistrates' court, the person liable to make the payments shall, until he is given the prescribed notice to that effect, be deemed to comply with the order if he makes payments in accordance with the order and any order under subsection (6ZA)(b) of this section of which he has received such notice.

(6A) In this section—

"High Court order" includes a maintenance order deemed to be made by the High Court by virtue of section 1(2) above, and

"magistrates' court order" includes a maintenance order deemed to be made by a magistrates' court by virtue of that subsection.

(7) In this section "certified copy" in relation to an order of a court means a copy certified by the proper officer of the court to be a true copy of the order or of the official record thereof.

[Maintenance Orders Act 1958, s 2, as amended by the Administration of Justice Act 1977, Sch 3, the Civil Jurisdiction and Judgments Act 1982, Sch 11, the Maintenance Enforcement Act 1991, Sch 1, the Access to Justice Act 1999, Schs 13 and 15 and the Ocurts Act 2003, Sch 8.]

1. A High Court order is registered in a magistrates' court in accordance with the Family Proceedings Rules 1991, rr 7.22–7.24, this PART, post. As to appeal against a magistrates' court varying or refusing to vary such an order, see s 4(7), post. It is our view that the entire maintenance element of an order ought to be registered and not (for example) registering the children's payment in one court and leaving the wife's payments to be made as directed under the original order of another court. Even if the order were considered in law divisible (which is doubtful) such a division would lead to confusion in collection, accounting, variation and enforcement.

2. For meaning of "High Court order", "county court order" and "magistrates' court order", "original court", see s 1(3), ante. For procedure for registration of a maintenance order in a magistrates' court, see the Family Proceedings Rules 1991, rr 7.22–7.24, this PART, post, and for the duties of the justices' chief executive of a magistrates' court in the matter, see Magistrates' Courts (Maintenance Orders Act 1958) Rules 1959, r 4, this PART, post.

3. See *Practice Direction (maintenance: registration of orders)* [1980] 1 All ER 1007, [1980] 1 WLR 354 which discourages orders for payment direct to a child where no benefit would accrue to the parties, and registration of nominal orders and orders for maintenance pending suit and interim orders.

4. "Prescribed" means prescribed by rules of court (see s 21(1), post). The prescribed period is 14 days (see the Family Proceedings Rules 1991, r 7.23(2), this PART, post).

5. Ie, the person entitled to receive payments: see sub-s (1), supra.

6. "Magistrates' court" has the meaning assigned to it by the Magistrates' Courts Act 1980 (see ss 148 and 150 thereof) (s 21(1), post).

7. "Defendant" means the person liable to make payments (see s 21(1), post).

8. That is, a person entitled to receive payments either directly or through another person or for transmission to another person (see s 21(2), post); this includes the justices' chief executive of a magistrates' court, but he may not apply for registration of an order unless he is so requested in writing by the person entitled to receive payments through him (see s 20(1), post).

9. Ie, registration in the High Court.

10. Ie, the court in which the order was made (see s 1(3), ante).

11. "Prescribed" means prescribed by rules of court (see s 21(1), post). See Magistrates' Courts (Maintenance Orders Act 1958) Rules 1959, r 2, this PART, post.

12. "Certified copy" is defined in sub-s (3), infra.

6–374 2A. Interest on sums recoverable under certain orders registered in the High Court.

(1) Where, in connection with an application under section 2(3) of this Act for the registration of a magistrates' court order, the applicant shows in accordance with rules of court—

(a) that the order, though deemed for the purposes of section 1 of this Act to have been made by a magistrates' court in England, was in fact made in another part of the United Kingdom or in a country or territory outside the United Kingdom; and

(b) that, as regards any sum for whose payment the order provides, interest on that sum at a particular rate is, by the law of that part or of that country or territory, recoverable under the order from a particular date or time,

then, if the original court grants the application and causes a certified copy of the order to be sent to the prescribed officer of the High Court under section 2(4)(c) of this Act, it shall also cause to be sent to him a certificate in the prescribed form showing, as regards that sum, the rate of interest so recoverable and the date or time from which it is so recoverable.

(2) The officer of the court who receives a certificate sent to him under the preceding subsection shall cause the certificate to be registered in that court together with the order to which it relates.

(3) Where an order is registered together with a certificate under this section, then, subject to any provision made under the next following subsection, sums payable under the order shall carry interest at the rate specified in the certificate from the date or time so specified.

(4) Provision may be made by rules of court as to the manner in which and the periods by reference to which any interest payable by virtue of subsection (3) is to be calculated and paid, including provision for such interest to cease to accrue as from a prescribed date.

(5) Except as provided by this section sums payable under registered orders shall not carry interest.
[Maintenance Orders Act 1958, s 2A, as inserted by the Civil Jurisdiction and Judgments Act 1982, Sch 11.]

6–375 3. Enforcement of registered orders.   (1) Subject to the provisions of section 2A of this Act and this section, a registered order shall be enforceable in all respects as if it had been made by the court of registration and as if that court had had jurisdiction to make it; and proceedings for or with respect to the enforcement of a registered order may be taken accordingly[1].

(2) Subject to the provisions of subsections (2A) to (3) of this section, an order registered in a magistrates' court shall be enforceable as a magistrates' court maintenance order within the meaning of section 150(1) of the Magistrates' Courts Act 1980[2].

(2A) Where an order registered in a magistrates' court is an order other than one deemed to be made by the High Court by virtue of section 1(2) of this Act, section 76 of the Magistrates' Courts Act 1980 (enforcement of sums adjudged to be paid) shall have effect as if for subsections (4) to (6) there were substituted the following subsections—

"(4) Where proceedings are brought for the enforcement of a magistrates' court maintenance order under this section, the court may vary the order by exercising one of its powers under paragraphs (a) to (d) of section 59(3) above.

(5) In deciding which of the powers under paragraphs (a) to (d) of section 59(3) above it is to exercise, the court shall have regard to any representations made by the debtor and the creditor (which expressions have the same meaning as they have in section 59 above).

(6) Subsection (4) of section 59 above shall apply for the purposes of subsection (4) above as it applies for the purposes of that section."

(2B) Where an order registered in a magistrates' court is an order deemed to be made by the High Court by virtue of section 1(2) of this Act, sections 76 and 93 of the Magistrates' Courts Act 1980 (enforcement of sums adjudged to be paid and complaint for arrears) shall have effect subject to the modifications specified in subsections (2ZA) and (2ZB) of section 18 of the Maintenance Orders Act 1950 (enforcement of registered orders).

(3) Where an order remains or becomes registered after the discharge of the order, no proceedings shall be taken by virtue of that registration except in respect of arrears which were due under the order at the time of the discharge and have not been remitted.

(3A) Any person under an obligation to make payments under an order registered in a magistrates' court shall give notice of any change of address to the designated officer for the court; and any person who without reasonable excuse fails to give such a notice shall be liable on summary conviction to a fine not exceeding **level 2** on the standard scale.

(4) Except as provided by this section, no proceedings shall be taken for or with respect to the enforcement of a registered order.
[Maintenance Orders Act 1958, s 3 as amended by the Civil Jurisdiction and Judgments Act 1982, Sch 11, the Matrimonial and Family Proceedings Act 1984, Sch 1, the Family Law Reform Act 1987, Sch 2, the Maintenance Enforcement Act 1991, Sch 1, the Statute Law (Repeals) Act 1993, Sch 1, the Access to Justice Act 1999, Sch 13 and the Courts Act 2003, Sch 8.]

---

1. Statutory procedure appropriate to the court of registration is the only machinery available for the enforcement of the order (see sub-s (4), infra).
2. See PART I: MAGISTRATES' COURTS, PROCEDURE, ante.

6–376 4. Variation of orders registered in magistrates' courts.   (1) The provisions of this section shall have effect with respect to the variation[1] of orders registered in magistrates' courts, and references in this section to registered orders shall be construed accordingly.

(2) Subject to the following provisions of this section—

(*a*) the court of registration may exercise the same jurisdiction to vary any rate of payments specified by a registered order (other than jurisdiction in a case where a party to the order is not present in England[2] when the application for variation is made) as is exercisable, apart from this subsection, by the original court[3]; and

(*b*) a rate of payments specified by a registered order shall not[4] be varied except by the court of registration or any other magistrates' court to which the jurisdiction conferred by the foregoing paragraph is extended by rules of court.

(2A) The power of a magistrates' court to vary a registered order under subsection (2) of this section shall include power, if the court is satisfied that payment has not been made in accordance with the order, to vary the order by exercising one of its powers under paragraphs (*a*) to (*d*) of section 59(3) of the Magistrates' Courts Act 1980.

(2B) Subsection (4) of section 59 of that Act shall apply for the purposes of subsection (2A) of this section as it applies for the purposes of that section.

(2C) In deciding which of the powers under paragraphs (*a*) to (*d*) of section 59(3) of that Act it is to exercise, the court shall have regard to any representations made by the debtor and the creditor (which expressions have the same meaning as they have in section 59 of that Act).

(4) If it appears to the court to which an application is made by virtue of subsection (2) of this section for the variation of a rate of payments specified by a registered order that it is for any reason[5] appropriate to remit the application to the original court, the first-mentioned court shall so remit the application, and the original court shall thereupon deal with the application as if the order were not registered.

(5) Nothing in subsection (2) of this section shall affect the jurisdiction of the original court to vary a rate of payments specified by a registered order if an application for the variation of that rate is made to that court—

(*a*) in proceedings for a variation of provisions of the order which do not specify a rate of payments; or

(*b*) at a time when a party to the order is not present in England[2].

(5A) Subject to the following provisions of this section, subsections (4) to (11) of section 60 of the Magistrates' Courts Act 1980 (power of clerk and court to vary maintenance orders) shall apply in relation to a registered order (other than one deemed to be made by the High Court by virtue of section 1(2) of this Act) as they apply in relation to a maintenance order made by a magistrates' court (disregarding section 23(2) of the Domestic Proceedings and Magistrates' Courts Act 1978 and section 15(2) of the Children Act 1989) but—*

(*a*) as if in subsection (8) after the words "the court which may" there were inserted "subject to subsection (10) below"; and

(*b*) as if for subsections (9) and (10) there were substituted the following subsections—

"(9) Subsection (4) of section 59 above shall apply for the purposes of subsection (8) above as it applies for the purposes of that section.

(10) In deciding which of the powers under paragraphs (*a*) to (*d*) of section 59(3) above it is to exercise, the court shall have regard to any representations made by the debtor and the creditor."

(5B) Subject to the following provisions of this section, subsections (4) to (11) of section 60 of the Magistrates' Courts Act 1980 (power of clerk and court to vary maintenance orders) shall apply in relation to a registered order deemed to be made by the High Court by virtue of section 1(2) of this Act as they apply in relation to a maintenance order made by a magistrates' court (disregarding section 23(2) of the Domestic Proceedings and Magistrates' Courts Act 1978 and section 15(2) of the Children Act 1989) but—*

(*a*) as if in subsection (4) for paragraph (*b*) there were substituted—

"(*b*) payments under the order are required to be made to the designated officer for the court or any other magistrates' court by any method of payment falling within section 59(6) above (standing order, etc)";

(*b*) as if in subsection (5) for the words "to the designated officer for the court" there were substituted "in accordance with paragraph (*a*) of subsection (9) below";

(*c*) as if in subsection (7), paragraph (*c*) and the word "and" immediately preceding it were omitted;

(*d*) as if in subsection (8) for the words "paragraphs (*a*) to (*d*) of section 59(3) above" there were substituted "subsection (9) below";

(*e*) as if for subsections (9) and (10) there were substituted the following subsections—

"(9) The powers of the court are—

(*a*) the power to order that payments under the order be made directly to the designated officer for the court or any other magistrates' court;

(*b*) the power to order that payments under the order be made to the designated officer for the court or any other magistrates' court by such method of payment falling within section 59(6) above (standing order, etc) as may be specified;

(c) the power to make an attachment of earnings order under the Attachment of Earnings Act 1971 to secure payments under the order.

(10) In deciding which of the powers under subsection (9) above it is to exercise, the court shall have regard to any representations made by the debtor.

(10A) Subsection (4) of section 59 above (power of court to require debtor to open account) shall apply for the purposes of subsection (9) above as it applies for the purposes of that section but as if for paragraph (a) there were substituted—

'(a) the court proposes to exercise its power under paragraph (b) of section 60(9) below'."

(6) No application for any variation of a registered order shall be made to any court while proceedings for any variation of the order are pending in any other court.

(6A) Except as provided by subsection (5B) of this section, no application for any variation in respect of a registered order shall be made to any court in respect of an order made by the Court of Session or the High Court in Northern Ireland and registered in that court in accordance with the provisions of this Part of this Act by virtue of section 1(2) above.

(6B) No application for any variation of a registered order shall be made to any court in respect of an order for periodical or other payments made under Part III of the Matrimonial and Family Proceedings Act 1984.*

(7) Where a magistrates' court, in exercise of the jurisdiction conferred by subsection (2) of this section, varies or refuses to vary a registered order, an appeal[6] from the variation or refusal shall lie to the High Court[7].

[Maintenance Orders Act 1958, s 4, as amended by Maintenance Orders Act 1968, the Administration of Justice Act 1970, s 48 and Sch 11, the Administration of Justice Act 1977, Schs 3 and 5, the Matrimonial and Family Proceedings Act 1984, Sch 1, the Maintenance Enforcement Act 1991, Sch 1, the Access to Justice Act 1999, Schs 13 and 15 and the Courts Act 2003, Sch 8.]

---

*Amended by the Civil Partnership Act 2004, Sch 27 from a date to be appointed.

1. Note that the section does not refer to revocation or revival of an order or any variation of the order other than as to the rate of payments (*Miller v Miller* [1961] P 1, [1960] 3 All ER 115, 124 JP 413). Representation may be granted in proceedings under this section; see Sch 2 to the Legal Aid Act 1988, ante. See the Family Proceedings Rules 1991, r 7.27, this PART, post, as to variation or discharge of registered orders.

2. England includes Wales (s 21(1)).

3. In the case of an order registered in a magistrates' court, the original court will be the High Court or a county court (see s 1, ante). The magistrates' court shall act on the same principles and considerations that would have operated in the High Court or county court if the application had been made there (*Miller v Miller*, supra). The powers of the original court as respects variation are contained in s 31 of the Matrimonial Causes Act 1973, which by sub-s (7) provides: "In exercising the powers conferred by this section the court shall have regard to all the circumstances of the case, including any change in any of the matters to which the court was required to have regard when making the order to which the application relates . . .". The court, therefore, is not confined to looking at changes in the means of the parties since the order was made, but must have regard to changes in any of the matters effectively mentioned in s 25 of the Matrimonial Causes Act 1973, post. It is right for the court hearing an application for a variation to look at the matter as it stands at that time and to make an order which is reasonable in the circumstances of the case from the point of view of both parties (*Lewis v Lewis* [1977] 3 All ER 992). In deciding whether or not to vary a periodical payments order, the court is entitled to look *de novo* at all the circumstances of the case and is not restricted to looking solely at what the wife reasonably requires in order to maintain herself and the children on a day-to-day basis. The court is entitled to conclude that because the husband's income has increased substantially since the original periodical payments order was granted the wife is entitled to an increased proportion of the husband's income for the benefit of the wife and children (*Cornick v Cornick (No 2)* [1996] 1 FCR 179, CA).

It is not open to one bench of justices to sit in appeal upon a decision of another bench of justices. Where justices on an application to vary realised they were being invited to come to a different conclusion on the same facts to one reached only 3 months earlier, but nevertheless reduced the earlier order, it was held that they should have declined to vary the order (*Bromiley v Bromiley* [1987] 2 FLR 207, [1987] Fam Law 165). Magistrates have jurisdiction to backdate to the date of complaint a variation in the rate of periodical payments under a registered order (*Moon v Moon* (1979) 2 FLR 115, 10 Fam Law 114).

There is jurisdiction under s 31(1) and (2)(b) of the 1973 Act to vary an order for periodical payments notwithstanding that it contains an undertaking by the wife not to apply to increase the husband's liability (*Jessel v Jessel* [1979] 3 All ER 645).

4. Exceptions to this are mentioned in sub-s (5), infra.

5. In *Gsell v Gsell* [1971] 1 All ER 559, 135 JP 163, PAYNE J, suggested that an application which would involve the consideration of a large number of documents and would take some time (ie, a day or so) to hear would be a suitable case to remit to the High Court. In cases where an order for discovery is relevant, justices should consider whether the proper course is not to remit the application to the original court where the power of discovery is available; see *Goodall v Jolly* (1983) 147 JP 513, [1984] FLR 143.

6. This right of appeal does not cover a decision under s 95 of the Magistrates' Courts Act 1980 as to remission of arrears; such a decision may be challenged only by case stated under s 111 of the 1980 Act, see *Berry v Berry* [1987] Fam 1, [1986] 2 All ER 948, 150 JP 319, CA.

7. The Family Proceedings Rules 1991, r 7.28 provides for the hearing and determining of the appeal by a Divisional Court of the Family Division, and r 8.2 (The Family Proceedings Rules 1991), applies as it applies in relation to an appeal from a magistrates' court under the Domestic Proceedings and Magistrates' Courts Act 1978.

6–377 4A. Variation etc of orders registered in the High Court.   (1) The provisions of this section shall have effect with respect to orders registered in the High Court other than maintenance orders deemed to be made by a magistrates' court by virtue of section 1(4) of this Act, and the reference in subsection (2) of this section to a registered order shall be construed accordingly.

(2) The High Court may exercise the same powers in relation to a registered order as are

exercisable by the High Court under section 1 of the Maintenance Enforcement Act 1991 in relation to a qualifying periodical maintenance order (within the meaning of that section) which has been made by the High Court, including the power under subsection (7) of that section to revoke, suspend, revive or vary—

(a) any such order as is referred to in paragraph (a) of section 2(6) of this Act which continues to have effect by virtue of that paragraph; and

(b) any means of payment order (within the meaning of section 1(7) of that Act of 1991) made by virtue of the provisions of this section.

[Maintenance Orders Act 1958, s 4A added by the Maintenance Enforcement Act 1991, Sch 1.]

6–378 5. Cancellation of registration. (1) If a person entitled to receive payments[1] under a registered order desires the registration to be cancelled, he may give notice[2] under this section.

(2) Where the original court varies or discharges an order registered in a magistrates' court, the original court may, if it thinks fit, give notice under this section.

(3) Where the original court discharges an order registered in the High Court and it appears to the original court, whether by reason of the remission of arrears by that court or otherwise, that no arrears under the order remain to be recovered, the original court shall give notice under this section.

(4) Notice under this section shall be given to the court of registration; and where such notice is given—

(a) no proceedings for the enforcement of the registered order shall be begun before the cancellation of the registration and no writ, warrant or other process for the enforcement thereof shall be issued in consequence of any such proceedings begun before the giving of the notice;

(b) ... and

(c) the court of registration shall cancel the registration on being satisfied in the prescribed[3] manner—

(i) that no process for the enforcement of the registered order issued before the giving of the notice remains in force; and

(ii) in the case of an order registered in a magistrates' court, that no proceedings for the variation of the order are pending in a magistrates' court.

(4A) For the purposes of a notice under subsection (2) or (3) above—

"court of registration" includes any court in which an order is registered under Part II of the Maintenance Orders Act 1950, and

"registration" includes registration under that Act.

(5) On the cancellation of the registration of a High Court or county court order—

(a) any order which requires payments under the order in question to be made (otherwise than to the designated officer for a magistrates' court) by any method of payment falling within section 59(6) of the Magistrates' Courts Act 1980 or section 1(5) of the Maintenance Enforcement Act 1991 (standing order, etc) shall continue to have effect; and

(b) any order made under section 2(6ZA)(b) of this Act or by virtue of the powers conferred by section 3(2A) or (2B) or section 4(2A), (5A) or (5B) of this Act and which requires payments under the order in question to be made to the designated officer for a magistrates' court (whether or not by any method of payment falling within section 59(6) of the Magistrates' Courts Act 1980) shall cease to have effect;

but, in a case falling within paragraph (b) of this subsection, until the defendant receives the prescribed notice of the cancellation he shall be deemed to comply with the High Court or county court order if he makes payment in accordance with any such order as is referred to in paragraph (b) of this subsection which was in force immediately before the cancellation and of which he has notice.

(6) On the cancellation of the registration of a magistrates' court order—

(a) any order which requires payments under the magistrates' court order to be made by any method of payment falling within section 59(6) of the Magistrates' Courts Act 1980 or section 1(5) of the Maintenance Enforcement Act 1991 (standing order, etc) shall continue to have effect; and

(b) in any other case, payments shall become payable to the designated officer for the original court;

but, in a case falling within paragraph (b) of this subsection, until the defendant[4] receives the prescribed[3] notice of the cancellation he shall be deemed to comply with the magistrates' court order if he makes payments in accordance with any order which was in force immediately before the cancellation and of which he has notice.

(7) In subsections (5) and (6) of this section "High Court order" and "magistrates' court order" shall be construed in accordance with section 2(6A) of this Act.

[Maintenance Orders Act 1958, s 5, as amended by the Administration of Justice Act 1977, Sch 3, the Maintenance Enforcement Act 1991, Sch 1, the Access to Justice Act 1999, Schs 13 and 15 and the Courts Act 2003, Sch 8.]

1. That is, a person entitled to receive payments either directly or through another person or for transmission to another person (see s 21(2), post): this includes the justices' chief executive of a magistrates' court, but he may not give notice under this section unless he is so requested in writing by the person entitled to receive payments through him (see s 20(1), post). As to the procedure to be followed by the collecting officer where the parties persist in making and receiving payments direct despite an order that they be made through the collecting officer, see the Maintenance Orders Act 1950, s 19(3) and note thereto, ante.

2. See the Family Proceedings Rules 1991, r 7.29, this PART, post, as to cancellation of the registration of an order in the High Court or in a magistrates' court. As to cancellation of the registration in a magistrates' court of a county court order, see the County Court Rules 1981, Ord 36, r 11.

3. "Prescribed" means prescribed by rules of court (s 21(1), post); see Magistrates' Courts (Maintenance Orders Act 1958) Rules 1959, r 2, this PART, post.

4. "Defendant" means the person liable to make payments under the maintenance order (s 21(1), post).

PART III
MISCELLANEOUS AND SUPPLEMENTAL

Miscellaneous

6–379   17. Prohibition of committal more than once in respect of same arrears.   Where a defendant has been imprisoned or otherwise detained under an order or warrant of commitment issued in respect of his failure to pay a sum due under a maintenance order, then, notwithstanding anything in this Act, no such order or warrant (other than a warrant of which the issue has been postponed under paragraph (ii)[1] of subsection (5) of the next following section) shall thereafter be issued in respect of that sum or any part thereof.
[Maintenance Orders Act 1958, s 17.]

1. This is a postponement on the application of a defendant who has obtained relief while undergoing imprisonment or detention under the warrant (see s 18(4), (5), post).

6–380   18. Power of magistrates to review committals, etc.   (1) Where, for the purpose of enforcing a maintenance order, a magistrates' court has exercised its power under s 77(2) of the Magistrates' Courts Act 1980[1], or this section[2] to postpone the issue of a warrant of commitment and under the terms of the postponement the warrant falls to be issued, then—

(*a*)   the warrant shall not be issued except in pursuance of subsection (2) or paragraph (*a*) of subsection (3) of this section; and

(*b*)   the designated officer for the court shall give notice to the defendant[3] stating that if the defendant considers there are grounds for not issuing the warrant he may make an application to the court in the prescribed[4] manner requesting that the warrant shall not be issued and stating those grounds.

(2)   If no such application is received by the designated officer for the court within the prescribed[4] period, any justice of the peace acting in the same local justice area as the court may issue the warrant of commitment at any time after the expiration of that period; and if such an application is so received any such justice may, after considering the statements contained in the application—

(*a*)   if he is of opinion that the application should be further considered, refer[5] it to the court;

(*b*)   if he is not of that opinion, issue the warrant forthwith[6];

and when an application is referred to the court under this subsection, the deisgnated officer for the court shall give to the defendant and the person in whose favour the maintenance order in question was made notice[3] of the time and place appointed for the consideration of the application by the court.

(3)   On considering an application referred to it under the last foregoing subsection the court shall, unless in pursuance of subsection (6) of this section it remits[7] the whole of the sum in respect of which the warrant could otherwise be issued, either—

(*a*)   issue the warrant; or

(*b*)   further postpone the issue thereof until such time and on such conditions, if any, as the court thinks just; or

(*c*)   if in consequence of any change in the circumstances of the defendant the court considers it appropriate so to do, order that the warrant shall not be issued in any event.

(4)   A defendant who is for the time being imprisoned or otherwise detained under a warrant of commitment issued by a magistrates' court for the purpose of enforcing a maintenance order, and who is not detained otherwise than for the enforcement of such an order, may make an application to the court in the prescribed[4] manner requesting that the warrant shall be cancelled and stating the grounds of the application; and thereupon any justice of the peace acting in the same local justice areaas the court may, after considering the statements contained in the application—

(*a*)   if he is of opinion that the application should be further considered, refer it to the court;

(*b*)   if he is not of that opinion, refuse the application[8];

and when an application is referred to the court under this subsection, the designated officer for the court shall give to the person in charge of the prison or other place in which the defendant is detained and the person[9] in whose favour the maintenance order in question was made notice of the time and place appointed for the consideration of the application by the court.

(5) On considering an application referred to it under the last foregoing subsection, the court shall, unless in pursuance of the next following subsection it remits the whole of the sum in respect of which the warrant was issued or such part thereof as remains to be paid, either—

(*a*) refuse the application; or

(*b*) if the court is satisfied that the defendant is unable to pay, or to make any payment or further payment towards, the sum aforesaid and if it is of opinion that in all the circumstances of the case the defendant ought not to continue to be detained under warrant, order that the warrant shall cease to have effect when the person in charge of the prison or other place aforesaid is informed of the making of the order;

and where the court makes an order under paragraph (*b*) of this subsection, it may if it thinks fit also—

(i) fix a term of imprisonment in respect of the sum aforesaid or such part thereof as remains to be paid, being a term not exceeding so much of the term of the previous warrant as, after taking into account any reduction thereof by virtue of the next following subsection, remained to be served at the date of the order; and

(ii) postpone the issue of a warrant for the commitment of the defendant for that term until such time and on such conditions, if any, as the court thinks just.

(6) On considering an application under this section in respect of a warrant or a postponed warrant, the court may, if the maintenance order in question is an affiliation order or an order enforceable[10] as an affiliation order, remit the whole or any part of the sum due under the order; and where the court remits the sum or part of the sum in respect of which the warrant was issued or the postponed warrant could have been issued, s 79 of the Magistrates' Courts Act 1980[11] (which provides that on payment of the sum for which imprisonment has been ordered by a magistrates' court the order shall cease to have effect and that on payment of part of that sum the period of detention shall be reduced proportionately) shall apply as if payment of that sum or part had been made as therein mentioned.

(7) Where notice of the time and place appointed for the consideration of an application is required by this section to be given to the defendant or the person in whose favour the maintenance order in question was made and the defendant or, as the case may be, that person does not appear at that time and place, the court may proceed with the consideration of the application in his absence.

(8) A notice required by this section to be given by the designated officer for a magistrates' court to any person shall be deemed to be given to that person if it is sent by registered post[12] addressed to him at his last known address, notwithstanding that the notice is returned as undelivered or is for any other reason not received by that person.

[Maintenance Orders Act 1958, s 18, amended by the Magistrates' Courts Act 1980, Sch 7, the Access to Justice Act 1999, Sch 13 and the Courts Act 2003, Sch 8.]

---

1. This is a general power to postpone the issue of a warrant of commitment after fixing a term of imprisonment.
2. Under this section a warrant of commitment may be postponed before its issue (sub-s (3), para (*b*), infra) or after its execution (sub-s (5), para (*b*)(ii), infra).
3. "Defendant" means the person liable to make payments under the order (s 21(1), post). If notice is sent by registered post or recorded delivery service to any person at his last known address service is complete even if, in fact, the notice does not reach him (see sub-s (8), infra). If having served a notice under this subsection, the defendant is subsequently informed that the warrant will not be issued, a fresh notice must be served before the warrant of commitment can at a later date be issued (*Slater v Calder Justices* (1984) 148 JP 274).
4. "Prescribed" means prescribed by rules of court (s 21(1), post); see Magistrates' Courts (Maintenance Orders Act 1958) Rules 1959, r 22, this PART, post.
5. A justice should *always* refer the matter to the court wherever there is a *prima facie* change in the defendant's circumstances (*Wood v Warley Justices* (1974) 4 Fam Law 130).
6. Note that the discretion of the justice, as such, is limited: he may issue the warrant forthwith or may refer the application for relief to the court.
7. The court has power to remit the arrears in whole or in part.
8. Note that the discretion of the justice, as such, is limited: he may refuse the application or refer it to the court.
9. This, usually, will be the complainant in the original proceedings. The definition seems not to be wide enough to include the Department of Social Security who, by an arrangement with the person in whose favour the order was made, may be entitled to receive the money in reimbursement of a grant. If notice is sent by registered post to any person at his last known address service is complete even if, in fact, the notice does not reach him (see sub-s (8), infra).
10. This will include an order registered in a magistrates' court under s 3, ante.
11. This will enable a magistrates' court to remit such an amount as will secure the defendant's immediate release from prison or other detention.
12. Or by recorded delivery service (Recorded Delivery Service Act 1962).

6–381   **19.** *Revocation and variation of Orders in Council under the Maintenance Orders (Facilities for Enforcement) Act 1920, s 12*[1].

---

1. See this title, ante.

Supplemental

6–382   **20. Special provisions as to magistrates' courts.** (1) Notwithstanding anything in this Act, the designated officer for a magistrates' court who is entitled to receive payments under a maintenance order for transmission to another person shall not apply for the registration of the maintenance order under Part I of this Act or give notice in relation to the order in pursuance of subsection (1) of section five[1] thereof unless he is requested in writing to do so by a person entitled to receive the payments through him; and where the designated officer is requested as aforesaid—

(i)   he shall comply with the request unless it appears to him unreasonable in the circumstances to do so;

(ii) the person by whom the request was made shall have the same liabilities for all the costs properly incurred in or about any proceedings taken in pursuance of the request as if the proceedings had been taken by that person.

(2) An application to a magistrates' court by virtue of subsection (2) of section four of this Act for the variation of a maintenance order shall be made by complaint.

(8) For the avoidance of doubt it is hereby declared that a complaint may be made to enforce payment of a sum due and unpaid under a maintenance order notwithstanding that a previous complaint has been made in respect of that sum or a part thereof and whether or not an order was made in pursuance of the previous complaint.

[Maintenance Orders Act 1958, s 20, as amended by the Attachment of Earnings Act 1971, Sch 5, the Magistrates' Courts Act 1980, Sch 9, the Access to Justice Act 1999, Sch 13 and the Courts Act 2003, Sch 8.]

---

1. This relates to the cancellation of registration.

6–383   21. Interpretation.   (1) In this Act, unless the context otherwise requires, the following expressions have the following meanings—

"magistrates' court" has the meaning assigned to it by the Magistrates' Courts Act 1980[1] and the reference to that Act in s 148(2) thereof shall be construed as including a reference to this Act;

"defendant", in relation to a maintenance order or a related attachment of earnings order, means the person liable to make payments under the maintenance order;

"England" includes Wales;

"prescribed" means prescribed by rules of court.

(2) Any reference in this Act to a person entitled to receive payments under a maintenance order is a reference to a person entitled to receive such payments either directly or through another person or for transmission to another person.

(3) Any reference in this Act to proceedings relating to an order includes a reference to proceedings in which the order may be made.

(4) Any reference in this Act to costs incurred in proceedings relating to a maintenance order shall be construed, in the case of a maintenance order made by the High Court, as a reference to such costs as are included in an order for costs relating solely to that maintenance order.

(6) Any reference in this Act to any enactment is a reference to that enactment as amended by or under any subsequent enactment.

[Maintenance Orders Act 1958, s 21, as amended by the Administration of Justice Act 1970, Sch 11, the Magistrates' Courts Act 1980, Sch 7, the Family Law Reform Act 1987, Sch 4, the Access to Justice Act 1999, Sch 10, the Access to Justice Act 1999, Sch 15 and the Courts Act 2003, Sch 8.]

---

1. See definition in s 148 thereof.
2. The rule-making power is now under s 144 of the Magistrates' Courts Act 1980.

6–384   22. *Legislative powers of Parliament of Northern Ireland.*

6–385   23. Short title, extent, commencement and repeals.   (1) This Act may be cited as the Maintenance Orders Act 1958.

(2) The following provisions of this Act, namely—

section 2, section 2A;

section 5(2), (3), (4) and (4A);

extend to Scotland and Northern Ireland.

(2A) Section 20(3)(*a*)[1] above extends to Northern Ireland.

(2B) Subject to subsections (2) and (2A) above, this Act extends only to England.

[Maintenance Orders Act 1958, s 23, amended by the Statute Law (Repeals) Act 1975, the Administration of Justice Act 1977, Sch 3 and the Civil Jurisdiction and Judgments Act 1982, Sch 12.]

---

1. Section 20(3)(*a*), enables a summons for discharge or variation of an attachment of earnings order to be served on the person to whom it is addressed in Scotland or Northern Ireland.

Married Women's Property Act 1964
(1964 c 19)

6–490   Money and property derived from housekeeping allowance.   If any question arises as to the right of a husband or wife to money derived from any allowance made by the husband for the

expenses of the matrimonial home or for similar purposes, or to any property acquired out of such money, the money or property shall, in the absence of any agreement between them to the contrary, be treated as belonging to the husband and the wife in equal shares.
[Married Women's Property Act 1964, s 1.]

Family Law Reform Act 1969

(1969 c 46)

PART I

REDUCTION OF AGE OF MAJORITY AND RELATED PROVISIONS

6–502   **1. Reduction of age of majority from 21 to 18.**   (1) As from the date on which this section comes into force a person shall attain full age on attaining the age of eighteen instead of on attaining the age of twenty-one; and a person shall attain full age on that date if he has then already attained the age of eighteen but not the age of twenty-one.

(2) The foregoing subsection applies for the purposes of any rule of law, and, in the absence of a definition or of any indication of a contrary intention, for the construction of "full age", "infant", "infancy", "minor", "minority" and similar expressions in—

(*a*) any statutory provision, whether passed or made before, on or after the date on which this section comes into force; and

(*b*) any deed, will or other instrument of whatever nature (not being a statutory provision) made on or after that date.

(3) *Amendment of other provisions.*

(4) This section does not affect the construction of any such expression as is referred to in subsection (2) of this section in any of the statutory provisions described in Schedule 2[1] to this Act, and the transitional provisions and savings contained in Schedule 3 to this Act shall have effect in relation to this section.

(5) *Power to make Statutory Instruments.*

(6) In this section "statutory provision" means any enactment (including, except where the context otherwise requires, this Act) and any order, rule, regulation, byelaw or other instrument made in the exercise of a power conferred by any enactment.

(7) *Relates to wills.*
[Family Law Reform Act 1969, s 1.]

---

1. These include the Representation of the People Acts and subsidiary legislation thereunder.

6–503   **8. Consent by person over 16 to surgical, medical and dental treatment[1].**   (1) The consent of a minor who has attained the age of sixteen years to any surgical, medical or dental treatment which, in the absence of consent, would constitute a trespass to his person, shall be as effective as it would be if he were of full age; and where a minor has by virtue of this section given an effective consent to any treatment it shall not be necessary to obtain any consent for it from his parent or guardian.

(2) In this section "surgical, medical or dental treatment" includes any procedure undertaken for the purposes of diagnosis, and this section applies to any procedure (including, in particular, the administration of an anaesthetic) which is ancillary to any treatment as it applies to that treatment.

(3) Nothing in this section shall be construed as making ineffective any consent which would have been effective if this section had not been enacted.
[Family Law Reform Act 1969, s 8.]

---

1. A consent given by a minor who has attained the age of 16 cannot be overridden by those with parental responsibility, but it can be overridden by the court. Section 8 of this Act does not operate to prevent parental consent remaining effective, as well in the case of a child aged 16 or 17 as in the case of a child under 16. The powers of the High Court, exercising its inherent jurisdiction, are wider than those of a parent and enable it to consent to a minor receiving medical treatment, overriding the refusal of both the minor and the parent; see *Re W (a minor) medical treatment: court's jurisdiction* [1992] 4 All ER 627, [1992] 3 WLR 758, [1992] 2 FCR 785.

An application under the Children Act 1989, s 8, by an area health authority in respect of children, in care needing medical treatment is unnecessary (*Re K, W and H (minors) (consent to treatment)* [1993] 1 FCR 240).

6–504   **9. Time at which a person attains a particular age.**   (1) The time at which a person attains a particular age expressed in years shall be the commencement of the relevant anniversary of the date of his birth.

(2) This section applies only where the relevant anniversary falls on a date after that on which this section comes into force, and, in relation to any enactment, deed, will or other instrument, has effect subject to any provision therein.
[Family Law Reform Act 1969, s 9.]

6–505 12. Persons under full age may be described as minors instead of infants. A person who is not of full age may be described as a minor instead of as an infant, and accordingly in this Act "minor" means such a person as aforesaid.
[Family Law Reform Act 1969, s 12.]

Part III

PROVISIONS FOR USE OF SCIENTIFIC TESTS IN DETERMINING PARENTAGE[1]

6–506 20. Power of court to require use of scientific tests. (1) In any civil proceedings in which the parentage of any person falls to be determined, the court may, either of its own motion or on an application[2] by any party to the proceedings, give a direction[3]—

 (*a*) for the use of scientific tests to ascertain whether such tests show that a party to the proceedings is or is not the father or mother of that person; and
 (*b*) for the taking, within a period specified in the direction, of bodily samples from all or any of the following, namely, that person, any party who is alleged to be the father or mother of that person and any other party to the proceedings;

and the court may at any time revoke or vary a direction previously given by it under this subsection.

 (2) The individual carrying out scientific tests in pursuance of a direction under subsection (1) above shall make to the court a report in which he shall state—

 (*a*) the results of the tests;
 (*b*) whether any party to whom the report relates is or is not excluded by the results from being the father or mother of the person whose parentage is to be determined; and
 (*c*) in relation to any party who is not so excluded, the value, if any, of the results in determining whether that party is the father or mother of that person;

and the report shall be received by the court as evidence in the proceedings of the matters stated in it.

 (2A) Where the proceedings in which the parentage of any person falls to be determined are proceedings on an application under section 55A or 56 of the Family Law Act 1986, any reference in subsection (1) or (2) of this section to any party to the proceedings shall include a reference to any person named in the application.

 (3) A report under subsection (2) of this section shall be in the form prescribed by regulations[4] made under section 22 of this Act.

 (4) Where a report has been made to a court under subsection (2) of this section, any party may, with the leave of the court, or shall, if the court so directs, obtain from the tester a written statement explaining or amplifying any statement made in the report, and that statement shall be deemed for the purposes of this section (except subsection (3) thereof) to form part of the report made to the court.

 (5) Where a direction is given under this section in any proceedings, a party to the proceedings, unless the court otherwise directs, shall not be entitled to call as a witness the tester, or any other person by whom any thing necessary for the purpose of enabling those tests to be carried out was done, unless within fourteen days after receiving a copy of the report he serves notice on the other parties to the proceedings, or on such of them as the court may direct, of his intention to call the tester or that other person; and where [the tester or] any such person is called as a witness the party who called him shall be entitled to cross-examine him.

 (6) Where a direction is given under this section the party on whose application the direction is given shall pay the cost[5] of taking and testing bodily samples for the purpose of giving effect to the direction (including any expenses reasonably incurred by any person in taking any steps required of him for the purpose), and of making a report to the court under this section, but the amount paid shall be treated as costs incurred by him in the proceedings.
[Family Law Reform Act 1969, s 20 as amended by the Children Act 1989, s 89, the Courts and Legal Services Act 1990, Sch 16, the Family Law Reform Act 1987, Sch 2 and the Child Support, Pensions and Social Security Act 2000, s 82.]

---

 1. See Home Office Circular 248/1971, amended by Home Office Circulars Nos 55/1979 and 23/1980, for guidance as to these provisions and the procedure to be followed.
 2. Application may be made either orally at the hearing or in writing before the hearing date. For power of court to deal with an application made before the hearing date see rr 4 and 5 of the Magistrates' Courts (Blood Test) Rules 1971, this PART, post.
 3. For procedure to be followed when a direction is given see rr 7–15 of the Magistrates' Courts (Blood Test) Rules 1971, this PART, post.
 The court has a judicial discretion whether to order that blood tests shall be taken and the discretion must be exercised on the principles set out in *S v McC; W v W* [1972] AC 24, [1970] 3 All ER 107, [1970] 3 WLR 366, HL. While a refusal to undergo blood testing is a factor to be taken into account, it cannot be determinative of an application for a direction (*Re H (Paternity: Blood Test)* [1996] 2 FLR 65, [1996] 3 WLR 506, [1996] 3 FCR 201, [1996] 2 FLR 65). The power to grant a direction for blood tests is available on an application under s 27 of the Child Support Act 1991, this PART, post, when the principles in *S v McC; W v W*, supra, will also apply (*Re E (a minor) (child support: blood test)* [1995] 1 FCR 245, [1994] 2 FLR 548.
 Although the issue of a direction for the use of blood tests must be separately considered from an application under s 8 of the Children Act 1989 and the welfare requirements of s 1 of that Act, the interests of the child are fundamental to the application. Where a child is conceived and brought up in an existing marriage as a child of the family, and the association of the mother with a man who claims to be the father has terminated well before the birth of the child and such association

coexisted with sexual relations with the husband, a court should decline to exercise its discretion to make a direction for the use of blood tests (*Re F (a minor: paternity test)* [1993] 3 All ER 596, [1993] 1 FCR 932, [1993] 1 FLR 598, [1993] 3 All ER 596). Where the interests of the child require the ordering of DNA tests, these must be balanced against the mother's and her husband's right to respect for private life under art 8(2) of the European Convention on Human Rights but where there is serious conflict between the child and one of its parents, the interests of the child have to prevail under art 8(2) (*Re T (a child) (DNA tests: paternity)* [2001] 3 FCR 577, [2001] 2 FLR 1190, FD). An order for blood tests was refused where the mother had waited until the child was three years old and had divorced the husband before denying that he was the father. The motive for applying for blood tests was to prevent the contact which the court found was in the interests of the child (*O v L (Blood Tests)* [1995] 2 FLR 930 sub nom *Re L (a minor) (Blood Tests)* [1996] 2 FCR 649, CA).
 4. See the Blood Tests (Evidence of Paternity) Regulations 1971 this PART, post.
 5. See r 8 of the Magistrates' Courts (Blood Test) Rules 1971 this PART, post, for requirement that the applicant, unless legally aided, shall pay a sum to meet this cost to the justices' chief executive.

6–507   21. Consents, etc, required for taking of bodily samples.   (1) Subject to the provisions of subsections (3) and (4) of this section, a bodily sample which is required to be taken from any person for the purpose of giving effect to a direction under section 20 of this Act shall not be taken from that person except with his consent.
 (2) The consent of a minor who has attained the age of sixteen years to the taking from himself of a bodily sample shall be as effective as it would be if he were of full age; and where a minor has by virtue of this subsection given an effective consent to the taking of a bodily sample it shall not be necessary to obtain any consent for it from any other person.
 (3) A bodily sample may be taken from a person under the age of sixteen years, not being such a person as is referred to in subsection (4) of this section,

 (*a*) if the person who has the care and control of him consents[1]; or
 (*b*) where that person does not consent, if the court considers that it would be in his best interests for the sample to be taken[2].

 (4) A bodily sample may be taken from a person who is suffering from mental disorder within the meaning of the Mental Health Act 1983, and is incapable of understanding the nature and purpose of scientific tests if the person who has the care and control of him consents and the medical practitioner in whose care he is has certified that the taking of a bodily sample from him will not be prejudicial to his proper care and treatment.
 (5) The foregoing provisions of this section are without prejudice to the provisions of section 23 of this Act.
[Family Law Reform Act 1969, s 21 as amended by the Mental Health Act 1983, Sch 4, the Family Law Reform Act 1987, Sch 2 and the Child Support, Pensions and Social Security Act 2000, s 82.]

 1. The decision in *re O; Re J (children) (blood tests: constraint)* [2000] 2 All ER 29, [2000] 2 WLR 1284, [2000] 1 FCR 330, that 'may' was to be read as 'may only' and that the person with care and control of the child had the absolute right to refuse to allow a blood sample to be taken from the child for the purpose of establish paternity was effectively reversed by the insertion of clause (b) below by the Child Support, Pensions and Social Security Act 2000 (*Re H and A (paternity: blood tests)* [2002] EWCA Civ 383, [2002] 1 FLR 1145, [2002] 2 FCR 469).
 2. The 2 key principles established by the authorities are that: (1) the interests of justice are best served by ascertaining the truth; and (2) the court should be furnished with the best available science and not confined to such unsatisfactory alternatives as presumptions and inferences (*Re H and A (Paternity: Blood Tests*, supra)

6–508   22. *Power to make regulations.*

6–509   23. Failure to comply with direction for taking scientific tests.   (1) Where a court gives a direction under section 20 of this Act and any person fails to take any step[1] required of him for the purpose of giving effect to the direction, the court may draw such inferences[2], if any, from that fact as appear proper in the circumstances.
 (2) Where in any proceedings in which the parentage of any person falls to be determined by the court hearing the proceedings there is a presumption of law that that person is legitimate, then if—

 (*a*) a direction is given under section 20 of this Act in those proceedings, and
 (*b*) any party who is claiming any relief in the proceedings and who for the purpose of obtaining that relief is entitled to rely on the presumption fails to take any step required of him for the purpose of giving effect to the direction,

the court may adjourn the hearing for such period as it thinks fit to enable that party to take that step, and if at the end of that period he has failed without reasonable cause to take it the court may, without prejudice to subsection (1) of this section, dismiss his claim for relief notwithstanding the absence of evidence to rebut the presumption.
 (3) Where any person named in a direction under section 20 of this Act fails to consent to the taking of a bodily sample from himself or from any person named in the direction of whom he has the care and control, he shall be deemed for the purposes of this section to have failed to take a step required of him for the purpose of giving effect to the direction.
[Family Law Reform Act 1969, s 23, as amended by the Family Law Reform Act 1987, Sch 2.]

 1. See rr 8, 9 and 12 of the Magistrates' Courts (Blood Tests) Rules 1971 this PART, post, for steps to be taken when a direction is given.
 2. For consideration of this provision and in particular the effect of a refusal to take part in DNA profiling, see *Re A (a*

minor) (paternity: refusal of blood test) [1994] 2 FCR 908, [1994] 2 FLR 463, CA. See also *Re CB (a minor) (blood tests)* [1994] 2 FCR 925, [1994] 2 FLR 762, and *Secretary of State for Work and Pensions v Jones* [2003] EWHC 2163 (Fam) [2004] 1 FLR 282. An inference adverse to the refusing party may be drawn irrespective of whether the refusal was made before or after the direction, although the inference to be drawn from a refusal before a direction may not be as strong as when the court's direction is flouted; see *Re H (Paternity : Blood Test)* [1996] 2 FLR 65, [1996] 3 WLR 506, [1996] 3 FCR 201. The court should find proven forensically what the person, by his refusal, had prevented from being established scientifically. The proper inference permitted by s 23 is a forensic inference and the forensic process is advanced by presenting the truth to the court (*Re G (a minor) (paternity: blood tests)* [1997] 2 FCR 325 and see *R v Secretary of State for Social Security, ex p G* [1997] 3 FCR 728).

6–510   24. Penalty for personating another, etc, for purpose of providing bodily sample.   If for the purpose of providing a bodily sample for a test required to give effect to a direction under section 20 of this Act any person personates another, or proffers a child knowing that it is not the child named in the direction, he shall be liable—

> (*a*)   on conviction on indictment, to imprisonment for a term not exceeding two years, or
> (*b*)   on summary conviction, to a fine not exceeding the statutory maximum.

[Family Law Reform Act 1969, s 24, as amended by the Criminal Law Act 1977, s 28 and the Family Law Reform Act 1987, Sch 2.]

6–511   25. Interpretation of Part III.   In this Part of this Act the following expressions have the meanings hereby respectively assigned to them, that is to say—

> "bodily samples" means a sample of bodily fluid or bodily tissue taken for the purpose of scientific tests;
> "excluded" means excluded subject to the occurrence of mutation, to section 27 of the Family Law Reform Act 1987 and to sections 27 to 29 of the Human Fertilisation and Embryology Act 1990;
> "scientific tests" means scientific tests carried out under this Act and made with the object of ascertaining the inheritable characteristics of bodily fluids or bodily tissue.

[Family Law Reform Act 1969, s 25 as amended by the Human Fertilisation and Embryology Act 1990, Sch 4 and the Family Law Reform Act 1987, s 23.]

PART IV
MISCELLANEOUS AND GENERAL

6–512   26. Rebuttal of presumption as to legitimacy and illegitimacy.   Any presumption of law as to the legitimacy or illegitimacy of any person may in any civil proceedings be rebutted by evidence which shows that it is more probable than not[1] that that person is illegitimate or legitimate, as the case may be, and it shall not be necessary to prove that fact beyond reasonable doubt in order to rebut the presumption.

[Family Law Reform Act 1969, s 26.]

---

1.   The standard to be applied is not a mere balance of probabilities, but a standard commensurate with the seriousness of the issue involved: where the issue is the paternity of a child it is an issue of great gravity (*Serio v Serio* (1983) 4 FLR 756). See also *W v K (proof of paternity)* (1986) 151 JP 589, [1988] 1 FLR 86.

Marriage (Registrar General's Licence) Act 1970
(1970 c 34)

6–620   This Act, which is to be construed as one with the Marriage Acts 1949 to 1960, permits marriages to be solemnised on unregistered premises on the authority of certificates issued by the Registrar General in cases where one of the parties to be married is seriously ill and is not expected to recover and cannot be moved. Provision is made for the giving of notices and the production of evidence of capacity and consents and for the manner of solemnisation. Section 16 of the Act which creates certain offences is reproduced below.

6–621   16. Offences.   (1)   It shall be an offence knowingly and wilfully—

> (*a*)   to solemnise a marriage by Registrar General's licence in any place other than the place specified in the licence;
> (*b*)   to solemnise a marriage by Registrar General's licence without the presence of a registrar except in the case of a marriage according to the usages of the Society of Friends or a marriage between two persons professing the Jewish religion according to the usages of the Jews;
> (*c*)   to solemnise a marriage by Registrar General's licence after the expiration of one month from the date of entry of the notice of marriage in the marriage notice book;
> (*d*)   to give false information by way of evidence as required by section 3 of this Act[1];
> (*e*)   to give a false certificate as provided for in section three (1)(*d*) of this Act[2];

and any person found guilty of any of the above-mentioned offences shall be liable on summary conviction to a fine not exceeding **the statutory maximum** or on indictment to a fine or to imprisonment not exceeding three years or to both such fine and such imprisonment[3].

(2) A superintendent registrar who knowingly and wilfully solemnises or permits to be solemnised in his presence, or a registrar who knowingly and wilfully registers a marriage by Registrar General's licence which is void by virtue of Part III of the principal Act as amended by this Act shall be guilty of an offence and shall be liable on summary conviction to a fine not exceeding **the statutory maximum** or on indictment to a fine or to imprisonment not exceeding three years or to both such fine and such imprisonment[3].

(3) No prosecution under this section shall be commenced after the expiration of three years from the commission of the offence.

(4) The provisions of section 75(1)(*a*) and 75(2)(*a*) of the principal Act shall not apply to a marriage solemnised on the authority of the Registrar General's licence.

[Marriage (Registrar General's Licence) Act 1970, s 16, as amended by the Criminal Law Act 1977, ss 28 and 32.]

---

1. This relates to evidence that there is no lawful impediment to the marriage, that the required consents have been duly given and that there is sufficient reason why a licence under this Act should be granted.

2. Namely that one of the persons to be married is seriously ill and is not expected to recover and cannot be moved to a place at which a marriage could otherwise be solemnised and that such a person understands the nature and purport of the marriage ceremony.

3. For procedure in respect of this offence triable either way, see the Magistrates' Courts Act 1980, ss 18–21, in PART I, ante.

Maintenance Orders (Reciprocal Enforcement) Act 1972
(1972 c 18)

PART I
RECIPROCAL ENFORCEMENT OF MAINTENANCE ORDERS MADE IN UNITED KINGDOM OR RECIPROCATING COUNTRY

Designation of reciprocating countries

6–781 1. Orders in Council designating reciprocating countries. (1) Her Majesty, if satisfied that, in the event of the benefits conferred by this Part of this Act being applied to, or to particular classes of, maintenance orders made by the courts of any country or territory outside the United Kingdom, similar benefits will in that country or territory be applied to, or to those classes of, maintenance orders made by the courts of the United Kingdom, may by Order in Council designate that country or territory as a reciprocating country[1] for the purposes of this Part of this Act; and, subject to subsection (2) below, in this part of this Act "reciprocating country" means a country or territory that is for the time being so designated.

(2) A country or territory may be designated under subsection (1) above as a reciprocating country either as regards maintenance orders generally, or as regards maintenance orders other than those of any specified class, or as regards maintenance orders of one or more specified classes only; and a country or territory which is for the time being so designated otherwise than as regards maintenance orders generally shall for the purposes of this Part of this Act be taken to be a reciprocating country only as regards maintenance orders of the class to which the designation extends.

[Maintenance Orders (Reciprocal Enforcement) Act 1972, s 1.]

---

1. Several Orders in Council have been made, and are printed in this PART, post. These should be referred to because, in some instances, they effect substantial modifications to the Act in relation to its operation for the particular countries.

Orders made by courts in the United Kingdom

6–782 2. Transmission of maintenance order made in United Kingdom for enforcement in reciprocating country. (1) Subject to subsection (2) below, where the payer under a maintenance order made, whether before or after the commencement of this Part of this Act, by a court in the United Kingdom is residing or has assets in a reciprocating country, the payee under the order may apply for the order to be sent to that country for enforcement.

(2) Subsection (1) above shall not have effect in relation to a provisional order or to an order made by virtue of a provision of Part II of this Act.

(3) Every application under this section shall be made in the prescribed manner[1] to the prescribed officer[1] of the court which made the maintenance order to which the application relates.

(4) If, on application duly made under this section to the prescribed officer[1] of a court in the United Kingdom, that officer is satisfied that the payer under the maintenance order to which the applicant relates is residing or has assets in a reciprocating country, the following documents, that is to say—

(*a*) a certified copy of the maintenance order;

(b) a certificate signed by that officer certifying that the order is enforceable in the United Kingdom;

(c) a certificate of arrears so signed;

(d) a statement giving such information as the officer possesses as to the whereabouts of the payer and the nature and location of his assets in that country;

(e) a statement giving such information as the officer possesses for facilitating the identification of the payer; and

(f) where available, a photograph of the payer;

shall be sent by that officer to the Secretary of State[2] with a view to their being transmitted by the Secretary of State[2] to the responsible authority in the reciprocating country if he is satisfied that the statement relating to the whereabouts of the payer and the nature and location of his assets in that country gives sufficient information to justify that being done.

(5) Nothing in this section shall be taken as affecting any jurisdiction of a court in the United Kingdom with respect to a maintenance order to which this section applies, and any such order may be enforced, varied or revoked accordingly.

[Maintenance Orders (Reciprocal Enforcement) Act 1972, s 2, as amended by the Civil Jurisdiction and Judgments Act 1982, Sch 11.]

---

1. See the Magistrates' Courts (Reciprocal Enforcement of Maintenance Orders) Rules 1974, this PART, post.

2. Reference to the Secretary of State is to be construed as reference to the Lord Chancellor: SI 1992/709, art 4(1).

6–783 3. Power of magistrates' court to make provisional maintenance order against person residing in reciprocating country. (1) Where an application is made to a magistrates' court for a maintenance order against a person residing in a reciprocating country and the court would have jurisdiction to determine the application under the Domestic Proceedings and Magistrates' Courts Act 1978 or the Children Act 1989 if that person—

(a) were residing in England and Wales, and

(b) received reasonable notice of the date of the hearing of the application,

the court shall (subject to subsection (2) below) have jurisdiction to determine the application.

(2) A maintenance order made by virtue of this section shall be a provisional order.

(3) (*Repealed*).

(4) No enactment (or provision made under an enactment) requiring or enabling—

(a) a court to transfer proceedings from a magistrates' court to a county court or the High Court, or

(b) a magistrates' court to refuse to make an order on an application on the ground that any matter in question is one that would be more conveniently dealt with by the High Court,

shall apply in relation to an application to which subsection (1) above applies.

(5) Where a court makes a maintenance order which is by virtue of this section a provisional order, the following documents, that is to say—

(a) a certified copy of the maintenance order;

(b) a document, authenticated in the prescribed manner[1], setting out or summarising the evidence given in the proceedings;

(c) a certificate signed by the prescribed officer[1] of the court certifying that the grounds stated in the certificate are the grounds on which the making of the order might have been opposed by the payer under the order;

(d) a statement giving such information as was available to the court as to the whereabouts of the payer;

(e) a statement giving such information as the officer possesses for facilitating the identification of the payer; and

(f) where available, a photograph of the payer;

shall be sent by that officer to the Secretary of State[2] with a view to their being transmitted by the Secretary of State[2] to the responsible authority in the reciprocating country in which the payer is residing if he is satisfied that the statement relating to the whereabouts of the payer gives sufficient information to justify that being done.

(6) A maintenance order made by virtue of this section which has been confirmed by a competent court in a reciprocating country shall be treated for all purposes as if the magistrates' court which made the order had made it in the form in which it was confirmed and as if the order had never been a provisional order, and subject to section 5 of this Act, any such order may be enforced, varied or revoked accordingly.

(7) In the application of this section to Northern Ireland—

(a) for subsection (1) there shall be substituted—

"(1) Where an application is made to a magistrates' court against a person residing in a reciprocating country and the court would have jurisdiction to determine the application under the Domestic Proceedings (Northern Ireland) Order 1980 or the Children (Northern Ireland) Order 1995 if that person—

    (*a*)   were residing in Northern Ireland, and

    (*b*)   received reasonable notice of the date of the hearing of the application,

the court shall (subject to subsection (2) below) have jurisdiction to determine the application.";

    (*b*)   in subsection (4), for references to the High Court there shall be substituted references to the High Court of Justice in Northern Ireland.

[Maintenance Orders (Reciprocal Enforcement) Act 1972, s 3 as amended by the Family Law Reform Act 1987, Sch 4, the Maintenance Orders (Reciprocal Enforcement) Act 1992, Sch 1 and SI 1995/755.]

---

1.   See the Magistrates' Courts (Reciprocal Enforcement of Maintenance Orders) Rules 1974, this PART, *post*.
2.   Reference to the Secretary of State is to be construed as reference to the Lord Chancellor: SI 1992/709, art 4(1).

6–784   **5. Variation and revocation of maintenance order made in United Kingdom.**
(1) This section applies to a maintenance order a certified copy of which has been sent to a reciprocating country in pursuance of section 2 of this Act and to a maintenance order made by virtue of section 3 or 4 thereof which has been confirmed by a competent court in such a country.

(2) A court in the United Kingdom having power to vary a maintenance order to which this section applies shall have power to vary that order by a provisional order.

(3) Where the court hearing an application for the variation of a maintenance order to which this section applies proposes to vary it by increasing the rate of the payments under the order then unless either—

    (*a*)   both the payer and the payee under the order appear in the proceedings, or

    (*b*)   the applicant appears and the appropriate process has been duly served on the other party,

the order varying the order shall be a provisional order.

(3A) Where subsection (1) of section 60 of the Magistrates' Courts Act 1980 (revocation, variation etc of orders for periodical payment) applies in relation to a maintenance order to which this section applies, that subsection shall have effect as if for the words "by order on complaint," there were substituted "on an application being made, by order".

(3B) *Northern Ireland.*

(4) Where a court in the United Kingdom makes a provisional order varying a maintenance order to which this section applies, the prescribed officer[1] of the court shall send in the prescribed manner[1] to the court in a reciprocating country having power to confirm the provisional order a certified copy of the provisional order together with a document, authenticated in the prescribed manner[1], setting out or summarising the evidence given in the proceedings.

(5) Where a certified copy of a provisional order made by a court in a reciprocating country, being an order varying or revoking a maintenance order to which this section applies, together with a document, duly authenticated, setting out or summarising the evidence given in the proceedings in which the provisional order was made, is received by the court in the United Kingdom which made the maintenance order, that court may confirm or refuse to confirm[2] the provisional order and, if that order is an order varying the maintenance order, confirm it either without alteration or with such alterations as it thinks reasonable.

(6) For the purpose of determining whether a provisional order should be confirmed under subsection (5) above, the court shall proceed as if an application for the variation or revocation, as the case may be, of the maintenance order in question had been made to it.

(7) Where a maintenance order to which this section applies has been varied by an order (including a provisional order which has been confirmed) made by a court in the United Kingdom or by a competent court in a reciprocating country, the maintenance order shall, as from the date on which under the provisions of the order the variation is to take effect, have effect as varied by that order and, where that order was a provisional order, as if that order had been made in the form in which it was confirmed, and as if it had never been a provisional order.

(8) Where a maintenance order to which this section applies has been revoked by an order made by a court in the United Kingdom or by a competent court in a reciprocating country, including a provisional order made by the last-mentioned court which has been confirmed by a court in the United Kingdom, the maintenance order shall, as from the date on which under the provisions of the order the revocation is to take effect, be deemed to have ceased to have effect except as respects any arrears due under the maintenance order at that date.

(9) Where before a maintenance order made by virtue of section 3 or 4 of this Act is confirmed a document, duly authenticated, setting out or summarising evidence taken in a reciprocating country for the purpose of proceedings relating to the confirmation of the order is received by the court, in the United Kingdom which made the order, or that court, in compliance with a request made to it by a court in such a country, takes the evidence of a person residing in the United Kingdom for the purpose of such proceedings, the court in the United Kingdom which made the order shall consider that evidence and if, having done so, it appears to it that the order ought not to have been made—

    (*a*)   it shall, in such manner as may be prescribed[1] give to the person on whose application the maintenance order was made an opportunity to consider that evidence, to make representations with respect to it and to adduce further evidence; and (*b*) after considering all the evidence and any representations made by that person, it may revoke the maintenance order.

(10) *Scotland.*

[Maintenance Orders (Reciprocal Enforcement) Act 1972, s. 5, as amended by the Domestic Proceedings and Magistrates' Courts Act 1978, s 54, the Maintenance Orders (Reciprocal Enforcement) Act 1992, Sch 1 and SI 1995/755.]

---

1. See the Magistrates' Courts (Reciprocal Enforcement of Maintenance Orders) Rules 1974, this PART, post.
2. This section gives the court a wide discretion either to confirm or refuse to confirm or to vary and confirm the provisional order as if the application to vary had been made to that court (*Horn v Horn* [1985] FLR 984, [1985] Fam Law 260).

Orders made by courts in reciprocating countries[1]

6–785   6. Registration in United Kingdom court of maintenance order made in reciprocating country.   (1) This section applies to a maintenance order made, whether before or after the commencement of this Part of this Act, by a court in a reciprocating country, including such an order made by such a court which has been confirmed by a court in another reciprocating country but excluding a provisional order which has not been confirmed.

(2) Where a certified copy of an order to which this section applies is received by the Secretary of State[2] from the responsible authority in a reciprocating country, and it appears to the Secretary of State[2] that the payer under the order is residing or has assets in the United Kingdom, he shall send the copy of the order to the prescribed officer[1] of the appropriate court.

(3) Where the prescribed officer[1] of the appropriate court receives from the Secretary of State[2] a certified copy of an order to which this section applies, he shall, subject to subsection (4) below, register the order in the prescribed manner[1] in that court.

(4) Before registering an order under this section an officer of a court shall take such steps as he thinks fit for the purpose of ascertaining whether the payer under the order is residing or has assets within the jurisdiction of the court, and if after taking those steps he is satisfied that the payer is not residing and has no assets within the jurisdiction of the court he shall return the certified copy of the order to the Secretary of State[2] with a statement giving such information as he possesses as to the whereabouts of the payer and the nature and location of his assets.

[Maintenance Orders (Reciprocal Enforcement) Act 1972, s 6 as amended by the Civil Jurisdiction and Judgments Act 1982, Sch 11.]

---

1. Legal aid (under the Legal Aid Act 1988) may be granted for proceedings under Pt I of this Act relating to a maintenance order made by a court of a country outside the United Kingdom.
2. Reference to the Secretary of State is to be construed as reference to the Lord Chancellor: SI 1992/709, art 4(1).

6–786   7. Confirmation by United Kingdom court of provisional maintenance order made in reciprocating country.   (1) This section applies to a maintenance order made, whether before or after the commencement of this Part of this Act, by a court in a reciprocating country being a provisional order.

(2) Where a certified copy of an order to which this section applies together with—

(*a*) a document, duly authenticated, setting out or summarising the evidence given in the proceedings in which the order was made; and
(*b*) a statement of the grounds on which the making of the order might have been opposed by the payer under the order,

is received by the Secretary of State[1] from the responsible authority in a reciprocating country, and it appears to the Secretary of State[1] that the payer under the order is residing in the United Kingdom, he shall send the copy of the order and documents which accompanied it to the prescribed officer[2] of the appropriate court, and that court shall—

(i) if the payer under the order establishes any grounds on which he might have opposed the making of the order in the proceedings in which the order was made, refuse to confirm the order; and
(ii) in any other case, confirm the order either without alteration or with such alterations[3] as it thinks reasonable.

(3) In any proceedings for the confirmation under this section of a provisional order, the statement received from the court which made the order of the grounds on which the making of the order might have been opposed by the payer under the order shall be conclusive[4] evidence that the payer might have opposed the making of the order on any of those grounds.

(4) For the purpose of determining whether a provisional order should be confirmed under this section a magistrates' court in Northern Ireland shall proceed as if an application for a maintenance order against the payer under the provisional order had been made to it.

(5) The prescribed officer[2] of a court having power under this section to confirm a provisional order shall, if the court confirms the order, register the order in the prescribed manner[2] in that court,

and shall, if the court refuses to confirm the order, return the certified copy of the order and the documents which accompanied it to the Secretary of State.

(5A) Where a magistrates' court in England and Wales confirms a provisional order under this section, it shall at the same time exercise one of its powers under subsection (5B) below.

(5B) The powers of the court are—

(a) the power to order that payments under the order be made directly to the designated officer for the court or for any other magistrates' court in England and Wales;

(b) the power to order that payments under the order be made to the designated officer for the court or for any other magistrates' court in England and Wales by such method of payment falling within section 59(6) of the Magistrates' Courts Act 1980 (standing order, etc) as may be specified;

(c) the power to make an attachment of earnings order under the Attachment of Earnings Act 1971 to secure payments under the order.

(5C) In deciding which of the powers under subsection (5B) above it is to exercise, the court shall have regard to any representations made by the payer under the order.

(5D) Subsection (4) of section 59 of the Magistrates' Courts Act 1980 (power of court to require debtor to open account) shall apply for the purposes of subsection (5B) above as it applies for the purposes of that section but as if for paragraph (a) there were substituted—

"(a) the court proposes to exercise its power under paragraph (b) of section 7(5B) of the Maintenance Orders (Reciprocal Enforcement) Act 1972, and".

(6) If notice of the proceedings for the confirmation of the provisional order cannot be duly served on the payer under that order the officer by whom the certified copy of the order was received shall return that copy and the documents which accompanied it to the Secretary of State[1] with a statement giving such information as he possesses as to the whereabouts of the payer.

(7) *Scotland.*

(8) *Repealed.*

[Maintenance Orders (Reciprocal Enforcement) Act 1972, s 7 amended by the Maintenance Enforcement Act 1991, Sch 1, the Maintenance Orders (Reciprocal Enforcement) Act 1992, Sch 1, SI 1995/755, the Access to Justice Act 1999, Sch 13 and the Courts Act 2003, Sch 8.]

---

1. Reference to the Secretary of State is to be construed as reference to the Lord Chancellor: SI 1992/709, art 4(1).
2. See the Magistrates' Courts (Reciprocal Enforcement of Maintenance Orders) Rules 1974, this PART, post.
3. The order is made in accordance with the laws of the reciprocating country (*Peagram v Peagram* [1926] 2 KB 165, 90 JP 136; *Harris v Harris* [1949] 2 All ER 318, 113 JP 495).
4. This does not prevent the person summoned from raising any defence not included in these grounds (*Re Wheat* [1932] 2 KB 716, 96 JP 399); as, for instance, that the court had no jurisdiction to make the order (*Harris v Harris* [1949] 2 All ER 318, 113 JP 495).

6–787   **8. Enforcement of maintenance order registered in United Kingdom court.**   (1) Subject to subsection (2) below, a registered order may be enforced in the United Kingdom as if it had been made by the registering court and as if that court had had jurisdiction to make it; and proceedings for or with respect to the enforcement of any such order may be taken accordingly.

(2) Subsection (1) above does not apply to an order which is for the time being registered in the High Court under Part I of the Maintenance Orders Act 1958 or to an order which is for the time being registered in the High Court of Justice in Northern Ireland under Part II of the Maintenance and Affiliation Orders Act (Northern Ireland) 1966.

(3) Any person for the time being under an obligation to make payments in pursuance of a registered order shall give notice of any change of address to the appropriate officer of the registering court, and any person failing without reasonable excuse to give such a notice shall be liable on summary conviction to a fine not exceeding **level 2** on the standard scale.

(3A) In subsection (3) above "appropriate officer" means—

(a) in relation to a magistrates' court in England and Wales, the designated officer for the court; and

(b) in relation to a court elsewhere, the clerk of the court.

(4) An order which by virtue of this section is enforceable by a magistrates' court shall subject to the modifications of sections 76 and 93 of the Magistrates' Courts Act 1980 specified in subsections (4A) and (4B) below be enforceable as if it were a magistrates' court maintenance order made by that court.

In this subsection "magistrates' court maintenance order" has the same meaning as in section 150(1) of the Magistrates' Courts Act 1980.

(4A) Section 76 (enforcement of sums adjudged to be paid) shall have effect as if for subsections (4) to (6) there were substituted the following subsections—

"(4) Where proceedings are brought for the enforcement of a magistrates' court maintenance order under this section, the court may vary the order by exercising one of its powers under subsection (5) below.

(5) The powers of the court are—

(a)   the power to order that payments under the order be made directly to the designated officer for the court or for any other magistrates' court;

(b)   the power to order that payments under the order be made to the designated officer for the court or for any other magistrates' court by such method of payment falling within section 59(6) above (standing order, etc) as may be specified;

(c)   the power to make an attachment of earnings order under the Attachment of Earnings Act 1971 to secure payments under the order.

(6) In deciding which of the powers under subsection (5) above it is to exercise, the court shall have regard to any representations made by the debtor (within the meaning of section 59 above).

(7) Subsection (4) of section 59 above (power of court to require debtor to open account) shall apply for the purposes of subsection (5) above as it applies for the purposes of that section but as if for paragraph (a) there were substituted—

"(a) the court proposes to exercise its power under paragraph (b) of section 76(5) below, and".

(4B) In section 93 (complaint for arrears), subsection (6) (court not to impose imprisonment in certain circumstances) shall have effect as if for paragraph (b) there were substituted—

"(b) if the court is of the opinion that it is appropriate—

(i)   to make an attachment of earnings order; or

(ii) to exercise its power under paragraph (b) of section 76(5) above."

(5) The magistrates' court by which an order is enforceable by virtue of this section, and the officers thereof, shall take all such steps for enforcing or facilitating the enforcement of the order as may be prescribed[1].

(6) In any proceedings for or with respect to the enforcement of an order which is for the time being registered in any court under this Part of this Act a certificate of arrears sent to the prescribed officer[1] of the court shall be evidence of the facts stated therein.

(7) Subject to subsection (8) below, sums of money payable under a registered order shall be payable in accordance with the order as from the date on which they are required to be paid under the provisions of the order.

(8) The court having power under section 7 of this Act to confirm a provisional order may, if it decides to confirm the order, direct that the sums of money payable under it shall be deemed to have been payable in accordance with the order as from the date on which they are required to be paid under the provisions of the order or such later date as it may specify; and subject to any such direction, a maintenance order registered under the said section 7 shall be treated as if it had been made in the form in which it was confirmed and as if it had never been a provisional order.

(9) *Scotland.*

(10) *Northern Ireland.*

[Maintenance Orders (Reciprocal Enforcement) Act 1972, s 8, as amended by the Domestic Proceedings and Magistrates' Courts Act 1978, s 54 and Sch 2, the Criminal Justice Act 1982, s 46, the Civil Jurisdiction and Judgments Act 1982, Sch 11, the Family Law Reform Act 1987, Sch 2, the Maintenance Enforcement Act 1991, Sch 1, the Access to Justice Act 1999, Sch 13 and the Courts Act 2003, Sch 8.]

---

1. See the Magistrates' Courts (Reciprocal Enforcement of Maintenance Orders) Rules 1974 this PART, post.

6–788   9. Variation and revocation of maintenance order registered in United Kingdom court.   (1) Subject to the provisions of this section, the registering court—

(a)   shall have the like power, on an application made by the payer or payee under a registered order, to vary or revoke the order as if it had been made by the registering court and as if that court had had jurisdiction to make it; and

(b)   shall have power to vary or revoke a registered order by a provisional order.

(1ZA) Where the registering court is a magistrates' court in England and Wales, section 60 of the Magistrates' Courts Act 1980 (revocation, variation etc of orders for periodical payment) shall have effect in relation to the registered order—

(za) as if in subsection (1) for the words "by order on complaint," there were substituted "on an application being made, by order";

(a)   as if in subsection (3) for the words "paragraphs (a) to (d) of section 59(3) above" there were substituted "subsection (3A) below" and after that subsection there were inserted—

"(3A) The powers of the court are—

(a)   the power to order that payments under the order be made directly to the designated officer for the court or for any other magistrates' court;

(b)   the power to order that payments under the order be made to the designated officer for the court or for any other magistrates' court by such method of payment falling within section 59(6) above (standing order, etc) as may be specified;

(c)   the power to make an attachment of earnings order under the Attachment of Earnings Act 1971 to secure payments under the order.";

(b)   as if in subsection (4) for paragraph (b) there were substituted—

"(*b*) payments under the order are required to be made to the designated officer for the court or for any other magistrates' courtby any method of payment falling within section 59(6) above (standing order, etc)";

(*c*) as if in subsection (5) for the words "to the designated officer for the court" there were substituted "in accordance with paragraph (*a*) of subsection (3A) above";

(*d*) as if in subsection (7), paragraph (*c*) and the word "and" immediately preceding it were omitted;

(*e*) as if in subsection (8) for the words "paragraphs (*a*) to (*d*) of section 59(3) above" there were substituted "subsection (3A) above";

(*f*) as if for subsections (9) and (10) there were substituted the following subsections—

"(9) In deciding, for the purposes of subsections (3) and (8) above, which of the powers under subsection (3A) above it is to exercise, the court shall have regard to any representations made by the debtor.

(10) Subsection (4) of section 59 above (power of court to require debtor to open account) shall apply for the purposes of subsection (3A) above as it applies for the purposes of that section but as if for paragraph (*a*) there were substituted—

'(*a*) the court proposes to exercise its power under paragraph (*b*) of section 60(3A) below, and'."

(1A) The powers conferred by subsection (1) above are not exercisable in relation to so much of a registered order as provides for the payment of a lump sum.

(1B) The registering court shall not vary or revoke a registered order if neither the payer nor the payee under the order is resident in the United Kingdom.

(2) The registering court shall not vary a registered order otherwise than by a provisional order unless—

(*a*) both the payer and the payee under the registered order are for the time being residing in the United Kingdom; or

(*b*) the application is made by the payee under the registered order; or

(*c*) the variation consists of a reduction in the rate of the payments under the registered order and is made solely on the ground that there has been a change in the financial circumstances of the payer since the registered order was made or, in the case of an order registered under section 7 of this Act, since the registered order was confirmed, and the courts in the reciprocating country in which the maintenance order in question was made do not have power, according to the law in force in that country, to confirm provisional orders varying maintenance orders.

(3) The registering court shall not revoke a registered order otherwise than by a provisional order unless both the payer and the payee under the registered order are for the time being residing in the United Kingdom.

(4) On an application for the revocation of a registered order the registering court shall, unless both the payer and the payee under the registered order are for the time being residing in the United Kingdom, apply the law applied by the reciprocating country in which the registered order was made; but where by virtue of this subsection the registering court is required to apply that law, that court may make a provisional order if it has reason to believe that the ground on which the application is made is a ground on which the order could be revoked according to the law applied by the reciprocating country, notwithstanding that it has not been established that it is such a ground.

(5) Where the registering court makes a provisional order varying or revoking a registered order the prescribed officer[1] of the court shall send in the prescribed manner[1] to the court in the reciprocating country which made the registered order a certified copy of the provisional order together with a document, authenticated in the prescribed manner, setting out or summarising the evidence given in the proceedings.

(6) Where a certified copy of a provisional order made by a court in a reciprocating country, being an order varying a registered order, together with a document, duly authenticated, setting out or summarising the evidence given in the proceedings in which the provisional order was made, is received by the registering court, that court may confirm the order either without alteration or with such alterations as it thinks reasonable or refuse to confirm the order.

(7) For the purpose of determining whether a provisional order should be confirmed under subsection (6) above the court shall proceed as if an application for the variation of the registered order had been made to it.

(8) Where a registered order has been varied by an order (including a provisional order which has been confirmed) made by a court in the United Kingdom or by a competent court in a reciprocating country, the registered order shall, as from the date on which under the provisions of the order the variation is to take effect, have effect as varied by that order and where that order was a provisional order, as if that order had been made in the form in which it was confirmed and as if it had never been a provisional order.

(9) Where a registered order has been revoked by an order made by a court in the United Kingdom or by a competent court in a reciprocating country, including a provisional order made by the first-mentioned court which has been confirmed by a competent court in a reciprocating country, the registered order shall, as from the date on which under the provisions of the order the revocation

is to take effect, be deemed to have ceased to have effect except as respects any arrears due under the registered order at that date.

(10) The prescribed officer[1] of the registering court shall register in the prescribed manner[1] any order varying a registered order other than a provisional order which is not confirmed.

(11) *Scotland.*

[Maintenance Orders (Reciprocal Enforcement) Act 1972, s 9, as amended by the Domestic Proceedings and Magistrates' Courts Act 1978, s 54, the Civil Jurisdiction and Judgments Act 1982, Sch 11, the Maintenance Enforcement Act 1991, Sch 1, the Maintenance Orders (Reciprocal Enforcement) Act 1992, Sch 1 and the Access to Justice Act 1999, Sch 15 and the Courts Act 2003, Sch 8.]

---

1. See the Magistrates' Courts (Reciprocal Enforcement of Maintenance Orders) Rules 1974, this PART, post.

6–789   10. Cancellation of registration and transfer of order.   (1) Where—

(a)   a registered order is revoked by an order made by the registering court; or

(b)   a registered order is revoked by a provisional order made by that court which has been confirmed by a court in a reciprocating country and notice of the confirmation is received by the registering court; or

(c)   a registered order is revoked by an order made by a court in such a country and notice of the revocation is received by the registering court,

the prescribed officer[1] of the registering court shall cancel the registration; but any arrears due under the registered order at the date when its registration is cancelled by virtue of this subsection shall continue to be recoverable as if the registration had not been cancelled.

(2) Where the prescribed officer[1] of the registering court is of opinion that the payer under a registered order is not residing within the jurisdiction of that court and has no assets within that jurisdiction against which the order can be effectively enforced, he shall cancel the registration of the order and, subject to subsection (3) below, shall send the certified copy of the order to the Secretary of State[2].

(3) Where the prescribed officer[1] of the registering court, being a magistrates' court, is of opinion that the payer is residing or has assets within the jurisdiction of another magistrates' court in that part of the United Kingdom in which the registering court is, he shall transfer the order to that other court by sending the certified copy of the order to the prescribed officer[1] of that other court.

(4) On the transfer of an order under subsection (3) above, the prescribed officer[1] of the court to which it is transferred shall, subject to subsection (6) below, register the order in the prescribed manner[1] in that court.

(5) Where the certified copy of an order is received by the Secretary of State[2] under this section and it appears to him that the payer under the order is residing or has assets in the United Kingdom, he shall transfer the order to the appropriate court by sending the certified copy of the order together with the related documents to the prescribed officer[1] of the appropriate court and, subject to subsection (6) below, that officer shall register the order in the prescribed manner[1] in that court.

(6) Before registering an order in pursuance of subsection (4) or (5) above an officer of a court shall take such steps as he thinks fit for the purpose of ascertaining whether the payer is residing or has assets within the jurisdiction of the court, and if after taking those steps he is satisfied that the payer is not residing and has no assets within the jurisdiction of the court he shall send the certified copy of the order to the Secretary of State[2].

(7) The officer of a court who is required by any of the foregoing provisions of this section to send to the Secretary of State[2] or to the prescribed officer[1] of another court the certified copy of an order shall send with that copy—

(a)   a certificate of arrears signed by him;

(b)   a statement giving such information as he possesses as to the whereabouts of the payer and the nature and location of his assets; and

(c)   any relevant documents in his possession relating to the case.

(8) *Scotland.*

[Maintenance Orders (Reciprocal Enforcement) Act 1972, s 10 as amended by the Civil Jurisdiction and Judgments Act 1982, Sch 11.]

---

1. See the Magistrates' Courts (Reciprocal Enforcement of Maintenance Orders) Rules 1974, this PART, post.
2. Reference to the Secretary of State is to be construed as reference to the Lord Chancellor: SI 1992/709, art 4(1).

6–790   11. Steps to be taken by Secretary of State[1] where payer under certain orders is not residing in the United Kingdom.   (1) If at any time it appears to the Secretary of State[1] that the payer under a maintenance order, a certified copy of which has been received by him from a reciprocating country, is not residing and has no assets in the United Kingdom, he shall send to the responsible authority in that country or, if having regard to all the circumstances he thinks it proper to do so, to the responsible authority in another reciprocating country—

(a)   the certified copy of the order in question and a certified copy of any order varying that order;

(b) if the order has at any time been a registered order, a certificate of arrears signed by the prescribed officer[2];

(c) a statement giving such information as the Secretary of State[1] possesses as to the whereabouts of the payer and the nature and location of his assets; and

(d) any other relevant documents in his possession relating to the case.

(2) Where the documents mentioned in subsection (1) above are sent to the responsible authority in a reciprocating country other than that in which the order in question was made, the Secretary of State[1] shall inform the responsible authority in the reciprocating country in which that order was made of what he has done.

[Maintenance Orders (Reciprocal Enforcement) Act 1972, s 11 as amended by the Civil Jurisdiction and Judgments Act 1982, Sch 11.]

---

1. Reference to the Secretary of State is to be construed as reference to the Lord Chancellor: SI 1992/709, art 4(1).
2. See the Magistrates' Courts (Reciprocal Enforcement of Maintenance Orders) Rules 1974, this PART, post.

Appeals

6–791 12. Appeals. (1) No appeal shall lie from a provisional order made in pursuance of any provision of this Part of this Act by a court in the United Kingdom.

(2) Where in pursuance of any such provision any such court confirms or refuses to confirm a provisional order made by a court in a reciprocating country, whether a maintenance order or an order varying or revoking a maintenance order, the payer or payee under the maintenance order shall have the like right of appeal (if any) from the confirmation of, or refusal to confirm, the provisional order as he would have if that order were not a provisional order and the court which confirmed or refused to confirm it had made or, as the case may be, refused to make it.

(3) Where in pursuance of any such provision any such court makes, or refuses to make, an order, varying or revoking a maintenance order made by a court in a reciprocating country, then, subject to subsection (1) above, the payer or payee under the maintenance order shall have the like right of appeal (if any) from that order or from the refusal to make it as he would have if the maintenance order had been made by the first-mentioned court.

(4) Nothing in this section (except subsection (1)) shall be construed as affecting any right of appeal conferred by any other enactment.

[Maintenance Orders (Reciprocal Enforcement) Act 1972, s 12.]

Evidence

6–792 13. Admissibility of evidence given in reciprocating country. (1) A statement contained in—

(a) a document, duly authenticated, which purports to set out or summarise evidence given in proceedings in a court in a reciprocating country; or

(b) a document, duly authenticated, which purports to set out or summarise evidence taken in such a country for the purpose of proceedings in a court in the United Kingdom under this Part of this Act, whether in response to a request made by such a court or otherwise; or

(c) a document, duly authenticated, which purports to have been received in evidence in proceedings in a court in such a country or to be a copy of a document so received,

shall in any proceedings in a court in the United Kingdom relating to a maintenance order to which this Part of this Act applies be admissible as evidence of any fact stated therein to the same extent as oral evidence of that fact is admissible in those proceedings.

(2) A document purporting to set out or summarise evidence given as mentioned in subsection (1)(a) above, or taken as mentioned in subsection (1)(b) above, shall be deemed to be duly authenticated for the purposes of that subsection if the document purports to be certified by the judge, magistrate or other person before whom the evidence was given, or, as the case may be, by whom it was taken, to be the original document containing or recording, or, as the case may be, summarising, that evidence or a true copy of that document.

(3) A document purporting to have been received in evidence as mentioned in subsection (1)(c) above, or to be a copy of a document so received, shall be deemed to be duly authenticated for the purposes of that subsection if the document purports to be certified by a judge, magistrate or officer of the court in question to have been, or to be a true copy of a document which has been, so received.

(4) It shall not be necessary in any such proceedings to prove the signature or official position of the person appearing to have given such a certificate.

(5) Nothing in this section shall prejudice the admission in evidence of any document which is admissible in evidence apart from this section.

[Maintenance Orders (Reciprocal Enforcement) Act 1972, s 13.]

6–793 14. Obtaining of evidence needed for purpose of certain proceedings. (1) Where for the purpose of any proceedings in a court in a reciprocating country relating to a maintenance order to which this Part of this Act applies a request is made by or on behalf of that court for the taking in the United Kingdom of the evidence of a person residing therein relating to matters specified in the request, such court in the United Kingdom as may be prescribed[1] shall have power to take that evidence and, after giving notice of the time and place at which the evidence is to be taken to such persons and in such manner as it thinks fit, shall take the evidence in such manner as may be prescribed[1].

Evidence taken in compliance with such a request shall be sent in the prescribed manner[1] by the prescribed officer[1] of the court to the court in the reciprocating country or by or on behalf of which the request was made.

(2) Where any person, not being the payer or the payee under the maintenance order to which the proceedings in question relate, is required by virtue of this section to give evidence before a court in the United Kingdom, the court may order that there shall be paid—

(a) if the court is a court in England, Wales or Scotland, out of moneys provided by Parliament; and

(b) if the court is a court in Northern Ireland, out of moneys provided by the Parliament of Northern Ireland,

such sums as appear to the court reasonably sufficient to compensate that person for the expense, trouble or loss of time properly incurred in or incidental to his attendance.

(3) Section 97(1), (3) and (4) of the Magistrates' Courts Act 1980 (which provide for compelling the attendance of witnesses, etc) shall apply in relation to a magistrates' court having power under subsection (1) above to take the evidence of any person as if the proceedings in the court in a reciprocating country for the purpose of which a request for the taking of the evidence has been made were proceedings in the magistrates' court and had been begun by complaint.

(4) *Scotland.*

(5) A court in the United Kingdom may for the purposes of any proceedings in that court under this Part of this Act relating to a maintenance order to which this Part of this Act applies request a court in a reciprocating country to take or provide evidence relating to such matters as may be specified in the request and may remit the case to that court for that purpose.

(6) *Northern Ireland.*

[Maintenance Orders (Reciprocal Enforcement) Act 1972, s 14, amended by the Magistrates' Courts Act 1980, Sch 7.]

---

1. See the Magistrates' Courts (Reciprocal Enforcement of Maintenance Orders) Rules 1974, this PART, post.

6–794   15. Order, etc made abroad need not be proved.   For the purposes of this Part of this Act, unless the contrary is shown—

(a) any order made by a court in a reciprocating country purporting to bear the seal of that court or to be signed by any person in his capacity as a judge, magistrate or officer of the court, shall be deemed without further proof to have been duly sealed or, as the case may be, to have been signed by that person;

(b) the person by whom the order was signed shall be deemed without further proof to have been a judge, magistrate or officer, as the case may be, of that court when he signed it and, in the case of an officer, to have been authorised to sign it; and

(c) a document purporting to be a certified copy of an order made by a court in a reciprocating country shall be deemed without further proof to be such a copy.

[Maintenance Orders (Reciprocal Enforcement) Act 1972, s 15.]

Supplemental

6–795   16. Payment of sums under orders made abroad: conversion of currency.   (1) Payment of sums due under a registered order shall, while the order is registered in a court in England, Wales or Northern Ireland, be made in such manner and to such person as may be prescribed[1].

(2) Where the sums required to be paid under a registered order are expressed in a currency other than the currency of the United Kingdom, then, as from the relevant date, the order shall be treated as if it were an order requiring the payment of such sums in the currency of the United Kingdom as, on the basis of the rate of exchange prevailing at that date, are equivalent to the sums so required to be paid.

(3) Where the sum specified in any statement, being a statement of the amount of any arrears due under a maintenance order made by a court in a reciprocating country, is expressed in a currency other than the currency of the United Kingdom, that sum shall be deemed to be such sum in the currency of the United Kingdom as, on the basis of the rate of exchange prevailing at the relevant date, is equivalent to the sum so specified.

(4) For the purposes of this section a written certificate purporting to be signed by an officer of any bank in the United Kingdom certifying that a specified rate of exchange prevailed between currencies at a specified date and that at such rate a specified sum in the currency of the United Kingdom is equivalent to a specified sum in another specified currency shall be evidence of the rate of exchange so prevailing on that date and of the equivalent sums in terms of the respective currencies.

(5) In this section "the relevant date" means—

(a) in relation to a registered order or to a statement of arrears due under a maintenance order made by a court in a reciprocating country, the date on which the order first becomes a registered order or (if earlier) the date on which it is confirmed by a court in the United Kingdom;

(b) in relation to a registered order which has been varied, the date on which the last order varying that order is registered in a court in the United Kingdom or (if earlier) the date on which the last order varying that order is confirmed by such a court.

(6) *Scotland.*

[Maintenance Orders (Reciprocal Enforcement) Act 1972, s 16.]

---

1. See the Magistrates' Courts (Reciprocal Enforcement of Maintenance Orders) Rules 1974, this PART, post.

6–796 17. Proceedings in magistrates' courts. (1)–(3) *Repealed.*

(4) Anything authorised or required by this Part of this Act to be done by, to or before the magistrates' court by, to or before which any other thing was done may be done by, to or before any magistrates' court acting in the same local justice area (or, in Northern Ireland, acting for the same petty sessions district) as that court.

(5) *Repealed.*

(5A) Where the respondent to an application for the variation or revocation of—

(a) a maintenance order made by a magistrates' court in England and Wales, being an order to which section 5 of this Act applies; or

(b) a registered order which is registered in such a court,

is residing in a reciprocating country, a magistrates' court in England and Wales shall have jurisdiction to hear the application (where it would not have such jurisdiction apart from this subsection) if it would have had jurisdiction to hear it had the respondent been residing in England and Wales.

(6) *Northern Ireland.*

(7) Where the respondent to an application for the variation or revocation—

(a) of a maintenance order made by a magistrates' court, being an order to which section 5 of this Act applies; or

(b) of a registered order registered in a magistrates' court,

does not appear at the time and place appointed for the hearing of the application, but the court is satisfied that the respondent is residing in a reciprocating country, the court may proceed to hear and determine the application at the time and place appointed for the hearing or for any adjourned hearing in like manner as if the respondent had appeared at that time and place.

(7A) *Repealed.*

[Maintenance Orders (Reciprocal Enforcement) Act 1972, s 17, as amended by the Affiliation Proceedings (Amendment) Act 1972, s 3, the Domestic Proceedings and Magistrates' Courts Act 1978, Sch 3, the Maintenance Orders (Reciprocal Enforcement) Act 1992, Sch 1, SI 1995/755 and the Courts Act 2003, Sch 8.]

6–797 18. Magistrates' court rules. (1) Rules of court may make provision with respect to—

(a) the circumstances in which anything authorised or required by this Part of this Act to be done by, to or before a magistrates' court acting in a particular local justice area or by, to or before an officer of that court may be done by, to or before a magistrates' court acting in such other local justice area as the rules may provide or by, to or before an officer of that court;

(b) the orders made, or other things done, by a magistrates' court, or an officer of such a court, under this Part of this Act, or by a court in a reciprocating country, notice of which is to be given to such persons as the rules may provide and the manner in which such notice shall be given;

(c) the cases and manner in which courts in reciprocating countries are to be informed of orders made, or other things done, by a magistrates' court under this Part of this Act;

(d) the cases and manner in which a justices' clerk may take evidence needed for the purposes of proceedings in a court in a reciprocating country relating to a maintenance order to which this Part of this Act applies;

(e) the circumstances and manner in which cases may be remitted by the magistrates' courts to courts in reciprocating countries;

(f) the circumstances and manner in which magistrates' courts may for the purposes of this Part of this Act communicate with courts in reciprocating countries.

(1A) For the purpose of giving effect to this Part of this Act, rules of court may make, in relation to any proceedings brought under or by virtue of this Part of this Act, any provision not covered by subsection (1) above which—

(a) falls within subsection (2) of section 93 of the Children Act 1989, and

(b) may be made in relation to relevant proceedings under that section.

(2)–(2A) *Northern Ireland.*

[Maintenance Orders (Reciprocal Enforcement) Act 1972, s 18, amended by the Magistrates' Courts Act 1980, Sch 7, the Maintenance Orders (Reciprocal Enforcement) Act 1992, Sch 1, SI 1995/755 and the Courts Act 2003, Sch 8.]

6–798   20. *Restriction on enforcement of arrears under maintenance order registered in Scotland.*

6–799   21. Interpretation of Part I.   (1) In this Part of this Act—

"affiliation order" means an order (however described) adjudging, finding or declaring a person to be the father of a child, whether or not it also provides for the maintenance of the child;

"the appropriate court", in relation to a person residing or having assets in England and Wales or in Northern Ireland means a magistrates' court, and in relation to a person residing or having assets in Scotland means a sheriff court, within the jurisdiction of which that person is residing or has assets;

"certificate of arrears", in relation to a maintenance order, means a certificate certifying that the sum specified in the certificate is to the best of the information or belief of the officer giving the certificate the amount of the arrears due under the order at the date of the certificate or, as the case may be, that to the best of his information or belief there are no arrears due thereunder at that date;

"certified copy", in relation to an order of a court, means a copy of the order certified by the proper officer of the court to be a true copy;

"court" includes any tribunal or person having power to make, confirm, enforce, vary or revoke a maintenance order;

"maintenance order" means an order (however described) of any of the following descriptions, that is to say—

(a) an order (including an affiliation order or order consequent upon an affiliation order) which provides for the payment of a lump sum or the making of periodical payments towards the maintenance of any person, being a person whom the person liable to make payments under the order is, according to the law applied in the place where the order was made, liable to maintain;

(aa) an order which has been made in Scotland, on or after the granting of a decree of divorce, for the payment of a periodical allowance by one party to the marriage to the other party; and

(b) an affiliation order or order consequent upon an affiliation order, being an order which provides for the payment by a person adjudged, found or declared to be a child's father of expenses incidental to the child's birth or, where the child has died, of his funeral expenses,

and, in the case of a maintenance order which has been varied, means that order as varied;

"order", as respects Scotland, includes any interlocutor, and any decree or provision contained in an interlocutor;

"payee", in relation to a maintenance order, means the person entitled to the payments for which the order provides;

"payer", in relation to a maintenance order, means the person liable to make payments under the order;

"prescribed", in relation to a magistrates' court in Northern Ireland, means prescribed by rules made in accordance with Article 13 of the Magistrates' Courts (Northern Ireland) Order 1981, as the case may be, and in relation to any other court means prescribed by rules of court;

"provisional order" means (according to the context)—

(a) an order made by a court in the United Kingdom which is provisional only and has no effect unless and until confirmed, with or without alteration, by a competent court in a reciprocating country; or

(b) an order made by a court in a reciprocating country which is provisional only and has no effect unless and until confirmed, with or without alteration, by a court in the United Kingdom having power under this Part of this Act to confirm it;

"reciprocating country" has the meaning assigned to it by section 1 of this Act;

"registered order" means a maintenance order which is for the time being registered in a court in the United Kingdom under this Part of this Act;

"registering court", in relation to a registered order, means the court in which that order is for the time being registered under this Part of the Act;

"the responsible authority", in relation to a reciprocating country, means any person who in that country has functions similar to those of the Secretary of State under this Part of this Act;

"revoke" and "revocation" include discharge.

(2) For the purposes of this Part of this Act an order shall be taken to be a maintenance order so far (but only so far) as it relates to the payment of a lump sum or the making of periodical payments as mentioned in paragraph (a) of the definition of "maintenance order" in subsection (1) above, or to the payment of a periodical allowance as mentioned in paragraph (aa) of that definition, or to the payment by a person adjudged, found or declared to be a child's father of any such expenses as are mentioned in paragraph (b) of that definition.

(3) Any reference in this Part of this Act to the payment of money for the maintenance of a child shall be construed as including a reference to the payment of money for the child's education.

[Maintenance Orders (Reciprocal Enforcement) Act 1972, s 21, as amended by the Domestic Proceedings and Magistrates' Courts Act 1978, s 55, the Magistrates' Courts Act 1980, Sch 7, the Civil Jurisdiction and Judgments Act 1982, Sch 11, the Maintenance Orders (Reciprocal Enforcement) Act 1992, Sch 1 and the Courts Act 2003, Sch 8.]

Amendments, repeals and transitional provisions

6–800 22. Amendments and repeals.   (1) The enactments mentioned in the Schedule to this Act shall have effect to the minor and consequential amendments specified therein.

(2)[1] The following are hereby repealed—

(*a*) the Maintenance Orders (Facilities for Enforcement) Act 1920;

(*b*) *Repealed.*

(*c*) in the Maintenance Orders Act 1958, section 19 and, in section 23(2), the words "section nineteen";

(*d*) in the South Africa Act 1962, paragraph of Sch 2.

[Maintenance Orders (Reciprocal Enforcement) Act 1972, s 22, amended by the Magistrates' Courts Act 1980, Sch 9.]

---

1. This subsection has not yet been brought into force.

6–801 23. Maintenance order registered in High Court under the Maintenance Orders etc Act 1920.   (1) Where a country or territory, being a country or territory to which at the commencement of section 1 of this Act the Maintenance Orders (Facilities for Enforcement) Act 1920 extended, becomes a reciprocating country, then, if immediately before the Order in Council made under section 12 of that Act extending that Act to that country or territory was revoked any maintenance order made by a court in that country or territory was registered in the High Court under section 1 of that Act, the High Court may, on an application by the payer or the payee under the order or of its own motion, transfer the order to such magistrates' court as having regard to the place where the payer is residing and to all the circumstances it thinks most appropriate, with a view to the order being registered in that court under this Part of this Act.

(2) Where the High Court transfers an order to a magistrates' court under this section it shall—

(*a*) cause a certified copy of the order to be sent to the appropriate officer of that court, and

(*b*) cancel the registration of the order in the High Court.

(3) The appropriate officer of the court who receives a certified copy of an order sent to him under this section shall register the order in the prescribed manner[1] in that court.

(4) On registering a maintenance order in a magistrates' court by virtue of this section the appropriate officer of the court shall, if the order is registered in that court under Part I of the Maintenance Orders Act 1958, cancel that registration.

(5) In the application of this section to Northern Ireland, for references to the High Court there shall be substituted references to the High Court of Justice in Northern Ireland.

(6) In this section "appropriate officer" means—

(*a*) in relation to a magistrates' court in England and Wales, the the designated officer for the court; and

(*b*) in relation to a magistrates' court in Northern Ireland, the clerk of the court.

[Maintenance Orders (Reciprocal Enforcement) Act 1972, s 23 as amended by the Access to Justice Act 1999, Sch 13 and the Courts Act 2003, Sch 8.]

---

1. See the Magistrates' Courts (Reciprocal Enforcement of Maintenance Orders) Rules 1974, this PART, post.

6–802 24. Application of Part I to certain orders and proceedings under the Maintenance Orders etc Act 1920.   Where Her Majesty proposes by an Order in Council under section 1 of this Act to designate as a reciprocating country a country or territory to which at the commencement of that section the Maintenance Orders (Facilities for Enforcement) Act 1920 extended, that Order[1] in Council may contain such provisions as Her Majesty considers expedient for the purpose of securing—

(*a*) that the provisions of this Part of this Act apply, subject to such modifications as may be specified in the Order, to maintenance orders, or maintenance orders of a specified class—

(i) made by a court in England, Wales or Northern Ireland against a person residing or having assets in that country or territory, or

(ii) made by a court in that country or territory against a person residing or having assets in England, Wales or Northern Ireland,

being orders to which immediately before the date of the coming into operation of the Order in Council the said Act of 1920 applied, except any order which immediately before that date is registered in the High Court or the High Court of Justice in Northern Ireland under section 1 of that Act;

   (*b*) that any maintenance order, or maintenance order of a specified class, made by a court in that country or territory which has been confirmed by a court in England, Wales or Northern Ireland under section 4 of the said Act of 1920 and is in force immediately before that date is registered under section 7 of this Act;

   (*c*) that any proceedings brought under or by virtue of a provision of the said Act of 1920 in a court in England, Wales or Northern Ireland which are pending at that date, being proceedings affecting a person resident in that country or territory, are continued as if they had been brought under or by virtue of the corresponding provision of this Part of this Act.

[Maintenance Orders (Reciprocal Enforcement) Act 1972, s 24 as amended by the Civil Jurisdiction and Judgments Act 1982, Sch 11.]

---

   1. See the Reciprocal Enforcement of Maintenance Orders (Designation of Reciprocating Countries) Order 1974, this PART, post. 6-4590

PART II[1]
RECIPROCAL ENFORCEMENT OF CLAIMS FOR THE RECOVERY OF MAINTENANCE

Convention countries

6–803   25. Convention countries.   (1) Her Majesty may by Order in Council[2] declare that any country or territory specified in the Order, being a country or territory outside the United Kingdom to which the Maintenance Convention extends, is a convention country for the purposes of this Part of this Act.

   (2) In this section "the Maintenance Convention" means the United Nations Convention on the Recovery Abroad of Maintenance done at New York on 20th June, 1956.

[Maintenance Orders (Reciprocal Enforcement) Act 1972, s 25.]

---

   1. For guidance as to the operation of this Part of the Act see Notes for Guidance with Home Office Circular No 54/1975. See also the Magistrates' Courts (Recovery Abroad of Maintenance) Rules 1975, this PART, post for procedure.

   2. The countries to which Pt II of the Act have been applied are specified in the Recovery Abroad of Maintenance (Convention Countries) Order 1975 and the Recovery of Maintenance (United States of America) Order 1993 this PART, post.

Application by person in the United Kingdom for recovery, etc of maintenance in convention country

6–804   26. Application by person in United Kingdom for recovery, etc of maintenance in convention country.   (1) Where a person in the United Kingdom ("the applicant") claims to be entitled to recover in a convention country maintenance from another person, and that other person is for the time being subject to the jurisdiction of that country, the applicant may apply to the Secretary of State, in accordance with the provisions of this section, to have his claim for the recovery of maintenance from that other person transmitted to that country.

   (2) Where the applicant seeks to vary any provision made in a convention country for the payment by any other person of maintenance to the applicant, and that other person is for the time being subject to the jurisdiction of that country, the applicant may apply to the Secretary of State[1], in accordance with the provisions of this section, to have his application for the variation of that provision transmitted to that country.

   (3) An application to the Secretary of State[1] under subsection (1) or (2) above shall be made through the appropriate officer, and that officer shall assist the applicant in completing an application[2] which will comply with the requirements of the law applied by the convention country and shall send the application to the Secretary of State[1], together with such other documents, if any, as are required by that law.

   (3A) An application under subsection (1) or (2) above, for the purpose of recovering maintenance from a person in a specified State within the meaning of the Recovery of Maintenance (United States of America) Order 1993, and a certificate signed by a justice of the peace or, where the applicant is residing in Scotland, the sheriff, to the effect that the application sets forth facts from which it may be determined that the respondent owes a duty to maintain the applicant and any other person named in the application and that a court in the specified State may obtain jurisdiction of the respondent or his property, shall be registered in the court in the prescribed manner by the appropriate officer or, in Scotland, by the sheriff clerk in the Maintenance Orders (Reciprocal Enforcement) Act 1972 register.

   (4) On receiving an application from the appropriate officer the Secretary of State[1] shall transmit it, together with any accompanying documents, to the appropriate authority in the convention country, unless he is satisfied that the application is not made in good faith or that it does not comply with the requirements of the law applied by that country.

   (5) The Secretary of State[1] may request the appropriate officer to obtain from the court of which he is an officer such information relating to the application as may be specified in the request, and it shall be the duty of the court to furnish the Secretary of State[1] with the information he requires.

   (6) The appropriate officer for the purposes of this section is—

(a) where the applicant is residing in England and Wales, the designated officer for the local justice area in which the applicant is residing;

(b) where the applicant is residing in Northern Ireland, the clerk of the court for the petty sessions district in which the applicant is residing; and

(c) where the applicant is residing in Scotland, the sheriff clerk or sheriff clerk depute of the sheriff court within the jurisdiction of which the applicant is residing.

[Maintenance Orders (Reciprocal Enforcement) Act 1972, s 26, amended by SI 1993/591,the Access to Justice Act 1999, Sch 13 and the Courts Act 2003, Sch 8.]

---

1. Reference to the Secretary of State is to be construed as reference to the Lord Chancellor: SI 1992/709, art 4(1).

2. Recommended forms of application and evidence are set out immediately following the Schedule to the Magistrates' Courts (Recovery Abroad of Maintenance) Rules 1975, this PART, post.

Application by person in convention country for recovery of maintenance in England, Wales or Northern Ireland

6–805   27A. Applications for recovery of maintenance in England and Wales.   (1) This section applies to any application which—

(a) is received by the Lord Chancellor from the appropriate authority in a convention country, and

(b) is an application by a person in that country for the recovery of maintenance from another person who is for the time being residing in England and Wales.

(2) Subject to sections 27B to 28B of this Act, an application to which this section applies shall be treated for the purposes of any enactment as if it were an application for a maintenance order under the relevant Act, made at the time when the application was received by the Lord Chancellor.

(3) In the case of an application for maintenance for a child (or children) alone, the relevant Act is the Children Act 1989.

(4) In any other case, the relevant Act is the Domestic Proceedings and Magistrates' Courts Act 1978.

(5) In subsection (3) above, "child" means the same as in Schedule 1 to the Children Act 1989.

[Maintenance Orders (Reciprocal Enforcement) Act 1972, s 27A, as inserted by the Maintenance Orders (Reciprocal Enforcement) Act 1992, Sch 1.]

6–806   27B. Sending application to the appropriate magistrates' court.   (1) On receipt of an application to which section 27A of this Act applies, the Lord Chancellor shall send it, together with any accompanying documents, to the designated officer for a magistrates' court which is acting in the local justice area justices' chief executive for a magistrates' court acting for the petty sessions area in which the respondent is residing.

(2) Subject to subsection (4) below, if notice of the hearing of the application by a magistrates' court having jurisdiction to hear it cannot be duly served on the respondent, the designated officer for the court shall return the application and the accompanying documents to the Lord Chancellor with a statement giving such information as he possesses as to the whereabouts of the respondent.

(3) If the application is returned to the Lord Chancellor under subsection (2) above, then, unless he is satisfied that the respondent is not residing in the United Kingdom, he shall deal with it in accordance with subsection (1) above or section 28D(1) of this Act or send it to the Secretary of State to be dealt with in accordance with section 31 of this Act (as the circumstances of the case require).

(4) If the designated officer for a court to whom the application is sent under this section is satisfied that the respondent is residing within another local justice area, he shall send the application and accompanying documents to the designated officer for a magistrates' court acting in that other area and shall inform the Lord Chancellor that he has done so.

(5) If the application is sent to the designated officer for a court under subsection (4) above, he shall proceed as if it had been sent to him under subsection (1) above.

[Maintenance Orders (Reciprocal Enforcement) Act 1972, s 27B, as inserted by the Maintenance Orders (Reciprocal Enforcement) Act 1992, Sch 1 and amended by SI 1995/756 and the Access to Justice Act 1999, Sch 13.]

6–807   27C. Applications to which section 27A applies: general.   (1) This section applies where a magistrates' court makes an order on an application to which section 27A of this Act applies.

(2) Section 59 of the Magistrates' Courts Act 1980 (orders for periodical payment: means of payment) shall not apply.

(3) The court shall, at the same time that it makes the order, exercise one of its powers under subsection (4) below.

(4) Those powers are—

(a) the power to order that payments under the order be made directly to the designated officer for the court or for any other magistrates' court in England and Wales;

(b) the power to order that payments under the order be made to the designated officer for the court or for any other magistrates' court in England and Walesby such method of payment falling within section 59(6) of the Magistrates' Courts Act 1980 (standing order, etc) as may be specified;

(c) the power to make an attachment of earnings order under the Attachment of Earnings Act 1971 to secure payments under the order.

(5) In deciding which of the powers under subsection (4) above it is to exercise, the court shall have regard to any representations made by the person liable to make payments under the order.

(6) Subsection (4) of section 59 of the Magistrates' Courts Act 1980 (power of court to require debtor to open account) shall apply for the purposes of subsection (4) above as it applies for the purposes of that section, but as if for paragraph (*a*) there were substituted—

"(*a*) the court proposes to exercise its power under paragraph (*b*) of section 27C(4) of the Maintenance Orders (Reciprocal Enforcement) Act 1972, and".

(7) The designated officer for the court shall register the order in the prescribed manner in the court.

[Maintenance Orders (Reciprocal Enforcement) Act 1972, s 27C, as inserted by the Maintenance Orders (Reciprocal Enforcement) Act 1992, Sch 1 and amended by the Access to Justice Act 1999, Sch 13 and the Courts Act 2003, Sch 8.]

6–808   28. Applications by spouses under the Domestic Proceedings and Magistrates' Courts Act 1978.   (1) The magistrates' court hearing an application which by virtue of section 27A of this Act is to be treated as if it were an application for a maintenance order under the Domestic Proceedings and Magistrates' Courts Act 1978 may make any order on the application which it has power to make under section 2 or 19(1) of that Act.

(2) Part I of that Act shall apply in relation to such an application, and to any order made on such an application, with the following modifications—

(a) sections 6 to 8, 16 to 18, 20ZA, 25 to 27 and 28(2) shall be omitted,

(b) in section 30(1), for the words "either the applicant or the respondent ordinarily resides" there shall be substituted "the respondent resides", and

(c) section 32(2) shall be omitted.

(3) Subsections (1) and (2) above do not apply where section 28A of this Act applies.

[Maintenance Orders (Reciprocal Enforcement) Act 1972, s 28, as substituted by the Maintenance Orders (Reciprocal Enforcement) Act 1992, Sch 1.]

6–809   28A. Applications by former spouses under the Domestic Proceedings and Magistrates' Courts Act 1978.   (1) This section applies where in the case of any application which by virtue of section 27A of this Act is to be treated as if it were an application for a maintenance order under the Domestic Proceedings and Magistrates' Courts Act 1978 ("the 1978 Act")—

(a) the applicant and respondent were formerly married,

(b) their marriage was dissolved or annulled in a country or territory outside the United Kingdom by a divorce or annulment which is recognised as valid by the law of England and Wales,

(c) an order for the payment of maintenance for the benefit of the applicant or a child of the family has, by reason of the divorce or annulment, been made by a court in a convention country, and

(d) where the order for the payment of maintenance was made by a court of a different country from that in which the divorce or annulment was obtained, either the applicant or the respondent was resident in the convention country whose court made that order at the time that order was applied for.

(2) Any magistrates' court that would have jurisdiction to hear the application under section 30 of the 1978 Act (as modified in accordance with subsection (6) below) if the applicant and the respondent were still married shall have jurisdiction to hear it notwithstanding the dissolution or annulment of the marriage.

(3) If the magistrates' court hearing the application is satisfied that the respondent has failed to comply with the provisions of any order such as is mentioned in subsection (1)(*c*) above, it may (subject to subsections (4) and (5) below) make any order which it has power to make under section 2 or 19(1) of the 1978 Act.

(4) The court shall not make an order for the making of periodical payments for the benefit of the applicant or any child of the family unless the order made in the convention country provides for the making of periodical payments for the benefit of the applicant or, as the case may be, that child.

(5) The court shall not make an order for the payment of a lump sum for the benefit of the applicant or any child of the family unless the order made in the convention country provides for the payment of a lump sum to the applicant or, as the case may be, to that child.

(6) Part I of the 1978 Act shall apply in relation to the application, and to any order made on the application, with the following modifications—

(a) section 1 shall be omitted,

(b) for the reference in section 2(1) to any ground mentioned in section 1 of that Act there shall be substituted a reference to non-compliance with any such order as is mentioned in subsection (1)(c) of this section,

(c) for the references in section 3(2) and (3) to the occurrence of the conduct which is alleged as the ground of the application there shall be substituted references to the breakdown of the marriage,

(d) the reference in section 4(2) to the subsequent dissolution or annulment of the marriage of the parties affected by the order shall be omitted,

(e) sections 6 to 8, 16 to 18, 20ZA and 25 to 28 shall be omitted,

(f) in section 30(1), for the words "either the applicant or the respondent ordinarily resides" there shall be substituted "the respondent resides", and

(g) section 32(2) shall be omitted.

(7) A divorce or annulment obtained in a country or territory outside the United Kingdom shall be presumed for the purposes of this section to be one the validity of which is recognised by the law of England and Wales, unless the contrary is proved by the respondent.

(8) In this section, "child of the family" has the meaning given in section 88 of the 1978 Act.

[Maintenance Orders (Reciprocal Enforcement) Act 1972, s 28A, as substituted by the Maintenance Orders (Reciprocal Enforcement) Act 1992, Sch 1.]

6–810   28B. Applications under the Children Act 1989.   No provision of an order made under Schedule 11 to the Children Act 1989 requiring or enabling a court to transfer proceedings from a magistrates' court to a county court or the High Court shall apply in relation to an application which by virtue of section 27A of this Act is to be treated as if it were an application for a maintenance order under that Act.

[Maintenance Orders (Reciprocal Enforcement) Act 1972, s 28B, as inserted by the Maintenance Orders (Reciprocal Enforcement) Act 1992, Sch 1.]

6–811   28C–28E. Applications for recovery of maintenance in Northern Ireland.   *Applies where the Lord Chancellor receives from the appropriate authority in a convention country an application by a person in that country for the recovery of maintenance from another person who is for the time being residing in Northern Ireland.*

Transfer, enforcement, variation and revocation of registered orders

6–819   32. Transfer of orders.   (1) Where the prescribed officer of the registering court is of opinion that the payer under a registered order has ceased to reside within the jurisdiction of that court, then, unless he is of opinion that the payer has ceased to reside in the United Kingdom, he shall, subject to subsection (2) below, send a certified copy of the order and the related documents to the Secretary of State[1], and if he is of opinion that the payer has ceased to reside in the United Kingdom he shall send a notice to that effect to the Secretary of State[1].

(2) Where the appropriate officer of the registering court, being a magistrates' court, is of opinion that the payer is residing within the jurisdiction of another magistrates' court in that part of the United Kingdom in which the registering court is, he shall transfer the order to that other court by sending a certified copy of the order and the related documents to the appropriate officer of that other court and, subject to subsection (4) below, that appropriate officer shall register the order in the prescribed manner in that court.

(2A) In subsection (2) above the "appropriate officer" means—

(a) in relation to a court in England and Wales, the designated officer for the court; and

(b) in relation to a court in Northern Ireland, the clerk of the court.

(3) Where a certified copy of an order is received by the Secretary of State[1] under this section and it appears to him that the payer under the order is still residing in the United Kingdom, he shall transfer the order to the appropriate court by sending the copy of the order and the related documents to the prescribed officer of the appropriate court and, subject to subsection (4) below, that officer shall register the order in the prescribed manner in that court.

(4) Before registering an order in pursuance of subsection (2) or (3) above an officer of a court shall take such steps as he thinks fit for the purpose of ascertaining whether the payer under the order is residing within the jurisdiction of the court, and if after taking those steps he is satisfied that the payer is not so residing he shall return the certified copy of the order and the related documents to the officer of the court or the Secretary of State[1], as the case may be, from whom he received them, together with a statement giving such information as he possesses as to the whereabouts of the payer.

(5) Where a certified copy of an order is received by the Secretary of State[1] under this section and it appears to him that the payer under the order has ceased to reside in the United Kingdom he shall return the copy of the order and the related documents to the registering court.

(6) An officer of a court on registering an order in the court in pursuance of subsection (2) or (3) above shall give notice of the registration in the prescribed manner to the prescribed officer of the court in which immediately before its registration under this section the order was registered.

(7) The officer to whom notice is given under subsection (6) above shall on receiving the notice cancel the registration of the order in that court.

(7A)–(7B) *Scotland.*

(8) In this section—

"the appropriate court", in relation to a person residing in England and Wales or in Northern Ireland, means a magistrates' court within the jurisdiction of which that person is residing;

"certificate of arrears" and "certified copy" have the same meanings respectively as in Part I of this Act;

"payer", in relation to a registered order, means the person liable to make payments under the order; and

"related documents" means—

    (*a*) the application on which the order was made;
    (*b*) a certificate of arrears signed by the prescribed officer of the registering court;
    (*c*) a statement giving such information as he possesses as to the whereabouts of the payer; and
    (*d*) any relevant documents in his possession relating to the case.

(9) *Scotland.*

[Maintenance Orders (Reciprocal Enforcement) Act 1972, s 32, amended by the Legal Aid (Scotland) Act 1986, Schs 3 and 5, the Access to Justice Act 1999, Sch 13 and the Courts Act 2003. Sch 8.]

---

1. Reference to the Secretary of State is to be construed as reference to the Lord Chancellor: SI 1992/709, art 4(1).

6–820 33. Enforcement of orders. (1) Subject to subsection (2) below, a registered order which is registered in a court other than the court by which the order was made may be enforced as if it had been made by the registering court and as if that court had had jurisdiction to make it; and proceedings for or with respect to the enforcement of any such order may be taken in accordance with this subsection but not otherwise.

(2) Subsection (1) above does not apply to an order which is for the time being registered in the High Court under Part I of the Maintenance Orders Act 1958 or to an order which is for the time being registered in the High Court of Justice in Northern Ireland under Part II of the Maintenance and Affiliation Orders Act (Northern Ireland) 1966.

(3) An order which by virtue of subsection (1) above is enforceable by a magistrates' court shall, subject to the modifications of sections 76 and 93 of the Magistrates' Courts Act 1980 (enforcement of sums adjudged to be paid and complaint for arrears) specified in subsections (4A) and (4B) of section 8 of this Act, be enforceable as if it were a magistrates' court maintenance order made by that court.

In this subsection "magistrates' court maintenance order" has the same meaning as in section 150(1) of the Magistrates' Courts Act 1980[1].

(3A) Where, by virtue of being registered in the magistrates' court in which it was made, a registered order is enforceable as a magistrates' court maintenance order, sections 76 and 93 of the Magistrates' Courts Act 1980 shall have effect subject to the modifications specified in subsections (4A) and (4B) of section 8 of this Act.

(4) A magistrates' court in which an order is registered under this Part of this Act, and the officers thereof, shall take all such steps for enforcing the order as may be prescribed.

(5) In any proceedings for or with respect to the enforcement of an order which is for the time being registered in any court under this Part of this Act a certificate of arrears sent under section 32 of this Act to the prescribed officer of the court shall be evidence of the facts stated therein.

(6) Part II of the Maintenance Orders 1950 (enforcement of certain orders throughout the United Kingdom) shall not apply to a registered order.

[Maintenance Orders (Reciprocal Enforcement) Act 1972, s 33 as amended by the Family Law Reform Act 1987, Sch 2 and the Maintenance Enforcement Act 1991, Sch 1.]

---

1. See PART I: MAGISTRATES' COURTS, PROCEDURE, ante.

6–821 34. Variation and revocation of orders. (1) Subject to subsection (3A) below and section 34A of this Act, where a registered order is registered in a court other than the court by which the order was made, the registering court shall have the like power to vary or revoke the order as if it had been made by the registering court and as if that court had had jurisdiction to make it; and no court other than the registering court shall have power to vary or revoke a registered order.

(2) Where the registering court revokes a registered order it shall cancel the registration.

(3) Where the Secretary of State[1] receives from the appropriate authority in a convention country an application by a person in that country for the variation of a registered order, he shall, if the registering court is a magistrates' court, send the application together with any documents accompanying it to—

    (*a*) the designated officer for the court, if the court is in England and Wales; or
    (*b*) the clerk of the court, if the court is in Northern Ireland.

(3A) Where subsection (1) of section 60 of the Magistrates' Courts Act 1980 (revocation, variation etc of orders for periodical payment) applies in relation to a registered order, that subsection shall have effect as if for the words "by order on complaint," there were substituted "on an application being made, by order".

(3B) *Northern Ireland.*

(4) Where a court in a part of the United Kingdom makes, or refuses to make, an order varying or revoking a registered order made by a court in another part thereof, any person shall have the like right of appeal (if any) against the order or refusal as he would have if the registered order had been made by the first-mentioned court.

(5) *Scotland.*

[Maintenance Orders (Reciprocal Enforcement) Act 1972, s 34, amended by the Legal Aid (Scotland) Act 1986, Sch 3, the Maintenance Enforcement Act 1991, Sch 1, the Maintenance Orders (Reciprocal Enforcement) Act 1992, Sch 1, SI 1995/755, the Access to Justice Act 1999, Sch 13 and the Courts Act 2003, Sch 8.]

---

1. Reference to the Secretary of State is to be construed as reference to the Lord Chancellor: SI 1992/709, art 4(1).

6–822 34A. Variation of orders by magistrates' courts in England and Wales. (1) The provisions of this section shall have effect in relation to a registered order which is registered in a magistrates' court in England and Wales (whether or not the court made the order) in place of the following enactments, that is to say—

(*a*) subsections (3) to (11) of section 60 of the Magistrates' Courts Act 1980;
(*b*) section 20ZA of the Domestic Proceedings and Magistrates' Courts Act 1978; and
(*c*) paragraph 6A of Schedule 1 to the Children Act 1989.

(2) The power of a magistrates' court in England and Wales to vary a registered order shall include power, if the court is satisfied that payment has not been made in accordance with the order, to exercise one of its powers under subsection (3) below.

(3) The powers of the court are—

(*a*) the power to order that payments under the order be made directly to the designated officer for the court or for any other magistrates' court in England and Wales;
(*b*) the power to order that payments under the order be made to the designated officer for the court or for any other magistrates' court in England and Wales, by such method of payment falling within section 59(6) of the Magistrates' Courts Act 1980 (standing order, etc) as may be specified;
(*c*) the power to make an attachment of earnings order under the Attachment of Earnings Act 1971 to secure payments under the order.

(4) In any case where—

(*a*) a registered order is registered in a magistrates' court in England and Wales, and
(*b*) payments under the order are required to be made to the designated officer for the court or for any other magistrates' court in England and Wales by any method of payment falling within section 59(6) of the Magistrates' Courts Act 1980 (standing order, etc),

an interested party may apply in writing to the court in which the order is registered for the order to be varied as mentioned in subsection (5) below.

(5) Subject to subsection (8) below, where an application has been made under subsection (4) above, a justices' clerk, after giving written notice (by post or otherwise) of the application to any other interested party and allowing that party, within the period of 14 days beginning with the date of the giving of that notice, an opportunity to make written representations, may vary the order to provide that payments under the order shall be made in accordance with paragraph (*a*) of subsection (3) above.

(6) The clerk may proceed with an application under subsection (4) above notwithstanding that any such interested party as is referred to in subsection (5) above has not received written notice of the application.

(7) In subsections (4) to (6) above "interested party", in relation to an order, means the debtor or the creditor.

(8) Where an application has been made under subsection (4) above, the clerk may, if he considers it inappropriate to exercise his power under subsection (5) above, refer the matter to the court which may vary the order by exercising one of its powers under subsection (3) above.

(9) In deciding, for the purposes of subsections (2) and (8) above, which of the powers under subsection (3) above it is to exercise, the court shall have regard to any representations made by the debtor.

(10) Subsection (4) of section 59 of the Magistrates' Courts Act 1980 (power of court to require debtor to open account) shall apply for the purposes of subsection (3) above as it applies for the purposes of that section but as if for paragraph (*a*) there were substituted—

"(*a*) the court proposes to exercise its power under paragraph (*b*) of section 34A(3) of the Maintenance Orders (Reciprocal Enforcement) Act 1972, and".

(11) In this section "creditor" and "debtor" have the same meaning as they have in section 59 of the Magistrates' Courts Act 1980.

[Maintenance Orders (Reciprocal Enforcement) Act 1972, s 34A added by the Maintenance Enforcement Act 1991, Sch 1 and amended y the Access to Justice Act 1999, Sch 13 and the Courts Act 2003, Sch 8.]

6–823   35. Further provisions with respect to variation, etc of orders by magistrates' courts in England and Wales.   (1) Notwithstanding anything in section 28(2) or 28A(6)(*e*) of this Act, a magistrates' court in England and Wales shall have jurisdiction to hear an application—

(*a*)   for the variation or revocation of a registered order registered in that court, and

(*b*)   made by the person against whom or on whose application the order was made,

notwithstanding that the person by or against whom the application is made is residing outside England and Wales.

(2) None of the powers of the court, or of the clerk of the court, under section 34A of this Act shall be exercisable in relation to such an application.

(3) Where the respondent to an application for the variation or revocation of a registered order which is registered in a magistrates' court in England and Wales does not appear at the time and place appointed for the hearing of the application, but the court is satisfied—

(*a*)   that the respondent is residing outside England and Wales, and

(*b*)   that the prescribed notice of the making of the application and of the time and place appointed for the hearing has been given to the respondent in the prescribed manner,

the court may proceed to hear and determine the application at the time and place appointed for the hearing or for any adjourned hearing in like manner as if the respondent had appeared at that time and place.

[Maintenance Orders (Reciprocal Enforcement) Act 1972, s 35, as substituted by the Maintenance Orders (Reciprocal Enforcement) Act 1992, Sch 1.]

6–824   35A.   *Further provisions with respect to variation etc of orders by magistrates' courts in Northern Ireland.*

Supplemental

6–825   36. Admissibility of evidence given in convention country.   (1) A statement contained in—

(*a*)   a document, duly authenticated, which purports to set out or summarise evidence given in proceedings in a court in a convention country; or

(*b*)   a document, duly authenticated, which purports to set out or summarise evidence taken in such a country for the purpose of proceedings in a court in the United Kingdom under this Part of this Act, whether in response to a request made on behalf of such court or otherwise; or

(*c*)   a document, duly authenticated, which purports to have been received in evidence in proceedings in a court in such a country, or to be a copy of a document so received,

shall, in any proceedings in a magistrates' court or in, or remitted from, a sheriff court arising out of an application to which section 27A(1) of this Act applies, an application to which section 28C(1) of this Act applies, an application received by the Secretary of State as mentioned in section 31(1) of this Act or an application made by any person for the variation or revocation of a registered order or in proceedings on appeal from any such proceedings, be admissible as evidence of any fact stated therein to the same extent as oral evidence of that fact is admissible in those proceedings.

(2) A document purporting to set out or summarise evidence given as mentioned in subsection (1)(*a*) above, or taken as mentioned in subsection (1)(*b*) above, shall be deemed to be duly authenticated for the purposes of that subsection if the document purports to be certified by the judge, magistrate or other person before whom the evidence was given or, as the case may be, by whom it was taken, to be the original document containing or recording, or, as the case may be, summarising, that evidence or a true copy of that document.

A document purporting to have been received in evidence as mentioned in subsection (1)(*c*) above, or to be a copy of a document so received, shall be deemed to be duly authenticated for the purposes of that subsection if the document purports to be certified by a judge, magistrate or officer of the court in question to have been, or to be a true copy of a document which has been, so received.

(4) It shall not be necessary in any such proceedings to prove the signature or official position of the person appearing to have given such a certificate.

(5) Nothing in this section shall prejudice the admission in evidence of any document which is admissible in evidence apart from this section.

[Maintenance Orders (Reciprocal Enforcement) Act 1972, s 36, as amended by the Domestic Proceedings and Magistrates' Courts Act 1978, s 60, the Maintenance Orders (Reciprocal Enforcement) Act 1992, Sch 1 and SI 1995/755.]

6–826   37. Obtaining of evidence for purpose of proceedings in United Kingdom court.

(1) A court in the United Kingdom may for the purpose of any proceedings in that court under this

Part of this Act arising out of an application received by the Secretary of State[1] from a convention country request the Secretary of State[1] to make to the appropriate authority or court in the convention country a request for the taking in that country of the evidence of a person residing therein relating to matters connected with the application.

(2) A request made by a court under this section shall—

(a) give details of the application in question;
(b) state the name and address of the person whose evidence is to be taken; and
(c) specify the matters relating to which the evidence of that person is required.

(3) If the Secretary of State[1] is satisfied that a request made to him under this section contains sufficient information to enable the evidence of the person named in the request relating to the matters specified therein to be taken by a court or person in the convention country, he shall transmit the request to the appropriate authority or court in that country.
[Maintenance Orders (Reciprocal Enforcement) Act 1972, s 37.]

----

1. Reference to the Secretary of State is to be construed as reference to the Lord Chancellor: SI 1992/709, art 4(1).

6–827   38. Taking of evidence at request of court in convention country.   (1) Where a request is made to the Secretary of State[1] by or on behalf of a court in a convention country to obtain the evidence of a person residing in the United Kingdom relating to matters connected with an application to which section 26 of this Act applies, the Secretary of State[1] shall request such court, or such officer of a court, as he may determine to take the evidence of that person relating to such matters connected with that application as may be specified in the request.

(2) The court by which or officer by whom a request under subsection (1) above is received from the Secretary of State[1] shall have power to take the evidence and, after giving notice of the time and place at which the evidence is to be taken to such persons and in such manner as it or he thinks fit, shall take the evidence of the person named in the request relating to the matters specified therein in such manner as may be prescribed; and the evidence so taken shall be sent in the prescribed manner by the prescribed officer to the court in the convention country by or on behalf of which the request referred to in subsection (1) above was made.

(3) Where any person, not being the person by whom the application mentioned in subsection (1) above was made, is required by virtue of this section to give evidence before a court in the United Kingdom, the court may order that there shall be paid—

(a) if the court is a court in England, Wales or Scotland, out of moneys provided by Parliament; and
(b) if the court is a court in Northern Ireland, out of moneys provided by the Parliament of Northern Ireland,

such sums as appear to the court reasonably sufficient to compensate that person for the expense, trouble or loss of time properly incurred in or incidental to his attendance.

(4) Section 97(1), (3) and (4) of the Magistrates' Courts Act 1980 (which provide for compelling the attendance of witnesses, etc) shall apply in relation to a magistrates' court to which a request under subsection (1) above is made as if the application to which the request relates were a complaint to be heard by that court.
[Maintenance Orders (Reciprocal Enforcement) Act 1972, s 38, as amended by the Magistrates' Courts Act 1980, Sch 7.]

----

1. Reference to the Secretary of State is to be construed as reference to the Lord Chancellor: SI 1992/709, art 4(1).

6–828   38A. Rules of court[1].   (1) Rules of court may make provision with respect to the orders made or other things done by a magistrates' court, or an officer of such a court, by virtue of this Part of this Act, notice of which is to be given to such persons as the rules may provide and the manner in which such notice shall be given.

(2) For the purpose of giving effect to this Part of this Act, rules of court may make, in relation to any proceedings brought under or by virtue of this Part of this Act, any provision not covered by subsection (1) above which—

(a) falls within subsection (2) of section 93 of the Children Act 1989, and
(b) may be made in relation to relevant proceedings under that section.

(3)–(4) *Northern Ireland.*
[Maintenance Orders (Reciprocal Enforcement) Act 1972, s 38A, as inserted by the Maintenance Orders (Reciprocal Enforcement) Act 1992, Sch 1 and amended by SI 1995/755 and SI 2004/2035.]

----

1. The amendment of this provision by the Courts Act 2003 (Consequential Amendments) Order 2004, SI 2004/2035 so far as it relates to Family Procedure Rules, does not affect the operation of the enactment amended in relation to rules of court other than Family Procedure Rules during the period between the coming into force of the order on 1 September 2004 and the coming into force of the first Family Procedure Rules made under s 75 of the Courts Act 2003 (SI 2004/2035, art 2).

6–829   39. Interpretation of Part II.   In this Part of this Act—

"maintenance", as respects Scotland, includes aliment and any sums which are payable, following divorce, by one former spouse for the support of the other;

"maintenance order" has the same meaning as in Part I of this Act;

"order", as respects Scotland, includes any interlocutor, and any decree or provision contained in an interlocutor;

"prescribed" has the same meaning as in Part I of this Act;

"registered order" means an order which is for the time being registered in a court in the United Kingdom under this Part of this Act;

"registering court", in relation to a registered court, means the court in which that order is for the time being registered under this Part of this Act;

"revoke" and "revocation" include discharge.

[Maintenance Orders (Reciprocal Enforcement) Act 1972, s 39, as amended by the Domestic Proceedings and Magistrates' Courts Act 1978, s 60, the Family Law (Scotland) Act 1985, s 28 and Sch 1 and the Maintenance Orders (Reciprocal Enforcement) Act 1992, Sch 1.]

PART III

MISCELLANEOUS AND SUPPLEMENTAL

Further provisions relating to enforcement of maintenance orders and to applications for recovery of maintenance

6–830   40. Power to apply Act to maintenance orders and applications for recovery of maintenance made in certain countries.   Where Her Majesty is satisfied—

(a)   that arrangements have been or will be made in a country or territory outside the United Kingdom to ensure that maintenance orders made by courts in the United Kingdom can be enforced in that country or territory or that applications by persons in the United Kingdom for the recovery of maintenance from persons in that country or territory can be entertained by courts in that country or territory; and

(b)   that in the interest of reciprocity it is desirable to ensure that maintenance orders made by courts in that country or territory can be enforced in the United Kingdom or, as the case may be, that applications by persons in that country or territory for the recovery of maintenance from persons in the United Kingdom can be entertained by courts in the United Kingdom,

Her Majesty may by Order in Council[1] make provision for applying the provisions of this Act with such exceptions, adaptations and modifications as may be specified in the Order, to such orders or applications as are referred to in paragraphs (a) and (b) above and to maintenance and other orders made in connection with such applications by courts in the United Kingdom or in that country or territory.

[Maintenance Orders (Reciprocal Enforcement) Act 1972, s 40 as amended by the Civil Jurisdiction and Judgments Act 1982, Schs 11 and 14.]

---

1. A number of Orders are printed in this PART, post.

Provisions with respect to certain orders of magistrates' courts

6–831   42. Provisional order for maintenance of party to marriage made by magistrates' court to cease to have effect on remarriage of party.   (1) Where a magistrates' court has, by virtue of section 3 of this Act, made a provisional maintenance order consisting of, or including, a provision such as is mentioned in section 2(1)(a) of the Domestic Proceedings and Magistrates' Courts Act 1978 (making of periodical payments by husband or wife) or Article 4(1)(a) of the Domestic Proceedings (Northern Ireland) Order 1980 and the order has been confirmed by a competent court in a reciprocating country, then, if after the making of that order the marriage of the parties to the proceedings in which the order was made is dissolved or annulled but the order continues in force, that order or, as the case may be, that provision thereof shall cease to have effect on the remarriage of the party in whose favour it was made, except in relation to any arrears due under it on the date of such remarriage and shall not be capable of being revived.

(2) For the avoidance of doubt it is hereby declared that references in this section to remarriage include references to a marriage which is by law void or voidable.

[Maintenance Orders (Reciprocal Enforcement) Act 1972, s 42, as amended by the Domestic Proceedings and Magistrates' Courts Act 1978, Sch 2 and the Maintenance Orders (Northern Ireland Consequential Amendments) Order 1980, SI 1980/564.]

Supplemental provisions

6–840   44. Exclusion of certain enactments relating to evidence.   (1) Section 20 of the Family Law Reform Act 1969 (power of court hearing certain proceedings to require use of blood tests to determine paternity) and any corresponding enactment of the Parliament of Northern Ireland shall not apply to any proceedings under this Act, but the foregoing provision is without prejudice to the power of a court to allow the report of any person who has carried out such tests to be given in evidence in those proceedings.

(2) The Evidence (Proceedings in Other Jurisdictions) Act 1975 shall not apply to the taking of evidence in the United Kingdom for the taking of which section 14 or section 38 of this Act provides.
[Maintenance Orders (Reciprocal Enforcement) Act 1972, s 44, as amended by the Evidence (Proceedings in Other Jurisdictions) Act 1975, Sch 1.]

6–841 47. Interpretation: general. (2) References in this Act to a part of the United Kingdom are references to England and Wales, to Scotland, or to Northern Ireland.

(3) Any reference in this Act to the jurisdiction of a court, where the reference is to assets being located or to a person residing, within the jurisdiction of a court, shall be construed—

(a) in relation to a magistrates' court in England and Wales as a reference to the local justice area in which the court acts, and

(b) in relation to a magistrates' court in Northern Ireland as a reference to the petty sessions district for which the court acts.

(4) Any reference in this Act to any other enactment is a reference thereto as amended, and includes a reference thereto as extended or applied, by or under any other enactment.
[Maintenance Orders (Reciprocal Enforcement) Act 1972, s 47 as amended by the Civil Jurisdiction and Judgments Act 1982, Schs 11 and 14 and the Courts Act 2003, Sch 8.]

Matrimonial Causes Act 1973
(1973 c 18)

6–960 25. Matters to which court is to have regard in deciding how to exercise its powers under ss 23, 24 and 24A. (1) It shall be the duty of the court[1] in deciding whether to exercise its powers under section 23, 24 or 24A or 24B★ above and, if so, in what manner, to have regard to all the circumstances of the case[2], first consideration[3] being given to the welfare while a minor of any child of the family[4] who has not attained the age eighteen.

(2) As regards the exercise of the powers of the court under section 23(1)(a), (b) or (c), 24 or 24A or 24B★ above in relation to a party to the marriage, the court shall in particular have regard to the following matters—

(a) the income, earning capacity, property and other financial resources[5] which each of the parties to the marriage has or is likely to have in the foreseeable future[6], including in the case of earning capacity any increase in that capacity which it would in the opinion of the court be reasonable to expect a party to the marriage to take steps to acquire;

(b) the financial needs, obligations and responsibilities[7] which each of the parties to the marriage has or is likely to have in the foreseeable future;

(c) the standard of living enjoyed by the family before the breakdown of the marriage;

(d) the age of each party to the marriage and the duration of the marriage;

(e) any physical or mental disability of either of the parties to the marriage;

(f) the contributions which each of the parties has made or is likely in the foreseeable future to make to the welfare of the family, including any contribution by looking after the home or caring for the family;

(g) the conduct of each of the parties, if that conduct is such that it would in the opinion of the court be inequitable to disregard it;

(h) in the case of proceedings for divorce or nullity of marriage,★★ the value to each of the parties to the marriage of any benefit (for example, a pension)★★★ which, by reason of the dissolution or annulment of the marriage, that party will lose the chance of acquiring.

(3) As regards the exercise of the powers of the court under section 23(1)(d), (e) or (f), (2) or (4), 24 or 24A★ above in relation to a child of the family[4], the court shall in particular have regard to the following matters—

(a) the financial needs of the child;

(b) the income, earning capacity (if any), property and other financial resources of the child;

(c) any physical or mental disability of the child;

(d) the manner in which he was being and in which the parties to the marriage expected him to be educated or trained;

(e) the considerations mentioned in relation to the parties to the marriage in paragraphs (a), (b), (c) and (e) of subsection (2) above.

(4) As regards the exercise of the powers of the court under section 23(1)(d), (e) or (f), (2) or (4), 24 or 24A★ above against a party to a marriage in favour of a child of the family who is not the child of that party, the court shall also have regard—

(a) to whether that party assumed any responsibility for the child's maintenance, and, if so, to the extent to which, and the basis upon which, that party assumed such responsibility and to the length of time for which that party discharged such responsibility;

(b) to whether in assuming and discharging such responsibility that party did so knowing that the child was not his or her own;

(c) to the liability of any other person to maintain the child.*

[Matrimonial Causes Act 1973, s 25, as substituted by the Matrimonial and Family Proceedings Act 1984, s 3 and as amended by the Welfare Reform and Pensions Act 1999, Sch 3.]

---

*Amended by the Family Law Act 1996, Schs 8 and 10, this PART, POST, WHEN IN FORCE.
**Repealed by the Family Law Act 1996, Sch 8, when in force.
***Repealed by the Pensions Act 1996, s 166, when in force.

1. "The court" (except where the context otherwise requires) means the High Court or, where a county court has jurisdiction by virtue of the Matrimonial Causes Act 1967, a county court (s 52(1)).

2. While s 25 requires the court to have regard to all the circumstances of the case, including the specific criteria set out in sub-ss (2), (3) and (4), there is nothing to require the court in the case of a child attending university to have regard to what from time to time might be the level of grant calculated in accordance with the Education (Mandatory Awards) Regulations 1995 (*B v B (financial provision for child)* [1998] 1 FCR 49). A long lapse of time between the parties last living together and the application for maintenance is a relevant circumstance (*Lombardi v Lombardi* [1973] 3 All ER 625).

3. The welfare of minor children is not however the paramount consideration overriding all others; see *Suter v Suter and Jones* [1987] Fam 111, [1987] 2 All ER 336, 151 JP 593, CA (but as to magistrates' courts proceedings see the Domestic Proceedings and Magistrates' Courts Act 1978, s 15.

4. "Child of the family", in relation to the parties to a marriage, means—(a) a child of both of those parties; and (b) any other child, not being a child who is placed with those parties as foster parents by a local authority or voluntary organisation, who has been treated by both of those parties as a child of their family (s 52(1)).

5. These are not confined to family assets; see *Daubney v Daubney* [1976] Fam 267, [1976] 2 All ER 453.

6. There is no reason in principle why the court, when exercising its jurisdiction under s 25, should not make an order in respect of an undischarged bankrupt provided there is a clear picture of that person's assets and liabilities and the expenses of the bankruptcy (*Hellyer v Hellyer* [1997] 1 FCR 340).

7. The fact that the husband has undertaken the legal responsibility of maintaining a new wife must be fully borne in mind and be given the same degree and weight as his responsibilities in any other financial respect (*Barnes v Barnes* [1972] 3 All ER 872).

6–961 25A. Exercise of court's powers in favour of party to marriage on decree of divorce or nullity of marriage. (1) Where on or after the grant of a decree of divorce or nullity of marriage the court decides to exercise its powers under section 23(1)(a), (b) or (c), 24 or 24A or 24B above in favour of a party to the marriage*, it shall be the duty of the court to consider whether it would be appropriate so to exercise those powers that the financial obligations of each party towards the other will be terminated as soon after the grant of the decree as the court considers just and reasonable[1].

(2) Where the court decides in such a case to make a periodical payments or secured periodical payments order in favour of a party to the marriage, the court shall in particular consider whether it would be appropriate to require those payments to be made or secured only for such term as would in the opinion of the court be sufficient to enable the party in whose favour the order is made to adjust without undue hardship[2] to the termination of his or her financial dependence on the other party[3].

(3) Where on or after the grant of a decree of divorce or nullity of marriage an application is made by a party to the marriage for a periodical payments or secured periodical payments order in his or her favour, then, if the court considers that no continuing obligation should be imposed on either party to make or secure periodical payments in favour of the other, the court may dismiss the application with a direction that the applicant shall not be entitled to make any further application in relation to that marriage for an order under section 23(1)(a) or (b) above.**

[Matrimonial Causes Act 1973, s 25A, as inserted by the Matrimonial and Family Proceedings Act 1984, s 3 and as amended by the Welfare Reform and Pensions Act 1999, Sch 3.]

---

*Amended by the Family Law Act 1996, Sch 8, this PART, POST, WHEN IN FORCE.
**Sub-section (3) substituted for a new sub-s (3) and (3A) by the Family Law Act 1996, Sch 8, when in force.

1. The application of the principle of a "clean break" was considered in *Morris v Morris* (1985) 150 JP 7, [1985] FLR 1176, [1986] Fam Law 24, CA, where, on a variation by a county court, a provision terminating periodical payments in 5 years time was held to be wrong because it was too early having regard to the circumstances of the parties to reach such a conclusion. The "clean break" approach should be applied to applicants of acutely limited means to avoid the necessity of their returning to court at regular intervals when any adjustment in the amount payable would make no difference to the payee; see *Ashley v Blackman* [1988] Fam 85, [1988] 3 WLR 222, [1988] FCR 699.

2. The court must inquire whether the position has been reached in which a limited term order is appropriate and, if, but only if, the court is so satisfied then to devise a programme of adjustment which will achieve partial or total financial viability without undue hardship. Where a wife gave birth to a child of whom the husband was not the father, it was held that it would be wrong to ignore the wife's responsibility to her child (then aged 7) because he was not a child of the family, and that the wife's dependence on the husband, although it should not be permitted to continue for very many more years, it would be premature to consider a limited term order (*Fisher v Fisher* [1989] FCR 309, [1989] 1 FLR 423, CA).

3. If it is not possible to say what period will be sufficient for a party to adjust without undue hardship, the appropriate order is one for joint lives until further order or remarriage (*Barrett v Barrett* [1988] FCR 707, [1988] 2 FLR 516, CA).

6–961A 25B–25D. *Pensions.*

Maintenance agreements

6–962 34. Validity of maintenance agreements. (1) If a maintenance agreement includes a provision purporting to restrict any right to apply to a court for an order containing financial arrangements, then—

(a) that provision shall be void[1]; but

(b) any other financial arrangements contained in the agreement shall not thereby be rendered void or unenforceable[2] and shall, unless they are void or unenforceable for any other reason (and subject to sections 35 and 36 below), be binding on the parties to the agreement.

(2) In this section and in section 35 below—

"maintenance agreement" means any agreement in writing made, whether before or after the commencement of this Act, between the parties to a marriage, being—

(a) an agreement containing financial arrangements, whether made during the continuance or after the dissolution or annulment of the marriage; or

(b) a separation agreement which contains no financial arrangements in a case where no other agreement in writing between the same parties contains such arrangements;

"financial arrangements" means provisions governing the rights and liabilities towards one another when living separately of the parties to a marriage (including a marriage which has been dissolved or annulled) in respect of the making or securing of payments or the disposition or use of any property, including such rights and liabilities with respect to the maintenance or education of any child, whether or not a child of the family.

[Matrimonial Causes Act 1973, s 34.]

---

1. This enacts a principle already well settled in case law (see *Hyman v Hyman* [1929] AC 601, 93 JP 209, HL; *Hughes v Hughes* [1929] P 1, 93 JP 3).

2. *Bennett v Bennett* [1951] 2 KB 572, [1951] 1 All ER 1088, 115 JP 355; affd [1952] 1 KB 249, [1952] 1 All ER 413, CA, to the extent that it decided otherwise, is no longer good law.

6–963 35. Alteration of agreements by court during lives of parties. (1) Where a maintenance agreement is for the time being subsisting and each of the parties to the agreement is for the time being either domiciled or resident in England and Wales, then, subject to subsection (3) below, either party may apply to the court or to a magistrates'[1] court[2] for an order under this section.

(2) If the court to which the application is made is satisfied either—

(a) that by reason of a change in the circumstances[3] in the light of which any financial arrangements contained in the agreement were made or, as the case may be, financial arrangements were omitted from it (including a change foreseen by the parties when making the agreement), the agreement should be altered so as to make different, or, as the case may be, so as to contain, financial arrangements, or

(b) that the agreement does not contain proper financial arrangements with respect to any child of the family,

then subject to subsections (3), (4) and (5) below, that court may by order make such alterations in the agreement—

(i) by varying or revoking any financial arrangements contained in it, or

(ii) by inserting in it financial arrangements for the benefit of one of the parties to the agreement or of a child of the family,

as may appear to that court to be just[4] having regard to all the circumstances, including, if relevant, the matters mentioned in section 25(4) above; and the agreement shall have effect thereafter as if any alteration made by the order had been made by agreement between the parties and for valuable consideration.

(3) A magistrates' court shall not entertain an application under subsection (1) above unless both the parties to the agreement are resident in England and Wales and the court acts in, or is authorised by the Lord Chancellor to act for, a local justice area in which at least one of the parties is resident and shall not have power to make any order on such an application except—

(a) in a case where the agreement includes no provision for periodical payments by either of the parties, an order inserting provision for the making by one of the parties of periodical payments for the maintenance of the other party or for the maintenance of any child of the family;

(b) in a case where the agreement includes provision for the making by one of the parties of periodical payments, an order increasing or reducing the rate of, or terminating, any of those payments.

(4) Where a court decides to alter, by order under this section, an agreement by inserting provision for the making or securing by one of the parties to the agreement of periodical payments for the maintenance of the other party or by increasing the rate of the periodical payments which the agreement provides shall be made by one of the parties for the maintenance of the other, the term for which the payments or, as the case may be, the additional payments attributable to the increase are to be made under the agreement as altered by the order shall be such term as the court may specify, subject to the following limits, that is to say—

(a) where the payments will not be secured, the term shall be so defined as not to extend beyond the death of either of the parties to the agreement or the remarriage of the party to whom the payments are to be made;

(*b*)　where the payments will be secured, the term shall be so defined as not to extend beyond the death or remarriage of that party.★

(5)　Where a court decides to alter, by order under this section, an agreement by inserting provision for the making or securing by one of the parties to the agreement of periodical payments for the maintenance of a child of the family or by increasing the rate of the periodical payments which the agreement provides shall be made or secured by one of the parties for the maintenance of such a child, then, in deciding the term for which under the agreement as altered by the order the payments, or as the case may be, the additional payments attributable to the increase are to be made or secured for the benefit of the child, the court shall apply the provisions of section 29(2) and (3) above as to age limits as if the order in question were a periodical payment or secured periodical payments order in favour of the child.

(6)　For the avoidance of doubt it is hereby declared that nothing in this section or in section 34 above affects any power of a court before which are proceedings between the parties to a maintenance agreement are brought under any other enactment (including a provision of this Act) to make an order[5] containing financial arrangements or any right of either party to apply for such an order in such proceedings.★★

[Matrimonial Causes Act 1973, s 35 as amended by the Matrimonial and Family Proceedings Act 1984, Sch 1, the Justices of the Peace Act 1997, Sch 5, the Access to Justice Act 1999, Sch 15 and the Courts Act 2003, Sch 8.]

★**Amended by the Civil Partnership Act 2004, Sch 27 from a date to be appointed.**

★★**Amended by the insertion of a new sub-s (7) by the Family Law Act 1996, Sch 8, this Part, post, when in force.**

1. The jurisdiction of a magistrates' court under this section is unaffected by s 2 of the Matrimonial Causes Act 1967 (Matrimonial Causes Act 1967, s 2(4)).

2. An application under this section is to be by way of complaint and summons; see Magistrates' Courts Rules 1981, r 105 and note thereto in Part I: Magistrates' Courts, Procedure, ante.

3. The expressions used in this paragraph were considered by the Court of Appeal in *K v K* [1961] 2 All ER 266, and in *Ratcliffe v Ratcliffe* [1962] 3 All ER 993. In the former case it was decided that the occurrence of an event during the currency of the agreement, contemplated by the parties when the agreement was made, is not within the intent of the paragraph: in the latter it was held that although there was a change in the circumstances it was not just that by reason of the change there should be an alteration in the financial arrangements (change brought about by husband's voluntary and unilateral action). And see *Gorman v Gorman* [1964] 3 All ER 739, in which it was held that a case for altering the agreement was not made out because, *inter alia*, a wife for whose maintenance no provision had been made was not debarred from instituting proceedings against her husband for his wilful neglect to provide reasonable maintenance for her.

4. This may include back-dating the variation (*Warden v Warden* [1982] Fam 10, [1981] 3 All ER 193).

5. This gives statutory effect to the decisions in *Tulip v Tulip* [1951] P 378, [1951] 2 All ER 91; *Dowell v Dowell* [1952] 2 All ER 141, 116 JP 350.

6–964　47. Matrimonial relief in respect of polygamous marriages.　(1)　A court in England and Wales shall not be precluded from granting matrimonial relief or making a declaration concerning the validity of a marriage by reason only that either party to the marriage is, or has during the subsistence of the marriage been, married to more than one person.

(2)　In this section "matrimonial relief" means—

(*a*), (*b*)　divorce, nullity, etc

(*c*)　an order under section 35 above altering a maintenance agreement;

(*d*)　divorce, nullity, etc

(*dd*)　an order under Part III of the Matrimonial and Family Proceedings Act 1984;

(*e*)　an order under Part I of the Domestic Proceedings and Magistrates' Courts Act 1978.★

(3)　*Declarations of validity.*

(4)　Provision may be made by rules of court—

(*a*)　for requiring notice of proceedings brought by virtue of this section to be served on any additional spouse of a party to the marriage in question; and

(*b*)　for conferring on any such additional spouse the right to be heard in the proceedings,

in such cases as may be specified in the rules.

[Matrimonial Causes Act 1973, s 47, as amended by the Domestic Proceedings and Magistrates' Courts Act 1978, Sch 2, the Matrimonial and Family Proceedings Act 1984, Sch 1, the Family Law Act 1986, Sch 1 and the Private International Law (Miscellaneous Provisions) Act 1995, Sch.]

★**Amended by the Family Law Act 1996, Sch 8, this Part, post, when in force.**

Legitimacy Act 1976

(1976 c 31)

6–1320　1. Legitimacy of children of certain void marriages.　(1)　The child of a void marriage[1], whenever born, shall, subject to subsection (2) below and Schedule 1[2] to this Act, be treated as the legitimate child of his parents if at the time of the insemination resulting in the birth or, where there was no such insemination, the child's conception (or at the time of the celebration of the marriage if later) both or either of the parties reasonably believed that the marriage was valid.

(2) This section only applies where the father of the child was domiciled in England and Wales at the time of the birth or, if he died before the birth, was so domiciled immediately before his death.

(3) It is hereby declared for the avoidance of doubt that subsection (1) above applies notwithstanding that the belief that the marriage was valid was due to a mistake as to law.

(4) In relation to a child born after the coming into force of section 28 of the Family Law Reform Act 1987, it shall be presumed for the purposes of subsection (1) above, unless the contrary is shown, that one of the parties to the void marriage reasonably believed at the time of the insemination resulting in the birth or, where there was no such insemination, the child's conception (or at the time of the celebration of the marriage if later) that the marriage was valid.

[Legitimacy Act 1976, s 1 as amended by the Family Law Reform Act 1987, s 28.]

---

1. "Void marriage" means a marriage, not being voidable only, in respect of which the High Court has or had jurisdiction to grant a decree of nullity, or would have or would have had such jurisdiction if the parties were domiciled in England and Wales (Legitimacy Act 1976, s 10(1)).
2. The Schedule refers to savings.

6–1321   2. Legitimation by subsequent marriage of parents[1]. Subject to the following provisions of this Act, where the parents of an illegitimate person marry one another, the marriage shall, if the father of the illegitimate person is at the date of marriage domiciled in England and Wales, render that person, if living, legitimate from the date of the marriage.

[Legitimacy Act 1976, s 2.]

---

1. Notwithstanding the repeal by this Act of corresponding provisions, namely ss 1 and 8 of the Legitimacy Act 1926, persons legitimated or recognised as legitimate under that Act shall continue to be legitimated or recognised as legitimated by virtue of ss 1 or 8 of that Act (Legitimacy Act 1976, Sch 1).

6–1322   3. Legitimation by extraneous law[1]. Subject to the following provisions of this Act, where the parents of an illegitimate person marry one another and the father of the illegitimate person is not at the time of the marriage domiciled in England and Wales but is domiciled in a country by the law of which the illegitimate person became legitimated by virtue of such subsequent marriage, that person, if living, shall in England and Wales be recognised as having been so legitimated from the date of the marriage notwithstanding that, at the time of his birth, his father was domiciled in a country the law of which did not permit legitimation by subsequent marriage.

[Legitimacy Act 1976, s 3.]

---

1. Notwithstanding the repeal by this Act of corresponding provisions, namely ss 1 and 8 of the Legitimacy Act 1926, persons legitimated or recognised as legitimate under that Act shall continue to be legitimated or recognised as legitimated by virtue of ss 1 or 8 of that Act (Legitimacy Act 1976, Sch 1).

6–1323   4. Legitimation of adopted child. (1) Section 39 of the Adoption Act 1976 or section 67 of the Adoption and Children Act 2002 does not prevent an adopted child being legitimated under section 2 or 3 above if either natural parent is the sole adoptive parent.

(2) Where an adopted child (with a sole adoptive parent) is legitimated—

(a) subsection (2) of the said section 39 or subsection (3)(b) of the said section 67 shall not apply after the legitimation to the natural relationship with the other natural parent, and

(b) revocation of the adoption order in consequence of the legitimation shall not affect section 39, 41 or 42 of the Adoption Act 1976 or section 67, 68 or 69 of the Adoption and Children Act 2002 as it applies to any instrument made before the date of legitimation.

[Legitimacy Act 1976, s 4 as amended by the Adoption Act 1976, Sch 3 and the Adoption and Children Act 2002, Sch 3.]

6–1324   5. *Rights of legitimated persons and others to take interests in property.*

6–1325   6. *Dispositions depending on date of birth.*

6–1326   7. *Protection of trustees and personal representatives.*

6–1327   8. Personal rights and obligations. A legitimated person[1] shall have the same rights, and shall be under the same obligations in respect of the maintenance and support of himself or of any other person as if he had been born legitimate, and, subject to the provisions of this Act, the provisions of any Act relating to claims for damages, compensation, allowance, benefit or otherwise by or in respect of a legitimate child shall apply in like manner in the case of a legitimated person.

[Legitimacy Act 1976, s 8.]

---

1. "Legitimated person" means a person legitimated or recognised as legitimated (a) under s 2 or 3 above; or (b) under ss 1 or 8 of the Legitimacy Act 1926; or (c) except in s 8, by a legitimation (whether or not by virtue of the subsequent marriage of his parents) recognised by the law of England and Wales and effected under the law of any other country; and

cognate expressions shall be construed accordingly. For the purposes of the Act "legitimated person" includes, where the context admits, a person legitimated, or recognised as legitimated, before the passing of the Children Act 1975 (Legitimacy Act 1976, s 10).

6–1328   9.   Re-registration of birth of legitimated person.   (1) It shall be the duty of the parents of a legitimated person or, in cases where re-registration can be effected on information furnished by one parent and one of the parents is dead, of the surviving parent to furnish to the Registrar General information with a view to obtaining the re-registration of the birth of that person within 3 months after the date of the marriage by virtue of which he was legitimated.

(2) The failure of the parents or either of them to furnish information as required by subsection (1) above in respect of any legitimated person shall not affect the legitimation of that person.

(3) This section does not apply in relation to a person who was legitimated otherwise than by virtue of the subsequent marriage of his parents.

(4) Any parent who fails to give information as required by this section shall be liable on summary conviction to a fine not exceeding **level 1** on the standard scale.

[Legitimacy Act 1976, s 9, as amended by the Criminal Law Act 1977, s 31 and the Criminal Justice Act 1982, s 46.]

Adoption Act 1976[1]

(1976 c 36)

PART I[2]
THE ADOPTION SERVICE

The Adoption Service

6–1340   1–11.   *Repealed.*

PART II[1]
ADOPTION ORDERS

The making of adoption orders

6–1349   12.   Adoption orders[2].   (1) An adoption order is an order giving parental responsibility[3] for a child to the adopters, made on their application[4] by an authorised court[5].

(2) The order does not affect parental responsibility so far as it relates to any period before the making of the order.

(3) The making of an adoption order operates to extinguish—

(a) the parental responsibility which any person has for the child immediately before the making of the order;

(aa) any order under the Children Act 1989;

(b) any duty arising by virtue of an agreement or the order of a court to make payments, so far as the payments are in respect of the child's maintenance or upbringing for any period after the making of the order.

(4) Subsection (3)(b) does not apply to a duty arising by virtue of an agreement—

(a) which constitutes a trust, or

(b) which expressly provides that the duty is not to be extinguished by the making of an adoption order.

(5) An adoption order may not be made in relation to a child who is or has been married.

(6) An adoption order may contain such terms and conditions[6] as the court thinks fit.

(7) An adoption order may be made notwithstanding that the child is already an adopted child.★

[Adoption Act 1976, s 12 as amended by the Children Act 1989, Sch 10.]

★Repealed by the Adoption and Children Act 2002, s 139(3), Sch 5 as from 30 December 2005, except in relation to any application for an adoption order where the application has been made and has not been disposed of immediately before that date, and the child in relation to whom the application is made has his home immediately before this repeal with a person with whom he has been placed for adoption by an adoption agency.

1. Part II contains ss 12–26.

2. Any interference with a parent's right (here father's) that would result from the making of an adoption order must be necessary and proportionate in accordance with art 8(2) of the Convention; adoption is inappropriate where the child has a strong relationship with the paternal family and is a member both of his foster mother's family and of his father's family: *Re B (a child)(adoption order)* [2001] EWCA Civ 347, [2001] 2 FCR 89, [2001] 2 FLR 26, CA.

3. "Parental responsibility" has the same meaning as in the Children Act 1989 (s 72(1), post); see s 3 of the Children Act 1989, this PART, post.

4. For procedure, see the Magistrates' Courts (Adoption) Rules 1984, this PART, post. In Home Office Circular No 52/59, dated March 25th 1959, it is suggested that it might be desirable for courts to provide applicants, through the guardian ad litem or otherwise, with a simple statement about the effect of an adoption order; such an explanatory memorandum is attached as an appendix to the circular.

Representation may be granted for proceedings in a magistrates' court where the application for an adoption order is opposed by any party; see Sch 2 to the Legal Aid Act 1988 in **PART I: MAGISTRATES' COURTS, PROCEDURE**, ante.

5. For meaning of "authorised court", see ss 62 and 72(1), post.

6. The court has power, when making an adoption order, to impose a term or condition as to future contact of the child with a member of his natural family, whether a natural parent or a brother or sister. In normal circumstances it is desirable that there should be a complete break on the making of an adoption order, but each case must be considered on its own particular facts. The court should not, except in the most exceptional case, impose a term or condition regarding access to members of the child's natural family to which the adopting parents do not agree; see *Re C (a minor) (adoption order: conditions)* [1989] AC 1, [1988] 1 All ER 705, [1988] FCR 484, HL, and see also *Re S (a minor) (adoption order: conditions)* [1995] 2 All ER 122, [1995] 2 FCR 177, CA. The question of contact, even indirect contact, should not be re-opened after the making of an adoption order unless there is some fundamental change in circumstances (*Re S (adopted child: contact)* [1993] 2 FCR 234).

6–1350 13–17. *Repealed.*

Freeing for adoption

6–1355 18. Freeing child for adoption. (1) Where, on an application by an adoption agency[1], an authorised court[2] is satisfied[3] in the case of each parent[4] or guardian[5] of the child that—

(a) he freely, and with full understanding of what is involved, agrees generally and unconditionally to the making of an adoption order[6], or

(b) his agreement to the making of an adoption order should be dispensed[7] with on a ground specified in section 16(2),

the court shall make an order declaring the child[8] free for adoption[9].

(2) No application shall be made under subsection (1) unless—

(a) it is made with the consent of a parent or guardian of a child, or

(b) the adoption agency is applying for dispensation under subsection (1)(b) of the agreement of each parent or guardian of the child, and the child is in the care of the adoption agency.

(2A) For the purposes of subsection (2) a child is in the care of an adoption agency if the adoption agency is a local authority and he is in their care.

(3) No agreement required under subsection (1)(a) shall be dispensed with under subsection (1)(b) unless the child is already placed for adoption or the court is satisfied that it is likely that the child will be placed for adoption.

(4) An agreement by the mother of the child is ineffective for the purposes of this section if given less than 6 weeks after the child's birth.

(5) On the making of an order under this section, parental responsibility[10] for the child is given to the adoption agency, and subsections (2) to (4) of section 12 apply as if the order were an adoption order and the agency were the adopters.

(6) Before making an order under this section, the court shall satisfy itself, in relation to each parent or guardian of the child who can be found, that he has been given an opportunity of making, if he so wishes, a declaration that he prefers not to be involved in future questions concerning the adoption of the child; and any such declaration shall be recorded[11] by the court.

(7) Before making an order under this section in the case of a child whose father does not have parental responsibility for him, the court shall satisfy itself in relation to any person claiming to be the father that—

(a) he has no intention of applying for—

(i) an order under section 4(1) of the Children Act 1989, or

(ii) a residence order under section 10 of that Act, or

(b) if he did make any such application, it would be likely to be refused.

(8) Subsections (5) and (7) of section 12 apply in relation to the making of an order under this section as they apply in relation to the making of an order under that section.*

[Adoption Act 1976, s 18, as amended by the Health and Social Services and Social Security Adjudications Act 1983, s 9 and Sch 2, the Family Law Reform Act 1987, s 7 and Sch 2 and the Children Act 1989, Sch 10.]

---

*Repealed by the Adoption and Children Act 2002, s 139(3), Sch 5 as from 30 December 2005, except in relation to any application for an adoption order where the application has been made and has not been disposed of immediately before that date, and the child in relation to whom the application is made has his home immediately before this repeal with a person with whom he has been placed for adoption by an adoption agency.

1. For meaning of "adoption agency", see s 1(4), ante and s 72(1), post.

2. For meaning of "authorised court", see ss 62 and 72(1), post.

3. Before considering whether to dispense with parental consent the court must consider whether freeing for adoption will promote the welfare of the child (*Re U (application to free for adoption)* [1993] 2 FCR 64, [1993] 2 FLR 919, CA; following *Re E (a minor) (adoption: parental agreement)* [1989] FCR 118). The court is required to consider the promotion of the child's welfare under s 6 even though an adoption agency is similarly charged; the adoption agency's view does not bind the court (*Re U*, ibid).

4. See note 3 to s 16(1)(b), ante.

5. For meaning of "guardian", see s 72(1) post.

6. The distinction between 'freeing for adoption' and 'an adoption order' must be scrupulously observed in letters and forms sent to a parent whose consent is being sought, these concepts being complex in their interrelationship; the

consequences of consent to a freeing order could not be starker and the degree of understanding and the quality of consent must, therefore, be commensurate: *Re A (a child)(adoption: consent)* [2001] 2 FCR 174, [2001] 2 FLR 455, CA.

7. See note 5 to s 16(1)(*b*)(ii), ante. In seeking to determine whether a parent's refusal to give consent to an order freeing a child for adoption is reasonable, the court must ask itself whether, having regard to the evidence and applying the current values of our society, the advantages of adoption for the welfare of the child appear sufficiently strong to justify overriding the views and interests of the objecting parent (*Re F (children) (adoption: freeing order)* [2000] 3 FCR 337, [2000] 2 FLR 505, CA, followed in *Re B-M (a child)(adoption: parental agreement)* [2001] 1 FCR 1, CA).

Where both parents were heroin addicts with extensive criminal histories and domestic violence issues, the child was made the subject of an interim care order when only 2 months old and, thereafter, there was a rapid downhill spiral, the threshold criteria for a care order were clearly established and the history was deadly to any optimistic assessment for the future; adoption was an incalculably better prospect than care and the views and interests of the parents should have been set aside: *Re D (grant of care order: refusal of freeing order)* [2001] 1 FCR 501, [2001] 1 FLR 862, CA.)

8. Where the child is a ward of court, leave of the court should be sought before applying for an order under this section or where a local authority wishes to place a ward with long term foster parents with a view to adoption; see *Practice Direction* [1985] 2 All ER 832, [1985] 1 WLR 924, amended by *Practice Direction* [1986] 1 All ER 652, [1986] 1 WLR 286.

9. In spite of the restrictive definition of 'adoption order' in s 72, post, s 18 extends to a prospective adoption order in a foreign jurisdiction (*Re S (a child) (adoption: procedure)* [2002] EWCA Civ 798, [2002] 3 FCR 171, [2002] 2 FLR 681.

10. "Parental responsibility" has the same meaning as in the Children Act 1989 (s 72(1), post); see s 3 of Children Act 1989, this PART, post.

The effect of this provision is that a freeing order divests the natural parents of their parenthood, as well as parental responsibility (*M v C and Calderdale Metropolitan Borough Council* [1993] 1 FCR 431, [1993] 1 FLR 505, [1993] 3 All ER 313—as a consequence of a freeing order held that the father was not entitled to apply for a residence order under s 8 of the Children Act 1989). However, the Court of Appeal has, in *Re A (a minor) (adoption: contact)* [1993] 2 FLR 645, upheld the making of a contact order to a natural mother at the same time as an order freeing for adoption; such an order preserves contact between the child and the natural family pending adoption. Moreover, while a contact order cannot survive the adoption order, a further contact order may, theoretically, be imposed on adopters after the making of the adoption order as an alternative to the making of an adoption order with conditions (*Re A (a minor) (adoption contact)* ibid).

11. We suggest that the declaration should be recorded in the register of adoptions.

6–1356   19. Progress reports to former parents.   (1) This section and section 20 apply to any person ("the former parent"), who was required to be given an opportunity of making a declaration under section 18(6) but did not do so.

(2) Within the 14 days following the date 12 months after the making of the order under section 18 the adoption agency to which parental responsibility was given on the making of the order, unless it has previously by notice[1] to the former parent informed him that an adoption order has been made in respect of the child, shall by notice to the former parent inform him—

(*a*)   whether an adoption order has been made in respect of the child, and (if not)

(*b*)   whether the child has his home with a person with whom he has been placed for adoption.

(3) If at the time when the former parent is given notice under subsection (2) an adoption order has not been made in respect of the child, it is thereafter the duty of the adoption agency to give notice to the former parent of the making of an adoption order (if and when made), and meanwhile to give the former parent notice[2] whenever the child is placed for adoption or ceases to have his home with a person with whom he has been placed for adoption.

(4) If at any time the former parent by notice makes a declaration to the adoption agency that he prefers not to be involved in future questions concerning the adoption of the child—

(*a*)   the agency shall secure that the declaration is recorded[3] by the court which made the order under section 18, and

(*b*)   the agency is released from the duty of complying further with subsection (3) as respects that former parent.★

[Adoption Act 1976, s 19 as amended by the Children Act 1989, Sch 10.]

★**Repealed, except in so far as this section continues to have effect in relation to orders made under s 18 hereof, by the Adoption and Children Act 2002, s 139(2), (3), Sch 4, para 7(1)(a), Sch 5.**

1. "Notice" means a notice in writing (s 72(1) post), and may be given by post (s 69, post).
2. Notice should be given within as short a time as possible, and having regard to the limit specified in s 19(2), 14 days would be a reasonable time for the purpose of s 19(3). If notice is not given as required any subsequent placement of a child for adoption will be invalid (*R v Derbyshire County Council, ex p T* [1990] Fam 164, [1990] 1 All ER 792, [1989] FCR 713, CA).
3. See note 9 to s 18, ante.

6–1357   20. Revocation of s 18 order.   (1) The former parent[1], at any time more than 12 months after the making of the order under section 18 when—

(*a*)   no adoption order has been made in respect of the child, and

(*b*)   the child does not have his home with a person with whom he has been placed for adoption,

may apply to the court which made the order for a further order revoking it on the ground that he wishes to resume parental responsibility[2].

(2) While the application is pending the adoption agency[3] having parental responsibility[2] shall not place the child for adoption without the leave of the court.

(3) The revocation of an order under section 18 ("a section 18 order") operates—

(*a*)   to extinguish the parental responsibility given to the adoption agency under the section 18 order;

(*b*)   to give parental responsibility for the child to—

  (i)   the child's mother; and
  (ii) where the child's father and mother were married to each other at the time of his birth, the father; and

(*c*)   to revive—

  (i)   any parental responsibility agreement,
  (ii) any order under section 4(1) of the Children Act 1989, and
  (iii) any appointment of a guardian in respect of the child (whether made by a court or otherwise),

  extinguished by the making of the section 18 order.

(3A) Subject to subsection (3)(*c*), the revocation does not—

(*a*) operate to revive—

  (i)   any order under the Children Act 1989, or
  (ii) any duty referred to in section 12(3)(*b*),

  extinguished by the making of the section 18 order; or

(*b*) affect any person's parental responsibility so far as it relates to the period between the making of the section 18 order and the date of revocation of that order.

(4) Subject to subsection (5), if the application is dismissed on the ground that to allow it would contravene the principle embodied in section 6—

(*a*) the former parent who made the application shall not be entitled to make any further application under subsection (1) in respect of the child, and
(*b*) the adoption agency is released from the duty of complying further with section 19(3) as respects that parent.

(5) Subsection (4)(*a*) shall not apply where the court which dismissed the application gives leave to the former parent to make a further application under subsection (1), but such leave shall not be given unless it appears to the court that because of a change in circumstances or for any other reason it is proper to allow the application to be made.*

[Adoption Act 1976, s 20 as amended by the Children Act 1989, Sch 10.]

---

*Repealed, except in so far as this section continues to have effect in relation to orders made under s 18 hereof, by the Adoption and Children Act 2002, s 139(2), (3), Sch 4, para 7(1)(a), Sch 5.

1. Since s 19(1), ante, defines a "former parent" as one who has not signed a s 18(6) declaration, neither a mother who has renounced her right to further involvement nor a local authority seeking to share parental authority with the mother may apply for revocation of the freeing order under s 20. However, in such circumstances, the High Court may consider exercising its inherent jurisdiction to revoke the freeing order (*In re C (a minor) (adoption: freeing order)* [1999] Fam 240, [1999] 2 WLR 1079). The High Court may exercise its inherent jurisdiction to revoke the freeing order even where the application is made within the first 12 months after the making of the freeing order (*Re J (adoption: revocation of freeing order)* [2000] 2 FCR 133, [2000] 2 FLR 58).

2. See note 8 to s 18(5) ante. Where it is clear that an adoption order is not likely to take place within a short period, the freeing order may be revoked so as to restore the parent to his or her normal rights and to ensure that the child does not remain in an adoption limbo. Even if the former parent is not, at the date of revocation, fit to have sole and unfettered responsibility of the child, the court has jurisdiction to make a revocation order, provided the welfare of the child can be protected whether by making the revocation of the freeing order conditional upon such consequential orders as are appropriate under the Children Act 1989 or in some other way (*Re G (a minor) (adoption: freeing order)* [1997] 2 All ER 534, [1997] 2 WLR 747, [1997] 2 FCR 289, [1997] 2 FLR 202, HL).

3. For meaning of "adoption agency", see s 1(4), ante and s 72(1), post.

6–1358   21. Variation of section 18 order so as to substitute one adoption agency for another.
(1) On an application to which this section applies, an authorised court may vary an order under section 18 so as to give parental responsibility for the child to another adoption agency ("the substitute agency") in place of the agency for the time being having parental responsibility for the child under the order ("the existing agency").

(2) This section applies to any application made jointly by—

(*a*) the existing agency; and
(*b*) the would-be substitute agency.

(3) Where an order under section 18 is varied under this section, section 19 shall apply as if the substitute agency had been given responsibility for the child on the making of the order.*

[Adoption Act 1976, s 21, as substituted by the Children Act 1989, Sch 10.]

---

*Repealed, except in so far as this section continues to have effect in relation to orders made under s 18 hereof, by the Adoption and Children Act 2002, s 139(2), (3), Sch 4, para 7(1)(a), Sch 5.

Supplemental

6–1359   22–25. *Repealed.*

PART III[1]

CARE AND PROTECTION OF CHILDREN AWAITING ADOPTION

6-1370   27-37.   *Repealed.*

PART IV[1]

STATUS OF ADOPTED CHILDREN

6-1381   38. Meaning of "adoption" in Part IV.   (1) In this Part "adoption" means adoption—

- (*a*)   by an adoption order;
- (*b*)   by an order made under the Children Act 1975, the Adoption Act 1958, the Adoption Act 1950 or any enactment repealed by the Adoption Act 1950;
- (*c*)   by an order made in Scotland, Northern Ireland, the Isle of Man or in any of the Channel Islands;
- (*cc*)   which is a Convention adoption[2];
- (*d*)   which is an overseas adoption[3]; or
- (*e*)   which is an adoption recognised by the law of England and Wales and effected under the law of any other country,

and cognate expressions shall be construed accordingly.

(2) The definition of adoption includes, where the context admits, an adoption effected before the passing of the Children Act 1975 but does not include an adoption of a kind mentioned in paragrpahs (*c*) to (*e*) of subsection (1) effected on or after the day which is the apppointed day for the purposes of Chapter 4 of Part 1 of the Adoption and Children Act 2002, and the date of an adoption effected by an order is the date of the making of the order.

[Adoption Act 1976, s 38 as amended by the Adoption (Intercountry Aspects) Act 1999, ss 4 and 17 and the Adoption and Children Act 2002, Sch 3.]

---

1.   Part IV contains ss 38–49.
2.   See the Adoption (Intercountry Aspects) Act 2002, s 17, for savings for adoptions etc under the 1965 Convention.
3.   For meaning of "overseas adoption", see s 72(2), post.

6-1382   39. Status conferred by adoption.   (1) An adopted child shall be treated in law—

- (*a*)   where the adopters are a married couple, as if he had been born as a child of the marriage (whether or not he was in fact born after the marriage was solemnised);
- (*b*)   in any other case, as if he had been born to the adopter in wedlock (but not as a child of any actual marriage of the adopter).

(2) An adopted child shall, subject to subsections (3) and (3A), be treated in law as if he were not the child of any person other than the adopters or adopter.

(3) In the case of a child adopted by one of its natural parents as sole adoptive parent, subsection (2) has no effect as respects entitlement to property depending on relationship to that parent, or as respects anything else depending on that relationship.

(3A) Where, in the case of a Convention adoption, the High Court is satisfied, on an application under this subsection—

- (*a*)   that under the law of the country in which the adoption was effected the adoption is not a full adoption;
- (*b*)   that the consents referred to in Article 4(c) and (d) of the Convention have not been given for a full adoption, or that the United Kingdom is not the receiving State (within the meaning of Article 2 of the Convention); and
- (*c*)   that it would be more favourable to the adopted child for a direction to be given under this subsection,

the Court may direct that subsection (2) shall not apply, or shall not apply to such extent as may be specified in the direction.

In this subsection "full adoption" means an adoption by virtue of which the adopted child falls to be treated in law as if he were not the child of any person other than the adopters or adopter.

(3B) The following provisions of the Family Law Act 1986—

- (*a*)   section 59 (provisions relating to the Attorney General); and
- (*b*)   section 60 (supplementary provision as to declarations), shall apply in relation to, and to an application for, a direction under subsection (3A) as they apply in relation to, and to an application for, a declaration under Part III of that Act.[1]

(4) It is hereby declared that this section prevents an adopted child from being illegitimate.

(5) This section has effect—

- (*a*)   in the case of an adoption before 1st January 1976, from that date, and
- (*b*)   in the case of any other adoption, from the date of the adoption.

(6) Subject to the provisions of this Part, this section—

(a) applies for the construction of enactments or instruments passed or made before the adoption or later, and so applies subject to any contrary indication; and

(b) has effect as respects things done, or events occurring, after the adoption, or after 31st December 1975, whichever is the later.

[Adoption Act 1976, s 39 as amended by the Adoption (Intercountry Aspects) Act 1999, ss 4 and 17.]

---

1. See the Adoption (Intercountry Aspects) Act 2002, s 17, for savings for adoptions etc under the 1965 Convention.

6–1383   40. Citizenship. *Repealed.*

6–1384   41. Adoptive relatives.   (1) A relationship existing by virtue of section 39 may be referred to as an adoptive relationship, and—

(a) a male adopter may be referred to as the adoptive father;

(b) a female adopter may be referred to as the adoptive mother;

(c) any other relative of any degree under an adoptive relationship may be referred to as an adoptive relative of that degree,

but this section does not prevent the term "parent", or any other term not qualified by the word "adoptive" being treated as including an adoptive relative.

[Adoption Act 1976, s 41.]

6–1385   42–46. *Instruments concerning property; dispositions; property devolving with peerages etc; protection of trustees and personal representatives.*

6–1386   47. Miscellaneous enactments.   (1) Section 39 does not apply for the purposes of section 1 of and Schedule 1 to the Marriage Act 1949 or Schedule 1 to the Civil Partnership Act 2004 (prohibited degrees of kindred and affinity) or sections 10 and 11 (incest) of the Sexual Offences Act 1956.

(2) Section 39 does not apply for the purposes of any provision of—

(a) the British Nationality Act 1981,

(b) the Immigration Act 1971,

(c) any instrument having effect under an enactment within paragraph (a) or (b), or

(d) any other provision of the law for the time being in force which determines British citizenship, British overseas territories citizenship or British Overseas citizenship.

(3)–(5) *Repealed.*

[Adoption Act 1976, s 47 as amended by the British Nationality Act 1981, Schs 7 and 9, SI 1986/948, the Social Security Act 1986, s 86(2) and Sch 11, the Social Security Act 1988, Sch 5, the British Overseas Territories Act 2002, s 2(3) and SI 2005/3129.]

6–1387   48. Pensions. Section 39 (2) does not affect entitlement to a pension which is payable to or for the benefit of a child and is in payment at the time of his adoption.

[Adoption Act 1976, s 48.]

6–1388   49. Insurance.   Where a child is adopted whose natural parent has effected an insurance with a friendly society or a collecting society or an industrial insurance company for the payment on the death of the child of money for funeral expenses, the rights and liabilities under the policy shall by virtue of the adoption be transferred to the adoptive parents who shall for the purposes of the enactments relating to such societies and companies be treated as the person who took out the policy.

[Adoption Act 1976, s 49.]

PART V[1]
REGISTRATION AND REVOCATION OF ADOPTION ORDERS AND CONVENTION ADOPTIONS

6–1389   50–54. *Repealed.*

PART VI[1]
MISCELLANEOUS AND SUPPLEMENTAL

6–1400   55–71. *Repealed.*

6–1423   72. Interpretation.   (1) In this Act, unless the context otherwise requires—

"adoption agency" in sections 11, 13, 18 to 23 and 27 to 31 includes an adoption agency within the meaning of—

(a) section 1 of the Adoption (Scotland) Act 1978; and

(b) Article 3 of the Adoption (Northern Ireland) Order 1987.

"adoption order"—

(a) means an order under section 12(1); and

(b) in sections 12(3) and (4), 18 to 20, 27, 28 and 30 to 32 and in the definition of 'British adoption order' in this subsection includes an order under section 12 of the Adoption (Scotland) Act 1978 and Article 12 of the Adoption (Northern Ireland) Order 1987 (adoption orders in Scotland and Northern Ireland respectively); and

(c) in sections 27, 28 and 30 to 32 includes an order under section 55, section 49 of the Adoption (Scotland) Act 1978 and Article 57 of the Adoption (Northern Ireland) Order 1987 (orders in relation to children being adopted abroad).

"adoption society" means a body of persons whose functions consist of or include the making of arrangements for the adoption of children;

"appropriate voluntary organisation" has the meaning assigned by section 1(5);

"authorised court" shall be construed in accordance with section 62;

"body of persons" means any body of persons, whether incorporated or unincorporated;

"British adoption order" means—

(a) an adoption order as defined in this subsection, and

(b) an order under any provision for the adoption of a child effected under the law of any British territory outside the United Kingdom;

"British territory" means, for the purposes of any provision of this Act, any of the following countries, that is to say, Great Britain, Northern Ireland, the Channel Islands, the Isle of Man and a colony, being a country designated for the purposes of that provision by order of the Secretary of State or, if no country is so designated, any of those countries;

"child", except where used to express a relationship, means a person who has not attained the age of 18 years;

"the Convention" means the Convention on Protection of Children and Co-operation in respect of Intercountry Adoption, concluded at the Hague on 29th May 1993;

"Convention adoption" means an adoption effected under the law of a Convention country outside the British Islands, and certified in pursuance of Article 23(1) of the Convention;

"Convention adoption order" means an adoption order made in accordance with section 17;

"Convention country" means any country or territory in which the Convention is in force;

"existing", in relation to an enactment or other instrument, means one passed or made at any time before 1st January 1976;

"guardian" has the same meaning as in the Children Act 1989;

"internal law" has the meaning assigned by section 71;

"local authority" means the council of a county (other than a metropolitan county), a metropolitan district, a London borough or the Common Council of the City of London but, in relation to Wales, means the council of a county or county borough;

"notice" means a notice in writing;

"order freeing a child for adoption" means an order under section 18 and in sections 27(2) and 59 includes an order under—

(a) section 18 of the Adoption (Scotland) Act 1978; and

(b) Article 17 or 18 of the Adoption (Northern Ireland) Order 1987;

"overseas adoption" has the meaning assigned by subsection (2);

"parent" means, in relation to a child, any parent who has parental responsibility for the child under the Children Act 1989[1];

"parental responsibility" and "parental responsibility agreement" have the same meaning as in the Children Act 1989;

"prescribed" means prescribed by Family Procedure Rules;

"relative" in relation to a child means a grandparent, brother, sister, uncle or aunt, whether of the full blood or half-blood or by affinity and includes, where the child is illegitimate, the father of the child and any person who would be a relative within the meaning of this definition if the child were the legitimate child of his mother and father[2];

"United Kingdom national" means, for the purposes of any provision of this Act, a citizen of the United Kingdom and colonies satisfying such conditions, if any, as the Secretary of State may by order specify for the purposes of that provision;

"upbringing" has the same meaning as in the Children Act 1989;

"voluntary organisation" means a body other than a public or local authority the activities of which are not carried on for profit.

(1A) In this Act, in determining with what person, or where, a child has his home, any absence of the child at a hospital or boarding school and any other temporary absence shall be disregarded.

(1B) In this Act, references to a child who is in the care of or looked after by a local authority have the same meaning as in the Children Act 1989.

(2) In this Act "overseas adoption" means an adoption of such a description as the Secretary of State may by order specify[3], being a description of adoptions of children appearing to him to be effected under the law of any country outside the British Islands[4]; and an order under this subsection may contain provision as to the manner in which evidence of an overseas adoption may be given.

(3) For the purposes of this Act, a person shall be deemed to make arrangements for the adoption

of a child if he enters into or makes any agreement or arrangement for, or for facilitating, the adoption of the child by any other person[5], whether the adoption is effected, or is intended to be effected, in Great Britain or elsewhere, or if he initiates or takes part in any negotiations of which the purpose or effect is the conclusion of any agreement or the making of any arrangement therefor, and if he causes another person to do so.

(3A) In this Act, in relation to the proposed adoption of a child resident outside the British Islands, references to arrangements for the adoption of a child include references to arrangements for an assessment for the purpose of indicating whether a person is suitable to adopt a child or not.

(3B) *(Repealed)*.

(4) Except so far as the context otherwise requires, any reference in this Act to an enactment shall be construed as a reference to that enactment as amended by or under any other enactment, including this Act.

(5) In this Act, except where otherwise indicated—

(a) a reference to a numbered Part, section or Schedule is a reference to the Part or section of, or the Schedule to, this Act so numbered, and

(b) a reference in a section to a numbered subsection is a reference to the subsection of that section so numbered, and

(c) a reference in a section, subsection or Schedule to a numbered paragraph is a reference to the paragraph of that section, subsection or Schedule so numbered.★

[Adoption Act 1976, s 72, as amended by the Magistrates' Courts Act 1980, s 154 and Sch 7, the Health and Social Services and Social Security Adjudications Act 1983, Sch 2, the Family Law Reform Act 1987, s 7 and Sch 2, the Children Act 1989, Schs 10 and 15, the Local Government (Wales) Act 1994, Sch 10, the Care Standards Act 2000, Sch 4, the Adoption (Intercountry Aspects) Act 1999, ss 8, 13, 17 and Schs 2 and 3, the Adoption and Children Act 2002, s 139 and Schs 4 and 5 and SI 2004/2035.]

★Repealed, except in so far as this section relates to ss 18–21, 38–49 and Sch 2, para 6, by the Adoption and Children Act 2002, s 139(2), (3), Sch 4, paras 6, 7, Sch 5.

1 The effect of this definition is to give the term "parent" a narrower meaning in this Act than it has in the Children Act 1989 where the term "parent" will ordinarily include a putative father without parental responsibility; see *M v C and Calderdale Metropolitan Borough Council* [1993] 3 All ER 313, [1993] 1 FCR 431, [1993] 1 FLR 505. Nor does the term "parent" in the context of the Adoption Act embrace "step-parent" (*Re M W (adoption: surrogacy)* [1995] 2 FLR 759).

2. This definition is clear and precise; accordingly the reference to "uncle" may not be extended to include a great-uncle (*Re C (minors) (wardship: adoption)* [1989] 1 All ER 395, [1989] 1 WLR 61, CA).

3. See the Adoption (Designation of Overseas Adoptions) Order 1973, this PART, post.

4. See the Adoption (Intercountry Aspects) Act 1999, s 17, for savings in relation to a 1965 Convention order.

5. A properly constituted adoption agency cannot be "any other person", therefore s 11(1) of the Act does not render unlawful arrangements made between an individual and an adoption agency for the placement of the child by the latter (*Re W (a minor) (adoption: mother under disability)* [1995] 4 All ER 282, [1995] 1 FCR 714, [1995] 1 FLR 163).

6–1424 **73. Transitional provisions, amendments and repeals.** (1) The transitional provisions contained in Schedule 2[1] shall have effect.

(2)–(3) *Amendments and repeals.*★

[Adoption Act 1976, s 73.]

★Repealed, except in so far as this section relates to ss 18–21, 38–49 and Sch 2, para 6, by the Adoption and Children Act 2002, s 139(2), (3), Sch 4, paras 6, 7, Sch 5.

1. See, post.

6–1425 **74. Short title, commencement and extent.** (1) This Act may be cited as the Adoption Act 1976.

(2) This Act shall come into force on such date as the Secretary of State may by order[1] appoint and different dates may be appointed for different provisions.

(3) This Act extends to England and Wales only.★

[Adoption Act 1976, s 74, as amended by the British Nationality Act 1981, s 52(8) and Sch 9 and the Children Act 1989, Sch 10.]

★Repealed, except in so far as this section relates to ss 18–21, 38–49 and Sch 2, para 6, by the Adoption and Children Act 2002, s 139(2), (3), Sch 4, paras 6, 7, Sch 5.

1. For commencement orders made under this section, see note 1 to the short title to this Act ante.

SCHEDULES
SCHEDULE 1
REGISTRATION OF ADOPTIONS

6–1426 *Repealed.*

SCHEDULE 2
TRANSITIONAL PROVISIONS AND SAVINGS

6–1429 *Repealed.*

Domestic Proceedings and Magistrates' Courts Act 1978[1]

(1978 c 22)

PART I[2]
MATRIMONIAL PROCEEDINGS IN MAGISTRATES' COURTS

Powers of court to make orders for financial provision for parties to a marriage and children of the family

6–1491   1. Grounds of application for financial provision.   Either party to a marriage may apply to a magistrates' court[3] for an order under section 2 of this Act on the ground that the other party to the marriage—

    (a) has failed to provide reasonable maintenance[4] for the applicant; or

    (b) has failed to provide, or to make a proper contribution towards, reasonable maintenance[4] for any child of the family[5]; or

    (c) has behaved[4] in such a way that the applicant cannot reasonably be expected to live with[6] the respondent[7]; or

    (d) has deserted[4] the applicant.★

[Domestic Proceedings and Magistrates' Courts Act 1978, s 1 as amended by the Matrimonial and Family Proceedings Act 1984, Sch 1.]

  ★**Paragraphs 3 and 4 of s 1 are repealed by the Family Law Act 1996, s 18 and Sch 10, this PART, POST, WHEN IN FORCE.**

  1. The Act was brought into force as follows: ss 86, 88 (5), 89 (except para (a) of subsection (2)), 90, Sch 1, and so much of Sch 3 as relates to s 2 of the Administration of Justice Act 1964 were brought into force on 18th July 1978 (Domestic Proceedings and Magistrates' Courts Act 1978 (Commencement No 1) Order 1978, SI 1978 No 997); ss 73, 74, 87, para (a) of s 89(2) and certain minor and consequential amendments and repeals were brought into force on 20th November 1978 (Domestic Proceedings and Magistrates' Courts Act 1978 (Commencement No 2) Order 1978, SI 1978 No 1489); s 40 and paras 30 and 31 of Sch 2 were brought into force on 17th September 1979, and ss 16, 17, 18, 28, 29 (1), (2) and (5), 30, Pt IV (ss 75–83), ss 84 and 85, the remainder of s 88 and consequential amendments and repeals were brought into force on 1st November 1979 (Domestic Proceedings and Magistrates' Courts Act 1978 (Commencement No 3) Order 1979, SI 1979/731); Pts I and II (other than provisions of those parts brought into force earlier), sections 49 to 63, section 72, and consequential amendments and repeals contained in Schs 2 and 3, were brought into force on the 1st February 1981 (Domestic Proceedings and Magistrates' Courts Act 1978 (Commencement No 4) Order, SI 1980/1478).

  For transitional provisions, see Sch 1 to this Act, post, and the commencement orders.

  2. Part I contains ss 1–35.

  3. Any magistrates' court within the commission area has jurisdiction; see the Magistrates' Courts Act 1980, s 52, ante.

  4. The grounds of application are examined in detail in the General Notes at the beginning of this section on *Matrimonial Proceedings*.

  5. "Child of the family" is defined in s 88, post.

  6. "Live with" should be construed in accordance with s 88 (2), post.

  7. Section 127 of the Magistrates' Courts Act 1980 (limitation of time) may apply here.

6–1492   2. Powers of court to make orders for financial provision.   (1) Where on an application for an order[1] under this section the applicant satisfies[2] the court of any ground mentioned in section 1 of this Act, the court[3] may[4], subject to the provisions of this Part of this Act, make any one or more of the following orders[5], that is to say—

    (a) an order that the respondent shall make to the applicant such periodical payments[6], and for such term, as may be specified in the order;

    (b) an order that the respondent shall pay to the applicant such lump sum[7] as may be so specified;

    (c) an order[8] that the respondent shall make to the applicant for the benefit of a child of the family[9] to whom the application relates[10], or to such a child, such periodical payments[6], and for such term, as may be so specified;

    (d) an order that the respondent shall pay to the applicant for the benefit of a child of the family[9] to whom the application relates, or to such a child, such lump sum[7] as may be so specified.

  (2) Without prejudice to the generality of subsection (1)(b) or (d) above, an order[11] under this section for the payment of a lump sum may be made for the purpose of enabling any liability or expenses reasonably incurred in maintaining the applicant, or any child of the family to whom the application relates, before the making of the order to be met.

  (3) The amount of any lump sum required to be paid by an order under this section shall not exceed £1,000 or such larger amount as the Lord Chancellor may from time to time by order fix for the purposes of this subsection.

  Any order made by the Lord Chancellor under this subsection shall be made by statutory instrument and shall be subject to annulment in pursuance of a resolution of either House of Parliament.★

[Domestic Proceedings and Magistrates' Courts Act 1978, s 2 as amended by SI 1988/1069 and SI 1992/709.]

  ★**Repealed and new sub-ss (4) and (5) inserted by the Constitutional Reform Act 2005, Sch 4 from a date to be apoointed.**

  1. For procedure on an application, see the Family Proceedings Courts (Matrimonial Proceedings etc) Rules 1991, this PART, post. The order may be made in the respondent's absence if it is proved to the satisfaction of the Court that he received reasonable notice of the hearing, or the circumstances justify proceeding with the hearing in his absence (Family

Proceedings Courts (Matrimonial Proceedings etc) Rules 1991 r 8, this PART, post). Where the husband does not appear but sends written details of his finances, which his wife cannot agree, the court should adjourn so he can be required to attend and deal with those matters (*Whittingstall v Whittingstall* [1989] FCR 759). Where an application in a case between husband and wife is withdrawn at the hearing justices have jurisdiction to allow a fresh application to be made founded on the same ground, provided that application is made within the statutory time limit (*Land v Land* [1949] P 405, [1949] 2 All ER 218, 113 JP 403).

2. If the court is not satisfied, it must not dismiss the application before deciding whether it should exercise its powers under the Children Act 1989 in relation to any child; see s 8, post. Note also the power in s 27, post, to refuse an order in a case more suitable for the High Court.

3. As to the examination of witnesses where the parties are not legally represented, see the Magistrates' Courts Act 1980, s 73, ante.

4. The word "may", although permissive, is coupled with a duty to exercise this power to enforce the legal right of an applicant who has proved a case (*Dawson v Dawson* (1929) 93 JP 187; *Hill v Hill* (1972) 116 Sol Jo 565).

Before deciding whether to exercise its powers under this section the court shall consider whether there is any possibility of reconciliation between the parties (s 26, post).

5. Any order should include a statement that the ground of the application is found to be true (*Brown v Brown* (1898) 62 JP 568, 711; *Wilcox v Wilcox* (1902) 66 JP 166; *Bullivant v Bullivant* (1902) 18 TLR 317; *Dodd v Dodd* [1906] P 189, 70 JP 163). In the case of desertion the date upon which desertion is found to have commenced should appear in the order (*Fengl v Fengl* [1914] P 274).

A written statement of wages shall be *prima facie* evidence of the facts stated therein (Magistrates' Courts Act 1980, s 100, ante). Investigation of means may be made by a probation officer; see ibid, s 60, ante, and *Higgs v Higgs* [1941] P 27, [1941] 1 All ER 214, 105 JP 119.

Guidance on the making of an order against a member of Her Majesty's forces is given in Home Office Circular No 251/1970 and Home Office Circular No 25/1986, dated 4 April 1986. For orders against members of the Royal Navy and the Royal Marines, see Home Office Circular No 12/1982, dated 10th February 1982. See also the Army Act 1955, ss 144 and 150 to 152, the Air Force Act 1955, ss 144 and 150 to 152, post; and *Barnish v Barnish* (1976) 6 Fam Law 174, 120 Sol Jo 450.

For the effect on an order under this section of the parties living together, see s 25, post.

Because of the restrictive terms of s 20 (variation etc) post, it may be necessary for courts not wishing to order periodical payments or lump sums to consider ordering a nominal payment to preserve future powers.

6. Payment may be made to the juices' chief executive of the court or of any magistrates' court; see the Magistrates' Courts Act 1980, s 59, and the Magistrates' Courts Rules 1981, r 39 et seq. As to the effect of parties living together, see s 25, post. For enforcement see s 32, post.

7. A lump sum may be made payable by instalments (Magistrates' Courts Act 1980, s 75, ante) which may be varied subsequently under s 22, post. It may be made payable through the justices' chief executive: see the Magistrates' Courts Rules 1981, r 48, in PART I: MAGISTRATES' COURTS, PROCEDURE, ante.

8. An order for periodical payments for a child may be made whether or not an order for custody under s 8, post, is made. Note power under s 11 (1) and (2) to make an order for maintenance of a child whether or not a s 1 ground is proved.

9. "Child of the family" is defined in s 88, post. Where it is desired to have an order for tax advantage, (cf *Sherdley v Sherdley* [1988] AC 213, [1987] 2 All ER 54, 151 JP 715, HL) it should be observed that this section does not seem to allow orders against a parent in whose favour a residence order is in force; s 6 post would however seem to allow this.

10. It would seem that the court may only order maintenance for a child in respect of whom an application has been made.

11. Provided magistrates have regard to the respondent's capacity to pay a lump sum out of income or potential income, they may make a lump sum order against the respondent notwithstanding his lack of capital resources (*Burridge v Burridge* [1983] Fam 9, [1982] 3 All ER 80).

6–1493   3. Matters to which court is to have regard in exercising its powers under s 2[1].

(1) Where an application is made for an order under section 2 of this Act, it shall be the duty of the court, in deciding whether to exercise its powers under that section and, if so, in what manner, to have regard to all the circumstances of the case, first consideration being given to the welfare while a minor of any child of the family who has not attained the age of eighteen.

(2) As regards the exercise of its powers under subsection (1)(*a*) or (*b*) of section 2, the court shall in particular have regard to the following matters—

  (*a*) the income, earning capacity[2], property and other financial resources[3] which each of the parties[4] to the marriage has or is likely to have in the foreseeable future, including in the case of earning capacity any increase in that capacity which it would in the opinion of the court be reasonable to expect a party to the marriage to take steps to acquire;

  (*b*) the financial needs[5], obligations[6] and responsibilities[7] which each of the parties to the marriage has or is likely to have in the foreseeable future;

  (*c*) the standard of living[8] enjoyed by the parties to the marriage before the occurrence of the conduct which is alleged as the ground of the application;

  (*d*) the age of each party to the marriage and the duration of the marriage[9];

  (*e*) any physical or mental disability of either of the parties to the marriage;

  (*f*) the contributions which each of the parties has made or is likely in the foreseeable future to make to the welfare of the family, including any contribution by looking after the home or caring for the family;

  (*g*) the conduct[10] of each of the parties, if that conduct is such that it would in the opinion of the court be inequitable to disregard it.

(3) As regards the exercise of its powers under subsection (1)(*c*) or (*d*) of section 2, the court shall in particular have regard to the following matters—

  (*a*) the financial needs of the child;

  (*b*) the income, earning capacity (if any), property and other financial resources of the child;

(c)   any physical or mental disability of the child;

(d)   the standard of living enjoyed by the family before the occurrence of the conduct which is alleged as the ground of the application;

(e)   the manner in which the child was being and in which the parties to the marriage expected him to be educated or trained;

(f)   the matters mentioned in relation to the parties to the marriage in paragraphs (a) and (b) of subsection (2) above.

(4)   As regards the exercise of its powers under section 2 in favour of a child of the family who is not the child of the respondent, the court shall also have regard—

(a)   to whether the respondent had assumed any responsibility for the child's maintenance and, if he did, to the extent[11] to which, and the basis on which, he assumed that responsibility and to the length of time during which, he discharged that responsibility;

(b)   to whether in assuming and discharging that responsibility the respondent did so knowing that the child was not his own child;

(c)   to the liability of any other person to maintain the child.

[Domestic Proceedings and Magistrates' Courts Act 1978, s 3, as substituted by the Matrimonial and Family Proceedings Act 1984, s 9.]

---

1. This section reproduces, as far as possible, the guidelines contained in s 25 of the Matrimonial Causes Act 1973, post, (as substituted by the Matrimonial and Family Proceedings Act 1984, s 3), modifying them only so far as is necessary to reflect the different circumstances of a matrimonial case before magistrates, and in particular excluding the guideline contained in s 25(2)(h) of the 1973 Act. Accordingly, justices' discretion as to quantum of maintenance should be exercised on the same principles as those adopted in the divorce courts (*Macey v Macey* (1982) 3 FLR 7). Guidance as to general principles may be found in the cases referred to below, but these cases must be considered having regard also to the amendments made to s 3 of this Act by the Matrimonial and Family Proceedings Act 1984, s 9. The court should make findings *seriatim* upon each of the matters set out in s 3 and then balance the factors one against another so as to arrive at an order which is just and reasonable (*Vasey v Vasey* (1984) 149 JP 219, [1985] FLR 596, CA).

One-third guideline.—The "one-third guideline" should be adopted by magistrates' courts as a flexible starting point for assessing maintenance for a spouse (*Brasman v Brasman* (1975) 5 Fam Law 85), but it must be recognised that it is merely a guideline, not a rule. It serves in cases where the marriage has lasted for many years and the wife has been in the home bringing up the children. It may not be applicable when the marriage has lasted only a short time, or where there are no children and she can go out to work (*Wachtel v Wachtel* [1973] Fam 72, [1973] 1 All ER 829). In applying the guideline that a wife should have one-third of the joint income of the parties, the joint income should be assessed by adding the wife's gross income to the gross income of the husband (*Rodewald v Rodewald* [1977] Fam 192, [1977] 2 All ER 609). Where the parties have no earnings and live on small retirement pensions the one-third guideline is inappropriate (*Cann v Cann* [1977] 3 All ER 957). The question of maintenance must be considered in conjunction with any capital asset or lump sum that may have been awarded and regard must be had to the totality of the order made in the wife's favour; see *Hunter v Hunter* [1973] 3 All ER 362. But it is wrong to approach the matter on a strictly arithmetical one-third basis using gross income figures; the court must have regard to the needs of the parties, their outgoings and examine the net effect of the order it proposes to make (*Furniss v Furniss* (1981) 3 FLR 46). See also *Stockford v Stockford* (1982) 3 FLR 58 and *Titheradge v Titheradge* (1982) 4 FLR 552.

Income support.—It may be helpful, particularly when dealing with people on low incomes, to take into account the Department of Social Security formula when assessing maintenance, if only as a starting point. Income support is intended to fill the gap between financial resources, and the claimant's needs ("applicable amount"). If the latter exceed the former, then the balance will be made up by benefit. The total disposable income comprises gross earnings less income tax and National Insurance contributions, plus net weekly earning of wife/cohabitant, plus educational grants, social security benefits, maintenance payments, and other sources of income. There are certain "earnings disregards": the first £5 earned by each partner is disregarded as is the first £5 of wages earned by a dependent child under 19 who has left school: in some instances (eg, lone parent, disability pensions, special occupations) the disregard may be £15 for a couple.

Some special types of income are completely ignored (eg, work expenses, occasional gifts) or partly ignored (eg, child-minding income, lodgers or boarders' payments). However, if an employer pays an employee in kind instead of cash, then a value may be attributed and taken fully into account as if the person were earning a wage.

Capital up to £3,000 is ignored, and partly taken into account up to £8,000: above that, a claimant is not eligible for income support. The value of a claimant's home is ignored.

Cases which discuss the application of the former supplementary benefit formula are *Smethurst v Smethurst* [1978] Fam 52, [1977] 3 All ER 1110; and *Shallow v Shallow* [1979] Fam 1, [1977] 2 All ER 483. See also *Tovey v Tovey* (1978) 8 Fam Law 80. But see *Stockford v Stockford* (1981) 3 FLR 58, where the Court of Appeal emphasised that the statutory provisions, such as those in s 3 of this Act, must be applied without superimposed judicial glosses. Income support rates appear from time to time by statutory instrument of which a Queen's Printer's copy is admissible (see PART II: EVIDENCE—*Public Documents*, ante). The DSS leaflet IS 1 which describes the various benefits can be produced in civil proceedings if agreed by the parties. As to the incidence of benefit where there is a second family, see post, *Second Family*. Similar provisions will apply to other benefits under the Social Security Contributions and Benefits Act 1992.

Where the husband is receiving the full income support, the justices should take into account the fact that the Department of Social Security must have accepted that he was genuinely unable to obtain employment (*Williams v Williams* [1974] Fam 55 [1974] 3 All ER 377, followed in *Chase v Chase* (1983) 13 Fam Law 21); but, although a weighty factor, the continuance of benefit is not conclusive evidence that the husband is unable to obtain employment; see *Bromilow v Bromilow* (1976) 7 Fam Law 16 and *Munt v Munt* (1983) 13 Fam Law 81. Attendance and mobility allowances should not be taken into the calculations of figures that are available for the payment of maintenance (*Claxton v Claxton* (1983) 147 JP 94, 3 FLR 415). As regards a mobility component, note also the Social Security Contributions and Benefits Act 1992, s 73(14), which provides that "A payment to or in respect of any person which is attributable to his entitlement to the mobility component, and the right to receive such a payment, shall (except in prescribed circumstances and for prescribed purposes) be disregarded in applying any enactment or instrument under which regard is to be had to a person's means." There is no rule of law that the husband's residual income should not be reduced below a "subsistence level" of the amount he receives as income support, by an order for periodical payments. Courts should ask "how much of his earnings does the husband need?" and order accordingly: the rates are no more than a guide (*Freeman v Swatridge and Swatridge* (1984) 148 JP 619, [1984] FLR 762, CA). In such cases, justices may usefully consider what the Child Support

Agency assessment would be in the particular circumstances (*E v C (calculation of child maintenance)* [1996] 1 FCR 612, [1996] 1 FLR 472).

Nominal order.—A nominal order is now virtually a term of art: it has been construed as meaning (in 1984) 50p or £1 a year, as opposed to £1 a week which, for someone on income support, was found not to be a nominal order (*Freeman v Swatridge and Swatridge* (1984) 148 JP 619, [1984] FLR 762, CA). *Incidence of income tax.*—See PART VIII title TAX AND DUTIES, post, sub-title "Income tax and maintenance orders" and the provisions of the Income and Corporation Taxes Act 1988, ss 347A and 347B, and the Finance Act 1988, ss 38, 39 and 40, in that PART.

Child benefit.—Child benefit has replaced family allowances and child tax allowances. It is not means tested, and it is suggested that it would not be inconsistent with the principle of the scheme for a woman to receive child benefit in addition to any sum payable under an order, rather than to give the payer under the order the benefit by reducing his liability to support his dependants. Nevertheless, child benefit and the single parent allowance are resources to which the court shall have regard; see *Stockford v Stockford* (1981) 3 FLR 58.

Second family.—Where the husband has acquired a second family, the criterion may not necessarily be to order proper maintenance for the first family and disregard the second. Where this happens, it might cause the husband and his second family undue hardship, because although the first wife's income could always be made up by the DSS to the appropriate maximum income support figure, the income of the second family could not, because benefit is not payable to a wife or common law wife if a man in full employment is living in the house. For a full discussion of the implications see the note on *Winter v Winter* (1972) Times, 14 November, printed in 1976 at 140 JP Jo 597.

2. "Earning capacity" includes the ability to earn higher wages by working overtime (*Klucinski v Klucinski* [1953] 1 All ER 683, 117 JP 187). Although the court must have regard to all the resources of the wife, it does not follow that the husband is entitled to have the whole of her income or capacity to earn taken into account in assessing her maintenance. Each case depends on its own facts; see *Attwood v Attwood* [1968] P 591, [1968] 3 All ER 385. A husband who, on application to vary a maintenance order, alleges that the wife should be working must make that allegation in the application so that the wife has notice (*Adams v Adams* (1978) 8 Fam Law 141).

3. These are not confined to family assets; see *Daubney v Daubney* [1976] Fam 267, [1976] 2 All ER 453. The fact that a husband was living free with his parents was not to be taken as a financial resource of his (*Wills v Wills* [1984] FLR 672).

Where a wife is in receipt of state benefits, the amount she so receives is not to be regarded as "financial resources". It is, therefore, an irrelevant factor in assessing the amount the husband should pay that the wife would receive no benefit from the order as her state benefits would be reduced by that amount. But where the available financial resources of the husband are so modest that an order making adequate contribution for the wife would leave him with a sum quite inadequate to enable him to meet his own financial requirements, then the court can have regard to the fact that state benefits will be available to the wife; see *Barnes v Barnes* [1972] 3 All ER 872, [1972] 1 WLR 1381. Courts should bear in mind both the principle in *Barnes v Barnes*, referred to above, and the "clean break" objective, and strike whatever balance—or if need be make whatever choice—between them that the requirements of justice in the particular circumstances appear to dictate; see *Ashley v Blackman* [1988] Fam 85, [1988] 3 WLR 222, [1988] FCR 699.

4. Note that this refers to the parties to the marriage and not to third parties, eg mistresses or second wives; consequently, a financial provision order must be for payment out of the respondent's resources and not out of the capital or income of a second spouse or cohabitee (*Macey v Macey* (1982) 3 FLR 7). See also *Brown v Brown* (1981) 11 Fam Law 247.

5. The fact that a husband was living free with his parents because he could not afford to pay was not in itself a ground for saying there was no need for an order (*Wills v Wills* [1984] FLR 672).

6. This will include not only obligations to a former wife or to children of a former marriage, but also moral obligations to make voluntary payments for the upkeep of an illegitimate child; see *Roberts v Roberts* [1970] P 1, [1968] 3 All ER 479, 133 JP 8. While outgoings are not wholly irrelevant, the essential starting point, when determining maintenance for a spouse or a child, is to take the actual earnings of the parties in gross terms and to make basic calculations on that footing without being unduly influenced by detailed calculations of the outgoings on either side, see *Moon v Moon* (1980) 2 FLR 115. There is nothing in this provision which restricts its application to obligations or responsibilities which are legally enforceable (*Blower v Blower* [1986] 1 FLR 292, [1986] Fam Law 56). A court which disregards items in an absent husband's completed means questionnaire because his wife does not agree with them, will be failing in its duty to give proper consideration to the matters under s 3 (*Whittingstall v Whittingstall* [1989] FCR 759, [1990] 2 FLR 368).

7. The fact that the husband has undertaken the responsibility of maintaining a new wife must be fully borne in mind and be given the same degree and weight as his responsibilities in any other financial respect (*Barnes v Barnes* [1972] 3 All ER 872).

8. Although the standard of living may have to be lower than before the occurrence of the conduct alleged, in general the wife and children should not be relegated to a significantly lower standard than that of the husband (*Attwood v Attwood* [1968] P 591, [1968] 3 All ER 385, 132 JP 554; *Kershaw v Kershaw* [1966] P 13, [1964] 3 All ER 635, 128 JP 589); but the court must ensure that the result of its order is not to depress the husband below subsistence level (*Ashley v Ashley* [1968] P 582, [1965] 3 All ER 554, 130 JP 1). See also *Chase v Chase* (1983) 13 Fam Law 21.

9. In *S v S* [1977] Fam 127, [1977] 1 All ER 56, a case involving a marriage of a little over two years, ORMROD LJ said: "I think it is of importance, with these short marriages, particularly where the people concerned are not young, to look very closely to see what the effect of the marriage has been, mainly on the wife, but of course also on the husband". In *Krystman v Krystman* [1973] 3 All ER 247, a divorce case in which there had been a "shotgun" marriage, no child, cohabitation for a fortnight, separation for 26 years and no previous application for maintenance, the Court of Appeal said the husband should not be required to maintain the wife. See also *Graves v Graves* (1973) 4 Fam Law 124, in which it was held that where a marriage was of short duration and the parties were young, a nominal order was the appropriate order unless there were children or the wife was handicapped in some way so as to prevent her from working; followed in *Frisby v Frisby* [1984] Fam Law 19. In *Khan v Khan* [1980] 1 All ER 497, a young wife, who had not previously worked, was allowed maintenance at rather less than one-third of the joint incomes for a period of 12 months to enable her to train herself and obtain satisfactory employment, and at a reduced level thereafter. In *Campbell v Campbell* [1976] Fam 347, [1977] 1 All ER 1, where there was a short marriage of just over 2 years, Sir GEORGE BAKER P, held that the rights, duties and obligations of marriage commenced with the marriage and periods of pre-marital cohabitation could not be taken into account when calculating the length of the marriage; but in certain circumstances it may be appropriate to take into account the conduct of the parties prior to the ceremony of marriage (*Kokosinski v Kokosinski* [1980] Fam 72, [1980] 1 All ER 1106); and it is within the discretion of the court to consider what weight shall be given to the years of cohabitation (*Foley v Foley* [1981] Fam 160, [1981] 2 All ER 857). For consideration of relevant factors when af0ter a long delay application is made for a variation in maintenance, see *McGrady v McGrady* (1980) 1 FLR 67, 8 Fam Law 15. On an application to vary, long-term cohabitation with another person is an important change in circumstances which has to be taken into account, but it should not be equated with marriage (*Hepburn v Hepburn* [1989] FCR 618, [1989] FLR 618, CA).

10. In *Kyte v Kyte* [1988] Fam 145, [1987] 3 All ER 1041, [1988] FCR 325, where the similarly worded para (*g*) in s 25(2) of the Matrimonial Causes Act 1973 was considered, the Court of Appeal ruled that in deciding whether to take the conduct of the parties into account the court was not restricted to conduct contributing to the breakdown of the

marriage, nor to the conduct of one party where the other was blameless. The court is entitled to look at the whole of the picture, including the conduct during the marriage and after the marriage which may or may not have contributed to the breakdown of the marriage or which in some other way makes it inequitable to ignore the conduct of each of the parties.

11. "Extent" has no temporal significance: where it continued for only four months before the separation of the parties it was held to be a full responsibility (*Roberts v Roberts* [1962] P 212, [1962] 2 All ER 967, 126 JP 438).

6–1494   4. Duration of orders for financial provision for a party to a marriage.   (1) The term[1] to be specified in any order made under section 2(1)(*a*) of this Act shall be such term as the court thinks fit except that the term shall not begin earlier than the date of the making of the application for the order and shall not extend beyond the death of either of the parties to the marriage.

(2) Where an order is made under the said section 2(1)(*a*) and the marriage of the parties affected by the order is subsequently dissolved or annulled but the order continues in force, the order shall, notwithstanding anything in it, cease to have effect on the remarriage[2] of the party in whose favour it was made, except in relation to any arrears due under the order on the date of the remarriage.
[Domestic Proceedings and Magistrates' Courts Act 1978, s 4.]

---

1. When considering making an order for a finite term, it should be noted that there is no provision for revival of an order. It is therefore safer practice to stipulate an order to have effect "until further order be made".
2. See provision for transferring to an "agreed order" in s 6(4), post.

6–1495   5. Age limit on making orders for financial provision for children and duration of such orders.   (1) Subject to subsection (3) below, no order shall be made under section 2(1)(*c*) or (*d*) of this Act in favour of a child who has attained the age of eighteen.

(2) The term to be specified in an order made under section 2(1)(*c*) of this Act in favour of a child may begin with the date of the making of an application for the order in question or any later date or a date ascertained in accordance with subsection (5) or (6) below, but—

(*a*)   shall not in the first instance extend beyond the date of the birthday of the child next following his attaining the upper limit of the compulsory school age (construed in accordance with section 8 of the Education Act 1996) unless the court considers that in the circumstances of the case the welfare of the child requires that it should extend to a later date;* and

(*b*)   shall not in any event, subject to subsection (3) below, extend beyond the date of the child's eighteenth birthday.

(3) The court—

(*a*)   may make an order under section 2(1)(*c*) or (*d*) of this Act in favour of a child who has attained the age of eighteen, and

(*b*)   may include in an order made under section 2(1)(*c*) of this Act in relation to a child who has not attained that age a provision for extending beyond the date when the child will attain that age the term for which by virtue of the order any payments are to be made to or for the benefit of that child,

if it appears to the court—

(i)   that the child is, or will be, or if such an order or provision were made would be, receiving instruction at an educational establishment or undergoing training for a trade, profession or vocation, whether or not he is also, or will also be, in gainful employment; or

(ii)   that there are special circumstances which justify the making of the order or provision.

(4) Any order made under section 2(1)(*c*) of this Act in favour of a child shall, notwithstanding anything in the order, cease to have effect on the death of the person liable to make payments under the order.

(5) Where—

(*a*)   a maintenance assessment ("the current assessment") is in force with respect to a child; and

(*b*)   an application is made for an order under section 2(1)(*c*) of this Act—

(i)   in accordance with section 8 of the Child Support Act 1991; and

(ii)   before the end of the period of 6 months beginning with the making of the current assessment,

the term to be specified in any such order made on that application may be expressed to begin on, or at any time after, the earliest permitted date.

(6) For the purposes of subsection (5) above, "the earliest permitted date" is whichever is the later of—

(*a*)   the date 6 months before the application is made; or

(*b*)   the date on which the current assessment took effect or, where successive maintenance assessments have been continuously in force with respect to a child, on which the first of those assessments took effect.

(7) Where—

(*a*)   a maintenance assessment ceases to have effect or is cancelled by or under any provision of the Child Support Act 1991; and

(b) an application is made, before the end of the period of 6 months beginning with the relevant date, for an order under section 2(1)(c) of this Act in relation to a child with respect to whom that maintenance assessment was in force immediately before it ceased to have effect or was cancelled,

the term to be specified in any such order, or in any interim order under section 19 of this Act, made on that application, may begin with the date on which that maintenance assessment ceased to have effect or, as the case may be, the date with effect from which it was cancelled, or any later date.

(8) In subsection (7)(b) above—

(a) where the maintenance assessment ceased to have effect, the relevant date is the date on which it so ceased; and

(b) where the maintenance assessment was cancelled, the relevant date is the later of—

(i)   the date on which the person who cancelled it did so, and
(ii) the date from which the cancellation first had effect.

[Domestic Proceedings and Magistrates' Courts Act 1978, s 5 as amended by the Matrimonial and Family Proceedings Act 1984, s 9, SI 1993/623 and the Education Act 1996, Sch 37.]

6–1496   6. Orders for payments which have been agreed by the parties.   (1) Either party to a marriage may apply to a magistrates' court for an order under this section on the ground that either the party making the application or the other party to the marriage has agreed to make such financial provision as may be specified in the application[1] and, subject to subsection (3) below, the court on such an application may, if—

(a) it is satisfied that the applicant or the respondent, as the case may be, has agreed to make that provision, and

(b) it has no reason to think that it would be contrary to the interests of justice to exercise its powers hereunder,

order that the applicant or the respondent, as the case may be, shall make the financial provision specified in the application.

(2) In this section "financial provision" means the provision mentioned in any one or more of the following paragraphs, that is to say—

(a) the making of periodical payments[2] by one party to the other,

(b) the payment of a lump sum[3] by one party to the other,

(c) the making of periodical payments[2] by one party to a child of the family[4] or to the other party for the benefit of such a child,

(d) the payment by one party of a lump sum[3] to a child of the family[4] or to the other party for the benefit of such a child,

and any reference in this section to the financial provision specified in an application made under subsection (1) above or specified by the court under subsection (5) below is a reference to the type of provision specified in the application or by the court, as the case may be, to the amount so specified as the amount of any payment to be made thereunder and, in the case of periodical payments, to the term so specified as the term for which the payments are to be made.

(3) Where the financial provision specified in an application under subsection (1) above includes or consists of provision in respect of a child of the family, the court shall not make an order under that subsection unless it considers that the provision which the applicant or the respondent, as the case may be, has agreed to make in respect of that child provides for, or makes a proper contribution towards, the financial needs of the child.

(4) A party to a marriage who has applied for an order under section 2 of this Act shall not be precluded at any time before the determination of that application, from applying for an order under this section; but if an order is made under this section on the application of either party and either of them has also made an application for an order under section 2 of this Act, the application made for the order under section 2 shall be treated as if it had been withdrawn.

(5) Where on an application under subsection (1) above the court decides—

(a) that it would be contrary to the interests of justice to make an order for the making of the financial provision specified in the application, or

(b) that any financial provision which the applicant or the respondent, as the case may be, has agreed to make in respect of a child of the family does not provide for, or make a proper contribution towards, the financial needs of that child,

but is of the opinion—

(i)   that it would not be contrary to the interests of justice to make an order for the making of some other financial provision specified by the court, and

(ii) that, in so far as that other financial provision contains any provision for a child of the family, it provides for, or makes a proper contribution towards, the financial needs of that child,

then, if both the parties agree, the court may order that the applicant or the respondent, as the case may be, shall make that other financial provision.

(6) Subject to subsection (8) below, the provisions of section 4 of this Act shall apply in relation

to an order under this section which requires periodical payments to be made to a party to a marriage for his own benefit as they apply in relation to an order under section 2(1)(*a*) of this Act.

(7) Subject to subsection (8) below, the provisions of section 5 of this Act shall apply in relation to an order under this section for the making of financial provision in respect of a child of the family as they apply in relation to an order under section 2(1)(*c*) or (*d*) of this Act.

(8) Where the court makes an order under this section which contains provision for the making of periodical payments and, by virtue of subsection (4) above, an application for an order under section 2 of this Act is treated as if it had been withdrawn, then the term which may be specified as the term for which the payments are to be made may begin with the date of the making of the application for the order under section 2 or any later date.

(9) Where the respondent is not present or represented by counsel or solicitor at the hearing of an application for an order under subsection (1) above, the court shall not make an order under this section unless there is produced to the court such evidence as may be prescribed[5] by rules of court of—

(*a*) the consent of the respondent to the making of the order,
(*b*) the financial resources of the respondent, and.
(*c*) in a case where the financial provision specified in the application includes or consists of provision in respect of a child of the family to be made by the applicant to the respondent for the benefit of the child or to the child, the financial resources of the child.

[Domestic Proceedings and Magistrates' Courts Act 1978, s 6, as substituted by the Matrimonial and Family Proceedings Act 1984, s 10 and amended by the Courts Act 2003, Sch 8.]

---

1. For form of application and procedure, see the Family Proceedings Courts (Matrimonial Proceedings etc) Rules 1991, r 3, this PART, post.

2. Payment may be made to the justices' chief executive or of any magistrates' court: see Magistrates' Courts Act 1980, s 59, and Magistrates' Courts Rules 1981, r 39 et seq. As to the effect of parties living together, see s 25, post. For enforcement, see s 32, post.

3. There is no upper limit fixed to the amount of any such lump sum under s 6, unlike an order under s 2. A lump sum may be payable by instalments (Magistrates' Courts Act 1980, s 75, ante) which may be varied subsequently under s 22, post. It may be made payable through the justices' chief executive; see Magistrates' Courts Rules 1981, r 48, in PART I: MAGISTRATES' COURTS, PROCEDURE, ante.

4. "Child of the family" is defined in s 88, post. This section would seem to enable someone to apply for an order to be made against himself for tax advantage (cf *Sherdley v Sherdley* [1988] AC 213, [1987] 2 All ER 54, HL), unlike ss 2 or 7; it may also be supplemented by s 11(2A) post.

5. See the Family Proceedings Courts (Matrimonial Proceedings etc) Rules 1991, r 17, this PART, post.

6–1497   7. Powers of court where parties are living apart by agreement.   (1) Where the parties to a marriage have been living apart for a continuous period exceeding three months, neither party having deserted the other,* and one of the parties has been making periodical payments for the benefit of the other party or of a child of the family, that other party may apply to a magistrates' court for an order under this section, and any application made under this subsection shall specify the aggregate amount of the payments so made during the period of three months immediately preceding the date of the making of the application.

(2) Where on an application for an order under this section the court is satisfied that the respondent has made the payments specified in the application, the court may, subject to the provisions of this Part of this Act, make one or both of the following orders, that is to say—

(*a*) an order that the respondent shall make to the applicant such periodical payments[1], and for such term, as may be specified in the order;
(*b*) an order that the respondent shall make to the applicant for the benefit of a child of the family[2] to whom the application relates, or to such a child, such periodical payments[1], and for such term, as may be so specified.

(3) The court in the exercise of its powers under this section—

(*a*) shall not require the respondent to make payments which exceed in aggregate during any period of three months the aggregate amount paid by him for the benefit of the applicant or a child of the family during the period of three months immediately preceding the date of the making of the application;
(*b*) shall not require the respondent to make payments to or for the benefit of any person which exceed in amount the payments which the court considers that it would have required the respondent to make to or for the benefit of that person on an application under section 1 of this Act;
(*c*) shall not require payments to be made to or for the benefit of a child of the family[2] who is not a child of the respondent unless the court considers that it would have made an order in favour of that child on an application under section 1 of this Act.

(4) Where on an application under this section the court considers that the orders which it has the power to make under this section—

(*a*) would not provide reasonable maintenance for the applicant, or
(*b*) if the application relates to a child of the family, would not provide, or make a proper contribution towards reasonable maintenance for that child,

the court shall refuse to make an order under this section, but the court may treat the application as if it were an application for an order under section 2 of this Act.

(5) The provisions of section 3 of this Act shall apply in relation to an application for an order under this section as they apply in relation to an application for an order under section 2 of this Act subject to the modification that for the reference in subsection (2)(c) of the said section 3 to the occurrence of the conduct which is alleged as the ground of the application there shall be substituted a reference to the living apart of the parties to the marriage.

(6) The provisions of section 4 of this Act shall apply in relation to an order under this section which requires periodical payments to be made to the applicant for his own benefit as they apply in relation to an order under section 2(1)(a) of this Act.

(7) The provisions of section 5 of this Act shall apply in relation to an order under this section for the making of periodical payments in respect of a child of the family as they apply in relation to an order under section 2(1)(c) of this Act.

[Domestic Proceedings and Magistrates' Courts Act 1978, s 7 as amended by the Matrimonial and Family Proceedings Act 1984, Sch 1.]

---

*Repealed by the Family Law Act 1996, Sch 10, this PART, POST, WHEN IN FORCE.

1. Payment may be made to the justices' chief executive or of any magistrates' court; see the Magistrates' Courts Act 1980, s 59, and Magistrates' Courts Rules 1981, r 39 et seq. As to the effect of parties living together, see s 25, post. For enforcement, see s 32, post.

2. "Child of the family" is defined in s 88, post.

Powers of court as to the custody etc of children[1]

6–1498   8. Restrictions on making of orders under this Act: welfare of children. Where an application is made by a party to a marriage for an order under section 2, 6 or 7 of this Act, then, if there is a child of the family[1] who is under the age of eighteen, the court shall not dismiss or make a final order on the application until it has decided whether to exercise any of its powers under the Children Act 1989[2] with respect to the child.

[Domestic Proceedings and Magistrates' Courts Act 1978, s 8, as substituted by the Children Act 1989, Sch 13.]

---

1. "Child of the family" is defined in s 88(1), post.
2. See this PART, post.

Interim orders

6–1519   19. Interim orders.   (1) Where an application is made for an order under section 2, 6 or 7 of this Act—

(a) the magistrates' court at any time before making a final order on, or dismissing, the application or on refusing to make an order on the application by virtue of section 27 of this Act, and

(b) the High Court on ordering the application to be reheard by a magistrates' court (either after the refusal of an order under section 27 of this Act or on an appeal under section 29 of this Act),

shall, subject to the provisions of this Part of this Act, have the—

(i) power to make an order (in this Part of this Act referred to as an "interim maintenance order") which requires the respondent to make to the applicant or to any child of the family who is under the age of eighteen, or to the applicant for the benefit of such a child, such periodical payments as the court thinks reasonable;

(ii) *Repealed.*

(2) *Repealed.*

(3) An interim maintenance order may provide for payments to be made from such date as the court may specify, except that, subject to section 5(5) and (6) of this Act, the date shall not be earlier than the date of the making of the application for an order under section 2, 6 or 7 of this Act; and where such an order made by the High Court on an appeal under section 29 of this Act provides for payments to be made from a date earlier than the date of the making of the order, the interim order may provide that payments made by the respondent under an order made by a magistrates' court shall, to such extent and in such manner as may be provided by the interim order, be treated as having been paid on account of any payment provided for by the interim order.

(3A) Where an application is made for an order under section 6 of this Act by the party to the marriage who has agreed to make the financial provision specified in the application—

(a) subsection (1) shall apply as if the reference in paragraph (i) to the respondent were a reference to the applicant and the references to the applicant were references to the respondent; and

(b) subsection (3) shall apply accordingly.

(4) *Repealed.*

(5) Subject to subsection (6) below, an interim order made on an application for an order under

section 2, 6 or 7 of this Act shall cease to have effect[1] on whichever of the following dates occurs first, that is to say—

(a) the date, if any, specified for the purpose in the interim order;
(b) the date of the expiration of the period of three months[2] beginning with the date of the making of the interim order;
(c) the date on which a magistrates' court either makes a final order on or dismisses the application.

(6) Where an interim order made under subsection (1) above would, but for this subsection, cease to have effect by virtue of subsection (5)(a) or (b) above, the magistrates' court which made the order or, in the case of an interim order made by the High Court, the magistrates' court by which the application for an order under section 2, 6 or 7 of this Act is to be reheard, shall have power by order to provide that the interim order shall continue in force for a further period, and any order continued in force under this subsection shall cease to have effect on whichever of the following dates occurs first, that is to say—

(a) the date, if any, specified for the purpose in the order made under this subsection;
(b) the date of the expiration of the period of three months[3] beginning with the date of the making of the order under this subsection or, if more than one order has been made under this subsection with respect to the application, beginning with the date of the making of the first of those orders;
(c) the date on which the court either makes a final order on, or dismisses, the application.

(7) Not more than one interim maintenance order may be made with respect to any application for an order under section 2, 6 or 7 of this Act, but without prejudice to the powers of a court under this section on any further such application.

(8) No appeal shall lie from the making of or refusal to make, the variation of or refusal to vary, or the revocation of or refusal to revoke, an interim maintenance order.

(9) An interim order made by the High Court under this section on ordering that an application be reheard by a magistrates' court shall, for the purpose of its enforcement and for the purposes of section 20 of this Act, be treated as if it were an order of that magistrates' court and not of the High Court.

[Domestic Proceedings and Magistrates' Courts Act 1978, s 19 as amended by the Matrimonial and Family Proceedings Act 1984, Sch 1, the Children Act 1989, Schs 13 and 15 and SI 1993/623.]

---

1. As to the effect of parties living together, see s 25, post.
2. Note that an interim order can run for longer than three months by operation of the extension provisions in sub-s (6), post.
3. In theory, if an extension period of three months is ordered on the last day of an interim order under sub-s (5) (b), the total period of the interim order could be six months.

Variation, revocation and cessation of orders etc

6–1520 **20. Variation, revival[1] and revocation of orders for periodical payments.** (1) Where a magistrates' court has made an order under section 2(1)(a) or (c) of this Act for the making of periodical payments the court shall have power, on an application made under this section, to vary[2] or revoke that order and also to make an order under section 2(1)(b) or (d) of this Act[3].

(2) Where a magistrates' court has made an order under section 6 of this Act for the making of periodical payments by a party to a marriage the court shall have power, on an application made under this section, to vary or revoke that order and also to make an order for the payment of a lump sum by that party either—

(a) to the other party to the marriage, or
(b) to a child of the family or to that other party for the benefit of that child.

(3) Where a magistrates' court has made an order under section 7 of this Act for the making of periodical payments, the court shall have power, on an application made under this section, to vary or revoke that order.

(4) *Repealed.*

(5) Where a magistrates' court has made an interim maintenance order under section 19 of this Act, the court, on an application made under this section, shall have power to vary or revoke that order, except that the court shall not by virtue of this subsection extend the period for which the order is in force.

(6) The power of the court under this section to vary an order for the making of periodical payments shall include power to suspend any provision thereof temporarily and to revive any provision so suspended.

(7) Where the court has power by virtue of this section to make an order for the payment of a lump sum, the amount of the lump sum shall not exceed the maximum amount that may at that time be required to be paid under section 2(3) of this Act, but the court may make an order for the payment of a lump sum not exceeding that amount notwithstanding that the person required to pay the lump sum was required to pay a lump sum by a previous order under this Part of this Act.

(8) Where the court has power by virtue of subsection (2) above to make an order for the payment

of a lump sum and the respondent or the applicant, as the case may be, has agreed to pay a lump sum of an amount exceeding the maximum amount that may at that time be required to be paid under section 2(3) of this Act, the court may, notwithstanding anything in subsection (7) above, make an order for the payment of a lump sum of that amount.

(9) An order made by virtue of this section which varies an order for the making of periodical payments may provide that the payments as so varied shall be made from such date as the court may specify, except that, subject to subsections (9A) and (9B) below, the date shall not be earlier than the date of the making of the application under this section.

(9A) Where—

(a) there is in force an order ("the order")—

(i) under section 2(1)(c) of this Act,

(ii) under section 6(1) of this Act making provision of a kind mentioned in paragraph (c) of section 6(2) of this Act (regardless of whether it makes provision of any other kind mentioned in that paragraph),

(iii) under section 7(2)(b) of this Act, or

(iv) which is an interim maintenance order under which the payments are to be made to a child or to the applicant for the benefit of a child;

(b) the order requires payments specified in it to be made to or for the benefit of more than one child without apportioning those payments between them;

(c) a maintenance assessment* ("the assessment"*) is made with respect to one or more, but not all, of the children with respect to whom those payments are to be made; and

(d) an application is made, before the end of the period of 6 months beginning with the date on which the assessment* was made, for the variation or revocation of the order,

the court may, in exercise of its powers under this section to vary or revoke the order, direct that the variation or revocation shall take effect from the date on which the assessment* took effect or any later date.

(9B) Where—

(a) an order ("the child order") of a kind prescribed for the purposes of section 10(1) of the Child Support Act 1991 is affected by a maintenance assessment*;

(b) on the date on which the child order became so affected there was in force an order ("the spousal order")—

(i) under section 2(1)(a) of this Act,

(ii) under section 6(1) of this Act making provision of a kind mentioned in section 6(2)(a) of this Act (regardless of whether it makes provision of any other kind mentioned in that paragraph),

(iii) under section 7(2)(a) of this Act, or

(iv) which is an interim maintenance order under which the payments are to be made to the applicant (otherwise than for the benefit of a child); and

(c) an application is made, before the end of the period of 6 months beginning with the date on which the maintenance assessment was made, for the spousal order to be varied or revoked,

the court may, in exercise of its powers under this section to vary or revoke the spousal order, direct that the variation or revocation shall take effect from the date on which the child order became so affected or any later date.

(9C) For the purposes of subsection (9B) above, an order is affected if it ceases to have effect or is modified by or under section 10 of the Child Support Act 1991.

(10) *Repealed.*

(11) In exercising the powers conferred by this section the court shall, so far as it appears to the court just to do so, give effect to any agreement[4] which has been reached between the parties in relation to the application and, if there is no such agreement or if the court decides not to give effect to the agreement, the court shall have regard to all the circumstances of the case, first consideration being given to the welfare while a minor of any child of the family who has not attained the age of eighteen, and the circumstances of the case shall include any change in any of the matters[5] to which the court was required to have regard when making the order to which the application relates or, in the case of an application for the variation or revocation of an order made under section 6 of this Act or on an appeal under section 29 of this Act, to which the court would have been required to have regard if that order had been made under section 2 of this Act.

(12) An application under this section may be made—

(a) where it is for the variation or revocation of an order under section 2, 6, 7 or 19 of this Act for periodical payments, by either party to the marriage in question; and

(b) where it is for the variation of an order under section 2(1)(c), 6 or 7 of this Act for periodical payments to or in respect of a child, also by the child himself, if he has attained the age of sixteen.

(13) *Repealed.*

[Domestic Proceedings and Magistrates' Courts Act 1978, s 20 as amended by the Matrimonial and Family

Proceedings Act 1984, ss 9 and 11 and Sch 1, the Family Law Reform Act 1987, Sch 4, the Children Act 1989, Schs 13 and 15 and SI 1993/623.]

---

*Amended by the Child Support, Pensions and Social Security Act 2000, Sch 3, from a date to be appointed.
1. Subject to the transitional provisions, in respect of orders made before 1 April 1989, referred to in note 4, infra, the power of revival is confined to revival of a provision temporarily suspended under s 20(6), and revival of orders for periodical payments on an application made by a child in accordance with s 20A, post.
2. Note the requirements of sub-s (11) below that the court shall have regard to all the circumstances of the case including a change in any s 3 matters; see *Riley v Riley* (1986) 151 JP 650.
3. It would seem that where the court did not originally make an order for periodical payments, there can be no variation to commence payments; likewise if there was no order originally for periodical payments, there can be no subsequent order for a lump sum.
4. A solicitor's letter saying that his client did not oppose an application to reduce the amount of periodical payments and remission of arrears and consented to the order being reduced to a nominal order was held to amount to an agreement to such reduction and remission within the meaning of this section. Provided there is no question of injustice to the parties, the court must give effect to any agreement (*Whitton v Devizes Magistrates' Court* (1984) 150 JP 330).
5. See s 3, ante. The court must consider all appropriate circumstances under s 3 *de novo* (*Riley v Riley* (1986) 151 JP 650).

6–1521　20ZA. Variation of orders for periodical payments: further provisions.　(1) Subject to subsections (7) and (8) below, the power of the court under section 20 of this Act to vary an order for the making of periodical payments shall include power, if the court is satisfied that payment has not been made in accordance with the order, to exercise one of its powers under paragraphs (*a*) to (*d*) of section 59(3) of the Magistrates' Courts Act 1980.

(2) In any case where—

(*a*)　a magistrates' court has made an order under this Part of this Act for the making of periodical payments, and

(*b*)　payments under the order are required to be made by any method of payment falling within section 59(6) of the Magistrates' Courts Act 1980 (standing order, etc),

an application may be made under this subsection to the court for the order to be varied as mentioned in subsection (3) below.

(3) Subject to subsection (5) below, where an application is made under subsection (2) above, a justices' clerk, after giving written notice (by post or otherwise) of the application to the respondent and allowing the respondent, within the period of 14 days beginning with the date of the giving of that notice, an opportunity to make written representations, may vary the order to provide that payments under the order shall be made to the designated officer for the court.

(4) The clerk may proceed with an application under subsection (2) above notwithstanding that the respondent has not received written notice of the application.

(5) Where an application has been made under subsection (2) above, the clerk may, if he considers it inappropriate to exercise his power under subsection (3) above, refer the matter to the court which, subject to subsections (7) and (8) below, may vary the order by exercising one of its powers under paragraphs (*a*) to (*d*) of section 59 (3) of the Magistrates' Courts Act 1980.

(6) Subsection (4) of section 59 of the Magistrates' Courts Act 1980 (power of court to order that account be opened) shall apply for the purposes of subsections (1) and (5) above as it applies for the purposes of that section.

(7) Before varying the order by exercising one of its powers under paragraphs (*a*) to (*d*) of section 59(3) of the Magistrates' Courts Act 1980, the court shall have regard to any representations made by the parties to the application.

(8) If the court does not propose to exercise its power under paragraph (*c*), (*cc*) or (*d*) of subsection (3) of section 59 of the Magistrates' Courts Act 1980, the court shall, unless upon representations expressly made in that behalf by the person to whom payments under the order are required to be made it is satisfied that it is undesirable to do so, exercise its power under paragraph (*b*) of that subsection.

(9) Subsection (12) of section 20 of this Act shall have effect for the purposes of applications under subsection (2) above as it has effect for the purposes of applications under that section.

(10) None of the powers of the court, or of a justices' clerk, conferred by this section shall be exercisable in relation to an order under this Part of this Act for the making of periodical payments which is not a qualifying maintenance order (within the meaning of section 59 of the Magistrates' Courts Act 1980).
[Domestic Proceedings and Magistrates' Courts Act 1978, s 20ZA as added by the Maintenance Enforcement Act 1991, s 5 and amended by SI 1994/731, the Access to Justice Act 1999, Sch 13 and the Courts Act 2003, Sch 8.]

6–1522　20A. Revival of orders for periodical payments[1].　(1) Where an order made by a magistrates' court under this Part of this Act for the making of periodical payments to or in respect of a child (other than an interim maintenance order) ceases to have effect—

(*a*)　on the date on which the child attains the age of sixteen, or

(*b*)　at any time after that date but before or on the date on which he attains the age of eighteen,

the child may apply to the court which made the order for an order for its revival.

(2) If on such an application it appears to the court that—

    (*a*) the child is, will be or (if an order were made under this subsection) would be receiving instruction at an educational establishment or undergoing training for a trade, profession or vocation, whether or not while in gainful employment, or

    (*b*) there are special circumstances which justify the making of an order under this subsection,

the court shall have power by order to revive the order from such date as the court may specify, not being earlier than the date of the making of the application.

    (3) Any order revived under this section may be varied or revoked under section 20 in the same way as it could have been varied or revoked had it continued in being.

[Domestic Proceedings and Magistrates' Courts Act 1978, s 20A, as inserted by the Family Law Reform Act 1987, Sch 2 and substituted by the Children Act 1989, Sch 13.]

---

   1. This section shall not have effect in relation to the revival of orders made under Pt I of this Act before 1 April 1989 (Family Law Reform Act 1987 (Commencement No 2) Order 1989, SI 1989/382, Sch 2). For revival of such orders, see s 20 and notes thereto, ante.

6–1523   **22. Variation of instalments of lump sum.**   Where in the exercise of its powers under section 75 of the Magistrates' Courts Act 1980 a magistrates' court orders that a lump sum required to be paid under this Part of this Act shall be paid by instalments[1], the court, on an application made by either the person liable to pay or the person entitled to receive that sum, shall have power to vary that order by varying the number of instalments payable, the amount of any instalment payable and the date on which any instalment becomes payable.

[Domestic Proceedings and Magistrates' Courts Act 1978, s 22, amended by the Magistrates' Courts Act 1980, Sch 7.]

---

   1. Note the Magistrates' Courts Rules 1981, r 48, for payment to the clerk of the court unless the court otherwise directs.

6–1524   **23. Supplementary provisions with respect to variation and revocation of orders.**
    (1) *Repealed.*

    (2) The powers of a magistrates' court to revoke, revive or vary an order for the periodical payment of money and the power of the clerk of a magistrates' court to vary such an order under section 60 of the Magistrates' Courts Act 1980 and the power of a magistrates' court to suspend or rescind certain other orders under section 63(2) of that Act shall not apply in relation to an order made under this Part of this Act.

[Domestic Proceedings and Magistrates' Courts Act 1978, s 23, amended by the Magistrates' Courts Act 1980, Sch 7, the Courts and Legal Services Act 1990, Sch 20 and the Maintenance Enforcement Act 1991, Sch 2.]

6–1525   **25. Effect on certain orders of parties living together.**   (1) Where—

    (*a*) periodical payments are required to be made to one of the parties to a marriage (whether for his own benefit or for the benefit of a child of the family) by an order made under section 2 or 6 of this Act or by an interim maintenance order made under section 19 of this Act (otherwise than on an application under section 7 of this Act),

    (*b*) *Repealed,*

the order shall be enforceable notwithstanding that the parties to the marriage are living with each other[1] at the date of the making of the order or that, although they are not living with each other at that date, they subsequently resume living with each other; but the order shall cease to have effect if after that date the parties continue to live with each other, or resume living with each other, for a continuous period exceeding six months.

    (2) Where any of the following orders is made under this Part of this Act, that is to say—

    (*a*) an order under section 2 or 6 of this Act which requires periodical payments to be made to a child of the family, or

    (*b*) an interim maintenance order under section 19 of this Act (otherwise than on an application under section 7 of this Act) which requires periodical payments to be made to a child of the family,

    (*c*)–(*d*) *Repealed,*

then, unless the court otherwise directs, the order shall continue to have effect and be enforceable notwithstanding that the parties to the marriage in question are living with each other[1] at the date of the making of the order or that, although they are not living with each other at that date, they subsequently resume living with each other.

    (3) Any order made under section 7 of this Act, and any interim maintenance order made on an application for an order under that section, shall cease to have effect if the parties to the marriage resume living with each other[1].

    (4) Where an order made under this Part of this Act ceases to have effect by virtue of subsection (1) or (3) above or by virtue of a direction given under subsection (2) above, a magistrates' court may, on an application made by either party to the marriage, make an order declaring that the first mentioned order ceased to have effect from such date as the court may specify.

[Domestic Proceedings and Magistrates' Courts Act 1978, s 25 as amended by the Children Act 1989, Schs 13 and 15.]

---

1. "Living with each other" must be construed in accordance with s 88(2), post.

Reconciliation

6–1526   26. Reconciliation.   (1) Where an application is made for an order under section 2 of this Act the court, before deciding whether to exercise its powers under that section, shall consider whether there is any possibility of reconciliation between the parties to the marriage in question; and if at any stage of the proceedings on that application it appears to the court that there is a reasonable possibility of such a reconciliation, the court may adjourn the proceedings for such period as it thinks fit to enable attempts to be made to effect a reconciliation.

(2) Where the court adjourns any proceedings under subsection (1) above, it may request an officer of the Service (within the meaning of the Criminal Justice and Court Services Act 2000), a Welsh family proceedings officer (within the meaning given by section 35 of the Children Act 2004) or any other person to attempt to effect a reconciliation between the parties to the marriage, and where any such request is made, that officer or other person shall report in writing to the court whether the attempt has been successful or not, but shall not include in that report any other information.

[Domestic Proceedings and Magistrates' Courts Act 1978, s 26, as amended by the Criminal Justice and Court Services Act 2000, Sch 7 and the Children Act 2004, Sch 3.]

Provisions relating to High Court and county court

6–1527   27. Refusal of order in case more suitable for High Court.   Where on hearing an application for an order under section 2 of this Act a magistrates' court is of the opinion that any of the matters[1] in question between the parties would be more conveniently dealt with by the High Court, the magistrates' court shall refuse[2] to make any order on the application, and no appeal[3] shall lie from that refusal; but if in any proceedings in the High Court relating to or comprising the same subject matter as that application the High Court so orders, the application shall be reheard and determined by a magistrates' court acting in the same local justice area as the first mentioned court.

[Domestic Proceedings and Magistrates' Courts Act 1978, s 27 as amended by the Courts Act 2003, Sch 8.]

---

1. This means matters in which the High Court has concurrent jurisdiction (*Perks v Perks* [1946] P 1, [1945] 2 All ER 580, 110 JP 94; *Smyth v Smyth*, infra): not in cases where the High Court has no jurisdiction to grant relief, eg desertion of short duration (*Davies v Davies* [1957] P 357, [1957] 2 All ER 444, 121 JP 369). It is not proper for a magistrates' court to hear the evidence and then refer to the High Court under this section the question whether or not an order should be made, and, if so, what order (*Davies v Davies*, supra). A complaint for the revocation of an order under s 28, post, may not be disposed of under this section (*Smyth v Smyth* [1956] P 427, [1956] 2 All ER 476, 120 JP 307).
2. For power to make an interim order where an order is refused under this section, see s 19, ante.
3. But appeal lies on the question whether the High Court has concurrent jurisdiction (*Davies v Davies* [1957] P 357, [1957] 2 All ER 444, 121 JP 369).

6–1528   28. Powers of High Court and county court in relation to certain orders under Part I.   (1) Where after the making by a magistrates' court of an order under this Part of this Act proceedings between, and relating to the marriage of, the parties to the proceedings in which that order was made have been commenced in the High Court or a county court, then, except in the case of an order for the payment of a lump sum, the court in which the proceedings or any application made therein are or is pending may, if it thinks fit, direct that the order made by a magistrates' court shall cease[1] to have effect on such date as may be specified in the direction.*

(2) *Repealed.*

(3) Nothing in this section shall be taken as prejudicing the effect of any order made by the High Court or a county court so far as it implicitly supersedes or revokes an order or part of an order made by a magistrates' court.

[Domestic Proceedings and Magistrates' Courts Act 1978, s 28 as amended by the Matrimonial Homes Act 1983, Sch 2 and the Family Law Act 1996, Sch 10.]

---

*Amended by the Family Law Act 1996, Sch 8, this PART, POST, WHEN IN FORCE.
1. Where the High Court or a county court discharges a magistrates' court's order, a copy of the High Court or county court order must be sent to the clerk to the magistrates' court (Registrar's Direction, 11 March 1974, annexed to Home Office Circular 78/1974).

6–1529   29. Appeals.   (1) Subject to section 27 of this Act, where a magistrates' court makes or refuses to make, varies or refuses to vary, revokes or refuses to revoke an order (other than an interim maintenance order) under this Part of this Act, an appeal[1] shall lie to the High Court.

(2) On an appeal under this section the High Court shall have power[2] to make such orders as may be necessary to give effect to its determination of the appeal, including such incidental or consequential orders as appear to the court to be just, and, in the case of an appeal from a decision of a magistrates' court made on an application for or in respect of an order for the making of periodical payments, the High Court shall have power to order that its determination of the appeal shall have effect from such

date as the court thinks fit, not being earlier than the date of the making of the application to the magistrates' court or, in a case where there was made to the magistrates' court an application for an order under section 2 and an application under section 6 and the term of the periodical payments was or might have been ordered to begin on the date of the making of the application for an order under section 2, the date of the making of that application.

(3) Without prejudice to the generality of subsection (2) above, where, on an appeal under this section in respect of an order of a magistrates' court requiring any person to make periodical payments, the High Court reduces the amount of those payments or discharges the order, the High Court shall have power to order the person entitled to payments under the order of the magistrates' court to pay to the person liable to make payments under that order such sum in respect of payments already made in compliance with the order as the court thinks fit and, if any arrears are due under the order of the magistrates' court, the High Court shall have power to remit the payment of those arrears or any part thereof.

(4) *Repealed.*

(5) Any order of the High Court made on an appeal under this section (other than an order directing that an application shall be reheard by a magistrates' court) shall for the purposes of the enforcement of the order and for the purposes of section 20 of this Act be treated as if it were an order of the magistrates' court from which the appeal was brought and not of the High Court.

[Domestic Proceedings and Magistrates' Courts Act 1978, s 29 as amended by the Matrimonial and Family Proceedings Act 1984, Sch 1 and the Children Act 1989, Schs 13 and 15.]

---

1. There is no right of appeal under this section against a decision by magistrates under s 95 of the Magistrates' Courts Act 1980 as to remission of arrears; such a decision may be challenged only by case stated under s 111 of the 1980 Act, see *Berry v Berry* [1987] Fam 1, [1986] 2 All ER 948, 150 JP 319.

2. See also the Rules of the Supreme Court 1965, Ord 55, rr 6 and 7, in PART I: MAGISTRATES' COURTS, PROCEDURE, ante.

Provisions relating to procedure, jurisdiction and enforcement

6–1531   30. Provisions as to jurisdiction and procedure. (1) A magistrates' court shall, subject to section 2 of the Family Law Act 1986 and section 70 of the Magistrates' Courts Act 1980 and any determination of the Lord Chancellor thereunder, have jurisdiction to hear an application for an order under this Part of this Act if it acts in, or is authorised by the Lord Chancellor to act for, a local justice area in which either the applicant or the respondent ordinarily resides[1] at the date of the making of the application.

(2)–(4) *Repealed.*

(5) It is hereby declared that any jurisdiction conferred on a magistrates' court by this Part of this Act is exercisable notwithstanding that any party to the proceedings is not domiciled in England.

[Domestic Proceedings and Magistrates' Courts Act 1978, s 30, amended by the Magistrates' Courts Act 1980, Sch 7, the Family Law Act 1986, Sch 1, the Courts and Legal Services Act 1990, Sch 20, the Police and Magistrates' Courts Act 1994, Sch 8 and the Courts Act 2003, Sch 8.]

---

1. Ordinary residence can be changed in a day: where there are indications that a place to which a person has moved is intended as his home for an indefinite period, he is ordinarily resident there (*Macrae v Macrae* [1949] P 397, [1949] 2 All ER 34, 113 JP 342; applied in *Hopkins v Hopkins* [1951] P 116, [1950] 2 All ER 1035; *Stransky v Stransky* [1954] P 428, [1954] 2 All E R 536; *Lewis v Lewis* [1956] 1 All ER 375).

6–1532   31. Constitution of courts. (1) Where the hearing of an application under section 1 of this Act is adjourned after the court has decided that it is satisfied of any ground mentioned in that section, the court which resumes the hearing of that application may include justices who were not sitting when the hearing began if—

(*a*) the parties to the proceedings agree; and

(*b*) at least one of the justices composing the court which resumes the hearing was sitting when the hearing of the application began.

(2) Where, by virtue of subsection (1) above, among the justices composing the court which resumes the hearing of an application under section 1 of this Act there are any justices who were not sitting when the hearing of the application began, the court which resumes the hearing shall before making any order on the application make such inquiry into the facts and circumstances of the case as will enable the justices who were not sitting when the hearing began to be fully acquainted with those facts and circumstances.

[Domestic Proceedings and Magistrates' Courts Act 1978, s 31.]

6–1543   32. Enforcement etc of orders for payment of money. (1) An order[1] for the payment[2] of money made by a magistrates' court under this Part of this Act shall be enforceable[3] as a magistrates' court maintenance order.

(2) Without prejudice to section 59 of the Magistrates' Courts Act 1980 (which relates to the power of a magistrates' court to direct periodical payments to be made through the designated officer for a magistrates' court), a magistrates' court making an order under this Part of this Act for the making of a periodical payment by one person to another may direct that it shall be made to some

third party on that other person's behalf instead of directly to that other person[4]; and, for the purposes of any order made under this Part of this Act, the said section 59 shall have effect as if, in subsection (2) thereof, for the words "the applicant for the order" there were substituted the words "the person to whom the payments under the order fall to be made"[5].

(3) Any person for the time being under an obligation to make payments in pursuance of any order for the payment of money made under this Part of this Act shall give notice of any change of address[6] to such person, if any, as may be specified in the order; and any person who without reasonable excuse fails to give such a notice shall be liable on summary conviction to a fine not exceeding **level 2** on the standard scale.

(4) A person shall not be entitled to enforce through the High Court or any county court the payment of any arrears due under an order made by virtue of this Part of this Act without the leave of that court if those arrears became due more than twelve months before proceedings to enforce the payment of them are begun.

(5) The court hearing an application for the grant of leave under subsection (4) above may refuse leave, or may grant leave subject to such restrictions and conditions (including conditions as to the allowing of time for payment or the making of payment by instalments) as that court thinks proper, or may remit the payment of such arrears or any part thereof.

(6) An application for the grant of leave under subsection (4) above shall be made in such manner as may be prescribed by rules.

[Domestic Proceedings and Magistrates' Courts Act 1978, s 32, amended by the Magistrates' Courts Act 1980, Sch 7, the Criminal Justice Act 1982, s 46, the Family Law Reform Act 1987, Sch 2, the Access to Justice Act 1999, Sch 13 and the Courts Act 2003, Sch 8.]

---

1. An order of the High Court made on appeal shall for the purposes of this section be treated as if it were an order of the magistrates' court from which the appeal was brought (s 29 (5), ante).

2. Members of visiting forces have no immunity under the Visiting Forces Act 1952 from the ordinary process of law in respect of payments under orders. The service authorities of Canada and the United States of America are prepared to assist in securing compliance. It is recommended that a copy of any summons issued shall be supplied to the defendant's commanding officer. The Under Secretary of State, Home Office (C Division) should be informed before a member of a visiting force is committed to prison. See generally, Home Office Circular No 122/1954, dated June 9th 1954, at 118 JP Jo 560.

3. As to enforcement of arrears which became due more than a year before enforcement proceedings are begun, see sub-s (4) and Magistrates' Courts Act 1980, s 95 and note thereto. A wife cannot claim arrears of maintenance as a creditor of her deceased husband's estate, see *Re Hedderwick, Morton v Brinsley* [1933] Ch 669; *Re Woolgar, Woolgar v Hopkins* [1942] Ch 318, [1942] 1 All ER 583; *Re Bidie, Bidie v General Accident Fire and Life Assurance Corpn Ltd* [1948] Ch 697, [1948] 1 All ER 885, 112 JP 257; affd [1949] Ch 121, [1948] 2 All ER 995, 113 JP 22, CA. The order must not be enforced earlier than the fifteenth day after the making thereof (Magistrates' Courts Act 1980, s 93(2), ante).

If defendant does not appear to a summons the application must not be heard in his absence and a warrant may be issued. See Magistrates' Courts Act 1980, s 99, ante, as to evidence of non-payment. As to the investigation of means by a probation officer, see Magistrates' Courts Act 1980, s 72, ante. The provisions of the Magistrates' Courts Act 1980, Sch 4, ante, as to the scale of imprisonment for non-payment, and of ss 76, 77 and 78 of that Act, ante, as to procedure on the execution of the distress warrant, apply. As to enforcement in England and Ireland of maintenance orders made in other countries, see Maintenance Orders (Facilities for Enforcement) Act 1920 and the Maintenance Orders (Reciprocal Enforcement) Act 1972, this PART, ante. For enforcement of an order made under Part I of the Domestic Proceedings and Magistrates' Courts Act 1978 where the respondent resides in Scotland or Northern Ireland, see Pt II of the Maintenance Orders Act 1950, this PART, ante.

4. This would appear to facilitate payment by means of a standing order to a bank account, or to the Department of Social Security, for example.

5. The substitution of s 59 by the Maintenance Enforcement Act 1991 would seem to have nullified this provision.

6. The Secretary of State for Social Services may provide an address otherwise unobtainable: see the Social Security Administration Act 1992, s 133.

6–1546   35. Orders for repayment in certain cases of sums paid after cessation of order by reason of remarriage[1].   (1) Where—

(a) an order made under section 2(1)(a), 6 or 7 of this Act has, by virtue of section 4(2) of this Act, ceased to have effect by reason of the remarriage of the party in whose favour it was made, and

(b) the person liable to make payments under the order made payments in accordance with it in respect of a period after the date of that remarriage in the mistaken belief that the order was still subsisting,

no proceedings in respect of a cause of action arising out of the circumstances mentioned in paragraphs (a) and (b) above shall be maintainable by the person so liable or his personal representatives against the person so entitled or his personal representatives, but on an application made under this section the court may exercise the powers conferred on it by subsection (2) below.

(2) The court[2] may order the respondent to an application made under this section to pay to the applicant a sum equal to the amount of the payments made in respect of the period mentioned in subsection (1)(b) above or, if it appears to the court that it would be unjust to make that order, it may either order the respondent to pay to the applicant such lesser sum as it thinks fit or dismiss the application.

(3) An application under this section may be made by the person liable to make payments under the order made under section 2(1)(a), 6 or 7 of this Act or his personal representatives and may be made against the person entitled to payments under that order or his personal representatives.

Domestic Proceedings and Magistrates' Courts Act 1978

(4) An application under this section shall be made to a county court, except that such an application may be made in proceedings in the High Court or a county court for leave to enforce, or the enforcement of, the payment of arrears under an order made under section 2(1)(*a*), 6 or 7 of this Act; and accordingly references in this section to the court are references to the High Court or a county court, as the circumstances require.

(5) An order under this section for the payment of any sum may provide for the payment of that sum by instalments of such amount as may be specified in the order.

(6) The jurisdiction conferred on a county court by this section shall be exercisable by a county court notwithstanding that by reason of the amount claimed in an application under this section the jurisdiction would not but for this subsection be exercisable by a county court.

(7) The designated officer for a magistrates' court to whom any payments under an order made under section 2(1)(*a*), 6 or 7 of this Act are required to be made, and the collecting officer under an attachment of earnings order made to secure payments under the first mentioned order, shall not be liable—

(*a*) in the case of the designated officer, for any act done by him in pursuance of the mentioned order after the date on which that order ceased to have effect by reason of the remarriage of the person entitled to payments under it, and

(*b*) in the case of the collecting officer, for any act done by him after that date in accordance with any enactment or rule of court specifying how payments made to him in compliance with the attachment of earnings order are to be dealt with,

if, but only if, the act was one which he would have been under a duty to do had the first mentioned order not ceased to have effect by reason of the remarriage and the act was done before notice in writing of the fact that the person so entitled had remarried was given to him by or on behalf of that person, the person liable to make payments under the first mentioned order or the personal representatives of either of those persons.

(8) In this section "collecting officer", in relation to an attachment of earnings order, means the officer of the High Court or the officer designated by the Lord Chancellor to whom a person makes payments in compliance with the order.

[Domestic Proceedings and Magistrates' Courts Act 1978, s 35, as amended by the Access to Justice Act 1999, Sch 13 and the Courts Act 2003, Sch 8.]

---

1. Appeals on questions of fact from such orders are governed by the Supreme Court Act 1981, ss 19(2) and 28(3).
2. This will be the county court in most cases: see subsection (4), post.

PART V[f]
SUPPLEMENTARY PROVISIONS

6-1550 88. Interpretation. (1) In this Act—

"child", in relation to one or both of the parties to a marriage, includes a child whose father and mother were not married to each other at the time of his birth;

"child of the family"[2], in relation to the parties to a marriage, means—

(*a*) a child of both of those parties; and

(*b*) any other child, not being a child who is placed with those parties as foster parents by a local authority or voluntary organisation, who has been treated by both of those parties as a child of their family;

"family proceedings" has the meaning assigned to it by section 65 of the Magistrates' Courts Act 1997;

"local authority" means the council of a county (other than a metropolitan county), of a metropolitan district or of a London borough or the Common Council of the City of London;

"magistrates' court maintenance order" has the same meaning as in section 150(1) of the Magistrates' Courts Act 1980;

"maintenance assessment*" has the same meaning as it has in the Child Support Act 1991 by virtue of section 54 of that Act as read with any regulations in force under that section;

"rules" means rules made under section 144 of the Magistrates' Courts Act 1980.

(2) References in this Act to the parties to a marriage living with each other shall be construed as references to their living with each other in the same household.

(3) For the avoidance of doubt it is hereby declared that references in this Act to remarriage include references to a marriage which is by law void or voidable.

(4) Anything authorised or required by this Act to be done by, to or before the magistrates' court by, to or before which any other thing was done, or is to be done, may be done by, to or before any magistrates' court acting in the same local justice area as that court.

(5) Any reference in this Act to an enactment shall be construed as a reference to that enactment as amended or extended by or under any subsequent enactment, including this Act.

[Domestic Proceedings and Magistrates' Courts Act 1978, s 88, as amended by the Justices of the Peace Act 1979, Sch 2, the Magistrates' Courts Act 1980, Sch 7, the Local Government Act 1985, s 12, the Family Law Reform

Act 1987, Sch 2, the Children Act 1989, Schs 11, 13 and 15, SI 1993/623, the Justices of the Peace Act 1997, Sch 5, the Access to Justice Act 1999, Sch 15 and the Courts Act 2003, Sch 8.]

---

*Amended by the Child Support, Pensions and Social Security Act 2000, Sch 3, from a date to be appointed.
1. Part V contains ss 86–90.
2. This definition is similar to that contained in s 52(1) of the Matrimonial Causes Act 1973. To establish that a child is a child of the family it is sufficient to show that the child was treated by both parties as a child of the family. The knowledge, or lack of knowledge, possessed by one or both parties of the facts relating to the child, for example as to the identity of its parents is not material in determining whether it is a child of the family (*W (RJ) v W (SJ)* [1972] Fam 152, [1971] 3 All ER 303). Whether a child has been treated by both parties to the marriage as a child of the family is a broad question of fact to be decided by looking at all the circumstances of the case (*D v D* (1980) 2 FLR 93). The test is an objective one; the court has to consider *inter alia* the extent to which responsibility has been assumed for the child's maintenance and the length of time that responsibility has been discharged; contrast *W v W (child of the family)* [1984] FLR 796, CA, and *Teeling v Teeling* [1984] FLR 808, CA. Whether grandparents have treated their grandchild as a child of the family depends on whether they have simply provided emergency or secondary cover, or whether the parent or parents have irrevocably abdicated leaving the grandparent to assume primary responsibility for their child for the foreseeable future (*Re A (a minor) (child of the family)* [1998] 1 FCR 458, [1998] 1 FLR 347). The parties to a marriage cannot treat an unborn child as a child of their family (*A v A* [1974] Fam 6, [1974] 1 All ER 755). "Family" should be construed using the word in its ordinary sense; see *M v M* (1980) 2 FLR 39, 10 Fam Law 184.

6–1551   89. Transitional provisions, amendments, repeals and commencement. (1) The transitional provisions contained in Schedule 1 to this Act shall have effect.

(2) Subject to the transitional provisions contained in Schedule 1 to this Act—

(*a*) the enactments specified in Schedule 2 to this Act shall have effect subject to the amendments specified in that Schedule (being minor amendments and amendments consequential on the preceding provisions of this Act), and

(*b*) the enactments specified in Schedule 3 to this Act are hereby repealed to the extent specified in the third column of that Schedule.

(3) *Commencement.*

(4) Without prejudice to the transitional provisions contained in Schedule 1 to this Act, an order under subsection (3) above may make such further transitional provision as appears to the Secretary of State to be necessary or expedient in connection with the provisions thereby brought into force, including adaptations of the provisions thereby brought into force or any provision of this Act then in force as appear to him to be necessary or expedient in consequence of the partial operation of this Act or the Children Act 1975.

(5) An order under subsection (3) above may repeal any provision of this Act which has ceased to have effect by reason of the coming into force of the Adoption Act 1976.

(6) The inclusion in this Act of any express transitional provision or amendment shall not be taken as prejudicing the general application of ss 16(1) and 17(2) of the Interpretation Act 1978 with regard to the effect of repeals.
[Domestic Proceedings and Magistrates' Courts Act 1978, s 89.]

6–1552   90. Short title and extent. (1) This Act may be cited as the Domestic Proceedings and Magistrates' Courts Act 1978.

(2) Except for the following provisions, that is to say—

(*a*) sections 54, 55, 60, 61, 74(1) and (3), 87, 88(5), 89(2)(*a*), (3) and (4) and this section, and
(*b*) paragraphs 1, 12, 13, 14, 17 and 18 of Schedule 2,

this Act does not extend to Scotland.

(3) Except for the following provisions, that is to say—

(*a*) sections 54, 59, 74(5), 88(5), 89(2), (3) and (4) and this section, and
(*b*) paragraphs 12, 13, 14 and 33 of Schedule 2 and Schedule 3,

this Act does not extend to Northern Ireland, and in section 88(5) of this Act any reference to an enactment includes a reference to an enactment contained in an Act of Parliament of Northern Ireland or a Measure of the Northern Ireland Assembly.
[Domestic Proceedings and Magistrates' Courts Act 1978, s 90 as amended by the Maintenance Orders (Reciprocal Enforcement) Act 1992, Sch 2.]

Section 89   SCHEDULE 1
                          TRANSITIONAL PROVISIONS

(*As amended by the Magistrates' Courts Act 1980, Sch 9, the Matrimonial and Family Proceedings Act 1984, Sch 1, and the Family Law Reform Act 1987, Sch 2.*)

6–1553   1. This Act (including the repeals and amendments made by it) shall not have effect in relation to any application made under any enactment repealed or amended by this Act if that application is pending at the time when the provision of this Act which repeals or amends that enactment comes into force.
2. Any order made or other thing done under the Matrimonial Proceedings (Magistrates' Courts) Act 1960 which is in force immediately before the coming into force of Part I of this Act shall not be affected by the repeal by this Act of that Act, and the provisions of that Act shall after the coming into force of the said Part I apply in

relation to such an order, and to an order made under that Act by virtue of paragraph 1 above, subject to the following modifications—

(a) on a complaint for the revocation of the order the court shall not be bound under section 8 of that Act to revoke the order by reason of an act of adultery committed by the person on whose complaint the order was made;

(b) on a complaint for the variation, revival or revocation of the order, the court, in exercising its powers under the said section 8 in relation to a provision of the order requiring the payment of money, shall have regard to any change in any of the matters to which the court would have been required to have regard when making that order if the order had been made on an application under section 2 of this Act;

(bb) on a complaint after the coming into force of paragraph 27 of Schedule 1 to the Matrimonial and Family Proceedings Act 1984 for the variation, revival or revocation of the order, the court, in exercising its powers under the said section 8 in relation to any provision of the order requiring the payment of money, shall have power to order that payments required to be made for the maintenance of a child of the family shall be made to the child himself;

(c) where the order contains a provision for the legal custody of a child, the court shall have power, on a complaint made by a grandparent of the child, to vary that order under the said section 8 by the addition to the order of a provision requiring access to the child to be given to that grandparent;

(d) where the court, by virtue of paragraph (c) above, varies the order by the addition of a provision requiring access to a child to be given to a grandparent, the court shall have power to vary or revoke that provision on a complaint made—

    (i) by that grandparent, or

    (ii) by either party to the marriage in question, or

    (iii) where the child is not a child of both the parties to the marriage, by any person who though not a party to the marriage is a parent of the child, or

    (iv) where under the order a child is for the time being committed to the legal custody of some person other than one of the parents or a party to the marriage, by the person to whose legal custody the child is committed by the order.

3. The amendment by this Act of any enactment shall not affect the operation of that enactment in relation to any order made or having effect as if made under the Matrimonial Proceedings (Magistrates' Courts) Act 1960 (including an order made under that Act by virtue of paragraph 1 above) or in relation to any decision of a magistrates' court made on an application for such an order or for the variation, revival or revocation of such an order but as respects enactments amended by this Act in their application in relation to orders made or decisions on applications for orders or for the variation, revival or revocation of orders made or having effect as if made under other Acts those enactments shall apply as amended by this Act.

3A. Any order for the payment of money in force under the Matrimonial Proceedings (Magistrates' Courts) Act 1960 (including any such order made under that Act by virtue of paragraph 1 above) shall be enforceable as a magistrates' court maintenance order.

4. Any reference in paragraph 1 above to an application made under an enactment repealed by this Act shall be construed as including a reference to an application which is treated as a complaint under section 1 of the Matrimonial Proceedings (Magistrates' Courts) Act 1960 by virtue of section 27 of the Maintenance Orders (Reciprocal Enforcement) Act 1972 and any reference in paragraph 2, 3 or 3A above to an order made under the Matrimonial Proceedings (Magistrates' Courts) Act 1960 shall be construed as including a reference to an order which is made under that Act by virtue of section 28 of the Maintenance Orders (Reciprocal Enforcement) Act 1972.

5. A provision contained in section 72 of this Act shall not apply in relation to proceedings commenced before the coming into force of that provision.

6. *Repealed.*

7. *Repealed.*

8. A provision of Schedule 2 to this Act which relates to the punishment by way of fine which may be imposed for any offence shall not affect the punishment which may be imposed for an offence which is committed before the date on which that provision comes into force.

Civil Jurisdiction and Judgments Act 1982[1]

(1982 c 27)

PART I[2]

IMPLEMENTATION OF THE CONVENTIONS

Main implementing provisions

6–1640   1. Interpretation of references to the Conventions and Contracting States.   (1) In this Act—

"the 1968 Convention" means the Convention on jurisdiction and the enforcement of judgments in civil and commercial matters (including the Protocol annexed to that Convention), signed at Brussels on 27th September 1968;

"the 1971 Protocol" means the Protocol on the interpretation of the 1968 Convention by the European Court, signed at Luxembourg on 3rd June 1971;

"the Accession Convention" means the Convention on the accession to the 1968 Convention and the 1971 Protocol of Denmark, the Republic of Ireland and the United Kingdom, signed at Luxembourg on 9th October 1978;

"the 1982 Accession Convention" means the Convention on the accession of the Hellenic Republic to the 1968 Convention and the 1971 Protocol, with the adjustments made to them by the Accession Convention, signed at Luxembourg on 25th October 1982;

"the 1989 Accession Convention" means the Convention on the accession of the Kingdom of Spain and the Portuguese Republic to the 1968 Convention and the 1971 Protocol, with the adjustments made to them by the Accession Convention and the 1982 Accession Convention, signed at Donostia—San Sebastián on 26th May 1989;

"the 1996 Accession Convention" means the Convention on the accession of the Republic of Austria, the Republic of Finland and the Kingdom of Sweden to the 1968 Convention and the 1971 Protocol, with the adjustments made to them by the Accession Convention, the 1982 Accession Convention and the 1989 Accession Convention, signed at Brussels on 29th November 1996*;

"the Brussels Conventions" means the 1968 Convention, the 1971 Protocol, the Accession Convention, the 1982 Accession Convention and the 1989 Accession Convention;**

"the Lugano Convention" means the Convention on jurisdiction and the enforcement of judgments in civil and commercial matters (including the Protocols annexed to that Convention) opened for signature at Lugano on 16th September 1988 and signed by the United Kingdom on 18th September 1989[3]

"the Regulation" means Council Regulation (EC) No 44/2001 of 22nd December 2000 on juridiction and the recognition and enforcement of judgments in civil and commercial matters.

(2) In this Act, unless the context otherwise requires—

(*a*) references to, or to any provision of, the 1968 Convention or the 1971 Protocol are references to that Convention, Protocol or provision as amended by the Accession Convention, the 1982 Accession Convention and the 1989 Accession Convention**,***; and

(*b*) any reference in any provision to a numbered Article without more is a reference—

  (i) to the Article so numbered of the 1968 Convention, in so far as the provision applies in relation to that Convention, and

  (ii) to the Article so numbered of the Lugano Convention, in so far as the provision applies in relation to that Convention,

and any reference to a sub-division of a numbered Article shall be construed accordingly.

(3) In this Act—

"Contracting State", without more, in any provision means—

(*a*) in the application of the provision in relation to the Brussels Conventions, a Brussels Contracting State, and

(*b*) in the application of the provision in relation to the Lugano Convention, a Lugano Contracting State;

"Brussels Contracting State" means Denmark (which is not bound by the Regulation, but was one of the parties acceding to the 1968 Convention under the Accession Convention),

"Lugano contracting State" means one of the original parties to the Lugano Convention, that is to say—

  Austria, Belgium, Denmark, Finland, France, the Federal Republic of Germany, the Hellenic Republic, Iceland, the Republic of Ireland, Italy, Luxembourg, the Netherlands, Norway, Portugal, Spain, Sweden, Switzerland and the United Kingdom,**

  being a State in relation to which that Convention has taken effect in accordance with paragraph 3 or 4 of Article 61.

"Regulation State" in any provision, in the application of that provision in relation to the Regulation, has the same meaning as "Member State" in the Regulation, that is all Members States except Denmark.

(4) Any question arising as to whether it is the Regulation, any of the Brussels Conventions, or the Lugano Convention which applies in the circumstances of a particular case shall be determined as follows—

(*a*) in accordance with Article 54B of the Lugano Convention (which determines the relationship between the Brussels Conventions and the Lugano Convention); and

(*b*) in accordance with Article 68 of the Regulation (which determines the relationship between the Brussels Conventions and the Regulation).

[Civil Jurisdiction and Judgments Act 1982, s 1 amended by SI 1989/1346, SI 1990/2591, the Civil Jurisdiction and Judgments Act 1991, s 2 and SI 2001/3929.]

***Definition inserted by SI 2000/1824, from a date to be appointed.**
****Amended by SI 2000/1824, from a date to be appointed.**
*****Sub-section (2): new para (*aa*) inserted by SI 2000/1824, from a date to be appointed.**
1. Only those provisions of this Act which are likely to be of concern to magistrates' courts are included in this work.
2. Part I contains ss 1–15.
3. OJ 1988 No L319/9 and Cm 1362.

6–1641   2. The Brussels Conventions to have the force of law.   (1) The Brussels Conventions shall have the force of law in the United Kingdom, and judicial notice shall be taken of them.

(2) For convenience of reference there are set out in Schedules 1, 2, 3, 3A and 3B* respectively the English texts of—

(a) the 1968 Convention as amended by Titles II and III of the Accession Convention, by Titles II and III of the 1982 Accession Convention and** by Titles II and III of, and Annex I(d) to, the 1989 Accession Convention*;

(b) the 1971 Protocol as amended by Title IV of the Accession Convention, by Title IV of the 1982 Accession Convention and* by Title IV of the 1989 Accession Convention;

(c) Titles V and VI of the Accession Convention (transitional and final provisions) as amended by Title V of the 1989 Accession Convention;

(d) Titles V and VI of the 1982 Accession Convention (transitional and final provisions); and

(e) Titles VI and VII of the 1989 Accession Convention (transitional and final provisions),***

being texts prepared from the authentic English texts referred to in Articles 37 and 41 of the Accession Convention, in Article 17 of the 1982 Accession Convention and in Article 34 of the 1989 Accession Convention.

[Civil Jurisdiction and Judgments Act 1982, s 2 amended by SI 1989/1346, SI 1990/2591 and the Civil Jurisdiction and Judgments Act 1991, Sch 2.]

---

*Section 2 is amended by SI 2000/1824, when in force.
**Repealed by SI 2000/1824, from a date to be appointed.
***A new s 2(2)(f) is inserted by SI 2000/1824, when in force.

6–1642   3. Interpretation of the Brussels Conventions.   (1) Any question as to the meaning or effect of any provision of the Brussels Conventions shall, if not referred to the European Court in accordance with the 1971 Protocol, be determined in accordance with the principles laid down by and any relevant decision of the European Court.

(2) Judicial notice shall be taken of any decision of, or expression of opinion by, the European court on any such question.

(3) Without prejudice to the generality of subsection (1), the following reports (which are reproduced in the Official Journal of the Communities), namely—

(a) the reports by Mr P Jenard on the 1968 Convention and the 1971 Protocol[1]; and

(b) the report by Professor Peter Schlosser on the Accession Convention[2]; and

(c) the report by Professor Demetrios I Evrigenis and Professor K D Kerameus on the 1982 Accession Convention;

(d) the report by Mr Martinho de Almeida Cruz, Mr Manuel Desantes Real and Mr P Jenard on the 1989 Accession Convention,

may be considered in ascertaining the meaning or effect of any provision of the Brussels Conventions and shall be given such weight as is appropriate in the circumstances.

[Civil Jurisdiction and Judgments Act 1982, s 3 amended by SI 1989/1346, SI 1990/2591 and the Civil Jurisdiction and Judgments Act 1991, Sch 2.]

---

1. OJ 1979 No C59/1 and 66.
2. OJ 1979 No C59/71.

6–1643   3A. The Lugano Convention to have the force of law.   (1) The Lugano Convention shall have the force of law in the United Kingdom, and judicial notice shall be taken of it.

(2) For convenience of reference there is set out in Schedule 3C the English text of the Lugano Convention.*

[Civil Jurisdiction and Judgments Act 1982, s 3A, as inserted by the Civil Jurisdiction and Judgments Act 1991, s 1.]

---

*Section 3A(2) is amended by SI 2000/1824, when in force.

6–1644   3B. Interpretation of the Lugano Convention.   (1) In determining any question as to the meaning or effect of a provision of the Lugano Convention, a court in the United Kingdom shall, in accordance with Protocol No 2 to that Convention, take account of any principles laid down in any relevant decision delivered by a court of any other Lugano Contracting State concerning provisions of the Convention.

(2) Without prejudice to any practice of the courts as to the matters which may be considered apart from this section, the report on the Lugano Convention by Mr P Jenard and Mr G Möller (which is reproduced in the Official Journal of the Communities of 28th July 1990)[1] may be considered in ascertaining the meaning or effect of any provision of the Convention and shall be given such weight as is appropriate in the circumstances.

[Civil Jurisdiction and Judgments Act 1982, s 3B, as inserted by the Civil Jurisdiction and Judgments Act 1991, s 1.]

1. OJ 1990 No C 189/07.

Supplementary provisions as to recognition and enforcement of judgments

6–1653   4. *Enforcement of judgments other than maintenance orders.*

6–1654   5. Recognition and enforcement of maintenance orders.   (1) The function of transmitting to the appropriate court an application under Article 31 for the recognition or enforcement in the United Kingdom of a maintenance order shall be discharged—

(*a*)   as respects England and Wales and Northern Ireland, by Lord Chancellor; and
(*b*)   as respects Scotland, by the Secretary of State.

In this subsection "the appropriate court" means the magistrates' court or sheriff court having jurisdiction in the matter in accordance with the second paragraph of Article 32.

(2) Such an application shall be determined in the first instance by the prescribed officer of that court.

(3) Where on such an application the enforcement of the order is authorised to any extent, the order shall to that extent be registered in the prescribed manner in that court.

(4) A maintenance order registered under this section shall, for the purposes of its enforcement, be of the same force and effect, the registering court shall have in relation to its enforcement the same powers, and proceedings for or with respect to its enforcement may be taken, as if the order had been originally made by the registering court.

(5) Subsection (4) is subject to Article 39 (restriction on enforcement where appeal pending or time for appeal unexpired), to section 7 and to any provision made by rules of court as to the manner in which and conditions subject to which an order registered under this section may be enforced.

(5A) A maintenance order which by virtue of this section is enforceable by a magistrates' court in England and Wales shall, subject to the modifications of sections 76 and 93 of the Magistrates' Courts Act 1980 specified in subsections (5B) and (5C) below, be enforceable in the same manner as a magistrates' court maintenance order made by that court.

In this subsection "magistrates' court maintenance order" has the same meaning as in section 150(1) of the Magistrates' Courts Act 1980.

(5B) Section 76 (enforcement of sums adjudged to be paid) shall have effect as if for subsections (4) to (6) there were substituted the following subsections—

"(4) Where proceedings are brought for the enforcement of a magistrates' court maintenance order under this section, the court may vary the order by exercising one of its powers under subsection (5) below.

(5) The powers of the court are—

(*a*)   the power to order that payments under the order be made directly to the designated officer for thre court or for any other magistrates' court;
(*b*)   the power to order that payments under the order be made to the designated officer for thre court or for any other magistrates' court by such method of payment falling within section 59(6) above (standing order, etc) as may be specified;
(*c*)   the power to make an attachment of earnings order under the Attachment of Earnings Act 1971 to secure payments under the order.

(6) In deciding which of the powers under subsection (5) above it is to exercise, the court shall have regard to any representations made by the debtor (within the meaning of section 59 above).

(7) Subsection (4) of section 59 above (power of court to require debtor to open account) shall apply for the purposes of subsection (5) above as it applies for the purposes of that section but as if for paragraph (*a*) there were substituted—

"(*a*) the court proposes to exercise its power under paragraph (*b*) of section 76(5) below, and."

(5C) In section 93 (complaint for arrears), subsection (6) (court not to impose imprisonment in certain circumstances) shall have effect as if for paragraph (*b*) there were substituted—

"(*b*) if the court is of the opinion that it is appropriate—

(i)   to make an attachment of earnings order; or
(ii)   to exercise its power under paragraph (*b*) of section 76(5) above."

(6) A maintenance order which by virtue of this section is enforceable by a magistrates' court in Northern Ireland shall be enforceable in the same manner as an affiliation order made by that court.

(7) The payer under a maintenance order registered under this section in a magistrates' court in England and Wales or Northern Ireland shall give notice of any change of address to the proper officer of that court.

A person who without reasonable excuse fails to comply with this subsection shall be guilty of an offence and liable on summary conviction to a fine not exceeding **level 2** on the standard scale.

(8) In subsection (7) "proper officer" means—

(*a*) in relation to a magistrates' court in England and Wales, the designated officer for the court; and

(*b*) in relation to a magistrates' court in Northern Ireland, the clerk of the court.

[Civil Jurisdiction and Judgments Act 1982, s 5, as amended by the Criminal Justice Act 1982, s 46, the Family Law Reform Act 1987, Sch 2 the Maintenance Enforcement Act 1991, Sch 1, SI 1992/709, the Access to Justice Act 1999, Sch 13 and the Courts Act 2003.]

6–1655   6. Appeals under Article 37, second paragraph and Article 41. (1) The single further appeal on a point of law referred to in the 1968 Convention and the Lugano Convention in Article 37, second paragraph and Article 41 in relation to the recognition or enforcement of a judgment other than a maintenance order lies—

(*a*) in England and Wales or Northern Ireland, to the Court of Appeal or to the House of Lords in accordance with Part II of the Administration of Justice Act 1969 (appeals direct from the High Court to the House of Lords);

(*b*) in Scotland, to the Inner House of the Court of Session.

(2) Paragraph (*a*) of subsection (1) has effect notwithstanding section 15(2) of the Administration of Justice Act 1969 (exclusion of direct appeal to the House of Lords in cases where no appeal to that House lies from a decision of the Court of Appeal).

(3) The single further appeal on a point of law referred to in each of those Conventions in Article 37, second paragraph and Article 41 in relation to the recognition or enforcement of a maintenance order lies—

(*a*) in England and Wales, to the High Court by way of case stated in accordance with section 111 of the Magistrates' Courts Act 1980;

(*b*) in Scotland, to the Inner House of the Court of Session;

(*c*) in Northern Ireland, to the Court of Appeal.

[Civil Jurisdiction and Judgments Act 1982, s 6 as amended by the Civil Jurisdiction and Judgments Act 1991, Sch 2.]

6–1656   7. Interest on registered judgments. (1) Subject to subsection (4), where in connection with an application for registration of a judgment under section 4 or 5 the applicant shows—

(*a*) that the judgment provides for the payment of a sum of money; and

(*b*) that in accordance with the law of the Contracting State in which the judgment was given interest on that sum is recoverable under the judgment from a particular date or time,

the rate of interest and the date or time from which it is so recoverable shall be registered with the judgment and, subject to any provision made under subsection (2), the debt resulting, apart from section 4(2), from the registration of the judgment shall carry interest in accordance with the registered particulars.

(2) Provision may be made by rules of court as to the manner in which and the periods by reference to which any interest payable by virtue of subsection (1) is to be calculated and paid, including provision for such interest to cease to accrue as from a prescribed date.

(3) Costs or expenses recoverable by virtue of section 4(2) shall carry interest as if they were the subject of an order for the payment of costs or expenses made by the registering court on the date of registration.

(4) Interest on arrears of sums payable under a maintenance order registered under section 5 in a magistrates' court in England and Wales or Northern Ireland shall not be recoverable in that court, but without prejudice to the operation in relation to any such order of section 2A of the Maintenance Orders Act 1958 or section 11A of the Maintenance and Affiliation Orders Act (Northern Ireland) 1966 (which enable interest to be recovered if the order is re-registered for enforcement in the High Court).

(5) Except as mentioned in subsection (4), debts under judgments registered under section 4 or 5 shall carry interest only as provided by this section.

[Civil Jurisdiction and Judgments Act 1982, s 7.]

6–1657   8. Currency of payment under registered maintenance orders. (1) Sums payable in the United Kingdom under a maintenance order by virtue of its registration under section 5, including any arrears so payable, shall be paid in the currency of the United Kingdom.

(2) Where the order is expressed in any other currency, the amounts shall be converted on the basis of the exchange rate prevailing on the date of registration of the order.

(3) For the purposes of this section, a written certificate purporting to be signed by an officer of any bank in the United Kingdom and stating the exchange rate prevailing on a specified date shall be evidence, and in Scotland sufficient evidence, of the facts stated.

[Civil Jurisdiction and Judgments Act 1982, s 8.]

6–1658   11. Proof and admissibility of certain judgments and related documents. (1) For the purposes of the 1968 Convention and the Lugano Convention—

(*a*)   a document, duly authenticated, which purports to be a copy of a judgment given by a court of a Contracting State other than the United Kingdom shall without further proof be deemed to be a true copy, unless the contrary is shown; and

(*b*)   the original or a copy of any such document as is mentioned in Article 46(2) or 47 (supporting documents to be produced by a party seeking recognition or enforcement of a judgment) shall be evidence, and in Scotland sufficient evidence, of any matter to which it relates.

(2)   A document purporting to be a copy of a judgment given by any such court as is mentioned in subsection (1)(*a*) is duly authenticated for the purposes of this section if it purports—

(*a*)   to bear the seal of that court; or

(*b*)   to be certified by any person in his capacity as a judge or officer of that court to be a true copy of a judgment given by that court.

(3)   Nothing in this section shall prejudice the admission in evidence of any document which is admissible apart from this section.

[Civil Jurisdiction and Judgments Act 1982, s 11 as amended by the Civil Jurisdiction and Judgments Act 1991, Sch 2.]

6–1659   12. Provision for issue of copies of, and certificates in connection with, UK judgments.   Rules[1] of court may make provision for enabling any interested party wishing to secure under the 1968 Convention or the Lugano Convention the recognition or enforcement in another Contracting State of a judgment given by a court in the United Kingdom to obtain, subject to any conditions specified in the rules—

(*a*)   a copy of the judgment; and

(*b*)   a certificate giving particulars relating to the judgment and the proceedings in which it was given.

[Civil Jurisdiction and Judgments Act 1982, s 12 as amended by the Civil Jurisdiction and Judgments Act 1991, Sch 2.]

---

1. So far as magistrates' courts are concerned, see the Magistrates' Courts (Civil Jurisdiction and Judgments Act 1982) Rules 1986, this PART, post.

6–1660   13. Modifications to cover authentic instruments and court settlements.   (1)   Her Majesty may by Order in Council[1] provide that—

(*a*)   any provision of this Act relating to the recognition or enforcement in the United Kingdom or elsewhere of judgments to which the 1968 Convention or the Lugano Convention applies; and

(*b*)   any other statutory provision, whenever passed or made, so relating,

shall apply, with such modifications as may be specified in the Order, in relation to documents and settlements within Title IV of the 1968 Convention or, as the case may be, Title IV of the Lugano Convention (authentic instruments and court settlements enforceable in the same manner as judgments) as if they were judgments to which the Convention in question applies.

(2)   An Order in Council under this section may make different provision in relation to different descriptions of documents and settlements.

(3)   Any Order in Council under this section shall be subject to annulment in pursuance of a resolution of either House of Parliament.

[Civil Jurisdiction and Judgments Act 1982, s 13 as amended by the Civil Jurisdiction and Judgments Act 1991, Sch 2.]

---

1. The Civil Jurisdiction and Judgments (Authentic Instruments and Court Settlements) Order 1993, SI 1993/604 has been made. This applies specified provisions of the 1982 Act to authentic instruments and court settlements from Contracting States other than the United Kingdom. Authentic instruments usually take the form of agreements containing obligations, which are drawn up by the parties before a notary public. Court settlements are settlements of legal proceedings agreed by the parties and approved by the court, and which are enforceable without having to be drawn up as judgments.

6–1661   14. Modifications consequential on revision of the Conventions.   (1)   If at any time it appears to Her Majesty in Council that Her Majesty's Government in the United Kingdom have agreed to a revision of the Lugano Convention or any of the Brussels Conventions, including in particular the Lugano Convention or the 1968 Convention of one or more further states, Her Majesty may by Order in Council make such modifications of this Act or any other statutory provision, whenever passed or made, as Her Majesty considers appropriate in consequence of the revision.

(2)   An Order in Council under this section shall not be made unless a draft of the Order has been laid before Parliament and approved by a resolution of each House of Parliament.

(3)   In this section "revision" means an omission from, addition to or alteration of the Lugano Convention or any of the Brussels Conventions and includes replacement of the Lugano Convention or any of the Brussels Conventions to any extent by another Convention, protocol or other description of international agreement.

[Civil Jurisdiction and Judgments Act 1982, s 14 as amended by the Civil Jurisdiction and Judgments Act 1991, Sch 2.]

6–1662   15. Interpretation of Part I and consequential amendments. (1) In this Part, unless the context otherwise requires—

"judgment" has the meaning given by Article 25;

"maintenance order" means a maintenance judgment within the meaning of the 1968 Convention or, as the case may be, the Lugano Convention;

"payer", in relation to a maintenance order means the person liable to make the payments for which the order provides;

"prescribed" means prescribed by rules of court.

(2) References in this Part to a judgment registered under section 4 or 5 include, to the extent of its registration, references to a judgment so registered to a limited extent only.

(3) Anything authorised or required by the 1968 Convention, the Lugano Convention or this Part to be done by, to or before a particular magistrates' court may be done by, to or before any magistrates' court acting in the same local justice area (or, in Northern Ireland, for the same petty sessions district) as that court.

(4) The enactments specified in Part I of Schedule 12 shall have effect with the amendments specified there, being amendments consequential on this Part.

[Civil Jurisdiction and Judgments Act 1982, s 15 as amended by the Civil Jurisdiction and Judgments Act 1991, Sch 2 and the Courts Act 2003, Sch 8.]

PART IV¹

MISCELLANEOUS PROVISIONS

Provisions relating to recognition and enforcement of judgments

6–1663   36. Registration of maintenance orders in Northern Ireland. (1) Where—

(*a*) a High Court order or a Court of Session order has been registered in the High Court of Justice in Northern Ireland ("the Northern Ireland High Court") under Part II of the Maintenance Orders Act 1950; or

(*b*) a county court order, a magistrates' court order or a sheriff court order has been registered in a court of summary jurisdiction in Northern Ireland under that Part,

an application may be made to the original court for the registration of the order in, respectively, a court of summary jurisdiction in Northern Ireland or the Northern Ireland High Court.

(2) In subsection (1) "the original court", in relation to an order, means the court by which the order was made.

(3) Section 2 (except subsection (6A)) and section 2A of the Maintenance Orders Act 1958 shall have effect for the purposes of an application under subsection (1), and subsections (2), (3), (4) and (4A) of section 5 of that Act shall have effect for the purposes of the cancellation of a registration made on such an application, as if—

(*a*) "registration" in those provisions included registration in the appropriate Northern Ireland court ("registered" being construed accordingly);

(*b*) any reference in those provisions to a High Court order or a magistrates' court order included, respectively, a Court of Session order or a sheriff court order; and

(*c*) any other reference in those provisions to the High Court or a magistrates' court included the Northern Ireland High Court or a court of summary jurisdiction in Northern Ireland.

(4) Where an order is registered in Northern Ireland under this section, Part II of the Maintenance and Affiliation Orders Act (Northern Ireland) 1966, except sections 11, 11A and 14(2) and (3), shall apply as if the order had been registered in accordance with the provisions of that Part.

(5) A court of summary jurisdiction in Northern Ireland shall have jurisdiction to hear an application by or against a person residing outside Northern Ireland for the discharge or variation of an order registered in Northern Ireland under this section; and where such an application is made against a person residing outside Northern Ireland, then, if he resides in England and Wales or Scotland, section 15 of the Maintenance Orders Act 1950 (which relates to the service of process on persons residing in those countries) shall have effect in relation to the application as it has effect in relation to the proceedings therein mentioned.

(5A) Article 165 of the Children (Northern Ireland) Order 1995 (provision which may be made by magistrates' courts rules, etc.) shall apply for the purpose of giving effect to subsection (5) above as it applies for the purpose of giving effect to that Order, except that in the application of that Article by virtue of this subsection "relevant proceedings" means any application made, or proceedings brought, by virtue of that subsection and any part of such proceedings.

(6) The enactments specified in Part III of Schedule 12 shall have effect with the amendments specified there, being amendments consequential on this section.

[Civil Jurisdiction and Judgments Act 1982, s 36 as amended by SI 1995/755.]

---

1. Part IV contains ss 26–40.

PART V[1]
SUPPLEMENTARY AND GENERAL PROVISIONS

General

6–1665 **50. Interpretation: general.** In this Act, unless the context otherwise requires—

"the Accession Convention", "the 1982 Accession Convention" and "the 1989 Accession Convention"* have the meaning given by section 1(1);

"Article" and references to sub-divisions of numbered Articles are to be construed in accordance with section 1(2)(*b*);

"association" means an unincorporated body of persons;

"Brussels Contracting State" has the meaning given by section 1(3);

"the Brussels Conventions" has the meaning given by section 1(1);

"Contracting State" has the meaning given by section 1(3);

"the 1968 Convention" has the meaning given by section 1(1), and references to that Convention and to provisions of it are to be construed in accordance with section 1(2)(*a*);

"corporation" means a body corporate, and includes a partnership subsisting under the law of Scotland;

"court", without more, includes a tribunal;

"court of law", in relation to the United Kingdom, means any of the following courts, namely—

(*a*) the House of Lords,
(*b*) in England and Wales or Northern Ireland, the Court of Appeal, the High Court, the Crown Court, a county court and a magistrates' court,
(*c*) in Scotland, the Court of Session and a sheriff court;

"the Crown" is to be construed in accordance with section 51(2);

"enactment" includes an enactment comprised in Northern Ireland legislation;

"judgment", subject to sections 15(1) and 18(2) and to paragraph 1 of Schedules 6 and 7, means any judgment or order (by whatever name called) given or made by a court in any civil proceedings;

"Lugano Contracting State" has the meaning given by section 1(3);

"the Lugano Convention" has the meaning given by section 1(1);

"magistrates' court", in relation to Northern Ireland, means a court of summary jurisdiction;

"modifications" includes additions, omissions and alterations;

"overseas country" means any country or territory outside the United Kingdom;

"part of the United Kingdom" means England and Wales, Scotland or Northern Ireland;

"the 1971 Protocol" has the meaning given by section 1(1), and references to that Protocol and to provisions of it are to be construed in accordance with section 1(2)(*a*);

"the Regulation" has the meaning given by section 1(1);

"Regulation State" has the meaning given by section 1(3);

"rules of court", in relation to any court, means rules, orders or regulations made by the authority having power to make rules, orders or regulations regulating the procedure of that court, and includes—

(*a*) in Scotland, Acts of Sederunt;
(*b*) in Northern Ireland, Judgment Enforcement Rules;

"statutory provision" means any provision contained in an Act, or in any Northern Ireland legislation, or in—

(*a*) subordinate legislation (as defined in section 21(1) of the Interpretation Act 1978); or
(*b*) any instrument of a legislative character made under any Northern Ireland legislation;

"tribunal"—

(*a*) means a tribunal of any description other than a court of law;
(*b*) in relation to an overseas country, includes, as regards matters relating to maintenance within the meaning of the 1968 Convention, any authority having power to give, enforce, vary or revoke a maintenance order.*

[Civil Jurisdiction and Judgments Act 1982, s 50 amended by SI 1990/2591, the Civil Jurisdiction and Judgments Act 1991, Sch 2 an SI 2001/3929.]

---

*Section 50 is amended by SI 2000/1824, when in force.
1. Part V contains ss 41–55.

6–1666 **51. Application to Crown.** (1) This Act binds the Crown.

(2) In this section and elsewhere in this Act references to the Crown do not include references to Her Majesty in Her private capacity or to Her Majesty in right of Her Duchy of Lancaster or to the Duke of Cornwall.

[Civil Jurisdiction and Judgments Act 1982, s 51.]

6–1667 **52. Extent.** (1) This Act extends to Northern Ireland.

(2) Without prejudice to the power conferred by section 39, Her Majesty may by Order in Council

direct that all or any of the provisions of this Act apart from that section shall extend, subject to such modifications as may be specified in the Order, to any of the following territories, that is to say—

(a) the Isle of Man;
(b) any of the Channel Islands;
(c) any colony;
(d) the Sovereign Base Areas of Akrotiri and Dhekelia (that is to say the areas mentioned in section 2(1) of the Cyprus Act 1960).

[Civil Jurisdiction and Judgments Act 1982, s 52 amended by SI 1990/2591.]

6–1668 **53–55.** *Commencement, transitional provisions and savings; repeals; short title.*

6–1670
SCHEDULES
SCHEDULE 1
TEXT OF 1968 CONVENTION, AS AMENDED[1]
ARRANGEMENT OF PROVISIONS

(Set out below are those provisions of the Convention which are relevant to matters relating to maintenance and the jurisdiction of magistrates' courts.)

Section 2(2)

ARRANGEMENT OF PROVISIONS

TITLE 1. SCOPE (Article 1)
TITLE II. JURISDICTION

Section 1. General provisions (Articles 2–4)
Section 2. Special jurisdiction (Articles 5–6A).
Section 3. Jurisdiction in matters relating to insurance (Articles 7–12A).
Section 4. Jurisdiction over consumer contracts (Articles 13–15).
Section 5. Exclusive jurisdiction (Article 16).
Section 6. Prorogation of jurisdiction (Articles 17 and 18).
Section 7. Examination as to jurisdiction and admissibility (Articles 19 and 20).
Section 8. Lis pendens—Related actions (Articles 21–23).
Section 9. Provisional, including protective, measures (Article 24).

TITLE III. RECOGNITION AND ENFORCEMENT

Definition of judgment (Article 25).
Section 1. Recognition (Articles 26–30).
Section 2. Enforcement (Articles 31–45).
Section 3. Common provisions (Articles 46–49).

TITLE IV. AUTHENTIC INSTRUMENTS AND COURT SETTLEMENTS (Articles 50 and 51).
TITLE V. GENERAL PROVISIONS (Articles 52 and 53).
TITLE VI. TRANSITIONAL PROVISIONS (Article 54 and 54A).
TITLE VII. RELATIONSHIP TO OTHER CONVENTIONS (Articles 55–59).
TITLE VIII. FINAL PROVISIONS (Articles 60–68).

---

*Schedule 1 is repealed by SI 2000/1824, when in force.
1. This Schedule was substituted by SI 1990/2591. For the procedure to be followed in magistrates' courts in dealing with claims for the recognition and enforcement of maintenance orders under the Convention, see the Magistrates' Courts (Civil Jurisdiction and Judgments Act 1982) Rules 1986 this PART, post.

6–1671
CONVENTION
ON JURISDICTION AND THE ENFORCEMENT OF JUDGMENTS IN CIVIL AND COMMERCIAL MATTERS
PREAMBLE

THE HIGH CONTRACTING PARTIES TO THE TREATY ESTABLISHING THE EUROPEAN ECONOMIC COMMUNITY,

Desiring to implement the provisions of Article 220 of that Treaty by virtue of which they undertook to secure the simplification of formalities governing the reciprocal recognition and enforcement of judgments of courts or tribunals;

Anxious to strengthen in the Community the legal protection of persons therein established;

Considering that it is necessary for this purpose to determine the international jurisdiction of their courts, to facilitate recognition and to introduce an expeditious procedure for securing the enforcement of judgments, authentic instruments and court settlements;

Have decided to conclude this Convention and to this end have designated as their Plenipotentiaries:

(*Designations of Plenipotentiaries of the original six Contracting States*)

WHO, meeting within the Council, having exchanged their Full Powers, found in good and due form,

HAVE AGREED AS FOLLOWS:*

---

*Schedule 1 is substituted by SI 2000/1824, when in force.

TITLE I
SCOPE

6-1672   Article 1.   This Convention shall apply in civil and commercial matters whatever the nature of the court or tribunal. It shall not extend, in particular, to revenue, customs or administrative matters.

The Convention shall not apply to:

1.   the status or legal capacity of natural persons, rights in property arising out of a matrimonial relationship, wills and succession;
2.   bankruptcy, proceedings relating to the winding-up of insolvent companies or other legal persons, judicial arrangements, compositions and analogous proceedings;
3.   social security;
4.   arbitration.*

*Schedule 1 is substituted by SI 2000/1824, when in force.

TITLE II
JURISDICTION
SECTION 1
GENERAL PROVISIONS

6-1673   Article 2.   Subject to the provisions of this Convention, persons domiciled in a Contracting State shall, whatever their nationality, be sued in the courts of that State.

Persons who are not nationals of the State in which they are domiciled shall be governed by the rules of jurisdiction applicable to nationals of that State.*

*Schedule 1 is substituted by SI 2000/1824, when in force.

6-1674   Article 3.   Persons domiciled in a Contracting State may be sued in the courts of another Contracting State only by virtue of the rules set out in Sections 2 to 6 of this Title.

In particular the following provisions shall not be applicable as against them:

—   in Belgium: Article 15 of the civil code (Code civil—Burgerlijk Wetboek) and Article 638 of the judicial code (Code judiciaire—Gerechtelijk Wetboek),
—   in Denmark: Article 246(2) and (3) of the law on civil procedure (Lov om rettens pleje),
—   In the Federal Republic of Germany: Article 23 of the code of civil procedure (Zivilprozeßordnung),
—   in Greece, Article 40 of the code of civil procedure (Κώδικας Πολιτικής Δικουομίας);
—   in France: Articles 14 and 15 of the civil code (Code civil),
—   in Ireland: the rules which enable jurisdiction to be founded on the document instituting the proceedings having been served on the defendant during his temporary presence in Ireland,
—   in Italy: Articles 2 and 4, Nos 1 and 2 of the code of civil procedure (Codice di procedura civile),
—   in Luxembourg: Articles 14 and 15 of the civil code (Code civil),
—   in the Netherlands: Articles 126(3) and 127 of the code of civil procedure (Wetboek van Burgerlijke Rechtsvordering),
—   in Portugal: Article 65(1)(c), article 65(2) and Article 65A(c) of the code of civil procedure (Código de Processo Civil) and Article 11 of the code of labour procedure (Código de Processo de Trabalho),
—   in the United Kingdom: the rules which enable jurisdiction to be founded on:

(a)   the document instituting the proceedings having been served on the defendant during his temporary presence in the United Kingdom, or
(b)   the presence within the United Kingdom of property belonging to the defendant; or
(c)   the seizure by the plaintiff of property situated in the United Kingdom.*

*Schedule 1 is substituted by SI 2000/1824, when in force.

6-1675   Article 4.   If the defendant is not domiciled in a Contracting State, the jurisdiction of the courts of each Contracting State shall, subject to the provisions of Article 16, be determined by the law of that State.

As against such a defendant, any person domiciled in a Contracting State may, whatever his nationality, avail himself in that State of the rules of jurisdiction there in force, and in particular those specified in the second paragraph of Article 3, in the same way as the nationals of that State.*

*Schedule 1 is substituted by SI 2000/1824, when in force.

SECTION 2
SPECIAL JURISDICTION

6-1676   Article 5.   A person domiciled in a Contracting State may, in another Contracting State, be sued:

1.   . . .
2.   in matters relating to maintenance[1], in the courts for the place where the maintenance creditor is domiciled or habitually resident or, if the matter is ancillary to proceedings concerning the status of a person, in the court which, according to its own law, has jurisdiction to entertain those proceedings, unless that jurisdiction is based solely on the nationality of one of the parties;
3–7. . . .*

*Schedule 1 is substituted by SI 2000/1824, when in force.

1. 'Maintenance' excludes rights in property arising out of a matrimonial relationship (art 1, ante) and see para **6–230 Civil Jurisdiction and Judgments Act 1982** ante.

4217 Civil Jurisdiction and Judgments Act 1982 6–1684

6–1677   Article 6.   A person domiciled in a Contracting State may also be sued:

1.   where he is one of a number of defendants, in the courts for the place where any one of them is domiciled;
2.   as a third party in an action on a warranty or guarantee or in any other third party proceedings, in the court seised of the original proceedings, unless these were instituted solely with the object of removing him from the jurisdiction of the court which would be competent in his case;
3.   on a counter-claim arising from the same contract or facts on which the original claim was based, in the court in which the original claim is pending.★

Schedule 1 is substituted by SI 2000/1824, when in force.

6–1678   Article 6a.   Where by virtue of this Convention a court of a Contracting State has jurisdiction in actions relating to liability arising from the use or operation of a ship, that court, or any other court substituted for this purpose by the internal law of that State, shall also have jurisdiction over claims for limitation of such liability.★

Schedule 1 is substituted by SI 2000/1824, when in force.

TITLE III
RECOGNITION AND ENFORCEMENT

6–1679   Article 25.   For the purposes of this Convention, "judgment" means any judgment given by a court or tribunal of a Contracting State, whatever the judgment may be called, including a decree, order, decision or writ of execution, as well as the determination of costs or expenses by an officer of the court.★

Schedule 1 is substituted by SI 2000/1824, when in force.

SECTION 1
RECOGNITION

6–1680   Article 26.   A judgment given in a Contracting State shall be recognised in the other Contracting States without any special procedure being required.

Any interested party who raises the recognition of a judgment as the principal issue in a dispute may, in accordance with the procedures provided for in Sections 2 and 3 of this Title, apply for a decision that the judgment be recognised.

If the outcome of proceedings in a court of a Contracting State depends on the determination of an incidental question of recognition that court shall have jurisdiction over that question.★

Schedule 1 is substituted by SI 2000/1824, when in force.

6–1681   Article 27.   A judgment shall not be recognized:

1.   if such recognition is contrary to public policy in the State in which recognition is sought;
2.   where it was given in default of appearance, if the defendant was not duly served with the document which instituted the proceedings or with an equivalent document in sufficient time to enable him to arrange for his defence;
3.   if the judgment is irreconcilable with a judgment given in a dispute between the same parties in the State in which recognition is sought;
4.   if the court of the State of origin, in order to arrive at its judgment, has decided a preliminary question concerning the status or legal capacity of natural persons, rights in property arising out of a matrimonial relationship, wills or succession in a way that conflicts with a rule of the private international law of the State in which the recognition is sought, unless the same result would have been reached by the application of the rules of private international law of that State;
5.   if the judgment is irreconcilable with an earlier judgment given in a non-contracting State involving the same cause of action and between the same parties, provided that this latter judgment fulfils the conditions necessary for its recognition in the State addressed.★

Schedule 1 is substituted by SI 2000/1824, when in force.

6–1682   Article 28.   Moreover, a judgment shall not be recognised if it conflicts with the provisions of Sections 3, 4 or 5 of Title II, or in a case provided for in Article 59.

In its examination of the grounds of jurisdiction referred to in the foregoing paragraph, the court or authority applied to shall be bound by the findings of fact on which the court of the State of origin based its jurisdiction.

Subject to the provisions of the first paragraph, the jurisdiction of the court of the State of origin may not be reviewed; the test of public policy referred to in point 1 of Article 27 may not be applied to the rules relating to jurisdiction.★

Schedule 1 is substituted by SI 2000/1824, when in force.

6–1683   Article 29.   Under no circumstances may a foreign judgment be reviewed as to its substance.★

Schedule 1 is substituted by SI 2000/1824, when in force.

6–1684   Article 30.   A court of a Contracting State in which recognition is sought of a judgment given in another Contracting State may stay the proceedings if an ordinary appeal against the judgment has been lodged.

A court of a Contracting State in which recognition is sought of a judgment given in Ireland or the United Kingdom may stay the proceedings if enforcement is suspended in the State of origin by reason of an appeal.*

---

*Schedule 1 is substituted by SI 2000/1824, when in force.

SECTION 2
ENFORCEMENT

6–1685 Article 31.   A judgment given in a Contracting State and enforceable in that State shall be enforced in another Contracting State when, on the application of any interested party, it has been declared enforceable there.

However, in the United Kingdom, such a judgment shall be enforced in England and Wales, in Scotland, or in Northern Ireland when, on the application of any interested party, it has been registered for enforcement in that part of the United Kingdom.*

---

*Schedule 1 is substituted by SI 2000/1824, when in force.

6–1686 Article 32.   1. The application shall be submitted:

— in Belgium, to the tribunal de première instance or rechtbank van eerste aanleg,
— in Denmark, to the byret,
— in the Federal Republic of Germany, to the presiding judge of a chamber of the Landgericht,
— in Greece, to the Μονομελές Πρωτοδικείο,
— in Spain, to the Juzgado de Primera Instancia,
— in France, to the presiding judge of the tribunal de grande instance,
— in Ireland, to the High Court,
— in Italy, to the corte d'appello,
— in Luxembourg, to the presiding judge of the tribunal d'arrondissement,
— in the Netherlands, to the presiding judge of the arrondissementsrechtbank,
— in Portugal, to the Tribunal Judicial de Círculo,
— in the United Kingdom:

   (a) in England and Wales, to the High court of Justice, or in the case of a maintenance judgment to the Magistrates' Court on transmission by the Secretary of State;
   (b) in Scotland, to the Court of Session, or in the case of a maintenance judgment to the Sheriff Court on transmission by the Secretary of State;
   (c) in Northern Ireland, to the High Court of Justice, or in the case of a maintenance judgment to the Magistrates' Court on transmission by the Secretary of State.

2 The jurisdiction of local courts shall be determined by reference to the place of domicile of the party against whom enforcement is sought. If he is not domiciled in the State in which enforcement is sought, it shall be determined by reference to the place of enforcement.*

---

*Schedule 1 is substituted by SI 2000/1824, when in force.

6–1687 Article 33.   The procedure for making the application shall be governed by the law of the State in which enforcement is sought.

The applicant must give an address for service of process within the area of jurisdiction of the court applied to. However, if the law of the State in which enforcement is sought does not provide for the furnishing of such an address, the applicant shall appoint a representative *ad litem*.

The documents referred to in Articles 46 and 47 shall be attached to the application.*

---

*Schedule 1 is substituted by SI 2000/1824, when in force.

6–1688 Article 34.   The court applied to shall give its decision without delay; the party against whom enforcement is sought shall not at this stage of the proceedings be entitled to make any submissions on the application.

The application may be refused only for one of the reasons specified in Articles 27 and 28.

Under no circumstances may the foreign judgment be reviewed as to its substance.*

---

*Schedule 1 is substituted by SI 2000/1824, when in force.

6–1689 Article 35 The appropriate officer of the court shall without delay bring the decision given on the application to the notice of the applicant in accordance with the procedure laid down by the law of the State in which enforcement is sought.*

---

*Schedule 1 is substituted by SI 2000/1824, when in force.

6–1690

   Article 36.   If enforcement is authorised, the party against whom enforcement is sought may appeal against the decision within one month of service thereof.

If that party is domiciled in a Contracting State other than that in which the decision authorising enforcement was given, the time for appealing shall be two months and shall run from the date of service, either on him in person or at his residence. No extension of time may be granted on account of distance.*

---

*Schedule 1 is substituted by SI 2000/1824, when in force.

6–1691   Article 37.   1 An appeal against the decision authorising enforcement shall be lodged in accordance with the rules governing procedure in contentious matters:

— in Belgium, with the tribunal de première instance or rechtbank van eerste aanleg,
— in Denmark, with the landsret,
— in the Federal Republic of Germany, with the Oberlandesgericht,
— in Greece, with the Åñåôåßß,
— in Spain, with the Audiencia Provincial,
— in France, with the cour d'appel;
— in Ireland, with the High Court,
— in Italy, with the corte d'appello,
— in Luxembourg, with the Cour supérieure de justice sitting as a court of civil appeal,
— in the Netherlands, with the arrondissementsrechtbank,
— in Portugal, with the Tribunal de Relaçãao,
— in the United Kingdom:

    (*a*) in England and Wales, with the High Court of Justice, or in the case of a maintenance judgment with the Magistrates' Court;
    (*b*) in Scotland, with the Court of Session, or in the case of a maintenance judgment with the Sheriff Court;
    (*c*) in Northern Ireland, with the High Court of Justice, or in the case of a maintenance judgment with the Magistrates' Court.

2 The judgment given on the appeal may be contested only:

— in Belgium, Greece, Spain, France, Italy, Luxembourg and in the Netherlands, by an appeal in cassation,
— in Denmark, by an appeal to the højesteret, with the leave of the Minister of Justice,
— in the Federal Republic of Germany, by a Rechtsbeschwerde,
— in Ireland, by an appeal on a point of law to the Supreme Court,
— in Portugal, by an appeal on a point of law,
— in the United Kingdom, by a single further appeal on a point of law.*

*Schedule 1 is substituted by SI 2000/1824, when in force.

6–1692   Article 38.   The court with which the appeal under Article 37(1) is lodged may, on the application of the appellant, stay the proceedings if an ordinary appeal has been lodged against the judgment in the State of origin or if the time for such an appeal has not yet expired; in the latter case, the court may specify the time within which such an appeal is to be lodged.

Where the judgment was given in Ireland or the United Kingdom, any form of appeal available in the State of origin shall be treated as an ordinary appeal for the purposes of the first paragraph.

The court may also make enforcement conditional on the provision of such security as it shall determine.*

*Schedule 1 is substituted by SI 2000/1824, when in force.

6–1693   Article 39.   During the time specified for an appeal pursuant to Article 36 and until any such appeal has been determined, no measures of enforcement may be taken other than protective measures taken against the property of the party against whom enforcement is sought.

The decision authorising enforcement shall carry with it the power to proceed to any such protective measures.*

*Schedule 1 is substituted by SI 2000/1824, when in force.

6–1694   Article 40.   1 If the application for enforcement is refused, the applicant may appeal:

— in Belgium, to the cour d'appel or hof van beroep,
— in Denmark, to the landsret,
— in the Federal Republic of Germany, to the Oberlandesgericht,
— in Greece, to the Åñåôåßß,
— in Spain, to the Audiencia Provincial,
— in France, to the cour d'appel,
— in Ireland, to the High Court,
— in Italy, to the corte d'appello,
— in Luxembourg, to the Cour supérieure de justice sitting as a court of civil appeal,
— in the Netherlands, to the gerechtshof,
— in Portugal, to the Tribunal da Relação,
— in the United Kingdom:

    (*a*) in England and Wales, to the High Court of Justice, or in the case of a maintenance judgment to the Magistrates' Court;
    (*b*) in Scotland, to the Court of Session, or in the case of a maintenance judgment to the Sheriff Court;
    (*c*) in Northern Ireland, to the High Court of Justice, or in the case of a maintenance judgment to the Magistrates' Court.

2 The party against whom enforcement is sought shall be summoned to appear before the appellate court. If he fails to appear, the provisions of the second and third paragraphs of Article 20 shall apply even where he is not domiciled in any of the Contracting States.*

*Schedule 1 is substituted by SI 2000/1824, when in force.

6–1695   Article 41.   A judgment given on an appeal provided for in Article 40 may be contested only:

— in Belgium, Greece, Spain, France, Italy, Luxembourg and in the Netherlands, by an appeal in cassation,
— in Denmark, by an appeal to the højesteret, with the leave of the Minister of Justice,
— in the Federal Republic of Germany, by a Rechtsbeschwerde,
— in Ireland, by an appeal on a point of law to the Supreme Court,
— in Portugal, by an appeal on a point of law,
— in the United Kingdom, by a single further appeal on a point of law.*

*Schedule 1 is substituted by SI 2000/1824, when in force.

6–1696   Article 42.   Where a foreign judgment has been given in respect of several matters and enforcement cannot be authorised for all of them, the court shall authorise enforcement for one or more of them.

An applicant may request partial enforcement of a judgment.*

*Schedule 1 is substituted by SI 2000/1824, when in force.

6–1697   Article 43.   A foreign judgment which orders a periodic payment by way of a penalty shall be enforceable in the State in which enforcement is sought only if the amount of the payment has been finally determined by the courts of the State of origin.*

*Schedule 1 is substituted by SI 2000/1824, when in force.

6–1698   Article 44.   An applicant who, in the State of origin, has benefited from complete or partial legal aid or exemption from costs or expenses, shall be entitled, in the procedures provided for in Articles 32 to 35, to benefit from the most favourable legal aid or the most extensive exemption from costs or expenses provided for by the law of the State addressed.

However, an applicant who requests the enforcement of a decision given by an administrative authority in Denmark in respect of a maintenance order may, in the State addressed, claim the benefits referred to in the first paragraph if he presents a statement from the Danish Ministry of Justice to the effect that he fulfils the economic requirements to qualify for the grant of complete or partial legal aid or exemption from costs or expenses.*

*Schedule 1 is substituted by SI 2000/1824, when in force.

6–1699   Article 45.   No security, bond or deposit, however described, shall be required of a party who in one Contracting State applies for enforcement of a judgment given in another Contracting State on the ground that he is a foreign national or that he is not domiciled or resident in the State in which enforcement is sought.*

*Schedule 1 is substituted by SI 2000/1824, when in force.

SECTION 3
COMMON PROVISIONS

6–1700   Article 46.   A party seeking recognition or applying for enforcement of a judgment shall produce:

1.   a copy of the judgment which satisfies the conditions necessary to establish its authenticity;
2.   in the case of a judgment given in default, the original or a certified true copy of the document which establishes that the party in default was served with the document instituting the proceedings or with an equivalent document.*

*Schedule 1 is substituted by SI 2000/1824, when in force.

6–1701   Article 47.   A party applying for enforcement shall also produce:

1.   documents which establish that, according to the law of the State of origin, the judgment is enforceable and has been served;
2.   where appropriate, a document showing that the applicant is in receipt of legal aid in the State of origin.*

*Schedule 1 is substituted by SI 2000/1824, when in force.

6–1702   Article 48.   If the documents specified in point 2 of Articles 46 and 47 are not produced, the court may specify a time for their production, accept equivalent documents or, if it considers that it has sufficient information before it, dispense with their production.

If the court so requires, a translation of the documents shall be produced; the translation shall be certified by a person qualified to do so in one of the Contracting States.*

*Schedule 1 is substituted by SI 2000/1824, when in force.

6–1703   Article 49.   No legalisation or other similar formality shall be required in respect of the documents referred to in Articles 46 or 47 or the second paragraph of Article 48, or in respect of a document appointing a representative *ad litem*.*

*Schedule 1 is substituted by SI 2000/1824, when in force.

TITLE IV
AUTHENTIC INSTRUMENTS AND COURT SETTLEMENTS

6–1704   Article 50.   A document which has been formally drawn up or registered as an authentic instrument and is enforceable in one Contracting State shall, in another Contracting State, be declared enforceable there, on application made in accordance with the procedures provided for in Article 31 *et seq.* The application may be refused only if enforcement of the instrument is contrary to public policy in the State addressed.

The instrument produced must satisfy the conditions necessary to establish its authenticity in the State of origin. The provisions of Section 3 of Title III shall apply as appropriate.*

---

*Schedule 1 is substituted by SI 2000/1824, when in force.

6–1705   Article 51.   A settlement which has been approved by a court in the course of proceedings and is enforceable in the State in which it was concluded shall be enforceable in the State addressed under the same conditions as authentic instruments.*

---

*Schedule 1 is substituted by SI 2000/1824, when in force.

TITLE V
GENERAL PROVISIONS

6–1706   Article 52.   In order to determine whether a party is domiciled in the Contracting State whose courts are seised of a matter, the Court shall apply its internal law.

If a party is not domiciled in the State whose courts are seised of the matter, then, in order to determine whether the party is domiciled in another Contracting State, the court shall apply the law of that State.*

---

*Schedule 1 is substituted by SI 2000/1824, when in force.

6–1707   Article 53.   For the purposes of this Convention, the seat of a company or other legal person or association of natural or legal persons shall be treated as its domicile. However, in order to determine that seat, the court shall apply its rules of private international law.

In order to determine whether a trust is domiciled in the Contracting State whose courts are seised of the matter, the court shall apply its rules of private international law.*

---

*Schedule 1 is substituted by SI 2000/1824, when in force.

TITLE VI
TRANSITIONAL PROVISIONS

6–1708   Article 54.   The provisions of the Convention shall apply only to legal proceedings instituted and to documents formally drawn up or registered as authentic instruments after its entry into force in the State of origin and, where recognition or enforcement of a judgment or authentic instruments is sought, in the State addressed.

However, judgments given after the date of entry into force of this Convention between the State of origin and the State addressed in proceedings instituted before that date shall be recognised and enforced in accordance with the provisions of Title III if jurisdiction was founded upon rules which accorded with those provided for either in Title II of this Convention or in a convention concluded between the State of origin and the State addressed which was in force when the proceedings were instituted.*

---

*Schedule 1 is substituted by SI 2000/1824, when in force.

6–1708A

TITLE VII
RELATIONSHIP TO OTHER CONVENTIONS
Articles 55–59*

---

*Schedule 1 is substituted by SI 2000/1824, when in force.

6–1708B

TITLE VIII
FINAL PROVISIONS
Articles 60–68*

---

*Schedule 1 is substituted by SI 2000/1824, when in force.

6–1709   SCHEDULE 2

Text of 1971 Protocol, as amended

6–1710   SCHEDULE 3

Text of Titles V and VI of Accession Convention

6–1711   SCHEDULE 3B

Text of Titles VI and VII of 1989 Accession Convention

6–1712

Section 3A(2)
SCHEDULE 3C
TEXT OF THE LUGANO CONVENTION
ARRANGEMENT OF PROVISIONS

(As inserted by the Civil Jurisdiction and Judgments Act 1991, Sch 1)

TITLE I. SCOPE (Article 1)
TITLE II. JURISDICTION

Section 1. General provisions (Articles 2–4).
Section 2. Special jurisdiction (Articles 5–6A).
Section 3. Jurisdiction in matters relating to insurance (Articles 7–12A).
Section 4. Jurisdiction over consumer contracts (Articles 13–15).
Section 5. Exclusive jurisdiction (Article 16).
Section 6. Prorogation of jurisdiction (Articles 17–18).
Section 7. Examination as to jurisdiction and admissibility (Articles 19–20).
Section 8. *Lis pendens*—related actions (Articles 21–23).
Section 9. Provisional, including protective, measures (Article 24).

TITLE III. RECOGNITION AND ENFORCEMENT

Definition of "judgment" (Article 25).
Section 1. Recognition (Articles 26–30).
Section 2. Enforcement (Articles 31–45).
Section 3. Common provisions (Articles 46–49).

TITLE IV. AUTHENTIC INSTRUMENTS AND COURT SETTLEMENTS (Articles 50–51)
TITLE V. GENERAL PROVISIONS (Articles 52–53)
TITLE VI. TRANSITIONAL PROVISIONS (Articles 56–54A)
TITLE VII. RELATIONSHIP TO THE BRUSSELS CONVENTION AND TO OTHER CONVENTIONS (Articles 54B–59)
TITLE VIII. FINAL PROVISIONS (Articles 60–68)
PROTOCOL NO 1—ON CERTAIN QUESTIONS OF JURISDICTION, PROCEDURE AND EN-FORCEMENT
PROTOCOL NO 2—ON THE UNIFORM INTERPRETATION OF THE CONVENTION
PROTOCOL NO 3—ON THE APPLICATION OF ARTICLE 57

6–1713
CONVENTION
ON JURISDICTION AND THE ENFORCEMENT OF JUDGMENTS IN CIVIL AND COMMERCIAL MATTERS
PREAMBLE

The High Contracting Parties to this Convention,

Anxious to strengthen in their territories the legal protection of persons therein established,

Considering that it is necessary for this purpose to determine the international jurisdiction of their courts, to facilitate recognition and to introduce an expeditious procedure for securing the enforcement of judgments, authentic instruments and court settlements,

Aware of the links between them, which have been sanctioned in the economic field by the free trade agreements concluded between the European Economic Community and the States members of the European Free Trade Association,

Taking into account the Brussels Convention of 27 September 1968 on jurisdiction and the enforcement of judgments in civil and commercial matters, as amended by the Accession Conventions under the successive enlargements of the European Communities,

Persuaded that the extension of the principles of that Convention to the States parties to this instrument will strengthen legal and economic co-operation in Europe,

Desiring to ensure as uniform an interpretation as possible of this instrument,

Have in this spirit decided to conclude this Convention and

Have agreed as follows:

TITLE I
SCOPE

6–1714 **Article 1.** This Convention shall apply in civil and commercial matters whatever the nature of the court or tribunal. It shall not extend, in particular, to revenue, customs or administrative matters.

The Convention shall not apply to:

1. the status or legal capacity of natural persons, rights in property arising out of a matrimonial relationship, wills and succession;
2. bankruptcy, proceedings relating to the winding-up of insolvent companies or other legal persons, judicial arrangements, compositions and analogous proceedings;
3. social security;
4. arbitration.

TITLE II
JURISDICTION

SECTION 1
GENERAL PROVISIONS

6–1715 Article 2. Subject to the provisions of this Convention, persons domiciled in a Contracting State shall, whatever their nationality, be sued in the courts of that State.

Persons who are not nationals of the State in which they are domiciled shall be governed by the rules of jurisdiction applicable to nationals of that State.

6–1716 Article 3. Persons domiciled in a Contracting State may be sued in the courts of another Contracting State only by virtue of the rules set out in Sections 2 to 6 of this Title.

In particular the following provisions shall not be applicable as against them:

— in Belgium: Article 15 of the civil code (Code civil—Burgerlijk Wetboek) and Article 638 of the judicial code (Code judiciaire—Gerechtelijk Wetboek),
— in Denmark: Article 246(2) and (3) of the law on civil procedure (Lov om rettens pleje),
— in the Federal Republic of Germany: Article 23 of the code of civil procedure (Zivilprozeßordnung),
— in Greece: Article 40 of the code of civil procedure (Κώδικας Πολιτικής Δικουομίας),
— in France: Articles 14 and 15 of the civil code (Code civil),
— in Ireland: the rules which enable jurisdiction to be founded on the document instituting the proceedings having been served on the defendant during his temporary presence in Ireland,
— in Iceland: Article 77 of the Civil Proceedings Act (lög um meðferð einkamála ß héraði),
— in Italy: Articles 2 and 4, Nos 1 and 2 of the code of civil procedure (Codice di procedura civile),
— in Luxembourg: Articles 14 and 15 of the civil code (Code civil),
— in the Netherlands: Articles 126(3) and 127 of the code of civil procedure (Wetboek van Burgerlijke Rechtsvordering),
— in Norway: Section 32 of the Civil Proceedings Act (tvistemÅlsloven),
— in Austria: Article 99 of the Law on Court Jurisdiction (Jurisdiktionsnorm),
— in Portugal: Articles 65(1)(*c*), 65(2) and 65A(*c*) of the code of civil procedure (Código de Processo Civil) and Article 11 of the code of labour procedure (Código de Processo de Trabalho),
— in Switzerland: le for du lieu du séquestre/Gerichtsstand des Arrestortes /foro del luogo del sequestro within the meaning of Article 4 of the loi fédérale sur le droit international privé/Bundesgesetz über das internationale Privatrecht /legge federale sul diritto internazionale privato,
— in Finland: the second, third and fourth sentences of Section 1 of Chapter 10 of the Code of Judicial Procedure (oikeudenkäymiskaari/rättegångsbalken),
— in Sweden: the first sentence of Section 3 of Chapter 10 of the Code of Judicial Procedure (Rättegångsbalken),
— in the United Kingdom: the rules which enable jurisdiction to be founded on:
  (*a*) the document instituting the proceedings having been served on the defendant during his temporary presence in the United Kingdom; or
  (*b*) the presence within the United Kingdom of property belonging to the defendant; or
  (*c*) the seizure by the plaintiff of property situated in the United Kingdom.*

---

*Paragraph 3 is amended by SI 2000/1824, when in force.

6–1717 Article 4. If the defendant is not domiciled in a Contracting State, the jurisdiction of the courts of each Contracting State shall, subject to the provisions of Article 16, be determined by the law of that State.

As against such a defendant, any person domiciled in a Contracting State may, whatever his nationality, avail himself in that State of the rules of jurisdiction there in force, and in particular those specified in the second paragraph of Article 3, in the same way as the nationals of that State.

SECTION 2
SPECIAL JURISDICTION

6–1718 Article 5. A person domiciled in a Contracting State may, in another Contracting State, be sued:

1. . . .
2. in matters relating to maintenance[1], in the courts for the place where the maintenance creditor is domiciled or habitually resident or, if the matter is ancillary to proceedings concerning the status of a person, in the court which, according to its own law, has jurisdiction to entertain those proceedings, unless that jurisdiction is based solely on the nationality of one of the parties;
3–7. . . .

---

1. 'Maintenance' excludes rights in property arising out of a matrimonial relationship (art 1, ante) and see para **6–230 Civil Jurisdiction and Judgments Act 1982** ante.

6–1719 Article 6. A person domiciled in a Contracting State may also be sued:

1. where he is one of a number of defendants, in the courts for the place where any one of them is domiciled;
2. as a third party in an action on a warranty or guarantee or in any other third party proceedings, in the court seised of the original proceedings, unless these were instituted solely with the object of removing him from the jurisdiction of the court which would be competent in his case;
3. on a counterclaim arising from the same contract or facts on which the original claim was based, in the court in which the original claim is pending;
4. in matters relating to a contract, if the action may be combined with an action against the same defendant in matters relating to rights *in rem* in immovable property, in the court of the Contracting State in which the property is situated.

6–1720   Article 6A.   Where by virtue of this Convention a court of a Contracting State has jurisdiction in actions relating to liability arising from the use or operation of a ship, that court, or any other court substituted for this purpose by the internal law of that State, shall also have jurisdiction over claims for limitation of such liability.

SECTION 6
PROROGATION OF JURISDICTION

6–1721   Article 17.   1 If the parties, one or more of whom is domiciled in a Contracting State, have agreed that a court or the courts of a Contracting State are to have jurisdiction to settle any disputes which have arisen or which may arise in connection with a particular legal relationship, that court or those courts shall have exclusive jurisdiction. Such an agreement conferring jurisdiction shall be either:

  (*a*) in writing or evidenced in writing, or
  (*b*) in a form which accords with practices which the parties have established between themselves, or
  (*c*) in international trade or commerce, in a form which accords with a usage of which the parties are or ought
       to have been aware and which in such trade or commerce is widely known to, and regularly observed by,
       parties to contracts of the type involved in the particular trade or commerce concerned.

Where such an agreement is concluded by parties, none of whom is domiciled in a Contracting State, the courts of other Contracting States shall have no jurisdiction over their disputes unless the court or courts chosen have declined jurisdiction.

2 The court or courts of a Contracting State on which a trust instrument has conferred jurisdiction shall have exclusive jurisdiction in any proceedings brought against a settlor, trustee or beneficiary, if relations between these persons or their rights or obligations under the trust are involved.

3 Agreements or provisions of a trust instrument conferring jurisdiction shall have no legal force if they are contrary to the provisions of Article 12 or 15, or if the courts whose jurisdiction they purport to exclude have exclusive jurisdiction by virtue of Article 16.

4 If an agreement conferring jurisdiction was concluded for the benefit of only one of the parties, that party shall retain the right to bring proceedings in any other court which has jurisdiction by virtue of this Convention.

5 In matters relating to individual contracts of employment an agreement conferring jurisdiction shall have legal force only if it is entered into after the dispute has arisen.

6–1722   Article 18.   Apart from jurisdiction derived from other provisions of this Convention, a court of a Contracting State before whom a defendant enters an appearance shall have jurisdiction. This rule shall not apply where appearance was entered solely to contest the jurisdiction, or where another court has exclusive jurisdiction by virtue of Article 16.

SECTION 7
EXAMINATION AS TO JURISDICTION AND ADMISSIBILITY

6–1723   Article 19.   Where a court of a Contracting State is seised of a claim which is principally concerned with a matter over which the courts of another Contracting State have exclusive jurisdiction by virtue of Article 16, it shall declare of its own motion that it has no jurisdiction.

6–1724   Article 20.   Where a defendant domiciled in one Contracting State is sued in a court of another Contracting State and does not enter an appearance, the court shall declare of its own motion that it has no jurisdiction unless its jurisdiction is derived from the provisions of this Convention.

The court shall stay the proceedings so long as it is not shown that the defendant has been able to receive the document instituting the proceedings or an equivalent document in sufficient time to enable him to arrange for his defence, or that all necessary steps have been taken to this end.

The provisions of the foregoing paragraph shall be replaced by those of Article 15 of the Hague Convention of 15 November 1965 on the service abroad of judicial and extrajudicial documents in civil or commercial matters, if the document instituting the proceedings or notice thereof had to be transmitted abroad in accordance with that Convention.

SECTION 8
LIS PENDENS—RELATED ACTIONS

6–1725   Article 21.   Where proceedings involving the same cause of action and between the same parties are brought in the courts of different Contracting States, any court other than the court first seised shall of its own motion stay its proceedings until such time as the jurisdiction of the court first seised is established.

Where the jurisdiction of the court first seised is established, any court other than the court first seised shall decline jurisdiction in favour of that court.

6–1726   Article 22.   Where related actions are brought in the courts of different Contracting States, any court other than the court first seised may, while the actions are pending at first instance, stay its proceedings.

A court other than the court first seised may also, on the application of one of the parties, decline jurisdiction if the law of that court permits the consolidation of related actions and the court first seised has jurisdiction over both actions.

For the purposes of this Article, actions are deemed to be related where they are so closely connected that it is expedient to hear and determine them together to avoid the risk of irreconcilable judgments resulting from separate proceedings.

6–1727   Article 23.   Where actions come within the exclusive jurisdiction of several courts, any court other than the court first seised shall decline jurisdiction in favour of that court.

SECTION 9
PROVISIONAL, INCLUDING PROTECTIVE, MEASURES

6–1728 Article 24.   Application may be made to the courts of a Contracting State for such provisional, including protective, measures as may be available under the law of that State, even if, under this Convention, the courts of another Contracting State have jurisdiction as to the substance of the matter.

TITLE III
RECOGNITION AND ENFORCEMENT

6–1729 Article 25.   For the purposes of this Convention, 'judgment' means any judgment given by a court or tribunal of a Contracting State, whatever the judgment may be called, including a decree, order, decision or writ of execution, as well as the determination of costs or expenses by an officer of the court.

SECTION 1
RECOGNITION

6–1730 Article 26.   A judgment given in a Contracting State shall be recognised in the other Contracting States without any special procedure being required.

Any interested party who raises the recognition of a judgment as the principal issue in a dispute may, in accordance with the procedures provided for in Sections 2 and 3 of this Title, apply for a decision that the judgment be recognised.

If the outcome of proceedings in a court of a Contracting State depends on the determination of an incidental question of recognition that court shall have jurisdiction over that question.

6–1731 Article 27.   A judgment shall not be recognised:

1. if such recognition is contrary to public policy in the State in which recognition is sought;
2. where it was given in default of appearance, if the defendant was not duly served with the document which instituted the proceedings or with an equivalent document in sufficient time to enable him to arrange for his defence;
3. if the judgment is irreconcilable with a judgment given in a dispute between the same parties in the State in which recognition is sought;
4. if the court of the State of origin, in order to arrive at its judgment, has decided a preliminary question concerning the status or legal capacity of natural persons, rights in property arising out of a matrimonial relationship, wills or succession in a way that conflicts with a rule of the private international law of the State in which the recognition is sought, unless the same result would have been reached by the application of the rules of private international law of that State;
5. if the judgment is irreconcilable with an earlier judgment given in a non-contracting State involving the same cause of action and between the same parties, provided that this latter judgment fulfils the conditions necessary for its recognition in the State addressed.

6–1732 Article 28.   Moreover, a judgment shall not be recognised if it conflicts with the provisions of Section 3, 4 or 5 of Title II or in a case provided for in Article 59.

A judgment may furthermore be refused recognition in any case provided for in Article 54B(3) or 57(4).

In its examination of the grounds of jurisdiction referred to in the foregoing paragraphs, the court or authority applied to shall be bound by the findings of fact on which the court of the State of origin based its jurisdiction.

Subject to the provisions of the first and second paragraphs, the jurisdiction of the court of the State of origin may not be reviewed; the test of public policy referred to in Article 27(1) may not be applied to the rules relating to jurisdiction.

6–1733 Article 29.   Under no circumstances may a foreign judgment be reviewed as to its substance.

6–1734 Article 30.   A court of a Contracting State in which recognition is sought of a judgment given in another Contracting State may stay the proceedings if an ordinary appeal against the judgment has been lodged.

A court of a Contracting State in which recognition is sought of a judgment given in Ireland or the United Kingdom may stay the proceedings if enforcement is suspended in the State of origin by reason of an appeal.

SECTION 2
ENFORCEMENT

6–1735 Article 31.   A judgment given in a Contracting State and enforceable in that State shall be enforced in another Contracting State when, on the application of any interested party, it has been declared enforceable there.

However, in the United Kingdom, such a judgment shall be enforced in England and Wales, in Scotland, or in Northern Ireland when, on the application of any interested party, it has been registered for enforcement in that part of the United Kingdom.

6–1736 Article 32.   1 The application shall be submitted:

— in Belgium, to the tribunal de première instance or rechtbank van eerste aanleg,
— in Denmark, to the byret,
— in the Federal Republic of Germany, to the presiding judge of a chamber of the Landgericht,
— in Greece, to the Μονομελές Πρωτοδικείο,
— in Spain, to the Juzgado de Primera Instancia,
— in France, to the presiding judge of the tribunal de grande instance,
— in Ireland, to the High Court,
— in Iceland, to the héraðsdómari,
— in Italy, to the corte d'appello,

— in Luxembourg, to the presiding judge of the tribunal d'arrondissement,
— in the Netherlands, to the presiding judge of the arrondissementsrechtbank,
— in Norway, to the herredsrett or byrett as namsrett,
— in Austria, to the Landesgericht or the Kreisgericht,
— in Portugal, to the Tribunal Judicial de Círculo,
— in Switzerland:

   (a) in respect of judgments ordering the payment of a sum of money, to the juge de la mainlevée/ Rechtsöffnungsrichter/giudice competente a pronunciare sul rigetto dell'opposizione, within the framework of the procedure governed by Articles 80 and 81 of the loi fédérale sur la poursuite pour dettes et la faillite/Bundesgesetz über Schuldbetreibung und Konkurs/legge federale sulla esecuzione e sul fallimento;
   (b) in respect of judgments ordering a performance other than the payment of a sum of money, to the juge cantonal d'exequatur compétent/zuständiger kantonaler Vollstreckungsrichter/giudice cantonale competente a pronunciare l'exequatur,

— in Finland, to the ulosotonhaltija/överexekutor,
— in Sweden, to the Svea hovrätt,
— in the United Kingdom:

   (a) in England and Wales, to the High Court of Justice, or in the case of a maintenance judgment to the Magistrates' Court on transmission by the Secretary of State;
   (b) in Scotland, to the Court of Session, or in the case of a maintenance judgment to the Sheriff Court on transmission by the Secretary of State;
   (c) in Northern Ireland, to the High Court of Justice, or in the case of a maintenance judgment to the Magistrates' Court on transmission by the Secretary of State.

2 The jurisdiction of local courts shall be determined by reference to the place of domicile of the party against whom enforcement is sought. If he is not domiciled in the State in which enforcement is sought, it shall be determined by reference to the place of enforcement.*

---

*Paragraph 32 is amended by SI 2000/1824, when in force.

6–1737   Article 33.   The procedure for making the application shall be governed by the law of the State in which enforcement is sought.
The applicant must give an address for service of process within the area of jurisdiction of the court applied to. However, if the law of the State in which enforcement is sought does not provide for the furnishing of such an address, the applicant shall appoint a representative *ad litem*.
The documents referred to in Articles 46 and 47 shall be attached to the application.

6–1738   Article 34.   The court applied to shall give its decision without delay; the party against whom enforcement is sought shall not at this stage of the proceedings be entitled to make any submissions on the application.
The application may be refused only for one of the reasons specified in Articles 27 and 28.
Under no circumstances may the foreign judgment be reviewed as to its substance.

6–1739   Article 35.   The appropriate officer of the court shall without delay bring the decision given on the application to the notice of the applicant in accordance with the procedure laid down by the law of the State in which enforcement is sought.

6–1740   Article 36.   If enforcement is authorised, the party against whom enforcement is sought may appeal against the decision within one month of service thereof.
If that party is domiciled in a Contracting State other than that in which the decision authorising enforcement was given, the time for appealing shall be two months and shall run from the date of service, either on him in person or at his residence. No extension of time may be granted on account of distance.

6–1741   Article 37.   1 An appeal against the decision authorising enforcement shall be lodged in accordance with the rules governing procedure in contentious matters:

— in Belgium, with the tribunal de première instance or rechtbank van eerste aanleg,
— in Denmark, with the landsret,
— in the Federal Republic of Germany, with the Oberlandesgericht,
— in Greece, with the Åñåôáâ,
— in Spain, with the Audiencia Provincial,
— in France, with the cour d'appel,
— in Ireland, with the High Court,
— in Iceland, with the héraðsdómari,
— in Italy, with the corte d'appello,
— in Luxembourg, with the Cour supérieure de justice sitting as a court of civil appeal,
— in the Netherlands, with the arrondissementsrechtbank,
— in Norway, with the lagmannsrett,
— in Austria, with the Landesgericht or the Kreisgericht,
— in Portugal, with the Tribunal da Relçatao,
— in Switzerland, with the tribunal cantonal /Kantonsgericht /tribunale cantonale,
— in Finland, with the hovioikeus/hovrätt,
— in Sweden, with the Svea hovrätt,
— in the United Kingdom:

    (a) in England and Wales, with the High Court of Justice, or in the case of a maintenance judgment with the Magistrates' Court;

    (b) in Scotland, with the Court of Session, or in the case of a maintenance judgment with the Sheriff Court;

    (c) in Northern Ireland, with the High Court of Justice, or in the case of a maintenance judgment with the Magistrates' Court.

2 The judgment given on the appeal may be contested only:

— in Belgium, Greece, Spain, France, Italy, Luxembourg and in the Netherlands, by an appeal in cassation,
— in Denmark, by an appeal to the højesteret, with the leave of the Minister of Justice,
— in the Federal Republic of Germany, by a Rechtsbeschwerde,
— in Ireland, by an appeal on a point of law to the Supreme Court,
— in Iceland, by an appeal to the Hæstiréttur,
— in Norway, by an appeal (kjæremål or anke) to the Hoyesteretts Kjæremålsutvalg or Hoyesterett,
— in Austria, in the case of an appeal, by a Revisionsrekurs and, in the case of opposition proceedings, by a Berufung with the possibility of a Revision,
— in Portugal, by an appeal on a point of law,
— in Switzerland, by a recours de droit public devant le tribunal fédéral /staatsrechtliche Beschwerde beim Bundesgericht /ricorso di diritto pubblico davanti al tribunale federale,
— in Finland, by an appeal to the korkein oikeus /högsta domstolen,
— in Sweden, by an appeal to the högsta domstolen,
— in the United Kingdom, by a single further appeal on a point of law.*

---

*Paragraph 37 is amended by SI 2000/1824, when in force.

6–1742   Article 38.   The court with which the appeal under the first paragraph of Article 37 is lodged may, on the application of the appellant, stay the proceedings if an ordinary appeal has been lodged against the judgment in the State of origin or if the time for such an appeal has not yet expired; in the latter case, the court may specify the time within which such an appeal is to be lodged.

    Where the judgment was given in Ireland or the United Kingdom, any form of appeal available in the State of origin shall be treated as an ordinary appeal for the purposes of the first paragraph.

    The court may also make enforcement conditional on the provision of such security as it shall determine.

6–1743   Article 39.   During the time specified for an appeal pursuant to Article 36 and until any such appeal has been determined, no measures of enforcement may be taken other than protective measures taken against the property of the party against whom enforcement is sought.

    The decision authorising enforcement shall carry with it the power to proceed to any such protective measures.

6–1744   Article 40.   1 If the application for enforcement is refused, the applicant may appeal:

— in Belgium, to the cour d'appel or hof van beroep,
— in Denmark, to the landsret,
— in the Federal Republic of Germany, to the Oberlandesgericht,
— in Greece, to the Åñåôåßö,
— in Spain, to the Audiencia Provincial,
— in France, to the cour d'appel,
— in Ireland, to the High Court,
— in Iceland, to the héraðsdómari,
— in Italy, to the corte d'appello,
— in Luxembourg, to the Cour supérieure de justice sitting as a court of civil appeal,
— in the Netherlands, to the gerechtshof,
— in Norway, to the lagmannsrett,
— in Austria, to the Landesgericht or the Kreisgericht,
— in Portugal, to the Tribunal da Relaçatao,
— in Switzerland, to the tribunal cantonal /Kantonsgericht /tribunale cantonale,
— in Finland, to the hovioikeus /hovrätt,
— in Sweden, to the Svea hovrätt,
— in the United Kingdom:

    (a) in England and Wales, to the High Court of Justice, or in the case of a maintenance judgment to the Magistrates' Court;

    (b) in Scotland, to the Court of Session, or in the case of a maintenance judgment to the Sheriff Court;

    (c) in Northern Ireland, to the High Court of Justice, or in the case of a maintenance judgment to the Magistrates' Court.

2 The party against whom enforcement is sought shall be summoned to appear before the appellate court. If he fails to appear, the provisions of the second and third paragraphs of Article 20 shall apply even where he is not domiciled in any of the Contracting States.*

---

*Paragraph 40 is amended by SI 2000/1824, when in force.

6–1745   Article 41.   A judgment given on an appeal provided for in Article 40 may be contested only:

— in Belgium, Greece, Spain, France, Italy, Luxembourg and in the Netherlands, by an appeal in cassation,
— in Denmark, by an appeal to the højesteret, with the leave of the Minister of Justice,
— in the Federal Republic of Germany, by a Rechtsbeschwerde,
— in Ireland, by an appeal on a point of law to the Supreme Court,
— in Iceland, by an appeal to the Hæstiréttur,

- — in Norway, by an appeal (kjæremål or anke) to the Hoyesteretts kjæremålsutvalg or Hoyesterett,
- — in Austria, by a Revisionsrekurs,
- — in Portugal, by an appeal on a point of law,
- — in Switzerland, by a recours de droit public devant le tribunal fédéral /staatsrechtliche Beschwerde beim Bundesgericht /ricorso di diritto pubblico davanti al tribunale federale,
- — in Finland, by an appeal to the korkein oikeus /högsta domstolen,
- — in Sweden, by an appeal to the högsta domstolen,
- — in the United Kingdom, by a single further appeal on a point of law.*

---

*Paragraph 41 is amended by SI 2000/1824, when in force.

6–1746 Article 42. Where a foreign judgment has been given in respect of several matters and enforcement cannot be authorised for all of them, the court shall authorise enforcement for one or more of them.

An applicant may request partial enforcement of a judgment.

6–1747 Article 43. A foreign judgment which orders a periodic payment by way of a penalty shall be enforceable in the State in which enforcement is sought only if the amount of the payment has been finally determined by the courts of the State of origin.

6–1748 Article 44. An applicant who, in the State of origin, has benefited from complete or partial legal aid or exemption from costs or expenses, shall be entitled, in the procedures provided for in Articles 32 to 35, to benefit from the most favourable legal aid or the most extensive exemption from costs or expenses provided for by the law of the State addressed.

However, an applicant who requests the enforcement of a decision given by an administrative authority in Denmark or in Iceland in respect of a maintenance order may, in the State addressed, claim the benefits referred to in the first paragraph if he presents a statement from, respectively, the Danish Ministry of Justice or the Icelandic Ministry of Justice to the effect that he fulfils the economic requirements to qualify for the grant of complete or partial legal aid or exemption from costs or expenses.

6–1749 Article 45. No security, bond or deposit, however described, shall be required of a party who in one Contracting State applies for enforcement of a judgment given in another Contracting State on the ground that he is a foreign national or that he is not domiciled or resident in the State in which enforcement is sought.

SECTION 3
COMMON PROVISIONS

6–1750 Article 46. A party seeking recognition or applying for enforcement of a judgment shall produce:

1. a copy of the judgment which satisfies the conditions necessary to establish its authenticity;
2. in the case of a judgment given in default, the original or a certified true copy of the document which establishes that the party in default was served with the document instituting the proceedings or with an equivalent document.

6–1751 Article 47. A party applying for enforcement shall also produce:

1. documents which establish that, according to the law of the State of origin, the judgment is enforceable and has been served;
2. where appropriate, a document showing that the applicant is in receipt of legal aid in the State of origin.

6–1752 Article 48. If the documents specified in Article 46(2) and Article 47(2) are not produced, the court may specify a time for their production, accept equivalent documents or, if it considers that it has sufficient information before it, dispense with their production.

If the court so requires, a translation of the documents shall be produced; the translation shall be certified by a person qualified to do so in one of the Contracting States.

6–1753 Article 49. No legalisation or other similar formality shall be required in respect of the documents referred to in Article 46 or 47 or the second paragraph of Article 48, or in respect of a document appointing a representative *ad litem*.

TITLE IV
AUTHENTIC INSTRUMENTS AND COURT SETTLEMENTS

6–1754 Article 50. A document which has been formally drawn up or registered as an authentic instrument and is enforceable in one Contracting State shall, in another Contracting State, be declared enforceable there, on application made in accordance with the procedures provided for in Articles 31 *et seq*. The application may be refused only if enforcement of the instrument is contrary to public policy in the State addressed.

The instrument produced must satisfy the conditions necessary to establish its authenticity in the State of origin.

The provisions of Section 3 of Title III shall apply as appropriate.

6–1755 Article 51. A settlement which has been approved by a court in the course of proceedings and is enforceable in the State in which it was concluded shall be enforceable in the State addressed under the same conditions as authentic instruments.

TITLE V
GENERAL PROVISIONS

6–1756 Article 52. In order to determine whether a party is domiciled in the Contracting State whose courts are seised of a matter, the court shall apply its internal law.

If a party is not domiciled in the State whose courts are seised of the matter, then, in order to determine whether the party is domiciled in another Contracting State, the court shall apply the law of that State.

6–1757 Article 53. For the purposes of this Convention, the seat of a company or other legal person or association of natural or legal persons shall be treated as its domicile. However, in order to determine that seat, the court shall apply its rules of private international law.

In order to determine whether a trust is domiciled in the Contracting State whose courts are seised of the matter, the court shall apply its rules of private international law.

TITLE VI
TRANSITIONAL PROVISIONS

6–1758 Article 54. The provisions of this Convention shall apply only to legal proceedings instituted[1] and to documents formally drawn up or registered as authentic instruments after its entry into force in the State of origin and, where recognition or enforcement of a judgment or authentic instrument is sought, in the State addressed.

However, judgments given after the date of entry into force of this Convention between the State of origin and the State addressed in proceedings instituted before that date shall be recognised and enforced in accordance with the provisions of Title III if jurisdiction was founded upon rules which accorded with those provided for either in Title II of this Convention or in a convention concluded between the State of origin and the State addressed which was in force when the proceedings were instituted.

If the parties to a dispute concerning a contract had agreed in writing before the entry into force of this Convention that the contract was to be governed by the law of Ireland or of a part of the United Kingdom, the courts of Ireland or of that part of the United Kingdom shall retain the right to exercise jurisdiction in the dispute.

---

1. The applicability of the Convention is determined by the date on which proceedings are instituted and not the date of the hearing to challenge the jurisdiction of the court, *Davy International Ltd v Voest* [1999] 1 All ER 103, CA.

TITLE VII
RELATIONSHIP TO THE BRUSSELS CONVENTION AND TO OTHER CONVENTIONS

TITLE VIII
FINAL PROVISIONS

Child Abduction Act 1984[1]

(1984 c 37)

PART I[2]
OFFENCES UNDER LAW OF ENGLAND AND WALES

6–1760 1. Offence of abduction of child by parent, etc. (1) Subject to subsections (5) and (8) below, a person connected with a child under the age of sixteen commits an offence if he takes or sends the child out of the United Kingdom without the appropriate consent[3].

(2) A person is connected with a child for the purposes of this section if—

(*a*) he is a parent of the child; or
(*b*) in the case of a child whose parents were not married to each other at the time of his birth, there are reasonable grounds for believing that he is the father of the child; or
(*c*) he is a guardian of the child; or
(*ca*) he is a special guardian of the child; or
(*d*) he is a person in whose favour a residence order is in force with respect to the child; or
(*e*) he has custody of the child.

(3) In this section "the appropriate consent", in relation to a child, means—

(*a*) the consent of each of the following—

(i) the child's mother;
(ii) the child's father, if he has parental responsibility for him;
(iii) any guardian of the child;
(iiia) any special guardian of the child;
(iv) any person in whose favour a residence order is in force with respect to the child;
(v) any person who has custody of the child; or

(*b*) the leave of the court granted under or by virtue of any provision of Part II of the Children Act 1989; or
(*c*) if any person has custody of the child, the leave of the court which awarded custody to him.

(4) A person does not commit an offence under this section by taking or sending a child out of the United Kingdom without obtaining the appropriate consent if—

(*a*) he is a person in whose favour there is a residence order in force with respect to the child and he takes or sends the child out of the United Kingdom for a period of less than one month; or

(*b*) he is a special guardian of the child and he takes or sends the child out of the United Kingdom for a period of less than three months.

(4A) Subsection (4) above does not apply if the person taking or sending the child out of the United Kingdom does so in breach of an order under Part II of the Children Act 1989.

(5) A person does not commit an offence under this section by doing anything without the consent of another person whose consent is required under the foregoing provisions if—

(*a*) he does it in the belief that the other person—

(i) has consented; or

(ii) would consent if he was aware of all the relevant circumstances; or

(*b*) he has taken all reasonable steps to communicate with the other person but has been unable to communicate with him; or

(*c*) the other person has unreasonably refused to consent,

(5A) Subsection (5)(*c*) above does not apply if—

(*a*) the person who refused to consent is a person—

(i) in whose favour there is a residence order in force with respect to the child; or

(ia) who is a speical guardian of the child; or

(ii) who has custody of the child; or

(*b*) the person taking or sending the child out of the United Kingdom is, by so acting, in breach of an order made by a court in the United Kingdom.

(6) Where, in proceedings for an offence under this section, there is sufficient evidence to raise an issue as to the application of subsection (5) above, it shall be for the prosecution to prove that that subsection does not apply.

(7) For the purposes of this section—

(*a*) "guardian of a child", "special guardian", "residence order" and "parental responsibility" have the same meaning as in the Children Act 1989; and

(*b*) a person shall be treated as having custody of a child if there is in force an order of a court in the United Kingdom awarding him (whether solely or jointly with another person) custody, legal custody or care and control of the child.

(8) This section shall have effect subject to the provisions of the Schedule to this Act in relation to a child who is in the care of a local authority detained in a place of safety, remanded to a local authority accommodation or the subject of proceedings or an order relating to adoption.

[Child Abduction Act 1984, s 1 as amended by the Family Law Act 1986, s 65, the Children Act 1989, Sch 12 and the Adoption and Children Act 2002, Sch 3.]

---

1. This Act came into force on 12 October 1984, (s 13(2)).
2. Part I contains ss 1–5.
3. The *Practice Direction* [1986] 1 All ER 983, [1986] 1 WLR 475 states the procedure to be followed in order to ask the police to institute a port alert where there is a real and imminent danger of removal from the jurisdiction.

6–1761 2. Offence of abduction of child by other persons. (1) Subject to subsection (3) below, a person, other than one mentioned in subsection (2) below commits an offence[1] if, without lawful authority or reasonable excuse, he takes[2] or detains a child under the age of sixteen—

(*a*) so as to remove him from the lawful control[3] of any person having[4] lawful control of the child; or

(*b*) so as to keep him out of the lawful control of any person entitled to lawful control of the child.

(2) The persons are—

(*a*) where the father and mother of the child in question were married to each other at the time of his birth, the child's father and mother;

(*b*) where the father and mother of the child in question were not married to each other at the time of his birth, the child's mother; and

(*c*) any other person mentioned in section 1(2)(*c*) to (*e*) above.

(3) In proceedings against any person for an offence under this section, it shall be a defence for that person to prove—

(*a*) where the father and mother of the child in question were not married to each other at the time of his birth—

(i) that he is the child's father; or

(ii) that, at the time of the alleged offence, he believed, on reasonable grounds, that he was the child's father; or (*b*) that, at the time of the alleged offence, he believed that the child had attained the age of sixteen.

[Child Abduction Act 1984, s 2 as amended by the Children Act 1989, Sch 12.]

1. This is an offence requiring *mens rea* ie an intention, when taking the child, to keep them out of control of someone known to be entitled to such control. 'So as to' in sub-ss (*a*) and (*b*) means 'with the intention of' rather than merely 'with the effect of' although it will not always be necessary to prove just who does have, or is entitled to lawful control, *Re Owens* [2000] 1 Cr App Rep 195, DC.

2. A person "takes" a child within the meaning of s 2(1)(*b*) so as to keep him or her out of the lawful control of, say, his or her mother if his actions are an effective cause of the child accompanying him, but it is not necessary that the defendant should be the sole cause of the child accompanying him. The consent or otherwise of the child is wholly irrelevant (*R v A* [2000] 2 All ER 177, [2000] 1 WLR 1879, [2000] 1 Cr App Rep 418, [2000] Crim LR 169, CA).

3. Whether a child has been removed from "lawful control" will be a question of fact; see *R v Mousir* [1987] Crim LR 561, and commentary thereto. "Control" does not have a necessary spatial element; thus, no geographical element is contemplated in the words "so as to remove him from the lawful control". What these words do require is the removal of the *control* of the child from the parent to the defendant. Therefore, the test is whether the child was deflected by some action of the defendant from that which he would with parental consent have otherwise been doing (*R v Leather* [1994] 1 FCR 877, 98 Cr App Rep 179, [1993] Crim LR 516).

4. "Having" means that the child must be in the lawful control of someone when he/she is taken or detained; the form of the offence in para (*b*) is, therefore, the appropriate one where the child has run away from lawful control before the taking or detaining occurs: *Foster v DPP* [2004] EWHC 2955, [2005] 1 FCR 153, [2005] Crim LR 639.

6–1762 3. Construction of references to taking, sending and detaining. For the purposes of this Part of this Act—

(*a*) a person shall be regarded as taking a child if he causes or induces the child to accompany him or any other person or causes the child to be taken;
(*b*) a person shall be regarded as sending a child if he causes the child to be sent;
(*c*) a person shall be regarded as detaining a child if he causes the child to be detained or induces the child to remain with him or any other person; and
(*d*) references to a child's parents and to a child whose parents were (or were not) married to each other at the time of his birth shall be construed in accordance with section 1 of the Family Law Reform Act 1987 (which extends their meaning).

[Child Abduction Act 1984, s 3 as amended by the Children Act 1989, Schs 12 and 15.]

6–1763 4. Penalties and prosecutions. (1) A person guilty of an offence under this Part of this Act shall be liable[1]—

(*a*) on summary conviction, to imprisonment for a term not exceeding **six months** or to a fine not exceeding **the statutory maximum**, or to both such imprisonment and fine;
(*b*) on conviction on indictment, to imprisonment for a term not exceeding **seven years**.

(2) No prosecution for an offence under section 1 above shall be instituted except by or with the consent of the Director of Public Prosecutions.

[Child Abduction Act 1984, s 4 as amended by the Statute Law (Repeals) Act 1993, Sch 1.]

1. For procedure in respect of this offence which is triable either way, see the Magistrates' Courts Act 1980, ss 18–21, in PART I: MAGISTRATES' COURTS, PROCEDURE, ante.

6–1764 5. Restriction on prosecutions for offence of kidnapping. Except by or with the consent of the Director of Public Prosecutions no prosecution shall be instituted for an offence of kidnapping if it was committed—

(*a*) against a child under the age of sixteen; and
(*b*) by a person connected with the child, within the meaning of s 1 above.

[Child Abduction Act 1984, s 5.]

6–1765

PART II[1]
OFFENCE UNDER LAW OF SCOTLAND

1. Part II contains ss 6–10.

PART III[1]
SUPPLEMENTARY

6–1766 11. *Consequential amendments and repeals.*

1. Part III contains ss 11–13.

6–1767 12. *Enactment of corresponding provision for Northern Ireland.*

6–1768   13. Short title, commencement and extent.   (1) This Act may be cited as the Child Abduction Act 1984.

(2) This Act shall come into force at the end of the period of three months beginning with the day on which it is passed.

(3) Part I of this Act extends to England and Wales only, Part II extends to Scotland only and in Part III ss 11(1) and (5)(*a*) and s 12 do not extend to Scotland and ss 11(1), (2) and (5)(*a*) and (*c*) does not extend to Northern Ireland.
[Child Abduction Act 1984, s 13.]

Section 1(1)   SCHEDULE
                 Modifications of Section 1 for Children in Certain Cases

(*As amended by the Children Act 1989, Schs 12 and 15, the Justices of the Peace Act 1997, Sch 5, the Access to Justice Act 1999, Sch 15, the Powers of Criminal Courts (Sentencing) Act 2000, Sch 9 and the Adoption and Children Act 2002, Sch 3.*)

Children in care of local authorities and voluntary organisations

6–1769   1. (1) This paragraph applies in the case of a child who is in the care of a local authority within the meaning of the Children Act 1989 in England or Wales.

(2) Where this paragraph applies, section 1 of this Act shall have effect as if—

(*a*) the reference in subsection (1) to the appropriate consent were a reference to the consent of the local authority in whose care the child is; and
(*b*) subsections (3) to (6) were omitted.

Children in places of safety

6–1770   2. (1) This paragraph applies in the case of a child who is—

(*a*) detained in a place of safety under paragraph 7(4) of Schedule 7 to the Powers of Criminal Courts (Sentencing) Act 2000; or
(*b*) remanded to local authority accommodation under section 23 of the Children and Young Persons Act 1969.

(2) Where this paragraph applies, section 1 of this Act shall have effect as if—

(*a*) the reference in subsection (1) to the appropriate consent were a reference to the leave of any magistrates' court acting for the area in which the place of safety is; and
(*b*) subsections (3) to (6) were omitted.

Adoption and custodianship

6–1771   3. (1) This paragraph applies where—

(*a*) a child is placed for adoption by an adoption agency under section 19 of the Adoption and Children Act 2002, or an adoption agency is authorised to place the child for adoption under that section; or
(*b*) a placement order is in force in respect of the child; or
(*c*) an application for such an order has been made in respect of the child and has not been disposed of; or
(*d*) an application for an adoption order has been made in respect of the child and has not been disposed of; or
(*e*) an order under section 84 of the Adoption and Children Act 2002 (giving parental responsibility prior to adoption abroad) has been made in respect of the child, or an application for such an order in respect of him has been made and has not been disposed of.

(2) Where this paragraph applies, section 1 of this Act shall have effect as if—

(*a*) the reference in subsection (1) to the appropriate consent were—

(i)   in a case within sub-paragraph (1)(*a*) above, a reference to the consent of each person who has parental responsibility for the child or to the leave of the High Court;
(ii) in a case within sub-paragraph (1)(*b*) above, a reference to the leave of the court which made the placement order;
(iii) in a case within sub-paragraph (1)(*c*) or (*d*) above, a reference to the leave of the court to which the application was made;
(iv) in a case within sub-paragraph (1)(*e*) above, a reference to the leave of the court which made the order or, as the case may be, to which the application was made;

(*b*) subsection (3) were omitted;
(*c*) in subsection (4), in paragraph (*a*), for the words from "in whose favour" to the first mention of "child" there were substituted "who provides the child's home in a case falling within sub-paragraph (1)(*a*) or (*b*) of paragraph 3 of the Schedule to this Act"; and
(*d*) subsections (4A), (5), (5A) and (6) were omitted.

Cases within paragraphs 1 and 3

6–1772   4. In the case of a child falling within both para 1 and para 3 above, the provisions of para 3 shall apply to the exclusion of those in para 1.

Interpretation

6–1773   **5.** In this Schedule—

(*a*) "adoption agency" , "adoption order", "placed for adoption by an adoption agency" and "placement order" have the same meaning as in the Adoption and Children Act 2002; and

(*b*) "area", in relation to a magistrates' court, means the petty sessions area for which the court is appointed.

Surrogacy Arrangements Act 1985
(1985 c 49)

6–1774   A surrogate mother is a woman who carries a child in pursuance of an arrangement made before she began to carry the child and made with a view to the child being handed over to another person or persons together with parental responsibility being met by that other person (s 1, amended by the Children Act 1989, Sch 13 and the Human Fertilisation and Embryology Act 1990, s 36—*SUMMARISED*.) No surrogacy arrangement is enforceable by or against any of the persons making it (s 1A inserted by the Human Fertilisation and Embryology Act 1990, s 36). Negotiations, offers, agreements, compiling of information with a view to surrogacy arrangements on a commercial basis are offences (s 2—*SUMMARISED*). Advertisements about surrogacy arrangements may not be published or conveyed or distributed (s 3—*SUMMARISED*). An offence under s 2 carries a maximum fine not exceeding **level 5** on the standard scale or imprisonment not exceeding **3 months, or both**; an offence under s 3 carries a maximum fine not exceeding **level 5** on the standard scale; consent of the Director of Public Prosecutions is required for proceedings; a director, manager, secretary or other similar officer of a body corporate may be liable as well as the body corporate; in proceedings under s 2 proof of things done or of words written, spoken or published by a person in management is admissible as evidence of the activities of the body; there is a time limit of two years in place of six months under Magistrates' Courts Act 1980, s 127(1) for offences under this Act (s 4—*SUMMARISED*).

Child Abduction and Custody Act 1985[1]
(1985 c 60)

PART I[2]
INTERNATIONAL CHILD ABDUCTION

6–1775   **1. The Hague Convention[3].**   (1) In this Part of this Act "the Convention" means the Convention on the Civil Aspects of International Child Abduction which was signed at The Hague on 25th October 1980.

(2) Subject to the provisions of this Part of this Act, the provisions of that Convention set out in Schedule 1 to this Act shall have the force of law in the United Kingdom.

(3) But—

(*a*) those provisions of the Convention,

(*b*) this Part of this Act, and

(*c*) rules of court under section 10 of this Act,

are subject to Article 60 of the Council Regulation (by virtue of which the Regulation takes precedence over the Hague Convention, in so far as it concerns matters governed by the Regulation).

(4) "The Council Regulation" means Council Regulation (EC) No 2201/2003 of 27th November 2003 concerning jurisdiction and the recognition and enforcement of judgments in matrimonial matters and matters of parental responsibility.

[Child Abduction and Custody Act 1985, s 1 as amended by SI 2005/265.]

---

1. This Act enables the United Kingdom to ratify two international Conventions relating respectively to the civil aspects of international child abduction and to the recognition and enforcement of custody decisions. As only the High Court has jurisdiction to consider applications under the Act, only those provisions of the Act that may be relevant to applications pending in or orders made by magistrates' courts are printed in this manual.

2. Part I contains ss 1–11.

3. The concepts of the Hague Convention are not to be applied by analogy in a non-Convention case. The welfare of the child is the paramount consideration. In such a case, where the choice lies between deciding the question in England or deciding it in a foreign country, differences between the legal systems cannot be irrelevant, but their relevance will depend upon the facts of the individual case. In practice it will be for the party resisting return to show that there is a difference which may be detrimental to the child's welfare: *Re J (a child) (return to foreign jurisdiction: convention rights)* [2005] UKHL 40, [2005] 2 FCR 281, [2005] 2 FLR 802.

6–1776   **2. Contracting States.** *Contracting States shall be those for the time being specified by Order in Council[1].*

---

1. See the Child Abduction and Custody (Parties to Convention) Order 1986, SI 1986/1159 amended by SI 2005/1260, Sch 1 of which specifies as Contracting States: Argentina, Australia (Australian States and mainland Territories), Austria, The Bahamas, Belarus, Belgium, Belize, Bosnia and Herzegovina, Brazil, Burkina Faso, Canada (Ontario, New Brunswick,

British Columbia, Manitoba, Nova Scotia, Newfoundland, Prince Edward Island, Quebec, Yukon Territory, Saskatchewan, Alberta, Northwest Territories), Chile, China (Hong Kong Special Administrative Region, Macau Special Administrative Region), Colombia, Croatia, Cyprus, Czech Republic, Denmark, Ecuador, Estonia, Fiji, Finland, France, Georgia, Germany, Greece, Honduras, Hungary, Iceland, Ireland, Israel, Italy, Latvia, Lithuania, Luxembourg, Macedonia, Malta, Mauritius, Mexico, Monaco, Netherlands, New Zealand, Norway, Panama, Peru, Poland, Portugal, Romania, St Kitts and Nevis, Serbia and Montenegro, Slovakia, Slovenia, South Africa, Spain, Sweden, Switzerland, Turkey, Turkmenistan, United States of America, Uruguay, Uzbekistan, Venezuela, Zimbabwe.

6–1777　3. Central Authorities.　*The functions under the Convention of a Central Authority shall be discharged in England and Wales by the Lord Chancellor.*

6–1778　4. Judicial Authorities.　*The court having jurisdiction to entertain applications under the Convention shall be in England and Wales the High Court.*

6–1779　5. Interim powers[1].　Where an application has been made to a court in the United Kingdom under the Convention, the court may, at any time before the application is determined, give such interim directions as it thinks fit for the purpose of securing the welfare of the child concerned or of preventing changes in the circumstances relevant to the determination of the application.
[Child Abduction and Custody Act 1985, s 5.]

---

[1] The terms of s 5 and the Convention on the Civil Aspects of International Child Abduction are sufficiently wide to impose a duty on the court to co-operate with all other contracting states and to act expeditiously in making orders which will ensure the return of wrongfully abducted children. The court's jurisdiction is not limited to a child already in the United Kingdom and an order may be made where there are substantial grounds for expecting the child to be in England in a few days (*Re N (child abduction: jurisdiction)* [1995] 2 All ER 417, [1995] 2 WLR 233, [1995] 2 FCR 605). In respect of countries which are not signatories to the Hague Convention, the courts in England, if the child is not habitually resident in this country and there are legal procedures in the country of habitual residence available to achieve a fair hearing of competing parental claims, will decline jurisdiction except for the purpose of making whatever orders are necessary to ensure a peaceful and speedy return of the child to the country of habitual residence (*Re M (jurisdiction: forum conveniens)* [1996] 1 FCR 40, CA). See also *Re Z (a minor) (abduction: non-Convention country)* [1999] 1 FCR 251, [1999] 1 FLR 1270, FD. Where, however, the choice lies between deciding the question of what is best for any individual child here or deciding it in a foreign country, differences between the legal systems cannot be irrelevant. If there is a genuine issue between the parents as to whether it is in the best interests of the child to live in this country or elsewhere it must be relevant whether that issue is capable of being tried in the courts of the country to which he is to be returned, and if those courts have no choice but to do as one parent wishes, so that the other cannot ask them to decide, with an open mind, whether the child will be better off living here or there, then the domestic courts must ask themselves whether it is in the interests of the child to enable that dispute to be heard. The absence of a relocation jurisdiction may be a decisive factor, but if it appears that the mother will be unable to make a good cause for relocation, that factor may not be decisive; there are also bound to be many cases where the connection of the child and all the family with the other country is so strong that any difference between the legal systems here and there should carry little weight: *Re J (a child) (return to foreign jurisdiction: convention rights)* [2005] UKHL 40, [2005] 3 All ER 291 (which concerned an application to remove a child to a non-Hague Convention country).

6–1780　6. Reports.　Where the Lord Chancellor or the Secretary of State is requested to provide information relating to a child under Article 7(*d*) of the Convention he may—

(*a*)　request a local authority or an officer of the Service to make a report to him in writing with respect to any matter which appears to him to be relevant;

(*b*)　*Northern Ireland*;

(*c*)　request any court to which a written report relating to the child has been made to send him a copy of the report;

and such a request shall be duly complied with.
[Child Abduction and Custody Act 1985, s 6, as amended by the Criminal Justice and Court Services Act 2000, Sch 7]

6–1781　7. Proof of documents and evidence.　(1) For the purposes of Article 14 of the Convention a decision or determination of a judicial or administrative authority outside the United Kingdom may be proved by a duly authenticated copy of the decision or determination; and any document purporting to be such a copy shall be deemed to be a true copy unless the contrary is shown.

(2) For the purposes of subsection (1) above a copy is duly authenticated if it bears the seal, or is signed by a judge or officer, of the authority in question.

(3) For the purposes of Articles 14 and 30 of the Convention any such document as is mentioned

in Article 8 of the Convention, or a certified copy of any such document, shall be sufficient evidence of anything stated in it.
[Child Abduction and Custody Act 1985, s 7.]

6–1782   8. Declarations by United Kingdom courts[1]**.** The High Court or Court of Session may, on an application made for the purposes of Article 15 of the Convention by any person appearing to the court to have an interest in the matter, make a declaration or declarator that the removal of any child from, or his retention outside, the United Kingdom was wrongful within the meaning of Article 3 of the Convention.
[Child Abduction and Custody Act 1985, s 8.]

---

1. The court has jurisdiction to make a declaration under s 8 in the absence of a request from the central authority of the country to which the child was removed: *Re G (abduction: rights of custody)* [2002] 2 FLR 703.

6–1783   9. Suspension of court's powers in cases of wrongful removal. The reference in Article 16 of the Convention to deciding on the merits of rights of custody shall be construed as a reference to—

(*a*) making, varying or revoking a custody order, or a supervision order under section 31 of the Children Act 1989 or Article 50 of the Children (Northern Ireland) Order 1995;
(*aa*) enforcing under section 29 of the Family Law Act 1986 a custody order within the meaning of Chapter V of Part I of that Act;
(*b*) registering or enforcing a decision under Part II of this Act;
(*c*) *Repealed*;
(*d*) *(Scotland)*;
(*e*) *Repealed*.

[Child Abduction and Custody Act 1985, s 9 as amended by the Family Law Act 1986, Sch 1, the Children Act 1989, Schs 13 and 15 and SI 1995/756.]

6–1784   10. Rules of court[1]**.**

---

1. See the Magistrates' Courts (Child Abduction and Custody) Rules 1986, this PART, post.

6–1785   11. *Cost of applications.*

PART II[1]
RECOGNITION AND ENFORCEMENT OF CUSTODY DECISIONS

6–1786   12. The European Convention[2]**.** (1) In this Part of this Act "the Convention" means the European Convention on Recognition and Enforcement of Decisions concerning Custody of Children and on the Restoration of Custody of Children which was signed in Luxembourg on 20th May 1980.
   (2) Subject to the provisions of this Part of this Act, the provisions of that Convention set out in Schedule 2 to this Act (which include Articles 9 and 10 as they have effect in consequence of a reservation made by the United Kingdom under Article 17) shall have the force of law in the United Kingdom.
   (3) But—

(*a*) those provisions of the Convention,
(*b*) this Part of this Act, and
(*c*) rules of court under section 24 of this Act,

are subject to Article 60 of the Council Regulation (by virtue of which the Regulation takes precedence over the European Convention, in so far as it concerns matters governed by the Regulation).
   (4) "The Council Regulation" means Council Regulation (EC) No 2201/2003 of 27th November 2003 concerning jurisdiction and the recognition and enforcement of judgments in matrimonial matters and matters of parental responsibility.
[Child Abduction and Custody Act 1985, s 12, as amended by SI 2001/310 and SI 2005/265.]

---

1. Part II contains ss 12–24.
2. For the principles applicable to an application to return to a non convention country, see *Re P (a minor) (child abduction: non convention country)* [1997] Fam 45, [1997] 1 FLR 780, CA.
3. For an example of the Regulation taking priority over the Convention see *In re G (Children) (Foreign Contact Order: Enforcement)* [2003] EWCA Civ 1607, [2004] 1 WLR 521, [2004] 1 FLR 378.

6–1787   13. Contracting States. *Contracting States shall be those for the time being specified by Order in Council*[1].

---

1. See the Child Abduction and Custody (Parties to Convention) Order 1986, SI 1986/1159, amended by SI 2005/1260, Sch 2 of which specifies as Contracting States: Austria, Belgium, Bulgaria, Cyprus, Czech Republic, Denmark, Estonia,

Finland, France, Germany, Greece, Hungary, Iceland, Republic of Ireland, Italy, Latvia, Liechtenstein, Lithuania, Luxembourg, Macedonia, Malta, Moldova, Netherlands, Norway, Poland, Portugal, Romania, Serbia and Montenegro, Slovakia Spain, Sweden, Switzerland and Turkey.

6–1788   14. Central Authorities.   *The functions under the Convention of a Central Authority shall be discharged in England and Wales by the Lord Chancellor.*

6–1789   15. Recognition of decisions[1].   (1) Articles 7 and 12 of the Convention shall have effect in accordance with this section.

(2) A decision to which either of those Articles applies which was made in a Contracting State other than the United Kingdom shall be recognised in each part of the United Kingdom as if made by a court having jurisdiction to make it in that part but—

(*a*)   the appropriate court in any part of the United Kingdom may, on the application of any person appearing to it to have an interest in the matter, declare on any of the grounds specified in Article 9 or 10 of the Convention that the decision is not to be recognised in any part of the United Kingdom; and

(*b*)   the decision shall not be enforceable in any part of the United Kingdom unless registered in the appropriate court under section 16 below.

(3) The references in Article 9(1)(*c*) of the Convention to the removal of the child are to his improper removal within the meaning of the Convention.
[Child Abduction and Custody Act 1985, s 15.]

---

1. By virtue of the terms of s 15 of this Act and Article 7 of the European Convention (set out in Sch 2 to the Act) a decision relating to custody and access given in a contracting State is to be recognised and made enforceable in every other contracting State. By Article 10(1)(*b*) of the Convention a court may refuse recognition and enforcement on grounds which include a finding that "... by reason of a change in circumstances including the passage of time but not including a mere change in the residence of the child after an improper removal, the effects of the original decision are manifestly no longer in accordance with the welfare of the child. ..."; see *Re A (minors) (foreign access order: enforcement)* [1996] 3 FCR 165, CA.

6–1790   16. Registration of decisions.   (1) A person on whom any rights are conferred by a decision relating to custody made by an authority in a Contracting State other than the United Kingdom may make an application for the registration of the decision in an appropriate court in the United Kingdom.

(2) The Central Authority in the United Kingdom shall assist such a person in making such an application if a request for such assistance is made by him or on his behalf by the Central Authority of the Contracting State in question.

(3) An application under subsection (1) above or a request under subsection (2) above shall be treated as a request for enforcement for the purposes of Articles 10 and 13 of the Convention.

(4) The High Court or Court of Session shall refuse to register a decision if—

(*a*)   the court is of the opinion that on any of the grounds specified in Article 9 or 10 of the Convention the decision should not be recognised in any part of the United Kingdom;

(*b*)   the court is of the opinion that the decision is not enforceable in the Contracting State where it was made and is not a decision to which Article 12 of the Convention applies; or

(*c*)   an application in respect of the child under Part I of this Act is pending.

(5) Where the Lord Chancellor is requested to assist in making an application under this section to the Court of Session he shall transmit the request to the Secretary of State and the Secretary of State shall transmit to the Lord Chancellor any such request to assist in making an application to the High Court.

(6) In this section "decision relating to custody" has the same meaning as in the Convention.
[Child Abduction and Custody Act 1985, s 16.]

6–1791   17. Variation and revocation of registered decisions.   (1) Where a decision which has been registered under section 16 above is varied or revoked by an authority in the Contracting State in which it was made, the person on whose behalf the application for registration of the decision was made shall notify the court in which the decision is registered of the variation or revocation.

(2) Where a court is notified under subsection (1) above of the revocation of a decision, it shall—

(*a*)   cancel the registration, and

(*b*)   notify such persons as may be prescribed by rules of court of the cancellation.

(3) Where a court is notified under subsection (1) above of the variation of a decision, it shall—

(*a*)   notify such persons as may be prescribed by rules of court of the variation; and

(*b*)   subject to any conditions which may be so prescribed, vary the registration.

(4) The court in which a decision is registered under section 16 above may also, on the application of any person appearing to the court to have an interest in the matter, cancel or vary the registration

if it is satisfied that the decision has been revoked or, as the case may be, varied by an authority in the Contracting State in which it was made.
[Child Abduction and Custody Act 1985, s 17.]

6–1792   18. Enforcement of decisions.   Where a decision relating to custody has been registered under section 16 above, the court in which it is registered shall have the same powers for the purpose of enforcing the decision as if it had been made by that court; and proceedings for or with respect to enforcement may be taken accordingly.
[Child Abduction and Custody Act 1985, s 18.]

6–1793   19. Interim powers.   Where an application has been made to a court for the registration of a decision under section 16 above or for the enforcement of such a decision, the court may, at any time before the application is determined, give such interim directions as it thinks fit for the purpose of securing the welfare of the child concerned or of preventing changes in the circumstances relevant to the determination of the application or, in the case of an application for registration, to the determination of any subsequent application for the enforcement of the decision.
[Child Abduction and Custody Act 1985, s 19.]

6–1794   20. Suspension of court's powers.   (1) Where it appears to any court in which such proceedings as are mentioned in subsection (2) below are pending in respect of a child that—

    (*a*)   an application has been made for the registration of a decision in respect of the child under section 16 above (other than a decision mentioned in subsection (3) below) or that such a decision is registered; and

    (*b*)   the decision was made in proceedings commenced before the proceedings which are pending,

the powers of the court with respect to the child in those proceedings shall be restricted as mentioned in subsection (2) below unless, in the case of an application for registration, the application is refused.

    (2)   Where subsection (1) above applies the court shall not—

    (*a*)   in the case of custody proceedings, make, vary or revoke any custody order, or a supervision order under section 31 of the Children Act 1989 or Article 50 of the Children (Northern Ireland) Order 1995;

    (*aa*)   in the case of proceedings under section 29 of the Family Law Act 1986 for the enforcement of a custody order within the meaning of Chapter V of Part I of that Act, enforce that order; or

    (*b*)–(*c*)   *Repealed*;

    (*d*)   *Scotland*;

    (*e*)   *Repealed*.

    (2A)   Where it appears to the Secretary of State—

    (*a*)   that an application has been made for the registration of a decision in respect of a child under section 16 above (other than a decision mentioned in subsection (3) below); or

    (*b*)   that such a decision is registered,

the Secretary of State shall not make, vary or revoke any custody order in respect of the child unless, in the case of an application for registration, the application is refused.

    (3)   The decision referred to in subsection (1) or (2A) above is a decision which is only a decision relating to custody within the meaning of section 16 of this Act by virtue of being a decision relating to rights of access.

    (4)   Paragraph (*b*) of Article 10(2) of the Convention shall be construed as referring to custody proceedings within the meaning of this Act.

    (5)   *Scotland.*
[Child Abduction and Custody Act 1985, s 20 as amended by the Family Law Act 1986, s 67 and Sch 1, the Children Act 1989, Schs 13 and 15 and SI 1995/756.]

6–1795   21. Reports.   Where the Lord Chancellor or the Secretary of State is requested to make enquiries about a child under Article 15(1)(*b*) of the Convention he may—

    (*a*)   request a local authority or an officer of the Service to make a report to him in writing with respect to any matter relating to the child concerned which appears to him to be relevant;

    (*b*)   request the Department of Health and Social Services for Northern Ireland to arrange for a suitably qualified person to make such a report to him;

    (*c*)   request any court to which a written report relating to the child has been made to send him a copy of the report;

and any such request shall be duly complied with.
[Child Abduction and Custody Act 1985, s 21, as amended by the Criminal Justice and Court Services Act 2000, Sch 7.]

6–1796   22. Proof of documents and evidence.   (1) In any proceedings under this Part of this Act a decision of an authority outside the United Kingdom may be proved by a duly authenticated copy of the decision; and any document purporting to be such a copy shall be deemed to be a true copy unless the contrary is shown.

(2) For the purposes of subsection (1) above a copy is duly authenticated if it bears the seal, or is signed by a judge or officer, of the authority in question.

(3) In any proceedings under this Part of this Act any such document as is mentioned in Article 13 of the Convention, or a certified copy of any such document, shall be sufficient evidence of anything stated in it.

[Child Abduction and Custody Act 1985, s 22.]

6–1797　23. Decisions of United Kingdom courts.　(1) Where a person on whom any rights are conferred by a decision relating to custody made by a court in the United Kingdom makes an application to the Lord Chancellor or the Secretary of State under Article 4 of the Convention with a view to securing its recognition or enforcement in another Contracting State, the Lord Chancellor or the Secretary of State may require the court which made the decision to furnish him with all or any of the documents referred to in Article 13(1)(*b*), (*c*) and (*d*) of the Convention.

(2) Where in any custody proceedings a court in the United Kingdom makes a decision relating to a child who has been removed from the United Kingdom, the court may also, on an application made by any person for the purposes of Article 12 of the Convention, declare the removal to have been unlawful if it is satisfied that the applicant has an interest in the matter and that the child has been taken from or sent or kept out of the United Kingdom without the consent of the person (or, if more than one, all the persons) having the right to determine the child's place of residence under the law of the part of the United Kingdom in which the child was habitually resident.

(3) In this section "decision relating to custody" has the same meaning as in the Convention.

[Child Abduction and Custody Act 1985, s 23.]

6–1798　24. *Rules of court.*—[1].

---

1. See the Magistrates' Courts (Child Abduction and Custody) Rules 1986, this Part, post.

PART III[1]
SUPPLEMENTARY

6–1799　24A. Power to order disclosure of child's whereabouts.　(1) Where—

(*a*)　in proceedings for the return of a child under Part I of this Act; or

(*b*)　on an application for the recognition, registration or enforcement of a decision in respect of a child under Part II of this Act,

there is not available to the court adequate information as to where the child is, the court may order[2] any person who it has reason to believe may have relevant information to disclose it to the court.

(2) A person shall not be excused from complying with an order under subsection (1) above by reason that to do so may incriminate him or his spouse of an offence; but a statement or admission made in compliance with such an order shall not be admissible in evidence against either of them in proceedings for any offence other than perjury.

[Child Abduction and Custody Act 1985, s 24A, as inserted by the Family Law Act 1986, s 67.]

---

1. Part III contains ss 24A–29.
2. For consideration of this power, see *Re D (child abduction)* [1988] FCR 585, [1989] 1 FLR 97n.

6–1800　25. Termination of existing custody orders, etc.　(1) Where—

(*a*)　an order is made for the return of a child under Part I of this Act; or

(*b*)　a decision with respect to a child (other than a decision mentioned in subsection (2) below) is registered under section 16 of this Act,

any custody order relating to him shall cease to have effect.

(2) The decision referred to in subsection (1)(*b*) above is a decision which is only a decision relating to custody within the meaning of section 16 of this Act by virtue of being a decision relating to rights of access.

(3), (4), (5) and (7) *Repealed.*

(6) *Consequential amendments.*

[Child Abduction and Custody Act 1985, s 25 amended by the Children Act 1989, Sch 15 and SI 1995/756.]

6–1801　26. *Expenses.*

6–1802　27. Interpretation.　(1) In this Act "custody order" means (unless the contrary intention appears) any such order or authorisation as is mentioned in Schedule 3 to this Act and "custody proceedings" means proceedings in which an order within paragraphs 1, 2, 5, 6, 8 or 9 of that Schedule may be made, varied or revoked.

(2) For the purposes of this Act "part of the United Kingdom" means England and Wales,

Scotland or Northern Ireland and "the appropriate court", in relation to England and Wales or Northern Ireland means the High Court and, in relation to Scotland, the Court of Session.

(3) In this Act "local authority" means—

(a) in relation to England and Wales, the council of a non-metropolitan county, a metropolitan district, a London borough or the Common Council of the City of London; and

(b) Scotland.

(4) In this Act a decision relating to rights of access in England and Wales or Scotland or Northern Ireland means a decision as to the contact which a child may, or may not, have with any person.

(5) In this Act "officer of the Service" has the same meaning as in the Criminal Justice and Court Services Act 2000.

[Child Abduction and Custody Act 1985, s 27 as amended by the Family Law Act 1986, s 67 and Sch 1, the Children Act 1989, Sch 13, SI 1995/756, the Children (Scotland) Act 1995, Sch 4 and the Criminal Justice and Court Services Act 2000, Sch 7.]

6–1803   28. *Application as respects British Islands and colonies.*

6–1804   29. *Short title, commencement and extent.*

6–1805

Section 1(2)

SCHEDULES

SCHEDULE 1

CONVENTION ON THE CIVIL ASPECTS OF INTERNATIONAL CHILD ABDUCTION[1]

1. Only those provisions of the Convention that may be relevant to the work of magistrates' courts are included in this manual.

CHAPTER 1—SCOPE OF THE CONVENTION

Article 3

6–1805A   The removal or the retention of a child is to be considered wrongful[1] where—

(a) it is in breach of rights of custody[2] attributed to a person, an institution or any other body, either jointly or alone, under the law of the State in which the child was habitually resident[3] immediately before the removal or retention; and

(b) at the time of removal or retention those rights were actually exercised, either jointly or alone, or would have been so exercised but for the removal or retention.

The rights of custody mentioned in sub-paragraph (a) above may arise in particular by operation of law or by reason of a judicial or administrative decision, or by reason of an agreement having legal effect under the law of that State.

1. The concept and ambit of "wrongful retention" extends the aim of the Convention way beyond a "snatch", and can apply even after a child has been in a country for a substantial period of time. While child abduction is a specialist branch of family law, and any one involved in children cases in England and Wales must be alert to the possibility of international child abduction whenever the child has formerly lived abroad in a Convention country and a parent wishes to return to that country with him; see *Re H (child abduction: wrongful retention)* [2000] 3 FCR 412, [2000] 2 FLR 294. It is essential to read this Article in conjunction with art 5. A foreign court seized of the issue of custody and access was held to be an institution or other body which had the right to determine a child's place of residence; removal whilst such foreign proceedings were at an interim stage was wrongful *(Re NB (a minor) (abduction)* [1993] 1 FCR 271, [1993] 1 FLR 864, CA).

A mother who disobeyed an English court and obtained an order in a foreign court could not then claim that her husband's subsequent removal of the child to England was wrongful *(Re R (wardship: child abduction) (No 2)* [1993] 1 FLR 249).

In order to establish wrongful retention of a child under art 3 a parent must prove an act of wrongful retention on a specific occasion and not merely a continuing state of affairs *(Re S (minors) (abduction: wrongful detention)* [1994] 1 All ER 237).

Consent falls to be considered, not for the purpose of establishing the wrongfulness of a removal or a breach of rights of custody pursuant to art 3 of the Hague Convention, but only for the purpose of invoking an exercise of the court's discretion pursuant to Art 13 *(Re P (Abduction: Consent)* [2004] EWCA Civ 971, [2004] 2 FLR 1057).

2. "Rights of custody" are normally to be interpreted in a wide sense if the court is to protect children from being taken away from their primary carers; and once such rights of custody arise they have force and can be exercised against any other person, including a parent who otherwise in law can alone exercise parental rights: *Re G (abduction: rights of custody)* [2002] 2 FLR 703 (where such rights were found to have been gained by an unmarried father and his mother). See also *Re P (Abduction: Consent)* [2004] EWCA Civ 971, [2004] 2 FLR 1057), in which it was held that "rights of custody" under the Hague Convention was to be given an autonomous interpretation which was to be purposive and effective, and it did not matter that the domestic order being relied on, which was made in the state where the child had his or her habitual residual residence, was not recognised in that jurisdiction as conferring "rights of custody" for domestic or Hague Convention purposes. However, it was held in *In re C (a child) (unmarried father: custody rights)* [2002] EWHC 2219 (Fam), [2003] 1 WLR 493, [2003] 1 FLR 25 that although both unmarried parents had shared primary care of the child, since the mother had at no point relinquished her care responsibility for the child the father had not acquired "rights of custody" within the meaning of arts 3 and 5 of the Convention. See also *Re J (abduction: acquiring custody rights by caring for child)* [2005] 2 FLR 791.

There are circumstances in which a person who is not related by blood to the child who has been in his care may nonetheless be found to have inchoate rights of custody; it is not the blood relationship of parent or grandparent who does not have parental responsibility but the situation of the exclusivity of the care of the child (*Re F (abduction: unmarried father: sole carer)* [2002] EWHC 2896 (Fam) [2003] 1 FLR 839).

A court may be an "institution or any other body" to which rights of custody may be attributed within the meaning of Article 3. For the court to be held to have a right of custody the application to the court must raise matters of custody within the meaning of the Convention, which will require in every case a consideration of the terms of the application (*Re H (child abduction: rights of custody* [2000] 2 All ER 1, [2000] 2 WLR 337, [2000] 1 FCR 225, [2000] 1 FLR 374, HL). In *Re J* [1999] 3 FCR 577, [1999] 2 FLR 653 an urgent, ex parte application by the father for a parental responsibility order and a prohibited steps order was held to be sufficient to invest the court with custody rights even though the court decided that the applications should proceed on notice and the mother left the jurisdiction with the child that day before notice of the proceedings could be served. However, in *In re C*, supra it was held that the mere making of application for a residence order, where the mother left the jurisdiction before service could be effected, did not invest custody rights in the court; the matter must as a minimum come before a judge who exercises a judicial discretion as to the future conduct of the proceedings, though he need not make a substantive order or give directions. See also *In re B (abduction) (rights of custody)* [1997] 2 FLR 594.

In *Re H (child abduction) (unmarried father: rights of custody)* [2003] EWHC 492 (Fam), [2003] 2 FLR 153, removal of the child of unmarried parents occurred before the first listing of the father's applications for contact and parental responsibility, but there had been an exchange of letters between the parties' solicitors in which the mother's solicitors stated that she had no plans to leave the jurisdiction and would not do so in the foreseeable future and in reliance on that the father did not seek urgent relief; it was held that the letters exchanged between the solicitors had the effect of attributing to the father a right of custody within the meaning of art 5 of the Hague Convention on the Civil Aspects of International Child Abduction 1980.

3. See *Re J (a minor) (abduction: custody rights)* [1990] 2 AC 562, sub nom *C v S (a minor) (abduction: illegitimate child)* [1990] 2 FLR 442, *Re M (abduction: habitual residence)* [1996] 1 FLR 887, CA and *Re S (a minor) (custody: habitual residence)* [1997] 4 All ER 251, [1997] 3 WLR 597, [1997] 3 FCR 293, HL, as to the meaning of habitually resident; mere presence within a jurisdiction prior to the making of a foreign order is insufficient to establish "habitual residence" (*Re O (a minor) (abduction: habitual residence)* [1993] 2 FLR 594, [1995] 2 FCR 649). The place of habitual residence of a young child of parents living together is the same as that of the parents and is a question of fact to be determined by reference to all the circumstances of the case (*In re A (minors) (abduction: habitual residence)* [1996] 1 All ER 24, [1996] 1 WLR 25). A child does not lose his habitual residence in one country when taken to another for a short period while his parents attempt a reconciliation (*Re B (a minor) (child abduction: habitual residence)* [1995] 1 FCR 273. The test for habitual residence is whether the residence is for a settled purpose, which may be either a purpose of short duration or conditional upon future events; the test is not, 'that one does not lose one's habitual residence in a particular country absent a settled intention not to return there', since such a test comes perilously close to confusing the question of habitual residence with the question of domicile (*Re R (abduction: habitual residence)* [2003] EWHC 1968 (Fam), [2004] 1 FLR 216). The powers conferred on a person by s 3(5) of the Children Act 1989 (to do what is reasonable for the purpose of safeguarding or promoting the child's welfare) do not include the power to change habitual residence merely by taking him out of the jurisdiction (*Re S (a minor) (custody: habitual residence)* supra.

Article 4

6–1805B The Convention shall apply to any child who was habitually resident in a Contracting State immediately before any breach of custody or access rights. The Convention shall cease to apply when the child attains the age of sixteen years[1].

Article 5

6–1805C For the purposes of this Convention—

  (a) "rights of custody" shall include rights relating to the care of the person of the child and, in particular, the right to determine the child's place of residence[2];
  (b) "rights of access" shall include the right to take a child for a limited period of time to a place other than the child's habitual residence.

---

1. Article 4 must be construed at face value and does not apply when the child concerned has reached the age of 16 (*Re H (child abduction: child of sixteen)* [2000] 3 FCR 404, [2000] 2 FLR 51).
2. The meaning of the term "rights of custody" is to be drawn from the definitions, structure and purposes of the convention and is not dependent on the meaning in any one legal system. For the rights of custody of unmarried fathers see *Practice Note – The Central Authority for England and Wales – Child Abduction and Custody Act 1985 – Hague Convention on the Civil Aspects of International Child Abduction – Applications for return orders by unmarried fathers* [1998] 1 FCR 253, [1998] 1 FLR 491. Where a mother had been granted sole custody by a Dutch District Court, the father's right to be informed and consulted about any important decisions relating to the children did not amount to a right relating to the care of the person or the child and was not a right of "custody" (*Re V–B (minors) (abduction: rights of custody)* [1999] 2 FCR 371, [1999] 2 FLR 192, CA).

CHAPTER II—CENTRAL AUTHORITIES

Article 7

CHAPTER III—RETURN OF CHILDREN

Articles 8–11
Article 12

6–1805D Where a child has been wrongfully removed or retained[1] in terms of Article 3 and, at the date of the commencement of the proceedings before the judicial or administrative authority of the Contracting State where the child is, a period of less than one year[2] has elapsed from the date of the wrongful removal or retention, the authority concerned shall[3] order the return of the child forthwith[4].

The judicial or administrative authority, even where the proceedings have been commenced after the expiration of the period of one year referred to in the preceding paragraph, shall also order the return of the child, unless it is demonstrated that the child is now settled[5] in its new environment[6].

Where the judicial or administrative authority in the requested state has reason to believe that the child has been taken to another State, it may stay the proceedings or dismiss the application for the return of the child.

1. 'Removal' and 'retention' can both occur on the facts in relation to the same child at different times. An initial lawful retention can become a wrongful retention where for example a parent who at the time the child was removed and retained, subsequently acquires those rights and demands the child's return (*Re S (a minor) (custody: habitual residence)* [1997] 4 All ER 251, [1997] 3 WLR 597, [1997] 3 FCR 293, HL).

2. The procedures under the Convention are intended to be applied expeditiously. A wrongful removal does not determine the child's status irrespective of what happens subsequently so that where a parent subsequently brings the child back into the country from which he was originally wrongfully removed more than a year before there may be a second wrongful removal such that the procedures of the Convention may be invoked (*Re S (child abduction)* [1998] 1 FCR 17, [1998] 1 FLR 651).

3. The court is under a duty to order return subject only to art 13 exceptions; the fact that an application was based on facts inconsistent with the applicant's case is not material once wrongful removal or retention is established under art 3 (*Re N (child abduction: habitual residence)* [1993] 2 FCR 330, [1993] 2 FLR 124, CA). Courts in England and Wales will normally assume that a fair hearing would be provided in the courts of another jurisdiction (*Re M (minors) (abduction: peremptory return orders)* (1995) Times, 20 November). While the approach of the Hague Convention is directed at the welfare of the child, the welfare test is generally to be applied in such a way as to enable the courts of the child's habitual residence to make decisions as to what are his best interests. Exceptionally, provision is made for specific consideration of the welfare of the particular child where the threshold of art 13 has been crossed and the needs of the child require the court to take another course than the summary return. It is only in exceptional cases that the discretion will be exercised not to order the return of the child and in exercising that discretion, the behaviour of the offending parent is of crucial importance and in most cases, determinative. Nevertheless, in rare cases the court will have to look past the parent's conduct to the manifest needs of the child, see *Re M (minors) (abduction: psychological harm)* [1998] 2 FCR 488, CA (mother wrongly retained children in England in breach of order of Greek court. Court declined to order return in view of cogent evidence of grave risk of psychological harm to the children if they were returned summarily to their father in Greece.)

There remains a residual power in the Court of Appeal to deal with an exceptional change of circumstance which renders an order impracticable to enforce or impossible to implement: *Re B (children)(abduction: new evidence)* [2001] EWCA Civ 625, [2001] 2 FCR 531.

4. Return under the Hague Convention is to the jurisdiction of habitual residence and not to a particular person or situation, and where it would be unacceptable to return a child to the situation pertaining when the child left the other jurisdiction the court may delay the return to resolve certain issues, such as housing and welfare support in the other jurisdiction, while the child is still in England (*Re H (abduction: grave risk)* [2003] EWCA Civ 355, [2003] 2 FLR 141).

5. Each case should be considered on its own facts, but it will be very difficult indeed for a parent who has hidden a child away to demonstrate that it is settled in its new environment and thus overcome the real obligation to order a return. It is not enough to have regard only to the physical characteristics of settlement. Equal regard must be paid to the emotional and psychological elements. In cases of concealment and subterfuge the burden of demonstrating the necessary elements of emotional and psychological settlement is much increased: *Cannon v Cannon* [2004] EWCA Civ 1330, [2005] 1 FLR 169. Even if settlement is established on the facts the court retains a residual discretion to order a return under the Hague Convention: *Cannon v Cannon*, supra.

6. See *Re N (minors) (abduction)* [1991] 1 FLR 413. In determining whether the child "is now settled in its new environment", it is necessary to consider the reason for any delay in the commencement of proceedings to ensure that the abducting parent cannot rely on evading the wronged parent to argue that the child has settled in the new jurisdiction and should not be returned to the original jurisdiction (*Re H (child abduction – child of sixteen)* [2000] 3 FCR 404, [2000] 2 FLR 51).

Article 13

6–1805E   Notwithstanding the provisions of the preceding Article, the judicial or administrative authority of the requested State is not bound[1] to order the return of the child if the person, institution or other body which opposes its return establishes that—

    (*a*)   the person, institution or other body having the care of the person of the child was not actually exercising the custody rights at the time of removal or retention, or had consented[2] to or subsequently acquiesced[3] in the removal or retention; or

    (*b*)   there is a grave[4] risk that his or her return would expose the child to physical or psychological harm[5] or otherwise place the child in an intolerable situation.

The judicial or administrative authority may also refuse to order the return of the child if it finds that the child objects[6] to being returned and has attained an age and degree of maturity at which it is appropriate to take account[7] of its views.

In considering the circumstances referred to in this Article, the judicial and administrative authorities shall take into account the information relating to the social background of the child provided by the Central Authority or other competent authority of the child's habitual residence.

1. Nothing in Council Regulation (EC) No 1347/2000 on Jurisdiction and the Recognition and Enforcement of Judgments in Matrimonial Matters and in Matters of Parental Responsibility for Children of Both Spouses ("Brussels II") prevents the hearing and determination of an application for the immediate return of a child in a case of wrongful removal nor the exercise of the discretion whether to return the child (*Re L (abduction: jurisdiction)* [2002] EWHC 1864 (Fam), [2002] 1 WLR 3208). "The principle that it would be wrong to allow the abducting parent to rely upon adverse conditions brought about by a situation which she has herself created by her own conduct is born of the proposition that it would drive a coach and horses through the 1985 Act idf that were not accepted as the broad and instinctive approach to a defence raised under Art 13(b) of the Convention. However, it is not a principle articulated in the Convention or the Act and should not be applied to the effective exclusion of the very defence itself, which is in terms directed to the question of risk of harm to the child and not the wrongful conduct of the abducting parent. By reason of the provisions of Arts 3 and 12, such wrongful conduct is a 'given', in the context of which the defence is nonetheless made available if its constituents can be established" (per Sir Mark Potter P in *S v B (abduction: human rights)* [2005] EWHC 733 (Fam), [2005] 2 FLR 878, at para 49. (See further in *R v B* consideration of Art 8 human rights issues with regard to a sibling who is not included within the application.)

2. The evidence for establishing consent must be clear and compelling; a party wishing to retain or remove a child would be well advised to get written consent (*Re M (a minor) (abduction: consent or acquiescence)* [1999] 1 FCR 5, [1999] 1 FLR 171, FD). Consent must be read in the sense that it is not based on a misunderstanding or non-disclosure (*T v T (child abduction: consent)* [1999] 2 FCR 2, [1999] 2 FLR 912, FD).

3. A wronged parent will have "acquiesced" in the removal or retention of a child if he in fact has consented to the child's continued presence in the jurisdiction to which he has been abducted. Whether the parent has so acquiesced depends on his actual state of mind and subjective intention and is a question of fact to be determined by the judge, the burden of proof being on the abducting parent. However, even if the wronged parent has not in fact acquiesced, he will be held to have done so if his words or actions clearly and unequivocally showed (and have led the other parent to believe) that he was not asserting or going to assert his right to the summary return of the child and were inconsistent with such return (*Re H (minors) (abduction: acquiescence)* [1997] 2 All ER 225, [1997] 2 WLR 563, [1997] 2 FCR 257, [1997] 1 FLR 872, HL).

4. For an example where economic hardship to a mother who removed her child was held to be insufficient for the purpose of this Article see (*Re NB (a minor) (abduction)* [1993] 1 FCR 271, CA). The grave risk must be associated with the child's return and not with the merits of the custody application (*Re L (a minor) (abduction)* [1993] 2 FCR 509). The court is entitled to weigh the risk of psychological harm of return against the psychological consequences of refusing return. Where both risks are substantial the court must give due weight to the purpose of the Convention to ensure the return of abducted children (*N v N (abduction: Article 13 defence)* [1995] 1 FLR 107).

5. The word "harm" is capable of including harm caused by the deterioration in the mother's condition and consequently her ability to care for the children. However, in evaluating the gravity of the risk of harm, account must be taken of any protection that the courts of the requesting state can offer and any medical assistance that will available to the mother in that state: *TB v JB (abduction: grave risk of harm)* [2001] 2 FCR 497, CA. It has been held " . . . the court should require clear and compelling evidence of the grave risk of harm or other intolerability which must be measured as substantial, not trivial, and of a severity which is much more than is inherent in the inevitable disruption, uncertainty and anxiety which follows an unwelcome return to the jurisdiction of the court of habitual residence" (*Re C (abduction: grave risk of psychological harm)* [1999] 1 FLR 1145, per Ward LJ at 1154). See also *S v B (abduction: human rights)* [2005] EWHC 733 (Fam), [2005] 2 FLR 878.

6. As to the meaning of "objects" see *S v S (child abduction)* [1993] 1 FCR 12; *B v K (child abduction)* [1993] 1 FCR 383 [1993] Fam Law 17. Where a child is old enough to object the court should take his views into account but is not obliged to give effect to that preference (*Re R (child abduction: acquiescence)* [1995] 1 FLR 716) and *Re K (child abduction: child's objections)* [1995] 3 FCR 473. In *B v K* it was held that a child not old enough to be competent to object could suffer psychological harm, within paragraph (*b*) of the article, if he were separated from siblings who did themselves object. See also *Re T (abduction: child's objection to return)* [2000] 2 FCR 159, [2000] 2 FLR 192, CA (followed in *Re J (children) (abduction: child's objections to return)* [2004] EWCA Civ 428, [2004] 1 FCR 737, [2004] 2 FLR 64). In exceptional circumstances where it is inappropriate for a child's wishes and feelings to be represented either by one of the parties or the court welfare officer, and there is an arguable case that the discretion under art 13 will be exercised, the court may allow the child to be separately represented (*Re S (abduction: separate representation of children)* [1997] 2 FCR 342).

7. "Take account" does not have a different meaning to the words "have regard to" in s 1(3) of the Children Act 1989: *Re J and K (abduction: objections of child)* [2004] EWHC 1985 (Fam), [2005] 1 FLR 273.

Articles 14 and 15

Article 16

6–1805F   After receiving notice of a wrongful removal or retention of a child in the sense of Article 3, the judicial or administrative authorities of the Contracting State to which the child has been removed or in which it has been retained shall not decide on the merits of rights of custody until it has been determined that the child is not to be returned under this Convention or unless an application under this Convention is not lodged within a reasonable time following receipt of the notice.

Articles 17–19

CHAPTER IV—RIGHTS OF ACCESS

Article 21

CHAPTER V—GENERAL PROVISIONS

Articles 22–32

6–1806

Section 12(2)   SCHEDULE 2
EUROPEAN CONVENTION ON RECOGNITION AND ENFORCEMENT OF DECISIONS CONCERNING CUSTODY OF CHILDREN

6–1807

Section 27(1)   SCHEDULE 3
CUSTODY ORDERS

(*As amended by the Family Law Reform Act 1987, Sch 2, the Children Act 1989, Schs 13 and 15, SI 1995/756 and the Adoption and Children Act 2002, Sch 3.*)

PART I
ENGLAND AND WALES

1. The following are the orders referred to in section 27(1) of this Act—

(*a*) a care order under the Children Act 1989 (as defined by section 31(11) of that Act, read with section 105(1) and Schedule 14);

(*b*) a residence order (as defined by section 8 of the Act of 1989);

(*bb*) a special guardianship order (within the meaning of the Act of 1989); and

(c)   any order made by a court in England and Wales under any of the following enactments—

    (i)   section 9(1), 10(1)(a) or 11(a) of the Guardianship of Minors Act 1971;
    (ii)   section 42(1) or (2) or 43(1) of the Matrimonial Causes Act 1973;
    (iii)   section 2(2)(b), 4(b) or (5) of the Guardianship Act 1973 as applied by section 34(5) of the Children Act 1975;
    (iv)   section 8(2)(a), 10(1) or 19(1)(ii) of the Domestic Proceedings and Magistrates' Courts Act 1978;
    (v)   *repealed.*

2. An order made by the High Court in the exercise of its jurisdiction relating to wardship so far as it gives the care and control of a child to any person.

3. *Repealed.*

4. An authorisation given by the Secretary of State under section 26(2) of the Children and Young Persons Act 1969 (except where the relevant order, within the meaning of that section, was made by virtue of the court which made it being satisfied that the child was guilty of an offence).

PARTS II AND III

(Scotland and Northern Ireland)

Family Law Act 1986[1]

(1986 c 55)

PART I[2]
CHILD CUSTODY

CHAPTER I
PRELIMINARY

6–1810   1. Orders to which Part I applies.   (1) Subject to the following provisions of this section, in this Part "Part I order" means—

    (a)   a section 8 order[3] made by a court in England and Wales under the Children Act 1989, other than an order varying or discharging such an order;
    (aa)   a special guardianship order made by a court in England and Wales under the Children Act 1989;
    (ab)   an order made under section 26 of the Adoption and Children Act 2002 (contact), other than an order varying or revoking such an order;
    (b)   an order made by a court of civil jurisdiction in Scotland under any enactment or rule of law with respect to the residence, custody, care or control of a child, contact with or, access to a child or the education or upbringing of a child, excluding—

        (i)   an order committing the care of a child to a local authority or placing a child under the supervision of a local authority;
        (ii)   an adoption order as defined in section 12(1) of the Adoption (Scotland) Act 1978;
        (iii)   an order freeing a child for adoption made under section 18 of the said Act of 1978;
        (iv)   an order giving parental responsibilities and parental rights in relation to a child made in the course of proceedings for the adoption of the child (other than an order made following the making of a direction under section 53(1) of the Children Act 1975);
        (v)   an order made under the Education (Scotland) Act 1980;
        (vi)   an order made under Part II or III of the Social Work (Scotland) Act 1968;
        (vii)   an order made under the Child Abduction and Custody Act 1985;
        (viii) an order for the delivery of a child or other order for the enforcement of a Part I order,
        (ix)   an order relating to the tutory or curatory of a child;

    (c)   an Article 8 order made by a court in Northern Ireland under the Children (Northern Ireland) Order 1995, other than an order varying or discharging such an order;
    (d)   an order made by a court in England and Wales in the exercise of the inherent jurisdiction of the High Court with respect to children—

        (i)   so far as it gives care of a child to any person or provides for contact with, or the education of, a child; but
        (ii)   excluding an order varying or revoking such an order;

    (e)   an order made by the High Court in Northern Ireland in the exercise of its inherent jurisdiction with respect to children—

        (i)   so far as it gives care of a child to any person or provides for contact with, or the education of, a child; but
        (ii)   excluding an order varying or discharging such an order;

(2) In this Part, "Part I order" does not include—

(a)–(c) *Repealed.*

(3) In this Part, "Part I order"—

(*a*)   includes any order which would have been a custody order by virtue of this section in any form in which it was in force at any time before its amendment by the Children Act 1989 or the Children (Northern Ireland) Order 1995, as the case may be; and

(*b*)   (subject to sections 32 and 40 of this Act) excludes any order which would have been excluded from being a custody order by virtue of this section in any such form.

(4)–(5)   *Repealed.*

(6)   Provision may be made by act of sederunt prescribing, in relation to orders within subsection (1)(*b*) above, what constitutes an application for the purposes of this Part.

[Family Law Act 1986, s 1 as amended by the Family Law Reform Act 1987, Sch 2, the Children Act 1989, Schs 13 and 15, SI 1995/756, the Children (Scotland) Act 1995, Sch 4 and the Adoption and Children Act 2002, Sch 3.]

---

1. This Act is to be brought into force in accordance with s 69, post. Sections 66–67 were brought into force on 7 January 1987 by s 69(2), and the remainder of the Act, except para 10(3) of Sch 1, was brought into force on 4 April 1988 by the Family Law Act 1986 (Commencement No 1) Order 1988, SI 1988/375.

2. Part I contains Chapter I, s 1, Chapter II, ss 2–7, Chapter III, ss 8–18, Chapter IV, ss 19–24, Chapter V, ss 25–32, and Chapter VI, ss 33–43.

3. Whilst there is no direct indication as to jurisdiction in proceedings under the Children Act 1989, and the references in s 31(8) of that Act to the local authority to be designated in a care order are illustrative rather than defining, there are strong policy reasons for adopting the widest possible approach. Accordingly, it has been held that the jurisdictional basis for an application under Part IV is effectively the same as that in relation to section 8 orders (*Re R (care proceedings: jurisdiction)* [1995] 3 FCR 305, [1995] 1 FLR 712). As applications under s 4 of the Children Act 1989 are not mentioned in s 1 of the 1986 Act, the court does have jurisdiction to hear a parental responsibility application in respect of a child who is permanently out of the jurisdiction (*In re S (a minor) (parental responsibility: jurisdiction)* [1998] 1 WLR 1701, [1999] 2 FCR 27, [1998] 2 FLR 921, CA).

CHAPTER II

JURISDICTION OF COURTS IN ENGLAND AND WALES

6–1811   2. Jurisdiction: general.   (1) A court in England and Wales shall not make a section 1(1)(*a*) order with respect to a child unless—

(*a*)   it has jurisdiction under the Council Regulation, or

(*b*)   the Council Regulation does not apply but—

(i)   the question of making the order arises in or in connection with matrimonial proceedings or civil partnership proceedings and the condition in section 2A of this Act is satisfied, or

(ii)   the condition in section 3 of this Act is satisfied.

(2A)   A court in England and Wales shall not have jurisdiction to make a special guardianship order under the Children Act 1989 unless the condition in section 3 of this Act is satisfied.

(2B)   A court in England and Wales shall not have jurisdiction to make an order under section 26 of the Adoption and Children Act 2002 unless the condition in section 3 of this Act is satisfied.

(3)   A court in England and Wales shall not make a section 1(1)(*d*) order unless—

(*a*)   it has jurisdiction under the Council Regulation, or

(*b*)   the Council Regulation does not apply but—

(i)   the condition in section 3 of this Act is satisfied, or

(ii)   the child concerned is present in England and Wales on the relevant date and the court considers that the immediate exercise of its powers is necessary for his protection.

[Family Law Act 1986, s 2, as substituted by the Children Act 1989, Sch 13 and amended by SI 2001/310, SI 2005/265, the Adoption and Children Act 2002, Sch 3 and SI 2005/3336.]

6–1812   2A. Jurisdiction in or in connection with matrimonial proceedings or civil partnership proceedings.   (1) The condition referred to in section 2(1) of this Act is that the proceedings or civil partnership proceedings are proceedings in respect of the marriage of the parents of the child concerned and—

(*a*)   the proceedings—

(i)   are proceedings for divorce or nullity of marriage, or dissolution or annulment of a civil partnership, and

(ii)   are continuing;

(*b*)   the proceedings—

(i)   are proceedings for judicial separation or legal separation of civil partners,

(ii)   are continuing,

and the jurisdiction of the court is not excluded by subsection (2) below; or

(*c*)   the proceedings have been dismissed after the beginning of the trial but—

(i)   the section 1(1)(*a*) order is being made forthwith, or

(ii)   the application for the order was made on or before the dismissal.*

(2)   For the purposes of subsection (1)(*b*) above, the jurisdiction of the court is excluded if—

(*a*) after the grant of a decree of judicial separation, on the relevant date, proceedings for divorce or nullity in respect of the marriage, or

(*b*) after the making of a separation order, on the relevant date, proceedings for dissolution or annulment in respect of the civil partnership,

are continuing in Scotland or Northern Ireland.

(3) Subsection (2) above shall not apply if the court in which the other proceedings there referred to are continuing has made—

(*a*) an order under section 13(6) or 19A(4) of this Act (not being an order made by virtue of section 13(6)(*a*)(i)), or

(*b*) an order under section 14(2) or 22(2) of this Act which is recorded as being made for the purpose of enabling Part I proceedings to be taken in England and Wales with respect to the child concerned.

(4) Where a court—

(*a*) has jurisdiction to make a section 1(1)(*a*) order by virtue of section 2(1)(*b*)(i) of this Act but

(*b*) considers that it would be more appropriate for Part I matters relating to the child to be determined outside England and Wales,

the court may by order direct that, while the order under this subsection is in force, no section 1(1)(*a*) order shall be made by any court by virtue of section 2(1)(*b*)(i) of this Act.★

[Family Law Act 1986, s 2A, as inserted by the Children Act 1989, Sch 13 and amended by SI 1995/756, SI 2005/265 and SI 2005/3336.]

★**Amended by the Family Law Act 1996, Sch 8, this PART, POST, WHEN IN FORCE.**

6–1813 3. Habitual residence or presence of child[1]. (1) The condition referred to in section 2(1)(*b*)(ii) of this Act is that on the relevant date the child concerned—

(*a*) is habitually resident[2] in England and Wales, or

(*b*) is present[3] in England and Wales and is not habitually resident in any part of the United Kingdom,

and, in either case, the jurisdiction of the court is not excluded by subsection (2) below★.

(2) For the purposes of subsection (1) above, the jurisdiction of the court is excluded if, on the relevant date, matrimonial proceedings or civil partnership proceedings are continuing[4] in a court in Scotland or Northern Ireland in respect of the marriage or civil partnership of the parents of the child concerned.

(3) Subsection (2) above shall not apply if the court in which the other proceedings there referred to are continuing has made—

(*a*) an order under section 13(6) or 19A(4) of this Act (not being an order made by virtue of section 13(6)(*a*)(i)), or

(*b*) an order under section 14(2) or 22(2) of this Act which is recorded as made for the purpose of enabling Part I proceedings with respect to the child concerned to be taken in England and Wales,

and that order is in force.

(4)–(6) *Repealed*.

[Family Law Act 1986, s 3 as amended by the Family Law Reform Act 1987, Sch 2, the Children Act 1989, Schs 13 and 15, SI 1995/756 and SI 2005/3336.]

★**Amended by the Family Law Act 1996, Sch 8, this PART, POST, WHEN IN FORCE.**

1. For the effect which removal, with consent, of a child under the age of 16 outside part of the United Kingdom has on habitual residence, see s 41, post. Part I of the Family Law Act 1986 does not apply to public law proceedings under Parts IV and V of the Children Act 1989. Nevertheless the Court has jurisdiction to hear cases where the child is present within the jurisdiction when the application is made whether or not he is habitually resident either abroad or in another part of the United Kingdom, *Re M (a minor) (care orders: jurisdiction)* [1997] Fam 67, [1997] 1 All ER 263, [1997] 2 WLR 314, [1997] 1 FLR 456.

2. For consideration of the provisions of this Act and authorities on the concept of "habitual residence", see *D v D (custody jurisdiction)* [1996] 3 FCR, [1996] 1 FLR 574. See also *B v H (habitual residence: wardship)* [2002] 2 FCR 329, [2002] 1 FLR 388: children do not lose their habitual residence in the UK when they leave the jurisdiction with their mother on a trip presented to her by the father as a temporary visit; and a newly born child can be habitually resident in the UK even though he/she has never been physically present in the UK.

3. Before accepting jurisdiction courts should be satisfied that the application was: (*a*) not a device to avoid immigration controls, and (*b*) that the facts of the case were exceptional or most exceptional so that the jurisdiction is exercised sparingly (*Re M (a minor) (immigration: residence)* [1993] 2 FLR 858). See also *Re F (residence order: jurisdiction)* [1996] 1 FCR 577.

4. Proceedings that have been stayed are not "continuing" for the purposes of s 3: *Re B (court's jurisdiction)* [2004] EWCA Civ 681, [2004] 2 FLR 741.

6–1814 5. Power of court to refuse application or stay proceedings. (1) A court in England and Wales which has jurisdiction to make a Part I order may refuse an application for the order in any case where the matter in question has already been determined in proceedings outside England and Wales.

(2) Where, at any stage of the proceedings on an application made to a court in England and Wales for a Part I order, or for the variation of a Part I order, it appears to the court—

(a) that proceedings with respect to the matters to which the application relates are continuing outside England and Wales, or

(b) that it would be more appropriate for those matters to be determined in proceedings to be taken outside England and Wales, or

(c) that it should exercise its powers under Article 15 of the Council Regulation (transfer to a court better placed to hear the case),]

the court may stay the proceedings on the application or (as the case may be) exercise its powers under Article 15.

(3) The court may remove a stay granted [by virtue of subsection (2)(a) or (b) above if it appears to the court that there has been unreasonable delay in the taking or prosecution of the other proceedings referred to in that subsection, or that those proceedings are stayed, sisted or concluded.

(3A) The court may remove a stay granted under Article 15 of the Council Regulation only in accordance with that Article.

(4) Nothing in this section so far as it relates to proceedings not governed by the Council Regulation shall affect any power exercisable apart from this section to refuse an application or to grant or remove a stay.

[Family Law Act 1986, s 5 as amended by the Children Act 1989, Sch 13, SI 2001/310 and SI 2005/265.]

6–1815   6. Duration and variation of Part I orders.   (1) If a Part I order made by a court in Scotland or Northern Ireland (or a variation of such an order) comes into force with respect to a child at a time when a Part I order made by a court in England and Wales has effect with respect to him, the latter order shall cease to have effect so far as it makes provision for any matter for which the same or different provision is made by (or by the variation of) the order made by the court in Scotland or Northern Ireland.

(2) Where by virtue of subsection (1) above a Part I order has ceased to have effect so far as it makes provision for any matter, a court in England or Wales shall not have jurisdiction to vary that order so as to make provision for that matter.

(3) A court in England and Wales shall not have jurisdiction to vary a Part I order if, on the relevant date, matrimonial proceedings or civil partnership proceedings are continuing in Scotland or Northern Ireland in respect of the marriage or civil partnership of the parents of the child concerned.

(3A) Subsection (3) shall not apply if—

(a) the Part 1 order was made in or in connection with proceedings—

(i) for divorce or nullity in England and Wales in respect of the marriage of the parents of the child concerned; or

(ii) for dissolution or annulment in England and Wales in respect of the civil partnership of the parents of the child concerned; and

(b) those proceedings are continuing.

(3B) Subsection (3) shall not apply if—

(a) the Part 1 order was made in or in connection with proceedings—

(i) for judicial separation in England and Wales; or

(ii) for a separation order in England and Wales; and

(b) those proceedings are continuing; and

(c) as the case may be, the decree of judicial separation has not yet been granted or the separation order has not yet been made.

(4) Subsection (3) above shall not apply if the court in which the proceedings there referred to are continuing has made—

(a) an order under section 13(6) or 19A(4) of this Act (not being an order made by virtue of section 13(6)(a)(i)), or

(b) an order under section 14(2) or 22(2) of this Act which is recorded as made for the purpose of enabling Part I proceedings with respect to the child concerned to be taken in England and Wales,

and that order is in force.

(5) Subsection (3) above shall not apply in the case of a variation of a section 1(1)(d) order if the child concerned is present in England and Wales on the relevant date and the court considers that the immediate exercise of its powers is necessary for his protection.

(6) Subsection (7) below applies where a Part I order which is—

(a) a residence order (within the meaning of the Children Act 1989) in favour of a person with respect to a child,

(b) an order made in the exercise of the High Court's inherent jurisdiction with respect to children by virtue of which a person has care of a child, or

(c) an order—

(i) of a kind mentioned in section 1(3)(a) of this Act,

(ii) under which a person is entitled to the actual possession of a child,

ceases to have effect in relation to that person by virtue of subsection (1) above.

(7) Where this subsection applies, any family assistance order made under section 16 of the Children Act 1989 with respect to the child shall also cease to have effect.

(8) For the purposes of subsection (7) above the reference to a family assistance order under section 16 of the Children Act 1989 shall be deemed to include a reference to an order for the supervision of a child made under—

(a) section 7(4) of the Family Law Reform Act 1969,

(b) section 44 of the Matrimonial Causes Act 1973,

(c) section 2(2)(a) of the Guardianship Act 1973,

(d) section 34(5) or 36(3)(b) of the Children Act 1975, or

(e) section 9 of the Domestic Proceedings and Magistrates' Courts Act 1978;

but this subsection shall cease to have effect once all such orders for the supervision of children have ceased to have effect in accordance with Schedule 14 to the Children Act 1989.

[Family Law Act 1986, s 6 as amended by the Children Act 1989, Sch 13, SI 1995/756 and SI 2005/3336.]

---

*Amended by the Family Law Act 1996, Sch 8, this PART, POST, WHEN IN FORCE.

6–1816 7. Interpretation of Chapter II. In this Chapter—

(a) "child" means a person who has not attained the age of eighteen;

(aa) "civil partnership proceedings" means proceedings for the dissolution or annulment of a civil partnership or for legal separation of the civil partners;

(b) "matrimonial proceedings" means proceedings for divorce, nullity of marriage or judicial separation;

(c) "the relevant date" means, in relation to the making or variation of an order—

(i) where an application is made for an order to be made or varied, the date of the application (or first application, if two or more are determined together), and

(ii) where no such application is made, the date on which the court is considering whether to make or, as the case may be, vary the order; and

(d) "section 1(1)(a) order" and "section 1(1)(d) order" mean orders falling within section 1(1)(a) and (d) of this Act respectively.

[Family Law Act 1986, s 7, as substituted by the Children Act 1989, Sch 13 and SI 2005/3336.]

6–1817

CHAPTER III[1]

JURISDICTION OF COURTS IN SCOTLAND

---

1. Chapter III which contains ss 8–18 extends to Scotland only (s 69(6)).

6–1818

CHAPTER IV[1]

JURISDICTION OF COURTS IN NORTHERN IRELAND

---

1. Chapter IV which contains ss 19–24 extends to Northern Ireland only (s 69(7)).

CHAPTER V

RECOGNITION AND ENFORCEMENT

6–1819 25. Recognition of Part I orders: general. (1) Where a Part I order made by a court in any part of the United Kingdom is in force with respect to a child who has not attained the age of sixteen, then, subject to subsection (2) below, the order shall be recognised in any other part of the United Kingdom as having the same effect in that other part as if it had been made by the appropriate court in that other part and as if that court had had jurisdiction to make it.

(2) Where a Part I order includes provision as to the means by which rights conferred by the order are to be enforced, subsection (1) above shall not apply to that provision.

(3) A court in a part of the United Kingdom in which a Part I order is recognised in accordance with subsection (1) above shall not enforce the order unless it has been registered in that part of the United Kingdom under section 27 of this Act and proceedings for enforcement are taken in accordance with section 29 of this Act.

[Family Law Act 1986, s 25 as amended by the Children Act 1989, Sch 13.]

6–1820   26. Recognition: special Scottish rule.   (1) An order relating to parental responsibilities or parental rights in relation to a child which is made outside the United Kingdom shall be recognised in Scotland if the order was made in the country where the child was habitually resident.

(2) Subsection (1) above shall not apply to an order as regards which provision as to recognition is made by Articles 21 to 27, 41(1) and 42(1) of the Council Regulation.

[Family Law Act 1986, s 26, as substituted by the Children (Scotland) Act 1995, Sch 4 and amended by SSI 2001/36 and SSI 2005/42.]

6–1821   27. Registration.   (1) Any person on whom any rights are conferred by a Part I order may apply to the court which made it for the order to be registered in another part of the United Kingdom under this section.

(2) An application under this section shall be made in the prescribed[1] manner and shall contain the prescribed information and be accompanied by such documents as may be prescribed.

(3) On receiving an application under this section the court which made the Part I order shall, unless it appears to the court that the order is no longer in force, cause the following documents to be sent to the appropriate court in the part of the United Kingdom specified in the application, namely—

(*a*) a certified copy of the order, and
(*b*) where the order has been varied, prescribed particulars of any variation which is in force, and
(*c*) a copy of the application and of any accompanying documents.

(4) Where the prescribed officer of the appropriate court receives a certified copy of a Part I order under subsection (3) above, he shall forthwith cause the order, together with particulars of any variation, to be registered in that court in the prescribed manner.

(5) An order shall not be registered under this section in respect of a child who has attained the age of sixteen, and the registration of an order in respect of a child who has not attained the age of sixteen shall cease to have effect on the attainment by the child of that age.

[Family Law Act 1986, s 27 as amended by the Children Act 1989, Sch 13.]

---

1. For procedure on an application under this section for the registration of a Part I order made by a magistrates' court in England and Wales, see the Magistrates' Courts (Family Law Act 1986) Rules 1988, this PART, post.

6–1822   28. Cancellation and variation of registration.   (1) A court which revokes, recalls or varies an order registered under section 27 of this Act shall cause notice of the revocation, recall or variation to be given in the prescribed manner to the prescribed officer of the court in which it is registered and, on receiving the notice, the prescribed officer—

(*a*) in the case of the revocation or recall of the order, shall cancel the registration, and
(*b*) in the case of the variation of the order, shall cause particulars of the variation to be registered in the prescribed manner.

(2) Where—

(*a*) an order registered under section 27 of this Act ceases (in whole or in part) to have effect in the part of the United Kingdom in which it was made, otherwise than because of its revocation, recall or variation, or
(*b*) an order registered under section 27 of this Act in Scotland ceases (in whole or in part) to have effect there as a result of the making of an order in proceedings outside the United Kingdom,

the court in which the order is registered may, of its own motion or on the application of any person who appears to the court to have an interest in the matter, cancel the registration (or, if the order has ceased to have effect in part, cancel the registration so far as it relates to the provisions which have ceased to have effect).

[Family Law Act 1986, s 28.]

6–1823   29. Enforcement.   (1) Where a Part I order has been registered under section 27 of this Act, the court in which it is registered shall have the same powers for the purpose of enforcing the order as it would have if it had itself made the order and had jurisdiction to make it; and proceedings for or with respect to enforcement may be taken accordingly.

(2) Where an application has been made to any court for the enforcement of an order registered in that court under section 27 of this Act, the court may, at any time before the application is determined, give such interim directions as it thinks fit for the purpose of securing the welfare of the child concerned or of preventing changes in the circumstances relevant to the determination of the application.

(3) The references in subsection (1) above to a Part I order do not include references to any provision of the order as to the means by which rights conferred by the order are to be enforced.

[Family Law Act 1986, s 29 as amended by the Children Act 1989, Sch 13.]

6–1824   30. Staying or sisting of enforcement proceedings.   (1) Where in accordance with section 29 of this Act proceedings are taken in any court for the enforcement of an order registered in that court, any person who appears to the court to have an interest in the matter may apply for the proceedings to be stayed or sisted on the ground that he has taken or intends to take other proceedings (in the United Kingdom or elsewhere) as a result of which the order may cease to have effect, or may have a different effect, in the part of the United Kingdom in which it is registered.

(2) If after considering an application under subsection (1) above the court considers that the proceedings for enforcement should be stayed or sisted in order that other proceedings may be taken or concluded, it shall stay or sist the proceedings for enforcement accordingly.

(3) The court may remove a stay or recall a sist granted in accordance with subsection (2) above if it appears to the court—

(a) that there has been unreasonable delay in the taking or prosecution of the other proceedings referred to in that subsection, or

(b) that those other proceedings are concluded and that the registered order, or a relevant part of it, is still in force.

(4) Nothing in this section shall affect any power exercisable apart from this section to grant, remove or recall a stay or sist.
[Family Law Act 1986, s 30.]

6–1825 31. Dismissal of enforcement proceedings. (1) Where in accordance with section 29 of this Act proceedings are taken in any court for the enforcement of an order registered in that court, any person who appears to the court to have an interest in the matter may apply for those proceedings to be dismissed on the ground that the order has (in whole or in part) ceased to have effect in the part of the United Kingdom in which it was made.

(2) Where in accordance with section 29 of this Act proceedings are taken in the Court of Session for the enforcement of an order registered in that court, any person who appears to the court to have an interest in the matter may apply for those proceedings to be dismissed on the ground that the order has (in whole or in part) ceased to have effect in Scotland as a result of the making of an order in proceedings outside the United Kingdom.

(3) If, after considering an application under subsection (1) or (2) above, the court is satisfied that the registered order has ceased to have effect, it shall dismiss the proceedings for enforcement (or, if it is satisfied that the order has ceased to have effect in part, it shall dismiss the proceedings so far as they relate to the enforcement of provisions which have ceased to have effect).
[Family Law Act 1986, s 31.]

6–1826 32. Interpretation of Chapter V. (1) In this Chapter—

"the appropriate court", in relation to England and Wales or Northern Ireland, means the High Court and, in relation to Scotland, means the Court of Session;

"Part I order" includes (except where the context otherwise requires) any order within section 1(3) of this Act which, on the assumptions mentioned in subsection (3) below—

(a) could have been made notwithstanding the provisions of this Part;

(b) would have been a Part I order for the purposes of this Part; and

(c) would not have ceased to have effect by virtue of section 6, 15 or 23 of this Act.

(2) In the application of this Chapter to Scotland, "Part I order" also includes (except where the context otherwise requires) any order within section 1(3) of this Act which, on the assumptions mentioned in subsection (3) below—

(a) would have been a Part I order for the purposes of this Part; and

(b) would not have ceased to have effect by virtue of section 6 or 23 of this Act,

and which, but for the provisions of this Part, would be recognised in Scotland under any rule of law.

(3) The said assumptions are—

(a) that this Part had been in force at all material times; and

(b) that any reference in section 1 of this Act to any enactment included a reference to any corresponding enactment previously in force.
[Family Law Act 1986, s 32 as amended by the Children Act 1989, Sch 13.]

CHAPTER VI
MISCELLANEOUS AND SUPPLEMENTAL

6–1827 33. Power to order disclosure of child's whereabouts. (1) Where in proceedings for or relating to a Part I order in respect of a child there is not available to the court adequate information as to where the child is, the court may order any person[1] who it has reason to believe may have relevant information to disclose it to the court.

(2) A person shall not be excused from complying with an order under subsection (1) above by reason that to do so may incriminate him or his spouse of an offence; but a statement or admission made in compliance with such an order shall not be admissible in evidence against either of them in proceedings for any offence other than perjury.

(3) A court in Scotland before which proceedings are pending for the enforcement of an order relating to parental responsibilities or parental rights in relation to a child made outside the United

Kingdom which is recognised in Scotland shall have the same powers as it would have under subsection (1) above if the order were its own.

[Family Law Act 1986, s 33 as amended by the Children Act 1989, Sch 13 and the Children (Scotland) Act 1995, Sch 4.]

---

1. Although s 33 extends to the police, the police ought not to be asked to divulge the whereabouts of a child to the court in response to a s 33 application other than in exceptional circumstances.(*S v S* [1999] 1 All ER 281, [1998] 1 WLR 1716, sub nom *S v S (Chief Constable of West Yorkshire intervening)* [1999] 1 FCR 244, CA.

6–1828 34. Power to order recovery of child. (1) Where—

(*a*) a person is required by a Part I order, or an order for the enforcement of a Part I order, to give up a child to another person ("the person concerned"), and

(*b*) the court which made the order imposing the requirement is satisfied that the child has not been given up in accordance with the order,

the court may make an order authorising an officer of the court or a constable to take charge of the child and deliver him to the person concerned.

(2) The authority conferred by subsection (1) above includes authority—

(*a*) to enter and search any premises where the person acting in pursuance of the order has reason to believe the child may be found, and

(*b*) to use such force as may be necessary to give effect to the purpose of the order.

(3) Where by virtue of—

(*a*) section 14 of the Children Act 1989, or

(*b*) Article 14 (enforcement of residence orders) of the Children (Northern Ireland) Order 1995,

a Part I order (or a provision of a Part I order) may be enforced as if it were an order requiring a person to give up a child to another person, subsection (1) above shall apply as if the Part I order had included such a requirement.

(4) This section is without prejudice to any power conferred on a court by or under any other enactment or rule of law.

[Family Law Act 1986, s 34 as amended by the Children Act 1989, Sch 13 and SI 1995/756.]

6–1829 35. Powers to restrict removal of child from jurisdiction. (1) *Repealed.*

(2) *Repealed.*

(3) A court in Scotland—

(*a*) at any time after the commencement of proceedings in connection with which the court would have jurisdiction to make a Part I order, or

(*b*) in any proceedings in which it would be competent for the court to grant an interdict prohibiting the removal of a child from its jurisdiction,

may, on an application by any of the persons mentioned in subsection (4) below, grant interdict or interim interdict prohibiting the removal of the child from the United Kingdom or any part of the United Kingdom, or out of the control of the person in whose care the child is.

(4) The said persons are—

(*a*) any party to the proceedings,

(*b*) the tutor or curator of the child concerned, and

(*c*) any other person who has or wishes to obtain the care of the child.

(5) In subsection (3) above "the court" means the Court of Session or the sheriff; and for the purposes of subsection (3)(*a*) above, proceedings shall be held to commence—

(*a*) in the Court of Session, when a summons is signed or a petition is presented;

(*b*) in the sheriff court, when the warrant of citation is signed.

[Family Law Act 1986, s 35 as amended by the Children Act 1989, Schs 13 and 15, SI 1995/755 and the Children (Scotland) Act 1995, Schs 4 and 5.]

6–1830 36. Effect of orders restricting removal. (1) This section applies to any order made by a court in the United Kingdom prohibiting the removal of a child from the United Kingdom or from any specified part of it.

(2) An order to which this section applies shall have effect in each part of the United Kingdom other than the part in which it was made—

(*a*) as if it had been made by the appropriate court in the other part, and

(*b*) in the case of an order which has the effect of prohibiting the child's removal to that other part, as if it had included a prohibition on his further removal to any place except one to which he could be removed consistently with the order.

(3) The references in subsections (1) and (2) above to prohibitions on a child's removal include references to prohibitions subject to exceptions; and in a case where removal is prohibited except with the consent of the court, nothing in subsection (2) above shall be construed as affecting the identity of the court whose consent is required.

(4) In this section "child" means a person who has not attained the age of sixteen; and this section shall cease to apply to an order relating to a child when he attains the age of sixteen.
[Family Law Act 1986, s 36.]

6–1831   37. Surrender of passports.   (1) Where there is in force an order prohibiting or otherwise restricting the removal of a child from the United Kingdom or from any specified part of it, the court by which the order was in fact made, or by which it is treated under section 36 of this Act as having been made, may require any person to surrender any United Kingdom passport which has been issued to, or contains particulars of, the child.

(2) In this section "United Kingdom passport" means a current passport issued by the Government of the United Kingdom.
[Family Law Act 1986, s 37.]

6–1832   38. Automatic restriction on removal of wards of court.   (1) The rule of law which (without any order of the court) restricts the removal of a ward of court from the jurisdiction of the court shall, in a case to which this section applies, have effect subject to the modifications in subsection (3) below.

(2) This section applies in relation to a ward of court if—

(*a*) proceedings for divorce, nullity or judicial separation in respect of the marriage of his parents are continuing in a court in another part of the United Kingdom (that is to say, in a part of the United Kingdom outside the jurisdiction of the court of which he is a ward), or

(*aa*) proceedings for dissolution or annulment or legal separation in respect of the civil partnership of his parents are continuing in a court in another part of the United Kingdom (that is to say, in a part of the United Kingdom outside the jurisdiction of the court of which he is a ward), or

(*b*) he is habitually resident in another part of the United Kingdom,

except where that other part is Scotland and he has attained the age of sixteen.

(3) Where this section applies, the rule referred to in subsection (1) above shall not prevent—

(*a*) the removal of the ward of court, without the consent of any court, to the other part of the United Kingdom mentioned in subsection (2) above, or

(*b*) his removal to any other place with the consent of either the appropriate court in that other part of the United Kingdom or the court mentioned in subsection (2)(*a*) or (*aa*) above .*
[Family Law Act 1986, s 38 as amended by SI 2005/3336.]

*Amended by the insertion of a new sub-s (4) by the Family Law Act 1996, Sch 8, this PART, POST, WHEN IN FORCE.

6–1833   39. Duty to furnish particulars of other proceedings.   Parties to proceedings for or relating to a Part I order shall, to such extent and in such manner as may be prescribed[1], give particulars of other proceedings known to them which relate to the child concerned (including proceedings instituted abroad and proceedings which are no longer continuing).
[Family Law Act 1986, s 39 as amended by the Children Act 1989, Sch 13.]

1. For the prescribed procedure in relation to proceedings in magistrates' courts, see the Magistrates' Courts (Family Law Act 1986) Rules 1988, this PART, post.

6–1834   40. Interpretation of Chapter VI.   (1) In this Chapter—

"the appropriate court" has the same meaning as in Chapter V;
"Part I order" includes (except where the context otherwise requires) any such order as is mentioned in section 32(1) of this Act.

(2) In the application of this Chapter to Scotland, "Part I order" also includes (except where the context otherwise requires) any such order as is mentioned in section 32(2) of this Act.
[Family Law Act 1986, s 40 as amended by the Children Act 1989, Sch 13.]

6–1835   41. Habitual residence after removal without consent, etc[1].   (1) Where a child who—

(*a*) has not attained the age of sixteen, and
(*b*) is habitually resident in a part of the United Kingdom,

becomes habitually resident outside that part of the United Kingdom in consequence of circumstances of the kind specified in subsection (2) below, he shall be treated for the purposes of this Part as continuing to be habitually resident in that part of the United Kingdom for the period of one year beginning with the date on which those circumstances arise.

(2) The circumstances referred to in subsection (1) above exist where the child is removed from or retained outside, or himself leaves or remains outside, the part of the United Kingdom in which he was habitually resident before his change of residence—

(a) without the agreement of the person or all the persons having, under the law of that part of the United Kingdom, the right to determine where he is to reside, or

(b) in contravention of an order made by a court in any part of the United Kingdom.

(3) A child shall cease to be treated by virtue of subsection (1) above as habitually resident in a part of the United Kingdom if, during the period there mentioned—

(a) he attains the age of sixteen, or

(b) he becomes habitually resident outside that part of the United Kingdom with the agreement of the person or persons mentioned in subsection (2)(a) above and not in contravention of an order made by a court in any part of the United Kingdom.

[Family Law Act 1986, s 41.]

---

1. An order made less than one year after the removal of a child and, consequently, without jurisdiction due to lack of habitual reference is not a nullity, but remains in force until set aside; moreover, there is no basis in the argument that jurisdiction wrongly taken at the start of proceedings taints all subsequent proceedings with that lack of jurisdiction: *Re B (court's jurisdiction)* [2004] EWCA Civ 681, [2004] 2 FLR 741.

6–1836 42. General interpretation of Part I. (1) In this Part—

"certified copy", in relation to an order of any court, means a copy certified by the prescribed officer of the court to be a true copy of the order or of the official record of the order;

"parental responsibilities" and "parental rights" have the meanings respectively given by sections 1(3) and 2(4) of the Children (Scotland) Act 1995;

"part of the United Kingdom" means England and Wales, Scotland or Northern Ireland;

"prescribed"[1] means prescribed by rules of court or act of sederunt;

"the Council Regulation" means Council Regulation (EC) No 2201/2003 of 27th November 2003 concerning jurisdiction and the recognition and enforcement of judgments in matrimonial matters and matters of parental responsibility,

(2) For the purposes of this Part proceedings in England and Wales or in Northern Ireland for divorce, nullity or judicial separation in respect of the marriage of the parents of a child shall, unless they have been dismissed, be treated as continuing until the child concerned attains the age of eighteen (whether or not a decree has been granted and whether or not, in the case of a decree of divorce or nullity of marriage, that decree has been made absolute).* be treated as continuing (irrespective of whether a divorce order, separation order or decree of nullity has been made)—

(a) from the time when a statement of marital breakdown under section 5 of the Family Law Act 1996 with respect to the marriage is received by the court in England and Wales until such time as the court may designate or, if earlier, until the time when—

(i) the child concerned attains the age of eighteen; or

(ii) it ceases, by virtue of section 5(3) or 7(9) of that Act (lapse of divorce or separation process) to be possible for an application for a divorce order, or for a separation order, to be made by reference to that statement; and

(b) from the time when a petition for nullity is presented in relation to the marriage in England and Wales or a petition for divorce, judicial separation or nullity is presented in relation to the marriage in Northern Ireland or a specified British overseas territory, until the time when—

(i) the child concerned attains the age of eighteen; or

(ii) if earlier, proceedings on the petition are dismissed.

(2A) For the purposes of this Part proceedings in England and Wales or in Northern Ireland for dissolution, annulment or legal separation in respect of the civil partnership of the parents of the child shall, unless they have been dismissed, be treated as continuing until the child concerned attains the age of eighteen (whether or not a dissolution, nullity or separation order has been made and whether or not, in the case of a dissolution or nullity order, that order has been made final).

(3) For the purposes of this Part, matrimonial proceedings or civil partnership proceedings in a court in Scotland which has jurisdiction in those proceedings to make a Part I order with respect to a child shall, unless they have been dismissed or decree of absolvitor has been granted therein, be treated as continuing until the child concerned attains the age of sixteen.

(4) Any reference in this Part to proceedings in respect of the marriage or civil partnership of the parents of a child shall, in relation to a child who, although not a child of both parties to the marriage or civil partnership, is a child of the family of those parties, be construed as a reference to proceedings in respect of that marriage or civil partnership; and for this purpose "child of the family"—

(a) if the proceedings are in England and Wales, means any child who has been treated by both parties as a child of their family, except a child who is placed with those parties as foster parents by a local authority or a voluntary organisation;

(b) if the proceedings are in Scotland, means any child who has been treated by both parties as a child of their family, except a child who has been placed with those parties as foster parents by a local authority or a voluntary organisation; who has been accepted as one of the family by the other party;

(c) if the proceedings are in Northern Ireland, means any child who has been treated by both parties as a child of their family, except a child who is placed with those parties as foster parents by an authority within the meaning of the Children (Northern Ireland) Order 1995 or a voluntary organisation.

(4A) Any reference in this Part to proceedings in respect of the civil partnership of the parents of a child shall, in relation to a child who, although not a child of the civil partners, is a child of the family of the civil partners, be construed as a reference to proceedings in respect of that civil partnership; and for this purpose "child of the family" has the meaning given in paragraphs (a) to (c) of subsection (4) (but substituting references to the civil partners for references to the parties to the marriage).

(5) References in this Part to Part I orders include (except where the context otherwise requires) references to Part I orders as varied.

(6) For the purposes of this Part each of the following orders shall be treated as varying the Part I order to which it relates—

(a) an order which provides for a person to be allowed contact with or to be given access to a child who is the subject of a Part I order, or which makes provision for the education of such a child,

(b)–(d) *Repealed.*

(7) In this Part—

(a) references to Part I proceedings in respect of a child are references to any proceedings for a Part I order or an order corresponding to a Part I order and include, in relation to proceedings outside the United Kingdom, references to proceedings before a tribunal or other authority having power under the law having effect there to determine Part I matters; and

(b) references to Part I matters are references to matters that might be determined by a Part I order or an order corresponding to a Part I order.

[Family Law Act 1986, s 42 as amended by the Children Act 1989, Schs 13 and 15, SI 1995/756, the Children (Scotland) Act 1995, Sch 4, SI 2001/310, the British Overseas Territories Act 2000, s 1, SSI 2005/42, SI 2005/265 and SI 2005/3336.]

---

*Repealed by the Family Law Act 1996, Sch 8, this Part, post, when in force.
1. In relation to magistrates' courts, see the Magistrates' Courts (Family Law Act 1986) Rules 1988, this Part, post.

6–1837   **43.** *Application of Part I to dependent territories.*

6–1838

PART II[1]
Recognition of Divorces, Annulments and Legal Separations

---

1. Part II contains ss 44–54.

PART III[1]
Declarations of Status

6–1839   **55. Declarations as to marital status.** (1) Subject to the following provisions of this section, any person may apply to the High Court or a county court for one or more of the following declarations in relation to a marriage specified in the application, that is to say—

(a) a declaration that the marriage was at its inception a valid marriage;
(b) a declaration that the marriage subsisted on a date specified in the application;
(c) a declaration that the marriage did not subsist on a date so specified;
(d) a declaration that the validity of a divorce, annulment or legal separation obtained in any country outside England and Wales in respect of the marriage is entitled to recognition in England and Wales;
(e) a declaration that the validity of a divorce, annulment or legal separation so obtained in respect of the marriage is not entitled to recognition in England and Wales.

(2) A court shall have jurisdiction to entertain an application under subsection (1) above if, and only if, either of the parties to the marriage to which the application relates—

(a) is domiciled in England and Wales on the date of the application, or
(b) has been habitually resident in England and Wales throughout the period of one year ending with that date, or
(c) died before that date and either—

(i) was at death domiciled in England and Wales, or
(ii) had been habitually resident in England and Wales throughout the period of one year ending with the date of death.

(3) Where an application under section (1) above is made to a court by any person other than a party to the marriage to which the application relates, the court shall refuse to hear the application if

it considers that the applicant does not have a sufficient interest in the determination of that application.

[Family Law Act 1986, s 55 as amended by the Child Support, Pensions and Social Security Act 2000, Sch 8 .]

1. Part III contains ss 55–63.

6–1839A   55A. Declarations of parentage.   (1) Subject to the following provisions of this section, any person may apply to the High Court, a county court or a magistrates' court for a declaration as to whether or not a person named in the application is or was the parent of another person so named.

(2) A court shall have jurisdiction to entertain an application under subsection (1) above if, and only if, either of the persons named in it for the purposes of that subsection—

(*a*)   is domiciled in England and Wales on the date of the application, or

(*b*)   has been habitually resident in England and Wales throughout the period of one year ending with that date, or

(*c*)   died before that date and either—

(i)   was at death domiciled in England and Wales, or

(ii)   had been habitually resident in England and Wales throughout the period of one year ending with the date of death.

(3) Except in a case falling within subsection (4) below, the court shall refuse to hear an application under subsection (1) above unless it considers that the applicant has a sufficient personal interest in the determination of the application (but this is subject to section 27 of the Child Support Act 1991).

(4) The excepted cases are where the declaration sought is as to whether or not—

(*a*)   the applicant is the parent of a named person;

(*b*)   a named person is the parent of the applicant; or

(*c*)   a named person is the other parent of a named child of the applicant.

(5) Where an application under subsection (1) above is made and one of the persons named in it for the purposes of that subsection is a child, the court may refuse to hear the application if it considers that the determination of the application would not be in the best interests of the child.

(6) Where a court refuses to hear an application under subsection (1) above it may order that the applicant may not apply again for the same declaration without leave of the court.

(7) Where a declaration is made by a court on an application under subsection (1) above, the prescribed officer of the court shall notify the Registrar General, in such a manner and within such period as may be prescribed, of the making of that declaration.

[Family Law Act 1986, s 55A as inserted by the Child Support, Pensions and Social Security Act 2000, Sch 8.]

6–1840   56. Declarations of parentage, legitimacy or legitimation.   (1) Any person may apply to the High Court or a county court for a declaration—

(*a*)   that a person named in the application is or was his parent; or

(*b*)   that he is the legitimate child of his parents.

(2) Any person may apply to the High Courtor a county court for one (or for one or, in the alternative, the other) of the following declarations, that is to say—

(*a*)   a declaration that he has become a legitimated person;

(*b*)   a declaration that he has not become a legitimated person.

(3) A court shall have jurisdiction to entertain an application under this section if, and only if, the applicant—

(*a*)   is domiciled in England and Wales on the date of the application; or

(*b*)   has been habitually resident in England and Wales throughout the period of one year ending with that date.

(4) Where a declaration is made by a court on an application under subsection (1) above, the prescribed officer of the court shall notify the Registrar General, in such a manner and within such period as may be prescribed, of the making of that declaration.

(5) In this section "legitimated person" means a person legitimated or recognised as legitimated—

(*a*)   under section 2 or 3 of the Legitimacy Act 1976;

(*b*)   under section 1 or 8 of the Legitimacy Act 1926; or

(*c*)   by a legitimation (whether or not by virtue of the subsequent marriage of his parents) recognised by the law of England and Wales and effected under the law of another country.

[Family Law Act 1986, s 56, as substituted by the Family Law Reform Act 1987, s 22 and as amended by the Child Support, Pensions and Social Security Act 2000, Sch 8.]

6–1841   57. Declarations as to adoptions effected overseas.   (1) Any person whose status as an adopted child of any person depends on whether he has been adopted by that person by either—

(*a*)   a Convention adoption, or an overseas adoption, within the meaning of the Adoption and Children Act 2002, or

(b) an adoption recognised by the law of England and Wales and effected under the law of any country outside the British Islands,

may apply to the High Court or a county court for one (or for one or, in the alternative, the other) of the declarations mentioned in subsection (2) below.

(2) The said declarations are—

(a) a declaration that the applicant is for the purposes of section 39 of the Adoption Act 1976 or section 67 of the Adoption and Children Act 2002 the adopted child of that person;

(b) a declaration that the applicant is not for the purposes of that section the adopted child of that person.

(3) A court shall have jurisdiction to entertain an application under subsection (1) above if, and only if, the applicant—

(a) is domiciled in England and Wales on the date of the application, or

(b) has been habitually resident in England and Wales throughout the period of one year ending with that date.

(4) (*Spent*).

[Family Law Act 1986, s 57, as amended by the Child Support, Pensions and Social Security Act 2000, Sch 8, the Adoption (Intercountry Aspects) Act 1999, Sch 2 and the Adoption and Children Act 2002, Sch 3.]

---

*Section 57(1) and (2) are amended by the Adoption and Children Act 2002, Sch 3, from a date to be appointed.

6–1842   58. General provisions as to the making and effect of declarations.   (1) Where on an application to a court for a declaration under this Part the truth of the proposition to be declared is proved to the satisfaction of the court, the court shall make that declaration unless to do so would manifestly be contrary to public policy.

(2) Any declaration made under this Part shall be binding on Her Majesty and all other persons.

(3) A court, on the dismissal of an application for a declaration under this Part, shall not have power to make any declaration for which an application has not been made.

(4) No declaration which may be applied for under this Part may be made otherwise than under this Part by any court.

(5) No declaration may be made by any court, whether under this Part or otherwise—

(a) that a marriage was at its inception void;

(b) *repealed*

(6) Nothing in this section shall affect the powers of any court to grant a decree of nullity of marriage.

[Family Law Act 1986, s 58 as amended by the Child Support, Pensions and Social Security Act 2000, Schs 8 and 9.]

6–1843   59. Provisions relating to the Attorney-General.   (1) On an application to a court for a declaration under this Part the court may at any stage of the proceedings, of its own motion or on the application of any party to the proceedings, direct that all necessary papers in the matter be sent to the Attorney-General.

(2) The Attorney-General, whether or not he is sent papers in relation to an application to a court for a declaration under this Part, may–

(a) intervene in the proceedings on that application in such manner as he thinks necessary or expedient, and

(b) argue before the court any question in relation to the application which the court considers it necessary to have fully argued.

(3) Where any costs are incurred by the Attorney-General in connection with any application to a court for a declaration under this Part, the court may make such order as it considers just as to the payment of those costs by parties to the proceedings.

[Family Law Act 1986, s 59 as amended by the Child Support, Pensions and Social Security Act 2000, Sch 8.]

6–1844   60. Supplementary provisions as to declarations.   (1) Any declaration made under this Part, and any application for such a declaration, shall be in the form prescribed by rules of court.

(2) Rules of court may make provision—

(a) as to the information required to be given by any applicant for a declaration under this Part;

(b) as to the persons who are to be parties to proceedings on an application under this Part;

(c) requiring notice of an application under this Part to be served on the Attorney-General and on persons who may be affected by any declaration applied for.

(3) No proceedings under this Part shall affect any final judgment or decree already pronounced or made by any court of competent jurisdiction.

(4) The court hearing an application under this Part may direct that the whole or any part of the

proceedings shall be heard in camera, and an application for a direction under this subsection shall be heard in camera unless the court otherwise directs.

(5) An appeal shall lie to the High Court against—

(*a*) the making by a magistrates' court of a declaration under section 55A above,

(*b*) any refusal by a magistrates' court to make such a declaration, or

(*c*) any order under subsection (6) of that section made on such a refusal."

[Family Law Act 1986, s 60 as amended by the Family Law Reform Act 1987, Sch 2 and the Child Support, Pensions and Social Security Act 2000, s 83.]

6–1845   63. Interpretation of Part III.   *Repealed.*

Part IV[1]

Miscellaneous and General

6–1846   68. Minor and consequential amendments, repeals and savings.   (1) The enactments and orders mentioned in Schedule 1 to this Act shall have effect subject to the amendments specified in that Schedule, being minor amendments and amendments consequential on the provisions of this Act.

(2) The enactments mentioned in Schedule 2 to this Act (which include some that are spent or no longer of practical utility) are hereby repealed to the extent specified in the third column of that Schedule.

(3) Nothing in this Act shall affect—

(*a*) any proceedings under section 45 of the Matrimonial Causes Act 1973 begun before the date of the commencement of Part III of this Act;

(*b*) any proceedings for jactitation of marriage begun before that date; or

(*c*) any proceedings for a declaration begun in the High Court before that date by virtue of rules of court relating to declaratory judgments.

(4) The repeal of section 2 of the Legitimacy Declaration Act (Ireland) 1868 shall not affect any proceedings under that section begun before the commencement of that repeal.
[Family Law Act 1986, s 68.]

---

1. Part IV contains ss 66–69.

6–1847   69. Short title, commencement and extent.   (1) This Act may be cited as the Family Law Act 1986.

(2) Sections 64 to 67 of this Act shall come into force at the end of the period of two months beginning with the day on which this Act is passed.

(3) Subject to subsection (2) above, this Act shall come into force on such day as the relevant Minister or Ministers may by order[1] made by statutory instrument appoint; and different days may be so appointed for different provisions or for different purposes.

(4) In subsection (3) above "the relevant Minister or Ministers" means—

(*a*) in the case of an order which appoints a day only for Part III of this Act and its associated amendments and repeals, the Lord Chancellor;

(*b*) in any other case, the Lord Chancellor and the Lord Advocate.

(5) The following provisions of this Act, namely—

Chapter II of Part I;
section 53;
Part III;
sections 64 and 65;
section 68(3); and
paragraphs 9 to 17, 19 and 23 to 27 of Schedule 1 and section 68(1) so far as relating to those
    paragraphs,

extend to England and Wales only.

(6) The following provisions of this Act, namely—

Chapter III of Part I;
section 26; and
paragraphs 1, 3 to 8, 18, 21 and 22 of Schedule 1 and section 68(1) so far as relating to those
    paragraphs,

extend to Scotland only; and sections 34 and 38 of this Act do not extend to Scotland.

(7) The following provisions of this Act, namely—

Chapter IV of Part I;
section 68(4); and
paragraphs 2 and 32 to 34 of Schedule 1 and section 68(1) so far as relating to those paragraphs,

extend to Northern Ireland only; and paragraph 20 of Schedule 1 to this Act and section 68(1) of this Act so far as relating to that paragraph do not extend to Northern Ireland.
[Family Law Act 1986, s 69 as amended by SI 1995/755.]

---

1. The Family Law Act 1986 (Commencement No 1) Order 1988, SI 1988/375, brought the whole of the remaining provisions of the Act into force on 4 April 1988.

Family Law Reform Act 1987[1]
(1987 c 42)

PART I[2]
GENERAL PRINCIPLE

6–1950   1. General principle.   (1) In this Act and enactments passed and instruments made after the coming into force of this section, references (however expressed) to any relationship between two persons shall, unless the contrary intention appears, be construed without regard to whether or not the father and mother of either of them, or the father and mother of any person through whom the relationship is deduced, have or had been married to each other at any time.

(2) In this Act and enactments passed after the coming into force of this section, unless the contrary intention appears—

  (a)   references to a person whose father and mother were married to each other at the time of his birth include; and
  (b)   references to a person whose father and mother were not married to each other at the time of his birth do not include,

references to any person to whom subsection (3) below applies, and cognate references shall be construed accordingly.

(3) This subsection applies to any person who—

  (a)   is treated as legitimate by virtue of section 1 of the Legitimacy Act 1976[3];
  (b)   is a legitimated person within the meaning of section 10 of that Act;
  (c)   is an adopted person within the meaning of Chapter 4 of Part 1 of the Adoption and Children Act 2002.
  (d)   is otherwise treated in law as legitimate.

(4) For the purpose of construing references falling within subsection (2) above, the time of a person's birth shall be taken to include any time during the period beginning with—

  (a)   the insemination resulting in his birth; or
  (b)   where there was no such insemination, his conception,

and (in either case) ending with his birth.
[Family Law Reform Act 1987, s 1 as amended by the Adoption and Children Act 2002, Sch 3.]

---

1. This Act reforms the law relating to the consequences of birth outside marriage, and makes further provision with respect to the rights and duties of parents and the determination of parentage.
   The Act shall come into force on such day or days as the Lord Chancellor may by order appoint (s 34(2), post). At the date of going to press the Family Law Reform Act 1987 (Commencement No 1) Order 1988, SI 1988/425, and (Commencement No 2) Order 1989, SI 1989/382, had been made, bringing into force on 4 April 1988 and 1 April 1989 respectively, all provisions of the Act except: ss 23 and 32, Sch 1 and paras 21–25 of Sch 2.
2. Part I contains s 1.
3. See this title, ante.

PART II[1]
RIGHTS AND DUTIES OF PARENTS ETC
Parental rights and duties: general

6–1951   2. Construction of enactments relating to parental rights and duties.   (1) In the following enactments, namely—

  (a)   section 42(1) of the National Assistance Act 1948;
  (b)   section 6 of the Family Law Reform Act 1969;
  (c)   the Guardianship of Minors Act 1971 (in this Act referred to as "the 1971 Act");
  (d)   Part I of the Guardianship Act 1973 (in this Act referred to as "the 1973 Act");
  (e)   Part II of the Children Act 1975;
  (f)   the Child Care Act 1980 except Part I and sections 13, 24, 64 and 65;
  (g)   *Repealed,*

references (however expressed) to any relationship between two persons shall be construed in accordance with section 1 above.

(2) *Consequential amendment.*

[Family Law Reform Act 1987, s 2 as amended by the Social Security (Consequential Provisions) Act 1992, Sch 1.]

1. Part II contains ss 2–17.

PART III[1]
PROPERTY RIGHTS

1. Part III which is not printed in this work contains ss 18–21.

PART IV[1]
DETERMINATION OF RELATIONSHIPS

6–1957   23. Provisions as to scientific tests.   *This section amends the Family Law Reform Act 1969, ss 20(1), (2), 25.*

1. Part IV contains ss 22 and 23.

PART V[1]
REGISTRATION OF BIRTHS

6–1958

1. Part V contains ss 26–26.

PART VI[1]
MISCELLANEOUS AND SUPPLEMENTAL

Miscellaneous

6–1959   27. Artificial insemination.   (1) Where after the coming into force of this section a child is born in England and Wales as the result of the artificial insemination of a woman who—

(a) was at the time of the insemination a party to a marriage (being a marriage which had not at that time been dissolved or annulled); and

(b) was artificially inseminated with the semen of some person other than the other party to that marriage,

then, unless it is proved to the satisfaction of any court by which the matter has to be determined that the other party to that marriage did not consent to the insemination, the child shall be treated in law as the child of the parties to that marriage and shall not be treated as the child of any person other than the parties to that marriage.

(2) Any reference in this section to a marriage includes a reference to a void marriage if at the time of the insemination resulting in the birth of the child both or either of the parties reasonably believed that the marriage was valid; and for the purposes of this section it shall be presumed, unless the contrary is shown, that one of the parties so believed at that time that the marriage was valid.

(3) Nothing in this section shall affect the succession to any dignity or title of honour or render any person capable of succeeding to or transmitting a right to succeed to any such dignity or title.
[Family Law Reform Act 1987, s 27.]

1. Part VI contains ss 27–34.

Supplemental

6–1960   30. Orders applying section 1 to other enactments.   (1) The Lord Chancellor may by order make provision for the construction in accordance with section 1 above of such enactments passed before the coming into force of that section as may be specified in the order.

(2) An order under this section shall so amend the enactments to which it relates as to secure that (so far as practicable) they continue to have the same effect notwithstanding the making of the order.

(3) An order under this section shall be made by statutory instrument which shall be subject to annulment in pursuance of a resolution of either House of Parliament.
[Family Law Reform Act 1987, s 30.]

6–1961   31. Interpretation.   In this Act—

"the 1953 Act" means the Births and Deaths Registration Act 1953;
"the 1971 Act" means the Guardianship of Minors Act 1971;
"the 1973 Act" means the Guardianship Act 1973.
[Family Law Reform Act 1987, s 31.]

6–1962   33. *Amendments, transitional provisions, savings and repeals.*

6–1963 **34. Short title, commencement and extent.** (1) This Act may be cited as the Family Law Reform Act 1987.

(2) This Act shall come into force on such day as the Lord Chancellor may by order made by statutory instrument appoint; and different days may be so appointed for different provisions or different purposes.

(3) Without prejudice to the transitional provisions contained in Schedule 3 to this Act, an order under subsection (2) above may make such further transitional provisions as appear to the Lord Chancellor to be necessary or expedient in connection with the provisions brought into force by the order, including—

(a) such adaptations of the provisions so brought into force; and
(b) such adaptations of any provisions of this Act then in force,

as appear to him necessary or expedient in consequence of the partial operation of this Act.

(4) The following provisions of this Act extend to Scotland and Northern Ireland, namely—

(a) section 33(1) and paragraphs 12, 13 and 74 of Schedule 2;
(b) section 33(2) and paragraph 7 of Schedule 3 so far as relating to the operation of the Maintenance Orders Act 1950;
(c) section 33(4) and Schedule 4 so far as relating to that Act and the Interpretation Act 1978; and
(d) this section.

(5) Subject to subsection (4) above, this Act extends to England and Wales only.

[Family Law Reform Act 1987, s 34.]

SCHEDULES

Section 33(2)　　　　　　　SCHEDULE 3
TRANSITIONAL PROVISIONS AND SAVINGS[1]

(*Amended by the Children Act 1989, Sch 15 and the Adoption and Children Act 2004, Sch 5.*)

Applications pending under amended or repealed enactments

6–1969 **1.** This Act (including the repeals and amendments made by it) shall not have effect in relation to any application made under any enactment repealed or amended by this Act if that application is pending at the time when the provision of this Act which repeals or amends that enactment comes into force.

---

1. In addition to the transitional provisions set out in Sch 3, the Family Law Reform Act 1987 (Commencement No 2) Order 1989, SI 1989/382, contains the following transitional provisions which are likely to be of long standing application—

"SCHEDULE 2
TRANSITIONAL PROVISIONS
1. The Act (including the repeals and amendments made by it) shall not have effect in relation to the variation, discharge, revival or enforcement of—

(a) orders made under the Guardianship of Minors Acts 1971 and 1973 before 1st April 1989; or
(b) orders made under the said Acts by virtue of paragraph 1 of Schedule 3 to the Act.

2. Paragraph 62 of Schedule 2 to the Act shall not have effect in relation to the revival of orders made under section 34(1)(b) of the Children Act 1975 before 1st April 1989.
3. Paragraph 69 of Schedule 2 to the Act, and the repeals made by Schedule 4 to the Act in section 20 of the Domestic Proceedings and Magistrates' Courts Act 1978, shall not have effect in relation to the revival of orders made under Part I of that Act before 1st April 1989."

References to provisions of Adoption Act 1976

6–1970 **2–5.** *Repealed.*

Affiliation orders

6–1974 **6.** (1) Neither section 17[1] of this Act nor any associated amendment or repeal shall affect, or affect the operation of any enactment in relation to—

(a) any affiliation order made under the Affiliation Proceedings Act 1957[2] which is in force immediately before the coming into force of that section; or
(b) any affiliation order made under that Act by virtue of paragraph 1 above.

(2) Any reference in this paragraph or paragraph 7 below to an affiliation order made under the Affiliation Proceedings Act 1957 includes a reference to—

(a) an affiliation order made, by virtue of section 44 of the National Assistance Act 1948, section 19 of the Supplementary Benefits Act 1976, section 49 or 50 of the Child Care Act 1980 or section 25 of the Social Security Act 1986; and
(b) any order made in relation to such an order.

---

1. Section 17, which provides that the Affiliation Proceedings Act 1957 shall cease to have effect, was brought into force on 1 April 1989 (SI 1989/382).
2. As a consequence of its repeal, the Affiliation Proceedings Act 1957 is no longer printed in this Manual. In view,

however, of the provisions of this Schedule and the continued application of the 1957 Act to orders made before 1 April 1989, it is suggested that users may care to refer to the 1989, or earlier, edition of this Manual for the text of that Act.

6–1975 7. Where—

(a)   an application is made to the High Court or a county court for an order under section 11B of the 1971 Act in respect of a child whose parents were not married to each other at the time of his birth, and

(b)   an affiliation order made under the Affiliation Proceedings Act 1957 and providing for periodical payments is in force in respect of the child by virtue of this Schedule,

the court may, if it thinks fit, direct that the affiliation order shall cease to have effect on such date as may be specified in the direction.

Property rights

6–1976 8. The repeal by this Act of section 14 of the Family Law Reform Act 1969 shall not affect any rights arising under the intestacy of a person dying before the coming into force of the repeal.

6–1977 9. The repeal by this Act of section 15 of the Family Law Reform Act 1969 shall not affect, or affect the operation of section 33 of the Trustee Act 1925 in relation to—

(a)   any disposition inter vivos made before the date on which the repeal comes into force; or

(b)   any disposition by will or codicil executed before that date.

6–1978 10. The repeal by this Act of section 17 of the Family Law Reform Act 1969 shall not affect the liability of trustees or personal representatives in respect of any conveyance or distribution made before the coming into force of the repeal.

Children Act 1989[1]

(1989 c 41)

PART I[2]

INTRODUCTORY

6–2100 1. Welfare of the child. (1) When a court determines any question with respect to—

(a)   the upbringing[3] of a child; or

(b)   the administration of a child's property or the application of any income arising from it,

the child's welfare shall be the court's paramount consideration[4].

(2) In any proceedings in which any question with respect to the upbringing of a child arises, the court shall have regard to the general principle that any delay[5] in determining the question is likely to prejudice the welfare of the child.

(3) In the circumstances mentioned in subsection (4), a court shall have regard[6] in particular to—

(a)   the ascertainable wishes[7] and feelings of the child concerned (considered in the light of his age and understanding);

(b)   his physical, emotional and educational needs;

(c)   the likely effect on him of any change in his circumstances;

(d)   his age, sex, background and any characteristics of his which the court considers relevant;

(e)   any harm which he has suffered or is at risk of suffering;

(f)   how capable each of his parents, and any other person in relation to whom the court considers the question to be relevant, is of meeting his needs;

(g)   the range of powers available to the court under this Act in the proceedings in question.

(4) The circumstances are that—

(a)   the court is considering whether to make, vary or discharge a section 8 order, and the making, variation or discharge of the order is opposed by any party to the proceedings; or

(b)   the court is considering whether to make, vary or discharge a special guardianship order or an order under Part IV.

(5) Where a court is considering whether or not to make one or more orders under this Act with respect to a child, it shall not make the order or any of the orders unless it considers that doing so would be better for the child than making no order[8] at all.

[Children Act 1989, s 1 as amended by the Adoption and Children Act 2002, s 115.]

---

1. This Act reforms the law relating to children; provides for local authority services for children in need and others; amends the law with respect to children's homes, community homes, voluntary homes and voluntary organisations; makes provision with respect to fostering, child minding and day care for young children and adoption. The Children Act 1989 and Part IV in particular, is compliant with the European Convention on Human Rights: *Re V (a child) (care proceedings: human rights claims)* [2004] EWCA Civ 54, [2004] 1 All ER 997, [2004] 1 WLR 1433, [2004] 1 FCR 338, [2004] 1 FLR.

Commencement: Sections 89 and 96(3)–(7), and para 35 of Sch 12, came into force on the passing of this Act on the 16th November 1989. Paragraph 36 of Sch 12 came into force on the 16 January 1990. All other provisions of the Act shall come into force on such day or days as may be appointed by order made by the Lord Chancellor or the Secretary of State, or by both acting jointly (s 108(2), post). The Children Act 1989 (Commencement and Transitional Provisions) Order 1991, SI 1991/828, amended by SI 1991/1990, brought para 21 of Sch 10 to the Act into force on 1 May 1991, all remaining provisions of the Act, except s 5(11) and (12), not already in force, into force on 14 October 1991, and s 5(11) and (12) into force on 1 February 1992.

2. Part I contains ss 1–7.

3. In determining whether an interview of a child, who had been the subject of anti-social behaviour order proceedings, and his mother should be broadcast on television, the court was not considering a matter with respect to the child's upbringing, therefore s 1(1) of the Children Act 1989 did not apply (*Medway Council v BBC* [2002] 1 FLR 104).

4. Although under art 8 of the European Convention on Human Rights, the interests of all the family members are to be taken into account, case law suggests that the best interests of the child are crucial: See *Whitear v United Kingdom* (1997) EHRLR 291.

As to cases involving challenges to decisions of public authorities – whether proceedings should be brought by way of judicial review or wardship, the principles by reference to which such cases should be decided and whether public or private law is involved – see *A (a patient) v A Health Authority; Re J: R (on the application of S) v Secretary of State for the Home Department* [2002] EWHC 18 (Fam/Admin), [2002] 1 FLR 845, where it was held that the crucial issue was what test was to be a applied as a matter of substantive law. If the task of the court is to come to a decision for and on behalf of a child (or an incompetent adult), then the welfare of that person must be the paramount consideration. If, however, the task is to review the decision of a public authority taken in the exercise of some statutory power, then the governing principles are those of public law.

5. While delay is ordinarily inimical to the welfare of the child, a planned and purposeful delay to enable an assessment to be undertaken may well be beneficial; in such cases a delay of the final decision for the purpose of ascertaining the result of an assessment is proper delay and is to be encouraged (*Re C (a minor) (care proceedings)* [1992] 2 FCR 341). See also *C v Solihull Metropolitan Borough Council* [1993] 1 FLR 290 and *Hounslow London Borough Council v A* [1993] 1 WLR 291, [1993] 1 FLR 702.

When exercising the discretion to adjourn or not to adjourn, the existence of consent between the parties is a factor not lightly to be disregarded. However, the need to decide children's cases within as short a space of time as possible is a more important factor; in weighing the one against the other, the argument that the case is not ready should be looked at with considerable caution; see *Re G (child case: avoiding delay)* [1991] FCR 562. Unnecessary delay which is detrimental to the welfare of the child will justify the court in refusing an adjournment to enable a psychological assessment to be completed where the court already has sufficient information contained in the statements, reports and plans already before it to make a final decision (*Re S (minors) care order: delay principle*) [1997] 1 FCR 490. Contending parties should be confined to material facts with emphasis on the present situation and its bearing on the future. Opinion evidence should be confined and witnesses discouraged from giving their view of the desirable result (*Re L (minors)* (1989) Times, 12 October). The profundity of the court's investigation into proposals must reflect the reality where there is consensus between the parties; where possible it helps if the advocates place a draft order before the court; if the magistrates consider the terms are in some respect deficient they should tell the parties so they can make submissions (*Devon County Council v S* [1992] 1 FCR 550). For a case where a decision to proceed to hear an application to deny contact to an absent mother was upheld, see *Re SW (a minor) (care proceedings)* [1993] 2 FLR 609.

The no delay principle does not place CAFCASS under a duty to make provision to enable it, immediately on request by the court, to make available an officer of the service for appointment as a guardian; the relevant statutory provisions imply that, while CAFCASS should respond as soon as practicable after a request is made, there can be a gap between the request made by the court and CAFCASS making an officer available for appointment (*R v Children and Family Court Advisory and Support Service* [2003] EWHC 235 Admin, [2003] 1 FLR 953).

6. Whilst it is not the court's function to judge religious beliefs, tenets, doctrines or rules, the impact of these factors upon a child must be a relevant consideration (*Re R (a minor) (residence: religion)* [1993] 2 FCR 525, [1993] 2 FLR 163 a case concerning the Exclusive Brethren sect). Although a child's religious and cultural heritage is a relevant factor in considering a child's welfare, it is merely one factor to be weighed in the balance; the 1989 Act contains no presumption which can displace the welfare of the child as the paramount consideration (*R v P (a child) (residence order: restriction order)* [1999] 3 All ER 734, [1999] 3 WLR 1164, [1999] 2 FCR 289, CA).

7. A child's religious beliefs are a feature the court must consider, but the child's wishes are not the paramount consideration (*Re R (a minor) (residence: religion)* [1993] 2 FCR 525, [1993] 2 FLR 163, CA). Justices should not normally see a child privately but should put questions to the guardian ad litem or court welfare officer appointed (*Re M (a minor) (justices' discretion)* [1993] 2 FCR 721, [1993] 2 FLR 706); see also para **6–142 Welfare checklist**.

8. Nevertheless, the court should draw up a form of order to show the determination: (*S v R (parental responsibility)* [1993] 1 FCR 331). For the "no order principle" see para **6–143**, ante.

6–2101   2. Parental responsibility for children.

(1) Where a child's father and mother were married to each other at the time of his birth, they shall each have parental responsibility for the child.

(2) Where a child's father and mother were not married to each other at the time of his birth—

(*a*) the mother shall have parental responsibility for the child;

(*b*) the father shall have parental responsibility for the child if he has acquired it (and has not ceased to have it) in accordance with the provisions of this Act.

(3) References in this Act to a child whose father and mother were, or (as the case may be) were not, married to each other at the time of his birth must be read with section 1 of the Family Law Reform Act 1987 (which extends their meaning).

(4) The rule of law that a father is the natural guardian of his legitimate child is abolished.

(5) More than one person may have parental responsibility for the same child at the same time.

(6) A person who has parental responsibility for a child at any time shall not cease to have that responsibility solely because some other person subsequently acquires parental responsibility for the child.

(7) Where more than one person has parental responsibility for a child, each of them may act alone and without the other (or others) in meeting that responsibility; but nothing in this Part shall be taken to affect the operation of any enactment which requires the consent of more than one person in a matter affecting the child.

(8) The fact that a person has parental responsibility for a child shall not entitle him to act in any way which would be incompatible with any order made with respect to the child under this Act.

(9) A person who has parental responsibility for a child may not surrender or transfer any part of

that responsibility to another but may arrange for some or all of it to be met by one or more persons acting on his behalf.

(10) The person with whom any such arrangement is made may himself be a person who already has parental responsibility for the child concerned.

(11) The making of any such arrangement shall not affect any liability of the person making it which may arise from any failure to meet any part of his parental responsibility for the child concerned.

[Children Act 1989, s 2, as amended by the Adoption and Children Act 2002, s 111.]

6–2102 3. Meaning of "parental responsibility". (1) In this Act "parental responsibility" means all the rights, duties, powers, responsibilities and authority which by law a parent of a child has in relation to the child and his property.

(2) It also includes the rights, powers and duties which a guardian of the child's estate (appointed, before the commencement of section 5, to act generally) would have had in relation to the child and his property.

(3) The rights referred to in subsection (2) include, in particular, the right of the guardian to receive or recover in his own name, for the benefit of the child, property of whatever description and wherever situated which the child is entitled to receive or recover.

(4) The fact that a person has, or does not have, parental responsibility for a child shall not affect—

(a) any obligation which he may have in relation to the child (such as a statutory duty to maintain the child); or

(b) any rights which, in the event of the child's death, he (or any other person) may have in relation to the child's property.

(5) A person who—

(a) does not have parental responsibility for a particular child; but

(b) has care of the child,

may (subject to the provisions of this Act) do what is reasonable in all the circumstances of the case for the purpose of safeguarding or promoting the child's welfare.

[Children Act 1989, s 3.]

6–2103 4. Acquisition of parental responsibility by father. (1) Where a child's father and mother were not married to each other at the time of his birth, the father shall acquire parental responsibility for the child if—

(a) he becomes registered as the child's father under any of the enactments specified in subsection (1A);

(b) he and the child's mother make an agreement (a "parental responsibility agreement") providing for him to have parental responsibility for the child; or

(c) the court, on his application, orders that he shall have parental responsibility for the child.

(1A) The enactments referred to in subsection (1)(a) are—

(a) paragraphs (a), (b) and (c) of section 10(1) and of section 10A(1) of the Births and Deaths Registration Act 1953;

(b) paragraphs (a), (b)(i) and (c) of section 18(1), and sections 18(2)(b) and 20(1)(a) of the Registration of Births, Deaths and Marriages (Scotland) Act 1965; and

(c) sub-paragraphs (a), (b) and (c) of Article 14(3) of the Births and Deaths Registration (Northern Ireland) Order 1976.

(1B) The Secretary of State may by order amend subsection (1A) so as to add further enactments to the list in that subsection.

(2) No parental responsibility agreement shall have effect for the purposes of this Act unless—

(a) it is made in the form prescribed[3] by regulations made by the Lord Chancellor; and

(b) where regulations are made by the Lord Chancellor prescribing the manner in which such agreements must be recorded, it is recorded in the prescribed[2] manner.

(2A) A person who has acquired parental responsibility under subsection (1) shall cease to have that responsibility only if the court so orders.

(3) The court may make an order under subsection (2A) on the application—

(a) of any person who has parental responsibility for the child; or

(b) with the leave of the court, of the child himself,

subject, in the case of parental responsibility acquired under subsection (1)(c), to section 12(4).

(4) The court may only grant leave under subsection (3)(b) if it is satisfied that the child has sufficient understanding to make the proposed application.★

[Children Act 1989, s 4, as amended by the Adoption and Children Act 2002, s 111 and SI 2003/3191.]

---

1. On an application for a parental responsibility order the court must consider, amongst other things, the degree of commitment which the father has shown to the child, the degree of attachment between the father and the child, and the

reasons for the father applying for the order; see *Re H (a minor) (contact and parental responsibility)* [1993] 1 FCR 85, [1993] 1 FLR 484. See also *Re CB (a minor) (parental responsibility order)* [1993] 1 FLR 920.

2. In making an agreement with the father, the mother is not exercising her parental responsibility and therefore, in the case where a local authority shares parental responsibility under a care order, it may not prevent her entering into an agreement by determining the extent to which she could meet her parental responsibility for the child under s 33(3) of the 1989 Act, *Re X (minors) (care proceedings: parental responsibility)* [2000] Fam 156, [2000] 2 All ER 66, [2000] 2 WLR 1031, [2000] 1 FLR 379, FD.

3. See the Parental Responsibility Agreement Regulations 1991, SI 1991/1478, as amended by SI 1994/3157 and SI 2005/2808, which contain the relevant forms for applications under ss 4 and 4A and require that a form be recorded by filing the agreement together with two copies in the Principal Registry.

6–2103A 4A. Acquisition of parental responsibility by step-parent. (1) Where a child's parent ("parent A") who has parental responsibility for the child is married to a person who is not the child's parent ("the step-parent")—

> (a) parent A or, if the other parent of the child also has parental responsibility for the child, both parents may by agreement with the step-parent provide for the step-parent to have parental responsibility for the child; or
> (b) the court may, on the application of the step-parent, order that the step-parent shall have parental responsibility for the child.

(2) An agreement under subsection (1)(a) is also a "parental responsibility agreement", and section 4(2) applies in relation to such agreements as it applies in relation to parental responsibility agreements under section 4.

(3) A parental responsibility agreement under subsection (1)(a), or an order under subsection (1)(b), may only be brought to an end by an order of the court made on the application—

> (a) of any person who has parental responsibility for the child; or
> (b) with the leave of the court, of the child himself.

(4) The court may only grant leave under subsection (3)(b) if it is satisfied that the child has sufficient understanding to make the proposed application.
[Children Act 1989, s 4A as inserted by the Adoption and Children Act 2002, s 112.]

6–2104 5. Appointment of guardians. (1) Where an application with respect to a child is made to the court by any individual, the court may by order appoint that individual to be the child's guardian if—

> (a) the child has no parent with parental responsibility for him; or
> (b) a residence order has been made with respect to the child in favour of a parent , guardian or special guardian of his who has died while the order was in force; or
> (c) paragraph (b) does not apply, and the child's only or last surviving special guardian dies.

(2) The power conferred by subsection (1) may also be exercised in any family proceedings if the court considers that the order should be made even though no application has been made for it.

(3) A parent who has parental responsibility for his child may appoint another individual to be the child's guardian in the event of his death.

(4) A guardian of a child may appoint another individual to take his place as the child's guardian in the event of his death; and a special guardian of a child may appoint another individual to be the child's guardian in the event of his death.

(5) An appointment under subsection (3) or (4) shall not have effect unless it is made in writing, is dated and is signed by the person making the appointment or—

> (a) in the case of an appointment made by a will which is not signed by the testator, is signed at the direction of the testator in accordance with the requirements of section 9 of the Wills Act 1837; or
> (b) in any other case, is signed at the direction of the person making the appointment, in his presence and in the presence of two witnesses who each attest the signature.

(6) A person appointed as a child's guardian under this section shall have parental responsibility for the child concerned.

(7) Where—

> (a) on the death of any person making an appointment under subsection (3) or (4), the child concerned has no parent with parental responsibility for him; or
> (b) immediately before the death of any person making such an appointment, a residence order in his favour was in force with respect to the child or he was the child's only (or last surviving) special guardian,

the appointment shall take effect on the death of that person.⋆

(8) Where, on the death of any person making an appointment under subsection (3) or (4)—

> (a) the child concerned has a parent with parental responsibility for him; and
> (b) subsection (7)(b) does not apply,

the appointment shall take effect when the child no longer has a parent who has parental responsibility for him.

(9) Subsections (1) and (7) do not apply if the residence order referred to in paragraph (*b*) of those subsections was also made in favour of a surviving parent of the child.

(10) Nothing in this section shall be taken to prevent an appointment under subsection (3) or (4) being made by two or more persons acting jointly.

(11) Subject to any provision made by rules of court, no court shall exercise the High Court's inherent jurisdiction to appoint a guardian of the estate of any child.

(12) Where rules of court are made under subsection (11) they may prescribe the circumstances in which, and conditions subject to which, an appointment of such a guardian may be made.

(13) A guardian of a child may only be appointed in accordance with the provisions of this section.
[Children Act 1989, s 5 as amended by the Adoption and Children Act 2002, s 115.]

6–2105   6. Guardians: revocation and disclaimer.   (1) An appointment under section 5(3) or (4) revokes an earlier such appointment (including one made in an unrevoked will or codicil) made by the same person in respect of the same child, unless it is clear (whether as the result of an express provision in the later appointment or by any necessary implication) that the purpose of the later appointment is to appoint an additional guardian.

(2) An appointment under section 5(3) or (4) (including one made in an unrevoked will or codicil) is revoked if the person who made the appointment revokes it by a written and dated instrument which is signed—

(*a*) by him; or

(*b*) at his direction, in his presence and in the presence of two witnesses who each attest the signature.

(3) An appointment under section 5(3) or (4) (other than one made in a will or codicil) is revoked if, with the intention of revoking the appointment, the person who made it—

(*a*) destroys the instrument by which it was made; or

(*b*) has some other person destroy that instrument in his presence.

(3A) An appointment under section 5(3) or (4) (including one made in an unrevoked will or codicil) is revoked if the person appointed is the spouse of the person who made the appointment and either—

(*a*) a decree of a court of civil jurisdiction in England and Wales dissolves or annuls the marriage, or*

(*b*) the marriage is dissolved or annulled and the divorce or annulment is entitled to recognition in England and Wales by virtue of Part II of the Family Law Act 1986,

unless a contrary intention appears by the appointment.

(3B) An appointment under section 5(3) or (4) (including one made in an unrevoked will or codicil) is revoked if the person appointed is the civil partner of the person who made the appointment and either—

(*a*) an order of a court of civil jurisdiction in England and Wales dissolves or annuls the civil partnership, or

(*b*) the civil partnership is dissolved or annulled and the dissolution or annulment is entitled to recognition in England and Wales by virtue of Chapter 3 of Part 5 of the Civil Partnership Act 2004,

unless a contrary intention appears by the appointment.

(4) For the avoidance of doubt, an appointment under section 5(3) or (4) made in a will or codicil is revoked if the will or codicil is revoked.

(5) A person who is appointed as a guardian under section 5(3) or (4) may disclaim his appointment by an instrument in writing signed by him and made within a reasonable time of his first knowing that the appointment has taken effect.

(6) Where regulations are made by the Lord Chancellor prescribing the manner in which such disclaimers must be recorded, no such disclaimer shall have effect unless it is recorded in the prescribed manner.

(7) Any appointment of a guardian under section 5 may be brought to an end at any time by order of the court—

(*a*) on the application of any person who has parental responsibility for the child;

(*b*) on the application of the child concerned, with leave of the court; or

(*c*) in any family proceedings, if the court considers that it should be brought to an end even though no application has been made.
[Children Act 1989, s 6 as amended by the Law Reform (Succession) Act 1995, s 4 and the Civil Partnership Act 2004, s 76.]

---

*Amended by the Family Law Act 1996, s 66(1), Sch 8, when in force.

6–2106 **7. Welfare reports[1].** (1) A court considering any question with respect to a child under this Act may—

(*a*) ask an officer of the Service or a Welsh family proceedings officer; or

(*b*) ask a local authority to arrange for—

(i) an officer of the authority; or

(ii) such other person (other than an officer of the Service) or a Welsh family proceedings officer the authority considers appropriate[2],

to report to the court[3] on such matters relating to the welfare of that child as are required to be dealt with in the report.

(2) The Lord Chancellor may make regulations specifying matters which, unless the court orders otherwise, must be dealt with in any report under this section.

(3) The report may be made in writing, or orally, as the court requires.

(4) Regardless of any enactment or rule of law which would otherwise prevent it from doing so, the court may take account[4] of—

(*a*) any statement contained in the report; and

(*b*) any evidence given in respect of the matters referred to in the report,

in so far as the statement or evidence is, in the opinion of the court, relevant to the question which it is considering.

(5) It shall be the duty of the authority or an officer of the Service or a Welsh family proceedings officer to comply with any request for a report under this section.
[Children Act 1989, s 7, as amended by the Criminal Justice and Court Services Act 2000, Sch 7 and the Children Act 2004, Sch 3.]

---

1. Where professional witnesses have been asked to advise the court by way of a s 7 report, the court cannot depart from their recommendations without clearly explaining its reasons: *Re J (children)(residence: expert evidence)* [2001] 2 FCR 44, CA. See also *Re E (children)(residence order)* [2001] EWCA Civ 567, [2001] 2 FCR 662 where the court welfare officer had been given a full opportunity to express her concerns, the judge had given clear reasons for disagreeing with her and, reviewing the evidence, the judge based been entitled to come to a different view of the facts from the welfare officer.

Evidence may not be given in proceedings under the Children Act 1989 of statements made by one or other of the parties in the course of meetings held or communications made for the purpose of conciliation save in the very unusual case where a statement is made clearly indicating that the maker has in the past caused or is likely in the future to cause serious harm to the well-being of a child. In such exceptional case, it will be for the court to exercise a discretion and only admit the evidence where the public interest in protecting the child's interests outweighs the public interest in preserving the confidentiality of attempted conciliation (*Re D (minors) (conciliation: disclosure of information)* [1993] 2 WLR 721, [1993] 1 FLR 932).

2. In private law proceedings a local authority should not be required to become involved unless they consider that it is a case where care or supervision might be required. Therefore the court was wrong to seek to impose a requirement on a local authority to produce a report by a psychiatrist especially as the discretion to nominate a person under s 7(1)(*b*)(ii) is that of the authority. The better course would be for the parties themselves jointly to instruct an expert (*Re K (contact; psychiatric report* [1996] 1 FCR 474).

3. Where, however, a guardian ad litem has also been appointed the observations in *Re S (a minor) (care proceedings: reports)* [1992] 2 FCR 554, [1993] 1 FLR 110 discouraging the seeking of a welfare report in the absence of special circumstances, should be borne in mind.

4. The fundamental rule that all the evidence upon which a court relies is to be disclosed to the parties, applies also to the contents of a welfare report, and the rule shall be departed from only in the most exceptional circumstances where the court is satisfied that real harm to the child would ensue from disclosure. Moreover, it is not open to a welfare officer to give assurances of confidentiality to informants; see *Re G (minors) (welfare report: disclosure)* [1993] 2 FLR 293.

PART II[1]
ORDERS WITH RESPECT TO CHILDREN IN FAMILY PROCEEDINGS
General

6–2107 **8. Residence, contact and other orders with respect to children.** (1) [2]In this Act—

"a contact order"[3] means an order requiring the person with whom a child lives, or is to live, to allow the child to visit or stay with the person named in the order, or for that person and the child otherwise to have contact with each other[4];

"a prohibited steps order"[5] means an order that no step which could be taken by a parent in meeting his parental responsibility[6] for a child, and which is of a kind specified in the order, shall be taken by any person without the consent of the court;

"a residence order" means an order settling the arrangements to be made as to the person with whom a child is to live[7]; and

"a specific issue order" means an order giving directions for the purpose of determining a specific question which has arisen, or which may arise, in connection with any aspect of parental responsibility[8] for a child.

(2) In this Act "a section 8 order" means any of the orders mentioned in subsection (1) and any order varying or discharging such an order.

(3) For the purposes of this Act "family proceedings"[9] means any proceedings—

(*a*) under the inherent jurisdiction of the High Court in relation to children; and

(*b*) under the enactments mentioned in subsection (4),

but does not include proceedings on an application for leave under section 100(3).

(4) The enactments are—

(a) Parts I, II and IV of this Act;

(b) the Matrimonial Causes Act 1973;

(ba) Schedule 5 to the Civil Partnership Act 2004;

(c) (*Repealed*);

(d) the Adoption and Children Act 2002;(*e*)the Domestic Proceedings and Magistrates' Courts Act 1978;

(ea) Schedule 6 to the Civil Partnership Act 2004;

(f) (*Repealed*);

(g) Part III of the Matrimonial and Family Proceedings Act 1984;

(h) the Family Law Act 1996;

(i) sections 11 and 12 of the Crime and Disorder Act 1998.★

[Children Act 1989, s 8, as amended by the Family Law Act 1996, Schs 8 and 10 and the Crime and Disorder Act 1998, Sch 8 and the Adoption and Children Act 2002, Sch 3 and the Civil Partnership Act 2004, Sch 27.]

★Sub-section (5) inserted by the Family Law Act 1996, Sch 9, this PART, POST, WHEN IN FORCE.

1. Part II contains ss 8–16.

2. Where leave had been granted to allow a child to leave the jurisdiction subject to an undertaking by the mother to return the child by a specified date, with which she failed to comply, it was held that the court was empowered to grant a specific issue order for the return of the child to the jurisdiction and a prohibited steps order for the non-removal of the child out of the jurisdiction, notwithstanding that the application was made ex parte or that the party on whom the orders would be directed was not within the jurisdiction and had no assets within the jurisdiction (*Re D (a minor)* [1992] 1 All ER 892, [1992] 1 WLR 315, CA).

3. For consideration of the general principles which should be applied by the court when hearing an application for a contact order, see para **6–151**, ante. As a general principle, a child should not be denied the opportunity of contact with either parent unless the court is wholly satisfied that it is in the interests of the child that contact should cease. The implacable hostility of a mother towards contact with the father is a factor which is capable, according to the circumstances, of supplying a cogent reason for departing from the general principle (*Re D (a minor) (contact)* [1993] 1 FCR 964).

Where there are competing adoption and contact applications pending, it is desirable that all available options should be open to the court and, therefore, the court should hear the two applications concurrently (*G v G (children: concurrent applications)* [1993] 2 WLR 837, [1993] 2 FCR 27, [1993] 2 FLR 306).

Where a child's father had had no contact for 3 years and a mother would not prepare the child for initial contact, the Court of Appeal sought the involvement of the Official Solicitor, as guardian ad litem in order to explore the question of the child being prepared for contact by a child psychiatrist (*Re R (a minor) (contact)* [1993] 2 FLR 762, CA).

4. An order stating that there shall be no contact is nevertheless a contact order (*Nottinghamshire County Council v P* [1993] 3 All ER 815, [1993] 2 FLR 134, CA).

5. For consideration of the general principles which should be applied when hearing an application for a prohibited steps order, see para **6–152 Prohibited Steps Order**, ante.

6. It has been held that a prohibited steps order does not allow a court to make an order prohibiting the parents from having contact with each other because such contact is not a step which can be taken by a parent in meeting his parental responsibility towards his child (*Croydon London Borough Council v A* [1992] 3 All ER 788, [1992] 3 WLR 267).

7. There is no presumption of law that a child of any given age is better off with one parent or another, but no court can be ignorant of the natural position if other things are equal; a baby of under four week old would normally be with his or her mother (*Re W (residence order: baby)* [1992] 2 FCR 603).

Where an application for a residence order is made in circumstances to which Part I of the Child Abduction and Custody Act 1985 apply (abduction) the philosophy of the Hague Convention should be followed even where the foreign country involved is not a convention country (*G v G (minors) (abduction)* [1991] FCR 12; *Re F (a minor) (abduction)* [1990] 3 All ER 97, 3 WLR 1272, [1991] FCR 227); see also *Re S (minors) (abduction)* [1993] 2 FCR 499, CA and *S v S (child abduction: non-Convention country)* [1995] 1 FCR 188.

8. An application under this section by an area health authority in respect of children in care who needed medical treatment is misconceived and unnecessary, since consent may be given by a competent child (see *Gillick v West Norfolk and Wisbech Area Health Authority* [1986] AC 112), or by a person having parental responsibility or, if this is not possible, by the High Court (*Re K, W and H (minors) (consent to treatment)* [1993] 1 FCR 240, [1993] 1 FLR 854).

However, a specific issue order on the application of a local authority has been held appropriate to secure a blood transfusion; the application should be made to a High Court judge to allow for proceedings to be transferred to the inherent jurisdiction if this becomes necessary (*Camden London Borough Council v R (a minor) (blood transfusion)* [1993] 2 FCR 544).

9. But see s 92(2) post which extends family proceedings to include proceedings under the Children Act 1989 in magistrates' courts.

6–2108 9. Restrictions on making section 8 orders. (1) No court shall make any section 8 order, other than a residence order, with respect to a child who is in the care of a local authority.

(2) No application may be made by a local authority for a residence order or contact order and no court shall make such an order in favour of a local authority.

(3) A person who is, or was at any time within the last six months, a local authority foster parent of a child may not apply for leave[1] to apply for a section 8 order with respect to the child unless—

(a) he has the consent of the authority;

(b) he is a relative of the child; or

(c) the child has lived with him for at least one year preceding the application.

(4) *Repealed.*

(5) No court shall exercise its powers[2] to make a specific issue order or prohibited steps order—

(a) with a view to achieving a result which could be achieved by making a residence or contact order; or

(b) in any way which is denied to the High Court (by section 100(2)) in the exercise of its inherent jurisdiction with respect to children.

(6) Subject to section 12(5) court shall make any section 8 order which is to have effect for a period which will end after the child has reached the age of sixteen unless it is satisfied that the circumstances of the case are exceptional.

(7) No court shall make any section 8 order, other than one varying or discharging such an order, with respect to a child who has reached the age of sixteen unless it is satisfied that the circumstances of the case are exceptional.

[Children Act 1989, s 9 as amended by the Adoption and Children Act 2002, s 113 and 114.]

---

1. In ordinary circumstances it is not appropriate to join foster parents as parties to the proceedings; see *Re G (minors) (interim care order)* [1993] 2 FCR 557, [1993] 2 FLR 839, CA.

2. This prohibition applies to an application by a local authority notwithstanding s 9(2) which prevents an application for a residence or contact order (*Nottinghamshire County Council v P* [1994] Fam 18, [1993] 3 All ER 815, [1994] 1 FCR 624, CA).

6–2109   10. Power of court to make section 8 orders.   (1) In any family proceedings[1] in which a question arises with respect to the welfare of any child, the court may make a section 8 order with respect to the child if—

(a) an application for the order has been made by a person who—

(i)   is entitled to apply for a section 8 order with respect to the child; or
(ii) has obtained the leave[2] of the court to make the application; or

(b) the court considers[3] that the order should be made even though no such application has been made[4].

(2) The court may also make a section 8 order with respect to any child on the application of a person who—

(a) is entitled to apply for a section 8 order with respect to the child; or
(b) has obtained the leave of the court to make the application.

(3) This section is subject to the restrictions[5] imposed by section 9.

(4) The following persons are entitled to apply to the court for any section 8 order with respect to a child—

(a) any parent[6], guardian or special guardian of the child;
(aa) any person who by virtue of section 4A has parental responsibility for the child;
(b) any person in whose favour a residence order is in force with respect to the child.

(5) The following persons are entitled to apply for a residence or contact order with respect to a child—

(a) any party to a marriage (whether or not subsisting) in relation to whom the child is a child of the family;
(aa) any civil partner in a civil partnership (whether or not subsisting) in relation to whom the child is a child of the family;
(b) any person with whom the child has lived for a period of at least three years;
(c) any person who—

(i)   in any case where a residence order is in force with respect to the child, has the consent of each of the persons in whose favour the order was made;
(ii) in any case where the child is in the care of a local authority, has the consent of that authority; or
(iii) in any other case, has the consent of each of those (if any) who have parental responsibility for the child.

(5A) A local authority foster parent is entitled to apply for a residence order with respect to a child if the child has lived with him for a period of at least one year immediately preceding the application.

(6) A person who would not otherwise be entitled (under the previous provisions of this section) to apply for the variation or discharge of a section 8 order shall be entitled to do so if—

(a) the order was made on his application; or
(b) in the case of a contact order, he is named in the order.

(7) Any person who falls within a category of person prescribed by rules of court is entitled to apply for any such section 8 order as may be prescribed in relation to that category of person.

(7A) If a special guardianship order is in force with respect to a child, an application for a residence order may only be made with respect to him, if apart from this subsection the leave of the court is not required, with such leave.

(8) Where the person applying[7] for leave to make an application for a section 8 order is the child concerned, the court may only grant leave if it is satisfied that he has sufficient understanding to make the proposed application for the section 8 order.

(9) Where the person applying for leave[8] to make an application for a section 8 order is not the child concerned, the court shall, in deciding whether or not to grant leave, have particular regard to[9]—

(a) the nature of the proposed application for the section 8 order;
(b) the applicant's connection with the child;
(c) any risk there might be of that proposed application disrupting the child's life to such an extent that he would be harmed by it; and
(d) where the child is being looked after by a local authority—

    (i) the authority's plans for the child's future; and
    (ii) the wishes and feelings of the child's parents.

(10) The period of three years mentioned in subsection (5)(b) need not be continuous but must not have begun more than five years before, or ended more than three months before, the making of the application.

[Children Act 1989, s 10 as amended by the Adoption and Children Act 2002, Sch 3 and the Civil Partnership Act 2004, s 77.]

---

1. A court which is considering an application for an order under ss 8 and 10 has the power, in its discretion, to receive and act on evidence adduced by one party, or emanating from a welfare officer, which is not disclosed to the other party. Such power, however, should be exercised only in most exceptional circumstances, and where the court is satisfied that disclosure of the evidence would be so detrimental to the welfare of the child as to outweigh the normal requirements for a fair trial that all evidence must be disclosed (*Re B (a minor)* [1992] 2 FCR 617, [1993] 1 FLR 1991, [1993] 1 All ER 931, CA).

2. As to the procedural requirements, see r 3(2) of the Family Proceedings Courts (Children Act 1989) Rules 1991, in this PART, post. Section 10(9) sets out the considerations to which the court should have particular regard; the welfare of the child is not at this stage the paramount consideration (*Re M (prohibited steps order: application for leave)* [1993] 1 FCR 78, [1993] 1 FLR 275). The same consideration applies if a party seeks leave to join care proceedings in order to advocate a s 8 order (*G v Kirklees Metropolitan Borough Council* [1993] 1 FCR 357, [1993] 1 FLR 805).

3. Before making an order under this provision, the justices must inform the parties of the order which they intend or are minded to make and allow the parties to make representations; see *Croydon London Borough Council v A* [1992] 3 All ER 788, [1992] 3 WLR 267.

4. Section 10(1)(b) enables the court to make a residence order ex parte, but such power should be exercised only occasionally where there are exceptional circumstances (In *Re B (minors)* [1992] 3 All ER 867, [1992] 3 WLR 113.) The rarity of *ex parte* residence orders was again emphasised in *Re G (minors) (ex p residence order)* [1992] 2 FCR 720 where it was said by Butler Sloss, LJ that "snatch" situations were the only situations where the *ex parte* procedure was thought appropriate. *Re G* was followed in *Re P (a minor) (ex p residence order)* [1993] 2 FCR 417 which also decided that the proper procedure to challenge an *ex parte* residence order was in *inter partes* application to vary or rescind the order. An *ex parte* residence order for as long as three months is wrong in principle (*Re Y (a minor) (ex p residence order)* [1993] 2 FCR 422). It is almost always wrong in principle to make a residence order in favour of an individual who has not sought such an order and does not consent to the making of it, see *Re K (care of residence order)* [1996] 1 FCR 365.

5. The restrictions in s 9(3) are procedural in nature in regulating who can apply for an order, not the content of an order and do not prevent the court of its own motion making a section 8 order in favour of local authority foster parents (*Gloucestershire County Council v C* [1999] 3 WLR 685, [1999] 3 FCR 114, [1999] 2 FLR 61, CA).

6. The term "parent" will ordinarily include a putative father without parental responsibility, but does not include a natural parent who has lost parenthood through adoption or an order freeing the child for adoption (*M v C and Calderdale Metropolitan Borough Council* [1993] 1 FCR 431, [1993] 1 FLR 505, [1993] 3 All ER 313).

An application for leave by the natural parent of a child in respect of whom an adoption order has been made should be transferred to the Family Division of the High Court. In most cases it will be appropriate for the Official Solicitor to be made a respondent and for the local authority involved in the adoption proceedings to be notified of the application, but the adoptive parents should only be informed of the application if the court is satisfied that the mother has a prima facie case for leave; see *Re C (a minor) (adopted child: contact)* [1993] 3 All ER 259, [1993] 3 WLR 85, [1993] 2 FLR 431. Similarly where leave is sought for contact where an informal arrangement has broken down (*Re T (minors) (adopted children: contact)* [1996] 1 All ER 215, [1995] 3 WLR 793, [1995] 2 FLR 792, CA).

7. An application by the child concerned for a s 8 order is likely to raise issues which are more appropriate for determination in the High Court and should be transferred there for the hearing of the application (*Practice Direction (family proceedings orders: applications by children)* [1993] 1 All ER 820, [1993] 1 FCR 584, [1993] 1 FLR 668). See also *Re AD (a minor)* [1993] 1 FCR 573. The principles in s 10(9) do not apply to an application for leave by a child; in dealing with such an application by a child, the best interests of the child are important, but they are not paramount; see *Re C (residence: child's application for leave)* [1995] 1 FLR 927, [1996] 1 FCR 461. "The child concerned" is the child with respect to whom the court might make an order so that where a sibling makes an application subsection (9) will apply and for the application of the criteria in that subsection to the grant of leave in such a situation, see *Re S (a minor) (adopted child: contact)* [1999] 1 All ER 648, [1999] 3 WLR 504, [1999] 1 FCR 169, FD.

8. On such an application the court is not determining a question as to the child's upbringing and so the child's welfare is not the paramount consideration (*JR v Merton London Borough* [1992] 2 FCR 174).

The grant of leave is a substantial judicial decision and notice of an application for leave should generally be given to all parties likely to be affected if leave is given. In almost all cases it is appropriate for the respondent along with the applicant to be invited to attend the hearing. Justices should record their reasons for deciding to proceed in the absence of the respondent and for granting leave *Re W (a child) (contact: leave to apply)* [2000] 1 FCR 185, [2000] 1 FLR 263, FD.

The court should not, on an application for leave, hold a full and detailed investigation of the case. However, where the facts are disputed the justices should hear evidence from the main parties in order that they may form a view on the disputed facts broadly as to the merits of the application and as to any risk that there might be of the proposed application disrupting the child's life to such an extent that he would be harmed by it (*Re F and R (Section 8 Order: grandparent's application)* [1995] 1 FLR 524).

9. Since s 10(9) stipulates the particular matters to which the court is to have regard, s 1(1), ante, does not apply so as to make the child's welfare the paramount consideration on an application for leave (*Re A (minors) (residence orders: leave to apply)* [1992] 3 All ER 872, [1992] 3 WLR 422, [1992] 2 FLR 154, CA; *North Yorkshire County Council v G* [1993] 2 FLR 732). Nevertheless, s 10(9) in enjoining the court to have particular regard to the factors referred to in paragraphs (a)–(d) does not exclude consideration of other potentially relevant circumstances or matters (*A v A and Newham London Borough Council* [1993] 1 FCR 870). (See also *Re J (leave to issue application for residence order)* [2003] 1 FLR 114 in which

it was held it was not appropriate to substitute the test "has the applicant satisfied the court that he or she has a good arguable case" for the test that Parliament set out in s 10(9) of the Children Act 1989.)

6–2110 11. General principles and supplementary provisions. (1) In proceedings in which any question of making a section 8 order, or any other question with respect to such an order, arises, the court shall (in the light of any rules made by virtue of subsection (2))—

(*a*) draw up a timetable with a view to determining the question without delay; and

(*b*) give such directions as it considers appropriate for the purpose of ensuring, so far as is reasonably practicable, that that timetable is adhered to.

(2) Rules of court may—

(*a*) specify periods within which specified steps must be taken in relation to proceedings in which such questions arise; and

(*b*) make other provision with respect to such proceedings for the purpose of ensuring, so far as is reasonably practicable, that such questions are determined without delay.

(3) Where a court has power to make a section 8 order, it may do so at any time during the course of the proceedings in question even though it is not in a position to dispose finally of those proceedings.

(4) Where a residence order is made in favour of two or more persons who do not themselves all live together, the order may specify the periods during which the child is to live in the different households concerned[1].

(5) Where—

(*a*) a residence order has been made with respect to a child; and

(*b*) as a result of the order the child lives, or is to live, with one of two parents who each have parental responsibility for him,

the residence order shall cease to have effect if the parents live together for a continuous period of more than six months.

(6) A contact order which requires the parent with whom a child lives to allow the child to visit, or otherwise have contact with, his other parent shall cease to have effect if the parents live together for a continuous period of more than six months.

(7) A section 8 order may[2]—

(*a*) contain directions about how it is to be carried into effect[3];

(*b*) impose conditions[4] which must be complied with by any person—

(i) in whose favour the order is made;

(ii) who is a parent of the child concerned;

(iii) who is not a parent of his but who has parental responsibility for him; or

(iv) with whom the child is living,

and to whom the conditions are expressed to apply;

(*c*) be made to have effect for a specified period, or contain provisions which are to have effect for a specified period;

(*d*) make such incidental, supplemental or consequential provision as the court thinks fit[5].

[Children Act 1989, s 11.]

---

1. It will be wrong to make a shared residence order under this provision solely to give an applicant parental responsibility; see *N v B (children: orders as to residence)* [1993] 1 FCR 231. It will rarely be appropriate for a shared residence order to be made and the making of such an order will depend on exceptional circumstances (*Re H (a minor) (residence order)* [1993] 1 FCR 671). However, if it was planned or had turned out that children were spending substantial amounts of time with each of their parents then a shared residence order was an appropriate order to make; there was no need to show exceptional circumstances or a positive benefit to the children: *Re D (children)(shared residence orders)* [2001] 1 FCR 147, [2001] 1 FLR 495, CA, explaining *Re H*, supra.

2. Section 11(7) does not enable the court to impose obligations and conditions upon persons other than those referred to in s 11(7)(*b*) and a local authority is not included in that category. Accordingly, it has been held that it was wrong for a court to direct under s 11(7) that contact be supervised by the local authority; such a result may, however, be achieved by an order under s 16 of the Act (*Leeds City Council v C* [1993] 1 FCR 585, [1993] 1 FLR 269).

3. Directions contained in a residence order, including an interim residence order made ex parte, may require a child who has been removed or abducted to be restored to his home; see *Re B (minors)* [1992] 3 All ER 867, [1992] 3 WLR 113, [1992] 1 FCR 555).

4. It is inappropriate and beyond the powers of the court to impose conditions under this provision in the nature of injunctive orders to protect a parent from molestation or intimidation. If such orders are required, the proceedings should be transferred to the High Court which may make any necessary injunctions in exercising its inherent jurisdiction (*Re D (a minor) (contact: conditions)* [1997] 3 FCR 721, sub nom *D v N (contact order: conditions)* [1997] 2 FLR 797. A condition of residence imposed on a primary carer is highly exceptional as it could lead to quite unsustainable restrictions on ordinary adult liberties. Whilst the effect of the statute is to impose express restrictions where the primary carer seeks to remove a child from the jurisdiction, the court will not ordinarily seek to dictate the primary carer's place of residence (*Re S (a child) (residence order: condition)* [2001] EWCA Civ 847, [2001] 3 FCR 154. However, for an exceptional case where the court (by means of a prohibited steps order) prevented the removal of the children by their father to Northern Ireland, see *Re H (children)(residence order: condition)* [2001] EWCA Civ 1338, [2001] 3 FCR 182. See also *B v B (residence: condition limiting geographic area)* [2004] 2 FLR 979, where exceptional circumstances existed in the form of two previous applications by the mother to relocate to Australia motivated by a desire to get away from the father, and a proposed move now to the

north of England with good reason to doubt that she would promote contact as would be necessary for contact to take place.

5. It has been noted that although the court has no power to make a "stay" as such, an order under this section may stipulate when a s 8 order is to come into effect (*Re J (a minor) (residence)* [1993] 2 FCR 636, [1994] 1 FLR 369).

6–2111 12. Residence orders and parental responsibility.   (1) Where the court makes a residence order in favour of the father of a child it shall, if the father would not otherwise have parental responsibility for the child, also make an order under section 4 giving him that responsibility.

(2) Where the court makes a residence order in favour of any person who is not the parent or guardian of the child concerned that person shall have parental responsibility for the child while the residence order remains in force.

(3) Where a person has parental responsibility for a child as a result of subsection (2), he shall not have the right—

(a) repealed;
(b) to agree, or refuse to agree, to the making of an adoption order, or an order under section 84 of the Adoption and Children Act 2002, with respect to the child; or
(c) to appoint a guardian for the child.

(4) Where subsection (1) requires the court to make an order under section 4 in respect of the father of a child, the court shall not bring that order to an end at any time while the residence order concerned remains in force.

(5) The power of a court to make a residence order in favour of any person who is not the parent or guardian of the child concerned includes power to direct, at the request of that person, that the order continue in force until the child reaches the age of eighteen (unless the order is brought to an end earlier); and any power to vary a residence order is exercisable accordingly.

(6) Where a residence order includes such a direction, an application to vary or discharge the order may only be made, if apart from this subsection the leave of the court is not required, with such leave.

[Children Act 1989, s 12 as amended by the Adoption and Children Act 2002, s 114 and Sch 3.]

6–2112 13. Change of child's name or removal from jurisdiction.   (1) Where a residence order is in force with respect to a child, no person may—

(a) cause the child to be known by a new surname; or
(b) remove him from the United Kingdom[1];

without either the written consent of every person who has parental responsibility for the child or the leave of the court[2].

(2) Subsection (1)(b) does not prevent the removal of a child, for a period of less than one month, by the person in whose favour the residence order is made.

(3) In making a residence order with respect to a child the court may grant the leave required by subsection (1)(b), either generally or for specified purposes.

[Children Act 1989, s 13.]

---

1. "United Kingdom", in this context, includes Northern Ireland; however, whilst a primary carer may not need to apply under s 13(1)(b) where he/she seeks to remove a child to Northern Ireland, he/she may still have to meet the challenge of an application for a prohibited steps order or for the imposition, under s 11(7), of a condition to the residence order to prevent such a removal: *Re H (children)(residence order: condition)* [2001] EWCA Civ 1338, [2001] 3 FCR 182.

2. Welfare of the child being the paramount consideration, leave should not be withheld unless the interests of the child and those of the parent with whom the child is living are shown to be incompatible (*K v K (removal of child from jurisdiction)* [1992] 2 FCR 161). Regard may be had to the reasonableness of the parent's plans and the effect of a refusal of leave (*M v A (removal of children from jurisdiction)* [1994] 2 FCR 57) (see also *Re H (application to remove from jurisdiction)* [1999] 2 FCR 34 CA and *Re G-A (a child)(removal from jurisdiction: human rights)* [2001] 1 FCR 43, CA). The section does not create any presumptions in favour of the applicant parent and the implementation of the European Convention on Human Rights has not affected the principles of domestic law (*Payne v Payne* [2001] EWCA Civ 166, [2001] Fam 473, [2001] 2 WLR 1826, [2001] 1 FCR 425. Applications to remove a child to a country which is not a signatory to the Hague Convention on the Civil Aspects of International Child Abduction should be heard before a judge of the Family Division of the High Court (*Re K (removal from jurisdiction: practice)* [1999] 3 FCR 673, CA).

Where the choice lies between deciding the question of what is best for any individual child here or deciding it in a foreign country, differences between the legal systems cannot be irrelevant. If there is a genuine issue between the parents as to whether it is in the best interests of the child to live in this country or elsewhere it must be relevant whether that issue is capable of being tried in the courts of the country to which he is to be returned, and if those courts have no choice but to do as one parent wishes, so that the other cannot ask them to decide, with an open mind, whether the child will be better off living here or there, then the domestic courts must ask themselves whether it is in the interests of the child to enable that dispute to be heard. The absence of a relocation jurisdiction may be a decisive factor, but if it appears that the mother will be unable to make a good cause for relocation, that factor may not be decisive; there are also bound to be many cases where the connection of the child and all the family with the other country is so strong that any difference between the legal systems here and there should carry little weight: *Re J (a child) (return to foreign jurisdiction: convention rights)* [2005] UKHL 40, [2005] 3 All ER 291 (which concerned an application to remove a child to a non-Hague Convention country).

6–2113 14. Enforcement of residence orders.   (1) Where—

(a) a residence order is in force with respect to a child in favour of any person; and (*b*)   any other person (including one in whose favour the order is also in force) is in breach of the arrangements settled by that order,

the person mentioned in paragraph (*a*) may, as soon as the requirement in subsection (2) is complied with, enforce the order under section 63(3) of the Magistrates' Courts Act 1980 as if it were an order requiring the other person to produce the child to him.

(2)   The requirement is that a copy of the residence order has been served on the other person.

(3)   Subsection (1) is without prejudice to any other remedy open to The person in whose favour the residence order is in force.

[Children Act 1989, s 14.]

Special guardianship

6–2113A   14A.   Special guardianship orders.   (1)   A "special guardianship order" is an order appointing one or more individuals to be a child's "special guardian" (or special guardians).

(2)   A special guardian—

(*a*)   must be aged eighteen or over; and
(*b*)   must not be a parent of the child in question,

and subsections (3) to (6) are to be read in that light.

(3)   The court may make a special guardianship order with respect to any child on the application of an individual who—

(*a*)   is entitled to make such an application with respect to the child; or
(*b*)   has obtained the leave of the court to make the application,

or on the joint application of more than one such individual.

(4)   Section 9(3) applies in relation to an application for leave to apply for a special guardianship order as it applies in relation to an application for leave to apply for a section 8 order.

(5)   The individuals who are entitled to apply for a special guardianship order with respect to a child are—

(*a*)   any guardian of the child;
(*b*)   any individual in whose favour a residence order is in force with respect to the child;
(*c*)   any individual listed in subsection (5)(*b*) or (*c*) of section 10 (as read with subsection (10) of that section);
(*d*)   a local authority foster parent with whom the child has lived for a period of at least one year immediately preceding the application.

(6)   The court may also make a special guardianship order with respect to a child in any family proceedings in which a question arises with respect to the welfare of the child if—

(*a*)   an application for the order has been made by an individual who falls within subsection (3)(*a*) or (*b*) (or more than one such individual jointly); or
(*b*)   the court considers that a special guardianship order should be made even though no such application has been made.

(7)   No individual may make an application under subsection (3) or (6)(*a*) unless, before the beginning of the period of three months ending with the date of the application, he has given written notice of his intention to make the application—

(*a*)   if the child in question is being looked after by a local authority, to that local authority, or
(*b*)   otherwise, to the local authority in whose area the individual is ordinarily resident.

(8)   On receipt of such a notice, the local authority must investigate the matter and prepare a report for the court dealing with—

(*a*)   the suitability of the applicant to be a special guardian;
(*b*)   such matters (if any) as may be prescribed[1] by the Secretary of State; and
(*c*)   any other matter which the local authority consider to be relevant.

(9)   The court may itself ask a local authority to conduct such an investigation and prepare such a report, and the local authority must do so.

(10)   The local authority may make such arrangements as they see fit for any person to act on their behalf in connection with conducting an investigation or preparing a report referred to in subsection (8) or (9).

(11)   The court may not make a special guardianship order unless it has received a report dealing with the matters referred to in subsection (8).

(12)   Subsections (8) and (9) of section 10 apply in relation to special guardianship orders as they apply in relation to section 8 orders.

(13)   This section is subject to section 29(5) and (6) of the Adoption and Children Act 2002.

[Children Act 1989, s 14A as inserted by the Adoption and Children Act 2002, s 115.]

---

1.   The Special Guardianship Regulations 2005, SI 2005/1109 and the Special Guardianship (Wales) Regulations 2005, SI 2005/1513 have been made.

6–2113B   14B. Special guardianship orders: making.   (1) Before making a special guardianship order, the court must consider whether, if the order were made—

(*a*) a contact order should also be made with respect to the child, and

(*b*) any section 8 order in force with respect to the child should be varied or discharged.

(2) On making a special guardianship order, the court may also—

(*a*) give leave for the child to be known by a new surname;

(*b*) grant the leave required by section 14C(3)(*b*), either generally or for specified purposes.

[Children Act 1989, s 14B as inserted by the Adoption and Children Act 2002, s 115.]

6–2113C   14C. Special guardianship orders: effect.   (1) The effect of a special guardianship order is that while the order remains in force—

(*a*) a special guardian appointed by the order has parental responsibility for the child in respect of whom it is made; and

(*b*) subject to any other order in force with respect to the child under this Act, a special guardian is entitled to exercise parental responsibility to the exclusion of any other person with parental responsibility for the child (apart from another special guardian).

(2) Subsection (1) does not affect—

(*a*) the operation of any enactment or rule of law which requires the consent of more than one person with parental responsibility in a matter affecting the child; or

(*b*) any rights which a parent of the child has in relation to the child's adoption or placement for adoption.

(3) While a special guardianship order is in force with respect to a child, no person may—

(*a*) cause the child to be known by a new surname; or

(*b*) remove him from the United Kingdom,

without either the written consent of every person who has parental responsibility for the child or the leave of the court.

(4) Subsection (3)(*b*) does not prevent the removal of a child, for a period of less than three months, by a special guardian of his.

(5) If the child with respect to whom a special guardianship order is in force dies, his special guardian must take reasonable steps to give notice of that fact to—

(*a*) each parent of the child with parental responsibility; and

(*b*) each guardian of the child,

but if the child has more than one special guardian, and one of them has taken such steps in relation to a particular parent or guardian, any other special guardian need not do so as respects that parent or guardian.

(6) This section is subject to section 29(7) of the Adoption and Children Act 2002.

[Children Act 1989, s 14C as inserted by the Adoption and Children Act 2002, s 115.]

6–2113D   14D. Special guardianship orders: variation and discharge.   (1) The court may vary or discharge a special guardianship order on the application of—

(*a*) the special guardian (or any of them, if there are more than one);

(*b*) any parent or guardian of the child concerned;

(*c*) any individual in whose favour a residence order is in force with respect to the child;

(*d*) any individual not falling within any of paragraphs (*a*) to (*c*) who has, or immediately before the making of the special guardianship order had, parental responsibility for the child;

(*e*) the child himself; or

(*f*) a local authority designated in a care order with respect to the child.

(2) In any family proceedings in which a question arises with respect to the welfare of a child with respect to whom a special guardianship order is in force, the court may also vary or discharge the special guardianship order if it considers that the order should be varied or discharged, even though no application has been made under subsection (1).

(3) The following must obtain the leave of the court before making an application under subsection (1)—

(*a*) the child;

(*b*) any parent or guardian of his;

(*c*) any step-parent of his who has acquired, and has not lost, parental responsibility for him by virtue of section 4A;

(*d*) any individual falling within subsection (1)(*d*) who immediately before the making of the special guardianship order had, but no longer has, parental responsibility for him.

(4) Where the person applying for leave to make an application under subsection (1) is the child, the court may only grant leave if it is satisfied that he has sufficient understanding to make the proposed application under subsection (1).

(5) The court may not grant leave to a person falling within subsection (3)(*b*)(*c*) or (*d*) unless it is satisfied that there has been a significant change in circumstances since the making of the special guardianship order.
[Children Act 1989, s 14D as inserted by the Adoption and Children Act 2002, s 115.]

6–2113E 14E. Special guardianship orders: supplementary. (1) In proceedings in which any question of making, varying or discharging a special guardianship order arises, the court shall (in the light of any rules made by virtue of subsection (3))—

(*a*) draw up a timetable with a view to determining the question without delay; and
(*b*) give such directions as it considers appropriate for the purpose of ensuring, so far as is reasonably practicable, that the timetable is adhered to.

(2) Subsection (1) applies also in relation to proceedings in which any other question with respect to a special guardianship order arises.
(3) The power to make rules in subsection (2) of section 11 applies for the purposes of this section as it applies for the purposes of that.
(4) A special guardianship order, or an order varying one, may contain provisions which are to have effect for a specified period.
(5) Section 11(7) (apart from paragraph (*c*)) applies in relation to special guardianship orders and orders varying them as it applies in relation to section 8 orders.
[Children Act 1989, s 14E as inserted by the Adoption and Children Act 2002, s 115.]

6–2113F 14F. Special guardianship support services. (1) Each local authority must make arrangements for the provision within their area of special guardianship support services, which means—

(*a*) counselling, advice and information; and
(*b*) such other services as are prescribed[1],

in relation to special guardianship.
(2) The power to make regulations under subsection (1)(*b*) is to be exercised so as to secure that local authorities provide financial support.
(3) At the request of any of the following persons—

(*a*) a child with respect to whom a special guardianship order is in force;
(*b*) a special guardian;
(*c*) a parent;
(*d*) any other person who falls within a prescribed description,

a local authority may carry out an assessment of that person's needs for special guardianship support services (but, if the Secretary of State so provides in regulations, they must do so if he is a person of a prescribed description, or if his case falls within a prescribed description, or if both he and his case fall within prescribed descriptions).
(4) A local authority may, at the request of any other person, carry out an assessment of that person's needs for special guardianship support services.
(5) Where, as a result of an assessment, a local authority decide that a person has needs for special guardianship support services, they must then decide whether to provide any such services to that person.
(6) If—

(*a*) a local authority decide to provide any special guardianship support services to a person, and
(*b*) the circumstances fall within a prescribed description,

the local authority must prepare a plan in accordance with which special guardianship support services are to be provided to him, and keep the plan under review.
(7) The Secretary of State may by regulations[1] make provision about assessments, preparing and reviewing plans, the provision of special guardianship support services in accordance with plans and reviewing the provision of special guardianship support services.
(8) The regulations may in particular make provision—

(*a*) about the type of assessment which is to be carried out, or the way in which an assessment is to be carried out;
(*b*) about the way in which a plan is to be prepared;
(*c*) about the way in which, and the time at which, a plan or the provision of special guardianship support services is to be reviewed;
(*d*) about the considerations to which a local authority are to have regard in carrying out an assessment or review or preparing a plan;
(*e*) as to the circumstances in which a local authority may provide special guardianship support services subject to conditions (including conditions as to payment for the support or the repayment of financial support);
(*f*) as to the consequences of conditions imposed by virtue of paragraph (*e*) not being met (including the recovery of any financial support provided);

    (*g*) as to the circumstances in which this section may apply to a local authority in respect of persons who are outside that local authority's area;

    (*h*) as to the circumstances in which a local authority may recover from another local authority the expenses of providing special guardianship support services to any person.

  (9) A local authority may provide special guardianship support services (or any part of them) by securing their provision by—

    (*a*) another local authority; or

    (*b*) a person within a description prescribed in regulations of persons who may provide special guardianship support services,

and may also arrange with any such authority or person for that other authority or that person to carry out the local authority's functions in relation to assessments under this section.

  (10) A local authority may carry out an assessment of the needs of any person for the purposes of this section at the same time as an assessment of his needs is made under any other provision of this Act or under any other enactment.

  (11) Section 27 (co-operation between authorities) applies in relation to the exercise of functions of a local authority under this section as it applies in relation to the exercise of functions of a local authority under Part 3.

[Children Act 1989, s 14F as inserted by the Adoption and Children Act 2002, s 115.]

---

   1. The Special Guardianship Regulations 2005, SI 2005/1109 and the Special Guardianship (Wales) Regulations 2005, SI 2005/1513 have been made.

6–2113G 14G. Special guardianship support services: representations *Repealed.*

Financial relief

6–2114 15. Orders for financial relief with respect to children. (1) Schedule 1 (which consists primarily of the re-enactment, with consequential amendments and minor modifications, of provisions of section 6 of the Family Law Reform Act 1969, the Guardianship of Minors Acts 1971 and 1973[1], the Children Act 1975 and of sections 15 and 16 of the Family Law Reform Act 1987) makes provision in relation to financial relief for children.

  (2) The powers of a magistrates' court under section 60 of the Magistrates' Courts Act 1980 to revoke, revive or vary an order for the periodical payment of money and the power of the clerk of a magistrates' court to vary such an order shall not apply in relation to an order made under Schedule 1.

[Children Act 1989, s 15 as amended by the Courts and Legal Services Act 1990, Sch 16 and the Maintenance Enforcement Act 1991, Sch 2.]

---

   1. Section 16(1) of the Interpretation Act 1978, in PART II: EVIDENCE, ante, enables an applicant for the variation of an order made under the Guardianship of Minors Act 1971 to be made notwithstanding the repeal of that Act. Section 60 of the Magistrates' Courts Act 1980 has no application in these circumstances, as the power contained therein applies only to orders made under current legislation. Any appeal arising from such variation proceedings should be by way of notice of motion and not under s 94 of this Act (*B v B (children: periodical payments*) [1995] 1 WLR 440, [1995] 1 FCR 763, [1995] 1 FLR 459).

Family assistance orders

6–2115 16. Family assistance orders. (1) Where, in any family proceedings, the court has power to make an order under this Part with respect to any child, it may (whether or not it makes such an order) make an order requiring—

    (*a*) an officer of the Service or a Welsh family proceedings officer to be made available; or

    (*b*) a local authority to make an officer of the authority available,

to advise, assist and (where appropriate) befriend any person named in the order.

  (2) The persons who may be named in an order under this section ("a family assistance order") are—

    (*a*) any parent, guardian or special guardian of the child;

    (*b*) any person with whom the child is living or in whose favour a contact order is in force with respect to the child;

    (*c*) the child himself.

  (3) No court may make a family assistance order unless—

    (*a*) it is satisfied that the circumstances of the case are exceptional; and

    (*b*) it has obtained the consent of every person to be named in the order other than the child.

  (4) A family assistance order may direct—

    (*a*) the person named in the order; or

    (*b*) such of the persons named in the order as may be specified in the order, to take such steps as may be so specified with a view to enabling the officer concerned to be kept informed of the address of any person named in the order and to be allowed to visit any such person.

(5) Unless it specifies a shorter period, a family assistance order shall have effect for a period of six months beginning with the day on which it is made.

(6) Where—

(a) a family assistance order is in force with respect to a child; and

(b) a section 8 order is also in force with respect to the child,

the officer concerned may refer to the court the question whether the section 8 order should be varied or discharged.

(7) A family assistance order shall not be made so as to require a local authority to make an officer of theirs available unless—

(a) the authority agree; or

(b) the child concerned lives or will live within their area.

(8)–(9) (*Repealed*).

[Children Act 1989, s 16, as amended by the Criminal Justice and Court Services Act 2000, Sch 7 and the Children Act 2004, Sch 3 and the Adoption and Children Act 2002, Sch 3.]

PART III[1]

LOCAL AUTHORITY SUPPORT FOR CHILDREN AND FAMILIES

Provision of services for children and their families

6–2116   17. Provision of services for children in need, their families and others[2]. (1) It shall be the general duty of every local authority (in addition to the other duties imposed on them by this Part)—

(a) to safeguard and promote[3] the welfare of children within their area[4] who are in need; and

(b) so far as is consistent with that duty, to promote the upbringing of such children by their families,

by providing a range and level of services appropriate to those children's needs.

(2) For the purpose principally of facilitating the discharge of their general duty under this section, every local authority shall have the specific duties and powers set out in Part 1 of Schedule 2.

(3) Any service provided by an authority in the exercise of functions conferred on them by this section may be provided for the family of a particular child in need or for any member of his family, if it is provided with a view to safeguarding or promoting the child's welfare.

(4) The Secretary of State may by order[5] amend any provision of Part I of Schedule 2 or add any further duty or power to those for the time being mentioned there.

(4A) Before determining what (if any) services to provide for a particular child in need in the exercise of functions conferred on them by this section, a local authority shall, so far as is reasonably practicable and consistent with the child's welfare—

(a) ascertain the child's wishes and feelings regarding the provision of those services; and

(b) give due consideration (having regard to his age and understanding) to such wishes and feelings of the child as they have been able to ascertain.

(5) Every local authority—

(a) shall facilitate the provision by others (including in particular voluntary organisations) of services which the authority have power to provide by virtue of this section, or section 18, 20, 23, 23B to 23D, 24A or 24B; and

(b) may make such arrangements as they see fit for any person to act on their behalf in the provision of any such service.

(6) The services provided by a local authority in the exercise of functions conferred on them by this section may include providing accommodation[6] and giving assistance in kind or, in exceptional circumstances, in cash.

(7) Assistance may be unconditional or subject to conditions as to the repayment of the assistance or of its value (in whole or in part).

(8) Before giving any assistance or imposing any conditions, a local authority shall have regard to the means of the child concerned and of each of his parents.

(9) No person shall be liable to make any repayment of assistance or of its value at any time when he is in receipt of income support under Part VII of the Social Security Contributions and Benefits Act 1992, of any element of child tax credit other than the family element, of working tax credit or of an income-based jobseeker's allowance.

(10) For the purposes of this Part a child shall be taken to be in need if—

(a) he is unlikely to achieve or maintain, or to have the opportunity of achieving or maintaining, a reasonable standard of health or development without the provision for him of services by a local authority under this Part;

(b) his health or development is likely to be significantly impaired, or further impaired, without the provision for him of such services; or (*c*) he is disabled,

and "family", in relation to such a child, includes any person who has parental responsibility for the child and any other person with whom he has been living.

(11) For the purposes of this Part, a child is disabled if he is blind, deaf or dumb or suffers from mental disorder of any kind or is substantially and permanently handicapped by illness, injury or congenital deformity or such other disability as may be prescribed; and in this Part—

"development" means physical, intellectual, emotional, social or behavioural development; and "health" means physical or mental health.

(12) The Treasury may by regulations[7] prescribe circumstances in which a person is to be treated for the purposes of this Part (or for such of those purposes as are prescribed) as in receipt of any element of child tax credit other than the family element or of working tax credit.

[Children Act 1989, s 17 as amended by the Disability Living Allowance and Disability Working Allowance Act 1991, Sch 3, the Social Security (Consequential Provisions) Act 1992, Sch 2, the Jobseekers Act 1995, Sch 2 the Tax Credits Act 1999, Sch 1, the Children (Leaving Care) Act 2000, s 7, the Adoption and Children Act 2002, s 116, the Tax Credit Acts 2002, Sch 3 and the Children Act 2004, s 53.]

1. Part III contains ss 17–30.

2. As to the framework and nature of the assessment required to be undertaken by local authorities for children in need see the Secretary of State's guidance issued in March 2000 entitled "Framework for the Assessment of Children in Need and Their Families" and *R (on the application of AB and SB) v Nottingham City Council* [2001] EWHC Admin 235, [2001] 3 FCR 50. Although the Act does not apply to the Prison Service or its institutions, the duty of a local authority under s 17 or s 47 does not cease when a child is detained although, subject to compliance with the Human Rights Act 1998 and the facts of each case, it is unlikely that the High Court or a local authority can properly override or interfere with the Home Secretary's exercise of the powers and duties conferred on him in relation to a child lawfully detained (*R (Howard League for Penal Reform) v Secretary of State for the Home Department* [2002] EWHC 2479 (Admin) [2003] 1 FLR 484).

3. For commentary on the scope of this duty see *Nottinghamshire County Council v P* [1993] 3 All ER 815, [1993] 2 FLR 134, CA.

4. Physical presence is sufficient to found the duty under this section (*R (Stewart) v London Borough of Wandsworth* [2001] EWHC Admin 709, [2002] 1 FLR 469.

5. The Children Act 1989 (Amendment) (Children's Services Planning) Order 1996, SI 1996/785 has been made.

6. This sub-section was amended by the Adoption and Children Act 2002, s 116 to clarify the position after the decisions of the Court of Appeal in *A v Lambeth London Borough Council* [2001[EWCA Civ 1624, [2001] 3 FCR 673, [2002] 1 FLR 353 sub nom *R (on the application of W) v Lambeth London Borough Council* [2001] EWCA Civ 613, [2002] 2 All ER 901, [2002] 2 FCR 289, [2002] 2 FLR 327 sub nom (on appeal sub nom *R (on the application of G) v Lambeth London Borough Council* [2003] UKHL 57, [2004] 1 All ER 97, [2003] 3 FCR 419).

7. The Children Act 1989, s 17(12) Regulations 2003, SI 2003/2077 have been made.

6–2116A 17A. Direct payments. (1) The Secretary of State may by regulations[1] make provision for and in connection with requiring or authorising the responsible authority in the case of a person of a prescribed description who falls within subsection (2) to make, with that person's consent, such payments to him as they may determine in accordance with the regulations in respect of his securing the provision of the service mentioned in that subsection.

(2) A person falls within this subsection if he is—

(*a*) a person with parental responsibility for a disabled child,

(*b*) a disabled person with parental responsibility for a child, or

(*c*) a disabled child aged 16 or 17,

and a local authority ("the responsible authority") have decided for the purposes of section 17 that the child's needs (or, if he is such a disabled child, his needs) call for the provision by them of a service in exercise of functions conferred on them under that section.

(3) Subsections (3) to (5) and (7) of section 57 of the 2001 Act shall apply, with any necessary modifications, in relation to regulations[1] under this section as they apply in relation to regulations under that section.

(4) Regulations under this section shall provide that, where payments are made under the regulations[1] to a person falling within subsection (5)—

(*a*) the payments shall be made at the rate mentioned in subsection (4)(*a*) of section 57 of the 2001 Act (as applied by subsection (3)); and

(*b*) subsection (4)(*b*) of that section shall not apply.

(5) A person falls within this subsection if he is—

(*a*) a person falling within subsection (2)(*a*) or (*b*) and the child in question is aged 16 or 17, or

(*b*) a person who is in receipt of income support, under Part 7 of the Social Security Contributions and Benefits Act 1992 (c 4) or of an income-based jobseeker's allowance.

(6) In this section—

"the 2001 Act" means the Health and Social Care Act 2001;

"disabled" in relation to an adult has the same meaning as that given by section 17(11) in relation to a child;

"prescribed" means specified in or determined in accordance with regulations under this section (and has the same meaning in the provisions of the 2001 Act mentioned in subsection (3) as they apply by virtue of that subsection).

[Children Act 1989, s 17A, as substituted by the Health and Social Care Act 2001, s 58 and amended by the Tax Credits Act 2002, Schs 3 and 6.]

---

1. The Community Care, Services for Carers and Children's Services (Direct Payments) (England) Regulations 2003, SI 2003/762 amended by SI 2005/2114 and the Community Care, Services for Carers and Children's Services (Direct Payments) (Wales) Regulations 2004, SI 2004/1748 amended by SI 2005/3302 have been made.

6–2116B   17B. Vouchers for persons with parental responsibility for disabled children[1].
(1) The Secretary of State may by regulations make provision for the issue by a local authority of vouchers to a person with parental responsibility for a disabled child.

(2) "Voucher" means a document whereby, if the local authority agrees with the person with parental responsibility that it would help him care for the child if the person with parental responsibility had a break from caring, that person may secure the temporary provision of services for the child under section 17.

(3) The regulations may, in particular, provide—

(a) for the value of a voucher to be expressed in terms of money, or of the delivery of a service for a period of time, or both;

(b) for the person who supplies a service against a voucher, or for the arrangement under which it is supplied, to be approved by the local authority;

(c) for a maximum period during which a service (or a service of a prescribed description) can be provided against a voucher.*

[Children Act 1989, s 17B, as inserted by the Carers and Disabled Children Act 2000, s 7.]

---

*Section 17B as inserted by the Carers and Disabled Children Act 2000, s 7, when in force.
1. At the date of going to press, s 17B which is to be inserted by the Carers and Disabled Children Act 2000, s 7, had not been brought into force.

6–2117   18. Day care for pre-school and other children.   (1) Every local authority shall provide such day care for children in need within their area who are—

(a) aged five or under; and
(b) not yet attending schools,

as is appropriate.

(2) A local authority may provide day care for children within their area who satisfy the conditions mentioned in subsection (1)(a) and (b) even though they are not in need.

(3) A local authority may provide facilities (including training, advice, guidance and counselling) for those—

(a) caring for children in day care; or
(b) who at any time accompany such children while they are in day care.

(4) In this section "day care" means any form of care or supervised activity provided for children during the day (whether or not it is provided on a regular basis).

(5) Every local authority shall provide for children in need within their area who are attending any school such care or supervised activities as is appropriate—

(a) outside school hours; or
(b) during school holidays.

(6) A local authority may provide such care or supervised activities for children within their area who are attending any school even though those children are not in need.

(7) In this section "supervised activity" means an activity supervised by a responsible person.
[Children Act 1989, s 18.]

6–2118   19. Review of provision for day care, child minding etc.   *Repealed.*

Provision of accommodation for children

6–2119   20. Provision of accommodation for children: general.   (1) Every local authority shall provide accommodation for any child in need within their area who appears to them to require accommodation as a result of—

(a) there being no person who has parental responsibility for him;
(b) his being lost or having been abandoned; or
(c) the person who has been caring for him being prevented (whether or not permanently, and for whatever reason) from providing him with suitable accommodation or care.

(2) Where a local authority provide accommodation under subsection (1) for a child who is ordinarily resident in the area of another local authority, that other local authority may take over the provision of accommodation for the child within—

(a) three months of being notified in writing that the child is being provided with accommodation; or

(b)   such other longer period as may be prescribed.

(3) Every local authority shall provide accommodation for any child in need within their area who has reached the age of sixteen and whose welfare the authority consider is likely to be seriously prejudiced if they do not provide him with accommodation.

(4) A local authority may provide accommodation for any child within their area (even though a person who has parental responsibility for him is able to provide him with accommodation) if they consider that to do so would safeguard or promote the child's welfare.

(5) A local authority may provide accommodation for any person who has reached the age of sixteen but is under twenty-one in any community home which takes children who have reached the age of sixteen if they consider that to do so would safeguard or promote his welfare.

(6) Before providing accommodation under this section, a local authority shall, so far as is reasonably practicable and consistent with the child's welfare—

(a)   ascertain the child's wishes and feelings regarding the provision of accommodation; and
(b)   give due consideration (having regard to his age and understanding) to such wishes and feelings of the child as they have been able to ascertain.

(7) A local authority may not provide accommodation under this section for any child if any person who—

(a)   has parental responsibility for him; and
(b)   is willing and able to—

(i)   provide accommodation for him; or
(ii) arrange for accommodation to be provided for him,

objects[1].

(8) Any person who has parental responsibility for a child may at any time remove the child from accommodation provided by or on behalf of the local authority under this section.

(9) Subsections (7) and (8) do not apply while any person—

(a)   in whose favour a residence order is in force with respect to the child; or
(aa) who is a special guardian of the child; or
(b)   who has care of the child by virtue of an order made in the exercise of the High Court's inherent jurisdiction with respect to children,

agrees to the child being looked after in accommodation provided by or on behalf of the local authority.

(10) Where there is more than one such person as is mentioned in subsection (9), all of them must agree.

(11) Subsections (7) and (8) do not apply where a child who has reached the age of sixteen agrees to being provided with accommodation under this section.

[Children Act 1989, s 20 as amended by the Adoption and Children Act 2002, Sch 3 and the Children Act 2004, s 67.]

---

1. Whilst a local authority accommodates a child pursuant to a voluntary arrangement under s 20 is able to exercise mundane day-to-day powers of management as to provision of that accommodation, this power does not override the wishes of a parent with parental responsibility and does not include the power to place a child with foster parents against the wishes of the parents. (*R v Tameside Metropolitan Borough Council, ex p J* [2000] 1 FCR 173, [2000] 1 FLR 942, QBD).

6–2130   21. Provision of accommodation for children in police protection or detention or on remand, etc.   (1) Every local authority shall make provision for the reception and accommodation of children who are removed or kept away from home under Part V.

(2) Every local authority shall receive, and provide accommodation for, children—

(a)   in police protection whom they are requested to receive under section 46(3)(f);
(b)   whom they are requested to receive under section 38(6) of the Police and Criminal Evidence Act 1984;
(c)   who are—

(i)   on remand (within the meaning of the section) under paragraph 7(5) of Schedule 7 to the Powers of Criminal Courts (Sentencing) Act 2000 or section 23(1) of the Children and Young Persons Act 1969; or
(ii) the subject of a supervision order imposing a local authority residence requirement under paragraph 5 of Schedule 6 to that Act of 2000 or a foster parent residence requirement under paragraph 5A of that Schedule,

and with respect to whom they are the designated authority.

(3) Where a child has been—

(a)   removed under Part V; or
(b)   detained under section 38 of the Police and Criminal Evidence Act 1984,

and he is not being provided with accommodation by a local authority or in a hospital vested in the Secretary of State or a Primary Care Trust, or otherwise made available pursuant to arrangements

made by a Health Authority or Primary Care Trust, any reasonable expenses of accommodating him shall be recoverable from the local authority in whose area he is ordinarily resident.
[Children Act 1989, s 21 as amended by the National Health Service and Community Care Act 1990, Sch 9, the Courts and Legal Services Act 1990, Sch 16, the Health Authorities Act 1995, Sch 1, SI 2000/90 and the Powers of Criminal Courts (Sentencing) Act 2000, Sch 9 and the Anti-social Behaviour Act 2003, Sch 2.]

Duties of local authorities in relation to children looked after by them

6–2131   22. General duty of local authority in relation to children looked after by them.
(1) In this Act, any reference to a child who is looked after by a local authority is a reference to a child who is—

(a) in their care; or

(b) provided with accommodation by the authority in the exercise of any functions (in particular those under this Act) which are social services functions within the meaning of the Local Authority Social Services Act 1970, apart from functions under sections 17, 23B and 24B.

(2) In subsection (1) "accommodation" means accommodation which is provided for a continuous period of more than 24 hours.

(3) It shall be the duty of a local authority looking after any child—

(a) to safeguard and promote his welfare; and

(b) to make such use of services available for children cared for by their own parents as appears to the authority reasonable in his case.

(3A) The duty of a local authority under subsection (3)(a) to safeguard and promote the welfare of a child looked after by them includes in particular a duty to promote the child's educational achievement.

(4) Before making any decision with respect to a child whom they are looking after, or proposing to look after, a local authority shall, so far as is reasonably practicable, ascertain the wishes and feelings of—

(a) the child;

(b) his parents;

(c) any person who is not a parent of his but who has parental responsibility for him; and

(d) any other person whose wishes and feelings the authority consider to be relevant,

regarding the matter to be decided.

(5) In making any such decision a local authority shall give due consideration—

(a) having regard to his age and understanding, to such wishes and feelings of the child as they have been able to ascertain;

(b) to such wishes and feelings of any person mentioned in subsection (4)(b) to (d) as they have been able to ascertain; and

(c) to the child's religious persuasion, racial origin and cultural and linguistic background.

(6) If it appears to a local authority that it is necessary, for the purpose of protecting members of the public from serious injury, to exercise their powers with respect to a child whom they are looking after in a manner which may not be consistent with their duties under this section, they may do so.

(7) If the Secretary of State considers it necessary, for the purpose of protecting members of the public from serious injury, to give directions to a local authority with respect to the exercise of their powers with respect to a child whom they are looking after, he may give such directions to the authority.

(8) Where any such directions are given to an authority they shall comply with them even though doing so is inconsistent with their duties under this section.
[Children Act 1989, s 22 as amended by the Children (Leaving Care) Act 2000, s 2, the Local Government Act 2000, s 107 and the Adoption and Children Act 2002, s 116 and the Children Act 2004, s 52.]

6–2132   23. Provision of accommodation and maintenance by local authority for children whom they are looking after.   (1) It shall be the duty of any local authority looking after a child—

(a) when he is in their care, to provide accommodation for him; and

(b) to maintain him in other respects apart from providing accommodation for him.

(2) A local authority shall provide accommodation and maintenance for any child whom they are looking after by—

(a) placing him (subject to subsection (5) and any regulations[1] made by the Secretary of State) with—

(i) a family;

(ii) a relative of his; or

(iii) any other suitable person,

on such terms as to payment by the authority and otherwise as the authority may determine;

(aa) maintaining him in an appropriate children's home; or

(f) making such other arrangements as—

(i)   seem appropriate to them; and

(ii) comply with any regulations[2] made by the Secretary of State.

(2A) Where under subsection (2)(aa) a local authority maintains a child in a home provided, equipped and maintained by the Secretary of State under section 82(5), it shall do so on such terms as the Secretary of State may from time to time determine.

(3) Any person with whom a child has been placed under subsection (2)(a) is referred to in this Act as a local authority foster parent unless he falls within subsection (4).

(4) A person falls within this subsection if he is—

(a) a parent of the child;

(b) a person who is not a parent of the child but who has parental responsibility for him; or

(c) where the child is in care and there was a residence order in force with respect to him immediately before the care order was made, a person in whose favour the residence order was made.

(5) Where a child is in the care of a local authority, the authority may only allow him to live[3] with a person who falls within subsection (4) in accordance with regulations[4] made by the Secretary of State.

(5A) For the purposes of subsection (5) a child shall be regarded as living with a person if he stays with that person for a continuous period of more than 24 hours.

(6) Subject to any regulations made by the Secretary of State for the purposes of this subsection, any local authority looking after a child shall make arrangements to enable him to live with—

(a) a person falling within subsection (4); or

(b) a relative, friend or other person connected with him,

unless that would not be reasonably practicable or consistent with his welfare.

(7) Where a local authority provide accommodation for a child whom they are looking after, they shall, subject to the provisions of this Part and so far as is reasonably practicable and consistent with his welfare, secure that—

(a) the accommodation is near his home; and

(b) where the authority are also providing accommodation for a sibling of his, they are accommodated together.

(8) Where a local authority provide accommodation for a child whom they are looking after and who is disabled, they shall, so far as is reasonably practicable, secure that the accommodation is not unsuitable to his particular needs.

(9) Part II of Schedule 2 shall have effect for the purposes of making further provision as to children looked after by local authorities and in particular as to the regulations that may be made under subsections (2)(a) and (f) and (5).

(10) In this Act—

"appropriate children's home" means a children's home in respect of which a person is registered under Part II of the Care Standards Act 2000; and

"children's home" has the same meaning as in that Act.

[Children Act 1989, s 23 as amended by the Courts and Legal Services Act 1990, Sch 16 and the Care Standards Act 2000, Sch 4.]

1. See the Arrangements for Placement of Children (General) Regulations 1991, SI 1991/890 amended by SI 1991/2033, SI 1993/3069, SI 1995/2015, 1997/647, SI 2002/546 (E), 2469, 2935 (W) and 3013 (W) and SI 2005/774 (W); the Fostering Services Regulations 2002, SI 2002/57 amended by SI 2002/865; the Fostering Services (Wales) Regulations 2003, SI 2003/237 amended by SI 2003/896 and SI 2005/3302. For disqualification as a foster parent, see *Re S (Foster Placement (Children) Regulations 1991)* [2000] 1 FLR 648, FD.

2. See the Arrangements for Placement of Children (General) Regulations 1991, SI 1991/890 amended by SI 1991/2033, SI 1993/3069, SI 1995/2015, SI 1997/649, SI 2002/546 (England), 2469, 2935 (Wales) and 3013 (Wales) and SI 2005/774 (W).

3. A local authority which permits a child to remain living at home under an interim care order is not "providing accommodation" for the child within s 23(1)(a) (*Hackney London Borough Council v C* [1997] 1 FCR 509, [1997] 1 FLR 544).

4. See the Arrangements for Placement of Children (General) Regulations 1991, SI 1991/890 amended by SI 1991/2033, SI 1993/3069, SI 1995/2015 and the Placement of Children with Parents Regulations 1991, SI 1991/893 amended by SI 1995/2015, SI 1997/649, SI 2002/546 (England), 2469, 2935 (Wales) and 3013 (Wales) and SI 2005/774 (W).

6–2132A   23A. The responsible authority and relevant children.   (1) The responsible local authority shall have the functions set out in section 23B in respect of a relevant child.

(2) In subsection (1) "relevant child" means (subject to subsection (3)) a child who—

(a) is not being looked after by any local authority;

(b) was, before last ceasing to be looked after, an eligible child for the purposes of paragraph 19B of Schedule 2; and

(c) is aged sixteen or seventeen.

(3) The Secretary of State may prescribe[1]—

(a) additional categories of relevant children; and

(b) categories of children who are not to be relevant children despite falling within subsection (2).

(4) In subsection (1) the "responsible local authority" is the one which last looked after the child.

(5) If under subsection (3)(a) the Secretary of State prescribes a category of relevant children which includes children who do not fall within subsection (2)(b) (for example, because they were being looked after by a local authority in Scotland), he may in the regulations also provide for which local authority is to be the responsible local authority for those children.

[Children Act 1989, s 23A as inserted by the Children (Leaving Care) Act 2000, s 2.]

1. See the Children Leaving Care (Wales) Regulations 2001, SI 2001/2189 amended by SI 2002/1855 and 2935 and SI 2004/1732 and the Children Leaving Care (England) Regulations 2001, SI 2001/2874 amended by SI 2002/546.

6–2132B 23B. Additional functions of the responsible authority in respect of relevant children. (1) It is the duty of each local authority to take reasonable steps to keep in touch with a relevant child for whom they are the responsible authority, whether he is within their area or not.

(2) It is the duty of each local authority to appoint a personal adviser[1] for each relevant child (if they have not already done so under paragraph 19C of Schedule 2).

(3) It is the duty of each local authority, in relation to any relevant child who does not already have a pathway plan prepared for the purposes of paragraph 19B of Schedule 2—

(a) to carry out an assessment of his needs with a view to determining what advice, assistance and support it would be appropriate for them to provide him under this Part; and

(b) to prepare a pathway plan for him.

(4) The local authority may carry out such an assessment at the same time as any assessment of his needs is made under any enactment referred to in sub-paragraphs (a) to (c) of paragraph 3 of Schedule 2, or under any other enactment.

(5) The Secretary of State may by regulations[2] make provision as to assessments for the purposes of subsection (3).

(6) The regulations[1] may in particular make provision about—

(a) who is to be consulted in relation to an assessment;

(b) the way in which an assessment is to be carried out, by whom and when;

(c) the recording of the results of an assessment;

(d) the considerations to which the local authority are to have regard in carrying out an assessment.

(7) The authority shall keep the pathway plan under regular review.

(8) The responsible local authority shall safeguard and promote the child's welfare and, unless they are satisfied that his welfare does not require it, support him by—

(a) maintaining him;

(b) providing him with or maintaining him in suitable accommodation; and

(c) providing support of such other descriptions as may be prescribed[1].

(9) Support under subsection (8) may be in cash.

(10) The Secretary of State may by regulations[1] make provision about the meaning of "suitable accommodation" and in particular about the suitability of landlords or other providers of accommodation.

(11) If the local authority have lost touch with a relevant child, despite taking reasonable steps to keep in touch, they must without delay—

(a) consider how to re-establish contact; and

(b) take reasonable steps to do so,

and while the child is still a relevant child must continue to take such steps until they succeed.

(12) Subsections (7) to (9) of section 17 apply in relation to support given under this section as they apply in relation to assistance given under that section.

(13) Subsections (4) and (5) of section 22 apply in relation to any decision by a local authority for the purposes of this section as they apply in relation to the decisions referred to in that section.

[Children Act 1989, s 23B as inserted by the Children (Leaving Care) Act 2000, s 2.]

1. It is not unlawful to appoint an officer or employee of the local authority as the personal adviser to a child in care. However, if such a person is appointed, it is essential that all those involved recognise that he or she is acting as personal adviser and not as some other role: *R (J) v Caerphilly County Borough Council* [2005] EWHC 586 (Admin), [2005] 2 FLR 860.

2. See the Children Leaving Care (Wales) Regulations 2001, SI 2001/2189 amended by SI 2002/1855 and 2935 and the Children Leaving Care (England) Regulations 2001, SI 2001/2874 amended by SI 2002/546.

6–2132C 23C. Continuing functions in respect of former relevant children. (1) Each local authority shall have the duties provided for in this section towards—

(a) a person who has been a relevant child for the purposes of section 23A (and would be one if he were under eighteen), and in relation to whom they were the last responsible authority; and

(b) a person who was being looked after by them when he attained the age of eighteen, and immediately before ceasing to be looked after was an eligible child, and in this section such a person is referred to as a "former relevant child".

(2) It is the duty of the local authority to take reasonable steps—

(a) to keep in touch with a former relevant child whether he is within their area or not; and
(b) if they lose touch with him, to re-establish contact.

(3) It is the duty of the local authority—

(a) to continue the appointment of a personal adviser for a former relevant child; and
(b) to continue to keep his pathway plan under regular review.

(4) It is the duty of the local authority to give a former relevant child—

(a) assistance of the kind referred to in section 24B(1), to the extent that his welfare requires it;
(b) assistance of the kind referred to in section 24B(2), to the extent that his welfare and his educational or training needs require it;
(c) other assistance, to the extent that his welfare requires it.

(5) The assistance given under subsection (4)(c) may be in kind or, in exceptional circumstances, in cash.

(6) Subject to subsection (7), the duties set out in subsections (2), (3) and (4) subsist until the former relevant child reaches the age of twenty-one.

(7) If the former relevant child's pathway plan sets out a programme of education or training which extends beyond his twenty-first birthday—

(a) the duty set out in subsection (4)(b) continues to subsist for so long as the former relevant child continues to pursue that programme; and
(b) the duties set out in subsections (2) and (3) continue to subsist concurrently with that duty.

(8) For the purposes of subsection (7)(a) there shall be disregarded any interruption in a former relevant child's pursuance of a programme of education or training if the local authority are satisfied that he will resume it as soon as is reasonably practicable.

(9) Section 24B(5) applies in relation to a person being given assistance under subsection (4)(b) as it applies in relation to a person to whom section 24B(3) applies.

(10) Subsections (7) to (9) of section 17 apply in relation to assistance given under this section as they apply in relation to assistance given under that section.
[Children Act 1989, s 23C as inserted by the Children (Leaving Care) Act 2000, s 2.]

Personal advisers and pathway plans

6–2132D   23D. Personal advisers.   (1) The Secretary of State may by regulations[1] require local authorities to appoint a personal adviser for children or young persons of a prescribed description who have reached the age of sixteen but not the age of twenty-one who are not—

(a) children who are relevant children for the purposes of section 23A;
(b) the young persons referred to in section 23C; or
(c) the children referred to in paragraph 19C of Schedule 2.

(2) Personal advisers appointed under or by virtue of this Part shall (in addition to any other functions) have such functions as the Secretary of State prescribes[1].
[Children Act 1989, s 23D as inserted by the Children (Leaving Care) Act 2000, s 3.]

---

1. See the Children (Leaving Care) (Wales) Regulations 2001, SI 2001/2189 amended by SI 2002/1855 and 2935 and the Children Leaving Care (England) Regulations 2001, SI 2001/2874 amended by SI 2002/546.

6–2132E   23E. Pathway plans.   (1) In this Part, a reference to a "pathway plan" is to a plan setting out—

(a) in the case of a plan prepared under paragraph 19B of Schedule 2—
  (i) the advice, assistance and support which the local authority intend to provide a child under this Part, both while they are looking after him and later; and
  (ii) when they might cease to look after him; and
(b) in the case of a plan prepared under section 23B, the advice, assistance and support which the local authority intend to provide under this Part,

and dealing with such other matters (if any) as may be prescribed.

(2) The Secretary of State may by regulations make provision about pathway plans and their review.
[Children Act 1989, s 23E as inserted by the Children (Leaving Care) Act 2000, s 3.]

Advice and assistance for certain children

6–2133   24. Persons qualifying for advice and assistance.   (1) In this Part "a person qualifying for advice and assistance" means a person to whom subsection (1A) or (1B) applies.

(1A) This subsection applies to a person—

(a) who has reached the age of sixteen but not the age of twenty-one;

(b) with respect to whom a special guardianship order is in force (or, if he has reached the age of eighteen, was in force when he reached that age); and

(c) who was, immediately before the making of that order, looked after by a local authority.

(1B) This subsection applies to a person to whom subsection (1A) does not apply, and who—

(a) is under twenty-one; and

(b) at any time after reaching the age of sixteen but while still a child was, but is no longer, looked after, accommodated or fostered.

(2) In subsection (1B)(b), "looked after, accommodated or fostered" means—

(a) looked after by a local authority;

(b) accommodated by or on behalf of a voluntary organisation;

(c) accommodated in a private children's home;

(d) accommodated for a consecutive period of at least three months—

   (i) by any Health Authority, Special Health Authority, Primary Care Trust or local education authority, or

   (ii) in any care home or independent hospital or in any accommodation provided by a National Health Service trust or an NHS foundation trust; or

(e) privately fostered.

(3) Subsection (2)(d) applies even if the period of three months mentioned there began before the child reached the age of sixteen.

(4) In the case of a person qualifying for advice and assistance by virtue of subsection (2)(a), it is the duty of the local authority which last looked after him to take such steps as they think appropriate to contact him at such times as they think appropriate with a view to discharging their functions under sections 24A and 24B.

(5) In each of sections 24A and 24B, the local authority under the duty or having the power mentioned there ("the relevant authority") is—

(za) in the case of a person to whom subsection (1A) applies, a local authority determined in accordance with regulations[1] made by the Secretary of State;

(a) in the case of a person qualifying for advice and assistance by virtue of subsection (2)(a), the local authority which last looked after him; or

(b) in the case of any other person qualifying for advice and assistance, the local authority within whose area the person is (if he has asked for help of a kind which can be given under section 24A or 24B).

[Children Act 1989, s 24 as amended by the Children (Leaving Care) Act 2000, s 4, the Health and Social Care (Community Health and Standards) Act 2003, Sch 4 and the Adoption and Children Act 2002, Sch 3.]

---

1. The Special Guardianship Regulations 2005, SI 2005/1109 and the Special Guardianship (Wales) Regulations 2005, SI 2005/1513 have been made.

6–2133A 24A. Advice and assistance. (1) The relevant authority shall consider whether the conditions in subsection (2) are satisfied in relation to a person qualifying for advice and assistance.

(2) The conditions are that—

(a) he needs help of a kind which they can give under this section or section 24B; and

(b) in the case of a person to whom section 24(1A) applies, or to whom section 24(1B) applies and who was not being looked after by any local authority, they are satisfied that the person by whom he was being looked after does not have the necessary facilities for advising or befriending him.

(3) If the conditions are satisfied—

(a) they shall advise and befriend him if he is a person to whom section 24(1A) applies, or he is a person to whom section 24(1B) applies and he was being looked after by a local authority or was accommodated by or on behalf of a voluntary organisation; and

(b) in any other case they may do so.

(4) Where as a result of this section a local authority are under a duty, or are empowered, to advise and befriend a person, they may also give him assistance.

(5) The assistance may be in kind and, in exceptional circumstances, assistance may be given—

(a) by providing accommodation, if in the circumstances assistance may not be given in respect of the accommodation under section 24B, or

(b) in cash.

(6) Subsections (7) to (9) of section 17 apply in relation to assistance given under this section or section 24B as they apply in relation to assistance given under that section.

[Children Act 1989, s 24A as inserted by the Children (Leaving Care) Act 2000, s 4 and amended by the Adoption and Children Act 2002, s 116 and the Adoption and Children Act 2002, Sch 3.]

6–2133B   24B. Employment, education and training.   (1) The relevant local authority may give assistance to any person who qualifies for advice and assistance by virtue of section 24(1A) or section 24(2)(*a*) by contributing to expenses incurred by him in living near the place where he is, or will be, employed or seeking employment.

(2) The relevant local authority may give assistance to a person to whom subsection (3) applies by—

(*a*)   contributing to expenses incurred by the person in question in living near the place where he is, or will be, receiving education or training; or

(*b*)   making a grant to enable him to meet expenses connected with his education or training.

(3) This subsection applies to any person who—

(*a*)   is under twenty-four; and

(*b*)   qualifies for advice and assistance by virtue of section 24(1A) or section 24(2)(*a*), or would have done so if he were under twenty-one.

(4) Where a local authority are assisting a person under subsection (2) they may disregard any interruption in his attendance on the course if he resumes it as soon as is reasonably practicable.

(5) Where the local authority are satisfied that a person to whom subsection (3) applies who is in full-time further or higher education needs accommodation during a vacation because his term-time accommodation is not available to him then, they shall give him assistance by—

(*a*)   providing him with suitable accommodation during the vacation; or

(*b*)   paying him enough to enable him to secure such accommodation himself.

(6) The Secretary of State may prescribe the meaning of "full-time", "further education", "higher education" and "vacation" for the purposes of subsection (5).
[Children Act 1989, s 24B as inserted by the Children (Leaving Care) Act 2000, s 4 and the Adoption and Children Act 2002, Sch 3.]

6–2133C   24C. Information.   (1) Where it appears to a local authority that a person—

(*a*)   with whom they are under a duty to keep in touch under section 23B, 23C or 24; or

(*b*)   whom they have been advising and befriending under section 24A; or

(*c*)   to whom they have been giving assistance under section 24B,

proposes to live, or is living, in the area of another local authority, they must inform that other authority.

(2) Where a child who is accommodated—

(*a*)   by a voluntary organisation or in a private children's home;

(*b*)   by any Health Authority, Special Health Authority, Primary Care Trust or local education authority; or

(*c*)   in any care home or independent hospital or any accommodation provided by a National Health Service trust or an NHS foundation trust,

ceases to be so accommodated, after reaching the age of sixteen, the organisation, authority or (as the case may be) person carrying on the home shall inform the local authority within whose area the child proposes to live.

(3) Subsection (2) only applies, by virtue of paragraph (*b*) or (*c*), if the accommodation has been provided for a consecutive period of at least three months.
[Children Act 1989, s 24C as inserted by the Children (Leaving Care) Act 2000, s 4 and amended by the Health and Social Care (Community Health and Standards) Act 2003, Sch 4.]

6–2133D   24D. Representations: sections 23A to 24B.   (1) Every local authority shall establish a procedure for considering representations (including complaints) made to them by—

(*a*)   a relevant child for the purposes of section 23A or a young person falling within section 23C;

(*b*)   a person qualifying for advice and assistance; or

(*c*)   a person falling within section 24B(2),

about the discharge of their functions under this Part in relation to him.

(1A) Regulations may be made by the Secretary of State imposing time limits on the making of representations under subsection (1).

(2) In considering representations under subsection (1), a local authority shall comply with regulations[1] (if any) made by the Secretary of State for the purposes of this subsection.
[Children Act 1989, s 24D as inserted by the Children (Leaving Care) Act 2000, s 5 and the Adoption and Children Act 2002, s 117.]

---

1. The following regulations have been made under this provision which also make any necessary amendments to the Representations Procedure (Children) Regulations 1991, SI 1991/894 as amended (revoked in relation to Wales by SI 2005/3365): in relation to England, the Advocacy Services and Representations Procedure (Children) (Amendment) Regulations 2004, SI 2004/719; in relation to Wales, the Advocacy Services and Representations Procedure (Children) (Wales) Regulations 2004, SI 2004/1448, the Representations Procedure (Children) (Wales) Regulations 2005, SI 2005/3365.

Secure accommodation

6–2134 **25. Use of accommodation for restricting liberty**[1]. (1) Subject to the following provisions of this section, a child[2] who is being looked after[3] by a local authority may not be placed, and, if placed, may not be kept, in accommodation provided for the purpose of restricting liberty[4] ("secure accommodation[5]") unless it appears[6]—

    (*a*) that—

        (i) he has a history of absconding and is likely[7] to abscond from any other description of accommodation[8]; and

        (ii) if he absconds, he is likely[7] to suffer significant harm; or

    (*b*) that if he is kept in any other description of accommodation[8] he is likely to injure himself or other persons.

    (2) The Secretary of State may by regulations[9]—

    (*a*) specify a maximum period—

        (i) beyond which a child may not be kept in secure accommodation without the authority of the court; and

        (ii) for which the court may authorise a child to be kept in secure accommodation;

    (*b*) empower the court from time to time to authorise a child to be kept in secure accommodation for such further period as the regulations may specify; and

    (*c*) provide that applications to the court under this section shall be made only by local authorities.

    (3) It shall be the duty of a court[10] hearing an application[11] under this section to determine whether any relevant criteria for keeping a child in secure accommodation are satisfied in his case.

    (4) If a court determines that any such criteria are satisfied, it shall[12] make an order[13] authorising the child to be kept in secure accommodation and specifying the maximum period[14] for which he may be so kept.

    (5) On any adjournment of the hearing of an application under this section, a court may make an interim order permitting the child to be kept during the period of the adjournment in secure accommodation.

    (6) No court shall exercise the powers conferred by this section in respect of a child who is not legally represented[15] in that court unless, having been informed of his right to apply for representation funded by the Legal Services Commission as part of the Community Legal Service or Criminal Defence Service and having had the opportunity to do so, he refused or failed to apply.

    (7) The Secretary of State may by regulations provide that—

    (*a*) this section shall or shall not apply to any description of children specified in the regulations;

    (*b*) this section shall have effect in relation to children of a description specified in the regulations subject to such modifications as may be so specified;

    (*c*) such other provisions as may be so specified shall have effect for the purpose of determining whether a child of a description specified in the regulations may be placed or kept in secure accommodation.

    (8) The giving of an authorisation under this section shall not prejudice any power of any court in England and Wales or Scotland to give directions relating to the child to whom the authorisation relates.

    (9) This section is subject to section 20(8).

[Children Act 1989, s 25 as amended by the Access to Justice Act 1999, Sch 4.]

---

    1. For further consideration of the provisions of s 25 which may give rise to an application for a secure accommodation order to a youth court, see para **5–30** Secure accommodation et seq, in PART V: YOUTH COURTS, post. The inter-relationship between s 25 and reg 6(1)(*b*) of the Children (Secure Accommodation) Regulations 1991 was considered in *Re G (secure accommodation order)* [2001] 3 FCR 47, [2001] 1 FLR 884, where it was held that where a child had previously been remanded to local authority accommodation and had not committed a further offence, the conditions specified in reg 6(1)(*b*) had not been met, but the Youth Court could nonetheless make a secure accommodation order if it was satisfied under s 25(3) that all the criteria specified in s 25(1) had been met and, indeed, had to do so. Secure accommodation order is a deprivation of liberty within the meaning of art 5 of the European Convention on Human Rights, it comes within the exception to the right to liberty in arti 5(1)(*d*) as it is a lawful order and, in the light of the compulsory education requirements of the Education Act 1996 which is embraced in the exercise by a local authority of parental rights for the benefit and protection of the child concerned, is for the purpose of educational supervision *(K (a child) (secure accommodation order: Right to liberty* [2001] 2 All ER 719, [2001] 2 WLR 1141, [2001] 1 FCR 249, CA).

    Although an application for a secure accommodation order is not to be classified as a criminal charge within the meaning of the Convention, a child facing such an application should be afforded the 5 minimum rights set out in art 6(2): *Re C (secure accommodation order: representation)* [2001] EWCA Civ 458, [2001] 2 FLR 169.

    2. While on an application for a secure accommodation order the court must be satisfied that the criteria in s 25(1) are met and that the duration of the order proposed is not in excess of that specified under s 25(2), there is no inhibition on the court making in the case of a child aged 15 a secure accommodation order that will extend beyond the child's 16th birthday (*Re G (a child) (secure accommodation order)* [2000] 2 FCR 386, [2000] 2 FLR 259, CA).

    3. This may include a child who is being looked after by the local authority pursuant to the conditions of bail *(Re C (secure accommodation: bail)* [1994] 2 FCR 1153, [1994] 2 FLR 922). In these circumstances application for a secure accommodation order may be made to a family proceedings court *(Re W (a minor) (secure accommodation: jurisdiction)* [1995] 2 FCR 708).

4. It is the restriction of liberty which is the essential factor in determining what is secure accommodation; accordingly, a hospital ward may be "secure accommodation" (*A Metropolitan Borough Council v DB* [1997] 1 FLR 767).

5. To constitute "secure accommodation" a place does not have to be so designated; each case will turn on its own facts. It is relevant to consider the extent to which liberty is restricted. Accordingly, a unit for the treatment of mentally disturbed children was secure accommodation as its purpose was to restrict the liberty of children there with a view to modifying their behaviour (*R v Northampton Juvenile Court, ex p London Borough of Hammersmith* [1985] FLR 193 and, on the facts, the maternity wing of a hospital where access was regulated by a key/pass system where trained staff were instructed to keep the minor confined to the ward (*Re B (a minor) (treatment and secure accommodation)* [1997] 1 FCR 618).

6. The grounds in paras (*a*) and (*b*) on which a child may be placed in secure accommodation are disjunctive rather conjunctive; see *Re D (secure accommodation order)* [1997] 1 FLR 197.

A local authority may only lawfully keep a child in secure accommodation for so long as (i) it is within the maximum period permitted without the authority of the court, or the maximum period specified in an order under s 25(4); and (ii) it continues to appear to the local authority themselves that the criteria in s 25(1) are satisfied. Accordingly, if it appears to the local authority that the criteria are no longer satisfied, they must cease to keep the child in secure accommodation (*LM v Essex County Council* [1999] 1 FCR 673, [1999] 1 FLR 988).

7. "Likely" in s 25(*a*)(i), (ii) means a real possibility that cannot sensibly be ignored (*S v Knowsley Borough Council* [2004] EWHC 491 (Fam), [2004] 2 FLR 716).

8. The guardian ad litem is entitled to enquire into alternative local authority placements and the court is required to do so; the position is quite distinct from the making of a care order (*Hereford and Worcester County Council v S* [1993] 1 FCR 653, [1993] 2 FLR 360).

9. See the Children (Secure Accommodation) Regulations 1991 and the Children (Secure Accommodation) (No 2) Regulations 1991, post.

10. The Criminal Justice Act 1991, s 60(3) provides that in the case of a child or young person who has been remanded or committed to local authority accommodation by a youth court or a magistrates' court other than a youth court, any application under s 25 of the Children Act 1989 (use of accommodation for restricting liberty) shall, notwithstanding anything in s 92(2) of that Act or s 65 of the Magistrates' Courts Act 1980, be made to that court. In the transitional period "youth court" is construed as meaning "juvenile court" (Criminal Justice Act 1991, Sch 12, para 23).

11. It is essential in an application for a secure accommodation order that there is a clear recording of the facts as found by the court, and in order to reach those conclusions it is necessary for there to be sworn evidence unless the matters proceed by agreement between all parties, in which case the statements which have been filed will constitute the agreed evidence (*Re AS (secure accommodation order)* [1999] 1 FLR 103).

12. In considering any relevant criteria for the making of a secure accommodation order, the court will have regard to the duty of a local authority to safeguard and promote the welfare of children accommodated by them. However, the principles in s 1 of the Act and in particular the paramountcy of the child's welfare are not applicable to such applications and if any relevant criteria are satisfied, there is a mandatory duty on the court to make an order: *Re M (a minor) (secure accommodation order)* [1995] 3 All ER 407, [1995] 2 WLR 302, [1995] 2 FCR 373, CA.

13. Natural justice does not demand that the child shall be present in court before the order is made. While the court may allow the child to be in court, the court must always bear in mind that attendance in court is likely to be harmful to the child, and the court should only allow the child to attend if is satisfied that attendance is in the interests of the child (*Re W (secure accommodation order: attendance at court)* [1994] 3 FCR 248, [1994] 2 FLR 1092). It is important to read sub-s (5) with sub-s (4); an order should be no longer than is necessary and unavoidable, and if further enquiries are indicated before the length of an order can be assessed an interim order is appropriate (*Hereford and Worcester County Council v S* [1993] 1 FCR 653, [1993] 2 FLR 360).

Once a family proceedings court has made a secure accommodation order, the court is *functus officio* in relation to that order and cannot subsequently discharge it or set it aside; nor can any higher court save, in appropriate circumstances, on appeal under s 94, post. Accordingly, where the local authority are themselves in agreement that the criteria are no longer satisfied, an application for, and the grant of, a writ of *habeas corpus* is the correct remedy (*LM v Essex County Council* [1999] 1 FCR 673, [1999] 1 FLR 988). Otherwise judicial review is the appropriate remedy in most cases and it can be combined with points made under the Human Rights Act 1998 (*S v Knowsley Borough Council* [2004] EWHC 491 (Fam), [2004] 2 FLR 716).

14. It is important that the order should be for no longer than is necessary, the court must make findings of the fact and give reasons for the length of the order chosen (*Re W (a minor) (secure accommodation order)* [1993] 1 FLR 692, *sub nom W v North Yorkshire County Council* [1993] FCR 693). See also *C v Humberside County Council* [1995] 1 FCR 110, [1994] 2 FLR 759. The period of time specified runs from the date of authorisation and not from the date of placement (*Re B (a minor) (secure accommodation)* [1995] 1 WLR 232, [1995] 1 FCR 142, [1994] 2 FLR 707).

15. It is implicit in this provision that legal representation, in order to be effective, must involve the taking of instructions. Accordingly, the local authority must inform the child of an application which is to be made to the court; the child must have the opportunity to be legally represented and to give instructions to the legal representative. Moreover in all save for the most exceptional circumstances, it is appropriate for a guardian ad litem to be appointed (*Re AS (secure accommodation order)* [1999] 1 FLR 103).

Supplemental

6–2135 26. Review of cases and inquiries into representations. (1) The Secretary of State may make regulations[1] requiring the case of each child who is being looked after by a local authority to be reviewed in accordance with the provisions of the regulations.

(2) The regulations may, in particular, make provision—

(*a*) as to the manner in which each case is to be reviewed;

(*b*) as to the considerations to which the local authority are to have regard in reviewing each case;

(*c*) as to the time when each case is first to be reviewed and the frequency of subsequent reviews;

(*d*) requiring the authority, before conducting any review, to seek the views of—

(i) the child;

(ii) his parents;

(iii) any person who is not a parent of his but who has parental responsibility for him; and

(iv) any other person whose views the authority consider to be relevant,

including, in particular, the views of those persons in relation to any particular matter which is to be considered in the course of the review;

(e) requiring the authority, in the case of a child who is in their care—

    (i) to keep the section 31A plan for the child under review and, if they are of the opinion that some change is required, to revise the plan, or make a new plan, accordingly,

    (ii) to consider, whether an application should be made to discharge the care order;

(f) requiring the authority, in the case of a child in accommodation provided by the authority—

    (i) if there is no plan for the future care of the child, to prepare one,

    (ii) if there is such a plan for the child, to keep it under review and, if they are of the opinion that some change is required, to revise the plan or make a new plan, accordingly,

    (iii) to consider, whether the accommodation accords with the requirements of this Part;

(g) requiring the authority to inform the child, so far as is reasonably practicable, of any steps he may take under this Act;

(h) requiring the authority to make arrangements, including arrangements with such other bodies providing services as it considers appropriate, to implement any decision which they propose to make in the course, or as a result, of the review;

(i) requiring the authority to notify details of the result of the review and of any decision taken by them in consequence of the review to—

    (i) the child;

    (ii) his parents;

    (iii) any person who is not a parent of his but who has parental responsibility for him; and

    (iv) any other person whom they consider ought to be notified;

(j) requiring the authority to monitor the arrangements which they have made with a view to ensuring that they comply with the regulations.

(k) for the authority to appoint a person in respect of each case to carry out in the prescribed manner the functions mentioned in subsection (2A) and any prescribed function.

(2A) The functions referred to in subsection (2)(k) are—

(a) participating in the review of the case in question,

(b) monitoring the performance of the authority's functions in respect of the review,

(c) referring the case to an officer of the Children and Family Court Advisory and Support Service or a Welsh family proceedings officer, if the person appointed under subsection (2)(k) considers it appropriate to do so.

(2B) A person appointed under subsection (2)(k) must be a person of a prescribed description.

(2C) In relation to children whose cases are referred to officers under subsection (2A)(c), the Lord Chancellor may by regulations[3]—

(a) extend any functions of the officers in respect of family proceedings (within the meaning of section 12 of the Criminal Justice and Court Services Act 2000) to other proceedings,

(b) require any functions of the officers to be performed in the manner prescribed by the regulations.

(2D) The power to make regulations in subsection (2C) is exercisable in relation to functions of Welsh family proceedings officers only with the consent of the National Assembly for Wales.

(3) Every local authority shall establish a procedure for considering any representations (including any complaint) made to them by—

(a) any child who is being looked after by them or who is not being looked after by them but is in need;

(b) a parent of his;

(c) any person who is not a parent of his but who has parental responsibility for him;

(d) any local authority foster parent;

(e) such other person as the authority consider has a sufficient interest in the child's welfare to warrant his representations being considered by them,

about the discharge by the authority of any of their qualifying functions in relation to the child.

(3A) The following are qualifying functions for the purposes of subsection (3)—

(a) functions under this Part,

(b) such functions under Part 4 or 5 as are specified by the Secretary of State in regulations.

(3B) The duty under subsection (3) extends to representations (including complaints) made to the authority by—

(a) any person mentioned in section 3(1) of the Adoption and Children Act 2002 (persons for whose needs provision is made by the Adoption Service) and any other person to whom arrangements for the provision of adoption support services (within the meaning of that Act) extend,

(b) such other person as the authority consider has sufficient interest in a child who is or may be adopted to warrant his representations being considered by them,

about the discharge by the authority of such functions under the Adoption and Children Act 2002 as are specified by the Secretary of State in regulations.

(3C) The duty under subsection (3) extends to any representations (including complaints) which are made to the authority by—

(a) a child with respect to whom a special guardianship order is in force,

(b) a special guardian or a parent of such a child,

(c) any other person the authority consider has a sufficient interest in the welfare of such a child to warrant his representations being considered by them, or

(d) any person who has applied for an assessment under section 14F(3) or (4),

about the discharge by the authority of such functions under section 14F as may be specified by the Secretary of State in regulations.

(4) The procedure shall ensure that at least one person who is not a member or officer of the authority takes part in—

(a) the consideration; and

(b) any discussions which are held by the authority about the action (if any) to be taken in relation to the child in the light of the consideration,

but this subsection is subject to subsection (5A).

(4A) Regulations may be made by the Secretary of State imposing time limits on the making of representations under this section.

(5) In carrying out any consideration of representations under this section a local authority shall comply with any regulations[2] made by the Secretary of State for the purposes of regulating the procedure to be followed.

(5A) Regulations under subsection (5) may provide that subsection (4) does not apply in relation to any consideration or discussion which takes place as part of a procedure for which provision is made by the regulations for the purpose of resolving informally the matters raised in the representations.

(6) The Secretary of State may make regulations[2] requiring local authorities to monitor the arrangements that they have made with a view to ensuring that they comply with any regulations made for the purposes of subsection (5).

(7) Where any representation has been considered under the procedure established by a local authority under this section, the authority shall—

(a) have due regard to the findings of those considering the representation; and

(b) take such steps as are reasonably practicable to notify (in writing)—

(i) the person making the representation;

(ii) the child (if the authority consider that he has sufficient understanding); and

(iii) such other persons (if any) as appear to the authority to be likely to be affected,

of the authority's decision in the matter and their reasons for taking that decision and of any action which they have taken, or propose to take.

(8) Every local authority shall give such publicity to their procedure for considering representations under this section as they consider appropriate.

[Children Act 1989, s 26 as amended by the Adoption and Children Act 2002, s 117 and the Health and Social Care (Community Health and Standards) Act 2003, s 117.]

---

1. See the Review of Children's Cases Regulations 1991, SI 1991/895 amended by SI 1991/2033, SI 1993/3069, SI 1995/2015, SI 1997/649, SI 2002/546 (England), 2935 (Wales) and 3013 (Wales), SI 2004/1419 (E), 1448 (W) and 2253 (E) and SI 2005/774 (W). See also the Adoption Agencies (Wales) Regulations 2005, SI 2005/1313. For procedures where a child is to be placed for adoption, see the Adoption Agencies Regulations 2005, in this PART, STATUTORY INSTRUMENTS AND PRACTICE DIRECTIONS ON FAMILY LAW, post.

2. See the Representations Procedure (Children) Regulations 1991, SI 1991/894 amended by SI 1991/2033, SI 1993/3069, SI 2002/546 (England), 2469 and 2935 (Wales), SI 2004/719 (E) and 1448 (W) and SI 2005/3482.

3. The Children and Family Court Advisory and Support Service (Reviewed Case Referral) Regulations 2004, SI 2004/2187 amended by SI 2005/605 have been made.

6–2135ZA   26ZA. Representations: further consideration. *Secretary of State may by regulations make provision for the further consideration of representations which have been considered by a local authority in England under section 24D or section 26.*

6–2135ZB   26ZB. Representations: further consideration (Wales). *Secretary of State may by regulations[1] make provision for the further consideration of representations which have been considered by a local authority in Wales under section 24D or section 26.*

---

1. The Social Services Complaints Procedure (Wales) Regulations 2005, SI 2005/3366 have been made.

6–2135A   26A. Advocacy services. (1) Every local authority shall make arrangements for the provision of assistance to—

(a) persons who make or intend to make representations under section 24D; and

(b) children who make or intend to make representations under section 26.

(2) The assistance provided under the arrangements shall include assistance by way of representation.*

(2A) The duty under subsection (1) includes a duty to make arrangements for the provision of assistance where representations under section 24D or 26 are further considered under section 26ZA or 26ZB.

(3) The arrangements—

(a) shall secure that a person may not provide assistance if he is a person who is prevented from doing so by regulations¹ made by the Secretary of State; and

(b) shall comply with any other provision made by the regulations¹ in relation to the arrangements.

(4) The Secretary of State may make regulations requiring local authorities to monitor the steps that they have taken with a view to ensuring that they comply with regulations¹ made for the purposes of subsection (3).

(5) Every local authority shall give such publicity to their arrangements for the provision of assistance under this section as they consider appropriate.

[Children Act 1989, s 26A, as inserted by the Adoption and Children Act 2002, s 119 and amended by the Health and Social Care (Community Health and Standards) Act 2003, s 116.]

1. The following regulations have been made under this provision which also make any necessary amendments to the Representations Procedure (Children) Regulations 1991, SI 1991/894 as amended: in relation to England, the Advocacy Services and Representations Procedure (Children) (Amendment) Regulations 2004, SI 2004/719; in relation to Wales, the Advocacy Services and Representations Procedure (Children) (Wales) Regulations 2004, SI 2004/1448; Social Services Complaints Procedure (Wales) Regulations 2005, SI 2005/3366.

6–2136   27. Co-operation between authorities. (1) Where it appears to a local authority that any authority mentioned in subsection (3) could, by taking any specified action, help in the exercise of any of their functions under this Part, they may request the help of that other authority, specifying the action in question.

(2) An authority whose help is so requested shall comply with the request if it is compatible with their own statutory or other duties and obligations and does not unduly prejudice the discharge of any of their functions.

(3) The authorities are—

(a) any local authority;

(b) any local education authority;

(c) any local housing authority;

(d) any Health Authority, Special Health Authority, Primary Care Trust, National Health Service trust or NHS foundation trust; and

(e) any person authorised by the Secretary of State for the purposes of this section.

(4) *Repealed.*

[Children Act 1989, s 27 as amended by the Courts and Legal Services Act 1990, Schs 16 and 20, the Education Act 1993, Schs 19 and 21, the Health Authorities Act 1995, Sch 1, SI 2000/90 and the Health and Social Care (Community Health and Standards) Act 2003, s 199.]

6–2137   28. Consultation with local education authorities. (1) Where—

(a) a child is being looked after by a local authority; and

(b) the authority propose to provide accommodation for him in an establishment at which education is provided for children who are accommodated there,

they shall, so far as is reasonably practicable, consult the appropriate local education authority before doing so.

(2) Where any such proposal is carried out, the local authority shall, as soon as is reasonably practicable, inform the appropriate local education authority of the arrangements that have been made for the child's accommodation.

(3) Where the child ceases to be accommodated as mentioned in subsection (1)(b), the local authority shall inform the appropriate local education authority.

(4) In this section "the appropriate local education authority" means—

(a) the local education authority within whose area the local authority's area falls; or,

(b) where the child has special educational needs and a statement of his needs is maintained under Part IV of the Education Act 1996, the local education authority who maintain the statement.

[Children Act 1989, s 28 as amended by the Education Act 1993, Sch 19 and the Education Act 1996, Sch 37.]

6–2138   29. Recoupment of cost of providing services etc. (1) Where a local authority provide any service under section 17 or 18, other than advice, guidance or counselling, they may recover from a person specified in subsection (4) such charge for the service as they consider reasonable.

(2) Where the authority are satisfied that the person's means are insufficient for it to be reasonably practicable for him to pay the charge, they shall not require him to pay more than he can reasonably be expected to pay.

(3) No person shall be liable to pay any charge under subsection (1) for a service provided under

section 17 or 18(1) or (5) at any time when he is in receipt of income support under Part VII of the Social Security Contributions and Benefits Act 1992, of any element of child tax credit other than the family element, of working tax credit or of an income-based jobseeker's allowance.

(3A) No person shall be liable to pay any charge under subsection (1) for a service provided under section 18(2) or (6) at any time when he is in receipt of income support under Part VII of the Social Security Contributions and Benefits Act 1992 or of an income-based jobseeker's allowance.

(3B) No person shall be liable to pay any charge under subsection (1) for a service provided under section 18(2) or (6) at any time when—

(a) he is in receipt of guarantee state pension credit under section 1(3)(a) of the State Pension Credit Act 2002, or

(b) he is a member of a married or unmarried couple (within the meaning of that Act) the other member of which is in receipt of guarantee state pension credit.

(4) The persons are—

(a) where the service is provided for a child under sixteen, each of his parents;

(b) where it is provided for a child who has reached the age of sixteen, the child himself; and

(c) where it is provided for a member of the child's family, that member.

(5) Any charge under subsection (1) may, without prejudice to any other method of recovery, be recovered summarily as a civil debt.

(6) Part III of Schedule 2 makes provision in connection with contributions towards the maintenance of children who are being looked after by local authorities and consists of the re-enactment with modifications of provisions in Part V of the Child Care Act 1980.

(7) Where a local authority provide any accommodation under section 20(1) for a child who was (immediately before they began to look after him) ordinarily resident within the area of another local authority, they may recover from that other authority any reasonable expenses incurred by them in providing the accommodation and maintaining him.

(8) Where a local authority provide accommodation under section 21(1) or (2)(a) or (b) for a child who is ordinarily resident within the area of another local authority and they are not maintaining him in—

(a) a community home provided by them;

(b) a controlled community home; or

(c) a hospital vested in the Secretary of State or a Primary Care Trust, or any other hospital made available pursuant to arrangements made by a Strategic Health Authority, a Health Authority or a Primary Care Trust,

they may recover from that other authority any reasonable expenses incurred by them in providing the accommodation and maintaining him.

(9) Except where subsection (10) applies, where a local authority comply with any request under section 27(2) in relation to a child or other person who is not ordinarily resident within their area, they may recover from the local authority in whose area the child or person is ordinarily resident any reasonable expenses incurred by them in respect of that person.*

(10) Where a local authority ("authority A") comply with any request under section 27(2) from another local authority ("authority B") in relation to a child or other person—

(a) whose responsible authority is authority B for the purposes of section 23B or 23C; or

(b) whom authority B are advising or befriending or to whom they are giving assistance by virtue of section 24(5)(a),

authority A may recover from authority B any reasonable expenses incurred by them in respect of that person.

[Children Act 1989, s 29 as amended by the National Health Service and Community Care Act 1990, Sch 9, the Courts and Legal Services Act 1990, Sch 16, the Disability Living Allowance and Disability Working Allowance Act 1991, Sch 3, the Social Security (Consequential Provisions) Act 1992, Sch 2, the Health Authorities Act 1995, Sch 1, the Jobseekers Act 1995, Sch 2, the Tax Credits Act 1999, Sch 1, SI 2000/90, the Children (Leaving Care) Act 2000, s 7, the Local Government Act 2000, s 103, SI 2002/2469, the Tax Credits Act 2002, Sch 3 and the State Pension Credits Act 2002, s 11.]

6–2139   30. Miscellaneous.   (1) Nothing in this Part shall affect any duty imposed on a local authority by or under any other enactment.

(2) Any question arising under section 20(2), 21(3) or 29(7) to (9) as to the ordinary residence of a child shall be determined by agreement between the local authorities concerned or, in default of agreement, by the Secretary of State.

(3) Where the functions conferred on a local authority by this Part and the functions of a local education authority are concurrent, the Secretary of State may by regulations provide by which authority the functions are to be exercised.

(4) The Secretary of State may make regulations for determining, as respects any local education authority functions specified in the regulations, whether a child who is being looked after by a local authority is to be treated, for purposes so specified, as a child of parents of sufficient resources or as a child of parents without resources.

[Children Act 1989, s 30.]

General

6–2140 **31. Care and supervision orders**[2]. (1) On the application of any local authority or authorised person, the court may make[3] an order[4]—

(a) placing the child with respect to whom the application is made in the care of a designated local authority; or

(b) putting him under the supervision of a designated local.

(2) A court may only make a care order or supervision order if it is satisfied[5]—

(a) that the child concerned is suffering, or is likely to suffer, significant harm; and

(b) that the harm, or likelihood of harm, is attributable to—

(i) the care given to the child, or likely to be given to him if the order were not made, not being what it would be reasonable to expect a parent to give to him; or

(ii) the child's being beyond parental control.

(3) No care order or supervision order may be made with respect to a child who has reached the age of seventeen (or sixteen, in the case of a child who is married).

(3A) No care order may be made with respect to a child until the court has considered a section 31A plan.

(4) An application under this section may be made on its own or in any other family proceedings.

(5) The court may—

(a) on an application for a care order, make a supervision order;

(b) on an application for a supervision order, make a care order[6].

(6) Where an authorised person proposes to make an application under this section he shall—

(a) if it is reasonably practicable to do so; and

(b) before making the application,

consult the local authority appearing to him to be the authority in whose area the child concerned is ordinarily resident.

(7) An application made by an authorised person shall not be entertained by the court if, at the time when it is made, the child concerned is—

(a) the subject of an earlier application for a care order, or supervision order, which has not been disposed of; or

(b) subject to—

(i) a care order or supervision order;

(ii) an order under section 63(1) of the Powers of Criminal Courts (Sentencing) Act 2000; or

(iii) a supervision requirement within the meaning of Part II of the Children (Scotland) Act 1995.

(8) The local authority designated in a care order must be—

(a) the authority within whose area the child is ordinarily resident[7]; or

(b) where the child does not reside[8] in the area of a local authority, the authority within whose area any circumstances[9] arose in consequence of which the order is being made.

(9) In this section—

"authorised person" means—

(a) the National Society for the Prevention of Cruelty to Children and any of its officers; and

(b) any person authorised by order of the Secretary of State to bring proceedings under this section and any officer of a body which is so authorised;

"harm" means ill-treatment or the impairment of health or development including, for example, impairment suffered from seeing or hearing the ill-treatment of another;

"development" means physical, intellectual, emotional, social or behavioural development;

"health" means physical or mental health; and

"ill-treatment" includes sexual abuse and forms of ill-treatment which are not physical.

(10) Where the question of whether harm suffered by a child is significant turns on the child's health or development, his health or development shall be compared with that which could reasonably be expected of a similar child.

(11) In this Act—

"a care order" means (subject to section 105(1)) an order under subsection (1)(a) and (except where express provision to the contrary is made) includes an interim care order made under section 38; and

"a supervision order" means an order under subsection (1)(b) and (except where express provision to the contrary is made) includes an interim supervision order made under section 38.

[Children Act 1989, s 31 as amended by the Children (Scotland) Act 1995, Sch 4, the Powers of Criminal Courts (Sentencing) Act 2000, Sch 9, the Criminal Justice and Court Services Act 2000, Sch 7 and the Adoption and Children Act 2002, s 120.]

1. Part IV contains ss 31–42.

2. There is an important partnership to be played between the court and the local authority in considering applications under this Part of the Act. The part played by the court is to consider all the facts that are presented to it by the local authority and to make a decision finally disposing of the case when all of those facts are as clearly known to the court as can be hoped. A delay of a final decision for the purpose of ascertaining the result of a programme of assessment is proper delay and is to be encouraged. It is for the local authority to put all material facts before the court, including the results of an assessment, before inviting the court to pass to them the responsibility of the management of a full care order. The court must be slow to abdicate its responsibility until all the facts are known; see *Hounslow London Borough Council v A* [1993] 1 WLR 291, [1993] 1 FLR 702. The local authority should produce to the court a care plan which should accord so far as was reasonably practicable with para 2.62 of Vol 3 of the D of H *Guide to the Children Act 1989 (Re R (minors) (care proceedings care plan)* [1994] 2 FCR 136).

The proper forum for a challenge to the care plan is in the care proceedings, rather than by way of judicial review; only in the event of a failure by a local authority to amend its proposals for the child so as to accord with the court's determination of the child's interests is it proper for the guardian to consider taking proceedings for judicial review (*Re C (adoption: religious observance)* [2002] 1 FLR 1119).

3. Justices do not have an inherent jurisdiction to grant a stay of a care order pending an appeal; application should instead be made to the High Court (*Re O (a minor) (care proceedings: education)* [1992] 4 All ER 905).

4. For comparison of the relative merits of a local authority having the parental responsibility obligation resulting from a care order as against supervisory obligations, see *Re S (J) (a minor) (care or supervision order)* [1993] 2 FCR 193, [1993] 2 FLR 919 and *Re O (minors) (care or supervision order)* [1997] 2 FCR 17.

5. For the application of the threshold criteria, see para **6–165 Care and supervision orders: test to be applied**.

6. This provision does not extend to the making of a care order on an application under para 6(3) of Sch 3, post, for the extension of a supervision order (*Re A (a minor) (supervision order: extension*[1995] 2 FCR 114, [1995] 1 FLR 335).

7. For the purpose of designating particular local authorities in care orders, a simple test should be applied having regard to s 31(8) and s 105(6) (as to the latter provision, see infra). This will enable the court to make a rapid designation of the authority upon which is to fall the administrative, professional and financial responsibility for implementing the care order and the care plan. To ensure that s 31(8) provides a test applicable in all cases, it is legitimate to construe s 31(8)(*b*) as though it reads "where the child does not ordinarily reside" in a local authority area inserting the word "ordinarily". The preferred approach to periods which must be disregarded under s 105 (6), post, is notionally to extend the child's residence in the authority's area, where he or she had been ordinarily resident immediately before the commencement of the disregard period. Developments affecting the family during the period to be disregarded, such as the movement of the entire family into a different authority area, may be considered but only in exceptional circumstances (*Northamptonshire County Council v Islington London Borough Council* [1999] 3 FCR 385, [1999] 2 FLR 881). In relation to a newborn baby, ordinary residence is necessarily dependent on the residence of the mother (*C v Plymouth City Council* [2000] 2 FCR 289, [2000] 2 FLR 875, CA). Pursuant to s 105(6), post, in determining ordinary residence, any period during which the child has been provided with accommodation by a local authority must be disregarded. This will include any time during which the child was subject to an interim care order (*Re BC (a minor) (care order: appropriate local authority)* [1995] 3 FCR 598).

Where, during the pendency of care proceedings, a child becomes resident in the area of another authority, consideration should be given to joining that authority as a party or to that authority taking over the proceedings. There is the need for early and full cooperation and the care plan should be prepared as a joint document; any points of disagreement between the authorities should be clearly identified in the plan (*L v London Borough of Bexley* [1996] 2 FLR 595). The provisions of s 31(8) are mandatory and it is not open to a local authority to refuse to "consent" to the making of a care order by which it is the designated authority (*Hackney London Borough Council v C* [1997] 1 FCR 509, [1997] 1 FLR 544). However, where a local authority fulfils its duty under s 23(6) of the Act to make arrangements to enable a looked-after child to live with a person or family to whom he is closely related, or with whom he is closely connected, the child ceases to be "provided with accommodation" within the meaning of s 105(6)(*c*) and begins to live with the relative or family arranged by the local authority: *In re H (A Child) (Care Order: Appropriate Local Authority)* [2003] EWCA Civ 1629, [2004] Fam 89.

8. The subsection should be construed to include the word "ordinarily" between "not" and "reside" in order to rectify a parliamentary slip (*Gateshead Metropolitan Borough Council v L* [1996] 3 All ER 264, [1996] 2 FLR 179, FD, per Wilson J; followed in *Northamptonshire County Council v Islington London Borough Council* [1999] 3 FCR 385, [1999] 2 FLR 881).

9. The "circumstances" to which the court should have regard are the primary circumstances that carry the case over the s 31 threshold (*Northamptonshire County Council v Islington London Borough Council* [1999] 3 FCR 385, [1999] 2 FLR 881).

6–2140A   31A. Care orders: care plans.   (1) Where an application is made on which a care order might be made with respect to a child, the appropriate local authority must, within such time as the court may direct, prepare a plan ("a care plan") for the future care of the child.

(2) While the application is pending, the authority must keep any care plan prepared by them under review and, if they are of the opinion some change is required, revise the plan, or make a new plan, accordingly.

(3) A care plan must give any prescribed information and do so in the prescribed manner.

(4) For the purposes of this section, the appropriate local authority, in relation to a child in respect of whom a care order might be made, is the local authority proposed to be designated in the order.

(5) In section 31(3A) and this section, references to a care order do not include an interim care order.

(6) A plan prepared, or treated as prepared, under this section is referred to in this Act as a "section 31A plan".

[Children Act 1989, s 31A as inserted by the Adoption and Children Act 2002, s 121.]

6–2141   32. Period within which application for order under this Part must be disposed of.
(1) A court hearing an application for an order under this Part shall (in the light of any rules made by virtue of subsection (2))—

(a) draw up a timetable with a view to disposing of the application without delay; and

(b) give such directions as it considers appropriate for the purpose of ensuring, so far as is reasonably practicable, that that timetable is adhered to.

(2) Rules of court may—

(a) specify periods within which specified steps must be taken in relation to such proceedings; and

(b) make other provision with respect to such proceedings for the purpose of ensuring, so far as is reasonably practicable, that they are disposed of without delay.

[Children Act 1989, s 32.]

Care orders[1]

6–2142 33. Effect of care order. (1) Where a care order is made with respect to a child it shall be the duty[2] of the local authority designated by the order to receive the child into their care and to keep him in their care while the order remains in force[1].

(2) Where—

(a) a care order has been made with respect to a child on the application of an authorised person; but

(b) the local authority designated by the order was not informed that that person proposed to make the application,

the child may be kept in the care of that person until received into the care of the authority.

(3) While a care order is in force with respect to a child, the local authority designated by the order shall—

(a) have parental responsibility for the child; and

(b) have the power (subject to the following provisions of this section) to determine the extent to which—

(i) a parent, guardian or special guardian of the child; or

(ii) a person who by virtue of section 4A has parental responsibility for the child,

may meet his parental responsibility for him.

(4) The authority may not exercise the power in subsection (3)(b) unless they are satisfied that it is necessary to do so in order to safeguard or promote the child's welfare.

(5) Nothing in subsection (3)(b) shall prevent a person mentioned in that provision who has care of the child from doing what is reasonable in all the circumstances of the case for the purpose of safeguarding or promoting his welfare.

(6) While a care order is in force with respect to a child, the local authority designated by the order shall not—

(a) cause the child to be brought up in any religious persuasion other than that in which he would have been brought up if the order had not been made; or

(b) have the right—

(i) *repealed*;

(ii) to agree or refuse to agree to the making of an adoption order, or an order under section 84 of the Adoption and Children Act 2002, with respect to the child; or

(iii) to appoint a guardian for the child.

(7) While a care order is in force with respect to a child, no person may—

(a) cause the child to be known by a new surname; or

(b) remove him from the United Kingdom,

without either the written consent of every person who has parental responsibility for the child or the leave[3] of the court.

(8) Subsection (7)(b) does not—

(a) prevent the removal of such a child, for a period of less than one month, by the authority in whose care he is; or

(b) apply to arrangements for such a child to live outside England and Wales (which are governed by paragraph 19 of Schedule 2).

(9) The power in subsection (3)(b) is subject (in addition to being subject to the provisions of this section) to any right, duty, power, responsibility or authority which a person mentioned in that provision has in relation to the child and his property by virtue of any other enactment.

[Children Act 1989, s 33 as amended by the Adoption and Children Act 2002, Sch 3.]

---

1. A family proceedings court does not have power to stay a care order pending appeal to the High Court. However, an application may be made to the High Court immediately for a stay; see *Re O (a minor)* [1992] 4 All ER 905, [1992] 1 WLR 912. For provisions generally as to appeals, see s 94, post, and the Family Proceedings Rules 1991, r 4.22, post.

2. Once a care order is made responsibility for the care of the child is firmly with the local authority and the responsibilities of the court cease; accordingly, there is no power for the court to direct that the guardian ad litem should

have a continuing involvement in the case (*Kent County Council v C* [1992] 3 WLR 808, [1993] 1 FLR 308, sub nom *Re C N* [1992] 2 FCR 401).

3. By virtue of r 2(2)(*b*) of the Family Proceedings Courts (Children Act 1989) Rules 1991, this PART, post, applications under s 33(7) are specified proceedings for the purposes of s 41 of the Act. Accordingly, on such an application the court must appoint a guardian ad litem for the child unless it is satisfied that it is not necessary to do so in order to safeguard his interests; see also *Re J (a minor) (change of name)* [1993] 1 FCR 74, [1993] 1 FLR 699.

In exceptional circumstances and when the welfare of the child demands it, an application for a change of the child's surname to enable the child to use another surname may be made *ex parte* and without notice to his or her parents; see *Re J (a minor) (change of name)* [1993] 1 FCR 74, [1993] 1 FLR 699. In determining an application by a *Gillick* competent child to change his surname the welfare of the child is the paramount consideration and the court should give very careful consideration to the wishes, feelings, needs and objectives of the child (*Re S (a minor) (change of name)* [1999] 1 FCR 304, [1999] 1 FLR 672, CA).

6–2143   34. Parental contact etc with children in care[1]. (1) Where a child is in the care of a local authority, the authority shall (subject to the provisions of this section) allow the child reasonable[2] contact with—

  (*a*) his parents;
  (*b*) any guardian or special guardian of his;
  (*ba*) any person who by virtue of section 4A has parental responsibility for him;
  (*c*) where there was a residence order in force with respect to the child immediately before the care order was made, the person in whose favour the order was made; and
  (*d*) where, immediately before the care order was made, a person had care of the child by virtue of an order made in the exercise of the High Court's inherent jurisdiction with respect to children, that person.

(2) On an application made by the authority or the child, the court may make such order[3] as it considers appropriate with respect to the contact which is to be allowed between the child and any named person.

(3) On an application made by—

  (*a*) any person mentioned in paragraphs (*a*) to (*d*) of subsection (1); or
  (*b*) any person who has obtained the leave of the court to make the application,

the court may make such order[4] as it considers appropriate with respect to the contact which is to be allowed between the child and that person.

(4) On an application made by the authority or the child, the court may make an order[5] authorising the authority to refuse to allow contact between the child and any person who is mentioned in paragraphs (*a*) to (*d*) of subsection (1) and named in the order.

(5) When making a care order with respect to a child, or in any family proceedings in connection with a child who is in the care of a local authority, the court may make an order under this section, even though no application for such an order has been made with respect to the child, if it considers that the order should be made[6].

(6) An authority may refuse to allow the contact that would otherwise be required by virtue of subsection (1) or an order under this section if—

  (*a*) they are satisfied that it is necessary to do so in order to safeguard or promote the child's welfare; and
  (*b*) the refusal—

    (i) is decided upon as a matter of urgency; and
    (ii) does not last for more than seven days.

(7) An order under this section may impose such conditions as the court considers appropriate.
(8) The Secretary of State may by regulations[7] make provision as to—

  (*a*) the steps to be taken by a local authority who have exercised their powers under subsection (6);
  (*b*) the circumstances in which, and conditions subject to which, the terms of any order under this section may be departed from by agreement between the local authority and the person in relation to whom the order is made;
  (*c*) notification by a local authority of any variation or suspension of arrangements made (otherwise than under an order under this section) with a view to affording any person contact with a child to whom this section applies.

(9) The court may vary or discharge any order made under this section on the application of the authority, the child concerned or the person named in the order.
(10) An order under this section may be made either at the same time as the care order itself or later.
(11) Before making a care order with respect to any child the court shall—

  (*a*) consider the arrangements which the authority have made, or propose to make, for affording any person contact with a child to whom this section applies; and
  (*b*) invite the parties to the proceedings to comment on those arrangements.

[Children Act 1989, s 34 as amended by the Adoption and Children Act 2002, Sch 3.]

1. For consideration of the provisions of s 34 generally, see para **6-173 Parental contact with children in care**.

2. "Reasonable" is not the same as "at the discretion of the local authority"; reasonable implies that which is agreed between the local authority and the parents or, if there is no such agreement, that which is objectively reasonable (*Re P (contact with children in care)* [1993] 2 FLR 156). For the position under the European Convention on Human Rights see *B v United Kingdom* (1988) 10 EHRR 87, *Eriksson v Sweden* (1990) 12 EHRR 183 and *Johansen v Norway* (1996) 23 EHRR 33.

3. Section 34(2), when read in conjunction with sub-s (7), is sufficiently wide to enable the court to make what is, in effect, an interim contact order with a specific provision for a further hearing with a view to making some more enduring provision for contact at the later hearing (*Cheshire County Council v B* [1992] 2 FCR 572). However, the jurisdiction under s 34 is not to be deployed so as to inhibit the local authority in the performance of their statutory duty by preventing contact which the local authority considers advantageous to welfare. (*Re W (a child) (parental contact: prohibition)* [2000] 2 WLR 1276, [2000] 1 FCR 752, [2000] 1 FLR 502, CA.

4. For considerations applying where an application is made which is inconsistent with a wardship decision see *Cheshire County Council v M* [1992] 2 FCR 817; *Re W (children in care) (contact and parental responsibility orders)* [1993] 2 FCR 427.

5. The order may be for as short or as long a period as is considered to be for the child's welfare; in this sense it is wrong to say there is no power to make an "interim" order (*West Glamorgan County Council v P* [1992] 2 FCR 378).

6. It would appear that this power extends to making an order for no contact, but in most cases such an order will be ill-advised; see *Kent County Council v C* [1992] 3 WLR 808, [1993] 1 FLR 308, sub nom *Re C N* [1992] 2 FCR 401.

7. See the Contact with Children Regulations 1991, SI 1991/891. By virtue of reg 3 of the Contact with Children Regulations 1991, the local authority may depart from the terms of any order under s 34 by agreement between the local authority and the person in relation to whom the order is made, and where the child is of sufficient understanding, subject to agreement also with him; and subject also to appropriate written notice being given in accordance with the Regulations.

Supervision orders

6-2144   35. Supervision orders.   (1) While a supervision order is in force it shall be the duty of the supervisor—

(*a*)   to advise, assist and befriend the supervised child;

(*b*)   to take such steps as are reasonably necessary to give effect to the order; and

(*c*)   where—

(i)   the order is not wholly complied with; or

(ii)   the supervisor considers that the order may no longer be necessary,

to consider whether or not to apply to the court for its variation or discharge.

(2)   Parts I and II of Schedule 3 make further provision with respect to supervision orders.

[Children Act 1989, s 35.]

6-2145   36. Education supervision orders.   (1) On the application[1] of any local education authority, the court may make an order[2] putting the child with respect to whom the application is made under the supervision of a designated local education authority.

(2)   In this Act "an education supervision order" means an order under subsection (1).

(3)   A court may only make an education supervision order if it is satisfied that the child concerned is of compulsory school age and is not being properly educated.

(4)   For the purposes of this section, a child is being properly educated only if he is receiving efficient full-time education suitable to his age, ability and aptitude and any special educational needs he may have.

(5)   Where a child is—

(*a*)   the subject of a school attendance order which is in force under section 437 of the Education Act 1996 and which has not been complied with; or

(*b*)   is not attending regularly within the meaning of section 444 of that Act—

(i)   a school at which he is a registered pupil,

(ii)   any place at which education is provided for him in the circumstances mentioned in subsection (1) of section 444ZA of that Act, or

(iii)   any place which he is required to attend in the circumstances mentioned in subsection (2) of that section,

then, unless it is proved that he is being properly educated, it shall be assumed that he is not.

(6)   An education supervision order may not be made with respect to a child who is in the care of a local authority.

(7)   The local education authority designated in an education supervision order must be—

(*a*)   the authority within whose area the child concerned is living or will live; or

(*b*)   where—

(i)   the child is a registered pupil at a school; and

(ii)   the authority mentioned in paragraph (*a*) and the authority within whose area the school is situated agree,

the latter authority.

(8)   Where a local education authority propose to make an application for an education supervision order they shall, before making the application, consult the appropriate local authority.

(9)   The appropriate local authority is—

(a) in the case of a child who is being provided with accommodation by, or on behalf of, a local authority, that authority; and

(b) in any other case, the local authority within whose area the child concerned lives, or will live.

(10) Part III of Schedule 3 makes further provision with respect to education supervision orders.
[Children Act 1989, s 36 as amended by the Education Act 1993, Schs 19 and 21 and the Education Act 1996, Sch 37.]

---

1. Applications under this section are not "specified proceedings" for the purposes of s 41, post; accordingly, there is no power to appoint a guardian ad litem in such applications; see *Essex County Council v B* [1993] 1 FCR 145.

2. On making or refusing to make an education supervision order, the justices must, in accordance with r 21(5) of the Family Proceedings Courts (Children Act 1989) Rules 1991, record the reasons for the court's decision and any findings of fact; see *Essex County Council v B* [1993] 1 FCR 145.

Powers of court

6–2146 37. Powers of court in certain family proceedings.   (1) Where, in any family proceedings in which a question arises with respect to the welfare of any child, it appears to the court that it may be appropriate for a care or supervision order to be made with respect to him, the court may direct[1] the appropriate authority to undertake an investigation of the child's circumstances.

(2) Where the court gives a direction under this section the local authority concerned shall, when undertaking the investigation, consider whether they should—

(a) apply for a care order or for a supervision order with respect to the child;

(b) provide services or assistance for the child or his family; or

(c) take any other action with respect to the child.

(3) Where a local authority undertake an investigation under this section, and decide not to apply for a care order or supervision order with respect to the child concerned, they shall inform the court of—

(a) their reasons for so deciding;

(b) any service or assistance which they have provided, or intend to provide, for the child and his family; and

(c) any other action which they have taken, or propose to take, with respect to the child.

(4) The information shall be given to the court before the end of the period of eight weeks beginning with the date of the direction, unless the court otherwise directs.

(5) The local authority named in a direction under subsection (1) must be—

(a) the authority in whose area the child is ordinarily resident; or

(b) where the child is not ordinarily resident in the area of a local authority, the authority within whose area any circumstances arose in consequence of which the direction is being given.

(6) If, on the conclusion of any investigation or review under this section, the authority decide not to apply for a care order or supervision order with respect to the child—

(a) they shall consider whether it would be appropriate to review the case at a later date; and

(b) if they decide that it would be, they shall determine the date on which that review is to begin.
[Children Act 1989, s 37 as amended by the Courts and Legal Services Act 1990, Sch 16.]

---

1. For consideration of the power of the court to make a direction under this section, see *Re H (child's circumstances direction to investigate)* [1993] 2 FCR 277.

6–2147 38. Interim orders[1].   (1) Where—

(a) in any proceedings on an application for a care order or supervision order, the proceedings are adjourned; or

(b) the court gives a direction under section 37(1),

the court may make an interim care order[2] or an interim supervision order with respect to the child concerned.

(2) A court shall not make an interim care order or interim supervision order under this section unless it is satisfied[3] that there are reasonable grounds for believing that the circumstances with respect to the child are as mentioned in section 31(2)[4].

(3) Where, in any proceedings on an application for a care order or supervision order, a court makes a residence order with respect to the child concerned, it shall also make an interim supervision order with respect to him unless satisfied that his welfare will be satisfactorily safeguarded without an interim order being made.

(4) An interim order made under or by virtue of this section shall have effect for such period as may be specified in the order, but shall in any event cease to have effect on whichever of the following events first occurs[5]—

(a) the expiry of the period of eight weeks beginning with the date on which the order is made;

(b) if the order is the second or subsequent such order made with respect to the same child in the same proceedings, the expiry of the relevant period;

(c) in a case which falls within subsection (1)(*a*), the disposal of the application;

(d) in a case which falls within subsection (1)(*b*), on the disposal of an application for a care order or supervision order made by the authority with respect to the child;

(e) in a case which falls within subsection (1)(*b*) and in which—

(i) the court has given a direction under section 37(4), but

(ii) no application for a care order or supervision order has been made with respect to the child,

the expiry of the period fixed by that direction.

(5) In subsection (4)(*b*) "the relevant period" means—

(a) the period of four weeks beginning with the date on which the order in question is made; or

(b) the period of eight weeks beginning with the date on which the first order was made if that period ends later than the period mentioned in paragraph (*a*).

(6) Where the court makes an interim care order, or interim supervision order, it may give such directions[6] (if any) as it considers appropriate with regard to the medical or psychiatric examination or other assessment of the child; but if the child is of sufficient understanding to make an informed decision he may refuse[7] to submit to the examination or other assessment.

(7) A direction under subsection (6) may be to the effect that there is to be—

(a) no such examination or assessment; or

(b) no such examination or assessment unless the court directs otherwise.

(8) A direction under subsection (6) may be—

(a) given when the interim order is made or at any time while it is in force; and

(b) varied at any time on the application of any person falling within any class of person prescribed by rules of court for the purposes of this subsection.

(9) Paragraphs 4 and 5 of Schedule 3 shall not apply in relation to an interim supervision order.

(10) Where a court makes an order under or by virtue of this section it shall, in determining the period for which the order is to be in force, consider whether any party who was, or might have been, opposed to the making of the order was in a position to argue his case against the order in full.
[Children Act 1989, s 38.]

---

1. It is wrong to contemplate a series of interim care orders to allow a child's placement to be shown as permanent; it is the court's duty to determine current issues and, if the conditions are established, to make the appropriate order (*Re P (minors) (interim order)* [1993] 2 FLR 742, CA, *sub nom Cheshire County Council v P* [1993] 2 FCR 397, CA).

2. Guidelines to justices on hearing applications for interim care orders were given, with the approval of the President of the Family Division, by Cazalet J in *Hampshire County Council v S* [1993] 1 FLR 559, [1993] 1 All ER 944; see **Interim Care and Supervision Orders** in para **6–170**.
See also *Hertfordshire County Council v W* [1992] 2 FCR 885.
When making an interim order the court must be careful not to determine the case by deciding issues not necessarily arising with the interim order; in particular contact should only be denied in exceptional circumstances (*A v M and Walsall Metropolitan Borough Council* [1993] 2 FLR 244).

3. A court must look at the evidence and determine whether there is potentially credible evidence and whether it gives the court grounds for believing that the threshold criteria under s 31(2) exist; if there are such reasonable grounds the court must then consider the welfare principle set out in s 1(3) so that it may exercise its discretion as to the order to be made (*F v Kent County Council* [1993] 1 FCR 217).

4. See s 31, Children Act 1989, for criteria to be applied and notes thereto, ante. However, it does not follow that when the statutory conditions under s 38(2) are satisfied an interim care order automatically ensues; the court has to address the further question of whether an interim care order should now be made for the welfare of the children: *Re A (children)(interim care order)* [2001] 3 FCR 402.

5. There is no limit on the number of interim orders that may be made nor on the aggregate period for which such orders can be in force; sub-ss (4) and (5) provide that the first such order may extend to eight weeks and any second or subsequent orders may last for up to four weeks (*Gateshead Metropolitan Borough Council v N* [1993] 1 FCR 400, [1993] 1 FLR 811).

6. As to the jurisdiction of the court to order or prohibit an assessment, see para **4-170 Interim Care and Supervision Orders**, ante. Such directions are appealable under s 94(1) and are mandatory; a local authority having the care of the child must obey them; magistrates must give clear reasons for directions (*Re O (minors) (medical examination)* [1992] 2 FCR 394, [1993] 1 FLR 860). The question of whether there should be an HIV test of a child should come before a High Court judge, and any such application should lead to the transfer of the substantive application to the High Court (*Re HIV Tests (Note)* [1994] 2 FLR 116).

7. The High Court, under its inherent jurisdiction, may override in a proper case the wishes of a child and give consent for medical assessment (*South Glamorgan County Council v B* [1993] 1 FCR 626).

6–2147A   38A. Power to include exclusion requirement in interim care order.   (1) Where—

(a) on being satisfied that there are reasonable grounds for believing that the circumstances with respect to a child are as mentioned in section 31(2)(*a*) and (*b*)(i), the court makes an interim care order with respect to a child, and

(b) the conditions mentioned in subsection (2) are satisfied,

the court may include an exclusion requirement in the interim care order.

(2) The conditions are—

(a) that there is reasonable cause to believe that, if a person ("the relevant person") is excluded from a dwelling-house in which the child lives, the child will cease to suffer, or cease to be likely to suffer, significant harm, and

(b) that another person living in the dwelling-house (whether a parent of the child or some other person)—

(i) is able and willing to give to the child the care which it would be reasonable to expect a parent to give him, and

(ii) consents to the inclusion of the exclusion requirement.

(3) For the purposes of this section an exclusion requirement is any one or more of the following—

(a) a provision requiring the relevant person to leave a dwelling-house in which he is living with the child,

(b) a provision prohibiting the relevant person from entering a dwelling-house in which the child lives, and

(c) a provision excluding the relevant person from a defined area in which a dwelling-house in which the child lives is situated.

(4) The court may provide that the exclusion requirement is to have effect for a shorter period than the other provisions of the interim care order.

(5) Where the court makes an interim care order containing an exclusion requirement, the court may attach a power of arrest to the exclusion requirement.

(6) Where the court attaches a power of arrest to an exclusion requirement of an interim care order, it may provide that the power of arrest is to have effect for a shorter period than the exclusion requirement.

(7) Any period specified for the purposes of subsection (4) or (6) may be extended by the court (on one or more occasions) on an application to vary or discharge the interim care order.

(8) Where a power of arrest is attached to an exclusion requirement of an interim care order by virtue of subsection (5), a constable may arrest without warrant any person whom he has reasonable cause to believe to be in breach of the requirement.

(9) Sections 47(7), (11) and (12) and 48 of, and Schedule 5 to, the Family Law Act 1996 shall have effect in relation to a person arrested under subsection (8) of this section as they have effect in relation to a person arrested under section 47(6) of that Act.

(10) If, while an interim care order containing an exclusion requirement is in force, the local authority have removed the child from the dwelling-house from which the relevant person is excluded to other accommodation for a continuous period of more than 24 hours, the interim care order shall cease to have effect in so far as it imposes the exclusion requirement.

[Children Act 1989, s 38A, as inserted by the Family Law Act 1996, Sch 6.]

6–2147B   38B. Undertakings relating to interim care orders.   (1) In any case where the court has power to include an exclusion requirement in an interim care order, the court may accept an undertaking from the relevant person.

(2) No power of arrest may be attached to any undertaking given under subsection (1).

(3) An undertaking given to a court under subsection (1)—

(a) shall be enforceable as if it were an order of the court, and

(b) shall cease to have effect if, while it is in force, the local authority have removed the child from the dwelling-house from which the relevant person is excluded to other accommodation for a continuous period of more than 24 hours.

(4) This section has effect without prejudice to the powers of the High Court and county court apart from this section.

(5) In this section "exclusion requirement" and "relevant person" have the same meaning as in section 38A.

[Children Act 1989, s 38B, as inserted by the Family Law Act 1996, Sch 6.]

6–2148   39. Discharge and variation etc of care orders and supervision orders.   (1) A care order may be discharged by the court on the application of—

(a) any person who has parental responsibility for the child;

(b) the child himself[1]; or

(c) the local authority designated by the order.

(2) A supervision order may be varied or discharged by the court on the application of—

(a) any person who has parental responsibility for the child;

(b) the child himself; or

(c) the supervisor.

(3) On the application of a person who is not entitled to apply for the order to be discharged, but who is a person with whom the child is living, a supervision order may be varied by the court in so far as it imposes a requirement which affects that person.

(3A) On the application of a person who is not entitled to apply for the order to be discharged, but who is a person to whom an exclusion requirement contained in the order applies, an interim care order may be varied or discharged by the court in so far as it imposes the exclusion requirement.

(3B) Where a power of arrest has been attached to an exclusion requirement of an interim care order, the court may, on the application of any person entitled to apply for the discharge of the order so far as it imposes the exclusion requirement, vary or discharge the order in so far as it confers a power of arrest (whether or not any application has been made to vary or discharge any other provision of the order).

(4) Where a care order is in force with respect to a child the court may, on the application of any person entitled to apply for the order to be discharged, substitute a supervision order for the care order.

(5) When a court is considering whether to substitute one order for another under subsection (4) any provision of this Act which would otherwise require section 31(2) to be satisfied at the time when the proposed order is substituted or made shall be disregarded.
[Children Act 1989, s 39 as amended by the Family Law Act 1996, Sch 6.]

---

1. There is no requirement for the child first to apply for leave before making an application *(Re A (care: discharge application by child)* [1995] 2 FCR 686, [1995] 1 FLR 599).

6–2149   40. Orders pending appeals in cases about care or supervision orders.   (1) Where—

(*a*) a court dismisses an application for a care order; and
(*b*) at the time when the court dismisses the application, the child concerned is the subject of an interim care order,

the court[1] may make a care order with respect to the child to have effect subject to such directions (if any) as the court may see fit to include in the order.

(2) Where—

(*a*) a court dismisses an application for a care order, or an application for a supervision order; and
(*b*) at the time when the court dismisses the application, the child concerned is the subject of an interim supervision order,

the court may make a supervision order with respect to the child to have effect subject to such directions (if any) as the court may see fit to include in the order.

(3) Where a court grants an application to discharge a care order or supervision order, it may order that—

(*a*) its decision is not to have effect; or
(*b*) the care order, or supervision order, is to continue to have effect but subject to such directions as the court sees fit to include in the order.

(4) An order made under this section shall only have effect for such period, not exceeding the appeal period, as may be specified in the order.

(5) Where—

(*a*) an appeal is made against any decision of a court under this section; or
(*b*) any application is made to the appellate court in connection with a proposed appeal against that decision,

the appellate court may extend the period for which the order in question is to have effect, but not so as to extend it beyond the end of the appeal period.

(6) In this section "the appeal period" means—

(*a*) where an appeal is made against the decision in question, the period between the making of that decision and the determination of the appeal; and
(*b*) otherwise, the period during which an appeal may be made against the decision.
[Children Act 1989, s 40.]

---

1. The High Court has no power to make a care order pending the determination of the appeal, but can make an interim care order under s 38 of the Act (*Croydon London Borough Council v A (No 2)* [1992] 1 WLR 984, [1992] 2 FCR 858).

Guardians ad litem

6–2160   41. Representation of child and of his interests in certain proceedings.   (1) For the purpose of any specified[1] proceedings, the court shall appoint an officer of the Service or a Welsh family proceedings officer for the child concerned unless satisfied that it is not necessary to do so in order to safeguard his interests[2].

(2) The officer of the Service or Welsh family proceedings officer shall—

(*a*) be appointed in accordance with rules of court; and
(*b*) be under a duty[3] to safeguard the interests of the child in the manner prescribed by such rules.

(3) Where—

(*a*) the child concerned is not represented by a solicitor; and

(b)   any of the conditions mentioned in subsection (4) is satisfied,

the court may appoint a solicitor to represent him.

(4)   The conditions are that—

(a)   no officer of the Service or Welsh family proceedings officer has been appointed for the child;
(b)   the child has sufficient understanding to instruct a solicitor and wishes to do so;
(c)   it appears to the court that it would be in the child's best interests for him to be represented by a solicitor.

(5)   Any solicitor appointed under or by virtue of this section shall be appointed, and shall represent the child, in accordance with rules of court.

(6)   In this section "specified proceedings" means any proceedings—

(a)   on an application for a care order or supervision order;
(b)   in which the court has given a direction under section 37(1) and has made, or is considering whether to make, an interim care order;
(c)   on an application for the discharge of a care order or the variation or discharge of a supervision order;
(d)   on an application under section 39(4);
(e)   in which the court is considering whether to make a residence order with respect to a child who is the subject of a care order;
(f)   with respect to contact between a child who is the subject of a care order and any other person;
(g)   under Part V;
(h)   on an appeal against—

(i)   the making of, or refusal to make, a care order, supervision order or any order under section 34;
(ii)   the making of, or refusal to make, a residence order with respect to a child who is the subject of a care order; or
(iii)   the variation or discharge, or refusal of an application to vary or discharge, an order of a kind mentioned in sub-paragraph (i) or (ii);
(iv)   the refusal of an application under section 39(4);
(v)   the making of, or refusal to make, an order under Part V; or

(hh)   on an application for the making or revocation of a placement order (within the meaning of section 21 of the Adoption and Children Act 2002);
(i)   which are specified for the time being, for the purposes of this section, by rules of court.

(6A)   The proceedings which may be specified under subsection (6)(i) include (for example) proceedings for the making, varying or discharging of a section 8 order.

(7)–(9)   (*Repealed*).

(10)   Rules of court may make provision as to—

(a)   the assistance which any officer of the Service or Welsh family proceedings officer may be required by the court to give to it;
(b)   the consideration to be given by any officer of the Service or Welsh family proceedings officer, where an order of a specified kind has been made in the proceedings in question, as to whether to apply for the variation or discharge of the order;
(c)   the participation of officers of the Service or Welsh family proceedings officers in reviews, of a kind specified in the rules, which are conducted by the court.

(11)   Regardless of any enactment or rule of law which would otherwise prevent it from doing so, the court may take account of—

(a)   any statement contained in a report made by an officer of the Service or a Welsh family proceedings officer who is appointed under this section for the purpose of the proceedings in question; and
(b)   any evidence given in respect of the matters referred to in the report,

in so far as the statement or evidence is, in the opinion of the court, relevant to the question which the court is considering.

(12)   (*Repealed*).

[Children Act 1989, s 41 as amended by the Courts and Legal Services Act 1990, Sch 16, the Criminal Justice and Court Services Act 2000, Sch 7, the Children Act 2004, Sch 3 and the Adoption and Children Act 2002, s 122.]

---

1.   Specified proceedings are listed in sub-s (6); they do not include an application under s 8 of the Act for a prohibited steps order: (*Re M (prohibited steps order: application for leave)* [1993] 1 FCR 78, [1993] 1 FLR 275).

2.   However, CAFCASS is not under a duty to make provision to enable it, immediately on request by the court, to make available an officer of the service for appointment as a guardian; the relevant statutory provisions imply that, while CAFCASS should respond as soon as practicable after a request is made, there can be a gap between the request made by the court and CAFCASS making an officer available for appointment (*R v Children And Family Court Advisory And Support Service* [2003] EWHC 235 (Admin), [2003] 1 FLR 953).

3.   A statement made to a guardian ad litem [officer of the Service] in the course of an investigation is as confidential as the report itself. Accordingly, an admission by a mother that she had been responsible for the injuries to a child should not

have been disclosed to a social worker without the leave of the court (*Oxfordshire County Council v P*) [1995] Fam 161 [1995] 2 All ER 225, [1995] 2 WLR 543).

6–2161 **42. Right of officer of the Service to have access to local authority records.** (1) Where an officer of the Service or Welsh family proceedings officer has been appointed under section 41 he shall have the right at all reasonable times to examine and take copies of—

(a) any records[1] of, or held by, a local authority or an authorised person which were compiled in connection with the making, or proposed making, by any person of any application under this Act with respect to the child concerned;

(b) any records of, or held by, a local authority which were compiled in connection with any functions which are social services functions within the meaning of the Local Authority Social Services Act 1970, so far as those records[2] relate[3] to that child; or

(c) any records of, or held by, an authorised person which were compiled in connection with the activities of that person, so far as those records relate[3] to that child[4].

(2) Where an officer of the Service or Welsh family proceedings officer takes a copy of any record which he is entitled to examine under this section, that copy or any part of it shall be admissible as evidence of any matter referred to in any—

(a) report which he makes to the court in the proceedings in question; or

(b) evidence which he gives in those proceedings.

(3) Subsection (2) has effect regardless of any enactment or rule of law which would otherwise prevent the record in question being admissible in evidence.

(4) In this section "authorised person" has the same meaning as in section 31.

[Children Act 1989, s 42 as amended by the Courts and Legal Services Act 1990, Schs 16 and 20, the Criminal Justice and Court Services Act 2000, Sch 7, the Local Government Act 2000, Sch 5 and the Children Act 2004, Sch 3.]

---

1. This includes the case record relating to prospective adopters (*Re T (a minor) (guardian ad litem: case record)* [1994] 2 All ER 526, [1994] 2 WLR 594, [1994] 1 FLR 632).

2. This includes a document prepared by an Area Child Protection Committee for a 'Part 8 Review' (Part 8 of *Working Together under the Children Act 1989*) (*Re R (care proceedings : disclosure)* [2000] 3 FCR 721, [2000] 2 FLR 751, CA).

3. If the document the guardian wishes to examine and take copies of falls within CA 1989 s 42, as s 42(3) makes clear pubic interest immunity simply does not arise so far as the guardian's inspection is concerned (*Re J (care proceedings: disclosure)* [2003] EWHC 976 (Fam), [2003] 2 FLR 522).

4. The test is not whether the main focus or primary subject of the document is the child who is the subject of the proceedings; it is wider than that (*Re R (care proceedings: disclosure)* [2000] 3 FCR 721). (See also *Re J (care proceedings: disclosure)*, infra.)

PART V[1]
PROTECTION OF CHILDREN

6–2162 **43. Child assessment orders.** (1) On the application of a local authority or authorised person for an order to be made under this section with respect to a child, the court may make the order if, but only if, it is satisfied that—

(a) the applicant has reasonable cause to suspect that the child is suffering, or is likely to suffer, significant harm;

(b) an assessment of the state of the child's health or development, or of the way in which he has been treated, is required to enable the applicant to determine whether or not the child is suffering, or is likely to suffer, significant harm; and

(c) it is unlikely that such an assessment will be made, or be satisfactory, in the absence of an order under this section.

(2) In this Act "a child assessment order" means an order under this section.

(3) A court may treat an application under this section as an application for an emergency protection order.

(4) No court shall make a child assessment order if it is satisfied—

(a) that there are grounds for making an emergency protection order with respect to the child; and

(b) that it ought to make such an order rather than a child assessment order.

(5) A child assessment order shall—

(a) specify the date by which the assessment is to begin; and

(b) have effect for such period, not exceeding 7 days beginning with that date, as may be specified in the order.

(6) Where a child assessment order is in force with respect to a child it shall be the duty of any person who is in a position to produce the child—

(a) to produce him to such person as may be named in the order; and

(b) to comply with such directions relating to the assessment of the child as the court thinks fit to specify in the order.

(7) A child assessment order authorises any person carrying out the assessment, or any part of the assessment, to do so in accordance with the terms of the order.

(8) Regardless of subsection (7), if the child is of sufficient understanding to make an informed decision he may refuse to submit to a medical or psychiatric examination or other assessment.

(9) The child may only be kept away from home—

(*a*) in accordance with directions specified in the order;

(*b*) if it is necessary for the purposes of the assessment; and

(*c*) for such period or periods as may be specified in the order.

(10) Where the child is to be kept away from home, the order shall contain such directions as the court thinks fit with regard to the contact that he must be allowed to have with other persons while away from home.

(11) Any person making an application for a child assessment order shall take such steps as are reasonably practicable to ensure that notice of the application is given to—

(*a*) the child's parents;

(*b*) any person who is not a parent of his but who has parental responsibility for him;

(*c*) any other person caring for the child;

(*d*) any person in whose favour a contact order is in force with respect to the child;

(*e*) any person who is allowed to have contact with the child by virtue of an order under section 34; and

(*f*) the child,

before the hearing of the application.

(12) Rules of court may make provision as to the circumstances in which—

(*a*) any of the persons mentioned in subsection (11); or

(*b*) such other person as may be specified in the rules,

may apply to the court for a child assessment order to be varied or discharged.

(13) In this section "authorised person" means a person who is an authorised person for the purposes of section 31.

[Children Act 1989, s 43.]

---

1. Part V contains ss 43–52.

6–2163   44. Orders for emergency protection of children[1]. (1) Where any person ("the applicant") applies to the court for an order to be made under this section with respect to a child, the court may make the order if, but only if, it is satisfied that—

(*a*) there is reasonable cause to believe that the child is likely to suffer significant harm if—

(i) he is not removed to accommodation provided by or on behalf of the applicant; or

(ii) he does not remain in the place in which he is then being accommodated;

(*b*) in the case of an application made by a local authority—

(i) enquiries are being made with respect to the child under section 47(1)(*b*); and

(ii) those enquiries are being frustrated by access to the child being unreasonably refused to a person authorised to seek access and that the applicant has reasonable cause to believe that access to the child is required as a matter of urgency; or

(*c*) in the case of an application made by an authorised person—

(i) the applicant has reasonable cause to suspect that a child is suffering, or is likely to suffer, significant harm;

(ii) the applicant is making enquiries with respect to the child's welfare; and

(iii) those enquiries are being frustrated by access to the child being unreasonably refused to a person authorised to seek access and the applicant has reasonable cause to believe that access to the child is required as a matter of urgency.

(2) In this section—

(*a*) "authorised person" means a person who is an authorised person for the purposes of section 31; and

(*b*) "a person authorised to seek access" means—

(i) in the case of an application by a local authority, an officer of the local authority or a person authorised by the authority to act on their behalf in connection with the enquiries; or

(ii) in the case of an application by an authorised person, that person.

(3) Any person—

(*a*) seeking access to a child in connection with enquiries of a kind mentioned in subsection (1); and

(*b*) purporting to be a person authorised to do so,

shall, on being asked to do so, produce some duly authenticated document as evidence that he is such a person.

(4) While an order under this section ("an emergency protection order") is in force it—

(a) operates as a direction to any person who is in a position to do so to comply with any request to produce the child to the applicant;

(b) authorises—

(i) the removal of the child at any time to accommodation provided by or on behalf of the applicant and his being kept there; or

(ii) the prevention of the child's removal from any hospital, or other place, in which he was being accommodated immediately before the making of the order; and

(c) gives the applicant parental responsibility for the child.

(5) Where an emergency protection order is in force with respect to a child, the applicant—

(a) shall only exercise the power given by virtue of subsection (4)(b) in order to safeguard the welfare of the child;

(b) shall take, and shall only take, such action in meeting his parental responsibility for the child as is reasonably required to safeguard or promote the welfare of the child (having regard in particular to the duration of the order); and

(c) shall comply with the requirements of any regulations made by the Secretary of State for the purposes of this subsection.

(6) Where the court makes an emergency protection order, it may give such directions (if any) as it considers appropriate with respect to—

(a) the contact which is, or is not, to be allowed between the child and any named person;

(b) the medical or psychiatric examination or other assessment of the child.

(7) Where any direction is given under subsection (6)(b), the child may, if he is of sufficient understanding to make an informed decision, refuse to submit to the examination or other assessment.

(8) A direction under subsection (6)(a) may impose conditions and one under subsection (6)(b) may be to the effect that there is to be—

(a) no such examination or assessment; or

(b) no such examination or assessment unless the court directs otherwise.

(9) A direction under subsection (6) may be—

(a) given when the emergency protection order is made or at any time while it is in force; and

(b) varied at any time on the application of any person falling within any class of person prescribed by rules of court for the purposes of this subsection.

(10) Where an emergency protection order is in force with respect to a child and—

(a) the applicant has exercised the power given by subsection (4)(b)(i) but it appears to him that it is safe for the child to be returned; or

(b) the applicant has exercised the power given by subsection (4)(b)(ii) but it appears to him that it is safe for the child to be allowed to be removed from the place in question,

he shall return the child or (as the case may be) allow him to be removed.

(11) Where he is required by subsection (10) to return the child the applicant shall—

(a) return him to the care of the person from whose care he was removed; or

(b) if that is not reasonably practicable, return him to the care of—

(i) a parent of his;

(ii) any person who is not a parent of his but who has parental responsibility for him; or

(iii) such other person as the applicant (with the agreement of the court) considers appropriate.

(12) Where the applicant has been required by subsection (10) to return the child, or to allow him to be removed, he may again exercise his powers with respect to the child (at any time while the emergency protection order remains in force) if it appears to him that a change in the circumstances of the case makes it necessary for him to do so.

(13) Where an emergency protection order has been made with respect to a child, the applicant shall, subject to any direction given under subsection (6), allow the child reasonable contact with—

(a) his parents;

(b) any person who is not a parent of his but who has parental responsibility for him;

(c) any person with whom he was living immediately before the making of the order;

(d) any person in whose favour a contact order is in force with respect to him;

(e) any person who is allowed to have contact with the child by virtue of an order under section 34; and

(f) any person acting on behalf of any of those persons.

(14) Wherever it is reasonably practicable to do so, an emergency protection order shall name the child; and where it does not name him it shall describe him as clearly as possible.

(15) A person shall be guilty of an offence if he intentionally obstructs any person exercising the power under subsection (4)(*b*) to remove, or prevent the removal of, a child.

(16) A person guilty of an offence under subsection (15) shall be liable on summary conviction to a fine not exceeding **level 3** on the standard scale.

[Children Act 1989, s 44.]

---

1. Where a grave emergency, such as the use of a blood transfusion in respect of a child whose parents oppose such a course on religious grounds, occurs the inherent jurisdiction of the High Court should be invoked; where proceedings are commenced under the Children Act 1989 they should be transferred to the Family Division urgently (*Re O (a minor) (medical treatment)* [1993] 1 FCR 925). However, for comment on the use of s 8 in such cases, see *Camden London Borough Council v R (a minor) (blood transfusion)* [1993] 2 FCR 544. In *X Council v B (Emergency Protection Orders)* [2004] EWHC 2015 (Fam), [2005] 1 FLR 341, the court took the opportunity to give the following guidance in relation to EPO applications. (i) An order summarily removing a child from his parents is "draconian" and requires "exceptional justification" and "extraordinarily compelling reasons". It should not be made unless the FPC has been satisfied that it is both necessary and proportionate and that no other less radical form of order will promote the welfare of the child. Separation is only to be contemplated if immediate separation is essential to secure the child's safety: "imminent danger" must be "actually established". (ii) If the real purpose of the local authority's application is to facilitate assessment of the child then consideration should be given to whether that objective cannot equally effectively, and more proportionately, be achieved by a CAO under s 43. (iii) No EPO should be made for any longer than is absolutely necessary to protect the child. (iv) The evidence in support of the application for an EPO has to be full, detailed, precise and compelling. (v) Save in wholly exceptional cases, parents must be given adequate prior notice of the date, time and place of any application for an EPO, and of the evidence being relied upon. (vi) An ex parte application is normally appropriate only if the case is genuinely one of emergency or other great urgency (and even then it should normally be possible to give some kind of informal notice to the parents) or if there are compelling reasons to believe that the child's welfare will be compromised if the parents are alerted in advance. (vii) The FPC must comply meticulously with the mandatory requirements of rr 20 and 21(5)(6) of the Family Proceedings Courts (Children Act 1989) Rules 1991, keeping a note of the substance of the oral evidence and recording in writing not merely its reasons but also any findings of fact. (viii) Parents against whom an EPO has been made ex parte are entitled to be given, if they ask, proper information as to what happened at the hearing and to be told, if they ask, exactly what documents, bundles or other evidential materials were lodged with the FPC and what legal authorities were cited to the FPC. Those acting for the local authority in such a case ought to keep a proper note of the proceedings, to enable the authority to meet any proper request for information. (ix) The local authority, even after it has obtained an EPO, is under an obligation to consider less drastic alternatives to emergency removal. It would be prudent for local authorities to have procedures to ensure both that the required decision-making actually took place and that it was appropriately documented. (x) Section 44 imposes on the local authority a continuing duty to keep the case under review day by day to ensure that parent and child are separated for no longer than is necessary to secure the child's safety. (xi) Arrangements for "reasonable contact", required under s 44(13), subject only to any direction given by the FPC under s 44(6), must be driven by the needs of the family and not stunted by lack of resources.

6–2163A　44A. Power to include exclusion requirement in emergency protection order.

(1) Where—

   (*a*) on being satisfied as mentioned in section 44(1)(*a*), (*b*) or (*c*), the court makes an emergency protection order with respect to a child, and

   (*b*) the conditions mentioned in subsection (2) are satisfied,

the court may include an exclusion requirement in the emergency protection order.

(2) The conditions are—

   (*a*) that there is reasonable cause to believe that, if a person ("the relevant person") is excluded from a dwelling-house in which the child lives, then—

   　　(i) in the case of an order made on the ground mentioned in section 44(1)(*a*), the child will not be likely to suffer significant harm, even though the child is not removed as mentioned in section 44(1)(*a*)(i) or does not remain as mentioned in section 44(1)(*a*)(ii), or

   　　(ii) in the case of an order made on the ground mentioned in paragraph (*b*) or (*c*) of section 44(1), the enquiries referred to in that paragraph will cease to be frustrated, and

   (*b*) that another person living in the dwelling-house (whether a parent of the child or some other person)—

   　　(i) is able and willing to give to the child the care which it would be reasonable to expect a parent to give him, and

   　　(ii) consents to the inclusion of the exclusion requirement.

(3) For the purposes of this section an exclusion requirement is any one or more of the following—

   (*a*) a provision requiring the relevant person to leave a dwelling-house in which he is living with the child,

   (*b*) a provision prohibiting the relevant person from entering a dwelling-house in which the child lives, and

   (*c*) a provision excluding the relevant person from a defined area in which a dwelling-house in which the child lives is situated.

(4) The court may provide that the exclusion requirement is to have effect for a shorter period than the other provisions of the order.

(5) Where the court makes an emergency protection order containing an exclusion requirement, the court may attach a power of arrest to the exclusion requirement.

(6) Where the court attaches a power of arrest to an exclusion requirement of an emergency

protection order, it may provide that the power of arrest is to have effect for a shorter period than the exclusion requirement.

(7) Any period specified for the purposes of subsection (4) or (6) may be extended by the court (on one or more occasions) on an application to vary or discharge the emergency protection order.

(8) Where a power of arrest is attached to an exclusion requirement of an emergency protection order by virtue of subsection (5), a constable may arrest without warrant any person whom he has reasonable cause to believe to be in breach of the requirement.

(9) Sections 47(7), (11) and (12) and 48 of, and Schedule 5 to, the Family Law Act 1996 shall have effect in relation to a person arrested under subsection (8) of this section as they have effect in relation to a person arrested under section 47(6) of that Act.

(10) If, while an emergency protection order containing an exclusion requirement is in force, the applicant has removed the child from the dwelling-house from which the relevant person is excluded to other accommodation for a continuous period of more than 24 hours, the order shall cease to have effect in so far as it imposes the exclusion requirement.

[Children Act 1989, s 44A, as inserted by the Family Law Act 1996, Sch 6.]

6–2163B   44B. Undertakings relating to emergency protection orders.   (1) In any case where the court has power to include an exclusion requirement in an emergency protection order, the court may accept an undertaking from the relevant person.

(2) No power of arrest may be attached to any undertaking given under subsection (1).

(3) An undertaking given to a court under subsection (1)—

(*a*) shall be enforceable as if it were an order of the court, and

(*b*) shall cease to have effect if, while it is in force, the applicant has removed the child from the dwelling-house from which the relevant person is excluded to other accommodation for a continuous period of more than 24 hours.

(4) This section has effect without prejudice to the powers of the High Court and county court apart from this section.

(5) In this section "exclusion requirement" and "relevant person" have the same meaning as in section 44A.

[Children Act 1989, s 44B, as inserted by the Family Law Act 1996, Sch 6.]

6–2164   45. Duration of emergency protection orders and other supplemental provisions.

(1) An emergency protection order shall have effect for such period, not exceeding eight days, as may be specified in the order.

(2) Where—

(*a*) the court making an emergency protection order would, but for this subsection, specify a period of eight days as the period for which the order is to have effect; but

(*b*) the last of those eight days is a public holiday (that is to say, Christmas Day, Good Friday, a Bank Holiday or a Sunday),

the court may specify a period which ends at noon on the first later day which is not such a holiday.

(3) Where an emergency protection order is made on an application under section 46(7), the period of eight days mentioned in subsection (1) shall begin with the first day on which the child was taken into police protection under section 46.

(4) Any person who—

(*a*) has parental responsibility for a child as the result of an emergency protection order; and

(*b*) is entitled to apply for a care order with respect to the child,

may apply to the court for the period during which the emergency protection order is to have effect to be extended.

(5) On an application under subsection (4) the court may extend the period during which the order is to have effect by such period, not exceeding seven days, as it thinks fit, but may do so only if it has reasonable cause to believe that the child concerned is likely to suffer significant harm if the order is not extended.

(6) An emergency protection order may only be extended once.

(7) Regardless of any enactment or rule of law which would otherwise prevent it from doing so, a court hearing an application for, or with respect to, an emergency protection order may take account of—

(*a*) any statement contained in any report made to the court in the course of, or in connection with, the hearing; or

(*b*) any evidence given during the hearing,

which is, in the opinion of the court, relevant to the application.

(8) Any of the following may apply to the court for an emergency protection order to be discharged—

(*a*) the child;

(*b*) a parent of his;

(*c*)　any person who is not a parent of his but who has parental responsibility for him; or

(*d*)　any person with whom he was living immediately before the making of the order.

(8A)　On the application of a person who is not entitled to apply for the order to be discharged, but who is a person to whom an exclusion requirement contained in the order applies, an emergency protection order may be varied or discharged by the court in so far as it imposes the exclusion requirement.

(8B)　Where a power of arrest has been attached to an exclusion requirement of an emergency protection order, the court may, on the application of any person entitled to apply for the discharge of the order so far as it imposes the exclusion requirement, vary or discharge the order in so far as it confers a power of arrest (whether or not any application has been made to vary or discharge any other provision of the order).

(9)　No application for the discharge of an emergency protection order shall be heard by the court before the expiry of the period of 72 hours beginning with the making of the order.

(10)　No appeal may be made against—

(*a*)　the making of, or refusal to make, an emergency protection order;

(*b*)　the extension of, or refusal to extend, the period during which such an order is to have effect;

(*c*)　the discharge of, or refusal to discharge, such an order; or

(*d*)　the giving of, or refusal to give, any direction in connection with such an order.

(11)　Subsection (8) does not apply—

(*a*)　where the person who would otherwise be entitled to apply for the emergency protection order to be discharged—

(i)　was given notice (in accordance with rules of court) of the hearing at which the order was made; and

(ii)　was present at that hearing; or

(*b*)　to any emergency protection order the effective period of which has been extended under subsection (5).

(12)　A court making an emergency protection order may direct that the applicant may, in exercising any powers which he has by virtue of the order, be accompanied by a registered medical practitioner, registered nurse or registered midwife, if he so chooses.

(13)　The reference in subsection (12) to a registered midwife is to such a midwife who is also registered in the Specialist Community Public Health Nurses' Part of the register maintianed under article 5 of the Nursing and Midwifery Order 2001.

[Children Act 1989, s 45 as amended by the Courts and Legal Services Act 1990, Sch 16, the Family Law Act 1996, Sch 6, SI 2002/253 and SI 2004/1771.]

6–2165　46. Removal and accommodation of children by police in cases of emergency.

(1)　Where a constable has reasonable cause to believe that a child would otherwise be likely to suffer significant harm, he may[1]—

(*a*)　remove the child to suitable accommodation and keep him there; or

(*b*)　take such steps as are reasonable to ensure that the child's removal from any hospital, or other place, in which he is then being accommodated is prevented.

(2)　For the purposes of this Act, a child with respect to whom a constable has exercised his powers under this section is referred to as having been taken into police protection.

(3)　As soon as is reasonably practicable after taking a child into police protection, the constable concerned shall—

(*a*)　inform the local authority within whose area the child was found of the steps that have been, and are proposed to be, taken with respect to the child under this section and the reasons for taking them;

(*b*)　give details to the authority within whose area the child is ordinarily resident ("the appropriate authority") of the place at which the child is being accommodated;

(*c*)　inform the child (if he appears capable of understanding)—

(i)　of the steps that have been taken with respect to him under this section and of the reasons for taking them; and

(ii)　of the further steps that may be taken with respect to him under this section;

(*d*)　take such steps as are reasonably practicable to discover the wishes and feelings of the child;

(*e*)　secure that the case is inquired into by an officer designated for the purposes of this section by the chief officer of the police area concerned; and

(*f*)　where the child was taken into police protection by being removed to accommodation which is not provided—

(i)　by or on behalf of a local authority; or

(ii)　as a refuge, in compliance with the requirements of section 51,

secure that he is moved to accommodation which is so provided.

(4) As soon as is reasonably practicable after taking a child into police protection, the constable concerned shall take such steps as are reasonably practicable to inform—

(a) the child's parents;

(b) every person who is not a parent of his but who has parental responsibility for him; and

(c) any other person with whom the child was living immediately before being taken into police protection,

of the steps that he has taken under this section with respect to the child, the reasons for taking them and the further steps that may be taken with respect to him under this section.

(5) On completing any inquiry under subsection (3)(e), the officer conducting it shall release the child from police protection unless he considers that there is still reasonable cause for believing that the child would be likely to suffer significant harm if released.

(6) No child may be kept in police protection for more than 72 hours.

(7) While a child is being kept in police protection, the designated officer may apply on behalf of the appropriate authority for an emergency protection order to be made under section 44 with respect to the child.

(8) An application may be made under subsection (7) whether or not the authority know of it or agree to its being made.

(9) While a child is being kept in police protection—

(a) neither the constable concerned nor the designated officer shall have parental responsibility for him; but

(b) the designated officer shall do what is reasonable in all the circumstances of the case for the purpose of safeguarding or promoting the child's welfare (having regard in particular to the length of the period during which the child will be so protected).

(10) Where a child has been taken into police protection, the designated officer shall allow—

(a) the child's parents;

(b) any person who is not a parent of the child but who has parental responsibility for him;

(c) any person with whom the child was living immediately before he was taken into police protection;

(d) any person in whose favour a contact order is in force with respect to the child;

(e) any person who is allowed to have contact with the child by virtue of an order under section 34; and

(f) any person acting on behalf of any of those persons,

to have such contact (if any) with the child as, in the opinion of the designated officer, is both reasonable and in the child's best interests.

(11) Where a child who has been taken into police protection is in accommodation provided by, or on behalf of, the appropriate authority, subsection (10) shall have effect as if it referred to the authority rather than to the designated officer.

[Children Act 1989, s 46.]

---

1. A constable is not precluded from using this power where the statutory criteria are satisfied because an emergency protection order is in force (*Langley v Liverpool City Council* [2005] EWCA Civ 1173, [2006] 1 WLR 375, [2005] 3 FCR 303).

6–2166 47. Local authority's duty to investigate. (1) Where a local authority—

(a) are informed that a child who lives, or is found, in their area—

(i) is the subject of an emergency protection order; or

(ii) is in police protection; or

(iii) has contravened a ban imposed by a curfew notice within the meaning of Chapter I of Part I of the Crime and Disorder Act 1998; or

(b) have reasonable cause to suspect that a child who lives, or is found, in their area is suffering, or is likely to suffer, significant harm,

the authority shall make, or cause to be made, such enquiries as they consider necessary to enable them to decide whether they should take any action to safeguard or promote the child's welfare. In the case of a child falling within paragraph (a)(iii) above, the enquiries shall be commenced as soon as practicable and, in any event, within 48 hours of the authority receiving the information.

(2) Where a local authority have obtained an emergency protection order with respect to a child, they shall make, or cause to be made, such enquiries as they consider necessary to enable them to decide what action they should take to safeguard or promote the child's welfare.

(3) The enquiries shall, in particular, be directed towards establishing—

(a) whether the authority should make any application to the court, or exercise any of their other powers under this Act or section 11 of the Crime and Disorder Act 1998 (child safety orders), with respect to the child;

(b) whether, in the case of a child—

(i) with respect to whom an emergency protection order has been made; and

(ii) who is not in accommodation provided by or on behalf of the authority,

it would be in the child's best interests (while an emergency protection order remains in force) for him to be in such accommodation; and

(c) whether, in the case of a child who has been taken into police protection, it would be in the child's best interests for the authority to ask for an application to be made under section 46(7).

(4) Where enquiries are being made under subsection (1) with respect to a child, the local authority concerned shall (with a view to enabling them to determine what action, if any, to take with respect to him) take such steps as are reasonably practicable—

(a) to obtain access to him; or
(b) to ensure that access to him is obtained, on their behalf, by a person authorised by them for the purpose,

unless they are satisfied that they already have sufficient information with respect to him.

(5) Where, as a result of any such enquiries, it appears to the authority that there are matters connected with the child's education which should be investigated, they shall consult the relevant local education authority.*

(6) Where, in the course of enquiries made under this section—

(a) any officer of the local authority concerned; or
(b) any person authorised by the authority to act on their behalf in connection with those enquiries—

(i) is refused access to the child concerned; or
(ii) is denied information as to his whereabouts,

the authority shall apply for an emergency protection order, a child assessment order, a care order or a supervision order with respect to the child unless they are satisfied that his welfare can be satisfactorily safeguarded without their doing so.

(7) If, on the conclusion of any enquiries or review made under this section, the authority decide not to apply for an emergency protection order, a child assessment order, a care order or a supervision order they shall—

(a) consider whether it would be appropriate to review the case at a later date; and
(b) if they decide that it would be, determine the date on which that review is to begin.

(8) Where, as a result of complying with this section, a local authority conclude[1] that they should take action to safeguard or promote the child's welfare they shall take that action (so far as it is both within their power and reasonably practicable for them to do so).

(9) Where a local authority are conducting enquiries under this section, it shall be the duty of any person mentioned in subsection (11) to assist them with those enquiries (in particular by providing relevant information and advice) if called upon by the authority to do so.

(10) Subsection (9) does not oblige any person to assist a local authority where doing so would be unreasonable in all the circumstances of the case.

(11) The persons are—

(a) any local authority;
(b) any local education authority;
(c) any local housing authority;
(d) any Health Authority, Special Health Authority, Primary Care Trust, National Health Service trust or NHS foundation trust; and (e)any person authorised by the Secretary of State for the purposes of this section.

(12) Where a local authority are making enquiries under this section with respect to a child who appears to them to be ordinarily resident within the area of another authority, they shall consult that other authority, who may undertake the necessary enquiries in their place.
[Children Act 1989, s 47 as amended by the Courts and Legal Services Act 1990, Sch 16, the Health Authorities Act 1995, Sch 1, the Crime and Disorder Act 1998, s 15 and Sch 8, SI 2000/90 and the Health and Social Care (Community Health and Standards) Act 2003, Sch 4.]

---

*New sub-s (5A) inserted by the the Children Act 2004, s 53 from a date to be appointed.
1. What triggers the local authority's duty under this section is having reasonable cause *to suspect* and a local authority is not required to make a finding on the balance of probabilities as to past conduct before assessing risk and taking any necessary steps (*Re S (sexual abuse allegations: local authority response)* [2001] EWHC Admin 334, [2001] 3 FCR 702, [2001] 2 FLR 776.

6–2167 48. Powers to assist in discovery of children who may be in need of emergency protection. (1) Where it appears to a court making an emergency protection order that adequate information as to the child's whereabouts—

(a) is not available to the applicant for the order; but
(b) is available to another person,

it may include in the order a provision requiring that other person to disclose, if asked to do so by the applicant, any information that he may have as to the child's whereabouts.

(2) No person shall be excused from complying with such a requirement on the ground that complying might incriminate him or his spouse of an offence; but a statement or admission made in complying shall not be admissible in evidence against either of them in proceedings for any offence other than perjury.*

(3) An emergency protection order may authorise the applicant to enter premises specified by the order and search for the child with respect to whom the order is made.

(4) Where the court is satisfied that there is reasonable cause to believe that there may be another child on those premises with respect to whom an emergency protection order ought to be made, it may make an order authorising the applicant to search for that other child on those premises.

(5) Where—

(a) an order has been made under subsection (4);
(b) the child concerned has been found on the premises; and
(c) the applicant is satisfied that the grounds for making an emergency protection order exist with respect to him,

the order shall have effect as if it were an emergency protection order.

(6) Where an order has been made under subsection (4), the applicant shall notify the court of its effect.

(7) A person shall be guilty of an offence if he intentionally obstructs any person exercising the power of entry and search under subsection (3) or (4).

(8) A person guilty of an offence under subsection (7) shall be liable on summary conviction to a fine not exceeding **level 3** on the standard scale.

(9) Where, on an application made by any person for a warrant under this section, it appears to the court—

(a) that a person attempting to exercise powers under an emergency protection order has been prevented from doing so by being refused entry to the premises concerned or access to the child concerned; or
(b) that any such person is likely to be so prevented from exercising any such powers,

it may issue a warrant authorising any constable to assist the person mentioned in paragraph (a) or (b) in the exercise of those powers, using reasonable force if necessary.

(10) Every warrant issued under this section shall be addressed to, and executed by, a constable who shall be accompanied by the person applying for the warrant if—

(a) that person so desires; and
(b) the court by whom the warrant is issued does not direct otherwise.

(11) A court granting an application for a warrant under this section may direct that the constable concerned may, in executing the warrant, be accompanied by a registered medical practitioner, registered nurse or registered midwife if he so chooses.

(11A) The reference in subsection (11) to a registered midwife is to such a midwife who is also registered in the Specialist Community Public Health Nurses' Part of the register maintianed under article 5 of the Nursing and Midwifery Order 2001.

(12) An application for a warrant under this section shall be made in the manner and form prescribed by rules of court.

(13) Wherever it is reasonably practicable to do so, an order under subsection (4), an application for a warrant under this section and any such warrant shall name the child; and where it does not name him it shall describe him as clearly as possible.

[Children Act 1989, s 48 as amended by SI 2002/253 and SI 2004/1771.]

---

*Amended by the Civil Partnership Act 2004, Sch 27 from a date to be appointed.

6–2168   49. Abduction of children in care etc.   (1) A person shall be guilty of an offence if, knowingly and without lawful authority or reasonable excuse, he—

(a) takes a child to whom this section applies away from the responsible person;
(b) keeps such a child away from the responsible person; or
(c) induces, assists or incites such a child to run away or stay away from the responsible person.

(2) This section applies in relation to a child who is—

(a) in care;
(b) the subject of an emergency protection order; or
(c) in police protection,

and in this section "the responsible person" means any person who for the time being[1] has care of him by virtue of the care order, the emergency protection order, or section 46, as the case may be.

(3) A person guilty of an offence under this section shall be liable on summary conviction to

imprisonment for a term not exceeding six months, or to a fine not exceeding **level 5** on the standard scale, or to both.
[Children Act 1989, s 49.]

---

1. When a child is in care, the local authority may change the identity of the "responsible person" without giving notice to the parent or carer, although it is good practice to do so. Where a local authority had substituted foster parents for a natural parent as the "responsible person", once the parent knew of the change she was unlawfully keeping the child away from the "responsible person" (*Re R (a minor) (recovery order)* [1998] 3 FCR 321, [1998] 2 FLR 401).

6–2169　50. Recovery of abducted children etc.　(1) Where it appears to the court that there is reason to believe that a child to whom this section applies—

(*a*)　has been unlawfully taken away or is being unlawfully kept away from the responsible person;
(*b*)　has run away or is staying away from the responsible person; or
(*c*)　is missing,

the court may make an order under this section ("a recovery order").

(2)　This section applies to the same children to whom section 49 applies and in this section "the responsible person" has the same meaning as in section 49.

(3)　A recovery order—

(*a*)　operates as a direction to any person who is in a position to do so to produce the child on request to any authorised person;
(*b*)　authorises the removal of the child by any authorised person;
(*c*)　requires any person who has information as to the child's whereabouts to disclose that information, if asked to do so, to a constable or an officer of the court;
(*d*)　authorises a constable to enter any premises specified in the order and search for the child, using reasonable force[1] if necessary.

(4)　The court may make a recovery order only on the application of—

(*a*)　any person who has parental responsibility for the child by virtue of a care order or emergency protection order; or
(*b*)　where the child is in police protection, the designated officer.

(5)　A recovery order shall name the child and—

(*a*)　any person who has parental responsibility for the child by virtue of a care order or emergency protection order; or
(*b*)　where the child is in police protection, the designated officer.

(6)　Premises may only be specified under subsection (3)(*d*) if it appears to the court that there are reasonable grounds for believing the child to be on them.

(7)　In this section—

"an authorised person" means—

(*a*)　any person specified by the court;
(*b*)　any constable;
(*c*)　any person who is authorised—

(i)　after the recovery order is made; and
(ii)　by a person who has parental responsibility for the child by virtue of a care order or an emergency protection order,

to exercise any power under a recovery order; and

"the designated officer" means the officer designated for the purposes of section 46.

(8)　Where a person is authorised as mentioned in subsection (7)(*c*)—

(*a*)　the authorisation shall identify the recovery order; and
(*b*)　any person claiming to be so authorised shall, if asked to do so, produce some duly authenticated document showing that he is so authorised.

(9)　A person shall be guilty of an offence if he intentionally obstructs an authorised person exercising the power under subsection (3)(*b*) to remove a child.

(10)　A person guilty of an offence under this section shall be liable on summary conviction to a fine not exceeding **level 3** on the standard scale.

(11)　No person shall be excused from complying with any request made under subsection (3)(*c*) on the ground that complying with it might incriminate him or his spouse or civil partner of an offence; but a statement or admission made in complying shall not be admissible in evidence against either of them in proceedings for an offence other than perjury.

(12)　Where a child is made the subject of a recovery order whilst being looked after by a local authority, any reasonable expenses incurred by an authorised person in giving effect to the order shall be recoverable from the authority.

(13)　A recovery order shall have effect in Scotland as if it had been made by the Court of Session and as if that court had had jurisdiction to make it.

(14) In this section "the court", in relation to Northern Ireland, means a magistrates' court within the meaning of the Magistrates' Courts (Northern Ireland) Order 1981.
[Children Act 1989, s 50 as amended by the Civil Partnership Act 2004, Sch 27.]

---

1. The use of reasonable force authorised by the order is not limited to the process of entering the premises and searching for the child but extends to the removal of the child (*Re R (a minor) (recovery order)* [1998]3 FCR 321, [1998] 2 FLR 401).

6–2170 51. Refuges for children at risk. (1) Where it is proposed to use a voluntary home or private children's home to provide a refuge for children who appear to be at risk of harm, the Secretary of State may issue a certificate under this section with respect to that home.

(2) Where a local authority or voluntary organisation arrange for a foster parent to provide such a refuge, the Secretary of State may issue a certificate under this section with respect to that foster parent.

(3) In subsection (2) "foster parent" means a person who is, or who from time to time is, a local authority foster parent or a foster parent with whom children are placed by a voluntary organisation.

(4) The Secretary of State may by regulations[1]—

(a) make provision as to the manner in which certificates may be issued;
(b) impose requirements which must be complied with while any certificate is in force; and
(c) provide for the withdrawal of certificates in prescribed circumstances.

(5) Where a certificate is in force with respect to a home, none of the provisions mentioned in subsection (7) shall apply in relation to any person providing a refuge for any child in that home.

(6) Where a certificate is in force with respect to a foster parent, none of those provisions shall apply in relation to the provision by him of a refuge for any child in accordance with arrangements made by the local authority or voluntary organisation.

(7) The provisions are—

(a) section 49;
(b) sections 82 (recovery of certain fugitive children) and 83 (harbouring) of the Children (Scotland) Act 1995, so far as they apply in relation to anything done in England and Wales;
(c) section 32(3) of the Children and Young Persons Act 1969 (compelling, persuading, inciting or assisting any person to be absent from detention, etc), so far as it applies in relation to anything done in England and Wales;
(d) section 2 of the Child Abduction Act 1984.

[Children Act 1989, s 51 as amended by the Children (Scotland) Act 1995, Sch 4 and the Care Standards Act 2000, Sch 4.]

---

1. See the Refuges (Children's Homes and Foster Placements) Regulations 1991, SI 1991/1507 amended by SI 2002/546 (England) and 2935 (Wales).

6–2171 52. Rules and regulations. (1) Without prejudice to section 93 or any other power to make such rules, rules of court may be made with respect to the procedure to be followed in connection with proceedings under this Part.

(2) The rules may, in particular make provision—

(a) as to the form in which any application is to be made or direction is to be given;
(b) prescribing the persons who are to be notified of—

(i) the making, or extension, of an emergency protection order; or
(ii) the making of an application under section 45(4) or (8) or 46(7); and

(c) as to the content of any such notification and the manner in which, and person by whom, it is to be given.

(3) The Secretary of State may by regulations[1] provide that, where—

(a) an emergency protection order has been made with respect to a child;
(b) the applicant for the order was not the local authority within whose area the child is ordinarily resident; and
(c) that local authority are of the opinion that it would be in the child's best interests for the applicant's responsibilities under the order to be transferred to them,

that authority shall (subject to their having complied with any requirements imposed by the regulations) be treated, for the purposes of this Act, as though they and not the original applicant had applied for, and been granted, the order.

(4) Regulations made under subsection (3) may, in particular, make provision as to—

(a) the considerations to which the local authority shall have regard in forming an opinion as mentioned in subsection (3)(c); and
(b) the time at which responsibility under any emergency protection order is to be treated as having been transferred to a local authority.

[Children Act 1989, s 52.]

1. See the Emergency Protection Order (Transfer of Responsibility) Order 1991, post.

PART VI[1]
COMMUNITY HOMES

6–2172 53. Provision of community homes by local authorities. (1) Every local authority shall make such arrangements as they consider appropriate for securing that homes ("community homes") are available—

(a) for the care and accommodation of children looked after by them; and

(b) for purposes connected with the welfare of children (whether or not looked after by them),

and may do so jointly with one or more other local authorities.

(2) In making such arrangements, a local authority shall have regard to the need for ensuring the availability of accommodation—

(a) of different descriptions; and

(b) which is suitable for different purposes and the requirements of different descriptions of children.

(3) A community home may be a home—

(a) provided, equipped, maintained and (subject to subsection (3A)) managed by a local authority[2]; or

(b) provided by a voluntary organisation but in respect of which a local authority and the organisation—

   (i) propose that, in accordance with an instrument of management, the equipment, maintenance and (subject to subsection (3B)) management of the home shall be the responsibility of the local authority; or

   (ii) so propose that the management, equipment and maintenance of the home shall be the responsibility of the voluntary organisation.

(3A) A local authority may make arrangements for the management by another person of accommodation provided by the local authority for the purpose of restricting the liberty of children.

(3B) Where a local authority are to be responsible for the management of a community home provided by a voluntary organisation, the local authority may, with the consent of the body of managers constituted by the instrument of management for the home, make arrangements for the management by another person of accommodation provided for the purpose of restricting the liberty of children.

(4) Where a local authority are to be responsible for the management of a community home provided by a voluntary organisation, the authority shall designate the home as a controlled community home.

(5) Where a voluntary organisation are to be responsible for the management of a community home provided by the organisation, the local authority shall designate the home as an assisted community home.

(6) Schedule 4 shall have effect for the purpose of supplementing the provisions of this Part.
[Children Act 1989, s 53 as amended by the Criminal Justice and Public Order Act 1994, s 22.]

1. Part VI contains ss 53–59.
2. A local authority may authorise another person, or that person's employees, to exercise the function of managing community homes for children which are provided by that local authority, other than homes or parts of homes providing secure accommodation: Contracting Out (Management Functions in relation to certain Community Homes) Order 1996, SI 1996/586.

6–2173 54. (*Repealed*).

PART VII[1]
VOLUNTARY HOMES AND VOLUNTARY ORGANISATIONS

6–2178 59. Provision of accommodation by voluntary organisations. (1) Where a voluntary organisation provide accommodation for a child, they shall do so by—

(a) placing him (subject to subsection (2)) with—

   (i) a family;

   (ii) a relative of his; or

   (iii) any other suitable person,

   on such terms as to payment by the organisation and otherwise as the organisation may determine (subject to section 49 of the Children Act 2004);

(aa) maintaining him in an appropriate children's home; or

(f) making such other arrangements (subject to subsection (3)) as seem appropriate to them.

(1A) Where under subsection (1)(aa) a local authority maintains a child in a home provided, equipped and maintained by the Secretary of State under section 82(5), it shall do so on such terms as the Secretary of State may from time to time determine.

(2) The Secretary of State may make regulations[2] as to the placing of children with foster parents

by voluntary organisations and the regulations may, in particular, make provision which (with any necessary modifications) is similar to the provision that may be made under section 23(2)(a).

(3) The Secretary of State may make regulations[3] as to the arrangements which may be made under subsection (1)(f) and the regulations may in particular make provision which (with any necessary modifications) is similar to the provision that may be made under section 23(2)(f).

(4) The Secretary of State may make regulations[4] requiring any voluntary organisation who are providing accommodation for a child—

(a) to review his case; and

(b) to consider any representations (including any complaint) made to them by any person falling within a prescribed class of person,

in accordance with the provisions of the regulations.

(5) Regulations[4] under subsection (4) may in particular make provision which (with any necessary modifications) is similar to the provision that may be made under section 26.

(6) Regulations under subsections (2) to (4) may provide that any person who, without reasonable excuse, contravenes or fails to comply with a regulation shall be guilty of an offence and liable on summary conviction to a fine not exceeding **level 4** on the standard scale.

[Children Act 1989, s 59 as amended by the Care Standards Act 2000, Sch 4 and the Children Act 2004, s 49.]

---

1. Part VII contains ss 59–62.

2. See the Arrangements for Placement of Children (General) Regulations 1991, SI 1991/890 amended by SI 1991/2033, SI 1993/3069, SI 1995/2015, SI 1997/649, SI 2002/546 (England), 2469 and 2935 (Wales) and 3013 (W) and SI 2005/774 (W), the Fostering Services Regulations 2002, SI 2002/57 amended by SI 2002/865; the Fostering Services (Wales) Regulations 2003, SI 2003/237 amended by SI 2003/896 and SI 2005/3302.

3. See the Arrangements for Placement of Children (General) Regulations 1991, SI 1991/890 amended by SI 1991/2033, SI 1993/3069, SI 1995/2015, SI 1997/649, SI 2002/546 (England), 2469 and 2935 (Wales) and 3013 (W) and SI 2005/774 (W).

4. See the Representations Procedure (Children) Regulations 1991, SI 1991/894 amended by SI 1991/2033, SI 1993/3069, SI 2002/546 (England), 2469 and 2935 (Wales), SI 2004/719 (E) and 1448 (W) and SI 2005/3482, the Review of Children's Cases Regulations 1991, SI 1991/895 amended by SI 1991/2033, SI 1993/3069, SI 1995/2015, SI 1997/649, SI 2002/546 (England), 2935 (Wales), 3013 (Wales), SI 2004/1419 (E) and 1448 (W) and 2253 (E) and SI 2005/774 (W); the Adoption Agencies (Wales) Regulations 2005, SI 2005/1313. For procedures where a child is to be placed for adoption, see the Adoption Agencies Regulations 2005, in this PART, STATUTORY INSTRUMENTS AND PRACTICE DIRECTIONS ON FAMILY LAW, post.

6–2179 60. Voluntary homes. (1) *Repealed.*

(2) *Repealed.*

(3) In this Act "voluntary home" means a children's home which is carried on by a voluntary organisation but does not include a community home.

(4) Schedule 5 shall have effect for the purpose of supplementing the provisions of this Part.

[Children Act 1989, s 60 as amended by the Registered Homes (Amendment) Act 1991, s 2 and the Care Standards Act 2000, Sch 4.]

6–2190 61. Duties of voluntary organisations. (1) Where a child is accommodated by or on behalf of a voluntary organisation, it shall be the duty of the organisation—

(a) to safeguard and promote his welfare;

(b) to make such use of the services and facilities available for children cared for by their own parents as appears to the organisation reasonable in his case; and

(c) to advise, assist and befriend him with a view to promoting his welfare when he ceases to be so accommodated.

(2) Before making any decision with respect to any such child the organisation shall, so far as is reasonably practicable, ascertain the wishes and feelings of—

(a) the child;

(b) his parents;

(c) any person who is not a parent of his but who has parental responsibility for him; and

(d) any other person whose wishes and feelings the organisation consider to be relevant,

regarding the matter to be decided.

(3) In making any such decision the organisation shall give due consideration—

(a) having regard to the child's age and understanding, to such wishes and feelings of his as they have been able to ascertain;

(b) to such other wishes and feelings mentioned in subsection (2) as they have been able to ascertain; and

(c) to the child's religious persuasion, racial origin and cultural and linguistic background.

[Children Act 1989, s 61.]

6–2191 62. Duties of local authorities. (1) Every local authority shall satisfy themselves that any voluntary organisation providing accommodation—

(a) within the authority's area for any child; or

(*b*)　outside that area for any child on behalf of the authority,

are satisfactorily safeguarding and promoting the welfare of the children so provided with accommodation.

(2)　Every local authority shall arrange for children who are accommodated within their area by or on behalf of voluntary organisations to be visited, from time to time, in the interests of their welfare.

(3)　The Secretary of State may make regulations[1]—

(*a*)　requiring every child who is accommodated within a local authority's area, by or on behalf of a voluntary organisation, to be visited by an officer of the authority—

(i)　in prescribed circumstances; and
(ii)　on specified occasions or within specified periods; and

(*b*)　imposing requirements which must be met by any local authority, or officer of a local authority, carrying out functions under this section.

(4)　Subsection (2) does not apply in relation to community homes.

(5)　Where a local authority are not satisfied that the welfare of any child who is accommodated by or on behalf of a voluntary organisation is being satisfactorily safeguarded or promoted they shall—

(*a*)　unless they consider that it would not be in the best interests of the child, take such steps as are reasonably practicable to secure that the care and accommodation of the child is undertaken by—

(i)　a parent of his;
(ii)　any person who is not a parent of his but who has parental responsibility for him; or
(iii)　a relative of his; and

(*b*)　consider the extent to which (if at all) they should exercise any of their functions with respect to the child.

(6)　Any person authorised by a local authority may, for the purpose of enabling the authority to discharge their duties under this section—

(*a*)　enter, at any reasonable time, and inspect any premises in which children are being accommodated as mentioned in subsection (1) or (2);
(*b*)　inspect any children there;
(*c*)　require any person to furnish him with such records of a kind required to be kept by regulations made under section 22 of the Care Standards Act 2000 (in whatever form they are held), or allow him to inspect such records, as he may at any time direct.

(7)　Any person exercising the power conferred by subsection (6) shall, if asked to do so, produce some duly authenticated document showing his authority to do so.

(8)　Any person authorised to exercise the power to inspect records conferred by subsection (6)—

(*a*)　shall be entitled at any reasonable time to have access to, and inspect and check the operation of, any computer and any associated apparatus or material which is or has been in use in connection with the records in question; and
(*b*)　may require—

(i)　the person by whom or on whose behalf the computer is or has been so used; or
(ii)　any person having charge of, or otherwise concerned with the operation of, the computer, apparatus or material,

to afford him such assistance as he may reasonably require.

(9)　Any person who intentionally obstructs another in the exercise of any power conferred by subsections (6) or (8) shall be guilty of an offence and liable on summary conviction to a fine not exceeding **level 3** on the standard scale.

(10)　This section does not apply in relation to any voluntary organisation which is an institution within the further education sector, as defined in section 91 of the Further and Higher Education Act 1992, or a school.

[Children Act 1989, s 62, as amended by the Care Standards Act 2000, Sch 4.]

---

*Sub-section(10) inserted by the Care Standards Act 2000, Sch 4. In force in relation to England, with regard to Wales, in force from a date to be appointed: see the Care Standards Act 2000, s 122.

1. See the Foster Placement (Children) Regulations 1991, SI 1991/910 amended by SI 1995/2015, SI 1997/2308, SI 1999/2768 and SI 2001/2992 (England) and 3443 (Wales (Foster Placement (Children) Regulations 1991 revoked in so far as they apply to England by the Fostering Services Regulations 2002 and the Fostering Services Regulations 2002, SI 2002/57 amended by SI 2002/865 (England).

PART VIII[1]
REGISTERED CHILDREN'S HOMES

6–2192　63.　Private children's homes etc.　(1)–(10)　(*Repealed*).

(11)　Schedule 6 shall have effect with respect to private children's homes.

(12)　Schedule 7 shall have effect for the purpose of setting out the circumstances in which a

person may foster more than three children without being treated, for the purposes of this Act and the Care Standards Act 2000, as carrying on a children's home.
[Children Act 1989, s 63 as amended by the Registered Homes (Amendment) Act 1991, s 2, the Education Act 1993, s 292, the Education Act 1996, Sch 37 and the Care Standards Act 2000, Schs 4 and 6.]

1. Part VIII contains ss 63–65.

6–2193　64. Welfare of children in children's homes.　(1) Where a child is accommodated in a private children's home, it shall be the duty of the person carrying on the home to—

(a) safeguard and promote the child's welfare;
(b) make such use of the services and facilities available for children cared for by their own parents as appears to that person reasonable in the case of the child; and
(c) advise, assist and befriend him with a view to promoting his welfare when he ceases to be so accommodated.

(2) Before making any decision with respect to any such child the person carrying on the home shall, so far as is reasonably practicable, ascertain the wishes and feelings of—

(a) the child;
(b) his parents;
(c) any other person who is not a parent of his but who has parental responsibility for him; and
(d) any person whose wishes and feelings the person carrying on the home considers to be relevant,

regarding the matter to be decided.
(3) In making any such decision the person concerned shall give due consideration—

(a) having regard to the child's age and understanding, to such wishes and feelings of his as he has been able to ascertain;
(b) to such other wishes and feelings mentioned in subsection (2) as he has been able to ascertain; and
(c) to the child's religious persuasion, racial origin and cultural and linguistic background.

(4) Section 62, except subsection (4), shall apply in relation to any person who is carrying on a private children's home as it applies in relation to any voluntary organisation.
[Children Act 1989, s 64, as amended by the Care Standards Act 2000, Sch 4.]

6–2194　65. Persons disqualified from carrying on, or being employed in, children's homes.
(1) A person who is disqualified (under section 68) from fostering a child privately shall not carry on, or be otherwise concerned in the management of, or have any financial interest in, a children's home unless he has—

(a) disclosed to the appropriate authority the fact that he is so disqualified; and
(b) obtained its written consent.

(2) No person shall employ a person who is so disqualified in a children's home unless he has—

(a) disclosed to the appropriate authority the fact that that person is so disqualified; and
(b) obtained its written consent.

(3) Where the appropriate authority refuses to give its consent under this section, it shall inform the applicant by a written notice which states—

(a) the reason for the refusal;
(b) the applicant's right to appeal under section 65A against the refusal to the Tribunal established under section 9 of the Protection of Children Act 1999; and
(c) the time within which he may do so.

(4) Any person who contravenes subsection (1) or (2) shall be guilty of an offence and liable on summary conviction to imprisonment for a term not exceeding **six months** or to a fine not exceeding **level 5** on the standard scale or to both.
(5) Where a person contravenes subsection (2) he shall not be guilty of an offence if he proves that he did not know, and had no reasonable grounds for believing, that the person whom he was employing was disqualified under section 68.
(6) In this section and section 65A "appropriate authority" means—

(a) in relation to England, the National Care Standards Commission; and
(b) in relation to Wales, the National Assembly for Wales.
[Children Act 1989, s 65, as amended by the Care Standards Act 2000, Sch 4.]

6–2194A　65A. Appeal against refusal of authority to give consent under section 65.　(1) An appeal against a decision of an appropriate authority under section 65 shall lie to the Tribunal established under section 9 of the Protection of Children Act 1999.

(2) On an appeal the Tribunal may confirm the authority's decision or direct it to give the consent in questions.

[Children Act 1989, s 65A as inserted by the Care Standards Act 2000, s 116, Sch 4, para 14(1), (14).]

Part IX[1]
Private Arrangements For Fostering Children

6–2195   66. Privately fostered children.   (1) In this Part—

(a) "a privately fostered child" means a child who is under the age of sixteen and who is cared for, and provided with accommodation in their own home by, someone other than—

  (i) a parent of his;
  (ii) a person who is not a parent of his but who has parental responsibility for him; or
  (iii) a relative of his; and

(b) "to foster a child privately" means to look after the child in circumstances in which he is a privately fostered child as defined by this section.

(2) A child is not a privately fostered child if the person caring for and accommodating him—

(a) has done so for a period of less than 28 days; and
(b) does not intend to do so for any longer period.

(3) Subsection (1) is subject to—

(a) the provisions of section 63; and
(b) the exceptions made by paragraphs 1 to 5 of Schedule 8.

(4) In the case of a child who is disabled, subsection (1)(a) shall have effect as if for "sixteen" there were substituted "eighteen".

(4A) The Secretary of State may by regulations make provision as to the circumstances in which a person who provides accommodation to a child is, or is not, to be treated as providing him with accommodation in the person's own home.

(5) Schedule 8 shall have effect for the purposes of supplementing the provision made by this Part.

[Children Act 1989, s 66, as amended by the Care Standards Act 2000, Sch 4.]

---

1. Part IX contains ss 66–70.

6–2196   67. Welfare of privately fostered children.   (1) It shall be the duty of every local authority to satisfy themselves that the welfare of children who are privately fostered within their area is being satisfactorily safeguarded and promoted and to secure that such advice is given to those caring for them as appears to the authority to be needed.

(2) The Secretary of State may make regulations[1]—

(a) requiring every child who is privately fostered within a local authority's area to be visited by an officer of the authority—

  (i) in prescribed circumstances; and
  (ii) on specified occasions or within specified periods; and

(b) imposing requirements which are to be met by any local authority, or officer of a local authority, in carrying out functions under this section.

(3) Where any person who is authorised by a local authority to visit privately fostered children has reasonable cause to believe that—

(a) any privately fostered child is being accommodated in premises within the authority's area; or
(b) it is proposed to accommodate any such child in any such premises,

he may at any reasonable time inspect those premises and any children there.

(4) Any person exercising the power under subsection (3) shall, if so required, produce some duly authenticated document showing his authority to do so.

(5) Where a local authority are not satisfied that the welfare of any child who is privately fostered within their area is being satisfactorily safeguarded or promoted they shall—

(a) unless they consider that it would not be in the best interests of the child, take such steps as are reasonably practicable to secure that the care and accommodation of the child is undertaken by—

  (i) a parent of his;
  (ii) any person who is not a parent of his but who has parental responsibility for him; or
  (iii) a relative of his; and

(b) consider the extent to which (if at all) they should exercise any of their functions under this Act with respect to the child.*

[Children Act 1989, s 67.]

*Section amended by the Children Act 2004, s 67 from a date to be appointed.
1. The Children (Private Arrangements for Fostering) Regulations 1991, SI 1991/2050 amended by SI 1998/646 revoked in relation to England by SI 2005/1533 and the Children (Private Arrangements for Fostering) Regulations 2005, SI 2005/1533 have been made.

6–2197 68. Persons disqualified from being private foster parents. (1) Unless he has disclosed the fact to the appropriate local authority and obtained their written consent, a person shall not foster a child privately if he is disqualified from doing so by regulations made by the Secretary of State for the purposes of this section.

(2) The regulations may, in particular, provide for a person to be so disqualified where—

(a) an order of a kind specified in the regulations has been made at any time with respect to him;

(b) an order of a kind so specified has been made at any time with respect to any child who has been in his care;

(c) a requirement of a kind so specified has been imposed at any time with respect to any such child, under or by virtue of any enactment;

(d) he has been convicted of any offence of a kind so a probation order has been made in respect of him or he has been discharged absolutely or conditionally for any such offence;

(e) a prohibition has been imposed on him at any time under section 69 or under any other specified enactment;

(f) his rights and powers with respect to a child have at any time been vested in a specified authority under a specified enactment.

(3) Unless he has disclosed the fact to the appropriate local authority and obtained their written consent, a person shall not foster a child privately if—

(a) he lives in the same household as a person who is himself prevented from fostering a child by subsection (1); or

(b) he lives in a household at which any such person is employed.

(4) Where an authority refuse to give their consent under this section, they shall inform the applicant by a written notice which states—

(a) the reason for the refusal;

(b) the applicant's right under paragraph 8 of Schedule 8 to appeal against the refusal; and

(c) the time within which he may do so.

(5) In this section—

"the appropriate authority" means the local authority within whose area it is proposed to foster the child in question; and

"enactment" means any enactment having effect, at any time, in any part of the United Kingdom.
[Children Act 1989, s 68, as amended by the Criminal Justice and Court Services Act 2000, Sch 7.]

---

1. See the Disqualification for Caring for Children (England) Regulations 2002, SI 2002/635 and the Disqualification for Caring for Children (Wales) Regulations 2004, SI 2004/2695.

6–2198 69. Power to prohibit private fostering. (1) This section applies where a person—

(a) proposes to foster a child privately; or

(b) is fostering a child privately.

(2) Where the local authority for the area within which the child is proposed to be, or is being, fostered are of the opinion that—

(a) he is not a suitable person to foster a child;

(b) the premises in which the child will be, or is being, accommodated are not suitable; or

(c) it would be prejudicial to the welfare of the child for him to be, or continue to be, accommodated by that person in those premises,

the authority may impose a prohibition on him under subsection (3).

(3) A prohibition imposed on any person under this subsection may prohibit him from fostering privately—

(a) any child in any premises within the area of the local authority; or

(b) any child in premises specified in the prohibition;

(c) a child identified in the prohibition, in premises specified in the prohibition.

(4) A local authority who have imposed a prohibition on any person under subsection (3) may, if they think fit, cancel the prohibition—

(a) of their own motion; or

(b) on an application made by that person,

if they are satisfied that the prohibition is no longer justified.

(5) Where a local authority impose a requirement of any person under paragraph 6 of Schedule 8, they may also impose a prohibition on him under subsection (3).

(6) Any prohibition imposed by virtue of subsection (5) shall not have effect unless—

(a) the time specified for compliance with the requirement has expired; and
(b) the requirement has not been complied with.

(7) A prohibition imposed under this section shall be imposed by notice in writing addressed to the person on whom it is imposed and informing him of—

(a) the reason for imposing the prohibition;
(b) his right under paragraph 8 of Schedule 8 to appeal against the prohibition; and
(c) the time within which he may do so.
[Children Act 1989, s 69.]

6–2199 70. Offences. (1) A person shall be guilty of an offence if—

(a) being required, under any provision made by or under this Part, to give any notice or information—

(i) he fails without reasonable excuse to give the notice within the time specified in that provision; or
(ii) he fails without reasonable excuse to give the information within a reasonable time; or
(iii) he makes, or causes or procures another person to make, any statement in the notice or information which he knows to be false or misleading in a material particular;

(b) he refuses to allow a privately fostered child to be visited by a duly authorised officer of a local authority;
(c) he intentionally obstructs another in the exercise of the power conferred by section 67(3);
(d) he contravenes section 68;
(e) he fails without reasonable excuse to comply with any requirement imposed by a local authority under this Part;
(f) he accommodates a privately fostered child in any premises in contravention of a prohibition imposed by a local authority under this Part;
(g) he knowingly causes to be published, or publishes, an advertisement which he knows contravenes paragraph 10 of Schedule 8.

(2) Where a person contravenes section 68(3), he shall not be guilty of an offence under this section if he proves that he did not know, and had no reasonable ground for believing, that any person to whom section 68(1) applied was living or employed in the premises in question.

(3) A person guilty of an offence under subsection (1)(a) shall be liable on summary conviction to a fine not exceeding **level 5** on the standard scale.

(4) A person guilty of an offence under subsection (1)(b), (c) or (g) shall be liable on summary conviction to a fine not exceeding **level 3** on the standard scale.

(5) A person guilty of an offence under subsection (1)(d) or (f) shall be liable on summary conviction to imprisonment for a term not exceeding **six months**, or to a fine not exceeding **level 5** on the standard scale, or to both.

(6) A person guilty of an offence under subsection (1)(e) shall be liable on summary conviction to a fine not exceeding **level 4** on the standard scale.

(7) If any person who is required, under any provision of this Part, to give a notice fails to give the notice within the time specified in that provision, proceedings for the offence may be brought at any time within six months from the date when evidence of the offence came to the knowledge of the local authority.

(8) Subsection (7) is not affected by anything in section 127(1) of the Magistrates' Courts Act 1980 (time limit for proceedings).
[Children Act 1989, s 70.]

PART X
CHILD MINDING AND DAY CARE FOR YOUNG CHILDREN

6–2200 71–79. (*Repealed*).

PART XA[1]
CHILD MINDING AND DAY CARE FOR CHILDREN IN ENGLAND AND WALES

Introductory

6–2208A 79A. Child minders and day care providers. (1) This section and section 79B apply for the purposes of this Part.

(2) "Act as a child minder" means (subject to the following subsections) look after one or more children under the age of eight on domestic premises for reward; and "child minding" shall be interpreted accordingly.

(3) A person who—

(a) is the parent, or a relative, of a child;
(b) has parental responsibility for a child;
(c) is a local authority foster parent in relation to a child;
(d) is a foster parent with whom a child has been placed by a voluntary organisation; or

(*e*) fosters a child privately,

does not act as a child minder when looking after that child.

(4) Where a person—

(*a*) looks after a child for the parents ("P1"), or

(*b*) in addition to that work, looks after another child for different parents ("P2"),

and the work consists (in a case within paragraph (*a*)) of looking after the child wholly or mainly in P1's home or (in a case within paragraph (*b*)) of looking after the children wholly or mainly in P1's home or P2's home or both, the work is not to be treated as child minding.

(5) In subsection (4), "parent", in relation to a child, includes—

(*a*) a person who is not a parent of the child but who has parental responsibility for the child;

(*b*) a person who is a relative of the child.

(6) "Day care" means care provided at any time for children under the age of eight on premises other than domestic premises.

(7) This Part does not apply in relation to a person who acts as a child minder, or provides day care on any premises, unless the period, or the total of the periods, in any day which he spends looking after children or (as the case may be) during which the children are looked after on the premises exceeds two hours.

(8) In determining whether a person is required to register under this Part for child minding, any day on which he does not act as a child minder at any time between 2am and 6pm is to be disregarded.
[Children Act 1989, s 79A as inserted by the Care Standards Act 2000, s 79(1).]

---

1. Part XA comprises ss 79A to 79X.

6–2208B   79B. Other definitions, etc. (1) The registration authority in relation to England is Her Majesty's Chief Inspector of Schools in England (referred to in this Part as the Chief Inspector) and references to the Chief Inspector's area are references to England.

(2) The registration authority in relation to Wales is the National Assembly for Wales (referred to in this Act as "the Assembly").

(3) A person is qualified for registration for child minding if—

(*a*) he, and every other person looking after children on any premises on which he is or is likely to be child minding, is suitable to look after children under the age of eight;

(*b*) every person living or employed on the premises in question is suitable to be in regular contact with children under the age of eight;

(*c*) the premises in question are suitable to be used for looking after children under the age of eight, having regard to their condition and the condition and appropriateness of any equipment on the premises and to any other factor connected with the situation, construction or size of the premises; and

(*d*) he is complying with regulations under section 79C and with any conditions imposed by the registration authority.

(4) A person is qualified for registration for providing day care on particular premises if—

(*a*) every person looking after children on the premises is suitable to look after children under the age of eight;

(*b*) every person living or working on the premises is suitable to be in regular contact with children under the age of eight;

(*c*) the premises are suitable to be used for looking after children under the age of eight, having regard to their condition and the condition and appropriateness of any equipment on the premises and to any other factor connected with the situation, construction or size of the premises; and

(*d*) he is complying with regulations under section 79C and with any conditions imposed by the registration authority.

(5) For the purposes of subsection (4)(*b*) a person is not treated as working on the premises in question if—

(*a*) none of his work is done in the part of the premises in which children are looked after; or

(*b*) he does not work on the premises at times when children are looked after there.

(5A) Where, for the purposes of determining a person's qualification for registration under this Part—

(*a*) the registration authority requests any person ("A") to consent to the disclosure to the authority by another person ("B") of any information relating to A which is held by B and is of a prescribed description, and

(*b*) A does not give his consent (or withdraws it after having given it),

the registration authority may, if regulations[1] so provide and it thinks it appropriate to do so, regard A as not suitable to look after children under the age of eight, or not suitable to be in regular contact with such children.

(6) "Domestic premises" means any premises which are wholly or mainly used as a private dwelling and "premises" includes any area and any vehicle.

(7) "Regulations" means—

(*a*) in relation to England, regulations made by the Secretary of State;

(*b*) in relation to Wales, regulations made by the Assembly.

(8) "Tribunal" means the Tribunal established by section 9 of the Protection of Children Act 1999.

(9) Schedule 9A (which supplements the provisions of this Part) shall have effect.★

[Children Act 1989, s 79B as inserted by the Care Standards Act 2000, s 79(1) and amended by the Education Act 2002, Sch 13.]

★Section amended by the Children Act 2004, s 67 from a date to be appointed.

1. See the Day Care and Child Minding (Disqualification) (England) Regulations 2005, SI 2005/2296.

Regulations

6–2208C   79C. Regulations etc governing child minders and day care providers.   (1) The Secretary of State may, after consulting the Chief Inspector and any other person he considers appropriate, make regulations[1] governing the activities of registered persons who act as child minders, or provide day care, on premises in England.

(2) The Assembly may make regulations[2] governing the activities of registered persons who act as child minders, or provide day care, on premises in Wales.

(3) The regulations under this section may deal with the following matters (among others)—

(*a*) the welfare and development of the children concerned;

(*b*) suitability to look after, or be in regular contact with, children under the age of eight;

(*c*) qualifications and training;

(*d*) the maximum number of children who may be looked after and the number of persons required to assist in looking after them;

(*e*) the maintenance, safety and suitability of premises and equipment;

(*f*) the keeping of records;

(*g*) the provision of information.

(4) In relation to activities on premises in England, the power to make regulations under this section may be exercised so as to confer powers or impose duties on the Chief Inspector in the exercise of his functions under this Part.

(5) In particular they may be exercised so as to require or authorise the Chief Inspector, in exercising those functions, to have regard to or meet factors, standards and other matters prescribed by or referred to in the regulations.

(6) If the regulations require any person (other than the registration authority) to have regard to or meet factors, standards and other matters prescribed by or referred to in the regulations, they may also provide for any allegation that the person has failed to do so to be taken into account—

(*a*) by the registration authority in the exercise of its functions under this Part, or

(*b*) in any proceedings under this Part.

(7) Regulations may provide—

(*a*) that a registered person who without reasonable excuse contravenes, or otherwise fails to comply with, any requirement of the regulations shall be guilty of an offence; and

(*b*) that a person guilty of the offence shall be liable on summary conviction to a fine not exceeding level 5 on the standard scale.

[Children Act 1989, s 79C as inserted by the Care Standards Act 2000, s 79(1).]

---

1. The Child Minding and Day Care (Wales) Regulations 2002, SI 2002/812 amended by SI 2002/2171 and 2622, SI 2003/2708, SI 2004/2414 and SI 2005/2929 and the Day Care and Child Minding (National Standards) (England) Regulations 2003, SI 2003/1996 amended by SI 2005/2303 and the Day Care and Child Minding (Disqualification) (England) Regulations 2005, SI 2005/2296 have been made.

2. The Disqualification from Caring for Children (Wales) Regulations 2004, SI 2004/2695 have been made.

Registration

6–2208D   79D. Requirement to register.   (1) No person shall—

(*a*) act as a child minder in England unless he is registered under this Part for child minding by the Chief Inspector; or

(*b*) act as a child minder in Wales unless he is registered under this Part for child minding by the Assembly.

(2) Where it appears to the registration authority that a person has contravened subsection (1), the authority may serve a notice ("an enforcement notice") on him.

(3) An enforcement notice shall have effect for a period of one year beginning with the date on which it is served.

(4) If a person in respect of whom an enforcement notice has effect contravenes subsection (1) without reasonable excuse (whether the contravention occurs in England or Wales), he shall be guilty of an offence.

(5) No person shall provide day care on any premises unless he is registered under this Part for providing day care on those premises by the registration authority.

(6) If any person contravenes subsection (5) without reasonable excuse, he shall be guilty of an offence.

(7) A person guilty of an offence under this section shall be liable on summary conviction to a fine not exceeding level 5 on the standard scale.

[Children Act 1989, s 79D as inserted by the Care Standards Act 2000, s 79(1).]

6–2208E   79E. Applications for registration.   (1) A person who wishes to be registered under this Part shall make an application to the registration authority.

(2) The application shall—

(a)   give prescribed[1] information about prescribed matters;

(b)   give any other information which the registration authority reasonably requires the applicant to give.*

(3) Where a person provides, or proposes to provide, day care on different premises, he shall make a separate application in respect of each of them.

(4) Where the registration authority has sent the applicant notice under section 79L(1) of its intention to refuse an application under this section, the application may not be withdrawn without the consent of the authority.

(5) A person who, in an application under this section, knowingly makes a statement which is false or misleading in a material particular shall be guilty of an offence and liable, on summary conviction, to a fine not exceeding level 5 on the standard scale.

[Children Act 1989, s 79E as inserted by the Care Standards Act 2000, s 79(1).]

---

*Paragraph (c) inserted by the Children Act 2004 s 48 from a date to be appointed.
1. See the Child Minding and Day Care (Applications for Registration (England) Regulations 2001, SI 2001/1829 amended by SI 2003/1995 and SI 2005/2448, the Registration of Social Care and Independent Health Care (Wales) Regulations 2002, SI 2002/919 amended by SI 2002/2622 and 2935, SI 2003/710 and 2527, SI 2004/219 and 1756 and 3302 and the Day Care and Child Minding (Registration Fees) (England) Regulations 2005, SI 2005/2301.

6–2208F   79F. Grant or refusal of registration.   (1) If, on an application by a person for registration for child minding—

(a)   the registration authority is of the opinion that the applicant is, and will continue to be, qualified for registration for child minding (so far as the conditions of section 79B(3) are applicable); and

(b)   the applicant pays the prescribed fee,

the authority shall grant the application; otherwise, it shall refuse it.

(2) If, on an application by any person for registration for providing day care on any premises—

(a)   the registration authority is of the opinion that the applicant is, and will continue to be, qualified for registration for providing day care on those premises (so far as the conditions of section 79B(4) are applicable); and

(b)   the applicant pays the prescribed fee,

the authority shall grant the application; otherwise, it shall refuse it.

(3) An application may, as well as being granted subject to any conditions the authority thinks necessary or expedient for the purpose of giving effect to regulations under section 79C, be granted subject to any other conditions the authority thinks fit to impose.

(4) The registration authority may as it thinks fit vary or remove any condition to which the registration is subject or impose a new condition.

(5) Any register kept by a registration authority of persons who act as child minders or provide day care shall be open to inspection by any person at all reasonable times.

(6) A registered person who without reasonable excuse contravenes, or otherwise fails to comply with, any condition imposed on his registration shall be guilty of an offence.

(7) A person guilty of an offence under subsection (6) shall be liable on summary conviction to a fine not exceeding level 5 on the standard scale.*

[Children Act 1989, s 79F as inserted by the Care Standards Act 2000, s 79(1).]

---

*Section amended by the Children Act 2004, s 48 from a date to be appointed.

6–2208G   79G. Cancellation of registration.   (1) The registration authority may cancel the registration of any person if—

(a)   in the case of a person registered for child minding, the authority is of the opinion that the person has ceased or will cease to be qualified for registration for child minding;

(b) in the case of a person registered for providing day care on any premises, the authority is of the opinion that the person has ceased or will cease to be qualified for registration for providing day care on those premises,

or if an annual fee which is due from the person has not been paid.

(2) Where a requirement to make any changes or additions to any services, equipment or premises has been imposed on a registered person under section 79F(3), his registration shall not be cancelled on the ground of any defect or insufficiency in the services, equipment or premises if—

(a) the time set for complying with the requirements has not expired; and
(b) it is shown that the defect or insufficiency is due to the changes or additions not having been made.

(3) Any cancellation under this section must be in writing.
[Children Act 1989, s 79G as inserted by the Care Standards Act 2000, s 79(1).]

---

*Section amended by the Children Act 2004, s 48 from a date to be appointed.

6–2208H 79H. Suspension of registration. (1) Regulations[1] may provide for the registration of any person for acting as a child minder or providing day care to be suspended for a prescribed period by the registration authority in prescribed circumstances.

(2) Any regulations made under this section shall include provision conferring on the person concerned a right of appeal to the Tribunal against suspension.

(3) A person registered under this Part for child minding by the Chief Inspector shall not act as a child minder in England at a time when that registration is suspended in accordance with regulations under this section.

(4) A person registered under this Part for child minding by the Assembly shall not act as a child minder in Wales at a time when that registration is so suspended.

(5) A person registered under this Part for providing day care on any premises shall not provide day care on those premises at any time when that registration is so suspended.

(6) If any person contravenes subsection (3), (4) or (5) without reasonable excuse, he shall be guilty of an offence and liable on summary conviction to a fine not exceeding level 5 on the standard scale.
[Children Act 1989, s 79H as inserted by the Care Standards Act 2000, s 79(1) and amended by the Education Act 2002, Sch 13.]

---

1. The Child Minding and Day Care (Suspension of Registration) (England) Regulations 2003, SI 2003/332 and the Suspension of Day Care Providers and Child Minders (Wales) Regulations 2004, SI 2004/3282 have been made.

6–2208J 79J. Resignation of registration. (1) A person who is registered for acting as a child minder or providing day care may by notice in writing to the registration authority resign his registration.

(2) But a person may not give a notice under subsection (1)—

(a) if the registration authority has sent him a notice under section 79L(1) of its intention to cancel the registration, unless the authority has decided not to take that step; or
(b) if the registration authority has sent him a notice under section 79L(5) of its decision to cancel the registration and the time within which an appeal may be brought has not expired or, if an appeal has been brought, it has not been determined.
[Children Act 1989, s 79J as inserted by the Care Standards Act 2000, s 79(1).]

6–2208K 79K. Protection of children in an emergency. (1) If, in the case of any person registered for acting as a child minder or providing day care—

(a) the registration authority applies to a justice of the peace for an order—

(i) cancelling the registration;
(ii) varying or removing any condition to which the registration is subject; or
(iii) imposing a new condition; and

(b) it appears to the justice that a child who is being, or may be, looked after by that person, is (as the case may be) in accordance with the provision for day care made by that person, is suffering, or is likely to suffer, significant harm,

the justice may make the order.

(2) The cancellation, variation, removal or imposition shall have effect from the time when the order is made.

(3) An application under subsection (1) may be made without notice.

(4) An order under subsection (1) shall be made in writing.

(5) Where an order is made under this section, the registration authority shall serve on the registered person, as soon as is reasonably practicable after the making of the order—

(a) a copy of the order;

(b)   a copy of any written statement of the authority's reasons for making the application for the order which supported that application; and

(c)   notice of any right of appeal conferred by section 79M.

(6)   Where an order has been so made, the registration authority shall, as soon as is reasonably practicable after the making of the order, notify the local authority in whose area the person concerned acts or acted as a child minder, or provides or provided day care, of the making of the order.
[Children Act 1989, s 79K as inserted by the Care Standards Act 2000, s 79(1).]

6–2208L   79L. Notice of intention to take steps.   (1) Not less than 14 days before—

(a)   refusing an application for registration;

(b)   cancelling a registration;

(c)   removing or varying any condition to which a registration is subject or imposing a new condition; or

(d)   refusing to grant an application for the removal or variation of any condition to which a registration is subject,

the registration authority shall send to the applicant, or (as the case may be) registered person, notice in writing of its intention to take the step in question.

(2)   Every such notice shall—

(a)   give the authority's reasons for proposing to take the step; and

(b)   inform the person concerned of his rights under this section.

(3)   Where the recipient of such a notice informs the authority in writing of his desire to object to the step being taken, the authority shall afford him an opportunity to do so.

(4)   Any objection made under subsection (3) may be made orally or in writing, by the recipient of the notice or a representative.

(5)   If the authority, after giving the person concerned an opportunity to object to the step being taken, decides nevertheless to take it, it shall send him written notice of its decision.

(6)   A step of a kind mentioned in subsection (1)(b) or (c) shall not take effect until the expiry of the time within which an appeal may be brought under section 79M or, where such an appeal is brought, before its determination.

(7)   Subsection (6) does not prevent a step from taking effect before the expiry of the time within which an appeal may be brought under section 79M if the person concerned notifies the registration authority in writing that he does not intend to appeal.
[Children Act 1989, s 79L as inserted by the Care Standards Act 2000, s 79(1).]

6–2208M   79M. Appeals.   (1) An appeal against—

(a)   the taking of any step mentioned in section 79L(1);

(b)   an order under section 79K, or

(c)   a determination made by the registration authority under this Part (other than one falling within paragraph (a) or (b)) which is of a prescribed[1] description,

shall lie to the Tribunal.

(2)   On an appeal, the Tribunal may—

(a)   confirm the taking of the step or the making of the order or determination or direct that it shall not have, or shall cease to have, effect; and

(b)   impose, vary or cancel any condition.
[Children Act 1989, s 79M as inserted by the Care Standards Act 2000, s 79(1) and amended by the Education Act 2002, ss 148 and 215(2).]

---

1. The Disqualification from Caring for Children (Wales) Regulations 2004, SI 2004/2695 and the Day Care and Child Minding (Disqualification) (England) Regulations 2005, SI 2005/2296 have been made.

Inspection: England

6–2208N   79N. General functions of the Chief Inspector.   (1) The Chief Inspector has the general duty of keeping the Secretary of State informed about the quality and standards of child minding and day care provided by registered persons in England.

(2)   When asked to do so by the Secretary of State, the Chief Inspector shall give advice or information to the Secretary of State about such matters relating to the provision of child minding or day care by registered persons in England as may be specified in the Secretary of State's request.

(3)   The Chief Inspector may at any time give advice to the Secretary of State, either generally or in relation to provision by particular persons or on particular premises, on any matter connected with the provision of child minding or day care by registered persons in England.

(4)   The Chief Inspector may secure the provision of training for persons who provide or assist in providing child minding or day care, or intend to do so.

(5)   Regulations[1] may confer further functions on the Chief Inspector relating to child minding and day care provided in England.

(6)   The annual reports of the Chief Inspector required by subsection (7)(a) of section 2 of the

School Inspections Act 1996 to be made to the Secretary of State shall include an account of the exercise of the Chief Inspector's functions under this Part, and the power conferred by subsection (7)(b) of that section to make other reports to the Secretary of State includes a power to make reports with respect to matters which fall within the scope of his functions by virtue of this Part.
[Children Act 1989, s 79N as inserted by the Care Standards Act 2000, s 79(1).]

1. The Child Minding and Day Care (Disclosure Functions) (England) Regulations 2004, SI 2004/3136 prescribe the circumstances for the disclosure by the Chief Inspector of certain information gathered while regulating childcare to parents, the police and various organisations concerned with the provision of care for, or with protecting, children.

6–2208P   79P. Early years child care inspectorate. *Repealed.*

6–2208Q   79Q. Inspection of provision of child minding and day care in England. (1) The Chief Inspector may at any time require any registered person to provide him with any information connected with the person's activities as a child minder, or provider of day care, which the Chief Inspector considers it necessary to have for the purposes of his functions under this Part.

(2) The Chief Inspector shall at prescribed intervals inspect any child minding provided in England by a registered person[1].

(3) The Chief Inspector shall at prescribed intervals inspect any day care provided by a registered person on any premises in England[1].

(4) *Repealed.*

(5) In prescribing the intervals mentioned in subsection (2) or (3) the Secretary of State may make provision as to the period within which the first inspection of child minding or day care provided by any person or at any premises is to take place.

(5A) Regulations[1] may make provision requiring a registered person, except in prescribed cases, to notify prescribed persons of the fact that any child minding or day care provided by the registered person is to be inspected under this section.

(6) When conducting an inspection under this section the Chief Inspector shall report in writing on—

(a) the quality and standards of the child minding or day care provided,

(b) how far the child minding or day care meets the needs of the range of children for whom it is provided,

(c) the contribution made by the child minding or day care to the well-being of the children for whom it is provided, and

(d) in the case of day care, the quality of leadership and management in connection with its provision.

(6A) In subsection (6)(c), the reference to well-being is a reference to well-being having regard to the matters mentioned in section 10(2) of the Children Act 2004.

(7) *Repealed.*

[Children Act 1989, s 79Q as inserted by the Care Standards Act 2000, s 79(1) and amended by the Education Act 2002, Sch 13 and the Education Act 2005, Sch 7.]

1. See the Day Care and Child Minding (Inspection) (England) Regulations 2005, SI 2005/2300.

6–2208R   79R. Reports of inspections. (1) A person who has conducted an inspection under section 79Q shall report in writing on the matters inspected to the Chief Inspector within the prescribed[1] period.

(2) The period mentioned in subsection (1) may, if the Chief Inspector considers it necessary, be extended by up to three months.

(3) Once the report of an inspection has been made to the Chief Inspector under subsection (1) he—

(a) may send a copy of it to the Secretary of State, and shall do so without delay if the Secretary of State requests a copy;

(b) shall send a copy of it, or of such parts of it as he considers appropriate, to any prescribed[1] authorities or persons; and

(c) may arrange for the report (or parts of it) to be further published in any manner he considers appropriate.

(4) Subsections (2) to (4) of section 42A of the School Inspections Act 1996 shall apply in relation to the publication of any report under subsection (3) as they apply in relation to the publication of a report under any of the provisions mentioned in subsection (2) of section 42A.

[Children Act 1989, s 79R as inserted by the Care Standards Act 2000, s 79(1).]

1. See the Day Care and Child Minding (Inspection) (England) Regulations 2005, SI 2005/2300.

Inspection: Wales

6–2208S   79S. General functions of the Assembly. (1) The Assembly may secure the provision of training for persons who provide or assist in providing child minding or day care, or intend to do so.

(2) In relation to child minding and day care provided in Wales, the Assembly shall have any additional function specified in regulations made by the Assembly; but the regulations may only specify a function corresponding to a function which, by virtue of section 79N(5), is exercisable by the Chief Inspector in relation to child minding and day care provided in England.
[Children Act 1989, s 79S as inserted by the Care Standards Act 2000, s 79(1).]

6–2208T 79T. Inspection: Wales.   (1) The Assembly may at any time require any registered person to provide it with any information connected with the person's activities as a child minder or provision of day care which the Assembly considers it necessary to have for the purposes of its functions under this Part.

(2) The Assembly may by regulations make provision—

(a) for the inspection of the quality and standards of child minding provided in Wales by registered persons and of day care provided by registered persons on premises in Wales;

(b) for the publication of reports of the inspections in such manner as the Assembly considers appropriate.

(3) The regulations may provide for the inspections to be organised by—

(a) the Assembly; or

(b) Her Majesty's Chief Inspector of Education and Training in Wales, or any other person, under arrangements made with the Assembly.

(4) The regulations may provide for subsections (2) to (4) of section 42A of the School Inspections Act 1996 to apply with modifications in relation to the publication of reports under the regulations.
[Children Act 1989, s 79T as inserted by the Care Standards Act 2000, s 79(1).]

Supplementary

6–2208U 79U. Rights of entry etc.   (1) Any person authorised for the purposes of this subsection by the registration authority may at any reasonable time enter any premises in England or Wales on which child minding or day care is at any time provided.

(2) Where a person who is authorised for the purposes of this subsection by the registration authority has reasonable cause to believe that a child is being looked after on any premises in contravention of this Part, he may enter those premises at any reasonable time.

(2A) Authorisation under subsection (1) or (2)—

(a) may be given for a particular occasion or period;

(b) may be given subject to conditions.*

(3) A person entering premises under this section may (subject to any conditions imposed under subsection (2A)(b)—

(a) inspect the premises;

(b) inspect, and take copies of—

(i) any records kept by the person providing the child minding orday care; and

(ii) any other documents containing information relating to its provision;

(c) seize and remove any document or other material or thing found there which he has reasonable grounds to believe may be evidence of a failure to comply with any condition or requirement imposed by or under this Part;

(d) require any person to afford him such facilities and assistance with respect to matters within the person's control as are necessary to enable him to exercise his powers under this section;

(e) take measurements and photographs or make recordings;

(f) inspect any children being looked after there, and the arrangements made for their welfare;

(g) interview in private the person providing the child minding or day care; and

(h) interview in private any person looking after children, or living or working, there who consents to be interviewed.

(4) Section 42 of the School Inspections Act 1996 (inspection of computer records for purposes of Part I of that Act) shall apply for the purposes of subsection (3) as it applies for the purposes of Part I of that Act.

(5) (*Repealed*).

(6) A person exercising any power conferred by this section shall, if so required, produce some duly authenticated document showing his authority to do so.

(7) It shall be an offence wilfully to obstruct a person exercising any such power.

(8) Any person guilty of an offence under subsection (7) shall be liable on summary conviction to a fine not exceeding level 4 on the standard scale.

(9) In this section—

"documents" and "records" each include information recorded in any form.
[Children Act 1989, s 79U as inserted by the Care Standards Act 2000, s 79(1) and amended by the Education Act 2002, s 216(4).]

6–2208V   79V. Function of local authorities.   Each local authority shall, in accordance with regulations[1], secure the provision—

(*a*) of information and advice about child minding and day care; and
(*b*) of training for persons who provide or assist in providing child minding or day care.

[Children Act 1989, s 79V as inserted by the Care Standards Act 2000, s 79(1).]

---

1. The Day Care and Child Minding (Functions of Local Authorities: Information, Advice and Training) (England) Regulations 2001, SI 2001/2746 amended by SI 2005/2302 have been made.

Checks on suitability of persons working with children over the age of seven

6–2208W   79W. Requirement for certificate of suitability.   (1) This section applies to any person not required to register under this Part who looks after, or provides care for, children and meets the following conditions.

References in this section to children are to those under the age of 15 or (in the case of disabled children) 17.

(2) The first condition is that the period, or the total of the periods, in any week which he spends looking after children or (as the case may be) during which the children are looked after exceeds five hours.

(3) The second condition is that he would be required to register under this Part (or, as the case may be, this Part if it were subject to prescribed modifications) if the children were under the age of eight.

(4) Regulations may require a person to whom this section applies to hold a certificate issued by the registration authority as to his suitability, and the suitability of each prescribed person, to look after children.

(5) The regulations may make provision about—

(*a*) applications for certificates;
(*b*) the matters to be taken into account by the registration authority in determining whether to issue certificates;
(*c*) the information to be contained in certificates;
(*d*) the period of their validity.

(6) The regulations may provide that a person to whom this section applies shall be guilty of an offence—

(*a*) if he does not hold a certificate as required by the regulations; or
(*b*) if, being a person who holds such a certificate, he fails to produce it when reasonably required to do so by a prescribed person.

(7) The regulations may provide that a person who, for the purpose of obtaining such a certificate, knowingly makes a statement which is false or misleading in a material particular shall be guilty of an offence.

(8) The regulations may provide that a person guilty of an offence under the regulations shall be liable on summary conviction to a fine not exceeding level 5 on the standard scale.

[Children Act 1989, s 79W as inserted by the Care Standards Act 2000, s 79(1).]

Time limit for proceedings

6–2208X   79X. Time limit for proceedings.   Proceedings for an offence under this Part or regulations made under it may be brought within a period of six months from the date on which evidence sufficient in the opinion of the prosecutor to warrant the proceedings came to his knowledge; but no such proceedings shall be brought by virtue of this section more than three years after the commission of the offence.

[Children Act 1989, s 79X as inserted by the Care Standards Act 2000, s 79(1).]

PART XI[1]
SECRETARY OF STATE'S SUPERVISORY FUNCTIONS AND RESPONSIBILITIES

6–2209   80. Inspection of children's homes etc by persons authorised by Secretary of State.

(1) The Secretary of State may cause to be inspected from time to time any—

(*a*) private children's home;
(*b*) premises in which a child who is being looked after by a local authority is living;
(*c*) premises in which a child who is being accommodated by or on behalf of a local education authority or voluntary organisation is living;
(*d*) premises in which a child who is being accommodated by or on behalf of a Health Authority, Special Health Authority, Primary Care Trust or National Health Service trust*** is living;
(*e*) *repealed*;
(*f*) *repealed*;
(*g*) premises in which a privately fostered child, or child who is treated as a foster child by virtue of paragraph 9 of Schedule 8, is living or in which it is proposed that he will live;
(*h*) premises on which any person is acting as a child minder;
(*i*) premises with respect to which a person is registered under section 71(1)(*b*);

- (j)　care home or independent hospital used to accommodate children;★
- (k)　premises which are provided by a local authority and in which any service is provided by that authority under Part III;
- (l)　school or college★ providing accommodation for any child.

(2) An inspection under this section shall be conducted by a person authorised to do so by the Secretary of State.

(3) An officer of a local authority shall not be so authorised except with the consent of that authority.

(4) The Secretary of State may require any person of a kind mentioned in subsection (5) to furnish him with such information, or allow him to inspect such records (in whatever form they are held), relating to—

- (a)　any premises to which subsection (1) or, in relation to Scotland, subsection (1)(h) or (i) applies;
- (b)　any child who is living in any such premises;
- (c)　the discharge by the Secretary of State of any of his functions under this Act;
- (d)　the discharge by any local authority of any of their functions under this Act,

as the Secretary of State may at any time direct.

(5) The persons are any—

- (a)　local authority;
- (b)　voluntary organisation;
- (c)　person carrying on a private★ children's home;
- (d)　proprietor of an independent school or governing body of any other school★;
- (da)　governing body of an institution designated under section 28 of the Further and Higher Education Act 1992;★
- (db)　further education corporation;★
- (e)　person fostering any privately fostered child or providing accommodation for a child on behalf of a local authority, local education authority, Health Authority, Special Health Authority, Primary Care Trust, National Health Service trust, NHS foundation trust or voluntary organisation;
- (f)　local education authority providing accommodation for any child;
- (g)　person employed in a teaching or administrative capacity at any educational establishment (whether or not maintained by a local education authority) at which a child is accommodated on behalf of a local authority or local education authority;
- (h)　person who is the occupier of any premises in which any person acts as a child minder (within the meaning of Part X) or provides day care for young children (within the meaning of that Part);
- (hh)　person who is the occupier of any premises—

  - (i)　in which any person required to be registered for child minding under Part XA acts as a child minder (within the meaning of that Part); or
  - (ii)　with respect to which a person is required to be registered under that Part for providing day care;

- (i)　person carrying on any home of a kind mentioned in subsection (1)(j);
- (j)　person carrying on a fostering agency.

(6) Any person inspecting any home or other premises under this section may—

- (a)　inspect the children there; and
- (b)　make such examination into the state and management of the home or premises and the treatment of the children there as he thinks fit.

(7) Any person authorised by the Secretary of State to exercise the power to inspect records conferred by subsection (4)—

- (a)　shall be entitled at any reasonable time to have access to, and inspect and check the operation of, any computer and any associated apparatus or material which is or has been in use in connection with the records in question; and
- (b)　may require—

  - (i)　the person by whom or on whose behalf the computer is or has been so used; or
  - (ii)　any person having charge of, or otherwise concerned with the operation of, the computer, apparatus or material,

  to afford him such reasonable assistance as he may require.

(8) A person authorised to inspect any premises under this section shall have a right to enter the premises for that purpose, and for any purpose specified in subsection (4), at any reasonable time.

(9) Any person exercising that power shall, if so required, produce some duly authenticated document showing his authority to do so.

(10) Any person who intentionally obstructs another in the exercise of that power shall be guilty of an offence and liable on summary conviction to a fine not exceeding **level 3** on the standard scale.

(11) The Secretary of State may by order provide for subsections (1), (4) and (6) not to apply in relation to such homes, or other premises, as may be specified in the order.

(12) Without prejudice to section 104, any such order may make different provision with respect to each of those subsections.★★

(13) In this section—

"college" means an institution within the further education sector as defined in section 91 of the Further and Higher Education Act 1992;

"fostering agency" has the same meaning as in the Care Standards Act 2000;

"further education corporation" has the same meaning as in the Further and Higher Education Act 1992.★

[Children Act 1989, s 80 as amended by the National Health Service and Community Care Act 1990, Sch 9, the Health Authorities Act 1995, Sch 1, the Care Standards Act 2000, Sch 4, the Adoption and Children Act 2002, Sch 3 and the Health and Social Care (Community Health and Standards) Act 2003, Sch 4.]

★Printed as amended by the Care Standards Act 2000, Sch 4. In force in relation to England, with regards Wales, in force from a date to be appointed: see the Care Standards Act 2000, s 122.

★★Repealed in relation to Scotland by the Regulation of Care (Scotland) Act 2000, Sch 4, from a date to be appointed.

1. Part XI contains ss 80–84.

6–2220 81. Inquiries. *Repealed.*

6–2221 82. Financial support by Secretary of State. (1) The Secretary of State may (with the consent of the Treasury) defray or contribute towards—

(a) any fees or expenses incurred by any person undergoing approved child care training;

(b) any fees charged, or expenses incurred, by any person providing approved child care training or preparing material for use in connection with such training; or

(c) the cost of maintaining any person undergoing such training.

(2) The Secretary of State may make grants to local authorities in respect of expenditure incurred by them in providing secure accommodation in community homes other than assisted community homes.

(3) Where—

(a) a grant has been made under subsection (2) with respect to any secure accommodation; but

(b) the grant is not used for the purpose for which it was made or the accommodation is not used as, or ceases to be used as, secure accommodation,

the Secretary of State may (with the consent of the Treasury) require the authority concerned to repay the grant, in whole or in part.

(4) The Secretary of State may make grants to voluntary organisations towards—

(a) expenditure incurred by them in connection with the establishment, maintenance or improvement of voluntary homes which, at the time when the expenditure was incurred—

(i) were assisted community homes; or
(ii) were designated as such; or

(b) expenses incurred in respect of the borrowing or money to defray any such expenditure.

(5) The Secretary of State may arrange for the provision, equipment and maintenance of homes for the accommodation of children who are in need of particular facilities and services which—

(a) are or will be provided in those homes; and

(b) in the opinion of the Secretary of State, are unlikely to be readily available in community homes.

(6) In this Part—

"child care training" means training undergone by any person with a view to, or in the course of—

(a) his employment for the purposes of any of the functions mentioned in section 83(9) or in connection with the adoption of children or with the accommodation of children in a care home or independent hospital; or

(b) his employment by a voluntary organisation for similar purposes;

"approved child care training" means child care training which is approved by the Secretary of State; and

"secure accommodation" means accommodation provided for the purpose of restricting the liberty of children.

(7) Any grant made under this section shall be of such amount, and shall be subject to such conditions, as the Secretary of State may (with the consent of the Treasury) determine.

[Children Act 1989, s 82, as amended by the Care Standards Act 2000, Sch 4.]

6–2222   83. Research and returns of information.   (1) The Secretary of State may conduct, or assist other persons in conducting, research into any matter connected with—

(*a*)   his functions, or the functions of local authorities, under the enactments mentioned in subsection (9);
(*b*)   the adoption of children; or
(*c*)   the accommodation of children in a care home or independent hospital.

(2) Any local authority may conduct, or assist other persons in conducting, research into any matter connected with—

(*a*)   their functions under the enactments mentioned in subsection (9);
(*b*)   the adoption of children; or
(*c*)   the accommodation of children in a care home or independent hospital.

(3) Every local authority shall, at such times and in such form as the Secretary of State may direct, transmit to him such particulars as he may require with respect to—

(*a*)   the performance by the local authority of all or any of their functions—

(i)   under the enactments mentioned in subsection (9); or
(ii)   in connection with the accommodation of children in a care home or independent hopsital; and

(*b*)   the children in relation to whom the authority have exercised those functions.

(4) Every voluntary organisation shall, at such times and in such form as the Secretary of State may direct, transmit to him such particulars as he may require with respect to children accommodated by them or on their behalf.

(4A) Particulars required to be transmitted under subsection (3) or (4) may include particulars relating to and identifying individual children.

(5) The Secretary of State may direct the justices' chief executive for each magistrates' court to which the direction is expressed to relate to transmit—

(*a*)   to such person as may be specified in the direction; and
(*b*)   at such times and in such form as he may direct,

such particulars as he may require with respect to proceedings of the court which relate to children.

(6) The Secretary of State shall in each year lay before Parliament a consolidated and classified abstract of the information transmitted to him under subsections (3) to (5).

(7) The Secretary of State may institute research designed to provide information on which requests for information under this section may be based.

(8) The Secretary of State shall keep under review the adequacy of the provision of child care training and for the purpose shall receive and consider any information from or representations made by—

(*a*)   the Central Council for Education and Training in Social Work;
(*b*)   such representatives of local authorities as appear to him to be appropriate; or
(*c*)   such other persons or organisations as appear to him to be appropriate,

concerning the provision of such training.

(9) The enactments are—

(*a*)   this Act;
(*b*)   the Children and Young Persons Acts 1933 to 1969;
(*c*)   section 116 of the Mental Health Act 1983 (so far as it relates to children looked after by local authorities);
(*d*)   section 10 of the Mental Health (Scotland) Act 1984 (so far as it relates to children for whom local authorities have responsibility).★

[Children Act 1989, s 83, as amended by the Access to Justice Act 1999, Sch 13, the Care Standards Act 2000, Sch 4 and the Children Act 2004, s 54.]

6–2223   84. Local authority failure to comply with statutory duty: default power of Secretary of State.   (1) If the Secretary of State is satisfied that any local authority has failed, without reasonable excuse, to comply with any of the duties imposed on them by or under this Act he may make an order declaring that authority to be in default with respect to that duty.

(2) An order under subsection (1) shall give the Secretary of State's reasons for making it.

(3) An order under subsection (1) may contain such directions for the purpose of ensuring that the duty is complied with, within such period as may be specified in the order, as appears to the Secretary of State to be necessary.

(4) Any such directions shall, on the application of the Secretary of State, be enforceable by mandamus.

[Children Act 1989, s 84.]

PART XII[1]

MISCELLANEOUS AND GENERAL

Notification of children accommodated in certain establishments

6–2224   85. Children accommodated by health authorities and local education authorities.
(1) Where a child is provided with accommodation by any Health Authority, Special Health Authority, Primary Care Trust, National Health Service trust, NHS foundatin trust or local education authority ("the accommodating authority")—

    (*a*) for a consecutive period of at least three months; or

    (*b*) with the intention, on the part of that authority, of accommodating him for such a period,

the accommodating authority shall notify the responsible authority.

(2) Where subsection (1) applies with respect to a child, the accommodating authority shall also notify the responsible authority when they cease to accommodate the child.

(3) In this section "the responsible authority" means—

    (*a*) the local authority appearing to the accommodating authority to be the authority within whose area the child was ordinarily resident immediately before being accommodated; or

    (*b*) where it appears to the accommodating authority that a child was not ordinarily resident within the area of any local authority, the local authority within whose area the accommodation is situated.

(4) Where a local authority have been notified under this section, they shall—

    (*a*) take such steps as are reasonably practicable to enable them to determine whether the child's welfare is adequately safeguarded and promoted while he is accommodated by the accommodating authority; and

    (*b*) consider the extent to which (if at all) they should exercise any of their functions under this Act with respect to the child.

[Children Act 1989, s 85 as amended by the National Health Service and Community Care Act 1990, Sch 9, the Health Authorities Act 1995, Sch 1 and SI 2000/90 and the Health and Social Care (Community Health and Standards) Act 2003, Sch 4.]

---

  1. Part XII contains ss 85–108

6–2225   86. Children accommodated in care homes or independent hospitals.   (1) Where a child is provided with accommodation in any care homes or independent hospital—

    (*a*) for a consecutive period of at least three months; or

    (*b*) with the intention, on the part of the person taking the decision to accommodate him, of accommodating him for such period,

the person carrying on the home shall notify the local authority within whose area the home is carried on.

(2) Where subsection (1) applies with respect to a child, the person carrying on the home shall also notify that authority when he ceases to accommodate the child in the home.

(3) Where a local authority have been notified under this section, they shall—

    (*a*) take such steps as are reasonably practicable to enable them to determine whether the child's welfare is adequately safeguarded and promoted while he is accommodated in the home; and

    (*b*) consider the extent to which (if at all) they should exercise any of their functions under this Act with respect to the child.

(4) If the person carrying on any home fails, without reasonable excuse, to comply with this section he shall be guilty of an offence.

(5) A person authorised by a local authority may enter any care homes or independent hospital within the authority's area for the purpose of establishing whether the requirements of this section have been complied with.

(6) Any person who intentionally obstructs another in the exercise of the power of entry shall be guilty of an offence.

(7) Any person exercising the power of entry shall, if so required, produce some duly authenticated document showing his authority to do so.

(8) Any person committing an offence under this section shall be liable on summary conviction to a fine not exceeding **level 3** on the standard scale.

[Children Act 1989, s 86, as amended by the Care Standards Act 2000, Sch 4.]

6–2226   87. Welfare of children in boarding schools and colleges.   (1) Where a school or college provides accommodation for any child, it shall be the duty of the relevant person to safeguard and promote the child's welfare.★

(2) Subsection (1) does not apply in relation to a school or college which is a children's home or care home.

(3) Where accommodation is provided for a child by any school or college the appropriate authority shall take such steps as are reasonably practicable to enable them to determine whether the

child's welfare is adequately safeguarded and promoted while he is accommodated by the school[1] or college.

(4) Where the Commission are of the opinion that there has been a failure to comply with subsection (1) in relation to a child provided with accommodation by a school or college, they shall—

    (a)   in the case of a school other than an independent school or a special school, notify the local education authority for the area in which the school is situated;

    (b)   in the case of a special school which is maintained by a local education authority, notify that authority;

    (c)   in any other case, notify the Secretary of State.

(4A) Where the National Assembly for Wales are of the opinion that there has been a failure to comply with subsection (1) in relation to a child provided with accommodation by a school or college, they shall—

    (a)   in the case of a school other than an independent school or a special school, notify the local education authority for the area in which the school is situated;

    (b)   in the case of a special school which is maintained by a local education authority, notify that authority.

(5) Where accommodation is, or is to be, provided for a child by any school or college, a person authorised by the appropriate authority may, for the purpose of enabling that authority to discharge its duty under this section, enter at any time premises which are, or are to be, premises of the school or college.

(6) Any person exercising the power conferred by subsection (5) may carry out such inspection of premises, children and records as is prescribed by regulations[2] made by the Secretary of State for the purposes of this section.

(7) Any person exercising that power shall, if asked to do so, produce some duly authenticated document showing his authority to do so.

(8) Any person authorised by the regulations to inspect records—

    (a)   shall be entitled at any reasonable time to have access to, and inspect and check the operation of, any computer and any associated apparatus or material which is or has been in use in connection with the records in question; and

    (b)   may require—

        (i)   the person by whom or on whose behalf the computer is or has been so used; or

        (ii) any person having charge of, or otherwise concerned with the operation of, the computer, apparatus or material,

    to afford him such assistance as he may reasonably require.

(9) Any person who intentionally obstructs another in the exercise of any power conferred by this section or the regulations shall be guilty of an offence and liable on summary conviction to a fine not exceeding level 3 on the standard scale.

(9A) Where the Commission or the National Assembly for Wales exercises the power conferred by subsection (5) in relation to a child, it must publish a report on whether the child's welfare is adequately safeguarded and promoted while he is accommodated by the school or college.

(9B) Where the Commission or the National Assembly for Wales publishes a report under this section, it must—

    (a)   send a copy of the report to the school or college concerned; and

    (b)   make copies of the report available for inspection at its offices by any person at any reasonable time.

(9C) Any person who requests a copy of a report published under this section is entitled to have one on payment of such reasonable fee (if any) as the Commission or the National Assembly for Wales (as the case may be) considers appropriate.

(10) In this section and sections 87A to 87D—

"the 1992 Act" means the Further and Higher Education Act 1992;

"appropriate authority" means—

    (a)   in relation to England, the National Care Standards Commission;

    (b)   in relation to Wales, the National Assembly for Wales;

"college" means an institution within the further education sector as defined in section 91 of the 1992 Act;

"the Commission" means the Commission for Social Care Inspection;

"further education corporation" has the same meaning as in the 1992 Act;

"local education authority" and "proprietor" have the same meanings as in the Education Act 1996".

(11) In this section and sections 87A and 87D "relevant person" means—

    (a)   in relation to an independent school, the proprietor of the school;

    (b)   in relation to any other school, or an institution designated under section 28 of the 1992 Act, the governing body of the school or institution;

(c) in relation to an institution conducted by a further education corporation, the corporation.

(12) Where a person other than the proprietor of an independent school is responsible for conducting the school, references in this section to the relevant person include references to the person so responsible.
[Children Act 1989, s 87 as amended by the Registered Homes (Amendment) Act 1991, s 2, the Education Act 1996, Sch 37 and the Care Standards Act 2000, s 105, Sch 4 and the Health and Social Care (Community Health and Standards) Act 2003, Sch 4.]

1. See the National Care Standards Commission (Inspection of Schools and Colleges) Regulations 2002, SI 2002/552.
2. See the Inspection of Premises, Children and Records (Independent Schools) Regulations 1991, SI 1991/975 and the Inspection of Boarding Schools and Colleges (Powers and Fees) (Wales) Regulations 2002, SI 2002/3161.

6–2226A 87A. Suspension of duty under section 87(3).   (1) The Secretary of State may appoint a person to be an inspector for the purposes of this section if—

(a) that person already acts as an inspector for other purposes in relation to schools or colleges to which section 87(1) applies, and
(b) the Secretary of State is satisfied that the person is an appropriate person to determine whether the welfare of children provided with accommodation by such schools or colleges is adequately safeguarded and promoted while they are accommodated by them.

(2) Where—

(a) the relevant person enters into an agreement in writing with a person appointed under subsection (1),
(b) the agreement provides for the person so appointed to have in relation to the school or college the function of determining whether section 87(1) is being complied with, and
(c) the appropriate authority receive from the person mentioned in paragraph (b) ("the inspector") notice in writing that the agreement has come into effect,

the appropriate authority's duty under section 87(3) in relation to the school or college shall be suspended.

(3) Where the appropriate authority's duty under section 87(3) in relation to any school or college is suspended under this section, it shall cease to be so suspended if the appropriate authority receive—

(a) a notice under subsection (4) relating to the inspector, or
(b) a notice under subsection (5) relating to the relevant agreement.

(4) The Secretary of State shall terminate a person's appointment under subsection (1) if—

(a) that person so requests, or
(b) the Secretary of State ceases, in relation to that person, to be satisfied that he is such a person as is mentioned in paragraph (b) of that subsection,

and shall give notice of the termination of that person's appointment to the appropriate authority.

(5) Where—

(a) the appropriate authority's duty under section 87(3) in relation to any school or college is suspended under this section, and
(b) the relevant agreement ceases to have effect,

the inspector shall give to the appropriate authority notice in writing of the fact that it has ceased to have effect.

(6) In this section references to the relevant agreement, in relation to the suspension of the appropriate authority's duty under section 87(3) as regards any school or college, are to the agreement by virtue of which the appropriate authority's duty under that provision as regards that school or college is suspended.
[Children Act 1989, s 87A, as inserted by the Deregulation and Contracting Out Act 1994, s 38 and amended by the Education Act 1996, Sch 37 and the Care Standards Act 2000, s 106(1).]

6–2226B 87B. Duties of inspectors under section 87A.   (1) The Secretary of State may impose on a person appointed under section 87A(1) ("an authorised inspector") such requirements relating to, or in connection with, the carrying out under substitution agreements of the function mentioned in section 87A(2)(b) as the Secretary of State thinks fit.

(2) Where, in the course of carrying out under a substitution agreement the function mentioned in section 87A(2)(b), it appears to an authorised inspector that there has been a failure to comply with section 87(1) in the case of a child provided with accommodation by the school or college to which the agreement relates, the inspector shall give notice of that fact

(*a*) in the case of a school other than an independent school or a special school, to the local education authority for the area in which the school is situated;
(*b*) in the case of a special school which is maintained by a local education authority, to that authority;
(*c*) in any other case, to the Secretary of State.*

4333 6-2230

(3) Where, in the course of carrying out under a substitution agreement the function mentioned in section 87A(2)(*b*), it appears to an authorised inspector that a child provided with accommodation by the school or college to which the agreement relates is suffering, or is likely to suffer, significant harm, the inspector shall—

(*a*) give notice of that fact to the local authority in whose area the school or college is situated, and
(*b*) where the inspector is required to make inspection reports to the Secretary of State, supply that local authority with a copy of the latest inspection report to have been made by the inspector to the Secretary of State in relation to the school or college.

(4) In this section "substitution agreement" means an agreement by virtue of which the duty of the appropriate authority under section 87(3) in relation to a school or college is suspended.
[Children Act 1989, s 87B, as inserted by the Deregulation and Contracting Out Act 1994, s 38 and amended by the Education Act 1996, Sch 37 and the Care Standards Act 2000, s 106, Sch 4.]

6-2226C 87C. Boarding schools: national minimum standards. (1) The Secretary of State may prepare and publish statements of national minimum standards for safeguarding and promoting the welfare of children for whom accommodation is provided in a school or college.

(2) The Secretary of State shall keep the standards set out in the statements under review and may publish amended statements whenever he considers it appropriate to do so.

(3) Before issuing a statement, or an amended statement which in the opinion of the Secretary of State effects a substantial change in the standards, the Secretary of State shall consult any persons he considers appropriate.

(4) The standards shall be taken into account—

(*a*) in the making by the appropriate authority of any determination under section 87(4) or (4A);
(*b*) in the making by a person appointed under section 87A(1) of any determination under section 87B(2); and
(*c*) in any proceedings under any other enactment in which it is alleged that the person has failed to comply with section 87(1).

[Children Act 1989, s 87C, as inserted by the Care Standards Act 2000, s 107.]

6-2226D 87D. Annual fee for boarding school inspections. (1) Regulations under subsection (2) may be made in relation to any school or college in respect of which the appropriate authority is required to take steps under section 87(3).

(2) The Secretary of State may by regulations[1] require the relevant person to pay the appropriate authority an annual fee of such amount, and within such time, as the regulations may specify.

(3) A fee payable by virtue of this section may, without prejudice to any other method of recovery, be recovered summarily as a civil debt.
[Children Act 1989, s 87C, as inserted by the Care Standards Act 2000, s 108.]

---

1. The National Care Standards Commission (Fees and Frequency of Inspections) Regulations 2001, SI 2001/3980 amended by SI 2002/1505 and 2070, SI 2003/368 and SI 2005/575

Adoption

6-2227 88. *Amendments of adoption legislation.*

Paternity tests

6-2228 89. *Tests to establish paternity.*

Criminal care and supervision orders

6-2229 90. Care and supervision orders in criminal proceedings. (1) The power of a court to make an order under subsection (2) of section 1 of the Children and Young Persons Act 1969 (care proceedings in juvenile courts) where it is of the opinion that the condition mentioned in paragraph (*f*) of that subsection ("the offence condition") is satisfied is hereby abolished.

(2) The powers of the court to make care orders—

(*a*) under section 7(7)(*a*) of the Children and Young Persons Act 1969 (alteration in treatment of young offenders etc); and
(*b*) under section 15(1) of that Act, on discharging a supervision order made under section 7(7)(*b*) of that Act,

are hereby abolished.

(3) The powers given by that Act to include requirements in supervision orders shall have effect subject to amendments made by Schedule 12.
[Children Act 1989, s 90.]

Effect and duration of orders etc

6-2230 91. Effect and duration of orders etc. (1) The making of a residence order with respect to a child who is the subject of a care order discharges the care order.

(2) The making of a care order with respect to a child who is the subject of any section 8 order discharges that order[1].

(3) The making of a care order with respect to a child who is the subject of a supervision order discharges that other order.

(4) The making of a care order with respect to a child who is a ward of court brings that wardship to an end.

(5) The making of a care order with respect to a child who is the subject of a school attendance order made under section 437 of the Education Act 1996 discharges the school attendance order.

(5A) The making of a special guardianship order with respect to a child who is the subject of—

(*a*) a care order; or

(*b*) an order under section 34,

discharges that order.

(6) Where an emergency protection order is made with respect to a child who is in care, the care order shall have effect subject to the emergency protection order.

(7) Any order made under section 4(1), 4A(1) or 5(1) shall continue in force until the child reaches the age of eighteen, unless it is brought to an end earlier.

(8) Any—

(*a*) agreement under section 4 or 4A; or

(*b*) appointment under section 5(3) or (4),

shall continue in force until the child reaches the age of eighteen, unless it is brought to an end earlier.★

(9) An order under Schedule 1 has effect as specified in that Schedule.

(10) A section 8 order shall, if it would otherwise still be in force, cease to have effect when the child reaches the age of sixteen, unless it is to have effect beyond that age by virtue of section 9(6) or 12(5).

(11) Where a section 8 order has effect with respect to a child who has reached the age of sixteen, it shall, if it would otherwise still be in force, cease to have effect when he reaches the age of eighteen.

(12) Any care order, other than an interim care order, shall continue in force until the child reaches the age of eighteen, unless it is brought to an end earlier.

(13) Any order made under any other provision of this Act in relation to a child shall, if it would otherwise still be in force, cease to have effect when he reaches the age of eighteen.

(14) On disposing of any application for an order under this Act, the court may (whether or not it makes any other order in response to the application) order that no application for an order under this Act of any specified kind may be made with respect to the child concerned by any person named in the order without leave of the court[2].

(15) Where an application ("the previous application") has been made for—

(*a*) the discharge of a care order;

(*b*) the discharge of a supervision order;

(*c*) the discharge of an education supervision order;

(*d*) the substitution of a supervision order for a care order; or

(*e*) a child assessment order,

no further application of a kind mentioned in paragraphs (*a*) to (*e*) may be made with respect to the child concerned, without leave of the court, unless the period between the disposal of the previous application and the making of the further application exceeds six months.

(16) Subsection (15) does not apply to applications made in relation to interim orders.

(17) Where—

(*a*) a person has made an application for an order under section 34;

(*b*) the application has been refused; and

(*c*) a period of less than six months has elapsed since the refusal,

that person may not make a further application for such an order with respect to the same child, unless he has obtained the leave of the court.

[Children Act 1989, s 91 as amended by the Education Act 1996, Sch 37 and the Adoption and Children Act 2002, s 148.]

---

1. Where a family proceedings court heard an application for a care order, when there was a pending application by the father for a residence order before it, and proceeded to make a care order, but made no order on the application for a residence order, it was held that the application for the residence order was deemed to have been dismissed by the justices because it was an application which was inconsistent with the care order; see *Hounslow London Borough Council v A* [1993] 1 WLR 291, [1993] 1 FLR 702.

2. Though there will be cases where when it is necessary for an order under s 91(14) to be made without prior notice to the parties, it is wrong in principle, save in exceptional cases, to place a litigant in person in the position, at short notice, of an order that bars him from dealing with any aspect of the case relating to his children, particularly relating to contact (*Re C (prohibition on further applications)* [2002] EWCA Civ 292, [2002] 3 FCR 183, [2002] 1 FLR 1136). See also *Re G (a child) (contempt: committal order)* [2003] EWCA Civ 489, [2003] 1 WLR 2051, [2003] 2 FCR 231.

On an application for leave to make an application, under s 91(14), it has been suggested that the test is whether there is an arguable case and not whether there is a reasonable likelihood of success; see *Re G (child case: parental involvement)* [1996] 2 FCR 1, [1996] 1 FLR 857, CA. The power in s 91(14) should be used sparingly; it will be a desirable power where applications are being made too often and there is evidence that the other party and the child are suffering or likely to suffer if such applications continue. The power may also be appropriately used in other exceptional circumstances where for example, although there have not been repeated applications, the applicant has sought to pursue litigation in an unreasonable fashion and in a fashion which is damaging to the interests of the child: see *C v W (a minor) (contact: leave to apply)* [1998] 1 FCR 618, [1999] 1 FLR 916 (father failed to attend court, to comply with the directions of the court, give evidence and give any explanations to the court and it was contrary to the child's interests to allow the father to continue litigation until he had demonstrated some sort of seriousness about his commitment to the litigation and his son). However, in suitable circumstances (and on clear evidence) a court may impose the leave restriction in cases where the welfare of the child requires it, although there is no history of making unreasonable applications. The court will need to be satisfied first, that the facts go beyond the commonly encountered need for a time to settle to a regime ordered by the court and the situation where there is animosity between the adults in dispute and secondly that there is a serious risk that, without the restriction, the child or the carers will be subject to unacceptable strain; see *Re P (a child) (residence order: restriction order)* [1999] 3 All ER 734, [1999] 3 WLR 1164, [1999] 2 FCR 289, CA). The exercise of the power should be confined to such cases and not used as a run of the mill type order (*Re F (child orders: restricting applications)* [1992] 2 FCR 433, [1993] 1 FLR 432) and see *Re F (contact: restraint Order)*[1996] 1 FCR 81. For an example of the proper use of this power see *Re T (a minor) (parental responsibility and contact)* [1993] 1 FCR 973, [1993] 2 FLR 450, *Re G and M (child orders: restricting applications)* [1995] 2 FLR 416 and *Re R (a minor) (leave to make applications)* [1998] 2 FCR 129, [1998] 1 FLR 749, CA (third application for residence order during the child's first three and a half years of life with no prospect of success). Applications for leave to commence proceedings should be heard inter partes (*Re M (care orders: restricting applications)* [1999] 3 FCR 400; *Re N (section 91 (14) order)* [1996] 2 FCR 377, [1996] 1 FLR 356, CA). Justices should give their reasons for imposing a leave restriction under s 91(14) and a failure to do so is a serious omission (*Re C (contact: no order for contact)* [2000] 2 FLR 723, FD) When considering an application for leave to apply for a s 8 order, the s 91(14) application is not to be subjected to the statutory criteria in s 10(9), ante, (*Re A (application for leave)* [1999] 1 FCR 127, [1998] 1 FLR 1).

Jurisdiction and procedure etc

6–2231 92. Jurisdiction[1] of courts. (1) The name "domestic proceedings", given to certain proceedings in magistrates' courts, is hereby changed to "family proceedings" and the names "domestic court" and "domestic court panel" are hereby changed to "family proceedings court" and "family panel", respectively.

(2) Proceedings under this Act shall be treated as family proceedings in relation to magistrates' courts[2].

(3) Subsection (2) is subject to the provisions of section 65(1) and (2) of the Magistrates' Courts Act 1980 (proceedings which may be treated as not being family proceedings), as amended by this Act.

(4) A magistrates' court shall not be competent to entertain any application, or make any order, involving the administration or application of—

(*a*) any property belonging to or held in trust for a child; or
(*b*) the income of any such property.

(5) The powers of a magistrates' court under section 63(2) of the Act of 1980 to suspend or rescind orders shall not apply in relation to any order made under this Act.

(6) Part I of Schedule 11 makes provision, including provision for the Lord Chancellor to make orders, with respect to the jurisdiction of courts and justices of the peace in relation to—

(*a*) proceedings under this Act; and
(*b*) proceedings under certain other enactments.

(7) For the purposes of this Act "the court" means the High Court, a county court or a magistrates' court.

(8) Subsection (7) is subject to the provision made by or under Part I of Schedule 11 and to any express provision as to the jurisdiction of any court made by any other provision of this Act.

(9) The Lord Chancellor may by order[3] make provision for the principal registry of the Family Division of the High Court to be treated as if it were a county court for such purposes of this Act, or of any provision made under this Act, as may be specified in the order.

(10) Any order under subsection (9) may make such provision as the Lord Chancellor thinks expedient for the purpose of applying (with or without modifications) provisions which apply in relation to the procedure in county courts to the principal registry when it acts as if it were a county court.

(11) Part II of Schedule 11 makes amendments consequential on this section.
[Children Act 1989, s 92.]

---

1. As to the court's jurisdiction in respect of foreign nationals, see the Family Law Act 1986, ss 2, 3, in this PART, ante, and the cases noted thereto. Whilst jurisdiction can be based on the physical presence of a child, immigration controls apply to children as well as adults and courts should be slow to intervene (*Re M (a minor) (immigration: residence)* [1993] 2 FLR 858).

2. But any application under s 25 (use of accommodation for restricting liberty) shall be made to a youth court or magistrates' court (Criminal Justice Act 1991, s 60(3)) in PART III, ante. Hearsay evidence in proceedings for a secure accommodation order is thus admissible, despite the terms of s 8(3) which purports to exclude matters other than arising under Pts I, II and IV from the definition of family proceedings. See the Children (Admissibility of Hearsay Evidence) Order 1991 post, and *R (J) v Oxfordshire County Council* [1992] 3 All ER 660, [1992] 3 WLR 88.

3. See the Children (Allocation of Proceedings) Order 1991, post.

6–2232 93. Rules of court. (1) An authority having power to make rules of court may make such provision for giving effect to—

(*a*)   this Act;

(*b*)   the provisions of any statutory instrument made under this Act; or

(*c*)   any amendment made by this Act in any other enactment,

as appears to that authority to be necessary or expedient.

(2)   The rules may, in particular, make provision—

(*a*)   with respect to the procedure to be followed in any relevant proceedings (including the manner in which any application is to be made or other proceedings commenced);

(*b*)   as to the persons entitled to participate in any relevant proceedings, whether as parties to the proceedings or by being given the opportunity to make representations to the court;

(*bb*)   for children to be separately represented in relevant proceedings,

(*c*)   with respect to the documents and information to be furnished, and notices to be given, in connection with any relevant proceedings;

(*d*)   applying (with or without modification) enactments which govern the procedure to be followed with respect to proceedings brought on a complaint made to a magistrates' court to relevant proceedings in such a court brought otherwise than on a complaint;

(*e*)   with respect to preliminary hearings;

(*f*)   for the service outside England and Wales, in such circumstances and in such manner as may be prescribed, of any notice of proceedings in a magistrates' court;

(*g*)   for the exercise by magistrates' courts, in such circumstances as may be prescribed, of such powers as may be prescribed (even though a party to the proceedings in question is or resides outside England and Wales);

(*h*)   enabling the court, in such circumstances as may be prescribed, to proceed on any application even though the respondent has not been given notice of the proceedings;

(*i*)   authorising a single justice to discharge the functions of a magistrates' court with respect to such relevant proceedings as may be prescribed;

(*j*)   authorising a magistrates' court to order any of the parties to such relevant proceedings as may be prescribed, in such circumstances as may be prescribed, to pay the whole or part of the costs of all or any of the other parties.

(3)   In subsection (2)—

"notice of proceedings" means a summons or such other notice of proceedings as is required; and "given", in relation to a summons, means "served";

"prescribed" means prescribed by the rules; and

"relevant proceedings" means any application made, or proceedings brought, under any of the provisions mentioned in paragraphs (*a*) to (*c*) of subsection (1) and any part of such proceedings.

(4)   This section and any other power in this Act to make rules of court are not to be taken as in any way limiting any other power of the authority in question to make rules of court.

(5)   When making any rules under this section an authority shall be subject to the same requirements as to consultation (if any) as apply when the authority makes rules under its general rule making power.

[Children Act 1989, s 93 as amended by the Courts and Legal Services Act 1990, Sch 16 and the Adoption and Children Act 2002, s 122.]

6–2233   94. Appeals[1].   (1)   Subject to any express provisions to the contrary made by or under this Act, an appeal[2] shall lie to the High Court[3] against—

(*a*)   the making by a magistrates' court of any order[4] under this Act or the Adoption and Children Act 2002; or

(*b*)   any refusal by a magistrates' court to make such an order.★

(2)   Where a magistrates' court has power, in relation to any proceedings under this Act or the Adoption and Children Act 2002, to decline jurisdiction because it considers that the case can more conveniently be dealt with by another court, no appeal shall lie against any exercise by that magistrates' court of that power.★

(3)   Subsection (1) does not apply in relation to an interim order for periodical payments made under Schedule 1.

(4)   On an appeal under this section, the High Court may make such orders[5] as may be necessary to give effect to its determination of the appeal.

(5)   Where an order is made under subsection (4) the High Court may also make such incidental or consequential orders as appear to it to be just.

(6)   Where an appeal from a magistrates' court relates to an order for the making of periodical payments, the High Court may order that its determination of the appeal shall have effect from such date as it thinks fit to specify in the order.

(7)   The date so specified must not be earlier than the earliest date allowed in accordance with rules of court made for the purposes of this section.

(8)   Where, on an appeal under this section in respect of an order requiring a person to make periodical payments, the High Court reduces the amount of those payments or discharges the order—

(*a*) it may order the person entitled to the payments to pay to the person making them such sum in respect of payments already made as the High Courts thinks fit; and

(*b*) if any arrears are due under the order for periodical payments, it may remit payment of the whole, or part, of those arrears.

(9) Any order of the High Court made on an appeal under this section (other than one directing that an application be re-heard by a magistrates' court) shall, for the purposes—

(*a*) of the enforcement of the order; and

(*b*) of any power to vary, revive or discharge orders[6],

be treated as if it were an order of the magistrates' court from which the appeal was brought and not an order of the High Court.

(10) The Lord Chancellor may by order[7] make provision as to the circumstances in which appeals may be made against decisions taken by courts on questions arising in connection with the transfer, or proposed transfer, of proceedings by virtue of any order under paragraph 2 of Schedule 11.★

(11) Except to the extent provided for in any order made under subsection (10), no appeal may be made against any decision of a kind mentioned in that subsection.★

[Children Act 1989, s 94 as amended by the Courts and Legal Services Act 1990, Sch 16 and the Adoption and Children Act 2002, s 100.]

★**Amended by the Constitutional Reform Act 2005, Sch 4 from a date to be appointed.**

1. For consideration generally of the procedure on appeals to the High Court in family proceedings, see para **6–43**.

2. On such appeal a party is not entitled to call evidence unless there are exceptional circumstances and leave is given. Where the matter is one of discretion the High Court will not interfere with the discretion of the court below unless it considers that the court was plainly wrong or it has erred in principle (*Croydon London Borough Council v A* [1992] 3 All ER 788, [1992] 3 WLR 267).

3. The appeal is regulated by *Practice Direction* [1992] 1 All ER 864, [1992] 1 WLR 261. The President of the Family Division has issued a Direction clarifying the position with regard to appeals from magistrates' courts to the High Court under s 94 (*Children Act 1989—Appeals* [1992] 2 FLR 503).

It has been held not to be a valid ground to appeal out of time where a mother accepted a decision for a care order where the local authority proposed that the children remain with the mother but subsequently removed the children (*Re M (minors) (Interim care order)* [1993] 2 FCR 182, [1993] 2 FLR 406). Appeal may lie against a consent order where the respondent to the application for a consent order gave that consent after a judicial warning that he was at risk of an order for costs if he continued to oppose the application (*Re R (contact: consent order)* [1995] 1 FLR 123, CA).

4. It would appear that there is no power for a magistrates' court to stay an order under this Act pending appeal. However, application for a stay may be made to the High Court; see *Re O (a minor)* [1992] 4 All ER 905, [1992] 1 WLR 912 and *Re J (a minor) (residence)* [1993] 2 FCR 636, [1994] 1 FLR 369. For further provisions as to appeals, see the Family Proceedings Rules 1991, r 4.22, post.

An appeal to the High Court against a decision on an application to vary an order for financial provision made under the repealed Guardianship of Minors Act 1971 should be by way of notice of motion and not under this section (*B v B (children: periodical payments)* [1995] 1 WLR 440, [1995] 1 FCR 763, [1995] 1 FLR 459).

5. The combined effect of s 94(4) and (5), and arts 13 and 18(2) of the Children (Allocation of Proceedings) Order 1991, this PART, post, is that on an appeal from a family proceedings court, at the same time as the High Court remits the matter for re-hearing, it may also transfer it from the family proceedings court to any county court which is a care centre (*Suffolk County Council v C* [1999] 1 FCR 473n, [1999] 1 FLR 259n).

6. "Order" includes a direction made under s 38(6) (*Re O (minors) (medical examination)* [1993] 1 FLR 860).

7. The Children (Allocation of Proceedings) (Appeals) Order 1991, SI 1991/1801 has been made; the order provides for an appeal against a district judge's transfer of proceedings to a magistrates' court under Article 11 of the Children (Allocation of Proceedings) Order 1991, this PART, post.

6–2234 95. Attendance of child at hearing under Part IV or V. (1) In any proceedings in which a court is hearing an application for an order under Part IV or V, or is considering whether to make any such order, the court may order the child concerned to attend such stage or stages of the proceedings as may be specified in the order.

(2) The power conferred by subsection (1) shall be exercised in accordance with rules of court.

(3) Subsections (4) to (6) apply where—

(*a*) an order under subsection (1) has not been not complied with; or

(*b*) the court has reasonable cause to believe that it will not be complied with.

(4) The court may make an order authorising a constable, or such person as may be specified in the order—

(*a*) to take charge of the child and to bring him to the court; and

(*b*) to enter and search any premises specified in the order if he has reasonable cause to believe that the child may be found on the premises.

(5) The court may order any person who is in a position to do so to bring the child to the court.

(6) Where the court has reason to believe that a person has information about the whereabouts of the child it may order him to disclose it to the court.

[Children Act 1989, s 95.]

6–2235 96. Evidence given by, or with respect to, children. (1) Subsection (2) applies where a child who is called as a witness in any civil proceedings does not, in the opinion of the court, understand the nature of an oath.

(2) The child's evidence may be heard by the court if, in its opinion—

(*a*) he understands that it is his duty to speak the truth; and

(*b*) he has sufficient understanding to justify his evidence being heard.

(3) The Lord Chancellor may by order[1] make provision for the admissibility of evidence which would otherwise be inadmissible under any rule of law relating to hearsay.

(4) An order under subsection (3) may only be made with respect to—

(*a*) civil proceedings in general or such civil proceedings, or class of civil proceedings, as may be prescribed; and

(*b*) evidence in connection with the upbringing, maintenance or welfare of a child.

(5) An order under subsection (3)—

(*a*) may, in particular, provide for the admissibility of statements which are made orally or in a prescribed form or which are recorded by any prescribed method of recording;

(*b*) may make different provision for different purposes and in relation to different descriptions of court; and

(*c*) may make such amendments and repeals in any enactment relating to evidence (other than in this Act) as the Lord Chancellor considers necessary or expedient in consequence of the provision made by the order.

(6) Subsection (5)(*b*) is without prejudice to section 104(4).

(7) In this section—

"civil proceedings" means civil proceedings, before any tribunal, in relation to which the strict rules of evidence apply, whether as a matter of law or by agreement of the parties, and references to "the court" shall be construed accordingly; and

"prescribed" means prescribed by an order under subsection (3).
[Children Act 1989, s 96 as amended by the Civil Evidence Act 1995, Sch 1.]

---

1. See the Children (Admissibility of Hearsay Evidence) Order 1993, this PART, *post.*

6–2236 97. Privacy for children involved in certain proceedings. (1) Rules made under section 144 of the Magistrates' Courts Act 1980* may make provision for a magistrates' court to sit in private in proceedings in which any powers under this Act or the Adoption and Children Act 2002 may be exercised by the court with respect to any child.

(2) No person[1] shall publish any material which is intended, or likely, to identify—

(*a*) any child as being involved in any proceedings before the High Court, a county court or a magistrates' court in which any power under this Act or the Adoption and Children Act 2002 may be exercised by the court with respect to that or any other child; or

(*b*) an address or school as being that of a child involved in any such proceedings.

(3) In any proceedings for an offence under this section it shall be a defence for the accused to prove that he did not know, and had no reason to suspect, that the published material was intended, or likely, to identify the child.

(4) The court or the Lord Chancellor may, if satisfied that the welfare of the child requires it, by order dispense with the requirements of subsection (2) to such extent as may be specified in the order.**

(5) For the purposes of this section—

"publish" includes—

(*a*) include in a programme service (within the meaning of the Broadcasting Act 1990); or

(*b*) cause to be published; and

"material" includes any picture or representation.

(6) Any person who contravenes this section shall be guilty of an offence and liable, on summary conviction, to a fine not exceeding **level 4** on the standard scale.

(7) Subsection (1) is without prejudice to—

(*a*) the generality of the rule making power in section 144 of the Act of 1980; or*

(*b*) any other power of a magistrates' court to sit in private.

(8) Sections 69 (sittings of magistrates' courts for family proceedings) and 71 (newspaper reports of certain proceedings) of the Act of 1980 shall apply in relation to any proceedings (before a magistrates' court) to which this section applies subject to the provisions of this section.**
[Children Act 1989, s 97 as amended by the Broadcasting Act 1990, Sch 20, the Courts and Legal Services Act 1990, Sch 16, SI 1992/709, the Access to Justice Act 1999, s 72 and the Adoption and Children Act 2002, s 101.]

---

*Amended by the Courts Act 2003, Sch 8 from a date to be appointed.

**Subsection (4) amended and new sub-s (9) inserted by the Consitutional Reform Act 2005, Sch 4 from a date to be appointed.

1. Section 97 does not impose an absolute prohibition on publicity and the court can be asked to exercise its discretion to allow the identity of the child to be published; if the court is not so asked or refuses to give its permission s 97(2) bites and no material that is intended or is likely to identify the child can be published: *P v BW (children cases: hearings in public)* [2003] EWHC 1541 (Fam), [2004] 2 WLR 509, [2004] 1 FLR 171.

6–2237   98. Self-incrimination[1].   (1) In any proceedings in which a court is hearing an application for an order under Part IV or V[2], no person shall be excused from—

(a)   giving evidence on any matter; or

(b)   answering any question put to him in the course of his giving evidence,

on the ground that doing so might incriminate him or his spouse or civil partner of an offence.

(2) A statement or admission made in such proceedings[3] shall not be admissible in evidence against[4] the person making it or his spouse or civil partner in proceedings for an offence other than perjury.

[Children Act 1989, s 98 as amended by the Civil Partnership Act 2004, s 263.]

---

1. For consideration of the relevance of s 98 on an application for leave to disclose evidence for use in criminal proceedings, see *Re K (minors) (disclosure)* [1994] 3 All ER 230, [1994] 1 FLR 377.

2. Section 98(2) of the Children Act 1989 does not apply to private law proceedings, in deciding whether or not to grant leave to disclose the need to encourage candour has to be balanced against other factors, such as the gravity of the offence concerned, any risk to children, and issues of public policy, and the court should also have regard to the welfare of the children concerned and to the factors set out in *Re C (A Minor) (Care Proceedings: Disclosure)* (infra), but in carrying out this balancing exercise the court should bear in mind that the need to encourage frankness ought to be given greater weight in private law proceedings than in public law proceedings (*Re D and M (disclosure: private law)* [2002] EWHC 2820 (Fam), [2003] 1 FLR 647).

3. The words "a statement or admission made in such proceedings" cover anything a person says in the witness box and anything a person says in his or her own statement filed in the proceedings. The privilege not only extends to an oral admission made by a mother to the guardian ad litem, but also extends to oral statements made to social workers who are charged with carrying out the local authority's duties of investigation in a child protection case, once the proceedings have begun (*Cleveland County Council v F* [1995] 1 WLR 785, [1995] 3 FCR 174, [1995] 1 FLR 797). However, in *Re G (a minor) (social worker: disclosure)* [1996] 2 All ER 65, [1996] 3 FCR 77, [1996] 1 FLR 276 the Court of Appeal in comments which were obiter, expressed doubt whether s 98(2) extended to protecting admissions made in advance of care proceedings to a social worker. Nothing in s 98(2) detracts from the power of the court to order disclosure of any part of the proceedings in appropriate circumstances, eg for a police inquiry, including disclosure of material covered by s 98(2) (*Re C (a minor) (care proceedings: disclosure)* [1997] Fam 76, [1997] 2 WLR 322, [1996] 3 FCR 521. See also *Re I (disclosure: police investigation)* [2002] All ER (D) 540 (May), [2002] JPN 499 (applying *Re EC*, supra, and holding that the use of the information was a matter for the Crown Court not a family court. The topic of disclosure is discussed more fully at para **4-29 Disclosure**, ante.

4. Putting an inconsistent statement made in care proceedings to a witness in criminal proceedings in order to challenge their evidence or attack their credibility does not amount to those statements being used "against" them (*Re K (minors) (disclosure)* [1994] 3 All ER 230, [1994] 1 FLR 377) nor when one co defendant may use such a statement to cross examine a co-accused (*Re L (care: confidentiality)* [1999] 1 FLR 165, FD)).

6–2238   99. Legal aid.   *Repealed.*

6–2239   100. Restrictions on use of wardship jurisdiction[1].   (1) Section 7 of the Family Law Reform Act 1969 (which gives the High Court power to place a ward of court in the care, or under the supervision, of a local authority) shall cease to have effect.

(2) No court shall exercise the High Court's inherent jurisdiction with respect to children—

(a)   so as to require a child to be placed in the care, or put under the supervision, of a local authority;

(b)   so as to require a child to be accommodated by or on behalf of a local authority;

(c)   so as to make a child who is the subject of a care order a ward of court; or

(d)   for the purpose of conferring on any local authority[2] power to determine any question which has arisen, or which may arise, in connection with any aspect of parental responsibility for a child.

(3) No application for any exercise of the court's inherent jurisdiction with respect to children may be made by a local authority unless the authority have obtained the leave of the court.

(4) The court may only grant leave if it is satisfied that—

(a)   the result which the authority wish to achieve could not be achieved through the making of any order of a kind to which subsection (5) applies; and

(b)   there is reasonable cause to believe that if the court's inherent jurisdiction is not exercised with respect to the child he is likely to suffer significant harm.

(5) This subsection applies to any order—

(a)   made otherwise than in the exercise of the court's inherent jurisdiction; and

(b)   which the local authority is entitled to apply for (assuming, in the case of any application which may only be made with leave, that leave is granted).

[Children Act 1989, s 100.]

---

1. As to the principles governing the subsequent use of material introduced in wardship proceedings see *Re Manda (wardship: disclosure of evidence)* [1993] 1 All ER 733, [1993] 2 WLR 161, [1993] 1 FLR 205.

2. Accordingly, the restriction on making an application does not apply where the local authority is inviting the court to exercise its inherent jurisdiction to protect children rather than to have protective powers conferred on itself (*Devon County Council v S* [1994] Fam 169, [1995] 1 All ER 243, [1994] 3 WLR 183).

6–2250   101. Effect of orders as between England and Wales and Northern Ireland, the Channel Islands or the Isle of Man.   (1) The Secretary of State may make regulations[1] providing—

(a) for prescribed orders which—

   (i)   are made by a court in Northern Ireland; and
   (ii) appear to the Secretary of State to correspond in their effect to orders which may be made under any provision of this Act,

   to have effect in prescribed circumstances, for prescribed purposes of this Act, as if they were orders of a prescribed kind made under this Act;

(b) for prescribed orders which—

   (i)   are made by a court in England and Wales; and
   (ii) appear to the Secretary of State to correspond in their effect to orders which may be made under any provision in force in Northern Ireland,

   to have effect in prescribed circumstances, for prescribed purposes of the law of Northern Ireland, as if they were orders of a prescribed kind made in Northern Ireland.

(2) Regulations under subsection (1) may provide for the order concerned to cease to have effect for the purposes of the law of Northern Ireland, or (as the case may be) the law of England and Wales, if prescribed conditions are satisfied.

(3) The Secretary of State may make regulations providing for prescribed orders which—

(a) are made by a court in the Isle of Man or in any of the Channel Islands; and
(b) appear to the Secretary of State to correspond in their effect to orders which may be made under this Act,

to have effect in prescribed circumstances for prescribed purposes of this Act, as if they were orders of a prescribed kind made under this Act.

(4) Where a child who is in the care of a local authority is lawfully taken to live in Northern Ireland, the Isle of Man or any of the Channel Islands, the care order in question shall cease to have effect if the conditions prescribed in regulations made by the Secretary of State are satisfied.

(5) Any regulations made under this section may—

(a) make such consequential amendments (including repeals) in—

   (i)   section 25 of the Children and Young Persons Act 1969 (transfers between England and Wales and Northern Ireland); or
   (ii) section 26 (transfers between England and Wales and Channel Islands or Isle of Man) of that Act,

   as the Secretary of State considers necessary or expedient; and

(b) modify any provision of this Act, in its application (by virtue of the regulations) in relation to an order made otherwise than in England and Wales.

[Children Act 1989, s 101.]

---

1. See the Children (Prescribed Orders—Northern Ireland, Guernsey and Isle of Man) Regulations 1991, SI 1991/2032.

Search warrants

6–2251   102. Power of constable to assist in exercise of certain powers to search for children or inspect premises.   (1) Where, on an application made by any person for a warrant under this section, it appears to the court—

(a) that a person attempting to exercise powers under any enactment mentioned in subsection (6) has been prevented from doing so by being refused entry to the premises concerned or refused access to the child concerned; or
(b) that any such person is likely to be so prevented from exercising any such powers,

it may issue a warrant authorising any constable to assist that person in the exercise of those powers using reasonable force if necessary.

(2) Every warrant issued under this section shall be addressed to, and executed by, a constable who shall be accompanied by the person applying for the warrant if—

(a) that person so desires; and
(b) the court by whom the warrant is issued does not direct otherwise.

(3) A court granting an application for a warrant under this section may direct that the constable concerned may, in executing the warrant, be accompanied by a registered medical practitioner, registered nurse or registered midwife if he so chooses.

(3A) The reference in subsection (3) to a registered midwife is to such a midwife who is also registered in the Specialist Community Public Health Nurses' Part of the register maintianed under article 5 of the Nursing and Midwifery Order 2001.

(4) An application for a warrant under this section shall be made in the manner and form prescribed by rules of court.

(5) Where—

(*a*) an application for a warrant under this section relates to a particular child; and
(*b*) it is reasonably practicable to do so,

the application and any warrant granted on the application shall name the child; and where it does not name him it shall describe him as clearly as possible.

(6) The enactments are—

(*a*) sections 62, 64, 67, 76,* 80, 86 and 87;
(*b*) paragraph 8(1)(*b*) and (2)(*b*) of Schedule 3;
(*c*) *repealed.*

[Children Act 1989, s 102 as amended by SI 2002/253 and the Adoption and Children Act 2002, Sch 3.]

*Section 102(6)(*a*) is amended by the Care Standards Act 2000, Sch 4, when in force.

General

6–2252 103. Offences by bodies corporate. (1) This section applies where any offence under this Act is committed by a body corporate.

(2) If the offence is proved to have been committed with the consent or connivance of or to be attributable to any neglect on the part of any director, manager, secretary or other similar officer of the body corporate, or any person who was purporting to act in any such capacity, he (as well as the body corporate) shall be guilty of the offence and shall be liable to be proceeded against and punished accordingly.

[Children Act 1989, s 103.]

6–2253 104. Regulations and orders. (1) Any power of the Lord Chancellor, the Treasury or the Secretary of State under this Act to make an order, regulations, or rules, except an order under section 56(4)(*a*), 57(3), 84 or 97(4) or paragraph 1(1) of Schedule 4, shall be exercisable by statutory instrument.

(2) Any such statutory instrument, except one made under section 4(1B), 17(4), 107 or 108(2), shall be subject to annulment in pursuance of a resolution of either House of Parliament.

(3) An order under section 4(1B) or 17(4) shall not be made unless a draft of it has been laid before, and approved by a resolution of, each House of Parliament.

(4) Any statutory instrument made under this Act may—

(*a*) make different provision for different cases;
(*b*) provide for exemptions from any of its provisions; and
(*c*) contain such incidental, supplemental and transitional provisions as the person making it considers expedient.

[Children Act 1989, s 104, as amended by the Care Standards Act 2000, s 117(2), Sch 6, the Tax Credits Act 2002, Sch 3 and the Adoption and Children Act 2002, s 111.]

6–2254 105. Interpretation. (1) In this Act—

"adoption agency" means a body which may be referred to as an adoption agency by virtue of section 2 of the Adoption and Children Act 2002;

"appropriate children's home" has the meaning given by section 23;

"bank holiday" means a day which is a bank holiday under the Banking and Financial Dealings Act 1971;

"care home" has the same meaning as in the Care Standards Act 2000;

"care order" has the meaning given by section 31(11) and also includes any order which by or under any enactment has the effect of, or is deemed to be, a care order for the purposes of this Act; and any reference to a child who is in the care of an authority is a reference to a child who is in their care by virtue of a care order;

"child" means, subject to paragraph 16 of Schedule 1, a person under the age of eighteen;

"child assessment order" has the meaning given by section 43(2);

"child minder" has the meaning given by section 71;*

"child of the family", in relation to the parties to a marriage, or to two people who are civil partners of each other, means—

(*a*) a child of both of them;
(*b*) any other child, not being a child who is placed with those parties as foster parents by a local authority or voluntary organisation, who has been treated by both of them as a child of their family;

"children's home" has the meaning given by section 23;

"community home" has the meaning given by section 53;

"contact order" has the meaning given by section 8(1);

"day care" (except in Part XA) has the same meaning as in section 18;

"disabled", in relation to a child, has the same meaning as in section 17(11);

"domestic premises" has the meaning given by section 71(12);

"dwelling-house" includes—

    (a) any building or part of a building which is occupied as a dwelling;

    (b) any caravan, house-boat or structure which is occupied as a dwelling;

    and any yard, garden, garage or outhouse belonging to it and occupied with it;

"education supervision order" has the meaning given in section 36;

"emergency protection order" means an order under section 44;

"family assistance order" has the meaning given in section 16(2);

"family proceedings" has the meaning given by section 8(3);

"functions" includes powers and duties;

"guardian of a child" means a guardian (other than a guardian of the estate of a child) appointed in accordance with the provisions of section 5;

"harm" has the same meaning as in section 31(9) and the question of whether harm is significant shall be determined in accordance with section 31(10);

"Health Authority" means a Health Authority established under section 8 of the National Health Service Act 1977;

"health service hospital" has the same meaning as in the National Health Service Act 1977;

"hospital" (except in Schedule 9A) has the same meaning as in the Mental Health Act 1983, except that it does not include a hospital at which high security psychiatric services within the meaning of that Act are provided;

"ill-treatment" has the same meaning as in section 31(9);

"income-based jobseeker's allowance" has the same meaning as in the Jobseekers Act 1995;

"independent hospital" has the same meaning as in the Care Standards Act 2000;

"independent school" has the same meaning as in the Education Act 1996;

"local authority" means, in relation to England, the council of a county, a metropolitan district, a London Borough or the Common Council of the City of London, in relation to Wales, the council of a county or a county borough and, in relation to Scotland, a local authority within the meaning of section 1(2) of the Social Work (Scotland) Act 1968;

"local authority foster parent" has the same meaning as in section 23(3);

"local education authority" has the same meaning as in the Education Act 1996;

"local housing authority" has the same meaning as in the Housing Act 1985;

"officer of the Service" has the same meaning as in the Criminal Justice and Court Services Act 2000;

"parental responsibility" has the meaning given in section 3;

"parental responsibility agreement" has the meaning given in sections 4(1) and 4A(2);

"prescribed" means prescribed by regulations made under this Act;

"private children's home" means a children's home in respect of which a person is registered under Part II of the Care Standards Act 2000 which is not a community home or a voluntary home;

"Primary Care Trust" means a Primary Care Trust established under section 16A of the National Health Service Act 1977;

"privately fostered child" and "to foster a child privately" have the same meaning as in section 66;

"prohibited steps order" has the meaning given by section 8(1);

"registered pupil" has the same meaning as in the Education Act 1996;

"relative", in relation to a child, means a grandparent, brother, sister, uncle or aunt (whether of the full blood or half blood or by affinity) or by marriage or civil partnership or step-parent;

"residence order" has the meaning given by section 8(1);

"responsible person", in relation to a child who is the subject of a supervision order, has the meaning given in paragraph 1 of Schedule 3;

"school" has the same meaning as in the Education Act 1996 or, in relation to Scotland, in the Education (Scotland) Act 1980;★

"section 31A plan" has the meaning given by section 31A(6);

"service", in relation to any provision made under Part III, includes any facility;

"signed", in relation to any person, includes the making by that person of his mark;

"special educational needs" has the same meaning as in the Education Act 1996;

"special guardian" and "special guardianship order" have the meaning given by section 14A;

"Special Health Authority" means a Special Health Authority established under section 11 of the National Health Service Act 1977;

"specific issue order" has the meaning given by section 8(1);

"Strategic Health Authority" means a Strategic Health Authority established under section 8 of the National Health Service 1977;

"supervision order" has the meaning given by section 31(11);

"supervised child" and "supervisor", in relation to a supervision order or an education supervision order, mean respectively the child who is (or is to be) under supervision and the person under whose supervision he is (or is to be) by virtue of the order;

"upbringing", in relation to any child, includes the care of the child but not his maintenance;

"voluntary home" has the meaning given by section 60;

"voluntary organisation" means a body (other than a public or local authority) whose activities are not carried on for profit;

"Welsh family proceedings officer" has the meaning given by section 35 of the Children Act 2004.

(2) References in this Act to a child whose father and mother were, or (as the case may be) were not, married to each other at the time of his birth must be read with section 1 of the Family Law Reform Act 1987 (which extends the meaning of such references).

(3) References in this Act to—

(a) a person with whom a child lives, or is to live, as the result of a residence order; or
(b) a person in whose favour a residence order is in force,

shall be construed as references to the person named in the order as the person with whom the child is to live.

(4) References in this Act to a child who is looked after by a local authority have the same meaning as they have (by virtue of section 22) in Part III.

(5) References in this Act to accommodation provided by or on behalf of a local authority are references to accommodation so provided in the exercise of functions of that or any other local authority which are social services functions within the meaning of the Local Authority Social Services Act 1970.

(5A) References in this Act to a child minder shall be construed—

(a) *repealed*;
(b) in relation to England and Wales, in accordance with section 79A

(5B) References in this Act to acting as a child minder and to a child minder shall be construed, in relation to Scotland, in accordance with section 2(17) of the Regulation of Care (Scotland) Act 2001 (asp 8).

(6) In determining the "ordinary residence" of a child for any purpose of this Act, there shall be disregarded any period in which he lives in any place—

(a) which is a school or other institution;
(b) in accordance with the requirements of a supervision order under this Act or an order under section 63(1) of the Powers of Criminal Courts (Sentencing) Act 2000; or
(c) while he is being provided with accommodation[1] by or on behalf of a local authority.

(7) References in this Act to children who are in need shall be construed in accordance with section 17.

(8) Any notice or other document required under this Act to be served on any person may be served on him by being delivered personally to him, or being sent by post to him in a registered letter or by the recorded delivery service at his proper address.

(9) Any such notice or other document required to be served on a body corporate or a firm shall be duly served if it is served on the secretary or clerk of that body or a partner of that firm.

(10) For the purposes of this section, and of section 7 of the Interpretation Act 1978 in its application to this section, the proper address of a person—

(a) in the case of a secretary or clerk of a body corporate, shall be that of the registered or principal office of that body;
(b) in the case of a partner of a firm, shall be that of the principal office of the firm; and
(c) in any other case, shall be the last known address of the person to be served.

[Children Act 1989, s 105 as amended by the Registered Homes (Amendment) Act 1991, s 2, the Education Act 1993, Sch 19, the Local Government (Wales) Act 1994, Sch 10, the Health Authorities Act 1995, Schs 1 and 3, the Jobseekers Act 1995, Sch 2, the Education Act 1996, Sch 37, the Family Law Act 1996, Sch 6, SI 2000/90, the Local Government Act 2000, s 107, the Powers of Criminal Courts (Sentencing) Act 2000, Sch 9, the Care Standards Act 2000, Schs 4 and 6, SI 2002/2469, the Children Act 2004, Sch 3, the Adoption and Children Act 2002, Sch 3 and the Civil Partnership Act 2004, s 75.]

---

*Repealed by the Care Standards Act 2000, Sch 6. In force in relation to Wales from 1 April 2002, with regards to England, in force from a date to be appointed.

1. Where a local authority fulfils its duty under s 23(6) of the Act to make arrangements to enable a looked-after child to live with a person or family to whom he is closely related, or with whom he is closely connected, the child ceases to be "provided with accommodation" within the meaning of s 105(6)(c) and begins to live with the relative or family arranged by the local authority: *In re H (A Child) (Care Order: Appropriate Local Authority)* [2003] EWCA Civ 1629, [2004] Fam 89, [2004] 2 WLR 419, [2004] 1 FLR 534.

6–2255   106. *Financial provisions.*

6–2256   107. Application to Channel Islands.   Her Majesty may by Order in Council direct that any of the provisions of this Act shall extend to any of the Channel Islands with such exceptions and modifications as may be specified in the Order.
[Children Act 1989, s 107.]

6–2257   108. Short title, commencement, extent etc.   (1) This Act may be cited as the Children Act 1989.

(2) Sections 89 and 96(3) to (7), and paragraph 35 of Schedule 12, shall come into force on the passing of this Act and paragraph 36 of Schedule 12 shall come into force at the end of the period of two months beginning with the day on which this Act is passed but otherwise this Act shall come into force on such date as may be appointed by order[1] made by the Lord Chancellor or the Secretary of State, or by both acting jointly.

(3) Different dates may be appointed for different provisions of this Act and in relation to different cases.

(4) The minor amendments set out in Schedule 12 shall have effect.

(5) The consequential amendments set out in Schedule 13 shall have effect.

(6) The transitional provisions and savings set out in Schedule 14 shall have effect.

(7) The repeals set out in Schedule 15 shall have effect.

(8) An order under subsection (2) may make such transitional provisions or savings as appear to the person making the order to be necessary or expedient in connection with the provisions brought into force by the order, including—

(a) provisions adding to or modifying the provisions of Schedule 14; and
(b) such adaptations—

(i) of the provisions brought into force by the order; and
(ii) of any provisions of this Act then in force,

as appear to him necessary or expedient in consequence of the partial operation of this Act.

(9) The Lord Chancellor may by order make such amendments or repeals, in such enactments as may be specified in the order, as appear to him to be necessary or expedient in consequence of any provision of this Act.

(10) This Act shall, in its application to the Isles of Scilly, have effect subject to such exceptions, adaptations and modifications as the Secretary of State may by order prescribe.

(11) The following provisions of this Act extend to Scotland—

section 19;
section 25(8);
section 50(13);
section 88;
section 104 (so far as necessary);
section 105 (so far as necessary);
subsections (1) to (3), (8) and (9) and this subsection;
in Schedule 2, paragraph 24;
in Schedule 12, paragraphs 1, 7 to 10, 18, 27, 30(a) and 41 to 44;
in Schedule 13, paragraphs 18 to 23, 32, 46, 47, 50, 57, 62, 63, 68(a) and (b) and 71;
in Schedule 14, paragraphs 1, 33 and 34;
in Schedule 15, the entries relating to—

(a) the Custody of Children Act 1891;
(b) the Nurseries and Child Minders Regulation Act 1948;
(c) section 53(3) of the Children and Young Persons Act 1963;
(d) section 60 of the Health Services and Public Health Act 1968;
(e) the Social Work (Scotland) Act 1968;
(f) the Adoption (Scotland) Act 1978;
(g) the Child Care Act 1980;
(h) the Foster Children (Scotland) Act 1984;
(i) the Child Abduction and Custody Act 1985; and
(j) the Family Law Act 1986.

(12) The following provisions of this Act extend to Northern Ireland—

section 50;
section 101(1)(b), (2) and (5)(a)(i);
subsections (1) to (3), (8) and (9) and this subsection;
in Schedule 2, paragraph 24;
in Schedule 12, paragraphs 7 to 10, 18 and 27;
in Schedule 13, paragraphs 21, 22, 46, 47, 57, 62, 63, 68(c) to (e), and 69 to 71;
in Schedule 14, paragraphs 28 to 30 and 38(a); and
in Schedule 15, the entries relating to the Guardianship of Minors Act 1971, the Children Act 1975, the Child Care Act 1980, and the Family Law Act 1986.

[Children Act 1989, s 108 as amended by the Courts and Legal Services Act 1990, Schs 16 and 20.]

---

1. See the Children Act 1989 (Commencement and Transitional Provisions) Order 1991, SI 1991/828, amended by SI 1991/1990.

SCHEDULES

Section 15(1)   SCHEDULE 1

FINANCIAL PROVISION FOR CHILDREN

(*As amended by the Courts and Legal Services Act 1990, Sch 16, the Maintenance Enforcement Act 1991 s 6, the Child Support Act 1991, s 58, SI 1992/709, SI 1993/623, SI 1994/731, the Justices of the Peace Act 1997, Sch 5 and the Access to Justice Act 1999, Sch 15, the Adoption and Children Act 2002, Sch 3 and the Civil Partnership Act 2004, s 78.*)

Orders for financial relief against parents

6–2258   **1.** (1) On an application made by a parent, guardian or special guardian of a child, or by any person in whose favour a residence order is in force with respect to a child, the court may[1]—

     (*a*) in the case of an application to the High Court or a county court, make one or more of the orders mentioned in sub-paragraph (2);

     (*b*) in the case of an application to a magistrates' court, make one or both of the orders mentioned in paragraphs (*a*) and (*c*) of that sub-paragraph.

     (2) The orders referred to in sub-paragraph (1) are—

     (*a*) an order requiring either or both parents of a child—

         (i)   to make to the applicant for the benefit of the child; or
         (ii)   to make to the child himself,

     such periodical payments, for such term, as may be specified in the order;

     (*b*) an order requiring either or both parents of a child—

         (i)   to secure to the applicant for the benefit of the child; or
         (ii)   to secure to the child himself,

     such periodical payments, for such term, as may be so specified;

     (*c*) an order requiring either or both parents of a child—

         (i)   to pay to the applicant for the benefit of the child; or
         (ii)   to pay to the child himself,

     such lump sum[2] as may be so specified;

     (*d*) an order requiring a settlement to be made for the benefit of the child, and to the satisfaction of the court, of property—

         (i)   to which either parent is entitled (either in possession or in reversion); and
         (ii)   which is specified in the order;

     (*e*) an order requiring either or both parents of a child—

         (i)   to transfer[3] to the applicant, for the benefit of the child; or
         (ii)   to transfer to the child himself,

     such property to which the parent is, or the parents are, entitled (either in possession or in reversion) as may be specified in the order.

     (3) The powers conferred by this paragraph may be exercised at any time.

     (4) An order under sub-paragraph (2)(*a*) or (*b*) may be varied or discharged by a subsequent order made on the application of any person by or to whom payments were required to be made under the previous order.

     (5) Where a court makes an order under this paragraph—

     (*a*) it may at any time make a further such order under sub-paragraph (2)(*a*), (*b*) or (*c*) with respect to the child concerned if he has not reached the age of eighteen;

     (*b*) it may not make more than one order under sub-paragraph (2)(*d*) or (*e*) against the same person in respect of the same child[4].

     (6) On making, varying or discharging a residence order or a special guardianship order the court may exercise any of its powers under this Schedule even though no application has been made to it under this Schedule.

     (7) Where a child is a ward of court, the court may exercise any of its powers under this Schedule even though no application has been made to it.

---

1. When considering an application for financial relief for a child, the welfare of the child is not the court's paramount consideration. Since a child's upbringing is defined by s 105(1) of the Children Act 1989 as not including questions of maintenance, s 1(1) of the Act does not apply to an application for a financial provision under Sch 1. Nevertheless, the welfare of the child is a relevant consideration, even if not paramount or the first consideration (*J v C (child: financial provision)* [1999] 1 FLR 152). Section 1(5) of the Act, ante, has no relevance to an application under this Schedule (*K v H (financial provision for child)* [1993] 1 FCR 683, [1993] 2 FLR 61). The court has jurisdiction to make an order for financial relief under Sch 1 notwithstanding the parent's bankruptcy (*Re G (Children Act 1989, Sch 1)* [1996] 2 FLR 171).

2. A lump sum may only be ordered to meet a particular item of capital expenditure and not to provide for regular support of a child which would otherwise have been provided by way of periodic payments (*Phillips v Peace* [1996] 2 FCR 237, [1996] 2 FLR 230).

3. It may be possible to rely on this provision to achieve what is in effect an ouster order in circumstances where such an order is not available under the Domestic Violence and Matrimonial Proceedings Act 1976; see *Pearson v Franklin* [1994] 2 All ER 137, [1994] 1 WLR 370, [1994] 1 FLR 246.

4. The "or" is disjunctive and a transfer of property order is precluded where a settlement of property has already been made. It is also a misuse of the court's power to make a lump sum order as a means of circumventing this restriction, *Phillips v Peace* [2004] EWHC 3180 (Fam), [2005] 1 WLR 3246, [2005] 2 FCR 264, [2005] 2 FLR 1212.

Orders for financial relief for persons over eighteen

6–2259   **2.**—(1) If, on an application by a person who has reached the age of eighteen, it appears to the court—

(a) that the applicant is, will be or (if an order were made under this paragraph) would be receiving instruction at an educational establishment or undergoing training for a trade, profession or vocation, whether or not while in gainful employment; or

(b) that there are special circumstances which justify the making of an order under this paragraph,

the court may make one or both of the orders mentioned in sub-paragraph (2).

(2) The orders are—

(a) an order requiring either or both of the applicant's parents to pay to the applicant such periodical payments, for such term, as may be specified in the order;

(b) an order requiring either or both of the applicant's parents to pay to the applicant such lump sum as may be so specified.

(3) An application may not be made under this paragraph by any person if, immediately before he reached the age of sixteen, a periodical payments order was in force with respect to him.

(4) No order shall be made under this paragraph at a time when the parents of the applicant are living with each other in the same household.

(5) An order under sub-paragraph (2)(a) may be varied or discharged by a subsequent order made on the application of any person by or to whom payments were required to be made under the previous order.

(6) In sub-paragraph (3) "periodical payments order" means an order made under—

(a) this Schedule;

(b) *repealed*;

(c) section 23 or 27 of the Matrimonial Causes Act 1973;

(d) Part I of the Domestic Proceedings and Magistrates' Courts Act 1978;

(e) Part 1 or 9 of Schedule 5 to the Civil Partnership Act 2004 (financial relief in the High Court or a county court etc);

(f) Schedule 6 to the 2004 Act (financial relief in the magistrates' courts etc),

for the making or securing of periodical payments.

(7) The powers conferred by this paragraph shall be exercisable at any time.

(8) Where the court makes an order under this paragraph it may from time to time while that order remains in force make a further such order.

Duration of orders for financial relief

6–2260   **3.**—(1) The term to be specified in an order for periodical payments made under paragraph 1(2)(a) or (b) in favour of a child may begin with the date of the making of an application for the order in question or any later date or a date ascertained in accordance with sub-paragraph (5) or (6) but—

(a) shall not in the first instance extend beyond the child's seventeenth birthday unless the court thinks it right in the circumstances of the case to specify a later date; and

(b) shall not in any event extend beyond the child's eighteenth birthday.

(2) Paragraph (b) of sub-paragraph (1) shall not apply in the case of a child if it appears to the court that—

(a) the child is, or will be or (if an order were made without complying with that paragraph) would be receiving instruction at an educational establishment or undergoing training for a trade, profession or vocation, whether or not while in gainful employment; or

(b) there are special circumstances[1] which justify the making of an order without complying with that paragraph.

(3) An order for periodical payments made under paragraph 1(2)(a) or 2(2)(a) shall, notwithstanding anything in the order, cease to have effect on the death of the person liable to make payments under the order.

(4) Where an order is made under paragraph 1(2)(a) or (b) requiring periodical payments to be made or secured to the parent of a child, the order shall cease to have effect if—

(a) any parent making or securing the payments; and

(b) any parent to whom the payments are made or secured,

live together for a period of more than six months.

(5) Where—

(a) a maintenance assessment★ ("the current assessment★") is in force with respect to a child; and

(b) an application is made for an order under paragraph 1(2)(a) or (b) of this Schedule for periodical payments in favour of that child—

(i) in accordance with section 8 of the Child Support Act 1991; and

(ii) before the end of the period of 6 months beginning with the making of the current assessment★,

the term to be specified in any such order made on that application may be expressed to begin on, or at any time after, the earliest permitted date.

(6) For the purposes of subsection (5) above, "the earliest permitted date" is whichever is the later of—

(a) the date 6 months before the application is made; or

(b) the date on which the current assessment★ took effect or, where successive maintenance assessments★ have been continuously in force with respect to a child, on which the first of those assessments★ took effect.

(7) Where—

(a) a maintenance assessment★ ceases to have effect or is cancelled by or under any provision of the Child Support Act 1991, and

(b) an application is made, before the end of the period of 6 months beginning with the relevant date, for an order for periodical payments under paragraph 1(2)(a) or (b) in favour of a child with respect to whom that maintenance assessment★ was in force immediately before it ceased to have effect or was cancelled★★, the term to be specified in any such order, or in any interim order under paragraph 9, made on that application may begin with the date on which that maintenance assessment★ ceased to have effect or, as the case may be, the date with effect from which it was cancelled,★★ or any later date.

(8) In sub-paragraph (7)(*b*)—

(*a*) where the maintenance assessment★ ceased to have effect, the relevant date is the date on which it so ceased; and★★

(*b*) where the maintenance assessment★ was cancelled, the relevant date is the later of—

(i) the date on which the person who cancelled it did so, and

(ii) the date from which the cancellation first had effect.★★

★Paragraph 3 is amended by the Child Support, Pensions and Social Security Act 2000, Sch 3, when in force.
★★Repealed by the Child Support, Pensions and Social Security Act 2000, Sch 9, when in force.
1. The "special circumstances" ordinarily will relate to the children, such for example, as some physical or other handicap. Special circumstances will not include a father's seeming unwillingness to make an accurate disclosure of his present means, or his prospects for the future, or the difficulty, if not impossibility, of the mother or the children being able to establish in the future his then resources or prospects (*T v S (financial provision for children)* [1994] 1 FCR 743).

Matters to which court is to have regard in making orders for financial relief

6–2261 **4.**—(1) In deciding whether to exercise its powers under paragraph 1 or 2, and if so in what manner, the court shall have regard to all the circumstances[1] including—

(*a*) the income, earning capacity, property and other financial resources[2] which each person mentioned in sub-paragraph (4) has or is likely to have in the foreseeable future;

(*b*) the financial needs, obligations and responsibilities which each person mentioned in sub-paragraph (4) has or is likely to have in the foreseeable future;

(*c*) the financial needs of the child;

(*d*) the income, earning capacity (if any), property and other financial resources of the child;

(*e*) any physical or mental disability of the child;

(*f*) the manner in which the child was being, or was expected to be, educated or trained.

(2) In deciding whether to exercise its powers under paragraph 1 against a person who is not the mother or father of the child, and if so in what manner, the court shall in addition have regard to—

(*a*) whether that person had assumed responsibility for the maintenance of the child and, if so, the extent to which and basis on which he assumed that responsibility and the length of the period during which he met that responsibility;

(*b*) whether he did so knowing that the child was not his child;

(*c*) the liability of any other person to maintain the child.

(3) Where the court makes an order under paragraph 1 against a person who is not the father of the child, it shall record in the order that the order is made on the basis that the person against whom the order is made is not the child's father.

(4) The persons mentioned in sub-paragraph (1) are—

(*a*) in relation to a decision whether to exercise its powers under paragraph 1, any parent of the child;

(*b*) in relation to a decision whether to exercise its powers under paragraph 2, the mother and father of the child;

(*c*) the applicant for the order;

(*d*) any other person in whose favour the court proposes to make the order.

---

1. Although the court must have regard to all the circumstances, no great significance should be attached to the issue of whether a pregnancy was planned or otherwise (*J v C (child: financial provision)* [1999] 1 FLR 152).
2. A child is entitled to be brought up in circumstances which bear some sort of relationship with the father's current resources and the father's present standard of living. The acquisition of wealth after the breakdown of the marriage does not affect that proposition (*J v C (child: financial provision)* [1999] 1 FLR 152). Where one or both of the parents' means lie somewhere on the spectrum from affluent to fabulously rich, the starting point for the judge should be to decide, at least generically, the home that the respondent should provide for the child (see *Re P (a child) (financial provisions)* [2003] EWCA Civ 837, [2003] 2 FCR 481).

Provisions relating to lump sums

6–2262 **5.**—(1) Without prejudice to the generality of paragraph 1, an order under that paragraph for the payment of a lump sum may be made for the purpose of enabling any liabilities or expenses—

(*a*) incurred in connection with the birth of the child or in maintaining the child; and

(*b*) reasonably incurred before the making of the order,

to be met.

(2) The amount of any lump sum required to be paid by an order made by a magistrates' court under paragraph 1 or 2 shall not exceed £1000 or such larger amount as the Lord Chancellor may from time to time by order fix for the purposes of this sub-paragraph.★

(3) The power of the court under paragraph 1 or 2 to vary or discharge an order for the making or securing of periodical payments by a parent shall include power to make an order under that provision for the payment of a lump sum by that parent.

(4) The amount of any lump sum which a parent may be required to pay by virtue of sub-paragraph (3) shall not, in the case of an order made by a magistrates' court, exceed the maximum amount that may at the time of the making of the order be required to be paid under sub-paragraph (2), but a magistrates' court may make an order

for the payment of a lump sum not exceeding that amount even though the parent was required to pay a lump sum by a previous order under this Act.

(5) An order made under paragraph 1 or 2 for the payment of a lump sum may provide for the payment of that sum by instalments.

(6) Where the court provides for the payment of a lump sum by instalments the court, on an application made either by the person liable to pay or the person entitled to receive that sum, shall have power to vary that order by varying—

(*a*) the number of instalments payable;

(*b*) the amount of any instalment payable;

(*c*) the date on which any instalment becomes payable.★

★Paragraph 5(2) amended and new sub-para (7) inserted by the Constitutional Reform Act, Sch 4, from a date to be appointed.

Variation etc of orders for periodical payments

6–2263   **6.** (1) In exercising its powers under paragraph 1 or 2 to vary or discharge an order for the making or securing of periodical payments the court shall have regard to all the circumstances of the case, including any change in any of the matters to which the court was required to have regard when making the order.

(2) The power of the court under paragraph 1 or 2 to vary an order for the making or securing of periodical payments shall include power to suspend any provision of the order temporarily and to revive any provision so suspended.

(3) Where on an application under paragraph 1 or 2 for the variation or discharge of an order for the making or securing of periodical payments the court varies the payments required to be made under that order, the court may provide that the payments as so varied shall be made from such date as the court may specify, except that, subject to sub-paragraph (9), the date shall not be earlier than the date of the making of the application.

(4) An application for the variation of an order made under paragraph 1 for the making or securing of periodical payments to or for the benefit of a child may, if the child has reached the age of sixteen, be made by the child himself.

(5) Where an order for the making or securing of periodical payments made under paragraph 1 ceases to have effect on the date on which the child reaches the age of sixteen, or at any time after that date but before or on the date on which he reaches the age of eighteen, the child may apply to the court which made the order for an order for its revival.

(6) If on such an application it appears to the court that—

(*a*) the child is, will be or (if an order were made under this sub-paragraph) would be receiving instruction at an educational establishment or undergoing training for a trade, profession or vocation, whether or not while in gainful employment; or

(*b*) there are special circumstances which justify the making of an order under this paragraph,

the court shall have power by order to revive the order from such date as the court may specify, not being earlier than the date of the making of the application.

(7) Any order which is revived by an order under sub-paragraph (5) may be varied or discharged under that provision, on the application of any person by whom or to whom payments are required to be made under the revived order.

(8) An order for the making or securing of periodical payments made under paragraph 1 may be varied or discharged, after the death of either parent, on the application of a guardian or special guardian of the child concerned.

(9) Where—

(*a*) an order under paragraph 1(2)(*a*) or (*b*) for the making or securing of periodical payments in favour of more than one child ("the order") is in force;

(*b*) the order requires payments specified in it to be made to or for the benefit of more than one child without apportioning those payments between them;

(*c*) a maintenance assessment★ ("the assessment★") is made with respect to one or more, but not all, of the children with respect to whom those payments are to be made; and

(*d*) an application is made, before the end of the period of 6 months beginning with the date on which the assessment★ was made, for the variation or discharge of the order,

the court may, in exercise of its powers under paragraph 1 to vary or discharge the order direct that the variation or discharge shall take effect from the date on which the assessment★ took effect or any later date.

★Paragraph 6 is amended by the Child Support, Pensions and Social Security Act 2000, Sch 3, when in force.

Variation of orders for periodical payments etc made by magistrates' courts

6–2264   **6A.** (1) Subject to sub-paragraphs (7) and (8), the power of a magistrates' court—

(*a*) under paragraph 1 or 2 to vary an order for the making of periodical payments, or

(*b*) under paragraph 5(6) to vary an order for the payment of a lump sum by instalments,

shall include power, if the court is satisfied that payment has not been made in accordance with the order, to exercise one of its powers under paragraphs (*a*) to (*d*) of section 59(3) of the Magistrates' Courts Act 1980.

(2) In any case where—

(*a*) a magistrates' court has made an order under this Schedule for the making of periodical payments or for the payment of a lump sum by instalments, and

(*b*) payments under the order are required to be made by any method of payment falling within section 59(6) of the Magistrates' Courts Act 1980 (standing order, etc), any person entitled to make an application under this Schedule for the variation of the order (in this paragraph referred to as "the applicant") may apply to the clerk to the justices for the petty sessions area for which the court is acting for the order to be varied as mentioned in sub-paragraph (3).

(3) Subject to sub-paragraph (5), where an application is made under sub-paragraph (2), the clerk, after giving written notice (by post or otherwise) of the application to any interested party and allowing that party, within the period of 14 days beginning with the date of the giving of that notice, an opportunity to make written representations, may vary the order to provide that payments under the order shall be made to the justices' chief executive for the court.

(4) The clerk may proceed with an application under sub-paragraph (2) notwithstanding that any such interested party as is referred to in sub-paragraph (3) has not received written notice of the application.

(5) Where an application has been made under sub-paragraph (2), the clerk may, if he considers it inappropriate to exercise his power under sub-paragraph (3), refer the matter to the court which, subject to sub-paragraphs (7) and (8), may vary the order by exercising one of its powers under paragraphs (*a*) to (*d*) of section 59(3) of the Magistrates' Courts Act 1980.

(6) Subsection (4) of section 59 of the Magistrates' Courts Act 1980 (power of court to order that account be opened) shall apply for the purposes of sub-paragraphs (1) and (5) as it applies for the purposes of that section.

(7) Before varying the order by exercising one of its powers under paragraphs (*a*) to (*d*)) of section 59(3) of the Magistrates' Courts Act 1980, the court shall have regard to any representations made by the parties to the application.

(8) If the court does not propose to exercise its power under paragraph (*c*), (*cc*) or (*d*) of subsection (3) of section 59 of the Magistrates' Courts Act 1980, the court shall, unless upon representations expressly made in that behalf by the applicant for the order it is satisfied that it is undesirable to do so, exercise its power under paragraph (*b*) of that subsection.

(9) None of the powers of the court, or of the clerk to the justices, conferred by this paragraph shall be exercisable in relation to an order under this Schedule for the making of periodical payments, or for the payment of a lump sum by instalments, which is not a qualifying maintenance order (within the meaning of section 59 of the Magistrates' Courts Act 1980).

(10) In sub-paragraphs (3) and (4) "interested party", in relation to an application made by the applicant under sub-paragraph (2), means a person who would be entitled to be a party to an application for the variation of the order made by the applicant under any other provision of this Schedule if such an application were made.

Variation of orders for secured periodical payments after death of parent

6–2265 **7.** (1) Where the parent liable to make payments under a secured periodical payments order has died, the persons who may apply for the variation or discharge of the order shall include the personal representatives of the deceased parent.

(2) No application for the variation of the order shall, except with the permission of the court, be made after the end of the period of six months from the date on which representation in regard to the estate of that parent is first taken out.

(3) The personal representatives of a deceased person against whom a secured periodical payments order was made shall not be liable for having distributed any part of the estate of the deceased after the end of the period of six months referred to in sub-paragraph (2) on the ground that they ought to have taken into account the possibility that the court might permit an application for variation to be made after that period by the person entitled to payments under the order.

(4) Sub-paragraph (3) shall not prejudice any power to recover any part of the estate so distributed arising by virtue of the variation of an order in accordance with this paragraph.

(5) Where an application to vary a secured periodical payments order is made after the death of the parent liable to make payments under the order, the circumstances to which the court is required to have regard under paragraph 6(1) shall include the changed circumstances resulting from the death of the parent.

(6) In considering for the purposes of sub-paragraph (2) the question when representation was first taken out, a grant limited to settled land or to trust property shall be left out of account and a grant limited to real estate or to personal estate shall be left out of account unless a grant limited to the remainder of the estate has previously been made or is made at the same time.

(7) In this paragraph "secured periodical payments order" means an order for secured periodical payments under paragraph 1(2)(*b*).

Financial relief under other enactments

6–2266 **8.** (1) This paragraph applies where a residence order[1] or a special guardianship order is made with respect to a child at a time when there is in force an order ("the financial relief order") made under any enactment other than this Act and requiring a person to contribute to the child's maintenance.

(2) Where this paragraph applies, the court may, on the application of—

(*a*) any person required by the financial relief order to contribute to the child's maintenance; or

(*b*) any person in whose favour a residence order or a special guardianship order with respect to the child is in force,

make an order revoking the financial relief order, or varying it by altering the amount of any sum payable under that order or by substituting the applicant for the person to whom any such sum is otherwise payable under that order.

---

1. The making of a residence order is not a condition precedent to the continuing validity of financial provision orders. An order under the Guardianship of Minors Act 1971 may be varied under s 11(*b*) of the 1971 Act by virtue of the Interpretation Act 1978 s 16(1) (*B v B (children: periodical payments)* [1995] 1 WLR 440, [1995] 1 FCR 763, [1995] 1 FLR 459).

Interim orders

6–2267 **9.** (1) Where an application is made under paragraph 1 or 2 the court may, at any time before it disposes of the application, make an interim order—

(a) requiring either or both parents to make such periodical payments, at such times and for such term as the court thinks fit; and

(b) giving any direction which the court thinks fit.

(2) An interim order made under this paragraph may provide for payments to be made from such date as the court may specify, except that, subject to paragraph 3(5) and (6), the date shall not be earlier than the date of the making of the application under paragraph 1 or 2.

(3) An interim order made under this paragraph shall cease to have effect when the application is disposed of or, if earlier, on the date specified for the purposes of this paragraph in the interim order.

(4) An interim order in which a date has been specified for the purposes of sub-paragraph (3) may be varied by substituting a later date.

Alteration of maintenance agreements

6–2268　10. (1) In this paragraph and in paragraph 11 "maintenance agreement" means any agreement in writing made with respect to a child, whether before or after the commencement of this paragraph, which—

(a) is or was made between the father and mother of the child; and

(b) contains provision with respect to the making or securing of payments, or the disposition or use of any property, for the maintenance or education of the child,

and any such provisions are in this paragraph, and paragraph 11, referred to as "financial arrangements".

(2) Where a maintenance agreement is for the time being subsisting and each of the parties to the agreement is for the time being either domiciled or resident in England and Wales, then, either party may apply to the court for an order under this paragraph.

(3) If the court to which the application is made is satisfied either—

(a) that, by reason of a change in the circumstances in the light of which any financial arrangements contained in the agreement were made (including a change foreseen by the parties when making the agreement), the agreement should be altered so as to make different financial arrangements; or

(b) that the agreement does not contain proper financial arrangements with respect to the child,

then that court may by order make such alterations in the agreement by varying or revoking any financial arrangements contained in it as may appear to it to be just having regard to all the circumstances.

(4) If the maintenance agreement is altered by an order under this paragraph, the agreement shall have effect thereafter as if the alteration had been made by agreement between the parties and for valuable consideration.

(5) Where a court decides to make an order under this paragraph altering the maintenance agreement—

(a) by inserting provision for the making or securing by one of the parties to the agreement of periodical payments for the maintenance of the child; or

(b) by increasing the rate of periodical payments required to be made or secured by one of the parties for the maintenance of the child,

then, in deciding the term for which under the agreement as altered by the order the payments or (as the case may be) the additional payments attributable to the increase are to be made or secured for the benefit of the child, the court shall apply the provisions of sub-paragraphs (1) and (2) of paragraph 3 as if the order were an order under paragraph 1(2)(a) or (b).

(6) A magistrates' court shall not entertain an application under sub-paragraph (2) unless both the parties to the agreement are resident in England and Wales and at least one of the parties is resident in the commission area for which the court is appointed, and shall not have power to make any order on such an application except—

(a) in a case where the agreement contains no provision for periodical payments by either of the parties, an order inserting provision for the making by one of the parties of periodical payments for the maintenance of the child;

(b) in a case where the agreement includes provision for the making by one of the parties of periodical payments, an order increasing or reducing the rate of, or terminating, any of those payments.

(7) For the avoidance of doubt it is hereby declared that nothing in this paragraph affects any power of a court before which any proceedings between the parties to a maintenance agreement are brought under any other enactment to make an order containing financial arrangements or any right of either party to apply for such an order in such proceedings.

6–2269　11. (1) Where a maintenance agreement provides for the continuation, after the death of one of the parties, of payments for the maintenance of a child and that party dies domiciled in England and Wales, the surviving party or the personal representatives of the deceased party may apply to the High Court or a county court for an order under paragraph 10.

(2) If a maintenance agreement is altered by a court on an application under this paragraph, the agreement shall have effect thereafter as if the alteration had been made, immediately before the death, by agreement between the parties and for valuable consideration.

(3) An application under this paragraph shall not, except with leave of the High Court or a county court, be made after the end of the period of six months beginning with the day on which representation in regard to the estate of the deceased is first taken out.

(4) In considering for the purposes of sub-paragraph (3) the question when representation was first taken out, a grant limited to settled land or to trust property shall be left out of account and a grant limited to real estate or to personal estate shall be left out of account unless a grant limited to the remainder of the estate has previously been made or is made at the same time.

(5) A county court shall not entertain an application under this paragraph, or an application for leave to make an application under this paragraph, unless it would have jurisdiction to hear and determine proceedings for an order under section 2 of the Inheritance (Provision for Family and Dependants) Act 1975 in relation to the deceased's estate by virtue of section 25 of the County Courts Act 1984 (jurisdiction under the Act of 1975).

(6) The provisions of this paragraph shall not render the personal representatives of the deceased liable for having distributed any part of the estate of the deceased after the expiry of the period of six months referred to in

sub-paragraph (3) on the ground that they ought to have taken into account the possibility that a court might grant leave for an application by virtue of this paragraph to be made by the surviving party after that period.

(7) Sub-paragraph (6) shall not prejudice any power to recover any part of the estate so distributed arising by virtue of the making of an order in pursuance of this paragraph.

Enforcement of orders for maintenance

6–2270   **12.** (1) Any person for the time being under an obligation to make payments in pursuance of any order for the payment of money made by a magistrates' court under this Act shall give notice of any change of address to such person (if any) as may be specified in the order.

(2) Any person failing without reasonable excuse to give such a notice shall be guilty of an offence and liable on summary conviction to a fine not exceeding **level 2** on the standard scale.

(3) An order for the payment of money made by a magistrates' court under this Act shall be enforceable as a magistrates' court maintenance order within the meaning of section 150(1) of the Magistrates' Courts Act 1980.

Direction for settlement of instrument by conveyancing counsel

6–2280   **13.** Where the High Court or a county court decides to make an order under this Act for the securing of periodical payments or for the transfer or settlement of property, it may direct that the matter be referred to one of the conveyancing counsel of the court to settle a proper instrument to be executed by all necessary parties.

Financial provision for child resident in country outside England and Wales

6–2281   **14.** (1) Where one parent of a child lives in England and Wales and the child lives outside England and Wales with—

(*a*)   another parent of his;
(*b*)   a guardian or special guardian of his; or
(*c*)   a person in whose favour a residence order is in force with respect to the child,

the court shall have power, on an application made by any of the persons mentioned in paragraphs (*a*) to (*c*), to make one or both of the orders mentioned in paragraph 1(2)(*a*) and (*b*) against the parent living in England and Wales.

(2) Any reference in this Act to the powers of the court under paragraph 1(2) or to an order made under paragraph 1(2) shall include a reference to the powers which the court has by virtue of sub-paragraph (1) or (as the case may be) to an order made by virtue of sub-paragraph (1).

Local authority contribution to child's maintenance

6–2282   **15.** (1) Where a child lives, or is to live, with a person as the result of a residence order, a local authority may make contributions to that person towards the cost of the accommodation and maintenance of the child.

(2) Sub-paragraph (1) does not apply where the person with whom the child lives, or is to live, is a parent of the child or the husband or wife or civil partner of a parent of the child.

Interpretation

6–2283   **16.** (1) In this Schedule "child" includes, in any case where an application is made under paragraph 2 or 6 in relation to a person who has reached the age of eighteen, that person.

(2) In this Schedule, except paragraphs 2 and 15, "parent" includes—

(*a*)   any party to a marriage (whether or not subsisting) in relation to whom the child concerned is a child of the family, and
(*b*)   any civil partner in a civil partnership (whether or not subsisting) in relation to whom the child concerned is a child of the family;

and for this purpose any reference to either parent or both parents shall be read as a reference to any parent of his and to all of his parents.

(3) In this Schedule, "maintenance assessment*" has the same meaning as it has in the Child Support Act 1991 by virtue of section 54 of that Act as read with any regulations in force under that section.

---

*Paragraph 16 is amended by the Child Support, Pensions and Social Security Act 2000, Sch 3, when in force.

Sections 17, 23 and 29   SCHEDULE 2
LOCAL AUTHORITY SUPPORT FOR CHILDREN AND FAMILIES

(As amended by the Courts and Legal Services Act 1990, Sch 16, the Disability Living Allowance and Disability Working Allowance Act 1991, Sch 3, the Social Security (Consequential Provisions) Act 1992, Sch 2, the Education Act 1993, Sch 19, the Jobseekers Act 1995, Sch 2, SI 1996/785, the Education Act 1996, Sch 37, the Tax Credits Act 1999, Sch 1, 2000/90, the Powers of Criminal Courts (Sentencing) Act 2000, Sch 9, the Children Leaving Care Act 2000, s 7, the Health and Social Care (Community Health and Standards) Act 2003, Sch 9 and the Adoption and Children Act 2002, Sch 3.)

PART I
PROVISION OF SERVICES FOR FAMILIES

Identification of children in need and provision of information

6–2284   **1.** (1) Every local authority shall take reasonable steps to identify the extent to which there are children in need within their area.

(2) Every local authority shall—

(a)　publish information—

    (i)　about services provided by them under sections 17, 18, 20 and 24; and
    (ii)　where they consider it appropriate, about the provision by others (including, in particular, voluntary organisations) of services which the authority have power to provide under those sections; and

(b)　take such steps as are reasonably practicable to ensure that those who might benefit from the services receive the information relevant to them.

Children's services plans

6–2284A　1A. (1)　Every local authority shall on or before 31st March 1997—

(a)　review their provision of services under sections 17, 20, 21, 23 and 24; and
(b)　having regard to that review and to their most recent review under section 19, prepare and publish a plan for the provision of services under Part III.

(2)　Every local authority—

(a)　shall, from time to time review the plan prepared by them under sub-paragraph (1)(b) (as modified or last substituted under this sub-paragraph), and
(b)　may, having regard to that review and to their most recent review under section 19, prepare and publish—

    (i)　modifications (or, as the case may be, further modifications) to the plan reviewed; or
    (ii)　a plan in substitution for that plan.

(3)　In carrying out any review under this paragraph and in preparing any plan or modifications to a plan, a local authority shall consult—

(a)　every Health Authority and Primary Care Trust the whole or any part of whose area lies within the area of the local authority;
(b)　every National Health Service trust which manages a hospital, establishment or facility (within the meaning of the National Health Service and Community Care Act 1990) in the authority's area;*
(c)　if the local authority is not itself a local education authority, every local education authority the whole or any part of whose area lies within the area of the local authority;
(d)　any organisation which represents schools in the authority's area which are grant-maintained schools or grant-maintained special schools (within the meaning of the Education Act 1993);
(e)　the governing body of every such school in the authority's area which is not so represented;
(f)　such voluntary organisations as appear to the local authority—

    (i)　to represent the interests of persons who use or are likely to use services provided by the local authority under Part III; or
    (ii)　to provide services in the area of the local authority which, were they to be provided by the local authority, might be categorised as services provided under that Part.

(g)　the chief constable of the police force for the area;
(h)　the probation committee for the area;
(i)　such other persons as appear to the local authority to be appropriate; and
(j)　such other persons as the Secretary of State may direct.

(4)　Every local authority shall, within 28 days of receiving a written request from the Secretary of State, submit to him a copy of—

(a)　the plan prepared by them under sub-paragraph (l); or
(b)　where that plan has been modified or substituted, the plan as modified or last substituted.

---

*New sub-para (ba) inserted by the Health and Social Care (Community Health and Standards) Act 2003, Sch 4, as from a date to be appointed.

Maintenance of a register of disabled children

6–2285　2. (1)　Every local authority shall open and maintain a register of disabled children within their area.
    (2)　The register may be kept by means of a computer.

Assessment of children's needs

6–2286　3.　Where it appears to a local authority that a child within their area is in need, the authority may assess his needs for the purposes of this Act at the same time as any assessment of his needs is made under—

(a)　the Chronically Sick and Disabled Persons Act 1970;
(b)　Part IV of the Education Act 1996;
(c)　the Disabled Persons (Services, Consultation and Representation) Act 1986; or
(d)　any other enactment.

Prevention of neglect and abuse

6–2287　4. (1)　Every local authority shall take reasonable steps, through the provision of services under Part III of this Act, to prevent children within their area suffering ill-treatment or neglect.
    (2)　Where a local authority believe that a child who is at any time within their area—

(a)　is likely to suffer harm; but
(b)　lives or proposes to live in the area of another local authority

they shall inform that other local authority.
    (3)　When informing that other local authority they shall specify—

(a)　the harm that they believe he is likely to suffer; and

(b) (if they can) where the child lives or proposes to live.

Provision of accommodation in order to protect child

6–2288   5. (1) Where—

(a) it appears to a local authority that a child who is living on particular premises is suffering, or is likely to suffer, ill treatment at the hands of another person who is living on those premises; and
(b) that other person proposes to move from the premises,

the authority may assist that other person to obtain alternative accommodation.

(2) Assistance given under this paragraph may be in cash.

(3) Subsections (7) to (9) of section 17 shall apply in relation to assistance given under this paragraph as they apply in relation to assistance given under that section.

Provision for disabled children

6–2289   6. Every local authority shall provide services designed—

(a) to minimise the effect on disabled children within their area of their disabilities; and
(b) to give such children the opportunity to lead lives which are as normal as possible.

Provision to reduce need for care proceedings etc

6–2290   7. Every local authority shall take reasonable steps designed—

(a) to reduce the need to bring—

(i) proceedings for care or supervision orders with respect to children within their area;
(ii) criminal proceedings against such children;
(iii) any family or other proceedings with respect to such children which might lead to them being placed in the authority's care; or
(iv) proceedings under the inherent jurisdiction of the High Court with respect to children;

(b) to encourage children within their area not to commit criminal offences; and
(c) to avoid the need for children within their area to be placed in secure accommodation.

Provision for children living with their families

6–2291   8. Every local authority shall make such provision as they consider appropriate for the following services to be available with respect to children in need within their area while they are living with their families—

(a) advice, guidance and counselling[1];
(b) occupational, social, cultural or recreational activities;
(c) home help (which may include laundry facilities);
(d) facilities for, or assistance with, travelling to and from home for the purpose of taking advantage of any other service provided under this Act or of any similar service;
(e) assistance to enable the child concerned and his family to have a holiday.

---

1. For commentary on the scope of this duty, see *Nottinghamshire County Council v P* [1993] 3 All ER 815, [1993] 2 FLR 134, CA.

Family centres

6–2292   9. (1) Every local authority shall provide such family centres as they consider appropriate in relation to children within their area.

(2) "Family centre" means a centre at which any of the persons mentioned in sub-paragraph (3) may—

(a) attend for occupational, social, cultural or recreational activities;
(b) attend for advice, guidance or counselling; or
(c) be provided with accommodation while he is receiving advice, guidance or counselling.

(3) The persons are—

(a) a child;
(b) his parents;
(c) any person who is not a parent of his but who has parental responsibility for him;
(d) any other person who is looking after him.

Maintenance of the family home

6–2293   10. Every local authority shall take such steps as are reasonably practicable, where any child within their area who is in need and whom they are not looking after is living apart from his family—

(a) to enable him to live with his family; or
(b) to promote contact between him and his family,

if, in their opinion, it is necessary to do so in order to safeguard or promote his welfare.

Duty to consider racial groups to which children in need belong

6–2294   11. Every local authority shall, in making any arrangements—

(a) for the provision of day care within their area; or
(b) designed to encourage persons to act as local authority foster parents,

have regard to the different racial groups to which children within their area who are in need belong.

PART II
CHILDREN LOOKED AFTER BY LOCAL AUTHORITIES

Regulations as to placing of children with local authority foster parents

6–2295   12. Regulations[1] under section 23(2)(*a*) may, in particular, make provision—

(*a*) with regard to the welfare of children placed with local authority foster parents;
(*b*) as to the arrangements to be made by local authorities in connection with the health and education of such children;
(*c*) as to the records to be kept by local authorities;
(*d*) for securing that a child is not placed with a local authority foster parent unless that person is for the time being approved as a local authority foster parent by such local authority as may be prescribed;
(*e*) for securing that where possible the local authority foster parent with whom a child is to be placed is—

   (i) of the same religious persuasion as the child; or
   (ii) gives an undertaking that the child will be brought up in that religious persuasion;

(*f*) for securing that children placed with local authority foster parents, and the premises in which they are accommodated, will be supervised and inspected by a local authority and that the children will be removed from those premises if their welfare appears to require it;
(*g*) as to the circumstances in which local authorities may make arrangements for duties imposed on them by the regulations to be discharged, on their behalf.

---

1. See the Arrangements for Placement of Children (General) Regulations 1991, SI 1991/890 amended by SI 1991/2033, SI 1993/3069 and SI 1995/2015, SI 1997/649, SI 2002/546 (England), 2469 and 2935 (Wales) and 3013 (W) and SI 2005/774 (W); the Fostering Services Regulations 2002, SI 2002/57 amended by SI 2002/865; the Fostering Services (Wales) Regulations 2003, SI 2003/237 amended by SI 2003/896 and SI 2005/3302. For disqualification as a foster parent, see *Re S (Foster Placement (Children) Regulations 1991)* [2000] 1 FLR 648, FD.

Regulations as to arrangements under section 23(2)(f)

6–2296   13. Regulations[1] under section 23(2)(*f*) may, in particular, make provision as to—

(*a*) the persons to be notified of any proposed arrangements;
(*b*) the opportunities such persons are to have to make representations in relation to the arrangements proposed;
(*c*) the persons to be notified of any proposed changes in arrangements;
(*d*) the records to be kept by local authorities;
(*e*) the supervision by local authorities of any arrangements made.

---

1. See the Arrangements for Placement of Children (General) Regulations 1991, SI 1991/890 amended by SI 1991/2033, SI 1993/3069 and SI 1995/2015, SI 1997/649, SI 2002/546 (England), 2469 and 2935 (Wales) and 3013 (W) and SI 2005/774 (W).

Regulations as to conditions under which child in care is allowed to live with parent, etc

6–2297   14. Regulations[1] under section 23(5) may, in particular, impose requirements on a local authority as to—

(*a*) the making of any decision by a local authority to allow a child to live with any person falling within section 23(4) (including requirements as to those who must be consulted before the decision is made, and those who must be notified when it has been made);
(*b*) the supervision or medical examination of the child concerned;
(*c*) the removal of the child, in such circumstances as may be prescribed, from the care of the person with whom he has been allowed to live;
(*d*) the records to be kept by local authorities.

---

1. See the Arrangements for Placement of Children (General) Regulations 1991, SI 1991/890 amended by SI 1991/2033, SI 1993/3069 and SI 1995/2015, SI 1991/649, SI 2002/546 (England) 2469 and 2935 (Wales) and the Placement of Children with Parents Regulations 1991, SI 1991/893 amended by SI 1995/2015 and SI 2002/546 (England), 2469 and 2935 (Wales) and 3013 (W) and SI 2005/774 (W).

Promotion and maintenance of contact between child and family

6–2298   15. (1) Where a child is being looked after by a local authority, the authority shall, unless it is not reasonably practicable or consistent with his welfare, endeavour to promote contact between the child and—

(*a*) his parents;
(*b*) any person who is not a parent of his but who has parental responsibility for him; and
(*c*) any relative, friend or other person connected with him.

(2) Where a child is being looked after by a local authority—

(*a*) the authority shall take such steps as are reasonably practicable to secure that—

   (i) his parents; and
   (ii) any person who is not a parent of his but who has parental responsibility for him,

   are kept informed of where he is being accommodated; and

(*b*) every such person shall secure that the authority are kept informed of his or her address.

(3) Where a local authority ("the receiving authority") take over the provision of accommodation for a child from another local authority ("the transferring authority") under section 20(2)—

(*a*) the receiving authority shall (where reasonably practicable) inform—

(i)   the child's parents; and
(ii) any person who is not a parent of his but who has parental responsibility for him;

(b) sub-paragraph (2)(a) shall apply to the transferring authority, as well as the receiving authority, until at least one such person has been informed of the change; and

(c) sub-paragraph (2)(b) shall not require any person to inform the receiving authority of his address until he has been so informed.

(4) Nothing in this paragraph requires a local authority to inform any person of the whereabouts of a child if—

(a) the child is in the care of the authority; and

(b) the authority has reasonable cause to believe that informing the person would prejudice the child's welfare.

(5) Any person who fails (without reasonable excuse) to comply with sub-paragraph (2)(b) shall be guilty of an offence and liable on summary conviction to a fine not exceeding **level 2** on the standard scale.

(6) It shall be a defence in any proceedings under sub-paragraph (5) to prove that the defendant was residing at the same address as another person who was the child's parent or had parental responsibility for the child and had reasonable cause to believe that the other person had informed the appropriate authority that both of them were residing at that address.

Visits to, or by, children: expenses

6–2299 **16.** (1) This paragraph applies where—

(a) a child is being looked after by a local authority; and
(b) the conditions mentioned in sub-paragraph (3) are satisfied.

(2) The authority may—

(a) make payments to—

(i)   a parent of the child;
(ii)   any person who is not a parent of his but who has parental responsibility for him; or
(iii) any relative, friend or other person connected with him,

in respect of travelling, subsistence or other expenses incurred by that person visiting the child; or

(b) make payments to the child, or to any person on his behalf, in respect of travelling, subsistence or other expenses incurred by or on behalf of the child in his visiting—

(i)   a parent of his;
(ii)   any person who is not a parent of his but who has parental responsibility for him; or
(iii) any relative, friend or other person connected with him.

(3) The conditions are that—

(a) it appears to the authority that the visit in question could not otherwise be made without undue financial hardship; and

(b) the circumstances warrant the making of the payments.

Appointment of visitor for child who is not being visited

6–2310 **17.** (1) Where it appears to a local authority in relation to any child that they are looking after that—

(a) communication between the child and—

(i)   a parent of his, or
(ii)   any person who is not a parent of his but who has parental responsibility for him,

has been infrequent; or

(b) he has not visited or been visited by (or lived with) any such person during the preceding twelve months,

and that it would be in the child's best interests for an independent person to be appointed to be his visitor for the purposes of this paragraph, they shall appoint such a visitor.

(2) A person so appointed shall—

(a) have the duty of visiting, advising and befriending the child; and

(b) be entitled to recover from the authority who appointed him any reasonable expenses incurred by him for the purposes of his functions under this paragraph.

(3) A person's appointment as a visitor in pursuance of this paragraph shall be determined if—

(a) he gives notice in writing to the authority who appointed him that he resigns the appointment; or

(b) the authority give him notice in writing that they have terminated it.

(4) The determination of such an appointment shall not prejudice any duty under this paragraph to make a further appointment.

(5) Where a local authority propose to appoint a visitor for a child under this paragraph, the appointment shall not be made if—

(a) the child objects to it; and

(b) the authority are satisfied that he has sufficient understanding to make an informed decision.

(6) Where a visitor has been appointed for a child under this paragraph, the local authority shall determine the appointment if—

(a) the child objects to its continuing; and

(b) the authority are satisfied that he has sufficient understanding to make an informed decision.

(7) The Secretary of State may make regulations[1] as to the circumstances in which a person appointed as a visitor under this paragraph is to be regarded as independent of the local authority appointing him.

1. See the Definition of Independent Visitors (Children) Regulations 1991, SI 1991/892 amended by SI 2001/2237.

Power to guarantee apprenticeship deeds etc

6–2311   18. (1) While a child is being looked after by a local authority, or is a person qualifying for advice and assistance, the authority may undertake any obligation by way of guarantee under any deed of apprenticeship or articles of clerkship which he enters into.

(2) Where a local authority have undertaken any such obligation under any deed or articles they may at any time (whether or not they are still looking after the person concerned) undertake the like obligation under any supplemental deed or articles.

Arrangements to assist children to live abroad

6–2312   19. (1) A local authority may only arrange for, or assist in arranging for, any child in their care to live outside England and Wales with the approval of the court[1].

(2) A local authority may, with the approval of every person who has parental responsibility for the child arrange for, or assist in arranging for, any other child looked after by them to live outside England and Wales.

(3) The court shall not give its approval under sub-paragraph (1) unless it is satisfied that—

(*a*) living outside England and Wales would be in the child's best interests;
(*b*) suitable arrangements have been, or will be, made for his reception and welfare in the country in which he will live;
(*c*) the child has consented to living in that country; and
(*d*) every person who has parental responsibility for the child has consented to his living in that country.

(4) Where the court is satisfied that the child does not have sufficient understanding to give or withhold his consent, it may disregard sub-paragraph (3)(*c*) and give its approval if the child is to live in the country concerned with a parent, guardian, special guardian or other suitable person.

(5) Where a person whose consent is required by sub-paragraph (3)(*d*) fails to give his consent, the court may disregard that provision and give its approval if it is satisfied[2] that that person—

(*a*) cannot be found;
(*b*) is incapable of consenting; or
(*c*) is withholding his consent unreasonably.

(6) Section 85 of the Adoption and Children Act 2002 (which imposes restrictions on taking children out of the United Kingdom) shall not apply in the case of any child who is to live outside England and Wales with the approval of the court given under this paragraph.[3]

(7) Where a court decides to give its approval under this paragraph it may order that its decision is not to have effect during the appeal period.

(8) In sub-paragraph (7) "the appeal period" means—

(*a*) where an appeal is made against the decision, the period between the making of the decision and the determination of the appeal; and
(*b*) otherwise, the period during which an appeal may be made against the decision.

(9) This paragraph does not apply to a local authority placing a child for adoption with prospective adopters.

1. For consideration of the application of this provision and the principles to be applied by the court, see *Re G (child in care: arrangements to live abroad)* [1994] 2 FCR 359, CA.
2. In determining whether or not parental consent is being withheld unreasonably the court must apply the test laid down in *Re W (an infant)* [1971] AC 682, *(Re G (child in care: arrangements to live abroad)* [1994] 2 FCR 359, CA).
3. The effect of paras 19(1) and 19(6) is that a local authority can place for adoption abroad a child in their care only if they obtain the approval of the court, such approval being necessary under para 19(1); court approval is necessary even if all those with parental responsibility for the child agreed and, thus, it must still be obtained even though the children in question have been freed for adoption (which vests sole parental authority in the local authority): *Re A (Adoption: Placement outside Jurisdiction)* [2004] EWCA 515, [2005] Fam 105, [2004] 3 WLR 1207 (sub nom *Re B (children) (adoption: removal from jurisdiction)* [2004] FCR 129.

Preparation for ceasing to be looked after

6–2312A   19A. It is the duty of the local authority looking after a child to advise, assist and befriend him with a view to promoting his welfare when they have ceased to look after him.

6–2312B   19B. (1) A local authority shall have the following additional functions in relation to an eligible child whom they are looking after.

(2) In sub-paragraph (1) "eligible child" means, subject to sub-paragraph (3), a child who—

(*a*) is aged sixteen or seventeen; and
(*b*) has been looked after by a local authority for a prescribed[1] period, or periods amounting in all to a prescribed period, which began after he reached a prescribed age and ended after he reached the age of sixteen.

(3) The Secretary of State may prescribe[1]—

(*a*) additional categories of eligible children; and
(*b*) categories of children who are not to be eligible children despite falling within sub-paragraph (2).

(4) For each eligible child, the local authority shall carry out an assessment of his needs with a view to determining what advice, assistance and support it would be appropriate for them to provide him under this Act—

(*a*) while they are still looking after him; and
(*b*) after they cease to look after him,

and shall then prepare a pathway plan for him[1].

(5) The local authority shall keep the pathway plan under regular review.

(6) Any such review may be carried out at the same time as a review of the child's case carried out by virtue of section 26.

(7) The Secretary of State may by regulations[1] make provision as to assessments for the purposes of sub-paragraph (4).

(8) The regulations[2] may in particular provide for the matters set out in section 23B(6).

---

1. This duty is mandatory and a local authority may not substitute an alternative process whatever its merits, *R (P) v London Borough of Newham* [2004] EWHC 2210 (Admin), [2005] 1 FCR 170.

1. Children Leaving Care (Wales) Regulations 2001, SI 2001/2189 amended by SI 2002/1855 and 2935 and the Children Leaving Care (England) Regulations 2001, SI 2001/2874 amended by SI 2002/546.

Personal advisers

6–2312C 19C. A local authority shall arrange for each child whom they are looking after who is an eligible child for the purposes of paragraph 19B to have a personal adviser.

Death of children being looked after by local authorities

6–2313 20. (1) If a child who is being looked after by a local authority dies, the authority—

(a) shall notify the Secretary of State and the Commission for Social Care Inspection;

(b) shall, so far as is reasonably practicable, notify the child's parents and every person who is not a parent of his but who has parental responsibility for him;

(c) may, with the consent (so far as it is reasonably practicable to obtain it) of every person who has parental responsibility for the child, arrange for the child's body to be buried or cremated; and

(d) may, if the conditions mentioned in sub-paragraph (2) are satisfied, make payments to any person who has parental responsibility for the child, or any relative, friend or other person connected with the child, in respect of travelling, subsistence or other expenses incurred by that person in attending the child's funeral.

(2) The conditions are that—

(a) it appears to the authority that the person concerned could not otherwise attend the child's funeral without undue financial hardship; and

(b) that the circumstances warrant the making of the payments.

(3) Sub-paragraph (1) does not authorise cremation where it does not accord with the practice of the child's religious persuasion.

(4) Where a local authority have exercised their power under sub-paragraph (1)(c) with respect to a child who was under sixteen when he died, they may recover from any parent of the child any expenses incurred by them.

(5) Any sums so recoverable shall, without prejudice to any other method of recovery, be recoverable summarily as a civil debt.

(6) Nothing in this paragraph affects any enactment regulating or authorising the burial, cremation or anatomical examination of the body of a deceased person.

PART III
CONTRIBUTIONS TOWARDS MAINTENANCE OF CHILDREN
LOOKED AFTER BY LOCAL AUTHORITIES
Liability to contribute

6–2314 21. (1) Where a local authority are looking after a child (other than in the cases mentioned in sub-paragraph (7)) they shall consider whether they should recover contributions towards the child's maintenance from any person liable to contribute ("a contributor").

(2) An authority may only recover contributions from a contributor if they consider it reasonable to do so.

(3) The persons liable to contribute are—

(a) where the child is under sixteen, each of his parents;

(b) where he has reached the age of sixteen, the child himself.

(4) A parent is not liable to contribute during any period when he is in receipt of income support under Part VII of the Social Security Contributions and Benefits Act 1992, of any element of child tax credit other than the family element, of working tax credit or of an income-based jobseeker's allowance.*

(5) A person is not liable to contribute towards the maintenance of a child in the care of a local authority in respect of any period during which the child is allowed by the authority (under section 23(5)) to live with a parent of his.

(6) A contributor is not obliged to make any contribution towards a child's maintenance except as agreed or determined in accordance with this Part of this Schedule[1].

(7) The cases are where the child is looked after by a local authority under—

(a) section 21;

(b) an interim care order;

(c) section 92 of the Powers of Criminal Courts (Sentencing) Act 2000.

---

*Sub-section (4) printed as prospectively amended by the Tax Credits Act 2002, s 47, when in force.

1. It should be noted that, unlike the provisions in Sch 1, para 4, *ante*, there is no reference in Sch 2 to the requirement for the court to have regard to the child's needs nor even of the local authority's expenditure on behalf of the child; see *Re C (a minor) (contribution notice)* [1994] 2 FCR 165, [1994] 1 FLR 111.

Agreed contributions

6–2315 **22.** (1) Contributions towards a child's maintenance may only be recovered if the local authority have served a notice ("a contribution notice") on the contributor specifying—

(*a*) the weekly sum which they consider that he should contribute; and
(*b*) arrangements for payment.

(2) The contribution notice must be in writing and dated.
(3) Arrangements for payment shall, in particular, include—

(*a*) the date on which liability to contribute begins (which must not be earlier than the date of the notice);
(*b*) the date on which liability under the notice will end (if the child has not before that date ceased to be looked after by the authority); and
(*c*) the date on which the first payment is to be made.

(4) The authority may specify in a contribution notice a weekly sum which is a standard contribution determined by them for all children looked after by them[1].
(5) The authority may not specify in a contribution notice a weekly sum greater than that which they consider—

(*a*) they would normally be prepared to pay if they had placed a similar child with local authority foster parents; and
(*b*) it is reasonably practicable for the contributor to pay (having regard to his means).

(6) An authority may at any time withdraw a contribution notice (without prejudice to their power to serve another).
(7) Where the authority and the contributor agree—

(*a*) the sum which the contributor is to contribute; and
(*b*) arrangements for payment,

(whether as specified in the contribution notice or otherwise) and the contributor notifies the authority in writing that he so agrees, the authority may recover summarily as a civil debt any contribution which is overdue and unpaid.

(8) A contributor may, by serving a notice in writing on the authority, withdraw his agreement in relation to any period of liability falling after the date of service of the notice.
(9) Sub-paragraph (7) is without prejudice to any other method of recovery.

---

1. Paragraph 22(4) is permissive only and not mandatory (*Re C (a minor) (contribution notice)* [1994] 1 FLR 111).

Contribution orders

6–2316 **23.** (1) Where a contributor has been served with a contribution notice and has—

(*a*) failed to reach any agreement with the local authority as mentioned in paragraph 22(7) within the period of one month beginning with the day on which the contribution notice was served; or
(*b*) served a notice under paragraph 22(8) withdrawing his agreement,

the authority may apply to the court for an order under this paragraph.

(2) On such an application the court may make an order ("a contribution order") requiring the contributor to contribute a weekly sum towards the child's maintenance in accordance with arrangements for payment specified by the court[1].
(3) A contribution order—

(*a*) shall not specify a weekly sum greater than that specified in the contribution notice; and
(*b*) shall be made with due regard to the contributor's means[2].

(4) A contribution order shall not—

(*a*) take effect before the date specified in the contribution notice; or
(*b*) have effect while the contributor is not liable to contribute (by virtue of paragraph 21); or
(*c*) remain in force after the child has ceased to be looked after by the authority who obtained the order.

(5) An authority may not apply to the court under sub-paragraph (1) in relation to a contribution notice which they have withdrawn.
(6) Where—

(*a*) a contribution order is in force;
(*b*) the authority serve another contribution notice; and
(*c*) the contributor and the authority reach an agreement under paragraph 22(7) in respect of that other contribution notice,

the effect of the agreement shall be to discharge the order from the date on which it is agreed that the agreement shall take effect.

(7) Where an agreement is reached under sub-paragraph (6) the authority shall notify the court—

(*a*) of the agreement; and
(*b*) of the date on which it took effect.

(8) A contribution order may be varied or revoked on the application of the contributor or the authority.
(9) In proceedings for the variation of a contribution order, the authority shall specify—

(*a*) the weekly sum which, having regard to paragraph 22, they propose that the contributor should contribute under the order as varied; and
(*b*) the proposed arrangements for payment.

(10) Where a contribution order is varied, the order—

(a) shall not specify a weekly sum greater than that specified by the authority in the proceedings for variation; and

(b) shall be made with due regard to the contributor's means.

(11) An appeal shall lie in accordance with rules of court from any order made under this paragraph.

---

1. As these are proceedings under the Children Act 1989, the magistrates are required to state their findings of fact and the reasons for the court's decision (*Re C (a minor) (contribution notice)* 2 FCR 165, [1994] 1 FLR 111).

2. There is no requirement for the court to have regard to the child's needs nor to the local authority's expenditure on behalf of the child. The court should assess the contributor's income and expenditure. Whilst not ignoring wholly unreasonable expenditure, there is no prior duty to maintain which entitles the justices to reduce the contributor's financial outgoings by reference to what ought to be set aside to contribute to the local authority (*Re C (a minor) (contribution notice)* [1994] 2 FCR 165, [1994] 1 FLR 111).

Enforcement of contribution orders etc

6–2317 **24.** (1) A contribution order made by a magistrates' court shall be enforceable as a magistrates' court maintenance order (within the meaning of section 150(1) of the Magistrates' Courts Act 1980).

(2) Where a contributor has agreed, or has been ordered, to make contributions to a local authority, any other local authority within whose area the contributor is for the time being living may—

(a) at the request of the local authority who served the contribution notice; and
(b) subject to agreement as to any sum to be deducted in respect of services rendered,

collect from the contributor any contributions due on behalf of the authority who served the notice.

(3) In sub-paragraph (2) the reference to any other local authority includes a reference to—

(a) a local authority within the meaning of section 1(2) of the Social Work (Scotland) Act 1968; and
(b) a Health and Social Services Board established under Article 16 of the Health and Personal Social Services (Northern Ireland) Order 1972.

(4) The power to collect sums under sub-paragraph (2) includes the power to—

(a) receive and give a discharge for any contributions due; and
(b) (if necessary) enforce payment of any contributions,

even though those contributions may have fallen due at a time when the contributor was living elsewhere.

(5) Any contribution collected under sub-paragraph (2) shall be paid (subject to any agreed deduction) to the local authority who served the contribution notice.

(6) In any proceedings under this paragraph, a document which purports to be—

(a) a copy of an order made by a court under or by virtue of paragraph 23; and
(b) certified as a true copy by the justices' chief executive for the court,

shall be evidence of the order.

(7) In any proceedings under this paragraph, a certificate which—

(a) purports to be signed by the clerk or some other duly authorised officer of the local authority who obtained the contribution order; and
(b) states that any sum due to the authority under the order is overdue and unpaid,

shall be evidence that the sum is overdue and unpaid.

Regulations

6–2318 **25.** The Secretary of State may make regulations—

(a) as to the considerations which a local authority must take into account in deciding—

   (i) whether it is reasonable to recover contributions; and
   (ii) what the arrangements for payment should be;

(b) as to the procedures they must follow in reaching agreements with—

   (i) contributors (under paragraphs 22 and 23); and
   (ii) any other local authority (under paragraph 23).

Sections 35 and 36.	**SCHEDULE 3**

SUPERVISION ORDERS

(*As amended by the Courts and Legal Services Act 1990, Schs 16 and 20, the Education Act 1993, Sch 19, the Probation Service Act 1993, Sch 3, the Education Act 1996, Sch 37, the Powers of Criminal Courts (Sentencing) Act 2000, Sch 9 and the Care Standards Act 2000, Sch 4.*)

PART I
GENERAL

Meaning of "responsible person"

6–2319 **1.** In this Schedule, "the responsible person", in relation to a supervised child, means—

(a) any person who has parental responsibility for the child; and
(b) any other person with whom the child is living.

Power of supervisor to give directions to supervised child

6–2320 **2.** (1) A supervision order may require[1] the supervised child to comply with any directions given from time to time by the supervisor which require him to do all or any of the following things—

(a) to live at a place or places specified in the directions for a period or periods so specified;
(b) to present himself to a person or persons specified in the directions at a place or places and on a day or days so specified;
(c) to participate in activities specified in the directions on a day or days so specified.

(2) It shall be for the supervisor to decide whether, and to what extent, he exercises his power to give directions and to decide the form of any directions which he gives.

(3) Sub-paragraph (1) does not confer on a supervisor power to give directions in respect of any medical or psychiatric examination or treatment (which are matters dealt with in paragraphs 4 and 5).

---

1. Where a requirement is imposed under a supervision order, the requirement must be apparent on the face of the order (*Re T (a minor) (care order: conditions)* [1994] 2 FLR 423), sub nom *Re KDT (a minor) (care order: conditions)* [1994] 2 FCR 721.

It would seem that, apart from bringing the matter back to the court under s 35, ante, or applying for a variation of the supervision order, there is no way in which the direction can be directly enforced either by the supervising officer or by the court (*Hereford and Worcester County Council v R and G* [1994] 2 FCR 981).

Imposition of obligations on responsible person

6–2321   3. (1) With the consent of any responsible person, a supervision order may include a requirement—

(a) that he take all reasonable steps to ensure that the supervised child complies with any direction given by the supervisor under paragraph 2;
(b) that he take all reasonable steps to ensure that the supervised child complies with any requirement included in the order under paragraph 4 or 5;
(c) that he comply with any directions[1] given by the supervisor requiring him to attend at a place specified in the directions for the purpose of taking part in activities so specified.

(2) A direction given under sub-paragraph (1)(c) may specify the time at which the responsible person is to attend and whether or not the supervised child is required to attend with him.

(3) A supervision order may require any person who is a responsible person in relation to the supervised child to keep the supervisor informed of his address, if it differs from the child's.

---

1. A responsible person may under this provision be required to comply with directions to attend for treatment; however, such directions are entirely a matter for the supervisor and may not be imposed by the court (*Re H (minors) (terms of supervision order)* [1994] 2 FCR 1, [1994] 2 FLR 979).

Psychiatric and medical examinations

6–2322   4. (1) A supervision order may require the supervised child—

(a) to submit to a medical or psychiatric examination; or
(b) to submit to any such examination from time to time as directed by the supervisor.

(2) Any such examination shall be required to be conducted—

(a) by, or under the direction of, such registered medical practitioner as may be specified in the order;
(b) at a place specified in the order and at which the supervised child is to attend as a non-resident patient; or
(c) at—

(i)   a health service hospital; or
(ii) in the case of a psychiatric examination, a hospital, independent hospital or care home,

at which the supervised child is, or is to attend as, a resident patient.

(3) A requirement of a kind mentioned in sub-paragraph (2)(c) shall not be included unless the court is satisfied, on the evidence of a registered medical practitioner, that—

(a) the child may be suffering from a physical or mental condition that requires, and may be susceptible to, treatment; and
(b) a period as a resident patient is necessary if the examination is to be carried out properly.

(4) No court shall include a requirement under this paragraph in a supervision order unless it is satisfied that—

(a) where the child has sufficient understanding to make an informed decision, he consents to its inclusion; and
(b) satisfactory arrangements have been, or can be, made for the examination.

Psychiatric and medical treatment

6–2323   5. (1) Where a court which proposes to make or vary a supervision order is satisfied, on the evidence of a registered medical practitioner approved for the purposes of section 12 of the Mental Health Act 1983, that the mental condition of the supervised child—

(a) is such as requires, and may be susceptible to, treatment; but
(b) is not such as to warrant his detention in pursuance of a hospital order under Part III of that Act,

the court may include in the order a requirement that the supervised child shall, for a period specified in the order, submit to such treatment as is so specified.

(2) The treatment specified in accordance with sub-paragraph (1) must be—

(a) by, or under the direction of, such registered medical practitioner as may be specified in the order;
(b) as a non-resident patient at such a place as may be so specified; or
(c) as a resident patient in a hospital, independednt hospital or care home.

(3) Where a court which proposes to make or vary a supervision order is satisfied, on the evidence of a registered medical practitioner, that the physical condition of the supervised child is such as requires, and may be susceptible

to, treatment, the court may include in the order a requirement that the supervised child shall, for a period specified in the order, submit to such treatment as is so specified.

(4) The treatment specified in accordance with sub-paragraph (3) must be—

(a) by, or under the direction of, such registered medical practitioner as may be specified in the order;

(b) as a non-resident patient at such place as may be so specified; or

(c) as a resident patient in a health service hospital.

(5) No court shall include a requirement under this paragraph in a supervision order unless it is satisfied—

(a) where the child has sufficient understanding to make an informed decision, that he consents to its inclusion; and

(b) that satisfactory arrangements have been, or can be, made for the treatment.

(6) If a medical practitioner by whom or under whose direction a supervised person is being treated in pursuance of a requirement included in a supervision order by virtue of this paragraph is unwilling to continue to treat or direct the treatment of the supervised child or is of the opinion that—

(a) the treatment should be continued beyond the period specified in the order;

(b) the supervised child needs different treatment;

(c) he is not susceptible to treatment; or

(d) he does not require further treatment,

the practitioner shall make a report in writing to that effect to the supervisor.

(7) On receiving a report under this paragraph the supervisor shall refer it to the court, and on such a reference the court may make an order cancelling or varying the requirement.

PART II
MISCELLANEOUS

Life of supervision order

6–2324 **6.** (1) Subject to sub-paragraph (2) and section 91, a supervision order shall cease to have effect at the end of the period of one year beginning with the date on which it was made[1].

(2) A supervision order shall also cease to have effect if an event mentioned in section 25(1)(a) or (b) of the Child Abduction and Custody Act 1985 (termination of existing orders) occurs with respect to the child.

(3) Where the supervisor applies to the court to extend, or further extend, a supervision order the court may extend the order for such period as it may specify[2].

(4) A supervision order may not be extended so as to run beyond the end of the period of three years beginning with the date on which it was made.

---

1. The court has jurisdiction to make a supervision order for a period of less than 12 months (*M v Warwickshire County Council*) [1994] 2 FCR 121, [1994] 2 FLR 593).

2. There is no requirement for the threshold conditions of s 31(2), ante, to be satisfied upon an application to extend a supervision order during the period of its currency. There is no jurisdiction, on such an application, to make an interim care order under s 31(5)(b), ante, to replace the supervision order (*Re A (a minor) (supervision order: extension)* [1995] 3 All ER 401, [1995] 1 WLR 482, [1995] 2 FCR 114, [1995] 1 FLR 335, CA.)

Limited life of directions

6–2325 **7.** (*Repealed*).

Information to be given to supervisor etc

6–2326 **8.** (1) A supervision order may require the supervised child—

(a) to keep the supervisor informed of any change in his address; and

(b) to allow the supervisor to visit him at the place where he is living.

(2) The responsible person in relation to any child with respect to whom a supervision order is made shall—

(a) if asked by the supervisor, inform him of the child's address (if it is known to him); and

(b) if he is living with the child, allow the supervisor reasonable contact with the child.

Selection of supervisor

6–2327 **9.** (1) A supervision order shall not designate a local authority as the supervisor unless—

(a) the authority agree; or

(b) the supervised child lives or will live within their area.

(2) A court shall not place a child under the supervision of a probation officer unless—

(a) the appropriate authority so request; and

(b) a probation officer is already exercising or has exercised, in relation to another member of the household to which the child belongs, duties imposed on probation officers by section 14 or by rules under section 25(2)(c) of the Probation Service Act 1993.

(3) In sub-paragraph (2) "the appropriate authority" means the local authority appearing to the court to be the authority in whose area the supervised child lives or will live.

(4) Where a supervision order places a person under the supervision of a probation officer, the officer shall be selected in accordance with arrangements made by the probation committee for the area in question.

(5) If the selected probation officer is unable to carry out his duties, or dies, another probation officer shall be selected in the same manner.

Effect of supervision order on earlier orders

6–2328   10. The making of a supervision order with respect to any child brings to an end any earlier care or supervision order which—

(a) was made with respect to that child; and

(b) would otherwise continue in force.

Local authority functions and expenditure

6–2329   11. (1) The Secretary of State may make regulations with respect to the exercise by a local authority of their functions where a child has been placed under their supervision by a supervision order.

(2) Where a supervision order requires compliance with directions given by virtue of this section, any expenditure incurred by the supervisor for the purposes of the directions shall be defrayed by the local authority designated in the order.

PART III
EDUCATION SUPERVISION ORDERS

Effect of orders

6–2340   12. (1) Where an education supervision order is in force with respect to a child, it shall be the duty of the supervisor—

(a) to advise, assist and befriend, and give directions to—

(i)   the supervised child; and

(ii) his parents;

in such a way as will, in the opinion of the supervisor, secure that he is properly educated;

(b) where any such directions given to—

(i)   the supervised child; or

(ii) a parent of his,

have not been complied with, to consider what further steps to take in the exercise of the supervisor's powers under this Act.

(2) Before giving any directions under sub-paragraph (1) the supervisor shall, so far as is reasonably practicable, ascertain the wishes and feelings of—

(a) the child; and

(b) his parents;

including, in particular, their wishes as to the place at which the child should be educated.

(3) When settling the terms of any such directions, the supervisor shall give due consideration—

(a) having regard to the child's age and understanding, to such wishes and feelings of his as the supervisor has been able to ascertain; and

(b) to such wishes and feelings of the child's parents as he has been able to ascertain.

(4) Directions may be given under this paragraph at any time while the education supervision order is in force.

6–2341   13. (1) Where an education supervision order is in force with respect to a child, the duties of the child's parents under sections 7 and 444 of the Education Act 1996 (duties to secure education of children and to secure regular attendance of registered pupils) shall be superseded by their duty to comply with any directions in force under the education supervision order.

(2) Where an education supervision order is made with respect to a child—

(a) any school attendance order—

(i)   made under section 437 of the Education Act 1996 with respect to the child; and

(ii) in force immediately before the making of the education supervision order,

shall cease to have effect; and

(b) while the education supervision order remains in force, the following provisions shall not apply with respect to the child—

(i)   section 437 of that Act (school attendance orders);

(ii) section 9 of that Act (pupils to be educated in accordance with wishes of their parents);

(iii) the Education Act 1996 (parental preference and appeals against admission decisions);

(c) a supervision order made with respect to the child in criminal proceedings, while the education supervision order is in force, may not include an education requirement of the kind which could otherwise be included under paragraph 7 of Schedule 6 to the Powers of Criminal Courts (Sentencing) Act 2000;

(d) any education requirement of a kind mentioned in paragraph (c), which was in force with respect to the child immediately before the making of the education supervision order, shall cease to have effect.

Effect where child also subject to supervision order

6–2342   14. (1) This paragraph applies where an education supervision order and a supervision order, or order under section 63(1) of the Powers of Criminal Courts (Sentencing) Act 2000, are in force at the same time with respect to the same child.

(2) Any failure to comply with a direction given by the supervisor under the education supervision order shall be disregarded if it would not have been reasonably practicable to comply with it without failing to comply with a direction given under the other order.

Duration of orders

6–2343 **15.** (1) An education supervision order shall have effect for a period of one year, beginning with the date on which it is made.

(2) An education supervision order shall not expire if, before it would otherwise have expired, the court has (on the application of the authority in whose favour the order was made) extended the period during which it is in force.

(3) Such an application may not be made earlier than three months before the date on which the order would otherwise expire.

(4) The period during which an education supervision order is in force may be extended under sub-paragraph (2) on more than one occasion.

(5) No one extension may be for a period of more than three years.

(6) An education supervision order shall cease to have effect on—

(a) the child's ceasing to be of compulsory school age; or
(b) the making of a care order with respect to the child;

and sub-paragraphs (1) to (4) are subject to this sub-paragraph.

Information to be given to supervisor etc

6–2344 **16.** (1) An education supervision order may require the child—

(a) to keep the supervisor informed of any change in his address; and
(b) to allow the supervisor to visit him at the place where he is living.

(2) A person who is the parent of a child with respect to whom an education supervision order has been made shall—

(a) if asked by the supervisor, inform him of the child's address (if it is known to him); and
(b) if he is living with the child, allow the supervisor reasonable contact with the child.

Discharge of orders

6–2345 **17.** (1) The court may discharge any education supervision order on the application of—

(a) the child concerned;
(b) a parent of his; or
(c) the local education authority concerned.

(2) On discharging an education supervision order, the court may direct the local authority within whose area the child lives, or will live, to investigate the circumstances of the child.

Offences

6–2346 **18.** (1) If a parent of a child with respect to whom an education supervision order is in force persistently fails to comply with a direction given under the order he shall be guilty of an offence.

(2) It shall be a defence for any person charged with such an offence to prove that—

(a) he took all reasonable steps to ensure that the direction was complied with;
(b) the direction was unreasonable; or
(c) he had complied with—

(i) a requirement included in a supervision order made with respect to the child; or
(ii) directions given under such a requirement,

and that it was not reasonably practicable to comply both with the direction and with the requirement or directions mentioned in this paragraph.

(3) A person guilty of an offence under this paragraph shall be liable on summary conviction to a fine not exceeding **level 3** on the standard scale.

Persistent failure of child to comply with directions

6–2347 **19.** (1) Where a child with respect to whom an education supervision order is in force persistently fails to comply with any direction given under the order, the local education authority concerned shall notify the appropriate local authority.

(2) Where a local authority have been notified under sub-paragraph (1) they shall investigate the circumstances of the child.

(3) In this paragraph "the appropriate local authority" has the same meaning as in section 36.

Miscellaneous

6–2348 **20.** The Secretary of State may by regulations make provision modifying, or displacing, the provisions of any enactment about education in relation to any child with respect to whom an education supervision order is in force to such extent as appears to the Secretary of State to be necessary or expedient in consequence of the provision made by this Act with respect to such orders.

Interpretation

6–2349 **21.** In this Part of this Schedule "parent" has the same meaning as in the Education Act 1996.

Section 53(6)

SCHEDULE 4
MANAGEMENT AND CONDUCT OF COMMUNITY HOMES

(As amended by the Courts and Legal Services Act 1990, Schs 16 and 20, the Criminal Justice and Public Order Act 1994, s 22 and the Care Standards Act 2000, Sch 6.)

PART I
INSTRUMENTS OF MANAGEMENT

6–2350 **1–2.** *Instruments of management for controlled and assisted community homes.*

PART II

6–2352 **3.** *Management of controlled and assisted community homes.*

PART III
REGULATIONS

6–2353 **4.** (1) The Secretary of State may make regulations[1]—

(*a*) as to the placing of children in community homes;

(2) *(Repealed)*.
(3) *(Repealed)*.

---

1. See the Arrangements for Placement of Children (General) Regulations 1991, SI 1991/890, amended by SI 1991/2033, SI 1993/3069 SI 1995/2015, SI 1997/649, SI 2002/546 (England), 2469 and 2935 (Wales) and 3013 (W) and SI 2005/774 (W) and the Secure Accommodation Regulations 1991, post.

Section 60(4)

SCHEDULE 5
VOLUNTARY HOMES AND VOLUNTARY ORGANISATIONS

(As amended by the Criminal Justice and Public Order Act 1994, s 19 and Sch 11 and the Care Standards Act 2000, s 41 and Sch 4.)

PART II
REGULATIONS AS TO VOLUNTARY HOMES

Regulations as to conduct of voluntary homes

6–2370 **7.** (1) The Secretary of State may make regulations[1]—

(*a*) as to the placing of children in voluntary homes;
(*b*)–(*c*) *(repealed)*.

(2)–(3) *(Repealed)*.
(4) Any person guilty of such an offence shall be liable to a fine not exceeding **level 4** on the standard scale.

---

1. See the Arrangements for Placement of Children (General) Regulations 1991, SI 1991/890, amended by SI 1991/2033, SI 1993/3069 SI 1995/2015, SI 1997/649, SI 2002/546 (England), 2469 and 2935 (Wales) and 3013 (W) and SI 2005/774 (W) and the Secure Accommodation Regulations 1991, post.

Disqualification

6–2371 **8** *(Repealed)*.

Section 63(11)

SCHEDULE 6
PRIVATE CHILDREN'S HOMES

(As amended by the Courts and Legal Services Act 1990, Sch 16, the Criminal Justice and Public Order Act 1994, s 19 and Sch 11 and the Care Standards Act 2000, Sch 4 and 6.)

PART II
REGULATIONS

6–2381 **10.** (1) The Secretary of State may make regulations[1]—

(*a*) as to the placing of children in private children's homes;
(*b*)–(*c*) *(repealed)*.

(2) The regulations may in particular—

(*a*)–(k) *(repealed)*.
(*l*) make provision similar to that made by regulations under section 26.

(3)–(4) *(Repealed)*.

---

1. See the Arrangements for Placement of Children (General) Regulations 1991, SI 1991/890, amended by SI 1991/2033, SI 1993/3069, SI 1995/2015, SI 1997/649, SI 2002/546 (England), 2469 and 2935 (Wales) and 3013 (W) and SI 2005/774 (W) and the Secure Accommodation Regulations 1991, post.

SCHEDULE 7
FOSTER PARENTS: LIMITS ON NUMBER OF FOSTER CHILDREN
(As amended by the Care Standards Act 2000, Sch 4.)

Interpretation

6–2382　**1.** For the purposes of this Schedule, a person fosters a child if—

  (*a*)　he is a local authority foster parent in relation to the child;
  (*b*)　he is a foster parent with whom the child has been placed by a voluntary organisation; or
  (*c*)　he fosters the child privately.

The usual fostering limit

6–2383　**2.** Subject to what follows, a person may not foster more than three children ("the usual fostering limit").

Siblings

6–2384　**3.** A person may exceed the usual fostering limit if the children concerned are all siblings with respect to each other.

Exemption by local authority

6–2385　**4.** (1) A person may exceed the usual fostering limit if he is exempted from it by the local authority within whose area he lives.
　　(2) In considering whether to exempt a person, a local authority shall have regard, in particular, to—

  (*a*)　the number of children whom the person proposes to foster;
  (*b*)　the arrangements which the person proposes for the care and accommodation of the fostered children;
  (*c*)　the intended and likely relationship between the person and the fostered children;
  (*d*)　the period of time for which he proposes to foster the children; and
  (*e*)　whether the welfare of the fostered children (and of any other children who are or will be living in the accommodation) will be safeguarded and promoted.

　　(3) Where a local authority exempt a person, they shall inform him by notice in writing—

  (*a*)　that he is so exempted;
  (*b*)　of the children, described by name, whom he may foster; and
  (*c*)　of any condition to which the exemption is subject.

　　(4) A local authority may at any time by notice in writing—

  (*a*)　vary or cancel an exemption; or
  (*b*)　impose, vary or cancel a condition to which the exemption is subject,

and, in considering whether to do so, they shall have regard in particular to the considerations mentioned in sub-paragraph (2).
　　(5) The Secretary of State may make regulations amplifying or modifying the provisions of this paragraph in order to provide for cases where children need to be placed with foster parents as a matter of urgency.

Effect of exceeding fostering limit

6–2386　**5.** (1) A person shall cease to be treated as fostering and shall be treated, for the purposes of this Act and the Care Standards Act 2000 as carrying on a children's home if—

  (*a*)　he exceeds the usual fostering limit; or
  (*b*)　where he is exempted under paragraph 4,—

    (i)　he fosters any child not named in the exemption; and
    (ii)　in so doing, he exceeds the usual fostering limit.

　　(2) Sub-paragraph (1) does not apply if the children concerned are all siblings in respect of each other.

Complaints etc

6–2387　**6.** (1) Every local authority shall establish a procedure for considering any representations (including any complaint) made to them about the discharge of their functions under paragraph 4 by a person exempted or seeking to be exempted under that paragraph.
　　(2) In carrying out any consideration or representations under sub-paragraph (1), a local authority shall comply with any regulations[1] made by the Secretary of State for the purposes of this paragraph.

---

1. See the Representations Procedure (Children) Regulations 1991, SI 1991/894 amended by SI 1991/2033, SI 1993/3069, SI 2002/546 (E), 2469 and 2935 (W), SI 2004, SI 2004/719 (E) and 1448 (W) and SI 2005/3482.

Section 66(5)

SCHEDULE 8
PRIVATELY FOSTERED CHILDREN

(As amended by the Registered Homes (Amendment) Act 1991, s 2, the Children (Scotland) Act 1995, Sch 4, the Powers of Criminal Courts (Sentencing) Act 2000, Sch 9, the Care Standards Act 2000, Schs 4 and 6, the Education Act 2002, s 21, the Adoption and Children Act 2002, Sch 3 and the Children Act 2004, s 67.)

Exemptions

6–2388   **1.** A child is not a privately fostered child while he is being looked after by a local authority.

6–2389   **2.** (1) A child is not a privately fostered child while he is in the care of any person—

     (a) in premises in which any—

         (i)   parent of his;
         (ii)   person who is not a parent of his but who has parental responsibility for him; or
         (iii)   person who is a relative of his and who has assumed responsibility for his care,

     is for the time being living;

     (b) *repealed*;
     (c) in accommodation provided by or on behalf of any voluntary organisation;
     (d) in any school in which he is receiving full-time education;
     (e) in any health service hospital;
     (f) in any care home or independent hospital; or
     (g) in any home or institution not specified in this paragraph but provided, equipped and maintained by the Secretary of State.

(2) Sub-paragraph (1)(c) to (g) does not apply where the person caring for the child is doing so in his personal capacity and not in the course of carrying out his duties in relation to the establishment mentioned in the paragraph in question.

6–2400   **3.** A child is not a privately fostered child while he is in the care of any person in compliance with—

     (a) an order under section 63(1) of the Powers of Criminal Courts (Sentencing) Act 2000; or
     (b) a supervision requirement within the meaning of Part II of the Children (Scotland) Act 1995.

6–2401   **4.** A child is not a privately fostered child while he is liable to be detained, or subject to guardianship, under the Mental Health Act 1983.

6–2402   **5.** A child is not a privately fostered child while he is placed in the care of a person who proposes to adopt him under arrangements made by an adoption agency within the meaning of—

     (a) section 2 of the Adoption and Children Act 2002;
     (b) section 1 of the Adoption (Scotland) Act 1978; or
     (c) Article 3 of the Adoption (Northern Ireland) Order 1987.

Power of local authority to impose requirements

6–2403   **6.** (1) Where a person is fostering any child privately, or proposes to foster any child privately, the appropriate local authority may impose on him requirements as to—

     (a) the number, age and sex of the children who may be privately fostered by him;
     (b) the standard of the accommodation and equipment to be provided for them;
     (c) the arrangements to be made with respect to their health and safety; and
     (d) particular arrangements which must be made with respect to the provision of care for them,

and it shall be his duty to comply with any such requirement before the end of such period as the authority may specify unless, in the case of a proposal, the proposal is not carried out.

(2) A requirement may be limited to a particular child, or class of child.

(3) A requirement (other than one imposed under sub-paragraph (1)(a)) may be limited by the authority so as to apply only when the number of children fostered by the person exceeds a specified number.

(4) A requirement shall be imposed by notice in writing addressed to the person on whom it is imposed and informing him of—

     (a) the reason for imposing the requirement;
     (b) his right under paragraph 8 to appeal against it; and
     (c) the time within which he may do so.

(5) A local authority may at any time vary any requirement, impose any additional requirement or remove any requirement.

(6) In this Schedule—

     (a) "the appropriate local authority" means—

         (i)   the local authority within whose area the child is being fostered; or
         (ii)   in the case of a proposal to foster a child, the local authority within whose area it is proposed that he will be fostered; and

(*b*) "requirement", in relation to any person, means a requirement imposed on him under this paragraph.

Regulations requiring notification of fostering etc

6–2404 **7.**—(1) The Secretary of State may by regulations[1] make provision as to—

(*a*) the circumstances in which notification is required to be given in connection with children who are, have been or are proposed to be fostered privately; and

(*b*) the manner and form in which such notification is to be given.

(2) The regulations may, in particular—

(*a*) require any person who is, or proposes to be, involved (whether or not directly) in arranging for a child to be fostered privately to notify the appropriate authority;

(*b*) require any person who is—

(i) a parent of a child; or

(ii) a person who is not a parent of his but who has parental responsibility for a child,

and who knows that it is proposed that the child should be fostered privately, to notify the appropriate authority;

(*c*) require any parent of a privately fostered child, or person who is not a parent of such a child but who has parental responsibility for him, to notify the appropriate authority of any change in his address;

(*d*) require any person who proposes to foster a child privately, to notify the appropriate authority of his proposal;

(*e*) require any person who is fostering a child privately, or proposes to do so, to notify the appropriate authority of—

(i) any offence of which he has been convicted;

(ii) any disqualification imposed on him under section 68; or

(iii) any prohibition imposed on him under section 69;

(*f*) require any person who is fostering a child privately, to notify the appropriate authority of any change in his address;

(*g*) require any person who is fostering a child privately to notify the appropriate authority in writing of any person who begins, or ceases, to be part of his household;

(*h*) require any person who has been fostering a child privately, but has ceased to do so, to notify the appropriate authority (indicating, where the child has died, that that is the reason).

---

1. The Children (Private Arrangements for Fostering) Regulations 1991, SI 1991/2050 amended by 1998/646 revoked in relation to England by SI 2005/1533 and the Children (Private Arrangements for Fostering) Regulations 2005, SI 2005/1533 have been made.

6–2404A **7A.** Every local authority must promote public awareness in their area of requirements as to notification for which provision is made under paragraph 7.★

★In force in England 1 July 2005, in Wales from a date to be appointed.

Appeals

6–2405 **8.**—(1) A person aggrieved by—

(*a*) a requirement imposed under paragraph 6;

(*b*) a refusal of consent under section 68;

(*c*) a prohibition imposed under section 69;

(*d*) a refusal to cancel such a prohibition;

(*e*) a refusal to make an exemption under paragraph 4 of Schedule 7;

(*f*) a condition imposed in such an exemption; or

(*g*) a variation or cancellation of such an exemption,

may appeal to the court.

(2) The appeal must be made within fourteen days from the date on which the person appealing is notified of the requirement, refusal, prohibition, condition, variation or cancellation.

(3) Where the appeal is against—

(*a*) a requirement imposed under paragraph 6;

(*b*) a condition of an exemption imposed under paragraph 4 of Schedule 7; or

(*c*) a variation or cancellation of such an exemption,

the requirement, condition, variation or cancellation shall not have effect while the appeal is pending.

(4) Where it allows an appeal against a requirement or prohibition, the court may, instead of cancelling the requirement or prohibition—

(*a*) vary the requirement, or allow more time for compliance with it; or

(*b*) if an absolute prohibition has been imposed, substitute for it a prohibition on using the premises after such time as the court may specify unless such specified requirements as the local authority had power to impose under paragraph 6 are complied with.

(5) Any requirement or prohibition specified or substituted by a court under this paragraph shall be deemed for the purposes of Part IX (other than this paragraph) to have been imposed by the local authority under paragraph 6 or (as the case may be) section 69.

(6) Where it allows an appeal against a refusal to make an exemption, a condition imposed in such an exemption or a variation or cancellation of such an exemption, the court may—

(a) make an exemption;
(b) impose a condition; or
(c) vary the exemption.

(7) Any exemption made or varied under sub-paragraph (6), or any condition imposed under that sub-paragraph, shall be deemed for the purposes of Schedule 7 (but not for the purposes of this paragraph) to have been made, varied or imposed under that Schedule.

(8) Nothing in sub-paragraph (1)(e) to (g) confers any right of appeal on—

(a) a person who is, or would be if exempted under Schedule 7, a local authority foster parent; or
(b) a person who is, or would be if so exempted, a person with whom a child is placed by a voluntary organisation.

Extension of Part IX to certain school children during holidays

6–2406   9. (1) Where a child under sixteen who is a pupil at a school lives at the school during school holidays for a period of more than two weeks, Part IX shall apply in relation to the child as if—

(a) while living at the school, he were a privately fostered child; and
(b) paragraphs 2(1)(c) and (d) and 6 were omitted.

But this sub-paragraph does not apply to a school which is an appropraite children's home.

(2) Sub-paragraph (3) applies to any person who proposes to care for and accommodate one or more children at a school in circumstances in which some or all of them will be treated as private foster children by virtue of this paragraph.

(3) That person shall, not less than two weeks before the first of those children is treated as a private foster child by virtue of this paragraph during the holiday in question, give written notice of his proposal to the local authority within whose area the child is ordinarily resident ("the appropriate authority"), stating the estimated number of the children.

(4) A local authority may exempt any person from the duty of giving notice under sub-paragraph (3).

(5) Any such exemption may be granted for a special period or indefinitely and may be revoked at any time by notice in writing given to the person exempted.

(6) Where a child who is treated as a private foster child by virtue of this paragraph dies, the person caring for him at the school shall, not later than 48 hours after the death, give written notice of it—

(a) to the appropriate local authority; and
(b) where reasonably practicable, to each parent of the child and to every person who is not a parent of his but who has parental responsibility for him.

(7) Where a child who is treated as a foster child by virtue of this paragraph ceases for any other reason to be such a child, the person caring for him at the school shall give written notice of the fact to the appropriate local authority.

Prohibition of advertisements relating to fostering

6–2407   10. No advertisement indicating that a person will undertake, or will arrange for, a child to be privately fostered shall be published, unless it states that person's name and address.

Avoidance of insurances on lives of privately fostered children

6–2408   11. A person who fosters a child privately and for reward shall be deemed for the purposes of the Life Assurance Act 1774 to have no interest in the life of the child.

Section 71(16)   SCHEDULE 9A
          CHILD MINDING AND DAY CARE FOR YOUNG CHILDREN

(*As inserted by the Care Standards Act 2000 and amended by the Education Act 2002, Sch 21, the Criminal Justice Act, Sch 32 and the Children Act 2004, Sch 4*)

Exemption of certain schools

6–2416A   1. (1) Except in prescribed[1] circumstances, Part XA does not apply to provision of day care within sub-paragraph (2) for any child looked after in—

(a) a maintained school;
(b) a school assisted by a local education authority;
(c) a school in respect of which payments are made by the Secretary of State or the Assembly under section 485 of the Education Act 1996;
(d) an independent school.

(2) The provision mentioned in sub-paragraph (1) is provision of day care made by—

(a) the person carrying on the establishment in question as part of the establishment's activities; or
(b) a person employed to work at that establishment and authorised to make that provision as part of the establishment's activities.

(3) In sub-paragraph (1)—

"assisted" has the same meaning as in the Education Act 1996;
"maintained school" has the meaning given by section 20(7) of the School Standards and Framework Act 1998.

---

1. See the Day Care (Application to Schools) Regulations 2003, SI 2003/1992 and the Day Care (Application to Schools) (Wales) Regulations 2005, SI 2005/118.

Exemption for other establishments

6–2416B **2.** (1) Part XA does not apply to provision of day care within sub-paragraph (2) for any child looked after—

- (*a*) in an appropriate children's home;
- (*b*) in a care home;
- (*c*) as a patient in a hospital (within the meaning of the Care Standards Act 2000);
- (*d*) in a residential family centre.

(2) The provision mentioned in sub-paragraph (1) is provision of day care made by—

- (*a*) the department, authority or other person carrying on the establishment in question as part of the establishment's activities; or
- (*b*) a person employed to work at that establishment and authorised to make that provision as part of the establishment's activities.

6–2416C **2A.** (1) Part XA does not apply to provision of day care in a hotel, guest house or other similar establishment for children staying in that establishment where—

- (*a*) the provision takes place only between 6pm and 2 am; and
- (*b*) the person providing the care is doing so for no more than two different clients at the same time.

(2) For the purposes of sub-paragraph (1)(*b*), a "client" is a person at whose request (or persons at whose joint request) day care is provided for a child.

---

*In force in England 1 March 2005, in Wales from a date to be appointed.

Exemption for occasional facilities

6–2416C **3.** (1) Where day care is provided on particular premises on less than six days in any year, that provision shall be disregarded for the purposes of Part XA if the person making it has notified the registration authority in writing before the first occasion on which the premises concerned are so used in that year.

(2) In sub-paragraph (1) "year" means the year beginning with the day (after the commencement of paragraph 5 of Schedule 9) on which the day care in question was or is first provided on the premises concerned and any subsequent year.

Disqualification for registration

6–2416D **4.** (1) Regulations[1] may provide for a person to be disqualified for registration for child minding or providing day care.

(2) The regulations may, in particular, provide for a person to be disqualified where—

- (*a*) he is included in the list kept under section 1 of the Protection of Children Act 1999;
- (*b*) he is subject to a direction under section 142 of the Education Act 2002, given on the grounds that he is unsuitable to work with children;
- (*c*) an order of a prescribed kind has been made at any time with respect to him;
- (*d*) an order of a prescribed kind has been made at any time with respect to any child who has been in his care;
- (*e*) a requirement of a prescribed kind has been imposed at any time with respect to such a child, under or by virtue of any enactment;
- (*f*) he has at any time been refused registration under Part X or Part XA or any prescribed enactment or had any such registration cancelled;
- (*g*) he has been convicted of any offence of a prescribed kind, or has been discharged absolutely or conditionally for any such offence;
- (*h*) he has at any time been disqualified from fostering a child privately;
- (*j*) a prohibition has been imposed on him at any time under section 69, section 10 of the Foster Children (Scotland) Act 1984 or any prescribed enactment;
- (*k*) his rights and powers with respect to a child have at any time been vested in a prescribed authority under a prescribed enactment.

(3) Regulations may provide for a person who lives—

- (*a*) in the same household as a person who is himself disqualified for registration for child minding or providing day care; or
- (*b*) in a household at which any such person is employed,

to be disqualified for registration for child minding or providing day care.

(3A) Regulations under this paragraph may provide for a person not to be disqualified for registration (and may in particular provide for a person not to be disqualified for registration for the purposes of sub-paragraphs (4) and (5)) by reason of any fact which would otherwise cause him to be disqualified if—

- (*a*) he has disclosed the fact to the registration authority, and
- (*b*) the registration authority has consented in writing and has not withdrawn that consent.*

(4) A person who is disqualified for registration for providing day care shall not provide day care, or be directly concerned in the management of any provision of day care.*

(5) No person shall employ, in connection with the provision of day care, a person who is disqualified for registration for providing day care.

(6) In this paragraph "enactment" means any enactment having effect, at any time, in any part of the United Kingdom.

(7) A conviction in respect of which a probation order was made before 1st October 1992 (which would not otherwise be treated as a conviction) is to be treated as a conviction for the purposes of this paragraph.

*Sub-paras (3A) and (4) reproduced as in force in England 1 March 2005, in force in Wales from a date to be appointed.
1. See the Disqualification for Caring for Children (England) Regulations 2002, SI 2002/635, the Disqualification for Caring for Children (Wales) Regulations 2004, 2004/2695 and the Day Care and Child Minding (Disqualification) (England) Regulations 2005, SI 2005/2296.

6–2416E   5. (1) If any person—

(*a*) acts as a child minder at any time when he is disqualified for registration for child minding; or
(*b*) contravenes any of sub-paragraphs (3) to (5) of paragraph 4,

he shall be guilty of an offence.

(2) Where a person contravenes sub-paragraph (3) of paragraph 4, he shall not be guilty of an offence under this paragraph if he proves that he did not know, and had no reasonable grounds for believing, that the person in question was living or employed in the household.

(3) Where a person contravenes sub-paragraph (5) of paragraph 4, he shall not be guilty of an offence under this paragraph if he proves that he did not know, and had no reasonable grounds for believing, that the person whom he was employing was disqualified.

(4) A person guilty of an offence under this paragraph shall be liable on summary conviction to imprisonment for a term not exceeding six months, or to a fine not exceeding level 5 on the standard scale, or to both.

6–2416EA
Provision of day care: unincorporated associations

5A. (1) References in Part XA to a person, so far as relating to the provision of day care, include an unincorporated association.

(2) Proceedings for an offence under Part XA which is alleged to have been committed by an unincorporated association must be brought in the name of the association (and not in that of any of its members).

(3) For the purpose of any such proceedings, rules of court relating to the service of documents are to have effect as if the association were a body corporate.

(4) In proceedings for an offence under Part XA brought against an unincorporated association, section 33 of the Criminal Justice Act 1925 and Schedule 3 to the Magistrates' Courts Act 1980 (procedure) apply as they do in relation to a body corporate.

(5) A fine imposed on an unincorporated association on its conviction of an offence under Part XA is to be paid out of the funds of the association.

(6) If an offence under Part XA committed by an unincorporated association is shown—

(*a*) to have been committed with the consent or connivance of an officer of the association or a member of its governing body, or
(*b*) to be attributable to any neglect on the part of such an officer or member,

the officer or member as well as the association is guilty of the offence and liable to proceeded against and punished accordingly.*

*In force in England 1 March 2005, in Wales from a date to be appointed.

Certificates of registration

6–2416F   6. (1) If an application for registration is granted, the registration authority shall give the applicant a certificate of registration.

(2) A certificate of registration shall give prescribed[1] information about prescribed matters.

(3) Where, due to a change of circumstances, any part of the certificate requires to be amended, the registration authority shall issue an amended certificate.

(4) Where the registration authority is satisfied that the certificate has been lost or destroyed, the authority shall issue a copy, on payment by the registered person of any prescribed fee.

(5) For the purposes of Part XA, a person is—

(*a*) registered for providing child minding (in England or in Wales); or
(*b*) registered for providing day care on any premises,

if a certificate of registration to that effect is in force in respect of him.

1. The Child Minding and Day Care (Certificates of Registration) (England) Regulations 2001, SI 2001/1830, the Registration of Social Care and Independent Health Care (Wales) Regulations 2002, SI SI 2002/919 amended by SI 2002/2622 and 2935, SI 2003/710 and 2527, SI 2004/219 and 1756 and 3302 and the Day Care and Child Minding (Registration Fees) (England) Regulations 2005, SI 2005/2301 have been made.

Fees*

6–2416G   7. Regulations may require registered persons to pay to the registration authority, at or by the prescribed times, fees of the prescribed[1] amounts in respect of the discharge by the registration authority of its functions under Part XA *.

*Reproduced as in force in relation to England 3 October 2005, in Wales from a date to be appointed.
1. See the Day Care and Child Minding (Registration Fees) (England) Regulations 2005, SI 2005/2301.

Co-operation between authorities

6–2416H   8. (1) Where it appears to the Chief Inspector that any local authority in England could, by taking any specified action, help in the exercise of any of his functions under Part XA, he may request the help of that authority specifying the action in question.

(2) Where it appears to the Assembly that any local authority in Wales could, by taking any specified action, help in the exercise of any of its functions under Part XA, the Assembly may request the help of that authority specifying the action in question.

(3) An authority whose help is so requested shall comply with the request if it is compatible with their own statutory or other duties and obligations and does not unduly prejudice the discharge of any of their functions.]

6–2417

Section 88

SCHEDULE 10
AMENDMENTS OF ADOPTION LEGISLATION

(*As amended by the National Health Service and Community Care Act 1990, Sch 9 and the Adoption and Children Act 2002, Sch 3.*)

6–2418

Section 92

SCHEDULE 11
JURISDICTION

(*As amended by the Child Support Act 1991, s 45, the Family Law Act 1996, Schs 8 and 10 and the Adoption and Children Act 2002, Sch 3.*)

PART I[1]
GENERAL

Commencement of proceedings

6–2493 **1.** (1) The Lord Chancellor may by order specify proceedings under this Act or the Adoption and Children Act 2002 which may only be commenced in—

(a) a specified level of court;
(b) a court which falls within a specified class of court; or
(c) a particular court determined in accordance with, or specified in, the order.

(2) The Lord Chancellor may by order specify circumstances in which specified proceedings under this Act or the Adoption and Children Act 2002 (which might otherwise be commenced elsewhere) may only be commenced in—

(a) a specified level of court;
(b) a court which falls within a specified class of court; or
(c) a particular court determined in accordance with, or specified in, the order.

(2A) Sub-paragraphs (1) and (2) shall also apply in relation to proceedings—

(a) under section 55A of the Family Law Act 1986 (declarations of parentage); or
(b) which are to be dealt with in accordance with an order made under section 45 of the Child Support Act 1991 (jurisdiction of courts in certain proceedings under that Act).

(3) The Lord Chancellor may by order make provision by virtue of which, where specified proceedings with respect to a child under—

(a) this Act;
(b) the Adoption and Children Act 2002; or
(bb) section 20 (appeals) or 27 (reference to court for declaration of parentage) of the Child Support Act 1991,
(c) the High Court's inherent jurisdiction with respect to children,

have been commenced in or transferred to any court (whether or not by virtue of an order under this Schedule), any other specified family proceedings which may affect, or are otherwise connected with, the child may, in specified circumstances, only be commenced in that court.

(4) A class of court specified in an order under this Schedule may be described by reference to a description of proceedings and may include different levels of court.

---

1. See generally the Children (Allocation of Proceedings) Order 1991, post.

Transfer of proceedings

6–2494 **2.** (1) The Lord Chancellor may by order provide that in specified circumstances the whole, or any specified part of, specified proceedings to which this paragraph applies shall be transferred to—

(a) a specified level of court;
(b) a court which falls within a specified class of court; or
(c) a particular court determined in accordance with, or specified in, the order.

(2) Any order under this paragraph may provide for the transfer to be made at any stage, or specified stage, of the proceedings and whether or not the proceedings, or any part of them, have already been transferred.

(3) The proceedings to which this paragraph applies are—

(a) any proceedings under this Act;
(b) any proceedings under the Adoption and Children Act 2002;
(ba) any proceedings under section 55A of the Family Law Act 1986;
(bb) any proceedings under section 20 (appeals) of the Child Support Act 1991;
(c) any other proceedings which—

(i) are family proceedings for the purposes of this Act, other than proceedings under the inherent jurisdiction of the High Court; and
(ii) may affect, or are otherwise connected with, the child concerned.

(4) Proceedings to which this paragraph applies by virtue of sub-paragraph (3)(c) may only be transferred in

accordance with the provisions of an order made under this paragraph for the purpose of consolidating them with proceedings under—

    (a) this Act;
    (b) the Adoption and Children Act 2002; or
    (c) the High Court's inherent jurisdiction with respect to children.

(5) An order under this paragraph may make such provision as the Lord Chancellor thinks appropriate for excluding proceedings to which this paragraph applies from the operation of any enactment which would otherwise govern the transfer of those proceedings, or any part of them.

Hearings by single justice

6–2495   **3.** (1) In such circumstances as the Lord Chancellor may by order specify—

    (a) the jurisdiction of a magistrates' court to make an emergency protection order;
    (b) any specified question with respect to the transfer of specified proceedings to or from a magistrates' court in accordance with the provisions of an order under paragraph 2,

may be exercised by a single justice.
(2) Any provision made under this paragraph shall be without prejudice to any other enactment or rule of law relating to the functions which may be performed by a single justice of the peace.

General

6–2496   **4.** (1) For the purposes of this Schedule—

    (a) the commencement of proceedings under this Act includes the making of any application under this Act in the course of proceedings (whether or not those proceedings are proceedings under this Act); and
    (b) there are three levels of court, that is to say the High Court, any county court and any magistrates' court.

(2) In this Schedule "specified" means specified by an order made under this Schedule.
(3) Any order under paragraph 1 may make provision as to the effect of commencing proceedings in contravention of any of the provisions of the order.
(4) An order under paragraph 2 may make provision as to the effect of a failure to comply with any of the provisions of the order.
(5) An order under this Schedule may—

    (a) make such consequential, incidental or transitional provision as the Lord Chancellor considers expedient, including provision amending any other enactment so far as it concerns the jurisdiction of any court or justice of the peace;
    (b) make provision for treating proceedings which are—

      (i) in part proceedings of a kind mentioned in paragraph (a) or (b) of paragraph 2(3); and
      (ii) in part proceedings of a kind mentioned in paragraph (c) of paragraph 2(3),

    as consisting entirely of proceedings of one or other of those kinds, for the purposes of the application of any order made under paragraph 2.

PART II
CONSEQUENTIAL AMENDMENTS

6–2681

  Section 108(4)

SCHEDULE 12
MINOR AMENDMENTS

6–2682

  Section 108(5)

SCHEDULE 13
CONSEQUENTIAL AMENDMENTS

  (*Repealed*).

  Section 108(6)

SCHEDULE 14
TRANSITIONALS AND SAVINGS

(*As amended by the Courts and Legal Services Act 1990, Schs 16 and 20, the Armed Forces Act 1991, Sch 3 and the Access to Justice Act 1999, Sch 15 and modified by SI 1991/828, SI 1991/1990.*)

Pending proceedings, etc

6–2683   **1.** (1) Subject to sub-paragraphs (1A) and (4), nothing in any provision of this Act (other than the repeals mentioned in sub-paragraph (2)) shall affect any proceedings which are pending immediately before the commencement of that provision.
(1A) Proceedings pursuant to section 7(2) of the Family Law Reform Act 1969 (committal of wards of court to care of local authority) or in the exercise of the High Court's inherent jurisdiction with respect to children which are pending in relation to a child who has been placed or allowed to remain in the care of a local authority shall not be treated as pending proceedings after 13th October 1992 for the purposes of this Schedule if no final order has been made by that date pursuant to section 7(2) of the 1969 Act or in the exercise of the High Court's inherent jurisdiction in respect of the child's care.
(2) The repeals are those of—

    (a) section 42(3) of the Matrimonial Causes Act 1973 (declaration by court that party to marriage unfit to have custody of children of family); and

(b)   section 38 of the Sexual Offences Act 1956 (power of court to divest person of authority over girl or boy in cases of incest).

(3)   For the purposes of the following provisions of this Schedule, any reference to an order in force immediately before the commencement of a provision of this Act shall be construed as including a reference to an order made after that commencement in proceedings pending before that commencement.

(4)   Sub-paragraph (3) is not to be read as making the order in question have effect from a date earlier than that on which it was made.

(5)   An order under section 96(3) may make such provision with respect to the application of the order in relation to proceedings which are pending when the order comes into force as the Lord Chancellor considers appropriate.

6–2684   **2.** Where, immediately before the date on which Part IV comes into force, there was in force an order under section 3(1) of the Children and Young Persons Act 1963 (order directing a local authority to bring a child or young person before a juvenile court under section 1 of the Children and Young Persons Act 1969), the order shall cease to have effect on that day.

CUSTODY ORDERS, ETC

Cessation of declarations of unfitness, etc

6–2685   **3.** Where, immediately before the day on which Parts I and II come into force, there was in force—

(a)   a declaration under section 42(3) of the Matrimonial Causes Act 1973 (declaration by court that party to marriage unfit to have custody of children of family); or

(b)   an order under section 38(1) of the Sexual Offences Act 1956 divesting a person of authority over a girl or boy in a case of incest;

the declaration or, as the case may be, the order shall cease to have effect on that day.

The Family Law Reform Act 1987 (c 42)

Conversion of orders under section 4

6–2686   **4.** Where, immediately before the day on which Parts I and II come into force, there was in force an order under section 4(1) of the Family Law Reform Act 1987 (order giving father parental rights and duties in relation to a child), then, on and after that day, the order shall be deemed to be an order under section 4 of this Act giving the father parental responsibility for the child.

Orders to which paragraphs 6 to 11 apply

6–2687   **5.** (1)   In paragraphs 6 to 11 "an existing order" means any order which—

(a)   as in force immediately before the commencement of Parts I and II;
(b)   was made under any enactment mentioned in sub-paragraph (2);
(c)   determines all or any of the following—

(i)   who is to have custody of a child;
(ii)   who is to have care and control of a child;
(iii)   who is to have access to a child;
(iv)   any matter with respect to a child's education or upbringing; and

(d)   is not an order of a kind mentioned in paragraph 15(1).

(2)   The enactments are—

(a)   the Domestic Proceedings and Magistrates' Courts Act 1978;
(b)   the Children Act 1975;
(c)   the Matrimonial Causes Act 1973;
(d)   the Guardianship of Minors Acts 1971 and 1973;
(e)   the Matrimonial Causes Act 1965;
(f)   the Matrimonial Proceedings (Magistrates' Courts) Act 1960.

(3)   For the purposes of this paragraph and paragraphs 6 to 11 "custody" includes legal custody and joint as well as sole custody but does not include access.

Parental responsibility of parents

6–2688   **6.** (1)   Where—

(a)   a child's father and mother were married to each other at the time of his birth; and
(b)   there is an existing order with respect to the child,

each parent shall have parental responsibility for the child in accordance with section 2 as modified by sub-paragraph (3).

(2)   Where—

(a)   a child's father and mother were not married to each other at the time of his birth; and
(b)   there is an existing order with respect to the child,

section 2 shall apply as modified by sub-paragraphs (3) and (4).

(3)   The modification is that for section 2(8) there shall be substituted—

"(8)   The fact that a person has parental responsibility for a child does not entitle him to act in a way which would be incompatible with any existing order or any order made under this Act with respect to the child".

(4)   The modifications are that—

(a) for the purposes of section 2(2), where the father has custody or care and control of the child by virtue of any existing order, the court shall be deemed to have made (at the commencement of that section) an order under section 4(1) giving him parental responsibility for the child; and

(b) where by virtue of paragraph (a) a court is deemed to have made an order under section 4(1) in favour of a father who has care and control of a child by virtue of an existing order, the court shall not bring the order under section 4(1) to an end at any time while he has care and control of the child by virtue of the order.

Persons who are not parents but who have custody or care and control

6–2689   7. (1) Where a person who is not the parent or guardian of a child has custody or care and control of him by virtue of an existing order, that person shall have parental responsibility for him so long as he continues to have that custody or care and control by virtue of the order.

(2) Where sub-paragraph (1) applies, Parts I and II and paragraph 15 of Schedule 1 shall have effect as modified by this paragraph.

(3) The modifications are that—

(a) for section 2(8) there shall be substituted—

"(8) The fact that a person has parental responsibility for a child does not entitle him to act in a way which would be incompatible with any existing order or with any order made under this Act with respect to the child";

(b) at the end of section 10(4) there shall be inserted—

"(c) any person who has custody or care and control of a child by virtue of any existing order"; and

(c) at the end of section 34(1)(c) there shall be inserted—

"(cc)where immediately before the care order was made there was an existing order by virtue of which a person had custody or care and control of the child, that person."

(d) for paragraph 15 of Schedule 1 there shall be substituted—

"**15.** Where a child lives with a person as the result of a custodianship order within the meaning of section 33 of the Children Act 1975, a local authority may make contributions to that person towards the cost of the accommodation and maintenance of the child so long as that person continues to have legal custody of that child by virtue of the order."

Persons who have care and control

6–2690   8. (1) Sub-paragraphs (2) to (6) apply where a person has care and control of a child by virtue of an existing order, but they shall cease to apply when that order ceases to have effect.

(2) Section 5 shall have effect as if—

(a) for any reference to a residence order in favour of a parent or guardian there were substituted a reference to any existing order by virtue of which the parent or guardian has care and control of the child; and

(b) for subsection (9) there were substituted—

"(9) Subsections (1) and (7) do not apply if the existing order referred to in paragraph (b) of those subsections was one by virtue of which a surviving parent of the child also had care and control of him."

(3) Section 10 shall have effect as if for subsection (5)(c)(i) there were substituted—

"(i) in any case where by virtue of an existing order any person or persons has or have care and control of the child, has the consent of that person or each of those persons".

(4) Section 20 shall have effect as if for subsection (9)(a) there were substituted "who has care and control of the child by virtue of an existing order."

(5) Section 23 shall have effect as if for subsection (4)(c) there were substituted—

"(c) where the child is in care and immediately before the care order was made there was an existing order by virtue of which a person had care and control of the child, that person."

(6) In Schedule 1, paragraphs 1(1) and 14(1) shall have effect as if for the words "in whose favour a residence order is in force with respect to the child" there were substituted "who has been given care and control of the child by virtue of an existing order".

Persons who have access

6–2691   9. (1) Sub-paragraphs (2) to (4) apply where a person has access by virtue of an existing order.

(2) Section 10 shall have effect as if after subsection (5) there were inserted—

"(5A) Any person who has access to a child by virtue of an existing order is entitled to apply for a contact order."

(3) Section 16(2) shall have effect as if after paragraph (b) there were inserted—

"(bb)any person who has access to the child by virtue of an existing order."

(4) Sections 43(11), 44(13) and 46(10), shall have effect as if in each case after paragraph (d) there were inserted—

"(dd)any person who has been given access to him by virtue of an existing order."

Enforcement of certain existing orders

6–2692   10. (1) Sub-paragraph (2) applies in relation to any existing order which, but for the repeal by this Act of—

(a) section 13(1) of the Guardianship of Minors Act 1971;

(b)   section 43(1) of the Children Act 1975; or

(c)   section 33 of the Domestic Proceedings and Magistrates' Courts Act 1978,

(provisions concerning the enforcement of custody orders) might have been enforced as if it were an order requiring a person to give up a child to another person.

(2) Where this sub-paragraph applies, the existing order may, after the repeal of the enactments mentioned in sub-paragraph (1)(a) to (c), be enforced under section 14 as if—

(a)   any reference to a residence order were a reference to the existing order; and

(b)   any reference to a person in whose favour the residence order is in force were a reference to a person to whom actual custody of the child is given by an existing order which is in force.

(3) In sub-paragraph (2) "actual custody", in relation to a child, means the actual possession of his person.

Discharge of existing orders

6–2693 11. (1) The making of a residence order or a care order with respect to a child who is the subject of an existing order discharges the existing order.

(2) Where the court makes any section 8 order (other than a residence order) with respect to a child with respect to whom any existing order is in force, the existing order shall have effect subject to the section 8 order.

(3) The court may discharge an existing order which is in force with respect to a child—

(a)   in any family proceedings relating to the child or in which any question arises with respect to the child's welfare; or

(b)   on the application of—

(i)   any parent or guardian of the child;

(ii) the child himself; or

(iii) any person named in the order.

(4) A child may not apply for the discharge of an existing order except with the leave of the court.

(5) The power in sub-paragraph (3) to discharge an existing order includes the power to discharge any part of the order.

(6) In considering whether to discharge an order under the power conferred by sub-paragraph (3) the court shall, if the discharge of the order is opposed by any party to the proceedings, have regard in particular to the matters mentioned in section 1(3).

GUARDIANS

Existing guardians to be guardians under this Act

6–2694 12[1]. (1) Any appointment of a person as guardian of a child which—

(a)   was made—

(i)   under sections 3 to 5 of the Guardianship of Minors Act 1971;

(ii) under section 38(3) of the Sexual Offences Act 1956; or

(iii) under the High Court's inherent jurisdiction with respect to children; and

(b)   has taken effect before the commencement of section 5,

shall (subject to sub-paragraph (2)) be deemed, on and after the commencement of section 5, to be an appointment made and having effect under that section.

(2) Where an appointment of a person as guardian of a child has effect under section 5 by virtue of sub-paragraph (1)(a)(ii), the appointment shall not have effect for a period which is longer than any period specified in the order.

---

1. References in paras 12, 13 and 14 to the commencement of s 5 shall be construed as references to the commencement of subs-s (1)–(10) and (13) of that section except in relation to the appointment of a guardian of the estate of any child in which case they shall be construed as a reference to the commencement of subss (11) and (12) of that section (Children Act 1989 (Commencement and Transitional Provisions) Order 1991, SI 1991/828 amended by SI 1991/1990, art 1C).

Appointment of guardian not yet in effect

6–2695 13[1]. Any appointment of a person to be a guardian of a child—

(a)   which was made as mentioned in paragraph 12(1)(a)(i); but

(b)   which, immediately before the commencement of section 5, had not taken effect,

shall take effect in accordance with section 5 (as modified, where it applies, by paragraph 8(2)).

---

1. See note 1 to para 12 in para **6–2694**, ante.

Persons deemed to be appointed as guardians under existing wills

6–2696 14[1]. For the purposes of the Wills Act 1837 and of this Act any disposition by will and testament or devise of the custody and tuition of any child, made before the commencement of section 5 and paragraph 1 of Schedule 13, shall be deemed to be an appointment by will of a guardian of the child.

---

1. See note 1 to para 12 in para **6–2694**, ante.

Children in care

Children in compulsory care

6–2697 15.—(1) Sub-paragraph (2) applies where, immediately before the day on which Part IV comes into force, a person was—

(*a*) in care by virtue of—

    (i)   a care order under section 1 of the Children and Young Persons Act 1969;
    (ii) a care order under section 15 of that Act, on discharging a supervision order made under section 1 of that Act; or
    (iii) an order or authorisation under section 25 or 26 of that Act;

(*b*) (*Repealed*);
(*c*) in care—

    (i)   under section 2 of the Child Care Act 1980; or
    (ii) by virtue of paragraph 1 of Schedule 4 to that Act (which extends the meaning of a child in care under section 2 to include children in care under section 1 of the Children Act 1948),

and a child in respect of whom a resolution under section 3 of the Act of 1980 or section 2 of the Act of 1948 was in force;

(*d*) a child in respect of whom a resolution had been passed under section 65 of the Child Care Act 1980;
(*e*) in care by virtue of an order under—

    (i)   section 2(1)(*e*) of the Matrimonial Proceedings (Magistrates' Courts) Act 1960;
    (ii) section 7(2) of the Family Law Reform Act 1969;
    (iii) section 43(1) of the Matrimonial Causes Act 1973; or
    (iv) section 2(2)(*b*) of the Guardianship Act 1973;
    (v) section 10 of the Domestic Proceedings and Magistrates' Courts Act 1978,

(orders having effect for certain purposes as if the child had been received into care under section 2 of the Child Care Act 1980);

(*f*) in care by virtue of an order made, on the revocation of a custodianship order, under section 36 of the Children Act 1975;
(*g*) in care by virtue of an order made, on the refusal of an adoption order, under section 26 of the Adoption Act 1976 or any order having effect (by virtue of paragraph 1 of Schedule 2 to that Act) as if made under that section; or
(*h*) in care by virtue of an order of the court made in the exercise of the High Court's inherent jurisdiction with respect to children.

(2) Where this sub-paragraph applies, then, on and after the day on which Part IV commences—

(*a*) the order or resolution in question shall be deemed to be a care order;
(*b*) the authority in whose care the person was immediately before that commencement shall be deemed to be the authority designated in that deemed care order; and
(*c*) any reference to a child in the care of a local authority shall include a reference to a person who is the subject of such a deemed care order,

and the provisions of this Act shall apply accordingly, subject to paragraph 16.

Modifications

6–2698 16.—(1) Sub-paragraph (2) only applies where a person who is the subject of a care order by virtue of paragraph 15(2) is a person falling within sub-paragraph (1)(*a*) of that paragraph.

(2) Where the person would otherwise have remained in care until reaching the age of nineteen, by virtue of—

(*a*) section 20(3)(*a*) or 21(1) of the Children and Young Persons Act 1969;
(*b*) (*Repealed*);

(3) (*Repealed*).

(3A) Where in respect of a child who has been placed or allowed to remain in the care of a local authority pursuant to section 7(2) of the Family Law Reform Act 1969 or in the exercise of the High Court's inherent jurisdiction and the child is still in the care of a local authority, proceedings have ceased by virtue of paragraph 1(1A) to be treated as pending, paragraph 15(2) shall apply on 14th October 1992 as if the child was in care pursuant to an order as specified in paragraph 15(1)(*e*)(ii) or (*h*) as the case may be.

(4) Sub-paragraphs (5) and (6) only apply where a child who is the subject of a care order by virtue of paragraph 15(2) is a person falling within sub-paragraph (1)(*e*) to (*h*) of that paragraph.

(5) Subject to sub-paragraph (6), where a court, on making the order, or at any time thereafter, gave directions—

(*a*) under section 4(4)(*a*) of the Guardianship Act 1973;
(*b*) under section 43(5)(*a*) of the Matrimonial Causes Act 1973; or
(*c*) in the exercise of the High Court's inherent jurisdiction with respect to children,

as to the exercise by the authority of any powers, those directions shall, subject to the provisions of section 25 of this Act and of any regulations made under that section, continue to have effect (regardless of any conflicting provision in this Act other than section 25) until varied or discharged by a court under this sub-paragraph.

(6) Where directions referred to in sub-paragraph (5) are to the effect that a child be placed in accommodation provided for the purpose of restricting liberty then the directions shall cease to have effect upon the expiry of the maximum period specified by regulations under section 25(2)(*a*) in relation to children of his description, calculated from 14th October 1991.

Cessation of wardship where ward in care

6–2699   16A. (1) Where a child who is a ward of court is in care by virtue of—

(a)   an order under section 7(2) of the Family Law Reform Act 1969; or
(b)   an order made in the exercise of the High Court's inherent jurisdiction with respect to children,

he shall, on the day on which Part IV commences, cease to be a ward of court.

(2) Where immediately before the day on which Part IV commences a child was in the care of a local authority and as a result of an order—

(a)   pursuant to section 7(2) of the Family Law Reform Act 1969; or
(b)   made in the exercise of the High Court's inherent jurisdiction with respect to children,

continued to be in the care of a local authority and was made a ward of court, he shall on the day on which Part IV commences, cease to be a ward of court.

(3) Sub-paragraphs (1) and (2) do not apply in proceedings which are pending.

Children placed with parent etc while in compulsory care

6–2700   17. (1) This paragraph applies where a child is deemed by paragraph 15 to be in the care of a local authority under an order or resolution which is deemed by that paragraph to be a care order.

(2) If, immediately before the day on which Part III comes into force, the child was allowed to be under the charge and control of—

(a)   a parent or guardian under section 21(2) of the Child Care Act 1980; or
(b)   a person who, before the child was in the authority's care, had care and control of the child by virtue of an order falling within paragraph 5,

on and after that day the provision made by and under section 23(5) shall apply as if the child had been placed with the person in question in accordance with that provision.

Orders for access to children in compulsory care

6–2701   18. (1) This paragraph applies to any access order—

(a)   made under section 12C of the Child Care Act 1980 (access orders with respect to children in care of local authorities); and
(b)   in force immediately before the commencement of Part IV.

(2) On and after the commencement of Part IV, the access order shall have effect as an order made under section 34 in favour of the person named in the order.

6–2702   18A. (1) This paragraph applies to any decision of a local authority to terminate arrangements for access or to refuse to make such arrangements—

(a)   of which notice has been given under, and in accordance with, section 12B of the Child Care Act 1980 (termination of access); and
(b)   which is in force immediately before the commencement of Part IV.

(2) On and after the commencement of Part IV, a decision to which this paragraph applies shall have effect as a court order made under section 34(4) authorising the local authority to refuse to allow contact between the child and the person to whom notice was given under section 12B of the Child Care Act 1980.

6–2703   19. (1) This paragraph applies where, immediately before the commencement of Part IV, an access order made under section 12C of the Act of 1980 was suspended by virtue of an order made under section 12E of that Act (suspension of access orders in emergencies).

(2) The suspending order shall continue to have effect as if this Act had not been passed.

(3) If—

(a)   before the commencement of Part IV; and
(b)   during the period for which the operation of the access order is suspended,

the local authority concerned made an application for its variation or discharge to an appropriate juvenile court, its operation shall be suspended until the date on which the application to vary or discharge it is determined or abandoned.

Children in voluntary care

6–2712   20. (1) This paragraph applies where, immediately before the day on which Part III comes into force—

(a)   a child was in the care of a local authority—

(i)   under section 2(1) of the Child Care Act 1980; or
(ii)   by virtue of paragraph 1 of Schedule 4 to that Act (which extends the meaning of references to children in care under section 2 to include references to children in care under section 1 of the Children Act 1948); and

(b)   he was not a person in respect of whom a resolution under section 3 of the Act of 1980 or section 2 of the Act of 1948 was in force.

(2) Where this paragraph applies, the child shall, on and after the day mentioned in sub-paragraph (1), be treated for the purposes of this Act as a child who is provided with accommodation by the local authority under Part III, but he shall cease to be so treated once he ceases to be so accommodated in accordance with the provisions of Part III.

(3) Where—

(a)   this paragraph applies; and

(b) the child, immediately before the day mentioned in sub-paragraph (1), was (by virtue of section 21(2) of the Act of 1980) under the charge and control of a person falling within paragraph 17(2)(a) or (b),

the child shall not be treated for the purposes of this Act as if he were being looked after by the authority concerned.

Boarded out children

6–2713　21. (1) Where, immediately before the day on which Part III comes into force, a child in the care of a local authority—

    (a) was—

        (i) boarded out with a person under section 21(1)(a) of the Child Care Act 1980; or
        (ii) placed under the charge and control of a person, under section 21(2) of that Act; and

    (b) the person with whom he was boarded out, or (as the case may be) placed, was not a person falling within paragraph 17(2)(a) or (b),

on and after that day, he shall be treated (subject to sub-paragraph (2)) as having been placed with a local authority foster parent and shall cease to be so treated when he ceases to be placed with that person in accordance with the provisions of this Act.

(2) Regulations made under section 23(2)(a) shall not apply in relation to a person who is a local authority foster parent by virtue of sub-paragraph (1) before the end of the period of twelve months beginning with the day on which Part III comes into force and accordingly that person shall for that period be subject—

    (a) in a case falling within sub-paragraph (1)(a)(i), to terms and regulations mentioned in section 21(1)(a) of the Act of 1980; and

    (b) in a case falling within sub-paragraph (1)(a)(ii), to terms fixed under section 21(2) of that Act and regulations made under section 22A of that Act,

as if that Act had not been repealed by this Act.

Children in care to qualify for advice and assistance

6–2714　22. Any reference in Part III to a person qualifying for advice and assistance shall be construed as including a reference to a person within the area of the local authority in question who is under twenty-one and who was, at any time after reaching the age of sixteen but while still a child—

    (a) a person falling within—

        (i) any of paragraphs (a) to (h) of paragraph 15(1); or
        (ii) paragraph 20(1); or

    (b) the subject of a criminal care order (within the meaning of paragraph 34).

Emigration of children in care

6–2715　23. Where—

    (a) the Secretary of State has received a request in writing from a local authority that he give his consent under section 24 of the Child Care Act 1980 to the emigration of a child in their care; but

    (b) immediately before the repeal of the Act of 1980 by this Act, he has not determined whether or not to give his consent,

section 24 of the Act of 1980 shall continue to apply (regardless of that repeal) until the Secretary of State has determined whether or not to give his consent to the request.

Contributions for maintenance of children in care

6–2716　24. (1) Where, immediately before the day on which Part III of Schedule 2 comes into force, there was in force an order made (or having effect as if made) under any of the enactments mentioned in sub-paragraph (2), then, on and after that day—

    (a) the order shall have effect as if made under paragraph 23(2) of Schedule 2 against a person liable to contribute; and

    (b) Part III of Schedule 2 shall apply to the order, subject to the modifications in sub-paragraph (3).

(2) The enactments are—

    (a) section 11(4) of the Domestic Proceedings and Magistrates' Courts Act 1978;
    (b) section 26(2) of the Adoption Act 1976;
    (c) section 36(5) of the Children Act 1975;
    (d) section 2(3) of the Guardianship Act 1973;
    (e) section 2(1)(h) of the Matrimonial Proceedings (Magistrates' Courts) Act 1960,

(provisions empowering the court to make an order requiring a person to make periodical payments to a local authority in respect of a child in care).

(3) The modifications are that, in paragraph 23 of Schedule 2—

    (a) in sub-paragraph (4), paragraph (a) shall be omitted;
    (b) for sub-paragraph (6) there shall be substituted—

"(6) Where—

    (a) a contribution order is in force;
    (b) the authority serve a contribution notice under paragraph 22; and
    (c) the contributor and the authority reach an agreement under paragraph 22(7) in respect of the contribution notice,

the effect of the agreement shall be to discharge the order from the date on which it is agreed that the agreement shall take effect"; and

(c)　at the end of sub-paragraph (10) there shall be inserted—

"and

(c)　where the order is against a person who is not a parent of the child, shall be made with due regard to—

(i)　whether that person had assumed responsibility for the maintenance of the child, and, if so, the extent to which and basis on which he assumed that responsibility and the length of the period during which he met that responsibility;

(ii)　whether he did so knowing that the child was not his child;

(iii)　the liability of any other person to maintain the child."

SUPERVISION ORDERS

Orders under section 1(3)(b) or 21(2) of the 1969 Act

6–2717　**25.** (1)　This paragraph applies to any supervision order—

(a)　made—

(i)　under section 1(3)(b) of the Children and Young Persons Act 1969; or

(ii)　under section 21(2) of that Act on the discharge of a care order made under section 1(3)(c) of that Act; and

(b)　in force immediately before the commencement of Part IV.

(2)　On and after the commencement of Part IV, the order shall be deemed to be a supervision order made under section 31 and—

(a)　any requirement of the order that the child reside with a named individual shall continue to have effect while the order remains in force, unless the court otherwise directs;

(b)　any other requirement imposed by the court, or directions given by the supervisor, shall be deemed to have been imposed or given under the appropriate provisions of Schedule 3.

(3)　Where, immediately before the commencement of Part IV, the order had been in force for a period of six months or more, it shall cease to have effect at the end of the period of six months beginning with the day on which Part IV comes into force unless—

(a)　the court directs that it shall cease to have effect at the end of a different period (which shall not exceed three years);

(b)　it ceases to have effect earlier in accordance with section 91; or

(c)　it would have ceased to have had effect earlier had this Act not been passed.

(4)　Where sub-paragraph (3) applies, paragraph 6 of Schedule 3 shall not apply.

(5)　Where, immediately before the commencement of Part IV, the order had been in force for less than six months it shall cease to have effect in accordance with section 91 and paragraph 6 of Schedule 3 unless—

(a)　the court directs that it shall cease to have effect at the end of a different period (which shall not exceed three years); or

(b)　it would have ceased to have had effect earlier had this Act not been passed.

Other supervision orders

6–2718　**26.** (1)　This paragraph applies to any order for the supervision of a child which was in force immediately before the commencement of Part IV and was made under—

(a)　section 2(1)(f) of the Matrimonial Proceedings (Magistrates' Courts) Act 1960;

(b)　section 7(4) of the Family Law Reform Act 1969;

(c)　section 44 of the Matrimonial Causes Act 1973;

(d)　section 2(2)(a) of the Guardianship Act 1973;

(e)　section 34(5) or 36(3)(b) of the Children Act 1975;

(f)　section 26(1)(a) of the Adoption Act 1976; or

(g)　section 9 of the Domestic Proceedings and Magistrates' Courts Act 1978.

(2)　The order shall not be deemed to be a supervision order made under any provision of this Act but shall nevertheless continue in force for a period of one year beginning with the day on which Part IV comes into force unless—

(a)　the court directs that it shall cease to have effect at the end of a lesser period; or

(b)　it would have ceased to have had effect earlier had this Act not been passed.

PLACES OF SAFETY ORDERS

6–2719　**27.** (1)　This paragraph applies to—

(a)　any order or warrant authorising the removal of a child to a place of safety which—

(i)　was made, or issued, under any of the enactments mentioned in sub-paragraph (2); and

(ii)　was in force immediately before the commencement of Part IV; and

(b)　any interim order made under section 23(5) of the Children and Young Persons Act 1963 or section 28(6) of the Children and Young Persons Act 1969.

(2)　The enactments are—

(a)　section 40 of the Children and Young Persons Act 1933 (warrant to search for or remove child);

(b)　section 28(1) of the Children and Young Persons Act 1969 (detention of child in place of safety);

(*c*) section 34(1) of the Adoption Act 1976 (removal of protected children from unsuitable surroundings);
(*d*) section 12(1) of the Foster Children Act 1980 (removal of foster children kept in unsuitable surroundings).

(3) The order or warrant shall continue to have effect as if this Act had not been passed.
(4) Any enactment repealed by this Act shall continue to have effect in relation to the order or warrant so far as is necessary for the purposes of securing that the effect of the order is what it would have been had this Act not been passed.
(5) Sub-paragraph (4) does not apply to the power to make an interim order or further interim order given by section 23(5) of the Children and Young Persons Act 1963 or section 28(6) of the Children and Young Persons Act 1969.
(6) Where, immediately before section 28 of the Children and Young Persons Act 1969 is repealed by this Act, a child is being detained under the powers granted by that section, he may continue to be detained in accordance with that section but subsection (6) shall not apply.

RECOVERY OF CHILDREN

6–2730 **28.** The repeal by this Act of subsection (1) of section 16 of the Child Care Act 1980 (arrest of child absent from compulsory care) shall not affect the operation of that section in relation to any child arrested before the coming into force of the repeal.

6–2731 **29.** (1) This paragraph applies where—

(*a*) a summons has been issued under section 15 or 16 of the Child Care Act 1980 (recovery of children in voluntary or compulsory care); and
(*b*) the child concerned is not produced in accordance with the summons before the repeal of that section by this Act comes into force.

(2) The summons, any warrant issued in connection with it and section 15 or (as the case may be) section 16, shall continue to have effect as if this Act had not been passed.

6–2732 **30.** The amendment by paragraph 27 of Schedule 12 of section 32 of the Children and Young Persons Act 1969 (detention of absentees) shall not affect the operation of that section in relation to—

(*a*) any child arrested; or
(*b*) any summons or warrant issued,

under that section before the coming into force of that paragraph.

VOLUNTARY ORGANISATIONS: PARENTAL RIGHTS RESOLUTIONS

6–2733 **31.** (1) This paragraph applies to a resolution—

(*a*) made under section 64 of the Child Care Act 1980 (transfer of parental rights and duties to voluntary organisations); and
(*b*) in force immediately before the commencement of Part IV.

(2) The resolution shall continue to have effect until the end of the period of six months beginning with the day on which Part IV comes into force unless it is brought to an end earlier in accordance with the provisions of the Act of 1980 preserved by this paragraph.
(3) While the resolution remains in force, any relevant provisions of, or made under, the Act of 1980 shall continue to have effect with respect to it.
(4) Sub-paragraph (3) does not apply to—

(*a*) section 62 of the Act of 1980 and any regulations made under that section (arrangements by voluntary organisations for emigration of children); or
(*b*) section 65 of the Act of 1980 (duty of local authority to assume parental rights and duties).

(5) Section 5(2) of the Act of 1980 (which is applied to resolutions under Part VI of that Act by section 64(7) of that Act) shall have effect with respect to the resolution as if the reference in paragraph (*c*) to an appointment of a guardian under section 5 of the Guardianship of Minors Act 1971 were a reference to an appointment of a guardian under section 5 of this Act.

FOSTER CHILDREN

6–2734 **32.** (1) This paragraph applies where—

(*a*) immediately before the commencement of Part VIII, a child was a foster child within the meaning of the Foster Children Act 1980; and
(*b*) the circumstances of the case are such that, had Parts VIII and IX then been in force, he would have been treated for the purposes of this Act as a child who was being provided with accommodation in a children's home and not as a child who was being privately fostered.

(2) If the child continues to be cared for and provided with accommodation as before, section 63(1) and (10) shall not apply in relation to him if—

(*a*) an application for registration of the home in question is made under section 63 before the end of the period of three months beginning with the day on which Part VIII comes into force; and
(*b*) the application has not been refused or, if it has been refused—

(i) the period for an appeal against the decision has not expired; or
(ii) an appeal against the refusal has been made but has not been determined or abandoned.

(3) While section 63(1) and (10) does not apply, the child shall be treated as a privately fostered child for the purposes of Part IX.

NURSERIES AND CHILD MINDING

6–2735 33. (1) Sub-paragraph (2) applies where, immediately before the commencement of Part X, any premises are registered under section 1(1)(*a*) of the Nurseries and Child-Minders Regulation Act 1948 (registration of premises, other than premises wholly or mainly used as private dwellings, where children are received to be looked after).

(2) During the transitional period, the provisions of the Act of 1948 shall continue to have effect with respect to those premises to the exclusion of Part X.

(3) Nothing in sub-paragraph (2) shall prevent the local authority concerned from registering any person under section 71(1)(*b*) with respect to the premises.

(4) In this paragraph "the transitional period" means the period ending with—

(*a*) the first anniversary of the commencement of Part X; or

(*b*) if earlier, the date on which the local authority concerned registers any person under section 71(1)(*b*) with respect to the premises.

6–2736 34. (1) Sub-paragraph (2) applies where, immediately before the commencement of Part X—

(*a*) a person is registered under section 1(1)(*b*) of the Act of 1948 (registration of persons who for reward receive into their homes children under the age of five to be looked after); and

(*b*) all the children looked after by him as mentioned in section 1(1)(*b*) of that Act are under the age of five.

(2) During the transitional period, the provisions of the Act of 1948 shall continue to have effect with respect to that person to the exclusion of Part X.

(3) Nothing in sub-paragraph (2) shall prevent the local authority concerned from registering that person under section 71(1)(*a*).

(4) In this paragraph "the transitional period" means the period ending with—

(*a*) the first anniversary of the commencement of Part X; or

(*b*) if earlier, the date on which the local authority concerned registers that person under section 71(1)(*a*).

CHILDREN ACCOMMODATED IN CERTAIN ESTABLISHMENTS

6–2737 35. In calculating, for the purposes of section 85(1)(*a*) or 86(1)(*a*), the period of time for which a child has been accommodated any part of that period which fell before the day on which that section came into force shall be disregarded.

CRIMINAL CARE ORDERS

6–2738 36. (1) This paragraph applies where, immediately before the commencement of section 90(2) there was in force an order ("a criminal care order") made—

(*a*) under section 7(7)(*a*) of the Children and Young Persons Act 1969 (alteration in treatment of young offenders etc); or

(*b*) under section 15(1) of that Act, on discharging a supervision order made under section 7(7)(*b*) of that Act.

(2) The criminal care order shall continue to have effect until the end of the period of six months beginning with the day on which section 90(2) comes into force unless it is brought to an end earlier in accordance with—

(*a*) the provisions of the Act of 1969 preserved by sub-paragraph (3)(*a*); or

(*b*) this paragraph.

(3) While the criminal care order remains in force, any relevant provisions—

(*a*) of the Act of 1969; and

(*b*) of the Child Care Act 1980,

shall continue to have effect with respect to it.

(4) While the criminal care order remains in force, a court may, on the application of the appropriate person, make—

(*a*) a residence order;

(*b*) a care order or a supervision order under section 31;

(*c*) an education supervision order under section 36 (regardless of subsection (6) of that section); or

(*d*) an order falling within sub-paragraph (5),

and shall, on making any of those orders, discharge the criminal care order.

(5) The order mentioned in sub-paragraph (4)(*d*) is an order having effect as if it were a supervision order of a kind mentioned in section 12AA of the Act of 1969 (as inserted by paragraph 23 of Schedule 12), that is to say, a supervision order—

(*a*) imposing a requirement that the child shall live for a specified period in local authority accommodation; but

(*b*) in relation to which the conditions mentioned in subsection (6) of section 12AA are not required to be satisfied.

(6) The maximum period which may be specified in an order made under sub-paragraph (4)(*d*) is six months and such an order may stipulate that the child shall not live with a named person.

(7) Where this paragraph applies, section 5 of the Rehabilitation of Offenders Act 1974 (rehabilitation periods for particular sentences) shall have effect regardless of the repeals in it made by this Act.

(8) In sub-paragraph (4) "appropriate person" means—

(a) in the case of an application for a residence order, any person (other than a local authority) who has the leave of the court;
(b) in the case of an application for an education supervision order, a local education authority; and
(c) in any other case, the local authority to whose care the child was committed by the order.

MISCELLANEOUS
Consents under the Marriage Act 1949 (c 76)

6–2739   **37.** (1) In the circumstances mentioned in sub-paragraph (2), section 3 of and Schedule 2 to the Marriage Act 1949 (consents to marry) shall continue to have effect regardless of the amendment of that Act by paragraph 5 of Schedule 12.

(2) The circumstances are that—

(a) immediately before the day on which paragraph 5 of Schedule 12 comes into force, there is in force—

    (i) an existing order, as defined in paragraph 5(1); or
    (ii) an order of a kind mentioned in paragraph 16(1); and

(b) section 3 of and Schedule 2 to the Act of 1949 would, but for this Act, have applied to the marriage of the child who is the subject of the order.

The Children Act 1975 (c 72)

6–2740   **38.** The amendments of other enactments made by the following provisions of the Children Act 1975 shall continue to have effect regardless of the repeal of the Act of 1975 by this Act—

(a) section 68(4), (5) and (7) (amendments of section 32 of the Children and Young Persons Act 1969); and
(b) in Schedule 3—

    (i) paragraph 13 (amendments of Births and Deaths Registration Act 1953);
    (ii) paragraph 43 (amendment of Perpetuities and Accumulations Act 1964);
    (iii) paragraphs 46 and 47 (amendments of Health Services and Public Health Act 1968); and
    (iv) paragraph 77 (amendment of Parliamentary and Other Pensions Act 1972).

The Child Care Act 1980 (c 5)

6–2741   **39.** The amendment made to section 106(2)(a) of the Children and Young Persons Act 1963 by paragraph 26 of Schedule 5 to the Child Care Act 1980 shall continue to have effect regardless of the repeal of the Act of 1980 by this Act.

Legal aid

6–2742   **40.** (*Repealed*)

6–2743

Section 108(7)   SCHEDULE 15
                        REPEALS

Human Fertilisation and Embryology Act 1990[1]
(1990 c 37)

Principal terms used

6–2800   **1. Meaning of "embryo", "gamete" and associated expressions.** (1) In this Act, except where otherwise stated—

(a) embryo means a live human embryo where fertilisation is complete[2], and
(b) references to an embryo include an egg in the process of fertilisation,

and, for this purpose, fertilisation is not complete until the appearance of a two cell zygote.

(2) This Act, so far as it governs bringing about the creation of an embryo, applies only to bringing about the creation of an embryo outside the human body; and in this Act—

(a) references to embryos the creation of which was brought about *in vitro* (in their application to those where fertilisation is complete) are to those where fertilisation began outside the human body whether or not it was completed there, and
(b) references to embryos taken from a woman do not include embryos whose creation was brought about *in vitro*.

(3) This Act, so far as it governs the keeping or use of an embryo, applies only to keeping or using an embryo outside the human body.

(4) References in this Act to gametes, eggs or sperm, except where otherwise stated, are to live human gametes, eggs or sperm but references below in this Act to gametes or eggs do not include eggs in the process of fertilisation.
[Human Fertilisation and Embryology Act 1990, s 1.]

---

1. This Act makes provision in connection with human embryos and any subsequent development of such embryos; prohibits certain practices in connection with embryos and gametes; establishes a Human Fertilisation and Embryology Authority, and makes provision about the persons who in certain circumstances are to be treated in law as the parents of a child.

The Act has been brought into force in accordance with s 49(2), post; for commencement orders, see Human Fertilisation and Embryology Act 1990 (Commencement No 1) Order 1990, SI 1990/2165 (Commencement No 2 and Transitional Provision) Order 1991, SI 1991/480 (Commencement No 3 and Transitional Provisions) Order 1991, SI 1991/1400, (Commencement No 4—Amendment of Transitional Provisions) Order 1991, SI 1991/1781 and (Commencement No 5) Order 1994, SI 1994/1776.

2. Sub-section (1) is directed to live human embryos created outside the human body, not to the manner of their creation. Accordingly, an embryo created by Cell Nuclear Replacement (cloning) comes within the definition of embryo in the 1990 Act: *R (Quintavalle) v Secretary of State for Health* [2005] UKHL 28, [2005] 2 AC 561, [2005] 2 All ER 555, [2005] 2 WLR 1061, [2005] 1 FCR 134, see now the Human Reproductive Cloning Act 2001, post.

6–2801 2. Other terms. (1) In this Act—

"the Authority" means the Human Fertilisation and Embryology Authority established under section 5 of this Act,

"directions" means directions under section 23 of this Act,

"licence" means a licence under Schedule 2 to this Act and, in relation to a licence, "the person responsible" has the meaning given by section 17 of this Act, and

"treatment services" means medical, surgical or obstetric services provided to the public or a section of the public for the purpose of assisting women to carry children.

(2) References in this Act to keeping, in relation to embryos or gametes, include keeping while preserved, whether preserved by cryopreservation or in any other way; and embryos or gametes so kept are referred to in this Act as "stored" (and "store" and "storage" are to be interpreted accordingly).

(3) For the purposes of this Act, a woman is not to be treated as carrying a child until the embryo has become implanted.
[Human Fertilisation and Embryology Act 1990, s 2.]

Activities governed by the Act

6–2802 3. Prohibitions in connection with embryos. (1) No person shall—

(a) bring about the creation of an embryo, or
(b) keep or use an embryo,

except in pursuance of a licence[1].

(2) No person shall place in a woman—

(a) a live embryo other than a human embryo, or
(b) any live gametes other than human gametes.

(3) A licence cannot authorise—

(a) keeping[2] or using an embryo after the appearance of the primitive streak,
(b) placing an embryo in any animal,
(c) keeping or using an embryo in any circumstances in which regulations prohibit its keeping or use, or
(d) replacing a nucleus of a cell of an embryo with a nucleus taken from a cell of any person, embryo or subsequent development of an embryo.

(4) For the purposes of subsection (3)(a) above, the primitive streak is to be taken to have appeared in an embryo not later than the end of the period of 14 days beginning with the day when the gametes are mixed, not counting any time during which the embryo is stored.
[Human Fertilisation and Embryology Act 1990, s 3.]

---

1. The Human Fertilisation Embryology Authority was right to grant a licence authorising IVF treatment with Pre-implantation Genetic Diagnosis for the purpose of tissue typing, subject to such conditions as the Authority thought appropriate (*R (on the application of Quintavalle) v Human Fertilisation and Embryology Authority* [2005] UKHL 28, [2005] 2 AC 561, [2005] 2 All ER 555, [2005] 2 WLR 1061, [2005] 1 FCR 134).

2. The offence under s 3(1) does not extend to an individual who, notwithstanding his statutory responsibilities, does not in fact keep the embryo; and the person named in the licence as the 'person responsible' with duties defined by s 17(1) of the Act, including making proper arrangements for the keeping of gametes and embryos, is not deemed to be the keeper of an embryo solely by virtue of his appointment: *A-G's Reference (No 2 of 2003)* [2004] EWCA Crim 785, [2004] 1 WLR 2062, [2004] 17 LS Gaz R 30.

6–2803   3A. Prohibition in connection with germ cells.   (1) No person shall, for the purpose of providing fertility services for any woman, use female germ cells taken or derived from an embryo or a foetus or use embryos created by using such cells.

(2) In this section—

"female germ cells" means cells of the female germ line and includes such cells at any stage of maturity and accordingly includes eggs; and

"fertility services" means medical, surgical or obstetric services provided for the purpose of assisting women to carry children.

[Human Fertilisation and Embryology Act 1990, s 3A, as inserted by the Criminal Justice and Public Order Act 1994, s 156.]

6–2804   4. Prohibitions in connection with gametes.   (1) No person shall—

(a)   store any gametes, or

(b)   in the course of providing treatment services for any woman, use the sperm of any man unless the services are being provided for the woman and the man together or use the eggs of any other woman, or

(c)   mix gametes with the live gametes of any animal,

except in pursuance of a licence.

(2) A licence cannot authorise storing or using gametes in any circumstances in which regulations prohibit their storage or use.

(3) No person shall place sperm and eggs in a woman in any circumstances specified in regulations except in pursuance of a licence.

(4) Regulations made by virtue of subsection (3) above may provide that, in relation to licences only to place sperm and eggs in a woman in such circumstances, sections 12 to 22 of this Act shall have effect with such modifications as may be specified in the regulations.

(5) Activities regulated by this section or section 3 of this Act are referred to in this Act as "activities governed by this Act".

[Human Fertilisation and Embryology Act 1990, s 4.]

6–2805   5–26.   *The Human Fertilisation and Embryology Authority, its functions and procedure; scope of licences; licence conditions; grant, revocation and suspension of licences; directions and guidance.*

Status

6–2806   27. Meaning of "mother".   (1) The woman who is carrying or has carried a child as a result of the placing in her of an embryo or of sperm and eggs, and no other woman, is to be treated as the mother of the child.

(2) Subsection (1) above does not apply to any child to the extent that the child is treated by virtue of adoption as not being the woman's child.

(3) Subsection (1) above applies whether the woman was in the United Kingdom or elsewhere at the time of the placing in her of the embryo or the sperm and eggs.

[Human Fertilisation and Embryology Act 1990, s 27 as amended by the Adoption and Children Act 2002, Sch 3.]

6–2807   28. Meaning of "father".   (1) Subject to subsections (5A) to (5I) below, this section applies in the case of a child who is being or has been carried by a woman as the result of the placing in her of an embryo or of sperm and eggs or her artificial insemination.

(2) If—

(a)   at the time of the placing in her of the embryo or the sperm and eggs or of her insemination, the woman was a party to a marriage, and

(b)   the creation of the embryo carried by her was not brought about with the sperm of the other party to the marriage,

then, subject to subsection (5) below, the other party to the marriage shall be treated as the father of the child unless it is shown that he did not consent to the placing in her of the embryo or the sperm and eggs or to her insemination (as the case may be).

(3) If no man is treated, by virtue of subsection (2) above, as the father of the child but—

(a)   the embryo or the sperm and eggs were placed in the woman, or she was artificially inseminated, in the course of treatment services[1] provided for her and a man together by a person to whom a licence applies, and

(b)   the creation of the embryo carried by her was not brought about with the sperm of that man,

then, subject to subsection (5) below, that man shall be treated as the father of the child[2].

(4) Where a person is treated as the father of the child by virtue of subsection (2) or (3) above, no other person is to be treated as the father of the child.

(5) Subsections (2) and (3) above do not apply—

(a) in relation to England and Wales and Northern Ireland, to any child who, by virtue of the rules of common law, is treated as the legitimate child of the parties to a marriage,

(b) in relation to Scotland, to any child who, by virtue of any enactment or other rule of law, is treated as the child of the parties to a marriage, or

(c) to any child to the extent that the child is treated by virtue of adoption as not being the man's child.

(5A) If—

(a) a child has been carried by a woman as the result of the placing in her of an embryo or of sperm and eggs or her artificial insemination,

(b) the creation of the embryo carried by her was brought about by using the sperm of a man after his death, or the creation of the embryo was brought about using the sperm of a man before his death but the embryo was placed in the woman after his death,

(c) the woman was a party to a marriage with the man immediately before his death,

(d) the man consented in writing (and did not withdraw the consent)—

(i) to the use of his sperm after his death which brought about the creation of the embryo carried by the woman or (as the case may be) to the placing in the woman after his death of the embryo which was brought about using his sperm before his death, and

(ii) to being treated for the purpose mentioned in subsection (5I) below as the father of any resulting child,

(e) the woman has elected in writing not later than the end of the period of 42 days from the day on which the child was born for the man to be treated for the purpose mentioned in subsection (5I) below as the father of the child, and

(f) no-one else is to be treated as the father of the child by virtue of subsection (2) or (3) above or by virtue of adoption or the child being treated as mentioned in paragraph (a) or (b) of subsection (5) above,

then the man shall be treated for the purpose mentioned in subsection (5I) below as the father of the child.

(5B) If—

(a) a child has been carried by a woman as the result of the placing in her of an embryo or of sperm and eggs or her artificial insemination,

(b) the creation of the embryo carried by her was brought about by using the sperm of a man after his death, or the creation of the embryo was brought about using the sperm of a man before his death but the embryo was placed in the woman after his death,

(c) the woman was not a party to a marriage with the man immediately before his death but treatment services were being provided for the woman and the man together before his death either by a person to whom a licence applies or outside the United Kingdom,

(d) the man consented in writing (and did not withdraw the consent)—

(i) to the use of his sperm after his death which brought about the creation of the embryo carried by the woman or (as the case may be) to the placing in the woman after his death of the embryo which was brought about using his sperm before his death, and

(ii) to being treated for the purpose mentioned in subsection (5I) below as the father of any resulting child,

(e) the woman has elected in writing not later than the end of the period of 42 days from the day on which the child was born for the man to be treated for the purpose mentioned in subsection (5I) below as the father of the child, and

(f) no-one else is to be treated as the father of the child by virtue of subsection (2) or (3) above or by virtue of adoption or the child being treated as mentioned in paragraph (a) or (b) of subsection (5) above,

then the man shall be treated for the purpose mentioned in subsection (5I) below as the father of the child.

(5C) If—

(a) a child has been carried by a woman as the result of the placing in her of an embryo,

(b) the embryo was created at a time when the woman was a party to a marriage,

(c) the creation of the embryo was not brought about with the sperm of the other party to the marriage,

(d) the other party to the marriage died before the placing of the embryo in the woman,

(e) the other party to the marriage consented in writing (and did not withdraw the consent)—

(i) to the placing of the embryo in the woman after his death, and

(ii) to being treated for the purpose mentioned in subsection (5I) below as the father of any resulting child,

(f) the woman has elected in writing not later than the end of the period of 42 days from the day on which the child was born for the other party to the marriage to be treated for the purpose mentioned in subsection (5I) below as the father of the child, and

(g) no-one else is to be treated as the father of the child by virtue of subsection (2) or (3) above or by virtue of adoption or the child being treated as mentioned in paragraph (a) or (b) of subsection (5) above,

then the other party to the marriage shall be treated for the purpose mentioned in subsection (5I) below as the father of the child.

(5D) If—

(a) a child has been carried by a woman as the result of the placing in her of an embryo,

(b) the embryo was not created at a time when the woman was a party to a marriage but was created in the course of treatment services provided for the woman and a man together either by a person to whom a licence applies or outside the United Kingdom,

(c) the creation of the embryo was not brought about with the sperm of that man,

(d) the man died before the placing of the embryo in the woman,

(e) the man consented in writing (and did not withdraw the consent)—

  (i) to the placing of the embryo in the woman after his death, and

  (ii) to being treated for the purpose mentioned in subsection (5I) below as the father of any resulting child,

(f) the woman has elected in writing not later than the end of the period of 42 days from the day on which the child was born for the man to be treated for the purpose mentioned in subsection (5I) below as the father of the child, and

(g) no-one else is to be treated as the father of the child by virtue of subsection (2) or (3) above or by virtue of adoption or the child being treated as mentioned in paragraph (a) or (b) of subsection (5) above,

then the man shall be treated for the purpose mentioned in subsection (5I) below as the father of the child.

(5E) In the application of subsections (5A) to (5D) above to Scotland, for any reference to a period of 42 days there shall be substituted a reference to a period of 21 days.

(5F) The requirement under subsection (5A), (5B), (5C) or (5D) above as to the making of an election (which requires an election to be made either on or before the day on which the child was born or within the period of 42 or, as the case may be, 21 days from that day) shall nevertheless be treated as satisfied if the required election is made after the end of that period but with the consent of the Registrar General under subsection (5G) below.

(5G) The Registrar General may at any time consent to the making of an election after the end of the period mentioned in subsection (5F) above if, on an application made to him in accordance with such requirements as he may specify, he is satisfied that there is a compelling reason for giving his consent to the making of such an election.

(5H) In subsections (5F) and (5G) above "the Registrar General" means the Registrar General for England and Wales, the Registrar General of Births, Deaths and Marriages for Scotland or (as the case may be) the Registrar General for Northern Ireland.

(5I) The purpose referred to in subsections (5A) to (5D) above is the purpose of enabling the man's particulars to be entered as the particulars of the child's father in (as the case may be) a register of live-births or still-births kept under the Births and Deaths Registration Act 1953 or the Births and Deaths Registration (Northern Ireland) Order 1976 or a register of births or still-births kept under the Registration of Births, Deaths and Marriages (Scotland) Act 1965.

(6) Where—

(a) the sperm of a man who had given such consent as is required by paragraph 5 of Schedule 3 to this Act was used for a purpose for which such consent was required, or

(b) the sperm of a man, or any embryo the creation of which was brought about with his sperm, was used after his death,

he is not, subject to subsections (5A) and (5B) above, to be treated as the father of the child.

(7) The references in subsection (2) above subsections (5A) to (5D) above to the parties to a marriage at the time there referred to—

(a) are to the parties to a marriage subsisting at that time, unless a judicial separation was then in force, but

(b) include the parties to a void marriage if either or both of them reasonably believed at that time that the marriage was valid; and for the purposes of this subsection it shall be presumed, unless the contrary is shown, that one of them reasonably believed at that time that the marriage was valid.

(8) This section applies whether the woman was in the United Kingdom or elsewhere at the time of the placing in her of the embryo or the sperm and eggs or her artificial insemination.

(9) In subsection (7)(a) above, "judicial separation" includes a legal separation obtained in a country outside the British Islands and recognised in the United Kingdom.

[Human Fertilisation and Embryology Act 1990, s 28, as amended by the Human Fertilisation and Embryology (Deceased Fathers) Act 2003, ss 1 and 2 and the Adoption and Children Act 2002, Sch 3.]

---

1. In *Re Q (parental order)* [1996] 2 FCR 345, [1996] 1 FLR 369, Johnson J noted the conundrum posed by sub-s (3) in that the subsection envisages a situation in which the man involved himself receives medical treatment although the

subsection refers to a man whose sperm was not used in the procedure. Applying a robust interpretation of the words "treatment . . . together" adopted in *Re B (parentage)* [1996] 2 FLR 15 and *R v Human Fertilization and Embryology Authority, ex p Blood* [1997] 2 All ER 687, [1997] 2 WLR 806, [1997] 2 FCR 501, [1997] 2 FLR 758, CA, Wilson J in *U v W (A-G intervening)* [1997] 3 WLR 739, [1998] 1 FCR 526, [1997] 2 FLR 282, was of the view that there is a mental element inherent in the notion of "treatment . . . together" and that what is relevant is that it has to be demonstrated that, in the provision of treatment services with donor sperm, the doctor has responded to a request for that form of treatment made by the woman and the man as a couple, notwithstanding the absence in the man of any physical role in such treatment.

Where a married couple consented to the use of the husband's sperm and the wife's eggs, but the clinic in error fertilised the wife's eggs with the sperm of another man and twins were born as a result, such a fundamental error vitiated the whole concept of "treated together" and took the case outside the scope s 28(3) (even if that subsection could apply to a married couple); lack of consent by the husband meant that s 28(2) could not apply and it was, therefore, the man whose sperm was used who was the father of the twins, and while this interfered with the husband's rights under art 8, and the rights of the children under art 8 were also engaged, the remedy of adoption was available to cure any violation (*Leeds Teaching Hospital NHS Trust v A* [2003] EWHC 259 (QB), [2003] 1 FCR 599, [2003] 1 FLR 413 and 1092).

2. Where a couple engaged in IVF treatment together, but it was unsuccessful, the couple then separated and the mother found a new partner, and the mother subsequently returned for further IVF treatment (the hospital being unaware of the change of partner) and became pregnant from the implantation of embryos that had been fertilised from the earlier treatment and frozen, the concession made on behalf of the mother and the child in parental responsibility and contact proceedings brought by the first partner that he was the "father" of the child might or might not have been well founded: *Re D (a child)(IVF treatment)* [2001] EWCA Civ 230, [2001] 1 FCR 481, [2001] 1 FLR 972, CA. In further litigation between the parties, the Court of Appeal confirmed that the time at which legal paternity is created is when the embryo or the sperm and eggs are placed in the woman and that in this case, as the man and the woman were not undergoing treatment together, he could not claim paternity: *Re R (a child)* [2003] EWCA Civ 182, [2003] 2 All ER 131, [2003] 2 WLR 1485, [2003] 1 FCR 481 *affd* [2005] UKHL 33, [2005] 2 AC 621, [2005] 4 All ER 433, [2005] 2 WLR 1158, [2005] 2 FLR 843, sub nom *Re D (a child)* [2005] 2 FCR 222.

6–2808   29. Effect of sections 27 and 28. (1) Where by virtue of section 27 or 28 of this Act a person is to be treated as the mother or father of a child, that person is to be treated in law as the mother or, as the case may be, father of the child for all purposes.

(2) Where by virtue of section 27 or 28 of this Act a person is not to be treated as the mother or father of a child, that person is to be treated in law as not being the mother or, as the case may be, father of the child for any purpose.

(3) Where subsection (1) or (2) above has effect, references to any relationship between two people in any enactment, deed or other instrument or document (whenever passed or made) are to be read accordingly.

(3A) Subsections (1) to (3) above do not apply in relation to the treatment in law of a deceased man in a case to which section 28(5A), (5B), (5C) or (5D) of this Act applies.

(3B) Where subsection (5A), (5B), (5C) or (5D) of section 28 of this Act applies, the deceased man—

(a) is to be treated in law as the father of the child for the purpose referred to in that subsection, but

(b) is to be treated in law as not being the father of the child for any other purpose.

(3C) Where subsection (3B) above has effect, references to any relationship between two people in any enactment, deed or other instrument or document (whenever passed or made) are to be read accordingly.

(3D) In subsection (3C) above "enactment" includes an enactment comprised in, or in an instrument made under, an Act of the Scottish Parliament or Northern Ireland legislation.

(4) In relation to England and Wales and Northern Ireland, nothing in the provisions of section 27(1) or 28(2) to (4) or (5A) to (5I), read with this section, affects—

(a) the succession to any dignity or title of honour or renders any person capable of succeeding to or transmitting a right to succeed to any such dignity or title, or

(b) the devolution of any property limited (expressly or not) to devolve (as nearly as the law permits) along with any dignity or title of honour.

(5) In relation to Scotland—

(a) those provisions do not apply to any title, coat of arms, honour or dignity transmissible on the death of the holder thereof or affect the succession thereto or the devolution thereof, and

(b) where the terms of any deed provide that any property or interest in property shall devolve along with a title, coat of arms, honour or dignity, nothing in those provisions shall prevent that property or interest from so devolving.

[Human Fertilisation and Embryology Act 1990, s 29, as amended by the Human Fertilisation and Embryology (Deceased Fathers) Act 2003, ss 1 and 2.]

6–2809   30. Parental orders in favour of gamete donors[1]. (1) The court may make an order providing for a child to be treated in law as the child of the parties to a marriage (referred to in this section as "the husband" and "the wife") if—

(a) the child has been carried by a woman other than the wife as the result of the placing in her of an embryo or sperm and eggs or her artificial insemination,

(b) the gametes of the husband or the wife, or both, were used to bring about the creation of the embryo, and (*c*) the conditions in subsections (2) to (7) below are satisfied.

(2) The husband and the wife must apply for the order within six months of the birth of the child or, in the case of a child born before the coming into force of this Act, within six months of such coming into force.

(3) At the time of the application and of the making of the order—

(*a*) the child's home must be with the husband and the wife, and

(*b*) the husband or the wife, or both of them, must be domiciled in a part of the United Kingdom or in the Channel Islands or the Isle of Man.

(4) At the time of the making of the order both the husband and the wife must have attained the age of eighteen.

(5) The court must be satisfied that both the father of the child (including a person who is the father by virtue of section 28 of this Act), where he is not the husband, and the woman who carried the child have freely, and with full understanding of what is involved, agreed unconditionally to the making of the order.

(6) Subsection (5) above does not require the agreement of a person who cannot be found or is incapable of giving agreement and the agreement of the woman who carried the child is ineffective for the purposes of that subsection if given by her less than six weeks after the child's birth.

(7) The court must be satisfied that no money or other benefit (other than for expenses reasonably incurred) has been given or received by the husband or the wife for or in consideration of—

(*a*) the making of the order,

(*b*) any agreement required by subsection (5) above,

(*c*) the handing over of the child to the husband and the wife, or

(*d*) the making of any arrangements with a view to the making of the order,

unless authorised[2] by the court.

(8) For the purposes of an application under this section—

(*a*) in relation to England and Wales, section 92(7) to (10) of, and Part I of Schedule 11 to, the Children Act 1989 (jurisdiction of courts) shall apply for the purposes of this section to determine the meaning of "the court" as they apply for the purposes of that Act and proceedings on the application shall be "family proceedings" for the purposes of that Act,

(*b*) in relation to Scotland, "the court" means the Court of Session or the sheriff court of the sheriffdom within which the child is, and

(*c*) in relation to Northern Ireland, "the court" means the High Court or any county court within whose division the child is.

(9) Regulations[3] may provide—

(*a*) for any provision of the enactments about adoption to have effect, with such modifications (if any) as may be specified in the regulations, in relation to orders under this section, and applications for such orders, as it has effect in relation to adoption, and applications for adoption orders, and

(*b*) for references in any enactment to adoption, an adopted child or an adoptive relationship to be read (respectively) as references to the effect of an order under this section, a child to whom such an order applies and a relationship arising by virtue of the enactments about adoption, as applied by the regulations, and for similar expressions in connection with adoption to be read accordingly,

and the regulations may include such incidental or supplemental provision as appears to the Secretary of State necessary or desirable in consequence of any provision made by virtue of paragraph (*a*) or (*b*) above.

(10) In this section "the enactments about adoption" means the Adoption Act 1976*, the Adoption (Scotland) Act 1978 and the Adoption (Northern Ireland) Order 1987.

(11) Subsection (1)(*a*) above applies whether the woman was in the United Kingdom or elsewhere at the time of the placing in her of the embryo or the sperm and eggs or her artificial insemination.
[Human Fertilisation and Embryology Act 1990, s 30.]

---

*Words "Adoption and Children Act 2002" substituted by the Adoption and Children Act 2002, Sch 3 from a date to be appointed.

1. For the procedure to be followed in connection with an application for a parental order in a magistrates' court see the Family Proceedings Courts (Children Act 1989) Rules 1991, this PART, STATUTORY INSTRUMENTS ON FAMILY LAW, post.

2. Where a sum has been paid that was in excess of expenses reasonably incurred (because it included an element for loss of earnings when the surrogate mother was, in fact, on income support), the court has a discretion retrospectively to authorise that payment and in exercising that discretion the court will balance all the circumstances of the case with the welfare of the child as the first consideration against the degree of taint of the transaction for which authorisation is being sought (*Re C: Application by Mr and Mrs X under s 30 of the Human Fertilisation and Embryology Act 1990* [2002] EWHC 157 (Fam), [2002] 1 FLR 909).

3. The Parental Orders (Human Fertilisation and Embryology) Regulations 1994, SI 1994/2767, have been made; see this PART, post.

Information

6–2810   31. The Authority's register of information.   (1) The Authority shall keep a register which shall contain any information obtained by the Authority which falls within subsection (2) below.

(2) Information falls within this subsection if it relates to—

(*a*)   the provision of treatment services for any identifiable individual, or

(*b*)   the keeping or use of the gametes of any identifiable individual or of an embryo taken from any identifiable woman,

or if it shows that any identifiable individual was, or may have been, born in consequence of treatment services.

(3) A person who has attained the age of eighteen ("the applicant") may by notice to the Authority require the Authority to comply with a request under subsection (4) below, and the Authority shall do so if—

(*a*)   the information contained in the register shows that the applicant was, or may have been, born in consequence of treatment services, and

(*b*)   the applicant has been given a suitable opportunity to receive proper counselling about the implications of compliance with the request.

(4) The applicant may request the Authority to give the applicant notice stating whether or not the information contained in the register shows that a person other than a parent of the applicant would or might, but for sections 27 to 29 of this Act, be a parent of the applicant and, if it does show that—

(*a*)   giving the applicant so much of that information as relates to the person concerned as the Authority is required by regulations[1] to give (but no other information), or

(*b*)   stating whether or not that information shows that, but for sections 27 to 29 of this Act, the applicant, and a person specified in the request as a person whom the applicant proposes to marry, would or might be related.

(5) Regulations cannot require the Authority to give any information as to the identity of a person whose gametes have been used or from whom an embryo has been taken if a person to whom a licence applied was provided with the information at a time when the Authority could not have been required to give information of the kind in question.

(6) A person who has not attained the age of eighteen ("the minor") may by notice to the Authority specifying another person ("the intended spouse") as a person whom the minor proposes to marry require the Authority to comply with a request under subsection (7) below, and the Authority shall do so if—

(*a*)   the information contained in the register shows that the minor was, or may have been, born in consequence of treatment services, and

(*b*)   the minor has been given a suitable opportunity to receive proper counselling about the implications of compliance with the request.

(7) The minor may request the Authority to give the minor notice stating whether or not the information contained in the register shows that, but for sections 27 to 29 of this Act, the minor and the intended spouse would or might be related.

[Human Fertilisation and Embryology Act 1990, s 31.]

---

1. The Human Fertilisation and Embryology Authority (Disclosure of Donor Information) Regulations 2004, SI 2004/1511 have been made.

6–2811   32. Information to be provided to Registrar General.   (1) This section applies where a claim is made before the Registrar General that a man is or is not the father of a child and it is necessary or desirable for the purpose of any function of the Registrar General to determine whether the claim is or may be well-founded.

(2) The Authority shall comply with any request made by the Registrar General by notice to the Authority to disclose whether any information on the register kept in pursuance of section 31 of this Act tends to show that the man may be the father of the child by virtue of section 28 of this Act and, if it does, disclose that information.

(3) In this section and section 33 of this Act, "the Registrar General" means the Registrar General for England and Wales, the Registrar General of Births, Deaths and Marriages for Scotland or the Registrar General for Northern Ireland, as the case may be.

[Human Fertilisation and Embryology Act 1990, s 32.]

6–2812   33. Restrictions on disclosure of information.   (1) No person who is or has been a member or employee of the Authority shall disclose any information mentioned in subsection (2) below which he holds or has held as such a member or employee.

(2) The information referred to in subsection (1) above is—

(a) any information contained or required to be contained in the register kept in pursuance of section 31 of this Act, and

(b) any other information obtained by any member or employee of the Authority on terms or in circumstances requiring it to be held in confidence.

(3) Subsection (1) above does not apply to any disclosure of information mentioned in subsection (2)(a) above made—

(a) to a person as a member or employee of the Authority,
(b) to a person to whom a licence applies for the purposes of his functions as such,
(c) so that no individual to whom the information relates can be identified,
(d) in pursuance of an order of a court under section 34 or 35 of this Act,
(e) to the Registrar General in pursuance of a request under section 32 of this Act, or
(f) in accordance with section 31 of this Act.

(4) Subsection (1) above does not apply to any disclosure of information mentioned in subsection (2)(b) above—

(a) made to a person as a member or employee of the Authority,
(b) made with the consent of the person or persons whose confidence would otherwise be protected, or
(c) which has been lawfully made available to the public before the disclosure is made.

(5) No person who is or has been a person to whom a licence applies and no person to whom directions have been given shall disclose any information falling within section 31(2) of this Act which he holds or has held as such a person.

(6) Subsection (5) above does not apply to any disclosure of information made—

(a) to a person as a member or employee of the Authority,
(b) to a person to whom a licence applies for the purposes of his functions as such,
(c) so far as it identifies a person who, but for sections 27 to 29 of this Act, would or might be a parent of a person who instituted proceedings under section 1A of the Congenital Disabilities (Civil Liability) Act 1976, but only for the purpose of defending such proceedings, or instituting connected proceedings for compensation against that parent,
(d) so that no individual to whom the information relates can be identified,
(e) in pursuance of directions given by virtue of section 24(5) or (6) of this Act,
(f) necessarily—
   (i) for any purpose preliminary to proceedings, or
   (ii) for the purposes of, or in connection with, any proceedings,
(g) for the purpose of establishing, in any proceedings relating to an application for an order under subsection (1) of section 30 of this Act, whether the condition specified in paragraph (a) or (b) of that subsection is met, or
(h) under section 3 of the Access to Health Records Act 1990 (right of access to health records).

(6A) Paragraph (f) of subsection (6) above, so far as relating to disclosure for the purposes of, or in connection with, any proceedings, does not apply—

(a) to disclosure of information enabling a person to be identified as a person whose gametes were used in accordance with consent given under paragraph 5 of Schedule 3 to this Act, for the purposes of treatment services in consequence of which an identifiable individual was, or may have been, born, or
(b) to disclosure, in circumstances in which subsection (1) of section 34 of this Act applies, of information relevant to the determination of the question mentioned in that subsection.

(6B) In the case of information relating to the provision of treatment services for any identifiable individual—

(a) where one individual is identifiable, subsection (5) above does not apply to disclosure with the consent of that individual;
(b) where both a woman and a man treated together with her are identifiable, subsection (5) above does not apply—
   (i) to disclosure with the consent of them both, or
   (ii) if disclosure is made for the purpose of disclosing information about the provision of treatment services for one of them, to disclosure with the consent of that individual.

(6C) For the purposes of subsection (6B) above, consent must be to disclosure to a specific person, except where disclosure is to a person who needs to know—

(a) in connection with the provision of treatment services, or any other description of medical, surgical or obstetric services, for the individual giving the consent,
(b) in connection with the carrying out of an audit of clinical practice, or
(c) in connection with the auditing of accounts.

(6D) For the purposes of subsection (6B) above, consent to disclosure given at the request of another shall be disregarded unless, before it is given, the person requesting it takes reasonable steps to explain to the individual from whom it is requested the implications of compliance with the request.

(6E) In the case of information which relates to the provision of treatment services for any identifiable individual, subsection (5) above does not apply to disclosure in an emergency, that is to say, to disclosure made—

(a) by a person who is satisfied that it is necessary to make the disclosure to avert an imminent danger to the health of an individual with whose consent the information could be disclosed under subsection (6B) above, and

(b) in circumstances where it is not reasonably practicable to obtain that individual's consent.

(6F) In the case of information which shows that any identifiable individual was, or may have been, born in consequence of treatment services, subsection (5) above does not apply to any disclosure which is necessarily incidental to disclosure under subsection (6B) or (6E) above.

(6G) Regulations may provide for additional exceptions from subsection (5) above, but no exception may be made under this subsection—

(a) for disclosure of a kind mentioned in paragraph (a) or (b) of subsection (6A) above, or

(b) for disclosure, in circumstances in which section 32 of this Act applies, of information having the tendency mentioned in subsection (2) of that section.

(7) This section does not apply to the disclosure to any individual of information which—

(a) falls within section 31(2) of this Act by virtue of paragraph (a) or (b) of that subsection, and

(b) relates only to that individual or, in the case of an individual treated together with another, only to that individual and that other.

(8) (*Repealed*).

(9) In subsection 6(*f*) above, references to proceedings include any formal procedure for dealing with a complaint.

[Human Fertilisation and Embryology Act 1990, s 33 as amended by the Human Fertilisation and Embryology (Disclosure of Information) Act 1992, s 1 and the Data Protection Act 1998, Sch 16.]

6–2813　34. Disclosure in interests of justice.　(1) Where in any proceedings before a court the question whether a person is or is not the parent of a child by virtue of sections 27 to 29 of this Act falls to be determined, the court may on the application of any party to the proceedings make an order requiring the Authority—

(a) to disclose whether or not any information relevant to that question is contained in the register kept in pursuance of section 31 of this Act, and

(b) if it is, to disclose so much of it as is specified in the order,

but such an order may not require the Authority to disclose any information falling within section 31(2)(b) of this Act.

(2) The court must not make an order under subsection (1) above unless it is satisfied that the interests of justice require it to do so, taking into account—

(a) any representations made by any individual who may be affected by the disclosure, and

(b) the welfare of the child, if under 18 years old, and of any other person under that age who may be affected by the disclosure.

(3) If the proceedings before the court are civil proceedings, it—

(a) may direct that the whole or any part of the proceedings on the application for an order under subsection (2) above shall be heard in camera, and

(b) if it makes such an order, may then or later direct that the whole or any part of any later stage of the proceedings shall be heard in camera.

(4) An application for a direction under subsection (3) above shall be heard in camera unless the court otherwise directs.

[Human Fertilisation and Embryology Act 1990, s 34.]

Conscientious objection

6–2814　38. Conscientious objection.　(1) No person who has a conscientious objection to participating in any activity governed by this Act shall be under any duty, however arising, to do so.

(2) In any legal proceedings the burden of proof of conscientious objection shall rest on the person claiming to rely on it.

(3) *Scotland*.

[Human Fertilisation and Embryology Act 1990, s 38.]

Enforcement

6–2815　39. Powers of members and employees of Authority.　(1) Any member or employee of the Authority entering and inspecting premises to which a licence relates may—

(a) take possession of anything which he has reasonable grounds to believe may be required—

      (i)   for the purpose of the functions of the Authority relating to the grant, variation, suspension and revocation of licences, or

      (ii) for the purpose of being used in evidence in any proceedings for an offence under this Act,

and retain it for so long as it may be required for the purpose in question, and

    (b) for the purpose in question, take such steps as appear to be necessary for preserving any such thing or preventing interference with it, including requiring any person having the power to do so to give such assistance as may reasonably be required.

    (2) In subsection (1) above—

    (a) the references to things include information recorded in any form, and

    (b) the reference to taking possession of anything includes, in the case of information recorded otherwise than in legible form, requiring any person having the power to do so to produce a copy of the information in legible form and taking possession of the copy.

    (3) Nothing in this Act makes it unlawful for a member or employee of the Authority to keep any embryo or gametes in pursuance of that person's functions as such.

[Human Fertilisation and Embryology Act 1990, s 39.]

6–2816   40. Power to enter premises. (1) A justice of the peace (including, in Scotland, a sheriff) may issue a warrant under this section if satisfied by the evidence on oath of a member or employee of the Authority that there are reasonable grounds for suspecting that an offence under this Act is being, or has been, committed on any premises.

    (2) A warrant under this section shall authorise any named member or employee of the Authority (who must, if so required, produce a document identifying himself), together with any constables—

    (a) to enter the premises specified in the warrant, using such force as is reasonably necessary for the purpose, and

    (b) to search the premises and—

      (i)   take possession of anything which he has reasonable grounds to believe may be required to be used in evidence in any proceedings for an offence under this Act, or

      (ii) take such steps as appear to be necessary for preserving any such thing or preventing interference with it, including requiring any person having the power to do so to give such assistance as may reasonably be required.

    (3) A warrant under this section shall continue in force until the end of the period of one month beginning with the day on which it is issued.

    (4) Anything of which possession is taken under this section may be retained—

    (a) for a period of six months, or

    (b) if within that period proceedings to which the thing is relevant are commenced against any person for an offence under this Act, until the conclusion of those proceedings[1].

    (5) In this section—

    (a) the references to things include information recorded in any form, and

    (b) the reference in subsection (2)(b)(i) above to taking possession of anything includes, in the case of information recorded otherwise than in legible form, requiring any person having the power to do so to produce a copy of the information in legible form, or in a form from which it can readily be produced in visible and legible form and taking possession of the copy.

[Human Fertilisation and Embryology Act 1990, s 40 as amended by the Criminal Justice and Police Act 2001, Sch 2.]

---

   1. See the Criminal Justice and Police Act 2001, Part 2 (PART I, *ante*). These provisions (summarised at para **1–180**, *ante*) confer, by ss 50 and 51, additional powers of seizure of property in relation to searches carried out under existing powers. However, s 57 (retention of seized items) does not authorise the retention of any property which could not be retained under the provisions listed in s 57(1), which include s 40(4) of the Human Fertilisation and Embryology Act 1990, if the property was seized under the new powers (ie those conferred by ss 50 and 51) in reliance on one of those powers (ie those conferred by the provisions listed in s 57(1)). Section 57(4) further provides that nothing in any of the provisions listed in s 57(1) authorises the retention of anything after an obligation to return it has arisen under Part 2.

Offences

6–2817   41. Offences. (1) A person who—

    (a) contravenes section 3(2), 3A or 4(1)(c) of this Act, or

    (b) does anything which, by virtue of section 3(3) of this Act, cannot be authorised by a licence,

is guilty of an offence and liable on conviction on indictment to imprisonment for a term not exceeding **ten years** or a **fine** or both.

    (2) A person who—

    (a) contravenes section 3(1) of this Act, otherwise than by doing something which, by virtue of section 3(3) of this Act, cannot be authorised by a licence,

(b) keeps or uses any gametes in contravention of section 4(1)(a) or (b) of this Act,
(c) contravenes section 4(3) of this Act, or
(d) fails to comply with any directions given by virtue of section 24(7)(a) of this Act,

is guilty of an offence.

(3) If a person—

(a) provides any information for the purposes of the grant of a licence, being information which is false or misleading in a material particular, and
(b) either he knows the information to be false or misleading in a material particular or he provides the information recklessly,

he is guilty of an offence.

(4) A person guilty of an offence under subsection (2) or (3) above is liable[1]—

(a) on conviction on indictment, to imprisonment for a term not exceeding **two years** or a **fine** or both, and
(b) on summary conviction, to imprisonment for a term not exceeding **six months** or a **fine** not exceeding **the statutory maximum** or both.

(5) A person who discloses any information in contravention of section 33 of this Act is guilty of an offence and liable[1]—

(a) on conviction on indictment, to imprisonment for a term not exceeding **two years** or a **fine** or both, and
(b) on summary conviction, to imprisonment for a term not exceeding **six months** or a **fine** not exceeding **the statutory maximum** or both.

(6) A person who—

(a) fails to comply with a requirement made by virtue of section 39(1)(b) or (2)(b) or 40(2)(b)(ii) or (5)(b) of this Act, or
(b) intentionally obstructs the exercise of any rights conferred by a warrant issued under section 40 of this Act,

is guilty of an offence.

(7) A person who without reasonable excuse fails to comply with a requirement imposed by regulations made by virtue of section 10(2)(a) of this Act is guilty of an offence.

(8) Where a person to whom a licence applies or the nominal licensee gives or receives any money or other benefit, not authorised by directions, in respect of any supply of gametes or embryos, he is guilty of an offence.

(9) A person guilty of an offence under subsection (6), (7) or (8) above is liable on summary conviction to imprisonment for a term not exceeding **six months** or a fine not exceeding **level five** on the standard scale or both.

(10) It is a defence for a person ("the defendant") charged with an offence of doing anything which, under section 3(1) or 4(1) of this Act, cannot be done except in pursuance of a licence to prove—

(a) that the defendant was acting under the direction of another, and
(b) that the defendant believed on reasonable grounds—

(i) that the other person was at the material time the person responsible under a licence, a person designated by virtue of section 17(2)(b) of this Act as a person to whom a licence applied, or a person to whom directions had been given by virtue of section 24(9) of this Act, and
(ii) that the defendant was authorised by virtue of the licence or directions to do the thing in question.

(11) It is a defence for a person charged with an offence under this Act to prove—

(a) that at the material time he was a person to whom a licence applied or to whom directions had been given, and
(b) that he took all such steps as were reasonable and exercised all due diligence to avoid committing the offence.

[Human Fertilisation and Embryology Act 1990, s 41 as amended by the Criminal Justice and Public Order Act 1994, s 156.]

---

1. For procedure in respect of this offence which is triable either way, see the Magistrates' Courts Act 1980, ss 18–21, in PART I: MAGISTRATES' COURTS, PROCEDURE, ante.

6–2818   42. Consent to prosecution.   No proceedings for an offence under this Act shall be instituted—

(a) in England and Wales, except by or with the consent of the Director of Public Prosecutions, and
(b) *Northern Ireland.*

[Human Fertilisation and Embryology Act 1990, s 42.]

Miscellaneous and General

6–2819 43. Keeping and examining gametes and embryos in connection with crime, etc.
(1) Regulations[1] may provide—

(a) for the keeping and examination of gametes or embryos, in such manner and on such conditions (if any) as may be specified in regulations, in connection with the investigation of, or proceedings for, an offence (wherever committed), or

(b) for the storage of gametes, in such manner and on such conditions (if any) as may be specified in regulations, where they are to be used only for such purposes, other than treatment services, as may be specified in regulations.

(2) Nothing in this Act makes unlawful the keeping or examination of any gametes or embryos in pursuance of regulations made by virtue of this section.

(3) In this section "examination" includes use for the purposes of any test.
[Human Fertilisation and Embryology Act 1990, s 43.]

---

1. See the Human Fertilisation and Embryology (Special Exemptions) Regulations 1991, SI 1991/1588.

6–2820 45. *Regulations*[1].

---

1. The Human Fertilisation and Embryology (Statutory Storage Period for Embryos) Regulations 1996, SI 1996/375; the Human Fertilisation and Embryology (Research Purposes) Regulations 2001, SI 2001/188; Human Fertilisation and Embryology Authority (Disclosure of Donor Information) Regulations 2004, SI 2004/1511 have been made.

6–2821 46. Notices. (1) This section has effect in relation to any notice required or authorised by this Act to be given to or served on any person.

(2) The notice may be given to or served on the person—

(a) by delivering it to the person,

(b) by leaving it at the person's proper address, or

(c) by sending it by post to the person at that address.

(3) The notice may—

(a) in the case of a body corporate, be given to or served on the secretary or clerk of the body,

(b) in the case of a partnership, be given to or served on any partner, and

(c) in the case of an unincorporated association other than a partnership, be given to or served on any member of the governing body of the association.

(4) For the purposes of this section and section 7 of the Interpretation Act 1978 (service of documents by post) in its application to this section, the proper address of any person is the person's last known address and also—

(a) in the case of a body corporate, its secretary or its clerk, the address of its registered or principal office, and

(b) in the case of an unincorporated association or a member of its governing body, its principal office.

(5) Where a person has notified the Authority of an address or a new address at which notices may be given to or served on him under this Act, that address shall also be his proper address for the purposes mentioned in subsection (4) above or, as the case may be, his proper address for those purposes in substitution for that previously notified.
[Human Fertilisation and Embryology Act 1990, s 46.]

6–2822 47. Index. The expressions listed in the left-hand column below are respectively defined or (as the case may be) are to be interpreted in accordance with the provisions of this Act listed in the right-hand column in relation to those expressions.

Expression	Relevant provision
Activities governed by this Act	Section 4(5)
Authority	Section 2(1)
Carry, in relation to a child	Section 2(3)
Directions	Section 2(1)
Embryo	Section 1
Gametes, eggs or sperm	Section 1
Keeping, in relation to embryos or gametes	Section 2(2)
Licence	Section 2(1)
Licence committee	Section 9(1)
Nominal licence	Section 17(3)
Person responsible	Section 17(1)
Person to whom a licence applies	Section 17(2)
Statutory storage period	Section 14(3) to (5)
Store, and similar expressions, in relation to embryos or gametes	Section 2(2)
Treatment services	Section 2(1)

[Human Fertilisation and Embryology Act 1990, s 47.]

6–2823 49. Short title, commencement, etc. (1) This Act may be cited as the Human Fertilisation and Embryology Act 1990.

(2) This Act shall come into force on such day as the Secretary of State may by order[1] made by statutory instrument appoint and different days may be appointed for different provisions and for different purposes.

(3) Sections 27 to 29 of this Act shall have effect only in relation to children carried by women as a result of the placing in them of embryos or of sperm and eggs, or of their artificial insemination (as the case may be), after the commencement of those sections.

(4) Section 27 of the Family Law Reform Act 1987 (artificial insemination) does not have effect in relation to children carried by women as the result of their artificial insemination after the commencement of sections 27 to 29 of this Act.

(5) Schedule 4 to this Act (which makes minor and consequential amendments) shall have effect.

(6) *An order under this section may make such transitional provision as the Secretary of State considers necessary or desirable.*

(7) Her Majesty may by Order in Council direct that any of the provisions of this Act shall extend, with such exceptions, adaptations and modifications (if any) as may be specified in the Order, to any of the Channel Islands.

[Human Fertilisation and Embryology Act 1990, s 49.]

---

1. For commencement orders, see note to the title of this Act, ante.

6–2824
SCHEDULES
SCHEDULE 1
The Authority: Supplementary Provisions

6–2825
SCHEDULE 2
Activities for which licences may be granted

6–2826
SCHEDULE 3
Consents to use of gametes or embryos

Child Support Act 1991[1]
(1991 c 48)

The basic principles

6–2900 1. The duty to maintain. (1) For the purposes of this Act, each parent of a qualifying child is responsible for maintaining him.

(2) For the purposes of this Act, a non-resident parent shall be taken to have met his responsibility to maintain any qualifying child of his by making periodical payments of maintenance with respect to the child of such amount, and at such intervals, as may be determined in accordance with the provisions of this Act.

(3) Where a maintenance calculation made under this Act requires the making of periodical payments, it shall be the duty of the non-resident parent with respect to whom the calculation was made to make those payments.

[Child Support Act 1991, s 1 as amended by the Child Support, Pensions and Social Security Act 2000, Sch 3.]

---

1. This Act makes provision for the assessment, collection and enforcement of periodical maintenance payable by certain parents with respect to children of theirs who are not in their care; for the collection and enforcement of certain other kinds of maintenance and for connected purposes. The 1991 Act replaces, save as expressly retained by the provisions of the Act itself, pre-existing rights of a child or a parent to periodical payments for the maintenance of a child. Therefore a claimant only has such rights as are a necessary consequence of the provisions of the Act and a claimant has no right to exercise against the other parent and is unable to assert an arguable civil right under art 6(1) of the European Convention on Human Rights which entitles him or her to a determination by a court (*R (Kehoe) v Secretary of State for Work and Pensions* [2005] UKHL 48, [2006] 1 AC 42, [2005] 4 All ER 905, [2005] 2 FCR 682).

The Act shall come into force on such dates as may be appointed by order made by the Lord Chancellor or Secretary of State (s 58, post). At the date of going to press, most provisions of the Act had been brought into force by the Child Support Act 1991 (Commencement No 1) Order 1992, SI 1992/1431, (Commencement No 2) Order 1992, SI 1992/1938 and the Child Support Act 1991 (Commencement No 3 and Transitional Provisions) Order 1992, SI 1992/2644.

6–2901 2. Welfare of children: the general principle. Where, in any case which falls to be dealt with under this Act, the Secretary of State is considering the exercise of any discretionary power conferred by this Act, he shall have regard to the welfare[1] of any child likely to be affected by his decision.

[Child Support Act 1991, s 2 as amended by the Social Security Act 1998, Schs 7 and 8.]

---

1. The calculation of a liability order is according to a strict mathematical formula. The principle of welfare has no influence on the quantification of liability but the Child Support Agency is not at liberty to decide whether to issue a

deduction of earnings order without giving considerable weight to the welfare principle (*R v Secretary of State for Social Security, ex p Biggin* [1995] 2 FCR 595, [1995] 1 FLR 851, per THORPE J).

6–2902   3. Meaning of certain terms used in this Act.   (1) A child is a "qualifying child" if—

(*a*)   one of his parents is, in relation to him, a non-resident parent; or

(*b*)   both of his parents are, in relation to him, non-resident parents

(2)   The parent of any child is a non-resident parent, in relation to him, if—

(*a*)   that parent is not living in the same household with the child; and

(*b*)   the child has his home with a person who is, in relation to him, a person with care.

(3)   A person is a "person with care", in relation to any child, if he is a person—

(*a*)   with whom the child has his home;

(*b*)   who usually provides day to day care for the child (whether exclusively or in conjunction with any other person); and

(*c*)   who does not fall within a prescribed category[1] of person.

(4)   The Secretary of State shall not, under subsection (3)(*c*), prescribe as a category—

(*a*)   parents;

(*b*)   guardians;

(*c*)   persons in whose favour residence orders under section 8 of the Children Act 1989 are in force;

(*d*)   in Scotland, persons with whom a child is to live by virtue of a residence order under section 11 of the Children (Scotland) Act 1995.

(5)   For the purposes of this Act there may be more than one person with care in relation to the same qualifying child.

(6)   Periodical payments which are required to be paid in accordance with a maintenance calculation are referred to in this Act as "child support maintenance".

(7)   Expressions are defined in this section only for the purposes of this Act.

[Child Support Act 1991, s 3 as amended by the Children (Scotland) Act 1995, Sch 4 and the Child Support, Pensions and Social Security Act 2000, Sch 3.]

---

1. See reg 21 of the Child Support (Maintenance Calculation Procedure) Regulations 2000, SI 2001/157 amended by SI 2002/1204, SI 2003/328, 347 and 2779, 2004/2415 and SI 2005/785 (CD Rom only); the prescribed categories for England and Wales are local authorities and persons with whom a child looked after by a local authority is placed by that authority under the provisions of the Children Act 1989.

6–2903   4. Child support maintenance.   (1) A person who is, in relation to any qualifying child or any qualifying children, either the person with care or the non-resident parent may apply to the Secretary of State for a maintenance calculation to be made under this Act with respect to that child, or any of those children.

(2)   Where a maintenance calculation has been made in response to an application under this section the Secretary of State may, if the person with care or non-resident parent with respect to whom the calculation was made applies to him under this subsection, arrange for—

(*a*)   the collection of the child support maintenance payable in accordance with the calculation;

(*b*)   the enforcement of the obligation to pay child support maintenance in accordance with the calculation.

(3)   Where an application under subsection (2) for the enforcement of the obligation mentioned in subsection (2)(*b*) authorises the Secretary of State to take steps to enforce that obligation whenever he considers it necessary to do so, the Secretary of State may act accordingly.

(4)   A person who applies to the Secretary of State under this section shall, so far as that person reasonably can, comply with such regulations[1] as may be made by the Secretary of State with a view to the Secretary of State being provided with the information which is required to enable—

(*a*)   the non-resident parent to be identified or traced (where that is necessary);

(*b*)   the amount of child support maintenance payable by the non-resident parent to be calculated; and

(*c*)   that amount to be recovered from the non-resident parent.

(5)   Any person who has applied to the Secretary of State under this section may at any time request him to cease acting under this section.

(6)   It shall be the duty of the Secretary of State to comply with any request made under subsection (5) (but subject to any regulations made under subsection (8)).

(7)   The obligation to provide information which is imposed by subsection (4)—

(*a*)   shall not apply in such circumstances as may be prescribed; and

(*b*)   may, in such circumstances as may be prescribed, be waived by the Secretary of State.

(8)   The Secretary of State may by regulations make such incidental, supplemental or transitional provision as he thinks appropriate with respect to cases in which he is requested to cease to act under this section.

(9) No application may be made under this section if there is in force with respect to the person with care and non-resident parent in question a maintenance calculation made in response to an application treated as made under section 6.

(10)[2] No application may be made at any time under this section with respect to a qualifying child or any qualifying children if—

(a) there is in force a written maintenance agreement made before 5th April 1993, or a maintenance order made before a prescribed date[3], in respect of that child or those children and the person who is, at that time, the non-resident parent; or

(aa) a maintenance order made on or after the date prescribed for the purposes of paragraph (a) is in force in respect of them, but has been so for less than the period of one year beginning with the date on which it was made; or

(b) benefit is being paid[4] to, or in respect of, a parent with care of that child or those children.

(11) In subsection (10) "benefit" means any benefit which is mentioned in, or prescribed by regulations under, section 6(1).
[Child Support Act 1991, s 4 as amended by the Child Support Act 1995, s 18, the Social Security Act 1998, Schs 7 and 8 and the Child Support, Pensions and Social Security Act 2000, Sch 3.]

---

1. See Pt II of the Child Support (Information, Evidence and Disclosure) Regulations 1992, SI 1992/1812 amended by SI 1995/123, 1045 and 3261, SI 1996/1945 and 2907, SI 1998/58, SI 1999/977 and 1510, SI 2001/161, the Child Support, Pensions and Social Security Act 2000, s 1, SI 2003/328, SI 2004/1823 and 2415 and SI 2005/2877 (CD Rom only).
2. Section 4(10) does not apply in relation to a maintenance order made in the circumstances mentioned in s 8(7) or (8), post (Child Support Act 1995, s 18(6), this PART, post).
3. The prescribed date is 3 March 2003, see the Child Support (Applications: Prescribed Date) Regulations 2003, SI 2003/194.
4. The word "paid" is to be construed as meaning "actually paid". Therefore, whether an application may be made by the parent with care under s 4 depends on whether or not benefit is being paid to, or in respect of, a parent with care; it does not depend on whether the benefit in question is benefit to which she is entitled (*Secretary of State for Social Security v Harmon* [1999] 1 FCR 213, [1998] 2 FLR 598).

6–2904 5. Child support maintenance: supplemental provisions. (1) Where—

(a) there is more than one person with care of a qualifying child; and

(b) one or more, but not all, of them have parental responsibility for the child;

no application may be made for a maintenance calculation with respect to the child by any of those persons who do not have parental responsibility for the child.

(2) Where more than one application for a maintenance calculation is made with respect to the child concerned, only one of them may be proceeded with.

(3) The Secretary of State may by regulations[1] make provision as to which of two or more applications for a maintenance calculation with respect to the same child is to be proceeded with.
[Child Support Act 1991, s 5 as amended by the Children (Scotland) Act 1995, Schs 4 and 5 and the Child Support, Pensions and Social Security Act 2000, Sch 3.]

---

1. See reg 4 of, and Sch 2 to, the Child Support (Maintenance Calculation Procedure) Regulations 2000, SI 2001/157 amended by SI 2002/1204 and SI 2003/328, 347 and 2779, SI 2004/2415 and SI 2005/785 (CD Rom only).

6–2905 6. Applications by those claiming or receiving benefit. (1) This section applies where income support, an income-based jobseeker's allowance or any other benefit of a prescribed kind is claimed by or in respect of, or paid to or in respect of, the parent of a qualifying child who is also a person with care of the child.

(2) In this section, that person is referred to as "the parent".

(3) The Secretary of State may—

(a) treat the parent as having applied for a maintenance calculation with respect to the qualifying child and all other children of the non-resident parent in relation to whom the parent is also a person with care; and

(b) take action under this Act to recover from the non-resident parent, on the parent's behalf, the child support maintenance so determined.

(4) Before doing what is mentioned in subsection (3), the Secretary of State must notify the parent in writing of the effect of subsections (3) and (5) and section 46.

(5) The Secretary of State may not act under subsection (3) if the parent asks him not to (a request which need not be in writing).

(6) Subsection (1) has effect regardless of whether any of the benefits mentioned there is payable with respect to any qualifying child.

(7) Unless she has made a request under subsection (5), the parent shall, so far as she reasonably can, comply with such regulations as may be made by the Secretary of State with a view to the Secretary of State's being provided with the information which is required to enable—

(a) the non-resident parent to be identified or traced;

(b) the amount of child support maintenance payable by him to be calculated; and

(c) that amount to be recovered from him.

(8) The obligation to provide information which is imposed by subsection (7)—

(a) does not apply in such circumstances as may be prescribed; and

(b) may, in such circumstances as may be prescribed, be waived by the Secretary of State.

(9) If the parent ceases to fall within subsection (1), she may ask the Secretary of State to cease acting under this section, but until then he may continue to do so.

(10) The Secretary of State must comply with any request under subsection (9) (but subject to any regulations made under subsection (11)).

(11) The Secretary of State may by regulations make such incidental or transitional provision as he thinks appropriate with respect to cases in which he is asked under subsection (9) to cease to act under this section.

(12) The fact that a maintenance calculation is in force with respect to a person with care does not prevent the making of a new maintenance calculation with respect to her as a result of the Secretary of State's acting under subsection (3).

[Child Support Act 1991, s 6 as substituted by the Child Support, Pensions and Social Security Act 2000, ss 1 and 3.]

_____

1. The word "paid" is to be construed as meaning "actually paid". Therefore, whether an application may be made by the parent with care under s 4 depends on whether or not benefit is being paid to, or in respect of, a parent with care; it does not depend on whether the benefit in question is benefit to which she is entitled (*Secretary of State for Social Security v Harmon* [1999] 1 FCR 213, [1998] 2 FLR 598). An application can be made under s 6 notwithstanding a court maintenance order is in force. When an assessment is made, any court order ceases to have effect.

An application under s 6 is the triggering factor for the Secretary of State to take action under the Child Support Act. There is no balancing provision to stop matters proceedings to the point where the child support officer has to make an assessment. Therefore a mother who made an application when she was in receipt of benefit, and who subsequently remarried and ceased to receive income support, remained entitled to take the benefit of the legislation (*R v Secretary of State for Social Security, ex p Harris* [1999] 1 FLR 837, QBD).

2. Before reaching a decision, the Secretary of State is not required to make enquiries of the father whether there is anything he wishes to say (*R v Secretary of State for Social Security, ex p Lloyd* [1995] 3 FCR 97, [1995] 1 FLR 856).

3. See Pt II of the Child Support (Information, Evidence and Disclosure) Regulations 1992, SI 1992/1812 amended by SI 1995/123, 1045 and 3261, SI 1996/1945 and 2907, SI 1998/58, SI 1999/977 and 1510, SI 2001/161, the Child Support, Pensions and Social Security Act 2000, s 1, SI 2003/328, SI 2004/1823 and 2415 and SI 2005/2877 (CD Rom only).

6–2906   7. *Right of child in Scotland to apply for calculation.*

6–2907   8. Role of the courts with respect to maintenance for children. (1) This subsection applies in any case where the Secretary of State would have jurisdiction to make a maintenance calculation with respect to a qualifying child and a non-resident parent of his on an application duly made (or treated as made) by a person entitled to apply for such an calculation with respect to that child.

(2) Subsection (1) applies even though the circumstances of the case are such that the Secretary of State would not make an calculation if it were applied for.

(3) Except as provided in subsection (3A), in any case where subsection (1) applies, no court shall exercise any power which it would otherwise have to make, vary or revive any maintenance order in relation to the child and non-resident parent concerned[1].

(3A) Unless a maintenance calculation has been made with respect to the child concerned, subsection (3) does not prevent a court from varying a maintenance order in relation to that child and the non-resident parent concerned—

(a) if the maintenance order was made on or after the date prescribed for the purposes of section 4(10)(a) or 7(10)(a); or

(b) where the order was made before then, in any case in which section 4(10) or 7(10) prevents the making of an application for a maintenance calculation with respect to or by that child.

(4) Subsection (3) does not prevent a court from revoking a maintenance order.

(5) The Lord Chancellor or in relation to Scotland the Lord Advocate may by order[2] provide that, in such circumstances as may be specified by the order, this section shall not prevent a court from exercising any power which it has to make a maintenance order in relation to a child if—

(a) a written agreement (whether or not enforceable) provides for the making, or securing, by a non-resident parent of the child of periodical payments to or for the benefit of the child; and

(b) the maintenance order which the court makes is, in all material respects, in the same terms as that agreement.*

(6) This section shall not prevent a court from exercising any power which it has to make a maintenance order in relation to a child if—

(a) a maintenance calculation is in force with respect to the child;

(b) the non-resident parent's net weekly income exceeds the figure referred to in paragraph 10(3) of Schedule 1 (as it has effect from time to time pursuant to regulations made under paragraph 10A(1)(b)); and

(c) the court is satisfied that the circumstances of the case make it appropriate for the non-resident parent to make or secure the making of periodical payments under a maintenance order in addition to the child support maintenance payable by him in accordance with the maintenance calculation.

(7) This section shall not prevent a court from exercising any power which it has to make a maintenance order in relation to a child if—

(a) the child is, will be or (if the order were to be made) would be receiving instruction at an educational establishment or undergoing training for a trade, profession or vocation (whether or not while in gainful employment); and

(b) the order is made solely for the purposes of requiring the person making or securing the making of periodical payments fixed by the order to meet some or all of the expenses incurred in connection with the provision of the instruction or training.   *Edu*

(8) This section shall not prevent a court from exercising any power which it has to make a maintenance order in relation to a child if—   *— disability*

(a) a disability living allowance is paid to or in respect of him; or

(b) no such allowance is paid but he is disabled,

and the order[3] is made solely for the purpose of requiring the person making or securing the making of periodical payments fixed by the order to meet some or all of any expenses attributable to the child's disability.

(9) For the purposes of subsection (8), a child is disabled if he is blind, deaf or dumb or is substantially and permanently handicapped by illness, injury, mental disorder or congenital deformity or such other disability as may be prescribed.

(10) This section shall not prevent a court from exercising any power which it has to make a maintenance order in relation to a child if the order is made against a person with care of the child.

(11) In this Act "maintenance order"[4], in relation to any child, means an order which requires the making or securing of periodical payments to or for the benefit of the child and which is made under—

(a) Part II of the Matrimonial Causes Act 1973;

(b) the Domestic Proceedings and Magistrates' Courts Act 1978;

(c) Part III of the Matrimonial and Family Proceedings Act 1984;

(d) the Family Law (Scotland) Act 1985;

(e) Schedule 1 to the Children Act 1989; or

(f) any other prescribed[5] enactment,

and includes any order varying or reviving such an order.*

[Child Support Act 1991, s 8 as amended by the Child Support Act 1995, s 18, the Social Security Act 1998, Sch 7 and the Child Support, Pensions and Social Security Act 2000, Sch 3.]

---

   *Subsections (5A) and (12) inserted by the Constitutional Reform Act 2005, Sch 4 from a date to be appointed.

   1. Where, under the Child Support Act 1991, the absent parent is possessed of capital assets but no income so that a nil assessment is made, the court may not make an order for a lump sum under Sch 1 to the Children Act 1989 to provide for regular support of the child which would ordinarily have been provided by way of periodic payments. A lump sum may only be ordered to meet a particular item of capital expenditure (*Phillips v Peace* [1996] 2 FCR 237, [1996] 2 FLR 230).

   2. The Child Maintenance (Written Agreements) Order 1993, SI 1993/620 has been made. This provides that s 8 shall not prevent a court from exercising any power which it has to make a maintenance order in relation to a child in any circumstances in which paragraphs (a) and (b) of s 8(5) apply.

   3. The embargo in s 8(3) on the court making maintenance orders in respect of children does not apply in specified circumstances and under s 8(8) a court may make a maintenance order in respect of a disabled child when payments are required solely to meet some or all of any expenses attributable to the child's disability (*C v F (disabled child: maintenance orders)* [1999] 1 FCR 39, [1998] 2 FLR 1). Although generally an order for periodical payments under Sch 1 to the Children Act 1989, ante, will not extend beyond the child's 18th birthday, para 3(2)(b) of Sch 1 gives jurisdiction to extend such payments beyond the child's birthday if there are special circumstances such as physical or other handicap. Section 55 of the Child Support Act 1991, post, defines a child for the purposes of the Act as a person under the age of 16, or under the age of 19 if he is receiving full time education, but that age restriction does not apply to those maintenance orders, including those for disabled children, which the court is not precluded by s 8 from making. Therefore, the court may make an order for such a child beyond the age of 19 (*C v F (disabled child: maintenance orders)* [1999] 1 FCR 39, [1998] 2 FLR 1).

   4. An order which made capital provision for a child rather than the commutation of periodical payments into a lump sum was held not to be a "maintenance order" within the meaning of s 8(11) (*AMS v Child Support Officer* [1998] 2 FCR 622, [1998] 1 FLR 955).

   5. The Affiliation Proceedings Act 1957 is prescribed for the purposes of s 8(11) by the Child Support (Maintenance Arrangements and Jurisdiction) Regulations 1992, SI 1992/2645 in this PART, STATUTORY INSTRUMENTS ON FAMILY LAW, post.

6–2908   9. Agreements about maintenance.   (1) In this section "maintenance agreement" means any agreement for the making, or for securing the making, of periodical payments by way of maintenance, or in Scotland aliment, to or for the benefit of any child.

(2) Nothing in this Act shall be taken to prevent any person from entering into a maintenance agreement.

(3) Subject to section 4(10)(a) and section 7(10) the existence of a maintenance agreement shall not prevent any party to the agreement, or any other person, from applying for a maintenance

calculation with respect to any child to or for whose benefit periodical payments are to be made or secured under the agreement.

(4) Where any agreement contains a provision which purports to restrict the right of any person to apply for a maintenance calculation, that provision shall be void.

(5) Where section 8 would prevent any court from making a maintenance order in relation to a child and a non-resident parent of his, no court shall exercise any power that it has to vary any agreement so as—

(a) to insert a provision requiring that non-resident parent to make or secure the making of periodical payments by way of maintenance, or in Scotland aliment, to or for the benefit of that child; or

(b) to increase the amount payable under such a provision.

(6) In any case in which section 4(10) or 7(10) prevents the making of an application for a maintenance calculation, and—

(a) no application has been made for a maintenance calculation under section 6, or

(b) such an application has been made but no maintenance calculation has been made in response to it,

subsection (5) shall have effect with the omission of paragraph (b).

[Child Support Act 1991, s 9 as amended by the Child Support Act 1995, s 18 and the Child Support, Pensions and Social Security Act 2000, Sch 3.]

6–2909   10. Relationship between maintenance calculations and certain court orders and related matters.   (1) Where an order of a kind prescribed[1] for the purposes of this subsection is in force with respect to any qualifying child with respect to whom a maintenance calculation is made, the order—

(a) shall, so far as it relates to the making or securing of periodical payments, cease to have effect to such extent as may be determined in accordance with regulations made by the Secretary of State; or

(b) where the regulations so provide, shall, so far as it so relates, have effect subject to such modifications as may be so determined.

(2) Where an agreement of a kind prescribed[2] for the purposes of this subsection is in force with respect to any qualifying child with respect to whom a maintenance calculation is made, the agreement—

(a) shall, so far as it relates to the making or securing of periodical payments, be unenforceable to such extent as may be determined in accordance with regulations made by the Secretary of State; or

(b) where the regulations so provide, shall, so far as it so relates, have effect subject to such modifications as may be so determined.

(3) Any regulations under this section may, in particular, make such provision with respect to—

(a) any case where any person with respect to whom an order or agreement of a kind prescribed for the purposes of subsection (1) or (2) has effect applies to the prescribed court, before the end of the prescribed period, for the order or agreement to be varied in the light of the maintenance calculation and of the provisions of this Act;

(b) the recovery of any arrears under the order or agreement which fell due before the coming into force of the maintenance calculation,

as the Secretary of State considers appropriate and may provide that, in prescribed circumstances, an application to any court which is made with respect to an order of a prescribed kind relating to the making or securing of periodical payments to or for the benefit of a child shall be treated by the court as an application for the order to be revoked.

(4) The Secretary of State may by regulations[3] make provision for—

(a) notification to be given by the Secretary of State concerned to the prescribed person in any case where he considers that the making of a maintenance calculation has affected, or is likely to affect, any order of a kind prescribed for the purposes of this subsection;

(b) notification to be given by the prescribed person to the Secretary of State in any case where a court makes an order which it considers has affected, or is likely to affect, a maintenance calculation.

(5) Rules may be made under section 144 of the Magistrates' Courts Act 1980 (rules of procedure) requiring any person who, in prescribed circumstances, makes an application to a magistrates' court for a maintenance order to furnish the court with a statement in a prescribed form, and signed by an officer of the Secretary of State, as to whether or not, at the time when the statement is made, there is a maintenance calculation in force with respect to that person or the child concerned.

In this subsection—

"maintenance order" means an order of a prescribed kind for the making or securing of periodical payments to or for the benefit of a child; and

"prescribed" means prescribed by the rules.
[Child Support Act 1991, s 10, as amended by the Social Security Act 1998, Sch 7 and the Child Support, Pensions and Social Security Act 2000, Sch 3.]

---

1. For orders made under enactments which are prescribed for the purposes of s 10(1) see reg 3 of the Child Support (Maintenance Arrangements and Jurisdiction) Regulations 1992, SI 1992/2645 in this PART, STATUTORY INSTRUMENTS ON FAMILY LAW, post. For transitional relief see the Child Support (Miscellaneous Amendments and Transitional Provisions) Regulations 1994, SI 1994/227 amended by SI 1995/1045 and 3261, SI 1999/1510 and the Child Support, Pensions and Social Security Act 2000, s 1 and Sch 3 (CD Rom only).
2. For prescribed agreements see reg 4 of the Child Support (Maintenance Arrangements and Jurisdiction) Regulations 1992, SI 1992/2645 in this PART, STATUTORY INSTRUMENTS ON FAMILY LAW, post.
3. See the Child Support (Maintenance Arrangements and Jurisdiction) Regulations 1992, SI 1992/2645 in this PART, STATUTORY INSTRUMENTS ON FAMILY LAW, post.

Maintenance assessments

6–2910   11. Maintenance calculations.   (1) An application for a maintenance calculation made to the Secretary of State shall be dealt with by him in accordance with the provision made by or under this Act.

(2) The Secretary of State shall (unless he decides not to make a maintenance calculation in response to the application, or makes a decision under section 12) determine the application by making a decision under this section about whether any child support maintenance is payable and, if so, how much.

(3) Where—

(*a*) a parent is treated under section 6(3) as having applied for a maintenance calculation; but
(*b*) the Secretary of State becomes aware before determining the application that the parent has ceased to fall within section 6(1),

he shall, subject to subsection (4), cease to treat that parent as having applied for a maintenance calculation.

(4) If it appears to the Secretary of State that subsection (10) of section 4 would not have prevented the parent with care concerned from making an application for a maintenance calculation under that section he shall—

(*a*) notify her of the effect of this subsection; and
(*b*) if, before the end of the period of one month beginning with the day on which notice was sent to her, she asks him to do so, treat her as having applied not under section 6 but under section 4.

(5) Where subsection (3) applies but subsection (4) does not, the Secretary of State shall notify—

(*a*) the parent with care concerned; and
(*b*) the non-resident parent (or alleged non-resident parent), where it appears to him that that person is aware that the parent with care has been treated as having applied for a maintenance calculation.

(6) The amount of child support maintenance to be fixed by a maintenance calculation shall be determined in accordance with Part I of Schedule 1 unless an application for a variation has been made and agreed.

(7) If the Secretary of State has agreed to a variation, the amount of child support maintenance to be fixed shall be determined on the basis he determines under section 28F(4).

(8) Part II of Schedule 1 makes further provision with respect to maintenance calculations.
[Child Support Act 1991, s 11 as amended by the Child Support Act 1995, s 19, the Social Security Act 1998, Sch 7 and the Child Support, Pensions and Social Security Act 2000, Sch 3.]

---

1. For transitional relief where there is an existing court order see the Child Support (Miscellaneous Amendments and Transitional Provisions) Regulations 1994, SI 1994/227 amended by SI 1995/1045 and 3261, SI 1999/1510 and the Child Support, Pensions and Social Security Act 2000, s 1 and Sch 3 (CD Rom only).

6–2911   12. Default and interim maintenance decisions.   (1) Where the Secretary of State—

(*a*) is required to make a maintenance calculation; or
(*b*) is proposing to make a decision under section 16 or 17,

and it appears to him that he does not have sufficient information to enable him to do so, he may make a default maintenance decision.

(2) Where an application for a variation has been made under section 28A(1) in connection with an application for a maintenance calculation (or in connection with such an application which is treated as having been made), the Secretary of State may make an interim maintenance decision.

(3) The amount of child support maintenance fixed by an interim maintenance decision shall be determined in accordance with Part I of Schedule 1.

(4) The Secretary of State may by regulations make provision as to default and interim maintenance decisions.

(5) The regulations may, in particular, make provision as to—

(*a*)   the procedure to be followed in making a default or an interim maintenance decision; and

(*b*)   a default rate of child support maintenance to apply where a default maintenance decision is made.

[Child Support Act 1991, s 12 as substituted by the Child Support, Pensions and Social Security Act 2000, s 4.]

---

1. See reg 7 of the Child Support (Maintenance Calculation Procedure) Regulations 2000, SI 2001/157 amended by SI 2002/1204, SI 2003/328, 347 and 2779, SI 2004/2415 and SI 2005/785 (CD Rom only).

Child support officers

6–2912   13.   Child support officers.   *Repealed.*

Information

6–2913   14.   Information required by Secretary of State.   (1) The Secretary of State may make regulations[1] requiring any information or evidence needed for the determination of any application made or treated as made under this Act, or any question arising in connection with such an application (or application treated as made), or needed for the making of any decision or in connection with the imposition of any condition or requirement under this Act, or needed in connection with the collection or enforcement of child support or other maintenance under this Act, to be furnished—

(*a*)   by such persons as may be determined in accordance with regulations made by the Secretary of State; and

(*b*)   in accordance with the regulations.

(1A) Regulations under subsection (1) may make provision for notifying any person who is required to furnish any information or evidence under the regulations of the possible consequences of failing to do so.

(2)–(2A) *Repealed.*

(3) The Secretary of State may by regulations[2] make provision authorising the disclosure by him, in such circumstances as may be prescribed, of such information held by him for purposes of this Act as may be prescribed.

(4) The provisions of Schedule 2 (which relate to information which is held for purposes other than those of this Act but which is required by the Secretary of State) shall have effect.

[Child Support Act 1991, s 14 as amended by the Child Support Act 1995, Sch 3, the Jobseekers Act 1995, Sch 2 and the Social Security Act 1998, Sch 7 and the Child Support, Pensions and Social Security Act 2000, Sch 3.]

---

1. See the Child Support (Information, Evidence and Disclosure) Regulations 1992, SI 1992/1812 amended by SI 1995/123, 1045 and 3261, SI 1996/1945 and 2907, SI 1998/58, SI 1999/977 and 1510, SI 2001/161, the Child Support, Pensions and Social Security Act 2000, s 1, SI 2003/328, SI 2004/2415 and SI 2005/2877 (CD Rom only).

2. By reg 8 of the Child Support (Information, Evidence and Disclosure) Regulations 1992, SI 1992/1812 amended by SI 1995/123, 1045 and 3261, SI 1996/1945 and 2907, SI 1998/58, SI 1999/977 and 1510, SI 2001/161, the Child Support, Pensions and Social Security Act 2000, s 1, SI 2003/328 and SI 2004/2415 (CD Rom only), disclosure may be made by the Secretary of State or a child support officer to a court for the purposes of proceedings relating to the Act or to the benefit Acts.

6–2913A   14A.   Information – Offences.   (1) This section applies to—

(a)   persons who are required to comply with regulations under section 4(4) or 7(5); and

(b)   persons specified in regulations under section 14(1)(a).

(2) Such a person is guilty of an offence if, pursuant to a request for information under or by virtue of those regulations—

(a)   he makes a statement or representation which he knows to be false; or

(b)   he provides, or knowingly causes or knowingly allows to be provided, a document or other information which he knows to be false in a material particular.

(3) Such a person is guilty of an offence if, following such a request, he fails to comply with it.

(4) It is a defence for a person charged with an offence under subsection (3) to prove that he had a reasonable excuse for failing to comply.

(5) A person guilty of an offence under this section is liable on summary conviction to a fine not exceeding level 3 on the standard scale.]

[Child Support Act 1991, s 14A, as inserted by the Child Support, Pensions and Social Security Act 2000, s 13.]

6–2914   15.   Powers of inspectors.   (1) The Secretary of State may appoint, on such terms as he thinks fit, persons to act as inspectors under this section.

(2) The function of inspectors is to acquire information which the Secretary of State needs for any of the purposes of this Act.

(3) Every inspector is to be given a certificate of his appointment.

(4) An inspector has power, at any reasonable time and either alone or accompanied by such other persons as he thinks fit, to enter any premises which—

(*a*)   are liable to inspection under this section; and

(b)   are premises to which it is reasonable for him to require entry in order that he may exercise his functions under this section,

and may there make such examination and inquiry as he considers appropriate.

(4A)   Premises liable to inspection under this section are those which are not used wholly as a dwelling house and which the inspector has reasonable grounds for suspecting are—

(a)   premises at which a non-resident parent is or has been employed;

(b)   premises at which a non-resident parent carries out, or has carried out, a trade, profession, vocation or business;

(c)   premises at which there is information held by a person ("A") whom the inspector has reasonable grounds for suspecting has information about a non-resident parent acquired in the course of A's own trade, profession, vocation or business.

(5)   An inspector exercising his powers may question any person aged 18 or over whom he finds on the premises.

(6)   If required to do so by an inspector exercising his powers, any such person shall furnish to the inspector all such information and documents as the inspector may reasonably require.
shall furnish to the inspector all such information and documents as the inspector may reasonably require.

(7)   No person shall be required under this section to answer any question or to give any evidence tending to incriminate himself or, in the case of a person who is married or is a civil partner, his or her spouse or civil partner.

(8)   On applying for admission to any premises in the exercise of his powers, an inspector shall, if so required, produce his certificate.

(9)   If any person—

(a)   intentionally delays or obstructs any inspector exercising his powers; or

(b)   without reasonable excuse, refuses or neglects to answer any question or furnish any information or to produce any document when required to do so under this section,

he shall be guilty of an offence and liable on summary conviction to a fine not exceeding **level 3** on the standard scale.

(10)   In this section—

"certificate" means a certificate of appointment issued under this section;
"inspector" means an inspector appointed under this section;
"powers" means powers conferred by this section;

(11)   In this section, "premises" includes—

(a)   moveable structures and vehicles, vessels, aircraft and hovercraft;

(b)   installations that are offshore installations for the purposes of the Mineral Workings (Offshore Installations) Act 1971; and

(c)   places of all other descriptions whether or not occupied as land or otherwise,

and references in this section to the occupier of premises are to be construed, in relation to premises that are not occupied as land, as references to any person for the time being present at the place in question.
[Child Support Act 1991, s 15, as amended by the Social Security Act 1998, Schs 7 and 8, the Child Support, Pensions and Social Security Act 2000, s 14 and the Civil Partnership Act 2004, Sch 24.]

Reviews and appeals

6–2915   16.   Revision of decisions.   (1)   Any decision of the Secretary of State to which subsection (1A) applies may be revised by the Secretary of State—

(a)   either within the prescribed period or in prescribed cases or circumstances; and

(b)   either on an application made for the purpose or on his own initiative;

and regulations[1] may prescribe the procedure by which a decision of the Secretary of State may be so revised.

(1A)   This subsection applies to—

(a)   a decision of the Secretary of State under section 11, 12 or 17;

(b)   a reduced benefit decision under section 46;

(c)   a decision of an appeal tribunal on a referral under section 28D(1)(b).

(1B)   Where the Secretary of State revises a decision under section 12(1)—

(a)   he may (if appropriate) do so as if he were revising a decision under section 11; and

(b)   if he does that, his decision as revised is to be treated as one under section 11 instead of section 12(1) (and, in particular, is to be so treated for the purposes of an appeal against it under section 20).

(2)   In making a decision under subsection (1), the Secretary of State need not consider any issue that is not raised by the application or, as the case may be, did not cause him to act on his own initiative.

(3) Subject to subsections (4) and (5) and section 28ZC, a revision under this section shall take effect as from the date on which the original decision took (or was to take) effect.

(4) Regulations may provide that, in prescribed cases or circumstances, a revision under this section shall take effect as from such other date as may be prescribed.

(5) Where a decision is revised under this section, for the purpose of any rule as to the time allowed for bringing an appeal, the decision shall be regarded as made on the date on which it is so revised.

(6) Except in prescribed circumstances, an appeal against a decision of the Secretary of State shall lapse if the decision is revised under this section before the appeal is determined.
[Child Support Act 1991, s 16 as amended by the Social Security Act 1998, s 40 and the Child Support, Pensions and Social Security Act 2000, s 8.]

---

1. The Child Support (Decisions and Appeals) Regulations 1999, SI 1999/991 amended by SI 2000/3185, SI 2002/1204, SI 2003/328 and SI 2004/2415 have been made.

6–2916   17. Decisions superseding earlier decisions.   (1) Subject to subsection (2), the following, namely—

   (a)   any decision of the Secretary of State under section 11 or 12 or this section, whether as originally made or as revised under section 16;
   (b)   any decision of an appeal tribunal under section 20;
   (c)   any reduced benefit decision under section 46;
   (d)   any decision of an appeal tribunal on a referral under section 28D(1)(b);
   (e)   any decision of a Child Support Commissioner on an appeal from such a decision as is mentioned in paragraph (b) or (d),

may be superseded by a decision made by the Secretary of State, either on an application made for the purpose or on his own initiative.

(2) In making a decision under subsection (1), the Secretary of State need not consider any issue that is not raised by the application or, as the case may be, did not cause him to act on his own initiative.

(3) Regulations may prescribe the cases and circumstances in which, and the procedure by which, a decision may be made under this section.

(4) Subject to subsection (5) and section 28ZC, a decision under this section shall take effect as from the beginning of the maintenance period in which it is made or, where applicable, the beginning of the maintenance period in which the application was made.

(4A) In subsection (4), a "maintenance period" is (except where a different meaning is prescribed for prescribed cases) a period of seven days, the first one beginning on the effective date of the first decision made by the Secretary of State under section 11 or (if earlier) his first default or interim maintenance decision (under section 12) in relation to the non-resident parent in question, and each subsequent one beginning on the day after the last day of the previous one.

(5) Regulations may provide that, in prescribed cases or circumstances, a decision under this section shall take effect as from such other date as may be prescribed.
[Child Support Act 1991, s 17 as amended by the Social Security Act 1998, s 41 and the Child Support, Pensions and Social Security Act 2000, s 9(1), (2).]

6–2917   18–19. *Repealed.*

6–2918   20. Appeals to appeal tribunals.   (1) A qualifying person has a right of appeal to an appeal tribunal against—

   (a)   a decision of the Secretary of State under section 11, 12 or 17 (whether as originally made or as revised under section 16);
   (b)   a decision of the Secretary of State not to make a maintenance calculation under section 11 or not to supersede a decision under section 17;
   (c)   a reduced benefit decision under section 46;
   (d)   the imposition (by virtue of section 41A) of a requirement to make penalty payments, or their amount;
   (e)   the imposition (by virtue of section 47) of a requirement to pay fees.

(2) In subsection (1), "qualifying person" means—

   (a)   in relation to paragraphs (a) and (b)—

      (i)   the person with care, or non-resident parent, with respect to whom the Secretary of State made the decision, or
      (ii)   in a case relating to a maintenance calculation which was applied for under section 7, either of those persons or the child concerned;

   (b)   in relation to paragraph (c), the person in respect of whom the benefits are payable;
   (c)   in relation to paragraph (d), the parent who has been required to make penalty payments; and
   (d)   in relation to paragraph (e), the person required to pay fees.

(3) A person with a right of appeal under this section shall be given such notice as may be prescribed of—

(*a*) that right; and

(*b*) the relevant decision, or the imposition of the requirement.

(4) Regulations[1] may make—

(*a*) provision as to the manner in which, and the time within which, appeals are to be brought; and

(*b*) such provision with respect to proceedings before appeal tribunals as the Secretary of State considers appropriate.

(5) The regulations may in particular make any provision of a kind mentioned in Schedule 5 to the Social Security Act 1998.

(6) No appeal lies by virtue of subsection (1)(*c*) unless the amount of the person's benefit is reduced in accordance with the reduced benefit decision; and the time within which such an appeal may be brought runs from the date of notification of the reduction.

(7) In deciding an appeal under this section, an appeal tribunal—

(*a*) need not consider any issue that is not raised by the appeal; and

(*b*) shall not take into account any circumstances not obtaining at the time when the Secretary of State made the decision or imposed the requirement.

(8) If an appeal under this section is allowed, the appeal tribunal may—

(*a*) itself make such decision as it considers appropriate; or

(*b*) remit the case to the Secretary of State, together with such directions (if any) as it considers appropriate.

[Child Support Act 1991, s 20, as substituted by the Child Support, Pensions and Social Security Act 2000, s 10.]

---

1. Article 4 of the Child Support appeals (Jurisdiction of courts) Order 2002, SI 2002/1915 provides that an appeal under section 20 of the Act shall be made to a court instead of to an appeal tribunal in the circumstances mentioned in article 4.

    "4. The circumstances are that—

    (a) the appeal will be an appeal under section 20(1)(a) or (b) of the Act;

    (b) the determination made by the Secretary of State in making the decision to be appealed against included a determination that a particular person (whether the applicant or some other person) either was, or was not, a parent of the qualifying child in question ("a parentage determination"); and

    (c) the ground of the appeal will be that the decision to be appealed against should not have included that parentage determination."

In considering an appeal under s 20 the role of the court is to determine the correctness of the decision by the CSA that X is the father on the basis of which it proceeded to make a maintenance assessment.

A family proceedings court seised of a s 20 appeal has power to order a DNA test. The result of that scientific test will show whether or not Z is in fact the father. If the test shows that Z is *not* the father, then his appeal under s 20 will be allowed; if it shows that he *is* the father, then his appeal will be dismissed. Where the appeal is unsuccessful, the parentage determination originally made by the CSA will stand. The matter is referred back to the CSA to be dealt with in accordance with the court's decision on the appeal. If his appeal fails Z will have to continue paying maintenance; if his appeal succeeds the CSA will have to refund him any money he has paid as maintenance.

There is no power in a family proceedings court to make a declaration of parentage in the course of hearing such an appeal. Not only is there no need to do so but any child in question has not been made a party and has not received notice, *Re L (Family Proceedings Court) (Appeal: jurisdiction)* [2004] EWHC 1682 (Fam), [2005] 1 FLR 210 (proceedings under the version of s 20 prior to amendment where the appeal of the child was allowed under s 60(5) of the Family Law Act 1986 in default of any provision for appeal in s 20 of the 1001 Act).

Regulations 31 and 32 of the Social Security and Child Support (Decisions and Appeals) Regulations 1999, SI 1999/991, as amended by SI 1999/2570 apply to appeals brought under this Order with the following modifications—

    (a) for the words "an appeal tribunal" shall be substituted "a court";

    (b) for the words "legally qualified panel member" and "panel member" shall be substituted "justices' clerk or the court"; and

    (c) in regulation 32(10) for the words "such written form as has been approved by the President" shall be substituted "written form".

6–2919   20A–21. *Repealed.*

6–2920   22. *Child Support Commissioners.*

6–2921   23. *Child Support Commissioners for Northern Ireland.*

6–2921A   23A. Redetermination of appeals.   (1) This section applies where an application is made to a person under section 24(6)(*a*) for leave to appeal from a decision of an appeal tribunal.

(2) If the person who constituted, or was the chairman of, the appeal tribunal considers that the decision was erroneous in law, he may set aside the decision and refer the case either for redetermination by the tribunal or for determination by a differently constituted tribunal.

(3) If each of the principal parties to the case expresses the view that the decision was erroneous in point of law, the person shall set aside the decision and refer the case for determination by a differently constituted tribunal.

(4) The "principal parties" are—

(a) the Secretary of State; and

(b) those who are qualifying persons for the purposes of section 20(2) in relation to the decision in question.

[Child Support Act 1991, s 23A, as inserted by the Child Support, Pensions and Social Security Act 2000, s 11.]

6–2922 24. Appeal to Child Support Commissioner.   (1) Any person who is aggrieved by a decision of an appeal tribunal, and the Secretary of State, may appeal to a Child Support Commissioner on a question of law.

(1A) *Repealed.*

(2) Where, on an appeal under this section, a Child Support Commissioner holds that the decision appealed against was wrong in law he shall set it aside.

(3) Where a decision is set aside under subsection (2), the Child Support Commissioner may—

(a) if he can do so without making fresh or further findings of fact, give the decision which he considers should have been given by the appeal tribunal;

(b) if he considers it expedient, make such findings and give such decision as he considers appropriate in the light of those findings; or

(c) on an appeal by the Secretary of State, refer the case to an appeal tribunal with directions for its determination; or

(d) on any other appeal, refer the case to the Secretary of State or, if he considers it appropriate, to an appeal tribunal with directions for its determination.

(4) The reference under subsection (3) to the Secretary of State shall, subject to any direction of the Child Support Commissioner, be to an officer of his, or a person providing him with services, who has taken no part in the decision originally appealed against.

(5) On a reference under subsection (3) to an appeal tribunal, the tribunal shall, subject to any direction of the Child Support Commissioner, consist of persons who were not members of the tribunal which gave the decision which has been appealed against.

(6) No appeal lies under this section without the leave—

(a) of the person who constituted, or was the chairman of, the appeal tribunal when the decision appealed against was given or of such other person as may be determined in accordance with regulations made by the Lord Chancellor; or

(b) subject to and in accordance with regulations so made, of a Child Support Commissioner.

(7) The Lord Chancellor may by regulations[1] make provision as to the manner in which, and the time within which, appeals under this section are to be brought and applications for leave under this section are to be made.

(8) Where a question which would otherwise fall to be determined by the Secretary of State first arises in the course of an appeal to a Child Support Commissioner, he may, if he thinks fit, determine it even though it has not been considered by the Secretary of State.

(9) Before making any regulations under subsection (6) or (7), the Lord Chancellor shall consult the Secretary of State.

[Child Support Act 1991, s 24 as amended by the Child Support Act 1995, Sch 3 and the Social Security Act 1998, Schs 7 and 8 and SI 1999/678.]

---

1. The Child Support Commissioners (Procedure) Regulations 1999, SI 1999/1305, have been made.

6–2923 25. Appeal from Child Support Commissioner on question of law.   (1) An appeal on a question of law shall lie to the appropriate court from any decision of a Child Support Commissioner.

(2) No such appeal may be brought except—

(a) with leave of the Child Support Commissioner who gave the decision or, where regulations made by the Lord Chancellor so provide, of a Child Support Commissioner selected in accordance with the regulations; or

(b) if the Child Support Commissioner refuses leave, with the leave of the appropriate court.

(3) An application for leave to appeal under this section against a decision of a Child Support Commissioner ("the appeal decision") may only be made by—

(a) a person who was a party to the proceedings in which the original decision, or appeal decision, was given;

(b) the Secretary of State; or

(c) any other person who is authorised to do so by regulations made by the Lord Chancellor.

(3A) The Child Support Commissioner to whom an application for leave to appeal under this section is made shall specify as the appropriate court either the Court of Appeal or the Court of Session.

(3B) In determining the appropriate court, the Child Support Commissioner shall have regard to the circumstances of the case, and in particular the convenience of the persons who may be parties to the appeal.

(4) In this section—

"appropriate court", except in subsections (3A) and (3B), means the court specified in accordance with those subsections; and

"original decision" means the decision to which the appeal decision in question relates.

(5) The Lord Chancellor may by regulations[1] make provision with respect to—

(a) the manner in which and the time within which applications must be made to a Child Support Commissioner for leave under this section; and

(b) the procedure for dealing with such applications.

(6) Before making any regulations under subsection (2), (3) or (5), the Lord Chancellor shall consult the Secretary of State.

[Child Support Act 1991, s 25 as amended by the Child Support Act 1995, Sch 3 and SI 1999/678.]

---

1. The Child Support Commissioners (Procedure) Regulations 1999, SI 1999/1305, have been made.

6–2924 **26. Disputes about parentage.** (1) Where a person who is alleged to be a parent of the child with respect to whom an application for a maintenance calculation has been made or treated as made ("the alleged parent") denies that he is one of the child's parents, the Secretary of State shall not make a maintenance calculation on the assumption that the alleged parent is one of the child's parents unless the case falls within one of those set out in subsection (2).

(2) The Cases are—

CASE **A1**

Where—

(a) the child is habitually resident in England and Wales;

(b) the Secretary of State is satisfied that the alleged parent was married to the child's mother at some time in the period beginning with the conception and ending with the birth of the child; and

(c) the child has not been adopted.

CASE A2

Where—

(a) the child is habitually resident in England and Wales;

(b) the alleged parent has been registered as father of the child under section 10 or 10A of the Births and Deaths Registration Act 1953, or in any register kept under section 13 (register of births and still-births) or section 44 (Register of Corrections Etc) of the Registration of Births, Deaths and Marriages (Scotland) Act 1965, or under Article 14 or 18(1)(b)(ii) of the Births and Deaths Registration (Northern Ireland) Order 1976; and

(c) the child has not subsequently been adopted.

CASE **A3**

Where the result of a scientific test (within the meaning of section 27A) taken by the alleged parent would be relevant to determining the child's parentage, and the alleged parent—

(a) refuses to take such a test; or

(b) has submitted to such a test, and it shows that there is no reasonable doubt that the alleged parent is a parent of the child.

CASE A

Where the alleged parent is a parent of the child in question by virtue of having adopted him.

CASE B

Where the alleged parent is a parent of the child in question by virtue of an order under section 30 of the Human Fertilisation and Embryology Act 1990 (parental orders in favour of gamete donors).

CASE B1

Where the Secretary of State is satisfied that the alleged parent is a parent of the child in question by virtue of section 27 or 28 of that Act (meaning of "mother" and of "father" respectively).

CASE C

Where—

(a) either—

(i) a declaration that the alleged parent is a parent of the child in question (or a declaration which has that effect) is in force under section 56 of the Family Law Act 1986 or Article 32 of the Matrimonial and Family Proceedings (Northern Ireland) Order 1989 (declarations of parentage); or

(ii) a declarator by a court in Scotland that the alleged parent is a parent of the child in question (or a declarator which has that effect) is in force; and

(b) the child has not subsequently been adopted.

CASE D

Repealed.

CASE E

Where—

(a) the child is habitually resident in Scotland;

(b) the Secretary of State is satisfied that one or other of the presumptions set out in section 5(1) of the Law Reform (Parent and Child) (Scotland) Act 1986 applies; and

(c) the child has not subsequently been adopted.

CASE F

Where—

(a) the alleged parent has been found, or adjudged[1], to be the father of the child in question—

(i) in proceedings before any court in England and Wales which are relevant proceedings for the purposes of section 12 of the Civil Evidence Act 1968 or in proceedings before any court in Northern Ireland which are relevant proceedings for the purposes of section 8 of the Civil Evidence Act (Northern Ireland) 1971; or

(ii) in affiliation proceedings before any court in the United Kingdom,

(whether or not he offered any defence to the allegation of paternity) and that finding or adjudication still subsists; and

(b) the child has not subsequently been adopted.

(3) In this section—

"adopted" means adopted within the meaning of Part IV of the Adoption Act 1976 or Chapter 4 of Part 1 of the Adoption and Children Act 2002 or, in relation to Scotland, Part IV of the Adoption (Scotland) Act 1978; and

"affiliation proceedings", in relation to Scotland, means any action of affiliation and aliment.

[Child Support Act 1991, s 26 as amended by SI 1995/756, the Social Security Act 1998, Sch 7, the Child Support, Pensions and Social Security Act 2000, ss 1 and 15 and the Adoption and Children Act 2002, Sch 3.]

---

1. A man in respect of whom a parental responsibility order had been made, was "adjudged" to be the father of the child even where the order was discharged subsequently on the basis that it was inappropriate in all the circumstances (*R v Secretary of State for Social Security, ex p West* [1999] 3 FCR 574, [1999] 1 FLR 1233, CA, (application for leave); *R v Secretary of State for Social Security, ex p W* [1999] 3 FCR 693, [1999] 2 FLR 604, FD (substantive hearing)).

6–2925 **27. Reference to court for declaration of parentage.**   (1) Subsection (1A) applies in any case where—

(a) an application for a maintenance calculation has been made, or a maintenance calculation is in force, with respect to a person ("the alleged parent") who denies that he is a parent[1] of a child with respect to whom the application or assessment was made; and

(b) the Secretary of State is not satisfied that the case falls within one of those set out in section 26(2).

(1A) In any case where this subsection applies, the Secretary of State or the person with care may apply to the court for a declaration as to whether or not the alleged parent is one of the child's parents[2].

(2) If, on hearing any application under subsection (1A), the court is satisfied that the alleged parent is, or is not, a parent of the child in question it shall make a declaration to that effect[3].

(3) A declaration under this section shall have effect only for the purposes of—

(a) this Act; and

(b) proceedings in which a court is considering whether to make a maintenance order in the circumstances mentioned in subsection (6), (7) or (8) of section 8.

(4) In this section "court" means, subject to any provision made under Schedule 11 to the Children Act 1989 (jurisdiction of courts with respect to certain proceedings relating to children) the High Court, a county court or a magistrates' court.

(5) In the definition of "relevant proceedings" in section 12(5) of the Civil Evidence Act 1968 (findings of paternity etc as evidence in civil proceedings) the following paragraph shall be added at the end—

"(*d*) section 27 of the Child Support Act 1991."

(6) This section does not apply to Scotland.

[Child Support Act 1991, s 27 as amended by the Child Support Act 1995, s 20, the Social Security Act 1998, Sch 7 and the Child Support, Pensions and Social Security Act 2000, Sch 3.]

---

1. "Parent", in relation to any child, means any person who is in law the mother or father of the child (s 54, post). "Parent" therefore includes a biological parent. Also a child conceived as a result of consensual AID and born between 4 April 1988 and 31 July 1991 (inclusive) by virtue of s 27 of the Family Law Reform Act 1987 (now repealed) or after 1 August 1991 by virtue of s 28(2) of the Human Fertilisation and Embryology Act 1990, is treated as a child of both spouses. See further paras **6–2806** and **6–2807** ante and *Re M (Child Support Act: parentage)* [1997] 3 FCR 383, [1997] 2 FLR 90.

2. On an application for a declaration of parentage under this section, the court may make a direction for blood tests to be taken pursuant to s 20(1) of the Family Law Reform Act 1969, this PART, ante (*Re E (a minor) (child support: blood test)* [1995] 1 FCR 245, [1994] 2 FLR 548).

There is no right of appeal to the High Court from a declaration of paternity under s 27 made by a family proceedings court, since no right of appeal is conferred by the Act either expressly or pursuant to powers delegated to the Lord Chancellor under s 45(1)(*b*) post. However, if following a s 27 declaration medical evidence establishes conclusively that a person cannot be the father of a child, the High Court can, in the absence of any other available relief, make a declaration to that effect under RSC Ord 15, r 16 (*T v Child Support Agency* [1997] 4 All ER 27, [1998] 1 FCR 62, [1997] 2 FLR 875).

3. For the purposes of a reference under this section, a putative father's refusal to comply with a court order to provide a blood test sample may result in an adverse inference being drawn sufficient to rebut the presumption of legitimacy (*F v Child Support Agency* [1999] 2 FCR 385, [1999] 2 FLR 244).

6–2926   27A. Recovery of fees for scientific tests.   (1) This section applies in any case where—

(*a*)   an application for a maintenance calculation has been made or a maintenance calculation is in force;

(*b*)   scientific tests have been carried out (otherwise than under a direction or in response to a request) in relation to bodily samples obtained from a person who is alleged to be a parent of a child with respect to whom the application or calculation is made or, as the case may be, treated as made;

(*c*)   the results of the tests do not exclude the alleged parent from being one of the child's parents; and

(*d*)   one of the conditions set out in subsection (2) is satisfied.

(2) The conditions are that—

(*a*)   the alleged parent does not deny that he is one of the child's parents;

(*b*)   in proceedings under section 55A of the Family Law Act 1986, a court has made a declaration that the alleged parent is a parent of the child in question; or

(*c*)   Scotland.

(3) In any case to which this section applies, any fee paid by the Secretary of State in connection with scientific tests may be recovered by him from the alleged parent as a debt due to the Crown.

(4) In this section—

"bodily sample" means a sample of bodily fluid or bodily tissue taken for the purpose of scientific tests;

"direction" means a direction given by a court under section 20 of the Family Law Reform Act 1969 (tests to determine paternity);

"request" means a request made by a court under section 70 of the Law Reform (Miscellaneous Provisions) (Scotland) Act 1990 (blood and other samples in civil proceedings); and

"scientific tests" means scientific tests made with the object of ascertaining the inheritable characteristics of bodily fluids or bodily tissue.

(5) Any sum recovered by the Secretary of State under this section shall be paid by him into the Consolidated Fund.

[Child Support Act 1991, s 27A, as inserted by the Child Support Act 1995, s 21 and amended by the Child Support, Pensions and Social Security Act 2000, s 1 and Sch 8.]

6–2927   28. *Power of Secretary of State to initiate or defend actions of declarator: Scotland.*

Decisions and appeals dependent on other case

6–2928   28ZA. *Decisions involving issues that arise on appeal in other cases*

6–2929   28ZB. *Appeals involving issues that arise on appeal in other cases*

Cases of error

6–2930　28ZC. *Restrictions on liability in certain cases of error*

6–2931　28ZD. *Correction of errors and setting aside of decisions*

6–2932　28A. Application for a departure direction. (1) Where an application for a maintenance calculation is made under section 4 or 7, or treated as made under section 6, the person with care or the non-resident parent or (in the case of an application under section 7) either of them or the child concerned may apply to the Secretary of State for the rules by which the calculation is made to be varied[1] in accordance with this Act.

(2) Such an application is referred to in this Act as an "application for a variation".

(3) An application for a variation may be made at any time before the Secretary of State has reached a decision (under section 11 or 12(1)) on the application for a maintenance calculation (or the application treated as having been made under section 6).

(4) A person who applies for a variation—

(a) need not make the application in writing unless the Secretary of State directs in any case that he must; and

(b) must say upon what grounds the application is made.

(5) In other respects an application for a variation is to be made in such manner as may be prescribed[2].

(6) Schedule 4A has effect in relation to applications for a variation.

[Child Support Act 1991, s 28A as substituted by the Child Support, Pensions and Social Security Act 2000, s 5.]

---

1. Regulations for handling an application for a variation made after a maintenance calculation has been completed, have been made; see the Child Support (Variations) (Modification of Statutory Provisions) Regulations 2000, SI 2000/3173 amended by SI 2002/1204.

2. See the Child Support (Variations) Regulations 2001, SI 2000/156 amended by SI 2002/1204, SI 2003/328 and 347, SI 2004/2415 and SI 2005/785 (CD Rom only).

6–2933　28B. Preliminary consideration of applications. (1) Where an application for a departure direction has been duly made to the Secretary of State, he may give the application a preliminary consideration.

(2) Where the Secretary of State does so he may, on completing the preliminary consideration, reject the application if it appears to him—

(a) that there are no grounds on which a departure direction could be given in response to the application; or

(b) that the difference between the current amount and the revised amount is less than an amount to be calculated in accordance with regulations[1] made by the Secretary of State for the purposes of this subsection and section 28F(4).

(3) In subsection (2)—

"the current amount" means the amount of the child support maintenance fixed by the current assessment; and

"the revised amount" means the amount of child support maintenance which, but for subsection (2)(b), would be fixed if a fresh maintenance assessment were to be made as a result of a departure direction allowing the departure applied for.

(4)–(5) *Repealed.*

(6) Where a decision as to a maintenance assessment is revised or superseded under section 16 or 17, the Secretary of State—

(a) shall notify the applicant and such other persons as may be prescribed that the decision has been revised or superseded; and

(b) may direct that the application is to lapse unless, before the end of such period as may be prescribed, the applicant notifies the Secretary of State that he wishes it to stand.

[Child Support Act 1991, s 28B, as inserted by the Child Support Act 1995, s 2 and amended by the Social Security Act 1998, Schs 7 and 8.]

---

1. See the Child Support (Variations) Regulations 2001, SI 2000/156 amended by SI 2002/1204, SI 2003/328 and 347, SI 2004/2415 and SI 2005/785 (CD Rom only).

6–2934　28C. Imposition of regular payments condition. (1) Where—

(a) an application for a variation is made by the non-resident parent; and

(b) the Secretary of State makes an interim maintenance decision,

the Secretary of State may also, if he has completed his preliminary consideration (under section 28B) of the application for a variation and has not rejected it under that section, impose on the non-resident parent one of the conditions mentioned in subsection (2) (a "regular payments condition").

(2) The conditions are that—

(*a*) the non-resident parent must make the payments of child support maintenance specified in the interim maintenance decision;

(*b*) the non-resident parent must make such lesser payments of child support maintenance as may be determined in accordance with regulations made by the Secretary of State.

(3) Where the Secretary of State imposes a regular payments condition, he shall give written notice of the imposition of the condition and of the effect of failure to comply with it to—

(*a*) the non-resident parent;

(*b*) all the persons with care concerned; and

(*c*) if the application for the maintenance calculation was made under section 7, the child who made the application.

(4) A regular payments condition shall cease to have effect—

(*a*) when the Secretary of State has made a decision on the application for a maintenance calculation under section 11 (whether he agrees to a variation or not);

(*b*) on the withdrawal of the application for a variation.

(5) Where a non-resident parent has failed to comply with a regular payments condition, the Secretary of State may in prescribed circumstances refuse to consider the application for a variation, and instead reach his decision under section 11 as if no such application had been made.

(6) The question whether a non-resident parent has failed to comply with a regular payments condition is to be determined by the Secretary of State.

(7) Where the Secretary of State determines that a non-resident parent has failed to comply with a regular payments condition he shall give written notice of his determination to—

(*a*) that parent;

(*b*) all the persons with care concerned; and

(*c*) if the application for the maintenance calculation was made under section 7, the child who made the application.

[Child Support Act 1991, s 28C, as inserted by the Child Support, Pensions and Social Security Act 2000, s 5.]

6–2935 28D. Determination of applications. (1) Where an application for a variation has not failed, the Secretary of State shall, in accordance with the relevant provisions of, or made under, this Act—

(*a*) either agree or not to a variation, and make a decision under section 11 or 12(1); or

(*b*) refer the application to an appeal tribunal for the tribunal to determine what variation, if any, is to be made.

(2) For the purposes of subsection (1), an application for a variation has failed if—

(*a*) it has lapsed or★ been withdrawn; or

(*b*) the Secretary of State has refused to consider it under section 28C(5).

(3) In dealing with an application for a variation which has been referred to it under subsection (1)(*b*), an appeal tribunal shall have the same powers, and be subject to the same duties, as would the Secretary of State if he were dealing with the application.

[Child Support Act 1991, s 28D, as inserted by the Child Support Act 1995, s 4, the Social Security Act 1998, Sch 7 and the Child Support, Pensions and Social Security Act 2000, s 5.]

★Repealed by the Child Support, Pensions and Social Security Act 2000, Sch 9, when in force.

6–2936 28E. Matters to be taken into account. (1) In determining whether to agree to a variation, the Secretary of State shall have regard both to the general principles set out in subsection (2) and to such other considerations as may be prescribed[1].

(2) The general principles are that—

(*a*) parents should be responsible for maintaining their children whenever they can afford to do so;

(*b*) where a parent has more than one child, his obligation to maintain any one of them should be no less of an obligation than his obligation to maintain any other of them.

(3) In determining whether to agree to a variation, the Secretary of State shall take into account any representations made to him—

(*a*) by the person with care or non-resident parent concerned; or

(*b*) where the application for the current calculation was made under section 7, by either of them or the child concerned.

(4) In determining any application for a whether to agree to a variation, no account shall be taken of the fact that—

(*a*) any part of the income of the person with care concerned is, or would be if the Secretary of State agreed to a variation, derived from any benefit; or (*b*) some or all of any child support maintenance might be taken into account in any manner in relation to any entitlement to benefit.

(5) In this section "benefit" has such meaning as may be prescribed[1].
[Child Support Act 1991, s 28E, as inserted by the Child Support Act 1995, s 5 and amended by the Child Support, Pensions and Social Security Act 2000, Sch 3.]

---

1. See the Child Support (Variations) Regulations 2000, SI 2001/156 amended by SI 2002/1204, SI 2003/328 and 347, SI 2004/2415 and SI 2005/785 and 2877 (CD Rom only).

6–2937   28F.   Agreement to a variation.   (1) The Secretary of State may agree to a variation if—

(*a*) he is satisfied that the case is one which falls within one or more of the cases set out in Part I of Schedule 4B or in regulations made under that Part; and

(*b*) it is his opinion that, in all the circumstances of the case, it would be just and equitable to agree to a variation.

(2) In considering whether it would be just and equitable in any case to agree to a variation, the Secretary of State—

(*a*) must have regard, in particular, to the welfare of any child likely to be affected if he did agree to a variation; and

(*b*) must, or as the case may be must not, take any prescribed factors into account, or must take them into account (or not) in prescribed circumstances.

(3) The Secretary of State shall not agree to a variation (and shall proceed to make his decision on the application for a maintenance calculation without any variation) if he is satisfied that—

(*a*) he has insufficient information to make a decision on the application for the maintenance calculation under section 11, and therefore that his decision would be made under section 12(1); or

(*b*) other prescribed circumstances apply.

(4) Where the Secretary of State agrees to a variation, he shall—

(*a*) determine the basis on which the amount of child support maintenance is to be calculated in response to the application for a maintenance calculation (including an application treated as having been made); and

(*b*) make a decision under section 11 on that basis.

(5) If the Secretary of State has made an interim maintenance decision, it is to be treated as having been replaced by his decision under section 11, and except in prescribed circumstances any appeal connected with it (under section 20) shall lapse.

(6) In determining whether or not to agree to a variation, the Secretary of State shall comply with regulations made under Part II of Schedule 4B.
[Child Support Act 1991, s 28F, as substituted by the Child Support, Pensions and Social Security Act 2000, s 5.]

---

1. See the Child Support (Variations) Regulations 2000, SI 2001/156 amended by SI 2002/1204, SI 2003/328 and 347, SI 2004/2415 and SI 2005/785 and 2877 (CD Rom only).

6–2938   28G.   Variations: revision and supersession.   (1) An application for a variation may also be made when a maintenance calculation is in force.

(2) The Secretary of State may by regulations[1] provide for—

(*a*) sections 16, 17 and 20; and

(*b*) sections 28A to 28F and Schedules 4A and 4B,

to apply with prescribed modifications in relation to such applications.

(3) The Secretary of State may by regulations[2] provide that, in prescribed[1] cases (or except in prescribed cases), a decision under section 17 made otherwise than pursuant to an application for a variation may be made on the basis of a variation agreed to for the purposes of an earlier decision without a new application for a variation having to be made.
[Child Support Act 1991, s 28G, as amended by the Child Support, Pensions and Social Security Act 2000, s 5.]

---

1. See the Child Support (Variations) (Modification of Statutory Provisions) Regulations 2000, SI 2000/3173 amended by SI 2002/1204.
2. See the Child Support (Variations) Regulations 2000, SI 2001/156 amended by SI 2002/1204, SI 2003/328 and 347, SI 2004/2415 and SI 2005/785 and 2877 (CD Rom only).

6–2939   28H.   Departure directions: decisions and appeals.   Schedule 4C shall have effect for applying sections 16, 17, 20 and 28ZA to 28ZC to decisions with respect to departure directions.*
[Child Support Act 1991, s 28H, as substituted by the Social Security Act 1998, Sch 7.]

---

*Repealed by the Child Support, Pensions and Social Security Act 2000, Sch 3, partly in force 3 March 2003, for remaining purposes from a date to be appointed.

6–2940 28I. Transitional provisions. (1)[1] In the case of an application for a departure direction relating to a maintenance calculation which was made before the coming into force of section 28A, the period within which the application must be made shall be such period as may be prescribed.

(2)[1] The Secretary of State may by regulations make provision for applications for departure directions to be dealt with according to an order determined in accordance with the regulations.

(3)[1] The regulations may, for example, provide for—

(a) applications relating to prescribed descriptions of maintenance calculation, or

(b) prescribed descriptions of application,

to be dealt with before applications relating to other prescribed descriptions of calculation or (as the case may be) other prescribed descriptions of application.

(4) The Secretary of State may by regulations make provision—

(a) enabling applications for departure directions made before the coming into force of section 28A to be considered even though that section is not in force;

(b) for the determination of any such application as if section 28A and the other provisions of this Act relating to departure directions were in force; and

(c) as to the effect of any departure direction given before the coming into force of section 28A.

(5) Regulations under section 28G(4) may not provide for a departure direction to have effect from a date earlier than that on which that section came into force.*

[Child Support Act 1991, s 28I, as inserted by the Child Support Act 1995, s 9 and amended by the Child Support, Pensions and Social Security Act 2000, Sch 3.]

---

*Repealed by the Child Support, Pensions and Social Security Act 2000, Sch 3, partly in force 3 March 2003, for remaining purposes from a date to be appointed.

1. At the date of going to press, s 28I(1)–(3) had not been brought into force; see SI 1995/3262 and SI 1996/2630.

6–2940J 28J. Voluntary payments. (1) This section applies where—

(a) a person has applied for a maintenance calculation under section 4(1) or 7(1), or is treated as having applied for one by virtue of section 6;

(b) the Secretary of State has neither made a decision under section 11 or 12 on the application, nor decided not to make a maintenance calculation; and

(c) the non-resident parent makes a voluntary payment.

(2) A "voluntary payment" is a payment—

(a) on account of child support maintenance which the non-resident parent expects to become liable to pay following the determination of the application (whether or not the amount of the payment is based on any estimate of his potential liability which the Secretary of State has agreed to give); and

(b) made before the maintenance calculation has been notified to the non-resident parent or (as the case may be) before the Secretary of State has notified the non-resident parent that he has decided not to make a maintenance calculation.

(3) In such circumstances and to such extent as may be prescribed—

(a) the voluntary payment may be set off against arrears of child support maintenance which accrued by virtue of the maintenance calculation taking effect on a date earlier than that on which it was notified to the non-resident parent;

(b) the amount payable under a maintenance calculation may be adjusted to take account of the voluntary payment.

(4) A voluntary payment shall be made to the Secretary of State unless he agrees, on such conditions as he may specify, that it may be made to the person with care, or to or through another person.

(5) The Secretary of State may by regulations make provision as to voluntary payments, and the regulations may in particular—

(a) prescribe what payments or descriptions of payment are, or are not, to count as "voluntary payments";

(b) prescribe the extent to which and circumstances in which a payment, or a payment of a prescribed description, counts.

[Child Support Act 1991, s 28J as inserted by the Child Support, Pensions and Social Security Act 2000, 20.]

Collection and enforcement

6–2941 29. Collection of child support maintenance. (1) The Secretary of State may arrange for the collection of any child support maintenance payable in accordance with a maintenance calculation where—

(a) the calculation is made by virtue of section 6; or

(b) an application has been made to the Secretary of State under section 4(2) or 7(3) for him to arrange for its collection.

(2) Where a maintenance calculation is made under this Act, payments of child support maintenance under the calculation shall be made in accordance with regulations[1] made by the Secretary of State.

(3) The regulations may, in particular, make provision—

(a) for payments of child support maintenance to be made—

    (i)   to the person caring for the child or children in question;

    (ii) to, or through, the Secretary of State; or

    (iii) to, or through, such other person as the Secretary of State may, from time to time, specify;

(b) as to the method by which payments of child support maintenance are to be made;

(c) as to the intervals at which such payments are to be made;

(d) as to the method and timing of the transmission of payments which are made, to or through the Secretary of State or any other person, in accordance with the regulations;

(e) empowering the Secretary of State to direct any person liable to make payments in accordance with the calculation—

    (i)   to make them by standing order or by any other method which requires one person to give his authority for payments to be made from an account of his to an account of another's on specific dates during the period for which the authority is in force and without the need for any further authority from him;

    (ii) to open an account from which payments under the calculation may be made in accordance with the method of payment which that person is obliged to adopt;

(f) providing for the making of representations with respect to matters with which the regulations are concerned.

[Child Support Act 1991, s 29 as amended by the Child Support, Pensions and Social Security Act 2000, Sch 3.]

---

1. See the Child Support (Collection and Enforcement) Regulations 1992, SI 1992/1989 in this PART, STATUTORY INSTRUMENTS ON FAMILY LAW, post.

6–2942 30. Collection and enforcement of other forms of maintenance. (1) Where the Secretary of State is arranging for the collection of any payments under section 29 or subsection (2), he may also arrange for the collection of any periodical payments, or secured periodical payments, of a prescribed[1] kind which are payable to or for the benefit of any person who falls within a prescribed[1] category.

(2) The Secretary of State may, except in prescribed cases, arrange for the collection of any periodical payments, or secured periodical payments, of a prescribed[1] kind which are payable for the benefit of a child even though he is not arranging for the collection of child support maintenance with respect to that child.

(3) Where—

(a) the Secretary of State is arranging, under this Act, for the collection of different payments ("the payments") from the same non-resident parent;

(b) an amount is collected by the Secretary of State from the non-resident parent which is less than the total amount due in respect of the payments; and

(c) the non-resident parent has not stipulated how that amount is to be allocated by the Secretary of State as between the payments,

the Secretary of State may allocate that amount as he sees fit.

(4) In relation to England and Wales, the Secretary of State may by regulations[2] make provision for sections 29 and 31 to 40 to apply, with such modifications (if any) as he considers necessary or expedient, for the purpose of enabling him to enforce any obligation to pay any amount which he is authorised to collect under this section.

(5) In relation to Scotland, the Secretary of State may by regulations make provision for the purpose of enabling him to enforce any obligation to pay any amount which he is authorised to collect under this section—

(a) empowering him to bring any proceedings or take any other steps (other than diligence against earnings) which could have been brought or taken by or on behalf of the person to whom the periodical payments are payable;

(b) applying sections 29, 31 and 32 with such modifications (if any) as he considers necessary or expedient.*

[Child Support Act 1991, s 30 as amended by the Child Support, Pensions and Social Security Act 2000, Sch 3.]

---

*Section 30 is amended by the insertion of a new sub-s (5A) by the Child Support Act 1995, Sch 3, this PART, POST, WHEN IN FORCE.

1. See reg 2 of the Child Support (Collection and Enforcement of Other Forms of Maintenance) Regulations 1992, SI 1992/2643 in this PART, STATUTORY INSTRUMENTS ON FAMILY LAW, post.

2. See reg 3 of the Child Support (Collection and Enforcement of Other Forms of Maintenance) Regulations 1992, SI 1992/2643 in this PART, STATUTORY INSTRUMENTS ON FAMILY LAW, post.

6–2943　31. Deduction from earnings orders.　(1) This section applies where any person ("the liable person") is liable to make payments of child support maintenance.

(2) The Secretary of State may make an order ("a deduction from earnings order") against a liable person to secure the payment of any amount due under the maintenance calculation in question.

(3) A deduction from earnings order may be made so as to secure the payment of—

(a) arrears[1] of child support maintenance payable under the calculation;

(b) amounts of child support maintenance which will become due under the calculation; or

(c) both such arrears and such future amounts.

(4) A deduction from earnings order—

(a) shall be expressed to be directed at a person ("the employer") who has the liable person in his employment; and

(b) shall have effect from such date as may be specified in the order.

(5) A deduction from earnings order shall operate as an instruction to the employer to—

(a) make deductions from the liable person's earnings; and

(b) pay the amounts deducted to the Secretary of State.

(6) The Secretary of State shall serve a copy of any deduction from earnings order which he makes under this section on—

(a) the person who appears to the Secretary of State to have the liable person in question in his employment; and

(b) the liable person.

(7) Where—

(a) a deduction from earnings order has been made; and

(b) a copy of the order has been served on the liable person's employer,

it shall be the duty of that employer to comply with the order; but he shall not be under any liability for non-compliance before the end of the period of 7 days beginning with the date on which the copy was served on him.

(8) In this section and in section 32 "earnings" has such meaning as may be prescribed[2].

[Child Support Act 1991, s 31 as amended by the Child Support, Pensions and Social Security Act 2000, Sch 3.]

---

1. Voluntary overpayments made in the past are not to be set off against arrears in payments required to be made in determining whether the payer is in arrears for the purpose of making a deduction from earnings order (*R v Secretary of State for Social Security, ex p Newmarch Singh* [2000] 2 FLR 664, QBD).

2. See the Child Support (Collection and Enforcement) Regulations 1992, SI 1992/1989 in this PART, STATUTORY INSTRUMENTS ON FAMILY LAW, post.

6–2944　32. Regulations about deduction from earnings orders.　(1) The Secretary of State may by regulations[1] make provision with respect to deduction from earnings orders.

(2) The regulations may, in particular, make provision—

(a) as to the circumstances in which one person is to be treated as employed by another;

(b) requiring any deduction from earnings under an order to be made in the prescribed manner;

(bb) for the amount or amounts which are to be deducted from the liable person's earnings not to exceed a prescribed proportion of his earnings (as determined by the employer);

(c) requiring an order to specify the amount or amounts to which the order relates and the amount or amounts which are to be deducted from the liable person's earnings in order to meet his liabilities under the maintenance calculation in question;

(d) requiring the intervals between deductions to be made under an order to be specified in the order;

(e) as to the payment of sums deducted under an order to the Secretary of State;

(f) allowing the person who deducts and pays any amount under an order to deduct from the liable person's earnings a prescribed sum towards his administrative costs;

(g) with respect to the notification to be given to the liable person of amounts deducted, and amounts paid, under the order;

(h) requiring any person on whom a copy of an order is served to notify the Secretary of State in the prescribed manner and within a prescribed period if he does not have the liable person in his employment or if the liable person ceases to be in his employment;

(i) as to the operation of an order where the liable person is in the employment of the Crown;

(j) for the variation of orders;

(k) similar to that made by section 31(7), in relation to any variation of an order;

(l) for an order to lapse when the employer concerned ceases to have the liable person in his employment;

(m) as to the revival of an order in such circumstances as may be prescribed;

(n) allowing or requiring an order to be discharged;

(o) as to the giving of notice by the Secretary of State to the employer concerned that an order has lapsed or has ceased to have effect.

(3) The regulations may include provision that while a deduction from earnings order is in force—

(a) the liable person shall from time to time notify the Secretary of State, in the prescribed manner and within a prescribed period, of each occasion on which he leaves any employment or becomes employed, or re-employed, and shall include in such a notification a statement of his earnings and expected earnings from the employment concerned and of such other matters as may be prescribed;

(b) any person who becomes the liable person's employer and knows that the order is in force shall notify the Secretary of State, in the prescribed manner and within a prescribed period, that he is the liable person's employer, and shall include in such a notification a statement of the liable person's earnings and expected earnings from the employment concerned and of such other matters as may be prescribed.

(4) The regulations may include provision with respect to the priority as between a deduction from earnings order and—

(a) any other deduction from earnings order;

(b) any order under any other enactment relating to England and Wales which provides for deductions from the liable person's earnings;

(c) any diligence against earnings.

(5) The regulations may include a provision that a liable person may appeal[2] to a magistrates' court (or in Scotland to the sheriff) if he is aggrieved by the making of a deduction from earnings order against him, or by the terms of any such order, or there is a dispute as to whether payments constitute earnings or as to any other prescribed matter relating to the order.

(6) On an appeal under subsection (5) the court or (as the case may be) the sheriff shall not question the maintenance calculation by reference to which the deduction from earnings order was made.

(7) Regulations made by virtue of subsection (5) may include provision as to the powers of a magistrates' court, or in Scotland of the sheriff, in relation to an appeal (which may include provision as to the quashing of a deduction from earnings order or the variation of the terms of such an order).

(8) If any person fails to comply with the requirements of a deduction from earnings order, or with any regulation under this section which is designated for the purposes of this subsection, he shall be guilty of an offence.

(9) In subsection (8) "designated" means designated by the regulations.

(10) It shall be a defence for a person charged with an offence under subsection (8) to prove that he took all reasonable steps to comply with the requirements in question.

(11) Any person guilty of an offence under subsection (8) shall be liable on summary conviction to a fine not exceeding level two on the standard scale.

[Child Support Act 1991, s 32 as amended by the Child Support, Pensions and Social Security Act 2000, Sch 3.]

---

1. See the Child Support (Collection and Enforcement) Regulations 1992, SI 1992/1989 in this PART, STATUTORY INSTRUMENTS ON FAMILY LAW, *post*.

2. Regulation 22(3) of the Child Support (Collection and Enforcement) Regulations provides

"An appeal may be made only on one or both of the following grounds—

(a) that the deduction from earnings order is defective;

(b) that the payments in question do not constitute earnings."

All matters relating to the quantification or validity of a maintenance assessment are to be dealt with through the review and appeal structure created by the Act. With regard to enforcement, the magistrates' court is given a limited jurisdiction. The right of appeal given by reg 22 to the person liable to pay under an assessment is restricted to two technical grounds. Section 32(6) precludes any challenge to the quantification or validity of the maintenance assessment. The word "defective" in reg 22(3)(a) means a defect in form, namely a failure to comply with the requirements of regs 9, 10 and 11 (form of deduction from earnings order and the matters to be included in it; what rate of deduction and what protected earnings rate should be inserted in the order). The sole question for magistrates is whether or not payments have become payable by the liable person and have not been paid. If that is established, the magistrates are bound to make a liability order (*R v Secretary of State for Social Security, ex p Biggin* [1995] 2 FCR 595, [1995] 1 FLR 851 and *Secretary of State for Social Security v Shotton* [1996] 3 FCR 346, [1996] 2 FLR 241). Even where it is conceded that the attachment of earnings order is defective, justices have no power to require the Secretary of State to repay the sums paid under the order (*Department of Social Services v Taylor* (1996) Times, 8 February, DC).

6–2945   33. Liability orders[1]. (1) This section applies where—

(a) a person who is liable to make payments of child support maintenance ("the liable person") fails to make one or more of those payments; and

(b) it appears to the Secretary of State that—

(i) it is inappropriate to make a deduction from earnings order against him (because, for example, he is not employed); or

(ii) although such an order has been made against him, it has proved ineffective as a means of securing that payments are made in accordance with the maintenance calculation in question.

(2) The Secretary of State may apply to a magistrates' court or, in Scotland, to the sheriff for an order ("a liability order") against the liable person[2].

(3) Where the Secretary of State applies for a liability order, the magistrates' court or (as the case

may be) sheriff shall make the order if satisfied that the payments in question have become payable by the liable person and have not been paid.

(4) On an application under subsection (2), the court or (as the case may be) the sheriff shall not question[3] the maintenance calculation under which the payments of child support maintenance fell to be made.

(5) If the Secretary of State designates a liability order for the purposes of this subsection it shall be treated as a judgment entered in a county court for the purposes of section 73 of the County Courts Act 1984 (register of judgments and orders).

[Child Support Act 1991, s 33 as amended by the Child Support Act 1995, Sch 3 and the Child Support, Pensions and Social Security Act 2000, Sch 3.]

---

1. A liability order is merely a "gateway" to further enforcement action at the discretion of the Child Support Agency, and it does not engage art 8 of the Convention at all as it does not in any way impinge on the parent's private life (*R (on the application of Denson) v Child Support Agency* [2002] EWHC 154 (Admin), [2002] 1 FCR 460, [2002] 1 FLR 938).

2. The Child Support Act 1991 and the accompanying regulations provide a comprehensive code for the collection of payments due under maintenance assessments and the enforcement of liability orders. These provisions indicate that Parliament intended that all questions concerning the enforcement of maintenance assessments should be determined exclusively by the Secretary of State, a magistrates' court or a county court. The civil jurisdiction of the High Court is necessarily excluded and, accordingly, there is no power for the High Court to grant a *Mareva* injunction preventing disposal of assets before a liability order is obtained in the magistrates' court. However, once a liability order has been obtained, the county court will have jurisdiction to grant any *Mareva* injunction which the circumstances require (*Department of Social Security v Butler* [1996] 1 FCR 63, [1996] 1 FLR 65).

3. Although they may not question the amount of any arrears, justices have jurisdiction to determine whether a non-resident parent was a liable person in the first place and are required to receive evidence, where it is appropriate, that the parent with care was claiming a benefit unless there is a concession making this unnecessary (*Farley v Secretary of State for Work and Pensions* [2005] EWCA Civ 778, [2005] 3 FLR 327, [2005] 2 FLR 1059, and *Farley v Child Support Agency and Secretary of State for Work and Pensions* [2005] EWCA Civ 869, [2005] 3 FCR 343, [2005] 2 FLR 1075 setting aside the judgment in the above case but granting judicial review and a declaration to the same effect))..

6–2946 34. Regulations about liability orders. (1) The Secretary of State may make regulations[1] in relation to England and Wales—

(*a*) prescribing the procedure to be followed in dealing with an application by the Secretary of State for a liability order;

(*b*) prescribing the form and contents of a liability order; and

(*c*) providing that where a magistrates' court has made a liability order, the person against whom it is made shall, during such time as the amount in respect of which the order was made remains wholly or partly unpaid, be under a duty to supply relevant information to the Secretary of State.

(2) In subsection (1) "relevant information" means any information of a prescribed description which is in the possession of the liable person and which the Secretary of State has asked him to supply.

[Child Support Act 1991, s 34.]

---

1. See the Child Support (Collection and Enforcement) Regulations 1992, SI 1992/1989 in this PART, STATUTORY INSTRUMENTS ON FAMILY LAW, post.

6–2947 35. Enforcement of liability orders by distress. (1) Where a liability order has been made against a person ("the liable person"), the Secretary of State may levy the appropriate amount by distress and sale of the liable person's goods.

(2) In subsection (1), "the appropriate amount" means the aggregate of—

(*a*) the amount in respect of which the order was made, to the extent that it remains unpaid; and

(*b*) an amount, determined in such manner as may be prescribed[1], in respect of the charges connected with the distress.

(3) The Secretary of State may, in exercising his powers under subsection (1) against the liable person's goods, seize—

(*a*) any of the liable person's goods except—

(i) such tools, books, vehicles and other items of equipment as are necessary to him for use personally by him in his employment, business or vocation;

(ii) such clothing, bedding, furniture, household equipment and provisions as are necessary for satisfying his basic domestic needs; and

(*b*) any money, banknotes, bills of exchange, promissory notes, bonds, specialties or securities for money belonging to the liable person.

(4) For the purposes of subsection (3), the liable person's domestic needs shall be taken to include those of any member of his family with whom he resides.

(5) No person levying a distress under this section shall be taken to be a trespasser—

(*a*) on that account; or

(*b*) from the beginning, on account of any subsequent irregularity in levying the distress.

(6) A person sustaining special damage by reason of any irregularity in levying a distress under this section may recover full satisfaction for the damage (and no more) by proceedings in trespass or otherwise.

(7) The Secretary of State may make regulations supplementing the provisions of this section.

(8) The regulations may, in particular—

(a) provide that a distress under this section may be levied anywhere in England and Wales;

(b) provide that such a distress shall not be deemed unlawful on account of any defect or want of form in the liability order;

(c) provide for an appeal to a magistrates' court by any person aggrieved by the levying of, or an attempt to levy, a distress under this section;

(d) make provision as to the powers of the court on an appeal (which may include provision as to the discharge of goods distrained or the payment of compensation in respect of goods distrained and sold).

[Child Support Act 1991, s 35.]

---

1. See the Child Support (Collection and Enforcement) Regulations 1992, SI 1992/1989 in this PART, STATUTORY INSTRUMENTS ON FAMILY LAW, post.

6–2948 36. Enforcement in county courts. (1) Where a liability order has been made against a person, the amount in respect of which the order was made, to the extent that it remains unpaid, shall, if a county court so orders, be recoverable by means of garnishee proceedings or a charging order, as if it were payable under a county court order.

(2) In subsection (1) "charging order" has the same meaning as in section 1 of the Charging Orders Act 1979.

[Child Support Act 1991, s 36.]

6–2949 37. *Regulations about liability orders: Scotland.*

6–2950 38. *Enforcement of liability orders by diligence: Scotland.*

6–2951 39. Liability orders: enforcement throughout United Kingdom. (1) The Secretary of State may by regulations[1] provide for—

(a) any liability order made by a court in England and Wales; or

(b) any corresponding order made by a court in Northern Ireland, to be enforced in Scotland as if it had been made by the sheriff.

(2) The power conferred on the Court of Session by section 32 of the Sheriff Courts (Scotland) Act 1971 (power of Court of Session to regulate civil procedure in the sheriff court) shall extend to making provision for the registration in the sheriff court for enforcement of any such order as is referred to in subsection (1).

(3) The Secretary of State may by regulations make provision for, or in connection with, the enforcement in England and Wales of—

(a) any liability order made by the sheriff in Scotland; or

(b) any corresponding order made by a court in Northern Ireland,

as if it had been made by a magistrates' court in England and Wales.

(4) Regulations under subsection (3) may, in particular, make provision for the registration of any such order as is referred to in that subsection in connection with its enforcement in England and Wales.

[Child Support Act 1991, s 39.]

---

1. See the Child Support (Collection and Enforcement) Regulations 1992, SI 1992/1989 in this PART, STATUTORY INSTRUMENTS ON FAMILY LAW, post.

6–2951A 39A. Commitment to prison and disqualification from driving. (1) Where the Secretary of State has sought—

(a) in England and Wales to levy an amount by distress under this Act; or

(b) to recover an amount by virtue of section 36 or 38,

and that amount, or any portion of it, remains unpaid he may apply to the court under this section.

(2) An application under this section is for whichever the court considers appropriate in all the circumstances of—

(a) the issue of a warrant committing the liable person to prison; or

(b) an order for him to be disqualified from holding or obtaining a driving licence.

(3) On any such application the court shall (in the presence of the liable person) inquire as to—

(a) whether he needs a driving licence to earn his living;

(b) his means; and

(c)   whether there has been wilful refusal or culpable neglect on his part.

(4)   The Secretary of State may make representations to the court as to whether he thinks it more appropriate to commit the liable person to prison or to disqualify him from holding or obtaining a driving licence; and the liable person may reply to those representations.

(5)   In this section and section 40B, "driving licence" means a licence to drive a motor vehicle granted under Part III of the Road Traffic Act 1988.

(6)   In this section "the court" means—

(a)   in England and Wales, a magistrates' court;

(b)   in Scotland, the sheriff.

[Child Support Act 1991, s 39A, as inserted by the Child Support, Pensions and Social Security Act 2000, s 16(1).]

6–2952   40. Commitment to prison.   (1) *Repealed.*

(2)   *Repealed.*

(3)   If, but only if, the court is of the opinion that there has been wilful refusal or culpable neglect on the part of the liable person it may—

(a)   issue a warrant of commitment against him; or

(b)   fix a term of imprisonment and postpone the issue of the warrant until such time and on such conditions (if any) as it thinks just.

(4)   Any such warrant—   (scan in (c))

(a)   shall be made in respect of an amount equal to the aggregate of—

(i)   the amount mentioned in section 35(1) or so much of it as remains outstanding; and

(ii)   an amount (determined in accordance with regulations[1] made by the Secretary of State) in respect of the costs of commitment; and

(b)   shall state that amount.

(5)   No warrant may be issued under this section against a person who is under the age of 18.

(6)   A warrant issued under this section shall order the liable person—

(a)   to be imprisoned for a specified period; but

(b)   to be released (unless he is in custody for some other reason) on payment of the amount stated in the warrant.

(7)   The maximum period of imprisonment which may be imposed by virtue of subsection (6) shall be calculated in accordance with Schedule 4 to the Magistrates' Courts Act 1980 (maximum periods of imprisonment in default of payment) but shall not exceed six weeks.

(8)   The Secretary of State may by regulations make provision for the period of imprisonment specified in any warrant issued under this section to be reduced where there is part payment of the amount in respect of which the warrant was issued.

(9)   A warrant issued under this section may be directed to such person or persons as the court issuing it thinks fit.

(10)   Section 80 of the Magistrates' Courts Act 1980 (application of money found on defaulter) shall apply in relation to a warrant issued under this section against a liable person as it applies in relation to the enforcement of a sum mentioned in subsection (1) of that section.

(11)   The Secretary of State may by regulations make provision—

(a)   as to the form of any warrant issued under this section;

(b)   allowing an application under this section to be renewed where no warrant is issued or term of imprisonment is fixed;

(c)   that a statement in writing to the effect that wages of any amount have been paid to the liable person during any period, purporting to be signed by or on behalf of his employer, shall be evidence of the facts stated;

(d)   that, for the purposes of enabling an inquiry to be made as to the liable person's conduct and means, a justice of the peace may issue a summons to him to appear before a magistrates' court and (if he does not obey) may issue a warrant for his arrest;

(e)   that for the purpose of enabling such an inquiry, a justice of the peace may issue a warrant for the liable person's arrest without issuing a summons;

(f)   as to the execution of a warrant for arrest.

(12)   This section does not apply to Scotland.

[Child Support Act 1991, s 40, amended by the Child Support, Pensions and Social Security Act 2000, Schs 3 and 9.]

---

1.   See the Child Support (Collection and Enforcement) Regulations 1992, SI 1992/1989 in this PART, STATUTORY INSTRUMENTS ON FAMILY LAW, post.

6–2952A   40A.   *Commitment to prison: Scotland*

6–2952B 40B. Disqualification from driving: further provision. (1) If, but only if, the court is of the opinion that there has been wilful refusal or culpable neglect on the part of the liable person, it may—

(a) order him to be disqualified, for such period specified in the order but not exceeding two years as it thinks fit, from holding or obtaining a driving licence (a "disqualification order"); or

(b) make a disqualification order but suspend its operation until such time and on such conditions (if any) as it thinks just.

(2) The court may not take action under both section 40 and this section.

(3) A disqualification order must state the amount in respect of which it is made, which is to be the aggregate of—

(a) the amount mentioned in section 35(1), or so much of it as remains outstanding; and

(b) an amount (determined in accordance with regulations made by the Secretary of State) in respect of the costs of the application under section 39A.

(4) A court which makes a disqualification order shall require the person to whom it relates to produce any driving licence held by him, and its counterpart (within the meaning of section 108(1) of the Road Traffic Act 1988).

(5) On an application by the Secretary of State or the liable person, the court—

(a) may make an order substituting a shorter period of disqualification, or make an order revoking the disqualification order, if part of the amount referred to in subsection (3) (the "amount due") is paid to any person authorised to receive it; and

(b) must make an order revoking the disqualification order if all of the amount due is so paid.

(6) The Secretary of State may make representations to the court as to the amount which should be paid before it would be appropriate to make an order revoking the disqualification order under subsection (5)(a), and the person liable may reply to those representations.

(7) The Secretary of State may make a further application under section 39A if the amount due has not been paid in full when the period of disqualification specified in the disqualification order expires.

(8) Where a court—

(a) makes a disqualification order;

(b) makes an order under subsection (5); or

(c) allows an appeal against a disqualification order,

it shall send notice of that fact to the Secretary of State; and the notice shall contain such particulars and be sent in such manner and to such address as the Secretary of State may determine.

(9) Where a court makes a disqualification order, it shall also send the driving licence and its counterpart, on their being produced to the court, to the Secretary of State at such address as he may determine.

(10) Section 80 of the Magistrates' Courts Act 1980 (application of money found on defaulter) shall apply in relation to a disqualification order under this section in relation to a liable person as it applies in relation to the enforcement of a sum mentioned in subsection (1) of that section.

(11) The Secretary of State may by regulations make provision in relation to disqualification orders corresponding to the provision he may make under section 40(11).

(12) In the application to Scotland of this section—

(a) in subsection (2) for "section 40" substitute "section 40A";

(b) in subsection (3) for paragraph (a) substitute—
"(a) the appropriate amount under section 38;";

(c) subsection (10) is omitted; and

(d) for subsection (11) substitute—
"(11)The power of the Court of Session by Act of Sederunt to regulate the procedure and practice in civil proceedings in the sheriff court shall include power to make, in relation to disqualification orders, provision corresponding to that which may be made by virtue of section 40A(8).".]

[Child Support Act 1991, s 40B, as inserted by the Child Support, Pensions and Social Security Act 2000, s 16(3).]

6–2953 41. Arrears of child support maintenance. (1) This section applies where—

(a) the Secretary of State is authorised under section 4, 6 or 7 to recover child support maintenance payable by an non-resident parent in accordance with a maintenance calculation; and

(b) the non-resident parent has failed to make one or more payments of child support maintenance due from him in accordance with that calculation.

(2) Where the Secretary of State recovers any such arrears he may, in such circumstances as may be prescribed[1] and to such extent as may be prescribed[1], retain them if he is satisfied that the amount of any benefit paid to or in respect of the person with care of the child or children in question would

have been less had the non-resident parent made the payment or payments of child support maintenance in question.

(2A) In determining for the purposes of subsection (2) whether the amount of any benefit paid would have been less at any time than the amount which was paid at that time, in a case where the maintenance calculation had effect from a date earlier than that on which it was made, the calculation shall be taken to have been in force at that time.

(3)–(5) *Repealed.*

(6) Any sums retained by the Secretary of State by virtue of this section shall be paid by him into the Consolidated Fund.

[Child Support Act 1991, s 41 as amended by the Child Support Act 1995, Sch 3 and the Child Support, Pensions and Social Security Act 2000, Schs 3 and 9.]

---

1. See the Child Support (Arrears, Interest and Adjustment of Maintenance Assessments) Regulations 1992, SI 1992/1816 amended by SI 1998/1129, SI 2000/3185 and SI 2001/162 and 3649.

Special cases

6–2954 42. Special cases. (1) The Secretary of State may by regulations[1] provide that in prescribed circumstances a case is to be treated as a special case for the purposes of this Act.

(2) Those regulations may, for example, provide for the following to be special cases—

(a) each parent of a child is an non-resident parent in relation to the child;

(b) there is more than one person who is a person with care in relation to the same child;

(c) there is more than one qualifying child in relation to the same non-resident parent but the person who is the person with care in relation to one of those children is not the person who is the person with care in relation to all of them;

(d) a person is an non-resident parent in relation to more than one child and the other parent of each of those children is not the same person;

(e) the person with care has care of more than one qualifying child and there is more than one non-resident parent in relation to those children;

(f) a qualifying child has his home in two or more separate households.

(3) The Secretary of State may by regulations make provision with respect to special cases.

(4) Regulations made under subsection (3) may, in particular—

(a) modify any provision made by or under this Act, in its application to any special case or any special case falling within a prescribed category;

(b) make new provision for any such case; or

(c) provide for any prescribed provision made by or under this Act not to apply to any such case.

[Child Support Act 1991, s 42 as amended by the Child Support, Pensions and Social Security Act 2000, Sch 3.]

---

1. See the Child Support (Maintenance Calculation and Special Cases) Regulations 2000, SI 2001/155 amended by SI 2002/1204 and 2497, SI 2003/328, 347 and 2779, SI 2004/2415 and 3168 (E) and SI 2005/785, 2078, 2877 and 2929 (W) (CD Rom only).

6–2955 43. Recovery of child support maintenance by deduction from benefit. (1) This section applies where—

(a) a non-resident parent is liable to pay a flat rate of child support maintenance (or would be so liable but for a variation having been agreed to), and that rate applies (or would have applied) because he falls within paragraph 4(1)(b) or (c) or 4(2) of Schedule 1; and

(b) such conditions as may be prescribed for the purposes of this section are satisfied.

(2) The power of the Secretary of State to make regulations under section 5 of the Social Security Administration Act 1992 by virtue of subsection (1)(p) (deductions from benefits) may be exercised in relation to cases to which this section applies with a view to securing that payments in respect of child support maintenance are made or that arrears of child support maintenance are recovered.

(3) For the purposes of this section, the benefits to which section 5 of the 1992 Act applies are to be taken as including war disablement pensions and war widows' pensions (within the meaning of section 150 of the Social Security Contributions and Benefits Act 1992 (interpretation)).

[Child Support Act 1991, s 43 as substituted by the Child Support, Pensions and Social Security Act 2000, s 21.]

---

1. See the Child Support (Maintenance Calculation and Special Cases) Regulations 2000, SI 2001/155 amended by SI 2002/1204 and 2497, SI 2003/328, 347 and 2779, SI 2004/2415 and 3168 (E) and SI 2005/785, 2078, 2877 and 2929 (W) (CD Rom only).

2. The Social Security (Claims and Payments) Regulations 1987, SI 1987/1968 as amended by SI 1993/478 provide that where a person in receipt of income support, either alone or in conjunction with certain other benefits, has a liability to make payments in place of child support maintenance under s 43(1), a deduction may be made from those benefits towards satisfying that liability, subject to certain restrictions.

Jurisdiction

6–2956 44. Jurisdiction. (1) The Secretary of State shall have jurisdiction to make a maintenance calculation with respect to a person who is—

  (*a*) a person with care;
  (*b*) an non-resident parent; or
  (*c*) a qualifying child,

only if that person is habitually resident in the United Kingdom, except in the case of a non-resident parent who falls within subsection (2A).

(2) Where the person with care is not an individual, subsection (1) shall have effect as if paragraph (*a*) were omitted.

(2A) A non-resident parent falls within this subsection if he is not habitually resident in the United Kingdom, but is—

  (*a*) employed in the civil service of the Crown, including Her Majesty's Diplomatic Service and Her Majesty's Overseas Civil Service;
  (*b*) a member of the naval, military or air forces of the Crown, including any person employed by an association established for the purposes of Part XI of the Reserve Forces Act 1996;
  (*c*) employed by a company of a prescribed description registered under the Companies Act 1985 in England and Wales or in Scotland, or under the Companies (Northern Ireland) Order 1986; or
  (*d*) employed by a body of a prescribed description.

(3) *Repealed.*
[Child Support Act 1991, s 44, as amended by the Social Security Act 1998, Sch 7 and the Child Support, Pensions and Social Security Act 2000, Schs 3 and 9.]

---

1. See reg 7 of the Child Support (Maintenance Arrangements and Jurisdiction) Regulations 1992, SI 1992/2645 in this PART, STATUTORY INSTRUMENTS ON FAMILY LAW, post.

6–2957 45. Jurisdiction of courts in certain proceedings under this Act. (1) The Lord Chancellor or, in relation to Scotland, the Secretary of State may by order[1] make such provision as he considers necessary to secure that appeals, or such class of appeals as may be specified in the order—

  (*a*) shall be made to a court instead of being made to an appeal tribunal; or
  (*b*) shall be so made in such circumstances as may be so specified.

(2) In subsection (1), "court" means—

  (*a*) in relation to England and Wales and subject to any provision made under Schedule 11 to the Children Act 1989 (jurisdiction of courts with respect to certain proceedings relating to children) the High Court, a county court or a magistrates' court; and
  (*b*) in relation to Scotland, the Court of Session or the sheriff.

(3) Schedule 11 to the Act of 1989 shall be amended in accordance with subsections (4) and (5).
(4)–(5) *Amendment of the Children Act 1989.*
(6) Where the effect of any order under subsection (1) is that there are no longer any appeals which fall to be dealt with by appeal tribunals, the Lord Chancellor after consultation with the Secretary of State may by order provide for the abolition of those tribunals.
(7) Any order under subsection (1) or (6) may make—

  (*a*) such modifications of any provision of this Act or of any other enactment; and
  (*b*) such transitional provision,

as the Minister making the order considers appropriate in consequence of any provision made by the order.*
[Child Support Act 1991, s 45, as amended by the Social Security Act 1998, Sch 7.]

---

*Subsections (58A) and (9) inserted by the Constitutional Reform Act 2005, Sch 4 from a date to be appointed.
1. The Child Support Appeals (Jurisdiction of Courts) Order 1993, SI 1993/961 has been made. Articles 3 and 4 provide as follows:
  "Parentage appeals to be made to courts
    3. An appeal under s 20 of the Act shall be made to a court instead of to a child support appeal tribunal in the circumstances mentioned in art 4.
    4. The circumstances are that—
  (*a*) the decision against which the appeal is brought was made on the basis that a particular person (whether the applicant or some other person) either was, or was not, a parent of a child in question, and
  (*b*) the ground of the appeal will be that the decision should not have been made on that basis".

Miscellaneous and supplemental

6–2958 46. Reduced benefit decisions . (1) This section applies where any person ("the parent")—

  (*a*) has made a request under section 6(5);
  (*b*) fails to comply with any regulation made under section 6(7); or
  (*c*) having been treated as having applied for a maintenance calculation under section 6, refuses to take a scientific test (within the meaning of section 27A).

(2) The Secretary of State may serve written notice on the parent requiring her, before the end of a specified period—

(a) in a subsection (1)(a) case, to give him her reasons for making the request;

(b) in a subsection (1)(b) case, to give him her reasons for failing to do so; or

(c) in a subsection (1)(c) case, to give him her reasons for her refusal.

(3) When the specified period has expired, the Secretary of State shall consider whether, having regard to any reasons given by the parent, there are reasonable grounds for believing that—

(a) in a subsection (1)(a) case, if the Secretary of State were to do what is mentioned in section 6(3);

(b) in a subsection (1)(b) case, if she were to be required to comply; or

(c) in a subsection (1)(c) case, if she took the scientific test,

there would be a risk of her, or of any children living with her, suffering harm or undue distress as a result of his taking such action, or her complying or taking the test.

(4) If the Secretary of State considers that there are such reasonable grounds, he shall—

(a) take no further action under this section in relation to the request, the failure or the refusal in question; and

(b) notify the parent, in writing, accordingly.

(5) If the Secretary of State considers that there are no such reasonable grounds, he may, except in prescribed circumstances, make a reduced benefit decision with respect to the parent.

(6) In a subsection (1)(a) case, the Secretary of State may from time to time serve written notice on the parent requiring her, before the end of a specified period—

(a) to state whether her request under section 6(5) still stands; and

(b) if so, to give him her reasons for maintaining her request,

and subsections (3) to (5) have effect in relation to such a notice and any response to it as they have effect in relation to a notice under subsection (2)(a) and any response to it.

(7) Where the Secretary of State makes a reduced benefit decision he must send a copy of it to the parent.

(8) A reduced benefit decision is to take effect on such date as may be specified in the decision.

(9) Reasons given in response to a notice under subsection (2) or (6) need not be given in writing unless the Secretary of State directs in any case that they must.

(10) In this section—

(a) "comply" means to comply with the requirement or with the regulation in question; and "complied" and "complying" are to be construed accordingly;

(b) "reduced benefit decision" means a decision that the amount payable by way of any relevant benefit to, or in respect of, the parent concerned be reduced by such amount, and for such period, as may be prescribed;

(c) "relevant benefit" means income support or an income-based jobseeker's allowance or any other benefit of a kind prescribed for the purposes of section 6; and

(d) "specified", in relation to a notice served under this section, means specified in the notice; and the period to be specified is to be determined in accordance with regulations made by the Secretary of State.

[Child Support Act 1991, s 46 as as substituted by the Child Support, Pensions and Social Security Act 2000, Sch 3.]

---

1. See Part IV of the Child Support (Maintenance Calculation Procedure) Regulations 2000, SI 2001/155 amended by SI 2002/1204 and 2497, SI 2003/328, 347 and 2779, SI 2004/2415 and 3168 (E) and SI 2005/785, 2078, 2877 and 2929 (W) (CD Rom only).

6–2959 46A–46B. *Regulations about finality of decisions and appeals generally*

6–2960 47. Fees. The Secretary of State may by regulations provide for the payment, by the non-resident parent or the person with care (or by both), of such fees as may be prescribed in cases where the Secretary of State takes any action under section 4 or 6.

[Child Support Act 1991, s 47 amended by the Child Support Act 1995, Sch 3, the Jobseekers Act 1995, Sch 2, the Tax Credits Act 2002, Sch 3 and the Child Support, Pensions and Social Security Act 2000, Sch 3—summarised.]

6–2961 48. Right of audience. (1) Any officer of the Secretary of State who is authorised by the Secretary of State for the purposes of this section shall have, in relation to any proceedings under this Act before a magistrates' court, a right of audience and the right to conduct litigation.

(2) In this section "right of audience" and "right to conduct litigation" have the same meaning as in section 119 of the Courts and Legal Services Act 1990.

[Child Support Act 1991, s 48 as amended by the Child Support Act 1995, Sch 3.]

6–2962 49. *Right of audience: Scotland.*

6–2963 50. Unauthorised disclosure of information. (1) Any person who is, or has been, employed in employment to which this section applies is guilty of an offence if, without lawful authority, he discloses any information which—

(*a*) was acquired by him in the course of that employment; and

(*b*) relates to a particular person.

(2) It is not an offence under this section—

(*a*) to disclose information in the form of a summary or collection of information so framed as not to enable information relating to any particular person to be ascertained from it; or

(*b*) to disclose information which has previously been disclosed to the public with lawful authority.

(3) It is a defence for a person charged with an offence under this section to prove that at the time of the alleged offence—

(*a*) he believed that he was making the disclosure in question with lawful authority and had no reasonable cause to believe otherwise; or

(*b*) he believed that the information in question had previously been disclosed to the public with lawful authority and had no reasonable cause to believe otherwise.

(4) A person guilty of an offence under this section shall be liable[1]—

(*a*) on conviction on indictment, to imprisonment for a term not exceeding **two years** or a **fine** or both; or

(*b*) on summary conviction, to imprisonment for a term not exceeding **six months** or a fine not exceeding **the statutory maximum** or both.

(5) This section applies to employment as—

(*a*) the Chief Child Support Officer;

(*b*) any other child support officer;

(*c*) any clerk to, or other officer of, an appeal tribunal or a child support appeal tribunal;

(*d*) any member of the staff of such a tribunal;

(*e*) a civil servant in connection with the carrying out of any functions under this Act,

and to employment of any other kind which is prescribed[2] for the purposes of this section.

(6) For the purposes of this section a disclosure is to be regarded as made with lawful authority if, and only if, it is made—

(*a*) by a civil servant in accordance with his official duty; or

(*b*) by any other person either—

(i) for the purposes of the function in the exercise of which he holds the information and without contravening any restriction duly imposed by the responsible person; or

(ii) to, or in accordance with an authorisation duly given by, the responsible person;

(*c*) in accordance with any enactment or order[3] of a court;

(*d*) for the purpose of instituting, or otherwise for the purposes of, any proceedings before a court or before any tribunal or other body or person mentioned in this Act; or

(*e*) with the consent of the appropriate person.

(7) "The responsible person" means—

(*a*) the Lord Chancellor;

(*b*) the Secretary of State;

(*c*) any person authorised by the Lord Chancellor, or Secretary of State, for the purposes of this subsection; or

(*d*) any other prescribed person, or person falling within a prescribed category.

(8) "The appropriate person" means the person to whom the information in question relates, except that if the affairs of that person are being dealt with—

(*a*) under a power of attorney;

(*b*) by a receiver appointed under section 99 of the Mental Health Act 1983;

(*c*) by a Scottish mental health custodian, that is to say a guardian or other person entitield to act on behalf of the person under the Adults with Incapacity (Scotland) Act 2000 (asp 4); or

(*d*) by a mental health appointee, that is to say—

(i) a person directed or authorised as mentioned in sub-paragraph (*a*) of rule 41(1) of the Court of Protection Rules 1984; or

(ii) a receiver ad interim appointed under sub-paragraph (*b*) of that rule;

the appropriate person is the attorney, receiver, custodian or appointee (as the case may be) or, in a case falling within paragraph (*a*), the person to whom the information relates.*

[Child Support Act 1991, s 50 and the Social Security Act 1998, Sch 7 and the Adults with Incapacity (Scotland) Act 2000, Sch 5.]

---

*Subsection (8) amended and sub-ss (9) inserted by the Mental Capacity Act 2005, Sch 6 from a date to be appointed.

1. For procedure in respect of an offence which is triable either way, see ss 18–21 of the Magistrates' Courts Act 1980, in PART I: MAGISTRATES' COURTS PROCEDURE, ante.

2. See reg 11 of the Child Support (Information Evidence and Disclosure) Regulations 1992, SI 1992/1812 amended by SI 1995/123, 1045 and 3261, SI 1996/1945 and 2907, SI 1998/58, SI 1999/977 and 1510, SI 2001/161, the Child Support, Pensions and Social Security Act 2000, s 1, SI 2003/328, SI 2004/ 1823 and 2415 and SI 2005/2877 (CD Rom only).

3. It is not open to a court to make an order or direction under s 50 giving leave to, or directing, the Secretary of State, to provide information which is held by the Child Support Agency (*Re C (a minor) (disclosure of address)* [1995] 1 FCR 202, [1995] 1 FLR 201). However, under *Registrar's Direction (disclosure of addresses)* [1988] 1 WLR 573, an arrangement exists whereby the High Court may request disclosure of addresses by government departments.

6–2964 51. Supplementary powers to make regulations. (1) The Secretary of State may by regulations make such incidental, supplemental and transitional provision as he considers appropriate in connection with any provision made by or under this Act.

(2) The regulations may, in particular, make provision—

(*a*) as to the procedure to be followed with respect to—

(i) the making of applications for maintenance calculations;
(ii) the making of decisions under section 11;
(iii) the making of decisions under section 16 or 17;

(*b*) extending the categories of case to which section 16, 17 or 20 applies;
(*c*) as to the date on which an application for a maintenance calculation is to be treated as having been made;
(*d*) for attributing payments made under maintenance calculations to the payment of arrears;
(*e*) for the adjustment, for the purpose of taking account of the retrospective effect of a maintenance calculation, of amounts payable under the calculation;
(*f*) for the adjustment, for the purpose of taking account of over-payments or under-payments of child support maintenance, of amounts payable under a maintenance calculation;
(*g*) as to the evidence which is to be required in connection with such matters as may be prescribed;
(*h*) as to the circumstances in which any official record or certificate is to be conclusive (or in Scotland, sufficient) evidence;
(i) with respect to the giving of notices or other documents;
(*j*) for the rounding up or down of any amounts calculated, estimated or otherwise arrived at in applying any provision made by or under this Act.

(3) No power to make regulations conferred by any other provision of this Act shall be taken to limit the powers given to the Secretary of State by this section.

[Child Support Act 1991, s 51 as amended by the Social Security Act 1998, Sch 7 and the Child Support, Pensions and Social Security Act 2000, Sch 3.]

6–2965 52. *Regulations and orders.*

6–2966 53. *Financial provisions.*

6–2967 54. Interpretation. In this Act—

"non-resident parent has the meaning given in section 3(2);
"appeal tribunal" means an appeal tribunal constituted under Chapter I of Part I of the Social Security Act 1998;
"application for a variation" means an application under section 28A;
"benefit Acts" means the Social Security Contributions and Benefits Act 1992 and the Social Security Administration Act 1992;
"child benefit" has the same meaning as in the Child Benefit Act 1975;
"child support maintenance" has the meaning given in section 3(6);
"deduction from earnings order" has the meaning given in section 31(2);
"default maintenance decision" has the meaning given in section 12;
"disability living allowance" has the same meaning as in the benefit Acts;
"general qualification" shall be construed in accordance with section 71 of the Courts and Legal Services Act 1990 (qualification for judicial appointments);
"income support" has the same meaning as in the benefit Acts;
"income-based jobseeker's allowance" has the same meaning as in the Jobseekers Act 1995;
"interim maintenance decision" has the meaning given in section 12;
"liability order" has the meaning given in section 33(2);
"maintenance agreement" has the meaning given in section 9(1);
"maintenance calculation" means a calculation of maintenance made under this Act and, except in prescribed circumstances, includes a default maintenance decision and an interim maintenance decision;
"maintenance order" has the meaning given in section 8(11);
"parent", in relation to any child, means any person who is in law the mother or father of the child;

"parent with care" means a person who is, in relation to a child, both a parent and a person with care;

"parental responsibility", in the application of this Act—

    (a) to England and Wales, has the same meaning as in the Children Act 1989; and

    (b) to Scotland, shall be construed as a reference to "parental responsibilities" within the meaning given by section 1(3) of the Children (Scotland) Act 1995;

"parent with care" means a person who is, in relation to a child, both a parent and a person with care

"person with care" has the meaning given in section 3(3);

"prescribed" means prescribed by regulations made by the Secretary of State;

"qualifying child" has the meaning given in section 3(1);

"voluntary payment" has the meaning given in section 28J.

[Child Support Act 1991, s 54 amended by the Social Security (Consequential Provisions) Act 1992, Sch 3, the Child Support Act 1995, Sch 3, the Children (Scotland) Act 1995, Schs 4 and 5, and the Jobseekers Act 1995, Sch 2, the Social Security Act 1998, Schs 7 and 8, the Tax Credits Act 2002, Sch 6 and the Child Support, Pensions and Social Security Act 2000, Sch 3.]

6–2968   **55. Meaning of "child".**   (1) For the purposes of this Act a person is a child if—

    (a) he is under the age of 16;

    (b) he is under the age of 19 and receiving full-time education (which is not advanced education)—

        (i) by attendance at a recognised educational establishment; or

        (ii) elsewhere, if the education is recognised by the Secretary of State; or

    (c) he does not fall within paragraph (a) or (b) but—

        (i) he is under the age of 18, and

        (ii) prescribed conditions are satisfied with respect to him.

(2) A person is not a child for the purposes of this Act if he—

    (a) is or has been married or a civil partner;

    (b) has celebrated a marriage, or been a party to a civil partnership, which is void; or

    (c) has celebrated a marriage in respect of which a decree of nullity has been granted or has been a party to a civil partnership in respect of which a nullity order has been made.

(3) In this section—

"advanced education" means education of a prescribed description; and

"recognised educational establishment" means an establishment recognised by the Secretary of State for the purposes of this section as being, or as comparable to, a university, college or school.

(4) Where a person has reached the age of 16, the Secretary of State may recognise education provided for him otherwise than at a recognised educational establishment only if the Secretary of State is satisfied that education was being so provided for him immediately before he reached the age of 16.

(5) The Secretary of State may provide that in prescribed circumstances education is or is not to be treated for the purposes of this section as being full-time.

(6) In determining whether a person falls within subsection (1)(b), no account shall be taken of such interruptions in his education as may be prescribed.

(7) The Secretary of State may by regulations provide that a person who ceases to fall within subsection (1) shall be treated as continuing to fall within that subsection for a prescribed period.

(8) No person shall be treated as continuing to fall within subsection (1) by virtue of regulations made under subsection (7) after the end of the week in which he reaches the age of 19.

[Child Support Act 1991, s 55 as amended by the Civil Partnership Act 2004, Sch 24.]

6–2969   **56.** *Corresponding provision for and co-ordination with Northern Ireland.*

6–2970   **57. Application to Crown.**   (1) The power of the Secretary of State to make regulations under section 14 requiring prescribed persons to furnish information may be exercised so as to require information to be furnished by persons employed in the service of the Crown or otherwise in the discharge of Crown functions.

(2) In such circumstances, and subject to such conditions, as may be prescribed, an inspector appointed under section 15 may enter any Crown premises for the purpose of exercising any powers conferred on him by that section.

(3) Where such an inspector duly enters any Crown premises for those purposes, section 15 shall apply in relation to persons employed in the service of the Crown or otherwise in the discharge of Crown functions as it applies in relation to other persons.

(4) Where a liable person is in the employment of the Crown, a deduction from earnings order may be made under section 31 in relation to that person; but in such a case subsection (8) of section

32 shall apply only in relation to the failure of that person to comply with any requirement imposed on him by regulations made under section 32.
[Child Support Act 1991, s 57.]

6–2971   58. Short title, commencement and extent, etc.   (1) This Act may be cited as the Child Support Act 1991.

(2) Section 56(1) and subsections (1) to (11) and (14) of this section shall come into force on the passing of this Act but otherwise this Act shall come into force on such date as may be appointed by order[1] made by the Lord Chancellor, the Secretary of State or Lord Advocate, or by any of them acting jointly.

(3) Different dates may be appointed for different provisions of this Act and for different purposes (including, in particular, for different cases or categories of case).

(4) An order under subsection (2) may make such supplemental, incidental or transitional provision as appears to the person making the order to be necessary or expedient in connection with the provisions brought into force by the order, including such adaptations or modifications of—

(a)   the provisions so brought into force;
(b)   any provisions of this Act then in force; or
(c)   any provision of any other enactment,

as appear to him to be necessary or expedient.

(5) Different provision may be made by virtue of subsection (4) with respect to different periods.

(6) Any provision made by virtue of subsection (4) may, in particular, include provision for—

(a)   the enforcement of a maintenance calculation (including the collection of sums payable under the calculation) as if the calculation were a court order of a prescribed kind;
(b)   the registration of maintenance calculations with the appropriate court in connection with any provision of a kind mentioned in paragraph (a);
(c)   the variation, on application made to a court, of the provisions of a maintenance calculation relating to the method of making payments fixed by the calculation or the intervals at which such payments are to be made;
(d)   a maintenance calculation, or an order of a prescribed kind relating to one or more children, to be deemed, in prescribed circumstances, to have been validly made for all purposes or for such purposes as may be prescribed.

In paragraph (c) "court" includes a single justice.

(7) The Lord Chancellor, the Secretary of State or the Lord Advocate may by order make such amendments or repeals in, or such modifications of, such enactments as may be specified in the order, as appear to him to be necessary or expedient in consequence of any provision made by or under this Act (including any provision made by virtue of subsection (4)).

(8) This Act shall, in its application to the Isles of Scilly, have effect subject to such exceptions, adaptations and modifications as the Secretary of State may by order prescribe.

(9) Sections 27, 35, 40A and 48 and paragraph 7 of Schedule 5 do not extend to Scotland.

(10) Sections 7, 28, 40A and 49 extend only to Scotland.

(11) With the exception of sections 23 and 56(1), subsections (1) to (3) of this section and Schedules 2 and 4, and (in so far as it amends any enactment extending to Northern Ireland) Schedule 5, this Act does not extend to Northern Ireland.

(12) Until Schedule 1 to the Disability Living Allowance and Disability Working Allowance Act 1991 comes into force, paragraph 1(1) of Schedule 3 shall have effect with the omission of the words "and disability appeal tribunals" and the insertion, after "social security appeal tribunals", of the word "and".

(13) The consequential amendments set out in Schedule 5 shall have effect.

(14) *Repeals.*
[Child Support Act 1991, s 58 as amended by the Child Support, Pensions and Social Security Act 2000, Sch 3.]

1. As to commencement of this Act, see note 1 to the short title of the Act, ante.

Children (Scotland) Act 1995[1]

(1995 c 36)

PART II[2]

PROMOTION OF CHILDREN'S WELFARE BY LOCAL AUTHORITIES AND BY CHILDREN'S HEARINGS
ETC.

CHAPTER I
SUPPORT FOR CHILDREN AND THEIR FAMILIES

Miscellaneous and General

6–3051   33. Effect of orders etc. made in different parts of the United Kingdom.   (1) The
Secretary of State may make regulations providing for a prescribed order which is made by a court in
England and Wales or in Northern Ireland, if that order appears to him to correspond generally to an
order of a kind which may be made under this Part of this Act or to a supervision requirement, to
have effect in prescribed circumstances and for prescribed purposes of the law of Scotland as if it
were an order of that kind or, as the case may be, as if it were a supervision requirement.

(2) The Secretary of State may make regulations[3] providing—

(a)   for a prescribed order made under this Part of this Act by a court in Scotland; or
(b)   for a supervision requirement,

if that order or requirement appears to him to correspond generally to an order of a kind which may
be made under any provision of law in force in England and Wales or in Northern Ireland, to have
effect in prescribed circumstances and for prescribed purposes of the law of England and Wales, or
as the case may be of Northern Ireland, as if it were an order of that kind.

(3) Regulations under subsection (1) or (2)(a) above may provide for the order given effect for
prescribed purposes to cease to have effect for those purposes, or for the purposes of the law of the
place where the order was made, if prescribed conditions are satisfied.

(4) Where a child who is subject to a supervision requirement is lawfully taken to live in England
and Wales or in Northern Ireland, the requirement shall cease to have effect if prescribed conditions
are satisfied.

(5) Regulations under this section may modify any provision of—

(a)   the Social Work (Scotland) Act 1968 or this Act in any application which the Acts may
respectively have, by virtue of the regulations, in relation to an order made otherwise than in
Scotland;
(b)   the Children Act 1989 or the Children and Young Persons Act 1969 or sections 63 to 67 of
and Schedules 6 and 7 to the Powers of Criminal Courts (Sentencing) Act 2000 in any
application which those Acts may respectively have, by virtue of the regulations, in relation to
an order prescribed under subsection (2)(a) above or to a supervision requirement; or
(c)   (*Northern Ireland*).

[Children (Scotland) Act 1995, s 33 as amended by the Powers of Criminal Courts (Sentencing) Act 2000, Sch 9.]

---

1. Only provisions of this Act which extend to England and Wales are set out in this work.
2. Part II contains ss 16–93; Chapter 1 contains ss 16–38.
3. See the Children (Reciprocal Enforcement of Prescribed Orders etc (England and Wales and Northern Ireland))
(Scotland) Regulations 1996, this PART, post.

CHAPTER 2[1]
CHILDREN'S HEARINGS

Conduct of proceedings at and in connection with children's hearing

6–3052   44. Prohibition of publication of proceedings at children's hearing.   (1) No person
shall publish any matter in respect of a case about which the Principal Reporter has from any source
received information or any matter in respect of proceedings at a children's hearing, or before a
sheriff on an application under section 57, section 60(7), section 65(7) or (9), section 76(1) or
section 85(1) of this Act, or on any appeal under this Part of this Act, which is intended to, or is likely
to, identify—

(a)   the child concerned in, or any other child connected (in any way) with, the case, any child
concerned in the proceedings or appeal; or
(b)   an address or school as being that of any such child.

(2) Any person who contravenes subsection (1) above shall be guilty of an offence and shall be
liable on summary conviction to a fine not exceeding **level 4** on the standard scale in respect of each
such contravention.

(3) It shall be a defence in proceedings for an offence under this section for the accused to prove
that he did not know, and had no reason to suspect, that the published matter was intended, or was
likely, to identify the child or, as the case may be, the address or school.

(4) In this section "to publish" includes, without prejudice to the generality of that expression—

(a) to publish matter in a programme service, as defined by section 201 of the Broadcasting Act 1990 (definition of programme service); and
(b) to cause matter to be published.

(5) The requirements of subsection (1) above may, in the interests of justice, be dispensed with by—

(a) the sheriff in any proceedings before him;
(b) the Court of Session in any appeal under section 51(11) of this Act; or
(c) the Secretary of State in relation to any proceedings at a children's hearing,

to such extent as the sheriff, the Court or the Secretary of State as the case may be considers appropriate.
[Children (Scotland) Act 1995, s 44, as amended by the Criminal Justice (Scotland) Act 2003, s 52.]

---

1. Chapter 2 contains ss 39–51.

CHAPTER 3[1]
PROTECTION AND SUPERVISION OF CHILDREN
Fugitive children and harbouring

6–3053 **82. Recovery of certain fugitive children.** (1) A child who absconds—

(a) from a place of safety in which he is being kept under or by virtue of this Part of this Act;
(b) from a place (in this section referred to as a "relevant place") which, though not a place of safety such as is mentioned in paragraph (a) above, is a residential establishment in which he is required to reside by virtue of section 70(3)(a) of this Act or a hospital or other institution in which he is temporarily residing while subject to such a requirement; or
(c) from a person who, by virtue of a supervision requirement or of section 74 of this Act, has control over him while he is being taken to, is awaiting being taken to, or (whether or not by reason of being on leave) is temporarily away from, such place of safety or relevant place,

may be arrested without warrant in any part of the United Kingdom and taken to the place of safety or as the case may be the relevant place; and a court which is satisfied that there are reasonable grounds for believing that the child is within any premises may, where there is such power of arrest, grant a warrant authorising a constable to enter those premises and search for the child using reasonable force if necessary.

(2) Without prejudice to the generality of subsection (1) above, a child who at the end of a period of leave from a place of safety or relevant place fails to return there shall, for the purposes of this section, be taken to have absconded.

(3) A child who absconds from a person who, not being a person mentioned in paragraph (c) of subsection (1) above, is a person who has control over him by virtue of a supervision requirement may, subject to the same provisions as those to which an arrest under that subsection is subject, be arrested as is mentioned in that subsection and returned to that person; and the provision in that subsection for a warrant to be granted shall apply as respects such a child as it applies as respects a child mentioned in that subsection.

(4) If a child—

(a) is taken under subsection (1) above to a place of safety or relevant place; or
(b) is returned under subsection (3) above to a person,

but the occupier of that place of safety or of that relevant place, or as the case may be that person, is unwilling or unable to receive him, that circumstance shall be intimated forthwith to the Principal Reporter.

(5) Where intimation is required by subsection (4) above as respects a child, he shall be kept in a place of safety until—

(a) in a case where he is subject to a supervision requirement, he can be brought before a children's hearing for that requirement to be reviewed; or
(b) in any other case, the Principal Reporter has, in accordance with section 56(6) of this Act, considered whether compulsory measures of supervision are required in respect of him.
[Children (Scotland) Act 1995, s 82.]

---

1. Chapter 3 contains ss 52–85.

6–3054 **83. Harbouring.** A person who—

(a) knowingly assists or induces a child to abscond in circumstances which render the child liable to arrest under subsection (1) or (3) of section 82 of this Act;
(b) knowingly and persistently attempts to induce a child so to abscond;
(c) knowingly harbours or conceals a child who has so absconded; or
(d) knowingly prevents a child from returning—

(i) to a place mentioned in paragraph (a) or (b) of the said subsection (1);

(ii) to a person mentioned in paragraph (*c*) of that subsection, or in the said subsection (3),

shall, subject to section 38(3) and (4) of this Act, to section 51(5) and (6) of the Children Act 1989 and to Article 70(5) and (6) of the Children (Northern Ireland) Order 1995 (analogous provision for England and Wales and for Northern Ireland), be guilty of an offence and liable on summary conviction to a fine not exceeding **level 5** on the standard scale or to imprisonment for a term not exceeding **six months** or to **both** such fine and such imprisonment.
[Children (Scotland) Act 1995, s 83.]

CHAPTER 4[1]
PARENTAL RESPONSIBILITIES ORDERS, ETC.

Interpretation of Part II

6–3055   93. Interpretation of Part II.   (1) In this Part of this Act, unless the context otherwise requires—

"accommodation" shall be construed in accordance with section 25(8) of this Act;

"chief social work officer" means an officer appointed under section 3 of the Social Work (Scotland) Act 1968;

"child assessment order" has the meaning given by section 55(1) of this Act;

"child protection order" has the meaning given by section 57(1) of this Act;

"children's hearing" shall be construed in accordance with section 39(3), but does not include a business meeting arranged under section 64, of this Act;

"compulsory measures of supervision" means, in respect of a child, such measures of supervision as may be imposed upon him by a children's hearing;

"constable" means a constable of a police force within the meaning of the Police (Scotland) Act 1967;

"contact order" has the meaning given by section 11(2)(*d*) of this Act;

"disabled" has the meaning given by section 23(2) of this Act;

"education authority" has the meaning given by section 135(1) of the Education (Scotland) Act 1980 (c 44)

"exclusion order" has the meaning given by section 76(12) of this Act;

"family", in relation to a child, includes—

(*a*) any person who has parental responsibility for the child; and

(*b*) any other person with whom the child has been living;

"local authority" means a council constituted under section 2 of the Local Government etc. (Scotland) Act 1994;

"local government area" shall be construed in accordance with section 1 of the said Act of 1994;

"parental responsibilities" has the meaning given by section 1(3) of this Act;

"parental responsibilities order" has the meaning given by section 86(1) of this Act;

"parental rights" has the meaning given by section 2(4) of this Act;

"place of safety", in relation to a child, means—

(*a*) a residential or other establishment provided by a local authority;

(*b*) a community home within the meaning of section 53 of the Children Act 1989;

(*c*) a police station; or

(*d*) a hospital, or surgery, the person or body of persons responsible for the management of which is willing temporarily to receive the child;

(*e*) the dwelling-house of a suitable person who is so willing; or

(*f*) any other suitable place the occupier of which is so willing;

"the Principal Reporter" means the Principal Reporter appointed under section 127 of the said Act of 1994 or any officer of the Scottish Children's Reporter Administration to whom there is delegated, under section 131(1) of that Act, any function of the Principal Reporter under this Act;

"relevant local authority", in relation to a child who is subject to a warrant granted under this Part of this Act or to a supervision requirement, means the local authority for whose area there is established the children's panel from which the children's hearing which granted the warrant or imposed the supervision requirement was constituted;

"residence order" has the meaning given by section 11(2)(*c*) of this Act;

"residential establishment"—

(*a*) in relation to a place in Scotland, means an establishment (whether managed by a local authority, by a voluntary organisation or by any other person) which provides residential accommodation for children for the purposes of this Act or the Social Work (Scotland) Act 1968;

(*b*) in relation to a place in England and Wales, means a community home, voluntary home or private* children's home (within the meaning of the Children Act 1989); and

(*c*) in relation to a place in Northern Ireland, means a home provided under Part VIII of the Children (Northern Ireland) Order 1995, or a voluntary home, or a registered children's home (which have respectively the meanings given by that Order);

"school age" shall be construed in accordance with section 31 of the Education (Scotland) Act 1980;

"secure accommodation" means accommodation provided in a residential establishment, approved by the Scottish Ministers in accordance with regulations made under section 29(9)(a) of the Regulation of Care (Scotland) Act 2001 (asp 8) or by the Secretary of State in accordance with regulations made under section 22(8)(a) of the Care Standards Act 2000, for the purpose of restricting the liberty of children;*

"supervision requirement" has the meaning given by section 70(1) of this Act, and includes any condition contained in such a requirement or related to it;

"voluntary organisation" means a body (other than a public or local authority) whose activities are not carried on for profit; and

"working day" means every day except—

    (a) Saturday and Sunday;

    (b) December 25th and 26th; and

    (c) January 1st and 2nd

(2) For the purposes of—

(a) Chapter 1 and this Chapter (except this section) of this Part and section 44, "child" means a person under the age of eighteen years; and

(b) Chapter 2 (except section 44) and Chapter 3 (except section 75A) of this Part—

    "child" means—

        (i) a child who has not attained the age of sixteen years;

        (ii) a child over the age of sixteen years who has not attained the age of eighteen years and in respect of whom a supervision requirement is in force; or

        (iii) a child whose case has been referred to a children's hearing by virtue of section 33 of this Act;

and for the purposes of the application of those Chapters to a person who has failed to attend school regularly without reasonable excuse includes a person who is over sixteen years of age but is not over school age; and

"relevant person" in relation to a child means—

    (a) any parent enjoying parental responsibilities or parental rights under Part I of this Act;

    (b) any person in whom parental responsibilities or rights are vested by, under or by virtue of this Act; and

    (c) any person who appears to be a person who ordinarily (and other than by reason only of his employment) has charge of, or control over, the child.

(3) Where, in the course of any proceedings under Chapter 2 or 3 of this Part, a child ceases to be a child within the meaning of subsection (2) above, the provisions of those Chapters of this Part and of any statutory instrument made under those provisions shall continue to apply to him as if he had not so ceased to be a child.

(4) Any reference in this Part of this Act to a child—

(a) being "in-need", is to his being in need of care and attention because—

        (i) he is unlikely to achieve or maintain, or to have the opportunity of achieving or maintaining, a reasonable standard of health or development unless there are provided for him, under or by virtue of this Part, services by a local authority;

        (ii) his health or development is likely significantly to be impaired, or further impaired, unless such services are so provided;

        (iii) he is disabled; or

        (iv) he is affected adversely by the disability of any other person in his family;

(b) who is "looked after" by a local authority, shall be construed in accordance with section 17(6) of this Act.

(5) Any reference to any proceedings under this Part of this Act, whether or an application or on appeal, being heard by the sheriff, shall be construed as a reference to such proceedings being heard by the sheriff in chambers.

[Children (Scotland) Act 1995, s 93, as amended by the Regulation of Care (Scotland) Act 2001, s 74, the Care Standards Act 2000, Sch 4, the Criminal Justice (Scotland) Act 2003, s 52 and the Antisocial Behaviour etc (Scotland) Act 2004, s 137.]

---

*Printed as amended by the Care Standards Act 2000, Sch 4. In force in relation to England, with regards Wales, in force from a date to be appointed: see the Care Standards Act 2000, s 122.

1. Chapter 4 contains ss 86–93.

PART IV[1]
GENERAL AND SUPPLEMENTAL

6–3056 105. Extent, short title, minor and consequential amendments, repeals and commencement. (1) This Act, which subject to subsections (8) to (10) below extends to Scotland only—

(a) may be cited as the Children (Scotland) Act 1995; and

(b) except for subsections (1), (2) and (6) to (10) of this section, shall come into force on such day as the Secretary of State may by order made by statutory instrument appoint;

and different days may be appointed under paragraph (b) above for different purposes.

(2) An order under subsection (1)(b) above may contain such transitional and consequential provisions and savings as appear to the Secretary of State to be necessary or expedient in connection with the provisions brought into force.

(3) The transitional provisions and savings contained in Schedule 3 to this Act shall have effect but are without prejudice to sections 16 and 17 of the Interpretation Act 1978 (effect of repeals).

(4) Schedule 4 to this Act, which contains minor amendments and amendments consequential upon the provisions of this Act, shall have effect.

(5) The enactments mentioned in Schedule 5 to this Act (which include spent provisions) are hereby repealed to the extent specified in the third column of that Schedule.

(6) The Secretary of State may by order made by statutory instrument make such further amendments or repeals, in such enactments as may be specified in the order, as appear to him to be necessary or expedient in consequence of any provision of this Act.

(7) A statutory instrument containing an order under subsection (6) above shall be subject to annulment in pursuance of a resolution of either House of Parliament.

(8) Sections 18, 26(2), 33, 44, 70(4), 74, 82, 83, 93 and 104 of this Act and this section extend to England and Wales, and those sections and this section (except section 70(4)) also extend to Northern Ireland; but—

(a) subsection (4) of this section so extends—

  (i) to England and Wales, only in so far as it relates to paragraphs 8, 10, 19, 31, 37, 41(1), (2) and (7) to (9), 48 to 52, 54 and 55 of Schedule 4; and

  (ii) to Northern Ireland, only in so far as it relates to paragraphs 31, 37, 41(1), (2) and (7) to (9), 54, 55 and 58 of that Schedule; and

(b) subsection (5) of this section so extends—

  (i) to England and Wales, only in so far as it relates to the entries in Schedule 5 in respect of Part V of the Social Work (Scotland) Act 1968, the Maintenance Orders (Reciprocal Enforcement) Act 1972, section 35(4)(c) of the Family Law Act 1986, the Children Act 1989, the Child Support Act 1991 and the Education Act 1993; and

  (ii) to Northern Ireland, only in so far as it relates to the entries in that Schedule in respect of Part V of the Social Work (Scotland) Act 1968, the Maintenance Orders (Reciprocal Enforcement) Act 1972 and section 35(4)(c) of the Family Law Act 1986.

(9) This section, so far as it relates to the repeal of Part V of the Social Work (Scotland) Act 1968, also extends to the Channel Islands.

(10) Her Majesty may by Order in Council direct that any of the relevant provisions specified in the Order shall extend, with such exceptions, adaptations and modifications (if any) as may be specified in the Order, to any of the Channel Islands; and in this subsection "the relevant provisions" means sections 74, 82, 83 and 93 of this Act and any regulations made under section 74 of this Act.
[Children (Scotland) Act 1995, s 105.]

---

1. Part IV contains ss 99–105.

Family Law Act 1996[1]
(1996 c 27)

PART I[2]
PRINCIPLES OF PARTS II AND III

6–3071 1. The general principles underlying Parts II and III.   (1) The court and any person, in exercising functions under or in consequence of Parts II and III, shall have regard to the following general principles—

(a) that the institution of marriage is to be supported;

(b) that the parties to a marriage which may have broken down are to be encouraged to take all practicable steps, whether by marriage counselling or otherwise, to save the marriage;

(c) that a marriage which has irretrievably broken down and is being brought to an end should be brought to an end—

  (i) with minimum distress to the parties and to the children affected;

  (ii) with questions dealt with in a manner designed to promote as good a continuing relationship between the parties and any children affected as is possible in the circumstances; and

  (iii) without costs being unreasonably incurred in connection with the procedures to be followed in bringing the marriage to an end; and

(*d*) that any risk to one of the parties to a marriage, and to any children, of violence from the other party should, so far as reasonably practicable, be removed or diminished.
[Family Law Act 1996, s 1.]

---

1. The Family Law Act 1996 is to be brought into force in accordance with the provisions of s 67, post; commencement orders which had been made at the date of going to press are noted thereto.
2. Part I contains s 1.

PART II[1]
DIVORCE AND SEPARATION

6–3072 18. Grounds for financial provision orders in magistrates' courts. (1) In section 1 of the Domestic Proceedings and Magistrates' Courts Act 1978, omit paragraphs (*c*) and (*d*) (which provide for behaviour and desertion to be grounds on which an application for a financial provision order may be made).

(2) In section 7(1) of that Act (powers of magistrates' court where spouses are living apart by agreement), omit "neither party having deserted the other".
[Family Law Act 1996, s 18.]

---

1. Part II contains ss 2–25.

PART IV[1]
FAMILY HOMES AND DOMESTIC VIOLENCE

Rights to occupy matrimonial home

6–3078 30. Rights concerning matrimonial home where one spouse has no estate, etc.
(1) This section applies if—

(*a*) one spouse is entitled to occupy a dwelling-house by virtue of

(i) a beneficial estate or interest or contract; or
(ii) any enactment giving that spouse the right to remain in occupation; and

(*b*) the other spouse is not so entitled.

(2) Subject to the provisions of this Part, the spouse not so entitled has the following rights ("matrimonial home rights")—

(*a*) if in occupation, a right not to be evicted or excluded from the dwelling-house or any part of it by the other spouse except with the leave of the court given by an order under section 33;
(*b*) if not in occupation, a right with the leave of the court so given to enter into and occupy the dwelling-house.

(3) If a spouse is entitled under this section to occupy a dwelling-house or any part of a dwelling-house, any payment or tender made or other thing done by that spouse in or towards satisfaction of any liability of the other spouse in respect of rent, mortgage payments or other outgoings affecting the dwelling-house is, whether or not it is made or done in pursuance of an order under section 40, as good as if made or done by the other spouse.

(4) A spouse's occupation by virtue of this section—

(*a*) is to be treated, for the purposes of the Rent (Agriculture) Act 1976 and the Rent Act 1977 (other than Part V and sections 103 to 106 of that Act), as occupation by the other spouse as the other spouse's residence, and
(*b*) if the spouse occupies the dwelling-house as that spouse's only or principal home, is to be treated, for the purposes of the Housing Act 1985, Part I of the Housing Act 1988 and Chapter I of Part V of the Housing Act 1996, as occupation by the other spouse as the other spouse's only or principal home.

(5) If a spouse ("the first spouse")—

(*a*) is entitled under this section to occupy a dwelling-house or any part of a dwelling-house, and
(*b*) makes any payment in or towards satisfaction of any liability of the other spouse ("the second spouse") in respect of mortgage payments affecting the dwelling-house,

the person to whom the payment is made may treat it as having been made by the second spouse, but the fact that that person has treated any such payment as having been so made does not affect any claim of the first spouse against the second spouse to an interest in the dwelling-house by virtue of the payment.

(6) If a spouse is entitled under this section to occupy a dwelling-house or part of a dwelling-house by reason of an interest of the other spouse under a trust, all the provisions of subsections (3) to (5) apply in relation to the trustees as they apply in relation to the other spouse.

(7) This section does not apply to a dwelling-house which has at no time been, and which was at no time intended by the spouses to be, a matrimonial home of theirs.

(8) A spouse's matrimonial home rights continue—

(a) only so long as the marriage subsists, except to the extent that an order under section 33(5) otherwise provides; and

(b) only so long as the other spouse is entitled as mentioned in subsection (1) to occupy the dwelling-house, except where provision is made by section 31 for those rights to be a charge on an estate or interest in the dwelling-house.

(9) It is hereby declared that a spouse—

(a) who has an equitable interest in a dwelling-house or in its proceeds of sale, but

(b) is not a spouse in whom there is vested (whether solely or as joint tenant) a legal estate in fee simple or a legal term of years absolute in the dwelling-house,

is to be treated, only for the purpose of determining whether he has matrimonial home rights, as not being entitled to occupy the dwelling-house by virtue of that interest.
[Family Law Act 1996, s 30 amended by SI 1997/74.]

---

1. Pt IV contains ss 30–63. The whole of Part IV, except s 60, was brought into force on 1 October 1997 (SI 1997/1892).

6–3079   31. Effect of matrimonial home rights as charge on dwelling-house. (1) Subsections (2) and (3) apply if, at any time during a marriage, one spouse is entitled to occupy a dwelling-house by virtue of a beneficial estate or interest.

(2) The other spouse's matrimonial home rights are a charge on the estate or interest.

(3) The charge created by subsection (2) has the same priority as if it were an equitable interest created at whichever is the latest of the following dates—

(a) the date on which the spouse so entitled acquires the estate or interest;

(b) the date of the marriage; and

(c) 1st January 1968 (the commencement date of the Matrimonial Homes Act 1967).

(4) Subsections (5) and (6) apply if, at any time when a spouse's matrimonial home rights are a charge on an interest of the other spouse under a trust, there are, apart from either of the spouses, no persons, living or unborn, who are or could become beneficiaries under the trust.

(5) The rights are a charge also on the estate or interest of the trustees for the other spouse.

(6) The charge created by subsection (5) has the same priority as if it were an equitable interest created (under powers overriding the trusts) on the date when it arises.

(7) In determining for the purposes of subsection (4) whether there are any persons who are not, but could become, beneficiaries under the trust, there is to be disregarded any potential exercise of a general power of appointment exercisable by either or both of the spouses alone (whether or not the exercise of it requires the consent of another person).

(8) Even though a spouse's matrimonial home rights are a charge on an estate or interest in the dwelling-house, those rights are brought to an end by—

(a) the death of the other spouse, or

(b) the termination (otherwise than by death) of the marriage,

unless the court directs otherwise by an order made under section 33(5).

(9) If—

(a) a spouse's matrimonial home rights are a charge on an estate or interest in the dwelling-house, and

(b) that estate or interest is surrendered to merge in some other estate or interest expectant on it in such circumstances that, but for the merger, the person taking the estate or interest would be bound by the charge,

the surrender has effect subject to the charge and the persons thereafter entitled to the other estate or interest are, for so long as the estate or interest surrendered would have endured if not so surrendered, to be treated for all purposes of this Part as deriving title to the other estate or interest under the other spouse or, as the case may be, under the trustees for the other spouse, by virtue of the surrender.

(10) If the title to the legal estate by virtue of which a spouse is entitled to occupy a dwelling-house (including any legal estate held by trustees for that spouse) is registered under the Land Registration Act 2002 or any enactment replaced by that Act—

(a) registration of a land charge affecting the dwelling-house by virtue of this Part is to be effected by registering a notice under that Act; and

(b) a spouse's matrimonial home rights are not to be capable of falling within paragraph 2 of Schedule 1 or 3 to that Act.

(11) (*Repealed*).

(12) If—

(a) a spouse's matrimonial home rights are a charge on the estate of the other spouse or of trustees of the other spouse, and

(b) that estate is the subject of a mortgage,

then if, after the date of the creation of the mortgage ("the first mortgage"), the charge is registered under section 2 of the Land Charges Act 1972, the charge is, for the purposes of section 94 of the

Law of Property Act 1925 (which regulates the rights of mortgagees to make further advances ranking in priority to subsequent mortgages), to be deemed to be a mortgage subsequent in date to the first mortgage.

(13) It is hereby declared that a charge under subsection (2) or (5) is not registrable under subsection (10) or under section 2 of the Land Charges Act 1972 unless it is a charge on a legal estate.

[Family Law Act 1996, s 31, as amended by the Land Registration Act 2002, ss 133 and 135.]

6–3080   32. Further provisions relating to matrimonial home rights.   Schedule 4 re-enacts with consequential amendments and minor modifications provisions of the Matrimonial Homes Act 1983.

[Family Law Act 1996, s 32.]

Occupation orders

6–3081   33. Occupation orders where applicant has estate or interest etc. or has matrimonial home rights.   (1) If—

   (*a*) a person ("the person entitled")—

      (i) is entitled to occupy a dwelling-house by virtue of a beneficial estate or interest or contract or by virtue of any enactment giving him the right to remain in occupation, or

      (ii) has matrimonial home rights in relation to a dwelling-house, and

   (*b*) the dwelling-house—

      (i) is or at any time has been the home of the person entitled and of another person with whom he is associated, or

      (ii) was at any time intended by the person entitled and any such other person to be their home,

the person entitled may apply to the court for an order containing any of the provisions specified in subsections (3), (4) and (5).

(2) If an agreement to marry is terminated, no application under this section may be made by virtue of section 62(3)(*e*) by reference to that agreement after the end of the period of three years beginning with the day on which it is terminated.

(3) An order under this section may—

   (*a*) enforce the applicant's entitlement to remain in occupation as against the other person ("the respondent");

   (*b*) require the respondent to permit the applicant to enter and remain in the dwelling-house or part of the dwelling-house;

   (*c*) regulate the occupation of the dwelling-house by either or both parties;

   (*d*) if the respondent is entitled as mentioned in subsection (1)(*a*)(i), prohibit, suspend or restrict the exercise by him of his rights to occupy the dwelling-house;

   (*e*) if the respondent has matrimonial home rights in relation to the dwelling-house and the applicant is the other spouse, restrict or terminate those rights;

   (*f*) require the respondent to leave the dwelling-house or part of the dwelling-house; or

   (*g*) exclude the respondent from a defined area in which the dwelling-house is included.

(4) An order under this section may declare that the applicant is entitled as mentioned in subsection (1)(*a*)(i) or has matrimonial home rights.

(5) If the applicant has matrimonial home rights and the respondent is the other spouse, an order under this section made during the marriage may provide that those rights are not brought to an end by—

   (*a*) the death of the other spouse; or

   (*b*) the termination (otherwise than by death) of the marriage.

(6) In deciding whether to exercise its powers under subsection (3) and (if so) in what manner, the court shall have regard to all the circumstances including—

   (*a*) the housing needs and housing resources of each of the parties and of any relevant child;

   (*b*) the financial resources of each of the parties;

   (*c*) the likely effect of any order, or of any decision by the court not to exercise its powers under subsection (3), on the health, safety or well-being of the parties and of any relevant child; and

   (*d*) the conduct of the parties in relation to each other and otherwise.

(7) If it appears to the court that the applicant or any relevant child is likely to suffer significant harm attributable to conduct of the respondent if an order under this section containing one or more of the provisions mentioned in subsection (3) is not made, the court shall make the order unless it appears to it that—

   (*a*) the respondent or any relevant child is likely to suffer significant harm if the order is made; and

(b) the harm likely to be suffered by the respondent or child in that event is as great as, or greater than, the harm attributable to conduct of the respondent which is likely to be suffered by the applicant or child if the order is not made.

(8) The court may exercise its powers under subsection (5) in any case where it considers that in all circumstances it is just and reasonable to do so.

(9) An order under this section—

(a) may not be made after the death of either of the parties mentioned in subsection (1); and

(b) except in the case of an order made by virtue of subsection (5)(a), ceases to have effect on the death of either party.

(10) An order under this section may, in so far as it has continuing effect, be made for a specified period, until the occurrence of a specified event or until further order.

[Family Law Act 1996, s 33.]

6–3082   34. Effect of order under s 33 where rights are charge on dwelling-house. (1) If a spouse's matrimonial home rights are a charge on the estate or interest of the other spouse or of trustees for the other spouse—

(a) an order under section 33 against the other spouse has, except so far as a contrary intention appears, the same effect against persons deriving title under the other spouse or under the trustees and affected by the charge, and

(b) sections 33(1), (3), (4) and (10) and 30(3) to (6) apply in relation to any person deriving title under the other spouse or under the trustees and affected by the charge as they apply in relation to the other spouse.

(2) The court may make an order under section 33 by virtue of subsection (1)(b) if it considers that in all the circumstances it is just and reasonable to do so.

[Family Law Act 1996, s 34.]

6–3083   35. One former spouse with no existing right to occupy. (1) This section applies if—

(a) one former spouse is entitled to occupy a dwelling-house by virtue of a beneficial estate or interest or contract, or by virtue of any enactment giving him the right to remain in occupation;

(b) the other former spouse is not so entitled; and

(c) the dwelling-house was at any time their matrimonial home or was at any time intended by them to be their matrimonial home.

(2) The former spouse not so entitled may apply to the court for an order under this section against the other former spouse ("the respondent").

(3) If the applicant is in occupation, an order under this section must contain provision—

(a) giving the applicant the right not to be evicted or excluded from the dwelling-house or any part of it by the respondent for the period specified in the order; and

(b) prohibiting the respondent from evicting or excluding the applicant during that period.

(4) If the applicant is not in occupation, an order under this section must contain provision—

(a) giving the applicant the right to enter into and occupy the dwelling-house for the period specified in the order; and

(b) requiring the respondent to permit the exercise of that right.

(5) An order under this section may also—

(a) regulate the occupation of the dwelling-house by either or both of the parties;

(b) prohibit, suspend or restrict the exercise by the respondent of his right to occupy the dwelling-house;

(c) require the respondent to leave the dwelling-house or part of the dwelling-house; or

(d) exclude the respondent from a defined area in which the dwelling-house is included.

(6) In deciding whether to make an order under this section containing provision of the kind mentioned in subsection (3) or (4) and (if so) in what manner, the court shall have regard to all the circumstances including—

(a) the housing needs and housing resources of each of the parties and of any relevant child;

(b) the financial resources of each of the parties;

(c) the likely effect of any order, or of any decision by the court not to exercise its powers under subsection (3) or (4), on the health, safety or well-being of the parties and of any relevant child;

(d) the conduct of the parties in relation to each other and otherwise;

(e) the length of time that has elapsed since the parties ceased to live together;

(f) the length of time that has elapsed since the marriage was dissolved or annulled; and

(g) the existence of any pending proceedings between the parties—

(i) for an order under section 23A or 24 of the Matrimonial Causes Act 1973 (property adjustment orders in connection with divorce proceedings etc.);

(ii) for an order under paragraph 1(2)(*d*) or (*e*) of Schedule 1 to the Children Act 1989 (orders for financial relief against parents); or

(iii) relating to the legal or beneficial ownership of the dwelling-house.

(7) In deciding whether to exercise its power to include one or more of the provisions referred to in subsection (5) ("a subsection (5) provision") and (if so) in what manner, the court shall have regard to all the circumstances including the matters mentioned in subsection (6)(*a*) to (*e*).

(8) If the court decides to make an order under this section and it appears to it that, if the order does not include a subsection (5) provision, the applicant or any relevant child is likely to suffer significant harm attributable to conduct of the respondent, the court shall include the subsection (5) provision in the order unless it appears to the court that—

(*a*) the respondent or any relevant child is likely to suffer significant harm if the provision is included in the order; and

(*b*) the harm likely to be suffered by the respondent or child in that event is as great as or greater than the harm attributable to conduct of the respondent which is likely to be suffered by the applicant or child if the provision is not included.

(9) An order under this section—

(*a*) may not be made after the death of either of the former spouses; and

(*b*) ceases to have effect on the death of either of them.

(10) An order under this section must be limited so as to have effect for a specified period not exceeding six months, but may be extended on one or more occasions for a further specified period not exceeding six months.

(11) A former spouse who has an equitable interest in the dwelling-house or in the proceeds of sale of the dwelling-house but in whom there is not vested (whether solely or as joint tenant) a legal estate in fee simple or a legal term of years absolute in the dwelling-house is to be treated (but only for the purpose of determining whether he is eligible to apply under this section) as not being entitled to occupy the dwelling-house by virtue of that interest.

(12) Subsection (11) does not prejudice any right of such a former spouse to apply for an order under section 33.

(13) So long as an order under this section remains in force, subsections (3) to (6) of section 30 apply in relation to the applicant—

(*a*) as if he were the spouse entitled to occupy the dwelling-house by virtue of that section; and

(*b*) as if the respondent were the other spouse.

[Family Law Act 1996, s 35.]

6–3084 36. One cohabitant or former cohabitant with no existing right to occupy. (1) This section applies if—

(*a*) one cohabitant or former cohabitant is entitled to occupy a dwelling-house by virtue of a beneficial estate or interest or contract or by virtue of any enactment giving him the right to remain in occupation;

(*b*) the other cohabitant or former cohabitant is not so entitled; and

(*c*) that dwelling-house is the home in which they cohabit or a home in which they at any time cohabited or intended to cohabit.

(2) The cohabitant or former cohabitant not so entitled may apply to the court for an order under this section against the other cohabitant or former cohabitant ("the respondent").

(3) If the applicant is in occupation, an order under this section must contain provision—

(*a*) giving the applicant the right not to be evicted or excluded from the dwelling-house or any part of it by the respondent for the period specified in the order; and

(*b*) prohibiting the respondent from evicting or excluding the applicant during that period.

(4) If the applicant is not in occupation, an order under this section must contain provision—

(*a*) giving the applicant the right to enter into and occupy the dwelling-house for the period specified in the order; and

(*b*) requiring the respondent to permit the exercise of that right.

(5) An order under this section may also—

(*a*) regulate the occupation of the dwelling-house by either or both of the parties;

(*b*) prohibit, suspend or restrict the exercise by the respondent of his right to occupy the dwelling-house;

(*c*) require the respondent to leave the dwelling-house or part of the dwelling-house; or

(*d*) exclude the respondent from a defined area in which the dwelling-house is included.

(6) In deciding whether to make an order under this section containing provision of the kind mentioned in subsection (3) or (4) and (if so) in what manner, the court shall have regard to all the circumstances including—

(*a*) the housing needs and housing resources of each of the parties and of any relevant child;

   (b)   the financial resources of each of the parties;

   (c)   the likely effect of any order, or of any decision by the court not to exercise its powers under subsection (3) or (4), on the health, safety or well-being of the parties and of any relevant child;

   (d)   the conduct of the parties in relation to each other and otherwise;

   (e)   the nature of the parties' relationship and in particular the level of commitment involved in it;

   (f)   the length of time during which they have cohabited;

   (g)   whether there are or have been any children who are children of both parties or for whom both parties have or have had parental responsibility;

   (h)   the length of time that has elapsed since the parties ceased to live together; and

   (i)   the existence of any pending proceedings between the parties—

      (i)   for an order under paragraph 1(2)(d) or (e) of Schedule 1 to the Children Act 1989 (orders for financial relief against parents); or

      (ii)   relating to the legal or beneficial ownership of the dwelling-house.

(7) In deciding whether to exercise its powers to include one or more of the provisions referred to in subsection (5) ("a subsection (5) provision") and (if so) in what manner, the court shall have regard to all the circumstances including—

   (a)   the matters mentioned in subsection (6)(a) to (d); and

   (b)   the questions mentioned in subsection (8).

(8) The questions are—

   (a)   whether the applicant or any relevant child is likely to suffer significant harm attributable to conduct of the respondent if the subsection (5) provision is not included in the order; and

   (b)   whether the harm likely to be suffered by the respondent or child if the provision is included is as great as or greater than the harm attributable to conduct of the respondent which is likely to be suffered by the applicant or child if the provision is not included.

(9) An order under this section—

   (a)   may not be made after the death of either of the parties; and

   (b)   ceases to have effect on the death of either of them.

(10) An order under this section must be limited so as to have effect for a specified period not exceeding six months, but may be extended on one occasion for a further specified period not exceeding six months.

(11) A person who has an equitable interest in the dwelling-house or in the proceeds of sale of the dwelling-house but in whom there is not vested (whether solely or as joint tenant) a legal estate in fee simple or a legal term of years absolute in the dwelling-house is to be treated (but only for the purpose of determining whether he is eligible to apply under this section) as not being entitled to occupy the dwelling-house by virtue of that interest.

(12) Subsection (11) does not prejudice any right of such a person to apply for an order under section 33.

(13) So long as the order remains in force, subsections (3) to (6) of section 30 apply in relation to the applicant—

   (a)   as if he were B (the person entitled to occupy the dwelling-house by virtue of that section); and

   (b)   as if the respondent were A (the person entitled as mentioned in subsection (1)(a) of that section)..

[Family Law Act 1996, s 36 as amended by the Domestic Violence, Crime and Victims Act 2004, Sch 10 and the Civil Partnership Act 2004, Sch 9.]

6-3085 37. Neither spouse entitled to occupy. (1) This section applies if—

   (a)   one spouse or former spouse and the other spouse or former spouse occupy a dwelling-house which is or was the matrimonial home; but

   (b)   neither of them is entitled to remain in occupation—

      (i)   by virtue of a beneficial estate or interest or contract; or

      (ii)   by virtue of any enactment giving him the right to remain in occupation.

(2) Either of the parties may apply to the court for an order against the other under this section.

(3) An order under this section may—

   (a)   require the respondent to permit the applicant to enter and remain in the dwelling-house or part of the dwelling-house;

   (b)   regulate the occupation of the dwelling-house by either or both of the spouses;

   (c)   require the respondent to leave the dwelling-house or part of the dwelling-house; or

   (d)   exclude the respondent from a defined area in which the dwelling-house is included.

(4) Subsections (6) and (7) of section 33 apply to the exercise by the court of its powers under this section as they apply to the exercise by the court of its powers under subsection (3) of that section.

(5) An order under this section must be limited so as to have effect for a specified period not exceeding six months, but may be extended on one or more occasions for a further specified period not exceeding six months.
[Family Law Act 1996, s 37.]

6–3086 38. Neither cohabitant or former cohabitant entitled to occupy. (1) This section applies if—

- (a) one cohabitant or former cohabitant and the other cohabitant or former cohabitant occupy a dwelling-house which is the home in which they cohabit or cohabited or civil partnership (2)(a) or (aa) above and SI 2005/3336; but
- (b) neither of them is entitled to remain in occupation—
  - (i) by virtue of a beneficial estate or interest or contract; or
  - (ii) by virtue of any enactment giving him the right to remain in occupation.

(2) Either of the parties may apply to the court for an order against the other under this section.
(3) An order under this section may—

- (a) require the respondent to permit the applicant to enter and remain in the dwelling-house or part of the dwelling-house;
- (b) regulate the occupation of the dwelling-house by either or both of the parties;
- (c) require the respondent to leave the dwelling-house or part of the dwelling-house; or
- (d) exclude the respondent from a defined area in which the dwelling-house is included.

(4) In deciding whether to exercises its powers to include one or more of the provisions referred to in subsection (3) ("a subsection (3) provision") and (if so) in what manner, the court shall have regard to all the circumstances including—

- (a) the housing needs and housing resources of each of the parties and of any relevant child;
- (b) the financial resources of each of the parties;
- (c) the likely effect of any order, or of any decision by the court not to exercise its powers under subsection (3), on the health, safety or well-being of the parties and of any relevant child;
- (d) the conduct of the parties in relation to each other and otherwise; and
- (e) the questions mentioned in subsection (5).

(5) The questions are—

- (a) whether the applicant or any relevant child is likely to suffer significant harm attributable to conduct of the respondent if the subsection (3) provision is not included in the order; and
- (b) whether the harm likely to be suffered by the respondent or child if the provision is included is as great as or greater than the harm attributable to conduct of the respondent which is likely to be suffered by the applicant or child if the provision is not included.

(6) An order under this section shall be limited so as to have effect for a specified period not exceeding six months, but may be extended on one occasion for a further specified period not exceeding six months.
[Family Law Act 1996, s 38 as amended by the Domestic Violence, Crime and Victims Act 2004, Sch 10.]

6–3087 39. Supplementary provisions. (1) In this Part an "occupation order" means an order under section 33, 35, 36, 37 or 38.
(2) An application for an occupation order may be made in other family proceedings or without any other family proceedings being instituted.
(3) If—

- (a) an application for an occupation order is made under section 33, 35, 36, 37 or 38, and
- (b) the court considers that it has no power to make the order under the section concerned, but that it has power to make an order under one of the other sections,

the court may make an order under that other section.
(4) The fact that a person has applied for an occupation order under sections 35 to 38, or that an occupation order has been made, does not affect the right of any person to claim a legal or equitable interest in any property in any subsequent proceedings (including subsequent proceedings under this Part).
[Family Law Act 1996, s 39.]

6–3088 40. Additional provisions that may be included in certain occupation orders.
(1) The court may on, or at any time after, making an occupation order under section 33, 35 or 36—

- (a) impose on either party obligations as to—
  - (i) the repair and maintenance of the dwelling-house; or
  - (ii) the discharge of rent, mortgage payments or other outgoings affecting the dwelling-house;
- (b) order a party occupying the dwelling-house or any part of it (including a party who is entitled to do so by virtue of a beneficial estate or interest or contract or by virtue of any enactment giving him the right to remain in occupation) to make periodical payments to the other party

in respect of the accommodation, if the other party would (but for the order) be entitled to occupy the dwelling-house by virtue of a beneficial estate or interest or contract or by virtue of any such enactment;

(*c*) grant either party possession or use of furniture or other contents of the dwelling-house;
(*d*) order either party to take reasonable care of any furniture or other contents of the dwelling-house;
(*e*) order either party to take reasonable steps to keep the dwelling-house and any furniture or other contents secure.

(2) In deciding whether and, if so, how to exercise its powers under this section, the court shall have regard to all the circumstances of the case including—

(*a*) the financial needs and financial resources of the parties; and
(*b*) the financial obligations which they have, or are likely to have in the foreseeable future, including financial obligations to each other and to any relevant child.

(3) An order under this section ceases to have effect when the occupation order to which it relates ceases to have effect.
[Family Law Act 1996, s 40.]

6–3089 41. Additional considerations if parties are cohabitants or former cohabitants. *Repealed.*

Non-molestation orders

6–3090 42. Non-molestation orders[1]. (1) In this Part a "non-molestation order" means an order containing either or both of the following provisions—

(*a*) provision prohibiting a person ("the respondent") from molesting another person who is associated with the respondent;
(*b*) provision prohibiting the respondent from molesting a relevant child.

(2) The court may make a non-molestation order—

(*a*) if an application for the order has been made (whether in other family proceedings or without any other family proceedings being instituted) by a person who is associated with the respondent; or
(*b*) if in any family proceedings to which the respondent is a party the court considers that the order should be made for the benefit of any other party to the proceedings or any relevant child even though no such application has been made.

(3) In subsection (2) "family proceedings" includes proceedings in which the court has made an emergency protection order under section 44 of the Children Act 1989 which includes an exclusion requirement (as defined in section 44A(3) of that Act).
(4) Where an agreement to marry is terminated, no application under subsection (2)(*a*) may be made by virtue of section 62(3)(*e*) by reference to that agreement after the end of the period of three years beginning with the day on which it is terminated.
(5) In deciding whether to exercise its powers under this section and, if so, in what manner, the court shall have regard to all the circumstances including the need to secure the health, safety and well-being—

(*a*) of the applicant or, in a case falling within subsection (2)(*b*), the person for whose benefit the order would be made; and
(*b*) of any relevant child.

(6) A non-molestation order may be expressed so as to refer to molestation in general, to particular acts of molestation, or to both.
(7) A non-molestation order may be made for a specified period or until further order.
(8) A non-molestation order which is made in other family proceedings ceases to have effect if those proceedings are withdrawn or dismissed.
[Family Law Act 1996, s 42.]

---

1. For further consideration of s 42 and the meaning of "molestation", see para **6–130**, ante.

Further provisions relating to occupation and non-molestation orders

6–3091 43. Leave of court required for applications by children under sixteen. (1) A child under the age of sixteen may not apply for an occupation order or a non-molestation order except with the leave of the court.
(2) The court may grant leave for the purposes of subsection (1) only if it is satisfied that the child has sufficient understanding to make the proposed application for the occupation order or non-molestation order.
[Family Law Act 1996, s 43.]

6–3092   44. Evidence of agreement to marry. (1) Subject to subsection (2), the court shall not make an order under section 33 or 42 by virtue of section 62(3)(*e*) unless there is produced to it evidence in writing of the existence of the agreement to marry.

(2) Subsection (1) does not apply if the court is satisfied that the agreement to marry was evidenced by—

(*a*) the gift of an engagement ring by one party to the agreement to the other in contemplation of their marriage, or

(*b*) a ceremony entered into by the parties in the presence of one or more other persons assembled for the purpose of witnessing the ceremony.

[Family Law Act 1996, s 44.]

6–3093   45. *Ex parte* orders. (1) The court may, in any case where it considers that it is just and convenient to do so, make an occupation order or a non-molestation order even though the respondent has not been given such notice of the proceedings as would otherwise be required by rules of court.

(2) In determining whether to exercise its powers under subsection (1), the court shall have regard to all the circumstances including—

(*a*) any risk of significant harm to the applicant or a relevant child, attributable to conduct of the respondent, if the order is not made immediately;

(*b*) whether it is likely that the applicant will be deterred or prevented from pursuing the application if the order is not made immediately; and

(*c*) whether there is reason to believe that the respondent is aware of the proceedings but is deliberately evading service and that the applicant or a relevant child will be seriously prejudiced by the delay involved—

(i) where the court is a magistrates' court, in effecting service of proceedings; or

(ii) in any other case, in effecting substituted service.

(3) If the court makes an order by virtue of subsection (1) it must afford the respondent an opportunity to make representations relating to the order as soon as just and convenient at a full hearing.

(4) If, at a full hearing, the court makes an occupation order ("the full order"), then—

(*a*) for the purposes of calculating the maximum period for which the full order may be made to have effect, the relevant section is to apply as if the period for which the full order will have effect began on the date on which the initial order first had effect; and

(*b*) the provisions of section 36(10) or 38(6) as to the extension of orders are to apply as if the full order and the initial order were a single order.

(5) In this section—

"full hearing" means a hearing of which notice has been given to all the parties in accordance with rules of court;

"initial order" means an occupation order made by virtue of subsection (1); and

"relevant section" means section 33(10), 35(10), 36(10), 37(5) or 38(6).

[Family Law Act 1996, s 45.]

6–3094   46. Undertakings. (1) In any case where the court has power to make an occupation order or non-molestation order, the court may accept an undertaking from any party to the proceedings.

(2) No power of arrest may be attached to any undertaking given under subsection (1).

(3) The court shall not accept an undertaking under subsection (1) in any case where apart from this section a power of arrest would be attached to the order.

(4) An undertaking given to a court under subsection (1) is enforceable as if it were an order of the court.

(5) This section has effect without prejudice to the powers of the High Court and the county court apart from this section.

[Family Law Act 1996, s 46.]

6–3095   47. Arrest for breach of order[1]. (1) In this section "a relevant order" means an occupation order or a non-molestation order.

(2) If—

(*a*) the court makes a relevant order; and

(*b*) it appears to the court that the respondent has used or threatened violence against the applicant or a relevant child,

it shall attach a power of arrest to one or more provisions of the order unless satisfied that in all the circumstances of the case the applicant or child will be adequately protected without such a power of arrest[2].

(3) Subsection (2) does not apply in any case where the relevant order is made by virtue of section 45(1), but in such a case the court may attach a power of arrest to one or more provisions of the order if it appears to it—

(a) that the respondent has used or threatened violence against the applicant or a relevant child; and

(b) that there is a risk of significant harm to the applicant or child, attributable to conduct of the respondent, if the power of arrest is not attached to those provisions immediately.

(4) If, by virtue of subsection (3), the court attaches a power of arrest to any provisions of a relevant order[3], it may provide that the power of arrest is to have effect for a shorter period than the other provisions of the order.

(5) Any period specified for the purposes of subsection (4) may be extended by the court (on one or more occasions) on an application to vary or discharge the relevant order.

(6) If, by virtue of subsection (2) or (3), a power of arrest is attached to certain provisions of an order, a constable may arrest without warrant a person whom he has reasonable cause for suspecting to be in breach of any such provision.

(7) If a power of arrest is attached under subsection (2) or (3) to certain provisions of the order and the respondent is arrested under subsection (6)—

(a) he must be brought[4] before the relevant judicial authority within the period of 24 hours beginning at the time of his arrest; and

(b) if the matter is not then disposed of forthwith, the relevant judicial authority before whom he is brought may remand him.

In reckoning for the purposes of this subsection any period of 24 hours, no account is to be taken of Christmas Day, Good Friday or any Sunday.

(8) If the court has made a relevant order but—

(a) has not attached a power of arrest under subsection (2) or (3) to any provisions of the order, or

(b) has attached that power only to certain provisions of the order,

then, if at any time the applicant considers that the respondent has failed to comply with the order, he may apply to the relevant judicial authority for the issue of a warrant for the arrest of the respondent.

(9) The relevant judicial authority shall not issue a warrant on an application under subsection (8) unless—

(a) the application is substantiated on oath; and

(b) the relevant judicial authority has reasonable grounds for believing that the respondent has failed to comply with the order.

(10) If a person is brought before a court by virtue of a warrant issued under subsection (9) and the court does not dispose of the matter forthwith, the court may remand him.

(11) Schedule 5 (which makes provision corresponding to that applying in magistrates' courts in civil cases under sections 128 and 129 of the Magistrates' Courts Act 1980) has effect in relation to the powers of the High Court and a county court to remand a person by virtue of this section.

(12) If a person remanded under this section is granted bail (whether in the High Court or a county court under Schedule 5 or in a magistrates' court under section 128 or 129 of the Magistrates' Courts Act 1980), he may be required by the relevant judicial authority to comply, before release on bail or later, with such requirements as appear to that authority to be necessary to secure that he does not interfere with witnesses or otherwise obstruct the course of justice.
[Family Law Act 1996, s 47.]

---

1. For full discussion of this provision see para **6–134** Arrest for breach order made under Part IV, ante.
2. Although s 47(2) does not contain the same express permission that is found in s 47(4), post, in relation to orders made at a with-notice hearing, there is nothing in the Act to prohibit the court from attaching a power of arrest for a shorter period than the order to which it is attached (*Re B – J (a child) (non-molestation order: power of arrest)* [2000] 2 FCR 599, [2000] 2 FLR 443, CA).
3. The power to attach a power of arrest for a shorter period than the other provisions of the order only applies to proceedings under s 45, ante, ie ex parte orders (*M v W (Non-molestation orders: duration)* [2000] 1 FLR 107, FD).
4. When the arrested person is brought before the relevant authority the attendance of the arresting officer will not be necessary, unless the arrest itself is in issue; see the *President's Direction (Family Law Act 1996: attendance of arresting officer)* [2000] 1 WLR 83, [2000] 1 FCR 86, [2000] 1 FLR 270, and notes thereto in para **6–134** Arrest for breach of order made under Part IV.

6–3096 48. Remand for medical examination and report. (1) If the relevant judicial authority has reason to consider that a medical report will be required, any power to remand a person under section 47(7)(b) or (10) may be exercised for the purpose of enabling a medical examination and report to be made.

(2) If such a power is so exercised, the adjournment must not be for more than 4 weeks at a time unless the relevant judicial authority remands the accused in custody.

(3) If the relevant judicial authority so remands the accused, the adjournment must not be for more than 3 weeks at a time.

(4) If there is reason to suspect that a person who has been arrested—

(a) under section 47(6), or

(*b*)   under a warrant issued on an application made under section 47(8),

is suffering from mental illness or severe mental impairment, the relevant judicial authority has the same power to make an order under section 35 of the Mental Health Act 1983 (remand for report on accused's mental condition) as the Crown Court has under section 35 of the Act of 1983 in the case of an accused person within the meaning of that section.
[Family Law Act 1996, s 48.]

6–3097   49. Variation and discharge of orders.   (1) An occupation order or non-molestation order may be varied or discharged by the court on an application by—

(*a*)   the respondent, or
(*b*)   the person on whose application the order was made.

(2)   In the case of a non-molestation order made by virtue of section 42(2)(*b*) the order may be varied or discharged by the court even though no such application has been made.

(3)   If a spouse's matrimonial home rights are a charge on the estate or interest of the other spouse or of trustees for the other spouse, an order under section 33 against the other spouse may also be varied or discharged by the court on an application by any person deriving title under the other spouse or under the trustees and affected by the charge.

(4)   If, by virtue of section 47(3), a power of arrest has been attached to certain provisions of an occupation order or non-molestation order, the court may vary or discharge the order under subsection (1) in so far as it confers a power of arrest (whether or not any application has been made to vary or discharge any other provision of the order).
[Family Law Act 1996, s 49.]

Enforcement powers of magistrates' courts

6–3098   50. Power of magistrates' court to suspend execution of committal orders.   (1) If, under section 63(3) of the Magistrates' Courts Act 1980, a magistrates' court has power to commit a person to custody for breach of a relevant requirement, the court may by order direct that the execution of the order of committal is to be suspended for such period or on such terms and conditions as it may specify.

(2)   In subsection (1) "a relevant requirement" means—

(*a*)   an occupation order or non-molestation order;
(*b*)   an exclusion requirement included by virtue of section 38A of the Children Act 1989 in an interim care order made under section 38 of that Act; or
(*c*)   an exclusion requirement included by virtue of section 44A of the Children Act 1989 in an emergency protection order under section 44 of that Act.
[Family Law Act 1996, s 50.]

6–3099   51. Power of magistrates' court to order hospital admission or guardianship.   (1) A magistrates' court has the same power to make a hospital order or guardianship order under section 37 of the Mental Health Act 1983 or an interim hospital order under section 38 of that Act in the case of a person suffering from mental illness or severe mental impairment who could otherwise be committed to custody for breach of a relevant requirement as a magistrates' court has under those sections in the case of a person convicted of an offence punishable on summary conviction with imprisonment.

(2)   In subsection (1) "a relevant requirement" has the meaning given by section 50(2).
[Family Law Act 1996, s 51.]

Interim care orders and emergency protection orders

6–3100   52. Amendments of Children Act 1989.   Schedule 6 makes amendments of the provisions of the Children Act 1989 relating to interim care orders and emergency protection orders.
[Family Law Act 1996, s 52.]

Transfer of tenancies

6–3101   53. Transfer of certain tenancies.   Schedule 7 makes provision in relation to the transfer of certain tenancies on divorce, etc. or on separation of cohabitants.
[Family Law Act 1996, s 53.]

Dwelling-house subject to mortgage

6–3102   54. Dwelling-house subject to mortgage.   (1) In determining for the purposes of this Part whether a person is entitled to occupy a dwelling-house by virtue of an estate or interest, any right to possession of the dwelling-house conferred on a mortgagee of the dwelling-house under or by virtue of his mortgage is to be disregarded.

(2)   Subsection (1) applies whether or not the mortgagee is in possession.

(3)   Where a person ("A") is entitled to occupy a dwelling-house by virtue of an estate or interest, a connected person does not by virtue of—

(a) any matrimonial home rights conferred by section 30, or

(b) any rights conferred by an order under section 35 or 36,

have any larger right against the mortgagee to occupy the dwelling-house than A has by virtue of his estate or interest and of any contract with the mortgagee.

(4) Subsection (3) does not apply, in the case of matrimonial home rights, if under section 31 those rights are a charge, affecting the mortgagee, on the estate or interest mortgaged.

(5) In this section "connected person", in relation to any person, means that person's spouse, former spouse, cohabitant or former cohabitant.

[Family Law Act 1996, s 54.]

6–3103   55. Actions by mortgagees: joining connected persons as parties.   (1) This section applies if a mortgagee of land which consists of or includes a dwelling-house brings an action in any court for the enforcement of his security.

(2) A connected person who is not already a party to the action is entitled to be made a party in the circumstances mentioned in subsection (3).

(3) The circumstances are that—

(a) the connected person is enabled by section 30(3) or (6) (or by section 30(3) or (6) as applied by section 35(13) or 36(13)), to meet the mortgagor's liabilities under the mortgage;

(b) he has applied to the court before the action is finally disposed of in that court; and

(c) the court sees no special reason against his being made a party to the action and is satisfied—

   (i)   that he may be expected to make such payments or do such other things in or towards satisfaction of the mortgagor's liabilities or obligations as might affect the outcome of the proceedings; or

   (ii) that the expectation of it should be considered under section 36 of the Administration of Justice Act 1970.

(4) In this section "connected person" has the same meaning as in section 54.

[Family Law Act 1996, s 55.]

6–3104   56. Actions by mortgagees: service of notice on certain persons.   (1) This section applies if a mortgagee of land which consists, or substantially consists, of a dwelling-house brings an action for the enforcement of his security, and at the relevant time there is—

(a) in the case of unregistered land, a land charge of Class F registered against the person who is the estate owner at the relevant time or any person who, where the estate owner is a trustee, preceded him as trustee during the subsistence of the mortgage; or

(b) in the case of registered land, a subsisting registration of—

   (i)   a notice under section 31(10);

   (ii) a notice under section 2(8) of the Matrimonial Homes Act 1983; or

   (iii) a notice or caution under section 2(7) of the Matrimonial Homes Act 1967.

(2) If the person on whose behalf—

(a) the land charge is registered, or

(b) the notice or caution is entered,

is not a party to the action, the mortgagee must serve notice of the action on him.

(3) If—

(a) an official search has been made on behalf of the mortgagee which would disclose any land charge of Class F, notice or caution within subsection (1)(a) or (b),

(b) a certificate of the result of the search has been issued, and

(c) the action is commenced within the priority period,

the relevant time is the date of the certificate.

(4) In any other case the relevant time is the time when the action is commenced.

(5) The priority period is, for both registered and unregistered land, the period for which, in accordance with section 11(5) and (6) of the Land Charges Act 1972, a certificate on an official search operates in favour of a purchaser.

[Family Law Act 1996, s 56.]

Jurisdiction and procedure etc.

6–3105   57. Jurisdiction of courts.   (1) For the purposes of this Part "the court" means the High Court, a county court or a magistrates' court.

(2) Subsection (1) is subject to the provision made by or under the following provisions of this section, to section 59 and to any express provision as to the jurisdiction of any court made by any other provision of this Part.

(3) The Lord Chancellor may by order specify proceedings under this Part which may only be commenced in—

(a) s specified level of court;

(*b*)   a court which falls within a specified class of court; or

(*c*)   a particular court determined in accordance with, or specified in, the order.

(4) The Lord Chancellor may by order specify circumstances in which specified proceedings under this Part may only be commenced in—

(*a*)   a specified level of court;

(*b*)   a court which falls within a specified class of court; or

(*c*)   a particular court determined in accordance with, or specified in, the order.

(5) The Lord Chancellor may by order provide that in specified circumstances the whole, or any specified part of any specified proceedings under this Part is to be transferred to—

(*a*)   a specified level of court;

(*b*)   a court which falls within a specified class of court; or

(*c*)   a particular court determined in accordance with, or specified in, the order.

(6) An order under subsection (5) may provide for the transfer to be made at any stage, or specified stage, of the proceedings and whether or not the proceedings, or any part of them, have already been transferred.

(7) An order under subsection (5) may make such provision as the Lord Chancellor thinks appropriate for excluding specified proceedings from the operation of section 38 or 39 of the Matrimonial and Family Proceedings Act 1984 (transfer of family proceedings) or any other enactment which would otherwise govern the transfer of those proceedings, or any part of them.

(8) For the purposes of subsections (3), (4) and (5), there are three levels of Court—

(*a*)   the High Court;

(*b*)   any county court; and

(*c*)   any magistrates' court.

(9) The Lord Chancellor may by order make provision for the principal registry of the Family Division of the High Court to be treated as if it were a county court for specified purposes of this Part, or of any provision made under this Part.

(10) Any order under subsection (9) may make such provision as the Lord Chancellor thinks expedient for the purpose of applying (with or without modifications) provisions which apply in relation to the procedure in county courts to the principal registry when it acts as if it were a county court.

(11) In this section "specified" means specified by an order under this section.*

[Family Law Act 1996, s 57.]

---

*Amended by the Constitutional Reform Act 2005, Sch 4 from a date to be appointed.

6–3106   58. Contempt proceedings.   The powers of the court in relation to contempt of court arising out of a person's failure to comply with an order under this Part may be exercised by the relevant judicial authority.

[Family Law Act 1996, s 58.]

6–3107   59. Magistrates' courts.   (1) A magistrates' court shall not be competent to entertain any application, or make any order, involving any disputed question as to a party's entitlement to occupy any property by virtue of a beneficial estate or interest or contract or by virtue of any enactment giving him the right to remain in occupation, unless it is unnecessary to determine the question in order to deal with the application or make the order.

(2) A magistrates' court may decline jurisdiction in any proceedings under this Part if it considers that the case can more conveniently be dealt with by another court.

(3) The powers of a magistrates' court under section 63(2) of the Magistrates' Courts Act 1980 to suspend or rescind orders shall not apply in relation to any order made under this Part.

[Family Law Act 1996, s 59.]

6–3108   60. Provision for third parties to act on behalf of victims of domestic violence[1].

(1) Rules of court may provide for a prescribed person, or any person in a prescribed category, ("a representative") to act on behalf of another in relation to proceedings to which this Part applies.

(2) Rules made under this section may, in particular, authorise a representative to apply for an occupation order or for a non-molestation order for which the person on whose behalf the representative is acting could have applied.

(3) Rules made under this section may prescribe—

(*a*)   conditions to be satisfied before a representative may make an application to the court on behalf of another; and

(*b*)   considerations to be taken into account by the court in determining whether, and if so how, to exercise any of its powers under this Part when a representative is acting on behalf of another.

(4) Any rules made under this section may be made so as to have effect for a specified period and may make consequential or transitional provision with respect to the expiry of the specified period.

(5) Any such rules may be replaced by further rules made under this section.
[Family Law Act 1996, s 60.]

---

1. At the date of going to press, s 60 had not been brought into force.

6–3109 61. Appeals. (1) An appeal shall lie to the High Court against—

(a) the making by a magistrates' court of any order under this Part, or
(b) any refusal by a magistrates' court to make such an order,

but no appeal shall lie against any exercise by a magistrates' court of the power conferred by section 59(2).

(2) On an appeal under this section, the High Court may make such orders as may be necessary to give effect to its determination of the appeal.

(3) Where an order is made under subsection (2), the High Court may also make such incidental or consequential orders as appear to it to be just.

(4) Any order of the High Court made on an appeal under this section (other than one directing that an application be re-heard by a magistrates' court) shall, for the purposes—

(a) of the enforcement of the order, and
(b) of any power to vary, revive or discharge orders,

be treated as if it were an order of the magistrates' court from which the appeal was brought and not an order of the High Court.

(5) The Lord Chancellor may by order make provision as to the circumstances in which appeals may be made against decisions taken by courts on questions arising in connection with the transfer, or proposed transfer, of proceedings by virtue of any order under section 57(5).

(6) Except to the extent provided for in any order made under subsection (5), no appeal may be made against any decision of a kind mentioned in that subsection.*
[Family Law Act 1996, s 61.]

---

*Subsection (5) amended and new subs (7) inserted by the Constitutional Reform Act 2005, Sch 4 from a date to be appointed.

General

6–3110 62. Meaning of "cohabitants", "relevant child" and "associated persons". (1) For the purposes of this Part—

(a) "cohabitants" are two persons who are neither married to each other nor civil partners of each other but are living together as husband and wife or as if they were civil partners; and
(b) "cohabit" and "former cohabitants" are to be read accordingly, but the latter expression does not include cohabitants who have subsequently married each other or become civil partners of each other.

(2) In this Part, "relevant child", in relation to any proceedings under this Part, means—

(a) any child who is living with or might reasonably be expected to live with either party to the proceedings;
(b) any child in relation to whom an order under the Adoption Act 1976, the Adoption and Children Act 2002 or the Children Act 1989 is in question in the proceedings; and
(c) any other child whose interests the court considers relevant.

(3) For the purposes of this Part, a person is associated[1] with another person if—

(a) they are or have been married to each other;
(aa) they are or have been civil partners of each other;
(b) they are cohabitants or former cohabitants;
(c) they live or have lived in the same household, otherwise than merely by reason of one of them being the other's employee, tenant, lodger or boarder;
(d) they are relatives;
(e) they have agreed to marry one another (whether or not that agreement has been terminated);
(eza) they have entered into a civil partnership agreement (as defined by section 73 of the Civil Partnership Act 2004) (whether or not that agreement has been terminated);*
(f) in relation to any child, they are both persons falling within subsection (4); or
(g) they are parties to the same family proceedings (other than proceedings under this Part).

(4) A person falls within this subsection in relation to a child if—

(a) he is a parent of the child; or
(b) he has or has had parental responsibility for the child.

(5) If a child has been adopted or falls within subsection (7), two persons are also associated with each other for the purposes of this Part if—

(a) one is a natural parent of the child or a parent of such a natural parent; and
(b) the other is the child or any person—

(i) who has become a parent of the child by virtue of an adoption order or has applied for an adoption order, or

(ii) with whom the child has at any time been placed for adoption.

(6) A body corporate and another person are not, by virtue of subsection (3)(*f*) or (*g*), to be regarded for the purposes of this Part as associated with each other.

(7) A child falls within this subsection if—

(*a*) an adoption agency, within the meaning of section 2 of the Adoption and Children Act 2002, has power to place him for adoption under section 19 of that Act (placing children with parental consent) or he has become the subject of an order under section 21 of that Act (placement orders), or

(*b*) he is freed for adoption by virtue of an order made—

(i) in England and Wales, under section 18 of the Adoption Act 1976,

(ii) in Scotland, under section 18 of the Adoption (Scotland) Act 1978, or

(iii) in Northern Ireland, under Article 17(1) or 18(1) of the Adoption (Northern Ireland) Order 1987.

[Family Law Act 1996, s 62 as amended by the Adoption and Children Act 2002, Sch 3, the Civil Partnership Act 2004, Sch 9 and the Domestic Violence, Crime and Victims Act 2004, Sch 10.]

---

*New para (*ea*) inserted by the Domestic Violence, Crime and Victims Act 2004, s 4 from a date to be appointed.

1. Since Part IV of the Act is designed to provide swift and accessible protective remedies to persons of both sexes who are the victims of domestic violence, s 62(3) should be given a purposive construction and courts should not decline jurisdiction unless the facts of the case are plainly incapable of being brought within the statute (*G v F (non-molestation order: jurisdiction)* [2000] 2 FCR 638, [2000] 2 FLR 533).

6–3111 63. Interpretation of Part IV. (1) In this Part—

"adoption order" means an adoption order within the meaning of section 72(1) of the Adoption Act 1976 or section 46(1) of the Adoption and Children Act 2002;

"associated", in relation to a person, is to be read with section 62(3) to (6);

"child" means a person under the age of eighteen years;

"cohabit", "cohabitant" and "former cohabitant" have the meaning given by section 62(1);

"the court" is to be read with section 57;

"development" means physical, intellectual, emotional, social or behavioural development;

"dwelling-house" includes (subject to subsection (4))—

(*a*) any building or part of a building which is occupied as a dwelling;

(*b*) any caravan, house-boat or structure which is occupied as a dwelling,

and any yard, garden, garage or outhouse belonging to it and occupied with it;

"family proceedings" means any proceedings—

(*a*) under the inherent jurisdiction of the High Court in relation to children; or

(*b*) under the enactments mentioned in subsection (2);

"harm"—

(*a*) in relation to a person who has reached the age of eighteen years, means ill-treatment or the impairment of health; and

(*b*) in relation to a child, means ill-treatment or the impairment of health or development;

"health" includes physical or mental health;

"home" rights" has the meaning given by section 30;

"ill-treatment" includes forms of ill-treatment which are not physical and, in relation to a child, includes sexual abuse;

"mortgage", "mortgagor" and "mortgagee" have the same meaning as in the Law of Property Act 1925;

"mortgage payments" includes any payments which, under the terms of the mortgage, the mortgagor is required to make to any person;

"non-molestation order" has the meaning given by section 42(1);

"occupation order" has the meaning given by section 39;

"parental responsibility" has the same meaning as in the Children Act 1989;

"relative", in relation to a person, means—

(*a*) the father, mother, stepfather, stepmother, son, daughter, stepson, stepdaughter, grandmother, grandfather, grandson or granddaughter of that person or of that person's spouse or former spouse, or

(*b*) the brother, sister, uncle, aunt, niece, nephew or first cousin (whether of the full blood or of the half blood or by marriage or civil partnership) of that person or of that person's spouse, former spouse civil partner or former civil partner, and includes, in relation to a person who is cohabiting or has cohabited with another person, any person who would fall within paragraph (*a*) or (*b*) if the parties were married to each other or were civil partners of each other;

"relevant child", in relation to any proceedings under this Part, has the meaning given by section 62(2);

"the relevant judicial authority", in relation to any order under this Part, means—

(*a*) where the order was made by the High Court, a judge of that court;

(*b*) where the order was made by the county court, a judge or district judge of that or any other county court; or

(*c*) where the order was made by a magistrates' court, any magistrates' court.

(2) The enactments referred to in the definition of "family proceedings" are—

(*a*) Part II;

(*b*) this Part;

(*c*) the Matrimonial Causes Act 1973;

(*d*) the Adoption Act 1976;

(*e*) the Domestic Proceedings and Magistrates' Courts Act 1978;

(*f*) Part III of the Matrimonial and Family Proceedings Act 1984;

(*g*) Parts I, II and IV of the Children Act 1989;

(*h*) section 30 of the Human Fertilisation and Embryology Act 1990;

(*i*) the Adoption and Children Act 2002;

(*j*) Schedules 5 to 7 of the Civil Partnership Act 2004.

(3) Where the question of whether harm suffered by a child is significant turns on the child's health or development, his health or development shall be compared with that which could reasonably be expected of a similar child.

(4) For the purposes of sections 31, 32, 53 and 54 and such other provisions of this Part (if any) as may be prescribed, this Part is to have effect as if paragraph (*b*) of the definition of "dwelling-house" were omitted.

(5) It is hereby declared that this Part applies as between the parties to a marriage even though either of them is, or has at any time during the marriage been, married to more than one person.

[Family Law Act 1996, s 63 as amended by the Adoption and Children Act 2002, Sch 3, the Civil Partnership Act 2004, Sch 9 and the Domestic Violence, Crime and Victims Act 2004, Sch 10.]

PART V[1]
SUPPLEMENTAL

6–3112   64. Provision for separate representation for children.   (1) The Lord Chancellor may by regulations provide for the separate representation of children in proceedings in England and Wales which relate to any matter in respect of which a question has arisen, or may arise, under—

(*a*) Part II;

(*b*) Part IV;

(*c*) the 1973 Act; or

(*d*) the Domestic Proceedings and Magistrates' Courts Act 1978.

(2) The regulations may provide for such representation only in specified circumstances.

[Family Law Act 1996, s 64.]

---

1. Part V contains ss 66–67.

6–3113   65. Rules, regulations and orders.   (1) Any power to make rules, orders or regulations which is conferred by this Act is exercisable by statutory instrument.

(2) Any statutory instrument made under this Act may—

(*a*) contain such incidental, supplemental, consequential and transitional provision as the Lord Chancellor considers appropriate; and

(*b*) make different provision for different purposes.

(3) Any statutory instrument containing an order, rules or regulations made under this Act, other than an order made under section 5(8) or 67(3), shall be subject to annulment by a resolution of either House of Parliament.

(4) No order shall be made under section 5(8) unless a draft of the order has been laid before, and approved by a resolution of, each House of Parliament.

(5) This section does not apply to rules of court made, or any power to make rules of court, for the purposes of this Act.*

[Family Law Act 1996, s 65.]

***Amended by the Constitutional Reform Act 2005, Sch 4 from a date to be appointed.**

6–3114   66. Consequential amendments, transitional provisions and repeals. (1) Schedule 8 makes minor and consequential amendments.

(2) Schedule 9 provides for the making of other modifications consequential on provisions of this Act, makes transitional provisions and provides for savings.

(3) Schedule 10 repeals certain enactments.

[Family Law Act 1996, s 66.]

6–3115   67. Short title, commencement and extent. (1) This Act may be cited as the Family Law Act 1996.

(2) Section 65 and this section come into force on the passing of this Act.

(3) The other provisions of this Act come into force on such day as the Lord Chancellor may by order[1] appoint; and different days may be appointed for different purposes.

(4) This Act, other than section 17, extends only to England and Wales, except that—

    (*a*)   in Schedule 8—

        (i)   the amendments of section 38 of the Family Law Act 1986 extend also to Northern Ireland;

        (ii)   the amendments of the Judicial Proceedings (Regulation of Reports) Act 1926 extend also to Scotland; and

        (iii)   the amendments of the Maintenance Orders Act 1950, the Civil Jurisdiction and Judgments Act 1982, the Finance Act 1985 and sections 42 and 51 of the Family Law Act 1986 extend also to both Northern Ireland and Scotland; and

    (*b*)   in Schedule 10, the repeal of section 2(1)(*b*) of the Domestic and Appellate Proceedings (Restriction of Publicity) Act 1968 extends also to Scotland.

[Family Law Act 1996, s 67.]

---

1. At the date of going to press, the Family Law Act 1996 (Commencement No 1) Order 1997, SI 1997/1077, the Family Law Act 1996 (Commencement No 2) Order 1997, SI 1997/1892, and the Family Law Act 1996 (Commencement No 3) Order 1998, SI 1998/2572 had been made.

SCHEDULES

Section 32

SCHEDULE 4
PROVISIONS SUPPLEMENTARY TO SECTIONS 30 AND 31

(*As amended by the Land Registration Act 2002, s 133.*)

Interpretation

6–3116   1. (1)   In this Schedule—

    (*a*)   any reference to a solicitor includes a reference to a licensed conveyancer or a recognised body, and

    (*b*)   any reference to a person's solicitor includes a reference to a licensed conveyancer or recognised body acting for that person.

(2)   In sub-paragraph (1)—

"licensed conveyancer" has the meaning given by section 11(2) of the Administration of Justice Act 1985;

"recognised body" means a body corporate for the time being recognised under section 9 (incorporated practices) or section 32 (provision of conveyancing by recognised bodies) of that Act.

Restriction on registration where spouse entitled to more than one charge

6–3117   2. Where one spouse is entitled by virtue of section 31 to a registrable charge in respect of each of two or more dwelling-houses, only one of the charges to which that spouse is so entitled shall be registered under section 31(10) or under section 2 of the Land Charges Act 1972 at any one time, and if any of those charges is registered under either of those provisions the Chief Land Registrar, on being satisfied that any other of them is so registered, shall cancel the registration of the charge first registered.

Contract for sale of house affected by registered charge to include term requiring cancellation of registration before completion

6–3118   3. (1)   Where one spouse is entitled by virtue of section 31 to a charge on an estate in a dwelling-house and the charge is registered under section 31(10) or section 2 of the Land Charges Act 1972, it shall be a term of any contract for the sale of that estate whereby the vendor agrees to give vacant possession of the dwelling-house on completion of the contract that the vendor will before such completion procure the cancellation of the registration of the charge at his expense.

(2)   Sub-paragraph (1) shall not apply to any such contract made by a vendor who is entitled to sell the estate in the dwelling-house freed from any such charge.

(3)   If, on the completion of such a contract as is referred to in sub-paragraph (1), there is delivered to the purchaser or his solicitor an application by the spouse entitled to the charge for the cancellation of the registration of that charge, the term of the contract for which sub-paragraph (1) provides shall be deemed to have been performed.

(4)   This paragraph applies only if and so far as a contrary intention is not expressed in the contract.

(5)   This paragraph shall apply to a contract for exchange as it applies to a contract for sale.

(6) This paragraph shall, with the necessary modifications, apply to a contract for the grant of a lease or underlease of a dwelling-house as it applies to a contract for the sale of an estate in a dwelling-house.

Cancellation of registration after termination of marriage, etc

6–3119 **4.** (1) Where a spouse's matrimonial home rights are a charge on an estate in the dwelling-house and the charge is registered under section 31(10) or under section 2 of the Land Charges Act 1972, the Chief Land Registrar shall, subject to sub-paragraph (2), cancel the registration of the charge if he is satisfied—

  (a) by the production of a certificate or other sufficient evidence, that either spouse is dead, or
  (b) by the production of an official copy of a decree or order of a court, that the marriage in question has been terminated otherwise than by death, or
  (c) by the production of an order of the court, that the spouse's matrimonial home rights constituting the charge have been terminated by the order.

(2) Where—

  (a) the marriage in question has been terminated by the death of the spouse entitled to an estate in the dwelling-house or otherwise than by death, and
  (b) an order affecting the charge of the spouse not so entitled had been made under section 33(5),

then if, after the making of the order, registration of the charge was renewed or the charge registered in pursuance of sub-paragraph (3), the Chief Land Registrar shall not cancel the registration of the charge in accordance with sub-paragraph (1) unless he is also satisfied that the order has ceased to have effect.

(3) Where such an order has been made, then, for the purposes of sub-paragraph (2), the spouse entitled to the charge affected by the order may—

  (a) if before the date of the order the charge was registered under section 31(10) or under section 2 of the Land Charges Act 1972, renew the registration of the charge, and
  (b) if before the said date the charge was not so registered, register the charge under section 31(10) or under section 2 of the Land Charges Act 1972.

(4) Renewal of the registration of a charge in pursuance of sub-paragraph (3) shall be effected in such manner as may be prescribed, and an application for such renewal or for registration of a charge in pursuance of that sub-paragraph shall contain such particulars of any order affecting the charge made under section 33(5) as may be prescribed.

(5) The renewal in pursuance of sub-paragraph (3) of the registration of a charge shall not affect the priority of the charge.

(6) In this paragraph "prescribed" means prescribed by rules made under section 16 of the Land Charges Act 1972 or under land registration rules under the Land Registration Act 2002, as the circumstances of the case require.

Release of matrimonial home rights

6–3120 **5.** (1) A spouse entitled to matrimonial home rights may by a release in writing release those rights or release them as respects part only of the dwelling-house affected by them.

(2) Where a contract is made for the sale of an estate or interest in a dwelling-house, or for the grant of a lease or underlease of a dwelling-house, being (in either case) a dwelling-house affected by a charge registered under section 31(10) or under section 2 of the Land Charges Act 1972, then, without prejudice to sub-paragraph (1), the matrimonial home rights constituting the charge shall be deemed to have been released on the happening of whichever of the following events first occurs—

  (a) the delivery to the purchaser or lessee, as the case may be, or his solicitor on completion of the contract of an application by the spouse entitled to the charge for the cancellation of the registration of the charge; or
  (b) the lodging of such an application at Her Majesty's Land Registry.

Postponement of priority of charge

6–3121 **6.** A spouse entitled by virtue of section 31 to a charge on an estate or interest may agree in writing that any other charge on, or interest in, that estate or interest shall rank in priority to the charge to which that spouse is so entitled.

Section 47(11)   SCHEDULE 5
              POWERS OF HIGH COURT AND COUNTY COURT TO REMAND

Interpretation

6–3122 **1.** In this Schedule "the court" means the High Court or a county court and includes—

  (a) in relation to the High Court, a judge of that court, and
  (b) in relation to a county court, a judge or district judge of that court.

Remand in custody or on bail

6–3123 **2.** (1) Where a court has power to remand a person under section 47, the court may—

  (a) remand him in custody, that is to say, commit him to custody to be brought before the court at the end of the period of remand or at such earlier time as the court may require, or
  (b) remand him on bail—

    (i) by taking from him a recognizance (with or without sureties) conditioned as provided in sub-paragraph (3), or

(ii) by fixing the amount of the recognizances with a view to their being taken subsequently in accordance with paragraph 4 and in the meantime committing the person to custody in accordance with paragraph (*a*).

(2) Where a person is brought before the court after remand, the court may further remand him.

(3) Where a person is remanded on bail under sub-paragraph (1), the court may direct that his recognizance be conditioned for his appearance—

(*a*) before that court at the end of the period of remand, or
(*b*) at every time and place to which during the course of the proceedings the hearing may from time to time be adjourned.

(4) Where a recognizance is conditioned for a person's appearance in accordance with sub-paragraph (1)(*b*), the fixing of any time for him next to appear shall be deemed to be a remand; but nothing in this sub-paragraph or sub-paragraph (3) shall deprive the court of power at any subsequent hearing to remand him afresh.

(5) Subject to paragraph 3, the court shall not remand a person under this paragraph for a period exceeding 8 clear days, except that—

(*a*) if the court remands him on bail, it may remand him for a longer period if he and the other party consent, and
(*b*) if the court adjourns a case under section 48(1), the court may remand him for the period of the adjournment.

(6) Where the court has power under this paragraph to remand a person in custody it may, if the remand is for a period not exceeding 3 clear days, commit him to the custody of a constable.

Further remand

6–3124 **3.** (1) If the court is satisfied that any person who has been remanded under paragraph 2 is unable by reason of illness or accident to appear or be brought before the court at the expiration of the period for which he was remanded, the court may, in his absence, remand him for a further time; and paragraph 2(5) shall not apply.

(2) Notwithstanding anything in paragraph 2(1), the power of the court under sub-paragraph (1) to remand a person on bail for a further time may be exercised by enlarging his recognizance and those of any sureties for him to a later time.

(3) Where a person remanded on bail under paragraph 2 is bound to appear before the court at any time and the court has no power to remand him under sub-paragraph (1), the court may in his absence enlarge his recognizance and those of any sureties for him to a later time; and the enlargement of his recognizance shall be deemed to be a further remand.

Postponement of taking of recognizance

6–3125 **4.** Where under paragraph 2(1)(*b*)(ii) the court fixes the amount in which the principal and his sureties, if any, are to be bound, the recognizance may thereafter be taken by such person as may be prescribed by rules of court, and the same consequences shall follow as if it had been entered into before the court.

6–3126

Section 52 | SCHEDULE 6
AMENDMENTS OF CHILDREN ACT 1989

6–3127

Section 53 | SCHEDULE 7
TRANSFER OF CERTAIN TENANCIES ON DIVORCE ETC. OR ON SEPARATION OF COHABITANTS

6–3128

Section 66(1) | SCHEDULE 8
MINOR AND CONSEQUENTIAL AMENDMENTS

(*As amended by the Access to Justice Act 1999, Sch 15 and the Welfare Reform and Pensions Act 1999, Sch 12.*)
This Schedule is reproduced in an abridged form and contains only those consequential amendments which relate to enactments contained in this Manual.

PART I
AMENDMENTS CONNECTED WITH PART II

(*Repealed*)

Section 66(2) | SCHEDULE 9
MODIFICATIONS, SAVING AND TRANSITIONAL

Transitional arrangements for those who have been living apart

6–3147 **1.** (1) The Lord Chancellor may by order provide for the application of Part II to marital proceedings which—

(*a*) are begun during the transitional period, and
(*b*) relate to parties to a marriage who immediately before the beginning of that period were living apart,

subject to such modifications (which may include omissions) as may be prescribed.

(2) An order made under this paragraph may, in particular, make provision as to the evidence which a party who claims to have been living apart from the other party immediately before the beginning of the transitional period must produce to the court.

(3) In this paragraph—

"marital proceedings" has the same meaning as in section 24;

"prescribed" means prescribed by the order; and

"transitional period" means the period of two years beginning with the day on which section 3 is brought into force."

Modifications of enactments etc.

6–3148   **2.** (1) The Lord Chancellor may by order make such consequential modifications of any enactment or subordinate legislation as appear to him necessary or expedient in consequence of Part II in respect of any reference (in whatever terms) to—

  (*a*) a petition;
  (*b*) the presentation of a petition;
  (*c*) the petitioner or respondent in proceedings on a petition;
  (*d*) proceedings on a petition;
  (*e*) proceedings in connection with any proceedings on a petition;
  (*f*) any other matrimonial proceedings
  (*g*) a decree; or
  (*h*) findings of adultery in any proceedings.

  (2) An order under sub-paragraph (1) may, in particular—

  (*a*) make provision applying generally in relation to enactments and subordinate legislation of a description specified in the order;
  (*b*) modify the effect of sub-paragraph (3) in relation to documents and agreements of a description so specified.

  (3) Otherwise a reference (in whatever terms) in any instrument or agreement to the presentation of a petition or to a decree has effect, in relation to any time after the coming into force of this paragraph—

  (*a*) in the case of a reference to the presentation of a petition, as if it included a reference to the making of a statement; and
  (*b*) in the case of a reference to a decree, as if it included a reference to a divorce order or (as the case may be) a separation order.

6–3149   **3.** If an Act or subordinate legislation—

  (*a*) refers to an enactment repealed or amended by or under this Act, and
  (*b*) was passed or made before the repeal or amendment came into force,

the Lord Chancellor may by order make such consequential modifications of any provision contained in the Act or subordinate legislation as appears to him necessary or expedient in respect of the reference.

Expressions used in paragraphs 2 and 3

6–3150   **4.** In paragraphs 2 and 3—

"decree" means a decree of divorce (whether a decree nisi or a decree which has been made absolute) or a decree of judicial separation;

"instrument" includes any deed, will or other instrument or document;

"petition" means a petition for a decree of divorce or a petition for a decree of judicial separation; and

"subordinate legislation" has the same meaning as in the Interpretation Act 1978.

Proceedings under way

6–3151   **5.** (1) Except for paragraph 6 of this Schedule, nothing in any provision of Part II, Part I of Schedule 8 or Schedule 10—

  (*a*) applies to, or affects—

    (i)   any decree granted before the coming into force of the provision;
    (ii) any proceedings begun, by petition or otherwise, before that time; or
    (iii) any decree granted in any such proceedings;

  (*b*) affects the operation of—

    (i)   the 1973 Act,
    (ii) any other enactment, or
    (iii) any subordinate legislation,

in relation to any such proceedings or decree or to any proceedings in connection with any such proceedings or decree; or

  (*c*) without prejudice to paragraph (*b*), affects any transitional provision having effect under Schedule 1 to the 1973 Act.

  (2) In this paragraph, "subordinate legislation" has the same meaning as in the Interpretation Act 1978.

6–3152   **6.** (1) Section 31 of the 1973 Act has effect as amended by this Act in relation to any order under Part II of the 1973 Act made after the coming into force of the amendments.

  (2) Subsections (7) to (7F) of that section also have effect as amended by this Act in relation to any order made before the coming into force of the amendments.

Interpretation

6–3153   **7.** In paragraphs 8 to 15 "the 1983 Act" means the Matrimonial Homes Act 1983.

Pending applications for orders relating to occupation and molestation

6–3154   **8.** (1) In this paragraph and paragraph 10 "the existing enactments" means—

     (*a*)   the Domestic Violence and Matrimonial Proceedings Act 1976;

     (*b*)   sections 16 to 18 of the Domestic Proceedings and Magistrates' Courts Act 1978; and

     (*c*)   sections 1 and 9 of the 1983 Act.

   (2) Nothing in Part IV, Part III of Schedule 8 or Schedule 10 affects any application for an order or injunction under any of the existing enactments which is pending immediately before the commencement of the repeal of that enactment.

Pending applications under Schedule 1 to the Matrimonial Homes Act 1983

6–3155   **9.** Nothing in Part IV, Part III of Schedule 8 or Schedule 10 affects any application for an order under Schedule 1 to the 1983 Act which is pending immediately before the commencement of the repeal of that Schedule.

Existing orders relating to occupation and molestation

6–3156   **10.** (1) In this paragraph "an existing order" means any order or injunction under any of the existing enactments which—

     (*a*)   is in force immediately before the commencement of the repeal of that enactment; or

     (*b*)   was made or granted after that commencement in proceedings brought before that commencement.

   (2) Subject to sub-paragraphs (3) and (4), nothing in Part IV, Part III of Schedule 8 or Schedule 10—

     (*a*)   prevents an existing order from remaining in force; or

     (*b*)   affects the enforcement of an existing order.

   (3) Nothing in Part IV, Part III of Schedule 8 or Schedule 10 affects any application to extend, vary or discharge an existing order, but the court may, if it thinks it just and reasonable to do so, treat the application as an application for an order under Part IV.

   (4) The making of an order under Part IV between parties with respect to whom an existing order is in force discharges the existing order.

Matrimonial home rights

6–3157   **11.** (1) Any reference (however expressed) in any enactment, instrument or document (whether passed or made before or after the passing of this Act) to rights of occupation under, or within the meaning of, the 1983 Act shall be construed, so far as is required for continuing the effect of the instrument or document, as being or as the case requires including a reference to matrimonial home rights under, or within the meaning of, Part IV.

   (2) Any reference (however expressed) in this Act or in any other enactment, instrument or document (including any enactment amended by Schedule 8) to matrimonial home rights under, or within the meaning of, Part IV shall be construed as including, in relation to times, circumstances and purposes before the commencement of sections 30 to 32, a reference to rights of occupation under, or within the meaning of, the 1983 Act.

6–3158   **12.** (1) Any reference (however expressed) in any enactment, instrument or document (whether passed or made before or after the passing of this Act) to registration under section 2(8) of the 1983 Act shall, in relation to any time after the commencement of sections 30 to 32, be construed as being or as the case requires including a reference to registration under section 31(10).

   (2) Any reference (however expressed) in this Act or in any other enactment, instrument or document (including any enactment amended by Schedule 8) to registration under section 31(10) shall be construed as including a reference to—

     (*a*)   registration under section 2(7) of the Matrimonial Homes Act 1967 or section 2(8) of the 1983 Act, and

     (*b*)   registration by caution duly lodged under section 2(7) of the Matrimonial Homes Act 1967 before 14th February 1983 (the date of the commencement of section 4(2) of the Matrimonial Homes and Property Act 1981).

6–3159   **13.** In sections 30 and 31 and Schedule 4—

     (*a*)   any reference to an order made under section 33 shall be construed as including a reference to an order made under section 1 of the 1983 Act, and

     (*b*)   any reference to an order made under section 33(5) shall be construed as including a reference to an order made under section 1 of the 1983 Act by virtue of section 2(4) of that Act.

6–3160   **14.** Neither section 31(11) nor the repeal by the Matrimonial Homes and Property Act 1981 of the words "or caution" in section 2(7) of the Matrimonial Homes Act 1967, affects any caution duly lodged as respects any estate or interest before 14th February 1983.

6–3161   **15.** Nothing in this Schedule is to be taken to prejudice the operation of sections 16 and 17 of the Interpretation Act 1978 (which relate to the effect of repeals).

SCHEDULE 10
REPEALS

This Schedule is reproduced in an abridged form and contains only those repeals which affect enactments contained in this Manual.

Chapter	Short title	Extent of repeal
1973 c 18	The Matrimonial Causes Act 1973	In section 25(2)(h), the words "in the case of proceedings for divorce or nullity of marriage,"
1978 c 22	The Domestic Proceedings and Magistrates' Court Act 1978.	In section 7(1), the words "neither party having deserted the other"
		Sections 16 to 18
		Section 28(2)
		Section 63(3)
		In Schedule 2, paragraphs 38 and 53
1980 c 43	The Magistrates' Court Act 1980.	In section 18(1)(d), the words "divorce or"
1989 c 41	The Children Act 1989.	In Schedule 11, paragraph 6(b)
		In Schedule 13, paragraphs 33
1990 c 41	The Courts and Legal Services Act 1990.	In Schedule 18, paragraph 21

Adoption (Intercountry Aspects) Act 1999
(1999 c 18)

6-3163 This Act regulates intercountry adoptions and gives effect to the Convention on Protection of Children and Co-operation in respect of Intercountry Adoption concluded at the Hague on 29 May 1993 by making amendments to the Adoption Act 1976 (now repealed and replaced by the Adoption and Children Act 2002), and effect is given to the Convention by the Intercountry Adoption (Hague Convention) Regulations 2003, SI 2003/118 amended by SI 2004/1868 made under s 1 of the 1999 Act. Jurisdiction is conferred on the High Court and county courts (but not magistrates' courts) by s 62(4) of the 1976 Act.

Human Reproductive Cloning Act 2001[1]
(2001 c 23)

6-3190 **1. The offence.** (1) A person who places in a woman a human embryo which has been created otherwise than by fertilisation is guilty of an offence.

(2) A person who is guilty of the offence is liable on conviction on indictment to imprisonment for a term not exceeding 10 years or a fine or both.

(3) No proceedings for the offence may be instituted—

(a) in England and Wales, except with the consent of the Director of Public Prosecutions;

(b) in Northern Ireland, except with the consent of the Director of Public Prosecutions for Northern Ireland.

---

1. This Act was passed because the High Court held (in a ruling later reversed by the Court of Appeal (see *R (on the application of Quantavalle) v Secretary of State for Health* [2002] EWCA Civ 29, [2002] 2 All ER 625, [2002] 2 WLR 550, [2002] 2 FCR 140) that embryos created by cell nuclear replacement were not governed by the Human Fertilisation and Embryology Act 1990 Act. It puts the ban on human reproductive cloning on a statutory footing by rendering it a criminal offence.

6-3191 **2. Short title and extent.** (1) This Act may be cited as the Human Reproductive Cloning Act 2001.

(2) This Act extends to Northern Ireland.

(3) Her Majesty may by Order in Council direct that any of the provisions of this Act are to extend, with such exceptions, adaptations and modifications (if any) as may be specified in the Order, to any of the Channel Islands.

Adoption and Children Act 2002[1]
(2002 c 38)

PART 1
ADOPTION[2]

CHAPTER 1
INTRODUCTORY[3]

6-3195A **1. Considerations applying to the exercise of powers.** (1) This section applies whenever a court or adoption agency is coming to a decision relating to the adoption of a child.

(2) The paramount consideration of the court or adoption agency must be the child's welfare, throughout his life.

(3) The court or adoption agency must at all times bear in mind that, in general, any delay in coming to the decision is likely to prejudice the child's welfare.

(4) The court or adoption agency must have regard to the following matters (among others)—

(a) the child's ascertainable wishes and feelings regarding the decision (considered in the light of the child's age and understanding),

(b) the child's particular needs,

(c) the likely effect on the child (throughout his life) of having ceased to be a member of the original family and become an adopted person,

(d) the child's age, sex, background and any of the child's characteristics which the court or agency considers relevant,

(e) any harm (within the meaning of the Children Act 1989 (c 41)) which the child has suffered or is at risk of suffering,

(f) the relationship which the child has with relatives, and with any other person in relation to whom the court or agency considers the relationship to be relevant, including—

(i) the likelihood of any such relationship continuing and the value to the child of its doing so,

(ii) the ability and willingness of any of the child's relatives, or of any such person, to provide the child with a secure environment in which the child can develop, and otherwise to meet the child's needs,

(iii) the wishes and feelings of any of the child's relatives, or of any such person, regarding the child.

(5) In placing the child for adoption, the adoption agency must give due consideration to the child's religious persuasion, racial origin and cultural and linguistic background.

(6) The court or adoption agency must always consider the whole range of powers available to it in the child's case (whether under this Act or the Children Act 1989); and the court must not make any order under this Act unless it considers that making the order would be better for the child than not doing so.

(7) In this section, "coming to a decision relating to the adoption of a child", in relation to a court, includes—

(a) coming to a decision in any proceedings where the orders that might be made by the court include an adoption order (or the revocation of such an order), a placement order (or the revocation of such an order) or an order under section 26 (or the revocation or variation of such an order),

(b) coming to a decision about granting leave in respect of any action (other than the initiation of proceedings in any court) which may be taken by an adoption agency or individual under this Act,

but does not include coming to a decision about granting leave in any other circumstances.

(8) For the purposes of this section—

(a) references to relationships are not confined to legal relationships,

(b) references to a relative, in relation to a child, include the child's mother and father.

[Adoption and Children Act 2002, s 1.]

---

1. The Act received the Royal Assent on 7 November 2002, but only ss 116 and 117, and Sch 6 came into immediate effect. By December 2005, however, nearly all of the Act's provisions had been brought into force in relation to England, and most of its provisions had been brought into force in relation to Wales.

The purpose of the Act is to reform adoption law, to implement the proposals in the white paper *Adoption – a new approach* (2000) Cm 5017 (Dept of Health), to underpin the government's programme to improve the performance of the adoption service and to promote greater use of adoption.

The Act replaces the Adoption Act 1976 (except provisions about the status of children already adopted) and reforms the existing legal framework for domestic and intercountry adoptions in England and Wales. It also consolidates some of the provisions of the Adoption (Intercountry Aspects) Act 1999.

The Act affects all adoptions/arrangements to adopt children in England and Wales and all adoption applications from persons resident and settled in England and Wales who seek to adopt children living abroad.

The Act is in three parts. Part 1 of the Act (ss 1–110) is concerned with the framework of adoption law in England and Wales. Chapter 1 (s 1 only) aligns adoption law with the relevant provisions of the Children Act 1989 by ensuring that the child's welfare is the paramount consideration in all decisions relating to adoption. Chapter 2 (ss 2–17) covers the adoption service. Principally, it places a duty on local authorities in England and Wales to maintain an adoption service. Chapter 3 (ss 18–65) covers placement for adoption and adoption orders. It introduces placement by consent and placement orders, provides for the removal of children who are or may be placed for adoption and provides for adoption orders. It also provides for disclosure of information prior to and following a person's adoption (as to providing information in relation to pre-commencement adoptions, see s 98). Chapter 4 (ss 66–76) deals with the status of adopted children. Chapter 5 (ss 77–82) provides for the Adopted Children Register. Chapter 6 (ss 83–91) deals with intercountry adoption. Chapter 7 (ss 92–110) contains miscellaneous provisions. These include provision for offences relating to arranging adoptions, reports and making certain payments.

Part 2 (ss 111–122) makes amendments to the Children Act 1989. It provides for the automatic acquisition of parental responsibility where an unmarried father registers the child's birth jointly with the mother; introduces a more straightforward process for step-parents to acquire parental responsibility; provides for a local authority foster parent to apply for a s 8 order after the child has lived with him for 1 year rather than 3 years; provides for enhanced residence orders and special guardianship; makes provision in respect of local authorities' powers to provide accommodation for children in need; amends the complaints procedure, inter alia, by allowing for regulations to impose time limits for the making of representations; provides for care plans and the review of care plans for looked after children; places a duty on local authorities to provide for the arrangement of advocacy services for looked after children and young people leaving care that wish to make a complaint under the Children Act 1989; amends the definition of "harm" in s 31 of the Children Act 1989 by inserting at the end, as an example, "impairment suffered from seeing or hearing the ill-treatment of another"; and provides for the representation of children in proceedings.

Part 3 (ss 123–150 and the Schedules) provides, in Chapter 1, for restrictions on advertising, an Adoption and Children Act register, and makes other miscellaneous provisions. Chapter 2 contains final provisions. Schedules 1–6 are concerned, respectively, with the registration of adoptions; disclosure of birth records; minor and consequential amendments; transitional and transitory provisions and savings; repeals; and glossary of terms.

    2. Part 1 contains ss 1–110.

    3. Chapter 1 contains only s 1.

CHAPTER 2

THE ADOPTION SERVICE[1]

The Adoption Service

6–3195B 2. Basic definitions. (1) The services maintained by local authorities under section 3(1) may be collectively referred to as "the Adoption Service", and a local authority or registered adoption society may be referred to as an adoption agency.

(2) In this Act, "registered adoption society" means a voluntary organisation which is an adoption society registered under Part 2 of the Care Standards Act 2000 (c 14); but in relation to the provision of any facility of the Adoption Service, references to a registered adoption society or to an adoption agency do not include an adoption society which is not registered in respect of that facility.

(3) A registered adoption society is to be treated as registered in respect of any facility of the Adoption Service unless it is a condition of its registration that it does not provide that facility.

(4) No application for registration under Part 2 of the Care Standards Act 2000 may be made in respect of an adoption society which is an unincorporated body.

(5) In this Act—

"the 1989 Act" means the Children Act 1989 (c 41),

"adoption society" means a body whose functions consist of or include making arrangements for the adoption of children,

"voluntary organisation" means a body other than a public or local authority the activities of which are not carried on for profit.

(6) In this Act, "adoption support services" means—

(*a*) counselling, advice and information, and

(*b*) any other services prescribed by regulations[2],

in relation to adoption.

(7) The power to make regulations under subsection (6)(*b*) is to be exercised so as to secure that local authorities provide financial support.[3]

(8) In this Chapter, references to adoption are to the adoption of persons, wherever they may be habitually resident, effected under the law of any country or territory, whether within or outside the British Islands.[3]

[Adoption and Children Act 2002, s 2.]

    [1.] Chapter 2 contains ss 2–17.

    2. The Adoption Support Services Regulations 2005, SI 2005/691 amended by SI 2005/3482, the Adoption Support Services (Local Authorities) (Wales) Regulations 2005, SI 2005/1512, the Adoption Support Agencies (Wales) Regulations 2005, SI 2005/1514, the Adoption Support Agencies (England) and Adoption Agencies (Miscellaneous Amendments) Regulations 2005, SI 2005/2720 and the Adoption Information and Intermediary Services (Pre-Commencement Adoptions) (Wales) Regulations 2005, SI 2005/2701 amended by SI 2005/3293 have been made.

    3. Subsections (7) and (8) in force in Wales from 28 November 2003 for the purposes of para 3 of Sch 4: SI 2003/3079.

6–3195C 3. Maintenance of Adoption Service. (1) Each local authority must continue to maintain within their area a service designed to meet the needs, in relation to adoption, of—

(*a*) children who may be adopted, their parents and guardians,

(*b*) persons wishing to adopt a child, and

(*c*) adopted persons, their parents, natural parents and former guardians;

and for that purpose must provide the requisite facilities.

(2) Those facilities must include making, and participating in, arrangements—

(*a*) for the adoption of children, and

(*b*) for the provision of adoption support services.

(3) As part of the service, the arrangements made for the purposes of subsection (2)(*b*)—

(*a*) must extend to the provision of adoption support services to persons who are within a description prescribed by regulations[1],

(*b*) may extend to the provision of those services to other persons.

(4) A local authority may provide any of the requisite facilities by securing their provision by—

(*a*) registered adoption societies, or

(*b*) other persons who are within a description prescribed by regulations[2] of persons who may provide the facilities in question.

(5) The facilities of the service must be provided in conjunction with the local authority's other social services and with registered adoption societies in their area, so that help may be given in a co-ordinated manner without duplication, omission or avoidable delay.

(6) The social services referred to in subsection (5) are the functions of a local authority which are social services functions within the meaning of the Local Authority Social Services Act 1970 (c 42) (which include, in particular, those functions in so far as they relate to children).

[Adoption and Children Act 2002, s 3.]

---

1. See the Adoption Support Services Regulations 2005, SI 2005/691 amended by SI 2005/3482 and the Adoption Support Services (Local Authorities) (Wales) Regulations 2005, SI 2005/1512.

2. See the Adoption Support Services Regulations 2005, SI 2005/691 amended by SI 2005/3482, the Adoption Support Services (Local Authorities) (Wales) Regulations 2005, SI 2005/1512 and the Local Authority (Adoption) (Miscellaneous Provisions) Regulations 2005, SI 2005/3390.

6–3195D **4. Assessments etc for adoption support services.**   (1) A local authority must at the request of—

(*a*) any of the persons mentioned in paragraphs (*a*) to (*c*) of section 3(1), or

(*b*) any other person who falls within a description prescribed by regulations (subject to subsection (7)(*a*)),

carry out an assessment of that person's needs for adoption support services.

(2) A local authority may, at the request of any person, carry out an assessment of that person's needs for adoption support services.

(3) A local authority may request the help of the persons mentioned in paragraph (*a*) or (*b*) of section 3(4) in carrying out an assessment.

(4) Where, as a result of an assessment, a local authority decide that a person has needs for adoption support services, they must then decide whether to provide any such services to that person.

(5) If—

(*a*) a local authority decide to provide any adoption support services to a person, and

(*b*) the circumstances fall within a description prescribed by regulations,

the local authority must prepare a plan in accordance with which adoption support services are to be provided to the person and keep the plan under review.

(6) Regulations[1] may make provision about assessments, preparing and reviewing plans, the provision of adoption support services in accordance with plans and reviewing the provision of adoption support services.

(7) The regulations may in particular make provision—

(*a*) as to the circumstances in which a person mentioned in paragraph (*b*) of subsection (1) is to have a right to request an assessment of his needs in accordance with that subsection,

(*b*) about the type of assessment which, or the way in which an assessment, is to be carried out,

(*c*) about the way in which a plan is to be prepared,

(*d*) about the way in which, and time at which, a plan or the provision of adoption support services is to be reviewed,

(*e*) about the considerations to which a local authority are to have regard in carrying out an assessment or review or preparing a plan,

(*f*) as to the circumstances in which a local authority may provide adoption support services subject to conditions,

(*g*) as to the consequences of conditions imposed by virtue of paragraph (*f*) not being met (including the recovery of any financial support provided by a local authority),

(*h*) as to the circumstances in which this section may apply to a local authority in respect of persons who are outside that local authority's area,

(*i*) as to the circumstances in which a local authority may recover from another local authority the expenses of providing adoption support services to any person.

(8) A local authority may carry out an assessment of the needs of any person under this section at the same time as an assessment of his needs is made under any other enactment.

(9) If at any time during the assessment of the needs of any person under this section, it appears to a local authority that—

(*a*) there may be a need for the provision of services to that person by a Primary Care Trust (in Wales, a Health Authority or Local Health Board), or

(*b*) there may be a need for the provision to him of any services which fall within the functions of a local education authority (within the meaning of the Education Act 1996 (c 56)), the local authority must notify that Primary Care Trust, Health Authority, Local Health Board or local education authority.

(10) Where it appears to a local authority that another local authority could, by taking any specified action, help in the exercise of any of their functions under this section, they may request the help of that other local authority, specifying the action in question.

(11) A local authority whose help is so requested must comply with the request if it is consistent with the exercise of their functions.

[Adoption and Children Act 2002, s 4.]

---

1. The Adoption Support Services Regulations 2005, SI 2005/691 amended by SI 2005/3482 and the Adoption Support Services (Local Authorities) (Wales) Regulations 2005, SI 2005/1512 have been made.

6–3195E   5. Local authority plans for adoption services.   (1) Each local authority must prepare a plan for the provision of the services maintained under section 3(1) and secure that it is published.

(2) The plan must contain information of a description prescribed by regulations (subject to subsection (4)(b)).

(3) The regulations may make provision requiring local authorities—

(a)   to review any plan,

(b)   in the circumstances prescribed by the regulations, to modify that plan and secure its publication or to prepare a plan in substitution for that plan and secure its publication.

(4) The appropriate Minister may direct—

(a)   that a plan is to be included in another document specified in the direction,

(b)   that the requirements specified in the direction as to the description of information to be contained in a plan are to have effect in place of the provision made by regulations under subsection (2).

(5) Directions may be given by the appropriate Minister for the purpose of making provision in connection with any duty imposed by virtue of this section including, in particular, provision as to—

(a)   the form and manner in which, and the time at which, any plan is to be published,

(b)   the description of persons who are to be consulted in the preparation of any plan,

(c)   the time at which any plan is to be reviewed.

(6) Subsections (2) to (5) apply in relation to a modified or substituted plan (or further modified or substituted plan) as they apply in relation to a plan prepared under subsection (1).

(7) Directions given under this section may relate—

(a)   to a particular local authority,

(b)   to any class or description of local authorities, or

(c)   except in the case of a direction given under subsection (4)(b), to local authorities generally,

and accordingly different provision may be made in relation to different local authorities or classes or descriptions of local authorities.

[Adoption and Children Act 2002, s 5.]

6–3195F   6. Arrangements on cancellation of registration.   Where, by virtue of the cancellation of its registration under Part 2 of the Care Standards Act 2000 (c 14), a body has ceased to be a registered adoption society, the appropriate Minister may direct the body to make such arrangements as to the transfer of its functions relating to children and other transitional matters as seem to him expedient.

[Adoption and Children Act 2002, s 6.]

6–3195G   7. Inactive or defunct adoption societies etc.   (1) This section applies where it appears to the appropriate Minister that—

(a)   a body which is or has been a registered adoption society is inactive or defunct, or

(b)   a body which has ceased to be a registered adoption society by virtue of the cancellation of its registration under Part 2 of the Care Standards Act 2000 has not made such arrangements for the transfer of its functions relating to children as are specified in a direction given by him.

(2) The appropriate Minister may, in relation to such functions of the society as relate to children, direct what appears to him to be the appropriate local authority to take any such action as might have been taken by the society or by the society jointly with the authority.

(3) A local authority are entitled to take any action which—

(a)   apart from this subsection the authority would not be entitled to take, or would not be entitled to take without joining the society in the action, but

(b)   they are directed to take under subsection (2).

(4) The appropriate Minister may charge the society for expenses necessarily incurred by him or on his behalf in securing the transfer of its functions relating to children.

(5) Before giving a direction under subsection (2) the appropriate Minister must, if practicable, consult both the society and the authority.

[Adoption and Children Act 2002, s 7.]

6–3195H   8. Adoption support agencies.   (1) In this Act, "adoption support agency" means an undertaking the purpose of which, or one of the purposes of which, is the provision of adoption support services; but an undertaking is not an adoption support agency—

(*a*)   merely because it provides information in connection with adoption other than for the purpose mentioned in section 98(1), or

(*b*)   if it is excepted by virtue of subsection (2).

"Undertaking" has the same meaning as in the Care Standards Act 2000 (c 14).

(2) The following are excepted—

(*a*)   a registered adoption society, whether or not the society is registered in respect of the provision of adoption support services,

(*b*)   a local authority,

(*c*)   a local education authority (within the meaning of the Education Act 1996 (c 56)),

(*d*)   a Special Health Authority, Primary Care Trust (in Wales, a Health Authority or Local Health Board) or NHS trust,

(*e*)   the Registrar General,

(*f*)   any person, or description of persons, excepted by regulations[1].

(3) In section 4 of the Care Standards Act 2000 (basic definitions)—

(*a*)   after subsection (7) there is inserted—

"(7A) "Adoption support agency" has the meaning given by section 8 of the Adoption and Children Act 2002.",

(*b*)   in subsection (9)(*a*) (construction of references to descriptions of agencies), for "or a voluntary adoption agency" there is substituted "a voluntary adoption agency or an adoption support agency".

[Adoption and Children Act 2002, s 8.]

---

1. The Adoption Support Agencies (England) and Adoption Agencies (Miscellaneous Amendments) Regulations 2005, SI 2005/2720 have been made.

Regulations

6–3195I   9. General power to regulate adoption etc agencies.   (1) Regulations may make provision for any purpose relating to—

(*a*)   the exercise by local authorities or voluntary adoption agencies of their functions in relation to adoption, or

(*b*)   the exercise by adoption support agencies of their functions in relation to adoption.

(2) The extent of the power to make regulations under this section is not limited by sections 10 to 12, 45, 54, 56 to 65 and 98 or by any other powers exercisable in respect of local authorities, voluntary adoption agencies or adoption support agencies.

(3) Regulations may provide that a person who contravenes or fails to comply with any provision of regulations under this section is to be guilty of an offence and liable on summary conviction to a fine not exceeding level 5 on the standard scale.

(4) In this section and section 10, "voluntary adoption agency" means a voluntary organisation which is an adoption society.

[Adoption and Children Act 2002, s 9.]

6–3195J   10. Management etc of agencies.   (1) In relation to local authorities, voluntary adoption agencies and adoption support agencies, regulations[1] under section 9 may make provision as to—

(*a*)   the persons who are fit to work for them for the purposes of the functions mentioned in section 9(1),

(*b*)   the fitness of premises,

(*c*)   the management and control of their operations,

(*d*)   the number of persons, or persons of any particular type, working for the purposes of those functions,

(*e*)   the management and training of persons working for the purposes of those functions,

(*f*)   the keeping of information.

(2) Regulations made by virtue of subsection (1)(*a*) may, in particular, make provision for prohibiting persons from working in prescribed positions unless they are registered in, or in a particular part of, one of the registers maintained under section 56(1) of the Care Standards Act 2000 (c 14) (registration of social care workers).

(3) In relation to voluntary adoption agencies and adoption support agencies, regulations under section 9 may—

(a) make provision as to the persons who are fit to manage an agency, including provision prohibiting persons from doing so unless they are registered in, or in a particular part of, one of the registers referred to in subsection (2),

(b) impose requirements as to the financial position of an agency,

(c) make provision requiring the appointment of a manager,

(d) in the case of a voluntary adoption agency, make provision for securing the welfare of children placed by the agency, including provision as to the promotion and protection of their health,

(e) in the case of an adoption support agency, make provision as to the persons who are fit to carry on the agency.

(4) Regulations under section 9 may make provision as to the conduct of voluntary adoption agencies and adoption support agencies, and may in particular make provision—

(a) as to the facilities and services to be provided by an agency,

(b) as to the keeping of accounts,

(c) as to the notification to the registration authority of events occurring in premises used for the purposes of an agency,

(d) as to the giving of notice to the registration authority of periods during which the manager of an agency proposes to be absent, and specifying the information to be given in such a notice,

(e) as to the making of adequate arrangements for the running of an agency during a period when its manager is absent,

(f) as to the giving of notice to the registration authority of any intended change in the identity of the manager,

(g) as to the giving of notice to the registration authority of changes in the ownership of an agency or the identity of its officers,

(h) requiring the payment of a prescribed fee to the registration authority in respect of any notification required to be made by virtue of paragraph (g),

(i) requiring arrangements to be made for dealing with complaints made by or on behalf of those seeking, or receiving, any of the services provided by an agency and requiring the agency or manager to take steps for publicising the arrangements.

[Adoption and Children Act 2002, s 10.]

---

1. The following regulations have been made:

Adoption Agencies Regulations 2005, in this Part, Statutory Instruments and Practice Directions on Family Law, post;
Adoption Support Services Regulations 2005, SI 2005/691 amended by SI 2005/3482;
Disclosure of Adoption Information (Post-commencement Adoptions) Regulations 2005, SI 2005/888 amended by SI 2005/3482;
Adoption Information and Intermediary Services (Pre-Commencement Adoptions) Regulations 2005, SI 2005/890 amended by SI 2005/2720 (E) and 3482;
Adoption Agencies (Wales) Regulations 2005, SI 2005/1313;
Adoption Support Services (Local Authorities) (Wales) Regulations 2005, SI 2005/1512;
Adoption Support Agencies (Wales) Regulations 2005, SI 2005/1514;
Suitability of Adopters Regulations 2005, SI 2005/1712; Independent Review of Determinations (Adoption) (Wales) Regulations 2005, SI 2005/1819;
Access to Information (Post-commencement Adoptions) (Wales) Regulations 2005, SI 2005/2689;
Adoption Support Agencies (England) and Adoption Agencies (Miscellaneous Amendments) Regulations 2005, SI 2005/2720;
Adoption Information and Intermediary Services (Pre-Commencement Adoptions) (Wales) Regulations 2005, SI 2005/2701 amended by SI 2005/3293;
Local Authorities (Prescribed Fees) (Adoptions with a Foreign Element) (Wales) Regulations 2005, SI 2005/3114;
Local Authority (Non-agency) Adoptions (Wales) Regulations 2005, SI 2005/3113;
Local Authority Adoption Service (Wales) Regulations 2005, SI 2005/3115;
Independent Review of Determinations (Adoption) Regulations 2005, SI 2005/3332;
Local Authority (Adoption) (Miscellaneous Provisions) Regulations 2005, SI 2005/3390.

6–3195K   11. Fees.   (1) Regulations under section 9 may prescribe—

(a) the fees which may be charged by adoption agencies in respect of the provision of services to persons providing facilities as part of the Adoption Service (including the Adoption Services in Scotland and Northern Ireland),

(b) the fees which may be paid by adoption agencies to persons providing or assisting in providing such facilities.

(2) Regulations under section 9 may prescribe the fees which may be charged by local authorities in respect of the provision of prescribed facilities of the Adoption Service where the following conditions are met.

(3) The conditions are that the facilities are provided in connection with—

(a) the adoption of a child brought into the United Kingdom for the purpose of adoption, or (*b*)   a Convention adoption, an overseas adoption or an adoption effected under the law of a country or territory outside the British Islands.

(4) Regulations under section 9 may prescribe the fees which may be charged by adoption agencies in respect of the provision of counselling, where the counselling is provided in connection with the disclosure of information in relation to a person's adoption.

[Adoption and Children Act 2002, s 11.]

6–3195L   12. Independent review of determinations.   *Provision for regulations made under s 9.*

Supplemental

6–3195M   13. Information concerning adoption.   (1) Each adoption agency must give to the appropriate Minister any statistical or other general information he requires about—

(*a*)   its performance of all or any of its functions relating to adoption,
(*b*)   the children and other persons in relation to whom it has exercised those functions.

(2) The following persons—

(*a*)   the justices' chief executive for each magistrates' court,
(*b*)   the relevant officer of each county court,
(*c*)   the relevant officer of the High Court,

must give to the appropriate Minister any statistical or other general information he requires about the proceedings under this Act of the court in question.

(3) In subsection (2), "relevant officer", in relation to a county court or the High Court, means the officer of that court who is designated to act for the purposes of that subsection by a direction given by the Lord Chancellor.

(4) The information required to be given to the appropriate Minister under this section must be given at the times, and in the form, directed by him.

(5) The appropriate Minister may publish from time to time abstracts of the information given to him under this section.

[Adoption and Children Act 2002, s 13.]

6–3195N   14. Default power of appropriate Minister.   (1) If the appropriate Minister is satisfied that any local authority have failed, without reasonable excuse, to comply with any of the duties imposed on them by virtue of this Act or of section 1 or 2(4) of the Adoption (Intercountry Aspects) Act 1999 (c 18), he may make an order declaring that authority to be in default in respect of that duty.

(2) An order under subsection (1) must give the appropriate Minister's reasons for making it.

(3) An order under subsection (1) may contain such directions as appear to the appropriate Minister to be necessary for the purpose of ensuring that, within the period specified in the order, the duty is complied with.

(4) Any such directions are enforceable, on the appropriate Minister's application, by a mandatory order.

[Adoption and Children Act 2002, s 14.]

6–3195O   15. Inspection of premises etc.   (1) The appropriate Minister may arrange for any premises in which—

(*a*)   a child is living with a person with whom the child has been placed by an adoption agency, or
(*b*)   a child in respect of whom a notice of intention to adopt has been given under section 44 is, or will be, living,

to be inspected from time to time.

(2) The appropriate Minister may require an adoption agency—

(*a*)   to give him any information, or
(*b*)   to allow him to inspect any records (in whatever form they are held),

relating to the discharge of any of its functions in relation to adoption which the appropriate Minister specifies.

(3) An inspection under this section must be conducted by a person authorised by the appropriate Minister.

(4) An officer of a local authority may only be so authorised with the consent of the authority.

(5) A person inspecting any premises under subsection (1) may—

(*a*)   visit the child there,
(*b*)   make any examination into the state of the premises and the treatment of the child there which he thinks fit.

(6) A person authorised to inspect any records under this section may at any reasonable time have access to, and inspect and check the operation of, any computer (and associated apparatus) which is being or has been used in connection with the records in question.

(7) A person authorised to inspect any premises or records under this section may—

(a) enter the premises for that purpose at any reasonable time,
(b) require any person to give him any reasonable assistance he may require.

(8) A person exercising a power under this section must, if required to do so, produce a duly authenticated document showing his authority.

(9) Any person who intentionally obstructs another in the exercise of a power under this section is guilty of an offence and liable on summary conviction to a fine not exceeding level 3 on the standard scale.
[Adoption and Children Act 2002, s 15.]

6–3195P   16. Distribution of functions in relation to registered adoption societies[1]

___

1. Section 16 inserts a new s 36A in the Care Standards Act 2000.

6–3195Q   17. Inquiries.   (1) The appropriate Minister may cause an inquiry to be held into any matter connected with the functions of an adoption agency.

(2) Before an inquiry is begun, the appropriate Minister may direct that it is to be held in private.
(3) Where no direction has been given, the person holding the inquiry may if he thinks fit hold it, or any part of it, in private.
(4) Subsections (2) to (5) of section 250 of the Local Government Act 1972 (c 70) (powers in relation to local inquiries) apply in relation to an inquiry under this section as they apply in relation to a local inquiry under that section.
[Adoption and Children Act 2002, s 17.]

CHAPTER 3
PLACEMENT FOR ADOPTION AND ADOPTION ORDERS[1]
Placement of children by adoption agency for adoption

6–3195R   18. Placement for adoption by agencies.   (1) An adoption agency may—

(a) place a child for adoption with prospective adopters, or
(b) where it has placed a child with any persons (whether under this Part or not), leave the child with them as prospective adopters,

but, except in the case of a child who is less than six weeks old, may only do so under section 19 or a placement order.

(2) An adoption agency may only place a child for adoption with prospective adopters if the agency is satisfied that the child ought to be placed for adoption.
(3) A child who is placed or authorised to be placed for adoption with prospective adopters by a local authority is looked after by the authority.
(4) If an application for an adoption order has been made by any persons in respect of a child and has not been disposed of—

(a) an adoption agency which placed the child with those persons may leave the child with them until the application is disposed of, but
(b) apart from that, the child may not be placed for adoption with any prospective adopters.

"Adoption order" includes a Scottish or Northern Irish adoption order.

(5) References in this Act (apart from this section) to an adoption agency placing a child for adoption—

(a) are to its placing a child for adoption with prospective adopters, and
(b) include, where it has placed a child with any persons (whether under this Act or not), leaving the child with them as prospective adopters;

and references in this Act (apart from this section) to a child who is placed for adoption by an adoption agency are to be interpreted accordingly.

(6) References in this Chapter to an adoption agency being, or not being, authorised to place a child for adoption are to the agency being or (as the case may be) not being authorised to do so under section 19 or a placement order.
(7) This section is subject to sections 30 to 35 (removal of children placed by adoption agencies).
[Adoption and Children Act 2002, s 18.]

___

1. Chapter 3 contains ss 18–65.

6–3195S   19. Placing children with parental consent.   (1) Where an adoption agency is satisfied that each parent or guardian of a child has consented to the child—

(a) being placed for adoption with prospective adopters identified in the consent, or
(b) being placed for adoption with any prospective adopters who may be chosen by the agency,

and has not withdrawn the consent, the agency is authorised to place the child for adoption accordingly.

(2) Consent to a child being placed for adoption with prospective adopters identified in the consent may be combined with consent to the child subsequently being placed for adoption with any prospective adopters who may be chosen by the agency in circumstances where the child is removed from or returned by the identified prospective adopters.

(3) Subsection (1) does not apply where—

(*a*)　an application has been made on which a care order might be made and the application has not been disposed of, or

(*b*)　a care order or placement order has been made after the consent was given.

(4) References in this Act to a child placed for adoption under this section include a child who was placed under this section with prospective adopters and continues to be placed with them, whether or not consent to the placement has been withdrawn.

(5) This section is subject to section 52 (parental etc consent).

[Adoption and Children Act 2002, s 19.]

6–3195T　20.　Advance consent to adoption.　(1) A parent or guardian of a child who consents to the child being placed for adoption by an adoption agency under section 19 may, at the same or any subsequent time, consent to the making of a future adoption order.

(2) Consent under this section—

(*a*)　where the parent or guardian has consented to the child being placed for adoption with prospective adopters identified in the consent, may be consent to adoption by them, or

(*b*)　may be consent to adoption by any prospective adopters who may be chosen by the agency.

(3) A person may withdraw any consent given under this section.

(4) A person who gives consent under this section may, at the same or any subsequent time, by notice given to the adoption agency—

(*a*)　state that he does not wish to be informed of any application for an adoption order, or

(*b*)　withdraw such a statement.

(5) A notice under subsection (4) has effect from the time when it is received by the adoption agency but has no effect if the person concerned has withdrawn his consent.

(6) This section is subject to section 52 (parental etc consent).

[Adoption and Children Act 2002, s 20.]

6–3195U　21.　Placement orders.　(1) A placement order is an order made by the court authorising a local authority to place a child for adoption with any prospective adopters who may be chosen by the authority.

(2) The court may not make a placement order in respect of a child unless—

(*a*)　the child is subject to a care order,

(*b*)　the court is satisfied that the conditions in section 31(2) of the 1989 Act (conditions for making a care order) are met, or

(*c*)　the child has no parent or guardian.

(3) The court may only make a placement order if, in the case of each parent or guardian of the child, the court is satisfied—

(*a*)　that the parent or guardian has consented to the child being placed for adoption with any prospective adopters who may be chosen by the local authority and has not withdrawn the consent, or

(*b*)　that the parent's or guardian's consent should be dispensed with.

This subsection is subject to section 52 (parental etc consent).

(4) A placement order continues in force until—

(*a*)　it is revoked under section 24,

(*b*)　an adoption order is made in respect of the child, or

(*c*)　the child marries or attains the age of 18 years.

"Adoption order" includes a Scottish or Northern Irish adoption order.

[Adoption and Children Act 2002, s 21.]

6–3195V　22.　Applications for placement orders.　(1) A local authority must apply to the court for a placement order in respect of a child if—

(*a*)　the child is placed for adoption by them or is being provided with accommodation by them,

(*b*)　no adoption agency is authorised to place the child for adoption,

(*c*)　the child has no parent or guardian or the authority consider that the conditions in section 31(2) of the 1989 Act are met, and

(*d*)　the authority are satisfied that the child ought to be placed for adoption.

(2) If—

    (*a*) an application has been made (and has not been disposed of) on which a care order might be made in respect of a child, or

    (*b*) a child is subject to a care order and the appropriate local authority are not authorised to place the child for adoption,

the appropriate local authority must apply to the court for a placement order if they are satisfied that the child ought to be placed for adoption.

    (3) If—

    (*a*) a child is subject to a care order, and

    (*b*) the appropriate local authority are authorised to place the child for adoption under section 19,

the authority may apply to the court for a placement order.

    (4) If a local authority—

    (*a*) are under a duty to apply to the court for a placement order in respect of a child, or

    (*b*) have applied for a placement order in respect of a child and the application has not been disposed of,

the child is looked after by the authority.

    (5) Subsections (1) to (3) do not apply in respect of a child—

    (*a*) if any persons have given notice of intention to adopt, unless the period of four months beginning with the giving of the notice has expired without them applying for an adoption order or their application for such an order has been withdrawn or refused, or

    (*b*) if an application for an adoption order has been made and has not been disposed of.

"Adoption order" includes a Scottish or Northern Irish adoption order.

    (6) Where—

    (*a*) an application for a placement order in respect of a child has been made and has not been disposed of, and

    (*b*) no interim care order is in force,

the court may give any directions it considers appropriate for the medical or psychiatric examination or other assessment of the child; but a child who is of sufficient understanding to make an informed decision may refuse to submit to the examination or other assessment.

    (7) The appropriate local authority—

    (*a*) in relation to a care order, is the local authority in whose care the child is placed by the order, and

    (*b*) in relation to an application on which a care order might be made, is the local authority which makes the application.

[Adoption and Children Act 2002, s 22.]

6–3195W 23. Varying placement orders. (1) The court may vary a placement order so as to substitute another local authority for the local authority authorised by the order to place the child for adoption.

    (2) The variation may only be made on the joint application of both authorities.

[Adoption and Children Act 2002, s 23.]

6–3195X 24. Revoking placement orders. (1) The court may revoke a placement order on the application of any person.

    (2) But an application may not be made by a person other than the child or the local authority authorised by the order to place the child for adoption unless—

    (*a*) the court has given leave to apply, and

    (*b*) the child is not placed for adoption by the authority.

    (3) The court cannot give leave under subsection (2)(*a*) unless satisfied that there has been a change in circumstances since the order was made.

    (4) If the court determines, on an application for an adoption order, not to make the order, it may revoke any placement order in respect of the child.

    (5) Where—

    (*a*) an application for the revocation of a placement order has been made and has not been disposed of, and

    (*b*) the child is not placed for adoption by the authority,

the child may not without the court's leave be placed for adoption under the order.

[Adoption and Children Act 2002, s 24.]

6–3195Y 25. Parental responsibility. (1) This section applies while—

    (*a*) a child is placed for adoption under section 19 or an adoption agency is authorised to place a child for adoption under that section, or

    (*b*) a placement order is in force in respect of a child.

(2) Parental responsibility for the child is given to the agency concerned.

(3) While the child is placed with prospective adopters, parental responsibility is given to them.

(4) The agency may determine that the parental responsibility of any parent or guardian, or of prospective adopters, is to be restricted to the extent specified in the determination.

[Adoption and Children Act 2002, s 25.]

6–3195Z 26. Contact. (1) On an adoption agency being authorised to place a child for adoption, or placing a child for adoption who is less than six weeks old, any provision for contact under the 1989 Act ceases to have effect.

(2) While an adoption agency is so authorised or a child is placed for adoption—

(*a*) no application may be made for any provision for contact under that Act, but

(*b*) the court may make an order under this section requiring the person with whom the child lives, or is to live, to allow the child to visit or stay with the person named in the order, or for the person named in the order and the child otherwise to have contact with each other.

(3) An application for an order under this section may be made by—

(*a*) the child or the agency,

(*b*) any parent, guardian or relative,

(*c*) any person in whose favour there was provision for contact under the 1989 Act which ceased to have effect by virtue of subsection (1),

(*d*) if a residence order was in force immediately before the adoption agency was authorised to place the child for adoption or (as the case may be) placed the child for adoption at a time when he was less than six weeks old, the person in whose favour the order was made,

(*e*) if a person had care of the child immediately before that time by virtue of an order made in the exercise of the High Court's inherent jurisdiction with respect to children, that person,

(*f*) any person who has obtained the court's leave to make the application.

(4) When making a placement order, the court may on its own initiative make an order under this section.

(5) This section does not prevent an application for a contact order under section 8 of the 1989 Act being made where the application is to be heard together with an application for an adoption order in respect of the child.

(6) In this section, "provision for contact under the 1989 Act" means a contact order under section 8 of that Act or an order under section 34 of that Act (parental contact with children in care).

[Adoption and Children Act 2002, s 26.]

6–3196 27. Contact: supplementary. (1) An order under section 26—

(*a*) has effect while the adoption agency is authorised to place the child for adoption or the child is placed for adoption, but

(*b*) may be varied or revoked by the court on an application by the child, the agency or a person named in the order.

(2) The agency may refuse to allow the contact that would otherwise be required by virtue of an order under that section if—

(*a*) it is satisfied that it is necessary to do so in order to safeguard or promote the child's welfare, and

(*b*) the refusal is decided upon as a matter of urgency and does not last for more than seven days.

(3) Regulations[1] may make provision as to—

(*a*) the steps to be taken by an agency which has exercised its power under subsection (2),

(*b*) the circumstances in which, and conditions subject to which, the terms of any order under section 26 may be departed from by agreement between the agency and any person for whose contact with the child the order provides,

(*c*) notification by an agency of any variation or suspension of arrangements made (otherwise than under an order under that section) with a view to allowing any person contact with the child.

(4) Before making a placement order the court must—

(*a*) consider the arrangements which the adoption agency has made, or proposes to make, for allowing any person contact with the child, and

(*b*) invite the parties to the proceedings to comment on those arrangements.

(5) An order under section 26 may provide for contact on any conditions the court considers appropriate.

[Adoption and Children Act 2002, s 27.]

---

1. See the Adoption Agencies Regulations 2005, in this PART, STATUTORY INSTRUMENTS AND PRACTICE DIRECTIONS ON FAMILY LAW, post and the Adoption Agencies (Wales) Regulations 2005, SI 2005/1313.

6–3196A   28. Further consequences of placement.   (1) Where a child is placed for adoption under section 19 or an adoption agency is authorised to place a child for adoption under that section—

(*a*)   a parent or guardian of the child may not apply for a residence order unless an application for an adoption order has been made and the parent or guardian has obtained the court's leave under subsection (3) or (5) of section 47,

(*b*)   if an application has been made for an adoption order, a guardian of the child may not apply for a special guardianship order unless he has obtained the court's leave under subsection (3) or (5) of that section.

(2)   Where—

(*a*)   a child is placed for adoption under section 19 or an adoption agency is authorised to place a child for adoption under that section, or

(*b*)   a placement order is in force in respect of a child,

then (whether or not the child is in England and Wales) a person may not do either of the following things, unless the court gives leave or each parent or guardian of the child gives written consent.

(3)   Those things are—

(*a*)   causing the child to be known by a new surname, or

(*b*)   removing the child from the United Kingdom.

(4)   Subsection (3) does not prevent the removal of a child from the United Kingdom for a period of less than one month by a person who provides the child's home.

[Adoption and Children Act 2002, s 28.]

6–3196B   29. Further consequences of placement orders.   (1) Where a placement order is made in respect of a child and either—

(*a*)   the child is subject to a care order, or

(*b*)   the court at the same time makes a care order in respect of the child,

the care order does not have effect at any time when the placement order is in force.

(2)   On the making of a placement order in respect of a child, any order mentioned in section 8(1) of the 1989 Act, and any supervision order in respect of the child, ceases to have effect.

(3)   Where a placement order is in force—

(*a*)   no prohibited steps order, residence order or specific issue order, and

(*b*)   no supervision order or child assessment order,

may be made in respect of the child.

(4)   Subsection (3)(*a*) does not apply in respect of a residence order if—

(*a*)   an application for an adoption order has been made in respect of the child, and

(*b*)   the residence order is applied for by a parent or guardian who has obtained the court's leave under subsection (3) or (5) of section 47 or by any other person who has obtained the court's leave under this subsection.

(5)   Where a placement order is in force, no special guardianship order may be made in respect of the child unless—

(*a*)   an application has been made for an adoption order, and

(*b*)   the person applying for the special guardianship order has obtained the court's leave under this subsection or, if he is a guardian of the child, has obtained the court's leave under section 47(5).

(6)   Section 14A(7) of the 1989 Act applies in respect of an application for a special guardianship order for which leave has been given as mentioned in subsection (5)(*b*) with the omission of the words "the beginning of the period of three months ending with".

(7)   Where a placement order is in force—

(*a*)   section 14C(1)(*b*) of the 1989 Act (special guardianship: parental responsibility) has effect subject to any determination under section 25(4) of this Act,

(*b*)   section 14C(3) and (4) of the 1989 Act (special guardianship: removal of child from UK etc) does not apply.

[Adoption and Children Act 2002, s 29.]

Removal of children who are or may be placed by adoption agencies

6–3196C   30. General prohibitions on removal.   (1) Where—

(*a*)   a child is placed for adoption by an adoption agency under section 19, or

(*b*)   a child is placed for adoption by an adoption agency and either the child is less than six weeks old or the agency has at no time been authorised to place the child for adoption,

a person (other than the agency) must not remove the child from the prospective adopters.

(2)   Where—

(*a*) a child who is not for the time being placed for adoption is being provided with accommodation by a local authority, and

(*b*) the authority have applied to the court for a placement order and the application has not been disposed of,

only a person who has the court's leave (or the authority) may remove the child from the accommodation.

(3) Where subsection (2) does not apply, but—

(*a*) a child who is not for the time being placed for adoption is being provided with accommodation by an adoption agency, and

(*b*) the agency is authorised to place the child for adoption under section 19 or would be so authorised if any consent to placement under that section had not been withdrawn,

a person (other than the agency) must not remove the child from the accommodation.

(4) This section is subject to sections 31 to 33 but those sections do not apply if the child is subject to a care order.

(5) This group of sections (that is, this section and those sections) apply whether or not the child in question is in England and Wales.

(6) This group of sections does not affect the exercise by any local authority or other person of any power conferred by any enactment, other than section 20(8) of the 1989 Act (removal of children from local authority accommodation).

(7) This group of sections does not prevent the removal of a child who is arrested.

(8) A person who removes a child in contravention of this section is guilty of an offence and liable on summary conviction to imprisonment for a term not exceeding three months, or a fine not exceeding level 5 on the standard scale, or both.

[Adoption and Children Act 2002, s 30.]

6–3196D   31. Recovery by parent etc where child not placed or is a baby.   (1) Subsection (2) applies where—

(*a*) a child who is not for the time being placed for adoption is being provided with accommodation by an adoption agency, and

(*b*) the agency would be authorised to place the child for adoption under section 19 if consent to placement under that section had not been withdrawn.

(2) If any parent or guardian of the child informs the agency that he wishes the child to be returned to him, the agency must return the child to him within the period of seven days beginning with the request unless an application is, or has been, made for a placement order and the application has not been disposed of.

(3) Subsection (4) applies where—

(*a*) a child is placed for adoption by an adoption agency and either the child is less than six weeks old or the agency has at no time been authorised to place the child for adoption, and

(*b*) any parent or guardian of the child informs the agency that he wishes the child to be returned to him,

unless an application is, or has been, made for a placement order and the application has not been disposed of.

(4) The agency must give notice of the parent's or guardian's wish to the prospective adopters who must return the child to the agency within the period of seven days beginning with the day on which the notice is given.

(5) A prospective adopter who fails to comply with subsection (4) is guilty of an offence and liable on summary conviction to imprisonment for a term not exceeding three months, or a fine not exceeding level 5 on the standard scale, or both.

(6) As soon as a child is returned to an adoption agency under subsection (4), the agency must return the child to the parent or guardian in question.

[Adoption and Children Act 2002, s 31.]

6–3196E   32. Recovery by parent etc where child placed and consent withdrawn.   (1) This section applies where—

(*a*) a child is placed for adoption by an adoption agency under section 19, and

(*b*) consent to placement under that section has been withdrawn,

unless an application is, or has been, made for a placement order and the application has not been disposed of.

(2) If a parent or guardian of the child informs the agency that he wishes the child to be returned to him—

(*a*) the agency must give notice of the parent's or guardian's wish to the prospective adopters, and

(*b*) the prospective adopters must return the child to the agency within the period of 14 days beginning with the day on which the notice is given.

(3) A prospective adopter who fails to comply with subsection (2)(*b*) is guilty of an offence and liable on summary conviction to imprisonment for a term not exceeding three months, or a fine not exceeding level 5 on the standard scale, or both.

(4) As soon as a child is returned to an adoption agency under this section, the agency must return the child to the parent or guardian in question.

(5) Where a notice under subsection (2) is given, but—

(*a*) before the notice was given, an application for an adoption order (including a Scottish or Northern Irish adoption order), special guardianship order or residence order, or for leave to apply for a special guardianship order or residence order, was made in respect of the child, and

(*b*) the application (and, in a case where leave is given on an application to apply for a special guardianship order or residence order, the application for the order) has not been disposed of,

the prospective adopters are not required by virtue of the notice to return the child to the agency unless the court so orders.

[Adoption and Children Act 2002, s 32.]

6–3196F   33. Recovery by parent etc where child placed and placement order refused.
(1) This section applies where—

(*a*) a child is placed for adoption by a local authority under section 19,
(*b*) the authority have applied for a placement order and the application has been refused, and
(*c*) any parent or guardian of the child informs the authority that he wishes the child to be returned to him.

(2) The prospective adopters must return the child to the authority on a date determined by the court.

(3) A prospective adopter who fails to comply with subsection (2) is guilty of an offence and liable on summary conviction to imprisonment for a term not exceeding three months, or a fine not exceeding level 5 on the standard scale, or both.

(4) As soon as a child is returned to the authority, they must return the child to the parent or guardian in question.

[Adoption and Children Act 2002, s 33.]

6–3196G   34. Placement orders: prohibition on removal.   (1) Where a placement order in respect of a child—

(*a*) is in force, or
(*b*) has been revoked, but the child has not been returned by the prospective adopters or remains in any accommodation provided by the local authority,

a person (other than the local authority) may not remove the child from the prospective adopters or from accommodation provided by the authority.

(2) A person who removes a child in contravention of subsection (1) is guilty of an offence.

(3) Where a court revoking a placement order in respect of a child determines that the child is not to remain with any former prospective adopters with whom the child is placed, they must return the child to the local authority within the period determined by the court for the purpose; and a person who fails to do so is guilty of an offence.

(4) Where a court revoking a placement order in respect of a child determines that the child is to be returned to a parent or guardian, the local authority must return the child to the parent or guardian as soon as the child is returned to the authority or, where the child is in accommodation provided by the authority, at once.

(5) A person guilty of an offence under this section is liable on summary conviction to imprisonment for a term not exceeding three months, or a fine not exceeding level 5 on the standard scale, or both.

(6) This section does not affect the exercise by any local authority or other person of a power conferred by any enactment, other than section 20(8) of the 1989 Act.

(7) This section does not prevent the removal of a child who is arrested.

(8) This section applies whether or not the child in question is in England and Wales.

[Adoption and Children Act 2002, s 34.]

6–3196H   35. Return of child in other cases.   (1) Where a child is placed for adoption by an adoption agency and the prospective adopters give notice to the agency of their wish to return the child, the agency must—

(*a*) receive the child from the prospective adopters before the end of the period of seven days beginning with the giving of the notice, and
(*b*) give notice to any parent or guardian of the child of the prospective adopters' wish to return the child.

(2) Where a child is placed for adoption by an adoption agency, and the agency—

(a) is of the opinion that the child should not remain with the prospective adopters, and

(b) gives notice to them of its opinion,

the prospective adopters must, not later than the end of the period of seven days beginning with the giving of the notice, return the child to the agency.

(3) If the agency gives notice under subsection (2)(b), it must give notice to any parent or guardian of the child of the obligation to return the child to the agency.

(4) A prospective adopter who fails to comply with subsection (2) is guilty of an offence and liable on summary conviction to imprisonment for a term not exceeding three months, or a fine not exceeding level 5 on the standard scale, or both.

(5) Where—

(a) an adoption agency gives notice under subsection (2) in respect of a child,

(b) before the notice was given, an application for an adoption order (including a Scottish or Northern Irish adoption order), special guardianship order or residence order, or for leave to apply for a special guardianship order or residence order, was made in respect of the child, and

(c) the application (and, in a case where leave is given on an application to apply for a special guardianship order or residence order, the application for the order) has not been disposed of,

prospective adopters are not required by virtue of the notice to return the child to the agency unless the court so orders.

(6) This section applies whether or not the child in question is in England and Wales.

[Adoption and Children Act 2002, s 35.]

Removal of children in non-agency cases

6–3196I   **36. Restrictions on removal.**   (1) At any time when a child's home is with any persons ("the people concerned") with whom the child is not placed by an adoption agency, but the people concerned—

(a) have applied for an adoption order in respect of the child and the application has not been disposed of,

(b) have given notice of intention to adopt, or

(c) have applied for leave to apply for an adoption order under section 42(6) and the application has not been disposed of,

a person may remove the child only in accordance with the provisions of this group of sections (that is, this section and sections 37 to 40).

The reference to a child placed by an adoption agency includes a child placed by a Scottish or Northern Irish adoption agency.

(2) For the purposes of this group of sections, a notice of intention to adopt is to be disregarded if—

(a) the period of four months beginning with the giving of the notice has expired without the people concerned applying for an adoption order, or

(b) the notice is a second or subsequent notice of intention to adopt and was given during the period of five months beginning with the giving of the preceding notice.

(3) For the purposes of this group of sections, if the people concerned apply for leave to apply for an adoption order under section 42(6) and the leave is granted, the application for leave is not to be treated as disposed of until the period of three days beginning with the granting of the leave has expired.

(4) This section does not prevent the removal of a child who is arrested.

(5) Where a parent or guardian may remove a child from the people concerned in accordance with the provisions of this group of sections, the people concerned must at the request of the parent or guardian return the child to the parent or guardian at once.

(6) A person who—

(a) fails to comply with subsection (5), or

(b) removes a child in contravention of this section,

is guilty of an offence and liable on summary conviction to imprisonment for a term not exceeding three months, or a fine not exceeding level 5 on the standard scale, or both.

(7) This group of sections applies whether or not the child in question is in England and Wales.

[Adoption and Children Act 2002, s 36.]

6–3196J   **37. Applicants for adoption.**   If section 36(1)(a) applies, the following persons may remove the child—

(a) a person who has the court's leave,

(b) a local authority or other person in the exercise of a power conferred by any enactment, other than section 20(8) of the 1989 Act.

[Adoption and Children Act 2002, s 37.]

6–3196K   38. Local authority foster parents.   (1) This section applies if the child's home is with local authority foster parents.

(2) If—

(a)   the child has had his home with the foster parents at all times during the period of five years ending with the removal and the foster parents have given notice of intention to adopt, or

(b)   an application has been made for leave under section 42(6) and has not been disposed of,

the following persons may remove the child.

(3) They are—

(a)   a person who has the court's leave,

(b)   a local authority or other person in the exercise of a power conferred by any enactment, other than section 20(8) of the 1989 Act.

(4) If subsection (2) does not apply but—

(a)   the child has had his home with the foster parents at all times during the period of one year ending with the removal, and

(b)   the foster parents have given notice of intention to adopt,

the following persons may remove the child.

(5) They are—

(a)   a person with parental responsibility for the child who is exercising the power in section 20(8) of the 1989 Act,

(b)   a person who has the court's leave,

(c)   a local authority or other person in the exercise of a power conferred by any enactment, other than section 20(8) of the 1989 Act.

[Adoption and Children Act 2002, s 38.]

6–3196L   39. Partners of parents[1].   (1) This section applies if a child's home is with a partner of a parent and the partner has given notice of intention to adopt.

(2) If the child's home has been with the partner for not less than three years (whether continuous or not) during the period of five years ending with the removal, the following persons may remove the child—

(a)   a person who has the court's leave,

(b)   a local authority or other person in the exercise of a power conferred by any enactment, other than section 20(8) of the 1989 Act.

(3) If subsection (2) does not apply, the following persons may remove the child—

(a)   a parent or guardian,

(b)   a person who has the court's leave,

(c)   a local authority or other person in the exercise of a power conferred by any enactment, other than section 20(8) of the 1989 Act.

[Adoption and Children Act 2002, s 39.]

---

1. See the definition of "partner" in s 144(7), post.

6–3196M   40. Other non-agency cases.   (1) In any case where sections 37 to 39 do not apply but—

(a)   the people concerned have given notice of intention to adopt, or

(b)   the people concerned have applied for leave under section 42(6) and the application has not been disposed of,

the following persons may remove the child.

(2) They are—

(a)   a person who has the court's leave,

(b)   a local authority or other person in the exercise of a power conferred by any enactment, other than section 20(8) of the 1989 Act.

[Adoption and Children Act 2002, s 40.]

Breach of restrictions on removal

6–3196N   41. Recovery orders.   (1) This section applies where it appears to the court—

(a)   that a child has been removed in contravention of any of the preceding provisions of this Chapter or that there are reasonable grounds for believing that a person intends to remove a child in contravention of those provisions, or

(b)   that a person has failed to comply with section 31(4), 32(2), 33(2), 34(3) or 35(2).

(2) The court may, on the application of any person, by an order—

(a) direct any person who is in a position to do so to produce the child on request to any person mentioned in subsection (4),
(b) authorise the removal of the child by any person mentioned in that subsection,
(c) require any person who has information as to the child's whereabouts to disclose that information on request to any constable or officer of the court,
(d) authorise a constable to enter any premises specified in the order and search for the child, using reasonable force if necessary.

(3) Premises may only be specified under subsection (2)(d) if it appears to the court that there are reasonable grounds for believing the child to be on them.

(4) The persons referred to in subsection (2) are—

(a) any person named by the court,
(b) any constable,
(c) any person who, after the order is made under that subsection, is authorised to exercise any power under the order by an adoption agency which is authorised to place the child for adoption.

(5) A person who intentionally obstructs a person exercising a power of removal conferred by the order is guilty of an offence and liable on summary conviction to a fine not exceeding level 3 on the standard scale.

(6) A person must comply with a request to disclose information as required by the order even if the information sought might constitute evidence that he had committed an offence.

(7) But in criminal proceedings in which the person is charged with an offence (other than one mentioned in subsection (8))—

(a) no evidence relating to the information provided may be adduced, and
(b) no question relating to the information may be asked,

by or on behalf of the prosecution, unless evidence relating to it is adduced, or a question relating to it is asked, in the proceedings by or on behalf of the person.

(8) The offences excluded from subsection (7) are—

(a) an offence under section 2 or 5 of the Perjury Act 1911 (c 6) (false statements made on oath otherwise than in judicial proceedings or made otherwise than on oath),
(b) an offence under section 44(1) or (2) of the Criminal Law (Consolidation) (Scotland) Act 1995 (c 39) (false statements made on oath or otherwise than on oath).

(9) An order under this section has effect in relation to Scotland as if it were an order made by the Court of Session which that court had jurisdiction to make.
[Adoption and Children Act 2002, s 41.]

Preliminaries to adoption

6–3196O 42. Child to live with adopters before application.   (1) An application for an adoption order may not be made unless—

(a) if subsection (2) applies, the condition in that subsection is met,
(b) if that subsection does not apply, the condition in whichever is applicable of subsections (3) to (5) applies.

(2) If—

(a) the child was placed for adoption with the applicant or applicants by an adoption agency or in pursuance of an order of the High Court, or
(b) the applicant is a parent of the child,

the condition is that the child must have had his home with the applicant or, in the case of an application by a couple, with one or both of them at all times during the period of ten weeks preceding the application.

(3) If the applicant or one of the applicants is the partner of a parent of the child, the condition is that the child must have had his home with the applicant or, as the case may be, applicants at all times during the period of six months preceding the application.

(4) If the applicants are local authority foster parents, the condition is that the child must have had his home with the applicants at all times during the period of one year preceding the application.

(5) In any other case, the condition is that the child must have had his home with the applicant or, in the case of an application by a couple, with one or both of them for not less than three years (whether continuous or not) during the period of five years preceding the application.

(6) But subsections (4) and (5) do not prevent an application being made if the court gives leave to make it.

(7) An adoption order may not be made unless the court is satisfied that sufficient opportunities to see the child with the applicant or, in the case of an application by a couple, both of them together in the home environment have been given—

(a) where the child was placed for adoption with the applicant or applicants by an adoption agency, to that agency, (*b*) in any other case, to the local authority within whose area the home is.

(8) In this section and sections 43 and 44(1)—

(*a*) references to an adoption agency include a Scottish or Northern Irish adoption agency,

(*b*) references to a child placed for adoption by an adoption agency are to be read accordingly.

[Adoption and Children Act 2002, s 42.]

6–3196P 43. Reports where child placed by agency. Where an application for an adoption order relates to a child placed for adoption by an adoption agency, the agency must—

(*a*) submit to the court a report on the suitability of the applicants and on any other matters relevant to the operation of section 1, and

(*b*) assist the court in any manner the court directs.

[Adoption and Children Act 2002, s 43.]

6–3196Q 44. Notice of intention to adopt. (1) This section applies where persons (referred to in this section as "proposed adopters") wish to adopt a child who is not placed for adoption with them by an adoption agency.

(2) An adoption order may not be made in respect of the child unless the proposed adopters have given notice to the appropriate local authority of their intention to apply for the adoption order (referred to in this Act as a "notice of intention to adopt").

(3) The notice must be given not more than two years, or less than three months, before the date on which the application for the adoption order is made.

(4) Where—

(*a*) if a person were seeking to apply for an adoption order, subsection (4) or (5) of section 42 would apply, but

(*b*) the condition in the subsection in question is not met,

the person may not give notice of intention to adopt unless he has the court's leave to apply for an adoption order.

(5) On receipt of a notice of intention to adopt, the local authority must arrange for the investigation of the matter and submit to the court a report of the investigation.

(6) In particular, the investigation must, so far as practicable, include the suitability of the proposed adopters and any other matters relevant to the operation of section 1 in relation to the application.

(7) If a local authority receive a notice of intention to adopt in respect of a child whom they know was (immediately before the notice was given) looked after by another local authority, they must, not more than seven days after the receipt of the notice, inform the other local authority in writing that they have received the notice.

(8) Where—

(*a*) a local authority have placed a child with any persons otherwise than as prospective adopters, and

(*b*) the persons give notice of intention to adopt,

the authority are not to be treated as leaving the child with them as prospective adopters for the purposes of section 18(1)(*b*).

(9) In this section, references to the appropriate local authority, in relation to any proposed adopters, are—

(*a*) in prescribed cases, references to the prescribed local authority,

(*b*) in any other case, references to the local authority for the area in which, at the time of giving the notice of intention to adopt, they have their home,

and "prescribed" means prescribed by regulations[1].

[Adoption and Children Act 2002, s 44.]

1. The Local Authority (Non-agency Adoptions) Regulations 2005, SI 2005/3113 and the Local Authority (Adoption) (Miscellaneous Provisions) Regulations 2005, SI 2005/3390 have been made.

6–3196R 45. Suitability of adopters. (1) Regulations under section 9 may make provision as to the matters to be taken into account by an adoption agency in determining, or making any report in respect of, the suitability of any persons to adopt a child.

(2) In particular, the regulations may make provision for the purpose of securing that, in determining the suitability of a couple to adopt a child, proper regard is had to the need for stability and permanence in their relationship.

[Adoption and Children Act 2002, s 45.]

The making of adoption orders

6–3196S 46. Adoption orders. (1) An adoption order is an order made by the court on an application under section 50 or 51 giving parental responsibility for a child to the adopters or adopter.

(2) The making of an adoption order operates to extinguish—

(a) the parental responsibility which any person other than the adopters or adopter has for the adopted child immediately before the making of the order,

(b) any order under the 1989 Act or the Children (Northern Ireland) Order 1995 (SI 1995/755 (NI 2)),

(c) any order under the Children (Scotland) Act 1995 (c 36) other than an excepted order, and

(d) any duty arising by virtue of an agreement or an order of a court to make payments, so far as the payments are in respect of the adopted child's maintenance or upbringing for any period after the making of the adoption order.

"Excepted order" means an order under section 9, 11(1)(d) or 13 of the Children (Scotland) Act 1995 or an exclusion order within the meaning of section 76(1) of that Act.

(3) An adoption order—

(a) does not affect parental responsibility so far as it relates to any period before the making of the order, and

(b) in the case of an order made on an application under section 51(2) by the partner of a parent of the adopted child, does not affect the parental responsibility of that parent or any duties of that parent within subsection (2)(d).

(4) Subsection (2)(d) does not apply to a duty arising by virtue of an agreement—

(a) which constitutes a trust, or

(b) which expressly provides that the duty is not to be extinguished by the making of an adoption order.

(5) An adoption order may be made even if the child to be adopted is already an adopted child.

(6) Before making an adoption order, the court must consider whether there should be arrangements for allowing any person contact with the child; and for that purpose the court must consider any existing or proposed arrangements and obtain any views of the parties to the proceedings.
[Adoption and Children Act 2002, s 46.]

6–3196T 47. Conditions for making adoption orders. (1) An adoption order may not be made if the child has a parent or guardian unless one of the following three conditions is met; but this section is subject to section 52 (parental etc consent).

(2) The first condition is that, in the case of each parent or guardian of the child, the court is satisfied—

(a) that the parent or guardian consents to the making of the adoption order,

(b) that the parent or guardian has consented under section 20 (and has not withdrawn the consent) and does not oppose the making of the adoption order, or

(c) that the parent's or guardian's consent should be dispensed with.

(3) A parent or guardian may not oppose the making of an adoption order under subsection (2)(b) without the court's leave.

(4) The second condition is that—

(a) the child has been placed for adoption by an adoption agency with the prospective adopters in whose favour the order is proposed to be made,

(b) either—

(i) the child was placed for adoption with the consent of each parent or guardian and the consent of the mother was given when the child was at least six weeks old, or

(ii) the child was placed for adoption under a placement order, and

(c) no parent or guardian opposes the making of the adoption order.

(5) A parent or guardian may not oppose the making of an adoption order under the second condition without the court's leave.

(6) The third condition is that the child is free for adoption by virtue of an order made—

(a) in Scotland, under section 18 of the Adoption (Scotland) Act 1978 (c 28), or

(b) in Northern Ireland, under Article 17(1) or 18(1) of the Adoption (Northern Ireland) Order 1987 (SI 1987/2203 (NI 22)).

(7) The court cannot give leave under subsection (3) or (5) unless satisfied that there has been a change in circumstances since the consent of the parent or guardian was given or, as the case may be, the placement order was made.

(8) An adoption order may not be made in relation to a person who is or has been married.

(9) An adoption order may not be made in relation to a person who has attained the age of 19 years.
[Adoption and Children Act 2002, s 47.]

6–3196U 48. Restrictions on making adoption orders. (1) The court may not hear an application for an adoption order in relation to a child, where a previous application to which subsection (2) applies made in relation to the child by the same persons was refused by any court, unless it appears to the court that, because of a change in circumstances or for any other reason, it is proper to hear the application.

(2) This subsection applies to any application—

(a) for an adoption order or a Scottish or Northern Irish adoption order, or

(b) for an order for adoption made in the Isle of Man or any of the Channel Islands.

[Adoption and Children Act 2002, s 48.]

6–3196V 49. Applications for adoption. (1) An application for an adoption order may be made by—

(a) a couple[1], or

(b) one person,

but only if it is made under section 50 or 51 and one of the following conditions is met.

(2) The first condition is that at least one of the couple (in the case of an application under section 50) or the applicant (in the case of an application under section 51) is domiciled in a part of the British Islands.

(3) The second condition is that both of the couple (in the case of an application under section 50) or the applicant (in the case of an application under section 51) have been habitually resident in a part of the British Islands for a period of not less than one year ending with the date of the application.

(4) An application for an adoption order may only be made if the person to be adopted has not attained the age of 18 years on the date of the application.

(5) References in this Act to a child, in connection with any proceedings (whether or not concluded) for adoption, (such as "child to be adopted" or "adopted child") include a person who has attained the age of 18 years before the proceedings are concluded.

[Adoption and Children Act 2002, s 49.]

---

1. See the definition of "couple" in s 144(4), post.

6–3196W 50. Adoption by couple. (1) An adoption order may be made on the application of a couple where both of them have attained the age of 21 years.

(2) An adoption order may be made on the application of a couple where—

(a) one of the couple is the mother or the father of the person to be adopted and has attained the age of 18 years, and

(b) the other has attained the age of 21 years.

[Adoption and Children Act 2002, s 50.]

6–3196X 51. Adoption by one person. (1) An adoption order may be made on the application of one person who has attained the age of 21 years and is not married.

(2) An adoption order may be made on the application of one person who has attained the age of 21 years if the court is satisfied that the person is the partner of a parent of the person to be adopted.

(3) An adoption order may be made on the application of one person who has attained the age of 21 years and is married if the court is satisfied that—

(a) the person's spouse cannot be found,

(b) the spouses have separated and are living apart, and the separation is likely to be permanent, or

(c) the person's spouse is by reason of ill-health, whether physical or mental, incapable of making an application for an adoption order.

(4) An adoption order may not be made on an application under this section by the mother or the father of the person to be adopted unless the court is satisfied that—

(a) the other natural parent is dead or cannot be found,

(b) by virtue of section 28 of the Human Fertilisation and Embryology Act 1990 (c 37) (disregarding subsections (5A) to (5I), there is no other parent, or

(c) there is some other reason justifying the child's being adopted by the applicant alone,

and, where the court makes an adoption order on such an application, the court must record that it is satisfied as to the fact mentioned in paragraph (a) or (b) or, in the case of paragraph (c), record the reason.

[Adoption and Children Act 2002, s 51, as amended by the Human Fertilisation and Embryology (Deceased Fathers) Act 2003, Schedule.].]

Placement and adoption: general

6–3196Y 52. Parental etc consent. (1) The court cannot dispense with the consent of any parent or guardian of a child to the child being placed for adoption or to the making of an adoption order in respect of the child unless the court is satisfied that—

(a) the parent or guardian cannot be found or is incapable of giving consent, or

(b) the welfare[1] of the child requires the consent to be dispensed with.

(2) The following provisions apply to references in this Chapter to any parent or guardian of a child giving or withdrawing—

(a) consent to the placement of a child for adoption, or

(b) consent to the making of an adoption order (including a future adoption order).

(3) Any consent given by the mother to the making of an adoption order is ineffective if it is given less than six weeks after the child's birth.

(4) The withdrawal of any consent to the placement of a child for adoption, or of any consent given under section 20, is ineffective if it is given after an application for an adoption order is made.

(5) "Consent" means consent given unconditionally and with full understanding of what is involved; but a person may consent to adoption without knowing the identity of the persons in whose favour the order will be made.

(6) "Parent" (except in subsections (9) and (10) below) means a parent having parental responsibility.

(7) Consent under section 19 or 20 must be given in the form prescribed by rules, and the rules may prescribe forms in which a person giving consent under any other provision of this Part may do so (if he wishes).

(8) Consent given under section 19 or 20 must be withdrawn—

(a) in the form prescribed by rules, or

(b) by notice given to the agency.

(9) Subsection (10) applies if—

(a) an agency has placed a child for adoption under section 19 in pursuance of consent given by a parent of the child, and

(b) at a later time, the other parent of the child acquires parental responsibility for the child.

(10) The other parent is to be treated as having at that time given consent in accordance with this section in the same terms as those in which the first parent gave consent.

[Adoption and Children Act 2002, s 52.]

---

1. Section 1, ante, applies to a decision about whether or not to dispense with the consent of a parent to a placement order or an adoption order; the child's interests are the paramount consideration.

6–3196Z   53. Modification of 1989 Act in relation to adoption. (1) Where—

(a) a local authority are authorised to place a child for adoption, or

(b) a child who has been placed for adoption by a local authority is less than six weeks old,

regulations[1] may provide for the following provisions of the 1989 Act to apply with modifications, or not to apply, in relation to the child.

(2) The provisions are—

(a) section 22(4)(b), (c) and (d) and (5)(b) (duty to ascertain wishes and feelings of certain persons),

(b) paragraphs 15 and 21 of Schedule 2 (promoting contact with parents and parents' obligation to contribute towards maintenance).

(3) Where a registered adoption society is authorised to place a child for adoption or a child who has been placed for adoption by a registered adoption society is less than six weeks old, regulations may provide—

(a) for section 61 of that Act to have effect in relation to the child whether or not he is accommodated by or on behalf of the society,

(b) for subsections (2)(b) to (d) and (3)(b) of that section (duty to ascertain wishes and feelings of certain persons) to apply with modifications, or not to apply, in relation to the child.

(4) Where a child's home is with persons who have given notice of intention to adopt, no contribution is payable (whether under a contribution order or otherwise) under Part 3 of Schedule 2 to that Act (contributions towards maintenance of children looked after by local authorities) in respect of the period referred to in subsection (5).

(5) That period begins when the notice of intention to adopt is given and ends if—

(a) the period of four months beginning with the giving of the notice expires without the prospective adopters applying for an adoption order, or

(b) an application for such an order is withdrawn or refused.

(6) In this section, "notice of intention to adopt" includes notice of intention to apply for a Scottish or Northern Irish adoption order.

[Adoption and Children Act 2002, s 53.]

1. See the Adoption Agencies Regulations 2005, in this PART, STATUTORY INSTRUMENTS AND PRACTICE DIRECTIONS ON FAMILY LAW, post and the Adoption Agencies (Wales) Regulations 2005, SI 2005/1313.

6–3197   54. Disclosing information during adoption process.   Regulations under section 9 may require adoption agencies in prescribed circumstances to disclose in accordance with the regulations prescribed information to prospective adopters.
[Adoption and Children Act 2002, s 54.]

6–3197A   55. Revocation of adoptions on legitimation.   (1) Where any child adopted by one natural parent as sole adoptive parent subsequently becomes a legitimated person on the marriage of the natural parents, the court by which the adoption order was made may, on the application of any of the parties concerned, revoke the order.
(2) In relation to an adoption order made by a magistrates' court, the reference in subsection (1) to the court by which the order was made includes a court acting for the same petty sessions area.
[Adoption and Children Act 2002, s 55.]

Disclosure of information in relation to a person's adoption

6–3197B   56. Information to be kept about a person's adoption.   (1) In relation to an adopted person, regulations[1] may prescribe—

(a) the information which an adoption agency must keep in relation to his adoption,
(b) the form and manner in which it must keep that information.

(2) Below in this group of sections (that is, this section and sections 57 to 65), any information kept by an adoption agency by virtue of subsection (1)(a) is referred to as section 56 information.
(3) Regulations[1] may provide for the transfer in prescribed circumstances of information held, or previously held, by an adoption agency to another adoption agency.
[Adoption and Children Act 2002, s 56.]

1. See the Disclosure of Adoption Information (Post-commencement Adoptions) Regulations 2005, SI 2005/888 amended by SI 2005/3482 and the Access to Information (Post-commencement Adoptions) (Wales) Regulations 2005, SI 2005/2689.

6–3197C   57. Restrictions on disclosure of protected etc information.   (1) Any section 56 information kept by an adoption agency which—

(a) is about an adopted person or any other person, and
(b) is or includes identifying information about the person in question,

may only be disclosed by the agency to a person (other than the person the information is about) in pursuance of this group of sections.
(2) Any information kept by an adoption agency—

(a) which the agency has obtained from the Registrar General on an application under section 79(5) and any other information which would enable the adopted person to obtain a certified copy of the record of his birth, or
(b) which is information about an entry relating to the adopted person in the Adoption Contact Register,

may only be disclosed to a person by the agency in pursuance of this group of sections.
(3) In this group of sections, information the disclosure of which to a person is restricted by virtue of subsection (1) or (2) is referred to (in relation to him) as protected information.
(4) Identifying information about a person means information which, whether taken on its own or together with other information disclosed by an adoption agency, identifies the person or enables the person to be identified.
(5) This section does not prevent the disclosure of protected information in pursuance of a prescribed agreement to which the adoption agency is a party.
(6) Regulations may authorise or require an adoption agency to disclose protected information to a person who is not an adopted person.
[Adoption and Children Act 2002, s 57.]

6–3197D   58. Disclosure of other information.   (1) This section applies to any section 56 information other than protected information.
(2) An adoption agency may for the purposes of its functions disclose to any person in accordance with prescribed arrangements any information to which this section applies.
(3) An adoption agency must, in prescribed[1] circumstances, disclose prescribed[1] information to a prescribed[1] person.
[Adoption and Children Act 2002, s 58.]

1. See the Disclosure of Adoption Information (Post-commencement Adoptions) Regulations 2005, SI 2005/888 amended by SI 2005/3482 and the Access to Information (Post-commencement Adoptions) (Wales) Regulations 2005, SI 2005/2689.

6–3197E   59. Offence. Regulations[1] may provide that a registered adoption society which discloses any information in contravention of section 57 is to be guilty of an offence and liable on summary conviction to a fine not exceeding level 5 on the standard scale.
[Adoption and Children Act 2002, s 59.]

1. See the Disclosure of Adoption Information (Post-commencement Adoptions) Regulations 2005, SI 2005/888 amended by SI 2005/3482 and the Access to Information (Post-commencement Adoptions) (Wales) Regulations 2005, SI 2005/2689.

6–3197F   60. Disclosing information to adopted adult. (1) This section applies to an adopted person who has attained the age of 18 years.
(2) The adopted person has the right, at his request, to receive from the appropriate adoption agency—

(a) any information which would enable him to obtain a certified copy of the record of his birth, unless the High Court orders otherwise,
(b) any prescribed[1] information disclosed to the adopters by the agency by virtue of section 54.

(3) The High Court may make an order under subsection (2)(a), on an application by the appropriate adoption agency, if satisfied that the circumstances are exceptional.
(4) The adopted person also has the right, at his request, to receive from the court which made the adoption order a copy of any prescribed document or prescribed order relating to the adoption.
(5) Subsection (4) does not apply to a document or order so far as it contains information which is protected information.
[Adoption and Children Act 2002, s 60.]

1. See the Disclosure of Adoption Information (Post-commencement Adoptions) Regulations 2005, SI 2005/888 amended by SI 2005/3482 and the Access to Information (Post-commencement Adoptions) (Wales) Regulations 2005, SI 2005/2689.

6–3197G   61. Disclosing protected information about adults. (1) This section applies where—

(a) a person applies to the appropriate adoption agency for protected information to be disclosed to him, and
(b) none of the information is about a person who is a child at the time of the application.

(2) The agency is not required to proceed with the application unless it considers it appropriate to do so.
(3) If the agency does proceed with the application it must take all reasonable steps to obtain the views of any person the information is about as to the disclosure of the information about him.
(4) The agency may then disclose the information if it considers it appropriate to do so.
(5) In deciding whether it is appropriate to proceed with the application or disclose the information, the agency must consider—

(a) the welfare of the adopted person,
(b) any views obtained under subsection (3),
(c) any prescribed matters,

and all the other circumstances of the case.
(6) This section does not apply to a request for information under section 60(2) or to a request for information which the agency is authorised or required to disclose in pursuance of regulations made by virtue of section 57(6).
[Adoption and Children Act 2002, s 61.]

6–3197H   62. Disclosing protected information about children. (1) This section applies where—

(a) a person applies to the appropriate adoption agency for protected information to be disclosed to him, and
(b) any of the information is about a person who is a child at the time of the application.

(2) The agency is not required to proceed with the application unless it considers it appropriate to do so.
(3) If the agency does proceed with the application, then, so far as the information is about a person who is at the time a child, the agency must take all reasonable steps to obtain—

(a) the views of any parent or guardian of the child, and
(b) the views of the child, if the agency considers it appropriate to do so having regard to his age and understanding and to all the other circumstances of the case,

as to the disclosure of the information.

(4) And, so far as the information is about a person who has at the time attained the age of 18 years, the agency must take all reasonable steps to obtain his views as to the disclosure of the information.

(5) The agency may then disclose the information if it considers it appropriate to do so.

(6) In deciding whether it is appropriate to proceed with the application, or disclose the information, where any of the information is about a person who is at the time a child—

(*a*) if the child is an adopted child, the child's welfare must be the paramount consideration,

(*b*) in the case of any other child, the agency must have particular regard to the child's welfare.

(7) And, in deciding whether it is appropriate to proceed with the application or disclose the information, the agency must consider—

(*a*) the welfare of the adopted person (where subsection (6)(*a*) does not apply),

(*b*) any views obtained under subsection (3) or (4),

(*c*) any prescribed matters,

and all the other circumstances of the case.

(8) This section does not apply to a request for information under section 60(2) or to a request for information which the agency is authorised or required to disclose in pursuance of regulations made by virtue of section 57(6).

[Adoption and Children Act 2002, s 62.]

6–3197I 63. Counselling.   (1) Regulations[1] may require adoption agencies to give information about the availability of counselling to persons—

(*a*) seeking information from them in pursuance of this group of sections,

(*b*) considering objecting or consenting to the disclosure of information by the agency in pursuance of this group of sections, or

(*c*) considering entering with the agency into an agreement prescribed for the purposes of section 57(5).

(2) Regulations[1] may require adoption agencies to make arrangements to secure the provision of counselling for persons seeking information from them in prescribed circumstances in pursuance of this group of sections.

(3) The regulations[1] may authorise adoption agencies—

(*a*) to disclose information which is required for the purposes of such counselling to the persons providing the counselling,

(*b*) where the person providing the counselling is outside the United Kingdom, to require a prescribed fee to be paid.

(4) The regulations[1] may require any of the following persons to provide counselling for the purposes of arrangements under subsection (2)—

(*a*) a local authority, a council constituted under section 2 of the Local Government etc (Scotland) Act 1994 (c 39) or a Health and Social Services Board established under Article 16 of the Health and Personal Social Services (Northern Ireland) Order 1972 (SI 1972/1265 (NI 14)),

(*b*) a registered adoption society, an organisation within section 144(3)(*b*) or an adoption society which is registered under Article 4 of the Adoption (Northern Ireland) Order 1987 (SI 1987/2203 (NI 22)),

(*c*) an adoption support agency in respect of which a person is registered under Part 2 of the Care Standards Act 2000 (c 14).

(5) For the purposes of subsection (4), where the functions of a Health and Social Services Board are exercisable by a Health and Social Services Trust, the reference in sub-paragraph (*a*) to a Board is to be read as a reference to the Health and Social Services Trust.

[Adoption and Children Act 2002, s 63.]

---

1. See the Disclosure of Adoption Information (Post-commencement Adoptions) Regulations 2005, SI 2005/888 amended by SI 2005/3482 and the Access to Information (Post-commencement Adoptions) (Wales) Regulations 2005, SI 2005/2689.

6–3197J 64. Other provision to be made by regulations.   (1) Regulations may make provision for the purposes of this group of sections, including provision as to—

(*a*) the performance by adoption agencies of their functions,

(*b*) the manner in which information may be received, and

(*c*) the matters mentioned below in this section.

(2) Regulations may prescribe—

(*a*) the manner in which agreements made by virtue of section 57(5) are to be recorded,

(*b*) the information to be provided by any person on an application for the disclosure of information under this group of sections.

(*d*) an overseas adoption, or

(*e*) an adoption recognised by the law of England and Wales and effected under the law of any other country;

and related expressions are to be interpreted accordingly.

(2) But references in this Chapter to adoption do not include an adoption effected before the day on which this Chapter comes into force (referred to in this Chapter as "the appointed day").

(3) Any reference in an enactment to an adopted person within the meaning of this Chapter includes a reference to an adopted child within the meaning of Part 4 of the Adoption Act 1976 (c 36).

[Adoption and Children Act 2002, s 66.]

---

1. Chapter 4 contains ss 66–76.

6–3197M 67. Status conferred by adoption. (1) An adopted person is to be treated in law as if born as the child of the adopters or adopter.

(2) An adopted person is the legitimate child of the adopters or adopter and, if adopted by—

(*a*) a couple, or

(*b*) one of a couple under section 51(2),

is to be treated as the child of the relationship of the couple in question.

(3) An adopted person—

(*a*) if adopted by one of a couple under section 51(2), is to be treated in law as not being the child of any person other than the adopter and the other one of the couple, and

(*b*) in any other case, is to be treated in law, subject to subsection (4), as not being the child of any person other than the adopters or adopter;

but this subsection does not affect any reference in this Act to a person's natural parent or to any other natural relationship.

(4) In the case of a person adopted by one of the person's natural parents as sole adoptive parent, subsection (3)(*b*) has no effect as respects entitlement to property depending on relationship to that parent, or as respects anything else depending on that relationship.

(5) This section has effect from the date of the adoption.

(6) Subject to the provisions of this Chapter and Schedule 4, this section—

(*a*) applies for the interpretation of enactments or instruments passed or made before as well as after the adoption, and so applies subject to any contrary indication, and

(*b*) has effect as respects things done, or events occurring, on or after the adoption.

[Adoption and Children Act 2002, s 67.]

6–3197N 68. Adoptive relatives. (1) A relationship existing by virtue of section 67 may be referred to as an adoptive relationship, and—

(*a*) an adopter may be referred to as an adoptive parent or (as the case may be) as an adoptive father or adoptive mother,

(*b*) any other relative of any degree under an adoptive relationship may be referred to as an adoptive relative of that degree.

(2) Subsection (1) does not affect the interpretation of any reference, not qualified by the word "adoptive", to a relationship.

(3) A reference (however expressed) to the adoptive mother and father of a child adopted by—

(*a*) a couple of the same sex, or

(*b*) a partner of the child's parent, where the couple are of the same sex,

is to be read as a reference to the child's adoptive parents.

[Adoption and Children Act 2002, s 68.]

6–3197O 69. Rules of interpretation for instruments concerning property. (1) The rules of interpretation contained in this section apply (subject to any contrary indication and to Schedule 4) to any instrument so far as it contains a disposition of property.

(2) In applying section 67(1) and (2) to a disposition which depends on the date of birth of a child or children of the adoptive parent or parents, the disposition is to be interpreted as if—

(*a*) the adopted person had been born on the date of adoption,

(*b*) two or more people adopted on the same date had been born on that date in the order of their actual births;

but this does not affect any reference to a person's age.

(3) Examples of phrases in wills on which subsection (2) can operate are—

1 Children of A "living at my death or born afterwards".

2 Children of A "living at my death or born afterwards before any one of such children for the time being in existence attains a vested interest and who attain the age of 21 years".

3 As in example 1 or 2, but referring to grandchildren of A instead of children of A.

4 A for life "until he has a child", and then to his child or children.

Note Subsection (2) will not affect the reference to the age of 21 years in example 2.

(4) Section 67(3) does not prejudice—

(*a*) any qualifying interest, or

(*b*) any interest expectant (whether immediately or not) upon a qualifying interest.

"Qualifying interest" means an interest vested in possession in the adopted person before the adoption.

(5) Where it is necessary to determine for the purposes of a disposition of property effected by an instrument whether a woman can have a child—

(*a*) it must be presumed that once a woman has attained the age of 55 years she will not adopt a person after execution of the instrument, and

(*b*) if she does so, then (in spite of section 67) that person is not to be treated as her child or (if she does so as one of a couple) as the child of the other one of the couple for the purposes of the instrument.

(6) In this section, "instrument" includes a private Act settling property, but not any other enactment.

[Adoption and Children Act 2002, s 69.]

6–3197P 70. Dispositions depending on date of birth. (1) Where a disposition depends on the date of birth of a person who was born illegitimate and who is adopted by one of the natural parents as sole adoptive parent, section 69(2) does not affect entitlement by virtue of Part 3 of the Family Law Reform Act 1987 (c 42) (dispositions of property).

(2) Subsection (1) applies for example where—

(*a*) a testator dies in 2001 bequeathing a legacy to his eldest grandchild living at a specified time,

(*b*) his unmarried daughter has a child in 2002 who is the first grandchild,

(*c*) his married son has a child in 2003,

(*d*) subsequently his unmarried daughter adopts her child as sole adoptive parent.

In that example the status of the daughter's child as the eldest grandchild of the testator is not affected by the events described in paragraphs (*c*) and (*d*).

[Adoption and Children Act 2002, s 70.]

6–3197Q 71. Property devolving with peerages etc. (1) An adoption does not affect the descent of any peerage or dignity or title of honour.

(2) An adoption does not affect the devolution of any property limited (expressly or not) to devolve (as nearly as the law permits) along with any peerage or dignity or title of honour.

(3) Subsection (2) applies only if and so far as a contrary intention is not expressed in the instrument, and has effect subject to the terms of the instrument.

[Adoption and Children Act 2002, s 71.]

6–3197R 72. Protection of trustees and personal representatives. (1) A trustee or personal representative is not under a duty, by virtue of the law relating to trusts or the administration of estates, to enquire, before conveying or distributing any property, whether any adoption has been effected or revoked if that fact could affect entitlement to the property.

(2) A trustee or personal representative is not liable to any person by reason of a conveyance or distribution of the property made without regard to any such fact if he has not received notice of the fact before the conveyance or distribution.

(3) This section does not prejudice the right of a person to follow the property, or any property representing it, into the hands of another person, other than a purchaser, who has received it.

[Adoption and Children Act 2002, s 72.]

6–3197S 73. Meaning of disposition. (1) This section applies for the purposes of this Chapter.

(2) A disposition includes the conferring of a power of appointment and any other disposition of an interest in or right over property; and in this subsection a power of appointment includes any discretionary power to transfer a beneficial interest in property without the furnishing of valuable consideration.

(3) This Chapter applies to an oral disposition as if contained in an instrument made when the disposition was made.

(4) The date of death of a testator is the date at which a will or codicil is to be regarded as made.

(5) The provisions of the law of intestate succession applicable to the estate of a deceased person are to be treated as if contained in an instrument executed by him (while of full capacity) immediately before his death.

[Adoption and Children Act 2002, s 73.]

6–3197T   74. Miscellaneous enactments.   (1) Section 67 does not apply for the purposes of—

(a) the table of kindred and affinity in Schedule 1 to the Marriage Act 1949 (c 76), or
(b) sections 64 and 65 of the Sexual Offences Act 2003 (sex with an adult relative).

(2) Section 67 does not apply for the purposes of any provision of—

(a) the British Nationality Act 1981 (c 61),
(b) the Immigration Act 1971 (c 77),
(c) any instrument having effect under an enactment within paragraph (a) or (b), or
(d) any other provision of the law for the time being in force which determines British citizenship, British overseas territories citizenship, the status of a British National (Overseas) or British Overseas citizenship.

[Adoption and Children Act 2002, s 74 as amended by the Sexual Offences Act 2003, Sch 6.]

6–3197U   75. Pensions.   Section 67(3) does not affect entitlement to a pension which is payable to or for the benefit of a person and is in payment at the time of the person's adoption.
[Adoption and Children Act 2002, s 75.]

6–3197V   76. Insurance.   (1) Where a child is adopted whose natural parent has effected an insurance with a friendly society or a collecting society or an industrial insurance company for the payment on the death of the child of money for funeral expenses, then—

(a) the rights and liabilities under the policy are by virtue of the adoption transferred to the adoptive parents, and
(b) for the purposes of the enactments relating to such societies and companies, the adoptive parents are to be treated as the person who took out the policy.

(2) Where the adoption is effected by an order made by virtue of section 51(2), the references in subsection (1) to the adoptive parents are to be read as references to the adopter and the other one of the couple.
[Adoption and Children Act 2002, s 76.]

CHAPTER 5
THE REGISTERS[1]

Adopted Children Register etc

6–3197W   77. Adopted Children Register.   (1) The Registrar General must continue to maintain in the General Register Office a register, to be called the Adopted Children Register.
(2) The Adopted Children Register is not to be open to public inspection or search.
(3) No entries may be made in the Adopted Children Register other than entries—

(a) directed to be made in it by adoption orders, or
(b) required to be made under Schedule 1.

(4) A certified copy of an entry in the Adopted Children Register, if purporting to be sealed or stamped with the seal of the General Register Office, is to be received as evidence of the adoption to which it relates without further or other proof.
(5) Where an entry in the Adopted Children Register contains a record—

(a) of the date of birth of the adopted person, or
(b) of the country, or the district and sub-district, of the birth of the adopted person,

a certified copy of the entry is also to be received, without further or other proof, as evidence of that date, or country or district and sub-district, (as the case may be) in all respects as if the copy were a certified copy of an entry in the registers of live-births.
(6) Schedule 1 (registration of adoptions and the amendment of adoption orders) is to have effect.
[Adoption and Children Act 2002, s 77.]

---

1. Chapter 5 contains ss 77–82.

6–3197X   78. Searches and copies.   (1) The Registrar General must continue to maintain at the General Register Office an index of the Adopted Children Register.
(2) Any person may—

(a) search the index,
(b) have a certified copy of any entry in the Adopted Children Register.

(3) But a person is not entitled to have a certified copy of an entry in the Adopted Children Register relating to an adopted person who has not attained the age of 18 years unless the applicant has provided the Registrar General with the prescribed particulars.
"Prescribed" means prescribed by regulations[1] made by the Registrar General with the approval of the Chancellor of the Exchequer.
(4) The terms, conditions and regulations as to payment of fees, and otherwise, applicable under

the Births and Deaths Registration Act 1953 (c 20), and the Registration Service Act 1953 (c 37), in respect of—

(a) searches in the index kept in the General Register Office of certified copies of entries in the registers of live-births,

(b) the supply from that office of certified copies of entries in those certified copies,

also apply in respect of searches, and supplies of certified copies, under subsection (2).

[Adoption and Children Act 2002, s 78.]

---

1. The Adopted Children and Adoption Contact Registers Regulations 2005, SI 2005/924 have been made.

6–3197Y   79. Connections between the register and birth records. (1) The Registrar General must make traceable the connection between any entry in the registers of live-births or other records which has been marked "Adopted" and any corresponding entry in the Adopted Children Register.

(2) Information kept by the Registrar General for the purposes of subsection (1) is not to be open to public inspection or search.

(3) Any such information, and any other information which would enable an adopted person to obtain a certified copy of the record of his birth, may only be disclosed by the Registrar General in accordance with this section.

(4) In relation to a person adopted before the appointed day the court may, in exceptional circumstances, order the Registrar General to give any information mentioned in subsection (3) to a person.

(5) On an application made in the prescribed manner by the appropriate adoption agency in respect of an adopted person a record of whose birth is kept by the Registrar General, the Registrar General must give the agency any information relating to the adopted person which is mentioned in subsection (3).

"Appropriate adoption agency" has the same meaning as in section 65.

(6) In relation to a person adopted before the appointed day, Schedule 2 applies instead of subsection (5).

(7) On an application made in the prescribed manner by an adopted person a record of whose birth is kept by the Registrar General and who—

(a) is under the age of 18 years, and

(b) intends to be married,

the Registrar General must inform the applicant whether or not it appears from information contained in the registers of live-births or other records that the applicant and the person whom the applicant intends to marry may be within the prohibited degrees of relationship for the purposes of the Marriage Act 1949 (c 76).

(8) Before the Registrar General gives any information by virtue of this section, any prescribed fee which he has demanded must be paid.

(9) In this section—

"appointed day" means the day appointed for the commencement of sections 56 to 65,

"prescribed" means prescribed by regulations[1] made by the Registrar General with the approval of the Chancellor of the Exchequer.

[Adoption and Children Act 2002, s 79.]

---

1. The Adopted Children and Adoption Contact Registers Regulations 2005, SI 2005/924 have been made.

Adoption Contact Register

6–3197Z   80. Adoption Contact Register. (1) The Registrar General must continue to maintain at the General Register Office in accordance with regulations a register in two Parts to be called the Adoption Contact Register.

(2) Part 1 of the register is to contain the prescribed[1] information about adopted persons who have given the prescribed[1] notice expressing their wishes as to making contact with their relatives.

(3) The Registrar General may only make an entry in Part 1 of the register for an adopted person—

(a) a record of whose birth is kept by the Registrar General,

(b) who has attained the age of 18 years, and

(c) who the Registrar General is satisfied has such information as is necessary to enable him to obtain a certified copy of the record of his birth.

(4) Part 2 of the register is to contain the prescribed[1] information about persons who have given the prescribed[1] notice expressing their wishes, as relatives of adopted persons, as to making contact with those persons.

(5) The Registrar General may only make an entry in Part 2 of the register for a person—

(a) who has attained the age of 18 years, and

(b) who the Registrar General is satisfied is a relative of an adopted person and has such information as is necessary to enable him to obtain a certified copy of the record of the adopted person's birth.

(6) Regulations[1] may provide for—

(a) the disclosure of information contained in one Part of the register to persons for whom there is an entry in the other Part,

(b) the payment of prescribed[1] fees in respect of the making or alteration of entries in the register and the disclosure of information contained in the register.

[Adoption and Children Act 2002, s 80.]

---

1. See the Adopted Children and Adoption Contact Registers Regulations 2005, SI 2005/924.

6–3198   81. Adoption Contact Register: supplementary.   (1) The Adoption Contact Register is not to be open to public inspection or search.

(2) In section 80, "relative", in relation to an adopted person, means any person who (but for his adoption) would be related to him by blood (including half-blood) or marriage.

(3) The Registrar General must not give any information entered in the register to any person except in accordance with subsection (6)(a) of that section or regulations made by virtue of section 64(4)(b).

(4) In section 80, "regulations" means regulations made by the Registrar General with the approval of the Chancellor of the Exchequer, and "prescribed" means prescribed by such regulations.

[Adoption and Children Act 2002, s 81.]

General

6–3198A   82. Interpretation.   (1) In this Chapter—

"records" includes certified copies kept by the Registrar General of entries in any register of births, "registers of live-births" means the registers of live-births made under the Births and Deaths Registration Act 1953 (c 20).

(2) Any register, record or index maintained under this Chapter may be maintained in any form the Registrar General considers appropriate; and references (however expressed) to entries in such a register, or to their amendment, marking or cancellation, are to be read accordingly.

[Adoption and Children Act 2002, s 82.]

CHAPTER 6
ADOPTIONS WITH A FOREIGN ELEMENT[1]

Bringing children into and out of the United Kingdom

6–3198B   83. Restriction on bringing children in.   (1) This section applies where a person who is habitually resident in the British Islands (the "British resident")—

(a) brings, or causes another to bring, a child who is habitually resident outside the British Islands into the United Kingdom for the purpose of adoption by the British resident, or

(b) at any time brings, or causes another to bring, into the United Kingdom a child adopted by the British resident under an external adoption effected within the period of six months ending with that time.

The references to adoption, or to a child adopted, by the British resident include a reference to adoption, or to a child adopted, by the British resident and another person.

(2) But this section does not apply if the child is intended to be adopted under a Convention adoption order[2].

(3) An external adoption means an adoption, other than a Convention adoption, of a child effected under the law of any country or territory outside the British Islands, whether or not the adoption is—

(a) an adoption within the meaning of Chapter 4, or

(b) a full adoption (within the meaning of section 88(3)).

(4) Regulations[3] may require a person intending to bring, or to cause another to bring, a child into the United Kingdom in circumstances where this section applies—

(a) to apply to an adoption agency (including a Scottish or Northern Irish adoption agency) in the prescribed manner for an assessment of his suitability to adopt the child, and

(b) to give the agency any information it may require for the purpose of the assessment.

(5) Regulations[3] may require prescribed conditions to be met in respect of a child brought into the United Kingdom in circumstances where this section applies.

(6) In relation to a child brought into the United Kingdom for adoption in circumstances where this section applies, regulations[3] may—

(a) provide for any provision of Chapter 3 to apply with modifications or not to apply, (b)　if notice of intention to adopt has been given, impose functions in respect of the child on the local authority to which the notice was given.

(7) If a person brings, or causes another to bring, a child into the United Kingdom at any time in circumstances where this section applies, he is guilty of an offence if—

(a)　he has not complied with any requirement imposed by virtue of subsection (4), or
(b)　any condition required to be met by virtue of subsection (5) is not met,

before that time, or before any later time which may be prescribed[3].

(8) A person guilty of an offence under this section is liable—

(a)　on summary conviction to imprisonment for a term not exceeding six months, or a fine not exceeding the statutory maximum, or both,
(b)　on conviction on indictment, to imprisonment for a term not exceeding twelve months, or a fine, or both.

(9) In this section, "prescribed" means prescribed by regulations and "regulations" means regulations made by the Secretary of State, after consultation with the Assembly.

[Adoption and Children Act 2002, s 83.]

---

1. Chapter 6 contains ss 83–91. The provisions in this Chapter incorporate many of the measures of the Adoption (Intercountry Aspects) Act 1999 and extend those measures with new safeguards and penalties.
2. "Convention adoption order" is defined in s 144(1), post.
3. See the Adoptions with a Foreign Element Regulations 2005, SI 2005/392 amended by SI 2005/3482.

6–3198C　84. Giving parental responsibility prior to adoption abroad.　(1) The High Court may, on an application by persons who the court is satisfied intend to adopt a child under the law of a country or territory outside the British Islands, make an order giving parental responsibility for the child to them.

(2) An order under this section may not give parental responsibility to persons who the court is satisfied meet those requirements as to domicile, or habitual residence, in England and Wales which have to be met if an adoption order is to be made in favour of those persons.

(3) An order under this section may not be made unless any requirements prescribed by regulations are satisfied.

(4) An application for an order under this section may not be made unless at all times during the preceding ten weeks the child's home was with the applicant or, in the case of an application by two people, both of them.

(5) Section 46(2) to (4) has effect in relation to an order under this section as it has effect in relation to adoption orders.

(6) Regulations may provide for any provision of this Act which refers to adoption orders to apply, with or without modifications, to orders under this section.

(7) In this section, "regulations" means regulations[1] made by the Secretary of State, after consultation with the Assembly.

[Adoption and Children Act 2002, s 84.]

---

1. The Adoptions with a Foreign Element Regulations 2005, SI 2005/392 amended by SI 2005/3482 have been made.

6–3198D　85. Restriction on taking children out.　(1) A child who—

(a)　is a Commonwealth citizen, or
(b)　is habitually resident in the United Kingdom,

must not be removed from the United Kingdom to a place outside the British Islands for the purpose of adoption unless the condition in subsection (2) is met.

(2) The condition is that—

(a)　the prospective adopters have parental responsibility for the child by virtue of an order under section 84, or
(b)　the child is removed under the authority of an order under section 49 of the Adoption (Scotland) Act 1978 (c 28) or Article 57 of the Adoption (Northern Ireland) Order 1987 (SI 1987/2203 (NI 22)).

(3) Removing a child from the United Kingdom includes arranging to do so; and the circumstances in which a person arranges to remove a child from the United Kingdom include those where he—

(a)　enters into an arrangement for the purpose of facilitating such a removal of the child,
(b)　initiates or takes part in any negotiations of which the purpose is the conclusion of an arrangement within paragraph (a), or

An arrangement includes an agreement (whether or not enforceable).

(4) A person who removes a child from the United Kingdom in contravention of subsection (1) is guilty of an offence.

(5) A person is not guilty of an offence under subsection (4) of causing a person to take any step

mentioned in paragraph (*a*) or (*b*) of subsection (3) unless it is proved that he knew or had reason to suspect that the step taken would contravene subsection (1).

But this subsection only applies if sufficient evidence is adduced to raise an issue as to whether the person had the knowledge or reason mentioned.

(6) A person guilty of an offence under this section is liable—

(*a*) on summary conviction to imprisonment for a term not exceeding six months, or a fine not exceeding the statutory maximum, or both,

(*b*) on conviction on indictment, to imprisonment for a term not exceeding twelve months, or a fine, or both.

(7) In any proceedings under this section—

(*a*) a report by a British consular officer or a deposition made before a British consular officer and authenticated under the signature of that officer is admissible, upon proof that the officer or the deponent cannot be found in the United Kingdom, as evidence of the matters stated in it, and

(*b*) it is not necessary to prove the signature or official character of the person who appears to have signed any such report or deposition.

[Adoption and Children Act 2002, s 85.]

6–3198E 86. Power to modify sections 83 and 85. (1) Regulations may provide for section 83 not to apply if—

(*a*) the adopters or (as the case may be) prospective adopters are natural parents, natural relatives or guardians of the child in question (or one of them is), or

(*b*) the British resident in question is a partner of a parent of the child,

and any prescribed conditions are met.

(2) Regulations may provide for section 85(1) to apply with modifications, or not to apply, if—

(*a*) the prospective adopters are parents, relatives or guardians of the child in question (or one of them is), or

(*b*) the prospective adopter is a partner of a parent of the child,

and any prescribed conditions are met.

(3) On the occasion of the first exercise of the power to make regulations under this section—

(*a*) the statutory instrument containing the regulations is not to be made unless a draft of the instrument has been laid before, and approved by a resolution of, each House of Parliament, and

(*b*) accordingly section 140(2) does not apply to the instrument.

(4) In this section, "prescribed" means prescribed by regulations and "regulations" means regulations made by the Secretary of State after consultation with the Assembly.

[Adoption and Children Act 2002, s 86.]

Overseas adoptions

6–3198F 87. Overseas adoptions. (1) In this Act, "overseas adoption"—

(*a*) means an adoption of a description specified in an order made by the Secretary of State, being a description of adoptions effected under the law of any country or territory outside the British Islands, but

(*b*) does not include a Convention adoption.

(2) Regulations may prescribe the requirements that ought to be met by an adoption of any description effected after the commencement of the regulations for it to be an overseas adoption for the purposes of this Act.

(3) At any time when such regulations have effect, the Secretary of State must exercise his powers under this section so as to secure that subsequently effected adoptions of any description are not overseas adoptions for the purposes of this Act if he considers that they are not likely within a reasonable time to meet the prescribed requirements.

(4) In this section references to this Act include the Adoption Act 1976 (c 36).

(5) An order under this section may contain provision as to the manner in which evidence of any overseas adoption may be given.

(6) In this section—

"adoption" means an adoption of a child or of a person who was a child at the time the adoption was applied for,

"regulations" means regulations made by the Secretary of State after consultation with the Assembly.

[Adoption and Children Act 2002, s 87.]

Miscellaneous

6–3198G   88. Modification of section 67 for Hague Convention adoptions.   (1) If the High Court is satisfied, on an application under this section, that each of the following conditions is met in the case of a Convention adoption, it may direct that section 67(3) does not apply, or does not apply to any extent specified in the direction.

(2) The conditions are—

(*a*)   that under the law of the country in which the adoption was effected, the adoption is not a full adoption,

(*b*)   that the consents referred to in Article 4(*c*) and (*d*) of the Convention have not been given for a full adoption or that the United Kingdom is not the receiving State (within the meaning of Article 2 of the Convention),

(*c*)   that it would be more favourable to the adopted child for a direction to be given under subsection (1).

(3) A full adoption is an adoption by virtue of which the child is to be treated in law as not being the child of any person other than the adopters or adopter.

(4) In relation to a direction under this section and an application for it, sections 59 and 60 of the Family Law Act 1986 (c 55) (declarations under Part 3 of that Act as to marital status) apply as they apply in relation to a direction under that Part and an application for such a direction.

[Adoption and Children Act 2002, s 88.]

6–3198H   89. Annulment etc of overseas or Hague Convention adoptions.   (1) The High Court may, on an application under this subsection, by order annul a Convention adoption or Convention adoption order on the ground that the adoption is contrary to public policy.

(2) The High Court may, on an application under this subsection—

(*a*)   by order provide for an overseas adoption or a determination under section 91 to cease to be valid on the ground that the adoption or determination is contrary to public policy or that the authority which purported to authorise the adoption or make the determination was not competent to entertain the case, or

(*b*)   decide the extent, if any, to which a determination under section 91 has been affected by a subsequent determination under that section.

(3) The High Court may, in any proceedings in that court, decide that an overseas adoption or a determination under section 91 is to be treated, for the purposes of those proceedings, as invalid on either of the grounds mentioned in subsection (2)(*a*).

(4) Subject to the preceding provisions, the validity of a Convention adoption, Convention adoption order or overseas adoption or a determination under section 91 cannot be called in question in proceedings in any court in England and Wales.

[Adoption and Children Act 2002, s 89.]

6–3198I   90. Section 89: supplementary.   (1) Any application for an order under section 89 or a decision under subsection (2)(*b*) or (3) of that section must be made in the prescribed manner and within any prescribed period.

"Prescribed" means prescribed by rules.

(2) No application may be made under section 89(1) in respect of an adoption unless immediately before the application is made—

(*a*)   the person adopted, or

(*b*)   the adopters or adopter,

habitually reside in England and Wales.

(3) In deciding in pursuance of section 89 whether such an authority as is mentioned in section 91 was competent to entertain a particular case, a court is bound by any finding of fact made by the authority and stated by the authority to be so made for the purpose of determining whether the authority was competent to entertain the case.

[Adoption and Children Act 2002, s 90.]

6–3198J   91. Overseas determinations and orders.   (1) Subsection (2) applies where any authority of a Convention country (other than the United Kingdom) or of the Channel Islands, the Isle of Man or any British overseas territory has power under the law of that country or territory—

(*a*)   to authorise, or review the authorisation of, an adoption order made in that country or territory, or

(*b*)   to give or review a decision revoking or annulling such an order or a Convention adoption.

(2) If the authority makes a determination in the exercise of that power, the determination is to have effect for the purpose of effecting, confirming or terminating the adoption in question or, as the case may be, confirming its termination.

(3) Subsection (2) is subject to section 89 and to any subsequent determination having effect under that subsection.

[Adoption and Children Act 2002, s 91.]

CHAPTER 7
MISCELLANEOUS[1]

Restrictions

6–3198K   92. Restriction on arranging adoptions etc.   (1) A person who is neither an adoption agency nor acting in pursuance of an order of the High Court must not take any of the steps mentioned in subsection (2).

(2) The steps are—

(a) asking a person other than an adoption agency to provide a child for adoption,
(b) asking a person other than an adoption agency to provide prospective adopters for a child,
(c) offering to find a child for adoption,
(d) offering a child for adoption to a person other than an adoption agency,
(e) handing over a child to any person other than an adoption agency with a view to the child's adoption by that or another person,
(f) receiving a child handed over to him in contravention of paragraph (e),
(g) entering into an agreement with any person for the adoption of a child, or for the purpose of facilitating the adoption of a child, where no adoption agency is acting on behalf of the child in the adoption,
(h) initiating or taking part in negotiations of which the purpose is the conclusion of an agreement within paragraph (g),
(i) causing another person to take any of the steps mentioned in paragraphs (a) to (h).

(3) Subsection (1) does not apply to a person taking any of the steps mentioned in paragraphs (d), (e), (g), (h) and (i) of subsection (2) if the following condition is met.

(4) The condition is that—

(a) the prospective adopters are parents, relatives or guardians of the child (or one of them is), or
(b) the prospective adopter is the partner of a parent of the child.

(5) References to an adoption agency in subsection (2) include a prescribed person outside the United Kingdom exercising functions corresponding to those of an adoption agency, if the functions are being exercised in prescribed circumstances in respect of the child in question.

(6) The Secretary of State may, after consultation with the Assembly, by order make any amendments of subsections (1) to (4), and any consequential amendments of this Act, which he considers necessary or expedient.

(7) In this section—

(a) "agreement" includes an arrangement (whether or not enforceable),
(b) "prescribed" means prescribed by regulations made by the Secretary of State after consultation with the Assembly.

[Adoption and Children Act 2002, s 92.]

---

1. Chapter 7 contains ss 92–110.

6–3198L   93. Offence of breaching restrictions under section 92.   (1) If a person contravenes section 92(1), he is guilty of an offence; and, if that person is an adoption society, the person who manages the society is also guilty of the offence.

(2) A person is not guilty of an offence under subsection (1) of taking the step mentioned in paragraph (f) of section 92(2) unless it is proved that he knew or had reason to suspect that the child was handed over to him in contravention of paragraph (e) of that subsection.

(3) A person is not guilty of an offence under subsection (1) of causing a person to take any of the steps mentioned in paragraphs (a) to (h) of section 92(2) unless it is proved that he knew or had reason to suspect that the step taken would contravene the paragraph in question.

(4) But subsections (2) and (3) only apply if sufficient evidence is adduced to raise an issue as to whether the person had the knowledge or reason mentioned.

(5) A person guilty of an offence under this section is liable on summary conviction to imprisonment for a term not exceeding six months, or a fine not exceeding £10,000, or both.

[Adoption and Children Act 2002, s 93.]

6–3198M   94. Restriction on reports.   (1) A person who is not within a prescribed description may not, in any prescribed circumstances, prepare a report for any person about the suitability of a child for adoption or of a person to adopt a child or about the adoption, or placement for adoption, of a child.

"Prescribed" means prescribed by regulations[1] made by the Secretary of State after consultation with the Assembly.

(2) If a person—

(*a*) contravenes subsection (1), or

(*b*) causes a person to prepare a report, or submits to any person a report which has been prepared, in contravention of that subsection,

he is guilty of an offence.

(3) If a person who works for an adoption society—

(*a*) contravenes subsection (1), or

(*b*) causes a person to prepare a report, or submits to any person a report which has been prepared, in contravention of that subsection,

the person who manages the society is also guilty of the offence.

(4) A person is not guilty of an offence under subsection (2)(*b*) unless it is proved that he knew or had reason to suspect that the report would be, or had been, prepared in contravention of subsection (1).

But this subsection only applies if sufficient evidence is adduced to raise an issue as to whether the person had the knowledge or reason mentioned.

(5) A person guilty of an offence under this section is liable on summary conviction to imprisonment for a term not exceeding six months, or a fine not exceeding level 5 on the standard scale, or both.

[Adoption and Children Act 2002, s 94.]

---

1. The Restriction on the Preparation of Adoption Reports Regulations 2005, SI 2005/1711 have been made. The Restriction on the Preparation of Adoption Reports Regulations 2005, SI 2005/1711 have been made. The Local Authority (Non-agency Adoptions) Regulations 2005, SI 2005/3113 and the Local Authority (Adoption) (Miscellaneous Provisions) Regulations 2005, SI 2005/3390 have been made.

6–3198N 95. Prohibition of certain payments. (1) This section applies to any payment (other than an excepted payment) which is made for or in consideration of—

(*a*) the adoption of a child,

(*b*) giving any consent required in connection with the adoption of a child,

(*c*) removing from the United Kingdom a child who is a Commonwealth citizen, or is habitually resident in the United Kingdom, to a place outside the British Islands for the purpose of adoption,

(*d*) a person (who is neither an adoption agency nor acting in pursuance of an order of the High Court) taking any step mentioned in section 92(2),

(*e*) preparing, causing to be prepared or submitting a report the preparation of which contravenes section 94(1).

(2) In this section and section 96, removing a child from the United Kingdom has the same meaning as in section 85.

(3) Any person who—

(*a*) makes any payment to which this section applies,

(*b*) agrees or offers to make any such payment, or

(*c*) receives or agrees to receive or attempts to obtain any such payment,

is guilty of an offence.

(4) A person guilty of an offence under this section is liable on summary conviction to imprisonment for a term not exceeding six months, or a fine not exceeding £10,000, or both.

[Adoption and Children Act 2002, s 95.]

6–3198O 96. Excepted payments. (1) A payment is an excepted payment if it is made by virtue of, or in accordance with provision made by or under, this Act, the Adoption (Scotland) Act 1978 (c 28) or the Adoption (Northern Ireland) Order 1987 (SI 1987/2203 (NI 22)).

(2) A payment is an excepted payment if it is made to a registered adoption society by—

(*a*) a parent or guardian of a child, or

(*b*) a person who adopts or proposes to adopt a child,

in respect of expenses reasonably incurred by the society in connection with the adoption or proposed adoption of the child.

(3) A payment is an excepted payment if it is made in respect of any legal or medical expenses incurred or to be incurred by any person in connection with an application to a court which he has made or proposes to make for an adoption order, a placement order, or an order under section 26 or 84.

(4) A payment made as mentioned in section 95(1)(*c*) is an excepted payment if—

(*a*) the condition in section 85(2) is met, and

(*b*) the payment is made in respect of the travel and accommodation expenses reasonably incurred in removing the child from the United Kingdom for the purpose of adoption.

[Adoption and Children Act 2002, s 96.]

6-3198P 97. Sections 92 to 96: interpretation. In sections 92 to 96—

  (*a*) "adoption agency" includes a Scottish or Northern Irish adoption agency,
  (*b*) "payment" includes reward,
  (*c*) references to adoption are to the adoption of persons, wherever they may be habitually resident, effected under the law of any country or territory, whether within or outside the British Islands.

[Adoption and Children Act 2002, s 97.]

Information

6-3198Q 98. Pre-commencement adoptions: information. (1) Regulations[1] under section 9 may make provision for the purpose of—

  (*a*) assisting persons adopted before the appointed day who have attained the age of 18 to obtain information in relation to their adoption, and
  (*b*) facilitating contact between such persons and their relatives.

  (2) For that purpose the regulations may confer functions on—

  (*a*) registered adoption support agencies,
  (*b*) the Registrar General,
  (*c*) adoption agencies.

  (3) For that purpose the regulations may—

  (*a*) authorise or require any person mentioned in subsection (2) to disclose information,
  (*b*) authorise or require the disclosure of information contained in records kept under section 8 of the Public Records Act 1958 (c 51) (court records),

and may impose conditions on the disclosure of information, including conditions restricting its further disclosure.

  (4) The regulations may authorise the charging of prescribed fees by any person mentioned in subsection (2) or in respect of the disclosure of information under subsection (3)(*b*).

  (5) An authorisation or requirement to disclose information by virtue of subsection (3)(*a*) has effect in spite of any restriction on the disclosure of information in Chapter 5.

  (6) The making of regulations by virtue of subsections (2) to (4) which relate to the Registrar General requires the approval of the Chancellor of the Exchequer.

  (7) In this section—

"appointed day" means the day appointed for the commencement of sections 56 to 65,
"registered adoption support agency" means an adoption support agency in respect of which a person is registered under Part 2 of the Care Standards Act 2000 (c 14),
"relative", in relation to an adopted person, means any person who (but for his adoption) would be related to him by blood (including half-blood) or marriage.

[Adoption and Children Act 2002, s 98.]

---

1. The Adoption Information and Intermediary Services (Pre-Commencement Adoptions) Regulations 2005, SI 2005/890 amended by SI 2005/2720 (E) and 3482 and the Adoption Information and Intermediary Services (Pre-Commencement Adoptions) (Wales) Regulations 2005, SI 2005/2701 amended by SI 2005/3293 have been made.

Proceedings

6-3198R 99. Proceedings for offences. Proceedings for an offence by virtue of section 9 or 59 may not, without the written consent of the Attorney General, be taken by any person other than the National Care Standards Commission or the Assembly.

[Adoption and Children Act 2002, s 99.]

6-3198S 100. Appeals. *Amends s 94 of the Children Act 1989.*

6-3198T 101. Privacy. (1) Proceedings under this Act in the High Court or a County Court may be heard and determined in private.

  (2) In section 12 of the Administration of Justice Act 1960 (c 65) (publication of information relating to proceedings in private), in subsection (1)(*a*)(ii), after "1989" there is inserted "or the Adoption and Children Act 2002".

  (3) *Amends s 97 of the Children Act 1989.*

[Adoption and Children Act 2002, s 101.]

The Children and Family Court Advisory and Support Service

6-3198U 102. Officers of the Service. (1) For the purposes of—

  (*a*) any relevant application,
  (*b*) the signification by any person of any consent to placement or adoption,

rules must provide for the appointment in prescribed cases of an officer of the Children and Family Court Advisory and Support Service ("the Service").

(2) The rules may provide for the appointment of such an officer in other circumstances in which it appears to the Lord Chancellor to be necessary or expedient to do so.

(3) The rules may provide for the officer—

(a) to act on behalf of the child upon the hearing of any relevant application, with the duty of safeguarding the interests of the child in the prescribed manner,

(b) where the court so requests, to prepare a report on matters relating to the welfare of the child in question,

(c) to witness documents which signify consent to placement or adoption,

(d) to perform prescribed functions.

(4) A report prepared in pursuance of the rules on matters relating to the welfare of a child must—

(a) deal with prescribed matters (unless the court orders otherwise), and

(b) be made in the manner required by the court.

(5) A person who—

(a) in the case of an application for the making, varying or revocation of a placement order, is employed by the local authority which made the application,

(b) in the case of an application for an adoption order in respect of a child who was placed for adoption, is employed by the adoption agency which placed him, or

(c) is within a prescribed description,

is not to be appointed under subsection (1) or (2).

(6) In this section, "relevant application" means an application for—

(a) the making, varying or revocation of a placement order,

(b) the making of an order under section 26, or the varying or revocation of such an order,

(c) the making of an adoption order, or

(d) the making of an order under section 84.

(7) Rules may make provision as to the assistance which the court may require an officer of the Service to give to it.

[Adoption and Children Act 2002, s 102.]

6–3198V   103. Right of officers of the Service to have access to adoption agency records.
(1) Where an officer of the Service has been appointed to act under section 102(1), he has the right at all reasonable times to examine and take copies of any records of, or held by, an adoption agency which were compiled in connection with the making, or proposed making, by any person of any application under this Part in respect of the child concerned.

(2) Where an officer of the Service takes a copy of any record which he is entitled to examine under this section, that copy or any part of it is admissible as evidence of any matter referred to in any—

(a) report which he makes to the court in the proceedings in question, or

(b) evidence which he gives in those proceedings.

(3) Subsection (2) has effect regardless of any enactment or rule of law which would otherwise prevent the record in question being admissible in evidence.

[Adoption and Children Act 2002, s 103.]

Evidence

6–3198W   104. Evidence of consent.   (1) If a document signifying any consent which is required by this Part to be given is witnessed in accordance with rules, it is to be admissible in evidence without further proof of the signature of the person by whom it was executed.

(2) A document signifying any such consent which purports to be witnessed in accordance with rules is to be presumed to be so witnessed, and to have been executed and witnessed on the date and at the place specified in the document, unless the contrary is proved.

[Adoption and Children Act 2002, s 104.]

Scotland, Northern Ireland and the Islands

6–3198X   105. Effect of certain Scottish orders and provisions.   (1) A Scottish adoption order or an order under section 25 of the Adoption (Scotland) Act 1978 (c 28) (interim adoption orders) has effect in England and Wales as it has in Scotland, but as if references to the parental responsibilities and the parental rights in relation to a child were to parental responsibility for the child.

(2) An order made under section 18 of the Adoption (Scotland) Act 1978 (freeing orders), and the revocation or variation of such an order under section 20 or 21 of that Act, have effect in England and Wales as they have effect in Scotland, but as if references to the parental responsibilities and the parental rights in relation to a child were to parental responsibility for the child.

(3) Any person who—

(*a*)   contravenes section 27(1) of that Act (removal where adoption agreed etc), or

(*b*)   contravenes section 28(1) or (2) of that Act (removal where applicant provided home),

is guilty of an offence and liable on summary conviction to imprisonment for a term not exceeding three months, or a fine not exceeding level 5 on the standard scale, or both.

(4)   Orders made under section 29 of that Act (order to return or not to remove child) are to have effect in England and Wales as if they were orders of the High Court under section 41 of this Act.

[Adoption and Children Act 2002, s 105.]

6–3198Y   106. Effect of certain Northern Irish orders and provisions.   (1) A Northern Irish adoption order or an order under Article 26 of the Adoption (Northern Ireland) Order 1987 (SI 1987/2203 (NI 22)) (interim orders) has effect in England and Wales as it has in Northern Ireland.

(2)   An order made under Article 17 or 18 of the Adoption (Northern Ireland) Order 1987 (freeing orders), or the variation or revocation of such an order under Article 20 or 21 of that Order, have effect in England and Wales as they have in Northern Ireland.

(3)   Any person who—

(*a*)   contravenes Article 28(1) or (2) of the Adoption (Northern Ireland) Order 1987 (removal where adoption agreed etc), or

(*b*)   contravenes Article 29(1) or (2) of that Order (removal where applicant provided home),

is guilty of an offence and liable on summary conviction to imprisonment for a term not exceeding three months, or a fine not exceeding level 5 on the standard scale, or both.

(4)   Orders made under Article 30 of that Order (order to return or not to remove child) are to have effect in England and Wales as if they were orders of the High Court under section 41 of this Act.

[Adoption and Children Act 2002, s 106.]

6–3198Z   107. Use of adoption records from other parts of the British Islands.   Any document which is receivable as evidence of any matter—

(*a*)   in Scotland under section 45(2) of the Adoption (Scotland) Act 1978 (c 28),

(*b*)   in Northern Ireland under Article 63(1) of the Adoption (Northern Ireland) Order 1987, or

(*c*)   in the Isle of Man or any of the Channel Islands under an enactment corresponding to section 77(3) of this Act,

is also receivable as evidence of that matter in England and Wales.

[Adoption and Children Act 2002, s 107.]

6–3199   108. Channel Islands and the Isle of Man.   (1) Regulations may provide—

(*a*)   for a reference in any provision of this Act to an order of a court to include an order of a court in the Isle of Man or any of the Channel Islands which appears to the Secretary of State to correspond in its effect to the order in question,

(*b*)   for a reference in any provision of this Act to an adoption agency to include a person who appears to the Secretary of State to exercise functions under the law of the Isle of Man or any of the Channel Islands which correspond to those of an adoption agency and for any reference in any provision of this Act to a child placed for adoption by an adoption agency to be read accordingly,

(*c*)   for a reference in any provision of this Act to an enactment (including an enactment contained in this Act) to include a provision of the law of the Isle of Man or any of the Channel Islands which appears to the Secretary of State to correspond in its effect to the enactment,

(*d*)   for any reference in any provision of this Act to the United Kingdom to include the Isle of Man or any of the Channel Islands.

(2)   Regulations may modify any provision of this Act, as it applies to any order made, or other thing done, under the law of the Isle of Man or any of the Channel Islands.

(3)   In this section, "regulations" means regulations made by the Secretary of State after consultation with the Assembly.

[Adoption and Children Act 2002, s 108.]

General

6–3199A   109. Avoiding delay.   (1) In proceedings in which a question may arise as to whether an adoption order or placement order should be made, or any other question with respect to such an order, the court must (in the light of any rules made by virtue of subsection (2))—

(*a*)   draw up a timetable with a view to determining such a question without delay, and

(*b*)   give such directions as it considers appropriate for the purpose of ensuring that the timetable is adhered to.

(2)   Rules may—

(a) prescribe periods within which prescribed steps must be taken in relation to such proceedings, and

(b) make other provision with respect to such proceedings for the purpose of ensuring that such questions are determined without delay.

[Adoption and Children Act 2002, s 109.]

6–3199B   **110. Service of notices etc.**   Any notice or information required to be given by virtue of this Act may be given by post.

[Adoption and Children Act 2002, s 110.]

PART 2
AMENDMENTS OF THE CHILDREN ACT 1989[1]

6–3199C   **111. Parental responsibility of unmarried father.**   (1) Section 4 of the 1989 Act (acquisition of responsibility by the father of a child who is not married to the child's mother) is amended as follows.

(2) In subsection (1) (cases where parental responsibility is acquired), for the words after "birth" there is substituted

", the father shall acquire parental responsibility for the child if—

(a) he becomes registered as the child's father under any of the enactments specified in subsection (1A);

(b) he and the child's mother make an agreement (a "parental responsibility agreement") providing for him to have parental responsibility for the child; or

(c) the court, on his application, orders that he shall have parental responsibility for the child."

(3) After that subsection there is inserted—

"(1A) The enactments referred to in subsection (1)(a) are—

(a) paragraphs (a), (b) and (c) of section 10(1) and of section 10A(1) of the Births and Deaths Registration Act 1953;

(b) paragraphs (a), (b)(i) and (c) of section 18(1), and sections 18(2)(b) and 20(1)(a) of the Registration of Births, Deaths and Marriages (Scotland) Act 1965; and

(c) sub-paragraphs (a), (b) and (c) of Article 14(3) of the Births and Deaths Registration (Northern Ireland) Order 1976.

(1B) The Lord Chancellor may by order amend subsection (1A) so as to add further enactments to the list in that subsection."

(4) For subsection (3) there is substituted—

"(2A) A person who has acquired parental responsibility under subsection (1) shall cease to have that responsibility only if the court so orders.

(3) The court may make an order under subsection (2A) on the application—

(a) of any person who has parental responsibility for the child; or

(b) with the leave of the court, of the child himself,

subject, in the case of parental responsibility acquired under subsection (1)(c), to section 12(4)."

(5) Accordingly, in section 2(2) of the 1989 Act (a father of a child who is not married to the child's mother shall not have parental responsibility for the child unless he acquires it in accordance with the provisions of the Act), for the words from "shall not" to "acquires it" there is substituted "shall have parental responsibility for the child if he has acquired it (and has not ceased to have it)".

(6) In section 104 of the 1989 Act (regulations and orders)—

(a) in subsection (2), after "section" there is inserted "4(1B),", and

(b) in subsection (3), after "section" there is inserted "4(1B) or".

(7) Paragraph (a) of section 4(1) of the 1989 Act, as substituted by subsection (2) of this section, does not confer parental responsibility on a man who was registered under an enactment referred to in paragraph (a), (b) or (c) of section 4(1A) of that Act, as inserted by subsection (3) of this section, before the commencement of subsection (3) in relation to that paragraph[2].

[Adoption and Children Act 2002, s 111.]

---

1. Part 2 contains ss 111–122.
2. Section 111 is in force from 1 December 2003: see Adoption and Children Act 2002 (Commencement No 4) Order 2003, SI 2003/3079.

6–3199D   **112. Acquisition of parental responsibility by step-parent.**   *Inserts new s 4A into the Children Act 1989.*

6–3199E   **113. Section 8 orders: local authority foster parents.**   *Amends s 9 of the Children Act 1989.*

6–3199F   114. Residence orders: extension to age of 18. *Amends s 9, 12 and 91 of the Children Act 1989.*

6–3199G   115. Special guardianship. *Amends ss 1 and 5 and inserts new ss 14A–14G into the Children Act 1989.*

6–3199H   116. Accommodation of children in need etc. *Amends ss 17, 22 and 24A of the Children Act 1989.*

6–3199I   117. Inquiries by local authorities into representations. *Amends ss 24D and 26 of the Children Act 1989.*

6–3199J   118. Review of cases of looked after children. *Makes various amendments to s 26 of the Children Act 1989.*

6–3199K   119. Advocacy services. *Inserts new s 26A into the Children Act 1989.*

6–3199L   120. Meaning of "harm" in the 1989 Act. *Amends s 31 of the Children Act 1989.*

6–3199M   121. Care plans. *Amends s 31 of and inserts new s 31A into the Children Act 1989.*

6–3199N   122. Interests of children in proceedings. *Amend ss 41 and 93 of the Children Act 1989.*

PART 3

MISCELLANEOUS AND FINAL PROVISIONS[1]

CHAPTER 1

MISCELLANEOUS[2]

Advertisements in the United Kingdom

6–3199O   123. Restriction on advertisements etc.   (1) A person must not—

(*a*)   publish or distribute an advertisement or information to which this section applies, or

(*b*)   cause such an advertisement or information to be published or distributed.

(2) This section applies to an advertisement indicating that—

(*a*)   the parent or guardian of a child wants the child to be adopted,

(*b*)   a person wants to adopt a child,

(*c*)   a person other than an adoption agency is willing to take any step mentioned in paragraphs (*a*) to (*e*), (*g*) and (*h*) and (so far as relating to those paragraphs) (*i*) of section 92(2),

(*d*)   a person other than an adoption agency is willing to receive a child handed over to him with a view to the child's adoption by him or another, or

(*e*)   a person is willing to remove a child from the United Kingdom for the purposes of adoption.

(3) This section applies to—

(*a*)   information about how to do anything which, if done, would constitute an offence under section 85 or 93, section 11 or 50 of the Adoption (Scotland) Act 1978 (c 28) or Article 11 or 58 of the Adoption (Northern Ireland) Order 1987 (SI 1987/2203 (NI 22)) (whether or not the information includes a warning that doing the thing in question may constitute an offence),

(*b*)   information about a particular child as a child available for adoption.

(4) For the purposes of this section and section 124—

(*a*)   publishing or distributing an advertisement or information means publishing it or distributing it to the public and includes doing so by electronic means (for example, by means of the internet),

(*b*)   the public includes selected members of the public as well as the public generally or any section of the public.

(5) Subsection (1) does not apply to publication or distribution by or on behalf of an adoption agency.

(6) The Secretary of State may by order make any amendments of this section which he considers necessary or expedient in consequence of any developments in technology relating to publishing or distributing advertisements or other information by electronic or electro-magnetic means.

(7) References to an adoption agency in this section include a prescribed person outside the United Kingdom exercising functions corresponding to those of an adoption agency, if the functions are being exercised in prescribed circumstances.

"Prescribed" means prescribed by regulations made by the Secretary of State.

(8) Before exercising the power conferred by subsection (6) or (7), the Secretary of State must consult the Scottish Ministers, the Department of Health, Social Services and Public Safety and the Assembly.

(9) In this section—

(a) "adoption agency" includes a Scottish or Northern Irish adoption agency,

(b) references to adoption are to the adoption of persons, wherever they may be habitually resident, effected under the law of any country or territory, whether within or outside the British Islands.

[Adoption and Children Act 2002, s 123.]

---

1. Part 3 contains ss 123–150 and Schedules 1–6.
2. Chapter 1 contains ss 123–139.

6–3199P   124. Offence of breaching restriction under section 123.   (1) A person who contravenes section 123(1) is guilty of an offence.

(2) A person is not guilty of an offence under this section unless it is proved that he knew or had reason to suspect that section 123 applied to the advertisement or information.

But this subsection only applies if sufficient evidence is adduced to raise an issue as to whether the person had the knowledge or reason mentioned.

(3) A person guilty of an offence under this section is liable on summary conviction to imprisonment for a term not exceeding three months, or a fine not exceeding level 5 on the standard scale, or both.

[Adoption and Children Act 2002, s 124.]

Adoption and Children Act Register

6–3199Q   125. Adoption and Children Act Register.   (1) Her Majesty may by Order in Council make provision for the Secretary of State to establish and maintain a register, to be called the Adoption and Children Act Register, containing—

(a) prescribed information about children who are suitable for adoption and prospective adopters who are suitable to adopt a child,

(b) prescribed information about persons included in the register in pursuance of paragraph (a) in respect of things occurring after their inclusion.

(2) For the purpose of giving assistance in finding persons with whom children may be placed for purposes other than adoption, an Order under this section may—

(a) provide for the register to contain information about such persons and the children who may be placed with them, and

(b) apply any of the other provisions of this group of sections (that is, this section and sections 126 to 131), with or without modifications.

(3) The register is not to be open to public inspection or search.

(4) An Order under this section may make provision about the retention of information in the register.

(5) Information is to be kept in the register in any form the Secretary of State considers appropriate.

[Adoption and Children Act 2002, s 125.]

6–3199R   126. Use of an organisation to establish the register.   (1) The Secretary of State may make an arrangement with an organisation under which any function of his under an Order under section 125 of establishing and maintaining the register, and disclosing information entered in, or compiled from information entered in, the register to any person is performed wholly or partly by the organisation on his behalf.

(2) The arrangement may include provision for payments to be made to the organisation by the Secretary of State.

(3) If the Secretary of State makes an arrangement under this section with an organisation, the organisation is to perform the functions exercisable by virtue of this section in accordance with any directions given by the Secretary of State and the directions may be of general application (or general application in any part of Great Britain) or be special directions.

(4) An exercise of the Secretary of State's powers under subsection (1) or (3) requires the agreement of the Scottish Ministers (if the register applies to Scotland) and of the Assembly (if the register applies to Wales).

(5) References in this group of sections to the registration organisation are to any organisation for the time being performing functions in respect of the register by virtue of arrangements under this section.

[Adoption and Children Act 2002, s 126.]

6–3199S   127. Use of an organisation as agency for payments.   (1) An Order under section 125 may authorise an organisation with which an arrangement is made under section 126 to act as agent for the payment or receipt of sums payable by adoption agencies to other adoption agencies and may require adoption agencies to pay or receive such sums through the organisation.

(2) The organisation is to perform the functions exercisable by virtue of this section in accordance with any directions given by the Secretary of State; and the directions may be of general application (or general application in any part of Great Britain) or be special directions.

(3) An exercise of the Secretary of State's power to give directions under subsection (2) requires the agreement of the Scottish Ministers (if any payment agency provision applies to Scotland) and of the Assembly (if any payment agency provision applies to Wales).

[Adoption and Children Act 2002, s 127.]

6–3199T 128. Supply of information for the register. (1) An Order under section 125 may require adoption agencies to give prescribed information to the Secretary of State or the registration organisation for entry in the register.

(2) Information is to be given to the Secretary of State or the registration organisation when required by the Order and in the prescribed form and manner.

(3) An Order under section 125 may require an agency giving information which is entered on the register to pay a prescribed fee to the Secretary of State or the registration organisation.

(4) But an adoption agency is not to disclose any information to the Secretary of State or the registration organisation—

(a) about prospective adopters who are suitable to adopt a child, or persons who were included in the register as such prospective adopters, without their consent,

(b) about children suitable for adoption, or persons who were included in the register as such children, without the consent of the prescribed person.

(5) Consent under subsection (4) is to be given in the prescribed form.

[Adoption and Children Act 2002, s 128.]

6–3199U 129. Disclosure of information. (1) Information entered in the register, or compiled from information entered in the register, may only be disclosed under subsection (2) or (3).

(2) Prescribed information entered in the register may be disclosed by the Secretary of State or the registration organisation—

(a) where an adoption agency is acting on behalf of a child who is suitable for adoption, to the agency to assist in finding prospective adopters with whom it would be appropriate for the child to be placed,

(b) where an adoption agency is acting on behalf of prospective adopters who are suitable to adopt a child, to the agency to assist in finding a child appropriate for adoption by them.

(3) Prescribed information entered in the register, or compiled from information entered in the register, may be disclosed by the Secretary of State or the registration organisation to any prescribed person for use for statistical or research purposes, or for other prescribed purposes.

(4) An Order under section 125 may prescribe the steps to be taken by adoption agencies in respect of information received by them by virtue of subsection (2).

(5) Subsection (1) does not apply—

(a) to a disclosure of information with the authority of the Secretary of State, or

(b) to a disclosure by the registration organisation of prescribed information to the Scottish Ministers (if the register applies to Scotland) or the Assembly (if the register applies to Wales).

(6) Information disclosed to any person under subsection (2) or (3) may be given on any prescribed terms or conditions.

(7) An Order under section 125 may, in prescribed circumstances, require a prescribed fee to be paid to the Secretary of State or the registration organisation—

(a) by a prescribed adoption agency in respect of information disclosed under subsection (2), or

(b) by a person to whom information is disclosed under subsection (3).

(8) If any information entered in the register is disclosed to a person in contravention of subsection (1), the person disclosing it is guilty of an offence.

(9) A person guilty of an offence under subsection (8) is liable on summary conviction to imprisonment for a term not exceeding three months, or a fine not exceeding level 5 on the standard scale, or both.

[Adoption and Children Act 2002, s 129.]

6–3199V 130. Territorial application. (1) In this group of sections, "adoption agency" means—

(a) a local authority in England,

(b) a registered adoption society whose principal office is in England.

(2) An Order under section 125 may provide for any requirements imposed on adoption agencies in respect of the register to apply—

(a) to Scottish local authorities and to voluntary organisations providing a registered adoption service,

(b)   to local authorities in Wales and to registered adoption societies whose principal offices are in Wales,

and, in relation to the register, references to adoption agencies in this group of sections include any authorities or societies mentioned in paragraphs (a) and (b) to which an Order under that section applies those requirements.

(3) For the purposes of this group of sections, references to the register applying to Scotland or Wales are to those requirements applying as mentioned in paragraph (a) or, as the case may be, (b) of subsection (2).

(4) An Order under section 125 may apply any provision made by virtue of section 127—

(a)   to Scottish local authorities and to voluntary organisations providing a registered adoption service,

(b)   to local authorities in Wales and to registered adoption societies whose principal offices are in Wales.

(5) For the purposes of this group of sections, references to any payment agency provision applying to Scotland or Wales are to provision made by virtue of section 127 applying as mentioned in paragraph (a) or, as the case may be, (b) of subsection (4).

[Adoption and Children Act 2002, s 130.]

6–3199W   131. Supplementary.   (1) In this group of sections—

(a)   "organisation" includes a public body and a private or voluntary organisation,

(b)   "prescribed" means prescribed by an Order under section 125,

(c)   "the register" means the Adoption and Children Act Register,

(d)   "Scottish local authority" means a local authority within the meaning of the Regulation of Care (Scotland) Act 2001 (asp 4),

(e)   "voluntary organisation providing a registered adoption service" has the same meaning as in section 144(3).

(2) For the purposes of this group of sections—

(a)   a child is suitable for adoption if an adoption agency is satisfied that the child ought to be placed for adoption,

(b)   prospective adopters are suitable to adopt a child if an adoption agency is satisfied that they are suitable to have a child placed with them for adoption.

(3) Nothing authorised or required to be done by virtue of this group of sections constitutes an offence under section 93, 94 or 95.

(4) No recommendation to make an Order under section 125 is to be made to Her Majesty in Council unless a draft has been laid before and approved by resolution of each House of Parliament.

(5) If any provision made by an Order under section 125 would, if it were included in an Act of the Scottish Parliament, be within the legislative competence of that Parliament, no recommendation to make the Order is to be made to Her Majesty in Council unless a draft has been laid before, and approved by resolution of, the Parliament.

(6) No recommendation to make an Order under section 125 containing any provision in respect of the register is to be made to Her Majesty in Council if the register applies to Wales or the Order would provide for the register to apply to Wales, unless a draft has been laid before, and approved by resolution of, the Assembly.

(7) No recommendation to make an Order under section 125 containing any provision by virtue of section 127 is to be made to Her Majesty in Council if any payment agency provision applies to Wales or the Order would provide for any payment agency provision to apply to Wales, unless a draft has been laid before, and approved by resolution of, the Assembly.

[Adoption and Children Act 2002, s 131.]

Other miscellaneous provisions

6–3199X   132. Amendment of Adoption (Scotland) Act 1978: contravention of sections 30 to 36 of this Act

6–3199Y   133. Scottish restriction on bringing children into or out of United Kingdom

6–3199Z   134. Amendment of Adoption (Scotland) Act 1978: overseas adoptions

6–3200   135. Adoption and fostering: criminal records.   *Amends ss 113 and 115 of the Police Act 1997.*

6–3200A   136. Payment of grants in connection with welfare services.   *Amends ss 113 and 115 of the Police Act 1997.*

6–3200B **137. Extension of the Hague Convention to British overseas territories.** (1) Her Majesty may by Order in Council provide for giving effect to the Convention in any British overseas territory.

(2) An Order in Council under subsection (1) in respect of any British overseas territory may, in particular, make any provision corresponding to provision which in relation to any part of Great Britain is made by the Adoption (Intercountry Aspects) Act 1999 (c 18) or may be made by regulations under section 1 of that Act.

(3) The British Nationality Act 1981 (c 61) is amended as follows.

(4) In section 1 (acquisition of British citizenship by birth or adoption)—

(a) in subsection (5), at the end of paragraph (b) there is inserted "effected under the law of a country or territory outside the United Kingdom",

(b) at the end of subsection (5A)(b) there is inserted "or in a designated territory",

(c) in subsection (8), the words following "section 50" are omitted.

(5) In section 15 (acquisition of British overseas territories citizenship)—

(a) after subsection (5) there is inserted—

"(5A) Where—

(a) a minor who is not a British overseas territories citizen is adopted under a Convention adoption,

(b) on the date on which the adoption is effected—

(i) the adopter or, in the case of a joint adoption, one of the adopters is a British overseas territories citizen, and

(ii) the adopter or, in the case of a joint adoption, both of the adopters are habitually resident in a designated territory, and

(c) the Convention adoption is effected under the law of a country or territory outside the designated territory,

the minor shall be a British overseas territories citizen as from that date.",

(b) in subsection (6), after "order" there is inserted "or a Convention adoption".

(6) In section 50 (interpretation), in subsection (1)—

(a) after the definition of "company" there is inserted—

""Convention adoption" means an adoption effected under the law of a country or territory in which the Convention is in force, and certified in pursuance of Article 23(1) of the Convention",

(b) after the definition of "Crown service under the government of the United Kingdom" there is inserted—

""designated territory" means a qualifying territory, or the Sovereign Base Areas of Akrotiri and Dhekelia, which is designated by Her Majesty by Order in Council under subsection (14)".

(7) After subsection (13) of that section there is inserted—

"(14) For the purposes of the definition of "designated territory" in subsection (1), an Order in Council may—

(a) designate any qualifying territory, or the Sovereign Base Areas of Akrotiri and Dhekelia, if the Convention is in force there, and

(b) make different designations for the purposes of section 1 and section 15;

and, for the purposes of this subsection and the definition of "Convention adoption" in subsection (1), "the Convention" means the Convention on the Protection of Children and Co-operation in respect of Intercountry Adoption, concluded at the Hague on 29th May 1993.

An Order in Council under this subsection shall be subject to annulment in pursuance of a resolution of either House of Parliament."

[Adoption and Children Act 2002, s 137.]

6–3200C **138. Proceedings in Great Britain.** Proceedings for an offence by virtue of section 9, 59, 93, 94, 95 or 129—

(a) may not be brought more than six years after the commission of the offence but, subject to that,

(b) may be brought within a period of six months from the date on which evidence sufficient in the opinion of the prosecutor to warrant the proceedings came to his knowledge.

In relation to Scotland, "the prosecutor" is to be read as "the procurator fiscal".

[Adoption and Children Act 2002, s 138.]

Amendments etc

6–3200D 139. Amendments, transitional and transitory provisions, savings and repeals.
(1) Schedule 3 (minor and consequential amendments) is to have effect[1].
(2) Schedule 4 (transitional and transitory provisions and savings) is to have effect.
(3) The enactments set out in Schedule 5 are repealed to the extent specified[2].
[Adoption and Children Act 2002, s 139.]

---

1. Subsection 139(1) in force from 28 November 2003 in so far as it relates to paras 103, 105, 106, 110 and 118 of Sch 3; in force from 1 December 2003 in England for the purposes of making regulations, s 139(2), in so far as it relates to Sch 4, para 5; in force from 1 December 2003 in so far as it relates to Sch 3, paras 6 and 7: see Adoption and Children Act 2002 (Commencement No 4) Order 2003, SI 2003/3079.
2. Subsection 139(3) in force from 28 November 2003 in so far as it relates to the repeal of s 12(5)(*b*) of the Criminal Justice and Court Services Act 2000.

CHAPTER 2
FINAL PROVISIONS[1]

6–3200E 140. Orders, rules and regulations. (1) Any power to make subordinate legislation conferred by this Act on the Lord Chancellor, the Secretary of State, the Scottish Ministers, the Assembly or the Registrar General is exercisable by statutory instrument.
(2) A statutory instrument containing subordinate legislation made under any provision of this Act (other than section 14 or 148 or an instrument to which subsection (3) applies) is to be subject to annulment in pursuance of a resolution of either House of Parliament.
(3) A statutory instrument containing subordinate legislation—

(*a*) under section 9 which includes provision made by virtue of section 45(2),
(*b*) under section 92(6), 94 or 123(6), or
(*c*) which adds to, replaces or omits any part of the text of an Act,

is not to be made unless a draft of the instrument has been laid before, and approved by resolution of, each House of Parliament.
(4) Subsections (2) and (3) do not apply to an Order in Council or to subordinate legislation made—

(*a*) by the Scottish Ministers, or
(*b*) by the Assembly, unless made jointly by the Secretary of State and the Assembly.

(5) A statutory instrument containing regulations under section 63(2) made by the Scottish Ministers is to be subject to annulment in pursuance of a resolution of the Scottish Parliament.
(6) The power of the Department of Health, Social Services and Public Safety to make regulations under section 63(2) is to be exercisable by statutory rule for the purposes of the Statutory Rules (Northern Ireland) Order 1979 (SI 1979/ 1573 (NI 12)); and any such regulations are to be subject to negative resolution within the meaning of section 41(6) of the Interpretation Act (Northern Ireland) 1954 (c 33 (NI)) as if they were statutory instruments within the meaning of that Act.
(7) Subordinate legislation made under this Act may make different provision for different purposes.
(8) A power to make subordinate legislation under this Act (as well as being exercisable in relation to all cases to which it extends) may be exercised in relation to—

(*a*) those cases subject to specified exceptions, or
(*b*) a particular case or class of case.

(9) In this section, "subordinate legislation" does not include a direction.
[Adoption and Children Act 2002, s 140.]

---

1. Chapter 2 contains ss 140–150.

6–3200F 141. Rules of procedure. (1) The Lord Chancellor may make rules in respect of any matter to be prescribed by rules made by virtue of this Act and dealing generally with all matters of procedure.
(2) Subsection (1) does not apply in relation to proceedings before magistrates' courts, but the power to make rules conferred by section 144 of the Magistrates' Courts Act 1980 (c 43) includes power to make provision in respect of any of the matters mentioned in that subsection.
(3) In the case of an application for a placement order, for the variation or revocation of such an order, or for an adoption order, the rules must require any person mentioned in subsection (4) to be notified—

(*a*) of the date and place where the application will be heard, and
(*b*) of the fact that, unless the person wishes or the court requires, the person need not attend.

(4) The persons referred to in subsection (3) are—

(*a*) in the case of a placement order, every person who can be found whose consent to the making of the order is required under subsection (3)(*a*) of section 21 (or would be required but for subsection (3)(*b*) of that section) or, if no such person can be found, any relative prescribed by rules who can be found,

(*b*)   in the case of a variation or revocation of a placement order, every person who can be found whose consent to the making of the placement order was required under subsection (3)(*a*) of section 21 (or would have been required but for subsection (3)(*b*) of that section),

(*c*)   in the case of an adoption order—

   (i)   every person who can be found whose consent to the making of the order is required under subsection (2)(*a*) of section 47 (or would be required but for subsection (2)(*c*) of that section) or, if no such person can be found, any relative prescribed by rules who can be found,

   (ii)   every person who has consented to the making of the order under section 20 (and has not withdrawn the consent) unless he has given a notice under subsection (4)(*a*) of that section which has effect,

   (iii) every person who, if leave were given under section 47(5), would be entitled to oppose the making of the order.

(5)   Rules made in respect of magistrates' courts may provide—

(*a*)   for enabling any fact tending to establish the identity of a child with a child to whom a document relates to be proved by affidavit, and

(*b*)   for excluding or restricting in relation to any facts that may be so proved the power of a justice of the peace to compel the attendance of witnesses.

[Adoption and Children Act 2002, s 141.]

6–3200G   142. Supplementary and consequential provision.   (1) The appropriate Minister may by order make—

(*a*)   any supplementary, incidental or consequential provision,

(*b*)   any transitory, transitional or saving provision,

which he considers necessary or expedient for the purposes of, in consequence of or for giving full effect to any provision of this Act.

(2)   For the purposes of subsection (1), where any provision of an order extends to England and Wales, and Scotland or Northern Ireland, the appropriate Minister in relation to the order is the Secretary of State.

(3)   Before making an order under subsection (1) containing provision which would, if included in an Act of the Scottish Parliament, be within the legislative competence of that Parliament, the appropriate Minister must consult the Scottish Ministers.

(4)   Subsection (5) applies to any power of the Lord Chancellor, the Secretary of State or the Assembly to make regulations, rules or an order by virtue of any other provision of this Act or of Her Majesty to make an Order in Council by virtue of section 125.

(5)   The power may be exercised so as to make—

(*a*)   any supplementary, incidental or consequential provision,

(*b*)   any transitory, transitional or saving provision,

which the person exercising the power considers necessary or expedient.

(6)   The provision which may be made under subsection (1) or (5) includes provision modifying Schedule 4 or amending or repealing any enactment or instrument.

In relation to an Order in Council, "enactment" in this subsection includes an enactment comprised in, or in an instrument made under, an Act of the Scottish Parliament.

(7)   The power of the Registrar General to make regulations under Chapter 5 of Part 1 may, with the approval of the Chancellor of the Exchequer, be exercised so as to make—

(*a*)   any supplementary, incidental or consequential provision,

(*b*)   any transitory, transitional or saving provision,

which the Registrar General considers necessary or expedient.

[Adoption and Children Act 2002, s 142.]

6–3200H   143. Offences by bodies corporate and unincorporated bodies.   (1) Where an offence under this Act committed by a body corporate is proved to have been committed with the consent or connivance of, or to be attributable to any neglect on the part of, any director, manager, secretary or other similar officer of the body, or a person purporting to act in any such capacity, that person as well as the body is guilty of the offence and liable to be proceeded against and punished accordingly.

(2)   Where the affairs of a body corporate are managed by its members, subsection (1) applies in relation to the acts and defaults of a member in connection with his functions of management as it applies to a director of a body corporate.

(3)   Proceedings for an offence alleged to have been committed under this Act by an unincorporated body are to be brought in the name of that body (and not in that of any of its members) and, for the

purposes of any such proceedings in England and Wales or Northern Ireland, any rules of court relating to the service of documents have effect as if that body were a corporation.

(4) A fine imposed on an unincorporated body on its conviction of an offence under this Act is to be paid out of the funds of that body.

(5) If an unincorporated body is charged with an offence under this Act—

(a) in England and Wales, section 33 of the Criminal Justice Act 1925 (c 86) and Schedule 3 to the Magistrates' Courts Act 1980 (c 43) (procedure on charge of an offence against a corporation),

(b) in Northern Ireland, section 18 of the Criminal Justice Act (Northern Ireland) 1945 (c 15 (NI)) and Schedule 4 to the Magistrates' Courts (Northern Ireland) Order 1981 (SI 1981/1675 (NI 26)) (procedure on charge of an offence against a corporation),

have effect in like manner as in the case of a corporation so charged.

(6) Where an offence under this Act committed by an unincorporated body (other than a partnership) is proved to have been committed with the consent or connivance of, or to be attributable to any neglect on the part of, any officer of the body or any member of its governing body, he as well as the body is guilty of the offence and liable to be proceeded against and punished accordingly.

(7) Where an offence under this Act committed by a partnership is proved to have been committed with the consent or connivance of, or to be attributable to any neglect on the part of, a partner, he as well as the partnership is guilty of the offence and liable to be proceeded against and punished accordingly.

[Adoption and Children Act 2002, s 143.]

6–3200I   144. General interpretation etc.   (1)   In this Act—

"appropriate Minister" means—

(a) in relation to England, Scotland or Northern Ireland, the Secretary of State,
(b) in relation to Wales, the Assembly,

and in relation to England and Wales means the Secretary of State and the Assembly acting jointly,

"the Assembly" means the National Assembly for Wales,

"body" includes an unincorporated body,

"by virtue of" includes "by" and "under",

"child", except where used to express a relationship, means a person who has not attained the age of 18 years,

"the Convention" means the Convention on Protection of Children and Co-operation in respect of Intercountry Adoption, concluded at the Hague on 29th May 1993,

"Convention adoption order" means an adoption order which, by virtue of regulations under section 1 of the Adoption (Intercountry Aspects) Act 1999 (c 18) (regulations giving effect to the Convention), is made as a Convention adoption order,

"Convention country" means a country or territory in which the Convention is in force,

"court" means, subject to any provision made by virtue of Part 1 of Schedule 11 to the 1989 Act, the High Court, a county court or a magistrates' court,

"enactment" includes an enactment comprised in subordinate legislation,

"fee" includes expenses,

"guardian" has the same meaning as in the 1989 Act and includes a special guardian within the meaning of that Act,

"information" means information recorded in any form,

"local authority" means any unitary authority, or any county council so far as they are not a unitary authority,

"Northern Irish adoption agency" means an adoption agency within the meaning of Article 3 of the Adoption (Northern Ireland) Order 1987 (SI 1987/2203 (NI 22)),

"Northern Irish adoption order" means an order made, or having effect as if made, under Article 12 of the Adoption (Northern Ireland) Order 1987,

"notice" means a notice in writing,

"registration authority" (in Part 1) has the same meaning as in the Care Standards Act 2000 (c 14),

"regulations" means regulations made by the appropriate Minister, unless they are required to be made by the Lord Chancellor, the Secretary of State or the Registrar General,

"relative", in relation to a child, means a grandparent, brother, sister, uncle or aunt, whether of the full blood or half-blood or by marriage,

"rules" means rules made under section 141(1) or made by virtue of section 141(2) under section 144 of the Magistrates' Courts Act 1980 (c 43),

"Scottish adoption order" means an order made, or having effect as if made, under section 12 of the Adoption (Scotland) Act 1978 (c 28),

"subordinate legislation" has the same meaning as in the Interpretation Act 1978 (c 30),

"unitary authority" means—

(a)   the council of any county so far as they are the council for an area for which there are no district councils,

(b)   the council of any district comprised in an area for which there is no county council,

(c)   the council of a county borough,

(d)   the council of a London borough,

(e)   the Common Council of the City of London.

(2) Any power conferred by this Act to prescribe a fee by Order in Council or regulations includes power to prescribe—

(a)   a fee not exceeding a prescribed amount,

(b)   a fee calculated in accordance with the Order or, as the case may be, regulations,

(c)   a fee determined by the person to whom it is payable, being a fee of a reasonable amount.

(3) In this Act, "Scottish adoption agency" means—

(a)   a local authority, or

(b)   a voluntary organisation providing a registered adoption service;

but in relation to the provision of any particular service, references to a Scottish adoption agency do not include a voluntary organisation unless it is registered in respect of that service or a service which, in Scotland, corresponds to that service.

Expressions used in this subsection have the same meaning as in the Regulation of Care (Scotland) Act 2001 (asp 4) and "registered" means registered under Part 1 of that Act.

(4) In this Act, a couple means—

(a)   a married couple, or

(b)   two people (whether of different sexes or the same sex) living as partners in an enduring family relationship.

(5) Subsection (4)(b) does not include two people one of whom is the other's parent, grandparent, sister, brother, aunt or uncle.

(6) References to relationships in subsection (5)—

(a)   are to relationships of the full blood or half blood or, in the case of an adopted person, such of those relationships as would exist but for adoption, and

(b)   include the relationship of a child with his adoptive, or former adoptive, parents,

but do not include any other adoptive relationships.

(7) For the purposes of this Act, a person is the partner of a child's parent if the person and the parent are a couple but the person is not the child's parent.

[Adoption and Children Act 2002, s 144.]

6–3200J 145. Devolution: Wales.   (1) The references to the Adoption Act 1976 (c 36) and to the 1989 Act in Schedule 1 to the National Assembly for Wales (Transfer of Functions) Order 1999 (SI 1999/672) are to be treated as referring to those Acts as amended by virtue of this Act.

(2) This section does not affect the power to make further Orders varying or omitting those references.

(3) In Schedule 1 to that Order, in the entry for the Adoption Act 1976, "9" is omitted.

(4) The functions exercisable by the Assembly under sections 9 and 9A of the Adoption Act 1976 (by virtue of paragraphs 4 and 5 of Schedule 4 to this Act) are to be treated for the purposes of section 44 of the Government of Wales Act 1998 (c 38) (parliamentary procedures for subordinate legislation) as if made exercisable by the Assembly by an Order in Council under section 22 of that Act.

[Adoption and Children Act 2002, s 145.]

6–3200K 146. Expenses.   There shall be paid out of money provided by Parliament—

(a)   any expenditure incurred by a Minister of the Crown by virtue of this Act,

(b)   any increase attributable to this Act in the sums payable out of money so provided under any other enactment.

[Adoption and Children Act 2002, s 146.]

6–3200L 147. Glossary.   Schedule 6 (glossary) is to have effect.

[Adoption and Children Act 2002, s 147.]

6–3200M 148. Commencement.   (1) This Act (except sections 116 and 136, this Chapter and the provisions mentioned in subsections (5) and (6)) is to come into force on such day as the Secretary of State may by order[1] appoint.

(2) Before making an order under subsection (1) (other than an order bringing paragraph 53 of Schedule 3 into force) the Secretary of State must consult the Assembly.

(3) Before making an order under subsection (1) bringing sections 123 and 124 into force, the Secretary of State must also consult the Scottish Ministers and the Department of Health, Social Services and Public Safety.

(4) Before making an order under subsection (1) bringing sections 125 to 131 into force, the Secretary of State must also consult the Scottish Ministers.

(5) The following are to come into force on such day as the Scottish Ministers may by order appoint—

  (*a*) section 41(5) to (9), so far as relating to Scotland,

  (*b*) sections 132 to 134,

  (*c*) paragraphs 21 to 35 and 82 to 84 of Schedule 3,

  (*d*) paragraphs 15 and 23 of Schedule 4,

  (*e*) the entries in Schedule 5, so far as relating to the provisions mentioned in paragraphs (*c*) and (*d*),

  (*f*) section 139, so far as relating to the provisions mentioned in the preceding paragraphs.

(6) Sections 2(6), 3(3) and (4), 4 to 17, 27(3), 53(1) to (3), 54, 56 to 65 and 98, paragraphs 13, 65, 66 and 111 to 113 of Schedule 3 and paragraphs 3 and 5 of Schedule 4 are to come into force on such day as the appropriate Minister may by order appoint.

[Adoption and Children Act 2002, s 148.]

---

1. At the time of going to press the following commencement orders have been made: Adoption and Children Act 2002 (Commencement No 1) (Wales) Order 2003, SI 2003/181; Adoption and Children Act 2002; (Commencement No 2) Order 2003, SI 2003/288; Adoption and Children Act 2002; (Commencement No 3) Order 2003, SI 2003/366; Adoption and Children Act 2002; (Commencement No 4) Order 2003, SI 2003/3079; Adoption and Children Act 2002; (Commencement No 5) (Wales) Order 2004, SI 2004/252; Adoption and Children Act 2002; (Commencement No 6) Order 2004, SI 2004/1403; Adoption and Children Act 2002; (Commencement No 7) Order 2004, SI 2004/3203; Adoption and Children Act 2002; (Commencement No 8) (Wales) Order 2005, SI 2005/1206; Adoption and Children Act 2002; (Commencement No 9) Order 2005, SI 2005/2213; and Adoption and Children Act 2002 (Commencement No 10 Transitional and Savings Provisions) Order 2005, SI 2005/2897.

6–3200N 149. Extent. (1) The amendment or repeal of an enactment has the same extent as the enactment to which it relates.

(2) Subject to that and to the following provisions, this Act except section 137 extends to England and Wales only.

(3) The following extend also to Scotland and Northern Ireland—

  (*a*) sections 63(2) to (5), 65(2)(*a*) and (*b*) and (3), 123 and 124,

  (*b*) this Chapter, except sections 141 and 145.

(4) The following extend also to Scotland—

  (*a*) section 41(5) to (9),

  (*b*) sections 125 to 131,

  (*c*) section 138,

  (*d*) section 139, so far as relating to provisions extending to Scotland.

(5) In Schedule 4, paragraph 23 extends only to Scotland.

[Adoption and Children Act 2002, s 149.]

6–3200O 150. Short title. This Act may be cited as the Adoption and Children Act 2002.

[Adoption and Children Act 2002, s 150.]

Section 77(6)

SCHEDULE 1
REGISTRATION OF ADOPTIONS

Registration of adoption orders

6–3200P 1. (1) Every adoption order must contain a direction to the Registrar General to make in the Adopted Children Register an entry in the form prescribed by regulations[1] made by the Registrar General with the approval of the Chancellor of the Exchequer.

(2) Where, on an application to a court for an adoption order in respect of a child, the identity of the child with a child to whom an entry in the registers of live-births or other records relates is proved to the satisfaction of the court, any adoption order made in pursuance of the application must contain a direction to the Registrar General to secure that the entry in the register or, as the case may be, record in question is marked with the word "Adopted".

(3) Where an adoption order is made in respect of a child who has previously been the subject of an adoption order made by a court in England or Wales under Part 1 of this Act or any other enactment—

  (*a*) sub-paragraph (2) does not apply, and

  (*b*) the order must contain a direction to the Registrar General to mark the previous entry in the Adopted Children Register with the word "Re-adopted".

(4) Where an adoption order is made, the prescribed officer of the court which made the order must communicate the order to the Registrar General in the prescribed manner; and the Registrar General must then comply with the directions contained in the order.

"Prescribed" means prescribed by rules.

Registration of adoptions in Scotland, Northern Ireland, the Isle of Man and the Channel Islands

2. (1) Sub-paragraphs (2) and (3) apply where the Registrar General is notified by the authority maintaining a register of adoptions in a part of the British Islands outside England and Wales that an order has been made in that part authorising the adoption of a child.

(2) If an entry in the registers of live-births or other records (and no entry in the Adopted Children Register) relates to the child, the Registrar General must secure that the entry is marked with—

(a) the word "Adopted", followed by

(b) the name, in brackets, of the part in which the order was made.

(3) If an entry in the Adopted Children Register relates to the child, the Registrar General must mark the entry with—

(a) the word "Re-adopted", followed by

(b) the name, in brackets, of the part in which the order was made.

(4) Where, after an entry in either of the registers or other records mentioned in sub-paragraphs (2) and (3) has been so marked, the Registrar General is notified by the authority concerned that—

(a) the order has been quashed,

(b) an appeal against the order has been allowed, or

(c) the order has been revoked,

the Registrar General must secure that the marking is cancelled.

(5) A copy or extract of an entry in any register or other record, being an entry the marking of which is cancelled under sub-paragraph (4), is not to be treated as an accurate copy unless both the marking and the cancellation are omitted from it.

Registration of other adoptions

3. (1) If the Registrar General is satisfied, on an application under this paragraph, that he has sufficient particulars relating to a child adopted under a registrable foreign adoption to enable an entry to be made in the Adopted Children Register for the child he must make the entry accordingly.

(2) If he is also satisfied that an entry in the registers of live-births or other records relates to the child, he must—

(a) secure that the entry is marked "Adopted", followed by the name, in brackets, of the country in which the adoption was effected, or

(b) where appropriate, secure that the overseas registers of births are so marked.

(3) An application under this paragraph must be made, in the prescribed manner, by a prescribed person and the applicant must provide the prescribed documents and other information.

(4) An entry made in the Adopted Children Register by virtue of this paragraph must be made in the prescribed form.

(5) In this Schedule "registrable foreign adoption" means an adoption which satisfies prescribed requirements and is either—

(a) adoption under a Convention adoption, or

(b) adoption under an overseas adoption.

(6) In this paragraph—

(a) "prescribed" means prescribed by regulations[1] made by the Registrar General with the approval of the Chancellor of the Exchequer,

(b) "overseas register of births" includes—

(i) a register made under regulations made by the Secretary of State under section 41(1)(g), (h) or (i) of the British Nationality Act 1981 (c 61),

(ii) a record kept under an Order in Council made under section 1 of the Registration of Births, Deaths and Marriages (Special Provisions) Act 1957 (c 58) (other than a certified copy kept by the Registrar General).

Amendment of orders and rectification of Registers and other records

4. (1) The court by which an adoption order has been made may, on the application of the adopter or the adopted person, amend the order by the correction of any error in the particulars contained in it.

(2) The court by which an adoption order has been made may, if satisfied on the application of the adopter or the adopted person that within the period of one year beginning with the date of the order any new name—

(a) has been given to the adopted person (whether in baptism or otherwise), or

(b) has been taken by the adopted person,

either in place of or in addition to a name specified in the particulars required to be entered in the Adopted Children Register in pursuance of the order, amend the order by substituting or, as the case may be, adding that name in those particulars.

(3) The court by which an adoption order has been made may, if satisfied on the application of any person concerned that a direction for the marking of an entry in the registers of live-births, the Adopted Children Register or other records included in the order in pursuance of paragraph 1(2) or (3) was wrongly so included, revoke that direction.

(4) Where an adoption order is amended or a direction revoked under sub-paragraphs (1) to (3), the prescribed officer of the court must communicate the amendment in the prescribed manner to the Registrar General.

"Prescribed" means prescribed by rules.

(5) The Registrar General must then—

(a) amend the entry in the Adopted Children Register accordingly, or

(b) secure that the marking of the entry in the registers of live-births, the Adopted Children Register or other records is cancelled,

as the case may be.

(6) Where an adoption order is quashed or an appeal against an adoption order allowed by any court, the court must give directions to the Registrar General to secure that—

(a) any entry in the Adopted Children Register, and

(b) any marking of an entry in that Register, the registers of live-births or other records as the case may be, which was effected in pursuance of the order,

is cancelled.

(7) Where an adoption order has been amended, any certified copy of the relevant entry in the Adopted Children Register which may be issued pursuant to section 78(2)(b) must be a copy of the entry as amended, without the reproduction of—

(a) any note or marking relating to the amendment, or

(b) any matter cancelled in pursuance of it.

(8) A copy or extract of an entry in any register or other record, being an entry the marking of which has been cancelled, is not to be treated as an accurate copy unless both the marking and the cancellation are omitted from it.

(9) If the Registrar General is satisfied—

(a) that a registrable foreign adoption has ceased to have effect, whether on annulment or otherwise, or

(b) that any entry or mark was erroneously made in pursuance of paragraph 3 in the Adopted Children Register, the registers of live-births, the overseas registers of births or other records,

he may secure that such alterations are made in those registers or other records as he considers are required in consequence of the adoption ceasing to have effect or to correct the error.

"Overseas register of births" has the same meaning as in paragraph 3.

(10) Where an entry in such a register is amended in pursuance of sub-paragraph (9), any copy or extract of the entry is not to be treated as accurate unless it shows the entry as amended but without indicating that it has been amended.

Marking of entries on re-registration of birth on legitimation

5. (1) Without prejudice to paragraphs 2(4) and 4(5), where, after an entry in the registers of live-births or other records has been marked in accordance with paragraph 1 or 2, the birth is re-registered under section 14 of the Births and Deaths Registration Act 1953 (c 20) (re-registration of births of legitimated persons), the entry made on the re-registration must be marked in the like manner.

(2) Without prejudice to paragraph 4(9), where an entry in the registers of live-births or other records is marked in pursuance of paragraph 3 and the birth in question is subsequently re-registered under section 14 of that Act, the entry made on re-registration must be marked in the like manner.

Cancellations in registers on legitimation

6. (1) This paragraph applies where an adoption order is revoked under section 55(1).

(2) The prescribed officer of the court must communicate the revocation in the prescribed manner to the Registrar General who must then cancel or secure the cancellation of—

(a) the entry in the Adopted Children Register relating to the adopted person, and

(b) the marking with the word "Adopted" of any entry relating to the adopted person in the registers of live-births or other records.

"Prescribed" means prescribed by rules.

(3) A copy or extract of an entry in any register or other record, being an entry the marking of which is cancelled under this paragraph, is not to be treated as an accurate copy unless both the marking and the cancellation are omitted from it.

---

1. The Adopted Children and Adoption Contact Registers Regulations 2005, SI 2005/924 have been made.

Section 79(6)   SCHEDULE 2
     DISCLOSURE OF BIRTH RECORDS BY REGISTRAR GENERAL

6–3200Q 1. On an application made in the prescribed manner by an adopted person—

(a) a record of whose birth is kept by the Registrar General, and

(b) who has attained the age of 18 years,

the Registrar General must give the applicant any information necessary to enable the applicant to obtain a certified copy of the record of his birth.

"Prescribed" means prescribed by regulations[1] made by the Registrar General with the approval of the Chancellor of the Exchequer.

2. (1) Before giving any information to an applicant under paragraph 1, the Registrar General must inform the applicant that counselling services are available to the applicant—

(a) from a registered adoption society, an organisation within section 144(3)(b) or an adoption society which is registered under Article 4 of the Adoption (Northern Ireland) Order 1987 (SI 1987/2203 (NI 22)),

(b) if the applicant is in England and Wales, at the General Register Office or from any local authority or registered adoption support agency,

(c) if the applicant is in Scotland, from any council constituted under section 2 of the Local Government etc (Scotland) Act 1994 (c 39), or

(d) if the applicant is in Northern Ireland, from any Board.

(2) In sub-paragraph (1)(b), "registered adoption support agency" means an adoption support agency in respect of which a person is registered under Part 2 of the Care Standards Act 2000 (c 14).

(3) In sub-paragraph (1)(d), "Board" means a Health and Social Services Board established under Article 16

of the Health and Personal Social Services (Northern Ireland) Order 1972 (SI 1972/1265 (NI 14)); but where the functions of a Board are exercisable by a Health and Social Services Trust, references in that sub-paragraph to a Board are to be read as references to the Health and Social Services Trust.

(4) If the applicant chooses to receive counselling from a person or body within sub-paragraph (1), the Registrar General must send to the person or body the information to which the applicant is entitled under paragraph 1.

3. (1) Where an adopted person who is in England and Wales—

(a) applies for information under paragraph 1 or Article 54 of the Adoption (Northern Ireland) Order 1987, or

(b) is supplied with information under section 45 of the Adoption (Scotland) Act 1978 (c 28),

the persons and bodies mentioned in sub-paragraph (2) must, if asked by the applicant to do so, provide counselling for the applicant.

(2) Those persons and bodies are—

(a) the Registrar General,

(b) any local authority,

(c) a registered adoption society, an organisation within section 144(3)(b) or an adoption society which is registered under Article 4 of the Adoption (Northern Ireland) Order 1987.

4. (1) Where a person—

(a) was adopted before 12th November 1975, and

(b) applies for information under paragraph 1,

the Registrar General must not give the information to the applicant unless the applicant has attended an interview with a counsellor arranged by a person or body from whom counselling services are available as mentioned in paragraph 2.

(2) Where the Registrar General is prevented by sub-paragraph (1) from giving information to a person who is not living in the United Kingdom, the Registrar General may give the information to any body which—

(a) the Registrar General is satisfied is suitable to provide counselling to that person, and

(b) has notified the Registrar General that it is prepared to provide such counselling.

---

1. The Adopted Children and Adoption Contact Registers Regulations 2005, SI 2005/924 have been made.

Section 139

SCHEDULE 3
MINOR AND CONSEQUENTIAL AMENDMENTS

The Marriage Act 1949 (c 76)

6–3200R   1–5. *Amend s 3 of the Marriage Act 1949.*

The Births and Deaths Registration Act 1953 (c 20)

6. In section 10 of the Births and Deaths Registration Act 1953 (registration of father where parents not married)—

(a) in subsection (1)(d)(i), for "a parental responsibility agreement made between them in relation to the child" there is substituted "any agreement made between them under section 4(1)(b) of the Children Act 1989 in relation to the child",

(b) in subsection (1)(d)(ii), for "the Children Act 1989" there is substituted "that Act",

(c) in subsection (3), the words following "the Family Law Reform Act 1987" are omitted[1].

7. In section 10A of the Births and Deaths Registration Act 1953 (re-registration of father where parents not married)—

(a) in subsection (1)(d)(i), for "a parental responsibility agreement made between them in relation to the child" there is substituted "any agreement made between them under section 4(1)(b) of the Children Act 1989 in relation to the child",

(b) in subsection (1)(d)(ii), for "the Children Act 1989" there is substituted "that Act".

The Sexual Offences Act 1956 (c 69)

8. In section 28 of the Sexual Offences Act 1956 (causing or encouraging prostitution of, intercourse with, or indecent assault on, girl under sixteen), in subsection (4), the "or" at the end of paragraph (a) is omitted, and after that paragraph there is inserted—

"(aa) a special guardianship order under that Act is in force with respect to her and he is not her special guardian; or".[1]

---

1. Paragraphs 6 and 7 in force from 1 December 2003: see Adoption and Children Act 2002 (Commencement No 4) Order 2003, SI 2003/3079.

The Health Services and Public Health Act 1968 (c 46)

9. The Health Services and Public Health Act 1968 is amended as follows.

10. In section 64 (financial assistance by the Secretary of State to certain voluntary organisations), in subsection (3)(a)(xviii), for "the Adoption Act 1976" there is substituted "the Adoption and Children Act 2002".

11. In section 65 (financial and other assistance by local authorities to certain voluntary organisations), in subsection (3)(b), for "the Adoption Act 1976" there is substituted "the Adoption and Children Act 2002".

The Local Authority Social Services Act 1970 (c 42)

12. The Local Authority Social Services Act 1970 is amended as follows.

13. In section 7D (default powers of Secretary of State as respects social services functions of local authorities), in subsection (1), after "the Children Act 1989" there is inserted "section 1 or 2(4) of the Adoption (Intercountry Aspects) Act 1999 or the Adoption and Children Act 2002".

14. In Schedule 1 (enactments conferring functions assigned to social services committee)—

(a) the entry relating to the Adoption Act 1976 is omitted,
(b) in the entry relating to the Children Act 1989, after "Consent to application for residence order in respect of child in care" there is inserted "Functions relating to special guardianship orders",
(c) in the entry relating to the Adoption (Intercountry Aspects) Act 1999—

   (i) in the first column, for "Section" there is substituted "Sections 1 and",
   (ii) in the second column, for "Article 9(a) to (c) of" there is substituted "regulations made under section 1 giving effect to" and at the end there is inserted "and functions under Article 9(a) to (c) of the Convention",

and at the end of the Schedule there is inserted—

"Adoption and Children Act 2002   Maintenance of Adoption Service; functions of local authority as adoption agency."

The Immigration Act 1971 (c 77)

15. In section 33(1) of the Immigration Act 1971 (interpretation)—

(a) in the definition of "Convention adoption", after "1978" there is inserted "or in the Adoption and Children Act 2002",
(b) in the definition of "legally adopted", for "section 72(2) of the Adoption Act 1976" there is substituted "section 87 of the Adoption and Children Act 2002".

The Legitimacy Act 1976 (c 31)

16–18. *Amend ss 4 and 6 of the Legitimacy Act 1976.*

The Adoption Act 1976 (c 36)

19. In section 38 of the Adoption Act 1976 (meaning of "adoption" in Part 4), in subsection (2), after "1975" there is inserted "but does not include an adoption of a kind mentioned in paragraphs (c) to (e) of subsection (1) effected on or after the day which is the appointed day for the purposes of Chapter 4 of Part 1 of the Adoption and Children Act 2002".

The National Health Service Act 1977 (c 49)

20. In section 124A(3) of the National Health Service Act 1977 (information provided by the Registrar General to the Secretary of State), the "or" at the end of paragraph (a) is omitted and after that paragraph there is inserted—

"(aa) entered in the Adopted Children Register maintained by the Registrar General under the Adoption and Children Act 2002; or".

The Adoption (Scotland) Act 1978 (c 28)

The Magistrates' Courts Act 1980 (c 43)

36. The Magistrates' Courts Act 1980 is amended as follows.

37. In section 65 (meaning of family proceedings), in subsection (1), for paragraph (h) there is substituted—

"(h) the Adoption and Children Act 2002;".

38. In section 69 (sitting of magistrates' courts for family proceedings), in subsections (2) and (3), for "the Adoption Act 1976" there is substituted "the Adoption and Children Act 2002".

39. In section 71 (newspaper reports of family proceedings)—

(a) in subsection (1), "(other than proceedings under the Adoption Act 1976)" is omitted,
(b) in subsection (2)—

   (i) for "the Adoption Act 1976" there is substituted "the Adoption and Children Act 2002",
   (ii) the words following "(a) and (b)" are omitted.

40. In Part 1 of Schedule 6 (fees to be taken by justices' chief executives), in the entry relating to family proceedings—

(a) for "the Adoption Act 1976, except under section 21 of that Act", there is substituted "the Adoption and Children Act 2002, except under section 23 of that Act",
(b) in paragraph (c), for "section 21 of the Adoption Act 1976" there is substituted "section 23 of the Adoption and Children Act 2002".

The Mental Health Act 1983 (c 20)

41. *Amends s 28 of the Mental Health Act 1983.*

The Child Abduction Act 1984 (c 37)

42. *Amends s 1 of the Child Abduction Act 1984.*

43. Amends the Schedule to the Child Abduction Act 1984.

The Matrimonial and Family Proceedings Act 1984 (c 42)

44. In section 40 of the Matrimonial and Family Proceedings Act 1984 (family proceedings rules), in subsection (2), in paragraph (*a*), after "the Adoption Act 1968" the "or" is omitted and after "the Adoption Act 1976" there is inserted "or section 141(1) of the Adoption and Children Act 2002".

The Child Abduction and Custody Act 1985 (c 60)

45. *Amends Schedule 3 to the Child Abduction and Custody Act 1985.*

The Family Law Act 1986 (c 55)

46. The Family Law Act 1986 is amended as follows.

47. *Amends s 1 of the Family Law Act 1986.*

48. *Amends s 2 of the Family Law Act 1986.*

49. *Amends s 57 of the Family Law Act 1986.*

The Family Law Reform Act 1987 (c 42)

50. The Family Law Reform Act 1987 is amended as follows.

51. *Amends s 1 of the Family Law Reform Act 1987.*

52. In section 19 (dispositions of property), in subsection (5), after "1976" there is inserted "or section 69 of the Adoption and Children Act 2002".

The Adoption (Northern Ireland) Order 1987 (SI 1987/2203 (NI 22))

53. In Article 2(2) (interpretation), in the definition of "prescribed", for "Articles 54" there is substituted "Articles 53(3B) and (3D), 54".

The Children Act 1989 (c 41)

54. The Children Act 1989 is amended as follows.

55. *Amends s 8 of the Children Act 1989.*

56. *Amends s 10 of the Children Act 1989.*

57. *Amends s 12 of the Children Act 1989.*

58. *Amends s 16 of the Children Act 1989.*

59. *Amends s 20 of the Children Act 1989.*

60. *Amends s 24 of the Children Act 1989.*

61. *Amends s 24A of the Children Act 1989.*

62. *Amends s 24B of the Children Act 1989.*

63. *Amends s 33 of the Children Act 1989.*

64. *Amends s 34 of the Children Act 1989.*

65. *Amends s 80 of the Children Act 1989.*

66. *Amends s 81 of the Children Act 1989.*

67. *Amends s 88 of the Children Act 1989.*

68. *Amends s 91 of the Children Act 1989.*

69. *Amends s 102 of the Children Act 1989.*

70. *Amends s 105 of the Children Act 1989.*

71. *Amends Sch 1 to the Children Act 1989.*

72. *Amends Sch 2 to the Children Act 1989.*

73. *Amends Sch 8 to the Children Act 1989.*

74. Part 1 of Schedule 10 is omitted.

75. *Amends Sch 8 to the Children Act 1989.*

The Human Fertilisation and Embryology Act 1990 (c 37)

76–79. *Sections 27, 28 and 30 of the Human Fertilisation and Embryology Act 1990 amended.*

79. In section 30 (parental orders in favour of gamete donors), in subsection (10) for "Adoption Act 1976" there is substituted "Adoption and Children Act 2002".

The Courts and Legal Services Act 1990 (c 41)

80. In section 58A of the Courts and Legal Services Act 1990 (conditional fee agreements: supplementary), in subsection (2), for paragraph (*b*) there is substituted—

"(*b*) the Adoption and Children Act 2002;".

The Child Support Act 1991 (c 48)

81. *Amends s 26 of the Child Support Act 1991.*

The Family Law Act 1996 (c 27)

85. The Family Law Act 1996 is amended as follows.

86, 87. *Amend s 62 of the Family Law Act 1996.*

88. In section 63 (interpretation of Part 4)—

(*a*) in subsection (1), for the definition of "adoption order", there is substituted—

""adoption order" means an adoption order within the meaning of section 72(1) of the Adoption Act 1976 or section 46(1) of the Adoption and Children Act 2002;",

(*b*) in subsection (2), after paragraph (*h*) there is inserted—

"(i) the Adoption and Children Act 2002."

The Housing Act 1996 (c 52)

89. Section 178 of the Housing Act 1996 (meaning of associated person) is amended as follows.

90. In subsection (2), for the words from "has been freed" to "1976" there is substituted "falls within subsection (2A)".

91. After that subsection there is inserted—

"(2A) A child falls within this subsection if—

(*a*) an adoption agency, within the meaning of section 2 of the Adoption and Children Act 2002, is authorised to place him for adoption under section 19 of that Act (placing children with parental consent) or he has become the subject of an order under section 21 of that Act (placement orders), or

(*b*) he is freed for adoption by virtue of an order made—

(i) in England and Wales, under section 18 of the Adoption Act 1976,

(ii) in Scotland, under section 18 of the Adoption (Scotland) Act 1978, or

(iii) in Northern Ireland, under Article 17(1) or 18(1) of the Adoption (Northern Ireland) Order 1987."

92. In subsection (3), for the definition of "adoption order", there is substituted—

""adoption order" means an adoption order within the meaning of section 72(1) of the Adoption Act 1976 or section 46(1) of the Adoption and Children Act 2002;".

The Police Act 1997 (c 50)

93. In section 115 of the Police Act 1997 (enhanced criminal records), in subsection (5)(*h*), for "section 11 of the Adoption Act 1976" there is substituted "section 2 of the Adoption and Children Act 2002".

The Protection of Children Act 1999 (c 14)

94. In section 2B of the Protection of Children Act 1999 (individuals named in the findings of certain inquiries), in subsection (7), after paragraph (*a*) there is inserted—

"(vi)section 17 of the Adoption and Children Act 2002;".

The Adoption (Intercountry Aspects) Act 1999 (c 18)

95. The following provisions of the Adoption (Intercountry Aspects) Act 1999 cease to have effect in relation to England and Wales: sections 3, 6, 8, 9 and 11 to 13.

96. Section 2 of that Act (accredited bodies) is amended as follows.

97. In subsection (2A)—

(*a*) for the words from the beginning to "2000" there is substituted "A registered adoption society",

(*b*) for "agency" there is substituted "society".

98. For subsection (5) there is substituted—

"(5) In this section, "registered adoption society" has the same meaning as in section 2 of the Adoption and Children Act 2002 (basic definitions); and expressions used in this section in its application to England and Wales which are also used in that Act have the same meanings as in that Act."

99. In subsection (6)—

(*a*) the words "in its application to Scotland" are omitted,

(*b*) after "expressions" there is inserted "used in this section in its application to Scotland".

100. Section 14 (restriction on bringing children into the United Kingdom for adoption) is omitted.

101. In section 16(1) (devolution: Wales), the words ", or section 17 or 56A of the 1976 Act," are omitted.

The Access to Justice Act 1999 (c 22)

102. Amends Schedule 2 to the Access to Justice Act 1999.

The Care Standards Act 2000 (c 14)

103. The Care Standards Act 2000 is amended as follows[1].

104. In section 4 (basic definitions), in subsection (7), for "the Adoption Act 1976" there is substituted "the Adoption and Children Act 2002".

105. At the end of section 5 (registration authorities) there is inserted—

"(2) This section is subject to section 36A."[1]

106. In section 11 (requirement to register), in subsection (3), for "reference in subsection (1) to an agency does" there is substituted "references in subsections (1) and (2) to an agency do".[1]

107. In section 14 (2) (offences conviction of which may result in cancellation of registration), for paragraph (*d*) there is substituted—

"(*d*) an offence under regulations under section 1(3) of the Adoption (Intercountry Aspects) Act 1999, (*e*)   an offence under the Adoption and Children Act 2002 or regulations made under it".

108. In section 16(2) (power to make regulations providing that no application for registration may be made in respect of certain agencies which are unincorporated bodies), "or a voluntary adoption agency" is omitted.

109. In section 22(10) (disapplication of power to make regulations in the case of voluntary adoption agencies), at the end there is inserted "or adoption support agencies".

110. In section 23 (standards), at the end of subsection (4)(*d*) there is inserted "or proceedings against a voluntary adoption agency for an offence under section 9(4) of the Adoption Act 1976 or section 9 of the Adoption and Children Act 2002"[1].

111. In section 31 (inspections by authorised persons), in subsection (3)(*b*), for "section 9(2) of the Adoption Act 1976", there is substituted "section 9 of the Adoption and Children Act 2002".

112. In section 43 (introductory), in subsection (3)(*a*)—

(*a*)   for "the Adoption Act 1976" there is substituted "the Adoption and Children Act 2002",
(*b*)   after "children" there is inserted "or the provision of adoption support services (as defined in section 2(6) of the Adoption and Children Act 2002)".

113. In section 46 (inspections: supplementary), in subsection (7)(*c*), for "section 9(3) of the Adoption Act 1976" there is substituted "section 9 of the Adoption and Children Act 2002".

114. In section 48 (regulation of fostering functions), at the end of subsection (1) there is inserted—

    "(*f*) as to the fees or expenses which may be paid to persons assisting local authorities in making decisions in the exercise of such functions".

115. In section 55(2)(*b*) (definition of "social care worker"), for "or a voluntary adoption agency" there is substituted ", a voluntary adoption agency or an adoption support agency".

116. In section 121 (general interpretation)—

(*a*)   in subsection (1), in the definition of "voluntary organisation", for "the Adoption Act 1976" there is substituted "the Adoption and Children Act 2002",
(*b*)   in subsection (13), in the appropriate place in the table there is inserted—

"Adoption support agency   Section 4".

117. In Schedule 4 (minor and consequential amendments), paragraph 27(*b*) is omitted.

The Criminal Justice and Court Services Act 2000 (c 43)

118. In section 12(5) of the Criminal Justice and Court Services Act 2000 (meaning of "family proceedings" in relation to CAFCASS), paragraph (*b*) (supervision orders under the 1989 Act) and the preceding "and" are omitted[2].

---

[1] Paragraphs 105, 106 and 110 in so far as that paragraph relates to the Adoption Act 1976, and para 103 in force in Wales from 28 November 2003: SI 2003/3079.
[2] Paragraph 118 in force from 28 November 2003: SI 2003/3079.

Section 139   SCHEDULE 4
TRANSITIONAL AND TRANSITORY PROVISIONS AND SAVINGS

General rules for continuity

6–3200S   **1.** (1) Any reference (express or implied) in Part 1 or any other enactment, instrument or document to—

(*a*)   any provision of Part 1, or
(*b*)   things done or falling to be done under or for the purposes of any provision of Part 1,

must, so far as the nature of the reference permits, be construed as including, in relation to the times, circumstances or purposes in relation to which the corresponding provision repealed by this Act had effect, a reference to that corresponding provision or (as the case may be) to things done or falling to be done under or for the purposes of that corresponding provision.

(2) Any reference (express or implied) in any enactment, instrument or document to—

(*a*)   a provision repealed by this Act, or
(*b*)   things done or falling to be done under or for the purposes of such a provision,

must, so far as the nature of the reference permits, be construed as including, in relation to the times, circumstances or purposes in relation to which the corresponding provision of Part 1 has effect, a reference to that corresponding provision or (as the case may be) to things done or falling to be done under or for the purposes of that corresponding provision.

General rule for old savings

2. (1) The repeal by this Act of an enactment previously repealed subject to savings does not affect the continued operation of those savings.

(2) The repeal by this Act of a saving made on the previous repeal of an enactment does not affect the operation of the saving in so far as it is not specifically reproduced in this Act but remains capable of having effect.

Adoption support services

3. (1) The facilities to be provided by local authorities as part of the service maintained under section 1(1) of the Adoption Act 1976 (c 36) include such arrangements as the authorities may be required by regulations[1] to make for the provision of adoption support services to prescribed persons.

(2) Regulations under sub-paragraph (1) may require a local authority—

(*a*)   at the request of a prescribed person, to carry out an assessment of his needs for adoption support services, (*b*) if, as a result of the assessment, the authority decide that he has such needs, to decide whether to provide any such services to him,

(*c*) if the authority decide to provide any such services to a person, and the circumstances fall within a description prescribed by the regulations, to prepare a plan in accordance with which the services are to be provided to him and keep the plan under review.

(3) Subsections (6) and (7) (except paragraph (*a*)) of section 4 of this Act apply to regulations under sub-paragraph (1) as they apply to regulations made by virtue of that section.

(4) Section 57(1) of the Adoption Act 1976 (prohibited payments) does not apply to any payment made in accordance with regulations under sub-paragraph (1).

---

1. The Adoption Support Service (Local Authorities) (England) Regulations 2003, SI 2003/1348 and the Adoption Support Services (Local Authorities) (Wales) Regulations 2004, SI 2004/1011 have been made.

Regulation of adoption agencies

4. (1) In section 9 of the Adoption Act 1976—

(*a*) for "Secretary of State" in subsections (2) and (3) there is substituted "appropriate Minister", and

(*b*) at the end of that section there is inserted—

"(5) In this section and section 9A, "the appropriate Minister" means—

(*a*) in relation to England, the Secretary of State,

(*b*) in relation to Wales, the National Assembly for Wales,

and in relation to England and Wales, means the Secretary of State and the Assembly acting jointly."

(2) Until the commencement of the repeal by this Act of section 9(2) of the Adoption Act 1976, section 36A of the Care Standards Act 2000 (c 14) (inserted by section 16 of this Act) is to have effect as if, after "2002", there were inserted "or under section 9(2) of the Adoption Act 1976".

Independent review mechanism

5. After section 9 of the Adoption Act 1976 (c 36) there is inserted—

"**9A. Independent review of determinations.** (1) Regulations under section 9 may establish a procedure under which any person in respect of whom a qualifying determination has been made by an adoption agency may apply to a panel constituted by the appropriate Minister for a review of that determination.

(2) The regulations must make provision as to the description of determinations which are qualifying determinations for the purposes of subsection (1).

(3) The regulations may include provision as to—

(*a*) the duties and powers of a panel (including the power to recover the costs of a review from the adoption agency by which the determination reviewed was made),

(*b*) the administration and procedures of a panel,

(*c*) the appointment of members of a panel (including the number, or any limit on the number, of members who may be appointed and any conditions for appointment),

(*d*) the payment of expenses of members of a panel,

(*e*) the duties of adoption agencies in connection with reviews conducted under the regulations,

(*f*) the monitoring of any such reviews.

(4) The appropriate Minister may make an arrangement with an organisation under which functions in relation to the panel are performed by the organisation on his behalf.

(5) If the appropriate Minister makes such an arrangement with an organisation, the organisation is to perform its functions under the arrangement in accordance with any general or special directions given by the appropriate Minister.

(6) The arrangement may include provision for payments to be made to the organisation by the appropriate Minister.

(7) Where the appropriate Minister is the National Assembly for Wales, subsections (4) and (6) also apply as if references to an organisation included references to the Secretary of State.

(8) In this section, "organisation" includes a public body and a private or voluntary organisation."[1]

---

1. This para in force from 1 December 2003 for the purposes of making of regulations, and from 1 April 2004 for remaining purposes: see Adoption and Children Act 2002 (Commencement No 4) Order 2003, SI 2003/3079.

Pending applications for freeing orders

6. Nothing in this Act affects any application for an order under section 18 of the Adoption Act 1976 (freeing for adoption) where—

(*a*) the application has been made and has not been disposed of immediately before the repeal of that section, and

(*b*) the child in relation to whom the application is made has his home immediately before that repeal with a person with whom he has been placed for adoption by an adoption agency.

Freeing orders

7. (1) Nothing in this Act affects any order made under section 18 of the Adoption Act 1976 (c 36) and—

(*a*) sections 19 to 21 of that Act are to continue to have effect in relation to such an order, and

(*b*) Part 1 of Schedule 6 to the Magistrates' Courts Act 1980 (c 43) is to continue to have effect for the purposes of an application under section 21 of the Adoption Act 1976 in relation to such an order.

(2) Section 20 of that Act, as it has effect by virtue of this paragraph, is to apply as if, in subsection (3)(c) after "1989" there were inserted—

"(iia)any care order, within the meaning of that Act".

(3) Where a child is free for adoption by virtue of an order made under section 18 of that Act, the third condition in section 47(6) is to be treated as satisfied.

Pending applications for adoption orders

8. Nothing in this Act affects any application for an adoption order under section 12 of the Adoption Act 1976 where—

(a) the application has been made and has not been disposed of immediately before the repeal of that section, and

(b) the child in relation to whom the application is made has his home immediately before that repeal with a person with whom he has been placed for adoption by an adoption agency.

Notification of adoption applications

9. Where a notice given in respect of a child by the prospective adopters under section 22(1) of the Adoption Act 1976 is treated by virtue of paragraph 1(1) as having been given for the purposes of section 44(2) in respect of an application to adopt the child, section 42(3) has effect in relation to their application for an adoption order as if for "six months" there were substituted "twelve months".

Adoptions with a foreign element

10. In section 13 of the Adoption Act 1976 (child to live with adopters before order is made)—

(a) in subsection (1)(a), at the beginning there is inserted "(subject to subsection (1A))",

(b) after subsection (1) there is inserted—

"(1A) Where an adoption is proposed to be effected by a Convention adoption order, the order shall not be made unless at all times during the preceding six months the child had his home with the applicants or one of them.",

(c) in subsection (2), after "subsection (1)" there is inserted "or (1A)",

(d) subsection (4) is omitted.

11. In section 56 of the Adoption Act 1976 (restriction on removal of children for adoption outside Great Britain)—

(a) in subsection (1), "not being a parent or guardian or relative of the child" is omitted,

(b) at the end of that section there is inserted—

"(4) Regulations may provide for subsection (1) to apply with modifications, or not to apply, if—

(a) the prospective adopters are parents, relatives or guardians of the child in question (or one of them is), or

(b) the prospective adopter is a step-parent of the child,

and any prescribed conditions are met.

(5) On the occasion of the first exercise of the power to make regulations under subsection (4)—

(a) the regulations shall not be made unless a draft of the regulations has been approved by a resolution of each House of Parliament, and

(b) accordingly section 67(2) does not apply to the statutory instrument containing the regulations.

(6) In this section, "prescribed" means prescribed by regulations and "regulations" means regulations made by the Secretary of State, after consultation with the National Assembly for Wales."

12. (*This paragraph substitutes a new s 56A of the Adoption Act 1976.*)

13. In section 72 of the Adoption Act 1976 (c 36) (interpretation), subsection (3B) is omitted.

Advertising

14. In section 58 of the Adoption Act 1976 (c 36) (restrictions on advertisements)—

(a) after subsection (1) there is inserted—

"(1A) Publishing an advertisement includes doing so by electronic means (for example, by means of the internet).",

(b) in subsection (2), for the words following "conviction" there is substituted "to imprisonment for a term not exceeding three months, or a fine not exceeding level 5 on the standard scale, or both".

15. In section 52 of the Adoption (Scotland) Act 1978 (c 28) (restriction on advertisements)—

(a) after subsection (1) there is inserted—

"(1A) Publishing an advertisement includes doing so by electronic means (for example, by means of the internet).",

(b) in subsection (2), for the words following "conviction" there is substituted "to imprisonment for a term not exceeding three months, or a fine not exceeding level 5 on the standard scale, or both".

16. (1) The Secretary of State may make regulations providing for the references to an adoption agency in—

(a) section 58(1)(c) of the Adoption Act 1976, and

(*b*) section 52(1)(*c*) of the Adoption (Scotland) Act 1978,

to include a prescribed person outside the United Kingdom exercising functions corresponding to those of an adoption agency, if the functions are being exercised in prescribed circumstances.

"Prescribed" means prescribed by the regulations.

(2) Before exercising the power conferred by sub-paragraph (1) in relation to the Adoption (Scotland) Act 1978, the Secretary of State must consult the Scottish Ministers.

Status

17. (1) Section 67—

(*a*) does not apply to a pre-1976 instrument or enactment in so far as it contains a disposition of property, and
(*b*) does not apply to any public general Act in its application to any disposition of property in a pre-1976 instrument or enactment.

(2) Section 73 applies in relation to this paragraph as if this paragraph were contained in Chapter 4 of Part 1; and an instrument or enactment is a pre-1976 instrument or enactment for the purposes of this Schedule if it was passed or made at any time before 1st January 1976.

18. Section 69 does not apply to a pre-1976 instrument.

19. In section 70(1), the reference to Part 3 of the Family Law Reform Act 1987 (c 42) includes Part 2 of the Family Law Reform Act 1969 (c 46).

Registration of adoptions

20. (1) The power of the court under paragraph 4(1) of Schedule 1 to amend an order on the application of the adopter or adopted person includes, in relation to an order made before 1st April 1959, power to make any amendment of the particulars contained in the order which appears to be required to bring the order into the form in which it would have been made if paragraph 1 of that Schedule had applied to the order.

(2) In relation to an adoption order made before the commencement of the Adoption Act 1976 (c 36), the reference in paragraph 4(3) of that Schedule to paragraph 1(2) or (3) is to be read—

(*a*) in the case of an order under the Adoption of Children Act 1926 (c 29), as a reference to section 12(3) and (4) of the Adoption of Children Act 1949 (c 98),
(*b*) in the case of an order under the Adoption Act 1950 (c 26), as a reference to section 18(3) and (4) of that Act,
(*c*) in the case of an order under the Adoption Act 1958 (c 5), as a reference to section 21(4) and (5) of that Act.

The Child Abduction Act 1984 (c 37)

21. Paragraph 43 of Schedule 3 does not affect the Schedule to the Child Abduction Act 1984 in its application to a child who is the subject of—

(*a*) an order under section 18 of the Adoption Act 1976 freeing the child for adoption,
(*b*) a pending application for such an order, or
(*c*) a pending application for an order under section 12 of that Act.

The Courts and Legal Services Act 1990 (c 41)

22. Paragraph 80 of Schedule 3 does not affect section 58A(2)(*b*) of the Courts and Legal Services Act 1990 in its application to proceedings under the Adoption Act 1976 (c 36).

The Children (Scotland) Act 1995 (c 36)

23. Paragraph 84 of Schedule 3 does not affect section 86(6) of the Children (Scotland) Act 1995 in its application to a child who becomes the subject of an order under section 18 or 55 of the Adoption Act 1976 by virtue of an application made before the repeal of that section.

Section 139	SCHEDULE 5
	REPEALS

6–3200T

Short title and chapter	Extent of repeal
Births and Deaths Registration Act 1953 (c 20)	In section 10(3), the words following "the Family Law Reform Act 1987".
Sexual Offences Act 1956 (c 69)	In section 28(4), the "or" at the end of paragraph (*a*).
Local Authority Social Services Act 1970 (c 42)	In Schedule 1, the entry relating to the Adoption Act 1976.
Adoption Act 1976 (c 36)	The whole Act, except Part 4 and paragraph 6 of Schedule 2.
Criminal Law Act 1977 (c 45)	In Schedule 12, the entries relating to the Adoption Act 1976.
National Health Service Act 1977 (c 49)	In section 124A(3), the "or" at the end of paragraph (*a*).
Domestic Proceedings and Magistrates' Courts Act 1978 (c 22)	Sections 73(2), 74(2) and 74(4).
Adoption (Scotland) Act 1978 (c 28)	In section 50, the words "not being a parent or guardian or relative of the child". Section 52. In section 53(2), the words "England and Wales or".

Short title and chapter	Extent of repeal
Magistrates' Courts Act 1980 (c 43)	In section 65(1), in the definition of "order freeing a child for adoption", paragraph (*a*) and the word "and" immediately following that paragraph. In section 71(1) the words "(other than proceedings under the Adoption Act 1976)". In section 71(2) the words following "(*a*) and (*b*)". In Schedule 7, paragraphs 141 and 142.
British Nationality Act 1981 (c 61)	In section 1(8), the words following "section 50".
Mental Health Act 1983 (c 20)	In Schedule 4, paragraph 45.
Health and Social Services and Social Security Adjudications Act 1983 (c 41)	In Schedule 2, paragraphs 29 to 33, 35 and 36.
County Courts Act 1984 (c 28)	In Schedule 9, paragraph 19.
Child Abduction Act 1984 (c 37)	In Schedule 2, paragraph 58.
Matrimonial and Family Proceedings Act 1984 (c 42)	In section 1(5A)(*a*), the "or" at the end of sub-paragraph (i). In section 40(2)(*a*), after "the Adoption Act 1968", the word "or".
Child Abduction and Custody Act 1985 (c 60)	In Schedule 1, paragraph 20. In Schedule 3, in paragraph 1, the "and" at the end of paragraph (*b*). In Schedule 3, in paragraph 1(*c*), paragraph (v).
Family Law Reform Act 1987 (c 42)	In Schedule 3, paragraphs 2 to 5.
Children Act 1989 (c 41)	Section 9(4). Section 12(3)(*a*). In section 20(9), the "or" at the end of paragraph (*a*). In section 26(2)(*e*) and (*f*), the words "to consider". Section 33(6)(*b*)(i). Section 80(1)(*e*) and (*f*). Section 81(1)(*b*). Section 88(1). Section 102(6)(*c*). In section 105(1), the definition of "protected child". In Schedule 10, Part 1.
National Health Service and Community Care Act 1990 (c 19)	In Schedule 9, paragraph 17.
Human Fertilisation and Embryology Act 1990 (c 37)	In Schedule 4, paragraph 4.
Courts and Legal Services Act 1990 (c 41)	In Schedule 16, paragraph 7.
Local Government (Wales) Act 1994 (c 19)	In Schedule 10, paragraph 9.
Health Authorities Act 1995 (c 17)	In Schedule 1, paragraph 101.
Adoption (Intercountry Aspects) Act 1999 (c 18)	In section 2(6), the words "in its application to Scotland". Section 7(3). Section 14. In section 16(1), the words ", or section 17 or 56A of the 1976 Act,". In Schedule 2, paragraph 3.
Access to Justice Act 1999 (c 22)	In Schedule 13, paragraph 88.
Care Standards Act 2000 (c 14)	In section 16(2), the words "or a voluntary adoption agency". In Schedule 4, paragraphs 5 and 27(*b*).
Local Government Act 2000 (c 22)	In Schedule 5, paragraph 16.
Criminal Justice and Court Services Act 2000 (c 43)	Section 12(5)(*b*) and the preceding "and"[1].
This Act	In Schedule 7, paragraphs 51 to 53. In Schedule 4, paragraphs 3 to 5 and 10 to 16.

1. Section 139(3) in so far as it relates to the Criminal Justice and Court Services Act 2000 in force from 28 November 2003 see Adoption and Children Act 2002 (Commencement No 4) Order 2003, SI 2003/3079.

Section 147

SCHEDULE 6
GLOSSARY

6-3200U   In this Act, the expressions listed in the left-hand column below have the meaning given by, or are to be interpreted in accordance with, the provisions of this Act or (where stated) of the 1989 Act listed in the right-hand column.

Expression	Provision
the 1989 Act	section 2(5)
Adopted Children Register	section 77
Adoption and Children Act Register	section 125
adoption (in relation to Chapter 4 of Part 1)	section 66
adoption agency	section 2(1)
adoption agency placing a child for adoption	section 18(5)
Adoption Contact Register	section 80
adoption order	section 46(1)

Expression	Provision
Adoption Service	section 2(1)
adoption society	section 2(5)
adoption support agency	section 8
adoption support services	section 2(6)
appointed day (in relation to Chapter 4 of Part 1)	section 66(2)
appropriate Minister	section 144
Assembly	section 144
body	section 144
by virtue of	section 144
care order	section 105(1) of the 1989 Act
child	sections 49(5) and 144
child assessment order	section 43(2) of the 1989 Act
child in the care of a local authority	section 105(1) of the 1989 Act
child looked after by a local authority	section 22 of the 1989 Act
child placed for adoption by an adoption agency	section 18(5)
child to be adopted, adopted child	section 49(5)
consent (in relation to making adoption orders or placing for adoption)	section 52
the Convention	section 144
Convention adoption	section 66(1)(c)
Convention adoption order	section 144
Convention country	section 144
couple	section 144(4)
court	section 144
disposition (in relation to Chapter 4 of Part 1)	section 73
enactment	section 144
fee	section 144
guardian	section 144
information	section 144
interim care order	section 38 of the 1989 Act
local authority	section 144
local authority foster parent	section 23(3) of the 1989 Act
Northern Irish adoption agency	section 144
Northern Irish adoption order	section 144
notice	section 144
notice of intention to adopt	section 44(2)
overseas adoption	section 87
parental responsibility	section 3 of the 1989 Act
partner, in relation to a parent of a child	section 144(7)
placement order	section 21
placing, or placed, for adoption	sections 18(5) and 19(4)
prohibited steps order	section 8(1) of the 1989 Act
records (in relation to Chapter 5 of Part 1)	section 82
registered adoption society	section 2(2)
registers of live-births (in relation to Chapter 5 of Part 1)	section 82
registration authority (in Part 1)	section 144
regulations	section 144
relative	section 144, read with section 1(8)
residence order	section 8(1) of the 1989 Act
rules	section 144
Scottish adoption agency	section 144(3)
Scottish adoption order	section 144
specific issue order	section 8(1) of the 1989 Act
subordinate legislation	section 144
supervision order	section 31(11) of the 1989 Act
unitary authority	section 144
voluntary organisation	section 2(5)

Human Fertilisation and Embryology (Deceased Fathers) Act 2003[1]

(2003 c 24)

6–3200V   1. Certain deceased men to be registered as fathers[2]

---

1. This Act makes provision about the circumstances in which, and the extent to which, a man is to be treated as the father of a child where the child was conceived by certain fertility treatment undertaken after the man's death. The Act also deals with certain consequential and supplementary matters.
   Where the Act inserts new provisions in, or otherwise amends, existing legislation that is reproduced in this work, the relevant changes will be set out in the legislation concerned when they take effect.
   The whole of the Act is in force: see Human Fertilisation and Embryology (Deceased Fathers) Act 2003 (Commencement) Order 2003, SI 2003/3095.
2. This section inserts new provisions after s 28(5) of the Human Fertilisation and Embryology Act 1990; see this PART, *ante*.

6–3200W **2. Consequential and supplementary provision.** (1) The Schedule (which contains consequential amendments) shall have effect.

(2) Section 1 of the Regulatory Reform Act 2001 (c 6) (power by order to make provision reforming law which imposes burdens) shall have effect, for the purposes of making a relevant calculation in relation to any amendment made to the Births and Deaths Registration Act 1953 (c 20) by or under this Act, as if this Act and any order made under this Act were passed or made more than two years before it was passed or made.

(3) In subsection (2) "relevant calculation" means a calculation as to whether any period is a period of, or of more or less than, two years.

[Human Fertilisation and Embryology (Deceased Fathers) Act 2003, s 2.]

6–3200X **3. Retrospective, transitional and transitory provision.** (1) This Act shall (in addition to any case where the sperm or embryo is used on or after the coming into force of section 1) apply to any case where the sperm of a man, or any embryo the creation of which was brought about with the sperm of a man, was used on or after 1st August 1991 and before the coming into force of that section.

(2) Where the child concerned was born before the coming into force of section 1 of this Act, section 28(5A) or (as the case may be) (5B) of the Human Fertilisation and Embryology Act 1990 (c 37) shall have effect as if for paragraph (e) there were substituted—

> "(e) the woman has elected in writing not later than the end of the period of six months beginning with the coming into force of this subsection for the man to be treated for the purpose mentioned in subsection (5I) below as the father of the child,".

(3) Where the child concerned was born before the coming into force of section 1 of this Act, section 28(5C) of the Act of 1990 shall have effect as if for paragraph (f) there were substituted—

> "(f) the woman has elected in writing not later than the end of the period of six months beginning with the coming into force of this subsection for the other party to the marriage to be treated for the purpose mentioned in subsection (5I) below as the father of the child,".

(4) Where the child concerned was born before the coming into force of section 1 of this Act, section 28(5D) of the Act of 1990 shall have effect as if for paragraph (f) there were substituted—

> "(f) the woman has elected in writing not later than the end of the period of six months beginning with the coming into force of this subsection for the man to be treated for the purpose mentioned in subsection (5I) below as the father of the child,".

(5) Where the child concerned was born before the coming into force of section 1 of this Act, section 28 of the Act of 1990 shall have effect as if—

(a) subsection (5E) were omitted; and
(b) in subsection (5F) for the words from " (which requires" to "that day)" there were substituted " (which requires an election to be made not later than the end of a period of six months)".

(6) Where the man who might be treated as the father of the child died before the passing of this Act—

(a) subsections (5A) and (5B) of section 28 of the Act of 1990 shall have effect as if paragraph (d) of each subsection were omitted;
(b) subsections (5C) and (5D) of that section of that Act shall have effect as if paragraph (e) of each subsection were omitted; and
(c) sections 10ZA(3)(a) of the Births and Deaths Registration Act 1953 (c 20) and 18ZA(3)(a) of the Registration of Births, Deaths and Marriages (Scotland) Act 1965 (c 49), and Article 14A(3)(a) of the Births and Deaths Registration (Northern Ireland) Order 1976 (SI 1976/1041 (NI 14)), shall have effect as if the words "consent in writing and" were omitted.

(7) Section 15(3)(a) of the Adoption Act 1976 (c 36) (adoption by one person where no other parent) shall have effect as if after "1990" there were inserted " (disregarding subsections (5A) to (5I) of that section)".

(8) Subsection (7) shall cease to apply when, and to the extent that, the repeal of section 15(3)(a) of the Act of 1976 by the Adoption and Children Act 2002 (c 38) comes into force.

[Human Fertilisation and Embryology (Deceased Fathers) Act 2003, s 3.]

6–3200Y **4. Short title, commencement and extent[1].** (1) This Act may be cited as the Human Fertilisation and Embryology (Deceased Fathers) Act 2003.

(2) This Act (apart from this section) shall come into force on such day as the Secretary of State may by order appoint; and different days may be appointed for different purposes.

(3) An order under subsection (2)—

(a) shall be made by statutory instrument; and
(b) may make such transitory, transitional or saving provision as the Secretary of State considers appropriate.

(4) Any amendment by the Schedule of an enactment has the same extent as the enactment amended.

(5) Subject to that, this Act extends to England and Wales, Scotland and Northern Ireland.
[Human Fertilisation and Embryology (Deceased Fathers) Act 2003, s 4.]

---

1. The whole of the Act is in force: see Human Fertilisation and Embryology (Deceased Fathers) Act 2003 (Commencement) Order 2003, SI 2003/3095.

6–3200Z   SCHEDULE[1]
CONSEQUENTIAL AMENDMENTS

---

1. The amendments to provisions reproduced in this work will be shown in the statutes concerned when they take effect.

Gender Recognition Act 2004
(2004 c 7)

6–3201   Sections 1–8[1]

---

1. Sections 1–8 deal with applications for a gender recognition certificate made on the basis that the applicant, who must be aged at least 18, is living in the other gender or has changed gender under the law of a country or territory outside the UK.

6–3201A   9. General.   (1) Where a full gender recognition certificate is issued to a person, the person's gender becomes for all purposes the acquired gender (so that, if the acquired gender is the male gender, the person's sex becomes that of a man and, if it is the female gender, the person's sex becomes that of a woman).

(2) Subsection (1) does not affect things done, or events occurring, before the certificate is issued; but it does operate for the interpretation of enactments passed, and instruments and other documents made, before the certificate is issued (as well as those passed or made afterwards).

(3) Subsection (1) is subject to provision made by this Act or any other enactment or any subordinate legislation.
[Gender Recognition Act 2004, s 9.]

6–3201B   10. Registration.   (1) Where there is a UK birth register entry in relation to a person to whom a full gender recognition certificate is issued, the Secretary of State must send a copy of the certificate to the appropriate Registrar General.

(2) In this Act "UK birth register entry", in relation to a person to whom a full gender recognition certificate is issued, means—

(a) an entry of which a certified copy is kept by a Registrar General, or
(b) an entry in a register so kept,

containing a record of the person's birth or adoption (or, if there would otherwise be more than one, the most recent).

(3) "The appropriate Registrar General" means whichever of—

(a) the Registrar General for England and Wales,
(b) the Registrar General for Scotland, or
(c) the Registrar General for Northern Ireland,

keeps a certified copy of the person's UK birth register entry or the register containing that entry.

(4) Schedule 3 (provisions about registration) has effect.
[Gender Recognition Act 2004, s 10.]

6–3201C   11. Marriage.   Schedule 4 (amendments of marriage law) has effect.
[Gender Recognition Act 2004, s 11.]

6–3201D   12. Parenthood.   The fact that a person's gender has become the acquired gender under this Act does not affect the status of the person as the father or mother of a child.
[Gender Recognition Act 2004, s 12.]

6–3201E   13. Social security benefits and pensions .   Schedule 5 (entitlement to benefits and pensions) has effect.
[Gender Recognition Act 2004, s 13.]

6–3201F   14. Discrimination.   Schedule 6 (amendments of Sex Discrimination Act 1975 (c 65) and Sex Discrimination (Northern Ireland) Order 1976 (SI 1976/1042 (NI 15))) has effect.
[Gender Recognition Act 2004, s 14.]

6–3201G   **15. Succession etc.**   The fact that a person's gender has become the acquired gender under this Act does not affect the disposal or devolution of property under a will or other instrument made before the appointed day.
[Gender Recognition Act 2004, s 15.]

6–3201H   **16. Peerages etc.**   The fact that a person's gender has become the acquired gender under this Act—

     (*a*)   does not affect the descent of any peerage or dignity or title of honour, and
     (*b*)   does not affect the devolution of any property limited (expressly or not) by a will or other instrument to devolve (as nearly as the law permits) along with any peerage or dignity or title of honour unless an intention that it should do so is expressed in the will or other instrument.

[Gender Recognition Act 2004, s 16.]

6–3201I   **17. Trustees and personal representatives**

6–3201J   **18. Orders where expectations defeated**

6–3201K   **19. Report**

6–3201L   **20. Gender-specific offences.**   (1) Where (apart from this subsection) a relevant gender-specific offence could be committed or attempted only if the gender of a person to whom a full gender recognition certificate has been issued were not the acquired gender, the fact that the person's gender has become the acquired gender does not prevent the offence being committed or attempted.
     (2) An offence is a "relevant gender-specific offence" if—

     (*a*)   either or both of the conditions in subsection (3) are satisfied, and
     (*b*)   the commission of the offence involves the accused engaging in sexual activity.

     (3) The conditions are—

     (*a*)   that the offence may be committed only by a person of a particular gender, and
     (*b*)   that the offence may be committed only on, or in relation to, a person of a particular gender,

and the references to a particular gender include a gender identified by reference to the gender of the other person involved.
[Gender Recognition Act 2004, s 20.]

6–3201M   **21. Foreign gender change and marriage.**   (1) A person's gender is not to be regarded as having changed by reason only that it has changed under the law of a country or territory outside the United Kingdom.
     (2) Accordingly, a person is not to be regarded as being married by reason of having entered into a foreign post-recognition marriage.
     (3) But if a full gender recognition certificate is issued to a person who has entered into a foreign post-recognition marriage, after the issue of the certificate the marriage is no longer to be regarded as being void on the ground that (at the time when it was entered into) the parties to it were not respectively male and female.
     (4) However, subsection (3) does not apply to a foreign post-recognition marriage if a party to it has entered into a later (valid) marriage or civil partnership before the issue of the full gender recognition certificate.
     (5) For the purposes of this section a person has entered into a foreign post-recognition marriage if (and only if)—

     (*a*)   the person has entered into a marriage in accordance with the law of a country or territory outside the United Kingdom,
     (*b*)   before the marriage was entered into the person had changed gender under the law of that or any other country or territory outside the United Kingdom,
     (*c*)   the other party to the marriage was not of the gender to which the person had changed under the law of that country or territory, and
     (*d*)   by virtue of subsection (1) the person's gender was not regarded as having changed under the law of any part of the United Kingdom.

     (6) Nothing in this section prevents the exercise of any enforceable Community right.
[Gender Recognition Act 2004, s 21 as amended by the Civil Partnership Act 2004, s 250.]

Supplementary

6–3201N   **22. Prohibition on disclosure of information.**   (1) It is an offence for a person who has acquired protected information in an official capacity to disclose the information to any other person.
     (2) "Protected information" means information which relates to a person who has made an application under section 1(1) and which—

(a) concerns that application or any application by the person under section 5(2), 5A(2) or 6(1), or

(b) if the application under section 1(1) is granted, otherwise concerns the person's gender before it becomes the acquired gender.

(3) A person acquires protected information in an official capacity if the person acquires it—

(a) in connection with the person's functions as a member of the civil service, a constable or the holder of any other public office or in connection with the functions of a local or public authority or of a voluntary organisation,

(b) as an employer, or prospective employer, of the person to whom the information relates or as a person employed by such an employer or prospective employer, or

(c) in the course of, or otherwise in connection with, the conduct of business or the supply of professional services.

(4) But it is not an offence under this section to disclose protected information relating to a person if—

(a) the information does not enable that person to be identified,

(b) that person has agreed to the disclosure of the information,

(c) the information is protected information by virtue of subsection (2)(b) and the person by whom the disclosure is made does not know or believe that a full gender recognition certificate has been issued,

(d) the disclosure is in accordance with an order of a court or tribunal,

(e) the disclosure is for the purpose of instituting, or otherwise for the purposes of, proceedings before a court or tribunal,

(f) the disclosure is for the purpose of preventing or investigating crime,

(g) the disclosure is made to the Registrar General for England and Wales, the Registrar General for Scotland or the Registrar General for Northern Ireland,

(h) the disclosure is made for the purposes of the social security system or a pension scheme,

(i) the disclosure is in accordance with provision made by an order under subsection (5), or

(j) the disclosure is in accordance with any provision of, or made by virtue of, an enactment other than this section.

(5) The Secretary of State may by order[1] make provision prescribing circumstances in which the disclosure of protected information is not to constitute an offence under this section.

(6) The power conferred by subsection (5) is exercisable by the Scottish Ministers (rather than the Secretary of State) where the provision to be made is within the legislative competence of the Scottish Parliament.

(7) An order under subsection (5) may make provision permitting—

(a) disclosure to specified persons or persons of a specified description,

(b) disclosure for specified purposes,

(c) disclosure of specified descriptions of information, or

(d) disclosure by specified persons or persons of a specified description.

(8) A person guilty of an offence under this section is liable on summary conviction to a fine not exceeding level 5 on the standard scale.

[Gender Recognition Act 2004, s 22 as amended by the Civil Partnership Act 2004, s 250.]

---

1. The Gender Recognition (Disclosure of Information) (England, Wales and Northern Ireland) (No 2) Order 2005, SI 2005/916 has been made which includes disclosure for the purpose of obtaining legal advice, disclosure for religious purposes or medical purposes, disclosure by or on behalf of a credit reference agency and disclosure for purposes in relation to insolvency or bankruptcy.

6–3201O   23. Power to modify statutory provisions

6–3201P   24. Orders and Regulations

6–3201Q   25. Interpretation

6–3201R   26. Commencement[1]. Apart from sections 23 to 25, this section and sections 28 and 29, this Act does not come into force until such day as the Secretary of State may appoint by order made after consulting the Scottish Ministers and the Department of Finance and Personnel in Northern Ireland.

[Gender Recognition Act 2004, s 26.]

---

1. The Gender Recognition Act 2004 (Commencement) Order 2005, SI 2005/54 has been made, bringing the whole of the Act (except those provision in force from Royal Assent) in force from 1 April 2005

6–3201S   27. Applications within two years of commencement

6–3201T   28. Extent

6–3201U   29. Short title.   This Act may be cited as the Gender Recognition Act 2004.
[Gender Recognition Act 2004, s 29.]

6–3201V   SCHEDULE 1
                           GENDER RECOGNITION PANELS

6–3201W   SCHEDULE 2
                           INTERIM CERTIFICATES: MARRIAGE

6–3201X   SCHEDULE 3
                           REGISTRATION

6–3201Y

Section 11   SCHEDULE 4
                           EFFECT ON MARRIAGE

PART 1
ENGLAND AND WALES

Marriage Act 1949 (c 76)

1. The Marriage Act 1949 is amended as follows.
2. In section 1 (restrictions on marriage), insert at the end—

"(6) Subsection (5) of this section and Parts 2 and 3 of the First Schedule to this Act have effect subject to the following modifications in the case of a party to a marriage whose gender has become the acquired gender under the Gender Recognition Act 2004 ("the relevant person").
    (7) Any reference in those provisions to a former wife or former husband of the relevant person includes (respectively) any former husband or former wife of the relevant person.
    (8) And—
    (a) the reference in paragraph (b) of subsection (5) of this section to the relevant person's son's mother is to the relevant person's son's father if the relevant person is the son's mother; and
    (b) the reference in paragraph (d) of that subsection to the relevant person's daughter's father is to the relevant person's daughter's mother if the relevant person is the daughter's father."
3. After section 5A insert—

"5B Marriages involving person of acquired gender
(1) A clergyman is not obliged to solemnise the marriage of a person if the clergyman reasonably believes that the person's gender has become the acquired gender under the Gender Recognition Act 2004.
(2) A clerk in Holy Orders of the Church in Wales is not obliged to permit the marriage of a person to be solemnised in the church or chapel of which the clerk is the minister if the clerk reasonably believes that the person's gender has become the acquired gender under that Act."
Matrimonial Causes Act 1973 (c 18)
4. The Matrimonial Causes Act 1973 is amended as follows.
5. In section 12 (grounds on which a marriage celebrated after 31st July 1971 is voidable), insert at the end—

"(h) that the respondent is a person whose gender at the time of the marriage had become the acquired gender under the Gender Recognition Act 2004."
6. In section 13(2), (3) and (4) (bars to relief), for "or (f)" substitute ", (f) or (h)".

PART 2
SCOTLAND

PART 3
NORTHERN IRELAND

6–3201Z   SCHEDULE 5
                           BENEFITS AND PENSIONS
                           SCHEDULE 6
                           SEX DISCRIMINATION

Domestic Violence, Crime and Victims Act 2004[1]
(2004 c 28)

PART 1
DOMESTIC VIOLENCE ETC[2]

Amendments to Part 4 of the Family Law Act 1996

6–3202   1. Breach of non-molestation order to be a criminal offence.   In Part 4 of the Family Law Act 1996 (c 27) (family homes and domestic violence), after section 42 insert—

"**42A Offence of breaching non-molestation order.**   (1) A person who without reasonable excuse does anything that he is prohibited from doing by a non-molestation order is guilty of an offence.
    (2) In the case of a non-molestation order made by virtue of section 45(1), a person can be

guilty of an offence under this section only in respect of conduct engaged in at a time when he was aware of the existence of the order.

(3) Where a person is convicted of an offence under this section in respect of any conduct, that conduct is not punishable as a contempt of court.

(4) A person cannot be convicted of an offence under this section in respect of any conduct which has been punished as a contempt of court.

(5) A person guilty of an offence under this section is liable—

(a) on conviction on indictment, to imprisonment for a term not exceeding five years, or a fine, or both;

(b) on summary conviction, to imprisonment for a term not exceeding 12 months, or a fine not exceeding the statutory maximum, or both.

(6) A reference in any enactment to proceedings under this Part, or to an order under this Part, does not include a reference to proceedings for an offence under this section or to an order made in such proceedings.

"Enactment" includes an enactment contained in subordinate legislation within the meaning of the Interpretation Act 1978 (c 30)."

[Domestic Violence, Crime and Victims Act 2004, s 1.]

---

1. This Act amends previous legislation concerning domestic violence, makes provision about homicide, makes common assault arrestable, makes provision about alternative verdicts, changes certain Crown Court procedures regarding sample counts and findings of unfitness to plead, makes provision about the execution of warrants and the enforcement of orders made on conviction, amends certain provisions of the Criminal Justice Act 2003 and makes various other provisions for victims and witnesses including the establishment of a new commissioner.

The Act has 4 Parts and 12 Schedules. It will be brought into force in accordance with commencement orders made under s 60. At the time of going to press the Domestic Violence, Crime and Victims Act 2004 (Commencement No 1) Order 2005, SI 2005/579, had been made. However, mot of the Act remains unimplemented.

2. Part 1 contains ss 1–9.

6–3202A 2. Additional considerations if parties are cohabitants or former cohabitants.
(1) Section 41 of the Family Law Act 1996 (c 27) (which requires a court, when considering the nature of the relationship of cohabitants or former cohabitants, to have regard to their non-married status) is repealed.

(2) In section 36(6)(e) of that Act (court to have regard to nature of parties' relationship when considering whether to give right to occupy to cohabitant or former cohabitant with no existing right), after "relationship" insert "and in particular the level of commitment involved in it".

[Domestic Violence, Crime and Victims Act 2004, s 2.]

6–3202B 3. "Cohabitants" in Part 4 of 1996 Act to include same-sex couples. In section 62(1)(a) of the Family Law Act 1996 (definition of "cohabitant" for the purposes of Part 4 of that Act), for the words after " "cohabitants" are" substitute "two persons who, although not married to each other, are living together as husband and wife or (if of the same sex) in an equivalent relationship; and".

[Domestic Violence, Crime and Victims Act 2004, s 3.]

6–3202C 4. Extension of Part 4 of 1996 Act to non-cohabiting couples. In section 62(3) of the Family Law Act 1996 (definition of "associated" persons for the purposes of Part 4 of that Act), after paragraph (e) insert—

"(ea)they have or have had an intimate personal relationship with each other which is or was of significant duration;" .

[Domestic Violence, Crime and Victims Act 2004, s 4.]

or allowing the death of a child or vulnerable adult

6–3202D 5. The offence. (1) A person ("D") is guilty of an offence if—

(a) a child or vulnerable adult ("V") dies as a result of the unlawful act of a person who—

(i) was a member of the same household as V, and

(ii) had frequent contact with him,

(b) D was such a person at the time of that act,

(c) at that time there was a significant risk of serious physical harm being caused to V by the unlawful act of such a person, and

(d) either D was the person whose act caused V's death or—

(i) D was, or ought to have been, aware of the risk mentioned in paragraph (c),

(ii) D failed to take such steps as he could reasonably have been expected to take to protect V from the risk, and

(iii) the act occurred in circumstances of the kind that D foresaw or ought to have foreseen.

(2) The prosecution does not have to prove whether it is the first alternative in subsection (1)(d) or the second (sub-paragraphs (i) to (iii)) that applies.

(3) If D was not the mother or father of V—

(a) D may not be charged with an offence under this section if he was under the age of 16 at the time of the act that caused V's death;

(b) for the purposes of subsection (1)(d)(ii) D could not have been expected to take any such step as is referred to there before attaining that age.

(4) For the purposes of this section—

(a) a person is to be regarded as a "member" of a particular household, even if he does not live in that household, if he visits it so often and for such periods of time that it is reasonable to regard him as a member of it;

(b) where V lived in different households at different times, "the same household as V" refers to the household in which V was living at the time of the act that caused V's death.

(5) For the purposes of this section an "unlawful" act is one that—

(a) constitutes an offence, or

(b) would constitute an offence but for being the act of—

(i) a person under the age of ten, or
(ii) a person entitled to rely on a defence of insanity.

Paragraph (b) does not apply to an act of D.

(6) In this section—

"act" includes a course of conduct and also includes omission;

"child" means a person under the age of 16;

"serious" harm means harm that amounts to grievous bodily harm for the purposes of the Offences against the Person Act 1861 (c 100);

"vulnerable adult" means a person aged 16 or over whose ability to protect himself from violence, abuse or neglect is significantly impaired through physical or mental disability or illness, through old age or otherwise.

(7) A person guilty of an offence under this section is liable on conviction on indictment to imprisonment for a term not exceeding 14 years or to a fine, or to both.

[Domestic Violence, Crime and Victims Act 2004, s 5.]

6–3202E   6. Evidence and procedure: England and Wales.   (1) Subsections (2) to (4) apply where a person ("the defendant") is charged in the same proceedings with an offence of murder or manslaughter and with an offence under section 5 in respect of the same death ("the section 5 offence").

(2) Where by virtue of section 35(3) of the Criminal Justice and Public Order Act 1994 (c 33) a court or jury is permitted, in relation to the section 5 offence, to draw such inferences as appear proper from the defendant's failure to give evidence or refusal to answer a question, the court or jury may also draw such inferences in determining whether he is guilty—

(a) of murder or manslaughter, or

(b) of any other offence of which he could lawfully be convicted on the charge of murder or manslaughter,

even if there would otherwise be no case for him to answer in relation to that offence.

(3) The charge of murder or manslaughter is not to be dismissed under paragraph 2 of Schedule 3 to the Crime and Disorder Act 1998 (c 37) (unless the section 5 offence is dismissed).

(4) At the defendant's trial the question whether there is a case for the defendant to answer on the charge of murder or manslaughter is not to be considered before the close of all the evidence (or, if at some earlier time he ceases to be charged with the section 5 offence, before that earlier time).

(5) An offence under section 5 is an offence of homicide for the purposes of the following enactments—

sections 24 and 25 of the Magistrates' Courts Act 1980 (c 43) (mode of trial of child or young person for indictable offence);

section 51A of the Crime and Disorder Act 1998 (sending cases to the Crown Court: children and young persons);

section 8 of the Powers of Criminal Courts (Sentencing) Act 2000 (c 6) (power and duty to remit young offenders to youth courts for sentence).

[Domestic Violence, Crime and Victims Act 2004, s 6.]

6–3202F   7. Evidence and procedure: Northern Ireland

6–3202G   8. Evidence and procedure: courts-martial

Domestic homicide reviews

6–3202H   9. Establishment and conduct of reviews

PART 2
CRIMINAL JUSTICE[1]

Assault, harassment etc

6–3202I   10. Common assault to be an arrestable offence.   (1) *Repealed.*

(2) In Article 26(2) of the Police and Criminal Evidence (Northern Ireland) Order 1989 (SI 1989/1341 (NI 12)) (specific offences which are arrestable offences), after paragraph (m) insert—

"(n) an offence under section 42 of the Offences against the Person Act 1861 (c 100) (common assault etc)."

[Domestic Violence, Crime and Victims Act 2004, s 10 as amended by the Serious Organised Crime and Police Act 2005, Sch 17.]

---

1. Part 2 contains ss 10–31.

6–3202J   11. Common assault etc as alternative verdict.   In section 6 of the Criminal Law Act 1967 (c 58) (trial of offences), after subsection (3) (alternative verdicts on trial on indictment) insert—

"(3A) For the purposes of subsection (3) above an offence falls within the jurisdiction of the court of trial if it is an offence to which section 40 of the Criminal Justice Act 1988 applies (power to join in indictment count for common assault etc), even if a count charging the offence is not included in the indictment.

(3B) A person convicted of an offence by virtue of subsection (3A) may only be dealt with for it in a manner in which a magistrates' court could have dealt with him."

[Domestic Violence, Crime and Victims Act 2004, s 11.]

6–3202K   12. Restraining orders: England and Wales.   (1) In section 5 of the Protection from Harassment Act 1997 (c 40) (power to make restraining order where defendant convicted of offence under section 2 or 4 of that Act), in subsection (1) omit "under section 2 or 4".

(2) After subsection (3) of that section insert—

"(3A) In proceedings under this section both the prosecution and the defence may lead, as further evidence, any evidence that would be admissible in proceedings for an injunction under section 3."

(3) After subsection (4) of that section insert—

"(4A) Any person mentioned in the order is entitled to be heard on the hearing of an application under subsection (4)."

(4) After subsection (6) of that section insert—

"(7) A court dealing with a person for an offence under this section may vary or discharge the order in question by a further order."

(5) After that section insert—

"5A Restraining orders on acquittal.   (1) A court before which a person ("the defendant") is acquitted of an offence may, if it considers it necessary to do so to protect a person from harassment by the defendant, make an order prohibiting the defendant from doing anything described in the order.

(2) Subsections (3) to (7) of section 5 apply to an order under this section as they apply to an order under that one.

(3) Where the Court of Appeal allow an appeal against conviction they may remit the case to the Crown Court to consider whether to proceed under this section.

(4) Where—

(a) the Crown Court allows an appeal against conviction, or

(b) a case is remitted to the Crown Court under subsection (3),

the reference in subsection (1) to a court before which a person is acquitted of an offence is to be read as referring to that court.

(5) A person made subject to an order under this section has the same right of appeal against the order as if—

(a) he had been convicted of the offence in question before the court which made the order, and

(b) the order had been made under section 5."

[Domestic Violence, Crime and Victims Act 2004, s 12.]

6–3202L   13. Restraining orders: Northern Ireland

Surcharges

6–3202M 14. Surcharge payable on conviction. (1) In Chapter 1 of Part 12 of the Criminal Justice Act 2003 (c 44) (general provisions about sentencing), after section 161 insert—

"Surcharges

161A. Court's duty to order payment of surcharge. (1) A court when dealing with a person for one or more offences must also (subject to subsections (2) and (3)) order him to pay a surcharge.

(2) Subsection (1) does not apply in such cases as may be prescribed by an order made by the Secretary of State.

(3) Where a court dealing with an offender considers—

(a) that it would be appropriate to make a compensation order, but
(b) that he has insufficient means to pay both the surcharge and appropriate compensation,

the court must reduce the surcharge accordingly (if necessary to nil).

(4) For the purposes of this section a court does not "deal with" a person if it—

(a) discharges him absolutely, or
(b) makes an order under the Mental Health Act 1983 in respect of him.

161B Amount of surcharge. (1) The surcharge payable under section 161A is such amount as the Secretary of State may specify by order.

(2) An order under this section may provide for the amount to depend on—

(a) the offence or offences committed,
(b) how the offender is otherwise dealt with (including, where the offender is fined, the amount of the fine),
(c) the age of the offender.

This is not to be read as limiting section 330(3) (power to make different provision for different purposes etc)."

(2) In section 164 of that Act (fixing of fines), after subsection (4) insert—

"(4A) In applying subsection (3), a court must not reduce the amount of a fine on account of any surcharge it orders the offender to pay under section 161A, except to the extent that he has insufficient means to pay both."

(3) In Part 1 of Schedule 9 to the Administration of Justice Act 1970 (c 31) (cases where payment enforceable as on summary conviction), after paragraph 12 insert—

"**13.** Where under section 161A of the Criminal Justice Act 2003 a court orders the payment of a surcharge."

(4) In Schedule 5 to the Courts Act 2003 (c 39) (collection of fines), in paragraph 1(1) (application of Schedule), after "a fine" insert "or a surcharge imposed under section 161A of the Criminal Justice Act 2003".

(5) The Secretary of State may by order—

(a) make provision amending Schedule 5 (collection of fines) or Schedule 6 (discharge of fines by unpaid work) to the Courts Act 2003 in its application by virtue of subsection (3) or (4) to surcharges;
(b) make provision for any part of Schedule 5, or the whole or any part of Schedule 6, not to apply to surcharges;
(c) make amendments to any enactment that are consequential on provision made under paragraph (a) or (b).

[Domestic Violence, Crime and Victims Act 2004, s 14.]

6–3202N 15. Increase in maximum on-the-spot penalty for disorderly behaviour. (1) In Chapter 1 of Part 1 of the Criminal Justice and Police Act 2001 (c 16) (on-the-spot penalties for disorderly behaviour), section 3 is amended as follows.

(2) In subsection (2) (maximum penalty that may be prescribed), at the end insert "plus a half of the relevant surcharge".

(3) After that subsection insert—

"(2A) The "relevant surcharge", in relation to a person of a given age, is the amount payable by way of surcharge under section 161A of the Criminal Justice Act 2003 by a person of that age who is fined the maximum amount for the offence."

[Domestic Violence, Crime and Victims Act 2004, s 15.]

6–3202O 16. Higher fixed penalty for repeated road traffic offences. (1) The Road Traffic Offenders Act 1988 (c 53) is amended as follows.

(2) In section 53 (amount of fixed penalty), after subsection (2) insert—

"(3) In particular, in relation to England and Wales an order made under subsection (1)(a) may prescribe a higher fixed penalty in a case where, in the period of three years ending with the date of the offence in question, the offender committed an offence for which—

    (a) he was disqualified from driving, or

    (b) penalty points were endorsed on the counterpart of any licence held by him."

  (3) At the end of section 84 (regulations) (which becomes subsection (1)) insert—

    "(2) The Secretary of State may by regulations provide that where—

    (a) a conditional offer has been issued under section 75 of this Act,

    (b) the amount of the penalty stated in the offer is not the higher amount applicable by virtue of section 53(3) of this Act, and

    (c) it subsequently appears that that higher amount is in fact applicable,

the fixed penalty clerk may issue a further notice (a "surcharge notice") requiring payment of the difference between the two amounts.

    (3) Regulations under subsection (2) above may—

    (a) provide for this Part of this Act to have effect, in cases to which the regulations apply, with such modifications as may be specified;

    (b) make provision for the collection and enforcement of amounts due under surcharge notices."

[Domestic Violence, Crime and Victims Act 2004, s 16.]

Trial by jury of sample counts only

6–3202P   **17. Application by prosecution for certain counts to be tried without a jury**

6–3202Q   **18. Procedure for applications under section 17**

6–3202R   **19. Effect of order under section 17(2)**

6–3202S   **20. Rules of court**

6–3202T   **21. Application of sections 17 to 20 to Northern Ireland**

Unfitness to plead and insanity

6–3202U   **22. Procedure for determining fitness to plead: England and Wales**

6–3202V   **23. Procedure for determining fitness to be tried: Northern Ireland**

6–3202W   **24. Powers of court on finding of insanity or unfitness to plead etc**

6–3202X   **25. Appeal against order made on finding of insanity or unfitness to plead etc**

6–3202Y   **26. Courts-martial etc**

Miscellaneous

6–3202Z   **27. Powers of authorised officers executing warrants.**   (1) *Inserts new s 125B into the Magistrates' Courts Act 1980.*
    (2) After Schedule 4 to that Act insert the Schedule set out in Schedule 4 to this Act.
[Domestic Violence, Crime and Victims Act 2004, s 27.]

6–3203   **28. Disclosure orders for purpose of executing warrants.**   *Inserts new ss 125CA and 125CB into the Magistrates' Courts Act 1980.*

6–3203A   **29. Procedure on breach of community penalty etc.**   Schedule 5 (procedure on breach of community penalty etc) has effect.
[Domestic Violence, Crime and Victims Act 2004, s 29.]

6–3203B   **30. Prosecution appeals**

6–3203C   **31. Intermittent custody.**   Schedule 6 (intermittent custody) has effect.
[Domestic Violence, Crime and Victims Act 2004, s 31.]

PART 3[1]
VICTIMS ETC

CHAPTER 1[2]
The Victims' Code

6–3203D   32. Code of practice for victims

6–3203E   33. Procedure

6–3203F   34. Effect of non-compliance.   (1) If a person fails to perform a duty imposed on him by a code issued under section 32, the failure does not of itself make him liable to criminal or civil proceedings.

(2) But the code is admissible in evidence in criminal or civil proceedings and a court may take into account a failure to comply with the code in determining a question in the proceedings.
[Domestic Violence, Crime and Victims Act 2004, s 34.]

[1.] Part 3 contains ss 32–57.
2. Chapter 1 contains ss 32–34.

CHAPTER 2[1]
Representations and Information

Imprisonment or detention

6–3203G   35. Victims' rights to make representations and receive information.   (1) This section applies if—

   (a) a court convicts a person ("the offender") of a sexual or violent offence, and
   (b) a relevant sentence is imposed on him in respect of the offence.

(2) But section 39 applies (instead of this section) if a hospital direction and a limitation direction are given in relation to the offender.

(3) The local probation board for the area in which the sentence is imposed must take all reasonable steps to ascertain whether a person who appears to the board to be the victim of the offence or to act for the victim of the offence wishes—

   (a) to make representations about the matters specified in subsection (4);
   (b) to receive the information specified in subsection (5).

(4) The matters are—

   (a) whether the offender should be subject to any licence conditions or supervision requirements in the event of his release;
   (b) if so, what licence conditions or supervision requirements.

(5) The information is information about any licence conditions or supervision requirements to which the offender is to be subject in the event of his release.

(6) If a person whose wishes have been ascertained under subsection (3) makes representations to the local probation board mentioned in that subsection or the relevant local probation board about a matter specified in subsection (4), the relevant local probation board must forward those representations to the persons responsible for determining the matter.

(7) If a local probation board has ascertained under subsection (3) that a person wishes to receive the information specified in subsection (5), the relevant local probation board must take all reasonable steps—

   (a) to inform the person whether or not the offender is to be subject to any licence conditions or supervision requirements in the event of his release,
   (b) if he is, to provide the person with details of any licence conditions or supervision requirements which relate to contact with the victim or his family, and
   (c) to provide the person with such other information as the relevant local probation board considers appropriate in all the circumstances of the case.

(8) The relevant local probation board is—

   (a) in a case where the offender is to be supervised on release by an officer of a local probation board, that local probation board;
   (b) in any other case, the local probation board for the area in which the prison or other place in which the offender is detained is situated.
[Domestic Violence, Crime and Victims Act 2004, s 35.]

[1.] Chapter 2 contains ss 35–46.

Hospital orders

6–3203H   36. Victims' rights: preliminary.   (1) This section applies if the conditions in subsections (2) and (3) are met.

(2) The first condition is that one of these applies in respect of a person ("the patient") charged with a sexual or violent offence—

  (a)　the patient is convicted of the offence;

  (b)　a verdict is returned that the patient is not guilty of the offence by reason of insanity;

  (c)　a finding is made—

    (i)　under section 4 of the Criminal Procedure (Insanity) Act 1964 (c 84) that the patient is under a disability, and

    (ii)　under section 4A of that Act that he did the act or made the omission charged against him as the offence.

(3) The second condition is that a hospital order with a restriction order is made in respect of the patient by a court dealing with him for the offence.

(4) The local probation board for the area in which the determination mentioned in subsection (2)(a), (b) or (c) is made must take all reasonable steps to ascertain whether a person who appears to the board to be the victim of the offence or to act for the victim of the offence wishes—

  (a)　to make representations about the matters specified in subsection (5);

  (b)　to receive the information specified in subsection (6).

(5) The matters are—

  (a)　whether the patient should be subject to any conditions in the event of his discharge from hospital;

  (b)　if so, what conditions.

(6) The information is information about any conditions to which the patient is to be subject in the event of his discharge from hospital.

[Domestic Violence, Crime and Victims Act 2004, s 36.]

6–3203I　37. Representations. (1) This section applies if section 36 applies.

  (2) If—

  (a)　a person makes representations about a matter specified in section 36(5) to the local probation board mentioned in section 36(4) or the relevant local probation board, and

  (b)　it appears to the relevant local probation board that the person is the victim of the offence or acts for the victim of the offence,

the relevant local probation board must forward the representations to the persons responsible for determining the matter.

(3) The duty in subsection (2) applies only while the restriction order made in respect of the patient is in force.

(4) The Secretary of State must inform the relevant local probation board if he is considering—

  (a)　whether to give a direction in respect of the patient under section 42(1) of the Mental Health Act 1983 (c 20) (directions lifting restrictions),

  (b)　whether to discharge the patient under section 42(2) of that Act, either absolutely or subject to conditions, or

  (c)　if the patient has been discharged subject to conditions, whether to vary the conditions.

(5) A Mental Health Review Tribunal must inform the relevant local probation board if—

  (a)　an application is made to the tribunal by the patient under section 69, 70 or 75 of the Mental Health Act 1983 (applications concerning restricted patients), or

  (b)　the Secretary of State refers the patient's case to the tribunal under section 71 of that Act (references concerning restricted patients).

(6) Subsection (7) applies if—

  (a)　the relevant local probation board receives information under subsection (4) or (5), and

  (b)　a person who appears to the relevant local probation board to be the victim of the offence or to act for the victim of the offence—

    (i)　when his wishes were ascertained under section 36(4), expressed a wish to make representations about a matter specified in section 36(5), or

    (ii)　has made representations about such a matter to the relevant local probation board or the local probation board mentioned in section 36(4).

(7) The relevant local probation board must provide the information to the person.

(8) The relevant local probation board is—

  (a)　if the patient is to be discharged subject to a condition that he reside in a particular area, the local probation board for the area;

  (b)　in any other case, the local probation board for the area in which the hospital in which the patient is detained is situated.

[Domestic Violence, Crime and Victims Act 2004, s 37.]

6–3203J   38. Information.   (1) This section applies if section 36 applies.

(2) Subsection (3) applies if a person who appears to the relevant local probation board to be the victim of the offence or to act for the victim of the offence—

(a) when his wishes were ascertained under section 36(4), expressed a wish to receive the information specified in section 36(6), or

(b) has subsequently informed the relevant local probation board that he wishes to receive that information.

(3) The relevant local probation board must take all reasonable steps—

(a) to inform that person whether or not the patient is to be subject to any conditions in the event of his discharge;

(b) if he is, to provide that person with details of any conditions which relate to contact with the victim or his family;

(c) if the restriction order in respect of the patient is to cease to have effect, to notify that person of the date on which it is to cease to have effect;

(d) to provide that person with such other information as the board considers appropriate in all the circumstances of the case.

(4) The Secretary of State must inform the relevant local probation board—

(a) whether the patient is to be discharged;

(b) if he is, whether he is to be discharged absolutely or subject to conditions;

(c) if he is to be discharged subject to conditions, what the conditions are to be;

(d) if he has been discharged subject to conditions—

(i) of any variation of the conditions by the Secretary of State;

(ii) of any recall to hospital under section 42(3) of the Mental Health Act 1983 (c 20);

(e) if the restriction order is to cease to have effect by virtue of action to be taken by the Secretary of State, of the date on which the restriction order is to cease to have effect.

(5) Subsections (6) and (7) apply (instead of subsection (4)) if—

(a) an application is made to a Mental Health Review Tribunal by the patient under section 69, 70 or 75 of the Mental Health Act 1983 (c 20) (applications concerning restricted patients), or

(b) the Secretary of State refers the patient's case to a Mental Health Review Tribunal under section 71 of that Act (references concerning restricted patients).

(6) The tribunal must inform the relevant local probation board—

(a) of the matters specified in subsection (4)(a) to (c);

(b) if the patient has been discharged subject to conditions, of any variation of the conditions by the tribunal;

(c) if the restriction order is to cease to have effect by virtue of action to be taken by the tribunal, of the date on which the restriction order is to cease to have effect.

(7) The Secretary of State must inform the relevant local probation board of the matters specified in subsection (4)(d) and (e).

(8) The duties in subsections (3) to (7) apply only while the restriction order is in force.

(9) The relevant local probation board has the meaning given in section 37(8).

[Domestic Violence, Crime and Victims Act 2004, s 38.]

Hospital directions

6–3203K   39. Victims' rights: preliminary.   (1) This section applies if—

(a) a person ("the offender") is convicted of a sexual or violent offence,

(b) a relevant sentence is imposed on him in respect of the offence, and

(c) a hospital direction and a limitation direction are given in relation to him by a court dealing with him for the offence.

(2) The local probation board for the area in which the hospital direction is given must take all reasonable steps to ascertain whether a person who appears to the board to be the victim of the offence or to act for the victim of the offence wishes—

(a) to make representations about the matters specified in subsection (3);

(b) to receive the information specified in subsection (4).

(3) The matters are—

(a) whether the offender should, in the event of his discharge from hospital, be subject to any conditions and, if so, what conditions;

(b) whether the offender should, in the event of his release from hospital, be subject to any licence conditions or supervision requirements and, if so, what licence conditions or supervision requirements;

(c) if the offender is transferred to a prison or other institution in which he might have been detained if he had not been removed to hospital, whether he should, in the event of his release from prison or another such institution, be subject to any licence conditions or supervision requirements and, if so, what licence conditions or supervision requirements.

(4) The information is—

(a) information about any conditions to which the offender is to be subject in the event of his discharge;

(b) information about any licence conditions or supervision requirements to which the offender is to be subject in the event of his release.

[Domestic Violence, Crime and Victims Act 2004, s 39.]

6–3203L   40. Representations.   (1) This section applies if section 39 applies.

(2) If—

(a) a person makes representations about a matter specified in section 39(3) to the local probation board mentioned in section 39(2) or the relevant local probation board, and

(b) it appears to the relevant local probation board that the person is the victim of the offence or acts for the victim of the offence,

the relevant local probation board must forward the representations to the persons responsible for determining the matter.

(3) If the representations are about a matter specified in section 39(3)(a), the duty in subsection (2) applies only while the limitation direction given in relation to the offender is in force.

(4) The Secretary of State must inform the relevant local probation board if he is considering—

(a) whether to give a direction in respect of the offender under section 42(1) of the Mental Health Act 1983 (c 20) (directions lifting restrictions),

(b) whether to discharge the offender under section 42(2) of that Act, either absolutely or subject to conditions, or

(c) if the offender has been discharged subject to conditions, whether to vary the conditions.

(5) A Mental Health Review Tribunal must inform the relevant local probation board if—

(a) an application is made to the tribunal by the offender under section 69, 70 or 75 of the Mental Health Act 1983 (applications concerning restricted patients), or

(b) the Secretary of State refers the offender's case to the tribunal under section 71 of that Act (references concerning restricted patients).

(6) Subsection (7) applies if—

(a) the relevant local probation board receives information under subsection (4) or (5), and

(b) a person who appears to the relevant local probation board to be the victim of the offence or to act for the victim of the offence—

   (i) when his wishes were ascertained under section 39(2), expressed a wish to make representations about a matter specified in section 39(3)(a), or

   (ii) has made representations about such a matter to the relevant local probation board or the local probation board mentioned in section 39(2).

(7) The relevant local probation board must provide the information to the person.

(8) The relevant local probation board is—

(a) if the offender is to be discharged from hospital subject to a condition that he reside in a particular area, the local probation board for the area;

(b) if the offender is to be supervised on release by an officer of a local probation board, that local probation board;

(c) in any other case, the local probation board for the area in which the hospital, prison or other place in which the offender is detained is situated.

[Domestic Violence, Crime and Victims Act 2004, s 40.]

6–3203M   41. Information.   (1) This section applies if section 39 applies.

(2) Subsection (3) applies if a person who appears to the relevant local probation board to be the victim of the offence or to act for the victim of the offence—

(a) when his wishes were ascertained under section 39(2), expressed a wish to receive the information specified in section 39(4), or

(b) has subsequently informed the relevant local probation board that he wishes to receive that information.

(3) The relevant local probation board must take all reasonable steps—

(a) to inform that person whether or not the offender is to be subject to any conditions in the event of his discharge;

(b) if he is, to provide that person with details of any conditions which relate to contact with the victim or his family;

(c) if the limitation direction in respect of the offender is to cease to have effect, to notify that person of the date on which it is to cease to have effect;

(d) to inform that person whether or not the offender is to be subject to any licence conditions or supervision requirements in the event of his release;

(e) if he is, to provide that person with details of any licence conditions or supervision requirements which relate to contact with the victim or his family;

(f) to provide that person with such other information as the board considers appropriate in all the circumstances of the case.

(4) The Secretary of State must inform the relevant local probation board—

(a) whether the offender is to be discharged;

(b) if he is, whether he is to be discharged absolutely or subject to conditions;

(c) if he is to be discharged subject to conditions, what the conditions are to be;

(d) if he has been discharged subject to conditions—

(i) of any variation of the conditions by the Secretary of State;

(ii) of any recall to hospital under section 42(3) of the Mental Health Act 1983 (c 20);

(e) if the limitation direction is to cease to have effect by virtue of action to be taken by the Secretary of State, of the date on which the limitation direction is to cease to have effect.

(5) Subsections (6) and (7) apply (instead of subsection (4)) if—

(a) an application is made to a Mental Health Review Tribunal by the offender under section 69, 70 or 75 of the Mental Health Act 1983 (c 20) (applications concerning restricted patients), or

(b) the Secretary of State refers the offender's case to a Mental Health Review Tribunal under section 71 of that Act (references concerning restricted patients).

(6) The tribunal must inform the relevant local probation board—

(a) of the matters specified in subsection (4)(a) to (c);

(b) if the offender has been discharged subject to conditions, of any variation of the conditions by the tribunal;

(c) if the limitation direction is to cease to have effect by virtue of action to be taken by the tribunal, of the date on which the limitation direction is to cease to have effect.

(7) The Secretary of State must inform the relevant local probation board of the matters specified in subsection (4)(d) and (e).

(8) The duties in subsections (3)(a) to (c) and (4) to (7) apply only while the limitation direction is in force.

(9) The relevant local probation board has the meaning given in section 40(8).
[Domestic Violence, Crime and Victims Act 2004, s 41.]

Transfer directions

6–3203N 42. Victims' rights: preliminary. (1) This section applies if—

(a) a person ("the offender") is convicted of a sexual or violent offence,

(b) a relevant sentence is imposed on him in respect of the offence, and

(c) while the offender is serving the sentence, the Secretary of State gives a transfer direction and a restriction direction in respect of him.

(2) The local probation board for the area in which the hospital specified in the transfer direction is situated must take all reasonable steps to ascertain whether a person who appears to the board to be the victim of the offence or to act for the victim of the offence wishes—

(a) to make representations about the matters specified in subsection (3);

(b) to receive the information specified in subsection (4).

(3) The matters are—

(a) whether the offender should be subject to any conditions in the event of his discharge from hospital;

(b) if so, what conditions.

(4) The information is information about any conditions to which the offender is to be subject in the event of his discharge from hospital.
[Domestic Violence, Crime and Victims Act 2004, s 42.]

6–3203O 43. Representations. (1) This section applies if section 42 applies.

(2) If—

(a) a person makes representations about a matter specified in section 42(3) to the local probation board mentioned in section 42(2) or the relevant local probation board, and

(b) it appears to the relevant local probation board that the person is the victim of the offence or acts for the victim of the offence, the relevant local probation board must forward the representations to the persons responsible for determining the matter.

(3) The duty in subsection (2) applies only while the restriction direction given in respect of the offender is in force.

(4) The Secretary of State must inform the relevant local probation board if he is considering—

(a) whether to give a direction in respect of the offender under section 42(1) of the Mental Health Act 1983 (c 20) (directions lifting restrictions),

(b) whether to discharge the offender under section 42(2) of that Act, either absolutely or subject to conditions, or

(c) if the offender has been discharged subject to conditions, whether to vary the conditions.

(5) A Mental Health Review Tribunal must inform the relevant local probation board if—

(a) an application is made to the tribunal by the offender under section 69, 70 or 75 of the Mental Health Act 1983 (applications concerning restricted patients), or

(b) the Secretary of State refers the offender's case to the tribunal under section 71 of that Act (references concerning restricted patients).

(6) Subsection (7) applies if—

(a) the relevant local probation board receives information under subsection (4) or (5), and

(b) a person who appears to the relevant local probation board to be the victim of the offence or to act for the victim of the offence—

(i) when his wishes were ascertained under section 42(2), expressed a wish to make representations about a matter specified in section 42(3), or

(ii) has made representations about such a matter to the relevant local probation board or the local probation board mentioned in section 42(2).

(7) The relevant local probation board must provide the information to the person.

(8) The relevant local probation board is—

(a) if the offender is to be discharged subject to a condition that he reside in a particular area, the local probation board for the area;

(b) in any other case, the local probation board for the area in which the hospital in which the offender is detained is situated.

[Domestic Violence, Crime and Victims Act 2004, s 43.]

6–3203P   44. Information.   (1) This section applies if section 42 applies.

(2) Subsection (3) applies if a person who appears to the relevant local probation board to be the victim of the offence or to act for the victim of the offence—

(a) when his wishes were ascertained under section 42(2), expressed a wish to receive the information specified in section 42(4), or

(b) has subsequently informed the relevant local probation board that he wishes to receive that information.

(3) The relevant local probation board must take all reasonable steps—

(a) to inform that person whether or not the offender is to be subject to any conditions in the event of his discharge;

(b) if he is, to provide that person with details of any conditions which relate to contact with the victim or his family;

(c) if the restriction direction in respect of the offender is to cease to have effect, to notify that person of the date on which it is to cease to have effect;

(d) to provide that person with such other information as the board considers appropriate in all the circumstances of the case.

(4) The Secretary of State must inform the relevant local probation board—

(a) whether the offender is to be discharged;

(b) if he is, whether he is to be discharged absolutely or subject to conditions;

(c) if he is to be discharged subject to conditions, what the conditions are to be;

(d) if he has been discharged subject to conditions—

(i) of any variation of the conditions by the Secretary of State;

(ii) of any recall to hospital under section 42(3) of the Mental Health Act 1983 (c 20);

(e) if the restriction direction is to cease to have effect by virtue of action to be taken by the Secretary of State, of the date on which the restriction direction is to cease to have effect.

(5) Subsections (6) and (7) apply (instead of subsection (4)) if—

(a) an application is made to a Mental Health Review Tribunal by the offender under section 69, 70 or 75 of the Mental Health Act 1983 (applications concerning restricted patients), or

(b) the Secretary of State refers the offender's case to a Mental Health Review Tribunal under section 71 of that Act (references concerning restricted patients).

(6) The tribunal must inform the relevant local probation board—

(a) of the matters specified in subsection (4)(a) to (c);

(b) if the offender has been discharged subject to conditions, of any variation of the conditions by the tribunal;

(c) if the restriction direction is to cease to have effect by virtue of action to be taken by the tribunal, of the date on which the restriction direction is to cease to have effect.

(7) The Secretary of State must inform the relevant local probation board of the matters specified in subsection (4)(d) and (e).

(8) The duties in subsections (3) to (7) apply only while the restriction direction is in force.

(9) The relevant local probation board has the meaning given in section 43(8).

[Domestic Violence, Crime and Victims Act 2004, s 44.]

Interpretation

6–3203Q   45. Interpretation: sections 35 to 44.   (1) In sections 35 to 44—

"court" does not include a court-martial or the Courts-Martial Appeal Court;

"hospital direction" has the meaning given in section 45A(3)(a) of the Mental Health Act 1983 (c 20);

"hospital order" has the meaning given in section 37(4) of that Act;

"licence condition" means a condition in a licence;

"limitation direction" has the meaning given in section 45A(3)(b) of the Mental Health Act 1983;

"local probation board" means a local probation board established under section 4 of the Criminal Justice and Court Services Act 2000 (c 43);

"relevant sentence" means any of these—

(a) a sentence of imprisonment for a term of 12 months or more;

(b) a sentence of detention during Her Majesty's pleasure;

(c) a sentence of detention for a period of 12 months or more under section 91 of the Powers of Criminal Courts (Sentencing) Act 2000 (c 6) (offenders under 18 convicted of certain serious offences);

(d) a detention and training order for a term of 12 months or more;

"restriction direction" has the meaning given in section 49(2) of the Mental Health Act 1983;

"restriction order" has the meaning given in section 41(1) of that Act;

"supervision requirements" means requirements specified in a notice under section 103(6) of the Powers of Criminal Courts (Sentencing) Act 2000;

"transfer direction" has the meaning given in section 47(1) of the Mental Health Act 1983.

(2) For the purposes of sections 35 to 44, an offence is a sexual or violent offence if it is any of these—

(a) murder or an offence specified in Schedule 15 to the Criminal Justice Act 2003 (c 44);

(b) an offence in respect of which the patient or offender is subject to the notification requirements of Part 2 of the Sexual Offences Act 2003 (c 42));

(c) an offence against a child within the meaning of Part 2 of the Criminal Justice and Court Services Act 2000.

[Domestic Violence, Crime and Victims Act 2004, s 45.]

Northern Ireland

6–3203R   46. Victims of mentally disordered persons.   (1) The Justice (Northern Ireland) Act 2002 (c 26) is amended as follows.

(2) After section 69 (views on temporary release) insert—

"69A Information about discharge and leave of absence of mentally disordered persons.

(1) The Secretary of State must make a scheme requiring the Secretary of State to make available to persons falling within subsection (2) information about—

(a) the discharge from hospital of, or

(b) the grant of leave of absence from hospital to,

persons in respect of whom relevant determinations have been made.

(2) The persons referred to in subsection (1) are victims of the offences in respect of which the determinations were made who wish to receive the information.

(3) A relevant determination is made in respect of a person if—

(a) a hospital order with a restriction order is made in respect of him by a court dealing with him for an offence, or

(b) a transfer direction and a restriction direction are given in respect of him while he is serving a sentence of imprisonment in respect of an offence.

(4) The Secretary of State may from time to time make a new scheme or alterations to a scheme.

(5) The information to be made available under a scheme must include information as to any relevant conditions to which a person in respect of whom a relevant determination has been made is to be subject in the event of—

(a) his discharge from hospital, or
(b) the grant of leave of absence from hospital to him.

(6) A condition is relevant for the purposes of subsection (5) if it appears to the Secretary of State that it might affect a victim of an offence in respect of which the determination was made.

(7) A scheme may require the Secretary of State to take all reasonable steps to ascertain whether a person who appears to him to be the victim of an offence in respect of which a relevant determination has been made wishes to make representations about the matters specified in subsection (8).

(8) The matters are—

(a) whether the person in respect of whom the determination has been made should be subject to any conditions in the event of his discharge from hospital or the grant of leave of absence from hospital to him;
(b) if so, what conditions.

(9) A scheme that includes provision such as is mentioned in subsection (7) must specify how the representations are to be made.

(10) A scheme may require other information in relation to the discharge of, or the grant of leave of absence to, persons in respect of whom relevant determinations are made to be made available under the scheme.

(11) The other information may include, in cases of a description specified by the scheme or in which the Secretary of State considers it appropriate, the date on which it is anticipated that a person in respect of whom a relevant determination has been made will be discharged or granted leave of absence from hospital.

(12) Subsections (5) to (8) of section 68 apply in relation to a scheme made under this section as they apply in relation to a scheme made under that section.

(13) A scheme may make different provision in relation to different descriptions of persons in respect of whom a relevant determination is made.

69B Views on leave of absence. (1) If a person who is the victim of an offence in respect of which a relevant determination has been made makes to the Secretary of State representations falling within subsection (2) the Secretary of State has the obligations specified in subsection (3).

(2) Representations fall within this subsection if they are to the effect that the grant of leave of absence to the person in respect of whom the determination has been made would threaten the safety, or otherwise adversely affect the well-being, of—

(a) the actual victim of the offence in respect of which the determination was made, or
(b) a person who is regarded for the purposes of a scheme under section 69A as a victim of that offence by virtue of section 68(5) (as applied by section 69A(12)).

(3) The Secretary of State must—

(a) have regard to the representations in deciding whether he should give his consent to leave of absence being granted, and
(b) inform the victim of any such decision.

(4) Section 69A(3) (relevant determination) applies for the purposes of this section."
(3) In section 70 (supplementary), after subsection (3) insert—

"(4) In sections 68 and 69 references to a person serving a sentence of imprisonment in Northern Ireland include a person detained in hospital pursuant to a transfer direction and a restriction direction.

(5) In subsection (4) and section 69A(3)—

"restriction direction" has the meaning given in Article 55(2) of the Mental Health (Northern Ireland) Order 1986;
"transfer direction" has the meaning given in Article 53(2) of that Order.

(6) In section 69A(3)—

"hospital order" has the meaning given in Article 44(1) of the Mental Health (Northern Ireland) Order 1986;
"restriction order" has the meaning given in Article 47(1) of that Order;
"sentence of imprisonment" has the meaning given in Article 53(5) of that Order.

(7) In sections 69A and 69B "leave of absence" means leave of absence under Article 15 of the Mental Health (Northern Ireland) Order 1986."
(4) In section 90(5) (statutory rules), in paragraph (b) after "section 68" insert "or 69A".

[Domestic Violence, Crime and Victims Act 2004, s 46.]

CHAPTER 3[1]

Other Matters Relating to Victims etc

Parliamentary Commissioner

6–3203S   **47. Investigations by Parliamentary Commissioner.**   Schedule 7 (which amends the Parliamentary Commissioner Act 1967 (c 13)) has effect.

[Domestic Violence, Crime and Victims Act 2004, s 47.]

-----

1. Chapter 3 contains ss 47–57.

Commissioner for Victims and Witnesses

6–3203T   **48. Commissioner for Victims and Witnesses.**   (1) The Secretary of State must appoint a Commissioner for Victims and Witnesses (referred to in this Part as the Commissioner).

(2) Before appointing the Commissioner the Secretary of State must consult the Attorney General and the Lord Chancellor as to the person to be appointed.

(3) The Commissioner is a corporation sole.

(4) The Commissioner is not to be regarded—

(a) as the servant or agent of the Crown, or

(b) as enjoying any status, immunity or privilege of the Crown.

(5) The Commissioner's property is not to be regarded as property of, or held on behalf of, the Crown.

(6) Schedule 8 (which make further provision in connection with the Commissioner) has effect.

[Domestic Violence, Crime and Victims Act 2004, s 48.]

6–3203U   **49. General functions of Commissioner.**   (1) The Commissioner must—

(a) promote the interests of victims and witnesses;

(b) take such steps as he considers appropriate with a view to encouraging good practice in the treatment of victims and witnesses;

(c) keep under review the operation of the code of practice issued under section 32.

(2) The Commissioner may, for any purpose connected with the performance of his duties under subsection (1)—

(a) make proposals to the Secretary of State for amending the code (at the request of the Secretary of State or on his own initiative);

(b) make a report to the Secretary of State;

(c) make recommendations to an authority within his remit;

(d) undertake or arrange for or support (financially or otherwise) the carrying out of research;

(e) consult any person he thinks appropriate.

(3) If the Commissioner makes a report to the Secretary of State under subsection (2)(b)—

(a) the Commissioner must send a copy of the report to the Attorney General and the Lord Chancellor;

(b) the Secretary of State must lay a copy of the report before Parliament and arrange for the report to be published.

[Domestic Violence, Crime and Victims Act 2004, s 49.]

6–3203V   **50. Advice.**   (1) If he is required to do so by a Minister of the Crown, the Commissioner must give advice to the Minister of the Crown in connection with any matter which—

(a) is specified by the Minister, and

(b) relates to victims or witnesses.

(2) If he is required to do so by or on behalf of an authority within his remit, the Commissioner must give advice to the authority in connection with the information provided or to be provided by or on behalf of the authority to victims or witnesses.

(3) In this section "Minister of the Crown" includes the Treasury.

[Domestic Violence, Crime and Victims Act 2004, s 50.]

6–3203W   **51. Restrictions on exercise of functions.**   The Commissioner must not exercise any of his functions in relation to—

(a) a particular victim or witness;

(b) the bringing or conduct of particular proceedings;

(c) anything done or omitted to be done by a person acting in a judicial capacity or on the instructions of or on behalf of such a person.

[Domestic Violence, Crime and Victims Act 2004, s 51.]

6–3203X   **52. "Victims" and "witnesses".**   (1) This section applies for the purposes of sections 48 to 51.

(2) "Victim" means—

(a) a victim of an offence, or

(b) a victim of anti-social behaviour.

(3) It is immaterial for the purposes of subsection (2)(a) that—

(a) no complaint has been made about the offence;

(b) no person has been charged with or convicted of the offence.

(4) "Witness" means a person (other than a defendant)—

(a) who has witnessed conduct in relation to which he may be or has been called to give evidence in relevant proceedings;

(b) who is able to provide or has provided anything which might be used or has been used as evidence in relevant proceedings; or

(c) who is able to provide or has provided anything mentioned in subsection (5) (whether or not admissible in evidence in relevant proceedings).

(5) The things referred to in subsection (4)(c) are—

(a) anything which might tend to confirm, has tended to confirm or might have tended to confirm evidence which may be, has been or could have been admitted in relevant proceedings;

(b) anything which might be, has been or might have been referred to in evidence given in relevant proceedings by another person;

(c) anything which might be, has been or might have been used as the basis for any cross examination in the course of relevant proceedings.

(6) For the purposes of subsection (4)—

(a) a person is a defendant in relation to any criminal proceedings if he might be, has been or might have been charged with or convicted of an offence in the proceedings;

(b) a person is a defendant in relation to any other relevant proceedings if he might be, has been or might have been the subject of an order made in those proceedings.

(7) In subsections (4) to (6) "relevant proceedings" means—

(a) criminal proceedings;

(b) proceedings of any other kind in respect of anti-social behaviour.

(8) For the purposes of this section—

(a) "anti-social behaviour" means behaviour by a person which causes or is likely to cause harassment, alarm or distress to one or more persons not of the same household as the person;

(b) a person is a victim of anti-social behaviour if the behaviour has caused him harassment, alarm or distress and he is not of the same household as the person who engages in the behaviour.

[Domestic Violence, Crime and Victims Act 2004, s 52.]

6–3203Y   53. Authorities within Commissioner's remit.   (1) For the purposes of this Part the authorities within the Commissioner's remit are those specified in Schedule 9.

(2) An authority specified in Schedule 9 that has functions in relation to an area outside England and Wales is within the Commissioner's remit only to the extent that it discharges its functions in relation to England and Wales.

(3) Subsection (2) does not apply in relation to the Foreign and Commonwealth Office.

(4) The Secretary of State may by order amend Schedule 9 by—

(a) adding an authority appearing to him to exercise functions of a public nature;

(b) omitting an authority;

(c) changing the description of an authority.

(5) In preparing a draft of an order under subsection (4) the Secretary of State must consult the Attorney General and the Lord Chancellor.

[Domestic Violence, Crime and Victims Act 2004, s 53.]

Disclosure of information

6–3203Z   54. Disclosure of information.   (1) A person may disclose information to a relevant authority for a purpose specified in subsection (2).

(2) The purposes are purposes connected with any of these—

(a) compliance with the code issued under section 32;

(b) compliance with sections 35 to 44;

(c) the carrying out of the functions of the Commissioner.

(3) These are relevant authorities—

(a) a person required to do anything under the code issued under section 32;

(b) a local probation board established under section 4 of the Criminal Justice and Court Services Act 2000 (c 43);

(c) the Commissioner;

(d) an authority within the Commissioner's remit.

(4) The Secretary of State may by order—

(a) amend subsection (2) by adding any purpose appearing to him to be connected with the assistance of victims of offences or anti-social behaviour, witnesses of offences or anti-social behaviour or other persons affected by offences or anti-social behaviour;

(b) amend subsection (3) by adding any authority appearing to him to exercise functions of a public nature.

(5) The reference in subsection (4)(a) to persons affected by offences does not include persons accused or convicted of offences.

(6) The Secretary of State may exercise the power in subsection (4) only after consulting the Attorney General and the Lord Chancellor.

(7) Nothing in this section authorises the making of a disclosure which contravenes the Data Protection Act 1998 (c 29).

(8) This section does not affect a power to disclose which exists apart from this section.

[Domestic Violence, Crime and Victims Act 2004, s 54.]

Victims' Advisory Panel

6–3204 55. Victims' Advisory Panel. (1) The Secretary of State must appoint persons to form a panel, to be known as the Victims' Advisory Panel.

(2) The Secretary of State must consult the Attorney General and the Lord Chancellor before—

(a) appointing a person to the Panel, or

(b) removing a person from the Panel.

(3) The Secretary of State must consult the Panel at such times and in such manner as he thinks appropriate on matters appearing to him to relate to victims of offences or anti-social behaviour or witnesses of offences or anti-social behaviour.

(4) The Secretary of State may reimburse the members of the Panel for such of their travelling and other expenses as he thinks appropriate.

(5) If the Secretary of State consults the Panel under subsection (3) in a particular year, he must arrange for the Panel to prepare a report for the year—

(a) summarising what the Panel has done in response to the consultation, and

(b) dealing with such other matters as the Panel consider appropriate.

(6) If a report is prepared under subsection (5), the Secretary of State must—

(a) arrange for it to be published, and

(b) lay it before Parliament.

(7) The non-statutory Victims' Advisory Panel is to be treated as having been established in accordance with this section.

(8) If the Secretary of State consults the non-statutory Victims' Advisory Panel on a matter mentioned in subsection (3) before the date on which this section comes into force, the consultation is to be treated as taking place under subsection (3).

(9) The non-statutory Victims' Advisory Panel is the unincorporated body of persons known as the Victims' Advisory Panel established by the Secretary of State before the date on which this section comes into force.

(10) In this section "year" means a period of 12 months beginning on 1 April.

[Domestic Violence, Crime and Victims Act 2004, s 55.]

Grants

6–3204A 56. Grants for assisting victims, witnesses etc

Criminal injuries compensation

6–3204B 57. Recovery of criminal injuries compensation from offenders. (1) The Criminal Injuries Compensation Act 1995 (c 53) is amended as follows.

(2) After section 7 insert—

"7A Recovery of compensation from offenders: general. (1) The Secretary of State may, by regulations made by statutory instrument, make provision for the recovery from an appropriate person of an amount equal to all or part of the compensation paid in respect of a criminal injury.

(2) An appropriate person is a person who has been convicted of an offence in respect of the criminal injury.

(3) The amount recoverable from a person under the regulations must be determined by reference only to the extent to which the criminal injury is directly attributable to an offence of which he has been convicted.

(4) The regulations may confer functions in respect of recovery on—

(a) claims officers;

(b) if a Scheme manager has been appointed, persons appointed by the Scheme manager under section 3(4)(a).

(5) The regulations may not authorise the recovery of an amount in respect of compensation from a person to the extent that the compensation has been repaid in accordance with the Scheme.

7B Recovery notices. (1) If, under regulations made under section 7A(1), an amount has been determined as recoverable from a person, he must be given a notice (a "recovery notice") in accordance with the regulations which—

(a) requires him to pay that amount, and

(b) contains the information mentioned in subsection (2).

(2) The information is—

(a) the reasons for the determination that an amount is recoverable from the person;

(b) the basis on which the amount has been determined;

(c) the way in which and the date before which the amount is required to be paid;

(d) the means by which the amount may be recovered if it is not paid in accordance with the notice;

(e) the grounds on which and the procedure by means of which he may seek a review if he objects to—

(i) the determination that an amount is recoverable from him;

(ii) the amount determined as recoverable from him.

(3) The Secretary of State may by order made by statutory instrument amend subsection (2) by—

(a) adding information;

(b) omitting information;

(c) changing the description of information.

7C Review of recovery determinations. (1) Regulations under section 7A(1) shall include provision for the review, in such circumstances as may be prescribed by the regulations, of—

(a) a determination that an amount is recoverable from a person;

(b) the amount determined as recoverable from a person.

(2) A person from whom an amount has been determined as recoverable under the regulations may seek such a review only on the grounds—

(a) that he has not been convicted of an offence to which the injury is directly attributable;

(b) that the compensation paid was not determined in accordance with the Scheme;

(c) that the amount determined as recoverable from him was not determined in accordance with the regulations.

(3) Any such review must be conducted by a person other than the person who made the determination under review.

(4) The person conducting any such review may—

(a) set aside the determination that the amount is recoverable;

(b) reduce the amount determined as recoverable;

(c) increase the amount determined as recoverable;

(d) determine to take no action under paragraphs (a) to (c).

(5) But the person conducting any such review may increase the amount determined as recoverable if (but only if) it appears to that person that the interests of justice require the amount to be increased.

7D Recovery proceedings. (1) An amount determined as recoverable from a person under regulations under section 7A(1) is recoverable from him as a debt due to the Crown if (but only if)—

(a) he has been given a recovery notice in accordance with the regulations which complies with the requirements of section 7B, and

(b) he has failed to pay the amount in accordance with the notice.

(2) In any proceedings for the recovery of the amount from a person, it is a defence for the person to show—

(a) that he has not been convicted of an offence to which the injury is directly attributable;

(b) that the compensation paid was not determined in accordance with the Scheme; or

(c) that the amount determined as recoverable from him was not determined in accordance with regulations under section 7A.

(3) In any such proceedings, except for the purposes of subsection (2)(b), no question may be raised or finding made as to the amount that was, or ought to have been, the subject of an award.

(4) For the purposes of section 9 of the Limitation Act 1980 (time limit for actions for sums recoverable by statute to run from date on which cause of action accrued) the cause of action to recover that amount shall be taken to have accrued—

(a) on the date on which the compensation was paid; or

(b) if later, on the date on which a person from whom an amount is sought to be recovered was convicted of an offence to which the injury is directly attributable.

(5) If that person is convicted of more than one such offence and the convictions are made on different dates, the reference in subsection (4)(b) to the date on which he was convicted of such an offence shall be taken to be a reference to the earlier or earliest (as the case may be) of the dates on which he was convicted of such an offence.".

(3) In section 9(7) (financial provisions: sums payable into Consolidated Fund), after "section 3(1)(c)" insert ", or by virtue of regulations made under section 7A(1),".

(4) In section 11, after subsection (8) insert—

"(8A) No regulations under section 7A(1) or order under section 7B(3) shall be made unless a draft of the regulations or order has been laid before Parliament and approved by a resolution of each House."

[Domestic Violence, Crime and Victims Act 2004, s 57.]

PART 4[1]
SUPPLEMENTARY

6-3204C 58. Amendments and repeals. (1) Schedule 10 (minor and consequential amendments) has effect.

(2) The provisions mentioned in Schedule 11 are repealed or revoked to the extent specified.

[Domestic Violence, Crime and Victims Act 2004, s 58.]

[1.] Part 4 contains ss 58–62.

6-3204D 59. Transitional and transitory provisions. Schedule 12 (transitional and transitory provisions) has effect.

[Domestic Violence, Crime and Victims Act 2004, s 59.]

6-3204E 60. Commencement. The preceding provisions of this Act come into force in accordance with provision made by the Secretary of State by order[1].

[Domestic Violence, Crime and Victims Act 2004, s 60.]

[1.] At the time of going to press the Domestic Violence, Crime and Victims Act 2004 (Commencement No 1) Order 2005, SI 2005/579, had been made. However, mot of the Act remains unimplemented.

6-3204F 61. Orders. (1) An order under this Act—

(a) may make different provision for different purposes;

(b) may include supplementary, incidental, saving or transitional provisions.

(2) Any power to make an order under this Act is exercisable by statutory instrument.

(3) A statutory instrument containing an order under section 9(6) or 33(7) is subject to annulment in pursuance of a resolution of either House of Parliament.

(4) No order may be made under section 14(5), 53(4) or 54(4) unless a draft of the order has been laid before Parliament and approved by a resolution of each House.

[Domestic Violence, Crime and Victims Act 2004, s 61.]

6-3204G 62. Extent. (1) Subject to the following provisions of this section, Parts 1 to 3 extend to England and Wales only.

(2) The following provisions extend also to Northern Ireland—

section 5;
section 9;
sections 17 to 21;
Schedule 1;
section 56;

(3) The following provisions extend to Northern Ireland only—

section 7;
section 10(2);
section 13;
section 23;
section 46.

(4) Section 8, so far as relating to proceedings before courts-martial constituted under a particular Act mentioned in subsection (2) of that section, has the same extent as that Act.

(5) An amendment, repeal or revocation in Schedule 3, 7, 8, 10 or 11 has the same extent as the provision to which it relates.

[Domestic Violence, Crime and Victims Act 2004, s 62.]

6–3204H   63. Short title.   This Act may be cited as the Domestic Violence, Crime and Victims Act 2004.

[Domestic Violence, Crime and Victims Act 2004, s 63.]

6–3204I SCHEDULE 1
MODIFICATION OF SECTIONS 17 TO 20 FOR NORTHERN IRELAND

6–3204J SCHEDULE 2
SUPERVISION ORDERS ON FINDING OF INSANITY OR UNFITNESS TO PLEAD ETC

6–3204K SCHEDULE 3
UNFITNESS TO STAND TRIAL AND INSANITY: COURTS-MARTIAL ETC

Section 27 SCHEDULE 4
POWERS OF AUTHORISED OFFICERS EXECUTING WARRANTS

6–3204L   *Inserts new Schedule 4A to the Magistrates' Courts Act 1980.*

Section 29 SCHEDULE 5
PROCEDURE ON BREACH OF COMMUNITY PENALTY ETC

(As amended by SI 2005/886.)

6–3204M

Interpretation

1. In this Schedule—

"the Sentencing Act" means the Powers of Criminal Courts (Sentencing) Act 2000 (c 6);
"the 2003 Act" means the Criminal Justice Act 2003 (c 44).

Detention and training orders

2. (1) Section 104 of the Sentencing Act (breach of supervision requirements of detention and training order) is amended as follows.

(2) In subsection (1) (issue of summons or warrant by justice of the peace)—

(a) omit the words "acting in a relevant local justice area";

(b) in paragraph (a), omit the words "before a youth court acting in the area";

(c) in paragraph (b), omit the words "requiring him to be brought before such a court".

(3) For subsection (2) substitute—

"(2) Any summons or warrant issued under this section shall direct the offender to appear or be brought—

(a) before a youth court in the local justice area in which the offender resides; or

(b) if it is not known where the offender resides, before a youth court acting in the same local justice area as the justice who issued the summons or warrant."

Suspended sentence supervision orders

3. (1) Section 123 of the Sentencing Act (breach of requirement of suspended sentence supervision order) is amended as follows.

(2) In subsection (1) (issue of summons or warrant by justice of the peace) omit the words "acting for the local justice area for the time being specified in the order".

(3) For subsection (2) substitute—

"(2) Any summons or warrant issued under this section shall direct the offender to appear or be brought—

(a) before a magistrates' court for the local justice area in which the offender resides; or

(b) if it is not known where the offender resides, before a magistrates' court acting in the local justice area for the time being specified in the suspended sentence supervision order."

(4) After subsection (4) insert—

"(5) Where a magistrates' court dealing with an offender under this section would not otherwise have the power to amend the suspended sentence supervision order under section 124(3) below (amendment by reason of change of residence), that provision has effect as if the reference to a magistrates' court acting in the local justice area for the time being specified in the suspended sentence supervision order were a reference to the court dealing with the offender."

Community orders under the Sentencing Act

4. (1) Schedule 3 to the Sentencing Act (breach, revocation and amendment of certain community orders), as it has effect on the day on which this Act is passed, is amended as follows.

(2) In paragraph 3(1) (issue of summons or warrant by justice of the peace) omit the words "acting in the local justice area concerned".

(3) In paragraph 3(2) (court before which offender to appear or be brought), for paragraph (c) substitute—

"(c) in the case of a relevant order which is not an order to which paragraph (a) or (b) applies, before a magistrates' court acting in the local justice area in which the offender resides or, if it is not known where he resides, before a magistrates' court acting in the local justice area concerned."

(4) In paragraph 4 (powers of magistrates' court to deal with breach), after sub-paragraph (3) insert—

"(3A) Where a magistrates' court dealing with an offender under sub-paragraph (1)(a), (b) or (c) above would not otherwise have the power to amend the relevant order under paragraph 18 below (amendment by reason of change of residence), that paragraph has effect as if the reference to a magistrates' court acting in the local justice area concerned were a reference to the court dealing with the offender."

Curfew orders and exclusion orders

5. (1) Schedule 3 to the Sentencing Act (breach, revocation and amendment of curfew orders and exclusion orders), as substituted by paragraph 125 of Schedule 32 to the 2003 Act, is amended as follows.

(2) In paragraph 3(1) (issue of summons or warrant by justice of the peace) omit the words "acting in the local justice area concerned".

(3) In paragraph 3(2) (court before which offender to appear or be brought), for paragraph (b) substitute—

"(b) in the case of a relevant order which is not an order to which paragraph (a) above applies, before a magistrates' court acting in the local justice in which the offender resides or, if it is not known where he resides, before a magistrates' court acting in the local justice area concerned."

(4) In paragraph 4 (powers of magistrates' court to deal with breach), after sub-paragraph (4) insert—

"(4A) Where a magistrates' court dealing with an offender under sub-paragraph (2)(a) or (b) above would not otherwise have the power to amend the relevant order under paragraph 15 below (amendment by reason of change of residence), that paragraph has effect as if the reference to a magistrates' court acting in the local justice area concerned were a reference to the court dealing with the offender."

Attendance centre orders

6. (1) Schedule 5 to the Sentencing Act (breach, revocation and amendment of attendance centre orders) is amended as follows.

(2) In paragraph 1(1) (issue of summons or warrant by justice of the peace), omit the words—

(a) "acting for a relevant local justice area";
(b) "before a magistrates' court acting in the area";
(c) "requiring him to be brought before such a court".

(3) For paragraph 1(2) substitute—

"(2) Any summons or warrant issued under this paragraph shall direct the offender to appear or be brought—

(a) before a magistrates' court acting in the local justice area in which the offender resides; or
(b) if it is not known where the offender resides, before a magistrates' court acting in the local justice area in which is situated the attendance centre which the offender is required to attend by the order or by virtue of an order under paragraph 5(1)(b) below."

(4) In paragraph 2 (powers of magistrates' court to deal with breach), after sub-paragraph (5) insert—

"(5A) Where a magistrates' court dealing with an offender under sub-paragraph (1)(a) above would not otherwise have the power to amend the order under paragraph 5(1)(b) below (substitution of different attendance centre), that paragraph has effect as if references to an appropriate magistrates' court were references to the court dealing with the offender."

Community orders under the 2003 Act

7. (1) Schedule 8 to the 2003 Act (breach, revocation or amendment of community order) is amended as follows.

(2) In paragraph 7(2) (issue of summons or warrant by justice of the peace) omit the words "acting in the local justice area concerned".

(3) In paragraph 7(3) (court before which offender to appear or be brought), for paragraph (b) substitute—

"(b) in any other case, before a magistrates' court acting in the local justice area in which the offender resides or, if it is not known where he resides, before a magistrates' court acting in the local justice area concerned."

(4) In paragraph 9 (powers of magistrates' court to deal with breach), after sub-paragraph (5) insert—

"(5A) Where a magistrates' court dealing with an offender under sub-paragraph (1)(a) would not otherwise have the power to amend the community order under paragraph 16 (amendment by reason of change of residence), that paragraph has effect as if the references to the appropriate court were references to the court dealing with the offender."

(5) In paragraph 27 (provision of copies of orders), at the end of sub-paragraph (1)(c) insert

", and
(d) where the court acts in a local justice area other than the one specified in the order prior to the revocation or amendment, provide a copy of the revoking or amending order to a magistrates' court acting in the area so specified."

Suspended sentence orders under the 2003 Act

8. (1) Schedule 12 to the 2003 Act (breach or amendment of suspended sentence order, and effect of further conviction) is amended as follows.

(2) In paragraph 6(2) (issue of summons or warrant by justice of the peace) omit the words "acting in the local justice area concerned".

(3) In paragraph 6(3) (court before which offender to appear or be brought), for paragraph (b) substitute—

"(b) in any other case, before a magistrates' court acting in the local justice area in which the offender resides or, if it is not known where he resides, before a magistrates' court acting in the local justice area concerned."

(4) In paragraph 8 (powers of magistrates' court to deal with breach), after sub-paragraph (4) insert—

"(4A) Where a magistrates' court dealing with an offender under sub-paragraph (2)(c) would not otherwise have the power to amend the suspended sentence order under paragraph 14 (amendment by reason of change of residence), that paragraph has effect as if the references to the appropriate court were references to the court dealing with the offender."

(5) In paragraph 22 (provision of copies of orders), at the end of sub-paragraph (1)(c) insert

", and
(d) where the court acts in a local justice area other than the one specified in the order prior to the revocation or amendment, provide a copy of the revoking or amending order to a magistrates' court acting in the area so specified."

9. In Schedule 13 to the 2003 Act (transfer of suspended sentence orders to Scotland or Northern Ireland), in paragraph 12 (modifications of Schedule 12), after sub-paragraph (5) insert—

"(5A) In paragraph 6(3)(b), the words "before a magistrates' court acting for the petty sessions area in which the offender resides or, if it is not known where he resides," are omitted."

Local justice areas

10. The power conferred by section 109(5)(b) of the Courts Act 2003 (c 39) to amend or repeal any enactment, other than one contained in an Act passed in a later session, includes power to amend any such enactment as amended by this Schedule, but only for the purpose of making consequential provision in connection with the establishment of local justice areas under section 8 of that Act.

Section 31   SCHEDULE 6
                                      INTERMITTENT CUSTODY

6–3204N **1.** The Criminal Justice Act 2003 (c 44) is amended as follows.
        2. In section 244 (duty to release prisoners), in subsection (3)—

(a) in paragraph (c), for the words from "which is not" to "section 183(3)" substitute "which for the purposes of section 183 (as read with section 263(2) or 264A(2) in the case of concurrent or consecutive sentences) is not a licence period";
(b) in paragraph (d), after "consecutive sentences" insert "none of which falls within paragraph (c)".

3. In section 246 (power to release prisoners on licence before required to do so), in the definition of "the required custodial days" in subsection (6)—

(a) in paragraph (b), after "custody" insert "which are consecutive";
(b) at the end of that paragraph insert

", or
(c) in the case of two or more sentences of intermittent custody which are wholly or partly concurrent, the aggregate of the numbers so specified less the number of days that are to be served concurrently;".

4. In section 249 (duration of licence), at the end of subsection (3) insert "and subsection (2) has effect subject to section 264A(3) (consecutive terms: intermittent custody)".
5. In section 250 (licence conditions), in subsection (7), for "and section 264(3) and (4) (consecutive terms)" substitute ", section 264(3) and (4) (consecutive terms) and section 264A(3) (consecutive terms: intermittent custody)".
6. In section 264 (consecutive terms), in subsection (1), after paragraph (b) insert

", and
(c) none of those terms is a term to which an intermittent custody order relates."

7. After that section insert—

"264A Consecutive terms: intermittent custody. (1) This section applies where—

(a) a person ("the offender") has been sentenced to two or more terms of imprisonment which are to be served consecutively on each other,
(b) the sentences were passed on the same occasion or, where they were passed on different occasions, the person has not been released under this Chapter at any time during the period beginning with the first and ending with the last of those occasions, and
(c) each of the terms is a term to which an intermittent custody order relates.

(2) The offender is not to be treated as having served all the required custodial days in relation to any of the terms of imprisonment until he has served the aggregate of all the required custodial days in relation to each of them.

(3) After the number of days served by the offender in prison is equal to the aggregate of the required custodial days in relation to each of the terms of imprisonment, the offender is to be on licence until the relevant time and subject to such conditions as are required by this Chapter in respect of any of the terms of imprisonment, and none of the terms is to be regarded for any purpose as continuing after the relevant time.

(4) In subsection (3) "the relevant time" means the time when the offender would, but for his release, have served a term equal in length to the aggregate of—

(a) all the required custodial days in relation to the terms of imprisonment, and

(b) the longest of the total licence periods in relation to those terms.

(5) In this section—

"total licence period", in relation to a term of imprisonment to which an intermittent custody order relates, means a period equal in length to the aggregate of all the licence periods as defined by section 183 in relation to that term;

"the required custodial days", in relation to such a term, means the number of days specified under that section."

6–3204O
SCHEDULE 7
INVESTIGATIONS BY PARLIAMENTARY COMMISSIONER

6–3204P
SCHEDULE 8
COMMISSIONER FOR VICTIMS AND WITNESSES

6–3204Q
SCHEDULE 9
AUTHORITIES WITHIN COMMISSIONER'S REMIT

6–3204R
SCHEDULE 10[1]
MINOR AND CONSEQUENTIAL AMENDMENTS

---

1. Amendments of provisions that appear in this work will be shown when the amendments come into force.

6–3204S
SCHEDULE 11[1]
REPEALS

---

1. Repeals of provisions reproduced in this work will be shown when they take effect.

Section 59
SCHEDULE 12
TRANSITIONAL AND TRANSITORY PROVISIONS

6–3204T **1.** (1) Section 1 and paragraphs 37 to 39 of Schedule 10 apply only in relation to conduct occurring on or after the commencement of that section.

(2) In relation to an offence committed before the commencement of section 154(1) of the Criminal Justice Act 2003 (c 44), the reference to 12 months in subsection (5)(b) of section 42A of the Family Law Act 1996 (inserted by section 1 of this Act) is to be read as a reference to six months.

2. In section 5, the reference in subsection (1)(a) to an unlawful act does not include an act that (or so much of an act as) occurs before the commencement of that section.

3. (1) This paragraph has effect, in relation to any time before the commencement of the repeal (by paragraph 51 of Schedule 3 to the Criminal Justice Act 2003) of section 6 of the Magistrates' Courts Act 1980 (c 43), where—

(a) a magistrates' court is considering under subsection (1) of that section whether to commit a person ("the accused") for trial for an offence of murder or manslaughter, and

(b) the accused is charged in the same proceedings with an offence under section 5 above in respect of the same death.

(2) If there is sufficient evidence to put the accused on trial by jury for the offence under section 5, there is deemed to be sufficient evidence to put him on trial by jury for the offence of murder or manslaughter.

4. Section 10 applies only in relation to offences committed on or after the commencement of that section.

5. (1) Section 12(1) and paragraphs 43(3) and 48 of Schedule 10 do not apply where the conviction occurs before the commencement of those provisions.

(2) Section 12(2) applies only in relation to applications made on or after the commencement of that provision.

(3) Section 12(4) and paragraphs 43(2) and 44 of Schedule 10 do not apply where the acquittal (or, where subsection (5) of the inserted section 5A applies, the allowing of the appeal) occurs before the commencement of those provisions.

6. (1) Section 13(1) and paragraph 47(3) of Schedule 10 do not apply where the conviction occurs before the commencement of those provisions.

(2) Section 13(2) applies only in relation to applications made on or after the commencement of that provision.

(3) Section 13(4) and paragraph 47(2) of Schedule 10 do not apply where the acquittal (or, where paragraph (5) of the inserted Article 7A applies, the allowing of the appeal) occurs before the commencement of those provisions.

7. Section 14 applies only in relation to offences committed on or after the commencement of that section.

8. (1) The provisions mentioned in sub-paragraph (2) do not apply—

(a) in relation to proceedings before the Crown Court or a court-martial, where the accused was arraigned before the commencement of those provisions;

(b) in relation to proceedings before the Court of Appeal or the Courts-Martial Appeal Court, where the hearing of the appeal began before that commencement.

(2) The provisions are—

(a) sections 22 and 23;

(b) section 24 and Schedule 2;

(c) section 26 and Schedule 3;

(d) paragraphs 5, 6, 8, 17 to 21, 45, 60 and 61 of Schedule 10

9. The Schedule inserted by Schedule 2 has effect in relation to any time before the commencement of sections 8 and 37 of the Courts Act 2003 (c 39)—

    (a) as if a reference to a local justice area were to a petty sessions area;

    (b) as if a reference to a designated officer were to a justices' chief executive.

10. Each entry in Schedule 11 applies in the same way as the provision of this Act to which it corresponds.

Children Act 2004[1]

(2004 c 31)

PART 1[2]
Children's Commissioner

6–3205 1. Establishment. (1) There is to be an office of Children's Commissioner.

    (2) Schedule 1 has effect with respect to the Children's Commissioner.

[Children Act 2004, s 1.]

---

1. The purpose of this Act is to create clear accountability for children's services, and to enable better joint working and to secure a better focus on safeguarding children. Pursuant to this, the Act establishes the post of Children's Commissioner whose role is to promote awareness of the views and interests of children. The Commissioner is also able to hold enquiries either on the direction of the Secretary of State or on his own initiative. Other matters provided for include the devolution of CAFCASS functions in Wales to the Assembly, stronger notification arrangements for private fostering, clarification and simplification of the registration of child minders and providers of day care, changes in local authorities' obligations towards children in need, changes to the defence of "lawful chastisement" of a child, and changes to the publication of material from family proceedings.

The Act has 6 Parts and 5 Schedules. Sections 1–9 came into force on enactment. The remaining provisions are to be brought into force in accordance with commencement orders made under s 6. At the time of going to press the following commencement orders had been made: Children Act 2004 (Commencement No 1) Order 2005, SI 2005/394; Children Act 2004 (Commencement No 2) Order 2005, SI 2005/700; and Children Act 2004 (Commencement No 3) Order 2005, SI 2005/847. The (Commencement No 1) Order applies only to England. It brought the following provisions into force on 1 March 2005: s 11 (for the purposes of making an order under s 11(1); ss 13–14; s 17; ss 20–23; s 46 and para 1 of Sch 4 (in so far as they related to paras 2, 5 and 7–9 of Sch 4); s 50; ss 53–54, s 57; s 60; paras 2, 5 and 7–9 of Sch 4; Part 1 of Sch 5; and Part 2 of Sch 5 (in so far as it relates to s 79G(2) of, and para 4(3A)(*b*) of Sch 9A to, the Children Act 1989. The Order brought the following provisions into force on 1 April 2005: s 10; s 18; s 24; s 44 (for the purposes of making regulations); s 51; s 55; and Parts 3 and 4 of Sch 5. The Order will bring the following provisions into force on 1 July 2005: s 44 (in so far as not already in force); and s 52. Finally, the Order will bring into force on 1 October 2005 s 11 (in so far as not already in force).

2. Part 1 contains ss 1–9.

6–3205A 2. General function. (1) The Children's Commissioner has the function of promoting awareness of the views and interests of children in England.

    (2) The Children's Commissioner may in particular under this section—

    (a) encourage persons exercising functions or engaged in activities affecting children to take account of their views and interests;

    (b) advise the Secretary of State on the views and interests of children;

    (c) consider or research the operation of complaints procedures so far as relating to children;

    (d) consider or research any other matter relating to the interests of children;

    (e) publish a report on any matter considered or researched by him under this section.

    (3) The Children's Commissioner is to be concerned in particular under this section with the views and interests of children so far as relating to the following aspects of their well-being—

    (a) physical and mental health and emotional well-being;

    (b) protection from harm and neglect;

    (c) education, training and recreation;

    (d) the contribution made by them to society;

    (e) social and economic well-being.

    (4) The Children's Commissioner must take reasonable steps to involve children in the discharge of his function under this section, and in particular to—

    (a) ensure that children are made aware of his function and how they may communicate with him; and

    (b) consult children, and organisations working with children, on the matters he proposes to consider or research under subsection (2)(c) or (d).

    (5) Where the Children's Commissioner publishes a report under this section he must, if and to the extent that he considers it appropriate, also publish the report in a version which is suitable for children (or, if the report relates to a particular group of children, for those children).

    (6) The Children's Commissioner must for the purposes of subsection (4) have particular regard to groups of children who do not have other adequate means by which they can make their views known.

(7) The Children's Commissioner is not under this section to conduct an investigation of the case of an individual child.

(8) The Children's Commissioner or a person authorised by him may for the purposes of his function under this section at any reasonable time—

(a) enter any premises, other than a private dwelling, for the purposes of interviewing any child accommodated or cared for there; and

(b) if the child consents, interview the child in private.

(9) Any person exercising functions under any enactment must supply the Children's Commissioner with such information in that person's possession relating to those functions as the Children's Commissioner may reasonably request for the purposes of his function under this section (provided that the information is information which that person may, apart from this subsection, lawfully disclose to him).

(10) Where the Children's Commissioner has published a report under this section containing recommendations in respect of any person exercising functions under any enactment, he may require that person to state in writing, within such period as the Children's Commissioner may reasonably require, what action the person has taken or proposes to take in response to the recommendations.

(11) In considering for the purpose of his function under this section what constitutes the interests of children (generally or so far as relating to a particular matter) the Children's Commissioner must have regard to the United Nations Convention on the Rights of the Child.

(12) In subsection (11) the reference to the United Nations Convention on the Rights of the Child is to the Convention on the Rights of the Child adopted by the General Assembly of the United Nations on 20th November 1989, subject to any reservations, objections or interpretative declarations by the United Kingdom for the time being in force.
[Children Act 2004, s 2.]

6–3205B **3. Inquiries initiated by Commissioner.** (1) Where the Children's Commissioner considers that the case of an individual child in England raises issues of public policy of relevance to other children, he may hold an inquiry into that case for the purpose of investigating and making recommendations about those issues.

(2) The Children's Commissioner may only conduct an inquiry under this section if he is satisfied that the inquiry would not duplicate work that is the function of another person (having consulted such persons as he considers appropriate).

(3) Before holding an inquiry under this section the Children's Commissioner must consult the Secretary of State.

(4) The Children's Commissioner may, if he thinks fit, hold an inquiry under this section, or any part of it, in private.

(5) As soon as possible after completing an inquiry under this section the Children's Commissioner must—

(a) publish a report containing his recommendations; and

(b) send a copy to the Secretary of State.

(6) The report need not identify any individual child if the Children's Commissioner considers that it would be undesirable for the identity of the child to be made public.

(7) Where the Children's Commissioner has published a report under this section containing recommendations in respect of any person exercising functions under any enactment, he may require that person to state in writing, within such period as the Children's Commissioner may reasonably require, what action the person has taken or proposes to take in response to the recommendations.

(8) Subsections (2) and (3) of section 250 of the Local Government Act 1972 (c 70) apply for the purposes of an inquiry held under this section with the substitution for references to the person appointed to hold the inquiry of references to the Children's Commissioner.
[Children Act 2004, s 3.]

6–3205C **4. Other inquiries held by Commissioner.** (1) Where the Secretary of State considers that the case of an individual child in England raises issues of relevance to other children, he may direct the Children's Commissioner to hold an inquiry into that case.

(2) The Children's Commissioner may, if he thinks fit, hold an inquiry under this section, or any part of it, in private.

(3) The Children's Commissioner must, as soon as possible after the completion of an inquiry under this section, make a report in relation to the inquiry and send a copy to the Secretary of State.

(4) The Secretary of State must, subject to subsection (5), publish each report received by him under this section as soon as possible.

(5) Where a report made under this section identifies an individual child and the Secretary of State considers that it would be undesirable for the identity of the child to be made public—

(a) the Secretary of State may make such amendments to the report as are necessary to protect the identity of the child and publish the amended report only; or

(b) if he considers that it is not possible to publish the report without identifying the child, he need not publish the report.

4545 Children Act 2004 6–3205I

(6) The Secretary of State must lay a copy of each report published by him under this section before each House of Parliament.

(7) Subsections (2) to (5) of section 250 of the Local Government Act 1972 (c 70) apply for the purposes of an inquiry held under this section.

[Children Act 2004, s 4.]

6–3205D 5. Functions of Commissioner in Wales. (1) The Children's Commissioner has the function of promoting awareness of the views and interests of children in Wales, except in so far as relating to any matter falling within the remit of the Children's Commissioner for Wales under section 72B, 73 or 74 of the Care Standards Act 2000 (c 14).

(2) Subsections (2) to (12) of section 2 apply in relation to the function of the Children's Commissioner under subsection (1) above as in relation to his function under that section.

(3) In discharging his function under subsection (1) above the Children's Commissioner must take account of the views of, and any work undertaken by, the Children's Commissioner for Wales.

(4) Where the Children's Commissioner considers that the case of an individual child in Wales raises issues of public policy of relevance to other children, other than issues relating to a matter referred to in subsection (1) above, he may hold an inquiry into that case for the purpose of investigating and making recommendations about those issues.

(5) Subsections (2) to (8) of section 3 apply in relation to an inquiry under subsection (4) above.

(6) Where the Secretary of State considers that the case of an individual child in Wales raises issues of relevance to other children, other than issues relating to a matter referred to in subsection (1) above, he may direct the Children's Commissioner to hold an inquiry into that case.

(7) Subsections (2) to (7) of section 4 apply in relation to an inquiry under subsection (6) above.

[Children Act 2004, s 5.]

6–3205E 6. Functions of Commissioner in Scotland

6–3205F 7. Functions of Commissioner in Northern Ireland

6–3205G 8. Annual reports

6–3205H 9. Care leavers and young persons with learning disabilities

PART 2[1]
CHILDREN'S SERVICES IN ENGLAND

General

6–3205I 10. Co-operation to improve well-being. (1) Each children's services authority in England must make arrangements to promote co-operation between—

(a) the authority;

(b) each of the authority's relevant partners; and

(c) such other persons or bodies as the authority consider appropriate, being persons or bodies of any nature who exercise functions or are engaged in activities in relation to children in the authority's area.

(2) The arrangements are to be made with a view to improving the well-being of children in the authority's area so far as relating to—

(a) physical and mental health and emotional well-being;

(b) protection from harm and neglect;

(c) education, training and recreation;

(d) the contribution made by them to society;

(e) social and economic well-being.

(3) In making arrangements under this section a children's services authority in England must have regard to the importance of parents and other persons caring for children in improving the well-being of children.

(4) For the purposes of this section each of the following is a relevant partner of a children's services authority in England—

(a) where the authority is a county council for an area for which there is also a district council, the district council;

(b) the police authority and the chief officer of police for a police area any part of which falls within the area of the children's services authority;

(c) a local probation board for an area any part of which falls within the area of the authority;

(d) a youth offending team for an area any part of which falls within the area of the authority;

(e) a Strategic Health Authority and Primary Care Trust for an area any part of which falls within the area of the authority;

(f) a person providing services under section 114 of the Learning and Skills Act 2000 (c 21) in any part of the area of the authority;

(g) the Learning and Skills Council for England.

(5) The relevant partners of a children's services authority in England must co-operate with the authority in the making of arrangements under this section.

(6) A children's services authority in England and any of their relevant partners may for the purposes of arrangements under this section—

(a) provide staff, goods, services, accommodation or other resources;
(b) establish and maintain a pooled fund.

(7) For the purposes of subsection (6) a pooled fund is a fund—

(a) which is made up of contributions by the authority and the relevant partner or partners concerned; and
(b) out of which payments may be made towards expenditure incurred in the discharge of functions of the authority and functions of the relevant partner or partners.

(8) A children's services authority in England and each of their relevant partners must in exercising their functions under this section have regard to any guidance given to them for the purpose by the Secretary of State.

(9) Arrangements under this section may include arrangements relating to—

(a) persons aged 18 and 19;
(b) persons over the age of 19 who are receiving services under sections 23C to 24D of the Children Act 1989 (c 41);
(c) persons over the age of 19 but under the age of 25 who have a learning difficulty, within the meaning of section 13 of the Learning and Skills Act 2000, and are receiving services under that Act.

[Children Act 2004, s 10.]

---

1. Part 2 contains ss 10–24.

6–3205J 11. Arrangements to safeguard and promote welfare. (1) This section applies to each of the following—

(a) a children's services authority in England;
(b) a district council which is not such an authority;
(c) a Strategic Health Authority;
(d) a Special Health Authority, so far as exercising functions in relation to England, designated by order[1] made by the Secretary of State for the purposes of this section;
(e) a Primary Care Trust;
(f) an NHS trust all or most of whose hospitals, establishments and facilities are situated in England;
(g) an NHS foundation trust;
(h) the police authority and chief officer of police for a police area in England;
(i) the British Transport Police Authority, so far as exercising functions in relation to England;
(j) a local probation board for an area in England;
(k) a youth offending team for an area in England;
(l) the governor of a prison or secure training centre in England (or, in the case of a contracted out prison or secure training centre, its director);
(m) any person to the extent that he is providing services under section 114 of the Learning and Skills Act 2000 (c 21).

(2) Each person and body to whom this section applies must make arrangements for ensuring that—

(a) their functions are discharged having regard to the need to safeguard and promote the welfare of children; and
(b) any services provided by another person pursuant to arrangements made by the person or body in the discharge of their functions are provided having regard to that need.

(3) In the case of a children's services authority in England, the reference in subsection (2) to functions of the authority does not include functions to which section 175 of the Education Act 2002 (c 32) applies.

(4) Each person and body to whom this section applies must in discharging their duty under this section have regard to any guidance given to them for the purpose by the Secretary of State.

[Children Act 2004, s 11.]

---

1. NHS Direct has been designated by the Children Act 2004 (Designation of NHS Direct) Order 2005, SI 2005/2411.

6–3205K 12. Information databases. (1) The Secretary of State may for the purpose of arrangements under section 10 or 11 above or under section 175 of the Education Act 2002—

(a) by regulations require children's services authorities in England to establish and operate databases containing information in respect of persons to whom such arrangements relate;

(b) himself establish and operate, or make arrangements for the operation and establishment of, one or more databases containing such information.

(2) The Secretary of State may for the purposes of arrangements under subsection (1)(b) by regulations establish a body corporate to establish and operate one or more databases.

(3) A database under this section may only include information falling within subsection (4) in relation to a person to whom arrangements specified in subsection (1) relate.

(4) The information referred to in subsection (3) is information of the following descriptions in relation to a person—

(a) his name, address, gender and date of birth;

(b) a number identifying him;

(c) the name and contact details of any person with parental responsibility for him (within the meaning of section 3 of the Children Act 1989 (c 41)) or who has care of him at any time;

(d) details of any education being received by him (including the name and contact details of any educational institution attended by him);

(e) the name and contact details of any person providing primary medical services in relation to him under Part 1 of the National Health Service Act 1977 (c 49);

(f) the name and contact details of any person providing to him services of such description as the Secretary of State may by regulations specify;

(g) information as to the existence of any cause for concern in relation to him;

(h) information of such other description, not including medical records or other personal records, as the Secretary of State may by regulations specify.

(5) The Secretary of State may by regulations make provision in relation to the establishment and operation of any database or databases under this section.

(6) Regulations under subsection (5) may in particular make provision—

(a) as to the information which must or may be contained in any database under this section (subject to subsection (3));

(b) requiring a person or body specified in subsection (7) to disclose information for inclusion in the database;

(c) permitting a person or body specified in subsection (8) to disclose information for inclusion in the database;

(d) permitting or requiring the disclosure of information included in any such database;

(e) permitting or requiring any person to be given access to any such database for the purpose of adding or reading information;

(f) as to the conditions on which such access must or may be given;

(g) as to the length of time for which information must or may be retained;

(h) as to procedures for ensuring the accuracy of information included in any such database;

(i) in a case where a database is established by virtue of subsection (1)(b), requiring children's services authorities in England to participate in the operation of the database.

(7) The persons and bodies referred to in subsection (6)(b) are—

(a) the persons and bodies specified in section 11(1);

(b) the Learning and Skills Council for England;

(c) the governing body of a maintained school in England (within the meaning of section 175 of the Education Act 2002 (c 32));

(d) the governing body of an institution in England within the further education sector (within the meaning of that section);

(e) the proprietor of an independent school in England (within the meaning of the Education Act 1996 (c 56));

(f) a person or body of such other description as the Secretary of State may by regulations specify.

(8) The persons and bodies referred to in subsection (6)(c) are—

(a) a person registered in England for child minding or the provision of day care under Part 10A of the Children Act 1989 (c 41);

(b) a voluntary organisation exercising functions or engaged in activities in relation to persons to whom arrangements specified in subsection (1) relate;

(c) the Commissioners of Inland Revenue;

(d) a registered social landlord;

(e) a person or body of such other description as the Secretary of State may by regulations specify.

(9) The Secretary of State may provide information for inclusion in a database under this section.

(10) The provision which may be made under subsection (6)(e) includes provision for a person of a description specified in the regulations to determine what must or may be done under the regulations.

(11) Regulations under subsection (5) may also provide that anything which may be done under regulations under subsection (6)(c) to (e) or (9) may be done notwithstanding any rule of common law which prohibits or restricts the disclosure of information.

(12) Any person or body establishing or operating a database under this section must in the establishment or operation of the database have regard to any guidance, and comply with any direction, given to that person or body by the Secretary of State.

(13) Guidance or directions under subsection (12) may in particular relate to—

(a) the management of a database under this section;
(b) the technical specifications for any such database;
(c) the security of any such database;
(d) the transfer and comparison of information between databases under this section;
(e) the giving of advice in relation to rights under the Data Protection Act 1998 (c 29).

[Children Act 2004, s 12.]

Local Safeguarding Children Boards

6–3205L   13. Establishment of LSCBs.   (1) Each children's services authority in England must establish a Local Safeguarding Children Board for their area.

(2) A Board established under this section must include such representative or representatives of—

(a) the authority by which it is established, and
(b) each Board partner of that authority,

as the Secretary of State may by regulations[1] prescribe.

(3) For the purposes of this section each of the following is a Board partner of a children's services authority in England—

(a) where the authority is a county council for an area for which there is also a district council, the district council;
(b) the chief officer of police for a police area any part of which falls within the area of the authority;
(c) a local probation board for an area any part of which falls within the area of the authority;
(d) a youth offending team for an area any part of which falls within the area of the authority;
(e) a Strategic Health Authority and a Primary Care Trust for an area any part of which falls within the area of the authority;
(f) an NHS trust and an NHS foundation trust all or most of whose hospitals, establishments and facilities are situated in the area of the authority;
(g) a person providing services under section 114 of the Learning and Skills Act 2000 (c 21) in any part of the area of the authority;
(h) the Children and Family Court Advisory and Support Service;
(i) the governor of any secure training centre in the area of the authority (or, in the case of a contracted out secure training centre, its director);
(j) the governor of any prison in the area of the authority which ordinarily detains children (or, in the case of a contracted out prison, its director).

(4) A children's services authority in England must take reasonable steps to ensure that the Local Safeguarding Children Board established by them includes representatives of relevant persons and bodies of such descriptions as may be prescribed by the Secretary of State in regulations.

(5) A Local Safeguarding Children Board established under this section may also include representatives of such other relevant persons or bodies as the authority by which it is established consider, after consulting their Board partners, should be represented on it.

(6) For the purposes of subsections (4) and (5), relevant persons and bodies are persons and bodies of any nature exercising functions or engaged in activities relating to children in the area of the authority in question.

(7) In the establishment and operation of a Local Safeguarding Children Board under this section—

(a) the authority establishing it must co-operate with each of their Board partners; and
(b) each Board partner must co-operate with the authority.

(8) Two or more children's services authorities in England may discharge their respective duties under subsection (1) by establishing a Local Safeguarding Children Board for their combined area (and where they do so, any reference in this section or sections 14 to 16 to the authority establishing the Board shall be read as a reference to the authorities establishing it).

[Children Act 2004, s 13.]

---

1. The Local Safeguarding Children Boards Regulations 2006, SI 2006/90 have been made.

6–3205M   14. Functions and procedure of LSCBs.   (1) The objective of a Local Safeguarding Children Board established under section 13 is—

(a) to co-ordinate what is done by each person or body represented on the Board for the purposes of safeguarding and promoting the welfare of children in the area of the authority by which it is established; and
(b) to ensure the effectiveness of what is done by each such person or body for those purposes.

(2) A Local Safeguarding Children Board established under section 13 is to have such functions in relation to its objective as the Secretary of State may by regulations[1] prescribe (which may in particular include functions of review or investigation).

(3) The Secretary of State may by regulations[1] make provision as to the procedures to be followed by a Local Safeguarding Children Board established under section 13.
[Children Act 2004, s 14.]

---

1. The Local Safeguarding Children Boards Regulations 2006, SI 2006/90 have been made.

6–3205N   15. Funding of LSCBs.   (1) Any person or body specified in subsection (3) may make payments towards expenditure incurred by, or for purposes connected with, a Local Safeguarding Children Board established under section 13—

(a) by making the payments directly; or
(b) by contributing to a fund out of which the payments may be made.

(2) Any person or body specified in subsection (3) may provide staff, goods, services, accommodation or other resources for purposes connected with a Local Safeguarding Children Board established under section 13.

(3) The persons and bodies referred to in subsections (1) and (2) are—

(a) the children's services authority in England by which the Board is established;
(b) any person who is a Board partner of the authority under section 13(3)(a) to (h);
(c) in a case where the governor of a secure training centre or prison is a Board partner of the authority, the Secretary of State; and
(d) in a case where the director of a contracted out secure training centre or prison is a Board partner of the authority, the contractor.
[Children Act 2004, s 15.]

6–3205O   16. LSCBs: supplementary.   (1) The Secretary of State may by regulations[1] make provision as to the functions of children's services authorities in England relating to Local Safeguarding Children Boards established by them.

(2) A children's services authority in England and each of their Board partners must, in exercising their functions relating to a Local Safeguarding Children Board, have regard to any guidance given to them for the purpose by the Secretary of State.
[Children Act 2004, s 16.]

---

1. The Local Safeguarding Children Boards Regulations 2006, SI 2006/90 have been made.

Local authority administration

6–3205P   17. Children and young people's plans.   (1) The Secretary of State may by regulations[1] require a children's services authority in England from time to time to prepare and publish a plan setting out the authority's strategy for discharging their functions in relation to children and relevant young persons.

(2) Regulations under this section may in particular make provision as to—

(a) the matters to be dealt with in a plan under this section;
(b) the period to which a plan under this section is to relate;
(c) when and how a plan under this section must be published;
(d) keeping a plan under this section under review;
(e) consultation to be carried out during preparation of a plan under this section.

(3) The matters for which provision may be made under subsection (2)(a) include in particular—

(a) the arrangements made or to be made under section 10 by a children's services authority in England;
(b) the strategy or proposals in relation to children and relevant young persons of any person or body with whom a children's services authority in England makes or proposes to make such arrangements.

(4) The power to make regulations conferred by this section shall, for the purposes of subsection (1) of section 100 of the Local Government Act 2003 (c 26), be regarded as included among the powers mentioned in subsection (2) of that section.

(5) In this section "relevant young persons" means persons, other than children, in relation to whom arrangements under section 10 may be made.
[Children Act 2004, s 17.]

---

1. The Children and Young People's Plan (England) Regulations 2005, SI 2005/2149 have been made.

6–3205Q   18. Director of children's services.   (1) A children's services authority in England may, and with effect from the appointed day must, appoint an officer for the purposes of—

(a)   the functions conferred on or exercisable by the authority which are specified in subsection (2); and

(b)   such other functions conferred on or exercisable by the authority as may be prescribed by the Secretary of State by regulations.

(2)   The functions referred to in subsection (1)(a) are—

(a)   functions conferred on or exercisable by the authority in their capacity as a local education authority;

(b)   functions conferred on or exercisable by the authority which are social services functions (within the meaning of the Local Authority Social Services Act 1970 (c 42)), so far as those functions relate to children;

(c)   the functions conferred on the authority under sections 23C to 24D of the Children Act 1989 (c 41) (so far as not falling within paragraph (b));

(d)   the functions conferred on the authority under sections 10 to 12 and 17 of this Act; and

(e)   any functions exercisable by the authority under section 31 of the Health Act 1999 (c 8) on behalf of an NHS body (within the meaning of that section), so far as those functions relate to children.

(3)   Subsection (2)(a) does not include—

(a)   functions under section 120(3) of the Education Reform Act 1988 (c 40) (functions of LEAs with respect to higher and further education);

(b)   functions under section 85(2) and (3) of the Further and Higher Education Act 1992 (c 13) (finance and government of locally funded further and higher education);

(c)   functions under section 15B of the Education Act 1996 (c 56) or section 23 of the Learning and Skills Act 2000 (c 21) (education for persons who have attained the age of 19);

(d)   functions under section 22 of the Teaching and Higher Education Act 1998 (c 30) (financial support to students);

(e)   such other functions conferred on or exercisable by a children's services authority in England in their capacity as a local education authority as the Secretary of State may by regulations prescribe.

(4)   An officer appointed by a children's services authority in England under this section is to be known as their "director of children's services".

(5)   The director of children's services appointed by a children's services authority in England may also have responsibilities relating to such functions conferred on or exercisable by the authority, in addition to those specified in subsection (1), as the authority consider appropriate.

(6)   The functions in relation to which a director of children's services may have responsibilities by virtue of subsection (5) include those referred to in subsection (3)(a) to (e).

(7)   A children's services authority in England must have regard to any guidance given to them by the Secretary of State for the purposes of this section.

(8)   Two or more children's services authorities in England may for the purposes of this section, if they consider that the same person can efficiently discharge, for both or all of them, the responsibilities of director of children's services, concur in the appointment of a person as director of children's services for both or all of them.

(9)   The amendments in Schedule 2—

(a)   have effect, in relation to any authority which appoint a director of children's services before the appointed day, from the day of his appointment; and

(b)   on and after the appointed day have effect for all purposes.

(10)   In this section, "the appointed day" means such day as the Secretary of State may by order appoint.
[Children Act 2004, s 18.]

6–3205R   19. Lead member for children's services.   (1) A children's services authority in England must, in making arrangements for the discharge of—

(a)   the functions conferred on or exercisable by the authority specified in section 18(1)(a) and (b), and

(b)   such other functions conferred on or exercisable by the authority as the authority consider appropriate,

designate one of their members as their "lead member for children's services".

(2)   A children's services authority in England must have regard to any guidance given to them by the Secretary of State for the purposes of subsection (1).
[Children Act 2004, s 19.]

Inspections of children's services

6–3205S   20. Joint area reviews.   (1) Any two or more of the persons and bodies to which this section applies must, at the request of the Secretary of State—

(a) conduct, in accordance with a timetable drawn up by them and approved by the Secretary of State, a review of children's services provided in—

    (i) the area of every children's services authority in England;

    (ii) the areas of such children's services authorities in England as may be specified in the request;

(b) conduct a review of such children's services provided in the area of such children's services authority in England as may be specified in the request.

(2) Any two or more of the persons and bodies to which this section applies may conduct a review of any children's services provided in the area of a particular children's services authority in England.

(3) The purpose of a review under this section is to evaluate the extent to which, taken together, the children's services being reviewed improve the well-being of children and relevant young persons (and in particular to evaluate how those services work together to improve their well-being).

(4) The persons and bodies to which this section applies are—

(a) the Chief Inspector of Schools;

(b) the Adult Learning Inspectorate;

(c) the Commission for Social Care Inspection;

(d) the Commission for Healthcare Audit and Inspection;

(e) the Audit Commission for Local Authorities and the National Health Service in England and Wales;

(f) the chief inspector of constabulary;

(g) Her Majesty's Chief Inspector of the National Probation Service for England and Wales;

(h) Her Majesty's Chief Inspector of Court Administration; and

(i) the Chief Inspector of Prisons.

(5) Reviews under this section are to be conducted in accordance with arrangements made by the Chief Inspector of Schools.

(6) Before making arrangements for the purposes of reviews under this section the Chief Inspector of Schools must consult such of the other persons and bodies to which this section applies as he considers appropriate.

(7) The annual report of the Chief Inspector of Schools required by subsection (7)(a) of section 2 of the School Inspections Act 1996 (c 57) to be made to the Secretary of State must include an account of reviews under this section; and the power conferred by subsection (7)(b) of that section to make other reports to the Secretary of State includes a power to make reports about such reviews.

(8) The Secretary of State may by regulations[1] make provision for the purposes of reviews under this section and in particular provision—

(a) requiring or facilitating the sharing or production of information for the purposes of a review under this section (including provision for the creation of criminal offences);

(b) authorising any person or body conducting a review under this section to enter any premises for the purposes of the review (including provision for the creation of criminal offences);

(c) imposing requirements as to the making of a report on each review under this section;

(d) for the making by such persons as may be specified in or under the regulations of written statements of proposed action in the light of the report and the period within which any such action must or may be taken;

(e) for the provision to members of the public of copies of reports and statements made under paragraphs (c) and (d), and for charging in respect of any such provision;

(f) for the disapplication, in consequence of a requirement under this section, of any requirement under any other enactment to conduct an assessment or to do anything in connection with an assessment.

(9) Regulations under subsection (8) may in particular make provision by applying enactments falling within subsection (10), with or without modification, for the purposes of reviews under this section.

(10) The enactments falling within this subsection are enactments relating to the powers of persons and bodies to which this section applies for the purposes of assessments other than reviews under this section.

(11) Regulations under subsection (8) may make provision authorising or requiring the doing of anything by reference to the determination of a person of a description specified in the regulations. [Children Act 2004, s 20.]

---

1. The Children Act 2004 (Joint Area Reviews) Regulations 2005, SI 2005/1973 have been made.

6–3205U 21. Framework. (1) The Chief Inspector of Schools must devise a Framework for Inspection of Children's Services ("the Framework").

(2) The Framework must, for the purpose specified in subsection (3), set out principles to be applied by any person or body conducting a relevant assessment.

(3) The purpose referred to in subsection (2) is to ensure that relevant assessments properly

evaluate and report on the extent to which children's services improve the well-being of children and relevant young persons.

(4) The principles in the Framework may—

(a) include principles relating to the organisation of the results of any relevant assessment;

(b) make different provision for different cases.

(5) For the purposes of subsections (2) to (4) a relevant assessment is an assessment conducted under any enactment in relation to any children's services.

(6) When devising the Framework, the Chief Inspector of Schools must consult the other persons and bodies to which section 20 applies.

(7) The Chief Inspector of Schools must publish the Framework, but before doing so must—

(a) consult such persons and bodies, other than those referred to in subsection (6), as he thinks fit; and

(b) obtain the consent of the Secretary of State.

(8) The Chief Inspector of Schools may at any time revise the Framework (and subsections (6) and (7) apply in relation to revisions to the Framework as to the original Framework).
[Children Act 2004, s 21.]

6–3205V 22. Co-operation and delegation. (1) Each person or body with functions under any enactment of conducting assessments of children's services must for the purposes of those assessments co-operate with other persons or bodies with such functions.

(2) A person or body with functions under any enactment of conducting assessments of children's services may delegate any of those functions to any other person or body with such functions.
[Children Act 2004, s 22.]

6–3205W 23. Sections 20 to 22: interpretation. (1) This section applies for the purposes of sections 20 to 22.

(2) "Assessment" includes an inspection, review, investigation or study.

(3) "Children's services" means—

(a) anything done for or in relation to children and relevant young persons (alone or with other persons)—

(i)   in respect of which, apart from section 20, a person or body to which that section applies conducts any kind of assessment, or secures that any kind of assessment is conducted; and

(ii) which is specified in, or is of a description prescribed by, regulations[1] made by the Secretary of State;

(b) any function under sections 10 and 13 to 19; and

(c) any function conferred on a children's services authority under section 12.

(4) "Relevant young persons" means persons, other than children, in relation to whom arrangements under section 10 may be made.

(5) "The Chief Inspector of Schools" means Her Majesty's Chief Inspector of Schools in England.
[Children Act 2004, s 23.]

---

1. The Children Act 2004 (Children's Services) Regulations 2005, SI 2005/1972 have been made.

6–3205X 24. Performance rating of social services. (1) In section 79(2) of the Health and Social Care (Community Health and Standards) Act 2003 (c 43) (duty of Commission for Social Care Inspection to award a performance rating to a local authority), for the words from "a performance rating" to the end substitute—

"(a) a performance rating to that authority in respect of all the English local authority social services provided by, or pursuant to arrangements made by, that authority—

(i) to or so far as relating to persons under the age of eighteen; or

(ii) under sections 23C to 24D of the Children Act 1989; and

(b) a performance rating to that authority in respect of all other English local authority social services provided by, or pursuant to arrangements made by, that authority."

(2) In section 81(2) of that Act (duty of the Commission to inform the Secretary of State where it awards the lowest performance rating under section 79), for "section 79" substitute "section 79(2)(a) or (b)".
[Children Act 2004, s 24.]

PART 3[1]
CHILDREN'S SERVICES IN WALES
General

6–3205Y 25. Co-operation to improve well-being: Wales. (1) Each children's services authority in Wales must make arrangements to promote co-operation between—

(a) the authority;
(b) each of the authority's relevant partners; and
(c) such other persons or bodies as the authority consider appropriate, being persons or bodies of any nature who exercise functions or are engaged in activities in relation to children in the authority's area.

(2) The arrangements are to be made with a view to improving the well-being of children in the authority's area so far as relating to—

(a) physical and mental health and emotional well-being;
(b) protection from harm and neglect;
(c) education, training and recreation;
(d) the contribution made by them to society;
(e) social and economic well-being.

(3) In making arrangements under this section a children's services authority in Wales must have regard to the importance of parents and other persons caring for children in improving the well-being of children.

(4) For the purposes of this section each of the following is the relevant partner of a children's services authority in Wales—

(a) the police authority and the chief officer of police for a police area any part of which falls within the area of the children's services authority;
(b) a local probation board for an area any part of which falls within the area of the authority;
(c) a youth offending team for an area any part of which falls within the area of the authority;
(d) a Local Health Board for an area any part of which falls within the area of the authority;
(e) an NHS trust providing services in the area of the authority;
(f) the National Council for Education and Training for Wales.

(5) The relevant partners of a children's services authority in Wales must co-operate with the authority in the making of arrangements under this section.

(6) A children's services authority in Wales and any of their relevant partners may for the purposes of arrangements under this section—

(a) provide staff, goods, services, accommodation or other resources;
(b) establish and maintain a pooled fund.

(7) For the purposes of subsection (6) a pooled fund is a fund—

(a) which is made up of contributions by the authority and the relevant partner or partners concerned; and
(b) out of which payments may be made towards expenditure incurred in the discharge of functions of the authority and functions of the relevant partner or partners.

(8) A children's services authority in Wales and each of their relevant partners must in exercising their functions under this section have regard to any guidance given to them for the purpose by the Assembly.

(9) The Assembly must obtain the consent of the Secretary of State before giving guidance under subsection (8) at any time after the coming into force of any of paragraphs (a) to (c) of subsection (4).

(10) Arrangements under this section may include arrangements relating to—

(a) persons aged 18 and 19;
(b) persons over the age of 19 who are receiving—

    (i) services under sections 23C to 24D of the Children Act 1989 (c 41); or
    (ii) youth support services (within the meaning of section 123 of the Learning and Skills Act 2000 (c 21)).

[Children Act 2004, s 25.]

---

1. Part 3 contains ss 25–34.

6–3205Z   26. Children and young people's plans: Wales.   (1) The Assembly may by regulations require a children's services authority in Wales from time to time to prepare and publish a plan setting out the authority's strategy for discharging their functions in relation to children and relevant young persons.

(2) Regulations under this section may in particular make provision as to—

(a) the matters to be dealt with in a plan under this section;
(b) the period to which a plan under this section is to relate;
(c) when and how a plan under this section must be published;
(d) keeping a plan under this section under review;
(e) consultation to be carried out before a plan under this section is published;
(f) implementation of a plan under this section.

(3) The matters for which provision may be made under subsection (2)(a) include in particular—

(a) the arrangements made or to be made under section 25 by a children's services authority in Wales;

(b) the strategy or proposals in relation to children and relevant young persons of any person or body with whom a children's services authority in Wales makes or proposes to make such arrangements.

(4) Regulations under this section may require a children's services authority in Wales to obtain the Assembly's approval before publishing a plan under this section; and may provide that the Assembly may modify a plan before approving it.

(5) A children's services authority in Wales must have regard to any guidance given to them by the Assembly in relation to how they are to discharge their functions under regulations under this section.

(6) In this section "relevant young persons" means the persons, in addition to children, in relation to whom arrangements under section 25 may be made.

[Children Act 2004, s 26.]

6–3206 27. Responsibility for functions under sections 25 and 26. (1) A children's services authority in Wales must—

(a) appoint an officer, to be known as the "lead director for children and young people's services", for the purposes of co-ordinating and overseeing arrangements made under sections 25 and 26; and

(b) designate one of their members, to be known as the "lead member for children and young people's services", to have as his special care the discharge of the authority's functions under those sections.

(2) A Local Health Board must—

(a) appoint an officer, to be known as the Board's "lead officer for children and young people's services", for the purposes of the Board's functions under section 25; and

(b) designate one of the Board's members who is not an officer as its "lead member for children and young people's services" to have the discharge of those functions as his special care.

(3) An NHS trust to which section 25 applies must—

(a) appoint an executive director, to be known as the trust's "lead executive director for children and young people's services", for the purposes of the trust's functions under that section; and

(b) designate one of the trust's non-executive directors as its "lead non-executive director for children and young people's services" to have the discharge of those functions as his special care.

(4) Each children's services authority in Wales, Local Health Board and NHS trust to which section 25 applies must have regard to any guidance given to them by the Assembly in relation to—

(a) their functions under this section;

(b) the responsibilities of the persons appointed or designated by them under this section.

[Children Act 2004, s 27.]

6–3206A 28. Arrangements to safeguard and promote welfare: Wales. (1) This section applies to each of the following—

(a) a children's services authority in Wales;

(b) a Local Health Board;

(c) an NHS trust all or most of whose hospitals, establishments and facilities are situated in Wales;

(d) the police authority and chief officer of police for a police area in Wales;

(e) the British Transport Police Authority, so far as exercising functions in relation to Wales;

(f) a local probation board for an area in Wales;

(g) a youth offending team for an area in Wales;

(h) the governor of a prison or secure training centre in Wales (or, in the case of a contracted out prison or secure training centre, its director);

(i) any person to the extent that he is providing services pursuant to arrangements made by a children's services authority in Wales under section 123(1)(b) of the Learning and Skills Act 2000 (c 21) (youth support services).

(2) Each person and body to whom this section applies must make arrangements for ensuring that—

(a) their functions are discharged having regard to the need to safeguard and promote the welfare of children; and

(b) any services provided by another person pursuant to arrangements made by the person or body in the discharge of their functions are provided having regard to that need.

(3) In the case of a children's services authority in Wales, the reference in subsection (2) to functions of the authority does not include functions to which section 175 of the Education Act 2002 (c 32) applies.

(4) The persons and bodies referred to in subsection (1)(a) to (c) and (i) must in discharging their duty under this section have regard to any guidance given to them for the purpose by the Assembly.

(5) The persons and bodies referred to in subsection (1)(d) to (h) must in discharging their duty under this section have regard to any guidance given to them for the purpose by the Secretary of State after consultation with the Assembly.

[Children Act 2004, s 28.]

6–3206B 29. Information databases: Wales. (1) The Assembly may for the purpose of arrangements under section 25 or 28 above or under section 175 of the Education Act 2002—

(a) by regulations require children's services authorities in Wales to establish and operate databases containing information in respect of persons to whom such arrangements relate;

(b) itself establish and operate, or make arrangements for the operation and establishment of, one or more databases containing such information.

(2) The Assembly may for the purposes of arrangements under subsection (1)(b) by regulations establish a body corporate to establish and operate one or more databases.

(3) A database under this section may only include information falling within subsection (4) in relation to a person to whom arrangements specified in subsection (1) relate.

(4) The information referred to in subsection (3) is information of the following descriptions in relation to a person—

(a) his name, address, gender and date of birth;

(b) a number identifying him;

(c) the name and contact details of any person with parental responsibility for him (within the meaning of section 3 of the Children Act 1989 (c 41)) or who has care of him at any time;

(d) details of any education being received by him (including the name and contact details of any educational institution attended by him);

(e) the name and contact details of any person providing primary medical services in relation to him under Part 1 of the National Health Service Act 1977 (c 49);

(f) the name and contact details of any person providing to him services of such description as the Assembly may by regulations specify;

(g) information as to the existence of any cause for concern in relation to him;

(h) information of such other description, not including medical records or other personal records, as the Assembly may by regulations specify.

(5) The Assembly may by regulations make provision in relation to the establishment and operation of any database or databases under this section.

(6) Regulations under subsection (5) may in particular make provision—

(a) as to the information which must or may be contained in any database under this section (subject to subsection (3));

(b) requiring a person or body specified in subsection (7) to disclose information for inclusion in the database;

(c) permitting a person or body specified in subsection (8) to disclose information for inclusion in the database;

(d) permitting or requiring the disclosure of information included in any such database;

(e) permitting or requiring any person to be given access to any such database for the purpose of adding or reading information;

(f) as to the conditions on which such access must or may be given;

(g) as to the length of time for which information must or may be retained;

(h) as to procedures for ensuring the accuracy of information included in any such database;

(i) in a case where a database is established by virtue of subsection (1)(b), requiring children's services authorities in Wales to participate in the operation of the database.

(7) The persons and bodies referred to in subsection (6)(b) are—

(a) the persons and bodies specified in section 28(1);

(b) the National Council for Education and Training for Wales;

(c) the governing body of a maintained school in Wales (within the meaning of section 175 of the Education Act 2002 (c 32));

(d) the governing body of an institution in Wales within the further education sector (within the meaning of that section);

(e) the proprietor of an independent school in Wales (within the meaning of the Education Act 1996 (c 56));

(f) a person or body of such other description as the Assembly may by regulations specify.

(8) The persons and bodies referred to in subsection (6)(c) are—

(a) a person registered in Wales for child minding or the provision of day care under Part 10A of the Children Act 1989 (c 41);

(b) a voluntary organisation exercising functions or engaged in activities in relation to persons to whom arrangements specified in subsection (1) relate;

(c) the Commissioners of Inland Revenue;

(d) a registered social landlord;

(e) a person or body of such other description as the Assembly may by regulations specify.

(9) The Assembly and the Secretary of State may provide information for inclusion in a database under this section.

(10) The provision which may be made under subsection (6)(e) includes provision for a person of a description specified in the regulations to determine what must or may be done under the regulations.

(11) Regulations under subsection (5) may also provide that anything which may be done under regulations under subsection (6)(c) to (e) or (9) may be done notwithstanding any rule of common law which prohibits or restricts the disclosure of information.

(12) Regulations under subsections (1)(a) and (5) may only be made with the consent of the Secretary of State.

(13) Any person or body establishing or operating a database under this section must in the establishment or operation of the database have regard to any guidance, and comply with any direction, given to that person by the Assembly.

(14) Guidance or directions under subsection (13) may in particular relate to—

(a) the management of a database under this section;

(b) the technical specifications for any such database;

(c) the security of any such database;

(d) the transfer and comparison of information between databases under this section;

(e) the giving of advice in relation to rights under the Data Protection Act 1998 (c 29).

[Children Act 2004, s 29.]

6–3206C   30. Inspection of functions under this Part.   (1) Chapter 6 of Part 2 of the Health and Social Care (Community Health and Standards) Act 2003 (c 43) (functions of the Assembly in relation to social services) shall apply as if anything done by a children's services authority in Wales in the exercise of functions to which this section applies were a Welsh local authority social service within the meaning of that Part.

(2) This section applies to the following functions of a children's services authority—

(a) the authority's functions under section 25 or 26, except so far as relating to education, training or youth support services (within the meaning of section 123 of the Learning and Skills Act 2000 (c 21));

(b) the authority's functions under section 28;

(c) any function conferred on the authority under section 29.

[Children Act 2004, s 30.]

Local Safeguarding Children Boards

6–3206D   31. Establishment of LSCBs in Wales.   (1) Each children's services authority in Wales must establish a Local Safeguarding Children Board for their area.

(2) A Board established under this section must include such representative or representatives of—

(a) the authority by which it is established, and

(b) each Board partner of that authority,

as the Assembly may by regulations prescribe.

(3) For the purposes of this section each of the following is a Board partner of a children's services authority in Wales—

(a) the chief officer of police for a police area any part of which falls within the area of the authority;

(b) a local probation board for an area any part of which falls within the area of the authority;

(c) a youth offending team for an area any part of which falls within the area of the authority;

(d) a Local Health Board for an area any part of which falls within the area of the authority;

(e) an NHS trust providing services in the area of the authority;

(f) the governor of any secure training centre within the area of the authority (or, in the case of a contracted out secure training centre, its director);

(g) the governor of any prison in the area of the authority which ordinarily detains children (or, in the case of a contracted out prison, its director).

(4) Regulations under subsection (2) that make provision in relation to a Board partner referred to in subsection (3)(a) to (c), (f) or (g) may only be made with the consent of the Secretary of State.

(5) A children's services authority in Wales must take reasonable steps to ensure that the Local Safeguarding Children Board established by them includes representatives of relevant persons and bodies of such descriptions as may be prescribed by the Assembly in regulations.

(6) A Local Safeguarding Children Board established under this section may also include

representatives of such other relevant persons or bodies as the authority by which it is established consider, after consulting their Board partners, should be represented on it.

(7) For the purposes of subsections (5) and (6), relevant persons and bodies are persons and bodies of any nature exercising functions or engaged in activities relating to children in the area of the authority in question.

(8) In the establishment and operation of a Local Safeguarding Children Board under this section—

(a) the authority establishing it must co-operate with each of their Board partners; and
(b) each Board partner must co-operate with the authority.

(9) Two or more children's services authorities in Wales may discharge their respective duties under subsection (1) by establishing a Local Safeguarding Children Board for their combined area (and where they do so, any reference in this section and sections 32 to 34 to the authority establishing the Board shall be read as a reference to the authorities establishing it).
[Children Act 2004, s 31.]

6–3206E 32. Functions and procedure of LSCBs in Wales.   (1) The objective of a Local Safeguarding Children Board established under section 31 is—

(a) to co-ordinate what is done by each person or body represented on the Board for the purposes of safeguarding and promoting the welfare of children in the area of the authority by which it is established; and
(b) to ensure the effectiveness of what is done by each such person or body for those purposes.

(2) A Local Safeguarding Children Board established under section 31 is to have such functions in relation to its objective as the Assembly may by regulations prescribe (which may in particular include functions of review or investigation).

(3) The Assembly may by regulations make provision as to the procedures to be followed by a Local Safeguarding Children Board established under section 31.
[Children Act 2004, s 32.]

6–3206F 33. Funding of LSCBs in Wales.   (1) Any person or body specified in subsection (3) may make payments towards expenditure incurred by, or for purposes connected with, a Local Safeguarding Children Board established under section 31—

(a) by making the payments directly; or
(b) by contributing to a fund out of which the payments may be made.

(2) Any person or body specified in subsection (3) may provide staff, goods, services, accommodation or other resources for purposes connected with a Local Safeguarding Children Board established under section 31.

(3) The persons and bodies referred to in subsections (1) and (2) are—

(a) the children's services authority in Wales by which the Board is established;
(b) any person who is a Board partner of the authority under section 31(3)(a) to (e);
(c) in a case where the governor of a secure training centre or prison is a Board partner of the authority, the Secretary of State; and
(d) in a case where the director of a contracted out secure training centre or prison is a Board partner of the authority, the contractor.
[Children Act 2004, s 33.]

6–3206G 34. LSCBs in Wales: supplementary.   (1) The Assembly may by regulations make provision as to the functions of children's services authorities in Wales relating to Local Safeguarding Children Boards established by them.

(2) A children's services authority in Wales and each of their Board partners must, in exercising their functions relating to a Local Safeguarding Children Board, have regard to any guidance given to them for the purpose by the Assembly.

(3) The Assembly must obtain the consent of the Secretary of State before giving guidance under subsection (2) at any time after the coming into force of any of paragraphs (a) to (c), (f) or (g) of section 31(3).
[Children Act 2004, s 34.]

PART 4[1]
ADVISORY AND SUPPORT SERVICES FOR FAMILY PROCEEDINGS

CAFCASS functions in Wales

6–3206H 35. Functions of the Assembly relating to family proceedings.   (1) In respect of family proceedings in which the welfare of children ordinarily resident in Wales is or may be in question, it is a function of the Assembly to—

(a) safeguard and promote the welfare of the children;
(b) give advice to any court about any application made to it in such proceedings;

(c) make provision for the children to be represented in such proceedings;

(d) provide information, advice and other support for the children and their families.

(2) The Assembly must also make provision for the performance of the functions conferred on Welsh family proceedings officers by virtue of any enactment (whether or not they are exercisable for the purposes of subsection (1)).

(3) In subsection (1), "family proceedings" has the meaning given by section 12 of the Criminal Justice and Court Services Act 2000 (c 43).

(4) In this Part, "Welsh family proceedings officer" means—

(a) any member of the staff of the Assembly appointed to exercise the functions of a Welsh family proceedings officer; and

(b) any other individual exercising functions of a Welsh family proceedings officer by virtue of section 36(2) or (4).

[Children Act 2004, s 35.]

---

1. Part 2 contains ss 35–43.

6–3206I 36. Ancillary powers of the Assembly. (1) The Assembly may make arrangements with organisations under which the organisations perform the functions of the Assembly under section 35 on its behalf.

(2) Arrangements under subsection (1) may provide for the organisations to designate individuals who may perform functions of Welsh family proceedings officers.

(3) The Assembly may only make an arrangement under subsection (1) if it is of the opinion—

(a) that the functions in question will be performed efficiently and to the required standard; and

(b) that the arrangement represents good value for money.

(4) The Assembly may make arrangements with individuals under which they may perform functions of Welsh family proceedings officers.

(5) The Assembly may make arrangements with an organisation or individual under which staff of the Assembly engaged in the exercise of its functions under section 35 may work for the organisation or individual.

(6) The Assembly may make arrangements with an organisation or individual under which any services provided by the Assembly's staff to the Assembly in the exercise of its functions under section 35 are also made available to the organisation or individual.

(7) The Assembly may charge for anything done under arrangements under subsection (5) and (6).

(8) In this section, references to organisations include public bodies and private or voluntary organisations.

[Children Act 2004, s 36.]

6–3206J 37. Welsh family proceedings officers. (1) The Assembly may authorise a Welsh family proceedings officer of a description prescribed in regulations made by the Secretary of State—

(a) to conduct litigation in relation to any proceedings in any court,

(b) to exercise a right of audience in any proceedings in any court,

in the exercise of his functions.

(2) A Welsh family proceedings officer exercising a right to conduct litigation by virtue of subsection (1)(a) who would otherwise have such a right by virtue of section 28(2)(a) of the Courts and Legal Services Act 1990 (c 41) is to be treated as having acquired that right solely by virtue of this section.

(3) A Welsh family proceedings officer exercising a right of audience by virtue of subsection (1)(b) who would otherwise have such a right by virtue of section 27(2)(a) of the Courts and Legal Services Act 1990 is to be treated as having acquired that right solely by virtue of this section.

(4) A Welsh family proceedings officer may, subject to rules of court, be cross-examined in any proceedings to the same extent as any witness.

(5) But a Welsh family proceedings officer may not be cross-examined merely because he is exercising a right to conduct litigation or a right of audience granted in accordance with this section.

(6) In this section, "right to conduct litigation" and "right of audience" have the same meanings as in section 119 of the Courts and Legal Services Act 1990.

[Children Act 2004, s 37.]

6–3206K 38. Inspections. (1) Her Majesty's Inspectorate of Court Administration must at the request of the Assembly inspect, and report to the Assembly on—

(a) the discharge by the Assembly of its functions under this Part; and

(b) the discharge by Welsh family proceedings officers of their functions under this Part and any other enactment.

(2) The Assembly may only make a request under subsection (1) with the consent of the Secretary of State.
[Children Act 2004, s 38.]

6–3206L   39. Protection of children.   (1) The Protection of Children Act 1999 (c 14) ("the 1999 Act") shall have effect as if the Assembly, in performing its functions under sections 35 and 36, were a child care organisation within the meaning of that Act.

(2) Arrangements which the Assembly makes with an organisation under section 36(1) must provide that, before selecting an individual to be employed under the arrangements in a child care position, the organisation—

   (a)   must ascertain whether the individual is included in any of the lists mentioned in section 7(1) of the 1999 Act, and

   (b)   if he is included in any of those lists, must not select him for that employment.

(3) Such arrangements must provide that, if at any time the organisation has power to refer an individual who is or has been employed in a child care position under the arrangements to the Secretary of State under section 2 of the 1999 Act (inclusion in list on reference following disciplinary actions etc), the organisation must so refer him.

(4) In this section, "child care position" and "employment" have the same meanings as in the 1999 Act.
[Children Act 2004, s 39.]

6–3206M   40. Advisory and support services for family proceedings: supplementary. Schedule 3 (which makes supplementary and consequential provision relating to this Part, including provision relating to functions of Welsh family proceedings officers) has effect.
[Children Act 2004, s 40.]

6–3206N   41. Sharing of information.   (1) The Assembly and the Children and Family Court Advisory and Support Service may provide any information to each other for the purposes of their respective functions under this Part and Part 1 of the Criminal Justice and Court Services Act 2000 (c 43).

(2) A Welsh family proceedings officer and an officer of the Service (within the meaning given by section 11(3) of that Act) may provide any information to each other for the purposes of any of their respective functions.
[Children Act 2004, s 41.]

Transfers

6–3206O   42. Transfer of property from CAFCASS to Assembly

6–3206P   43. Transfer of staff from CAFCASS to Assembly

PART 5[1]
MISCELLANEOUS
Private fostering

6–3206Q   44. Amendments to notification scheme.   *Amends s 67 of the Children Act 1989: see this* PART, *ante.*

6–3206R   45. Power to establish registration scheme in England.   (1) The Secretary of State may by regulations require any person who fosters a child privately in the area of a children's services authority in England to be registered for private fostering by that authority in accordance with the regulations.

(2) Regulations under this section may make supplementary provision relating to the registration of persons for private fostering, including provision as to—

   (a)   how a person applies for registration and the procedure to be followed in considering an application;

   (b)   the requirements to be satisfied before a person may be registered;

   (c)   the circumstances in which a person is disqualified from being registered;

   (d)   the circumstances in which an application for registration may or must be granted or refused;

   (e)   the payment of a fee on the making or granting of an application for registration;

   (f)   the imposition of conditions on registration and the variation or cancellation of such conditions;

   (g)   the circumstances in which a person's registration may be, or be regarded as, cancelled;

   (h)   the making of appeals against any determination of a children's services authority in England in relation to a person's registration;

   (i)   temporary registration, or circumstances in which a person may be regarded as registered;

(j) requirements to be complied with by a children's services authority in England or a person registered under the regulations.

(3) The provision which may be made under subsection (2)(a) includes provision that any person who, in an application for registration under the regulations, knowingly makes a statement which is false or misleading in a material particular is guilty of an offence and liable on summary conviction to a fine not exceeding level 5 on the standard scale.

(4) The requirements for which provision may be made under subsection (2)(b) include requirements relating to—

(a) the suitability of the applicant to foster children privately;

(b) the suitability of the premises in which it is proposed to foster children privately (including their suitability by reference to any other person living there).

(5) The provision which may be made under subsection (2)(c) includes provision that a person may be disqualified where—

(a) an order of a kind specified in the regulations has been made at any time with respect to him;

(b) an order of a kind so specified has been made at any time with respect to any child who has been in his care;

(c) a requirement of a kind so specified has been imposed at any time with respect to any such child, under or by virtue of any enactment;

(d) he has been convicted of a criminal offence of a kind so specified, or a probation order has been made in respect of him for any such offence or he has been discharged absolutely or conditionally for any such offence;

(e) a prohibition has been imposed on him under any specified enactment;

(f) his rights and powers with respect to a child have at any time been vested in a specified authority under a specified enactment;

(g) he lives in the same household as a person who is himself disqualified from being registered or in a household in which such a person is employed.

(6) The provision which may be made under subsection (2)(c) also includes provision for a children's services authority in England to determine whether a person is or is not to be disqualified.

(7) The conditions for which provision may be made under subsection (2)(f) include conditions relating to—

(a) the maintenance of premises in which children are, or are proposed to be, privately fostered;

(b) any other persons living at such premises.

(8) The provision which may be made under subsection (2)(j) includes—

(a) a requirement that a person registered under the regulations obtain the consent of the children's services authority in England by whom he is registered before privately fostering a child;

(b) provision relating to the giving of such consent (including provision as to the circumstances in which, or conditions subject to which, it may or must be given).

(9) The provision which may be made under subsection (2)(j) also includes—

(a) a requirement for a children's services authority in England to undertake annual inspections in relation to persons registered under the regulations (whether in fact privately fostering children or not); and

(b) provision for the payment of a fee by registered persons in respect of such inspections.

(10) Regulations under this section may—

(a) authorise a children's services authority in England to issue a notice to any person whom they believe to be fostering a child privately in their area without being registered in accordance with the regulations; and

(b) provide that a person who, without reasonable excuse, fosters a child privately without being registered in accordance with the regulations while such a notice is issued in respect of him is guilty of an offence and liable on summary conviction to a fine not exceeding level 5 on the standard scale.

(11) Regulations under this section may provide that a person registered under the regulations who without reasonable excuse contravenes or otherwise fails to comply with any requirement imposed on him in the regulations is guilty of an offence and liable on summary conviction to a fine not exceeding level 5 on the standard scale.

(12) Regulations under this section may provide that a person who fosters a child privately while he is disqualified from being registered is guilty of an offence unless—

(a) he is disqualified by virtue of the fact that he lives in the same household as a person who is himself disqualified from being registered or in a household in which such a person is employed; and

(b) he did not know, and had no reasonable grounds for believing, that that person was so disqualified.

(13) Where regulations under this section make provision under subsection (12), they must provide that a person who is guilty of the offence referred to in that subsection is liable on summary conviction to—

(a) a fine not exceeding level 5 on the standard scale, or

(b) a term of imprisonment not exceeding 51 weeks (or, in the case of an offence committed before the commencement of section 281(5) of the Criminal Justice Act 2003 (c 44), not exceeding six months), or

(c) both.

(14) Regulations under this section may—

(a) make consequential amendments (including repeals) to sections 67(2) to (6) and 68 to 70 of, and paragraphs 6 to 9 of Schedule 8 to, the Children Act 1989 (c 41);

(b) amend Schedule 1 to the Local Authority Social Services Act 1970 (c 42) (social services functions) as to add functions of a children's services authority in England under this section to the functions listed in that Schedule.

(15) Nothing in this section affects the scope of section 66(1).

(16) For the purposes of this section references to a person fostering a child privately have the same meaning as in the Children Act 1989.
[Children Act 2004, s 45.]

---

1. Part 5 contains ss 46–63.

6–3206S   46. Power to establish registration scheme in Wales. (1) The Assembly may by regulations require any person who fosters a child privately in the area of a children's services authority in Wales to be registered for private fostering by that authority in accordance with the regulations.

(2) Subsections (2) to (15) of section 45 apply in relation to regulations under this section as they apply in relation to regulations under that section with the substitution for references to a children's services authority in England of references to a children's services authority in Wales.

(3) Subsection (16) of that section applies for the purposes of this section.
[Children Act 2004, s 46.]

6–3206T   47. Expiry of powers in sections 45 and 46. (1) If no regulations have been made under section 45 by the relevant time, that section shall (other than for the purposes of section 46(2) and (3)) cease to have effect at that time.

(2) If no regulations have been made under section 46 by the relevant time, that section shall cease to have effect at that time.

(3) In this section, the relevant time is the end of the period of four years beginning with the day on which this Act is passed.
[Children Act 2004, s 47.]

Child minding and day care

6–3206U   48. Child minding and day care. Schedule 4 (which makes provision amending Part 10A of the Children Act 1989 (c 41) in relation to child minding and day care) has effect.
[Children Act 2004, s 48.]

Local authority services

6–3206V   49. Payments to foster parents. (1) The appropriate person may by order make provision as to the payments to be made—

(a) by a children's services authority in England or Wales or a person exercising functions on its behalf to a local authority foster parent with whom any child is placed by that authority or person under section 23(2)(a) of the Children Act 1989;

(b) by a voluntary organisation to any person with whom any child is placed by that organisation under section 59(1)(a) of that Act.

(2) In subsection (1)—

"appropriate person" means—

(a) the Secretary of State, in relation to a children's services authority in England;

(b) the Assembly, in relation to a children's services authority in Wales;

"local authority foster parent" and "voluntary organisation" have the same meanings as in the Children Act 1989.

(3) In section 23(2)(a) of the Children Act 1989, at the end insert "(subject to section 49 of the Children Act 2004)".

(4) In section 59(1)(a) of that Act, at the end insert "(subject to section 49 of the Children Act 2004)".
[Children Act 2004, s 49.]

6–3206W 50. Intervention. (1) Section 497A of the Education Act 1996 (c 56) (power to secure proper performance of a local education authority's functions) applies in relation to—

(a) the relevant functions of a children's services authority in England, and
(b) the relevant functions of a children's services authority in Wales,

as it applies in relation to the functions of a local education authority referred to in subsection (1) of that section.

(2) For the purposes of this section, the relevant functions of a children's services authority in England or Wales are—

(a) functions conferred on or exercisable by the authority which are social services functions, so far as those functions relate to children;
(b) the functions conferred on the authority under sections 23C to 24D of the Children Act 1989 (so far as not falling within paragraph (a)); and
(c) the functions conferred on the authority under sections 10, 12 and 17 above (in the case of a children's services authority in England) or under sections 25, 26 and 29 above (in the case of a children's services authority in Wales).

(3) In subsection (2)(a) "social services functions" has the same meaning as in the the Local Authority Social Services Act 1970 (c 42).

(4) Sections 497AA and 497B of the Education Act 1996 apply accordingly where powers under section 497A of that Act are exercised in relation to any of the relevant functions of a children's services authority in England or Wales.

(5) In the application of sections 497A(2) to (7), 497AA and 497B of that Act in relation to the relevant functions of a children's services authority in England or Wales, references to the local education authority are to be read as references to the children's services authority in England or Wales.

(6) In subsection (5) of section 497A of that Act, the reference to functions to which that section applies includes (for all purposes) relevant functions of a children's services authority in England or Wales.
[Children Act 2004, s 50.]

6–3206X 51. Inspection of local education authorities. *Amends s 38 of the Education Act 1997, which is not reproduced in this work.*

6–3206Y 52. Duty of local authorities to promote educational achievement. *Inserts new subs (3A) in s 22 of the Children Act 1989: see this PART, ante.*

6–3206Z 53. Ascertaining children's wishes. *Inserts new subs (4A) in s 17 of the Children Act 1989, amends s 20 and inserts new subs (5A) in that Act: see this PART, ante.*

6–3207 54. Information about individual children. *Inserts new subs (4A) in s 83 of the Children Act 1989: see this PART, ante.*

6–3207A 55. Social services committees

6–3207B 56. Social services functions

Other provisions

6–3207C 57. Fees payable to adoption review panel members

6–3207D 58. Reasonable punishment. (1) In relation to any offence specified in subsection (2), battery of a child cannot be justified on the ground that it constituted reasonable punishment.

(2) The offences referred to in subsection (1) are—

(a) an offence under section 18 or 20 of the Offences against the Person Act 1861 (c 100) (wounding and causing grievous bodily harm);
(b) an offence under section 47 of that Act (assault occasioning actual bodily harm);
(c) an offence under section 1 of the Children and Young Persons Act 1933 (c 12) (cruelty to persons under 16).

(3) Battery of a child causing actual bodily harm to the child cannot be justified in any civil proceedings on the ground that it constituted reasonable punishment.

(4) For the purposes of subsection (3) "actual bodily harm" has the same meaning as it has for the purposes of section 47 of the Offences against the Person Act 1861.

(5) In section 1 of the Children and Young Persons Act 1933, omit subsection (7).
[Children Act 2004, s 58.]

6–3207E   59. Power to give financial assistance.   *Amends s 14, and the heading to* PART 2, *of the Education Act 2002, which are not reproduced in this work.*

6–3207F   60. Child safety orders.   *Amends ss 8, 11 and 12 of the Crime and Disorder Act 1998.*

6–3207G   61. Children's Commissioner for Wales: powers of entry.   *Amends s 76 of the Care Standards Act 2000, which is not reproduced in this work.*

6–3207H   62. Publication of material relating to legal proceedings.   (1) In section 97(2) of the Children Act 1989 (c 41) (privacy for children involved in certain proceedings), after "publish" insert "to the public at large or any section of the public".

(2) In section 12(4) of the Administration of Justice Act 1960 (c 65) (publication of information relating to proceedings in private), at the end insert "(and in particular where the publication is not so punishable by reason of being authorised by rules of court)".

(3) In section 66 of the Adoption Act 1976 (c 36) (rules of procedure), after subsection (5) insert—

> "(5A) Rules may, for the purposes of the law relating to contempt of court, authorise the publication in such circumstances as may be specified of information relating to proceedings held in private involving children."

(4) In section 145(1) of the Magistrates' Courts Act 1980 (c 43) (rules: supplementary), after paragraph (g) insert—

> "(ga) authorising, for the purposes of the law relating to contempt of court, the publication in such circumstances as may be specified of information relating to proceedings referred to in section 12(1)(a) of the Administration of Justice Act 1960 which are held in private;".

(5) In section 40(4) of the Matrimonial and Family Proceedings Act 1984 (c 42) (family proceedings rules), in paragraph (a) after "County Courts Act 1984;" insert—

> "(aa) authorise, for the purposes of the law relating to contempt of court, the publication in such circumstances as may be specified of information relating to family proceedings held in private;".

(6) In section 141 of the Adoption and Children Act 2002 (c 38) (rules of procedure) at the end insert—

> "(6) Rules may, for the purposes of the law relating to contempt of court, authorise the publication in such circumstances as may be specified of information relating to proceedings held in private involving children."

(7) In section 76 of the Courts Act 2003 (c 39) (Family Procedure Rules: further provision) after subsection (2) insert—

> "(2A) Family Procedure Rules may, for the purposes of the law relating to contempt of court, authorise the publication in such circumstances as may be specified of information relating to family proceedings held in private."

[Children Act 2004, s 62.]

6–3207I   63. Disclosure of information by Inland Revenue.   *Inserts new para 10A in Schedule 5 to the Tax Credits Act 2002.*

PART 6[1]
GENERAL

6–3207J   64. Repeals.   The enactments specified in Schedule 5 are repealed to the extent specified.
[Children Act 2004, s 64.]

---

1. Part 6 contains ss 66–69.

6–3207K   65. Interpretation.   (1) In this Act—

"the Assembly" means the National Assembly for Wales;

"child" means, subject to section 9, a person under the age of eighteen (and "children" is to be construed accordingly);

"children's services authority in England" means—

    (a) a county council in England;
    (b) a metropolitan district council;
    (c) a non-metropolitan district council for an area for which there is no county council;
    (d) a London borough council;

    (e) the Common Council of the City of London;

    (f) the Council of the Isles of Scilly;

"children's services authority in Wales" means a county council or county borough council in Wales.

(2) This Act applies in relation to the Isles of Scilly subject to such modifications as may be specified by order made by the Secretary of State.

(3) In this Act—

    (a) references to a prison include a young offender institution;

    (b) references to a contracted out secure training centre, and to the contractor in relation to such a secure training centre, have the meanings given by section 15 of the Criminal Justice and Public Order Act 1994 (c 33);

    (c) references to a contracted out prison, and to the contractor in relation to such a prison, have the meanings given by section 84(4) of the Criminal Justice Act 1991 (c 53).

(4) Where—

    (a) a contract under section 7 of the Criminal Justice and Public Order Act 1994 is for the time being in force in relation to part of a secure training centre, or

    (b) a contract under section 84 of the Criminal Justice Act 1991 is for the time being in force in relation to part of a prison,

this Act has effect as if each part of the secure training centre or prison were a separate institution.
[Children Act 2004, s 65.]

6–3207L 66. Regulations and orders. (1) Any power to make regulations or an order under this Act includes power—

    (a) to make different provision for different purposes;

    (b) to make different provision for different cases or areas;

    (c) to make incidental, supplementary, consequential or transitional provision or savings.

(2) Any power to make regulations or an order under this Act, other than an order under section 42 or 43, is exercisable by statutory instrument.

(3) The Secretary of State may not make a statutory instrument containing regulations under section 12 or 45 unless a draft of the instrument has been laid before, and approved by resolution of, each House of Parliament.

(4) The Secretary of State may not make a statutory instrument containing the first order under section 49 unless a draft of the instrument has been laid before, and approved by resolution of, each House of Parliament.

(5) A statutory instrument containing—

    (a) any regulations made by the Secretary of State under this Act to which subsection (3) does not apply,

    (b) an order made by the Secretary of State under section 49 to which subsection (4) does not apply, or

    (c) an order made by the Secretary of State under section 11(1)(d) or section 65(2),

is subject to annulment in pursuance of a resolution of either House of Parliament.

(6) Subsection (5) does not apply to regulations made by the Secretary of State jointly with the Assembly under section 43(7).
[Children Act 2004, s 66.]

6–3207M 67. Commencement[1]. (1) Part 1 comes into force on the day on which this Act is passed.

(2) Part 2 comes into force in accordance with provision made by order by the Secretary of State.

(3) Part 3 comes into force in accordance with provision made by order by the Assembly subject to subsections (4) and (5).

(4) The Assembly must obtain the consent of the Secretary of State before making provision under subsection (3) in relation to section 25(4)(a) to (c) or 31(3)(a) to (c), (f) or (g).

(5) In section 28, the following provisions come into force in accordance with provision made by order by the Secretary of State after consulting the Assembly—

    (a) subsection (1)(d) to (h);

    (b) subsection (2), so far as relating to the persons and bodies referred to in subsection (1)(d) to (h);

    (c) subsection (5).

(6) Part 4 comes into force in accordance with provision made by order by the Assembly with the consent of the Secretary of State.

(7) In Part 5—

(a) section 44 so far as relating to England comes into force in accordance with provision made by order by the Secretary of State, and so far as relating to Wales in accordance with provision made by order by the Assembly;

(b) sections 45 to 47 come into force at the end of the period of two months beginning with the day on which this Act is passed;

(c) section 48 and Schedule 4 so far as relating to England come into force in accordance with provision made by order by the Secretary of State, and so far as relating to Wales in accordance with provision made by order by the Assembly;

(d) section 49 comes into force at the end of the period of two months beginning with the day on which this Act is passed;

(e) sections 50 to 57 so far as relating to England come into force in accordance with provision made by order by the Secretary of State, and so far as relating to Wales in accordance with provision made by order by the Assembly;

(f) section 58 comes into force at the end of the period of two months beginning with the day on which this Act is passed;

(g) section 59 comes into force on the day on which this Act is passed;

(h) section 60 comes into force in accordance with provision made by order by the Secretary of State;

(i) section 61 comes into force in accordance with provision made by order by the Assembly;

(j) section 62 comes into force in accordance with provision made by order by the Lord Chancellor;

(k) section 63 comes into force on the day on which this Act is passed.

(8) This Part comes into force on the day on which this Act is passed except that Schedule 5 comes into force in accordance with the commencement provisions set out in that Schedule.
[Children Act 2004, s 67.]

---

1. At the time of going to press the following commencement orders had been made: Children Act 2004 (Commencement No 1) Order 2005, SI 2005/394; Children Act 2004 (Commencement No 2) Order 2005, SI 2005/700; and Children Act 2004 (Commencement No 3) Order 2005, SI 2005/847.

6–3207N 68. Extent. (1) Part 1 extends to the whole of the United Kingdom (unless otherwise specifically provided).

(2) Parts 2 to 4 extend to England and Wales only.

(3) In Part 5—

(a) sections 44 to 62 extend to England and Wales only;
(b) section 63 extends to the whole of the United Kingdom.

(4) In this Part—

(a) section 64 and Schedule 5 extend to England and Wales only; and
(b) the remaining provisions extend to the whole of the United Kingdom.
[Children Act 2004, s 68.]

6–3207O 69. Short title. This Act may be cited as the Children Act 2004.
[Children Act 2004, s 69.]

Section 1   SCHEDULE 1
                          CHILDREN'S COMMISSIONER

6–3207P *Evidence*
   9. (1) A document purporting to be duly executed under the seal of the Children's Commissioner or to be signed by him or on his behalf is to be received in evidence and, unless the contrary is proved, taken to be so executed or signed.
   (2) This paragraph does not extend to Scotland.

6–3207Q   SCHEDULE 2[1]
          DIRECTOR OF CHILDREN'S SERVICES: CONSEQUENTIAL AMENDMENTS

---

1. Amendments of provisions that appear in this work will be shown when the amendments come into force.

6–3207R   SCHEDULE 3[1]
          ADVISORY AND SUPPORT SERVICES FOR FAMILY PROCEEDINGS

---

1. Amends various enactments. Amendments of provisions that appear in this work will be shown when the amendments come into force.

6–3207S   SCHEDULE 4[1]
               CHILD MINDING AND DAY CARE

---

1. Amends Part 10A of, and Schedule 9A to, the Children Act 1989.

SCHEDULE 5[1]
REPEALS

1. Repeals of provisions reproduced in this work will be shown when they take effect.

Civil Partnership Act 2004[1]

(2004 c 33)

PART 1[2]
Introduction

6–3208 1. Civil partnership. (1) A civil partnership is a relationship between two people of the same sex ("civil partners")—

(a) which is formed when they register as civil partners of each other—

    (i) in England or Wales (under Part 2),

    (ii) in Scotland (under Part 3),

    (iii) in Northern Ireland (under Part 4), or

    (iv) outside the United Kingdom under an Order in Council made under Chapter 1 of Part 5 (registration at British consulates etc or by armed forces personnel), or

(b) which they are treated under Chapter 2 of Part 5 as having formed (at the time determined under that Chapter) by virtue of having registered an overseas relationship.

(2) Subsection (1) is subject to the provisions of this Act under or by virtue of which a civil partnership is void.

(3) A civil partnership ends only on death, dissolution or annulment.

(4) The references in subsection (3) to dissolution and annulment are to dissolution and annulment having effect under or recognised in accordance with this Act.

(5) References in this Act to an overseas relationship are to be read in accordance with Chapter 2 of Part 5.

[Civil Partnership Act 2004, s 1.]

1. This Act enables two people of the same sex who are in a relationship to register as civil partners. Various rights and obligations stem from such registrations.

The Act will be brought into force in accordance with commencement orders made under s 263. At the time of going to press the following commencement order had been made: Civil Partnership Act 2004 (Commencement No 1) Order 2005, SI 2005/1112.

The Act contains 8 Parts and 30 Schedules.

2. Part 1 contains s 1.

PART 2[1]
CIVIL PARTNERSHIP: ENGLAND AND WALES

CHAPTER 1[2]
Registration

Formation, eligibility and parental etc consent

6–3208A 2. Formation of civil partnership by registration. (1) For the purposes of section 1, two people are to be regarded as having registered as civil partners of each other once each of them has signed the civil partnership document—

(a) at the invitation of, and in the presence of, a civil partnership registrar, and

(b) in the presence of each other and two witnesses.

(2) Subsection (1) applies regardless of whether subsections (3) and (4) are complied with.

(3) After the civil partnership document has been signed under subsection (1), it must also be signed, in the presence of the civil partners and each other, by—

(a) each of the two witnesses, and

(b) the civil partnership registrar.

(4) After the witnesses and the civil partnership registrar have signed the civil partnership document, the relevant registration authority must ensure that—

(a) the fact that the two people have registered as civil partners of each other, and

(b) any other information prescribed by regulations[3],

is recorded in the register as soon as is practicable.

(5) No religious service is to be used while the civil partnership registrar is officiating at the signing of a civil partnership document.

(6) "The civil partnership document" has the meaning given by section 7(1).

(7) "The relevant registration authority" means the registration authority in whose area the registration takes place.
[Civil Partnership Act 2004, s 2.]

---

1. Part 2 contains ss 2–84.
2. Chapter 1 contains ss 2–36.
3. The Civil Partnership (Registration Provisions) Regulations 2005, SI 2005/3176 have been made.

6–3208B   3. Eligibility.   (1) Two people are not eligible to register as civil partners of each other if—

   (a) they are not of the same sex,
   (b) either of them is already a civil partner or lawfully married,
   (c) either of them is under 16, or
   (d) they are within prohibited degrees of relationship.

  (2) Part 1 of Schedule 1 contains provisions for determining when two people are within prohibited degrees of relationship.
[Civil Partnership Act 2004, s 3.]

6–3208C   4. Parental etc consent where proposed civil partner under 18.   (1) The consent of the appropriate persons is required before a child and another person may register as civil partners of each other.
  (2) Part 1 of Schedule 2 contains provisions for determining who are the appropriate persons for the purposes of this section.
  (3) The requirement of consent under subsection (1) does not apply if the child is a surviving civil partner.
  (4) Nothing in this section affects any need to obtain the consent of the High Court before a ward of court and another person may register as civil partners of each other.
  (5) In this Part "child", except where used to express a relationship, means a person who is under 18.
[Civil Partnership Act 2004, s 4.]

Registration procedure: general

6–3208D   5. Types of pre-registration procedure.   (1) Two people may register as civil partners of each other under—

   (a) the standard procedure;
   (b) the procedure for house-bound persons;
   (c) the procedure for detained persons;
   (d) the special procedure (which is for cases where a person is seriously ill and not expected to recover).

  (2) The procedures referred to in subsection (1)(a) to (c) are subject to—

   (a) section 20 (modified procedures for certain non-residents);
   (b) Schedule 3 (former spouses one of whom has changed sex).

  (3) The procedures referred to in subsection (1) (including the procedures as modified by section 20 and Schedule 3) are subject to—

   (a) Part 2 of Schedule 1 (provisions applicable in connection with prohibited degrees of relationship), and
   (b) Parts 2 and 3 of Schedule 2 (provisions applicable where proposed civil partner is under 18).

  (4) This section is also subject to section 249 and Schedule 23 (immigration control and formation of civil partnerships).
[Civil Partnership Act 2004, s 5.]

6–3208E   6. Place of registration.   (1) The place at which two people may register as civil partners of each other—

   (a) must be in England or Wales,
   (b) must not be in religious premises, and
   (c) must be specified in the notices, or notice, of proposed civil partnership required by this Chapter.

  (2) "Religious premises" means premises which—

   (a) are used solely or mainly for religious purposes, or
   (b) have been so used and have not subsequently been used solely or mainly for other purposes.

  (3) Subsections (3A) and (3B) apply in the case of registration under the standard procedure (including that procedure modified as mentioned in section 5).
  (3A) The place must be—

   (a) on approved premises, or

(b) in a register office.

(3B) If it is in a register office, the place must be open to any person wishing to attend the registration.

(3C) In this Chapter "register office" means a register office provided under section 10 of the Registration Service Act 1953.

(4) *Repealed.*

(5) *Repealed.*

[Civil Partnership Act 2004, s 6 as amended by SI 2005/2000.]

6–3208EA 6A. Power to approve premises. (1) The Chancellor of the Exchequer may by regulations[1] make provision for and in connection with the approval by registration authorities of premises for the purposes of section 6(3A)(a).

(2) The matters dealt with by regulations may include—

(a) the kind of premises in respect of which approvals may be granted;

(b) the procedure to be followed in relation to applications for approval;

(c) the considerations to be taken into account by a registration authority in determining whether to approve any premises;

(d) the duration and renewal of approvals;

(e) the conditions that must or may be imposed by a registration authority on granting or renewing an approval;

(f) the determination and charging by registration authorities of fees in respect of applications for the approval of premises and in respect of the renewal of approvals;

(g) the circumstances in which a registration authority must or may revoke an approval;

(h) the review of any decision to refuse an approval or the renewal of an approval, to impose conditions on granting or renewing an approval or to revoke an approval;

(i) the notification to the Registrar General of all approvals granted, renewed or revoked;

(j) the keeping by registration authorities of registers of approved premises;

(k) the issue by the Registrar General of guidance supplementing the provision made by the regulations.

(3) Without prejudice to the width of subsection (2)(e), the Chancellor of the Exchequer must exercise his power to provide for the imposition of conditions as mentioned there so as to secure that members of the public are permitted to attend when two people sign the civil partnership schedule on approved premises in accordance with section 6(3A)(a).

[Civil Partnership Act 2004, s 6A as inserted by SI 2005/2000.]

---

1. The Marriages and Civil Partnerships (Approved Premises) Regulations 2005, SI 2005/3168 have been made.

6–3208F 7. The civil partnership document. (1) In this Part "the civil partnership document" means—

(a) in relation to the special procedure, a Registrar General's licence, and

(b) in relation to any other procedure, a civil partnership schedule.

(2) Before two people are entitled to register as civil partners of each other—

(a) the civil partnership document must be delivered to the civil partnership registrar, and

(b) the civil partnership registrar may then ask them for any information required (under section 2(4)) to be recorded in the register.

[Civil Partnership Act 2004, s 7.]

The standard procedure

6–3208G 8. Notice of proposed civil partnership and declaration. (1) For two people to register as civil partners of each other under the standard procedure, each of them must—

(a) give a notice of proposed civil partnership to a registration authority, and

(b) have resided in England or Wales for at least 7 days immediately before giving the notice.*

(2) A notice of proposed civil partnership must contain such information as may be prescribed by regulations[1].

(3) A notice of proposed civil partnership must also include the necessary declaration, made and signed by the person giving the notice—

(a) at the time when the notice is given, and

(b) in the presence of an authorised person;

and the authorised person must attest the declaration by adding his name, description and place of residence.

(4) The necessary declaration is a solemn declaration in writing—

(a) that the proposed civil partner believes that there is no impediment of kindred or affinity or other lawful hindrance to the formation of the civil partnership;

    (b) that each of the proposed civil partners has had a usual place of residence in England or Wales for at least 7 days immediately before giving the notice.*

    (5) Where a notice of proposed civil partnership is given to a registration authority in accordance with this section, the registration authority must ensure that the following information is recorded in the register as soon as possible—

    (a) the fact that the notice has been given and the information in it;
    (b) the fact that the authorised person has attested the declaration.

    (6) "Authorised person" means an employee or officer or other person provided by a registration authority who is authorised by that authority to attest notices of proposed civil partnership.

    (7) For the purposes of this Chapter, a notice of proposed civil partnership is recorded when subsection (5) is complied with.
[Civil Partnership Act 2004, s 8.]

---

    *Subsection (1) and (4)(*b*) substituted by SI 2005/2000 from 5 December 2005.
    1. The Civil Partnership (Registration Provisions) Regulations 2005, SI 2005/3176 have been made.

6–3208H   9. Power to require evidence of name etc.   (1) The registration authority to which a notice of proposed civil partnership is given may require the person giving the notice to provide it with specified evidence—

    (a) relating to that person, or
    (b) if the registration authority considers that the circumstances are exceptional, relating not only to that person but also to that person's proposed civil partner.

    (2) Such a requirement may be imposed at any time before the registration authority issues the civil partnership schedule under section 14.

    (3) "Specified evidence", in relation to a person, means such evidence as may be specified in guidance issued by the Registrar General—

    (a) of the person's name and surname,
    (b) of the person's age,
    (c) as to whether the person has previously formed a civil partnership or a marriage and, if so, as to the ending of the civil partnership or marriage,
    (d) of the person's nationality, and
    (e) as to the person's residence in England or Wales during the period of 7 days preceding the giving of a notice of proposed civil partnership by that person.*
[Civil Partnership Act 2004, s 9.]

---

    *Amended by SI 2005/2000 from 5 December 2005.

6–3208I   10. Proposed civil partnership to be publicised.   (1) Where a notice of proposed civil partnership has been given to a registration authority, the relevant information must be publicised during the waiting period—

    (a) by that registration authority,
    (b) by any registration authority in whose area the person giving the notice has resided during the period of 7 days preceding the giving of the notice,
    (c) by any registration authority in whose area the proposed civil partner of the person giving the notice has resided during the period of 7 days preceding the giving of that notice,
    (d) by the registration authority in whose area the place specified in the notice as the place of proposed registration is located, and
    (e) by the Registrar General.

    (2) "The relevant information" means—

    (a) the name of the person giving the notice,
    (b) the name of that person's proposed civil partner, and
    (c) such other information as may be prescribed by regulations.*
[Civil Partnership Act 2004, s 10.]

---

    *Amended by SI 2005/2000 from 5 December 2005.

6–3208J   11. Meaning of "the waiting period".   In this Chapter "the waiting period", in relation to a notice of proposed civil partnership, means the period—

    (a) beginning the day after the notice is recorded, and
    (b) subject to section 12, ending at the end of the period of 15 days beginning with that day.
[Civil Partnership Act 2004, s 11.]

6–3208K   12. Power to shorten the waiting period.   (1) If the Registrar General, on an application being made to him, is satisfied that there are compelling reasons because of the exceptional circumstances of the case for shortening the period of 15 days mentioned in section 11(b), he may shorten it to such period as he considers appropriate.

(2) Regulations[1] may make provision with respect to the making, and granting, of applications under subsection (1).

(3) Regulations under subsection (2) may provide for—

(a) the power conferred by subsection (1) to be exercised by a registration authority on behalf of the Registrar General in such classes of case as are prescribed by the regulations;

(b) the making of an appeal to the Registrar General against a decision taken by a registration authority in accordance with regulations made by virtue of paragraph (a).

[Civil Partnership Act 2004, s 12.]

1. The Civil Partnership (Registration Provisions) Regulations 2005, SI 2005/3176 have been made.

6–3208L 13. Objection to proposed civil partnership. (1) Any person may object to the issue of a civil partnership schedule under section 14 by giving any registration authority notice of his objection.

(2) A notice of objection must—

(a) state the objector's place of residence and the ground of objection, and

(b) be signed by or on behalf of the objector.

(3) If a notice of objection is given to a registration authority, it must ensure that the fact that it has been given and the information in it are recorded in the register as soon as possible.

[Civil Partnership Act 2004, s 13.]

6–3208M 14. Issue of civil partnership schedule. (1) As soon as the waiting period in relation to each notice of proposed civil partnership has expired, the registration authority in whose area it is proposed that the registration take place is under a duty, at the request of one or both of the proposed civil partners, to issue a document to be known as a "civil partnership schedule".

(2) Regulations[1] may make provision as to the contents of a civil partnership schedule.

(3) The duty in subsection (1) does not apply if the registration authority is not satisfied that there is no lawful impediment to the formation of the civil partnership.

(4) If an objection to the issue of the civil partnership schedule has been recorded in the register, no civil partnership schedule is to be issued until—

(a) the relevant registration authority has investigated the objection and is satisfied that the objection ought not to obstruct the issue of the civil partnership schedule, or

(b) the objection has been withdrawn by the person who made it.

(5) "The relevant registration authority" means the authority which first records that a notice of proposed civil partnership has been given by one of the proposed civil partners.

[Civil Partnership Act 2004, s 14.]

1. The Civil Partnership (Registration Provisions) Regulations 2005, SI 2005/3176 have been made.

6–3208N 15. Appeal against refusal to issue civil partnership schedule. (1) If the registration authority refuses to issue a civil partnership schedule—

(a) because an objection to its issue has been made under section 13, or

(b) in reliance on section 14(3),

either of the proposed civil partners may appeal to the Registrar General.

(2) On an appeal under this section the Registrar General must either confirm the refusal or direct that a civil partnership schedule be issued.

[Civil Partnership Act 2004, s 15.]

6–3208O 16. Frivolous objections and representations: liability for costs etc. (1) Subsection (3) applies if—

(a) a person objects to the issue of a civil partnership schedule, but

(b) the Registrar General declares that the grounds on which the objection is made are frivolous and ought not to obstruct the issue of the civil partnership schedule.

(2) Subsection (3) also applies if—

(a) in reliance on section 14(3), the registration authority refuses to issue a civil partnership schedule as a result of a representation made to it, and

(b) on an appeal under section 15 against the refusal, the Registrar General declares that the representation is frivolous and ought not to obstruct the issue of the civil partnership schedule.

(3) The person who made the objection or representation is liable for—

(a) the costs of the proceedings before the Registrar General, and

(b) damages recoverable by the proposed civil partner to whom the objection or representation relates.

(4) For the purpose of enabling any person to recover any such costs and damages, a copy of a declaration of the Registrar General purporting to be sealed with the seal of the General Register Office is evidence that the Registrar General has made the declaration.
[Civil Partnership Act 2004, s 16.]

6–3208P   17. Period during which registration may take place. (1) The proposed civil partners may not register as civil partners of each other on the production of the civil partnership schedule until the waiting period in relation to each notice of proposed civil partnership has expired.

(2) Subject to subsection (1), under the standard procedure, they may register as civil partners by signing the civil partnership schedule at any time during the applicable period.*

(3) If they do not register as civil partners by signing the civil partnership schedule before the end of the applicable period—

(a) the notices of proposed civil partnership and the civil partnership schedule are void, and
(b) no civil partnership registrar may officiate at the signing of the civil partnership schedule by them.

(4) The applicable period, in relation to two people registering as civil partners of each other, is the period of 12 months beginning with—

(a) the day on which the notices of proposed civil partnership are recorded, or
(b) if the notices are not recorded on the same day, the earlier of those days.
[Civil Partnership Act 2004, s 17.]

---

*Amended by SI 2005/2000 from 5 December 2005.

The procedures for house-bound and detained persons

6–3208Q   18. House-bound persons. (1) This section applies if two people wish to register as civil partners of each other at the place where one of them is house-bound.

(2) A person is house-bound at any place if, in relation to that person, a statement is made by a registered medical practitioner that, in his opinion—

(a) because of illness or disability, that person ought not to move or be moved from the place where he is at the time when the statement is made, and
(b) it is likely to be the case for at least the following 3 months that because of the illness or disability that person ought not to move or be moved from that place.

(3) The procedure under which the two people concerned may register as civil partners of each other is the same as the standard procedure, except that—

(a) each notice of proposed civil partnership must be accompanied by a statement under subsection (2) ("a medical statement"), which must have been made not more than 14 days before the day on which the notice is recorded,
(b) the fact that the registration authority to whom the notice is given has received the medical statement must be recorded in the register, and
(c) the applicable period (for the purposes of section 17) is the period of 3 months beginning with—

(i) the day on which the notices of proposed civil partnership are recorded, or
(ii) if the notices are not recorded on the same day, the earlier of those days.

(4) A medical statement must contain such information and must be made in such manner as may be prescribed by regulations[1].

(5) A medical statement may not be made in relation to a person who is detained as described in section 19(2).

(6) For the purposes of this Chapter, a person in relation to whom a medical statement is made is to be treated, if he would not otherwise be so treated, as resident and usually resident at the place where he is for the time being.
[Civil Partnership Act 2004, s 18.]

---

1. The Civil Partnership (Registration Provisions) Regulations 2005, SI 2005/3176 have been made.

6–3208R   19. Detained persons. (1) This section applies if two people wish to register as civil partners of each other at the place where one of them is detained.

(2) "Detained" means detained—

(a) as a patient in a hospital (but otherwise than by virtue of section 2, 4, 5, 35, 36 or 136 of the Mental Health Act 1983 (c 20) (short term detentions)), or
(b) in a prison or other place to which the Prison Act 1952 (c 52) applies.

(3) The procedure under which the two people concerned may register as civil partners of each other is the same as the standard procedure, except that—

(a) each notice of proposed civil partnership must be accompanied by a supporting statement, which must have been made not more than 21 days before the day on which the notice is recorded,

(b) the fact that the registration authority to whom the notice is given has received the supporting statement must be recorded in the register, and

(c) the applicable period (for the purposes of section 17) is the period of 3 months beginning with—

  (i) the day on which the notices of proposed civil partnership are recorded, or

  (ii) if the notices are not recorded on the same day, the earlier of those days.

(4) A supporting statement, in relation to a detained person, is a statement made by the responsible authority which—

(a) identifies the establishment where the person is detained, and

(b) states that the responsible authority has no objection to that establishment being specified in a notice of proposed civil partnership as the place at which the person is to register as a civil partner.

(5) A supporting statement must contain such information and must be made in such manner as may be prescribed by regulations[1].

(6) "The responsible authority" means—

(a) if the person is detained in a hospital, the hospital's managers;

(b) if the person is detained in a prison or other place to which the 1952 Act applies, the governor or other officer for the time being in charge of that prison or other place.

(7) "Patient" and "hospital" have the same meaning as in Part 2 of the 1983 Act and "managers", in relation to a hospital, has the same meaning as in section 145(1) of the 1983 Act.

(8) For the purposes of this Chapter, a detained person is to be treated, if he would not otherwise be so treated, as resident and usually resident at the place where he is for the time being.
[Civil Partnership Act 2004, s 19.]

---

  1. The Civil Partnership (Registration Provisions) Regulations 2005, SI 2005/3176 have been made.

Modified procedures for certain non-residents

6–3208S   20. Modified procedures for certain non-residents. (1) Subsection (5) applies in the following three cases.

(2) The first is where—

(a) two people wish to register as civil partners of each other in England and Wales, and

(b) one of them ("A") resides in Scotland and the other ("B") resides in England or Wales.

(3) The second is where—

(a) two people wish to register as civil partners of each other in England and Wales, and

(b) one of them ("A") resides in Northern Ireland and the other ("B") resides in England or Wales.

(4) The third is where—

(a) two people wish to register as civil partners of each other in England and Wales, and

(b) one of them ("A") is a member of Her Majesty's forces who is serving outside the United Kingdom and the other ("B") resides in England or Wales.

(5) For the purposes of the standard procedure, the procedure for house-bound persons and the procedure for detained persons—

(a) A is not required to give a notice of proposed civil partnership under this Chapter;

(b) B may give a notice of proposed civil partnership and make the necessary declaration without regard to the requirement that would otherwise apply that A must reside in England or Wales;

(c) the waiting period is calculated by reference to the day on which B's notice is recorded;

(d) the civil partnership schedule is not to be issued by a registration authority unless A or B produces to that registration authority a certificate of no impediment issued to A under the relevant provision;

(e) the applicable period is calculated by reference to the day on which B's notice is recorded and, where the standard procedure is used in the first and second cases, is the period of 3 months beginning with that day;

(f) section 31 applies as if in subsections (1)(a) and (2)(c) for "each notice" there were substituted "B's notice".

(6) "The relevant provision" means—

(a) if A resides in Scotland, section 97;

(b) if A resides in Northern Ireland, section 150;

(c) if A is a member of Her Majesty's forces who is serving outside the United Kingdom, section 239.

(7) "Her Majesty's forces" has the same meaning as in the Army Act 1955 (3 & 4 Eliz 2 c 18).*
[Civil Partnership Act 2004, s 20.]

---

*Amended by SI 2005/2000 from 5 December 2005.

The special procedure

6–3208T   21. Notice of proposed civil partnership.   (1) For two people to register as civil partners of each other under the special procedure, one of them must—

  (a)   give a notice of proposed civil partnership to the registration authority for the area in which it is proposed that the registration take place, and

  (b)   comply with any requirement made under section 22.

(2) The notice must contain such information as may be prescribed by regulations[1].

(3) Subsections (3) to (6) of section 8 (necessary declaration etc), apart from paragraph (b) of subsection (4), apply for the purposes of this section as they apply for the purposes of that section.
[Civil Partnership Act 2004, s 21.]

---

1. The Civil Partnership (Registration Provisions) Regulations 2005, SI 2005/3176 have been made.

6–3208U   22. Evidence to be produced.   (1) The person giving a notice of proposed civil partnership to a registration authority under the special procedure must produce to the authority such evidence as the Registrar General may require to satisfy him—

  (a)   that there is no lawful impediment to the formation of the civil partnership,

  (b)   that the conditions in subsection (2) are met, and

  (c)   that there is sufficient reason why a licence should be granted.

(2) The conditions are that one of the proposed civil partners—

  (a)   is seriously ill and not expected to recover, and

  (b)   understands the nature and purport of signing a Registrar General's licence.*

(3) The certificate of a registered medical practitioner is sufficient evidence of any or all of the matters referred to in subsection (2).
[Civil Partnership Act 2004, s 22.]

---

*Substituted by SI 2005/2000 from 5 December 2005.

6–3208V   23. Application to be reported to Registrar General.   On receiving a notice of proposed civil partnership under section 21 and any evidence under section 22, the registration authority must—

  (a)   inform the Registrar General, and

  (b)   comply with any directions the Registrar General may give for verifying the evidence given.
[Civil Partnership Act 2004, s 23.]

6–3208W   24. Objection to issue of Registrar General's licence.   (1) Any person may object to the Registrar General giving authority for the issue of his licence by giving the Registrar General or any registration authority notice of his objection.

(2) A notice of objection must—

  (a)   state the objector's place of residence and the ground of objection, and

  (b)   be signed by or on behalf of the objector.

(3) If a notice of objection is given to a registration authority, it must ensure that the fact that it has been given and the information in it are recorded in the register as soon as possible.
[Civil Partnership Act 2004, s 24.]

6–3208X   25. Issue of Registrar General's licence.   (1) This section applies where a notice of proposed civil partnership is given to a registration authority under section 21.

(2) The registration authority may issue a Registrar General's licence if, and only if, given authority to do so by the Registrar General.

(3) The Registrar General—

  (a)   may not give his authority unless he is satisfied that one of the proposed civil partners is seriously ill and not expected to recover, but

  (b)   if so satisfied, must give his authority unless a lawful impediment to the issue of his licence has been shown to his satisfaction to exist.

(4) A licence under this section must state that it is issued on the authority of the Registrar General.

(5) Regulations[1] may (subject to subsection (4)) make provision as to the contents of a licence under this section.

(6) If an objection has been made to the Registrar General giving authority for the issue of his licence, he is not to give that authority until—

(a) he has investigated the objection and decided whether it ought to obstruct the issue of his licence, or

(b) the objection has been withdrawn by the person who made it.

(7) Any decision of the Registrar General under subsection (6)(a) is final.
[Civil Partnership Act 2004, s 25.]

---

1. The Civil Partnership (Registration Provisions) Regulations 2005, SI 2005/3176 have been made.

6–3208Y 26. Frivolous objections: liability for costs. (1) This section applies if—

(a) a person objects to the Registrar General giving authority for the issue of his licence, but

(b) the Registrar General declares that the grounds on which the objection is made are frivolous and ought not to obstruct the issue of his licence.

(2) The person who made the objection is liable for—

(a) the costs of the proceedings before the Registrar General, and

(b) damages recoverable by the proposed civil partner to whom the objection relates.

(3) For the purpose of enabling any person to recover any such costs and damages, a copy of a declaration of the Registrar General purporting to be sealed with the seal of the General Register Office is evidence that the Registrar General has made the declaration.
[Civil Partnership Act 2004, s 26.]

6–3208Z 27. Period during which registration may take place. (1) If a Registrar General's licence has been issued under section 25, the proposed civil partners may register as civil partners by signing it at any time within 1 month from the day on which the notice of proposed civil partnership was given.

(2) If they do not register as civil partners by signing the licence within the 1 month period—

(a) the notice of proposed civil partnership and the licence are void, and

(b) no civil partnership registrar may officiate at the signing of the licence by them.
[Civil Partnership Act 2004, s 27.]

Supplementary

6–3209 28. Registration authorities. In this Chapter "registration authority" means—

(a) in relation to England, a county council, the council of any district comprised in an area for which there is no county council, a London borough council, the Common Council of the City of London or the Council of the Isles of Scilly;

(b) in relation to Wales, a county council or a county borough council.
[Civil Partnership Act 2004, s 28.]

6–3209A 29. Civil partnership registrars. (1) A civil partnership registrar is an individual who is designated by a registration authority as a civil partnership registrar for its area.

(2) It is the duty of each registration authority to ensure that there is a sufficient number of civil partnership registrars for its area to carry out in that area the functions of civil partnership registrars.

(3) Each registration authority must inform the Registrar General as soon as is practicable—

(a) of any designation it has made of a person as a civil partnership registrar, and

(b) of the ending of any such designation.

(4) The Registrar General must make available to the public a list—

(a) of civil partnership registrars, and

(b) of the registration authorities for which they are designated to act.*
[Civil Partnership Act 2004, s 29.]

*****Repealed by SI 2005/2000 from 5 December 2005.**

6–3209B 30. The Registrar General and the register. (1) In this Chapter "the Registrar General" means the Registrar General for England and Wales.

(2) The Registrar General must provide a system for keeping any records that relate to civil partnerships and are required by this Chapter to be made.

(3) The system may, in particular, enable those records to be kept together with other records kept by the Registrar General.

(4) In this Chapter "the register" means the system for keeping records provided under subsection (2).
[Civil Partnership Act 2004, s 30.]

6–3209C   31. Offences relating to civil partnership schedule.   (1) A person commits an offence if he issues a civil partnership schedule knowing that he does so—

(a)   before the waiting period in relation to each notice of proposed civil partnership has expired,

(b)   after the end of the applicable period, or

(c)   at a time when its issue has been forbidden under Schedule 2 by a person entitled to forbid its issue.

(2) A person commits an offence if, in his actual or purported capacity as a civil partnership registrar, he officiates at the signing of a civil partnership schedule by proposed civil partners knowing that he does so—

(a)   at a place other than the place specified in the notices of proposed civil partnership and the civil partnership schedule,

(b)   in the absence of a civil partnership registrar,

(c)   before the waiting period in relation to each notice of proposed civil partnership has expired, or

(d)   even though the civil partnership is void under section 49(b) or (c).

(3) A person guilty of an offence under subsection (1) or (2) is liable on conviction on indictment to imprisonment for a term not exceeding 5 years or to a fine (or both).

(4) A prosecution under this section may not be commenced more than 3 years after the commission of the offence.*

[Civil Partnership Act 2004, s 31.]

---

*Amended by SI 2005/2000 from 5 December 2005.

6–3209D   32. Offences relating to Registrar General's licence.   (1) A person commits an offence if—

(a)   he gives information by way of evidence in response to a requirement under section 22(1), knowing that the information is false;

(b)   he gives a certificate as provided for by section 22(3), knowing that the certificate is false.

(2) A person commits an offence if, in his actual or purported capacity as a civil partnership registrar, he officiates at the signing of a Registrar General's licence by proposed civil partners knowing that he does so—

(a)   at a place other than the place specified in the licence,

(b)   in the absence of a civil partnership registrar,

(c)   after the end of 1 month from the day on which the notice of proposed civil partnership was given, or

(d)   even though the civil partnership is void under section 49(b) or (c).

(3) A person guilty of an offence under subsection (1) or (2) is liable—

(a)   on conviction on indictment, to imprisonment not exceeding 3 years or to a fine (or both);

(b)   on summary conviction, to a fine not exceeding the statutory maximum.

(4) A prosecution under this section may not be commenced more than 3 years after the commission of the offence.

[Civil Partnership Act 2004, s 32.]

6–3209E   33. Offences relating to the recording of civil partnerships.   (1) A civil partnership registrar commits an offence if he refuses or fails to comply with the provisions of this Chapter or of any regulations made under section 36.

(2) A civil partnership registrar guilty of an offence under subsection (1) is liable—

(a)   on conviction on indictment, to imprisonment for a term not exceeding 2 years or to a fine (or both);

(b)   on summary conviction, to a fine not exceeding the statutory maximum;

and on conviction shall cease to be a civil partnership registrar.

(3) A person commits an offence if—

(a)   under arrangements made by a registration authority for the purposes of section 2(4), he is under a duty to record information required to be recorded under section 2(4), but

(b)   he refuses or without reasonable cause omits to do so.

(4) A person guilty of an offence under subsection (3) is liable on summary conviction to a fine not exceeding level 3 on the standard scale.

(5) A person commits an offence if he records in the register information relating to the formation of a civil partnership by the signing of a civil partnership schedule, knowing that the civil partnership is void under section 49(b) or (c).

(6) A person guilty of an offence under subsection (5) is liable on conviction on indictment, to imprisonment for a term not exceeding 5 years or to a fine (or both).

(7) A person commits an offence if he records in the register information relating to the formation

of a civil partnership by the signing of a Registrar General's licence, knowing that the civil partnership is void under section 49(b) or (c).

(8) A person guilty of an offence under subsection (7) is liable—

(a) on conviction on indictment, to imprisonment for a term not exceeding 3 years or to a fine (or both);

(b) on summary conviction, to a fine not exceeding the statutory maximum.

(9) A prosecution under subsection (5) or (7) may not be commenced more than 3 years after the commission of the offence.
[Civil Partnership Act 2004, s 33.]

6–3209F   34. Fees

6–3209G   35. Power to assimilate provisions relating to civil registration

6–3209H   36. Regulations and orders. (1) Regulations may make provision supplementing the provisions of this Chapter.

(2) Regulations may in particular make provision—

(a) relating to the use of Welsh in documents and records relating to civil partnerships;

(b) with respect to the retention of documents relating to civil partnerships;

(c) prescribing the duties of civil partnership registrars;

(d) prescribing the duties of persons in whose presence any declaration is made for the purposes of this Chapter;

(e) for the issue by the Registrar General of guidance supplementing any provision made by the regulations.

(f) for the issue by registration authorities or the Registrar General of certified copies of entries in the register and for such copies to be received in evidence.

(3) In this Chapter, except in section 6A, "regulations" means regulations made by the Registrar General with the approval of the Chancellor of the Exchequer.

(4) Any power to make regulations or an order under this Chapter is exercisable by statutory instrument.

(5) A statutory instrument containing regulations under section 6A or an order under section 34 is subject to annulment in pursuance of a resolution of either House of Parliament.

(6) No order may be made under section 35 unless a draft of the statutory instrument containing the order has been laid before, and approved by a resolution of, each House of Parliament.
[Civil Partnership Act 2004, s 36 as amended by SI 2005/2000.]

CHAPTER 2[1]
Dissolution, Nullity and other Proceedings

---

1. Chapter 2 contains ss 37–64. Chapter 2 enables the High Court, or a county court with jurisdiction by virtue of Part 5 of the Matrimonial Proceedings Act 1984, to make a "dissolution order", a "nullity order" a "presumption of death order" or a "separation order" in relation to a civil partnership. The provisions of this chapter are not reproduced in this work.

CHAPTER 3[1]
Property and Financial Arrangements

6–3209I   72. Financial relief for civil partners and children of family. (1) Schedule 5 makes provision for financial relief in connection with civil partnerships that corresponds to provision made for financial relief in connection with marriages by Part 2 of the Matrimonial Causes Act 1973 (c 18).

(2) Any rule of law under which any provision of Part 2 of the 1973 Act is interpreted as applying to dissolution of a marriage on the ground of presumed death is to be treated as applying (with any necessary modifications) in relation to the corresponding provision of Schedule 5.

(3) Schedule 6 makes provision for financial relief in connection with civil partnerships that corresponds to provision made for financial relief in connection with marriages by the Domestic Proceedings and Magistrates' Courts Act 1978 (c 22).

(4) Schedule 7 makes provision for financial relief in England and Wales after a civil partnership has been dissolved or annulled, or civil partners have been legally separated, in a country outside the British Islands.
[Civil Partnership Act 2004, s 72.]

---

1. Chapter 3 contains ss 65–72.

CHAPTER 4[1]
Civil Partnership Agreements

---

1. Chapter 4 contains ss 73 and 74.

CHAPTER 5[1]

Children

6–3209J   75. Parental responsibility, children of the family and relatives.   (1) Amend the Children Act 1989 (c 41) ("the 1989 Act") as follows.

(2) In section 4A(1) (acquisition of parental responsibility by step-parent) after "is married to" insert ", or a civil partner of,".

(3) In section 105(1) (interpretation), for the definition of "child of the family" (in relation to the parties to a marriage) substitute—

> ""child of the family", in relation to parties to a marriage, or to two people who are civil partners of each other, means—
>
> > (a) a child of both of them, and
> >
> > (b) any other child, other than a child placed with them as foster parents by a local authority or voluntary organisation, who has been treated by both of them as a child of their family."

(4) In the definition of "relative" in section 105(1), for "by affinity)" substitute "by marriage or civil partnership)".

[Civil Partnership Act 2004, s 75.]

---

1. Chapter 5 contains ss 75–79.

6–3209K   76. Guardianship.   *Amends s 6 of the Children Act1989 Act.*

6–3209L   77. Entitlement to apply for residence or contact order.   *Amends s 10 of the Children Act 1989.*

6–3209M   78. Financial provision for children.   *Amends Schedule 1 to the Children Act 1989.*

79. Adoption.   (1) Amend the Adoption and Children Act 2002 (c 38) as follows.

(2) In section 21 (placement orders), in subsection (4)(c), after "child marries" insert ", forms a civil partnership".

(3) In section 47 (conditions for making adoption orders), after subsection (8) insert—

> "(8A) An adoption order may not be made in relation to a person who is or has been a civil partner."

(4) In section 51 (adoption by one person), in subsection (1), after "is not married" insert "or a civil partner".

(5) After section 51(3) insert—

> "(3A) An adoption order may be made on the application of one person who has attained the age of 21 years and is a civil partner if the court is satisfied that—
>
> > (a) the person's civil partner cannot be found,
> >
> > (b) the civil partners have separated and are living apart, and the separation is likely to be permanent, or
> >
> > (c) the person's civil partner is by reason of ill-health, whether physical or mental, incapable of making an application for an adoption order."

(6) In section 64 (other provision to be made by regulations), in subsection (5) for "or marriage" substitute ", marriage or civil partnership".

(7) In section 74(1) (enactments for whose purposes section 67 does not apply), for paragraph (a) substitute—

> "(a) section 1 of and Schedule 1 to the Marriage Act 1949 or Schedule 1 to the Civil Partnership Act 2004 (prohibited degrees of kindred and affinity)," .

(8) In section 79 (connections between the register and birth records), in subsection (7)—

> (a) in paragraph (b), after "intends to be married" insert "or form a civil partnership", and
>
> (b) for "the person whom the applicant intends to marry" substitute "the intended spouse or civil partner".

(9) In section 81 (Adoption Contact Register: supplementary), in subsection (2) for "or marriage" substitute ", marriage or civil partnership".

(10) In section 98 (pre-commencement adoptions: information), in subsection (7), in the definition of "relative" for "or marriage" substitute ", marriage or civil partnership".

(11) In section 144 (interpretation), in the definition of "relative" in subsection (1), after "by marriage" insert "or civil partnership".

(12) In section 144(4) (meaning of "couple"), after paragraph (a) insert—

> "(aa) two people who are civil partners of each other, or" .

[Civil Partnership Act 2004, s 79.]

CHAPTER 6[1]
Miscellaneous

6–3209O   80. False statements etc with reference to civil partnerships.   (1)   A person commits an offence if—

(a)   for the purpose of procuring the formation of a civil partnership, or a document mentioned in subsection (2), he—

(i)   makes or signs a declaration required under this Part or Part 5, or
(ii)   gives a notice or certificate so required,

knowing that the declaration, notice or certificate is false,

(b)   for the purpose of a record being made in any register relating to civil partnerships, he—

(i)   makes a statement as to any information which is required to be registered under this Part or Part 5, or
(ii)   causes such a statement to be made,

knowing that the statement is false,

(c)   he forbids the issue of a document mentioned in subsection (2)(a) or (b) by representing himself to be a person whose consent to a civil partnership between a child and another person is required under this Part or Part 5, knowing the representation to be false, or
(d)   with respect to a declaration made under paragraph 5(1) of Schedule 1 he makes a statement mentioned in paragraph 6 of that Schedule which he knows to be false in a material particular.

(2)   The documents are—

(a)   a civil partnership schedule or a Registrar General's licence under Chapter 1;
(b)   a document required by an Order in Council under section 210 or 211 as an authority for two people to register as civil partners of each other;
(c)   a certificate of no impediment under section 240.

(3)   A person guilty of an offence under subsection (1) is liable—

(a)   on conviction on indictment, to imprisonment for a term not exceeding 7 years or to a fine (or both);
(b)   on summary conviction, to a fine not exceeding the statutory maximum.

(4)   The Perjury Act 1911 (c 6) has effect as if this section were contained in it.
[Civil Partnership Act 2004, s 80.]

---

1.   Chapter 6 contains ss 80–84.

6–3209P   81. Housing and tenancies

6–3209Q   82. Family homes and domestic violence.   Schedule 9 amends Part 4 of the Family Law Act 1996 (c 27) and related enactments so that they apply in relation to civil partnerships as they apply in relation to marriages.
[Civil Partnership Act 2004, s 82.]

6–3209R   83. Fatal accidents claims

6–3209S   84. Evidence.   (1)   Any enactment or rule of law relating to the giving of evidence by a spouse applies in relation to a civil partner as it applies in relation to the spouse.
(2)   Subsection (1) is subject to any specific amendment made by or under this Act which relates to the giving of evidence by a civil partner.
(3)   For the avoidance of doubt, in any such amendment, references to a person's civil partner do not include a former civil partner.
(4)   References in subsections (1) and (2) to giving evidence are to giving evidence in any way (whether by supplying information, making discovery, producing documents or otherwise).
(5)   Any rule of law—

(a)   which is preserved by section 7(3) of the Civil Evidence Act 1995 (c 38) or section 118(1) of the Criminal Justice Act 2003 (c 44), and
(b)   under which in any proceedings evidence of reputation or family tradition is admissible for the purpose of proving or disproving the existence of a marriage,

is to be treated as applying in an equivalent way for the purpose of proving or disproving the existence of a civil partnership.
[Civil Partnership Act 2004, s 84.]

PART 3

CIVIL PARTNERSHIP: SCOTLAND

PART 4

CIVIL PARTNERSHIP: NORTHERN IRELAND

PART 5[1]

CIVIL PARTNERSHIP FORMED OR DISSOLVED ABROAD ETC

CHAPTER 1

REGISTRATION OUTSIDE UK UNDER ORDER IN COUNCIL

CHAPTER 2

OVERSEAS RELATIONSHIPS TREATED AS CIVIL PARTNERSHIPS

---

1. Part 5 contains ss 210–245.

CHAPTER 3[1]

Dissolution etc: Jurisdiction and Recognition

Introduction

6–3209T   219. Power to make provision corresponding to EC Regulation 2201/2003. (1) The Lord Chancellor may by regulations make provision—

(a) as to the jurisdiction of courts in England and Wales or Northern Ireland in proceedings for the dissolution or annulment of a civil partnership or for legal separation of the civil partners in cases where a civil partner—

    (i) is or has been habitually resident in a member State,

    (ii) is a national of a member State, or

    (iii) is domiciled in a part of the United Kingdom or the Republic of Ireland, and

(b) as to the recognition in England and Wales or Northern Ireland of any judgment of a court of another member State which orders the dissolution or annulment of a civil partnership or the legal separation of the civil partners.

(2) The Scottish Ministers may by regulations make provision—

(a) as to the jurisdiction of courts in Scotland in proceedings for the dissolution or annulment of a civil partnership or for legal separation of the civil partners in such cases as are mentioned in subsection (1)(a), and

(b) as to the recognition in Scotland of any such judgment as is mentioned in subsection (1)(b).

(3) The regulations may in particular make provision corresponding to that made by Council Regulation (EC) No 2201/2003 of 27th November 2003 in relation to jurisdiction and the recognition and enforcement of judgments in matrimonial matters.

(4) The regulations may provide that for the purposes of this Part and the regulations "member State" means—

(a) all member States with the exception of such member States as are specified in the regulations, or

(b) such member States as are specified in the regulations.

(5) The regulations may make provision under subsections (1)(b) and (2)(b) which applies even if the date of the dissolution, annulment or legal separation is earlier than the date on which this section comes into force.

(6) Regulations under subsection (1) are to be made by statutory instrument and may only be made if a draft has been laid before and approved by resolution of each House of Parliament.

(7) Regulations under subsection (2) are to be made by statutory instrument and may only be made if a draft has been laid before and approved by resolution of the Scottish Parliament.

(8) In this Part "section 219 regulations" means regulations made under this section.

[Civil Partnership Act 2004, s 219.]

---

1. Chapter 3 contains ss 219–238.

Recognition of dissolution, annulment and separation

6–3209U   233. Effect of dissolution, annulment or separation obtained in the UK. (1) No dissolution or annulment of a civil partnership obtained in one part of the United Kingdom is effective in any part of the United Kingdom unless obtained from a court of civil jurisdiction.

(2) Subject to subsections (3) and (4), the validity of a dissolution or annulment of a civil partnership or a legal separation of civil partners which has been obtained from a court of civil jurisdiction in one part of the United Kingdom is to be recognised throughout the United Kingdom.

(3) Recognition of the validity of a dissolution, annulment or legal separation obtained from a

court of civil jurisdiction in one part of the United Kingdom may be refused in any other part if the dissolution, annulment or separation was obtained at a time when it was irreconcilable with a decision determining the question of the subsistence or validity of the civil partnership—

    (a)   previously given by a court of civil jurisdiction in the other part, or

    (b)   previously given by a court elsewhere and recognised or entitled to be recognised in the other part.

    (4) Recognition of the validity of a dissolution or legal separation obtained from a court of civil jurisdiction in one part of the United Kingdom may be refused in any other part if the dissolution or separation was obtained at a time when, according to the law of the other part, there was no subsisting civil partnership.

[Civil Partnership Act 2004, s 233.]

6–3209V   234. Recognition in the UK of overseas dissolution, annulment or separation.
    (1) Subject to subsection (2), the validity of an overseas dissolution, annulment or legal separation is to be recognised in the United Kingdom if, and only if, it is entitled to recognition by virtue of sections 235 to 237.

    (2) This section and sections 235 to 237 do not apply to an overseas dissolution, annulment or legal separation as regards which provision as to recognition is made by section 219 regulations.

    (3) For the purposes of subsections (1) and (2) and sections 235 to 237, an overseas dissolution, annulment or legal separation is a dissolution or annulment of a civil partnership or a legal separation of civil partners which has been obtained outside the United Kingdom (whether before or after this section comes into force).

[Civil Partnership Act 2004, s 234.]

6–3209W   235. Grounds for recognition.   (1) The validity of an overseas dissolution, annulment or legal separation obtained by means of proceedings is to be recognised if—

    (a)   the dissolution, annulment or legal separation is effective under the law of the country in which it was obtained, and

    (b)   at the relevant date either civil partner—

        (i)   was habitually resident in the country in which the dissolution, annulment or legal separation was obtained,

        (ii)   was domiciled in that country, or

        (iii)   was a national of that country.

    (2) The validity of an overseas dissolution, annulment or legal separation obtained otherwise than by means of proceedings is to be recognised if—

    (a)   the dissolution, annulment or legal separation is effective under the law of the country in which it was obtained,

    (b)   at the relevant date—

        (i)   each civil partner was domiciled in that country, or

        (ii)   either civil partner was domiciled in that country and the other was domiciled in a country under whose law the dissolution, annulment or legal separation is recognised as valid, and

    (c)   neither civil partner was habitually resident in the United Kingdom throughout the period of 1 year immediately preceding that date.

    (3) In this section "the relevant date" means—

    (a)   in the case of an overseas dissolution, annulment or legal separation obtained by means of proceedings, the date of the commencement of the proceedings;

    (b)   in the case of an overseas dissolution, annulment or legal separation obtained otherwise than by means of proceedings, the date on which it was obtained.

    (4) Where in the case of an overseas annulment the relevant date fell after the death of either civil partner, any reference in subsection (1) or (2) to that date is to be read in relation to that civil partner as a reference to the date of death.

[Civil Partnership Act 2004, s 235.]

6–3209X   236. Refusal of recognition.   (1) Recognition of the validity of an overseas dissolution, annulment or legal separation may be refused in any part of the United Kingdom if the dissolution, annulment or separation was obtained at a time when it was irreconcilable with a decision determining the question of the subsistence or validity of the civil partnership—

    (a)   previously given by a court of civil jurisdiction in that part of the United Kingdom, or

    (b)   previously given by a court elsewhere and recognised or entitled to be recognised in that part of the United Kingdom.

    (2) Recognition of the validity of an overseas dissolution or legal separation may be refused in any part of the United Kingdom if the dissolution or separation was obtained at a time when, according to the law of that part of the United Kingdom, there was no subsisting civil partnership.

(3) Recognition of the validity of an overseas dissolution, annulment or legal separation may be refused if—

    (a) in the case of a dissolution, annulment or legal separation obtained by means of proceedings, it was obtained—

        (i) without such steps having been taken for giving notice of the proceedings to a civil partner as, having regard to the nature of the proceedings and all the circumstances, should reasonably have been taken, or

        (ii) without a civil partner having been given (for any reason other than lack of notice) such opportunity to take part in the proceedings as, having regard to those matters, he should reasonably have been given, or

    (b) in the case of a dissolution, annulment or legal separation obtained otherwise than by means of proceedings—

        (i) there is no official document certifying that the dissolution, annulment or legal separation is effective under the law of the country in which it was obtained, or

        (ii) where either civil partner was domiciled in another country at the relevant date, there is no official document certifying that the dissolution, annulment or legal separation is recognised as valid under the law of that other country, or

    (c) in either case, recognition of the dissolution, annulment or legal separation would be manifestly contrary to public policy.

(4) In this section—

"official", in relation to a document certifying that a dissolution, annulment or legal separation is effective, or is recognised as valid, under the law of any country, means issued by a person or body appointed or recognised for the purpose under that law;

"the relevant date" has the same meaning as in section 235.

[Civil Partnership Act 2004, s 236.]

6–3209Y 237. Supplementary provisions relating to recognition of dissolution etc. (1) For the purposes of sections 235 and 236, a civil partner is to be treated as domiciled in a country if he was domiciled in that country—

    (a) according to the law of that country in family matters, or

    (b) according to the law of the part of the United Kingdom in which the question of recognition arises.

(2) The Lord Chancellor or the Scottish Ministers may by regulations[1] make provision—

    (a) applying sections 235 and 236 and subsection (1) with modifications in relation to any country whose territories have different systems of law in force in matters of dissolution, annulment or legal separation;

    (b) applying sections 235 and 236 with modifications in relation to—

        (i) an overseas dissolution, annulment or legal separation in the case of an overseas relationship (or an apparent or alleged overseas relationship);

        (ii) any case where a civil partner is domiciled in a country or territory whose law does not recognise legal relationships between two people of the same sex;

    (c) with respect to recognition of the validity of an overseas dissolution, annulment or legal separation in cases where there are cross-proceedings;

    (d) with respect to cases where a legal separation is converted under the law of the country or territory in which it is obtained into a dissolution which is effective under the law of that country or territory;

    (e) with respect to proof of findings of fact made in proceedings in any country or territory outside the United Kingdom.

(3) The power to make regulations under subsection (2) is exercisable by statutory instrument.

(4) A statutory instrument containing such regulations—

    (a) if made by the Lord Chancellor, is subject to annulment in pursuance of a resolution of either House of Parliament;

    (b) if made by the Scottish Ministers, is subject to annulment in pursuance of a resolution of the Scottish Parliament.

(5) In this section (except subsection (4)) and sections 233 to 236 and 238—

"annulment" includes any order annulling a civil partnership, however expressed;

"part of the United Kingdom" means England and Wales, Scotland or Northern Ireland;

"proceedings" means judicial or other proceedings.

(6) Nothing in this Chapter is to be read as requiring the recognition of any finding of fault made in proceedings for dissolution, annulment or legal separation or of any maintenance, custody or other ancillary order made in any such proceedings.

[Civil Partnership Act 2004, s 237.]

1. The Civil Partnership (Supplementary Provisions Relating to the Recognition of Overseas Dissolutions, Annulments or Legal Separations) (England and Wales and Northern Ireland) Regulations 2005, SI 2005/3104 have been made.

6–3209Z   238. Non-recognition elsewhere of dissolution or annulment.   (1) This section applies where, in any part of the United Kingdom—

    (a)   a dissolution or annulment of a civil partnership has been granted by a court of civil jurisdiction, or

    (b)   the validity of a dissolution or annulment of a civil partnership is recognised by virtue of this Chapter.

(2) The fact that the dissolution or annulment would not be recognised outside the United Kingdom does not—

    (a)   preclude either party from forming a subsequent civil partnership or marriage in that part of the United Kingdom, or

    (b)   cause the subsequent civil partnership or marriage of either party (wherever it takes place) to be treated as invalid in that part.

[Civil Partnership Act 2004, s 238.]

CHAPTER 4[1]
Miscellaneous and Supplementary

6–3210   245. Interpretation.   (1) In this Part "United Kingdom national" means a person who is—

    (a)   a British citizen, a British overseas territories citizen, a British Overseas citizen or a British National (Overseas),

    (b)   a British subject under the British Nationality Act 1981 (c 61), or

    (c)   a British protected person, within the meaning of that Act.

(2) In this Part "Her Majesty's forces" has the same meaning as in the Army Act 1955 (3 & 4
[Civil Partnership Act 2004, s 245.]

1. Chapter 4 contains ss 239–245.

PART 6[1]
RELATIONSHIPS ARISING THROUGH CIVIL PARTNERSHIP

6–3210A   246. Interpretation of statutory references to stepchildren etc.   (1) In any provision to which this section applies, references to a stepchild or step-parent of a person (here, "A"), and cognate expressions, are to be read as follows—

A's stepchild includes a person who is the child of A's civil partner (but is not A's child);
A's step-parent includes a person who is the civil partner of A's parent (but is not A's parent);
A's stepdaughter includes a person who is the daughter of A's civil partner (but is not A's daughter);
A's stepson includes a person who is the son of A's civil partner (but is not A's son);
A's stepfather includes a person who is the civil partner of A's father (but is not A's parent);
A's stepmother includes a person who is the civil partner of A's mother (but is not A's parent);
A's stepbrother includes a person who is the son of the civil partner of A's parent (but is not the son of either of A's parents);
A's stepsister includes a person who is the daughter of the civil partner of A's parent (but is not the daughter of either of A's parents).

(2) For the purposes of any provision to which this section applies—

"brother-in-law" includes civil partner's brother,
"daughter-in-law" includes daughter's civil partner,
"father-in-law" includes civil partner's father,
"mother-in-law" includes civil partner's mother,
"parent-in-law" includes civil partner's parent,
"sister-in-law" includes civil partner's sister, and
"son-in-law" includes son's civil partner.

[Civil Partnership Act 2004, s 246.]

1. Part 6 contains ss 246–248.

6–3210B   247. Provisions to which section 246 applies: Acts of Parliament etc.   (1) Section 246 applies to—

    (a)   any provision listed in Schedule 21 (references to stepchildren, in-laws etc in existing Acts),

    (b)   except in so far as otherwise provided, any provision made by a future Act, and

    (c)   except in so far as otherwise provided, any provision made by future subordinate legislation.

(2) A Minister of the Crown may by order[1]—

(a) amend Schedule 21 by adding to it any provision of an existing Act;
(b) provide for section 246 to apply to prescribed provisions of existing subordinate legislation.

(3) The power conferred by subsection (2) is also exercisable—
(a) by the Scottish Ministers, in relation to a relevant Scottish provision;
(b) by a Northern Ireland department, in relation to a provision which deals with a transferred matter;
(c) by the National Assembly for Wales, if the order is made by virtue of subsection (2)(b) and deals with matters with respect to which functions are exercisable by the Assembly.

(4) Subject to subsection (5), the power to make an order under subsection (2) is exercisable by statutory instrument.
(5) Any power of a Northern Ireland department to make an order under subsection (2) is exercisable by statutory rule for the purposes of the Statutory Rules (Northern Ireland) Order 1979 (SI 1979/1573 (NI 12)).
(6) A statutory instrument containing an order under subsection (2) made by a Minister of the Crown is subject to annulment in pursuance of a resolution of either House of Parliament.
(7) A statutory instrument containing an order under subsection (2) made by the Scottish Ministers is subject to annulment in pursuance of a resolution of the Scottish Parliament.
(8) A statutory rule containing an order under subsection (2) made by a Northern Ireland department is subject to negative resolution (within the meaning of section 41(6) of the Interpretation Act (Northern Ireland) 1954 (c 33 (NI))).
(9) In this section—
"Act" includes an Act of the Scottish Parliament;
"existing Act" means an Act passed on or before the last day of the Session in which this Act is passed;
"existing subordinate legislation" means subordinate legislation made before the day on which this section comes into force;
"future Act" means an Act passed after the last day of the Session in which this Act is passed;
"future subordinate legislation" means subordinate legislation made on or after the day on which this section comes into force;
"Minister of the Crown" has the same meaning as in the Ministers of the Crown Act 1975 (c 26);
"prescribed" means prescribed by the order;
"relevant Scottish provision" means a provision that would be within the legislative competence of the Scottish Parliament if it were included in an Act of that Parliament;
"subordinate legislation" has the same meaning as in the Interpretation Act 1978 (c 30) except that it includes an instrument made under an Act of the Scottish Parliament;
"transferred matter" has the meaning given by section 4(1) of the Northern Ireland Act 1998 (c 47) and "deals with" in relation to a transferred matter is to be construed in accordance with section 98(2) and (3) of the 1998 Act.
[Civil Partnership Act 2004, s 247.]

1. The Civil Partnership Act 2004 (Relationships Arising Through Civil Partnership) Order 2005, SI 2005/3137 has been made.

6–3210C   248. Provisions to which section 246 applies: Northern Ireland

PART 7[1]
MISCELLANEOUS

6–3210D   249. Immigration control and formation of civil partnerships.   Schedule 23 contains provisions relating to the formation of civil partnerships in the United Kingdom by persons subject to immigration control.
[Civil Partnership Act 2004, s 249.]

1. Part 7 contains ss 249–251.

6–3210E   250. Gender recognition where applicant a civil partner.   (1) Amend the Gender Recognition Act 2004 (c 7) as follows.
(2) In—
(a) section 3 (evidence), in subsection (6)(a), and
(b) section 4 (successful applications), in subsections (2) and (3),
after "is married" insert "or a civil partner".
(3) In section 5 (subsequent issue of full certificates)—
(a) in subsection (2), after "is again married" insert "or is a civil partner",
(b) in subsection (6)(a), for "is not married" substitute "is neither married nor a civil partner", and
(c) for the heading substitute "Issue of full certificates where applicant has been married".

(4) After section 5 insert—

"5A. Issue of full certificates where applicant has been a civil partner. (1) A court which—

(a) makes final a nullity order made on the ground that an interim gender recognition certificate has been issued to a civil partner, or

(b) (in Scotland) grants a decree of dissolution on that ground,

must, on doing so, issue a full gender recognition certificate to that civil partner and send a copy to the Secretary of State.

(2) If an interim gender recognition certificate has been issued to a person and either—

(a) the person's civil partnership is dissolved or annulled (otherwise than on the ground mentioned in subsection (1)) in proceedings instituted during the period of six months beginning with the day on which it was issued, or

(b) the person's civil partner dies within that period,

the person may make an application for a full gender recognition certificate at any time within the period specified in subsection (3) (unless the person is again a civil partner or is married).

(3) That period is the period of six months beginning with the day on which the civil partnership is dissolved or annulled or the death occurs.

(4) An application under subsection (2) must include evidence of the dissolution or annulment of the civil partnership and the date on which proceedings for it were instituted, or of the death of the civil partner and the date on which it occurred.

(5) An application under subsection (2) is to be determined by a Gender Recognition Panel.

(6) The Panel—

(a) must grant the application if satisfied that the applicant is neither a civil partner nor married, and

(b) otherwise must reject it.

(7) If the Panel grants the application it must issue a full gender recognition certificate to the applicant."

(5) In—

(a) section 7 (applications: supplementary), in subsection (1),

(b) section 8 (appeals etc), in subsections (1) and (5), and

(c) section 22 (prohibition on disclosure of information), in subsection (2)(a),

after "5(2)" insert ", 5A(2)".

(6) In section 21 (foreign gender change and marriage), in subsection (4), after "entered into a later (valid) marriage" insert "or civil partnership".

(7) In section 25 (interpretation), in the definition of "full gender recognition certificate" and "interim gender recognition certificate", for "or 5" substitute ", 5 or 5A".

(8) In Schedule 1 (Gender Recognition Panels), in paragraph 5, after "5(2)" insert ", 5A(2)".

(9) In Schedule 3 (registration), in paragraphs 9(1), 19(1) and 29(1), for "or 5(2)" substitute ", 5(2) or 5A(2)".

[Civil Partnership Act 2004, s 250.]

6–3210F   251. Discrimination against civil partners in employment field. (1) Amend the Sex Discrimination Act 1975 (c 65) as follows.

(2) For section 3 (discrimination against married persons in employment field) substitute—

"3. Discrimination against married persons and civil partners in employment field.
(1) In any circumstances relevant for the purposes of any provision of Part 2, a person discriminates against a person ("A") who fulfils the condition in subsection (2) if—

(a) on the ground of the fulfilment of the condition, he treats A less favourably than he treats or would treat a person who does not fulfil the condition, or

(b) he applies to A a provision, criterion or practice which he applies or would apply equally to a person who does not fulfil the condition, but—

(i) which puts or would put persons fulfilling the condition at a particular disadvantage when compared with persons not fulfilling the condition, and

(ii) which puts A at that disadvantage, and

(iii) which he cannot show to be a proportionate means of achieving a legitimate aim.

(2) The condition is that the person is—

(a) married, or

(b) a civil partner.

(3) For the purposes of subsection (1), a provision of Part 2 framed with reference to discrimination against women is to be treated as applying equally to the treatment of men, and for that purpose has effect with such modifications as are requisite."

(3) In section 5 (interpretation), for subsection (3) substitute—

"(3) Each of the following comparisons, that is—

(a) a comparison of the cases of persons of different sex under section 1(1) or (2),

(b) a comparison of the cases of persons required for the purposes of section 2A, and

(c) a comparison of the cases of persons who do and who do not fulfil the condition in section 3(2),

must be such that the relevant circumstances in the one case are the same, or not materially different, in the other.";

and omit section 1(4).

(4) In section 7 (exception where sex is a genuine occupational qualification), in subsection (2)(h) for "by a married couple" substitute

"—

(i) by a married couple,

(ii) by a couple who are civil partners of each other, or

(iii) by a married couple or a couple who are civil partners of each other".

(5) In section 65 (remedies on complaint under section 63), in subsection (1B) for "or marital status as the case may be" substitute "or (as the case may be) fulfilment of the condition in section 3(2)".

[Civil Partnership Act 2004, s 251.]

6–3210G   252. Discrimination against civil partners in employment field: Northern Ireland

6–3210H   253. Civil partners to have unlimited insurable interest in each other

6–3210I   254. Social security, child support and tax credits

6–3210J   255. Power to amend enactments relating to pensions

6–3210K   256. Amendment of certain enactments relating to pensions

6–3210L   257. Amendment of certain enactments relating to the armed forces

PART 8[1]
SUPPLEMENTARY

6–3210M   258. Regulations and orders.   (1) This section applies to any power conferred by this Act to make regulations or an order (except a power of a court to make an order).

(2) The power may be exercised so as to make different provision for different cases and different purposes.

(3) The power includes power to make any supplementary, incidental, consequential, transitional, transitory or saving provision which the person making the regulations or order considers expedient.

[Civil Partnership Act 2004, s 258.]

---

1. Part 8 contains ss 258–264.

6–3210N   259. Power to make further provision in connection with civil partnership.   (1) A Minister of the Crown may by order[1] make such further provision (including supplementary, incidental, consequential, transitory, transitional or saving provision) as he considers appropriate—

(a) for the general purposes, or any particular purpose, of this Act,

(b) in consequence of any provision made by or under this Act, or

(c) for giving full effect to this Act or any provision of it.

(2) The power conferred by subsection (1) is also exercisable—

(a) by the Scottish Ministers, in relation to a relevant Scottish provision;

(b) by a Northern Ireland department, in relation to a provision which deals with a transferred matter;

(c) by the National Assembly for Wales, in relation to a provision which is made otherwise than by virtue of subsection (3) and deals with matters with respect to which functions are exercisable by the Assembly.

(3) An order under subsection (1) may—

(a) amend or repeal any enactment contained in an Act passed on or before the last day of the Session in which this Act is passed, including an enactment conferring power to make subordinate legislation where the power is limited by reference to persons who are or have been parties to a marriage;

(b) amend, repeal or (as the case may be) revoke any provision contained in Northern Ireland legislation passed or made on or before the last day of the Session in which this Act is passed, including a provision conferring power to make subordinate legislation where the power is limited by reference to persons who are or have been parties to a marriage;

(c) amend, repeal or (as the case may be) revoke any Church legislation.

(4) An order under subsection (1) may—

(a) provide for any provision of this Act which comes into force before another such provision has come into force to have effect, until that other provision has come into force, with such modifications as are specified in the order;

(b) amend or revoke any subordinate legislation.

(5) The power to make an order under subsection (1) is not restricted by any other provision of this Act.

(6) Subject to subsection (7), the power to make an order under subsection (1) is exercisable by statutory instrument.

(7) Any power of a Northern Ireland department to make an order under this section is exercisable by statutory rule for the purposes of the Statutory Rules (Northern Ireland) Order 1979 (SI 1979/1573 (NI 12)).

(8) An order under subsection (1) which contains any provision (whether alone or with other provisions) made by virtue of subsection (3) may not be made—

(a) by a Minister of the Crown, unless a draft of the statutory instrument containing the order has been laid before, and approved by a resolution of, each House of Parliament;

(b) by the Scottish Ministers, unless a draft of the statutory instrument containing the order has been laid before, and approved by a resolution of, the Scottish Parliament;

(c) by a Northern Ireland department, unless a draft of the statutory rule containing the order has been laid before, and approved by a resolution of, the Northern Ireland Assembly.

(9) A statutory instrument containing an order under subsection (1) to which subsection (8) does not apply—

(a) if made by a Minister of the Crown, is subject to annulment in pursuance of a resolution of either House of Parliament;

(b) if made by the Scottish Ministers, is subject to annulment in pursuance of a resolution of the Scottish Parliament.

(10) A statutory rule made by a Northern Ireland department and containing an order to which subsection (8) does not apply is subject to negative resolution (within the meaning of section 41(6) of the Interpretation Act (Northern Ireland) 1954 (c 33 (NI))).

(11) In this section—

"Act" includes an Act of the Scottish Parliament;

"Church legislation" has the same meaning as in section 255;

"Minister of the Crown" has the same meaning as in the Ministers of the Crown Act 1975 (c 26);

"relevant Scottish provision" means a provision that would be within the legislative competence of the Scottish Parliament if it were included in an Act of that Parliament;

"subordinate legislation" has the same meaning as in the Interpretation Act 1978 (c 30) except that it includes any instrument made under an Act of the Scottish Parliament and any instrument within the meaning of section 1(c) of the Interpretation Act (Northern Ireland) 1954 (c 33 (NI));

"transferred matter" has the meaning given by section 4(1) of the Northern Ireland Act 1998 (c 47) and "deals with" in relation to a transferred matter is to be construed in accordance with section 98(2) and (3) of the 1998 Act.

[Civil Partnership Act 2004, s 259.]

---

1. The Civil Partnerships (Pensions and Benefit Payments) (Consequential etc. Provisions) Order 2005, SI 2005/2053 and the Civil Partnerships (Treatment of Overseas Relationships) (No 2) Order 2005, SI 2005/3284 have been made.

6–3210O   260. Community obligations and civil partners. (1) Subsection (2) applies where any person, by Order in Council or regulations under section 2(2) of the European Communities Act 1972 (c 68) (general implementation of Treaties)—

(a) is making provision for the purpose of implementing, or for a purpose concerning, a Community obligation of the United Kingdom which relates to persons who are or have been parties to a marriage, or

(b) has made such provision and it has not been revoked.

(2) The appropriate person may by Order in Council or (as the case may be) by regulations make provision in relation to persons who are or have been civil partners in a civil partnership that is the same or similar to the provision referred to in subsection (1).

(3) "Marriage" and "civil partnership" include a void marriage and a void civil partnership respectively.

(4) "The appropriate person" means—

(a) if subsection (1)(a) applies, the person making the provision referred to there;
(b) if subsection (1)(b) applies, any person who would have power to make the provision referred to there if it were being made at the time of the exercise of the power under subsection (2).

(5) The following provisions apply in relation to the power conferred by subsection (2) to make an Order in Council or regulations as they apply in relation to the power conferred by section 2(2) of the 1972 Act to make an Order in Council or regulations—

(a) paragraph 2 of Schedule 2 to the 1972 Act (procedure etc in relation to making of Orders in Council and regulations: general);
(b) paragraph 15(3)(c) of Schedule 8 to the Scotland Act 1998 (c 46) (modifications of paragraph 2 in relation to Scottish Ministers and to Orders in Council made on the recommendation of the First Minister);
(c) paragraph 3 of Schedule 2 to the 1972 Act (modifications of paragraph 2 in relation to Northern Ireland departments etc) and the Statutory Rules (Northern Ireland) Order 1979 (SI 1979/1573 (NI 12)) (treating the power conferred by subsection (2) as conferred by an Act passed before 1st January 1974 for the purposes of the application of that Order);
(d) section 29(3) of the Government of Wales Act 1998 (c 38) (modifications of paragraph 2 in relation to the National Assembly for Wales).

[Civil Partnership Act 2004, s 260.]

6–3210P   261. Minor and consequential amendments, repeals and revocations. (1) Schedule 27 contains minor and consequential amendments.
(2) Schedule 28 contains consequential amendments of enactments relating to Scotland.
(3) Schedule 29 contains minor and consequential amendments relating to Northern Ireland.
(4) Schedule 30 contains repeals and revocations.

[Civil Partnership Act 2004, s 261.]

6–3210Q   262. Extent. (1) Part 2 (civil partnership: England and Wales), excluding section 35 but including Schedules 1 to 9, extends to England and Wales only.
(2) Part 3 (civil partnership: Scotland), including Schedules 10 and 11, extends to Scotland only.
(3) Part 4 (civil partnership: Northern Ireland), including Schedules 12 to 19, extends to Northern Ireland only.
(4) In Part 5 (civil partnerships formed or dissolved abroad etc)—

(a) sections 220 to 224 extend to England and Wales only;
(b) sections 225 to 227 extend to Scotland only;
(c) sections 228 to 232 extend to Northern Ireland only.

(5) In Part 6—

(a) any amendment made by virtue of section 247(1)(a) and Schedule 21 has the same extent as the provision subject to the amendment;
(b) section 248 and Schedule 22 extend to Northern Ireland only.

(6) Section 251 extends to England and Wales and Scotland only.
(7) Section 252 extends to Northern Ireland only.
(8) Schedule 28 extends to Scotland only.
(9) Schedule 29 extends to Northern Ireland only.
(10) Any amendment, repeal or revocation made by Schedules 24 to 27 and 30 has the same extent as the provision subject to the amendment, repeal or revocation.

[Civil Partnership Act 2004, s 262.]

6–3210R   263. Commencement[1]. (1) Part 1 comes into force in accordance with provision made by order by the Secretary of State, after consulting the Scottish Ministers and the Department of Finance and Personnel.
(2) Part 2, including Schedules 1 to 9, comes into force in accordance with provision made by order by the Secretary of State.
(3) Part 3, including Schedules 10 and 11, comes into force in accordance with provision made by order by the Scottish Ministers, after consulting the Secretary of State.
(4) Part 4, including Schedules 12 to 19, comes into force in accordance with provision made by order by the Department of Finance and Personnel, after consulting the Secretary of State.
(5) Part 5, excluding section 213(2) to (6) but including Schedule 20, comes into force in accordance with provision made by order by the Secretary of State, after consulting the Scottish Ministers and the Department of Finance and Personnel.
(6) Section 213(2) to (6) comes into force on the day on which this Act is passed.
(7) In Part 6—

(a) sections 246 and 247(1) and Schedule 21 come into force in accordance with provision made by order by the Secretary of State, after consulting the Scottish Ministers and the Department of Finance and Personnel,

(b)   section 248(1) and Schedule 22 come into force in accordance with provision made by order by the Department of Finance and Personnel, after consulting the Secretary of State, and

(c)   sections 247(2) to (7) and 248(2) to (5) come into force on the day on which this Act is passed.

(8)   In Part 7—

(a)   sections 249, 251, 253, 256 and 257 and Schedules 23, 25 and 26 come into force in accordance with provision made by order by the Secretary of State,

(b)   section 250 comes into force in accordance with provision made by order by the Secretary of State, after consulting the Scottish Ministers and the Department of Finance and Personnel,

(c)   section 252 comes into force in accordance with provision made by the Department of Finance and Personnel, after consulting the Secretary of State,

(d)   subject to paragraph (e), section 254(1) and Schedule 24 come into force in accordance with provision made by order by the Secretary of State,

(e)   the provisions of Schedule 24 listed in subsection (9), and section 254(1) so far as relating to those provisions, come into force in accordance with provision made by the Department of Finance and Personnel, after consulting the Secretary of State, and

(f)   sections 254(2) to (6) and 255 come into force on the day on which this Act is passed.

(9)   The provisions are—

(a)   Part 2;

(b)   in Part 5, paragraphs 67 to 85, 87, 89 to 99 and 102 to 105;

(c)   Part 6;

(d)   Parts 9 and 10;

(e)   Part 15.

(10)   In this Part—

(a)   sections 258, 259, 260 and 262, this section and section 264 come into force on the day on which this Act is passed,

(b)   section 261(1) and Schedule 27 and, except so far as relating to any Acts of the Scottish Parliament or any provision which extends to Northern Ireland only, section 261(4) and Schedule 30 come into force in accordance with provision made by order by the Secretary of State,

(c)   section 261(2) and Schedule 28 and, so far as relating to any Acts of the Scottish Parliament, section 261(4) and Schedule 30 come into force in accordance with provision made by order by the Scottish Ministers, after consulting the Secretary of State,

(d)   section 261(3) and Schedule 29 and, so far as relating to any provision which extends to Northern Ireland only, section 261(4) and Schedule 30 come into force in accordance with provision made by order by the Department of Finance and Personnel, after consulting the Secretary of State.

(11)   The power to make an order under this section is exercisable by statutory instrument.
[Civil Partnership Act 2004, s 263.]

---

1. At the time of going to press no commencement orders had been made.

6–3210S   264. Short title.   This Act may be cited as the Civil Partnership Act 2004.
[Civil Partnership Act 2004, s 264.]

Sections 3(2) and 5(3)   SCHEDULE 1
PROHIBITED DEGREES OF RELATIONSHIP: ENGLAND AND WALES

PART 1
THE PROHIBITIONS

Absolute prohibitions

6–3210T   1. (1)   Two people are within prohibited degrees of relationship if one falls within the list below in relation to the other.

Adoptive child
Adoptive parent
Child
Former adoptive child
Former adoptive parent
Grandparent
Grandchild
Parent
Parent's sibling
Sibling
Sibling's child

(2)   In the list "sibling" means a brother, sister, half-brother or half-sister.

Qualified prohibitions

2. (1) Two people are within prohibited degrees of relationship if one of them falls within the list below in relation to the other, unless—

(a) both of them have reached 21 at the time when they register as civil partners of each other, and
(b) the younger has not at any time before reaching 18 been a child of the family in relation to the other.

> Child of former civil partner
> Child of former spouse
> Former civil partner of grandparent
> Former civil partner of parent
> Former spouse of grandparent
> Former spouse of parent
> Grandchild of former civil partner
> Grandchild of former spouse

(2) "Child of the family", in relation to another person, means a person who—

(a) has lived in the same household as that other person, and
(b) has been treated by that other person as a child of his family.

3. Two people are within prohibited degrees of relationship if one falls within column 1 of the table below in relation to the other, unless—

(a) both of them have reached 21 at the time when they register as civil partners of each other, and
(b) the persons who fall within column 2 are dead.

Relationship	Relevant deaths
Former civil partner of child	The child
	The child's other parent
Former spouse of child	The child
	The child's other parent
Parent of former civil partner	The former civil partner
	The former civil partner's other parent
Parent of former spouse	The former spouse
	The former spouse's other parent

PART 2
SPECIAL PROVISIONS RELATING TO QUALIFIED PROHIBITIONS

6–3210U

Provisions relating to paragraph 2

4. Paragraphs 5 to 7 apply where two people are subject to paragraph 2 but intend to register as civil partners of each other by signing a civil partnership schedule.

5. (1) The fact that a notice of proposed civil partnership has been given must not be recorded in the register unless the registration authority—

(a) is satisfied by the production of evidence that both the proposed civil partners have reached 21, and
(b) has received a declaration made by each of the proposed civil partners—

     (i) specifying their affinal relationship, and
     (ii) declaring that the younger of them has not at any time before reaching 18 been a child of the family in relation to the other.

(2) Sub-paragraph (1) does not apply if a declaration is obtained under paragraph 7.

(3) A declaration under sub-paragraph (1)(b) must contain such information and must be signed and attested in such manner as may be prescribed by regulations[1].

(4) The fact that a registration authority has received a declaration under sub-paragraph (1)(b) must be recorded in the register.

(5) A declaration under sub-paragraph (1)(b) must be filed and kept by the registration authority.

6. (1) Sub-paragraph (2) applies if—

(a) a registration authority receives from a person who is not one of the proposed civil partners a written statement signed by that person which alleges that a declaration made under paragraph 5 is false in a material particular, and
(b) the register shows that such a statement has been received.

(2) The registration authority in whose area it is proposed that the registration take place must not issue a civil partnership schedule unless a High Court declaration is obtained under paragraph 7.

7. (1) Either of the proposed civil partners may apply to the High Court for a declaration that, given that—

(a) both of them have reached 21, and
(b) the younger of those persons has not at any time before reaching 18 been a child of the family in relation to the other,

there is no impediment of affinity to the formation of the civil partnership.

(2) Such an application may be made whether or not any statement has been received by the registration authority under paragraph 6.

8. Section 13 (objection to proposed civil partnership) does not apply in relation to a civil partnership to which paragraphs 5 to 7 apply, except so far as an objection to the issue of a civil partnership schedule is made under that section on a ground other than the affinity between the proposed civil partners.

Provisions relating to paragraph 3

9. (1) This paragraph applies where two people are subject to paragraph 3 but intend to register as civil partners of each other by signing a civil partnership schedule.

(2) The fact that a notice of proposed civil partnership has been given must not be recorded in the register unless the registration authority is satisfied by the production of evidence—

(a) that both the proposed civil partners have reached 21, and
(b) that the persons referred to in paragraph 3(b) are dead.

---

1. The Civil Partnership (Registration Provisions) Regulations 2005, SI 2005/3176 have been made.

Sections 4(2) and 5(3)   SCHEDULE 2
CIVIL PARTNERSHIPS OF PERSONS UNDER 18: ENGLAND AND WALES

PART 1
APPROPRIATE PERSONS

6–3210V   **1.** Column 2 of the table specifies the appropriate persons (or person) to give consent to a child whose circumstances fall within column 1 and who intends to register as the civil partner of another—

Case	Appropriate persons
1 The circumstances do not fall within any of items 2 to 8.	Each of the following— (a) any parent of the child who has parental responsibility for him, and (b) any guardian of the child.
2 A special guardianship order is in force with respect to the child and the circumstances do not fall within any of items 3 to 7.	Each of the child's special guardians.
3 A care order has effect with respect to the child and the circumstances do not fall within item 5.	Each of the following— (a) the local authority designated in the order, and (b) each parent, guardian or special guardian (in so far as their parental responsibility has not been restricted under section 33(3) of the 1989 Act).
4 A residence order has effect with respect to the child and the circumstances do not fall within item 5.	Each of the persons with whom the child lives, or is to live, as a result of the order.
5 An adoption agency is authorised to place the child for adoption under section 19 of the 2002 Act.	Either— (a) the adoption agency, or (b) if a care order has effect with respect to the child, the local authority designated in the order.
6 A placement order is in force with respect to the child.	The local authority authorised by the placement order to place the child for adoption.
7 The child has been placed for adoption with prospective adopters.	The prospective adopters (in so far as their parental responsibility has not been restricted under section 25(4) of the 2002 Act), in addition to any person specified in relation to item 5 or 6.
8 The circumstances do not fall within any of items 2 to 7, but a residence order was in force with respect to the child immediately before he reached 16.	The persons with whom the child lived, or was to live, as a result of the order.

2. In the table—

"the 1989 Act" means the Children Act 1989 (c 41) and "guardian of a child", "parental responsibility", "residence order", "special guardian", "special guardianship order" and "care order" have the same meaning as in that Act;

"the 2002 Act" means the Adoption and Children Act 2002 (c 38) and "adoption agency", "placed for adoption", "placement order" and "local authority" have the same meaning as in that Act;

"appropriate local authority" means the local authority authorised by the placement order to place the child for adoption.

PART 2
OBTAINING CONSENT: GENERAL

6–3210W

Consent of appropriate person unobtainable

3. (1) This paragraph applies if—

(a) a child and another person intend to register as civil partners of each other under any procedure other than the special procedure, and
(b) the registration authority to whom the child gives a notice of proposed civil partnership is satisfied that the consent of a person whose consent is required ("A") cannot be obtained because A is absent, inaccessible or under a disability.

(2) If there is any other person whose consent is also required, the registration authority must dispense with the need for A's consent.

(3) If no other person's consent is required—

(a) the Registrar General may dispense with the need for any consent, or

(b) the court may, on an application being made to it, consent to the child registering as the civil partner of the person mentioned in sub-paragraph (1)(a).

(4) The consent of the court under sub-paragraph (3)(b) has the same effect as if it had been given by A.

Consent of appropriate person refused

4. (1) This paragraph applies if—

(a) a child and another person intend to register as civil partners of each other under any procedure other than the special procedure, and

(b) any person whose consent is required refuses his consent.

(2) The court may, on an application being made to it, consent to the child registering as the civil partner of the person mentioned in sub-paragraph (1)(a).

(3) The consent of the court under sub-paragraph (2) has the same effect as if it had been given by the person who has refused his consent.

Declaration

5. If one of the proposed civil partners is a child and is not a surviving civil partner, the necessary declaration under section 8 must also—

(a) state in relation to each appropriate person—

    (i) that that person's consent has been obtained,

    (ii) that the need to obtain that person's consent has been dispensed with under paragraph 3, or

    (iii) that the court has given consent under paragraph 3 or 4, or

(b) state that no person exists whose consent is required to a civil partnership between the child and another person.

Forbidding proposed civil partnership

6. (1) This paragraph applies if it has been recorded in the register that a notice of proposed civil partnership between a child and another person has been given.

(2) Any person whose consent is required to a child and another person registering as civil partners of each other may forbid the issue of a civil partnership schedule by giving any registration authority written notice that he forbids it.

(3) A notice under sub-paragraph (2) must specify—

(a) the name of the person giving it,

(b) his place of residence, and

(c) the capacity, in relation to either of the proposed civil partners, in which he forbids the issue of the civil partnership schedule.

(4) On receiving the notice, the registration authority must as soon as is practicable record in the register the fact that the issue of a civil partnership schedule has been forbidden.

(5) If the issue of a civil partnership schedule has been forbidden under this paragraph, the notice of proposed civil partnership and all proceedings on it are void.

(6) Sub-paragraphs (2) and (5) do not apply if the court has given its consent under paragraph 3 or 4.

Evidence

7. (1) This paragraph applies if, for the purpose of obtaining a civil partnership schedule, a person declares that the consent of any person or persons whose consent is required under section 4 has been given.

(2) The registration authority may refuse to issue the civil partnership schedule unless satisfied by the production of written evidence that the consent of that person or those persons has in fact been given.

Issue of civil partnership schedule

8. The duty in section 14(1) to issue a civil partnership schedule does not apply if its issue has been forbidden under paragraph 6.

9. If a proposed civil partnership is between a child and another person, the civil partnership schedule must contain a statement that the issue of the civil partnership schedule has not been forbidden under paragraph 6.

PART 3
OBTAINING CONSENT: SPECIAL PROCEDURE

6–3210X

Consent of appropriate person unobtainable or refused

10. (1) Sub-paragraph (2) applies if—

(a) a child and another person intend to register as civil partners of each other under the special procedure, and

(b) the Registrar General is satisfied that the consent of a person ("A") whose consent is required cannot be obtained because A is absent, inaccessible, or under a disability.

(2) If this sub-paragraph applies—

(a) the Registrar General may dispense with the need for A's consent (whether or not there is any other person whose consent is also required), or

(b) the court may, on application being made, consent to the child registering as the civil partner of the person mentioned in sub-paragraph (1)(a).

(3) The consent of the court under sub-paragraph (2)(b) has the same effect as if it had been given by A.

(4) Sub-paragraph (5) applies if—

(a) a child and another person intend to register as civil partners of each other under the special procedure, and

(b) any person whose consent is required refuses his consent.

(5) The court may, on application being made, consent to the child registering as the civil partner of the person mentioned in sub-paragraph (4)(a).

(6) The consent of the court under sub-paragraph (5) has the same effect as if it had been given by the person who has refused his consent.

Declaration

11. If one of the proposed civil partners is a child and is not a surviving civil partner, the necessary declaration under section 8 must also—

(a) state in relation to each appropriate person—

(i) that that person's consent has been obtained,

(ii) that the need to obtain that person's consent has been dispensed with under paragraph 10(2), or

(iii) that the court has given consent under paragraph 10(2) or (5), or

(b) state that no person exists whose consent is required to a civil partnership between the child and another person.

Forbidding proposed civil partnership

12. Paragraph 6 applies in relation to the special procedure as if—

(a) any reference to forbidding the issue of a civil partnership schedule were a reference to forbidding the Registrar General to give authority for the issue of his licence, and

(b) sub-paragraph (6) referred to the court giving its consent under paragraph 10(2) or (5).

Evidence

13. (1) This paragraph applies—

(a) if a child and another person intend to register as civil partners of each other under the special procedure, and

(b) the consent of any person ("A") is required to the child registering as the civil partner of that person.

(2) The person giving the notice (under section 21) of proposed civil partnership to the registration authority must produce to the authority such evidence as the Registrar General may require to satisfy him that A's consent has in fact been given.

(3) The power to require evidence under sub-paragraph (2) is in addition to the power to require evidence under section 22.

Issue of Registrar General's licence

14. The duty of the Registrar General under section 25(3)(b) to give authority for the issue of his licence does not apply if he has been forbidden to do so by virtue of paragraph 12.

PART 4
PROVISIONS RELATING TO THE COURT

6–3210Y **15.** (1) For the purposes of Parts 2 and 3 of this Schedule, "the court" means—

(a) the High Court,

(b) the county court of the district in which any applicant or respondent resides, or

(c) a magistrates' court acting in the local justice area in which any applicant or respondent resides.

(2) Rules of court may be made for enabling applications under Part 2 or 3 of this Schedule—

(a) if made to the High Court, to be heard in chambers;

(b) if made to the county court, to be heard and determined by the district judge subject to appeal to the judge;

(c) if made to a magistrates' court, to be heard and determined otherwise than in open court.

(3) Rules of court must provide that, where an application is made in consequence of a refusal to give consent, notice of the application is to be served on the person who has refused consent.

Section 5(2)   **SCHEDULE 3**
REGISTRATION BY FORMER SPOUSES ONE OF WHOM HAS CHANGED SEX

(As amended by SI 2005/2000.)

Application of Schedule

6–3210Z **1.** This Schedule applies if—

(a) a court—

(i) makes absolute a decree of nullity granted on the ground that an interim gender recognition certificate has been issued to a party to the marriage, or

(ii) (in Scotland) grants a decree of divorce on that ground,

and, on doing so, issues a full gender recognition certificate (under section 5(1) of the Gender Recognition Act 2004 (c 7)) to that party, and

(b)   the parties wish to register in England or Wales as civil partners of each other without being delayed by the waiting period.

The relevant period

2. For the purposes of this Schedule the relevant period is the period—

(a)   beginning with the issue of the full gender recognition certificate, and
(b)   ending at the end of 1 month from the day on which it is issued.

Modifications of standard procedure and procedures for house-bound and detained persons

3. If—

(a)   each of the parties gives a notice of proposed civil partnership during the relevant period, and
(b)   on doing so, each makes an election under this paragraph,

Chapter 1 of Part 2 applies with the modifications given in paragraphs 4 to 6.

4. (1) Omit—

(a)   section 10 (proposed civil partnership to be publicised);
(b)   section 11 (meaning of "the waiting period");
(c)   section 12 (power to shorten the waiting period).

(2) In section 14 (issue of civil partnership schedule), for subsection (1) substitute—

"(1) As soon as the notices of proposed civil partnership have been given, the registration authority in whose area it is proposed that the registration take place must, at the request of one or both of the proposed civil partners, issue a document to be known as a "civil partnership schedule"."

(3) For section 17 (period during which registration may take place) substitute—

"17. Period during which registration may take place. (1) The proposed civil partners may register as civil partners by signing the civil partnership schedule at any time during the applicable period.

(2) If they do not register as civil partners by signing the civil partnership schedule before the end of the applicable period—

(a)   the notices of proposed civil partnership and the civil partnership schedule are void, and
(b)   no civil partnership registrar may officiate at the signing of the civil partnership schedule by them.

(3) The applicable period, in relation to two people registering as civil partners of each other, is the period of 1 month beginning with—

(a)   the day on which the notices of proposed civil partnership are given, or
(b)   if the notices are not given on the same day, the earlier of those days."

5. In section 18 (house-bound persons), in subsection (3)—

(a)   treat the reference to the standard procedure as a reference to the standard procedure as modified by this Schedule, and
(b)   omit paragraph (c) (which provides for a 3 month registration period).

6. In section 19 (detained persons), in subsection (3)—

(a)   treat the reference to the standard procedure as a reference to the standard procedure as modified by this Schedule, and
(b)   omit paragraph (c) (which provides for a 3 month registration period).

Modified procedures for certain non-residents

7. (1) Sub-paragraphs (5) to (8) apply (in place of section 20) in the following two cases.
(2) The first is where—

(a)   two people wish to register as civil partners of each other in England and Wales, and
(b)   one of them ("A") resides in Scotland and the other ("B") resides in England or Wales.

(3) *Repealed.*
(4) The second is where—

(a)   two people wish to register as civil partners of each other in England and Wales, and
(b)   one of them ("A") is an officer, seaman or marine borne on the books of one of Her Majesty's ships at sea and the other ("B") resides in England or Wales.

(5) A is not required to give a notice of proposed civil partnership to a registration authority in England or Wales in order to register in England or Wales as B's civil partner.

(6) B may make the necessary declaration without reference to A's usual place of residence for any period.

(7) If, on giving such notice, B makes an election under this paragraph, Chapter 1 of Part 2 applies with the modifications given in paragraphs 4 to 6 and the further modifications in sub-paragraph (8).

(8) The further modifications are that—

(a)   the civil partnership schedule is not to be issued by a registration authority unless A or B produces to that registration authority a certificate of no impediment issued to A under the relevant provision;
(b)   the applicable period is the period of one month beginning with the day on which B's notice is given;
(c)   section 31 applies as if in subsections (1)(a) and (2)(c) for "each notice" there were substituted "B's notice".

(9) "The relevant provision" means—

(a)   if A resides in Scotland, section 97;
(b)   *repealed*;

(c) if A is an officer, seaman or marine borne on the books of one of Her Majesty's ships at sea, section 239.

(10) *Repealed.*

SCHEDULE 6
FINANCIAL RELIEF IN MAGISTRATES' COURTS ETC
PART 1
FAILURE TO MAINTAIN ETC: FINANCIAL PROVISION

Circumstances in which orders under this Part may be made

6–3211 **1.** (1) On an application to it by one of the civil partners, a magistrates' court may make any one or more of the orders set out in paragraph 2 if it is satisfied that the other civil partner—

(a) has failed to provide reasonable maintenance for the applicant,
(b) has failed to provide, or to make a proper contribution towards, reasonable maintenance for any child of the family,
(c) has behaved in such a way that the applicant cannot reasonably be expected to live with the respondent, or
(d) has deserted the applicant.

(2) The power of the court under sub-paragraph (1) is subject to the following provisions of this Schedule.

The orders: periodical and secured periodical payments and lump sums

2. (1) The orders are—

(a) an order that the respondent must make to the applicant such periodical payments for such term as may be specified;
(b) an order that the respondent must pay to the applicant such lump sum as may be specified;
(c) an order that the respondent must make—

  (i) to the applicant for the benefit of a child of the family to whom the application relates, or
  (ii) to a child of the family to whom the application relates;

  such periodical payments for such term as may be specified;

(d) an order that the respondent must pay such lump sum as may be specified—

  (i) to the applicant for the benefit of a child of the family to whom the application relates, or
  (ii) to such a child of the family to whom the application relates.

(2) The amount of a lump sum required to be paid under sub-paragraph (1)(b) or (d) must not exceed—

(a) £1,000, or
(b) such larger amount as the Lord Chancellor may from time to time by order fix for the purposes of this sub-paragraph.

(3) The power to make an order under sub-paragraph (2) is exercisable by statutory instrument which is subject to annulment in pursuance of a resolution of either House of Parliament.

(4) "Specified" means specified in the order.

Particular provision that may be made by lump sum orders

3. (1) An order under this Part for the payment of a lump sum may be made for the purpose of enabling any liability or expenses reasonably incurred in maintaining the applicant or any child of the family to whom the application relates before the making of the order to be met.

(2) Sub-paragraph (1) does not restrict the power to make the orders set out in paragraph 2(1)(b) and (d).

Matters to which court is to have regard in exercising its powers under this Part—general

4. If an application is made for an order under this Part, the court, in deciding—

(a) whether to exercise its powers under this Part, and
(b) if so, in what way,

must have regard to all the circumstances of the case, giving first consideration to the welfare while under 18 of any child of the family who has not reached 18.

Particular matters to be taken into account when exercising powers in relation to civil partners

5. (1) This paragraph applies in relation to the exercise by the court of its power to make an order by virtue of paragraph 2(1)(a) or (b).

(2) The court must in particular have regard to—

(a) the income, earning capacity, property and other financial resources which each civil partner—

  (i) has, or
  (ii) is likely to have in the foreseeable future,

  including, in the case of earning capacity, any increase in that capacity which it would in the opinion of the court be reasonable to expect a civil partner in the civil partnership to take steps to acquire;

(b) the financial needs, obligations and responsibilities which each civil partner has or is likely to have in the foreseeable future;
(c) the standard of living enjoyed by the civil partners before the occurrence of the conduct which is alleged as the ground of the application;
(d) the age of each civil partner and the duration of the civil partnership;
(e) any physical or mental disability of either civil partner;

(f) the contributions which each civil partner has made or is likely in the foreseeable future to make to the welfare of the family, including any contribution by looking after the home or caring for the family;
(g) the conduct of each civil partner, if that conduct is such that it would in the opinion of the court be inequitable to disregard it.

Particular matters to be taken into account when exercising powers in relation to children

6. (1) This paragraph applies in relation to the exercise by the court of its power to make an order by virtue of paragraph 2(1)(c) or (d).
(2) The court must in particular have regard to—

(a) the financial needs of the child;
(b) the income, earning capacity (if any), property and other financial resources of the child;
(c) any physical or mental disability of the child;
(d) the standard of living enjoyed by the family before the occurrence of the conduct which is alleged as the ground of the application;
(e) the way in which the child was being and in which the civil partners expected the child to be educated or trained;
(f) the considerations mentioned in relation to the civil partners in paragraph 5(2)(a) and (b).

(3) In relation to the exercise of its power to make an order in favour of a child of the family who is not the respondent's child, the court must also have regard to—

(a) whether the respondent has assumed any responsibility for the child's maintenance;
(b) if so, the extent to which, and the basis on which, the respondent assumed that responsibility and the length of time during which the respondent discharged that responsibility;
(c) whether in assuming and discharging that responsibility the respondent did so knowing that the child was not the respondent's child;
(d) the liability of any other person to maintain the child.

Reconciliation

7. (1) If an application is made for an order under this Part—

(a) the court, before deciding whether to exercise its powers under this Part, must consider whether there is any possibility of reconciliation between the civil partners, and
(b) if at any stage of the proceedings on that application it appears to the court that there is a reasonable possibility of such a reconciliation, the court may adjourn the proceedings for such period as it thinks fit to enable attempts to be made to effect a reconciliation.

(2) If the court adjourns any proceedings under sub-paragraph (1), it may request—

(a) an officer of the Children and Family Court Advisory and Support Service, or
(b) any other person,

to attempt to effect a reconciliation between the civil partners.
(3) If any such request is made, the officer or other person—

(a) must report in writing to the court whether the attempt has been successful, but
(b) must not include in the report any other information.

Refusal of order in case more suitable for High Court

8. (1) If on hearing an application for an order under this Part a magistrates' court is of the opinion that any of the matters in question between the civil partners would be more conveniently dealt with by the High Court, the magistrates' court must refuse to make any order on the application.
(2) No appeal lies from a refusal under sub-paragraph (1).
(3) But, in any proceedings in the High Court relating to or comprising the same subject matter as an application in respect of which a magistrates' court has refused to make any order, the High Court may order the application to be reheard and determined by a magistrates' court acting for the same local justice area as the court which refused to make any order.

PART 2
ORDERS FOR AGREED FINANCIAL PROVISION

6–3211A

Orders for payments which have been agreed by the parties

9. (1) Either civil partner may apply to a magistrates' court for an order under this Part on the ground that that civil partner or the other civil partner has agreed to make such financial provision as may be specified in the application.
(2) On such an application, the court may order that the applicant or the respondent (as the case may be) is to make the financial provision specified in the application, if—

(a) it is satisfied that the applicant or the respondent (as the case may be) has agreed to make that provision, and
(b) it has no reason to think that it would be contrary to the interests of justice to do so.

(3) Sub-paragraph (2) is subject to paragraph 12.

Meaning of "financial provision" and of references to specified financial provision

10. (1) In this Part "financial provision" means any one or more of the following—

(a) the making of periodical payments by one civil partner to the other;

(b) the payment of a lump sum by one civil partner to the other;

(c) the making of periodical payments by one civil partner to a child of the family or to the other civil partner for the benefit of such a child;

(d) the payment by one party of a lump sum to a child of the family or to the other civil partner for the benefit of such a child.

(2) Any reference in this Part to the financial provision specified in an application or specified by the court is a reference—

(a) to the type of provision specified in the application or by the court,

(b) to the amount so specified as the amount of any payment to be made under the application or order, and

(c) in the case of periodical payments, to the term so specified as the term for which the payments are to be made.

Evidence to be produced where respondent not present etc

11. (1) This paragraph applies if—

(a) the respondent is not present, or

(b) is not represented by counsel or a solicitor,

at the hearing of an application for an order under this Part.

(2) The court must not make an order under this Part unless there is produced to it such evidence as may be prescribed by rules of court of—

(a) the consent of the respondent to the making of the order,

(b) the financial resources of the respondent, and

(c) if the financial provision specified in the application includes or consists of provision in respect of a child of the family to be made by the applicant to the respondent for the benefit of the child or to the child, the financial resources of the child.

Exercise of powers in relation to children

12. (1) This paragraph applies if the financial provision specified in an application under this Part—

(a) includes, or

(b) consists of,

provision in respect of a child of the family.

(2) The court must not make an order under this Part unless it considers that the provision which the applicant or the respondent (as the case may be) has agreed to make in respect of the child provides for, or makes a proper contribution towards, the financial needs of the child.

Power to make alternative orders

13. (1) This paragraph applies if on an application under this Part the court decides—

(a) that it would be contrary to the interests of justice to make an order for the making of the financial provision specified in the application, or

(b) that any financial provision which the applicant or the respondent (as the case may be) has agreed to make in respect of a child of the family does not provide for, or make a proper contribution towards, the financial needs of that child.

(2) If the court is of the opinion—

(a) that it would not be contrary to the interests of justice to make an order for the making of some other financial provision specified by the court, and

(b) that, in so far as that other financial provision contains any provision for a child of the family, it provides for, or makes a proper contribution towards, the financial needs of that child,

then, if both the civil partners agree, the court may order that the applicant or the respondent (as the case may be) is to make that other financial provision.

Relationship between this Part and Part 1

14. (1) A civil partner who has applied for an order under Part 1 is not precluded at any time before the determination of the application from applying for an order under this Part.

(2) If—

(a) an order is made under this Part on the application of either civil partner, and

(b) either of them has also made an application for a Part 1 order,

the application for the Part 1 order is to be treated as if it had been withdrawn.

PART 3

ORDERS OF COURT WHERE CIVIL PARTNERS LIVING APART BY AGREEMENT

6–3211B

Powers of court where civil partners are living apart by agreement

15. (1) If—

(a) the civil partners have been living apart for a continuous period exceeding 3 months, neither civil partner having deserted the other, and

(b) one of the civil partners has been making periodical payments for the benefit of the other civil partner or of a child of the family,

the other civil partner may apply to a magistrates' court for an order under this Part.

(2) An application made under sub-paragraph (1) must specify the total amount of the payments made by the respondent during the period of 3 months immediately preceding the date of the making of the application.

(3) If on an application for an order under this Part the court is satisfied that the respondent has made the payments specified in the application, the court may make one or both of the orders set out in paragraph 16.

(4) Sub-paragraph (3) is subject to the provisions of this Schedule.

The orders that may be made under this Part

16. (1) The orders are—

(a) an order that the respondent is to make to the applicant such periodical payments for such term as may be specified;

(b) an order that the respondent is to make—

(i) to the applicant for the benefit of a child of the family to whom the application relates, or
(ii) to a child of the family to whom the application relates.

such periodical payments for such term as may be specified.

(2) "Specified" means specified in the order.

Restrictions on orders under this Part

17. The court in the exercise of its powers under this Part must not require—

(a) the respondent to make payments whose total amount during any period of 3 months exceeds the total amount paid by him for the benefit of—

(i) the applicant, or
(ii) a child of the family,

during the period of 3 months immediately preceding the date of the making of the application;

(b) the respondent to make payments to or for the benefit of any person which exceed in amount the payments which the court considers that it would have required the respondent to make to or for the benefit of that person on an application under Part 1;

(c) payments to be made to or for the benefit of a child of the family who is not the respondent's child, unless the court considers that it would have made an order in favour of that child on an application under Part 1.

Relationship with powers under Part 1

18. (1) Sub-paragraph (2) applies if on an application under this Part the court considers that the orders which it has the power to make under this Part—

(a) would not provide reasonable maintenance for the applicant, or
(b) if the application relates to a child of the family, would not provide, or make a proper contribution towards, reasonable maintenance for that child.

(2) The court—

(a) must refuse to make an order under this Part, but
(b) may treat the application as if it were an application for an order under Part 1.

Matters to be taken into consideration

19. Paragraphs 4 to 6 apply in relation to an application for an order under this Part as they apply in relation to an application for an order under Part 1, subject to the modification that for the reference in paragraph 5(2)(c) to the occurrence of the conduct which is alleged as the ground of the application substitute a reference to the living apart of the civil partners.

PART 4

INTERIM ORDERS

6–3211C

Circumstances in which interim orders may be made

20. (1) This paragraph applies if an application has been made for an order under Part 1, 2 or 3.

(2) A magistrates' court may make an interim order—

(a) at any time before making a final order on, or dismissing, the application, or
(b) on refusing (under paragraph 8) to make on order on the application.

(3) The High Court may make an interim order on ordering the application to be reheard by a magistrates' court (either after the refusal of an order under paragraph 8 or on an appeal made by virtue of paragraph 46).

(4) Not more than one interim order may be made with respect to an application for an order under Part 1, 2 or 3.

(5) Sub-paragraph (4) does not affect the power of a court to make an interim order on a further application under Part 1, 2 or 3.

Meaning of interim order

21. (1) An interim order is an order requiring the respondent to make such periodical payments as the court thinks reasonable—

   (a) to the applicant,
   (b) to any child of the family who is under 18, or
   (c) to the applicant for the benefit of such a child.

   (2) In relation to an interim order in respect of an application for an order under Part 2 by the civil partner who has agreed to make the financial provision specified in the application, sub-paragraph (1) applies as if—

   (a) the reference to the respondent were a reference to the applicant, and
   (b) the references to the applicant were references to the respondent.

When interim order may start

   22. (1) An interim order may provide for payments to be made from such date as the court may specify, except that the date must not be earlier than the date of the making of the application for an order under Part 1, 2 or 3.
   (2) Sub-paragraph (1) is subject to paragraph 27(7) and (8).

Payments which can be treated as having been paid on account

   23. (1) If an interim order made by the High Court on an appeal made by virtue of paragraph 46 provides for payments to be made from a date earlier than the date of the making of the order, the interim order may provide that payments made by the respondent under an order made by a magistrates' court are to be treated, to such extent and in such manner as may be provided by the interim order, as having been paid on account of any payment provided for by the interim order.
   (2) In relation to an interim order in respect of an application for an order under Part 2 by the civil partner who has agreed to make the financial provision specified in the application, sub-paragraph (1) applies as if the reference to the respondent were a reference to the applicant.

When interim order ceases to have effect

   24. (1) Subject to sub-paragraphs (2) and (3), an interim order made on an application for an order under Part 1, 2 or 3 ceases to have effect on the earliest of the following dates—

   (a) the date, if any, specified for the purpose in the interim order;
   (b) the date on which the period of 3 months beginning with the date of the making of the interim order ends;
   (c) the date on which a magistrates' court either makes a final order on, or dismisses, the application.

   (2) If an interim order made under this Part would, but for this sub-paragraph, cease to have effect under sub-paragraph (1)(a) or (b)—

   (a) the magistrates' court which made the order, or
   (b) in the case of an interim order made by the High Court, the magistrates' court by which the application for an order under Part 1, 2 or 3 is to be reheard,

may by order provide that the interim order is to continue in force for a further period.
   (3) An order continued in force under sub-paragraph (2) ceases to have effect on the earliest of the following dates—

   (a) the date, if any, specified for the purpose in the order continuing it;
   (b) the date on which ends the period of 3 months beginning with—

     (i) the date of the making of the order continuing it, or
     (ii) if more than one such order has been made with respect to the application, the date of the making of the first such order;

   (c) the date on which the court either makes a final order on, or dismisses, the application.

Supplementary

   25. (1) An interim order made by the High Court under paragraph 20(3) on ordering an application to be reheard by a magistrates' court is to be treated for the purposes of—

   (a) its enforcement, and
   (b) Part 6 (variation etc of orders),

as if it were an order of that magistrates' court (and not of the High Court).
   (2) No appeal lies from the making of or refusal to make, the variation of or refusal to vary, or the revocation of or refusal to revoke, an interim order.

PART 5
COMMENCEMENT AND DURATION OF ORDERS UNDER PARTS 1, 2 AND 3

6–3211D

Duration of periodical payments order for a civil partner

   26. (1) The court may specify in a periodical payments order made under paragraph 2(1)(a) or Part 3 in favour of a civil partner such term as it thinks fit, except that the term must not—

   (a) begin before the date of the making of the application for the order, or
   (b) extend beyond the death of either of the civil partners.

   (2) If—

   (a) a periodical payments order is made under paragraph 2(1)(a) or Part 3 in favour of one of the civil partners, and
   (b) the civil partnership is subsequently dissolved or annulled but the order continues in force,

the periodical payments order ceases to have effect (regardless of anything in it) on the formation of a subsequent civil partnership or marriage by that civil partner, except in relation to any arrears due under the order on the date of that event.

Age limit on making orders for financial provision for children and duration of such orders

27. (1) Subject to sub-paragraph (5), no order is to be made under paragraph 2(1)(c) or (d) or Part 3 in favour of a child who has reached 18.

(2) The term to be specified in a periodical payments order made under paragraph 2(1)(c) or Part 3 in favour of a child may begin with—

(a) the date of the making of an application for the order or a later date, or

(b) a date ascertained in accordance with sub-paragraph (7) or (8).

(3) The term to be specified in such an order—

(a) must not in the first instance extend beyond the date of the birthday of the child next following his reaching the upper limit of the compulsory school age unless the court considers that in the circumstances of the case the welfare of the child requires that it should extend to a later date, and

(b) must not in any event, subject to sub-paragraph (5), extend beyond the date of the child's 18th birthday.

(4) Sub-paragraph (3)(a) must be read with section 8 of the Education Act 1996 (c 56) (which applies to determine for the purposes of any enactment whether a person is of compulsory school age).

(5) Sub-paragraphs (1) and (3)(b) do not apply in the case of a child if it appears to the court that—

(a) the child is, or will be, or, if such an order were made without complying with either or both of those provisions, would be—

(i)   receiving instruction at an educational establishment, or

(ii) undergoing training for a trade, profession or vocation,

whether or not also the child is, will be or would be, in gainful employment, or

(b) there are special circumstances which justify the making of the order without complying with either or both of sub-paragraphs (1) and (3)(b).

(6) Any order made under paragraph 2(1)(c) or Part 3 in favour of a child, regardless of anything in the order, ceases to have effect on the death of the person liable to make payments under the order.

(7) If—

(a) a maintenance calculation ("current calculation") is in force with respect to a child, and

(b) an application is made for an order under paragraph 2(1)(c) or Part 3—

(i)   in accordance with section 8 of the Child Support Act 1991 (c 48), and

(ii) before the end of 6 months beginning with the making of the current calculation,

the term to be specified in any such order made on that application may be expressed to begin on, or at any time after, the earliest permitted date.

(8) "The earliest permitted date" is whichever is the later of—

(a) the date 6 months before the application is made, or

(b) the date on which the current calculation took effect or, where successive maintenance calculations have been continuously in force with respect to a child, on which the first of those calculations took effect.

(9) If—

(a) a maintenance calculation ceases to have effect by or under any provision of the 1991 Act, and

(b) an application is made, before the end of 6 months beginning with the relevant date, for a periodical payments order under paragraph 2(1)(c) or Part 3 in favour of a child with respect to whom that maintenance calculation was in force immediately before it ceased to have effect,

the term to be specified in any such order, or in any interim order under Part 4, made on that application, may begin with the date on which that maintenance calculation ceased to have effect or any later date.

(10) "The relevant date" means the date on which the maintenance calculation ceased to have effect.

(11) In this Schedule "maintenance calculation" has the same meaning as it has in the 1991 Act by virtue of section 54 of the 1991 Act as read with any regulations in force under that section.

Application of paragraphs 26 and 27 to Part 2 orders

28. (1) Subject to sub-paragraph (3), paragraph 26 applies in relation to an order under Part 2 which requires periodical payments to be made to a civil partner for his own benefit as it applies in relation to an order under paragraph 2(1)(a).

(2) Subject to sub-paragraph (3), paragraph 27 applies in relation to an order under Part 2 for the making of financial provision in respect of a child of the family as it applies in relation to an order under paragraph 2(1)(c) or (d).

(3) If—

(a) the court makes an order under Part 2 which contains provision for the making of periodical payments, and

(b) by virtue of paragraph 14, an application for an order under Part 1 is treated as if it had been withdrawn,

the term which may be specified under Part 2 as the term for which the payments are to be made may begin with the date of the making of the application for the order under Part 1 or any later date.

Effect on certain orders of parties living together

29. (1) Sub-paragraph (2) applies if periodical payments are required to be made to a civil partner (whether for the civil partner's own benefit or for the benefit of a child of the family)—

(a) by an order made under Part 1 or 2, or

(b) by an interim order made under Part 4 (otherwise than on an application under Part 3).

(2) The order is enforceable even though—

(a) the civil partners are living with each other at the date of the making of the order, or
(b) if they are not living with each other at that date, they subsequently resume living with each other;

but the order ceases to have effect if after that date the parties continue to live with each other, or resume living with each other, for a continuous period exceeding 6 months.

(3) Sub-paragraph (4) applies if—

(a) an order is made under Part 1 or 2 which requires periodical payments to be made to a child of the family, or
(b) an interim order is made under Part 4 (otherwise than on an application under Part 3) which requires periodical payments to be made to a child of the family.

(4) Unless the court otherwise directs, the order continues to have effect and is enforceable even if—

(a) the civil partners are living with each other at the date of the making of the order, or
(b) if they are not living with each other at that date, they subsequently resume living with each other.

(5) An order made under Part 3, and any interim order made on an application for an order under that Part, ceases to have effect if the civil partners resume living with each other.

(6) If an order made under this Schedule ceases to have effect under—

(a) sub-paragraph (2) or (5), or
(b) a direction given under sub-paragraph (4),

a magistrates' court may, on an application made by either civil partner, make an order declaring that the order ceased to have effect from such date as the court may specify.

PART 6
VARIATION ETC OF ORDERS

6–3211E

Power to vary, revoke, suspend or revive order

30. (1) If a magistrates' court has made an order for the making of periodical payments under Part 1, 2 or 3, the court may, on an application made under this Part—

(a) vary or revoke the order,
(b) suspend any provision of it temporarily, or
(c) revive any provision so suspended.

(2) If a magistrates' court has made an interim order under Part 4, the court may, on an application made under this Part—

(a) vary or revoke the order,
(b) suspend any provision of it temporarily, or
(c) revive any provision so suspended,

except that it may not by virtue of this sub-paragraph extend the period for which the order is in force.

Powers to order lump sum on variation

31. (1) If a magistrates' court has made an order under paragraph 2(1)(a) or (c) for the making of periodical payments, the court may, on an application made under this Part, make an order for the payment of a lump sum under paragraph 2(1)(b) or (d).

(2) If a magistrates' court has made an order under Part 2 for the making of periodical payments by a civil partner the court may, on an application made under this Part, make an order for the payment of a lump sum by that civil partner—

(a) to the other civil partner, or
(b) to a child of the family or to that other civil partner for the benefit of that child.

(3) Where the court has power by virtue of this paragraph to make an order for the payment of a lump sum—

(a) the amount of the lump sum must not exceed the maximum amount that may at that time be required to be paid under Part 1, but
(b) the court may make an order for the payment of a lump sum not exceeding that amount even if the person required to pay it was required to pay a lump sum by a previous order under this Schedule.

(4) Where—

(a) the court has power by virtue of this paragraph to make an order for the payment of a lump sum, and
(b) the respondent or the applicant (as the case may be) has agreed to pay a lump sum of an amount exceeding the maximum amount that may at that time be required to be paid under Part 1,

the court may, regardless of sub-paragraph (3), make an order for the payment of a lump sum of that amount.

Power to specify when order as varied is to take effect

32. An order made under this Part which varies an order for the making of periodical payments may provide that the payments as so varied are to be made from such date as the court may specify, except that, subject to paragraph 33, the date must not be earlier than the date of the making of the application under this Part.

33. (1) If—

(a) there is in force an order ("the order")—

(i) under paragraph 2(1)(c),

   (ii) under Part 2 making provision of a kind set out in paragraph 10(1)(c) (regardless of whether it makes provision of any other kind mentioned in paragraph 10(1)(c)),

   (iii) under paragraph 16(1)(b), or

   (iv) which is an interim order under Part 4 under which the payments are to be made to a child or to the applicant for the benefit of a child,

 (b) the order requires payments specified in it to be made to or for the benefit of more than one child without apportioning those payments between them,

 (c) a maintenance calculation ("the calculation") is made with respect to one or more, but not all, of the children with respect to whom those payments are to be made, and

 (d) an application is made, before the end of 6 months beginning with the date on which the calculation was made, for the variation or revocation of the order,

the court may, in exercise of its powers under this Part to vary or revoke the order, direct that the variation or revocation is to take effect from the date on which the calculation took effect or any later date.

 (2) If—

 (a) an order ("the child order") of a kind prescribed for the purposes of section 10(1) of the Child Support Act 1991 is affected by a maintenance calculation,

 (b) on the date on which the child order became so affected there was in force an order ("the civil partner's order")—

   (i) under paragraph 2(1)(a),

   (ii) under Part 2 making provision of a kind set out in paragraph 10(1)(a) (regardless of whether it makes provision of any other kind mentioned in paragraph 10(1)(a)),

   (iii) under paragraph 16(1)(a), or

   (iv) which is an interim order under Part 4 under which the payments are to be made to the applicant (otherwise than for the benefit of a child), and

 (c) an application is made, before the end of 6 months beginning with the date on which the maintenance calculation was made, for the civil partner's order to be varied or revoked,

the court may, in exercise of its powers under this Part to vary or revoke the civil partner's order, direct that the variation or revocation is to take effect from the date on which the child order became so affected or any later date.

 (3) For the purposes of sub-paragraph (2), an order is affected if it ceases to have effect or is modified by or under section 10 of the 1991 Act.

Matters to which court is to have regard in exercising powers under this Part

 34. (1) In exercising the powers conferred by this Part the court must, so far as it appears to the court just to do so, give effect to any agreement which has been reached between the civil partners in relation to the application.

 (2) If—

 (a) there is no such agreement, or

 (b) if the court decides not to give effect to the agreement,

the court must have regard to all the circumstances of the case, giving first consideration to the welfare while under 18 of any child of the family who has not reached 18.

 (3) Those circumstances include any change in any of the matters—

 (a) to which the court was required to have regard when making the order to which the application relates, or

 (b) in the case of an application for the variation or revocation of an order made under Part 2 or on an appeal made by virtue of paragraph 46, to which the court would have been required to have regard if that order had been made under Part 1.

Variation of orders for periodical payments: further provisions

 35. (1) The power of the court under paragraphs 30 to 34 to vary an order for the making of periodical payments includes power, if the court is satisfied that payment has not been made in accordance with the order, to exercise one of its powers under section 59(3)(a) to (d) of the Magistrates' Courts Act 1980 (c 43).

 (2) Sub-paragraph (1) is subject to paragraph 37.

 36. (1) If—

 (a) a magistrates' court has made an order under this Schedule for the making of periodical payments, and

 (b) payments under the order are required to be made by any method of payment falling within section 59(6) of the 1980 Act (standing order, etc),

an application may be made under this sub-paragraph to the court for the order to be varied as mentioned in sub-paragraph (2).

 (2) Subject to sub-paragraph (4), if an application is made under sub-paragraph (1), a justices' clerk, after—

 (a) giving written notice (by post or otherwise) of the application to the respondent, and

 (b) allowing the respondent, within the period of 14 days beginning with the date of the giving of that notice, an opportunity to make written representations,

may vary the order to provide that payments under the order are to be made to the designated officer for the court.

 (3) The clerk may proceed with an application under sub-paragraph (1) even if the respondent has not received written notice of the application.

 (4) If an application has been made under sub-paragraph (1), the clerk may, if he considers it inappropriate to exercise his power under sub-paragraph (2), refer the matter to the court which, subject to paragraph 37, may vary the order by exercising one of its powers under section 59(3)(a) to (d) of the 1980 Act.

 37. (1) Before varying the order by exercising one of its powers under section 59(3)(a) to (d) of the 1980 Act, the court must have regard to any representations made by the parties to the application.

 (2) If the court does not propose to exercise its power under section 59(3)(c), (cc) or (d) of the 1980 Act, the

court must, unless upon representations expressly made in that behalf by the person to whom payments under the order are required to be made it is satisfied that it is undesirable to do so, exercise its power under section 59(3)(b).

38. (1) Section 59(4) of the 1980 Act (power of court to order that account be opened) applies for the purposes of paragraphs 35 and 36(4) as it applies for the purposes of section 59.

(2) None of the powers of the court, or of a justices' clerk, conferred by paragraphs 35 to 37 and sub-paragraph (1) is exercisable in relation to an order under this Schedule for the making of periodical payments which is not a qualifying maintenance order (within the meaning of section 59 of the 1980 Act).

Persons who may apply under this Part

39. An application under paragraph 30, 31 or 36 may be made—

(a) if it is for the variation or revocation of an order under Part 1, 2, 3 or 4 for periodical payments, by either civil partner, and

(b) if it is for the variation of an order under paragraph 2(1)(c) or Part 2 or 3 for periodical payments to or in respect of a child, also by the child himself, if he has reached 16.

Revival of orders for periodical payments

40. (1) If an order made by a magistrates' court under this Schedule for the making of periodical payments to or in respect of a child (other than an interim order) ceases to have effect—

(a) on the date on which the child reaches 16, or

(b) at any time after that date but before or on the date on which he reaches 18,

the child may apply to the court which made the order for an order for its revival.

(2) If on such an application it appears to the court that—

(a) the child is, will be or (if an order were made under this sub-paragraph) would be receiving instruction at an educational establishment or undergoing training for a trade, profession or vocation, whether or not while in gainful employment, or

(b) there are special circumstances which justify the making of an order under this sub-paragraph,

the court may by order revive the order from such date as the court may specify, not being earlier than the date of the making of the application.

(3) Any order revived under this paragraph may be varied or revoked under paragraphs 30 to 34 in the same way as it could have been varied or revoked had it continued in being.

Variation of instalments of lump sum

41. If in the exercise of its powers under section 75 of the 1980 Act a magistrates' court orders that a lump sum required to be paid under this Schedule is to be paid by instalments, the court, on an application made by either the person liable to pay or the person entitled to receive that sum, may vary that order by varying—

(a) the number of instalments payable,

(b) the amount of any instalment payable, and

(c) the date on which any instalment becomes payable.

Supplementary provisions with respect to variation and revocation of orders

42. None of the following powers apply in relation to an order made under this Schedule—

(a) the powers of a magistrates' court to revoke, revive or vary an order for the periodical payment of money and the power of a justices' clerk to vary such an order under section 60 of the 1980 Act;

(b) the power of a magistrates' court to suspend or rescind certain other orders under section 63(2) of the 1980 Act.

PART 7
ARREARS AND REPAYMENTS

Enforcement etc of orders for payment of money

43. Section 32 of the Domestic Proceedings and Magistrates' Courts Act 1978 (c 22) applies in relation to orders under this Schedule as it applies in relation to orders under Part 1 of that Act.

Orders for repayment after cessation of order because of subsequent civil partnership etc

44. (1) Sub-paragraphs (3) and (4) apply if—

(a) an order made under paragraph 2(1)(a) or Part 2 or 3 has, under paragraph 26(2), ceased to have effect because of the formation of a subsequent civil partnership or marriage by the party ("R") in whose favour it was made, and

(b) the person liable to make payments under the order ("P") made payments in accordance with it in respect of a relevant period in the mistaken belief that the order was still subsisting.

(2) "Relevant period" means a period after the date of the formation of the subsequent civil partnership or marriage.

(3) No proceedings in respect of a cause of action arising out of the circumstances mentioned in sub-paragraph (1)(a) and (b) is maintainable by P (or P's personal representatives) against R (or R's personal representatives).

(4) But on an application made under this paragraph by P (or P's personal representatives) against R (or R's personal representatives) the court—

(a) may order the respondent to pay to the applicant a sum equal to the amount of the payments made in respect of the relevant period, or

(b) if it appears to the court that it would be unjust to make that order, may—

(i) order the respondent to pay to the applicant such lesser sum as it thinks fit, or
(ii) dismiss the application.

(5) An order under this paragraph for the payment of any sum may provide for the payment of that sum by instalments of such amount as may be specified in the order.

(6) An application under this paragraph—

(a) may be made in proceedings in the High Court or a county court for leave to enforce, or the enforcement of, the payment of arrears under an order made under paragraph 2(1)(a) or Part 2 or 3, but

(b) if not made in such proceedings, must be made to a county court,

and accordingly references in this paragraph to the court are references to the High Court or a county court, as the circumstances require.

(7) The jurisdiction conferred on a county court by this paragraph is exercisable by a county court even though, because of the amount claimed in an application under this paragraph, the jurisdiction would not but for this sub-paragraph be exercisable by a county court.

(8) Subject to sub-paragraph (9)—

(a) the designated officer for a magistrates' court to whom any payments under an order made under paragraph 2(1)(a), or Part 2 or 3, are required to be made is not liable for any act done by him in pursuance of the order after the date on which that order ceased to have effect because of the formation of a subsequent civil partnership or marriage by the person entitled to payments under it, and

(b) the collecting officer under an attachment of earnings order made to secure payments under the order under paragraph 2(1)(a), or Part 2 or 3, is not liable for any act done by him after that date in accordance with any enactment or rule of court specifying how payments made to him in compliance with the attachment of earnings order are to be dealt with.

(9) Sub-paragraph (8) applies if (but only if) the act—

(a) was one which he would have been under a duty to do had the order under paragraph 2(1)(a) or Part 2 or 3 not ceased to have effect, and

(b) was done before notice in writing of the formation of the subsequent civil partnership or marriage was given to him by or on behalf of—

(i) the person entitled to payments under the order,
(ii) the person liable to make payments under it, or
(iii) the personal representatives of either of them.

(10) In this paragraph "collecting officer", in relation to an attachment of earnings order, means—

(a) the officer of the High Court, or
(b) the officer designated by the Lord Chancellor,

to whom a person makes payments in compliance with the order.

PART 8
SUPPLEMENTARY

6–3211G

Restrictions on making of orders under this Schedule: welfare of children

45. If—

(a) an application is made by a civil partner for an order under Part 1, 2 or 3, and
(b) there is a child of the family who is under 18,

the court must not dismiss or make a final order on the application until it has decided whether to exercise any of its powers under the Children Act 1989 (c 41) with respect to the child.

Constitution of courts, powers of High Court and county court in relation to orders and appeals

46. The following provisions of the Domestic Proceedings and Magistrates' Courts Act 1978 (c 22) apply in relation to an order under this Schedule relating to a civil partnership as they apply in relation to an order under Part 1 of that Act relating to a marriage—

(a) section 28 (powers of the High Court and a county court in relation to certain orders),
(b) section 29 (appeals), and
(c) section 31 (constitution of courts).

Provisions as to jurisdiction and procedure

47. (1) Subject to section 2 of the Family Law Act 1986 (c 55) and section 70 of the Magistrates' Courts Act 1980 (c 43) and any determination of the Lord Chancellor, a magistrates' court has jurisdiction to hear an application for an order under this Schedule if it acts in, or is authorised by the Lord Chancellor to act for, a local justice area in which either the applicant or the respondent ordinarily resides at the date of the making of the application.

(2) Any jurisdiction conferred on a magistrates' court by this Schedule is exercisable even if any party to the proceedings is not domiciled in England and Wales.

Meaning of "child of the family"

48. In this Schedule "child of the family", in relation to two people who are civil partners of each other, means—

(a) a child of both of them, and

(b) any other child, other than a child placed with them as foster parents by a local authority or voluntary organisation, who has been treated by both the civil partners as a child of their family.

6–3211H

SCHEDULE 9[1]

FAMILY HOMES AND DOMESTIC VIOLENCE

_____

1. This Schedule amends various legislation, including the Family Law Act 1996. Where these amendments affect provisions reproduced in this work they will be shown when the amendments take effect.

Section 247   SCHEDULE 21

REFERENCES TO STEPCHILDREN ETC IN EXISTING ACTS

(Amended by SI 2005/3137)

6–3211I   **1** The Declinature Act 1681 (c 79) (Senators of College of Justice not to sit in causes of persons related to them).

2 Section 21 of the Small Landholders (Scotland) Act 1911 (c 49) (assignment of holding).

2A Section 4(3) of the Workmen's Compensation Act 1925 (c 84) (Member of a family).

3 Section 68(2)(e) of the Marriage Act 1949 (c 76) (solemnisation of marriages of stepchildren of servicemen in naval, military and air force chapels etc).

4 Section 7(7) of the Leasehold Reform Act 1967 (c 88) (rights of members of family succeeding to tenancy on death: member of another's family).

5 Section 18(3) of that Act (residential rights and exclusion of enfranchisement or extension: adult member of another's family).

6 Section 2(2) of the Employers' Liability (Compulsory Insurance) Act 1969 (c 57) (employees to be covered).

7 Section 27(5) of the Parliamentary and other Pensions Act 1972 (c 48) (pensions for dependants of Prime Minister or Speaker).

8 Section 184(5) of the Consumer Credit Act 1974 (c 39) (associates).

9 Section 1(5) of the Fatal Accidents Act 1976 (c 30) (right of action for wrongful act causing death: who are dependants).

10 The definition of "relative" in section 31(1) of the Credit Unions Act 1979 (c 34) (interpretation, etc).

11 Section 32(3) of the Estate Agents Act 1979 (c 38) ("associate": meaning of relative).

12 Section 13(1) of the Administration of Justice Act 1982 (c 53) (deduction of relationships).

13 Section 12(5) of the Mental Health Act 1983 (c 20) (general provisions as to medical recommendations: persons who may not give recommendations).

14 Section 25C(10) of that Act (supervision applications: meaning of "close relative").

15 Section 5(3) of the Mobile Homes Act 1983 (c 34) (interpretation: member of another's family).

15A Section 11(6) of the Inheritance Tax Act 1984 (c 51) (dispositions for maintenance of family).

15B Section 22(2) of that Act (gifts in consideration of marriage).

15C Section 71(8) of that Act (accumulation and maintenance trusts).

16 Section 153(4) of the Companies Act 1985 (c 6) (transactions not prohibited by section 151).

17 Section 203(1) of that Act (notification of family and corporate interests: person interested in shares).

18 Section 327(2) of that Act (extension of section 323 to spouses and children).

19 Section 328(8) of that Act (extension of section 324 to spouses and children).

20 Section 346(2) of that Act ("connected persons").

21 Section 430E(8) of that Act (associates).

22 Section 742A(6) of that Act (meaning of "offer to the public").

22A Section 743(b) of that Act ("employees' share scheme").

23 Section 74(4)(a) of the Bankruptcy (Scotland) Act 1985 (c 66) (meaning of "associate").

24 Section 113(2) of the Housing Act 1985 (c 68) (members of a person's family).

25 Section 186(2) of that Act (members of a person's family).

26 Section 105(2) of the Housing Associations Act 1985 (c 69) (members of a person's family).

27 Section 20(6) of the Airports Act 1986 (c 31) (powers of investment and disposal in relation to public airport companies).

28 Section 435(8) of the Insolvency Act 1986 (c 45) (meaning of "associate").

29 Section 70(2)(a) and (c), (3)(a) and (4) of the Building Societies Act 1986 (c 53) (interpretation).

30 Section 83(2)(c) of the Housing (Scotland) Act 1987 (c 26) (members of a person's family).

31 Section 4(6) of the Landlord and Tenant Act 1987 (c 31) (relevant disposals).

31A Paragraph 2(5) of Schedule 14 to the Income and Corporation Taxes Act 1988 (c 1) (life assurance premiums payable to friendly societies and industrial assurance companies).

32 Section 52(2)(a) of the Companies Act 1989 (c 40) (meaning of "associate").

33 The definition of "relative" in section 105(1) of the Children Act 1989 (c 41) (interpretation).

34 Paragraph 1(2) of Schedule 2 to the Broadcasting Act 1990 (c 42) (restrictions on the holding of licences).

35 Section 11(1) of the Agricultural Holdings (Scotland) Act 1991 (c 55) (bequest of lease).

35A Paragraphs 2(7), 2A(10) and 9(11) of Schedule 5 to the Taxation of Chargeable Gains Act 1992 (c 12) (attribution of gains to settlors with interest in non-resident or dual resident settlement).

36 Section 77(3)(c) of the Friendly Societies Act 1992 (c 40) (information on appointed actuary to be annexed to balance sheet).

37 The definitions of "son" and "daughter" in section 119A(2) of that Act (meaning of "associate").

38 Paragraph 2(1) of Schedule 5 to the Charities Act 1993 (c 10) (meaning of "connected person" for purposes of section 36(2)).

39 Section 10(5) of the Leasehold Reform, Housing and Urban Development Act 1993 (c 28) (premises with a resident landlord: adult member of another's family).

40 Section 61(2) of the Crofters (Scotland) Act 1993 (c 44) (member of family).

41 Section 2 of the Criminal Law (Consolidation) (Scotland) Act 1995 (c 39) (intercourse with stepchild).

42 Section 161(1) of the Employment Rights Act 1996 (c 18) (domestic servants).

43 The definition of "relative" in section 63(1) of the Family Law Act 1996 (c 27) (interpretation of Part 4 of the 1996 Act).

44 Section 62(2) of the Housing Act 1996 (c 52) (members of a person's family: Part 1).

45 Section 140(2) of that Act (members of a person's family: Chapter 1).

46 Section 143P(3) of that Act (members of a person's family: Chapter 1A).

47 The definition of "relative" in section 178(3) of that Act (meaning of associated person).

48 Section 422(4)(b) of the Financial Services and Markets Act 2000 (c 8) (controller).

49 Paragraph 16(2) of Schedule 11 to that Act (offers of securities).

49A Section 80(4A) of the Care Standards Act 2000 (c 14) (basic definitions).

50 Section 108(2)(c) of the Housing (Scotland) Act 2001 (asp 10) (meaning of certain terms).

51 Section 1(3) of the Mortgage Rights (Scotland) Act 2001 (asp 11) (application to suspend enforcement of standard security).

52 Paragraph 3(8) of Schedule 6 to the Commonhold and Leasehold Reform Act 2002 (c 15) (premises excluded from right to manage).

53 Section 127(6) of the Enterprise Act 2002 (c 40) (associated persons).

54 Section 242(2) of the Income Tax (Earnings and Pensions) Act 2003 (c 1) (works transport services).

55 Section 270A(3)(a) of that Act (limited exemption for qualifying childcare vouchers).

56 Section 318(3) of that Act (childcare: exemption for employer-provided care).

57 Section 318A(3) of that Act (childcare: limited exemption for other care).

58 Section 318C(8) of that Act (childcare: meaning of "qualifying child care").

59 Section 371(7) of that Act (travel costs and expenses where duties performed abroad: visiting spouse's or child's travel).

60 Section 374(9) of that Act (non-domiciled employee's spouse's or child's travel costs and expenses where duties performed in UK).

61 Section 27(3)(a) and (c) of the Sexual Offences Act 2003 (c 42) (family relationships).

62 Section 27(4) of the Human Tissue Act 2004 (c 30) (provision with respect to consent).

63 Section 54(9) of that Act (general interpretation).

Section 249

SCHEDULE 23
IMMIGRATION CONTROL AND FORMATION OF CIVIL PARTNERSHIPS

PART 1
INTRODUCTION

6–3211J

Application of Schedule

1. (1) This Schedule applies if—

(a) two people wish to register as civil partners of each other, and
(b) one of them is subject to immigration control.

(2) For the purposes of this Schedule a person is subject to immigration control if—

(a) he is not an EEA national, and
(b) under the Immigration Act 1971 (c 77) he requires leave to enter or remain in the United Kingdom (whether or not leave has been given).

(3) "EEA national" means a national of a State which is a contracting party to the Agreement on the European Economic Area signed at Oporto on 2nd May 1992 (as it has effect from time to time).

The qualifying condition

2. (1) For the purposes of this Schedule the qualifying condition, in relation to a person subject to immigration control, is that the person—

(a) has an entry clearance granted expressly for the purpose of enabling him to form a civil partnership in the United Kingdom,
(b) has the written permission of the Secretary of State to form a civil partnership in the United Kingdom, or
(c) falls within a class specified for the purpose of this paragraph by regulations[1] made by the Secretary of State.

(2) "Entry clearance" has the meaning given by section 33(1) of the Immigration Act 1971.

(3) Section 25 of the Asylum and Immigration (Treatment of Claimants, etc) Act 2004 (c 19) (regulations about applications for permission to marry) applies in relation to the permission referred to in sub-paragraph (1)(b) as it applies in relation to permission to marry under sections 19(3)(b), 21(3)(b) and 23(3)(b) of that Act.

---

1. The Immigration (Procedure for Formation of Civil Partnerships) Regulations 2005, SI 2005/2917 have been made.

PART 2

ENGLAND AND WALES

6–3211K

Application of this Part

3. This Part of this Schedule applies if the civil partnership is to be formed in England and Wales by signing a civil partnership schedule.

Procedure for giving notice of proposed civil partnership

4. (1) Each notice of proposed civil partnership under Chapter 1 of Part 2 of this Act—

(a) must be given to a registration authority specified for the purposes of this paragraph by regulations made by the Secretary of State, and

(b) must be delivered to the relevant individual in person by the two proposed civil partners.

(2) "The relevant individual" means such employee or officer or other person provided by the specified registration authority as is determined in accordance with regulations[1] made by the Secretary of State for the purposes of this sub-paragraph.

(3) Regulations under sub-paragraph (2) may, in particular, describe a person by reference to the location or office where he works.

(4) Before making any regulations under this paragraph the Secretary of State must consult the Registrar General.

Declaration

5. The necessary declaration under section 8 must include a statement that the person subject to immigration control fulfils the qualifying condition (and the reason why).

Recording of notice

6. (1) The fact that a notice of proposed civil partnership has been given must not be recorded in the register unless the registration authority is satisfied by the production of specified evidence that the person fulfils the qualifying condition.

(2) "Specified evidence" means such evidence as may be specified in guidance issued by the Registrar General.

Supplementary

7. (1) Part 2 of this Act has effect in any case where this Part of this Schedule applies subject to any necessary modification.

(2) In particular section 52 has effect as if the matters proof of which is not necessary in support of the civil partnership included compliance with this Part of this Schedule.

(3) An expression used in this Part of this Schedule and in Chapter 1 of Part 2 of this Act has the same meaning as in that Chapter.

---

1. The Immigration (Procedure for Formation of Civil Partnerships) Regulations 2005, SI 2005/2917 have been made.

6–3211L   SCHEDULE 27[1]

MINOR AND CONSEQUENTIAL AMENDMENTS: GENERAL

---

1. Where these amendments affect provisions reproduced in this work they will be shown when the amendments take effect.

6–3211M   SCHEDULE 30[1]

REPEALS AND REVOCATIONS

---

1. The repeals of provisions reproduced in this work will be shown when the repeals take effect.

Statutory Instruments on Family Law
Adoption and Parental Orders

Adoption (Designation of Overseas Adoptions) Order 1973[1]
(SI 1973/19 as amended by SI 1993/690)

6–3280   1, 2. *Citation, commencement and application of Interpretation Act* [1978].

---

1. Now having effect under s 72(2) of the Adoption Act 1976.

6–3281   3. (1) An adoption of an infant is hereby specified as an overseas adoption if it is an adoption effected in a place in relation to which this Article applies and under the law in force in that place.

(2) As respects any adoption effected before the date on which this Order comes into operation, this Article applies in relation to any place which, at that date, forms part of a country or territory

described in Part I or II of the Schedule to this Order and as respects any adoption effected on or after that date, this Article applies in relation to any place which, at the time the adoption is effected, forms part of a country or territory which at that time is a country or territory described in Part I or II of the Schedule to this Order.

(3) In this Article the expression—

"infant" means a person who at the time when the application for adoption was made had not attained the age of 18 years and had not been married;

"law" does not include customary or common law.

6–3282   **4.** (1) Evidence that an overseas adoption had been effected may be given by the production of a document purporting to be—

(*a*) a certified copy of an entry made, in accordance with the law of the country or territory concerned, in a public register relating to the recording of adoptions and showing that the adoption has been effected; or

(*b*) a certificate that the adoption has been effected, signed or purporting to be signed by a person authorised by the law of the country or territory concerned to sign such a certificate, or a certified copy of such certificate.

(2) Where a document produced by virtue of paragraph (1) of this Article is not in English, the Registrar General or the Register General of Births, Deaths and Marriages for Scotland, as the case may be, may require the production of an English translation of the document before satisfying himself of the matters specified in section 8 of the Adoption Act 1968.

(3) Nothing in this Article shall be construed as precluding proof, in accordance with the Evidence (Foreign, Dominion and Colonial Documents) Act 1933, or the Oaths and Evidence (Overseas Authorities and Countries) Act 1963, or otherwise, that an overseas adoption has been effected.

6–3283

SCHEDULE

PART I

COMMONWEALTH COUNTRIES AND UNITED KINGDOM DEPENDENT TERRITORIES

Australia	Malaysia
Bahamas	Malta
Barbados	Mauritius
Bermuda	Montserrat
Botswana	New Zealand
British Honduras	Nigeria
British Virgin Islands	Pitcairn
Canada	St. Christopher, Nevis and Anguilla
Cayman Islands	St. Vincent
The Republic of Cyprus	Seychelles
Dominica	Singapore
Fiji	Southern Rhodesia
Ghana	Sri Lanka
Gibraltar	Swaziland
Guyana	Tanzania
Hong Kong	Tonga
Jamaica	Trinidad and Tobago
Kenya	Uganda
Lesotho	Zambia
Malawi	

PART II

OTHER COUNTRIES AND TERRITORIES

Austria
Belgium
China
Denmark (including Greenland and the Faroes)
Finland
France (including Réunion, Martinique, Guadeloupe and French Guyana)
The Federal Republic of Germany and Land Berlin (West Berlin)
Greece
Iceland
The Republic of Ireland
Israel
Italy
Luxembourg
The Netherlands (including Surinam and the Antilles)
Norway
Portugal (including the Azores and Madeira)
South Africa and South West Africa
Spain (including the Balearics and the Canary Islands)
Sweden
Switzerland
Turkey
The United States of America
Yugoslavia

Magistrates' Courts (Adoption) Rules 1984[1]

(SI 1984/611 amended by SI 1989/384, SI 1991/1991, SI 1992/709, SI 2001/820 and 615, and SI 2005/617)

PART I
INTRODUCTORY

6–3410 **1.** *Citation, operation and revocations.*

1. Made by the Lord Chancellor in exercise of the power conferred on him by s 144 of the Magistrates' Courts Act 1980.

These rules are revoked by the Courts Act 2003 (Revocations, Savings and Transitional Provisions) Order 2005, SI 2005/2804. Notwithstanding their revocation, art 4 provides that the following rules continue to apply: rr 32(1), (3) and (6).

Notwithstanding their revocation, art 5 provides that these rules continue to apply on a transitional basis to an application under: s 12 (adoption order); s 18 (freeing for adoption); s 20 (revocation of a section 18 order); s 21 (variation of a section 18 order so as to substitute one adoption agency for another); s 27(1) or (2) (restriction on removal of child where adoption pending or application made under section 18); s 29 (return of child taken away in breach of section 27); s 53 (annulment etc. of overseas adoptions); and s 55 (adoption of children abroad).

Article 6 provides that while s19 of the Adoption Act 1976 has effect, r 32(2) (requirement to record declaration that parent of a child prefers not to be involved in future questions concerning adoption of child in court register) continues to apply.

In *Re J S (an infant)* [1959] 3 All ER 856, 124 JP 89, the High Court directed that a note should be taken of the evidence at the hearing; that the guardian ad litem's report need not be disclosed to the parties, but on appeal must be forwarded to the judge's clerk. See note 3 to r 6(10), post.

Interpretation

6–3411 **2.** (1) In these Rules, the following expressions shall, unless the context otherwise requires, have the meaning hereby respectively assigned to them, that is to say—

"the 1976 Act" means the Adoption Act 1976;

"the 1989 Act" means the Children Act 1989;

"adoption agency" means a local authority or approved adoption society;

"the child" means the person whom the applicant for an adoption order proposes to adopt or, as the case may be, the person the adoption agency proposes should be freed for adoption;

"children's guardian" means an officer of the service appointed to act on behalf of the child in accordance with section 65(1)(*a*) of the 1976 Act;

"interim order" means an order under section 25 of the 1976 Act;

"regular armed forces of the Crown" means the Royal Navy, the regular forces as defined by section 225 of the Army Act 1955, the regular air force as defined by section 223 of the Air Force Act 1955, the Queen Alexandra's Royal Naval Nursing Service and the Women's Royal Naval Service;

"reporting officer" means an officer of the service appointed in accordance with section 65(1)(*b*) of the 1976 Act.

(2) Expressions which are used in these Rules which are used in the 1976 Act and the 1989 Act have the same meaning as in those Acts.

(3) In these Rules, unless the context otherwise requires, any reference to a rule or to a Schedule shall be construed as a reference to a rule contained in these Rules or to a Schedule hereto, and any reference in a rule to a paragraph shall be construed as a reference to a paragraph of that rule.

(4) In these Rules, any reference to a form shall be construed as a reference to the form so numbered in Schedule 1 to these Rules or to a form substantially to the like effect, with such variations as the circumstances may require.

Extent

6–3412 **3.** These Rules shall apply only to proceedings under the 1976 Act.

PART II
FREEING FOR ADOPTION

The application

6–3423 **4.** (1) An application to free a child for adoption shall be in Form 1 and shall be made to a family proceedings court acting for the area within which either the child or a parent or guardian of the child is at the date of the application by delivering it, or sending it by post to that court, together with all documents referred to in the application.

(2) The applicant shall be the adoption agency and the respondents shall be—

(*a*) each parent[1] or guardian of the child;

(*b*) any local authority or voluntary organisation which has parental responsibility for, is looking after, or which is caring for, the child;

(*c*)–(*e*) Revoked.

(f)   any person liable by virtue of any order or agreement to contribute to the maintenance of the child.

(3) The court may at any time direct that any other person or body, except the child, be made a respondent to the application.

(4) The applicant shall supply to the designated officer for the court three copies of—

(a)   Form 1, together with any other documents required to be supplied, and

(b)   a report in writing covering all the relevant matters specified in Schedule 2.

---

1. By virtue of r 2(2), ante, "parent" has the same meaning as in s 72(1) of the Adoption Act 1976, ante; accordingly, where the natural father of a child does not have parental responsibility for the child, it is not mandatory that he be joined as a party to the proceedings. Nevertheless, the court has a discretion, in such cases, to direct that the father be joined as a respondent; see *Re C (adoption: parties)* [1996] 2 FCR 129, CA. As a matter of general practice, directions should be given to inform unmarried fathers of adoption proceedings unless the court decides it is not appropriate to do so; the weight to be attributed to the mother's desire for confidentiality would depend on the facts of each case, as would the application of art 8(1): *Re H (a child)(adoption: disclosure), Re G (a child)(adoption: disclosure)* [2001] 1 FCR 726, [2001] 1 FLR 646, CA. See also *Re J (adoption: contacting father)* [2003] EWHC 199 (Fam), [2003] 1 FLR 933, where it was held that it was lawful for a local authority not to inform the father (then aged 17) of the child's existence or to consult him regarding adoption; his relationship with the mother had ended shortly after she had become pregnant, the parties had never cohabited and had not seen each other since the relationship ended, there was no "family life" for the purposes of art 8, the child had severe cystic fibrosis and the mother did not want the father to be informed.

Appointment and duties of reporting officer

6–3424   **5.** (1) As soon as practicable after the application has been made or at any stage thereafter, if it appears that a parent or guardian of the child is willing to agree to the making of an adoption order and is in England or Wales, the court shall appoint a reporting officer in respect of that parent or guardian, and shall send to him a copy of the application and any documents attached thereto and of the report supplied by the applicant.

(2) The same person may be appointed as reporting officer in respect of two or more parents or guardians of the child.

(3) The reporting officer shall not be a member or employee of the applicant or any respondent body nor have been involved in the making of any arrangements for the adoption of the child.

(4) The reporting officer shall—

(a)   ensure so far as is reasonably practicable that any agreement to the making of an adoption order is given freely and unconditionally and with full understanding of what is involved;

(b)   confirm that the parent or guardian has been given an opportunity of making a declaration under section 18(6) of the 1976 Act that he prefers not to be involved in future questions concerning the adoption of the child;

(c)   assess the signature by the parent or guardian of the written agreement to the making of an adoption order;

(d)   investigate all the circumstances relevant to that agreement and any such declaration;

(e)   where it is proposed to free a child whose mother and father were not married at the time of his birth for adoption and his father is not his guardian, interview any person claiming to be the father in order to be able to advise the court on the matters listed in section 18(7) of the 1976 Act; but if more than one reporting officer has been appointed, the court shall nominate one of them to conduct the interview; and

(f)   on completing his investigations make a report in writing to the court, drawing attention to any matters which, in his opinion, may be of assistance to the court in considering the application.

(5) With a view to obtaining the directions of the court on any matter, the reporting officer may at any time make such interim report to the court as appears to him to be necessary; and in particular, the reporting officer shall make a report if a parent or guardian of the child is unwilling to agree to the making of an adoption order, and in such a case the designated officer for the court shall notify the applicant.

(6) The court may, at any time before the final determination of the application, require the reporting officer to perform such further duties as the court considers necessary.

(7) The reporting officer shall attend any hearing of the application if so required by the court.

(8) Any report made to the court under this rule shall be confidential.

(9) The powers of the court to appoint a reporting officer under paragraph (1), to nominate one reporting officer to conduct an interview under paragraph (4)(e), to give directions following the making of an interim report in accordance with paragraph (5) and to require the reporting officer to perform further duties under paragraph (6) shall also be exercisable, before the hearing of the application, by a single justice or by the justices' clerk.

Appointment and duties of children's guardian

6–3425   **6.** (1) As soon as practicable after the application has been made, or after receipt of the statement of facts supplied under rule 7, if it appears that a parent or guardian of the child is unwilling to agree to the making of an adoption order, the court shall appoint a childrens' guardian[1] of the child and shall send to him a copy of the application, together with any documents attached thereto, the statement of facts and the report supplied by the applicant.

(2) Where there are special circumstances and it appears to the court that the welfare of the child requires it, the court may at any time appoint a children's guardian of the child, and where such an appointment is made the court shall indicate any particular matters which it requires the children's guardian to investigate, and the court shall send the children's guardian a copy of the application, together with any documents attached thereto, and the report supplied by the applicant.

(3) The same person may be appointed as reporting officer under rule 5(1) in respect of a parent or guardian who appears to be willing to agree to the making of an adoption order, and as children's guardian of the child under this rule; and, whether or not so appointed as reporting officer, the children's guardian may be appointed as reporting officer in respect of a parent or guardian of the child who originally was unwilling to agree to the making of an adoption order but who later signifies his or her agreement.

Children's guardian

(4) The children's guardian shall not be a member or employee of the applicant or any respondent body nor have been involved in the making of any arrangements for the adoption of the child.

(5) With a view to safeguarding the interests of the child before the court, the children's guardian shall, so far as is reasonably practicable—

(a) investigate—

(i) so far as he considers necessary, the matters alleged in the application, the report supplied by the applicant and, where appropriate, the statement of facts supplied under rule 7, and

(ii) any other matters which appear to him to be relevant to the making of an order freeing the child for adoption;

(b) advise whether, in his opinion, the child should be present at the hearing of the application; and

(c) perform such other duties as appear to him to be necessary or as the court may direct.

(6) On completing his investigations the children's guardian shall make a report in writing to the court, drawing attention to any matters which, in his opinion, may be of assistance to the court in considering the application.

(7) With a view to obtaining the directions of the court on any matter, the children's guardian may at any time make such interim report to the court as appears to him to be necessary.

(8) The court may, at any time before the final determination of the application, require the children's guardian to perform such further duties as the court considers necessary.

(9) The children's guardian shall attend any hearing of the application unless the court otherwise orders.

(10) Any report made to the court under this rule shall be confidential[2].

(11) The powers of the court to appoint a children's guardian under paragraph (1) or (2), to require the performance by the children's guardian of particular duties in accordance with paragraph (2), (5)(c) or (8), and to give directions following the making of an interim report in accordance with paragraph (7), shall also be exercisable, before the hearing of the application, by a single justice or by the justices' clerk.

---

1. The children's guardian is appointed as a matter of public policy; it is desirable to appoint a person experienced in such matters rather than a person nominated by the applicant (*Re A B* [1948] 2 All ER 727).

2. A party who is an individual and is referred to in a confidential report supplied to the court may, for the purposes of the hearing, be supplied with a copy of that part of any such report which refers to him, subject to any direction given by the court; see r 32(4), post, and notes thereto. Since disclosure of any part of a report is a matter for the court, the guardian ad litem has no power to give the child an unqualified promise of confidentiality; see *Re D (minors) (adoption reports: confidentiality)* [1995] 4 All ER 385, [1995] 3 WLR 483, HL.

It is undesirable that the report should be confined to answering questions on a printed form (*Re H (minors)* (1975) 5 Fam Law 54).

Statement of facts in dispensation cases

6–3426 7. (1) Where the adoption agency applying for an order freeing a child for adoption intends to request the court to dispense with the agreement of a parent or guardian of the child on any of the grounds specified in section 16(2) of the 1976 Act[1], the request shall, unless otherwise directed, be made in the application, or, if made subsequently, by notice to the designated officer for the court, and there shall be attached to the application or notice three copies of the statement of facts on which the applicant intends to rely.

(2) Where the applicant has been informed by a person with whom the child has been placed for adoption that he wishes his identity to remain confidential, the statement of facts supplied under paragraph (1) shall be framed in such a way as not to disclose the identity of that person.

(3) Where a statement of facts has been supplied under paragraph (1), the designated officer for the court shall, where and as soon as practicable, inform the parent or guardian of the request to dispense with his agreement and shall send to him a copy of the statement supplied under paragraph (1).

(4) The designated officer for the court shall also send a copy of the statement supplied under paragraph (1) to the children's guardian and to the reporting officer if a different person.

---

1. For method of service of notices, see r 29, post.

Agreement

6–3427   **8.** (1) Any document signifying the agreement of a person to the making of an adoption order may be in Form 2, and, if executed by a person outside England and Wales before the commencement of the proceedings, shall be filed with the application.

(2) If the document is executed in Scotland it shall be witnessed by a Justice of the Peace or a Sheriff.

(3) If the document is executed in Northern Ireland it shall be witnessed by a Justice of the Peace.

(4) If the document is executed outside the United Kingdom it shall be witnessed by one of the following persons—

(a) any person for the time being authorised by law in the place where the document is executed to administer an oath for any judicial or other legal purpose;

(b) a British consular officer;

(c) a notary public; or

(d) if the person executing the document is serving in any of the regular armed forces of the Crown, an officer holding a commission in any of those forces.

Notice of hearing

6–3428   **9.** (1) As soon as practicable after the application has been made, the justices' clerk shall fix a time for the hearing of the application and the designated officer for the court shall serve[1] notice of the hearing on all the parties, the reporting officer and the children's guardian (if appointed) in Form 3.

(2) The reporting officer and the children's guardian (if appointed), but no other person, shall be served with a copy of the application and the report supplied by the applicant, and that report shall be confidential.

---

1. For method of service of notices, see r 29, post.

The hearing

6–3429   **10.** (1) On the hearing of the application any person upon whom notice is required to be served under rule 9 may attend and be heard on the question whether an order freeing the child for adoption should be made.

(2) Any member or employee of a party which is a local authority, adoption agency or other body may address the court if he is duly authorised in that behalf.

(3) Where the court has been informed by the applicant that the child has been placed with a person (whether alone or jointly with another) for adoption and that person wishes his identity to remain confidential, the proceedings shall be conducted with a view to securing that any such person is not seen by or made known to any respondent who is not already aware of his identity except with his consent.

(4) Subject to paragraph (5), the court shall not make an order freeing the child for adoption except after the personal attendance before the court of a representative of the applicant duly authorised in that behalf and of the child.

(5) If there are special circumstances which, having regard to the report of the children's guardian (if any), appear to the court to make the attendance of the child unnecessary, the court may direct that the child need not attend.

(6) If there are special circumstances which appear to the court to make the attendance of any other party necessary, the court may direct that that party shall attend.

Proof of identity of child, etc

6–3430   **11.** (1) Where proof of the identity of the child is required for any purpose, any fact tending to establish his identity with a child to whom a document relates may be proved by affidavit.

(2) Where any such fact is proved by affidavit, the attendance of a witness at the hearing to prove that fact shall not be compelled unless the fact is disputed or for some special reason his attendance is required by the court.

(3) Where the precise date of the child's birth is not proved to the satisfaction of the court, the court shall determine the probable date of his birth and the date so determined may be specified in the order freeing the child for adoption as the date of his birth.

(4) Where the place of birth of the child cannot be proved to the satisfaction of the court but it appears probable that the child was born in the United Kingdom, the Channel Islands or the Isle of Man, he may be treated as having been born in the registration district and sub-district in which the court sits, and in any other case (where the country of birth is not proved) the particulars of the country of birth may be omitted from the order freeing the child for adoption.

Application for revocation of order freeing a child for adoption

6–3431   12. (1) An application by a former parent for an order revoking an order freeing the child for adoption shall be made in Form 4 to the court which made the order to which the application relates by delivering it, or sending it by post to that court, together with all documents referred to in the application.

(2) Notice of the application shall be served on all persons who were parties to the proceedings in which the order freeing the child for adoption was made and on any adoption agency which has parental responsibility for the child by virtue of section 21 of the 1976 Act, save that notice shall not be served on a party to the earlier proceedings who was joined as a party by virtue of rule 4(2)(*b*).

(3) As soon as practicable after the application has been made, the justices' clerk shall fix a time for the hearing of the application and the court (or a single justice or the designated officer for the court) shall appoint a children's guardian of the child in accordance with rule 6(4) and shall send to him a copy of the application and any documents attached thereto.

(4) The children's guardian shall have the same duties as if he had been appointed under rule 6 but as if in that rule—

(*a*)   the reference to an order freeing the child for adoption was a reference to the revocation of an order freeing the child for adoption; and

(*b*)   each reference to the report supplied by the applicant was omitted.

Joint application for parental responsibility by adoption agencies

6–3432   13. (1) An application by two adoption agencies under section 21(1) of the 1976 Act shall be made in the appropriate form prescribed in Schedule 1 to these Rules to a court acting for the area within which the child is at the date of the application by delivering it, or sending it by post, to that court, together with all documents referred to in the application.

(2) Notice of any order made under section 21 of the 1976 Act shall be sent by the court to the court which made the order under section 18 of the 1976 Act (if a different court) and to any former parent (as defined in section 19(1) of the 1976 Act) of the child.

PART III
ADOPTION ORDERS

Application for a serial number

6–3433   14. If any person proposing to apply to a domestic court for an adoption order wishes his identity to be kept confidential[1], he may, before making his application, apply to the designated officer for the court for a serial number to be assigned to him for the purposes of identifying him in connection with the proposed application, and a number shall be assigned to him accordingly.

---

1. Where a serial number is used it will be for the court to consider whether material in a report should be given to a respondent; whilst the respondent has a right to object to the applicants as well as to the principle of adoption this needs to be balanced with the applicants' right to confidentiality (*Re S (adoption application: disclosure of information)* [1993] 2 FCR 16, sub nom *Re S (a minor) (adoption)* [1993] 2 FLR 204, CA).

The applicant

6–3434   15. (1) An application for an adoption order shall be in Form 6 and shall be made to a family proceedings court acting in the area within which the child is at the date of the application by delivering it, or sending it by post to that court, together with all documents referred to in the application.

(2) The applicant shall be the proposed adopter and the respondents shall be—

(*a*)   each parent[1] or guardian (not being an applicant) of the child, unless the child is free for adoption;

(*b*)   any adoption agency having parental responsibility for the child by virtue of section 18 or 21 of the 1976 Act;

(*c*)   any adoption agency named in the application or in any form of agreement to the making of the adoption order as having taken part in the arrangements for the adoption of the child;

(*d*)   any local authority to whom the applicant has given notice under section 18 of the 1975 Act of his intention to apply for an adoption order;

(*e*)   any local authority or voluntary organisation which has parental responsibility for, is looking after, or is caring for, the child;

(*f*)–(*i*)   Revoked.

(*j*)   where the applicant proposes to rely on section 15(1)(*b*)(ii) of the 1976 Act, the spouse of the applicant.

(3) The court may at any time direct that any other person to body, except the child, be made a respondent to the application[2].

(4) The applicant shall supply to the designated officer for the court three copies of—

(*a*)   Form 6, together with any other documents required to be supplied, and (*b*)   where the child was not placed for adoption with the applicant by an adoption agency, save where the applicant or one of the applicants is a parent of the child, reports by a registered medical practitioner made not more than three months earlier on the health of the child and of each applicant, covering the matters specified in Schedule 3.

1. By virtue of r 2(2), ante, "parent" has the same meaning as in s 72(1) of the Adoption Act 1976, ante; accordingly, where the natural father of a child does not have parental responsibility for the child, it is not mandatory that he be joined as a party to the proceedings. Nevertheless, the court has a discretion, in such cases, to direct that the father be joined as a respondent; *see Re C (adoption: parties)* [1996] 2 FCR 129, CA. As a matter of general practice, directions should be given to inform unmarried fathers of adoption proceedings unless the court decides it is not appropriate to do so; the weight of the mother's desire for confidentiality would depend on the facts of each case, as would the application of art 8(1): *Re H (a child)(adoption: disclosure), Re G (a child)(adoption: disclosure)* [2001] 1 FCR 726, [2001] 1 FLR 646, CA.

2. The Court has an unfettered discretion and the European Convention on Human Rights is a factor to be considered although in any event the climate has shifted towards according greater involvement of unmarried fathers, see *Re S (a child) (adoption proceedings: joinder of father)* [2001] 1 FCR 158, sub nom *Re R (adoption: father's involvement* [2001] 1 FLR 302, CA; and see *Re B (a child) (sole adoption by unmarried father)* [2001] 1 FCR 600, CA.

Preliminary examination of application

6–3435   **16.** If it appears to the designated officer for the court on receipt of the application for an adoption order that the court—

(*a*)   may be precluded, by virtue of section 24(1) of the 1976 Act, from proceeding to hear the application, or

(*b*)   may, for any other reason appearing in the application, have no jurisdiction to make an adoption order,

he shall bring the relevant matter to the attention of the court and the application shall not be proceeded with unless the court gives directions as to the further conduct of the application.

Appointment and duties of reporting officer

6–3436   **17.** (1) As soon as practicable after the application has been made or at any stage thereafter, if the child is not free for adoption and if it appears that a parent or guardian of the child is willing to agree to the making of an adoption order and is in England and Wales, the court shall appoint a reporting officer in respect of that parent or guardian, and shall send to him a copy of the application and any documents attached thereto.

(2) The same person may be appointed as reporting officer in respect of two or more parents or guardians of the child.

(3) The reporting officer shall not be a member or employee of the applicant or any respondent body (except where a local authority is made a respondent only under rule 15(2)(*d*)) nor have been involved in the making of any arrangements for the adoption of the child.

(4) The reporting officer shall—

(*a*)   ensure so far as is reasonably practicable that any agreement to the making of the adoption order is given freely and unconditionally and with full understanding of what is involved;

(*b*)   witness the signature by the parent or guardian of the written agreement to the making of the adoption order;

(*c*)   investigate all the circumstances relevant to that agreement; and

(*d*)   on completing his investigations make a report in writing to the court, drawing attention to any matters which, in his opinion, may be of assistance to the court in considering the application.

(5) Paragraphs (5) to (8) of rule 5 shall apply to a reporting officer appointed under this rule as they apply to a reporting officer appointed under that rule; and paragraph (9) of rule 5 shall apply in relation to the appointment of a reporting officer under this rule as it applies in relation to such an appointment made under that rule.

Appointment and duties of children's guardian

6–3437   **18.** (1) As soon as practicable after the application has been made, or after receipt of the statement of facts supplied under rule 19, if the child is not free for adoption and if it appears that a parent or guardian of the child is unwilling to agree to the making of the adoption order, the court shall appoint a childrens' guardian ad litem of the child and shall send him a copy of the application together with any documents attached thereto.

(2) Where there are special circumstances and it appears to the court that the welfare of the child requires it, the court may at any time appoint a childrens' guardian of the child and where such an appointment is made the court shall indicate any particular matters which it requires the guardian ad litem to investigate and the court shall send the guardian ad litem a copy of the application together with any documents attached thereto.

(3) The same person may be appointed as reporting officer under rule 17(1) in respect of a parent or guardian who appears to be willing to agree to the making of the adoption order, and as childrens' guardian of the child under this rule; and, whether or not so appointed as reporting officer, the childrens' guardian may be appointed as reporting officer in respect of a parent or

guardian of the child who originally was unwilling to agree to the making of an adoption order but who later signifies his or her agreement.

guardian ad litem

(4) The children's guardian shall not be a member or employee of the applicant or any respondent body (except where a local authority is made a respondent only under rule 15(2)(*d*)) nor have been involved in the making of any arrangements for the adoption of the child.

(5) With a view to safeguarding the interests of the child before the court the children' guardian shall so far as is reasonably practicable—

(*a*) investigate—

    (i) so far as he considers necessary, the matters alleged in the application, any report supplied under rule 22(1) or (2) and, where appropriate, the statement of facts supplied under rule 19;

    (ii) any other matters which appear to him to be relevant to the making of an adoption order;

(*b*) advise whether, in his opinion, the child should be present at the hearing of the application; and

(*c*) perform such other duties as appear to him to be necessary or as the court may direct.

(6) Paragraphs (6) to (10) of rule 6 shall apply to a guardian ad litem appointed under this rule as they apply to a children's guardian appointed under that rule; and paragraph (11) of rule 6 shall apply in relation to the appointment of a children's guardian under this rule as it applies in relation to such an appointment made under that rule.

Statement of facts in dispensation cases

6–3438   19. (1) Where the child is not free for adoption and the applicant for the adoption order intends to request the court to dispense with the agreement of a parent or guardian of the child on any of the grounds specified in section 16(2) of the 1976 Act, the request shall, unless otherwise directed, be made in the application or, if made subsequently, by notice to the designated officer for the court and there shall be attached to the application or notice three copies of the statement of facts on which the applicant intends to rely.

(2) Where a serial number has been assigned to the applicant under rule 14, the statement of facts supplied under paragraph (1) shall be framed in such a way as not to disclose the identity of the applicant.

(3) Where a statement of facts has been supplied under paragraph (1), the designated officer for the court shall, where and as soon as practicable, inform the parent or guardian of the request to dispense with his agreement and shall send to him a copy of the statement supplied under paragraph (1).

(4) The designated officer for the court shall also send a copy of the statement supplied under paragraph (1) to the children's guardian and to the reporting officer if a different person.

Agreement

6–3439   20. (1) Any document signifying the agreement of a person to the making of the adoption order may be in Form 7, and, if executed by a person outside England and Wales before the commencement of the proceedings, shall be filed with the application.

(2) If the document is executed outside England and Wales it shall be witnessed by one of the persons specified in rule 8(2), (3) or (4), according to the country in which it is executed.

Notice of hearing

6–3450   21. (1) Subject to paragraph (4), as soon as practicable after the application has been made the designated officer for the court shall fix a time for the hearing of the application and shall serve[1] notice of the hearing on all the parties, the reporting officer and the children's (if appointed) in Form 8.

(2) In a case where section 18 of the 1975 Act[2] applies, the designated officer for the court shall send a copy of the application and, where appropriate, of the report supplied under rule 15(4), to the local authority to whom notice under that section was given.

(3) No person other than the reporting officer, the children's guardian (if appointed) and, in cases where section 18 of the 1975 Act[2] applies, the local authority to whom notice under that section was given, shall be served with a copy of the application.

(4) Where section 18 of the 1975 Act[2] applies, the justices' chief executive shall fix a time for the hearing so that the hearing takes place on a date not less than three months from the date of the notice given to the local authority under that section.

---

1. Where it is impossible to comply with this Rule, the court retains jurisdiction to deal with the matter. Cf *Re R (adoption)* [1966] 3 All ER 613, 131 JP 1. For method of service of notices, see r 29, post.

2. See now s 22 of the Adoption Act 1976.

Reports by adoption agency or local authority

6–3451   22. (1) Where the child was placed for adoption with the applicant by an adoption agency, that agency shall supply, within six weeks of receipt of the notice of hearing under rule 21, three copies of a report in writing covering the matters specified in Schedule 2.

(2) Where the child was not placed for adoption with the applicant by an adoption agency, the local authority to whom the notice under section 18 of the 1975 Act[1] was given shall supply, within six weeks of receipt of the notice of hearing under rule 21, three copies of a report in writing covering the matters specified in Schedule 2.

(3) The court may request a further report under paragraph (1) or (2) and may indicate any particular matters it requires such a further report to cover.

(4) The designated officer for the court shall send a copy of any report supplied under paragraph (1) or (2) to the reporting officer and to the children's guardian (if appointed).

(5) No other person shall be supplied with a copy of any report supplied under paragraph (1) or (2) and any such report shall be confidential.

---

1. See now s 22 of the Adoption Act 1976.

The hearing

6–3452   23. (1) On the hearing of the application any person upon whom notice is required to be served under rule 21 may attend and be heard on the question whether an adoption order should be made.

(2) Any member or employee of a party which is a local authority, adoption agency or other body may address the court if he is duly authorised in that behalf.

(3) If a serial number has been assigned to the applicant under rule 14, the proceedings shall be conducted with a view to securing that he is not seen by or made known to any respondent who is not already aware of the applicant's identity except with his consent.

(4) Subject to paragraphs (5) and (7), the court shall not make an adoption order or an interim order except after the personal attendance before the court of the applicant and the child[1].

(5) If there are special circumstances which, having regard to the report of the children's guardian (if any), appear to the court to make the attendance of the child unnecessary, the court may direct that the child need not attend.

(6) If there are special circumstances which appear to the court to make the attendance of any other party necessary, the court may direct that that party shall attend.

(7) In the case of an application under section 14(1A) or (1B) of the 1976 Act, the court may in special circumstances make an adoption order or an interim order after the personal attendance of one only of the applicants, if the application is verified by a declaration made by the applicant who does not attend and witnessed by a justice of the peace, a justices' clerk within the meaning of section 70 of the Justices of the Peace Act 1979, or, if made outside the United Kingdom, by any of the persons specified in rule 8(4).

---

1. A decision not to make an order may be reached without seeing the infant (*Re G (TJ) (an infant)* [1963] 2 QB 73, [1963] 1 All ER 20, 127 JP 144).

Proof of identity of child, etc

6–3453   24. (1) Where proof of the identity of the child is required for any purpose, any fact tending to establish his identity with a child to whom a document relates may be proved by affidavit.

(2) Where any such fact is proved by affidavit, the attendance of a witness at the hearing to prove that fact shall not be compelled unless the fact is disputed or for some special reason his attendance is required by the court.

(3) Subject to paragraph (5), where the precise date of the child's birth is not proved to the satisfaction of the court, the court shall determined the probable date of his birth and the date so determined may be specified in the adoption order as the date of his birth.

(4) Subject to paragraph (5), where the place of birth of the child cannot be proved to the satisfaction of the court but it appears probable that the child was born in the United Kingdom, the Channel Islands or the Isle of Man, he may be treated as having been born in the registration district and sub-district in which the court sits, and in any other case (where the country of birth is not proved) the particulars of the country of birth may be omitted from the adoption order.

(5) Where the child is free for adoption, any order made identifying the probable date and place of birth of the child in the proceedings under section 14 of the 1975 Act[1] shall be sufficient proof of the date and place of birth of the child in proceedings to which this rule applies.

---

1. See now s 18 of the Adoption Act 1976.

Further proceedings after interim order

6–3454   25. Where the court has made an interim order, the justices' clerk shall fix a time for the further hearing of the application, such hearing to be on a date before the order expires, and shall send notice in Form 8 of the date of the hearing to all the parties and to the children's guardian (if appointed) not less than one month before that date.

Committal of child to care on refusal of adoption order

6–3455   26. *Revoked.*

PART IV
MISCELLANEOUS
Application for removal, return etc, of child

6–3456   **27.** (1) An application—

(a)   for leave under section 27 or 28 of the 1976 Act to remove a child from the home of a person with whom the child lives,

(b)   under section 29(1) of the 1976 Act for an order for the return of a child who has been removed from the home of a person with whom the child lives,

(c)   under section 29(2) of the 1976 Act for an order directing a person not to remove a child from the home of a person with whom the child lives,

(d)   under section 30(2) of the 1976 Act, for leave to give notice of an intention not to allow a child to remain in a person's home, or

(e)   under section 20(2) of the 1976 Act, for leave to place a child for adoption,

shall be made in accordance with paragraph (2).

(2)   The application under paragraph (1) above shall be made by complaint—

(a)   if an application for an adoption order or an order under section 18 or 20 of the 1976 Act is pending, to the family proceedings court in which the application is pending; or

(b)   if no such application is pending, to the family proceedings court in whose area the applicant lives or, in the case of an application made under section 28 of the 1976 Act, the court in whose area the child is:

> Provided that if an application is pending under paragraph (1) above, any further application concerning the home of the child shall be made to the family proceedings court in which that original application is pending.

(3)   The respondents shall be—

(a)   in a case where proceedings for an adoption order or an order under sections 18 or 20 of the 1976 Act are pending (or where such proceedings have subsequently been commenced), all the parties to those proceedings;

(b)   in any other case, any person against whom an order is sought in the application and the local authority to whom the prospective adopter has given notice under section 22 of the 1976 Act; and

(c)   in any case, such other person or body, not being the child, as the court thinks fit.

(4)   If in any application under this rule a serial number has been assigned to a person who has applied or who proposes to apply for adoption order, or such a person applies to the designated officer for the court in that behalf before making that application and a serial number is assigned accordingly—

(a)   the designated officer for the court shall ensure that a summons directed to any of the respondents does not disclose the identity of that person to any respondent to the application under this rule who is not already aware of that person's identity, and

(b)   the proceedings on the application under this rule shall be conducted with a view to securing that he is not seen by or made known to any party who is not already aware of his identity except with his consent.

(5)   The designated officer for the court shall serve notice of the time fixed for the hearing on the reporting officer and children's guardian (if any), together with a copy of the complaint, and on the hearing of the application the reporting officer and children's guardian may attend and be heard on the question of whether the application made should be granted.

(6)   Unless otherwise directed, any prospective adopter who is a respondent under this rule and who wishes to oppose the application shall make his application for an adoption order within 14 days of the service upon him of the summons or before or at the time of the hearing of the application under this rule, whichever is the sooner.

(7)   The court may at any time give directions, and if giving directions under paragraph (6) shall give directions, as to the conduct of any application under this rule and in particular as to the appointment of a children's guardian of the child.

(8)   Any member or employee of a party which is a local authority, adoption agency or other body may address the court at the hearing of an application under this rule if he is duly authorised in that behalf.

(9)   Where an application under paragraph (1)(a) or (d) is granted or an application under paragraph (1)(b) or (c) is refused, the court may thereupon, if application for an adoption order has been made, treat the hearing of the application as the hearing of the application for an adoption order and refuse an adoption order accordingly.

(10)   Where an application under this rule is determined the designated officer for the court shall serve notice of the effect of the determination on all the parties.

(11)   A search warrant issued by a justice of the peace under section 29(4) of the 1976 Act (which relates to premises specified in an information to which an order made under the said section 29(1) relates, authorising a constable to search the said premises and if he finds the child to return the child to the person on whose application the said order was made) shall be in a warrant form as per section 102 of the 1989 Act (warrant to search for or remove a child) or a form to the like effect.

Amendment and revocation of orders

6–3457   **28.** (1) Any application made under paragraph 4 of Schedule 1 to the 1976 Act for the amendment of an adoption order or the revocation of a direction to the Registrar General, or under section 52 of, and Schedule 2 to, the 1976 Act for the revocation of an adoption order, shall be in Form 9, and shall be made to a family proceedings court acting in the same local justice area as the family proceedings court which made the adoption order, by delivering it or sending it by post to the designated officer for the court.

(2) Notice of the application shall be given by the designated officer for the court to such persons (if any) as the court thinks fit.

(3) Where the application is granted, the designated officer for the court shall send to the Registrar General a notice specifying the amendments or informing him of the revocation and shall give sufficient particulars of the order to enable the Registrar General to identify the case.

Power of court to limit cross-examination

6–3457A   **28A.** The court may limit the issues on which a children's guardian or a reporting officer may be cross-examined.

Service of documents

6–3458   **29.** (1) Unless otherwise directed, any document under these rules may be served—

    (*a*)   on a corporation or body of persons, by delivering it at, or sending it by post to, the registered or principal office of the corporation or body;

    (*b*)   on any other person, by delivering it to him, or by sending it by post to him at his usual or last known address.

(2) A note of service or non-service shall be endorsed on a copy of Form 3 or Form 8.

(3) In the case of a document sent by post to a person's usual or last known address in accordance with paragraph (1)(*b*), the court may treat service as having been effected notwithstanding that the document has been returned undelivered.

Costs

6–3459   **30.** (1) On the determination of an application or on the making of an interim order, the court may make such order as to the costs as it thinks just and, in particular, may order the applicant to pay—

    (*a*)   the expenses incurred by the reporting officer and the children's guardian (if appointed), and

    (*b*)   the expenses incurred by any respondent in attending the hearing,

or such part of those expenses as the court thinks proper.

(2) Determination of an application in this rule includes a refusal to proceed with the application or withdrawal of the application.

Notice and copies of orders etc

6–3460   **31.** (1) In applications to which these rules apply orders[1] shall be made in the form indicated in this paragraph—

Description of order	Form
(*a*) order under section 18 of the 1976 Act	10
(*b*) order under section 20 of the 1976 Act	11
(*c*) interim order	12
(*d*) adoption order	13

(2) Where an adoption order is made by a court sitting in Wales in respect of a child who was born in Wales (or is treated under rule 24(4) as having been born in the registration district and sub-district in which that court sits) and the adopter so requests before the order is drawn up, the designated officer for the court shall supply a translation into Welsh of the particulars set out in the order.

(3) Within 7 days of the making of an order in an application to which these rules apply, the designated officer for the court shall send a copy of the order (and of any translation into Welsh required to be supplied under paragraph (2)) to the applicant.

(4) Within 7 days of the making of an adoption order, the designated officer for the court shall send a copy of the order (and of any translation into Welsh supplied under paragraph (2)) to the Registrar General; where a translation into Welsh under paragraph (2) has been supplied, the English text shall prevail.

(5) Where an order to which paragraph 1(*a*), (*b*) or (*d*) applies is made or refused or an order to which paragraph 1(*c*) applies is made, the designated officer for the court shall serve notice to that effect on every respondent.

(6) *Revoked.*

(7) The designated officer for the court shall serve notice of the making of an order to which paragraph 1(*a*), (*b*) or (*d*) applies on any court in Great Britain which appears to him to have made

any such order as is referred to in section 12(3) of the 1976 Act (orders relating to parental responsibility for, and the maintenance of, the child).

(8) A copy of any order may be supplied to the Registrar General at his request.

(9) A copy of any order may be supplied to the applicant.

(10) A copy of any order may be supplied to any other person with the leave of the court.

---

1. The size and format of the order is not specified by the Rules, but international metric size A4 is preferred. See Department of Health and Social Security Circular 40/1973.

Keeping of registers, custody, inspection and disclosure of documents and information

6-3461 **32.** (1) Such part of the register kept in pursuance of rules made under the Magistrates' Courts Act 1980 as relates to proceedings under Part II of the 1976 Act shall be kept in a separate book and shall contain the particulars shown in Form 14 and the book shall not contain particulars of any other proceedings except proceedings under the 1976 Act (or under any previous enactment relating to adoption).

(2) Any declaration by a parent or guardian or a former parent of a child that he prefers not to be involved in future questions concerning the adoption of the child which is required to be recorded by the court in accordance with section 18(6) or 19(4) of the 1976 Act shall be recorded in the book kept in pursuance of paragraph (1).

(3) The book kept in pursuance of paragraph (1) and all other documents relating to proceedings mentioned in that paragraph shall, while they are in the custody of the court, be kept in a place of special security.

(4) A party who is an individual and is referred to in a confidential report supplied to the court by an adoption agency, a local authority, a reporting officer or a children's guardian may, for the purposes of the hearing, be supplied with a copy of that part of any such report which refers to him, subject to any direction[1] given by the court that—

(a) no part of one or any of the reports shall be revealed to that party, or

(b) the part of one or any of the reports referring to that party shall be revealed only to that party's legal advisers, or

(c) the whole or any other part of one or any of the reports be revealed to that party.

(5) Any person who obtains any information in the course of, or relating to, any proceedings mentioned in paragraph (1), shall treat that information as confidential and shall only disclose it if—

(a) the disclosure is necessary for the proper exercise of his duties, or

(b) the information is requested—

(i) by a court or public authority (whether in Great Britain or not) having power to determine adoptions and related matters, for the purpose of the discharge of its duties in that behalf, or

(ii) by the Registrar General, or a person authorised in writing by him, where the information requested relates only to the identity of any adoption agency which made the arrangements for placing the child for adoption in the actual custody of the applicants, and of any local authority which was notified of the applicant's intention to apply for an adoption order in respect of the child, or

(iii) by a person who is authorised in writing by the Lord Chancellor to obtain the information for the purposes of research.

(5A) Nothing in this rule shall prevent the disclosure of a document prepared by an officer of the service for the purpose of—

(a) enabling a person to perform functions required under section 62(3A) of the Justices of the Peace Act 1997; and

(b) assisting an officer of the service who is appointed by the court under any enactment to perform his functions.

(5B) Nothing in this rule shall prevent the disclosure of any document relating to proceedings by an officer of the service to any other officer of the service unless that other officer is involved in the same proceedings but on behalf of a different party.

(6) Save as required or authorised by a provision of any enactment or of these Rules or with the leave of the court, no document or order held by or lodged with the court in proceedings under the 1976 Act (or under any previous enactment relating to adoption) shall be open to inspection by any person, and no copy of any such document or order, or of an extract from any such document or order, shall be taken by or issued to any person.

---

1. The fundamental principle of fairness that a party is entitled to the disclosure of all materials which may be taken into account by the court when reaching an adverse decision applies with particular force to adoption proceedings. When deciding whether to direct that notwithstanding r 32(4) a party referred to in a confidential report should not be entitled to inspect the part of the report referring to him or her, the court should consider whether disclosure would involve a real possibility of significant harm to the child. If it would, the court should next consider whether the overall interests of the child would benefit from non-disclosure, weighing on the one hand the interest of the child in having material properly tested, and on the other both the magnitude and the risk that harm will occur and the gravity of the harm if it does occur. If the court is satisfied that the interests of the child point towards non-disclosure, the next and final step is for the court to weigh that consideration, and

its strength in the circumstances of the case, against the interest of the parent or other party in having an opportunity to see and respond to the material. In the latter regard the court should take into account the importance of the material to the issues in the case. Non-disclosure should be the exception and not the rule. The court should be rigorous in its examination of the risk and gravity of the feared harm to the child, and should order non-disclosure only when the case for doing so is compelling (*Re D (minors) (adoption reports: confidentiality)* [1995] 4 All ER 385, [1996] 1 FCR 205, [1995] 2 FLR 687, HL, see also *Re X (children) (adoption: confidentiality)* [2002] EWCA Civ 828, [2002] 3 FCR 648, [2002] 2 FLR 476).

Proceedings to be by way of complaint, etc

6–3462 33. Save in so far as special provision is made by these Rules, proceedings on an application shall be regulated in the same manner as proceedings on complaint[1], and accordingly for the purposes of this rule the application shall be deemed to be a complaint, the applicant to be a complainant, the respondents to be defendants and any notice served under these rules to be a summons; but nothing in this rule shall be construed as enabling a warrant of arrest to be issued for failure to appear in answer to any such notice.

1. For observations on the procedure to be followed in contested cases, see *Re M (an infant)* [1973] QB 108, [1972] 3 All ER 321.

6–3463 SCHEDULE 1

Forms[1]

1. The prescribed forms are not printed here, but are comprehensively set out in Schedule 1 to the Rules.

Rule 4(4) SCHEDULE 2
MATTERS TO BE COVERED IN REPORTS SUPPLIED UNDER RULES 4(4), 22(1) OR 22(2)

6–3464 So far as is practicable[1], the report supplied by the adoption agency or, in the case of a report supplied under rule 22(2), the local authority shall include all the following particulars—
1. *The Child*

(a) Name, sex, date and place of birth and address;
(b) whether the child's father and mother were married to each other at the time of his birth;
(c) nationality;
(d) physical description;
(e) personality and social development;
(f) religion, including details of baptism, confirmation or equivalent ceremonies;
(g) details of any wardship proceedings and of any court orders relating to parental responsibility for the child or to maintenance and residence;
(h) details of any brothers and sisters, including dates of birth, arrangements concerning with whom they are to live and whether any brother or sister is the subject of a parallel application;
(i) extent of contact with members of the child's natural family and, if the father and mother were not married to each other at the time of his birth, his father, and in each case the nature of the relationship enjoyed;
(j) if the child has been looked after by or is in the care of a local authority or has been cared for by a voluntary organisation, details (including dates) of any placements with foster parents, or other arrangements in respect of the care of the child, including particulars of the persons with whom the child has had his home and observations on the care provided;
(k) date and circumstances of placement with prospective adopter;
(l) names, addresses and types of schools attended, with dates, and educational attainments;
(m) any special needs in relation to the child's health (whether physical or mental) and his emotional and behavioural development and whether he is subject to a statement under the Education Act 1981;[2]
(n) what, if any, rights to or interests in property or any claim to damages, under the Fatal Accidents Act 1976 or otherwise, the child stands to retain or lose if adopted;
(o) wishes and feelings in relation to adoption and the application, including any wishes in respect of religious and cultural upbringing; and
(p) any other relevant information which might assist the court.

2. *Each Natural Parent, including where appropriate the father who was not married to the child's mother at the time of his birth*[3]

(a) Name, date and place of birth and address;
(b) marital status and date and place of marriage (if any);
(c) past and present relationship (if any) with the other natural parent, including comments on its stability;
(d) physical description;
(e) personality;
(f) religion;
(g) educational attainments;
(h) past and present occupations and interests;
(i) so far as available, names and brief details of the personal circumstances of the parents and any brothers and sisters of the natural parent, with their ages or ages at death;
(j) wishes and feelings in relation to adoption and the application, including any wishes in respect of the child's religious and cultural upbringing;
(k) reasons why any of the above information is unavailable; and
(l) any other relevant information which might assist the court.

3. *Guardian*
Give the details required under paragraph 2(a), (f), (j) and (l).
4. *Prospective Adopter*

(a) Name, date and place of birth and address;
(b) relationship (if any) to the child;
(c) marital status, date and place of marriage (if any) and comments on stability of relationship;
(d) details of any previous marriage;
(e) if a parent and step-parent are applying, the reason why they prefer adoption to a residence order;
(f) if a natural parent is applying alone, the reasons for the exclusion of the other parent;
(g) if a married person is applying alone, the reasons for this;
(h) physical description;
(i) personality;
(j) religion, and whether willing to follow any wishes of the child or his parents or guardian in respect of the child's religious and cultural upbringing;
(k) educational attainments;
(l) past and present occupations and interests;
(m) particulars of the home and living conditions (and particulars of any home where the prospective adopter proposes to live with the child, if different);
(n) details of income and comments on the living standards of the household;
(o) details of other members of the household (including any children of the prospective adopter even if not resident in the household);
(p) details of the parents and any brothers or sisters of the prospective adopter, with their ages or ages at death;
(q) attitudes to the proposed adoption of such other members of the prospective adopter's household and family as the adoption agency or, as the case may be, the local authority considers appropriate;
(r) previous experience of caring for children as step-parent, foster parent, child-minder or prospective adopter and assessment of ability in this respect, together where appropriate with assessment of ability in bringing up the prospective adopter's own children;
(s) reasons for wishing to adopt the child and extent of understanding of the nature and effect of adoption;
(t) any hopes and expectations for the child's future;
(u) assessment of ability to bring up the child throughout his childhood;
(v) details of any adoption allowance payable;
(w) confirmation that any referees have been interviewed, with a report of their views and opinion of the weight to be placed thereon; and
(x) any other relevant information which might assist the court.

5. *Actions of the adoption agency or local authority supplying the report*

(a) Reports under rules 4(4) or 22(1)—

   (i) brief account of the agency's actions in the case, with particulars and dates of all written information and notices given to the child, his natural parents and the prospective adopter;
   (ii) details of alternatives to adoption considered;
   (iii) reasons for considering that adoption would be in the child's best interests (with date of relevant decision); and
   (iv) reasons for considering that the prospective adopter would be suitable to be an adoptive parent and that he would be suitable for this child (with dates of relevant decisions) or, if the child has not yet been placed for adoption, reasons for considering that he is likely to be so placed;

   OR

(b) Reports under rule 22(2)—

   (i) confirmation that notice was given under section 22 of the 1976 Act, with the date of that notice;
   (ii) brief account of the local authority's action in these; and
   (iii) account of investigations whether child was placed in contravention of section 11 of the 1976 Act.

6. *Generally*

(a) Whether any respondent appears to be under the age of majority or under a mental disability; and
(b) whether, in the opinion of the body supplying the report, any other person should be made a respondent (for example, a person who was not married to the mother of the child at the time of his birth and who claims to be the father of the child, a spouse, or ex-spouse of a natural parent, a relative of a deceased parent, or a person with parental responsibility).

7. *Conclusions*
(This part of the report should contain more than a simple synopsis of the information above. As far as possible, the court should be given a fuller picture of the child, his natural parents and, where appropriate, the prospective adopter).

(a) Except where the applicant or one of them is a parent of the child, a summary by the medical adviser to the body supplying the report, of the health history and state of health of the child, his natural parents and, if appropriate, the prospective adopter, with comments on the implications for the order sought and on how any special health needs of the child might be met;
(b) opinion on whether making the order sought would be in the child's best long-term interests, and on how any special emotional, behavioural and educational needs of the child might be met;
(c) opinion on the effect on the child's natural parents of making the order sought;
(d) if the child has been placed for adoption, opinion on the likelihood of full integration of the child into the household, family and community of the prospective adopter, and on whether the proposed adoption would be in the best long-term interests of the prospective adopter;
(e) opinion, if appropriate, on the relative merits of adoption and a residence order; and
(f) final conclusions and recommendations whether the order sought should be made (and, if not, alternative proposals).

---

1. The word "practicable" imports a consideration of the consequences of the action. Accordingly, if ascertaining the wishes and feelings of the father would be detrimental for the child, then it is not practicable to obtain them (*Re P (adoption) (natural father's rights)* [1995] 2 FCR 58).
2. See now the Education Act 1996, Pt IV, Chapter I, ss 312–336, in PART VIII: EDUCATION, *post*.

3. This will be appropriate only if the putative father is a parent or guardian within the meaning of s 16(1) of the Adoption Act 1976, ante: see *Re L (a minor) (adoption application)* [1991] FCR 297, [1991] 1 FLR 171, CA.

Rule 15(4)   SCHEDULE 3
REPORTS ON THE HEALTH OF THE CHILD AND OF THE APPLICANT(S)

6–3465 This information is required for reports on the health of a child and of his prospective adopter(s). Its purpose is to build up a full picture of their health history and current state of health, including strengths and weaknesses. This will enable the local authority's medical adviser to base his advice to the court on the fullest possible information, when commenting on the health implications of the proposed adoption. The reports made by the examining doctor should cover, as far as practicable, the following matters.

1. *The Child*
Name, date of birth, sex, weight and height.

A. A health history of each natural parent, so far as is possible, including:
    (i) name, date of birth, sex, weight and height;
    (ii) a family health history, covering the parents, the brothers and sisters and the other children of the natural parent, with details of any serious physical or mental illness and inherited and congenital disease;
    (iii) past health history, including details of any serious physical or mental illness, disability, accident, hospital admission or attendance at an out-patient department, and in each case any treatment given;
    (iv) a full obstetric history of the mother, including any problems in the ante-natal, labour and post-natal periods, with the results of any tests carried out during or immediately after pregnancy;
    (v) details of any present illness including treatment and prognosis;
    (vi) any other relevant information which might assist the medical adviser, and
    (vii) the name and address of any doctor(s) who might be able to provide further information about any of the above matters.

B. A neo-natal report on the child, including—
    (i) details of the birth, and any complications;
    (ii) results of a physical examination and screening tests;
    (iii) details of any treatment given;
    (iv) details of any problem in management and feeding;
    (v) any other relevant information which might assist the medical adviser; and
    (vi) the name and address of any doctor(s) who might be able to provide further information about any of the above matters;

C. A full health history and examination of the child, including—
    (i) details of any serious illness, disability, accident, hospital admission or attendance at an out-patient department, and in each case any treatment given;
    (ii) details and dates of immunisations;
    (iii) a physical and developmental assessment according to age, including an assessment of vision and hearing and of neurological, speech and language development and any evidence of emotional disorder;
    (iv) for a child over five years of age, the school health history (if available);
    (v) any other relevant information which might assist the medical adviser; and
    (vi) the name and address of any doctor(s) who might be able to provide further information about any of the above matters.

D. The signature, name, address and qualifications of the registered medical practitioner who prepared the report, and the date of the report and of the examinations carried out.

2. *The Applicant*
(If there is more than one applicant, a report on each applicant should be supplied covering all the matters listed below.)

A.
    (i) name, date of birth, sex, weight and height;
    (ii) a family health history, covering the parents, the brothers and sisters and the children of the applicant, with details of any serious physical or mental illness and inherited and congenital disease;
    (iii) marital history, including (if applicable) reasons for inability to have children;
    (iv) past health history, including details of any serious physical or mental illness, disability, accident, hospital admission or attendance at an out-patient department, and in each case any treatment given;
    (v) obstetric history (if applicable);
    (vi) details of any present illness, including treatment and prognosis;
    (vii) a full medical examination;
    (viii) details of any daily consumption of alcohol, tobacco and habit-forming drugs;
    (ix) any other relevant information which might assist the medical adviser; and
    (x) the name and address of any doctor(s) who might be able to provide further information about any of the above matters.

B. The signature, name, address and qualifications of the registered medical practitioner who prepared the report, and the date of the report and of the examinations carried out.

Parental Orders (Human Fertilisation and Embryology) Regulations 1994[1]

(SI 1994/2767 amended by SI 2005/2897)

Citation, commencement, interpretation and extent

6–3470 1. (1) These Regulations may be cited as the Parental Orders (Human Fertilisation and Embryology) Regulations 1994 and shall come into force on 1st November 1994.

(2) In these Regulations unless the context otherwise requires—

"the 1990 Act" means the Human Fertilisation and Embryology Act 1990;

"the 1976 Act" means the Adoption Act 1976[2] and references to sections are to sections of the 1976 Act;

"the Order" means the Adoption (Northern Ireland) Order 1987 and references to articles are to articles of the Order;

"parental order" means an order under section 30 of the 1990 Act[3] (parental orders in favour of gamete donors) providing for a child to be treated in law as a child of the parties to a marriage.

(3) These Regulations extend to England and Wales and Northern Ireland.

---

1. Made by the Secretary of State in exercise of powers conferred by ss 30(9) and 45(1) and (3) of the Human Fertilisation and Embryology Act 1990.
2. For the Adoption Act 1976, see this PART, ante.
3. For the Human Fertilisation and Embryology Act 1990, see this PART, ante.

Application of Adoption Act 1976 provisions with modifications to parental orders and applications for such orders

6–3471   2. The provisions of the 1976 Act set out in column 1 of Schedule 1 to these Regulations shall have effect with the modifications (if any) set out in column 2 of that Schedule in relation to parental orders made in England and Wales and applications for such orders, as they had effect, prior to 30th December 2005, in relation to adoption and applications for adoption orders.

6–3472   3. *Application of Adoption (Northern Ireland) Order 1987 provisions with modifications to parental orders and applications for such orders.*

Reference in enactments to be read as references to parental orders etc

6–3473   4. Schedule 3 shall have effect so that the references mentioned in column 2, where they appear in the enactments mentioned in relation to them in column 1, shall be read in relation to parental orders and applications for such orders as provided for in column 2.

6–3474

Regulation 2   SCHEDULE 1
APPLICATION OF ADOPTION ACT 1976 PROVISIONS WITH MODIFICATIONS TO PARENTAL ORDERS AND APPLICATIONS FOR SUCH ORDERS

Column 1 provisions of the 1976 Act	Column 2 modifications
Applications by Gamete Donors for a parental order 1 (a) Section 6 (duty to promote the welfare of the child)	(i) As if for the words "the adoption of a child" there were substituted the words "an application for a parental order"; and (ii) as if the words "or adoption agency" were omitted.
(b) Section 12(1) to (3)[1] (adoption orders)	(i) As if for the words "an adoption order" on each occasion they appear there were substituted the words "a parental order"; (ii) as if in subsection (1) for the word "adopters" there were substituted the words "husband and wife" and as if for the words "an authorised" there were substituted the word "the".
(c) Section 24(1) (restrictions on making adoption orders)	(i) As if for the words "an adoption order" there were substituted the words "a parental order"; and (ii) as if for the words "a British adoption order" there were substituted the words "such an order".
(d) Section 27(1)[2] (restrictions on removal while application is pending)	As if for the words "an adoption order is pending in a case where a parent or guardian of the child has agreed to the making of the adoption order (whether or not he knows the identity of the applicant)" there were substituted the words "a parental order is pending".
(e) Section 29[3] (return of a child taken away in breach of section 27 or 28 of the 1976 Act)	(i) As if for paragraphs (a) to (c) of subsections (1) and (2) there were substituted the words "(a) section 27 as applied with modifications by regulation 2 of and paragraph 1(d) of Schedule 1 to the Parental Orders (Human Fertilisation and Embryology) Regulations 1994,

Column 1 provisions of the 1976 Act	Column 2 modifications
	(*b*) section 27 of the Adoption (Scotland) Act 1978 as applied with modifications by regulation 2 of and Schedule 1 to the Parental Orders (Human Fertilisation and Embryology) (Scotland) Regulations 1994,
	(*c*) Article 28 of the Adoption (Northern Ireland) Order 1987 as applied with modifications by regulation 3 of and paragraph 2(*d*) of Schedule 2 to the Parental Orders (Human Fertilisation and Embryology) Regulations 1994.''; and
	(ii) (ii) as if for the words "an authorised" there were substituted on each occasion they appear the word "the".

Effect of a parental order

2 Section 39(1)(*a*), (2), (4) and (6) (status conferred by adoption)	(i) As if for the words "an adopted child" there were substituted, on each occasion they appear, the words "a child who is the subject of a parental order";
	(ii) as if in section 39(1)(*a*) the words "where the adopters are a married couple," were omitted and for the words "child of the marriage" there were substituted the words "child of the marriage of the husband and wife";
	(iii) as if in section 39(2) for the word "adopters" there were substituted the words "persons who obtain the parental order" and the words "or adopter" and the words "subject to subsection (3)," were omitted;
	(iv) as if in section 39(6) for the word "adoption" there were substituted the words "the making of the parental order" and the words "Subject to the provisions of this Part," and ", or after 31st December 1975, whichever is the later" were omitted.

Interpretation of certain events consequent upon the making of a parental order

3 (*a*) Section 42 (rules of construction for instruments concerning property)	(i) As if in section 42(2) for the words "section 39(1)" there were substituted the words "section 39(1)(*a*) as applied with modifications by regulation 2 of and paragraph 2 of Schedule 1 to the Parental Orders (Human Fertilisation and Embryology) Regulations 1994";
	(ii) as if in section 42(2), for the words "of the adoptive parent or parents" there were substituted the words "in respect of whom the husband and wife have obtained a parental order";
	(iii) as if in section 42(2)(*a*) for the words "adopted child" there were substituted the words "child the subject of the parental order" and for the word "adoption" there were substituted the words "the parental order";
	(iv) as if in section 42(2)(*b*) for the words "adopted" there were substituted the words "in respect of whom parental orders were made";
	(v) as if in section 42(4) for the word "adoption" there were substituted the words "making of the parental order" and for the words "adopted child" there were substituted the words "child the subject of the parental order";
	(vi) as if in section 42(5) for the word "adopt" there were substituted the words "obtain a parental order in respect of" and as if after the words in section 42(4) "section 39(2)" and, in section 42(5) "section 39", there were inserted the words "as applied with modifications by regulation 2 of and paragraph 2 of Schedule 1 to the Parental Orders (Human Fertilisation and Embryology) Regulations 1994".
(*b*) Section 44 (property devolving with peerages etc)	As if for the words "an adoption" on each occasion they appear there were substituted the words "the making of a parental order".
(*c*) Section 45 (protection of trustees and personal representatives)	As if in section 45(1) for the words "adoption has been effected" there were substituted the words "parental order has been made".

Column 1 provisions of the 1976 Act	Column 2 modifications
(d) Section 46 (meaning of "disposition")	(i) As if for the words "this Part" on each occasion they appear and in section 46(5) the words "the Part", there were substituted the words "sections 39, 42, 44, 45 and 47 as applied with modifications by regulation 2 of and paragraphs 2 and 3(a), (b), (c) and (e) respectively of Schedule 1 to the Parental Orders (Human Fertilisation and Embryology) Regulations 1994"; and (ii) as if in section 46(2) for the word "applies" there were substituted the word "apply".
(e) Section 47[4] (miscellaneous enactments)	(i) As if for subsection (1) there were substituted the words "(1) Section 39(2) as applied with modifications by regulation 2 of and paragraph 2 of Schedule 1 to the Parental Orders (Human Fertilisation and Embryology) Regulations 1994 does not apply so as to prevent a child who is the subject of a parental order from continuing to be treated as the child of a person who was in law the child's mother or father before the order was made, for the purposes of the table of kindred and affinity in Schedule 1 to the Marriage Act 1949[5] and of Sections 10 and 11 (incest) of the Sexual Offences Act 1956" and (ii) as if in subsection (2) for the words "Section 39" there were substituted the words "Section 39 as applied with modifications by regulation 2 of and paragraph 2 of Schedule 1 to the Parental Orders (Human Fertilisation and Embryology) Regulations 1994".
Registration 4 (a) Section 50 (Adopted Children Register)	(i) As if for the words "Adopted Children Register" on each occasion they appear, except on the second occasion in section 50(3), there were substituted the words "Parental Order Register"; (ii) as if in section 50(1) for the words "adoption orders" there were substituted the words "parental orders"; (iii) as if in section 50(2) for the word "adoption" there were substituted the words "parental order"; (iv) as if in section 50(2) for the words "adopted person" there were substituted the words "person who is the subject of the parental order"; (v) as if in section 50(3) for the words "every person shall be entitled to search that index and to have a certified copy of any entry in the Adopted Children Register in all respects upon and subject to the same terms" there were substituted the following words: "the Registrar General shall— (a) cause a search to be made of that index on behalf of any person or permit that person to search that index himself, and (b) issue to any person a certified copy of any entry in the Parental Order Register, in all respects, except as to the entitlement of any person to search that index, upon and subject to the same terms"; (vi) as if in section 50(4) for the words "marked "Adopted"" there were substituted the words "marked "Re-registered by the Registrar General" pursuant to paragraph 1(3) of Schedule 1 as applied with modifications by regulation 2 of and paragraph 8(a) of Schedule 1 to the Parental Orders (Human Fertilisation and Embryology) Regulations 1994"; (vii) as if in section 50(5) after the words "section 51" there were inserted the words "as applied with modifications by regulation 2 of and paragraph 4(b) of Schedule 1 to the Parental Orders (Human Fertilisation and Embryology) Regulations 1994";

Column 1 provisions of the 1976 Act	Column 2 modifications
	(viii) as if in section 50(5)(*c*) and (6) for the words "an adoption order" on each occasion they appear there were substituted the words "a parental order"; and
	(ix) as if in section 50(7) for the words "adoptions and the amendment of adoption orders" there were substituted the words "parental orders and the amendment of such orders".
(*b*) Section 51(1) to (6) and (9)³(disclosure of birth records of adopted children)	(i) As if in section 51(1) for the words "an adopted person" there were substituted the words "a person who is the subject of a parental order";
	(ii) as if in section 51(2) for the words "an adopted person under the age of 18 years" there were substituted the words "a person who is the subject of a parental order and who is under the age of 18 years";
	(iii) as if section 51 (3)(*a*)(i) and (*d*) were omitted;
	(iv) as if in section 51(3)(*a*)(iii), (*b*)(ii) and (*c*)(ii) for the words "adoption order" there were substituted the words "parental order";
	(v) as if in section 51(4) for the words from "Where" to "1978" there were substituted the words "Where a person who is the subject of a parental order and who is in England and Wales applies for information under subsection (1),"; and
	(vi) as if section 51(5)(*a*) and (*c*) were omitted.

Procedure

5 (*a*) Section 61(1) (evidence of agreement and consent)	(i) As if for the words "this Act" there were substituted the words "section 30 of the Human Fertilisation and Embryology Act 1990";
	(ii) as if the words "(other than an order to which section 17(6) applies)" were omitted; and
	(iii) as if for the words "and, if the document signifying the agreement or consent is witnessed in accordance with rules, it" there were substituted "and any such written consent".
(*b*) Section 63(2)⁷ (appeals etc)	(i) As if the words "Subject to subsection (3)" were omitted; and
	(ii) as if for the words "this Act" there were substituted the words "section 30 of the Human Fertilisation and Embryology Act 1990".
(*c*) Section 64⁸ (proceedings to be in private)	As if for the words "under this Act" there were substituted the words "pursuant to section 30 of the Human Fertilisation and Embryology Act 1990".

Orders, rules and regulations

6 Section 67(1), (2), (5) and (6) (orders, rules and regulations)	(i) As if after the words "this Act" on each occasion they appear, there were inserted the words "as applied with modifications by regulation 2 of and Schedule 1 to the Parental Orders (Human Fertilisation and Embryology) Regulations 1994";
	(ii) as if in section 67(2) the words ", except section 3(1)," were omitted; and
	(iii) as if in section 67(6) after the words "paragraph 1(1)" there were inserted the words "as applied with modifications by regulation 2 of and paragraphs 4(*b*) and 8(*a*) respectively of Schedule 1 to the Parental Orders (Human Fertilisation and Embryology) Regulations 1994".

Interpretation

7 Section 72(1)⁹(interpretation)	(i) As if after the definition of "guardian" there were inserted the words ""husband and wife" means, in relation to the provisions of this Act as they have effect in relation to parental orders and applications for such orders, the husband and wife as defined in section 30 of the Human Fertilisation and Embryology Act 1990;"; and

Column 1	Column 2
provisions of the 1976 Act	modifications

| | (ii) as if after the definition of "parent" there were inserted the words """parental order" means an order under section 30 of the Human Fertilisation and Embryology Act 1990;". |

Schedule 1 to the 1976 Act (registration of adoptions)

8 (*a*) Schedule 1, paragraph 1	(i) As if in paragraph 1(1) for the words "adoption order" there were substituted the words "parental order";
	(ii) as if in paragraph 1(1) for the words "Adopted Children Register" there were substituted the words "Parental Order Register";
	(iii) as if paragraph 1(2) were omitted;
	(iv) as if in paragraph 1(3) for the words from "application to a court" to "time in force)" there were substituted the words "application to a court for a parental order";
	(v) as if in paragraph 1(3) for the words "any adoption order" there were substituted the words "any parental order";
	(vi) as if in paragraph 1(3) for the words "marked with the word "Adopted"" there were substituted the words "marked with the words "Re-registered by the Registrar General"";
	(vii) as if paragraph 1(4) were omitted; and
	(viii) as if in paragraph 1(5) for the words "an adoption order" there were substituted the words "a parental order".
(*b*) Schedule 1, paragraph 2	(i) As if in paragraph 2(1) for the words "an adoption order" there were substituted the words "a parental order";
	(ii) as if in paragraph 2(1) the words "or the Adopted Children Register" were omitted;
	(iii) as if in paragraph 2(1) for the words ""Adopted (Scotland)" or, as the case may be, "Re-adopted (Scotland)"" there were substituted the words ""Re-registered (Scotland)"";
	(iv) as if in paragraph 2(1) for the words from "and where, after an entry has been so marked" to the end of the sub-paragraph were omitted;
	(v) as if in paragraph 2(2) for the words "register of adoptions" there were substituted the words "register of parental orders";
	(vi) as if in paragraph 2(2) for the words "an order has been made in that country authorising the adoption of a child" there were substituted the words " a parental order has been made in that country in respect of a child";
	(vii) as if in paragraph 2(2) the words "or the Adopted Children Register" were omitted;
	(viii) as if in paragraph 2(2) for the words "marked with the word "Adopted" or "Re-adopted", as the case may require" there were substituted the words "marked with the word "Re-registered""; and
	(ix) as if in paragraph 2(3) for the words "so marked" there were substituted the words "marked in accordance with the provisions of sub-paragraph (1) or (2)"; and
	(x) as if paragraph 2(4) and (5) were omitted.
(*c*) Schedule 1, paragraph 4	(i) As if for the words "an adoption order" on each occasion they appear there were substituted the words "a parental order";
	(ii) as if for the words "Adopted Children Register" on each occasion they appear there were substituted the words "Parental Order Register";
	(iii) as if in paragraph 4(1) for the words "adopter or of the adopted person" there were substituted the words "husband or wife or of the person who is the subject of the parental order";
	(iv) as if in paragraph 4(1)(*a*) for the words "adopter or the adopted person" there were substituted the words "husband or wife or the child who is the subject of the parental order";

Column 1	Column 2
provisions of the 1976 Act	modifications

(v) as if in paragraph 4(1)(*a*) for the words "given to the adopted person" there were substituted the words "given to that child" and the words ", or taken by him," were omitted;

(vi) as if in paragraph 4(1)(*b*) the words "or (4)" were omitted;

(vii) as if in paragraph 4(4) after the words "section 50" there were inserted the words "as applied with modifications by regulation 2 of and paragraph 4(*a*) of Schedule 1 to the Parental Orders (Human Fertilisation and Embryology) Regulations 1994"; and

(viii) as if paragraph 4(5) were omitted.

---

1. Section 12(1), (2) and (3) have been amended by s 88(1) of and para 3 of Sch 10 to the Children Act 1989.
2. Section 27(1) has been amended by s 88(1) of and para 12 of Sch 10 to the Children Act 1989.
3. Section 29 has been amended by s 88(1) of and para 15 of Sch 10 to the Children Act 1989.
4. Section 47 has been amended by s 52 of and Sch 7 to the British Nationality Act 1981 and by art 8 of and the Schedule to the Hong Kong (British Nationality) Order 1986 (SI 1986/948).
5. Schedule 1 has been amended by s 1(6) of and Sch 1 to the Marriage (Prohibited Degrees of Relationship) Act 1986 and s 108(1)(*a*) of and Sch 3 to the Children Act 1975.
6. Section 51(1) was amended by s 88(1) of and para 20(1) of Sch 10 to the Children Act 1989; s 51(3) to (9) were substituted by para 20(2) of that Schedule.
7. Section 63(2) has been amended by s 30(1) of and Sch 10 to the Health and Social Services and Social Security Adjudications Act 1983 (c 41).
8. Section 64 has been amended by ss 73 and 89 of and Sch 3 to the Domestic Proceedings and Magistrates' Courts Act 1978.
9. Section 72 has been amended by s 154 of and para 142 of Sch 7 to the Magistrates' Courts Act 1980 and by s 9 of and para 37 of Sch 2 to the Health and Social Services and Social Security Adjudications Act 1983 and by ss 7 and 33 of and para 68 of Sch 2 to the Family Law Reform Act 1987 and by ss 88 and 108(7) of and para 30 of Sch 10 and Sch 15 of the Children Act 1989.

6–3475

Regulation 3   SCHEDULE 2
APPLICATION OF ADOPTION (NORTHERN IRELAND) ORDER 1987
PROVISIONS WITH MODIFICATIONS TO PARENTAL ORDERS AND APPLICATIONS FOR SUCH ORDERS

6–3476

Regulation 4   SCHEDULE 3
REFERENCES IN ENACTMENTS TO BE READ AS REFERENCES TO PARENTAL ORDERS ETC

Column 1	Column 2
1 Article 37 of the Birth and Deaths Registration (Northern Ireland) Order 1976	In article 37(1) the words "article 52(1)(*a*)" and "article 50" shall be read as though they were followed by the words "as applied with modifications by regulation 3 of and paragraph 5(*c*) of Schedule 2 to the Parental Orders (Human Fertilisation and Embryology) Regulations 1994." and the reference to "Adopted Children Register" shall be read as a reference to "Parental Order Register".
2 Paragraph 5(*a*) of Schedule 8 to the Children Act 1989	The reference in sub-paragraph (*a*) to a person who proposes to adopt a child under arrangements made by an adoption agency within the meaning of the Acts or Order mentioned in that sub-paragraph shall be read as including a reference to a person who proposes to be treated as the parent of a child by virtue of a parental order and the enactments about adoption as applied by these Regulations.
3 Sections 27(2) and 28(5)(*c*) of the 1990 Act	The references to a child who is treated by virtue of adoption as not being the child of any person other than the adopter or adopters shall be read as references to a child who is treated by virtue of the making of a parental order as not being the child of any person other than the husband and wife as defined by section 30 of the 1990 Act.

Adoption Agencies Regulations 2005[1]

(SI 2005/389 amended by SI 2004/3482)

6–3477   1. Citation, commencement and application.   (1) These Regulations may be cited as the Adoption Agencies Regulations 2005 and shall come into force on 30th December 2005.
(2) These Regulations apply to England only.

---

1. Made by the Secretary of State for Education and Skills, in exercise of the powers conferred on her by ss 26(1) to (2B), 59(4)(a) and (5) and 104(4) of the Children Act 1989 and ss 9(1)(a), 11(1)(b), 27(3), 53(1) to (3), 54, 140(7) and (8) and 142 (4) and (5) of the Adoption and Children Act 2002], and all other powers enabling her in that behalf.

6–3478   2. Interpretation.   (1) In these Regulations—

"the Act" means the Adoption and Children Act 2002;
"the 1989 Act" means the Children Act 1989;
"adoption panel" means a panel established in accordance with regulation 3;
"adoption placement plan" has the meaning given in regulation 35(2);
"adoption placement report" means the report prepared by the adoption agency in accordance with regulation 31(2)(d);
"adoption support services" has the meaning given in section 2(6)(a) of the Act and in any regulations made under section 2(6)(b) of the Act;
"adoptive family" has the meaning given in regulation 31(2)(a);
"CAFCASS" means the Children and Family Court Advisory and Support Service;
"child's case record" has the meaning given in regulation 12;
"child's health report" means the report obtained in accordance with regulation 15(2)(b);
"child's permanence report" means the report prepared by the adoption agency in accordance with regulation 17(1);
"independent member" in relation to an adoption panel has the meaning given in regulation 3(3)(e);
"independent review panel" means a panel constituted under section 12 of the Act;
"joint adoption panel" means an adoption panel established in accordance with regulation 3(5);
"medical adviser" means the person appointed as the medical adviser by the adoption agency in accordance with regulation 9(1);
"proposed placement" has the meaning given in regulation 31(1);
"prospective adopter's case record" has the meaning given in regulation 22(1);
"prospective adopter's report" means the report prepared by the adoption agency in accordance with regulation 25(5);
"prospective adopter's review report" means the report prepared by the adoption agency in accordance with regulation 29(4)(a);
"qualifying determination" has the meaning given in regulation 27(4)(a);
"registration authority" means the Commission for Social Care Inspection;
"relevant foreign authority" means a person, outside the British Islands performing functions in the country in which the child is, or in which the prospective adopter is, habitually resident which correspond to the functions of an adoption agency or to the functions of the Secretary of State in respect of adoptions with a foreign element;
"relevant post-qualifying experience" means post-qualifying experience in child care social work including direct experience in adoption work;
"section 83 case" means a case where a person who is habitually resident in the British Islands intends to bring, or to cause another to bring, a child into the United Kingdom in circumstances where section 83 of the Act (restriction on bringing children into the United Kingdom) applies;
"social worker" means a person who is registered as a social worker in a register maintained by the General Social Care Council or the Care Council for Wales under section 56 of the Care Standards Act 2000 or in a corresponding register maintained under the law of Scotland or Northern Ireland;
"vice chair" has the meaning given in regulation 3(4) or, as the case may be, (5)(c);
"working day" means any day other than a Saturday, Sunday, Christmas Day, Good Friday or a day which is a bank holiday within the meaning of the Banking and Financial Dealings Act 1971.

6–3479   3. Establishment of adoption panel.   (1) Subject to paragraph (5) and regulation 3A, an adoption agency must establish at least one panel, to be known as an adoption panel, in accordance with this regulation.

(2) The adoption agency must appoint to chair the panel a person, not being a disqualified person, who has the skills and experience necessary for chairing an adoption panel.

(3) Subject to paragraph (5), the adoption panel shall consist of no more than ten members, including the person appointed under paragraph (2), and shall include—

(a) two social workers each with at least three years' relevant post-qualifying experience;

(b) in the case of a registered adoption society, one person who is a director, manager or other officer and is concerned in the management of that society;

(c) in the case of a local authority, one member of that authority;

(d) the medical adviser to the adoption agency (or one of them if more than one medical adviser is appointed);

(e) at least three other persons (in this regulation referred to as "independent members") including where reasonably practicable at least two persons with personal experience of adoption.

(4) The adoption agency must appoint one member of the adoption panel as vice chair ("vice chair") who shall act as chair if the person appointed to chair the panel is absent or his office is vacant.

(5) An adoption panel may be established jointly by any two or more local authorities ("joint adoption panel") and if a joint adoption panel is established—

(a) the maximum number of members who may be appointed to that panel is eleven;

(b) by agreement between the local authorities there shall be appointed to that panel—

(i) a person to chair the panel, not being a disqualified person, who has the skills and experience necessary for chairing an adoption panel;

(ii) two social workers each with at least three years' relevant post-qualifying experience;

(iii) one member of any of the local authorities;

(iv) the medical adviser to one of the local authorities; and

(v) at least three independent members including where reasonably practicable at least two persons with personal experience of adoption;

(c) by agreement the local authorities must appoint one member of the panel as vice chair ("vice chair") who shall act as chair if the person appointed to chair the panel is absent or his office is vacant.

(6) A person shall not be appointed as an independent member of an adoption panel if—

(a) in the case of a registered adoption society, he is or has been within the last year a trustee or employee, or is related to an employee, of that society;

(b) in the case of a local authority, he—

(i) is or has been within the last year employed by that authority in their children and family social services;

(ii) is related to a person falling within head (i); or

(iii) is or has been within the last year a member of that authority; or

(c) he is the adoptive parent of a child who was—

(i) placed for adoption with him by the adoption agency ("agency A"); or

(ii) placed for adoption with him by another adoption agency where he had been approved as suitable to be an adoptive parent by agency A,

unless at least twelve months has elapsed since the adoption order was made in respect of the child.

(7) For the purposes of regulation 3(2) and (5)(b)(i) a person is a disqualified person if—

(a) in the case of a registered adoption society, he is or has been within the last year a trustee or employee, or is related to an employee, of that society; or

(b) in the case of a local authority, he—

(i) is or has been within the last year employed by that authority in their children and family social services;

(ii) is related to a person falling within head (i); or

(iii) is or has been within the last year a member of that authority.

(8) For the purposes of paragraphs (6)(a) and (b)(ii) and (7) a person ("person A") is related to another person ("person B") if person A is—

(a) a member of the household of, or married to or the civil partner of, person B;

(b) the son, daughter, mother, father, sister or brother of person B; or

(c) the son, daughter, mother, father, sister or brother of the person to whom person B is married or with whom B has formed a civil partnership.

3A. Where an adoption agency operates only for the purpose of putting persons into contact with other adoption agencies and for the purpose of putting such agencies into contact with each other or for either of such purposes, regulations 3, 8, 10 and, to the extent that it requires consultation with the adoption panel, regulation 7 shall not apply to such an agency.

6–3480   **4. Tenure of office of members of the adoption panel.**   (1) Subject to the provisions of this regulation and regulation 10, a member of an adoption panel shall hold office for a term not exceeding three years, and may not hold office for the adoption panel of the same adoption agency for more than three terms in total.

(2) The medical adviser member of the adoption panel shall hold office only for so long as he is the medical adviser.

(3) A member of an adoption panel may resign his office at any time by giving one month's notice in writing to the adoption agency.

(4) Where an adoption agency is of the opinion that any member of the adoption panel is unsuitable or unable to remain in office, it may terminate his office at any time by giving him notice in writing with reasons.

(5) If the member whose appointment is to be terminated under paragraph (4) is a member of a joint adoption panel, his appointment may only be terminated with the agreement of all the local authorities whose panel it is.

6–3481 5. Meetings of adoption panel. (1) Subject to paragraph (2), no business shall be conducted by the adoption panel unless at least five of its members, including the person appointed to chair the panel or the vice chair and at least one of the social workers and one of the independent members, meet as the panel.

(2) In the case of a joint adoption panel, no business shall be conducted unless at least six of its members, including the person appointed to chair the panel or the vice chair and at least one of the social workers and one of the independent members, meet as the panel.

(3) An adoption panel must make a written record of its proceedings, its recommendations and the reasons for its recommendations.

6–3482 6. Payment of fees to member of local authority adoption panel. A local authority may pay to any member of their adoption panel such fee as they may determine, being a fee of a reasonable amount.

6–3483 7. Adoption agency arrangements for adoption work. An adoption agency must, in consultation with the adoption panel and, to the extent specified in regulation 9(2) with the agency's medical adviser, prepare and implement written policy and procedural instructions governing the exercise of the functions of the agency and the adoption panel in relation to adoption and such instructions shall be kept under review and, where appropriate, revised by the agency.

6–3484 8. Requirement to appoint an agency adviser to the adoption panel. (1) The adoption agency must appoint a senior member of staff, or in the case of a joint adoption panel the local authorities whose panel it is must by agreement appoint a senior member of staff of one of them, (referred to in this regulation as the "agency adviser")—

   (a) to assist the agency with the appointment (including re-appointment), termination and review of appointment of members of the adoption panel;

   (b) to be responsible for the induction and training of members of the adoption panel;

   (c) to be responsible for liaison between the agency and the adoption panel, monitoring the performance of members of the adoption panel and the administration of the adoption panel; and

   (d) to give such advice to the adoption panel as the panel may request in relation to any case or generally.

(2) The agency adviser must be a social worker and have at least five years' relevant post-qualifying experience and, in the opinion of the adoption agency, relevant management experience.

6–3485 9. Requirement to appoint a medical adviser. (1) The adoption agency must appoint at least one registered medical practitioner to be the agency's medical adviser.

(2) The medical adviser shall be consulted in relation to the arrangements for access to, and disclosure of, health information which is required or permitted by virtue of these Regulations.

6–3486 10. Establishment of new adoption panels on 30 December 2005. (1) All members of an adoption panel established before 30th December 2005 (referred to in this regulation as the "old adoption panel") shall cease to hold office on that date.

(2) With effect from 30th December 2005 an adoption agency shall establish a new adoption panel in accordance with regulations 3 and 4.

(3) This paragraph applies where a person's term of office as a member of the old adoption panel was extended by the adoption agency in accordance with regulation 5A(1A) of the Adoption Agencies Regulations 1983.

(4) This paragraph applies where the person served only one term of office as a member of the old adoption panel.

(5) A person who has been at any time a member of an old adoption panel may not hold office as a member of the new adoption panel of the same adoption agency—

   (a) where paragraph (3) applies, for more than one term, not exceeding one year;

   (b) where paragraph (4) applies, for more than two terms, each term not exceeding three years;

   (c) in any other case, for more than one term, not exceeding three years.

6–3487   11. Application of regulations 11 to 17.   Regulations 12 to 17 apply where the adoption agency is considering adoption for a child.

6–3488   12. Requirement to open the child's case record.   (1) The adoption agency must set up a case record ("the child's case record") in respect of the child and place on it—

(a) the information and reports obtained by the agency by virtue of this Part;

(b) the child's permanence report;

(c) the written record of the proceedings of the adoption panel under regulation 18, its recommendation and the reasons for its recommendation and any advice given by the panel to the agency;

(d) the record of the agency's decision and any notification of that decision under regulation 19;

(e) any consent to placement for adoption under section 19 of the Act (placing children with parental consent);

(f) any consent to the making of a future adoption order under section 20 of the Act (advance consent to adoption);

(g) any form or notice withdrawing consent under section 19 or 20 of the Act or notice under section 20(4)(a) or (b) of the Act;

(h) a copy of any placement order in respect of the child; and

(i) any other documents or information obtained by the agency which it considers should be included in that case record.

(2) Where an adoption agency places on the child's case record a notice under section 20(4)(a) or (b) of the Act, the agency must send a copy of that notice to a court which has given the agency notice of the issue of an application for an adoption order.

6–3489   13. Requirement to provide counselling and information for, and ascertain wishes and feelings of, the child.   (1) The adoption agency must, so far as is reasonably practicable—

(a) provide a counselling service for the child;

(b) explain to the child in an appropriate manner the procedure in relation to, and the legal implications of, adoption for the child and provide him with appropriate written information about these matters; and

(c) ascertain the child's wishes and feelings regarding—

(i) the possibility of placement for adoption with a new family and his adoption;

(ii) his religious and cultural upbringing; and

(iii) contact with his parent or guardian or other relative or with any other person the agency considers relevant.

(2) Paragraph (1) does not apply if the adoption agency is satisfied that the requirements of that paragraph have been carried out in respect of the child by another adoption agency.

6–3490   14. Requirement to provide counselling and information for, and ascertain wishes and feelings of, the parent or guardian of the child and others.   (1) The adoption agency must, so far as is reasonably practicable—

(a) provide a counselling service for the parent or guardian of the child;

(b) explain to him—

(i) the procedure in relation to both placement for adoption and adoption;

(ii) the legal implications of—

(aa) giving consent to placement for adoption under section 19 of the Act;

(bb) giving consent to the making of a future adoption order under section 20 of the Act; and

(cc) a placement order; and

(iii) the legal implications of adoption,

and provide him with written information about these matters; and

(c) ascertain the wishes and feelings of the parent or guardian of the child and, of any other person the agency considers relevant, regarding—

(i) the child;

(ii) the placement of the child for adoption and his adoption, including any wishes and feelings about the child's religious and cultural upbringing; and

(iii) contact with the child if the child is authorised to be placed for adoption or the child is adopted.

(2) Paragraph (1) does not apply if the agency is satisfied that the requirements of that paragraph have been carried out in respect of the parent or guardian and any other person the agency considers relevant by another adoption agency.

(3) This paragraph applies where the father of the child does not have parental responsibility for the child and the father's identity is known to the adoption agency.

(4) Where paragraph (3) applies and the adoption agency is satisfied it is appropriate to do so, the agency must—

  (a) carry out in respect of the father the requirements of paragraph (1)(a), (b)(i) and (iii) and (c) as if they applied to him unless the agency is satisfied that the requirements have been carried out in respect of the father by another agency; and

  (b) ascertain so far as possible whether the father—

    (i) wishes to acquire parental responsibility for the child under section 4 of the 1989 Act (acquisition of parental responsibility by father); or

    (ii) intends to apply for a residence order or contact order with respect to the child under section 8 of the 1989 Act (residence, contact and other orders with respect to children) or, where the child is subject to a care order, an order under section 34 of the 1989 Act (parental contact etc with children in care).

6–3491   15. Requirement to obtain information about the child.   (1) The adoption agency must obtain, so far as is reasonably practicable, the information about the child which is specified in Part 1 of Schedule 1.

  (2) Subject to paragraph (4), the adoption agency must—

  (a) make arrangements for the child to be examined by a registered medical practitioner; and

  (b) obtain from that practitioner a written report ("the child's health report") on the state of the child's health which shall include any treatment which the child is receiving, any need for health care and the matters specified in Part 2 of Schedule 1,

unless the agency has received advice from the medical adviser that such an examination and report is unnecessary.

  (3) Subject to paragraph (4), the adoption agency must make arrangements—

  (a) for such other medical and psychiatric examinations of, and other tests on, the child to be carried out as are recommended by the agency's medical adviser; and

  (b) for written reports of such examinations and tests to be obtained.

  (4) Paragraphs (2) and (3) do not apply if the child is of sufficient understanding to make an informed decision and refuses to submit to the examinations or other tests.

6–3492   16. Requirement to obtain information about the child's family.   (1) The adoption agency must obtain, so far as is reasonably practicable, the information about the child's family which is specified in Part 3 of Schedule 1.

  (2) The adoption agency must obtain, so far as is reasonably practicable, the information about the health of each of the child's natural parents and his brothers and sisters (of the full blood or half-blood) which is specified in Part 4 of Schedule 1.

6–3493   17. Requirement to prepare child's permanence report for the adoption panel.   (1) The adoption agency must prepare a written report ("the child's permanence report") which shall include—

  (a) the information about the child and his family as specified in Parts 1 and 3 of Schedule 1;

  (b) a summary, written by the agency's medical adviser, of the state of the child's health, his health history and any need for health care which might arise in the future;

  (c) the wishes and feelings of the child regarding the matters set out in regulation 13(1)(c);

  (d) the wishes and feelings of the child's parent or guardian, and where regulation 14(4)(a) applies, his father, and any other person the agency considers relevant, regarding the matters set out in regulation 14(1)(c);

  (e) the views of the agency about the child's need for contact with his parent or guardian or other relative or with any other person the agency considers relevant and the arrangements the agency proposes to make for allowing any person contact with the child;

  (f) an assessment of the child's emotional and behavioural development and any related needs;

  (g) an assessment of the parenting capacity of the child's parent or guardian and, where regulation 14(4)(a) applies, his father;

  (h) a chronology of the decisions and actions taken by the agency with respect to the child;

  (i) an analysis of the options for the future care of the child which have been considered by the agency and why placement for adoption is considered the preferred option; and

  (j) any other information which the agency considers relevant.

  (2) Subject to paragraph (2A), the adoption agency must send—

  (a) the child's permanence report;

  (b) the child's health report and any other reports referred to in regulation 15; and

  (c) the information relating to the health of each of the child's natural parents,

to the adoption panel.

  (2A) The adoption agency shall only send the documents referred to in paragraph (2)(b) and (c) to the adoption panel if the agency's medical adviser advises it to do so.

  (3) The adoption agency must obtain, so far as is reasonably practicable, any other relevant

information which may be requested by the adoption panel and send that information to the panel.

6–3494   18. Function of the adoption panel in relation to a child referred by the adoption agency.
(1) The adoption panel must consider the case of every child referred to it by the adoption agency and make a recommendation to the agency as to whether the child should be placed for adoption.
(2) In considering what recommendation to make the adoption panel must have regard to the duties imposed on the adoption agency under section 1(2), (4), (5) and (6) of the Act (considerations applying to the exercise of powers in relation to the adoption of a child) and—

(a) must consider and take into account the reports and any other information passed to it in accordance with regulation 17;
(b) may request the agency to obtain any other relevant information which the panel considers necessary; and
(c) must obtain legal advice in relation to the case.

(3) Where the adoption panel makes a recommendation to the adoption agency that the child should be placed for adoption, it must consider and may at the same time give advice to the agency about—

(a) the arrangements which the agency proposes to make for allowing any person contact with the child; and
(b) where the agency is a local authority, whether an application should be made by the authority for a placement order in respect of the child.

6–3495   19. Adoption agency decision and notification.   (1) The adoption agency must take into account the recommendation of the adoption panel in coming to a decision about whether the child should be placed for adoption.
(2) No member of the adoption panel shall take part in any decision made by the adoption agency under paragraph (1).
(3) The adoption agency must, if their whereabouts are known to the agency, notify in writing the parent or guardian and, where regulation 14(3) applies and the agency considers it is appropriate, the father of the child of its decision.

6–3496   20. Request to appoint an officer of the Service or a Welsh family proceedings officer.
Where the parent or guardian of the child is prepared to consent to the placement of the child for adoption under section 19 of the Act and, as the case may be, to consent to the making of a future adoption order under section 20 of the Act, the adoption agency must request the CAFCASS to appoint an officer of the Service or the National Assembly for Wales to appoint a Welsh family proceedings officer for the purposes of the signification by that officer of the consent to placement or to adoption by that parent or guardian and send with that request the information specified in Schedule 2.

6–3497   20A. (1) Where the parent or guardian resides outside England and Wales and is prepared to consent to the placement of the child for adoption under section 19 of the Act and, as the case may be, to consent to the making of a future adoption order under section 20 of the Act, the adoption agency must arrange for the appointment of an authorised person to witness the execution of the form of consent to placement or to adoption by that parent or guardian and send to that person the information specified in Schedule 2.
(2) "Authorised person" for the purposes of this regulation means in relation to a form of consent executed—

(a) in Scotland, a Justice of the Peace or a Sheriff;
(b) in Northern Ireland, a Justice of the Peace;
(c) outside the United Kingdom, any person for the time being authorised by law in the place where the document is executed to administer an oath for any judicial or other legal purpose; a British Consular officer; a notary public; or, if the person executing the document is serving in any of the regular armed forces of the Crown, an officer holding a commission in any of those forces.

PART 4
DUTIES OF ADOPTION AGENCY IN RESPECT OF A PROSPECTIVE ADOPTER

6–3498   21. Requirement to provide counselling and information.   (1) Where an adoption agency is considering a person's suitability to adopt a child, the agency must—

(a) provide a counselling service for the prospective adopter;
(b) in a section 83 case, explain to the prospective adopter the procedure in relation to, and the legal implications of, adopting a child from the country from which the prospective adopter wishes to adopt;
(c) in any other case, explain to him the procedure in relation to, and the legal implications of, placement for adoption and adoption; and
(d) provide him with written information about the matters referred to in sub-paragraph (b) or, as the case may be, (c).

(2) Paragraph (1) does not apply if the adoption agency is satisfied that the requirements set out in that paragraph have been carried out in respect of the prospective adopter by another adoption agency.

6–3499   22. Requirement to consider application for an assessment of suitability to adopt a child.
(1) Where the adoption agency, following the procedures referred to in regulation 21, receives an application in writing in the form provided by the agency from a prospective adopter for an assessment of his suitability to adopt a child, the agency must set up a case record in respect of that prospective adopter ("the prospective adopter's case record") and consider his suitability to adopt a child.

(2) The adoption agency may ask the prospective adopter to provide any further information in writing the agency may reasonably require.

(3) The adoption agency must place on the prospective adopter's case record—

(a)   the application by the prospective adopter for an assessment of his suitability to adopt a child referred to in paragraph (1);

(b)   the information and reports obtained by the agency by virtue of this Part;

(c)   the prospective adopter's report and his observations on that report;

(d)   the written record of the proceedings of the adoption panel under regulation 26 (and, where applicable, regulation 27(6)), its recommendation and the reasons for its recommendation and any advice given by the panel to the agency;

(e)   the record of the agency's decision under regulation 27(3), (5) or, as the case may be, (9);

(f)   where the prospective adopter applied to the Secretary of State for a review by an independent review panel the recommendation of that review panel;

(g)   where applicable, the prospective adopter's review report and his observations on that report; and

(h)   any other documents or information obtained by the agency which it considers should be included in that case record.

6–3500   23. Requirement to carry out police checks.   (1) An adoption agency must take steps to obtain—

(a)   in respect of the prospective adopter, an enhanced criminal record certificate within the meaning of section 115 of the Police Act 1997 including the matters specified in subsection (6A) of that section; and

(b)   in respect of any other member of his household aged 18 or over, an enhanced criminal record certificate under section 115 of that Act including the matters specified in subsection (6A) of that section.

(2) An adoption agency may not consider a person suitable to adopt a child if he or any member of his household aged 18 or over—

(a)   has been convicted of a specified offence committed at the age of 18 or over; or

(b)   has been cautioned by a constable in respect of any such offence which, at the time the caution was given, he admitted.

(3) In paragraph (2), "specified offence" means—

(a)   an offence against a child;

(b)   an offence specified in Part 1 of Schedule 3;

(c)   an offence contrary to section 170 of the Customs and Excise Management Act 1979 in relation to goods prohibited to be imported under section 42 of the Customs Consolidation Act 1876 (prohibitions and restrictions relating to pornography) where the prohibited goods included indecent photographs of children under the age of 16;

(d)   any other offence involving bodily injury to a child, other than an offence of common assault or battery,

and the expression "offence against a child" has the meaning given to it by section 26(1) of the Criminal Justice and Court Services Act 2000 except that it does not include an offence contrary to section 9 of the Sexual Offences Act 2003 (sexual activity with a child) in a case where the offender was under the age of 20 and the child was aged 13 or over at the time the offence was committed.

(4) An adoption agency may not consider a person suitable to adopt a child if he or any member of his household aged 18 or over—

(a)   has been convicted of an offence specified in paragraph 1 of Part 2 of Schedule 3 committed at the age of 18 or over or has been cautioned by a constable in respect of any such offence which, at the time the caution was given, was admitted; or

(b)   falls within paragraph 2 or 3 of Part 2 of Schedule 3,

notwithstanding that the statutory offences specified in Part 2 of Schedule 3 have been repealed.

(5) Where an adoption agency becomes aware that a prospective adopter or a member of his household falls within paragraph (2) or (4), the agency must notify the prospective adopter as soon as possible that he cannot be considered suitable to adopt a child.

6–3501   24. Requirement to provide preparation for adoption.   (1) Where an adoption agency is considering a person's suitability to adopt a child, the agency must make arrangements for the prospective adopter to receive such preparation for adoption as the agency considers appropriate.

(2) In paragraph (1) "preparation for adoption" includes the provision of information to the prospective adopter about—

(a) the age range, sex, likely needs and background of children who may be placed for adoption by the adoption agency;
(b) the significance of adoption for a child and his family;
(c) contact between a child and his parent or guardian or other relatives where a child is authorised to be placed for adoption or is adopted;
(d) the skills which are necessary for an adoptive parent;
(e) the adoption agency's procedures in relation to the assessment of a prospective adopter and the placement of a child for adoption; and
(f) the procedure in relation to placement for adoption and adoption.

(3) Paragraph (1) does not apply if the adoption agency is satisfied that the requirements set out in that paragraph have been carried out in respect of the prospective adopter by another adoption agency.

6–3502 25. Prospective adopter's report. (1) This regulation applies where the adoption agency consider the prospective adopter may be suitable to adopt a child.

(2) The adoption agency must obtain the information about the prospective adopter which is specified in Part 1 of Schedule 4.

(3) The adoption agency must obtain—

(a) a written report from a registered medical practitioner about the health of the prospective adopter following a full examination which must include matters specified in Part 2 of Schedule 4 unless the agency has received advice from its medical adviser that such an examination and report is unnecessary; and
(b) a written report of each of the interviews with the persons nominated by the prospective adopter to provide personal references for him.

(4) The adoption agency must ascertain whether the local authority in whose area the prospective adopter has his home have any information about the prospective adopter which may be relevant to the assessment and if so obtain from that authority a written report setting out that information.

(5) The adoption agency must prepare a written report ("the prospective adopter's report") which shall include—

(a) the information about the prospective adopter and his family which is specified in Part 1 of Schedule 4;
(b) a summary, written by the agency's medical adviser, of the state of health of the prospective adopter;
(c) any relevant information the agency obtains under paragraph (4);
(d) any observations of the agency on the matters referred to in regulations 21, 23 and 24;
(e) the agency's assessment of the prospective adopter's suitability to adopt a child; and
(f) any other information which the agency considers to be relevant.

(6) In a section 83 case, the prospective adopter's report shall also include—

(a) the name of the country from which the prospective adopter wishes to adopt ("country of origin");
(b) confirmation that the prospective adopter meets the eligibility requirements to adopt from the country of origin;
(c) additional information obtained as a consequence of the requirements of the country of origin; and
(d) the agency's assessment of the prospective adopter's suitability to adopt a child who is habitually resident outside the British Islands.

(7) Where the adoption agency receives information under paragraph (2), (3) or (4) or other information in relation to the assessment of the prospective adopter and is of the opinion that a prospective adopter is unlikely to be considered suitable to adopt a child, it may make the prospective adopter's report under paragraph (5) notwithstanding that the agency may not have obtained all the information about the prospective adopter which may be required by this regulation.

(7A) The report shall not be completed until the adoption agency has carried out police checks in accordance with regulation 23 and made arrangements for the prospective adopter to receive preparation for adoption in accordance with regulation 24.

(8) The adoption agency must notify the prospective adopter that his application is to be referred to the adoption panel and give him a copy of the prospective adopter's report, inviting him to send any observations in writing to the agency within 10 working days, beginning with the date on which the notification is sent.

(9) At the end of the period of 10 working days referred to in paragraph (8) (or earlier if any observations made by the prospective adopter are received before that period has expired) the adoption agency must send—

(a) the prospective adopter's report and the prospective adopter's observations;
(b) the written reports referred to in paragraphs (3) and (4) but in the case of reports obtained in accordance with paragraph (3)(a), only if the agency's medical adviser advises it to do so; and

(c) any other relevant information obtained by the agency,

to the adoption panel.

(10) The adoption agency must obtain, so far as is reasonably practicable, any other relevant information which may be required by the adoption panel and send that information to the panel.

6–3503 26. Function of the adoption panel. (1) Subject to paragraphs (2) and (2A), the adoption panel must consider the case of the prospective adopter referred to it by the adoption agency and make a recommendation to the agency as to whether the prospective adopter is suitable to adopt a child.

(2) In considering what recommendation to make the adoption panel—

(a) must consider and take into account all the information and reports passed to it in accordance with regulation 25;
(b) may request the adoption agency to obtain any other relevant information which the panel considers necessary; and
(c) may obtain legal advice as it considers necessary in relation to the case.

(2A) In relation to the case of a prospective adopter in respect of whom a report has been prepared in accordance with regulation 25(7), the adoption panel must either—

(a) request the adoption agency to prepare a further prospective adopter's report, covering all the matters set out in regulation 25(5); or
(b) recommend that the prospective adopter is not suitable to adopt a child.

(3) Where the adoption panel makes a recommendation to the adoption agency that the prospective adopter is suitable to adopt a child, the panel may consider and give advice to the agency about the number of children the prospective adopter may be suitable to adopt, their age range, sex, likely needs and background.

(4) Before making any recommendation, the adoption panel must invite the prospective adopters to attend a meeting of the panel.

6–3504 27. Adoption agency decision and notification. (1) The adoption agency must make a decision about whether the prospective adopter is suitable to adopt a child.

(2) No member of the adoption panel shall take part in any decision made by the adoption agency under paragraph (1).

(3) Where the adoption agency decides to approve the prospective adopter as suitable to adopt a child, it must notify him in writing of its decision.

(4) Where the adoption agency considers that the prospective adopter is not suitable to adopt a child, it must—

(a) notify the prospective adopter in writing that it proposes not to approve him as suitable to adopt a child ("qualifying determination");
(b) send with that notification its reasons together with a copy of the recommendation of the adoption panel if that recommendation is different;
(c) advise the prospective adopter that within 40 working days beginning with the date on which the notification was sent he may—

(i) submit any representations he wishes to make to the agency; or
(ii) apply to the Secretary of State for a review by an independent review panel of the qualifying determination.

(5) If, within the period of 40 working days referred to in paragraph (4), the prospective adopter has not made any representations or applied to the Secretary of State for a review by an independent review panel, the adoption agency shall proceed to make its decision and shall notify the prospective adopter in writing of its decision together with the reasons for that decision.

(6) If, within the period of 40 working days referred to in paragraph (4), the adoption agency receives further representations from the prospective adopter, it may refer the case together with all the relevant information to the adoption panel for further consideration.

(7) The adoption panel must consider any case referred to it under paragraph (6) and make a fresh recommendation to the adoption agency as to whether the prospective adopter is suitable to adopt a child.

(8) The adoption agency must make a decision on the case but—

(a) if the case has been referred to the adoption panel under paragraph (6), the agency must make the decision only after taking into account the recommendations of the adoption panel made under both paragraph (7) and regulation 26; or
(b) if the prospective adopter has applied to the Secretary of State for a review by an independent review panel of the qualifying determination, the agency must make the decision only after taking into account the recommendation of the independent review panel and the recommendation of the adoption panel made under regulation 26.

(9) As soon as possible after making its decision under paragraph (8), the adoption agency must notify the prospective adopter in writing of its decision stating its reasons for that decision if they do not consider the prospective adopter suitable to adopt a child, and of the adoption panel's recommendation under paragraph (7), if this is different from the agency's decision.

(10) In a case where an independent review panel has made a recommendation, the adoption agency shall send to the Secretary of State a copy of the notification referred to in paragraph (9).

6–3505   **28. Information to be sent to the independent review panel.**   (1) If the adoption agency receives notification from the Secretary of State that a prospective adopter has applied for a review by an independent review panel of the qualifying determination, the agency must, within 10 working days of receipt of that notification, send to the Secretary of State the information specified in paragraph (2).

(2) The following information is specified for the purposes of paragraph (1)—

(a) all of the documents and information which were passed to the adoption panel in accordance with regulation 25;

(b) any relevant information in relation to the prospective adopter which was obtained by the agency after the date on which the documents and information referred to in sub-paragraph (a) were passed to the adoption panel; and

(c) the documents referred to in regulation 27(4)(a) and (b).

6–3506   **29. Review and termination of approval.**   (1) The adoption agency must review the approval of each prospective adopter in accordance with this regulation, unless—

(a) in a section 83 case, the prospective adopter has visited the child in the country in which the child is habitually resident and has confirmed in writing that he wishes to proceed with the adoption; and

(b) in any other case, a child is placed for adoption with the prospective adopter or the agency is considering placing a child with the prospective adopter in accordance with regulations 31 to 33.

(2) A review must take place whenever the adoption agency considers it necessary but otherwise not more than one year after approval and thereafter at intervals of not more than a year.

(3) When undertaking such a review the adoption agency must—

(a) make such enquiries and obtain such information as it considers necessary in order to review whether the prospective adopter continues to be suitable to adopt a child; and

(b) seek and take into account the views of the prospective adopter.

(4) If at the conclusion of the review, the adoption agency considers that the prospective adopter may no longer be suitable to adopt a child, it must—

(a) prepare a written report ("the prospective adopter's review report") which shall include the agency's reasons;

(b) notify the prospective adopter that his case is to be referred to the adoption panel; and

(c) give him a copy of the report inviting him to send any observations to the agency within 10 working days beginning with the date on which that report is given to him.

(5) At the end of the period of 10 working days referred to in paragraph (4)(c) (or earlier if the prospective adopter's comments are received before that period has expired), the adoption agency must send the prospective adopter's review report together with the prospective adopter's observations to the adoption panel.

(6) The adoption agency must obtain, so far as is reasonably practicable, any other relevant information which may be required by the adoption panel and send that information to the panel.

(7) The adoption panel must consider the prospective adopter's review report, the prospective adopter's observations and any other information passed to it by the adoption agency and make a recommendation to the agency as to whether the prospective adopter continues to be suitable to adopt a child.

(8) The adoption agency must make a decision as to whether the prospective adopter continues to be suitable to adopt a child and regulation 27(2) to (10) shall apply in relation to that decision by the agency.

6–3507   **30. Duties of the adoption agency in a section 83 case.**   Where the adoption agency decides in a section 83 case to approve a prospective adopter as suitable to adopt a child, the agency must send to the Secretary of State—

(a) written confirmation of the decision and any recommendation the agency may make in relation to the number of children the prospective adopter may be suitable to adopt, their age range, sex, likely needs and background;

(b) all the documents and information which were passed to the adoption panel in accordance with regulation 25;

(c) the record of the proceedings of the adoption panel, its recommendation and the reasons for its recommendation;

(d) if the prospective adopter applied to the Secretary of State for a review by an independent review panel of a qualifying determination, the record of the proceedings of that panel, its recommendation and the reasons for its recommendation; and

(e) any other information relating to the case which the Secretary of State or the relevant foreign authority may require.

PART 5

DUTIES OF ADOPTION AGENCY IN RESPECT OF PROPOSED PLACEMENT OF CHILD WITH PROSPECTIVE ADOPTER

6–3508   **31. Proposed placement.**   (1) Where an adoption agency is considering placing a child for adoption with a particular prospective adopter ("the proposed placement") the agency must—

(a) provide the prospective adopter with a copy of the child's permanence report and any other information the agency considers relevant;

(b) meet with the prospective adopter to discuss the proposed placement;

(c) ascertain the views of the prospective adopter about—

    (i) the proposed placement; and

    (ii) the arrangements the agency proposes to make for allowing any person contact with the child; and

(d) provide a counselling service for, and any further information to, the prospective adopter as may be required.

(2) Where the adoption agency considers that the proposed placement should proceed, the agency must—

(a) where the agency is a local authority, carry out an assessment of the needs of the child and the prospective adopter and any children of the prospective adopter ("the adoptive family") for adoption support services in accordance with regulations made under section 4(6) of the Act;

(b) where the agency is a registered adoption society, notify the prospective adopter that he may request the local authority in whose area he has his home ("the relevant authority") to carry out an assessment of his needs for adoption support services under section 4(1) of the Act and pass to the relevant authority, at their request, a copy of the child's permanence report and a copy of the prospective adopter's report;

(c) consider the arrangements for allowing any person contact with the child; and

(d) prepare a written report ("the adoption placement report") which shall include—

    (i) the agency's reasons for proposing the placement;

    (ii) the information obtained by the agency by virtue of paragraph (1);

    (iii) where the agency is a local authority, their proposals for the provision of adoption support services for the adoptive family;

    (iv) the arrangements the agency proposes to make for allowing any person contact with the child; and

    (v) any other relevant information.

(3) Where the adoption agency remains of the view that the proposed placement should proceed, it must notify the prospective adopter that the proposed placement is to be referred to the adoption panel and give him a copy of the adoption placement report, inviting him to send any observations in writing to the agency within 10 working days, beginning with the date on which the notification is sent.

(4) At the end of the period of 10 working days referred to in paragraph (3) (or earlier if observations are received before the 10 working days has expired) the adoption agency must send—

(a) the adoption placement report;

(b) the child's permanence report; and

(c) the prospective adopter's report and his observations,

to the adoption panel.

(5) The adoption agency must obtain so far as is reasonably practicable any other relevant information which may be requested by the adoption panel in connection with the proposed placement and send that information to the panel.

(6) This paragraph applies where an adoption agency ("agency A") intends to refer a proposed placement to the adoption panel and another agency ("agency B") made the decision (in accordance with these Regulations) that—

(a) the child should be placed for adoption; or

(b) the prospective adopter is suitable to be an adoptive parent.

(7) Where paragraph (6) applies agency A may only refer the proposed placement to the adoption panel if it has consulted agency B about the proposed placement.

(8) Agency A must—

(a) where paragraph (6)(a) applies, open a child's case record; or

(b) where paragraph (6)(b) applies, open a prospective adopter's case record,

and place on the appropriate record, the information and documents received from agency B.

6–3509 **32. Function of the adoption panel in relation to proposed placement.** (1) The adoption panel must consider the proposed placement referred to it by the adoption agency and make a recommendation to the agency as to whether the child should be placed for adoption with that particular prospective adopter.

(2) In considering what recommendation to make the adoption panel shall have regard to the duties imposed on the adoption agency under section 1(2), (4) and (5) of the Act (considerations applying to the exercise of powers in relation to the adoption of a child) and—

(a) must consider and take into account all information and the reports passed to it in accordance with regulation 31;

(b) may request the agency to obtain any other relevant information which the panel considers necessary; and

(c)   may obtain legal advice as it considers necessary in relation to the case.

(3)   The adoption panel must consider—

(a)   in a case where the adoption agency is a local authority, the authority's proposals for the provision of adoption support services for the adoptive family;

(b)   the arrangements the adoption agency proposes to make for allowing any person contact with the child; and

(c)   whether the parental responsibility of any parent or guardian or the prospective adopter should be restricted and if so the extent of any such restriction.

(4)   Where the adoption panel makes a recommendation to the adoption agency that the child should be placed for adoption with the particular prospective adopter, the panel may at the same time give advice to the agency about any of the matters set out in paragraph (3).

(5)   An adoption panel may only make the recommendation referred to in paragraph (1) if—

(a)   that recommendation is to be made at the same meeting of the adoption panel at which a recommendation has been made that the child should be placed for adoption; or

(b)   the adoption agency, or another adoption agency, has already made a decision in accordance with regulation 19 that the child should be placed for adoption,

and in either case that recommendation is to be made at the same meeting of the panel at which a recommendation has been made that the prospective adopter is suitable to adopt a child or the adoption agency, or another adoption agency, has made a decision in accordance with regulation 27 that the prospective adopter is suitable to adopt a child.

6–3510   **33. Adoption agency decision in relation to proposed placement.**   (1) The adoption agency must take into account the recommendation of the adoption panel in coming to a decision about whether the child should be placed for adoption with the particular prospective adopter.

(2)   No member of the adoption panel shall take part in any decision made by the adoption agency under paragraph (1).

(3)   As soon as possible after making its decision the adoption agency must notify in writing—

(a)   the prospective adopter of its decision; and

(b)   if their whereabouts are known to the agency, the parent or guardian and, where regulation 14(3) applies and the agency considers it is appropriate, the father of the child, of the fact that the child is to be placed for adoption.

(4)   If the adoption agency decides that the proposed placement should proceed, the agency must, in an appropriate manner and having regard to the child's age and understanding, explain its decision to the child.

(5)   The adoption agency must place on the child's case record—

(a)   the prospective adopter's report;

(b)   the adoption placement report and the prospective adopter's observations on that report;

(c)   the written record of the proceedings of the adoption panel under regulation 32, its recommendation, the reasons for its recommendation and any advice given by the panel to the agency; and

(d)   the record and notification of the agency's decision under this regulation.

6–3511   **34. Function of the adoption agency in a section 83 case.**   (1) This paragraph applies where in a section 83 case the adoption agency receives from the relevant foreign authority information about a child to be adopted by a prospective adopter.

(2)   Where paragraph (1) applies, the adoption agency must—

(a)   send a copy of the information referred to in paragraph (1) to the prospective adopter unless it is aware that the prospective adopter has received a copy;

(b)   consider that information and meet with the prospective adopter to discuss the information; and

(c)   if appropriate, provide a counselling service for, and any further information to, the prospective adopter as may be required.

PART 6

PLACEMENT AND REVIEWS

6–3512   **35. Requirements imposed on the adoption agency before the child may be placed for adoption.**   (1) This paragraph applies where the adoption agency—

(a)   has decided in accordance with regulation 33 to place a child for adoption with a particular prospective adopter; and

(b)   has met with the prospective adopter to consider the arrangements it proposes to make for the placement of the child with him.

(2)   Where paragraph (1) applies, the adoption agency must, as soon as possible, send the prospective adopter a placement plan in respect of the child which covers the matters specified in Schedule 5 ("the adoption placement plan").

(3)   Where the prospective adopter notifies the adoption agency that he wishes to proceed with the placement and the agency is authorised to place the child for adoption or, subject to paragraph

(4), the child is less than 6 weeks old, the agency may place the child for adoption with the prospective adopter.

(4) Unless there is a placement order in respect of the child, the adoption agency may not place for adoption a child who is less than six weeks old unless the parent or guardian of the child has agreed in writing with the agency that the child may be placed for adoption.

(5) Where the child already has his home with the prospective adopter, the adoption agency must notify the prospective adopter in writing of the date on which the child is placed for adoption with him by that agency.

(6) The adoption agency must before the child is placed for adoption with the prospective adopter—

(a) send to the prospective adopter's general practitioner written notification of the proposed placement and send with that notification a written report of the child's health history and current state of health;

(b) send to the local authority (if that authority is not the adoption agency) and Primary Care Trust or Local Health Board (Wales), in whose area the prospective adopter has his home, written notification of the proposed placement; and

(c) where the child is of compulsory school age, send to the local education authority, in whose area the prospective adopter has his home, written notification of the proposed placement and information about the child's educational history and whether he has been or is likely to be assessed for special educational needs under the Education Act 1996.

(7) The adoption agency must notify the prospective adopter in writing of any change to the adoption placement plan.

(8) The adoption agency must place on the child's case record—

(a) in the case of a child who is less than 6 weeks old and in respect of whom there is no placement order, a copy of the agreement referred to in paragraph (4); and

(b) a copy of the adoption placement plan and any changes to that plan.

6–3513 36. Reviews. (1) Where an adoption agency is authorised to place a child for adoption but the child is not for the time being placed for adoption the agency must carry out a review of the child's case—

(a) not more than 3 months after the date on which the agency first has authority to place; and

(b) thereafter not more than 6 months after the date of the previous review ("6 months review"),

until the child is placed for adoption.

(2) Paragraphs (3) and (4) apply where a child is placed for adoption.

(3) The adoption agency must carry out a review of the child's case—

(a) not more than 4 weeks after the date on which the child is placed for adoption ("the first review");

(b) not more than 3 months after the first review; and

(c) thereafter not more than 6 months after the date of the previous review,

unless the child is returned to the agency by the prospective adopter or an adoption order is made.

(4) The adoption agency must—

(a) ensure that the child and the prospective adopter are visited within one week of the placement and thereafter at least once a week until the first review and thereafter at such frequency as the agency decides at each review;

(b) ensure that written reports are made of such visits; and

(c) provide such advice and assistance to the prospective adopter as the agency considers necessary.

(5) When carrying out a review the adoption agency must consider each of the matters set out in paragraph (6) and must, so far as is reasonably practicable, ascertain the views of—

(a) the child, having regard to his age and understanding;

(b) if the child is placed for adoption, the prospective adopter; and

(c) any other person the agency considers relevant,

in relation to such of the matters set out in paragraph (6) as the agency considers appropriate.

(6) The matters referred to in paragraph (5) are—

(a) whether the adoption agency remains satisfied that the child should be placed for adoption;

(b) the child's needs, welfare and development, and whether any changes need to be made to meet his needs or assist his development;

(c) the existing arrangements for contact, and whether they should continue or be altered;

(d) the arrangements in relation to the exercise of parental responsibility for the child, and whether they should continue or be altered;

(e) where the child is placed for adoption, the arrangements for the provision of adoption support services for the adoptive family and whether there should be any re-assessment of the need for those services;

(f) in consultation with the appropriate agencies, the arrangements for assessing and meeting the child's health care and educational needs;

(g) subject to paragraphs (1) and (3), the frequency of the reviews.

(7) Where the child is subject to a placement order and has not been placed for adoption at the time of the first 6 months review, the local authority must at that review—

(a) establish why the child has not been placed for adoption and consider what further steps the authority should take in relation to the placement of the child for adoption; and
(b) consider whether it remains satisfied that the child should be placed for adoption.

(8) The adoption agency must, so far as is reasonably practicable, notify—

(a) the child, where the agency considers he is of sufficient age and understanding;
(b) the prospective adopter; and
(c) any other person whom the agency considers relevant,

any decision taken by the agency in consequence of that review.

(9) The adoption agency must ensure that—

(a) the information obtained in the course of a review or visit in respect of a child's case including the views expressed by the child;
(b) the details of the proceedings of any meeting arranged by the agency to consider any aspect of the review of the case; and
(c) details of any decision made in the course of or as a result of the review,

are recorded in writing and placed on the child's case record.

(10) Where the child is returned to the adoption agency in accordance with section 35(1) or (2) of the Act, the agency must conduct a review of the child's case no earlier than 28 days, or later than 42 days, after the date on which the child is returned to the agency and when carrying out that review the agency must consider the matters set out in paragraph (6)(a), (b), (c) and (f).

6–3514 **37. Independent reviewing officers.** (1) An adoption agency which is—

(a) a local authority; or
(b) a registered adoption society which is a voluntary organisation who provide accommodation for a child,

must appoint a person ("the independent reviewing officer") in respect of the case of each child authorised to be placed for adoption by the agency to carry out the functions mentioned in section 26(2A) of the 1989 Act.

(2) The independent reviewing officer must be registered as a social worker in a register maintained by the General Social Care Council or by the Care Council for Wales under section 56 of the Care Standards Act 2000 or in a corresponding register maintained under the law of Scotland or Northern Ireland.

(3) The independent reviewing officer must, in the opinion of the adoption agency, have sufficient relevant social work experience to undertake the functions referred to in paragraph (1) in relation to the case.

(4) A person who is an employee of the adoption agency may not be appointed as an independent reviewing officer in a case if he is involved in the management of the case or is under the direct management of—

(a) a person involved in the management of the case;
(b) a person with management responsibilities in relation to a person mentioned in sub-paragraph (a); or
(c) a person with control over the resources allocated to the case.

(5) The independent reviewing officer must—

(a) as far as is reasonably practicable attend any meeting held in connection with the review of the child's case; and
(b) chair any such meeting that he attends.

(6) The independent reviewing officer must, as far as is reasonably practicable, take steps to ensure that the review is conducted in accordance with regulation 36 and in particular to ensure—

(a) that the child's views are understood and taken into account;
(b) that the persons responsible for implementing any decision taken in consequence of the review are identified; and
(c) that any failure to review the case in accordance with regulation 36 or to take proper steps to make the arrangements agreed at the review is brought to the attention of persons at an appropriate level of seniority within the adoption agency.

(7) If the child whose case is reviewed wishes to take proceedings on his own account, for example, to apply to the court for revocation of a placement order, it is the function of the independent reviewing officer—

(a) to assist the child to obtain legal advice; or
(b) to establish whether an appropriate adult is able and willing to provide such assistance or bring the proceedings on the child's behalf.

(8) The adoption agency must inform the independent reviewing officer of—

(a) any significant failure to make the arrangements agreed at a review; and
(b) any significant change in the child's circumstances after a review.

6–3515 38. Withdrawal of consent. (1) This paragraph applies where consent given under section 19 or 20 of the Act in respect of a child is withdrawn in accordance with section 52(8) of the Act.

(2) Where paragraph (1) applies and the adoption agency is a local authority, on receipt of the form or notice given in accordance with section 52(8) of the Act the authority must immediately review their decision to place the child for adoption and where, in accordance with section 22(1) to (3) of the Act, the authority decide to apply for a placement order in respect of the child, they must notify as soon as possible—

(a) the parent or guardian of the child;
(b) where regulation 14(3) applies and the agency considers it is appropriate, the child's father; and
(c) if the child is placed for adoption, the prospective adopter with whom the child is placed.

(3) Where paragraph (1) applies and the adoption agency is a registered adoption society, the agency must immediately consider whether it is appropriate to inform the local authority in whose area the child is living.

PART 7
CASE RECORDS

6–3516 39. Storage of case records. The adoption agency must ensure that the child's case record and the prospective adopter's case record and the contents of those case records are at all times kept in secure conditions and in particular that all appropriate measures are taken to prevent the theft, unauthorised disclosure, loss or destruction of, or damage to, the case record or its contents.

6–3517 40. Preservation of case records. An adoption agency must keep the child's case record and the prospective adopter's case record for such period as it considers appropriate.

6–3518 41. Confidentiality of case records. Subject to regulation 42, the contents of the child's case record and the prospective adopter's case record shall be treated by the adoption agency as confidential.

6–3519 42. Access to case records and disclosure of information. (1) Subject to paragraph (3), an adoption agency shall provide such access to its case records and disclose such information in its possession, as may be required—

(a) to those holding an inquiry under sections 3 and 4 of the Children Act 2004 (inquiries held by the Children's Commissioner) or under the Inquiries Act 2005 for the purposes of such an inquiry;
(b) to the Secretary of State;
(c) to the registration authority;
(d) subject to the provisions of sections 29(7) and 32(3) of the Local Government Act 1974 (investigations and disclosure), to the Commission for Local Administration in England, for the purposes of any investigation conducted in accordance with Part 3 of that Act;
(e) to any person appointed by the agency for the purposes of the consideration by the agency of any representations (including complaints);
(f) by and to the extent specified in these Regulations;
(g) to an officer of the Service or a Welsh family proceedings officer for the purposes of the discharge of his duties under the Act; and
(h) to a court having power to make an order under the Act or the 1989 Act.

(2) Subject to paragraph (3), an adoption agency may provide such access to its case records and disclose such information in its possession, as it thinks fit for the purposes of carrying out its functions as an adoption agency.

(3) A written record shall be kept by an adoption agency of any access provided or disclosure made by virtue of this regulation.

6–3520 43. Transfer of case records. (1) An adoption agency may transfer a copy of a child's case record or prospective adopter's case record (or part of that record) to another adoption agency when it considers this to be in the interests of the child or prospective adopter to whom the record relates, and a written record shall be kept of any such transfer.

(2) Subject to paragraph (3), a registered adoption society which intends to cease to act or exist as such shall forthwith either transfer its case records to another adoption agency having first obtained the registration authority's approval for such transfer, or transfer its case records—

(a) to the local authority in whose area the society's principal office is situated; or
(b) in the case of a society which amalgamates with another registered adoption society to form a new registered adoption society, to the new body.

(3) An adoption agency to which case records are transferred by virtue of paragraph (2)(a) or (b) shall notify the registration authority in writing of such transfer.

6–3521   **44. Application of regulations 40 to 42.**   Nothing in this Part applies to the information which an adoption agency must keep in relation to an adopted person by virtue of regulations made under section 56 of the Act.

PART 8

MISCELLANEOUS

6–3522   **45. Modification of 1989 Act in relation to adoption.**   (1) This paragraph applies where—

(a)   a local authority are authorised to place a child for adoption; or

(b)   a child who has been placed for adoption by a local authority is less than 6 weeks old.

(2) Where paragraph (1) applies—

(a)   section 22(4)(b) of the 1989 Act shall not apply;

(b)   section 22(4)(c) of the 1989 Act shall apply as if for that sub-paragraph there were inserted "(c) any prospective adopter with whom the local authority has placed the child for adoption;";

(c)   section 22(5)(b) of the 1989 Act shall apply as if for the words "(4)(b) to (d)" there were inserted "(4)(c) and (d)"; and

(d)   paragraphs 15 and 21 of Schedule 2 to the 1989 Act shall not apply.

(3) This paragraph applies where a registered adoption society is authorised to place a child for adoption or a child who has been placed for adoption by a registered adoption society is less than 6 weeks old.

(4) Where paragraph (3) applies—

(a)   section 61 of the 1989 Act is to have effect in relation to the child whether or not he is accommodated by or on behalf of the society;

(b)   section 61(2)(b) of the 1989 Act shall not apply; and

(c)   section 61(2)(c) of the 1989 Act shall apply as if for that sub-paragraph there were inserted "(c) any prospective adopter with whom the registered adoption society has placed the child for adoption;".

6–3523   **46. Contact.**   (1) This paragraph applies where an adoption agency decides that a child should be placed for adoption.

(2) Where paragraph (1) applies and subject to paragraph (3), the adoption agency must consider what arrangements it should make for allowing any person contact with the child once the agency is authorised to place the child for adoption ("the contact arrangements").

(3) The adoption agency must—

(a)   take into account the wishes and feelings of the parent or guardian of the child and, where regulation 14(3) applies and the agency considers it is appropriate, the father of the child;

(b)   take into account any advice given by the adoption panel in accordance with regulation 18(3); and

(c)   have regard to the considerations set out in section 1(2) and (4) of the Act,

in coming to a decision in relation to the contact arrangements.

(4) The adoption agency must notify—

(a)   the child, if the agency considers he is of sufficient age and understanding;

(b)   if their whereabouts are known to the agency, the parent or guardian, and, where regulation 14(3) applies and the agency considers it is appropriate, the father of the child;

(c)   any person in whose favour there was a provision for contact under the 1989 Act which ceased to have effect by virtue of section 26(1) of the Act; and

(d)   any other person the agency considers relevant,

of the contact arrangements.

(5) Where an adoption agency decides that a child should be placed for adoption with a particular prospective adopter, the agency must review the contact arrangements in light of the views of the prospective adopter and any advice given by the adoption panel in accordance with regulation 32(3).

(6) If the adoption agency proposes to make any change to the contact arrangements which affects any person mentioned in paragraph (4), it must seek the views of that person and take those views into account in deciding what arrangements it should make for allowing any person contact with the child while he is placed for adoption with the prospective adopter.

(7) The adoption agency must—

(a)   set out the contact arrangements in the placement plan; and

(b)   keep the contact arrangements under review.

6–3524   **47. Contact: supplementary.**   (1) Where an adoption agency has decided under section 27(2) of the Act to refuse to allow the contact that would otherwise be required by virtue of an order under section 26 of the Act, the agency must, as soon as the decision is made, inform the persons specified in paragraph (3) and notify them of the decision, the date of the decision, the reasons for the decision and the duration of the period.

(2) The terms of an order under section 26 of the Act may be departed from by agreement

between the adoption agency and any person for whose contact with the child the order provides subject to the following conditions—

    (a) where the child is of sufficient age and understanding, subject to his agreement;

    (b) where the child is placed for adoption, subject to consultation before the agreement is reached, with the prospective adopter with whom the child is placed for adoption; and

    (c) written confirmation by the agency to the persons specified in paragraph (3) of the terms of that agreement.

(3) The following persons are specified for the purposes of paragraphs (1) and (2)—

    (a) the child, if the adoption agency considers he is of sufficient age and understanding;

    (b) the person in whose favour the order under section 26 was made; and

    (c) if the child is placed for adoption, the prospective adopter.

6–3525

SCHEDULE 1

INFORMATION

6–3526

PART 1

INFORMATION ABOUT THE CHILD

Regulation 15(1)

    1. Name, sex, date and place of birth and address including the local authority area.

    2. A photograph and physical description.

    3. Nationality.

    4. Racial origin and cultural and linguistic background.

    5. Religious persuasion (including details of baptism, confirmation or equivalent ceremonies).

    6. Whether the child is looked after or is provided with accommodation under section 59(1) of the 1989 Act.

    7. Details of any order made by a court with respect to the child under the 1989 Act including the name of the court, the order made and the date on which the order was made.

    8. Whether the child has any rights to, or interest in, property or any claim to damages under the Fatal Accidents Act 1976 or otherwise which he stands to retain or lose if he is adopted.

    9. A chronology of the child's care since birth.

    10. A description of the child's personality, his social development and his emotional and behavioural development.

    11. Whether the child has any difficulties with activities such as feeding, washing and dressing himself.

    12. The educational history of the child including—

    (a) the names, addresses and types of nurseries or schools attended with dates;

    (b) a summary of his progress and attainments;

    (c) whether he is subject to a statement of special educational needs under the Education Act 1996;

    (d) any special needs he has in relation to learning; and

    (e) where he is looked after, details of his personal education plan prepared by the local authority.

    13. Information about—

    (a) the child's relationship with—

        (i) his parent or guardian;

        (ii) any brothers or sisters or other relatives he may have; and

        (iii) any other person the agency considers relevant;

    (b) the likelihood of any such relationship continuing and the value to the child of its doing so; and

    (c) the ability and willingness of the child's parent or guardian or any other person the agency considers relevant, to provide the child with a secure environment in which he can develop, and otherwise to meet his needs.

    14. The current arrangements for and the type of contact between the child's parent or guardian or other person with parental responsibility for him, his father, and any relative, friend or other person.

    15. A description of the child's interests, likes and dislikes.

    16. Any other relevant information which might assist the adoption panel and the adoption agency.

    17. In this Part "parent" includes the child's father whether or not he has parental responsibility for the child.

6–3527

PART 2

MATTERS TO BE INCLUDED IN THE CHILD'S HEALTH REPORT

Regulation 15(2)

    1. Name, date of birth, sex, weight and height.

    2. A neo-natal report on the child, including—

    (a) details of his birth and any complications;

    (b) the results of a physical examination and screening tests;

    (c) details of any treatment given;

    (d) details of any problem in management and feeding;

    (e) any other relevant information which may assist the adoption panel and the adoption agency; and

    (f) the name and address of any registered medical practitioner who may be able to provide further information about any of the above matters.

    3. A full health history of the child, including—

    (a) details of any serious illness, disability, accident, hospital admission or attendance at an out-patient department, and in each case any treatment given;

(b) details and dates of immunisations;
(c) a physical and developmental assessment according to age, including an assessment of vision and hearing and of neurological, speech and language development and any evidence of emotional disorder;
(d) for a child over five years of age, the school health history (if available);
(e) how his physical and mental health and medical history have affected his physical, intellectual, emotional, social or behavioural development; and
(f) any other relevant information which may assist the adoption panel and the adoption agency.

6–3528

PART 3
INFORMATION ABOUT THE CHILD'S FAMILY AND OTHERS

Regulation 16(1)

Information about each parent of the child
1. Name, sex, date and place of birth and address including the local authority area.
2. A photograph, if available, and physical description.
3. Nationality.
4. Racial origin and cultural and linguistic background.
5. Religious persuasion.
6. A description of their personality and interests.
Information about the child's brothers and sisters
7. Name, sex, and date and place of birth.
8. A photograph, if available, and physical description.
9. Nationality.
10. Address, if appropriate.
11. If the brother or sister is under the age of 18—

(a) where and with whom he or she is living;
(b) whether he or she is looked after or is provided with accommodation under section 59(1) of the 1989 Act;
(c) details of any court order made with respect to him or her under the 1989 Act, including the name of the court, the order made, and the date on which the order was made; and
(d) whether he or she is also being considered for adoption.

Information about the child's other relatives and any other person the agency considers relevant
12. Name, sex and date and place of birth.
13. Nationality.
14. Address, if appropriate.
Family history and relationships
15. Whether the child's parents were married to each other at the time of the child's birth (or have subsequently married) and if so, the date and place of marriage and whether they are divorced or separated.
16. Where the child's parents are not married, whether the father has parental responsibility for the child and if so how it was acquired.
17. If the identity or whereabouts of the child's father are not known, the information about him that has been ascertained and from whom, and the steps that have been taken to establish paternity.
18. Where the child's parents have been previously married or formed a civil partnership, the date of the marriage or, as the case may be, the date and place of registration of the civil partnership.
19. So far as is possible, a family tree with details of the child's grandparents, parents and aunts and uncles with their age (or ages at death).
20. Where it is reasonably practicable, a chronology of each of the child's parents from birth.
21. The observations of the child's parents about their own experiences of being parented and how this has influenced them.
22. The past and present relationship of the child's parents.
23. Details of the wider family and their role and importance to—

(a) the child's parents; and
(b) any brothers or sisters of the child.

Other information about each parent of the child
24. Information about their home and the neighbourhood in which they live.
25. Details of their educational history.
26. Details of their employment history.
27. Information about the parenting capacity of the child's parents, particularly their ability and willingness to parent the child.
28. Any other relevant information which might assist the adoption panel and the adoption agency.
29. In this Part "parent" includes the father of the child whether or not he has parental responsibility for the child.

6–3529

PART 4
INFORMATION RELATING TO THE HEALTH OF THE CHILD'S NATURAL PARENTS AND BROTHERS AND SISTERS

Regulation 16(2)

1. Name, date of birth, sex, weight and height of each natural parent.
2. A health history of each of the child's natural parents, including details of any serious physical or mental illness, any hereditary disease or disorder, drug or alcohol misuse, disability, accident or hospital admission and in each case any treatment given where the agency consider such information to be relevant.
3. A health history of the child's brothers and sisters (of the full blood or half-blood), and the other children of each parent with details of any serious physical or mental illness and any hereditary disease or disorder.
4. A summary of the mother's obstetric history, including any problems in the ante-natal, labour and post-natal periods, with the results of any tests carried out during or immediately after the pregnancy.
5. Details of any present illness, including treatment and prognosis.

6. Any other relevant information which the adoption agency considers may assist the adoption panel and the agency.

6–3530

Regulation 20   SCHEDULE 2

INFORMATION AND DOCUMENTS TO BE PROVIDED TO THE CAFCASS OR THE NATIONAL ASSEMBLY FOR WALES

1. A certified copy of the child's birth certificate.
2. Name and address of the child's parent or guardian.
3. A chronology of the actions and decisions taken by the adoption agency with respect to the child.
4. Confirmation by the adoption agency that it has counselled, and explained to the parent or guardian the legal implications of both consent to placement under section 19 of the Act and, as the case may be, to the making of a future adoption order under section 20 of the Act and provided the parent or guardian with written information about this together with a copy of the written information provided to him.
5. Such information about the parent or guardian or other information as the adoption agency considers the officer of the Service or the Welsh family proceedings officer may need to know.

6–3531
6–3532

SCHEDULE 3

PART 1
OFFENCES SPECIFIED FOR THE PURPOSES OF REGULATION 23(3)(B)

Regulation 23(3)

Offences in England and Wales
1. Any of the following offences against an adult—

(a) an offence of rape under section 1 of the Sexual Offences Act 2003;
(b) an offence of assault by penetration under section 2 of that Act;
(c) an offence of causing a person to engage in sexual activity without consent under section 4 of that Act, if the activity fell within subsection (4) of that section;
(d) an offence of sexual activity with a person with a mental disorder impeding choice under section 30 of that Act, if the touching fell within subsection (3) of that section;
(e) an offence of causing or inciting a person with mental disorder impeding choice to engage in sexual activity under section 31of that Act, if the activity caused or incited fell within subsection (3) of that section;
(f) an offence of inducement, threat or deception to procure sexual activity with a person with a mental disorder under section 34 of that Act, if the touching involved fell within subsection (2) of that section; and
(g) an offence of causing a person with a mental disorder to engage in or agree to engage in sexual activity by inducement, threat or deception under section 35 of that Act, if the activity fell within subsection (2) of that section.

Offences in Scotland
2. An offence of rape.
3. An offence specified in Schedule 1 to the Criminal Procedure (Scotland) Act 1995 except, in a case where the offender was under the age of 20 at the time the offence was committed, an offence contrary to section 5 of the Criminal Law (Consolidation) (Scotland) Act 1995 (intercourse with a girl under 16), an offence of shameless indecency between men or an offence of sodomy.
4. An offence of plagium (theft of a child below the age of puberty).
5. Section 52 or 52A of the Civil Government (Scotland) Act 1982 (indecent photographs of children).
6. An offence under section 3 of the Sexual Offences (Amendment) Act 2000 (abuse of trust).
Offences in Northern Ireland
7. An offence of rape.
8. An offence specified in Schedule 1 to the Children and Young Person Act (Northern Ireland) 1968, except offences of common assault or battery or in the case where the offender was under the age of 20 at the time the offence was committed, an offence contrary to section 5 or 11 of the Criminal Law Amendment Act 1885 (unlawful carnal knowledge of a girl under 17 and gross indecency between males).
9. An offence under Article 3 of the Protection of Children (Northern Ireland) Order 1978 (indecent photographs).
10. An offence under Article 9 of the Criminal Justice (Northern Ireland) Order 1980 (inciting girl under 16 to have incestuous sexual intercourse).
11. An offence contrary to Article 15 of the Criminal Justice (Evidence, Etc) (Northern Ireland) Order 1988 (possession of indecent photographs of children).

6–3533

PART 2
REPEALED STATUTORY OFFENCES

Regulation 23(4)

1. (1) An offence under any of the following sections of the Sexual Offences Act 1956—

(a) section 1 (rape);
(b) section 5 (intercourse with a girl under 13);
(c) subject to paragraph 4, section 6 (intercourse with a girl under 16);
(d) section 19 or 20 (abduction of girl under 18 or 16);
(e) section 25 or 26 of that Act (permitting girl under 13, or between 13 and 16, to use premises for intercourse); and
(f) section 28 (causing or encouraging prostitution of, intercourse with or indecent assault on, girl under 16).

(2) An offence under section 1 of the Indecency with Children Act 1960 (indecent conduct towards young child).

(3) An offence under section 54 of the Criminal Law Act 1977 (inciting girl under sixteen to incest).

(4) An offence under section 3 of the Sexual Offences (Amendment) Act 2000 (abuse of trust).

2. A person falls within this paragraph if he has been convicted of any of the following offences against a child committed at the age of 18 or over or has been cautioned by a constable in respect of any such offence which, at the time the caution was given, he admitted—

(a) an offence under section 2 or 3 of the Sexual Offences Act 1956 Act (procurement of woman by threats or false pretences);

(b) an offence under section 4 of that Act (administering drugs to obtain or facilitate intercourse);

(c) an offence under section 14 or 15 of that Act (indecent assault);

(d) an offence under section 16 of that Act (assault with intent to commit buggery);

(e) an offence under section 17 of that Act (abduction of woman by force or for the sake of her property); and

(f) an offence under section 24 of that Act (detention of woman in brothel or other premises).

3. A person falls within this paragraph if he has been convicted of any of the following offences committed at the age of 18 or over or has been cautioned by a constable in respect of any such offence which, at the time the caution was given, he admitted—

(a) an offence under section 7 of the Sexual Offences Act 1956 (intercourse with defective) by having sexual intercourse with a child;

(b) an offence under section 9 of that Act (procurement of defective) by procuring a child to have sexual intercourse;

(c) an offence under section 10 of that Act (incest by a man) by having sexual intercourse with a child;

(d) an offence under section 11 of that Act (incest by a woman) by allowing a child to have sexual intercourse with her;

(e) subject to paragraph 4, an offence under section 12 of that Act by committing buggery with a child under the age of 16;

(f) subject to paragraph 4, an offence under section 13 of that Act by committing an act of gross indecency with a child;

(g) an offence under section 21 of that Act (abduction of defective from parent or guardian) by taking a child out of the possession of her parent or guardian;

(h) an offence under section 22 of that Act (causing prostitution of women) in relation to a child;

(i) an offence under section 23 of that Act (procuration of girl under 21) by procuring a child to have sexual intercourse with a third person;

(j) an offence under section 27 of that Act (permitting defective to use premise for intercourse) by inducing or suffering a child to resort to or be on premises for the purpose of having sexual intercourse;

(k) an offence under section 29 of that Act (causing or encouraging prostitution of defective) by causing or encouraging the prostitution of a child;

(l) an offence under section 30 of that Act (man living on earnings of prostitution) in a case where the prostitute is a child;

(m) an offence under section 31 of that Act (woman exercising control over prostitute) in a case where the prostitute is a child;

(n) an offence under section 128 of the Mental Health Act 1959 (sexual intercourse with patients) by having sexual intercourse with a child;

(o) an offence under section 4 of the Sexual Offences Act 1967 (procuring others to commit homosexual acts) by—

    (i) procuring a child to commit an act of buggery with any person; or

    (ii) procuring any person to commit an act of buggery with a child;

(p) an offence under section 5 of that Act (living on earnings of male prostitution) by living wholly or in part on the earnings of prostitution of a child; and

(q) an offence under section 9(1)(a) of the Theft Act 1968 (burglary), by entering a building or part of a building with intent to rape a child.

4. Paragraphs 1(c) and 3(e) and (f) do not include offences in a case where the offender was under the age of 20 at the time the offence was committed.

6–3534

6–3535

SCHEDULE 4

Part 1
INFORMATION ABOUT THE PROSPECTIVE ADOPTER

Regulation 25(2)

Information about the prospective adopter

1. Name, sex, date and place of birth and address including the local authority area.

2. A photograph and physical description.

3. Whether the prospective adopter is domiciled or habitually resident in a part of the British Islands and if habitually resident for how long he has been habitually resident.

4. Racial origin and cultural and linguistic background.

5. Religious persuasion.

6. Relationship (if any) to the child.

7. A description of his personality and interests.

8. If the prospective adopter is married or has formed a civil partnership and is applying alone for an assessment of his suitability to adopt, the reasons for this.

9. Details of any previous family court proceedings in which the prospective adopter has been involved.

10. Names and addresses of three referees who will give personal references on the prospective adopter, not more than one of whom may be a relative.

11. Name and address of the prospective adopter's registered medical practitioner.

12. If the prospective adopter—

(a) is married, the date and place of marriage;
(b) has formed a civil partnership, the date and place of registration of that partnership; or
(c) has a partner, details of that relationship.

13. Details of any previous marriage, civil partnership or relationship.
14. A family tree with details of the prospective adopter, his siblings and any children of the prospective adopter, with their ages (or ages at death).
15. A chronology of the prospective adopter from birth.
16. The observations of the prospective adopter about his own experience of being parented and how this has influenced him.
17. Details of any experience the prospective adopter has had of caring for children (including as a parent, step-parent, foster parent, child minder or prospective adopter) and an assessment of his ability in this respect.
18. Any other information which indicates how the prospective adopter and anybody else living in his household is likely to relate to a child placed for adoption with the prospective adopter.

Wider family

19. A description of the wider family of the prospective adopter and their role and importance to the prospective adopter and their likely role and importance to a child placed for adoption with the prospective adopter.

Information about the home etc of the prospective adopter

20. Information about the prospective adopter's home and the neighbourhood in which he lives.
21. Details of other members of the prospective adopter's household (including any children of the prospective adopter whether or not resident in the household).
22. Information about the local community of the prospective adopter, including the degree of the family's integration with its peer groups, friendships and social networks.

Education and employment

23. Details of the prospective adopter's educational history and attainments and his views about how this has influenced him.
24. Details of his employment history and the observations of the prospective adopter about how this has influenced him.
25. The current employment of the prospective adopter and his views about achieving a balance between employment and child care.

Income

26. Details of the prospective adopter's income and expenditure.

Other information

27. Information about the prospective adopter's capacity to—

(a) provide for a child's needs, particularly emotional and behavioural development needs;
(b) share a child's history and associated emotional issues; and
(c) understand and support a child through possible feelings of loss and trauma.

28. The prospective adopter's—

(a) reasons for wishing to adopt a child;
(b) views and feelings about adoption and its significance;
(c) views about his parenting capacity;
(d) views about parental responsibility and what it means;
(e) views about a suitable home environment for a child;
(f) views about the importance and value of education;
(g) views and feelings about the importance of a child's religious and cultural upbringing; and
(h) views and feelings about contact.

29. The views of other members of the prospective adopter's household and wider family in relation to adoption.
30. Any other relevant information which might assist the adoption panel or the adoption agency.

6–3536

PART 2
REPORT ON THE HEALTH OF THE PROSPECTIVE ADOPTER

Regulation 25(3)(a)

1. Name, date of birth, sex, weight and height.
2. A family health history of the parents, any brothers and sisters and the children of the prospective adopter, with details of any serious physical or mental illness and hereditary disease or disorder.
3. Infertility or reasons for deciding not to have children (if applicable).
4. Past health history, including details of any serious physical or mental illness, disability, accident, hospital admission or attendance at an out-patient department, and in each case any treatment given.
5. Obstetric history (if applicable).
6. Details of any present illness, including treatment and prognosis.
7. Details of any consumption of alcohol that may give cause for concern or whether the prospective adopter smokes or uses habit-forming drugs.
8. Any other relevant information which the adoption agency considers may assist the adoption panel and the adoption agency.

6–3537

Regulation 35(2)

SCHEDULE 5
ADOPTION PLACEMENT PLAN

1. Whether the child is placed under a placement order or with the consent of the parent or guardian.
2. The arrangements for preparing the child and the prospective adopter for the placement.
3. Date on which it is proposed to place the child for adoption with the prospective adopter.
4. The arrangements for review of the placement.

5. Whether parental responsibility of the prospective adopter for the child is to be restricted, and if so, the extent to which it is to be restricted.

6. Where the local authority has decided to provide adoption support services for the adoptive family, how these will be provided and by whom.

7. The arrangements which the adoption agency has made for allowing any person contact with the child, the form of contact, the arrangements for supporting contact and the name and contact details of the person responsible for facilitating the contact arrangements (if applicable).

8. The dates on which the child's life story book and later life letter are to be passed by the adoption agency to the prospective adopter.

9. Details of any other arrangements that need to be made.

10. Contact details of the child's social worker, the prospective adopter's social worker and out of hours contacts.

Family Procedure (Adoption) Rules 2005[1]
(SI 2005/2795)

PART 1
OVERRIDING OBJECTIVE

6–3550 1. The overriding objective. (1) These Rules are a new procedural code with the overriding objective of enabling the court to deal with cases justly, having regard to the welfare issues involved.

(2) Dealing with a case justly includes, so far as is practicable—

(a) ensuring that it is dealt with expeditiously and fairly;

(b) dealing with the case in ways which are proportionate to the nature, importance and complexity of the issues;

(c) ensuring that the parties are on an equal footing;

(d) saving expense; and

(e) allotting to it an appropriate share of the court's resources, while taking into account the need to allot resources to other cases.

---

1. Made by the Family Procedure Rule Committee in exercise of the powers conferred by ss 75 and 76 of the Courts Act 2003, ss 52(7) and (8), 60(4), 90(1), 102, 109(2) and 141(1) and (3) of, and paragraphs 1(4), 4(4) and 6(2) of Schedule 1 to, the Adoption and Children Act 2002 and s 54(1) of the Access to Justice Act 1999.

6–3550A 2. Application by the court of the overriding objective. The court must seek to give effect to the overriding objective when it—

(a) exercises any power given to it by these Rules; or

(b) interprets any rule.

6–3550B 3. Duty of the parties. The parties are required to help the court to further the overriding objective.

6–3550C 4. Court's duty to manage cases. (1) The court must further the overriding objective by actively managing cases.

(2) Active case management includes—

(a) encouraging the parties to co-operate with each other in the conduct of the proceedings;

(b) identifying at an early stage—

(i) the issues; and

(ii) who should be a party to the proceedings;

(c) deciding promptly—

(i) which issues need full investigation and hearing and which do not; and

(ii) the procedure to be followed in the case;

(d) deciding the order in which issues are to be resolved;

(e) encouraging the parties to use an alternative dispute resolution procedure if the court considers that appropriate and facilitating the use of such procedure;

(f) helping the parties to settle the whole or part of the case;

(g) fixing timetables or otherwise controlling the progress of the case;

(h) considering whether the likely benefits of taking a particular step justify the cost of taking it;

(i) dealing with as many aspects of the case as it can on the same occasion;

(j) dealing with the case without the parties needing to attend at court;

(k) making use of technology; and

(l) giving directions to ensure that the case proceeds quickly and efficiently.

PART 2
INTERPRETATION AND APPLICATION OF OTHER RULES

6–3550D 5. Extent and application of other rules. (1) Unless the context otherwise requires, these Rules apply to proceedings in—

(a)   the High Court;

(b)   a county court; and

(c)   a magistrates' court.

(2)   Rule 35.15 of the CPR shall apply in detailed assessment proceedings in the High Court and a county court.

(3)   Subject to paragraph (4), Parts 43, 44 (except rules 44.3(2) and (3) and 44.9 to 44.12A), 47 and 48 and rule 45.6 of the CPR apply to costs in proceedings, with the following modifications—

(a)   in rule 43.2(1)(c)(ii), "district judge" includes a district judge of the principal registry of the Family Division;

(b)   after rule 43.2(1)(d)(iv), insert—

"or

(v)   a magistrates' court."; and

(c)   in rule 48.7(1) after "section 51(6) of the Supreme Court Act 1981" insert "or section 145A of the Magistrates' Courts Act 1980".

(4)   Part 47 of the CPR does not apply to proceedings in a magistrates' court.

(5)   Parts 50 and 70 to 74 of, and Schedules 1 and 2 to, the CPR apply, as far as they are relevant, to the enforcement of orders made in proceedings in the High Court and county courts with necessary modifications.

6–3550E   6. Interpretation.   (1)   In these Rules—

"the Act" means Part 1 of the Adoption and Children Act 2002;

"the 1989 Act" means the Children Act 1989;

"adoption proceedings" means proceedings for the making of an adoption order under the Act;

"application notice" means a document in which the applicant states his intention to seek a court order in accordance with the procedure in Part 9;

"business day" means any day other than—

(a)   a Saturday, Sunday, Christmas Day or Good Friday; or

(b)   a bank holiday under the Banking and Financial Dealings Act 1971, in England and Wales;

"Central Authority" means, in relation to England, the Secretary of State for Education and Skills, and in relation to Wales, the National Assembly for Wales;

"child"—

(a)   means, subject to paragraph (b), a person under the age of 18 years who is the subject of the proceedings; and

(b)   in adoption proceedings, also includes a person who has attained the age of 18 years before the proceedings are concluded;

"children and family reporter" means an officer of the Service or a Welsh family proceedings officer who prepares a report on matters relating to the welfare of the child;

"children's guardian" means an officer of the Service or a Welsh family proceedings officer appointed to act on behalf of a child who is a party to the proceedings with the duty of safeguarding the interests of the child;

"civil restraint order" means an order restraining a party—

(a)   from making any further applications in current proceedings (a limited civil restraint order);

(b)   from making certain applications in specified courts (an extended civil restraint order); or

(c)   from making any application in specified courts (a general civil restraint order);

"court officer" means, in the High Court and a county court, a member of court staff, and in a magistrates' court, the designated officer;

"CPR" means the Civil Procedure Rules 1998;

"detailed assessment proceedings" means the procedure by which the amount of costs is decided in accordance with Part 47 of the CPR;

"filing", in relation to a document, means delivering it, by post or otherwise, to the court office;

"jurisdiction" means, unless the context requires otherwise, England and Wales and any part of the territorial waters of the United Kingdom adjoining England and Wales;

"legal representative" means a barrister or a solicitor, solicitor's employee or other authorised litigator (as defined in section 119 of the Courts and Legal Services Act 1990) who has been instructed to act for a party in relation to an application;

"litigation friend" has the meaning given by section 1 of Part 7;

"non-subject child" means a person under the age of 18 years who is a party to the proceedings but is not the subject of the proceedings;

"officer of the Service" has the meaning given by section 11(3) of the Criminal Justice and Court Services Act 2000;

"patient" means a party to proceedings who, by reason of mental disorder within the meaning of the Mental Health Act 1983, is incapable of managing and administering his property and affairs;

"placement proceedings" means proceedings for the making, varying or revoking of a placement order under the Act;

"proceedings" means, unless the context otherwise requires, proceedings brought under the Act (whether at first instance or appeal) or proceedings for the purpose of enforcing an order made in any proceedings under that Act, as the case may be;

"provision for contact" means a contact order under section 8 or 34 of the 1989 Act or a contact order under section 26;

"reporting officer" means an officer of the Service or a Welsh family proceedings officer appointed to witness the documents which signify a parent or guardian's consent to the placing of the child for adoption or to the making of an adoption order or a section 84 order;

"section 84 order" means an order made by the High Court under section 84 giving parental responsibility prior to adoption abroad;

"section 88 direction" means a direction given by the High Court under section 88 that section 67(3) (status conferred by adoption) does not apply or does not apply to any extent specified in the direction;

"section 89 order" means an order made by the High Court under section 89—

(a) annulling a Convention adoption or Convention adoption order;

(b) providing for an overseas adoption or determination under section 91 to cease to be valid; or

(c) deciding the extent, if any, to which a determination under section 91 has been affected by a subsequent determination under that section;

"the Service Regulation" means Council Regulation (EC) No 1348/2000 of 29 May 2000 on the service in the Member States of judicial and extrajudicial documents in civil or commercial matters;

"Welsh family proceedings officer" has the meaning given by section 35(4) of the Children Act 2004.

(2) A section or Schedule referred to by number alone means the section or Schedule so numbered in the Adoption and Children Act 2002.

(3) Any provision in these Rules—

(a) requiring or permitting directions to be given by the court is to be taken as including provision for such directions to be varied or revoked; and

(b) requiring or permitting a date to be set is to be taken as including provision for that date to be set aside.

6–3550F   **7. Power to perform functions of the court.**   (1) Where these Rules or a practice direction provide for the court to perform any act then, except where any rule or practice direction, any other enactment, or the Family Proceedings (Allocation to Judiciary) Directions, provides otherwise, that act may be performed—

(a) in relation to proceedings in the High Court or in a district registry, by any judge or district judge of that Court including a district judge of the principal registry of the Family Division;

(b) in relation to proceedings in a county court, by any judge or district judge including a district judge of the principal registry of the Family Division when the principal registry of the Family Division is treated as if it were a county court; and

(c) in relation to proceedings in a magistrates' court—

(i) by any family proceedings court constituted in accordance with sections 66 and 67 of the Magistrates' Courts Act 1980; or

(ii) by a single justice of the peace who is a member of the family panel—

(aa) where an application without notice is made under section 41(2) (recovery orders); and

(bb) in accordance with the relevant practice direction.

(The Justices' Clerks Rules 2005 make provision for a justices' clerk or assistant clerk to carry out certain functions of a single justice of the peace.)

(2) A deputy High Court judge and a district judge, including a district judge of the principal registry of the Family Division, may not try a claim for a declaration of incompatibility in accordance with section 4 of the Human Rights Act 1998.

6–3550G   **8. Court's discretion as to where it deals with cases.**   The court may deal with a case at any place that it considers appropriate.

6–3550H   **9. Court documents.**   (1) A court officer must seal, or otherwise authenticate with the stamp of the court, the following documents on issue—

(a) the application form;

(b) the order; and

(c) any other document which a rule or practice direction requires it to seal or stamp.

(2) The court officer may place the seal or the stamp on the document—

(a) by hand; or

(b) by printing a facsimile of the seal on the document whether electronically or otherwise.

(3) A document purporting to bear the court's seal or stamp will be admissible in evidence without further proof.

(4) The relevant practice direction contains provisions about court documents.

6–3550I   10. Computation of time.   (1) This rule shows how to calculate any period of time for doing any act which is specified—

(a) by these Rules;

(b) by a practice direction; or

(c) by a direction or order of the court.

(2) A period of time expressed as a number of days must be computed as clear days.

(3) In this rule "clear days" means that in computing the numbers of days—

(a) the day on which the period begins; and

(b) if the end of the period is defined by reference to an event, the day on which that event occurs

are not included.

(4) Where the specified period is 7 days or less and would include a day which is not a business day, that day does not count.

(5) When the period specified—

(a) by these Rules or a practice direction; or

(b) by any direction or order of the court,

for doing any act at the court office ends on a day on which the office is closed, that act will be in time if done on the next day on which the court office is open.

6–3550J   11. Dates for compliance to be calendar dates and to include time of day.   (1) Where the court makes an order or gives a direction which imposes a time limit for doing any act, the last date for compliance must, wherever practicable—

(a) be expressed as a calendar date; and

(b) include the time of day by which the act must be done.

(2) Where the date by which an act must be done is inserted in any document, the date must, wherever practicable, be expressed as a calendar date.

(3) Where "month" occurs in any order, direction or other document, it means a calendar month.

PART 3
GENERAL CASE MANAGEMENT POWERS

6–3550K   12. The court's general powers of management.   (1) The list of powers in this rule is in addition to any powers given to the court by any other rule or practice direction or by any other enactment or any powers it may otherwise have.

(2) Except where these Rules provide otherwise, the court may—

(a) extend or shorten the time for compliance with any rule, practice direction or court direction (even if an application for extension is made after the time for compliance has expired);

(b) adjourn or bring forward a hearing;

(c) require a party or a party's legal representative to attend the court;

(d) hold a hearing and receive evidence by telephone or by using any other method of direct oral communication;

(e) direct that part of any proceedings be dealt with as separate proceedings;

(f) stay the whole or part of any proceedings or judgment either generally or until a specified date or event;

(g) consolidate proceedings;

(h) hear two or more applications on the same occasion;

(i) direct a separate hearing of any issue;

(j) decide the order in which issues are to be heard;

(k) exclude an issue from consideration;

(l) dismiss or give judgment on an application after a decision on a preliminary issue;

(m) direct any party to file and serve an estimate of costs; and

(n) take any other step or give any other direction for the purpose of managing the case and furthering the overriding objective.

(3) The court may not extend the period within which a section 89 order must be made.

(4) Paragraph (2)(f) does not apply to proceedings in a magistrates' court.

6–3550L   13. Exercise of powers of court's own initiative.   (1) Except where an enactment provides otherwise, the court may exercise the powers in rule 12 on an application or of its own initiative. (Part 9 sets out the procedure for making an application.)

(2) Where the court proposes to exercise its powers of its own initiative—

(a) it may give any person likely to be affected an opportunity to make representations; and

(b) where it does so it must specify the time by and the manner in which the representations must be made.

(3) Where the court proposes to hold a hearing to decide whether to exercise its powers of its own initiative it must give each party likely to be affected at least 3 days' notice of the hearing.

(4) The court may exercise its powers of its own initiative, without hearing the parties or giving them an opportunity to make representations.

(5) Where the court has exercised its powers under paragraph (4)—

(a) a party affected by the direction may apply to have it set aside or varied; and
(b) the direction must contain a statement of the right to make such an application.

(6) An application under paragraph (5)(a) must be made—

(a) within such period as may be specified by the court; or
(b) if the court does not specify a period, within 7 days beginning with the date on which the order was served on the party making the application.

(7) If the High Court or a county court of its own initiative dismisses an application (including an application for permission to appeal) and it considers that the application is totally without merit—

(a) the court's order must record that fact; and
(b) the court must at the same time consider whether it is appropriate to make a civil restraint order.

6–3550M 14. Court officer's power to refer to the court. Where these Rules require a step to be taken by a court officer—

(a) the court officer may consult the court before taking that step;
(b) the step may be taken by the court instead of the court officer.

6–3550N 15. General power of the court to rectify matters where there has been an error of procedure. Where there has been an error of procedure such as a failure to comply with a rule or practice direction—

(a) the error does not invalidate any step taken in the proceedings unless the court so orders; and
(b) the court may make an order to remedy the error.

6–3550O 16. Power of the court to make civil restraint orders

PART 4
HOW TO START PROCEEDINGS

6–3550P 17. Forms. Subject to rule 28(2) and (3), the forms set out in the relevant practice direction or forms to the like effect must be used in the cases to which they apply.

6–3550Q 18. Documents to be attached to the application form. The application form must have attached to it any documents referred to in the application form.

6–3550R 19. How to start proceedings. (1) Proceedings are started when a court officer issues an application at the request of the applicant.

(2) An application is issued on the date entered in the application form by the court officer.

(Restrictions on where proceedings may be started are set out in the Children (Allocation of Proceedings) Order 1991.)

6–3550S 20. Application for a serial number. (1) This rule applies to any application in proceedings by a person who intends to adopt the child.

(2) If the applicant wishes his identity to be kept confidential in the proceedings, he may, before those proceedings have started, request a court officer to assign a serial number to him to identify him in connection with the proceedings, and a number will be assigned to him.

(3) The court may at any time direct that a serial number identifying the applicant in the proceedings referred to in paragraph (2) must be removed.

(4) If a serial number has been assigned to a person under paragraph (2)—

(a) the court officer will ensure that any application form or application notice sent in accordance with these Rules does not contain information which discloses, or is likely to disclose, the identity of that person to any other party to that application who is not already aware of that person's identity; and
(b) the proceedings on the application will be conducted with a view to securing that the applicant is not seen by or made known to any party who is not already aware of his identity except with his consent.

6–3550T 21. Personal details. (1) Unless the court directs otherwise, a party is not required to reveal—

(a) the address or telephone number of their private residence;

(b) the address of the child;
(c) the name of a person with whom the child is living, if that person is not the applicant; or
(d) in relation to an application under section 28(2) (application for permission to change the child's surname), the proposed new surname of the child.

(2) Where a party does not wish to reveal any of the particulars in paragraph (1), he must give notice of those particulars to the court and the particulars will not be revealed to any person unless the court directs otherwise.

(3) Where a party changes his home address during the course of proceedings, he must give notice of the change to the court.

PART 5
PROCEDURE FOR APPLICATIONS IN ADOPTION, PLACEMENT AND RELATED PROCEEDINGS

6–3550U 22. Application of this Part. The rules in this Part apply to the following proceedings—

(a) adoption proceedings;
(b) placement proceedings; or
(c) proceedings for—

    (i) the making of a contact order under section 26;
    (ii) the variation or revocation of a contact order under section 27;
    (iii) an order giving permission to change a child's surname or remove a child from the United Kingdom under section 28(2) and (3);
    (iv) a section 84 order;
    (v) a section 88 direction;
    (vi) a section 89 order; or
    (vii) any other order that may be referred to in a practice direction.

(Parts 9 and 10 set out the procedure for making an application in proceedings not dealt with in this Part.)

6–3550V 23. Who the parties are. (1) In relation to the proceedings set out in column 1 of each of the following tables, column 2 of Table 1 sets out who the application may be made by and column 2 of Table 2 sets out who the respondents to those proceedings will be.

TABLE 1

Proceedings for	Applicants
An adoption order (section 46)	The prospective adopters (section 50 and 51).
A section 84 order	The prospective adopters asking for parental responsibility prior to adoption abroad.
A placement order (section 21)	A local authority (section 22).
An order varying a placement order (section 23)	The joint application of the local authority authorised by the placement order to place the child for adoption and the local authority which is to be substituted for that authority (section 23).
An order revoking a placement order (section 24)	The child; the local authority authorised to place the child for adoption; or where the child is not placed for adoption by the authority, any other person who has the permission of the court to apply (section 24).
A contact order (section 26)	The child; the adoption agency; any parent, guardian or relative; any person in whose favour there was provision for contact under the 1989 Act which ceased to have effect on an adoption agency being authorised to place a child for adoption, or placing a child for adoption who is less than six weeks old (section 26(1)); a person in whose favour there was a residence order in force immediately before the adoption agency was authorised to place the child for adoption or placed the child for adoption at a time when he was less than six weeks old; a person who by virtue of an order made in the exercise of the High Court's inherent jurisdiction with respect to children had care of the child immediately before that time; or any person who has the permission of the court to make the application (section 26).
An order varying or revoking a contact order (section 27)	The child; the adoption agency; or any person named in the contact order (section 27(1)).

4655 Family Procedure (Adoption) Rules 2005 6–3550V

Proceedings for	Applicants
An order permitting the child's name to be changed or the removal of the child from the United Kingdom (section 28(2) and (3))	Any person including the adoption agency or the local authority authorised to place, or which has placed, the child for adoption (section 28(2)).
A section 88 direction	The adopted child; the adopters; any parent; or any other person.
A section 89 order	The adopters; the adopted person; any parent; the relevant Central Authority; the adoption agency; the local authority to whom notice under section 44 (notice of intention to adopt or apply for a section 84 order) has been given; the Secretary of State for the Home Department; or any other person.

TABLE 2

Proceedings for	Respondents
An adoption order (section 46) or a section 84 order	Each parent who has parental responsibility for the child or guardian of the child unless he has given notice under section 20(4)(a) (statement of wish not to be informed of any application for an adoption order) which has effect; any person in whose favour there is provision for contact; any adoption agency having parental responsibility for the child under section 25; any adoption agency which has taken part at any stage in the arrangements for adoption of the child; any local authority to whom notice under section 44 (notice of intention to adopt or apply for a section 84 order) has been given; any local authority or voluntary organisation which has parental responsibility for, is looking after, or is caring for, the child; and the child where— permission has been granted to a parent or guardian to oppose the making of the adoption order (section 47(3) or 47(5)); he opposes the making of an adoption order; a children and family reporter recommends that it is in the best interests of the child to be a party to the proceedings and that recommendation is accepted by the court; he is already an adopted child; any party to the proceedings or the child is opposed to the arrangements for allowing any person contact with the child, or a person not being allowed contact with the child after the making of the adoption order; the application is for a Convention adoption order or a section 84 order; he has been brought into the United Kingdom in the circumstances where section 83(1) applies (restriction on bringing children in); the application is for an adoption order other than a Convention adoption order and the prospective adopters intend the child to live in a country or territory outside the British Islands after the making of the adoption order; or —the prospective adopters are relatives of the child.
A placement order (section 21)	Each parent who has parental responsibility for the child or guardian of the child; any person in whose favour an order under the 1989 Act is in force in relation to the child;

Proceedings for	Applicants
	any adoption agency or voluntary organisation which has parental responsibility for, is looking after, or is caring for, the child; the child; and the parties or any persons who are or have been parties to proceedings for a care order in respect of the child where those proceedings have led to the application for the placement order.
An order varying a placement order (section 23)	The parties to the proceedings leading to the placement order which it is sought to have varied except the child who was the subject of those proceedings; and any person in whose favour there is provision for contact.
An order revoking a placement order (section 24)	The parties to the proceedings leading to the placement order which it is sought to have revoked; and any person in whose favour there is provision for contact.
A contact order (section 26)	The adoption agency authorised to place the child for adoption or which has placed the child for adoption; the person with whom the child lives or is to live; each parent with parental responsibility for the child or guardian of the child; and the child where— the adoption agency authorised to place the child for adoption or which has placed the child for adoption or a parent with parental responsibility for the child opposes the making of the contact order under section 26; he opposes the making of the contact order under section 26; existing provision for contact is to be revoked; relatives of the child do not agree to the arrangements for allowing any person contact with the child, or a person not being allowed contact with the child; or he is suffering or is at risk of suffering harm within the meaning of the 1989 Act.
An order varying or revoking a contact order (section 27)	The parties to the proceedings leading to the contact order which it is sought to have varied or revoked; and any person named in the contact order.
An order permitting the child's name to be changed or the removal of the child from the United Kingdom (section 28(2) and (3))	The parties to proceedings leading to any placement order; the adoption agency authorised to place the child for adoption or which has placed the child for adoption; any prospective adopters with whom the child is living; and each parent with parental responsibility for the child or guardian of the child.
A section 88 direction	The adopters; the parents; the adoption agency; the local authority to whom notice under section 44 (notice of intention to apply for a section 84 order) has been given; and the Attorney-General.
A section 89 order	The adopters; the parents; the adoption agency; and the local authority to whom notice under section 44 (notice of intention to adopt or apply for a section 84 order) has been given.

(2) The court may at any time direct that a child, who is not already a respondent to proceedings, be made a respondent to proceedings where—

(a) the child—

(i) wishes to make an application; or

(ii) has evidence to give to the court or a legal submission to make which has not been given or made by any other party; or

(b) there are other special circumstances.

(3) The court may at any time direct that—

(a) any other person or body be made a respondent to proceedings; or

(b) a respondent be removed.

(4) If the court makes a direction for the addition or removal of a party, it may give consequential directions about—

(a) serving a copy of the application form on any new respondent;

(b) serving relevant documents on the new party; and
(c) the management of the proceedings.

6–3550W   24. What the court or a court officer will do when the application has been issued.
(1) As soon as practicable after the application has been issued in proceedings—

(a) the court will—

   (i) if section 48(1) (restrictions on making adoption orders) applies, consider whether it is proper to hear the application;
   (ii) subject to paragraph (4), set a date for the first directions hearing;
   (iii) appoint a children's guardian in accordance with rule 59;
   (iv) appoint a reporting officer in accordance with rule 69;
   (v) consider whether a report relating to the welfare of the child is required, and if so, request such a report in accordance with rule 73;
   (vi) set a date for the hearing of the application; and
   (vii) do anything else that may be set out in a practice direction; and

(b) a court officer will—

   (i) subject to receiving confirmation in accordance with paragraph (2)(b)(ii), give notice of any directions hearing set by the court to the parties and to any children's guardian, reporting officer or children and family reporter;
   (ii) serve a copy of the application form (but, subject to sub-paragraphs (iii) and (iv), not the documents attached to it) on the persons referred to in the relevant practice direction;
   (iii) send a copy of the certified copy of the entry in the register of live-births or Adopted Children Register and any health report attached to an application for an adoption order to—

      (aa) any children's guardian, reporting officer or children and family reporter; and
      (bb) the local authority to whom notice under section 44 (notice of intention to adopt or apply for a section 84 order) has been given;

   (iv) if notice under rule 27 has been given (request to dispense with consent of parent or guardian), in accordance with that rule inform the parent or guardian of the request and send a copy of the statement of facts to—

      (aa) the parent or guardian;
      (bb) any children's guardian, reporting officer or children and family reporter;
      (cc) any local authority to whom notice under section 44 (notice of intention to adopt or apply for a section 84 order) has been given; and
      (dd) any adoption agency which has placed the child for adoption; and

   (v) do anything else that may be set out in a practice direction.

(2) In addition to the matters referred to in paragraph (1), as soon as practicable after an application for an adoption order or a section 84 order has been issued the court or the court officer will—

(a) where the child is not placed for adoption by an adoption agency—

   (i) ask either the Service or the Assembly to file any relevant form of consent to an adoption order or a section 84 order; and
   (ii) ask the local authority to prepare a report on the suitability of the prospective adopters if one has not already been prepared; and

(b) where the child is placed for adoption by an adoption agency, ask the adoption agency to—

   (i) file any relevant form of consent to—

      (aa) the child being placed for adoption;
      (bb) an adoption order;
      (cc) a future adoption order under section 20; or
      (dd) a section 84 order;

   (ii) confirm whether a statement has been made under section 20(4)(a) (statement of wish not to be informed of any application for an adoption order) and if so, to file that statement;
   (iii) file any statement made under section 20(4)(b) (withdrawal of wish not to be informed of any application for an adoption order) as soon as it is received by the adoption agency; and
   (iv) prepare a report on the suitability of the prospective adopters if one has not already been prepared.

(3) In addition to the matters referred to in paragraph (1), as soon as practicable after an application for a placement order has been issued—

(a) the court will consider whether a report giving the local authority's reasons for placing the child for adoption is required, and if so, will direct the local authority to prepare such a report; and

(b) the court or the court officer will ask either the Service or the Assembly to file any form of consent to the child being placed for adoption.

(4) Where it considers it appropriate the court may, instead of setting a date for a first directions hearing, give the directions provided for by rule 26.

6–3550X 25. Date for first directions hearing. Unless the court directs otherwise, the first directions hearing must be within 4 weeks beginning with the date on which the application is issued.

6–3550Y 26. The first directions hearing. (1) At the first directions hearing in the proceedings the court will—

(a) fix a timetable for the filing of—

(i) any report relating to the suitability of the applicants to adopt a child;
(ii) any report from the local authority;
(iii) any report from a children's guardian, reporting officer or children and family reporter;
(iv) if a statement of facts has been filed, any amended statement of facts;
(v) any other evidence, and

give directions relating to the reports and other evidence;

(b) consider whether an alternative dispute resolution procedure is appropriate and, if so, give directions relating to the use of such procedure;
(c) consider whether the child or any other person should be a party to the proceedings and, if so, give directions in accordance with rule 23(2) or (3) joining that child or person as a party;
(d) give directions relating to the appointment of a litigation friend for any patient or non-subject child unless a litigation friend has already been appointed;
(e) consider whether the case needs to be transferred to another court and, if so, give directions to transfer the proceedings to another court in accordance with any order made by the Lord Chancellor under Part I of Schedule 11 to the 1989 Act;
(f) give directions about—

(i) tracing parents or any other person the court considers to be relevant to the proceedings;
(ii) service of documents;
(iii) subject to paragraph (2), disclosure as soon as possible of information and evidence to the parties; and
(iv) the final hearing; and

(2) Rule 77(2) applies to any direction given under paragraph (1)(f)(iii) as it applies to a direction given under rule 77(1).

(3) In addition to the matters referred to in paragraph (1), the court will give any of the directions listed in the relevant practice direction in proceedings for—

(a) a Convention adoption order;
(b) a section 84 order;
(c) a section 88 direction;
(d) a section 89 order; or
(e) an adoption order where section 83(1) applies (restriction on bringing children in).

(4) The parties or their legal representatives must attend the first directions hearing unless the court directs otherwise.

(5) Directions may also be given at any stage in the proceedings—

(a) of the court's own initiative; or
(b) on the application of a party or any children's guardian or, where the direction concerns a report by a reporting officer or children and family reporter, the reporting officer or children and family reporter.

(6) For the purposes of giving directions or for such purposes as the court directs—

(a) the court may set a date for a further directions hearing or other hearing; and
(b) the court officer will give notice of any date so fixed to the parties and to any children's guardian, reporting officer or children and family reporter.

(7) After the first directions hearing the court will monitor compliance with the court's timetable and directions by the parties.

6–3550Z 27. Requesting the court to dispense with the consent of any parent or guardian.
(1) The following paragraphs apply where the applicant wants to ask the court to dispense with the consent of any parent or guardian of a child to—

(a) the child being placed for adoption;
(b) the making of an adoption order except a Convention adoption order; or
(c) the making of a section 84 order.

(2) The applicant requesting the court to dispense with the consent must—

(a) give notice of the request in the application form or at any later stage by filing a written request setting out the reasons for the request; and

(b) file a statement of facts setting out a summary of the history of the case and any other facts to satisfy the court that—

(i) the parent or guardian cannot be found or is incapable of giving consent; or

(ii) the welfare of the child requires the consent to be dispensed with.

(3) If a serial number has been assigned to the applicant under rule 20, the statement of facts supplied under paragraph (2)(b) must be framed so that it does not disclose the identity of the applicant.

(4) On receipt of the notice of the request—

(a) a court officer will—

(i) inform the parent or guardian of the request; and

(ii) send a copy of the statement of facts filed in accordance with paragraph (2)(b) to—

(aa) the parent or guardian;

(bb) any children's guardian, reporting officer or children and family reporter;

(cc) any local authority to whom notice under section 44 (notice of intention to adopt or apply for a section 84 order) has been given; and

(dd) any adoption agency which has placed the child for adoption; and

(b) if the applicant considers that the parent or guardian is incapable of giving consent, the court will consider whether to—

(i) appoint a litigation friend for the parent or guardian under rule 55(1); or

(ii) give directions for an application to be made under rule 55(3),

unless a litigation friend is already appointed for that parent or guardian.

6–3551 28. Consent.   (1) Consent of any parent or guardian of a child—

(a) under section 19, to the child being placed for adoption; and

(b) under section 20, to the making of a future adoption order

must be given in the form required by the relevant practice direction or a form to the like effect.

(2) Subject to paragraph (3), consent—

(a) to the making of an adoption order; or

(b) to the making of a section 84 order,

may be given in the form required by the relevant practice direction or a form to the like effect.

(3) Any consent to a Convention adoption order must be in a form which complies with the internal law relating to adoption of the Convention country of which the child is habitually resident.

(4) Any form of consent executed in Scotland must be witnessed by a Justice of the Peace or a Sheriff.

(5) Any form of consent executed in Northern Ireland must be witnessed by a Justice of the Peace.

(6) Any form of consent executed outside the United Kingdom must be witnessed by—

(a) any person for the time being authorised by law in the place where the document is executed to administer an oath for any judicial or other legal purpose;

(b) a British Consular officer;

(c) a notary public; or

(d) if the person executing the document is serving in any of the regular armed forces of the Crown, an officer holding a commission in any of those forces.

6–3551A 29. Reports by the adoption agency or local authority.   (1) The adoption agency or local authority must file the report on the suitability of the applicant to adopt a child within the timetable fixed by the court.

(2) A local authority that is directed to prepare a report on the placement of the child for adoption must file that report within the timetable fixed by the court.

(3) The reports must cover the matters specified in the relevant practice direction.

(4) The court may at any stage request a further report or ask the adoption agency or local authority to assist the court in any other manner.

(5) A court officer will send a copy of any report referred to in this rule to any children's guardian, reporting officer or children and family reporter.

(6) Any report to the court under this rule will be confidential.

6–3551B 30. Health reports.   (1) Reports by a registered medical practitioner ("health reports") made not more than three months earlier on the health of the child and of each applicant must be attached to an application for an adoption order or a section 84 order except where—

(a) the child was placed for adoption with the applicant by an adoption agency;

(b) the applicant or one of the applicants is a parent of the child; or

(c) the applicant is the partner of a parent of the child.

(2) Health reports must contain the matters set out in the relevant practice direction.

(3) Any health report will be confidential.

6–3551C   31. Notice of final hearing.   A court officer will give notice to the parties, any children's guardian, reporting officer or children and family reporter and to any other person that may be referred to in a practice direction—

    (a)   of the date and place where the application will be heard; and

    (b)   of the fact that, unless the person wishes or the court requires, the person need not attend.

6–3551D   32. The final hearing.   (1) Any person who has been given notice in accordance with rule 31 may attend the final hearing and, subject to paragraph (2), be heard on the question of whether an order should be made.

(2) A person whose application for the permission of the court to oppose the making of an adoption order under section 47(3) or (5) has been refused is not entitled to be heard on the question of whether an order should be made.

(3) Any member or employee of a party which is a local authority, adoption agency or other body may address the court at the final hearing if he is authorised to do so.

(4) The court may direct that any person must attend a final hearing.

(5) Paragraphs (6) and (7) apply to—

    (a)   an adoption order;

    (b)   a section 84 order; or

    (c)   a section 89 order.

(6) Subject to paragraphs (7) and (8), the court cannot make an order unless the applicant and the child personally attend the final hearing.

(7) The court may direct that the applicant or the child need not attend the final hearing.

(8) In a case of adoption by a couple under section 50 the court may make an adoption order after personal attendance of one only of the applicants if there are special circumstances.

(9) The court cannot make a placement order unless a legal representative of the applicant attends the final hearing.

6–3551E   33. Proof of identity of the child.   (1) Unless the contrary is shown, the child referred to in the application will be deemed to be the child referred to in the form of consent—

    (a)   to the child being placed for adoption;

    (b)   to the making of an adoption order; or

    (c)   to the making of a section 84 order

where the conditions in paragraph (2) apply.

(2) The conditions are—

    (a)   the application identifies the child by reference to a full certified copy of an entry in the registers of live-births;

    (b)   the form of consent identifies the child by reference to a full certified copy of an entry in the registers of live-births attached to the form; and

    (c)   the copy of the entry in the registers of live-births referred to in sub-paragraph (a) is the same or relates to the same entry in the registers of live-births as the copy of the entry in the registers of live-births attached to the form of consent.

(3) Where the child is already an adopted child paragraph (2) will have effect as if for the references to the registers of live-births there were substituted references to the Adopted Children Register.

(4) Subject to paragraph (7), where the precise date of the child's birth is not proved to the satisfaction of the court, the court will determine the probable date of birth.

(5) The probable date of the child's birth may be specified in the placement order, adoption order or section 84 order as the date of his birth.

(6) Subject to paragraph (7), where the child's place of birth cannot be proved to the satisfaction of the court—

    (a)   he may be treated as having been born in the registration district of the court where it is probable that the child may have been born in—

       (i)   the United Kingdom;

       (ii)   the Channel Islands; or

       (iii)   the Isle of Man; or

    (b)   in any other case, the particulars of the country of birth may be omitted from the placement order, adoption order or section 84 order.

(7) A placement order identifying the probable date and place of birth of the child will be sufficient proof of the date and place of birth of the child in adoption proceedings and proceedings for a section 84 order.

PART 6
SERVICE

SECTION 1
GENERAL RULES ABOUT SERVICE

6–3551F   34. Scope of this Part.   The rules in this Part apply to the service of documents, including a document that is required to be given or sent by these Rules or any practice direction, except where—

    (a)   any other enactment, a rule in another Part or a practice direction makes a different provision; or

    (b)   the court directs otherwise.

6–3551G   35. Methods of service.   (1) Subject to paragraph (2), a document may be served—

    (a)   where it is not known whether a solicitor is acting on behalf of a party—

        (i)   by delivering it to the party personally; or

        (ii)   by delivering it at, or by sending it by first class post to, the party's residence or last known residence; or

    (b)   where a solicitor is known to be acting on behalf of a party—

        (i)   by delivering the document at, or sending it by first class post to, the solicitor's address for service; or

        (ii)   through a document exchange in accordance with the relevant practice direction.

    (2) A notice of hearing must be served in accordance with paragraph (1)(a)(i) or (ii) irrespective of whether a solicitor is acting on behalf of a party.

    (3) Where it appears to the court that there is a good reason to authorise service by a method not permitted by paragraph (1), the court may direct that service is effected by an alternative method.

    (4) A direction that service is effected by an alternative method must specify—

    (a)   the method of service; and

    (b)   the date when the document will be deemed to be served.

6–3551H   36. Who is to serve.   (1) A document which has been issued or prepared by a court officer will be served by the court officer except where—

    (a)   a practice direction provides otherwise; or

    (b)   the court directs otherwise.

    (2) Where a court officer is to serve a document, it is for the court to decide which of the methods of service specified in rule 35(1) is to be used.

6–3551I   37. Service of documents on children and patients.   (1) The following table shows the person on whom a document must be served if it is a document which would otherwise be served on a child, non-subject child or patient—

Nature of party	Type of document	Person to be served
Child who is not also a patient	Any document	The solicitor acting for the child;
		where there is no such solicitor, the children's guardian or the children and family reporter.
Non-subject child who is not also a patient	Application form	One of the non-subject child's parents or guardians; if there is no parent or guardian, the person with whom the non-subject child resides or in whose care the non-subject child is.
Patient	Application form	The person authorised under Part VII of the Mental Health Act 1983 to conduct the proceedings in the name of the patient or on his behalf; if there is no person so authorised, the person with whom the patient resides or in whose care the patient is.

Nature of party	Type of document	Person to be served
Non-subject child or patient	Application for an order appointing a litigation friend, where the non-subject child or patient has no litigation friend	See rule 57.
	Any other document	The litigation friend who is conducting proceedings on behalf of the non-subject child or patient.

(2) Where a child is directed by the court to serve a document, service is to be effected by—

(a)   the solicitor acting for the child;
(b)   where there is no such solicitor, the children's guardian;
(c)   where there is neither a solicitor or children's guardian, the litigation friend; or
(d)   where there is neither a solicitor, children's guardian, or litigation friend, a court officer.

(3) Where a non-subject child or patient is directed by the court to serve a document, service is to be effected by—

(a)   the solicitor acting for the non-subject child or patient; or
(b)   where there is no such solicitor, the litigation friend.

(4) The court may give directions permitting a document to be served on the child, non-subject child or patient, or on some other person other than the person specified in the table in this rule.
(5) The court may direct that, although a document has been served on someone other than the person specified in the table, the document is to be treated as if it had been properly served.
(6) This rule does not apply where a non-subject child is conducting proceedings without a litigation friend in accordance with rule 51.

6–3551J 38. Deemed service.   (1) Unless the contrary is proved, a document which is served in accordance with these Rules or any relevant practice direction will be deemed to be served on the day shown in the following table—

Method of service	Deemed day of service
First class post	The second day after it was posted.
Document exchange	The second day after it was left at the document exchange.
Delivering the document to address	The day after the document was delivered to that address.

(2) If a document is served personally—

(a)   after 5 pm on a business day; or
(b)   at any time on a day which is not a business day

it will be treated as being served on the next business day.

6–3551K 39. Power of court to dispense with service.   Where a rule or practice direction requires a document to be served, the court may direct that the requirement is dispensed with.

6–3551L 40. Certificate of service.   (1) Where a rule, practice direction or court order requires a certificate of service, the certificate must state the details set out in the following table—

Method of service	Details to be certified
Post	Date of posting.
Personal	Date of personal service.
Document exchange	Date of delivery to the document exchange.
Delivery of document to address	Date when the document was delivered to the address.
Alternative method permitted by the court	As required by the court.

(2) Where an application form is to be served by the applicant he must file a certificate of service within 7 days beginning with the date on which the application form was served.

6–3551M 41. Notice of non-service.   Where a person fails to serve any document under these Rules or as directed by the court he must file a certificate of non-service stating the reason why service has not been effected.

SECTION 2
SERVICE OUT OF THE JURISDICTION

PART 7
LITIGATION FRIEND, CHILDREN'S GUARDIAN, REPORTING OFFICER AND CHILDREN AND FAMILY REPORTER

SECTION 1
LITIGATION FRIEND

6–3551N   49. Application of this Section.   (1) This Section—

    (a)   contains special provisions which apply in proceedings involving non-subject children and patients; and

    (b)   sets out how a person becomes a litigation friend.

  (2) The provisions of this Section also apply to a child who does not have a children's guardian, in which case, any reference to a "non-subject child" in these Rules is to be taken as including a child.

6–3551O   50. Requirement for litigation friend in proceedings.   (1) Subject to rule 51, a non-subject child must have a litigation friend to conduct proceedings on his behalf.

  (2) A patient must have a litigation friend to conduct proceedings on his behalf.

6–3551P   51. Circumstances in which the non-subject child does not need a litigation friend.   (1) A non-subject child may conduct proceedings without a litigation friend—

    (a)   where he has obtained the court's permission to do so; or

    (b)   where a solicitor—

        (i)   considers that the non-subject child is able, having regard to his understanding, to give instructions in relation to the proceedings; and

        (ii)   has accepted instructions from that child to act for him in the proceedings and, if the proceedings have begun, he is already acting.

  (2) An application for permission under paragraph (1)(a) may be made by the non-subject child without notice.

  (3) Where a non-subject child has a litigation friend in proceedings and he wishes to conduct the remaining stages of the proceedings without a litigation friend, the non-subject child may apply to the court, on notice to the litigation friend, for permission for that purpose and for the removal of the litigation friend.

  (4) Where the court is considering whether to—

    (a)   grant permission under paragraph (1)(a); or

    (b)   grant permission under paragraph (3) and remove a litigation friend

it will grant the permission sought and, as the case may be, remove the litigation friend if it considers that the non-subject child concerned has sufficient understanding to conduct the proceedings concerned or proposed without a litigation friend.

  (5) In exercising its powers under paragraph (4) the court may require the litigation friend to take such part in the proceedings as the court directs.

  (6) The court may revoke any permission granted under paragraph (1)(a) where it considers that the non-subject child does not have sufficient understanding to participate as a party in the proceedings concerned without a litigation friend.

  (7) Where a solicitor is acting for a non-subject child in proceedings without a litigation friend by virtue of paragraph (1)(b) and either of the conditions specified in paragraph (1)(b)(i) or (ii) cease to be fulfilled, he must inform the court immediately.

  (8) Where—

    (a)   the court revokes any permission under paragraph (6); or

    (b)   either of the conditions specified in paragraph (1)(b)(i) or (ii) is no longer fulfilled

the court may, if it considers it necessary in order to protect the interests of the non-subject child concerned, appoint a person to be that child's litigation friend.

6–3551Q   52. Stage of proceedings at which a litigation friend becomes necessary.   (1) This rule does not apply where a non-subject child is conducting proceedings without a litigation friend in accordance with rule 51.

  (2) A person may not without the permission of the court take any step in proceedings except—

    (a)   filing an application form; or

    (b)   applying for the appointment of a litigation friend under rule 55

until the non-subject child or patient has a litigation friend.

  (3) If a party becomes a patient during proceedings, no party may take any step in proceedings without the permission of the court until the patient has a litigation friend.

6–3551R   53. Who may be a litigation friend for a patient without a court order.   (1) This rule does not apply if the court has appointed a person to be a litigation friend.

  (2) A person authorised under Part VII of the Mental Health Act 1983 to conduct legal

proceedings in the name of a patient or on his behalf is entitled to be the litigation friend of the patient in any proceedings to which his authority extends.

(3) If nobody has been appointed by the court or, in the case of a patient, authorised under Part VII of the Mental Health Act 1983, a person may act as a litigation friend if he—

- (a) can fairly and competently conduct proceedings on behalf of the non-subject child or patient;
- (b) has no interest adverse to that of the non-subject child or patient; and
- (c) subject to paragraph (4), undertakes to pay any costs which the non-subject child or patient may be ordered to pay in relation to the proceedings, subject to any right he may have to be repaid from the assets of the non-subject child or patient.

(4) Paragraph (3)(c) does not apply to the Official Solicitor, an officer of the Service or a Welsh family proceedings officer.

6–3551S   54. How a person becomes a litigation friend without a court order.   (1) If the court has not appointed a litigation friend, a person who wishes to act as a litigation friend must follow the procedure set out in this rule.

(2) A person authorised under Part VII of the Mental Health Act 1983 must file an official copy of the order or other document which constitutes his authorisation to act.

(3) Any other person must file a certificate of suitability stating that he satisfies the conditions specified in rule 53(3).

(4) A person who is to act as a litigation friend must file—

- (a) the authorisation; or
- (b) the certificate of suitability

at the time when he first takes a step in the proceedings on behalf of the non-subject child or patient.

(5) A court officer will send the certificate of suitability to every person on whom, in accordance with rule 37(1) (service on parent, guardian etc), the application form should be served.

(6) This rule does not apply to the Official Solicitor, an officer of the Service or a Welsh family proceedings officer.

6–3551T   55. How a person becomes a litigation friend by court order.   (1) The court may make an order appointing—

- (a) the Official Solicitor;
- (b) in the case of a non-subject child, an officer of the Service or a Welsh family proceedings officer (if he consents); or
- (c) some other person (if he consents)

as a litigation friend.

(2) An order appointing a litigation friend may be made by the court of its own initiative or on the application of—

- (a) a person who wishes to be a litigation friend; or
- (b) a party to the proceedings.

(3) The court may at any time direct that a party make an application for an order under paragraph (2).

(4) An application for an order appointing a litigation friend must be supported by evidence.

(5) Unless the court directs otherwise, a person appointed under this rule to be a litigation friend for a non-subject child or patient will be treated as a party for the purpose of any provision in these Rules requiring a document to be served on, or sent to, or notice to be given to, a party to the proceedings.

(6) Subject to rule 53(4), the court may not appoint a litigation friend under this rule unless it is satisfied that the person to be appointed complies with the conditions specified in rule 53(3).

6–3551U   56. Court's power to change litigation friend and to prevent person acting as litigation friend.   (1) The court may—

- (a) direct that a person may not act as a litigation friend;
- (b) terminate a litigation friend's appointment; or
- (c) appoint a new litigation friend in substitution for an existing one.

(2) An application for an order under paragraph (1) must be supported by evidence.

(3) Subject to rule 53(4), the court may not appoint a litigation friend under this rule unless it is satisfied that the person to be appointed complies with the conditions specified in rule 53(3).

6–3551V   57. Appointment of litigation friend by court order—supplementary.   (1) A copy of the application for an order under rule 55 or 56 must be sent by a court officer to every person on whom, in accordance with rule 37(1) (service on parent, guardian etc), the application form should be served.

(2) Where an application for an order under rule 55 is in respect of a patient, the court officer must also send a copy of the application to the patient unless the court directs otherwise.

(3) A copy of an application for an order under rule 56 must also be sent to—

(a) the person who is the litigation friend, or who is purporting to act as the litigation friend, when the application is made; and

(b) the person who it is proposed should be the litigation friend, if he is not the applicant.

6–3551W 58. Procedure where appointment of litigation friend comes to an end. (1) When a non-subject child who is not a patient reaches the age of 18, a litigation friend's appointment comes to an end.

(2) When a party ceases to be a patient, the litigation friend's appointment continues until it is brought to an end by a court order.

(3) An application for an order under paragraph (2) may be made by—

(a) the former patient;

(b) the litigation friend; or

(c) a party.

(4) A court officer will send a notice to the other parties stating that the appointment of the non-subject child or patient's litigation friend to act has ended.

SECTION 2
CHILDREN'S GUARDIAN

6–3551X 59. Appointment of children's guardian. (1) In proceedings to which Part 5 applies, the court will appoint a children's guardian where the child is a party to the proceedings unless it is satisfied that it is not necessary to do so to safeguard the interests of the child.

(2) At any stage in proceedings where the child is a party to the proceedings—

(a) a party may apply, without notice to the other parties unless the court directs otherwise, for the appointment of a children's guardian; or

(b) the court may of its own initiative appoint a children's guardian.

(3) The court will grant an application under paragraph (2)(a) unless it considers that such an appointment is not necessary to safeguard the interests of the child.

(4) When appointing a children's guardian the court will consider the appointment of anyone who has previously acted as a children's guardian of the same child.

6–3551Y 60. What the court or a court officer will do once the court has made a decision about appointing a children's guardian. (1) Where the court refuses an application under rule 59(2)(a) it will give reasons for the refusal and the court or a court officer will—

(a) record the refusal and the reasons for it; and

(b) as soon as practicable, notify the parties and either the Service or the Assembly of a decision not to appoint a children's guardian.

(2) Where the court appoints a children's guardian under rule 59 a court officer will record the appointment and, as soon as practicable, will—

(a) inform the parties and either the Service or the Assembly; and

(b) unless it has already been sent, send the children's guardian a copy of the application and copies of any document filed with the court in the proceedings.

(3) A court officer also has a continuing duty to send the children's guardian a copy of any other document filed with the court during the course of the proceedings.

6–3551Z 61. Termination of the appointment of the children's guardian. (1) The appointment of a children's guardian under rule 59 continues for such time as is specified in the appointment or until terminated by the court.

(2) When terminating an appointment in accordance with paragraph (1), the court will give reasons for doing so, a note of which will be taken by the court or a court officer.

6–3552 62. Powers and duties of the children's guardian. (1) The children's guardian is to act on behalf of the child upon the hearing of any application in proceedings to which Part 5 applies with the duty of safeguarding the interests of the child.

(2) The children's guardian must also provide the court with such other assistance as it may require.

6–3552A 63. How the children's guardian exercises his duties—investigations and appointment of solicitor. (1) The children's guardian must make such investigations as are necessary for him to carry out his duties and must, in particular—

(a) contact or seek to interview such persons as he thinks appropriate or as the court directs; and

(b) obtain such professional assistance as is available to him which he thinks appropriate or which the court directs him to obtain.

(2) The children's guardian must—

(a) appoint a solicitor for the child unless a solicitor has already been appointed;

(b) give such advice to the child as is appropriate having regard to his understanding; and

(c) where appropriate instruct the solicitor representing the child on all matters relevant to the interests of the child, including possibilities for appeal, arising in the course of proceedings.

(3) Where the children's guardian is authorised in the terms mentioned by and in accordance with section 15(1) of the Criminal Justice and Court Services Act 2000 or section 37(1) of the Children Act 2004 (right of officer of the Service or Welsh family proceedings officer to conduct litigation or exercise a right of audience), paragraph (2)(a) will not apply if he intends to have conduct of the proceedings on behalf of the child unless—

(a) the child wishes to instruct a solicitor direct; and
(b) the children's guardian or the court considers that he is of sufficient understanding to do so.

6–3552B   64. Where the child instructs a solicitor or conducts proceedings on his own behalf.
(1) Where it appears to the children's guardian that the child—

(a) is instructing his solicitor direct; or
(b) intends to conduct and is capable of conducting the proceedings on his own behalf

he must inform the court of that fact.
(2) Where paragraph (1) applies, the children's guardian—

(a) must perform the duties set out in rules 62, 63, 65 to 67 and this rule, other than those duties in rule 63(2)(a) and (c), and such other duties as the court may direct;
(b) must take such part in the proceedings as the court may direct; and
(c) may, with the permission of the court, have legal representation in the conduct of those duties.

6–3552C   65. How the children's guardian exercises his duties—attendance at court, advice to the court and reports.   (1) The children's guardian or the solicitor appointed under section 41(3) of the 1989 Act or in accordance with rule 63(2)(a) must attend all directions hearings unless the court directs otherwise.
(2) The children's guardian must advise the court on the following matters—

(a) whether the child is of sufficient understanding for any purpose including the child's refusal to submit to a medical or psychiatric examination or other assessment that the court has the power to require, direct or order;
(b) the wishes of the child in respect of any matter relevant to the proceedings including his attendance at court;
(c) the appropriate forum for the proceedings;
(d) the appropriate timing of the proceedings or any part of them;
(e) the options available to it in respect of the child and the suitability of each such option including what order should be made in determining the application; and
(f) any other matter on which the court seeks his advice or on which he considers that the court should be informed.

(3) The advice given under paragraph (2) may, subject to any direction of the court, be given orally or in writing.
(4) The children's guardian must—

(a) unless the court directs otherwise, file a written report advising on the interests of the child in accordance with the timetable set by the court; and
(b) where practicable, notify any person the joining of whom as a party to those proceedings would be likely, in his opinion, to safeguard the interests of the child, of the court's power to join that person as a party under rule 23 and must inform the court—

(i) of any notification;
(ii) of anyone whom he attempted to notify under this paragraph but was unable to contact; and
(iii) of anyone whom he believes may wish to be joined to the proceedings.

(5) Any report to the court under this rule will be confidential.
(Part 9 sets out the procedure for making an application to be joined as a party in proceedings.)

6–3552D   66. How the children's guardian exercises his duties—service of documents and inspection of records.   (1) The children's guardian must—

(a) serve documents on behalf of the child in accordance with rule 37(2)(b); and
(b) accept service of documents on behalf of the child in accordance with the table in rule 37(1),

and, where the child has not himself been served and has sufficient understanding, advise the child of the contents of any document so served.
(2) Where the children's guardian inspects records of the kinds referred to in—

(a) section 42 of the 1989 Act (right to have access to local authority records); or
(b) section 103 (right to have access to adoption agency records)

he must bring all records and documents which may, in his opinion, assist in the proper determination of the proceedings to the attention of—

(i) the court; and

(ii) unless the court directs otherwise, the other parties to the proceedings.

6–3552E 67. How the children's guardian exercises his duties—communication of a court's decision to the child. The children's guardian must ensure that, in relation to a decision made by the court in the proceedings—

(a) if he considers it appropriate to the age and understanding of the child, the child is notified of that decision; and

(b) if the child is notified of the decision, it is explained to the child in a manner appropriate to his age and understanding.

6–3552F 68. Solicitor for child. (1) A solicitor appointed under section 41(3) of the 1989 Act or in accordance with rule 63(2)(a) must represent the child—

(a) in accordance with instructions received from the children's guardian unless the solicitor considers, having taken into account the views of the children's guardian and any direction of the court under rule 64(2)—

(i) that the child wishes to give instructions which conflict with those of the children's guardian; and

(ii) that he is able, having regard to his understanding, to give such instructions on his own behalf,

in which case the solicitor must conduct the proceedings in accordance with instructions received from the child;

(b) where no children's guardian has been appointed and the condition in section 41(4)(b) of the 1989 Act is satisfied, in accordance with instructions received from the child; or

(c) in default of instructions under sub-paragraph (a) or (b), in furtherance of the best interests of the child.

(2) A solicitor appointed under section 41(3) of the 1989 Act or in accordance with rule 63(2)(a) must—

(a) serve documents on behalf of the child in accordance with rule 37(2)(a); and

(b) accept service of documents on behalf of the child in accordance with the table in rule 37(1),

and, where the child has not himself been served and has sufficient understanding, advise the child of the contents of any document so served.

(3) Where the child wishes an appointment of a solicitor under section 41(3) of the 1989 Act or in accordance with rule 63(2)(a) to be terminated—

(a) he may apply to the court for an order terminating the appointment; and

(b) the solicitor and the children's guardian will be given an opportunity to make representations.

(4) Where the children's guardian wishes an appointment of a solicitor under section 41(3) of the 1989 Act or in accordance with rule 63(2)(a) to be terminated—

(a) he may apply to the court for an order terminating the appointment; and

(b) the solicitor and, if he is of sufficient understanding, the child, will be given an opportunity to make representations.

(5) When terminating an appointment in accordance with paragraph (3) or (4), the court will give its reasons for so doing, a note of which will be taken by the court or a court officer.

(6) The court or a court officer will record the appointment under section 41(3) of the 1989 Act or in accordance with rule 63(2)(a) or the refusal to make the appointment.

SECTION 3
REPORTING OFFICER

6–3552G 69. When the court appoints a reporting officer. In proceedings to which Part 5 applies, the court will appoint a reporting officer where—

(a) it appears that a parent or guardian of the child is willing to consent to the placing of the child for adoption, to the making of an adoption order or to a section 84 order; and

(b) that parent or guardian is in England or Wales.

6–3552H 70. Appointment of the same reporting officer in respect of two or more parents or guardians. The same person may be appointed as the reporting officer for two or more parents or guardians of the child.

6–3552I 71. The duties of the reporting officer. The reporting officer must witness the signature by a parent or guardian on the document in which consent is given to—

(a) the placing of the child for adoption;

(b) the making of an adoption order; or

(c) the making of a section 84 order.

6–3552J   72. How the reporting officer exercises his duties.   (1) The reporting officer must—

(a)   ensure so far as reasonably practicable that the parent or guardian is—

(i)   giving consent unconditionally; and
(ii)   with full understanding of what is involved;

(b)   investigate all the circumstances relevant to a parent's or guardian's consent to the placing of the child for adoption or to the making of an adoption order or a section 84 order; and

(c)   on completing his investigations the reporting officer must—

(i)   make a report in writing to the court in accordance with the timetable set by the court, drawing attention to any matters which, in his opinion, may be of assistance to the court in considering the application; or

(ii)   make an interim report to the court if a parent or guardian of the child is unwilling to consent to the placing of the child for adoption or to the making of an adoption order or section 84 order.

(2) On receipt of an interim report under paragraph (1)(c)(ii) a court officer must inform the applicant that a parent or guardian of the child is unwilling to consent to the placing of the child for adoption or to the making of an adoption order or section 84 order.

(3) The reporting officer may at any time before the final hearing make an interim report to the court if he considers necessary and ask the court for directions.

(4) The reporting officer must attend all directions hearings unless the court directs otherwise.

(5) Any report to the court under this rule will be confidential.

SECTION 4
CHILDREN AND FAMILY REPORTER

6–3552K   73. Request by court for a welfare report in respect of the child.   (1) In proceedings to which Part 5 applies, where the court is considering an application for an order in proceedings the court may ask a children and family reporter to prepare a report on matters relating to the welfare of the child.

(2) It is the duty of a children and family reporter to—

(a)   comply with any request for a report under this rule; and
(b)   provide the court with such other assistance as it may require.

(3) Any report to the court under this rule will be confidential.

6–3552L   74. How the children and family reporter exercises his powers and duties.   (1) The children and family reporter must make such investigations as may be necessary for him to perform his powers and duties and must, in particular—

(a)   contact or seek to interview such persons as he thinks appropriate or as the court directs; and

(b)   obtain such professional assistance as is available to him which he thinks appropriate or which the court directs him to obtain.

(2) The children and family reporter must—

(a)   notify the child of such contents of his report (if any) as he considers appropriate to the age and understanding of the child, including any reference to the child's own views on the application and his recommendation; and

(b)   if he does notify the child of any contents of his report, explain them to the child in a manner appropriate to his age and understanding.

(3) The children and family reporter must—

(a)   attend all directions hearings unless the court directs otherwise;
(b)   advise the court of the child's wishes and feelings;
(c)   advise the court if he considers that the joining of a person as a party to the proceedings would be likely to safeguard the interests of the child;
(d)   consider whether it is in the best interests of the child for the child to be made a party to the proceedings, and if so, notify the court of his opinion together with the reasons for that opinion; and
(e)   where the court has directed that a written report be made, file the report in accordance with the timetable set by the court.

SECTION 5
WHO CAN ACT AS CHILDREN'S GUARDIAN, REPORTING OFFICER AND CHILDREN AND FAMILY REPORTER

6–3552M   75. Persons who may not be appointed as children's guardian, reporting officer or children and family reporter.   (1) In adoption proceedings or proceedings for a section 84 order or a section 89 order, a person may not be appointed as a children's guardian, reporting officer or children and family reporter if he—

(a)   is a member, officer or servant of a local authority which is a party to the proceedings;
(b)   is, or has been, a member, officer or servant of a local authority or voluntary organisation who has been directly concerned in that capacity in arrangements relating to the care,

accommodation or welfare of the child during the five years prior to the commencement of the proceedings; or

  (c) is a serving probation officer who has, in that capacity, been previously concerned with the child or his family.

(2) In placement proceedings, a person described in paragraph (1)(b) or (c) may not be appointed as a children's guardian, reporting officer or children and family reporter.

6–3552N 76. Appointment of the same person as children's guardian, reporting officer and children and family reporter. The same person may be appointed to act as one or more of the following—

  (a) the children's guardian;
  (b) the reporting officer; and
  (c) the children and family reporter.

PART 8

DOCUMENTS AND DISCLOSURE OF DOCUMENTS AND INFORMATION

6–3552O 77. Confidential reports to the court and disclosure to the parties. (1) The court will consider whether to give a direction that a confidential report be disclosed to each party to the proceedings.

(2) Before giving such a direction the court will consider whether any information should be deleted including information which—

  (a) discloses, or is likely to disclose, the identity of a person who has been assigned a serial number under rule 20(2); or
  (b) discloses the particulars referred to in rule 21(1) where a party has given notice under rule 21(2) (disclosure of personal details).

(3) The court may direct that the report will not be disclosed to a party.

6–3552P 78. Communication of information relating to proceedings. (1) For the purposes of the law relating to contempt of court, information (whether or not it is recorded in any form) relating to proceedings held in private may be communicated—

  (a) where the court gives permission;
  (b) unless the court directs otherwise, in accordance with the relevant practice direction; or
  (c) where the communication is to—

    (i) a party;
    (ii) the legal representative of a party;
    (iii) a professional legal adviser;
    (iv) an officer of the Service or a Welsh family proceedings officer;
    (v) a welfare officer;
    (vi) the Legal Services Commission;
    (vii) an expert whose instruction by a party has been authorised by the court; or
    (viii) a professional acting in furtherance of the protection of children.

(2) In this rule—

"professional acting in furtherance of the protection of children" includes—

  (a) an officer of a local authority exercising child protection functions;
  (b) a police officer who is—

    (i) exercising powers under section 46 of the 1989 Act; or
    (ii) serving in a child protection unit or a paedophile unit of a police force;

  (c) any professional person attending a child protection conference or review in relation to a child who is the subject of the proceedings to which the information relates; or
  (d) an officer of the National Society for the Prevention of Cruelty to Children;

"professional legal adviser" means a barrister or a solicitor, solicitor's employee or other authorised litigator (as defined in section 119 of the Courts and Legal Services Act 1990) who is providing advice to a party but is not instructed to represent that party in the proceedings;

"welfare officer" means a person who has been asked to prepare a report under section 7(1)(b) of the 1989 Act.

6–3552Q 79. Orders for disclosure against a person not a party. (1) This rule applies where an application is made to the court under any Act for disclosure by a person who is not a party to the proceedings.

(2) The application must be supported by evidence.
(3) The court may make an order under this rule only where—

  (a) the documents of which disclosure is sought are likely to support the case of the applicant or adversely affect the case of one of the other parties to the proceedings; and
  (b) disclosure is necessary in order to dispose fairly of the application or to save costs.

(4) An order under this rule must—

(a) specify the documents or the classes of documents which the respondent must disclose; and

(b) require the respondent, when making disclosure, to specify any of those documents—

(i) which are no longer in his control; or
(ii) in respect of which he claims a right or duty to withhold inspection.

(5) Such an order may—

(a) require the respondent to indicate what has happened to any documents which are no longer in his control; and

(b) specify the time and place for disclosure and inspection.

(6) This rule does not apply to proceedings in a magistrates' court.

6-3552R   80. Rules not to limit other powers of the court to order disclosure.   (1) Rule 79 does not limit any other power which the court may have to order—

(a) disclosure before proceedings have started; and

(b) disclosure against a person who is not a party to proceedings.

(2) This rule does not apply to proceedings in a magistrates' court.

6-3552S   81. Claim to withhold inspection or disclosure of a document.   (1) A person may apply, without notice, for an order permitting him to withhold disclosure of a document on the ground that disclosure would damage the public interest.

(2) Unless the court orders otherwise, an order of the court under paragraph (1)—

(a) must not be served on any other person; and

(b) must not be open to inspection by any person.

(3) A person who wishes to claim that he has a right or a duty to withhold inspection of a document, or part of a document, must state in writing—

(a) that he has such a right or duty; and

(b) the grounds on which he claims that right or duty.

(4) The statement referred to in paragraph (3) must be made to the person wishing to inspect the document.

(5) A party may apply to the court to decide whether a claim made under paragraph (3) should be upheld.

(6) For the purpose of deciding an application under paragraph (1) (application to withhold disclosure) or paragraph (3) (claim to withhold inspection) the court may—

(a) require the person seeking to withhold disclosure or inspection of a document to produce that document to the court; and

(b) invite any person, whether or not a party, to make representations.

(7) An application under paragraph (1) or (5) must be supported by evidence.

(8) This rule does not affect any rule of law which permits or requires a document to be withheld from disclosure or inspection on the ground that its disclosure or inspection would damage the public interest.

(9) This rule does not apply to proceedings in a magistrates' court.

6-3552T   82. Custody of documents.   All documents relating to proceedings under the Act must, while they are in the custody of the court, be kept in a place of special security.

6-3552U   83. Inspection and copies of documents.   Subject to the provisions of these Rules, any practice direction or any direction given by the court—

(a) no document or order held by the court in proceedings under the Act will be open to inspection by any person; and

(b) no copy of any such document or order, or of an extract from any such document or order, will be taken by or given to any person.

6-3552V   84. Disclosing information to an adopted adult.   (1) The adopted person has the right, at his request, to receive from the court which made the adoption order a copy of the following—

(a) the application form for an adoption order (but not the documents attached to that form);

(b) the adoption order and any other orders relating to the adoption proceedings;

(c) orders allowing any person contact with the child after the adoption order was made; and

(d) any other document or order referred to in the relevant practice direction.

(2) The court will remove any protected information from any copy of a document or order referred to in paragraph (1) before the copies are given to the adopted person.

(3) This rule does not apply to an adopted person under the age of 18 years.

(4) In this rule "protected information" means information which would be protected information under section 57(3) if the adoption agency gave the information and not the court.

6–3552W   85. Translation of documents.   (1) Where a translation of any document is required for the purposes of proceedings for a Convention adoption order the translation must—

   (a)   unless the court directs otherwise, be provided by the applicant; and

   (b)   be signed by the translator to certify that the translation is accurate.

   (2)   This rule does not apply where the document is to be served in accordance with the Service Regulation.

PART 9

PROCEDURE FOR OTHER APPLICATIONS IN PROCEEDINGS

6–3552X   86. Types of application for which Part 9 procedure may be followed.   (1) The Part 9 procedure is the procedure set out in this Part.

   (2)   An applicant may use the Part 9 procedure if the application is made—

   (a)   in the course of existing proceedings;

   (b)   to commence proceedings other than those to which Part 5 applies; or

   (c)   in connection with proceedings which have been concluded.

   (Rule 22 lists the proceedings to which Part 5 applies.)

   (3)   Paragraph (2) does not apply—

   (a)   to applications made in accordance with—

      (i)   section 60(3) (order to prevent disclosure of information to an adopted person);

      (ii)   section 79(4) (order for Registrar General to give any information referred to in section 79(3));

      (iii)   rule 27 (request to dispense with consent);

      (iv)   rule 59(2) (appointment of children's guardian);

      (v)   rule 84 (disclosure of information to adopted adult);

      (vi)   rule 106 (withdrawal of application); or

      (vii) rule 107 (recovery orders); or

   (b)   if a practice direction provides that the Part 9 procedure may not be used in relation to the type of application in question.

   (4)   The following persons are to be respondents to an application under this Part—

   (a)   where there are existing proceedings or the proceedings have concluded, the parties to those proceedings;

   (b)   where there are no existing proceedings—

      (i)   if notice has been given under section 44 (notice of intention to adopt or apply for a section 84 order), the local authority to whom notice has been given; and

      (ii)   if an application is made in accordance with—

        (aa) section 26(3)(f) (permission to apply for contact order); or

        (bb) section 42(6) (permission to apply for adoption order),

      any person who, in accordance with rule 23, will be a party to the proceedings brought if permission is granted; and

   (c)   any other person as the court may direct.

6–3552Y   87. Application notice to be filed.   (1) Subject to paragraph (2), the applicant must file an application notice.

   (2)   An applicant may make an application without filing an application notice if—

   (a)   this is permitted by a rule or practice direction; or

   (b)   the court dispenses with the requirement for an application notice.

6–3552Z   88. Notice of an application.   (1) Subject to paragraph (2), a copy of the application notice will be served on each respondent.

   (2)   An application may be made without serving a copy of the application notice if this is permitted by—

   (a)   a rule;

   (b)   a practice direction; or

   (c)   the court.

   (Rule 91 deals with service of a copy of the application notice.)

6–3553   89. Time when an application is made.   Where an application must be made within a specified time, it is so made if the court receives the application notice within that time.

6–3553A   90. What an application notice must include.   (1) An application notice must state—

   (a)   what order the applicant is seeking; and

   (b)   briefly, why the applicant is seeking the order.

   (2)   The applicant may rely on the matters set out in his application notice as evidence if the application is verified by a statement of truth.

6–3553B **91. Service of a copy of an application notice.** (1) A court officer will serve a copy of the application notice—

(a) as soon as practicable after it is filed; and
(b) in any event at least 7 days before the court is to deal with the application.

(2) The applicant must, when he files the application notice, file a copy of any written evidence in support.

(3) When a copy of an application notice is served by a court officer it will be accompanied by—

(a) a notice of the date and place where the application will be heard;
(b) a copy of any witness statement in support; and
(c) a copy of any draft order which the applicant has attached to his application.

(4) If—

(a) an application notice is served; but
(b) the period of notice is shorter than the period required by these Rules or a practice direction,

the court may direct that, in the circumstances of the case, sufficient notice has been given and hear the application.

(5) This rule does not require written evidence—

(a) to be filed if it has already been filed; or
(b) to be served on a party on whom it has already been served.

6–3553C **92. Applications which may be dealt with without a hearing.** The court may deal with an application without a hearing if—

(a) the parties agree as to the terms of the order sought;
(b) the parties agree that the court should dispose of the application without a hearing; or
(c) the court does not consider that a hearing would be appropriate.

6–3553D **93. Service of application where application made without notice.** (1) This rule applies where the court has disposed of an application which it permitted to be made without service of a copy of the application notice.

(2) Where the court makes an order, whether granting or dismissing the application, a copy of the application notice and any evidence in support will, unless the court directs otherwise, be served with the order on all the parties in the proceedings.

(3) The order must contain a statement of the right to make an application to set aside or vary the order under rule 94.

6–3553E **94. Application to set aside or vary order made without notice.** (1) A person who was not served with a copy of the application notice before an order was made under rule 93 may apply to have the order set aside or varied.

(2) An application under this rule must be made within 7 days beginning with the date on which the order was served on the person making the application.

6–3553F **95. Power of the court to proceed in the absence of a party.** (1) Where the applicant or any respondent fails to attend the hearing of an application, the court may proceed in his absence.

(2) Where—

(a) the applicant or any respondent fails to attend the hearing of an application; and
(b) the court makes an order at the hearing,

the court may, on application or of its own initiative, re-list the application.

6–3553G **96. Dismissal of totally without merit applications.** If the High Court or a county court dismisses an application (including an application for permission to appeal) and it considers that the application is totally without merit—

(a) the court's order must record that fact; and
(b) the court must at the same time consider whether it is appropriate to make a civil restraint order.

Part 10
Alternative Procedure for Applications

6–3553H **97. Types of application for which Part 10 procedure may be followed.** (1) The Part 10 procedure is the procedure set out in this Part.

(2) An applicant may use the Part 10 procedure where the procedure set out in Part 9 does not apply and—

(a) there is no form prescribed by a rule or practice direction in which to make the application;
(b) he seeks the court's decision on a question which is unlikely to involve a substantial dispute of fact; or
(c) paragraph (5) applies.

(3) The court may at any stage direct that the application is to continue as if the applicant had

not used the Part 10 procedure and, if it does so, the court may give any directions it considers appropriate.

(4) Paragraph (2) does not apply—

(a) to applications made in accordance with—

(i) rule 27 (request to dispense with consent);
(ii) rule 59(2) (appointment of children's guardian);
(iii) rule 84 (disclosure of information to adopted adult);
(iv) rule 106 (withdrawal of application); or
(v) rule 107 (recovery orders); or

(b) if a practice direction provides that the Part 10 procedure may not be used in relation to the type of application in question.

(5) A rule or practice direction may, in relation to a specified type of proceedings—

(a) require or permit the use of the Part 10 procedure; and
(b) disapply or modify any of the rules set out in this Part as they apply to those proceedings.

6–3553I 98. Contents of the application. (1) In this Part "application" means an application made under this Part.

(2) Where the applicant uses the Part 10 procedure the application must state—

(a) that this Part applies;
(b)

(i) the question which the applicant wants the court to decide; or
(ii) the order which the applicant is seeking and the legal basis of the application for that order;

(c) if the application is being made under an enactment, what that enactment is;
(d) if the applicant is applying in a representative capacity, what that capacity is; and
(e) if the respondent appears or is to appear in a representative capacity, what that capacity is.

(3) A court officer will serve a copy of the application on the respondent.

6–3553J 99. Issue of application without naming respondents. (1) A practice direction may set out circumstances in which an application may be issued under this Part without naming a respondent.

(2) The practice direction may set out those cases in which an application for permission must be made before the application is issued.

(3) The application for permission—

(a) need not be served on any other person; and
(b) must be accompanied by a copy of the application that the applicant proposes to issue.

(4) Where the court gives permission it will give directions about the future management of the application.

6–3553K 100. Acknowledgement of service. (1) Subject to paragraph (2), each respondent must file an acknowledgement of service within 14 days beginning with the date on which the application is served.

(2) If the application is to be served out of the jurisdiction the respondent must file an acknowledgement of service within the period set out in the practice direction supplementing Part 6, section 2.

(3) A court officer will serve the acknowledgement of service on the applicant and any other party.

(4) The acknowledgement of service must—

(a) state whether the respondent contests the application;
(b) state, if the respondent seeks a different order from that set out in the application, what that order is; and
(c) be signed by the respondent or his legal representative.

6–3553L 101. Consequence of not filing an acknowledgement of service. (1) This rule applies where—

(a) the respondent has failed to file an acknowledgement of service; and
(b) the time period for doing so has expired.

(2) The respondent must attend the hearing of the application but may not take part in the hearing unless the court gives permission.

6–3553M 102. Filing and serving written evidence. (1) The applicant must file written evidence on which he intends to rely when he files his application.

(2) A court officer will serve the applicant's evidence on the respondent with the application.

(3) A respondent who wishes to rely on written evidence must file it when he files his acknowledgement of service.

(4) A court officer will serve the respondent's evidence, if any, on the other parties with the acknowledgement of service.

(5) The applicant may, within 14 days beginning with the date on which a respondent's evidence was served on him, file further written evidence in reply.

(6) If he does so, a court officer will serve a copy of that evidence on the other parties.

(7) The applicant may rely on the matters set out in his application as evidence under this rule if the application is verified by a statement of truth.

6–3553N   103. Evidence—general. (1) No written evidence may be relied on at the hearing of the application unless—

   (a) it has been served in accordance with rule 102; or
   (b) the court gives permission.

(2) The court may require or permit a party to give oral evidence at the hearing.

(3) The court may give directions requiring the attendance for cross-examination of a witness who has given written evidence.

6–3553O   104. Procedure where respondent objects to use of the Part 10 procedure. (1) Where a respondent contends that the Part 10 procedure should not be used because—

   (a) there is a substantial dispute of fact; and
   (b) the use of the Part 10 procedure is not required or permitted by a rule or practice direction,

he must state his reasons when he files his acknowledgement of service.

(2) When the court receives the acknowledgement of service and any written evidence it will give directions as to the future management of the case.

6–3553P   105. Applications under section 60(3) and 79(4) or rule 108. (1) The Part 10 procedure must be used in an application made in accordance with—

   (a) section 60(3) (order to prevent disclosure of information to an adopted person);
   (b) section 79(4) (order for Registrar General to give any information referred to in section 79(3)); and
   (c) rule 108 (directions of High Court regarding fathers without parental responsibility).

(2) The respondent to an application made in accordance with paragraph (1)(b) is the Registrar General.

PART 11
MISCELLANEOUS

6–3553Q   106. Withdrawal of application. (1) An application may be withdrawn with the permission of the court.

(2) Subject to paragraph (3), a person seeking permission to withdraw an application must file a written request for permission setting out the reasons for the request.

(3) The request under paragraph (2) may be made orally to the court if the parties and any children's guardian, reporting officer or children and family reporter are present.

(4) A court officer will notify the other parties and any children's guardian, reporting officer or children and family reporter of a written request.

(5) The court may deal with a written request under paragraph (2) without a hearing if the other parties and any children's guardian, reporting officer or children and family reporter have had an opportunity to make written representations to the court about the request.

6–3553R   107. Application for recovery orders. (1) An application for any of the orders referred to in section 41(2) (recovery orders) may—

   (a) in the High Court or a county court, be made without notice in which case the applicant must file the application—

      (i) where the application is made by telephone, the next business day after the making of the application; or
      (ii) in any other case, at the time when the application is made; and

   (b) in a magistrates' court, be made, with the permission of the court, without notice in which case the applicant must file the application at the time when the application is made or as directed by the court.

(2) Where the court refuses to make an order on an application without notice it may direct that the application is made on notice in which case the application will proceed in accordance with Part 5.

(3) The respondents to an application under this rule are—

   (a) in a case where—

      (i) placement proceedings;
      (ii) adoption proceedings; or
      (iii) proceedings for a section 84 order

      are pending, all parties to those proceedings;

(b) any adoption agency authorised to place the child for adoption or which has placed the child for adoption;

(c) any local authority to whom notice under section 44 (notice of intention to adopt or apply for a section 84 order) has been given;

(d) any person having parental responsibility for the child;

(e) any person in whose favour there is provision for contact;

(f) any person who was caring for the child immediately prior to the making of the application; and

(g) any person whom the applicant alleges to have effected or to have been or to be responsible for taking or keeping the child.

6–3553S   108. Inherent jurisdiction and fathers without parental responsibility. Where no proceedings have started an adoption agency or local authority may ask the High Court for directions on the need to give a father without parental responsibility notice of the intention to place a child for adoption.

6–3553T   109. Timing of applications for section 89 order. An application for a section 89 order must be made within 2 years beginning with the date on which—

(a) the Convention adoption or Convention adoption order; or

(b) the overseas adoption or determination under section 91

to which it relates was made.

6–3553U   110. Costs. The court may at any time make such order as to costs as it thinks just including an order relating to the payment of expenses incurred by any officer of the Service or a Welsh family proceedings officer.

(Rule 5(3) provides that Parts 43, 44 (except rules 44.3(2) and (3) and 44.9 to 44.12A), 47 and 48 and rule 45.6 of the CPR apply to costs in proceedings.)

6–3553V   111. Orders. (1) An order takes effect from the date when it is made, or such later date as the court may specify.

(2) In proceedings in Wales a party may request that an order be drawn up in Welsh as well as English.

6–3553W   112. Copies of orders. (1) Within 7 days beginning with the date on which the final order was made in proceedings or such shorter time as the court may direct a court officer will send—

(a) a copy of the order to the applicant;

(b) a copy, which is sealed, authenticated with the stamp of the court or certified as a true copy, of—

(i) an adoption order;
(ii) a section 89 order; or
(iii) an order quashing or revoking an adoption order or allowing an appeal against an adoption order

to the Registrar General;

(c) a copy of a Convention adoption order to the relevant Central Authority;

(d) a copy of a section 89 order relating to a Convention adoption order or a Convention adoption to the—

(i) relevant Central Authority;
(ii) adopters;
(iii) adoption agency; and
(iv) local authority;

(e) unless the court directs otherwise, a copy of a contact order or a variation or revocation of a contact order to the—

(i) person with whom the child is living;
(ii) adoption agency; and
(iii) local authority; and

(f) a notice of the making or refusal of—

(i) the final order; or
(ii) an order quashing or revoking an adoption order or allowing an appeal against an order in proceedings

to every respondent and, with the permission of the court, any other person.

(2) The court officer will also send notice of the making of an adoption order or a section 84 order to—

(a) any court in Great Britain which appears to him to have made any such order as is referred to in section 46(2) (order relating to parental responsibility for, and maintenance of, the child); and

(b) the principal registry of the Family Division, if it appears to him that a parental responsibility agreement has been recorded at the principal registry.

(3) A copy of any final order may be sent to any other person with the permission of the court.

(4) The court officer will send a copy of any order made during the course of the proceedings to all the parties to those proceedings unless the court directs otherwise.

(5) If an order has been drawn up in Welsh as well as English in accordance with rule 111(2) any reference in this rule to sending an order is to be taken as a reference to sending both the Welsh and English orders.

6–3553X   113. Amendment and revocation of orders.   (1) Subject to paragraph (2), an application under—

(a) section 55 (revocation of adoptions on legitimation); or
(b) paragraph 4 of Schedule 1 (amendment of adoption order and revocation of direction)

may be made without serving a copy of the application notice.

(2) The court may direct that an application notice be served on such persons as it thinks fit.

(3) Where the court makes an order granting the application, a court officer will send the Registrar General a notice—

(a) specifying the amendments; or
(b) informing him of the revocation,

giving sufficient particulars of the order to enable the Registrar General to identify the case.

(4) The court may at any time correct an accidental slip or omission in an order.

(5) A party may apply for a correction under paragraph (4) without notice to the other parties.

6–3553Y   114. Keeping of registers.   (1) A magistrates' court officer will keep a register in which there will be entered a minute or memorandum of every adjudication of the court in proceedings to which these Rules apply.

(2) The register may be stored in electronic form on the court computer system and entries in the register will include, where relevant, the following particulars—

(a) the name and address of the applicant;
(b) the name of the child including, in adoption proceedings, the name of the child prior to, and after, adoption;
(c) the age and sex of the child;
(d) the nature of the application; and
(e) the minute of adjudication.

(3) The part of the register relating to adoption proceedings will be kept separately to any other part of the register and will—

(a) not contain particulars of any other proceedings; and
(b) be kept by the court in a place of special security.

PART 12
DISPUTING THE COURT'S JURISDICTION

6–3553Z   115. Procedure for disputing the court's jurisdiction.   (1) A respondent who wishes to—

(a) dispute the court's jurisdiction to hear the application; or
(b) argue that the court should not exercise its jurisdiction

may apply to the court for an order declaring that it has no such jurisdiction or should not exercise any jurisdiction which it may have.

(2) An application under this rule must—

(a) be made within 14 days beginning with the date on which the notice of the directions hearing is sent to the parties; and
(b) be supported by evidence.

(3) If the respondent does not make an application within the period specified in paragraph (2) he is to be treated as having accepted that the court has jurisdiction to hear the application.

(4) An order containing a declaration that the court has no jurisdiction or will not exercise its jurisdiction may also make further provision including—

(a) setting aside the application form;
(b) discharging any order made before the application was commenced or, where applicable, before the application form was served; and
(c) staying the proceedings.

(5) If a respondent makes an application under this rule, he must file his written evidence in support with the application notice, but he need not before the hearing of the application file any other written evidence.

(6) Paragraph (4) does not apply to proceedings in a magistrates' court.

PART 13

HUMAN RIGHTS

6–3554   116. Human Rights Act 1998.   (1) A party who seeks to rely on any provision of or right arising under the Human Rights Act 1998 or seeks a remedy available under that Act must inform the court in his application or otherwise in writing specifying—

    (a)   the Convention right which it is alleged has been infringed and details of the alleged infringement; and

    (b)   the relief sought and whether this includes a declaration of incompatibility.

(2) The High Court may not make a declaration of incompatibility unless 21 days' notice, or such other period of notice as the court directs, has been given to the Crown.

(3) Where notice has been given to the Crown, a Minister, or other person permitted by that Act, will be joined as a party on giving notice to the court.

(4) Where a claim is made under section 7(1) of the Human Rights Act 1998 (claim that public authority acted unlawfully) in respect of a judicial act—

    (a)   that claim must be set out in the application form or the appeal notice; and

    (b)   notice must be given to the Crown.

(5) Where paragraph (4) applies and the appropriate person (as defined in section 9(5) of the Human Rights Act 1998) has not applied within 21 days, or such other period as the court directs, beginning with the date on which the notice to be joined as a party was served, the court may join the appropriate person as a party.

(6) On any application concerning a committal order, if the court ordering the release of the person concludes that his Convention rights have been infringed by the making of the order to which the application or appeal relates, the judgment or order should so state, but if the court does not do so, that failure will not prevent another court from deciding the matter.

(7) Where by reason of a rule, practice direction or court order the Crown is permitted or required—

    (a)   to make a witness statement;

    (b)   to swear an affidavit;

    (c)   to verify a document by a statement of truth; or

    (d)   to discharge any other procedural obligation,

that function will be performed by an appropriate officer acting on behalf of the Crown, and the court may if necessary nominate an appropriate officer.

(8) In this rule—

"Convention right" has the same meaning as in the Human Rights Act 1998; and

"declaration of incompatibility" means a declaration of incompatibility under section 4 of the Human Rights Act 1998.

(A practice direction makes provision for the notices mentioned in this rule.)

PART 14

INTERIM INJUNCTIONS

PART 15

ADMISSIONS AND EVIDENCE

6–3554A   122. Making an admission.   (1) A party may admit the truth of the whole or any part of another party's case by giving notice in writing.

(2) The court may allow a party to amend or withdraw an admission.

6–3554B   123. Power of court to control evidence.   (1) The court may control the evidence by giving directions as to—

    (a)   the issues on which it requires evidence;

    (b)   the nature of the evidence which it requires to decide those issues; and

    (c)   the way in which the evidence is to be placed before the court.

(2) The court may use its power under this rule to exclude evidence that would otherwise be admissible.

(3) The court may limit cross-examination.

6–3554C   124. Evidence of witnesses—general rule.   (1) The general rule is that any fact which needs to be proved by the evidence of witnesses is to be proved—

    (a)   at final hearing, by their oral evidence; and

    (b)   at any other hearing, by their evidence in writing.

(2) This is subject—

    (a)   to any provision to the contrary contained in these Rules or elsewhere; or

    (b)   to any order of the court.

6–3554D **125. Evidence by video link or other means.** The court may allow a witness to give evidence through a video link or by other means.

6–3554E **126. Service of witness statements for use at final hearing.** (1) A witness statement is a written statement signed by a person which contains the evidence which that person would be allowed to give orally.

(2) The court will give directions about the service of any witness statement of the oral evidence which a party intends to rely on in relation to any issues of fact to be decided at the final hearing on the other parties.

(3) The court may give directions as to—

(a) the order in which witness statements are to be served; and
(b) whether or not the witness statements are to be filed.

6–3554F **127. Use at final hearing of witness statements which have been served.** (1) If—

(a) a party has filed a witness statement which has been served on the other parties; and
(b) he wishes to rely at the final hearing on the evidence of the witness who made the statement,

he must call the witness to give oral evidence unless the court directs otherwise or he puts the statement in as hearsay evidence.

(2) Where a witness is called to give oral evidence under paragraph (1), his witness statement shall stand as his evidence in chief unless the court directs otherwise.

(3) A witness giving oral evidence at final hearing may with the permission of the court—

(a) amplify his witness statement; and
(b) give evidence in relation to new matters which have arisen since the witness statement was served on the other parties.

(4) The court will give permission under paragraph (3) only if it considers that there is good reason not to confine the evidence of the witness to the contents of his witness statement.

(5) If a party who has filed a witness statement which has been served on the other parties does not—

(a) call the witness to give evidence at final hearing; or
(b) put the witness statement in as hearsay evidence, any other party may put the witness statement in as hearsay evidence.

6–3554G **128. Evidence in proceedings other than at final hearing.** (1) Subject to paragraph (2), the general rule is that evidence at hearings other than the final hearing is to be by witness statement unless the court, a practice direction or any other enactment requires otherwise.

(2) At hearings other than the final hearing, a party may, rely on the matters set out in—

(a) his application form; or
(b) his application notice, if it is verified by a statement of truth.

6–3554H **129. Order for cross-examination.** (1) Where, at a hearing other than the final hearing, evidence is given in writing, any party may apply to the court for permission to cross-examine the person giving the evidence.

(2) If the court gives permission under paragraph (1) but the person in question does not attend as required by the order, his evidence may not be used unless the court gives permission.

6–3554I **130. Form of witness statement.** A witness statement must comply with the requirements set out in the relevant practice direction.

6–3554J **131. Witness summaries.** (1) A party who—

(a) is required to file a witness statement for use at final hearing; but
(b) is unable to obtain one, may apply, without notice, for permission to file a witness summary instead.

(2) A witness summary is a summary of—

(a) the evidence, if known, which would otherwise be included in a witness statement; or
(b) if the evidence is not known, the matters about which the party filing the witness summary proposes to question the witness.

(3) Unless the court directs otherwise, a witness summary must include the name and address of the intended witness.

(4) Unless the court directs otherwise, a witness summary must be filed within the period in which a witness statement would have had to be filed.

(5) Where a party files a witness summary, so far as practicable, rules 126 (service of witness statements for use at final hearing), 127(3) (amplifying witness statements), and 130 (form of witness statement) shall apply to the summary.

6–3554K 132. Cross-examination on a witness statement. Where a witness is called to give evidence at final hearing, he may be cross-examined on his witness statement whether or not the statement or any part of it was referred to during the witness's evidence in chief.

6–3554L 133. False statements. (1) Proceedings for contempt of court may be brought against a person if he makes, or causes to be made, a false statement in a document verified by a statement of truth without an honest belief in its truth.

(2) Proceedings under this rule may be brought only—

(a) by the Attorney General; or

(b) with the permission of the court.

(3) This rule does not apply to proceedings in a magistrates' court.

6–3554M 134. Affidavit evidence. Evidence must be given by affidavit instead of or in addition to a witness statement if this is required by the court, a provision contained in any other rule, a practice direction or any other enactment.

6–3554N 135. Form of affidavit. An affidavit must comply with the requirements set out in the relevant practice direction.

6–3554O 136. Affidavit made outside the jurisdiction. A person may make an affidavit outside the jurisdiction in accordance with—

(a) this Part; or

(b) the law of the place where he makes the affidavit.

6–3554P 137. Notarial acts and instruments. A notarial act or instrument may be received in evidence without further proof as duly authenticated in accordance with the requirements of law unless the contrary is proved.

6–3554Q 138. Use of plans, photographs and models as evidence. (1) This rule applies to evidence (such as a plan, photograph or model) which is not—

(a) contained in a witness statement, affidavit or expert's report; and

(b) to be given orally at the final hearing.

(2) This rule includes documents which may be received in evidence without further proof under section 9 of the Civil Evidence Act 1995.

(3) Unless the court orders otherwise the evidence shall not be receivable at the final hearing unless the party intending to put it in evidence has given notice to the court in accordance with this rule and the court will give directions about service of the notice on any other party.

(4) Where the party intends to use the evidence as evidence of any fact then, subject to paragraph (6), he must give notice not later than the latest date for filing witness statements.

(5) He must give notice at least 21 days before the hearing at which he proposes to put in the evidence, if—

(a) there are not to be witness statements; or

(b) he intends to put in the evidence solely in order to disprove an allegation made in a witness statement.

(6) Where the evidence forms part of expert evidence, he must give notice when the expert's report is filed.

(7) Where the evidence is being produced to the court for any reason other than as part of factual or expert evidence, he must give notice at least 21 days before the hearing at which he proposes to put in the evidence.

(8) Where a party has given notice that he intends to put in the evidence, the court may direct that every other party be given an opportunity to inspect it and to agree to its admission without further proof.

6–3554R 139. Evidence of finding on question of foreign law. (1) This rule sets out the procedure which must be followed by a party who intends to put in evidence a finding on a question of foreign law by virtue of section 4(2) of the Civil Evidence Act 1972.

(2) He must give the court notice of his intention—

(a) if there are to be witness statements, not later than the latest date for filing them; or

(b) otherwise, not less than 21 days before the hearing at which he proposes to put the finding in evidence

and the court will give directions about service of the notice on any other party.

(3) The notice must—

(a) specify the question on which the finding was made; and

(b) enclose a copy of a document where it is reported or recorded.

6–3554S   149. Use of deposition at a hearing.   (1) A deposition ordered under rule 146 may be given in evidence at a hearing unless the court orders otherwise.

(2) A party intending to put in evidence a deposition at a hearing must file notice of his intention to do so on the court and the court will make directions about serving the notice on every other party.

(3) He must file the notice at least 21 days before the day fixed for the hearing.

(4) The court may require a deponent to attend the hearing and give evidence orally.

PART 17
EXPERTS

6–3554T   154. Duty to restrict expert evidence.   Expert evidence shall be restricted to that which is reasonably required to resolve the proceedings.

6–3554U   155. Interpretation.   A reference to an "expert" in this Part—

(a) is a reference to an expert who has been instructed to give or prepare evidence for the purpose of court proceedings; and

(b) does not include—

(i) a person who is within a prescribed description for the purposes of section 94(1) of the Act (persons who may prepare a report for any person about the suitability of a child for adoption or of a person to adopt a child or about the adoption, or placement for adoption, of a child); or

(ii) an officer of the Service or a Welsh family proceedings officer when acting in that capacity.

(Regulation 3 of the Restriction on the Preparation of Adoption Reports Regulations 2005 (SI 2005/1711) sets out which persons are within a prescribed description for the purposes of section 94(1) of the Act.)

6–3554V   156. Experts—overriding duty to the court.   (1) It is the duty of an expert to help the court on the matters within his expertise.

(2) This duty overrides any obligation to the person from whom he has received instructions or by whom he is paid.

6–3554W   157. Court's power to restrict expert evidence.   (1) No party may call an expert or put in evidence an expert's report without the court's permission.

(2) When a party applies for permission under this rule he must identify—

(a) the field in which he wishes to rely on expert evidence; and

(b) where practicable the expert in that field on whose evidence he wishes to rely.

(3) If permission is granted under this rule it shall be in relation only to the expert named or the field identified under paragraph (2).

(4) The court may limit the amount of the expert's fees and expenses that the party who wishes to rely on the expert may recover from any other party.

6–3554X   158. General requirement for expert evidence to be given in a written report.   Expert evidence is to be given in a written report unless the court directs otherwise.

6–3554Y   159. Written questions to experts.   (1) A party may put to—

(a) an expert instructed by another party; or

(b) a single joint expert appointed under rule 160,

written questions about his report.

(2) Written questions under paragraph (1)—

(a) may be put once only;

(b) must be put within 5 days beginning with the date on which the expert's report was served; and

(c) must be for the purpose only of clarification of the report,

unless in any case—

(i) the court gives permission;

(ii) the other party agrees; or

(iii) any practice direction provides otherwise.

(3) An expert's answers to questions put in accordance with paragraph (1) shall be treated as part of the expert's report.

(4) Where—

(a) a party has put a written question to an expert instructed by another party in accordance with this rule; and

(b) the expert does not answer that question,

the court may make one or both of the following orders in relation to the party who instructed the expert—

(i) that the party may not rely on the evidence of that expert; or

(ii) that the party may not recover the fees and expenses of that expert from any other party.

6–3554Z 160. Court's power to direct that evidence is to be given by a single joint expert. (1) Where two or more parties wish to submit expert evidence on a particular issue, the court may direct that the evidence on that issue is to given by one expert only.

(2) The parties wishing to submit the expert evidence are called "the instructing parties".

(3) Where the instructing parties cannot agree who should be the expert, the court may—

(a) select the expert from a list prepared or identified by the instructing parties; or

(b) direct that the expert be selected in such other manner as the court may direct.

6–3555 161. Instructions to a single joint expert. (1) Where the court gives a direction under rule 160 for a single joint expert to be used, each instructing party may give instructions to the expert.

(2) When an instructing party gives instructions to the expert he must, at the same time, send a copy of the instructions to the other instructing parties.

(3) The court may give directions about—

(a) the payment of the expert's fees and expenses; and

(b) any inspection, examination or experiments which the expert wishes to carry out.

(4) The court may, before an expert is instructed, limit the amount that can be paid by way of fees and expenses to the expert.

(5) Unless the court otherwise directs, the instructing parties are jointly and severally liable for the payment of the expert's fees and expenses.

6–3555A 162. Power of court to direct a party to provide information. (1) Where a party has access to information which is not reasonably available to the other party, the court may direct the party who has access to the information to prepare and file a document recording the information.

(2) A court officer will send a copy of that document to the other party.

6–3555B 163. Contents of report. (1) An expert's report must comply with the requirements set out in the relevant practice direction.

(2) At the end of an expert's report there must be a statement that—

(a) the expert understands his duty to the court; and

(b) he has complied with that duty.

(3) The expert's report must state the substance of all material instructions, whether written or oral, on the basis of which the report was written.

(4) The instructions referred to in paragraph (3) shall not be privileged against disclosure.

6–3555C 164. Use by one party of expert's report disclosed by another. Where a party has disclosed an expert's report, any party may use that expert's report as evidence at the final hearing.

6–3555D 165. Discussions between experts. (1) The court may, at any stage, direct a discussion between experts for the purpose of requiring the experts to—

(a) identify and discuss the expert issues in the proceedings; and

(b) where possible, reach an agreed opinion on those issues.

(2) The court may specify the issues which the experts must discuss.

(3) The court may direct that following a discussion between the experts they must prepare a statement for the court showing—

(a) those issues on which they agree; and

(b) those issues on which they disagree and a summary of their reasons for disagreeing.

6–3555E 166. Consequence of failure to disclose expert's report. A party who fails to disclose an expert's report may not use the report at the final hearing or call the expert to give evidence orally unless the court gives permission.

6–3555F 167. Expert's right to ask court for directions. (1) An expert may file a written request for directions to assist him in carrying out his function as an expert.

(2) An expert must, unless the court directs otherwise, provide a copy of any proposed request for directions under paragraph (1)—

(a) to the party instructing him, at least 7 days before he files the request; and

(b) to all other parties, at least 4 days before he files it.

(3) The court, when it gives directions, may also direct that a party be served with a copy of the directions.

PART 18
CHANGE OF SOLICITOR

6–3555G 168. Change of solicitor—duty to give notice. (1) This rule applies where—

(a) a party for whom a solicitor is acting wants to change his solicitor;
(b) a party, after having conducted the application in person, appoints a solicitor to act on his behalf (except where the solicitor is appointed only to act as an advocate for a hearing); or
(c) a party, after having conducted the application by a solicitor, intends to act in person.

(2) Where this rule applies, the party or his solicitor (where one is acting) must—

(a) file notice of the change; and
(b) where paragraph (1)(a) or (c) applies, serve notice of the change on the former solicitor.

(3) The court will give directions about serving notice of the change on every other party.

(4) The notice filed at court must state that notice has been served as required by paragraph (2)(b).

(5) Subject to paragraph (6), where a party has changed his solicitor or intends to act in person, the former solicitor will be considered to be the party's solicitor unless and until—

(a) notice is filed and served in accordance with paragraphs (2) and (3); or
(b) the court makes an order under rule 169 and the order is served as required by paragraph (3) of that rule.

(6) Where the certificate of a LSC funded client or an assisted person is revoked or discharged—

(a) the solicitor who acted for that person will cease to be the solicitor acting in the case as soon as his retainer is determined under regulation 4 of the Community Legal Service (Costs) Regulations 2000; and
(b) if that person wishes to continue where he appoints a solicitor to act on his behalf, paragraph (2) will apply as if he had previously conducted the application in person;

(7) In this rule—

"assisted person" means an assisted person within the statutory provisions relating to legal aid;

"certificate" means a certificate issued under the Funding Code (approved under section 9 of the Access to Justice Act 1999);

"LSC funded client" means an individual who receives services funded by the Legal Services Commission as part of the Community Legal Service within the meaning of Part I of the Access to Justice Act 1999.

6–3555H 169. Order that a solicitor has ceased to act. (1) A solicitor may apply for an order declaring that he has ceased to be the solicitor acting for a party.

(2) Where an application is made under this rule—

(a) notice of the application must be given to the party for whom the solicitor is acting, unless the court directs otherwise; and
(b) the application must be supported by evidence.

(3) Where the court makes an order that a solicitor has ceased to act—

(a) the court will give directions about serving the order on every party to the proceedings; and
(b) if it is served by a party or the solicitor, the party or the solicitor (as the case may be) must file a certificate of service.

6–3555I 170. Removal of solicitor who has ceased to act on application of another party. (1) Where—

(a) a solicitor who has acted for a party—

(i) has died;
(ii) has become bankrupt;
(iii) has ceased to practice; or
(iv) cannot be found; and

(b) the party has not given notice of a change of solicitor or notice of intention to act in person as required by rule 168(2),

any other party may apply for an order declaring that the solicitor has ceased to be the solicitor acting for the other party in the case.

(2) Where an application is made under this rule, notice of the application must be given to the party to whose solicitor the application relates unless the court directs otherwise.

(3) Where the court makes an order made under this rule—

(a) the court will give directions about serving the order on every party to the proceedings; and

(b) where it is served by a party, that party must file a certificate of service.

PART 19
APPEALS

Scientific tests

Blood Tests (Evidence of Paternity) Regulations 1971[1]

(SI 1971/1861 amended by SI 1989/776, SI 1990/359 and 1025, SI 1991/2472, SI 1992/709 and 1369, SI 2001/773, SI 2004/596, 2033 and Si 2005/617)

6–3570 1. *Citation and commencement.*

1. Made in pursuance of s 22 of the Family Law Reform Act 1969.

Interpretation

6–3571 2. (1) In these Regulations, unless the context otherwise requires—

"the Act" means the Family Law Reform Act 1969;

"court" means a court which gives a direction for the use of scientific tests in pursuance of section 20(1) of the Act;

"direction" means a direction given as aforesaid;

"direction form" means Form 1 in Schedule 1 to these Regulations;

"photograph" means a recent photograph, taken full face without a hat, of the size required for insertion in a passport;

sample" means bodily fluid or bodily tissue taken for the purpose of scientific tests;

"sampler" means a registered medical practitioner, or a person who is under the supervision of such a practitioner and is either a registered nurse or a registered biomedical scientist, or a tester;

"subject" means a person from whom a court directs that bodily samples shall be taken;

"tester" means an individual employed to carry out tests by a body which has been accredited for the purposes of section 20 of the Act either by the Lord Chancellor or by a body appointed by him for those purposes and which has been nominated in a direction to carry out tests[1];

"tests" means scientific tests carried out under Part III of the Act and includes any test made with the object of ascertaining the inheritable characteristics of bodily fluids or bodily tissue.

(2) A reference in these Regulations to a person who is under a disability is a reference to a person who has not attained the age of 16 years or who is suffering from a mental disorder within the meaning of the Mental Health Act 1983 and is incapable of understanding the nature and purpose of scientific tests.

(3) The Interpretation Act 1978 shall apply to the interpretation of these Regulations as it applies to the interpretation of an Act of Parliament.

1. For list of persons so appointed, see Lord Chancellor's Department Circular, dated August 1998.

Direction form

6–3572 3. A sampler shall not take a sample from a subject unless Parts I and II of the direction form have been completed and the direction form purports to be signed by the proper officer of the court or some person on his behalf.

Subjects under disability to be accompanied to sampler

6–3573 4. A subject who is under a disability who attends a sampler for the taking of a sample shall be accompanied by a person of full age who shall identify him to the sampler.

6–3574 5–9. *Taking and testing of samples.*

Report by tester

6–3575 10. On completion of the tests in compliance with the direction, the tester shall forward to the court a report in Form 2 in Schedule 1 to these Regulations, together with the appropriate direction forms.

Procedure where tests not made

6–3576   **11.** If at any time it appears to a tester that he will be unable to make tests in accordance with the direction, he shall inform the court, giving his reasons, and shall return the direction forms in his possession to the court.

Fees

6–3577   **12.** (1) A sampler may charge £27.50 for making the arrangements to take a sample.

     (2) The charge in paragraph (1) is payable whether or not a sample is taken.

6–3578

Regulations 2(1) and 10   SCHEDULE 1
FORM 1
FAMILY LAW REFORM ACT, 1969

6–3579

FAMILY LAW REFORM ACT 1969

....
V
....
Reference No. of direction ....
Full name and date of birth of person .... to be tested to whom this form relates.
*(Insert title of proceedings.)

PART I

Notification of direction

The ....(*name and address of court*) on ....day of ....19 directed that scientific tests be carried out in respect of the persons whose names are set out below for the purpose of ascertaining the parentage of ....(*name of person whose parentage is in dispute*) and that bodily samples be taken from the persons named below on or before the ....day of .... 19 .

The name of the person appearing to the court to have the care and control of the person to whom this form relates who is under 16/suffering from a mental disorder within the meaning of the Mental Health Act 1959 and is incapable of understanding the nature and purpose of scientific tests, is ....

     ....(Signed)
     Proper Officer of the Court.

Name ....Address ....Age

*(Delete as appropriate.)

PART II

Request to sampler to take sample

To ....(*name and address of sampler*). You are hereby requested to take a bodily sample from .... (*name of person to whom form relates*).

The sample is to be taken notwithstanding the refusal to consent of the person with care and control of......(*name of person to whom form relates*). Delete if not applicable
*(Delete if sampler is also tester.)
[Other samples will be taken as follows:—*
Name of person from whom sample will be taken Name, address and telephone number of accredited body ....]

     ....(Signed)

(To be completed where all the samples from the parties named in Part I are not to be taken by the same sampler.)

[Being unable to comply with the request set out above, I have nominated ....(*name and address of nominee*) to take the sample.†
     ....(Signed)]

* To be completed where all the samples from the parties named in Part I are not to be taken by the same sampler.
† For use where sampler named above nominates another sampler.

FORM 2
REPORT BY TESTER

FAMILY LAW REFORM ACT 1969

Ref. No. of Proceedings ....
To: (High Court of Justice, Strand, London W.C.2.

(Court Manager, ...County Court
(Designated Officer, ...Magistrates' Court. (1)

PART I

I, ...,being employed to carry out scientific tests a by a body which has been accredited for the purposes of section 20 of the Family Law Reform Act 1969, certify that I have carried out scientific tests (the details of which are given in Part II of this Report) on samples provided by (the details of which are given in Part II of this Report) of the persons named in this direction, viz.,

From the results obtained Mr ....is excluded/is not excluded from possible parentage of ....
Reason for conclusion:—

Comments on value, if any, of tests in determining whether any person tested is the father or mother of the person whose parentage is in dispute:—

........Signed

........Status

........Address

....

PART II

Report of Scientific Tests

Regulation 12   SCHEDULE 2
                               CHARGES MADE BY SAMPLERS

6–3580   *Revoked.*

Magistrates' Courts (Blood Tests) Rules 1971[1]

(SI 1971/1991 amended by SI 1989/384, SI 2001/776, SI 2004/2033 and SI 2005/617)

6–3590   **1.** *Citation and commencement.*

----

1. Made under s 15 of the Justices of the Peace Act 1949 as extended by s 122 of the Magistrates' Courts Act 1952. See now Magistrates' Courts Act 1980, ss 144, 145 and 154.

6–3591   **2.** (1) In these Rules save where the context otherwise requires—

"the Act" means the Family Law Reform Act 1969;

"the applicant" means an applicant for a direction;

"bodily samples" and "scientific tests" have the same meaning as in Part III of the Act;

"complaint" means a complaint in the hearing of which the parentage of any person falls to be determined;

"court" means a magistrates' court;

"direction" means a direction given in accordance with the provisions of section 20(1) of the Act;

"direction form" means Form 1 in Schedule 1 to the Blood Tests (Evidence of Paternity) Regulations 1971[1],

"photograph" means a recent photograph, taken full face without a hat, of the size required for insertion in a passport;

"proceedings" means any proceedings in a magistrates' court for the hearing of a complaint;

"sampler" means a registered medical practitioner, or a person who is under the supervision of such a practitioner and is either a registered nurse or a registered biomedical scientist, or a tester;

"subject" means a person from whom a court directs that bodily samples shall be taken;

"tester" means an individual employed to carry out tests by a body which has been accredited for the purposes of section 20 of the Act either by the Lord Chancellor or by a body appointed by him for those purposes and which has been nominated in a direction to carry out tests.

(2) Any reference in these Rules to a form other than a direction form is a reference to a form contained in the Schedule to these Rules.

(3) Any reference in these Rules to a person who is under a disability is a reference to a person who has not attained the age of 16 years or who is suffering from a mental disorder within the meaning of the Mental Health Act [1983] and is incapable of understanding the nature and purpose of blood tests.

(4) The Interpretation Act [1978] shall apply to the interpretation of these Rules as it applies to the interpretation of an Act of Parliament.

----

1. See these Regulations, post.

6–3592   **3.** Form 1 shall be served on any person who makes a complaint in the hearing of which it appears to the justices' clerk that the paternity of any person falls to be determined and on any person who is served with a summons to answer such a complaint.

6–3593   **4.** A party to any proceedings may apply in writing to the court for a direction at any time after the making of the complaint, and, on, receipt of the application, the designated officer for the court shall inform the other party to the proceedings that the application has been made and that he may consent to the court giving a direction before the commencement of the hearing of the complaint.

6–3594 **5.** A court may give a direction in the absence of the applicant and the other party to the proceedings if it appears to the court that the other party, or, where he is under a disability, the person having the care and control of him has consented to the giving of the direction.

6–3595 **6.** The court, when giving a direction, shall name the person appearing to the court to have the care and control of any subject who is under a disability.

6–3596 **7.** A direction shall be in Form 2 and a copy of it shall be served on every subject or, where the subject is under a disability, on the person named in the direction as having the care and control of him.

6–3597 **8.** Within 14 days, or such longer period as the court may order, of the giving of the direction, the applicant, unless he has been granted legal aid under the Legal Aid and Advice Act 1949[1], shall pay to the designated officer for the court such sum as appears to the designated officer for the court to be sufficient to pay the fees of the sampler and tester in respect of taking and testing samples for the purpose of giving effect to the direction.

_____

1. See now Legal Aid Act 1988 in PART I: MAGISTRATES' COURTS, PROCEDURE.

6–3598 **9.** Within 14 days, or such longer period as the court may order, of service of a copy of the direction, each subject who is not under a disability and the person having the care and control of a subject who is under a disability but has attained the age of 12 months by the date of the direction shall furnish to the designated officer for the court a photograph of the subject.

6–3599 **10.** (1) If any person fails to comply with the provisions of Rule 8 or 9 of these Rules, the designated officer for the court shall not take any further steps required of him by these Rules without first informing the court and receiving its instructions to do so.

(2) If the court is informed by the designated officer for the court in accordance with paragraph (1) of this Rule, it may vary or revoke the direction or may make such order as to the hearing or the continuation of the hearing of the complaint as appears to the court to be appropriate in all the circumstances and shall cause the parties to be notified.

6–3600 **11.** Where a court has given a direction and the designated officer for the court is satisfied that the requirements of Rule 8 of these Rules (where applicable) have been met and he is in possession of a photograph (or a certificate under the proviso to Rule 9 of these Rules) in respect of each subject who has attained the age of 12 months by the date of the direction, the designated officer for the court shall arrange for blood sample to be taken and for bodily samples to be taken and for scientific tests to be made on those samples, or shall arrange for the parties' solicitors to make the arrangement on his behalf.

6–3601 **12.** When arrangements have been made for the taking of samples, the designated officer for the court shall—

(a) give notice in Form 3 to each subject or, where a subject is under a disability, the person having the care and control of the subject, of the arrangements made for the taking of samples from the subject and shall require him, or where he is under a disability, the person having the care and control of him, to comply with the arrangements;

(b) complete Parts I and II of a direction form in respect of each subject and send the direction form to the sampler who is to take the bodily sample from that subject.

6–3602 **13.** When a direction form is returned to the court by a sampler, or by a tester, unless it is accompanied by a report under section 20(2) of the Act, the court shall cause a copy of the form to be served on each party to the proceedings and shall consider any entries made on the direction form by the sampler, tester or any other person and may vary or revoke the direction or make such order as to the hearing or the continuation of the hearing of the complaint as appears to the court to be appropriate in all the circumstances.

6–3603 **14.** On receipt of the report by the tester under section 20(2) of the Act, the designated officer for the court shall serve a copy of the report on each of the parties to the proceedings.

6–3604 **15.** The designated officer for the court shall use any sum paid to him under Rule 8 of these Rules in paying the fees due to the sampler and shall repay the balance, if any, to the applicant.

6–3605 **16.** Service of any document required to be served by these Rules may be effected by delivering it to the person upon whom it is required to be served or to his solicitor or by sending it by first class post to him at his last known or usual place of abode or to his solicitor at his office.

6–3606

Rule 2(2)

SCHEDULE
FORM 1
FAMILY LAW REFORM ACT 1969

Revoked.

6–3607

FORM 2
FAMILY LAW REFORM ACT 1969

Blood test direction (MC (BT) Rules 1971, r 7.)

In the .... Magistrates' Court
.... Complainant
and
.... Defendant

By virtue of the power conferred upon the court by section 20(1) of the Family Law Reform Act 1969 and on the application of .... the court hereby directs that scientific tests be used to ascertain whether such tests show that .... is or is not excluded from being the father of .... and that for that purpose bodily samples shall be taken from:—

And it is further ordered that such samples shall be taken before the .... day of 19
....
.... By order of the court,
....
.... Justices' Clerk.
Dated .... 19 .... Address ....

The person appearing to the court to have the care and control of .... being a person who (has not attained the age of sixteen years) (is suffering from a mental disorder within the meaning of the Mental Health Act 1959 and is incapable of understanding the nature and purpose of scientific tests) is ....

NOTES[1]

1. If you ask the court to order the use of blood tests, you are reminded that, unless you have been granted legal aid, you must pay to the justices' clerk within fourteen days from the date of this direction the sum of £..... for the payment of fees in respect of taking and testing samples for the purpose of giving effect to this direction.

2. Within fourteen days of receiving this direction, whether or not you are the complainant or the defendant, you must send a photograph of yourself to the justices' clerk. If you are the person having care and control of the above named child, and the child has attained the age of 12 months, you must send a photograph of the child. Photographs should have been taken recently, should be taken full face without a hat, and of the size required for insertion in a passport[2].

3. Until these requirements have been satisfied, it will not be possible to arrange for the sampling and testing to take place.

---

1. These notes are not part of the prescribed Form but are suggested by Home Office Circular 38/1973.
2. Para 2 of the notes will need amendment if the subject is suffering from a mental disorder: see r 9.

6–3608

FORM 3
FAMILY LAW REFORM ACT 1969

Requirement to give blood sample (MC (BT) Rules 1971, r 12.)

To .... (Name of subject/person having care and control of subject).
Further to the direction for the carrying out of scientific tests given on .... 19 .... by the .... Magistrates' Court, a copy of which has been served on you, you are hereby required, for the purpose of giving effect to the direction, to attend on .... (*insert title and name of sampler*) at .... (*insert address at which sample is to be taken*) at .... am/pm on .... 19 .... for a bodily sample to be taken from you.
....
.... Designated Officer for the .... Magistrates' Court.
.... Address ....

Note.—Any travelling or other expenses reasonably incurred in complying with this requirement are payable in the first instance by the person who applied to the court for the direction, namely .... whose solicitors are .... of .... The court has power to deal with these expenses when it makes an order for costs at the end of the proceedings.

Children

Emergency Protection Order (Transfer of Responsibilities) Regulations 1991[1]
(SI 1991/1414)

6–3613   1. *Citation and commencement.*

---

1. Made by the Secretary of State under ss 52(3), (4) and 104(4) of the Children Act 1989.

Transfer of responsibilities under emergency protection orders

6–3614 **2.** Subject to regulation 5 of these Regulations, where—

(a) any emergency protection order has been made with respect to a child;

(b) the applicant for the order was not the local authority within whose area the child is ordinarily resident; and

(c) that local authority are of the opinion that it would be in the child's best interests for the applicant's responsibilities under the order to be transferred to them,

that authority shall (subject to their having complied with the requirements imposed by regulation 3(1) of these Regulations) be treated, for the purposes of the Children Act 1989, as though they and not the original applicant had applied for, and been granted, the order.

Requirements to be complied with by local authorities

6–3615 **3.** (1) In forming their opinion under regulation 2(c) of these Regulations the local authority shall consult the applicant for the emergency protection order and have regard to the following considerations—

(a) the ascertainable wishes and feelings of the child having regard to his age and understanding;

(b) the child's physical, emotional and educational needs for the duration of the emergency protection order;

(c) the likely effect on him of any change in his circumstances which may be caused by a transfer of responsibilities under the order;

(d) his age, sex family background;

(e) the circumstances which gave rise to the application for the emergency protection order;

(f) any directions of a court and other orders made in respect of the child;

(g) the relationship (if any) of the applicant for the emergency protection order to the child, and

(h) any plans which the applicant may have in respect of the child.

(2) The local authority shall give notice, as soon as possible after they form the opinion referred to in regulation 2(c), of the date and time of the transfer to—

(a) the court which made the emergency protection order,

(b) the applicant for the order, and

(c) those (other than the local authority) to whom the applicant for the order gave notice of it.

(3) A notice required under this regulation shall be given in writing and may be sent by post.

When responsibility under emergency protection order transfers

6–3616 **4.** The time at which responsibility under any emergency protection order is to be treated as having been transferred to a local authority shall be the time stated as the time of transfer in the notice given in accordance with regulation 3 of these Regulations by the local authority to the applicant for the emergency protection order or the time at which notice is given to him under that regulation, whichever is the later.

Exception for children in refuges

6–3617 **5.** These Regulations shall not apply where the child to whom the emergency protection order applies is in a refuge in respect of which there is in force a Secretary of State's certificate issued under section 51 of the Children Act 1989 (refuges for children at risk) and the person carrying on the home or, the foster parent providing the refuge, having taken account of the wishes and feelings of the child, has decided that the child should continue to be provided with the refuge for the duration of the order.

Children (Secure Accommodation) Regulations 1991[1]

(SI 1991/1505 amended by 1992/2117, SI 1995/1398, SI 1996/692, SI 2000/694, SI 2001/2337, SI 2002/546 and 2395 (Wales) and SI 2004/696)

6–3618 **1.** *Citation and commencement.*

---

1. Made by the Secretary of State for Health, in exercise of the powers conferred by ss 25(2) and (7) and 104(4) of and paras 4(1) and (2)(d) and (i) of Sch 4, 7(1) and (2)(f) and (3) of Sch 5 and 10(1) and (2)(j) and (3) of Sch 6 to the Children Act 1989.

Interpretation

6–3619 **2.** (1) In these Regulations, unless the context otherwise requires—

"the Act" means the Children Act 1989;

"children's home" means a private children's home, a community home or a voluntary home;

"independent visitor" means a person appointed under paragraph 17 of Schedule 2 to the Act;

"secure accommodation" means accommodation which is provided for the purpose of restricting the liberty of children to whom section 25 of the Act (use of accommodation for restricting liberty) applies.

(2) Any reference in these regulations to a numbered regulation shall be construed as a reference to the regulation bearing that number in these Regulations, and any reference in a regulation to a numbered paragraph is a reference to the paragraph bearing that number in that regulation.

Approval by Secretary of State of secure accommodation in a children's home

6–3620   **3.** Accommodation in a children's home shall not be used as secure accommodation unless it has been approved by the Secretary of State for such use and approval shall be subject to such terms and conditions as he sees fit.

Placement of a child aged under 13 in secure accommodation in a children's home

6–3621   **4.** A child under the age of 13 years shall not be placed in secure accommodation in a children's home without the prior approval of the Secretary of State to the placement of that child and such approval shall be subject to such terms and conditions as he sees fit.

Children to whom section 25 of the Act shall not apply

6–3622   **5.** (1) Section 25 of the Act shall not apply to a child who is detained[1] under any provision of the Mental Health Act 1983 or in respect of whom an order has been made under section 90 or 91 of the Powers of Criminal Courts (Sentencing) Act 2000 (detention at Her Majesty's pleasure or for specified period).

(2) Section 25 of the Act shall not apply to a child—

(a) to whom section 20(5) of the Act (accommodation of persons over 16 but under 21) applies and who is being accommodated under that section,

(b) in respect of whom an order has been made under section 43 of the Act (child assessment order) and who is kept away from home pursuant to that order[2].

---

1. "Detained" is to be given its literal meaning; a child subject to an order under s 2 of the Mental Health Act 1983 but released on leave is not detained and therefore can be the subject of an application under s 25 of the 1989 Act (*Hereford and Worcester County Council v S* [1993] 1 FCR 653, 1 [1993] 2 FLR 360).

2. Regulation 5(2) does not inhibit the making of a secure accommodation order in the case of a child aged 15 which would extend in duration beyond the child's 16th birthday (*Re G (a child) (secure accommodation order)* [2000] 2 FCR 385, [2000] 2 FLR 259, CA).

Detained and remanded children to whom section 25 of the Act shall have effect subject to modifications

6–3623   **6.** (1) Subject to regulation 5, section 25 of the Act shall have effect subject to the modification specified in paragraph (2) in relation to children who are being looked after by a local authority and are of the following descriptions—

(a) children detained under section 38(6) of the Police and Criminal Evidence Act 1984 (detained children), and

(b) children remanded to local authority accommodation under section 23 of the Children and Young Persons Act 1969 (remand to local authority accommodation) but only if—

(i) the child is charged with or has been convicted of a violent or sexual offence, or of an offence punishable in the case of an adult with imprisonment for a term of 14 years or more, or

(ii) the child has a recent history of absconding while remanded to local authority accommodation, and is charged with or has been convicted of an imprisonable offence alleged or found to have been committed while he was so remanded.

(2) The modification referred to in paragraph (1) is that, for the words "unless it appears" to the end of subsection (1), there shall be substituted the following words—

"unless it appears that any accommodation other than that provided for the purpose of restricting liberty is inappropriate because—

(a) the child is likely to abscond from such other accommodation, or

(b) the child is likely to injure himself or other people if he is kept in any such other accommodation".

Children to whom section 25 of the Act shall apply and have effect subject to modifications

6–3624   **7.** (1) Subject to regulation 5 and paragraphs (2) and (3) of this regulation section 25 of the Act shall apply (in addition to children looked after by a local authority)—

(a) to children, other than those looked after by a local authority, who are accommodated by health authorities, Primary Care Trusts, National Health Service trusts established under section 5 of the National Health Service and Community Care Act 1990, and NHS foundation trust or local education authorities, and (*b*)   to children, other than those looked after by a local authority, who are accommodated in care homes or independent hospitals.

(2)   In relation to the children of a description specified in paragraph (1)(*a*) section 25 of the Act shall have effect subject to the following modifications—

(*a*)   for the words "who is being looked after by a local authority" in subsection (1) there shall be substituted the words "who is being provided with accommodation by a health authority, a Primary Care Trust, a National Health Service trust established under section 5 of the National Health Service and Community Care Act 1990, and NHS foundation trust or a local education authority".

(*b*)   for the words "local authorities" in subsection (2)(*c*) there shall be substituted the words "health authorities, Primary Care Trusts, National Health Service trusts, and NHS foundation trust or local education authorities".

(3)   In relation to the children of a description specified in paragraph (1)(*b*), section 25 of the Act shall have effect subject to the following modifications—

(*a*)   for the words "who is being looked after by a local authority" in subsection (1) there shall be substituted the words "who is being provided with accommodation in a care home or independent hospital"; and

(*b*)   for the words "local authorities" in subsection (2)(*c*) there shall be substituted the words "care homes or independent hospitals".

Applications to court

6–3625   **8.** Subject to section 101 of the Local Government Act 1972 or to provisions in or under sections 14 to 20 of the Local Government Act 2000, applications to a court under section 25 of the Act in respect of a child shall be made only by the local authority which are looking after that child.

Duty to give information of placement in children's homes

6–3626   **9.** Where a child is placed in secure accommodation in a children's home which is managed by a person, organization or authority other than the local authority which is looking after him, the person who, or the organization or the authority which manages that accommodation shall inform the authority which are looking after him that he has been placed there, within 12 hours of his being placed there, with a view to obtaining their authority to continue to keep him there if necessary.

Maximum period in secure accommodation without court authority

6–3627   **10.** (1) Subject to paragraphs (2) and (3), the maximum period beyond which a child to whom section 25 of the Act applies may not be kept in secure accommodation without the authority of a court is an aggregate of 72 hours (whether or not consecutive) in any period of 28 consecutive days.

(2)   Where authority of a court to keep a child in secure accommodation has been given, any period during which the child has been kept in such accommodation before the giving of that authority shall be disregarded for the purposes of calculating the maximum period in relation to any subsequent occasion on which the child is placed in such accommodation after the period authorised by court has expired.

(3)   Where a child is in secure accommodation at any time between 12 midday on the day before and 12 midday on the day after a public holiday or a Sunday, and

(*a*)   during that period the maximum period specified in paragraph (1) expires, and

(*b*)   the child had, in the 27 days before the day on which he was placed in secure accommodation, been placed and kept in such accommodation for an aggregate of more than 48 hours,

the maximum period does not expire until 12 midday on the first day, which is not itself a public holiday or a Sunday, after the public holiday or Sunday.

Maximum initial period of authorisation by a court

6–3628   **11.** Subject to regulations 12 and 13 the maximum period for which a court may authorise a child to whom section 25 of the Act applies to be kept in secure accommodation is three months.

Further periods of authorisation by a court

6–3629   **12.** Subject to regulation 13 a court may from time to time authorise a child to whom section 25 of the Act applies to be kept in secure accommodation for a further period not exceeding 6 months at any one time.

Maximum periods of authorisation by court for remanded children

6–3630   **13.** (1) The maximum period for which a court may from time to time authorise a child who has been remanded to local authority accommodation under section 23 of the Children and

Young Persons Act 1969 to be kept in secure accommodation (whether the period is an initial period or a further period) is the period of the remand.

(2) Any period of authorisation in respect of such a child shall not exceed 28 days on any one occasion without further court authorisation.

Duty to inform parents and others in relation to children in secure accommodation in a children's home

6–3631   **14.** Where a child to whom section 25 of the Act applies is kept in secure accommodation in a children's home and it is intended that an application will be made to a court to keep the child in that accommodation, the local authority which are looking after the child shall if practicable inform of that intention as soon as possible—

    (a)   his parent,
    (b)   any person who is not a parent of his but who has parental responsibility for him,
    (c)   the child's independent visitor, if one has been appointed, and
    (d)   any other person who that local authority consider should be informed.

Appointment of persons to review placement in secure accommodation in a children's home

6–3632   **15.** Each local authority looking after a child in secure accommodation in a children's home shall appoint at least three persons, at least one of whom is neither a member nor an officer of the local authority by or on behalf of which the child is being looked after, who shall review the keeping of the child in such accommodation for the purposes of securing his welfare within one month of the inception of the placement and then at intervals not exceeding three months where the child continues to be kept in such accommodation.

Review of placement in secure accommodation in a children's home

6–3633   **16.** (1) The persons appointed under regulation 15 to review the keeping of a child in secure accommodation shall satisfy themselves as to whether or not—

    (a)   the criteria for keeping the child in secure accommodation continue to apply;
    (b)   the placement in such accommodation in a children's home continues to be necessary; and
    (c)   any other description of accommodation would be appropriate for him,

and in doing so shall have regard to the welfare of the child whose case is being reviewed.

(2) In undertaking the review referred to in regulation 15 the persons appointed shall, if practicable, ascertain and take into account the wishes and feelings of—

    (a)   the child,
    (b)   any parent of his,
    (c)   any person not being a parent of his but who has parental responsibility for him,
    (d)   any other person who has had the care of the child, whose views the persons appointed consider should be taken into account,
    (e)   the child's independent visitor if one has been appointed, and
    (f)   the person, organization or local authority managing the secure accommodation in which the child is placed if that accommodation is not managed by the authority which is looking after that child.

(3) The local authority shall, if practicable, inform all those whose views are required to be taken into account under paragraph (2) of the outcome of the review what action, if any, the local authority propose to take in relation to the child in the light of the review, and their reasons for taking or not taking such action.

6–3634   **17.** (*Records to be kept*).

6–3635   **18.** *Revoked.*

6–3636   **19.** (*Revocation*).

Children (Secure Accommodation) (No 2) Regulations 1991[1]
(SI 1991/2034 amended by SI 2000/694, SI 2002/546 and SI 2004/696)

6–3637   **1.** *Citation and commencement.*

---

1. Made by the Secretary of State for Health, in exercise of the powers conferred by s 25(2)(c) of the Children Act 1989.

Applications to court—special cases

6–3638   **2.** (1) Applications to a court under section 25 of the Children Act 1989 in respect of a child provided with accommodation by a health authority, a Primary Care Trust, a National Health

Service trust established under section 5 of the National Health Service and Community Care Act 1990, and NHS foundation trust or a local education authority shall, unless the child is looked after by a local authority, be made only by the health authority, Primary Care Trust, National Health Service trust, and NHS foundation trust or local education authority providing accommodation for the child.

(2) Applications to a court under section 25 of the Children Act 1989 in respect of a child provided with accommodation in a care home or independent hospital shall, unless the child is looked after by a local authority, be made only by the person carrying on the home in which accommodation is provided for the child.

Children (Admissibility of Hearsay Evidence) Order 1993[1]
(SI 1993/621)

6–3653 **1.** *Citation and Commencement.*

6–3654 **2.** *Admissibility of hearsay evidence.* In—

(*a*) civil proceedings before the High Court or a county court; and
(*b*)

    (i) family proceedings, and
    (ii) civil proceedings under the Child Support Act 1991 in a magistrates' court,

evidence given in connection with the upbringing, maintenance or welfare of a child shall be admissible notwithstanding any rule of law relating to hearsay.

6–3655 **3.** *Revocation.*

---

1. Made by the Lord Chancellor, in exercise of the powers conferred on him by s 96(3) of the Children Act 1989.

Family Proceedings Courts

Family Proceedings Courts (Children Act 1989) Rules 1991[1]
(SI 1991/1395 amended by SI 1991/1991, SI 1992/2068, SI 1993/627, SI 1994/809, 2166, 3156, SI 1997/1895, SI 2001/615, 818, SI 2003/2840, SI 2004/3376 and SI 2005/229, 413, 585, 1977 and 2930)

PART I
INTRODUCTORY

Citation, commencement and interpretation

6–4252 **1.** (1) These Rules may be cited as the Family Proceedings Courts (Children Act 1989) Rules 1991 and shall come into force on 14th October 1991.

(2) Unless a contrary intention appears—
a section or schedule referred to means the section or schedule in the Act of 1989,

"application" means an application made under or by virtue of the Act of 1989 or under these Rules, and "applicant" shall be construed accordingly,
"business day" means any day other than—

(*a*) a Saturday, Sunday, Christmas Day or Good Friday; or
(*b*) a bank holiday, that is to say, a day which is, or is to be observed as, a bank holiday, or a holiday, under the Banking and Financial Dealings Act 1971, in England and Wales,
"child"

(*a*) means, in relation to any relevant proceedings, subject to sub-paragraph (*b*), a person under the age of 18 with respect to whom the proceedings are brought, and
(*b*) where paragraph 16(1) of Schedule 1 applies[2]; also includes a person who has reached the age of 18;

"children and family reporter" means an officer of the service or a Welsh family proceedings officer who has been asked to prepare a welfare report under section 7(1)(*a*),
"children's guardian"—

(*a*) means an officer of the service or a Welsh family proceedings officer appointed under section 41 for the child with respect to whom the proceedings are brought; but
(*b*) does not include such an officer appointed in relation to proceedings specified by rule 21A,
"contribution order" has the meaning assigned to it by paragraph 23(2) of Schedule 2,

"the Council Regulation" means Council Regulation (EC) 2201/2003 of 27 November 2003 concerning jurisdiction and the recognition and enforcement of judgments in matrimonial matters and the matters of parental responsibility,

"court" means a family proceedings court constituted in accordance with sections 66 and 67 of the Magistrates' Courts Act 1980 or, in respect of those proceedings prescribed in rule 2(5), a single justice who is a member of a family panel,

"directions appointment" means a hearing for directions under rule 14(2),

"emergency protection order" means an order under section 44,

"file" means deposit with the justices' chief executive,

"form" means a form in Schedule 1[3] to these Rules with such variation as the circumstances of the particular case may require,

"justices' chief executive" means a justices' chief executive appointed under section 40 of the Justices of the Peace Act 1997;

"leave" includes approval,

"Member State" means—

    (a) those parties contracting to the Council Regulation, that is to say, Belgium, Cyprus, Czech Republic, Germany, Greece, Spain, Estonia, France, Hungary, Ireland, Italy, Latvia, Lithuania, Luxembourg, Malta, Netherlands, Austria, Poland, Portugal, Slovakia, Slovenia, Finland, Sweden and the United Kingdom.

    (b) a party which has subsequently adopted the Council Regulation,

"note" includes a record made by mechanical means,

"officer of the service" has the same meaning as in the Criminal Justice and Court Services Act 2000,

"parental responsibility" has the meaning assigned to it by section 3,

"parties" in relation to any relevant proceedings means the respondents specified for those proceedings in the third column of Schedule 2 to these Rules, and the applicant,

"recovery order" means an order under section 50,

"relevant proceedings" has the meaning assigned to it by section 93(3),

"section 8 order" has the meaning assigned to it by section 8(2),

"special guardianship order" has the meaning assigned to it by section 14A,

"specified proceedings" has the meaning assigned to it by section 41(6) and rule 2(2),

"the 1981 rules" means the Magistrates' Courts Rules 1981,

"the Act of 1989" means the Children Act 1989,

"welfare officer" means a person who has been asked to prepare a welfare report under section 7(1)(b),

"Welsh family proceedings officer" has the same meaning as in the Children Act 2004.

---

1. Made by the Lord Chancellor, in exercise of the powers conferred on him by s 144 of the Magistrates' Courts Act 1980.

2. The paragraph provides an extended definition in connection with applications for financial provision.

3. The Forms contained in Sch 1 to these Rules are printed in PART IX: PRECEDENTS AND FORMS, post.

Matters prescribed for the purposes of the Act of 1989

6–4253 **2.** (1) The parties to proceedings in which directions are given under section 38(6)[1], and any person named in such a direction, form the prescribed class for the purposes of section 38(8)(b) (application to vary directions made with interim care or interim supervision order).

(2) The following proceedings are specified for the purposes of section 41[2] in accordance with subsection (6)(i) thereof—

    (a) proceedings (in a family proceedings court) under section 25[3];
    (b) applications under section 33(7)[4];
    (c) proceedings under paragraph 19(1) of Schedule 2[5];
    (d) applications under paragraph 6(3) of Schedule 3[6].

(3) The applicant for an order that has been made under section 43(1)[7] and the persons referred to in section 43(11)[8] may, in any circumstances, apply under section 43(12) for a child assessment order to be varied or discharged.

(4) The following persons form the prescribed class for the purposes of section 44(9)(b) (application to vary directions[9])—

    (a) the parties to the application for the order in respect of which it is sought to vary the directions;
    (b) the children's guardian;
    (c) the local authority in whose area the child concerned is ordinarily resident;
    (d) any person who is named in the directions.

(5) The following proceedings are prescribed for the purposes of section 93(2)(i) as being proceedings with respect to which a single justice may discharge the functions of a family proceedings court, that is to say, proceedings—

    (a) where an ex parte application is made, under sections 10[10], 44(1)[11], 48(9)[12], 50(1)[13], 75(1)[14] or 102(1)[15],
    (b) subject to rule 28[16], under sections 11(3)[17] or 38(1)[18],

(c) under sections 4(3)(b)[19], 4A(3)(b), 7[20], 14[21], 34(3)(b)[22], 37[24], 41[25], 44(9)(b)[26] and (11)(b)(iii)[27], 48(4)[28], 91(15)[29] or (17)[30], or paragraph 11(4) of Schedule 14[31],

(d) in accordance with any Order made by the Lord Chancellor under Part I of Schedule 11[32], and

(e) in accordance with rules 3 to 8, 10 to 19, 21, 22, or 27.

---

1. The reference is to directions for medical or psychiatric examination or other assessment when an interim care or interim supervision order is made.

2. Such proceedings require the court to appoint a children's guardian unless it is satisfied that it is unnecessary to do so in order to safeguard the interests of the child.

3. An application to use secure accommodation.

4. An application to cause a child in care to be known by a new surname or to be removed from the jurisdiction.

5. A local authority application for the court to approve arrangements for a child in care to live outside England and Wales.

6. An application to extend the duration of a supervision order.

7. A child assessment order.

8. The full list is (a) the child's parents, (b) any person who is not a parent of the child but who has parental responsibility, (c) any other person caring for the child, (d) any person in whose favour a contact order is in force with respect to the child, (e) any person who is allowed to have contact with the child by virtue of an order under s 34, and (f) the child.

9. That is directions made on an emergency protection order in relation to contact or medical or psychiatric examination or other assessment.

10. Powers in relation to s 8 orders.

11. An emergency protection order.

12. A warrant to assist in discovery of child in need of emergency protection.

13. A recovery order.

14. Emergency orders in respect of registered child minders and those providing day care for young children.

15. Warrant to search for child or assist in inspection of premises.

16. See post, the qualification is essentially that an order be in the same terms as a previous order and be made on written request.

17. A s 8 order made otherwise than on disposal of the proceedings.

18. An interim care or interim supervision order.

19. Leave to allow a child to apply for termination of a parental responsibility order or agreement.

20. Arrangements for welfare reports.

21. The enforcement of a residence order.

22. Leave to apply for contact with a child in care.

24. Power to direct local authority investigation in family proceedings.

25. The appointment of a children's guardian.

26. Variation of directions made on an emergency protection order in relation to contact or medical or psychiatric examination or other assessment.

27. This refers to the courts agreement to arrangements for the return of a child removed under an emergency protection order who cannot be returned to a parent or someone with parental responsibility.

28. This provision allows a court making an emergency protection order and ordering the search of premises for that child to further authorise a search for any other child on premises who ought to be made the subject of an emergency protection order.

29. Leave to make a repeat application, within six months of a previous application, for: (a) the discharge of a supervision order; or (b) the discharge of a care order; or (c) the discharge of an education supervision order; or (d) for a child assessment order; or (e) for the substitution of a supervision order for a care order.

30. Leave to make a repeat application for contact with a child in care under s 34.

31. Leave for a child to apply to discharge an existing order under the transitional provisions.

32. See the Children (Allocation of Proceedings) Order 1991, post.

PART II

GENERAL

Application for leave to commence proceedings

6–4254 **3.**—(1) Where the leave of the court is required to bring any relevant proceedings, the person seeking leave shall file—

(a) a written[1] request for leave in Form C2 setting out the reasons for the application; and

(b) a draft of the application (being the documents referred to in rule 4(1A)) for the making of which leave is sought together with sufficient copies for one to be served on each respondent.

(2) On considering a request for leave[2] filed under paragraph (1), the court shall—

(a) grant the request, whereupon the justices' chief executive shall inform the person making the request and any local authority that is preparing, or has prepared, a report under section 14A(8) or (9) of the decision, or

(b) direct that a date be fixed for a hearing of the request, whereupon the justices' chief executive shall fix such a date and give such notice as the court directs to the person making the request and any local authority that is preparing, or has prepared, a report under section 14A(8) or (9) and to such other persons as the court requires to be notified, of the date so fixed.

(3) Where leave is granted to bring any relevant proceedings, the application shall proceed in accordance with rule 4; but paragraph (1)(a) of that rule shall not apply.

1. Failure to make written application in an emergency situation will not automatically invalidate a subsequent order and a hearing without written application may be justified (*Re O (residence order) (application for leave)* [1993] 2 FCR 482, [1994] 1 FLR 172).

2. The request for leave must be considered judicially, and, if for leave to make an application under s 8 of the Children Act 1989, must be considered having regard to s 10(9), Children Act 1989, ante. Normally, save in cases of urgency, or where there are other circumstances which make it right to grant either without giving the other parties an opportunity to adduce evidence or make representations, the court will decline the request for leave and direct an *inter partes* hearing of the request; see *Re M (prohibited steps order: application for leave)* [1993] 1 FCR 78, [1993] 1 FLR 275. Where contentious views are put before the court in writing, the court will normally require oral evidence to be given normally limited to the parties themselves to the extent that the court considers appropriate (*Re R (minors) (application for contact: evidence)* [1995] 1 FCR 565).

Application

6–4255 **4.** (1) Subject to paragraph (4), an applicant shall—

(*a*) file the documents referred to in paragraph (1A) below (which documents shall together be called the "application") together with sufficient copies for one to be served on each respondent, and

(*b*) serve a copy of the application, together with Form C6 and such (if any) of Forms C1A, C7 and C10A as are given to him by the justices' chief executive under paragraph 2(*b*), on each respondent such minimum number of days prior to the date fixed under paragraph (2)(*a*) as is specified in relation to that application in column (ii) of Schedule 2 to these Rules.

(1A) The documents to be filed under paragraph (1)(*a*) above are—

(*a*)

    (i)   whichever is appropriate of Forms C1, C2, C3, C4, C5 or C51, and

    (ii) such of the supplemental Forms C10 or C11 to C20 as may be appropriate, and

    (iii) in the case of an application for a section 8 order or an order under section 4(1)(*c*) where question 7 on Form C1, or question 4 on Form C2, is answered in the affirmative, supplemental Form C1A,

(*b*) where there is no appropriate form a statement in writing of the order sought,

and where the application is made in respect of more than one child, all the children shall be included in one application.

(2) On receipt by the justices' chief executive of the documents filed under paragraph (1)(*a*)—

(*a*) the justices' clerk shall fix the date, time and place for a hearing or a directions appointment, allowing sufficient time for the applicant to comply with paragraph (1)(*b*), and

(*b*) the justices' chief executive shall—

    (i)   endorse the date, time and place so fixed upon Form C6, and where appropriate, Form C6A, and

    (ii) return forthwith to the applicant the copies of the application and Form C10A if filed with it, together with Form C6, and such of Forms C6A and C7 as are appropriate, and, in the case of an application for a section 8 order or an order under section 4(1)(*c*), Form C1A.

(3) The applicant shall[1], at the same time as complying with paragraph (1)(*b*), serve Form C6A on the persons set out in relation to the relevant class of proceedings in column (iv) of Schedule 2 to these Rules.

(4) An application for—

(*a*) a section 8 order,

(*b*) an emergency protection order,

(*c*) a warrant under section 48(9)[2],

(*d*) a recovery order, or

(*e*) a warrant under section 102(1)[3],

may, with leave of the justices' clerk, be made ex parte[4] in which case the applicant shall—

    (i)   file with the justices' chief executive or the court the application in the appropriate form in Schedule 1 to these Rules at the time when the application is made or as directed by the justices' clerk, and

    (ii) in the case of an application for a prohibited steps order, or a specific issue order, under section 8 or an emergency protection order, and also in the case of an application for an order under section 75(1)[5] where the application is ex parte, serve a copy of the application on each respondent within 48 hours after the making of the order.

(5) Where the court refuses to make an order on an ex parte application it may direct that the application be made inter partes.

(6) In the case of proceedings under Schedule 1, the application under paragraph (1) shall be accompanied by a statement in Form C10A setting out the financial details which the applicant believes to be relevant to the application, together with sufficient copies for one to be served on each respondent

---

1. For the discretion to dispense with service, see r 8, post.
2. A warrant to assist in discovery of child in need of emergency protection.

3. Warrant to search for child or assist in inspection of premises.

4. *Ex parte* applications should rarely be made, and should rarely be granted, except in the most compelling of circumstances. Where the circumstances justify the making of an order *ex parte*, the order should provide for an early return date before the court, not a date two months ahead; see *M v C (children orders: reasons)* [1993] 1 FCR 264.

An ex parte interim residence order should only be made in exceptional circumstances where it is necessary for the protection of the child, for example in a "snatch"—child abduction (*Re G (minors) (ex p interim residence order)* [1993] 1 FLR 910), or when a child has to be protected from physical or moral danger by some immediate step taken by the court (*Re P (a minor) (ex p interim residence order)* [1993] 1 FLR 915).

5. Emergency orders in respect of registered child minders and those providing day care for young children.

Withdrawal of application

6–4256 **5.** (1) An application may be withdrawn only with leave[1] of the court.

(2) Subject to paragraph (3), a person seeking leave to withdraw an application shall file and serve on the parties a written request for leave setting out the reasons for the request.

(3) The request under paragraph (2) may be made orally to the court if the parties and, if appointed, the children's guardian or the welfare officer or children and family reporter are present[2].

(4) Upon receipt of a written request under paragraph (2), the court shall—

(a) if—

(i) the parties consent in writing,
(ii) any children's guardian has had an opportunity to make representations, and
(iii) the court thinks fit,

grant the request; in which case the justices' chief executive shall notify the parties, any local authority that is preparing, or has prepared, a report under section 14A(8) or (9), the children's guardian and the welfare officer or children and family reporter of the granting of the request; or

(b) the justices' chief executive shall fix a date for the hearing of the request and give at least 7 days' notice to the parties, any local authority that is preparing, or has prepared, a report under section 14A(8) or (9), the children's guardian and the welfare officer or children and family reporter of the date fixed.

---

1. In determining an application for leave, the welfare of the child is paramount and the checklist will be applied (*Re N (leave to withdraw care proceedings)* [2000] 1 FCR 258, [2000] 1 FLR 134, FD).

2. If the request to withdraw is made orally, the children's guardian must be present; it is not sufficient for the children's guardian to be represented (*Re F (a minor) (care proceedings: withdrawal)* [1993] 1 FCR 389, [1993] 2 FLR 9).

Transfer of proceedings

6–4257 **6.** (1) Where, in any relevant proceedings, the justices' chief executive or the court receives a request in writing from a party that the proceedings be transferred to another family proceedings court or to a county court, the justices' chief executive or court shall issue an order or certificate in the appropriate form in Schedule 1 to these Rules, granting or refusing the request in accordance with any Order[1] made by the Lord Chancellor under Part I of Schedule 11.

(2) Where a request is granted under paragraph (1), the justices' chief executive shall send a copy of the order—

(a) to the parties,
(aa) to any local authority that is preparing, or has prepared, a report under section 14A(8) or (9),
(b) to any children's guardian, and
(c) to the family proceedings court or to the county court to which the proceedings are to be transferred.

(3) Any consent given or refused by a justices' clerk in accordance with any Order[2] made by the Lord Chancellor under Part I of Schedule 11 shall be recorded in writing by the justices' clerk at the time it is given or refused or as soon as practicable thereafter.

(4) Where a request to transfer proceedings to a county court is refused under paragraph (1), the person who made the request may apply in accordance with rule 4.6 of the Family Proceedings Rules 1991 for an order under any Order[2] made by the Lord Chancellor under Part I of Schedule 11.

---

1. See the Children (Allocation of Proceedings) Order, post.

Parties

6–4258 **7.** (1) The respondents to relevant proceedings shall be those persons set out in the relevant entry in column (iii) of Schedule 2 to these Rules.

(2) In any relevant proceedings a person may file a request in Form C2 that he or another person—

(a) be joined as a party, or
(b) cease to be a party.

(3) On considering[1] a request under paragraph (2) the court shall, subject to paragraph (4)—

(*a*) grant it without a hearing or representations, save that this shall be done only in the case of a request under paragraph (2)(*a*), whereupon the justices' chief executive shall inform the parties and any local authority that is preparing, or has prepared, a report under section 14A(8) or (9) and the person making the request of that decision, or

(*b*) order that a date be fixed for the consideration of the request, whereupon the justices' chief executive shall give notice of the date so fixed, together with a copy of the request—

(i) in the case of a request under paragraph (2)(*a*), to the applicant and any local authority that is preparing, or has prepared, a report under section 14A(8) or (9), and

(ii) in the case of a request under paragraph (2)(*b*), to the parties and any local authority that is preparing, or has prepared, a report under section 14A(8) or (9), or

(*c*) invite the parties or any of them to make written representations, within a specified period, as to whether the request should be granted; and upon the expiry of the period the court shall act in accordance with sub-paragraph (*a*) or (*b*).

(4) Where a person with parental responsibility requests that he be joined under paragraph (2)(*a*), the court shall grant his request.

(5) In any relevant proceedings the court may direct—

(*a*) that a person who would not otherwise be a respondent under these Rules be joined as a party to the proceedings, or

(*b*) that a party to the proceedings cease to be a party[2].

---

1. Grandparents and others should not generally intervene in proceedings unless they have a separate point of view to put forward (*Re M (sexual abuse: evidence)* 1 FCR 253). Whilst the rule gives no guidance as to the criteria to be applied if the purpose of the leave is to seek an order under s 8 of the Act, the criteria in s 10(9) should be considered as should the applicant's prospect of success in a substantive application (*G v Kirklees Metropolitan Borough Council* [1993] 1 FCR 357, [1993] 1 FLR 805). The position of a person, such as a father, who may make an application in private law proceedings as of right or receive notice of care proceedings, is different. Whereas any other type of person has to show some justifiable reason why that person should be joined as a party, in the case of a father the onus is the other way round. The approach is that if a party wishes to participate in care proceedings, he should be permitted to do so unless there is some justifiable reason for not joining him as a party. It does not depend on his having an "arguable case" (*Re K (care proceedings: joinder of father)* [1999] 2 FCR 391, FD). The child has a need to obtain a resolution of proceedings so that where a father without parental responsibility made a very late application to be joined as a party the effect of which would be to disrupt and delay proceedings which had already been listed for trial, the court's denial of the father's application was proportionate to a legitimate aim and did not infringe his human rights (*Re P (care proceedings: father's application)* [2001] 1 FLR 781, FD. The grant of leave is a substantial judicial decision and notice of an application for leave should generally be given to all parties likely to be affected if leave is given. In almost all cases it is appropriate for the respondent along with the applicant to be invited to attend the hearing. Justices should record their reasons for deciding to proceed in the absence of the respondent and for granting leave: *Re W (a child) (contact: leave to apply)* [2000] 1 FCR 185, [2000] 1 FLR 263, FD. The criteria in s 10(9) of the Children Act 1989 apply also to applications to be joined as a party in care proceedings; the criteria are not exclusive and may include whether an applicant had any separate point to put forward and the test is the same where an applicant seeks party status without making or intending to make any application for a specific order: *In re W (a Child) (Care proceedings: Leave to apply)* (2004) Times 22 November, FD.

2. In such an application the welfare of the child is important but is not the paramount consideration. The court will not lightly accede to an application to prevent a natural parent from being a party to care proceedings or proceedings relating to a care order (*Re W (discharge of party to proceedings)* [1997] 2 FCR 190, [1997] 1 FLR 128).

Service

6–4259   8. (1) Where service of a document is required by these Rules (and not by a provision to which section 105(8) (service of notice or other document under the Act) applies) it may be effected—

(*a*) if the person to be served is not known by the person serving to be acting by solicitor—

(i) by delivering it to him personally, or

(ii) by delivering it at, or by sending it by first-class post to, his residence or his last known residence, or

(*b*) if the person to be served is known by the person serving to be acting by solicitor—

(i) by delivering the document at, or sending it by first-class post to, the solicitor's address for service,

(ii) where the solicitor's address for service includes a numbered box at a document exchange, by leaving the document at that document exchange or at a document exchange which transmits documents on every business day to that document exchange, or

(iii) by sending a legible copy of the document by facsimile transmission to the solicitor's office.

(2) In this rule, "first-class post" means first-class post which has been pre-paid or in respect of which pre-payment is not required.

(3) Where a child who is a party to any relevant proceedings is required by these Rules to serve a document, service shall be effected by—

(a) the solicitor acting for the child,
(b) where there is no such solicitor, the children's guardian, or
(c) where there is neither such a solicitor nor a children guardian, the justices' chief executive.

(4) Service of any document on a child shall, subject to any direction of the justices' chief executive or the court, be effected by service on—

(a) the solicitor acting for the child,
(b) where there is no such solicitor, the children's guardian, or
(c) where there is neither such a solicitor nor a children's guardian, with leave of the justices' clerk or the court, the child.

(5) Where the justices' clerk or the court refuses leave under paragraph (4)(c), a direction shall be given under paragraph (8).

(6) A document shall, unless the contrary is proved, be deemed to have been served—

(a) in the case of service by first-class post, on the second business day after posting, and
(b) in the case of service in accordance with paragraph (1)(b)(ii), on the second business day after the day on which it is left at the document exchange.

(7) At or before the first directions appointment in, or hearing of, relevant proceedings, whichever occurs first, the applicant shall file a statement in Form C9 that service of—

(a) a copy of the application and other documents referred to in rule 4(1)(b) has been effected on each respondent, and
(b) notice of the proceedings has been effected under rule 4(3);

and the statement shall indicate—

(i)   the manner, date, time and place of service, or
(ii) where service was effected by post, the date, time and place of posting.

(8) In any relevant proceedings, where these rules require a document to be served, the court or the justices' clerk may, without prejudice to any power under rule 14, direct that—

(a) the requirement shall not apply[1];
(b) the time specified by the rules for complying with the requirement shall be abridged to such extent as may be specified in the direction;
(c) a service shall be effected in such manner as may be specified in the direction.

---

1. The court has a general discretion to direct that the rule requiring service of notice of the proceedings be disapplied. Accordingly in determining whether service of notice of care proceedings shall be effected on a putative father, although the welfare of the child is not the paramount consideration, the court is entitled to consider the effect on the child's family and the long term well-being of the child (*Re X (care: notice of proceeding)* [1996] 3 FCR 91, [1996] 1 FLR 186).

Acknowledgement of application

6–4260   9. Within 14 days of service of an application for an order under section 4(1)(c), an application for a section 8 order, a special guardianship order or an application under Schedule 1, each respondent shall file and serve on the parties an acknowledgment of the application in Form C7 and, if both parts of question 6 or question 7 (or both) on Form C7 are answered in the affirmative, Form C1A.

Appointment of children's guardian

6–4261   10. (1) As soon as practicable after the commencement of specified proceedings or the transfer of such proceedings to the court, the justices' clerk or the court shall appoint a children's guardian unless—

(a) such an appointment has already been made by the court which made the transfer and is subsisting, or
(b) the justices' clerk or the court considers that such an appointment is not necessary to safeguard the interests of the child.

(2) At any stage in specified proceedings a party may apply, without notice to the other parties unless the justices' clerk or the court otherwise directs, for the appointment of a children's guardian.

(3) The justices' clerk or the court shall grant an application under paragraph (2) unless it is considered that such an appointment is not necessary to safeguard the interests of the child, in which case reasons shall be given; and a note of such reasons shall be taken by the justices' clerk.

(4) At any stage in specified proceedings the justices' clerk or the court may appoint a children's guardian even though no application is made for such an appointment.

(4A) The justices' chief executive or the court may, in specified proceedings, appoint more than one children's guardian in respect of the same child.

(5) The justices' chief executive shall, as soon as practicable, notify the parties and any welfare officer or children and family reporter of an appointment under this rule or, as the case may be, of a decision not to make such an appointment.

(6) Upon the appointment of a children's guardian the justices' chief executive shall, as soon

as practicable, notify him of the appointment and serve on him copies of the application and of documents filed under rule 17(1).

(7) A children's guardian appointed by the justices' chief executive or by the court under this rule shall not—

(a) be a member, officer or servant of a local authority which, or an authorised person (within the meaning of section 31(9)) who, is a party to the proceedings;

(b) be, or have been, a member, officer or servant of a local authority or voluntary organisation (within the meaning of section 105(1)) who has been directly concerned in that capacity in arrangements relating to the care, accommodation or welfare of the child during the five years prior to the commencement of the proceedings; or

(c) be a serving probation officer who has, in that capacity, been previously concerned with the child or his family.

(8) When appointing a children's guardian, the justices' clerk or the court shall consider[1] the appointment of anyone who has previously acted as children's guardian of the same child.

(9) The appointment of a children's guardian under this rule shall continue for such time as is specified in the appointment or until terminated by the court.

(10) When terminating[2] an appointment in accordance with paragraph (9), the court shall give reasons in writing for so doing, a note of which shall be taken by the justices' clerk.

(11) Where the justices' clerk or the court appoints a children's guardian in accordance with this rule or refuses to make such an appointment, the justices' clerk shall record the appointment or refusal in the appropriate form in Schedule 1 to these Rules.

---

1. However this principle is subject to the prohibition contained in r 10(7) (*Devon County Council v S and L* [1993] 2 FCR 36, [1993] 1 FLR 842).

2. For procedure in respect of termination of appointment in consequence of the receipt of a complaint, see *Re M (terminating appointment of guardian ad litem)* [1999] 2 FCR 625, [1999] 2 FLR 717, FD.

Powers and duties of officers of the service and Welsh family proceedings officers

6–4262   11. (1) In carrying out his duty under section 7(1)(a) or section 41(2)[1], the officer of the service or the Welsh family proceedings officer shall have regard to the principle set out in section 1(2) and the matters set out in section 1(3)(a) to (f) as if for the word "court" in that section there were substituted the words "officer of the service or Welsh family proceedings officer".

(2) The officer of the service or the Welsh family proceedings officer shall make such investigations as may be necessary for him to carry out his duties and shall, in particular—

(a) contact or seek to interview such persons as he thinks appropriate or as the court directs;

(b) obtain such professional assistance as is available to him which he thinks appropriate or which the justices' clerk or the court directs him to obtain.

(3) In addition to his duties, under other paragraphs of this rule, or rules 11A or 11B, the officer of the service or the Welsh family proceedings officer shall provide to the justices' chief executive, the justices' clerk and the court such other assistance as he or it may require.

(4) A party may question the officer of the service or the Welsh family proceedings officer about oral or written advice tendered by him to the justices' chief executive, the justices' clerk or the court.

---

1. This refers to the officer of the service's duty to safeguard the interests of the child in the manner prescribed by the rules.

Additional powers and duties of children's guardian

6–4262A   11A. (1) The children's guardian shall—

(a) appoint a solicitor to represent the child unless such a solicitor has already been appointed; and

(b) give such advice to the child as is appropriate having regard to his understanding and, subject to rule 12(1)(a), instruct the solicitor representing the child on all matters relevant to the interests of the child including possibilities for appeal, arising in the course of proceedings.

(2) Where it appears to the children's guardian that the child—

(a) is instructing his solicitor direct; or

(b) intends to conduct and is capable of conducting the proceedings on his own behalf,

he shall inform the court through the justices' chief executive and from then he—

(i) shall perform all of his duties set out in rule 11 and this rule, other than those duties under paragraph (1)(a) of this rule, and such other duties as the justices' clerk or the court may direct;

(ii) shall take such part in the proceedings as the justices' clerk or the court may direct; and

(iii) may, with the leave of the justices' clerk or the court, have legal representation in the conduct of those duties.

(3) Unless excused by the justices' clerk or the court, the children's guardian shall attend all

directions appointments in and hearings of the proceedings and shall advise the court on the following matters—

    (a) whether the child is of sufficient understanding for any purpose including the child's refusal to submit to a medical or psychiatric examination or other assessment that the court has the power to require, direct or order;

    (b) the wishes of the child in respect of any matter relevant to the proceedings including his attendance at court;

    (c) the appropriate forum for the proceedings;

    (d) the appropriate timing of the proceedings or any part of them;

    (e) the options available to it in respect of the child and the suitability of each such option including what order should be made in determining the application; and

    (f) any other matter concerning which the justices' chief executive, the justices' clerk or the court seeks his advice or concerning which he considers that the justices' chief executive, the justices' clerk or the court should be informed.

(4) The advice given under paragraph (3) may, subject to any order of the court, be given orally or in writing; and if the advice be given orally, a note of it shall be taken by the justices' clerk or the court.

(5) The children's guardian shall, where practicable, notify any person whose joinder as a party to those proceedings would be likely, in the opinion of the officer of the service or the Welsh family proceedings officer, to safeguard the interests of the child of that person's right to apply to be joined under rule 7(2) and shall inform the justices' chief executive or the court—

    (a) of any such notification given;

    (b) of anyone whom he attempted to notify under this paragraph but was unable to contact; and

    (c) of anyone whom he believes may wish to be joined to the proceedings.

(6) The children's guardian shall, unless the justices' clerk or the court otherwise directs, not less than 14 days before the date fixed for the final hearing of the proceedings—

    (a) file a written report advising on the interests of the child;

    (b) serve a copy of the filed report on the other parties and any local authority that is preparing, or has prepared, a report under section 14A(8) or (9).

(7) The children's guardian shall serve and accept service of documents on behalf of the child in accordance with rule 8(3)(b) and (4)(b) and, where the child has not himself been served, and has sufficient understanding, advise the child of the contents of any document so served.

(8) If the children's guardian inspects records of the kinds referred to in section 42, he shall bring to the attention of—

    (a) the court, through the justices' chief executive; and

    (b) unless the court or the justices' clerk otherwise directs, the other parties to the proceedings,

all records and documents which may, in his opinion, assist in the proper determination of the proceedings.

(9) The children's guardian shall ensure that, in relation to a decision made by the justices' clerk or the court in the proceedings—

    (a) if he considers it appropriate to the age and understanding of the child, the child is notified of that decision; and

    (b) if the child is notified of the decision, it is explained to the child in a manner appropriate to his age and understanding.

Additional powers and duties of a children and family reporter

6–4262B **11B.** (1) In addition to his duties under rule 11, the children and family reporter shall—

    (a) notify the child of such contents of his report (if any) as he considers appropriate to the age and understanding of the child, including any reference to the child's own views on the application and the recommendation of the children and family reporter; and

    (b) if he does notify the child of any contents of his report, explain them to the child in a manner appropriate to his age and understanding.

(2) Where the court has—

    (a) directed that a written report be made by a children and family reporter; and

    (b) notified the children and family reporter that his report is to be considered at a hearing,

the children and family reporter shall—

    (i) file his report; and

    (ii) serve a copy on the other parties, any local authority that is preparing, or has prepared, a report under section 14A(8) or (9) and on the children's guardian (if any),

by such time as the court may direct and if no direction is given, not less than 14 days before that hearing.

(3) The court may direct that the children and family reporter attend any hearing at which his report is to be considered.

(4) The children and family reporter shall advise the court if he considers that the joinder of a person as a party to the proceedings would be likely to safeguard the interests of the child.

(5) The children and family reporter shall consider whether it is in the best interests of the child for the child to be made a party to the proceedings.

(6) If the children and family reporter considers the child should be made a party to the proceedings he shall notify the court of his opinion together with the reasons for that opinion.

Solicitor for child

6–4263 **12.** (1) A solicitor appointed under section 41(3)[1] or in accordance with rule 11A(1)(*a*) shall represent the child—

(*a*) in accordance with instructions received from the children's guardian (unless the solicitor considers, having taken into account the views of the children's guardian and any direction of the court under rule 11(3), that the child wishes to give instructions which conflict with those of the children's guardian and that he is able, having regard to his understanding, to give such instructions on his own behalf in which case he shall conduct the proceedings in accordance with instructions received from the child), or

(*b*) where no children's guardian has been appointed for the child and the condition in section 41(4)(*b*)[2] is satisfied, in accordance with instructions received from the child, or

(*c*) in default of instructions under (*a*) or (*b*), in furtherance of the best interests of the child.

(2) A solicitor appointed under section 41(3)[1] or in accordance with rule 11A(1)(*a*) shall serve and accept service of documents on behalf of the child in accordance with rule 8(3)(*a*) and (4)(*a*) and, where the child has not himself been served and has sufficient understanding, advise the child of the contents of any document so served.

(3) Where the child wishes an appointment of a solicitor under section 41(3)[1] or in accordance with rule 11A(1)(*a*) to be terminated, he may apply to the court for an order terminating the appointment; and the solicitor and the children's guardian shall be given an opportunity to make representations.

(4) Where the children's guardian wishes an appointment of a solicitor under section 41(3)[1] to be terminated, he may apply to the court for an order terminating the appointment; and the solicitor and, if he is of sufficient understanding, the child, shall be given an opportunity to make representations.

(5) When terminating an appointment in accordance with paragraph (3) or (4), the court shall give reasons for so doing, a note of which shall be taken by the justices' clerk.

(6) Where the justices' clerk or the court appoints a solicitor under section 41(3)[1] or refuses to make such an appointment, the justices' clerk shall record the appointment or refusal in the appropriate form in Schedule 1 to these Rules and serve a copy on the parties and, where he is appointed, on the solicitor.

---

1. That is an appointment where a child is not represented and any of the following apply: (*a*) no children's guardian has been appointed; or (*b*) the child has sufficient understanding to instruct a solicitor and wishes to do so; or (*c*) it appears to the court that such representation would be in the child's best interests.
Re S (independent representation [1993] 3 All ER 36, [1993] 2 WLR 801, [1993] 2 FCR 1, [1993] 2 FLR 437, decided under the Family Proceedings Rules 1991, as amended, in respect of High Court proceedings, established that (1) when considering an application by a child to be represented independently of a children's guardian the court could in its discretion hear from any party; and (2) such applications are to be determined on the basis of the sufficiency of the child's understanding of the proceedings, the emotional complexity of the proceedings being a relevant factor. *Re T (a minor) (child: representation)* [1993] 4 All ER 518, [1993] 2 FCR 445, CA, established that a child's right to legal representation in wardship proceedings was the same as in proceedings under the Children Act 1989. A solicitor's view as to whether a child client could give instructions should rarely be disturbed, although the decision was ultimately for the court (*Re T (a minor) (child: representation)* [1993] 4 All ER 518, [1993] 2 FCR 445, CA).
2. That condition is that the child has sufficient understanding to instruct a solicitor and wishes to do so.

Welfare officer

6–4264 **13.** (1) Where the court or a justices' clerk has directed that a written report be made by a welfare officer in accordance with section 7(1)(*b*), the report shall be filed at or by such time as the court or justices' clerk directs or, in the absence of such a direction, at least 14 days before a relevant hearing; and the justices' chief executive shall, as soon as practicable, serve a copy of the report on the parties, any local authority that is preparing, or has prepared, a report under section 14A(8) or (9) and any children's guardian.

(2) In paragraph (1), a hearing is relevant if the justices' chief executive has given the welfare officer notice that his report is to be considered at it.

(3) After the filing of a written report by a welfare officer, the court or the justices' clerk may direct that the welfare officer attend any hearing at which the report is to be considered; and

(*a*) except where such a direction is given at a hearing attended by the welfare officer, the justices' chief executive shall inform the welfare officer of the direction; and

(*b*) at the hearing at which the report is considered any party may question the welfare officer about his report.

(3A) The welfare officer shall consider whether it is in the best interests of the child for the child to be made a party to the proceedings.

(3B) If the welfare officer considers the child should be made a party to the proceedings he shall notify the court of his opinion together with the reasons for that opinion.

(4) This rule is without prejudice to the court's power to give directions under rule 14.

Directions

6–4265 **14.**—(1) In this rule, "party" includes the children's guardian and, where a request or direction concerns a report under—

(a)   section 7, the welfare officer or children and family reporter; or
(b)   section 14A(8) or (9), the local authority preparing that report.

(2) In any relevant proceedings the justices' clerk or the court may, subject to paragraph (5), give, vary or revoke directions for the conduct of the proceedings, including—

(a)   the timetable for the proceedings;
(b)   varying the time within which or by which an act is required, by these Rules, to be done;
(c)   the attendance of the child;
(d)   the appointment of a children's guardian, or of a solicitor under section 41(3);
(e)   the service of documents;
(f)   the submission of evidence including experts' reports[1];
(g)   the preparation of welfare reports under section 7;
(h)   the transfer of the proceedings to another court in accordance with any order made by the Lord Chancellor under Part I of Schedule 11;
(i)   consolidation with other proceedings;
(j)   the preparation of reports under section 14A(8) or (9);
(k)   the attendance of the person who prepared the report under section 14A(8) or (9) at any hearing at which the report is to be considered;

and the justices' clerk shall, on receipt of an application by the justices' chief executive, or where proceedings have been transferred to his court, consider whether such directions need to be given.

(3) Where the justices' clerk or a single justice who is holding a directions appointment considers, for whatever reason, that it is inappropriate to give a direction on a particular matter, he shall refer the matter to the court which may give any appropriate direction.

(4) Where a direction is given under paragraph (2)(h), an order shall be issued in the appropriate form in Schedule 1 to these Rules and the justices' chief executive shall follow the procedure set out in rule 6(2).

(5) Directions under paragraph (2) may be given, varied or revoked either—

(a)   of the justices' chief executive or the court's own motion having given the parties notice of the intention to do so and an opportunity to attend and be heard or to make written representations,
(b)   on the written request in Form C2 of a party specifying the direction which is sought, filed and served on the other parties, or
(c)   on the written request in Form C2 of a party specifying the direction which is sought, to which the other parties consent and which they or their representatives have signed.

(6) In an urgent case, the request under paragraph (5)(b) may, with the leave of the justices' clerk or the court, be made—

(a)   orally,
(b)   without notice to the parties, or
(c)   both as in sub-paragraph (a) and as in sub-paragraph (b).

(7) On receipt of a request under paragraph (5)(b) the justices' chief executive shall fix a date for the hearing of the request and give not less than 2 days' notice in Form C6 to the parties of the date so fixed.

(8) On considering a request under paragraph (5)(c) the justices' chief executive or the court shall either—

(a)   grant the request, whereupon the justices' chief executive shall inform the parties of the decision, or
(b)   direct that a date be fixed for the hearing of the request, whereupon the justices' clerk shall fix such a date and give not less than 2 days' notice to the parties of the date so fixed.

(9) Subject to rule 28, a party may request, in accordance with paragraph 5(b) or (c), that an order be made under section 11(3)[2] or, if he is entitled to apply for such an order, under section 38(1)[4], and paragraphs (6), (7) and (8) shall apply accordingly.

(10) Where, in any relevant proceedings, the court has power to make an order of its own motion, the power to give directions under paragraph (2) shall apply.

(11) Directions of the justices' clerk or a court which are still in force immediately prior to the transfer of relevant proceedings to another court shall continue to apply following the transfer, subject to any changes of terminology which are required to apply those directions to the court to which the proceedings are transferred, unless varied or discharged by directions under paragraph (2).

(12) The justices' clerk or the court shall record the giving, variation or revocation of a direction under this rule in the appropriate form in Schedule 1 to these Rules and the justices' chief

executive shall serve, as soon as practicable, a copy of the form on any party who was not present at the giving, variation or revocation.

---

1. In children's cases, where relevant information must be made available to the court in order that it can arrive at a conclusion which is in the paramount interests of the welfare of the child, the court has power to override legal professional privilege in relation to experts' reports when it gives leave to the parties to obtain them (*Oxfordshire County Council v M* [1994] 2 All ER 269, [1994] 1 FCR 753, [1994] 1 FLR 175). Disclosure of a medical report to a party's legal representative, but not to the party instructing the representative, is inappropriate and prevents the party properly conducting his case (*Re NW (a minor) (medical reports)* [1994] 1 FCR 121, [1993] 2 FLR 591). See also *Essex County Council v R* [1993] 2 FLR 826.

2. A s 8 order made otherwise than on disposal of the proceedings.

3. An interim care or interim supervision order.

Timing of proceedings

6–4266 **15.** (1) Any period of time fixed by these Rules, or by any order or direction, for doing any act shall be reckoned in accordance with this rule.

(2) Where the period, being a period of 7 days or less, would include a day which is not a business day, that day shall be excluded.

(3) Where the time fixed for filing a document with the justices' chief executive expires on a day on which the office of the justices' chief executive is closed, and for that reason the document cannot be filed on that day, the document shall be filed in time if it is filed on the next day on which the office of the justices' chief executive is open.

(4) Where these Rules provide a period of time within which or by which a certain act is to be performed in the course of relevant proceedings, that period may not be extended otherwise than by a direction of the justices' clerk or the court under rule 14.

(5) At the—

(a) transfer to a court of relevant proceedings,

(b) postponement or adjournment of any hearing or directions appointment in the course of relevant proceedings, or

(c) conclusion of any such hearing or directions appointment other than one at which the proceedings are determined, or so soon thereafter as is practicable,

   (i) the justices' clerk shall fix a date upon which the proceedings shall come before him or the court again for such purposes as he or the court directs, which date shall, where paragraph (a) applies, be as soon as possible after the transfer, and

   (ii) the justices' chief executive shall give notice to the parties and to the children's guardian or the welfare officer of the date so fixed. The justices' chief executive shall give notice to the parties, any local authority that is preparing, or has prepared, a report under section 14A(8) or (9) and to the children's guardian or the welfare officer of the date so fixed.

Attendance at directions appointment and hearing

6–4267 **16.** (1) Subject to paragraph (2), a party shall attend a directions appointment of which he has been given notice in accordance with rule 14(5) unless the justices' clerk or the court otherwise directs.

(2) Relevant proceedings shall take place in the absence of any party including the child if—

(a) the court considers it in the interests of the child, having regard to the matters to be discussed or the evidence likely to be given, and

(b) the party is represented by a children's guardian or solicitor;

and when considering the interests of the child under sub-paragraph (a) the court shall give the children's guardian, solicitor for the child and, if he is of sufficient understanding, the child, an opportunity to make representations.

(3) Subject to paragraph (4) below, where at the time and place appointed for a hearing or directions appointment the applicant appears but one or more of the respondents do not, the justices' clerk or the court may proceed with the hearing or appointment.

(4) The court shall not begin to hear an application in the absence of a respondent unless—

(a) it is proved to the satisfaction of the court that he received reasonable notice of the date of the hearing; or

(b) the court is satisfied that the circumstances of the case justify proceeding with the hearing.

(5) Where, at the time and place appointed for a hearing or directions appointment, one or more respondents appear but the applicant does not, the court may refuse the application or, if sufficient evidence has previously been received, proceed in the absence of the applicant.

(6) Where at the time and place appointed for a hearing or directions appointment neither the applicant nor any respondent appears, the court may refuse the application.

(7) If the court considers it expedient in the interests of the child, it shall hear any relevant proceedings in private when only the officers of the court, the parties, their legal representatives and such other persons as specified by the court may attend.

Documentary evidence

6–4268 **17.** (1) Subject to paragraphs (4) and (5), in any relevant proceedings a party shall file and serve on the parties, any local authority that is preparing, or has prepared, a report under section

14A(8) or (9), any welfare officer or children and family reporter and any children's guardian of whose appointment he has been given notice under rule 10(5)—

(a) written statements of the substance of the oral evidence which the party intends to adduce at a hearing of, or a directions appointment in, those proceedings, which shall—

(i) be dated,
(ii) be signed by the person making the statement,
(iii) contain a declaration that the maker of the statement believes it to be true and understands that it may be placed before the court, and
(iv) show in the top right hand corner of the first page—

(a) the initials and surname of the person making the statement,
(b) the number of the statement in relation to the maker,
(c) the date on which the statement was made, and
(d) the party on whose behalf it is filed; and

(b) copies of any documents, including, subject to rule 18(3), experts' reports, upon which the party intends to rely, at a hearing of, or a directions appointment in, those proceedings,

at or by such time as the justices' clerk or the court directs or, in the absence of a direction, before the hearing or appointment.

(2) A party may, subject to any direction of the justices' clerk or the court about the timing of statements under this rule, file and serve on the parties a statement which is supplementary to a statement served under paragraph (1).

(3) At a hearing or directions appointment a party may not, without the leave of the justices' clerk, in the case of a directions appointment, or the court—

(a) adduce evidence, or
(b) seek to rely on a document,

in respect of which he has failed[1] to comply with the requirements of paragraph (1).

(4) In proceedings for a section 8 order or a special guardianship order a party shall—

(a) neither file nor serve any document other than as required or authorised by these Rules, and
(b) in completing a form prescribed by these Rules, neither give information, nor make a statement, which is not required or authorised by that form,

without the leave of the justices' clerk or the court.

(5) In proceedings for a section 8 order or a special guardianship order, no statement or copy may be filed under paragraph (1) until such time as the justices' clerk or the court directs.

---

1. If an adjournment is brought about by the late service of important documents or statements then the costs sanction should be employed; the exclusion of evidence would not generally be realistic (*R v Nottingham County Council* [1993] 1 FCR 576).

6–4268A　17A. Disclosure of report under section 14A(8) or (9).　(1) In proceedings for a special guardianship order, the local authority shall file the report under section 14A(8) or (9) within the timetable fixed by the court.

(2) The justices' clerk or the court shall consider whether to give a direction that the report under section 14A(8) or (9) be disclosed to each party to the proceedings.

(3) Before giving such a direction the justices' clerk or the court shall consider whether any information should be deleted including information which reveals the party's address in a case where he has declined to reveal it in accordance with rule 33A (disclosure of addresses).

(4) The justices' clerk or the court may direct that the report will not be disclosed to a party.

(5) The designated officer shall serve a copy of the report filed under paragraph (1)—

(a) in accordance with any direction given under paragraph (2); and
(b) on any children's guardian, welfare officer or children and family reporter.

Expert evidence—examination of child

6–4269　18. (1) No person may, without the leave[1] of the justices' clerk or the court, cause the child to be medically or psychiatrically examined, or otherwise assessed, for the purpose of the preparation of expert evidence for use in the proceedings[2].

(2) An application for leave under paragraph (1) shall, unless the justices' clerk or the court otherwise directs, be served on all the parties to the proceedings and on the children's guardian.

(3) Where the leave of the justices' clerk or the court has not been given under paragraph (1), no evidence arising out of an examination or assessment to which that paragraph applies may be adduced without the leave of the court[1].

---

1. For guidance on the grant of leave and consequential directions for expert evidence in children's cases, see para **6–35A**, ante.

2. Applications directed to the question of whether there should be HIV tests of children should come before a High Court judge, and should lead to the vertical transfer of the substantive application to the High Court (*Re HIV Tests (Note)* [1994] 2 FLR 116).

Amendment

6–4270   **19.** (1) Subject to rule 17(2), a document which has been filed or served in any relevant proceedings may not be amended without the leave of the justices' clerk or the court which shall, unless the justices' clerk or the court otherwise directs, be requested in writing.

(2) On considering a request for leave to amend a document the justices' clerk or the court shall either—

  (a) grant the request, whereupon the justices' chief executive shall inform the person making the request of that decision, or

  (b) invite the parties or any of them to make representations, within a specified period, as to whether such an order should be made.

(3) A person amending a document shall file it with the justices' chief executive and serve it on those persons on whom it was served prior to amendment; and the amendments shall be identified.

Oral evidence

6–4271   **20.** The justices' clerk or the court shall keep a note of the substance of the oral evidence given at a hearing of, or directions appointment in, relevant proceedings.

Hearing

6–4272   **21.** (1) Before the hearing, the justice or justices who will be dealing with the case shall read[1] any documents which have been filed under rule 17 in respect of the hearing.

(2) The justices' clerk at a directions appointment, or the court at a hearing or directions appointment, may give directions[2] as to the order of speeches and evidence.

(3) Subject to directions under paragraph (2), at a hearing of, or directions appointment in, relevant proceedings, the parties and the children's guardian shall adduce their evidence in the following order—

  (a) the applicant,

  (b) any party with parental responsibility for the child,

  (c) other respondents,

  (d) the children's guardian,

  (e) the child if he is a party to the proceedings and there is no children's guardian.

(3A) At the hearing at which the report under section 14A(8) or (9) is considered a party to whom the report, or part of it, has been disclosed may question the person who prepared the report about it.

(4) After the final hearing of relevant proceedings, the court shall make its decision as soon as is practicable.

(5) Before the court makes an order or refuses an application or request, the justices' clerk shall record in writing[3]—

  (a) the names of the justice or justices constituting the court by which the decision is made, and

  (b) in consultation with the justice or justices, the reasons[3] for the court's decision and any findings of fact.

(6) When making an order or when refusing an application, the court, or one of the justices constituting the court by which the decision is made shall

  (a) where it makes a finding of fact state such finding and complete Form C22; and

  (b) state the reasons for the court's decision[3].

(7) As soon as practicable after the court announces its decision—

  (a) the justices' clerk shall make a record of any order made in the appropriate form in Schedule 1 to these Rules or, where there is no such form, in writing; and

  (b) subject to paragraph (8), the justices' chief executive shall serve a copy of any order made on the parties to the proceedings and on any person with whom the child is living, and where applicable, on the local authority that prepared the report under section 14A(8) or (9).

(8) Within 48 hours after the making of an order under section 48(4)[4] or the making, ex parte, of—

  (a) a section 8 order, or

  (b) an order under section 44[5], 48(9)[6], 50[7] or 75(1)[8],

the applicant shall serve a copy of the order in the appropriate form in Schedule 1 to these Rules on—

  (i) each party,

  (ii) any person who has actual care of the child, or who had such care immediately prior to the making of the order, and

  (iii) in the case of an order referred to in sub-paragraph (b), the local authority in whose area the child lives or is found.

1. This is a mandatory requirement even when the application is for an interim order; see *Hampshire County Council v S* [1993] 1 FLR 559. Every effort should be made to enable courts at all levels to have the opportunity of reading the necessary papers in advance of the hearing. Justices should, where possible, be given the papers in advance so they may read them at their leisure, rather than under the pressure of the knowledge that the parties, their witnesses and the advocates in the case are waiting outside (*M v C (children orders: reasons)* [1993] 1 FCR 264, [1993] 2 FLR 584).

2. This power must be exercised judicially; it would be extremely rare for a court to decline to hear an advocate who wished to make a closing speech (*F v Kent County Council* [1993] 1 FCR 217); but see *M v Hampshire County Council* [1993] 1 FCR 23.

3. For the application of this rule as regards the record in writing and the reasons for the court's decision, see para **6–40 Reasons for decision**.

4. This provision allows a court making an emergency protection order and ordering the search of premises for that child to further authorise a search for any other child on premises who ought to be made the subject of an emergency protection order.

5. An emergency protection order.

6. A warrant to assist in discovery of child in need of emergency protection.

7. A recovery order.

8. Emergency orders in respect of registered child minders and those providing day care for young children.

PART IIA

PROCEEDINGS UNDER SECTION 30 OF THE HUMAN FERTILISATION AND EMBRYOLOGY ACT 1990

Interpretation

6–4273   21A. (1) In this Part of these Rules—

"the 1990 Act" means the Human Fertilisation and Embryology Act 1990;

"the birth father" means the father of the child, including a person who is treated as being the father of the child by section 28 of the 1990 Act where he is not the husband within the meaning of section 30 of the 1990 Act;

"the birth mother" means the woman who carried the child;

"the birth parents" means the birth mother and the birth father;

"the husband and wife" means the persons who may apply for a parental order where the conditions set out in section 30(1) of the 1990 Act are met;

"parental order" means an order under section 30 of the 1990 Act (parental orders in favour of gamete donors) providing for a child to be treated in law as a child of the parties to a marriage;

"parental order reporter" means an officer of the service or a Welsh family proceedings officer appointed under section 41 of the Children Act 1989 in relation to proceedings specified by paragraph (2).

(2) Applications under section 30 of the 1990 Act are specified proceedings for the purposes of section 41 of the Children Act 1989 in accordance with section 41(6)(i) of that Act.

Application of the remaining provisions of these Rules

6–4274   21B. Subject to the provisions of this Part, the remaining provisions of these Rules shall apply as appropriate with any necessary modifications to proceedings under this Part except that rules 7(1), 9, 10(1)(*b*), 10(11), 11(2), 11(3) and 12 shall not apply.

Parties

6–4275   21C. The applicants shall be the husband and wife and the respondents shall be the persons set out in the relevant entry in column (iii) of Schedule 2.

Acknowledgement

6–4276   21D. Within 14 days of the service of an application for a parental order, each respondent shall file and serve on all the other parties an acknowledgement in Form C52.

Appointment and duties of the parental order reporter

6–4277   21E. (1) As soon as practicable after the application has been filed, the justices' clerk shall consider the appointment of a parental order reporter in accordance with section 41(1) of the Children Act 1989.

(2) (*Revoked*)

(3) In addition to such of the matters set out in rules 11 and 11A as are appropriate, the parental order reporter shall—

(i)   investigate the matters set out in section 30(1) to (7) of the 1990 Act;

(ii) so far as he considers necessary, investigate any matter contained in the application form or other matter which appears relevant to the making of a parental order;

(iii) advise the court on whether there is any reason under section 6 of the Adoption Act 1976, as applied with modifications by the Parental Orders (Human Fertilisation and Embryology) Regulations 1994, to refuse the parental order.

Personal attendance of applicants

6–4278 21F. The court shall not make a parental order except upon the personal attendance before it of the applicants.

Copies of orders

6–4279 21G. (1) Where a parental order is made by a court sitting in Wales in respect of a child who was born in Wales and the applicants so request before the order is drawn up, the justices' chief executive shall obtain a translation into Welsh of the particulars set out in the order.

(2) Within 7 days after the making of a parental order, the justices' chief executive shall send a copy of the order to the Registrar General[1].

(3) A copy of any parental order may be supplied to the Registrar General at his request.

---

1. By the Registration Service Act 1953, s 1, the powers and duties conferred or imposed by or under any enactment on the Registrar General are to be exercised and performed by the Registrar General for England and Wales appointed under that section.

Amendment and revocation of orders

6–4280 21H. (1) Any application made under paragraph 4 of Schedule 1 to the Adoption Act 1976 as modified by the Parental Orders (Human Fertilisation and Embryology) Regulations 1994 for the amendment of a parental order or for the revocation of a direction to the Registrar General[1] shall be made to a family proceedings court for the same petty sessions area as the family proceedings court which made the parental order, by delivering it to or sending it by post to the justices' chief executive.

(2) Notice of the application shall be given by the justices' chief executive to such persons (if any) as the court thinks fit.

(3) Where the application is granted, the justices' chief executive shall send to the Registrar General a notice specifying the amendments or informing him of the revocation and shall give sufficient particulars of the order to enable the Registrar General to identify the case.

---

1. By s 50 of the Adoption Act 1976, a parental order may contain a direction to the Registrar General to make an entry in the Register of Births or the Parental Order Register.

Keeping of registers, custody, inspection and disclosure of documents and information

6–4281 21I. (1) Such part of the register kept in pursuance of rules made under the Magistrates' Courts Act 1980 as relates to proceedings for parental orders shall be kept in a separate book and the book shall not contain particulars of any other proceedings.

(2) The book kept in pursuance of paragraph (1) and all other documents relating to the proceedings for a parental order shall, while they are in the custody of the court, be kept in a place of special security.

(3) Any person who obtains information in the course of, or relating to proceedings for a parental order, shall treat that information as confidential and shall only disclose it if—

    (a) the disclosure is necessary for the proper exercise of his duties, or
    (b) the information is requested—

        (i) by a court or public authority (whether in Great Britain or not) having the power to determine proceedings for a parental order and related matters, for the purpose of the discharge of its duties in that behalf, or
        (ii) by a person who is authorised in writing by the Secretary of State to obtain the information for the purposes of research.

Application for removal, return etc of child

6–4282 21J. (1) An application under sections 27(1), 29(1) or 29(2) of the Adoption Act 1976 as applied with modifications by the Parental Orders (Human Fertilisation and Embryology) Regulations 1994 shall be made by complaint to the family proceedings court in which the application under section 30 of the 1990 Act is pending.

(2) The respondents shall be all the parties to the proceedings under section 30 and such other person or body, not being the child, as the court thinks fit.

(3) The justices' chief executive shall serve notice of the time fixed for the hearing, together with a copy of the complaint on the children's guardian who may attend on the hearing of the application and be heard on the question of whether the application should be granted.

(4) The court may at any time give directions as to the conduct of the application under this rule.

(5) Where an application under this rule is determined, the justices' chief executive shall serve notice of the determination on all the parties.

(6) A search warrant issued by a justice of the peace under section 29(4) of the Adoption Act 1976 (applied as above) (which relates to premises specified in an information to which an order made under the said section 29(1) relates, authorising a constable to search the said premises and if he finds the child to return the child to the person on whose application the said order was

made) shall be in a warrant form as if issued under section 102 of the Children Act 1989 (warrant to search for or remove a child) or a form to the like effect.

6–4282A   21K. Application by a party for transfer of proceedings to a court of another Member State.   (1) A party may make an application that proceedings, or a specific part of those proceedings, be heard in another Member State pursuant to Article 15 of the Council Regulation.
    (2) An application under paragraph (1) shall be made—

    (*a*)   to the court in which the relevant parental responsibility proceedings (within the meaning of the Council Regulation) are pending; and
    (*b*)   on notice in form C1; and
    (*c*)   such notice shall be filed and served on the respondents not less than 5 business days before the hearing of the application.

    (3) An application made under paragraph (1) must be supported by an affidavit, which should contain evidence of the child's particular connection to the other Member State in accordance with Article 15(3) of the Council Regulation. In this paragraph the child referred to is the child subject of the parental responsibility proceedings.
    (4) The respondents referred to in paragraph (2)(c) mean any other parties, the child and the Central Authority of the relevant Member State.

6–4282B   21L. Application by a court of another Member State for transfer of proceedings.   (1) A court of another Member State may make an application that proceedings, or a specific part of those proceedings, be heard in that Member State pursuant to Article 15 of the Council Regulation.
    (2) An application under paragraph (1) should be made in the first instance to the Central Authority of England and Wales.
    (3) The Central Authority will forward an application made under paragraph (1) to the court in which the parental responsibility proceedings are pending, or where there are no pending proceedings to the principal registry.
    (4) When a court receives the application the court shall serve all other parties in England and Wales not less than 5 business days before the hearing of the application.
    (5) A decision to accept or refuse jurisdiction under Article 15 of the Council Regulation is to be served on all parties, the Central Authority of the relevant Member State and the Central Authority of England and Wales. Service on a Central Authority or court of another Member State shall be made by the Central Authority of England and Wales.

6–4282C   21M. A certified copy of a judgment for enforcement in other Member States.   (1) An application for a certified copy of a judgment or certificate referred to in Article 37(1), 39 or 45(1) of the Council Regulation must be made to the court which made the order by witness statement or affidavit without notice being served on any other party.
    (2) A witness statement or affidavit by which an application for a certified copy of a judgment is made must—

    (*a*)   give particulars of the proceedings in which the judgment was obtained;
    (*b*)   have annexed to it—

       (i)   a copy of the petition or application by which the proceedings were begun;
       (ii)   evidence of service on the respondent;
       (iii) copies of the pleadings and particulars, if any; and
       (iv) a statement of the grounds on which the judgment was based together, where appropriate, with any document showing that the applicant is entitled to legal aid or assistance by way of representation for the purposes of the proceedings;

    (*c*)   state whether the respondent did or did not object to the jurisdiction, and if so, on what grounds;
    (*d*)   show that the judgment has been served in accordance with rule 8 and is not subject to any order for the stay of proceedings;
    (*e*)   state that the time for appealing has expired, or, as the case may be, the date on which it will expire and in either case whether notice of appeal against the judgment has been given; and
    (*f*)   state—

       (i)   whether the judgment provides for the payment of a sum of money;
       (ii)   whether interest is recoverable on the judgment or part thereof and if so, the rate of interest, the date from which interest is recoverable, and the date on which interest ceases to accrue.

    (3) A witness statement or affidavit by which an application for a certificate is made must give—

    (*a*)   particulars of the proceedings in which the judgment was obtained;
    (*b*)   the full name, country and place of birth and date of birth of the parties;
    (*c*)   details of the type of certificate applied for and the reasons for making the application; and
    (*d*)   where the application is for a certificate under Annex II to the Council Regulation—

       (i)   the full name and, if known, the address and the date and place of birth of any other persons with parental responsibility;

(ii) information as to whether or not the judgment entails the return of a child wrongfully removed or retained in another Member State and, if so, the full name and address of the person to whom the child should be returned.

(4) The certified copy of the judgment shall be an office copy sealed with the seal of the court and signed by the justices' clerk and there shall be issued with the copy of the judgment a certified copy of any order which has varied any of the terms of the original order.

6–4282D   21N. Application for a certificate in accordance with Article 41.   (1) An application for a certificate in accordance with Article 41 can be made, after judgment, by any party.

(2) An application under paragraph (1) should be made to the court in which the relevant judgment was made and must be supported by an affidavit, which should contain evidence of the cross-border character of the case.

6–4282E   21P. Rectification of certificates issued under Article 41.   (1) The court may rectify an error in a certificate issued under Article 41.

(2) The court may rectify the certificate of its own motion or pursuant to an application made by any party to the proceedings, or the court or Central Authority of another Member State.

6–4282F   23. Confidentiality of documents.   (1) Subject to rule 23A no document, other than a record of an order, held by the court and relating to relevant proceedings shall be disclosed, other than to—

(*a*) a party,
(*b*) the legal representative of a party,
(*c*) the children's guardian,
(*d*) the Legal Services Commission, or
(*e*) a welfare officer or children and family reporter, or
(*f*) an expert whose instruction by a party has been authorised by the court,

without leave of the justices' clerk or the court.

(2) Nothing in this rule shall prevent the notification by the Court or the justices' chief executive of a direction under section 37(1) to the authority concerned.

(3) Nothing in this rule shall prevent the disclosure of a document prepared by an officer of the service or a Welsh family proceedings officer for the purpose of—

(*a*) enabling a person to perform functions required under section 62(3A) of the Justices of the Peace Act 1997;
(*b*) enabling a person to perform functions required under section 38(1) of the Children Act 2004; or
(*c*) assisting an officer of the service or a Welsh family proceedings officer who is appointed by the court under any enactment to perform his functions.

(4) Nothing in this rule shall prevent the disclosure of any document relating to proceedings by an officer of the service or a Welsh family proceedings officer to any other officer of the service or Welsh family proceedings officer unless that other officer is involved in the same proceedings but on behalf of a different party.

6–4282FA   23A. Communication of information relating to proceedings.   (1) For the purposes of the law relating to contempt of court, information relating to relevant proceedings held in private (whether or not contained in a document filed with the court) may be communicated—

(*a*) where the justices' clerk or the court gives permission;
(*b*) subject to any direction of the justices' clerk or the court, in accordance with paragraphs (2) or (3) of this rule; or
(*c*) where the communication is to—

(i) a party,
(ii) the legal representative of a party,
(iii) a professional legal adviser,
(iv) an officer of the service or a Welsh family proceedings officer,
(v) the welfare officer,
(vi) the Legal Services Commission,
(vii) an expert whose instruction by a party has been authorised by the court, or
(viii) a professional acting in furtherance of the protection of children.

(2) A person specified in the first column of the following table may communicate to a person listed in the second column such information as is specified in the third column for the purpose or purposes specified in the fourth column.

Communication of information without permission of the court

Communicated by	To	Information	Purpose
A party	A lay adviser or a McKenzie Friend	Any information relating to the proceedings	To enable the party to obtain advice or assistance in relation to the proceedings.
A party	The party's spouse, civil partner, cohabitant or close family member		For the purpose of confidential discussions enabling the party to receive support from his spouse, civil partner, cohabitant or close family member.
A party	A health care professional or a person or body providing counselling services for children or families		To enable the party or any child of the party to obtain health care or counselling.
A party or any person lawfully in receipt of information	The Children's Commissioner or the Children's Commissioner for Wales		To refer an issue affecting the interests of children to the Children's Commissioner or the Children's Commissioner for Wales.
A party or a legal representative	A mediator		For the purpose of mediation in relation to the proceedings.
A party, any person lawfully in receipt of information or a designated officer	A person or body conducting an approved research project		For the purpose of an approved research project.
A party, a legal representative or a professional legal adviser	A person or body responsible for investigating or determining complaints in relation to legal representatives or professional legal advisers		For the purposes of making a complaint or the investigation or determination of a complaint in relation to a legal representative or a professional legal adviser.
A legal representative or a professional legal adviser	A person or body assessing quality assurance systems		To enable the legal representative or professional legal adviser to obtain a quality assurance assessment.
A legal representative or a professional legal adviser	An accreditation body	Any information relating to the proceedings providing that it does not, or is not likely to, identify any person involved in the proceedings	To enable the legal representative or professional legal adviser to obtain accreditation.
A party	An elected representative or peer	The text or summary of the whole or part of a judgment given in the proceedings	To enable the elected representative or peer to give advice, investigate any complaint or raise any question of policy or procedure.
A party	The General Medical Council		For the purpose of making a complaint to the General Medical Council.

Communicated by	To	Information	Purpose
A party	A police officer		For the purpose of a criminal investigation.
A party or any person lawfully in receipt of information	A member of the Crown Prosecution Service		To enable the Crown Prosecution Service to discharge its functions under any enactment.

(3) A person in the second column of the table in paragraph (3) may only communicate information relating to the proceedings received from a person in the first column for the purpose or purposes—

   (a) for which he received that information, or

   (b) of professional development or training, providing that any communication does not, or is not likely to, identify any person involved in the proceedings without that person's consent.

(4) In this rule—

"accreditation body" means—

   (a) The Law Society,

   (b) Resolution, or

   (c) The Legal Services Commission;

"approved research project" means a project of research—

   (a) approved in writing by a Secretary of State after consultation with the President of the Family Division,

   (b) approved in writing by the President of the Family Division,

   (c) conducted under section 83, or

   (d) conducted under section 13 of the Criminal Justice and Court Services Act 2000;

"body assessing quality assurance systems" includes—

   (a) The Law Society,

   (b) The Legal Services Commission, or

   (c) The General Council of the Bar;

"body or person responsible for investigating or determining complaints in relation to legal representatives or professional legal advisers" means—

   (a) The Law Society,

   (b) The General Council of the Bar,

   (c) The Institute of Legal Executives, or

   (d) The Legal Services Ombudsman;

"cohabitant" means one of two persons who are neither married to each other nor civil partners of each other but are living together as husband and wife or as if they were civil partners;

"criminal investigation" means an investigation conducted by police officers with a view to it being ascertained—

   (a) whether a person should be charged with an offence, or

   (b) whether a person charged with an offence is guilty of it;

"elected representative" means—

   (a) a member of the House of Commons,

   (b) a member of the National Assembly for Wales, or

   (c) a member of the European Parliament elected in England and Wales;

"health care professional" means—

   (a) a registered medical practitioner,

   (b) a registered nurse or midwife,

   (c) a clinical psychologist, or

   (d) a child psychotherapist;

"lay adviser" means a non-professional person who gives lay advice on behalf of an organisation in the lay advice sector;

"legal representative" means a barrister or a solicitor, solicitor's employee or other authorised litigator (as defined in the Courts and Legal Services Act 1990) who has been instructed to act for a party in relation to the proceedings;

"McKenzie Friend" means any person permitted by the court to sit beside an unrepresented litigant in court to assist that litigant by prompting, taking notes and giving him advice;

"mediator" means a family mediator who is—

   (a) undertaking, or has successfully completed, a family mediation training course approved by the United Kingdom College of Family Mediators, or

   (b) member of the Law Society's Family Mediation Panel;

"peer" means a member of the House of Lords as defined by the House of Lords Act 1999;

"professional acting in furtherance of the protection of children" includes—

(*a*) an officer of a local authority exercising child protection functions,
(*b*) a police officer who is—

   (i)   exercising powers under section 46, or
   (ii) serving in a child protection unit or a paedophile unit of a police force;

(*c*) any professional person attending a child protection conference or review in relation to a child who is the subject of the proceedings to which the information relates, or
(*d*) an officer of the National Society for the Prevention of Cruelty to Children;

"professional legal adviser" means a barrister or a solicitor, solicitor's employee or other authorised litigator (as defined in the Courts and Legal Services Act 1990) who is providing advice to a party but is not instructed to represent that party in the proceedings.

PART III
MISCELLANEOUS

Costs

6–4283 22. (1) In any relevant proceedings, the court may, at any time during the proceedings in that court, make an order that a party pay the whole or any part of the costs of any other party[1].
(2) A party against whom the court is considering making a costs order shall have an opportunity to make representations as to why the order should not be made.

---

1. For consideration of the exercise of the power to order costs against a local authority, see *Hillingdon London Borough Council v H* [1992] 3 WLR 521, [1992] 2 FCR 299. The court must assess the amount of any costs to be ordered; it is the duty of solicitors making a claim for a substantial amount to provide the court with a detailed statement of the costs and to make that statement available to the other parties well in advance of the hearing (*Hillingdon London Borough Council v H*, supra).

Power of court to limit cross-examination

6–4283A 22A. The court may limit the issues on which an officer of the service or a Welsh family proceedings officer may be cross-examined.

Confidentiality of documents

6–4284 23. (1) No document, other than a record of an order, held by the court and relating to relevant proceedings shall be disclosed, other than to—

(*a*) a party,
(*b*) the legal representative of a party,
(*c*) the children's guardian,
(*d*) the Legal Aid Board, or
(*e*) a welfare officer or children and family reporter, or
(*f*)   an expert whose instruction by a party has been authorised by the court.

without leave[1] of the justices' clerk or the court.
(2) Nothing in this rule shall prevent the notification by the court or the justices' chief executive of a direction under section 37(1)[2] to the authority concerned.
(3) Nothing in this rule shall prevent the disclosure of a document prepared by an officer of the service or a Welsh family proceedings officer for the purpose of—

(*a*) enabling a person to perform functions required under section 62(3A) of the Justices of the Peace Act 1997;
(*b*) enabling a person to perform functions required under section 38(1) of the Children Act 2004; or
(*c*) assisting an officer of the service or a Welsh family proceedings officer who is appointed by the court under any enactment to perform his functions.

(4) Nothing in this rule shall prevent the disclosure of any document relating to proceedings by [an officer of the service or a Welsh family proceedings officer to any other officer of the service or Welsh family proceedings officer unless that other officer is involved in the same proceedings but on behalf of a different party.

---

1. For commentary on disclosure of documents and information in family proceedings see para **6–29**, ante. The confidentiality of the report of the children's guardian must be strictly preserved; once the proceedings are at an end, the further distribution of the report of the children's guardian is a matter to be controlled by the court (*Re C (minors) guardian ad litem: disclosure of report*) [1995] 2 FCR 837).
2. A direction to the local authority to investigate.

Enforcement of residence order

6–4285 24. Where a person in whose favour a residence order or special guardianship order is in force wishes to enforce it he shall file a written statement describing the alleged breach of the arrangements settled by the order, whereupon the justices' clerk shall fix a date, time and place for a hearing of the proceedings and the justices' chief executive shall give notice, as soon as practicable, to the person wishing to enforce the residence order and to any person whom it is alleged is in breach of the arrangements settled by that order, of the date fixed.

Notification of consent

6–4286   **25.** (1) Consent for the purposes of—

   (*a*)   section 16(3)[1], or
   (*b*)   section 38A(2)(*b*)(ii) or 44A(2)(*b*)(ii)[3], or
   (*c*)   section 33(7)[2],

shall be given either—

     (i)   orally in court, or
     (ii)   in writing to the justices' chief executive or the court and signed by the person giving his consent.

(2) Any written consent given for the purposes of subsection (2) of section 38A or section 44A, shall include a statement that the person giving consent—

   (*a*)   is able and willing to give to the child the care which it would be reasonable to expect a parent to give him; and
   (*b*)   understands that the giving of consent could lead to the exclusion of the relevant person from the dwelling-house in which the child lives.

---

1. The making of a family assistance order.
2. An application to cause a child in care to be known by a new surname or to be removed from the jurisdiction.
3. The inclusion of an exclusion requirement in an interim care order or an emergency protection order.

Exclusion requirements: interim care orders and emergency protection orders

6–4286A   **25A.** (1) This rule applies where the court includes an exclusion requirement in an interim care order or an emergency protection order.

(2) The applicant for an interim care order or emergency protection order shall—

   (*a*)   prepare a separate statement[1] of the evidence in support of the application for an exclusion requirement;
   (*b*)   serve the statement personally on the relevant person with a copy of the order containing the exclusion requirement (and of any power of arrest which is attached to it);
   (*c*)   inform the relevant person of his right to apply to vary or discharge the exclusion requirement.

(3) Where a power of arrest is attached to an exclusion requirement in an interim care order or an emergency protection order, a copy of the order shall be delivered to the officer for the time being in charge of the police station for the area in which the dwelling-house in which the child lives is situated (or of such other station as the court may specify) together with a statement that the relevant person has been served with the order or informed of its terms (whether by being present when the order was made or by telephone or otherwise).

(4) Rules 12A(3), 20 (except paragraphs (1) and (3)) and 21 of the Family Proceedings Courts (Matrimonial Proceedings etc) Rules 1991 shall apply, with the necessary modifications, for the service, variation, discharge and enforcement of any exclusion requirement to which a power of arrest is attached as they apply to an order made on an application under Part IV of the Family Law Act 1996.

(5) The relevant person shall serve the parties to the proceedings with any application which he makes for the variation or discharge of the exclusion requirement.

(6) Where an exclusion requirement ceases to have effect whether—

   (*a*)   as a result of the removal of a child under section 38A(10) or 44A(10),
   (*b*)   because of the discharge of the interim care order or emergency protection order, or
   (*c*)   otherwise,

the applicant shall inform—

     (i)   the relevant person,
     (ii)   the parties to the proceedings,
     (iii)   any officer to whom a copy of the order was delivered under paragraph (3), and
     (iv)   (where necessary) the court.

(7) Where the court includes an exclusion requirement in an interim care order or an emergency protection order of its own motion, paragraph (2) shall apply with the omission of any reference to the statement of the evidence.

---

1. Best practice requires that the statement should be separate and free-standing, setting out concisely the factual material on which the applicant relies, the statutory requirements under s 38A(2) (interim care orders) or s 44A(2) (emergency protection orders) with a summary of evidence in support and make it clear that the requirement sought is that a particular person should leave the house and/or prohibit the person from entering the house and/or excluding him from a defined area surrounding the house where the child is living. See further and also where the court makes an exclusion order of its own motion *Re W (exclusion: statement of evidence)* [2000] 2 FLR 666, FD).

Secure accommodation

6–4287 26. In proceedings under section 25, the justices' chief executive shall, if practicable, arrange for copies of all written reports before the court to be made available before the hearing to—

   (a) the applicant,
   (b) the parent or guardian of the child,
   (c) any legal representative of the child,
   (d) the children's guardian, and
   (e) the child, unless the justices' chief executive or the court otherwise directs;

and copies of such reports may, if the court considers it desirable, be shown to any person who is entitled to notice of the proceedings in accordance with these Rules.

Investigation under section 37

6–4288 27. (1) This rule applies where a direction is given to an appropriate authority by a family proceedings court under section 37(1).

(2) On giving a direction the court shall adjourn the proceedings and the justices' clerk or the court shall record the direction in Form C40.

(3) A copy of the direction recorded under paragraph (2) shall, as soon as practicable after the direction is given, be served by the justices' chief executive on the parties to the proceedings in which the direction is given and, where the appropriate authority is not a party, on that authority.

(4) When serving the copy of the direction on the appropriate authority the justices' chief executive shall also serve copies of such of the documentary evidence which has been, or is to be, adduced in the proceedings as the court may direct.

(5) Where a local authority informs the court of any of the matters set out in section 37(3)(a) to (c) it shall do so in writing.

Limits on the power of a justices' clerk or a single justice to make an order under section 11(3) or section 38(1)

6–4289 28. A justices' clerk or single justice shall not make an order under section 11(3)[1] or section 38(1)[2] unless—

   (a) a written request for such an order has been made to which the other parties and any children's guardian consent and which they or their representatives have signed,
   (b) a previous such order has been made in the same proceedings, and
   (c) the terms of the order sought are the same as those of the last such order made.

---

  1. A s 8 order made otherwise than on disposal of the proceedings.
  2. An interim care or interim supervision order.

Appeals to a family proceedings court under section 77(6) and paragraph 8(1) of Schedule 8

6–4290 29. (1) An appeal under section 77(6)[1] or paragraph 8(1) of Schedule 8[1] shall be by application in accordance with rule 4.

(2) An appeal under section 77(6) shall be brought within 21 days from the date of the step to which the appeal relates.

---

  1. Section 77(6) related to appeals against certain local authority decisions in relation to child minders and the provision of day care for young children. Paragraph 8(1) related to appeals against certain local authority decisions in relation to private fostering arrangements. These provisions have been repealed and jurisdiction is now invested in the National Care Standards Commission and the National Assembly for Wales in accordance with the Care Standards Act 2000, in PART VIII: HEALTH AND SAFETY, post.

Contribution orders

6–4291 30. (1) An application for a contribution order under paragraph 23(1) of Schedule 2 shall be accompanied by a copy of the contribution notice served in accordance with paragraph 22(1) of that Schedule and a copy of any notice served by the contributor under paragraph 22(8) of that Schedule.

(2) Where a local authority notifies the court of an agreement reached under paragraph 23(6) of Schedule 2, it shall do so in writing through the justices' chief executive.

(3) An application for the variation or revocation of a contribution order under paragraph 23(8) of Schedule 2 shall be accompanied by a copy of the contribution order which it is sought to vary or revoke.

Direction to local education authority to apply for education supervision order

6–4292 31. (1) For the purposes of section 40(3) and (4) of the Education Act 1944, a direction by a magistrates' court to a local education authority to apply for an education supervision order shall be given in writing.

(2) Where, following such a direction, a local education authority informs the court that they have decided not to apply for an education supervision order, they shall do so in writing.

Applications and orders under sections 33 and 34 of the Family Law Act 1986

6–4292A   **31A.** (1) In this rule "the 1986 Act" means the Family Law Act 1986.

(2) An application under section 33 of the 1986 Act shall be in Form C4 and an order made under that section shall be in Form C30.

(3) An application under section 34 of the 1986 Act shall be in Form C3 and an order made under that section shall be in Form C31.

(4) An application under section 33 or section 34 of the 1986 Act may be made ex parte in which case the applicant shall file the application—

(*a*) where the application is made by telephone, within 24 hours after the making of the application, or

(*b*) in any other case at the time when the application is made,

and shall serve a copy of the application on each respondent 48 hours after the making of the order.

(5) Where the court refuses to make an order on an ex parte application it may direct that the application be make inter partes.

Delegation by justices' clerk

6–4293   **32.** (1) In this rule, "employed as a clerk in court" has the same meaning as in rule 2(1) of the Justices' Clerks (Qualifications of Assistants) Rules 1979.

(2) Anything authorised to be done by, to or before a justices' clerk under these Rules, or under paragraphs 13 to 15C of the Schedule to the Justices' Clerks Rules 1970 as amended by Schedule 3 to these Rules, may be done instead by, to or before a person employed as a clerk in court where that person is appointed by the magistrates' courts committee to assist him and where that person has been specifically authorised by the justices' clerk for that purpose.

(3) Any authorisation by the justices' clerk under paragraph (2) shall be recorded in writing at the time the authority is given or as soon as practicable thereafter.

Application of section 97 of the Magistrates' Courts Act 1980

6–4294   **33.** Section 97[1] of the Magistrates' Courts Act 1980 shall apply to relevant proceedings in a family proceedings court as it applies to a hearing of a complaint under that section.

---

1. Section 97 gives power to issue a summons or a warrant to secure the attendance of a witness.

Disclosure of addresses

6–4294A   **33A.** (1) Nothing in these rules shall be construed as requiring any party to reveal the address of their private residence (or that of any child) except by order of the court.

(2) Where a party declines to reveal an address in reliance upon paragraph (1) he shall give notice of that address to the court in Form C8 and that address shall not be revealed to any person except by order of the court.

Setting aside on failure of service

6–4294B   **33B.** Where an application has been sent to a respondent in accordance with rule 8(1) and, after an order has been made on the application, it appears to the court that the application did not come to the knowledge of the respondent in due time, the court may of its own motion set aside the order and may give such directions as it thinks fit for the rehearing of the application.

Consequential and minor amendments, savings and transitionals

6–4295   **34.** (1) Subject to paragraph (3) the consequential and minor amendments in Schedule 3 to these Rules shall have effect.

(2) Subject to paragraph (3), the provisions of the 1981 rules shall have effect subject to these Rules.

(3) Nothing in these Rules shall affect any proceedings which are pending (within the meaning of paragraph 1 of Schedule 14 to the Act of 1989) immediately before these Rules come into force.

6–4296   SCHEDULE 1
FORMS[1]

---

1. A selection of forms prescribed by these Rules is printed in PART IX: PRECEDENTS AND FORMS, post.

6–4356

Rules 4 and 7

SCHEDULE 2
RESPONDENTS AND NOTICE

(i) Provision under which proceedings brought	(ii) Minimum number of days prior to hearing or directions appointment for service under rule 4(1)(b)	(iii) Respondents	(iv) Persons to whom notice is to be given
All applications.	See separate entries below.	Subject to separate entries below, every person whom the applicant believes to have parental responsibility for the child; where the child is the subject of a care order, every person whom the applicant believes to have had parental responsibility immediately prior to the making of the care order; in the case of an application to extend, vary or discharge an order, the parties to the proceedings leading to the order which it is sought to have extended, varied or discharged; in the case of specified proceedings, the child.	Subject to separate entries below, the local authority providing accommodation for the child; persons who are caring for the child at the time when the proceedings are commenced; in the case of proceedings brought in respect of a child who is alleged to be staying in a refuge which is certificated under section 51(1) or (2), the person who is providing the refuge.
Section 4(1)(c), 4(3), 4A(1)(b), 4A(3), 5(1), 6(7), 8, 13(1), 14A, 14C(3), 14D, 16(6), 33(7), 77(6), Schedule 1, paragraph 19(1), 23(1) or 23(8) of Schedule 2, paragraph 8(1) of Schedule 8, or paragraph 11(3) or 16(5) of Schedule 14[1].	14 days	Except for proceedings under section 77(6)[2], Schedule 2, or paragraph 8(1) of Schedule 8[3], as for "all applications" above, and:	As for "all applications" above, and:
		in the case of proceedings under Schedule 1, those persons whom the applicant believes to be interested in or affected by the proceedings; in the case of an application under paragraph 11(3)(b)[4] or 16(5)[5] of Schedule 14, any person, other than the child, named in the order or directions which it is sought to discharge or vary; in the case of proceedings under section 77(6), the local authority against whose decision the appeal is made; in the case of an application under paragraph 23(1) of Schedule 2[6], the contributor; in the case of an application under paragraph 23(8) of Schedule 2[7]— (i) if the applicant is the local authority, the contributor, and (ii) if the applicant is the contributor, the local authority.	in the case of an application under paragraph 19(1) of Schedule 2[8], the parties to the proceedings leading to the care order; in the case of an application under section 5(1)[9], the father of the child if he does not have parental responsibility.

(i) *Provision under which proceedings brought*	(ii) *Minimum number of days prior to hearing or directions appointment for service under rule 4(1)(b)*	(iii) *Respondents*	(iv) *Persons to whom notice is to be given*
		In the case of an application under paragraph 8(1) of Schedule 8, the local authority against whose decision the appeal is made.	
		in the case of an application for a section 8 order, every person whom the applicant believes—	
		(i) to be named in a court order with respect to the same child, which has not ceased to have effect,	
		(ii) to be a party to pending proceedings in respect of the same child, or	
		(iii) to be a person with whom the child has lived for at least three years prior to the application, unless, in a case to which (i) or (ii) applies, the applicant believes that the court order or pending proceedings are not relevant to the application.	
		in the case of an application under section 14A, if a care order is in force with respect to the child, the child	in the case of an application under section 14A— (*a*) if the child is not being accommodated by the local authority, the local authority in whose area the applicant is ordinarily resident, and (*b*) every other person whom the applicant believes— (i) to be named in a court order with respect to that child which remains in force, (ii) to be a party to pending proceedings in respect of the same child, (iii) to be a person with whom the child has lived for at least 3 years prior to the application, unless, in a case to which (i) or (ii) applies, the applicant believes that the court order or pending proceedings are not relevant to the application; in the case of an application under section 14D— (*a*) as for applications under section 14A above, and (*b*) the local authority that prepared the report under section 14A(8) or (9) in the proceedings leading to the order which it is sought to have varied or discharged, if different from any local authority that will be otherwise be notified

1. The relevant applications are for: (i) an order conferring parental responsibility on a father who was not married to the child's mother at the time of his birth; or (ii) the termination of a parental responsibility agreement; or (iii) the appointment of a guardian; or (iv) the removal of a guardian; or (v) the removal of a child from the United Kingdom or for the child to be known by a new surname where a residence order is in force; or (vi) the variation or discharge of an order under s 8 by the officer concerned in a family assistance order; or (vii) leave for the removal of a child from the United Kingdom or for the child to be known by a new surname where a care order is in force; or (viii) appeal against a local authority's decision in respect of child minding or day care provision; or (ix) approval for local authority arrangements for a child to live outside England and Wales; or (x) a contribution order; or (xi) the variation or revocation of a contribution order; or (xii) appeal against a local authority's decision in respect of private fostering arrangements; or (xiii) the discharge of an existing order under transitional provisions; or (xiv) the variation or discharge of directions made in the County or High Court under repealed provisions.

2. An appeal against a local authority's decision in respect of child minding or day care provision.

3. Appeal against a local authority's decision in respect of private fostering arrangements.

4. The discharge of an existing order under transitional provisions.

5. The variation or discharge of directions made in the County or High Court under repealed provisions.

6. An application for a contribution order.

7. An application to vary or discharge a contribution order.

8. An application for approval for local authority arrangements for a child to live outside England and Wales.

9. An application for the appointment of a guardian.

6–4358

(i) Provision under which proceedings brought	(ii) Minimum number of days prior to hearing or directions appointment for service under rule 4(1)(b)	(iii) Respondents	(iv) Persons to whom notice is to be given
Section 36(1), 39(1), 39(2), 39(3), 39(4), 43(1), or paragraph 6(3), 15(2) or 17(1) of Schedule 3[1].	7 days	As for "all applications" above, and: in the case of an application under section 39(2) or (3)[2], the supervisor; in the case of proceedings under paragraph 17(1) of Schedule 3[3], the local education authority concerned; in the case of proceedings under section 36[4] or paragraph 15(2)[5]or 17(1) of Schedule 3[3], the child.	As for "all applications" above, and: in the case of an application for an order under section 43(1)[6]— (i) every person whom the applicant believes to be a parent of the child, (ii) every person whom the applicant believes to be caring for the child, (iii) every person in whose favour a contact order is in force with respect to the child, and (iv) every person who is allowed to have contact with the child by virtue of an order under section 34.

1. The relevant applications are for: (i) an education supervision order; or (ii) the discharge or variation of a care order; or (iii) the discharge or variation of a supervision order; or (iv) variation of a supervision order by person with whom child is living; or (v) a child assessment order; or (vi) the extension of a supervision order; or (vii) the extension of an education supervision order; or (viii) the discharge of an education supervision order.

2. An application for the variation of a supervision order.

3. An application for the discharge of an education supervision order.

4. An application for an education supervision order.

5. An application to extend an education supervision order.

6. A child assessment order.

6–4359

(i) Provision under which proceedings brought	(ii) Minimum number of days prior to hearing or directions appointment for service under rule 4(1)(b)	(iii) Respondents	(iv) Persons to whom notice is to be given
Section 31, 34(2), 34(3), 34(4), 34(9) or 38(8)(b)[1].	3 days	As for "all applications" above, and:	As for "all applications" above, and:

(i) Provision under which proceedings brought	(ii) Minimum number of days prior to hearing or directions appointment for service under rule 4(1)(b)	(iii) Respondents	(iv) Persons to whom notice is to be given
		in the case of an application under section 34, the person whose contact with the child is the subject of the application.	in the case of an application under section 31[2]— (i) every person whom the applicant believes to be a party to pending relevant proceedings in respect of the same child, and (ii) every person whom the applicant believes to be a parent[3] without parental responsibility for the child.

1. The relevant applications are for: (i) a care or supervision order; or (ii) a contact order in respect of a child in care; or (iii) an order refusing contact; or (iv) the variation or discharge of a contact order in respect of a child in care; or (v) the variation of a direction as to the medical or psychiatric examination or other assessment of a child the subject of an interim care order.

2. An application for a care or supervision order.

3. A father without parental responsibility is in a different position to others who require leave to be joined in care proceedings. Broadly, a father ought ordinarily to be given the opportunity to be heard before major decisions are taken in relation to his child, and if he wishes to participate as a party to care proceedings he should be permitted to do so unless there is some justifiable reason for not joining him as a party (*Re B (care proceedings: notification of father without parental responsibility)* [1999] 2 FLR 408).

6–4360

(i) Provision under which proceedings brought	(ii) Minimum number of days prior to hearing or directions appointment for service under rule 4(1)(b)	(iii) Respondents	(iv) Persons to whom notice is to be given
Section 43(12)[1].	2 days	As for "all applications" above.	Those of the persons referred to in section 43(11)(a) to (e) who were not party to the application for the order which it is sought to have varied or discharged.

1. An application for the variation or discharge of a child assessment order.

6–4361

(i) Provision under which proceedings brought	(ii) Minimum number of days prior to hearing or directions appointment for service under rule 4(1)(b)	(iii) Respondents	(iv) Persons to whom notice is to be given
Section 25, 44(1), 44(9)(b), 45(4), 45(8), 46(7), 48(9), 50(1), 75(1) or 102(1)[1].	1 day	Except for applications under section 75(1)[2] or 102(1)[3], as for "all applications" above, and: in the case of an application under section 44(9)(b)[4] (i) the parties to the application for the order in respect of which it is sought to vary the directions;	As for "all applications" above, and: in the case of an application under section 44(1)[6], every person whom the applicant believes to be a parent of the child; in the case of an application under section 44(9)(b)[4]—

(i) Provision under which proceedings brought	(ii) Minimum number of days prior to hearing or directions appointment for service under rule 4(1)(b)	(iii) Respondents	(iv) Persons to whom notice is to be given
		(ii) any person who was caring for the child prior to the making of the order; and (iii) any person whose contact with the child is affected by the direction which it is sought to have varied; in the case of an application under section 50[5], the person whom the applicant alleges to have effected or to have been or to be responsible for the taking or keeping of the child; in the case of an application under section 75(1)[2], the registered person; in the case of an application under section 102(1), the person referred to in section 102(1) and any person preventing or likely to prevent such a person from exercising powers under enactments mentioned in subsection (6) of that section.	(i) the local authority in whose area the child is living, and (ii) any person whom the applicant believes to be affected by the direction which it is sought to have varied.

1. The relevant applications are for: (i) the use of secure accommodation; or (ii) an emergency protection order; or (iii) the variation of a direction made with an emergency protection order; or (iv) to extend an emergency protection order; or (v) an application to discharge an emergency protection order; or (vi) an emergency protection order in respect of a child in police protection; or (vii) a warrant to assist in the discovery of a child in need of emergency protection; or (viii) a recovery order; or (ix) emergency protection in respect of registered child minders or day care provision; or (x) a warrant to search for child or assist in the inspection of premises.

2. An application for emergency protection in respect of registered child minders or day care provision.

3. An application for a warrant to search for child or assist in the inspection of premises.

4. An application for the variation of a direction made with an emergency protection order.

5. A recovery order.

6. An emergency protection order.

6–4361A

(i) Provision under which proceedings brought	(ii) Minimum number of days prior to hearing or directions appointment for service under rule 4(1)(b)	(iii) Respondents	(iv) Persons to whom notice is to be given
Section 30 of the Human Fertilisation and Embryology Act 1990[1].	14 days	The birth parents (except where the applicants seek to dispense with their agreement under section 30(6) of the Human Fertilisation and Embryology Act 1990) and any other persons or body with parental responsibility for the child at the date of the application	Any local authority or voluntary organisation that has at any time provided accommodation for the child.

1. An application for a parental order in respect of a child in favour of a married couple, at least one of whom is the genetic parent and where the child has been born as a result of a surrogacy arrangement satisfying certain conditions.

6–4362

Rule 34(1)

SCHEDULE 3

CONSEQUENTIAL AND MINOR AMENDMENTS

Children (Allocation of Proceedings) Order 1991[1]

(SI 1991/1677 amended by SI 1993/624, SI 1994/2164 and 3138, SI 1995/1649, SI 1997/1897, SI 1998/2166, SI 1999/524, SI 2000/2670, SI 2001/775 and 1656, SI 2003/331 and SI 2005/520 and 2797)

Citation, commencement and interpretation

6–4400   **1.** (1) This Order may be cited as the Children (Allocation of Proceedings) Order 1991 and shall come into force on 14th October 1991.

(2) In this Order, unless the context otherwise requires—

"child"—

    (a) means, subject to sub-paragraph (b), a person under the age of 18 with respect to whom proceedings are brought, and

    (b) where the proceedings are under Schedule 1, or are for adoption under the Adoption and Children Act 2002, also includes a person who has reached the age of 18,

"Convention adoption order" means an adoption order which, by virtue of regulations under section 1 of the Adoption (Intercountry Aspects) Act 1999 (regulations giving effect to the Convention), is made as a Convention adoption order;

"local justice area" has the same meaning as in the Courts Act 2003; and

"the Act" means the Children Act 1989, and a section, Part or Schedule referred to by number alone means the section, Part or Schedule so numbered in that Act.

---

1. Made by the Lord Chancellor in exercise of the powers conferred on him by s 92(9) and (10) of, and Pt I of Sch 11 to, the Children Act 1989.

Classes of county court

6–4401   **2.** For the purposes of this Order there shall be the following classes of county court:

    (a) designated county courts, being those courts designated for the time being—

        (i) as divorce county courts by an order under section 33 of the Matrimonial and Family Proceedings Act 1984;

        (ii) as civil partnership proceedings county courts by an order under section 36A of the Matrimonial and Family Proceedings Act 1984; or

        (iii) as both divorce county courts and civil partnership proceedings county courts by such orders;

    (b) family hearing centres, being those courts set out in Schedule 1 to this Order;

    (c) care centres, being those courts set out in column (ii) of Schedule 2 to this Order;

    (d) adoption centres, being those courts set out in Schedule 3 to this Order;

    (e) intercountry adoption centres, being those courts set out in Schedule 4 to this Order".

COMMENCEMENT OF PROCEEDINGS

Proceedings to be commenced in magistrates' court

6–4402   **3.** (1) Subject to paragraphs (2) and (3) and to article 4, proceedings under any of the following provisions shall be commenced in a magistrates' court:

    (a) section 25 (use of accommodation for restricting liberty);

    (b) section 31 (care and supervision orders);

    (c) section 33(7) (leave to change name of or remove from United Kingdom child in care);

    (d) section 34 (parental contact);

    (e) section 36 (education supervision orders);

    (f) section 43 (child assessment orders);

    (g) section 44 (emergency protection orders);

    (h) section 45 (duration of emergency protection orders etc);

    (i) section 46(7) (application for emergency protection order by police officer);

    (j) section 48 (powers to assist discovery of children etc);

    (k) section 50 (recovery orders);

    (l) section 75 (protection of children in an emergency);

    (m) section 77(6) (appeal against steps taken under section 77(1));

    (n) section 102 (powers of constable to assist etc);

(*o*) paragraph 19 of Schedule 2 (approval of arrangements to assist child to live abroad);
(*p*) paragraph 23 of Schedule 2 (contribution orders);
(*q*) paragraph 8 of Schedule 8 (certain appeals);
(*r*) section 23 of the Adoption and Children Act 2002 (varying placement orders);
(*t*) section 20 of the Child Support Act 1991 (appeals) where the proceedings are to be dealt with in accordance with the Child Support Appeals (Jurisdiction of Courts) Order 1993.
(*u*) section 30 of the Human Fertilisation and Embryology Act 1990 (parental orders in favour of gamete donors).

(2) Notwithstanding paragraph (1) and subject to paragraph (3), proceedings of a kind set out in sub-paragraphs (*b*), (*e*), (*f*), (*g*), (*i*) or (*j*) of paragraph (1), and which arise out of an investigation directed, by the High Court or a county court, under section 37(1), shall be commenced—

(*a*) in the court which directs the investigation, where that court is the High Court or a care centre, or
(*b*) in such care centre as the court which directs the investigation may order.

(3) Notwithstanding paragraphs (1) and (2), proceedings of a kind set out in sub-paragraph (*a*) to (*k*), (*n*) or (*o*) of paragraph (1) shall be made to a court in which are pending other proceedings, in respect of the same child, which are also of a kind set out in those sub-paragraphs.

Proceedings to be commenced in the High Court or a county court

6–4402A   3A. Proceedings for a Convention adoption order or an adoption order where section 83 of the Adoption and Children Act 2002 (restriction on bringing children in) applies shall be commenced in the High Court or in a county court.

Application where proceedings pending

6–4402B   3B. (1) Where an application has been made for an adoption order and has not been disposed of, an application for—

(*a*) leave to apply for a residence order under section 29(4)(b) of the Adoption and Children Act 2002;
(*b*) leave to apply for a special guardianship order under section 29(5)(b) of the Adoption and Children Act 2002;
(*c*) a residence order under section 8 where section 28(1)(a) or 29(4)(b) of the Adoption and Children Act 2002 applies (leave obtained to make application for a residence order);
(*d*) an order under section 14A where section 28(1)(b) or 29(5)(b) of the Adoption and Children Act 2002 applies (leave obtained to make application for a special guardianship order);
(*e*) leave to remove the child under section 37(a) of the Adoption and Children Act 2002; or
(*f*) leave to oppose the making of an adoption order under section 47(3) or (5) of the Adoption and Children Act 2002

shall be commenced in the court in which the adoption proceedings are pending.
(2) Where an application has been made for a placement order and has not been disposed of, an application for leave to remove a child from accommodation provided by the local authority under section 30(2)(b) of the Adoption and Children Act 2002 shall be commenced in the court in which the proceedings for the placement order are pending.
(3) Where an application has been made for leave under section 42(6) of the Adoption and Children Act 2002 and has not been disposed of, an application for leave to remove a child under section 38(3)(a) or 40(2)(a) of that Act shall be commenced in the court in which the proceedings under section 42(6) of that Act are pending.

Application where order already in force

6–4402C   3C. (1) Where a special guardianship order is in force in respect of a child, an application for leave to change child's name or remove child from United Kingdom under section 14C(3) shall be commenced in the court which made the special guardianship order.
(2) Where a placement order is in force in respect of a child, an application for—

(*a*) leave to apply to revoke the placement order under section 24(2)(a) of the Adoption and Children Act 2002;
(*b*) leave to place child for adoption under section 24(5) of that Act;
(*c*) leave to apply for a contact order under section 26(3)(f) of that Act;
(*d*) leave to apply to change child's name or remove child from United Kingdom under section 28(2)(b) of that Act; or
(*e*) a contact order under section 26 of that Act

shall be commenced in the court which made the placement order.

Application to extend, vary or discharge order

6–4403   4. (1) Subject to paragraphs (2) and (3), proceedings under the Act—

(*a*) to extend, vary or discharge an order, or
(*b*) the determination of which may have the effect of varying or discharging an order,

shall be made to the court which made the order[1].

(1A) Proceedings under the Adoption and Children Act 2002, save for proceedings under section 23 of that Act, to vary or revoke an order shall be commenced in the court which made the order.

(2) Notwithstanding paragraph (1), an application for an order under section 8, 14A or 14D which would have the effect of varying or discharging an order made, by a county court, in accordance with section 10(1)(*b*), 14A(6)(*b*) or 14D(2) respectively shall be made to a designated county court.

(3) Notwithstanding paragraph (1), an application to extend, vary or discharge an order made, by a county court, under section 38, or for an order which would have the effect of extending, varying or discharging such an order, shall be made to a care centre.

(4) A court may transfer proceedings made in accordance with paragraph (1) or (1A) to any other court in accordance with the provisions of articles 5 to 13.

---

1. Where an order has been made by the High Court before implementation of the Children Act 1989 on 14 October 1991, any application to vary the order, or which would have the effect of varying the order, is to be made to the High Court as the court which made the order (*Sunderland Borough Council v A* [1993] 1 FCR 396).

TRANSFER OF PROCEEDINGS

Disapplication of enactments about transfer

6–4404 **5.** Sections 38 and 39 of the Matrimonial and Family Proceedings Act 1984 shall not apply to proceedings under the Act or under the Adoption and Children Act 2002.

Transfer from one magistrates' court to another

6–4405 **6.** (1) A magistrates' court (the "transferring court") shall transfer proceedings to which this Article applies to another magistrates' court (the "receiving court") where—

(a) having regard to the principle set out in section 1(2) and, where applicable, section 1(3) of the Adoption and Children Act 2002, the transferring court considers that the transfer is in the interests of the child—

(i) because it is likely significantly to accelerate the determination of the proceedings,

(ii) because it would be appropriate for those proceedings to be heard together with other family proceedings which are pending in the receiving court, or

(iii) for some other reason, and

(b) the receiving court, by its justices' clerk (as defined by rule 1(2) of the Family Proceedings Courts (Children Act 1989) Rules 1991, consents to the transfer.

(2) This article applies to proceedings—

(a) under the Act;

(b) under the Adoption and Children Act 2002;

(c) of the kind mentioned in sub-paragraph (*t*) or (*u*) of article 3(1) and under section 55A of the Family Law Act 1986

(d) under section 11 of the Crime and Disorder Act 1998 (Child Safety Orders).

Transfer from magistrates' court to county court by magistrates' court

6–4406 **7.** (1) Subject to paragraphs (2), (3) and (4) and to articles 15 to 18, a magistrates' court may, upon application by a party or of its own motion, transfer to a county court proceedings of any of the kinds mentioned in article 3(1) or proceedings under section 55A of the Family Law Act 1986 where it considers it in the interests of the child to do so having regard, first, to the principle set out in section 1(2) and, where applicable, section 1(3) of the Adoption and Children Act 2002 and, secondly, to the following questions:

(a) whether the proceedings are exceptionally grave, important or complex[1], in particular—

(i) because of complicated or conflicting evidence about the risks involved to the child's physical or moral well-being or about other matters relating to the welfare of the child;

(ii) because of the number of parties;

(iii) because of a conflict with the law of another jurisdiction;

(iv) because of some novel and difficult point of law; or

(v) because of some question of general public interest;

(b) whether it would be appropriate for those proceedings to be heard together with other family proceedings which are pending in another court; and

(c) whether transfer is likely significantly to accelerate the determination of the proceedings, where—

(i) no other method of doing so, including transfer to another magistrates' court, is appropriate, and

(ii) delay would seriously prejudice the interests of the child who is the subject of the proceedings.

(2) Notwithstanding paragraph (1), proceedings of the kind mentioned in sub-paragraphs (*g*) to (*j*), (*l*), (*m*), (*p*) or (*q*) of article 3(1) shall not be transferred from a magistrates' court.

(3) Notwithstanding paragraph (1), proceedings of the kind mentioned in sub-paragraph (*a*) or

(*n*) of article 3(1) shall only be transferred from a magistrates' court to a county court in order to be heard together with other family proceedings which arise out of the same circumstances as gave rise to the proceedings to be transferred and which are pending in another court.

(4) Notwithstanding paragraphs (1) and (3), proceedings of the kind mentioned in article 3(1)(*a*) shall not be transferred from a magistrates' court which is not a family proceedings court within the meaning of section 92(1).

---

1. Where the estimate of the length of hearing is in excess of 2 or 3 days, magistrates should consider transferring the case to a district judge for consideration whether it should be heard by a circuit judge or a High Court judge. A case which seems to bristle with complexity at the outset should be transferred upwards, even if it simplifies as it progresses so as to justify a transfer back to the family proceedings court (*Re H (a minor) (care proceedings)* [1992] 2 FCR 330). The balancing of risk where the issue is whether or not to return a battered baby to the parents cannot be anything but exceptionally grave and important, with conflicting if not complex evidence as to where the balance or risk lies; responsibility for the decision in such cases should be carried by a judge and not by the justices; see *Re C (a minor) (care proceedings)* [1992] 2 FCR 341. Justices should consider transfer to a care centre where complex cases cannot be heard on consecutive days; cases extending beyond two or at the most three days are rarely appropriate for justices (*Re L (care proceedings: transfer)* [1993] 1 FCR 689). Cases which require a decision as to whether a child should be removed from the jurisdiction are not suitable for justices (*Re L (a minor) (removal from jurisdiction)* [1993] 1 FCR 325).

6–4407 **8.** Subject to articles 15 to 18, a magistrates' court may transfer to a county court proceedings under the Act or under the Adoption and Children Act 2002, being proceedings to which article 7 does not apply, where, having regard to the principle set out in section 1(2) and, where applicable, section 1(3) of the Adoption and Children Act 2002, it considers that in the interests of the child[1] the proceedings can be dealt with more appropriately in that county court.

---

1. When considering an application under art 8, although the family proceedings court has to have regard to the question of delay, its main function is to consider the interests of the child and to decide whether the proceedings can be more appropriately dealt with in a county court (*R v South East Hampshire Family Proceedings Court, ex p D* [1994] 2 All ER 445, [1994] 1 WLR 611, [1994] 1 FCR 620, [1994] 2 FLR 190). Where an application raises a question whether a child should be removed from the jurisdiction, questions of comity and mirror orders in a foreign court are likely to arise; such issues are more appropriately determined by the High Court. If such issues arise before a family proceedings court that court may transfer the case to the county court, which in turn may transfer the case to the High Court; see *N v B (children: orders as to residence)* [1993] 1 FCR 231, as explained in *M H v G P* [1995] 2 FLR 106, sub nom *Harris v Pinnington* [1995] 3 FCR 35; and *Re L (a minor) (removal from jurisdiction)* [1993] 1 FCR 325.

Transfer from magistrates' court following refusal of magistrates' court to transfer

6–4408 **9.** (1) Where a magistrates' court refuses to transfer proceedings under article 7, a party to those proceedings may apply to the care centre listed in column (ii) of Schedule 2 to this Order against the entry in column (i) for the local justice area in which the magistrates' court is situated for an order under paragraph (2).

(2) Upon hearing an application under paragraph (1) the court may transfer the proceedings to itself where, having regard to the principle set out in section 1(2) and, where applicable, section 1(3) of the Adoption and Children Act 2002 and the questions set out in article 7(1)(*a*) to (*c*), it considers it in the interests of the child to do so.

(3) Upon hearing an application under paragraph (1) the court may transfer the proceedings to the High Court where, having regard to the principle set out in section 1(2) and, where applicable, section 1(3) of the Adoption and Children Act 2002, it considers—

(*a*) that the proceedings are appropriate for determination in the High Court, and
(*b*) that such determination would be in the interests of the child.

(4) This article shall apply (with the necessary modifications) to proceedings brought under Parts I and II as it applies where a magistrates' court refuses to transfer proceedings under article 7.

Transfer from one county court to another

6–4409 **10.** (1) Subject to articles 15 and 16, a county court (the "transferring court") shall transfer proceedings to which this Article applies to another county court (the "receiving court") where—

(*a*) the transferring court, having regard to the principle set out in section 1(2), considers the transfer to be in the interests of the child, and
(*b*) the receiving court is—

(i) of the same class or classes, within the meaning of article 2, as the transferring court, or
(ii) to be presided over by a judge or district judge who is specified by directions under section 9 of the Courts and Legal Services Act 1990 for the same purposes as the judge or district judge presiding over the transferring court.

(2) This article applies to proceedings—

(*a*) under the Act;
(*b*) under the Adoption and Children Act 2002;

(c) of the kind mentioned in sub-paragraph (*t*) or (*u*) of article 3(1) and under section 55A of the Family Law Act 1986.

Transfer from county court to magistrates' court by county court[1]

6–4410 11. (1) A county court may transfer to a magistrates' court before trial proceedings which were transferred under article 7(1) where the county court, having regard to the principle set out in section 1(2) and, where applicable, section 1(3) of the Adoption and Children Act 2002 and the interests of the child, considers that the criterion cited by the magistrates' court as the reason for transfer—

(a) in the case of the criterion in article 7(1)(*a*), does not apply,
(b) in the case of the criterion in article 7(1)(*b*), no longer applies, because the proceedings with which the transferred proceedings were to be heard have been determined,
(c) in the case of the criterion in article 7(1)(*c*), no longer applies.

(2) Paragraph (1) shall apply (with the necessary modifications) to proceedings under Parts I and II brought in, or transferred to, a county court as it applies to proceedings transferred to a county court under article 7(1).

1. Where a district judge orders the transfer of proceedings to a magistrates' court in accordance with art 11, an appeal may be made against that decision—(*a*) to a judge of the Family Division of the High Court, or (*b*) except where the order was made by a district judge or deputy district judge of the principal registry of the Family Division, to a circuit judge (Children (Allocation of Proceedings) (Appeals) Order 1991, SI 1991/1801).

Transfer from county court to High Court by county court[1]

6–4411 12. (1) A county court may transfer proceedings to which this Article applies to the High Court where, having regard to the principle set out in section 1(2) and, where applicable, section 1(3) of the Adoption and Children Act 2002, it considers—

(a) that the proceedings are appropriate for determination in the High Court, and
(b) that such determination would be in the interests of the child.

(2) This article applies to proceedings—

(a) under the Act;
(b) under the Adoption and Children Act 2002;
(c) of the kind mentioned in sub-paragraph (*t*) or (*u*) of article 3(1) and under section 55A of the Family Law Act 1986.

1. For guidance on the transfer to the High Court of adoption proceedings concerning a child whose place of origin is outside the UK, see *Practice Direction* [1993] 4 All ER 960.

Transfer from High Court to county court

6–4412 13. (1) Subject to articles 15 to 18, the High Court may transfer to a county court proceedings to which this Article applies where, having regard to the principle set out in section 1(2) and, where applicable, section 1(3) of the Adoption and Children Act 2002, it considers that the proceedings are appropriate for determination in such a court and that such determination would be in the interests of the child.

(2) This article applies to proceedings—

(a) under the Act;
(b) under the Adoption and Children Act 2002;
(c) of the kind mentioned in sub-paragraph (*t*) or (*u*) of article 3(1) and under section 55A of the Family Law Act 1986.

ALLOCATION OF PROCEEDINGS TO PARTICULAR COUNTY COURTS

Commencement

6–4413 14. (1) Subject to articles 3B(*c*) and (*d*), 18 and 19 and to rule 2.40 of the Family Proceedings Rules 1991 (Application under Part I or II of the Children Act 1989 where cause is pending), an application under the Act which is to be commenced in a county court shall be commenced in a designated county court.

(2) Subject to paragraph (3), an application under the Adoption and Children Act 2002 which is to be made to a county court shall be commenced in an adoption centre.

(3) An application for a Convention adoption order or an adoption order where section 83 of the Adoption and Children Act 2002 applies which is to be made to a county court shall be commenced in an intercountry adoption centre.

Proceedings under Part I or II or Schedule I

6–4414 15. (1) Subject to paragraph (3), where an application under Part I or II or Schedule 1 is to be transferred from a magistrates' court to a county court, it shall be transferred to a designated county court.

(2) Subject to paragraph (3), where an application under Part I or II or Schedule 1, other than

an application for an order under section 8 or 14A, is to be transferred from the High Court to a county court, it shall be transferred to a designated county court.

(3) Where an application under Part I or II or Schedule 1, other than an application for an order under section 8 or 14A, is to be transferred to a county court for the purpose of consolidation with other proceedings, it shall be transferred to the court in which those other proceedings are pending.

Orders under section 8 of the Children Act 1989

6–4415 **16.** (1) An application for an order under section 8 or 14A in a designated county court, which is not also a family hearing centre, shall, if the court is notified that the application will be opposed, be transferred for trial to a family hearing centre.

(2) Subject to paragraph (3), where an application for an order under section 8 or 14A is to be transferred from the High Court to a county court it shall be transferred to a family hearing centre.

(3) Where an application for an order under section 8 or 14A is to be transferred to a county court for the purpose of consolidation with other proceedings, it may be transferred to the court in which those other proceedings are pending whether or not it is a family hearing centre; but paragraph (1) shall apply to the application following the transfer.

Application under the Adoption and Children Act 2002

6–4416 **17.** (1) Subject to paragraph (2), where proceedings under the Adoption and Children Act 2002, save for proceedings under section 23 of that Act, are to be transferred from the High Court or a magistrates' court to a county court, they shall be transferred to an adoption centre.

(2) Where proceedings for a Convention adoption order or an adoption order where section 83 of the Adoption and Children Act 2002 applies are to be transferred from the High Court to a county court, they shall be transferred to an intercountry adoption centre.

Applications under Part III, IV or V

6–4417 **18.** (1) An application under Part III, IV or V, if it is to be commenced in a county court, shall be commenced in a care centre.

(2) An application under Part III, IV or V which is to be transferred from the High Court to a county court shall be transferred to a care centre.

(3) An application under Part III, IV or V which is to be transferred from a magistrates' court to a county court shall be transferred to the care centre listed against the entry in column (i) of Schedule 2 to this Order for the local justicearea in which the relevant magistrates' court is situated.

Principal Registry of the Family Division

6–4418 **19.** The principal registry of the Family Division of the High Court shall be treated, for the purposes of this Order, as if it were a designated county court, a family hearing centre and a care centre listed against every entry in column (i) of Schedule 2 to this Order (in addition to the entries against which it is actually listed) and an adoption centre and intercountry adoption centr.

6–4419 **20.** Revoked.

MISCELLANEOUS

Contravention of provision of this Order

6–4420 **21.** Where proceedings are commenced or transferred in contravention of a provision of this Order, the contravention shall not have the effect of making the proceedings invalid; and no appeal shall lie against the determination of proceedings on the basis of such contravention alone.

6–4421 **22.** Revoked.

6–4422
Article 2

SCHEDULE 1
FAMILY HEARING CENTRES

London Region
Barnet County Court
Bow County Court
Brentford County Court
Bromley County Court
Croydon County Court
Edmonton County Court
Ilford County Court
Kingston-upon-Thames County Court
Romford County Court
Wandsworth County Court
Watford County Court

Midlands Region
　Birmingham County Court
　Coventry County Court
　Derby County Court
　Dudley County Court
　Leicester County Court
　Lincoln County Court
　Mansfield County Court
　Northampton County Court
　Nottingham County Court
　Stafford County Court
　Stoke-on-Trent County Court
　Telford County Court
　Walsall County Court
　Wolverhampton County Court

North West Region
　Worcester County Court
　Blackburn County Court
　Bolton County Court
　Carlisle County Court
　Lancaster County Court
　Liverpool County Court
　Manchester County Court
　Oldham County Court

North East Region
　Stockport County Court
　Barnsley County Court
　Bradford County Court
　Darlington County Court
　Dewsbury County Court
　Doncaster County Court
　Durham County Court
　Grimsby County Court
　Halifax County Court
　Harrogate County Court
　Huddersfield County Court
　Keighley County Court
　Kingston-upon-Hull County Court
　Leeds County Court
　Newcastle-upon-Tyne County Court
　Pontefract County Court
　Rotherham County Court
　Scarborough County Court
　Sheffield County Court
　Skipton County Court
　Sunderland County Court
　Teesside County Court
　Wakefield County Court
　York County Court

South East Region
　Bedford County Court
　Brighton County Court
　Cambridge County Court
　Canterbury County Court
　Chelmsford County Court
　Chichester County Court
　Colchester and Clacton County Court
　Dartford County Court
　Guildford County Court
　Hitchin County Court
　Ipswich County Court
　King's Lynn County Court
　Luton County Court
　Maidstone County Court
　Medway County Court
　Milton Keynes County Court
　Norwich County Court
　Oxford County Court
　Peterborough County Court
　Reading County Court
　Slough County Court
　Southend County Court
　Watford County Court

Wales and Chester Circuit
Aberystwyth County Court
Caernarfon County Court
Cardiff County Court
Carmarthen County Court
Chester County Court
Crewe County Court
Haverfordwest County Court
Llangefni County Court
Macclesfield County Court
Merthyr Tydfil County Court
Newport (Gwent) County Court
Pontypridd County Court
Rhyl County Court
Swansea County Court
Warrington County Court
Welshpool and Newtown County Court

South West Region
Barnstaple County Court
Wrexham County Court
Basingstoke County Court
Bath County Court
Bournemouth County Court
Bristol County Court
Exeter County Court
Gloucester County Court
Plymouth County Court
Portsmouth County Court
Salisbury County Court
Southampton County Court
Swindon County Court
Taunton County Court
Truro County Court
Weymouth County Court
Yeovil County Court

6–4422A

Article 2

SCHEDULE 3
ADOPTION CENTRES

Aberystwyth County Court
Birmingham County Court
Blackburn County Court
Bolton County Court
Bournemouth County Court
Bow County Court
Bradford County Court
Brentford County Court
Brighton County Court
Bristol County Court
Bromley County Court
Cambridge County Court
Canterbury County Court
Cardiff County Court
Carlisle County Court
Chelmsford County Court
Chester County Court
Coventry County Court
Croydon County Court
Derby County Court
Exeter County Court
Guildford County Court
Ipswich County Court
Kingston Upon Hull County Court
Lancaster County Court
Leeds County Court
Leicester County Court
Lincoln County Court
Liverpool County Court
Llangefni County Court
Luton County Court
Macclesfield County Court
Manchester County Court
Medway County Court
Middlesbrough County Court at Teesside Combined Court
Milton Keynes County Court
Newcastle upon Tyne County Court
Newport (Gwent) County Court
Northampton County Court

Norwich County Court
Nottingham County Court
Oxford County Court
Peterborough County Court
Plymouth County Court
Pontypridd County Court
Portsmouth County Court
Reading County Court
Rhyl County Court
Romford County Court
Sheffield County Court
Southampton County Court
Stockport County Court
Stoke On Trent County Court
Sunderland County Court
Swansea County Court
Swindon County Court
Taunton County Court
Teesside County Court
Telford County Court
Truro County Court
Warrington County Court
Watford County Court
Wolverhampton County Court
Worcester County Court
York County Court

6–4422B

Article 2   SCHEDULE 4
                    INTERCOUNTRY ADOPTION CENTRES

Birmingham County Court
Bournemouth County Court
Bristol County Court
Cardiff County Court
Chester County Court
Exeter County Court
Leeds County Court
Liverpool County Court
Manchester County Court
Newcastle upon Tyne County Court
Nottingham County Court
Portsmouth County Court

Family Proceedings Courts (Constitution) Rules 1991[1]
(SI 1991/1405 amended by SI 2000/1873, SI 2001/615 and SI 2003/3367)

Citation, commencement, revocations and savings

6–4450 **1.** (1) These Rules may be cited as the Family Proceedings Courts (Constitution) Rules 1991 and shall come into force on 14th October 1991, except that for the purposes of rules 4(1), 8, 11(2) and 12(1), these Rules shall come into force on 12th August 1991.

(2) Subject to paragraph (3), the Rules mentioned in the Schedule to these Rules are hereby revoked.

(3) Nothing in these Rules shall affect any proceedings which are pending (within the meaning of paragraph 1 of Schedule 14 to the Act of 1989) immediately before these Rules come into force.

---

1. Made by the Lord Chancellor in exercise of the powers conferred on him by s 144 of the Magistrates' Courts Act 1980. These rules are continued in force and have effect as if made under s 67 of the Magistrates' Courts Act 1980 by the Courts Act 2003 (Transitional Provisions, Savings and Consequential Provisions) Order 2005, SI 2005/911.

Interpretation

6–4451 **2.** (1) In these Rules, unless a contrary intention appears—

any reference to a rule shall be construed as a reference to a rule contained in these Rules and any reference in a rule to a paragraph shall be construed as a reference to a paragraph of that rule;

"commission area" has the meaning assigned to it by section 1 of the Act of 1979 but does not include the Greater London Commission Area;

"panel" means "family panel", within the meaning of section 92 of the Act of 1989;

"petty sessions area" has the meaning assigned to it by section 4 of the Act of 1979 but does not include the any petty sessions area within the Greater London Commission Area;

"District Judge (Magistrates' Courts)" means a District Judge (Magistrates' Courts) appointed under section 10A(1) of the Justices of the Peace Act 1997 or a Deputy District Judge (Magistrates' Courts) appointed under section 10B(1) of that Act;

"the Act of 1979" means the Justices of the Peace Act 1979;

"the Act of 1989" means the Children Act 1989.

(2) Any reference in these Rules to a justice for a petty sessions area shall be construed as a reference to a justice who ordinarily acts in and for that area.

Extent

6–4452　　3.　These Rules do not apply in the Greater London Commission Area.

Appointments and formation of panel

6–4453　　4.　(1) The justices for each petty sessions area shall, at a meeting held in October 1991, and before 14th October 1991, of which seven days' notice shall be given to each justice for that area, appoint, in accordance with the provisions of these Rules, justices to form a panel for that area who shall, subject to rule 5(4), serve thereon for a term commencing on 14th October 1991 and expiring on 31st December 1993.

(2) The justices for each petty sessions area shall, at the meeting held in October 1993 in accordance with rules made under section 18 of the Act of 1979 for the purpose of electing a chairman of the justices, and thereafter at the said meeting in every third year, appoint, in accordance with the provisions of these Rules, justices to form a panel for that area who shall, subject to rule 5(4), serve thereon for a term of three years commencing on 1st January in the following year.

(3) The number of justices appointed to the panel for a petty sessions area shall be such as the justices for that area at the time of appointment think sufficient for family proceedings courts in the area.

(4) Nominations shall be permitted but where voting is necessary it shall be by secret ballot.

(5) The justices for a petty sessions area may at any time, subject to rule 5(1), appoint one or more additional members of the panel who shall serve thereon until the end of the period for which the other members of the panel were appointed.

Eligibility

6–4454　　5.　(1) A justice shall not be appointed to a panel unless—

(a) he is a justice of the petty sessions area for which the panel is being formed;
(b) he has acted as a justice for a minimum period of one year;
(c) he has indicated that he is willing to serve as a member of the panel; and
(d) where he is appointed under rule 4(1), he will not attain the age of 70 years during the term of his appointment and has undertaken that he intends to serve as a member of the panel for the full term of the appointment.

(2) A justice shall be eligible for appointment to a panel whether or not he—

(a) has been a member of that panel before, or
(b) is, or has been, a member of any other panel.

(3) A District Judge (Magistrates' Courts) who has been nominated by the Lord Chancellor to hear family proceedings shall be a member of any panel for a petty sessions area or areas which is situated in the commission area or areas to which he is appointed and every such nomination shall be for a specified period and shall be revocable by the Lord Chancellor.

(4) The Lord Chancellor may remove from a panel any justice who, in the Lord Chancellor's opinion, is unsuitable to serve on a family proceedings court.

Vacancies in membership of panel

6–4455　　6.　If a vacancy occurs in the membership of a panel for a petty sessions area, the justices for that area shall, as soon as practicable, unless they consider that it is not necessary, and subject to rule 5, appoint a justice to fill the vacancy who shall serve on the panel until the end of the period for which the other members were appointed.

Temporary transfer of justices between panels

6–4456　　7.　[(1) A justices' chief executive for a petty sessions area may nominate a justice or justices from the panel for that area for temporary transfer to the panel for another petty sessions area within his commission area for the purpose of hearing family proceedings specified in his nomination if he is satisfied that the better administration of justice will be served by such transfer, and the justice or justices so nominated agree to be transferred.

(2) A justices' chief executive for one commission area ("the first commission area") may make a request to the justices' chief executive for another commission area ("the second commission area") for the temporary transfer of one or more justices from the panel for a petty sessions area within the second commission area to the panel for a petty sessions area within the first commission area for the purpose of hearing family proceedings specified in the request.

(3) The justices' chief executive for the second commission area shall grant a request under

paragraph (2) where he considers that the better administration of justice will be served by such transfer, and the justice or justices nominated by him for the transfer agree to be transferred.

(4) A justices' chief executive who grants a request under paragraph (2) shall do so in writing.

(5) The transfer of a justice or justices under this rule shall not prevent the justice or justices transferred from sitting in a family proceedings court in the petty sessions area from which he or they are transferred.

(6) A justice who is not a District Judge (Magistrates' Courts) shall only be transferred under this rule to a petty sessions area in a different commission area if the Lord Chancellor appoints the justice nominated for the transfer to the commission area within which the petty sessions area falls for the purpose of the proceedings specified in the request.

Chairman and deputy chairmen of panel

6–4457   8. (1) The members of each panel shall, in accordance with the provisions of this rule and rule 9, on the occasion of their appointment or as soon as practicable thereafter, meet and elect from amongst their number a chairman and as many deputy chairmen as will ensure, subject to rule 10(3), that each family proceedings court sits under the chairmanship of a person so elected.

(2) Nominations for chairman and one or more deputy chairmen may be made by the members of the panel to the justices' chief executive but, where voting is necessary, it shall be by secret ballot.

(3) If a vacancy occurs in the chairmanship or deputy chairmanship, the members of the panel shall, as soon as practicable, elect by secret ballot a chairman or, as the case may be, deputy chairman, to hold office for the remainder of the period for which the members serve.

Conduct of ballots generally

6–4458   9. (1) Where, under a ballot conducted under any provision of these Rules, there is an equality of votes between any candidates, and the addition of a vote would entitle one of them to be elected, the justices' chief executive shall forthwith decide between those candidates by lot.

(2) Where, under a ballot conducted under any provision of these Rules, a ballot paper is returned unmarked or it is marked in such a manner that there is a doubt as to the identity of the justice or justices for whom the vote is cast, the ballot paper or the vote, as the case may be, shall be rejected when the votes are counted.

Composition of family proceedings courts

6–4459   10. (1) The members of a panel shall meet as often as may be necessary but not less than twice a year to make arrangements connected with the sitting of family proceedings courts and to discuss questions connected with the work of those courts.

(2) The justices to sit in each family proceedings court shall be chosen from the panel in such manner as the panel may determine so as to ensure that section 66(1) of the Magistrates' Courts Act 1980 (which requires a family proceedings court to be composed of not more than three justices of the peace, including, so far as practicable, both a man and a woman), is complied with.

(3) Except as is provided by paragraph (4), where a District Judge (Magistrates' Courts) is chosen to sit in a family proceedings court under paragraph (2) he shall preside, but where a District Judge (Magistrates' Courts) is not so chosen, the court shall sit under the chairmanship of the chairman or a deputy chairman elected under rule 8.

(4) If, at any sitting of a family proceedings court, a District Judge (Magistrates' Courts), the chairman or a deputy chairman who was chosen to sit as a member of the court cannot do so owing to circumstances unforeseen when the justices to sit were chosen under paragraph (2), the members of that court shall choose one of their number to preside.

Combined panels

6–4460   11. (1) Where, immediately before 14th October 1991, there exists a combined domestic court panel ("the first panel") in respect of two or more petty sessions areas there shall, with effect from 14th October 1991, be a combined family panel ("the second panel") for those areas and in relation to the second panel these Rules shall have effect as if—

(a) a direction for its formation had, before 14th October 1991, been made under paragraph (2) by the magistrates' courts committee for the areas in question, save that paragraphs (4) and (5) shall not apply, and

(b) the direction stated under paragraph (6) that the number of justices to serve as members, and the number of members to be provided by each area, were to be the same as for the first panel.

(2) Subject to the provisions of this rule, a magistrates' courts committee may make a direction for the formation or dissolution of a combined panel in respect of two or more petty sessions areas in the same commission area, of which at least one is a petty sessions area for which the committee acts.

(3) A direction under paragraph (2) shall not be made unless the magistrates' courts committee has consulted the justices for each petty sessions area specified in the direction for which it acts.

(4) A direction under paragraph (2) shall be notified forthwith to the justices for each petty sessions area specified in the direction.

(5) If a magistrates' courts committee makes a direction under paragraph (2) which specifies a petty sessions area or petty sessions areas for which it does not act, the direction shall have no effect unless, before the date on which it is to come into effect, a corresponding direction has been made by the magistrates' courts committee or committees for the area or areas in question.

(6) A direction for the formation of a combined panel shall state—

(a) the number of justices who are to serve as members of the combined panel, which shall be such as the magistrates' courts committee thinks sufficient for family proceedings courts in the petty sessions areas specified in the direction; and

(b) the number of members thereof to be provided by each area, which shall, as nearly as may be, be the proportion which the number of justices for that area bears to the total number of justices for the petty sessions areas specified in the direction.

(7) A direction for the formation or dissolution of a combined panel under paragraph (2) shall have effect—

(a) where it is a direction for the formation of a combined panel and is made before 14th October 1991, on that date,

(b) where sub-paragraph (a) does not apply and the direction is consequential upon the making of an order under section 23 of the Act of 1979, on the date on which that order comes into force, and

(c) in any other case, on 1st January in the year following the next October meeting of the justices for each of the areas concerned held in accordance with rules made under section 18 of the Act of 1979 for the purpose of electing a chairman of the justices.

(8) For the purposes of paragraph (7)(b), a direction is consequential upon the making of an order under the said section 23 if it is made after that order is made (but before it comes into force) and specifies a petty sessions area which is the subject of such an order.

(9) A magistrates' courts committee which has made a direction for the formation of a combined panel may at any time make a further direction to increase the number of justices specified under paragraph (6)(a) and any such further direction shall state the petty sessions area or petty sessions areas by which the additional member or members is or are to be provided.

(10) A further direction in relation to a combined panel under paragraph (9) shall have effect forthwith or, in the case of a direction which specifies a petty sessions area or petty sessions areas for which the magistrates' courts committee does not act, as soon as corresponding further directions have been made under that paragraph by the magistrates' courts committee or committees for the area or areas in question.

(11) A combined panel formed by a direction made under paragraph (2), shall be the panel for the petty sessions areas specified in the direction and, in relation to any such combined panel, subject to rule 12(4), these Rules shall have effect accordingly.

(12) On the coming into effect of a direction made under this rule (other than a further direction under paragraph (9)), any existing panel in respect of any of the petty sessions areas specified in the direction shall dissolve and any appointments thereto shall cease.

Appointment of justices to combined panel

6–4461 **12.** (1) Where a magistrates' courts committee has made a direction for the formation of a combined panel under rule 11(2), the justices for each petty sessions area specified in the direction shall, at a meeting of the justices held in accordance with paragraph (2), appoint, subject to paragraph (3), such number of justices from the petty sessions areas in question as is stated in the direction, to serve as members of the combined panel, for a term commencing at the same time as the direction will have effect and expiring at the same time as will end the term of appointment of any justices for the time being appointed under rule 4(1) or, where that term has expired, rule 4(2), to form a panel which is not specified in the direction.

(2) The meeting referred to in paragraph (1) shall be—

(a) where the direction is made before 14th October 1991, the meeting referred to in rule 4(1);

(b) where sub-paragraph (a) does not apply and the direction is consequential upon the making of an order under section 23 of the Act of 1979, within the meaning of rule 11(8), a meeting held as soon as practicable after the direction has been made; and

(c) in any other case, the meeting referred to in rule 11(7)(c).

(3) In relation to the appointment of justices under paragraph (1), rules 4(4), 5(1)(b)–(d), (2) and (3), and 9 of these Rules shall apply as they apply in relation to appointments under rule 4.

(4) Subject to rule 13, after the first appointments to a combined panel have been made in accordance with paragraph (1), these Rules shall have effect in relation to the combined panel as if—

(a) in rule 4:

   (i) references to appointments to a panel in paragraph (2) of that rule were references to appointments to the combined panel of such number of justices from the petty sessions area as is stated in the direction; and

   (ii) paragraphs (3) and (5) thereof were omitted;

(b) for paragraph (1)(a) of rule 5 there were substituted the following paragraph—

"(1)

(a) The members of a combined panel provided by each petty sessions area for which the panel is formed shall be appointed from amongst the justices for that area.";

(c) for rule 6 there were substituted the following rule—

"**6.** If a vacancy occurs in the number of justices forming a combined panel or if a further direction is made under rule 11(9), the justices for the appropriate petty sessions area shall as soon as practicable appoint such a justice or justices as might have been appointed to the panel under rule 5.";

(d) in rule 7, where the first area or the second area is one of the petty sessions areas for which the combined panel has been formed, the references to those areas included the other petty sessions areas in respect of which the combined panel has been formed.

Appointments of justices to a panel as a consequence of a dissolution of a combined panel

6–4462 **13.** (1) Where a magistrates' courts committee makes a direction under rule 11(2), for the dissolution of a combined panel, the justices for each petty sessions area specified in the direction shall (unless the petty sessions area is also specified in a direction for the formation of a combined panel), at a meeting of the justices held in accordance with paragraph (2), appoint, subject to paragraph (3), justices to form a panel for that area for a term commencing at the same time as the direction will have effect and expiring at the same time as will end the term of appointment of any justices for the time being appointed under rule 4(1) or, where that term has expired, rule 4(2), to form a panel which is not specified in the direction.

(2) The meeting referred to in paragraph (1) shall be—

(a) where the direction is consequential upon the making of an order under section 23 of the 1979 Act, within the meaning of rule 11(8), a meeting held as soon as practicable after the direction has been made; and

(b) in any other case, the meeting of the justices referred to in rule 11(7)(c).

(3) In relation to the appointment of justices under paragraph (1), rules 4(3), (4) and (5), 5(1), (2) and (3) and 9 shall apply as they apply in relation to appointments under rule 4.

6–4463
Rule 1(2)

SCHEDULE
Revocations

Family Proceedings Courts (Matrimonial Proceedings etc) Rules 1991[1]

(SI 1991/1991 amended by SI 1992/2068, SI 1993/627, SI 1994/809, SI 1997/1894, SI 2001/778 and 615, and SI 2005/617 and 2930)

Part I
Introductory

Citation, commencement and transitional

6–4521 **1.** (1) These Rules may be cited as the Family Proceedings Courts (Matrimonial Proceedings etc) Rules 1991 and shall come into force on 14th October 1991 except that paragraph 3(7) of Schedule 2 to these Rules shall come into force on 7th October 1991.

(2) Nothing in these Rules shall affect any proceedings which are pending (within the meaning of paragraph 1 of Schedule 14 to the Children Act 1989) immediately before these Rules come into force.

---

1. Made by the Lord Chancellor in exercise of the powers conferred on him by s 144 of the Magistrates' Courts Act 1980.

Part II
Matrimonial Proceedings under the Domestic Proceedings and Magistrates' Courts Act 1978 Proceedings Under Section 55A of the Family Law Act 1986 and Proceedings under Part IV of the Family Law Act 1996

Interpretation, application and savings

6–4522 **2.** (1) In this Part of these Rules, unless a contrary intention appears—

any reference to a rule shall be construed as a reference to a rule contained in these Rules; and any reference in a rule to a paragraph shall be construed as a reference to a paragraph of that rule,

"application" means an application for an order made under or by virtue of the Act, the Act of 2004, the Family Law Act 1986 or the Family Law Act 1996, as the case may be and "applicant" shall be construed accordingly,

"business day" means any day other than—

(a) a Saturday, Sunday, Christmas Day or Good Friday; or

(*b*) a bank holiday, that is to say, a day which is, or is to be observed as, a bank holiday or a holiday under the Banking and Financial Dealings Act 1971, in England and Wales,

"court" means a family proceedings court constituted in accordance with sections 66 and 67 of the Magistrates' Courts Act 1980 or, in respect of those proceedings prescribed in rule 25, a single justice who is a member of a family panel,

"directions appointment" means a hearing for directions under rule 6(1),

"file" means deposit with the justices' chief executive,

"form" means a form in Schedule 1 to these Rules and, where a form is referred to by number, means the form so numbered in that Schedule, with such variation as the circumstances of the particular case may require;

"note" includes a record made by mechanical means,

"respondent" includes, as the case may be, more than one respondent,

"the Act" means the Domestic Proceedings and Magistrates' Courts Act 1978,

"the Act of 2004" means the Civil Partnership Act 2004.

(2) Expressions used in this Part of these Rules have the meaning which they bear in the Act, the Act of 2004, the Family Law Act 1986 or the Family Law Act 1996, as the case may be.

(3) This Part of these Rules shall not apply in relation to any such application or order as is referred to in paragraph 1 or 2 of Schedule 1 to the Domestic Proceedings and Magistrates' Courts Act 1978 (transitional provisions); and, accordingly, the Magistrates' Courts (Matrimonial Proceedings) Rules 1960 shall continue to apply in relation to any such application or order but with the following modification, that is to say, on any complaint made by virtue of paragraph 2(*d*) of the said Schedule 1 for the variation or revocation of a provision requiring access to a child to be given to a grandparent, rule 7 of the said Rules of 1960 shall be construed as applying to the complaint as it applies to a complaint made by virtue of section 8 of the Matrimonial Proceedings (Magistrates' Courts) Act 1960 and as if paragraph (5) of that rule included a reference to that grandparent.

(4) Subject to rule 1(2), the provisions of the Magistrates' Courts Rules 1981 shall have effect subject to this Part of these Rules.

Application

6–4523   **3.** (1) Subject to paragraph (3) and rule 3A, an applicant shall—

(*a*) file the application in the appropriate form in Schedule 1 to these Rules or, where there is no such form, in writing, together with sufficient copies for one to be served on the respondent, and

(*b*) serve a copy of the application, endorsed in accordance with paragraph (2)(*b*) on the respondent at least 21 days prior to the date fixed under paragraph (2)(*a*).

(2) [(2)On receipt by the designated officer for a magistrates' court of the documents filed under paragraph (1)(*a*)—

(*a*) the justices' clerk shall fix the date, time and place for a hearing or a directions appointment, allowing sufficient time for the applicant to comply with paragraph (1)(*b*), and

(*b*) the justices' chief executive shall—

   (i) endorse the date, time and place so fixed upon the copies of the application filed by the applicant, and

   (ii) return the copies to the applicant forthwith.

(3) A court may proceed on an application made orally where it is made by virtue of section 6(4) of the Act or paragraph 14 of Schedule 6 to the Act of 2004 and where an application is so made paragraph (1) shall not apply.

(4) *Revoked.*

Applications under Part IV of the Family Law Act 1996

6–4523A   **3A.** (1) An application for an occupation order or a non-molestation order under Part IV of the Family Law Act 1996 (family homes and domestic violence) shall be made in Form FL401.

(2) An application for an occupation order or a non-molestation order which is made in other proceedings which are pending shall be made in Form FL401.

(3) An application in Form FL401 shall be supported—

(*a*) by a statement which is signed and is declared to be true: or

(*b*) with the leave of the court, by oral evidence.

(4) An application in Form FL401 may, with the leave of the justices' clerk or of the court, be made ex parte, in which case—

(*a*) the applicant shall file with the justices' chief executive or the court the application at the time when the application is made or as directed by the justices' clerk; and

(*b*) the evidence in support of the application shall state the reasons why the application is made ex parte.

(5) An application made on notice (together with any statement supporting it and a notice in Form FL402) shall be served by the applicant on the respondent personally not less than 2 business days prior to the date on which the application will be heard.

(6) The court or the justices' clerk may abridge the period specified in paragraph (5).

(7) Where the applicant is acting in person, service of the application may, with the leave of the justices' clerk, be effected in accordance with rule 4.

(8) Where an application for an occupation order or a non-molestation order is pending, the court shall consider (on the application of either party or of its own motion) whether to exercise its powers to transfer the hearing of that application to another court and the justices' clerk or the court shall make an order for transfer in Form FL417 if it seems necessary or expedient to do so.

(9) Where an order for transfer is made, the justices' chief executive shall send a copy of the order—

(a) to the parties, and

(b) to the family proceedings court or to the county court to which the proceedings are to be transferred.

(10) A copy of an application for an occupation order under section 33, 35 or 36 of the Family Law Act 1996 shall be served by the applicant by first-class post on the mortgagee or, as the case may be, the landlord of the dwelling-house in question, with a notice in Form FL416 informing him of his right to make representations in writing or at any hearing.

(11) The applicant shall file a statement in Form FL415 after he has served the application.

(12) Rule 33A of the Family Proceedings Courts (Children Act 1989) Rules 1991 (disclosure of addresses) shall apply for the purpose of preventing the disclosure of addresses where an application is made in Form FL401 as it applies for that purpose in proceedings under the Children Act 1989.

Applications under section 55A of the Family Law Act 1986

6–4523B **3B.** (1) An application for a declaration of parentage under section 55A of the Family Law Act 1986 shall be made in Form FL 423.

(2) An application in Form FL 423 shall be supported by a statement which is signed and is declared to be true. Provided that if the applicant is under the age of 18, the statement shall, unless otherwise directed, be made by his next friend.

(3) A statement under paragraph (2) may contain statements of information or belief with the sources and grounds thereof.

(4) Within 14 days of service of the application the respondent shall file and serve on the parties an answer to the application in Form FL 423.

(5) Where the respondent or one of the respondents is a child, the justices' clerk or the court may at any stage in the proceedings appoint a guardian ad litem, but only if it considers that such an appointment is necessary to safeguard the interests of the child.

(6) The justices' chief executive shall send a copy of the application and every document accompanying it and of any answer to the Attorney General if he has notified the court that he wishes to intervene in the proceedings.

(7) When all answers to the application have been filed the applicant shall issue and serve on all respondents to the application a request for directions for the conduct of the proceedings, including directions as to any other persons who should be made respondents to the application or given notice of the proceedings.

(8) When giving directions in accordance with paragraph (7) the court shall consider whether it is desirable that the Attorney General should argue before it any question relating to the proceedings, and if it does so consider and the Attorney General agrees to argue that question—

(i) the justices' chief executive shall send a copy of the application and every document accompanying it and of any answer to the Attorney General;

(ii) the Attorney General need not file an answer; and

(iii) the court shall give him directions requiring him to serve on all parties to the proceedings a summary of his argument.

(9) Persons given notice of proceedings pursuant to directions given in accordance with paragraph (7) shall within 21 days after service of the notice upon them be entitled to apply to the court to be joined as parties.

(10) The Attorney General may file an answer to the application within 21 days after directions have been given in accordance with paragraph (7) and no directions for the hearing shall be given until that period and the period referred to in paragraph (9) have expired.

(11) The Attorney General, in deciding whether it is necessary or expedient to intervene in the proceedings, may have a search made for, and may inspect and obtain a copy of, any document filed in the court offices which relates to any other family proceedings referred to in the proceedings.

(12) Where the justices' clerk or the court is considering whether or not to transfer proceedings under section 55A of the Family Law Act 1986 to another court, rules 6, 14(2)(h), (4) and (11) and 32 of the Family Proceedings Courts (Children Act 1989) Rules 1991 shall apply as appropriate.

(13) A declaration made in accordance with section 55A of the Family Law Act 1986 shall be in form FL 424.

(14) The prescribed officer for the purposes of section 55A(7) of the Family Law Act 1986 shall be the justices' chief executive, who shall, within 21 days after a declaration of parentage has been made, send to the Registrar General a copy of the declaration and of the application.

Service

6–4524 4. (1) Where service of a document is required by these Rules it may be effected, unless the contrary is indicated—

(a) if the person to be served is not known by the person serving to be acting by solicitor—

(i) by delivering it to him personally, or
(ii) by delivering at, or by sending it by first-class post to, his residence or his last known residence, or

(b) if the person to be served is known by the person serving to be acting by solicitor—

(i) by delivering the document at, or sending it by first-class post to, the solicitor's address for service,
(ii) where the solicitor's address for service includes a numbered box at a document exchange, by leaving the document at that document exchange or at a document exchange which transmits documents on every business day to that document exchange, or
(iii) by sending a legible copy of the document by facsimile transmission to the solicitor's office.

(2) In this rule, "first-class post" means first-class post which has been pre-paid or in respect of which pre-payment is not required.

(3) A document shall, unless the contrary is proved, be deemed to have been served—

(a) in the case of service by first-class post, on the second business day after posting, and
(b) in the case of service in accordance with paragraph (1)(b)(ii), on the second business day after the day on which it is left at the document exchange.

(4) At or before the first directions appointment in, or hearing of, the proceedings, whichever occurs first, the applicant shall file a statement that service of a copy of the application has been effected on the respondent and the statement shall indicate—

(a) the manner, date, time and place of service, or
(b) where service was effected by post, the date, time and place of posting.

(5) In any proceedings under the Act, the justices' clerk or the court may direct that a requirement in this Part of these Rules to serve a document shall not apply or shall be effected in such manner as the justices' clerk or the court directs.

Answer to application

6–4525 5. Within 14 days of service of an application for an order under section 2, 6, 7 or 20 of the Act, or under Part 1, 2 or 3, or paragraphs 30 to 34, of Schedule 6 to the Act of 2004, the respondent shall file and serve on the parties an answer to the application in the appropriate form in Schedule 1 to these Rules.

Directions

6–4526 6. (1) In any proceedings under the Act, the justices' clerk or the court may, subject to paragraph (3), give, vary or revoke directions for the conduct of the proceedings, including—

(a) the timetable for the proceedings;
(b) varying the time within which or by which an act is required, by this Part of these Rules, to be done;
(c) the service of documents; and
(d) the submission of evidence;

and the justices' clerk shall, on receipt of an application by the justices' chief executive, consider whether such directions need to be given.

(2) Where the justices' clerk or a single justice who is holding a directions appointment considers, for whatever reason, that it is inappropriate to give a direction on a particular matter, he shall refer the matter to the court which may give any appropriate direction.

(3) Directions under paragraph (1) may be given, varied or revoked either—

(a) of the justices' clerk or the court's own motion the justices' chief executive having given the parties notice of the intention to do so and an opportunity to attend and be heard or to make written representations,
(b) on the written request of a party specifying the direction which is sought, which request has been filed and served on the other parties, or
(c) on the written request of a party specifying the direction which is sought, to which the other parties consent and which they or their representatives have signed.

(4) In an urgent case, the request under paragraph (3)(b) may, with the leave of the justices' clerk or the court, be made—

(a) orally,
(b) without notice to the other parties, or
(c) both as in sub-paragraph (a) and as in sub-paragraph (b).

(5) On receipt of a request under paragraph (3)(*b*) the justices' clerk shall fix a date for the hearing of the request and give not less than 2 days' notice to the parties of the date so fixed.

(6) On considering a request under paragraph (3)(*c*) the justices' clerk or the court shall either—

(*a*) grant the request, whereupon the justices' chief executive shall inform the parties of the decision, or

(*b*) direct that a date be fixed for the hearing of the request, whereupon the justices' chief executive shall fix such a date and give not less than 2 days' notice to the parties of the date so fixed.

(7) The justices' clerk or the court shall take a note of the giving, variation or revocation of a direction under this rule and the justices' chief executive shall serve, as soon as practicable, a copy of the note on any party who was not present at the giving, variation or revocation.

Timing of proceedings

6–4527   7. (1) Any period of time fixed by this Part of these Rules, or by any order or direction, for the doing of any act shall be reckoned in accordance with this rule.

(2) Where the period, being a period of 7 days or less, would include a day which is not a business day, that day shall be excluded.

(3) Where the time fixed for filing a document with the justices' chief executive expires on a day on which the office of the justices' chief executive is closed, and for that reason the document cannot be filed on that day, the document shall be filed in time if it is filed on the next day on which the office of the justices' chief executive is open.

(4) Where these Rules provide a period of time within which or by which a certain act is to be performed in the course of proceedings, that period may not be extended otherwise than by a direction of the justices' clerk or the court under rule 6(1).

(5) At the—

(*a*) postponement or adjournment of any hearing or directions appointment in the course of proceedings, or

(*b*) conclusion of any such hearing or directions appointment other than one at which the proceedings are determined, or as soon thereafter as is practicable,

the justices' clerk or the court shall—

(i) the justices' clerk shall fix a date upon which the proceedings shall come before him or the court again for such purposes as he or the court directs, and

(ii) the justices' chief executive shall serve, in accordance with these Rules, a copy of the order made on the parties to the proceedings.

Attendance at directions appointment and hearing

6–4528   8. (1) Subject to paragraph (2), a party shall attend a directions appointment of which he has been given notice in accordance with rule 6(3) unless the justices' clerk or the court otherwise directs.

(2) Subject to rules 18(2) and 22(2), the court shall not begin to hear an application in the absence of the respondent unless—

(*a*) it is proved to the satisfaction of the court that he received reasonable notice of the date of the hearing; or

(*b*) the court is satisfied that the circumstances of the case justify proceeding with the hearing.

(3) Where, at the time and place appointed for a hearing or directions appointment, the respondent appears but the applicant does not, the court may refuse the application or, if sufficient evidence has previously been received, proceed in the absence of the applicant.

(4) Where at the time and place appointed for a hearing or directions appointment neither the applicant nor the respondent appears, the court may refuse the application.

Documentary evidence

6–4529   9. (1) In any proceedings the parties shall file and serve on the other parties—

(*a*) written statements of the substance of the oral evidence which the party intends to adduce at a hearing of, or a directions appointment in, those proceedings, which shall—

(i) be dated,

(ii) be signed by the person making the statement, and

(iii) contain a declaration that the maker of the statement believes it to be true and understands that it may be placed before the court, and

(*b*) copies of any documents upon which the party intends to rely at a hearing of, or a directions appointment in, those proceedings,

at or by such time as the justices' clerk or the court directs or, in the absence of a direction, before the hearing or appointment.

(2) A party may, subject to any direction of the justices' clerk or the court about the timing of statements under this rule, file and serve on the parties a statement which is supplementary to a statement served under paragraph (1).

(3) At a hearing or directions appointment a party may not, without the leave of the justices' clerk in the case of a directions appointment, or the court—

(*a*) adduce evidence, or
(*b*) seek to rely on a document,

in respect of which he has failed to comply with the requirements of paragraph (1).

Amendment

6–4530 10. (1) Subject to rule 9(2), a copy of a document which has been filed or served in any proceedings may not be amended without the leave of the justices' clerk or the court which shall, unless the justices clerk or the court otherwise directs, be requested in writing.

(2) On considering a request for leave to amend a document the justices' clerk or the court shall either—

(*a*) grant the request, whereupon the justices' chief executive shall inform the person making the request of that decision, or
(*b*) invite the parties or any of them to make representations, within a specified period, as to whether such an order should be made.

(3) A person amending a document shall file it with the justices' chief executive and serve it on those persons on whom it was served prior to amendment; and the amendments shall be identified.

Oral evidence

6–4531 11. The justices' clerk or the court shall keep a note of the substance of the oral evidence given at a hearing of, or directions appointment in, any proceedings.

Hearing

6–4532 12. (1) Before the hearing, the justice or justices who will be dealing with the case shall read any documents which have been filed under rule 9 in respect of the hearing.

(2) The justices' clerk at a directions appointment or the court at a hearing or directions appointment, may give directions as to the order of speeches and evidence.

(3) Subject to directions under paragraph (2), at a hearing of, or directions appointment in, proceedings, the parties shall adduce their evidence in the following order—

(*a*) the applicant,
(*b*) the respondent other than the child, and
(*c*) the child if he is a respondent.

(4) After the final hearing of proceedings, the court shall make its decision as soon as is practicable.

(5) Before the court makes an order or refuses an application, the justices' clerk shall record in writing—

(*a*) the names of the justice or justices constituting the court by which the decision is made, and
(*b*) in consultation with the justice or justices, the reasons for the court's decision and any findings of fact.

(6) When making an order or when refusing an application, the court, or one of the justices constituting the court by which the decision is made, shall state any findings of fact and the reasons for the court's decision.

(7) After the court announces its decision—

(*a*) the justices' clerk shall, as soon as practicable, make a record of the order made in the appropriate form, in writing, and
(*b*) the justices' chief executive shall serve, in accordance with these Rules, a copy of the order made on the parties to the proceedings.

(8) The justices' clerk shall supply a copy of the record of the reasons for a decision made in pursuance of paragraph (5)(*b*) to any person on request, if satisfied that it is required in connection with an appeal or possible appeal.

Hearing of applications under Part IV of the Family Law Act 1996

6–4532A 12A. (1) This rule applies to the hearing of applications under Part IV of the Family Law Act 1996 and the following forms shall be used in connection with such hearings:

(*a*) a record of the hearing shall be made on Form FL405, and
(*b*) any order made on the hearing shall be issued in Form FL404.

(2) Where an order is made on an application made ex parte, a copy of the order together with a copy of the application and of any statement supporting it shall be served by the applicant on the respondent personally.

(3) Where the applicant is acting in person, service of a copy of an order made on an application made ex parte shall be effected by the justices' chief executive if the applicant so requests.

(4) Where the application is for an occupation order under section 33, 35 or 36 of the Family

Law Act 1996, a copy of any order made on the application shall be served by the applicant by first-class post on the mortgagee or, as the case may be, the landlord of the dwelling-house in question.

(5) A copy of an order made on an application heard inter partes shall be served by the applicant on the respondent personally.

(6) Where the applicant is acting in person, service of a copy of the order made on an application heard inter partes may, with the leave of the justices' clerk, be effected in accordance with rule 4.

(7) The court may direct that a further hearing be held in order to consider any representations made by a mortgagee or a landlord.

Applications to vary etc orders made under Part IV of the Family Law Act 1996

6–4532B   12B. An application to vary, extend or discharge an order made under Part IV of the Family Law Act 1996 shall be made in Form FL403 and rules 12 and 12A shall apply to the hearing of such an application.

Costs

6–4533   13. (1) In any proceedings, the court may at any time during the proceedings make an order that a party pay the whole or any part of the costs of any other party.

(2) A party against whom the court is considering making a costs order shall have an opportunity to make representations as to why the order should not be made.

Confidentiality of documents

6–4534   14. No document, other than a record of an order, held by the court and relating to proceedings shall be disclosed other than to—

(a) a party,
(b) the legal representative of a party, or
(c) the Legal Aid Board,

without leave of the justices' clerk or the court.

Delegation by Justices' clerk

6–4535   15. (1) In this rule, "employed as a clerk in court" has the same meaning as in rule 2(1) of the Justices' Clerks (Qualifications of Assistants) Rules 1979.

(2) Anything authorised to be done by, to or before a justices' clerk under this Part of these Rules, or under paragraph 15 or 15D of the Schedule to the Justices' Clerks Rules 1970 as amended by Schedule 2 to these Rules, may be done instead by, to or before a person employed as a clerk in court where that person is appointed by the Magistrates' Courts Committee to assist him and where that person has been specifically authorised by the justices' clerk for that purpose.

(3) Any authorisation by the justices' clerk under paragraph (2) shall be recorded in writing by the justices' chief executive at the time the authority is given or as soon as practicable thereafter.

Application of enactments governing procedure in proceedings brought on complaint

6–4536   16. (1) Section 53(3) of the Magistrates' Courts Act 1980 (orders with the consent of the defendant without hearing evidence) shall apply to applications under section 20 of the Act or paragraphs 30 to 34 of Schedule 6 to the Act of 2004, as the case may be, for the variation of orders for periodical payments, as it applies to complaints for the variation of the rate of any periodical payments ordered by a magistrates' court to be made.

(2) Section 97 of the Magistrates' Courts Act 1980 (issue of a witness summons) shall apply to proceedings as it applies to a hearing of a complaint under that section.

Orders made under section 6 of the Act or Part 2 of Schedule 6 to the Act of 2004 in the absence of the respondent

6–4537   17. For the purposes of subsection 9(a), (b) and (c) of section 6 of the Act or sub-paragraph (a), (b) or (c) of paragraph 11(2) of Schedule 6 to the Act of 2004, evidence of the consent of the respondent to the making of the order, of the financial resources of the respondent and of the financial resources of the child shall be by way of a written statement in the appropriate form in Schedule 1 to these Rules signed by the respondent or, where the application is in respect of financial provision for a child and the child has completed the appropriate form, the child.

Application under section 7 of the Act or Part 3 of Schedule 6 to the Act of 2004

6–4538   18. (1) Where, under subsection (4) of section 7 of the Act, a court decides to treat an application under section 7 as if it were an application for an order under section 2 of the Act, the court shall indicate orally which of grounds (a) and (b) in that subsection it considers applicable and a memorandum of the decision and the grounds therefor shall be entered in the court's register.

(1A) Where, under paragraph 18 of Schedule 6 to the Act of 2004, a court decides to treat an application under Part 3 of Schedule 6 as if it were an application for an order under Part 1 of that

Schedule, the court shall indicate orally which of grounds (a) and (b) in paragraph 18(1) it considers applicable and a memorandum of the decision and the grounds therefor shall be entered in the court's register.

(2) Where a court decides as aforesaid and the respondent is not then present or represented in court, or the respondent or his representative does not then agree to the continuance of the hearing, the court shall adjourn the hearing and the justices' chief executive shall serve notice of the decision and the ground therefor on the respondent in the appropriate form in Schedule 1 to these Rules.

Respondent on application under section 20 or section 20A

6–4539 19. (1) The respondent on an application for the variation or revocation of an order under section 20 of the Act shall be the parties to the marriage in question other than the applicant and, where the order requires payments to be made to or in respect of a child who is 16 years of age or over, that child.

(2) The respondents on an application for the revival of an order under section 20A of the Act shall be the parties to the proceedings leading to the order which it is sought to have revived.

Respondent on application under Part 6 of Schedule 6 to the Act of 2004

6–4539A 19A. (1) The respondent on an application for a variation or revocation of an order under paragraphs 30 to 34 of Schedule 6 to the Act of 2004 shall be the party to the civil partnership in question other than the applicant and, where the order requires payments to be made to or in respect of a child who is 16 years of age or over, that child.

(2) The respondents on an application for the revival of an order under paragraph 40 of Schedule 6 to the Act of 2004 shall be the parties to the proceedings leading to the order which it is sought to have revived.

Enforcement of orders made on applications under Part IV of the Family Law Act 1996

6–4540 20. (1) Where a power of arrest is attached to one or more of the provisions ("the relevant provisions") of an order made under Part IV of the Family Law Act 1996—

(a) the relevant provisions shall be set out in Form FL406 and the form shall not include any provisions of the order to which the power of arrest was not attached; and

(b) a copy of the form shall be delivered to the officer for the time being in charge of any police station for the applicant's address or of such other police station as the court may specify.

The copy of the form delivered under sub-paragraph (b) shall be accompanied by a statement showing that the respondent has been served with the order or informed of its terms (whether by being present when the order was made or by telephone or otherwise).

(2) Where an order is made varying or discharging the relevant provisions, the justices' chief executive shall—

(a) immediately inform the officer who received a copy of the form under paragraph (1) and, if the applicant's address has changed, the officer for the time being in charge of the police station for the new address; and

(b) deliver a copy of the order to any officer so informed.

(3) An application for the issue of a warrant for the arrest of the respondent shall be made in Form FL407 and the warrant shall be issued in Form FL408 and delivered by the justices' chief executive to the officer for the time being in charge of any police station for the respondent's address or of such other police station as the court may specify.

(4) The court before whom a person is brought following his arrest may—

(a) determine whether the facts, and the circumstances which led to the arrest, amounted to disobedience of the order, or

(b) adjourn the proceedings and, where such an order is made, the arrested person may be released and

(i) be dealt with within 14 days of the day on which he was arrested; and

(ii) be given not less than 2 business days' notice of the adjourned hearing.

Nothing in this paragraph shall prevent the issue of a notice under paragraph (8) if the arrested person is not dealt with within the period mentioned in sub-paragraph (b)(i) above.

(5) Paragraphs (6) to (13) shall apply for the enforcement of orders made on applications under Part IV of the Family Law Act 1996 by committal order.

(6) Subject to paragraphs (11) and (12), an order shall not be enforced by committal order unless—

(a) a copy of the order in Form FL404 has been served personally on the respondent; and

(b) where the order requires the respondent to do an act, the copy has been so served before the expiration of the time within which he was required to do the act and was accompanied by a copy of any order, made between the date of the order and the date of service, fixing that time.

(7) At the time when the order is drawn up, the justices' chief executive shall—

(a) where the order made is (or includes) a non-molestation order, and

(b) where the order made is an occupation order and the court so directs,

issue a copy of the order, indorsed with or incorporating a notice as to the consequences of disobedience, for service in accordance with paragraph (6).

(8) If the respondent fails to obey the order, the justices' chief executive shall, at the request of the applicant, issue a notice in Form FL418 warning the respondent that an application will be made for him to be committed and, subject to paragraph (12), the notice shall be served on him personally.

(9) The request for issue of the notice under paragraph (8) shall be treated as a complaint and shall—

(a) identify the provisions of the order or undertaking which it is alleged have been disobeyed or broken;

(b) list the ways in which it is alleged that the order or undertaking has been disobeyed or broken;

(c) be supported by a statement which is signed and is declared to be true and which states the grounds on which the application is made,

and, unless service is dispensed with under paragraph (12), a copy of the statement shall be served with the notice.

(10) If an order in Form FL419 (a committal order) is made, it shall include provision for the issue of a warrant of committal in Form FL420 and, unless the court otherwise orders—

(a) a copy of the order shall be served personally on the person to be committed either before or at the time of the execution of the warrant; or

(b) the order for the issue of the warrant may be served on the person to be committed at any time within 36 hours after the execution of the warrant.

(11) An order requiring a person to abstain from doing an act may be enforced by committal order notwithstanding that a copy of the order has not been served personally if the court is satisfied that, pending such service, the respondent had notice thereof either—

(a) by being present when the order was made;

(b) by being notified of the terms of the order whether by telephone or otherwise.

(12) The court may dispense with service of a copy of the order under paragraph (6) or a notice under paragraph (8) if the court thinks it just to do so.

(13) Where service of a notice to show cause is dispensed with under paragraph (12) and a committal order is made, the court may of its own motion fix a date and time when the person to be committed is to be brought before the court.

(14) Paragraphs (6) to (10), (12) and (13) shall apply to the enforcement of undertakings with the necessary modifications and as if—

(a) for paragraph (6) there were substituted the following—

"(6) A copy of Form FL422 recording the undertaking shall be delivered by the justices' chief executive to the party giving the undertaking—

(a) by handing a copy of the document to him before he leaves the court building; or

(b) where his place of residence is known, by posting a copy to him at his place of residence; or

(c) through his solicitor,

and, where delivery cannot be effected in this way, the justices' chief executive shall deliver a copy of the document to the party for whose benefit the undertaking is given and that party shall cause it to be served personally as soon as is practicable.";

(b) in paragraph (12), the words from "a copy" to "paragraph (6) or" were omitted.

(15) Where a person in custody under a warrant or order, desires to apply to the court for his discharge, he shall make his application in writing attested by the governor of the prison showing that he has purged or is desirous of purging his contempt and the justices' chief executive shall, not less than one day before the application is heard, serve notice of it on the party (if any) at whose instance the warrant or order was issued.

(16) The court by whom an order of committal is made may by order direct that the execution of the order of committal shall be suspended for such period or on such terms or conditions as it may specify.

(17) Where execution of an order of committal is suspended by an order under paragraph (16), the applicant for the order of committal must, unless the court otherwise directs, serve on the person against whom it was made a notice informing him of the making and terms of the order under that paragraph.

(18) The court may adjourn consideration of the penalty to be imposed for contempts found proved and such consideration may be restored if the respondent does not comply with any conditions specified by the court.

(19) Where the court makes a hospital order in Form FL413 or a guardianship order in Form FL414 under the Mental Health Act 1983¹, the justices' chief executive shall—

(a) send to the hospital any information which will be of assistance in dealing with the patient;

(b) inform the applicant when the respondent is being transferred to hospital.

(20) Where a transfer direction given by the Secretary of State under section 48 of the Mental

Health Act 1983 is in force in respect of a person remanded in custody by the court, the justices' clerk shall notify—

(a) the governor of the prison to which that person was remanded; and
(b) the hospital where he is detained.

of any committal hearing which that person is required to attend and the justices' clerk shall give notice in writing to the hospital where that person is detained of any further remand.

(21) An order for the remand of the respondent shall be in Form FL409 and an order discharging the respondent from custody shall be in Form FL421.

(22) In paragraph (4) "arrest" means arrest under a power of arrest attached to an order or under a warrant of arrest.

Applications under Part IV of the Family Law Act 1996: bail

6–4541   21. (1) An application for bail made by a person arrested under a power of arrest or a warrant of arrest may be made either orally or in writing.

(2) Where an application is made in writing, it shall contain the following particulars—

(a) the full name of the person making the application;
(b) the address of the place where the person making the application is detained at the time when the application is made;
(c) the address where the person making the application would reside if he were to be granted bail;
(d) the amount of the recognizance in which he would agree to be bound; and
(e) the grounds on which the application is made and, where a previous application has been refused, full particulars of any change in circumstances which has occurred since that refusal.

(3) An application made in writing shall be signed by the person making the application or by a person duly authorized by him in that behalf or, where the person making the application is a minor or is for any reason incapable of acting, by a guardian ad litem acting on his behalf and a copy shall be served by the person making the application on the applicant for the Part IV order.

(4) The following forms shall be used:

(a) the recognizance of the person making the application shall be in Form FL410 and that of a surety in Form FL411;
(b) a bail notice in Form FL412 shall be given to the respondent where he is remanded on bail.

Proceedings by or against a person outside England and Wales for variation or revocation of orders under section 20 of the Act or paragraphs 30 to 34 of Schedule 6 to the Act of 2004

6–4542   22. (1) The jurisdiction conferred on a court by virtue of section 20 of the Act or paragraphs 30 to 34 of Schedule 6 to the Act of 2004 shall, subject to the provisions of this rule, be exercisable even though the proceedings are brought by or against a person residing outside England and Wales.

(2) Subject to paragraph (3), where a court is satisfied that the respondent has been outside England and Wales for the whole of the period beginning one month before the making of the application and ending with the date of the hearing, it may proceed with an application made under section 20 of the Act or under paragraphs 30 to 34 of Schedule 6 to the Act of 2004 provided that—

(a) the applicant has taken steps to notify the respondent of the making of the application and of the time and place appointed for the hearing by—

(i) causing a notice in writing to that effect to be delivered to the respondent;
(ii) causing a notice in writing to that effect to be sent by post addressed to the respondent at his last known or usual place of abode or at his place of business or at such other address at which there is ground for believing that it will reach the respondent, in accordance with directions given for the purpose by a justice acting for the same petty sessions area as that of the court; or
(iii) causing a notice to that effect to be inserted in one or more newspapers, in accordance with directions given as aforesaid; and

(b) it is reasonable in all the circumstances to proceed in the absence of the respondent.

(3) The court shall not make the order for which the application is made unless it is satisfied that during the period of 6 months immediately preceding the making of the application the respondent was continuously outside England and Wales or was not in England and Wales on more than 30 days and that, having regard to any communication to the court in writing purporting to be from the respondent, it is reasonable in all the circumstances to do so.

(4) A court shall not exercise its powers under section 20 of the Act or under paragraphs 30 to 34 of Schedule 6 to the Act of 2004 so as to increase the amount of any periodical payments required to be made by any person under the Act unless the order under that section is made at a hearing at which that person appears or a statement has been filed under rule 4(4) that service of a copy of the application has been effected on the respondent.

(5) Paragraph (1) of rule 67 of the Magistrates' Courts Rules 1981 shall apply for the purpose of proving the delivery of a written notice in pursuance of paragraph (2)(a)(i) as it applies for the

purpose of proving the service of a summons. In relation to a solemn declaration made outside the United Kingdom, paragraph (1) of the said rule 67, as applied by this paragraph, shall have effect as if for the reference to the authorities mentioned in the said paragraph (1) there were substituted a reference to a consular officer of Her Majesty's Government in the United Kingdom or any person for the time being authorised by law, in the place where the declarant is, to administer an oath for any judicial or other legal purpose.

(6) Paragraph (2) of the said rule 67 shall apply for the purpose of proving the sending of a written notice in pursuance of paragraph (2)(*a*)(ii) or the insertion of a notice in a newspaper in pursuance of paragraph (2)(*a*)(iii) as it applies for the purpose of proving the service of any process, provided, as respects the insertion of a notice in a newspaper, that a copy of the newspaper containing the notice is annexed to the certificate.

Entries in court's registers

6–4543   23. (1) Where the justices' chief executive receives notice of any direction made by the High Court or a county court under section 28 of the Act by virtue of which an order made by the court under the Act ceases to have effect, particulars thereof shall be entered in the court's register.

(2) Where—

(*a*) in proceedings under the Act, the hearing of an application under section 2 of that Act is adjourned after the court has decided that it is satisfied of any ground mentioned in section 1; or

(*b*) in proceedings under the Act of 2004, the hearing of an application under Part 1 of Schedule 6 to that Act is adjourned after the court has decided that it is satisfied of any ground mentioned in paragraph 1,

and the parties to the proceedings agree to the resumption of the hearing in accordance with section 31 of the Act by a court which includes justices who were not sitting when the hearing began, particulars of the agreement shall be entered in the court's register.

Setting aside on failure of service

6–4544   24. Where an application has been sent to a respondent in accordance with rule 4(1) and, after an order has been made on the application, it appears to the court that the application did not come to the knowledge of the respondent in due time, the court may of its own motion set aside the order and may give such directions as it thinks fit for the rehearing of the application.

Proceedings with respect to which a single justice may discharge the functions of a court

6–4545   25. The following proceedings are prescribed as proceedings with respect to which a single justice may discharge the functions of a court, that is to say, proceedings—

(*a*) in which an application is made ex parte for an occupation order or a non-molestation order under Part IV of the Family Law Act 1996;

(*b*) in accordance with rules 3, 3A(2), (6) and (8), 4, 6 (except paragraph (2)), 7 to 14 and 20(4).

PART III
CONSEQUENTIAL AND MINOR AMENDMENTS

6–4546   26. *Consequential and minor amendments.*

PART IV
REVOCATIONS

6–4547   27. *Revocations.*

6–4548

SCHEDULE 1
FORMS

Family Proceedings Courts (Child Support Act 1991) Rules 1993[1]

(SI 1993/627 amended by SI 2001/615 and 778 and SI 2005/1977)

Citation, commencement, interpretation and transitional provision

6–4549   1. *Citation and commencement.*

---

1. Made by the Lord Chancellor, in exercise of the powers conferred on him by s 144 of the Magistrates' Courts Act 1980.

6–4549A   2. In these rules—

"the Act of 1991" means the Child Support Act 1991;

"court" means a family proceedings court constituted in accordance with section 66 and 67 of the Magistrates' Courts Act 1980 or a single justice who is a member of a family panel.

6–4549B   **3.** Rules 6 to 8 shall apply only to applications filed on or after 5th April 1993.

6–4549C   **4.** (1) Rules 2 to 16 of the Family Proceedings Courts (Matrimonial Proceedings etc) Rules 1991 shall apply as appropriate to an appeal under section 20 (appeal against decision of child support officer), where the proceedings are to be dealt with in accordance with the Child Support Appeals (Jurisdiction of Courts) Order 1993 and an application under section 27 of the Act of 1991 (reference to court for declaration of parentage).

(2) The respondent to an appeal under section 20 of the Act of 1991 shall be the Secretary of State.

(3) *(Revoked)*

(4) Where the justices' clerk or the court is considering whether or not to transfer proceedings under section 20 of the Act of 1991 to another court, rules 6, 14(2)(*h*), (4) and (11) and rule 32 of the Family Proceedings Courts (Children Act 1989) Rules 1991 shall also apply as appropriate.

Disclosure of information under the Act of 1991

6–4549D   **5.** Where the Secretary of State requires a person mentioned in regulation 2(2) or (3)(*a*) of the Child Support (Information, Evidence and Disclosure) Regulations 1992 to furnish information or evidence for a purpose mentioned in regulation 3(1) of those Regulations, nothing in rule 23 (confidentiality of documents) or rule 23A (communication of information relating to proceedings) of the Family Proceedings Courts (Children Act 1989) Rules 1991 or rule 14 of the Family Proceedings Courts (Matrimonial Proceedings etc) Rules 1991 (confidentiality of documents) shall prevent that person from furnishing the information or evidence sought or shall require him to seek leave of the court before doing so.

Applications for relief which is precluded by the Act of 1991

6–4549E   **6.** (1) Where an application is made for an order which, in the opinion of the justices' clerk, the court would be prevented from making by section 8 or 9 of the Act of 1991, the justices' chief executive may send a notice in the appropriate form to the applicant and the provisions of rule 4(1) to (3) of the Family Proceedings Courts (Matrimonial Proceedings etc) Rules 1991 (service) shall apply as appropriate.

(2) Where a notice is sent under paragraph (1), no requirement of any rules, except for those of this rule, as to the service of the application or as to any other procedural step applicable to the making of an application of the type in question, shall apply unless and until the court directs that such rules shall apply or that they shall apply to such extent and subject to such modifications as may be specified in the direction.

(3) Where an applicant who has been sent a notice under paragraph (1) informs the justices' chief executive in writing, within 14 days of the date of service of the notice, that he wishes to persist with his application, the justices' clerk shall give such directions as he considers appropriate for the matter to be heard and determined by the court and, without prejudice to the generality of the foregoing, such directions may provide for the hearing to be ex parte.

(4) Where directions are given under paragraph (3), the justices' chief executive shall inform the applicant of the directions and, in relation to the other parties,—

(*a*) where the hearing is to be ex parte, inform them briefly—

   (i) of the nature and effect of the notice under this rule,
   (ii) that the matter is being resolved ex parte, and
   (iii) that they will be informed of the result in due course; and

(*b*) where the hearing is to be inter partes, inform them of—

   (i) the circumstances which led to the directions being given, and
   (ii) the directions.

(5) Where a notice has been sent under paragraph (1) and the justices' chief executive is not informed under paragraph (3) the application shall be treated as having been withdrawn.

(6) Where the matter is heard pursuant to directions under paragraph (3) and the court determines that it would be prevented by section 8 or 9 of the Act of 1991 from making the order sought by the application, it shall dismiss the application.

(7) Where the court dismisses an application under this rule it shall give its reasons in writing, copies of which shall be sent to the parties by the justices' chief executive.

(8) In this rule, "the matter" means the question whether the making of an order in the terms sought by the application would be prevented by section 8 or 9 of the Act of 1991.

(9) Rule 15 of the Family Proceedings Courts (Matrimonial Proceedings etc) Rules 1991 (delegation by justices' clerk) shall apply as appropriate to anything authorised to be done by or to a justices' clerk under this rule or rule 7.

Modification of rule 6 in relation to non-free standing applications

6–4549F   **7.** Where a notice is sent under rule 6(1) in respect of an application which is contained in an application, answer or other document ("the document") which contains material extrinsic to the application—

(a) the document shall, until the contrary is directed under sub-paragraph (c) of this rule, be treated as if it did not contain the application in respect of which the notice was served;

(b) the justices' chief executive shall send to the respondents a copy of the notice under rule 6(1) and a notice informing the respondents of the effect of sub-paragraph (a) of this paragraph; and

(c) if it is determined, under rule 6, that the court would not be prevented by section 8 or 9 of the Act of 1991 from making the order sought by the application, the court shall direct that the document shall be treated as if it contained the application, and it may give such directions as it considers appropriate for the conduct of the proceedings in consequence of that direction.

Forms

6–4549G 8–12

Family Law Act 1996 (Part IV) (Allocation of Proceedings) Order 1997[1]

(SI 1997/1896 as amended by SI 2005/2924)

6–4550 1. (1) This Order may be cited as the Family Law Act 1996 (Part IV) (Allocation of Proceedings) Order 1997 and shall come into force on 1 October 1997.

(2) In this Order, unless the context otherwise requires—

"county court" means a county court of one of the classes specified in article 2;

"family proceedings" has the meaning assigned by section 63 and includes proceedings which are family business within the meaning of section 32 of the Matrimonial and Family Proceedings Act 1984;

"family proceedings court" has the meaning assigned by article 3;

"the Act" means the Family Law Act 1996 and a section, Part or Schedule referred to by number alone means the section, Part or Schedule so numbered in that Act.

---

1. Made by the Lord Chancellor in exercise of the powers conferred on him by s 57 of the Family Law Act 1996.

Classes of county court

6–4550A 2. The classes of county court specified for the purposes of this Order are—

(a) designated county courts, being those courts designated for the time being—

(i) as divorce county courts by an order under section 33 of the Matrimonial and Family Proceedings Act 1984;

(ii) as civil partnership proceedings county courts by an order under section 36A of the Matrimonial and Family Proceedings Act 1984; or

(iii) as both divorce county courts and civil proceedings county courts by such orders;

(b) family hearing centres, being those courts set out in Schedule 1 to the Children (Allocation of Proceedings) Order 1991; and

(c) care centres, being those courts set out in column (ii) of Schedule 2 to that Order.

Classes of magistrates' court

6–4550B 3. The classes of magistrates' court specified for the purposes of this Order are family proceedings courts, being those courts constituted in accordance with section 67 of the Magistrates' Courts Act 1980.

Commencement of Proceedings

Commencement of proceedings

6–4550C 4. (1) Subject to section 59, paragraph 1 of Schedule 7 and the provisions of this article, proceedings under Part IV may be commenced in a county court or in a family proceedings court.

(2) An application—

(a) under Part IV brought by an applicant who is under the age of eighteen; and

(b) for the grant of leave under section 43 (leave of court required for applications by children under sixteen),

shall be commenced in the High Court.

(3) Where family proceedings are pending in a county court or a family proceedings court, an application under Part IV may be made in those proceedings.

Application to extend, vary or discharge order

6–4550D 5. (1) Proceedings under Part IV—

(a) to extend, vary or discharge an order, or

(b) the determination of which may have the effect of varying or discharging an order,

shall be made to the court which made the order.

(2) A court may transfer proceedings made in accordance with paragraph (1) to any other court in accordance with the provisions of articles 6 to 14.

TRANSFER OF PROCEEDINGS

Disapplication of enactments about transfer

6–4550E   **6.** Sections 38 and 39 of the Matrimonial and Family Proceedings Act 1984 shall not apply to proceedings under Part IV.

Transfer from one family proceedings court to another

6–4550F   **7.** A family proceedings court ("the transferring court") shall (on application or of its own motion) transfer proceedings under Part IV to another family proceedings court ("the receiving court") where—

(a) the transferring court considers that it would be appropriate for those proceedings to be heard together with other family proceedings which are pending in the receiving court; and

(b) the receiving court, by its justices' clerk (as defined by rule 1(2) of the Family Proceedings Courts (Children Act 1989) Rules 1991, consents to the transfer.

Transfer from family proceedings court to county court

6–4550G   **8.** (1) A family proceedings court may, on application or of its own motion, transfer proceedings under Part IV to a county court where it considers that—

(a) it would be appropriate for those proceedings to be heard together with other family proceedings which are pending in that court; or

(b) the proceedings involve—

    (i) a conflict with the law of another jurisdiction;

    (ii) some novel and difficult point of law;

    (iii) some question of general public interest; or

(c) the proceedings are exceptionally complex.

(2) A family proceedings court must transfer proceedings under Part IV to a county court where—

(a) a child under the age of eighteen is the respondent to the application or wishes to become a party to the proceedings; or

(b) a party to the proceedings is a person who, by reason of mental disorder within the meaning of the Mental Health Act 1983, is incapable of managing and administering his property and affairs.

(3) Except where a transfer is ordered under paragraph (1)(a), the proceedings shall be transferred to the nearest county court.

Transfer from family proceedings court to High Court

6–4550H   **9.** A family proceedings court may, on application or of its own motion, transfer proceedings under Part IV to the High Court where it considers that it would be appropriate for those proceedings to be heard together with other family proceedings which are pending in that Court.

Transfer from one county court to another

6–4550I   **10.** A county court may, on application or of its own motion, transfer proceedings under Part IV to another county court where—

(a) it considers that it would be appropriate for those proceedings to be heard together with other family proceedings which are pending in that court;

(b) the proceedings involve the determination of a question of a kind mentioned in section 59(1) and the property in question is situated in the district of another county court; or

(c) it seems necessary or expedient so to do.

Transfer from county court to family proceedings court

6–4550J   **11.** A county court may, on application or of its own motion, transfer proceedings under Part IV to a family proceedings court where—

(a) it considers that it would be appropriate for those proceedings to be heard together with other family proceedings which are pending in that court; or

(b) it considers that the criterion—

    (i) in article 8(1)(a) no longer applies because the proceedings with which the transferred proceedings were to be heard have been determined;

    (ii) in article 8(1)(b) or (c) does not apply.

Transfer from county court to High Court

6–4550K   12. A county court may, on application or of its own motion, transfer proceedings under Part IV to the High Court where it considers that the proceedings are appropriate for determination in the High Court.

Transfer from High Court to family proceedings court

6–4550L   13. The High Court may, on application or of its own motion, transfer proceedings under Part IV to a family proceedings court where it considers that it would be appropriate for those proceedings to be heard together with other family proceedings which are pending in that court.

Transfer from High Court to county court

6–4550M   14. The High Court may, on application or of its own motion, transfer proceedings under Part IV to a county court where it considers that—

(a) it would be appropriate for those proceedings to be heard together with other family proceedings which are pending in that court;

(b) the proceedings are appropriate for determination in a county court; or

(c) it is appropriate for an application made by a child under the age of eighteen to be heard in a county court.

Disposal following arrest

6–4550N   15. Where a person is brought before—

(a) a relevant judicial authority in accordance with section 47(7)(a), or

(b) a court by virtue of a warrant issued under section 47(9),

and the matter is not disposed of forthwith, the matter may be transferred to be disposed of by the relevant judicial authority or court which issued the warrant or, as the case may be, which attached the power of arrest under section 47(2) or (3), if different.

MISCELLANEOUS

Principal Registry of the Family Division

6–4550O   16. (1) The principal registry of the Family Division of the High Court shall be treated, for the purposes of this Order, as if it were a designated county court, a family hearing centre and a care centre.

(2) Without prejudice to article 10, the principal registry may transfer an order made in proceedings which are pending in the principal registry to the High Court for enforcement.

Lambeth, Shoreditch and Woolwich County Courts

6–4550P   17. Proceedings under Part IV may be commenced in, transferred to and tried in Lambeth, Shoreditch or Woolwich County Court.

Contravention of provisions of this Order

6–4550Q   18. Where proceedings are commenced or transferred in contravention of a provision of this Order, the contravention shall not have the effect of making the proceedings invalid.

Family Proceedings Courts (Constitution) (Greater London) Rules 2003[1]

(SI 2003/2960)

6–4550R   1. Citation, commencement and application. (1) These Rules may be cited as the Family Proceedings Courts (Constitution) (Greater London) Rules 2003 and shall come into force on—

(a) for the purposes of rules 2, 9, and this rule on 15th December 2003; and

(b) for all other purposes on 1st January 2004.

(2) These Rules do not apply outside the Greater London area.

---

1. Made by the Lord Chancellor, in exercise of the powers conferred upon him by sections 67 and 144 of the Magistrates' Courts Act 1980. These rules are continued in force and have effect as if made under s 67 of the Magistrates' Courts Act 1980 by the Courts Act 2003 (Transitional Provisions, Savings and Consequential Provisions) Order 2005, SI 2005/911.

6–4550S   2. Interpretation. In these Rules—

"the 1989 Act" means the Children Act 1989;

"District Judge (Magistrates' Courts)" means a District Judge (Magistrates' Courts) appointed under section 10A(1) of the Justices of the Peace Act 1997;

"Greater London area" means the Commission Area of Greater London;

"justice" means a justice of the peace who is not a District Judge (Magistrates' Courts);

"petty sessions area" has the meaning assigned to it by section 4 of the Justices of the Peace Act 1997; and

"panel" means "family panel", within the meaning of section 92 of the 1989 Act.

6–4550T   3. Revocations.   (1) Subject to paragraph (2), the Family Proceedings Courts (Constitution) (Metropolitan Area) Rules 1991 are revoked.

(2) Nothing in these Rules shall affect any proceedings that are pending (within the meaning of paragraph 1 of Schedule 14 to the 1989 Act) immediately before these Rules come into force.

6–4550U   4. Formation of panel.   (1) There shall be one panel for the Greater London area and any justice who is a member of a family panel in any petty sessions area in the Greater London area on the 31st December 2003 shall be a member of the first panel.

(2) The panel shall thereafter be formed of justices who are nominated from time to time by the Lord Chancellor in accordance with these Rules.

(3) The justices who form the first panel constituted under paragraph (1) shall serve for a term commencing on 1st January 2004 and expiring on 31st December 2005 and succeeding justices shall, subject to paragraph (4), serve for a term of three years commencing on 1st January in the year following the expiry of the term of previous justices.

(4) The number of justices who are nominated under paragraph (2) shall be such as the Lord Chancellor thinks sufficient for family proceedings courts in the Greater London area and he may, at any time, subject to rule 5, nominate one or more additional justices to the panel who shall serve thereon for a term commencing on a date determined by the Lord Chancellor and ending at the end of the period for which the other justices to the panel were nominated.

6–4550V   5. Eligibility and removal.   (1) A justice shall not be nominated to the panel unless—

(a) he is a justice who acts for the Greater London area;
(b) he has acted as a justice for a minimum period of two years;
(c) he has indicated that he is willing to serve as a member of the panel; and
(d) he is suitable, in the opinion of the Lord Chancellor, to serve as a member of the panel.

(2) A justice shall be eligible for nomination to the panel whether or not he—

(a) has been a member of the panel before, or
(b) is, or has been, a member of any other panel.

(3) The Lord Chancellor may remove from the panel any justice who, in his opinion, is unsuitable to serve on the panel.

6–4550W   6. Vacancies in membership of panel.   If a vacancy occurs in the membership of the panel, the Lord Chancellor may, subject to rule 5(1), nominate a justice to fill the vacancy who shall serve on the panel for a term commencing on a date determined by the Lord Chancellor and ending at the end of the period for which the other justices to the panel were nominated.

6–4550X   7. Meetings.   The members of the panel shall meet as often as may be necessary but not less than twice a year to make arrangements connected with the sitting of family proceedings courts and to discuss questions connected with the work of those courts.

6–4550Y   8. Composition and chairmen of family proceedings courts.   (1) The justices to sit in each family proceedings court shall be chosen from the panel in such manner as the panel determines so as to ensure that section 66(1) and (2) of the Magistrates' Courts Act 1980 (which provides how a family proceedings court is to be constituted) is complied with (except where a single justice is authorised to discharge the functions of a magistrates' court).

(2) Subject to paragraph (3), the chairman of a family proceedings court which does not include a District Judge (Magistrates' Courts) (whether sitting alone or as chairman) shall be a justice nominated by the Lord Chancellor to act as a court chairman.

(3) Any justice who is eligible to act as a court chairman of a family proceedings court in any petty sessions area in the Greater London area on 31st December 2003 shall be entitled to continue to preside in a family proceedings court until 31st December 2005.

(4) If at any sitting of a family proceedings court which does not include a District Judge (Magistrates' Courts) (whether sitting alone or as chairman), a chairman is available to act as chairman but considers that it would be appropriate for another member of the court to act as chairman at that sitting, he may nominate that member to act as chairman at the sitting provided that the chairman who makes the nomination sits as a member of the court throughout the sitting.

(5) If, at any sitting of a family proceedings court, a District Judge (Magistrates' Courts) or the chairman who was chosen to preside in court cannot do so owing to circumstances unforeseen when the justices to sit were chosen under paragraph (1), the members of that court shall choose one of their number to preside.

6–4550Z   9. Transitional provisions.   (1) The justices who will be members of the first panel constituted in accordance with rule 4(1) may hold a meeting before 1st January 2004 in order to prepare to assume their functions on and after that date.

(2) If a meeting is held in accordance with paragraph (1) it shall be treated as if it were a meeting of the justices of the first panel despite the fact that the panel was not at that time in existence.

(3) The existing terms of appointment to a family panel in the Greater London area expire on 31st December 2003.

Guardianship and Custody

Magistrates' Courts (Guardianship of Minors) Rules 1974[1]

(SI 1974/706, amended by SI 1979/953, SI 1980/1585 and 1989/384, SI 1991/1991, SI 2005/617 and SI 2005/2930)

6–4551   1. *Citation and commencement.*

---

1. Made by the Lord Chancellor, in exercise of the powers conferred on him by s 3 of the Marriage Act 1949 and by s 15 of the Justices of the Peace Act 1949, as extended by s 122 of the Magistrates' Courts Act 1952, (see now Magistrates' Courts Act 1980, ss 144, 145 and 154) s 16(5) of the Guardianship of Minors Act 1971 and that section as applied by ss 1(6), 3(3) and 4(3) of the Guardianship Act 1973, and s 3(4) of the said Act of 1973.

Interpretation

6–4552   2. (1) In these Rules, the following expressions have the meanings hereby respectively assigned to them, that is to say:—

"the Act of 1949" means the Marriage Act 1949;

"court" means a magistrates' court, except as provided by rule 9(9);

"the Rules of 1968" means the Magistrates' Courts Rules 1968, as amended;

(2) In these Rules, unless the context otherwise requires, any reference to a rule shall be construed as a reference to a rule contained in these Rules and any reference in a rule to a paragraph shall be construed as a reference to a paragraph of that rule.

(3) *Revoked.*

(4) In these Rules, unless the context otherwise requires, any reference to any enactment shall be construed as a reference to that enactment, as amended, extended or applied by any subsequent enactment.

(5) The Interpretation Act [1978] shall apply for the interpretation of these Rules as it applies for the interpretation of an Act of Parliament.

6–4553   3. *Revocation.*

Applications under Guardianship of Minors Act 1971 and 1973 to be by complaint.

6–4554   4. *Revoked.*

Procedure for applications for consent to marriage or formation of civil partnership

6–4555   5. (1) An application for the consent of the court to the marriage of a child under section 3 of the Act of 1949 (marriages of persons under 18) may be made, either orally or in writing, to a justice of the peace.

(1A) An application for the consent of the court to the formation of a civil partnership by a child under paragraph 3, 4 or 10 of Schedule 2 to the Civil Partnership Act 2004 (obtaining consent etc) may be made, either orally or in writing, to a justice of the peace.

(2) Upon receiving such an application as is referred to in paragraph (1) or (1A) the justice shall, where the application was in consequence of a refusal to give consent to the marriage or to the civil partnership, as the case may be, give to any person whose consent is required and who has refused consent a notice of the application and of the date, time and place appointed for the hearing thereof.

(3) Rule 82 of the Rules of 1968 (service of summons, etc) shall apply in relation to the service of a notice given in accordance with paragraph (2) as it applies in relation to the service of a summons issued on a person other than a corporation.

(4) The provisions of Part II of the Magistrates' Courts Act 1952[1] relating to the hearing of a complaint and of rule 14 of the Rules of 1968 (order of evidence and speeches) shall apply to the hearing of such an application as is referred to in paragraph (1) or (1A) as if it were made by way of complaint but as if for any reference therein to the complainant, the complaint, the defendant and his defence there were substituted references, respectively, to the applicant, the application, the respondent and his case.

1. See now Pt II of the Magistrates' Courts Act 1980.

Provisions for certain hearings to be in camera

6–4556　6. *Revoked.*

Notice to local authority of proposal to commit minor to its care

6–4557　7. *Revoked.*

Substitution of new supervisor for minor

6–4558　8. *Revoked.*

Defendants to application for variation or discharge of order

6–4559　9. *Revoked.*

Defendants to applications regarding access to minors by grandparents

6–4559A　9A–9B. *Revoked.*

SCHEDULE

Forms

Magistrates' Courts (Child Abduction and Custody) Rules 1986[1]
(SI 1986/1141 amended by SI 1991/1991, SI 2001/615 and SI 2005/617)

6–4560　1. *Citation and commencement.*

1. These rules were made by the Lord Chancellor under s 144 of the Magistrates' Courts Act 1980 as extended by ss 10 and 24 of the Child Abduction and Custody Act 1985.

Interpretation

6–4561　2. In these Rules—

"complaint" includes an application under Rule 14 of the Magistrates' Courts (Children and Young Persons) Rules 1970.
"Contracting State" means a Contracting State defined in section 2 of the 1985 Act;
"the 1985 Act" means the Child Abduction and Custody Act 1985;
"the Hague Convention" means the Convention defined in section 1(1) of the 1985 Act;
"the High Court" means the High Court in England and Wales, the High Court in Northern Ireland or the High Court of Justice of the Isle of Man.

Stay of proceedings pending in a magistrates' court

6–4562　3. Where any proceedings in which a decision falls to be made on the merits of rights of custody (as construed under section 9 of the 1985 Act) are pending in a magistrates' court and that court receives notice from the High Court or the Court of Session that an application in respect of the child concerned has been made under the Hague Convention, the magistrates' courts shall order that all further proceedings in the proceedings pending before it shall be stayed, and shall cause notice to be given to the parties to the proceedings accordingly.

Dismissal of complaint

6–4563　4. Where a magistrates' court which has stayed any proceedings under Rule 3 above receives notice from the High Court or the Court of Session that an order has been made under Article 12 of the Hague Convention for the return of the child concerned, the court shall dismiss the complaint and cause notice to be given to the parties to the proceedings accordingly.

Resumption of proceedings after stay

6–4564　5. Where a magistrates' court which has stayed any proceedings under Rule 3 above receives notice from the High Court or Court of Session that an order for the return of the child concerned has been refused (other than in the circumstances set out in the third paragraph of Article 12 of the Hague Convention), the court shall order that the stay be lifted, shall so notify the parties to the proceedings, and shall proceed to deal with the complaint accordingly.

Further stay of proceedings or dismissal of complaint

6–4565　6. Where a magistrates' court which has stayed any proceedings under Rule 3 above receives notice from the High Court or Court of Session that an order has been made under the third paragraph of Article 12 of the Hague Convention staying or dismissing the application thereunder, the court shall continue the stay on the proceedings pending before it or, in a case where the High Court or Court of Session has dismissed the application, dismiss the complaint, and shall cause notice to be given to the parties accordingly.

Notice of registration of order in respect of a child

6–4566 7. Where any proceedings such as are mentioned in section 20(2)(*a*), (*b*) or (*c*) of the 1985 Act are pending in a magistrates' court and that court receives notice from the High Court or the Court of Session that an application has been made under section 16 of that Act for the registration of a decision made in respect of the child in proceedings commenced before the proceedings which are pending (other than a decision mentioned in section 20(3) of the 1985 Act) or that such a decision has been registered under the said section 16, the court shall cause notice to be given to the parties to those proceedings that it has received notice of the application or of the registration, as the case may be.

Authenticated copy of magistrates' court order

6–4567 8. (1) A person who wishes to make an application under the Hague Convention in a Contracting State other than the United Kingdom and who wishes to obtain from a magistrates' court an authenticated copy of a decision of that court relating to the child in respect of whom the application is to be made shall apply in writing to the designated officer for that court.

(2) An application under paragraph (1) above shall specify—

(*a*) the name and date or approximate date of birth of the child concerned;

(*b*) the date or approximate date of the proceedings in which the decision of the court was given, and the nature of those proceedings;

(*c*) the Contracting State in which the application in respect of the child is to be made;

(*d*) the relationship of the applicant to the child concerned;

(*e*) the postal address of the applicant.

(3) A designated officer who receives an application for an authenticated copy of a decision under this rule shall send by post to the applicant at the address indicated in the application for the purposes an authenticated copy of the decision concerned.

(4) For the purposes of paragraph (3) of this rule a copy of a decision shall be deemed to be authenticated if it is accompanied by a statement signed by the designated officer that it is a true copy of the decision concerned.

Application for declaration of unlawful removal of a child

6–4568 9. An application to a magistrates' court under section 23(2) of the 1985 Act (declaration that the removal of a child from the United Kingdom has been unlawful) may be made orally or in writing in the course of the custody proceedings (as defined in section 27 of that Act).

Registration and Enforcement

Maintenance Orders (Facilities for Enforcement) Rules 1922[1]

(SR & O 1922/1355, amended by SI 1970/762, SI 1989/384, SI 1992/457, SI 1993/617, SI 2000/1875, SI 2001/615 and 2005/617)

6–4570 1. The copy of an Order made by a court outside the United Kingdom and received by the Secretary of State[2] under section 1 of the Maintenance Orders (Facilities for Enforcement) Act 1920, shall, unless the Order was made by a Court of Superior Jurisdiction, be sent, to the designated officer for the local justice area in which the defendant is alleged to be living.

---

1. Made under the Maintenance Orders (Facilities for Enforcement) Act 1920, ante, and having effect as if made under s 15 of the Justices of the Peace Act 1949, which has itself been repealed; see now the Magistrates' Courts Act 1980, ss 144, 145 and 154.

2. Reference to the Secretary of State is to be construed as reference to the Lord Chancellor: SI 1992/709, art 4(1).

6–4571 2. The copy of a Provisional Order made by a court outside the United Kingdom and received by the Secretary of State[1] under section 4 of the Act shall be sent to a Court of Summary Jurisdiction in the manner provided by the foregoing Rule, with the accompanying documents and a requisition for the issue of a notice of hearing.

---

1. Reference to the Secretary of State is to be construed as reference to the Lord Chancellor: SI 1992/709, art 4(1).

6–4571A 2A. On receipt of an order in accordance with rule 2 above the designated officer for the local justice to whom it is sent shall serve upon the person against whom the order is made certified copies of the order and of the accompanying documents, together with the notice required to be served under section 4 of the Act.

6–4572   **3.** The designated officer for the local justice to whom any Order is sent in accordance with the above Rules shall enter it in his register on the date on which he receives it in the same manner as though the Order had been made at his court, distinguishing it from the other entries in such manner as he may find most convenient, so as to show that it is entered in pursuance of the Act.

6–4573   **4.** When an Order provisionally made outside the United Kingdom has been confirmed, with or without modification, under section 4 of the Act, by a Court of Summary Jurisdiction, or the court has decided not to confirm it, the designated officer for the court' shall send notice thereof to the court from which it issued, and also to the Secretary of State[1].

---

   1. Reference to the Secretary of State is to be construed as reference to the Lord Chancellor: SI 1992/709, art 4(1).

6–4574   **5.** When an order is registered in a Court of Summary Jurisdiction under section 1 of the Act, the court shall order that payments due thereunder shall be made to the designated officer for the court.

6–4575   **5A.** (1) This rule applies in respect of an order which is being or has been registered by a Court of Summary Jurisdiction under section 1 of the Act or in respect of a Provisional Order which is being or has been confirmed by a Court of Summary Jurisdiction under section 4 of the Act.

(2) Where, in the exercise of the duty imposed under rule 5 above, or in the exercise of the powers conferred by virtue of section 4(5A) or (6A) or section 6(2) of the Act, a Court of Summary Jurisdiction orders that payments under the order are to be made by a particular means, the clerk of the court shall record on the copy of the order the means of payment which the court has ordered and the designated officer for the court shall notify in writing, as soon as practicable, the person liable to make payments under the order of how payments are to be made.

(3) Where, in the exercise of any of the aforesaid powers, the court orders payment to the designated officer, or to the designated officer for any other magistrates' court, by a method of payment falling within section 59(6) of the Magistrates' Courts Act 1980 (standing order, etc), the designated officer for the court to whom payments are to be made shall notify the person liable to make the payments under the order of the number and location of the account into which the payments should be made.

(4) Where, under section 60(4) of the Magistrates' Courts Act 1980, as modified by section 4(6A) of the Act, the designated officer for a magistrates' court receives an application from an interested party for the method of payment to be varied, he shall notify in writing, as soon as practicable, that party and, where practicable, any other interested party, of the result of the application, including any decision to refer the matter to the court; where the clerk of the court grants the application, the designated officer for the court ve shall record the variation on the copy of the order.

6–4576   **6.** Where an Order has been registered in a Court of Summary Jurisdiction under section 1 of the Act, or a Provisional Order has been confirmed by a Court of Summary Jurisdiction under section 4 of the Act, the designated officer for the court to whom the payments are ordered to be made shall collect the moneys due under the Order in the same manner as though it were a magistrates' court maintenance order, and may take proceedings in his own name for enforcing payment, and shall send the moneys, when so collected, to the court from which the Order originally issued or to such other person or authority as that court or the Secretary of State[1] may from time to time direct[2]. Provided that if the court from which the Order originally issued is in Malta or in a Colony not possessing responsible Government or in a British Protectorate other than Northern or Southern Rhodesia, the moneys so collected shall be paid to the Crown Agents for the Colonies[3] for transmission to the person to whom they are due.

---

   1. Reference to the Secretary of State is to be construed as reference to the Lord Chancellor: SI 1992/709, art 4(1).

   2. The Secretary of State has directed, in Home Office Circular 139/1970, that any person collecting money, in accordance with a direction under r 5, which is due under an order of a New Zealand court shall send it to the Registrar or District Agent of the appropriate office of the New Zealand Department of Social Security as set out in the Appendix to the circular.

   3. Now the Crown Agents for Overseas Governments and Administrations, 4 Millbank, London SW1.

6–4576A   **6A.** (1) In this rule "an application" means—

     (*a*) an application under section 3 of the Act for a provisional order,

     (*b*) an application under section 4A of the Act for variation or revocation of a maintenance order made in the United Kingdom, or

     (*c*) an application under section 4A of the Act for variation or revocation of a maintenance order confirmed in the United Kingdom.

(2) An application shall be filed in an appropriate form.

(3) On receipt of such an application the designated officer for a magistrates' court shall—

(a) fix the date, time and place for a hearing or a directions appointment, and

(b) the designated officer for the court shall notify the applicant of the date, time and place so fixed.

6–4576B 6B. (1) The Schedule to these Rules shall apply to proceedings pursuant to rules 2A and 6A above.

(2) In the Schedule as it applies to rule 2A, "the resident party" and "the non-resident party" shall be taken to mean the payer and the payee respectively under the order in question.

(3) In the Schedule as it applies to rule 6A, "the resident party" and "the non-resident party" shall be taken to mean—

(a) in the case of an application under sub-paragraph (a) of rule 6A(1), the applicant and respondent respectively,

(b) in the case of an application under sub-paragraph (b) of rule 6A(1), the payee and payer respectively under the order in question, and

(c) in the case of an application under sub-paragraph (c) of rule 6A(1), the payer and payee respectively under the order in question.

6–4577 7. When a Provisional Order made under section 3 of the Act has been remitted under subsection (4) of that section to a Court of Summary Jurisdiction for the purpose of taking further evidence, notice specifying the further evidence required and the time and place fixed for taking it shall be sent by the designated officer for the court to the person on whose application the Provisional Order was made.

6–4578   SCHEDULE
                                   RULES OF PROCEDURE[1]

---

1. These are not reproduced here, but are as set out in Sch A1 to the Magistrates' Courts (Reciprocal Enforcement of Maintenance Orders) Rules 1974, SI 1974/668 this PART, post.

Maintenance Orders Act 1950 (Summary Jurisdiction) Rules 1950[1]
(SI 1950/2035 amended by SI 1980/1895, SI 1992/457, SI 2001/615, SI 2005/617 and SI 2005/2930)

PART I

Transfer of Wife Maintenance Proceedings[2]

6–4590 1. (1) Where proceedings under section 1 of the Matrimonial Proceedings (Magistrates' Courts) Act 1960, are begun against a defendant residing in Scotland or Northern Ireland, then, upon an application in that behalf made by the defendant in accordance with paragraph (2) of this Rule, a justice acting in the same place as that court may, if it appears that the case could be more conveniently heard in a court of summary jurisdiction having jurisdiction in the place where the parties last ordinarily resided together as man and wife, determine that the proceedings shall be removed into the last-mentioned court.

(1A) Where proceedings under Part 1 of Schedule 6 to the Civil Partnership Act 2004 are begun against a defendant residing in Scotland or Northern Ireland, then, upon an application in that behalf made by the defendant in accordance with paragraph (2) of this Rule, a justice acting in the same place as that court may, if it appears that the case could be more conveniently heard in a court of summary jurisdiction having jurisdiction in the place where the parties last ordinarily resided together as civil partners, determine that the proceedings shall be removed into the last-mentioned court.

(2) An application under the foregoing paragraphs may be made orally or in writing by or on behalf of the defendant and, unless the defendant applies in person, there shall be lodged with the designated officer for the court in which the proceedings under the said section 4 have been begun a statutory declaration by the defendant which shall state the grounds upon which the application is made and the address of the defendant to which notices may be sent.

(3) The justice adjudicating on an application made under paragraph (1) or (1A) of this Rule shall, unless he determines that the application shall be refused forthwith, afford to the complainant an opportunity of making representations, either orally or in writing, thereon.

(4) Where a justice determines under paragraph (1) or (1A) of this Rule that the proceedings under the said section 4 shall be removed into another court of summary jurisdiction, he shall cause the designated officer for the court in which the said proceedings have been begun to send to the clerk of that other court the complaint, a copy of the summons and any other relevant documents; and, on receipt thereof in that other court, the complaint shall be deemed to have been made in, and the summons to have been issued by, that other court, and any justice acting in the same place as that other court may appoint a time and place for the hearing of the

proceedings which, upon notice thereof being sent by registered post to the complainant and defendant, shall be deemed to have been the time and place appointed in the summons.

---

1. Made under s 29 of the Summary Jurisdiction Act 1879 (*since repealed*) as extended by the Maintenance Orders Act 1950, and having effect as if made under s 15 of the Justices of the Peace Act 1949, which has itself been repealed; see now the Magistrates' Courts Act 1980, ss 144, 145 and 154. See Home Office Circulars No 241/1950 (20 December 1950), and No 2/1952 (2 January 1952).

2. Under Maintenance Orders Act 1950, s 5; repealed by Matrimonial Proceedings (Magistrates' Courts) Act 1960, Sch, but not so as to affect the validity of rules made under the section (Matrimonial Proceedings (Magistrates' Courts) Act 1960, s 18(1)). See Home Office Circular No 241/1950, 20 December 1950, paras 14 and 15.

PART II

Procedure under Part II of the Act[1] in relation to Maintenance Orders made by Courts of Summary Jurisdiction in England.

6–4591 **2.** (1) An application for the registration in a court in Scotland or Northern Ireland under Part II of the Act of a maintenance order made by a court of summary jurisdiction in England may be made, either orally or in writing by or on behalf of the person entitled to the payments thereunder, to a justice acting in the same place as the court which made the order; and, unless the applicant appears in person, there shall be lodged with the designated officer for the court which made the order a statutory declaration by the applicant which shall contain the particulars specified in paragraph (2) of this Rule.

(2) A statutory declaration lodged under the foregoing paragraph shall state:—

(a) the address of the person liable to make the payments under the order;
(b) the reason why it is convenient that the order should be enforced in Scotland or Northern Ireland, as the case may be;
(c) unless a certificate of arrears is lodged under section 20 of the Act the amount of any arrears due under the order;
(d) that the order is not already registered under Part II of the Act.

(3) If it appears to the justice dealing with an application made as aforesaid that the person liable to make the payments under the order resides in Scotland or Northern Ireland, and that it is convenient that the order should be enforceable there, he shall cause the designated officer for the court which made the order to send to the sheriff-clerk of the sheriff court in Scotland[2], or, as the case may be, to the clerk of the court of summary jurisdiction in Northern Ireland[3], having jurisdiction in the place in which the person liable to make the payments under the order appears to be—

(a) a certified copy of the order;
(b) the certificate of arrears or statutory declaration (if any);
(c) if no statutory declaration has been lodged, written notice of the address of the person liable to make the payments under the order.

(4) A memorandum of any proceedings taken under the foregoing provisions of this Rule for the registration of a maintenance order in a court in Scotland or Northern Ireland shall be entered in the register, and on the receipt by the designated officer for the court which made the order (who shall be the prescribed officer of that court for the purposes of subsection (4) of section 17 of the Act) of notice under the said subsection (4) of the registration of the order he shall cause particulars of the notice to be registered in his court by means of a memorandum entered and signed by him in the register.

---

1. This Part relates to enforcement of orders.
2. A list of addresses of sheriff-clerks is appended to Home Office Circular No 241/1950 (20 December 1950).
3. The Home Office will provide the appropriate address on request.

6–4592 **3.** (1) An application to a court of summary jurisdiction in England under subsection (5) of section 22 of the Act to adduce evidence in connection with a maintenance order made by that court and registered in a court in Scotland or Northern Ireland may be made orally by or on behalf of the applicant and the proceedings may be *ex parte*.

(2) The court in which application is made under the last foregoing paragraph shall cause a transcript or summary of any evidence taken therein to be sent to the clerk of the court in which the order is registered.

(3) The designated officer for the court of summary jurisdiction in England by which a maintenance order registered in a court in Scotland or Northern Ireland was made shall be the prescribed officer to whom any transcript or summary of evidence adduced in the court in Scotland or Northern Ireland under the said subsection (5) shall be sent.

6–4593 **4.** (1) Where a maintenance order made by a court of summary jurisdiction in England and registered in a court in Scotland or Northern Ireland is varied under subsection (1) of section 22 of the Act by the court in which it is registered, the designated officer for the court which made the order shall be the prescribed officer to whom, under subsection (1) of section 23 of the Act, notice of the variation shall be given; and on receipt of such notice he shall cause particulars of the same to be registered in his court by means of a memorandum entered and signed by him in the register.

(2) Where a maintenance order made by a court of summary jurisdiction in England and registered in a court in Scotland or Northern Ireland is discharged or varied by the court which made it, the designated officer for that court shall give notice of the discharge or variation to the justices' chief executive for the court in which the order is registered by sending to him a certified copy of the order discharging or varying the maintenance order.

6–4594 5. (1) An application under subsection (2) of section 24 of the Act for the cancellation of the registration of a maintenance order made by a court of summary jurisdiction in England and registered in a court in Scotland or Northern Ireland may be made, either orally or in writing by or on behalf of the person liable to make the payments thereunder, to a justice acting in the same place as the court which made the order; and, unless the applicant appears in person, there shall be lodged with the designated officer for the court which made the order a statutory declaration by the applicant stating the facts upon which he relies in support of the application.

(2) If it appears to the justice dealing with an application made as aforesaid that the person liable to make the payments under the order has ceased to reside in Scotland or Northern Ireland, as the case may be, he shall cause the designated officer for the court which made the order to send notice to that effect to the clerk of the court in which the order is registered.

6–4595 6. On the cancellation under section 24 of the Act of the registration in a court in Scotland or Northern Ireland of a maintenance order made by a court of summary jurisdiction in England, the designated officer for the last-mentioned court shall be the prescribed officer to whom, under subsection (3) of the said section 24, notice of the cancellation shall be given; and on receipt of such notice he shall cause particulars of the same to be registered in his court by means of a memorandum entered and signed by him in the register.

PART III

Procedure in Courts of Summary Jurisdiction in England under Part II of the Act in relation to Maintenance Orders made by Courts in Scotland or Northern Ireland.

6–4596 7. The designated officer for the court of summary jurisdiction in England specified in paragraph (*b*) of subsection (3) of section 17 of the Act shall be the prescribed officer for the purpose of subsection (2) of the said section 17, and on receiving, in pursuance of that section, a certified copy of a maintenance order made by a court in Scotland or Northern Ireland he shall cause the order to be registered in his court by means of a memorandum entered and signed by him in the register and shall send written notice to the clerk of the court by which the order was made that it has been duly registered.

6–4597 8. An application for the variation under subsection (1) of section 22 of the Act of the rate of the payments under a maintenance order registered under Part II of the Act in a court of summary jurisdiction in England shall be made by way of complaint in accordance with the Magistrates' Courts Act 1980 and thereupon a summons may be issued directed to any person whom the justice to whom the complaint is made may consider proper to answer the same.

6–4598 9. (1) An application to a court of summary jurisdiction in England under subsection (5) of section 22 of the Act, to adduce evidence in connection with a maintenance order registered therein under Part II of the Act may be made orally by or on behalf of the applicant and the proceedings may be *ex parte*.

(2) The court in which application is made under the last foregoing paragraph shall cause a transcript or summary of any evidence taken therein to be sent to the clerk of the court in Scotland or Northern Ireland by which the order was made.

(3) The designated officer for the court of summary jurisdiction in England in which a maintenance order is registered under Part II of the Act shall be the prescribed officer to whom any transcript or summary of evidence adduced under the said subsection (5) in the court in Scotland or Northern Ireland by which the order was made shall be sent.

6–4599 9A. (1) An application to a magistrates' court under section 21(2) of the Act to adduce evidence in connection with a maintenance order made by the Court of Session and registered in the magistrates' court under Part I of the Act of 1958 by virtue of section 1(2) of the Act of 1958 may be made orally by or on behalf of the applicant and the proceedings may be *ex parte*.

(2) The court in which application is made under paragraph (1) above shall cause a transcript or summary of any evidence taken therein to be sent to the Deputy Principal Clerk of Session.

6–4600 9B. (1) Where, in the exercise of the duty imposed by section 19(2) of the Act or in the exercise of the powers conferred by virtue of section 18(2ZA) or section 22(1A) or (1E) of the Act, a court of summary jurisdiction orders that payments under a registered order are to be made by a particular means, the clerk of the court shall record on the copy of the order the means of payment which the court has ordered and the designated officer shall notify in writing, as soon as practicable, the person liable to make payments under the order of how payments are to be made.

(2) Where, in the exercise of any of the aforesaid powers, the court orders payment to the designated officer for the court, or to the designated officer for any other magistrates' court, by a method of payment falling within section 59(6) of the Magistrates' Courts Act 1980 (standing order, etc), the designated officer for the court to whom payments are to be made shall notify the person liable to make the payments under the order of the number and location of the account into which the payments should be made.

(3) Where, under section 60(4) of the Magistrates' Courts Act 1980, as modified by section 22(1E) of the Act, the designated officer for the court receives an application from an interested party for the method of payment to be varied, the designated officer shall notify in writing, as soon as practicable, that party and, where practicable, any other interested party, of the result of the application, including any decision to refer the matter to the court; where the clerk of the court grants the application, he shall record the variation on the copy of the order.

6–4601   **10.** (1) Where a maintenance order registered under Part II of the Act in a court of summary jurisdiction in England is varied under subsection (1) of section 22 of the Act by that court, the designated officer for the court shall

    (*a*) give notice of the variation to the clerk of the court in Scotland or Northern Ireland by which the order was made; and

    (*b*) if the order is registered in the High Court under Part I of the Act of 1958 by virtue of section 1(2) of the Act of 1958, give notice of the variation to the appropriate officer of the High Court,

by sending to the clerk of the court and, where necessary, the appropriate officer of the High Court, a certified copy of the order of variation to the clerk of the court in Scotland or Northern Ireland by which the order was made by sending to him a certified copy of the order of variation.

(2) Where a maintenance order registered under Part II of the Act in a court of summary jurisdiction in England is discharged or varied by any other court, the designated officer for the court in which it is registered shall be the prescribed officer to whom under section 23(1) of the Act notice of the discharge or variation shall be given; and on receipt of a certified copy of an order discharging or varying the registered order, he shall cause particulars of the same to be registered in his court by means of a memorandum entered and signed by him in the register.

6–4602   **11.** (1) An application under subsection (1) of section 24 of the Act for the cancellation of the registration of a maintenance order registered under Part II of the Act in a court of summary jurisdiction in England shall be made to the designated officer for that court by lodging with him a written application in that behalf (which shall state the date of the registration of the order) together with a copy of the order the registration of which it is sought to cancel.

(2) Where, in pursuance of an application made as aforesaid, the designated officer cancels the registration of the maintenance order he shall send written notice of the cancellation to the justices' chief executive for the court by which the order was made and, where the order is registered in the High Court under Part I of the Act of 1958 by virtue of section 1(2) of the Act of 1958, to the appropriate officer of the High Court.

6–4603   **12.** Where a maintenance order is registered under Part II of the Act in a court of summary jurisdiction in England, the designated officer for that court shall be the prescribed officer to whom notice shall be sent under subsection (2) of section 24 of the Act that the person liable to make the payments under the order has ceased to reside in England; and on receipt of such notice the clerk shall cancel the registration of the order and shall send written notice of the cancellation to the designated officer for the court by which the order was made and, where the order is registered in the High Court under Part I of the Act of 1958 by virtue of section 1(2) of the Act of 1958, to the appropriate officer of the High Court.

6–4604   **12A.** Where the designated officer for a magistrates' court in which a maintenance order is registered under Part I of the Act of 1958 receives a notice of cancellation under section 24(3) of the Act from the appropriate officer of the High Court, he shall—

    (*a*) cause the particulars of such notice to be entered in the register; and

    (*b*) cancel the registration under the said Part I; and

    (*c*) give notice of the cancellation to the appropriate officer of the court in Scotland or Northern Ireland, as the case may be, which made the order, that is to say either—

        (i) the Deputy Principal Clerk of Session, in the case of the Court of Session; or

        (ii) the Chief Registrar of the Queen's Bench Division (Matrimonial), in the case of the High Court of Justice in Northern Ireland.

PART IV

Forms

6–4605   **13.** (1) A notice under subsection (4) of section 19 of the Act that the payments under a maintenance order made by a sheriff court in Scotland or a court of summary jurisdiction in Northern Ireland have become payable through or to any officer or person shall be in the form number 1 in the Schedule to these Rules, or any form to the like effect, and shall be sent by registered post[1] by the designated officer for that court to the person liable to make the payments under the order at his last known address.

(2) A notice under the said subsection (4) that the payments under a maintenance order made by a court of summary jurisdiction in England have, on its registration under Part II of the Act in a court in Scotland or Northern Ireland, ceased to be payable through or to any officer or person shall be in the form number 2 in the Schedule to these Rules, or any form to the like effect, and shall be sent by registered post[1] by the designated officer for the first-mentioned court to the person liable to make the payments under the order at his last known address.

---

1. They may be sent by the recorded delivery service (Recorded Delivery Service Act 1962).

6–4606   14. A certificate lodged under subsection (1) of section 20 of the Act as to the amount of any arrears due under a maintenance order made by a court of summary jurisdiction in England shall be in the form number 3 in the Schedule to these Rules, or any form to the like effect.

6–4607   15. A notice under subsection (5) or subsection (5A) of section 24 of the Act of the cancellation of the registration under Part II of the Act of a maintenance order in a court of summary jurisdiction in England shall be in the form number 4 in the Schedule to these Rules, or any form to the like effect, and shall be sent by registered post[1] by the designated officer for that court to the person liable to make the payments under the order at his last known address.

---

1. They may be sent by the recorded delivery service (Recorded Delivery Service Act 1962).

PART V

Interpretation and Commencement

6–4608   16. (1) In Parts II to V of these Rules, unless the context otherwise requires, the following expressions have the meanings hereby respectively assigned to them:—

"maintenance order" has the same meaning as in Part II of the Act;
"the Act" means the Maintenance Orders Act 1950;
"the Act of 1958" means the Maintenance Orders Act 1958;
"appropriate officer of the High Court" means the Senior Registrar of the Principal Registry of the Family Division of the High Court or the district registrar of the relevant district registry;
"register" means the register kept in accordance with rule 54 of the Magistrates' Courts Rules 1968.

(2) References in Part III of these Rules to the clerk of the court by which the order was made shall be construed, in relation to a maintenance order made by a county court in Northern Ireland, as references to the Clerk of the Crown and Peace for the appropriate county in Northern Ireland.

(3) The Interpretation Act [1978] shall apply to the interpretation of these Rules as it applies to the interpretation of an Act of Parliament.

SCHEDULE OF FORMS

Magistrates' Courts (Maintenance Orders Act 1958) Rules 1959[1]

(SI 1959/3, amended by SI 1971/809, SI 1977/1890, SI 1980/1896, 1986/1962, SI 1989/384, SI 1992/457 and SI 2001/615)

PART I

PROCEDURE UNDER PART I OF THE ACT

6–4640   1. Applications for registration under section 2(3) of the Act. An application for the registration in the High Court of a magistrates' court order need not be in writing or on oath.

---

1. Made under s 15 of the Justices of the Peace Act 1949, as extended by s 122 of the Magistrates' Courts Act 1952; see now the Magistrates' Courts Act 1980, ss 144, 145 and 154. References in these Rules to the Magistrates' Courts Rules 1952 should now be read as a reference to the appropriate rule in the 1981 Rules.

6–4641   2. Manner in which magistrates' court is to be satisfied as to various matters. (1) An applicant wishing to show, in accordance with section 2A(1) of the Act, that the order to which the application relates, though deemed to have been made by the magistrates court in England, was in fact made in another part of the United Kingdom or a country or territory outside the United Kingdom and that by the law of that part or of that country or territory interest is recoverable under the order may do so by producing the original court order or an authenticated copy thereof showing the date or time from which and the rate at which interest is so recoverable.

(2) For the purposes of paragraph (1) of this Rule, a copy shall be deemed to be authenticated if it purports to be certified by a judge or official of the court which made the original order to be a true copy of the original order, but it shall not be necessary to prove the signature or official position of the person appearing to have given such a certificate.

(3) Where an application for the registration in the High Court of a magistrates' court order is

granted, the court shall be satisfied in the manner provided by paragraph (5) of this Rule that no process for the enforcement of the order issued before the grant of the application remains in force.

(4) Where the court receives notice given under section 5 of the Act (which relates to the cancellation of registration), the court shall be satisfied in the manner provided by paragraph (5) of this Rule that no process for the enforcement of the order issued before the giving of the notice remains in force and that no proceedings for the variation of the order are pending in a magistrates' court.

(5) For the purpose of satisfying the court as to the matters referred to in paragraphs (3) and (4) of this Rule—

(a) if the person through or to whom payments are ordered to be made is the justices' chief executive for a magistrates' court, there shall be produced a certificate in that behalf purporting to be signed by the justices' chief executive in the form numbered 1, 2 or 3, as the case may be, in the Schedule to these Rules;

(b) in any other case, there shall be produced a document purporting to be a statutory declaration in that behalf in the form numbered 5 or 6, as the case may be, in the Schedule to these Rules.

Receipt by magistrates' court of notice of registration in the High Court of order previously registered in magistrates' court

6–4642 2A. (1) Where a magistrates' court receives from the High Court notice of the registration in the High Court of an order made by a sheriff court in Scotland or a court of summary jurisdiction in Northern Ireland and previously registered in that magistrates' court in accordance with section 17(4) of the Act of 1950, the justices' chief executive for the court shall cause the particulars of such notice to be entered in the register.

(2) Where the court is satisfied in accordance with Rule 1A above that interest is recoverable under the order in respect of which the application has been granted the court shall, in accordance with section 2A(1) of the Act, cause the clerk to send, together with the certified copy of the order mentioned in paragraph (1) of this rule, a certificate in respect of the interest so recoverable in the form numbered 4 in the Schedule to these Rules to the appropriate officer of the High Court.

6–4643 3. Copy of magistrates' court order sent to the High Court for registration. Where an application for the registration of a magistrates' court order is granted and the court is satisfied that no process issued for the enforcement of the order before the grant of the application remains in force, the court shall, in accordance with paragraph (*c*) of subsection (4) of section two of the Act, cause the justices' chief executive to send a copy of the order, certified to be a true copy thereof in the form numbered 7 in the Schedule to these Rules to the appropriate officer of the High Court.

(2) Where the court is satisfied in accordance with Rule 1A above that interest is recoverable under the order in respect of which the application has been granted the court shall, in accordance with section 2A(1) of the Act, cause the justices' chief executive to send, together with the certified copy of the order mentioned in paragraph (1) of this rule, a certificate in respect of the interest so recoverable in the form numbered 4 in the Schedule to these Rules to the appropriate officer of the High Court.

6–4644 4. Registration of High Court or county court order in a magistrates' court. Where a justices' chief executive for a magistrates' court in accordance with paragraph (*b*) of subsection (2) of section two of the Act receives from an officer of the High Court or the registrar of a county court a certified copy of a High Court or county court order, he shall cause the order to be registered in his court by means of a memorandum entered and signed by him in the register and shall send written notice to that officer of the High Court or the registrar of the county court, as the case may be, that it has been duly registered.

Registration in magistrates' court of order made in Court of Session or High Court in Northern Ireland

6–4645 4A. Where a justices' chief executive for a magistrates' court, in pursuance of section 2(2)(*b*) of the Act, receives from the appropriate officer of the original court in Scotland or Northern Ireland a certified copy of an order made by the Court of Session or the High Court in Northern Ireland, he shall cause the order to be registered in his court by means of a memorandum entered and signed by him in the register and shall send written notice to the appropriate officer of the High Court and to the appropriate officer of the original court that the order has been duly registered.

6–4646 5. Notices as respects payments through a clerk of a magistrates' court. (1) A notice under subsection (6ZC) of section 2 of the Act, that the payments under a High Court or county court order or an order by the Court of Session or the High Court in Northern Ireland have, on its registration in a magistrates' court, become payable through the justices' chief executive for a magistrates' court shall be given by the justices' chief executive for the court of registration in the form numbered 8 in the Schedule to these Rules.

(2) A notice under subsection (6ZC) of section 2 of the Act, that the payments under a

magistrates' court order or an order made by a sheriff court in Scotland or a court of summary jurisdiction in Northern Ireland and registered in a magistrates' court under Part II of the Act of 1950 have, on its registration in the High Court, ceased to be payable to a justices' chief executive for a magistrates' court shall be given by the justices' chief executive for the administering court and shall be in the form numbered 9 in the Schedule to these Rules and, where payments have been payable through a justices' chief executive other than the clerk of the administering court, he shall send a copy of the said notice to that other justices' chief executive.

(3) A notice under subsection (5)(*b*) of section 5 of the Act, that the registration in a magistrates' court of a High Court or county court order or an order made by the Court of Session or the High Court in Northern Ireland has been cancelled and that payments thereunder have ceased to be payable through a justices' chief executive for a magistrates' court shall be given by the justices' chief executive for the court of registration and shall be in the form numbered 10 in the Schedule to these Rules and, where payments have been payable through a justices' chief executive other than the justices' chief executive for the court of registration, he shall send a copy of the said notice to that other justices' chief executive.

(4) A notice given in accordance with the preceding provisions of this Rule shall be delivered to the person liable to make payments under the order to which the notice relates or sent by post to that person at his last known address.

6–4647   5A. (1) Where, in the exercise of the duty imposed by section 2(6ZA)(*b*) of the Act or in the exercise of the powers conferred by section 3(2A) or (2B) or section 4(2A), (5A) or (5B) of the Act, a magistrates' court orders that payments under a registered order are to be made by a particular means, the clerk of the court shall record on the copy of the order the means of payment which the court has ordered and the justices' chief executive shall notify in writing, as soon as practicable, the person liable to make payments under the order of how payments are to be made.

(2) Where, in the exercise of any of the aforesaid powers, the court orders that payments be made by the debtor to the creditor or by the debtor to the justices' chief executive for the court, or to the justices' chief executive for any other magistrates' court by a method of payment falling within section 59(6) of the Magistrates' Courts Act 1980 (standing order, etc), the justices' chief executive for the court which makes the order to whom payments are to be made shall notify the person liable to make the payments under the order of the number and location of the account into which the payments should be made.

(3) Where, under section 60(4) of the Magistrates' Courts Act 1980, as applied by section 4(5A) of the Act, or as modified by section 4(5B) of the Act, the justices' chief executive for the court receives an application from an interested party for the method of payment to be varied, the justices' chief executive shall notify in writing, as soon as practicable, that party and, where practicable, any other interested party, of the result of the application, including any decision to refer the matter to the court; where the clerk of the court grants the application he shall record the variation on the copy of the order.

6–4657   6. Remission to the original court of application for variation of registered maintenance order. An order under subsection (4) of section four of the Act remitting an application for the variation of a High Court or county court order registered in a magistrates' court to the original court shall be in the form numbered 11 in the Schedule to these Rules.

6–4658   7. Notice of variation, remission, discharge or cancellation of registration by a magistrates' court of a registered order. (1) Where a High Court or county court order registered in a magistrates' court is, under subsection (2) of section four of the Act, varied by a magistrates' court, the justices' chief executive for the last-mentioned court shall give notice of the variation to the High Court or county court, as the case may be.

(2) Where an application for the variation of a High Court or county court order registered in a magistrates' court is, under subsection (4) of section four of the Act, remitted to the original court by a magistrates' court, the justices' chief executive for the last-mentioned court shall give notice of the remission to the High Court or county court, as the case may be.

(3) Where the registration of a High Court or county court order in a magistrates' court is, under subsection (4) of section five of the Act, cancelled by the court of registration, the justices' chief executive for the last-mentioned court shall give notice of cancellation to the High Court or county court, as the case may be, stating, if such be the case, that the cancellation is in consequence of a notice given under subsection (1) of the said section five.

(3A) Where the registration in a magistrates' court of an order made in the Court of Session or the High Court in Northern Ireland is cancelled under section 5(4) of the Act by that magistrates' court, the justices' chief executive for that magistrates' court shall give notice of the cancellation to the appropriate officer of the original court and to the appropriate officer of the High Court (where the order is registered by virtue of Part II of the Act of 1950).

(3B) Where the registration in a magistrates' court of an order under Part II of the Act of 1950 is cancelled by that magistrates' court by virtue of section 5(4) of the Act the justices' chief executive for the court shall give notice of the cancellation to the appropriate officer of the original court and to the appropriate officer of the High Court (where the order is registered under Part I of the Act).

(4) Where a magistrates' court order registered in the High Court is varied or discharged by a

magistrates' court, the justices' chief executive for the last-mentioned court shall give notice of the variation or discharge, as the case may be, to the High Court.

(5) Notice under the preceding provisions of this Rule shall be given by sending to the appropriate officer of the High Court or the registrar of the county court, as the case may be, a copy of the order of variation, remission, cancellation or discharge, as the case may be, certified to be a true copy thereof by the justices' chief executive for the magistrates' court and marked, in the case of a High Court maintenance order, with the title and cause number, if any, and in the case of a county court maintenance order, with the plaint or application number.

(6) For the purposes of the preceding paragraph the appropriate officer of the High Court shall be—

(a)   in relation to a High Court order registered in a magistrates' court, the officer to whom notice of registration was given under Rule 4 of these Rules;

(b)   in relation to a magistrates' court order registered in the High Court, the officer to whom a copy of the order was sent under Rule 3 of these Rules.

(7)   Where a magistrates' court order registered in the High Court is discharged by a magistrates' court and it appears to the last-mentioned court that no arrears remain to be recovered, notice under subsection (3) of section five of the Act shall be given by an endorsement in the form numbered 12 in the Schedule to these Rules on the certified copy of the order of discharge referred to in paragraph (5) of this Rule.

6–4659   8. Notices received from the High Court or a county court or from a person entitled to payments.   Subject to rule 8A below, where any notice is received—

(a)   of the registration in the High Court of a magistrates' court order;

(b)   of the discharge or variation by the High Court or a county court of a High Court or county court order registered in a magistrates' court;

(bb) of the discharge or variation by the Court of Session or High Court in Northern Ireland of an order made by such court and registered in a magistrates' court;

(c)   under subsection (1) or (2) of section five of the Act (which relates to the cancellation of registration);

the justices' chief executive for the magistrates' court shall cause particulars of the notice to be registered in his court by means of a memorandum entered and signed by him in the register and, in the case of a notice under subsection (1) or (2) of section five of the Act, shall cause the person in possession of any warrant of commitment, issued but not executed, for the enforcement of the order to be informed of the giving of the notice.

Notice of cancellation of registration in High Court under Part I of the Act

6–4660   8A. Where any notice is received by a court that the registration of an order in the High Court has been cancelled under section 5(4) of the Act, the justices' chief executive for the court shall cause the particulars of the notice to be entered in the register.

6–4661   9. Jurisdiction as respects complaints for variation of High Court maintenance orders. Rule 34 of the Magistrates' Courts Rules 1952[1] (which relates to jurisdiction to hear certain complaints), shall apply to a complaint for the variation of a High Court or county court order registered in a magistrates' court as if the order were a magistrates' court maintenance order made by the court of registration and as if in paragraph (4) of the said Rule for the words "shall cause" there were substituted the words "may cause".

---

1. See now r 41(4) of the Magistrates' Courts Rules 1981.

PART II

Revoked

PART III

MISCELLANEOUS AND SUPPLEMENTAL

6–4662   21. Administering court to be informed of proceedings in foreign court. Where any decision is reached, or warrant of distress or commitment is issued, in pursuance of a complaint or application relating to a maintenance order or the enforcement of a maintenance order (including an application under section twelve of the Act, which relates to the determination whether payments are earnings), being a complaint or application heard by a magistrates' court other than the administering court—

(a)   the justices' chief executive for the first-mentioned court shall forthwith send by post to the justices' chief executive for the administering court an extract from the register containing a minute or memorandum of the decision or of the issue of the warrant as the case may be;

(b)   on receipt of the extract the last-mentioned justices' chief executive shall enter the minute or memorandum in his register.

6–4663   22. Review of committals, etc.   (1) Where for the purpose of enforcing a maintenance order a magistrates' court has exercised its power under subsection (2) of section sixty-five of the Magistrates' Courts Act 1952[1], or subsection (3) or (5) of section eighteen of the Act to postpone the issue of a warrant of commitment and under the terms of the postponement the warrant falls to be issued, the justices' chief executive for the court shall give notice to the defendant in the form numbered 15 in the Schedule to these Rules and shall attach to the said notice a copy of the form numbered 16 in the said Schedule.

(2) An application under subsection (1) of the said section eighteen requesting that the warrant shall not be issued shall be in the form numbered 16 in the Schedule to these Rules and shall be delivered to the justices' chief executive for the court or sent to him by post.

(3) For the purposes of subsection (2) of the said section eighteen the period for the receipt by the justices' chief executive for an application under subsection (1) of the said section shall be the period of eight days beginning with the day on which the justices' chief executive sends to the defendant the notice referred to in paragraph (1) of this Rule.

(4) An application under subsection (4) of the said section eighteen requesting that a warrant of commitment which has been executed shall be cancelled shall be in the form numbered 17 in the Schedule to these Rules.

(5) Where an application by a defendant under subsection (1) or (4) of the said section eighteen is considered by the court the justices' chief executive for the court shall give notice of the decision of the court, if the person in question is not present—

(a) to the person in whose favour the maintenance order in question was made; and
(b) except where an application under subsection (1) of the said section eighteen is dismissed, to the defendant.

(6) Where on considering an application by a defendant under subsection (4) of the said section eighteen the court—

(a) makes an order under paragraph (b) of subsection (5) of the said section for the cancellation of the warrant of commitment; or
(b) remits under subsection (6) of the said section the whole or any part of the sum in respect of which the warrant was issued;

the justices' chief executive for the court shall forthwith give written notice of the decision to the person in charge of the prison or other place in which the defendant is detained.

---

1. See now the Magistrates' Courts Act 1980, ss 77(2).

6–4664   23. Warrants of commitment.   A warrant of commitment for the enforcement of a maintenance order, being an affiliation order or an order enforceable as an affiliation order, issued in pursuance of a complaint under section seventy-four of the Magistrates' Courts Act 1952[1], as amended by section sixteen of the Act, shall be in the form numbered 18 in the Schedule to these Rules:

Provided that where the issue of the warrant has been postponed under section sixty-five of the Magistrates' Courts Act 1952[2], or under section eighteen of the Act the warrant shall be in the form numbered 19 in the Schedule to these Rules.

---

1. See now the Magistrates' Courts Act 1980, s 93.
2. See now the Magistrates' Courts Act 1980, s 77.

6–4665   24. *Revocations.*

6–4666   25. Interpretation.   (1) Subsection (3) of section one of the Act shall apply to the interpretation of Part I of these Rules as it applies to the interpretation of Part I of the Act.

(2) Section twenty-one of the Act shall apply to the interpretation of these Rules as it applies to the interpretation of the Act.

(3) The Interpretation Act [1978] shall apply to the interpretation of these Rules as it applies to the interpretation of an Act of Parliament.

(4) In these rules—

"the Act" means the Maintenance Orders Act 1958;
"the Act of 1950" means the Maintenance Orders Act 1950;
"appropriate officer of the High Court" means the Senior Registrar of the Principal Registry of the Family Division of the High Court or such district registrar as may be specified by the applicant;
"appropriate officer of the original court" means—

(i) the Sheriff-clerk, in the case of a sheriff court in Scotland;
(ii) the clerk of petty sessions, in the case of a magistrates' court in Northern Ireland;
(iii) the Deputy Principal Clerk of Session, in the case of the Court of Session;
(iv) the Chief Registrar of the Queen's Bench Division (Matrimonial), in the case of the High Court of Justice in Northern Ireland.

(5) Any reference in these Rules to the administering court in relation to a maintenance order or a related attachment of earnings order is a reference to the magistrates' court—

(a) which made the maintenance order;

(b) in which the maintenance order is registered under the Act, under Part II of the Maintenance Orders Act, 1950, or under the Maintenance Orders (Facilities for Enforcement) Act 1920; or

(c) by which the maintenance order was confirmed under the Maintenance Orders (Facilities for Enforcement) Act 1920.

(6) Any reference in these Rules to the register is a reference to the register kept in accordance with Rule 54 of the Magistrates' Courts Rules 1968.

(7) Any reference in these Rules to a form in the Schedule to these Rules shall include a reference to a form to the like effect with such variations as the circumstances may require.

6–4667   26. *Citation and commencement.*

SCHEDULE
FORMS

6–4668

1. CERTIFICATE OF CLERK OF MAGISTRATES' COURT AS TO AMOUNT DUE AND UNPAID

(MO Act 1958, s 2(3))

I hereby certify that the amount due and unpaid at the date of this certificate under (insert particulars of maintenance order) made on the .... day of .... , 19 .. , by the Magistrates' Court sitting at ...., the payments whereunder are at present required to be made to me, is ....
Dated the .... day of ...., 19..
.... J C,
.... Justices' Chief Executive for the Magistrates' Court sitting at ....

4–4669

2. CERTIFICATE OF CLERK OF MAGISTRATES' COURT THAT NO PROCESS FOR ENFORCEMENT REMAINS IN FORCE

(MO Act 1958, s 2(4)(c))

I hereby certify that at the date of this certificate no process remains in force for the enforcement of (insert particulars of maintenance order) made on the .... day of .... , 19.. , by the Magistrates' Court sitting at .... , the payments whereunder are at present required to be made to me.
Dated the .... day of .... , 19..
.... J C,
.... Justices' Chief Executive for the Magistrates' Court sitting at ....

4–4670

3. CERTIFICATE OF CLERK OF MAGISTRATES' COURT THAT NO PROCESS FOR ENFORCEMENT REMAINS IN FORCE AND NO PROCEEDINGS FOR VARIATION ARE PENDING

(MO Act 1958, s 5(4)(c))

I hereby certify that at the date of this certificate no process remains in force for the enforcement and no proceedings are pending in a Magistrates' Court for the variation of (*insert particulars of maintenance order*) made on the .... day of .... , 19.. , by the (High Court) (.................. County Court) (Court of Session) (High Court in Northern Ireland) the payments whereunder are at present required to be made through me.
Dated the .... day of .... 19...
.... Justices' Chief Executive for the Magistrates' Court
.... sitting at ....]

4–4671

4. CERTIFICATE IN RESPECT OF INTEREST RECOVERABLE UNDER A MAINTENANCE ORDER

(MO Act 1958, s 2A(1))

I hereby certify that the rate of interest shown in accordance with sub-section (1) of section 2A of the Maintenance Order Act 1958 to be recoverable in respect of (insert particulars of maintenance order, or , if applicable relates only to a part of the order relating to a lump sum, insert particulars of that part of the order) is ....and that the date from which it is so recoverable is ....to ....
Dated the .... day of ...., 19 .... .
.... J C.
Justices' Chief Executive for the Magistrates' Court sitting at ....]

4–4672

5. DECLARATION THAT NO PROCESS FOR ENFORCEMENT REMAINS IN FORCE

(MO Act 1958, s 2(3))

I, G H, of ...., do solemnly and sincerely declare that at the date of this declaration no process remains in force for the enforcement of (insert particulars of maintenance order, or if application relates only to part of the order relating to a lump sum, insert particulars of that part of the order) made on the .... day of ...., 19.., by the Magistrates' Court sitting at ...., whereunder I am entitled to receive payment(s).

And I make this solemn declaration, conscientiously believing the same to be true by virtue of the provisions of the Statutory Declarations Act 1835.

Declared at ...., the .... day of ...., 19..,

before me,

.... J P,

.... Justice of the Peace for the (county) of

.... (Or other description)]

4–4673

6. DECLARATION THAT NO PROCESS FOR ENFORCEMENT REMAINS IN FORCE AND NO PROCEEDINGS FOR VARIATIONS ARE PENDING

(MO Act 1958, s 5(4)(c))

I, G H, of ...., do solemnly and sincerely declare that at the date of this declaration no process remains in force for the enforcement and no proceedings are pending in a Magistrates' Court for the variation of (insert particulars of maintenance order, or if application relates only to a part of the order relating to a lump sum, insert particulars of that part of the order) made on the .... day of .... 19.., by the (High Court) (.................. County Court) (Court of Session) (High Court in Northern Ireland) whereunder I am entitled to receive payment(s).

And I make this solemn declaration, conscientiously believing the same to be true by virtue of the provisions of the Statutory Declarations Act 1835.

.... G H

Declared at ...., the .... day of ...., 19..,

before me,

.... J P

.... Justice of the Peace for the (county) of ....

.... (or other description)]

4–4674

7. CERTIFICATE OF CLERK OF MAGISTRATES' COURT THAT COPY OF MAINTENANCE ORDER IS A TRUE COPY SENT FOR REGISTRATION

(MO Act 1958, s 2(4)(c))

I hereby certify that this is a true copy of (insert particulars of maintenance order) and that it is sent to .... in accordance with the provisions of paragraph (c) of subsection (4) of section two of the Maintenance Orders Act, 1958, and of Rule 3 of the Magistrates' Courts (Maintenance Orders Act, 1958) Rules, 1959.

Dated the .... day of ...., 19 ..

.... J C,

.... Justices' Chief Executive for the Magistrates' Court sitting at ....

4–4675

8. NOTICE THAT PAYMENTS HAVE BECOME PAYABLE THROUGH THE CLERK OF A MAGISTRATES' COURT

(MO Act 1958, s 2(6); MO Act, 1950, s 19(4))

..........Magistrates' Court (Code)

Date: ....

To: ....

Address: ....

You are hereby given notice that the sums payable by you under (insert particulars of maintenance order) made on the day of .... 19.., by the (High Court) (.................. County Court) (Court of Session) (High Court in Northern Ireland) and registered in this Court under Part I of the Maintenance Orders Act 1958, have under an order of this Court dated the .... day of .... 19.., become payable through (me) (the justices' chief executive for the Magistrates' Court sitting at ....).

Payments under the order (including payments in respect of any sums due at the date of the receipt by you of this notice) should henceforth be sent to the justices' chief executive for the Magistrates' Court at (state address).

.... Justices' Clerk]

4–4676

9. NOTICE THAT PAYMENTS HAVE CEASED TO BE PAYABLE THROUGH THE CLERK OF THE MAGISTRATES' COURT

(MO Act 1958, s 2(5); MO Act 1950, s 19(4))

..........Magistrates' Court (Code)

Date: ....

To: ....

Address: ....

You are hereby given notice that the sums payable by you under (insert particulars of maintenance order) made on the .... day of .... 19.. , by (this Court) ((state court in Scotland or Northern Ireland which made the order) and registered in this Court under Part II of the Maintenance Orders Act 1950) have by reason of the registration of the said order in the High Court ceased to be payable to (state justices' chief executive for Magistrates' Court to whom payments have hitherto been required to be made).

Payments under the order (including payments in respect of any sums due at the date of the receipt by you of this notice) should henceforth be paid to (state name and address of the person entitled to payments under the order).

.... Justices' Chief Executive]

4–4677

10. NOTICE OF CANCELLATION OF REGISTRATION

(MO Act 1958, s 5(5))

.... Magistrates' Court (*Code*)

Date: ....

To: ....

Address: ....

You are hereby given notice that the registration in this Court under Part I of the Maintenance Orders Act 1958, of (*insert particulars of maintenance order*) made on the .... day of .... 19.. , by the (High Court) (.................. County Court) (Court of Session) (High Court in Northern Ireland) has been cancelled.

Sums payable by you under the said order have by reason of the cancellation of the registration of the said order ceased to be payable ((through the justices' chief executive for (this court) (the magistrates' court at ....)), (by the following method of payment falling within section 59(6) of the Magistrates' Courts Act 1980 (standing order, etc) namely, ...), (by an attachment of earnings order) (by direct payment to ....).)

Payments under the order (including payments in respect of any sums due on the date of the receipt by you of this notice) should henceforth be paid to (*state name and address of person entitled to payments under the order*).

.... Justices' Chief Executive]

4–4678

11. ORDER REMITTING TO THE ORIGINAL COURT APPLICATION FOR VARIATION OF REGISTERED MAINTENANCE ORDER

(MO Act 1958, s 4(4))

In the (county of .... Petty Sessional Division of ....).

Before the Magistrates' Court sitting at ....

Complaint has been made by C D, of .... , (hereinafter called the complainant) who states that by (insert particulars of maintenance order) made on the .... day of .... , 19.., by the (High Court) (.................. County Court) and registered on the .... day of .... , 19..,n the Magistrates' Court sitting at .... , A.B. (hereinafter called the defendant) (or he/she) was ordered (state shortly terms of original order, and mention any subsequent order and effect thereof):

And the complainant has applied for the said order to be varied by an order requiring .... on the ground that ....

(And the said complaint has been sent to the Justices' Chief Executive for this Court in pursuance of Rule 34 of the Magistrates' Courts Rules 1952.)

It appearing to this Court that it is appropriate to remit the application to the (High Court) (.................. County Court), it is ordered that the application be so remitted.

Dated the .... day of .... , 19 ....

.... J P,

.... Justice of the Peace for the (county) first above mentioned.

4–4679

12. ENDORSEMENT THAT NO ARREARS REMAIN TO BE RECOVERED

(MO Act 1958, s 5(3))

In the (county of .... Petty Sessional Division of ....).

Before the Magistrates' Court sitting at ....

Whereas it appeared to this Court this day on discharging (insert particulars of maintenance order) that no arrears remain to be recovered thereunder notice is hereby given under subsection (3) of section five of the Maintenance Orders Act 1958.

Dated the .... day of .... 19...

.... J C,

.... Justices' Chief Executive for the Magistrates' Court sitting at ....

4–4680

15. NOTICE THAT WARRANT OF COMMITMENT FALLS TO BE ISSUED

(MO Act 1958, s 18(1))

In the (county of .... Petty Sessional Division of ....).

Before the Magistrates' Court sitting at ....

To A B, of ....

PLEASE READ THIS NOTICE CAREFULLY

On the .... day of .... .19.. this court postponed the issue of a warrant of commitment in your case for the enforcement of (insert particulars of maintenance order) (insert the terms of postponement).

You have failed to comply with these terms of postponement and the warrant committing you to prison for a term of .... now falls to be issued unless you pay under the maintenance order (the sum) (the net sum, after making deductions in respect of income tax,) of ....

If you consider that there are grounds for not issuing the warrant you may make an application to the Court on the attached form requesting that the warrant shall not be issued and stating those grounds.

If no such application is received by me on or before the .... day of .... 19.., and you fail to pay the sum referred to above the warrant will be issued.

If such an application is received by me on or before the .... day of .... , 19 .... it will be considered by a justice who may either refer it to the Court for further consideration or dismiss the application and issue the warrant forthwith.

Dated the .... day of .... 19..

.... J C,

.... Justices' Chief Executive for the Magistrates' Court sitting at ....

4–4681

16. APPLICATION REQUESTING THAT WARRANT SHOULD NOT BE ISSUED

(MO Act 1958, s 18(1))

To the Magistrates' Court sitting at ....

I, A B, of .... have received the notice sent to me by the Justices' Chief Executive for the Court and dated the .... day of .... , 19.. .

I hereby request that the warrant of commitment shall not be issued. The grounds of my request are as follows:—

Dated the .... day of .... , 19.. .

.... A B

NOTE. This application should be delivered or sent by post to the Justices' Chief Executive for the Court (insert address).

4–4682

17. APPLICATION REQUESTING THAT WARRANT SHOULD BE CANCELLED

(MO Act 1958, s 18(4))

To the Magistrates' Court sitting at ....

I, A B, hereby request that the warrant of commitment under which I am for the time being imprisoned (or otherwise detained) should be cancelled. The grounds of my request are as follows:—

Dated the .... day of .... , 19... .

.... A B.

4–4683

18. WARRANT OF COMMITMENT FOR THE ENFORCEMENT OF MAGISTRATES' COURT MAINTENANCE ORDER OR ORDER ENFORCEABLE AS AN AFFILIATION ORDER FOR USE IN CASE OF IMMEDIATE ISSUE

(MC Act 1952, ss 64, 74[1])

In the (county of .... Petty Sessional Division of ....).

To each and all of the constables of .... and to the Governor of Her Majesty's prison at .... (or the Police Officer in charge of ....).

Whereas on a complaint made by C D, of .... , that A B, of .... (hereinafter called the defendant) had made default in payment of the sums ordered to be paid by (insert particulars of maintenance order) it was proved to the Magistrates' Court sitting at .... , that the defendant did owe to .... , of .... , the sum of .... , under the order and the sum of .... for costs thereunder.

And whereas the Court having inquired in the presence of the defendant whether the default was due to his wilful refusal or culpable neglect is not of the opinion that it was not so due.

And whereas (the Court is of opinion that it is inappropriate to make an attachment of earnings order) (there is no power to make an attachment of earnings order).

It is ordered, the defendant not being absent, that he be committed to prison (or detained in police custody) for (state period) unless he sooner pays the said sums due from him as aforesaid (together with the costs of enforcement) as set out below.

You the said constables are hereby required to take the defendant and convey him to the Governor of Her Majesty's prison (or the Police Officer in charge of ....) at .... and you the said Governor (or Police Officer) to receive the defendant into your custody and keep him for (state period) from his arrest under this order or until he be sooner discharged in due course of law.

Dated the .... day of .... , 19 .... .

.... J P,

.... Justice of the Peace for the (county) first above mentioned.

	£	s	d
Amount found due – – – – –			
Deductions in respect of Income Tax – – – –			
Net amount – – – – –			
Enforcement costs payable – – – –			
Total sum payable by defendant – – – –			

(Endorsement of payments)

Date of Receipt	£	s	d	Signature

---

1. See now the Magistrates' Courts Act 1980, ss 76 and 93.

6–4684

19. WARRANT OF COMMITMENT FOR ENFORCEMENT OF AFFILIATION ORDER OR ORDER ENFORCEABLE AS A MAGISTRATES' COURT MAINTENANCE ORDER FOR USE WHERE ISSUE HAS BEEN POSTPONED

(MC Act 1952, ss 64, 65, 74[1]; MO Act 1958, s 18)

In the (county of .... Petty Sessional Division of ....).

To each and all of the constables of ....and to the Governor of Her Majesty's prison at .... (or the Police Officer in charge of ....)

Whereas on a complaint made by C D, of ...., that A B, of .... Hereinafter called the defendant) had made default in payment of the sums ordered to be paid by (insert particulars of maintenance order) it was proved to the Magistrates' Court sitting at ...., that the defendant did owe to ...., of ...., the sum of .... under the order and the sum of ....for costs thereunder.

And whereas the Court having inquired in the presence of the defendant whether the default was due to his wilful refusal or culpable neglect was not of the opinion that it was not so due.

And whereas (the Court was of opinion that it was inappropriate to make an attachment of earnings order) (there was no power to make an attachment of earnings order).

And whereas the Court, the defendant not being absent, on the ....day of ...., 19.., fixed a term of imprisonment (insert term) and postponed issue of the warrant of commitment (insert terms of postponement unless there has been a further postponement).

(And whereas on the application of the defendant the Court on the .... day of ...., 19.., further postponed the issue of the warrant (insert terms of further postponement):)

(And whereas on the application of the defendant the warrant having been executed the Court cancelled the warrant of commitment but fixed a further term of imprisonment (insert term) and postponed issue of the further warrant of commitment (insert terms of postponement):)

And whereas under the said terms of postponement the said warrant fell to be issued and the Justices' Chief Executive for the Court gave notice to the defendant that he might make an application to the Court requesting that the warrant should not be issued.

(And whereas no such application was received by the Justices' Chief Executive within the prescribed period.)

(And whereas such an application was made and considered by (me) (the Court).)

(And whereas by reason of part payment the said sums remaining due from the defendant as aforesaid are reduced in amount to ....)

It is ordered that the defendant be committed to prison (or detained in police custody) for (state period) unless he sooner pays the said sums (remaining) due from him as aforesaid (together with the costs of enforcement) as set out below.

You the said constables are hereby required to take the defendant and convey him to the Governor of Her Majesty's prison (or the Police Officer in charge of ....) and you the said Governor (or Police Officer) to receive the defendant into your custody and keep him for (state period) from his arrest under this order or until he be sooner discharged in due course of law.

Dated the .... day of ...., 19..

          .... J P,

          .... Justice of the Peace for the (county) first above mentioned.

	£	s	d
Amount found due			
Deductions in respect of Income Tax			
Net amount			
Paid			
Net amount remaining due			
Enforcement costs payable			
Total sum payable			

(Enforcement of payments)

Date of Receipt	£	s	d	Signature

1. See now the Magistrates' Courts Act 1980, s 76, 77 and 93.

Reciprocal Enforcement of Maintenance Orders (Designation of Reciprocating Countries) Order 1974[1]

(SI 1974/556, amended by SI 1979/115 and SI 1983/1125)

6–4690   **2.** (1) In this Order—

"the Act of 1972" means the Maintenance Orders (Reciprocal Enforcement) Act 1972;

"the Act of 1920" means the Maintenance Orders (Facilities for Enforcement) Act 1920;

"column (1)" and "column (2)" mean respectively columns (1) and (2) of the Schedule to this Order.

(2) The Interpretation Act [1978] shall apply for the interpretation of this Order as it applies for the interpretation of an Act of Parliament.

---

1. Made under ss 1 and 24 of the Maintenance Orders (Reciprocal Enforcement) Act 1972.

6–4691 **3.** Each of the countries and territories specified in column (1) is hereby designated as a reciprocating country for the purposes of Part I of the Act of 1972 as regards maintenance order of the description specified in respect of that country or territory in column (2).

6–4692 **4.** (1) Sections 5, 12 to 15, 17, 18 and 21 of the Act of 1972 shall apply in relation to a maintenance order transmitted under section 2 or 3 of the Act of 1920 to one of the countries and territories specified in column (1), being an order of the description specified in respect of that country or territory in column (2) to which immediately before the coming into operation of this Order the Act of 1920 applied, as they apply in relation to a maintenance order sent to that country or territory in pursuance of section 2 of the Act of 1972 or made by virtue of section 3 or 4 of the Act of 1972 and confirmed by a competent court in that country or territory.

(2) Sections 8 to 21 of the Act of 1972 shall apply in relation to a maintenance order made in one of the countries and territories specified in column (1), being an order of the description specified in respect of that country or territory in column (2) to which immediately before the coming into operation of this Order the Act of 1920 applied and not being an order which immediately before that date is registered in the High Court or the High Court of Justice in Northern Ireland under section 1 of the Act of 1920, as they apply in relation to a registered order.

(3) A maintenance order made by a court in one of the countries and territories specified in column (1) being an order of the description specified in respect of that country or territory in column (2) which has been confirmed by a court in England, Wales or Northern Ireland under section 4 of the Act of 1920 and is in force immediately before the coming into operation of this Order, shall be registered under section 7(5) of the Act of 1972 in like manner as if it had been confirmed by that court in England, Wales or Northern Ireland under subsection (2) of that section.

(4) Any proceedings brought under or by virtue of any provision of the Act of 1920 in a court in England, Wales or Northern Ireland which are pending immediately before the coming into operation of this Order, being proceedings affecting a person resident in one of the countries and territories specified in column (1), shall be continued as if they had been brought under or by virtue of the corresponding provision of the Act of 1972.

6–4693

Article 3

SCHEDULE[1]

COUNTRIES AND TERRITORIES DESIGNATED AS RECIPROCATING COUNTRIES

(1) Country or territory	(2) Description of maintenance orders to which designation extends
Australian Capital Territory	Maintenance orders other than— (a) *revoked* (b) orders obtained by or in favour of a public authority
British Columbia	Maintenance orders generally
Gibraltar	Maintenance orders generally
Manitoba (2)	Maintenance orders generally
New South Wales	Maintenance orders other than— (a) *revoked* (b) orders obtained by or in favour of a public authority
New Zealand	Maintenance orders generally
Northern Territory of Australia	Maintenance orders other than— (a) *revoked* (b) orders obtained by or in favour of a public authority
Nova Scotia	Maintenance orders other than— (a) maintenance orders of the description contained in paragraph (b) of the definition of "maintenance order" in section 21(1) of the Act of 1972 (orders for the payment of birth and funeral expenses of child), and (b) orders obtained by or in favour of a public authority
Ontario (2)	Maintenance orders other than— (a) *revoked* (b) maintenance orders of the description contained in the said paragraph (b), and (c) *revoked*
Queensland	Maintenance orders other than— (a) *revoked* (b) orders obtained by or in favour of a public authority
South Australia	Maintenance orders other than— (a) *revoked* (b) orders obtained by or in favour of a public authority
Tasmania	Maintenance orders other than— (a) *revoked* (b) orders obtained by or in favour of a public authority
Victoria	Maintenance orders other than— (a) *revoked* (b) orders obtained by or in favour of a public authority

1. The schedule is printed as extended by three further designation orders: SI 1975/2187, SI 1979/115 and SI 1983/1125.

2. Home Office Circular No 89/1984 warns that courts in Manitoba and Ontario require a photocopy of the relevant domestic legislation with the provisional maintenance order; the certificate referred to at s 3(5)(c) of the 1972 Act is no longer sufficient.

Magistrates' Courts (Reciprocal Enforcement of Maintenance Orders) Rules 1974[1]

(SI 1974/668, amended by SI 1975/2236, SI 1979/170, SI 1983/1148, 1986/1962, SI 1992/457, SI 1993/617, SI 2001/615 and SI 2002/1734)

6–4694　2. (1) In these Rules, unless the context requires—

"the Act" means the Maintenance Orders (Reciprocal Enforcement) Act 1972; and

"the court's register", in relation to a justices' chief executive, means the register kept by that justices' chief executive in pursuance of rule 54 of the Magistrates' Courts Rules 1968[2].

(2) The Interpretation Act [1978] shall apply for the interpretation of these Rules as it applies for the interpretation of an Act of Parliament.

---

1. Made under s 15 of the Justices of the Peace Act 1949 as extended by s 122 of the Magistrates' Courts Act 1952 and the Maintenance Orders (Reciprocal Enforcement) Act 1972; see now the Magistrates' Courts Act 1980, ss 144, 145 and 154.

References to the Secretary of State are to be construed as reference to the Lord Chancellor: SI 1992/709, art 4(5).

2. See now r 66 of the Magistrates' Courts Rules 1981.

6–4695　3. The officer of any court, by or in relation to whom anything is to be done in pursuance of any provision of Part I of the Act shall, where that court is a magistrates' court, be the justices' clerk.

6–4696　4. (1) An application under section 2 of the Act (transmission of maintenance order made in the United Kingdom for enforcement in reciprocating country) may, where the court which made the maintenance order to which the application relates is a magistrates' court be made in writing by or on behalf of the payee under the order.

(2) Any application made in pursuance of paragraph (1) above shall—

(a) specify the date on which the order was made;

(b) contain such particulars as are known to the applicant of the whereabouts of the payer and the nature and location of his assets;

(c) specify any matters likely to assist in the identification of the payer;

(d) where possible, be accompanied by a recent photograph of the payer.

(3) In this rule, "the payer" means the payer under the order to which the application relates.

6–4696A　4A. (1) In this rule "an application" means—

(a) an application under section 3 of the Act for a provisional maintenance order against a person residing in a reciprocating country,

(b) an application under section 5 of the Act for the variation or revocation of a maintenance order made in the United Kingdom, or

(c) an application under section 9 of the Act for the variation or revocation of a maintenance order registered by a court in the United Kingdom.

(2) An application shall be filed in an appropriate form.

(3) On receipt of such an application the justices' clerk shall—

(a) fix the date, time and place for a hearing or a directions appointment, and

(b) notify the applicant of the date, time and place so fixed.

(3) Where the justices' chief executive receives such an application—

(a) the justices' clerk shall fix the date, time and place for a hearing or a directions appointment, and

(b) the justices' chief executive shall notify the applicant of the date, time and place so fixed.

6–4696B　4B. (1) This rule applies to proceedings under section 5(5), 7 or 9(6) of the Act for the confirmation of a provisional order made in a reciprocating country.

(2) On receipt of the order and accompanying documents referred to in section 5(5), 7 or 9(6) of the Act—

(a) the justices' clerk shall fix the date, time and place for a hearing or a directions appointment allowing sufficient time for service under this rule to be effected at least 21 days before the date so fixed; and

(b) the justices' chief executive shall serve a copy of the order and documents on the resident party, together with a notice stating the date, time and place so fixed.

(3) Within 14 days of service under this rule the resident party shall file an answer to the provisional order in an appropriate form.

6–4696C 4C. (1) Schedule A1 to these Rules shall apply to proceedings pursuant to rules 4A and 4B above.

(2) In Schedule A1 as it appears to rule 4A, "the resident party" and "the non-resident party" shall be taken to mean—

(a) in the case of an application under sub-paragraph (a) of rule 4A(1), the applicant and the respondent respectively;

(b) in the case of an application under sub-paragraph (b) of rule 4A(1), the payee and the payer respectively under the order in question; and

(c) in the case of an application under sub-paragraph (c) of rule 4A(1), the payer and payee respectively under the order in question.

(3) In rule 4B and in Schedule A1 as it applies to that rule, "the resident party" and "non-resident party" shall be taken to mean the payer and the payee respectively under the order in question.

6–4697 5. A document setting out or summarising any evidence, required by section 3(5)(b), 5(4) or 9(5) of the Act (provisional orders) to be authenticated shall be authenticated by a certificate, signed by one of the justices before whom that evidence was given, that the document is the original document containing or recording or, as the case may be, summarising that evidence or a true copy of that document.

6–4698 6. (1) Subject to paragraph (2) below, any documents required by section 5(4) or 9(5) of the Act to be sent to a court in a reciprocating country shall be sent to that court by post.

(2) Where the court to which the documents are to be sent is in a country specified in Schedule 1 to these Rules, such documents shall be sent to the Secretary of State for transmission to that court.

6–4699 7. (1) For the purposes of compliance with section 5(9) of the Act (revocation by United Kingdom court of provisional order) there shall be served on the person on whose application the maintenance order was made a notice which shall—

(a) set out the evidence received or taken, as the case may be, in pursuance of that subsection;

(b) inform that person that it appears to the court that the maintenance order ought not to have been made; and

(c) inform that person that if he wishes to make representations with respect to the evidence set out in the notice he may do so orally or in writing and that if he wishes to adduce further evidence he should notify the justices' chief executive for the magistrates' court which made the maintenance order.

(2) Where a justices' chief executive receives notification that the person on whose application the maintenance order was made wishes to adduce further evidence—

(a) the justices' clerk shall fix a date for the hearing of such evidence; and

(b) the justices' chief executive shall send that person written notice of the date fixed.

6–4700 8. (1) Where a certified copy of an order, not being a provisional order, is received by a justices' chief executive who is required under any provision of Part I of the Act to register the order, he shall cause the order to be registered in his court by means of a minute or memorandum entered and signed by him in the court's register.

(2) Where any magistrates' court makes or confirms an order which is required under section 7(5) or 9(10) of the Act to be registered, the justices' chief executive shall enter and sign a minute or memorandum thereof in the court's register.

(3) Every minute or memorandum entered in pursuance of paragraph (1) or (2) above shall specify the section of the Act under which the order in question is registered.

6–4701 9. (1) When an order is registered under section 6(3) of the Act, the court shall order that payment of sums due thereunder shall be made to the justices' chief executive for the registering court during such hours and at such place as that justices' chief executive may direct.

(1A) A justices' chief executive to whom payments are ordered to be made (whether by virtue of an order under paragraph (1) above or by virtue of an order of the court under the Act) shall send those payments by post to the court which made the order or to such other person or authority as that court or the Secretary of State may from time to time direct;

Provided that if the court which made the order is in one of the countries or territories specified in Schedule 2 to these Rules, the justices' chief executive shall unless the Secretary of State otherwise directs send any such sums to the Crown Agents for Overseas Governments and Administrations for transmission to the person to whom they are due.

(2) Where it appears to a justices' chief executive to whom payments by way of periodical payments under any maintenance order are made that any sums payable under the order are in arrear he may and, if such sums are in arrear to an amount equal to four times the sum payable weekly under the order, he shall, whether the person for whose benefit the payment should have

been made requests him to do so or not, proceed in his own name for the recovery of those sums, unless it appears to him that it is unreasonable in the circumstances to do so.

6–4702 9A. Without prejudice to Rule 9 above, the justices' chief executive of the registering court shall take reasonable steps to notify the person to whom payments are due under a registered order of the means of enforcement available in respect of it, including, in an appropriate case, the possibility of registration of the whole or a part of the order in the High Court under Part I of the Maintenance Orders Act 1958.

6–4703 9B. (1) Where, in the exercise of the duty imposed under rule 9(1) above, or in the exercise of the powers conferred by virtue of section 7(5A), section 8(4A) or section 9(1ZA) of the Act, the court orders that payments under the order are to be made by a particular means, the clerk of the court shall record on the copy of the order the means of payment which the court has ordered and the justices' chief executive shall notify in writing, as soon as practicable, the person liable to make payments under the order of how payments are to be made.

(2) Where, in the exercise of any of the aforesaid powers, the court orders payment to the justices' chief executive for the court, or to the justices' chief executive for any other magistrates' court, by a method of payment falling within section 59(6) of the Magistrates' Courts Act 1980 (standing order, etc), the justices' chief executive for the court to whom payments are to be made shall notify the person liable to make the payments under the order of the number and location of the account into which the payments are to be made.

(3) Where, under section 60(4) of the Magistrates' Courts Act 1980, as modified by section 9(1ZA) of the Act, the justices' chief executive for the court receives an application from an interested party for the method of payment to be varied, the justices' chief executive shall notify in writing, as soon as practicable, that party and, where practicable, any other interested party, of the result of the application, including any decision to refer the matter to the court; where the clerk of the court grants the application, he shall record the variation on the copy of the order.

6–4704 10. (1) Subject to paragraph (2) below, where a request is made by or on behalf of a court in a reciprocating country for the taking in England and Wales of evidence of a person residing therein, the following magistrates' courts shall have power under section 14(1) of the Act (obtaining of evidence needed for purpose of certain proceedings) to take that evidence, that is to say—

(a) where the maintenance order to which the proceedings in the court in the reciprocating country relate was made by a magistrates' court, the court which made the order;

(b) where the maintenance order to which those proceedings relate is registered in a magistrates' court, the court in which the order is registered;

(c) a magistrates' court which has received such a request from the Secretary of State.

(2) The power conferred by paragraph (1) above may, with the agreement of a court having that power, be exercised by any other magistrates' court which, because the person whose evidence is to be taken resides within its jurisdiction or for any other reason, the first-mentioned court considers could more conveniently take the evidence; but nothing in this paragraph shall derogate from the power of any court specified in paragraph (1) above.

(3) Subject to paragraph (4) below, where the evidence of any person is to be taken by a magistrates' court under the foregoing provisions of this rule—

(a) the evidence shall be taken in the same manner as if that person were a witness in proceedings on a complaint;

(b) any oral evidence so taken shall be put into writing and read to the person who gave it, who shall be required to sign the document; and

(c) the justices by whom the evidence of any person is so taken shall certify at the foot of any document setting out the evidence of, or produced in evidence by, that person that such evidence was taken, or document received in evidence, as the case may be, by them.

(4) Where such a request as is mentioned in paragraph (1) above includes a request that the evidence be taken in a particular manner, the magistrates' court by which the evidence is taken shall, so far as circumstances permit, comply with that request.

(5) Any document such as is mentioned in paragraph (3)(c) above shall be sent—

(a) where the request for the taking of the evidence was made by or on behalf of a court in a country specified in Schedule 1 to these Rules, to the Secretary of State for transmission to that court;

(b) in any other case, to the court in the reciprocating country by or on behalf of which the request was made.

6–4705 11. Any request under section 14(5) of the Act for the taking or providing of evidence by a court in a reciprocating country shall, where made by a magistrates' court, be communicated in writing to the court in question.

6–4706 12. (1) Where a magistrates' court makes an order, not being a provisional order, varying a maintenance order to which section 5 of the Act (variation and revocation of maintenance order made in the United Kingdom) applies, the justices' chief executive shall send written notice of the making of the order to the Secretary of State; and where the order is made by virtue of paragraph (*a*) or (*b*) of subsection (3) of that section, he shall send such written notice to the court in a reciprocating country which would, if the order had been a provisional order, have had power to confirm the order.

(2) Where a magistrates' court revokes a maintenance order to which section 5 of the Act applies, the justices' chief executive shall send written notice of the revocation to the Secretary of State and to the court in a reciprocating country which has power to confirm that maintenance order, or by which the order has been confirmed, or in which the order is registered for enforcement, as the case may be.

(3) Where under section 9 of the Act (variation and revocation of maintenance order registered in United Kingdom court) a magistrates' court makes an order, not being a provisional order, varying or revoking a registered order, the justices' chief executive shall send written notice of the making of the order to the court in a reciprocating country which made the registered order.

(4) Where under section 7(2) of the Act (confirmation by United Kingdom court of provisional maintenance order made in reciprocating country) a magistrates' court confirms an order to which section 7 of the Act applies, the justices' chief executive shall send written notice of the confirmation to the court in a reciprocating country which made the order.

6–4707 **13.** (1) Where a justices' chief executive—

- (*a*) registers under section 6(3) of the Act (registration in United Kingdom court of maintenance order made in reciprocating country) an order to which section 6 of the Act applies; or
- (*b*) registers under section 7(5) of the Act an order which has been confirmed in pursuance of section 7(2) of the Act,

he shall send written notice to the Secretary of State that the order has been duly registered.

(2) *Revoked.*

(3) Where a justices' chief executive registers a maintenance order under section 10(4) of the Act, he shall send written notice to the Secretary of State that the order has been duly registered.

6–4708 **14.** (1) Where a justices' chief executive cancels the registration of a maintenance order under section 10(1) of the Act (cancellation of registration and transfer of order), he shall send written notice of the cancellation to the payer under the order.

(2) Where a justices' chief executive registers a maintenance order under section 6(3), 7(5), 9(10), 10(4), 10(5) or 23(2) of the Act, he shall send to the payer under the order written notice stating—

- (*a*) that the order has been duly registered;
- (*b*) that sums due under the order should be paid to the justices' chief executive; and
- (*c*) the hours during which and the place at which such payments should be made.

6–4708A
SCHEDULE A1
RULES OF PROCEDURE

1. In this Schedule, and in any rule where this Schedule applies to proceedings pursuant to that rule, unless the context otherwise requires—

"business day" means any day other than—

- (*a*) a Saturday, Sunday, Christmas or Good Friday; or
- (*b*) a bank holiday, that is to say, a day which is, or is to be observed as, a bank holiday, or a holiday, under the Banking and Financial Dealings Act 1971, in England and Wales,

"directions appointment" means a hearing for directions under paragraph 4 below,
"file" means deposit with the justices' chief executive,
"justices' chief executive" means a justices' chief executive appointed under section 40 of the Justices of the Peace Act 1997;
"justices' clerk" has the meaning assigned to it by section 70 of the Justices of the Peace Act 1979 and includes any person who performs a justices' clerk's functions by virtue of paragraph 12 below,
"leave" includes approval,
"note" includes a record made by mechanical or electronic means, and
"proceedings" means proceedings to which this Schedule applies.

Transfer of proceedings

2. (1) Where—

- (*a*) any proceedings are relevant proceedings within the meaning of section 93 of the Children Act 1989, and
- (*b*) the justices' chief executive or the court receives a request in writing from the resident party that the proceedings be transferred to another magistrates' court,

the justices' clerk or court shall issue a certificate in the appropriate form, granting or refusing the request in accordance with any Order made by the Lord Chancellor under Part I of Schedule 11 to the Children Act 1989.

(2) Where a request is granted under paragraph (1) the justices' chief executive shall send a copy of the certificate—

- (*a*) to the resident party,
- (*b*) to the Lord Chancellor's Department, and
- (*c*) to the magistrates' court to which the proceedings are to be transferred.

(3) Any consent given or refused by a justices' clerk in accordance with any Order made by the Lord

Chancellor under Part I of Schedule 11 shall be recorded in writing by the justices' clerk at the time it is given or refused or as soon as practicable thereafter.

Service

3. (1) Where service of a document is required by this Schedule or by a rule where this Schedule applies to proceedings pursuant to that rule it may be effected, unless the contrary is indicated—

(a) if the person to be served is not known by the person serving to be acting by solicitor—

(i) by delivering it to him personally, or
(ii) by delivering it at, or by sending it by first-class post to, his residence or last known residence, or

(b) if the person to be served is known by the person serving to be acting by solicitor—

(i) by delivering the document at, or sending it by first-class post to, the solicitor's address for service,
(ii) where the solicitor's address for service includes a numbered box at a document exchange, by leaving the document at that document exchange or at a document exchange which transmits documents on every business day to that document exchange, or
(iii) by sending a legible copy of the document by facsimile transmission to the solicitor's office.

(2) In this paragraph, "first-class post" means first-class post which has been pre-paid or in respect of which pre-payment is not required.

(3) A document shall, unless the contrary is proved, be deemed to have been served—

(a) in the case of service by first-class post, on the second business day after posting, and
(b) in the case of service in accordance with sub-paragraph (1)(b)(ii), on the second business day after the day on which it is left at the document exchange.

(4) In any proceedings where this Schedule, or a rule where this Schedule applies, requires a document to be served, the court or the justices' clerk may, without prejudice to any power under paragraph 4 below, direct that—

(a) the requirement shall not apply;
(b) the time specified by the rules for complying with the requirement shall be abridged to such extent as may be specified in the direction;
(c) service shall be effected in such manner as may be specified in the direction.

Directions

4. (1) The justices' clerk or the court may give, vary or revoke directions for the conduct of the proceedings, including—

(a) the timetable for the proceedings,
(b) varying the time within which or by which an act is required by this Schedule or by a rule where this Schedule applies to proceedings pursuant to that rule to be done,
(c) the service of documents, and
(d) the submission of evidence

and, where the justices' chief executive receives such an application or any other document by which proceedings are commenced, the justices' clerk shall consider whether such directions need to be given].

(2) Where the justices' clerk or a single justice who is holding a directions appointment considers, for whatever reason, that it is inappropriate to give a direction on a particular matter, he shall refer the matter to the court which may give any appropriate direction.

(3) Directions under sub-paragraph (1) may be given, varied or revoked either—

(a) of the justices' clerk's or the courts' own motion having given the resident party an opportunity to attend and be heard or to make written representations, or
(b) on the written request of either party specifying the direction which is sought.

(4) Where the justices' chief executive receives a request under sub-paragraph (3)(b) the justices' clerk shall—

(a) make the direction sought, or
(b) fix a date for a hearing to consider the request.

Timing of proceedings

5. (1) Any period of time fixed by this Schedule or by a rule where this Schedule applies to proceedings pursuant to that rule, or by any order or direction, for doing any act shall be reckoned in accordance with this rule.

(2) Where the period, being a period of 7 days or less, would include a day which is not a business day, that day shall be excluded.

(3) Where the time fixed for filing a document with the justices' chief executive expires on a day on which the office of the justices' chief executive is closed, and for that reason the document cannot be filed on that day, the document shall be filed in time if it is filed on the next day on which the office of the justices' chief executive is open.

(4) Where this Schedule or a rule where this Schedule applies to proceedings pursuant to that rule provides a period of time within which or by which a certain act is to be performed in the course of relevant proceedings, that period may not be extended otherwise than by a direction of the justices' chief executive or the court under paragraph 4(1) above.

(5) At the—

(a) transfer to a court of proceedings,
(b) postponement or adjournment of any hearing or directions appointment in the course of relevant proceedings, or
(c) conclusion of any such hearing or directions appointment other than one at which the proceedings are determined, or so soon thereafter as is practicable,

(i) the justices' clerk shall fix a date upon which the proceedings shall come before him or the court again for such purposes as he or the court directs, which date shall, where paragraph (a) applies, be as soon as possible after the transfer, and
(ii) the justices' chief executive shall give notice to the resident party of the date so fixed.

Attendance at directions appointment and hearing

6. (1) The resident party shall attend a directions appointment of which he has been given notice in accordance with paragraph 4 above unless the justices' clerk or the court otherwise directs.

(2) Where at the time and place appointed for a hearing or directions appointment the resident party does not appear the justices' clerk or the court shall not proceed with the hearing or appointment unless—

(*a*) the proceedings relate to an application filed by the resident party, or
(*b*) the court is satisfied that the resident party has received reasonable notice of the hearing or appointment.

(3) Where at the time and place appointed for a hearing or directions appointment the non-resident party does not appear the court may proceed with the hearing or appointment where the proceedings relate to an order or application sent by the Lord Chancellor to the court under the Act.

(4) Nothing in this Schedule shall be taken as preventing either party from appearing at any hearing or directions appointment.

Documentary evidence

7. (1) A party shall file, at or by such time as the justices' clerk or the court directs or, in the absence of a direction, before the hearing or appointment—

(*a*) written statements of the substance of the oral evidence which he intends to adduce at a hearing or a directions appointment, which shall—

(i) be dated,
(ii) be signed by the person making the statement,
(iii) contain a declaration that the maker of the statement believes it to be true and understands that it may be placed before the court, and
(iv) show in the top right-hand corner of the first page—

(*a*) the initials and surname of the person making the statement,
(*b*) the number of the statement in relation to the maker,
(*c*) the date on which the statement was made, and
(*d*) the party on whose behalf it is filed, and

(*b*) copies of any documents upon which he intends to rely at a hearing or a directions appointment.

(2) A party may, subject to any direction of the justices' clerk or the court about the timing of statements under this rule, file a statement which is supplementary to a statement served under sub-paragraph (1).

(3) Where a non-resident party files a statement or document under this rule, he shall also file a copy of it for service on the resident party; and the justices' chief executive shall on receipt of that copy serve it on the resident party.

(4) At a hearing or directions appointment a party may not without the leave of the justices' clerk, in the case of a directions appointment, or the court—

(*a*) adduce evidence, or
(*b*) seek to rely on a document,

in respect of which he has failed to comply with the requirements of sub-paragraphs (1) and, where applicable, (3).

Amendment

8. (1) A party amending a document shall file the amended document with the justices' chief executive; and the amendments shall be identified.

(2) Paragraph 7(3) above applies to an amended document filed under this paragraph.

Oral evidence

9. The justices' clerk or the court shall keep a note of the substance of any oral evidence given at a hearing or directions appointment.

Hearing

10. (1) Before the hearing, the justice or justices who will be dealing with the case shall read any documents which have been filed under paragraph 7 above in respect of the hearing.

(2) The justices' clerk at a directions appointment, or the court at a hearing or directions appointment, may give directions as to the order of speeches and evidence.

(3) After the final hearing, the court shall make its decision as soon as is practicable.

(4) Before the court makes an order or refuses an application, the justices' clerk shall record in writing—

(*a*) the names of the justice or justices constituting the court by which the decision is made, and
(*b*) in consultation with the justice or justices, the reasons for the court's decision and any findings of fact.

(5) After the court announces its decision, the justices' clerk shall as soon as practicable make a record in writing of any order.

(6) Where, under subsection (4) of section 7 of the Domestic Proceedings and Magistrates' Courts Act 1978, a court decides to treat an application under section 7 as if it were an application for an order under section 2 of that Act, the court shall indicate orally which of grounds (*a*) and (*b*) in that subsection it considers applicable and a memorandum of that decision and the grounds therefor shall be entered in the court's register.

Confidentiality of documents

11. (1) No document, other than a record of an order, held by the court and relating to any proceedings shall be disclosed, other than to—

(*a*) a party,
(*b*) the legal representative of a party,
(*c*) the Lord Chancellor's Department, or
(*d*) the Legal Aid Board,

without leave of the justices' clerk or the court.

Delegation by justices' clerk

12. (1) In this paragraph, "employed as a clerk in court" has the same meaning as in rule 2(1) of the Justices' Clerks (Qualifications of Assistants) Rules 1979.

(2) Anything authorised to be done by, to or before a justices' clerk under this Schedule or under a rule to which this Schedule applies may be done instead by, to or before a person employed as a clerk in court where that person is appointed by the magistrates' courts committee to assist him and where that person has been specifically authorised by the justices' clerk for that purpose.

(3) Any authorisation by the justices' clerk under sub-paragraph (2) shall be recorded in writing at the time the authority is given or as soon as practicable thereafter.

Application of section 97 of the Magistrates' Courts Act 1980

13. (1) Subject to sub-paragraph (2) below, section 97 of the Magistrates' Courts Act 1980 shall apply to proceedings to which this Schedule applies as it applies to a hearing of a complaint under that section.

(2) The power of a justice under section 97 of that Act to issue a witness summons may be exercised by a justices' clerk.

6–4709

Rules 6(2) and 10(5)   SCHEDULE 1

RECIPROCATING COUNTRIES TO WHICH DOCUMENTS ARE TRANSMITTED VIA THE SECRETARY OF STATE

(*Amended by SI 1975/2236, SI 1979/170, SI 1983/1148 and SI 2002/1734.*)

British Columbia
New Zealand
Nova Scotia
Ontario
Ghana
India
Kenya
New Brunswick
Northwest Territories of Canada
The Republic of South Africa
Alberta
Saskatchewan
Turks and Caicos Islands
United Republic of Tanzania (except Zanzibar)
Papua New Guinea
Zimbabwe
Nunavut

6–4710

Rule 9(1)   SCHEDULE 2

COUNTRIES AND TERRITORIES IN WHICH SUMS ARE PAYABLE THROUGH CROWN AGENTS FOR OVERSEAS GOVERNMENTS AND ADMINISTRATIONS

Gibraltar
Barbados
Bermuda
Ghana
Kenya
Fiji
Hong Kong
Singapore
Turks and Caicos Islands
United Republic of Tanzania (except Zanzibar)
Anguilla
Falkland Islands and Dependencies
St. Helena

Magistrates' Courts (Reciprocal Enforcement of Maintenance Orders) (Republic of Ireland) Rules 1975[1]

(SI 1975/286 amended by SI 1992/457, SI 1993/617 and SI 2001/615)

6–4720 1. *Citation.*

1. Made by the Lord Chancellor under s 15 of the Justice of the Peace Act 1949 as extended by s 122 of the Magistrates' Courts Act 1952 and ss 2, 3, 5, 6, 8, 9, 10, 14, 16 and 18 of the Maintenance Orders (Reciprocal Enforcement) Act 1972.

References to the Secretary of State are to be construed as reference to the Lord Chancellor: SI 1992/709, art 4(5).

6–4721 2. (1) In these rules, unless the context otherwise requires—

"the Act" means the Maintenance Orders (Reciprocal Enforcement) Act 1972 as applied with such exceptions, adaptations and modifications as are specified in the Reciprocal Enforcement of Maintenance Orders (Republic of Ireland) Order 1974; and "the court's register", in relation to a justices' chief executive, means the register kept by that justices' chief executive in pursuance of rule 54 of the Magistrates' Courts Rules 1968.

(2) The Interpretation Act [1978] shall apply to the interpretation of these Rules as it applies to the interpretation of an Act of Parliament.

6–4722   3. The officer of any court, by or in relation to whom anything is to be done in pursuance of any provision of Part I of the Act shall, where that court is a magistrates' court, be the justices' clerk.

6–4723   4. (1) An application under section 2 of the Act (transmission of maintenance order made in United Kingdom for enforcement in Republic of Ireland) may, where the court which made the maintenance order to which the application relates is a magistrates' court, be made in writing by or on behalf of the payee under the order.

(2) Any application made in pursuance of paragraph (1) above shall—

(a)   specify the date on which the order was made;
(b)   contain such particulars as are known to the applicant of the whereabouts of the payer;
(c)   specify any matters likely to assist in the identification of the payer;
(d)   where possible, be accompanied by a recent photograph of the payer.

(3) In this rule, "the payer" means the payer under the order to which the application relates.

6–4723A   4A. (1) An application under section 3 of the Act for a provisional order or under section 5 of the Act for the variation or revocation of a maintenance order or a provisional order made in the United Kingdom shall be filed in an appropriate form.

(2) Where the justices' chief executive receives such an application—

(a)   the justices clerk shall fix the date, time and place for a hearing or a directions appointment; and
(b)   the justices' chief executive shall notify the applicant of the date, time and place so fixed.

6–4723B   4B. (1) Schedule A1 to these Rules shall apply to proceedings pursuant to rule 4A above.

(2) In Schedule A1 as it applies to rule 4A, "the resident party" and "the non-resident party" shall be taken to mean—

(a)   in the case of an application for a provisional order, the applicant and the respondent respectively, and
(b)   in the case of an application for the variation or revocation of a maintenance order or a provisional order, the payee and the payer respectively under the order in question.

6–4724   5. A document setting out or summarising any evidence, required by section 3(5)(b) or 5(2) of the Act to be authenticated, shall be authenticated by a certificate, signed by one of the justices before whom that evidence was given, that the document is the original document setting out or, as the case may be, summarising that evidence or a true copy of that document.

6–4725   6. Where under section 3(6A) of the Act a person is required to be notified of the date fixed for the hearing at which confirmation of a provisional order is to be considered, the justices' chief executive for the magistrates' court which made the provisional order shall send that person written notice of the date fixed.

6–4726   7. Any documents required by section 5(4) of the Act to be sent to a court in the Republic of Ireland shall be sent to that court by post.

6–4727   8. (1) Where a justices' chief executive is required under any provision of Part I of the Act to register an order, he shall cause the order to be registered in his court by means of a minute or memorandum entered and signed by him in the court's register.

(2) Every minute or memorandum entered in pursuance of paragraph (1) above shall specify the section of the Act under which the order in question is registered.

6–4728   9. (1) Any notice required under section 6(6) of the Act (notice of registration in United Kingdom court of maintenance order made in Republic of Ireland) to be served on the payer under a maintenance order shall, where the order is registered in a magistrates' court, be in the form in Part I of the Schedule[1] to these Rules, or in a form to the like effect.

(2) Where a magistrates' court to which an appeal is made under section 6(7) of the Act sets aside the registration of a maintenance order, the justices' chief executive shall send written notice of the court's decision to the payee under the order.

(3) Any notice under section 6(10) of the Act (notice that maintenance order made in Republic of Ireland has not been registered in United Kingdom court) to be given to the payee under a maintenance order shall, where the appropriate court is a magistrates' court, be in the form in Part II of the Schedule to these Rules or in a form to the like effect.

---

1. SI 1993/617 inserts a new Sch A1 but does not formally number the pre-existing schedule.

6–4729 **10.** (1) When an order is registered under section 6(3) of the Act, the court shall order that payment of sums due thereunder shall be made to the justices' chief executive for the registering court during such hours and at such place as that justices' chief executive may direct.

(1A) A justices' clerk to whom payments are ordered to be made (whether by virtue of an order under paragraph (1) above or by virtue of an order of the court under the Act) shall send those payments by post to the payee under the order, or where a public authority has been authorised by the payee to receive the payments, to that public authority.

(2) Where it appears to a justices' chief executive to whom payments under any maintenance order are made that any sums payable under the order are in arrear he shall, if the person for whose benefit the payment should have been made so requests in writing, proceed in his own name for the recovery of those sums, unless it appears to him that it is unreasonable in the circumstances to do so.

(3) Where it appears to such a justices' chief executive that any sums payable under the order are in arrear to an amount equal to four times the sum payable weekly under the order he shall give to the person for whose benefit the payment should have been made notice in writing stating the particulars of the arrears.

6–4730 **10A.** (1) Where, in the exercise of the duty imposed under rule 10(1) above, or in the exercise of the powers conferred by virtue of section 8(4A) of the Act, the court orders that payments under the order are to be made by a particular means, the clerk of the court shall record on the copy of the order the means of payment which the court has ordered and notify in writing, as soon as practicable, the person liable to make payments under the order of how payments are to be made.

(2) Where, in the exercise of the aforesaid powers, the court orders payment to the justices' chief executive for the court, or to the justices' chief executive for any other magistrates' court, by a method of payment falling within section 59(6) of the Magistrates' Courts Act 1980 (standing order, etc), the justices' chief executive for the court to whom payments are to be made shall notify the person liable to make the payments under the order of the number and location of the account into which the payments are to be made.

6–4731 **11.** (1) Subject to paragraph (2) below, where a request is made by or on behalf of a court in the Republic of Ireland for the taking in England and Wales of the evidence of a person residing therein, the following magistrates' courts shall have power under section 14(1) of the Act (obtaining of evidence needed for purpose of certain proceedings) to take that evidence, that is to say:—

(a) where the maintenance order to which the proceedings in the court in the Republic of Ireland relate was made by a magistrates' court, the court which made the order;

(b) where the maintenance order to which those proceedings relate is registered in a magistrates' court, the court in which the order is registered;

(c) a magistrates' court which has received such a request from the Secretary of State.

(2) The power conferred by paragraph (1) above may, with the agreement of a court having that power, be exercised by any other magistrates' court which, because the person whose evidence is to be taken resides within its jurisdiction or for any reason, the first-mentioned court considers could more conveniently take the evidence; but nothing in this paragraph shall derogate from the power of any court specified in paragraph (1) above.

(3) Subject to paragraph (4) below, where the evidence of any person is to be taken by a magistrates' court under the foregoing provisions of this rule—

(a) the evidence shall be taken in the manner as if that person were a witness in proceedings on a complaint;

(b) any oral evidence so taken shall be put into writing and read to the person who gave it, who shall be required to sign the document; and

(c) the justices by whom the evidence of any person is so taken shall certify at the foot of any document setting out the evidence of, or produced in evidence by, that person that such evidence was taken, or document received in evidence, as the case may be, by them.

(4) Where such a request as is mentioned in paragraph (1) above includes a request that the evidence be taken in a particular manner, the magistrates' court by which the evidence is taken shall, so far as circumstances permit, comply with that request.

6–4732 **12.** Where a magistrates' court makes an order varying or revoking a maintenance order to which section 5 of the Act (variation and revocation of maintenance order made in United Kingdom) applies, the justices' chief executive shall send written notice of the making of the order to the Secretary of State.

6–4733 **13.** (1) Where a justices' chief executive registers under section 6(3) of the Act (registration in United Kingdom court of maintenance order made in Republic of Ireland an order to which section 6 of the Act applies), he shall send written notice to the Secretary of State that the order has been duly registered.

(2) Where a justices' clerk cancels the registration of a maintenance order under section 10(1) of the Act (cancellation of registration and transfer of order), he shall send written notice of the cancellation to the payer under the order.

(3) Where a justices' clerk registers a maintenance order under section 10(4) of the Act, he shall send written notice to the Secretary of State and to the payer under the order that the order has been duly registered.

6–4734   14. (1) Where the justices' chief executive for a magistrates' court receives from the Secretary of State a notice of the issue of the summons or other originating document in proceedings in the Republic of Ireland in relation to the making, variation or revocation of a maintenance order and it appears to that justices' chief executive that the person against whom those proceedings have been instituted is residing within the petty sessions area for which the court acts, the justices' chief executive shall serve the notice on that person by sending it by post in a registered letter addressed to him at his last known or usual place of abode.

(2) Where it appears to a justices' chief executive who has received such a notice from the Secretary of State that the person against whom the proceedings have been instituted is not so residing, the justices' chief executive shall send the notice to the Secretary of State.

(3) Where a justices' chief executive serves a notice in pursuance of paragraph (1) above he shall send a document which establishes that the notice was so served to the Secretary of State for transmission to the responsible authority in the Republic of Ireland.

6–4734A

SCHEDULE A1
RULES OF PROCEDURE[1]

---

1. These are not reproduced here, but are as set out in Sch A1 to the Magistrates' Courts (Reciprocal Enforcement of Maintenance) Rules 1974, SI 1974/668 this PART, ante.

6–4735

SCHEDULE[1]
PART I
NOTICE TO PAYER OF REGISTRATION OF MAINTENANCE ORDER

Rule 9(1)
To* ....
....

I hereby give notice that on.... day of...... .19.... I registered a maintenance order (copy attached) made by the..............court in the Republic of Ireland ordering you to pay†..........................the sum of‡................................

You are entitled to appeal to the..............magistrates' court within one calendar month from the date of service of this notice to set aside the registration of the order on one of the following grounds:—

(a) that the registration is contrary to public policy;
(b) if you did not appear in the proceedings in the Republic of Ireland, that you were not served with the summons or other notice of the proceedings either in sufficient time to enable you to arrange for your defence or in accordance with the law of the place where you were residing;
(c) that the order is irreconcilable with a judgment given in the United Kingdom in proceedings between you and the above-mentioned payee.

.... J.C.E.
.... Justices' Chief Executive

* Insert name and address of payer.
† Insert name and address of payee.
‡ Insert amount and period, eg, monthly.

PART II
NOTICE TO PAYEE THAT MAINTENANCE ORDER HAS NOT BEEN REGISTERED

Rule 9(3)
To* ....
....

I hereby give notice that I have not registered a maintenance order made by the..............court in the Republic of Ireland ordering†..................to pay you the sum of‡..........................on the ground thatÆ.........................

You are entitled to appeal against my decision to the.............. magistrates' court to have the order registered.

If you wish to appeal, you may do so by completing and returning to me the notice of appeal set out below. Unless you are present in court or legally represented when the appeal is heard, the court may dismiss the case. If you wish to be legally represented, you may apply to..legal aid and advice.

.... J.C.E.
.... Justices' Chief Executive

* Insert name and address of payee.
† Insert name and address of payer.
‡ Insert amount and period, eg, monthly.
Æ Insert one of the grounds specified in section 6(5) of the Maintenance Orders (Reciprocal Enforcement) Act 1972.
Æ Insert the name and address of the Secretary of the appropriate legal aid committee.

MAINTENANCE ORDERS (RECIPROCAL ENFORCEMENT) ACT 1972

Appeal by way of complaint

..............Magistrates' Court (Code)

Date:...

Defendant:...

Address:...

....

....

Matter of Complaint:

The..............Court at.............. in the Republic of Ireland having on.............. made a maintenance order requiring the defendant to pay to the undersigned complainant the sum of £.... . weekly or as the case may be and the order having been sent to the Justices' Clerk for the said Magistrates' Court for registration; the Justices' Clerk has refused to register the order on the ground that..

I hereby appeal to the said Magistrates' Court against the refusal to register this order.

.... Signed...............(Complainant)

---

1. SI 1993/617 inserts a new Sch A1 but does not formally number the pre-existing schedule.

RECOMMENDED FORMS[1]

Notice to payer that provisional maintenance order has been made

(1) Insert name and address of defendant	To ([1]) ....
	....
	....
	..............Magistrates' Court
(2) Insert name and address of complainant	On the complaint of ([2]).......................................
	....
	....
(3) Insert particulars of complaint	that (3) ....

the court on.......... day of.......... 19.. made a provisional order of complaint ordering you, the above-named defendant, to pay the following sums weekly/monthly; namely the sum of £.......... for the benefit of ....

I hereby give you notice that –

the provisional order has no effect unless and until it has been confirmed by the court;

the order may be confirmed with or without alteration;

in considering whether or not to confirm the order the court will take into account any representations made by you or any evidence adduced by you which reach the court within three weeks from the date on which this notice is served on you.

If you intend to defend or be represented at the hearing to consider whether or not to confirm the order, you should fill in and sign the attached form of defence and sent it by prepaid registered post to me at ...... before the expiration of ten days from the date of service of this notice upon you.

You may defend the proceedings in person or be legally represented at the hearing. Legal aid[2] is available if you wish to be represented and if you are financially eligible. I will arrange for a form of application for legal aid to be sent to you by the Legal Aid Board if you notify me of your wish.

If you wish to adduce evidence, but do not wish to attend the proceedings, the evidence may be set out in an affidavit sworn before a solicitor in the Republic of Ireland. If the affidavit is sent to me, I will produce it to the court.

If you do not wish to defend the proceedings, but would like certain matters to be brought to the attention of the court which is considering whether or not to confirm the provisional order, you may submit them to me and I will bring them to the attention of the court.

Whether or not you decide to defend or be represented in the proceedings, it will be helpful to the court, in considering whether or not to confirm the order, to have information about your income, resources and financial commitments. You should therefore complete the attached "Statement of Means" and return it to me.

Dated.................. ....

Justices' Clerk

Statement of Means

This form should be completed and returned to the court whether or not a form of defence is also completed and returned.

Full name

Income

What is your weekly gross pay, including all overtime and bonuses? (Do not deduct income tax or any other   £

Do you receive any weekly income from the State (eg social security, pension)?   £

What is the weekly take home pay of all other persons living with you as part of your family?   £

If you have any other source(s) of income please give details   £

Expenditure

What deductions are made from you pay, eg in respect of income tax? (Give details.)   £

What do you and other persons living with you as part of your family spend each week on the following items?

Rent (including rates if payable by you)   £
Mortgage repayments (including rates)   £
Household expenses (ie gas, electricity, etc)   £
Food   £
Household supplies   £
Clothes   £
School fees   £
School meals   £
Court orders (debts, maintenance etc)   £
Insurance premiums   £
Hire purchase payments   £
Travelling expenses   £
Other expenses (give details)   £
                                                    TOTAL   £

Form of Defence
This form should be completed and signed and returned to the court by prepaid registered post before the expiration of ten days from the date of service of the attached Notice.
I, of
Intend to defend or be represented at the hearing to consider whether or not to confirm the provisional order made against me on the complaint of (*insert name and address of complainant*)
I wish/do not wish (*Delete as appropriate*) to apply for legal aid for the purpose of the proceedings.
Further communications regarding these proceedings should be forwarded to me at
Signature
Date
The Clerk to the Justices
(*Address*)

1. The forms are annexed to Home Office Circular 102/1977; the first one has been slightly modified.
2. It is suggested that the clerk write to the Legal Aid Board asking him to send the defendant the necessary application forms, pointing out that the defendant will want to know where to submit the application form on completion, and what he should do about nominating a solicitor.

Recovery Abroad of Maintenance (Convention Countries) Order 1975[1]

(SI 1975/423 amended by SI 1978/279, SI 1982/1530, SI 1996/1925 and SI 2002/2839)

6–4740   1. *Citation.*

1. Made under s 25 of the Maintenance Orders (Reciprocal Enforcement) Act 1972.

6–4741   2. The countries and territories specified in the Schedule to this Order, being countries and territories outside the United Kingdom to which the United Nations Convention on the Recovery Abroad of Maintenance done at New York on 20th June 1956 extends, are hereby declared to be convention countries for the purposes of Part II of the Maintenance Orders (Reciprocal Enforcement) Act 1972.

6–4742
Article 2   SCHEDULE
                                     CONVENTION COUNTRIES

Algeria
Australia
Austria
Barbados
Belgium
Bosnia and Herzegovina
Brazil
Burkina Faso
Cape Verde
Central African Republic
Chile
Croatia
Cyprus
Czech Republic
Denmark
Ecuador
Finland
France (including the overseas departments of Guadeloupe, Guiana, Martinique and Reunion)

Comoro Archipelago
French Polynesia
New Caledonia and Dependencies St. Pierre and Miquelon

Germany
Greece
Guatemala
Haiti
Holy See
Hungary

Ireland
Israel
Italy
Luxembourg
Mexico
Monaco
Morocco
Netherlands (Kingdom in Europe, Netherlands Antilles and Aruba)
New Zealand
Niger
Norway
Pakistan
Philippines
Poland
Portugal
Romania
Slovakia
Slovenia
Spain
Sri Lanka
Suriname
Sweden
Switzerland
the former Yugoslav Republic of Macedonia
Tunisia
Turkey
Uruguay
Yugoslavia

Magistrates' Courts (Recovery Abroad of Maintenance) Rules 1975[1]

(SI 1975/488 amended by SI 1979/1561, SI 1980/1584, SI 1993/617 and SI 2001/615)

6–4743 **1.** *Citation.*

---

1. Made under s 15 of the Justices of the Peace Act 1949, as extended by s 122 of the Magistrates' Courts Act 1952, s 5(1) of the Justices of the Peace Act 1968 and ss 27(8) to (10), 32(1) to (3), (6) and (8), 33(4) and (5), 35(4) and 38(2) of the Maintenance Orders (Reciprocal Enforcement) Act 1972. See now the Magistrates' Courts Act 1980, ss 144, 145 and 154.

6–4744 **2.** (1) In these Rules, unless the context otherwise requires—

"the Act" means the Maintenance Orders (Reciprocal Enforcement) Act 1972; and
"the court's register", in relation to a justices' chief executive, means the register kept by the justices' chief executive in pursuance of rule 54 of the Magistrates' Courts Rules 1968[1].

(2) The Interpretation Act [1978] shall apply to the interpretation of these Rules as it applies to the interpretation of an Act of Parliament.

---

1. See now rule 66 of the Magistrates' Courts Rules 1981.

6–4745 **3.** The officer of any court, by or in relation to whom anything is to be done in pursuance of any provision of Part II of the Act, shall, where that court is a magistrates' court, be the justices' clerk.

6–4745A **3A.** (1) Where the justices' chief executive receives an application for the recovery of maintenance in England and Wales sent from the Lord Chancellor to a magistrates' court under section 27B of the Act—

(a) the justices' clerk shall fix the date, time and place for a hearing or a directions appointment, allowing sufficient time for service under this rule to be effected at least 21 days before the date so fixed; and
(b) the justices' chief executive shall serve copies of the application and any accompanying documents, together with a notice stating the date, time and place so fixed, on the respondent.]

(2) Within 14 days of service under this rule, the respondent shall file an answer to the application in the appropriate form.

6–4746 **4.** Where a magistrates' court dismisses an application under section 27A of the Act (application for recovery of maintenance), or an application by a person in a convention country for the variation of a registered order, the justices' chief executive shall send written notice of the courts' decision to the Secretary of State and any such notice shall include a statement of the justices' reasons for their decision.

6–4747   5. (1) Where a magistrates' court makes an order which is required under section 27C(7) of the Act to be registered, the justices' chief executive shall enter and sign a minute or memorandum of the order in the court's register.

(2) Where a justices' chief executive in pursuance of section 32(2) or (3) of the Act (transfer of orders), receives a certified copy of an order, he shall cause the order to be registered in his court by means of a minute or memorandum entered and signed by him in the court's register.

(3) Every minute or memorandum entered in pursuance of paragraph (1) or (2) above shall specify the section and subsection of the Act under which the order in question is registered.

6–4748   5A. Where an application under section 26(1) or (2) of the Act or a certificate under section 26(3A) of the Act is required to be registered in a magistrates' court in pursuance of the Recovery of Maintenance (United States of America) Order 1979, the justices' chief executive shall enter and sign a minute or memorandum of the application or certificate in his register.

6–4749   6. (1) Where a justices' chief executive registers an order in pursuance of section 27C(7) or 32(2) or (3) of the Act, he shall send written notice to the Secretary of State that the order has been duly registered.

(2) Where a justices' chief executive is required by section 32(6) of the Act to give notice of the registration of an order he shall do so by sending written notice to the officer specified in that subsection that the order has been duly registered.

6–4750   7. (1) A justices' chief executive to whom payments are made by virtue of section 27C, section 33(3A) or section 34A of the Act shall send those payments by post to such person or authority as the Lord Chancellor may from time to time direct.

(2) Where it appears to a justices' chief executive to whom payments under a registered order are made that any sums payable under the order are in arrear he may and, if such sums are in arrear to an amount equal

(a) in the case of payments to be made monthly or less frequently, to twice the sum payable periodically; or

(b) in any other case, to four times the sum payable periodically,

he shall, whether the person for whose benefit the payment should have been made requests him to do so or not, proceed in his own name for the recovery of those sums, unless it appears to him that it is unreasonable in the circumstances to do so.

6–4750A   7A. (1) Where, in the exercise of the duty imposed under section 27C of the Act, or in the exercise of the powers conferred by virtue of section 33(3A) or section 34A of the Act, the court orders that payments under the order are to be made by a particular means, the chief executive the court shall record on the copy of the order the means of payment which the court has ordered and the justices' chief executive notify in writing, as soon as practicable, the person liable to make payments under the order of how the payments are to be made.

(2) Where, in the exercise of any of the aforesaid powers, the court orders payment to the justices' chief executive for the court, or to the clerk of any other magistrates' court, by a method of payment falling within section 59(6) of the Magistrates' Courts Act 1980 (standing order, etc) the justices chief executive for the court to whom payments are to be made shall notify the person liable to make the payments under the order of the number and location of the account into which the payments are to be made.

(3) Where, under section 34A(4) of the Act, the justices' chief executive for the court receives an application from an interested party for the method of payment to be varied, the clerk shall notify in writing, as soon as practicable, that party and, where practicable, any other interested party, of the result of the application, including any decision to refer the matter to the court; where the clerk grants the application he shall record the variation on the copy of the order.

6–4750B   7B. (1) In this rule "an application" means an application under section 34 of the Act for the variation or revocation of a registered order.

(2) An application which is made directly to the registering court shall be filed in an appropriate form.

(3) Where the justices' chief executive receives an application, either filed in accordance with paragraph (2) or sent from the Lord Chancellor under section 34(3) of the Act—

(a) justices clerk shall fix the date, time and place for a hearing or a directions appointment; and

(b) the justices' chief Executive shall notify the applicant of the date, time and place so fixed.

6–4751   8. (1) Notice under section 35(4) of the Act (variation of orders by magistrates' courts) of the making of an application for the variation or revocation of a registered order and of the time and place appointed for the hearing of the application shall be in the form specified in the Schedule to these Rules and shall be sent by post by the justices' chief executive to the Secretary of State for onward transmission to the appropriate authority in the convention country in which the respondent is residing.

(2) The time for the hearing of the said application shall be not less than six weeks later than the date on which the said notice is sent to the Secretary of State.

6–4752　9. (1) Where a magistrates' court receives from the Secretary of State a request under section 38(1) of the Act (taking evidence at request of court in convention country) to take the evidence of any person, that evidence shall be taken in accordance with the provisions of this rule.

(2) Subject to paragraph (3) below—

(*a*)　the evidence shall be taken in the same manner as if the person concerned were a witness in proceedings on a complaint;

(*b*)　any oral evidence so taken shall be put into writing and read to the person who gave it, who shall be required to sign the document;

(*c*)　the justices by whom the evidence of any person is so taken shall certify at the foot of any document setting out the evidence of, or produced in evidence by, that person that such evidence was taken, or document received in evidence, as the case may be, by them.

(3) Where the request referred to in section 38(1) of the Act includes a request that the evidence be taken in a particular manner, the court by which the evidence is taken shall, so far as circumstances permit, comply with that request.

6–4753　10. (1) Where a justices' chief executive receives from the Secretary of State a request under section 38(1) of the Act to take the evidence of any person, that evidence shall be taken in accordance with the provisions of this rule.

(2) Subject to paragraph (3) below—

(*a*)　the person whose evidence is to be taken shall be examined on oath by or before the justices' clerk;

(*b*)　any oral evidence shall be put into writing and read to that person who shall be required to sign the document; and

(*c*)　the justices' clerk shall certify at the foot of any document setting out the evidence of, or produced in evidence by, that person that such evidence was taken, or document received in evidence, as the case may be, by him.

(3) Where the request referred to in section 38(1) of the Act includes a request that the evidence be taken in a particular manner the justices' clerk by whom the evidence is taken shall, so far as circumstances permit, comply with that request.

(4) For the purposes of this rule a justices' clerk shall have the like power to administer oaths as has a single justice of the peace.

6–4754　11. Any document such as is mentioned in paragraph (2)(*c*) of rule 9 or 10 of these Rules shall be sent to the Secretary of State for onward transmission to the appropriate authority in the convention country in which the request referred to in section 38(1) of the Act originated.

6–4754A　12. (1) Schedule 2 shall apply to proceedings pursuant to rules 3A and 7B above.

(2) In Schedule 2 as it applies to rule 3A, "the resident party" and "the non-resident party" shall be taken to mean the respondent and the applicant respectively.

(3) In Schedule 2 as it applies to rule 7B, "the resident party" and "the non-resident party" shall be taken to mean the payer and the payee under the order in question respectively.

6–4755

Rule 8 (1)　　　　　　　　　　　　SCHEDULE 1[1]
FORM OF NOTICE UNDER SECTION 35(4) OF THE MAINTENANCE ORDERS (RECIPROCAL ENFORCEMENT) ACT 1972

................Magistrates' Court (*Code*)

Date.................................:
To the defendant........................:
......of ....:
................Complaint has been made by
The complainant ....:
......of ....:
.... who states that by an order made on...
.... under the ....Act
.... by the .... Magistrates' Court
.... you were ordered as follows:—
.... and applies for that order to be [revoked]
.... [varied by an order requiring ....]
.... on the ground that
.... The hearing of the complaint will be on
Date of hearing　　　　　　　:　....................at　　　　　　　　　　　m.
　　　　　　　at the　　　　　:　....................Magistrates' Court.

J. C.E.
Justices' Chief Executive

NOTE: If you do not appear at the time and place specified above the court may proceed in your absence. If you wish to make written representations to the court you may do so on the enclosed form.

---

1. SI 1993/617 inserts a new Sch 2 but does not formally number this pre-existing schedule.

FORMS RECOMMENDED BY HOME OFFICE
(SEE HO CIRCULAR 54/1975)

Wife Maintenance
Child Maintenance

APPLICATION FOR THE RECOVERY OF MAINTENANCE FROM A PERSON SUBJECT TO THE JURISDICTION OF A STATE WHICH IS A CONTRACTING PARYT TO THE UNITED NATIONS CONVENTION ON THE RECOVERY ABROAD OF MAINTENANCE

..............Court
....

....
England and Wales/Scotland/ Northern Ireland

In the matter of
................/Claimant
against
................, Respondent

The claim of.. , who states that she is (state name of claimant) married to the said respondent and that she resides at .... in the County of ....

That the claimant is the mother and the said respondent is the father of the following dependent child(ren):
(1) .... born ....
(2) .... born ....
(3) .... born ....
(4) .... born ....

That the claimant is entitled to and seeks the recovery of maintenance from the said respondent for.....
(state whether maintenance sought for self, for child(ren)
.... or for both)
in the weekly amount of £...
(state separate amounts for self and for individual
.... child(ren), if maintenance sought for both)

That upon information and belief the respondent is now residing at .... in the State of .... and is subject to the jurisdiction of that State, which is a Contracting Party to the United Nations Convention on the Recovery Abroad of Maintenance done at New York on 20th June 1956. WHEREFORE, the claimant applies for such an order of maintenance directed to the said respondent as shall be deemed fair and reasonable.

Evidence in support of this application is attached.

The following documents are also attached:

an authority for the Receiving Agency in the said State to take on the claimant's behalf all appropriate steps for the recovery of maintenance;

documents establishing the family relationship of the claimant and respondent and their relationship to any dependent child(ren); namely,..
....
....
.........................(*list documents exhibited*)................

a photograph of the claimant [and a photograph of the respondent]
(*delete if none available*)
other documents as follows ....
....
....
................signed ....
(Claimant)

Taken before me this..dayof.............19...

Justices' Clerk.

Affiliation

APPLICATION FOR THE RECOVERY OF MAINTENANCE FROM A PERSON SUBJECT TO THE JURISDICTION OF STATE WHICH IS A CONTRACTING PARTY TOT HE UNITED NATIONS CONVENTION ON THE RECOVERY OF MAINTENANCE ABROAD

........Court
....

....
England and Wales/Scotland/ Northern Ireland

In the matter of
............./Claimant
against
............., Respondent

1. The claim of ...., who states that she is a single woman.
(state name of claimant)
and that she resides at ....
in the County of ....
That the claimant is the mother and the said respondent is the putative father of the following dependent child(ren):
(1) .... born ....
(2) .... born ....
(3) .... born ....
(4) .... born ....

That the claimant is entitled to and seeks the recovery of maintenance from the said respondent for the said child(ren) in the weekly amount of £.........
That upon information and belief the respondent is now residing at ....
.... in the State of ....

and is subject to the jurisdiction of that State, which is a Contracting party to the United Nations Convention on the Recovery Abroad of Maintenance done at New York on 20th June 1956. WHEREOF, the claimant applies for such an order of maintenance directed to the said respondent as shall be deemed fair and reasonable.

Evidence in support of this application is attached.

6. The following documents are also attached:

an authority for the Receiving Agency in the said State to take on the claimant's behalf all appropriate steps for the recovery of maintenance;

(2) a photograph of the claimant [and a photograph of the respondent]

(*delete if none available*)

(3) other documents as follows...

(signed)...................

(Claimant)

Taken before me this ....day of ....19..

Justices' Clerk.

SCHEDULE 2
                                   RULES OF PROCEDURE[1]

---

1. These are not reproduced here, but are as set out in Schedule A1 to the Magistrates' Courts (Reciprocal Enforcement of Maintenance) Rules 1974, SI 1974/668 this PART, *ante*.

Reciprocal Enforcement of Maintenance Orders (Designation of Reciprocating Countries) Order 1975[1]

(SI 1975/2187)

6–4760 1.   This Order may be cited as the Reciprocal Enforcement of Maintenance Orders (Designation of Reciprocating Countries) Order 1975 and shall come into operation on 28th January 1976.

---

1. Made under ss 1 and 24 of the Maintenance Orders (Reciprocal Enforcement) Act 1972.

6–4761 2.   (1) In this Order—

"the Act of 1972" means the Maintenance Orders (Reciprocal Enforcement) Act 1972;

"the Act of 1920" means the Maintenance Orders (Facilities for Enforcement) Act 1920;

"column (1)" and "column (2)" mean respectively columns (1) and (2) of the Schedule to this Order.

(2) The Interpretation Act 1889 shall apply for the interpretation of this Order as it applies for the interpretation of an Act of Parliament.

6–4762 3.   Each of the countries and territories specified in column (1) is hereby designated as a reciprocating country for the purposes of Part I of the Act of 1972 as regards maintenance orders of the description specified in respect of that country or territory in column (2).

6–4763 4.   (1) Sections 5, 12 to 15, 17, 18 and 21 of the Act of 1972 shall apply in relation to a maintenance order transmitted under section 2 or 3 of the Act of 1920 to one of the countries and territories specified in column (1), being an order of the description specified in respect of that country or territory in column (2) to which immediately before the coming into operation of this Order the Act of 1920 applied, as they apply in relation to a maintenance order sent to that country or territory in pursuance of section 2 of the Act of 1972 or made by virtue of section 3 or 4 of the Act of 1972 and confirmed by a competent court in that country or territory.

(2) Sections 8 to 21 of the Act of 1972 shall apply in relation to a maintenance order made in one of the countries and territories specified in column (1), being an order of the description specified in respect of that country or territory in column (2) to which immediately before the coming into operation of this Order the Act of 1920 applied and not being an order which immediately before that date is registered in the High Court or the High Court of Justice in Northern Ireland under section 1 of the Act of 1920, as they apply in relation to a registered order.

(3) A maintenance order made by a court in one of the countries and territories specified in column (1) being an order of the description specified in respect of that country or territory in column (2) which has been confirmed by a court in England, Wales or Northern Ireland under section 4 of the Act of 1920 and is in force immediately before the coming into operation of this Order, shall be registered under section 7(5) of the Act of 1972 in like manner as if it had been confirmed by that court in England, Wales or Northern Ireland under subsection (2) of that section.

(4) Any proceedings brought under or by virtue of any provision of the Act of 1920 in a court in England, Wales or Northern Ireland which are pending immediately before the coming into operation of this Order, being proceedings affecting a person resident in one of the countries and territories specified in column (1), shall be continued as if they had been brought under or by virtue of the corresponding provision of the Act of 1972.

6–4764

Article 3

SCHEDULE

<small>COUNTRIES AND TERRITORIES DESIGNATED AS RECIPROCATING COUNTRIES</small>

(1) Country or territory	(2) Description of maintenance orders to which designation extends
Barbados	Maintenance orders generally.
Bermuda	Maintenance orders generally.
Ghana	Maintenance order other than— (a) affiliation orders, and (b) maintenance orders of the description contained inparagraph (b) of the definition of "maintenance order"in the said section 21(1).
India	Maintenance orders other than— (a) affiliation orders; (b) maintenance orders of the description contained in paragraph (b) of the definition of "maintenance order" in the said section 21(1); and (c) orders obtained by or in favour of a public authority.
Kenya	Maintenance orders other than— (a) affiliation orders, and (b) maintenance orders of the description contained in paragraph (b) of the definition of "maintenance order", in the said section 21(1).
Malta	Maintenance orders generally.
New Brunswick	Maintenance orders other than— (a) affiliation orders; (b) maintenance orders of the description contained in paragraph (b) of the definition of "maintenance order" in the said section 21(1); and (c) orders obtained by or in favour of a public authority.
Northwest Territories of Canada	Maintenance orders other than— (a) affiliation orders; (b) maintenance orders of the description contained in paragraph (b) of the definitionof "maintenance order" in the said section 21(1); and (c) orders obtained by or in favour of a public authority.
The Republic of South Africa	Maintenance orders other than— (a) affiliation orders, and (b) maintenance orders of the description contained in paragraph (b) of the definition of "maintenance order" in the said section 21(1).

Reciprocal Enforcement of Maintenance Orders (Designation of Reciprocating Countries) Order 1979[1]

(SI 1979/115)

6–4770   **1.**   This Order may be cited as the Reciprocal Enforcement of Maintenance Orders (Designation of Reciprocating Countries) Order 1979 and shall come into operation on 1st April 1979.

---

1. Made under ss 1 and 24 of the Maintenance Orders (Reciprocal Enforcement) Act 1972.

6–4771   **2.**   In this Order—

"the Act of 1972" means the Maintenance Orders (Reciprocal Enforcement) Act 1972;
"the Act of 1920" means the Maintenance Orders (Facilities for Enforcement) Act 1920;
"the Order of 1974" means the Reciprocal Enforcement of Maintenance Orders (Designation of Reciprocating Countries) Order 1974;
"column (1)" and "column (2)" in Articles 3 and 6 below mean respectively columns (1) and (2) of the Schedule to this Order.

6–4772   **3.**   Each of the countries and territories specified in column (1) is hereby designated as a reciprocating country for the purposes of Part I of the Act of 1972 as regards maintenance orders of the description specified in respect of that country or territory in column (2).

6–4773   **4.**   *This article amends SI 1974/556.*

6–4774   **5.**   *This article amends SI 1974/556.*

6–4775   6. (1) Sections 5, 12 to 15, 17, 18 and 21 of the Act of 1972 shall apply in relation to a maintenance order transmitted under section 2 or 3 of the Act of 1920 to one of the countries and territories specified in column (1), being an order of the description specified in respect of that country or territory in column (2) to which immediately before the coming into operation of this Order the Act of 1920 applied, as they apply in relation to a maintenance order sent to that country or territory in pursuance of section 2 of the Act of 1972 or made by virtue of section 3 or 4 of the Act of 1972 and confirmed by a competent court in that country or territory.

(2) Sections 8 to 21 of the Act of 1972 shall apply in relation to a maintenance order made in one of the countries and territories specified in column (1), being an order of the description specified in respect of that country or territory in column (2) to which immediately before the coming into operation of this Order the Act of 1920 applied and not being an order which immediately before that date is registered in the High Court or the High Court of Justice in Northern Ireland under section 1 of the Act of 1920, as they apply in relation to a registered order.

(3) A maintenance order made by a court in one of the countries and territories specified in column (1) being an order of the description specified in respect of that country or territory in column (2) which has been confirmed by a court in England, Wales or Northern Ireland under section 4 of the Act of 1920 and is in force immediately before the coming into operation of this Order, shall be registered under section 7(5) of the Act of 1972 in like manner as if it had been confirmed by that court in England, Wales or Northern Ireland under subsection (2) of that section.

(4) Any proceedings brought under or by virtue of any provision of the Act of 1920 in a court in England, Wales or Northern Ireland which are pending immediately before the coming into operation of this Order, being proceedings affecting a person resident in one of the countries and territories specified in column (1), shall be continued as if they had been brought under or by virtue of the corresponding provision of the Act of 1972.

6–4776

Article 2

SCHEDULE

COUNTRIES AND TERRITORIES DESIGNATED AS RECIPROCATING COUNTRIES

(1) Country or territory	(2) Description of maintenance orders to which designation extends
Alberta	Maintenance orders other than— (a) provisional affiliation orders; (b) maintenance orders of the description contained in paragraph (b) of the definition of "maintenance order" in section 21(1)of the Act of 1972; (c) orders obtained by or in favour of a publicauthority.
Fiji	Maintenance orders generally.
Hong Kong	Maintenance orders generally.
Norfolk Island	Maintenance ordersother than orders obtained by or in favour of a public authority.
Saskatchewan	Maintenance orders other than— (a) provisional affiliation orders; and (b) maintenance orders of the description contained in the said paragraph (b).
Singapore	Maintenance orders generally.
Turks and Caicos Islands	Maintenance ordersother than— (a) affiliation orders; (b) maintenance orders of the description contained in the said paragraph (b); and (c) orders obtained by or in favour of a public authority.
United Republic of Tanzania (except Zanzibar)	Maintenance orders other than— (a) affiliation orders; (b) maintenance orders of the description contained in the said paragraph (b); and (c) orders obtained by or in favour of a publicauthority.
Western Australia	Maintenance orders other than orders obtained by or in favour of a public authority.

Magistrates' Courts (Reciprocal Enforcement of Maintenance Orders) (Hague Convention Countries) Rules 1980[1]

(SI 1980/108 amended by SI 1986/1962, SI 1992/457, SI 1993/617, SI 1999/2002 and SI 2001/615)

6–4789   **1.** *Citation and commencement.*

---

1. Made by the Lord Chancellor under s 15 of the Justices of the Peace Act 1949, and in exercise of powers conferred on him by the provisions specified in Schedule 1 to these Rules, post. See Home Office Circular No 15/1980, dated 26 February 1980, for guidance as to the provisions contained in these Rules.

References to the Secretary of State are to be construed as reference to the Lord Chancellor: SI 1992/709, art 4(5).

These Rules apply with the modifications set out in the Magistrates' Courts (Reciprocal Enforcement of Maintenance Orders) (United States of America) Rules 1995, post, to the matters prescribed under Part I of the Maintenance Orders (Reciprocal Enforcement) Act 1972 as set out in Sch 3 to the Reciprocal Enforcement of Maintenance Orders (United States of America) Order 1995, post.

6–4790   **2.** In these Rules, unless the context otherwise requires—

"the Act" means the Maintenance Orders (Reciprocal Enforcement) Act 1972 as applied with such exceptions, adaptations and modifications as are specified in the Reciprocal Enforcement of Maintenance Orders (Hague Convention Countries) Order 1979; and

"the court's register" in relation to a justices' chief executive means the register kept by the justices' chief executive in pursuance of Rule 54 of the Magistrates' Courts Rules 1968[1].

---

1. See now r 66 of the Magistrates' Courts Rules 1981.

6–4791   **3.** The officer of any court, by or in relation to whom anything is to be done in pursuance of any provision of Part I of the Act shall, where that court is a magistrates' court, be the justices' clerk.

6–4792   **4.** (1) An application under section 2 of the Act (transmission of maintenance order made in the United Kingdom for recognition and enforcement in Hague Convention country) shall where the court which made the maintenance order to which the application relates is a magistrates' court, be made in writing by or on behalf of the payee under the order.

(2) Any application made in pursuance of paragraph (1) above shall—

(a) specify the date on which the order was made;

(b) contain such particulars as are known to the applicant of the whereabouts of the payer and the nature and location of his assets;

(c) specify any matters likely to assist in the identification of the payer;

(d) where possible, be accompanied by a recent photograph of the payer.

(3) In this rule "the payer" means the payer under the order to which the application relates.

6–4792A   **4A.** (1) In this rule, "an application" means—

(a) an application under section 3 of the Act for a maintenance order against a person residing in a Hague Convention country,

(b) an application under section 5 of the Act for the variation or revocation of a maintenance order made in the United Kingdom, or

(c) an application under section 9 of the Act for the variation of a maintenance order registered by a court in the United Kingdom.

(2) An application shall be filed in an appropriate form.

(3) Where the justices' chief executive receives such an application—

(a) the justices' clerk shall fix the date, time and place for a hearing or a directions appointment; and

(b) the justices' chief executive shall notify the applicant of the date, time and place so fixed.

6–4792B   **4B.** (1) Schedule 1A to these Rules shall apply to proceedings pursuant to rule 4A above.

(2) In Schedule 1A as it applies to rule 4A, "the resident party" and "the non-resident party" shall be taken to mean—

(a) in the case of an application under sub-paragraph (a) of rule 4A(1), the applicant and the respondent respectively,

(b) in the case of an application under sub-paragraph (b) of rule 4A(1), the payee and payer respectively under the order in question, and

(c) in the case of an application under sub-paragraph (c) of rule 4A(1), the payer and payee respectively under the order in question.

6–4793   **5.** (1) Where a justices' chief executive is required under any provision of Part I of the Act to register a maintenance order, he shall cause the order to be registered in his court by means of a minute or memorandum entered and signed by him in the court's register.

(2) Every minute or memorandum entered in pursuance of paragraph (1) above shall specify the section of the Act under which the order in question is registered.

(3) Where a maintenance order is under any provision of Part I of the Act registered in a magistrates' court, the justices' chief executive shall send written notice of the registration to the Secretary of State.

6–4794   **6.** Where under section 5(4)(b) of the Act a copy of any representations made or evidence adduced by or on behalf of the payer in an application by the payee for the variation or revocation of a maintenance order to which section 5 of the Act applies, is required to be served on the payee before the hearing, the justices' chief executive for the magistrates' court to which the application is made shall arrange for a copy of such representations or evidence to be sent to the payee by post.

6–4795 **7.** (1) Any notice required under section 6(8) of the Act (notice of registration in United Kingdom court of maintenance order made in Hague Convention country) to be served on the payer under a maintenance order shall, where the order is registered in a magistrates' court, be in the form in Part I of Schedule 2 to these Rules, or in a form to the like effect.

(2) Where a magistrates' court to which an appeal is made under section 6(9) of the Act sets aside the registration of a maintenance order, the justices' chief executive shall send written notice of the court's decision to the Secretary of State.

(3) Any notice required under section 6(11) of the Act (notice that maintenance order made in Hague Convention country has not been registered in United Kingdom court) to be given to the payee under a maintenance order shall, where the appropriate court is a magistrates' court, be in the form in Part II of Schedule 2 to these Rules or in a form to the like effect.

6–4796 **8.** (1) When an order is registered under section 6(3) of the Act, the court shall order that payment of sums due thereunder shall be made to the justices' chief executive for the registering court during such hours and at such place as that justices' chief executive may direct.

(1A) A justices' chief executive to whom payments are ordered to be made (whether by virtue of an order under paragraph (1) above or by virtue of an order of the court under the Act) shall send those payments by post to the payee under the order.

(2) Where it appears to a justices' chief executive to whom payments by way of periodical payments under any maintenance order are to be made that any sums payable under the order are in arrear he may and, if such sums are in arrear to an amount equal to four times the sum payable weekly under the order, he shall, whether the person for whose benefit the payment should have been made requests him to do so or not, proceed in his own name for the recovery of those sums, unless it appears to him that it is unreasonable in the circumstances to do so.

6–4797 **8A.** Without prejudice to Rule 8 above, the justices' chief executive of the registering court shall take reasonable steps to notify the person to whom payments are due under a registered order of the means of enforcement available in respect of it, including, in an appropriate case, the possibility of registration of the whole or part of the order in the High Court under Part I of the Maintenance Orders Act 1958.

6–4798 **8B.** (1) Where, in the exercise of the duty imposed under rule 8(1) above, or in the exercise of the powers conferred by virtue of section 8(4A) or section 9(1ZA) of the Act, the court orders that payments under the order are to be made by a particular means, the clerk of the court shall record on the copy of the order the means of payment which the court has ordered and the justices' chief executive shall notify in writing, as soon as practicable, the person liable to make payments under the order of how payments are to be made.

(2) Where, in the exercise of any of the aforesaid powers, the court orders payment to the clerk of the court, or to the justices' chief executive for any other magistrates' court, by a method of payment falling within section 59(6) of the Magistrates' Courts Act 1980 (standing order, etc), the justices' chief executive for the court to whom payments are to be made shall notify the person liable to make the payments under the order of the number and location of the account into which the payments are to be made.

(3) Where, under section 60(4) of the Magistrates' Courts Act 1980, as modified by section 9(1ZA) of the Act, the justices' chief executive for the court receives an application from an interested party for the method of payment to be varied, the justices' chief executive shall notify in writing, as soon as practicable, that party and, where practicable, any other interested party, of the result of the application, including any decision to refer the matter to the court; where the clerk of the court then grants the application, he shall record the variation on the copy of the order.

6–4799 **9.** (1) Subject to paragraph (2) below, where a request is made by or on behalf of a court in a Hague Convention country for the taking in England and Wales of the evidence of a person residing therein, the following magistrates' courts shall have power under section 14(1) of the Act (obtaining of evidence needed for purpose of certain proceedings) to take that evidence, that is to say:—

(a) where the maintenance order to which the proceedings in the court in the Hague Convention country relate was made by a magistrates' court, the court which made the order;

(b) where the maintenance order to which those proceedings in the court in the Hague Convention country relate was made by a court in a Hague Convention country, the court in which the order is registered;

(c) a magistrates' court which has received such a request from the Secretary of State.

(2) The power conferred by paragraph (1) above may, with the agreement of a court having that power, be exercised by any other magistrates' court which, because the person whose evidence is to be taken resides within its jurisdiction or for any other reason, the first-mentioned

court considers could more conveniently take the evidence; but nothing in this paragraph shall derogate from the power of any court specified in paragraph (1) above.

(3) Subject to paragraph (4) below, where the evidence of any person is to be taken by a magistrates' court under the foregoing provisions of this Rule—

   (a) the evidence shall be taken in the same manner as if that person were a witness in proceedings on a complaint;

   (b) any oral evidence so taken shall be put into writing and read to the person who gave it who shall be required to sign the document; and

   (c) the justices by whom the evidence of any person is so taken shall certify at the foot of any document setting out the evidence of, or produced in evidence by, that person that such evidence was taken, or document received in evidence, as the case may be, by them.

(4) Where such a request as is mentioned in paragraph (1) above includes a request that the evidence be taken in a particular manner, the magistrates' court by which the evidence is taken shall, so far as circumstances permit, comply with that request.

6–4800 **10.** (1) Where a justices' chief executive cancels the registration of a maintenance order under section 10(1) of the Act (cancellation of registration and transfer of order) he shall send written notice of the cancellation to the payer under the order.

(2) Where a justices' chief executive registers a maintenance order under section 10(4) of the Act, he shall send written notice to the Secretary of State and to the payer under the order that the order has been duly registered.

6–4801 **11.** Where a justices' chief executive serves a notice on a payer under a maintenance order who resides in a Hague Convention country under any provision of Part I of the Act, he shall send a document which establishes that the notice was so served to the Secretary of State.

6–4802 **12.** (1) Where the justices' chief executive for a magistrates' court receives from the Secretary of State notice of the institution of proceedings, including notice of the substance of the claim, in a Hague Convention country in relation to the making, variation or revocation of a maintenance order and it appears to that justices' chief executive that the person against whom those proceedings have been instituted is residing within the petty sessions area for which the court acts, the justices' clerk shall serve the notice on that person by sending it by post in a registered letter addressed to him at his last known or usual place of abode.

(2) Where it appears to a justices' chief executive who has received such a notice from the Secretary of State that the person against whom the proceedings have been instituted is not so residing, the justices' clerk shall return the notice to the Secretary of State with an intimation to that effect.

6–4803   SCHEDULE 1

Enabling Powers

Section 15 of the Justices of the Peace Act 1949, as extended by section 122 of the Magistrates' Courts Act 1952;

The following provisions of the Maintenance Orders (Reciprocal Enforcement) Act 1972, as extended by Article 3 of the Reciprocal Enforcement of Maintenance Orders (Hague Convention Countries) Order 1979, namely,

   section 2(3) and (4) (see Rules 3 and 4[1]);
   section 3(5)(*b*), (6A), (6B) and (6D) (see Rule 3[1]);
   section 5(3), (4)(*c*), (6), (7) and (10) (see Rules 3 and 5[1]);
   section 5(4)(*b*) (see Rule 6[1]);
   section 6(2), (3), (5), (6), (7), (8), (10), (11) and (12) (see Rules 3, 5, 7 and Schedule 2[1]);
   section 8(5) (see Rule 8[1]);
   section 8(6) (see Rule 3[1]);
   section 9(3), (4)(*b*) and (*c*), (6), (7) and (8) (see Rules 3 and 5[1]);
   section 10(1), (2), (3), (4), (5) and (7) (see Rules 3, 5 and 10[1]);
   section 11(1)(*b*) (see Rule 3[1]);
   section 14(1) (see Rule 9[1]);
   section 16(1) (see Rule 8[1]);
   section 18(1) (see Rule 9[1]).

---

1. The references to Rules are to the Rules in this statutory instrument which give effect to the enabling powers to which the Rules relate.

6–4803A   SCHEDULE 1A
                                 RULES OF PROCEDURE[1]

---

1. These are not reproduced here, but are as set out in Schedule A1 to the Magistrates' Courts (Reciprocal Enforcement of Maintenance) Rules 1974, SI 1974/617 this PART, ante.

6–4804

SCHEDULE 2

PART I

Rule 7(1)

Notice to payer of registration of maintenance order.

To (1) ....

....

I hereby give notice that on........day of........19....I registered a maintenance order (copy attached) made by the.. ....court in (2) ....ordering you to pay (3) ....the sum of (4) ....

You are entitled to appeal to the........ magistrates' court within one calendar month from the date of the service of this notice to set aside the registration of the order on one of the following grounds:—

    (a) that the court making the order did not have jurisdiction to do so (5);

    (b) that the registration is contrary to public policy;

    (c) that the order was obtained by fraud in connection with a matter of procedure;

    (d) that proceedings between you and the payee and having the same purpose are pending before a court in the United Kingdom and those proceedings were instituted before these proceedings;

    (e) that the order is incompatible with a judgment given in proceedings between you and the payee and having the same purpose, either in the United Kingdom or in a Hague Convention country;

    (f) if you did not appear in the proceedings in the Hague Convention country, that you were not given notice of the institution of the proceedings, including notice of the substance of the claim, in accordance with the law of that country and in sufficient time to enable you to defend the proceedings.

                                      J.C.E.

                              Justices' Chief Executive

(1) Insert name and address of payer.

(2) Insert name of Hague Convention country.

(3) Insert name of payee.

(4) Insert amount in sterling and period, e.g. monthly.

(5) Jurisdiction may be based—

    (a) on the habitual residence of the payer or payee in that State;

    (b) on the payer and payee being nationals of that State;

    (c) on your submission to the jurisdiction of the court; or

    (d) in the case of an order made on divorce, etc. on any ground which is recognised by United Kingdom law.

PART II

Rule 7(3)

Notice to payee that maintenance order has not been registered.

To (1) ....

....

I hereby give notice that I have not registered a maintenance order made by the .... court in (2) ....ordering (3) .... to pay you the sum of (4) .... on the ground that (5) ....

You are entitled to appeal against my decision to the.......... magistrates' court within [two calendar months] from the date when this notice was given to have the order registered.

If you wish to appeal, you may do so by completing and returning to me the notice of appeal set out opposite. Unless you are present in court or legally represented when the appeal is heard the court may dismiss the case. If you wish to be legally represented and need legal aid or advice you may apply to the Area Secretary, the Law Society, 14 (London West) Legal Aid Area, Area Headquarters, 29–37 Red Lion Street, London WC1R 4PP.

                                      J.C.E.

                              Justices' Chief executive.

(1) Insert name and address of payee.

(2) Insert name of Hague Convention country.

(3) Insert name and address of payer.

(4) Insert amount in sterling and period e.g. monthly.

(5) Insert one of the grounds specified in section 6(5), (6) or (7) of the Maintenance Orders (Reciprocal Enforcement) Act 1972 (as extended by the Reciprocal Enforcement of Maintenance (Hague Convention Countries) Order 1979).

MAINTENANCE ORDERS (RECIPROCAL ENFORCEMENT) ACT 1972

Appeal by way of application

              ....Magistrates' Court (Code)

Date:..

Defendant:...

Address:..

....

Matter of Application:

The..........Court at......... in..........having on.......... made a maintenance order requiring the defendant to pay the undersigned applicant the sum of £...... weekly or as the case may be and the order having been sent to the Justices' Chief Executive for the said Magistrates' Court for registration; the Justices' Chief Executive has refused to register the order on the ground that................................... . I hereby appeal to the said Magistrates' Court against the refusal to register this order.

Signed..............(Applicant)

Reciprocal Enforcement of Maintenance Orders (Designation of Reciprocating Countries) Order 1983[1]

(SI 1983/1125)

6–4805   **1.**   This Order may be cited as the Reciprocal Enforcement of Maintenance Orders (Designation of Reciprocating Countries) Order 1983 and shall come into operation on 1st September 1983.

---

1. Made under ss 1 and 24 of the Maintenance Orders (Reciprocal Enforcement) Act 1972.

6–4806   **2.**   In this Order—

"the Act of 1972" means the Maintenance Orders (Reciprocal Enforcement) Act 1972;

"the Act of 1920" means the Maintenance Orders (Facilities for Enforcement) Act 1920;

"the Order of 1974" means the Reciprocal Enforcement of Maintenance Orders (Designation of Reciprocating Countries) Order 1974;

"column (1)" and "column (2)" in Articles 3 and 5 below means respectively columns (1) and (2) of the Schedule to this Order.

6–4807   **3.**   Each of the countries and territories specified in column (1) is hereby designated as a reciprocating country for the purposes of Part I of the Act of 1972 as regards maintenance orders of the description specified in respect of that country or territory in column (2).

6–4808   **4.**   *This article amends SI 1974/556, Sch.*

6–4809   **5.**   (1) Sections 5, 12 to 15, 17, 18 and 21 of the Act of 1972 shall apply in relation to a maintenance order transmitted under section 2 or 3 of the Act of 1920 to one of the countries and territories specified in column (1), being an order of the description specified in respect of that country or territory in column (2) to which immediately before the coming into operation of this Order the Act of 1920 applied, as they apply in relation to a maintenance order sent to that country or territory in pursuance of section 2 of the Act of 1972 or made by virtue of section 3 or 4 of the Act of 1972 and confirmed by a competent court in that country or territory.

(2) Sections 8 to 21 of the Act of 1972 shall apply in relation to a maintenance order made in one of the countries and territories specified in column (1), being an order of the description specified in respect of that country or territory in column (2) to which immediately before the coming into operation of this Order the Act of 1920 applied and not being an order which immediately before that date is registered in the High Court or the High Court of Justice in Northern Ireland under section 1 of the Act of 1920, as they apply in relation to a registered order.

(3) A maintenance order made by a court in one of the countries and territories specified in column (1) being an order of the description specified in respect of that country or territory in column (2) which has been confirmed by a court in England, Wales or Northern Ireland under section 4 of the Act of 1920 and is in force immediately before the coming into operation of this Order, shall be registered under section 7(5) of the Act of 1972 in like manner as if it had been confirmed by that court in England, Wales or Northern Ireland under subsection (2) of that section.

(4) Any proceedings brought under or by virtue of any provision of the Act of 1920 in a court in England, Wales or Northern Ireland which are pending immediately before the coming into operation of this Order, being proceedings affecting a person resident in one of the countries or territories specified in column (1), shall be continued as if they had been brought under or by virtue of the corresponding provision of the Act of 1972.

6–4809A

Article 3   SCHEDULE

COUNTRIES AND TERRITORIES DESIGNATED AS RECIPROCATING COUNTRIES

(1) Country or territory	(2) Description of maintenance orders to which designation extends
Anguilla	Maintenance orders generally
Falkland Islands and Dependencies	Maintenance orders generally
Isle of Man	Maintenance orders generally
Nauru	Maintenance orders generally
Papua New Guinea	Maintenance orders other than provisional affiliation orders
St. Helena	Maintenance orders generally
Zimbabwe	Maintenance orders other than— (a) affiliation orders; and (b) maintenance orders of the description contained in paragraph (b) of the definition of "maintenance order" in section 21(1) of the Act of 1972 (orders for the payment of birth and funeral expenses of child).

Magistrates' Courts (Civil Jurisdiction and Judgments Act 1982) Rules 1986[1]

(SI 1986/1962 amended by SI 1992/457, SI 1993/617 and SI 2001/615, SI 2002/194 and SI 2005/617)

PART I
CITATION, COMMENCEMENT AND INTERPRETATION

6–4810   1. *Citation and commencement.*

1. Made by the Lord Chancellor under s 144 of the Magistrates' Courts Act 1980 as extended by s 2A(1) of the Maintenance Orders Act 1958, ss 2(3), 8(5) and 33(4) of the Maintenance Orders (Reciprocal Enforcement) Act 1972 and ss 12 and 48 of the Civil Jurisdiction and Judgments Act 1982.

References to the Secretary of State in rr 3 to 14 have been changed to the Lord Chancellor following the transfer of ministerial responsibility in respect of England and Wales by SI 1992/709, art 4(6).

6–4811   2. In these Rules—

"the 1982 Act" means the Civil Jurisdiction and Judgments Act 1982;

"the court's register", in relation to the designated officer for a magistrates' court, means the register kept by the designated officer, means the register kept by that justices' chief executive in pursuance of Rule 66 of the Magistrates' Courts Rules 1981.

PART II
REGISTRATION OF MAINTENANCE ORDERS

The prescribed officer

6–4812   3. The prescribed officer of a magistrates' court for the purposes of the 1982 Act and the Civil Jurisdiction and Judgments Order 2001 shall be the justices' clerk.

Registration of maintenance orders

6–4813   4. (1) Where a designated officer for a magistrates' court receives an application under Article 31 of the 1968 Convention for enforcement of a maintenance order made in a Contracting State other than the United Kingdom he shall, subject to Articles 27 and 28 of that Convention and to paragraph (3) and (4) of this Rule, cause the order to be registered in his court by means of a minute or memorandum entered and signed by him in the court's register.

(1A) Where a designated officer for a magistrates' court receives an application under Article 38 of the Regulation for enforcement of a maintenance order made in a Regulation State other than the United Kingdom he shall, subject to Articles 34 and 35 of the Regulation and to paragraphs (3) and (4) of this Rule, cause the order to be registered in his court by means of a minute or memorandum entered and signed by him in the court's register.

(2) Before registering an order under paragraph (1) or (1A) of this Rule the designated officer for the court shall take such steps as he thinks fit for the purpose of ascertaining whether the payer under the order to which the application relates is residing within the jurisdiction of the court, and shall consider any information he possesses (whether provided by the applicant or otherwise) as to the nature and location of the payer's assets.

(3) If, after taking such steps and considering such information as are mentioned in paragraph (2) above, the designated officeris satisfied that the payer under the order is not residing within the jurisdiction of the court he shall, subject to paragraph (4) of this Rule, refuse the application and return the documents relating thereto to the Lord Chancellor with a statement giving such information as he possesses as to the whereabouts of the payer and the nature and location of his assets.

(4) If, after taking such steps and considering such information as are mentioned in paragraph (2) above, the designated officer is satisfied that the payer is not residing within the jurisdiction of the court but that there are assets against which, after registration in the High Court under Part I of the Maintenance Orders Act 1958, the order could be enforced, he shall cause the order to be registered in accordance with paragraph (1) of this Rule.

Provided that where the designated officer is of the opinion that the payer is residing within the jurisdiction of another magistrates court in England and Wales he may, if he thinks fit, and notwithstanding the provisions of this paragraph, refuse the application and return the documents relating thereto to the Lord Chancellor in accordance with paragraph (3) above.

(5) If the designated officer refuses an application made under Article 31 of the 1968 Convention or under Aricle 38 of the Regulation, he shall cause notice of his decision to be sent to the applicant, at the address provided by the applicant.

(6) Where an order has been registered under paragraph (1) or (1A) of this Rule the designated officer who was responsible for its registration shall cause a written notice stating that it has been duly registered in his court to be sent to:

(*a*)   the Lord Chancellor;
(*b*)   the payer under the order to which the registration relates;
(*c*)   the applicant, at the address provided by the applicant.

(7) Where an order has been registered under paragraph (1) or (1A) of this Rule and the designated officer who was responsible for its registration is of the opinion that the order, or a part thereof, is one which would be appropriate for enforcement in the High Court he shall notify the applicant accordingly and shall notify the applicant also of the possibility of an application by the applicant for registration of the whole or part of the order in the High Court under Part I of the Maintenance Orders Act 1958.

Appeals from decision as to registration

6–4814 5. An appeal under Article 36 or under Article 40 of the 1968 Convention or under Article 43 of the Regulation shall be by way of complaint to the magistrates' court in which the order is registered, or in which the application for its registration has been refused, as the case may be.

Payment of sums due under a registered order

6–4815 6. (1) When an order is registered under section 5(3) of the 1982 Act or under Article 43 of the Regulation, the court shall order that payment of sums due thereunder shall be made to the designated officer for the registering court during such hours and at such place as that designated officer may direct.

(1A) The designated officer to whom payments are ordered to be made (whether by virtue of an order under paragraph (1) above or by virtue of an order of the court under the 1982 Act) shall send those payments by post to the court which made the order or to such other person or authority as that court or the Lord Chancellor may from time to time direct.

(2) Where it appears to a designated officer to whom payments by way of periodical payments under any maintenance order are made that any sums payable under the order are in arrear he may and, if such sums are in arrear to an amount equal to four times the sum payable weekly, he shall, whether the person for whose benefit the payment should have been made requests him to do so or not, proceed in his own name for the recovery of those sums, unless it appears to him that it is unreasonable in the circumstances to do so.

(3) Without prejudice to the foregoing provisions of this Rule, the designated officer of the registering court shall take reasonable steps to notify the person to whom payments are due under a registered order of the means of enforcement available in respect of it, including, in an appropriate case, the possibility of registration of the whole or part of the order in the High Court under Part I of the Maintenance Orders Act 1958.

6–4816 6A. (1) Where, in the exercise of the duty imposed under rule 6(1) above, or in the exercise of the powers conferred by virtue of section 5(6B) of the Act of 1982, the court orders that payments under the order are to be made by a particular means, the clerk of the court shall record on the order the means of payment which the court has ordered and the designated officer for the court shall notify in writing, as soon as practicable, the person liable to make payments under the order of how payments are to be made.

(2) Where, in the exercise of any of the aforesaid powers, the court orders payment to the designated officer for the court, or to the justices' chief executive for any other magistrates' court, by a method of payment falling within section 59(6) of the Magistrates' Courts Act 1980 (standing order, etc), the designated officer for the court to whom payments are to be made shall notify the person liable to make the payments under the order of the number and location of the account into which the payments are to be made.

Variation and revocation of registered orders

6–4817 7. Where a maintenance order which has been registered for enforcement in a magistrates' court has been varied or revoked by an order made by a competent court in a Contracting State or a Regulation State the justices' chief executive the court in which the order is registered shall, on receiving notice of the variation or revocation, register the order of variation or revocation by means of a minute or memorandum entered and signed by him in his register, and shall cause notice of the same to be given in writing by post to the payee and to the payer under the order to which the variation or revocation relates.

Transfer of registered orders

6–4818 8. (1) Where the designated officer for the court where an order is registered is of the opinion that the payer under the registered order is residing within the jurisdiction of another magistrates' court in England and Wales he shall transfer the order to that other court by sending the information and documents relating to the registration of the order (that is, the information and documents required under Articles 46 and 47 of the Convention or under Article 53 of the Regulation, as appropriate) to the designated officer for that other court, and shall cause notice of the same to be given to the payee under the order to which the transfer relates, and to the Lord Chancellor.

Provided that where an application is pending in the registering court for the registration of the whole or part of the order in the High Court under Part I of the Maintenance Orders Act 1958, the designated officer shall not transfer the order, or such part of it to which the application relates, under this paragraph.

(2) On the transfer of an order under paragraph (1) above the designated officer for the court

to which it is transferred shall register the order in the like manner as if an application for registration had been received under Rule 4 of these Rules.

(3) The designated officer who is required by the foregoing provisions of this Rule to send to the designated officer for another court information and documents relating to the registration of an order shall send with that information and those documents—

(a) a certificate of arrears, if applicable, signed by him;

(b) a statement giving such information as he possesses as to the whereabouts of the payer and the nature and location of his assets; and

(c) any other relevant documents in his possession relating to the case.

Cancellation of registered orders

6–4819 9. Subject to Rule 8 of these Rules, where the designated officer for the court where an order is registered is of the opinion that the payer under the registered order is not residing within the jurisdiction of that court and has no assets against which, after registration in the High Court under Part I of the Maintenance Orders Act 1958, the order could be enforced he shall cancel the registration of the order and shall cause notice of the same to be given to the payee under the order to which the cancellation relates and shall send the information and documents relating to the registration of the order (that is, the information and documents required under Articles 46 and 47 of the Convention or under Article 53 of the Regulation, as appropriate) to the Lord Chancellor, together with such information and documents as are referred to in Rule 8(3)(a), (b) and (c) of these Rules.

PART III
APPLICATIONS FOR MAINTENANCE UNDER ARTICLE 5(2) OF THE 1968 CONVENTION

Complaint against a person residing outside the United Kingdom

6–4820 10. (1) This Rule applies where a complaint is made to a magistrates' court by a person who is domiciled or habitually resident in England and Wales against a person residing in a Contracting State or a Regulation State other than the United Kingdom, and the complaint is one in respect of which the court has jurisdiction to make a maintenance order by virtue of Article 5(2) of the 1968 Convention or Article 5(2) of the Regulation.

(2) On the making of a complaint to which paragraph (1) of this Rule applies, the following documents, that is to say—

(a) notice of the institution of the proceedings, including a statement of the grounds of the complaint;

(b) a statement signed by the designated officer for the court, giving such information as he possesses as to the whereabouts of the defendant;

(c) a statement giving such information as the designated officer for the court possesses for facilitating the identification of the defendant; and

(d) where available, a photograph of the defendant;

shall be sent by that clerk to the Lord Chancellor.

(3) The designated officer for the court shall give the defendant notice in writing of the date fixed for the hearing by sending the notice by post addressed to his last known or usual place of abode.

(4) Where the defendant makes any written representations or adduces any documentary evidence in advance of the hearing, a copy of the representations or evidence shall be served on the complainant by the designated officer for the court before the hearing.

(5) In considering whether or not to make a maintenance order pursuant to a complaint to which paragraph (1) of this Rule applies, where the defendant does not appear and is not represented at the hearing the court shall take into account any representations made and any evidence adduced by him or on his behalf under paragraph (4) above and, where the defendant does appear or is represented at the hearing, the court may take any such representations or evidence into account in addition to any oral representations made or evidence adduced at the hearing.

(6) Where a maintenance order has been made under this Rule in respect of a complaint in relation to which the court has jurisdiction by virtue of Article 5(2) of the 1968 Convention, the designated officer for the court shall cause notice thereof to be given to the defendant by sending a copy of the order by post addressed to his last known or usual place of abode and, on application by the complainant, shall give to the complainant the following documents, that is to say—

(a) a certified copy of the order;

(b) a written statement signed by the justices' clerk as to whether or not the defendant appeared in the proceedings in which the order was made, and, if he did not appear, the original or a certified copy of a document which establishes that the document mentioned in paragraph (2)(a) of this Rule had been served on the defendant;

(c) a document which establishes that notice of the order was sent to the defendant; and

(d) a written statement signed by the justices' clerk as to whether or not the complainant received legal aid in the proceedings;

with a view to an application being made by the complainant for registration and enforcement under Articles 31 and 32 of the 1968 Convention.

(7) Where a maintenance order has been made under this Rule in respect of a complaint in relation to which the court has jurisdiction by virtue of Article 5(2) of the Regulation, the designated officer for the court shall cause notice thereof to be given to the defendant by sending a copy of the order by post addressed to his last known or usual place of abode and, on application by the complainant, shall give to the complainant the following documents—

  (a) a certified copy of the order; and
  (b) a completed certificate in the form of Annex V to the Regulation;

with a view to an application being made by the complainant for registration and enforcement under Articles 38 and 39 of the Regulation.

Application for variation and revocation of a maintenance order

6–4821   **11.** (1) This Rule applies where an application is made to a magistrates' court for the variation or revocation of a maintenance order where the payer under the order is residing in a Contracting State or a Regulation State other than the United Kingdom.

(2) Where an application to which this Rule applies is made by the payee, the following documents, that is to say—

  (a) Notice of the institution of the proceedings, including a statement of the grounds of the application;
  (b) a statement signed by the designated officer for the court, giving such information as he possesses as to the whereabouts of the respondent;
  (c) a statement giving such information as the clerk possesses for facilitating the identification of the respondent; and
  (d) where available, a photograph of the respondent;

shall be sent by that designated officer to the Lord Chancellor.

(3) Where an application to which this Rule applies is made by the payee—

  (a) The designated officer for the court shall give the respondent notice in writing of the date fixed for the hearing by sending the notice by post addressed to his last known or usual place of abode;
  (b) where the respondent makes any written representations or adduces any documentary evidence in advance of the hearing, a copy of the representations or evidence shall be served on the applicant by the designated officer for the court before the hearing;
  (c) the court, in considering whether to vary or revoke the order, shall, where the payer does not appear and is not represented at the hearing, take into account any representations made and any evidence adduced by or on his behalf under sub-paragraph (b) above and, where the payer does appear or is represented at the hearing, the court may take any such representations or evidence into account, in addition to any oral representations or evidence adduced at the hearing.

(4) Where an application to which this Rule applies is made by the payer, the designated officer for the court shall arrange for the service of the document mentioned in paragraph (2)(a) of this Rule on the payee.

(5) Where upon an application to vary or revoke a maintenance order where the payer under the order is residing in a Contracting State the court varies or revokes the order, the designated officer for the court shall cause notice thereof to be given to the respondent by sending a copy of the order of variation or revocation by post addressed to his last known or usual place of abode and, on application by the applicant, shall give to the applicant the following documents, that is to say—

  (a) a certified copy of the order of variation or revocation;
  (b) a written statement, signed by the justices' clerk as to whether or not the respondent appeared in the proceedings for the variation or revocation of the order and if he did not appear the original or a certified copy of a document which establishes that the notice of the institution of the proceedings had been served on the respondent;
  (c) a document which establishes that notice of the order of variation or revocation was sent to the respondent; and
  (d) a written statement signed by the justices' clerk as to whether or not the applicant or the respondent received legal aid in the proceedings;

with a view to an application being made by the applicant for registration and enforcement of the order of variation or revocation under Articles 31 and 32 of the 1968 Convention.

(6) Where upon an application to vary or revoke a maintenance order where the payer under the order is residing in a Regulation State the court varies or revokes the order, the designated officer for the court shall cause notice thereof to be given to the respondent by sending a copy of the order of variation or revocation by post addressed to his last known or usual place of abode and, on application by the applicant, shall give to the applicant the following documents—

  (a) a certified copy of the order of variation or revocation; and
  (b) a completed certificate in the form of Annex V to the Regulation;

with a view to an application being made by the applicant for registration and enforcement of the order of variation or revocation under Articles 38 and 39 of the Regulation.

Copies of, and certificates in connection with, maintenance orders

6–4822   **12.** (1) Without prejudice to the provisions of Rules 10(6), 10(7), 11(5) and 11(6) of these Rules, a person wishing to obtain for the purposes of an application for recognition or enforcement in a Contracting State or a Regulation State a copy of a maintenance order made by a magistrates' court in England and Wales, and a certificate giving particulars relating to the order and the proceedings in which it was made may apply in writing to the designated officer for that court.

(2) An application under paragraph (1) above shall specify—

(a) the names of the parties to the proceedings in the magistrates' court;

(b) the date or approximate date of the proceedings in which the maintenance order was made, and the nature of those proceedings;

(c) the Contracting State or the Regulation State in which the application for recognition or enforcement has been made or is to be made;

(d) the postal address of the applicant.

(3) A designated officer who receives an application under paragraph (1) of this Rule shall send by post to the applicant at the address indicated in the application for the purposes an authenticated copy of the order concerned.

(4) For the purposes of paragraph (3) of this Rule a copy of an order shall be deemed to be authenticated if it is accompanied by a statement signed by the designated officer that it is a true copy of the order concerned and giving particulars of the proceedings in which it was made.

(5) A person wishing to obtain for the purposes of an application made or to be made in another Contracting State or in another Regulation State or in another part of the United Kingdom in connection with a maintenance order which is registered in a magistrates' court in England and Wales a certificate giving particulars of any payments made and any arrears which have accrued under the order while so registered may apply in writing to the designated officer for the registering court, and a designated officer who receives such an application shall send by post to the applicant at the address indicated in the application for the purposes a certificate giving the information so requested.

PART IV

EVIDENCE IN MAINTENANCE PROCEEDINGS

Admissibility of documents

6–4823   **13.** (1) Subject to paragraph (2) of this Rule, a statement contained in—

(a) a document which purports to set out or summarise evidence given in proceedings in a court in another part of the United Kingdom or another Contracting State or another Regulation State;

(b) a document which purports to have been received in evidence in proceedings in a court in another part of the United Kingdom or another Contracting State or another Regulation State;

(c) a document which purports to set out or summarise evidence taken in another part of the United Kingdom or in another Contracting State or another Regulation State for the purpose of proceedings in a court in England and Wales under the 1982 Act or the Regulation, whether in response to a request made by such a court or otherwise; or

(d) a document which purports to record information relating to the payments made under an order of a court in another part of the United Kingdom or another Contracting State or another Regulation State

shall, in any proceedings in a magistrates' court in England and Wales relating to a maintenance order to which the 1982 Act or the Regulation applies, be admissible as evidence of any fact stated therein to the same extent as oral evidence of that fact is admissible in those proceedings.

(2) Paragraph (1) of this Rule shall not apply unless the document concerned has been made or authenticated by the court in the other part of the United Kingdom or the other Contracting State or another Regulation State, as the case may be, or by a judge or official of that court, in accordance with paragraph (3), (4) or (5) of this Rule.

(3) A document purporting to set out or summarise evidence given as mentioned in paragraph (1)(a) above, or taken as mentioned in paragraph (1)(c) above, shall be deemed to be authenticated for the purposes of that paragraph if the document purports to be certified by the judge or official before whom the evidence was given or by whom it was taken, or to be the original document containing or recording or, as the case may be, summarising, the evidence or a true copy of that document.

(4) A document purporting to have been received in evidence as mentioned in paragraph (1)(b) above, or to be a copy of a document so received, shall be deemed to be authenticated for the purposes of that paragraph if the document purports to be certified by a judge or official of the court in question to be, or to be a true copy of, a document which has been so received.

(5) A document purporting to record information as mentioned in paragraph (1)(d) above shall be deemed to be authenticated for the purposes of that paragraph if the document purports to be

certified by a judge or official of the court in question to be a true record of the payments made under the order concerned.

(6) It shall not be necessary in any proceedings in which evidence is to be received under this Rule to prove the signature or official position of the person appearing to have given such a certificate.

(7) Nothing in this Rule shall prejudice the admission in evidence of any document which is admissible in evidence apart from this Rule.

(8) Any request by a magistrates' court in England and Wales for the taking or providing of evidence by a court in another part of the United Kingdom or another Contracting State or another Regulation State for the purpose of proceedings under the 1982 Act or the Regulation shall be communicated in writing to the court in question.

Evidence for the purposes of proceedings outside England and Wales

6–4824 **14.** (1) Subject to paragraph (2) below, where for the purposes of any proceedings in a court in another part of the United Kingdom or in a Contracting State or in a Regulation State other than the United Kingdom relating to a maintenance order a request is made by or on behalf of that court for the taking in England and Wales of evidence of a person residing therein relating to matters specified in the request, the following magistrates' courts shall have power to take that evidence, that is to say—

(a) where the maintenance order to which the proceedings in the court in the other part of the United Kingdom or Contracting State or Regulation State relate was made by a magistrates' court, the court which made the order;

(b) where the maintenance order to which those proceedings relate is registered in a magistrates' court, the court in which the order is registered;

(c) a magistrates' court which has received such a request from the Lord Chancellor.

(2) The power conferred by paragraph (1) above may, with the agreement of a court having that power, be exercised by any other magistrates' court which, because the person whose evidence is to be taken resides within its jurisdiction or for any other reason, the first mentioned court considers could more conveniently take the evidence; but nothing in this paragraph shall derogate from the power of any court specified in paragraph (1) above.

(3) Before taking the evidence of a person under paragraph (1) or (2) above, a magistrates' court shall give notice of the time and place at which the evidence is to be taken to such persons and in such manner as it thinks fit.

(4) Subject to paragraph (5) below, where the evidence of a person is to be taken by a magistrates' court under the foregoing provisions of this Rule—

(a) the evidence shall be taken in the same manner as if that person were a witness in proceedings on a complaint;

(b) any oral evidence so taken shall be put into writing and read to the person who gave it, who shall be required to sign the document; and

(c) the justices by whom the evidence of any person is so taken shall certify at the foot of any document setting out the evidence of, or produced in evidence by, that person that such evidence was taken, or a document received in evidence, as the case may be, by them.

(5) Where such a request as is mentioned in paragraph (1) above includes a request that the evidence be taken in a particular manner, the magistrates' court by which the evidence was taken shall, so far as circumstances permit, comply with that request.

(6) Any document such as is mentioned in paragraph (4)(c) above shall be sent to the court in the Contracting or Regulation State or on behalf of which the request was made.

Magistrates' Courts (Family Law Act 1986) Rules 1988[1]
(SI 1988/329 amended by SI 1991/1991, SI 2001/615 and SI 2005/617)

6–4840 **1.** *Citation and commencement.*

---

1. Made by the Lord Chancellor in exercise of the powers conferred upon him by s 144 of the Magistrates' Courts Act 1980.

Interpretation

6–4841 **2.** (1) In these Rules the following expressions have the meaning hereby respectively assigned to them—

"the Act" means the Family Law Act 1986;

"commission area" has the same meaning as in the Justices of the Peace Act 1979;

"Part I order" means a Part I order within the meaning of any of sections 1, 32, 40 and 42(5) and (6) of the Act;

"specified dependent territory" means a dependent territory specified in column 1 of Schedule 1 to the Family Law Act 1986 (Dependent Territories) Order 1991.

"the appropriate court" means, in relation to Scotland, the Court of Session and, in relation to Northern Ireland, the High Court and, in relation to a specified dependent territory, means the corresponding court in that territory;

"the Deputy Principal Clerk" means the Deputy Principal Clerk of Session;

"the Master" means the Master (Care and Protection) of the High Court in Northern Ireland.

(2) Any requirement in these Rules for any matter to be entered in the register of a magistrates' court is a requirement that it be entered in the register kept by the designated officer for that court in accordance with Rule 66 of the Magistrates' Courts Rules 1981.

Registration of Part I orders

6–4842　**3.**—(1) An application under section 27 of the Act for the registration in the appropriate court of a custody order made by a magistrates' court in England and Wales shall be made in writing in Form 1 in the Schedule to these Rules or in a similar form containing the information specified in the said Form 1, to the court which made the order.

(2) An application to which paragraph (1) above relates shall be accompanied by the following documents, namely—

(*a*)　a certified copy of the order;

(*b*)　where the order has been varied, a certified copy of any variation order which is in force;

(*c*)　any other document relevant to the application.

(3) Subject to paragraph (4) below, if it appears to the court to which an application is made in accordance with paragraphs (1) and (2) above that the order to which the application relates is in force it shall cause the designated officer for the court to send a copy of the application, together with copies of the documents set out in paragraph (2) above, to the Deputy Principal Clerk or the Master of the appropriate court, or the corresponding officer of the appropriate court in a specified dependent territory, or to more than one of those persons as the case may be.

(4) If it appears to the court to which an application is made in accordance with paragraphs (1) and (2) above that the order to which the application relates is no longer in force in respect of a child in respect of whom the order was made or that any such child has attained the age of 16, it shall refuse to send the documents referred to in paragraph (2) above to the appropriate court, or shall indicate thereon with respect to which child or children the order is not to be registered and the designated officer for the court shall notify the applicant of its refusal or indication accordingly.

(5) A memorandum of the granting of an application made in accordance with paragraphs (1) and (2) above shall be entered in the register of the court to which the application was made.

(6) Where the designated officer for the court which granted an application made in accordance with paragraphs (1) and (2) above receives notice of the registration in the appropriate court of the order he shall cause particulars of the notice to be entered in the register of his court.

Notice of revocation or variation of a registered order, and of cancellation of registration

6–4843　**4.**—(1) Where a custody order made by a magistrates' court in England and Wales and registered in the appropriate court in Scotland, Northern Ireland or a specified dependent territory is revoked or varied, the designated officer for the court making the order of revocation or variation shall cause a certified copy of that order to be sent to the Deputy Principal Clerk or the Master of the appropriate court, or the corresponding officer of the appropriate court in a specified dependent territory, or to more than one of those persons, as the case may be, and to the court which made the custody order, if that court is different from the court making the order of revocation or variation.

(2) Where the designated officer for the court which made an order revoking or varying a registered order receives notice of the registration in the appropriate court of the order of revocation or variation he shall cause particulars of the notice to be entered in the register of his court.

(3) Where the designated officer for the court which made a custody order receives, in accordance with paragraph (1) above, a certified copy of an order of revocation or variation of that order by another court, he shall cause notice thereof to be entered in the register of his court.

(4) Where the designated officer for a court which made a custody order receives notice of the registration in the appropriate court of an order revoking or varying the custody order he shall cause particulars of the notice to be entered in the register of his court.

(5) Where the designated officer for a court which made a custody order receives notice of the cancellation of the registration of that order in the appropriate court, he shall cause particulars of the notice to be entered in the register of his court.

Courts authorised to hear applications under the Guardianship of Minors Act 1971 and Part II of the Children Act 1975

6–4844　**5.** Revoked.

Duty to give statement of other proceedings

6–4845　**6.**—(1) A party to proceedings for or relating to a custody order in a magistrates' court in England and Wales who knows of other proceedings (including proceedings out of the jurisdiction and concluded proceedings) which relate to the child concerned shall provide to the court a statement giving the information set out in Form 2 in the Schedule to these Rules, and, for this purpose, the designated officer for a magistrates' court in which proceedings for or relating to a custody order are pending shall, as soon in those proceedings as may be practicable, notify the parties of the provisions of this rule by sending to each party a notice in the said Form 2 or in a similar form.

(2) Paragraph (1) above shall not apply in relation to proceedings commenced in a magistrates' court before 4th April 1988.

Stay of proceedings

6–4846   **7.** (1) Where under section 5(2) of the Act a magistrates' court stays proceedings on an application for a custody order it shall cause notice of the stay to be given to the parties to the proceedings.

(2) Where under section 5(3) of the Act a magistrates' court removes a stay granted in accordance with section 5(2) it shall cause notice of the removal of the stay to be given to the parties to the proceedings and shall proceed to deal with the application accordingly.

6–4847

Rule 3(1) and 6   SCHEDULE

FORM 1

APPLICATION FOR REGISTRATION IN SCOTLAND, NORTHERN IRELAND OR A SPECIFIED DEPENDANT TERRITORY OF A PART I ORDER
(SECTION 27 OF FAMILY LAW ACT 1986)

....Magistrates' Court (*Code*)

Date:

To the Justices' Chief Executive, ... Magistrates' Court, (*address*)

Name of applicant:

Address:

Order made on: .... (*date*)

To be registered in: (Scotland, Northern Ireland, specified dependent territory or more than one of these)

Name of child:

Date of birth:

Address (or suspected whereabouts) of child:

Name of person with whom child is presently residing (or suspected to be residing):

The applicant's interest under the order is ....

The following other persons have an interest under the order ....

....

(*State whether the order has been served on each person named*)

(The order is not registered in any other court)

(The order is already registered in ....)

To the best of the applicant's information and belief the order is in force and (no other order affecting the child is in force in the place where the order is to be registered) (the following other orders are in force in the place where the order is to be registered ....)

Signed by the applicant

....

Note:

This application must be accompanied by a certified copy of the order to which it relates, a certified copy of any variation order which is in force, and any other document which is relevant to the application.

FORM 2

NOTICE OF REQUIREMENT TO GIVE PARTICULARS OF OTHER PROCEEDINGS (S 39 FAMILY LAW ACT 1986)

....Magistrates' Court (*Code*)

Date:...

To:...

Address:..

....

Concerning the application of .... (name of applicant) under: .... (*statute*)

As a party to these proceedings you are required to inform the court if you know of any other proceedings (including proceedings out of the jurisdiction and concluded proceedings) relating to: .... (*name of child*).

The information you should provide, if known, is:

(*a*)   the place in which and the court in which the other proceedings were instituted;

(*b*)   the names of the parties to the proceedings and their relationship to the child;

(*c*)   the nature and current state of the proceedings and the relief claimed;

(*d*)   if the relief claimed in the proceedings before this court was not claimed in the other proceedings, the reasons why it was not claimed in the other proceedings.

The information should be provided in writing addressed to the Justices' Chief Executive, at the address below.

Justices' Chief Executive

.....................Magistrates' court

Address ....

Magistrates' Courts (Social Security Act 1986) (Transfer of Orders to maintain and Enforcement of Maintenance Orders) Rules 1990[1]
(SI 1990/1909 amended by SI 2001/615)

6–4848 **1.** (1) *Citation and commencement.*

(2) In these Rules, "personal allowance element", "the dependent parent" and "the liable parent" have the same meaning as in section 24A of the Social Security Act 1986 ("the 1986 Act")[2].

---

1. Made by the Lord Chancellor, in exercise of the powers conferred on him by s 144 of the Magistrates' Courts Act 1980 as extended by s 145 of that Act.
2. See now the Social Security Administration Act 1992, ss 106, 107.

6–4849 **2.** Where under section 24A of the 1986 Act[1] the Secretary of State gives notice in writing to a magistrates' court which has made an order under section 24(4) of that Act, transferring to a dependent parent (by virtue of subsection (3)) or transferring back from the dependent parent to himself (by virtue of subsection (7)) the right to receive the payments under the order (exclusive of any personal allowance element), the clerk of that court shall amend the order by substituting the name of the dependent parent for that of the Secretary of State or the name of the Secretary of State for that of the dependent parent, as appropriate.

---

1. See now the Social Security Administration Act 1992, ss 106–107.

6–4850 **3.** Where a clerk amends an order made under section 24(4) in accordance with rule 2 of these Rules—

(a) he shall make a written record of the fact that, the circumstances in which and the date on which, he has done so, and shall keep it with the register kept under rule 66 of the Magistrates' Courts Rules 1981; and
(b) the justices' chief executive shall send a copy of the amended order, as soon as practicable, to the Secretary of State, the liable parent and the dependent parent.

6–4851 **4.** Where an application within paragraph (a) or (b) of section 24B(5) of the 1986 Act[1] is made to a magistrates' court, the justices' chief exective for the court shall, after giving notice to the Secretary of State of any such application, notify the parties to the application that he has done so and that the Secretary of State is entitled to appear and be heard on the application.

---

1. See now the Social Security Administration Act 1992, ss 106, 107.

Child Support (Information, Evidence and Disclosure) Regulations 1992[1]
(SI 1992/1812 and amended by SI 1995/123, 1045 and 3261, SI 1996/1945 and 2907, SI 1998/58, SI 1999/977 and 1510, and SI 2001/161, the Child Support, Pensions and Social Security Act 2000, s 1, SI 2002/1204, SI 2003/3206, SI 2004/1823 and 2415 and SI 2005/2877)

The text of these regulations is reproduced in the CD Rom version.

Child Support (Collection and Enforcement) Regulations 1992[1]
(SI 1992/1989 amended by SI 1993/913, SI 1994/227, SI 1995/1045 and 3261, SI 1996/1945, SI 1998/58 and 2799, SI 1999/977 and 1510, and SI 2001/162 and by virtue of the Child Support, Pensions and Social Security Act 2000, s 1 and Sch 3 and SI 2005/2877)

PART I
GENERAL

Citation, commencement and interpretation

6–4941 **1.** (1) *Citation and commencement.*

(2) In these Regulations "the Act" means the Child Support Act 1991.*

(2A) Except in relation to regulation 8(3)(a) and Schedule 2, in these Regulations "fee" means an assessment fee or a collection fee, which for these purposes have the same meaning as in the Child Support Fees Regulations 1992 prior to their revocation by the Child Support (Collection and Enforcement and Miscellaneous Amendments) Regulations 2000.**

(3) Where under any provision of the Act or of these Regulations—

(a) any document or notice is given or sent to the Secretary of State, it shall be treated as having been given or sent on the day it is received by the Secretary of State; and

(b) any document or notice is given or sent to any other person, it shall, if sent by post to that person's last known or notified address, be treated as having been given or sent on the second day after the day of posting, excluding any Sunday or any day which is a bank holiday under the Banking and Financial Dealings Act 1971.***

(4) In these Regulations, unless the context otherwise requires, a reference—

(a) to a numbered Part is to the Part of these Regulations bearing that number;

(b) to a numbered regulation is to the regulation in these Regulations bearing that number;

(c) in a regulation to a numbered or lettered paragraph or sub-paragraph is to the paragraph or sub-paragraph in that regulation bearing that number or letter;

(d) in a paragraph to a lettered or numbered sub-paragraph is to the sub-paragraph in that paragraph bearing that letter or number;

(e) to a numbered Schedule is to the Schedule to these Regulations bearing that number.

---

*Subsection substituted by SI 2001/162 from a date to be appointed.
**Subsection inserted by SI 2001/162 from a date to be appointed.
***Amended by SI 2001/162 from a date to be appointed.
1. Made by the Secretary of State under ss 29(2) and (3), 31(8), 32(1) to (5) and (7) to (9), 34(1), 35(2), (7) and (8), 39(1), (3) and (4), 40(4), (8) and (11), 51, 52 and 54 of the Child Support Act 1991.

PART II
COLLECTION OF CHILD SUPPORT MAINTENANCE

PART III
DEDUCTION FROM EARNINGS ORDER[1]

Appeals against deduction from earnings orders

6–4941A   22. (1) A liable person in respect of whom a deduction from earnings order has been made may appeal to the magistrates' court, or in Scotland the sheriff, having jurisdiction in the area in which he resides.

(2) Any appeal shall—

(a) be by way of complaint for an order or, in Scotland, by way of application;

(b) be made within 28 days of the date on which the matter appealed against arose.

(3) An appeal may be made only on one or both of the following grounds—

(a) that the deduction from earnings order is defective[2];

(b) that the payments in question do not constitute earnings[3].

(4) Where the court or, as the case may be, the sheriff is satisfied that the appeal should be allowed the court or, sheriff, may—

(a) quash the deduction from earnings order; or

(b) specify which, if any, of the payments in question do not constitute earnings.

---

1. Part III contains regs 8–25, but we print only reg 22.
2. In this regulation "defective" in relation to a deduction from earnings order means that it does not comply with the requirements of the regulations and such failure to comply has made it impracticable for the employer to comply with his obligations (reg 8(1) as amended by SI 1995/1045).
3. In this regulation "earnings" are any sums payable to a person by way of (a) wages or salary (including any fees, bonus, commission, overtime pay or other emoluments payable in addition to wages or salary or payable under a contract of service); (b) pension (including an annuity in respect of past service, whether or not rendered to the person paying the annuity, and including periodical payments by way of compensation for the loss, abolition or relinquishment, or diminution in the emoluments, of any office or employment); (c) statutory sick pay. "Earnings" do not include (i) sums payable by any public department of the Government of Northern Ireland or of a territory outside the United Kingdom; (ii) pay or allowances payable to the liable person as a member of Her Majesty's forces; (iii) pension allowances or benefit payable under any enactment relating to social security; (iv) pension or allowances payable in respect of disablement or disability; (v) the guaranteed minimum pension within the meaning of the Social Security Pensions Act 1975 (reg 8(3) and (4)).

PART IV
LIABILITY ORDERS

Extent of this Part

6–4942   26. This Part, except regulation 29(2), does not apply to Scotland.

Notice of intention to apply for a liability order

6–4943   27. (1) The Secretary of State shall give the liable person at least 7 days notice of his intention to apply for a liability order under section 33(2) of the Act.

(2) Such notice shall set out the amount of child support maintenance which it is claimed has become payable by the liable person and has not been paid and the amount of any interest in respect of arrears payable under section 41(3) of the Act.*

(3) Payment by the liable person of any part of the amounts referred to in paragraph (2) shall not require the giving of a further notice under paragraph (1) prior to the making of the application.

---

*Amended by SI 2001/162 from a date to be appointed.

Application for a liability order

6–4944   **28.** (1) An application for a liability order shall be by way of complaint for an order to the magistrates' court having jurisdiction in the area in which the liable person resides.

(2) An application under paragraph (1) may not be instituted more than 6 years after the day on which payment of the amount in question became due.

(3) A warrant shall not be issued under section 55(2) of the Magistrates' Courts Act 1980 in any proceedings under this regulation.

Liability orders

6–4945   **29.** (1) A liability order shall be made in the form prescribed in Schedule 1.

(2) A liability order made by a court in England or Wales or any corresponding order made by a court in Northern Ireland may be enforced in Scotland as if it had been made by the sheriff.

(3) A liability order made by the sheriff in Scotland or any corresponding order made by a court in Northern Ireland may, subject to paragraph (4), be enforced in England and Wales as if it had been made by a magistrates' court in England and Wales.

(4) A liability order made by the sheriff in Scotland or a corresponding order made by a court in Northern Ireland shall not be enforced in England or Wales unless registered in accordance with the provisions of Part II of the Maintenance Orders Act 1950 and for this purpose—

(a) a liability order made by the sheriff in Scotland shall be treated as if it were a decree to which section 16(2)(*b*) of that Act applies (decree for payment of aliment);

(b) a corresponding order made by a court in Northern Ireland shall be treated as if it were an order to which section 16(2)(*c*) of that Act applies (order for alimony, maintenance or other payments).

Enforcement of liability orders by distress

6–4946   **30.** (1) A distress made pursuant to section 35(1) of the Act may be made anywhere in England and Wales.

(2) The person levying distress on behalf of the Secretary of State shall carry with him the written authorisation of the Secretary of State, which he shall show to the liable person if so requested, and he shall hand to the liable person or leave at the premises where the distress is levied—

(a) copies of this regulation, regulation 31 and Schedule 2;

(b) a memorandum setting out the amount which is the appropriate amount for the purposes of section 35(2) of the Act;

(c) a memorandum setting out details of any arrangement entered into regarding the taking of possession of the goods distrained; and

(d) a notice setting out the liable person's rights of appeal under regulation 31 giving the Secretary of State's address for the purposes of any appeal.

(3) A distress shall not be deemed unlawful on account of any defect or want of form in the liability order.

(4) If, before any goods are seized, the appropriate amount (including charges arising up to the time of the payment or tender) is paid or tendered to the Secretary of State, the Secretary of State shall accept the amount and the levy shall not be proceeded with.

(5) Where the Secretary of State has seized goods of the liable person in pursuance of the distress, but before sale of those goods the appropriate amount (including charges arising up to the time of the payment or tender) is paid or tendered to the Secretary of State, the Secretary of State shall accept the amount, the sale shall not be proceeded with and the goods shall be made available for collection by the liable person.

Appeals in connection with distress

6–4947   **31.** (1) A person aggrieved by the levy of, or an attempt to levy, a distress may appeal to the magistrates' court having jurisdiction in the area in which he resides.

(2) The appeal shall be by way of complaint for an order.

(3) If the court is satisfied that the levy was irregular, it may—

(a) order the goods distrained to be discharged if they are in the possession of the Secretary of State;

(b) order an award of compensation in respect of any goods distrained and sold of an amount equal to the amount which, in the opinion of the court, would be awarded by way of special damages in respect of the goods if proceedings under section 35(6) of the Act were brought in trespass or otherwise in connection with the irregularity.

(4) If the court is satisfied that an attempted levy was irregular, it may by order require the Secretary of State to desist from levying in the manner giving rise to the irregularity.

Charges connected with distress

6–4948 **32.** Schedule 2 shall have effect for the purpose of determining the amounts in respect of charges in connection with the distress for the purposes of section 35(2)(*b*) of the Act.

Application for warrant of commitment

6–4949 **33.** (1) For the purposes of enabling an inquiry to be made under section 39A of the Act as to the liable person's conduct and means, a justice of the peace having jurisdiction for the area in which the liable person resides may—

    (*a*) issue a summons to him to appear before a magistrates' court and (if he does not obey the summons) issue a warrant for his arrest; or

    (*b*) issue a warrant for his arrest without issuing a summons.

(2) In any proceedings under sections 39A and 40 of the Act, a statement in writing to the effect that wages of any amount have been paid to the liable person during any period, purporting to be signed by or on behalf of his employer, shall be evidence of the facts there stated.

(3) Where an application under section 39A of the Act has been made but no warrant of commitment is issued or term of imprisonment fixed, the application may be renewed on the ground that the circumstances of the liable person have changed.

Warrant of commitment

6–4950 **34.** (1) A warrant of commitment shall be in the form specified in Schedule 3, or in a form to the like effect.

(2) The amount to be included in the warrant under section 40(4)(*a*)(ii) of the Act in respect of costs shall be such amount as in the view of the court is equal to the costs reasonably incurred by the Secretary of State in respect of the costs of commitment.

(3) A warrant issued under section 40 of the Act may be executed anywhere in England and Wales by any person to whom it is directed or by any constable acting within his police area.

(4) A warrant may be executed by a constable notwithstanding that it is not in his possession at the time but such warrant shall, on the demand of the person arrested be shown to him as soon as possible.

(5) Where, after the issue of a warrant, part-payment of the amount stated in it is made, the period of imprisonment shall be reduced proportionately so that for the period of imprisonment specified in the warrant there shall be substituted a period of imprisonment of such number of days as bears the same proportion to the number of days specified in the warrant as the amount remaining unpaid under the warrant bears to the amount specified in the warrant.

(6) Where the part-payment is of such an amount as would, under paragraph (5), reduce the period of imprisonment to such number of days as have already been served (or would be so served in the course of the day of payment), the period of imprisonment shall be reduced to the period already served plus one day.

Disqualification from driving order

6–4950A **35.** (1) For the purposes of enabling an enquiry to be made under section 39A of the Act as to the liable person's livelihood, means and conduct, a justice of the peace having jurisdiction for the area in which the liable person resides may issue a summons to him to appear before a magistrates' court and to produce any driving licence held by him, and, where applicable, its counterpart, and, if he does not appear, may issue a warrant for his arrest.

(2) In any proceedings under sections 39A and 40B of the Act, a statement in writing to the effect that wages of any amount have been paid to the liable person during any period, purporting to be signed for or on behalf of his employer, shall be evidence of the facts there stated.

(3) Where an application under section 39A of the Act has been made but no disqualification order is made, the application may be renewed on the ground that the circumstances of the liable person have changed.

(4) A disqualification order shall be in the form prescribed in Schedule 4.

(5) The amount to be included in the disqualification order under section 40B(3)(*b*) of the Act in respect of the costs shall be such amount as in the view of the court is equal to the costs reasonably incurred by the Secretary of State in respect of the costs of the application for the disqualification order.

(6) An order made under section 40B(4) of the Act may be executed anywhere in England and Wales by any person to whom it is directed or by any constable acting within his police area, if the liable person fails to appear or produce or surrender his driving licence or its counterpart to the court.

(7) An order may be executed by a constable notwithstanding that it is not in his possession at the time but such order shall, if demanded, be shown to the liable person as soon as reasonably practicable.

(8) In this regulation "driving licence" means a licence to drive a motor vehicle granted under Part III of the Road Traffic Act 1988.

6–4951

Regulation 29(1)   SCHEDULE 1
                                   LIABILITY ORDER PRESCRIBED FORM

Section 33 of the Child Support Act 1991 and regulation 29(1) of the Child Support (Collection and Enforcement) Regulations 1992
....Magistrates'Court
Date:
Defendant:
Address:
On the complaint of the Secretary of State for Social Security that the sums specified below are due from the defendant under the Child Support Act 1991 and Part IV of the Child Support (Collection and Enforcement) Regulations 1992 and are outstanding, it is adjudged that the defendant is liable to pay the aggregate amount specified below.

Sum payable and outstanding   — child support maintenance
                                     — interest
                                     — other periodical payments collected by virtue of section 30 of the
                                     Child Support Act 1991
Aggregate amount in respect of which the liability order is made:
    Justice of the Peace
    (*or* by order of the Court Clerk of the Court)

––––––––––––––––––––––

*Amended by SI 2001/162 from a date to be appointed.

6–4952

Regulation 32   SCHEDULE 2
                                   CHARGES CONNECTED WITH DISTRESS

1. The sum in respect of charges connected with the distress which may be aggregated under section 35(2)(*b*) of the Act shall be set out in the following Table—

(1) Matter connected with distress	(2) Charge
A For making a visit to premises with a view to levying distress (whether the levy is made or not):	Reasonable costs and fees incurred, but not exceeding an amount which, when aggregated with charges under this head for any previous visits made with a view to levying distress in relation to an amount in respect of which the liability order concerned was made is not greater than the relevant amount calculated under paragraph 2(1) with respect to the visit.
B For levying distress:	An amount (if any) which, when aggregated with charges under head A for any visits made with a view to levying distress in relation to an amount in respect of which the liability order concerned was made, is equal to the relevant amount calculated under paragraph 2(1) with respect to the levy.
BB For preparing and sending a letter advising the liable person that the written authorisation of the Secretary of State is with the person levying the distress and requesting the total sum due:	£10.00.
C For the removal and storage of goods for the purposes of sale:	Reasonable costs and fees incurred.
D For the possession of goods as described in paragraph 2(3)—	
(i) for close possession (the person in possession on behalf of the Secretary of State to provide his own board):	£4.50 per day.
(ii) for walking possession:	10p per day.
E For appraisement of an item distrained, at the request in writing of the liable person:	Reasonable fees and expenses of the broker appraising.
F For other expenses of, and commission on, a sale by auction—	
(i) where the sale is held on the auctioneer's premises:	The auctioneer's commission fee and out-of-pocket expenses (but not exceeding in aggregate 15 per cent of the sum realised), together with reasonable costs and fees incurred in respect of advertising.
(ii) where the sale is held on the liable person's premises:	The auctioneer's commission fee (but not exceeding 7.5 per cent of the sum realised), together with the auctioneer's out-of-pocket expenses and reasonable costs and fees incurred in respect of advertising.
G For other expenses incurred in connection with a proposed sale where there is no buyer in relation to it:	Reasonable costs and fees incurred.

2. (1) In heads A and B of the Table to paragraph 1, "the relevant amount" with respect to a visit or a levy means—

   (*a*) where the sum due at the time of the visit or of the levy (as the case may be) does not exceed £100, £12.50;

   (*b*) where the sum due at the time of the visit or of the levy (as the case may be) exceeds £100, 12½ per cent on the first £100 of the sum due, 4 per cent on the next £400, 2½ per cent on the next £1,500, 1 per cent on the next £8,000 and ¼ per cent on any additional sum;

and the sum due at any time for these purposes means so much of the amount in respect of which the liability order concerned was made as is outstanding at the time.

(2) Where a charge has arisen under head B with respect to an amount, no further charge may be aggregated under heads A or B in respect of that amount.

(3) The Secretary of State takes close or walking possession of goods for the purposes of head D of the Table to paragraph 1 if he takes such possession in pursuance of an agreement which is made at the time that the distress is levied and which (without prejudice to such other terms as may be agreed) is expressed to the effect that, in consideration of the Secretary of State not immediately removing the goods distrained upon from the premises occupied by the liable person and delaying the sale of the goods, the Secretary of State may remove and sell the goods after a later specified date if the liable person has not by then paid the amount distrained for (including charges under this Schedule); and the Secretary of State is in close possession of goods on any day for these purposes if during the greater part of the day a person is left on the premises in physical possession of the goods on behalf of the Secretary of State under such an agreement.

3. (1) Where the calculation under this Schedule of a percentage of a sum results in an amount containing a fraction of a pound, that fraction shall be reckoned as a whole pound.

(2) In the case of dispute as to any charge under this Schedule, the amount of the charge shall be taxed.

(3) Such a taxation shall be carried out by the district judge of the county court for the district in which the distress is or is intended to be levied, and he may give such directions as to the costs of the taxation as he thinks fit; and any such costs directed to be paid by the liable person to the Secretary of State shall be added to the sum which may be aggregated under section 35(2) of the Act.

(4) References in the Table in paragraph 1 to costs, fees and expenses include references to amounts payable by way of value added tax with respect to the supply of goods or services to which the costs, fees and expenses relate.

6–4953

Regulation 34(1)   SCHEDULE 3
FORM OF WARRANT OF COMMITMENT

Section 40 of the Child Support Act 1991 and regulation 34(1) of the Child Support (Collection and Enforcement) Regulations 1992

....MagistratesCourt

Date:
Liable Person:
Address:
A liability order ("the order") was made against the liable person by the (.............) Magistrates' Court on (...................) under section 33 of the Child Support Act 1991 ("the Act") in respect of an amount of (...............).
The court is satisfied—

   (i) that the Secretary of State sought under section 35 of the Act to levy by distress the amount then outstanding in respect of which the order was made;

(and/or)

         that the Secretary of State sought under section 36 of the Act to recover through the (..........................) County Court, by means of (garnishee proceedings) or* (a charging order), the amount then outstanding in respect of which the order was made;

   (ii) that such amount, or any portion of it, remains unpaid; and

   (iii) having inquired in the liable person's presence as to his means and as to whether there has been (wilful refusal) or (culpable neglect) on his part, the court is of the opinion that there has been (wilful refusal) or* (culpable neglect) on his part.

The decision of the court is that the liable person be (committed to prison) (detained) for (.............) unless the aggregate amount mentioned below in respect of which this warrant is made is sooner paid. (*Note*: The period of imprisonment will be reduced as provided by regulation 34(5) and (6) of the Child Support (Collection and Enforcement) Regulations 1992 if part-payment is made of the aggregate amount.)

This warrant is made in respect of—
Amount outstanding (including any interest,** costs and charges):........................
Costs of commitment of the Secretary of State:............................
    Aggregate amount:........................
And you (*name of person or persons to whom warrant is directed*) are hereby required to take the liable person and convey him to (*name of prison or place of detention*) and there deliver him to the (governor) (officer in charge) thereof; and you, the (governor) (officer in charge), to receive the liable person into your custody and keep him for (*period of imprisonment*) from the date of his arrest under this warrant or until he be sooner discharged in due course of law.

    Justice of the Peace
    (*or* by order of the Court Clerk of the Court).

---

*Revoked by SI 2001/162 from a date to be appointed.
**Amended by SI 2001/162 from a date to be appointed.

6–4953A

Regulation 35(4)

SCHEDULE 4

FORM OF ORDER OF DISQUALIFICATION FROM HOLDING OR OBTAINING A DRIVING LICENCE

Sections 39A and 40B of the Child Support Act 1991 and regulation 35 of the Child Support (Collection and Enforcement) Regulations 1992.

..... Magistrates' Court

Date:

Liable Person:

Address:

A liability order ("the order") was made against the liable person by the [ ] Magistrates' Court on [ ] under section 33 of the Child Support Act 1991 ("the Act") in respect of an amount of [ ].

The court is satisfied—

(i) that the Secretary of State sought under section 35 of the Act to levy by distress the amount then outstanding in respect of which the order was made;

[and/or]

that the Secretary of State sought under section 36 of the Act to recover through [ ] County Court by means of [garnishee proceedings] [a charging order], the amount then outstanding in respect of which the order was made;

(ii) that such amount, or any proportion of it, remains unpaid; and

(iii) having inquired in the liable person's presence as to his means and whether there has been [wilful refusal] [culpable neglect] on his part.

The decision of the court is that the liable person be disqualified from [holding or obtaining] a driving licence from [date] for [period] unless the aggregate amount in respect of which this order is made is sooner paid*

This order is made in respect of—

Amount outstanding (including any interest, fees, penalty payments, costs and charges):

Aggregate amount:

And you [the liable person] shall surrender to the court any driving licence and counterpart held.

Justice of the Peace

or by order of the Court

Clerk of the Court

---

*Note: The period of disqualification may be reduced as provided by section 40B(5)(*a*) of the Act if part payment is made of the aggregate amount. The order will be revoked by section 40B(5)(*b*) of the Act if full payment is made of the aggregate amount.

Child Support (Collection and Enforcement of Other Forms of Maintenance) Regulations 1992[1]

(SI 1992/2643 amended by SI 1993/913, SI 2001/162 and SI 2005/2877)

Citation, commencement and interpretation

6–4954 **1.** (1) *Citation and commencement.*

(2) In these Regulations—

"the Act" means the Child Support Act 1991;

"child of the family" has the same meaning as in the Matrimonial Causes Act 1973 or, in Scotland, the Family Law (Scotland) Act 1985; and

"periodical payments" includes secured periodical payments.

---

1. Made by the Secretary of State for Social Security, in exercise of the powers conferred upon him by ss 30(1), (4) and (5), 51 and 54 of the Child Support Act 1991.

Periodical payments and categories of person prescribed for the purposes of section 30 of the Act

6–4955 **2.** The following periodical payments and categories of persons are prescribed for the purposes of section 30(1) of the Act—

(*a*) payments under a maintenance order made in relation to a child in accordance with the provisions of section 8(6) (periodical payments in addition to child support maintenance), 8(7) (periodical payments to meet expenses incurred in connection with the provision of instruction or training) or 8(8) of the Act (periodical payments to meet expenses attributable to disability);

(*b*) any periodical payments under a maintenance order or, in Scotland, registered minutes of agreement which are payable to or for the benefit of a spouse, civil partner, former spouse or former civil partner who is the person with care of a child who is a qualifying child in respect of whom a child support maintenance assessment* is in force in accordance with which the Secretary of State has arranged for the collection of child support maintenance under section 29 of the Act; and

(*c*) any periodical payments under a maintenance order payable to or for the benefit of a former child of the family of the person against whom the order is made, that child having his home with the person with care.

*Amended by SI 2001/162 from a date to be appointed.

Collection and enforcement—England and Wales

6–4956 3. In relation to England and Wales, sections 29(2) and (3) and 31 to 40 of the Act, and any regulations made under those sections, shall apply for the purpose of enabling the Secretary of State to enforce any obligation to pay any amount which he is authorised to collect under section 30 of the Act, with the modification that any reference in those sections or regulations to child support maintenance shall be read as a reference to any of the periodical payments mentioned in regulation 2 above, and any reference to a maintenance assessment* shall be read as a reference to any of the maintenance orders mentioned in that regulation.

*Amended by SI 2001/162 from a date to be appointed.

6–4957 4. *Collection and enforcement—Scotland.*

Collection and enforcement—supplementary

6–4958 5. Nothing in Regulations 3 or 4 applies to any periodical payment which falls due before the date specified by the Secretary of State by a notice in writing to the absent parent* that he is arranging for those payments to be collected, and that date shall be not earlier than the date the notice is given.

*Amended by SI 2001/162 from a date to be appointed.

Child Support (Maintenance Arrangements and Jurisdiction) Regulations 1992[1]

(SI 1992/2645 amended by SI 1993/913, SI 1995/123, 1995/1045 and 1995/3261, SI 1999/1510, SI 2001/161, SI 2002/2469, SI 2004/696 and SI 2005/785 and 2877)

Citation, commencement and interpretation

6–4959 1. (1) *Citation and commencement.*

(2) In these Regulations—

"the Act" means the Child Support Act 1991;

"Maintenance Assessment Procedure Regulations means the Child Support (Maintenance Assessment* Procedure) Regulations 1992;*

"Maintenance Assessments and Special Cases Regulations" means the Child Support (Maintenance Assessments and Special Cases) Regulations 1992;*

"effective date" means the date on which a maintenance assessment* takes effect for the purposes of the Act;

"maintenance order" has the meaning given in section 8(11) of the Act.

(3) In these Regulations, unless the context otherwise requires, a reference—

(*a*) to a numbered regulation is to the regulation in these Regulations bearing that number;

(*b*) in a regulation to a numbered paragraph is to the paragraph in that regulation bearing that number;

(*c*) in a paragraph to a lettered or numbered sub-paragraph is to the sub-paragraph in that paragraph bearing that letter or number.

*Amended by SI 2001/161 from a date to be appointed.
1. Made by the Secretary of State for Social Security, in exercise of the powers conferred upon him by ss 8(11), 10(1), (2) and (4), 44(3), 51, 52(4) and 54 of, and para 11 of Sch 1 to, the Child Support Act 1991.

Prescription of enactments for the purposes of section 8(11) of the Act

6–4960 2. The following enactments are prescribed for the purposes of section 8(11)(*f*) of the Act—

(*a*) the Conjugal Rights (Scotland) Amendment Act 1861;

(*b*) the Court of Session Act 1868;

(*c*) the Sheriff Courts (Scotland) Act 1907;

(*d*) the Guardianship of Infants Act 1925;

(*e*) the Illegitimate Children (Scotland) Act 1930;

(*f*) the Children and Young Persons (Scotland) Act 1932;

(*g*) the Children and Young Persons (Scotland) Act 1937;

(*h*) the Custody of Children (Scotland) Act 1939;

(*i*) the National Assistance Act 1948;

(*j*) the Affiliation Orders Act 1952;

(*k*) the Affiliation Proceedings Act 1957;

(*l*) the Matrimonial Proceedings (Children) Act 1958;

(*m*) the Guardianship of Minors Act 1971;

(*n*) the Guardianship Act 1973;
(*o*) the Children Act 1975;
(*p*) the Supplementary Benefits Act 1976;
(*q*) the Social Security Act 1986;
(*r*) the Social Security Administration Act 1992.

Relationship between maintenance assessments* and certain court orders

6–4961 **3.** (1) Orders made under the following enactments are of a kind prescribed for the purposes of section 10(1) of the Act—

(*a*) the Conjugal Rights (Scotland) Amendment Act 1861;
(*b*) the Court of Session Act 1868;
(*c*) the Sheriff Courts (Scotland) Act 1907;
(*d*) the Guardianship of Infants Act 1925;
(*e*) the Illegitimate Children (Scotland) Act 1930;
(*f*) the Children and Young Persons (Scotland) Act 1932;
(*g*) the Children and Young Persons (Scotland) Act 1937;
(*h*) the Custody of Children (Scotland) Act 1939;
(*i*) the National Assistance Act 1948;
(*j*) the Affiliation Orders Act 1952;
(*k*) the Affiliation Proceedings Act 1957;
(*l*) the Matrimonial Proceedings (Children) Act 1958;
(*m*) the Guardianship of Minors Act 1971;
(*n*) the Guardianship Act 1973;
(*o*) Part II of the Matrimonial Causes Act 1973;
(*p*) the Children Act 1975;
(*q*) the Supplementary Benefits Act 1976;
(*r*) the Domestic Proceedings and Magistrates' Courts Act 1978;
(*s*) Part III of the Matrimonial and Family Proceedings Act 1984;
(*t*) the Family Law (Scotland) Act 1985;
(*u*) the Social Security Act 1986;
(*v*) Schedule 1 to the Children Act 1989;
(*w*) the Social Security Administration Act 1992;
(*x*) Schedule 5, 6 or 7 to the Civil Partnership Act 2004.

(2) Subject to paragraphs (3) and (4), where a maintenance assessment* is made with respect to—

(*a*) all of the children with respect to whom an order falling within paragraph (1) is in force; or
(*b*) one or more but not all of the children with respect to whom an order falling within paragraph (1) is in force and where the amount payable under the order to or for the benefit of each child is separately specified,

that order shall, so far as it relates to the making or securing of periodical payments to or for the benefit of the children with respect to whom the maintenance assessment* has been made, cease to have effect.

(3) The provisions of paragraph (2) shall not apply where a maintenance order has been made in accordance with section 8(7) or (8) of the Act.

(4) In Scotland, where—

(*a*) an order has ceased to have effect by virtue of the provisions of paragraph (2) to the extent specified in that paragraph; and
(*b*) the Secretary of State no longer has jurisdiction to make a maintenance assessment* with respect to a child with respect to whom the order ceased to have effect,

that order shall, so far as it relates to that child, again have effect from the date the Secretary of State no longer has jurisdiction to make a maintenance assessment* with respect to that child.

(5) Subject to regulation 33(7) of the Maintenance Assessment Procedure Regulations, where a maintenance assessment is made with respect to children with respect to whom an order falling within paragraph (1) is in force, the effective date of that assessment shall be two days after the assessment is made.**

(6) Where the provisions of paragraph (2) apply to an order, that part of the order to which those provisions apply shall cease to have effect from the effective date of the maintenance assessment.**

(7) Where at the time an interim maintenance assessment was made there was in force with respect to children in respect of whom that interim maintenance assessment was made an order falling within paragraph (1), the effective date of a maintenance assessment subsequently made in accordance with Part I of Schedule 1 to the Act in respect of those children shall be the effective date of that interim maintenance assessment as determined under paragraph (5).**

(8) Subject to regulation 33(7) of the Maintenance Assessment Procedure Regulations, where—

(*a*) a maintenance assessment is made in accordance with Part I of Schedule 1 to the Act in respect of children with respect to whom an order falling within paragraph (1) was in force; and

(b) that order ceases to have effect on or after 18th April 1995, for reasons other than the making of an interim maintenance assessment, but prior to the date on which the maintenance assessment is made and after—

(i) the date on which a maintenance enquiry form referred to in regulation 5(2) of the Maintenance Assessment Procedure Regulations was given or sent to the absent parent where the application for a maintenance assessment was made by a person with care or a child under section 7 of the Act; or

(ii) the date on which a maintenance application which complies with the provisions of regulation 2 of the Maintenance Assessment Procedure Regulations was received by the Secretary of State from an absent parent,

the effective date of that maintenance assessment shall be the day following that on which the court order ceased to have effect.**

---

*Amended by SI 2001/161 from a date to be appointed.
**Revoked by SI 2001/161 from a date to be appointed.

Relationship between maintenance assessments* and certain agreements

6–4962 **4.** (1) Maintenance agreements within the meaning of section 9(1) of the Act are agreements of a kind prescribed for the purposes of section 10(2) of the Act.

(2) Where a maintenance assessment* is made with respect to—

(a) all of the children with respect to whom an agreement falling within paragraph (1) is in force; or

(b) one or more but not all of the children with respect to whom an agreement falling within paragraph (1) is in force and where the amount payable under the agreement to or for the benefit of each child is separately specified,

that agreement shall, so far as it relates to the making or securing of periodical payments to or for the benefit of the children with respect to whom the maintenance assessment* has been made, become unenforceable from the effective date of the assessment*.

(3) Where an agreement becomes unenforceable under the provisions of paragraph (2) to the extent specified in that paragraph, it shall remain unenforceable in relation to a particular child until such date as the Secretary of State no longer has jurisdiction to make a maintenance assessment* with respect to that child.

---

*Amended by SI 2001/161 from a date to be appointed.

Notifications by the Secretary of State

6–4963 **5.** (1) Where the Secretary of State is aware that an order of a kind prescribed in paragraph (2) is in force and considers that the making of a maintenance assessment* has affected, or is likely to affect, that order, he shall notify the persons prescribed in paragraph (3) in respect of whom that maintenance assessment* is in force, and the persons prescribed in paragraph (4) holding office in the court where the order in question was made or subsequently registered, of the assessment* and its effective date.

(2) The prescribed orders are those made under an enactment mentioned in regulation 3(1).

(3) The prescribed persons in respect of whom the maintenance assessment* is in force are—

(a) a person with care;

(b) an absent parent*;

(c) a person who is treated as an absent parent* under regulation 20 of the Maintenance Assessments* and Special Cases Regulations;

(d) a child who has made an application for a maintenance assessment* under section 7 of the Act.

(4) The prescribed person holding office in the court where the order in question was made or subsequently registered is—

(a) in England and Wales—

(i) in relation to the High Court, the senior district judge of the principal registry of the Family Division or, where proceedings were instituted in a district registry, the district judge;

(ii) in relation to a county court, the proper officer of that court within the meaning of Order 1, Rule 3 of the County Court Rules 1981;

(iii) in relation to a magistrates' court, the justices' chief executive for that court;

(b) (*Scotland*).

---

*Amended by SI 2001/161 from a date to be appointed.

Notification by the court

6–4964 **6.** (1) Where a court is aware that a maintenance assessment* is in force and makes an order mentioned in regulation 3(1) which it considers has affected, or is likely to affect, that assessment*, the person prescribed in paragraph (2) shall notify the Secretary of State to that effect.

(2) The prescribed person is the person holding the office specified below in the court where the order in question was made or subsequently registered—

(a) in England and Wales—

    (i) in relation to the High Court, the senior district judge of the principal registry of the Family Division or, where proceedings were instituted in a district registry, the district judge;

    (ii) in relation to a county court, the proper officer of that court within the meaning of Order 1, Rule 3 of the County Court Rules 1981;

    (iii) in relation to a magistrates' court, the justices' chief executive for that court;

(b) (*Scotland*).

---

*Amended by SI 2001/161 from a date to be appointed.

Cancellation of a maintenance assessment on grounds of lack of jurisdiction

6–4965   **7.** (1) Where—

(a) a person with care;
(b) an absent parent; or
(c) a qualifying child

with respect to whom a maintenance assessment is in force ceases to be habitually resident in the United Kingdom, the Secretary of State shall cancel that assessment.

(2) Where the person with care is not an individual, paragraph (1) shall apply as if subparagraph (a) were omitted.

(3) Where the Secretary of State cancels a maintenance assessment under paragraph (1) or by virtue of paragraph (2), the assessment shall cease to have effect from the date that the Secretary of State determines is the date on which—

(a) where paragraph (1) applies, the person with care, absent parent or qualifying child; or
(b) where paragraph (2) applies, the absent parent or qualifying child

with respect to whom the assessment was made ceases to be habitually resident in the United Kingdom.

(4) Where a parent is treated as an absent parent for the purposes of the Act and of the Maintenance Assessments and Special Cases Regulations by virtue of regulation 20 of those Regulations, he shall be treated as an absent parent for the purposes of paragraphs (1) to (3).*

---

*Revoked by SI 2001/161 from a date to be appointed.

Prescription for the purposes of jurisdiction

7A. (1) The companies prescribed for the purposes of section 44(2A)(c) of the Act (non-resident parents not habitually resident in the United Kingdom but employed by prescribed companies) are companies which employ employees to work outside the United Kingdom but make calculations and payment arrangements in relation to the earnings of those employees in the United Kingdom so that a deduction from earnings order may be made under section 31 of the Act in respect of the earnings of any such employee who is a liable person for the purposes of that section.

(2) The following bodies are prescribed for the purposes of section 44(2A)(d) of the Act (non-resident parents not habitually resident in the United Kingdom but employed by a prescribed body)—

(a) a National Health Service Trust established by order made under section 5 of the National Health Service and Community Care Act 1990 ("the 1990 Act") or under section 12A of the National Health Service (Scotland) Act 1978 ("the 1978 Act");

(aa) an NHS foundation trust within the meaning of section 1(1) of the Health and Social Care (Community Health and Standards) Act 2003;

(b) a Primary Care Trust established by order made under section 16A of the National Health Service Act 1977;

(c) a Health Authority established under section 8 of the National Health Service Act 1977 ("the 1977 Act");

(d) a Special Health Authority established under section 11 of the 1977 Act;

(da) a Strategic Health Authority established under section 8 of the 1977 Act;

(e) a local authority, and for this purpose "local authority" means, in relation to England, a county council, a district council, a London borough council, the Common Council of the City of London or the Council of the Isles of Scilly and, in relation to Wales, a county council or a county borough council and, in relation to Scotland, a council constituted under section 2 of the Local Government etc (Scotland) Act 1994;

(f) a Health and Social Service Trust established by order made under Article 10 of the Health and Personal Social Services (Northern Ireland) Order 1991;

(g) a Health and Social Services Board established by order made under Article 16 of the Health and Personal Social Services (Northern Ireland) Order 1972 ("the 1972 Order");
(h) the Central Services Agency established by order made under Article 26 of the 1972 Order;
(i) a Special Agency established by order made under Article 3 of the Health and Personal Social Services (Special Agencies) (Northern Ireland) Order 1990;
(j) a Health Board constituted under section 2 of the 1978 Act; and
(k) a Special Health Board constituted under section 2 of the 1978 Act.

Maintenance assessments and maintenance orders made in error

6–4966 8. (1) Where—

(a) at the time that a maintenance assessment* with respect to a qualifying child was made a maintenance order was in force with respect to that child;
(aa) the maintenance order has ceased to have effect by virtue of the provisions of regulation 3;
(b) the absent parent has made payments of child support maintenance due under that assessment*; and
(c) the Secretary of State cancels that assessment* on the grounds that it was made in error,

the payments of child support maintenance shall be treated as payments under the maintenance order and that order shall be treated as having continued in force.

(2) Where—

(a) at the time that a maintenance order with respect to a qualifying child was made a maintenance assessment* was in force with respect to that child;
(aa) the maintenance assessment* is cancelled or ceases to have effect;
(b) the absent parent* has made payments of maintenance due under that order; and
(c) the maintenance order is revoked by the court on the grounds that it was made in error,

the payments under the maintenance order shall be treated as payments of child support maintenance and the maintenance assessment* shall be treated as not having been cancelled or, as the case may be, as not having ceased to have effect.

---

*Amended by SI 2001/161 from a date to be appointed.

6–4966A 8A. Maintenance calculations and maintenance orders—payments. Where—

(a) a maintenance calculation has been made with respect to a qualifying child in response to an application made under section 4 or 7 of the Act;
(b) at the time that maintenance calculation was made a maintenance order was in force with respect to that child;
(c) the maintenance order has ceased to have effect by virtue of the provisions of regulation 3; and
(d) the non-resident parent has made payments of maintenance due under that order after the date on which the maintenance calculation took effect in accordance with regulation 26 of the Maintenance Calculation Procedure Regulations,

the payments made under the maintenance order shall be treated as payments of child support maintenance.

Cases in which application may be made under section 4 or 7 of the Act

6–4966A 9. The provisions of section 4(10) or 7(10) of the Act shall not apply to prevent an application being made under those sections after 22nd January 1996 where a decision has been made by the relevant court either that it has no power to vary or that it has no power to enforce a maintenance order in a particular case.

Recovery of Maintenance (United States of America) Order 1993[1]
(SI 1993/591)

6–4967 1. *Citation and commencement.*

---

1. Made in exercise of powers conferred by sections 40 and 45(1) of the Maintenance Orders (Reciprocal Enforcement) Act 1972. See Home Office Circular No 172/1979, dated 31 December 1979, for guidance as to the application of this order and the procedures to be followed.

6–4968 2. In this Order, unless the context otherwise requires—

"the Act" means the Maintenance Orders (Reciprocal Enforcement) Act 1972;
"specified State" means a State specified in the Schedule to this Order.

6–4969 3. (1) The provisions of Part II of the Act shall apply in relation to a specified State as they apply in relation to a convention country, subject to the modification set out in paragraph (2) below.

(2) After section 26(3) of the Act there shall be inserted—

"(3A) An application under subsection (1) or (2) above, for the purpose of recovering maintenance from a person in a specified State within the meaning of the Recovery of Maintenance (United States of America) Order 1993, and a certificate signed by a justice of the peace or, where the applicant is residing in Scotland, the sheriff, to the effect that the application sets forth facts from which it may be determined that the respondent owes a duty to maintain the applicant and any other person named in the application and that a court in the specified State may obtain jurisdiction of the respondent or his property, shall be registered in the court in the prescribed manner by the appropriate officer or, in Scotland, by the sheriff clerk in the Maintenance Orders (Reciprocal Enforcement) Act 1972 register.".

6–4969A   4. Revocations.

Article 2	SCHEDULE

Specified States	
Alaska	Montana
Arizona	Nebraska
Arkansas	Nevada
California	New Hampshire
Colorado	New Jersey
Connecticut	New Mexico
Delaware	New York
Florida	North Carolina
Georgia	North Dakota
Hawaii	Ohio
Idaho	Oklahoma
Illinois	Oregon
Indiana	Pennsylvania
Iowa	Rhode Island
Kansas	South Dakota
Kentucky	Tennessee
Louisiana	Texas
Maine	Utah
Maryland	Vermont
Massachusetts	Virginia
Michigan	Washington
Minnesota	Wisconsin
Missouri	Wyoming

Reciprocal Enforcement of Maintenance Orders (Hague Convention Countries) Order 1993[1]

(SI 1993/593 amended by SI 1994/1902, SI 1999/1318, SI 2001/410 and 2567 and SI 2002/2838)

6–4970   1. *Citation and commencement.*

1. Made in exercise of powers conferred by sections 40 and 45(1) of the Maintenance Orders (Reciprocal Enforcement) Act 1972. See Home Office Circular No 15/1980, dated 26 February 1980, for guidance as to the application of this order and the procedure to be followed.

6–4971   2. In this Order, unless the context otherwise requires—

"Act" means the Maintenance Orders (Reciprocal Enforcement) Act 1972;
"court in a Hague Convention country" includes any judicial or administrative authority in a Hague Convention country;
"Hague Convention" means the Convention on the Recognition and Enforcement of Decisions Relating to Maintenance Obligations concluded at The Hague on 2nd October 1973; and
"Hague Convention country" means a country or territory specified in Schedule 1 to this Order, being a country or territory (other than the United Kingdom) in which the Hague Convention is in force.

6–4972   3. (1) The provisions of Part I of the Act shall apply in relation to a Hague Convention country as they apply in relation to a reciprocating country, subject to the exceptions, adaptations and modifications set out in Schedule 2[1] to this Order.

(2) Accordingly, Part I of the Act shall, in relation to—

(a) maintenance orders made by courts in the United Kingdom against persons in a Hague Convention country, and

(b) maintenance orders made by courts in a Hague Convention country against persons in the United Kingdom,

have effect as set out in Schedule 3 to this Order.

---

1. We print only Sch 3, post. It should be noted that under Sch 2, ss 1, 7, 20, 22, 23, 24 of the Act do not apply.

6–4973 4. *Revocation.*

6–4974

SCHEDULE 1
HAGUE CONVENTION COUNTRIES

(Amended by SI 1994/1902, SI 1999/1318, SI 2001/2567 and SI 2002/2838)

Australia
Denmark
Federal Republic of Germany
Finland
France
Italy
Luxembourg
Netherlands (Kingdom in Europe and Netherlands Antilles)
Norway
Portugal
Republic of Estonia
Republic of Poland
Slovakia
Spain
Sweden
Switzerland
The Czech Republic
Turkey

SCHEDULE 3
PART I OF THE ACT AS MODIFIED BY SCHEDULE 2

(Amended by SI 1999/1318, and SI 2001/410)

Article 3(2)

Orders made by courts in the United Kingdom

6–4975 2. Transmission of maintenance order made in United Kingdom for recognition and enforcement in Hague Convention country. (1) Subject to subsection (2) below, where the payer under a maintenance order made, whether before, on or after 5th April 1993, by a court in the United Kingdom is residing in a Hague Convention country, the payee under the order may apply for the order to be sent to that country for recognition and enforcement.

(2) Subsection (1) above shall not have effect in relation to a maintenance order made under section 3 of this Act or to an order by virtue of a provision of Part II of this Act.

(3) Every application under this section shall be made in the prescribed manner to the prescribed officer of the court which made the maintenance order to which the application relates.

(4) If, on an application duly made under this section to the prescribed officer of a court in the United Kingdom, that officer is satisfied that the payer under the maintenance order to which the application relates is residing in a Hague Convention country, the following documents, that is to say—

(a) a certified copy of the maintenance order;
(b) a certificate signed by that officer certifying that the order is enforceable and that it is no longer subject to the ordinary forms of review;
(c) a certificate of arrears so signed;
(d) a statement giving such information as the officer possesses as to the whereabouts of the payer;
(e) a statement giving such information as the officer possesses for facilitating the identification of the payer;
(f) where available, a photograph of the payer;
(g) a written statement signed by that officer as to whether or not the payer appeared in the proceedings in which the maintenance order was made and, if he did not appear, the original or a certified copy of a document which establishes that notice of the institution of the proceedings, including notice of the substance of the claim, was served on the payer;
(h) a document which establishes that notice of the order was sent to the payer; and
(i) a written statement signed by that officer as to whether or not the payee received legal aid either in the said proceedings or in connection with the said application,

shall be sent by that officer, in the case of a court in England and Wales or Northern Ireland, to the Lord Chancellor, or, in the case of a court in Scotland, to the Secretary of State, with a view to their being transmitted by the Lord Chancellor, or, as the case may be, the Secretary of State, to the appropriate authority in the Hague Convention country if he is satisfied that the statement relating to the whereabouts of the payer gives sufficient information to justify that being done.

(5) Nothing in this section shall be taken as affecting any jurisdiction of a court in the United Kingdom with respect to a maintenance order to which this section applies, and subject to section 5 any such order may be enforced, varied or revoked accordingly.

3. Power of magistrates' court to make maintenance order against person residing in Hague Convention country. (1) Where an application is made to a magistrates' court for a maintenance order by a person who is habitually resident in England and Wales against a person residing in a Hague Convention country and the court would have jurisdiction to determine the application under the Domestic Proceedings and Magistrates' Courts Act 1978 or the Children Act 1989 if at any time when the proceedings were instituted that person—

(*a*) were residing in England and Wales, and

(*b*) received reasonable notice of the date of the hearing of the application,

the court shall subject to the following provisions of this section have jurisdiction to determine the application.

(4) No enactment (or provision made under an enactment) requiring or enabling—

(*a*) a court to transfer proceedings from a magistrates' court to a county court or the High Court, or

(*b*) a magistrates' court to refuse to make an order on an application on the ground that any matter in question is one that would be more conveniently dealt with by the High Court,

shall apply in relation to an application to which subsection (1) above applies.

(5) On the making of an application to which subsection (1) above applies, the following documents, that is to say—

(*a*) notice of the institution of the proceedings, including notice of the substance of the application;

(*b*) a statement signed by the prescribed officer of the court giving such information as he possesses as to the whereabouts of the respondent;

(*c*) a statement giving such information as the officer possesses for facilitating the identification of the respondent; and

(*d*) where available, a photograph of the respondent,

shall be sent by that officer to the Lord Chancellor with a view to their being transmitted by the Lord Chancellor to the appropriate authority in the Hague Convention country in which the respondent is residing for service on him of the document mentioned in paragraph (*a*) above if the Lord Chancellor is satisfied that the statement relating to the whereabouts of the respondent gives sufficient information to justify that being done.

(6) In considering whether or not to make a maintenance order pursuant to an application to which subsection (1) above applies the court shall take into account any representations made and any evidence adduced by or on behalf of the respondent.

(6A) Where the respondent makes any representations or adduces any evidence, a copy of the representations or evidence shall be served on the applicant by the prescribed officer of the court before the hearing.

(6B) The prescribed officer of the court shall give the respondent notice in writing of the date fixed for the hearing by sending the notice by post addressed to his last known or usual place of abode.

(6C) A maintenance order pursuant to an application to which subsection (1) above applies shall not be made unless the document mentioned in paragraph (*a*) of subsection (5) above has been served on the respondent in accordance with the law for the service of such documents in the Hague Convention country in which he is residing or in such other manner as may be authorised by the Lord Chancellor not less than six weeks previously.

(6D) Where a maintenance order has been made under this section, the prescribed officer of the court shall send the following documents, that is to say—

(*a*) a certified copy of the order;

(*b*) a certificate signed by that officer certifying that the order is enforceable and that it is no longer subject to the ordinary forms of review;

(*c*) a written statement, signed by that officer as to whether or not the respondent appeared in the proceedings in which the order was made, and, if he did not appear, the original or a certified copy of a document which establishes that the document mentioned in paragraph (*a*) of subsection (5) above has been served on the payer in accordance with subsection (6C) above;

(*d*) a document which establishes that notice of the order was sent to the respondent; and

(*e*) a written statement signed by that officer as to whether or not the applicant received legal aid in the proceedings,

to the Lord Chancellor with a view to their being transmitted by him to the appropriate authority in the Hague Convention country in which the respondent resides for recognition and enforcement of the order.

(6E) A maintenance order made under this section may, subject to section 5 of this Act, be enforced, varied or revoked in like manner as any other maintenance order made by a magistrates' court.

(7) *Northern Ireland.*

5. Variation and revocation of maintenance order made in United Kingdom. (1) This section applies to a maintenance order a certified copy of which has been sent to a Hague Convention country for recognition and enforcement of the order.

(2) The jurisdiction of a magistrates' court to revoke or vary a maintenance order shall be exercisable notwithstanding that the proceedings for the revocation or variation, as the case may be, of the order are brought by or against a person residing in a Hague Convention country.

(3) Where subsection (1) of section 60 of the Magistrates' Courts Act 1980 (revocation, variation etc of orders for periodical payment) applies in relation to a maintenance order to which this section applies, that subsection shall have effect as if for the words "by order on complaint," there were substituted "on an application being made, by order".

(4) Where an application is made by the payee to a court in England and Wales or Northern Ireland for the variation or revocation of an order to which this section applies, and the payer is residing in a Hague Convention country, the prescribed officer of the court shall send to the Lord Chancellor notice of the institution of the proceedings, including notice of the substance of the application, with a view to its being transmitted by him to the appropriate authority in the Hague Convention country for service on the payer.

(5) Where an application is made by the payee to a court in England and Wales or Northern Ireland for the variation or revocation of an order to which this section applies, and the payer is residing in a Hague Convention country—

(*a*) the court, in considering whether or not to vary or revoke the order, shall take into account any representations made and any evidence adduced by or on behalf of the payer;

(*b*) a copy of any such representations or evidence shall be served on the payee in the prescribed manner before the hearing;

(*c*) the prescribed officer of the court shall give the payer notice in writing of the date fixed for the hearing by sending the notice by post addressed to his last known or usual place of abode.

(6) Where an application is made by the payee to a court in England and Wales or Northern Ireland for the

variation or revocation of an order to which this section applies, and the payer is residing in a Hague Convention country, the order shall not be varied or revoked unless the document mentioned in subsection (4) above has been served on the payer in accordance with the law for the service of such a document in the Hague Convention country not less than six weeks previously.

(7) Where an application is made by the payer to a court in England and Wales or Northern Ireland for the variation or revocation of an order to which this section applies, the prescribed officer of the court shall arrange for the service of the document mentioned in subsection (4) above on the payee.

(8) Where an order to which this section applies has been varied or revoked by a court in the United Kingdom the prescribed officer of the court shall send the following documents, that is to say—

(a) a certified copy of the order of variation or revocation;

(b) a certificate signed by that officer certifying that the order of variation or revocation is enforceable and that it is no longer subject to the ordinary forms of review;

(c) a written statement, signed by that officer as to whether or not the respondent or, in Scotland the defender, appeared in the proceedings for the variation or revocation of the order, and, if he did not appear, the original or a certified copy of a document which establishes that notice of the institution of the proceedings has been served on the respondent, or, as the case may be, the defender, and

(d) a document which establishes that notice of the order of variation or revocation was sent to the respondent; and

(e) a written statement signed by that officer as to whether or not the payer or the payee received legal aid in the proceedings,

in the case of a court in England and Wales or Northern Ireland, to the Lord Chancellor, or, in the case of a court in Scotland, to the Secretary of State, with a view to their being transmitted by him to the appropriate authority in the Hague Convention country for recognition and enforcement of the order of variation or revocation.

(9) Where a maintenance order to which this section applies has been varied by an order made by a court in the United Kingdom the maintenance order shall, as from the date on which the order of variation took effect, have effect as varied by that order.

(10) Where a maintenance order to which this section applies has been revoked by an order made by a court in the United Kingdom the maintenance order shall, as from the date on which the order of revocation took effect, be deemed to have ceased to have effect except as respects any arrears due under the maintenance order at that date.

(11) *Revoked.*

(12) *Northern Ireland.*

Orders made by courts in Hague Convention countries

6–4976 6. Registration in United Kingdom court of maintenance order made in Hague Convention country.
(1) This section applies to a maintenance order made whether before, on or after 5th April 1993 by a competent court in a Hague Convention country.

(2) Where a certified copy of an order to which this section applies is received by the Lord Chancellor or the Secretary of State from a Hague Convention country, and it appears to him that the payer under the order is residing in the United Kingdom, he shall send the copy of the order and the accompanying documents to the prescribed officer of the appropriate court.

(3) Where the prescribed officer of the appropriate court receives from the Lord Chancellor or the Secretary of State a certified copy of an order to which this section applies, he shall, subject to the following subsections, register the order in the prescribed manner in that court.

(4) Before registering an order under this section an officer of a court shall take such steps as he thinks fit for the purpose of ascertaining whether the payer under the order is residing within the jurisdiction of the court, and if after taking those steps he is satisfied that the payer is not so residing he shall return the certified copy of the order and the accompanying documents to the Lord Chancellor or the Secretary of State, as the case may be, with a statement giving such information as he possesses as to the whereabouts of the payer.

(5)

(a) The prescribed officer of the appropriate court may refuse to authorise the registration of the order if the court in the Hague Convention country by or before which the order was made did not have jurisdiction to make the order; and for these purposes a court in a Hague Convention country shall be considered to have jurisdiction if—

(i) either the payer or the payee had his habitual residence in the Hague Convention country at the time when the proceedings were instituted; or

(ii) the payer and the payee were nationals of that country at that time; or

(iii) the respondent in those proceedings had submitted to the jurisdiction of the court, either expressly or by defending on the merits of the case without objecting to the jurisdiction; or

(iv) in the case of an order made by reason of a divorce or a legal separation or a declaration that a marriage is void or annulled, the court is recognised by the law of the part of the United Kingdom in which enforcement is sought as having jurisdiction to make the order.

(b) In deciding whether a court in a Hague Convention country had jurisdiction to make an order the prescribed officer shall be bound by any finding of fact on which the court based its jurisdiction.

(6) The prescribed officer of the appropriate court may refuse to authorise the registration of the order—

(a) if such registration is manifestly contrary to public policy[1];

(b) if the order was obtained by fraud in connection with a matter of procedure;

(c) if proceedings between the same parties and having the same purpose are pending before a court in the same part of the United Kingdom and those proceedings were the first to be instituted; or

(d) if the order is incompatible with an order made in proceedings between the same parties and having the same purpose, either in the United Kingdom or in another country, provided that the latter order itself fulfils the conditions necessary for its registration and enforcement under this Part of this Act.

(7) Without prejudice to subsection (6) above, if the payer did not appear in the proceedings in the Hague Convention country in which the order was made, the prescribed officer of the appropriate court shall refuse to authorise the registration of the order unless notice of the institution of the proceedings, including notice of the substance of the claim, was served on the payer in accordance with the law of that Hague Convention country

and if, having regard to the circumstances, the payer had sufficient time to enable him to defend the proceedings.

(8) If the order is registered under subsection (3) above, the prescribed officer of the appropriate court shall serve notice in a prescribed form on the payer and give notice to the payee that the order has been registered.

(9) The payer may, before the end of the period of one calendar month beginning with the date of service of the said notice, appeal to the court in which the order is registered to set aside the registration of the order on one of the grounds set out in paragraphs (5), (6) and (7) above.

(10) If the payer appeals to the court in which the order is registered to set aside the registration of the order, the prescribed officer of the court shall give notice to the payee of the appeal and of the date of the hearing of the appeal.

(11) If the prescribed officer refuses to register the order, he shall give notice to the payee in a prescribed form that registration has been refused.

(12) A payee to whom notice has been given by the prescribed officer of any court under subsection (11) above may, before the end of the period of two calendar months beginning with the date when notice was given, appeal to that court against the refusal to register the order.

(13) If the payee appeals to the court against the refusal to register the order, the prescribed officer of the court shall give notice to the payer of the appeal and of the date of the hearing of the appeal.

(14) *Scotland.*

(15) *Northern Ireland.*

---

1. For consideration of the question of public policy, see *Armitage v Nanchen* (1982) 4 FLR 293, 147 JP 53.

6–4976A   8. Enforcement of maintenance order registered in United Kingdom court. (1) Subject to subsections (2), (2A) and (2B) below, a registered order may be enforced in the United Kingdom as if it had been made by the registering court and as if that court had had jurisdiction to make it; and proceedings for or with respect to the enforcement of any such order may be taken accordingly.

(2) Subsection (1) above does not apply to an order which is for the time being registered in the High Court under Part I of the Maintenance Orders Act 1958 or to an order which is for time being registered in the High Court of Justice in Northern Ireland under Part II of the Maintenance and Affiliation Orders Act (Northern Ireland) 1966.

(2A) Where in a maintenance order made in a Hague Convention country there are provisions which are not enforceable under this Part of this Act, this section shall apply only to the remaining provisions of the order.

(2B) The payee under a registered order may request the partial enforcement of that order.

(3) Any person for the time being under an obligation to make payments in pursuance of a registered order shall give notice of any change of address to the [appropriate officer] of the registering court, and any person failing without reasonable excuse to give such a notice shall be liable on summary conviction to a fine not exceeding **level 2** on the standard scale.

(3A) In subsection (3) above "appropriate officer" means—

(a)   in relation to a magistrates' court in England and Wales, the justices' chief executive for the court; and

(b)   in relation to a court elsewhere, the clerk of the court.

(4) An order which by virtue of this section is enforceable by a magistrates' court in England and Wales shall, subject to the modifications of sections 76 and 93 of the Magistrates' Courts Act 1980 specified in subsections (4A) and (4B) below, be enforceable as if it were a magistrates' court maintenance order made by that court.

In this subsection, "magistrates' court maintenance order" has the same meaning as in section 150(1) of the Magistrates' Courts Act 1980.

(4A) Section 76 (enforcement of sums adjudged to be paid) shall have effect as if for subsections (4) to (6) there were substituted the following subsections—

"(4) Where proceedings are brought for the enforcement of a magistrates' court maintenance order under this section, the court may vary the order by exercising one of its powers under subsection (5) below.

(5) The powers of the court are—

(a)   the power to order that payments under the order be made directly to a justices' chief executive;

(b)   the power to order that payments under the order be made to a justices' chief executive by such method of payment falling within section 59(6) above (standing order, etc) as may be specified;

(c)   the power to make an attachment of earnings order under the Attachment of Earnings Act 1971 to secure payments under the order.

(6) In deciding which of the powers under subsection (5) above it is to exercise, the court shall have regard to any representations made by the debtor (within the meaning of section 59 above).

(7) Subsection (4) of section 59 above (power of court to require debtor to open account) shall apply for the purposes of subsection (5) above as it applies for the purposes of that section but as if for paragraph (a) there were substituted—

"(a) the court proposes to exercise its power under paragraph (b) of section 76(5) below, and"."

(4B) In section 93 (complaint for arrears), subsection (6) (court not to impose imprisonment in certain circumstances) shall have effect as if for paragraph (b) there were substituted—

"(b) if the court is of the opinion that it is appropriate—

(i)   to make an attachment of earnings order; or

(ii)   to exercise its power under paragraph (b) of section 76(5) above.".

(5) The magistrates' court by which an order is enforceable by virtue of this section, and the officers thereof, shall take all such steps for enforcing the order as may be prescribed.

(6) In any proceedings for or with respect to the enforcement of an order which is for the time being registered in any court under this Part of this Act a certificate of arrears sent to the prescribed officer of the court shall be evidence of the facts stated therein.

(7) Subject to subsection (8) below, a sum of money payable under a registered order shall be payable in accordance with the order, or such part thereof as the payee may have requested should be enforced, as from the date on which the order took effect.

(8) Where a registered order was made by a court in a Hague Convention country before the date of the

entry into force of the Hague Convention between the United Kingdom and that country, no sum of money falling due before that date shall be payable in accordance with the order.

(9) *Scotland.*

9. *Variation of maintenance order registered in United Kingdom court.*

(1) Subject to the provisions of this section—

(a) the registering court shall have the like power, on an application made by the payer or payee under a registered order, to vary the method of payment of the order as if it had been made by the registering court and as if that court had had jurisdiction to make it;

(b) the jurisdiction of a magistrates' court to vary the method of payment of a registered order shall be exercisable notwithstanding that the proceedings for the variation of the order are brought by or against a person residing in a Hague Convention country.

(1ZA) Where the registering court is a magistrates' court in England and Wales, section 60 of the Magistrates' Courts Act 1980 (revocation, variation etc of orders for periodical payment) shall have effect in relation to the registered order—

(za) as if in subsection (1) for the words "by order on complaint" there were substituted "on an application being made, by order and for the words "revoke, revive or vary the order", there were substituted "vary the order in accordance with subsection (3)'''";

(zab) as if subsection (2) were omitted;

(a) as if in subsection (3)—

(i) for the words "shall include", there were substituted "means the";

(ii) for the words "paragraphs (a) to (d) of section 59(3) above" there were substituted "subsection (3A) below"; and

(iii) after that subsection there were inserted—

"(3A) The powers of the court are—

(a) the power to order that payments under the order be made directly to a justices' chief executive;

(b) the power to order that payments under the order be made to a justices' chief executive, by such method of payment falling within section 59(6) above (standing order, etc) as may be specified;

(c) the power to make an attachment of earnings order under the Attachment of Earnings Act 1971 to secure payments under the order.";

(b) as if in subsection (4) for paragraph (b) there were substituted—

"(b) payments under the order are required to be made to a justices' chief executive, by any method of payment falling within section 59(6) above (standing order, etc)",

and as if after the words "the court" there were inserted "which made the order";

(c) as if in subsection (5) for the words "to the clerk" there were substituted "in accordance with paragraph (a) of subsection (3A) above";

(d) as if in subsection (7), paragraph (c) and the word "and" immediately preceding it were omitted;

(e) as if in subsection (8) for the words "paragraphs (a) to (d) of section 59(3) above" there were substituted "subsection (3A) above";

(f) as if for subsections (9) and (10) there were substituted the following subsections—

"(9) In deciding, for the purposes of subsections (3) and (8) above, which of the powers under subsection (3A) above it is to exercise, the court shall have regard to any representations made by the debtor.

(10) Subsection (4) of section 59 above (power of court to require debtor to open account) shall apply for the purposes of subsection (3A) above as it applies for the purposes of that section but as if for paragraph (a) there were substituted—

"(a) the court proposes to exercise its power under paragraph (b) of section 60(3A) below, and".".

(1ZB) Where the registering court is a court of summary jurisdiction in Northern Ireland, Article 86 of the Magistrates' Court (Northern Ireland) Order 1981 (revocation, variation etc, of orders for periodical payment) shall have effect in relation to the registered order—

(za) as if in paragraph (1) for the words "by order on complaint" there were substituted "on an application being made, by order" and for the words "revoke, revive or vary the order", there were substituted "vary the order in accordance with paragraph (3)";

(zab) as if paragraph (2) were omitted;

(a) as if in paragraph (3)—

(i) for the words "shall include", there were substituted "means the",

(ii) for the words "sub-paragraphs (a) to (d) of Article 85(3)" there were substituted "paragraph (3A)", and

(iii) after that paragraph there were inserted—

"(3A) The powers of the court are—

(a) the power to order that payments under the order be made directly to the collecting officer;

(b) the power to order that payments under the order be made to the collecting officer by such method of payment falling within Article 85(7) (standing order, etc) as may be specified;

(c) the power to make an attachment of earnings order under Part IX to secure payments under the order;"

(b) as if in paragraph (4) for sub-paragraph (b) there were substituted—

"(b) payments under the order are required to be made to the collecting officer by any method of payment falling within Article 85(7) (standing order, etc)";

and as if after the words "petty sessions" there were inserted "for the petty sessions district for which the court which made the order acts";

(c) as if in paragraph (5) for the words "to the collecting officer" there were substituted "in accordance with sub-paragraph (a) of paragraph (3A)";

(d) as if in paragraph (7), sub-paragraph (c) and the word "and" immediately preceding it were omitted;

(e) as if in paragraph (8) for the words "sub-paragraphs (a) to (d) of Article 85(3)" there were substituted "paragraph (3A)";

(*f*) as if for paragraphs (9) and (10) there were substituted the following paragraphs—

"(9) In deciding, for the purposes of paragraphs (3) and (8), which of the powers under paragraph (3A) it is to exercise, the court shall have regard to any representations made by the debtor.

(10) Paragraph (5) of Article 85 (power of court to require debtor to open account) shall apply for the purposes of paragraph (3A) as it applies for the purpose of that Article but as if for sub-paragraph (*a*) there were substituted—

"(*a*) the court proposes to exercise its power under sub-paragraph (*b*) of Article 86(3A), and".".

(2) The registering court shall not vary a registered order unless—

(*a*) the payer under the order had his habitual residence in the United Kingdom at the time when the proceedings to vary the order were instituted; or

(*b*) the respondent in those proceedings had submitted to the jurisdiction of the registering court, either expressly or by defending on the merits of the case without objecting to the jurisdiction.

(3)–(7) *Revoked.*

(8) Where a registered order has been varied by the registering court or by a court in a Hague Convention country, the prescribed officer of the registering court shall register the variation order in the prescribed manner.

(9) Where a registered order has been varied by the registering court or by a court in a Hague Convention country, the registered order shall, as from the date on which the variation order took effect, have effect as so varied.

(10) *Northern Ireland.*

(11) This section shall not apply to a court in Scotland.

10. Cancellation of registration and transfer of order. (1) Where a registered order is revoked by an order made by a court in a Hague Convention country and notice of the revocation is received by the registering court, the prescribed officer of the registering court shall cancel the registration; but any arrears due under the registered order at the date on which the order of revocation took effect, other than, in the case of a registered order made by a court in a Hague Convention country before the date of the entry into force of the Hague Convention between the United Kingdom and that country, arrears due before that date, shall continue to be recoverable as if the registration had not been cancelled.

(2) Where the prescribed officer of the registering court is of opinion that the payer under a registered order has ceased to reside within the jurisdiction of that court, he shall cancel the registration of the order and, subject to subsection (3) below, shall send the certified copy of the order to the Lord Chancellor.

(3) Where the prescribed officer of the registering court, being a magistrates' court, is of opinion that the payer is residing within the jurisdiction of another magistrates' court in that part of the United Kingdom in which the registering court is, he shall transfer the order to that other court by sending the certified copy of the order to the prescribed officer of that court.

(4) On the transfer of an order under subsection (3) above the prescribed officer of the court to which it is transferred shall, subject to subsection (6) below, register the order in the prescribed manner in that court.

(5) Where the certified copy of an order is received by the Lord Chancellor under this section and it appears to him that the payer under the order is still residing in the United Kingdom, he shall transfer the order to the appropriate court by sending the certified copy of the order together with the related documents to the prescribed officer of the appropriate court and, subject to subsection (6) below, that officer shall register the order in the prescribed manner in that court.

(6) Before registering an order in pursuance of subsection (4) or (5) above an officer of a court shall take such steps as he thinks fit for the purpose of ascertaining whether the payer is so residing, and if after taking those steps he is satisfied that the payer is not residing within the jurisdiction of the court he shall send the certified copy of the order to the Lord Chancellor.

(7) The officer of a court who is required by any of the foregoing provisions of this section to send to the Lord Chancellor or to the prescribed officer of another court the certified copy of an order shall send with that copy—

(*a*) a certificate of arrears signed by him;

(*b*) a statement giving such information as he possesses as to the whereabouts of the payer; and

(*c*) any relevant documents in his possession relating to the case.

(8) *Scotland.*

11. Steps to be taken by Lord Chancellor or Secretary of State where payer under certain orders is not residing in the United Kingdom. (1) If it appears to the Lord Chancellor or the Secretary of State that the payer under a maintenance order, a certified copy of which has been received by him from a Hague Convention country, is not residing in the United Kingdom or, in the case of an order which subsequently became a registered order, has ceased to reside therein, he shall send to the appropriate authority in that country—

(*a*) the certified copy of the order in question and a certified copy of any order varying that order;

(*b*) if the order has at any time been a registered order, a certificate of arrears signed by the prescribed officer;

(*c*) a statement giving such information as the Lord Chancellor or the Secretary of State possesses as to the whereabouts of the payer; and

(*d*) any other relevant documents in his possession relating to the case.

Appeals

6–4977 12. Appeals. Where in pursuance of section 9 above a registering court makes or refuses to make an order varying a registered order, the payer or the payee under the registered order shall have the like right of appeal (if any) from the order of variation or from the refusal to make it as he would have if the registered order had been made by the registering court.

Evidence

6–4978 13. Admissibility of evidence given in Hague Convention country. (1) A statement contained in—

(a) a document, duly authenticated, which purports to set out or summarise evidence given in proceedings in a court in a Hague Convention country; or

(b) a document, duly authenticated, which purports to set out or summarise evidence taken in that country for the purpose of proceedings in a court in the United Kingdom under this Part of this Act, whether in response to a request made by such a court or otherwise; or

(c) a document, duly authenticated, which purports to have been received in evidence in proceedings in a court in that country or to be a copy of a document so received; or

(d) a document purporting to be signed by a judicial officer, official or other competent person in a Hague Convention country which establishes that certain documents were served on a person,

shall in any proceedings in a court in the United Kingdom relating to a maintenance order to which this Part of this Act applies be admissible as evidence of any fact stated therein to the same extent as oral evidence of that fact is admissible in those proceedings.

(2) A document purporting to set out or summarise evidence given as mentioned in subsection (1)(a) above, or taken as mentioned in subsection (1)(b) above, shall be deemed to be duly authenticated for the purposes of that subsection if the document purports to be certified by the judicial officer or other person before whom the evidence was given, or, as the case may be, by whom it was taken, to be the original document containing or recording, or, as the case may be, summarising, that evidence or a true copy of that document.

(3) A document purporting to have been received in evidence as mentioned in subsection (1)(c) above, or to be a copy of a document so received, shall be deemed to be duly authenticated for the purposes of that subsection if the document purports to be certified by a judge or officer of the court in question to have been, or to be a true copy of a document which has been, so received.

(4) It shall not be necessary in any such proceedings to prove the signature or official position of the person appearing to have given such a certificate.

(5) Nothing in this section shall prejudice the admission in evidence of any document which is admissible in evidence apart from this section.

14. Obtaining of evidence needed for purpose of certain proceedings. (1) Where for the purpose of any proceedings in a court in a Hague Convention country relating to a maintenance order to which this Part of this Act applies a request is made by or on behalf of that court for the taking in the United Kingdom of the evidence of a person residing therein relating to matters specified in the request, such court in the United Kingdom as may be prescribed shall have power to take that evidence and, after giving notice of the time and place at which the evidence is to be taken to such persons and in such manner as it thinks fit, shall take the evidence in such manner as may be prescribed.

Evidence taken in compliance with such a request shall be sent by the prescribed officer of the court—)

(a) in England and Wales or Northern Ireland, to the Lord Chancellor, or

(b) in Scotland, to the Secretary of State,

for transmission to the appropriate authority in the Hague Convention country.

(2) Where any person, not being the payer or the payee under the maintenance order to which the proceedings in question relate, is required by virtue of this section to give evidence before a court in the United Kingdom, the court may order that there shall be paid out of moneys provided by Parliament such sums as appear to the court reasonably sufficient to compensate that person for the expense, trouble or loss of time properly incurred in or incidental to his attendance.

(3) Section 97(1), (3) and (4) of the Magistrates' Courts Act 1980 (which provide for compelling the attendance of witnesses, etc) shall apply in relation to a magistrates' court having power under subsection (1) above to take the evidence of any person as if the proceedings in the court in a Hague Convention country for the purpose of which a request for the taking of the evidence has been made were proceedings in the magistrates' court and had been begun by complaint.

(4) *Scotland.*

(5) A court in—

(a) England and Wales or Northern Ireland may for the purpose of any proceedings in that court under this Part of this Act relating to a maintenance order to which this Part of this Act applies send to the Lord Chancellor, or

(b) Scotland may for the purpose of such proceedings in that court relating to such an action, send to the Secretary of State,

for transmission to the appropriate authority in a Hague Convention country a request for a court in a Hague Convention country to take or provide evidence relating to such matters as may be specified in the request.

(6) *Northern Ireland.*

15. Order, etc made in Hague Convention country need not be proved. For the purposes of this Part of this Act, unless the contrary is shown—

(a) any order made by a court in a Hague Convention country purporting to bear the seal of that court or to be signed by any person in his capacity as a judge or officer of the court, shall be deemed without further proof to have been duly sealed or, as the case may be, to have been signed by that person;

(b) the person by whom the order was signed shall be deemed without further proof to have been a judge or officer, as the case may be, of that court when he signed it and, in the case of an officer, to have been authorised to sign it; and

(c) a document purporting to be a certified copy of an order made by a court in a Hague Convention country shall be deemed without further proof to be such a copy.

Supplemental

6–4979 16. Payment of sums under orders made in Hague Convention countries: conversion of currency.
(1) Payment of sums due under a registered order shall, while the order is registered in a court in England, Wales or Northern Ireland, be made in such manner and to such person as may be prescribed.

(2) Where the sum required to be paid under a registered order are expressed in a currency other than the currency of the United Kingdom, then, as from the relevant date, the order shall be treated as if it were an order requiring the payment of such sums in the currency of the United Kingdom as, on the basis of the rate of exchange prevailing at that date, are equivalent to the sums so required to be paid.

(3) Where the sum specified in any statement, being a statement of the amount of any arrears due under a maintenance order made by a court in a Hague Convention country, is expressed in a currency other than the currency of the United Kingdom, that sum shall be deemed to be such sum in the currency of the United Kingdom as, on the basis of the rate of exchange prevailing at the relevant date, is equivalent to the sum so specified.

(4) For the purposes of this section a written certificate purporting to be signed by an officer of any bank in the United Kingdom certifying that a specified rate of exchange prevailed between currencies at a specified date and that at such a rate a specified sum in the currency of the United Kingdom is equivalent to a specified sum in another specified currency shall be evidence of the rate of exchange so prevailing on that date and of the equivalent sums in terms of the respective currencies.

(5) In this section "the relevant date" means—

(a) in relation to a registered order or to a statement of arrears due under a maintenance order made by a court in a Hague Convention country, the date on which the order first becomes a registered order;

(b) in relation to a registered order which has been varied, the date on which the last order varying that order is registered in the registering court.

(6) *Scotland.*

17. Proceedings in magistrates' courts. (4) Anything authorised or required by this Part of this Act to be done by, to or before the magistrates' court by, to or before which any other thing was done may be done by, to or before any magistrates' court acting for the same petty sessions area (or, in Northern Ireland, petty sessions district) as that court.

(5) Any application which by virtue of a provision of this Part of this Act is made to a magistrates' court in Northern Ireland shall be made by complaint.

(5A) Where the respondent to an application for the variation or revocation of—

(a) a maintenance order made by a magistrates' court in England and Wales, being an order to which section 5 of this Act applies; or

(b) a registered order which is registered in such a court,

is residing in a Hague Convention country, a magistrates' court in England and Wales shall have jurisdiction to hear the application (where it would not have such jurisdiction apart from this subsection) if it would have had jurisdiction to hear it had the respondent been residing in England and Wales.

(6) *Northern Ireland.*

(7) Where the respondent to an application—

(a) for the variation or revocation of a maintenance order made by a magistrates' court, and to which section 5 of this Act applies; or

(b) for the variation of a registered order registered in a magistrates' court,

does not appear at the time and place appointed for the hearing of the application, but the court is satisfied that the respondent is residing in a Hague Convention country, and that the requirements of section 5(4), (6) or (7) or section 9(3), as the case may be, have been complied with, the court may proceed to hear and determine the application at the time and place appointed for the hearing or for any adjourned hearing as if the respondent had appeared at that time and place.

(7A) *Northern Ireland.*

18. Magistrates' courts rules. (1) Without prejudice to the generality of the power to make rules under section 144 of the Magistrates' Courts Act 1980 (magistrates' courts rules) provision may be made by such rules with respect to any of the following matters, namely—

(a) the circumstances in which anything authorised or required by this Part of this Act to be done by, to or before a magistrates' court acting for a particular petty sessions area or by, to or before an officer of that court may be done by, to or before a magistrates' court acting for such other petty sessions area as the rules may provide or by, to or before an officer of that court;

(b) the orders made, or other things done, by a magistrates' court, or an officer of such a court, under this Part of this Act, or by a court in a Hague Convention country, notice of which is to be given to such persons as the rules may provide and the manner in which such notice shall be given;

(c) the cases and manner in which courts in Hague Convention countries are to be informed of orders made, or other things done, by a magistrates' court under this Part of this Act;

(d) the cases and manner in which a justices' clerk may take evidence needed for the purpose of proceedings in court in a Hague Convention country relating to a maintenance order to which this Part of this Act applies;

(f) the circumstances and manner in which magistrates' courts may for the purposes of this Part of this Act communicate with courts in Hague Convention countries.

(1A) For the purpose of giving effect to this Part of this Act, rules made under section 144 of the Magistrates' Courts Act 1980 may make, in relation to any proceedings brought under or by virtue of this Part of this Act, any provision not covered by subsection (1) above which—

(a) falls within subsection (2) of section 93 of the Children Act 1989, and

(b) may be made in relation to relevant proceedings under that section.

(2) *Northern Ireland.*

21. Interpretation of Part I. (1) In this Part of this Act unless the context otherwise requires—

"affiliation order" means an order (however described) adjudging, finding or declaring a person to be the father of a child, whether or not it also provides for the maintenance of the child;

"the appropriate court", in relation to a person residing in England and Wales or in Northern Ireland means a magistrates' court, and in relation to a person residing in Scotland means the sheriff court, within the jurisdiction of which that person is residing;

"certificate of arrears", in relation to a maintenance order, means a certificate certifying that the sum specified in the certificate is to be the best of the information or belief of the officer giving the certificate the amount of the arrears due under the order at the date of the certificate except any arrears that accrued before the date of the entry into force of the Hague Convention between the United Kingdom and the Hague

Convention country in which the payer is residing, or, as the case may be, that to the best of his information or belief there are no arrears due thereunder at the date of the certificate;

"certified copy", in relation to an order of a court, means a copy of the order certified by the proper officer of the court to be a true copy;

"court" includes any tribunal or person having power to make, confirm, enforce, vary or revoke a maintenance order and "competent court in a Hague Convention country" means a court having jurisdiction on one of the grounds specified in section 6(5)(a) above;

"maintenance order" means an order (however described), including any settlement made by or before a competent court in a Hague Convention country, of any of the following descriptions, and in the case of an order which is not limited to the following descriptions, the part of the order which is so limited, that is to say—

(a) an order (including an affiliation order or order consequent upon an affiliation order) which provides for the periodical payment of sums of money towards the maintenance of any person, being a person whom the person liable to make payments under the order is, according to the law applied in the place where the order was made, liable to maintain;

(aa) an order which has been made in Scotland, on or after the granting of a decree of divorce, for the payment of a periodical allowance by one party to the marriage to the other party;

(b) an affiliation order or order consequent upon an affiliation order, being an order which provides for the payment by a person adjudged, found or declared to be a child's father of expenses incidental to the child's birth or, where the child has died, of his funeral expenses; and

(c) an order within the foregoing provisions of this definition made against a payer on the application of a public body which claims reimbursement of sums of money payable under the order with respect to the payee if the reimbursement can be obtained by the public body under the law to which it is subject,

and in the case of a maintenance order which has been varied (including a maintenance order which has been varied either by a court in the United Kingdom or by a competent court in a Hague Convention country whether or not the original order was made by such a court), means that order as varied:

Provided that the expression "maintenance order" shall not include an order made in a Hague Convention country of a description which that country or the United Kingdom has reserved the right under Article 26 of the Hague Convention not to recognise or enforce;

"order" means an order however described giving effect to a decision rendered by a court and, as respects Scotland, includes any interlocutor, and any decree or provision contained in an interlocutor;

"payee", in relation to a maintenance order, means the person entitled to the payments for which the order provides and includes a public body which has provided benefits for the payee and which is entitled *ipso jure* under the law to which it is subject to claim enforcement of the said order to the extent of the benefits so provided in place of the said person;

"payer", in relation to a maintenance order, means the person liable to make payments under the order;

"prescribed", in relation to a magistrates' court in England and Wales or in Northern Ireland, means prescribed by rules made under section 144 of the Magistrates' Courts Act 1980 or by rules made in accordance with Article 13 of the Magistrates' Courts (Northern Ireland) Order 1981, as the case may be, and in relation to any other court means prescribed by rules of court;

"registered order" means a maintenance order which is for the time being registered in a court in the United Kingdom under this Part of this Act and

"registered" and "registration" shall be construed accordingly;

"registering court", in relation to a registered order, means the court in which that order is for the time being registered under this Part of this Act;

"revoke" and "revocation" include discharge.

(2) Any reference in this Part of this Act to the payment of money for the maintenance of a child shall be construed as including a reference to the payment of money for the child's education.

Reciprocal Enforcement of Maintenance Orders (Republic of Ireland) Order 1993[1]

(SI 1993/594 amended by SI 2001/410)

6–4980   **1.** *Citation and commencement.*

---

1. Made in exercise of the powers conferred by ss 40 and 45(1) of the Maintenance Orders (Reciprocal Enforcement) Act 1972. See Home Office Circulars Nos 35/1975 and 102/1977 and see also Home Office Circular No 30/1988 (effect of Brussels Convention). For procedural rules, see Magistrates' Courts (Reciprocal Enforcement of Maintenance Orders) (Republic of Ireland) Rules 1975, this Part, ante.

6–4981   **2.** (1) The provisions of Part I of the Maintenance Orders (Reciprocal Enforcement) Act 1972 (in this Order referred to as "the Act") shall apply in relation to the Republic of Ireland as they apply in relation to a reciprocating country, subject to the exceptions, adaptations and modifications set out in Schedule 1[1] to this Order.

(2) Accordingly, Part I of the Act shall, in relation to—

(a) maintenance orders made by courts in the United Kingdom against persons in the Republic of Ireland, and

(b) maintenance orders made by courts in the Republic of Ireland against persons in the United Kingdom,

have effect as set out in Schedule 2 to this Order.

1. We print only Sch 2, *post*. It should be noted that under Sch 1, sections 1, 7, 20, 22, 23 and 24 of the Act do not apply.

6–4982 4. *Revocation.*

Article 2(2)

SCHEDULE 2

PART I OF THE ACT AS MODIFIED BY SCHEDULE 1

Orders made by courts in the United Kingdom

6–4983 2. Transmission of maintenance order made in United Kingdom for enforcement in the Republic of Ireland. (1) Subject to subsection (2) below, where the payer under a maintenance order made, whether before, on or after 5th April 1993, by a court in the United Kingdom is residing in the Republic of Ireland, the payee under the order may apply for the order to be sent to that country for enforcement.

(2) Subsection (1) above shall not have effect in relation to a provisional order or to an order made by virtue of a provision of Part II of this Act.

(3) Every application under this section shall be made in the prescribed manner to the prescribed officer of the court which made the maintenance order to which the application relates.

(4) If, on an application duly made under this section to the prescribed officer of a court in the United Kingdom, that officer is satisfied that the payer under the maintenance order to which the application relates is residing in the Republic of Ireland, the following documents, that is to say—

  (a) a certified copy of the maintenance order;
  (b) a certificate signed by that officer certifying that the order is enforceable in the United Kingdom;
  (c) a certificate of arrears so signed;
  (d) a statement giving such information as the officer possesses as to the whereabouts of the payer;
  (e) a statement giving such information as the officer possesses for facilitating the identification of the payer;
  (f) where available, a photograph of the payer;
  (g) if the payer did not appear in the proceedings in which the maintenance order was made, the original or a certified copy of a document which establishes that notice of the institution of the proceedings was served on the payer;
  (h) a document which establishes that notice of the order was sent to the payer; and
  (i) if the payee received legal aid in the proceedings, a written statement to that effect signed by that officer,

shall be sent by that officer, in the case of a court in England and Wales or Northern Ireland, to the Lord Chancellor, or, in the case of a court in Scotland, to the Secretary of State, with a view to their being transmitted by the Lord Chancellor, or, as the case may be, the Secretary of State, to the responsible authority in the Republic of Ireland if he is satisfied that the statement relating to the whereabouts of the payer gives sufficient information to justify that being done.

(5) Nothing in this section shall be taken as affecting any jurisdiction of a court in the United Kingdom with respect to a maintenance order to which this section applies, and any such order may be enforced, varied or revoked accordingly.

3. Power of magistrates' court to make and confirm provisional maintenance order against person residing in the Republic of Ireland. (1) Where an application is made to a magistrates' court for a maintenance order against a person residing in the Republic of Ireland and the court would have jurisdiction to determine the application under the Domestic Proceedings and Magistrates' Courts Act 1978 or the Children Act 1989 if that person—

  (a) were residing in England and Wales, and
  (b) received reasonable notice of the date of the hearing of the application,

the court shall (subject to subsection (2) below) have jurisdiction to determine the application.

(2) A maintenance order made by virtue of this section shall be a provisional order.

(4) No enactment (or provision made under an enactment) requiring or enabling—

  (a) a court to transfer proceedings from a magistrates' court to a county court or the High Court, or
  (b) a magistrates' court to refuse to make an order on an application on the ground that any matter in question is one that would be more conveniently dealt with by the High Court,

shall apply in relation to an application to which subsection (1) above applies.

(5) Where a court makes a maintenance order which is by virtue of this section a provisional order, the following documents, that is to say—

  (a) a certified copy of the maintenance order;
  (b) a document, authenticated in the prescribed manner, setting out or summarising the evidence given in the proceedings;
  (c) a certificate signed by the prescribed officer of the court certifying that the grounds stated in the certificate are the grounds on which the making of the order might have been opposed by the payer under the order;
  (ca) a notice addressed to the payer stating that a provisional order has been made, that it has no effect unless and until confirmed with or without alteration by the court making the order, and that in considering whether or not to confirm the provisional order the court will take into account any representations made or any evidence adduced by or on behalf of the payer within three weeks from the date of service of the notice;
  (d) a statement giving such information as was available to the court as to the whereabouts of the payer;
  (e) a statement giving such information as the officer possesses for facilitating the identification of the payer; and
  (f) where available, a photograph of the payer,

shall be sent by that officer to the Lord Chancellor with a view to their being transmitted by the Lord Chancellor to the responsible authority in the Republic of Ireland if he is satisfied that the statement relating to the whereabouts of the payer gives sufficient information to justify that being done.

(6) The court which made a provisional order by virtue of this section shall not earlier than three weeks after

the date of service of the notice referred to in paragraph (*ca*) of subsection (5) above consider whether or not to confirm the order and with or without alteration and shall take into account any representations made and any evidence adduced by or on behalf of the payer.

(6A) Where the payer makes any representations or adduces any evidence, a copy of the representations or evidence shall be served on the person on whose application the provisional order was made before the date of the hearing at which confirmation of the provisional order will be considered and that person shall be notified in the prescribed manner of the date fixed for the hearing.

(6B) The court shall not confirm such an order unless the documents mentioned in paragraphs (*a*), (*b*), (*c*) and (*ca*) of subsection (5) above have been served on the payer in accordance with the law for the service of such documents in the Republic of Ireland and in sufficient time to enable him to arrange for his defence.

(6C) Where an order has been confirmed under this section, the prescribed officer of the court shall—

(*a*) send to the payer by registered post notice of the confirmation of the order; and
(*b*) send the following documents, that is to say—

    (i) a certified copy of the maintenance order as confirmed;
    (ii) a certificate signed by that officer certifying that the order is enforceable in the United Kingdom;
    (iii) if the payer did not appear in the proceedings in which the order was confirmed, the original or a certified copy of a document which establishes that the documents mentioned in paragraphs (*a*), (*b*), (*c*) and (*ca*) of subsection (5) above have been served on the payer;
    (iv) a document which establishes that notice of the confirmation of the order has been sent to the payer by registered post;
    (v) if the payee received legal aid in the proceedings, a written statement to that effect signed by that officer,

to the Lord Chancellor with a view to their being transmitted by him to the responsible authority in the Republic of Ireland.

(6D) Where the court decides not to confirm a provisional order, it shall revoke the order.

(7) *Northern Ireland.*

5. Variation and revocation of maintenance order made in United Kingdom. (1) This section applies to a maintenance order a certified copy of which has been sent to the Republic of Ireland in pursuance of section 2 of this Act and to a provisional order made in pursuance of section 3 of this Act which has been confirmed by a court in England and Wales or Northern Ireland under that section.

(2) Where subsection (1) of section 60 of the Magistrates' Courts Act 1980 (revocation, variation etc of orders for periodical payment) applies in relation to a maintenance order to which this section applies, that subsection shall have effect as if for the words "by order on complaint," there were substituted "on an application being made, by order".

(3) Where an application is made to a court in England and Wales or Northern Ireland by the payee for the variation or revocation of an order to which this section applies, and the payer is residing in the Republic of Ireland, the prescribed officer of the court shall send to the Lord Chancellor a certified copy of the application, together with a document, authenticated in the prescribed manner, setting out or summarising the evidence in support of the application, with a view to their being transmitted by him to the responsible authority in the Republic of Ireland for service on the payer.

(4) A court in England and Wales or Northern Ireland shall not vary or revoke such an order before the expiry of three weeks from the date of service of the documents mentioned in subsection (3) above and before varying or revoking the order shall take into account any representations made and any evidence adduced by or on behalf of the payer.

(5) Where such an order is varied or revoked by a court in England and Wales or Northern Ireland a certified copy of the order of the court and a statement as to the service of the documents mentioned in subsection (3) above on the payer shall be sent to the court in the Republic of Ireland by which the order is being enforced.

(6) Where a maintenance order to which this section applies has been varied by an order made by a court in the United Kingdom, the maintenance order shall, as from the date on which the order of variation was made, have effect as varied by that order.

(7) Where a maintenance order to which this section applies has been revoked by an order made by a court in the United Kingdom, the maintenance order shall, as from the date on which the order of revocation was made, be deemed to have ceased to have effect except as respects any arrears due under the maintenance order at that date.

Orders made by the courts in the Republic of Ireland

6–4984   6. Registration in United Kingdom court of maintenance order made in the Republic of Ireland. (1) This section applies to a maintenance order made whether before, on or after 5th April 1993 by a court in the Republic of Ireland.

(2) Where a certified copy of an order to which this section applies is received by the Lord Chancellor or the Secretary of State from the responsible authority in the Republic of Ireland, and it appears to him that the payer under the order is residing in the United Kingdom, he shall send the copy of the order and the accompanying documents to the prescribed officer of the appropriate court.

(3) Where the prescribed officer of the appropriate court receives from the Lord Chancellor or the Secretary of State a certified copy of an order to which this section applies, he shall, subject to the following subsections, register the order in the prescribed manner in that court.

(4) Before registering an order under this section an officer of a court shall take such steps as he thinks fit for the purpose of ascertaining whether the payer under the order is residing within the jurisdiction of the court, and if after taking those steps he is satisfied that the payer is not so residing he shall return the certified copy of the order and the accompanying documents to the Lord Chancellor or, as the case may be, the Secretary of State with a statement giving such information as he possesses as to the whereabouts of the payer.

(5) The order shall not be registered—

(*a*) if such registration is contrary to public policy;
(*b*) if the payer did not appear in the proceedings in the Republic of Ireland and he was not served in accordance with the law of the place where he was residing with the summons or other notice of the institution of the proceedings in sufficient time to enable him to arrange for his defence;

(*c*) if the order is irreconcilable[1] with a judgment given in the United Kingdom in proceedings between the same parties.

(6) If the order is registered under this section, the prescribed officer of the appropriate court shall serve notice in a prescribed form on the payer and give notice to the payee that the order has been registered.

(7) The payer may within one calendar month from the date of service of the said notice appeal to the court in which the order is registered to set aside the registration of the order on one of the grounds set out in subsection (5) above.

(8) If the payer appeals to the appropriate court to set aside the registration of the order, the prescribed officer of the court shall give notice to the payee of the appeal and of the date of the hearing of the appeal.

(9) If the payer appeals to the appropriate court to set aside the registration of the order, the court may, on the application of the payer, stay, or in Scotland sist, the proceedings if either—

(*a*) enforcement of the maintenance order has been suspended in the Republic of Ireland pending the determination of any form of appeal; or

(*b*) the time for an appeal has not yet expired and enforcement has been suspended pending the making of an appeal,

and in the latter case the court may lay down the time within which the proceedings will be stayed or sisted.

(10) If the order is not registered by virtue of subsection (5) above, the prescribed officer shall give notice to the payee in a prescribed form that the order has not been registered.

(11) A payee to whom notice has been given by the officer of any court under subsection (10) above may within one calendar month of the date of the notice appeal to that court to set aside the decision not to register the order.

(12) *Scotland.*

---

1. An Irish maintenance order was held to be irreconcilable with a divorce decree absolute in England; only arrears falling due before the decree could be enforced (*R v West London Magistrates' Court, ex p Emmett*, [1994] 1 FCR 421, [1993] 2 FLR 663).

6–4984A   8. Enforcement of maintenance order registered in United Kingdom court. (1) Subject to subsections (1A), (2), (2A) and (2B) below, a registered order may be enforced in the United Kingdom as if it had been made by the registering court and as if that court had had jurisdiction to make it; and proceedings for or with respect to the enforcement of any such order may be taken accordingly.

(1A) During the period within which an appeal to set aside the registration of a registered order may be made under section 6(7) and until any such appeal has been determined, no measures of enforcement may be taken against the property of the payer other than those designed to protect the interests of the payee:

Provided that nothing in this subsection shall be construed as preventing a registered order from being registered as mentioned in subsection (2) below.

(2) Subsection (1) above does not apply to an order which is for the time being registered in the High Court under Part I of the Maintenance Orders Act 1958 or to an order which is for the time being registered in the High Court of Justice in Northern Ireland under Part II of the Maintenance and Affiliation Orders Act (Northern Ireland) 1966.

(2A) Where in a maintenance order made in the Republic of Ireland there are provisions which are not enforceable, this section shall apply only to the remaining provisions of the order.

(2B) The payee under a registered order may request the partial enforcement of that order.

(3) Any person for the time being under an obligation to make payments in pursuance of a registered order shall give notice of any change of address to the appropriate officer of the registering court, and any person failing without reasonable excuse to give such a notice shall be liable on summary conviction to a fine not exceeding **level 2** on the standard scale.

(3A) In subsection (3) above "appropriate officer" means—

(*a*) in relation to a magistrates' court in England and Wales, the justices' chief executive for the court; and

(*b*) in relation to a magistrates' court elsewhere, the clerk of the court.

(4) An order which by virtue of this section is enforceable by a magistrates' court in England and Wales shall subject to the modifications of sections 76 and 93 of the Magistrates' Courts Act 1980 specified in subsections (4A) and (4B) below be enforceable as if it were a magistrates' court maintenance order made by that court.

In this subsection, "magistrates' court maintenance order" has the same meaning as in section 150(1) of the Magistrates' Courts Act 1980.

(4A) Section 76 (enforcement of sums adjudged to be paid) shall have effect as if for subsections (4) to (6) there were substituted the following subsections—

"(4) Where proceedings are brought for the enforcement of a magistrates' court maintenance order under this section, the court may vary the order by exercising one of its powers under subsection (5) below.

(5) The powers of the court are—

(*a*) the power to order that payments under the order be made directly to the clerk of the court or a justices' chief executive;

(*b*) the power to order that payments under the order be made to a justices' chief executive, by such method of payment falling within section 59(6) above (standing order, etc) as may be specified;

(*c*) the power to make an attachment of earnings order under the Attachment of Earnings Act 1971 to secure payments under the order.

(6) In deciding which of the powers under subsection (5) above it is to exercise, the court shall have regard to any representations made by the debtor (within the meaning of section 59 above).

(7) Subsection (4) of section 59 above (power of court to require debtor to open account) shall apply for the purposes of subsection (5) above as it applies for the purposes of that section but as if for paragraph (*a*) there were substituted—

'(*a*) the court proposes to exercise its power under paragraph (*b*) of section 76(5) below, and'."

(4B) In section 93 (complaint for arrears), subsection (6) (court not to impose imprisonment in certain circumstances) shall have effect as if for paragraph (*b*) there were substituted—

"(*b*) if the court is of the opinion that it is appropriate—

(i)   to make an attachment of earnings order; or
(ii) to exercise its power under paragraph (*b*) of section 76(5) above.''

(5) The magistrates' court by which an order is enforceable by virtue of this section, and the officers thereof, shall take all such steps for enforcing the order as may be prescribed.

(6) In any proceedings for or with respect to the enforcement of an order which is for the time being registered in any court under this Part of this Act a certificate of arrears sent to the prescribed officer of the court shall be evidence of the facts stated therein.

(7) Subject to subsection (8) below, sums of money payable under a registered order shall be payable in accordance with the order, or such part thereof as the payee may have requested should be enforced, as from the date on which the order took effect.

(8) No sums of money accruing before 1st April 1975 under a registered order shall be payable in accordance with the order.

(9) *Scotland.*

9. Variation and revocation of maintenance order registered in United Kingdom court. (1) Where a registered order has been varied by a court in the Republic of Ireland, the registered order shall, as from the date on which the order of variation took effect or 1st April 1975, whichever is the later, have effect as varied by that order.

(2) Where a registered order has been revoked by a court in the Republic of Ireland, the registered order shall, as from the date on which the order of revocation took effect or 1st April 1975, whichever is the later, be deemed to have ceased to have effect except as respects any arrears due under the registered order at that date.

(3) The prescribed officer of the registering court shall register in the prescribed manner any order varying a registered order.

10. Cancellation of registration and transfer of order. (1) Where a registered order is revoked by an order made by a court in the Republic of Ireland and notice of the revocation is received by the registering court, the prescribed officer of the registering court shall cancel the registration; but any arrears due under the registered order at the date on which the order of revocation took effect or 1st April 1975, whichever is the later, shall continue to be recoverable as if the registration had not been cancelled.

(2) Where the prescribed officer of the registering court is of opinion that the payer under a registered order has ceased to reside within the jurisdiction of that court, he shall cancel the registration of the order and, subject to subsection (3) below, shall send the certified copy of the order to the Lord Chancellor.

(3) Where the prescribed officer of the registering court, being a magistrates' court, is of opinion that the payer is residing within the jurisdiction of another magistrates' court in that part of the United Kingdom in which the registering court is, he shall transfer the order to that other court by sending the certified copy of the order to the prescribed officer of that other court.

(4) On the transfer of an order under subsection (3) above the prescribed officer of the court to which it is transferred shall, subject to subsection (6) below, register the order in the prescribed manner in that court.

(5) Where the certified copy of an order is received by the Lord Chancellor under this section and it appears to him that the payer under the order is still residing in the United Kingdom, he shall transfer the order to the appropriate court by sending the certified copy of the order together with the related documents to the prescribed officer of the appropriate court and, subject to subsection (6) below, that officer shall register the order in the prescribed manner in that court.

(6) Before registering an order in pursuance of subsection (4) or (5) above an officer of a court shall take such steps as he thinks fit for the purpose of ascertaining whether the payer is so residing, and if after taking those steps he is satisfied that the payer is not residing within the jurisdiction of the court he shall send the certified copy of the order to the Lord Chancellor.

(7) The officer of a court who is required by any of the foregoing provisions of this section to send to the Lord Chancellor or to the prescribed officer of another court the certified copy of an order shall send with that copy—

(*a*) a certificate of arrears signed by him;
(*b*) a statement giving such information as he possesses as to the whereabouts of the payer; and
(*c*) any relevant documents in his possession relating to the case.

(8) *Scotland.*

11. Steps to be taken by Lord Chancellor or Secretary of State where payer under certain orders is not residing in the United Kingdom. (1) If it appears to the Lord Chancellor or the Secretary of State that the payer under a maintenance order, a certified copy of which has been received by him from the Republic of Ireland, is not residing in the United Kingdom, he shall send to the responsible authority in that country—

(*a*) the certified copy of the order in question;
(*b*) if the order has at any time been a registered order, a certificate of arrears signed by the prescribed officer;
(*c*) a statement giving such information as the Lord Chancellor or the Secretary of State possesses as to the whereabouts of the payer; and
(*d*) any other relevant documents in his possession relating to the case.

Appeals

6–4985   12. Appeals. (1) No appeal shall lie from a provisional order made in pursuance of section 3 of this Act by a court in England and Wales or Northern Ireland.

(2) Where in pursuance of that section any such court confirms or refuses to confirm such a provisional order, the payer or payee under the order shall have the like right of appeal (if any) from the confirmation of, or refusal to confirm, the provisional order as he would have if that order were not a provisional order and the court had made or, as the case may be, refused to make the order on the occasion on which it confirmed or, as the case may be, refused to confirm the order.

(3) Nothing in subsection (2) shall be construed as affecting any right of appeal conferred by any other enactment.

Evidence

6–4986 13. Admissibility of evidence given in the Republic of Ireland. (1) A statement contained in—

(a) a document, duly authenticated, which purports to set out or summarise evidence given in proceedings in a court in the Republic of Ireland; or

(b) a document, duly authenticated, which purports to set out or summarise evidence taken in that country for the purpose of proceedings in a court in the United Kingdom under this Part of this Act, whether in response to a request made by such a court or otherwise; or

(c) a document, duly authenticated, which purports to have been received in evidence in proceedings in a court in that country or to be a copy of a document so received; or

(d) a document purporting to be signed by a judge or officer of a court in the Republic of Ireland which establishes that certain documents were served on a person,

shall in any proceedings in a court in the United Kingdom relating to a maintenance order to which this Part of this Act applies be admissible as evidence of any facts stated therein to the same extent as oral evidence of that fact is admissible in those proceedings.

(2) A document purporting to set out or summarise evidence given as mentioned in subsection (1)(a) above, or taken as mentioned in subsection (1)(b) above, shall be deemed to be duly authenticated for the purposes of that subsection if the document purports to be certified by the judge or other person before whom the evidence was given or, as the case may be, by whom it was taken, to be the original document containing or recording, or, as the case may be, summarising, that evidence or a true copy of that document.

(3) A document purporting to have been received in evidence as mentioned in subsection (1)(c) above, or to be a copy of a document so received, shall be deemed to be duly authenticated for the purposes of that subsection if the document purports to be certified by a judge or officer of the court in question to have been, or to be a true copy of a document which has been, so received.

(4) It shall not be necessary in any such proceedings to prove the signature or official position of the person appearing to have given such a certificate.

(5) Nothing in this section shall prejudice the admission in evidence of any document which is admissible in evidence apart from this section.

14. Obtaining of evidence needed for purpose of certain proceedings. (1) Where for the purpose of any proceedings in a court in the Republic of Ireland relating to a maintenance order to which this Part of this Act applies a request is made by or on behalf of that court for the taking in the United Kingdom of the evidence of a person residing therein relating to matters specified in the request, such court in the United Kingdom as may be prescribed shall have power to take that evidence and, after giving notice of the time and place at which the evidence is to be taken to such persons and in such manner as it thinks fit, shall take the evidence in such manner as may be prescribed.

Evidence taken in compliance with such a request shall be sent by the prescribed officer of the court—

(a) In England and Wales or Northern Ireland, to the Lord Chancellor, or

(b) in Scotland, to the Secretary of State,

for transmission to the responsible authority in the Republic of Ireland.

(2) Where any person, not being the payer or the payee under the maintenance order to which the proceedings in question relate, is required by virtue of this section to give evidence before a court in the United Kingdom, the court may order that there shall be paid—

(a) if the court is a court in England, Wales or Scotland, out of moneys provided by Parliament; and

(b) if the court is a court in Northern Ireland, out of moneys provided by Parliament,

such sums as appear to the court reasonably sufficient to compensate that person for the expense, trouble or loss of time properly incurred in or incidental to his attendance.

(3) Section 97(1), (3) and (4) of the Magistrates' Courts Act 1980 (which provide for compelling the attendance of witnesses, etc) shall apply in relation to a magistrates' court having power under subsection (1) above to take the evidence of any person as if the proceedings in the court in the Republic of Ireland for the purpose of which a request for the taking of the evidence has been made were proceedings in the magistrates' court and had been begun by complaint.

(4) *Scotland.*

(5) A court in—

(a) England and Wales or Northern Ireland may for the purpose of any proceedings in that court under this Part of this Act relating to a maintenance order to which this Part of this Act applies, send to the Lord Chancellor, or

(b) Scotland may for the purpose of such proceedings in that court relating to such an action, send to the Secretary of State,

for transmission to the responsible authority in the Republic of Ireland a request for a court in the Republic of Ireland to take or provide evidence relating to such matters as may be specified in the request.

(6) *Northern Ireland.*

15. Order, etc made in the Republic of Ireland need not be proved. For the purposes of this Part of this Act, unless the contrary is shown—

(a) any order made by a court in the Republic of Ireland purporting to bear the seal of that court or to be signed by any person in his capacity as a judge or officer of the court, shall be deemed without further proof to have been duly sealed or, as the case may be, to have been signed by that person;

(b) the person by whom the order was signed shall be deemed without further proof to have been a judge or officer, as the case may be, of that court when he signed it and, in the case of an officer, to have been authorised to sign it; and

(c) a document purporting to be a certified copy of an order made by a court in the Republic of Ireland shall be deemed without further proof to be such a copy.

Supplemental

6–4987 16. Payment of sums under orders made in the Republic of Ireland. Payment of sums due under a registered order shall, while the order is registered in a court in England, Wales or Northern Ireland, be made in such manner and to such person as may be prescribed.

17. Proceedings in magistrates' courts. (4) Anything authorised or required by this Part of this Act to be done by, to or before the magistrates' court by, to or before which any other thing was done may be done by, to or before any magistrates' court acting for the same petty sessions area (or, in Northern Ireland, petty sessions district) as that court.

(5) Any application which by virtue of a provision of this Part of this Act is made to a magistrates' court in Northern Ireland shall be made by complaint.

(5A) Where the respondent to an application for the variation or revocation of—

(a) a maintenance order made by a magistrates' court in England and Wales, being an order to which section 5 of this Act applies; or

(b) a registered order which is registered in such a court,

is residing in the Republic of Ireland, a magistrates' court in England and Wales shall have jurisdiction to hear the application (where it would not have had such jurisdiction apart from this subsection) if it would have had jurisdiction to hear it had the respondent been residing in England and Wales.

(6) A magistrates' court in Northern Ireland shall have jurisdiction to hear a complaint for the variation or revocation of a maintenance order made by such a court, being an order to which section 5 of this Act applies, if the defendant to the complaint is residing in the Republic of Ireland and the court would have jurisdiction to hear the complaint had the defendant been residing in Northern Ireland.

(7) Where the respondent to an application for the variation or revocation of a maintenance order made by a magistrates' court, being an order to which section 5 of this Act applies, does not appear at the time and place appointed for the hearing of the application, but the court is satisfied that the respondent is residing in the Republic of Ireland, the court may proceed to hear and determine the application at the time and place appointed for the hearing or for any adjourned hearing in like manner as if the respondent had appeared at that time and place.

(7A) *Northern Ireland.*

18. Magistrates' courts rules. (1) Without prejudice to the generality of the power to make rules under section 144 of the Magistrates' Courts Act 1980 (magistrates' courts rules), provision may be made by such rules with respect to any of the following matters, namely—

(a) the circumstances in which anything authorised or required by this Part of this Act to be done by, to or before a magistrates' court acting for a particular petty sessions area or by, to or before an officer of that court may be done by, to or before a magistrates' court acting for such other petty sessions area as the rules may provide or by, to or before an officer of that court;

(b) the orders made, or other things done, by a magistrates' court, or an officer of such a court, under this Part of this Act, or by a court in the Republic of Ireland, notice of which is to be given to such persons as the rules may provide and the manner in which such notice shall be given;

(c) the cases and manner in which courts in the Republic of Ireland are to be informed of orders made, or other things done, by a magistrates' court under this Part of this Act;

(d) the cases and manner in which a justices' clerk may take evidence needed for the purpose of proceedings in a court in the Republic of Ireland relating to a maintenance order to which this Part of this Act applies;

(e) the circumstances and manner in which cases may be remitted by magistrates' courts to courts in the Republic of Ireland;

(f) the circumstances and manner in which magistrates' courts may for the purposes of this Part of this Act communicate with courts in the Republic of Ireland.

(1A) For the purpose of giving effect to this Part of this Act, rules made under section 144 of the Magistrates' Courts Act 1980 may make, in relation to any proceedings brought under or by virtue of this Part of this Act, any provision not covered by subsection (1) above which—

(a) falls within subsection (2) of section 93 of the Children Act 1989, and

(b) may be made in relation to relevant proceedings under that section.

(2) Rules with respect to the matters mentioned in subsection (1) above may be made in accordance with Article 13 of the Magistrates' Courts (Northern Ireland) Order 1981 in relation to proceedings or matters in magistrates' courts in Northern Ireland under this Part of this Act.

21. Interpretation of Part I. (1) In this Part of this Act—

"affiliation order" means an order (however described) adjudging, finding or declaring a person to be the father of a child, whether or not it also provides for the maintenance of the child;

"the appropriate court", in relation to a person residing in England and Wales or in Northern Ireland means a magistrates' court, and in relation to a person residing in Scotland means the sheriff court, within the jurisdiction of which that person is residing;

"certificate of arrears", in relation to a maintenance order, means a certificate certifying that the sum specified in the certificate is to the best of the information or belief of the officer giving the certificate the amount of the arrears due under the order at the date of the certificate except any arrears due under the order in respect of a period ending before 1st April 1975 or, as the case may be, that to the best of his information or belief there are no arrears due thereunder at the date of the certificate;

"certified copy", in relation to an order of a court, means a copy of the order certified by the proper officer of the court to be a true copy;

"court" includes any tribunal or person having power to make, confirm, enforce, vary or revoke a maintenance order;

"maintenance order" means an order (however described) of any of the following descriptions, that it is to say—

(a) an order (including an affiliation order or order consequent upon an affiliation order) which provides for the periodical payment of sums of money towards the maintenance of any person, being a person whom the person liable to make payments under the order is, according to the law applied in the place where the order was made, liable to maintain;

(aa) an order which has been made in Scotland, on or after the granting of a decree of divorce, for the payment of a periodical allowance by one party to the marriage to the other party; and

(b) an affiliation order or order consequent upon an affiliation order, being an order which provides for the payment by a person adjudged, found or declared to be a child's father of expenses incidental to the child's birth or, where the child has died, of his funeral expenses,

and, in the case of a maintenance order which has been varied, means that order as varied;

"order", as respects Scotland, includes any interlocutor, and any decree or provision contained in an interlocutor;

"payee", in relation to a maintenance order, means the person entitled to the payments for which the order provides;

"payer", in relation to a maintenance order, means the person liable to make payments under the order;

"prescribed", in relation to a magistrates' court in England and Wales or in Northern Ireland, means prescribed by rules made under section 144 of the Magistrates' Courts Act 1980 or by rules made in accordance with Article 13 of the Magistrates' Courts (Northern Ireland) Order 1981, as the case may be, and in relation to any other court means prescribed by rules of court;

"provisional order" means an order made by a court in England and Wales or Northern Ireland which is provisional only and has no effect unless and until confirmed, with or without alteration, by that court;

"registered order" means a maintenance order which is for the time being registered in a court in the United Kingdom under this Part of this Act;

"registering court", in relation to a registered order, means the court in which that order is for the time being registered under this Part of this Act;

"the responsible authority", in relation to the Republic of Ireland, means any person who in that country has functions similar to those of the Lord Chancellor or the Secretary of State under this Part of this Act; and

"revoke" and "revocation" include discharge.

(2) For the purposes of this Part of this Act an order shall be taken to be a maintenance order so far (but only so far) as it relates to the periodical payment of sums of money as mentioned in paragraph (a) of the definition of "maintenance order" in subsection (1) above, to the payment of a periodical allowance as mentioned in paragraph (aa) of that definition, or to the payment by a person adjudged, found or declared to be a child's father of any such expenses as are mentioned in paragraph (b) of that definition.

(3) Any reference in this Part of this Act to the payment of money for the maintenance of a child shall be construed as including a reference to the payment of money for the child's education.

Child Support (Miscellaneous Amendments and Transitional Provisions) Regulations 1994[1]

(SI 1994/227 amended by SI 1995/1045 and 3261, SI 1999/1510 and SI 2003/2779 and by virtue of the Child Support, Pensions and Social Security Act 2000, s 1 and Sch 3)
The text of these regulations is reproduced in the CD Rom version.

Reciprocal Enforcement of Maintenance Orders (United States of America) Order 1995[1]

(SI 1995/2709 amended by SI 2001/410 and SI 2003/776)

6–5021 1. *Citation and commencement.*

1. Made in the exercise of powers conferred by s 40 of the Maintenance Orders (Reciprocal Enforcement) Act 1972, ante.

6–5022 2. In this Order, unless the context otherwise requires—

"the Act" means the Maintenance Orders (Reciprocal Enforcement) Act 1972[2]; and
"specified State" means a State specified in Schedule 1 to this Order.

6–5023 3. The provisions of Part I of the Act shall apply, with the exceptions, adaptations, and modifications specified in Schedule 2 to this Order, to maintenance orders made by courts in the United Kingdom and to maintenance orders made by courts in a specified State, and accordingly Part I of the Act shall, in relation to such orders, have effect as set out in Schedule 3 to this Order.

6–5024

Article 2

SCHEDULE 1
SPECIFIED STATES

Alaska
Arizona
Arkansas
California
Colorado
Connecticut
Delaware
Florida
Georgia, Idaho and Illinois
Indiana
Iowa
Kansas
Kentucky

Louisiana
Maine
Maryland
Massachusetts
Michigan
Minnesota
Missouri
Montana
Nebraska
Nevada
New Jersey
New Mexico
New York
North Carolina
North Dakota
Ohio
Oklahoma
Oregon
Pennsylvania
South Dakota
Tennessee
Texas
Utah
Vermont
Virginia
Washington
West Virginia
Wisconsin
Wyoming

6–5025

Article 3

SCHEDULE 2
MODIFICATIONS TO PART I OF THE ACT[1]

1. Part I of the Maintenance Orders (Reciprocal Enforcement) Act 1972 as modified by Sch 2 of this Order is set out in full in Sch 3, post.

6–5026

Article 3

SCHEDULE 3
PART I OF THE ACT AS MODIFIED BY SCHEDULE 2

Orders made by courts in the United Kingdom

2. Transmission of maintenance order made in United Kingdom for enforcement in specified State.
(1) Subject to subsection (2) below, where the payer under a maintenance order made, whether before, on or after 1st December 1995, by a court in the United Kingdom is residing or has assets in a specified State, the payee under the order may apply for the order to be sent to that State for enforcement.

(2) Subsection (1) above shall not have effect in relation to an order made by virtue of a provision of Part II of this Act as applied to a specified State by the Recovery of Maintenance (United States of America) Order 1993.

(3) Every application under this section shall be made in the prescribed manner to the prescribed officer of the court which made the maintenance order to which the application relates.

(4) If, on an application duly made under this section to the prescribed officer of a court in the United Kingdom, that officer is satisfied that the payer under the maintenance order to which the application relates is residing or has assets in a specified State, the following documents, that is to say—

(a) three certified copies of the maintenance order;
(b) a certificate signed by that officer certifying that the order is enforceable in the United Kingdom;
(c) a certificate of arrears so signed or, in Scotland, signed by the applicant or his solicitor;
(d) a sworn statement signed by the payee giving the following information—

(i) the address of the payee;
(ii) such information as is known as to the whereabouts of the payer; and
(iii) a description, so far as is known, of the nature and location of any assets of the payer available for execution;

(e) a statement giving such information as the officer possesses for facilitating the identification of the payer; and
(f) where available, a photograph of the payer;

shall be sent by that officer, in the case of a court in England and Wales or Northern Ireland, to the Lord Chancellor, or, in the case of a court in Scotland, to the Secretary of State, with a view to their being transmitted by him to the appropriate authority in the specified State if he is satisfied that the statement relating to the whereabouts of the payer and the nature and location of his assets gives sufficient information to justify that being done.

(5) Nothing in this section shall be taken as affecting any jurisdiction of a court in the United Kingdom with respect to a maintenance order to which this section applies, and, subject to section 5 below, any such order may be enforced, varied or revoked accordingly.

5. Variation and revocation of maintenance order made in United Kingdom. (1) This section applies to a maintenance order certified copies of which have been sent in pursuance of section 2 to a specified State for enforcement.

(2) The jurisdiction of a court in the United Kingdom to revoke, revive or vary maintenance order shall be

exercisable notwithstanding that the proceedings for the revocation, revival or variation, as the case may be, of the order are brought by or against a person residing in a specified State.

(3) Where subsection (1) of section 60 of the Magistrates' Courts Act 1980 (revocation, variation, etc. of orders for periodical payment) applies in relation to a maintenance order to which this section applies, that subsection shall have effect as if for the words "by order on complaint" there were substituted "on an application being made, by order".

(4) Where an application is made by the payee to a court in the United Kingdom for the variation or revocation of an order to which this section applies, and the payer is residing in a specified State, the prescribed officer of the court shall—

(a)   in the case of a court in England and Wales or Northern Ireland, send to the Lord Chancellor, or, in the case of a court in Scotland, send to the Secretary of State, notice of the institution of the proceedings, including notice of the substance of the application, with a view to its being transmitted to the appropriate authority in the specified State for service on the payer; and

(b)   give the payer notice in writing of the date fixed for the hearing by sending the notice by post addressed to his last known or usual place of abode.

(5) Where such an application is made—

(a)   the order shall not be varied or revoked unless the document mentioned in subsection (4)(a) above has been served on the payer in accordance with the law for the service of such a document in the specified State;

(b)   the court, in considering whether or not to vary or revoke the order, shall take into account any representations made and any evidence adduced by or on behalf of the payer; and

(c)   a copy of any such representations or evidence shall be served on the payee in the prescribed manner before the hearing.

(6) Where an application is made by the payer to a court in the United Kingdom for the variation or revocation of an order to which this section applies, the prescribed officer of the court shall arrange for the service of notice of institution of the proceedings, including notice of the substance of the application, on the payee.

(7) Where an order to which this section applies is varied or revoked by a court in the United Kingdom the prescribed officer of the court shall send the following documents, that is to say—

(a)   three certified copies of the order of variation or revocation; and

(b)   a written statement, signed by that officer as to whether both the payer and the payee under the order appeared in the proceedings, and, if only the applicant appeared, the original or a certified copy of a document which establishes that notice of the institution of the proceedings had been served on the other party;

in the case of a court in England and Wales or Northern Ireland, to the Lord Chancellor, or, in the case of a court in Scotland, to the Secretary of State, with a view to their being transmitted by him to the appropriate authority in the specified State for registration and enforcement of the order of variation or revocation.

(8) Where a maintenance order to which this section applies has been varied by an order made by a court in the United Kingdom or by a court in a specified State, the maintenance order shall, as from the date on which the order of variation took effect, have effect as varied by that order.

(9) Where a maintenance order to which this section applies has been revoked by an order made by a court in the United Kingdom or by a court in a specified State, the maintenance order shall, as from the date on which the order of revocation took effect, be deemed to have ceased to have effect except in respect of any arrears due under the maintenance order at that date.

(10) Where a maintenance order to which this section applies has been varied or revoked by an order made by a court in a specified State, the prescribed officer of the court shall register the order of variation or revocation in the prescribed manner.

Orders made by courts in specified States

6. Registration in United Kingdom court of maintenance order made in a specified State. (1) This section applies to a maintenance order made, whether before, on or after 1st December 1995, by a court in a specified State.

(2) Where a certified copy of an order to which this section applies is received by the Lord Chancellor or the Secretary of State from the appropriate authority in a specified State, and it appears to him that the payer under the order is residing or has assets in the United Kingdom, he shall send the copy of the order to the prescribed officer of the appropriate court.

(3) Where the prescribed officer of the appropriate court receives from the Lord Chancellor or the Secretary of State a certified copy of an order to which this section applies, he shall, subject to subsection (4) below, register the order in the prescribed manner in that court.

(4) Before registering an order under this section an officer of a court shall take such steps as he thinks fit for the purpose of ascertaining whether the payer under the order is residing or has assets within the jurisdiction of the court, and if after taking those steps he is satisfied that the payer is not residing and has no assets within the jurisdiction of the court he shall return the certified copy of the order to the Lord Chancellor or the Secretary of State, as the case may be, with a statement giving such information as he possesses as to the whereabouts of the payer and the nature and location of his assets.

8. Enforcement of maintenance order registered in United Kingdom court. (1) Subject to subsection (2) below, a registered order may be enforced in the United Kingdom as if it had been made by the registering court and as if that court had had jurisdiction to make it; and proceedings for or with respect to the enforcement of any such order may be taken accordingly.

(2) Subsection (1) above does not apply to an order which is for the time being registered in the High Court under Part I of the Maintenance Orders Act 1958 or to an order which is for the time being registered in the High Court of Justice in Northern Ireland under Part II of the Maintenance and Affiliation Orders Act (Northern Ireland) 1966.

(3) Any person for the time being under an obligation to make payments in pursuance of a registered order shall give notice of any change of address to the appropriate officer of the registering court, and any person failing without reasonable excuse to give such a notice shall be liable on summary conviction to a fine not exceeding **level 2** on the standard scale.

(3A) In subsection (3) above "appropriate officer" means—

(a) in relation to a magistrates' court in England and Wales, the justices' chief executive for the court; and

(b) in relation to a magistrates' court elsewhere, the clerk of the court.

(4) An order which by virtue of this section is enforceable by a magistrates' court shall, subject to the modifications of sections 76 and 93 of the Magistrates' Courts Act 1980 specified in subsections (4A) and (4B) below, and subject to the modifications of Article 98 of the Magistrates' Courts (Northern Ireland) Order 1981 specified in subsection (4C) below, be enforceable as if it were a magistrates' courts maintenance order made by that court.

In this subsection "magistrates' court maintenance order" has the same meaning as in section 150(1) of the Magistrates' Courts Act 1980.

(4A) Section 76 (enforcement of sums adjudged to be paid) shall have effect as if for subsections (4) to (6) there were substituted the following subsections—

"(4) Where proceedings are brought for the enforcement of a magistrates' court maintenance order under this section, the court may vary the order by exercising one of its powers under subsection (5) below.

(5) The powers of the court are—

(a) the power to order that payments under the order be made directly to a justices' chief executive;

(b) the power to order that payments under the order be made a justices' chief executive, by such method of payment falling within section 59(6) above (standing order, etc.) as may be specified;

(c) the power to make an attachment of earnings order under the Attachment of Earnings Act 1971 to secure payments under the order.

(6) In deciding which of the powers under subsection (5) above it is to exercise, the court shall have regard to any representations made by the debtor (within the meaning of section 59 above).

(7) Subsection (4) of section 59 above (power of court to require debtor to open account) shall apply for the purposes of subsection (5) above as it applies for the purposes of that section but as if for paragraph (a) there were substituted—

"(a) the court proposes to exercise its power under paragraph (b) of section 76(5) below, and","

(4B) In section 93 (complaint for arrears)), subsection (6) (court not to impose imprisonment in certain circumstances) shall have effect as if for paragraph (b) there were substituted—

"(b) if the court is of the opinion that it is appropriate—

(i) to make an attachment of earnings order; or

(ii) to exercise its power under paragraph (b) of section 76(5) above."

(4C) Article 98 of the Magistrates' Courts (Northern Ireland) Order 1981 (enforcement of sums adjudged to be paid) shall have effect—

(a) as if for paragraph (7)(a) there were substituted the following paragraph—

"(a) if the court is of the opinion that it is appropriate—

(i) to make an attachment of earnings order; or

(ii) to exercise its power under paragraph (8C)(b)";

(b) as if for paragraphs (8B) to (8D) there were substituted the following paragraphs—

"(8B) Upon the appearance of a person or proof of service of the summons on him as mentioned in paragraph (4) for the enforcement of an order to which this Article applies, the court or resident magistrate may vary the order, by exercising one of the powers under paragraph (8C).

(8C) The powers mentioned in paragraph (8B) are—

(a) the power to order that payments under the order be made directly to the collecting officer;

(b) the power to order that payments under the order be made to the collecting officer, by such method of payment falling within Article 85(7) (standing order, etc.) as may be specified;

(c) the power to make an attachment of earnings order under Part IX to secure payments under the order.

(8D) In deciding which of the powers under paragraph (8C) is to be exercised, the court or, as the case may be, a resident magistrate shall have regard to any representations made by the debtor (within the meaning of Article 85).

(8E) Paragraph (5) of Article 85 (power of court to require debtor to open account) shall apply for the purposes of paragraph (8C) as it applies for the purposes of that Article but as if for sub-paragraph (a) there were substituted—

"(a) the court proposes to exercise its power under sub-paragraph (b) of Article 98(8C), and."

(5) The magistrates' court by which an order is enforceable by virtue of this section, and the officers thereof, shall take all such steps for enforcing or facilitating the enforcement of the order as may be prescribed.

(6) In any proceedings for or with respect to the enforcement of an order which is for the time being registered in any court under this Part of this Act a certificate of arrears sent to the prescribed officer of the court shall be evidence of the facts stated therein.

(7) Sums of money payable under a registered order shall be payable in accordance with the order as from the date on which the order was made.

(9) In the application of this section to Scotland—

(a) subsections (2) to (5) shall be omitted; and

(b) in subsection (6), for the word "evidence" there shall be substituted the words "sufficient evidence".

9. Variation of maintenance order registered in United Kingdom court. (1) Subject to the provisions of this section—

(a) the registering court shall have the like power, on an application made by the payer or payee under a registered order, to vary the order as if it had been made by the registering court and as if that court had had jurisdiction to make it;

(b) the jurisdiction of a magistrates' court to vary a registered order shall be exercisable notwithstanding that proceedings for the variation of the order are brought by or against a person residing in a specified State.

(1ZA) Where the registering court is a magistrates' court in England and Wales, section 60 of the Magistrates' Courts Act 1980 (revocation, variation, etc. of orders for periodical payment) shall have effect in relation to the registered order—

(za) as if in subsection (1) for the words "by order on complaint" there were substituted "on an application being made, by order";
(a) as if in subsection (3) for the words "paragraphs (a) to (d) of section 59(3) above" there were substituted "subsection (3A) below" and after that subsection there were inserted—

"(3A) The powers of the court are—

(a) the power to order that payments under the order be made directly to a justices' chief executive;
(b) the power to order that payments under the order be made to a justices' chief executive, by such method of payment falling within section 59(6) above (standing order, etc.) as may be specified;
(c) the power to make an attachment of earnings order under the Attachment of Earnings Act 1971 to secure payments under the order."
(b) as if in subsection (4) for paragraph (b) there were substituted—

"(b) payments under the order are required to be made to a justices' chief executive, by any method of payment falling within section 59(6) above (standing order, etc.)",

and as if after the words "the court" there were inserted "which made the order";

(c) as if in subsection (5) for the words "to the clerk" there were substituted "in accordance with paragraph (a) of subsection (3A) above";
(d) as if in subsection (7), paragraph (c) and the word "and" immediately preceding it were omitted;
(e) as if in subsection (8) for the words "paragraphs (a) to (d) of section 59 (3) above" there were substituted "subsection (3A) above";
(f) as if for subsections (9) and (10) there were substituted the following subsections—

"(9) In deciding, for the purposes of subsections (3) and (8) above, which of the powers under subsection (3A) above it is to exercise, the court shall have regard to any representations made by the debtor.
(10) Subsection (4) of section 59 above (power of court to require debtor to open account) shall apply for the purposes of subsection (3A) above as it applies for the purposes of that section but as if for paragraph (a) there were substituted—

"(a) the court proposes to exercise its power under paragraph (b) of section 60 (3A) below, and"."

(1ZB) Where the registering court is a court of summary jurisdiction in Northern Ireland, Article 86 of the Magistrates' Courts (Northern Ireland) Order 1981 (revocation, variation, etc. of orders for periodical payment) shall have effect in relation to the registered order—

(a) as if in paragraph (3) for the words "sub-paragraphs (a) to (d) of Article 85(3)" there were substituted "paragraph (3A) and after that paragraph there were inserted—

"(3A) The powers of the court are—

(a) the power to order that payments under the order be made directly to the collecting officer;
(b) the power to order that payments under the order be made to the collecting officer by such method of payment falling within Article 85(7) (standing order, etc.) as may be specified;
(c) the power to make an attachment of earnings order under Part IX to secure payments under the order.";
(b) as if in paragraph (4) for sub-paragraph (b) there were substituted—

"(b) payments under the order are required to be made to the collecting officer by any method of payment falling within Article 85(7) (standing order, etc.)",
and as if after the words "petty sessions" there were inserted "for the petty sessions district for which the court which made the order acts")

(c) as if in paragraph (5) for the words "to the collecting officer" there were substituted "in accordance with sub-paragraph (a) of paragraph (3A)";
(d) as if in paragraph (7), sub-paragraph (c) and the word "and" immediately preceding it were omitted;
(e) as if in paragraph (8) for the words "sub-paragraphs (a) to (d) of Article 85(3)" there were substituted "paragraph (3A)";
(f) as if for paragraphs (9) and (10) there were substituted the following paragraphs—

"(9) In deciding, for the purposes of paragraphs (3) and (8) above, which of the powers under paragraph (3A) it is to exercise, the court shall have regard to any representations made by the debtor.
(10) Paragraph (5) of Article 85 (power of court to require debtor to open account) shall apply for the purposes of paragraph (3A) as it applies for the purposes of that Article but as if for sub-paragraph (a) there were substituted—

"(a) the court proposes to exercise its power under sub-paragraph (b) of Article 86(3A), and"."

(1A) The powers conferred by subsection (1) above are not exercisable in relation to so much of a registered order as provides for the payment of a lump sum.
(1B) The registering court shall not vary a registered order if neither the payer nor the payee under the order is resident in the United Kingdom.
(2) Where an application is made by the payer to a registering court in the United Kingdom for the variation of a registered order, and the payee is residing in a specified State, the prescribed officer of the court shall—

(a) in the case of a court in England and Wales or Northern Ireland, send to the Lord Chancellor, or, in the case of a court in Scotland, send to the Secretary of State, notice of the institution of the proceedings with a view to its being transmitted by him to the appropriate authority in the specified State for service on the payee; and
(b) give the payee notice in writing of the date fixed for the hearing by sending the notice by post addressed to his last known or usual place of abode.

(3) Where such an application is made—

(a) the order shall not be varied unless the document mentioned in paragraph (a) of subsection (2) above has been served on the payee in accordance with the law for the service of such a document in the specified State;

(b) the court, in considering whether or not to make or vary the order, shall take into account any representations made and any evidence adduced by or on behalf of the payee; and

(c) a copy of any such representations and evidence shall be served on the payer by the prescribed officer of the court before the hearing.

(4) Where an application is made by the payee to a registering court in the United Kingdom for the variation of a registered order, and the payer is residing in the United Kingdom, the prescribed officer of the court shall serve the document mentioned in paragraph (a) of subsection (2) above on the payer.

(5) Where a registered order is varied by a registering court in the United Kingdom the prescribed officer of the court shall send the following documents, that is to say—

(a) three certified copies of the order of variation;

(b) a written statement signed by that officer as to whether both the payer and the payee under the order appeared in the proceedings for the variation of the order, and, if only the applicant appeared, the original or a certified copy of a document which establishes that notice of the institution of the proceedings had been served on the other party,

in the case of a court in England and Wales or Northern Ireland, to the Lord Chancellor, or, in the case of a court in Scotland, to the Secretary of State, with a view to their being transmitted by him to the appropriate authority in the specified State.

(6) Where a registered order has been varied by the registering court or by a court in a specified State, the prescribed officer of the registering court shall register the variation order in the prescribed manner.

(7) Where a registered order has been varied by the registering court or by a court in a specified State, the registered order shall, as from the date on which the variation order took effect, have effect as so varied.

10. Cancellation of registration and transfer of order. (1) Where a registered order is revoked by an order made by a court in a specified State and notice of the revocation is received by the registering court, the prescribed officer of the registering court shall cancel the registration; but any arrears due under the registered order at the date on which the order of revocation took effect, shall continue to be recoverable as if the registration had not been cancelled.

(2) Where the prescribed officer of the registering court is of opinion that the payer under a registered order is not residing within the jurisdiction of that court and has no assets within that jurisdiction against which the order can be effectively enforced, he shall cancel the registration of the order and, subject to subsection (3) below, shall send the certified copy of the order to the Lord Chancellor.

(3) Where the prescribed officer of the registering court, being a magistrates' court, is of opinion that the payer is residing or has assets within the jurisdiction of another magistrates' court in that part of the United Kingdom in which the registering court is, he shall transfer the order to that other court by sending the certified copy of the order to the prescribed officer of that other court.

(4) On the transfer of an order under subsection (3) above the prescribed officer of the court to which it is transferred shall, subject to subsection (6) below, register the order in the prescribed manner in that court.

(5) Where the certified copy of an order is received by the Lord Chancellor under this section and it appears to him that the payer under the order is residing or has assets in the United Kingdom, he shall transfer the order to the appropriate court by sending the certified copy of the order together with the related documents to the prescribed officer of the appropriate court and, subject to subsection (6) below, that officer shall register the order in the prescribed manner in that court.

(6) Before registering an order in pursuance of subsection (4) or (5) above an officer of a court shall take such steps as he thinks fit for the purpose of ascertaining whether the payer is residing or has assets within the jurisdiction of the court, and if after taking those steps he is satisfied that the payer is not residing and has no assets within the jurisdiction of the court he shall send the certified copy of the order to the Lord Chancellor.

(7) The officer of a court who is required by any of the foregoing provisions of this section to send to the Lord Chancellor or to the prescribed officer of another court the certified copy of an order shall send with that copy—

(a) a certificate of arrears signed by him or, in Scotland, by the applicant or his solicitor;

(b) a statement giving such information as he possesses as to the whereabouts of the payer and the nature and location of his assets; and

(c) any relevant documents in his possession relating to the case.

(8) In the application of this section to Scotland—

(a) in subsection (2), for the words "within the jurisdiction of that court" there shall be substituted the words "in Scotland";

(b) subsections (3) and (4) shall be omitted; and

(c) for the words "Lord Chancellor", in each place where they occur, there shall be substituted the words "Secretary of State".

11. Steps to be taken by Lord Chancellor or Secretary of State where payer under certain orders is not residing in United Kingdom. (1) If at any time it appears to the Lord Chancellor or the Secretary of State that the payer under a maintenance order, a certified copy of which has been received by him from a specified State, is not residing and has no assets in the United Kingdom, he shall send to the appropriate authority in that State or, if having regard to all the circumstances he thinks it proper to do so, to the appropriate authority in another specified State—

(a) the certified copy of the order in question and a certified copy of any order varying that order;

(b) if the order has at any time been a registered order, a certificate of arrears signed by the prescribed officer or, in Scotland, by the applicant or his solicitor;

(c) a statement giving such information as the Lord Chancellor or the Secretary of State possesses as to the whereabouts of the payer and the nature and location of his assets; and

(d) any other relevant documents in his possession relating to the case.

(2) Where the documents mentioned in subsection (1) are sent to the appropriate authority in a specified

State other than that in which the order in question was made, the Lord Chancellor or the Secretary of State shall inform the appropriate authority in the specified State in which that order was made of what he has done.

Appeals

12. Appeals. (1) Where in pursuance of section 9 a registering court makes, or refuses to make, an order varying a registered order, the payer or the payee under the registered order shall have the like right of appeal (if any) from the order of variation or from the refusal to make it as he would have if the registered order had been made by the registering court.

Evidence

13. Admissibility of evidence given in specified State. (1) A statement contained in—

  (a)   a document, duly authenticated, which purports to set out or summarise evidence given in proceedings in a court in a specified State; or

  (b)   a document, duly authenticated, which purports to set out or summarise evidence taken in such a State for the purpose of proceedings in a court in the United Kingdom under this Part of this Act, whether in response to a request made by such a court or otherwise; or

  (c)   a document, duly authenticated, which purports to have been received in evidence in proceedings in a court in such a State or to be a copy of a document so received.

shall in any proceedings in a court in the United Kingdom relating to a maintenance order to which this Part of this Act applies be admissible as evidence of any fact stated therein to the same extent as oral evidence of that fact is admissible in those proceedings.

(2) A document purporting to set out or summarise evidence given as mentioned in subsection (1)(*a*) above, or taken as mentioned in subsection (1)(*b*) above, shall be deemed to be duly authenticated for the purposes of that subsection if the document purports to be certified by the judge, magistrate or other person before whom the evidence was given, or, as the case may be, by whom it was taken, to be the original document containing or recording, or, as the case may be, summarising, that evidence or a true copy of that document.

(3) A document purporting to have been received in evidence as mentioned in subsection (1)(*c*) above, or to be a copy of a document so received, shall be deemed to be duly authenticated for the purposes of that subsection if the document purports to be certified by a judge, magistrate or other person before whom the evidence was given to have been, or to be a true copy of a document which has been, so received.

(4) It shall not be necessary in any such proceedings to prove the signature or official position of the person appearing to have given such a certificate.

(5) Nothing in this section shall prejudice the admission in evidence of any document which is admissible in evidence apart from this section.

14. Obtaining of evidence needed for purpose of certain proceedings. (1) Where for the purpose of any proceedings in a court in a specified State relating to a maintenance order to which this Part of this Act applies a request is made by or on behalf of that court for the taking in the United Kingdom of the evidence of a person residing therein relating to matters specified in the request, such court in the United Kingdom as may be prescribed shall have power to take that evidence and, after giving notice of the time and place at which the evidence is to be taken to such persons and in such manner as it thinks fit, shall take the evidence in such manner as may be prescribed.

Evidence taken in compliance with such a request shall be sent by the prescribed officer of the court—

  (a)   in England and Wales or Northern Ireland, to the Lord Chancellor; or

  (b)   in Scotland, to the Secretary of State,

for transmission to the appropriate authority in the specified State.

(2) Where any person, not being the payer or the payee under the maintenance order to which the proceedings in question relate, is required by virtue of this section to give evidence before a court in the United Kingdom, the court may order that there shall be paid out of moneys provided by Parliament such sums as appear to the court reasonably sufficient to compensate that person for the expense, trouble or loss of time properly incurred in or incidental to his attendance.

(3) Section 97(1), (3) and (4) of the Magistrates' Courts Act 1980 (which provide for compelling the attendance of witnesses, etc.) shall apply in relation to a magistrates' court having power under subsection (1) above to take the evidence of any person as if the proceedings in the court in a specified State for the purpose of which a request for the taking of the evidence has been made were proceedings in the magistrates' court and had been begun by complaint.

(4) Paragraphs 71 and 73 of Schedule 1 to the Sheriff Courts (Scotland) Act 1907 (which provide for the citation of witnesses, etc) shall apply in relation to a sheriff having power under subsection (1) above to take the evidence of any person as if the proceedings in the court in a specified State for the purpose of which a request for the taking of the evidence has been made were proceedings in the sheriff court.

(5) A court in—

  (a)   England and Wales or Northern Ireland may, for the purpose of any proceedings in that court under this Part of this Act relating to a maintenance order to which this Part of this Act applies, send to the Lord Chancellor; or

  (b)   Scotland may, for the purpose of such proceedings in that court relating to such an order, send to the Secretary of State,

for transmission to the appropriate authority in a specified State a request for a court in that State to take or provide evidence relating to such matters as may be specified in the request.

(6) In the application of this section to Northern Ireland, in subsection (3), for the reference to section 97(1), (3) and (4) of the Magistrates' Courts Act 1980 there shall be substituted a reference to Articles 118(1), (3) and (4), 119 and 120 of the Magistrates' Courts (Northern Ireland) Order 1981.

15. Order etc made in specified State need not be proved. For the purposes of this Part of this Act, unless the contrary is shown—

(a) any order made by a court in a specified State purporting to bear the seal of that court or to be signed by any person in his capacity as a judge, magistrate or officer of the court, shall be deemed without further proof to have been duly sealed or, as the case may be, to have been signed by that person;

(b) the person by whom the order was signed shall be deemed without further proof to have been a judge, magistrate or officer, as the case may be, of that court when he signed it and, in the case of an officer, to have been authorised to sign it; and

(c) a document purporting to be a certified copy of an order made by a court in a specified State shall be deemed without further proof to be such a copy.

Supplemental

16. Payment of sums due under orders made in specified State; conversion of currency. (1) Payment of sums due under a registered order shall, while the order is registered in a court in England, Wales or Northern Ireland, be made in such manner and to such person as may be prescribed.

(2) Where the sums required to be paid under a registered order are expressed in a currency other than the currency of the United Kingdom, then, as from the relevant date, the order shall be treated as if it were an order requiring the payment of such sums in the currency of the United Kingdom as, on the basis of the rate of exchange prevailing at that date, are equivalent to the sums so required to be paid.

(3) Where the sum specified in any statement, being a statement of the amount of any arrears due under a maintenance order made by a court in a specified State, is expressed in a currency other than the currency of the United Kingdom, that sum shall be deemed to be such sum in the currency of the United Kingdom as, on the basis of the rate of exchange prevailing at the relevant date, is equivalent to the sum so specified.

(4) For the purposes of this section a written certificate purporting to be signed by an officer of any bank in the United Kingdom certifying that a specified rate of exchange prevailed between currencies at a specified date and that at such rate a specified sum in the currency of the United Kingdom is equivalent to a specified sum in another specified currency shall be evidence of the rate of exchange so prevailing on that date and of the equivalent sums in terms of the respective currencies.

(5) In this section "the relevant date" means—

(a) in relation to a registered order or to a statement of arrears due under a maintenance order made by a court in a specified State, the date on which the order first becomes a registered order;

(b) in relation to a registered order which has been varied, the date on which the last order varying that order is registered in the registering court.

(6) In the application of this section to Scotland—

(a) subsection (1) shall not apply; and

(b) in subsection (4), for the word "evidence" there shall be substituted the words "sufficient evidence".

17. Proceedings in magistrates' courts. (4) Anything authorised or required by this Part of this Act to be done by, to or before the magistrates' court by, to or before which any other thing was done may be done by, to or before any magistrates' court acting for the same petty sessions area (or, in Northern Ireland, petty sessions district) as that court.

(5) Any application which by virtue of a provision of this Part of this Act is made to a magistrates' court in Northern Ireland shall be made by complaint.

(5A) Where the respondent to an application for the variation or revocation of—

(a) a maintenance order made by a magistrates' court in England and Wales, being an order to which section 5 of this Act applies; or

(b) a registered order which is registered in such a court,

is residing in a specified State, a magistrates' court in England and Wales shall have jurisdiction to hear the application (where it would not have such jurisdiction apart from this subsection) if it would have had jurisdiction to hear it had the respondent been residing in England and Wales.

(6) A magistrates' court in Northern Ireland shall have jurisdiction—

(a) to hear a complaint for the variation or revocation of a maintenance order made by such a court, and to which section 5 of this Act applies; or

(b) to hear a complaint for the variation of a registered order which is registered in that court,

if the defendant to the complaint is residing in a specified State and if the court would have had jurisdiction to hear the complaint had the defendant been residing in Northern Ireland and been served with a summons to appear before the court to answer the complaint.

(7) Where the respondent to an application—

(a) for the variation or revocation of a maintenance order made by a magistrates' court, and to which section 5 of this Act applies; or

(b) for the variation of a registered order registered in a magistrates' court,

does not appear at the time and place appointed for the hearing of the application, but the court is satisfied that the respondent is residing in a specified State, and that the requirements of section 5(4) or (6) or section 9(2) and (4), as the case may be, have been complied with, the court may proceed to hear and determine the application at the time and place appointed for the hearing or for any adjourned hearing as if the respondent had appeared at that time and place.

(7A) In the application of this section to Northern Ireland, in subsection (7)—

(a) for the word "respondent", in each place where it occurs, there shall be substituted "defendant"; and

(b) for the words "an application" and "the application", in each place where they occur, there shall be substituted "a complaint" and "the complaint" respectively.

18. Magistrates' courts rules. (1) Without prejudice to the generality of the power to make rules under section 144 of the Magistrates' Courts Act 1980 (magistrates' courts rules), provision may be made by such rules with respect to any of the following matters namely—

(a) the circumstances in which anything authorised or required by this Part of this Act to be done by, to or before a magistrates' court acting for a particular petty sessions area or by, to or before an officer of that court may be done by, to or before a magistrates' court acting for such other petty sessions area as the rules may provide or by, to or before an officer of that court;

(*b*) the orders made, or other things done, by a magistrates' court, or an officer of such a court, under this Part of this Act, or by a court in a specified State, notice of which is to be given to such persons as the rules may provide and the manner in which such notice shall be given;

(*c*) the cases and manner in which courts in specified States are to be informed of orders made, or other things done, by a magistrates' court under this Part of this Act;

(*d*) the cases and manner in which a justices' clerk may take evidence needed for the purpose of proceedings in a court in a specified State relating to a maintenance order to which this Part of this Act applies;

(*f*) the circumstances and manner in which magistrates' courts may for the purposes of this Part of this Act communicate with courts in specified States.

(1A) For the purpose of giving effect to this Part of this Act, rules made under section 144 of the Magistrates' Courts Act 1980 may make, in relation to any proceedings brought under or by virtue of this Part of this Act, any provision not covered by subsection (1) above which—

(*a*) falls within subsection (2) of section 93 of the Children Act 1980, and

(*b*) may be made in relation to relevant proceedings under that section.

(2) Rules with respect to the matters mentioned in subsection (1) above may be made in accordance with Article 13 of the Magistrates' Courts (Northern Ireland) Order 1981 in relation to proceedings or matters in magistrates' courts in Northern Ireland under this Part of this Act.

19. Rules for sheriff court. Without prejudice to the generality of the powers conferred on the Court of Session by section 32 of the Sheriff Courts (Scotland) Act 1971 to regulate by act of sederunt the procedure of the sheriff court, the said powers shall include power—

(*a*) to prescribe the decrees granted, or other things done, by the sheriff, or an officer of the sheriff court, under this Part of this Act, or by a court in a specified State, notice of which is to be given to such persons as the act of sederunt may provide and the manner in which such notice shall be given;

(*b*) to provide that evidence needed for the purpose of proceedings in a court in a specified State relating to a maintenance order to which this Part of this Act applies may, in such cases and manner as the act of sederunt may provide, be taken by a sheriff clerk or sheriff clerk depute;

(*c*) to prescribe the cases and manner in which courts in specified States are to be informed of decrees granted, or other things done, by the sheriff under this Part of this Act;

(*e*) to prescribe the circumstances and manner in which the sheriff may for the purposes of this Part of this Act communicate with courts in specified States.

21. Interpretation of Part I. (1) In this part of this Act unless the context otherwise requires—

"affiliation order" means an order (however described) adjudging, finding or declaring a person to be the father of a child, whether or not it also provides for the maintenance of the child;

"the appropriate court", in relation to a person residing or having assets in England and Wales or in Northern Ireland means a magistrates' court, and in relation to a person residing or having assets in Scotland means a sheriff court, within the jurisdiction of which that person is residing or has assets;

"certificate of arrears", in relation to a maintenance order, means a certificate certifying that the sum specified in the certificate is to the best of the information or belief of the officer or, in Scotland, the applicant or his solicitor giving the certificate the amount of the arrears due under the order at the date of the certificate or, as the case may be, that to the best of his information or belief there are no arrears due thereunder at that date;

"certified copy", in relation to an order of a court, means a copy of the order certified by the proper officer of the court to be a true copy;

"court" includes any tribunal or person having power to make, confirm, enforce, vary or revoke a maintenance order;

"maintenance order" means an order (however described) of any of the following descriptions, that is to say—

(*a*) an order (including an affiliation order or order consequent upon an affiliation order) which provides for the payment of a lump sum or the making of periodical payments towards the maintenance of any person, being a person whom the person liable to make payments under the order is, according to the law applied in the place where the order was made, liable to maintain;

(*aa*) an order which has been made in Scotland, on or after the granting of a decree of divorce, for the payment of a periodical allowance by one party to the marriage to the other party;

(*b*) an affiliation order or order consequent upon an affiliation order, being an order which provides for the payment by a person adjudged, found or declared to be a child's father of expenses incidental to the child's birth or, where the child has died, of his funeral expenses;

(*c*) an order within the foregoing provisions of this definition made against a payer on the application of a public body which claims reimbursement of sums of money payable under the order with respect to the payee if reimbursement can be obtained by the public body under the law to which it is subject,

and, in the case of a maintenance order which has been varied, means that order as varied;

"order", as respects Scotland, includes any interlocutor, and any decree or provision contained in an interlocutor;

"payee", in relation to a maintenance order, means the person entitled to the payments for which the order provides;

"payer", in relation to a maintenance order, means the person liable to make payments under the order;

"prescribed", in relation to a magistrates' court in England and Wales or in Northern Ireland, means prescribed by rules made under section 144 of the Magistrates' Courts Act 1980 or by rules made in accordance with Article 13 of the Magistrates' Courts (Northern Ireland) Order 1981, as the case may be, and in relation to any other court means prescribed by rules of court;

"registered order" means a maintenance order which is for the time being registered in a court in the United Kingdom under this Part of this Act and "registered" and "registration" shall be construed accordingly;

"registering court", in relation to a registered order, means the court in which that order is for the time being registered under this Part of this Act;

"revoke" and "revocation" include discharge;
"specified State" means a State specified in Schedule 1 to the Reciprocal Enforcement of Maintenance Orders (United State of America) Order 1995.

(3) Any reference in this Part of this Act to the payment of money for the maintenance of a child shall be construed as including a reference to the payment of money for the child's education.

Magistrates' Courts (Reciprocal Enforcement of Maintenance Orders) (United States of America) Rules 1995[1]

(SI 1995/2802)

6–5027 **1.** *Citation and commencement.*

1. Made by the Lord Chancellor in exercise of the powers conferred on him by s 144 of the Magistrates' Courts Act 1980.

Interpretation

6–5028 **2.** In these Rules "the 1980 Rules" means the Magistrates' Courts (Reciprocal Enforcement of Maintenance Orders) (Hague Convention Countries) Rules 1980 and any reference to a rule by number alone shall be construed as a reference to the rule so numbered in the 1980 Rules.

Application of the 1980 Rules

6–5029 **3.** Rules 2 to 12 of and Schedule 1A to the 1980 Rules shall apply in respect of the matters which are to be prescribed under Part I of the Maintenance Orders (Reciprocal Enforcement) Act 1972 as set out in Schedule 3 to the Reciprocal Enforcement of Maintenance Orders (United States of America) Order 1995 as if—

(a) for the reference in rule 2 to the Magistrates' Courts (Reciprocal Enforcement of Maintenance Orders) (Hague Convention Countries) Order 1979 there were substituted a reference to the Magistrates' Courts (Reciprocal Enforcement of Maintenance Orders) (United States of America) Order 1995;

(b) for rule 4(2)(b) there were substituted the following—

"(b) contain a sworn statement signed by the payee giving the following information—

(i) the address of the payee;
(ii) such information as is known as to the whereabouts of the payer; and
(iii) a description, so far as is known, of the nature and location of any assets of the payer available for execution;'';

(c) rules 4A(1)(a) and 4B(2)(a) were omitted;

(d) for the reference to section 5(4)(b) of the Act in rule 6 there were substituted a reference to rule 5(5)(c);

(e) rule 7 were omitted;

(f) for references in rules 4, 9, 11 and 12 to "Hague Convention country", wherever they appear, there were substituted references to "specified State".

Child Support (Maintenance Calculations and Special Cases) Regulations 2000[1]

(SI 2001/155 amended by SI 2002/1204, 2497 and 3019, SI 2003/328, 347, 1195 and 2779, SI 2004/2415 and 3168 (E) and SI 2005/785, 2078, 2929 (W) and 2877)

The text of these regulations is reproduced in the CD Rom version.

Child Support (Variations) Regulations 2000[1]

(SI 2001/156 amended by SI 2002/1204, SI 2003/238, 347 and 2779, SI 2004/2415, SI 2005/785 and 2877)

The text of these regulations is reproduced in the CD Rom version.

Child Support (Maintenance Calculation Procedure) Regulations 2000[1]

(SI 2001/157 as amended by SI 2002/1204, SI 2003/328 and 2779, SI 2004/2415 and SI 2005/785)

The text of these regulations is reproduced in the CD Rom version.

Reciprocal Enforcement of Maintenance Orders (Designation of Reciprocating Countries) Order 2001[1]

(SI 2001/3501)

6–5099F **1.** This Order may be cited as the Reciprocal Enforcement of Maintenance Orders (Designation of Reciprocating Countries) Order 2001 and shall come into force on 10th December 2001.

1. Made under s 1 of the Maintenance Orders (Reciprocal Enforcement) Act 1972.

6–5099G   **2.**   The territory specified in column (1) of the Schedule to this Order is hereby designated as a reciprocating country for the purposes of Part I of the Act as regards maintenance orders of the description specified in respect of that territory in column (2) of the Schedule to this Order.

6–5099H   SCHEDULE
              TERRITORY DESIGNATED AS A RECIPROCATING COUNTRY AND EXTENT OF DESIGNATION

(1) Territory	(2) Description of maintenance orders to which designation extends
Nunavut	Maintenance orders other than— (a) affiliation orders; (b) maintenance orders of the description contained in paragraph (b) of the definition of "maintenance order" in section 21(1) of the Act; and (c) orders obtained by or in favour of a public authority

Council Regulation (EC) No 44/2001 of 22 December 2000 on jurisdiction and the recognition and enforcement of judgments in civil and commercial matters

6–5099HA   THE COUNCIL OF THE EUROPEAN UNION, Having regard to the Treaty establishing the European Community, and in particular Article 61(c) and Article 67(1) thereof,

Having regard to the proposal from the Commission(1), Having regard to the opinion of the European Parliament(2), Having regard to the opinion of the Economic and Social Committee(3), Whereas:

(1) The Community has set itself the objective of maintaining and developing an area of freedom, security and justice, in which the free movement of persons is ensured. In order to establish progressively such an area, the Community should adopt, amongst other things, the measures relating to judicial cooperation in civil matters which are necessary for the sound operation of the internal market.

(2) Certain differences between national rules governing jurisdiction and recognition of judgments hamper the sound operation of the internal market. Provisions to unify the rules of conflict of jurisdiction in civil and commercial matters and to simplify the formalities with a view to rapid and simple recognition and enforcement of judgments from Member States bound by this Regulation are essential.

(3) This area is within the field of judicial cooperation in civil matters within the meaning of Article 65 of the Treaty.

(4) In accordance with the principles of subsidiarity and proportionality as set out in Article 5 of the Treaty, the objectives of this Regulation cannot be sufficiently achieved by the Member States and can therefore be better achieved by the Community. This Regulation confines itself to the minimum required in order to achieve those objectives and does not go beyond what is necessary for that purpose.

(5) On 27 September 1968 the Member States, acting under Article 293, fourth indent, of the Treaty, concluded the Brussels Convention on Jurisdiction and the Enforcement of Judgments in Civil and Commercial Matters, as amended by Conventions on the Accession of the New Member States to that Convention (hereinafter referred to as the "Brussels Convention")(4). On 16 September 1988 Member States and EFTA States concluded the Lugano Convention on Jurisdiction and the Enforcement of Judgments in Civil and Commercial Matters, which is a parallel Convention to the 1968 Brussels Convention. Work has been undertaken for the revision of those Conventions, and the Council has approved the content of the revised texts. Continuity in the results achieved in that revision should be ensured.

(6) In order to attain the objective of free movement of judgments in civil and commercial matters, it is necessary and appropriate that the rules governing jurisdiction and the recognition and enforcement of judgments be governed by a Community legal instrument which is binding and directly applicable.

(7) The scope of this Regulation must cover all the main civil and commercial matters apart from certain well-defined matters.

(8) There must be a link between proceedings to which this Regulation applies and the territory of the Member States bound by this Regulation. Accordingly common rules on jurisdiction should, in principle, apply when the defendant is domiciled in one of those Member States.

(9) A defendant not domiciled in a Member State is in general subject to national rules of jurisdiction applicable in the territory of the Member State of the court seised, and a defendant domiciled in a Member State not bound by this Regulation must remain subject to the Brussels Convention.

(10) For the purposes of the free movement of judgments, judgments given in a Member State

bound by this Regulation should be recognised and enforced in another Member State bound by this Regulation, even if the judgment debtor is domiciled in a third State.

(11) The rules of jurisdiction must be highly predictable and founded on the principle that jurisdiction is generally based on the defendant's domicile and jurisdiction must always be available on this ground save in a few well-defined situations in which the subject-matter of the litigation or the autonomy of the parties warrants a different linking factor. The domicile of a legal person must be defined autonomously so as to make the common rules more transparent and avoid conflicts of jurisdiction.

(12) In addition to the defendant's domicile, there should be alternative grounds of jurisdiction based on a close link between the court and the action or in order to facilitate the sound administration of justice.

(13) In relation to insurance, consumer contracts and employment, the weaker party should be protected by rules of jurisdiction more favourable to his interests than the general rules provide for.

(14) The autonomy of the parties to a contract, other than an insurance, consumer or employment contract, where only limited autonomy to determine the courts having jurisdiction is allowed, must be respected subject to the exclusive grounds of jurisdiction laid down in this Regulation.

(15) In the interests of the harmonious administration of justice it is necessary to minimise the possibility of concurrent proceedings and to ensure that irreconcilable judgments will not be given in two Member States. There must be a clear and effective mechanism for resolving cases of lis pendens and related actions and for obviating problems flowing from national differences as to the determination of the time when a case is regarded as pending. For the purposes of this Regulation that time should be defined autonomously.

(16) Mutual trust in the administration of justice in the Community justifies judgments given in a Member State being recognised automatically without the need for any procedure except in cases of dispute.

(17) By virtue of the same principle of mutual trust, the procedure for making enforceable in one Member State a judgment given in another must be efficient and rapid. To that end, the declaration that a judgment is enforceable should be issued virtually automatically after purely formal checks of the documents supplied, without there being any possibility for the court to raise of its own motion any of the grounds for non-enforcement provided for by this Regulation.

(18) However, respect for the rights of the defence means that the defendant should be able to appeal in an adversarial procedure, against the declaration of enforceability, if he considers one of the grounds for non-enforcement to be present. Redress procedures should also be available to the claimant where his application for a declaration of enforceability has been rejected.

(19) Continuity between the Brussels Convention and this Regulation should be ensured, and transitional provisions should be laid down to that end. The same need for continuity applies as regards the interpretation of the Brussels Convention by the Court of Justice of the European Communities and the 1971 Protocol(5) should remain applicable also to cases already pending when this Regulation enters into force.

(20) The United Kingdom and Ireland, in accordance with Article 3 of the Protocol on the position of the United Kingdom and Ireland annexed to the Treaty on European Union and to the Treaty establishing the European Community, have given notice of their wish to take part in the adoption and application of this Regulation.

(21) Denmark, in accordance with Articles 1 and 2 of the Protocol on the position of Denmark annexed to the Treaty on European Union and to the Treaty establishing the European Community, is not participating in the adoption of this Regulation, and is therefore not bound by it nor subject to its application.

(22) Since the Brussels Convention remains in force in relations between Denmark and the Member States that are bound by this Regulation, both the Convention and the 1971 Protocol continue to apply between Denmark and the Member States bound by this Regulation.

(23) The Brussels Convention also continues to apply to the territories of the Member States which fall within the territorial scope of that Convention and which are excluded from this Regulation pursuant to Article 299 of the Treaty.

(24) Likewise for the sake of consistency, this Regulation should not affect rules governing jurisdiction and the recognition of judgments contained in specific Community instruments.

(25) Respect for international commitments entered into by the Member States means that this Regulation should not affect conventions relating to specific matters to which the Member States are parties.

(26) The necessary flexibility should be provided for in the basic rules of this Regulation in order to take account of the specific procedural rules of certain Member States. Certain provisions of the Protocol annexed to the Brussels Convention should accordingly be incorporated in this Regulation.

(27) In order to allow a harmonious transition in certain areas which were the subject of special provisions in the Protocol annexed to the Brussels Convention, this Regulation lays down, for a transitional period, provisions taking into consideration the specific situation in certain Member States.

(28) No later than five years after entry into force of this Regulation the Commission will present a report on its application and, if need be, submit proposals for adaptations.

(29) The Commission will have to adjust Annexes I to IV on the rules of national jurisdiction,

the courts or competent authorities and redress procedures available on the basis of the amendments forwarded by the Member State concerned; amendments made to Annexes V and VI should be adopted in accordance with Council Decision 1999/468/EC of 28 June 1999 laying down the procedures for the exercise of implementing powers conferred on the Commission(6),
HAS ADOPTED THIS REGULATION:

CHAPTER I
SCOPE

Article 1. 2. The Regulation shall not apply to:

(a) the status or legal capacity of natural persons, rights in property arising out of a matrimonial relationship, wills and succession;

3. In this Regulation, the term "Member State" shall mean Member States with the exception of Denmark.

CHAPTER II
JURISDICTION

Section 1
General provisions

Article 2. 1. Subject to this Regulation, persons domiciled in a Member State shall, whatever their nationality, be sued in the courts of that Member State.

2. Persons who are not nationals of the Member State in which they are domiciled shall be governed by the rules of jurisdiction applicable to nationals of that State.
Article 3. 1. Persons domiciled in a Member State may be sued in the courts of another Member State only by virtue of the rules set out in Sections 2 to 7 of this Chapter.
Article 4. 1. If the defendant is not domiciled in a Member State, the jurisdiction of the courts of each Member State shall, subject to Articles 22 and 23, be determined by the law of that Member State.

2. As against such a defendant, any person domiciled in a Member State may, whatever his nationality, avail himself in that State of the rules of jurisdiction there in force, and in particular those specified in Annex I, in the same way as the nationals of that State.

Section 2
Special jurisdiction

Article 5. 2. In matters relating to maintenance, in the courts for the place where the maintenance creditor is domiciled or habitually resident or, if the matter is ancillary to proceedings concerning the status of a person, in the court which, according to its own law, has jurisdiction to entertain those proceedings, unless that jurisdiction is based solely on the nationality of one of the parties;

CHAPTER III
RECOGNITION AND ENFORCEMENT

Article 32. For the purposes of this Regulation, "judgment" means any judgment given by a court or tribunal of a Member State, whatever the judgment may be called, including a decree, order, decision or writ of execution, as well as the determination of costs or expenses by an officer of the court.

Section 1
Recognition

Article 33. 1. A judgment given in a Member State shall be recognised in the other Member States without any special procedure being required.

2. Any interested party who raises the recognition of a judgment as the principal issue in a dispute may, in accordance with the procedures provided for in Sections 2 and 3 of this Chapter, apply for a decision that the judgment be recognised.

3. If the outcome of proceedings in a court of a Member State depends on the determination of an incidental question of recognition that court shall have jurisdiction over that question.
Article 34. A judgment shall not be recognised:

1. if such recognition is manifestly contrary to public policy in the Member State in which recognition is sought;
2. where it was given in default of appearance, if the defendant was not served with the document which instituted the proceedings or with an equivalent document in sufficient time and in such a way as to enable him to arrange for his defence, unless the defendant failed to commence proceedings to challenge the judgment when it was possible for him to do so;
3. if it is irreconcilable with a judgment given in a dispute between the same parties in the Member State in which recognition is sought;
4. if it is irreconcilable with an earlier judgment given in another Member State or in a third State involving the same cause of action and between the same parties, provided that the earlier judgment fulfils the conditions necessary for its recognition in the Member State addressed.

Article 35.   1. Moreover, a judgment shall not be recognised if it conflicts with Sections 3, 4 or 6 of Chapter II, or in a case provided for in Article 72.

2. In its examination of the grounds of jurisdiction referred to in the foregoing paragraph, the court or authority applied to shall be bound by the findings of fact on which the court of the Member State of origin based its jurisdiction.

3. Subject to the paragraph 1, the jurisdiction of the court of the Member State of origin may not be reviewed. The test of public policy referred to in point 1 of Article 34 may not be applied to the rules relating to jurisdiction.

Article 36.   Under no circumstances may a foreign judgment be reviewed as to its substance.

Article 37.   1. A court of a Member State in which recognition is sought of a judgment given in another Member State may stay the proceedings if an ordinary appeal against the judgment has been lodged.

2. A court of a Member State in which recognition is sought of a judgment given in Ireland or the United Kingdom may stay the proceedings if enforcement is suspended in the State of origin, by reason of an appeal.

SECTION 2
ENFORCEMENT

Article 38.   1. A judgment given in a Member State and enforceable in that State shall be enforced in another Member State when, on the application of any interested party, it has been declared enforceable there.

2. However, in the United Kingdom, such a judgment shall be enforced in England and Wales, in Scotland, or in Northern Ireland when, on the application of any interested party, it has been registered for enforcement in that part of the United Kingdom.

Article 39.   1. The application shall be submitted to the court or competent authority indicated in the list in Annex II.

2. The local jurisdiction shall be determined by reference to the place of domicile of the party against whom enforcement is sought, or to the place of enforcement.

Article 40.   1. The procedure for making the application shall be governed by the law of the Member State in which enforcement is sought.

2. The applicant must give an address for service of process within the area of jurisdiction of the court applied to. However, if the law of the Member State in which enforcement is sought does not provide for the furnishing of such an address, the applicant shall appoint a representative ad litem.

3. The documents referred to in Article 53 shall be attached to the application.

Article 41.   The judgment shall be declared enforceable immediately on completion of the formalities in Article 53 without any review under Articles 34 and 35. The party against whom enforcement is sought shall not at this stage of the proceedings be entitled to make any submissions on the application.

Article 42.   1. The decision on the application for a declaration of enforceability shall forthwith be brought to the notice of the applicant in accordance with the procedure laid down by the law of the Member State in which enforcement is sought.

2. The declaration of enforceability shall be served on the party against whom enforcement is sought, accompanied by the judgment, if not already served on that party.

Article 43.   1. The decision on the application for a declaration of enforceability may be appealed against by either party.

2. The appeal is to be lodged with the court indicated in the list in Annex III.

3. The appeal shall be dealt with in accordance with the rules governing procedure in contradictory matters.

4. If the party against whom enforcement is sought fails to appear before the appellate court in proceedings concerning an appeal brought by the applicant, Article 26(2) to (4) shall apply even where the party against whom enforcement is sought is not domiciled in any of the Member States.

5. An appeal against the declaration of enforceability is to be lodged within one month of service thereof. If the party against whom enforcement is sought is domiciled in a Member State other than that in which the declaration of enforceability was given, the time for appealing shall be two months and shall run from the date of service, either on him in person or at his residence. No extension of time may be granted on account of distance.

Article 44.   The judgment given on the appeal may be contested only by the appeal referred to in Annex IV.

Article 45.   1. The court with which an appeal is lodged under Article 43 or Article 44 shall refuse or revoke a declaration of enforceability only on one of the grounds specified in Articles 34 and 35. It shall give its decision without delay.

2. Under no circumstances may the foreign judgment be reviewed as to its substance.

Article 46.   1. The court with which an appeal is lodged under Article 43 or Article 44 may, on the application of the party against whom enforcement is sought, stay the proceedings if an ordinary appeal has been lodged against the judgment in the Member State of origin or if the time for such an appeal has not yet expired; in the latter case, the court may specify the time within which such an appeal is to be lodged.

2. Where the judgment was given in Ireland or the United Kingdom, any form of appeal

available in the Member State of origin shall be treated as an ordinary appeal for the purposes of paragraph 1.

3. The court may also make enforcement conditional on the provision of such security as it shall determine.

Article 47. 1. When a judgment must be recognised in accordance with this Regulation, nothing shall prevent the applicant from availing himself of provisional, including protective, measures in accordance with the law of the Member State requested without a declaration of enforceability under Article 41 being required.

2. The declaration of enforceability shall carry with it the power to proceed to any protective measures.

3. During the time specified for an appeal pursuant to Article 43(5) against the declaration of enforceability and until any such appeal has been determined, no measures of enforcement may be taken other than protective measures against the property of the party against whom enforcement is sought.

Article 48. 1. Where a foreign judgment has been given in respect of several matters and the declaration of enforceability cannot be given for all of them, the court or competent authority shall give it for one or more of them.

2. An applicant may request a declaration of enforceability limited to parts of a judgment.

Article 49. A foreign judgment which orders a periodic payment by way of a penalty shall be enforceable in the Member State in which enforcement is sought only if the amount of the payment has been finally determined by the courts of the Member State of origin.

Article 50. An applicant who, in the Member State of origin has benefited from complete or partial legal aid or exemption from costs or expenses, shall be entitled, in the procedure provided for in this Section, to benefit from the most favourable legal aid or the most extensive exemption from costs or expenses provided for by the law of the Member State addressed.

Article 51. No security, bond or deposit, however described, shall be required of a party who in one Member State applies for enforcement of a judgment given in another Member State on the ground that he is a foreign national or that he is not domiciled or resident in the State in which enforcement is sought.

Article 52. In proceedings for the issue of a declaration of enforceability, no charge, duty or fee calculated by reference to the value of the matter at issue may be levied in the Member State in which enforcement is sought.

CHAPTER IV
AUTHENTIC INSTRUMENTS AND COURT SETTLEMENTS

Article 57

. 1. A document which has been formally drawn up or registered as an authentic instrument and is enforceable in one Member State shall, in another Member State, be declared enforceable there, on application made in accordance with the procedures provided for in Articles 38, et seq. The court with which an appeal is lodged under Article 43 or Article 44 shall refuse or revoke a declaration of enforceability only if enforcement of the instrument is manifestly contrary to public policy in the Member State addressed.

2. Arrangements relating to maintenance obligations concluded with administrative authorities or authenticated by them shall also be regarded as authentic instruments within the meaning of paragraph 1.

3. The instrument produced must satisfy the conditions necessary to establish its authenticity in the Member State of origin.

4. Section 3 of Chapter III shall apply as appropriate. The competent authority of a Member State where an authentic instrument was drawn up or registered shall issue, at the request of any interested party, a certificate using the standard form in Annex VI to this Regulation.

Article 58. A settlement which has been approved by a court in the course of proceedings and is enforceable in the Member State in which it was concluded shall be enforceable in the State addressed under the same conditions as authentic instruments. The court or competent authority of a Member State where a court settlement was approved shall issue, at the request of any interested party, a certificate using the standard form in Annex V to this Regulation.

CHAPTER V
GENERAL PROVISIONS

Article 59

. 1. In order to determine whether a party is domiciled in the Member State whose courts are seised of a matter, the court shall apply its internal law.

2. If a party is not domiciled in the Member State whose courts are seised of the matter, then, in order to determine whether the party is domiciled in another Member State, the court shall apply the law of that Member State.

CHAPTER VI
TRANSITIONAL PROVISIONS

Article 66

. 1. This Regulation shall apply only to legal proceedings instituted and to documents formally drawn up or registered as authentic instruments after the entry into force thereof.

2. However, if the proceedings in the Member State of origin were instituted before the entry

into force of this Regulation, judgments given after that date shall be recognised and enforced in accordance with Chapter III,

(a) if the proceedings in the Member State of origin were instituted after the entry into force of the Brussels or the Lugano Convention both in the Member State of origin and in the Member State addressed;

(b) in all other cases, if jurisdiction was founded upon rules which accorded with those provided for either in Chapter II or in a convention concluded between the Member State of origin and the Member State addressed which was in force when the proceedings were instituted.

This Regulation is binding in its entirety and directly applicable in the Member States in accordance with the Treaty establishing the European Community.

Done at Brussels, 22 December 2000.

For the Council

The President

C Pierret

_____

(1). OJ C 376, 28.12.1999, p 1.
(2). Opinion delivered on 21 September 2000 (not yet published in the Official Journal).
(3). OJ C 117, 26.4.2000, p 6.
(4). OJ L 299, 31.12.1972, p 32.

OJ L 304, 30.10.1978, p 1.
OJ L 388, 31.12.1982, p 1.
OJ L 285, 3.10.1989, p 1.
OJ C 15, 15.1.1997, p 1.
For a consolidated text, see OJ C 27, 26.1.1998, p 1.
(5). OJ L 204, 2.8.1975, p 28.
OJ L 304, 30.10.1978, p 1.
OJ L 388, 31.12.1982, p 1.
OJ L 285, 3.10.1989, p 1.
OJ C 15, 15.1.1997, p 1. For a consolidated text see OJ C 27, 26.1.1998, p 28.
(6). OJ L 184, 17.7.1999, p 23.

ANNEX II

The courts or competent authorities to which the application referred to in Article 39 may be submitted are the following:

– in Belgium, the "tribunal de première instance" or "rechtbank van eerste aanleg" or "erstinstanzliches Gericht",
– in Germany, the presiding judge of a chamber of the "Landgericht",
– in Greece, the ">ISO_7>ìïîîäëŸò ñûôïäéêâåßï",
– >ISO_1>in Spain, the "Juzgado de Primera Instancia",
– in France, the presiding judge of the "tribunal de grande instance",
– in Ireland, the High Court,
– in Italy, the "Corte d'appello",
– in Luxembourg, the presiding judge of the "tribunal d'arrondissement",
– in the Netherlands, the presiding judge of the "arrondissementsrechtbank";
– in Austria, the "Bezirksgericht",
– in Portugal, the "Tribunal de Comarca",
– in Finland, the "käräjäoikeus/tingsrätt",
– in Sweden, the "Svea hovrätt",
– in the United Kingdom:

(a) in England and Wales, the High Court of Justice, or in the case of a maintenance judgment, the Magistrate's Court on transmission by the Secretary of State;
(b) in Scotland, the Court of Session, or in the case of a maintenance judgment, the Sheriff Court on transmission by the Secretary of State;
(c) in Northern Ireland, the High Court of Justice, or in the case of a maintenance judgment, the Magistrate's Court on transmission by the Secretary of State;
(d) in Gibraltar, the Supreme Court of Gibraltar, or in the case of a maintenance judgment, the Magistrates' Court on transmission by the Attorney General of Gibraltar.

ANNEX III

The courts with which appeals referred to in Article 43(2) may be lodged are the following:

– in Belgium,

(a) as regards appeal by the defendant: the "tribunal de première instance" or "rechtbank van eerste aanleg" or "erstinstanzliches Gericht",
(b) as regards appeal by the applicant: the "Cour d'appel" or "hof van beroep",

– in the Federal Republic of Germany, the "Oberlandesgericht",
– in Greece, the ">ISO_7>Äöâôåßï",
– in Spain, the "Audiencia Provincial",
– in France, the "cour d'appel",

– in Ireland, the High Court,
– in Italy, the "corte d'appellocharacter.",
– in Luxembourg, the "Cour supérieure de Justice" sitting as a court of civil appeal,
– in the Netherlands:

    (a) for the defendant: the "arrondissementsrechtbank",
    (b) for the applicant: the "gerechtshof",

– in Austria, the "Bezirksgericht",
– in Portugal, the "Tribunal de Relação",
– in Finland, the "hovioikeus/hovrätt",
– in Sweden, the "Svea hovrätt",
– in the United Kingdom:

    (a) in England and Wales, the High Court of Justice, or in the case of a maintenance judgment, the Magistrate's Court;
    (b) in Scotland, the Court of Session, or in the case of a maintenance judgment, the Sheriff Court;
    (c) in Northern Ireland, the High Court of Justice, or in the case of a maintenance judgment, the Magistrate's Court;
    (d) in Gibraltar, the Supreme Court of Gibraltar, or in the case of a maintenance judgment, the Magistrates' Court.

Civil Jurisdiction and Judgments (Authentic Instruments and Court Settlements) Order 2001[1]
(SI 2001/3928)

6–5099I   **1.**   (1) This Order may be cited as the Civil Jurisdiction and Judgments (Authentic Instruments and Court Settlements) Order 2001 and shall come into force on 1st March 2002.
(2) In this Order—

"the Act" means the Civil Jurisdiction and Judgments Act 1982;
"the Regulation" means Council Regulation (EC) No 44/2001 of 22nd December 2000 on jurisdiction and the recognition and enforcement of judgments in civil and commercial matters;
"Regulation State" in any provision, in the application of that provision in relation to the Regulation, has the same meaning as "Member State" in the Regulation, that is all Member States except Denmark;
"the 2001 Order" means the Civil Jurisdiction and Judgments Order 2001.

(3) In this Order—

(a) references to authentic instruments and court settlements are references to those instruments and settlements referred to in Chapter IV of the Regulation; and
(b) references to judgments and maintenance orders are references to judgments and maintenance orders to which the Regulation applies.

---

1. Made in exercise of powers conferred by s 2(2) of the European Communities Act 1972.

6–5099J   **2.**   (1) Subject to the modifications specified in paragraphs (2) and (3), paragraphs 1 to 6 of Schedule 1 to the 2001 Order shall apply, as appropriate, to authentic instruments and court settlements which—

(a) do not concern maintenance as if they were judgments,
(b) concern maintenance as if they were maintenance orders.

(2) In the application of paragraph 2(2) of Schedule 1 to the 2001 Order to authentic instruments and court settlements, for the words "as if the judgment had been originally given" there shall be substituted "as if it was a judgment which had been originally given".
(3) In the application of paragraph 3(3) of Schedule 1 to the 2001 Order to authentic instruments and court settlements, for the words "as if the order had been originally made" there shall be substituted the words "as if it was an order which had been originally made".
(4) Paragraph 8 of Schedule 1 to the 2001 Order shall apply to authentic instruments as if they were judgments and in its application—

(a) for sub-paragraph (1)(b) there shall be substituted the following—

    "(b) a certificate obtained in accordance with Article 57 and Annex VI shall be evidence, and in Scotland sufficient evidence, that the authentic instrument is enforceable in the Regulation State of origin."; and
(b) for sub-paragraph (2) there shall be substituted the following—

    "(2) A document purporting to be a copy of an authentic instrument drawn up or registered, and enforceable, in a Regulation State other than the United Kingdom is duly authenticated for the purposes of this paragraph if it purports to be certified to be a true copy of such an instrument by a person duly authorised in that Regulation State to do so.".

(5) Paragraph 8 of Schedule 1 to the 2001 Order shall apply to court settlements as if they were judgments and in its application for "Article 54" there shall be substituted "Article 58".

6–5099K   **3.**   The disapplication of section 18 of the Act (enforcement of United Kingdom judgments in other parts of the United Kingdom) by section 18(7) will extend to authentic instruments and court settlements enforceable in a Regulation State outside the United Kingdom which will fall to be treated for the purposes of their enforcement as judgments of a court of law in the United Kingdom by virtue of registration under the Regulation.

6–5099I   **4.**   Section 48 of the Act (matters for which rules of court may provide) will apply to authentic instruments and court settlements as if they were judgments or maintenance orders, as appropriate, to which the Regulation applies.

Civil Jurisdiction and Judgments Order 2001[1]
(SI 2001/3929)

6–5099M   **1. Citation and commencement.**   This Order may be cited as the Civil Jurisdiction and Judgments Order 2001 and shall come into force—

     (*a*)   as to articles 1 and 2, paragraphs 1(a), 1(b)(ii) and 17 of Schedule 2 and, so far as it relates to those paragraphs, article 4, on 25th January 2002; and

     (*b*)   as to the remainder of this Order, on 1st March 2002.

---

1. Made under s 2(2) of the European Communities Act 1972.

6–5099N   **2. Interpretation.**   (1) In this Order—

"the Act" means the Civil Jurisdiction and Judgments Act 1982;

"the Regulation" means Council Regulation (EC) No 44/2001 of 22nd December 2000 on jurisdiction and the recognition and enforcement of judgments in civil and commercial matters;

"Regulation State" in any provision, in the application of that provision in relation to the Regulation, has the same meaning as "Member State" in the Regulation, that is all Member States except Denmark.

(2) In Schedule 2 to this Order, a section, Part, Schedule or paragraph referred to by number alone is a reference to the section, Part, Schedule or paragraph so numbered in the Act.

6–5099O   **3. The Regulation.**   Schedule 1 to this Order (which applies certain provisions of the Act with modifications for the purposes of the Regulation) shall have effect.

6–5099P   **4. Amendments to the Civil Jurisdiction and Judgments Act 1982.**   Schedule 2 to this Order (which makes amendments to the Act) shall have effect.

6–5099Q   **5. Consequential amendments.**   Schedule 3 to this Order (which makes consequential amendments) shall have effect.

6–5099R   **6. Transitional provisions.**   (1) Where proceedings are begun before 1st March 2002 in any part of the United Kingdom on the basis of jurisdiction determined in accordance with section 16 of, and Schedule 4 to, the Act, the proceedings may be continued as if the amendments made by paragraphs 3 and 4 of Schedule 2 to this Order had not been made and those amendments shall not apply in respect of any proceedings begun before that date.

(2) Where proceedings are begun before 1st March 2002 in any court in Scotland on the basis of jurisdiction determined in accordance with section 20 of, and Schedule 8 to, the Act, the proceedings may be continued as if the amendments made by paragraphs 6 and 7 of Schedule 2 to this Order had not been made and those amendments shall not apply in respect of any proceedings begun before that date.

Article 3   SCHEDULE 1
                            THE REGULATION

6–5099S

1   Interpretation
(1) In this Schedule—

"court", without more, includes a tribunal;

"judgment" has the meaning given by Article 32 of the Regulation;

"magistrates' court", in relation to Northern Ireland, means a court of summary jurisdiction;

"maintenance order" means a maintenance judgment within the meaning of the Regulation;

"part of the United Kingdom" means England and Wales, Scotland or Northern Ireland;

"payer", in relation to a maintenance order, means the person liable to make the payments for which the order provides;

''prescribed'' means prescribed by rules of court.

(2) In this Schedule, any reference to a numbered Article or Annex is a reference to the Article or Annex so numbered in the Regulation, and any reference to a sub-division of a numbered Article shall be construed accordingly.

(3) References in paragraphs 2 to 8 to a judgment registered under the Regulation include, to the extent of its registration, references to a judgment so registered to a limited extent only.

(4) Anything authorised or required by the Regulation or paragraphs 2 to 8 to be done by, to or before a particular magistrates' court may be done by, to or before any magistrates' court acting for the same petty sessions area (or, in Northern Ireland, petty sessions district) as that court.

2. Enforcement of judgments other than maintenance orders (section 4). (1) Where a judgment is registered under the Regulation, the reasonable costs or expenses of and incidental to its registration shall be recoverable as if they were sums recoverable under the judgment.

(2) A judgment registered under the Regulation shall, for the purposes of its enforcement, be of the same force and effect, the registering court shall have in relation to its enforcement the same powers, and proceedings for or with respect to its enforcement may be taken, as if the judgment had been originally given by the registering court and had (where relevant) been entered.

(3) Sub-paragraph (2) is subject to Article 47 (restriction on enforcement where appeal pending or time for appeal unexpired), to paragraph 5 and to any provision made by rules of court as to the manner in which and conditions subject to which a judgment registered under the Regulation may be enforced.

3. Recognition and enforcement of maintenance orders (section 5). (1) The Secretary of State's function (under Article 39 and Annex II) of transmitting an application for the recognition or enforcement in the United Kingdom of a maintenance order (made under Article 38) to a magistrates' court shall be discharged—

(*a*) as respects England and Wales and Northern Ireland, by the Lord Chancellor;
(*b*) as respects Scotland, by the Scottish Ministers.

(2) Such an application shall be determined in the first instance by the prescribed officer of the court having jurisdiction in the matter.

(3) A maintenance order registered under the Regulation shall, for the purposes of its enforcement, be of the same force and effect, the registering court shall have in relation to its enforcement the same powers, and proceedings for or with respect to its enforcement may be taken, as if the order had been originally made by the registering court.

(4) Sub-paragraph (3) is subject to Article 47 (restriction on enforcement where appeal pending or time for appeal unexpired), to paragraph 5 and to any provision made by rules of court as to the manner in which and conditions subject to which an order registered under the Regulation may be enforced.

(5) A maintenance order which by virtue of the Regulation is enforceable by a magistrates' court in England and Wales shall, subject to the modifications of sections 76 and 93 of the Magistrates' Courts Act 1980 specified in sections 5(5B) and 5(5C) of the Act, be enforceable in the same manner as a magistrates' court maintenance order made by that court.

In this sub-paragraph ''magistrates' court maintenance order'' has the same meaning as in section 150(1) of the Magistrates' Courts Act 1980.

(6) A maintenance order which by virtue of the Regulation is enforceable by a magistrates' court in Northern Ireland shall, subject to the modifications of Article 98 of the Magistrates' Courts (Northern Ireland) Order 1981 specified in section 5(6A) of the Act, be enforceable as an order made by that court to which that Article applies.

(7) The payer under a maintenance order registered under the Regulation in a magistrates' court in England and Wales or Northern Ireland shall give notice of any changes of address to the proper officer of that court.

A person who without reasonable excuse fails to comply with this sub-paragraph shall be guilty of an offence and liable on summary conviction to a fine not exceeding level 2 on the standard scale.

(8) In sub-paragraph (7) ''proper officer'' means—

(*a*) in relation to a magistrates' court in England and Wales, the justices' chief executive for the court; and
(*b*) in relation to a magistrates' court in Northern Ireland, the clerk of the court.

4. Appeals under Article 44 and Annex IV (section 6). (1) The single further appeal on a point of law referred to under Article 44 and Annex IV in relation to the recognition or enforcement of a judgment other than a maintenance order lies—

(*a*) in England and Wales or Northern Ireland, to the Court of Appeal or to the House of Lords in accordance with Part II of the Administration of Justice Act 1969 (appeals direct from the High Court to the House of Lords);
(*b*) in Scotland, to the Inner House of the Court of Session.

(2) Paragraph (*a*) of sub-paragraph (1) has effect notwithstanding section 15(2) of the Administration of Justice Act 1969 (exclusion of direct appeal to the House of Lords in cases where no appeal to that House lies from a decision of the Court of Appeal).

(3) The single further appeal on a point of law referred to in Article 44 and Annex IV in relation to the recognition or enforcement of a maintenance order lies—

(*a*) in England and Wales, to the High Court by way of case stated in accordance with section 111 of the Magistrates' Courts Act 1980;
(*b*) in Scotland, to the Inner House of the Court of Session;
(*c*) in Northern Ireland, to the Court of Appeal.

5. Interest on registered judgments (section 7). (1) Subject to sub-paragraph (3), where in connection with an application for registration of a judgment under the Regulation the applicant shows—

(*a*) that the judgment provides for the payment of a sum of money; and
(*b*) that in accordance with the law of the Regulation State in which the judgment was given interest on that sum is recoverable under the judgment from a particular date or time,

the rate of interest and the date or time from which it is so recoverable shall be registered with the judgment and, subject to rules of court, the debt resulting, apart from paragraph 2(1), from the registration of the judgment shall carry interest in accordance with the registered particulars.

(2) Costs or expenses recoverable by virtue of paragraph 2(1) shall carry interest as if they were the subject of an order for the payment of costs or expenses made by the registering court on the date of registration.

(3) Interest on arrears of sums payable under a maintenance order registered under the Regulation in a magistrates' court in England and Wales or Northern Ireland shall not be recoverable in that court, but without prejudice to the operation in relation to any such order of section 2A of the Maintenance Orders Act 1958 or section 11A of the Maintenance and Affiliation Orders Act (Northern Ireland) 1966 (which enable interest to be recovered if the order is re-registered for enforcement in the High Court).

(4) Except as mentioned in sub-paragraph (3), debts under judgments registered under the Regulation shall carry interest only as provided by this paragraph.

6. Currency of payment under registered maintenance orders (section 8). (1) Sums payable in the United Kingdom under a maintenance order by virtue of its registration under the Regulation, including any arrears so payable, shall be paid in the currency of the United Kingdom.

(2) Where the order is expressed in any other currency, the amounts shall be converted on the basis of the exchange rate prevailing on the date of registration of the order.

(3) For the purposes of this paragraph, a written certificate purporting to be signed by an officer of any bank in the United Kingdom and stating the exchange rate prevailing on a specified date shall be evidence, and in Scotland sufficient evidence, of the facts stated.

7. Allocation within United Kingdom of jurisdiction with respect to trusts and consumer contracts (section 10). (1) The provisions of this paragraph have effect for the purpose of allocating within the United Kingdom jurisdiction in certain proceedings in respect of which the Regulation confers jurisdiction on the courts of the United Kingdom generally and to which section 16 of the Act does not apply.

(2) Any proceedings which by virtue of Article 5(6) (trusts) are brought in the United Kingdom shall be brought in the courts of the part of the United Kingdom in which the trust is domiciled.

(3) Any proceedings which by virtue of the Article 16(1) (consumer contracts) are brought in the United Kingdom by a consumer on the ground that he is himself domiciled there shall be brought in the courts of the part of the United Kingdom in which he is domiciled.

8. Proof and admissibility of certain judgments and related documents (section 11). (1) For the purposes of the Regulation—

  (a) a document, duly authenticated, which purports to be a copy of a judgment given by a court of a Regulation State other than the United Kingdom shall without further proof be deemed to be a true copy, unless the contrary is shown; and

  (b) a certificate obtained in accordance with Article 54 and Annex V shall be evidence, and in Scotland sufficient evidence, that the judgment is enforceable in the Regulation State of origin.

(2) A document purporting to be a copy of a judgment given by any such court as is mentioned in sub-paragraph (1)(a) is duly authenticated for the purposes of this paragraph if it purports—

  (a) to bear the seal of that court; or

  (b) to be certified by any person in his capacity as a judge or officer of that court to be a true copy of a judgment given by that court.

(3) Nothing in this paragraph shall prejudice the admission in evidence of any document which is admissible apart from this paragraph.

9. Domicile of individuals (section 41). (1) Subject to Article 59 (which contains provisions for determining whether a party is domiciled in a Regulation State), the following provisions of this paragraph determine, for the purposes of the Regulation, whether an individual is domiciled in the United Kingdom or in a particular part of, or place in, the United Kingdom or in a state other than a Regulation State.

(2) An individual is domiciled in the United Kingdom if and only if—

  (a) he is resident in the United Kingdom; and

  (b) the nature and circumstances of his residence indicate that he has a substantial connection with the United Kingdom.

(3) Subject to sub-paragraph (5), an individual is domiciled in a particular part of the United Kingdom if and only if—

  (a) he is resident in that part; and

  (b) the nature and circumstances of his residence indicate that he has a substantial connection with that part.

(4) An individual is domiciled in a particular place in the United Kingdom if and only if he—

  (a) is domiciled in the part of the United Kingdom in which that place is situated; and

  (b) is resident in that place.

(5) An individual who is domiciled in the United Kingdom but in whose case the requirements of sub-paragraph (3)(b) are not satisfied in relation to any particular part of the United Kingdom shall be treated as domiciled in the part of the United Kingdom in which he is resident.

(6) In the case of an individual who—

  (a) is resident in the United Kingdom, or in a particular part of the United Kingdom; and

  (b) has been so resident for the last three months or more,

the requirements of sub-paragraph (2)(b) or, as the case may be, sub-paragraph (3)(b) shall be presumed to be fulfilled unless the contrary is proved.

(7) An individual is domiciled in a state other than a Regulation State if and only if—

  (a) he is resident in that state; and

  (b) the nature and circumstances of his residence indicate that he has a substantial connection with that state.

10. *Seat of company, or other legal person or association for purposes of Article 22(2) (section 43)*

11. *Persons deemed to be domiciled in the United Kingdom for certain purposes (section 44)*

12. *Domicile of trusts (section 45)*

Article 4

SCHEDULE 2
AMENDMENTS TO THE CIVIL JURISDICTION AND JUDGMENTS ACT 1982

6–5099T

PART I—
IMPLEMENTATION OF THE CONVENTIONS

PART II—
JURISDICTION, AND RECOGNITION AND ENFORCEMENT OF JUDGMENTS, WITHIN THE UNITED KINGDOM

4. For Schedule 4 (Title II of 1968 Convention as modified for allocation of jurisdiction within UK) substitute—

"SCHEDULE 4
CHAPTER II OF THE REGULATION AS MODIFIED: RULES FOR ALLOCATION OF JURISDICTION WITHIN UK

General

1. Subject to the rules of this Schedule, persons domiciled in a part of the United Kingdom shall be sued in the courts of that part.

2. Persons domiciled in a part of the United Kingdom may be sued in the courts of another part of the United Kingdom only by virtue of rules 3 to 13 of this Schedule.

Special jurisdiction

3. A person domiciled in a part of the United Kingdom may, in another part of the United Kingdom, be sued—

(a) in matters relating to a contract, in the courts for the place of performance of the obligation in question;

(b) in matters relating to maintenance, in the courts for the place where the maintenance creditor is domiciled or habitually resident or, if the matter is ancillary to proceedings concerning the status of a person, in the court which, according to its own law, has jurisdiction to entertain those proceedings, unless that jurisdiction is based solely on the nationality of one of the parties;

(c) in matters relating to tort, delict or quasi-delict, in the courts for the place where the harmful event occurred or may occur;

(d) as regards a civil claim for damages or restitution which is based on an act giving rise to criminal proceedings, in the court seised of those proceedings, to the extent that that court has jurisdiction under its own law to entertain civil proceedings;

(e) as regards a dispute arising out of the operations of a branch, agency or other establishment, in the courts for the place in which the branch, agency or other establishment is situated;

(f) as settlor, trustee or beneficiary of a trust created by the operation of a statute, or by a written instrument, or created orally and evidenced in writing, in the courts of the part of the United Kingdom in which the trust is domiciled;

(g) as regards a dispute concerning the payment of remuneration claimed in respect of the salvage of a cargo or freight, in the court under the authority of which the cargo or freight in question—

(i) has been arrested to secure such payment; or
(ii) could have been so arrested, but bail or other security has been given;

provided that this provision shall apply only if it is claimed that the defendant has an interest in the cargo or freight or had such an interest at the time of salvage;

(h) in proceedings—

(i) concerning a debt secured on immovable property; or
(ii) which are brought to assert, declare or determine proprietary or possessory rights, or rights of security, in or over movable property, or to obtain authority to dispose of movable property,

in the courts of the part of the United Kingdom in which the property is situated.

4. Proceedings which have as their object a decision of an organ of a company or other legal person or of an association of natural or legal persons may, without prejudice to the other provisions of this Schedule, be brought in the courts of the part of the United Kingdom in which that company, legal person or association has its seat.

5. A person domiciled in a part of the United Kingdom may, in another part of the United Kingdom, also be sued—

(a) where he is one of a number of defendants, in the courts for the place where any one of them is domiciled, provided the claims are so closely connected that it is expedient to hear and determine them together to avoid the risk of irreconcilable judgments resulting from separate proceedings;

(b) as a third party in an action on a warranty or guarantee or in any other third party proceedings, in the court seised of the original proceedings, unless these were instituted solely with the object of removing him from the jurisdiction of the court which would be competent in his case;

(c) on a counter-claim arising from the same contract or facts on which the original claim was based, in the court in which the original claim is pending;

(d) in matters relating to a contract, if the action may be combined with an action against the same defendant in matters relating to rights in rem in immovable property, in the court of the part of the United Kingdom in which the property is situated.

6. Where by virtue of this Schedule a court of a part of the United Kingdom has jurisdiction in actions relating to liability arising from the use or operation of a ship, that court, or any other court substituted for this purpose by the internal law of that part, shall also have jurisdiction over claims for limitation of such liability.

Jurisdiction over consumer contracts

7. (1) In matters relating to a contract concluded by a person, the consumer, for a purpose which can be regarded as being outside his trade or profession, jurisdiction shall be determined by this rule and rules 8 and 9, without prejudice to rule 3(e) and (h)(ii), if—

(a) it is a contract for the sale of goods on instalment credit terms; or
(b) it is a contract for a loan repayable by instalments, or for any other form of credit, made to finance the sale of goods; or
(c) in all other cases, the contract has been concluded with a person who pursues commercial or professional activities in the part of the United Kingdom in which the consumer is domiciled or, by any means, directs such activities to that part or to other parts of the United Kingdom including that part, and the contract falls within the scope of such activities.

(2) This rule shall not apply to a contract of transport other than a contract which, for an inclusive price, provides for a combination of travel and accommodation, or to a contract of insurance.

8. (1) A consumer may bring proceedings against the other party to a contract either in the courts of the part of the United Kingdom in which that party is domiciled or in the courts of the part of the United Kingdom in which the consumer is domiciled.

(2) Proceedings may be brought against a consumer by the other party to the contract only in the courts of the part of the United Kingdom in which the consumer is domiciled.

(3) The provisions of this rule shall not affect the right to bring a counter-claim in the court in which, in accordance with this rule and rules 7 and 9, the original claim is pending.

9. The provisions of rules 7 and 8 may be departed from only by an agreement—

(a) which is entered into after the dispute has arisen; or
(b) which allows the consumer to bring proceedings in courts other than those indicated in those rules; or
(c) which is entered into by the consumer and the other party to the contract, both of whom are at the time of conclusion of the contract domiciled or habitually resident in the same part of the United Kingdom, and which confers jurisdiction on the courts of that part, provided that such an agreement is not contrary to the law of that part.

Jurisdiction over individual contracts of employment

10. (1) In matters relating to individual contracts of employment, jurisdiction shall be determined by this rule, without prejudice to rule 3(e).

(2) An employer may be sued—

(a) in the courts of the part of the United Kingdom in which he is domiciled; or
(b) in the courts of the part of the United Kingdom where the employee habitually carries out his work or in the courts of that part where he last did so; or
(c) if the employee does not or did not habitually carry out his work in any one place, in the courts of the part of the United Kingdom where the business which engaged the employee is or was situated.

(3) An employer may bring proceedings only in the courts of the part of the United Kingdom in which the employee is domiciled.

(4) The provisions of this rule shall not affect the right to bring a counter-claim in the court in which, in accordance with this rule, the original claim is pending.

(5) The provisions of this rule may be departed from only by an agreement on jurisdiction—

(a) which is entered into after the dispute has arisen; or
(b) which allows the employee to bring proceedings in courts other than those indicated in this rule.

Exclusive jurisdiction

11. The following courts shall have exclusive jurisdiction, regardless of domicile:—

(a)

(i) in proceedings which have as their object rights *in rem* in immovable property or tenancies of immovable property, the courts of the part of the United Kingdom in which the property is situated;
(ii) however, in proceedings which have as their object tenancies of immovable property concluded for temporary private use for a maximum period of six consecutive months, the courts of the part of the United Kingdom in which the defendant is domiciled shall also have jurisdiction, provided that the tenant is a natural person and that the landlord and the tenant are domiciled in the same part of the United Kingdom;

(b) in proceedings which have as their object the validity of the constitution, the nullity or the dissolution of companies or other legal persons or associations of natural or legal persons, the courts of the part of the United Kingdom in which the company, legal person or association has its seat;
(c) in proceedings which have as their object the validity of entries in public registers, the courts of the part of the United Kingdom in which the register is kept;
(d) in proceedings concerned with the enforcement of judgments, the courts of the part of the United Kingdom in which the judgment has been or is to be enforced.

Prorogation of jurisdiction

12. (1) If the parties have agreed that a court or the courts of a part of the United Kingdom are to have jurisdiction to settle any disputes which have arisen or which may arise in connection with a particular legal relationship, and, apart from this Schedule, the agreement would be effective to confer jurisdiction under the law of that part, that court or those courts shall have jurisdiction.

(2) The court or courts of a part of the United Kingdom on which a trust instrument has conferred jurisdiction shall have jurisdiction in any proceedings brought against a settlor, trustee or beneficiary, if relations between these persons or their rights or obligations under the trust are involved.

(3) Agreements or provisions of a trust instrument conferring jurisdiction shall have no legal force if they

are contrary to the provisions of rule 9, or if the courts whose jurisdiction they purport to exclude have exclusive jurisdiction by virtue of rule 11.

13. (1) Apart from jurisdiction derived from other provisions of this Schedule, a court of a part of the United Kingdom before which a defendant enters an appearance shall have jurisdiction.

(2) This rule shall not apply where appearance was entered to contest the jurisdiction, or where another court has exclusive jurisdiction by virtue of rule 11.

Examination as to jurisdiction and admissibility

14. Where a court of a part of the United Kingdom is seised of a claim which is principally concerned with a matter over which the courts of another part of the United Kingdom have exclusive jurisdiction by virtue of rule 11, it shall declare of its own motion that it has no jurisdiction.

15. (1) Where a defendant domiciled in one part of the United Kingdom is sued in a court of another part of the United Kingdom and does not enter an appearance, the court shall declare of its own motion that it has no jurisdiction unless its jurisdiction is derived from the provisions of this Schedule.

(2) The court shall stay the proceedings so long as it is not shown that the defendant has been able to receive the document instituting the proceedings or an equivalent document in sufficient time to enable him to arrange for his defence, or that all necessary steps have been taken to this end.

Provisional, including protective, measures

16. Application may be made to the courts of a part of the United Kingdom for such provisional, including protective, measures as may be available under the law of that part, even if, under this Schedule, the courts of another part of the United Kingdom have jurisdiction as to the substance of the matter.".

PART III—
JURISDICTION IN SCOTLAND

PART IV—
MISCELLANEOUS PROVISIONS

PART V—
SUPPLEMENTARY AND GENERAL PROVISIONS

Reciprocal Enforcement of Maintenance Orders (Designation of Reciprocating Countries) Order 2002[1]
(SI 2002/788)

6-5100 1. This Order may be cited as the Reciprocal Enforcement of Maintenance Orders (Designation of Reciprocating Countries) Order 2002 and shall come into force on 28th May 2002.

---

1. Made under s 1 of the Maintenance Orders (Reciprocal Enforcement) Act 1972.

6-5100A 2. In this Order—

(a) "the 1920 Act" means the Maintenance Orders (Facilities for Enforcement) Act 1920;
(b) "the 1972 Act" means the Maintenance Orders (Reciprocal Enforcement) Act 1972;
(c) "column (1)" and "column (2)" mean respectively columns (1) and (2) of the Schedule to this Order.

6-5100B 3. The Country and the territory specified in column (1) is hereby designated as a reciprocating country for the purposes of Part I of the 1972 Act as regards maintenance orders of the description specified in respect of that Country or that territory in column (2).

6-5100C 4. (1) In this Article—

(a) "commencement date" means the date on which this Order comes into force;
(b) "registered" means registered in the High Court or the High Court of Justice in Northern Ireland under section 1 of the 1920 Act;
(c) "relevant maintenance order" means an order, other than an order of affiliation, for the periodic payments of sums of money.

(2) Paragraph (3) shall apply if—

(a) a relevant maintenance order is transmitted under section 2 or 3 of the 1920 Act to the Country or the territory specified in column (1); and
(b) immediately before the commencement date the 1920 Act applied to that order.

(3) Where this paragraph applies, sections 5, 12 to 15, 17, 18 and 21 of the 1972 Act shall apply in relation to a relevant maintenance order referred to in paragraph (1), as they apply in relation to a maintenance order of the same description—

(a) sent to the Country or territory specified in column (1) pursuant to section 2 of the 1972 Act;
(b) made under section 3 or 4 of the 1972 Act; and

(c) confirmed by a competent court in that Country or territory.

(4) Paragraph (5) shall apply if—

(a) a relevant maintenance order is transmitted under section 2 or 3 of the 1920 Act to the Country or territory specified in column (1); and

(b) immediately before the commencement date—

   (i) the 1920 Act applied to that order; and
   (ii) the order was not registered.

(5) Where this paragraph applies, sections 8 to 21 of the 1972 Act shall apply in relation to a relevant maintenance order referred to under paragraph (1), as they apply in relation to a maintenance order of the same description made under the 1972 Act which is so registered.

(6) Paragraph (7) shall apply if—

(a) a relevant maintenance order has been confirmed by a court in England, Wales or Northern Ireland under section 4 of the 1920 Act; and

(b) is in force immediately before the commencement date.

(7) Where this paragraph applies, a relevant maintenance order as referred to under paragraph (1) shall be registered under section 7(5) of the 1972 Act in the same manner as if it had been confirmed by that court in England, Wales or Northern Ireland under subsection (2) of that section.

(8) Any proceedings brought under or by virtue of any provision of the 1920 Act in a court in England, Wales or Northern Ireland which are pending immediately before the commencement date, being proceedings affecting a person resident in the Country or territory specified in column (1), shall be continued as if they had been brought under or by virtue of the corresponding provision of the 1972 Act.

SCHEDULE
COUNTRY AND TERRITORY DESIGNATED AS A RECIPROCATING COUNTRY AND EXTENT OF DESIGNATION

6–5100D

(1)	(2)
Country or territory	Description of maintenance orders to which designation extends
Brunei Darussalam	Maintenance orders other than lump sum orders
Newfoundland and Labrador (formerly known as Newfoundland)	Maintenance orders generally

Council Regulation (EC) No 2201/2003 of 27 November 2003 concerning jurisdiction and the recognition and enforcement of judgments in matrimonial matters and the matters of parental responsibility, repealing Regulation (EC) No 1347/2000

CHAPTER I
SCOPE AND DEFINITIONS

6–5100E Article 1. Scope. 1. This Regulation shall apply, whatever the nature of the court or tribunal, in civil matters relating to:

(a) divorce, legal separation or marriage annulment;
(b) the attribution, exercise, delegation, restriction or termination of parental responsibility.

2. The matters referred to in paragraph 1(b) may, in particular, deal with:

(a) rights of custody and rights of access;
(b) guardianship, curatorship and similar institutions;
(c) the designation and functions of any person or body having charge of the child's person or property, representing or assisting the child;
(d) the placement of the child in a foster family or in institutional care;
(e) measures for the protection of the child relating to the administration, conservation or disposal of the child's property.

3. This Regulation shall not apply to:

(a) the establishment or contesting of a parent-child relationship;
(b) decisions on adoption, measures preparatory to adoption, or the annulment or revocation of adoption;
(c) the name and forenames of the child;
(d) emancipation;
(e) maintenance obligations;
(f) trusts or succession;
(g) measures taken as a result of criminal offences committed by children.

6–5100F   Article 2. Definitions.   For the purposes of this Regulation:

1. the term "court" shall cover all the authorities in the Member States with jurisdiction in the matters falling within the scope of this Regulation pursuant to Article 1;

2. the term "judge" shall mean the judge or an official having powers equivalent to those of a judge in the matters falling within the scope of the Regulation;

3. the term "Member State" shall mean all Member States with the exception of Denmark;

4. the term "judgment" shall mean a divorce, legal separation or marriage annulment, as well as a judgment relating to parental responsibility, pronounced by a court of a Member State, whatever the judgment may be called, including a decree, order or decision;

5. the term "Member State of origin" shall mean the Member State where the judgment to be enforced was issued;

6. the term "Member State of enforcement" shall mean the Member State where enforcement of the judgment is sought;

7. the term "parental responsibility" shall mean all rights and duties relating to the person or the property of a child which are given to a natural or legal person by judgment, by operation of law or by an agreement having legal effect. The term shall include rights of custody and rights of access;

8. the term "holder of parental responsibility" shall mean any person having parental responsibility over a child;

9. the term "rights of custody" shall include rights and duties relating to the care of the person of a child, and in particular the right to determine the child's place of residence;

10. the term "rights of access" shall include in particular the right to take a child to a place other than his or her habitual residence for a limited period of time;

11. the term "wrongful removal or retention" shall mean a child's removal or retention where:

(a) it is in breach of rights of custody acquired by judgment or by operation of law or by an agreement having legal effect under the law of the Member State where the child was habitually resident immediately before the removal or retention; and

(b) provided that, at the time of removal or retention, the rights of custody were actually exercised, either jointly or alone, or would have been so exercised but for the removal or retention. Custody shall be considered to be exercised jointly when, pursuant to a judgment or by operation of law, one holder of parental responsibility cannot decide on the child's place of residence without the consent of another holder of parental responsibility.

CHAPTER II
JURISDICTION

SECTION 1
DIVORCE, LEGAL SEPARATION AND MARRIAGE ANNULMENT

6–5100G   Article 3. General jurisdiction.   1. In matters relating to divorce, legal separation or marriage annulment, jurisdiction shall lie with the courts of the Member State

(a) in whose territory:

- the spouses are habitually resident, or
- the spouses were last habitually resident, insofar as one of them still resides there, or
- the respondent is habitually resident, or
- in the event of a joint application, either of the spouses is habitually resident, or
- the applicant is habitually resident if he or she resided there for at least a year immediately before the application was made, or
- the applicant is habitually resident if he or she resided there for at least six months immediately before the application was made and is either a national of the Member State in question or, in the case of the United Kingdom and Ireland, has his or her "domicile" there;

(b) of the nationality of both spouses or, in the case of the United Kingdom and Ireland, of the "domicile" of both spouses.

2. For the purpose of this Regulation, "domicile" shall have the same meaning as it has under the legal systems of the United Kingdom and Ireland.

6–5100H   Article 4. Counterclaim.   The court in which proceedings are pending on the basis of Article 3 shall also have jurisdiction to examine a counterclaim, insofar as the latter comes within the scope of this Regulation.

6–5100I   Article 5. Conversion of legal separation into divorce.   Without prejudice to Article 3, a court of a Member State that has given a judgment on a legal separation shall also have jurisdiction for converting that judgment into a divorce, if the law of that Member State so provides.

6–5100J   Article 6. Exclusive nature of jurisdiction under Articles 3, 4 and 5.   A spouse who:

(a) is habitually resident in the territory of a Member State; or (*b*) is a national of a Member State, or, in the case of the United Kingdom and Ireland, has his or her "domicile" in the territory of one of the latter Member States,

may be sued in another Member State only in accordance with Articles 3, 4 and 5.

6–5100K   Article 7. Residual jurisdiction.   1. Where no court of a Member State has jurisdiction pursuant to Articles 3, 4 and 5, jurisdiction shall be determined, in each Member State, by the laws of that State.

2. As against a respondent who is not habitually resident and is not either a national of a Member State or, in the case of the United Kingdom and Ireland, does not have his "domicile" within the territory of one of the latter Member States, any national of a Member State who is habitually resident within the territory of another Member State may, like the nationals of that State, avail himself of the rules of jurisdiction applicable in that State.

SECTION 2

PARENTAL RESPONSIBILITY

6–5100L   Article 8. General jurisdiction.   1. The courts of a Member State shall have jurisdiction in matters of parental responsibility over a child who is habitually resident in that Member State at the time the court is seised.

2. Paragraph 1 shall be subject to the provisions of Articles 9, 10 and 12.

6–5100M   Article 9. Continuing jurisdiction of the child's former habitual residence.   1. Where a child moves lawfully from one Member State to another and acquires a new habitual residence there, the courts of the Member State of the child's former habitual residence shall, by way of exception to Article 8, retain jurisdiction during a three-month period following the move for the purpose of modifying a judgment on access rights issued in that Member State before the child moved, where the holder of access rights pursuant to the judgment on access rights continues to have his or her habitual residence in the Member State of the child's former habitual residence.

2. Paragraph 1 shall not apply if the holder of access rights referred to in paragraph 1 has accepted the jurisdiction of the courts of the Member State of the child's new habitual residence by participating in proceedings before those courts without contesting their jurisdiction.

6–5100N   Article 10. Jurisdiction in cases of child abduction.   In case of wrongful removal or retention of the child, the courts of the Member State where the child was habitually resident immediately before the wrongful removal or retention shall retain their jurisdiction until the child has acquired a habitual residence in another Member State and:

(*a*) each person, institution or other body having rights of custody has acquiesced in the removal or retention; or

(*b*) the child has resided in that other Member State for a period of at least one year after the person, institution or other body having rights of custody has had or should have had knowledge of the whereabouts of the child and the child is settled in his or her new environment and at least one of the following conditions is met:

   (i) within one year after the holder of rights of custody has had or should have had knowledge of the whereabouts of the child, no request for return has been lodged before the competent authorities of the Member State where the child has been removed or is being retained;

   (ii) a request for return lodged by the holder of rights of custody has been withdrawn and no new request has been lodged within the time limit set in paragraph (i);

   (iii) a case before the court in the Member State where the child was habitually resident immediately before the wrongful removal or retention has been closed pursuant to Article 11(7);

   (iv) a judgment on custody that does not entail the return of the child has been issued by the courts of the Member State where the child was habitually resident immediately before the wrongful removal or retention.

6–5100O   Article 11. Return of the child.   1. Where a person, institution or other body having rights of custody applies to the competent authorities in a Member State to deliver a judgment on the basis of the Hague Convention of 25 October 1980 on the Civil Aspects of International Child Abduction (hereinafter "the 1980 Hague Convention"), in order to obtain the return of a child that has been wrongfully removed or retained in a Member State other than the Member State where the child was habitually resident immediately before the wrongful removal or retention, paragraphs 2 to 8 shall apply.

2. When applying Articles 12 and 13 of the 1980 Hague Convention, it shall be ensured that the child is given the opportunity to be heard during the proceedings unless this appears inappropriate having regard to his or her age or degree of maturity.

3. A court to which an application for return of a child is made as mentioned in paragraph 1 shall act expeditiously in proceedings on the application, using the most expeditious procedures available in national law.

Without prejudice to the first subparagraph, the court shall, except where exceptional circumstances make this impossible, issue its judgment no later than six weeks after the application is lodged.

4. A court cannot refuse to return a child on the basis of Article 13b of the 1980 Hague Convention if it is established that adequate arrangements have been made to secure the protection of the child after his or her return.

5. A court cannot refuse to return a child unless the person who requested the return of the child has been given an opportunity to be heard.

6. If a court has issued an order on non-return pursuant to Article 13 of the 1980 Hague Convention, the court must immediately either directly or through its central authority, transmit a copy of the court order on non-return and of the relevant documents, in particular a transcript of the hearings before the court, to the court with jurisdiction or central authority in the Member State where the child was habitually resident immediately before the wrongful removal or retention, as determined by national law. The court shall receive all the mentioned documents within one month of the date of the non-return order.

7. Unless the courts in the Member State where the child was habitually resident immediately before the wrongful removal or retention have already been seised by one of the parties, the court or central authority that receives the information mentioned in paragraph 6 must notify it to the parties and invite them to make submissions to the court, in accordance with national law, within three months of the date of notification so that the court can examine the question of custody of the child.

Without prejudice to the rules on jurisdiction contained in this Regulation, the court shall close the case if no submissions have been received by the court within the time limit.

8. Notwithstanding a judgment of non-return pursuant to Article 13 of the 1980 Hague Convention, any subsequent judgment which requires the return of the child issued by a court having jurisdiction under this Regulation shall be enforceable in accordance with Section 4 of Chapter III below in order to secure the return of the child.

6–5100P   Article 12. Prorogation of jurisdiction.   1. The courts of a Member State exercising jurisdiction by virtue of Article 3 on an application for divorce, legal separation or marriage annulment shall have jurisdiction in any matter relating to parental responsibility connected with that application where:

(a)   at least one of the spouses has parental responsibility in relation to the child; and
(b)   the jurisdiction of the courts has been accepted expressly or otherwise in an unequivocal manner by the spouses and by the holders of parental responsibility, at the time the court is seised, and is in the superior interests of the child.

2. The jurisdiction conferred in paragraph 1 shall cease as soon as:

(a)   the judgment allowing or refusing the application for divorce, legal separation or marriage annulment has become final;
(b)   in those cases where proceedings in relation to parental responsibility are still pending on the date referred to in (a), a judgment in these proceedings has become final;
(c)   the proceedings referred to in (a) and (b) have come to an end for another reason.

3. The courts of a Member State shall also have jurisdiction in relation to parental responsibility in proceedings other than those referred to in paragraph 1 where:

(a)   the child has a substantial connection with that Member State, in particular by virtue of the fact that one of the holders of parental responsibility is habitually resident in that Member State or that the child is a national of that Member State; and
(b)   the jurisdiction of the courts has been accepted expressly or otherwise in an unequivocal manner by all the parties to the proceedings at the time the court is seised and is in the best interests of the child.

4. Where the child has his or her habitual residence in the territory of a third State which is not a contracting party to the Hague Convention of 19 October 1996 on jurisdiction, applicable law, recognition, enforcement and cooperation in respect of parental responsibility and measures for the protection of children, jurisdiction under this Article shall be deemed to be in the child's interest, in particular if it is found impossible to hold proceedings in the third State in question.

6–5100Q   Article 13. Jurisdiction based on the child's presence.   1. Where a child's habitual residence cannot be established and jurisdiction cannot be determined on the basis of Article 12, the courts of the Member State where the child is present shall have jurisdiction.

2. Paragraph 1 shall also apply to refugee children or children internationally displaced because of disturbances occurring in their country.

6–5100R   Article 14. Residual jurisdiction.   Where no court of a Member State has jurisdiction pursuant to Articles 8 to 13, jurisdiction shall be determined, in each Member State, by the laws of that State.

6–5100S   Article 15. Transfer to a court better placed to hear the case.   1. By way of exception, the courts of a Member State having jurisdiction as to the substance of the matter may, if they consider that a court of another Member State, with which the child has a particular connection, would be better placed to hear the case, or a specific part thereof, and where this is in the best interests of the child:

(a) stay the case or the part thereof in question and invite the parties to introduce a request before the court of that other Member State in accordance with paragraph 4; or

(b) request a court of another Member State to assume jurisdiction in accordance with paragraph 5.

2. Paragraph 1 shall apply:

(a) upon application from a party; or

(b) of the court's own motion; or

(c) upon application from a court of another Member State with which the child has a particular connection, in accordance with paragraph 3.

A transfer made of the court's own motion or by application of a court of another Member State must be accepted by at least one of the parties.

3. The child shall be considered to have a particular connection to a Member State as mentioned in paragraph 1, if that Member State:

(a) has become the habitual residence of the child after the court referred to in paragraph 1 was seised; or

(b) is the former habitual residence of the child; or

(c) is the place of the child's nationality; or

(d) is the habitual residence of a holder of parental responsibility; or

(e) is the place where property of the child is located and the case concerns measures for the protection of the child relating to the administration, conservation or disposal of this property.

4. The court of the Member State having jurisdiction as to the substance of the matter shall set a time limit by which the courts of that other Member State shall be seised in accordance with paragraph 1.

If the courts are not seised by that time, the court which has been seised shall continue to exercise jurisdiction in accordance with Articles 8 to 14.

5. The courts of that other Member State may, where due to the specific circumstances of the case, this is in the best interests of the child, accept jurisdiction within six weeks of their seisure in accordance with paragraph 1(a) or 1(b). In this case, the court first seised shall decline jurisdiction. Otherwise, the court first seised shall continue to exercise jurisdiction in accordance with Articles 8 to 14.

6. The courts shall cooperate for the purposes of this Article, either directly or through the central authorities designated pursuant to Article 53.

SECTION 3
COMMON PROVISIONS

6–5100T   Article 16. Seising of a Court.   1. A court shall be deemed to be seised:

(a) at the time when the document instituting the proceedings or an equivalent document is lodged with the court, provided that the applicant has not subsequently failed to take the steps he was required to take to have service effected on the respondent; or

(b) if the document has to be served before being lodged with the court, at the time when it is received by the authority responsible for service, provided that the applicant has not subsequently failed to take the steps he was required to take to have the document lodged with the court.

6–5100U   Article 17. Examination as to jurisdiction.   Where a court of a Member State is seised of a case over which it has no jurisdiction under this Regulation and over which a court of another Member State has jurisdiction by virtue of this Regulation, it shall declare of its own motion that it has no jurisdiction.

6–5100V   Article 18. Examination as to admissibility.   1. Where a respondent habitually resident in a State other than the Member State where the action was brought does not enter an appearance, the court with jurisdiction shall stay the proceedings so long as it is not shown that the respondent has been able to receive the document instituting the proceedings or an equivalent document in sufficient time to enable him to arrange for his defence, or that all necessary steps have been taken to this end.

2. Article 19 of Regulation (EC) No 1348/2000 shall apply instead of the provisions of paragraph 1 of this Article if the document instituting the proceedings or an equivalent document had to be transmitted from one Member State to another pursuant to that Regulation.

3. Where the provisions of Regulation (EC) No 1348/2000 are not applicable, Article 15 of the Hague Convention of 15 November 1965 on the service abroad of judicial and extrajudicial documents in civil or commercial matters shall apply if the document instituting the proceedings or an equivalent document had to be transmitted abroad pursuant to that Convention.

6–5100W   Article 19. Lis pendens and dependent actions.   1. Where proceedings relating to divorce, legal separation or marriage annulment between the same parties are brought before courts of different Member States, the court second seised shall of its own motion stay its proceedings until such time as the jurisdiction of the court first seised is established.

2. Where proceedings relating to parental responsibility relating to the same child and involving the same cause of action are brought before courts of different Member States, the court second seised shall of its own motion stay its proceedings until such time as the jurisdiction of the court first seised is established.

3. Where the jurisdiction of the court first seised is established, the court second seised shall decline jurisdiction in favour of that court.

In that case, the party who brought the relevant action before the court second seised may bring that action before the court first seised.

6–5100X   Article 20. Provisional, including protective, measures.   1. In urgent cases, the provisions of this Regulation shall not prevent the courts of a Member State from taking such provisional, including protective, measures in respect of persons or assets in that State as may be available under the law of that Member State, even if, under this Regulation, the court of another Member State has jurisdiction as to the substance of the matter.

2. The measures referred to in paragraph 1 shall cease to apply when the court of the Member State having jurisdiction under this Regulation as to the substance of the matter has taken the measures it considers appropriate.

CHAPTER III
RECOGNITION AND ENFORCEMENT

SECTION 1
RECOGNITION

6–5100Y   Article 21. Recognition of a judgment.   1. A judgment given in a Member State shall be recognised in the other Member States without any special procedure being required.

2. In particular, and without prejudice to paragraph 3, no special procedure shall be required for updating the civil-status records of a Member State on the basis of a judgment relating to divorce, legal separation or marriage annulment given in another Member State, and against which no further appeal lies under the law of that Member State.

3. Without prejudice to Section 4 of this Chapter, any interested party may, in accordance with the procedures provided for in Section 2 of this Chapter, apply for a decision that the judgment be or not be recognised.

The local jurisdiction of the court appearing in the list notified by each Member State to the Commission pursuant to Article 68 shall be determined by the internal law of the Member State in which proceedings for recognition or non-recognition are brought.

4. Where the recognition of a judgment is raised as an incidental question in a court of a Member State, that court may determine that issue.

6–5100Z   Article 22. Grounds of non-recognition for judgments relating to divorce, legal separation or marriage annulment.   A judgment relating to a divorce, legal separation or marriage annulment shall not be recognised:

(a) if such recognition is manifestly contrary to the public policy of the Member State in which recognition is sought;

(b) where it was given in default of appearance, if the respondent was not served with the document which instituted the proceedings or with an equivalent document in sufficient time and in such a way as to enable the respondent to arrange for his or her defence unless it is determined that the respondent has accepted the judgment unequivocally;

(c) if it is irreconcilable with a judgment given in proceedings between the same parties in the Member State in which recognition is sought; or

(d) if it is irreconcilable with an earlier judgment given in another Member State or in a non-Member State between the same parties, provided that the earlier judgment fulfils the conditions necessary for its recognition in the Member State in which recognition is sought.

6–5100ZA   Article 23. Grounds of non-recognition for judgments relating to parental responsibility.   A judgment relating to parental responsibility shall not be recognised:

(a) if such recognition is manifestly contrary to the public policy of the Member State in which recognition is sought taking into account the best interests of the child;

(b) if it was given, except in case of urgency, without the child having been given an opportunity to be heard, in violation of fundamental principles of procedure of the Member State in which recognition is sought;

(c) where it was given in default of appearance if the person in default was not served with the document which instituted the proceedings or with an equivalent document in sufficient time and in such a way as to enable that person to arrange for his or her defence unless it is determined that such person has accepted the judgment unequivocally;

(d) on the request of any person claiming that the judgment infringes his or her parental responsibility, if it was given without such person having been given an opportunity to be heard;

(e) if it is irreconcilable with a later judgment relating to parental responsibility given in the Member State in which recognition is sought;

(f) if it is irreconcilable with a later judgment relating to parental responsibility given in another Member State or in the non-Member State of the habitual residence of the child provided that the later judgment fulfils the conditions necessary for its recognition in the Member State in which recognition is sought; or

(g) if the procedure laid down in Article 56 has not been complied with.

6–5100ZB   Article 24. Prohibition of review of jurisdiction of the court of origin. The jurisdiction of the court of the Member State of origin may not be reviewed. The test of public policy referred to in Articles 22(a) and 23(a) may not be applied to the rules relating to jurisdiction set out in Articles 3 to 14.

6–5100ZC   Article 25. Differences in applicable law. The recognition of a judgment may not be refused because the law of the Member State in which such recognition is sought would not allow divorce, legal separation or marriage annulment on the same facts.

6–5100ZD   Article 26. Non-review as to substance. Under no circumstances may a judgment be reviewed as to its substance.

6–5100ZE   Article 27. Stay of proceedings. 1. A court of a Member State in which recognition is sought of a judgment given in another Member State may stay the proceedings if an ordinary appeal against the judgment has been lodged.

2. A court of a Member State in which recognition is sought of a judgment given in Ireland or the United Kingdom may stay the proceedings if enforcement is suspended in the Member State of origin by reason of an appeal.

SECTION 2
APPLICATION FOR A DECLARATION OF ENFORCEABILITY

6–5100ZF   Article 28. Enforceable judgments. 1. A judgment on the exercise of parental responsibility in respect of a child given in a Member State which is enforceable in that Member State and has been served shall be enforced in another Member State when, on the application of any interested party, it has been declared enforceable there.

2. However, in the United Kingdom, such a judgment shall be enforced in England and Wales, in Scotland or in Northern Ireland only when, on the application of any interested party, it has been registered for enforcement in that part of the United Kingdom.

6–5100ZG   Article 29. Jurisdiction of local courts. 1. An application for a declaration of enforceability shall be submitted to the court appearing in the list notified by each Member State to the Commission pursuant to Article 68.

2. The local jurisdiction shall be determined by reference to the place of habitual residence of the person against whom enforcement is sought or by reference to the habitual residence of any child to whom the application relates.

Where neither of the places referred to in the first subparagraph can be found in the Member State of enforcement, the local jurisdiction shall be determined by reference to the place of enforcement.

6–5100ZH   Article 30. Procedure. 1. The procedure for making the application shall be governed by the law of the Member State of enforcement.

2. The applicant must give an address for service within the area of jurisdiction of the court applied to. However, if the law of the Member State of enforcement does not provide for the furnishing of such an address, the applicant shall appoint a representative ad litem.

3. The documents referred to in Articles 37 and 39 shall be attached to the application.

6–5100ZI   Article 31. Decision of the court. 1. The court applied to shall give its decision without delay. Neither the person against whom enforcement is sought, nor the child shall, at this stage of the proceedings, be entitled to make any submissions on the application.

2. The application may be refused only for one of the reasons specified in Articles 22, 23 and 24.

3. Under no circumstances may a judgment be reviewed as to its substance.

6–5100ZJ   Article 32. Notice of the decision. The appropriate officer of the court shall without delay bring to the notice of the applicant the decision given on the application in accordance with the procedure laid down by the law of the Member State of enforcement.

6–5100ZK   Article 33. Appeal against the decision. 1. The decision on the application for a declaration of enforceability may be appealed against by either party.

2. The appeal shall be lodged with the court appearing in the list notified by each Member State to the Commission pursuant to Article 68.

3. The appeal shall be dealt with in accordance with the rules governing procedure in contradictory matters.

4. If the appeal is brought by the applicant for a declaration of enforceability, the party against whom enforcement is sought shall be summoned to appear before the appellate court. If such person fails to appear, the provisions of Article 18 shall apply.

5. An appeal against a declaration of enforceability must be lodged within one month of service thereof. If the party against whom enforcement is sought is habitually resident in a Member State other than that in which the declaration of enforceability was given, the time for appealing shall be two months and shall run from the date of service, either on him or at his residence. No extension of time may be granted on account of distance.

6–5100ZL   Article 34. Courts of appeal and means of contest.   The judgment given on appeal may be contested only by the proceedings referred to in the list notified by each Member State to the Commission pursuant to Article 68.

6–5100ZM   Article 35. Stay of proceedings.   1. The court with which the appeal is lodged under Articles 33 or 34 may, on the application of the party against whom enforcement is sought, stay the proceedings if an ordinary appeal has been lodged in the Member State of origin, or if the time for such appeal has not yet expired. In the latter case, the court may specify the time within which an appeal is to be lodged.

2. Where the judgment was given in Ireland or the United Kingdom, any form of appeal available in the Member State of origin shall be treated as an ordinary appeal for the purposes of paragraph 1.

6–5100ZN   Article 36. Partial enforcement.   1. Where a judgment has been given in respect of several matters and enforcement cannot be authorised for all of them, the court shall authorise enforcement for one or more of them.

2. An applicant may request partial enforcement of a judgment.

SECTION 3
PROVISIONS COMMON TO SECTIONS 1 AND 2

6–5100ZO   Article 37. Documents.   1. A party seeking or contesting recognition or applying for a declaration of enforceability shall produce:

(*a*) a copy of the judgment which satisfies the conditions necessary to establish its authenticity; and

(*b*) the certificate referred to in Article 39.

2. In addition, in the case of a judgment given in default, the party seeking recognition or applying for a declaration of enforceability shall produce:

(*a*) the original or certified true copy of the document which establishes that the defaulting party was served with the document instituting the proceedings or with an equivalent document; or

(*b*) any document indicating that the defendant has accepted the judgment unequivocally.

6–5100ZP   Article 38. Absence of documents.   1. If the documents specified in Article 37(1)(b) or (2) are not produced, the court may specify a time for their production, accept equivalent documents or, if it considers that it has sufficient information before it, dispense with their production.

2. If the court so requires, a translation of such documents shall be furnished. The translation shall be certified by a person qualified to do so in one of the Member States.

6–5100ZQ   Article 39. Certificate concerning judgments in matrimonial matters and certificate concerning judgments on parental responsibility.   The competent court or authority of a Member State of origin shall, at the request of any interested party, issue a certificate using the standard form set out in Annex I (judgments in matrimonial matters) or in Annex II (judgments on parental responsibility).

SECTION 4
ENFORCEABILITY OF CERTAIN JUDGMENTS CONCERNING RIGHTS OF ACCESS AND OF CERTAIN JUDGMENTS WHICH REQUIRE THE RETURN OF THE CHILD

6–5100ZR   Article 40. Scope.   1. This Section shall apply to:

(*a*) rights of access; and

(*b*) the return of a child entailed by a judgment given pursuant to Article 11(8).

2. The provisions of this Section shall not prevent a holder of parental responsibility from seeking recognition and enforcement of a judgment in accordance with the provisions in Sections 1 and 2 of this Chapter.

6–5100ZS   Article 41. Rights of access.   1. The rights of access referred to in Article 40(1)(a) granted in an enforceable judgment given in a Member State shall be recognised and enforceable in another Member State without the need for a declaration of enforceability and without any possibility of opposing its recognition if the judgment has been certified in the Member State of origin in accordance with paragraph 2.

Even if national law does not provide for enforceability by operation of law of a judgment granting access rights, the court of origin may declare that the judgment shall be enforceable, notwithstanding any appeal.

2. The judge of origin shall issue the certificate referred to in paragraph 1 using the standard form in Annex III (certificate concerning rights of access) only if:

(a) the judgment was given in default, the person defaulting was served with the document which instituted the proceedings or with an equivalent document in sufficient time and in such a way as to enable that person to arrange for his or her defense, or, the person has been served with the document but not in compliance with these conditions, it is nevertheless established that he or she accepted the decision unequivocally;

(b) all parties concerned were given an opportunity to be heard; and

(c) the child was given an opportunity to be heard, unless a hearing was considered inappropriate having regard to his or her age or degree of maturity.

The certificate shall be completed in the language of the judgment.

3. Where the rights of access involve a cross-border situation at the time of the delivery of the judgment, the certificate shall be issued ex officio when the judgment becomes enforceable, even if only provisionally. If the situation subsequently acquires a cross-border character, the certificate shall be issued at the request of one of the parties.

6–5100ZT   Article 42. Return of the child.   1. The return of a child referred to in Article 40(1)(b) entailed by an enforceable judgment given in a Member State shall be recognised and enforceable in another Member State without the need for a declaration of enforceability and without any possibility of opposing its recognition if the judgment has been certified in the Member State of origin in accordance with paragraph 2.

Even if national law does not provide for enforceability by operation of law, notwithstanding any appeal, of a judgment requiring the return of the child mentioned in Article 11(b)(8), the court of origin may declare the judgment enforceable.

2. The judge of origin who delivered the judgment referred to in Article 40(1)(b) shall issue the certificate referred to in paragraph 1 only if:

(a) the child was given an opportunity to be heard, unless a hearing was considered inappropriate having regard to his or her age or degree of maturity;

(b) the parties were given an opportunity to be heard; and

(c) the court has taken into account in issuing its judgment the reasons for and evidence underlying the order issued pursuant to Article 13 of the 1980 Hague Convention.

In the event that the court or any other authority takes measures to ensure the protection of the child after its return to the State of habitual residence, the certificate shall contain details of such measures.

The judge of origin shall of his or her own motion issue that certificate using the standard form in Annex IV (certificate concerning return of the child(ren)).

The certificate shall be completed in the language of the judgment.

6–5100ZU   Article 43. Rectification of the certificate.   1. The law of the Member State of origin shall be applicable to any rectification of the certificate.

2. No appeal shall lie against the issuing of a certificate pursuant to Articles 41(1) or 42(1).

6–5100ZV   Article 44. Effects of the certificate.   The certificate shall take effect only within the limits of the enforceability of the judgment.

6–5100ZW   Article 45. Documents.   1. A party seeking enforcement of a judgment shall produce:

(a) a copy of the judgment which satisfies the conditions necessary to establish its authenticity; and

(b) the certificate referred to in Article 41(1) or Article 42(1).

2. For the purposes of this Article,

– the certificate referred to in Article 41(1) shall be accompanied by a translation of point 12 relating to the arrangements for exercising right of access,

– the certificate referred to in Article 42(1) shall be accompanied by a translation of its point 14 relating to the arrangements for implementing the measures taken to ensure the child's return.

The translation shall be into the official language or one of the official languages of the Member State of enforcement or any other language that the Member State of enforcement expressly accepts. The translation shall be certified by a person qualified to do so in one of the Member States.

SECTION 5
AUTHENTIC INSTRUMENTS AND AGREEMENTS

6–5100ZX   Article 46. Authentic instruments and agreements.   Documents which have been formally drawn up or registered as authentic instruments and are enforceable in one Member

State and also agreements between the parties that are enforceable in the Member State in which they were concluded shall be recognised and declared enforceable under the same conditions as judgments.

SECTION 6
OTHER PROVISIONS

6–5100ZY **Article 47. Enforcement procedure.** 1. The enforcement procedure is governed by the law of the Member State of enforcement.

2. Any judgment delivered by a court of another Member State and declared to be enforceable in accordance with Section 2 or certified in accordance with Article 41(1) or Article 42(1) shall be enforced in the Member State of enforcement in the same conditions as if it had been delivered in that Member State.

In particular, a judgment which has been certified according to Article 41(1) or Article 42(1) cannot be enforced if it is irreconcilable with a subsequent enforceable judgment.

6–5100ZZ **Article 48. Practical arrangements for the exercise of rights of access.** 1. The courts of the Member State of enforcement may make practical arrangements for organising the exercise of rights of access, if the necessary arrangements have not or have not sufficiently been made in the judgment delivered by the courts of the Member State having jurisdiction as to the substance of the matter and provided the essential elements of this judgment are respected.

2. The practical arrangements made pursuant to paragraph 1 shall cease to apply pursuant to a later judgment by the courts of the Member State having jurisdiction as to the substance of the matter.

6–5100ZZA **Article 49. Costs.** The provisions of this Chapter, with the exception of Section 4, shall also apply to the determination of the amount of costs and expenses of proceedings under this Regulation and to the enforcement of any order concerning such costs and expenses.

6–5100ZZB **Article 50. Legal aid.** An applicant who, in the Member State of origin, has benefited from complete or partial legal aid or exemption from costs or expenses shall be entitled, in the procedures provided for in Articles 21, 28, 41, 42 and 48 to benefit from the most favourable legal aid or the most extensive exemption from costs and expenses provided for by the law of the Member State of enforcement.

6–5100ZZC **Article 51. Security, bond or deposit.** No security, bond or deposit, however described, shall be required of a party who in one Member State applies for enforcement of a judgment given in another Member State on the following grounds:

    (a) that he or she is not habitually resident in the Member State in which enforcement is sought; or

    (b) that he or she is either a foreign national or, where enforcement is sought in either the United Kingdom or Ireland, does not have his or her "domicile" in either of those Member States.

6–5100ZZD **Article 52. Legalisation or other similar formality.** No legalisation or other similar formality shall be required in respect of the documents referred to in Articles 37, 38 and 45 or in respect of a document appointing a representative ad litem.

CHAPTER IV
COOPERATION BETWEEN CENTRAL AUTHORITIES IN MATTERS OF PARENTAL RESPONSIBILITY

6–5100ZZE **Article 53. Designation.** Each Member State shall designate one or more central authorities to assist with the application of this Regulation and shall specify the geographical or functional jurisdiction of each. Where a Member State has designated more than one central authority, communications shall normally be sent direct to the relevant central authority with jurisdiction. Where a communication is sent to a central authority without jurisdiction, the latter shall be responsible for forwarding it to the central authority with jurisdiction and informing the sender accordingly.

6–5100ZZF **Article 54. General functions.** The central authorities shall communicate information on national laws and procedures and take measures to improve the application of this Regulation and strengthening their cooperation. For this purpose the European Judicial Network in civil and commercial matters created by Decision No 2001/470/EC shall be used.

6–5100ZZG **Article 55. Cooperation on cases specific to parental responsibility.** The central authorities shall, upon request from a central authority of another Member State or from a holder of parental responsibility, cooperate on specific cases to achieve the purposes of this Regulation. To this end, they shall, acting directly or through public authorities or other bodies, take all appropriate steps in accordance with the law of that Member State in matters of personal data protection to:

(a) collect and exchange information:
- (i) on the situation of the child;
- (ii) on any procedures under way; or
- (iii) on decisions taken concerning the child;

(b) provide information and assistance to holders of parental responsibility seeking the recognition and enforcement of decisions on their territory, in particular concerning rights of access and the return of the child;

(c) facilitate communications between courts, in particular for the application of Article 11(6) and (7) and Article 15;

(d) provide such information and assistance as is needed by courts to apply Article 56; and

(e) facilitate agreement between holders of parental responsibility through mediation or other means, and facilitate cross-border cooperation to this end.

6–5100ZZH   Article 56. Placement of a child in another Member State.   1. Where a court having jurisdiction under Articles 8 to 15 contemplates the placement of a child in institutional care or with a foster family and where such placement is to take place in another Member State, it shall first consult the central authority or other authority having jurisdiction in the latter State where public authority intervention in that Member State is required for domestic cases of child placement.

2. The judgment on placement referred to in paragraph 1 may be made in the requesting State only if the competent authority of the requested State has consented to the placement.

3. The procedures for consultation or consent referred to in paragraphs 1 and 2 shall be governed by the national law of the requested State.

4. Where the authority having jurisdiction under Articles 8 to 15 decides to place the child in a foster family, and where such placement is to take place in another Member State and where no public authority intervention is required in the latter Member State for domestic cases of child placement, it shall so inform the central authority or other authority having jurisdiction in the latter State.

6–5100ZZI   Article 57. Working method.   1. Any holder of parental responsibility may submit, to the central authority of the Member State of his or her habitual residence or to the central authority of the Member State where the child is habitually resident or present, a request for assistance as mentioned in Article 55. In general, the request shall include all available information of relevance to its enforcement. Where the request for assistance concerns the recognition or enforcement of a judgment on parental responsibility that falls within the scope of this Regulation, the holder of parental responsibility shall attach the relevant certificates provided for in Articles 39, 41(1) or 42(1).

2. Member States shall communicate to the Commission the official language or languages of the Community institutions other than their own in which communications to the central authorities can be accepted.

3. The assistance provided by the central authorities pursuant to Article 55 shall be free of charge.

4. Each central authority shall bear its own costs.

6–5100ZZJ   Article 58. Meetings.   1. In order to facilitate the application of this Regulation, central authorities shall meet regularly.

2. These meetings shall be convened in compliance with Decision No 2001/470/EC establishing a European Judicial Network in civil and commercial matters.

CHAPTER V
RELATIONS WITH OTHER INSTRUMENTS

6–5100ZZK   Article 59. Relation with other instruments.   1. Subject to the provisions of Articles 60, 63, 64 and paragraph 2 of this Article, this Regulation shall, for the Member States, supersede conventions existing at the time of entry into force of this Regulation which have been concluded between two or more Member States and relate to matters governed by this Regulation.

2.

(a) Finland and Sweden shall have the option of declaring that the Convention of 6 February 1931 between Denmark, Finland, Iceland, Norway and Sweden comprising international private law provisions on marriage, adoption and guardianship, together with the Final Protocol thereto, will apply, in whole or in part, in their mutual relations, in place of the rules of this Regulation. Such declarations shall be annexed to this Regulation and published in the Official Journal of the European Union. They may be withdrawn, in whole or in part, at any moment by the said Member States.

(b) The principle of non-discrimination on the grounds of nationality between citizens of the Union shall be respected.

(c) The rules of jurisdiction in any future agreement to be concluded between the Member States referred to in subparagraph (a) which relate to matters governed by this Regulation shall be in line with those laid down in this Regulation.

(d) Judgments handed down in any of the Nordic States which have made the declaration provided for in subparagraph (a) under a forum of jurisdiction corresponding to one of those laid down in Chapter II of this Regulation, shall be recognised and enforced in the other Member States under the rules laid down in Chapter III of this Regulation.

3. Member States shall send to the Commission:

(a) a copy of the agreements and uniform laws implementing these agreements referred to in paragraph 2(a) and (c);

(b) any denunciations of, or amendments to, those agreements or uniform laws.

6–5100ZZL Article 60. Relations with certain multilateral conventions. In relations between Member States, this Regulation shall take precedence over the following Conventions in so far as they concern matters governed by this Regulation:

(a) the Hague Convention of 5 October 1961 concerning the Powers of Authorities and the Law Applicable in respect of the Protection of Minors;

(b) the Luxembourg Convention of 8 September 1967 on the Recognition of Decisions Relating to the Validity of Marriages;

(c) the Hague Convention of 1 June 1970 on the Recognition of Divorces and Legal Separations;

(d) the European Convention of 20 May 1980 on Recognition and Enforcement of Decisions concerning Custody of Children and on Restoration of Custody of Children; and

(e) the Hague Convention of 25 October 1980 on the Civil Aspects of International Child Abduction.

6–5100ZZM Article 61. Relation with the Hague Convention of 19 October 1996 on Jurisdiction, Applicable law, Recognition, Enforcement and Cooperation in Respect of Parental Responsibility and Measures for the Protection of Children. As concerns the relation with the Hague Convention of 19 October 1996 on Jurisdiction, Applicable law, Recognition, Enforcement and Cooperation in Respect of Parental Responsibility and Measures for the Protection of Children, this Regulation shall apply:

(a) where the child concerned has his or her habitual residence on the territory of a Member State;

(b) as concerns the recognition and enforcement of a judgment given in a court of a Member State on the territory of another Member State, even if the child concerned has his or her habitual residence on the territory of a third State which is a contracting Party to the said Convention.

6–5100ZZN Article 62. Scope of effects. 1. The agreements and conventions referred to in Articles 59(1), 60 and 61 shall continue to have effect in relation to matters not governed by this Regulation.

2. The conventions mentioned in Article 60, in particular the 1980 Hague Convention, continue to produce effects between the Member States which are party thereto, in compliance with Article 60.

6–5100ZZO Article 63. Treaties with the Holy See. 1. This Regulation shall apply without prejudice to the International Treaty (Concordat) between the Holy See and Portugal, signed at the Vatican City on 7 May 1940.

2. Any decision as to the invalidity of a marriage taken under the Treaty referred to in paragraph 1 shall be recognised in the Member States on the conditions laid down in Chapter III, Section 1.

3. The provisions laid down in paragraphs 1 and 2 shall also apply to the following international treaties (Concordats) with the Holy See:

(a) "Concordato lateranense" of 11 February 1929 between Italy and the Holy See, modified by the agreement, with additional Protocol signed in Rome on 18 February 1984;

(b) Agreement between the Holy See and Spain on legal affairs of 3 January 1979.

4. Recognition of the decisions provided for in paragraph 2 may, in Italy or in Spain, be subject to the same procedures and the same checks as are applicable to decisions of the ecclesiastical courts handed down in accordance with the international treaties concluded with the Holy See referred to in paragraph 3.

5. Member States shall send to the Commission:

(a) a copy of the Treaties referred to in paragraphs 1 and 3;

(b) any denunciations of or amendments to those Treaties.

CHAPTER VI
TRANSITIONAL PROVISIONS

6–5100ZZP Article 64. 1. The provisions of this Regulation shall apply only to legal proceedings instituted, to documents formally drawn up or registered as authentic instruments and to agreements concluded between the parties after its date of application in accordance with Article 72.

2. Judgments given after the date of application of this Regulation in proceedings instituted before that date but after the date of entry into force of Regulation (EC) No 1347/2000 shall be

recognised and enforced in accordance with the provisions of Chapter III of this Regulation if jurisdiction was founded on rules which accorded with those provided for either in Chapter II or in Regulation (EC) No 1347/2000 or in a convention concluded between the Member State of origin and the Member State addressed which was in force when the proceedings were instituted.

3. Judgments given before the date of application of this Regulation in proceedings instituted after the entry into force of Regulation (EC) No 1347/2000 shall be recognised and enforced in accordance with the provisions of Chapter III of this Regulation provided they relate to divorce, legal separation or marriage annulment or parental responsibility for the children of both spouses on the occasion of these matrimonial proceedings.

4. Judgments given before the date of application of this Regulation but after the date of entry into force of Regulation (EC) No 1347/2000 in proceedings instituted before the date of entry into force of Regulation (EC) No 1347/2000 shall be recognised and enforced in accordance with the provisions of Chapter III of this Regulation provided they relate to divorce, legal separation or marriage annulment or parental responsibility for the children of both spouses on the occasion of these matrimonial proceedings and that jurisdiction was founded on rules which accorded with those provided for either in Chapter II of this Regulation or in Regulation (EC) No 1347/2000 or in a convention concluded between the Member State of origin and the Member State addressed which was in force when the proceedings were instituted.

CHAPTER VII
FINAL PROVISIONS

6–5100ZZQ Article 65. Review. No later than 1 January 2012, and every five years thereafter, the Commission shall present to the European Parliament, to the Council and to the European Economic and Social Committee a report on the application of this Regulation on the basis of information supplied by the Member States. The report shall be accompanied if need be by proposals for adaptations.

6–5100ZZR Article 66. Member States with two or more legal systems. With regard to a Member State in which two or more systems of law or sets of rules concerning matters governed by this Regulation apply in different territorial units:

   (a) any reference to habitual residence in that Member State shall refer to habitual residence in a territorial unit;
   (b) any reference to nationality, or in the case of the United Kingdom "domicile", shall refer to the territorial unit designated by the law of that State;
   (c) any reference to the authority of a Member State shall refer to the authority of a territorial unit within that State which is concerned;
   (d) any reference to the rules of the requested Member State shall refer to the rules of the territorial unit in which jurisdiction, recognition or enforcement is invoked.

6–5100ZZS Article 67. Information on central authorities and languages accepted. The Member States shall communicate to the Commission within three months following the entry into force of this Regulation:

   (a) the names, addresses and means of communication for the central authorities designated pursuant to Article 53;
   (b) the languages accepted for communications to central authorities pursuant to Article 57(2); and
   (c) the languages accepted for the certificate concerning rights of access pursuant to Article 45(2).

The Member States shall communicate to the Commission any changes to this information.
The Commission shall make this information publicly available.

6–5100ZZT Article 68. Information relating to courts and redress procedures. The Member States shall notify to the Commission the lists of courts and redress procedures referred to in Articles 21, 29, 33 and 34 and any amendments thereto.

The Commission shall update this information and make it publicly available through the publication in the Official Journal of the European Union and any other appropriate means.

6–5100ZZU Article 69. Amendments to the Annexes. Any amendments to the standard forms in Annexes I to IV shall be adopted in accordance with the consultative procedure set out in Article 70(2).

6–5100ZZV Article 70. Committee. 1. The Commission shall be assisted by a committee (committee).

2. Where reference is made to this paragraph, Articles 3 and 7 of Decision 1999/468/EC shall apply.

3. The committee shall adopt its rules of procedure.

6–5100ZZW Article 71. Repeal of Regulation (EC) No 1347/2000. 1. Regulation (EC) No 1347/2000 shall be repealed as from the date of application of this Regulation.

2. Any reference to Regulation (EC) No 1347/2000 shall be construed as a reference to this Regulation according to the comparative table in Annex V.

6–5100ZZX Article 72. Entry into force. This Regulation shall enter into force on 1 August 2004.

The Regulation shall apply from 1 March 2005, with the exception of Articles 67, 68, 69 and 70, which shall apply from 1 August 2004.

This Regulation shall be binding in its entirety and directly applicable in the Member States in accordance with the Treaty establishing the European Community.

6–5100ZZY

ANNEX I

CERTIFICATE REFERRED TO IN ARTICLE 39 CONCERNING JUDGMENTS IN MATRIMONIAL MATTERS[1]

1. Member State of origin
2. Court or authority issuing the certificate

2.1. Name
2.2. Address
2.3. Tel./fax/e-mail

3. Marriage

3.1. Wife

3.1.1. Full name
3.1.2. Address
3.1.3. Country and place of birth
3.1.4. Date of birth

3.2. Husband

3.2.1. Full name
3.2.2. Address
3.2.3. Country and place of birth
3.2.4. Date of birth

3.3. Country, place (where available) and date of marriage

3.3.1. Country of marriage
3.3.2. Place of marriage (where available)
3.3.3. Date of marriage

4. Court which delivered the judgment

4.1. Name of Court
4.2. Place of Court

5. Judgment

5.1. Date
5.2. Reference number
5.3. Type of judgment

5.3.1. Divorce
5.3.2. Marriage annulment
5.3.3. Legal separation

5.4. Was the judgment given in default of appearance?

5.4.1. No
5.4.2. Yes[2]

6. Names of parties to whom legal aid has been granted
7. Is the judgment subject to further appeal under the law of the Member State of origin?

7.1. No
7.2. Yes

8. Date of legal effect in the Member State where the judgment was given

8.1. Divorce
8.2. Legal separation

Done at ...., date ....
Signature and/or stamp

---

1. Council Regulation (EC) No 2201/2003 of 27 November 2003 concerning jurisdiction and the recognition and enforcement of judgments in matrimonial matters and the matters of parental responsibility, repealing Regulation (EC) No 1347/2000.
2. Documents referred to in Article 37(2) must be attached.

ANNEX II

CERTIFICATE REFERRED TO IN ARTICLE 39 CONCERNING JUDGMENTS ON PARENTAL RESPONSIBILITY[1]

1. Member State of origin
2. Court or authority issuing the certificate

2.1. Name
2.2. Address
2.3. Tel./Fax/e-mail

3. Person(s) with rights of access

3.1. Full name
3.2. Address
3.3. Date and place of birth (where available)

4. Holders of parental responsibility other than those mentioned under 3[2]

4.1.

    4.1.1. Full name
    4.1.2. Address
    4.1.3. Date and place of birth (where available)

4.2.

    4.2.1. Full Name
    4.2.2. Address
    4.2.3. Date and place of birth (where available)

4.3.

    4.3.1. Full name
    4.3.2. Address
    4.3.3. Date and place of birth (where available)

5. Court which delivered the judgment

5.1. Name of Court
5.2. Place of Court

6. Judgment

6.1. Date
6.2. Reference number
6.3. Was the judgment given in default of appearance?

    6.3.1. No
    6.3.2. Yes[3]

7. Children who are covered by the judgment[4]

7.1. Full name and date of birth
7.2. Full name and date of birth
7.3. Full name and date of birth
7.4. Full name and date of birth

8. Names of parties to whom legal aid has been granted
9. Attestation of enforceability and service

9.1. Is the judgment enforceable according to the law of the Member State of origin?

    9.1.1. Yes
    9.1.2. No

9.2. Has the judgment been served on the party against whom enforcement is sought?

    9.2.1. Yes

        9.2.1.1. Full name of the party
        9.2.1.2. Address
        9.2.1.3. Date of service

    9.2.2. No

10. Specific information on judgments on rights of access where "exequatur" is requested under Article 28. This possibility is foreseen in Article 40(2).

10.1 Practical arrangements for exercise of rights of access (to the extent stated in the judgment)

    10.1.1. Date and time

        10.1.1.1. Start
        10.1.1.2. End

    10.1.2. Place
    10.1.3. Specific obligations on holders of parental responsibility
    10.1.4. Specific obligations on the person with right of access

10.1.5. Any restrictions attached to the exercise of rights of access

11. Specific information for judgments on the return of the child in cases where the "exequatur" procedure is requested under Article 28. This possibility is foreseen under Article 40(2).

11.1. The judgment entails the return of the child
11.2. Person to whom the child is to be returned (to the extent stated in the judgment)

     11.2.1. Full name
     11.2.2. Address

Done at ...., date ....
Signature and/or stamp

1. Council Regulation (EC) No 2201/2003 of 27 November 2003 concerning jurisdiction and the recognition and enforcement of judgments in matrimonial matters and the matters of parental responsibility, repealing Regulation (EC) No 1347/2000.
2. In cases of joint custody, a person already mentioned under item 3 may also be mentioned under item 4.
3. Documents referred to in Article 37(2) must be attached.
4. If more than four children are covered, use a second form.

6–5100ZZZA

ANNEX III
CERTIFICATE REFERRED TO IN ARTICLE 41(1) CONCERNING JUDGMENTS ON RIGHTS OF ACCESS[1]

1. Member State of origin
2. Court or authority issuing the certificate

2.1. Name
2.2. Address
2.3. Tel./fax/e-mail

3. Person(s) with rights of access

3.1. Full name
3.2. Address
3.3. Date and place of birth (where available)

4. Holders of parental responsibility other than those mentioned under 3[2, 3]

4.1.

     4.1.1. Full name
     4.1.2. Address
     4.1.3. Date and place of birth (where available)

4.2.

     4.2.1. Full name
     4.2.2. Address
     4.2.3. Date and place of birth (where available)

4.3. Other

     4.3.1. Full name
     4.3.2. Address
     4.3.3. Date and place of birth (where available)

5. Court which delivered the judgment

5.1. Name of Court
5.2. Place of Court

6. Judgment

6.1. Date
6.2. Reference number

7. Children who are covered by the judgment[4]

7.1. Full name and date of birth
7.2. Full name and date of birth
7.3. Full name and date of birth
7.4. Full name and date of birth

8. Is the judgment enforceable in the Member State of origin?

8.1. Yes
8.2. No

9. Where the judgment was given in default of appearance, the person defaulting was served with the document which instituted the proceedings or with an equivalent document in sufficient time and in such a way as to enable that person to arrange for his or her defence, or the person has been served with the document but not in compliance with these conditions, it is nevertheless established that he or she accepted the decision unequivocally

10. All parties concerned were given an opportunity to be heard

11. The children were given an opportunity to be heard, unless a hearing was considered inappropriate having regard to their age or degree of maturity

12. Practical arrangements for exercise of rights of access (to the extent stated in the judgment)

12.1. Date and time

     12.1.1. Start
     12.1.2. End

12.2. Place
12.3. Specific obligations on holders of parental responsibility
12.4. Specific obligations on the person with right of access
12.5. Any restrictions attached to the exercise of rights of access

13. Names of parties to whom legal aid has been granted

Done at ...., date ....
Signature and/or stamp

---

1. Council Regulation (EC) No 2201/2003 of 27 November 2003 concerning jurisdiction and the recognition and enforcement of judgments in matrimonial matters and the matters of parental responsibility, repealing Regulation (EC) No 1347/2000.
2. In cases of joint custody, a person already mentioned under item 3 may also be mentioned in item 4.
3. Please put a cross in the box corresponding to the person against whom the judgment should be enforced.
4. If more than four children are concerned, use a second form.

6–5100ZZZB

ANNEX IV
CERTIFICATE REFERRED TO IN ARTICLE 42(1) CONCERNING THE RETURN OF THE CHILD[1]

1. Member State of origin
2. Court or authority issuing the certificate

2.1. Name
2.2. Address
2.3. Tel./fax/e-mail

3. Person to whom the child has to be returned (to the extent stated in the judgment)

3.1. Full name
3.2. Address
3.3. Date and place of birth (where available)

4. Holders of parental responsibility[2]

4.1. Mother

     4.1.1. Full name
     4.1.2. Address (where available)
     4.1.3. Date and place of birth (where available)

4.2. Father

     4.2.1. Full name
     4.2.2. Address (where available)
     4.2.3. Date and place of birth (where available)

4.3. Other

     4.3.1. Full name
     4.3.2. Address (where available)
     4.3.3. Date and place of birth (where available)

5. Respondent (where available)

5.1. Full name
5.2. Address (where available)

6. Court which delivered the judgment

6.1. Name of Court
6.2. Place of Court

7. Judgment

7.1. Date
7.2. Reference number

8. Children who are covered by the judgment[3]

8.1. Full name and date of birth
8.2. Full name and date of birth
8.3. Full name and date of birth
8.4. Full name and date of birth

9. The judgment entails the return of the child
10. Is the judgment enforceable in the Member State of origin?

10.1. Yes
10.2. No

11. The children were given an opportunity to be heard, unless a hearing was considered inappropriate having regard to their age or degree of maturity

12. The parties were given an opportunity to be heard

13. The judgment entails the return of the children and the court has taken into account in issuing its judgment the reasons for and evidence underlying the decision issued pursuant to Article 13 of the Hague Convention of 25 October 1980 on the Civil Aspects of International Child Abduction

14. Where applicable, details of measures taken by courts or authorities to ensure the protection of the child after its return to the Member State of habitual residence

15. Names of parties to whom legal aid has been granted

Done at ...., date ....
Signature and/or stamp

---

1. Council Regulation (EC) No 2201 of 27 November 2003 concerning jurisdiction and the recognition and enforcement of judgments in matrimonial matters and the matters of parental responsibility, repealing Regulation (EC) No 1347/2000.
2. This item is optional.
3. If more than four children are covered, use a second form.

6–5100ZZZC

ANNEX V
COMPARATIVE TABLE WITH REGULATION (EC) No 1347/2000

Articles repealed	Corresponding articles on new text		Articles repealed	Corresponding articles on new text
1	1, 2		27	34
2	3		28	35
3	12		29	36
4			30	50
5	4		31	51
6	5		32	37
7	6		33	39
8	7		34	38
9	17		35	52
10	18		36	59
11	16, 19		37	60, 61
12	20		38	62
13	2, 49, 46		39	
14	21		40	63
15	22, 23		41	66
16			42	64
17	24		43	65
18	25		44	68, 69
19	26		45	70
20	27		46	72
21	28		Annex I	68
22	21, 29		Annex II	68
23	30		Annex III	68

Articles repealed	Corresponding articles on new text		Articles repealed	Corresponding articles on new text
24	31		Annex IV	Annex I
25	32		Annex V	Annex II
26	33			

6–5100ZZZD

ANNEX VI

DECLARATIONS BY SWEDEN AND FINLAND PURSUANT TO ARTICLE 59(2)(A) OF THE COUNCIL REGULATION CONCERNING JURISDICTION AND THE RECOGNITION AND ENFORCEMENT OF JUDGMENTS IN MATRIMONIAL MATTERS AND MATTERS OF PARENTAL RESPONSIBILITY, REPEALING REGULATION (EC) No 1347/2000.

Declaration by Sweden:. Pursuant to Article 59(2)(a) of the Council Regulation concerning jurisdiction and the recognition and enforcement of judgments in matrimonial matters and matters of parental responsibility, repealing Regulation (EC) No 1347/2000, Sweden hereby declares that the Convention of 6 February 1931 between Denmark, Finland, Iceland, Norway and Sweden comprising international private law provisions on marriage, adoption and guardianship, together with the Final Protocol thereto, will apply in full in relations between Sweden and Finland, in place of the rules of the Regulation.

Declaration by Finland:. Pursuant to Article 59(2)(a) of the Council Regulation concerning jurisdiction and the recognition and enforcement of judgments in matrimonial matters and matters of parental responsibility, repealing Regulation (EC) No 1347/2000, Finland hereby declares that the Convention of 6 February 1931 between Finland, Denmark, Iceland, Norway and Sweden comprising international private law provisions on marriage, adoption and guardianship, together with the Final Protocol thereto, will apply in full in relations between Finland and Sweden, in place of the rules of the Regulation.

Practice Direction (Family Proceedings: Court Bundles)[1]

6–5101 **1.** The following practice direction applies to all hearings in family proceedings in the High Court, to all hearings of family proceedings in the Royal Courts of Justice and to hearings with a time estimate of half a day or more in all care centres, family hearing centres and divorce county courts (including the Principal Registry of the Family Division when so treated), except as specified in paragraph 2.3 below, and subject to specific directions given in any particular case. "Hearing" extends to all hearings before judges and district judges and includes the hearing of any application.

2.1. A bundle for the use of the court at the hearing shall be provided by the party in the position of applicant at the hearing or by any other party who agrees to do so. It shall contain copies of all documents relevant to the hearing in chronological order, paginated and indexed and divided into separate sections, as follows:

(a) applications and orders;
(b) statements and affidavits;
(c) experts' reports and other reports including those of a guardian ad litem, and
(d) other documents, divided into further sections as may be appropriate.

2.2. Where the nature of the hearing is such that a complete bundle of all documents is unnecessary, the bundle may comprise only those documents necessary for the hearing but the summary (paragraph 3.1(a) below) must commence with a statement that the bundle is limited or incomplete. The summary should be limited to those matters which the court needs to know for the purpose of the hearing and for management of the case.

2.3. The requirement to provide a bundle shall not apply to the hearing of any urgent application where the circumstances are such that it is not reasonably practicable for a bundle to be provided.

3.1. At the commencement of the bundle there shall be:

(a) a summary of the background to the hearing limited, if practicable, to one A4 page;
(b) a statement of the issue or issues to be determined;
(c) a summary of the order or directions sought by each party;
(d) a chronology if it is a final hearing or if the summary under (a) is insufficient;
(e) skeleton arguments as may be appropriate, with copies of all authorities relied on.

3.2. If possible the bundle shall be agreed. In all cases, the party preparing the bundle shall paginate it and provide an index to all other parties prior to the hearing.

3.3. The bundle should normally be contained in a ring binder or lever arch file (limited to 350 pages in each file). Where there is more than one bundle, each should be clearly distinguishable. Bundles shall be lodges, if practicable, two clear days prior to the hearing. For hearings in the Royal Courts of Justice bundles shall be lodged with the Clerk of the Rules. All bundles shall have clearly marked on the outside, the title and number of the case, the hearing date and time and, if known, the name of the judge hearing the case.

4. After each hearing which is not a final hearing, the party responsible for the bundle shall retrieve it from the court. The bundle with any additional documents shall be relodged for further hearings in accordance with the above provisions.

5. This direction replaces paragraphs 5 and 8 of Practice Direction (Family Proceedings: Case Management) [1995] 1 WLR 332, dated 31 January 1995, and shall have effect from 2 May 2000.

6. Issued with the approval and concurrence of the Lord Chancellor.

Dame Elizabeth Butler-Sloss P

10 March 2000

---

[1] [2000] 1 WLR 737, [2000] 1 FCR 521, [2000] 1 FLR 536, FD.

6–5102

Practice Direction (Care Cases: Judicial Continuity and Judicial Case Management)[1]

---

[1] [2003] 1 WLR 2209, [2003] 1 FLR 719.

1.1   This Practice Direction, which includes the annexed Principles and the annexed Protocol, is issued by the President of the Family Division with the concurrence of the Lord Chancellor. It is intended to implement the recommendations of the Final Report, published in May 2003, of the Lord Chancellor's Advisory Committee on Judicial Case Management in Public Law Children Act Cases chaired by Munby and Coleridge JJ.

1.2   The Practice Direction, Principles and Protocol apply to all Courts, including Family Proceedings Courts, hearing applications issued by local authorities under Part IV (Care and Supervision) of the Children Act 1989 ('care cases') where:

    (a) the application is issued on or after 1 November 2003; or

    (b) the proceedings are transferred on or after 1 November 2003 from the Family Proceedings Court to a Care Centre, or from a County Court to a Care Centre or from a Care Centre to the High Court.

1.3   *Practice Direction (family proceedings: court bundles)* [2000] 1 WLR 737, [2000] 1 FLR 536, remains in force and is to be complied with in all cases to which it applies, subject only to the Protocol and to any directions which may be given in any particular care case by the case management judge.

1.4   Paragraph 2 of the *President's Direction (judicial continuity)* [2002] 2 FLR 367 shall cease to have effect in any case to which this Practice Direction applies.

2   Purpose of the Practice Direction, Principles and Protocol

2.1   The purpose of the Practice Direction, Principles and Protocol is to ensure consistency in the application of best practice by all Courts dealing with care cases and, in particular, to ensure:

    (a) that care cases are dealt with in accordance with the overriding objective;

    (b) that there are no unacceptable delays in the hearing and determination of care cases; and

    (c) that save in exceptional or unforeseen circumstances every care case is finally determined within 40 weeks of the application being issued.

2.2   The Principles are the principles which govern the application of the Practice Direction and Protocol by the Courts and the parties.

3   The Overriding Objective

3.1   The overriding objective is to enable the Court to deal with every care case

    (a) justly, expeditiously, fairly and with the minimum of delay;

    (b) in ways which ensure, so far as is practicable, that

      (i) the parties are on an equal footing;

      (ii) the welfare of the children involved is safeguarded; and

      (iii) distress to all parties is minimised;

    (c) so far as is practicable, in ways which are proportionate

      (i) to the gravity and complexity of the issues; and

      (ii) to the nature and extent of the intervention proposed in the private and family life of the children and adults involved.

3.2   The Court should seek to give effect to the overriding objective when it exercises any power given to it by the Family Proceedings Courts (Children Act 1989) Rules 1991 or the Family Proceedings Rules 1991 (as the case may be) or interprets any rule.

3.3   The parties are required to help the Court to further the overriding objective.

3.4   The Court will further the overriding objective by actively managing cases as required by sections 11 and 32 of the Children Act 1989 and in accordance with the Practice Direction, Principles and Protocol.

4   Avoiding Delay

4.1   Section 1(2) of the Children Act 1989 requires the Court to 'have regard to the general principle that any delay in determining any question is likely to prejudice the welfare of the child'.

4.2   Decisions of the European Court of Human Rights emphasise the need under article 6 of the European Convention for the Protection of Human Rights and Fundamental Freedoms for 'exceptional diligence' in this context: *Johansen v Norway* (1996) 23 EHRR 33, para [88].

4.3   One of the most effective means by which unnecessary delay can be avoided in care cases is by active case management by a specialist judiciary.

5   Judicial Case Management

5.1   The key principles underlying the Practice Direction, Principles and Protocol are

    (a) **judicial continuity:** each care case will be allocated to one or not more than two case management judges, who will be responsible for every stage in the proceedings down to the final hearing and one of whom may be, and where possible should be, the judge who will conduct the final hearing;

    (b) **active case management:** each care case will be actively case managed by the case management judge(s) with a view at all times to furthering the overriding objective;

    (c) **consistency by standardisation of steps:** each care case will so far as possible be managed in a consistent way

      (i) in accordance with the standardised procedures laid down in the Protocol; and

      (ii) using, wherever possible, standardised forms of order and other standardised documents;

    (d) **the case management conference:** in each care case there will be a case management conference to enable the case management judge to actively case manage the case and, at the earliest practicable opportunity, to

      (i) identify the relevant issues; and

      (ii) fix the timetable for all further directions and other hearings (including the date of the final hearing).

6   Implementing the Protocol

6.1   The Protocol is based on, and is intended to promote the adoption in all Courts and in all care cases of, the best practice currently adopted by Courts dealing with care cases.

6.2   The Protocol will be implemented:

    (a) in each Care Centre by reference to the Care Centre Plan which will be drafted locally (see appendix E/1 to the Protocol); and

    (b) in each Family Proceedings Court by reference to the FPC Plan which will be drafted locally (see appendix E/2 to the Protocol).

6.3   The target times specified in the Protocol for the taking of each step should be adhered to wherever possible and treated as the maximum permissible time for the taking of that step. Save in exceptional or unforeseen circumstances every care case should be finally determined within 40 weeks of the application being issued. Simpler cases can often be finally determined within a shorter time.

6.4   Unless the case management judge is satisfied that some other direction is necessary in order to give effect to the overriding objective, the case management judge should, and, unless the case management judge has otherwise ordered, the parties and any expert who may be instructed in the case must (as the case may be):

    (a) use or require the parties to use the forms and standard documents referred to in Appendix A to the Protocol;

    (b) prepare or require the parties to prepare the documents referred to in Appendix B to the Protocol in accordance with that Appendix;

    (c) comply or require the parties and every expert to comply with the Code of Guidance for Expert Witnesses in Family Proceedings contained in Appendix C to the Protocol; and

    (d) make every order and direction in the form of any relevant form which may from time to time be approved by the President of the Family Division for this purpose.

6.5   Appendix D to the Protocol contains the text of the *President's Practice Direction (family proceedings: court bundles)* [2000] 1 WLR 737, [2000] 1 FLR 536.

6.6   Appendix F to the Protocol contains the Social Services Assessment and Care Planning Aide-Memoire, which is a summary of existing guidance relating to assessment and care planning.

6.7   Appendix G to the Protocol is a summary of best practice guidance relating to requests made under section 37 of the Children Act 1989.

6.8   Cases in which there are concurrent care proceedings and criminal proceedings are to be dealt with in accordance with the Care Centre Plan.

7   Monitoring and Compliance

7.1   It is the responsibility of the Designated Family Judge in conjunction with the Court Service and in consultation with the Family Division Liaison Judge:

    (a) to monitor the extent to which care cases in the Courts for which he is responsible are being conducted in compliance with the protocol and with directions previously given by the Court;

    (b) to arrange for the collection and collation of such statistical and other information and in such form as the Family Division Liaison Judge and the President of the Family Division may from time to time direct.

ANNEX TO THE PRACTICE DIRECTION: PRINCIPLES OF APPLICATION

The principles which govern the application of the Practice Direction and Protocol by the Courts and the parties

1   The **Aim** of the Practice Direction and Protocol is to reduce delay and improve the quality of justice for children and families by the following means:
- Proper Court control of proceedings
- Identifying and promoting best practice
- The consistent application of best practice by all Courts
- Providing predictable standards which the Courts will treat as the normal and reasonable approach to the conduct of proceedings by parties

2   In order to achieve the **Aim** the Practice Direction gives effect to:
- A **protocol** which sets out predictable standards as specific steps to be taken in all care proceedings by reference to identified best practice
- An **overriding objective** to provide consistency of case management decisions
- **Court plans** to maximise the use of judicial and administrative resources
- Best practice **guidance**

3   **Court Control:** Proper Court control of care proceedings requires forward planning so that:
- A specialist judiciary is identified and trained
- Arrangements are made for continuous case management in the High Court, and in each Care Centre and Family Proceedings Court
- The arrangements for continuous case management are supervised by the specialist judiciary in conjunction with dedicated court officers, in particular
- the matching and allocation of judicial and administrative resources to cases; and
- the allocation and listing of cases,
- There is continuous and active case management of each case by allocated case management judges / benches
- There is continuous monitoring of the progress of all proceedings against target times to help minimise delay

4   **Continuity of Case Management:** The continuity of case management is to be achieved:
- In the Care Centre and the High Court by a **care centre plan** (CCP); and
- In the Family Proceedings Courts, by a **family proceedings courts plan** (FPCP)
- By the **identification of the specialist judiciary** and the **dedicated court officers** in the plans

Guidelines for the preparation and implementation of the plans are set out at appendix E to the protocol.

5   **Active Case Management:** Active case management is to be achieved by giving directions to ensure that the determination of proceedings occurs quickly, efficiently and with the minimum of delay and risk to the child (and where appropriate other persons) by:
- Identifying the appropriate Court to conduct the proceedings and transferring the proceedings as early as possible to that Court
- Identifying all facts and matters that are in issue at the earliest stage and then at each case management step in the proceedings
- Deciding which issues need full investigation and hearing and which do not
- Considering whether the likely benefits of taking a particular social work or legal step justify the delay which will result and the cost of taking it
- Encouraging the parties to use an alternative dispute resolution procedure such as a family group conference and facilitating the use of such a procedure
- Helping the parties to reach agreement in relation to the whole or part of a case, quickly, fairly and with the minimum of hostility
- Encouraging the parties to co-operate with each other in the conduct of the proceedings
- Identifying the timetable for all legal and social work steps
- Fixing the dates for all appointments and hearings
- Standardising, simplifying and regulating:
- the use of case management documentation and forms
- the court's orders and directions
- Controlling:
- the use and cost of experts
- the nature and extent of the documents which are to be disclosed to the parties and presented to the Court
- whether and if so in what manner the documents disclosed are to be presented to the Court
- Monitoring the Court's timetable and directions against target times for the completion of each protocol step to prevent delay and non-compliance

6   **Standard Directions, Forms and Documents:** In order to simplify and provide consistency in the exchange of information: such standard variable directions, forms (appendix A) and standard documents (appendix B) as may be approved from time to time by the President are to be used unless otherwise directed by the Court.

7 **Controlling the Use and Cost of Experts:** Expert evidence should be proportionate to the issues in question and should relate to questions that are outside the skill and experience of the Court. To assist the Court in its control of the use and cost of experts a Code of Guidance is incorporated as appendix C to the protocol. The Code of Guidance is to be followed by the parties when a party proposes that the court gives permission for the use of an expert. The Code of Guidance should form part of every letter of instruction so that experts can adopt best practice guidance in the formulation of their reports and advices to the Court.

8 **Disclosure:** Disclosure of relevant documents should be encouraged at the earliest opportunity. Where disclosure is in issue the Court's control of the extent of disclosure will have regard to whether the disclosure proposed is proportionate to the issues in question and the continuing duty of each party to give full and frank disclosure of information to each other and the Court.

9 **Inter-Disciplinary Good Practice:** The Court's process and its reliance upon best practice should acknowledge and encourage inter-disciplinary best practice and in particular pre-application investigation, assessment, consultation and planning by statutory agencies (including local authorities) and other potential parties (an aide-memoire of local authority guidance is annexed to the protocol at appendix F).

10 **Target Time:** The target times specified in the protocol for the taking of each step should be adhered to wherever possible and treated as the maximum permissible time for the taking of that step. Where target times are expressed in days, the days are 'court business days' in accordance with the Rules. Save in exceptional or unforeseen circumstances every care case should be finally determined within 40 weeks of the application being issued. Simpler cases can often be finally determined within a shorter time. Target times should only be departed from at the direction of the Court and for good reason in accordance with the overriding objective.

11 **Monitoring and Compliance:** To facilitate directions being given to deal with a change of circumstances or to remedy a material non-compliance at the earliest opportunity the Court should consider requiring regular certification of compliance with the Court's timetable and directions by the parties, for example on interim care order renewal certificates. In addition the Court might consider other mechanisms to monitor the progress of a case without the need for the parties or their representatives to attend Court.

12 **Technology:** Where the facilities are available to the Court and the parties, the Court should consider making full use of technology including electronic information exchange and video or telephone conferencing.

6–5103

Protocol for Judicial Case Management in Public Law Children Act Cases

June 2003
FOREWORD
by the President of the Family Division, the Lord Chancellor and the Secretary of State for Education and Skills

After over a decade of otherwise successful implementation of the Children Act there remains a large cloud in the sky in the form of delay. Delay in care cases has persisted for too long. The average care case lasts for almost a year. This is a year in which the child is left uncertain as to his or her future, is often moved between several temporary care arrangements, and the family and public agencies are left engaged in protracted and complex legal wranglings. Though a fair and effective process must intervene before a child is taken from its parents, we believe it is essential that unnecessary delay is eliminated and that better outcomes for children and families are thereby achieved. This protocol sets a guideline of 40 weeks for the conclusion of care cases. Some cases will need to take longer than this, but many more cases should take less.

The causes of delay have become clear from the Scoping Study published by the Department in March 2002, and through the work of the Advisory Committee that finalised this protocol. There is now a real enthusiasm among all the agencies involved for tackling these causes. Other work has begun and the momentum is building. Overt efforts have been made locally, both by Care Centres and by Family Proceedings Courts. Additional judicial sitting days for care work are being found. Measures are being taken to help improve the performance of CAFCASS. This protocol will form the backbone of these other efforts.

The Advisory Committee has involved all of the agencies and organisations that have a significant role to play in the care process and has striven to produce a consensus as to the content of this protocol. We are grateful to all the members of the Committee and to everyone else who engaged with the consultation process.

This protocol has been prepared on the basis that a change in the whole approach to case management and a clarification of focus, among all those involved in care cases, is the best way forward. This protocol is not a fresh start – it is a collation and distillation of best practice – we do ask you to engage it wholeheartedly with all your usual enthusiasm and dedication.

Dame Elizabeth Butler-Sloss
President

Lord Falconer of Thoroton
Secretary of State for Constitutional Affairs and Lord Chancellor

Rt Hon Charles Clarke MP
Secretary of State for Education and Skills

THE PROTOCOL

Route Map – The 6 Steps
Reproduced following para **4–36A.**

DAYS
Where target times are expressed in days, the days are 'court business days' in accordance with the Rules (principles of application para 10)

STEP 1 – The Application

	OBJECTIVE		Target time: by DAY 3

OBJECTIVE
To provide sufficient information about the Local Authority's (LA) case to enable:
* **The parties and the Court to identify the issues**
* **The Court to make early welfare and case management decisions about the child**

	Action	Party	Timing
1.1	**LA Application** When a decision is made to apply for a care or supervision order the **LA** shall: • File with the Court an application in **form C1** • Set out in **form C13** under 'Reasons' a summary of all facts and matters relied upon, in particular, those necessary to satisfy the threshold criteria and / or • Refer in the Reasons to any annexed schedules setting out the facts and matters relied upon • **Not** state that the Reasons are those contained in the evidence filed or to be filed.	**LA**	**on DAY 1**
1.2	**Directions on Issue** On the day the application is filed (**DAY 1**) the **Court** shall: • Issue the application • Issue a notice in **form C6** to the LA fixing a time and a date for the First Hearing which shall be not later than on **DAY 6** • point a Guardian (unless satisfied that it is not necessary to do so to safeguard the child's interests) • Inform CAFCASS of the decision to appoint and the request to allocate a Guardian.	**Court**	**on DAY 1**
1.3	**Allocation of the Guardian by CAFCASS** Within **2 days** of issue (by **DAY 3**) CAFCASS shall inform the Court of: • The name of the allocated Guardian or • The likely date upon which an allocation will be made.	**CAFCASS**	**by DAY 3**
1.4	**Appointment of the Solicitor for the Child** When a Guardian is allocated the **Guardian** shall on that day: • Appoint a solicitor for the child • Inform the Court of the name of the solicitor appointed • In the event that the Guardian's allocation is delayed and the Court has already appointed a solicitor, ensure that effective legal representation is maintained	**Guardian**	**on DAY 3**
	Where a Guardian is not allocated within **2 days** of issue, the **Court** shall on **DAY 3**: • Consider when a Guardian will be allocated • Decide whether to appoint a solicitor for the child	**FPC**	**on DAY 3**

Action	Party	Timing
In any event on the day the appointment is made the Court shall: • Notify all parties on **form C46** of the names of the Guardian and/or the solicitor for the child who have been appointed.	**FPC**	**on DAY 3**

1.5   LA Documents   **LA**   **by DAY 3**

Within **2 days** of issue (by **DAY 3**) the **LA** shall file and serve on all parties, the solicitor for the child and CAFCASS the following documents:
- The **forms C1 and C13** and any supplementary forms and notices issued by the Court
- Any relevant **court orders** relating to the child (together with the relevant Justices Facts and Reasons in **form C22** and any relevant **judgments** that exist)
- The **initial social work statement (appendix B/3)**
- The **social work chronology (appendix B/2)**
- The **core or initial assessment** reports **(appendix F)**
- Any **section 37 report**
- Any other **additional evidence** including specialist assessments or reports which then exist and which are relied upon by the LA.

STEP 2 – The First Hearing in the FPC

OBJECTIVE   **Target time: by DAY 6**

To decide what immediate steps are necessary to safeguard the welfare of the child by:
- Determining contested interim care order applications/ with whom the child will live
- Identifying how to prevent delay
- Identifying the appropriate Court
- Transferring to the appropriate Court

Action	Party	Timing
2.1 The First Hearing The First Hearing shall take place in the Family Proceedings Court (FPC) on or before **DAY 6**. At every First Hearing the **FPC** shall: • Consider who should be a **party** to the proceedings (step 2.2) • Make arrangements for contested **interim care applications** to be determined (step 2.3) • Consider whether the proceedings should be **transferred** to the Care Centre or another FPC (step 2.4) • Where the proceedings are not transferred, make **initial case management** decisions (step 2.6).	**FPC**	**on DAY 6**
2.2 Parties and Service At the First Hearing the **FPC** shall: • Obtain confirmation that all those who are entitled to be parties have been served • Consider whether any other person should be joined as a party • Give directions relating to party status and the service of documents upon parties.	**FPC**	**on DAY 6**
2.3 Contested Interim Care Orders If any proceedings where the application for an interim care order (ICO) is not agreed at the First Hearing, the **FPC** shall: • Decide whether to grant an order and if so what order; or • List the application for an urgent contested interim hearing in an FPC prior to the Case Management Conference (CMC); and • Give such case management directions as are necessary to ensure that the interim hearing will be effective; or • Transfer the proceedings to be heard at the Care Centre.	**FPC**	**on DAY 6**

Action	Party	Timing

2.4   **Urgency and Transfer**   **FPC**   **on DAY 6**

At the First Hearing the **FPC** shall:

- Hear submissions as to complexity, gravity and urgency
- Consider whether transfer to another Court is appropriate and in any event determine any application made by a party for transfer
- Give reasons for any transfer decision made and record the information provided by the parties relating to transfer on **form C22** (including any intention to apply for transfer to the High Court)
- Send the court file and the Order of transfer in **form C49** to the receiving court within **1 day** of the First Hearing (by **DAY 7**).

2.5   **Proceedings Transferred to the Care Centre**   **FPC**   **on DAY 6**

Where a decision is made to transfer to the Care Centre, the **FPC** shall:

- In accordance with the arrangements set out in the **Care Centre Plan** (CCP) and the **FPC Plan** (FPCP) **(appendix E)**, immediately inform the court officer at the Care Centre of the transfer and of the reasons set out on **form C22**
- Obtain a date and time from the court officer for an **Allocation Hearing**/contested interim hearing in the Care Centre which shall be between **3** and **5 days** of the decision to transfer (by **DAY 11**)
- Notify the parties of the Care Centre to which the proceedings are transferred and of the date and time of the Allocation Hearing / contested interim hearing
- Direct the LA or the child's solicitor to prepare a **case synopsis (appendix B/1)** which shall be filed with the Care Centre and served within **2 days** of the First Hearing in the FPC (by **DAY 8**)
- Except as to disclosure of documents, make only those **case management directions upon transfer** as are agreed with the Care Centre as set out in the CCP and the FPCP.

2.6   **Case Management in the FPC**   **FPC**   **on DAY 6**

In any case where the proceedings are **NOT** transferred to the care centre the **FPC** shall at the First Hearing:

- Consider the **case management checklist (appendix A/3)**
- Fix a date and time for a **Case Management Conference** (CMC) in the FPC within **54 days** of the First Hearing (between **DAYS 15 and 60**) unless all of the case management decisions set out at step 4.8 of this protocol can be taken at the First Hearing and the application can be listed for Final Hearing
- Fix a date for the **Final Hearing** or if it is not possible to do so fix a hearing window (either of which shall be not later than in the **3 week** period commencing the **37th WEEK** after the application was issued)
- Consider whether a **Pre-Hearing Review** (PHR) is necessary and if so fix a PHR not later than **2 weeks** and no earlier than **8 weeks** before the Final Hearing date/window
- Give such **case management directions** as are necessary to ensure that all steps will have been taken prior to the CMC to enable it to be effective, in particular:
  - that a **statement of evidence** from each party (including the child where of sufficient age and understanding, but excluding the child's Guardian) is filed and served replying to the facts alleged and the proposals made by the LA in the initial social work statement

Action	Party	Timing

- whether directions as to full and frank **disclosure** of all relevant documents need to be given and in any event give directions where necessary to ensure that the disclosure of relevant documents by the LA occurs within **20 days** of the First Hearing (by **DAY 26**)
- whether a **core assessment (appendix F)** exists or should be directed to be undertaken by the LA before the CMC
- Record on the **Standard Directions Form (SDF) (appendix A/1)** the Court's case management decisions and reasons and serve the directions given on the parties

2.7   The **FPC** shall give a direction at the First Hearing that **no further documents** shall be filed without the Court's permission unless in support of a new application or in accordance with case management directions given at that hearing (the Court will consider directions relating to the filing of comprehensive evidence and documents at the CMC)

STEP 3 – Allocation Hearing & Directions

OBJECTIVE   **Target time: by DAY 11**
To make provision for continuous and consistent judicial case management

Action	Party	Timing

3.1   **Following Transfer**   **Care Centre**   **from DAY 6**
Following transfer to the **Care Centre** or to the **High Court** all further hearings in the proceedings shall be conducted:
- So as to ensure **judicial continuity of case management** in accordance with the protocol;
- By one or not more than 2 judges who are identified as **case management judges** in the CCP **(appendix E/1)**, one of whom may be and where possible should be the judge who will conduct the Final Hearing

3.2   **Allocation in the Care Centre**   **Court Officer**   **by DAY 8**
Within **2 days** of the order transferring proceedings to the Care Centre (normally by **DAY 8**) the **court officer** shall:
- Allocate one and not more than two **case management judges** (one of whom may be and where possible should be the Judge who will conduct the Final Hearing) to case manage the proceedings in accordance with the protocol and the CCP
- Where possible, identify the judge who is to be the **Final Hearing judge**
- Upon receipt of the court file from the FPC, attach to the file the **form C22** issued by the FPC, the **case synopsis (appendix B/1)** and a **Standard Directions Form (SDF) (appendix A/1)** and complete the SDF to the extent only of:
  - the names of the **allocated and identified judges**
  - the proposed date of the **CMC** (which shall be within **54 days** of the date of the First Hearing in the FPC ie between **DAYS 15 and 60**)
  - the proposed **Final Hearing** date or hearing window (which shall be not later than in the **3 week** period commencing the **37th WEEK** after the application was issued)
  - the proposed date of the **PHR** (which shall be not later than **2 weeks** and no earlier than **8 weeks** before the Final Hearing / trial window)
- Inform the case management judge in writing:
  - of any other circumstances of **urgency**
  - of any contested interim hearing for an **ICO**
  - **of any application to transfer to the High Court**

Action	Party	Timing

- of the date and time of the **Allocation Hearing** (which shall be between **3 and 5 days** of the First Hearing in the FPC ie by **DAY 11**)
- Notify the parties of the date, time and venue fixed for the Allocation Hearing, together with the identity of the allocated / nominated judges

	Party	Timing
3.3 Section 37 Request for a Report and Transfer to a Care Centre	Court Officer	within 2 days of the order of transfer

Where in any family proceedings a Court decides to direct an appropriate LA to investigate a child's circumstances, **the Court** shall follow the guidance set out at **appendix G**.

Where, following a section 37 request for a report, proceedings are transferred to the Care Centre:

- The **transferring court** shall make a record of the Court's reasons for the transfer on **form C22** and the **court officer** of the transferring court shall send the court file, the order of transfer in **form C49** and the record of reasons to the Care Centre within **1 day** of the order
- The **court officer** in the care centre shall within **2 days** of the order transferring the proceedings take the steps set out at paragraph 3.2 and shall also:
  - inform the case management judge in writing of the transfer (and such circumstances as are known)
  - request the case management judge to consider giving directions as to the **appointment of a Guardian and / or a solicitor for the child** at or before the Allocation Hearing
  - notify all parties on **form C46** of the names of the Guardian and / or the solicitor for the child when they are appointed
- inform the LA solicitor or the child's solicitor of the requirement that a **case synopsis (appendix B/1)** be prepared which shall be filed with the care centre and served not later than **2 days** before the date fixed for the Allocation Hearing.

	Party	Timing
3.4 Allocation Hearing	Case Management Judge	by DAY 11

The Allocation Hearing in the Case Centre shall take place between **3 and 5 days** of the First Hearing in the FPC (by **DAY 11**). At the Allocation Hearing the **case management judge** shall:

- Consider whether the proceedings should be **transferred to the High Court** or re-transferred to the FPC
- Determine any **contested interim application** for a care or supervision order
- Where **the proceedings have been transferred from a court following a section 37 request** consider:
  - whether directions should be given to **appoint a Guardian and / or a solicitor for the child** in accordance with steps 1.2 to 1.4 of the protocol
  - whether any directions need to be given for the filing and service of **LA documents** in accordance with step 1.5 of the protocol
- Consider the **case management checklist (appendix A/3)**
- Fix a date and time for a **CMC** which shall be within **54 days** of the First Hearing in the FPC (between **DAYS 15 and 60**)
- Fix a date for the **Final Hearing** and confirm the identity of the Final Hearing judge or if it is not possible to do so fix a hearing window (either of which shall be not later than in the **3 week** period commencing the **37th WEEK** after the application was issued)

Action	Party	Timing

- Fix a date and time for a **PHR** which shall be not later than **2 weeks** and no earlier than **8 weeks** before the Final Hearing date or window
- Give such **case management directions** as are necessary to ensure that all steps will have been taken prior to the CMC to enable it to be effective, in particular:
  - that a **statement of evidence from each party** (including the child where of sufficient age and understanding, but excluding the child's Guardian) is filed and served replying to the facts alleged and the proposals made by the LA in the initial social work statement
  - whether directions as to full and frank **disclosure** of all relevant documents need to be given and in any event give directions where necessary to ensure that the disclosure of relevant documents by the LA occurs within **20 days** of the First Hearing (by **DAY 26**)
  - whether a **core assessment (appendix F)** exists or should be directed to be undertaken by the LA before the CMC
- Having regard to the *Practice Direction (family proceedings: court bundles)* [2000] 1 FLR 536 (**appendix D**), if applicable, give directions to the LA setting out which of the following **case management documents** in addition to the **case management questionnaire** (**appendix A/2**) are to be filed and served for use at the CMC:
  - a **schedule of findings of fact** which the Court is invited to make (in particular so as to satisfy the threshold criteria)
  - any update to the **social work chronology (appendix B/2)** that may be required
  - the **initial care plan (appendix F)**
  - if there is a question of law: a **skeleton argument with authorities**
  - a **summary of the background** (only if necessary to supplement the case synopsis)
  - an **advocate's chronology** (only if necessary to supplement the social work chronology or the case synopsis)
- Having regard to **appendix D**, give directions to the LA setting out the form of **bundle or documents index** that the Court requires
- Complete the **SDF (appendix A/1)** to record the Court's case management decisions and reasons.

3.5   **Case Management Questionnaire**   **Court Officer**   **on DAY 12**
Within **1 day** of the Allocation Hearing (on **DAY 12**) the **court officer** shall serve on each party:
- the completed **SDF** together with a
- **case management questionnaire (appendix A/2)**.

3.6   **Allocation in the High Court**   **Court Officer**   **on DAY 12**
Where an application is transferred to the High Court, the **court officer** shall within **1 day** of the Allocation Hearing (on **DAY 12**):
- In consultation with the Family Division Liaison Judge (or if the proceedings are transferred to the RCJ, the Clerk of the Rules) allocate a judge of the High Court who shall be the **case management judge** (and who may be the judge who will conduct the final hearing) to case manage the proceedings in accordance with the protocol and the CCP
- If necessary to accord with the CCP, allocate a **second case management judge** in the Care Centre who shall be responsible to the allocated High Court judge for case management of the proceedings
- Where possible, identify a judge of the High Court to be the **Final Hearing judge**

Action	Party	Timing
• Attach to the court file the **form C22** issued by the FPC, the **case synopsis (appendix B/1)** and a **SDF (appendix A/1)** and complete the SDF to the extent only of:		
• the names of the **allocated judges**		
• the date of the CMC (which shall be within **54 days** of the date of the First Hearing in the FPC ie between **DAYS 15 and 60**)		
• the proposed **Final Hearing** date or window (which shall be not later than in the **3 week** period commencing the **37th WEEK** after the application was issued)		
• the proposed date of the **PHR** (which shall be not later than **2 weeks** and no earlier than **8 weeks** before the Final Hearing or window)		
• Inform the case management judge in writing of:		
• any other circumstance of **urgency**		
• any contested hearing for an **ICO**		
• Within **1 day** of receipt of the court file and **completed SDF** from the allocated High Court judge (by **DAY 16**), send to each party a copy of the completed SDF together with a **case management questionnaire (appendix A/2)**	Court Officer	on DAY 16

3.7 Allocation Directions in the High Court   Case Management Judge   by DAY 15

Within **3 days** of receipt of the court file (by **DAY 15**) the allocated **case management judge** shall:
- Consider the **case management checklist (appendix A/3)**
- Complete the **SDF (appendix A/1)** having regard to those matters set out at step 3.4
- Return the court file and the completed SDF to the court officer.

STEP 4 – The Case Management Conference

OBJECTIVE
To consider what case management directions are necessary:
- To ensure that a fair hearing of the proceedings takes place
- To timetable the proceedings so that the Final Hearing is completed within or before the recommended hearing window

Target time: between DAYS 15 and 60

Action	Party	Timing
4.1 LA Case Management Documents	LA	not later than 5 days before the CMC
In every case the **LA** shall not later than **5 days** before the CMC prepare, paginate, index, file and serve:		
• The **case management documents** for the CMC that have been directed at the Allocation Hearing / Directions (step 3.4) and		
• A **case management questionnaire (appendix A/2)**		
4.2 The Court Bundle	LA	not later than 5 days before the CMC
Not later than **5 days** before the date fixed for the CMC, the **LA** shall:		
• For hearings to which the *Practice Direction (family proceedings: court bundles)* [2000] 1 FLR 536 (**appendix D**) applies or in accordance with any direction given at a First Hearing or Allocation Hearing, file with the Court a **bundle**		
• Serve on each of the represented parties an **index** to the bundle		
• Serve on any un-represented party a copy indexed bundle		

Action	Party	Timing
• For hearings to which **appendix D does not apply**, serve on all parties an **index** of the documents that have been filed		

4.3 **Other Party's Case Management Documents** — All Parties except the LA — not later than 2 days before the CMC

Not later than **2 days** before the date of the CMC **each party other than the LA** shall:
• File with the Court and serve on the parties the following **case management documents**:
• a **position statement** which sets out that party's response to the case management documents filed by the LA indicating the issues that are agreed and those that are not agreed. (A Guardian's position statement on behalf of the child should comment on the LA's arrangements and plans for the child)
• a completed **case management questionnaire (appendix A/2)**
• **Not** file any other **case management documents** without the prior direction of the Court

4.4 **The Court's Preparation** — Court Officer — not later than 2 days before the CMC

Not later than **2 days** before the CMC the **court officer** shall:
• Place the **case management documents of all parties** at the front of the court file and at the front of any bundle that is filed by the LA
• Deliver the court file and bundle to the case management judge who is to conduct the CMC
• Ensure that any arrangements for video and telephone conferencing and with criminal and civil listing officers have been made

4.5 **Advocates Meeting** — Advocates — on or before the day of the CMC

Before **the day** fixed for the **CMC** or (where it has not been practicable to have an earlier meeting) not later than **1 hour** before the time fixed for the CMC, the **parties and / or their lawyers** shall:
• Meet to **identify and narrow the issues** in the case
• Consider the **case management checklist (appendix A/3)**
• Consider the **case management questionnaires (appendix A/2)**
• Consider in accordance with the **experts code of guidance (appendix C)** whether and if so why any application is to be made to instruct an **expert**
• Consider whether full and frank **disclosure** of all relevant documents has taken place
• Draft a composite **schedule of issues (appendix B/4)** which identifies:
• a summary of the issues in the case
• a summary of issues for determination at the CMC by reference to the case management questionnaires / case management checklist
• the timetable of legal and social work steps proposed
• the estimated length of hearing of the PHR and of the Final Hearing
• the order which the Court will be invited to make at the CMC — All Parties — on DAY 34

4.6 **Availability**
On **the day** of the CMC **the parties** shall complete and file with the Court:
• A **witness non-availability form (appendix A/4)**
• A schedule (so far as it is known) of the names and contact details (professional addresses, telephone, fax, DX and e-mail) of:

Action	Party	Timing

- the lead social worker and team manager
- the Guardian
- solicitors and counsel / advocates for each party
- un-represented litigants
- any experts upon whose evidence it is proposed to rely

4.7 Conduct of the CMC

The CMC shall be conducted by one of the allocated **case management judges** or as directed by the FPC **case management legal adviser** in accordance with the protocol. It is the essence of the protocol that case management through to Final Hearing must be consistently provided by the same case management judges / legal advisers / FPCs.

All advocates who are retained to have conduct of the final hearing shall:

- Use their best endeavours to attend the CMC and must do so if directed by the Court
- Bring to the CMC details of their own availability for the 12 month period following the CMC
- Attend the advocates meeting before the CMC

4.8 The Hearing

At the CMC the **case management judge / court** shall:

Case
Management
Judge

- Consider the parties' composite **schedule of issues** (appendix B/4)
- Consider the **case management checklist (appendix A/3)**
- Consider the parties' **case management questionnaires (appendix A/2)** and **case management documents** (steps 3.4 and 4.3)
- If not already fixed at the First or Allocation Hearing, fix the date of the Final Hearing which shall be not later than in the 3 week period commencing the 37th WEEK after the application was issued
- If not already fixed, fix the date and time of the **PHR** which shall be not later than **2 weeks** before and no earlier than **8 weeks** before the Final Hearing
- Give a **time estimate** for each hearing that has been fixed
- Consider whether any hearing can take place using video, telephone or other **electronic means**
- Consider any outstanding application of which notice has been given to the Court and to the parties in accordance with the rules
- Give all necessary **case management directions** to:
  - **timetable** all remaining legal and social work steps
  - ensure that full and frank **disclosure** of all relevant documents is complete
  - ensure that a **core assessment (appendix F)** or other appropriate assessments materials will be available to the Court
  - ensure that if any **expert** is to be instructed the expert and the parties will complete their work for the Court within the Court's timetable and in accordance with the **experts code of guidance (appendix C)**
  - provide for **regular monitoring** of the Court's case management directions to include certification of compliance at each ICO renewal and the notification to the Court by the Guardian and by each responsible party of any material non compliance
  - permit a **further directions hearing** before the allocated case management judge in the event of a change of circumstances or significant non compliance with the directions of the Court
  - update, file and serve such of the **existing case management documents** as are necessary

Action	Party	Timing

- update, file and serve a **court bundle / index** for the PHR and for the Final Hearing
- ensure that the PHR and Final Hearing will be effective

STEP 5 – The Pre-Hearing Review

OBJECTIVE

To identify and narrow the remaining issues between the parties and ensure that the Final Hearing is effective	Target time: by WEEK 37	
Action	**Party**	**Timing**

5.1 The Court's Preparation   Court Officer   from WEEK 28
The **court officer** shall:

- In circumstances where **no PHR direction** has been given, send the court file / bundle to the case management judge during **WEEK 28** with a request for confirmation that no PHR is necessary or for a direction that a PHR be listed
- **Notify** the parties of any **PHR direction** given by the case management judge
- **List a PHR** where directions have been given by the case management judge (not earlier than **8 weeks** and not later than **2 weeks** before the Final Hearing ie between **WEEKS 29 and 37**)
- Not later than **2 days** before the PHR:
  - place the **updated case management documents** directed at the CMC (if any) at the front of the court file and at the front of any bundle that is filed by the LA
  - deliver the court file / bundle to the judge / FPC nominated to conduct the PHR
  - ensure that any arrangements for video and telephone conferencing and with criminal and civil listing officers have been made

5.2 Advocates Meeting   Advocates   in the week before the PHR

In the **week** before the PHR **the advocates** who have conduct of the **Final Hearing** shall:

- Communicate with each other and if necessary meet to **identify and narrow the issues** to be considered by the Court at the PHR and the Final Hearing
- Consider the **pre-hearing review checklist (appendix A/5)**
- **2 days** before the PHR file a composite **schedule of issues (appendix B/4)** which shall set out:
  - a summary of issues in the case
  - a summary of issues for determination at the PHR
  - a draft witness template
  - the revised estimated length of hearing of the Final Hearing
  - whether the proceedings are ready to be heard and if not, what steps need to be taken at the PHR to ensure that the proceedings can be heard on the date fixed for the Final Hearing
  - the order which the Court will be invited to make at the PHR

5.3 Case Management Documents   Advocates   between WEEKS 29 and 30

No case management documents are to be filed for use at a PHR except:

- Any **updated case management documents** directed by the case management judge at the CMC (step 4.8)
- The composite **schedule of issues (appendix B/4)**
- Documents in support of a **new application**.

	Action	Party	Timing

5.4   Conduct of the PHR

The **PHR** (or any directions hearing in the FPC which immediately precedes a Final Hearing) shall be listed before the judge / FPC nominated to conduct the Final Hearing. In exceptional circumstances the Court may in advance approve the release of the PHR but only to one of the allocated case management judges.

The **advocates** who are retained to have conduct of the Final Hearing shall:
- Use their best endeavours to secure their release from any other professional obligation to enable them to attend the PHR
- Update the case management documents as directed at the CMC
- Attend the advocates meeting.

5.5   The Hearing   **Court   at the PHR**

At the PHR the **Court** shall:
- Consider the **pre-hearing review checklist (appendix A/5)**
- Consider the parties' composite **schedule of issues (appendix B/4)**
- Confirm or give a **revised time estimate** for the Final Hearing
- Confirm the **fixed dates, venues and the nominated judge** for the Final Hearing
- Give such directions as are necessary to **update the existing case management documents and the Court bundle / index** having regard to the application of the *Practice Direction (Family Proceedings: Court Bundles)* [2000] 1 FLR 536 **(appendix D)**
- Give such directions as are necessary to ensure that the Final Hearing will be effective

5.6   Dispensing with the PHR   **All Parties   before the PHR**

Where the requirements of an advocates meeting have been complied with and all parties certify (in the composite **schedule of issues**) that:
- The proceedings are ready to be heard
- There has been compliance with the directions of the Court and
- There is agreement by all parties to all of the directions proposed having regard to the **pre-hearing review checklist (appendix A/5)**

The Court may decide to **dispense with the PHR** or deal with it on paper or by electronic means, including computer, video or telephone conferencing

STEP 6 – The Final Hearing

OBJECTIVE   **Target time: by WEEK 40**
To determine the remaining issues between the parties

	Action	Party	Timing

6.1   The Hearing   Judge / FPC
                                                          nominated for
                                                          the Final Hear-
                                                          ing

The **Final Hearing** shall be conducted by:
- The judge or FPC identified in the allocation directions as confirmed at the PHR

Where one of the allocated case management judges or an FPC has heard a substantial factual issue or there has been a 'preliminary hearing' to determine findings of fact it is necessary for the same judge / magistrates who conducted the preliminary hearing to conduct the Final Hearing.

	Action	Party	Timing
6.2	**Case Management and Practice Direction Documents**	**All Parties**	**not later than 2 days before the Final Hearing**

Not later than **2 days** before the Final Hearing **the parties** shall:
* Prepare, file and serve the **case management documents** for the Final Hearing as directed by the Court at the PHR
* Prepare, file and serve the **court bundle or index of court documents** as directed by the Court at the PHR

6.3	**The Court's Preparation**	**Court Officer**	**not later than 2 days before the Final Hearing**

Not later than **2 days** before the Final Hearing the **court officer** shall:
* Place any **case management documents** at the front of the court file and at the front of any bundle that is filed by the LA
* Deliver the **court file / bundle** to the judge / FPC nominated to conduct the Final Hearing
* Ensure that any arrangements for the reception of evidence by video link and telephone conferencing, interpreters, facilities for disabled persons and special measures for vulnerable or intimidated witnesses have been made

6.4	**Orders and Reasons**	**Court**	**at the Final Hearing**

At the conclusion of the Final Hearing the **Court** shall:
* Set out the basis / reasons for the orders made or applications refused in a **judgment** and where appropriate in the form of **recitals** to the order or in the case of an FPC in **form C22**
* Annexe to the order the **agreed or approved documents** setting out the threshold criteria and the care plan for the child
* Where the judgment is not in writing give consideration to whether there should be a **transcript** and if so who will obtain and pay for it

6.5	**Reserved Judgment**	**Judge**	**at the end of submissions**

In a complex case a judge (but not an FPC) may decide to reserve judgment and take time for consideration. Where judgment is reserved the Court will endeavour to fix a date for judgment to be given or handed down within **20 days** (4 weeks) of the conclusion of submissions. Advocates may be invited to make oral or written submissions as to consequential orders and directions at the conclusion of submissions or when the draft judgment is released.

6.6	**Disclosure**	**Court**	**at the end of the Final Hearing**

At the end of every Final Hearing the **Court** shall consider whether to give directions for **disclosure of documents,** for example:
* In any case where it is proposed that the child should be placed for adoption and so that subsequent adoption proceedings are not delayed, to the LA adoption panel, specialist adoption agency and / or proposed adopters and their legal advisers for use in subsequent adoption proceedings
* For any medical or therapeutic purpose
* For a claim to be made to the CICA

THE APPENDICES

A Forms

A/1 – Standard Directions Form

IN THE HIGH COURT OF JUSTICE
FAMILY DIVISION

COUNTY COURT / FPC

Case Number

Application   of

Local Authority

Re

Child(ren)

STANDARD DIRECTIONS BY CASE MANAGEMENT JUDGE / MAGISTRATES / LEGAL ADVISER

Date of this order

Upon reading the papers filed by the applicant:
IT IS ORDERED by   **The Honourable**
His/Her Honour

District Judge
Magistrates/Justices
Clerk

ALLOCATION DIRECTIONS

This case is allocated for case management to:

The Honourable
His/Her Honour
District Judge   **and**

Magistrates/Justices
Clerk

Contact Telephone no

(Judge's Clerk / Court Officer / Legal Adviser)

The allocated judge(s) will be responsible for the continuous case management of this case

All future hearings in this case will be conducted by one of the allocated judges and *not* by the urgent applications judge or by any other judge unless on application to one of the allocated judges (if necessary in case of urgency by telephone) the allocated judge releases the case to another judge.

(Where it is possible to identify the Final Hearing Judge / Magistrates).

The judge who will be responsible for the PHR and the conduct of the Final Hearing is:

CASE MANAGEMENT CONFERENCE

There will be a
Case Management
Conference before   **The Honourable**
His/Her Honour
District Judge
Magistrates/Justices
Clerk

at   venue

on the   date

at   time

The parties and their lawyers shall consider each of the matters set out at Steps 1 to 4 of the Protocol and in the CMC Checklist.

The parties shall prepare, file and serve **the Evidence and Case Management Documents** listed below. No documents other than those identified shall thereafter be filed with the Court without the Court's permission, unless in support of a new application.

LOCAL AUTHORITY PREPARATION FOR THE CMC

The LOCAL AUTHORITY shall not later than **2pm 5 days before** the date of the Case Management Conference prepare and file with the Court the following:
(Delete as appropriate)

(a) a Bundle prepared in accordance with the [*Practice Direction (family proceedings: court bundles)* [2000] 1 FLR 536] [... or   *specify the form]*. The Local Authority shall at the same time serve on each of the Respondents an Index to the Bundle and on any unrepresented party a copy of the bundle;

(b) an Index of the Documents filed with the Court. The Local Authority shall at the same time serve on each of the Respondents a copy of the Index;

(c) the following case management documents *(delete if not required)*:

* A **case management questionnaire**
* A schedule of the **findings of fact** which the Court is to be invited to make (in particular so as to satisfy the threshold criteria)
* Any update to the **social work chronology**
* The **interim care plan**(s)
* A **skeleton argument** limited to legal questions with accompanying authorities
* A clear and concise **summary of the background** on one page of A4 paper (only where necessary to supplement the Case Synopsis)
* An **advocates** chronology (only where necessary to supplement the Case Synopsis or the social work chronology)

RESPONDENT'S PREPARATION FOR THE CMC

The RESPONDENTS shall not later than **2pm 2 working days before** the date of the Case Management Conference prepare and file with the Court and serve on the Local Authority copies of:

* A statement of evidence in **reply to** the local authorities **initial social work statement** (unless already filed)
* A **case management questionnaire**
* A **position statement** (setting out what is agreed and what is not agreed).

THE ADVOCATES MEETING

The parties lawyers and any un-represented party shall attend an **Advocates Meeting**:

at	venue
on the	date
at	time

to discuss those matters set out at Step 4.5 of the Protocol and shall prepare a composite **schedule of issues** which shall be filed with the Court:

not later than	time
on the	date

in default of the advocates meeting taking place and in any event, the lawyers for all parties and any un-represented party shall attend at Court on the day of the Case Management Conference NOT LATER THAN **1 hour before** the time fixed for the hearing so that they can all meet together to discuss the issues and draft the composite **schedule of issues**.

EXPERTS

Any party that proposes to ask the Court's permission to instruct an **expert witness** shall comply with the **experts code of guidance** and shall set out the required particulars in their case management questionnaire

AVAILABILITY AND CONTACT DETAILS

The parties' legal representatives shall bring to the advocates meeting and to the CMC:
* Their professional diaries for the next 12 months
* Details (so far as can be known) of the names and the availability of anybody who it is proposed should conduct any assessment of provide any expert evidence so that a **witness availability form** can be prepared and filed at the CMC

- Details (so far as can be known) of the names and contact details (professional addresses and telephone/fax/DX/e-mail numbers for) so that a **schedule** can be prepared and filed at the CMC with particulars of:
  - the lead social worker
  - the Children's Guardian
  - the solicitors and counsel/advocates for each party
  - any experts and assessors who have been or may be instructed

DISCLOSURE OF DOCUMENTS

Any outstanding disclosure of relevant documents between the parties shall take place:

by [ ] date

PRE-HEARING REVIEW

There will be a PHR before the Final Hearing Judge:

at [ ] venue

on the [ ] date

at [ ] time

with a time estimate of [ ] time estimate

FINAL HEARING

The Final Hearing will take place before the Final Hearing Judge:

at [ ] venue

on the [ ] date

at [ ] time

with a time estimate of [ ] time estimate

ADDITIONAL DIRECTIONS (if any)

OBSERVATIONS

Signed

Case Management Judge / Magistrates / Justices Clerk

A/2 – *Case Management Questionnaire*

This Questionnaire is completed [by][on behalf of],

[ ]

In the

Note: who is the [ ] [Applicant] [Respondent]
Please [ ] [other]
state in these proceedings.
your
party
status

[Family Proceedings Court]
[District Registry] [County Court]
[Principal Registry of the Family Division]
[The High Court of Justice]

Case Number

Please read the following notes before completing the Case Management Questionnaire.

- **The Local Authority** must file and serve this questionnaire (together with the other case management documents directed at steps 3.4 and 4.1 of the protocol) **not later than 5 days** before the date fixed for the Case Management Conference.

- **All other parties** must file and serve this questionnaire (together with the other case management documents listed at step 4.3 of the protocol) **not later than 2 days** before the date fixed for the Case Management Conference.
- Your answers to the following questions should be given **in summary form only**. However, if you need more space for your answers use a separate sheet of paper. Please put your full name and case number at the top of any additional sheet and mark clearly which question the information refers to. Please ensure that any additional sheets are firmly attached to the questionnaire.

Have you served a copy of the completed questionnaire [and the other documents required by the protocol] on the other [party][parties]?

Yes ☐   No ☐

A. COMPLEXITY / URGENCY

Are the proceedings complex?   Yes ☐   No ☐

Are there any urgent features that the Court should know about?   Yes ☐   No ☐

If **'Yes'**, to either question please explain briefly why the proceedings are complex and or what urgent features the Court should be aware of:

B. URGENT / PRELIMINARY HEARINGS

Do you wish there to be an urgent hearing?   Yes ☐   No ☐

Do you wish there to be a preliminary hearing?   Yes ☐   No ☐

If **'Yes'**, to either question please explain briefly why such a hearing is required and what question(s) the Court will be asked to answer at that hearing:

C. EVIDENCE

Part 1 – Witnesses / Reports

Are there any **witness statements** or **clinical reports** upon which you intend to rely?   Yes ☐   No ☐

If **'Yes'**, please provide the information requested in the box below:

Author:	Date of Report:	Nature of Evidence:

Part 2 – Further Assessments / Expert Evidence

Do you propose to ask for a further assessment?   Yes ☐   No ☐

Do you propose to seek permission to use expert evidence? Yes ☐   No ☐

If you answer 'Yes' to either of the above questions, for each further assessment or expert you propose please give those details required by the Experts Code of Guidance (step 2.3) on a separate sheet and attach it to this questionnaire.

D. OTHER EVIDENCE INCLUDING EVIDENCE OF ETHNICITY, LANGUAGE, RELIGION, CULTURE, GENDER AND VULNERABILITY

Is any other evidence needed for example, relating to the ethnicity, language, religion, culture, gender and vulnerability of the child or other significant person?

Yes ☐ No ☐

If **'Yes'**, please give brief details of the evidence that you propose:

E. LEGAL AND SOCIAL WORK TIMETABLE

Please give details of the Legal and Social Work timetable that is proposed:

Date Proposed:	Step Proposed:	Party Responsible:

F. HEARING AND READING TIME

How long do you think the Case Management Conference will take? ☐ hour(s) ☐ minutes

How long do you think the Pre-Hearing Review will take? ☐ hour(s) ☐ minutes

How long do you think the Final Hearing will take? ☐ day(s) ☐ minutes

Give details of the recommended reading list for the Case Management Conference:

G. PROPOSED DIRECTIONS

(Parties should agree directions at the Advocates Meeting. A list of proposed directions or orders should be attached to this questionnaire using the standard variable directions forms wherever possible.)

Have you attached a list of the directions (or orders) you wish the Court to consider at the CMC:

(a) to ensure that the matters set out in the protocol are complied with; and Yes ☐ No ☐

(b) that are required for any other purpose, in particular, compliance with the Experts Code of Guidance (Step 2.4) and to ensure that disclosure of relevant documents takes place. Yes ☐ No ☐

H. OTHER INFORMATION

In the space below, set out any other information you consider will help the judge or court to manage this case.

Signed: ☐ Date: ☐

[Counsel] [Solicitor] for the
[   ] [Applicant] [Respondent] [   ] [other]

Please enter your contact name, reference number and full postal address including (if appropriate) details of DX, fax or e-mail.

Name:	Reference:
Address:	Telephone number: Fax number: DX number: e-mail:

A/3 – Case Management Checklist

OBJECTIVE
The following checklist is to be used for the First Hearing in the FPC, the Allocation Hearing in the Care Centre, Allocation Directions in the High Court and for the CMC

Representation of the Child

1. Has CAFCASS been notified of any decision to appoint a Guardian. If so, has a Guardian been allocated or is the likely date of allocation known?
2. Are there any other relevant proceedings. If so, was a Guardian appointed and has CAFCASS been informed of the nature/number of the other/previous proceedings and the identity of the Guardian?
3. If a decision has been made to appoint a Guardian but no allocation has yet taken place by CAFCASS: are any directions necessary for the representation of the child including the appointment of a solicitor?
4. Have the parties been notified of the names of the Guardian and of the solicitor appointed in form C46?
5. Should consideration be given to the separate representation of the child?

Parties

6. Have all significant persons involved in the child's care been identified, in particular those persons who are automatically Respondents to the application. Are any directions required to ensure service upon a party?
7. Has consideration been given to notifying a father without parental responsibility and informing other significant adults in the extended family of the proceedings?
8. Should any other person be joined as a party to the proceedings (whether upon application or otherwise). Are any directions necessary for the service of documents. If so, which documents?

ICO

9. Are the grounds for making an ICO agreed. Have they been recorded on form C22 or in a document approved by the Court?
10. If the grounds for making an ICO are not agreed has a date been fixed for an urgent hearing of the contested interim application or are the proceedings to be transferred to the Care Centre?
11. Have all case management directions been given to ensure that the contested interim hearing will be effective?

Urgency, Transfer and Re-Transfer

12. Are there any features of particular urgency and if so what directions are necessary to provide for that urgency or to minimise delay, eg lateral or upwards transfer?
13. Have any circumstances of complexity, gravity and urgency been considered and has any decision to transfer the proceedings to the Care Centre / High Court been made and notified to the parties?
14. Have the directions that are set out in the CCP and the FPCP been made upon transfer?
15. After transfer, have the circumstances of complexity, gravity and urgency that remain been re-considered and is it appropriate to transfer back to the Care Centre or FPC?
16. In relation to any question of re-transfer, has the availability of the Court been ascertained and have the parties been notified?

Protocol Documents

17 **LA Documents on Issue of Application.** Are any directions necessary relating to the preparation, filing and service of those LA documents that are required by the protocol within 2 days of the proceedings being issued?

18 **Case Synopsis.** Are any directions necessary to ensure that the LA or the Child's solicitor prepares, files and serves a case synopsis?

19 **The Court Bundle / Index.** Are any directions necessary to ensure that a court bundle is prepared and filed or that an index to the Court documents is prepared, filed and served?

20 Have directions been given to update the court bundle / index, in particular the responsibility for, the format of and arrangements for updating (or the compilation of an application bundle) and whether updates can be provided to the Court / judge by e-mail?

21 **Local Authority Case Management Documents.** Are any directions necessary to ensure that the LA case management documents are prepared, filed and served?

22 **Other Party's Case Management Documents.** Are any directions necessary to ensure that the case management documents of other parties are prepared, filed and served?

23 **Case Management Questionnaires.** Are any directions necessary to ensure that the parties prepare, file and serve case management questionnaires?

24 **Recommended Reading List.** For any hearing where no case management questionnaire or schedule of issues will be available, are any directions necessary for the parties to provide the Court with a joint reading list?

25 **Witness Non-Availability Form.** Are any directions necessary to ensure that a witness availability form and schedule of contact details are completed / updated?

Preliminary Directions

26 **Statements of Evidence from Each Party.** Have directions been given for the parties other than the LA to prepare, file and serve evidence in reply to the LA's initial social work statement?

27 **Disclosure.** Have directions been given to ensure that all relevant documents are disclosed by the LA within 20 days of the First Hearing?

28 **Allocation.** Have all allocation directions been given?

29 **Standard Directions Form.** Has the SDF been completed and served?

Listing

30 **CMC.** Has a date and time been fixed for the CMC (between days 15 and 60). Is the date, time and time estimate recorded on the draft SDF?

31 If a CMC is not to be listed have all case management directions been given for the Final Hearing and are they recorded on the draft SDF?

32 **PHR.** Is a PHR necessary. Is the date, time and time estimate recorded on the draft SDF (not later then 2 weeks and no earlier than 8 weeks before the Final Hearing)?

33 If a PHR is not necessary have all case management directions set out in the PHR checklist been considered in giving directions for the Final Hearing?

34 **Final Hearing.** Has a date or hearing window been fixed for the Final Hearing (not later than in the 3 weeks commencing the 37th week after issue) and are the dates recorded on the draft SDF together with the time estimate?

35 **Venue / Technology.** Have directions been given for the venue of each hearing and whether video link, telephone conferencing or electronic communication with the Court can be used? If so, have arrangements been made for the same?

Evidence

36 **Other Proceedings.** Has consideration been given to the relevance of any other / previous proceedings and as to whether the Judgment / Reasons given or evidence filed should be admitted into evidence?

37 **Disclosure.** Has the Guardian read the social work files. If not when will that task be complete. Having read the files has the Guardian confirmed that either they contain no other relevant documents or that an application for specific disclosure is necessary?

38 Are there any applications relating to the disclosure of documents?

39   **The Child's Evidence.** Should evidence be prepared, filed and served concerning the child's wishes and feelings?

40   **The Issues.** What are the issues in the case

41   Are any directions necessary for the filing of further factual evidence (including clinical evidence of treatment) by any party and if so to which issue(s) is such evidence to be directed?

42   Are any directions necessary for any party to respond to the LA's factual evidence and/or to the LA's proposed threshold criteria and schedule of findings of fact sought?

43   **LA Core Assessment.** Has a core assessment been completed. If not, are any directions necessary for the preparation, service and filing of an assessment?

44   **Additional Assessments and Expert Evidence.** In respect of every question relating to a request for expert evidence, is the request in accordance with the Experts Code of Guidance?

45   What are the issues to which it is proposed expert evidence or further assessment should be directed?

46   Who is to conduct the assessment or undertake the report, what is the expert's discipline, has the expert confirmed availability, what is the timetable for the report, the responsibility for instruction and the likely costs on both an hourly and global basis, what is the proposed responsibility for or apportionment of costs of jointly instructed experts as between the LA and the publicly funded parties (including whether there should be a section 38(6) direction)?

47   Are any consequential directions necessary (eg to give permission for examination or interview)?

48   Are any directions necessary to provide the expert with documents / further documents?

49   Are any directions necessary for the conduct of experts meetings / discussions and the preparation, filing and service of statements of agreement and disagreement?

50   **Ethnicity, Language, Religion and Culture.** Has consideration been given to the ethnicity, language, religion and culture of the child and other significant persons and are any directions necessary to ensure that evidence about the same is available to the Court?

Care Plans and Final Evidence

51   **LA.** Have directions been given for the preparation, filing and service of the final proposals of the LA and in particular its final statements of evidence and care plan?

52   **Other Parties.** Have directions been given for the preparation, filing and service of the parents' and other parties' responses to the LA's proposals?

53   **Guardian.** Are any directions necessary for the preparation, filing and service of the Guardian's report?

Other Case Management Steps

54   **Advocates Meetings and Schedules of Issue.** Are any directions necessary to ensure that an advocates meeting takes place and that a composite Schedule of Issues is drafted?

55   **Preliminary / Split Hearing.** Is a finding of fact hearing necessary and if so, what is the discrete issue of fact that is to be determined, by whom and when?

56   **Family Group Conference / ADR.** Has consideration been given to whether a family group conference or alternative dispute resolution can be held and would any directions assist to facilitate the conference resolution?

57   **Twin Track Planning.** Are any directions necessary to ensure that in the appropriate case twin track planning has been considered and where appropriate, directions given in relation to any concurrent freeing for adoption proceedings and for the filing and service of evidence relating to placement options and their feasibility. In particular have dates been fixed for the filing of the parallel plan and in respect of the Adoption / Fostering / Permanent Placement Panel timetable?

58   **Adoption Directions.** Are any directions necessary to ensure that the Adoption Practice Direction is complied with and in particular that any proposed (concurrent) freeing proceedings have been commenced?

59   **Placement.** Are any directions necessary for the filing and service of evidence relating to placement options including extended family placements and their feasibility, information about the timetable for the assessment and planning processes and any proposed referrals to Adoption / Fostering and / or Permanence Panels?

60   **Court's Timetable.** Has a timetable of all legal and social work steps been agreed and is the timetable set out in the Court order or as an approved document annexed to the order?

61   **Monitoring and Compliance.** What directions are necessary to ensure that the Court's timetable and directions are monitored and complied with, in particular have directions been given for the certification of compliance upon ICO renewals and for any further directions or a return to Court in the event of significant non-compliance?

62   **Change of Circumstance.** What directions are necessary to make provision for the parties to return to court in the event of a significant change of circumstance?

63   **Preparation for Final Hearing.** Is any consideration necessary of the case management directions set out in the PHR checklist in particular:
• Use of interpreters?
• Special Measures for Vulnerable or intimidated witnesses?
• Children's evidence or attendance at court?
• Facilities for persons with a disability?
• Evidence or submissions by video or telephone conference or on paper or by e-mail?
• Video and audio recordings and transcripts?

A/4 – Witness Non-Availability

This Questionnaire is completed [by][on behalf of],

Note: who is the [ ] [Applicant] [Respondent]
Please [ ] [other]
state in these proceedings.
your
party
status

In the
and service,
and the preparation, filing and service

[Family Proceedings Court]
[District Registry] [County Court]
[Principal Registry of the Family Division]
[The High Court of Justice]

Case Number

Sheet No.   of

Note: This form may be used for a maximum of six witnesses. If you intend to ask for more than six witnesses to give evidence on your behalf, please continue on a second sheet. You should indicate how many sheets you have used by completing the box above.

Date of Final Hearing (where known)

Location of Final Hearing (where known)

Witness details:

Witness Number:	Witness Name:	Description:
1.		
2.		
3.		
4.		
5.		
6.		

Completion of the Non-Availability Grid:

NOTE:

Mark dates when Experts and other witnesses are NOT available. Codes for use in the grid are as follows: H = Holiday, C = Course, S = Sickness or medical appointment, T = Attendance at another trial/hearing, O = Other

The person signing this form must be fully familiar with all the details of non-availability given on the Grid overleaf. If there are other issues the Court should be aware of concerning witness availability please state these below:

Signed: [   ]   Date: [   ]

[Counsel] [Solicitor] for the
[   ] [Applicant] [Respondent] [   ]

Non-Availability Grid

The Non-Availability Grid cannot be reproduced for technical reasons. Please visit the LCD website at http://www.lcd.gov.uk/judicial/cap/jcmappendices.pdf to view the original document.

A/5 – PHR Checklist

OBJECTIVE
The following checklist is to be used for the Pre-Hearing Review

Representation of the Child

1   Have the protocol and other practice direction steps been complied with?

2   Have each of the directions given at the CMC and any subsequent hearing been complied with?

3   Have the issues to be determined at the Final Hearing been identified and recorded in the draft PHR order?

4   Which witnesses are to be called, by whom and in relation to what issues(s)?

5   Are any experts required to give oral evidence, if so why and in relation to what issue(s)?

6   What is the extent of the examination in chief and cross-examination of each witness that is proposed?

7   Has a witness template been completed and agreed?

8   What, if any, of the written evidence is agreed or not in issue (and accordingly is to be read by the Court on that basis)?

9   Are interpretation facilities necessary and if so have they been directed and / or arranged (Note the special arrangements to be made for deaf signing)?

10   Are any facilities needed for a party or witness with a disability. If so have arrangements been made?

11   Are any special measures or security measures applied for in relation to vulnerable or intimidated witnesses including, for example, live video link, screens or witness support. If so what are the arrangements, if any, that are directed to be made?

12   Is it intended that the child will attend to see the judge and / or give evidence at the Final Hearing and have the arrangements been agreed and made?

13   Is any evidence to be taken indirectly by live video link, eg for an expert or witness who is overseas or otherwise unable to attend Court. If so have the arrangements been made?

14   Are any video or audio recordings to be used and if so:
(a) have the relevant excerpts of the recordings been agreed?
(b) have agreed transcripts been obtained? and
(c) have the arrangements been made to view / listen to the recordings?

15   Are there questions of law to be determined, and if so when should the submissions be heard and what provision should be made for the consideration of the authorities and skeleton arguments that will be required?

16   Is there a recommended reading list for the Court?

17   What is the timetable for the Final Hearing including opening and closing submissions and judgment / reasons?

18   What is the estimated length of the Final Hearing?

19   Who is / are the judge / magistrates nominated to conduct the Final Hearing?

20   Where is the venue for the Final Hearing?

21   Does the *Practice Direction (family proceedings: court bundles)* [2000] 1 FLR 536 apply to the Final Hearing and / or are any other case management documents to be updated, prepared, filed and served by the parties and if so: by whom and when? ☐

22   Are the proceedings ready for Final Hearing and have all steps and directions been complied with so that the PHR can be dispensed with or considered by the Court in the absence of the parties? ☐

B   Standard Documents

The following documents are identified in the protocol and their contents are prescribed below

---

1   **Case Synopsis** shall contain such of the following information as is known in summary form for use at the Allocation Hearing and shall normally be limited to 2 sides of A4:
- The identities of the parties and other significant persons
- The applications that are before the Court
- A very brief summary of the precipitating incident(s) and background circumstances
- Any particular issue that requires a direction to be given at the Allocation Hearing (eg relating to a social services core assessment)
- Any intention to apply to transfer the proceedings to the High Court
- The parties interim proposals in relation to placement and contact
- The estimated length of the Allocation Hearing (to include a separate estimate relating to a contested ICO where relevant)
- A recommended reading list and a suggested reading time for the Allocation Hearing
- Advance notice of any other decisions or proceedings that may be relevant, to include: criminal prosecutions, family law proceedings, disciplinary, immigration and mental health adjudications

2   **Social Work Chronology** is a schedule containing a succinct summary of the significant dates and events in the child's life in chronological order. It is a running record ie it is to be updated during the proceedings. The schedule headings are:
- serial number
- date
- event-detail
- witness or document reference (where applicable)

3   **Initial Social Work Statement.** The initial social work statement filed by the LA within 2 days of the issue of an application is strictly limited to the following evidence:
- The precipitating incident(s) and background circumstances relevant to the grounds and reasons for making the application including a brief description of any referral and assessment processes that have already occurred
- Any facts and matters that are within the social worker's personal knowledge
- Any emergency steps and previous court orders that are relevant to the application
- Any decisions made by the LA that are relevant to the application
- Information relevant to the ethnicity, language, religion, culture, gender and vulnerability of the child and other significant persons in the form of a 'family profile' together with a narrative description and details of the social care services that are relevant to the same
- Where the LA is applying for an ICO and/or is proposing to remove or seeking to continue the removal of a child under emergency protection: the LA's initial proposals for the child including placement, contact with parents and other significant persons and the social care services that are proposed
- The LA's initial proposals for the further assessment of the parties during the proceedings including twin track planning
- The social work timetable, tasks and responsibilities so far as they are known.

4   **Schedule of Issues.** The composite schedule of issues produced by the advocates at the end of the advocates' meetings prior to the CMC and the PHR should be agreed so far as is possible and where not agreed should set out the differing positions as to the following:
- A summary of the issues in the case (including any diverse cultural or religious contexts)
- A summary of issues for determination at the CMC/PHR by reference to the questionnaires/checklists
- For the CMC: the timetable of legal and social work steps proposed
- The estimated length of hearing of the PHR and the Final Hearing
- For the PHR: whether the Final Hearing is ready to be heard and if not, what steps need to be taken
- The order which the Court will be invited to make at the CMC/PHR

C Code of Guidance for Expert Witnesses in Family Proceedings

OBJECTIVE

The objective of this Code of Guidance is to provide the Court with early information to enable it to determine whether it is necessary and / or practicable to ask an expert to assist the Court:

- **To identify, narrow and where possible agree the issues between the parties**
- **To provide an opinion about a question that is not within the skill and experience of the Court**
- **To encourage the early identification of questions that need to be answered by an expert**
- **To encourage disclosure of full and frank information between the parties, the Court and any expert instructed**

Action	Party	Timing

1 THE DUTIES OF EXPERTS

1.1 Overriding Duty: An **expert in family proceedings has an overriding duty to** the Court that takes precedence over any obligation to the person from whom he has received instructions or by whom he is paid.

1.2 Particular Duties: Among any other duties an expert may have, **an expert shall** have regard to the following duties:

- To assist the Court in accordance with the overriding duty
- To provide an opinion that is independent of the party or parties instructing the expert
- To confine an opinion to matters material to the issues between the parties and in relation only to questions that are within the expert's expertise (skill and experience). If a question is put which falls outside that expertise the expert must say so
- In expressing an opinion take into consideration all of the material facts including any relevant factors arising from diverse cultural or religious contexts at the time the opinion is expressed, indicating the facts, literature and any other material that the expert has relied upon in forming an opinion
- To indicate whether the opinion is provisional (or qualified, as the case may be) and the reason for the qualification, identifying what further information is required to give an opinion without qualification
- Inform those instructing the expert without delay of any change in the opinion and the reason for the change

2 PREPARATION FOR THE CMC

2.1 Preliminary Enquiries of the Expert: Not later than 10 days before the CMC the solicitor for the party proposing to instruct the expert (or lead solicitor / solicitor for the child if the instruction proposed is joint) shall approach the expert with the following information:

- The nature of the proceedings and the issues likely to require determination by the Court;
- The questions about which the expert is to be asked to give an opinion (including any diverse cultural or religious contexts)
- When the Court is to be asked to give permission for the instruction (if unusually permission has already been given the date and details of that permission)
- Whether permission is asked of the Court for the instruction of another expert in the same or any related field (i.e. to give an opinion on the same or related questions)
- The volume of reading which the expert will need to undertake
- Whether or not (in an appropriate case) permission has been applied for or given for the expert to examine the child
- Whether or not (in an appropriate case) it will be necessary for the expert to conduct interviews (and if so with whom)
- The likely timetable of legal and social work steps

Action	Party	Timing
• When the expert's opinion is likely to be required		
• Whether and if so what date has been fixed by the Court for any hearing at which the expert may be required to give evidence (in particular the Final Hearing).	Solicitor instructing the expert	in-10 days before the CMC

2.2 Expert's Response: Not later than 5 days before the CMC the solicitors intending to instruct the expert shall obtain the following information from the expert:

Action	Party	Timing
• That the work required is within the expert's expertise		
• That the expert is available to do the relevant work within the suggested time scale		
• When the expert is available to give evidence, the dates and/or times to avoid, and, where a hearing date has not been fixed, the amount of notice the expert will require to make arrangements to come to Court without undue disruption to their normal clinical routines.		
• The cost, including hourly and global rates, and likely hours to be spent, of attending at experts / professionals meetings, attending court and writing the report (to include any examinations and interviews).	Solicitor instructing the expert	in-5 days before the CMC

2.3 Case Management Questionnaire:

Any party who proposes to ask the Court for permission to instruct an expert shall not later than 2 days before the CMC (or any hearing at which the application is to be made) file and serve a case management questionnaire setting out the proposal to instruct the expert in the following detail:

- • The name, discipline, qualifications and expertise of the expert (by way of C.V. where possible)
- • The expert's availability to undertake the work
- • The relevance of the expert evidence sought to be adduced to the issues in the proceedings and the specific questions upon which it is proposed the expert should give an opinion (including the relevance of any diverse cultural or religious contexts)
- • The timetable for the report
- • The responsibility for instruction
- • Whether or not the expert evidence can properly be obtained by the joint instruction of the expert by two or more of the parties.
- • Whether the expert evidence can properly be obtained by only one party (eg on behalf of the child)
- • Whether it is necessary for more than one expert in the same discipline to be instructed by more than one party
- • Why the expert evidence proposed cannot be given by social services undertaking a core assessment or by the Guardian in accordance with their different statutory duties
- • The likely cost of the report on both an hourly and global basis.

Action	Party	Timing
• The proposed apportionment of costs of jointly instructed experts as between the Local Authority and the publicly funded parties.	The Party proposing to instruct the expert	not later than 2 days before the CMC

2.4 Draft Order for the CMC:

Any party proposing to instruct an **expert** shall in the draft order submitted at the CMC request the Court to give directions (among any others) as to the following:

- • The party who is to be responsible for drafting the letter of instruction and providing the documents to the expert
- • The issues identified by the Court and the questions about which the expert is to give an opinion
- • The timetable within which the report is to be prepared, filed and served

Action	Party	Timing
• The disclosure of the report to the parties and to any other expert		
• The conduct of an experts' discussion		
• The preparation of a statement of agreement and disagreement by the experts following an experts discussion		
• The attendance of the expert at the Final Hearing unless agreement is reached at or before the PHR about the opinions given by the expert.	**Any Party**	**not later than 2 days before the CMC**

3   LETTER OF INSTRUCTION

3.1   The solicitor instructing the expert shall within 5 days of the CMC prepare (agree with the other parties where appropriate) file and serve a letter of instruction to the expert which shall:

- Set out the context in which the expert's opinion is sought (including any diverse ethnic, cultural, religious or linguistic contexts)
- Define carefully the specific questions the expert is required to answer ensuring:
  - **that they are within the ambit of the expert's area of expertise and**
  - **that they do not contain unnecessary or irrelevant detail**
  - **that the questions addressed to the expert are kept to a manageable number and are clear, focused and direct**
  - **that the questions reflect what the expert has been requested to do by the Court**
- List the documentation provided or provide for the expert an indexed and paginated bundle which shall include:
  - **a copy of the order (or those parts of the order) which gives permission for the instruction of the expert immediately the order becomes available**
  - **an agreed list of essential reading**
  - **all new documentation when it is filed and regular updates to the list of documents provided or to the index to the paginated bundle**
  - **a copy of this code of guidance and of the protocol**
- Identify the relevant lay and professional people concerned with the proceedings (eg the treating clinicians) and inform the expert of his/her right to talk to the other professionals provided an accurate record is made of the discussion
- Identify any other expert instructed in the proceedings and advise the expert of his/her right to talk to the other experts provided an accurate record is made of the discussion
- Define the contractual basis upon which the expert is retained and in particular the funding mechanism including how much the expert will be paid (an hourly rate and overall estimate should already have been obtained) when the expert will be paid, and what limitation there might be on the amount the expert can charge for the work which he/she will have to do. There should also be a brief explanation of the 'detailed assessment process' in cases proceeding in the Care Centre or the High Court which are not subject to a high cost case contract

• In default of agreement the format of the letter of instruction shall be determined by the Court, which may determine the issue upon written application with representations from each party.	**Solicitor instructing expert**	**in-within 5 days of thethe CMC**

4   THE EXPERT'S REPORT

4.1   **Content of the Report:**
The expert's report shall be addressed to the Court and shall:

Action	Party	Timing
• Give details of the expert's qualifications and experience		
• Contain a statement setting out the substance of all material instructions (whether written or oral) summarising the facts stated and instructions given to the expert which are material to the conclusions and opinions expressed in the report		
• Give details of any literature or other research material upon which the expert has relied in giving an opinion		
• State who carried out any test, examination or interview which the expert has used for the report and whether or not the test, examination or interview has been carried out under the expert's supervision.		
• Give details of the qualifications of any person who carried out the test, examination or interview		

• Where there is a range of opinion on the question to be answered by the expert:
   – **summarise the range of opinion and**
   – **give reasons for the opinion expressed**		

• Contain a summary of the expert's conclusions and opinions		
• Contain a statement that the expert understands his duty to the Court and has complied with that duty		
• Where appropriate be verified by a statement of truth.	**The Expert**	**in accordance with the Court's timetable**

4.2 Supplementary Questions:

Any party wishing to ask supplementary questions of an expert for the purpose of clarifying the expert's report must put those questions in writing to the parties not later than 5 days after receipt of the report. Only those questions that are agreed by the parties or in default of agreement approved by the Court may be put to the expert. The Court may determine the issue upon written application with representations from each party.	**Any Party**	**within 5 days of the receipt of the report**

5 EXPERTS DISCUSSION (MEETING)

5.1 Experts Discussion (Meeting) Purpose:

The Court will give directions for the experts to meet or communicate:		
• To identify and narrow the issues in the case.		
• To reach agreement on the expert questions		
• To identify the reasons for disagreement on any expert question and to identify what if any action needs to be taken to resolve any outstanding disagreement/question		
• To obtain elucidation or amplification of relevant evidence in order to assist the Court to determine the issues		
• To limit, wherever possible, the need for experts to attend Court to give oral evidence.	**The Court**	**at the CMC**

5.2 The Arrangements for a Discussion/Meeting: In accordance with the directions given by the Court at the CMC, the solicitor for the child or such other professional who is given the responsibility by the Court shall make arrangements for there to be a discussion between the experts within 10 days of the filing of the experts reports. The following matters should be considered:

• Where permission has been given for the instruction of experts from different disciplines a global discussion may be held relating to those questions that concern all or most of them

Action	Party	Timing

- Separate discussions may have to be held among experts from the same or related disciplines but care should be taken to ensure that the discussions complement each other so that related questions are discussed by all relevant experts
- 7 days prior to a discussion or meeting the solicitor for the child or other nominated professional should formulate an agenda to include a list of the questions for consideration. This may usefully take the form of a list of questions to be circulated among the other parties in advance. The agenda should comprise all questions that each party wishes the experts to consider. The agenda and list of questions should be sent to each of the experts not later than 2 days before the discussion
- The discussion should usually be chaired by the child's solicitor or in exceptional cases where the parties have applied to the Court at the CMC, by an independent professional identified by the parties or the Court. In complex medical cases it may be necessary for the discussion to be jointly chaired by an expert. A minute must be taken of the questions answered by the experts, and a Statement of Agreement and Disagreement must be prepared which should be agreed and signed by each of the experts who participated in the discussion. The statement should be served and filed not later than 5 days after the discussion has taken place
- Consideration should be given in each case to whether some or all of the experts participate by telephone conference or video link to ensure that minimum disruption is caused to clinical schedules.

5.3   **Positions of the Parties:**

Where any party refuses to be bound by an agreement that has been reached at an experts' discussion that party must inform the Court at or before the PHR of the reasons for refusing to accept the agreement.	**Any Party**	**at the PHR**

5.4   **Professionals Meetings:**

In proceedings where the Court gives a direction that a professionals meeting shall take place between the Local Authority and any relevant named professionals for the purpose of providing assistance to the Local Authority in the formulation of plans and proposals for the child, the meeting shall be arranged, chaired and minuted in accordance with directions given by the Court.

6   **ARRANGING FOR THE EXPERT TO ATTEND COURT**

6.1   **Preparation:**

The party who is responsible for the instruction of an expert witness shall ensure:

- That a date and time is fixed for the Court to hear the expert's evidence that is if possible convenient to the expert and that the fixture is made substantially in advance of the Final Hearing and no later than at the PHR (ie no later than 2 weeks before the Final Hearing)
- That if the expert's oral evidence is not required the expert is notified as soon as possible

- That the witness template accurately indicates how long the expert is likely to be giving evidence, in order to avoid the inconvenience of the expert being delayed at Court.	**Every Party responsible for the instruction of an expert**	**by the PHR**

6.2   All parties shall ensure:

- That where expert witnesses are to be called the advocates attending the PHR have identified at the advocates meeting the issues which the experts are to address

Action	Party	Timing
• That wherever possible a logical sequence to the evidence is arranged with experts of the same discipline giving evidence on the same day(s) • That at the PHR the Court is informed of any circumstance where all experts agree but a party nevertheless does not accept the agreed opinion so that directions can be given for the proper consideration of the experts' evidence and the parties reasons for not accepting the same • That in the exceptional case the Court is informed of the need for a witness summons.	All Parties	at the PHR

7   POST HEARING ACTION

7.1 Within 10 days of the Final Hearing the solicitor instructing the expert should provide feedback to the expert by way of a letter informing the expert of the outcome of the case, and the use made by the Court of the expert's opinion. Where the Court directs that a copy of the transcript can be sent to the expert, the solicitor instructing the expert should obtain the transcript within 10 days of the Final Hearing.	Solicitor instructing the expert	in-within 10 days theof the Final Hearing

D   Practice Direction (Family Proceedings: Court Bundles)

Reproduced at para **6–5101**.

E   Court Plan Guidance

E/1 – The Care Centre Plan

E/2 – The Family Proceedings Court Plan

F   Social Services Assessment and Care Planning Aide-Memoire

DAYS

The reference in this appendix to 'DAYS' is independent of the 'DAYS' referred to in The 6 Steps

Recommenced Guidance	Recommended timetable
1 Referral A referral to a Council with Social Services Responsibilities (CSSR) in England and a Local Authority in Wales (ie a request for services including child protection) triggers the following Government guidance:	**On DAY 1**
2 Initial Decision Within 1 working day of a referral social services should make a decision about what response is required including a decision to take no action or to undertake an initial assessment. The parents or carers (the family), where appropriate, the child and (unless inappropriate) the referrer should be informed of the initial decision and its reasons by social services.	**On DAY 2**
3 Initial Assessment An initial assessment (if undertaken) should be completed by social services within a maximum of 7 working days of the date of the referral (ie 6 working days from the date of the decision about how to respond to a referral).	**By DAY 7**
**4 ** As part of an initial assessment social services should: • Obtain and collate information and reports from other agencies • Interview family members and the child • In any event, see the child.	
**5 ** At the conclusion of an initial assessment social services will make a decision about whether the child is a child in need and about further action including whether to undertake a core assessment. It will inform the family, the child and other relevant agencies of the decision and its reasons. Social services will record the response of each person and agency consulted.	

Recommenced Guidance	Recommended timetable

6   **Initial Assessment Record** Social services will make and keep a record of the initial assessment and decision making process. The Department of Health (DH) and Welsh Assembly Government (WAG) publish an 'Initial Assessment Record' for this purpose.

7   **Child in Need Plan** Where social services decide that the child is a child in need they will make a plan which sets out the services to be provided to meet the child's needs.

8   **Strategy Discussion/Record** Where social services has evidence that the child is suspected to be suffering or is likely to suffer significant harm it should ensure that an inter agency strategy discussion takes place to decide whether to initiate an enquiry under section 47 of the Children Act. This should also result in the child in need plan being updated. A record of the strategy discussion will be made.

9   **Achieving Best Evidence in Criminal Proceedings** Where a child is the victim of or witness to a suspected crime the strategy discussion shall include a discussion about how any interviews are to be conducted with the child. These may be as part of a police investigation and /or a section 47 enquiry initiated by social services. These interviews should be undertaken in accordance with Government guidance 'Achieving Best Evidence in Criminal Proceedings'.

10   **Complex Child Abuse Investigations** Where a complex child abuse investigation has been initiated by social services or the police there will be inter agency strategy discussions to make recommendations relating to the planning, co-ordination and management of the investigation and assessment processes in accordance with the guidance given in 'Working Together', 'Complex Child Abuse Investigations: Inter Agency Issues' (England only – to be published in Wales, Summer 2003).

11   **Section 47 Enquiries** If during a strategy discussion it is decided that there is reasonable cause to suspect that the child is suffering or is likely to suffer significant harm, section 47 enquiries will be initiated by social services. This means that a core assessment will be commenced under section 47 of the Children Act 1989. It should be completed within 35 working days of the completion of the initial assessment or the strategy discussion at which it was decided to initiate section 47 enquiries.   **By DAY 42 or within 35 days of the last strategy discussion**

12   **Core Assessment** Where social services decides to undertake a core assessment it should be completed within 35 working days of the initial assessment or the date of the subsequent strategy discussion. A timescale for completion of specialist assessments should be agreed with social services.   **By DAY 42 or within 15 days of the last strategy discussion**

13   At the conclusion of a core assessment social services should consult with the family, the child and all relevant agencies before making decisions about the plan for the child. Social Services will record the response of each person and agency consulted.

14   **Core Assessment Record** Social services will make and keep a record of the core assessment and decision making process. The DH and WAG publish a 'Core Assessment Record' for this purpose.

Recommended Guidance	Recommended timetable

15   Child Protection Conferences Where social services undertakes section 47 enquiries and it is concluded that a child is at continuing risk of suffering or is likely to suffer significant harm, social services will consider whether to convene a child protection conference. A child protection conference determines whether the child is at continuing risk of significant harm and therefore requires a child protection plan to be put in place when determining whether to place the child's name on the child protection register. It agrees an outline child protection plan. An initial child protection conference should take place within 15 working days of the last strategy discussion (ie by day 22) in accordance with the Government guidance given in 'Working Together to Safeguard Children: a guide to inter-agency working to safeguard and promote the welfare of children'.

By DAY 22 or within 15 days of the end of the last strategy discussion

16   Decision to Apply for a Care Order At the conclusion of the core assessment which may have been undertaken under section 47 of the Children Act and where no earlier decision has been made social services should decide whether to apply for a statutory order and should be able to identify by reference to the conclusions in the core assessment:
- The needs of the child (including for protection),
- The services that will be provided,
- The role of other professionals and agencies,
- Whether additional specialist assessments are to be undertaken,
- The timetable, and
- The responsibilities of those involved.

17   Plans At the conclusion of a core assessment social services will prepare one or more of the following plans:
- A children in need plan
- A child protection plan for a child whose name is on the child protection register
- A care plan (where the child is a looked after child)
The DH and WAG publish formats and / or guidance for each of these plans.

18   Interim Care Plans Where social services decide to make an application to the Court it will be necessary to satisfy the Court that an order would be better for the child than making no order at all. An interim care plan should be prepared, filed and served so as to be available to the Court for the CMC in accordance with steps 3.4 and 4.1 of the protocol.

19   In cases where no core assessment has been undertaken (eg because the interim care order had to be taken quickly before one could be begun/completed) it should be begun/completed as soon as possible. The interim care plan should be developed from the initial assessment information.

20   Care Plans Care Plans should be written so as to comply with the Government guidance given in **LAC(99) 29** in England and *Care Plans and Care Proceedings under the CA 1989* **NAFWC 1/2000** in Wales. While interim care plans will necessarily be in outline and contain less comprehensive information, the plan should include details of the following:
- The aim of the plan and a summary of the social work timetable
- A summary of the child's needs and how these are to be met including:
- placement
- contact with family and other significant persons
- education, healthcare and social care services

Recommenced Guidance   **Recommended timetable**

- the role of parents and other significant persons
- the views of others
- Implementation and management of the plan.

21   **Emergency Protection** Where at any time there is reasonable cause to believe that a child is suffering or is likely to suffer significant harm, an application for a child assessment order or an emergency protection order may be made (among others) by social services. The child may be removed or remain in a safe place under police powers of protection. In each case agency and/or court records of the application and reasons will exist.

22   **Adoption** Government guidance is given on the assessment and decision making process relating to adoption in England in **LAC (2001) 33** which from the 1st April 2003 incorporates the 'National Adoption Standards for England'. The processes and timescales of assessment and decision making for a child for whom adoption is identified as an option are set out in detail in the Standards.

G   Section 37 Request

OBJECTIVE

To provide a recommended procedure within the existing rules for the timely determination of section 37 requests by the Court

Target time: by DAY 40

Action	Party	Timing
1 **The Test** Where, in any family proceedings in which a question arises with respect to the welfare of any child, it appears to the Court that it may be appropriate for a	Court	on DAY 1
Action	Party	Timing

care or supervision order to be made with respect to the child, the **Court** may direct the appropriate local authority (LA) to undertake an investigation of the child's circumstances.

	Party	Timing
2 **The Court's Request** On the same day the Court shall: • Identify the LA that is to prepare the s 37 report • Fix the date for the next hearing • Specify the date for the s 37 report to be filed by the LA • Direct the court officer to give notice of the order and the form C40 to the LA court liaison manager / lawyer (as set out in the CCP) by fax on the day the order is made • Direct each party to serve upon the LA all further documents filed with the Court.	Court	on DAY 1
3 Where a s 37 report is required in less than 8 weeks, the **Court** should make direct enquiries of the Court liaison manager / lawyer of the LA to agree the period within which a report can be written.	Court	on DAY 1
4 Within 24 hours of the order being made (on **DAY 2**) the **court officer** shall serve on the LA a sealed copy of the order and such other documents as the Court has directed.	Court Officer	on DAY 1

5   **LA Responsibility** Within 24 hours of the receipt of the sealed order (on **DAY 3**) the Court liaison manager / lawyer of the **LA** shall ensure that the request is allocated to a social services team manager who shall:
- Be responsible for the preparation of the report and the allocation of a social worker/team to carry out any appropriate assessment

- Ensure that the request is treated and recorded as a formal referral by social services in respect of each child named in the order
- Notify the Court and the lawyers acting for all parties of his / her identity and contact details and the identity of the team that has been allocated
- Follow Government guidance in relation to referral and assessment processes (see appendix F).   **LA**   **on DAY 3**

6   Any **assessment** including a core assessment that is undertaken by social services should be completed within 35 days of the allocation above ie within 36 days of the service of the sealed court order.   **Social Services**   **by DAY 38**

7   At the conclusion of the social services enquiries **social services** shall:

- Consult with the family, the child and all relevant agencies before making decisions about a plan for the child. The LA will record the response of each person and agency consulted
- Decide whether to apply to the Court for a statutory
- File the section 37 report with the Court and serve it upon the parties on or before the date specified in the Court's order.   **Social Services**   **between DAYS 38 and 40**

8   Where social services decide not to apply for a care or supervision order they should as part of their report set out the decisions they have made and the reasons for those decisions and any plan they have made for the child (including the services to be provided) in accordance with Government guidance (see appendix F).

PART VII
TRANSPORT

AVIATION

7–5330 This title contains references to the following statutes—

and the following statutory instrument—

7–5331 European Communities Act 1972: regulations. Within the scope of the title AVIATION would logically fall the subject matter of a number of regulations made under the very wide enabling powers provided in s 2(2) of the European Communities Act 1972. Where such regulations create offences they are noted below:

Licensing of Air Carriers Regulations 1992, SI 1992/2992 amended by SI 1993/101 and SI 1998/1751;
Access for Community Air Carriers to Intra-Community Air Routes Regulations 1992, SI 1992/2993 amended by SI 1993/3040;
Air Fares Regulations 1992, SI 1992/2994 amended by SI 1993/100 and 3041.
Airports Slot Allocation Regulations 1993, SI 1993/1067 amended by SI 1993/3042.
Aeroplane Noise Regulations 1999, SI 1999/1452 amended by SI 1999/2253;
Air Carrier Liability Regulations 2004, SI 2004/1418 amended by SI 2004/1974.

Civil Aviation Act 1982[1]
(1982 c 16)

PART I[2]
ADMINISTRATION

Supplemental provisions in relation to CAA[3]

7–5370 18. Official secrets. (2) For the purposes of section 3(c) of the said Act of 1911 (under which the Secretary of State may by order declare any place belonging to Her Majesty to be a prohibited place for the purposes of that Act) a place belonging to or used for the purposes of the CAA shall be deemed to be a place belonging to Her Majesty.

(3) Subject to subsection (4) below, no person shall, except with the consent of and in accordance with any conditions imposed by the CAA, be entitled to exercise any right of entry (whether arising by virtue of a statutory provision or otherwise) upon a place which by virtue of subsection (2) above is a prohibited place for the purposes of the said Act of 1911.

(4) Subsection (3) above shall not apply to—

(a) a constable acting in the course of his duty as such; or

(b) an officer of customs and excise or inland revenue acting in the execution of his duty as such; or

(c) an officer of any government department specially authorised for the purpose by or on behalf of a Minister of the Crown;

(d) a member of the staff of the Scottish Administration specially authorised for the purpose by or on behalf of the Scottish Ministers;

and if the CAA refuses consent for or imposes conditions on the exercise by any person of a right of entry upon such a place as is mentioned in subsection (3) above and that person applies to the Secretary of State or the Scottish Ministers as the case may be for an authorisation to exercise the right, the Secretary of State or the Scottish Ministers may if he or they think fit authorise that person to exercise it subject to such conditions, if any, as the Secretary of State or the Scottish Ministers may determine.

[Civil Aviation Act 1982, s 18, as amended by the Official Secrets Act 1989, Sch 2 and SI 1999/1820 Sch 2.]

---

1. This Act consolidates certain enactments relating to civil aviation.
2. Part I contains ss 1–24. Sections 1–16 are concerned with the functions of the Secretary of State, the constitution and functions of the Civil Aviation Authority, and financial provisions in relation to the CAA.
3. "The CAA" means the Civil Aviation Authority (s 105(1)).

Disclosure of information

7–5371   23. Disclosure of information.   (1) Subject to subsection (4) below, no information which relates to a particular person and has been furnished to the CAA in pursuance of any provision of this Act to which this section applies or of an Air Navigation Order shall be disclosed by the CAA, or a member or employee of the CAA unless—

(a)   the person aforesaid has consented in writing to disclosure of the information; or

(b)   the CAA, after affording that person an opportunity to make representations about the information and considering any representation then made by that person about it, determines that the information may be disclosed; or

(c)   that person is an individual who is dead, or is a body corporate that has ceased to exist or, whether an individual or a body corporate, cannot be found after all reasonable inquiries have been made, and the CAA determines that the information may be disclosed; or

(d)   the CAA determines that the information is of the same kind as other information as respects which it has made a determination in pursuance of paragraph (b) or (c) above.

(2)   Subsection (1) above shall apply in relation to the disclosure by an officer of the Secretary of State of information furnished to the Secretary of State in pursuance of any provision of this Act to which this section applies or of an Air Navigation Order as it applies in relation to disclosure by the CAA or a member or employee of the CAA of information so furnished to the CAA, but with the substitution for references to the CAA in paragraphs (b) to (d) of references to the Secretary of State.

(3)   For the purposes of subsection (1) above, all reasonable inquiries to find a body corporate shall be deemed to have been made if—

(a)   in the case of a company within the meaning of the Companies Act 1985 or the Companies Act (Northern Ireland) 1960, inquiries have been made at its registered office; or

(b)   in the case of a company incorporated outside the United Kingdom and having a place of business within the United Kingdom, inquiries have been made at every address registered in respect of that company for the purposes of section 691(1)(b)(ii) of the said Act of 1985, or section 356(1)(c) of the said Act of 1960 (addresses for service of overseas companies).

(4)   Nothing in subsection (1) above prohibits the disclosure of any information—

(a)   by the CAA or a member or employee of the CAA to the Secretary of State or an officer of his or, with the consent of the Secretary of State, to an international organisation of which the United Kingdom is a member;

(b)   by an officer of the Secretary of State to the CAA or a member or employee of the CAA or to such an organisation or, in accordance with directions given by the Secretary of State—

(i)   to an officer of any government department; or

(ii)   in connection with negotiations conducted by officers of the Secretary of State with representatives of the government of any country or territory outside the United Kingdom; or

(iii)   in connection with the discharge of any obligation of the United Kingdom under international arrangements;

(c)   to a person to whom the information in question is required to be disclosed by regulations made in pursuance of section 7(2) above;

(d)   in pursuance of section 67(2) or (4) below;

(e)   by the CAA for the purpose of complying with any duty imposed on it by section 85(1) below;

(f)   with a view to the institution of, or otherwise for the purposes of, any criminal proceedings arising out of any enactment relating to civil aviation or for the purposes of any investigation undertaken in pursuance of regulations made by virtue of section 75 below.

(5)   If the CAA or a member or employee of the CAA or an officer of the Secretary of State discloses any information in contravention of subsection (1) above, it or he shall be liable[1]—

(a)   on summary conviction, to a fine not exceeding **the statutory maximum**[2]; and

(b)   on conviction on indictment, to a fine or, except in the case of the CAA, to imprisonment for a term not exceeding **two years** or to **both**.

(6)   This section applies to the following provisions of this Act, that is to say, sections 16, 17 and 28, section 36 (so far only as it relates to aerodromes owned or managed by the CAA) sections 64 to 72 (except section 69), sections 78 to 80 and sections 84 and 85.

[Civil Aviation Act 1982, s 23, as amended by the Companies Consolidation (Consequential Provisions) Act 1985, Sch 2 and the Airports Act 1986, Sch 4.]

---

1. For procedure in respect of this offence which is triable either way, see Magistrates' Courts Act 1980, ss 17A–21, in PART I: MAGISTRATES' COURTS, PROCEDURE, ante.

2. For meaning of "the statutory maximum", see s 105, post.

Eurocontrol

7–5372   24. Eurocontrol.   Schedule 4 to this Act shall have effect in relation to the European Organisation for the Safety of Air Navigation established by the International Convention relating to co-operation for the safety of air navigation (entitled Eurocontrol) concluded at Brussels on 13th December 1960 (copies of which Convention were laid before Parliament by Command of Her Majesty on 13th June 1961); and in this Act—

"Eurocontrol" means that organisation, including, except where the context otherwise requires, the Permanent Commission for the Safety of Air Navigation and the Air Traffic Services Agency comprised in that Organisation; and

"the Eurocontrol Convention" means that Convention as from time to time amended with the agreement of the contracting parties thereto.

[Civil Aviation Act 1982, s 24, as amended by the Civil Aviation (Eurocontrol) Act 1983, s 3.]

PART II[1]

AERODROMES AND OTHER LAND

Secretary of State's aerodromes

7–5373   25. *Secretary of State's power to provide aerodromes*

---

     1. Part II contains ss 25–59.

Other aerodromes

7–5374   39. Trespassing on licensed aerodromes.   (1) Subject to subsection (2) below, if any person trespasses on any land forming part of an aerodrome licensed in pursuance of an Air Navigation Order, he shall be liable on summary conviction to a fine not exceeding **level 3** on the standard scale.

(2) No person shall be liable under this section unless it is proved that, at the material time, notices warning trespassers of their liability under this section were posted so as to be readily seen and read by members of the public, in such positions on or near the boundary of the aerodrome as appear to the court to be proper.

[Civil Aviation Act 1982, s 39, as amended by the Criminal Justice Act 1982, ss 38 and 46 and the Anti-terrorism, Crime and Security Act 2001, s 83(1).]

Powers in relation to land exercisable in connection with civil aviation

7–5375   44. Power to obtain rights over land.   (1) The Secretary of State may make an order under this section if he is satisfied that it is expedient to do so in order—

   (*a*)   to secure the safe and efficient use for civil aviation purposes of any land which is vested in a relevant authority or which such an authority proposes to acquire; or

   (*b*)   to secure the provision of any services required in relation to any such land; or

   (*c*)   to secure that civil aircraft may be navigated with safety and efficiency.

(2) Such an order may provide for the creation—

   (*a*)   if it is made by virtue of paragraph (*a*) or (*b*) of subsection (1) above, in favour of the relevant authority in question or, where that authority is Eurocontrol, either of Eurocontrol or of the Secretary of State, or

   (*b*)   if it made by virtue of paragraph (*c*) of that subsection, in favour of the Secretary of State,

of easements or servitudes over land or of other rights in or in relation to land, including rights to carry out and maintain works on any land and to install and maintain structures and apparatus on, under, over or across any land.

(3) Any such order may contain such consequential, incidental and supplemental provisions as appear to the Secretary of State to be necessary or expedient for the purposes of the order, including, in particular, provisions for authorising persons to enter upon land for the purpose of carrying out, installing, maintaining or removing any works, structures or apparatus.

(4) Subject to subsection (5) below, no person shall, in the exercise of a power conferred by any such order, enter upon land which is occupied, unless, not less than seven days before the day upon which the entry is made, there has been served upon the occupier of the land a notice[1]—

   (*a*)   stating that an entry will be made upon the land upon that day in the exercise of powers conferred by the order; and

   (*b*)   specifying the purposes for which the entry will be made.

(5) Nothing in subsection (4) above shall restrict the right of any person to enter upon land in a case of emergency or for the purpose or performing any functions which are required to be performed from time to time in connection with the maintenance or use of any works, structures or apparatus.

(6) *Compensation for damage.*

(7) The ownership of anything shall not be affected by reason only that it is placed on or under, or affixed, to, any land in pursuance of any such order.

(7A) So long as any such order is in force, no person shall, except with the necessary consent, wilfully interfere—

   (*a*)   with any works carried out on any land in pursuance of the order, or (*b*)　with anything installed on, under, over or across any land in pursuance of the order.

(7B)　The necessary consent is—

(*a*)　if the relevant authority in whose favour the order is made is the Secretary of State or Eurocontrol, the consent of the Secretary of State,

(*b*)　if that relevant authority is the CAA, the consent of the Secretary of State or the CAA, and

(*c*)　if that relevant authority is a licence holder, the consent of the licence holder.

(8)　Subject to the special provisions of this Part of this Act relating to statutory undertakers, Schedule 7 to this Act shall have effect with respect to orders under this section.

(9)　Where an order under this section provides for the creation of an easement or servitude over land held by a statutory undertaker for the purposes of the carrying on of his undertaking, or of any other right in or in relation to such land, then, if on a representation made to the Secretary of State before the expiration of the time within which objections to the order may be made the Secretary of State is satisfied that the easement, servitude or right could not be enjoyed without serious detriment to the carrying on of the undertaking, and certifies accordingly, the order shall be subject to special parliamentary procedure.

(10)　If any person contravenes the provisions of subsection (7A) above he shall be liable, on summary conviction, to imprisonment for a term not exceeding **three months*** or to a fine not exceeding **level 5** on the standard scale or to both; and every person who wilfully obstructs any person in the exercise of any power of entry conferred by an order under this section shall be liable, on summary conviction, to a fine not exceeding **level 2** on the standard scale.

(11)　Proceedings for an offence under this section shall not be instituted—

(*a*)　in England and Wales, except by or with the consent of the Secretary of State or by or with the consent of the Director of Public Prosecutions;

(*b*)　*Northern Ireland*;

except that in England and Wales and in Northern Ireland such proceedings may be instituted by the CAA without such consent if the relevant authority in whose favour the order in question was made is the CAA.

(12)　The following are relevant authorities for the purposes of this section, that is to say—

(*a*)　the Secretary of State;

(*b*)　Eurocontrol;

(*c*)　the CAA; and

(*d*)　a licence holder;

and in this section and in Schedule 7 to this Act as it has effect with respect to orders under this section, references to land vested in or proposed to be acquired by a relevant authority shall include references to land occupied or, as the case may be, proposed to be occupied by Eurocontrol.
[Civil Aviation Act 1982, s 44, as amended by the Criminal Justice Act 1982, ss 38 and 46, the Transport Act 2000, Sch 31 and SI 2004/1755.]

---

*Words substituted by the Criminal Justice Act 2003, Sch 26, from a date to be appointed.
1.　For provisions as to service of notices, see s 56, post.

7–5376　45. Power to restrict use of land for purpose of securing safety at aerodromes.
(1)　Subject to subsection (2) below, the Secretary of State may by order impose such prohibitions or restrictions on the use of any area of land or water as a place for the arrival and departure of civil aircraft as he thinks expedient for the purpose of securing that aircraft may arrive and depart with safety at any aerodrome vested in him or under his control or at any aerodrome in the United Kingdom owned or managed by the CAA.

(2)　Nothing in subsection (1) above shall authorise the imposition of any such prohibition or restriction in relation to tidal waters beyond those of the territorial waters adjacent to the United Kingdom.

(3)　Part I of Schedule 7 to this Act shall have effect in relation to any order made under this section other than an order for the imposition of prohibitions or restrictions on the use of water; and in the case of an order for the imposition of prohibitions or restrictions on the use of water the Secretary of State—

(*a*)　shall, before making the order, publish notice of his intention to make the order in such manner as he thinks best calculated to bring his intention to the notice of persons who will be affected thereby; and

(*b*)　shall, immediately after the order has been made, publish in one or more newspapers circulating in the locality to which the order relates a notice stating that the order has been made and naming a place where a copy of the order may be seen at all reasonable hours, and shall serve a like notice upon any person who in his opinion will be affected thereby.

(4)　Part II of Schedule 7 to this Act and Schedule 8 to this Act shall have effect with respect to orders under this section; but where any aerodrome was first established as such after 31st July 1946 no compensation shall be payable by reason of the imposition under this section of prohibitions or restrictions upon the use of that aerodrome unless it was so established with the consent of the Secretary of State.

(5) Any person who contravenes the provisions of any order under this section shall be liable[1] in respect of each offence—

(*a*) on summary conviction to a fine which shall not exceed **the statutory maximum**[2] or to imprisonment for a term not exceeding **three months** or to **both**; and

(*b*) on conviction on indictment to a **fine** or to imprisonment for a term not exceeding **two years** or to **both**.

(6) Any offence against any order under this section committed on tidal waters outside the ordinary jurisdiction of a court of summary jurisdiction may be tried and punished by such a court as if it had been committed in the nearest part of the United Kingdom which is within the ordinary jurisdiction of such a court; but nothing in this subsection shall in its application to Scotland be construed as conferring jurisdiction on any court of summary jurisdiction other than the sheriff court.

(7) Proceedings for an offence against any order under this section shall not be instituted—

(*a*) in England and Wales, except by or with the consent of the Secretary of State or by or with the consent of the Director of Public Prosecutions;

(*b*) *Northern Ireland*;

except that in England and Wales and in Northern Ireland such proceedings may be instituted by the CAA without such consent if the order in question is made in respect of an aerodrome owned or managed by the CAA.

(8) In this section "aerodrome" includes part of an aerodrome; and, without prejudice to section 105(3) below, the reference in subsection (4) above to the Secretary of State shall, in relation to any time before the passing of this Act, have effect as a reference to whoever at that time was charged with exercising the functions which by virtue of this section are vested in the Secretary of State.

[Civil Aviation Act 1982, s 45.]

---

1. For procedure in respect of this offence which is triable either way, see the Magistrates' Courts Act 1980, ss 17A–21, in PART I: MAGISTRATES' COURTS, PROCEDURE, ante.
2. For meaning of "the statutory maximum", see s 105, post.

7–5377   47. Warning of presence of obstructions near licensed aerodromes.   (1) Subject to the provisions of this section, if the Secretary of State is satisfied with respect to any building, structure or erection in the vicinity of a licensed aerodrome that, in order to avoid danger to aircraft flying in that vicinity in darkness or conditions of poor visibility, provision ought to be made (whether by lighting or otherwise) for giving to such aircraft warning of the presence of that building, structure or erection, he may by order authorise (subject to any conditions specified in the order) the proprietor of the aerodrome, and any person acting under the proprietor's instructions—

(*a*) to execute, install, maintain, operate and, as occasion requires, to repair and alter, such works and apparatus as may be necessary for enabling such warning to be given in the manner specified in the order; and

(*b*) so far as may be necessary for exercising any of the powers conferred by the order to enter upon and pass over (with or without vehicles) any such land as may be specified in the order.

(2) An order shall not be made under this section in relation to any building, structure or erection if it appears to the Secretary of State that there have been made, and are being carried out, satisfactory arrangements for the giving of such warning as aforesaid of the presence of the building, structure or erection.

(3) The Secretary of State shall, before making an order under this section—

(*a*) cause to be published, in such manner as he thinks best for informing persons concerned, notice of the proposal to make the order and of the place where copies of the draft order may be obtained free of charge; and

(*b*) take into consideration any representations with respect to the order which may, within such period not being less than two months after the publication of the notice as may be specified therein, be made to him by any person appearing to him to have an interest in any land which would be affected by the order;

and at the end of that period the order may, subject to the provisions of this section, be made with such modifications (if any) of the original draft as the Secretary of State thinks proper.

(4) Every order under this section shall provide—

(*b*) that, except in a case of emergency, no works shall be executed on any land in pursuance of the order, unless, at least fourteen days previously, the proprietor of the aerodrome to which the order relates has served in the manner specified in the order on the occupier of that land, and on every other person known by the proprietor to have an interest therein, a written notice containing such particulars of the nature of the proposed works, and the manner in which and the time at which it is proposed to execute them, as may be specified in or in accordance with the order; and

(b)   that if, within fourteen days after service of the said notice on any person having such an interest, the proprietor of the aerodrome receives a written intimation of objection on the part of that person to the proposals contained in the notice, being an intimation which specifies the grounds of objection, then, unless and except in so far as the objection is withdrawn, no steps shall be taken in pursuance of the notice without the specific sanction of the Secretary of State;

and shall also provide for requiring the proprietor of the aerodrome to which the order relates to pay to any person having an interest in any land affected by the order such compensation for any loss or damage which that person may suffer in consequence of the order as may, in default of agreement, be determined from time to time by a single arbitrator appointed by the Lord Chief Justice or, in Scotland, by a single arbiter appointed by the Lord President of the Court of Session.

(5)   *Expenses.*

(6)   The ownership of anything shall not be taken to be affected by reason only that it is placed in, or affixed to, any land in pursuance of an order under this section; and (subject to the provisions of subsection (8) below) so long as any such order in respect of an aerodrome is in force, no person shall, except with the consent of the proprietor of the aerodrome, wilfully interfere with any works or things which, to the knowledge of that person, are works or things executed or placed, in, on or over any land in pursuance of the order.

(7)   If any person contravenes the provisions of subsection (6) above, he shall be liable, on summary conviction, to imprisonment for a term not exceeding **six months** or to a fine not exceeding **level 4** on the standard scale or to both; and every person who wilfully obstructs a person in the exercise of any of the powers conferred by an order under this section shall be liable, on summary conviction, to a fine not exceeding **level 3** on the standard scale.

(8)   Nothing in this section shall operate, in relation to any building, structure or erection, so as to restrict the doing of any work for the purpose of repairing, altering, demolishing or removing the building, structure or erection if—

(a)   notice of the doing of that work is given as soon as may be to the proprietor of the aerodrome; and

(b)   the giving or warning of the presence of the building, structure or erection in the manner provided by any order under this section in force in relation thereto is not interrupted.

(9)   *Consequential provisions for the protection of statutory undertakers.*

(10)   In this section—

"licensed aerodrome" means any premises which, by virtue of an Air Navigation Order, are for the time being licensed as an aerodrome for public use, but does not include any premises belonging to the Secretary of State;

"proprietor of the aerodrome" means, in relation to any premises used or appropriated for use as an aerodrome, the person carrying on or entitled to carry on the business of an aerodrome in those premises;

and nothing in section 104(1) below shall affect the construction of the reference in the definition in this subsection of "licensed aerodrome" to premises belonging to the Secretary of State.

[Civil Aviation Act 1982, s 47, as amended by the Criminal Justice Act 1982, ss 38 and 46.]

7–5378   50.   Power of entry for purposes of survey.   (1)   This section applies—

(a)   where the Secretary of State has confirmed or is considering the confirmation of an order authorising the CAA or a licence holder to acquire land in Great Britain compulsorily;

(b)   where the CAA or a licence holder proposes to acquire land in Northern Ireland compulsorily;

(c)   where the Secretary of State has made or has under consideration the making of an order under section 44 above providing for the creation in favour of the CAA or a licence holder of easements or servitudes over land or of other rights in or in relation to land;

(d)   where the Secretary of State has made, or has under consideration the making of, an order under section 46(1) above in respect of the CAA, a licence holder (within the meaning of section 105(1) below) or the licensee of an aerodrome licensed under an Air Navigation Order, being an order declaring that an area of land shall be subject to control by directions; and

(e)   in any case not falling within paragraphs (a) to (d) above where the Secretary of State has made, or has under consideration the making of, an order under or in pursuance of this Part of this Act, being—

(i)   an order authorising the compulsory purchase of land; or

(ii)   an order providing for the creation in favour of a particular person of easements or servitudes over land or of other rights in or in relation to land; or

(iii)   an order declaring that an area of land shall be subject to control by directions.

(2)   Where this section applies any person authorised in writing by the Secretary of State may at all reasonable times on producing if so required evidence of his authority for the purpose enter upon any of the land in question in order to make a relevant survey.

(3)   In subsection (2) above "a relevant survey" means—

(a) in a case falling within subsection (1)(*a*) above, any survey which the Secretary of State, the CAA or a licence holder requires to be made for the purpose of any steps to be taken in consequence of the order, or, as the case may be, for the purpose of determining whether the order should be confirmed;

(b) in a case falling within subsection (1)(*b*) above, any survey which the Secretary of State, the CAA or a licence holder requires to be made for the purpose of ascertaining whether the land would be suitable for the purposes for which it is proposed to acquire it;

(c) in a case falling within subsection (1)(*c*) above, any survey which the Secretary of State, the CAA or a licence holder requires to be made for the purpose of any steps to be taken in consequence of the order or, as the case may be, for the purpose of determining whether the order should be made;

(d) in a case falling within subsection (1)(*d*) above, any survey which the Secretary of State or the person in respect of whom the order under the said section 46(1) has been, or is to be, made requires to be made for the purpose of any steps to be taken in consequence of that order or, as the case may be, for the purpose of determining whether the order should be made;

(e) in a case falling within subsection (1)(*e*) above, any survey which the Secretary of State requires to be made for the purpose of any steps to be taken in consequence of the order in question or, as the case may be, for the purpose of determining whether the order should be made.

(4) Admission shall not, by virtue of subsection (2) above, be demanded as of right to any land which is occupied unless the following notice of the intended entry has been served on the occupier, that is to say—

(a) in a case falling within subsection (1)(*a*) to (*d*) above, eight days' notice; and

(b) in a case falling within subsection (1)(*e*) above, twenty-four hours' notice.

(5) If any person obstructs a person authorised as mentioned in subsection (2) above in the exercise of any power conferred by this section he shall be liable on summary conviction to a fine not exceeding **level 3** on the standard scale.

(6) Proceedings for an offence under this section shall not be instituted—

(a) in England and Wales, except by or with the consent of the Secretary of State or by or with the consent of the Director of Public Prosecutions;

(b) *Northern Ireland,*

except that in England and Wales and in Northern Ireland such proceedings may be instituted without such consent, in a case falling within subsection (1)(*a*) to (*c*) above, by the CAA and, in a case falling within subsection (1)(*d*) above, by the person in respect of whom the order in question has been, or is to be, made.

(7) *Compensation for damage.*

[Civil Aviation Act 1982, s 50, as amended by the Criminal Justice Act 1982, ss 38 and 46 and the Transport Act 2000, Sch 4.]

Supplemental

7–5379 56. Notices. (1) Any notice required to be served on any person for the purposes of any provision to which this section applies may be served on him either by delivering it to him or by leaving it at his proper address, or by post, so however that the notice shall not be duly served by post unless it is sent by registered letter or by the recorded delivery service.

(2) Any such notice required to be served upon an incorporated company or body shall be duly served if it is served on the secretary or clerk of the company or body.

(3) For the purposes of this section and of section 7 of the Interpretation Act 1978, the proper address of any person upon whom any such notice is to be served shall, in the case of the secretary or clerk of any incorporated company or body, be that of the registered or principal office of the company or body and in any other case be the last known address of he person to be served, except that, where the person to be served has furnished an address for service, that address shall be his proper address for those purposes.

(4) If it is not practicable after reasonable inquiry to ascertain the name or address of any owner, lessee or occupier of land on whom any such notice is to be served, the notice may be served by addressing it to him by the description of "owner", "lessee" or "occupier" of the land (describing it) to which the notice relates, and by delivering it to some person on the premises or, if there is no person on the premises to whom it can be delivered, by affixing it, or a copy of it, to some conspicuous part of the premises.

(5) In the application to Scotland of any provision to which this section applies and which requires notice to be served on the owners, lessees or occupiers of any land, that requirement shall be deemed to be complied with if notice is served on all the persons appearing from the valuation roll to have an interest in the land, and any reference in this Part of this Act to "owners", "lessees" or "occupiers" shall be construed accordingly.

(6) Service of a notice under subsection (5) above on any person appearing from the valuation roll to have an interest in land may be effected by sending the notice either—

(a) in a registered letter addressed to him at his address as entered in that roll; or

(b) by the recorded delivery service to him at that address.

(7) This section applies to any provision of this Part of this Act except section 42 above and so much of section 50 above as relates to the service of a notice under the said section 50 otherwise than by the Secretary of State.

(8) In this section "owner"—

(a) in relation to any land in England and Wales, means a person, other than a mortgagee not in possession, who is for the time being entitled to dispose of the fee simple of the land, whether in possession or in reversion, and includes also a person holding or entitled to the rents and profits under a lease or agreement, the unexpired term whereof exceeds three years;

(b) *Scotland or Northern Ireland.*

[Civil Aviation Act 1982, s 56.]

7–5380   57. Power to appoint special constables. (1) Any two justices of the peace may appoint such persons as may be nominated for the purpose by the Secretary of State to be special constables on any premises for the time being vested in or under the control of the Secretary of State.

(2) Every person so appointed shall be sworn in by the justices duly to execute the office of a constable on those premises and when so sworn in shall, on those premises, have the powers and privileges and be liable to the duties and responsibilities of a constable.

(3) Special constables appointed under this section shall be under the exclusive control of the Secretary of State, and the Secretary of State shall have power to suspend or terminate the appointment of any such special constable.

(4) *Scotland.*

[Civil Aviation Act 1982, s 57.]

PART III[1]
REGULATION OF CIVIL AVIATION
General

7–5381   60. Power to give effect to Chicago Convention and to regulate air navigation, etc.
(1) Subject to section 11(7) above, Her Majesty may by Order[2] in Council under this section (in this Act referred to as "an Air Navigation Order") make such provision as is authorised by subsections (2) and (3) below or otherwise by this Act or any other enactment.

(2) An Air Navigation Order[2] may contain such provision as appears to Her Majesty in Council to be requisite or expedient—

(a) for carrying out the Chicago Convention, any Annex thereto relating to international standards and recommended practices (being an Annex adopted in accordance with the Convention) and any amendment of the Convention or any such Annex made in accordance with the Convention; or

(b) generally for regulating air navigation.

(3)–(6) *Further provisions as to an Air Navigation Order.*

[Civil Aviation Act 1982, s 60, as amended by the Airports Act 1986, Sch 6, and the Aviation and Maritime Security Act 1990, Sch 4.]

---

1. Part III contains ss 60–84.
2. The Air Navigation (Cosmic Radiation) Order 2000, SI 2000/1104, the Air Navigation (Jersey) Order 2000, SI 2000/1346 amended by SI 2002/1078 and the Air Navigation (Environmental Standards) Order 2002, SI 2002/798 have been made. See also the Air Navigation Order 2005, SI 2005/1790, in this title, post.

7–5382   61. Air Navigation Orders etc: supplemental. (1) An Air Navigation Order may, for the purpose of securing compliance with its provisions, provide—

(a) subject to subsection (2) below, for persons to be guilty of offences in such circumstances as may be specified in the Order and to be liable on conviction of those offences to such penalties as may be so specified; and

(b) in the case of a provision having effect by virtue of paragraph (*l*) of subsection (3) of section 60 above, for the taking of such steps (including firing on aircraft) as may be specified in the Order.

(2) The power conferred by virtue of subsection (1)(a) above shall not include power—

(a) to provide for offences to be triable only on indictment;

(b) to authorise the imposition, on summary conviction of any offence, of any term of imprisonment or of a fine exceeding the statutory maximum;

(c) to authorise the imposition, on conviction on indictment of an offence, of a term of imprisonment exceeding two years.

(2A) Subsection (2)(c) above shall have effect with the substitution of "five years" for "two years" in the case of a provision about endangering an aircraft or a person in an aircraft.

(3) Without prejudice to section 127(2) of the Magistrates' Courts Act 1980 or to Article 19(2) of the Magistrates' Courts (Northern Ireland) Order 1981 (no time limit for offences triable either way), summary proceedings for an offence against an Air Navigation Order, or any regulations made by virtue of such an Order, may be instituted at any time within twelve months from the commission of the offence if—

(a)   it was committed in connection with the flight of an aircraft in the course of which an accident occurred; and

(b)   not more than six months after the commission of the offence—

     (i)   public notice has been given that an investigation into the accident is being carried out in accordance with regulations under section 75 below; or

     (ii)   the Secretary of State (acting alone or with any government department) has directed that a public inquiry into the accident be held in accordance with those regulations.

(4) In subsection (3) above "accident" has the same meaning as it has for the time being for the purposes of section 75 below; and for the purposes of that subsection, the flight of an aircraft shall be deemed to include any period from the moment when the power is applied for the purpose of the aircraft taking off on a flight until the moment when the landing run (if any) at the termination of that flight ends.

(5) The fact that any such direction as is mentioned in subsection (3)(b)(ii) above has been given on any date may be proved by the production of a certificate to that effect purporting to be signed by an officer of the Secretary of State.

(6) (Repealed).

(7)–(8) Financial provisions.

[Civil Aviation Act 1982, s 61, as amended by the Airports Act 1986, Sch 6 and the Aviation (Offences) Act 2003, s 2.]

War and emergencies

7–5383   62. Repealed.

7–5384   63. Repealed.

Air transport, etc

7–5385   64. Restriction of unlicensed carriage by air for reward.   (1) No aircraft shall be used for the carriage for reward of passengers or cargo on a flight to which this subsection applies unless—

(a)   the operator of the aircraft holds a licence granted to him by the CAA in pursuance of section 65 below (in this Act referred to as an "air transport licence") authorising him to operate aircraft on such flights as the flight in question; and

(b)   the terms of the licence are complied with so far as they relate to that flight and fall to be complied with before or during the flight.

(2) Subsection (1) above applies to any flight in any part of the world by an aircraft registered in the United Kingdom and to any flight beginning or ending in the United Kingdom by an aircraft registered in a relevant overseas territory or an associated state, except that it does not apply to—

(a)   a flight of a description specified in an instrument made by the CAA for the purposes of this paragraph and in force in accordance with subsection (3) below;

(b)   a particular flight or series of flights specified in an instrument made by the CAA for the purposes of this paragraph;

(c)   a flight by an aircraft of which the CAA is the operator;

(d)   a flight for the undertaking of carriage by air for which a valid operating licence issued in accordance with Council Regulation 2407/92 on licensing of air carriers is required.

(3) An instrument made in pursuance of paragraph (a) of subsection (2) above shall not come into force until it is published in the prescribed[1] manner, and it shall be the duty of the CAA forthwith after making an instrument in pursuance of paragraph (b) of that subsection to publish the instrument in the prescribed manner; and an instrument made in pursuance of paragraph (a) or (b) of that subsection may be revoked or varied by a subsequent instrument made in pursuance of that paragraph.

(4) Where an aircraft is used for the carriage of passengers or cargo in pursuance of an arrangement made between a member of an incorporated or unincorporated body of persons and that body or another member of it, then, if by reason of relationships arising from membership of the body the carriage is not apart from this subsection carriage for reward, it shall be treated for the purposes of this section as carriage for reward.

(5) Where an aircraft is used on a flight in contravention of subsection (1) above or, after an aircraft has been used in pursuance of an air transport licence on a flight to which that subsection applies, any term of the licence relating to the flight and falling to be complied with at or after the end of the flight by the operator of the aircraft or by another person who made available such accommodation as is mentioned in paragraph (b) of this subsection is contravened, then—

(a) if before the flight began the operator of the aircraft knew or ought to have known that the use of the aircraft on that flight was likely to be in contravention of that subsection or, as the case may be, that the term in question was likely to be contravened, he shall be guilty of an offence under this subsection; and

(b) if any other person, either by negotiating a contract or otherwise howsoever, made available accommodation for the carriage of passengers or cargo on the aircraft on the flight when he knew or ought to have known before the flight began that the accommodation was likely to be provided on an aircraft when used on a flight in contravention of the said subsection (1) or, as the case may be, that such a term as the term in question was likely to be contravened, that person shall be guilty of an offence under this subsection;

but a person shall not (except in pursuance of section 99(1) below or the law relating to persons who aid, abet, counsel or procure the commission of offences) be guilty of an offence by virtue of paragraph (b) above in consequence of the contravention by another person of a term of a licence.

(6) For the purpose of determining in pursuance of subsection (5) above whether an offence relating to a flight has been committed by the operator of the aircraft used on the flight, it is immaterial that the relevant contravention mentioned in that subsection occurred outside the United Kingdom if when it occurred the operator—

(a) was a United Kingdom national, or

(b) was a body incorporated under the law of any part of the United Kingdom or the law of a relevant overseas territory or an associated state, or

(c) was a person (other than a United Kingdom national or such a body) maintaining a place of business in the United Kingdom;

and for the purpose of determining in pursuance of that subsection whether an offence relating to a flight has been committed by a person who made available such accommodation as is mentioned in that subsection it is immaterial that the relevant contravention there mentioned occurred outside the United Kingdom and that at any relevant time that person was not a United Kingdom national or such a body as aforesaid if any part of the negotiations resulting in the making available of the accommodation in question took place, whether by means of the post or otherwise, in the United Kingdom.

(7) Where the CAA has reason to believe that an aircraft is intended to be used in contravention of subsection (1) above on a particular flight beginning in the United Kingdom or that any term of an air transport licence relating to such a flight and falling to be complied with at or after the end of the flight may not be complied with, the CAA may—

(a) give to the person appearing to it to be in command of the aircraft a direction that he shall not permit the aircraft to take off until it has informed him that the direction is cancelled;

(b) whether or not it has given such a direction, detain the aircraft until it is satisfied that the aircraft will not be used on the flight in contravention of the said subsection (1) or, as the case may be, that the term aforesaid will be complied with;

and a person who fails to comply with a direction given to him in pursuance of this subsection shall be guilty of an offence under this subsection.

(8) A person guilty of an offence under subsection (5) or (7) above shall be liable[2]—

(a) on summary conviction, to a fine not exceeding **the statutory maximum**[3]; and

(b) on conviction on indictment, to a **fine** or to imprisonment for a term not exceeding **two years** or to **both**.

[Civil Aviation Act 1982, s 64, as amended by SI 1992/2992.]

---

1. See the Civil Aviation Authority Regulations 1991, SI 1991/1672.
2. For procedure in respect of this offence which is triable either way, see the Magistrates' Courts Act 1980, ss 17A–21, in PART I: MAGISTRATES' COURTS, PROCEDURE, ante.
3. For meaning of "the statutory maximum", see s 105, post.

7–5386 65–66. *Grant and refusal of air transport licences; revocation, suspension and variation of air transport licences.*

7–5387 67. Supplementary provisions relating to air transport licensing. (1) Regulations made by the Secretary of State may make provision as to the circumstances in which an air transport licence shall or may be transferred or treated as if granted to a person other than the person to whom it was granted.

(2)–(4) *Supplementary provisions with respect to powers of CAA.*

(5) *Duty of Secretary of State to make regulations with respect to appeals from decisions of CAA.*

(6) A person who, for the purpose of obtaining for himself or another person either an air transport licence or a variation of an air transport licence or the cancellation of the suspension of an air transport licence, knowingly or recklessly furnishes the CAA or the Secretary of State with any information which is false in a material particular shall be guilty of an offence and liable[1]—

(a) on summary conviction, to a **fine** not exceeding **the statutory maximum**[2]; and

(b) on conviction on indictment, to a **fine** or to imprisonment for a term not exceeding **two years** or to **both**.
[Civil Aviation Act 1982, s 67.]

1. For procedure in respect of this offence which is triable either way, see the Magistrates' Courts Act 1980, ss 17A–21, in PART I: MAGISTRATES' COURTS, PROCEDURE, ante.
2. For meaning of "the statutory maximum", see s 105, post.

7–5388 71. Regulation of provision of accommodation in aircraft. (1) Provision may be made by regulations[1] made by the Secretary of State for securing that a person does not in the United Kingdom—

(a) make available, as a principal or an agent, accommodation for the carriage of persons or cargo on flights in any part of the world, or

(b) hold himself out as a person who, either as a principal or an agent or without disclosing his capacity, may make such accommodation available,

unless he is the operator of the relevant aircraft or holds and complies with the terms of a licence issued in pursuance of the regulations or is exempted by or under the regulations from the need to hold such a licence.

(2) *Consequential provisions with respect to regulations for the purposes of subsection (1).*
[Civil Aviation Act 1982, s 71.]

1. The Civil Aviation (Air Travel Organisers Licensing) Regulations 1995, SI 1995/1054 amended by SI 1996/1390, SI 1997/2912 and SI 2003/1741 have effect under this section.

Air navigation services

7–5389 73. *Repealed.*

7–5400 74. Provisions supplementary to s 73. (1) Any person who, without reasonable cause, fails to comply with any requirement of regulations made by virtue of subsection (7) of section 73 above shall be liable on summary conviction to a fine not exceeding **level 3** on the standard scale.

(2) Any person who, being in possession of information furnished to or obtained by him in pursuance of regulations under the said subsection (7), discloses that information otherwise than—

(a) with the consent of the person by whom it was furnished or from whom it was obtained, or

(b) for the purposes of the regulations, or

(c) for the purposes of any proceedings arising out of section 73 above, of proceedings brought by virtue of paragraph 3 of Schedule 4 to this Act or of any criminal proceedings whether or not arising out of this Act, or

(d) for the purposes of any public inquiry or Inspector's investigation held or carried out in pursuance of regulations made under section 75 below, or

(e) for the purpose of any report of any such proceedings, inquiry or investigation as aforesaid,

shall be liable on summary conviction to a fine not exceeding **level 3** on the standard scale or to imprisonment for a term not exceeding **three months** or to **both**.

(3) Any person who, in furnishing in pursuance of such regulations any such particulars as are described in paragraph *(c)* of the said subsection (7), furnishes any particulars which to his knowledge are false in any material particular, or recklessly furnishes any particulars which are false in any material particular, shall be liable[1]—

(a) on summary conviction, to a fine not exceeding **the statutory maximum**[2] or to imprisonment for a term not exceeding **three months** or to **both**; and

(b) on conviction on indictment, to a **fine** or to imprisonment for a term not exceeding **two years** or to **both**.

(4)–(6) *Regulations and charges.*

(7) In this section "record" has the same meaning as in section 73 above.
[Civil Aviation Act 1982, s 74, as amended by the Criminal Justice Act 1982, ss 38 and 46.]

1. For procedure in respect of this offence which is triable either way, see the Magistrates' Courts Act 1980, ss 17A–21, in PART I: MAGISTRATES' COURTS, PROCEDURE, ante.
2. For meaning of "the statutory maximum", see s 105, post.

7–5401 74A. *Enforcement of foreign judgments etc in respect of route charges.*

Investigation of accidents

7–5402 75. Investigation of accidents. (1) Without prejudice to section 60 above, the Secretary of State may by regulations[1] under this section make such provision as appears to him to be requisite or expedient—

    (*a*) for the investigation of any accident arising out of or in the course of air navigation and either occurring in or over the United Kingdom or occurring elsewhere to aircraft registered in the United Kingdom; and

    (*b*) for carrying out any Annex to the Chicago Convention (being an Annex adopted in accordance with the Convention and relating to the investigation of accidents involving aircraft) as it has effect from time to time with any amendment made in accordance with the Convention (hereafter in this section referred to as "the Annex").

  (1A) The power to make regulations under this section includes power to make provision—

    (*a*) for the purpose of implementing the Community obligations of the United Kingdom under Council Directive 94/56/EC of 21 November 1994 establishing the fundamental principles governing the investigation of civil aviation accidents and incidents;

    (*b*) for the purpose of dealing with matters arising out of or related to any such obligation.

  (2) Without prejudice to the generality of subsection (1)(*b*) above, the provision there authorised includes provision with respect to any of the following matters, that is to say—

    (*a*) the definition of "accident" for the purposes of this section so as to correspond to the meaning adopted for the time being in the Annex;

    (*b*) the participation of any persons authorised for the purpose in accordance with the regulations in any investigation held in accordance with the requirements of the Annex by the competent authorities of any other state; and

    (*c*) the investigation of any accident other than one to which subsection (1)(*a*) above applies for the purpose of securing any information, articles or other material which it is the duty of the United Kingdom in accordance with any requirements of the Annex to furnish to any other state.

  (3) Without prejudice to the generality of subsection (1) above, regulations under this section may contain provisions—

    (*a*) requiring notice to be given of any such accident as is mentioned in subsection (1)(*a*) above in such manner and by such persons as may be specified in the regulations;

    (*b*) applying any of the provisions of section 3 of the Notice of Accidents Act 1894 (with or without modifications) for the purposes of any investigations held in accordance with the regulations or any inquiries undertaken in accordance with the regulations with a view to determining whether any such investigation should be held;

    (*c*) prohibiting, pending investigation, access to or interference with aircraft to which an accident has occurred, and authorising any person so far as may be necessary for the purposes of an investigation, or for the purpose of determining whether an investigation should be held, to have access to, examine, remove, test, take measures for the preservation of, or otherwise deal with, any such aircraft and any other aircraft;

    (*d*) authorising or requiring the cancellation, suspension, endorsement or surrender of any licence or certificate granted under an Air Navigation Order or an order under section 62 above where it appears on an investigation that the licence or certificate ought to be cancelled, suspended, endorsed or surrendered and requiring the production of any such licence or certificate for the purpose of being so dealt with.

  (4) Without prejudice to subsection (2)(*a*) above, in this section "accident" shall be construed as including any fortuitous or unexpected event by which the safety of an aircraft or any person is threatened.

  (5) If any person contravenes or fails to comply with any regulations[1] under this section he shall be liable on summary conviction to a fine not exceeding **level 5** on the standard scale or to imprisonment for a term not exceeding **three months***.

  (6) Nothing in this section shall limit the powers of any authority under sections 245 to 247 and sections 252 to 254 of the Merchant Shipping Act 1995 or any enactment amending those sections. [Civil Aviation Act 1982, s 75, as amended by the Criminal Justice Act 1982, s 46, the Merchant Shipping Act 1995, Sch 13 and SI 1996/76.]

  ***Words substituted by the Criminal Justice Act 2003, Sch 26, from a date to be appointed.**
  1. See the Air Navigation (Investigation of Air Accidents Involving Civil and Military Aircraft or Installations) Regulations 1986, SI 1986/1953, the Civil Aviation (Investigation of Accidents and Incidents) Regulations 1996, SI 1996/2798 and the Civil Aviation (Investigation of Military Air Accidents at Civil Aerodromes) Regulations 2005, SI 2005/2693.

Trespass by aircraft and aircraft nuisance, noise, etc

7–5403 78. Regulation of noise and vibration from aircraft. (1)–(7) *Powers and duties for regulating noise and vibration.*

  (8) The Secretary of State may, after consultation with the person managing a designated aerodrome, by order require him at his own expense—

    (*a*) to provide in an area and within a period specified in the order, and to maintain and operate in accordance with any instructions so specified, such equipment for measuring noise in the vicinity of the aerodrome as is so specified; and (*b*) to make to the Secretary of State such reports as are so specified with respect to the noise measured by the equipment and to permit any person authorised by the Secretary of State for the purpose to inspect the equipment on demand at any time;

and it shall be the duty of the person for the time being managing the aerodrome to comply with the requirements of the order.

(9) If a person fails to perform any duty imposed on him by subsection (8) above the Secretary of State may, after affording him an opportunity of making representations to the Secretary of State with respect to the matter and after considering any representations then made by him—

(*a*) take such steps as the Secretary of State considers appropriate for remedying the failure, which may include steps to secure the provision, maintenance and operation of equipment by the Secretary of State or the CAA; and

(*b*) recover in any court of competent jurisdiction from the person aforesaid any expense attributable to the taking of those steps which is incurred by the Secretary of State from time to time;

and if a person fails to perform any duty imposed on him by virtue of paragraph (*b*) of subsection (8) above, then without prejudice to the preceding provisions of this subsection he shall—

(i) be guilty of an offence and liable on summary conviction to a fine not exceeding **level 3** on the standard scale; and

(ii) if the failure continues after his conviction of an offence under this subsection arising from the failure, be guilty of a separate offence under this subsection on each day on which the failure continues thereafter and liable to be fined accordingly.

(10) Paragraph (*b*) of subsection (9) above is without prejudice to the Secretary of State's power apart from that paragraph to recover the expenses mentioned therein.

(11) The Secretary of State may, after consultation with any local authority appearing to him to be concerned, by order repeal any provision of a local Act which he considers is unnecessary having regard to the provisions of this section and of section 79 below.

(12) *Notices.*

[Civil Aviation Act 1982, s 78, as amended by the Criminal Justice Act 1982, ss 38 and 46.]

7–5404 80. Designation of aerodromes for purposes of ss 78 and 79. In sections 78 and 79 above "designated aerodrome" means any aerodrome in Great Britain which is designated for the purposes of the section in which the expression is used by an order[1] made by the Secretary of State; and the Secretary of State may designate an aerodrome for the purposes of either or both of those sections.

[Civil Aviation Act 1982, s 80.]

---

1. See the Civil Aviation (Designation of Aerodromes) Order 1981, SI 1981/651.

7–5405 81. Dangerous flying. (1) Where an aircraft is flown in such a manner as to be the cause of unnecessary danger to any person or property on land or water, the pilot or the person in charge of the aircraft, and also the owner thereof, unless he proves to the satisfaction of the court that the aircraft was so flown without his actual fault or privity, shall be liable on summary conviction to a fine not exceeding **level 4** on the standard scale or to imprisonment for a term not exceeding **six months** or to **both**.

(2) In this section the expression "owner" in relation to an aircraft includes any person by whom the aircraft is hired at the time of the offence.

(3) The provisions of this section shall be in addition to and not in derogation of the powers conferred on Her Majesty in Council by section 60 above.

[Civil Aviation Act 1982, s 81, as amended by the Criminal Justice Act 1982, ss 38 and 46.]

7–5406 82. Prohibition of aerial advertising and propaganda. (1) Save in such circumstances as may be prescribed[1], no aircraft while in the air over any part of the United Kingdom shall be used, whether wholly or partly for emitting or displaying any advertisement or other communication in such a way that the advertisement or communication is audible or visible from the ground.

(2) Any person who uses an aircraft, or knowingly causes or permits an aircraft to be used, in contravention of subsection (1) above shall be guilty of an offence and liable on summary conviction to a fine not exceeding **level 4** on the standard scale or to imprisonment for a term not exceeding **three months** or to **both**.

[Civil Aviation Act 1982, s 82, as amended by the Criminal Justice Act 1982, ss 35, 38 and 46.]

---

1. See the Civil Aviation (Aerial Advertising) Regulations 1995, SI 1995/2943.

Records and provision of information, etc

7–5407 83. Recording and registration of births and deaths, etc. (1) The Secretary of State may by regulations[1] provide for requiring such persons as may be specified in the regulations to keep records and make returns to the CAA—

(a) of births and deaths occurring in any part of the world in any aircraft registered in the United Kingdom; and

(b) of the death, outside the United Kingdom, of any person who, being a traveller on such an aircraft, is killed on the journey in consequence of an accident;

and for the keeping by the CAA of a record of any returns made to it in accordance with any such requirement as aforesaid.

(2) Any person who fails to comply with any such requirement shall be liable on summary conviction to a fine not exceeding **level 3** on the standard scale.

(3) Proceedings for an offence under this section shall not be instituted—

(a) in England and Wales, except by or with the consent of the Secretary of State or by or with the consent of the Director of Public Prosecutions;

(b) *Northern Ireland.*

(4) Where regulations made under subsection (1) above provide for the keeping of records by the CAA in accordance with that subsection they shall also provide for the transmission of certified copies of those records to the Registrar General of Births, Deaths and Marriages in England and Wales, the Registrar General of Births, Deaths and Marriages in Scotland, or the Registrar General for Northern Ireland, as the case may require.

(5) The Registrar General to whom any such certified copies are sent shall cause them to be filed and preserved in a book to be kept by him for the purpose, and to be called the Air Register Book of Births and Deaths.

(6) Regulations made under subsection (1) above shall provide for the rectification of any records kept by the CAA in pursuance of the regulations and for the transmission of certified copies of any corrected entry in the records to the Registrar General of Births, Deaths and Marriages in England and Wales, the Registrar General of Births, Deaths and Marriages in Scotland, or the Registrar General for Northern Ireland, as the case may require.

(7) The Registrar General to whom a certified copy of any such corrected entry is sent in accordance with the regulations shall cause the corrected entry to be substituted for the corresponding entry for the time being made in the Air Register Book of Births and Deaths.

(8) The enactments relating to the registration of births and deaths in England and Wales, Scotland and Northern Ireland shall have effect as if the Air Register Book of Births and Deaths were a certified copy or duplicate register transmitted to the Registrar General in accordance with those enactments.

(9) The Secretary of State may by regulations provide—

(a) for the keeping by the CAA of a record of persons reported to him as missing, being persons with respect to whom there are reasonable grounds for believing that they have died in consequence of an accident to an aircraft registered in the United Kingdom;

(b) for the rectification of any such record; and

(c) for the transmission of information as to the matters for the time being entered on the record to the Registrar General of Births, Deaths and Marriages in England and Wales, the Registrar General of Births, Deaths and Marriages in Scotland or the Registrar General for Northern Ireland, as the case may require.

[Civil Aviation Act 1982, s 83, as amended by the Criminal Justice Act 1982, ss 38 and 46.]

1. The Civil Aviation (Births, Deaths and Missing Persons) Regulation 1948, SI 1948/1411 amended by SI 1972/323 have effect under this section.

7–5408 84. Provision by others of information for the CAA and Secretary of State. (1) The CAA may, by a notice in writing served in the prescribed[1] manner on a person of any of the following descriptions, that is to say—

(a) a holder of a licence issued by the CAA under this Act or a licence or certificate issued by the CAA under an Air Navigation Order or an operating licence granted by the CAA in accordance with Council Regulation 2407/92 on licensing of air carriers,

(b) a recipient of an approval given by the CAA under an Air Navigation Order,

(c) a person who in the United Kingdom has, at any time during the period of two years ending with the date of service of the notice, held himself out as one who may as a principal or otherwise enter into a contract to make available accommodation for the carriage or persons or cargo on flights in any part of the world in aircraft of which he is not the operator,

(d) a person carrying on business in the United Kingdom as a manufacturer of aircraft or engines or other equipment for aircraft or as an insurer of aircraft,

require him to furnish to the CAA, in such form and at such times as may be specified in the notice, information of such descriptions as may be so specified, being—

(i) in the case of such a holder or recipient as aforesaid (other than the holder of an aerodrome licence), descriptions of information which relates to his past, present or future activities as the holder or recipient of the licence, certificate or approval in question or his past activities as the holder or recipient of any similar licence, certificate or approval or is of a kind which the

CAA considers that it requires for the purpose of reviewing the licence, certificate or approval in question,

(ii) in the case of such a person as is mentioned in paragraph (c) of this subsection, descriptions of information which relates to his past, present or future activities in the United Kingdom connected with the making available of accommodation so mentioned,

(iii) in the case of such a person as is mentioned in paragraph (d) of this subsection or the holder of an aerodrome licence, descriptions of information which relates to his past, present or future activities (including, in the case of the holder of an aerodrome licence, information as to the numbers of aircraft and passengers and the quantity of cargo passing and expected to pass through the relevant aerodrome) and is of a kind which the CAA considers that it requires for the purpose of performing any of its functions.

In this subsection "aerodrome licence" means a licence to operate an aerodrome issued by the CAA under an Air Navigation Order.

(2) Without prejudice to the generality of subsection (1) above, the information relating to the activities of the holder of an air transport licence or operating licence which the CAA may require him to furnish in pursuance of that subsection includes particulars of any contract or arrangement—

(a) to which he is or was at any time a party and, if he is not or was not then an operator of aircraft registered in the United Kingdom or a relevant overseas territory or an associated state, to which such an operator is or was then a party; and

(b) which constitutes or relates to an agreement or understanding between operators of aircraft or such operators and other persons with respect to any of the following matters, that is to say—

(i) the provision of flights or of accommodation in aircraft,

(ii) the sharing or transfer of revenue from flights on particular routes,

(iii) the sale by a party to the contract or arrangement of tickets for flights in aircraft operated by another party to it,

(iv) the making available by a party to the contract or arrangement of staff, equipment or other facilities for use by another party to it.

(3) Provision may be made by regulations made by the Secretary of State for requiring a person of any description specified in subsection (1) above to furnish the Secretary of State, in such form and at such times as may be prescribed, with information of such descriptions as may be prescribed, being descriptions of information relating to civil aviation which the Secretary of State considers that he requires for the purpose of performing any of his functions or descriptions of information which he considers that he requires in order to facilitate the performance by the CAA of any of its functions.

(4) If a person required to furnish information by virtue of any of the preceding provisions of this section fails to comply with the requirement or in purported compliance with the requirement knowingly or recklessly furnishes information which is false in a material particular, then—

(a) in the case of a failure to comply with the requirement he shall be guilty of an offence and liable on summary conviction to a fine of an amount not exceeding **level 3** on the standard scale; and

(b) in any other case he shall be guilty of an offence and liable[2] on summary conviction to a fine not exceeding **the statutory maximum**[3] and on conviction on indictment to a **fine** or to imprisonment for a term not exceeding **two years** or to **both**; and

(c) if the requirement was made by virtue of subsection (1) or (2) above, the CAA may, whether or not any proceedings in respect of the requirement have been brought in pursuance of paragraph (a) or (b) of this subsection, revoke any licence or certificate or approval which was issued or given by the CAA and to which the requirement related;

and a person who fails to comply with a requirement imposed on him in pursuance of this section shall be guilty of an offence by virtue of paragraph (a) of this subsection notwithstanding that at any relevant time he is outside the United Kingdom and is neither a United Kingdom national nor a body incorporated under the law of a part of the United Kingdom or of a relevant overseas territory or an associated state.

[Civil Aviation Act 1982, s 84, as amended by the Criminal Justice Act 1982, ss 38 and 46, SI 1992/2992 and SI 1993/101 and 1327.]

---

1. See the Civil Aviation Regulations 1991, SI 1991/1672.
2. For procedure in respect of this offence which is triable either way, see the Magistrates' Courts Act 1980, ss 17A–21, in PART I: MAGISTRATES' COURTS, PROCEDURE, ante.
3. For meaning of "the statutory maximum", see s 105, post.

PART IV[1]

AIRCRAFT

Jurisdiction, etc

7–5409 **91.** *Jurisdiction in civil matters.*

---

1. Part IV contains ss 85–98.

7–5410   92. Application of criminal law to aircraft.   (1) Any act or omission taking place on board a British-controlled aircraft or (subject to subsection (1A) below) a foreign aircraft while in flight elsewhere than in or over the United Kingdom which, if taking place in, or in a part of, the United Kingdom, would constitute an offence under the law in force in, or in that part of, the United Kingdom shall constitute that offence; but this subsection shall not apply to any act or omission which is expressly or impliedly authorised by or under that law when taking place outside the United Kingdom.

(1A) Subsection (1) above shall only apply to an act or omission which takes place on board a foreign aircraft where—

(a)   the next landing of the aircraft is in the United Kingdom, and

(b)   in the case of an aircraft registered in a country other than the United Kingdom, the act or omission would, if taking place there, also constitute an offence under the law in force in that country.

(1B) Any act or omission punishable under the law in force in any country is an offence under that law for the purposes of subsection (1A) above, however it is described in that law.

(2) Subject to any provision to the contrary in any Act passed after 14th July 1967, no proceedings for any offence under the law in force in, or in a part of, the United Kingdom committed on board an aircraft while in flight elsewhere than in or over the United Kingdom (other than an offence under, or under any instrument made under, any of the air navigation enactments) shall be instituted—

(a)   in England and Wales, except by or with the consent of the Director of Public Prosecutions; or

(b)   in Northern Ireland, except by or with the consent of the Attorney General for Northern Ireland;

but, unless the Attorney General for Northern Ireland otherwise directs, paragraph (b) above shall be deemed to be complied with as respects the institution of any proceedings if the Director of Public Prosecutions for Northern Ireland gives his consent to the institution or carrying on of the proceedings.*

(2A) The requirement in subsection (1A)(b) above shall be taken to be met unless, not later than the rules of court may provide, the defence serve on the prosecution a notice—

(a)   stating that, on the facts as alleged with respect to the act or omission, the requirement is not in their opinion met;

(b)   showing the grounds for their opinion; and

(c)   requiring the prosecution to prove that it is met.

(2B) The court, if it thinks fit, may permit the defence to require the prosecution to prove that the requirement is met without the prior service of a notice under subsection (2A) above.

(2C) In the Crown Court the question whether the requirement is met is to be decided by the judge alone.

(3) For the purpose of conferring jurisdiction, any offence under the law in force in, or in a part of, the United Kingdom committed on board an aircraft in flight shall be deemed to have been committed in any place in the United Kingdom (or, as the case may be, in that part thereof) where the offender may for the time being be.

(4) For the purposes of this section the period during which an aircraft is in flight shall be deemed to include any period from the moment when power is applied for the purpose of the aircraft taking off on a flight until the moment when the landing run (if any) at the termination of that flight ends; and any reference in this section to an aircraft in flight shall include a reference to an aircraft during any period when it is on the surface of the sea or land but not within the territorial limits of any country.

(5) In this section, except where the context otherwise requires—

"aircraft" means any aircraft, whether or not a British-controlled aircraft, other than—

(a)   a military aircraft; or

(b)   subject to section 101(b) below, an aircraft which, not being a military aircraft, belongs to or is exclusively employed in the service of Her Majesty in right of the United Kingdom;

"the air navigation enactments" mean the enactments contained in sections 60 to 62, 72 to 77, 81 to 83, 87 and 97 of this Act;

"British-controlled aircraft" means an aircraft—

(a)   which is for the time being registered in the United Kingdom; or

(b)   which is not for the time being registered in any country but in the case of which either the operator of the aircraft or each person entitled as owner to any legal or beneficial interest in it satisfies the following requirements, namely—

    (i)   that he is a person qualified to be the owner of a legal or beneficial interest in an aircraft registered in the United Kingdom; and

    (ii)   that he resides or has his principal place of business in the United Kingdom; or

(c)   which, being for the time being registered in some other country, is for the time being chartered by demise to a person who, or to persons each of whom, satisfies the requirements aforesaid;

"foreign aircraft" means any aircraft other than a British-controlled aircraft;
"military aircraft" means—

  (a) an aircraft of the naval, military or air forces of any country; or
  (b) any other aircraft in respect of which there is in force a certificate issued in accordance with any Order in Council in force under section 60, 87, 89, 91, 101(1)(a) or 107(2) of this Act that the aircraft is to be treated for the purposes of that Order in Council as a military aircraft;

and a certificate of the Secretary of State that any aircraft is or is not a military aircraft for the purposes of this section shall be conclusive evidence of the fact certified.

(6) In subsection (2) above, the words from "but" onwards shall (notwithstanding their enactment in this Act) have effect subject to any question arising as to the validity, in relation to any such provision as is re-enacted in the preceding provisions of that subsection, of the provisions from which the words derive, that is to say, Article 7 of the Prosecution of Offences (Northern Ireland) Order 1972 and paragraphs 67 and 68 of Part II of Schedule 1 to the Criminal Justice (Northern Ireland) Order 1980.*

[Civil Aviation Act 1982, s 92, as amended by the Civil Aviation (Amendment) Act 1996, s 1.]

------

*Sub-section (2), words underlined and sub-s (6) repealed by the Justice (Northern Ireland) Act 2002, Sch 13, from a date to be appointed.

7–5411 93. *Repealed.*

Powers of commander of aircraft

7–5412 94. Powers of commander of aircraft.   (1) The provisions of subsections (2) to (5) below shall have effect for the purposes of any proceedings before any court in the United Kingdom.

(2) If the commander of an aircraft in flight, wherever that aircraft may be, has reasonable grounds to believe in respect of any person on board the aircraft—

  (a) that the person in question has done or is about to do any act on the aircraft while it is in flight which jeopardises or may jeopardise—
    (i) the safety of the aircraft or of persons or property on board the aircraft, or
    (ii) good order and discipline on board the aircraft, or
  (b) that the person in question has done on the aircraft while in flight any act which in the opinion of the commander is a serious offence under any law in force in the country in which the aircraft is registered, not being a law of a political nature or based on racial or religious discrimination,

then, subject to subsection (4) below, the commander may take with respect to that person such reasonable measures, including restraint of his person, as may be necessary—

  (i) to protect the safety of the aircraft or of persons or property on board the aircraft; or
  (ii) to maintain good order and discipline on board the aircraft; or
  (iii) to enable the commander to disembark or deliver that person in accordance with subsection (5) below,

and for the purposes of paragraph (b) of this subsection any British-controlled aircraft shall be deemed to be registered in the United Kingdom whether or not it is in fact so registered and whether or not it is in fact registered in some other country.

(3) Any member of the crew of an aircraft and any other person on board the aircraft may, at the request or with the authority of the commander of the aircraft, and any such member shall if so required by that commander, render assistance in restraining any person whom the commander is entitled under subsection (2) above to restrain; and at any time when the aircraft is in flight any such member or other person may, without obtaining the authority of the commander, take with respect to any person on board the aircraft any measures such as are mentioned in that subsection which he has reasonable grounds to believe are immediately necessary to protect the safety of the aircraft or of persons or property on board the aircraft.

(4) Any restraint imposed on any person on board an aircraft under the powers conferred by the preceding provisions of this section shall not be continued after the time when the aircraft first thereafter ceases to be in flight unless before or as soon as is reasonably practicable after that time the commander of the aircraft causes notification of the fact that a person on board the aircraft is under restraint and of the reasons therefor to be sent to an appropriate authority of the country in which the aircraft so ceases to be in flight, but subject to such notification may be continued after that time—

  (a) for any period (including the period of any further flight) between that time and the first occasion thereafter on which the commander is able with any requisite consent of the appropriate authorities to disembark or deliver the person under restraint in accordance with subsection (5) below; or
  (b) if the person under restraint agrees to continue his journey under restraint on board that aircraft.

(5) The commander of an aircraft—

(a) if in the case of any person on board the aircraft he has reasonable grounds—

    (i) to believe as mentioned in subsection (2)(a) above, and

    (ii) to believe that it is necessary so to do in order to protect the safety of the aircraft or of persons or property on board the aircraft or to maintain good order and discipline on board the aircraft,

may disembark that person in any country in which that aircraft may be; and

(b) if in the case of any person on board the aircraft he has reasonable grounds to believe as mentioned in subsection (2)(b) above, may deliver that person—

    (i) in the United Kingdom, to a constable or immigration officer; or

    (ii) in any other country which is a Convention country, to an officer having functions corresponding to the functions in the United Kingdom either of a constable or of an immigration officer.

(6) The commander of an aircraft—

(a) if he disembarks any person in pursuance of subsection (5)(a) above, in the case of a British-controlled aircraft, in any country or, in the case of any other aircraft, in the United Kingdom, shall report the fact of, and the reasons for, that disembarkation to—

    (i) an appropriate authority in the country of disembarkation; and

    (ii) the appropriate diplomatic or consular office of the country of nationality of that person;

(b) if he intends to deliver any person in accordance with subsection (5)(b) above in the United Kingdom or, in the case of a British-controlled aircraft, in any other country which is a Convention country, shall before or as soon as reasonably practicable after landing give notification of his intention and of the reasons therefor—

    (i) where the country in question is the United Kingdom, to a constable or immigration officer or, in the case of any other country, to an officer having functions corresponding to the functions in the United Kingdom either of a constable or of an immigration officer;

    (ii) in either case to the appropriate diplomatic or consular office of the country of nationality of that person;

and any commander of an aircraft who without reasonable cause fails to comply with the requirements of this subsection shall be liable on summary conviction to a fine not exceeding **level 3** on the standard scale.

(7) In this section—

"commander" in relation to an aircraft, means the member of the crew designated as commander of that aircraft by the operator thereof, or, failing such a person, the person who is for the time being the pilot in command of the aircraft; and

"pilot in command" in relation to an aircraft, means a person who for the time being is in charge of the piloting of the aircraft without being under the direction of any other pilot in the aircraft;

and, subject to subsection (8) below, subsections (4) and (5) of section 92 above shall apply for the purposes of this section as they apply for the purposes of that section.

(8) The time during which an aircraft is in flight shall, for the purposes of this section, be deemed to include, in addition to such a period as is mentioned in subsection (4) of section 92 above—

(a) any further period from the moment when all external doors, if any, of the aircraft are closed following embarkation for a flight until the moment when any such door is opened for disembarkation after that flight; and

(b) if the aircraft makes a forced landing, any period thereafter until the time when competent authorities of the country in which the forced landing takes place take over the responsibility for the aircraft and for the persons and property on board the aircraft (being, if the forced landing takes place in the United Kingdom, the time when a constable arrives at the place of landing).

[Civil Aviation Act 1982, s 94, as amended by the Criminal Justice Act 1982, ss 38 and 46.]

Evidence, etc

7–5413 95. Provisions as to evidence in connection with aircraft. (1) Where in any proceedings before a court in the United Kingdom for an offence committed on board an aircraft the testimony of any person is required and the court is satisfied that the person in question cannot be found in the United Kingdom, there shall be admissible in evidence before that court any deposition relating to the subject matter of those proceedings previously made on oath by that person outside the United Kingdom which was so made—

(a) in the presence of the person charged with the offence; and

(b) before a judge or magistrate of a country such as is mentioned in Schedule 3 to the British Nationality Act 1981 as for the time being in force or which was part of Her Majesty's dominions at the time the deposition was made or in which Her Majesty had jurisdiction at that time, or before a consular officer of Her Majesty's Government in the United Kingdom.

(2) Any such deposition shall be authenticated by the signature of the judge, magistrate or consular officer before whom it was made who shall certify that the person charged with the offence was present at the taking of the deposition.

(3) It shall not be necessary in any proceedings to prove the signature or official character of the person appearing so to have authenticated any such deposition or to have given such a certificate, and such a certificate shall, unless the contrary is proved, be sufficient evidence in any proceedings that the person charged with the offence was present at the making of the deposition.

(4) If a complaint is made to such a consular officer as aforesaid that

(a) any offence has been committed on a British-controlled aircraft while in flight elsewhere than in or over the United Kingdom, or

(b) there has taken place on board a foreign aircraft an act or omission which constitutes an offence by virtue of section 92(1) above,

that officer may inquire into the case upon oath.

(5) In this section—

"deposition" includes any affidavit, affirmation or statement made upon oath; and

"oath" includes an affirmation or declaration in the case of persons allowed by law to affirm or declare instead of swearing;

and subsections (4) and (5) of section 92 above shall apply for the purposes of this section as they apply for the purposes of that section.

(6) Nothing in this section shall prejudice the admission as evidence of any deposition which is admissible in evidence apart from this section.

[Civil Aviation Act 1982, s 95, as amended by the Civil Aviation (Amendment) Act 1996, s 2.]

7–5414 **96. Use of records and documentary evidence.** (1) In any legal proceedings—

(a) a document purporting to be certified by such authority or person as may be designated for the purpose by regulations[1] made by the Secretary of State as being, or being a true copy of, or of part of, a document issued or record kept in pursuance of—

(i) an Air Navigation Order, or

(ii) the Civil Aviation (Licensing) Act 1960,

by, or by the Minister in charge of, a government department, by an official of a government department specified for the purpose in an Air Navigation Order or by the Air Registration Board or the Air Transport Licensing Board, or

(b) a document printed by either Her Majesty's Stationery Office or the CAA and purporting to be the publication known as the "United Kingdom Air Pilot" or a publication of the series known as "Notam—United Kingdom",

shall be evidence, and in Scotland sufficient evidence, of the matters appearing from the document.

(2) In any legal proceedings any record made by any such authority or person as may be designated for the purposes of this subsection by regulations made by the Secretary of State, or by a person acting under the control of such an authority or person, being a record purporting to show—

(a) the position of an aircraft at any material time, or

(b) the terms or content of any message or signal transmitted to any aircraft, either alone or in common with other aircraft, or received from any aircraft, by the first-mentioned authority or person, or by a person acting under the control of that authority or person,

shall, if produced from the custody of that authority or person, be evidence, and in Scotland sufficient evidence, of the matters appearing from the record.

(3) The references in subsection (2) above to a record made by or under the control of any authority or person include references to a document or article purporting to be a copy of a record so made, and certified to be a true copy by or on behalf of that authority or person; and in relation to such a copy that subsection shall have effect as if the words "if produced from the custody of that authority or person" were omitted.

(4) Any person who wilfully certifies any document or article to be a true copy of any such record as is mentioned in subsection (2) above knowing it not to be a true copy shall be liable[2]—

(a) on summary conviction, to a fine not exceeding **the statutory maximum**[3] or to imprisonment for a term not exceeding **three months** or to **both**; and

(b) on conviction on indictment to a **fine** or to imprisonment for a term not exceeding **two years** or to **both**.

(5) In this section "record" has the same meaning as in section 73 above.

[Civil Aviation Act 1982, s 96.]

---

1. See the Civil Aviation (Documentary Evidence) Regulations 1972, SI 1972/187.

2. For procedure in respect of this offence which is triable either way, see the Magistrates' Courts Act 1980, ss 17A–21, in PART I: MAGISTRATES' COURTS, PROCEDURE, ante.

3. For meaning of "the statutory maximum", see s 105, post.

Seaplanes

7-5415   97. Seaplanes[1].

    1. The Collision Rules (Seaplanes) Order 1989, SI 1989/2005, amended by SI 1990/25, have been made.

Supplemental

7-5416   98. Construction of certain provisions of Part IV.   If the Secretary of State is satisfied that the requirements of Article 18 of the Tokyo Convention have been satisfied (which Article makes provision as to the country which is to be treated as the country of registration of certain aircraft operated by joint air transport organisations or international operating agencies established by two or more Convention countries) the Secretary of State may by order provide that for the purposes of sections 92 to 95 above such aircraft as may be specified in the order shall be treated as registered in such convention country as may be so specified.
[Civil Aviation Act 1982, s 98.]

PART V
MISCELLANEOUS AND GENERAL[1]

7-5417   99. Offences.   (1) Where an offence to which this subsection applies has been committed by a body corporate and is proved to have been committed with the consent or connivance of or to be attributable to any neglect on the part of any director, manager, secretary or other similar officer of the body corporate or any person who was purporting to act in any such capacity, he as well as the body corporate shall be guilty of that offence and be liable to be proceeded against and punished accordingly.

    (2) Where the affairs of a body corporate are managed by its members subsection (1) above shall apply in relation to the acts and defaults of a member in connection with his functions of management as if he were a director of the body corporate.

    (3) Any offence to which this subsection applies shall, for the purpose of conferring jurisdiction, be deemed to have been committed in any place where the offender may for the time being be.

    (4) Subsection (1) above applies to any offence under section 44, 45, 50, 64(5), 67(6), 82, 83 or 84(4) above or under regulations made by virtue of section 7(2)(b; or 71 above.

    (5) Subsection (3) above applies to any offence under any provision made by or under this Act, except, without prejudice to section 92(3) above—

    (a) Repealed;
    (b) an offence under section 44, 45, 50, 83 or 94(6) above;
    (c) an offence consisting in a contravention of an order made under section 62 above;
    (d) an offence consisting in a convention of an order made under section 63 above with respect to a British air transport undertaking;
    (e) an offence consisting in a contravention of an Order in Council under section 86 above.
[Civil Aviation Act 1982, s 99, as amended by the Airports Act 1986, Sch 6.]

    1. Part V contains ss 99–110.

7-5418   100. Application of Act to hovercraft.   The enactments and instruments with respect to which provision may be made by Order in Council in pursuance of section 1(1)(h) of the Hovercraft Act 1968 (power to apply enactments and instruments in relation to hovercraft etc) shall include this Act and any instrument made under it.
[Civil Aviation Act 1982, s 100.]

7-5419   101. Power to apply certain provisions to Crown aircraft.   (1) Her Majesty may by Order[1] in Council—

    (a) apply to any aircraft belonging to or exclusively employed in the service of Her Majesty, with or without modification, any of the provisions of this Act mentioned in subsection (2) below (being provisions which do not otherwise apply to such aircraft) or any Orders in Council, orders or regulations under those provisions;
    (b) apply the provisions of sections 92 to 95 above, with or without modifications, to aircraft such as are excluded from the definition of "aircraft" in subsection (5) of the said section 92 by paragraph (b) of the definition.

    (2) The provisions of this Act referred to in subsection (1)(a) above are sections 60 and 61, 75 to 77, 81, 87, 89, 91, 96 and 97 and Part III of Schedule 13.
[Civil Aviation Act 1982, s 101, as amended by SI 2001/4050.]

    1. The Civil Aviation (Crown Aircraft) Order 1970, SI 1970/289, has effect under this section.

7-5430   102. *Powers to make Orders in Council, orders and regulations.*

7–5431 105. General interpretation. (1) In this Act, except where the context otherwise requires—

"accounting year", in relation to the CAA, means the period of twelve months ending with 31st March in any year;

"aerodrome" means any area of land or water designed, equipped, set apart or commonly used for affording facilities for the landing and departure of aircraft and includes any area or space, whether on the ground, on the roof of a building or elsewhere, which is designed, equipped or set apart for affording facilities for the landing and departure of aircraft capable of descending or climbing vertically;

"Air Navigation Order" means an Order in Council under section 60 above;

"air navigation services" includes information, directions and other facilities furnished, issued or provided in connection with the navigation or movement of aircraft, and includes the control of movement of vehicles in any part of an aerodrome used for the movement of aircraft;

"air transport licence" has the meaning given by section 64(1)(*a*) above;

"air transport service" means a service for the carriage by air of passengers or cargo;

"the CAA" means the Civil Aviation Authority;

"cargo" includes mail;

"the Chicago Convention" means the convention on International Civil Aviation which was, on 7th December 1944, signed on behalf of the Government of the United Kingdom at the International Civil Aviation Conference held at Chicago;

"Convention country" means a country in which the Tokyo convention is for the time being in force; and Her Majesty may by Order[1] in Council certify that any country specified in the Order is for the time being a Convention country and any such Order in Council for the time being in force shall be conclusive evidence that the country in question is for the time being a Convention country;

"enactment" includes any enactment contained in an Act of the Parliament of Northern Ireland, an Order in Council under section 1(3) of the Northern Ireland (Temporary Provisions) Act 1972 or a Measure of the Northern Ireland Assembly;

"Eurocontrol" and "the Eurocontrol Convention" have the meanings given by section 24 above;

"flight" means a journey by air beginning when the aircraft in question takes off and ending when it next lands;

"functions" includes powers and duties;

"the initial debt" has the meaning given by section 9(1) above;

"the Land Compensation Act"—

    (*a*) in relation to England and Wales, means the Land Compensation Act 1961;

    (*b*) in relation to Scotland, means the Land Compensation (Scotland) Act 1963; and

    (*c*) in relation to Northern Ireland, means, subject to subsection (7) below, the Acquisition of Land (Assessment of Compensation) Act 1919;

"the Lands Tribunal" shall be construed subject to subsection (5) below;

"licence holder" means aperson who holds a licence under Chapter I of Part I of the Transport Act 2000 (air traffic services);

"local authority"—

    (*a*) in relation to England, means a county council, the council of a district or London borough or the Common Council of the City of London;

    (*aa*) in relation to Wales, means a county council or a county borough council;

    (*b*)–(*c*) *Scotland, Northern Ireland.*

"loss or damage" includes, in relation to persons, loss of life and personal injury;

"modifications" includes additions, omissions and amendments, and "modify" shall be construed accordingly;

"operator", in relation to an aircraft, means the person having the management of the aircraft for the time being or, in relation to a time, at that time;

"prescribed" means prescribed by regulations made by the Secretary of State;

"relevant overseas territory" means any of the Channel Islands, the Isle of Man, any colony;

"reward", in relation to a flight, includes any form of consideration received or to be received wholly or partly in connection with the flight irrespective of the person by whom or to whom the consideration has been or is to be given;

"statutory undertaker" means the CAA, a licence holder, a universal service provider in connection with the provision of a universal postal service, or any person (including a local authority) authorised by any Act (whether public general or local) or by any order or scheme made under or confirmed by any Act to construct, work or carry on—

    (*a*) any railway, light railway, tramway, road transport, water transport, canal, inland navigation, dock, harbour, pier or lighthouse undertaking;

    (*b*) any undertaking for the supply of hydraulic power[2];

    (*c*) *Repealed*;

and "statutory undertaking" shall be construed accordingly;

"subsidiary" shall be construed in accordance with section 736 of the Companies Act 1985; and

"Tokyo Convention" means the Convention on Offences and certain other Acts Committed on board Aircraft, which was signed at Tokyo on 14th September 1963;

"United Kingdom national" means an individual who is—

   (*a*) a British citizen, a British overseas territories citizen or a British Overseas citizen;

   (*b*) a person who under the British Nationality Act 1981 is a British subject; or

   (*c*) a British protected person (within the meaning of that Act);

"universal service provider" has the same meaning as in the Postal Services Act 2000; and references to the provision of a universal postal service shall be construed in accordance with that Act.

(1ZA) For the purposes of this Act—

   (*a*) a licence holder shall not be considered to be a statutory undertaker unless it is carrying out activities authorised by the licence;

   (*b*) the licence holder's undertaking shall not be considered to be a statutory undertaking except to the extent that it is its undertaking as licence holder; and references in this Act to a licence holder's undertaking shall be construed accordingly.

(1A) The undertaking of a universal service provider so far as relating to the provision of a universal postal service shall be taken to be his statutory undertaking for the purposes of this Act; and references in this Act to his undertaking shall be construed accordingly.

(2) Except where the context otherwise requires, any reference in this Act to the provisions of an Order in Council shall, if paragraph 3 of Part III of Schedule 13 to this Act (power to authorise making of regulations) applies to the power to make the Order in question, include a reference to the provisions of any regulations made, or directions given, under the Order in Council.

(3) Without prejudice to any transitional or transitory provision made by this Act or to section 17(2) of the Interpretation Act 1978 (repeal and re-enactment), any reference in any enactment contained in this Act (including a reference to a provision of that enactment or to any other enactment so contained) to a provision which is a re-enactment of a repealed enactment or to things done or falling to be done under such a provision shall, so far as the context permits, be construed as including, in relation to times, circumstances and purposes in relation to which the repealed enactment had effect, a reference to, or to things done or falling to be done under, that repealed enactment; and where the repealed enactment was itself a re-enactment of an earlier provision the reference shall extend in the same way to that earlier provision, and so on.

(4) Any reference in this Act to the re-enactment of a provision includes a reference to its re-enactment with modifications.

(5)–(8) *Scotland and Northern Ireland.*

[Civil Aviation Act 1982, s 105, as amended by the Telecommunications Act 1984 Sch 7, the Companies Consolidation (Consequential Provisions) Act 1985, Sch 2, the Local Government Act 1985, Sch 17, the Airports Act 1986, Sch 6, the Gas Act 1986, Sch 9, the Water Act 1989, Sch 27, the Electricity Act 1989, Sch 18, the Aviation and Maritime Security Act 1990, Sch 4, the Statute Law (Repeals) Act 1993, Sch 1, the Local Government (Wales) Act 1994, Sch 16, the Transport Act 2000, Sch 4, SI 2001/4050 and the British Overseas Territories Act 2002, s 2(3).]

---

1. See the Tokyo Convention (Certification of Countries) Order 1977, SI 1977/1258.

2. The Environment Agency, every water undertaker and every sewerage undertaker is deemed to be a statutory undertaker for the purposes of this Act (Water Act 1989, Sch 25, para 1).

7–5432 106. Application of Act to territorial waters. (1) Except where the context otherwise requires, in any provision of this Act to which this section applies a reference to a country or territory or to the territorial limits of any country shall be construed as including a reference to the territorial waters of the country or territory, as the case may be; and a reference to a part of the United Kingdom shall be construed as including a reference to so much of the territorial waters[1] of the United Kingdom as are adjacent to that part.

(2) This section applies to Parts III and IV of this Act, except sections 64 to 71 and 84.

(3) Nothing in this section shall prejudice the construction of any provision of this Act to which this section does not apply.

[Civil Aviation Act 1982, s 106, as amended by SI 2001/4050.]

---

1. See the Territorial Waters Jurisdiction Act 1878 and the Territorial Sea Act 1987 (12 miles).

Aviation Security Act 1982[1]

(1982 c 36)

PART I[2]
OFFENCES AGAINST THE SAFETY OF AIRCRAFT ETC

7–5433 1. Hijacking. (1) A person[3] on board an aircraft in flight who unlawfully, by the use of force or by threats of any kind, seizes the aircraft or exercises control of it commits the offence of hijacking, whatever his nationality, whatever the State in which the aircraft is registered and whether the aircraft is in the United Kingdom or elsewhere, but subject to subsection (2) below.

(2) If—

(a) the aircraft is used in military, customs or police service, or

(b) both the place of take-off and the place of landing are in the territory of the State in which the aircraft is registered,

subsection (1) above shall not apply unless—

(i) the person seizing or exercising control of the aircraft is a United Kingdom national; or

(ii) his act is committed in the United Kingdom; or

(iii) the aircraft is registered in the United Kingdom or is used in the military or customs service of the United Kingdom or in the service of any police force in the United Kingdom.

(3) A person who commits the offence of hijacking shall be liable, on conviction on indictment, to imprisonment for **life**.

(4) If the Secretary of State by order made by statutory instrument declares—

(a) that any two or more States named in the order have established an organisation or agency which operates aircraft; and

(b) that one of those States has been designated as exercising, for aircraft so operated, the powers of the State of registration,

the State declared under paragraph (b) of this subsection shall be deemed for the purposes of this section to be the State in which any aircraft so operated is registered; but in relation to such an aircraft subsection (2)(b) above shall have effect as if it referred to the territory of any one of the States named in the order.

(5) For the purposes of this section the territorial waters of any State shall be treated as part of its territory.

[Aviation Security Act 1982, s 1.]

---

1. For further provisions relating to aviation security, see the Aviation and Maritime Security Act 1990, ss 1 and 48, this PART, title MERCHANT SHIPPING, post.

2. Part I contains ss 1–9A.

3. The commander of an aircraft who collaborates with others who threaten or use force to the crew and/or passengers may be a party to the conspiracy of those others to hijack the aircraft (*R v Moussa Membar* [1983] Crim LR 618).

7–5434 **2. Destroying, damaging or endangering safety of aircraft.** (1) It shall, subject to subsection (4) below, be an offence for any person unlawfully and intentionally—

(a) to destroy an aircraft in service or so to damage such an aircraft as to render it incapable of flight or as to be likely to endanger its safety in flight; or

(b) to commit on board an aircraft in flight any act of violence which is likely to endanger the safety of the aircraft.

(2) It shall also, subject to subsection (4) below, be an offence for any person unlawfully and intentionally to place, or cause to be placed, on an aircraft in service any device or substance which is likely to destroy the aircraft, or is likely so to damage it as to render it incapable of flight or as to be likely to endanger its safety in flight; but nothing in this subsection shall be construed as limiting the circumstances in which the commission of any act—

(a) may constitute an offence under subsection (1) above, or

(b) may constitute attempting or conspiring to commit, or aiding, abetting, counselling or procuring, or being art and part in, the commission of such an offence.

(3) Except as provided by subsection (4) below, subsections (1) and (2) above shall apply whether any such act as is therein mentioned is committed in the United Kingdom or elsewhere, whatever the nationality of the person committing the act and whatever the State in which the aircraft is registered.

(4) Subsections (1) and (2) above shall not apply to any act committed in relation to an aircraft used in military, customs or police service unless—

(a) the act is committed in the United Kingdom, or

(b) where the act is committed outside the United Kingdom, the person committing it is a United Kingdom national.

(5) A person who commits an offence under this section shall be liable, on conviction on indictment, to imprisonment for **life**.

(6) In this section "unlawfully"—

(a) in relation to the commission of an act in the United Kingdom, means so as (apart from this Act) to constitute an offence under the law of the part of the United Kingdom in which the act is committed, and

(b) in relation to the commission of an act outside the United Kingdom, means so that the commission of the act would (apart from this Act) have been an offence under the law of England and Wales if it had been committed in England and Wales or of Scotland if it had been committed in Scotland.

(7) In this section "act of violence" means—

    (*a*) any act done in the United Kingdom which constitutes the offence of murder, attempted murder, manslaughter, culpable homicide or assault or an offence under section 18, 20, 21, 22, 23, 24, 28 or 29 of the Offences against the Person Act 1861 or under section 2 of the Explosive Substances Act 1883, and

    (*b*) any act done outside the United Kingdom which, if done in the United Kingdom, would constitute such an offence as is mentioned in paragraph (*a*) above.

[Aviation Security Act 1982, s 2.]

7–5435   3.   Other acts endangering or likely to endanger safety of aircraft.   (1) It shall, subject to subsections (5) and (6) below, be an offence for any person unlawfully and intentionally to destroy or damage any property to which this subsection applies, or to interfere with the operation of any such property, where the destruction, damage or interference is likely to endanger the safety of aircraft in flight.

(2) Subsection (1) above applies to any property used for the provision of air navigation facilities, including any land, building or ship so used, and including any apparatus or equipment so used, whether it is on board an aircraft or elsewhere.

(3) It shall also, subject to subsections (4) and (5) below, be an offence for any person intentionally to communicate any information which is false, misleading or deceptive in a material particular, where the communication of the information endangers the safety of an aircraft in flight or is likely to endanger the safety of aircraft in flight.

(4) It shall be a defence for a person charged with an offence under subsection (3) above to prove—

    (*a*) that he believed, and had reasonable grounds for believing, that the information was true; or

    (*b*) that, when he communicated the information, he was lawfully employed to perform duties which consisted of or included the communication of information and that he communicated the information in good faith in the performance of those duties.

(5) Subsections (1) and (3) above shall not apply to the commission of any act unless either the act is committed in the United Kingdom, or, where it is committed outside the United Kingdom—

    (*a*) the person committing it is a United Kingdom national; or

    (*b*) the commission of the act endangers or is likely to endanger the safety in flight of a civil aircraft registered in the United Kingdom or chartered by demise to a lessee whose principal place of business, or (if he has no place of business) whose permanent residence, is in the United Kingdom; or

    (*c*) the act is committed on board a civil aircraft which is so registered or so chartered; or

    (*d*) the act is committed on board a civil aircraft which lands in the United Kingdom with the person who committed the act still on board.

(6) Subsection (1) above shall also not apply to any act committed outside the United Kingdom and so committed in relation to property which is situated outside the United Kingdom and is not used for the provision of air navigation facilities in connection with international air navigation, unless the person committing the act is a United Kingdom national.

(7) A person who commits an offence under this section shall be liable, on conviction on indictment, to imprisonment for **life**.

(8) In this section "civil aircraft" means any aircraft other than an aircraft used in military, customs or police service and "unlawfully" has the same meaning as in section 2 of this Act.

[Aviation Security Act 1982, s 3.]

7–5436   4.   Offences in relation to certain dangerous articles.   (1) It shall be an offence for any person without lawful authority or reasonable excuse (the proof of which shall lie on him) to have with him—

    (*a*) in any aircraft registered in the United Kingdom, whether at a time when the aircraft is in the United Kingdom or not, or

    (*b*) in any other aircraft at a time when it is in, or in flight over, the United Kingdom, or

    (*c*) in any part of an aerodrome in the United Kingdom, or

    (*d*) in any air navigation installation in the United Kingdom which does not form part of an aerodrome,

any article to which this section applies.

(2) This section applies to the following articles, that is to say—

    (*a*) any firearm, or any article having the appearance of being a firearm, whether capable of being discharged or not;

    (*b*) any explosive, any article manufactured or adapted (whether in the form of a bomb, grenade or otherwise) so as to have the appearance of being an explosive, whether it is capable of producing a practical effect by explosion or not, or any article marked or labelled so as to indicate that it is or contains an explosive; and (*c*) any article (not falling within either of the preceding paragraphs) made or adapted for use for causing injury[1] to or incapacitating a person or for destroying or damaging property, or intended by the person having it with him for such use, whether by him or by any other person.

(3) For the purposes of this section a person who is for the time being in an aircraft, or in part of an aerodrome, shall be treated as having with him in the aircraft, or in that part of the aerodrome, as the case may be, an article to which this section applies if—

(*a*) where he is in an aircraft, the article, or an article in which it is contained, is in the aircraft and has been caused (whether by him or by any other person) to be brought there as being, or as forming part of, his baggage on a flight in the aircraft or has been caused by him to be brought there as being, or as forming part of, any other property to be carried on such a flight, or

(*b*) where he is in part of an aerodrome (otherwise than in an aircraft), the article, or an article in which it is contained, is in that or any other part of the aerodrome and has been caused (whether by him or by any other person) to be brought into the aerodrome as being, or as forming part of, his baggage on a flight from that aerodrome or has been caused by him to be brought there as being, or as forming part of, any other property to be carried on such a flight on which he is also to be carried,

notwithstanding that the circumstances may be such that (apart from this subsection) he would not be regarded as having the article with him in the aircraft or in a part of the aerodrome, as the case may be.

(4) A person guilty of an offence under this section shall be liable[2]—

(*a*) on summary conviction, to a fine not exceeding **the statutory maximum**[3] or to imprisonment for a term not exceeding **three months** or to **both**;

(*b*) on conviction on indictment, to a fine or to imprisonment for a term not exceeding **five years** or to **both**.

(5) Nothing in subsection (3) above shall be construed as limiting the circumstances in which a person would, apart from that subsection, be regarded as having an article with him as mentioned in subsection (1) above.

[Aviation Security Act 1982, s 4.]

---

1. A butterfly knife is a dangerous article *per se* and judicial notice should be taken of that fact (*DPP v Hynde* [1998] 1 All ER 649, [1998] 1 WLR 1222).

2. For procedure in respect of this offence which is triable either way, see the Magistrates' Courts Act 1980, ss 17A–21, in PART I: MAGISTRATES' COURTS, PROCEDURE, ante.

3. For meaning of "the statutory maximum", see s 38, post.

7–5437 5. Jurisdiction of courts in respect of air piracy. (1) Any court in the United Kingdom having jurisdiction in respect of piracy committed on the high seas shall have jurisdiction in respect of piracy committed by or against an aircraft, wherever that piracy is committed.

(2) In subsection (1) above, "aircraft" has the same meaning as in section 92 of the Civil Aviation Act 1982 (application of criminal law to aircraft); and, for the purposes of this definition, section 101 of that Act (Crown aircraft) shall apply to this section as it applies to the said section 92.

[Aviation Security Act 1982, s 5.]

7–5438 6. Ancillary offences. (1) Without prejudice to section 92 of the Civil Aviation Act 1982 (application of criminal law to aircraft) or to section 2(1)(*b*) of this Act, where a person (of whatever nationality) does on board any aircraft (wherever registered) and while outside the United Kingdom any act which, if done in the United Kingdom would constitute the offence of murder, attempted murder, manslaughter, culpable homicide or assault or an offence under section 18, 20, 21, 22, 23, 28 or 29 of the Offences against the Person Act 1861 or section 2 of the Explosive Substances Act 1883, his act shall constitute that offence if it is done in connection with the offence of hijacking committed or attempted by him on board that aircraft.

(2) It shall be an offence for any person in the United Kingdom to induce or assist the commission outside the United Kingdom of any act which—

(*a*) would, but for subsection (2) of section 1 of this Act, be an offence under that section; or

(*b*) would, but for subsection (4) of section 2 of this Act, be an offence under that section; or

(*c*) would, but for subsection (5) or (6) of section 3 of this Act, be an offence under that section.

(3) A person who commits an offence under subsection (2) above shall be liable, on conviction on indictment, to imprisonment for **life**.

(4) Subsection (2) above shall have effect without prejudice to the operation, in relation to any offence under section 1, 2 or 3 of this Act—

(*a*) in England and Wales, or in Northern Ireland, of section 8 of the Accessories and Abettors Act 1861; or

(*b*) Scotland.

[Aviation Security Act 1982, s 6.]

7–5439   7. Powers exercisable on suspicion of intended offence under Part I.   (1) Where a constable has reasonable cause to suspect that a person about to embark on an aircraft in the United Kingdom, or a person on board such an aircraft, intends to commit, in relation to the aircraft, an offence under any of the preceding provisions of this Part of this Act (other than section 4), the constable may prohibit him from travelling on board the aircraft, and for the purpose of enforcing that prohibition the constable—

(*a*)   may prevent him from embarking on the aircraft or, as the case may be, may remove him from the aircraft; and

(*b*)   may arrest him without warrant and detain him for so long as may be necessary for that purpose.

(2) Any person who intentionally obstructs a person acting in the exercise of a power conferred on him by subsection (1) above shall be guilty of an offence and liable[1]—

(*a*)   on summary conviction, to a fine not exceeding **the statutory maximum**[2];

(*b*)   on conviction on indictment, to a **fine** or to imprisonment for a term not exceeding **two years** or to **both**.

(3) Subsection (1) above shall have effect without prejudice to the operation in relation to any offence under this Act—

(*a*)   in England and Wales, of section 2 of the Criminal Law Act 1967 (which confers power to arrest without warrant) or of section 3 of that Act (use of force in making arrest etc); or

(*b*)–(*c*)   *Scotland, or Northern Ireland.*

[Aviation Security Act 1982, s 7, as amended by the Aviation and Maritime Security Act 1990, Sch 1.]

---

1. For procedure in respect of this offence which is triable either way, see the Magistrates' Courts Act 1980, ss 17A–21, in PART I: MAGISTRATES' COURTS, PROCEDURE, *ante*.

2. For meaning of "the statutory maximum", see s 38, *post*.

7–5440   8. Prosecution of offences and proceedings.   (1) Proceedings for an offence under any of the preceding provisions of this Part of this Act (other than sections 4 and 7) shall not be instituted—

(*a*)   in England and Wales, except by, or with the consent of, the Attorney General; and

(*b*)   *Northern Ireland.*

(2) *Scotland.*

[Aviation Security Act 1982, s 8.]

7–5441   9–9A. (*Repealed*).

PART II[1]

PROTECTION OF AIRCRAFT, AERODROMES AND AIR NAVIGATION INSTALLATIONS AGAINST ACTS OF VIOLENCE

General purposes

7–5442   10. Purposes to which Part II applies.   (1) The purposes to which this Part of this Act applies are the protection against acts of violence—

(*a*)   of aircraft, and of persons or property on board aircraft;

(*b*)   of aerodromes, and of such persons or property as (in the case of persons) are at any time present in any part of an aerodrome or (in the case of property) forms part of an aerodrome or is at any time (whether permanently or temporarily) in any part of an aerodrome; and

(*c*)   of air navigation installations which do not form part of an aerodrome.

(2) In this Part of this Act "act of violence" means any act (whether actual or potential, and whether done or to be done in the United Kingdom or elsewhere) which either—

(*a*)   being an act done in Great Britain, constitutes, or

(*b*)   if done in Great Britain would constitute,

the offence of murder, attempted murder, manslaughter, culpable homicide or assault, or an offence under section 18, 20, 21, 22, 23, 24, 28 or 29 of the Offences against the Person Act 1861, under section 2 of the Explosive Substances Act 1883 or under section 1 of the Criminal Damage Act 1971 or, in Scotland, the offence of malicious mischief.

[Aviation Security Act 1982, s 10.]

---

1. Part II contains ss 10–24 and is modified in its application to security approved air cargo agents by the Aviation Security (Air Cargo Agents) Regulations 1993, SI 1993/1073. Regulation 11 provides:

"**11.**—(1) Any provision in Part II of the 1982 Act which applies in relation to persons who are permitted to have access to a restricted zone of an aerodrome for the purposes of the activities of a business (including any provision which creates a criminal offence) shall also apply to any air cargo agent included on the list of security approved air cargo agents, subject to the modification set out in paragraph (2) of this regulation.

(2) In the application of section 14 of the 1982 Act to an air cargo agent in accordance with sub-paragraph (1)

above, paragraph (*d*) of subsection (1A) shall have effect as if for the words from "carried on by that person" onwards there were substituted "as are specified in the direction and are carried on by that person at any premises where relevant air cargo is handed by him."

Powers of Secretary of State

7–5443 11. Power for Secretary of State to require information. (1) The Secretary of State may, by notice in writing served on any person who—

(*a*) is the operator of one or more aircraft registered or operating in the United Kingdom,

(*b*) is the manager of an aerodrome in the United Kingdom,

(*c*) occupies any land forming part of an aerodrome in the United Kingdom, or

(*d*) is permitted to have access to a restricted zone of an aerodrome for the purposes of the activities of a business carried on by him,

require that person to provide the Secretary of State with such information specified in the notice as the Secretary of State may require in connection with the exercise by the Secretary of State of his functions under this Part of this Act.

(2) A notice under subsection (1) above shall specify a date (not being earlier than seven days from the date on which the notice is served) before which the information required by the notice in accordance with subsection (1) above is to be furnished to the Secretary of State.

(3) Any such notice may also require the person on whom it is served, after he has furnished to the Secretary of State the information required by the notice in accordance with subsection (1) above, to inform the Secretary of State if at any time the information previously furnished to the Secretary of State (including any information furnished in pursuance of a requirement imposed by virtue of this subsection) is rendered inaccurate by any change of circumstances (including the taking of any further measures for purposes to which this Part of this Act applies or the alteration or discontinuance of any measures already being taken).

(4) In so far as such a notice requires further information to be furnished to the Secretary of State in accordance with subsection (3) above, it shall require that information to be furnished to him before the end of such period (not being less than seven days from the date on which the change of circumstances occurs) as is specified in the notice for the purposes of this subsection.

(5) Any person who—

(*a*) without reasonable excuse, fails to comply with a requirement imposed on him by a notice under this section, or

(*b*) in furnishing any information so required, makes a statement which he knows to be false in a material particular, or recklessly makes a statement which is false in a material particular,

shall be guilty of an offence and liable[1]—

(i) on summary conviction, to a fine not exceeding **the statutory maximum**[2];

(ii) on conviction on indictment, to a **fine** or to imprisonment for a term not exceeding **two years** or to **both**.

(6) A notice served on a person under subsection (1) above may at any time—

(*a*) be revoked by a notice in writing served on him by the Secretary of State, or

(*b*) be varied by a further notice under subsection (1) above.

[Aviation Security Act 1982, s 11, as amended by the Aviation and Maritime Security Act 1990, Schs 1 and 4.]

---

1. For procedure in respect of this offence which is triable either way, see the Magistrates' Courts Act 1980, ss 17A–21, in PART I: MAGISTRATES' COURTS, PROCEDURE, ante.

2. For meaning of "the statutory maximum", see s 38, post.

7–5444 11A. Designation of restricted zones. (1) The manager of an aerodrome in the United Kingdom may, and shall if so requested in writing by the Secretary of State, apply to the Secretary of State for the designation of the whole or any part of the aerodrome as a restricted zone for the purposes of this Part of this Act.

(2) Where the aerodrome includes an air navigation installation, the manager:

(*a*) shall, before making any application under subsection (1) above, consult the authority responsible for the air navigation installation, and

(*b*) shall send a copy of the application to that authority.

(3) An application under subsection (1) above shall be in such form, and accompanied by such plans, as the Secretary of State may require.

(4) If the Secretary of State approves an application under subsection (1) above with or without modifications, he shall designate the restricted zone accordingly.

(5) Before approving an application with modifications, the Secretary of State shall consult—

(*a*) the manager of the aerodrome, and

(*b*) the authority responsible for any air navigation installation which forms part of the aerodrome.

(6) If the manager of an aerodrome is requested in writing by the Secretary of State to make an

application under subsection (1) above within a specified period but fails to do so within that period, the Secretary of State may designate the whole or any part of the aerodrome as a restricted zone.

(7) The whole or any part of an aerodrome may be designated as a restricted zone, or part of a restricted zone, for specified days or times of day only.

(8) The Secretary of State shall give notice of any designation under this section to—

(a) the manager of the aerodrome, and

(b) the authority responsible for any air navigation installation which forms part of the aerodrome,

and the designation of the restricted zone shall take effect on the giving of the notice.

(9) In relation to an air navigation installation in the United Kingdom which does not form part of an aerodrome, this section has effect as if any reference to an aerodrome were a reference to such an air navigation installation and any reference to the manager of an aerodrome were a reference to the authority responsible for such an air navigation installation.

(10) Where the whole or any part of an aerodrome has been designated under this section as a restricted zone—

(a) subsections (1) to (9) above also have effect in relation to any variation of the designation, and

(b) the designation may at any time be revoked by the Secretary of State.

[Aviation Security Act 1982, s 11A, as inserted by the Aviation and Maritime Security Act 1990, Sch 1.]

7–5445 12. Power to impose restrictions in relation to aircraft. (1) For purposes to which this Part of this Act applies, the Secretary of State may give a direction in writing to the operator of any one or more aircraft registered or operating in the United Kingdom, or to the manager of any aerodrome in the United Kingdom, requiring him—

(a) not to cause or permit persons or property to go or be taken on board any aircraft to which the direction relates, or to come or be brought into proximity to any such aircraft, unless such searches of those persons or that property as are specified in the direction have been carried out by constables or by other persons of a description specified in the direction, or

(b) not to cause or permit any such aircraft to fly unless such searches of the aircraft as are specified in the direction have been carried out by constables or by other persons of a description so specified.

(2) Subject to subsection (3) below, the Secretary of State may give a direction in writing to the operator of any one or more aircraft registered in the United Kingdom requiring him not to cause or permit the aircraft to fly unless such modifications or alterations of the aircraft or of apparatus or equipment installed in the aircraft, as are specified in the direction have first been carried out, or such additional apparatus or equipment as is so specified is first installed in the aircraft.

(3) Before giving any direction under subsection (2) above, the Secretary of State shall inform the Civil Aviation Authority of the modifications, alterations or additional apparatus or equipment proposed to be required, and shall take account of any advice given to him by that Authority with respect to those proposals.

(4) In giving any direction under subsection (2) above, the Secretary of State shall allow, and shall specify in the direction, such period as appears to him to be reasonably required for carrying out the modifications or alterations or installing the additional apparatus or equipment in question; and the direction shall not take effect before the end of the period so specified.

(5) Subject to the following provisions of this Part of this Act, a direction given to an operator of aircraft under subsection (1) above may be given so as to relate—

(a) either to all the aircraft registered or operating in the United Kingdom of which at the time when the direction is given or at any subsequent time he is the operator or only to one or more such aircraft, or to a class of such aircraft, specified in the direction;

(b) either to all persons or only to one or more persons, or persons of one or more descriptions, specified in the direction; and

(c) either to property of every description or only to particular property, or property of one or more descriptions, specified in the direction;

and a direction given to an operator of aircraft under subsection (2) above may be given so as to relate either to all aircraft registered in the United Kingdom of which at the time when the direction is given or at any subsequent time he is the operator or only to one or more such aircraft, or to a class of such aircraft, specified in the direction.

(6) Subject to the following provisions of this Part of this Act, a direction given to the manager of an aerodrome under subsection (1) above may be given so as to relate—

(a) either to all aircraft which at the time when the direction is given or at any subsequent time are in any part of the aerodrome, or to a class of such aircraft specified in the direction;

(b) either to all persons or only to one or more persons, or persons of one or more descriptions, specified in the direction; and

(c) either to property of every description or only to particular property, or property of one or more descriptions, specified in the direction.

(7) Subject to the following provisions of this Part of this Act, any direction given under this section to any person not to cause or permit anything to be done shall be construed as requiring him to take all such steps as in any particular circumstances are practicable and necessary to prevent that thing from being done.

(8) A direction may be given under this section to a person appearing to the Secretary of State to be about to become—

(*a*)   such an operator as is mentioned in subsection (1) or (2) above; or
(*b*)   such a manager as is mentioned in subsection (1) above;

but a direction given to a person by virtue of this subsection shall not take effect until he becomes such an operator or manager, and, in relation to a direction so given, the preceding provisions of this section shall apply with the necessary modifications.

(9) Any person who, without reasonable excuse, fails to comply with a direction given to him under this section shall be guilty of an offence and liable[1]—

(*a*)   on summary conviction, to a fine not exceeding **the statutory maximum**[2];
(*b*)   on conviction on indictment, to a **fine** or to imprisonment for a term not exceeding **two years** or to **both**.

(10) Where a person is convicted of an offence under subsection (9) above, then, if without reasonable excuse the failure in respect of which he was convicted is continued after the conviction, he shall be guilty of a further offence and liable on summary conviction to a fine not exceeding **one-tenth of level 5** on the standard scale for each day on which the failure continues.
[Aviation Security Act 1982, s 12, as amended by the Aviation and Maritime Security Act 1990, Sch 1.]

---

1. For procedure in respect of this offence which is triable either way, see the Magistrates' Courts Act 1980, ss 17A–21, in PART I: MAGISTRATES' COURTS, PROCEDURE, ante.
2. For meaning of "the statutory maximum", see s 38, post.

7–5446   13. Power to require aerodrome managers to promote searches at aerodromes.
(1) For purposes to which this Part of this Act applies, the Secretary of State may give a direction in writing to the manager of any aerodrome in the United Kingdom requiring him to use his best endeavours to secure that such searches to which this section applies as are specified in the direction are carried out by constables or by other persons of a description specified in the direction.

(2) The searches to which this section applies, in relation to an aerodrome, are searches—

(*a*)   of the aerodrome or any part of it;
(*b*)   of any aircraft which at the time when the direction is given or at any subsequent time is in any part of the aerodrome; and
(*c*)   of persons or property (other than aircraft) which may at any such time be in any part of the aerodrome.

(3) Without prejudice to section 7(1) of this Act, where a direction given under this section to the manager of an aerodrome is for the time being in force, then if a constable, or any other person specified in the direction in accordance with this section, has reasonable cause to suspect that an article to which section 4 of this Act applies is in, or may be brought into, any part of the aerodrome, he may, by virtue of this subsection and without a warrant, search any part of the aerodrome or any aircraft, vehicle, goods or other moveable property of any description which, or any person who, is for the time being in any part of the aerodrome, and for that purpose—

(*a*)   may enter any building or works in the aerodrome, or enter upon any land in the aerodrome, if need be by force, and
(*b*)   may stop any such aircraft, vehicle, goods, property or person and detain it or him for so long as may be necessary for that purpose.

(4) Any person who—

(*a*)   without reasonable excuse, fails to comply with a direction given to him under this section, or
(*b*)   intentionally obstructs a person acting in the exercise of a power conferred on him by subsection (3) above,

shall be guilty of an offence and liable[1]—

(i)   on summary conviction, to a fine not exceeding **the statutory maximum**[2];
(ii)   on conviction on indictment, to a **fine** or to imprisonment for a term not exceeding **two years** or to **both**.

(4A) Where a person is convicted of an offence under subsection (4)(*a*) above, then, if without reasonable excuse the failure in respect of which he was convicted is continued after the conviction, he shall be guilty of a further offence and liable on summary conviction to a fine not exceeding **one-tenth of level 5** on the standard scale for each day on which the failure continues.

(5) Subsection (3) above shall have effect without prejudice to the operation, in relation to any offence under this Act—

(a) in England and Wales, of sections 17, 24 and 25 of the Police and Criminal Evidence Act 1984 (which confer power to arrest without warrant and to enter premises for the purpose of making an arrest) or of section 3 of the Criminal Law Act 1967 (use of force in making arrest etc); or

(b)–(c) *Scotland, or Northern Ireland.*

[Aviation Security Act 1982, s 13, as amended by the Aviation and Maritime Security Act 1990, Sch 1.]

---

1. For procedure in respect of this offence which is triable either way, see the Magistrates' Courts Act 1980, ss 17A–21, in PART I: MAGISTRATES' COURTS, PROCEDURE, *ante.*
2. For meaning of "the statutory maximum", see s 38, *post.*

7–5447   13A. Power to require other persons to promote searches.   (1) For purposes to which this Part of this Act applies, the Secretary of State may give a direction in writing to any person (other than the manager of an aerodrome) who—

(a) occupies any land forming part of an aerodrome in the United Kingdom, or

(b) is permitted to have access to a restricted zone of such an aerodrome for the purposes of the activities of a business carried on by him,

requiring him to use his best endeavours to secure that such searches to which this section applies as are specified in the direction are carried out by constables or by other persons of a description specified in the direction.

(2) The searches to which this section applies are—

(a) in relation to a person falling within subsection (1)(a) above, searches—

    (i) of the land which he occupies within the aerodrome, and

    (ii) of persons or property which may at any time be on that land; and

(b) in relation to a person falling within subsection (1)(b) above, searches—

    (i) of any land which he occupies outside the aerodrome for the purposes of his business, and

    (ii) of persons or property which may at any time be on that land.

(3) Any person who, without reasonable excuse, fails to comply with a direction given to him under this section shall be guilty of an offence and liable[1]—

(a) on summary conviction, to a fine not exceeding **the statutory maximum**;

(b) on conviction on indictment, to a **fine** or to imprisonment for a term not exceeding **two years**, or to **both**.

(4) Where a person is convicted of an offence under subsection (3) above, then, if without reasonable excuse the failure in respect of which he was convicted is continued after the conviction, he shall be guilty of a further offence and liable on summary conviction to a fine not exceeding **one-tenth of level 5** on the standard scale for each day on which the failure continues.

[Aviation Security Act 1982, s 13A, as inserted by the Aviation and Maritime Security Act 1990, s 2.]

---

1. For procedure in respect of an offence which is triable either way, see the Magistrates' Courts Act 1980, ss 17A–21, in PART I: MAGISTRATES' COURTS, PROCEDURE, *ante.*

7–5448   14. General power to direct measures to be taken for purposes to which Part II applies[1].   (1) Subsection (1A) below applies to any person who—

(a) is the operator of one or more aircraft registered or operating in the United Kingdom,

(b) is the manager of an aerodrome in the United Kingdom,

(c) occupies any land forming part of an aerodrome in the United Kingdom, or

(d) is permitted to have access to a restricted zone of such an aerodrome for the purposes of the activities of a business carried on by him.

(1A) Subject to the following provisions of this section, the Secretary of State may give a direction in writing to any person to whom this subsection applies requiring him to take such measures for purposes to which this Part of this Act applies as are specified in the direction—

(a) in the case of a direction given to a person as the operator of any aircraft, in respect of all the aircraft registered or operating in the United Kingdom of which (at the time when the direction is given or at any subsequent time) he is the operator, or in respect of any such aircraft, or any class of such aircraft, specified in the direction;

(b) in the case of a direction given to a person as the manager of an aerodrome, in respect of that aerodrome;

(c) in the case of a direction given to a person as a person occupying any land forming part of an aerodrome, in respect of any such land as is specified in the direction; and

(d) in the case of a direction given to a person as a person who is permitted to have access to a restricted zone as mentioned in subsection (1)(d) above, in respect of such activities carried on by that person in that zone as are specified in the direction.

(2) Without prejudice to the generality of subsection (1A) above, the measures to be specified in a direction given under this section to any person to whom that subsection applies may include the provision by that person of persons charged with the duty (at such times as may be specified in the direction)—

(*a*) where the direction is given to a person as the operator of aircraft, of guarding the aircraft against acts of violence;

(*b*) where the direction is given to a person as the manager of an aerodrome, of guarding the aerodrome, or persons or property (including aircraft) in any part of the aerodrome, against acts of violence;

(*c*) where the direction is given to a person as falling within subsection (1)(*c*) above, of guarding against acts of violence any aircraft in the aerodrome which is for the time being under his control; or

(*d*) where the direction is given to a person as falling within subsection (1)(*d*) above, of guarding—

   (i)   any land outside the aerodrome occupied by him for the purposes of this business, any vehicles or equipment used for those purposes and any goods which are in his possession for those purposes, and

   (ii) any aircraft which is for the time being under his control,

for purposes to which this Part of this Act applies.

(3) A direction given under this section may be either of a general or of a specific character, and may require any measures specified in the direction to be taken at such time or within such period as may be so specified.

(4) *Repealed.*

(5) A direction under this section—

(*a*) shall not require any search (whether of persons or of property), and

(*b*) shall not require the modification or alteration of any aircraft, or of any of its apparatus or equipment, or the installation of additional apparatus or equipment, or prohibit any aircraft from being caused or permitted to fly without some modification or alteration of the aircraft or its apparatus or equipment or the installation of additional apparatus or equipment.

(6) A direction may be given under this section to a person appearing to the Secretary of State to be about to become a person to whom subsection (1A) above applies, but a direction given to a person by virtue of this subsection shall not take effect until he becomes such a person, and, in relation to a direction so given, the preceding provisions of this section shall apply with the necessary modifications.

(7) Any person—

(*a*) who without reasonable excuse, fails to comply with a direction given to him under this section, or

(*b*) intentionally interferes with any building constructed or works executed on any land in compliance with a direction under this section or with anything installed on, under, over or across any land in compliance with such a direction,

shall be guilty of an offence and liable[2]—

   (i)   on summary conviction, to a fine not exceeding **the statutory maximum**[3];

   (ii) on conviction on indictment, to a **fine** or to imprisonment for a term not exceeding **two years** or to **both**.

(7A) Where a person is convicted of an offence under subsection (7)(*a*) above, then, if without reasonable excuse the failure in respect of which he was convicted is continued after the conviction, he shall be guilty of a further offence and liable on summary conviction to a fine not exceeding **one-tenth of level 5** on the standard scale for each day on which the failure continues.

(8) The ownership of any property shall not be affected by reason only that it is placed on or under, or affixed to, any land in compliance with a direction under this section.

[Aviation Security Act 1982, s 14, as amended by the Aviation and Maritime Security Act 1990, s 3, Schs 1 and 4.]

---

1. See note to s 10 above.
2. For procedure in respect of this offence which is triable either way, see the Magistates' Courts Act 1980, ss 17A–21 in PART I: MAGISTRATES' COURTS, PROCEDURE, ante.
3. For meaning of "the statutory maximum", see s 38, post.

Supplemental provisions with respect to directions

7–5449 15. Matters which may be included in directions under ss 12 to 14.   (1) A direction under subsection (1) of section 12 or under section 13 or 13A of this Act may specify the minimum number of persons by whom any search to which the direction relates is to be carried out, the qualifications which persons carrying out any such search are to have, the manner in which any such search is to be carried out, and any apparatus, equipment or other aids to be used for the purpose of carrying out any such search.

(2) A direction under subsection (2) of section 12 of this Act must require all the persons carrying out any modifications or alterations, or the installation of any additional apparatus or equipment, to be persons approved by the Civil Aviation Authority.

(3) *Repealed.*

(4) A direction under section 14 of this Act may specify—

(a) the minimum number of persons to be employed for the purposes of any measures required by the direction to be taken by the person to whom it is given and the qualifications which persons employed for those purposes are to have, and

(b) any apparatus, equipment or other aids to be used for those purposes.

(5) Where a direction under any of the preceding provisions of this Part of this Act requires searches to be carried out, or other measures to be taken, by constables, the direction may require the person to whom it is given to inform the chief officer of police for the police area in which the searches are to be carried out or the other measures taken that the Secretary of State considers it appropriate that constables should be duly authorised to carry, and should carry, firearms when carrying out the searches or taking the measures in question.

(6) Nothing in subsections (1) to (5) above shall be construed as limiting the generality of any of the preceding provisions of this Part of this Act.

(7) In this section "qualifications" includes training and experience.

(8) *Northern Ireland.*

[Aviation Security Act 1982, s 15, as amended by the Aviation and Maritime Security Act 1990, Schs 1 and 4.]

7–5450 16. Limitations on scope of directions under ss 12 to 14. (1) Without prejudice to subsection (5) of section 15 of this Act, a direction shall not require or authorise any person to carry a firearm.

(2) A direction shall not have effect in relation to any aircraft used in military, customs or police service.

(3) A direction shall not have effect in relation to any aircraft of which the operator is the Government of a country outside the United Kingdom, or is a department or agency of such a Government, except at a time when any such aircraft is being used for the carriage of passengers or cargo for reward or is for the time being allocated by that Government, department or agency for such use.

(4) A direction (except in so far as it requires any building or other works to be constructed, executed, altered, demolished or removed) shall not be construed as requiring or authorising the person to whom the direction was given, or any person acting as his employee or agent, to do anything which, apart from the direction, would constitute an act of violence; but nothing in this subsection shall restrict the use of such force as is reasonable in the circumstances (whether at the instance of the person to whom the direction was given or otherwise) by a constable, or its use by any other person in the exercise of a power conferred by section 7(1) or 13(3) of this Act or by any of the following provisions of this Act.

(5) In so far as a direction requires anything to be done or not done at a place outside the United Kingdom—

(a) it shall not have effect except in relation to aircraft registered in the United Kingdom, and

(b) it shall not have effect so as to require anything to be done or not done in contravention of any provision of the law (whether civil or criminal) in force at that place, other than any such provision relating to breach of contract.

(6) In so far as a direction given to the manager of an aerodrome or to any person mentioned in section 14(1)(c) or (d) of this Act requires a building or other works to be constructed, executed, altered, demolished or removed on land outside the aerodrome, or requires any other measures to be taken on such land, the direction shall not confer on the person to whom it is given any rights as against a person having—

(a) an interest in that land, or

(b) a right to occupy that land, or

(c) a right restrictive of its use;

and accordingly the direction shall not be construed as requiring the person to whom it is given to do anything which would be actionable at the suit or instance of a person having such interest or right in his capacity as a person having that interest or right.

(7) Nothing in this section shall be construed as derogating from any exemption or immunity of the Crown in relation to the provisions of this Part of this Act.

(8) In this section "direction" means a direction under section 12, 13, 13A or 14 of this Act.

[Aviation Security Act 1982, s 16, as amended by the Aviation and Maritime Security Act 1990, Sch 1.]

7–5451 17. General or urgent directions under ss 12 and 14. (1) A direction given to any person under section 12, 13, 13A or 14 of this Act need not be addressed to that particular person, but may be framed in general terms applicable to all persons to whom such a direction may be given or to any class of such persons to which that particular person belongs.

(2) If it appears to the Secretary of State that an exception from any direction given under any of those sections is required as a matter of urgency in any particular case he may, by a notification given (otherwise than in writing) to the person for the time being subject to the direction, authorise that person to disregard the requirements of the direction—

(a) in relation to such aircraft or class of aircraft, in relation to such aerodrome or part of an aerodrome, in relation to such land outside an aerodrome, in relation to such activities, or in relation to such persons or property or such description of persons or property, and

(b) on such occasion or series of occasions, or for such period,

as he may specify; and the direction shall have effect in that case subject to any exceptions so specified.

(3) Any notification given to any person under subsection (2) above with respect to any direction shall cease to have effect (if it has not already done so)—

(a) if a direction in writing is subsequently given to that person varying or revoking the original direction; or

(b) if no such direction in writing is given within the period of thirty days beginning with the date on which the notification was given, at the end of that period.

(4) Any notification given under subsection (2) above shall be regarded as given to the person to whom it is directed if it is given—

(a) to any person authorised by that person to receive any such direction or notification;

(b) where that person is a body corporate, to the secretary, clerk or similar officer of the body corporate; and

(c) in any other case, to anyone holding a comparable office or position in that person's employment.

[Aviation Security Act 1982, s 17, as amended by the Aviation and Maritime Security Act 1990, Sch 1.]

7–5452 18. Objections to certain directions under s 14. *A person to whom a direction is given under s 14 may serve on the Secretary of State a notice in writing objecting to the direction.*

7–5453 18A. Enforcement notices. (1) Where an authorised person is of the opinion that any person has failed to comply with any general requirement of a direction given to him under section 12, 13, 13A or 14 of this Act, the authorised person may serve on that person a notice (in this Part of this Act referred to as an "enforcement notice")—

(a) specifying those general requirements of the direction with which he has, in the opinion of the authorised person, failed to comply, and

(b) specifying, subject to section 18B of this Act, the measures that ought to be taken in order to comply with those requirements.

(2) For the purposes of this section a requirement of a direction given by the Secretary of State under section 12, 13, 13A or 14 of this Act is a "general requirement" if the provision imposing the requirement—

(a) has been included in two or more directions given to different persons (whether or not at the same time), and

(b) is framed in general terms applicable to all the persons to whom those directions are given.

(3) Before serving any enforcement notice which relates to a direction given under section 12(2) of this Act, the authorised person shall inform the Civil Aviation Authority of the measures proposed to be specified in the notice, and shall take account of any advice given to him by that Authority with respect to those proposals.

[Aviation Security Act 1982, s 18A, as inserted by the Aviation and Maritime Security Act 1990, s 4.]

7–5454 18B. Contents of enforcement notice. (1) An enforcement notice may specify in greater detail measures which are described in general terms in those provisions of the direction to which it relates which impose general requirements, but may not impose any requirement which could not have been imposed by a direction given by the Secretary of State under the provision under which the direction was given.

(2) An enforcement notice may be framed so as to afford the person on whom it is served a choice between different ways of complying with the specified general requirements of the direction.

(3) Subject to subsection (4) below, an enforcement notice which relates to a direction given under section 12 of this Act must require the person to whom the direction was given not to cause or permit things to be done as mentioned in subsection (1)(a) or (b) or (2) of that section, as the case requires, until the specified measures have been taken.

(4) In serving an enforcement notice which relates to a direction under section 12(2) of this Act, the authorised person shall allow, and shall specify in the notice, such period as appears to him to be reasonably required for taking the measures specified in the notice; and the notice shall not take effect before the end of the period so specified.

(5) An enforcement notice which relates to a direction given under section 13, 13A or 14 of this Act must either—

(a) require the person to whom the direction was given to take the specified measures within a specified period which—

   (i) where the measures consist of or include the construction, execution, alteration, demolition or removal of a building or other works, must not be less than thirty days beginning with the date of service of the notice, and

   (ii) in any other case, must not be less than seven days beginning with that date; or

(b) require him not to do specified things, or cause or permit specified things to be done, until the specified measures have been taken.

(6) Subject to section 18E(2) of this Act, an enforcement notice requiring a person not to cause or permit anything to be done shall be construed as requiring him to take all such steps as in any particular circumstances are practicable and necessary to prevent that thing from being done.
[Aviation Security Act 1982, s 18B, as inserted by the Aviation and Maritime Security Act 1990, s 4.]

7–5455 18C. Offences relating to enforcement notices.   (1) Any person who, without reasonable excuse, fails to comply with an enforcement notice served on him shall be guilty of an offence and liable[1]—

(a) on summary conviction, to a fine not exceeding **the statutory maximum**;

(b) on conviction on indictment, to a **fine**.

(2) Where a person is convicted of an offence under subsection (1) above, then, if without reasonable excuse the failure in respect of which he was convicted is continued after the conviction, he shall be guilty of a further offence and liable on summary conviction to a fine not exceeding **one-tenth of level 5** on the standard scale for each day on which the failure continues.

(3) Any person who intentionally interferes with any building constructed or works executed on any land in compliance with an enforcement notice or with anything installed on, under, over or across any land in compliance with such a notice shall be guilty of an offence and liable[1]—

(a) on summary conviction, to a fine not exceeding **the statutory maximum**;

(b) on conviction on indictment, to a **fine**.

[Aviation Security Act 1982, s 18C, as inserted by the Aviation and Maritime Security Act 1990, s 4.]

---

1. For procedure in respect of an offence which is triable either way, see the Magistrates' Courts Act 1980, ss 17A–21, in PART I: MAGISTRATES' COURTS, PROCEDURE, ante.

7–5456 18D. Objections to enforcement notices.   (1) The person on whom an enforcement notice is served may serve on the Secretary of State a notice in writing of his objection to the enforcement notice, specifying the grounds of the objection.

(2) Any notice of objection under subsection (1) above must be served—

(a) where the enforcement notice specifies measures falling within section 18B(5)(a)(i) of this Act, before the end of the period of thirty days beginning with the date on which the enforcement notice was served, or

(b) in any other case, before the end of the period of seven days beginning with that date.

(3) The grounds of objection to an enforcement notice are—

(a) that the general requirements of the direction which are specified in the notice for the purposes of section 18A(1)(a) of this Act have been complied with,

(b) that the notice purports to impose a requirement which could not have been imposed by a direction given under the provision under which the direction to which the notice relates was given, or

(c) that any requirement of the notice—

   (i) is unnecessary for complying with the general requirements specified as mentioned in paragraph (a) above and should be dispensed with, or

   (ii) having regard to the terms of those general requirements, is excessively onerous or inconvenient and should be modified in a manner specified in the notice of objection under subsection (1) above.

(4) Where the person on whom an enforcement notice is served serves a notice under subsection (1) above objecting to the enforcement notice, the Secretary of State shall consider the grounds of the objection and, if so required by the objector, shall afford to him an opportunity of appearing before and being heard by a person appointed by the Secretary of State for the purpose, and shall then serve on the objector a notice in writing either—

(a) confirming the enforcement notice as originally served, or

(b) confirming it subject to one or more modifications specified in the notice under this subsection, or

(c) cancelling the enforcement notice.

(5) An enforcement notice to which an objection has been made under subsection (1) above—

(a) if it contains such a requirement as is mentioned in section 18B(3) or (5)(b) of this Act, shall continue to have effect as originally served until it has been cancelled, or it has been confirmed subject to modification by a notice under subsection (4) above, and

(b) in any other case, shall not take effect until it has been confirmed (with or without modification) by a notice under subsection (4) above.

[Aviation Security Act 1982, s 18D, as inserted by the Aviation and Maritime Security Act 1990, s 4.]

7–5457 18E. Enforcement notices: supplementary.   (1) An enforcement notice served on any person—

(a) may be revoked by a notice served on him by an authorised person, and

(b) may be varied by a further enforcement notice.

(2) Sections 15 and 16 of this Act apply to an enforcement notice as they apply to the direction to which the notice relates.

(3) The ownership of any property shall not be affected by reason only that it is placed on or under or affixed to any land in compliance with an enforcement notice.

(4) Where an authorised person has served an enforcement notice specifying the general requirements of a direction with which the person on whom it is served has, in the opinion of the authorised person, failed to comply, the person on whom the notice is served shall not be taken, for the purposes of section 12(9), 13(4), 13A(3) or 14(7) of this Act, to have failed to comply with the direction by reason of the matters specified in the notice.

(5) Subsection (4) above does not apply in relation to any proceedings commenced before the service of the enforcement notice.

(6) Where an enforcement notice has been served in relation to a direction, the fact that the notice specifies certain general requirements of the direction as those with which the person on whom the notice is served has, in the opinion of the authorised person, failed to comply shall not in any proceedings be evidence that any other requirement of the direction has been complied with.

(7) In this section "direction" means a direction under section 12, 13, 13A or 14 of this Act.

[Aviation Security Act 1982, s 18E, as inserted by the Aviation and Maritime Security Act 1990, s 4.]

7–5458   19. Operation of directions under Part II in relation to rights and duties under other laws.   (1) The following provisions of this section, where they refer to a direction under any of the preceding provisions of this Part of this Act, shall be construed as referring to that direction as it has effect subject to any limitation imposed on its operation—

(a) by section 16 of this Act, or

(b) by any exemption or immunity of the Crown;

and any reference in those provisions to compliance with such a direction shall be construed as a reference to compliance with it subject to any limitation so imposed.

(2) In so far as any such direction requires anything to be done or not done in the United Kingdom, the direction shall have effect notwithstanding anything contained in any contract (whether a United Kingdom contract or not) or contained in, or having effect by virtue of, any other Act or any rule of law; and accordingly no proceedings (whether civil or criminal) shall lie against any person in any United Kingdom court by reason of anything done or not done by him or on his behalf in compliance with such a direction.

(3) In so far as such a direction requires anything to be done or not done at a place outside the United Kingdom, the direction shall have effect notwithstanding anything contained in any contract (whether a United Kingdom contract or not); and accordingly, where such a direction is inconsistent with anything in such a contract, it shall (without prejudice to any proceedings in a court other than a United Kingdom court) be construed as requiring compliance with the direction notwithstanding that compliance would be in breach of that contract.

(4) No proceedings for breach of contract shall lie against any person in a United Kingdom court by reason of anything done or not done by him or on his behalf at a place outside the United Kingdom in compliance with any such direction, if the contract in question is a United Kingdom contract.

(4A) Any reference in this section to a direction under any of the preceding provisions of this Part of this Act includes a reference to an enforcement notice.

(5) In this section "United Kingdom court" means a court exercising jurisdiction in any part of the United Kingdom under the law of the United Kingdom or of part of the United Kingdom, and "United Kingdom contract" means a contract which is either expressed to have effect in accordance with the law of the United Kingdom or of part of the United Kingdom or (not being so expressed) is a contract of which the proper law is the law of the United Kingdom or of part of the United Kingdom.

[Aviation Security Act 1982, s 19, as amended by the Aviation and Maritime Security Act 1990, Sch 1.]

7–5459   20. Inspection of aircraft and aerodromes.   (1) For the purpose of enabling the Secretary of State to determine whether to give a direction to any person under any of the preceding provisions of this Part of this Act, or of ascertaining whether any such direction or any enforcement notice is being or has been complied with, an authorised person shall have power, on production (if required of his credentials, to inspect—

(a) any aircraft registered or operating in the United Kingdom, at a time when it is in the United Kingdom, or
(b) any part of any aerodrome in the United Kingdom, or
(c) any land outside an aerodrome which is occupied for the purposes of a business by a person who—

  (i) also occupies (or appears to the authorised person to be about to occupy) land within an aerodrome for the purposes of that business, or
  (ii) is permitted (or appears to the authorised person to be about to be permitted) to have access to a restricted zone of an aerodrome for the purposes of the activities of that business.

(2) An authorised person inspecting an aircraft, any part of an aerodrome or any land outside an aerodrome under subsection (1) above shall have power—

(a) to subject any property found by him in the aircraft (but not the aircraft itself or any apparatus or equipment installed in it) or, as the case may be, to subject that part of the aerodrome or any property found by him there or on that land, to such tests, or
(aa) to take such steps—

  (i) to ascertain what practice or procedures are being followed in relation to security, or
  (ii) to test the effectiveness of any practice or procedure relating to security,

(b) to require the operator of the aircraft, the manager of the aerodrome or the occupier of the land, to furnish to him such information,

as the authorised person may consider necessary for the purpose for which the inspection is carried out.

(3) Subject to subsection (4) below, an authorised person, for the purpose of exercising any power conferred on him by the preceding provisions of this section in relation to an aircraft, in relation to an aerodrome or in relation to any land outside an aerodrome, shall have power—

(a) for the purpose of inspecting an aircraft, to enter it and to take all such steps as are necessary to detain it, or
(b) for the purpose of inspecting any part of an aerodrome, to enter any building or works in the aerodrome or enter upon any land in the aerodrome, or
(c) for the purpose of inspecting any land outside an aerodrome, to enter upon the land and to enter any building or works on the land.

(4) The powers conferred by subsection (3) above shall not include power for an authorised person to use force for the purpose of entering any aircraft, building or works or entering upon any land.

(5) Any person who—

(a) (*Repealed*);
(b) without reasonable excuse, fails to comply with a requirement imposed on him under subsection (2)(b) above, or
(c) in furnishing any information so required, makes a statement which he knows to be false in a material particular, or recklessly makes a statement which is false in a material particular,

shall be guilty of an offence and liable[1]—

  (i) on summary conviction, to a fine not exceeding **the statutory maximum**[2];
  (ii) on conviction on indictment, to a **fine** or to imprisonment for a term not exceeding **two years** or to **both**.

[Aviation Security Act 1982, s 20, as amended by the Aviation and Maritime Security Act 1990, Schs 1 and 4.]

---

1. For procedure in respect of this offence which is triable either way, see the Magistrates' Courts Act 1980, ss 17A–21, in PART I: MAGISTRATES' COURTS, PROCEDURE, ante.
2. For meaning of "the statutory maximum", see s 38, post.

7–5459A 20A. Aviation security services: approved providers. (1) In this section "aviation security service" means a process or activity carried out for the purpose of—

(a) complying with a requirement of a direction under any of sections 12 to 14, or
(b) facilitating a person's compliance with a requirement of a direction under any of those sections.

(2) Regulations may provide for the Secretary of State to maintain a list of persons who are approved by him for the provision of a particular aviation security service.

(3) The regulations may—

(a) prohibit the provision of an aviation security service by a person who is not listed in respect of that service;

(b) prohibit the use or engagement for the provision of an aviation security service of a person who is not listed in respect of that service;

(c) create a criminal offence;

(d) make provision about application for inclusion in the list (including provision about fees);

(e) make provision about the duration and renewal of entries on the list (including provision about fees);

(f) make provision about training or qualifications which persons who apply to be listed or who are listed are required to undergo or possess;

(g) make provision about removal from the list which shall include provision for appeal;

(h) make provision about the inspection of activities carried out by listed persons;

(i) confer functions on the Secretary of State or on a specified person;

(j) confer jurisdiction on a court.

(4) Regulations under subsection (3)(c)—

(a) may not provide for a penalty on summary conviction greater than a fine not exceeding the statutory maximum,

(b) may not provide for a penalty of imprisonment on conviction on indictment greater than imprisonment for a term not exceeding two years (whether or not accompanied by a fine), and

(c) may create a criminal offence of purporting, with intent to deceive, to do something as a listed person or of doing something, with intent to deceive, which purports to be done by a listed person.

(5) A direction under any of sections 12 to 14 may—

(a) include a requirement to use a listed person for the provision of an aviation security service;

(b) provide for all or part of the direction not to apply or to apply with modified effect where a listed person provides an aviation security service.

(6) Regulations under this section—

(a) may make different provision for different cases,

(b) may include incidental, supplemental or transitional provision,

(c) shall be made by the Secretary of State by statutory instrument,

(d) shall not be made unless the Secretary of State has consulted organisations appearing to him to represent persons affected by the regulations, and

(e) shall be subject to annulment in pursuance of a resolution of either House of Parliament.

[Aviation Security Act 1982, s 20A, as inserted by the Anti-terrorism, Crime and Security Act 2001, s 85.]

7–5459B   20B. detention direction.   (1) An authorised person may give a detention direction in respect of an aircraft if he is of the opinion that—

(a) a person has failed to comply or is likely to fail to comply with a requirement of a direction under section 12 or 14 of this Act in respect of the aircraft,

(b) a person has failed to comply with a requirement of an enforcement notice in respect of the aircraft,

(c) a threat has been made to commit an act of violence against the aircraft or against any person or property on board the aircraft, or

(d) an act of violence is likely to be committed against the aircraft or against any person or property on board the aircraft.

(2) A detention direction in respect of an aircraft—

(a) shall be given in writing to the operator of the aircraft, and

(b) shall require him to take steps to ensure that the aircraft does not fly while the direction is in force.

(3) An authorised person who has given a detention direction in respect of an aircraft may do anything which he considers necessary or expedient for the purpose of ensuring that the aircraft does not fly while the direction is in force; in particular, the authorised person may—

(a) enter the aircraft;

(b) arrange for another person to enter the aircraft;

(c) arrange for a person or thing to be removed from the aircraft;

(d) use reasonable force;

(e) authorise the use of reasonable force by another person.

(4) The operator of an aircraft in respect of which a detention direction is given may object to the direction in writing to the Secretary of State.

(5) On receipt of an objection to a detention direction under subsection (4) the Secretary of State shall—

(a) consider the objection,

(b) allow the person making the objection and the authorised person who gave the direction an opportunity to make written or oral representations to the Secretary of State or to a person appointed by him,

(c) confirm, vary or cancel the direction, and

(d) give notice of his decision in writing to the person who made the objection and to the authorised person who gave the direction.

(6) A detention direction in respect of an aircraft shall continue in force until—

(a) an authorised person cancels it by notice in writing to the operator of the aircraft, or

(b) the Secretary of State cancels it under subsection (5)(c).

(7) A person commits an offence if—

(a) without reasonable excuse he fails to comply with a requirement of a detention direction, or

(b) he intentionally obstructs a person acting in accordance with subsection (3).

(8) A person who is guilty of an offence under subsection (7) shall be liable—

(a) on summary conviction, to a fine not exceeding the statutory maximum, or

(b) on conviction on indictment, to a fine, to imprisonment for a term not exceeding two years or to both.

(9) A detention direction may be given in respect of—

(a) any aircraft in the United Kingdom, and

(b) any aircraft registered or operating in the United Kingdom.

(10) A detention direction may be given in respect of a class of aircraft; and for that purpose—

(a) a reference to "the aircraft" in subsection (1) shall be treated as a reference to all or any of the aircraft within the class, and

(b) subsections (2) to (9) shall apply as if the direction were given in respect of each aircraft within the class.

[Aviation Security Act 1982, s 20B, as inserted by the Anti-terrorism, Crime and Security Act 2001, s 86(1).]

Air navigation installations

7–5460 21. Application of provisions of Part II to air navigation installations. (1) Sections 11, 13, 13A, 14, 15, 16 and 20 of this Act shall have effect in relation to air navigation installations in the United Kingdom in accordance with the following provisions of this section.

(2) In relation to any such air navigation installation which does not form part of an aerodrome, those sections shall have effect, subject to sub-section (5) below, as if in them any reference to an aerodrome were a reference to such an air navigation installation and any reference to the manager of an aerodrome were a reference to the authority responsible for such an air navigation installation.

(3) Where an air navigation installation forms part of an aerodrome in the United Kingdom, those sections shall have effect, subject to subsection (5) below, as if in them any reference to an aerodrome were a reference either—

(a) to an aerodrome, or

(b) to an air navigation installation which forms part of an aerodrome, or

(c) to so much of an aerodrome as does not consist of an air navigation installation;

and accordingly a notice under section 11 of this Act or a direction under section 13 or 14 of this Act may be served or given either in respect of the whole of the aerodrome, or in respect of the air navigation installation separately, or in respect of so much of the aerodrome as does not consist of an air navigation installation.

(4) For the purposes—

(a) of the service of a notice or the giving of a direction under section 11, 13 or 14 of this Act as modified by subsection (3) above, where the notice is to be served or the direction given in respect of an air navigation installation separately, and

(b) of the operation of section 16(6) of this Act in relation to a direction so given,

any reference in any of those sections to the manager of the aerodrome shall be construed as a reference to any person who is either the manager of the aerodrome or the authority responsible for the air navigation installation.

(5) Subsections (2) and (3) above shall not apply to section 13(3) of this Act; but where a direction given under section 13 of this Act, as applied or modified by the preceding provisions of this section, is for the time being in force—

(a) if it is a direction given in respect of an air navigation installation separately (whether that installation forms part of an aerodrome or not), the said section 13(3) shall have effect in relation to that direction as if the air navigation installation were an aerodrome and, where the direction was given to the authority responsible for the air navigation installation, as if it had been given to the manager of that aerodrome;

(*b*) if it is a direction given in respect of so much of an aerodrome as does not consist of an air navigation installation, the said section 13(3) shall have effect in relation to that direction as if any air navigation installation comprised in the aerodrome did not form part of the aerodrome.

(6) A direction under section 14 of this Act, as applied or modified by the preceding provisions of this section, may be given to the authority responsible for one or more air navigation installations so as to relate either—

(*a*) to all air navigation installations in the United Kingdom for which it is responsible at the time when the direction is given or at any subsequent time, or

(*b*) only to one or more such air navigation installations, or to a class of such air navigation installations, specified in the direction.

(7) Any reference in section 17, 18(1), 18A, 18B, 18E or 19(1) of this Act to a direction given under a provision therein mentioned shall be construed as including a reference to a direction given under that provision as applied or modified by the preceding provisions of this section.

(8) Notwithstanding anything in subsection (2)(*a*) of section 20 of this Act, a person inspecting an air navigation installation under that section (or under that section as applied or modified by the preceding provisions of this section) shall not be empowered thereby to test any apparatus or equipment which constitutes or forms part of the air navigation installation.

[Aviation Security Act 1982, s 21, as amended by the Aviation and Maritime Security Act 1990, Sch 1.]

Offences relating to security at aerodromes etc

7–5461 21A. False statements relating to baggage, cargo etc. (1) Subject to subsection (3) below, a person commits an offence if, in answer to a question which—

(*a*) relates to any baggage, cargo or stores (whether belonging to him or to another) that is or are intended for carriage by a civil aircraft registered or operating in the United Kingdom, and

(*b*) is put to him for purposes to which this Part of this Act applies—

  (i) by any of the persons mentioned in subsection (2) below,
  (ii) by any employee or agent of such a person in his capacity as employee or agent, or
  (iii) by a constable,

he makes a statement which he knows to be false in a material particular, or recklessly makes a statement which is false in a material particular.

(2) The persons referred to in subsection (1)(*b*) are—

(*a*) the manager of an aerodrome in the United Kingdom,

(*b*) the operator of one or more aircraft registered or operating in the United Kingdom,

(*c*) any person who—

  (i) is permitted to have access to a restricted zone of an aerodrome for the purposes of the activities of a business carried on by him, and
  (ii) has control in that restricted zone over the baggage, cargo or stores to which the question relates, and

(*d*) any air cargo agent who is included on the list of security approved air cargo agents maintained by the Secretary of State pursuant to regulations made under section 21F of this Act.

(3) Subsection (1) above does not apply in relation to any statement made by an authorised person in the exercise of the power conferred by section 20(2)(*aa*) of this Act.

(4) A person guilty of an offence under subsection (1) above shall be liable on summary conviction to a fine not exceeding **level 5** on the standard scale.

(5) In this section—

"cargo" includes mail;

"civil aircraft" has the same meaning as in section 3 of this Act; and

"stores" means any goods intended for sale or use on an aircraft, including spare parts and other articles of equipment, whether or not for immediate fitting.

[Aviation Security Act 1982, s 21A, as inserted by the Aviation and Maritime Security Act 1990, s 5 and as amended by the Aviation Security (Air Cargo Agents) Regulations 1993, SI 1993/1073.]

7–5462 21B. False statements in connection with identity documents. (1) Subject to subsection (4) below, a person commits an offence if—

(*a*) for the purpose of, or in connection with, an application made by him or another for the issue of an identity document to which this subsection applies, or

(*b*) in connection with the continued holding by him or another of any such document which has already been issued,

he makes to any of the persons specified in subsection (3) below, to any employee or agent of such a person or to a constable, a statement which he knows to be false in a material particular, or recklessly makes to any of those persons, to any such employee or agent or to a constable, a statement which is false in a material particular.

(2) Subsection (1) above applies to any identity document which is to be or has been issued by

any of the persons specified in subsection (3) below in accordance with arrangements the maintenance of which is required by a direction given by the Secretary of State under section 14 of this Act.

(3) The persons referred to in subsection (1) above are—

(a) the manager of an aerodrome in the United Kingdom,

(b) the authority responsible for an air navigation installation in the United Kingdom,

(c) the operator of one or more aircraft registered or operating in the United Kingdom,

(d) any person who is permitted to have access to a restricted zone of an aerodrome or air navigation installation for the purposes of the activities of a business carried on by him, and

(e) any air cargo agent who is included on the list of security approved air cargo agents maintained by the Secretary of State pursuant to regulations made under section 21F of this Act.

(4) Subsection (1) above does not apply in relation to any statement made by an authorised person in the exercise of the power conferred by section 20(2)(*aa*) of this Act.

(5) A person guilty of an offence under subsection (1) above shall be liable on summary conviction to a fine not exceeding **level 5** on the standard scale.

[Aviation Security Act 1982, s 21B, as inserted by the Aviation and Maritime Security Act 1990, s 5 and as amended by the Aviation Security (Air Cargo Agents) Regulations 1993, SI 1993/1073.]

7–5463   21C. Unauthorised presence in restricted zone.   (1) A person shall not—

(a) go, with or without a vehicle, onto any part of a restricted zone of—

(i) an aerodrome, or

(ii) an air navigation installation which does not form part of an aerodrome,

except with the permission of the manager of the aerodrome, the authority responsible for the air navigation installation or a person acting on behalf of that manager or authority, and in accordance with any conditions subject to which that permission is for the time being granted, or

(b) remain on any part of such a restricted zone after being requested to leave by the manager of the aerodrome, the authority responsible for the air navigation installation or a person acting on behalf of that manager or authority.

(2) Subsection (1)(a) above does not apply unless it is proved that, at the material time, notices stating that the area concerned was a restricted zone were posted so as to be readily seen and read by persons entering the restricted zone.

(3) A person who contravenes subsection (1) above without lawful authority or reasonable excuse shall be guilty of an offence and liable on summary conviction to a fine not exceeding **level 5** on the standard scale.

(4) A constable, the manager of an aerodrome or a person acting on his behalf may use reasonable force to remove a person who fails to comply with a request under subsection (1)(b) above.

[Aviation Security Act 1982, s 21C, as inserted by the Aviation and Maritime Security Act 1990, s 5 and amended by the Anti-terrorism, Crime and Security Act 2001, s 84.]

7–5464   21D. Unauthorised presence on board aircraft.   (1) A person shall not—

(a) get into or onto an aircraft at an aerodrome in the United Kingdom except with the permission of the operator of the aircraft or a person acting on his behalf, or

(b) remain on an aircraft at such an aerodrome after being requested to leave by the operator of the aircraft or a person acting on his behalf.

(2) A person who contravenes subsection (1) above without lawful authority or reasonable excuse shall be guilty of an offence and liable on summary conviction to a fine not exceeding **level 5** on the standard scale.

(3) A constable, the operator of an aircraft or a person acting on his behalf may use reasonable force to remove a person who fails to comply with a request under subsection (1)(b) above.

[Aviation Security Act 1982, s 21D, as inserted by the Aviation and Maritime Security Act 1990, s 5 and amended by the Anti-terrorism, Crime and Security Act 2001, s 84.]

7–5465   21E. Offences relating to authorised persons.   (1) A person who—

(a) intentionally obstructs an authorised person acting in the exercise of a power conferred on him by or under this Part of this Act, or

(b) falsely pretends to be an authorised person,

commits an offence.

(2) A person guilty of an offence under subsection (1)(a) above shall be liable[1]—

(a) on summary conviction, to a fine not exceeding **the statutory maximum**;

(b) on conviction on indictment, to a **fine** or to imprisonment for a term not exceeding **two years** or to **both**.

(3) A person guilty of an offence under subsection (1)(b) above shall be liable on summary conviction to a fine not exceeding **level 5** on the standard scale.

[Aviation Security Act 1982, s 21E, as inserted by the Aviation and Maritime Security Act 1990, s 5.]

Air cargo Agents

7–5466   21F. Air cargo agents.   (1) The Secretary of State may by regulations[1] made by statutory instrument make provision, for purposes to which this Part of this Act applies, in relation to persons (in this section referred to as "air cargo agents") who carry on a business of handling cargo which is to be delivered (whether by them or any other person) to the operator of any aircraft for carriage from any aerodrome in the United Kingdom by a civil aircraft.

(2)–(5) *Supplementary provisions as to regulations.*

(6) In this section—

"cargo" includes stores and mail; and

"stores" means any goods intended for sale or use on an aircraft, including spare parts and other articles of equipment, whether or not for immediate fitting.

[Aviation Security Act 1982, s 21F, as inserted by the Aviation and Maritime Security Act 1990, s 6.]

1. The Aviation Security (Air Cargo Agents) Regulations 1993, SI 1993/1073 amended by SI 1996/1607 and SI 1998/1152 have been made.

7–5466A   21FA. Air cargo agents: documents.   (1) A person commits an offence if with intent to deceive he issues a document which purports to be issued by a person on a list of approved air cargo agents maintained under section 21F(2)(*a*) of this Act.

(2) A person guilty of an offence under subsection (1) shall be liable on summary conviction to imprisonment for a term not exceeding six months or to a fine not exceeding level 5 on the standard scale or to both.

[Aviation Security Act 1982, s 21F, as inserted by the Anti-terrorism, Crime and Security Act 2001, s 87.]

Reporting of certain occurrences relating to aviation security

7–5467   21G. Duty to report certain occurrences.   For purposes to which this Part of this Act applies, the Secretary of State may by regulations made by statutory instrument require such persons as are specified in the regulations to make a report to him, in such manner and within such period as are so specified, of any occurrence of a description so specified.

[Aviation Security Act 1982, s 21G, as inserted by the Aviation and Maritime Security Act 1990, s 7—summarised.]

7–5468   24. Service of documents.   (1) This section has effect in relation to any notice, any document containing a direction and any other document authorised or required by any provision of this Part of this Act to be served on or given to any person.

(2) Any such document may be given to or served on any person

(*a*) by delivering it to him, or

(*b*) by leaving it at his proper address, or

(*c*) by sending it by post to him at that address, or

(*d*) by sending it to him at that address by telex or other similar means which produce a document containing the text of the communication.

(3) Any such document may, in the case of a body corporate, be given to or served on the secretary, clerk or similar officer of that body.

(4) For the purposes of this section and section 7 of the Interpretation Act 1978 (service of documents by post) in its application to this section, the proper address of any person to whom or on whom any document is to be given or served is his usual or last known address or place of business (whether in the United Kingdom or elsewhere), except that in the case of a body corporate or its secretary, clerk or similar officer, it shall be the address of the registered or principal office of that body in the United Kingdom (or, if it has no office in the United Kingdom, of its principal office, wherever it may be).

(5) If the person to or on whom any document mentioned in subsection (1) above is to be given or served has notified the Secretary of State of an address within the United Kingdom, other than his proper address within the meaning of subsection (4) above, as the one at which he or someone else on his behalf will accept documents of the same description as that document, that address shall also be treated for the purposes of this section and section 7 of the Interpretation Act 1978 as his proper address.

(6) Where an authorised person—

(*a*) intends to serve an enforcement notice on any person ("the intended recipient"), and

(*b*) is of the opinion that all the requirements of the notice could be complied with by an employee or agent of the intended recipient.

the authorised person may, after consulting that employee or agent, serve the notice on the intended recipient by delivering it to that employee or agent or by sending it to that employee or agent at the proper address of the employee or agent by such means as are mentioned in subsection (2)(*d*) above.

(7) An authorised person who serves an enforcement notice under subsection (6) above on an employee or agent of the intended recipient shall serve a copy of the notice on the intended recipient.

(8) Nothing in subsection (6) above shall be taken to impose on the employee or agent to whom the enforcement notice is delivered or sent any obligation to comply with it.

[Aviation Security Act 1982, s 24, as substituted by the Aviation and Maritime Security Act 1990, Sch 1.]

7–5469 24A. Interpretation of Part II.　(1) In this Part of this Act, except in so far as the context otherwise requires—

"act of violence" has the meaning given by section 10(2) of this Act,

"authorised person" means a person authorised in writing by the Secretary of State for the purposes of this Part of this Act,

"employee", in relation to a body corporate, includes officer,

"enforcement notice" has the meaning given by section 18A(1) of this Act, and

"restricted zone", in relation to an aerodrome or air navigation installation, means any part of the aerodrome or installation designated under section 11A of this Act or, where the whole of the aerodrome or installation is so designated, that aerodrome or installation.

(2) For the purposes of this Part of this Act a person is permitted to have access to a restricted zone of an aerodrome or air navigation installation if he is permitted to enter that zone or if arrangements exist for permitting any of his employees or agents to enter that zone.

[Aviation Security Act 1982, s 24A, as inserted by the Aviation and Maritime Security Act 1990, Sch 1.]

PART III[1]
POLICING OF AIRPORTS

7–5470 25. Designated airports.　(1) The Secretary of State may by order[2] designate for the purposes of this Part of this Act any aerodrome used for the purposes of civil aviation if he considers that the policing of that aerodrome should, in the interests of the preservation of the peace and the prevention of crime, be undertaken by constables under the direction and control of the chief officer of police for the police area in which the aerodrome is wholly or mainly situated.

(2)–(3) *Supplementary provisions with respect to an order under sub-s (1).*

[Aviation Security Act 1982, s 25.]

---

1. Part III contains ss 25–31.

2. The following airports have been designated: Heathrow (SI 1974/1671), Stansted (SI 1975/168), Gatwick (SI 1975/375), Birmingham (SI 1976/590), and Manchester (SI 1976/1045).

7–5471 26. Exercise of police functions at designated airports.　(1) So long as any aerodrome is a designated airport—

(*a*)　any relevant constable shall, when acting in the execution of his duty and, in particular, for the purpose of exercising the powers conferred on such a constable by or under the following provisions of this Part of this Act, be entitled as against the manager of the aerodrome to enter any part of the aerodrome; and

(*b*)　no member of any aerodrome constabulary maintained by the manager shall have the powers and privileges or be liable to the duties and responsibilities of a constable on the aerodrome or exercise there any power conferred by or under any enactment on members of that constabulary or on constables generally.

(2) Paragraph (*a*) of subsection (1) above is without prejudice to any right of entry existing apart from that paragraph.

(3) The manager of an aerodrome which is a designated airport shall—

(*a*)　make to the police authority for the relevant police area such payments in respect of the policing of the aerodrome, and

(*b*)　provide, for use in connection with the policing of the aerodrome, such accommodation and facilities,

as the manager and that authority may agree or as may, in default of agreement, be determined by the Secretary of State.

(4) *Repealed.*

[Aviation Security Act 1982, s 26, as amended by the Greater London Authority Act 1999, Schs 27 and 34.]

7–5472 27. Prevention of theft at designated airports.　(1) Any relevant constable may in any aerodrome which is a designated airport—

(*a*)　stop, and without warrant search and arrest, any airport employee whom he has reasonable grounds to suspect of having in his possession or of conveying in any manner anything stolen or unlawfully obtained on the aerodrome; and

(*b*)　if he has reasonable grounds to suspect that anything stolen or unlawfully obtained on the aerodrome may be found in or on any vehicle carrying an airport employee or in or on any aircraft, stop and without warrant search and detain the vehicle or, as the case may be, board and without warrant search the aircraft.

(2) Any relevant constable may—

(a) stop any person who is leaving a cargo area in an aerodrome which is a designated airport and inspect any goods carried by that person;

(b) stop and search any vehicle or aircraft which is leaving any such area and inspect the vehicle or aircraft and any goods carried on or in it; and

(c) detain in the area—

(i) any such goods as aforesaid for which there is not produced a document authorising their removal from the area signed by a person authorised in that behalf by the manager of the aerodrome; and

(ii) any such vehicle or aircraft as aforesaid so long as there are on or in it goods liable to detention under this paragraph.

(3) Nothing in subsection (2) above shall be construed as conferring a power to search any person.

(4) In any cargo area in an aerodrome which is a designated airport the powers of a constable under subsection (1)(b) above—

(a) extend to any vehicle whether or not it is carrying an airport employee; and

(b) include power, not only to board and search an aircraft, but also to stop and detain it.

(5) In this section "airport employee", in relation to any aerodrome, means any person in the employment of the manager of the aerodrome and any person employed otherwise than by the manager to work on the aerodrome.

(6) In this section "cargo area" means, subject to subsection (7) below, any area which appears to the Secretary of State to be used wholly or mainly for the storage or handling of cargo in an aerodrome and is designated by an order made by him for the purposes of this section.

(7) *Repealed.*

(8) Any power to make an order under this section shall be exercisable by statutory instrument subject to annulment in pursuance of a resolution of either House of Parliament.

(9) The powers conferred by this section on a relevant constable are without prejudice to any powers exercisable by him apart from this section.

[Aviation Security Act 1982, s 27, as amended by the Airports Act 1986, Sch 6.]

7–5473 28. Byelaws for designated airports. (1) So long as any aerodrome is a designated airport any power of the manager or the aerodrome to make aerodrome byelaws shall, if it would not otherwise do so—

(a) extend to the making of byelaws in respect of the whole of the aerodrome; and

(b) include power to make byelaws requiring any person, if so requested by a relevant constable, to leave the aerodrome or any particular part of it or to state his name and address and the purpose of his being on the aerodrome.

(2) A relevant constable may remove from any aerodrome which is a designated airport, or from any part of it—

(a) any person who, in contravention of any aerodrome byelaws, fails or refuses to leave the aerodrome or part after being requested by the constable to do so;

(b) any vehicle, animal or thing brought to or left within the aerodrome or part in contravention of any aerodrome byelaws and any vehicle, animal or thing likely to cause danger or obstruction.

(3) A relevant constable may without warrant arrest[1] a person within any aerodrome which is a designated airport—

(a) if he has reasonable cause to believe that the person has contravened any aerodrome byelaws and he does not know and cannot ascertain that person's name and address; or

(b) if that person, in contravention of any aerodrome bye-laws, fails or refuses to leave the aerodrome or any particular part of it after being requested by the constable to do so.

[Aviation Security Act 1982, s 28.]

---

1. The power of arrest under s 28(3) ceased to have effect on the enactment of s 26 of the Police and Criminal Evidence Act 1984, in PART I: MAGISTRATES' COURTS, PROCEDURE, ante; nevertheless a power of arrest may, subject to the general arrest conditions, be available under s 25 of that Act.

7–5474 29. Control of road traffic at designated airports. (1) So long as any aerodrome is a designated airport, the functions of a chief officer of police under any provisions applying in relation to the aerodrome under section 65 of the Airports Act 1986 (application to certain aerodromes of provisions relating to road traffic) shall, notwithstanding any order under that section, be exercisable by that officer to the exclusion of the chief officer of any aerodrome constabulary; and for the purposes of any functions of a chief officer of police under those provisions any part of the aerodrome which is not within the relevant police area shall be treated as if it were.

(2) So long as any aerodrome is a designated airport—

(a) traffic wardens appointed by the police authority for the relevant police area may exercise their functions on the aerodrome and shall be entitled, as against the manager of the aerodrome, to enter the aerodrome accordingly;

(b) *Repealed.*

(3) *Repealed.*

[Aviation Security Act 1982, s 29, as amended by the Airports Act 1986, Schs 4 and 6 and the Greater London Authority Act 1999, Schs 27 and 34.]

7–5475 30. Supplementary orders. The Secretary of State may by order make such provision as appears to him to be necessary or expedient in connection with, or in consequence of, any aerodrome becoming or ceasing to be a designated airport.

[Aviation Security Act 1982, s 30, as amended by the Airports Act 1986, Sch 6 and the Police and Magistrates' Courts Act 1994, Sch 9 and the Greater London Authority Act 1999, Sch 34—summarised.]

7–5476 31. Interpretation and application of Part III to Scotland and Northern Ireland.

(1) In this Part of this Act, subject to the following provisions of this section—

"aerodrome byelaws" means, in relation to any aerodrome, byelaws having effect under any enactment authorising the manager of the aerodrome to make byelaws in respect of the whole or any part of the aerodrome;

"aerodrome constabulary" means, in relation to any aerodrome, any body of constables which the manager of the aerodrome has power to maintain at the aerodrome;

"designated airport" means any aerodrome for the time being designated under section 25 of this Act;

"relevant police area" and "relevant constable", in relation to any aerodrome, mean respectively the police area in which the aerodrome is wholly or mainly situated and any constable under the direction and control of the chief officer of police for that area.

(2) *Scotland.*

(3) *Northern Ireland.*

[Aviation Security Act 1982, s 31, as amended by the Greater London Authority Act 1999, Sch 27.]

PART IV[1]
THE AVIATION SECURITY FUND

7–5477 32. The Aviation Security Fund. (1) There shall continue to be, under the control and management of the Secretary of State, a fund called the Aviation Security Fund out of which payments shall be made in accordance with this section.

(2) The Secretary of State may, out of the Aviation Security Fund, reimburse to any person who is—

(a) the operator of one or more aircraft registered or operating in the United Kingdom, or

(b) the manager of an aerodrome in the United Kingdom, or

(c) the authority responsible for an air navigation installation in the United Kingdom, or

(d) a person to whom a direction has been or could be given by the Secretary of State under section 14 of this Act by virtue of subsection (1)(c) or (d) of that section,

the whole or part of any expenses which, for purposes to which Part II of this Act applies, have, in the case of a person mentioned in paragraph (a), (b) or (c) above, been at any time on or after 1st June 1972 or, in the case of a person mentioned in paragraph (d) above, been at any time after the passing of the Aviation and Maritime Security Act 1990, incurred or may, in any case, be incurred by any such person in relation to those aircraft, to that aerodrome or air navigation installation or to the land or activities concerned, as the case may be, whether or not the expenses have been or are incurred in consequence of a direction given under Part II of this Act.

(3)–(7) *Supplementary provisions.*

[Aviation Security Act 1982, s 32, as amended by the Aviation and Maritime Security Act 1990, Sch 1.]

_____

1. Part IV contains ss 32–36.

7–5478 33. Contributions to the Fund. (1) The Secretary of State may make regulations containing such provisions as he considers appropriate for requiring managers of aerodromes to pay him, in respect of all aerodromes or of aerodromes of a prescribed class, contributions to the Aviation Security Fund calculated in accordance with the following provisions of this section.

(2) *Rate of payments.*

(3) Without prejudice to the generality of subsection (1) above, regulations under this section may—

(a) prescribe the time when any contribution is to be paid;

(b) charge interest at a rate prescribed with the consent of the Treasury on so much of any contribution as is overdue;

(c) require managers of aerodromes, in relation to the aerodromes under their management, to furnish the Secretary of State with such information, to keep such records and to make such returns to him about the matters mentioned in subsection (2) above as may be prescribed;

(d) provide that contravention of any prescribed provision of the regulations (other than a failure to pay a contribution or interest on any overdue contribution) shall be an offence, either triable on indictment or summarily or triable only summarily, and punishable in each case with a fine, not exceeding, in the case of a summary conviction—

  (i) in Great Britain, the statutory maximum if the offence is also triable on indictment or £1,000 if it is not;

  (ii) *Northern Ireland,*

(e) make such incidental, supplemental and transitional provision as the Secretary of State thinks fit; and

(f) make different provision for different cases.

(4) The Secretary of State shall pay into the Aviation Security Fund all money received by him by virtue of regulations made under this section.

(5) The power to make regulations under this section shall be exercisable by statutory instrument; and regulations shall not be made under this section unless a draft of the regulations has been laid before Parliament and approved by a resolution of each House of Parliament.

(6) In this section "prescribed" means prescribed by regulations under this section.

[Aviation Security Act 1982, s 33.]

PART V[1]
MISCELLANEOUS AND GENERAL

7–5479 37. Offences by bodies corporate.   (1) Where an offence under this Act (including any provision of Part II as applied by regulations made under section 21F of this Act) or under regulations made under section 21G of this Act has been committed by a body corporate and is proved to have been committed with the consent or connivance of, or to be attributable to any neglect on the part of, any director, manager, secretary or other similar officer of the body corporate, or any person who was purporting to act in any such capacity, he as well as the body corporate shall be guilty of that offence and shall be liable to be proceeded against and punished accordingly.

(2) Where the affairs of a body corporate are managed by its members, subsection (1) above shall apply in relation to the acts and defaults of a member in connection with his functions of management as if he were a director of the body corporate.

[Aviation Security Act 1982, s 37, as amended by the Aviation and Maritime Security Act 1990, Sch 1.]

---

1. Part V contains ss 37–41.

7–5480 38. Interpretation etc.   (1) In this Act, except in so far as the context otherwise requires—

"aerodrome" means the aggregate of the land, buildings and works comprised in an aerodrome within the meaning of the Civil Aviation Act 1982 and (if and so far as not comprised in an aerodrome as defined in that Act) any land, building or works situated within the boundaries of an area designated, by an order made by the Secretary of State which is for the time being in force, as constituting the area of an aerodrome for the purposes of this Act;

"air navigation installation" means any building, works, apparatus or equipment used wholly or mainly for the purpose of assisting air traffic control or as an aid to air navigation, together with any land contiguous or adjacent to any such building, works, apparatus or equipment and used wholly or mainly for purposes connected therewith;

"aircraft registered or operating in the United Kingdom" means any aircraft which is either—

  (a) an aircraft registered in the United Kingdom, or

  (b) an aircraft not so registered which is for the time being allocated for use on flights which (otherwise than in exceptional circumstances) include landing at or taking off from one or more aerodromes in the United Kingdom;

"article" includes any substance, whether in solid or liquid form or in the form of a gas or vapour;

"constable" includes any person having the powers and privileges of a constable;

"explosive" means any article manufactured for the purpose of producing a practical effect by explosion, or intended for that purpose by a person having the article with him;

"firearm" includes an airgun or air pistol;

"manager", in relation to an aerodrome, means the person (whether the Civil Aviation Authority, a local authority or any other person) by whom the aerodrome is managed;

"military service" includes naval and air force service;

"measures" (without prejudice to the generality of that expression) includes the construction, execution, alteration, demolition or removal of buildings of other works and also includes the institution or modification, and the supervision and enforcement, of any practice or procedure;

"operator" has the same meaning as in the Civil Aviation Act 1982;

"property" includes any land, buildings or works, any aircraft or vehicle and any baggage, cargo or other article of any description;

"United Kingdom national" means an individual who is—

(a) a British citizen, a British overseas territories citizen or a British Overseas citizen;

(b) a person who under the British Nationality Act 1981 is a British subject; or

(c) a British protected person (within the meaning of that Act).

(2) For the purposes of this Act—

(a) in the case of an air navigation installation provided by, or used wholly or mainly by, the Civil Aviation Authority, that Authority, and

(b) in the case of any other air navigation installation, the person by whom it is provided, or by whom it is wholly or mainly used,

shall be taken to be the authority responsible for that air navigation installation.

(3) For the purposes of this Act—

(a) the period during which an aircraft is in flight shall be deemed to include any period from the moment when all its external doors are closed following embarkation until the moment when any such door is opened for disembarkation, and, in the case of a forced landing, any period until the competent authorities take over responsibility for the aircraft and for persons and property on board; and

(b) an aircraft shall be taken to be in service during the whole of the period which begins with the pre-flight preparation of the aircraft for a flight and ends 24 hours after the aircraft lands having completed that flight, and also at any time (not falling within that period) while, in accordance with the preceding paragraph, the aircraft is in flight,

and anything done on board an aircraft while in flight over any part of the United Kingdom shall be treated as done in that part of the United Kingdom.

(4) For the purposes of this Act the territorial waters[1] adjacent to any part of the United Kingdom shall be treated as included in that part of the United Kingdom.

(5) Any power to make an order under subsection (1) above shall be exercisable by statutory instrument; and any statutory instrument containing any such order shall be subject to annulment in pursuance of a resolution of either House of Parliament.

(6) Any power to give a direction under any provision of this Act shall be construed as including power to revoke or vary any such direction by a further direction.

(7) Subject to section 18 of the Interpretation Act 1978 (which relates to offences under two or more laws), Part I of this Act shall not be construed as—

(a) conferring a right of action in any civil proceedings in respect of any contravention of this Act, or

(b) derogating from any right of action or other remedy (whether civil or criminal) in proceedings instituted otherwise than under this Act.

(8) *Northern Ireland.*

[Aviation Security Act 1982, s 38, as amended by the Airports Act 1986, Sch 6, the Aviation and Maritime Security Act 1990, Schs 1 and 4, the Statute Law (Repeals) Act 1993, Sch 1, SI 2001/4050 and the British Overseas Territories Act 2002, s 2(3).]

---

1. See the Territorial Waters Jurisdiction Act 1878 and the Territorial Sea Act 1987 (12 miles).

7–5481 **39. Extension of Act outside United Kingdom.** (1) *Repealed.*

(2) Section 8 of the Tokyo Convention Act 1967 (application to Channel Islands, Isle of Man and the United Kingdom dependencies) shall apply to section 5 of this Act as it applies to section 4 of that Act.

(3) Her Majesty may by Order in Council[1] make provision for extending any of the provisions of this Act (other than the provisions to which subsection (1) or (2) above applies and the provisions of Part III) with such exceptions, adaptations or modifications as may be specified in the Order, to any of the Channel Islands, the Isle of Man, any colony, for whose external relations a country other than the United Kingdom is responsible, or any country outside Her Majesty's dominions in which Her Majesty has jurisdiction in right of Her Majesty's Government in the United Kingdom.

(4) Except in pursuance of subsection (1) or (3) above, the provisions of this Act and, in particular, the repeal of the provisions which those subsections re-enact do not affect the law of any country or territory outside the United Kingdom.

[Aviation Security Act 1982, s 39, as amended by the Extradition Act 1989, Sch 2, the Aviation and Maritime Security Act 1990, Sch 4 and the Merchant Shipping and Maritime Security Act 1997, Sch 7.]

---

1. The Aviation Security (Jersey) Order 1993, SI 1993/1251 and the Aviation Security (Guernsey) Order, SI 1997/2989 have been made. See also the Aviation Security and Piracy (Overseas Territories) Order 2000, SI 2000/3059 which extends certain provisions of the Aviation Security Act 1982 and the Aviation and Maritime Security Act 1990, with adaptions and modifications, to the Territories specified in Sch 1 to the order.

Airports Act 1986[1]
(1986 c 31)

PART I[2]
TRANSFER OF UNDERTAKING OF BRITISH AIRPORTS AUTHORITY

1. This Act provides for the dissolution of the British Airports Authority and the vesting of its property, rights and liabilities in a company nominated by the Secretary of State; provides for the reorganisation of other airport undertakings in the public sector, the regulation of the use of airports and makes other amendments of the law relating to airports.

2. Part I contains ss 1–11. Sections 1–3, 4(1)–(4), 5, 9 and 11 have been repealed by the Statute Law (Repeals) Act 2004.

PART II[1]
TRANSFER OF AIRPORT UNDERTAKINGS OF LOCAL AUTHORITIES
Preliminary

7–5680A   12. Interpretation of Part II.   (1) In this Part—

"local authority"—

    (a) in relation to England and Wales, means a local authority within the meaning of the Local Government Act 1972 or the Common Council of the City of London; and

    (b) (*Scotland*); and

"principal council"—

    (a) in relation to England, means the council of a non-metropolitan county, of a district, or of a London borough; and

    (aa) in relation to Wales, means the council of a county or of a county borough; and

    (b) (*Scotland*).

(2) References in this Part to—

    (a) a public airport company;
    (b) the controlling authority of a public airport company;
    (c) a composite authority;
    (d) constituent councils of a composite authority; or
    (e) an associated company,

shall be read in accordance with the relevant provisions of section 16.

(3) For the purposes of this Part an airport shall be treated as controlled by a principal council or (as the case may be) by two or more principal councils jointly if it is for the time being owned—

    (a) by that council or jointly by those councils; or
    (b) by a subsidiary of that council or those councils; or
    (c) by that council or those councils jointly with any such subsidiary.

(4) Any reference in this Part, in relation to two or more principal councils, to a subsidiary of those councils shall be read as a reference to a body corporate which would, if those councils were a single body corporate, be a subsidiary of that body corporate.
[Airports Act 1986, s 12, as amended by the Local Government (Wales) Act 1994, Sch 16.]

---

1. Part II contains ss 12–28.

Transfer of airport undertakings of local authorities

7–5681   13. Transfer of airport undertakings of local authorities to companies owned by such authorities.   The Secretary of State may give to any principal council who control (whether alone or jointly with one or more other principal councils) an airport to which this section applies in accordance with section 14[1], a direction requiring the council to form a company for the purpose of carrying on—

    (a) the business of operating the airport as a commercial undertaking; and
    (b) any activities which appear to the council to be incidental to or connected with carrying on that business.
[Airports Act 1986, s 13—summarised.]

---

1. Section 13 applies to an airport if the annual turnover of the business carried on at the airport by the airport operator exceeded £1 million in the case of at least two of the last three financial years ending before the date of any direction given by the Secretary of State under s 13(1) (s 14).

Public airport companies

7–5682   16. Public airport companies and their controlling authorities.   (1) References in this Part to a public airport company are references to a company (whether formed under section 13 or not) which carries on the business of operating an airport as a commercial undertaking and is for the time being either—

(*a*)   a subsidiary of a single principal council, or

(*b*)   a subsidiary of two or more such councils.

(2) In this Part of this Act—

(*a*)   references to the controlling authority of a public airport company are references to the principal council or principal councils of whom it is for the time being a subsidiary as mentioned in subsection (1); and

(*b*)   references to a composite authority are references to a controlling authority consisting of two or more principal councils, the councils concerned being referred to as the constituent councils of that authority.

(3) For the purposes of this Part a public airport company is an associated company of a principal council if that council are its controlling authority or one of the constituent councils of a composite authority who are its controlling authority.

[Airports Act 1986, s 16.]

7–5683   17. Control over constitution and activities of public airport companies.   (1) Subject to subsection (2), it shall be the duty of the controlling authority of a public airport company to exercise their control over the company so as to ensure that at least three of the directors of the company, or at least one-quarter of their number (whichever is less), are full-time employees of the company who are suitably qualified to act as directors of the company by virtue of their experience in airport management.

(2) Where at any time it appears to the Secretary of State—

(*a*)   that a public airport company has made arrangements for the management of the airport operated by it to be carried on otherwise than through its officers or employees, and

(*b*)   that any such arrangements are adequate to secure that those participating in the management of the airport under the arrangements are suitably qualified to do so by virtue of their experience in airport management,

the Secretary of State may direct that subsection (1) shall not apply in relation to that company.

(3) Any direction given by the Secretary of State under subsection (2) may provide—

(*a*)   that it is to have effect only for such period, or in such circumstances, as may be specified in it, or

(*b*)   that its continuation in force is to be subject to compliance with such conditions specified in it as the Secretary of State thinks fit.

(4) It shall be the duty of the controlling authority of a public airport company to exercise their control over the company so as to ensure that the company does not—

(*a*)   engage in activities in which the controlling authority have no power to engage, or

(*b*)   permit any subsidiary of the company to engage in any such activities.

(5) Where the controlling authority of a public airport company are a composite authority, the duties imposed by subsections (1) and (4) are joint duties of both or all of the constituent councils of that authority; and subsection (4) shall apply in any such case as if it referred to activities in which none of the constituent councils have power to engage.

[Airports Act 1986, s 17.]

7–5684   18. Disabilities of directors of public airport companies.   (1) A director of a public airport company who is paid for acting as such, or who is an employee of the company or of a subsidiary of the company, shall be disqualified for being elected, or being, a member—

(*a*)   where the company's controlling authority is a single principal council, of that council; or

(*b*)   where the company's controlling authority are a composite authority, of any of the councils who are the constituent councils of that authority.

(2) Where a director of a public airport company is a member of any such council as is mentioned in subsection (1)(*a*) or (*b*) he shall not at any meeting of the council—

(*a*)   take part in the consideration or discussion of any contract or proposed contract between the company or a subsidiary of the company and the council; or

(*b*)   vote on any question with respect to any contract or proposed contract between the company or a subsidiary of the company and—

    (i)   the council, or

    (ii) (if they are a constituent council), any of the constituent councils, or with respect to any other matter relating to the activities of the company or such a subsidiary.

(2A) Where a director of a public airport company is a member of the executive of any such council as is mentioned in subsection (1)(*a*) or (*b*) above which are operating executive arrangements under Part II of the Local Government Act 2000, he shall not, in the course of the discharge of any function that is the responsibility of that executive, take any action in the consideration, or the making of any decision with respect to—

(*a*) any contract or proposed contract between the company or a subsidiary of the company and the council; or

(*b*) any matter relating to the activities of the company or such a subsidiary.

(3) Any person who contravenes paragraph (*a*) or (*b*) of subsection (2) or any person who contravenes subsection (2A) shall be guilty of an offence and liable on summary conviction to a fine not exceeding **the fourth level** on the standard scale, unless he proves that he did not know that the matter in relation to which the contravention occurred was such a contract or proposed contract as is mentioned in that paragraph or (as the case may be) was a matter otherwise relating to the activities of the company or subsidiary concerned.

(4) A prosecution for an offence under this section shall not, in England and Wales, be instituted except by or on behalf of the Director of Public Prosecutions.

(5) A principal council who are the controlling authority of a public airport company or one of the constituent councils of such an authority may by standing orders provide for the exclusion of a member of the council who is a director of the company from a meeting of the council while there is under consideration by the council—

(*a*) any contract or proposed contract between the company or a subsidiary of the company and the council, or

(*b*) any other matter relating to the activities of the company or such a subsidiary.

(6) Subsections (2) and (5) above shall apply in relation to members of—

(*a*) a committee of any principal council who are the controlling authority of a public airport company or one of the constituent councils of such an authority, or

(*b*) a joint committee of two or more local authorities one or more of whom are such a council,

(including, in either case, a sub-committee) as they apply in relation to members of any such council, but with the substitution of references to meetings of any such committee for references to meetings of the council.

(7) This section shall apply in relation to a director of a subsidiary of a public airport company as it applies in relation to a director of such a company.

[Airports Act 1986, s 18.]

7–5685 19. Prohibition on employment by public airport company of officers etc of controlling authority. (1) No person who is a full-time officer or employee of a principal council shall hold any office or employment under an associated company except as a director who is not also an employee of the company.

(2) Any person who contravenes subsection (1) shall be guilty of an offence and liable on summary conviction to a fine not exceeding **the fourth level** on the standard scale.

[Airports Act 1986, s 19.]

7–5686

PART III[1]

REGULATION OF USE OF AIRPORTS ETC

---

1. Part III contains ss 29–35.

PART IV[1]

ECONOMIC REGULATION OF AIRPORTS

Permissions

7–5687 37. Airports subject to economic regulation: requirement for permission to levy airport charges. Where an airport is subject to economic regulation under this Part no airport charges shall be levied at the airport unless—(*a*) they are levied by the airport operator, and (*b*) a permission to levy airport charges is for the time being in force in respect of the airport.

[Airports Act 1986, s 37—summarised.]

---

1. Part IV contains ss 36–56.

Conditions

7–5688 39. Imposition of conditions by CAA. So long as a permission is for the time being in force under this Part in respect of an airport, the airport operator shall comply with such conditions as are for the time being in force in relation to the airport by virtue of the provisions of this Part.

[Airports Act 1986, s 39—summarised.]

7–5689 40. Mandatory conditions in case of designated airports. Where an airport is designated for the purposes of this section by an order[1] made by the Secretary of State at a time when a permission under this Part is granted, or at the later time, the CAA shall impose in relation to the airport such conditions as to accounts and airport charges as are specified.
[Airports Act 1986, s 40—summarised.]

---

1. See the Economic Regulation of Airports (Designation) Order 1986, SI 1986/1502.

7–5690 41. Discretionary conditions. The CAA may, if it thinks fit in the case of any airport which is not a designated airport, impose in relation to the airport such conditions as are mentioned in section 40(2), either at the time of granting a permission under this Part in respect of the airport or at any other time while it is in force.
[Airports Act 1986, s 41—summarised.]

Enforcement of conditions

7–5691 50. Breach of accounts conditions: criminal penalties etc. (1) Any airport operator who fails to comply with any condition imposed in accordance with section 40(2)(*a*) (in pursuance of either section 40(1) or section 41(1)) shall be guilty of an offence and liable[1]—

(*a*) on summary conviction, to a fine not exceeding **the statutory maximum**;
(*b*) on conviction on indictment, to a **fine**.

(2) Any airport operator who, in the case of any condition imposed in accordance with section 40(2)(*b*) (in pursuance of either section 40(1) or section 41(1)), fails to comply with that condition before the end of the period allowed for compliance with it by virtue of that or any other such condition shall be guilty of an offence and liable—

(*a*) on summary conviction, to a fine not exceeding **the fifth level** on the standard scale; and
(*b*) on a second or subsequent summary conviction, to a fine of **one-tenth** of the amount corresponding to that level for each day on which the contravention is continued.

(3) Where an airport operator has failed to comply with any such condition as is mentioned in subsection (1) above, then (whether or not proceedings are brought under that subsection in respect of that contravention) the CAA may impose, in relation to the airport to which the contravention relates, such conditions as the CAA considers appropriate with respect to the publication of any matter to whose non-disclosure the contravention relates; and if the airport operator fails to comply with any condition so imposed before the end of the period allowed for compliance with it by virtue of that or any other such condition he shall be guilty of an offence and liable as mentioned in paragraphs (*a*) and (*b*) of subsection (2).

(4) In any proceedings for an offence under this section it shall be a defence for the person charged to prove—

(*a*) in the case of an offence under subsection (1), that he took all reasonable steps for securing compliance with the condition in question;
(*b*) in the case of an offence under subsection (2) or (3), that he took all reasonable steps for securing compliance with the condition in question before the end of the period mentioned in that subsection.

(5) Any reference in this section to an airport operator failing to comply with a condition is a reference to his failing to do so in contravention of section 39(1).
[Airports Act 1986, s 50.]

---

1. For procedure in respect of an offence which is triable either way, see the Magistrates' Courts Act 1980, ss 17A–21, in PART I: MAGISTRATES' COURTS, PROCEDURE, ante.

7–5692

PART V[1]
STATUS OF CERTAIN AIRPORT OPERATORS AS STATUTORY UNDERTAKERS ETC

---

1. Part V contains s 57–62.

PART VI[1]
MISCELLANEOUS AND SUPPLEMENTARY

Byelaws

7–5693 63. Airport byelaws. (1) Where an airport is either—

(*a*) designated[2] for the purposes of this section by an order made by the Secretary of State, or
(*b*) managed by the Secretary of State,

the airport operator (whether the Secretary of State or some other person) may make byelaws for regulating the use and operation of the airport and the conduct of all persons while within the airport.

(2) Any such byelaws may, in particular, include byelaws—

(a) for securing the safety of aircraft, vehicles and persons using the airport and preventing danger to the public arising from the use and operation of the airport;

(b) for controlling the operation of aircraft within, or directly above, the airport for the purpose of limiting or mitigating the effect of noise, vibration and atmospheric pollution caused by aircraft using the airport;

(c) for preventing obstruction within the airport;

(d) for regulating vehicular traffic anywhere within the airport, except on roads within the airport to which the road traffic enactments apply, and in particular (with that exception) for imposing speed limits on vehicles within the airport and for restricting or regulating the parking of vehicles or their use for any purpose or in any manner specified in the byelaws;

(e) for prohibiting waiting by hackney carriages except at standings appointed by such person as may be specified in the byelaws;

(f) for prohibiting or restricting access to any part of the airport;

(g) for preserving order within the airport and preventing damage to property within it;

(h) for regulating or restricting advertising within the airport;

(i) for requiring any person, if so requested by a constable or airport official, to leave the airport or any particular part of it, or to state his name and address and the purpose of his being within the airport;

(j) for securing the safe custody and redelivery of any property which, while not in proper custody, is found within the airport or in an aircraft within the airport, and in particular—

(i) for requiring charges to be paid in respect of any such property before it is redelivered; and

(ii) for authorising the disposal of any such property if it is not redelivered before the end of such period as may be specified in the byelaws;

(k) for restricting the area which is to be taken as constituting the airport for the purposes of the byelaws.

(3) In paragraph (d) of subsection (2) "the road traffic enactments" means the enactments (whether passed before or after this Act) relating to road traffic, including the lighting and parking of vehicles, and any order or other instrument having effect by virtue of any such enactment.

(4) In paragraph (i) of subsection (2) "airport official" means a person authorised by the airport operator; and any such official shall not exercise any power under a byelaw made by virtue of that paragraph without producing written evidence of his authority if required to do so.

(5)–(6) *Procedure for making byelaws.*

(7) Any byelaws made by the Secretary of State under this section shall be made by statutory instrument.

(8) Section 236(9) of the Local Government Act 1972[3] and section 202(13) of the Local Government (Scotland) Act 1973 (notice of byelaws made by one local authority to be given to another) and section 237 of the Act of 1972 and section 203 of the Act of 1973 (penalties) shall not apply to any byelaws made by a local authority under this section.

[Airports Act 1986, s 63.]

---

1. Part VI contains ss 63–85.

2. The following airports in England and Wales have been designated: Biggin Hill, Birmingham, Blackpool, Bournemouth (Hurn), Bristol, Cardiff-Wales, Coventry, East Midlands, Exeter, Humberside, Leeds/Bradford, Liverpool, London-Gatwick, London-Heathrow, London-Stansted, Luton, Manchester, Newcastle, Norwich, Southampton, Southend, Tees-side (Airport Byelaws (Designation) Order 1987, SI 1987/380), Bembridge, Carlisle, Gloucester/Cheltenham, Redhill and Swansea: (Airport Byelaws (Designation) (No 2) Order 1987, SI 1987/2246); Doncaster Sheffield Airport (Airport Byelaws (Designation) Order 2005, SI 2005/354.

3. See PART VIII title LOCAL GOVERNMENT, post.

7–5694 64. Byelaws: penalties and power to revoke in certain cases. (1) Any person contravening any byelaws made under section 63 shall be liable on summary conviction to a fine not exceeding such amount as, subject to subsection (2) of this section, may be specified by the byelaws in relation to the contravention.

(2) The maximum fines that byelaws may specify by virtue of subsection (1) are fines of an amount at the fourth level on the standard scale or of a lower amount.

(3) Where any person other than the Secretary of State has made any byelaw in relation to any airport by virtue of section 63(2)(b), the Secretary of State may, after consulting that person, by order—

(a) revoke or vary that byelaw if the Secretary of State considers it appropriate to do so by reason of his having designated the airport for the purposes of section 78 of the 1982 Act (regulation of noise and vibration from aircraft); or

(b) revoke or vary that byelaw to the extent that it appears to the Secretary of State to be inconsistent with the safety of persons or vehicles using the airport, of aircraft or of the general public or to be inconsistent with any international obligation of the United Kingdom.

[Airports Act 1986, s 64.]

Other provisions relating to airports

7–5695   65. Control of road traffic at designated airports.   (1) Subject to the provisions of this section, the road traffic enactments shall apply in relation to roads which are within a designated airport but to which the public does not have access as they apply in relation to roads to which the public has access.

(2) The Secretary of State may by order direct that in their application to roads within such an airport the road traffic enactments shall have effect subject to such modifications as appear to him necessary or expedient for the purpose of, or in consequence of, conferring—

(*a*)   on the airport operator functions exercisable under those enactments by a highway authority or local authority; or

(*b*)   on the chief officer of any airport constabulary functions so exercisable by a chief officer of police.

(3) An order under subsection (2) may exempt from the application of the road traffic enactments particular roads or lengths of road to which the public does not have access and may require the airport operator to indicate the roads or lengths of roads so exempted in such manner as may be specified in the order.

(4) Before making an order under this section in relation to any airport (other than one managed by the Secretary of State) the Secretary of State shall consult the airport operator.

(5) Any road or place within an airport in the metropolitan police district shall be deemed to be a street or place within the meaning of section 35 of the London Hackney Carriage Act 1831.

(6) In this section—

"airport constabulary" means, in relation to an airport owned or managed by the Secretary of State, the special constables appointed under section 57 of the 1982 Act and, in relation to any airport owned or managed by a local authority, any body of constables which the authority have power to maintain at that airport;

"designated airport" means an airport which is designated for the purposes of this section by an order made by the Secretary of State; and

"the road traffic enactments" has the meaning given by section 63(3).

(7) *Scotland.*
[Airports Act 1986, s 65.]

7–5696   66. Functions of operators of designated airports as respects abandoned vehicles.
(1) The Secretary of State may by order[1] direct that, in their application to land within any designated airport, the provisions of—

(*a*)   sections 3, 4 and 5 of the Refuse Disposal (Amenity) Act 1978 (powers and duties of local authorities to remove and dispose of vehicles abandoned on land in their area) and section 8 of that Act (powers of entry etc) so far as relating to section 3 of that Act, and

(*b*)   any regulations for the time being in force under any of those sections,

shall have effect subject to such modifications as appear to him necessary or expedient for the purpose of, or in consequence of, conferring on the airport operator the functions exercisable under those provisions by local authorities or local authorities of any description.

(2) In relation to the provisions of—

(*a*)   sections 99 to 102 of the Road Traffic Regulation Act 1984 (removal of vehicles from roads if illegally, obstructively or dangerously parked or broken down, and from roads or open land if abandoned), and

(*b*)   any regulations for the time being in force under any of those sections,

the powers of the Secretary of State under section 65(2) shall be exercisable not only as respects the application of those provisions to roads within an airport but also as respects their application to other land within the airport.

(3) Where the provisions of—

(*a*)   section 3 of the Refuse Disposal (Amenity) Act 1978,

(*b*)   section 99, 100 or 102 of the Road Traffic Regulation Act 1984, or

(*c*)   any regulations for the time being in force under any of those sections,

apply to any land within any airport in accordance with an order made under or by virtue of this section, those provisions shall have effect in relation to vehicles in a building on that land which is used for providing facilities for the parking of vehicles as they have effect in relation to vehicles on land in the open air.

(4) Before making an order under subsection (1) in relation to an airport (other than one managed by the Secretary of State) the Secretary of State shall consult the airport operator.

(5) In this section—

"designated airport" means an airport which is designated for the purposes of this section by an order made by the Secretary of State; and

"the road traffic enactments" has the meaning given by section 63(3).
[Airports Act 1986, s 66.]

---

1. The Airport (Designation) (Removal and Disposal of Vehicles) Order 1990, SI 1990/54 amended by SI 1993/2117 and SI 2000/707 has been made.

Supplementary

7-5697 73. Furnishing of information etc to CAA. (1) The CAA may by notice in writing served on any person require him at such time or times as may be specified in the notice—

(*a*) to produce to the CAA such documents or descriptions of documents specified in the notice, and

(*b*) to furnish to the CAA, in such form as may be specified in the notice, such accounts, estimates, returns or other information,

as the CAA may reasonably require for the purpose of performing its functions under this Act or for the purpose of giving any advice, assistance or information to the Secretary of State in connection with the performance by him of any functions under this Act.

(2) A person shall not by virtue of subsection (1) be compelled—

(*a*) to produce any documents which he could not be compelled to produce in civil proceedings before the High Court or (in Scotland) the Court of Session, or

(*b*) in complying with any requirement for the furnishing of information, to give any information which he could not be compelled to give in evidence in such proceedings.

(3) Any person who fails without reasonable excuse to comply with the requirements of a notice served on him under subsection (1) shall be guilty of an offence and liable on summary conviction to a fine not exceeding **the fifth level** on the standard scale.

(4) Any person who, in purported compliance with the requirements of any such notice, knowingly or recklessly furnishes information which is false in a material particular shall be guilty of an offence and liable[1]—

(*a*) on summary conviction, to a fine not exceeding **the statutory maximum**;

(*b*) on conviction on indictment, to a **fine**.
[Airports Act 1986, s 73.]

---

1. For procedure in respect of an offence which is traible either way, see the Magistrates' Courts Act 1980, ss 17A–21, in PART I: MAGISTRATES' COURTS, PROCEDURE, ante.

7-5698 74. Restriction on disclosure of information. (1) Subject to the following provisions of this section, no information with respect to any particular business which has been obtained under or by virtue of the provisions of this Act shall, so long as the business continues to be carried on, be disclosed without the consent of the person for the time being carrying it on.

(2) Subsection (1) does not apply to any disclosure of information which is made—

(*a*) for the purpose of facilitating the performance of any functions under this Act or any of the enactments or subordinate legislation specified in subsection (3) of any Minister, any Northern Ireland department, the head of any such department, the CAA, the Commission, the Director General of Fair Trading, the Water Services Regulation Authority, the Gas and Electricity Markets Authority, the Director General of Electricity Supply for Northern Ireland, the Office of Rail Regulation or a local weights and measures authority in Great Britain;

(*b*) in connection with the investigation of any criminal offence or for the purposes of any criminal proceedings;

(*c*) for the purposes of any civil proceedings brought under or by virtue of this Act or any of the enactments or subordinate legislation specified in subsection (3);

(*d*) in pursuance of any Community obligation.

(3) The enactments or subordinate legislation referred to in subsection (2) are—

(*a*) the Trade Descriptions Act 1968;

(*b*) the Fair Trading Act 1973;

(*c*) the Consumer Credit Act 1974;

(*d*) *Repealed*;

(*e*) *Repealed*;

(*f*) the Estate Agents Act 1979;

(*g*) the Competition Act 1980;

(*h*) the 1982 Act and any Order in Council made under section 60 of that Act (Air Navigation Orders);

(*i*) the Consumer Protection Act 1987;

(*j*) the Control of Misleading Advertisements Regulations 1988;

(*k*) the Water Act 1989, the Water Industry Act 1991 or any of the other consolidation Acts (within the meaning of section 206 of that Act of 1991);

(*l*) the Electricity Act 1989;

(*m*) Northern Ireland;

(*n*) the Railways Act 1993;

(*o*) the EC Competition Law (Articles 84 and 85) Enforcement Regulations 2001;

(*p*) the Competition Act 1998;

(*q*) Part I of the Transport Act 2000;

(*r*) the Enterprise Act 2002;

(*s*) the Railways Act 2005.

(4) Nothing in subsection (1) shall be construed—

(*a*) as limiting the matters which may be included in, or made public as part of, a report of the Commission under section 45; or

(*b*) as applying to any information which has been made public as part of such a report.

(5) Any person who discloses any information in contravention of this section shall be guilty of an offence and liable[1]—

(*a*) on summary conviction, to a fine not exceeding **the statutory maximum**;

(*b*) on conviction on indictment, to imprisonment for a term not exceeding **two years** or to a **fine**, or to **both**.

(6) In this section "the Commission" means the Competition Commission.

[Airports Act 1986, s 74, as amended by the Consumer Protection Act 1987, Schs 4 and 5 and the Water Act 1989, Sch 25, amended by SI 1988/915, the Electricity Act 1989, Sch 16, the Water Consolidation (Consequential Provisions) Act 1991, Sch 1, SI 1992/231, the Railways Act 1993, Sch 12, the Utilities Act 2000, s 3, SI 1996/2199, SI 1999/506, SI 2000/311, SI 2001/2916, SI 2001/4050, the Railways and Transport Safety Act 2003, Sch 2, the Water Act 2003, Sch 7 and the Railways Act 2005, Sch 12.]

---

*Words substituted by the Water Act 2003, s 105 from a date to be appointed.

1. For procedure in respect of an offence which is triable either way, see the Magistrates' Courts Act 1980, ss 17A–21, in PART I: MAGISTRATES' COURTS, PROCEDURE, ante.

7–5699 78. Offences by bodies corporate.   (1) Where a body corporate is guilty of an offence under this Act and that offence is proved to have been committed with the consent or connivance of, or to be attributable to any neglect on the part of, any director, manager, secretary or other similar officer of the body corporate or any person who was purporting to act in any such capacity he, as well as the body corporate, shall be guilty of an offence and shall be liable to be proceeded against and punished accordingly.

(2) Where the affairs of a body corporate are managed by its members, subsection (1) shall apply in relation to the acts and defaults of a member in connection with his functions of management as if he were a director of the body corporate.

[Airports Act 1986, s 78.]

7–5710 79. Orders and regulations.   *Power of the Secretary of State to make an order or regulations shall be exercisable by statutory instrument.*

7–5711 82. General interpretation.   (1) In this Act—

"the 1975 Act" means the Airports Authority Act 1975;

"the 1982 Act" means the Civil Aviation Act 1982;

"airport" means the aggregate of the land, buildings and works comprised in an aerodrome within the meaning of the 1982 Act;

"airport operator" means the person for the time being having the management of an airport, or, in relation to a particular airport, the management of that airport;

"air transport services" means services for the carriage by air of passengers or cargo;

"the appointed day" means the day appointed under section 2(1);

"the BAA" means the British Airports Authority;

"the CAA" means the Civil Aviation Authority;

"cargo" includes mail;

"debenture" includes debenture stock;

"functions" includes powers and duties;

"modifications" includes additions, omissions and amendments;

"operator", in relation to an aircraft, means the person for the time being having the management of the aircraft;

"the registrar of companies" has the same meaning as in the Companies Act 1985;

"securities", in relation to a company, includes shares, debentures, bonds and other securities of the company, whether or not constituting a charge on the assets of the company;

"shares" includes stock;

"subordinate legislation" has the same meaning as in the Interpretation Act 1978;

"subsidiary" has the meaning given by section 736 of the Companies Act 1985;

"the successor company" means the company nominated for the purposes of section 2;

"user", in relation to an airport, means—

(*a*) a person for whom any services or facilities falling within the definition of "relevant activities" in section 36(1) are provided at the airport, or

(*b*) a person using any of the air transport services operating from the airport.

(2) A company shall be regarded for the purposes of this Act as wholly owned by the Crown at any time when each of the issued shares in the company is held by, or by a nominee of, the Treasury or the Secretary of State.

(3) Any reference in section 14 or 37 to the business carried on at any airport by the airport operator shall, in a case where the person for the time being having the management of the airport has not had its management for the whole or any part of any period relevant for the purposes of that section, be construed as including a reference to the business carried on there by any other person who had the management of the airport for the whole or any part of that period.

(4) For the purposes of this Act a body corporate shall be treated as an associated company of an airport operator if either that body or the airport operator is a body corporate of which the other is a subsidiary or if both of them are subsidiaries of one and the same body corporate.

[Airports Act 1986, s 82, as amended by the Companies Act 1989, Sch 18.]

7–5712 85. *Short title, commencement and extent.*

Outer Space Act 1986[1]

(1986 c 38)

Note

7–5713

The Outer Space Act 1986 is not printed in this work. The Act confers licensing and other powers on the Secretary of State to secure compliance with the international obligations of the United Kingdom with respect to the launching and operation of space objects and the carrying on of other activities in outer space by United Kingdom nationals or bodies incorporated under the law of any part of the United Kingdom.

If a justice of the peace is satisfied by information on oath that there are reasonable grounds for believing that an activity to which the Act applies is being carried on by a person in contravention of the licensing requirements of section 3 of the Act, or in contravention of the conditions of a licence, he may, in certain circumstances, issue a warrant authorising a named person acting on behalf of the Secretary of State to do anything necessary to secure compliance with the international obligation of the United Kingdom or with the conditions of the licence. The warrant shall specify the action so authorised. A warrant remains in force for 1 month from the date of its issue (s 9).

It is an offence punishable on indictment to a fine or summarily to a fine not exceeding the statutory maximum to carry on an activity to which the Act applies without being licensed, knowingly or recklessly making a false statement to obtain a licence, failing to comply with the conditions of a licence or a direction of the Secretary of State, or intentionally obstructing a person in the exercise of powers conferred by warrant under s 9. Proceedings for an offence committed outside the United Kingdom may be taken and the offence may be treated as having been committed in any place in the United Kingdom. It is a defence for the accused to show he used all due diligence and took all reasonable precautions to avoid the commission of an offence (s 12).

For the full text of the Act, see Halsbury's Statutes, Fourth Edition, Vol 4, pp 415–427.

---

1. This Act was to be brought into force on such day as the Secretary of State might appoint (s 15(2)). The appointed day was 31 July 1989 (SI 1989/1097).

Transport Act 2000[1]

(2000 c 38)

PART I[2]
AIR TRAFFIC

CHAPTER I[3]
AIR TRAFFIC SERVICES

Restrictions

7–5714 3. Restrictions on providing services. (1) A person commits an offence if he provides air traffic services[4] in respect of a managed area[5].

(2) But subsection (1) is subject to subsections (3) to (5).

(3) Subsection (1) does not apply if the person—

(*a*) is authorised by an exemption to provide the services, or (*b*) acts as an employee or agent of a person who is authorised by an exemption to provide the services.

(4) Subsection (1) does not apply if the person—

(*a*) holds a licence authorising him to provide the services, or

(*b*) acts as an employee or agent of a person who is authorised by a licence to provide the services.

(5) Subsection (1) does not apply if the services are provided by the CAA in pursuance of directions under section 66(1).

(6) For the purposes of this section—

(*a*) air traffic services are to be treated as provided at the place from which they are provided;

(*b*) air traffic services may be provided in respect of a managed area whether or not the aircraft concerned is in that area when they are provided.

(7) A person who commits an offence under this section is liable⁶—

(*a*) on summary conviction, to a fine not exceeding the statutory maximum;

(*b*) on conviction on indictment, to a fine.

(8) No proceedings may be started in England and Wales or Northern Ireland for an offence under this section except by or on behalf of—

(*a*) the Secretary of State, or

(*b*) the CAA acting with his consent.

[Transport Act 2000, s 3.]

---

1. Part I of this Act makes provision for the provision of air traffic services in respect of a "managed area" (except where an exemption has been granted) under the authority of a licence issued by the Secretary of State. This Act is brought into force in accordance with orders made under s 275. At the date of going to press the following commencement orders have been made: (No 1 and Transitional Provisions) SI 2000/3229; (No 2) SI 2000/3376; (No 3) SI 2001/57 amended by SI 2001/115; (No 4) SI 2001/242; (No 5) SI 2001/869; (No 6) SI 2001/1498; (No 7) SI 2001/3342; (No 1) (Wales) SI 2001/2788; (No 8 and Transitional Provisions) SI 2002/846; (No 9 and Transitional Provisions) SI 2002/1014; (No 2) (Wales) SI 2002/1730; (No 10) SI 2003/1694; (No 11) SI 2005/2862. All of the provisions reproduced here have been brought into force.

2. Part I contains ss 1–107 and Schs 1–9.

3. Chapter I contains ss 1–40 and Schs 1–5.

4. Defined in s 98.

5. Defined in s 40, post.

6. For procedure in respect of this offence which is triable either way see the Magistrates' Courts Act 1980, ss 17A–21 in PART I MAGISTRATES' COURTS, PROCEDURE, ante.

7–5715　4. *Exemptions*

7–5716　5–19. *Licences*

7–5717　38. Directions in interests of national security etc. (1) The Secretary of State may give to a licence holder or to licence holders generally such directions of a general character as he thinks are necessary or expedient—

(*a*) in the interests of national security, or

(*b*) in the interests of encouraging or maintaining the United Kingdom's relations with another country or territory.

(2) The Secretary of State may give to a licence holder a direction requiring it to do or not to do a particular thing, if the Secretary of State thinks it necessary or expedient to give the direction in the interests of national security.

(3) The Secretary of State may give to a licence holder a direction requiring it—

(*a*) to do or not to do a particular thing in connection with anything authorised by the licence, or

(*b*) to secure that a particular thing is done or not done in connection with anything authorised by the licence,

if the Secretary of State thinks it necessary or expedient to give the direction in order to discharge or facilitate the discharge of an international obligation of the United Kingdom.

(4) In exercising his powers under subsections (1) to (3) the Secretary of State must have regard to the need to maintain a high standard of safety in the provision of air traffic services.

(5) In so far as a direction under this section conflicts with the requirements of section 93 or of an order under section 94, the direction is to be disregarded.

(6) In so far as a direction under this section conflicts with the requirements of an enactment or instrument other than section 93 or an order under section 94, the requirements are to be disregarded.

(7) Before giving a direction under this section to a particular licence holder (as opposed to licence holders generally) the Secretary of State must consult it.

(8) The Secretary of State must send a copy of a direction under this section to the CAA.

(9) The Secretary of State must lay before each House of Parliament a copy of a direction under this section unless he thinks its disclosure is against the interests of national security or the interests

of the United Kingdom's relations with another country or territory or the commercial interests of any person.

(10) A person must not disclose, and is not required by any enactment or otherwise to disclose, a direction given or other thing done by virtue of this section if the Secretary of State notifies him that he thinks disclosure is against the interests of national security or the interests of the United Kingdom's relations with another country or territory or the commercial interests of any person (other than the person notified).

(11) A person commits an offence if—

(a) without reasonable excuse he contravenes or fails to comply with a direction under this section, or

(b) he makes a disclosure in contravention of subsection (10).

(12) A person who commits an offence under this section is liable[1]—

(a) on summary conviction, to a fine not exceeding the statutory maximum;

(b) on conviction on indictment, to a fine or imprisonment for a term not exceeding two years or both.

[Transport Act 2000, s 38.]

---

1. For procedure in respect of this offence which is triable either way see the Magistrates' Courts Act 1980, ss 17A–21 in PART I MAGISTRATES' COURTS, PROCEDURE , ante.

Interpretation

7–5718　40. Interpretation. (1) This section defines these expressions (here listed alphabetically) for the purposes of this Chapter—

(a) aerodrome;

(b) condition of a licence;

(c) exemption;

(d) licence;

(e) licence holder;

(f) managed area;

(g) manager of an aerodrome;

(h) modification.

(2) An aerodrome is an aerodrome as defined in section 105(1) of the Civil Aviation Act 1982; and a manager of an aerodrome is a person who is in charge of it or holds a licence granted in respect of it by virtue of section 60 of that Act (Chicago Convention, regulation of air navigation etc).

(3) These are managed areas—

(a) the United Kingdom;

(b) any area which is outside the United Kingdom but in respect of which the United Kingdom has undertaken under international arrangements to provide air traffic services.

(4) An exemption is an exemption under this Chapter.

(5) A licence is a licence under this Chapter, and references to a licence holder must be construed accordingly.

(6) A condition of a licence is a provision of the licence which is expressed as a condition.

(7) "Modification" includes addition, alteration and omission, and cognate expressions are to be construed accordingly.

[Transport Act 2000, s 40.]

CHAPTER III[1]
AIR NAVIGATION

7–5719　66–70. *Functions of the CAA with regard to air navigation (summarised).*

---

1. Chapter III contains ss 66–72 and Schs 6 and 7.

7–5720　71. Information for purposes of Chapter III. (1) The CAA may, for any purpose connected with its air navigation functions, serve on a person who provides air traffic services a notice which—

(a) requires the person to produce any documents which are specified or described in the notice and are in his custody or under his control, and to produce them at a time and place so specified and to a person so specified, or

(b) requires the person to supply information specified or described in the notice, and to supply it at a time and place and in a form and manner so specified and to a person so specified.

(2) A requirement may be made under subsection (1)(b) only if the person is carrying on a business.

(3) No person may be required under this section—

(*a*) to produce documents which he could not be compelled to produce in civil proceedings in the court;

(*b*) to supply information which he could not be compelled to supply in such proceedings.

(4) If a person without reasonable excuse fails to do anything required of him by a notice under subsection (1) he is guilty of an offence and liable on summary conviction to a fine not exceeding level 5 on the standard scale.

(5) If a person intentionally alters, suppresses or destroys a document which he has been required to produce by a notice under subsection (1) he is guilty of an offence and liable[1]—

(*a*) on summary conviction, to a fine not exceeding the statutory maximum;

(*b*) on conviction on indictment, to a fine.

(6) If a person makes default in complying with a notice under subsection (1) the court may on the CAA's application make such order as the court thinks fit for requiring the default to be made good.

(7) An order under subsection (6) may provide that all the costs or expenses of and incidental to the application are to be borne—

(*a*) by the person in default, or

(*b*) if officers of a company or other association are responsible for its default, by those officers.

(8) A reference to producing a document includes a reference to producing a legible and intelligible copy of information recorded otherwise than in legible form.

(9) A reference to suppressing a document includes a reference to destroying the means of reproducing information recorded otherwise than in legible form.

(10) A reference to the court is to—

(*a*) the High Court in relation to England and Wales or Northern Ireland;

(*b*) the Court of Session in relation to Scotland.

[Transport Act 2000, s 71.]

---

1. For procedure in respect of this offence which is triable either way see the Magistrates' Courts Act 1980, ss 17A–21 in PART I MAGISTRATES' COURTS, PROCEDURE, ante.

7–5721 72. Interpretation. (1) This section applies for the purposes of this Chapter.

(2) The CAA's air navigation functions are the functions which the CAA is to perform in pursuance of directions under section 66(1).

(3) These are managed areas—

(*a*) the United Kingdom;

(*b*) any area which is outside the United Kingdom but in respect of which the United Kingdom has undertaken under international arrangements to carry out activities with regard to air navigation.

[Transport Act 2000, s 72.]

CHAPTER IV[1]
CHARGES FOR AIR SERVICES

Miscellaneous

7–5722 81. Records. (1) The Secretary of State may make regulations[2] in order to facilitate the assessment and collection of charges payable by virtue of section 73.

(2) The regulations may require operators or owners of aircraft or managers of aerodromes—

(*a*) to make such records of the movements of aircraft, and of such other particulars relating to aircraft, as are specified;

(*b*) to preserve the records for a specified period;

(*c*) to produce relevant records for inspection by specified persons at specified times;

(*d*) to provide specified particulars of relevant records to specified persons.

(3) Relevant records are records required to be preserved by the operators, owners or managers by the regulations or an Air Navigation Order.

(4) The persons who may be specified under subsection (2)(*c*) or (*d*) are—

(*a*) in the case of charges payable to Eurocontrol, officers of the CAA or of Eurocontrol;

(*b*) in the case of other charges, officers of the CAA or of the organisation, government or other person to whom the charges are payable.

(5) The requirements may be imposed on the operator or owner of an aircraft whether or not—

(*a*) it is registered in the United Kingdom;

(*b*) it is in the United Kingdom when the services concerned are provided;

(*c*) the services concerned are provided from a place in the United Kingdom.

(6) A record includes (in addition to a record in writing)—

(*a*) a disc, tape, sound-track or other device in which sounds or signals are embodied so as to be capable of being reproduced from it (with or without the aid of some other instrument);

(b) a film, tape or other device in which visual images are embodied so as to be capable of being reproduced from it (with or without the aid of some other instrument);

(c) a photograph.

(7) An Air Navigation Order is an Order in Council under section 60 of the Civil Aviation Act 1982.

(8) In subsection (4)—

(a) a reference to officers of the CAA includes a reference to persons authorised to act as such officers;

(b) a reference to officers of Eurocontrol includes a reference to persons authorised to act as such officers.

[Transport Act 2000, s 81.]

---

1. Chapter IV contains ss 73–84.
2. The Civil Aviation (Chargeable Air Services)(Records) Regulations 2001, SI 2001/399 have been made.

7–5723   82. Offences.   (1) A person commits an offence if without reasonable excuse he fails to comply with a requirement of regulations made under section 81.

(2) A person commits an offence if he is in possession of information provided to him or obtained by him under regulations made under section 81 and he discloses the information otherwise than—

(a) with the consent of the person by whom it was provided or from whom it was obtained,

(b) for the purposes of the regulations,

(c) for the purposes of any proceedings arising out of this Chapter,

(d) for the purposes of any criminal proceedings (however arising),

(e) for the purposes of any proceedings brought by virtue of paragraph 3 of Schedule 4 to the Civil Aviation Act 1982 (claims against Eurocontrol),

(f) for the purposes of a public inquiry or investigation held or carried out under regulations made under section 75 of the Civil Aviation Act 1982, or

(g) for the purposes of a report of any proceedings, inquiry or investigation mentioned above.

(3) A person commits an offence if in providing particulars under a provision contained in regulations by virtue of section 81(2)(d)—

(a) he provides particulars which he knows are false in a material particular, or

(b) he recklessly provides particulars which are false in a material particular.

(4) A person who commits an offence under subsection (1) is liable on summary conviction to a fine not exceeding level 3 on the standard scale.

(5) A person who commits an offence under subsection (2) is liable on summary conviction to a fine not exceeding level 3 on the standard scale or to imprisonment for a term not exceeding 3 months or to both.

(6) A person who commits an offence under subsection (3) is liable[1]—

(a) on summary conviction, to a fine not exceeding the statutory maximum or to imprisonment for a term not exceeding 3 months or to both;

(b) on conviction on indictment, to a fine or to imprisonment for a term not exceeding 2 years or to both.

[Transport Act 2000, s 82.]

---

1. For procedure in respect of this offence which is triable either way see the Magistrates' Courts Act 1980, ss 17A–21 in PART I MAGISTRATES' COURTS, PROCEDURE, ante.

Interpretation

7–5724   84. Interpretation.   (1) This section applies for the purposes of this Chapter.

(2) Eurocontrol has the meaning given by section 24 of the Civil Aviation Act 1982.

(3) The Eurocontrol agreement is the multilateral agreement relating to route charges signed at Brussels on 12 February 1981 or any agreement replacing it.

(4) An aerodrome is an aerodrome as defined in section 105(1) of the Civil Aviation Act 1982; and a manager of an aerodrome is a person who is in charge of it or holds a licence granted in respect of it by virtue of section 60 of that Act (Chicago Convention, regulation of air navigation etc).

(5) "Licence holder" has the meaning given by section 40.

[Transport Act 2000, s 84.]

CHAPTER VI[1]

MISCELLANEOUS AND GENERAL

General interpretation

7–5725   98. Air traffic services.   (1) For the purposes of this Part these are air traffic services—

(a) providing instructions, information or advice with a view to preventing aircraft colliding with other aircraft or with other obstructions (whether in the air or on the ground);

(b)　providing instructions, information or advice with a view to securing safe and efficient flying;
(c)　managing the flow of air traffic with a view to ensuring the most efficient use of airspace;
(d)　providing facilities for communicating with aircraft and for the navigation and surveillance of aircraft;
(e)　notifying organisations of aircraft needing search and rescue facilities, and assisting organisations to provide such facilities.

(2)　The Secretary of State may by order amend the meaning of air traffic services for the purposes of this Part.
[Transport Act 2000, s 98.]

1.　Chapter VI contains ss 90–107 and Schs 8 and 9.

7–5726　99. The CAA.　For the purposes of this Part the CAA is the Civil Aviation Authority.
[Transport Act 2000, s 99.]

Other general provisions

7–5727　100. Service of documents.　(1)　A document required or authorised by virtue of this Part to be served on a person may be served—

(a)　by delivering it to him or by leaving it at his proper address or by sending it by post to him at that address;
(b)　if the person is a body corporate, by serving it in accordance with paragraph (a) on the secretary of the body;
(c)　if the person is a partnership, by serving it in accordance with paragraph (a) on a partner or a person having the control or management of the partnership business.

(2)　For the purposes of this section and section 7 of the Interpretation Act 1978 (service of documents by post) in its application to this section, the proper address of a person on whom a document is to be served is his last known address, except that—

(a)　in the case of service on a body corporate or its secretary, it is the address of the registered or principal office of the body;
(b)　in the case of service on a partnership or a partner or a person having the control or management of a partnership business, it is the address of the principal office of the partnership.

(3)　For the purposes of subsection (2) the principal office of a company constituted under the law of a country or territory outside the United Kingdom or of a partnership carrying on business outside the United Kingdom is its principal office within the United Kingdom.

(4)　Subsection (5) applies if a person to be served under this Part with a document by another has specified to that other an address within the United Kingdom other than his proper address (as determined under subsection (2)) as the one at which he or someone on his behalf will accept documents of the same description as that document.

(5)　In relation to that document that address must be treated as his proper address for the purposes of this section and section 7 of the Interpretation Act 1978 in its application to this section, instead of that determined under subsection (2).

(6)　This section does not apply to a document if rules of court make provision about its service.

(7)　In this section references to serving include references to similar expressions (such as giving or sending).
[Transport Act 2000, s 100.]

7–5728　101. Making of false statements etc.　(1)　A person commits an offence if in giving information or making an application in relevant circumstances—

(a)　he makes a statement which he knows to be false in a material particular, or
(b)　he recklessly makes a statement which is false in a material particular.

(2)　A person gives information or makes an application in relevant circumstances if he gives or makes it in pursuance of—

(a)　a provision contained in or made under this Part, or
(b)　a direction given, notice served or other thing done in pursuance of such a provision.

(3)　A person who commits an offence under this section is liable—

(a)　on summary conviction, to a fine not exceeding the statutory maximum;
(b)　on conviction on indictment, to a fine.

(4)　No proceedings may be started in England and Wales for an offence under this section except by or with the consent of the Secretary of State or the Director of Public Prosecutions.

(5)　No proceedings may be started in Northern Ireland for an offence under this section except

by or with the consent of the Secretary of State or the Director of Public Prosecutions for Northern Ireland.
[Transport Act 2000, s 101.]

7-5729   102. *Disclosure of information*

7-5730   103. *Orders and regulations*

7-5731   107. *Extension outside United Kingdom*

Railways and Transport Safety Act 2003[1]
(2003 c 20)

PART 5[2]
AVIATION: ALCOHOL AND DRUGS

Offences

7-5732   93. Prescribed limit.   (1) A person commits an offence if—

(a) he performs an aviation function at a time when the proportion of alcohol in his breath, blood or urine exceeds the prescribed limit, or

(b) he carries out an activity which is ancillary to an aviation function at a time when the proportion of alcohol in his breath, blood or urine exceeds the prescribed limit.

(2) The prescribed limit of alcohol is (subject to subsection (3))—

(a) in the case of breath, 9 microgrammes of alcohol in 100 millilitres,

(b) in the case of blood, 20 milligrammes of alcohol in 100 millilitres, and

(c) in the case of urine, 27 milligrammes of alcohol in 100 millilitres.

(3) In relation to the aviation function specified in section 94(1)(h) the prescribed limit is—

(a) in the case of breath, 35 microgrammes of alcohol in 100 millilitres,

(b) in the case of blood, 80 milligrammes of alcohol in 100 millilitres, and

(c) in the case of urine, 107 milligrammes of alcohol in 100 millilitres.

(4) The Secretary of State may make regulations amending subsection (2) or (3).

(5) Section 94 defines "aviation function" and "ancillary activity" for the purposes of this Part.
[Railways and Transport Safety Act 2003, s 93.]

---

1. This Act makes provision about railways, including tramways and transport safety. Reproduced in this title are those provisions relating to aviation, alcohol and drugs. Part 1 relating to railways is reproduced in PART VII: TRANSPORT, title RAILWAYS, Part 3 relating to the British Transport Police is reproduced in PART VIII, title POLICE and Part 4 relating to shipping, alcohol and drugs is reproduced in PART VII: TRANSPORT, title MERCHANT SHIPPING.

Sections 104 and 114 came into force on the passing of the Act (10 July 2003) and ss 105 and 112 came into force on 10 September 2003. The remaining provisions come into force in accordance with orders made under s 120. At the date of going to press the following commencement orders had been made: (No 1) SI 2003/2681 which brought into force on 31 October ss 111 and 115; (No 2) SI 2004/827; (No 3) SI 2004/1572; (No 4) SI 2004/2759; (No 5) SI 2005/1991. Part 5 was brought fully into force on 30 March 2004, except s 96 (in force 29 March 2004 for certain purposes).

2. Part 5 comprises ss 92–102.

7-5733   94. Aviation functions.   (1) For the purposes of this Part the following (and only the following) are aviation functions—

(a) acting as a pilot of an aircraft during flight,

(b) acting as flight navigator of an aircraft during flight,

(c) acting as flight engineer of an aircraft during flight,

(d) acting as flight radio-telephony operator of an aircraft during flight,

(e) acting as a member of the cabin crew of an aircraft during flight,

(f) attending the flight deck of an aircraft during flight to give or supervise training, to administer a test, to observe a period of practice or to monitor or record the gaining of experience,

(g) acting as an air traffic controller in pursuance of a licence granted under or by virtue of an enactment (other than a licence granted to a student), and

(h) acting as a licensed aircraft maintenance engineer.

(2) For the purposes of subsection (1)(h) a person acts as a licensed aircraft maintenance engineer if—

(a) he issues a document relating to the maintenance, condition or use of an aircraft or equipment in reliance on a licence granted under or by virtue of an enactment relating to aviation, or

(b) he carries out or supervises work on an aircraft or equipment with a view to, or in connection with, the issue by him of a document of the kind specified in paragraph (a).

(3) For the purposes of this Part a reference to an activity which is ancillary to an aviation function is a reference to anything which falls to be treated as such by virtue of subsections (4) to (6).

(4) An activity shall be treated as ancillary to an aviation function if it is undertaken—

(*a*) by a person who has reported for a period of duty in respect of the function, and

(*b*) as a requirement of, for the purpose of or in connection with the performance of the function during that period of duty.

(5) A person who in accordance with the terms of an employment or undertaking holds himself ready to perform an aviation function if called upon shall be treated as carrying out an activity ancillary to the function.

(6) Where a person sets out to perform an aviation function, anything which he does by way of preparing to perform the function shall be treated as an activity ancillary to it.

(7) For the purposes of this Part it is immaterial whether a person performs a function or carries out an activity in the course of an employment or trade or otherwise.

(8) The Secretary of State may by regulations—

(*a*) amend this section;

(*b*) make an amendment of this Part which is consequential on an amendment under paragraph (a).

[Railways and Transport Safety Act 2003, s 94.]

Enforcement

7–5734 95. Penalty. A person guilty of an offence under this Part shall be liable—

(*a*) on conviction on indictment, to imprisonment for a term not exceeding two years, to a fine or to both, or

(*b*) on summary conviction, to a fine not exceeding the statutory maximum.

[Railways and Transport Safety Act 2003, s 95.]

7–5735 96. Specimens, &c. (1) The provisions specified in the first column of the table below, with the modifications specified in the third column and any other necessary modifications, shall have effect in relation to an offence under this Part.

Provision	Description	Modification
Road Traffic Act 1988[1] (c 52)		
Section 6	Power to administer preliminary tests	In place of subsections (2) to (5) the power to require a person to co-operate with a preliminary test shall apply where—
		(*a*) a constable in uniform reasonably suspects that the person is committing an offence under section 92 or 93,
		(*b*) a constable in uniform reasonably suspects that the person has committed an offence under section 92 or 93 and still has alcohol or a drug in his body or is still under the influence of a drug,
		(*c*) an aircraft is involved in an accident and a constable reasonably suspects that the person was undertaking an aviation function, or an activity ancillary to an aviation function, in relation to the aircraft at the time of the accident, or
		(*d*) an aircraft is involved in an accident and a constable reasonably suspects that the person has undertaken an aviation function, or an activity ancillary to an aviation function, in relation to the aircraft.
Sections 6A to 6E	Preliminary breath test, impairment test, and drug test	In place of sections 6A(2) and (3), 6B(4) and 6C(2), a preliminary breath test, preliminary impairment test or preliminary drug test may be administered by a constable—

Provision	Description	Modification
		(*a*) at or near the place where the requirement to co-operate with the test is imposed, or
		(*b*) at a police station specified by the constable.
		In section 6B(3) a reference to unfitness to drive shall be treated as a reference to having an impaired ability, because of drink or drugs, to perform an aviation function or to carry out an activity which is ancillary to an aviation function.
Section 7	Provision of specimen	In subsection (1) the reference to an offence under section 3A, 4 or 5 of the 1988 Act shall be treated as a reference to an offence under section 92 or 93 of this Act.
		In subsection (3)(c) the reference to an offence under section 3A or 4 of the 1988 Act shall be treated as a reference to an offence under section 92 of this Act.
Section 7A	Specimen of blood taken from person incapable of consenting	
Section 8	Choice of specimen of breath	In subsection (2) the reference to 50 microgrammes of alcohol shall, except in relation to the aviation function specified in section 94(1)(*h*), be treated as a reference to 15 microgrammes of alcohol.
Section 9	Protection for hospital patient	
Section 10	Detention of person affected by alcohol or drug	In subsection (1)—
		(*a*) the reference to driving or attempting to drive a mechanically propelled vehicle on a road shall be treated as a reference to performing an aviation function of the kind in respect of which the requirement to provide a specimen was imposed, and
		(*b*) the reference to an offence under section 4 or 5 of the 1988 Act shall be treated as a reference to an offence under section 92 or 93 of this Act.
		In subsection (2) the reference to driving a mechanically propelled vehicle shall be treated as a reference to performing an aviation function.
		In subsection (3) the reference to driving properly shall be treated as a reference to performing an aviation function.
Section 11	Interpretation	For the definition of "the prescribed limit" there shall be substituted the definition given in this Part.

Provision	Description	Modification
Road Traffic Offenders Act 1988¹ (c 53)		
Section 15	Use of specimens	In subsection (1), the reference to an offence under section 3A, 4 or 5 of the Road Traffic Act 1988 shall be treated as a reference to an offence under section 92 or 93 of this Act.
		The relevant time for the consumption of alcohol for the purpose of subsection (3)(*a*) shall be before providing the specimen and after the time of the alleged offence.
		In subsection (3)(*b*) the reference to driving shall be treated as a reference to undertaking an aviation function or an activity ancillary to an aviation function.
Section 16	Documentary evidence	

(2) The Secretary of State may by regulations amend the table in subsection (1) so as—

(*a*) to add a provision relating to an offence which concerns alcohol or drugs in relation to road traffic;

(*b*) to add, remove or amend a modification (whether or not in connection with an amendment of a provision specified in the table).

(3) For the purpose of the application by subsection (1) of a provision listed in the table in that subsection—

(*a*) the provision shall extend to the whole of the United Kingdom, and

(*b*) a reference to the provision shall be treated, unless the context otherwise requires, as including a reference to the provision as applied.

[Railways and Transport Safety Act 2003, s 96.]

---

1. In this PART, ante.

7–5736 97. Arrest without warrant.   (1) A constable may arrest a person without a warrant if the constable reasonably suspects that the person—

(*a*) is committing an offence under section 92, or

(*b*) has committed an offence under that section and is still under the influence of drink or drugs.

(2) But a person may not be arrested under this section while he is at a hospital as a patient.

(3) In subsection (2) "hospital" means an institution which provides medical or surgical treatment for in-patients or out-patients.

(4) Arrest under this section shall be treated as arrest for an offence for the purposes of—

(*a*) Part IV of the Police and Criminal Evidence Act 1984 (c 60) (detention), and

(*b*) Part V of the Police and Criminal Evidence (Northern Ireland) Order 1989 (SI 1989/1341 (NI 12)) (detention).

[Railways and Transport Safety Act 2003, s 97.]

7–5737 98. Right of entry.   (1) A constable in uniform may board an aircraft if he reasonably suspects that he may wish to exercise a power by virtue of section 96 or under section 97 in respect of a person who is or may be on the aircraft.

(2) A constable in uniform may enter any place if he reasonably suspects that he may wish to exercise a power by virtue of section 96 or under section 97 in respect of a person who is or may be in that place.

(3) For the purposes of boarding an aircraft or entering a place under this section a constable—

(*a*) may use reasonable force;

(*b*) may be accompanied by one or more persons.

[Railways and Transport Safety Act 2003, s 98.]

General

7–5738 99. Regulations

7–5739 100. Crown application.   (1) This Part shall apply to a function or activity performed or carried out in relation to an aircraft which belongs to or is employed in the service of the Crown.

(2) This section is subject to section 101.
[Railways and Transport Safety Act 2003, s 100.]

7–5740 101. Military application. (1) This Part shall not apply to a function or activity which is performed or carried out by a member of Her Majesty's air forces, military forces or naval forces, within the meaning given by section 225(1) of the Army Act 1955 (c 18), acting in the course of his duties.

(2) This Part shall not apply to a function or activity which is performed or carried out by—

(a) a member of a visiting force, within the meaning which that expression has in section 3 of the Visiting Forces Act 1952 (c 67) by virtue of section 12(1) of that Act, acting in the course of his duties, or

(b) a member of a civilian component of a visiting force, within that meaning, acting in the course of his duties.

(3) This Part shall not apply to a function or activity which is performed or carried out by a military or civilian member of a headquarters, within the meaning given by paragraphs 1 and 2 of the Schedule to the International Headquarters and Defence Organisations Act 1964 (c 5), acting in the course of his duties.
[Railways and Transport Safety Act 2003, s 101.]

7–5741 102. Territorial application. (1) This Part applies in relation to—

(a) a function or activity performed or carried out in the United Kingdom, and

(b) a flight function performed or flight activity carried out on a United Kingdom aircraft.

(2) In subsection (1)—

"flight function" means a function falling within section 94(1)(a) to (f),

"flight activity" means an activity which for the purposes of this Part is ancillary to a flight function, and

"United Kingdom aircraft" means an aircraft which is registered, in accordance with an enactment about aircraft, in the United Kingdom.

(3) Her Majesty may by Order in Council direct that a provision of this Part shall apply (with or without modification)—

(a) to a function or activity performed or carried out in any of the Channel Islands or a British overseas territory;

(b) to a function performed or activity carried out on an aircraft which is registered, in accordance with an enactment about aircraft, in any of the Channel Islands or a British overseas territory.

(4) Section 98 shall not extend to Scotland.

(5) Subsection (4) does not affect any rule of law or enactment concerning the right of a constable in Scotland to board an aircraft or enter any place for any purpose.
[Railways and Transport Safety Act 2003, s 102.]

Air Navigation Order 2005[1]
(SI 2005/1970)

7–5821 1. Citation and Commencement. This Order may be cited as the Air Navigation Order 2005 and shall come into force on 20th August 2005.

---

1. Made under s 2(2) of the European Communities Act 1972, ss 60 (other than sub-s (3)(r)), 61, 77, 101 and 102 and Schedule 13 to the Civil Aviation Act 1982 and s 35 of the Airports Act 1986.

2. Revocation

PART 1[1]
REGISTRATION AND MARKING OF AIRCRAFT

7–5822 3. Aircraft to be registered[2]. (1) Subject to paragraphs (2), (3) and (4) an aircraft shall not fly in or over the United Kingdom unless it is registered in—

(a) some part of the Commonwealth;

(b) a Contracting State; or

(c) some other country in relation to which there is in force an agreement between Her Majesty's Government in the United Kingdom and the Government of that country which makes provision for the flight over the United Kingdom of aircraft registered in that country.

(2) A non-EASA glider may fly unregistered, and shall be deemed to be registered in the United Kingdom for the purposes of articles 19, 20, 26 and 52, on any flight which—

(a) begins and ends in the United Kingdom without passing over any other country; and

(b) is not for the purpose of public transport or aerial work other than aerial work which consists of the giving of instruction in flying or the conducting of flying tests in a glider owned or operated by a flying club of which the person giving the instruction or conducting the test and the person receiving the instruction or undergoing the test are both members.

(3) Any non-EASA aircraft may fly unregistered on any flight which—

(a) begins and ends in the United Kingdom without passing over any other country, and
(b) is in accordance with the B Conditions.

(4) Paragraph (1) shall not apply to any non-EASA kite or non-EASA captive balloon.

(5) If an aircraft flies over the United Kingdom in contravention of paragraph (1) in such manner or circumstances that if the aircraft had been registered in the United Kingdom an offence against this Order or any regulations made thereunder would have been committed, the like offence shall be deemed to have been committed in respect of that aircraft.

---

1. Part 1 comprises arts 3–5.
2. Penalties for contraventions are contained in art 148 and Sch 14, post.

4. Registration of aircraft in the United Kingdom

7–5823   5. Nationality and registration marks[1]. (1) An aircraft (other than an aircraft permitted by or under this Order to fly without being registered) shall not fly unless it bears painted thereon or affixed thereto, in the manner required by the law of the country in which it is registered, the nationality and registration marks required by that law.

(2) The marks to be borne by aircraft registered in the United Kingdom shall comply with Part B of Schedule 2[2].

(3) Subject to paragraph (4), an aircraft shall not bear any marks which purport to indicate—

(a) that the aircraft is registered in a country in which it is not in fact registered; or
(b) that the aircraft is a State aircraft of a particular country if it is not in fact such an aircraft, unless the appropriate authority of that country has sanctioned the bearing of such marks.

(4) Marks approved by the CAA for the purposes of flight in accordance with the B Conditions shall be deemed not to purport to indicate that the aircraft is registered in a country in which it is not in fact registered.

---

1. Penalties for contraventions are contained in art 148 and Sch 14, post.
2. Schedule 2, Part B which contains provisions relating to the painting or affixing of nationality and registration marks, is not reproduced in this work.

PART 2[1]
AIR OPERATORS' CERTIFICATES

7–5824   6. Grant of air operators' certificates[2]. (1) Subject to article 7, an aircraft registered in the United Kingdom shall not fly on any flight for the purpose of public transport, otherwise than under and in accordance with the terms of an air operator's certificate granted to the operator of the aircraft under paragraph (2), certifying that the holder of the certificate is competent to secure that aircraft operated by him on such flights as that in question are operated safely.

(2) The CAA shall grant an air operator's certificate if it is satisfied that the applicant is competent, having regard in particular to—

(a) his previous conduct and experience; and
(b) his equipment, organisation, staffing, maintenance and other arrangements; to secure the safe operation of aircraft of the types specified in the certificate on flights of the description and for the purposes so specified.

---

1. Part 2 comprises arts 6–7.
2. Penalties for contraventions are contained in art 148 and Sch 14, post.

7–5825   7. Grant of police air operators' certificates[1]. (1) A flight by an aircraft registered in the United Kingdom in the service of a police authority shall, for the purposes of this Order, be deemed to be a flight for the purpose of public transport.

(2) If any passenger is carried on such a flight it shall be deemed to be for the purpose of public transport of passengers, and save as otherwise expressly provided, the provisions of this Order and of any regulations made thereunder shall be complied with in relation to a flight in the service of a police authority as if that flight was for the purpose of public transport or public transport of passengers as the case may be.

(3) An aircraft registered in the United Kingdom shall not fly on any flight in the service of a police authority otherwise than under and in accordance with either the terms of an air operator's certificate granted to the operator of the aircraft under article 6(2) or the terms of a police air operator's certificate granted to the operator of the aircraft under paragraph (4).

(4) The CAA shall grant a police air operator's certificate if it is satisfied that the applicant is competent, having regard in particular to—

(a) his previous conduct and experience; and

(*b*) his equipment, organisation, staffing, maintenance and other arrangements;

to secure that the operation of aircraft of the types specified in the certificate shall be as safe as is appropriate when flying on flights of the description and for the purposes so specified.

1. Penalties for contraventions are contained in art 148 and Sch 14, post.

PART 3[1]
AIRWORTHINESS AND EQUIPMENT OF AIRCRAFT

7–5826   8. Certificate of airworthiness to be in force.   (1) Subject to paragraph (2), an aircraft shall not fly unless there is in force in respect thereof a certificate of airworthiness duly issued or rendered valid under the law of the country in which the aircraft is registered or the State of the operator, and any conditions subject to which the certificate was issued or rendered valid are complied with.

(2) The foregoing prohibition shall not apply to flights, beginning and ending in the United Kingdom without passing over any other country, of—

(*a*) a non-EASA glider, if it is not being used for the public transport of passengers or aerial work other than aerial work which consists of the giving of instruction in flying or the conducting of flying tests in a glider owned or operated by a flying club of which the person giving the instruction or conducting the test and the person receiving the instruction or undergoing the test are both members;

(*b*) a non-EASA balloon flying on a private flight;

(*c*) a non-EASA kite;

(*d*) a non-EASA aircraft flying in accordance with the A Conditions or the B Conditions; or

(*e*) an aircraft flying in accordance with a national permit to fly, an EASA permit to fly issued by the CAA or a certificate of validation issued by the CAA under article 13.

(3) In the case of—

(*a*) a non-EASA aircraft registered in the United Kingdom the certificate of airworthiness referred to in paragraph (1) shall be a national certificate of airworthiness;

(*b*) an EASA aircraft registered in the United Kingdom the certificate of airworthiness referred to in paragraph (1) shall be an EASA certificate of airworthiness issued by the CAA.

(4) For the purposes of paragraph (1) a certificate of airworthiness—

(*a*) shall include an EASA restricted certificate of airworthiness issued by the CAA; and

(*b*) shall include an EASA restricted certificate of airworthiness issued by the competent authority of a State other than the United Kingdom which does not contain a condition restricting the aircraft to flight within the airspace of the issuing State; but

(*c*) shall not include an EASA restricted certificate of airworthiness issued by the competent authority of a State other than the United Kingdom which contains a condition restricting the aircraft to flight within the airspace of the issuing State.

(5) An aircraft registered in the United Kingdom with an EASA certificate of airworthiness shall not fly otherwise than in accordance with any conditions or limitations contained in its flight manual unless otherwise permitted by the CAA.

1. Part 3 comprises arts 8–24.
2. Penalties for contraventions are contained in art 148 and Sch 14, post.

9. Issue, renewal, etc, of national certificates of airworthiness

10. Validity of certificate of airworthiness

11. Issue, validity etc, of national permits to fly

12. Issue of EASA permits to fly

13. Issue etc of certificates of validation of permits to fly or equivalent documents

7–5827   14. Certificate of maintenance review[1]. (1) An aircraft registered in the United Kingdom—

(*a*) in respect of which a certificate of airworthiness is in force shall not fly unless the aircraft (including in particular its engines), together with its equipment and radio station, is maintained in accordance with a maintenance schedule approved by the CAA in relation to that aircraft;

(*b*) which is a public transport or an aerial work aircraft shall not fly unless there is in force a certificate (in this Order referred to as a "certificate of maintenance review") issued in respect of the aircraft in accordance with the provisions of this article and the certificate certifies the date on which the maintenance review was carried out and the date when the next review is due.

(2) A maintenance schedule approved under paragraph (1)(*a*) in relation to a public transport

or aerial work aircraft shall specify the occasions on which a review must be carried out for the purpose of issuing a certificate of maintenance review.

(3) A certificate of maintenance review may be issued for the purposes of this article only by—

(a) the holder of an aircraft maintenance engineer's licence—

   (i)   granted under this Order, being a licence which entitles him to issue that certificate;
   (ii) granted under the law of a country other than the United Kingdom and rendered valid under this Order in accordance with the privileges endorsed on the licence; or
   (iii) granted under the law of any such country as may be prescribed in accordance with the privileges endorsed on the licence and subject to any conditions which may be prescribed;

(b) a person whom the CAA has authorised to issue a certificate of maintenance review in a particular case, and in accordance with that authority;

(c) a person approved by the CAA as being competent to issue such a certificate, and in accordance with that approval; or

(d) the holder of an aircraft maintenance licence granted by the CAA under Part 66, in accordance with the privileges endorsed on the licence.

(4) In approving a maintenance schedule, the CAA may direct that certificates of maintenance review relating to that schedule, or to any part thereof specified in its direction, may be issued only by the holder of such a licence as is so specified.

(5) A person referred to in paragraph (3) shall not issue a certificate of maintenance review unless he has first verified that—

(a) maintenance has been carried out on the aircraft in accordance with the maintenance schedule approved for that aircraft;

(b) inspections and modifications required by the CAA as provided in article 10 have been completed as certified in the relevant certificate of release to service issued under this Order or under Part 145;

(c) defects entered in the technical log or approved record of the aircraft in accordance with article 15 have been rectified or the rectification thereof has been deferred in accordance with procedures approved by the CAA; and

(d) certificates of release to service have been issued:

   (i)   under this Order or in accordance with paragraph 21A. 163(d) of Part 21 in respect of an aircraft falling within article 16(1); or
   (ii) under Part 145 in respect of an aircraft required to be maintained in accordance with Part 145;

and for this purpose the operator of the aircraft shall make available to that person such information as is necessary.

(6) A certificate of maintenance review shall be issued in duplicate.

(7) One copy of the most recently issued certificate of maintenance review shall be carried in the aircraft when article 86 so requires, and the other shall be kept by the operator elsewhere than in the aircraft.

(8) Subject to article 91, each certificate of maintenance review shall be preserved by the operator of the aircraft for a period of at least 2 years after it has been issued.

---

1. Penalties for contraventions are contained in art 148 and Sch 14, post.

7–5828 15. Technical Log[1]. (1) This article applies to public transport and aerial work aircraft registered in the United Kingdom.

(2) Subject to paragraph (3), a technical log shall be kept in respect of every aircraft to which this article applies.

(3) In the case of an aircraft of which the maximum total weight authorised is 2,730 kg or less and which is not operated by the holder of an air operator's certificate granted by the CAA under article 6(2) a record approved by the CAA (in this article, article 14(5)(c) and in Schedule 6 called "an approved record") may be kept instead of a technical log.

(4) Subject to paragraph (5), at the end of every flight by an aircraft to which this article applies the commander shall enter in the technical log or the approved record as the case may be—

(a) the times when the aircraft took off and landed;

(b) particulars of any defect which is known to him and which affects the airworthiness or safe operation of the aircraft, or if no such defect is known to him, an entry to that effect; and

(c) such other particulars in respect of the airworthiness or operation of the aircraft as the CAA may require;

and he shall sign and date the entries.

(5) In the case of two or more consecutive flights each of which begins and ends—

(a) within the same period of 24 hours;

(b) at the same aerodrome, except where each such flight is for the purpose of dropping or projecting any material for agricultural, public health or similar purposes; and

(c) with the same person as commander of the aircraft;

the commander may, except where he becomes aware of a defect during an earlier flight, make the entries specified in paragraph (4) at the end of the last of such consecutive flights.

(6) Upon the rectification of any defect which has been entered in a technical log or approved record in accordance with paragraphs (4) and (5) a person issuing a certificate of release to service issued under this Order or under Part 145 in respect of that defect shall enter the certificate in the technical log or approved record in such a position as to be readily identifiable with the defect to which it relates.

(7) Subject to paragraph (8) the technical log or approved record shall be carried in the aircraft when article 86 so requires and copies of the entries required by this article shall be kept on the ground.

(8) In the case of an aeroplane of which the maximum total weight authorised is 2,730 kg or less, or a helicopter, if it is not reasonably practicable for the copy of the technical log or approved record to be kept on the ground it may be carried in the aeroplane or helicopter, as the case may be, in a container approved by the CAA for that purpose.

(9) Subject to article 91, a technical log or approved record required by this article shall be preserved by the operator of the aircraft to which it relates for a period of at least 2 years after the aircraft has been destroyed or has been permanently withdrawn from use, or for such shorter period as the CAA may permit in a particular case.

---

1. Penalties for contraventions are contained in art 148 and Sch 14, post.

7–5829 16. Requirement for a certificate of release to service[1]. (1) This article shall apply to any aircraft registered in the United Kingdom in respect of which a certificate of airworthiness is in force except any such aircraft which is required to be maintained in accordance with Part 145.

(2) Except as provided in paragraphs (3), (5), (6) and (8) an aircraft to which this article applies shall not fly unless there is in force a certificate of release to service issued under this Order if the aircraft or any part of the aircraft or such of its equipment as is necessary for the airworthiness of the aircraft has been overhauled, repaired, replaced, modified, maintained, or has been inspected as provided in article 10(*b*).

(3) If a repair or replacement of a part of a non-EASA aircraft or its equipment is carried out when the aircraft is at a place where it is not reasonably practicable—

(*a*) for the repair or replacement to be carried out in such a manner that a certificate of release to service under this Order can be issued; or

(*b*) for such a certificate to be issued while the aircraft is at that place;

it may fly to a place which satisfies the criteria in paragraph (4) and in such case the commander of the aircraft shall cause written particulars of the flight, and the reasons for making it, to be given to the CAA within 10 days thereafter.

(4) A place satisfies the criteria in this paragraph if it is—

(*a*) the nearest place at which a certificate of release to service under this Order can be issued;

(*b*) a place to which the aircraft can, in the reasonable opinion of the commander, safely fly by a route for which it is properly equipped; and

(*c*) a place to which it is reasonable to fly having regard to any hazards to the liberty or health of any person on board.

(5) A certificate of release to service shall not be required to be in force in respect of an aircraft to which this article applies of which the maximum total weight authorised does not exceed 2,730 kg if it is an aircraft in respect of which a certificate of airworthiness in the special category referred to in Part B of Schedule 3 is in force, unless the CAA gives a direction to the contrary in a particular case.

(6) A certificate of release to service shall not be required to be in force in respect of an aircraft to which this article applies of which the maximum total weight authorised does not exceed 2,730 kg and which is a private aircraft if it flies in the circumstances specified in paragraph (7).

(7) The circumstances referred to in paragraph (6) are—

(*a*) the only repairs or replacements in respect of which a certificate of release to service is not in force are of such a description as may be prescribed[2];

(*b*) such repairs or replacements have been carried out personally by the holder of a pilot's licence granted or rendered valid under this Order who is the owner or operator of the aircraft;

(*c*) the person carrying out the repairs or replacements shall keep in the aircraft log book kept in respect of the aircraft under article 22 a record which identifies the repairs or replacement and shall sign and date the entries; and

(*d*) any equipment or parts used in carrying out such repairs or replacements shall be of a type approved by EASA or the CAA either generally or in relation to a class of aircraft or one particular aircraft.

(8) A certificate of release to service issued under this Order shall not be required to be in force in respect of an aircraft to which this article applies if there is in force a certificate of release to service issued in accordance with paragraph 21A.163(*d*) of Part 21.

(9) Neither—

(a) equipment provided in compliance with Schedule 4 (except equipment specified in paragraph 4 of the Schedule); nor

(b) radio communication and radio navigation equipment provided for use in an aircraft or in any survival craft carried in an aircraft, whether or not such apparatus is provided in compliance with this Order or any regulations made thereunder;

shall be installed or placed on board for use in an aircraft to which this article applies after being overhauled, repaired, modified or inspected, unless there is in force in respect thereof at the time when it is installed or placed on board a certificate of release to service issued under this Order.

(10) A certificate of release to service issued under this Order shall—

(a) certify that the aircraft or any part thereof or its equipment has been overhauled, repaired, replaced, modified or maintained, as the case may be, in a manner and with material of a type approved by EASA or the CAA either generally or in relation to a class of aircraft or the particular aircraft and shall identify the overhaul, repair, replacement, modification or maintenance to which the certificate relates and shall include particulars of the work done; or

(b) certify in relation to any inspection required by the CAA that the aircraft or the part thereof or its equipment, as the case may be, has been inspected in accordance with the requirements of the CAA and that any consequential repair, replacement or modification has been carried out.

(11) A certificate of release to service issued under this Order may be issued only by—

(a) the holder of an aircraft maintenance engineer's licence—

(i) granted under this Order, being a licence which entitles him to issue that certificate; or

(ii) granted under the law of a country other than the United Kingdom and rendered valid under this Order, in accordance with the privileges endorsed on the licence.

(b) the holder of an aircraft maintenance engineer's licence or authorisation as such an engineer granted or issued by or under the law of any Contracting State other than the United Kingdom in which the overhaul, repair, replacement, modification, maintenance or inspection has been carried out, but only in respect of aircraft to which this article applies of which the maximum total weight authorised does not exceed 2,730 kg and in accordance with the privileges endorsed on the licence;

(c) a person approved by the CAA as being competent to issue such certification, and in accordance with that approval;

(d) a person whom the CAA has authorised to issue the certificate in a particular case, and in accordance with that authority;

(e) in relation only to the adjustment and compensation of direct reading magnetic compasses, the holder of a United Kingdom Airline Transport Pilot's Licence (Aeroplanes) or a JAR-FCL Airline Transport Pilot Licence (Aeroplane) or a Flight Navigator's Licence granted or rendered valid under this Order;

(f) a person approved in accordance with Part 145, and in accordance with that approval; or

(g) the holder of an aircraft maintenance licence granted by the CAA under Part 66, in accordance with the privileges endorsed on the licence.

(12) In this article, the expression "repair" includes in relation to a compass the adjustment and compensation thereof and the expression "repaired" shall be construed accordingly.

---

1. Penalties for contraventions are contained in art 148 and Sch 14, post.
2. See the Air Navigation (General) Regulations 2005, SI 2005/1980.

7–5830 17. Requirement for a certificate of release to service under Part 145[1]. An EASA aircraft to which Part 145 applies shall not fly when a certificate of release to service is required by or under Part 145 unless such a certificate is in force.

---

1. Penalties for contraventions are contained in art 148 and Sch 14, post.

7–5831 18. Licensing of maintenance engineers[1]. (1) The CAA shall grant an aircraft maintenance engineer's licence, subject to such conditions as it thinks fit, upon being satisfied that the applicant is a fit person to hold the licence and is qualified by reason of his knowledge, experience, competence and skill in aeronautical engineering, and for that purpose the applicant shall furnish such evidence and undergo such examinations and tests as the CAA may require of him.

(2) An aircraft maintenance engineer's licence shall authorise the holder, subject to such conditions as may be specified in the licence, to issue—

(a) certificates of maintenance review in respect of such aircraft as may be so specified;

(b) certificates of release to service under this Order in respect of such overhauls, repairs, replacements, modifications, maintenance and inspections of such aircraft and such equipment as may be so specified; or

(c) certificates of fitness for flight issued under paragraph 1(4) of the A Conditions in respect of such aircraft as may be so specified.

(3) A licence shall, subject to article 92, remain in force for the period specified therein, not

exceeding 5 years, but may be renewed by the CAA from time to time upon being satisfied that the applicant is a fit person and is qualified as aforesaid.

(4) The CAA may issue a certificate rendering valid for the purposes of this Order any licence as an aircraft maintenance engineer granted under the law of any country other than the United Kingdom.

(5) An aircraft maintenance engineer's licence granted under this article shall not be valid unless it bears the ordinary signature of the holder in ink or indelible pencil; provided that if the licence is annexed to an aircraft maintenance licence issued under Part 66 it shall be sufficient if that Part 66 licence bears such a signature.

(6) Without prejudice to any other provision of this Order the CAA may, for the purposes of this article—

(a) approve any course of training or instruction;
(b) authorise a person to conduct such examinations or tests as it may specify; and
(c) approve a person to provide or conduct any course of training or instruction.

(7) The holder of an aircraft maintenance engineer's licence granted under paragraph (1) or of an aircraft maintenance licence granted under Part 66 shall not exercise the privileges of such a licence if he knows or suspects that his physical or mental condition renders him unfit to exercise such privileges.

(8) The holder of an aircraft maintenance engineer's licence granted under paragraph (1) or of an aircraft maintenance licence granted under Part 66 shall not, when exercising the privileges of such a licence, be under the influence of drink or a drug to such an extent as to impair his capacity to exercise such privileges.

---

1. Penalties for contraventions are contained in art 148 and Sch 14, post.

7–5832   19. Equipment of aircraft[1]. (1) An aircraft shall not fly unless it is so equipped as to comply with the law of the country in which it is registered, and to enable lights and markings to be displayed, and signals to be made, in accordance with this Order and any regulations made thereunder.

(2) In the case of any aircraft registered in the United Kingdom the equipment required to be provided (in addition to any other equipment required by or under this Order) shall—

(a) be that specified in such parts of Schedule 4 as are applicable in the circumstances;
(b) comply with the provisions of that Schedule;
(c) except that specified in paragraph 4 of the said Schedule, be of a type approved by EASA or the CAA either generally or in relation to a class of aircraft or in relation to that aircraft; and
(d) be installed in a manner approved by EASA in the case of an EASA aircraft and the CAA in the case of a non-EASA aircraft.

(3) In any particular case the CAA may direct that an aircraft registered in the United Kingdom shall carry such additional or special equipment or supplies as it may specify for the purpose of facilitating the navigation of the aircraft, the carrying out of search and rescue operations, or the survival of the persons carried in the aircraft.

(4) The equipment carried in compliance with this article shall be so installed or stowed and kept stowed, and so maintained and adjusted, as to be readily accessible and capable of being used by the person for whose use it is intended.

(5) The position of equipment provided for emergency use shall be indicated by clear markings in or on the aircraft.

(6) In every public transport aircraft registered in the United Kingdom there shall be provided individually for each passenger or, if the CAA so permits in writing, exhibited in a prominent position in every passenger compartment, a notice which complies with paragraph (7).

(7) A notice complies with this paragraph if it—

(a) is relevant to the aircraft in question;
(b) contains pictorial instructions on the brace position to be adopted in the event of an emergency landing;
(c) contains pictorial instructions on the method of use of the safety belts and safety harnesses as appropriate;
(d) contains pictorial information as to where emergency exits are to be found and instructions as to how they are to be used; and
(e) contains pictorial information as to where the lifejackets, escape slides, life rafts and oxygen masks, if required to be provided by paragraph (2), are to be found and instructions as to how they are to be used.

(8) All equipment installed or carried in an aircraft, whether or not in compliance with this article, shall be so installed or stowed and so maintained and adjusted as not to be a source of danger in itself or to impair the airworthiness of the aircraft or the proper functioning of any equipment or services necessary for the safety of the aircraft.

(9) Without prejudice to paragraph (2), all navigational equipment capable of establishing the aircraft's position in relation to its position at some earlier time by computing and applying the resultant of the acceleration and gravitational forces acting upon it when carried in an aircraft registered in the United Kingdom (whether or not in compliance with this Order or any regulations

made thereunder) shall be of a type approved by EASA or the CAA either generally or in relation to a class of aircraft or in relation to that aircraft and shall be installed in a manner so approved.

(10) This article shall not apply in relation to radio communication and radio navigation equipment except any specified in Schedule 4.

---

1. Penalties for contraventions are contained in art 148 and Sch 14, post.

7–5833   **20. Radio equipment of aircraft**[1]. (1) An aircraft shall not fly unless it is so equipped with radio communication and radio navigation equipment as to comply with the law of the country in which the aircraft is registered or the State of the operator and to enable communications to be made and the aircraft to be navigated, in accordance with the provisions of this Order and any regulations made thereunder.

(2) Without prejudice to paragraph (1), the aircraft shall be equipped with radio communication and radio navigation equipment in accordance with Schedule 5.

(3) In any particular case the CAA may direct that an aircraft registered in the United Kingdom shall carry such additional or special radio communication or radio navigation equipment as it may specify for the purpose of facilitating the navigation of the aircraft, the carrying out of search and rescue operations or the survival of the persons carried in the aircraft.

(4) Subject to such exceptions as may be prescribed, the radio communication and radio navigation equipment provided in compliance with this article in an aircraft registered in the United Kingdom shall always be maintained in serviceable condition.

(5) All radio communication and radio navigation equipment installed in an aircraft registered in the United Kingdom or carried on such an aircraft for use in connection with the aircraft (whether or not in compliance with this Order or any regulations made thereunder) shall—

    (a)   be of a type approved by EASA or the CAA in relation to the purpose for which it is to be used; and

    (b)   except in the case of a non-EASA glider which is permitted by article 3(2) to fly unregistered, be installed in a manner approved by EASA in the case of an EASA aircraft and the CAA in the case of a non-EASA aircraft.

(6) Neither the equipment referred to in paragraph (5) nor the manner in which it is installed shall be modified except with the approval of EASA in the case of an EASA aircraft or the CAA in the case of a non-EASA aircraft.

---

1. Penalties for contraventions are contained in art 148 and Sch 14, post.

7–5834   **21. Minimum equipment requirements**[1]. (1) The CAA may grant in respect of any aircraft or class of aircraft registered in the United Kingdom a permission permitting such aircraft to commence a flight in specified circumstances notwithstanding that any specified item of equipment required by or under this Order to be carried in the circumstances of the intended flight is not carried or is not in a fit condition for use.

(2) An aircraft registered in the United Kingdom shall not commence a flight if any of the equipment required by or under this Order to be carried in the circumstances of the intended flight is not carried or is not in a fit condition for use unless—

    (a)   the aircraft does so under and in accordance with the terms of a permission under this article which has been granted to the operator; and

    (b)   in the case of an aircraft to which article 38 or 39 applies, the operations manual or police operations manual respectively contains particulars of that permission.

---

1. Penalties for contraventions are contained in art 148 and Sch 14, post.

7–5835   **22. Aircraft, engine and propeller log books**[1]. (1) In addition to any other log books required by or under this Order, the following log books shall be kept in respect of aircraft registered in the United Kingdom—

    (a)   an aircraft log book;

    (b)   a separate log book in respect of each engine fitted in the aircraft; and

    (c)   a separate log book in respect of each variable pitch propeller fitted to the aircraft.

(2) The log books shall include the particulars respectively specified in Schedule 6 and in the case of an aircraft having a maximum total weight authorised not exceeding 2,730 kg shall be of a type approved by the CAA.

(3) Each entry in the log book—

    (a)   other than such an entry as is referred to in paragraph 2(4)(b) or 3(4)(b) of Schedule 6, shall be made as soon as practicable after the occurrence to which it relates, but in no event more than 7 days after the expiration of the certificate of maintenance review (if any) in force in respect of the aircraft at the time of the occurrence;

    (b)   being such an entry as is referred to in paragraph 2(4)(b) or 3(4)(b) of Schedule 6 shall be made upon each occasion that any maintenance, overhaul, repair, replacement, modification or inspection is undertaken on the engine or propeller, as the case may be.

(4) Any document which is incorporated by reference in a log book shall be deemed, for the purposes of this Order, to be part of the log book.

(5) It shall be the duty of the operator of every aircraft in respect of which log books are required to be kept to keep them or cause them to be kept in accordance with the foregoing provisions of this article.

(6) Subject to article 91 every log book shall be preserved by the operator of the aircraft for a period of at least 2 years after the aircraft, the engine or the variable pitch propeller, as the case may be, has been destroyed or has been permanently withdrawn from use.

---

1. Penalties for contraventions are contained in art 148 and Sch 14, post.

7–5836   **23. Aircraft weight schedule[1].** (1) Every flying machine and glider in respect of which a certificate of airworthiness issued by the CAA or rendered valid under this Order is in force shall be weighed, and the position of its centre of gravity determined, at such times and in such manner as the CAA may require or approve in the case of that aircraft.

(2) Upon the aircraft being weighed the operator of the aircraft shall prepare a weight schedule showing—

    (a) either the basic weight of the aircraft, that is to say, the empty weight of the aircraft established in accordance with the type certification basis of the aircraft or such other weight as may be approved by the CAA or EASA in the case of that aircraft; and

    (b) either the position of the centre of gravity of the aircraft at its basic weight or such other position of the centre of gravity as may be approved by the CAA or EASA in the case of that aircraft.

(3) Subject to article 91 the weight schedule shall be preserved by the operator of the aircraft until the expiration of a period of six months following the next occasion on which the aircraft is weighed for the purposes of this article.

---

1. Penalties for contraventions are contained in art 148 and Sch 14, post.

24. Access and inspection for airworthiness purposes

PART 4[1]
AIRCRAFT CREW AND LICENSING

7–5837   **25. Composition of crew of aircraft[2].** (1) An aircraft shall not fly unless it carries a flight crew of the number and description required by the law of the country in which it is registered.

(2) An aircraft registered in the United Kingdom—

    (a) shall carry a flight crew adequate in number and description to ensure the safety of the aircraft;

    (b) which has a flight manual, shall carry a flight crew of at least the number and description specified in that flight manual;

    (c) which does not now have a flight manual but has done in the past, shall carry a flight crew of at least the number and description specified in that flight manual.

(3) A flying machine registered in the United Kingdom and flying for the purpose of public transport having a maximum total weight authorised exceeding 5,700 kg shall carry at least two pilots as members of the flight crew.

(4) Subject to paragraph (6) an aeroplane registered in the United Kingdom shall carry at least two pilots as members of its flight crew if it—

    (a) has a maximum total weight authorised of 5,700 kg or less;

    (b) is flying for the purpose of public transport;

    (c) is flying in circumstances where the commander is required to comply with the Instrument Flight Rules; and (d) comes within paragraph (5).

(5) For the purposes of paragraph (4)(d) an aeroplane comes with this paragraph if it has—

    (a) one or more turbine jets;

    (b) one or more turbine propeller engines and is provided with a means of pressurising the personnel compartments;

    (c) two or more turbine propeller engines and a maximum approved passenger seating configuration of more than nine;

    (d) two or more turbine propeller engines and a maximum approved passenger seating configuration of fewer than 10, and is not provided with a means of pressurising the personnel compartments; unless it is equipped with an autopilot which has been approved by the CAA for the purposes of this article and which is serviceable on take-off; or

    (e) two or more piston engines, unless it is equipped with an autopilot which has been approved by the CAA for the purposes of this article and which is serviceable on take-off.

(6) An aeroplane—

    (a) described in paragraph (5)(d) or (5)(e) which is equipped with an approved autopilot shall not be required to carry two pilots notwithstanding that before take-off the approved autopilot is found to be unserviceable, if the aeroplane flies in accordance with arrangements approved by the CAA;

(*b*)   described in paragraph (5)(*c*), (*d*) or (*e*) which is flying under and in accordance with the terms of a police air operator's certificate shall not be required to carry two pilots.

(7) Subject to paragraph (8), a helicopter registered in the United Kingdom shall carry at least two pilots as members of its flight crew if it—

(*a*)   has a maximum total weight authorised of 5,700 kg or less;
(*b*)   has a maximum approved passenger seating configuration of 9 or less;
(*c*)   is flying for the purpose of public transport; and
(*d*)   is flying in circumstances where the commander is required to comply with the Instrument Flight Rules or is flying by night with visual ground reference.

(8) A helicopter described in paragraph (7) shall not be required to carry two pilots if it—

(*a*)   is equipped with an autopilot with, at least, altitude hold and heading mode which is serviceable on take-off;
(*b*)   is equipped with such an autopilot notwithstanding that before take-off the approved autopilot is found to be unserviceable, if the helicopter flies in accordance with arrangements approved by the CAA; or
(*c*)   is flying under and in accordance with the terms of a police air operator's certificate.

(9) An aircraft registered in the United Kingdom engaged on a flight for the purpose of public transport shall carry—

(*a*)   a flight navigator as a member of the flight crew; or
(*b*)   navigational equipment suitable for the route to be flown; if on the route or any diversion therefrom, being a route or diversion planned before take-off, the aircraft is intended to be more than 500 nautical miles from the point of take-off measured along the route to be flown, and to pass over part of an area specified in Schedule 7.

(10) flight navigator carried in compliance with paragraph (9) shall be carried in addition to any person who is carried in accordance with this article to perform other duties.

(11) An aircraft registered in the United Kingdom which is required by article 20 to be equipped with radio communications apparatus shall carry a flight radiotelephony operator as a member of the flight crew.

(12) Paragraphs (13) and (14) apply to any flight for the purpose of public transport by an aircraft registered in the United Kingdom which has a maximum approved passenger seating configuration of more than 19 and on which at least one passenger is carried.

(13) The crew of an aircraft on a flight to which this paragraph applies shall include cabin crew carried for the purposes of performing in the interests of the safety of passengers, duties to be assigned by the operator or the commander of the aircraft but who shall not act as members of the flight crew.

(14) On a flight to which this paragraph applies—

(*a*)   there shall, subject to sub-paragraph (*b*), be carried not less than one member of the cabin crew for every 50 or fraction of 50 passenger seats installed in the aircraft;
(*b*)   the number of members of the cabin crew calculated in accordance with sub-paragraph (*a*) need not be carried if the CAA has granted written permission to the operator to carry a lesser number on that flight and the operator carries the number specified in that permission and complies with any other terms and conditions subject to which such permission is granted.

(15) The CAA may in the interests of safety direct the operator of any aircraft registered in the United Kingdom that all or any aircraft operated by him when flying in circumstances specified in the direction shall carry, in addition to the crew required to be carried therein by the foregoing provisions of this article, such additional persons as members of the flight crew or the cabin crew as it may specify in the direction.

---

1. Part 4 comprises arts 25–37.
2. Penalties for contraventions are contained in art 148 and Sch 14, post.

7–5838   26. Members of flight crew—requirement for licence[1]. (1) Subject to the provisions of this article, a person shall not act as a member of the flight crew of an aircraft registered in the United Kingdom unless he is the holder of an appropriate licence granted or rendered valid under this Order.

(2) A person may within the United Kingdom, the Channel Islands, and the Isle of Man without being the holder of such a licence—

(*a*)   act as a flight radiotelephony operator if—

(i)   he does so as the pilot of a glider on a private flight and he does not communicate by radiotelephony with any air traffic control unit; or
(ii)   he does so as a person being trained in an aircraft registered in the United Kingdom to perform duties as a member of the flight crew of an aircraft and—

(aa) he is authorised to operate the radiotelephony station by the holder of the licence granted in respect of that station under any enactment;

(*bb*)messages are transmitted only for the purposes of instruction, or of the safety or navigation of the aircraft;

(*cc*) messages are transmitted only on a frequency exceeding 60 MHz assigned by the CAA for the purposes of this sub-paragraph;

(*dd*)the operation of the transmitter requires the use only of external switches; and

(*ee*)the stability of the frequency radiated is maintained automatically by the transmitter.

(*b*) act as pilot in command of an aircraft for the purpose of becoming qualified for the grant or renewal of a pilot's licence or the inclusion or variation of any rating in a pilot's licence if—

(i) he is at least 16 years of age;

(ii) he is the holder of a valid medical certificate to the effect that he is fit so to act, issued by a person approved by the CAA;

(iii) he complies with any conditions subject to which that medical certificate was issued;

(iv) no other person is carried in the aircraft;

(v) the aircraft is not flying for the purpose of public transport or aerial work other than aerial work which consists of the giving of instruction in flying or the conducting of flying tests; and

(vi) he so acts in accordance with instructions given by a person holding a pilot's licence granted under this Order or a JAA licence, being a licence which includes a flight instructor rating, a flying instructor's rating or an assistant flying instructor's rating entitling him to give instruction in flying the type of aircraft being flown;

(*c*) act as pilot of an aircraft in respect of which the flight crew required to be carried by or under this Order does not exceed one pilot for the purpose of becoming qualified for the grant or renewal of a pilot's licence or the inclusion or variation of any rating in a pilot's licence if—

(i) the aircraft is not flying for the purpose of public transport or aerial work other than aerial work which consists of the giving of instruction in flying or the conducting of flying tests;

(ii) he so acts in accordance with instructions given by a person holding a pilot's licence granted under this Order or a JAA licence, being a licence which includes a flight instructor rating, a flying instructor's rating or an assistant flying instructor's rating entitling him to give instruction in flying the type of aircraft being flown; and

(iii) the aircraft is fitted with dual controls and he is accompanied in the aircraft by the said instructor who is seated at the other set of controls or the aircraft is fitted with controls designed for and capable of use by two persons and he is accompanied in the aircraft by the said instructor who is seated so as to be able to use the controls;

(*d*) act as pilot in command of a helicopter or gyroplane at night if—

(i) he is the holder of an appropriate licence granted or rendered valid under this Order in all respects save that the licence does not include an instrument rating and he has not within the immediately preceding 13 months carried out as pilot in command not less than 5 take-offs and 5 landings at a time when the depression of the centre of the sun was not less than 12° below the horizon;

(ii) he so acts in accordance with instructions given by a person holding a pilot's licence granted under this Order or a JAA licence, being a licence which includes a flight instructor rating, a flying instructor's rating or an assistant flying instructor's rating entitling him to give instruction in flying the type of helicopter or gyroplane being flown by night;

(iii) no person other than that specified in sub-paragraph (ii) is carried; and

(iv) the helicopter or gyroplane is not flying for the purpose of public transport or aerial work other than aerial work which consists of the giving of instruction in flying or the conducting of flying tests;

(*e*) act as pilot in command of a balloon if—

(i) he is the holder of an appropriate licence granted or rendered valid under this Order in all respects save that he has not within the immediately preceding 13 months carried out as pilot in command at least 5 flights each of not less than 5 minutes duration;

(ii) he so acts in accordance with instructions given by a person authorised by the CAA to supervise flying in the type of balloon being flown;

(iii) no person other than that specified in sub-paragraph (ii) is carried; and

(iv) the balloon is not flying for the purpose of public transport or aerial work other than aerial work which consists of the giving of instruction in flying or the conducting of flying tests.

(3) Subject as aforesaid, a person shall not act as a member of the flight crew required by or under this Order to be carried in an aircraft registered in a country other than the United Kingdom unless—

(*a*) in the case of an aircraft flying for the purpose of public transport or aerial work, he is the holder of an appropriate licence granted or rendered valid under the law of the country in which the aircraft is registered or the State of the operator; or

(b) in the case of any other aircraft, he is the holder of an appropriate licence granted or rendered valid under the law of the country in which the aircraft is registered or under this Order, and the CAA does not give a direction to the contrary.

(4) For the purposes of this Part of this Order—

(a) subject to sub-paragraph (b), a licence granted either under the law of a Contracting State other than the United Kingdom but which is not a JAA licence or a licence granted under the law of a relevant overseas territory; purporting in either case to authorise the holder to act as a member of the flight crew of an aircraft, not being a licence purporting to authorise him to act as a student pilot only, shall, unless the CAA gives a direction to the contrary, be deemed to be a licence rendered valid under this Order but does not entitle the holder—

(i) to act as a member of the flight crew of any aircraft flying for the purpose of public transport or aerial work or on any flight in respect of which he receives remuneration for his services as a member of the flight crew; or

(ii) in the case of a pilot's licence, to act as pilot of any aircraft flying in controlled airspace in circumstances requiring compliance with the Instrument Flight Rules or to give any instruction in flying;

(b) a JAA licence shall, unless the CAA gives a direction to the contrary, be deemed to be a licence rendered valid under this Order.

(5) Notwithstanding paragraph (1), a person may, unless the certificate of airworthiness in force in respect of the aircraft otherwise requires, act as pilot of an aircraft registered in the United Kingdom for the purpose of undergoing training or tests for the grant or renewal of a pilot's licence or for the inclusion, renewal or extension of a rating therein without being the holder of an appropriate licence, if the conditions specified in paragraph (6) are complied with.

(6) The conditions referred to in paragraph (5) are—

(a) no other person shall be carried in the aircraft or in an aircraft being towed thereby except—

(i) a person carried as a member of the flight crew in compliance with this Order;

(ii) a person authorised by the CAA to witness the training or tests or to conduct the tests; or

(iii) if the pilot in command of the aircraft is the holder of an appropriate licence, a person carried for the purpose of being trained or tested as a member of the flight crew of an aircraft; and

(b) the person acting as the pilot of the aircraft without being the holder of an appropriate licence either—

(i) within the period of six months immediately preceding was serving as a qualified pilot of an aircraft in any of Her Majesty's naval, military or air forces, and his physical condition has not, so far as he is aware, so deteriorated during that period as to render him unfit for the licence for which he intends to qualify; or

(ii) holds a pilot's, a flight navigator's or a flight engineer's licence granted under article 27 and the purpose of the training or test is to enable him to qualify under this Order for the grant of a pilot's licence or for the inclusion of an additional type in the aircraft rating in his licence, and he acts under the supervision of a person who is the holder of an appropriate licence.

(7) Notwithstanding paragraph (1), a person may act as a member of the flight crew (otherwise than as a pilot) of an aircraft registered in the United Kingdom for the purposes of undergoing training or tests for the grant or renewal of a flight navigator's or a flight engineer's licence or for the inclusion, renewal or extension of a rating therein, without being the holder of an appropriate licence, if he acts under the supervision and in the presence of another person who is the holder of the type of licence or rating for which the person undergoing the training or tests is being trained or tested.

(8) Notwithstanding paragraph (1), a person may act as a member of the flight crew of an aircraft registered in the United Kingdom without being the holder of an appropriate licence if, in so doing, he is acting in the course of his duty as a member of any of Her Majesty's naval, military or air forces.

(9) An appropriate licence for the purposes of this article means a licence which entitles the holder to perform the functions which he undertakes in relation to the aircraft concerned and the flight on which it is engaged.

(10) This article shall not require a licence to be held by a person by reason of his acting as a member of the flight crew of a glider unless—

(a) he acts as a flight radiotelephony operator otherwise than in accordance with paragraph (2)(a)(i); or

(b) the flight is for the purpose of public transport or aerial work, other than aerial work which consists of the giving of instruction in flying or the conducting of flying tests in a glider owned or operated by a flying club of which the person giving the instruction or conducting the test and the person receiving the instruction or undergoing the test are both members.

(11) Notwithstanding anything in this article—

(a) the holder of a licence granted or rendered valid under this Order, being a licence endorsed to the effect that the holder does not satisfy in full the relevant minimum standards established under the Chicago Convention, shall not act as a member of the flight crew of an aircraft registered in the United Kingdom in or over the territory of a Contracting State other than the United Kingdom, except in accordance with permission granted by the competent authorities of that State;

(b) the holder of a licence granted or rendered valid under the law of a Contracting State other than the United Kingdom, being a licence endorsed as aforesaid, shall not act as a member of the flight crew of any aircraft in or over the United Kingdom except in accordance with permission granted by the CAA, whether or not the licence is or is deemed to be rendered valid under this Order.

---

1. Penalties for contraventions are contained in art 148 and Sch 14, post.

27. Grant, renewal and effect of flight crew licences

7–5839 **28. Maintenance of privileges of aircraft ratings in United Kingdom licences for which there are no JAR-FCL equivalents except for Basic Commercial Pilot's Licences and Flight Engineer's Licences[1].** (1) This article applies to any United Kingdom licence for which there is no JAR-FCL equivalent other than a United Kingdom Basic Commercial Pilot's Licence and a United Kingdom Flight Engineer's Licence.

(2) Subject to paragraphs (3) and (4), the holder of a pilot's licence to which this article applies shall not be entitled to exercise the privileges of an aircraft rating contained in the licence on a flight unless the licence bears a valid certificate of test or a valid certificate of experience in respect of the rating, which certificate shall in either case be appropriate to the functions he is to perform on that flight in accordance with Section 1 of Part C of Schedule 8 and shall otherwise comply with that Section.

(3) The holder of a Private Pilot's Licence (Balloons and Airships) to which this article applies shall be entitled to exercise the privileges of an aircraft rating contained in the licence on a flight when the licence does not bear a certificate referred to in paragraph (2).

(4) The holder of a Microlight Licence, an SLMG Licence or a United Kingdom Private Pilot's Licence (Gyroplanes) shall not be entitled to exercise the privileges of an aircraft rating contained in the licence on a flight unless the certificate of test or certificate of experience required by paragraph (2) is included in the personal flying log book required to be kept by him under article 35.

(5) The holder of a flight navigator's licence to which this article applies shall not be entitled to perform functions on a flight to which article 25(9) applies unless the licence bears a valid certificate of experience which certificate shall be appropriate to the functions he is to perform on that flight in accordance with Section 1 of Part C of the said Schedule and shall otherwise comply with that Part.

---

1. Penalties for contraventions are contained in art 148 and Sch 14, post.

7–5840 **29. Maintenance of privileges of aircraft ratings in JAR-FCL licences, United Kingdom licences for which there are JAR-FCL equivalents, United Kingdom Basic Commercial Pilot's Licences and United Kingdom Flight Engineer's Licences[1].** (1) This article applies to—

(a) JAR-FCL licences;
(b) United Kingdom licences for which there are JAR-FCL equivalents;
(c) United Kingdom Basic Commercial Pilot's Licences; and
(d) United Kingdom Flight Engineer's Licences.

(2) The holder of a pilot's licence to which this article applies shall not be entitled to exercise the privileges of an aircraft rating contained in the licence on a flight unless—

(a) the licence bears a valid certificate of revalidation in respect of the rating; and
(b) the holder has undertaken differences training in accordance with paragraph 1.235 of Section 1 of JAR-FCL 1 in the case of an aeroplane and paragraph 2.235 of Section 1 of JAR-FCL 2 in the case of a helicopter and has had particulars thereof entered in his personal flying log book in accordance with the relevant paragraph.

(3) The holder of a United Kingdom Flight Engineer's Licence shall not be entitled to exercise the privileges of an aircraft rating contained in the licence on a flight unless the licence bears a valid certificate of revalidation in respect of the rating.

---

1. Penalties for contraventions are contained in art 148 and Sch 14, post.

7–5841 **30. Maintenance of privileges of aircraft ratings in National Private Pilot's Licences[1].** (1) The holder of a National Private Pilot's Licence (Aeroplanes) shall not be entitled to exercise the privileges of a simple single engine aeroplane (NPPL) class rating contained in the licence on a flight unless the rating is valid in accordance with Section 3 of Part C of Schedule 8.

(2) The holder of a National Private Pilot's Licence (Aeroplanes) shall not be entitled to exercise the privileges of an SLMG class rating or a Microlight class rating contained in the licence on a flight unless the licence includes a valid certificate of test or a valid certificate of experience in respect of the rating, which certificate shall in either case be appropriate to the functions he is to

perform on that flight in accordance with Section 1 of Part C of Schedule 8 and shall otherwise comply with that Section.

---

1. Penalties for contraventions are contained in art 148 and Sch 14, post.

7–5842   **31. Maintenance of privileges of other ratings**[1]. (1) A person shall not be entitled to perform the functions to which a flying instructor's rating (gyroplanes), an assistant flying instructor's rating (gyroplanes) or an instrument meteorological conditions rating (aeroplanes) relates unless his licence bears a valid certificate of test, which certificate shall be appropriate to the functions to which the rating relates in accordance with Section 1 of Part C of Schedule 8 and shall otherwise comply with that Part.

(2) A person shall not be entitled to perform the functions to which an instrument rating or an instructor's rating (other than a flying instructor's rating (gyroplanes) or an assistant flying instructor's rating (gyroplanes)) relates unless his licence bears a valid certificate of revalidation in respect of the rating.

---

1. Penalties for contraventions are contained in art 148 and Sch 14, post.

7–5843   **32. Medical requirements**[1]. (1) The holder of a licence granted under article 27, other than a Flight Radiotelephony Operator's Licence, shall not be entitled to perform any of the functions to which his licence relates unless it includes an appropriate valid medical certificate issued under paragraph (3).

(2) Every applicant for or holder of a licence granted under article 27 shall upon such occasions as the CAA may require submit himself to medical examination by a person approved by the CAA, either generally or in a particular case or class of cases, who shall make a report to the CAA in such form as the CAA may require.

(3) On the basis of such medical examination, the CAA or any person approved by it as competent to do so may issue a medical certificate subject to such conditions as it or he thinks fit to the effect that it or he has assessed the holder of the licence as meeting the requirements specified in respect of the certificate and the certificate shall, without prejudice to paragraph (6), be valid for such period as is therein specified and shall be deemed to form part of the licence.

(4) A person shall not be entitled to act as a member of the flight crew of an aircraft registered in the United Kingdom if he knows or suspects that his physical or mental condition renders him temporarily or permanently unfit to perform such functions or to act in such capacity.

(5) Every holder of a medical certificate issued under this article who—

(a) suffers any personal injury involving incapacity to undertake his functions as a member of the flight crew;

(b) suffers any illness involving incapacity to undertake those functions throughout a period of 21 days or more; or

(c) in the case of a woman, has reason to believe that she is pregnant;

shall inform the CAA in writing of such injury, illness or pregnancy, as soon as possible in the case of injury or pregnancy, and as soon as the period of 21 days has expired in the case of illness.

(6) The medical certificate shall be deemed to be suspended upon the occurrence of such injury or the expiry of such period of illness or the confirmation of the pregnancy; and—

(a) in the case of injury or illness the suspension shall cease upon the holder being medically examined under arrangements made by the CAA and pronounced fit to resume his functions as a member of the flight crew or upon the CAA exempting, subject to such conditions as it thinks fit, the holder from the requirement of a medical examination; and

(b) in the case of pregnancy, the suspension may be lifted by the CAA for such period and subject to such conditions as it thinks fit and shall cease upon the holder being medically examined under arrangements made by the CAA after the pregnancy has ended and pronounced fit to resume her functions as a member of the flight crew.

---

1. Penalties for contraventions are contained in art 148 and Sch 14, post.

7–5844   **33. Miscellaneous licensing provisions**[1]. (1) A person who, on the last occasion when he took a test for the purposes of article 28, 29, 30 or 31 failed that test shall not be entitled to fly in the capacity for which that test would have qualified him had he passed it.

(2) Nothing in this Order shall prohibit the holder of a pilot's licence from acting as pilot of an aircraft certificated for single pilot operation when, with the permission of the CAA, he is testing any person for the purposes of articles 27(1), 27(4), 28(2), 29(2) or 31, notwithstanding that—

(a) the type of aircraft in which the test is conducted is not specified in an aircraft rating included in his licence; or

(b) the licence or personal flying log book, as the case may be, does not include a valid certificate of test, experience or revalidation in respect of the type of aircraft.

(3) Without prejudice to any other provision of this Order the CAA may, for the purpose of this Part of this Order—

- (a) approve any course of training or instruction;
- (b) authorise a person to conduct such examinations or tests as it may specify; and
- (c) approve a person to provide any course of training or instruction.

---

1. Penalties for contraventions are contained in art 148 and Sch 14, post.

34. Validation of licences

35. Personal flying log book

7–5845   **36. Instruction in flying**[1]. (1) A person shall not give any instruction in flying to which this article applies unless—

- (a) he holds a licence, granted or rendered valid under this Order or a JAA licence, entitling him to act as pilot in command of the aircraft for the purpose and in the circumstances under which the instruction is to be given; and
- (b) his licence includes an instructor's rating entitling the holder to give the instruction.

(2) This article applies to instruction in flying given to any person flying or about to fly a flying machine or glider for the purpose of becoming qualified for—

- (a) the grant of a pilot's licence; and
- (b) the inclusion or variation of any rating or qualification in his licence.

---

1. Penalties for contraventions are contained in art 148 and Sch 14, post.

37. Glider pilot—minimum age

PART 5[1]
OPERATION OF AIRCRAFT

7–5845A   **38. Operations manual**[2]

---

1. Part 5 comprises arts 38–80.
2. Penalties for contraventions are contained in art 148 and Sch 14, post.

7–5846   **39. Police operations manual**[1]. (1) This article shall apply to aircraft flying, or intended by the operator of the aircraft to fly solely under and in accordance with the terms of a police air operator's certificate.

(2) An aircraft to which this article applies shall not fly except under and in accordance with the terms of Part I and Part II of a police operations manual, Part I of which shall have been approved in respect of the aircraft by the CAA.

(3) The operator of every aircraft to which this article applies shall—

- (a) make available to each member of its operating staff a police operations manual;
- (b) ensure that each copy of the operations manual is kept up to date; and
- (c) ensure that on each flight every member of the crew has access to a copy of every part of the operations manual which is relevant to his duties on the flight.

(4) Each police operations manual shall contain all such information and instructions as may be necessary to enable the operating staff to perform their duties as such.

(5) An aircraft to which this article applies shall not fly unless, not less than 30 days prior to such flight, the operator of the aircraft has furnished to the CAA a copy of Part II of the police operations manual for the time being in effect in respect of the aircraft.

(6) Subject to paragraph (7), any amendments or additions to Part II of the police operations manual shall be furnished to the CAA by the operator before or immediately after they come into effect.

(7) Where an amendment or addition relates to the operation of an aircraft to which the police operations manual did not previously relate, that aircraft shall not fly in the service of a police authority under and in accordance with the terms of a police operator's certificate until the amendment or addition has been furnished to the CAA.

(8) Without prejudice to paragraph (5), the operator shall make such amendments or additions to the police operations manual as the CAA may require for the purpose of ensuring the safety of the aircraft, or of persons or property carried therein, or the safety, efficiency or regularity of air navigation.

---

1. Penalties for contraventions are contained in art 148 and Sch 14, post.

7–5847   **40. Training manual**[1]. (1) Subject to paragraph (2), the operator of every aircraft registered in the United Kingdom and flying for the purpose of public transport shall—

- (a) make a training manual available to every person appointed by the operator to give or to supervise the training, experience, practice or periodical tests required under article 42(3); and

(b) ensure that each copy of that training manual is kept up to date.

(2) This article shall not apply to aircraft flying, or intended by the operator of the aircraft to fly solely under and in accordance with the terms of a police air operator's certificate.

(3) Each training manual shall contain all such information and instructions as may be necessary to enable a person appointed by the operator to give or to supervise the training, experience, practice and periodical tests required under article 42(3) to perform his duties as such including in particular information and instructions relating to the matters specified in Part B of Schedule 9.

(4) An aircraft to which this article applies shall not fly unless not less than 30 days prior to such flight the operator of the aircraft has furnished to the CAA a copy of the whole of his training manual relating to the crew of that aircraft.

(5) Subject to paragraph (6), any amendments or additions to the training manual shall be furnished to the CAA by the operator before or immediately after they come into effect.

(6) Where an amendment or addition relates to training, experience, practice or periodical tests on an aircraft to which the training manual did not previously relate, that aircraft shall not fly for the purpose of public transport until the amendment or addition has been furnished to the CAA.

(7) Without prejudice to paragraphs (4) and (5), the operator shall make such amendments or additions to the training manual as the CAA may require for the purpose of ensuring the safety of the aircraft, or of persons or property carried therein, or the safety, efficiency or regularity of air navigation.

---

1. Penalties for contraventions are contained in art 148 and Sch 14, post.

41. Flight data monitoring, accident prevention and flight safety programme

7–5848   **42. Public transport—operator's responsibilities[1].** (1) The operator of an aircraft registered in the United Kingdom shall not permit the aircraft to fly for the purpose of public transport without first—

(a) designating from among the flight crew a pilot to be the commander of the aircraft for the flight;

(b) satisfying himself by every reasonable means that the aeronautical radio stations and navigational aids serving the intended route or any planned diversion are adequate for the safe navigation of the aircraft; and

(c) subject to paragraph (2), satisfying himself by every reasonable means that—

   (i) every place (whether or not an aerodrome) at which it is intended to take off or land and any alternate place (whether or not an aerodrome) at which a landing may be made are suitable for the purpose; and

   (ii) in particular that they will be adequately manned and equipped at the time at which it is reasonably estimated such a take-off or landing will be made (including that those places will have such manning and equipment as may be prescribed[2]) to ensure so far as practicable the safety of the aircraft and its passengers.

(2) Without prejudice to any conditions imposed under article 6, the operator of an aircraft shall not be required for the purposes of this article to satisfy himself as to the adequacy of fire-fighting, search, rescue or other services which are required only after the occurrence of an accident.

(3) The operator of an aircraft registered in the United Kingdom shall not permit any person to be a member of the crew during any flight for the purpose of public transport (except a flight for the sole purpose of training persons to perform duties in aircraft) unless—

(a) such person has had the training, experience, practice and periodical tests specified in Part C of Schedule 9 in respect of the duties which he is to perform; and

(b) the operator has satisfied himself that such person is competent to perform his duties, and in particular to use the equipment provided in the aircraft for that purpose.

(4) The operator shall maintain, preserve, produce and furnish information respecting records relating to the matters specified in paragraph (3) in accordance with Part C of Schedule 9.

(5) The operator of an aircraft registered in the United Kingdom shall not permit any member of the flight crew, during any flight for the purpose of the public transport of passengers, to simulate emergency manoeuvres and procedures which the operator has reason to believe will adversely affect the flight characteristics of the aircraft.

---

1. Penalties for contraventions are contained in art 148 and Sch 14, post.
2. See the Air Navigation (General) Regulations 2005, SI 2005/1980.

7–5849   **43. Loading—public transport aircraft and suspended loads[1].** (1) The operator of an aircraft registered in the United Kingdom shall not cause or permit it to be loaded for a flight for the purpose of public transport, or any load to be suspended therefrom, except under the supervision of a person whom he has caused to be furnished with written instructions as to the distribution and securing of the load so as to ensure that—

    (*a*) the load may safely be carried on the flight; and

    (*b*) any conditions of the certificate of airworthiness or flight manual for the aircraft relating to the loading of the aircraft are complied with.

  (2) Subject to paragraph (3), the instructions shall indicate the weight of the aircraft prepared for service, that is to say the aggregate of the weight of the aircraft (shown in the weight schedule referred to in article 23) and the weight of such additional items in or on the aircraft as the operator thinks fit to include; and the instructions shall indicate the additional items included in the weight of the aircraft prepared for service, and show the position of the centre of gravity of the aircraft at that weight.

  (3) Paragraph (2) shall not apply in relation to a flight if—

    (*a*) the aircraft's maximum total weight authorised does not exceed 1,150 kg;

    (*b*) the aircraft's maximum total weight authorised does not exceed 2,730 kg and the flight is intended not to exceed 60 minutes in duration and is either—

      (i) a flight solely for training persons to perform duties in an aircraft; or

      (ii) a flight intended to begin and end at the same aerodrome; or

    (*c*) the aircraft is a helicopter the maximum total weight authorised of which does not exceed 3,000 kg, and the total seating capacity of which does not exceed 5 persons.

  (4) The operator of an aircraft registered in the United Kingdom shall not cause or permit it to be loaded for a flight for the purpose of public transport in contravention of the instructions referred to in paragraph (1).

  (5) Subject to paragraphs (6) and (7), the person supervising the loading of the aircraft shall, before the commencement of any such flight, prepare and sign a load sheet in duplicate conforming to the prescribed[2] requirements, and shall (unless he is himself the commander of the aircraft) submit the load sheet for examination by the commander of the aircraft who shall sign his name thereon.

  (6) The requirements of paragraph (5) shall not apply if—

    (*a*) the load and the distributing and securing thereof upon the next intended flight are to be unchanged from the previous flight; and

    (*b*) the commander of the aircraft makes and signs an endorsement to that effect upon the load sheet for the previous flight, indicating—

      (i) the date of the endorsement;

      (ii) the place of departure upon the next intended flight; and

      (iii) the next intended place of destination.

  (7) The requirements of paragraph (5) shall not apply if paragraph (2) does not apply in relation to the flight.

  (8) Subject to paragraph (9), one copy of the load sheet shall be carried in the aircraft when article 86 so requires until the flights to which it relates have been completed and one copy of that load sheet and of the instructions referred to in this article shall be preserved by the operator until the expiration of a period of six months thereafter and shall not be carried in the aircraft.

  (9) In the case of an aeroplane of which the maximum total weight authorised does not exceed 2,730 kg, or a helicopter, if it is not reasonably practicable for the copy of the load sheet to be kept on the ground it may be carried in the aeroplane or helicopter, as the case may be, in a container approved by the CAA for that purpose.

  (10) The operator of an aircraft registered in the United Kingdom and flying for the purpose of the public transport of passengers shall not cause or permit baggage to be carried in the passenger compartment of the aircraft unless—

    (*a*) such baggage can be properly secured; and

    (*b*) in the case of an aircraft capable of seating more than 30 passengers, such baggage (other than baggage carried in accordance with a permission issued under article 54(6)(*b*)) shall not exceed the capacity of the spaces in the passenger compartment approved by the CAA for the purpose of stowing baggage.

---

1. Penalties for contraventions are contained in art 148 and Sch 14, post.

2. See the Air Navigation (General) Regulations 2005, SI 2005/1980.

7–5850 **44. Public transport—aeroplanes—operating conditions and performance requirements[1].**

  (1) Subject to paragraph (4) an aeroplane registered in the United Kingdom and flying for the purpose of public transport shall comply with subpart F of Section 1 of JAR-OPS 1.

  (2) The assessment of the ability of an aeroplane to comply with paragraph (1) shall be based on the information as to its performance approved by the state of design and contained in the flight manual for the aeroplane.

  (3) In the event of the approved information in the flight manual being insufficient for that purpose such assessment shall be based on additional data acceptable to the CAA.

  (4) An aeroplane need not comply with paragraph (1) if it is flying under and in accordance with a permission granted to the operator by the CAA under paragraph (5).

  (5) The CAA may grant in respect of any aeroplane a permission authorising it to comply with the applicable provisions of Schedule 2 to the Air Navigation (General) Regulations 2005.

  (6) The applicable provisions for an aeroplane in respect of which such a permission has been

granted shall be those provisions of the said Schedule applicable to an aeroplane of the performance group specified in the permission.

(7) An aeroplane registered in the United Kingdom flying under and in accordance with a permission granted by the CAA under paragraph (5) when flying over water for the purpose of public transport shall fly, except as may be necessary for the purpose of take-off or landing, at such an altitude as would enable the aeroplane—

(a) if it has one engine only, in the event of the failure of that engine; or
(b) if it has more than one engine, in the event of the failure of one of those engines and with the remaining engine or engines operating within the maximum continuous power conditions specified in the certificate of airworthiness or flight manual for the aeroplane;

to reach a place at which it can safely land at a height sufficient to enable it to do so.

(8) Without prejudice to paragraph (7), an aeroplane flying under and in accordance with a permission granted by the CAA under paragraph (5) in respect of which either that permission or the certificate of airworthiness of the aeroplane designates the aeroplane as being of performance group X shall not fly over water for the purpose of public transport so as to be more than 60 minutes flying time from the nearest shore, unless the aeroplane has more than 2 power units.

(9) For the purposes of paragraph (8), flying time shall be calculated at normal cruising speed with one power unit inoperative.

---

1. Penalties for contraventions are contained in art 148 and Sch 14, post.

7–5851 45. Public transport—helicopters—operating conditions and performance requirements[1].
(1) A helicopter registered in the United Kingdom shall not fly for the purpose of public transport, except for the sole purpose of training persons to perform duties in a helicopter unless such requirements as may be prescribed[2] in respect of its weight and related performance and flight in specified meteorological conditions or at night are complied with.

(2) The assessment of the ability of a helicopter to comply with paragraph (1) shall be based on the information as to its performance approved by the state of design and contained in the flight manual for the helicopter.

(3) In the event of the approved information in the flight manual being insufficient for that purpose such assessment shall be based on additional data acceptable to the CAA.

(4) A helicopter registered in the United Kingdom when flying over water for the purpose of public transport shall fly, except as may be necessary for the purpose of take-off or landing, at such an altitude as would enable the helicopter—

(a) if it has one engine only, in the event of the failure of that engine; or
(b) if it has more than one engine, in the event of the failure of one of those engines and with the remaining engine or engines operating within the maximum continuous power conditions specified in the certificate of airworthiness or flight manual for the helicopter;

to reach a place at which it can safely land at a height sufficient to enable it to do so.

(5) Without prejudice to paragraph (4), a helicopter carrying out Performance Class 3 operations—

(a) shall not fly over water for the purpose of public transport in the specified circumstances unless it is equipped with the required apparatus;
(b) which is equipped with the required apparatus and which is flying under and in accordance with the terms of an air operator's certificate granted by the CAA under article 6(2), shall not fly in the specified circumstances on any flight for more than three minutes except with the permission in writing of the CAA;
(c) which is equipped with the required apparatus and which is flying under and in accordance with the terms of a police air operator's certificate—

(i) on which is carried any passenger who is not a permitted passenger, shall not fly in the specified circumstances on any flight for more than 20 minutes;
(ii) on which no passenger is carried other than a permitted passenger, shall not fly over water on any flight for more than 10 minutes so as to be more than 5 minutes from a point from which it can make an autorotative descent to land suitable for an emergency landing;

(d) shall not fly for the purpose of public transport over that part of the bed of the River Thames which lies between the following points—

(i) Hammersmith Bridge (512918N) (0001351W); and
(ii) Greenwich Reach (512906N) (0000043W)

between the ordinary high water marks on each of its banks unless it is equipped with the required apparatus.

(6) For the purposes of paragraph (5) flying time shall be calculated on the assumption that a helicopter is flying in still air at the speed specified in the flight manual for the helicopter as the speed for compliance with regulations governing flights over water.

(7) Without prejudice to paragraph (4), a helicopter carrying out Performance Class 1 or Performance Class 2 operations—

(a) which is flying under and in accordance with the terms of an air operator's certificate granted by the CAA under article 6(2), shall not fly over water for the purpose of public transport for more than 15 minutes during any flight unless it is equipped with the required apparatus;

(b) which is not equipped with the required apparatus and which is flying under and in accordance with the terms of a police air operator's certificate on which any passenger is carried who is not a permitted passenger, shall not fly over any water on any flight for more than 15 minutes.

(8) Notwithstanding paragraph (1), a helicopter specified in its flight manual as being in either Group A or Category A may fly for the purpose of public transport in accordance with the weight and related performance requirements prescribed for helicopters carrying out—

(a) Performance Class 2 operations if—

(i) the maximum total weight authorised of the helicopter is less than 5,700 kg; and
(ii) the total number of passengers carried on the helicopter does not exceed 15; or

(b) Performance Class 3 operations if—

(i) the maximum total weight authorised of the helicopter is less than 3,175 kg; and
(ii) the total number of passengers carried does not exceed 9.

(9) For the purposes of this article—

(a) "permitted passenger" means—

(i) a police officer;
(ii) an employee of a police authority in the course of his duty;
(iii) a medical attendant;
(iv) the holder of a valid pilot's licence who intends to act as a member of the flight crew of an aircraft flying under and in accordance with the terms of a police air operator's certificate and who is being carried for the purpose of training or familiarisation;
(v) a CAA Flight Operations Inspector;
(vi) a Home Office police aviation adviser;
(vii) an employee of a fire and rescue authority under the Fire and Rescue Services Act 2004;
(viii) an officer of revenue and customs;
(ix) an employee of the Ministry of Defence in the course of his duty; or
(x) such other person being carried for purposes connected with police operations as may be permitted in writing by the CAA;

(b) "required apparatus" means apparatus approved by the CAA enabling the helicopter to which it is fitted to land safely on water; and

(c) "specified circumstances" means circumstances in which a helicopter is more than 20 seconds flying time from a point from which it can make an autorotative descent to land suitable for an emergency landing.

---

1. Penalties for contraventions are contained in art 148 and Sch 14, post.
2. See the Air Navigation (General) Regulations 2005, SI 2005/1980.

7–5852 46. Public transport operations at night or in Instrument Meteorological Conditions by aeroplanes with one power unit which are registered elsewhere than in the United Kingdom[1]. An aeroplane which is registered elsewhere than in the United Kingdom and is powered by one power unit only shall not fly for the purpose of public transport at night or when the cloud ceiling or visibility prevailing at the aerodrome of departure or forecast for the estimated time of landing at the aerodrome at which it is intended to land or at any alternate aerodrome are less than 1,000 feet and 1 nautical mile respectively.

---

1. Penalties for contraventions are contained in art 148 and Sch 14, post.

7–5853 47. Public transport aircraft registered in the United Kingdom—aerodrome operating minima[1]. (1) This article shall apply to public transport aircraft registered in the United Kingdom.

(2) Subject to paragraph (3), the operator of every aircraft to which this article applies shall establish and include in the operations manual or the police operations manual relating to the aircraft the particulars (in this sub-article called "the said particulars") of the aerodrome operating minima appropriate to every aerodrome of intended departure or landing and every alternate aerodrome.

(3) In relation to any flight where—

(a) neither an operations manual nor a police operations manual is required by this Order; or
(b) it is not practicable to include the said particulars in the operations manual or the police operations manual;

the operator of the said aircraft shall, prior to the commencement of the flight, cause to be furnished in writing to the commander of the aircraft the said particulars calculated in accordance with the required data and instructions provided in accordance with paragraph (4) or (5) and the operator shall cause a copy of the said particulars to be retained outside the aircraft for at least three months after the flight.

(4) The operator of every aircraft to which this article applies for which an operations manual or a police operations manual is required by this Order, shall include in that operations manual such data and instructions (in this article called "the required data and instructions") as will enable the commander of the aircraft to calculate the aerodrome operating minima appropriate to aerodromes the use of which cannot reasonably have been foreseen by the operator prior to the commencement of the flight.

(5) The operator of every aircraft to which this article applies for which neither an operations manual nor a police operations manual is required by this Order shall, prior to the commencement of the flight, cause to be furnished in writing to the commander of the aircraft the required data and instructions; and the operator shall cause a copy of the required data and instructions to be retained outside the aircraft for at least three months after the flight.

(6) The specified aerodrome operating minima shall not permit a landing or take-off in circumstances where the relevant aerodrome operating minima declared by the competent authority would prohibit it, unless that authority otherwise permits in writing.

(7) In establishing aerodrome operating minima for the purposes of this article the operator of the aircraft shall take into account the following matters—

(a) the type and performance and handling characteristics of the aircraft and any relevant conditions in its certificate of airworthiness;

(b) the composition of its crew;

(c) the physical characteristics of the relevant aerodrome and its surroundings;

(d) the dimensions of the runways which may be selected for use; and

(e) whether or not there are in use at the relevant aerodrome any aids, visual or otherwise, to assist aircraft in approach, landing or take-off, being aids which the crew of the aircraft are trained and equipped to use, the nature of any such aids that are in use, and the procedures for approach, landing and take-off which may be adopted according to the existence or absence of such aids;

and shall establish in relation to each runway which may be selected for use such aerodrome operating minima as are appropriate to each set of circumstances which can reasonably be expected.

(8) An aircraft to which this article applies shall not commence a flight at a time when—

(a) the cloud ceiling or the runway visual range at the aerodrome of departure is less than the relevant minimum specified for take-off; or

(b) according to the information available to the commander of the aircraft it would not be able without contravening paragraph (9) or (10), to land at the aerodrome of intended destination at the estimated time of arrival there and at any alternate aerodrome at any time at which according to a reasonable estimate the aircraft would arrive there.

(9) An aircraft to which article 38 applies, when making a descent to an aerodrome, shall not descend from a height of 1,000 feet or more above the aerodrome to a height less than 1,000 feet above the aerodrome if the relevant runway visual range at the aerodrome is at the time less than the specified minimum for landing.

(10) An aircraft to which this article applies, when making a descent to an aerodrome, shall not—

(a) continue an approach to landing at any aerodrome by flying below the relevant specified decision height; or

(b) descend below the relevant specified minimum descent height;

unless in either case from such height the specified visual reference for landing is established and is maintained.

(11) If, according to the information available, an aircraft would as regards any flight be required by the Rules of the Air Regulations 1996 to be flown in accordance with the Instrument Flight Rules at the aerodrome of intended landing, the commander of the aircraft shall select prior to take-off an alternate aerodrome unless no aerodrome suitable for that purpose is available.

(12) In this article "specified" in relation to aerodrome operating minima means such particulars of aerodrome operating minima as have been specified by the operator in, or are ascertainable by reference to, the operations manual relating to that aircraft, or furnished in writing to the commander of the aircraft by the operator in accordance with paragraph (3).

---

1. Penalties for contraventions are contained in art 148 and Sch 14, post.

7–5854   48. Public transport aircraft registered elsewhere than in the United Kingdom—aerodrome operating minima[1]. (1) This article shall apply to public transport aircraft registered elsewhere than in the United Kingdom.

(2) An aircraft to which this article applies shall not fly in or over the United Kingdom unless the operator has made available to the flight crew, aerodrome operating minima which comply with paragraph (3) in respect of every aerodrome at which it is intended to land or take off and every alternate aerodrome.

(3) The aerodrome operating minima provided in accordance with paragraph (2) shall be no less restrictive than either—

(a) minima calculated in accordance with the notified method for calculating aerodrome operating minima; or

(b) minima which comply with the law of the country in which the aircraft is registered;

whichever are the more restrictive.

(4) An aircraft to which this article applies shall not:

(a) conduct a Category II, Category IIIA or Category IIIB approach and landing; or

(b) take off when the relevant runway visual range is less than 150 metres;

otherwise than under and in accordance with the terms of an approval so to do granted in accordance with the law of the country in which it is registered.

(5) An aircraft to which this article applies shall not take off from or land at an aerodrome in the United Kingdom in contravention of the specified aerodrome operating minima.

(6) Without prejudice to paragraphs (4) and (5), an aircraft to which this article applies, when making a descent to an aerodrome, shall not descend from a height of 1,000 feet or more above the aerodrome to a height of less than 1,000 feet above the aerodrome if the relevant runway visual range at the aerodrome is at the time less than the specified minimum for landing.

(7) Without prejudice to paragraphs (4) and (5), an aircraft to which this article applies, when making a descent to an aerodrome, shall not—

(a) continue an approach to landing at any aerodrome by flying below the relevant specified decision height; or

(b) descend below the relevant specified minimum descent height;

unless in either case from such height the specified visual reference for landing is established and is maintained.

(8) In this article—

(a) "specified" means specified by the operator in the aerodrome operating minima made available to the flight crew under paragraph (2);

(b) "a Category II approach and landing" means a landing following a precision approach using an Instrument Landing System or Microwave Landing System with—

(i) a decision height below 200 feet but not less than 100 feet; and

(ii) a runway visual range of not less than 300 metres;

(c) "a Category IIIA approach and landing" means a landing following a precision approach using an Instrument Landing System or Microwave Landing System with—

(i) a decision height lower than 100 feet; and

(ii) a runway visual range of not less than 200 metres; and

(d) "a Category IIIB approach and landing" means a landing following a precision approach using an Instrument Landing System or Microwave Landing System with—

(i) a decision height lower than 50 feet or no decision height; and

(ii) a runway visual range of less than 200 metres but not less than 75 metres.

---

1. Penalties for contraventions are contained in art 148 and Sch 14, post.

7–5855 49. Non-public transport aircraft—aerodrome operating minima[1]. (1) This article shall apply to any aircraft which is not a public transport aircraft.

(2) An aircraft to which this article applies shall not—

(a) conduct a Category II, Category IIIA or Category IIIB approach and landing; or

(b) take off when the relevant runway visual range is less than 150 metres;

otherwise than under and in accordance with the terms of an approval so to do granted in accordance with the law of the country in which it is registered.

(3) In the case of an aircraft registered in the United Kingdom, the approval referred to in paragraph (2) shall be issued by the CAA.

(4) Without prejudice to paragraph (2), an aircraft to which this article applies when making a descent at an aerodrome to a runway in respect of which there is a notified instrument approach procedure shall not descend from a height of 1,000 feet or more above the aerodrome to a height less than 1,000 feet above the aerodrome if the relevant runway visual range for that runway is at the time less than the specified minimum for landing.

(5) Without prejudice to paragraph (2), an aircraft to which this article applies when making a descent to a runway in respect of which there is a notified instrument approach procedure shall not—

(a) continue an approach to landing on such a runway by flying below the relevant specified decision height; or

(b) descend below the relevant specified minimum descent height;

unless in either case from such height the specified visual reference for landing is established and is maintained.

(6) If, according to the information available, an aircraft would as regards any flight be required

by the Rules of the Air Regulations 1996 to be flown in accordance with the Instrument Flight Rules at the aerodrome of intended landing, the commander of the aircraft shall select prior to take-off an alternate aerodrome unless no aerodrome suitable for that purpose is available.

(7) In this article "specified" in relation to aerodrome operating minima means such particulars of aerodrome operating minima as have been notified in respect of the aerodrome or if the relevant minima have not been notified such minima as are ascertainable by reference to the notified method for calculating aerodrome operating minima.

(8) In this article Category II, Category IIIA and Category IIIB approach and landing have the same meaning as in article 48(8).

---

1. Penalties for contraventions are contained in art 148 and Sch 14, post.

7–5856   50. Pilots to remain at controls[1]. (1) The commander of a flying machine or glider registered in the United Kingdom shall cause one pilot to remain at the controls at all times while it is in flight.

(2) If the flying machine or glider is required by or under this Order to carry two pilots, the commander shall cause both pilots to remain at the controls during take-off and landing.

(3) If the flying machine or glider carries two or more pilots (whether or not it is required to do so) and is engaged on a flight for the purpose of the public transport of passengers, the commander shall remain at the controls during take-off and landing.

(4) Each pilot at the controls shall be secured in his seat by either a safety belt with or without one diagonal shoulder strap, or a safety harness except that during take-off and landing a safety harness shall be worn if it is required by article 19 and Schedule 4 to be provided.

---

1. Penalties for contraventions are contained in art 148 and Sch 14, post.

51. Wearing of survival suits by crew

7–5857   52. Pre-flight action by commander of aircraft[1]. The commander of an aircraft registered in the United Kingdom shall take all reasonable steps to satisfy himself before the aircraft takes off—

(a)   that the flight can safely be made, taking into account the latest information available as to the route and aerodrome to be used, the weather reports and forecasts available and any alternative course of action which can be adopted in case the flight cannot be completed as planned;

(b)   either that—

  (i)   the equipment required by or under this Order to be carried in the circumstances of the intended flight is carried and is in a fit condition for use; or

  (ii)   the flight may commence under and in accordance with the terms of a permission granted to the operator under article 21;

(c)   that the aircraft is in every way fit for the intended flight, and that where a certificate of maintenance review is required by article 14(1) to be in force, it is in force and will not cease to be in force during the intended flight;

(d)   that the load carried by the aircraft is of such weight, and is so distributed and secured, that it may safely be carried on the intended flight;

(e)   in the case of a flying machine or airship, that sufficient fuel, oil and engine coolant (if required) are carried for the intended flight, and that a safe margin has been allowed for contingencies, and, in the case of a flight for the purpose of public transport, that the instructions in the operations manual relating to fuel, oil and engine coolant have been complied with;

(f)   in the case of an airship or balloon, that sufficient ballast is carried for the intended flight;

(g)   in the case of a flying machine, that having regard to the performance of the flying machine in the conditions to be expected on the intended flight, and to any obstructions at the places of departure and intended destination and on the intended route, it is capable of safely taking off, reaching and maintaining a safe height thereafter and making a safe landing at the place of intended destination;

(h)   that any pre-flight check system established by the operator and set out in the operations manual or elsewhere has been complied with by each member of the crew of the aircraft; and

(i)   in the case of a balloon, that the balloon will be able to land clear of any congested area.

---

1. Penalties for contraventions are contained in art 148 and Sch 14, post.

7–5858   53. Passenger briefing by commander[1]. (1) Subject to paragraph (2), the commander of an aircraft registered in the United Kingdom shall take all reasonable steps to ensure—

(a)   before the aircraft takes off on any flight, that all passengers are made familiar with the position and method of use of emergency exits, safety belts (with diagonal shoulder strap where required to be carried), safety harnesses and (where required to be carried) oxygen equipment, lifejackets and the floor path lighting system and all other devices required by or under this Order and intended for use by passengers individually in the case of an emergency occurring to the aircraft; and

(b) that in an emergency during a flight, all passengers are instructed in the emergency action which they should take.

(2) This article shall not apply to the commander of an aircraft registered in the United Kingdom in relation to a flight under and in accordance with the terms of a police air operator's certificate.

---

1. Penalties for contraventions are contained in art 148 and Sch 14, post.

7–5859   54. Public transport of passengers—additional duties of commander[1]. (1) This article applies to flights for the purpose of the public transport of passengers by aircraft registered in the United Kingdom other than flights under and in accordance with the terms of a police air operator's certificate.

(2) In the case of an aircraft which is not a seaplane, on a flight to which this article applies on which it is intended to reach a point more than 30 minutes flying time (while flying in still air at the speed specified in the relevant certificate of airworthiness or flight manual as the speed for compliance with regulations governing flights over water) from the nearest land, the commander shall, subject to paragraph (9), take all reasonable steps to ensure that before take-off all passengers are given a demonstration of the method of use of the lifejackets required by or under this Order for the use of passengers.

(3) In the case of an aircraft which is not a seaplane but is required by article 25(13) to carry cabin crew, the commander shall, subject to paragraph (9), take all reasonable steps to ensure that, before the aircraft takes off on a flight to which this article applies on which—

(a) it is intended to proceed beyond gliding distance from land; or

(b) in the event of any emergency occurring during the take-off or during the landing at the intended destination or any likely alternate destination it is reasonably possible that the aircraft would be forced to land onto water;

all passengers are given a demonstration of the method of use of the lifejackets required by or under this Order for the use of passengers.

(4) In the case of an aircraft which is a seaplane, the commander shall take all reasonable steps to ensure that before the aircraft takes off on a flight to which this article applies all passengers are given a demonstration of the method of use of the lifejackets required by or under this Order for the use of passengers.

(5) Before the aircraft takes off on a flight to which this article applies, and before it lands, the commander shall take all reasonable steps to ensure that the crew of the aircraft are properly secured in their seats and that any persons carried in compliance with article 25(13) and (14) are properly secured in seats which shall be in a passenger compartment and which shall be so situated that those persons can readily assist passengers.

(6) From the moment when, after the embarkation of its passengers for the purpose of taking off on a flight to which this article applies, it first moves until after it has taken off, and before it lands until it comes to rest for the purpose of the disembarkation of its passengers, and whenever by reason of turbulent air or any emergency occurring during the flight he considers the precaution necessary the commander shall take all reasonable steps to ensure that—

(a) all passengers of 2 years of age or more are properly secured in their seats by safety belts (with diagonal shoulder strap, where required to be carried) or safety harnesses and that all passengers under the age of 2 years are properly secured by means of a child restraint device; and

(b) those items of baggage in the passenger compartment which he reasonably considers ought by virtue of their size, weight or nature to be properly secured are properly secured and, in the case of an aircraft capable of seating more than 30 passengers, that such baggage is either stowed in the passenger compartment stowage spaces approved by the CAA for the purpose or carried in accordance with the terms of a permission granted by the CAA.

(7) In the case of aircraft in respect of which a certificate of airworthiness was first issued (whether in the United Kingdom or elsewhere) on or after 1st January 1989 except in a case where a pressure greater than 700 hectopascals is maintained in all passenger and crew compartments throughout the flight, the commander shall take all reasonable steps to ensure that on a flight to which this article applies—

(a) before the aircraft reaches flight level 100 the method of use of the oxygen provided in the aircraft in compliance with the requirements of article 19 and Schedule 4 is demonstrated to all passengers;

(b) when flying above flight level 120 all passengers and cabin crew are recommended to use oxygen; and

(c) during any period when the aircraft is flying above flight level 100 oxygen is used by all the flight crew of the aircraft.

(8) In the case of aircraft in respect of which a certificate of airworthiness was first issued (whether in the United Kingdom or elsewhere) prior to 1st January 1989, except in the case where a pressure greater than 700 hectopascals is maintained in all passenger and crew compartments

throughout the flight, the commander shall take all reasonable steps to ensure that on a flight to which this article applies—

(a) before the aircraft reaches flight level 130 the method of use of the oxygen provided in the aircraft in compliance with the requirements of article 19 and Schedule 4 is demonstrated to all passengers;

(b) when flying above flight level 130 all passengers and cabin crew are recommended to use oxygen; and

(c) during any period when the aircraft is flying above flight level 100 oxygen is used by all the flight crew of the aircraft;

provided that he may comply instead with paragraph (7).

(9) Where the only requirement to give a demonstration required by paragraph (2) or (3) arises because it is reasonably possible that the aircraft would be forced to land onto water at one or more of the likely alternate destinations the demonstration need not be given until after the decision has been taken to divert to such a destination.

---

1. Penalties for contraventions are contained in art 148 and Sch 14, post.

7–5860   55. Operation of radio in aircraft[1]. (1) A radio station in an aircraft shall not be operated, whether or not the aircraft is in flight, except in accordance with the conditions of the licence issued in respect of that station under the law of the country in which the aircraft is registered or the State of the operator and by a person duly licensed or otherwise permitted to operate the radio station under that law.

(2) Subject to paragraph (3), whenever an aircraft is in flight in such circumstances that it is required by or under this Order to be equipped with radio communications apparatus, a continuous radio watch shall be maintained by a member of the flight crew listening to the signals transmitted upon the frequency notified, or designated by a message received from an appropriate aeronautical radio station, for use by that aircraft.

(3) The radio watch—

(a) may be discontinued or continued on another frequency if a message from an appropriate aeronautical radio station permits;

(b) may be kept by a device installed in the aircraft if—

(i) the appropriate aeronautical radio station has been informed to that effect and has raised no objection; and

(ii) that station is notified, or in the case of a station situated in a country other than the United Kingdom, otherwise designated as transmitting a signal suitable for that purpose.

(4) Whenever an aircraft is in flight in such circumstances that it is required by or under this Order to be equipped with radio communication or radio navigation equipment a member of the flight crew shall operate that equipment in such a manner as he may be instructed by the appropriate air traffic control unit or as may be notified in relation to any notified airspace in which the aircraft is flying.

(5) The radio station in an aircraft shall not be operated so as to cause interference which impairs the efficiency of aeronautical telecommunications or navigational services, and in particular emissions shall not be made except as follows—

(a) emissions of the class and frequency for the time being in use, in accordance with general international aeronautical practice, in the airspace in which the aircraft is flying;

(b) distress, urgency and safety messages and signals, in accordance with general international aeronautical practice;

(c) messages and signals relating to the flight of the aircraft, in accordance with general international aeronautical practice; and

(d) such public correspondence messages as may be permitted by or under the aircraft radio station licence referred to in paragraph (1).

(6) In any flying machine registered in the United Kingdom which is engaged on a flight for the purpose of public transport the pilot and the flight engineer (if any) shall not make use of a hand-held microphone (whether for the purpose of radio communication or of intercommunication within the aircraft) whilst the aircraft is flying in controlled airspace below flight level 150 or is taking off or landing.

---

1. Penalties for contraventions are contained in art 148 and Sch 14, post.

7–5861   56. Minimum navigation performance[1]. (1) An aircraft registered in the United Kingdom shall not fly in North Atlantic Minimum Navigation Performance Specification airspace unless it is equipped with navigation systems which enable the aircraft to maintain the prescribed[2] navigation performance capability.

(2) The equipment required by paragraph (1) shall—

(a) be approved by EASA or the CAA;

(b) be installed in a manner approved by EASA in the case of an EASA aircraft and the CAA in the case of a non-EASA aircraft;

(c) be maintained in a manner approved by the CAA; and
(d) while the aircraft is flying in the said airspace, be operated in accordance with procedures approved by the CAA.

1. Penalties for contraventions are contained in art 148 and Sch 14, post.
2. See the Air Navigation (General) Regulations 2005, SI 2005/1980.

7–5862 57. Height keeping performance—aircraft registered in the United Kingdom[1]. (1) Unless otherwise authorised by the appropriate air traffic control unit, an aircraft registered in the United Kingdom shall not fly in reduced vertical separation minimum airspace notified for the purpose of this article, unless it is equipped with height keeping systems which enable the aircraft to maintain the prescribed[2] height keeping performance capability.

(2) The equipment required by paragraph (1) shall—

(a) be approved by EASA or the CAA;
(b) be installed in a manner approved by EASA in the case of an EASA aircraft and the CAA in the case of a non-EASA aircraft;
(c) be maintained in a manner approved by the CAA; and
(d) while the aircraft is flying in the said airspace, be operated in accordance with procedures approved by the CAA.

1. Penalties for contraventions are contained in art 148 and Sch 14, post.
2. See the Air Navigation (General) Regulations 2005, SI 2005/1980.

7–5863 58. Height keeping performance—aircraft registered elsewhere than in the United Kingdom[1]. Unless otherwise authorised by the appropriate air traffic control unit an aircraft registered elsewhere than in the United Kingdom shall not fly in United Kingdom reduced vertical separation minimum airspace unless—

(a) it is so equipped with height keeping systems as to comply with the law of the country in which the aircraft is registered in so far as that law requires it to be so equipped when flying in any specified areas; and
(b) the said equipment is capable of being operated so as to enable the aircraft to maintain the height keeping performance prescribed[2] in respect of the airspace in which the aircraft is flying, and it is so operated.

1. Penalties for contraventions are contained in art 148 and Sch 14, post.
2. See the Air Navigation (General) Regulations 2005, SI 2005/1980.

7–5864 59. Area navigation and required navigation performance capabilities—aircraft registered in the United Kingdom[1]. (1) Subject to paragraph (3) an aircraft registered in the United Kingdom shall not fly in designated required navigation performance airspace unless it is equipped with area navigation equipment which enables the aircraft to maintain the navigation performance capability specified in respect of that airspace.

(2) The equipment required by paragraph (1) shall—

(a) be approved by EASA or the CAA;
(b) be installed in a manner approved by EASA in the case of an EASA aircraft and the CAA in the case of a non-EASA aircraft;
(c) be maintained in a manner approved by the CAA; and
(d) while the aircraft is flying in the said airspace, be operated in accordance with procedures approved by the CAA.

(3) An aircraft need not comply with the requirements of paragraph (1) and (2) where the flight has been authorised by the appropriate air traffic control unit notwithstanding the lack of compliance and provided that the aircraft complies with any instructions the air traffic control unit may give in the particular case.

1. Penalties for contraventions are contained in art 148 and Sch 14, post.

7–5865 60. Area navigation and required navigation performance capabilities—aircraft registered elsewhere than in the United Kingdom[1]. (1) An aircraft registered elsewhere than in the United Kingdom shall not fly in designated required navigation performance airspace in the United Kingdom unless it is equipped with area navigation equipment so as to comply with the law of the country in which the aircraft is registered in so far as that law requires it to be so equipped when flying within designated required navigation performance airspace.

(2) Subject to paragraph (3), the said navigation equipment shall be capable of being operated so as to enable the aircraft to maintain the navigation performance capability notified in respect of the airspace in which the aircraft is flying, and shall be so operated.

(3) An aircraft need not comply with the requirements of paragraph (2) where the flight has been authorised by the appropriate United Kingdom air traffic control unit notwithstanding the lack of compliance and provided that the aircraft complies with any instructions the air traffic control unit may give in the particular case.

1. Penalties for contraventions are contained in art 148 and Sch 14, post.

7–5866 61. Use of airborne collision avoidance system[1]. On any flight on which an airborne collision avoidance system is required by article 20 and Schedule 5 to be carried in an aeroplane, the system shall be operated—

(a) in the case of an aircraft to which article 38 applies, in accordance with procedures contained in the operations manual for the aircraft;

(b) in the case of an aircraft registered in the United Kingdom to which article 38 does not apply, in accordance with procedures which are suitable having regard to the purposes of the equipment; or

(c) in the case of an aircraft which is registered elsewhere than in the United Kingdom, in accordance with any procedures with which it is required to comply under the law of the country in which the aircraft is registered.

1. Penalties for contraventions are contained in art 148 and Sch 14, post.

7–5867 62. Use of flight recording systems and preservation of records[1]. (1) On any flight on which a flight data recorder, a cockpit voice recorder or a combined cockpit voice recorder/flight data recorder is required by paragraph 5(4), (5), (6) or (7) of Schedule 4 to be carried in an aeroplane, it shall always be in use from the beginning of the take-off run to the end of the landing run.

(2) The operator of the aeroplane shall at all times, subject to article 91, preserve—

(a) the last 25 hours of recording made by any flight data recorder required by or under this Order to be carried in an aeroplane; and

(b) a record of not less than one representative flight, that is to say, a recording of a flight made within the last 12 months which includes a take-off, climb, cruise, descent, approach to landing and landing, together with a means of identifying the record with the flight to which it relates;

and shall preserve such records for such period as the CAA may in a particular case direct.

(3) On any flight on which a cockpit voice recorder, a flight data recorder or a combined cockpit voice recorder/flight data recorder is required by paragraph 5(16) of Schedule 4 to be carried in a helicopter, it shall always be in use from the time the rotors first turn for the purpose of taking off until the rotors are next stopped.

(4) The operator of the helicopter shall at all times, subject to article 91, preserve—

(a) the last 8 hours of recording made by any flight data recorder specified in paragraph (1) or (2) of Scale SS of paragraph 6 of Schedule 4 and required by or under this Order to be carried in the helicopter;

(b) in the case of a combined cockpit voice recorder/flight data recorder specified in paragraph (3) of the said Scale SS and required by or under this Order to be carried in a helicopter either—

(i) the last 8 hours of recording; or

(ii) the last 5 hours of recording or the duration of the last flight, whichever is the greater, together with an additional period of recording for either—

(aa) the period immediately preceding the last five hours of recording or the duration of the last flight, whichever is the greater; or

(bb) such period or periods as the CAA may permit in any particular case or class of cases or generally.

(5) The additional recording retained under sub-paragraphs (b)(ii)(aa) and (bb) of paragraph (4) shall, together with the recording required to be retained under sub-paragraph (b)(ii) of paragraph (4), total a period of 8 hours and shall be retained in accordance with arrangements approved by the CAA.

1. Penalties for contraventions are contained in art 148 and Sch 14, post.

7–5868 63. Towing of gliders[1]. (1) An aircraft in flight shall not tow a glider unless the flight manual for the towing aircraft includes an express provision that it may be used for that purpose.

(2) The length of the combination of towing aircraft, tow rope and glider in flight shall not exceed 150 metres.

(3) The commander of an aircraft which is about to tow a glider shall satisfy himself, before the towing aircraft takes off—

(a) that the tow rope is in good condition and is of adequate strength for the purpose, and that the combination of towing aircraft and glider, having regard to its performance in the conditions to be expected on the intended flight and to any obstructions at the place of departure and on the intended route, is capable of safely taking off, reaching and maintaining a safe height at which to separate the combination and that thereafter the towing aircraft can make a safe landing at the place of intended destination;

(b) that signals have been agreed and communication established with persons suitably stationed so as to enable the glider to take off safely; and

(c) that emergency signals have been agreed between the commander of the towing aircraft and the commander of the glider, to be used, respectively, by the commander of the towing aircraft to indicate that the tow should immediately be released by the glider, and by the commander of the glider to indicate that the tow cannot be released.

(4) The glider shall be attached to the towing aircraft by means of the tow rope before the aircraft takes off.

---

1. Penalties for contraventions are contained in art 148 and Sch 14, post.

64. Operation of self-sustaining gliders

7–5869   65. Towing, picking up and raising of persons and articles[1]. (1) Subject to the provisions of this article, an aircraft in flight shall not, by means external to the aircraft, tow any article, other than a glider, or pick up or raise any person, animal or article, unless there is a certificate of airworthiness issued or rendered valid in respect of that aircraft under the law of the country in which the aircraft is registered and that certificate or the flight manual for the aircraft includes an express provision that it may be used for that purpose.

(2) An aircraft shall not launch or pick up tow ropes, banners or similar articles other than at an aerodrome.

(3) An aircraft in flight shall not tow any article, other than a glider, at night or when flight visibility is less than one nautical mile.

(4) The length of the combination of towing aircraft, tow rope, and article in tow, shall not exceed 150 metres.

(5) A helicopter shall not fly at any height over a congested area of a city, town or settlement at any time when any article, person or animal is suspended from the helicopter.

(6) A passenger shall not be carried in a helicopter at any time when an article, person or animal is suspended therefrom, other than a passenger who has duties to perform in connection with the article, person or animal or a passenger who has been picked up or raised by means external to the helicopter or a passenger who it is intended shall be lowered to the surface by such means.

(7) Nothing in this article shall—

(a) prohibit the towing in a reasonable manner by an aircraft in flight of any radio aerial, any instrument which is being used for experimental purposes, or any signal, apparatus or article required or permitted by or under this Order to be towed or displayed by an aircraft in flight;

(b) prohibit the picking up or raising of any person, animal or article in an emergency or for the purpose of saving life;

(c) apply to any aircraft while it is flying in accordance with the B Conditions; or

(d) be taken to permit the towing or picking up of a glider otherwise than in accordance with article 63.

---

1. Penalties for contraventions are contained in art 148 and Sch 14, post.

7–5870   66. Dropping of articles and animals[1]. (1) Articles and animals (whether or not attached to a parachute) shall not be dropped, or permitted to drop, from an aircraft in flight so as to endanger persons or property.

(2) Subject to paragraph (3), except under and in accordance with the terms of an aerial application certificate granted under article 68, articles and animals (whether or not attached to a parachute) shall not be dropped, or permitted to drop, to the surface from an aircraft flying over the United Kingdom.

(3) Paragraph (2) shall not apply to the dropping of articles by, or with the authority of, the commander of the aircraft in any of the following circumstances—

(a) the dropping of articles for the purpose of saving life;

(b) the jettisoning, in case of emergency, of fuel or other articles in the aircraft;

(c) the dropping of ballast in the form of fine sand or water;

(d) the dropping of articles solely for the purpose of navigating the aircraft in accordance with ordinary practice or with the provisions of this Order;

(e) the dropping at an aerodrome of tow ropes, banners, or similar articles towed by aircraft;

(f) the dropping of articles for the purposes of public health or as a measure against weather conditions, surface icing or oil pollution, or for training for the dropping of articles for any such purposes, if the articles are dropped with the permission of the CAA; or

(g) the dropping of wind drift indicators for the purpose of enabling parachute descents to be made if the wind drift indicators are dropped with the permission of the CAA.

(4) For the purposes of this article "dropping" includes projecting and lowering.

(5) Nothing in this article shall prohibit the lowering of any article or animal from a helicopter to the surface, if there is a certificate of airworthiness issued or rendered valid in respect of the

helicopter under the law of the country in which it is registered and that certificate or the flight manual for the helicopter includes an express provision that it may be used for that purpose.

---

1. Penalties for contraventions are contained in art 148 and Sch 14, post.

7–5871 67. Dropping of persons and grant of parachuting permissions[1]. (1) A person shall not drop, be dropped or be permitted to drop to the surface or jump from an aircraft flying over the United Kingdom except under and in accordance with the terms of either a police air operator's certificate or a parachuting permission granted by the CAA under this article.

(2) For the purposes of this article "dropping" includes projecting and lowering.

(3) Notwithstanding the grant of a police air operator's certificate or a parachuting permission, a person shall not drop, be dropped or be permitted to drop from an aircraft in flight so as to endanger persons or property.

(4) An aircraft shall not be used for the purpose of dropping persons unless—

(a) there is a certificate of airworthiness issued or rendered valid in respect of that aircraft under the law of the country in which the aircraft is registered and that certificate or the flight manual for the aircraft includes an express provision that it may be used for that purpose and the aircraft is operated in accordance with a written permission granted by the CAA under this article; or

(b) the aircraft is operated under and in accordance with the terms of a police air operator's certificate.

(5) Every applicant for and every holder of a parachuting permission shall make available to the CAA if requested to do so a parachuting manual and shall make such amendments or additions to such manual as the CAA may require.

(6) The holder of a parachuting permission shall make the manual available to every employee or person who is or may engage in parachuting activities conducted by him.

(7) The manual shall contain all such information and instructions as may be necessary to enable such employees or persons to perform their duties.

(8) Nothing in this article shall apply to the descent of persons by parachute from an aircraft in an emergency.

(9) Nothing in this article shall prohibit the lowering of any person in an emergency or for the purpose of saving life.

(10) Nothing in this article shall prohibit the lowering of any person from a helicopter to the surface if there is a certificate of airworthiness issued or rendered valid in respect of the helicopter under the law of the country in which it is registered and that certificate or the flight manual for the helicopter includes an express provision that it may be used for that purpose.

---

1. Penalties for contraventions are contained in art 148 and Sch 14, post.

7–5872 68. Grant of aerial application certificates[1]. (1) An aircraft shall not be used for the dropping of articles for the purposes of agriculture, horticulture or forestry or for training for the dropping of articles for any of such purposes, otherwise than under and in accordance with the terms of an aerial application certificate granted to the operator of the aircraft under paragraph (2).

(2) The CAA—

(a) shall grant an aerial application certificate if it is satisfied that the applicant is a fit person to hold the certificate and is competent, having regard in particular to his previous conduct and experience, his equipment, organisation, staffing and other arrangements, to secure the safe operation of the aircraft specified in the certificate on flights for the purposes specified in paragraph (1);

(b) may grant such a certificate subject to such conditions as it thinks fit including, without prejudice to the generality of the foregoing, conditions for ensuring that the aircraft and any article dropped from it do not endanger persons or property in the aircraft or elsewhere.

(3) Every applicant for and holder of an aerial application certificate shall make available to the CAA upon application and to every member of his operating staff upon the certificate being granted, an aerial application manual.

(4) The manual shall contain all such information and instructions as may be necessary to enable the operating staff to perform their duties as such.

(5) The holder of an aerial application certificate shall make such amendments or additions to the manual as the CAA may require.

---

1. Penalties for contraventions are contained in art 148 and Sch 14, post.

7–5873 69. Carriage of weapons and of munitions of war[1]. (1) Subject to paragraph (6), an aircraft shall not carry any munition of war unless—

(a) such munition of war is carried with the permission of the CAA; and

(b) subject to paragraph (2), the commander of the aircraft is informed in writing by the operator before the flight commences of the type, weight or quantity and location of any such munition of war on board or suspended beneath the aircraft and any conditions of the permission of the CAA.

(2) In the case of an aircraft which is flying under and in accordance with the terms of a police air operator's certificate the commander of the aircraft shall be informed of the matters referred to in sub-paragraph (1)(b) but he need not be so informed in writing.

(3) Subject to paragraph (5), it shall be unlawful for an aircraft to carry any sporting weapon or munition of war in any compartment or apparatus to which passengers have access.

(4) Subject to paragraph (5), it shall be unlawful for a person to carry or have in his possession or take or cause to be taken on board an aircraft, to suspend or cause to be suspended beneath an aircraft or to deliver or cause to be delivered for carriage thereon any sporting weapon or munition of war unless—

(a) the sporting weapon or munition of war—

   (i) is either part of the baggage of a passenger on the aircraft or consigned as cargo to be carried thereby;

   (ii) is carried in a part of the aircraft, or in any apparatus attached to the aircraft inaccessible to passengers; and

   (iii) in the case of a firearm, is unloaded;

(b) particulars of the sporting weapon or munition of war have been furnished by that passenger or by the consignor to the operator before the flight commences; and

(c) without prejudice to paragraph (1), the operator consents to the carriage of such sporting weapon or munition of war by the aircraft.

(5) Paragraphs (3) and (4) shall not apply to or in relation to an aircraft which is flying under and in accordance with the terms of a police air operator's certificate.

(6) Nothing in this article shall apply to any sporting weapon or munition of war taken or carried on board an aircraft registered in a country other than the United Kingdom if the sporting weapon or munition of war, as the case may be, may under the law of the country in which the aircraft is registered be lawfully taken or carried on board for the purpose of ensuring the safety of the aircraft or of persons on board.

(7) For the purposes of this article—

(a) "munition of war" means—

   (i) any weapon or ammunition;

   (ii) any article containing an explosive, noxious liquid or gas; or

   (iii) any other thing which is designed or made for use in warfare or against persons, including parts, whether components or accessories, for such weapon, ammunition or article;

(b) "sporting weapon" means—

   (i) any weapon or ammunition;

   (ii) any article containing an explosive, noxious liquid or gas; or

   (iii) any other thing, including parts, whether components or accessories, for such weapon, ammunition or article;

   which is not a munition of war.

---

1. Penalties for contraventions are contained in art 148 and Sch 14, post.

7–5874   70. Carriage of dangerous goods[1]. (1) Without prejudice to any other provisions of this Order, the Secretary of State may make regulations[2] prescribing—

(a) the classification of certain articles and substances as dangerous goods;

(b) the categories of dangerous goods which an aircraft may not carry;

(c) the conditions which apply to the loading on, suspension beneath and carriage by an aircraft of dangerous goods;

(d) the manner in which dangerous goods must be packed, marked, labelled and consigned before being loaded on, suspended beneath or carried by an aircraft;

(e) any other provisions for securing the safety of aircraft and any apparatus attached thereto, and the safety of persons and property on the surface in relation to the loading on, suspension beneath or carriage by an aircraft of dangerous goods;

(f) the persons to whom information about the carriage of dangerous goods must be provided;

(g) the documents which must be produced to the CAA or an authorised person on request; and

(h) the powers to be conferred on an authorised person relating to the enforcement of the regulations made hereunder.

(2) It shall be an offence to contravene or permit the contravention of or fail to comply with any regulations made hereunder.

(3) The provisions of this article and of any regulations made thereunder shall be additional to and not in derogation from article 69.

---

1. Penalties for contraventions are contained in art 148 and Sch 14, post.
2. The Air Navigation (Dangerous Goods) Regulations 2002, SI 2002/2786 amended by SI 2004/3214 and SI 2005/3356 have been made.

7–5875   71. Method of carriage of persons[1]. (1) A person shall not—

(a) subject to paragraphs (2) and (3), be in or on any part of an aircraft in flight which is not a part designed for the accommodation of persons and in particular a person shall not be on the wings or undercarriage of an aircraft;

(b) be in or on any object, other than a glider or flying machine, towed by or attached to an aircraft in flight.

(2) A person may have temporary access to—

(a) any part of an aircraft for the purpose of taking action necessary for the safety of the aircraft or of any person, animal or goods therein; and

(b) any part of an aircraft in which cargo or stores are carried, being a part which is designed to enable a person to have access thereto while the aircraft is in flight.

(3) This article shall not apply to a passenger in a helicopter flying under and in accordance with a police air operator's certificate who is disembarking in accordance with a procedure contained in the police operations manual for the helicopter.

---

1. Penalties for contraventions are contained in art 148 and Sch 14, post.

7–5876   72. Exits and break-in markings[1]. (1) This article shall apply to every public transport aeroplane or helicopter registered in the United Kingdom.

(2) Whenever an aeroplane or helicopter to which this article applies is carrying passengers, every exit therefrom and every internal door in the aeroplane or helicopter shall be in working order, and, subject to paragraph (3), during take-off and landing and during any emergency, every such exit and door shall be kept free of obstruction and shall not be fastened by locking or otherwise so as to prevent, hinder or delay its use by passengers.

(3) In the case of—

(a) an exit which, in accordance with arrangements approved by the CAA either generally or in relation to a class of aeroplane or helicopter or a particular aeroplane or helicopter, is not required for use by passengers, the exit may be obstructed by cargo;

(b) a door between the flight crew compartment and any adjacent compartment to which passengers have access, the door may be locked or bolted if the commander of the aeroplane or helicopter so determines, for the purpose of preventing access by passengers to the flight crew compartment;

(c) any internal door which is so placed that it cannot prevent, hinder or delay the exit of passengers from the aeroplane or helicopter in an emergency if it is not in working order, paragraph (2) shall not apply.

(4) Every exit from the aeroplane or helicopter shall be marked with the words "Exit" or "Emergency Exit" in capital letters, which shall be red in colour and if necessary shall be outlined in white to contrast with the background.

(5) Every exit from the aeroplane or helicopter shall be marked with instructions in English and with diagrams to indicate the correct method of opening the exit, which shall be red in colour and located on a background which provides adequate contrast.

(6) The markings required by paragraph (5) shall be placed on or near the inside surface of the door or other closure of the exit and, if it is openable from the outside of the aeroplane or helicopter, on or near the exterior surface.

(7) An operator of an aeroplane or helicopter shall ensure that if areas of the fuselage suitable for break-in by rescue crews in emergency are marked on aeroplanes and helicopters, such areas shall be marked upon the exterior surface of the fuselage with markings to show the areas which can, for purposes of rescue in an emergency, be most readily and effectively broken into by persons outside the aeroplane or helicopter.

(8) The markings required by paragraph (7) shall—

(a) be red or yellow, and if necessary shall be outlined in white to contrast with the background;

(b) if the corner markings are more than 2 metres apart, have intermediate lines 9 centimetres x 3 centimetres inserted so that there is no more than 2 metres between adjacent marks.

(9) The markings required by this article shall—

(a) be painted, or affixed by other equally permanent means; and

(b) be kept at all times clean and unobscured.

(10) Subject to compliance with paragraph (11), if one, but not more than one, exit from an aeroplane or helicopter becomes inoperative at a place where it is not reasonably practicable for it to be repaired or replaced, nothing in this article shall prevent that aeroplane or helicopter from carrying passengers until it next lands at a place where the exit can be repaired or replaced.

(11) On any flight on which this paragraph must be complied with—

(a) the number of passengers carried and the position of the seats which they occupy shall be in accordance with arrangements approved by the CAA either in relation to the particular aeroplane or helicopter or to a class of aeroplane or helicopter; and

(b) in accordance with arrangements so approved, the exit shall be fastened by locking or otherwise, the words "Exit" or "Emergency Exit" shall be covered, and the exit shall be marked by a red disc at least 23 centimetres in diameter with a horizontal white bar across it bearing the words "No Exit" in red letters.

1. Penalties for contraventions are contained in art 148 and Sch 14, post.

7–5877 73. Endangering safety of an aircraft[1]. A person shall not recklessly or negligently act in a manner likely[2] to endanger an aircraft, or any person therein.

1. Penalties for contraventions are contained in art 148 and Sch 14, post.
2. "Likely" does not mean probably ie more than a 50 per cent chance of materialising but is to be construed as "is there a real risk, a risk that should not be ignored?" (*R v Whitehouse* [2000] Crim LR 172, CA).

7–5878 74. Endangering safety of any person or property[1]. A person shall not recklessly or negligently cause or permit an aircraft to endanger any person or property.

1. Penalties for contraventions are contained in art 148 and Sch 14, post.

7–5879 75. Drunkenness in aircraft[1]. (1) A person shall not enter any aircraft when drunk, or be drunk in any aircraft.
(2) A person shall not, when acting as a member of the crew of any aircraft or being carried in any aircraft for the purpose of so acting, be under the influence of drink or a drug to such an extent as to impair his capacity so to act.

1. Penalties for contraventions are contained in art 148 and Sch 14, post. This Article is intra vires s 60(3)(*h*) of the Civil Aviation Act 1982 and the fact that there might be an overlap between arts [73] and [75] does not make it otherwise. That there is no definition of drunkenness in the article does not mean that the article is so vague in its application as to breach art 5 of the European Convention on Human Rights (*R v Tagg* [2001] EWCA Crim 1230, [2001] Crim LR 900, [2002] 1 Cr App Rep 22, CA). "[D]runk in ordinary speech . . .refers to someone who has taken intoxicating liquor to an extent which affects his steady self-control" (*Neale v RMJE (a minor)* (1984) 80 Cr App Rep 20 *per* Goff LJ at p 23 applied in *R v Tagg*, ante).

7–5880 76. Smoking in aircraft[1]. (1) Notices indicating when smoking is prohibited shall be exhibited in every aircraft registered in the United Kingdom so as to be visible from each passenger seat therein.
(2) A person shall not smoke in any compartment of an aircraft registered in the United Kingdom at a time when smoking is prohibited in that compartment by a notice to that effect exhibited by or on behalf of the commander of the aircraft.

1. Penalties for contraventions are contained in art 148 and Sch 14, post.

7–5881 77. Authority of commander of an aircraft[1]. Every person in an aircraft shall obey all lawful commands which the commander of that aircraft may give for the purpose of securing the safety of the aircraft and of persons or property carried therein, or the safety, efficiency or regularity of air navigation.

1. Penalties for contraventions are contained in art 148 and Sch 14, post.

7–5882 78. Acting in a disruptive manner[1]. No person shall while in an aircraft—
   (*a*) use any threatening, abusive or insulting words towards a member of the crew of the aircraft;
   (*b*) behave in a threatening, abusive, insulting or disorderly manner towards a member of the crew of the aircraft; or
   (*c*) intentionally interfere with the performance by a member of the crew of the aircraft of his duties.

1. Penalties for contraventions are contained in art 148 and Sch 14, post.

7–5883 79. Stowaways[1]. A person shall not secrete himself for the purpose of being carried in an aircraft without the consent of either the operator or the commander or of any other person entitled to give consent to his being carried in the aircraft.

1. Penalties for contraventions are contained in art 148 and Sch 14, post.

7–5884 80. Flying displays[1]. (1) No person shall act as the organiser of a flying display (in this article referred to as "the flying display director") unless he has obtained the permission of the CAA under paragraph (5) for that flying display.
(2) The commander of an aircraft who is—
   (*a*) intending to participate in a flying display shall take all reasonable steps to satisfy himself before he participates that—

      (i) the flying display director has been granted an appropriate permission under paragraph (5);

      (ii) the flight can comply with any relevant conditions subject to which that permission may have been granted; and

      (iii) the pilot has been granted an appropriate pilot display authorisation; or

  (b) participating in a flying display for which a permission has been granted shall comply with any conditions subject to which that permission may have been granted.

(3) No person shall act as pilot of an aircraft participating in a flying display unless he holds an appropriate pilot display authorisation and he complies with any conditions subject to which the authorisation may have been given.

(4) The flying display director shall not permit any person to act as pilot of an aircraft which participates in a flying display unless such person holds an appropriate pilot display authorisation.

(5) The CAA—

  (a) shall grant a permission required by virtue of paragraph (1) if it is satisfied that the applicant is a fit and competent person, having regard in particular to his previous conduct and experience, his organisation, staffing and other arrangements, to safely organise the proposed flying display;

  (b) may grant such a permission subject to such conditions, which may include conditions in respect of military aircraft, as the CAA thinks fit.

(6) The CAA shall, for the purposes of this article—

  (a) grant a pilot display authorisation authorising the holder to act as pilot of an aircraft taking part in a flying display upon it being satisfied that the applicant is a fit person to hold the authorisation and is qualified by reason of his knowledge, experience, competence, skill, physical and mental fitness to fly in accordance therewith and for that purpose the applicant shall furnish such evidence and undergo such examinations and tests as the CAA may require; and

  (b) authorise a person to conduct such examinations or tests as it may specify.

(7) A pilot display authorisation granted in accordance with this article shall, subject to article 92, remain in force for the period indicated in the pilot display authorisation.

(8) Subject to paragraph (9), for the purposes of this article, an appropriate pilot display authorisation shall mean an authorisation which is valid and appropriate to the intended flight and which has been either—

  (a) granted by the CAA under paragraph (6)(a); or

  (b) granted by the competent authority of a JAA Full Member State.

(9) A pilot display authorisation granted by the competent authority of a JAA Full Member State shall not be an appropriate pilot display authorisation for the purposes of this article if the CAA has given a direction to that effect.

(10) A direction may be issued under paragraph (9) either in respect of a particular authorisation, a specified category of authorisations or generally.

(11) Paragraph (1) shall not apply to either—

  (a) a flying display which takes place at an aerodrome in the occupation of the Ministry of Defence or of any visiting force or any other premises in the occupation or under the control of the Ministry of Defence; or

  (b) a flying display at which the only participating aircraft are military aircraft.

(12) The flying display director shall not permit any military aircraft to participate in a flying display unless he complies with any conditions specified in respect of military aircraft subject to which permission for the flying display may have been granted.

(13) Nothing in this article shall apply to an aircraft race or contest or to an aircraft taking part in such a race or contest or to the commander or pilot whether or not such race or contest is held in association with a flying display.

---

1. Penalties for contraventions are contained in art 148 and Sch 14, post.

PART 6[1]

FATIGUE OF CREW AND PROTECTION OF CREW FROM COSMIC RADIATION

7–5885 81. Application and interpretation of Part 6. (1) Subject to paragraph (2), articles 82 and 83 shall apply to any aircraft registered in the United Kingdom which is either—

  (a) engaged on a flight for the purpose of public transport; or

  (b) operated by an air transport undertaking.

(2) Articles 82 and 83 shall not apply in relation to a flight made only for the purpose of instruction in flying given by or on behalf of a flying club or flying school, or a person who is not an air transport undertaking.

(3) For the purposes of this Part—

  (a) "flight time", in relation to any person, means all time spent by that person in—

    (i) a civil aircraft whether or not registered in the United Kingdom (other than such an aircraft of which the maximum total weight authorised does not exceed 1,600 kg and which is not flying for the purpose of public transport or aerial work); or

    (ii) a military aircraft (other than such an aircraft of which the maximum total weight authorised does not exceed 1,600 kg and which is flying on a military air experience flight);

    while it is in flight and he is carried as a member of the crew;

(b) "day" means a continuous period of 24 hours beginning at midnight Co-ordinated Universal Time;

(c) a helicopter shall be deemed to be in flight from the moment the helicopter first moves under its own power for the purpose of taking off until the rotors are next stopped; and

(d) a military air experience flight is a flight by a military aircraft operated under the auspices of the Royal Air Force Air Cadet Organisation for the purpose of providing air experience to its cadets.

---

1. Part 6 comprises arts 81–85.

7-5886　**82. Fatigue of crew—operator's responsibilities**[1]. (1) The operator of an aircraft to which this article applies shall not cause or permit that aircraft to make a flight unless—

(a) he has established a scheme for the regulation of flight times for every person flying in that aircraft as a member of its crew;

(b) the scheme is approved by the CAA;

(c) either—

    (i) the scheme is incorporated in the operations manual required by article 38; or

    (ii) in any case where an operations manual is not required by that article, the scheme is incorporated in a document, a copy of which has been made available to every person flying in that aircraft as a member of its crew; and

(d) he has taken all such steps as are reasonably practicable to ensure that the provisions of the scheme will be complied with in relation to every person flying in that aircraft as a member of its crew.

(2) The operator of an aircraft to which this article applies shall not cause or permit any person to fly therein as a member of its crew if he knows or has reason to believe that the person is suffering from, or, having regard to the circumstances of the flight to be undertaken, is likely to suffer from, such fatigue while he is so flying as may endanger the safety of the aircraft or of its occupants.

(3) The operator of an aircraft to which this article applies shall not cause or permit any person to fly therein as a member of its flight crew unless the operator has in his possession an accurate and up-to-date record in respect of that person and in respect of the 28 days immediately preceding the flight showing—

(a) all his flight times; and

(b) brief particulars of the nature of the functions performed by him in the course of his flight times.

(4) The record referred to in paragraph (3) shall, subject to article 91, be preserved by the operator of the aircraft until a date 12 months after the flight referred to in that paragraph.

---

1. Penalties for contraventions are contained in art 148 and Sch 14, post.

7-5887　**83. Fatigue of crew—responsibilities of crew**[1]. (1) A person shall not act as a member of the crew of an aircraft to which this article applies if he knows or suspects that he is suffering from, or, having regard to the circumstances of the flight to be undertaken, is likely to suffer from, such fatigue as may endanger the safety of the aircraft or of its occupants.

(2) A person shall not act as a member of the flight crew of an aircraft to which this article applies unless he has ensured that the operator of the aircraft is aware of his flight times during the period of 28 days preceding the flight.

---

1. Penalties for contraventions are contained in art 148 and Sch 14, post.

7-5888　**84. Flight times—responsibilities of flight crew**[1]. (1) Subject to paragraph (2), a person shall not act as a member of the flight crew of an aircraft registered in the United Kingdom if at the beginning of the flight the aggregate of all his previous flight times—

(a) during the period of 28 consecutive days expiring at the end of the day on which the flight begins exceeds 100 hours; or

(b) during the period of twelve months expiring at the end of the previous month exceeds 900 hours.

(2) This article shall not apply to a flight which is—

(a) a private flight in an aircraft of which the maximum total weight does not exceed 1,600 kg; or

(b) a flight which is not for the purpose of public transport and is not operated by an air transport undertaking where, at the time when the flight begins, the aggregate of all the flight times of the member of the flight crew concerned since he was last medically examined and found fit by a person approved by the CAA for the purpose of article 32(2) does not exceed 25 hours.

---

1. Penalties for contraventions are contained in art 148 and Sch 14, post.

7–5889 85. Protection of air crew from cosmic radiation[1]. (1) A relevant undertaking shall take appropriate measures to—

(a) assess the exposure to cosmic radiation when in flight of those air crew who are liable to be subject to cosmic radiation in excess of 1 milliSievert per year;

(b) take into account the assessed exposure when organising work schedules with a view to reducing the doses of highly exposed air crew; and

(c) inform the workers concerned of the health risks their work involves.

(2) A relevant undertaking shall ensure that in relation to a pregnant air crew member, the conditions of exposure to cosmic radiation when she is in flight are such that the equivalent dose to the foetus will be as low as reasonably achievable and is unlikely to exceed 1 milliSievert during the remainder of the pregnancy.

(3) Nothing in paragraph (2) shall require the undertaking concerned to take any action in relation to an air crew member until she has notified the undertaking in writing that she is pregnant.

(4) The definition in article 155 of "crew" shall not apply for the purposes of this article.

(5) In this article and in article 87—

(a) "air crew" has the same meaning as in article 42 of Council Directive 96/29/ Euratom of 13th May 1996; and

(b) "undertaking" includes a natural or legal person and "relevant undertaking" means an undertaking established in the United Kingdom which operates aircraft.

(6) In this article—

(a) "highly exposed air crew" and "milliSievert" have the same respective meanings as in article 42 of Council Directive 96/29/Euratom of 13th May 1996; and

(b) "year" means any period of twelve months.

---

1. Penalties for contraventions are contained in art 148 and Sch 14, post.

PART 7[1]
DOCUMENTS AND RECORDS

7–5890 86. Documents to be carried. (1) An aircraft shall not fly unless it carries the documents which it is required to carry under the law of the country in which it is registered.

(2) Subject to paragraph (3), an aircraft registered in the United Kingdom shall, when in flight, carry documents in accordance with Schedule 10[2].

(3) If the flight is intended to begin and end at the same aerodrome and does not include passage over the territory of any country other than the United Kingdom, the documents may be kept at that aerodrome instead of being carried in the aircraft.

---

1. Part 7 comprises arts 86–94.
2. Schedule 10 is not reproduced.

7–5891 87. Keeping and production of records of exposure to cosmic radiation[1]. (1) A relevant undertaking shall keep a record for the period and in the manner prescribed[2] of the exposure to cosmic radiation of air crew assessed under article 85 and the names of the air crew concerned.

(2) A relevant undertaking shall, within a reasonable period after being requested to do so by an authorised person, cause to be produced to that person the record required to be kept under paragraph (1).

(3) A relevant undertaking shall, within a reasonable period after being requested to do so by a person in respect of whom a record is required to be kept under paragraph (1), supply a copy of that record to that person.

---

1. Penalties for contraventions are contained in art 148 and Sch 14, post.
2. See the Air Navigation (Cosmic Radiation) (Keeping of Records) Regulations 2000, SI 2000/1380.

7–5892 88. Production of documents and records. (1) The commander of an aircraft shall, within a reasonable time after being requested to do so by an authorised person, cause to be produced to that person—

(a) the certificates of registration and airworthiness in force in respect of the aircraft;

(b) the licences of its flight crew; and

(c) such other documents as the aircraft is required by article 86 to carry when in flight.

(2) The operator of an aircraft registered in the United Kingdom shall, within a reasonable time after being requested to do so by an authorised person, cause to be produced to that person such of the following documents or records as have been requested by that person being documents or records which are required, by or under this Order, to be in force or to be carried, preserved or made available—

(a) the documents referred to in Schedule 10 as Documents A, B and G;

(b) the aircraft log book, engine log books and variable pitch propeller log books required under this Order to be kept;

(c) the weight schedule, if any, required to be preserved under article 23(3);

(d) in the case of a public transport aircraft or aerial work aircraft, the documents referred to in Schedule 10 as Documents D, E, F and H;

(e) any records of flight times, duty periods and rest periods which he is required by article 82(4) to preserve, and such other documents and information in the possession or control of the operator, as the authorised person may require for the purpose of determining whether those records are complete and accurate;

(f) any such operations manuals as are required to be made available under article 38(2)(a);

(g) the record made by any flight data recorder required to be carried by or under this Order.

(3) The holder of a licence granted or rendered valid under this Order or of a medical certificate required under article 26(2)(b)(ii) shall, within a reasonable time after being requested to do so by an authorised person, cause to be produced to that person his licence, including any certificate of validation.

(4) Every person required by article 35 to keep a personal flying log book shall cause it to be produced within a reasonable time to an authorised person after being requested to do so by him within a period of 2 years beginning with the date of the last entry.

7–5893 89. Production of air traffic service equipment documents and records. The holder of an approval under article 124 or 125 shall within a reasonable time after being requested to do so by an authorised person, cause to be produced to that person any documents and records relating to any air traffic service equipment used or intended to be used in connection with the provision of a service to an aircraft.

7–5894 90. Power to inspect and copy documents and records. An authorised person shall have the power to inspect and copy any certificate, licence, log book, document or record which he has the power under this Order or any regulations made thereunder to require to be produced to him.

7–5895 91. Preservation of documents, etc. (1) Subject to paragraphs (2), (3), (4) and (5), a person required by this Order to preserve any document or record by reason of his being the operator of an aircraft shall, if he ceases to be the operator of the aircraft, continue to preserve the document or record as if he had not ceased to be the operator, and in the event of his death the duty to preserve the document or record shall fall upon his personal representative.

(2) If another person becomes the operator of the aircraft, the first-mentioned operator or his personal representative shall deliver to that person upon demand the certificates of maintenance review and release to service, the log books and the weight schedule and any record made by a flight data recorder and preserved in accordance with article 62(2) and (4) which are in force or required to be preserved in respect of that aircraft.

(3) If an engine or variable pitch propeller is removed from the aircraft and installed in another aircraft operated by another person the first-mentioned operator or his personal representative shall deliver to that person upon demand the log book relating to that engine or propeller.

(4) If any person in respect of whom a record has been kept by the first-mentioned operator in accordance with article 82(4) becomes a member of the flight crew of a public transport aircraft registered in the United Kingdom and operated by another person the first-mentioned operator or his personal representative shall deliver those records to that other person upon demand.

(5) It shall be the duty of the other person referred to in paragraphs (2), (3) and (4) to deal with the document or record delivered to him as if he were the first-mentioned operator.

7–5896 92. Revocation, suspension and variation of certificates, licences and other documents.
(1) Subject to paragraphs (5) and (6), the CAA may, if it thinks fit, provisionally suspend or vary any certificate, licence, approval, permission, exemption, authorisation or other document issued, granted or having effect under this Order, pending inquiry into or consideration of the case.

(2) The CAA may, on sufficient ground being shown to its satisfaction after due inquiry, revoke, suspend or vary any such certificate, licence, approval, permission, exemption, authorisation or other document.

(3) The holder or any person having the possession or custody of any certificate, licence, approval, permission, exemption or other document which has been revoked, suspended or varied under this Order shall surrender it to the CAA within a reasonable time after being required to do so by the CAA.

(4) The breach of any condition subject to which any certificate, licence, approval, permission, exemption or other document, other than a licence issued in respect of an aerodrome, has been

granted or issued or which has effect under this Order shall, in the absence of provision to the contrary in the document, render the document invalid during the continuance of the breach.

(5) The provisions of article 93 shall have effect, in place of the provisions of this article, in relation to permits to which that article applies.

(6) Notwithstanding paragraph (1), a flight manual, performance schedule or other document incorporated by reference in a certificate of airworthiness may be varied on sufficient ground being shown to the satisfaction of the CAA, whether or not after due inquiry.

7–5897   93. Revocation, suspension and variation of permissions, etc granted under article 138 or article 140.   (1) Subject to the provisions of this article, the Secretary of State may revoke, suspend or vary any permit to which this article applies.

(2) Save as provided by paragraph (3), the Secretary of State may exercise his powers under paragraph (1) only after notifying the permit-holder of his intention to do so and after due consideration of the case.

(3) If, by reason of the urgency of the matter, it appears to the Secretary of State to be necessary for him to do so, he may provisionally suspend or vary a permit to which this article applies without complying with the requirements of paragraph (2); but he shall in any such case comply with those requirements as soon thereafter as is reasonably practicable and shall then, in the light of his due consideration of the case, either—

(a) revoke the provisional suspension or variation of the permit; or

(b) substitute therefor a definitive revocation, suspension or variation, which, if a definitive suspension, may be for the same or a different period as the provisional suspension (if any) or, if a definitive variation, may be in the same or different terms as the provisional variation (if any).

(4) The powers vested in the Secretary of State by paragraph (1) or paragraph (3) may be exercised by him whenever, in his judgement and whether or not by reason of anything done or omitted to be done by the permit-holder or otherwise connected with the permit-holder, it is necessary or expedient that the permit-holder should not enjoy, or should no longer enjoy, the rights conferred on him by a permit to which this article applies or should enjoy them subject to such limitations or qualifications as the Secretary of State may determine.

(5) In particular, and without prejudice to the generality of the foregoing, the Secretary of State may exercise his said powers if it appears to him that—

(a) the person to whom the permit was granted has committed a breach of any condition to which it is subject;

(b) any agreement between Her Majesty's Government in the United Kingdom and the Government of any other country in pursuance of which or in reliance on which the permit was granted is no longer in force or that that other Government has committed a breach thereof;

(c) the person to whom the permit was granted, or a Government of another country which is a party to an agreement referred to in sub-paragraph (b), or the aeronautical authorities of the country concerned, have—

(i) acted in a manner which is inconsistent with or prejudicial to the operation in good faith, and according to its object and purpose, of any such agreement as aforesaid; or

(ii) have engaged in unfair, discriminatory or restrictive practices to the prejudice of the holder of an Air Transport Licence granted under section 65 of the Civil Aviation Act 1982 or the holder of a route licence granted under that section as applied by section 69A of that Act in his operation of air services to or from points in the country concerned; and

(d) the person to whom the permit was granted, having been granted it as a person designated by the Government of a country other than the United Kingdom for the purposes of an agreement referred to in sub-paragraph (b), is no longer so designated or that that person has so conducted himself, or that such circumstances have arisen in relation to him, as to make it necessary or expedient to disregard or qualify the consequences of his being so designated.

(6) The permit-holder or any person having the possession or custody of any permit which has been revoked, suspended or varied under this article shall surrender it to the Secretary of State within a reasonable time of being required by him to do so.

(7) The breach of any condition subject to which any permit to which this article applies has been granted shall render the permit invalid during the continuance of the breach.

(8) The permits to which this article applies are permissions granted by the Secretary of State under article 138 or article 140 and any approvals or authorisations of, or consents to, any matter which the Secretary of State has granted, or is deemed to have granted, in pursuance of a permission which he has so granted.

(9) References in this article to the "permit-holder" are references to the person to whom any permit to which this article applies has been granted or is deemed to have been granted.

7–5898   94. Offences in relation to documents and records[1].   (1) A person shall not with intent to deceive—

(a) use any certificate, licence, approval, permission, exemption or other document issued or required by or under this Order or by or under Part 21, 66, 145, 147 or M which has been forged, altered, revoked or suspended, or to which he is not entitled;

(b) lend any certificate, licence, approval, permission, exemption or any other document issued or having effect or required by or under this Order or by or under Part 21, 66, 145, 147 or M to, or allow it to be used by, any other person; or

(c) make any false representation for the purpose of procuring for himself or any other person the grant, issue, renewal or variation of any such certificate, licence, approval, permission or exemption or other document;

and in this paragraph a reference to a certificate, licence, approval, permission, exemption or other document includes a copy or purported copy.

(2) A person shall not intentionally damage, alter or render illegible any log book or other record required by or under this Order or by or under Part 21, 66, 145, 147 or M to be maintained or any entry made therein, or knowingly make, or procure or assist in the making of, any false entry in or material omission from any such log book or record or destroy any such log book or record during the period for which it is required under this Order to be preserved.

(3) All entries made in writing in any log book or record referred to in paragraph (2) shall be made in ink or indelible pencil.

(4) A person shall not knowingly make in a load sheet any entry which is incorrect in any material particular, or any material omission from such a load sheet.

(5) A person shall not purport to issue any certificate for the purposes of this Order, of any regulations made thereunder or of Part 21, 66, 145, 147 or M unless he is authorised to do so under this Order or Part 21, 66, 145, 147 or M as the case may be.

(6) A person shall not issue any such certificate as aforesaid unless he has satisfied himself that all statements in the certificate are correct.

---

1. Penalties for contraventions are contained in art 148 and Sch 14, post.

PART 8[1]
MOVEMENT OF AIRCRAFT

7–5899 95. Rules of the Air[2]. (1) Without prejudice to any other provision of this Order, the Secretary of State may make regulations[3] (in this article called the "Rules of the Air") prescribing—

(a) the manner in which aircraft may move or fly including in particular provision for requiring aircraft to give way to military aircraft;

(b) the lights and other signals to be shown or made by aircraft or persons;

(c) the lighting and marking of aerodromes; and

(d) any other provisions for securing the safety of aircraft in flight and in movement and the safety of persons and property on the surface.

(2) Subject to paragraph (3), it shall be an offence to contravene, to permit the contravention of, or to fail to comply with, the Rules of the Air.

(3) It shall be lawful for the Rules of the Air to be departed from to the extent necessary—

(a) for avoiding immediate danger;

(b) for complying with the law of any country other than the United Kingdom within which the aircraft then is; or

(c) for complying with Military Flying Regulations (Joint Service Publication 550) or Flying Orders to Contractors (Aviation Publication 67) issued by the Secretary of State in relation to an aircraft of which the commander is acting as such in the course of his duty as a member of any of Her Majesty's naval, military or air forces.

(4) If any departure from the Rules of the Air is made for the purpose of avoiding immediate danger, the commander of the aircraft shall cause written particulars of the departure, and of the circumstances giving rise to it, to be given within 10 days thereafter to the competent authority of the country in whose territory the departure was made or if the departure was made over the high seas, to the CAA.

(5) Nothing in the Rules of the Air shall exonerate any person from the consequences of any neglect in the use of lights or signals or of the neglect of any precautions required by ordinary aviation practice or by the special circumstances of the case.

---

1. Part 8 comprises arts 95–99.
2. Penalties for contraventions are contained in art 148 and Sch 14, post.
3. Rules of the Air Regulations 1996, SI 1996/1393 amended by SI 1999/1323, SI 2000/1994, SI 2001/917, SI 2003/64 and SI 2005/1110 have been made.

7–5900 96. Power to prohibit or restrict flying[1]. (1) Where the Secretary of State deems it necessary in the public interest to restrict or prohibit flying by reason of—

(a) the intended gathering or movement of a large number of persons;

(b) the intended holding of an aircraft race or contest or of a flying display; or

(c) national defence or any other reason affecting the public interest;

the Secretary of State may make regulations[2] prohibiting, restricting or imposing conditions on flights by aircraft specified in paragraph (2) flying in the circumstances specified in paragraph (2).

(2) The aircraft and circumstances referred to in paragraph (1) are—

(a) aircraft, whether or not registered in the United Kingdom, in any airspace over the United Kingdom or in the neighbourhood of an offshore installation; and

(b) aircraft registered in the United Kingdom, in any other airspace, being airspace in respect of which Her Majesty's Government in the United Kingdom has in pursuance of international arrangements undertaken to provide navigation services for aircraft.

(3) Regulations made under this article may apply either generally or in relation to any class of aircraft.

(4) It shall be an offence to contravene or permit the contravention of or fail to comply with any regulations made hereunder.

(5) If the commander of an aircraft becomes aware that the aircraft is flying in contravention of any regulations which have been made for any of the reasons referred to in paragraph (1)(c) he shall, unless otherwise instructed under paragraph (6), cause the aircraft to leave the area to which the regulations relate by flying to the least possible extent over such area and the aircraft shall not begin to descend while over such an area.

(6) The commander of an aircraft flying either within an area for which regulations have been made for any of the reasons referred to in paragraph (1)(c) or within airspace notified as a Danger Area shall forthwith comply with instructions given by radio by the appropriate air traffic control unit or by, or on behalf of, the person responsible for safety within the relevant airspace.

---

1. Penalties for contraventions are contained in art 148 and Sch 14, post.
2. See the Air Navigation (Restriction of Flying) (Nuclear Installations) Regulations 2001, SI 2001/1607 and the Air Navigation (Restriction of Flying) (Prisons) Regulations 2001, SI 2001/1657.

7–5901   97. Balloons, kites, airships, gliders and parascending parachutes[1]. (1) The provisions of this article shall apply only to or in relation to aircraft within the United Kingdom.

(2) A balloon in captive or tethered flight shall not be flown within 60 metres of any vessel, vehicle or structure except with the permission of the person in charge of any such vessel, vehicle or structure.

(3) Without the permission of the CAA—

(a) a glider or parascending parachute shall not be launched by winch and cable or by ground tow to a height of more than 60 metres above ground level;

(b) a balloon in captive flight shall not be flown within the aerodrome traffic zone of a notified aerodrome during the notified operating hours of that aerodrome;

(c) a balloon in captive or tethered flight shall not be flown at a height measured to the top of the balloon of more than 60 metres above ground level;

(d) a kite shall not be flown at a height of more than 30 metres above ground level within the aerodrome traffic zone of a notified aerodrome during the notified operating hours of that aerodrome;

(e) a kite shall not be flown at a height of more than 60 metres above ground level; and

(f) a parascending parachute shall not be launched by winch and cable or by ground tow within the aerodrome traffic zone of a notified aerodrome during the notified operating hours of that aerodrome.

(4) An uncontrollable balloon in captive or released flight shall not be flown in airspace notified for the purposes of this paragraph without the permission of the CAA.

(5) A controllable balloon shall not be flown in free controlled flight—

(a) within airspace notified for the purposes of this paragraph; or

(b) within the aerodrome traffic zone of a notified aerodrome during the notified operating hours of that aerodrome;

except during the day and in visual meteorological conditions.

(6) A controllable balloon shall not be flown in tethered flight—

(a) within airspace notified for the purposes of this paragraph; or

(b) within the aerodrome traffic zone of a notified aerodrome;

except with the permission of the appropriate air traffic control unit.

(7) A balloon when in captive flight shall be securely moored and shall not be left unattended unless it is fitted with a device which ensures its automatic deflation if it breaks free of its moorings.

(8) An airship with a capacity exceeding 3,000 cubic metres shall not be moored other than on a notified aerodrome except with the permission of the CAA.

(9) An airship with a capacity not exceeding 3,000 cubic metres, unless it is moored on a notified aerodrome, shall not be moored—

(a) within 2 km of a congested area; or

(b) within the aerodrome traffic zone of a notified aerodrome;

except with the permission of the CAA.

(10) An airship when moored in the open shall be securely moored and shall not be left unattended.

(11) A person shall not cause or permit—

(a) a group of small balloons exceeding 1,000 in number to be simultaneously released at a single site wholly or partly within the aerodrome traffic zone of a notified aerodrome during the notified operating hours of that aerodrome unless that person has given to the CAA not less than 28 days previous notice in writing of the release;

(*b*) a group of small balloons exceeding 2,000 but not exceeding 10,000 in number to be simultaneously released at a single site—

(i) within airspace notified for the purposes of this sub-paragraph; or
(ii) within the aerodrome traffic zone of a notified aerodrome during the notified operating hours of that aerodrome;

without the permission of the CAA;

(*c*) a group of small balloons greater than 10,000 in number to be simultaneously released at a single site except with the permission of the CAA.

(12) For the purposes of this article—

(*a*) in paragraph (5) "day" means the time from half an hour before sunrise until half an hour after sunset (both times exclusive), sunset and sunrise being determined at surface level;
(*b*) the "notified operating hours" means the times notified in respect of an aerodrome during which rule 39 of the Rules of the Air Regulations 1996(*a*) applies;
(*c*) "simultaneously released at a single site" means the release of a specified number of balloons during a period not exceeding 15 minutes from within an area not exceeding 1 km square.

---

1. Penalties for contraventions are contained in art 148 and Sch 14, post.

7–5902 98. Regulation of small aircraft[1]. (1) A person shall not cause or permit any article or animal (whether or not attached to a parachute) to be dropped from a small aircraft so as to endanger persons or property.

(2) The person in charge of a small aircraft which weighs more than 7 kg without its fuel but including any articles or equipment installed in or attached to the aircraft at the commencement of its flight shall not fly such an aircraft—

(*a*) unless the person in charge of the aircraft has reasonably satisfied himself that the flight can safely be made;
(*b*) in Class A, C, D or E airspace unless the permission of the appropriate air traffic control unit has been obtained;
(*c*) within an aerodrome traffic zone during the notified hours of watch of the air traffic control unit (if any) at that aerodrome unless the permission of any such air traffic control unit has been obtained;
(*d*) at a height exceeding 400 feet above the surface unless it is flying in airspace described in sub-paragraph (*b*) or (*c*) and in accordance with the requirements thereof; or
(*e*) for aerial work purposes other than in accordance with a permission issued by the CAA.

---

1. Penalties for contraventions are contained in art 148 and Sch 14, post.

7–5903 99. Regulation of rockets[1]. (1) Subject to paragraph (2), this article applies to—

(*a*) small rockets of which the total impulse of the motor or combination of motors exceeds 160 Newton-seconds; and
(*b*) large rockets.

(2) This article shall not apply to—

(*a*) an activity to which the Outer Space Act 1986 applies; or
(*b*) a military rocket.

(3) No person shall launch a small rocket to which this article applies unless the condition in paragraph (4), and any of the conditions in paragraph (5) which are applicable, are satisfied.

(4) The condition first mentioned in paragraph (3) is that he has reasonably satisfied himself that—

(*a*) the flight can be safely made; and
(*b*) the airspace within which the flight will take place is, and will throughout the flight, remain clear of any obstructions including any aircraft in flight.

(5) The conditions mentioned secondly in paragraph (3) are that—

(*a*) for a flight within controlled airspace, he has obtained the permission of the appropriate air traffic control unit for aircraft flying in that airspace;
(*b*) for a flight within an aerodrome traffic zone at any of the times specified in Column 2 of the Table in rule 39(1) of the Rules of the Air Regulations 1996—

(i) he has obtained the permission of the air traffic control unit at the aerodrome; or
(ii) where there is no air traffic control unit, he has obtained from the aerodrome flight information service unit at that aerodrome information to enable the flight within the zone to be conducted safely; or
(iii) where there is no air traffic control unit and no aerodrome flight information service unit, he has obtained information from the air/ground communications service unit at that aerodrome to enable the flight to be conducted safely;

(c)　for a flight for aerial work purposes the flight is carried out under and in accordance with a permission granted by the CAA.

(6) No person shall launch a large rocket unless he does so under and in accordance with a permission granted by the CAA.

---

1. Penalties for contraventions are contained in art 148 and Sch 14, post.

Part 9[1]
Air Traffic Services

7–5904　100. Requirement for an air traffic control approval[2]. (1) No person in charge of the provision of an air traffic control service shall provide such a service in respect of United Kingdom airspace or airspace outside the United Kingdom for which the United Kingdom has, in pursuance of international arrangements, undertaken to provide air navigation services otherwise than under and in accordance with the terms of an air traffic control approval granted to him by the CAA.

(2) The CAA shall grant an air traffic control approval if it is satisfied that the applicant is competent, having regard to his organisation, staffing, equipment, maintenance and other arrangements, to provide a service which is safe for use by aircraft.

---

1. Part 9 comprises arts 100–106.
2. Penalties for contraventions are contained in art 148 and Sch 14, post.

7–5905　101. Duty of person in charge to satisfy himself as to competence of controllers[1]. The holder of an approval under article 100 shall not permit any person to act as an air traffic controller or a student air traffic controller in the provision of the service under the approval unless—

(a)　such person holds an appropriate licence; and
(b)　the holder has satisfied himself that such person is competent to perform his duties.

---

1. Penalties for contraventions are contained in art 148 and Sch 14, post.

7–5906　102. Manual of air traffic services. A person shall not provide an air traffic control service at any place unless—

(a)　the service is provided in accordance with the standards and procedures specified in a manual of air traffic services in respect of that place;
(b)　the manual is produced to the CAA within a reasonable time after a request for its production is made by the CAA; and
(c)　such amendments or additions have been made to the manual as the CAA may from time to time require.

7–5907　103. Provision of air traffic services[1]. In the case of an aerodrome (other than a Government aerodrome) in respect of which there is equipment for providing aid for holding, aid for let-down or aid for an approach to landing by radio or radar, the person in charge of the aerodrome shall—

(a)　inform the CAA in advance of the periods during and times at which any such equipment is to be in operation for the purpose of providing such aid as is specified by the said person; and
(b)　during any period and at such times as are notified, cause an approach control service to be provided.

---

1. Penalties for contraventions are contained in art 148 and Sch 14, post.

7–5908　104. Making of an air traffic direction in the interests of safety[1]. (1) The CAA may, in the interests of safety, direct the person in charge of an aerodrome that there shall be provided in respect of any aerodrome (other than a Government aerodrome) such an air traffic control service, a flight information service or a means of two way radio communication as the CAA considers appropriate.

(2) The CAA may, in the interests of safety, direct the holder of a licence to provide air traffic services granted under Part I of the Transport Act 2000 that there shall be provided, in respect of United Kingdom airspace or airspace outside the United Kingdom for which the United Kingdom has in pursuance of international arrangements undertaken to provide air navigation services, otherwise than in respect of an aerodrome, such an air traffic control service, a flight information service or a means of two way radio communication as the CAA considers appropriate.

(3) The CAA may specify in a direction made under this article the periods during which, the times at which, the manner in which and the airspace within which such service or such means shall be provided.

(4) The person who has been directed shall cause such a service or means to be provided in accordance with the direction.

(5) A provisional air traffic direction—

(a) may, if it thinks fit, be made by the CAA in accordance with paragraph (1) or (2) pending inquiry into or consideration of the case;

(b) shall have effect as though it were an air traffic direction made in accordance with paragraph (1) or (2) as the case may be.

1. Penalties for contraventions are contained in art 148 and Sch 14, post.

7–5909 105. Making of a direction for airspace policy purposes[1]. (1) After consultation with the Secretary of State the CAA may direct in accordance with paragraphs (2) and (3) any person in charge of the provision of air traffic services to provide air traffic services in respect of United Kingdom airspace or airspace outside the United Kingdom for which the United Kingdom has undertaken in pursuance of international arrangements to provide air traffic services.

(2) A direction under paragraph (1) may be made—

(a) in the interests of ensuring the efficient use of airspace; or

(b) to require that air traffic services are provided to a standard considered appropriate by the CAA for the airspace classification.

(3) The CAA may specify in a direction under paragraph (1) the air traffic services and the standard to which they are to be provided and the periods during which, the times at which, the manner in which, and the airspace within which such services shall be provided.

(4) The person who has been directed shall cause such a service to be provided in accordance with the direction.

1. Penalties for contraventions are contained in art 148 and Sch 14, post.

7–5910 106. Use of radio call signs at aerodromes[1]. The person in charge of an aerodrome provided with means of two-way radio communication shall not cause or permit any call sign to be used for a purpose other than a purpose for which that call sign has been notified.

1. Penalties for contraventions are contained in art 148 and Sch 14, post.

PART 10[1]
LICENSING OF AIR TRAFFIC CONTROLLERS

7–5911 107. Prohibition of unlicensed air traffic controllers and student air traffic controllers[2]. (1) Subject to paragraphs (3) and (4), a person shall not act as an air traffic controller or hold himself out, whether by use of a radio call sign or in any other way, as a person who may so act unless he is the holder of, and complies with the privileges and conditions of—

(a) a valid student air traffic controller's licence granted under this Order;

(b) an appropriate air traffic controller's licence granted under this Order; or

(c) a valid air traffic controller's licence so granted which is not appropriate but he is supervised as though he was the holder of a student air traffic controller's licence.

(2) A person shall not act as an air traffic controller unless he has identified himself in such a manner as may be notified.

(3) A licence shall not be required by any person who, acting in the course of his employment, passes on such instructions or advice as he has been instructed so to do by the holder of an air traffic controller's licence which entitles that holder to give such instructions or advice.

(4) A licence shall not be required by any person who acts in the course of his duty as a member of any of Her Majesty's naval, military or air forces or a visiting force.

1. Part 10 comprises arts 107–120.
2. Penalties for contraventions are contained in art 148 and Sch 14, post.

108. Grant and renewal of air traffic controller's and student air traffic controller's licences

109. Privileges of an air traffic controller's licence and a student air traffic controller's licence

110. Maintenance of validity of ratings and endorsements

111. Obligation to notify rating ceasing to be valid and change of unit

112. Requirement for medical certificate

113. Appropriate licence

114. Incapacity of air traffic controllers

7–5912 115. Fatigue of air traffic controllers—air traffic controllers' responsibilities[1]. A person shall not act as an air traffic controller if he knows or suspects that he is suffering from or, having regard to the circumstances of the period of duty to be undertaken, is likely to suffer from, such fatigue as may endanger the safety of any aircraft to which an air traffic control service may be provided.

_____

1. Penalties for contraventions are contained in art 148 and Sch 14, post.

7–5913   116. Prohibition of acting under the influence of drink or a drug[1]. A person shall not act as an air traffic controller or a student air traffic controller whilst under the influence of drink or a drug to such an extent as to impair his capacity to act as such.

_____

1. Penalties for contraventions are contained in art 148 and Sch 14, post.

117. Failing exams

118. Use of simulators

119. Approval of courses, persons and simulators

7–5914   120. Acting as an air traffic controller and a student air traffic controller.   For the purposes of this Part and Schedule 11—

- (a) "acting as an air traffic controller" shall mean either—

  - (i) giving an air traffic control service; or
  - (ii) the supervision of a student air traffic controller;

  or both; and

- (b) "acting as a student air traffic controller" shall mean giving an air traffic control service under the supervision of an air traffic controller.

PART 11[1]
FLIGHT INFORMATION SERVICES AND LICENSING OF FLIGHT INFORMATION SERVICE OFFICERS

7–5915   121. Prohibition of unlicensed flight information service officers[2]. (1) A person shall not act as a flight information service officer at any aerodrome or area control centre or hold himself out, whether by use of a radio call sign or in any other way, as a person who may so act unless he is the holder of and complies with the terms of a flight information service officer's licence granted under this Order authorising him to act as such at that aerodrome or area control centre.

(2) A person shall not act as a flight information service officer unless he has identified himself in such a manner as may be notified.

(3) For the purposes of this Part and Schedule 11 "acting as a flight information service officer" shall mean giving a flight information service.

_____

1. Part 11 comprises arts 121–123.
2. Penalties for contraventions are contained in art 148 and Sch 14, post.

122. Licensing of flight information service officers

7–5916   123. Flight information service manual[1]. A person shall not provide a flight information service at any aerodrome or area control centre unless—

- (a) the service is provided in accordance with the standards and procedures specified in a flight information service manual in respect of that aerodrome or area control centre;
- (b) the manual is produced to the CAA within a reasonable time after a request for its production is made by the CAA; and
- (c) such amendments or additions have been made to the manual as the CAA may from time to time require.

_____

1. Penalties for contraventions are contained in art 148 and Sch 14, post.

PART 12[1]
AIR TRAFFIC SERVICE EQUIPMENT

7–5917   124. Air traffic service equipment[2]. (1) A person shall not cause or permit any air traffic service equipment to be established or used in the United Kingdom otherwise than under and in accordance with an approval granted by the CAA to the person in charge of the equipment.

(2) An approval shall be granted under paragraph (1) upon the CAA being satisfied—

- (a) as to the intended purpose of the equipment;
- (b) that the equipment is fit for its intended purpose; and
- (c) that the person is competent to operate the equipment.

(3) The person in charge of an aeronautical radio station at an aerodrome for which a licence for public use has been granted shall cause to be notified in relation to that aeronautical radio

station the type and availability of operation of any service which is available for use by any aircraft.

(4) An approval granted under paragraph (1) may include a condition requiring a person in charge of an aeronautical radio station at any other aerodrome or place to cause the information specified in paragraph (3) to be notified.

(5) An approval granted under paragraph (1) may in addition to any other conditions which may be imposed include a condition requiring the person in charge of the equipment to use a person approved by the CAA under paragraph (6) for the provision of particular services in connection with the equipment and in particular but without limitation may include a condition requiring that the equipment be flight checked by such an approved person.

(6) The CAA may approve a person to provide particular services in connection with approved equipment.

(7) For the purpose of paragraphs (1) and (6) an approval may be granted in respect of one or more than one person or generally.

(8) The provisions of this article shall not apply in respect of any air traffic service equipment of which the person solely in charge is the Secretary of State.

---

1. Part 11 comprises arts 124 and 125.
2. Penalties for contraventions are contained in art 148 and Sch 14, post.

7–5918 **125. Air traffic service equipment records**[1]. (1) The person in charge of any air traffic service equipment and any associated apparatus required under paragraph (2) or (3) shall keep in respect of such equipment or apparatus records in accordance with Part A of Schedule 12, and shall preserve such records for a period of one year or such longer period as the CAA may in a particular case direct.

(2) The person in charge of an aeronautical radio station which is used for the provision of an air traffic control service by an air traffic control unit shall provide recording apparatus in accordance with paragraph (4).

(3) The CAA may direct the person in charge of any other air traffic service equipment to provide recording apparatus in accordance with paragraph (4).

(4) The person in charge of the air traffic service equipment in respect of which recording apparatus is required to be provided under paragraph (2) or (3) shall, subject to paragraph (7)—

(a) ensure that when operated the apparatus is capable of recording and replaying the terms or content of any message or signal transmitted or received by or through that equipment; or in the case of an aeronautical radio station the apparatus is capable of recording and replaying the terms or content of any voice radio message or signal transmitted to an aircraft either alone or in common with other aircraft or received from an aircraft by the air traffic control unit;

(b) ensure that the apparatus is in operation at all times when the equipment is being used in connection with the provision of a service provided for the purpose of facilitating the navigation of aircraft;

(c) ensure that each record made by the apparatus complies with Part B of Schedule 12;

(d) not cause or permit that apparatus to be used unless it is approved by the CAA; and

(e) comply with the terms of such an approval.

(5) The CAA may in considering whether or not to grant an approval, without limitation, have regard to the matters specified in Part C of Schedule 12.

(6) An approval may be granted—

(a) in addition to any other conditions which may be imposed, subject to conditions relating to the matters to which the CAA may have had regard to under paragraph (5);

(b) in respect of one or more than one person or generally.

(7) If any apparatus provided in compliance with paragraph (2) or (3) ceases to be capable of recording the matters required by this article to be included in the records, the person required to provide that apparatus shall ensure that, so far as practicable, a record is kept which complies with Part B of Schedule 12 and on which the particulars specified therein are recorded together with, in the case of apparatus provided in compliance with paragraph (2), a summary of voice communications exchanged between the aeronautical radio station and any aircraft.

(8) If any apparatus provided in compliance with paragraph (2) or (3) becomes unserviceable, the person in charge of the air traffic service equipment shall ensure that the apparatus is rendered serviceable again as soon as reasonably practicable.

(9) The person in charge of any air traffic service equipment shall preserve any record made in compliance with paragraph (4) or (7) for a period of 30 days from the date on which the terms or content of the message or signal were recorded or for such longer period as the CAA may in a particular case direct.

(10) Subject to paragraph (11), a person required by this article to preserve any record by reason of his being the person in charge of the air traffic service equipment shall, if he ceases to be such a person, continue to preserve the record as if he had not ceased to be such a person, and in the event of his death the duty to preserve the record shall fall upon his personal representative.

(11) If another person becomes the person in charge of the air traffic service equipment the previous person in charge or his personal representative shall deliver the record to that other

person on demand, and it shall be the duty of that other person to deal with any such record delivered to him as if he were the previous person in charge.

(12) The person in charge of any air traffic service equipment shall within a reasonable time after being requested to do so by an authorised person produce any record required to be preserved under this article to that authorised person.

(13) The provisions of this article shall not apply in respect of any air traffic service equipment of which the person solely in charge is the Secretary of State.

---

1. Penalties for contraventions are contained in art 148 and Sch 14, post.

PART 13[1]
AERODROMES, AERONAUTICAL LIGHTS AND DANGEROUS LIGHTS

7–5919   126.   Aerodromes—public transport of passengers and instruction in flying[2]. (1) An aircraft to which this paragraph applies shall not take off or land at a place in the United Kingdom other than—

(a)   an aerodrome licensed under this Order for the take-off and landing of such aircraft; or

(b)   a Government aerodrome notified as available for the take-off and landing of such aircraft, or in respect of which the person in charge of the aerodrome has given his permission for the particular aircraft to take off or land as the case may be;

and in accordance with any conditions subject to which the aerodrome may have been licensed or notified, or subject to which such permission may have been given.

(2) Subject to paragraph (4), paragraph (1) applies to—

(a)   any aeroplane of which the maximum total weight authorised exceeds 2,730 kg flying on a flight—

(i)   for the purpose of the public transport of passengers;

(ii)   for the purpose of instruction in flying given to any person for the purpose of becoming qualified for the grant of a pilot's licence or the inclusion of an aircraft rating, a night rating or a night qualification in a licence; or

(iii)   for the purpose of carrying out flying tests in respect of the grant of a pilot's licence or the inclusion of an aircraft rating or a night rating in a licence;

(b)   any aeroplane of which the maximum total weight authorised does not exceed 2,730 kg flying on a flight—

(i)   which is a scheduled journey for the purpose of the public transport of passengers;

(ii)   for the purpose of the public transport of passengers beginning and ending at the same aerodrome;

(iii)   for the purpose of—

(aa) instruction in flying given to any person for the purpose of becoming qualified for the grant of a pilot's licence or the inclusion of an aircraft rating, a night rating or a night qualification in a licence; or

(bb) a flying test in respect of the grant of a pilot's licence or the inclusion of an aircraft rating, a night rating or a night qualification in a licence; or

(iv)   for the purpose of the public transport of passengers at night;

(c)   any helicopter or gyroplane flying on a flight specified in sub-paragraph (b)(i) or (iii); and

(d)   any glider (other than a glider being flown under arrangements made by a flying club and carrying no person other than a member of the club) flying on a flight for the purpose of the public transport of passengers or for the purpose of instruction in flying.

(3) Subject to paragraph (4)—

(a)   the person in charge of any area in the United Kingdom intended to be used for the take off or landing of helicopters at night other than such a place as is specified in paragraph (1) shall cause to be in operation, whenever a helicopter flying for the purpose of the public transport of passengers is taking off or landing at that area by night, such lighting as will enable the pilot of the helicopter—

(i)   in the case of landing, to identify the landing area in flight, to determine the landing direction and to make a safe approach and landing; and

(ii)   in the case of taking off, to make a safe take-off;

(b)   a helicopter flying for the purpose of the public transport of passengers at night shall not take off or land at a place to which sub-paragraph (a) applies unless there is in operation such lighting.

(4) Paragraph (1) shall not apply to or in relation to an aircraft flying under and in accordance with the terms of a police air operator's certificate.

---

1. Part 11 comprises arts 126–137.
2. Penalties for contraventions are contained in art 148 and Sch 14, post.

127.   Use of Government aerodromes

7–5920 128. Licensing of aerodromes[1]. (1) The CAA shall grant a licence in respect of any aerodrome in the United Kingdom if it is satisfied that—

(a) the applicant is competent, having regard to his previous conduct and experience, his equipment, organisation, staffing, maintenance and other arrangements, to secure that the aerodrome and the airspace within which its visual traffic pattern is normally contained are safe for use by aircraft;

(b) the aerodrome is safe for use by aircraft, having regard in particular to the physical characteristics of the aerodrome and of its surroundings; and

(c) the aerodrome manual submitted under paragraph (6) is adequate.

(2) If the applicant so requests or if the CAA considers that an aerodrome should be available for the take-off or landing of aircraft to all persons on equal terms and conditions, it may grant a licence (in this Order referred to as "a licence for public use") which in addition to any other conditions which it may impose shall be subject to the condition that the aerodrome shall at all times when it is available for the take-off or landing of aircraft be so available to all persons on equal terms and conditions.

(3) The holder of an aerodrome licence granted under this Order (in this article called "an aerodrome licence holder") shall—

(a) furnish to any person on request information concerning the terms of the licence; and

(b) in the case of a licence for public use, cause to be notified the times during which the aerodrome will be available for the take-off or landing of aircraft engaged on flights for the purpose of the public transport of passengers or instruction in flying.

(4) An aerodrome licence holder shall not contravene or cause or permit to be contravened any condition of the aerodrome licence at any time in relation to an aircraft flying on a flight specified in article 126(2), but the licence shall not cease to be valid by reason only of such a contravention.

(5) An aerodrome licence holder shall take all reasonable steps to secure that the aerodrome and the airspace within which its visual traffic pattern is normally contained are safe at all times for use by aircraft.

(6) Upon making an application for an aerodrome licence the applicant shall submit to the CAA an aerodrome manual for that aerodrome.

(7) An aerodrome manual required under this article shall contain all such information and instructions as may be necessary to enable the aerodrome operating staff to perform their duties as such including, in particular, information and instructions relating to the matters specified in Schedule 13.

(8) Every aerodrome licence holder shall—

(a) furnish to the CAA any amendments or additions to the aerodrome manual before or immediately after they come into effect;

(b) without prejudice to sub-paragraph (a), make such amendments or additions to the aerodrome manual as the CAA may require for the purpose of ensuring the safe operation of aircraft at the aerodrome or the safety of air navigation; and

(c) maintain the aerodrome manual and make such amendments as may be necessary for the purposes of keeping its contents up to date.

(9) Every aerodrome licence holder shall make available to each member of the aerodrome operating staff a copy of the aerodrome manual, or a copy of every part of the aerodrome manual which is relevant to his duties and shall ensure that each such copy is kept up to date.

(10) Every aerodrome licence holder shall take all reasonable steps to secure that each member of the aerodrome operating staff—

(a) is aware of the contents of every part of the aerodrome manual which is relevant to his duties as such; and

(b) undertakes his duties as such in conformity with the relevant provisions of the manual.

(11) For the purposes of this article—

(a) "aerodrome operating staff" means all persons, whether or not the aerodrome licence holder and whether or not employed by the aerodrome licence holder, whose duties are concerned either with ensuring that the aerodrome and airspace within which its visual traffic pattern is normally contained are safe for use by aircraft, or whose duties require them to have access to the aerodrome manoeuvring area or apron;

(b) "visual traffic pattern" means the aerodrome traffic zone of the aerodrome, or, in the case of an aerodrome which is not notified for the purposes of rule 39 of the Rules of the Air Regulations 1996, the airspace which would comprise the aerodrome traffic zone of the aerodrome if it were so notified.

---

1. Penalties for contraventions are contained in art 148 and Sch 14, post.

129. Charges at aerodromes licensed for public use

130. Use of aerodromes by aircraft of Contracting States and of the Commonwealth

7–5921   131. Noise and vibration caused by aircraft on aerodromes. (1) The Secretary of State may prescribe[1] the conditions under which noise and vibration may be caused by aircraft (including military aircraft) on Government aerodromes, licensed aerodromes or on aerodromes at which the manufacture, repair or maintenance of aircraft is carried out by persons carrying on business as manufacturers or repairers of aircraft.

(2) Section 77(2) of the Civil Aviation Act 1982 shall apply to any aerodrome in relation to which the Secretary of State has prescribed conditions in accordance with paragraph (1).

---

1. See the Air Navigation (General) Regulations 2005, SI 2005/1980.

7–5922   132. Aeronautical lights[1]. (1) Except with the permission of the CAA and in accordance with any conditions subject to which the permission may be granted, a person shall not establish, maintain or alter the character of—

(a) an aeronautical beacon within the United Kingdom; or

(b) any aeronautical ground light (other than an aeronautical beacon) at an aerodrome licensed under this Order, or which forms part of the lighting system for use by aircraft taking off from or landing at such an aerodrome.

(2) In the case of an aeronautical beacon which is or may be visible from the waters within an area of a general lighthouse authority, the CAA shall not give its permission for the purpose of this article except with the consent of that authority.

(3) A person shall not intentionally or negligently damage or interfere with any aeronautical ground light established by or with the permission of the CAA.

---

1. Penalties for contraventions are contained in art 148 and Sch 14, post.

7–5923   133. Lighting of en-route obstacles[1]. (1) For the purposes of this article, an "en-route obstacle" means any building, structure or erection which is 150 metres or more above ground level, but it does not include a building, structure or erection—

(a) which is in the vicinity of a licensed aerodrome; and

(b) to which section 47 of the Civil Aviation Act 1982 applies.

(2) The person in charge of an en-route obstacle shall ensure that it is fitted with medium intensity steady red lights positioned as close as possible to the top of the obstacle and at intermediate levels spaced so far as practicable equally between the top lights and ground level with an interval not exceeding 52 metres.

(3) Subject to paragraph (4), the person in charge of an en-route obstacle shall ensure that, by night, the lights required to be fitted by this article shall be displayed.

(4) In the event of the failure of any light which is required by this article to be displayed by night the person in charge shall repair or replace the light as soon as is reasonably practicable.

(5) At each level on the obstacle where lights are required to be fitted, sufficient lights shall be fitted and arranged so as to show when displayed in all directions.

(6) In any particular case the CAA may direct that an en-route obstacle shall be fitted with and shall display such additional lights in such positions and at such times as it may specify.

(7) This article shall not apply to any en-route obstacle in respect of which the CAA has granted a permission for the purposes of this article to the person in charge.

(8) A permission may be granted for the purposes of this article in respect of a particular case or class of cases or generally.

---

1. Penalties for contraventions are contained in art 148 and Sch 14, post.

7–5924   134. Lighting of wind turbine generators in United Kingdom territorial waters[1]. (1) This article shall apply to any wind turbine generator which is situated in waters within or adjacent to the United Kingdom up to the seaward limits of the territorial sea and the height of which is 60 metres or more above the level of the sea at the highest astronomical tide.

(2) Subject to paragraph (3) the person in charge of a wind turbine generator to which this article applies shall ensure that it is fitted with at least one medium intensity steady red light positioned as close as reasonably practicable to the top of the fixed structure.

(3) Where four or more wind turbine generators to which this article applies are located together in the same group, with the permission of the CAA only those on the periphery of the group need be fitted with a light in accordance with paragraph (2).

(4) The light or lights required by paragraph (2) shall, subject to paragraph (5), be so fitted as to show when displayed in all directions without interruption.

(5) When displayed—

(a) the angle of the plane of the beam of peak intensity emitted by the light shall be elevated to between 3 and 4 degrees above the horizontal plane;

(b) not more than 45% or less than 20% of the minimum peak intensity specified for a light of this type shall be visible at the horizontal plane;

(c) not more than 10% of the minimum peak intensity specified for a light of this type shall be visible at a depression of 1.5 degrees or more below the horizontal plane.

(6) The person in charge of a wind turbine generator to which this article applies shall—

    (a) subject to sub-paragraph (b) ensure that by night, any light required to be fitted by this article shall be displayed;

    (b) in the event of the failure of the light which is required by this article to be displayed by night, repair or replace the light as soon as is reasonably practicable.

(7) When visibility in all directions from every wind turbine generator to which this article applies in a group is more than 5 km the light intensity for any light required by this article to be fitted to any generator in the group and displayed may be reduced to not less than 10% of the minimum peak intensity specified for a light of this type.

(8) In any particular case the CAA may direct that a wind turbine generator to which this article applies shall be fitted with and shall display such additional lights in such positions and at such times as it may specify.

(9) This article shall not apply to any wind turbine generator in respect of which the CAA has granted a permission for the purposes of this article to the person in charge.

(10) A permission may be granted for the purposes of this article in respect of a particular case or class of cases or generally.

(11) In this article—

    (a) ''wind turbine generator'' is a generating station which is wholly or mainly driven by wind;

    (b) the height of a wind turbine generator is the height of the fixed structure or if greater the maximum vertical extent of any blade attached to that structure; and

    (c) a wind turbine generator is in the same group as another wind turbine generator if the same person is in charge of both and—

        (i) it is within 2 km of that other wind turbine generator; or

        (ii) it is within 2 km of a wind turbine generator which is in the same group as that other wind turbine generator.

---

1. Penalties for contraventions are contained in art 148 and Sch 14, post.

7–5925 135. Dangerous lights[1]. (1) A person shall not exhibit in the United Kingdom any light which—

    (a) by reason of its glare is liable to endanger aircraft taking off from or landing at an aerodrome; or

    (b) by reason of its liability to be mistaken for an aeronautical ground light is liable to endanger aircraft.

(2) If any light which appears to the CAA to be such a light as aforesaid is exhibited the CAA may cause a notice to be served upon the person who is the occupier of the place where the light is exhibited or has charge of the light, directing that person, within a reasonable time to be specified in the notice, to take such steps as may be specified in the notice for extinguishing or screening the light and for preventing for the future the exhibition of any other light which may similarly endanger aircraft.

(3) The notice may be served either personally or by post, or by affixing it in some conspicuous place near to the light to which it relates.

(4) In the case of a light which is or may be visible from any waters within the area of a general lighthouse authority, the power of the CAA under this article shall not be exercised except with the consent of that authority.

---

1. Penalties for contraventions are contained in art 148 and Sch 14, post.

7–5926 136. Customs and Excise aerodromes. (1) The Secretary of State may, with the concurrence of the Commissioners of Revenue and Customs and subject to such conditions as they may think fit, by order designate any aerodrome to be a place for the landing or departure of aircraft for the purpose of the enactments for the time being in force relating to customs and excise.

(2) The Secretary of State may, with the concurrence of the Commissioners of Revenue and Customs, by order revoke any designation so made.

7–5927 137. Aviation fuel at aerodromes[1]. (1) Subject to paragraph (2), a person who has the management of any aviation fuel installation on an aerodrome in the United Kingdom shall not cause or permit any fuel to be delivered to that installation or from it to an aircraft unless—

    (a) when the aviation fuel is delivered into the installation he is satisfied that—

        (i) the installation is capable of storing and dispensing the fuel so as not to render it unfit for use in aircraft;

        (ii) the installation is marked in a manner appropriate to the grade of fuel stored or if different grades are stored in different parts each part is so marked; and

   (iii) in the case of delivery into the installation or part thereof from a vehicle or vessel, the fuel has been sampled and is of a grade appropriate to that installation or that part of the installation as the case may be and is fit for use in aircraft; and

  (b) when any aviation fuel is dispensed from the installation he is satisfied as the result of sampling that the fuel is fit for use in aircraft.

(2) Paragraph (1) shall not apply in respect of fuel which has been removed from an aircraft and is intended for use in another aircraft operated by the same operator as the aircraft from which it has been removed.

(3) A person to whom paragraph (1) applies shall keep a written record in respect of each installation of which he has the management, which record shall include—

  (a) particulars of the grade and quantity of aviation fuel delivered and the date of delivery;
  (b) particulars of all samples taken of the aviation fuel and of the results of tests of those samples; and
  (c) particulars of the maintenance and cleaning of the installation;

and he shall preserve the written record for a period of 12 months or such longer period as the CAA may in a particular case direct and shall, within a reasonable time after being requested to do so by an authorised person, produce such record to that person.

(4) A person shall not cause or permit any aviation fuel to be dispensed for use in an aircraft if he knows or has reason to believe that the aviation fuel is not fit for use in aircraft.

(5) If it appears to the CAA or an authorised person that any aviation fuel is intended or likely to be delivered in contravention of any provision of this article, the CAA or that authorised person may direct the person having the management of the installation not to permit aviation fuel to be dispensed from that installation until the direction has been revoked by the CAA or by an authorised person.

(6) In this article—

  (a) "aviation fuel" means fuel intended for use in aircraft; and
  (b) "aviation fuel installation" means any apparatus or container, including a vehicle, designed, manufactured or adapted for the storage of aviation fuel or for the delivery of such fuel to an aircraft.

PART 14[1]
GENERAL

7–5928 138. Restriction on carriage for valuable consideration in aircraft registered elsewhere than in the United Kingdom[2]. (1) An aircraft registered in a Contracting State other than the United Kingdom, or in a foreign country, shall not take on board or discharge any passengers or cargo in the United Kingdom where valuable consideration is given or promised in respect of the carriage of such persons or cargo unless—

  (a) it does so with the permission of the Secretary of State granted under this article to the operator or the charterer of the aircraft or to the Government of the country in which the aircraft is registered, and in accordance with any conditions to which such permission may be subject; or
  (b) it is exercising traffic rights permitted by virtue of Council Regulation 2408/92 on access for Community air carriers to intra-Community air routes (as that Regulation has effect in accordance with the EEA Agreement as amended by the Decision of the EEA Joint Committee No 7/94 of 21st March 1994).

(2) Without prejudice to article 93 or to paragraph (1), any breach by a person to whom a permission has been granted under this article of any condition to which that permission was subject shall constitute a contravention of this article.

---

1. Part 11 comprises arts 138–167.
2. Penalties for contraventions are contained in art 148 and Sch 14, post.

139. Filing and approval of tariffs

7–5929 140. Restriction on aerial photography, aerial survey and aerial work in aircraft registered elsewhere than in the United Kingdom[1]. (1) An aircraft registered in a Contracting State other than the United Kingdom, or in a foreign country, shall not fly over the United Kingdom for the purpose of aerial photography or aerial survey (whether or not valuable consideration is given or promised in respect of the flight or the purpose of the flight) or for the purpose of any other form of aerial work except with the permission of the Secretary of State granted under this article to the operator or the charterer of the aircraft and in accordance with any conditions to which such permission may be subject.

(2) Without prejudice to article 93 or to paragraph (1), any breach by a person to whom a permission has been granted under this article of any condition to which that permission was subject shall constitute a contravention of this article.

---

1. Penalties for contraventions are contained in art 148 and Sch 14, post.

7–5930 141. Flights over any foreign country[1]. (1) The operator and the commander of an aircraft registered in the United Kingdom (or, if the operator's principal place of business or permanent residence is in the United Kingdom, any other aircraft) which is being flown over any foreign country shall not allow that aircraft to be used for a purpose which is prejudicial to the security, public order or public health of, or to the safety of air navigation in relation to, that country.

(2) A person does not contravene paragraph (1) if he neither knew nor suspected that the aircraft was being or was to be used for a purpose referred to in paragraph (1).

(3) The operator and the commander of an aircraft registered in the United Kingdom (or, if the operator's principal place of business or permanent residence is in the United Kingdom, any other aircraft) which is being flown over any foreign country shall comply with any directions given by the appropriate aeronautical authorities of that country whenever—

(a) the flight has not been duly authorised; or

(b) there are reasonable grounds for the appropriate aeronautical authorities to believe that the aircraft is being or will be used for a purpose which is prejudicial to the security, public order or public health of, or to the safety of air navigation in relation to, that country;

unless the lives of persons on board or the safety of the aircraft would thereby be endangered.

(4) A person does not contravene paragraph (3) if he neither knew nor suspected that directions were being given by the appropriate aeronautical authorities.

(5) The requirement in paragraph (3) is without prejudice to any other requirement to comply with directions of an aeronautical authority.

(6) In this article "appropriate aeronautical authorities" includes any person, whether a member of a country's military or civil authorities, authorised under the law of the foreign country to issue directions to aircraft flying over that country.

---

1. Penalties for contraventions are contained in art 148 and Sch 14, post.

7–5931 142. Mandatory reporting of occurrences[1]. (1) The objective of this article is to contribute to the improvement of air safety by ensuring that relevant information on safety is reported, collected, stored, protected and disseminated.

(2) The sole objective of occurrence reporting is the prevention of accidents and incidents and not to attribute blame or liability.

(3) This article shall apply to occurrences which endanger or which, if not corrected, would endanger an aircraft, its occupants or any other person.

(4) Without prejudice to the generality of paragraph (3), a list of examples of these occurrences is set out in Annexes I and II (and their Appendices) of Directive 2003/42 of the European Parliament and of the Council of 13th June 2003 on occurrence reporting in civil aviation.

(5) Every person listed below shall report to the CAA any event which constitutes an occurrence for the purposes of paragraph (3) and which comes to his attention in the exercise of his functions—

(a) the operator and the commander of a turbine-powered aircraft which has a certificate of airworthiness issued by the CAA;

(b) the operator and the commander of an aircraft operated under an air operator's certificate granted by the CAA;

(c) a person who carries on the business of manufacturing a turbine-powered or a public transport aircraft, or any equipment or part thereof, in the United Kingdom;

(d) a person who carries on the business of maintaining or modifying a turbine-powered aircraft , which has a certificate of airworthiness issued by the CAA, and a person who carries on the business of maintaining or modifying any equipment or part of such an aircraft;

(e) a person who carries on the business of maintaining or modifying an aircraft, operated under an air operator's certificate granted by the CAA, and a person who carries on the business of maintaining or modifying any equipment or part of such an aircraft;

(f) a person who signs an airworthiness review certificate, or a certificate of release to service in respect of a turbine-powered aircraft, which has a certificate of airworthiness issued by the CAA, and a person who signs an airworthiness review certificate or a certificate of release to service in respect of any equipment or part of such an aircraft;

(g) a person who signs an airworthiness review certificate, or a certificate of release to service in respect of an aircraft, operated under an air operator's certificate granted by the CAA, and a person who signs an airworthiness review certificate or a certificate of release to service in respect of any equipment or part of such an aircraft;

(h) a person who performs a function which requires him to be authorised by the CAA as an air traffic controller or as a flight information service officer;

(i) a licensee and a manager of a licensed aerodrome or a manager of an airport to which Council Regulation (EEC) No 2408/92 of 23rd July 1992 on access for Community air carriers to intra-Community air routes applies;

(j) a person who performs a function in respect of the installation, modification, maintenance, repair, overhaul, flight-checking or inspection of air navigation facilities which are utilized by a person who provides an air traffic control service under an approval issued by the CAA;

(k)　a person who performs a function in respect of the ground-handling of aircraft, including fuelling, servicing, loadsheet preparation, loading, de-icing and towing at an airport to which Council Regulation (EEC) No 2408/92 of 23rd July 1992 on access for Community air carriers to intra-Community air routes applies.

(6) Reports of occurrences shall be made within such time, by such means and containing such information as may be prescribed[2] and shall be presented in such form as the CAA may in any particular case approve.

(7) A person listed in paragraph (5) shall make a report to the CAA within such time, by such means, and containing such information as the CAA may specify in a notice in writing served upon him, being information which is in his possession or control and which relates to an occurrence which has been reported by him or another person to the CAA in accordance with this article.

(8) A person shall not make any report under this article if he knows or has reason to believe that the report is false in any particular.

(9) The CAA shall put in place a mechanism to collect, evaluate, process and store occurrences reported in accordance with paragraphs (5) to (7).

(10) The CAA shall store in its databases the reports which it has collected of occurrences, accidents and serious incidents.

(11) The CAA shall make all relevant safety-related information stored in the databases mentioned in paragraph (10) available to the competent authorities of the other Member States and the Commission.

(12) The CAA shall ensure that the databases referred to in paragraph (10) are compatible with the software developed by the European Commission for the purpose of implementing Directive 2003/42 of the European Parliament and of the Council of 13th June 2003 on occurrence reporting in civil aviation.

(13) The CAA, having received an occurrence report, shall enter it into its databases and notify, whenever necessary: the competent authority of the Member State where the occurrence took place; where the aircraft is registered; where the aircraft was manufactured, and where the operator's air operator's certificate was granted.

(14) The CAA shall provide any entity entrusted with regulating civil aviation safety or with investigating civil aviation accidents and incidents within the Community with access to information on occurrences collected and exchanged in accordance with paragraphs (9) to (13) to enable it to draw the safety lessons from the reported occurrences.

(15) The CAA and the Chief Inspector of Air Accidents shall use any information received in accordance with the terms of this article solely for the purposes set out in this article.

(16) The names or addresses of individual persons shall not be recorded on the databases referred to in paragraph (10).

(17) Without prejudice to the rules of criminal law, no proceedings shall be instituted in respect of unpremeditated or inadvertent infringements of the law which come to the attention of the relevant authorities only because they have been reported under this article as required by Article 4 of Directive 2003/42 of the European Parliament and of the Council of 13th June 2003 on occurrence reporting in civil aviation, except in cases of gross negligence.

(18) The provisions in paragraphs (15) to (17) shall apply without prejudice to the right of access to information by judicial authorities.

(19) The CAA shall put in place a system of voluntary reporting to collect and analyse information on observed deficiencies in aviation which are not required to be reported under the system of mandatory reporting, but which are perceived by the reporter as an actual or potential hazard.

(20) Voluntary reports presented to the CAA under paragraph (19) shall be subjected to a process of disidentification by it where the person making the report requests that his identity is not recorded on the databases.

(21) The CAA shall ensure that relevant safety information deriving from the analysis of reports, which have been subjected to disidentification, are stored and made available to all parties so that they can be used for improving safety in aviation.

---

1. Penalties for contraventions are contained in art 148 and Sch 14, post.
2. See the Air Navigation (General) Regulations 2005, SI 2005/1980.

7–5932　143. Mandatory reporting of birdstrikes.　(1) Subject to the provisions of this article, the commander of an aircraft shall make a report to the CAA of any birdstrike occurrence which occurs whilst the aircraft is in flight within the United Kingdom.

(2) The report shall be made within such time, by such means and shall contain such information as may be prescribed[1] and it shall be presented in such form as the CAA may in any particular case approve.

(3) Nothing in this article shall require a person to report any occurrence which he has reported under article 142 or which he has reason to believe has been or will be reported by another person to the CAA in accordance with that article.

(4) A person shall not make any report under this article if he knows or has reason to believe that the report is false in any particular.

(5) In this article "birdstrike occurrence" means an incident in flight in which the commander of an aircraft has reason to believe that the aircraft has been in collision with one or more than one bird.

1. See the Air Navigation (General) Regulations 2005, SI 2005/1980.

7–5933 144. Power to prevent aircraft flying[1]. (1) If it appears to the CAA or an authorised person that any aircraft is intended or likely to be flown—

  (a) in such circumstances that any provision of article 3, 5, 6, 8, 25, 26, 43, 62, 69, 70 or 75(2) would be contravened in relation to the flight;

  (b) in such circumstances that the flight would be in contravention of any other provision of this Order, of any regulations made thereunder or of Part 21, 145 or M and be a cause of danger to any person or property whether or not in the aircraft; or

  (c) while in a condition unfit for the flight, whether or not the flight would otherwise be in contravention of any provision of this Order, of any regulations made thereunder or of Part 21, 145 or M;

the CAA or that authorised person may direct the operator or the commander of the aircraft that he is not to permit the aircraft to make the particular flight or any other flight of such description as may be specified in the direction, until the direction has been revoked by the CAA or by an authorised person, and the CAA or that authorised person may take such steps as are necessary to detain the aircraft.

(2) For the purposes of paragraph (1) the CAA or any authorised person may enter upon and inspect any aircraft.

(3) If it appears to the Secretary of State or an authorised person that any aircraft is intended or likely to be flown in such circumstances that any provision of article 138, 140 or 141 would be contravened in relation to the flight, the Secretary of State or that authorised person may direct the operator or the commander of the aircraft that he is not to permit the aircraft to make a particular flight or any other flight of such description as may be specified in the direction until the direction has been revoked by the Secretary of State or by an authorised person, and the Secretary of State or any authorised person may take such steps as are necessary to detain the aircraft.

(4) For the purposes of paragraph (3) the Secretary of State or any authorised person may enter upon any aerodrome and may enter upon and inspect any aircraft.

1. Penalties for contraventions are contained in art 148 and Sch 14, post.

7–5934 145. Right of access to aerodromes and other places. (1) Subject to paragraph (2), the CAA and any authorised person shall have the right of access at all reasonable times—

  (a) to any aerodrome for the purpose of inspecting the aerodrome;

  (b) to any aerodrome for the purpose of inspecting any aircraft on the aerodrome or any document which it or he has power to demand under this Order, or for the purpose of detaining any aircraft under the provisions of this Order;

  (c) to any place where an aircraft has landed, for the purpose of inspecting the aircraft or any document which it or he has power to demand under this Order and for the purpose of detaining the aircraft under the provisions of this Order; and

  (d) to any building or place from which an air traffic control service is being provided or where any air traffic service equipment requiring approval under article 124 is situated for the purpose of inspecting—

    (i) any equipment used or intended to be used in connection with the provision of a service to an aircraft in flight or on the ground; or

    (ii) any document or record which it or he has power to demand under this Order.

(2) Access to a Government aerodrome shall only be obtained with the permission of the person in charge of the aerodrome.

7–5935 146. Obstruction of persons[1]. A person shall not intentionally obstruct or impede any person acting in the exercise of his powers or the performance of his duties under this Order.

1. Penalties for contraventions are contained in art 148 and Sch 14, post.

7–5936 147. Directions. (1) Where any provision of this Order or any regulations made thereunder gives to a person the power to direct, the person to whom such a power is given shall also have the power to revoke or vary any such direction.

(2) Any person who without reasonable excuse fails to comply with any direction given to him under any provision of this Order or any regulations made thereunder shall be deemed for the purposes of this Order to have contravened that provision.

7–5937 148. Penalties. (1) If any provision of this Order, or any regulations made thereunder or of Part 21, 145 or M is contravened in relation to an aircraft, the operator of that aircraft and the commander and, in the case of a contravention of article 138, the charterer of that aircraft, shall (without prejudice to the liability of any other person for that contravention) be deemed for the purposes of the following provisions of this article to have contravened that provision unless he proves that the contravention occurred without his consent or connivance and that he exercised all due diligence to prevent the contravention.

(2) If it is proved that an act or omission of any person which would otherwise have been a contravention by that person of a provision of this Order, or any regulations made thereunder or of Part 21, 66, 145, 147 or M was due to any cause not avoidable by the exercise of reasonable care by that person the act or omission shall be deemed not to be a contravention by that person of that provision.

(3) Where a person is charged with contravening a provision of this Order or any regulations made thereunder by reason of his having been a member of the flight crew of an aircraft on a flight for the purpose of public transport or aerial work the flight shall be treated (without prejudice to the liability of any other person under this Order) as not having been for that purpose if he proves that he neither knew nor suspected that the flight was for that purpose.

(4) If any person contravenes any provision of this Order, or any regulations made thereunder or of Part 21, 66, 145, 147 or M not being a provision referred to in paragraph (5), (6) or (7), he shall be guilty of an offence and liable on summary conviction to a fine not exceeding level 3 on the standard scale.

(5) If any person contravenes any provision specified in Part A of Schedule 14 he shall be guilty of an offence and liable on summary conviction to a fine not exceeding level 4 on the standard scale.

(6) If any person contravenes any provision specified in Part B of the said Schedule he shall be guilty of an offence and liable on summary conviction to a fine not exceeding the statutory maximum and on conviction on indictment to a fine or imprisonment for a term not exceeding two years or both.

(7) If any person contravenes any provision specified in Part C of the said Schedule he shall be guilty of an offence and liable on summary conviction to a fine not exceeding the statutory maximum and on conviction on indictment to a fine or imprisonment for a term not exceeding five years or both.

7–5938　149. Extra-territorial effect of the Order.　(1) Except where the context otherwise requires, the provisions of this Order—

    (a)　in so far as they apply (whether by express reference or otherwise) to aircraft registered in the United Kingdom, shall apply to such aircraft wherever they may be;

    (b)　in so far as they apply as aforesaid to other aircraft shall apply to such other aircraft when they are within the United Kingdom or on or in the neighbourhood of an offshore installation;

    (c)　in so far as they prohibit, require or regulate (whether by express reference or otherwise) the doing of anything by persons in, or by any of the crew of, any aircraft registered in the United Kingdom, shall apply to such persons and crew, wherever they may be;

    (d)　in so far as they prohibit, require or regulate as aforesaid the doing of anything in relation to any aircraft registered in the United Kingdom by other persons shall, where such persons are Commonwealth citizens, British protected persons or citizens of the Republic of Ireland, apply to them wherever they may be; and

    (e)　in so far as they prohibit, require or regulate as aforesaid the doing of anything in relation to any aircraft on or in the neighbourhood of an offshore installation, shall apply to every person irrespective of his nationality or, in the case of a body corporate, of the law under which it was incorporated and wherever that person or body may be.

(2) Nothing in this article shall be construed as extending to make any person guilty of an offence in any case in which it is provided by section 3(1) of the British Nationality Act 1948 that that person shall not be guilty of an offence.

7–5939　150. Aircraft in transit over certain United Kingdom territorial waters.　(1) Where an aircraft, not being an aircraft registered in the United Kingdom, is flying over the territorial waters adjacent to the United Kingdom within part of a strait referred to in paragraph (4) solely for the purpose of continuous and expeditious transit of the strait, only the following articles and Schedules shall apply to that aircraft: article 20 and Schedule 5, to the extent necessary for the monitoring of the appropriate distress radio frequency, article 95(2), (3) and (4), together with the regulations made thereunder, article 148, article 153 and Part A of Schedule 14.

(2) The powers conferred by the provisions referred to in paragraph (1) shall not be exercised in a way which would hamper the transit of the strait by an aircraft not registered in the United Kingdom, but without prejudice to action needed to secure the safety of aircraft.

(3) In this article "transit of the strait" means overflight of the strait from an area of high seas at one end of the strait to an area of high seas at the other end, or flight to or from an area of high seas over some part of the strait for the purpose of entering, leaving or returning from a State bordering the strait and "an area of high seas" means any area outside the territorial waters of any State.

(4) The parts of the straits to which this article applies are specified in Schedule 15.

7–5940　151. Application of Order to British-controlled aircraft registered elsewhere than in the United Kingdom.　The CAA may direct that such of the provisions of this Order and of any regulations made or having effect thereunder as may be specified in the direction shall have effect as if reference in those provisions to aircraft registered in the United Kingdom included references to the aircraft specified in the direction, being an aircraft registered elsewhere than in the United Kingdom but for the time being under the management of a person who, or of persons each of whom, is qualified to hold a legal or beneficial interest by way of ownership in an aircraft registered in the United Kingdom.

7–5941 152. Application of Order to the Crown and visiting forces, etc. (1) Subject to the provisions of this article, the provisions of this Order shall apply to or in relation to aircraft belonging to or exclusively employed in the service of Her Majesty as they apply to or in relation to other aircraft.

(2) For the purposes of such application, the Department or other authority for the time being responsible on behalf of Her Majesty for the management of the aircraft shall be deemed to be the operator of the aircraft and, in the case of an aircraft belonging to Her Majesty, to be the owner of the interest of Her Majesty in the aircraft.

(3) Nothing in this article shall render liable to any penalty any Department or other authority responsible on behalf of Her Majesty for the management of any aircraft.

(4) Save as otherwise expressly provided the naval, military and air force authorities and members of any visiting force and any international headquarters and the members and property held or used for the purpose of such a force or headquarters shall be exempt from the provisions of this Order and of any regulations made thereunder to the same extent as if that force or headquarters formed part of the forces of Her Majesty raised in the United Kingdom and for the time being serving there.

(5) Save as otherwise provided by paragraph (6), article 80(5) and (12), article 81(3), article 95(1)(*a*) and article 131, nothing in this Order shall apply to or in relation to any military aircraft.

(6) Where a military aircraft is flown by a civilian pilot and is not commanded by a person who is acting in the course of his duty as a member of any of Her Majesty's naval, military or air forces or as a member of a visiting force or international headquarters, the following provisions of this Order shall apply on the occasion of that flight, that is to say, articles 73, 74, 75 and 96 and in addition article 95 (so far as applicable) shall apply unless the aircraft is flown in compliance with Military Flying Regulations (Joint Service Publication 550) or Flying Orders to Contractors (Aviation Publication 67) issued by the Secretary of State.

7–5942 153. Exemption from Order. The CAA may exempt from any of the provisions of this Order (other than article 85, 87, 93, 138, 139, 140, 141 or 154) or any regulations made thereunder, any aircraft or persons or classes of aircraft or persons, either absolutely or subject to such conditions as it thinks fit.

7–5943 154. Appeal to County Court or Sheriff Court. *Appeals against decision of CAA that a person is not a fit person to hold certain licences.*

7–5944 155. Interpretation. (1) In this Order—

"A Conditions" means the conditions so entitled set out in paragraph 1 of Part A of Schedule 3;

"Accident prevention and flight safety programme" means a programme designed to detect and eliminate or avoid hazards in order to improve the safety of flight operations;

"Aerial work" has the meaning assigned to it by article 157;

"Aerial work aircraft" means an aircraft (other than a public transport aircraft) flying, or intended by the operator to fly, for the purpose of aerial work;

"Aerial work undertaking" means an undertaking whose business includes the performance of aerial work;

"Aerobatic manoeuvres" includes loops, spins, rolls, bunts, stall turns, inverted flying and any other similar manoeuvre;

"Aerodrome" means any area of land or water designed, equipped, set apart or commonly used for affording facilities for the landing and departure of aircraft and includes any area or space, whether on the ground, on the roof of a building or elsewhere, which is designed, equipped or set apart for affording facilities for the landing and departure of aircraft capable of descending or climbing vertically, but shall not include any area the use of which for affording facilities for the landing and departure of aircraft has been abandoned and has not been resumed;

"Aerodrome control service" means an air traffic control service for any aircraft on the manoeuvring area or apron of the aerodrome in respect of which the service is being provided or which is flying in, or in the vicinity of, the aerodrome traffic zone of that aerodrome by visual reference to the surface or any aircraft transferred from approach control in accordance with procedures approved by the CAA;

"Aerodrome operating minima" in relation to the operation of an aircraft at an aerodrome means the cloud ceiling and runway visual range for take-off, and the decision height or minimum descent height, runway visual range and visual reference for landing, which are the minimum for the operation of that aircraft at that aerodrome;

"Aerodrome traffic zone" has the meaning assigned to it by article 156;

"Aeronautical beacon" means an aeronautical ground light which is visible either continuously or intermittently to designate a particular point on the surface of the earth;

"Aeronautical ground light" means any light specifically provided as an aid to air navigation, other than a light displayed on an aircraft;

"Aeronautical radio station" means a radio station on the surface, which transmits or receives signals for the purpose of assisting aircraft;

"Air control" means an aerodrome control service excluding that part of the aerodrome control service provided by ground movement control;

"Air/ground communications service" means a service provided from an aerodrome to give information to pilots of aircraft flying in the vicinity of the aerodrome by means of radio signals and 'air/ground communications service unit' shall be construed accordingly;

"Air traffic control service" means the giving of instructions, advice or information by means of radio signals to aircraft in the interests of safety;

"Air traffic control unit" means a person appointed by a person maintaining an aerodrome or place to provide an air traffic control service;

"Air traffic service equipment" means ground based equipment, including an aeronautical radio station, used or intended to be used in connection with the provision of a service to an aircraft in flight or on the ground which equipment is not otherwise approved by or under this Order but excluding—

(a) any public electronic communications network; and
(b) any equipment in respect of which the CAA has made a direction that it shall be deemed not to be air traffic service equipment for the purposes of articles 124 and 125;

"Air transport undertaking" means an undertaking whose business includes the undertaking of flights for the purpose of the public transport of passengers or cargo;

"Alternate aerodrome" means an aerodrome to which an aircraft may proceed when it becomes either impossible or inadvisable to proceed to or to land at the aerodrome of intended landing;

"Altitude hold and heading mode" mean aircraft autopilot functions which enable the aircraft to maintain an accurate height and an accurate heading;

"Annual costs" in relation to the operation of an aircraft means the best estimate reasonably practicable at the time of a particular flight in respect of the year commencing on the first day of January preceding the date of the flight, of the costs of keeping and maintaining and the indirect costs of operating the aircraft, such costs in either case excluding direct costs and being those actually and necessarily incurred without a view to profit;

"Annual flying hours" means the best estimate reasonably practicable at the time of a particular flight by an aircraft of the hours flown or to be flown by the aircraft in respect of the year commencing on the first day of January preceding the date of the flight;

"Approach control service" means an air traffic control service for any aircraft which is not receiving an aerodrome control service, which is flying in, or in the vicinity of the aerodrome traffic zone of the aerodrome in respect of which the service is being provided, whether or not the aircraft is flying by visual reference to the surface;

"Approach to landing" means that portion of the flight of the aircraft, when approaching to land, in which it is descending below a height of 1,000 feet above the relevant specified decision height or minimum descent height;

"Appropriate aeronautical radio station" means in relation to an aircraft an aeronautical radio station serving the area in which the aircraft is for the time being;

"Appropriate air traffic control unit" means in relation to an aircraft either the air traffic control unit serving the area in which the aircraft is for the time being or the air traffic control unit serving the area which the aircraft intends to enter and with which unit the aircraft is required to communicate prior to entering that area, as the context requires;

"Apron" means the part of an aerodrome provided for the stationing of aircraft for the embarkation and disembarkation of passengers, for loading and unloading of cargo and for parking;

"Area control centre" means an air traffic control unit established to provide an area control service to aircraft flying within a notified flight information region which are not receiving an aerodrome control service or an approach control service;

"Area control service" means an air traffic control service for any aircraft which is flying neither in nor in the vicinity of an aerodrome traffic zone;

"Area navigation equipment" means equipment carried on board an aircraft which enables the aircraft to navigate on any desired flight path within the coverage of appropriate ground based navigation aids or within the limits of that on-board equipment or a combination of the two;

"Authorised person" means—

(a) any constable;
(b) in article 144(3) and (4) any person authorised by the Secretary of State (whether by name, or by class or description) either generally or in relation to a particular case or class of cases; and
(c) in article 144(1) and (2) and in any article other than article 144, any person authorised by the CAA (whether by name or by class or description) either generally or in relation to a particular case or class of cases;

"B Conditions" means the conditions so entitled set out in paragraph 2 of Part A of Schedule 3;

"Basic EASA Regulation" means Regulation (EC) No 1592/2002 of the European Parliament and of the Council of 15th July 2002 on common rules in the field of civil aviation and establishing a European Aviation Safety Agency;

"Beneficial interest" includes interests arising under contract and other equitable interests;

"Cabin crew" in relation to an aircraft means those persons on a flight for the purpose of public transport carried for the purpose of performing in the interests of the safety of passengers duties to be assigned by the operator or the commander of the aircraft but who shall not act as a member of the flight crew;

"British protected person" has the same meaning as in section 50 of the British Nationality Act 1981;

"Captive balloon" means a balloon which when in flight is attached by a restraining device to the surface;

"Captive flight" means flight by an uncontrollable balloon during which it is attached to the surface by a restraining device;

"Cargo" includes mail and (for the avoidance of doubt) animals;

"Certificate of airworthiness" includes in the case of a national certificate of airworthiness any flight manual, performance schedule or other document, whatever its title, incorporated by reference in that certificate relating to the certificate of airworthiness;

"Certificate of maintenance review" has the meaning assigned to it by article 14(1)(*b*);

"Certificate of release to service issued under Part 145" means a certificate of release to service issued in accordance with Part 145;

"Certificate of release to service issued under this Order" means a certificate issued by a person specified in article 16(11) which conforms with article 16(10);

"Certificate of revalidation" means a certificate issued in accordance with Section 2 of Part C of Schedule 8 for the purpose of maintaining the privileges of a flight crew licence;

"Certificate of validation" means a certificate issued by the CAA rendering valid for the purposes of this Order a certificate of airworthiness or a permit to fly issued in respect of an aircraft registered elsewhere than in the United Kingdom or a flight crew licence granted under the law of a country other than the United Kingdom;

"Certificate of validity" means a certificate issued under article 11(6)(*d*) for the purpose of maintaining the validity of a permit to fly issued by the CAA;

"Certificated for single pilot operation" means an aircraft which is not required to carry more than one pilot by virtue of any one or more of the following—

(*a*) the certificate of airworthiness duly issued or rendered valid under the law of the country in which the aircraft is registered or the related flight manual;

(*b*) if no certificate of airworthiness is required to be in force, the certificate of airworthiness, if any, last in force in respect of the aircraft or the related flight manual;

(*c*) if no certificate of airworthiness is or has previously been in force but the aircraft is identical in design with an aircraft in respect of which such a certificate is or has been in force, the certificate of airworthiness which is or has been in force in respect of such an identical aircraft or the related flight manual; or

(*d*) in the case of an aircraft flying in accordance with the conditions of a permit to fly issued by the CAA, that permit to fly;

"Class A airspace", "Class B airspace", "Class C airspace", "Class D airspace" and "Class E airspace" mean airspace respectively notified as such;

"Class rating" in respect of aeroplanes has the meaning specified in paragraph 1.220 of Section 1 of JAR-FCL 1;

"Cloud ceiling" in relation to an aerodrome means the vertical distance from the elevation of the aerodrome to the lowest part of any cloud visible from the aerodrome which is sufficient to obscure more than one-half of the sky so visible;

"Commander" in relation to an aircraft means the member of the flight crew designated as commander of that aircraft by the operator, or, failing such a person, the person who is for the time being the pilot in command of the aircraft;

"the Commonwealth" means the United Kingdom, the Channel Islands, the Isle of Man, the countries mentioned in Schedule 3 to the British Nationality Act 1981 and all other territories forming part of Her Majesty's dominions or in which Her Majesty has jurisdiction and "Commonwealth citizen" shall be construed accordingly;

"Competent authority" means, subject to article 167 in relation to the United Kingdom, the CAA, and in relation to any other country the authority responsible under the law of that country for promoting the safety of civil aviation;

"Conditional sale agreement" has the same meaning as in section 189 of the Consumer Credit Act 1974;

"Congested area" in relation to a city, town or settlement, means any area which is substantially used for residential, industrial, commercial or recreational purposes;

"Contracting State" means any State (including the United Kingdom) which is party to the Chicago Convention;

"Controllable balloon" means a balloon, not being a small balloon, which is capable of free controlled flight;

"Controlled airspace" means airspace which has been notified as Class A, Class B, Class C, Class D or Class E airspace;

"Control area" means controlled airspace which has been further notified as a control area and which extends upwards from a notified altitude or flight level;

"Control zone" means controlled airspace which has been further notified as a control zone and which extends upwards from the surface;

"Co-pilot" in relation to an aircraft means a pilot who in performing his duties as such is subject to the direction of another pilot carried in the aircraft;

"Country" includes a territory;

"Crew" means a member of the flight crew, a person carried on the flight deck who is appointed by the operator of the aircraft to give or to supervise the training, experience, practice and periodical tests required in respect of the flight crew under article 42(3) or a member of the cabin crew;

"Critical power unit" means the power unit whose failure would most adversely affect the performance or handling qualities of an aircraft;

"Danger Area" means airspace which has been notified as such within which activities dangerous to the flight of aircraft may take place or exist at such times as may be notified;

"Decision height" in relation to the operation of an aircraft at an aerodrome means the height in a precision approach at which a missed approach must be initiated if the required visual reference to continue that approach has not been established;

"Declared distances" has the meaning which has been notified;

"Designated required navigation performance airspace" means airspace which has been notified, prescribed or otherwise designated by the competent authority for the airspace as requiring specified navigation performance capabilities to be met by aircraft flying within it;

"Direct costs" means, in respect of a flight, the costs actually and necessarily incurred in connection with that flight without a view to profit but excluding any remuneration payable to the pilot for his services as such;

"Director" has the same meaning as in section 53(1) of the Companies Act 1989;

"Disidentification" means removing from reports submitted all personal details pertaining to the reporter and technical details which might lead to the identity of the reporter, or of third parties, being inferred from the information;

"EASA" means the European Aviation Safety Agency;

"EASA aircraft" means an aircraft which is required by virtue of the Basic EASA Regulation and any implementing rules adopted by the Commission in accordance with that Regulation to hold an EASA certificate of airworthiness, an EASA restricted certificate of airworthiness or an EASA permit to fly;

"EASA certificate of airworthiness" means a certificate of airworthiness issued in respect of an EASA aircraft under and in accordance with subpart H of Part 21;

"EASA permit to fly" means a permit to fly issued in respect of an EASA aircraft under and in accordance with subpart H of Part 21;

"EASA restricted certificate of airworthiness" means a restricted certificate of airworthiness issued in respect of an EASA aircraft under and in accordance with subpart H of Part 21;

"European Aviation Safety Agency" means the Agency established under the Basic EASA Regulation;

"Flight" and "to fly" have the meanings respectively assigned to them by paragraph (2);

"Flight check" means a check carried out by an aircraft in flight of the accuracy and reliability of signals transmitted by an aeronautical radio station;

"Flight crew" in relation to an aircraft means those members of the crew of the aircraft who respectively undertake to act as pilot, flight navigator, flight engineer and flight radiotelephony operator of the aircraft;

"Flight data monitoring programme" means a programme of analysing recorded flight data in order to improve the safety of flight operations;

"Flight information service" means—

    (*a*) in the case of an aerodrome—

        (i) the giving of information by means of radio signals to aircraft flying in or intending to fly within the aerodrome traffic zone of that aerodrome; and

        (ii) the grant or refusal of a permission under Rule 35 or 36(2) of the Rules of the Air Regulations 1996;

    (*b*) in the case of an area control centre, the giving of information by means of radio signals to aircraft;

    and "aerodrome flight information service" shall be construed accordingly;

"Flight information service unit" means a person appointed by the CAA or by any other person maintaining an aerodrome or area control centre to provide a flight information service and "aerodrome flight information service unit" shall be construed accordingly;

"Flight level" means one of a series of levels of equal atmospheric pressure, separated by notified intervals and each expressed as the number of hundreds of feet which would be indicated at that level on a pressure altimeter calibrated in accordance with the International Standard Atmosphere and set to 1013.2 hectopascals;

"Flight manual" means a document provided for an aircraft stating the limitations within which the aircraft is considered airworthy as defined by the appropriate airworthiness requirements, and additional instructions and information necessary for the safe operation of the aircraft;

"Flight recording system" means a system comprising either a flight data recorder or a cockpit voice recorder or both;

"Flight simulator" means apparatus by means of which flight conditions in an aircraft are simulated on the ground;

"Flight visibility" means the visibility forward from the flight deck of an aircraft in flight;

"Flying display" means any flying activity deliberately performed for the purpose of providing an exhibition or entertainment at an advertised event open to the public;

"Flying machine" means an aeroplane, a powered lift tilt rotor aircraft, a self-launching motor glider, a helicopter or a gyroplane;

"Free balloon" means a balloon which when in flight is not attached by any form of restraining device to the surface;

"Free controlled flight" means flight during which a balloon is not attached to the surface by any form of restraining device (other than a tether not exceeding 5 metres in length which may be used as part of the take-off procedure) and during which the height of the balloon is controllable by means of a device attached to the balloon and operated by the commander of the balloon or by remote control;

"General lighthouse authority" has the same meaning as in section 193 of the Merchant Shipping Act 1995;

"Glider" means—

    (a) a non-power-driven heavier-than-air aircraft, deriving its lift in flight chiefly from aerodynamic reactions on surfaces which remain fixed under given conditions of flight;

    (b) a self-sustaining glider; and

    (c) a self-propelled hang-glider;

and a reference in this Order to a glider shall include a reference to a self-sustaining glider and a self-propelled hang-glider;

"Government aerodrome" means any aerodrome in the United Kingdom which is in the occupation of any Government Department or visiting force;

"Ground movement control" means that part of an aerodrome control service provided to an aircraft while it is on the manoeuvring area or apron of an aerodrome;

"Hire-purchase agreement" has the same meaning as in section 189 of the Consumer Credit Act 1974;

"Holding" means, in respect of an aircraft approaching an aerodrome to land, a manoeuvre in the air which keeps that aircraft within a specified volume of airspace;

"Instructor's rating" means a flying instructor's rating, an assistant flying instructor's rating, a flight instructor rating (aeroplane), a flight instructor rating (helicopter), a type rating instructor rating (multi-pilot aeroplane), a type rating instructor rating (helicopter), a class rating instructor rating (single pilot aeroplane), an instrument rating instructor rating (aeroplane) or an instrument rating instructor rating (helicopter);

"Instrument Flight Rules" means Instrument Flight Rules prescribed by Section VI of the Rules of the Air Regulations 1996;

"Instrument Landing System" means a ground-based radio system designed to transmit radio signals at very high frequency and ultra high frequency that allow the pilot of an aircraft to accurately determine the aircraft's position relative to a defined approach path whilst carrying out an approach to land;

"Instrument Meteorological Conditions" means weather precluding flight in compliance with the Visual Flight Rules;

"International headquarters" means an international headquarters designated by Order in Council under section 1 of the International Headquarters and Defence Organisations Act 1964;

"JAA" means the Joint Aviation Authorities, an associated body of the European Civil Aviation Conference;

"JAA Full Member State" means a State which is a full member of the JAA;

"JAA licence" means a flight crew licence granted under JAR-FCL 1 or 2 by the competent authority of a JAA Full Member State in accordance with a procedure which has been assessed as satisfactory following an inspection by a licensing and a medical standardisation team of the JAA;

"JAR-FCL 1" means the Joint Aviation Requirement of the JAA bearing that title including Amendment 3 adopted by the JAA on 1st July 2003;

"JAR-FCL 2" means the Joint Aviation Requirement of the JAA bearing that title including Amendment 3 adopted by the JAA on 1st September 2003;

"JAR-FCL licence" means a licence included in Section 2 of Part A of Schedule 8;

"JAR-OPS 1" means the Joint Aviation Requirement of the JAA bearing that title including Amendment 7 adopted by the JAA on 1st September 2004;

"JAR-OPS 3" means the Joint Aviation Requirement of the JAA bearing that title including Amendment 4 adopted by the JAA on 1st April 2004;

"Kg" means kilogramme or kilogrammes as the context requires;

"Km" means kilometre or kilometres as the context requires;

"To land" in relation to aircraft includes alighting on the water;

"Landing Decision Point" means the latest point in the course of a landing at which, following recognition of a power unit failure, the helicopter will be able to safely abort the landing and perform a go-around;

"Large rocket" means a rocket of which the total impulse of the motor or combination of motors is more than 10,240 Newton-seconds;

"Legal personal representative" means the person so constituted executor, administrator, or other representative, of a deceased person;

"Let down" means, in respect of an aircraft approaching an aerodrome to land a defined procedure designed to enable an aircraft safely to descend to a point at which it can continue the approach visually;

"Licence" in relation to a flight crew licence includes any certificate of competency or certificate of validity or revalidation issued with the licence or required to be held in connection with the licence by the law of the country in which the licence is granted;

"Licence for public use" has the meaning assigned to it by article 128(2);

"Licensed aerodrome" means an aerodrome licensed under this Order;

"Lifejacket" includes any device designed to support a person individually in or on the water;

"Log book" in the case of an aircraft log book, engine log book or variable pitch propeller log book, or personal flying log book, includes a record kept either in a book, or by any other means approved by the CAA in the particular case;

"Maintenance" means in relation to an aircraft any one or combination of overhaul, repair, inspection, replacement, modification or defect rectification of an aircraft or component, with the exception of pre-flight inspection;

"Manoeuvring area" means the part of an aerodrome provided for the take-off and landing of aircraft and for the movement of aircraft on the surface, excluding the apron and any part of the aerodrome provided for the maintenance of aircraft;

"Maximum approved passenger seating configuration" means—

    (a) in the case of an aircraft to which article 38 applies the maximum approved passenger seating configuration specified in the operations manual of the aircraft; and

    (b) in any other case, the maximum number of passengers which may be carried in the aircraft under and in accordance with its certificate of airworthiness, its flight manual and this Order;

"Maximum total weight authorised" in relation to an aircraft means the maximum total weight of the aircraft and its contents at which the aircraft may take off anywhere in the world, in the most favourable circumstances in accordance with the certificate of airworthiness in force in respect of the aircraft;

"Medical attendant" means a person carried on a flight for the purpose of attending to any person in the aircraft in need of medical attention, or to be available to attend to such a person;

"Medium intensity steady red light" means a red light which complies with the characteristics described for a medium intensity Type C light as specified in Volume 1 (Aerodrome Design and Operations) of Annex 14 (Fourth Edition July 2004) to the Chicago Convention;

"Microlight aeroplane" means an aeroplane designed to carry not more than two persons which has—

    (a) a maximum total weight authorised not exceeding—

        (i) 300 kg for a single seat landplane, (or 390 kg for a single seat landplane in respect of which a permit to fly or certificate of airworthiness issued by the CAA was in force prior to 1st January 2003);

        (ii) 450 kg for a two seat landplane;

        (iii) 330 kg for a single seat amphibian or floatplane; or

        (iv) 495 kg for a two seat amphibian or floatplane; and

    (b) a stalling speed at the maximum total weight authorised not exceeding 35 knots calibrated airspeed;

"Microwave Landing System" means a ground-based radio system designed to transmit radio signals at super high frequency that allow the pilot of an aircraft to accurately determine the aircraft's position within a defined volume of airspace whilst carrying out an approach to land;

"Military aircraft" means the naval, military or air force aircraft of any country and—

    (a) any aircraft being constructed for the naval, military or air force of any country under a contract entered into by the Secretary of State; and

    (b) any aircraft in respect of which there is in force a certificate issued by the Secretary of State that the aircraft is to be treated for the purposes of this Order as a military aircraft;

"Military rocket" means—

    (a) any rocket being constructed for the naval, military or air force of any country under a contract entered into by the Secretary of State; and

    (b) any rocket in respect of which there is in force a certificate issued by the Secretary of State that the rocket is to be treated for the purposes of this Order as a military rocket;

"Minimum descent height" in relation to the operation of an aircraft at an aerodrome means the height in a non-precision approach below which descent may not be made without the required visual reference;

"Multi-crew co-operation" means the functioning of the flight crew as a team of co-operating members led by the pilot in command;

"National certificate of airworthiness" means a certificate of airworthiness issued under and in accordance with Part 3 of this Order and which is not an EASA certificate of airworthiness;

"National permit to fly" means a permit to fly issued under and in accordance with Part 3 of this Order and which is not an EASA permit to fly;

"Nautical mile" means the International Nautical Mile, that is to say, a distance of 1,852 metres;

"Night" means the time from half an hour after sunset until half an hour before sunrise (both times inclusive), sunset and sunrise being determined at surface level;

"Non-EASA aircraft" means an aircraft which is not required by virtue of the Basic EASA Regulation and any implementing rules adopted by the Commission in accordance with that Regulation to hold an EASA certificate of airworthiness, an EASA restricted certificate of airworthiness or an EASA permit to fly; and a non-EASA balloon, a non-EASA glider and a non-EASA kite shall be construed accordingly;

"Non-precision approach" means an instrument approach using non-visual aids for guidance in azimuth or elevation but which is not a precision approach;

"Non-revenue flight" means—

(a) in the case of a flight by an aeroplane, any flight which the holder of a United Kingdom Private Pilot's Licence (Aeroplanes) may undertake under paragraph (2)(a) and (b) of the privileges of that licence set out in Section 1 of Part A of Schedule 8;

(b) in the case of a flight by a helicopter, any flight which the holder of a United Kingdom Private Pilot's Licence (Helicopters) may undertake under paragraph (2)(a) and (b) of the privileges of that licence set out in Section 1 of Part A of Schedule 8; and

(c) in the case of a flight by a gyroplane, any flight which the holder of a United Kingdom Private Pilot's Licence (Gyroplanes) may undertake under paragraph (2)(a) and (b) of the privileges of that licence set out in Section 1 of Part A of Schedule 8;

"North Atlantic Minimum Navigation Performance Specification airspace" means the airspace prescribed as such;

"Notified" means set out with the authority of the CAA in a document published by or under an arrangement entered into with the CAA and entitled "United Kingdom Notam" or "Air Pilot" and for the time being in force;

"Notified aerodrome" means an aerodrome which is notified for the purposes of rule 39 of the Rules of the Air Regulations 1996;

"Obstacle limitation surfaces" has the same meaning as in the document entitled "CAP 168 Licensing of aerodromes" published by the CAA in May 2004;

"Occurrence" means an operational interruption, defect, fault or other irregular circumstance that has or may have influenced flight safety and that has not resulted in an accident or serious incident as those terms are defined in regulation 2 of the Civil Aviation (Investigation of Air Accidents and Incidents) Regulations 1996;

"Offshore service" means an air traffic control service for any aircraft flying to or from offshore oil and gas installations and for other aircraft operating in the vicinity of these aircraft in airspace specified for this purpose in the manual of air traffic services;

"Operating staff" means the servants and agents employed by an operator an aircraft, whether or not as members of the crew, to ensure that flights of the aircraft are conducted in a safe manner, and includes an operator who himself performs those functions;

"Operational position" means a position provided and equipped for the purpose of providing a particular type of air traffic control service;

"Operator" has the meaning assigned to it by paragraph (3);

"Parascending parachute" means a parachute which is towed by cable in such a manner as to cause it to ascend;

"Part 21" means the annex so entitled to Commission Regulation (EC) No 1702/2003;

"Part 66" means annex III so entitled to Commission Regulation (EC) No 2042/2003;

"Part 145" means annex II so entitled to Commission Regulation (EC) No 2042/2003;

"Part 147" means annex IV so entitled to Commission Regulation (EC) No 2042/2003;

"Part M" means annex I so entitled to Commission Regulation (EC) No 2042/2003;

"Passenger" means a person other than a member of the crew;

"Performance Class 1 operations" means flights where, in the event of the failure of a power unit, the helicopter will be able to safely continue the flight and land at an appropriate landing area unless the power unit failure recognition occurs during take-off at or prior to reaching the take-off decision point in which case the helicopter will be able to safely land back within the area from which it has taken off;

"Performance Class 2 operations" means flights where, in the event of the failure of a power unit, the helicopter will be able to safely continue the flight to an appropriate landing area or, where the failure occurs at a point during the take-off manoeuvre or the landing manoeuvre when it cannot do so, the helicopter will be able to carry out a forced landing;

"Performance Class 3 operations" means flights where, in the event of the failure of a power unit at any time during the flight, the helicopter will be required to carry out a forced landing;

"Period of duty" means the period between the commencement and end of a shift during which an air traffic controller performs, or could be called upon to perform, any of the functions specified in respect of a rating included in his licence;

"Pilot in command" in relation to an aircraft means a person who for the time being is in charge of the piloting of the aircraft without being under the direction of any other pilot in the aircraft;

"Police air operator's certificate" means a certificate granted by the CAA under article 7(4);

"Police authority" means a Chief Officer of police for any area of England or Wales, a Chief Constable for any area of Scotland and the Chief Constable of the Northern Ireland Police Service;

"Police officer" means any person who is a member of a police force or of the Northern Ireland Police Service (including, for the avoidance of doubt, the Northern Ireland Police Service Reserve), and any special constable;

"Pre-flight inspection" means the inspection carried out before flight to ensure that the aircraft is fit for the intended flight;

"Precision approach" means an instrument approach using an Instrument Landing System, Microwave Landing System or precision approach radar for guidance in both azimuth and elevation;

"Precision approach radar" means radar equipment designed to enable an air traffic controller to determine accurately an aircraft's position whilst it is carrying out an approach to land so that the air traffic controller can provide instructions and guidance to the pilot to enable him to manoeuvre the aircraft relative to a defined approach path;

"Pressurised aircraft" means an aircraft provided with means of maintaining in any compartment a pressure greater than that of the surrounding atmosphere;

"Private aircraft" means an aircraft which is neither an aerial work nor a public transport aircraft;

"Private flight" means a flight which is neither for the purpose of aerial work nor public transport;

"Proficiency check" has the meaning specified in paragraph 1.001 of Section 1 of JAR-FCL 1 in respect of aeroplanes and paragraph 2.001 of Section 1 of JAR-FCL 2 in respect of helicopters;

"Public electronic communications network" has the same meaning as in section 151 of the Communications Act 2003;

"Public transport" has the meaning assigned to it by article 157;

"Public transport aircraft" means an aircraft flying, or intended by the operator of the aircraft to fly, for the purpose of public transport;

"Record" has the same meaning as in section 81(6) of the Transport Act 2000;

"Reduced vertical separation minimum airspace" means any airspace between flight level 290 and flight level 410 inclusive designated by the relevant competent authority as being airspace within which a vertical separation minimum of 1,000 feet or 300 metres shall be applied;

"Released flight" means flight by an uncontrollable balloon during which it is not attached to the surface by any form of restraining device;

"Relevant overseas territory" means any colony and any country or place outside Her Majesty's dominions in which for the time being Her Majesty has jurisdiction;

"Replacement" in relation to any part of an aircraft or its equipment includes the removal and replacement of that part whether or not by the same part, and whether or not any work is done on it, but does not include the removal and replacement of a part which is designed to be removable solely for the purpose of enabling another part to be inspected, repaired, removed or replaced or cargo to be loaded;

"Rocket" means a device which is propelled by ejecting expanding gasses generated in its motor from self contained propellant and which is not dependent on the intake of outside substances and includes any part of the device intended to become separated during operation;

"Runway visual range" in relation to a runway means the distance in the direction of take-off or landing over which the runway lights or surface markings may be seen from the touchdown zone as calculated by either human observation or instruments in—

    (a) the vicinity of the touchdown zone; or
    (b) where this is not reasonably practicable, in the vicinity of the midpoint of the runway;

and the distance, if any, communicated to the commander of an aircraft by or on behalf of the person in charge of the aerodrome as being the runway visual range shall be taken to be the runway visual range for the time being;

"Scheduled journey" means one of a series of journeys which are undertaken between the same two places and which together amount to a systematic service;

"Seaplane" has the same meaning as in section 97 of the Civil Aviation Act 1982;

"Sector" means part of the airspace controlled from an area control centre or other place;

"Self-launching motor glider" means an aircraft with the characteristics of a non-power-driven glider, which is fitted with one or more power units and which is designed or intended to take off under its own power;

"Self-propelled hang-glider" means an aircraft comprising an aerofoil wing and a mechanical propulsion device which—

    (a) is foot launched;
    (b) has a stall speed or minimum steady flight speed in the landing configuration not exceeding 35 knots calibrated airspeed;
    (c) carries a maximum of two persons;
    (d) has a maximum fuel capacity of 10 litres; and

(e) has a maximum unladen weight, including full fuel, of 60 kg for single place aircraft and 70 kg for two place aircraft;

"Self-sustaining glider" means an aircraft with the characteristics of a non-power-driven glider which is fitted with one or more power units capable of sustaining the aircraft in flight but which is not designed or intended to take off under its own power;

"Simple single engine aeroplane" means for the purposes of the National Private Pilot's Licence a single engine piston aeroplane with a maximum take off weight authorised not exceeding 2,000 kg and which is not a microlight aeroplane or a self-launching motor glider;

"Skill test" has the meaning specified in paragraph 1.001 of Section 1 of JAR-FCL 1 in respect of aeroplanes and paragraph 2.001 of Section 1 of JAR-FCL 2 in respect of helicopters;

"SLMG" means a self-launching motor glider;

"Small aircraft" means any unmanned aircraft, other than a balloon or a kite, weighing not more than 20 kg without its fuel but including any articles or equipment installed in or attached to the aircraft at the commencement of its flight;

"Small balloon" means a balloon not exceeding 2 metres in any linear dimension at any stage of its flight, including any basket or other equipment attached to the balloon;

"Small rocket" means a rocket of which the total impulse of the motor or combination of motors does not exceed 10,240 Newton-seconds;

"Special tasks service" means an air traffic control service—

(a) for any aircraft flying for the purposes of research and development of aircraft, aircraft equipment or aircraft systems which is not flying in accordance with normal aviation practice; and

(b) for other aircraft in the vicinity of any such aircraft;

"Special VFR flight" means a flight which is a special VFR flight for the purposes of the Rules of the Air Regulations 1996;

"State aircraft" means an aircraft engaged in military, customs, police or similar services;

"State of design" means the State having jurisdiction over the organisation responsible for the type design of an aircraft;

"State of the operator" means the State in which the operator of an aircraft has his principal place of business or, if he has no such place of business, his permanent residence, in circumstances where—

(a) that aircraft is registered in another Contracting State;

(b) the operator is operating that aircraft under an agreement for its lease, charter or interchange or any similar arrangement;

(c) the State in which that aircraft is registered has, by agreement with the State in which the operator of the aircraft has his principal place of business or, if he has no such place of business, his permanent residence, agreed to transfer to it its functions and duties as State of registry in respect of that aircraft in relation to, in the case of article 8(1), airworthiness, in the case of article 20(1), aircraft radio equipment, in the case of article 26(3), flight crew licensing or, in the case of article 55(1), radio licensing; and

(d) the agreement has been registered with the Council of the International Civil Aviation Organisation or the existence and scope of the agreement have been directly communicated to the CAA;

"Take-off decision point" means the latest point in the take-off at which, following recognition of a power unit failure, the helicopter will be able to carry out a rejected take-off;

"Technical log" means a record containing the information specified in paragraph 1.915 of Section 2 of JAR-OPS 1;

"Terminal control service" means an air traffic control service for any aircraft flying in, departing or intending to fly within a terminal control area while it is in the terminal control area or any sector adjacent thereto and is specified for this purpose in the manual of air traffic services;

"Tethered flight" means flight by a controllable balloon throughout which it is flown within limits imposed by a restraining device which attaches the balloon to the surface;

"Touring motor glider" has the meaning specified in paragraph 1.001 of Section 1 of JAR-FCL 1;

"Type rating" in respect of aeroplanes has the meaning specified in paragraph 1.215 of Section 1 of JAR-FCL 1;

"Type rating" in respect of helicopters has the meaning specified in paragraph 2.215 of Section 1 of JAR-FCL 2;

"Uncontrollable balloon" means a balloon, not being a small balloon, which is not capable of free controlled flight;

"United Kingdom licence" means a licence included in Section 1 of Part A of Schedule 8;

"United Kingdom licence for which there is a JAR-FCL equivalent" means the following licences included in Section 1 of Part A of Schedule 8—

Private Pilot's Licence (Aeroplanes);
Commercial Pilot's Licence (Aeroplanes);
Airline Transport Pilot's Licence (Aeroplanes);
Private Pilot's Licence (Helicopters);
Commercial Pilot's Licence (Helicopters and Gyroplanes);

Airline Transport Pilot's Licence (Helicopters and Gyroplanes);

"United Kingdom licence for which there is no JAR-FCL equivalent" means any licence included in Section 1 of Part A of Schedule 8 other than any such licence which is a United Kingdom licence for which there is a JAR-FCL equivalent;

"United Kingdom reduced vertical separation minimum airspace" means United Kingdom airspace which has been notified as reduced vertical separation minimum airspace for the purposes of article 58;

"Valuable consideration" means any right, interest, profit or benefit, forbearance, detriment, loss or responsibility accruing, given, suffered or undertaken under an agreement, which is of more than a nominal nature;

"Visiting force" means any such body, contingent or detachment of the forces of any country as is a visiting force for the purpose of the provisions of the Visiting Forces Act 1952—

    (a)   which apply to that country by virtue of paragraph (a) of section 1(1) of that Act; or

    (b)   which from time to time apply to that country by virtue of paragraph (b) of the said section 1(1) and of any Order in Council made or hereafter to be made under the said section 1 designating that country for the purposes of all the provisions of that Act following section 1(2) of that Act;

"Visual Flight Rules" means Visual Flight Rules prescribed by Section V of the Rules of the Air Regulations 1996;

"Visual Meteorological Conditions" means weather permitting flight in accordance with the Visual Flight Rules.

(2) An aircraft shall be deemed to be in flight—

    (a)   in the case of a piloted flying machine, from the moment when, after the embarkation of its crew for the purpose of taking off, it first moves under its own power until the moment when it next comes to rest after landing;

    (b)   in the case of a pilotless flying machine, or a glider, from the moment when it first moves for the purpose of taking off until the moment when it next comes to rest after landing;

    (c)   in the case of an airship, from the moment when it first becomes detached from the surface until the moment when it next becomes attached thereto or comes to rest thereon;

    (d)   in the case of a free balloon, from the moment when the balloon, including the canopy and basket, becomes separated from the surface until the moment it next comes to rest thereon; and

    (e)   in the case of a captive balloon, from the moment when the balloon, including the canopy and basket, becomes separated from the surface, apart from a restraining device attaching it to the surface, until the moment when it next comes to rest thereon;

and the expressions "a flight" and "to fly" shall be construed accordingly.

(3) Subject to paragraph (4), references in this Order to the operator of an aircraft are, for the purposes of the application of any provision of this Order in relation to any particular aircraft, references to the person who at the relevant time has the management of that aircraft.

(4) For the purposes of the application of any provision in Part 3 of this Order, when by virtue of any charter or other agreement for the hire or loan of an aircraft a person other than an air transport undertaking or an aerial work undertaking has the management of that aircraft for a period not exceeding 14 days, paragraph (3) shall have effect as if that agreement had not been entered into.

(5) References in this Order to—

    (a)   a certificate of airworthiness include both a national certificate of airworthiness and an EASA certificate of airworthiness unless otherwise stated;

    (b)   an aircraft, aeroplane, powered lift tilt rotor aircraft, self-launching motor glider, helicopter, gyroplane, airship, balloon or kite include both EASA and non-EASA examples unless otherwise stated.

(6) The expressions appearing in the "Classification of Aircraft" in Part A of Schedule 2 shall have the meanings thereby assigned to them.

7–5945   156. Meaning of aerodrome traffic zone.   (1) The aerodrome traffic zone of a notified aerodrome which is not on an offshore installation and at which the length of the longest runway is notified as 1,850 metres or less shall be, subject to paragraphs (2) and (5), the airspace extending from the surface to a height of 2,000 feet above the level of the aerodrome within the area bounded by a circle centred on the notified mid-point of the longest runway and having a radius of 2 nautical miles.

(2) Where the aerodrome traffic zone specified in paragraph (1) would extend less than 11/2 nautical miles beyond the end of any runway at the aerodrome and this paragraph is notified as being applicable, the aerodrome traffic zone shall be that specified in paragraph (3) as though the length of the longest runway at the aerodrome were notified as greater than 1,850 metres.

(3) The aerodrome traffic zone of a notified aerodrome which is not on an offshore installation and at which the length of the longest runway is notified as greater than 1,850 metres shall be, subject to paragraph (5), the airspace extending from the surface to a height of 2,000 feet above the level of the aerodrome within the area bounded by a circle centred on the notified midpoint of the longest runway and having a radius of 21/2 nautical miles.

(4) The aerodrome traffic zone of a notified aerodrome which is on an offshore installation shall be, subject to paragraph (5), the airspace extending from mean sea level to 2,000 feet above mean sea level and within 11/2 nautical miles of the offshore installation.

(5) The aerodrome traffic zone of a notified aerodrome shall exclude any airspace which is within the aerodrome traffic zone of another aerodrome which is notified for the purposes of this article as being the controlling aerodrome.

7–5946   157. Public transport and aerial work—general rules.   (1) Subject to the provisions of this article and articles 158 to 163, aerial work means any purpose (other than public transport) for which an aircraft is flown if valuable consideration is given or promised in respect of the flight or the purpose of the flight.

(2) If the only such valuable consideration consists of remuneration for the services of the pilot the flight shall be deemed to be a private flight for the purposes of Part 3 of this Order.

(3) Subject to the provisions of this article and articles 158 to 163, an aircraft in flight shall for the purposes of this Order be deemed to fly for the purpose of public transport—

(a) if valuable consideration is given or promised for the carriage of passengers or cargo in the aircraft on that flight;

(b) if any passengers or cargo are carried gratuitously in the aircraft on that flight by an air transport undertaking, not being persons in the employment of the undertaking (including, in the case of a body corporate, its directors and, in the case of the CAA, the members of the CAA), persons with the authority of the CAA either making any inspection or witnessing any training, practice or test for the purposes of this Order, or cargo intended to be used by any such passengers as aforesaid, or by the undertaking; or

(c) for the purposes of Part 3 of this Order (other than articles 19(2) and 20(2)), if valuable consideration is given or promised for the primary purpose of conferring on a particular person the right to fly the aircraft on that flight (not being a single-seat aircraft of which the maximum total weight authorised does not exceed 910 kg) otherwise than under a hire-purchase or conditional sale agreement.

(4) Notwithstanding that an aircraft may be flying for the purpose of public transport by reason of paragraph (3)(c), it shall not be deemed to be flying for the purpose of the public transport of passengers unless valuable consideration is given or promised for the carriage of those passengers.

(5) A glider shall not be deemed to fly for the purpose of public transport for the purposes of Part 3 of this Order by virtue of paragraph (3)(c) if the valuable consideration given or promised for the primary purpose of conferring on a particular person the right to fly the glider on that flight is given or promised by a member of a flying club and the glider is owned or operated by that flying club.

(6) Notwithstanding the giving or promising of valuable consideration specified in paragraph (3)(c) in respect of the flight or the purpose of the flight it shall—

(a) subject to sub-paragraph (b), for all purposes other than Part 3 of this Order; and

(b) for the purposes of articles 19(2) and 20(2);

be deemed to be a private flight.

(7) Where under a transaction effected by or on behalf of a member of an association of persons on the one hand and the association of persons or any member thereof on the other hand, a person is carried in, or is given the right to fly, an aircraft in such circumstances that valuable consideration would be given or promised if the transaction were effected otherwise than aforesaid, valuable consideration shall, for the purposes of this Order, be deemed to have been given or promised, notwithstanding any rule of law as to such transactions.

(8) For the purposes of—

(a) paragraph (3)(a), there shall be disregarded any valuable consideration given or promised in respect of a flight or the purpose of a flight by one company to another company which is—

(i) its holding company;

(ii) its subsidiary; or

(iii) another subsidiary of the same holding company;

(b) this article "holding company" and "subsidiary" have the meanings respectively specified in Section 736 of the Companies Act 1985.

7–5947   158. Public transport and aerial work—exceptions—flying displays etc.   (1) A flight shall, for the purposes of Part 4 of this Order, be deemed to be a private flight if—

(a) the flight is—

(i) wholly or principally for the purpose of taking part in an aircraft race, contest or flying display;

(ii) for the purpose of positioning the aircraft for such a flight as is specified in sub-paragraph (i) and is made with the intention of carrying out such a flight; or

(iii) for the purpose of returning after such a flight as is specified in sub-paragraph (i) to a place at which the aircraft is usually based; and

(b) the only valuable consideration in respect of the flight or the purpose of the flight other
     than—

     (i)   valuable consideration specified in article 157(3)(c); or
     (ii) in the case of an aircraft owned in accordance with article 162(2), valuable consideration
           which falls within article 162(3);

     falls within paragraph (2)(a) or (2)(b) or both.

(2) Valuable consideration falls within this paragraph if it either is—

(a) that given or promised to the owner or operator of an aircraft taking part in such a race,
     contest or flying display and such valuable consideration does not exceed the direct costs
     of the flight and a contribution to the annual costs of the aircraft which contribution shall
     bear no greater proportion to the total annual costs of the aircraft than the duration of the
     flight bears to the annual flying hours of the aircraft; or

(b) one or more prizes awarded to the pilot in command of an aircraft taking part in an aircraft
     race or contest to a value which shall not exceed £500 in respect of any one race or contest
     except with the permission of the CAA granted to the organiser of the race or contest; or
     falls within both sub-paragraphs (a) and (b).

(3) Any prize falling within paragraph (2)(b) shall be deemed for the purposes of this Order not
to constitute remuneration for services as a pilot.

7–5948   159. Public transport and aerial work—exceptions—charity flights.   (1) Subject to
paragraph (2), a flight shall be deemed to be a private flight if the only valuable consideration
given or promised in respect of the flight or the purpose of the flight other than—

(a) valuable consideration specified in article 157(3)(c); or
(b) in the case of an aircraft owned in accordance with article 162(2), valuable consideration
     which falls within article 162(3);

is given or promised to a registered charity which is not the operator of the aircraft and the flight
is made with the permission of the CAA and in accordance with any conditions therein specified.

(2) If valuable consideration specified in article 157(3)(c) is given or promised the flight shall
for the purposes of Part 3 of this Order (other than articles 19(2) and 20(2)) be deemed to be for
the purpose of public transport.

7–5949   160. Public transport and aerial work—exceptions—cost sharing.   (1) Subject to paragraph (4), a flight shall be deemed to be a private flight if the only valuable consideration given
or promised in respect of the flight or the purpose of the flight falls within paragraph (2) and the
criteria in paragraph (3) are satisfied.

(2) Valuable consideration falls within this paragraph if it is—

(a) valuable consideration specified in article 157(3)(c);
(b) in the case of an aircraft owned in accordance with article 162(2), valuable consideration
     which falls within article 162(3); or
(c) is a contribution to the direct costs of the flight otherwise payable by the pilot in command;

or falls within any two or all three sub-paragraphs.

(3) The criteria in this paragraph are satisfied if—

(a) no more than 4 persons (including the pilot) are carried;
(b) the proportion which the contribution referred to in paragraph (2)(c) bears to the direct
     costs shall not exceed the proportion which the number of persons carried on the flight
     (excluding the pilot) bears to the number of persons carried (including the pilot);
(c) no information shall have been published or advertised prior to the commencement of the
     flight other than, in the case of an aircraft operated by a flying club, advertising wholly
     within the premises of such a flying club in which case all the persons carried on such a
     flight who are aged 18 years or over shall be members of that flying club; and
(d) no person acting as a pilot shall be employed as a pilot by, or be a party to a contract for
     the provision of services as a pilot with, the operator of the aircraft which is being flown.

(4) If valuable consideration specified in article 157(3)(c) is given or promised the flight shall
for the purposes of Part 3 of this Order (other than articles 19(2) and 20(2)) be deemed to be for
the purpose of public transport.

7–5950   161. Public transport and aerial work—exceptions—recovery of direct costs.   (1) Subject
to paragraph (2), a flight shall be deemed to be a private flight if the only valuable consideration
given or promised in respect of the flight or the purpose of the flight other than—

(a) valuable consideration specified in article 157(3)(c); or
(b) in the case of an aircraft owned in accordance with article 162(2), valuable consideration
     which falls within article 162(3);

is the payment of the whole or part of the direct costs otherwise payable by the pilot in command
by or on behalf of the employer of the pilot in command, or by or on behalf of a body corporate
of which the pilot in command is a director, provided that neither the pilot in command nor any
other person who is carried is legally obliged, whether under a contract or otherwise, to be
carried.

(2) If valuable consideration specified in article 157(3)(c) is given or promised the flight shall for the purposes of Part 3 of this Order (other than articles 19(2) and 20(2)) be deemed to be for the purpose of public transport.

7–5951 162. Public transport and aerial work—exceptions—jointly owned aircraft. (1) A flight shall be deemed to be a private flight if the aircraft falls within paragraph (2) and the only valuable consideration given or promised in respect of the flight or the purpose of the flight falls within paragraph (3).

(2) An aircraft falls within this paragraph if it is owned—

(a) jointly by persons (each of whom is a natural person) who each hold not less than a 5% beneficial share and—

  (i) the aircraft is registered in the names of all the joint owners; or
  (ii) the aircraft is registered in the name or names of one or more of the joint owners as trustee or trustees for all the joint owners and written notice has been given to the CAA of the names of all the persons beneficially entitled to a share in the aircraft; or

(b) by a company in the name of which the aircraft is registered and the registered shareholders of which (each of whom is a natural person) each hold not less than 5% of the shares in that company.

(3) Valuable consideration falls within this paragraph if it is either—

(a) in respect of and is no greater than the direct costs of the flight and is given or promised by one or more of the joint owners of the aircraft or registered shareholders of the company which owns the aircraft; or

(b) in respect of the annual costs and given by one or more of such joint owners or shareholders (as aforesaid);

or falls within both sub-paragraphs (a) and (b).

7–5952 163. Public transport and aerial work—exceptions—parachuting. A flight shall be deemed to be for the purpose of aerial work if it is a flight in respect of which valuable consideration has been given or promised for the carriage of passengers and which is for the purpose of—

(a) the dropping of persons by parachute and which is made under and in accordance with the terms of a parachuting permission granted by the CAA under article 67;

(b) positioning the aircraft for such a flight as is specified in sub-paragraph (a) and which is made with the intention of carrying out such a flight and on which no person is carried who it is not intended shall be carried on such a flight and who may be carried on such a flight in accordance with the terms of a parachuting permission granted by the CAA under article 67; or

(c) returning after such a flight as is specified in sub-paragraph (a) to the place at which the persons carried on such a flight are usually based and on which flight no persons are carried other than persons carried on the flight specified in sub-paragraph (a).

7–5953 164. Exceptions from application of provisions of the Order for certain classes of aircraft. The provisions of this Order other than articles 68, 74, 96(1), 97, 98, 144(1)(b) and (c), 155(1) and (2) shall not apply to or in relation to—

(a) any small balloon;
(b) any kite weighing not more than 2 kg;
(c) any small aircraft; or
(d) any parachute including a parascending parachute.

7–5954 165. Approval of persons to furnish reports. In relation to any of its functions under any of the provisions of this Order the CAA may approve a person as qualified to furnish reports to it and may accept such reports.

7–5955 166. Certificates, authorisations, approvals and permissions. Wherever in this Order there is provision for the issue or grant of a certificate, authorisation, approval or permission by the CAA, unless otherwise provided, such a certificate, authorisation, approval or permission—

(a) shall be in writing;
(b) may be issued or granted subject to such conditions as the CAA thinks fit; and
(c) may be issued or granted, subject to article 92, for such periods as the CAA thinks fit.

7–5955A 167. Competent authority. (1) The CAA shall be—

(a) the national aviation authority of the United Kingdom for the purposes of Regulation (EC) No 1592/2002 of the European Parliament and of the Council of 15th July 2002 on common rules in the field of civil aviation and establishing a European Aviation Safety Agency; and

(b) the competent authority of the United Kingdom for the purposes of—

  (i) Commission Regulation (EC) No 1702/2003 of 24th September 2003 laying down implementing rules for the airworthiness and environmental certification of aircraft and related products, parts and appliances, as well as for the certification of design and production organisations; and

(ii) Commission Regulation (EC) No 2042/2003 of 20th November 2003 on the continuing airworthiness of aircraft and aeronautical products, parts and appliances, and on the approval of organisations and personnel involved in these tasks.

(2) The Secretary of State shall be the competent authority under article 15 of Council Directive 96/29/Euratom of 13th May 1996 for the purposes of article 42 of the Directive.

7–5955B 168. Saving. (1) Subject to articles 128 and 130, nothing in this Order or any regulations made thereunder shall confer any right to land in any place as against the owner of the land or other persons interested therein.

(2) Nothing in this Order shall oblige the CAA to accept an application from the holder of any current certificate, licence, approval, permission, exemption or other document, being an application for the renewal of that document, or for the granting of another document in continuation of or in substitution for the current document, if the application is made more than 60 days before the current document is due to expire.

7–5955C

SCHEDULE 2

CLASSIFICATION AND MARKING OF AIRCRAFT AND DEALER CERTIFICATION

PART A

CLASSIFICATION OF AIRCRAFT

Articles 4(6) and 155(6)

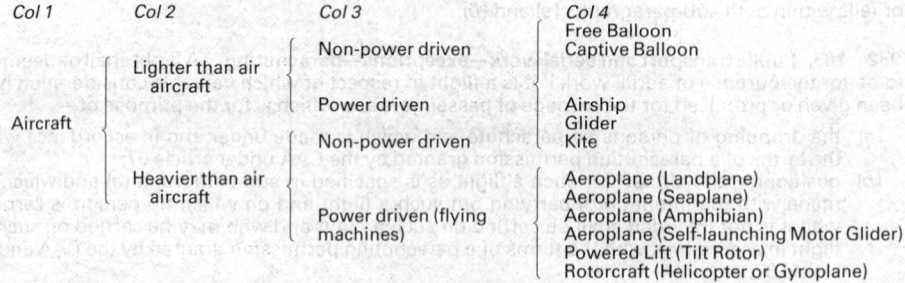

Col 1	Col 2	Col 3	Col 4
Aircraft	Lighter than air aircraft	Non-power driven	Free Balloon / Captive Balloon
		Power driven	Airship
	Heavier than air aircraft	Non-power driven	Glider / Kite
		Power driven (flying machines)	Aeroplane (Landplane) / Aeroplane (Seaplane) / Aeroplane (Amphibian) / Aeroplane (Self-launching Motor Glider) / Powered Lift (Tilt Rotor) / Rotorcraft (Helicopter or Gyroplane)

7–5955D

SCHEDULE 3

A AND B CONDITIONS AND CATEGORIES OF CERTIFICATE OF AIRWORTHINESS

PART A

A AND B CONDITIONS

Articles 3(3), 8(2) and 65(7)

A Conditions

1. (1) A non-EASA aircraft registered in the United Kingdom may fly for a purpose set out in paragraph (2) subject to the conditions contained in paragraphs (3) to (8) when either:

(a) it does not have a certificate of airworthiness duly issued or rendered valid under the law of the United Kingdom; or

(b) the certificate of airworthiness or certificate of validation issued in respect of the aircraft has ceased to be in force by virtue of any of the matters specified in article 10.

(2) The purposes referred to in paragraph (1) are—

(a) in the case of an aircraft falling within paragraph (1)(a) the aircraft shall fly only so as to enable it to—

(i) qualify for the issue, renewal or validation of a certificate of airworthiness after an application has been made for such issue, renewal or validation as the case may be, or carry out a functional check of a previously approved modification of the aircraft (and for the purpose of this Schedule "a previously approved modification" shall mean a modification which has previously been approved by the CAA or by an organisation approved for that purpose by the CAA in respect of that aircraft or another aircraft of the same type);

(ii) proceed to or from a place at which any inspection, repair, modification, maintenance, approval, test or weighing of, or the installation of equipment in, the aircraft is to take place or has taken place for a purpose referred to in sub-paragraph (i), after any relevant application has been made, or at which the installation of furnishings in, or the painting of, the aircraft is to be undertaken; or

(iii) proceed to or from a place at which the aircraft is to be or has been stored.

(b) in the case of an aircraft falling within paragraph (1)(b), the aircraft shall fly only so as to enable it to—

(i) proceed to a place at which any inspection or maintenance required by virtue of article 10(b)(ii) is to take place; or

    (ii) proceed to a place at which any inspection, maintenance or modification required by virtue of article 10(*b*)(i) or (*c*) is to take place and in respect of which flight the CAA has given permission in writing; or

    (iii) carry out a functional check, test or in-flight adjustment in connection with the carrying out in a manner approved by the CAA of any overhaul, repair, previously approved modification, inspection or maintenance required by virtue of article 10.

(3) The aircraft, including any modifications, shall be of a design which previously has been approved by the CAA, or by an organisation approved for that purpose by the CAA, as being compliant with a standard accepted by the CAA as appropriate for the issue of a national certificate of airworthiness.

(4) The aircraft and its engines shall be certified as fit for flight by the holder of an aircraft maintenance engineer's licence granted under this Order, being a licence which entitles him to issue that certificate or by a person approved by the CAA for the purpose of issuing certificates under this condition, and in accordance with that approval.

(5) The aircraft shall carry the minimum flight crew specified in any certificate of airworthiness or validation or flight manual which has previously been in force under the Order in respect of the aircraft, or is or has previously been in force in respect of any other aircraft of identical design.

(6) The aircraft shall not carry any persons or cargo except persons performing duties in the aircraft in connection with the flight or persons who are carried in the aircraft to perform duties in connection with a purpose referred to in paragraph (2).

(7) The aircraft shall not fly over any congested area of a city, town or settlement except to the extent that it is necessary to do so in order to take off or land.

B Conditions

2. (1) A non-EASA aircraft may fly for a purpose set out in paragraph (2) subject to the conditions set out in paragraphs (3) to (8) whether or not it is registered in accordance with article 3(1) and when there is not in force—

    (*a*) in the case of an aircraft which is so registered, a certificate of airworthiness duly issued or rendered valid under the law of the country in which the aircraft is registered; or

    (*b*) in the case of an aircraft which is not so registered, either a certificate of airworthiness duly issued or rendered valid under the law of the United Kingdom or a permit to fly issued by the CAA in respect of that aircraft.

(2) The purposes referred to in paragraph (1) are—

    (*a*) experimenting with or testing the aircraft (including any engines installed thereon) or any equipment installed or carried in the aircraft;

    (*b*) enabling the aircraft to qualify for the issue or validation of a certificate of airworthiness or the approval of a modification of the aircraft or the issue of a permit to fly;

    (*c*) demonstrating and displaying the aircraft, any engines installed thereon or any equipment installed or carried in the aircraft with a view to its sale or of other similar aircraft, engines or equipment;

    (*d*) demonstrating and displaying the aircraft to employees of the operator;

    (*e*) the giving of flying training to or the testing of flight crew employed by the operator or the training or testing of other persons employed by the operator and who are carried or are intended to be carried under paragraph (7)(*a*); or

    (*f*) proceeding to or from a place at which any experiment, inspection, repair, modification, maintenance, approval, test or weighing of the aircraft, the installation of equipment in the aircraft, demonstration, display or training is to take place for a purpose referred to in sub-paragraph (*a*), (*b*), (*c*), (*d*) or (*e*) or at which installation of furnishings in, or the painting of, the aircraft is to be undertaken.

(3) The flight shall be operated by a person approved by the CAA for the purposes of these Conditions and subject to any additional conditions which may be specified in such an approval.

(4) If not registered in the United Kingdom the aircraft shall be marked in a manner approved by the CAA for the purposes of these Conditions, and articles 20, 22, 52, 55, 86 and 88 shall be complied with in relation to the aircraft as if it were registered in the United Kingdom.

(5) If not registered in the United Kingdom, the aircraft shall carry such flight crew as may be necessary to ensure the safety of the aircraft.

(6) No person shall act as pilot in command of the aircraft except a person approved for the purpose by the CAA.

(7) The aircraft shall not carry any cargo, or any persons other than the flight crew except the following—

    (*a*) persons employed by the operator who during the flight carry out duties or are tested or receive training in connection with a purpose specified in paragraph (2);

    (*b*) persons acting on behalf of the manufacturers of component parts of the aircraft (including its engines) or of equipment installed in or carried in the aircraft for carrying out during the flight duties in connection with a purpose so specified;

    (*c*) persons approved by the CAA under article 165 as qualified to furnish reports for the purposes of article 9;

    (*d*) persons other than those carried under the preceding provisions of this paragraph who are carried in the aircraft in order to carry out a technical evaluation of the aircraft or its operation;

    (*e*) cargo which comprises equipment carried in connection with a purpose specified in paragraph (2)(*f*); or

    (*f*) persons employed by the operator or persons acting on behalf of the manufacturers of component parts of the aircraft (including its engines) or of equipment installed in or carried in the aircraft in connection with a purpose specified in paragraph (2)(*f*) which persons have duties in connection with that purpose.

(8) The aircraft shall not fly, except in accordance with procedures which have been approved by the CAA in relation to that flight, over any congested area of a city, town or settlement.

Article 148

SCHEDULE 14
PENALTIES

PART A
PROVISIONS REFERRED TO IN ARTICLE 148(5)

Article of order	Subject matter
3	Aircraft flying unregistered
5	Aircraft flying with false or incorrect markings
14(1)(*a*)	Flight without appropriate maintenance
14(1)(*b*)	Flight without a certificate of maintenance review
15	Failure to keep a technical log
16	Flight without a certificate of release to service issued under the Order or under paragraph 21A.163(*d*) of Part 21
17	Flight without a certificate of release to service issued under Part 145
18(7) and (8)	Exercise of privileges of aircraft maintenance engineer's licence or an aircraft maintenance licence whilst unfit or drunk etc
19	Flight without required equipment
20	Flight without required radio communication or radio navigation equipment
21	Minimum equipment requirements
22	Failure to keep log books
23	Requirement to weigh aircraft and keep weight schedule
25	Crew requirement
28, 30(2) and 31(1)	Requirement for appropriate certificate of test or experience
29 and 31(2)	Requirement for appropriate certificate of revalidation
30(1)	Requirement for valid rating
32(1)	Flight without valid medical certificate
32(4)	Flight in unfit condition
33(1)	Prohibition of flight after failure of test
36	Instruction in flying without appropriate licence and rating
38	Operations manual requirement
39	Police operations manual requirement
40	Training manual requirement
42	Operator's responsibilities in connection with crew
43	Requirements for loading aircraft
44 and 45	Operational restrictions on aeroplanes and helicopters
46	Prohibition on public transport flights at night or in Instrument Meteorological Conditions by non-United Kingdom registered single engined aeroplanes
47	Aerodrome operating minima—United Kingdom registered public transport aircraft
48	Aerodrome operating minima—public transport aircraft registered elsewhere than in the United Kingdom
49	Aerodrome operating minima—non-public transport aircraft
50	Requirement for pilot to remain at controls
52	Pre-flight action by commander of aircraft
53	Requirement for passenger briefing
54	Additional duties of commander on flight for public transport of passengers
55	Requirement for radio station in aircraft to be licensed and for operation of same
56	Requirement for minimum navigation performance equipment
57	Requirement for height keeping performance equipment—aircraft registered in the United Kingdom
58	Requirement for height keeping performance equipment—aircraft registered elsewhere than in the United Kingdom
59	Requirement for area navigation equipment and required navigation performance—aircraft registered in the United Kingdom
60	Requirement for area navigation equipment and required navigation performance—aircraft registered elsewhere than in the United Kingdom
61	Requirement for an airborne collision avoidance system
62	Use of flight recording systems and preservation of records
63	Towing of gliders
65	Towing, picking up and raising of persons and articles by aircraft
66	Dropping of articles and animals from aircraft
67	Dropping of persons and requirement for parachuting permission
68	Requirement for aerial application certificate
71	Carriage of persons in or on any part of an aircraft not designed for that purpose
72	Requirement for exits and break-in markings
76	Prohibition of smoking in aircraft
77	Requirement to obey lawful commands of aircraft commander
78(*a*) and (*b*)	Acting in a disruptive manner
79	Prohibition of stowaways
80	Flying displays
82(3)	Operator's obligation to obtain flight time records of flight crew
83(2)	Flight crew member's obligation to inform operator of flight times
84	Flight time limitations for flight crew
95	Breach of the Rules of the Air
96	Flight in contravention of restriction of flying regulations
97	Flight by balloons, kites, airships, gliders and parascending parachutes
98	Flight by small aircraft
99	Launching of rockets

Article of order	Subject matter
101	Requirement for an approved provider of air traffic services to be satisfied as to competence of air traffic controllers
103	Provision of air traffic services
104	Requirement to comply with an air traffic direction
105	Requirement to comply with an airspace policy direction
106	Use of radio call signs at aerodromes
107	Requirement for licensing of air traffic controllers
121	Requirement for licensing of flight information service officers
123	Requirement for flight information service manual
124	Use of air traffic service equipment
125	Requirement to keep air traffic service equipment records
126	Requirement for use of licensed aerodrome
128(4)	Contravention of conditions of aerodrome licence
132	Use of aeronautical lights
133	Requirement to light en-route obstacles
134	Requirement to light offshore wind turbine generators
135(1)	Prohibition of dangerous lights
135(2)	Failure to extinguish or screen dangerous lights
137(1) and (3)	Management of aviation fuel at aerodromes
146	Obstruction of persons performing duties under the Order

PART B
PROVISIONS REFERRED TO IN ARTICLE 148(6)

Article of order	Subject matter
6	Flight for the purpose of public transport without an air operator's certificate
7	Flight in the service of a police authority without a police air operator's certificate
8	Flight without a certificate of airworthiness
26	Requirement to hold an appropriate flight crew licence
69	Prohibition of carriage of weapons and munitions of war
70(2)	Requirements for the carriage of dangerous goods
74	Endangering safety of persons or property
75	Prohibition of drunkenness in aircraft
78(c)	Intentional interference
82(1)	Operator's obligation to regulate flight times of crew
82(2)	Operator's obligation not to allow flight by crew in dangerous state of fatigue
83(1)	Crew's obligation not to fly in dangerous state of fatigue
85	Protection of air crew from cosmic radiation
87	Keeping and production of records of exposure to cosmic radiation
94 (except (3)	Use of false or unauthorised documents and records
100	Provision of an air traffic control service without an approval
115	Controller's obligation not to act in a dangerous state of fatigue
116	Prohibition of acting under the influence of drink or a drug
137(4)	Use of aviation fuel which is unfit for use in aircraft
138	Restriction of carriage for valuable consideration by aircraft registered elsewhere than in the United Kingdom
140	Restriction of flights for aerial photography, aerial survey and aerial work by aircraft registered elsewhere than in the United Kingdom
141	Operators' or commanders' obligations in respect of flights over any foreign country
142(5), (6) and (7)	Failure to report an occurrence
142(8)	Making a false occurrence report
144	Flight in contravention of direction not to fly

PART C
PROVISIONS REFERRED TO IN ARTICLE 148(7)

Article of order	Subject matter
73	Endangering safety of aircraft

HIGHWAYS

7–5956   This title contains the following statutes—

Highway Act 1835
(5 & 6 Will 4 c 50)

7–5957 5. Interpretation of terms. . . . In the construction of this Act; and . . . the word "highways" shall be understood to mean all roads, bridges (not being county bridges), carriageways, cartways, horseways, bridleways, footways, causeways, churchways, and pavements . . .
[Highway Act 1835, s 5, as amended by the Statute Law Revision (No 2) Act 1888, the Highways Act 1959, Sch 25, the Statute Law (Repeals) Act 1975, Sch and the Statute Law (Repeals) Act 1989, Sch 1.]

7–5958 72. Riding or driving on footpath. TETHERING CATTLE.—If any person shall[1] wilfully ride upon any footpath or causeway by the side of any road[2] made or set apart for the use or accommodation of foot passengers; or shall wilfully lead or drive any horse, ass, sheep, mule, swine, cattle or carriage[3] of any description, or any truck or sledge, upon any such footpath[4] or causeway[5] or tether any horse, ass, mule, swine or cattle on any highway so as to suffer or permit the tethered animal to be thereon—*Penalty*, for every offence, not exceeding **level 2** on the standard scale above the damage occasioned thereby.
[Highway Act 1835, s 72, as amended by the Statute Law Revision (No 2) Act 1888, the Highways Act 1959, Sch 25, the Criminal Justice Act 1967, 3rd Sch and the Criminal Justice Act 1982, ss 39 and 46, and Sch 3.]

1. "Wilful" under this section means "purposely". See *Fearnley v Ormsby* (1879) 4 CPD 136, 43 JP 384.
2. This section does not apply to footpaths in general but only to a footpath or causeway which runs along the side of a road; see *Selby v DPP* (1989) 154 JP 566; DC. In the metropolitan court area, see Metropolitan Police Act 1839, s 54(7).
3. Bicycles, tricycles, velocipedes, and other similar machines are carriages within the meaning of the Highway Acts (Local Government Act 1888, s 85), as are motor vehicles and trailers (Road Traffic Act 1988, s 191). See *Taylor v Goodwin* (1879) 4 QBD 228, 43 JP 653; and *Cannan v Earl of Abingdon* [1900] 2 QB 66, 64 JP 504; *Simpson v Teignmouth and Shaldon Bridge Co* [1903] 1 KB 405, 67 JP 65; and *Smith v Kynnersley* [1903] 1 KB 788, 67 JP 125. Pedal cyclists guilty of dangerous, careless or inconsiderate riding or riding under the influence of drink may be prosecuted under the Road Traffic Act 1988, ss 28, 29, 30, in this PART; title ROAD TRAFFIC, ante.
4. The Road Traffic Act 1988, s 34 makes additional provision in respect of motor vehicles. Local authorities' vehicles cleansing, maintaining or improving footpaths may be exempt from this prohibition (Public Health Act 1961, s 49).
5. This relates to a "causeway by the side of any road" (*R v Pratt* (1867) LR 3 QB 64, 32 JP 246).

7–5959 78. Drivers of carts, etc, riding on any highway[1]. DAMAGE BY NEGLIGENCE—QUITTING THE ROAD—BEING AT A DISTANCE—OBSTRUCTING OTHERS—NOT KEEPING PROPER SIDE—DRIVING FURIOUSLY[2]—AND OTHER OFFENCES.—If the driver of any carriage[3] whatsoever on any part of a highway shall by negligence or wilful misbehaviour cause any[4] hurt or damage to any person, horse, cattle or goods conveyed in any carriage[5] passing or being upon such highway, or shall quit the same and go on the other side of the hedge or fence enclosing the same—or shall negligently or wilfully be at such distance from such carriage, or in such a situation whilst it shall be[6] passing upon such highway that he cannot have the direction and government of the horses or cattle drawing the same—or shall leave[7] any cart or carriage on such highway, so as to obstruct the passage thereof—or if the driver of any waggon, cart or other carriage whatsoever, or of any[8] horses, mules or other beasts of draught or burden, meeting any other waggon, cart or other carriage, or horses, mules or other beasts of burden, shall not keep his waggon, cart or carriage, or horses, mules or other beasts of burden on the left[9] or near side of the road—or if any person shall in any manner wilfully prevent any other person from passing him, or any waggon, cart or other carriage, or horses, mules or other beasts of burden, under his care upon such highway—or by negligence[10] or misbehaviour prevent, hinder or interrupt the free passage of any person, waggon, cart or other carriage, or horses, mules or other beasts of burden on any highway—or shall not keep his waggon, cart or other carriage, or horses, mules or other beasts of burden, on the left[9] or near side of the road for the purpose of[11] allowing such passage—or if any person riding any horse, or beast, or driving any sort of carriage, shall[12] ride or drive the same furiously so as to endanger the life or limb of any passenger—*Penalty*, not exceeding **level 1** on the standard scale.
[Highway Act 1835, s 78, as amended by the Statute Law Revision (No 2) Act 1888, the Highways Act 1959, Schs 23 and 25, the Criminal Justice Act 1967, 3rd Sch, the Statute Law (Repeals) Acts 1973, Sch 1 and 1975, Sch Part X, the Criminal Justice Act 1982, ss 38 and 46 and the Statute Law (Repeals) Act 1989, Sch 1.]

1. For application of this section to motor vehicles etc see note 3 below. The word "cart" does not include every kind of cart. The description seems to point to vehicles which carry heavy goods slowly along the road, and would exclude, eg a light spring cart (*Danby v Hunter* (1879) 5 QBD 20, 44 JP 283).
2. As to doing bodily harm by furious driving, see Offences against the Person Act 1861, s 35, post.
3. Bicycles, tricycles, velocipedes, and other similar machines, are declared to be carriages within the meaning of the Highway Acts, by the Local Government Act 1888, s 85. A motor vehicle or trailer is also a carriage (Road Traffic Act 1988, s 191, ante).
4. A conviction for assault by striking a horse ridden by the complainant after a conviction under this section for the same act was quashed (*Wemyss v Hopkins* (1875) 39 JP 549). This means negligence or misbehaviour in driving, not, eg in negligently opening the door of a stationary vehicle and thereby causing hurt to a passing cyclist (*Shears v Matthews* [1948] 2 All ER 1064, 113 JP 36). On similar facts, a defendant does not "wilfully" obstruct the free passage of the highway in contravention of s 72 of the Act when it is found as a fact that the obstruction was unintentional (*Eaton v Cobb* [1950] 1 All ER 1016, 114 JP 271). But in *Watson v Lowe* [1950] 1 All ER 100, 114 JP 85, applied in *Baldwin v Pearson* (1958) 122 JP 321, on similar facts, a person (whether driver or passenger) was rightly convicted under a later provision

of this section that by negligence he interrupted the free passage of a person on the highway. See also the Road Vehicles (Construction and Use) Regulations 1986, in this PART, title Road Traffic, ante.

5. The provision does not seem to apply where the damage is done to the carriage only.

6. It is no defence that the carriage was standing still upon the highway, and that no obstruction had been in fact caused, if the driver was absent (*Phythian v Baxendale* [1895] 1 QB 768, 59 JP 217).

7. An offence may be committed notwithstanding that the carriage was not at the time in question left unattended (*Hinde v Evans* (1906) 70 JP 548).

8. The singular number is to include the plural (s 5). No provision has been made for the converse; but see the Interpretation Act 1978, s 6.

9. That is, to the left side of the road, not necessarily close to the edge or kerb on the near side of the road (*Bolton v Everett* (1911) 75 JP 534; *Sleith v Godfrey* (1920) 85 JP 46). The driver need not keep on the near side of a clear road (*Finegan v London and North Western Rly Co* (1889) 53 JP 663), although he should always do so at night (*Cruden v Fentham* (1798) 2 Esp 685), and if he drives on the offside he must use more care and diligence and keep a better look out (*Pluckwell v Wilson* (1832) 5 C & P 375). See also *Hartley v Chadwick* (1904) 68 JP 512, and *Norton v Lees* (1921) 85 JP Jo 500; on appeal (1923) 87 JP Jo 675. See now Highway Code in this PART: title ROAD TRAFFIC, ante. As to penalty for neglect of traffic directions given by a police constable engaged in the regulation of traffic, or by any traffic sign, see the Road Traffic Act 1988, ss 36, 37, in this PART: title ROAD TRAFFIC, ante.

10. This does not include negligence in filling in excavations, which allowed a flagstone to protrude and to trip a foot passenger; the section is concerned with the activities of foot passengers (*Midlands Electricity Board v Stephenson* [1973] Crim LR 441).

11. It is no offence for the driver of a vehicle to allow a passing vehicle to pass on his near side there being no other traffic on the road (*Nuttall v Pickering* [1913] 1 KB 14, 77 JP 30).

12. This will include furiously riding, notwithstanding the penal part of the enactment omits all mention of a rider (*Williams v Evans* (1876) 1 Ex D 277, 41 JP 151). An offence was held to have been committed where defendant, who was in charge of a horse and trap of which he was the sole occupant, was asleep and the horse careered at a furious pace through a village, so that a police constable who was on the road might have been endangered as to life or limb (*Chatterton v Parker* [1914] WN 206, 78 JP 339). Where the Town Police Clauses Act 1847, is in force, the offence may be punished under that Statute.

National Parks and Access to the Countryside Act 1949
(12, 13 & 14 Geo 6 c 97)

PART IV
PUBLIC RIGHTS OF WAY

7–5961   57. Penalty for displaying on footpaths notices deterring public use.   (1) If any person places or maintains, on or near any way shown on a definitive map, or on a revised map prepared in definitive form, as a public path or road used as a public path, a notice containing any false or misleading statement likely to deter the public from using the way, he shall be liable on summary conviction to a fine not exceeding **level 1** on the standard scale.

(2) The court before whom a person is convicted of an offence under the last foregoing subsection may, in addition to or in substitution for the imposition of a fine, order him to remove the notice in respect of which he is convicted within such period, not being less than four days, as may be specified in the order; and if he fails to comply with the order he shall be liable on summary conviction to a fine not exceeding £2 for each day on which the failure continues.

(3) It shall be the duty of a highway authority to enforce the provisions of this section as respects any public path, or road used as a public path, for which they are the highway authority; and no proceedings in respect of an offence under those provisions shall be brought except by the authority required by this subsection to enforce those provisions as respects the path or road in question or by the council of the district or, where they are not the highway authority, the council of the Welsh county or county borough in which the notice is placed or maintained.

[National Parks and Access to the Countryside Act 1949, s 57, as amended by the Criminal Justice Act 1967, 3rd Sch, the Local Government Act 1972, Sch 21, the Criminal Justice Act 1982, ss 38 and 46 and the Local Government (Wales) Act 1994, Sch 6.]

PART V[1]
ACCESS TO OPEN COUNTRY

7–5962   68. Power of local planning authority to enforce access.   (1) If any person contravenes the provisions of section 66(1)[2], or any such restriction as is specified in paragraph (*c*) of section 67(2)[3], the local planning authority whose area comprises the land in respect of which the contravention occurred may serve on that person a notice requiring him, within such period as may be specified in the notice, to carry out such work so specified as may appear to the authority to be requisite for remedying the contravention, being work for restoring or re-opening any means of access to the land or for providing new means of access thereto.

(2) If within the period specified in a notice under the last foregoing subsection the person on whom the notice is served fails to comply therewith, the local planning authority may take all necessary steps for carrying out the work specified in the notice and may recover from that person any expenses reasonably incurred by them in carrying it out.

(3) Any person on whom a notice is served under subsection (1) of this section may, at any time within the period specified in the notice for carrying out the work so specified, complain to a court of

summary jurisdiction for the petty sessions area or place within which the land to which the notice relates is situated*—

(*a*)　that the period specified as aforesaid is too short;
(*b*)　that the work specified in the notice, or some of that work, is not requisite for remedying the contravention;
(*c*)　that he has not contravened the provisions or restriction in question; or
(*d*)　that the work specified in the notice, or so much of the work as is requisite for remedying the contravention, has been carried out.

(4)　Any summons issued on a complaint under the last foregoing subsection shall be served on the local planning authority.
(5)　On any such complaint the court, if satisfied of the grounds of the complaint, may—

(*a*)　extend the period within which the work was required to be carried out by the notice, or
(*b*)　quash the notice as respects the whole or any part of the work specified therein,

as the nature of the complaint may require; but is not so satisfied shall dismiss the complaint.
(6)　The Magistrates' Courts Act 1952[4] shall apply to the proceedings on any complaint under this section; and any person aggrieved[5] by the decision of the court on any such complaint may appeal to the Crown Court.
(7)　Where a complaint is made to the court under this section, the time between the making of the complaint and the determination thereof, and of any appeal from that determination, shall be disregarded in determining the period within which, in accordance with the notice, the work specified therein is to be carried out.
[National Parks and Access to the Countryside Act 1949, s 68, as amended by the Courts Act 1971, Sch 8 and the Access to Justice Act 1999, Sch 10.]

---

*Words repealed by the Courts Act 2003, Sch 8, from a date to be appointed.
1. Part V contains ss 59–82. Part V of this Act shall have effect, subject to modifications, as if the Broads Authority were a local planning authority (National Parks and Access to the Countryside Act 1949, s 111A, as inserted by the Norfolk and Suffolk Broads Act 1988, Sch 3).
2. Section 66(1) requires that a person interested in any land comprised in an access agreement or order shall not carry out any work thereon whereby the area to which the public are able to have access by virtue of the agreement or order is substantially reduced.
3. Section 67(2)(*c*) enables provision to be made by an access agreement or order for the imposition of restrictions on the destruction, removal, alteration or stopping-up of any means of access to the land, or the doing of any thing whereby the use of any such means of access by the public would be impeded.
4. Now the Magistrates' Courts Act 1980.
5. Note that the right of appeal is available to either party.

PART VI
GENERAL, FINANCIAL AND SUPPLEMENTARY

7–5963　　**108. Powers of entry.**　(1)　For the purpose of surveying land in connection with—

(*a*)　the acquisition thereof, or of any interest therein, whether by agreement or compulsorily, or
(*b*)　(*Repealed*).
(*c*)　the making of an access order with respect thereto,

in the exercise of any power conferred by this Act, any person duly authorised in writing by the Minister[1] or other authority having power so to acquire the land or to make the order, as the case may be, may enter upon the land.
(2)　For the purpose of surveying land, or of estimating its value, in connection with any claim for compensation payable under this Act by a Minister or other authority in respect of that or any other land, any person being an officer of the Valuation Office or a person duly authorised in writing by the authority from whom the compensation is claimed may enter upon the land.
(3)　A person authorised under this section to enter upon any land shall, if so required, produce evidence of his authority before entering; and a person shall not under this section demand admission as of right to any land which is occupied unless at least fourteen days' notice in writing of the intended entry has been given to the occupier.
(4)　Any person who wilfully obstructs a person in the exercise of his powers under this section shall be liable on summary conviction to a fine not exceeding **level 1** on the standard scale.
[National Parks and Access to the Countryside Act 1949, s 108, as amended by Highways Act 1959, 25th Sch, the Countryside Act 1968, s 46 and the Criminal Justice Act 1982, ss 38 and 46.]

---

1. "The Minister", as respects England and Wales, means the Minister of Housing and Local Government (s 114, amended, as to transfer of functions, by SI 1951/142 and SI 1951/1900).

Highways Act 1980[1]
(1980 c 66)

PART 1[2]

HIGHWAY AUTHORITIES AND AGREEMENTS BETWEEN AUTHORITIES

Highway authorities

7–5964   1. Highway authorities: general provision.   (1) The Minister[3] is the highway authority for—

(a)   any highway which is a trunk road;

(aa) any special road provided by him;

(b)   any highway as respects which an order made by him under any enactment expressly provides that he is to be the highway authority for it but does not direct that the highway is to be a trunk road;

(c)   any highway (not falling within paragraph (a) above) transferred to him by an order under section 14 or 18 below;

(d)   any other highway being a highway constructed by him, except where by virtue of section 2, 4(3) or 5(2) below or by virtue of some other enactment a local highway authority are the highway authority for it or where by means of an order made under section 14 or 18 below the highway is transferred to a local highway authority.

(2) Outside Greater London the council of a county or metropolitan district are the highway authority for all highways in the county or, as the case may be, the district, whether or not maintainable at the public expense, which are not highways for which under subsection (1) above the Minister is the highway authority.

(2A) Transport for London is the highway authority for all GLA roads.

(3) The council of a London borough or the Common Council are the highway authority for all highways in the borough or, as the case may be, in the City, whether or not maintainable at the public expense, which are not for the time being GLA roads or highways for which under subsection (1) above the Minister is the highway authority.

(3A) In Wales the council of a county or county borough are the highway authority for all highways in the county or, as the case may be, the county borough, whether or not maintainable at the public expense, which are not highways for which the Minister is the highway authority under subsection (1) above.

(4) Subsection (2) above is subject, as respects any highway outside Greater London for which the Minister is not the highway authority under subsection (1) above, to any provision of this Act, or of any order made under this or any other Act, by virtue of which a council other than the council of the county or, as the case may be, the metropolitan district in which the highway is situated are the highway authority therefore.

(5) Subsection (3A) above is subject to any provision of this Act, or of any order made under this or any other Act, by virtue of which a council other than the Welsh council for the area in which the highway is situated are the highway authority.

[Highways Act 1980, s 1 as amended by the Local Government Act 1985, Schs 4 and 17, the New Roads and Street Works Act 1991, s 21(2) and the Local Government (Wales) Act 1994, Sch 7 and the Greater London Authority Act 1999, s 259.]

---

1. This Act consolidates the Highways Acts 1959 to 1971 and related enactments. Many provisions of the Act are concerned with the functions of highway authorities and other bodies. Only those sections of the Act which are relevant to the work of magistrates' courts are contained in this Manual. The holder of a licence under s 6 of the Electricity Act 1989 who is entitled to exercise any power conferred by para 1 of Sch 4 of that Act (street works etc) shall be deemed to be a statutory undertaker and a public utility undertaker for the purposes of this Act (Electricity Act 1989, Sch 16, para 2(4) and (6)).

2. Part I contains ss 1–9.

3. Functions of the Minister, so far as exercisable in relation to Wales, have been transferred to the National Assembly for Wales, by the National Assembly for Wales (Transfer of Functions) Order 1999, SI 1999/672, art 2, Sch 1.

7–5965   2. Highway authority for road which ceases to be a trunk road.   (1) Where an order made under section 10 below directs that a trunk road shall cease to be a trunk road, then, as from the date specified in that behalf in the order, the following authority, that is to say—

(a)   where the road is situated outside Greater London, the council of the county or metropolitan district, and

(b)   where the road is situated in a Greater London, Transport for London,

shall become the highway authority for the road.

(2) In the case of a special road provided by the Minister, subsection (1) above has effect subject to any provision of the order directing that the Minister shall continue to be the highway authority for the road.

(3) Where Transport for London becomes the highway authority for a road by virtue of subsection (1) above, the road shall become a GLA road.

[Highways Act 1980, s 2 as amended by the Local Government Act 1985, Sch 4, the New Roads and Street Works Act 1991, s 21(3) and the Greater London Authority Act 1999, s 259.]

7–5966　**3. Highway authority for approaches to and parts of certain bridges.**　(1) Where a bridge carries a highway for which the Minister is not the highway authority and part of the bridge is situated in one county and part in another the highway authority for the highway carried by the bridge and the approaches thereto is such one of the councils of those counties as may be agreed between them before such a day as the Minister may by order made by statutory instrument appoint or, in default of such agreement, as may be determined by the Minister.

(2) Where the Minister has made a determination under subsection (1) above the determination—

(a)　may be varied at the request of the council of either of the counties concerned; and

(b)　shall be varied to give effect to any request made jointly to the Minister by those councils;

and any such variation shall take effect on the 1st April falling not less than 3 months, and not more than 15 months, after the date on which the determination is varied.

(3) Where a bridge carries a highway for which the Minister is not the highway authority and subsection (1) above does not apply, but some part of one or more of the approaches to the bridge lies in a county different from the bridge itself, the highway authority for the whole of that approach or those approaches is the council of the county in which the bridge is situated.

(4) For the purposes of this section, the approaches to a bridge consist of so much of the highway or highways on either side of the bridge as is situated within 100 yards of either end of the bridge. [Highways Act 1980, s 3.]

7–5967　**4–9.** *Agreements between authorities.*

7–5967A

PART II[1]

TRUNK ROADS, CLASSIFIED ROADS, METROPOLITAN ROADS, SPECIAL ROADS

---

1. Part II contains ss 10–23.

PART III[1]

CREATION OF HIGHWAYS

7–5968　**31. Dedication of way as highway presumed after public use for 20 years.**　(1) Where a way over any land[2], other than a way of such a character that use of it by the public could not give rise at common law to any presumption of dedication, has been actually enjoyed by the public as of right[3] and without interruption for a full period of 20 years, the way is to be deemed to have been dedicated as a highway unless there is sufficient evidence that there was no intention[3] during[4] that period to dedicate it.

(2) The period of 20 years referred to in subsection (1) above is to be calculated retrospectively from the date when the right of the public to use the way is brought into question, whether by a notice such as is mentioned in subsection (3) below or otherwise.

(3) Where the owner of the land over which any such way as aforesaid passes—

(a)　has erected in such manner as to be visible to persons using the way a notice inconsistent with the dedication of the way as a highway, and

(b)　has maintained the notice after the 1st January 1934, or any later date on which it was erected,

the notice, in the absence of proof of a contrary intention, is sufficient evidence to negative the intention to dedicate the way as a highway.

(4) In the case of land in the possession of a tenant for a term of years, or from year to year, any person for the time being entitled in reversion to the land shall, notwithstanding the existence of the tenancy, have the right to place and maintain such a notice as is mentioned in subsection (3) above, so, however, that no injury is done thereby to the business or occupation of the tenant.

(5) Where a notice erected as mentioned in subsection (3) above is subsequently torn down or defaced, a notice given by the owner of the land to the appropriate council that the way is not dedicated as a highway is, in the absence of proof of a contrary intention, sufficient evidence to negative the intention of the owner of the land to dedicate the way as a highway.

(6) An owner of land may at any time deposit with the appropriate council—

(a)　a map of the land on a scale of not less than 6 inches to 1 mile, and

(b)　a statement indicating what ways (if any) over the land he admits to have been dedicated as highways;

and, in any case in which such a deposit has been made, statutory declarations made by that owner or by his successors in title and lodged by him or them with the appropriate council at any time—

(i)　within ten years from the date of the deposit, or

(ii)　within ten years from the date on which any previous declaration was last lodged under this section, to the effect that no additional way (other than any specifically indicated in the declaration) over the land delineated on the said map has been dedicated as a highway since the date of the deposit, or since the date of the lodgment of such previous declaration, as the case may be, are, in the absence of proof of a contrary intention, sufficient evidence to negative the intention of the owner or his successors in title to dedicate any such additional way as a highway.

(7) For the purposes of the foregoing provisions of this section "owner", in relation to any land, means a person who is for the time being entitled to dispose of the fee simple in the land; and for the purposes of subsections (5) and (6) above "the appropriate council" means the council of the county, metropolitan district or London borough in which the way (in the case of subsection (5)) or the land (in the case of subsection (6)) is situated or, where the way or land is situated in the City, the Common Council.

(8) Nothing in this section affects any incapacity of a corporation or other body or person in possession of land for public or statutory purposes to dedicate a way over that land as a highway if the existence of a highway would be incompatible with those purposes.

(9) Nothing in this section operates to prevent the dedication of a way as a highway being presumed on proof of user for any less period than 20 years, or being presumed or proved in any circumstances in which it might have been presumed or proved immediately before the commencement of this Act.

(10) Nothing in this section or section 32 below affects section 56(1) of the Wildlife and Countryside Act 1981 (which provides that a definitive map and statement are conclusive evidence as to the existence of the highways shown on the map and as to certain particulars contained in the statement).

(11) For the purposes of this section "land" includes land covered with water.
[Highways Act 1980, s 31 as amended by the Wildlife and Countryside Act 1981, s 72 and Sch 17 and the Local Government Act 1985, Sch 4.]

---

1. Part III contains ss 24–35.

2. A right of navigation is equivalent to a right of way over land (*A-G (ex rel Yorkshire Derwent Trust Ltd) v Brotherton* [1991] Ch 185, [1992] 1 All ER 230, CA).

3. Evidence of a landowner's intention has to be overt and contemporaneous; he cannot assert later that he had no intention to dedicate. However, there is no requirement to publicise his intention and whether his acts were overt or not is a question of fact. Execution of a deed under s 193(2) of the Law of Property Act 1925, in PART VIII: COMMONS, post is such an overt act and persons using any way are doing so as licensees and not by right (*R v Secretary of State for the Environment, ex p Billson* [1998] 2 All ER 587, DC, [1998] 3 WLR 1240, applied in *R (on the application of Godmanchester Town Council) v Secretary of State for Environment, Food and Rural Affairs* [2004] EWHC 1217 (Admin), [2004] 4 All ER 342).

4. Nothing in the proviso requires there to be evidence not to dedicate for the whole of the 20-year period as the words "during the period" are not to be equated with "throughout that period" (*R v Secretary of State for the Environment, ex p Billson*, post).

7–5968A 31A. Register of maps, statements and declarations.   (1) The appropriate council shall keep, in such manner as may be prescribed[1], a register containing such information as may be prescribed[1] with respect to maps and statements deposited and declarations lodged with that council under section 31(6) above.

(2) Regulations[1] may make provision for the register to be kept in two or more parts, each part containing such information as may be prescribed with respect to such maps, statements and declarations.

(3) Regulations[1] may make provision as to circumstances in which an entry relating to a map, statement or declaration, or anything relating to it, is to be removed from the register or from any part of it.

(4) Every register kept under this section shall be available for inspection free of charge at all reasonable hours.

(5) In this section—

"appropriate council" has the same meaning as in section 31(6) above;

"prescribed" means prescribed by regulations[1];

"regulations" means regulations[1] made by the Secretary of State.
[Highways Act 1980, s 31A, as inserted by the Countryside and Rights of Way Act 2000, s 103(3) and amended by the Countryside and Rights of Way Act 2000, Sch 6.]

---

1. The Public Rights of Way (Registers) (Wales) Regulations 2006, SI 2006/42 have been made.

7–5969 32. Evidence of dedication of way as highway.   A court or other tribunal, before determining whether a way has or has not been dedicated as a highway, or the date on which such dedication, if any, took place, shall take into consideration any map, plan or history of the locality or other relevant document which is tendered in evidence, and shall give such weight thereto as the court or tribunal considers justified by the circumstances, including the antiquity of the tendered document, the status of the person by whom and the purpose for which it was made or compiled, and the custody in which it has been kept and from which it is produced.
[Highways Act 1980, s 32.]

PART IV[1]

MAINTENANCE OF HIGHWAYS

Highways maintainable at public expense

7–5970   **36. Highways maintainable at public expense.**   (1) All such highways as immediately before the commencement of this Act were highways maintainable at the public expense for the purposes of the Highways Act 1959 continue to be so maintainable (subject to this section and to any order of a magistrates' court under section 47 below) for the purposes of this Act.

(2) Without prejudice to any other enactment (whether contained in this Act or not) whereby a highway[2] may become for the purposes of this Act a highway maintainable at the public expense[3], and subject to this section and section 232(7) below, and to any order of a magistrates' court under section 47 below, the following highways (not falling within subsection (1) above) shall for the purposes of this Act be highways maintainable at the public expense—

(a) a highway constructed by a highway authority[4], otherwise than on behalf of some other person who is not a highway authority;

(b) a highway constructed by a council within their own area under Part II of the Housing Act 1985, other than one in respect of which the local highway authority are satisfied that it has not been properly constructed, and a highway constructed by a council outside their own area under the said Part II, being, in the latter case, a highway the liability to maintain which is, by virtue of the said Part II, vested in the council who are the local highway authority for the area in which the highway is situated;

(c) a highway that is a trunk road or a special road;

(d) a highway, being a footpath or bridleway, created in consequence of a public path creation order or a public path diversion order or in consequence of an order made by the Minister of Transport or the Secretary of State under section 247 of the Town and Country Planning Act 1990 or by a competent authority under section 257 of that Act, or dedicated in pursuance of a public path creation agreement;

(e) a highway, being a footpath or bridleway, created in consequence of a rail crossing diversion order, or of an order made under section 14 or 16 of the Harbours Act 1964, or of an order made under section 1 or 3 of the Transport and Works Act 1992;

(f) a highway, being a bridleway, a restricted byway or a way over which the public have a right of way for vehicular and all other kinds of traffic, created in consequence of a special diversion order or an SSSI diversion order.★

(3) Paragraph (c) of subsection (2) above is not to be construed as referring to a part of a trunk road or special road consisting of a bridge or other part which a person is liable to maintain under a charter or special enactment, or by reason of tenure, enclosure or prescription.

(3A) Paragraph (e) of subsection (2) above shall not apply to a footpath or bridleway, or to any part of a footpath or bridleway, which by virtue of an order of a kind referred to in that subsection is maintainable otherwise than at the public expense.

(4) Subject to subsection (5) below, where there occurs any event on the occurrence of which, under any rule of law relating to the duty of maintaining a highway by reason of tenure, enclosure or prescription, a highway would, but for the enactment which abrogated the former rule of law under which a duty of maintaining highways fell on the inhabitants at large (section 38(1) of the Highways Act 1959) or any other enactment, become, or cease to be, maintainable by the inhabitants at large of any area, the highway shall become, or cease to be, a highway which for the purposes of this Act is a highway maintainable at the public expense.

(5) A highway shall not by virtue of subsection (4) above become a highway which for the purposes of this Act is a highway maintainable at the public expense unless either—

(a) it was a highway before 31st August 1835; or

(b) it became a highway after that date and has at some time been maintainable by the inhabitants at large of any area or a highway maintainable at the public expense;

and a highway shall not by virtue of that subsection cease to be a highway maintainable at the public expense if it is a highway which under any rule of law would become a highway maintainable by reason of enclosure but is prevented from becoming such a highway by section 51 below.

(6) The council of every county, metropolitan district and London borough and the Common Council shall cause to be made, and shall keep corrected up to date, a list of the streets within their area which are highways maintainable at the public expense.

(7) Every list made under subsection (6) above shall be kept deposited at the offices of the council by whom it was made and may be inspected by any person free of charge at all reasonable hours and in the case of a list made by the council of a county in England, the county council shall supply to the council of each district in the county an up to date list of the streets within the area of the district that are highways maintainable at the public expense, and the list so supplied shall be kept deposited at the office of the district council and may be inspected by any person free of charge at all reasonable hours.

[Highways Act 1980, s 36 as amended by the Local Government Act 1985, Sch 4, the Housing (Consequential Provisions) Act 1985, Sch 2, the Planning (Consequential Provisions) Act 1990, Sch 2, the Transport and Works

Act 1992, s 64, the Local Government (Wales) Act 1994, Sch 7 and the Countryside and Rights of Way Act 200, s57.]

---

*Paragraph (f) in force in relation to England, except in relation to a highway created in consequence of a SSSI diversion order 12 February 2003, in force for certain purposes in relation to Wales 15 July 2005. Date in force for remaining purposes in England and Wales, to be appointed.
1. Part IV contains ss 36–61.
2. For meaning of "highway", see s 328, post.
3. For meaning of "highway maintainable at the public expense", see ss 328 and 329, post.
4. A footpath constructed by a council other than in its capacity as a highway authority which had subsequently become a highway as a result of public use for more than 20 years was not a "highway constructed by a highway authority" (*Gulliksen v Pembrokeshire County Council* [2002] EWCA Civ 968, [2003] QB 123, [2002] 4 All ER 401).

Methods whereby highways may become maintainable at public expense

7–5971 37. Provisions whereby highway created by dedication may become maintainable at public expense[1]. (1) A person who proposes to dedicate a way as a highway and who desires that the proposed highway[2] shall become maintainable at the public expense by virtue of this section shall give notice[3] of the proposal, not less than 3 months[4] before the date of the proposed dedication, to the council who would, if the way were a highway, be the highway authority therefor, describing the location and width of the proposed highway and the nature of the proposed dedication.

(2) If the council consider that the proposed highway will not be of sufficient utility to the public to justify its being maintained at the public expense, they may make a complaint[5] to a magistrates' court for an order to that effect.

(3) If the council certify that the way has been dedicated in accordance with the terms of the notice and has been made up in a satisfactory manner, and if—

(a) the person by whom the way was dedicated or his successor keeps it in repair for a period of 12 months from the date of the council's certificate, and

(b) the way has been used as a highway during that period,

then, unless an order has been made in relation to the highway under subsection (2) above, the highway shall, at the expiration of the period specified in paragraph (a) above, become for the purposes of this Act a highway maintainable at the public expense.

(4) If the council, on being requested by the person by whom the way was dedicated or his successor to issue a certificate under subsection (3) above, refuse to issue the certificate, that person may appeal[6] to a magistrates' court against the refusal, and the court, if satisfied that the certificate ought to have been issued, may make an order to the effect that subsection (3) above shall apply as if the certificate had been issued on a date specified in the order.

(5) Where a certificate has been issued by a council under subsection (3) above, or an order has been made under subsection (4) above, the certificate or a copy of the order, as the case may be, shall be deposited with the proper officer of the council and may be inspected by any person free of charge at all reasonable hours.
[Highways Act 1980, s 37.]

---

1. If the procedure prescribed in this section, re-enacting a similar provision in a repealed statute, has not been followed in relation to a road which came into existence after 1835, that road remains a private street (in the absence of proof that it had become repairable at the public expense in some other special way) (*Alsager UDC v Barratt* [1965] 2 QB 343, [1965] 1 All ER 889, 129 JP 218).
2. For meaning of "highway", see s 328, post; for meaning of "highway maintainable at the public expense", see ss 328 and 329, post.
3. For form of notice and its authentication and service, see ss 320–322, post.
4. For rule governing the reckoning of periods, see s 323, post.
5. See Magistrates' Courts Act 1980, s 51, in PART I: MAGISTRATES' COURTS, PROCEDURE, ante.
6. Procedure on appeal is by way of complaint for an order: see s 316, post; notice must be given to a prospective appellant of this right of appeal: see s 315, post.

7–5972 38. Power of highway authorities to adopt by agreement. (1) Subject to subsection (2) below, where any person is liable under a special enactment or by reason of tenure, enclosure or prescription to maintain a highway, the Minister, in the case of a trunk road, or a local highway authority, in any other case, may agree with that person to undertake the maintenance of that highway; and where an agreement is made under this subsection the highway to which the agreement relates shall, on such date as may be specified in the agreement, become for the purposes of this Act a highway maintainable at the public expense and the liability of that person to maintain the highway shall be extinguished.

(2) A local highway authority shall not have power to make an agreement under subsection (1) above with respect to a highway with respect to which they or any other highway authority have power to make an agreement under Part V or Part XII of this Act.

(3) A local highway authority may agree with any person to undertake the maintenance of a way—

(a) which that person is willing and has the necessary power to dedicate as a highway, or

(b) which is to be constructed by that person, or by a highway authority on his behalf, and which he proposes to dedicate as a highway;

and where an agreement is made under this subsection the way to which the agreement relates shall, on such date as may be specified in the agreement, become for the purposes of this Act a highway maintainable at the public expense.

(3A) The Minister may agree with any person to undertake the maintenance of a road—

(a) which that person is willing and has the necessary power to dedicate as a highway, or

(b) which is to be constructed by that person, or by a highway authority on his behalf, and which he proposes to dedicate as a highway,

and which the Minister proposes should become a trunk road; and where an agreement is made under this subsection the road shall become for the purposes of this Act a highway maintainable at the public expense on the date on which an order comes into force under section 10 directing that the road become a trunk road or, if later, the date on which the road is opened for the purposes of through traffic.

(4) Without prejudice to the provisions of subsection (3) above and subject to the following provisions of this section, a local highway authority may, by agreement with railway, canal or tramway undertakers, undertake to maintain as part of a highway maintainable at the public expense a bridge or viaduct which carries the railway, canal or tramway of the undertakers over such a highway or which is intended to carry such a railway, canal or tramway over such a highway and is to be constructed by those undertakers or by the highway authority on their behalf.

(5) (*Repealed*).

(6) An agreement under this section may contain such provisions as to the dedication as a highway of any road or way to which the agreement relates, the bearing of the expenses of the construction, maintenance or improvement of any highway, road, bridge or viaduct to which the agreement relates and other relevant matters as the authority making the agreement think fit.

[Highways Act 1980, s 38 as amended by the Local Government Act 1985, Sch 17 and the New Roads and Street Works Act 1991, s 22(1).]

7–5973   **40.** *Adoption of private streets.*

Maintenance of highways maintainable at public expense

7–5974   **41. Duty to maintain highways maintainable at public expense.**   (1) The authority who are for the time being the highway authority for a highway maintainable at the public expense are under a duty, subject to subsections (2) and (4) below, to maintain[1] the highway.

(1A) In particular, a highway authority are under a duty to ensure, so far as is reasonably practicable, that safe passage along a highway is not endangered by snow or ice.

(2) An order made by the Minister under section 10 above directing that a highway proposed to be constructed by him shall become a trunk road may, as regards—

(a) a highway to which this subsection applies which becomes a trunk road by virtue of the order, or

(b) a part of a highway to which this subsection applies, being a part which crosses the route of the highway to be so constructed,

contain such a direction as is specified in subsection (4) below.

(3) Subsection (2) above applies to—

(a) any highway maintainable at the public expense by a local highway authority, and

(b) any highway other than a highway falling within paragraph (a) above or a highway maintainable under a special enactment or by reason of tenure, enclosure or prescription.

(4) The direction referred to in subsection (2) above is—

(a) in a case where the highway or part of a highway falls within subsection (3)(a) above, a direction that, notwithstanding subsection (1) above, it shall be maintained by the highway authority for that highway until such date, not being later than the date on which the new route is opened for the purposes of through traffic, as may be specified in a notice given by the Minister to that authority; and

(b) in a case where the highway or part of a highway falls within subsection (3)(b) above, a direction that, notwithstanding subsection (1) above, the Minister is to be under no duty to maintain it until such date as aforesaid.

(5) Where an order under section 10 above contains a direction made in pursuance of subsections (2) to (4) above, then, until the date specified in the notice given by the Minister pursuant to the direction, in accordance with subsection (4) above, the powers of a highway authority under sections 97, 98, 270 and 301 below as respects the highway to which the direction relates are exercisable by the highway authority to whom the notice is required to be given, as well as by the Minister.

[Highways Act 1980, s 41, as amended by the Railways and Transport Safety Act 2003, s 111.]

---

1. The duty to maintain highways is wider in scope than a duty to repair or keep in repair. It includes taking preventative or clearance measures with regard to snow and ice which are sufficient to keep the surface reasonably safe (*Cross v Kirklees Borough Council* [1998] 1 All ER 564, CA).

7–5975   42. Power of district councils to maintain certain highways.   (1) Subject to Part I of Schedule 7 to this Act, the council of a non-metropolitan district may undertake the maintenance of any eligible highway in the district which is a highway maintainable at the public expense.

(2) For the purposes of subsection (1) above the following are eligible highways—

(a)   footpaths,

(b)   bridleways, and

(c)   roads (referred to in Schedule 7 to this Act as "urban roads") which are neither trunk roads nor classified roads and which—

(i)   are restricted roads for the purposes of section 81 of the Road Traffic Regulation Act 1984 (30 mph speed limit), or

(ii)   are subject to an order made by virtue of section 84(1)(a) of that Act imposing a speed limit not exceeding 40 mph, or

(iii)   are otherwise streets in an urban area.

(3) The county council who are the highway authority for a highway which is for the time being maintained by a non-metropolitan district council by virtue of this section shall reimburse to the district council any expenses incurred by them in carrying out on the highway works of maintenance necessary to secure that the duty to maintain the highway is performed, and Part II of Schedule 7 to this Act shall have effect for this purpose.

[Highways Act 1980, s 42 as amended by the Road Traffic Regulation Act 1984, Sch 13, the Local Government Act 1985, Sch 4 and the Road Traffic Act 1991, Sch 4.]

7–5976   43. Power of parish and community councils to maintain footpaths and bridleways.

(1) The council of a parish or community may undertake the maintenance of any footpath or bridleway within the parish or community which is, in either case, a highway maintainable at the public expense; but nothing in this subsection affects the duty of any highway authority or other person to maintain any such footpath or bridleway.

(2) The highway authority for any footpath or bridleway which a parish or community council have power to maintain under subsection (1) above, and a non-metropolitan district council for the time being maintaining any such footpath or bridleway by virtue of section 42 above, may undertake to defray the whole or part of any expenditure incurred by the parish or community council in maintaining the footpath or bridleway.

(3) The power of a parish or community council under subsection (1) above is subject to the restrictions for the time being imposed by any enactment on their expenditure, but for the purposes of any enactment imposing such a restriction their expenditure is to be deemed not to include any expenditure falling to be defrayed by a highway authority or district council by virtue of subsection (2) above.

[Highways Act 1980, s 43 as amended by the Local Government Act 1985, Sch 4.]

7–5977   44. Person liable to maintain highway may agree to maintain publicly maintainable highway.   Where any person is liable under a special enactment or by reason of tenure, enclosure or prescription to maintain a highway, he may enter into an agreement with the highway authority for that highway for the maintenance by him of any highway maintainable at the public expense by the highway authority; but nothing in this section affects the duty of a highway authority to maintain a highway as respects which any such agreement is made.

[Highways Act 1980, s 44.]

7–5978   45. Power to get materials for repair of publicly maintainable highways.   (1) For the purpose of repairing highways maintainable at the public expense[1] by them, a highway authority may exercise such powers with respect to the getting of materials as are mentioned in this section.

(2) Subject to subsection (3) below, the authority may search for, dig, get and carry away gravel[2], sand, stone and other materials in and from any waste or common land (including the bed of any river or brook flowing through such land).

(3) The authority—

(a)   shall not in the exercise of their powers under subsection (2) above divert or interrupt the course of any river or brook or dig or get materials out of any river or brook within 50 yards above or below a bridge, dam or weir;

(b)   shall not in the exercise of those powers remove such quantity of stones or other materials from any sea beach as to cause damage by inundation or increased danger of encroachment by the sea; and

(c)   shall not exercise those powers in any land forming part of a common to which section 20 of the Commons Act 1876 applies, except in accordance with that section.

(4) Subject to subsection (5) below, the authority may gather and carry away stones lying upon any land in the non-metropolitan county, metropolitan district or London borough within which the stones are to be used.

(5) The authority—

(a) shall not exercise the powers conferred by subsection (4) above in a garden, yard, avenue to a house, lawn, park, paddock or inclosed plantation, or in an inclosed wood not exceeding 100 acres in extent;

(b) shall not in the case of any other inclosed land[3] exercise those powers unless either they have obtained the consent of the owner[4] and of the occupier of that land, or a magistrates' court has made an order[5] authorising them to exercise those powers in the case of that land; and

(c) shall not in the exercise of those powers remove such quantity of stones or other materials from any sea beach as to cause damage by inundation or increased danger of encroachment by the sea.

(6) If the authority cannot get sufficient materials by the exercise of their powers under the foregoing provisions of this section, a magistrates' court may make an order[5] authorising them to search for, dig, get and carry away materials in and from any inclosed land in the non-metropolitan county, metropolitan district or London borough within which the materials are to be used, other than any such land as is mentioned in subsection (5)(a) above.

(7) For the purpose of repairing a bridge maintainable at the public expense and so much of a highway so maintainable as is carried by the bridge or forms the approaches to the bridge up to 100 yards from each end of the bridge, the authority may take and carry away the rubbish or refuse stones from any quarry in the non-metropolitan county or metropolitan district within which the materials are to be used or, if the materials are to be used in Greater London, from any quarry in Greater London.

(8) Subject to subsection (9) below, for the purpose of repairing or reconstructing a bridge maintainable at the public expense, the authority may be authorised by an order of a magistrates' court to quarry stone from any quarry in the non-metropolitan county or metropolitan district in which the bridge is or, if the bridge is in Greater London, from any quarry in Greater London.

(9) No order shall be made under subsection (8) above in relation to a quarry which has not been worked at any time during the 3 years immediately preceding the date on which a complaint for such an order is made; and no stone shall be taken from a quarry situated in a garden, yard, avenue to a house, lawn, paddock or inclosed plantation, or in land on which ornamental timber trees are growing, except with the consent of the owner of the quarry.

(10) An authority who exercise any of the powers conferred by this section shall pay compensation to persons interested in any land for any damage done thereto by the carriage of the materials obtained by the authority and also, in cases falling within subsection (6) or subsection (8) above, for the value of those materials.

(11) At least one month[6] before making a complaint to a magistrates' court for an order under subsection (5) or subsection (6) above the authority shall give notice[7] of their intention to make such a complaint to the owner, and to the occupier, of the land from which they propose to get materials.

(12) In relation to highways in respect of which a non-metropolitan district council's powers of maintenance under section 42 above are exercisable, references in this section and section 46 below to a highway authority include references to the district council; and for the purposes of this section—

"inclosed land" includes any land in the exclusive occupation of one or more persons for agricultural[8] purposes, though not separated by a fence or otherwise from adjoining land of another person, or from a highway; and

"London borough" includes the City of London.

[Highways Act 1980, s 45 as amended by the Local Government Act 1985, Sch 4.]

---

1. For the meaning of "highway maintainable at the public expense", see ss 328 and 329, post.
2. When a common is regulated by a provisional order of the Inclosure Comissioners or Act of Parliament, gravel, sand, etc, is not to be dug from any part not set apart for that purpose without consent of the conservators or two justices (Commons Act 1876, s 20; see Commons Act 1899, s 9). Justices have discretion to make or refuse the order, and may prescribe conditions as to the mode of working (*Hayes Common Conservators v Bromley RDC* [1897] 1 QB 321, 61 JP 104).
3. For the meaning of "inclosed land", see sub-s (12), infra.
4. For meaning of "owner", see s 329, post.
5. This order is made on complaint: see sub-s (11), infra, and Magistrates' Courts Act 1980, s 51, PART I, ante.
6. For the rule governing the reckoning of periods, see s 323, post.
7. For form of notice, its authentication and service, see ss 320–322, post.
8. For meaning of "agricultural", see s 329, post.

7–5979   46. Supplemental provisions with respect to the getting of materials under section 45. (1) Where an excavation is made by a highway authority in the exercise of powers conferred by section 45 above, the authority shall—

(a) while work is in progress, and thereafter so long as the excavation remains open, keep the excavation sufficiently fenced to prevent accidents to persons or animals,

(b) if no materials are found therein, fill up the excavation within 3 days from the date on which the excavation was made,

(c) if materials are found, then within 14 days[1] from the date on which sufficient materials have been obtained, fill up the excavation or slope it down and fence it off, if the owner or occupier of the land in question so requires, and thereafter keep it so fenced, and (*d*) when filling up an excavation, make good and level the ground and cover it with the turf or clod dug therefrom.

(2) An authority who fail to comply with any of the provisions of subsection (1) above are guilty of an offence and liable to a fine not exceeding **level 1** on the standard scale.

(3) If in the exercise of powers conferred by section 45 above materials are dug so as to damage or endanger a highway, occupation road, ford, dam, mine, building, works or apparatus, the authority are guilty of an offence and, without prejudice to any civil proceedings which may be available against them, liable to a fine not exceeding **level 1** on the standard scale.

(4) A person who, without the consent of the highway authority,—

(*a*) takes away any materials purchased, gotten or gathered by them for the repair of highways, or
(*b*) takes away any materials from a quarry or excavation opened by the authority before their workmen have ceased working thereat for 6 weeks,

is guilty of an offence and liable to a fine not exceeding **level 1** on the standard scale; but in the case of a quarry or excavation in private grounds, nothing in this subsection prevents the owner or occupier from getting materials therefrom for his own private use and not for sale.

[Highways Act 1980, s 46 as amended by the Criminal Justice Act 1982, s 46.]

---

1. For the rule governing the reckoning of periods, see s 323, post.

7–5980 47. Power of magistrates' court to declare unnecessary highway to be not maintainable at public expense. (1) Where a highway authority are of opinion that a highway maintainable at the public expense[1] by them is unnecessary for public use and therefore ought not to be maintained at the public expense, they may, subject to subsections (2) to (4) below, apply to a magistrates' court for an order declaring that the highway shall cease to be so maintained.

(2) No application shall be made under this section for an order relating to a trunk road[1], special road[1], metropolitan road[1], footpath[1] or bridleway[1].

(3) Where a county council, as highway authority, propose to make an application under this section for an order relating to any highway, they shall give notice[2] of the proposal to the council of the district in which the highway in England is situated, and the application shall not be made if, within 2 months[3] from the date of service of the notice by the county council, notice is given to the county council by the district council that the district council have refused to consent to the making of the application.

(4) If a highway authority propose to make an application under this section for an order relating to a highway situated in a parish or a community they shall give notice of the proposal—

(*a*) to the council of the parish or community, or
(*b*) in the case of a parish not having a separate parish council, to the chairman of the parish meeting,

and the application shall not be made if, within 2 months from the date of service of the notice by the highway authority, notice is given to the highway authority by the council of the parish or community or the chairman of the parish meeting, as the case may be, that the council or meeting have refused to consent to the making of the application.

(5) Where an application is made to a magistrates' court under this section, 2 or more justices of the peace acting for the petty sessions area for which the court acts shall together view the highway to which the application relates, and no further proceedings shall be taken on the application unless they are of opinion, after viewing the highway, that there was ground for making the application.

(6) The chief executive to the justices who view a highway in accordance with the provisions of subsection (5) above shall, as soon as practicable after the view, notify the highway authority by whom an application under this section relating to the highway was made of the decision of the justices and, if the justices decide that there was ground for making the application, of the time, not being less than 6 weeks[3] from the date of the notice, and place, at which the application is to be heard by a magistrates' court.

(7) A magistrates' court shall not hear an application under this section unless it is satisfied that the highway authority making the application have—

(*a*) not less than one month[3] before the date on which the application is to be heard by the court, given notice[4] to the owners and the occupiers of all lands[5] adjoining[5] the highway to which the application relates of the making of the application, and the purpose of it, and of the time and place at which the application is to be heard by the court, and
(*b*) given public notice in the terms and manner required by subsection (8) below.

(8) A highway authority making an application under this section shall publish once at least in each of the 4 weeks[3] immediately preceding the week in which the application is to be heard, in a local newspaper circulating in the area in which the highway to which the application relates is situated, a notice—

(*a*) stating that an application has been made to a magistrates' court under this section and the purpose of the application,
(*b*) describing the highway, and

(*c*) specifying the time and place at which the application is to be heard,

and shall cause a copy of the notice to be fixed, at least 14 days before the date on which the application is to be heard by the court, to the principal doors of every church and chapel in the parish or community in which the highway is situated, or in some conspicuous position near the highway.

(9) On the hearing of an application for an order under this section, a magistrates' court shall hear any person who objects to the order being made and may either dismiss the application or make an order declaring that the highway to which the application relates shall cease to be maintained at the public expense.

(10) Where an order is made under this section the highway to which the order relates shall cease to be a highway maintainable at the public expense.

(11) The highway authority on whose application an order is made under this section shall give notice of the making of the order to any public utility undertakers[5] having apparatus[5] under, in, upon, over, along or across the highway to which the order relates.
[Highways Act 1980, s 47 as amended by the Local Government (Wales) Act 1994, Sch 7 and the Access to Justice Act 1999, Sch 13.]

---

1. For meaning of "highway maintainable at the public expense", see ss 328 and 329, post; for meaning of "trunk road", "special road", "metropolitan road", "footpath", "bridleway", see s 329, post.
2. For form of notice, its authentication and service, see ss 320–322, post.
3. For the rule governing the reckoning of periods, see s 323, post.
4. For form of notice, its authentication and service, see ss 320–322, post.
5. For meaning of "land", "adjoining", "public utility undertakers" and "apparatus", see s 329, post.

7–5981   **48. Power of magistrates' court to order a highway to be again maintainable at public expense.**   (1) Subject to subsection (2) below, if it appears to a magistrates' court that, in consequence of any change of circumstances since the time at which an order was made under section 47 above, the highway to which the order relates has again become of public use and ought to be maintained at the public expense, the court may by order direct that the highway shall again become for the purposes of this Act a highway maintainable at the public expense.

(2) An order under this section shall not be made except on the application of a person interested in the maintenance of the highway to which the application relates, and on proof that not less than 1 month[1] before making the application he gave notice to the highway authority for the highway of his intention to make an application under this section.
[Highways Act 1980, s 48.]

---

1. For rule governing the reckoning of periods, see s 323, post.

Maintenance of privately maintainable highways

7–5982   **49. Maintenance of approaches to certain privately maintainable bridges.**   Where a person is liable to maintain the approaches to a bridge by reason of the fact that he is liable to maintain the bridge by reason of tenure or prescription, his liability to maintain the approaches extends to 100 yards from each end of the bridge.
[Highways Act 1980, s 49.]

7–5983   **50. Maintenance of privately maintainable footpaths and bridleways.**   (1) Where apart from section 41 above a person would under a special enactment or by reason of tenure, enclosure or prescription be under an obligation to maintain a footpath or bridleway, the operation of section 41(1) does not release him from the obligation.

(2) The council of a non-metropolitan district, parish or community may undertake by virtue of this subsection the maintenance of any footpath or bridleway within the district, parish or community (other than a footpath or bridleway the maintenance of which they have power to undertake under section 42 or, as the case may be, section 43 above) whether or not any other person is under a duty to maintain the footpath or bridleway; but nothing in this subsection affects the duty of any other person to maintain any such footpath or bridleway.

(3) The power of a district council under subsection (2) above is subject to Part I of Schedule 7 to this Act; and the power of a parish or community council under that subsection is subject to the restrictions for the time being imposed by any enactment on their expenditure.
[Highways Act 1980, s 50 as amended by the Local Government Act 1985, Sch 4.]

7–5984   **51. No liability to maintain by reason of enclosure if highway fenced with consent of highway authority.**   (1) If a person across whose land there is a highway maintainable at the public expense erects a fence between the highway and the adjoining land, and the fence is erected with the consent of the highway authority for the highway, he does not thereby become liable to maintain the highway by reason of enclosure.

(2) Nothing in subsection (1) above is to be construed as imposing on any person a liability to maintain a highway by reason of enclosure.
[Highways Act 1980, s 51.]

7–5985 **52. Power to get materials for repair of privately maintainable highways.** (1) A person liable to maintain a highway by reason of tenure, enclosure or prescription has, for the purpose of repairing it, the like powers with respect to the getting of materials as are conferred on a highway authority by section 45(2) to (6) above for the purpose of repairing highways maintainable at the public expense by them.

(2) A person on whom powers are conferred by this section is, with respect to the exercise of those powers, subject to the like duties and liabilities under section 45(10) and (11) above and under section 46(1) to (3) above as are a highway authority with respect to the exercise of the powers conferred on them by section 45.

[Highways Act 1980, s 52.]

7–5986 **53. Power of magistrates' court to extinguish liability to maintain privately maintainable highway.** (1) Where a person is liable by reason of tenure, enclosure or prescription to maintain a highway, a magistrates' court may, on a complaint[1] made either by that person or by the highway authority for the highway, make an order that the liability of that person to maintain the highway shall be extinguished, and on the extinguishment of that liability the highway, if it is not then a highway maintainable at the public expense, shall become for the purposes of this Act a highway maintainable at the public expense.

(2) Where a complaint is made to a magistrates' court under this section by a person liable as aforesaid to maintain a highway—

(a) the highway authority for the highway have a right to be heard by the court at the hearing of the complaint, and

(b) the court shall not make an order on the complaint unless it is satisfied that not less than 21 days[2] before the date on which the complaint is heard by the court the complainant gave notice[3] to the highway authority for the highway of the making of the complaint and of the time and place at which it was to be heard by the court.

(3) Where by virtue of an order under this section the liability of a person to maintain a highway is extinguished, that person is liable to pay to the highway authority for the highway such sum as may be agreed between him and that authority or, in default of agreement, as may be determined by arbitration to represent the value to him of the extinguishment of his liability.

(4) A sum payable by any person under subsection (3) above shall, at his option, be paid—

(a) as a lump sum, or

(b) by annual payments of such amount, and continuing for such number of years, as may be agreed between him and the highway authority or, in default of agreement, as may be determined by arbitration.

(5) Any matter which by virtue of subsection (3) or (4) above is to be determined by arbitration shall be determined by a single arbitrator appointed, in default of agreement between the parties concerned, by the Minister.

(6) Nothing in this section affects any exemption from rating under any enactment as continued by section 117 of the General Rate Act 1967[4].

[Highways Act 1980, s 53.]

---

1. See the Magistrates' Courts Act 1980, s 51, PART I: MAGISTRATES' COURTS, PROCEDURE, ante.
2. For rule governing the reckoning of periods, see s 323, post.
3. For form of notice, its authentication and service, see ss 320–322, post.
4. The General Rate Act 1967 has been repealed with effect from 31 March 1990 and replaced by the Local Government Finance Act 1988.

7–5987 **54. Extinguishment of liability to maintain privately maintainable highway diverted by order of magistrates' court.** (1) Where a highway which a person is liable to maintain under a special enactment or by reason of tenure, enclosure or prescription is diverted in accordance with an order made under section 116 below, then—

(a) the substituted highway becomes for the purposes of this Act a highway maintainable at the public expense, and

(b) the person liable as aforesaid to maintain the highway so diverted is liable to pay to the highway authority for the substituted highway such sum as may be agreed between him and that authority or, in default of agreement, as may be determined by arbitration to represent the value to him of the extinguishment of his liability.

(2) A sum payable by any person under subsection (1) above shall, at his option, be paid—

(a) as a lump sum, or

(b) by annual payments of such amount, and continuing for such number of years, as may be agreed between him and the highway authority or, in default of agreement, as may be determined by arbitration.

(3) Any matter which by virtue of subsection (1) or (2) above is to be determined by arbitration

shall be determined by a single arbitrator appointed, in default of agreement between the parties concerned, by the Minister.

[Highways Act 1980, s 54.]

7–5988 55. *Extinguishment of liability to maintain or improve bridges comprised in trunk roads and special roads.*

Enforcement of liability for maintenance

7–5989 56. Proceedings for an order to repair highway. (1) A person ("the complainant") who alleges that a way or bridge—

(a) is a highway maintainable at the public expense or a highway which a person is liable to maintain under a special enactment or by reason of tenure, enclosure or prescription, and

(b) is out of repair[1],

may serve a notice[2] on the highway authority or other person alleged to be liable to maintain the way or bridge ("the respondent") requiring the respondent to state whether he admits that the way or bridge is a highway and that he is liable to maintain it.

(2) If, within 1 month from the date of service on him of a notice under subsection (1) above, the respondent does not serve on the complainant a notice admitting both that the way or bridge in question is a highway and that the respondent is liable to maintain it, the complainant may apply to the Crown Court for an order requiring the respondent, if the court finds that the way or bridge is a highway which the respondent is liable to maintain and is out of repair, to put it in proper repair within such reasonable period as may be specified in the order.

(3) The complainant for an order under subsection (2) above shall give notice in writing of the application to the appropriate officer of the Crown Court and the notice shall specify—

(a) the situation of the way or bridge to which the application relates,

(b) the name of the respondent,

(c) the part of the way or bridge which is alleged to be out of repair, and

(d) the nature of the alleged disrepair;

and the complainant shall serve a copy of the notice on the respondent.

(4) If, within 1 month from the date of service on him of a notice under subsection (1) above, the respondent serves on the complainant a notice admitting both that the way or bridge in question is a highway and that the respondent is liable to maintain it, the complainant may, within 6 months from the date of service on him of that notice, apply to a magistrates' court for an order requiring the respondent, if the court finds that the highway is out of repair, to put it in proper repair within such reasonable period as may be specified in the order.

(5) A court in determining under this section whether a highway is out of repair shall not be required to view the highway unless it thinks fit, and any such view may be made by any 2 or more of the members of the court.

(6) If at the expiration of the period specified in an order made under subsection (2) or (4) above a magistrates' court is satisfied that the highway to which the order relates has not been put in proper repair, then, unless the court thinks fit to extend the period, it shall by order authorise the complainant (if he has not the necessary power in that behalf) to carry out such works as may be necessary to put the highway in proper repair.

(7) Any expenses which a complainant reasonably incurs in carrying out works authorised by an order under subsection (6) above are recoverable from the respondent summarily[3] as a civil debt.

(8) Where any expenses recoverable under subsection (7) above are recovered from the respondent, then, if the respondent would have been entitled to recover from some other person the whole or part of the expenses of repairing the highway in question if he had repaired it himself, he is entitled to recover from that other person the whole or the like part, as the case may be, of the expenses recovered from him.

(9) Where an application is made under this section for an order requiring the respondent to put in proper repair a footpath or bridleway which, in either case, is a highway maintainable at the public expense and some other person is liable to maintain the footpath or bridleway under a special enactment or by reason of tenure, enclosure or prescription, that other person has a right to be heard by the court which hears the application, but only on the question whether the footpath or bridleway is in proper repair.

[Highways Act 1980, s 56.]

---

1. An obstructed highway can be regarded as "out of repair" if its condition is the result of the failure of a highway authority to maintain it under s 44 (*Hereford and Worcester County Council v Newman* [1975] 2 All ER 673, [1975] 1 WLR 901, CA).

2. For form of notice, its authentication and service, see ss 320–322, post.

3. See the Magistrates' Courts Act 1980, s 58, PART I: MAGISTRATES' COURTS, PROCEDURE, ante.

7–5990 73. Power to prescribe improvement line for widening street. (1) Where in the opinion of a highway authority—

(a) a street which is a highway maintainable at the public expense by them is narrow or inconvenient, or without any sufficiently regular boundary line, or

(b) it is necessary or desirable that such a street should be widened,

the authority may prescribe in relation to either one side or both sides of the street, or at or within a distance of 15 yards from any corner of the street, a line to which the street is to be widened (in this section referred to as an "improvement line").

(2) Where an improvement line prescribed under this section in relation to any street is in force, then, subject to subsections (3) and (4) below, no new building shall be erected, and no permanent excavation below the level of the street shall be made, nearer to the centre line of the street than the improvement line, except with the consent of the authority who prescribed the line, and the authority may give a consent for such period and subject to such conditions as they may deem expedient.

(3) The prohibition imposed by subsection (2) above does not affect any right of statutory undertakers to make an excavation for the purpose of laying, altering, maintaining or renewing any main, sewer, pipe, electric line, cable, duct or other work or apparatus.

(4) Where an authority prescribe an improvement line under this section, a person aggrieved by the decision to prescribe the line or by the refusal of consent under subsection (2) above or by the period for which the consent is given or any conditions attached to it may appeal to the Crown Court.

(5) A condition imposed in connection with the giving of a consent under subsection (2) above is binding on the successor in title to every owner, and on every lessee and every occupier, of any land to which it relates.

(6) If a person contravenes the provisions of this section, or any condition imposed in connection with the giving of a consent under it, he is, without prejudice to any other proceedings which may be available against him, guilty of an offence[2] and liable to a fine not exceeding **level 1** on the standard scale; and if the offence is continued after conviction he is guilty of a further offence and liable to a fine not exceeding £2 for each day on which the offence is so continued.

(7) Where in the opinion of a highway authority an improvement line prescribed by them under this section, or any part of such a line, is no longer necessary or desirable and should be revoked, they may revoke the line or that part of it.

(8) Schedule 9 to this Act has effect in relation to the prescription of an improvement line under this section and to the revocation of such a line or any part of it.

(9) Any person whose property is injuriously affected by the prescribing of an improvement line under this section is, subject to the following provisions thereof, entitled to recover from the authority who prescribed the line compensation for the injury sustained.

(10) A person is not entitled to compensation on account of any building erected, contract made, or other thing done, after the date on which a plan showing the improvement line was deposited in accordance with the provisions of paragraph 5 of Schedule 9 to this Act, except as regards work done for the purpose of finishing a building the erection of which had begun before that date, or of carrying out a contract made before that date.

(11) Nothing in this section applies to or affects, without the consent of the undertakers concerned—

(a) any property occupied or used by railway undertakers for the purposes of a railway comprised in the railway undertaking; or

(b) any property belonging to any of the following undertakers and used by them for the following purposes respectively, that is to say, by canal undertakers for those of a canal comprised in the canal undertaking, by inland navigation undertakers for those of a navigation comprised in the inland navigation undertaking, by dock undertakers for those of a dock comprised in the dock undertaking, or by harbour undertakers for those of a harbour comprised in the harbour undertaking; or

(c) any land used by gas undertakers[3] for the manufacture or storage of gas, by electricity undertakers[4] for the generation of electricity by water undertakers as a pumping station or reservoir for water or by sewerage undertakers as a pumping station or sewage disposal works.

A consent required by this subsection shall not be unreasonably withheld, and any question whether the withholding of such a consent is unreasonable shall, except where the street in question is one for which the Minister is the highway authority, be determined by the Secretary of State.

(12) In relation to any prohibition or restriction on the use of land or buildings imposed by the Minister by the prescription of an improvement line under this section or by virtue of any condition imposed by him in connection with the giving of a consent under subsection (2) above, section 1(1)(c) of the Local Land Charges Act 1975 shall have effect as if the references to the date of the commencement of that Act were omitted.

(13) In this section "building" includes any erection however, and with whatever material, it is

constructed and any part of a building, and "new building" includes any addition to an existing building.

[Highways Act 1980, s 73 as amended by the Criminal Justice Act 1982, s 46 and the Water Act 1989, Schs 25 and 27.]

---

1. Part V contains ss 62–105.
2. Proceedings for an offence shall not, without the written consent of the Attorney-General, be taken by any person other than a person aggrieved, or a highway authority or council having an interest in the enforcement of the provision (s 312, *post*; Sch 22, *post*).
3. The Utilities Act 2000, s 76 provides that a reference to a public gas transporter shall have effect as a reference to a gas transporter.
4. The reference to "electricity undertakers" shall be construed as a reference to the holder of a licence under s 6(1)(*a*) of the Electricity Act 1989 (Electricity Act 1989, Sch 16, para 1(4)).

7–5991 74. Power to prescribe a building line.   (1) Subject to the provisions of this section, a highway authority may prescribe, in relation to either one side or both sides of a highway maintainable at the public expense for which they are the highway authority, a frontage line for building (in this section referred to as a "building line").

(2) Where a building line prescribed under this section in relation to any highway is in force, no new building, other than a boundary wall or fence, shall be erected, and no permanent excavation below the level of the highway shall be made, nearer to the centre line of the highway than the building line, except with the consent of the authority who prescribed the line; and the authority may give a consent for such period and subject to such conditions as they deem expedient.

(3) The prohibition imposed by subsection (2) above does not affect any right of light railway, tramway, electricity, gas, water undertakers or sewerage undertakers to make an excavation for the purpose of laying, altering, maintaining or renewing any main, sewer, pipe, electric line, duct or other apparatus.

(4) A condition imposed in connection with the giving of a consent under subsection (2) above is binding on the successor in title to every owner, and on every lessee and every occupier, of any land to which it relates.

(5) If a person contravenes the provisions of this section, or any condition imposed in connection with the giving of a consent under it, he is, without prejudice to any other proceedings which may be available against him, guilty of an offence and liable to a fine not exceeding **level 1** on the standard scale; and if the offence is continued after conviction, he is guilty of a further offence and liable to a fine not exceeding £2 for each day on which the offence is so continued.

(6) Where in the opinion of a highway authority a building line prescribed by them under this section, or any part of such a line, is no longer necessary or desirable and should be revoked, they may revoke the line or that part of it.

(7) Schedule 9 to this Act has effect in relation to the prescription of a building line under this section and to the revocation of such line or any part of it.

(8) Any person whose property is injuriously affected by the prescribing of a building line under this section is entitled, subject to subsection (9) below, to recover from the authority who prescribed the line compensation for the injury sustained.

(9) A person is not entitled to compensation under subsection (8) above—

(*a*) unless he made a claim within 6 months from the date on which the building line was prescribed or, if the claimant is a person to whom a notice of the prescribing of the line was required to be given by paragraph 8 of Schedule 9 to this Act, within 6 months from the date on which such a notice was given to him; or

(*b*) on account of anything done by him after the date on which a notice of the proposal to prescribe the line was served on him, except so far as it was done for the purpose of finishing a building the erection of which had begun before that date, or of carrying out a contract made before that date.

(10) Any two or more authorities on whom powers are conferred by this section may by agreement exercise those powers jointly, and the agreement may provide for the apportionment of any expenses incurred under it.

(11) Nothing in this section applies to or affects, without the consent of the undertakers concerned—

(*a*) any land belonging to any of the following undertakers, and held by them for the following purposes respectively, that is to say, by railway undertakers for those of a railway comprised in the railway undertaking, by canal undertakers for those of a canal comprised in the canal undertaking, by inland navigation undertakers for those of a navigation comprised in the inland navigation undertaking, by dock undertakers for those of a dock comprised in the dock undertaking, or by harbour undertakers for those of a harbour comprised in the harbour undertaking; or

(*b*) any land used by gas undertakers[1] for the manufacture or storage of gas, by electricity undertakers[2] for the generation of electricity by water undertakers as a pumping station or reservoir for water or by sewerage undertakers as a pumping station or sewage disposal works.

A consent required by this subsection shall not be unreasonably withheld, and any question whether the withholding of such a consent is unreasonable shall, except where the highway in question is one for which the Minister is the highway authority, be determined by the Minister.

(12) In relation to any prohibition or restriction on the use of land or buildings imposed by the Minister by the prescription of a building line under this section or by virtue of any condition imposed by him in connection with the giving of a consent under subsection (2) above, section 1(1)(c) of the Local Land Charges Act 1975 has effect as if the reference to the date of the commencement of that Act were omitted.

(13) In this section—

"building" and "new building" have the same meaning respectively as in section 73 above; and

"light railway undertakers" means persons authorised by any enactment to carry on a light railway undertaking.

[Highways Act 1980, s 74 as amended by the Criminal Justice Act 1982, s 46 and the Water Act 1989, Schs 25 and 27.]

---

1. The Utilities Act 2000, s 76 provides that a reference to a public gas transporter shall have effect as a reference to a gas transporter.

2. The reference to "electricity undertakers" shall be construed as a reference to the holder of a licence under s 6(1)(a) of the Electricity Act 1988 (Electricity Act 1989, Sch 16, para 1(4)).

7–5992 79. Prevention of obstruction to view at corners. (1) Where, in the case of a highway maintainable at the public expense, the highway authority for the highway deem it necessary for the prevention of danger arising from obstruction to the view of persons using the highway to impose restrictions with respect to any land at or near any corner or bend in the highway or any junction of the highway with a road to which the public has access, the authority may, subject to the provisions of this section, serve a notice, together with a plan showing the land to which the notice relates,—

(a) on the owner or occupier of the land, directing him to alter any wall (other than a wall forming part of the structure of a permanent edifice), fence, hoarding, paling, tree, shrub or other vegetation on the land so as to cause it to conform with any requirements specified in the notice; or

(b) on every owner, lessee and occupier of the land, restraining them either absolutely or subject to such conditions as may be specified in the notice from causing or permitting any building, wall, fence, hoarding, paling, tree, shrub or other vegetation to be erected or planted on the land.

(2) A notice under subsection (1) above may at any time be withdrawn by the authority by whom it was given.

(3) A notice restraining the erection of any building on land shall not be served by a highway authority except with the consent of the council of the non-metropolitan district in which the land is situated or if the land is situated in a London borough or the City and the highway authority concerned is the Minister, with the consent of the council of that London borough or the Common Council, as the case may require.

(3A) In relation to any land in Wales—

(a) subsection (3) above does not apply; but

(b) if the Minister is the highway authority, he shall not serve a notice restraining the erection of any building on the land except with the consent of the Welsh council in whose area the land is situated.

(4) A copy of a notice under subsection (1)(a) above shall be served on the owner or on the occupier of any land according as the notice was served on the occupier or on the owner of it.

(5) A notice under subsection (1)(b) above does not prevent any owner, lessee or occupier of any land from executing or permitting the reconstruction or repair, in such manner as not to create any new obstruction to the view of persons using the adjacent highways, of any building which was on the land before the service of the notice.

(6) A restriction imposed by a notice under subsection (1) above comes into force on the service of the notice and, while in force, is binding on the successor in title to every owner, and on every lessee and every occupier, of the land to which it relates.

(7) A person on whom a notice has been served under subsection (1) above may, within 14 days from the date of the receipt of the notice by him, give notice to the authority by whom the notice was given objecting to any requirement specified in it, or to any restriction imposed by it, and stating reasons for his objections.

(8) Where notice is given under subsection (7) above the question whether the notice under subsection (1) above is to be withdrawn as respects any requirement or restriction objected to shall be determined, if the parties so agree, by a single arbitrator appointed by them and, in default of agreement, shall be determined by a county court, and in determining a question under this subsection the arbitrator or court shall have power to order that the requirement or restriction objected to shall have effect subject to such modifications, if any, as the arbitrator or court may direct.

(9) A person on whom a notice is served under subsection (1) above may, notwithstanding

anything in any conveyance, or in any lease or other agreement, do all such things as may be necessary for complying with the requirements of the notice.

(10) Subject to the provisions of this section, if a person on whom a notice is served under subsection (1) above contravenes the provisions of the notice, he is, without prejudice to any other proceedings which may be available against him, guilty of an offence and liable to a fine not exceeding **level 1** on the standard scale; and if the offence is continued after conviction, he is guilty of a further offence and liable to a fine not exceeding £2 for each day on which the offence is so continued.

(11) Any person sustaining loss in direct consequence of any requirement of a notice served under subsection (1) above, and any person who proves that his property is injuriously affected by restrictions imposed by a notice served under that subsection, is entitled, if he makes a claim within 6 months from the date of service of the notice, to recover from the authority by whom the notice was served compensation for the injury sustained.

(12) A person on whom a notice is served under subsection (1) above is entitled to recover from the authority by whom the notice was served any expenses¹ reasonably incurred by him in carrying out any directions contained in the notice.

(13) If any question arises under subsection (12) above whether any expenses were reasonably incurred by any person as there provided, it shall be determined, if the parties so agree, by a single arbitrator appointed by them and, in default of agreement, shall be determined by a county court.

(14) Any two or more authorities on whom powers are conferred by this section may by agreement exercise those powers jointly, and the agreement may provide for the apportionment of any expenses incurred under it.

(15) Nothing in this section—

(a) authorises the service by a local highway authority of a notice under this section with respect to any wall forming part of an ancient monument or other object of archaeological interest, except with the consent of the Secretary of State; or

(b) applies with respect to a wall belonging to any of the following undertakers, that is to say, railway undertakers, canal undertakers, inland navigation undertakers, dock undertakers, or harbour undertakers, where the wall forms part of or is necessary for the maintenance of a railway comprised in the railway undertaking, a canal comprised in the inland navigation undertaking, a navigation comprised in the inland navigation undertaking, a dock comprised in the dock undertaking, or a harbour comprised in the harbour undertaking.

(16) In relation to any prohibition or restriction on the use of land or buildings imposed by the Minister by a notice served by him under this section, section 1(1)(c) of the Local Land Charges Act 1975 has effect as if the references to the date of the commencement of that Act were omitted.

(17) In this section—

"building" includes any erection however, and with whatever material, it is constructed, and any part of a building;

"wall" includes any partition, with whatever material it is constructed, and any bank.

[Highways Act 1980, s 79 as amended by the Criminal Justice Act 1982, s 46, the Local Government Act 1985, Sch 4 and the Local Government (Wales) Act 1994, Sch 7.]

---

1. For recovery of expenses, see s 305, post; and for limitation of time for summary proceedings therefore, see s 306, post; for power to include several sums in one complaint, see s 313, post.

7–5993 100. Drainage of highways.   (1) The highway authority for a highway may, for the purpose of draining it or of otherwise preventing surface water from flowing on to it, do all or any of the following:—

(a) construct or lay, in the highway or in land adjoining or lying near to the highway, such drains as they consider necessary;

(b) erect barriers in the highway or in such land as aforesaid to divert surface water into or through any existing drain;

(c) scour, cleanse and keep open all drains situated in the highway or in such land as aforesaid.

(2) Where under subsection (1) above a drain is constructed or laid, or barriers are erected, for the purpose of draining surface water from a highway or, as the case may be, diverting it into an existing drain, the water may be discharged into or through that drain and into any inland waters, whether natural or artificial, or any tidal waters.

(3) A highway authority shall pay compensation to the owner or occupier of any land who suffers damage by reason of the exercise by the authority of any power under subsection (1) or (2) above.

(4) If a person, without the consent of the highway authority, alters, obstructs or interferes with a drain or barrier which has been constructed, laid or erected by the authority in exercise of their powers under subsection (1) above, or which is under their control, then—

(a) the authority may carry out any work of repair or reinstatement necessitated by his action and may recover from him the expenses reasonably incurred by them in so doing, and

(b) without prejudice to their right to exercise that power, he is guilty of an offence and liable to a fine not exceeding three times the amount of those expenses.

(5) Without prejudice to their powers under the foregoing provisions of this section, a highway authority may, for the purpose of the drainage of a highway or proposed highway for which they are or, as the case may be, will be the highway authority, exercise any powers exercisable by a sewage undertaker under sections 158, 159, 163, 165 and 168 of the Water Industry Act 1991 for the purposes of the drainage of highways within the area of that undertaker.

(6) Where the highway authority are a county council they shall, before exercising any powers under sections 158, 159, 163, 165 and 168 of the Water Industry Act 1991 by virtue of subsection (5) above, give notice of their intention to do so to the district council, and the sewerage undertaker, within whose area the powers are proposed to be exercised; and where the highway authority are a metropolitan district council they shall, before so exercising any powers under that Act, give such notice to the sewerage undertaker within whose area the powers are proposed to be exercised.

(6A) In subsection (6) above, "the district council" shall be read, in relation to Wales, as "the Welsh council".

(6B) Where the highway authority are a Welsh council—

(a) subsection (6) above does not apply; but
(b) before exercising any powers under sections 158, 159, 163, 165 and 168 of the Water Industry Act 1991 by virtue of subsection (5) above, they shall give notice of their intention to do so—

(i) to the sewerage undertaker; and
(ii) where they propose to exercise those powers outside their county or county borough, to the Welsh council or, as the case may be, the district council

within whose area the powers are proposed to be exercised.

(7) A person who is liable to maintain a highway by reason of tenure, enclosure or prescription shall, for the purpose of draining it, have the like powers as are conferred on a highway authority by subsections (1) and (2) above for that purpose, and subsections (3) and (4) above shall have effect in relation to a highway so maintainable as if references therein to a highway authority and to subsection (1) or (2) above included references to the person liable to maintain that highway and to this subsection respectively.

(8) This section is without prejudice to any enactment the purpose of which is to protect water against pollution.

(9) In this section—

"drain" includes a ditch, gutter, watercourse, soak-away, bridge, culvert, tunnel and pipe; and
"owner", in relation to any land, means a person, other than a mortgagee not in possession, who is for the time being entitled to dispose of the fee simple in the land, whether in possession or in reversion, and includes also a person holding or entitled to the rents and profits of the land under a lease the unexpired term of which exceeds 3 years.

[Highways Act 1980, s 100 as amended by the Local Government Act 1985, Sch 4, the Water Act 1989, Sch 25, the Water Consolidation (Consequential Provisions) Act 1991, Sch 1 and the Local Government (Wales) Act 1994, Sch 7.]

7–5994 101. Power to fill in roadside ditches etc. (1) If it appears to the highway authority for any highway that a ditch on land adjoining or lying near to the highway constitutes a danger to users of the highway, the authority may—

(a) if they consider the ditch unnecessary for drainage purposes and any occupier of the land known to the authority agrees in writing that it is unnecessary for those purposes, fill it in; or
(b) place in the ditch, or in land adjoining or lying near to it, such pipes as they consider necessary in substitution for the ditch, and thereafter fill it in.

(2) A highway authority shall pay compensation to the owner or occupier of any land who suffers damage by reason of the exercise by the authority of any power under subsection (1) above.

(3) If a person, without the consent of the highway authority, opens up or keeps open any ditch which has been filled in under subsection (1) above (except as may be reasonably necessary for the purpose of doing work on any pipes placed in the ditch), then—

(a) the authority may carry out any work of repair or reinstatement necessitated by his action and may recover from him the expenses reasonably incurred by them in so doing; and
(b) without prejudice to their right to exercise that power, he is guilty of an offence and liable to a fine not exceeding three times the amount of those expenses.

(4) Nothing in section 263 of the Public Health Act 1936 (which prohibits the culverting of watercourses in certain districts without the approval of the local authority) applies to anything done under subsection (1) above.

(5) A highway authority shall not exercise their powers under subsection (1) above in such a manner as to be likely to cause damage to or affect the drainage of any land or works used for the purposes of a railway or canal undertaking, except—

(a) after giving not less than 14 days' notice to the undertakers of the manner in which it is proposed to exercise those powers; and
(b) in accordance with any reasonable requirements of the undertakers of which notice is given to the authority within 14 days from the date of service of the authority's notice;

and any question whether any such requirement is reasonable shall, in default of agreement, be determined by the Minister.

(6) In this section, "ditch" includes a watercourse and any part of a ditch or watercourse, and "pipes" including culverts, tunnels and other works.

[Highways Act 1980, s 101.]

7–5995

PART VI[1]

CONSTRUCTION OF BRIDGES OVER AND TUNNELS UNDER NAVIGABLE WATERS AND DIVERSION ETC OF WATERCOURSES

---

1. Part VI contains ss 106–111.

7–5996

PART VII[1]

PROVISION OF SPECIAL FACILITIES FOR HIGHWAYS

---

1. Part VII contains ss 112–115.

7–5997

PART VIIA[1]

PROVISION OF AMENITIES ON CERTAIN HIGHWAYS

---

1. Part VIIA which was inserted by the Local Government (Miscellaneous Provisions) Act 1982, Sch 5, contains ss 115A–115K.

PART VIII[1]

STOPPING UP AND DIVERSION OF HIGHWAYS AND STOPPING UP OF MEANS OF ACCESS TO HIGHWAYS

Stopping up and diversion of highways

7–5998   116. Power of magistrates' court to authorise stopping up or diversion of highway.
(1) Subject to the provisions of this section, if it appears to a magistrates' court, after a view, if the court thinks fits, by any two or more of the justices composing the court, that a highway (other than a trunk road or a special road) as respects which the highway authority have made an application under this section—

   (*a*)   is unnecessary[2], or
   (*b*)   can be diverted so as to make it nearer or more commodious to the public,

the court may by order authorise it to be stopped up or, as the case may be, to be so diverted.

(2) *(Repealed)*.

(3) If an authority propose to make an application under this section for an order relating to any highway (other than a classified road) they shall give notice[3] of the proposal to—

   (*a*)   if the highway is in a non-metropolitan district, the council of that district; and
   (*aa*) if the highway is in Wales, the Welsh council for the area in which it is situated if they are not the highway authority for it; and
   (*b*)   if the highway is in England, the council of the parish (if any) in which the highway is situated or, if the parish does not have a separate parish council, to the chairman of the parish meeting; and
   (*c*)   if the highway is in Wales, the council (if any) of the community in which the highway is situated;

and the application shall not be made if within 2 months from the date of service of the notice by the authority notice is given to the authority by the district council or Welsh council or by the parish or community council or, as the case may be, by the chairman of the parish meeting that the council or meeting have refused to consent to the making of the application.

(4) An application[4] under this section may be made, and an order under it may provide, for the stopping up or diversion of a highway for the purposes of all traffic, or subject to the reservation of a footpath or bridleway.

(5) An application or order under this section may include 2 or more highways which are connected with each other.

(6) A magistrates' court shall not make an order under this section unless it is satisfied that the applicant authority have given the notices required by Part I of Schedule 12 to this Act[5].

(7) On the hearing of an application under this section the applicant authority, any person[6] to whom notice is required to be given under paragraph 1 of Schedule 12, any person who uses the highway and any other person[6] who would be aggrieved by the making of the order applied for, have a right to be heard.

(8) An order under this section authorising the diversion of a highway—

(*a*) shall not be made unless the written consent of every person having a legal interest in the land over which the highway is to be diverted is produced to and deposited with the court; and

(*b*) except in so far as the carrying out of the diversion may necessitate temporary interference with the highway, shall not authorise the stopping up of any part of the highway until the new part to be substituted for the part to be stopped up (including, where a diversion falls to be carried out under orders of 2 different courts, any necessary continuation of the new part in the area of the other court) has been completed to the satisfaction of 2 justices of the peace acting for the same petty sessions area as the court by which the order was made and a certificate to that effect signed by them has been transmitted to the clerk of the applicant authority.

(9) Every order under this section shall have annexed to it a plan signed by the chairman of the court and shall be transmitted by the clerk of the court to the proper officer of the applicant authority, together with any written consents produced to the court under subsection (8) above.

(10) Part II of Schedule 12 to this Act applies where, in pursuance of an order under this section, a highway is stopped up or diverted and, immediately before the order is made, there is under, in, upon, over, along or across the highway any apparatus belonging to or used by any statutory undertakers for the purpose of their undertaking.

(11) In this section "statutory undertakers" includes operators of driver information systems.

[Highways Act 1980, s 116 as amended by the Local Government Act 1985, Schs 4 and 17, the Road Traffic (Driver Licensing and Information Systems) Act 1989, Sch 4 and the Local Government (Wales) Act 1994, Sch 7.]

1. Part VIII contains ss 116–129.

2. In deciding if a highway is unnecessary, justices should consider to whom the highway is unnecessary. If it is for the benefit of the public, the justices should ask themselves for what purpose the highway is unnecessary. Where there is evidence that the way is currently in use, it will be prima facie difficult for justices to come to the view that the way is unnecessary unless the public is going to be provided with an alternative (*Ramblers Association v Kent County Council* (1990) 154 JP 716, DC; applied in *Westley v Hertfordshire County Council* (1995) 160 JP 813).

3. For form of notice and its authentication and service, see ss 320–322, post.

4. Appeal lies to the Crown Court against the decision of a magistrates' court: s 317, post.

5. The requirements imposed by s 116(6) are mandatory and justices have no power to dispense with them (*Ramblers Association v Kent County Council* (1990) 154 JP 716, DC).

6. Part I of this Schedule, post, sets out detailed provisions for notices to be given to interested parties, displayed at the ends of the highway, and published in the London Gazette and a local newspaper.

7–5999 117. Application for order under section 116 on behalf of another person. A person who desires a highway to be stopped up or diverted but is not authorised to make an application for that purpose under section 116 above may request the highway authority to make such an application; and if the authority grant the request they may, as a condition of making the application, require him to make such provision for any costs to be incurred by them in connection with the matter as they deem reasonable.

[Highways Act 1980, s 117 as amended by the Local Government Act 1985, Sch 17.]

118B–119B. *Stopping up and diversion of certain highways for purposes of crime prevention, etc.*[1].

1. These sections (inserted by paras 8 and 12 of Sch 6 to the Countryside and Rights of Way Act 2000) enable a council (which is a highway authority), for the purposes of crime prevention, to make orders for the stopping up or diversion of certain highways within areas designated by the Secretary of State under s 118B(1)(*a*) of the 1980 Act. The following Crime (Designated Areas) Orders have been made: SI 2003/2208; SI 2004/1239; SI 2005/914; SI 2005/2463; SI 2006/302. Apart from crime prevention orders, the following regulations have also been made under various provisions of this Act including ss 118B(9), (10) and 119(12) and (13): Highways (Schools) (Special Extinguishment and Special Diversion Orders) (Wales) Regulations 2005, SI 2005/1809.

Stopping up of means of access to highways

7–6000 128. Penalty for using access which has been stopped up. Any person who uses an access which has been stopped up by virtue of section 124, 125 or 127 above[1] other than a person exercising a public right of way is guilty of an offence and liable to a fine not exceeding **level 3** on the standard scale.

[Highways Act 1980, s 128 as amended by the Criminal Justice Act 1982, ss 38 and 46.]

1. These sections provide a mechanism and procedure for stopping up private access to highways and to premises, with an entitlement to compensation from the appropriate authority.

PART IX[1]
LAWFUL AND UNLAWFUL INTERFERENCE WITH HIGHWAYS AND STREETS

Protection of public rights

7–6001 130. Protection of public rights. (1) It is the duty of the highway authority to assert and protect the rights of the public to the use and enjoyment of any highway for which they are the highway authority, including any roadside waste which forms part of it.

(2) Any council may assert and protect the rights of the public to the use and enjoyment of any highway in their area for which they are not the highway authority, including any roadside waste which forms part of it.

(3) Without prejudice to subsections (1) and (2) above, it is the duty of a council who are a highway authority to prevent, as far as possible, the stopping up or obstruction of—

(a) the highways for which they are the highway authority, and

(b) any highway for which they are not the highway authority, if, in their opinion, the stopping up or obstruction of that highway would be prejudicial to the interests of their area.

(4) Without prejudice to the foregoing provisions of this section, it is the duty of a local highway authority to prevent any unlawful encroachment on any roadside waste comprised in a highway for which they are the highway authority.

(5) Without prejudice to their powers under section 222 of the Local Government Act 1972, a council may, in the performance of their functions under the foregoing provisions of this section, institute legal proceedings in their own name, defend any legal proceedings and generally take such steps as they deem expedient.

(6) If the council of a parish or community or, in the case of a parish or community which does not have a separate parish or community council, the parish meeting or a community meeting, represent to a local highway authority—

(a) that a highway as to which the local highway authority have the duty imposed by subsection (3) above has been unlawfully stopped up or obstructed, or

(b) that an unlawful encroachment has taken place on a roadside waste comprised in a highway for which they are the highway authority,

it is the duty of the local highway authority, unless satisfied that the representations are incorrect, to take proper proceedings accordingly and they may do so in their own name.

(7) Proceedings or steps taken by a council in relation to an alleged right of way are not to be treated as unauthorised by reason only that the alleged right is found not to exist.

[Highways Act 1980, s 130.]

---

1. Part IX contains ss 130–185.

7–6001A   130A. Notices to enforce duty regarding public paths.

(1) Any person who alleges, as respects any highway for which a local highway authority other than an inner London authority are the highway authority—

(a) that the highway falls within subsection (2) below, and

(b) that it is obstructed by an obstruction to which this section applies,

may serve on the highway authority notice requesting them to secure the removal of the obstruction from the highway.

(2) A highway is within this subsection if it is—

(a) a footpath, bridleway, or restricted byway, or

(b) a way shown in a definitive map and statement as a restricted byway or a byway open to all traffic.

(3) Subject to subsection (4) below, this section applies to an obstruction of the highway if the obstruction is without lawful authority and either—

(a) the powers conferred by section 143, 149 or 154 below are exercisable in respect of it, or

(b) it is of a description prescribed by regulations made by the Secretary of State and the authority have power (otherwise than under any of those sections) to secure its removal.

(4) This section does not apply to an obstruction if—

(a) it is or forms part of—

(i) a building (whether temporary or permanent) or works for the construction of a building, or

(ii) any other structure (including a tent, caravan, vehicle or other temporary or movable structure) which is designed, adapted or used for human habitation,

(b) an order may be made in respect of it under section 56 above, or

(c) the presence of any person constitutes the obstruction.

(5) A person serving a notice under subsection (1) above must include in the notice the name and address, if known to him, of any person who it appears to him may be for the time being responsible for the obstruction.

(6) A highway authority on whom a notice under subsection (1) above is served shall, within one month from the date of service of the notice, serve—

(a) on every person whose name and address is, pursuant to subsection (5) above, included in the notice and, so far as reasonably practicable, on every other person who it appears to them may be for the time being responsible for the obstruction, a notice informing that person that a notice under subsection (1) above has been served in relation to the obstruction and stating what, if any, action the authority propose to take, and

(b) on the person who served the notice under subsection (1) above, a notice containing the name and address of each person on whom notice is served under paragraph (a) above and stating what, if any, action the authority propose to take in relation to the obstruction.

(7) For the purposes of this section the persons for the time being responsible for an obstruction include the owner and any other person who for the time being—

(a) has possession or control of it, or

(b) may be required to remove it.

(8) A notice under subsection (1) or (6) above shall be in such form and contain such information as may be prescribed by regulations[1] made by the Secretary of State.

(9) In this section "inner London authority" means Transport for London, the council of an inner London borough or the Common Council of the City of London.

(10) Subsection (2) above has effect until the commencement of section 47 of the Countryside and Rights of Way Act 2000 with the substitution for the references to a restricted byway and to a way shown in a definitive map and statement as a restricted byway of a reference to a way shown in a definitive map and statement as a road used as a public path.*

[Highways Act 1980, s 130A, as inserted by the Countryside and Rights of Way Act 2000, s 103(3).]

---

*Section 130A is printed as prospectively inserted by the Countryside and Rights of Way Act 2000, s 63.
1. The Removal of Obstructions from Highways (Wales) Regulations 2004, SI 2004/317 and the Removal of Obstructions from Highways (Notices etc) (England) Regulations 2004, SI 2004/370 have been made.

7–6001B 130B. Orders following notice under section 130A. (1) Where a notice under section 130A(1) above has been served on a highway authority in relation to any obstruction, the person who served it, if not satisfied that the obstruction has been removed, may apply to a magistrates' court in accordance with section 130C below for an order under this section.

(2) An order under this section is an order requiring the highway authority to take, within such reasonable period as may be fixed by the order, such steps as may be specified in the order for securing the removal of the obstruction.

(3) An order under this section shall not take effect—

(a) until the end of the period of twenty-one days from the day on which the order is made; or

(b) if an appeal is brought in respect of the order within that period (whether by way of appeal to the Crown Court or by way of case stated for the opinion of the High Court), until the final determination or withdrawal of the appeal.

(4) Subject to subsection (5) below, the court may make an order under this section if it is satisfied—

(a) that the obstruction is one to which section 130A above applies or, in a case falling within subsection (4)(a)(ii) of that section, is one to which that section would apply but for the obstruction having become used for human habitation since service of the notice relating to it under subsection (1) of that section,

(b) that the way obstructed is a highway within subsection (2) of that section, and

(c) that the obstruction significantly interferes with the exercise of public rights of way over that way.

(5) No order shall be made under this section if the highway authority satisfy the court—

(a) that the fact that the way obstructed is a highway within section 130A(2) above is seriously disputed,

(b) on any other grounds, that they have no duty under section 130(3) above to secure the removal of the obstruction, or

(c) that, under arrangements which have been made by the authority, its removal will be secured within a reasonable time, having regard to the number and seriousness of obstructions in respect of which they have such a duty.

(6) A highway authority against whom an order is made under this section shall, as soon as practicable after the making of the order, cause notice of the order and of the right to appeal against it to be displayed in such manner and at such places on the highway concerned as may be prescribed by regulations[1] made by the Secretary of State, and the notice shall be in such form and contain such information as may be so prescribed.

(7) An order under this section may be varied on the application of the highway authority to whom it relates.*

[Highways Act 1980, s 130B, as inserted by the Countryside and Rights of Way Act 2000, s 103(3).]

---

*Section 130B is printed as prospectively inserted by the Countryside and Rights of Way Act 2000, s 63.
1. The Removal of Obstructions from Highways (Wales) Regulations 2004, SI 2004/317 and the Removal of Obstructions from Highways (Notices etc.) (England) Regulations 2004, SI 2004/370 have been made.

7–6001C   130C. Section 130B: procedure.   (1) A person proposing to make an application under section 130B above shall before making the application serve notice of his intention to do so on the highway authority concerned.

(2) A notice under subsection (1) above shall be in such form and contain such information as may be prescribed by regulations[1] made by the Secretary of State.

(3) The notice may not be served before the end of two months beginning with the date of service on the highway authority of the notice under section 130A(1) above ("the request notice").

(4) An application in respect of which notice has been served under subsection (1) above may be made at any time—

(a)   after the end of five days beginning with the date of service of that notice, and

(b)   before the end of six months beginning with the date of service on the highway authority of the request notice.

(5) On making the application the applicant must give notice to the court of the names and addresses of which notice was given to the applicant under section 130A(6)(b) above.

(6) On the hearing of the application any person who is, within the meaning of section 130A above, a person for the time being responsible for the obstruction to which the application relates has a right to be heard as respects the matters mentioned in section 130B(4) above.

(7) Notice of the hearing, of the right to be heard under subsection (6) above and of the right to appeal against a decision on the application shall be given by the court to each person whose name and address is notified to the court under subsection (5) above.★

[Highways Act 1980, s 130C, as inserted by the Countryside and Rights of Way Act 2000, s 103(3).]

★**Section 130C is printed as prospectively inserted by the Countryside and Rights of Way Act 2000, s 63.**
1. The Removal of Obstructions from Highways (Wales) Regulations 2004, SI 2004/317 and the Removal of Obstructions from Highways (Notices etc.) (England) Regulations 2004, SI 2004/370 have been made.

7–6001D   130D. Section 130B: costs.   Where an application under section 130B above is dismissed by virtue of paragraph (a), (b) or (c) of subsection (5) of that section, the court, in determining whether and if so how to exercise its power under section 64(1) of the Magistrates' Courts Act 1980 (costs), shall have particular regard to any failure by the highway authority to give the applicant appropriate notice of, and information about, the grounds relied on by the authority under that paragraph.★

[Highways Act 1980, s 130D, as inserted by the Countryside and Rights of Way Act 2000, s 103(3).]

★**Section 130D is printed as prospectively inserted by the Countryside and Rights of Way Act 2000, s 63.**

Damage to highways, streets etc

7–6002   131. Penalty for damaging highway etc.   (1) If a person, without lawful authority or excuse—

(a)   makes a ditch or excavation in a highway which consists of or comprises a carriageway, or

(b)   removes any soil or turf from any part of a highway, except for the purpose of improving the highway and with the consent of the highway authority for the highway, or

(c)   deposits anything whatsoever on a highway so as to damage the highway, or

(d)   lights any fire, or discharges any firearm or firework, within 50 feet from the centre of a highway which consists of or comprises a carriageway, and in consequence thereof the highway is damaged,

he is guilty of an offence.

(2) If a person without lawful authority or excuse pulls down or obliterates a traffic sign placed on or over a highway, or a milestone or direction post (not being a traffic sign) so placed, he is guilty of an offence; but it is a defence in any proceedings under this subsection to show that the traffic sign, milestone or post was not lawfully so placed.

(3) A person guilty of an offence under this section is liable to a fine not exceeding **level 3** on the standard scale.

[Highways Act 1980, s 131 as amended by the Criminal Justice Act 1982, ss 35, 38 and 46.]

7–6003   131A. Disturbance of surface of certain highways.   (1) A person who, without lawful authority or excuse, so disturbs the surface of—

(a)   a footpath,

(b)   a bridleway, or

(c)   any other highway which consists of or comprises a carriageway other than a made-up carriageway,

as to render it inconvenient for the exercise of the public right of way is guilty of an offence and liable to a fine not exceeding **level 3** on the standard scale.

(2) Proceedings for an offence under this section shall be brought only by the highway authority or the council of the non-metropolitan district, parish or community in which the offence is

committed; and, without prejudice to section 130 (protection of public rights) above, it is the duty of the highway authority to ensure that where desirable in the public interest such proceedings are brought.
[Highways Act 1980, s 131A, added by the Rights of Way Act 1990, s 1.]

7–6004   132. Unauthorised marks on highways.   (1) A person who, without either the consent of the highway authority for the highway in question or an authorisation given by or under an enactment or a reasonable excuse, paints or otherwise inscribes or affixes any picture, letter, sign or other mark upon the surface of a highway or upon any tree, structure or works on or in a highway is guilty of an offence and liable to a fine not exceeding **level 4** on the standard scale.

(2) The highway authority for a highway may, without prejudice to their powers apart from this subsection and whether or not proceedings in respect of the matter have been taken in pursuance of subsection (1) above, remove any picture, letter, sign or other mark which has, without either the consent of the authority or an authorisation given by or under an enactment, been painted or otherwise inscribed or affixed upon the surface of the highway or upon any tree, structure or works on or in the highway.
[Highways Act 1980, s 132 as amended by the Criminal Justice Act 1982, ss 35, 38 and 46.]

7–6005   133. Damage to footways of streets by excavations.   If the footway of a street that is a highway maintainable at the public expense is damaged by or in consequence of any excavation or other work on land adjoining the street, the highway authority for the highway may make good the damage and recover the expenses reasonably incurred by them in so doing from the owner of the land in question or the person causing or responsible for the damage.
[Highways Act 1980, s 133.]

7–6006   134. Ploughing etc. of footpath or bridleway.   Where in the case of any footpath or bridleway (other than a field-edge path) which passes over a field or enclosure consisting of agricultural land, or land which is being brought into use for agriculture—

(a) the occupier of the field or enclosure desires in accordance with the rules of good husbandry to plough, or otherwise disturb the surface of, all or part of the land comprised in the field or enclosure, and

(b) it is not reasonably convenient in ploughing, or otherwise disturbing the surface of, the land to avoid disturbing the surface of the path or way so as to render it inconvenient for the exercise of the public right of way,

the public right of way shall be subject to the condition that the occupier has the right so to plough or otherwise disturb the surface of the path or way.

(2) Subsection (1) above does not apply in relation to any excavation or any engineering operation.

(3) Where the occupier has disturbed the surface of a footpath or bridleway under the right conferred by subsection (1) above he shall within the relevant period, or within an extension of that period granted under subsection (8) below,—

(a) so make good the surface of the path or way to not less than its minimum width as to make it reasonably convenient for the exercise of the right of way; and

(b) so indicate the line of the path or way on the ground to not less than its minimum width that it is apparent to members of the public wishing to use it.

(4) If the occupier fails to comply with the duty imposed by subsection (3) above he is guilty of an offence and liable to a fine not exceeding **level 3** on the standard scale.

(5) *Repealed.*

(6) Without prejudice to section 130 (protection of public rights) above, it is the duty of the highway authority to enforce the provisions of this section.

(7) For the purposes of this section "the relevant period",—

(a) where the disturbance of the surface of the path or way is the first disturbance for the purposes of the sowing of a particular agricultural crop, means fourteen days beginning with the day on which the surface of the path or way was first disturbed for those purposes; or

(b) in any other case, means twenty-four hours beginning with the time when it was disturbed.

(8) On an application made to the highway authority before the disturbance or during the relevant period, the authority may grant an extension of that period for an additional period not exceeding twenty-eight days.

(9) In this section "minimum width", in relation to a highway, has the same meaning as in Schedule 12A to this Act.
[Highways Act 1980, s 134 as substituted by the Rights of Way Act 1990, s 1 and amended by the Countryside and Rights of Way Act 2000, Sch 16.]

7–6007   135. Authorisation of other works disturbing footpath or bridleway.   (1) Where the occupier of any agricultural land, or land which is being brought into use for agriculture, desires to carry out in relation to that land an excavation or engineering operation, and the excavation or operation—

(*a*)　is reasonably necessary for the purposes of agriculture, but
(*b*)　will so disturb the surface of a footpath or bridleway which passes over that land as to render it inconvenient for the exercise of the public right of way,

he may apply to the highway authority for an order that the public right of way shall be subject to the condition that he has the right to disturb the surface by that excavation or operation during such period, not exceeding three months, as is specified in the order ("the authorisation period").

(2)　The highway authority shall make an order under subsection (1) above if they are satisfied either—

(*a*)　that it is practicable temporarily to divert the path or way in a manner reasonably convenient to users; or
(*b*)　that it is practicable to take adequate steps to ensure that the path or way remains sufficiently convenient, having regard to the need for the excavation or operation, for temporary use while it is being carried out.

(3)　An order made by a highway authority under subsection (1) above—

(*a*)　may provide for the temporary diversion of the path or way during the authorisation period, but shall not divert it on to land not occupied by the applicant unless written consent to the making of the order has been given by the occupier of that land, and by any other person whose consent is needed to obtain access to it;
(*b*)　may include such conditions as the authority reasonably think fit for the provision, either by the applicant or by the authority at the expense of the applicant, of facilities for the convenient use of any such diversion, including signposts and other notices, stiles, bridges, and gates;
(*c*)　shall not affect the line of a footpath or bridleway on land not occupied by the applicant;

and the authority shall cause notices of any such diversion, together with a plan showing the effect of the diversion and the line of the alternative route provided, to be prominently displayed throughout the authorisation period at each end of the diversion.

(4)　An order made by a highway authority under subsection (1) above may include such conditions as the authority reasonably think fit—

(*a*)　for the protection and convenience during the authorisation period of users of the path or way;
(*b*)　for making good the surface of the path or way to not more than its minimum width before the expiration of the authorisation period;
(*c*)　for the recovery from the applicant of expenses incurred by the authority in connection with the order.

(5)　An order under this section shall not authorise any interference with the apparatus or works of any statutory undertakers.

(6)　If the applicant fails to comply with a condition imposed under subsection (3)(*b*) or 4(*a*) or (*b*) above he is guilty of an offence and liable to a fine not exceeding **level 3** on the standard scale.

(7)　Proceedings for an offence under this section in relation to a footpath or bridleway shall be brought only by the highway authority or (with the consent of the highway authority) the council of the non-metropolitan district, parish or community in which the offence is committed.

(8)　Without prejudice to section 130 (protection of public rights) above, it is the duty of the highway authority to enforce the provisions of this section.

(9)　In this section "minimum width", in relation to a highway, has the same meaning as in Schedule 12A to this Act.

[Highways Act 1980, s 135 as substituted by the Rights of Way Act 1990, s 1.]

7–6007A　135A.　Temporary diversion for dangerous works.　　(1) Where works of a prescribed description are likely to cause danger to users of a footpath or bridleway which passes over any land, the occupier of the land may, subject to the provisions of this section, temporarily divert—

(*a*)　so much of the footpath or bridleway as passes over that land, and
(*b*)　so far as is requisite for effecting that diversion, so much of the footpath or bridleway as passes over other land occupied by him.

(2)　A person may not under this section divert any part of a footpath or bridleway if—

(*a*)　the period or periods for which that part has been diverted under this section, and
(*b*)　the period or periods for which any other part of the same footpath or bridleway passing over land occupied by him has been diverted under this section,

amount in aggregate to more than fourteen days in any one calendar year.

(3)　Where a person diverts a footpath or bridleway under this section—

(*a*)　he shall do so in a manner which is reasonably convenient for the exercise of the public right of way, and
(*b*)　where the diversion is by means of a temporary footpath or bridleway, he shall so indicate the line of the temporary footpath or bridleway on the ground to not less than the minimum width that it is apparent to members of the public wishing to use it.

(4) This section does not authorise a person—

(a) to divert a footpath or bridleway on to land not occupied by him without the consent of the occupier of that land and of any other person whose consent is needed to obtain access to it,

(b) to divert a footpath onto a highway other than a footpath or bridleway, or

(c) to divert a bridleway onto a highway other than a bridleway.

(5) The person by whom a footpath or bridleway is diverted under this section shall—

(a) at least fourteen days before the commencement of the diversion, give notice of the diversion in accordance with subsection (6) below,

(b) at least seven days before the commencement of the diversion, publish notice of the diversion in a local newspaper circulating in the area in which the footpath or bridleway is situated, and

(c) display such notices as may be prescribed at such places, in such manner and at such times before or during the diversion as may be prescribed.

(6) Notice under subsection (5)(a) above shall be given—

(a) to the highway authority for the footpath or bridleway,

(b) if the footpath or bridleway is on or contiguous with access land in England, to the Countryside Agency, and

(c) if the footpath or bridleway is on or contiguous with access land in Wales, to the Countryside Council for Wales.

(7) A notice under subsection (5)(a), (b) or (c) above shall be in such form and contain such information as may be prescribed.

(8) If a person—

(a) in a notice which purports to comply with the requirements of subsection (5)(a) or (b) above, makes a statement which he knows to be false in a material particular,

(b) by a notice displayed on or near a footpath or bridleway, falsely purports to be authorised under this section to divert the footpath or bridleway, or

(c) in diverting a footpath or bridleway under this section, fails to comply with subsection (3) above,

he shall be guilty of an offence and liable to a fine not exceeding level 3 on the standard scale.

(9) In this section—

"access land" has the same meaning as in Part I of the Countryside and Rights of Way Act 2000;

"minimum width" in relation to a temporary footpath or bridleway, means the minimum width, within the meaning of Schedule 12A to this Act, of the footpath or bridleway diverted;

"prescribed" means prescribed by regulations made by the Secretary of State.*

[Highways Act 1980, s 135A, as inserted by the Countryside and Rights of Way Act 2000, s 103(3).]

---

*Section 135A is printed as prospectively inserted by the Countryside and Rights of Way Act 2000, Sch 6 from a date to be appointed.

7–6007B   135B. Temporary diversion for dangerousworks: supplementary. (1) The person by whom a footpath or bridleway is diverted under section 135A above shall, before the diversion ceases to be authorised by that section, make good any damage to the footpath or bridleway resulting from the works mentioned in subsection (1) of that section, and remove from the footpath or bridleway any obstruction resulting from those works.

(2) Any person who fails to comply with the duty imposed on him by subsection (1) above is guilty of an offence and liable to a fine not exceeding level 3 on the standard scale.

(3) The highway authority may make good any damage, or remove any obstruction, in respect of which any person has failed to comply with that duty and recover from that person the amount of any expenses reasonably incurred by them in or in connection with doing so.

(4) Paragraph 3(1) of Schedule 12A to this Act does not apply in relation to any disturbance of the surface of a footpath or bridleway which subsection (1) above requires any person to make good; but paragraphs 7 and 8 of that Schedule apply for the purposes of subsection (3) above as if—

(a) references to the authority were references to the highway authority,

(b) references to the work were references to work carried out under subsection (3) above in relation to a footpath or bridleway, and

(c) references to the relevant land were references to the land over which the footpath or bridleway passes.

(5) The diversion of a footpath or bridleway under section 135A above does not—

(a) affect the liability of any person for anything done in relation to the path or way otherwise than for the purposes of or in consequence of the works mentioned in subsection (1) of that section, or

(b) authorise any interference with the apparatus or works of any statutory undertakers.

(6) Without prejudice to section 130 (protection of public rights of way) above, it is the duty of the highway authority to enforce the provisions of section 135A and this section.★

[Highways Act 1980, s 135, as inserted by the Countryside and Rights of Way Act 2000, s 103(3).]

★**Section 135B is printed as prospectively inserted by the Countryside and Rights of Way Act 2000, Sch 6.**

7–6008   136. Damage to highway consequent on exclusion of sun and wind.   (1) If a highway which consists of or comprises a carriageway is being damaged in consequence of the exclusion from it of the sun and wind by a hedge or tree (other than a tree planted for ornament or for shelter to a building, courtyard or hop ground), a magistrates' court may by order require the owner or occupier of the land on which the hedge or tree is growing, so to cut, prune or plash the hedge or prune or lop the tree as to remove the cause of damage.

(2) The power of a magistrates' court to make an order under subsection (1) above is exercisable on a complaint made by the highway authority for the highway, or, in the case of a highway maintainable by reason of tenure, enclosure or prescription, by the person liable to maintain the highway.

(3) If a person against whom an order under subsection (1) above is made fails to comply with it within 10 days from such date as may be specified in the order, he is guilty of an offence and liable to a fine not exceeding **level 1** on the standard scale, and the highway authority or other person on whose complaint the order was made may carry out the work required by the order and may recover the expenses reasonably incurred by them or him in so doing from the person in default.

(4) No person shall be required by an order made under this section, nor is any person permitted by subsection (3) above, to cut or prune a hedge at any time except between the last day of September and the first day of April.

[Highways Act 1980, s 136 as amended by the Wildlife and Countryside Act 1981, s 72 as amended by the Criminal Justice Act 1982, s 46.]

Obstruction of highways and streets

7–6009   137. Penalty for wilful obstruction.   (1) If a person, without lawful authority or excuse[1], in any way wilfully[2] obstructs[3] the free passage along a highway[4] he is guilty of an offence and liable to a fine not exceeding **level 3** on the standard scale.

(2)   (*Repealed*).

[Highways Act 1980, s 137 as amended by the Criminal Justice Act 1982, ss 38 and 46 and the Police and Criminal Evidence Act 1984, Sch 7.]

1. For the application of peaceful picketing in accordance with s 134 of the Industrial Relations Act 1971 (now the Trade Union and Labour Relations Act (Consolidation) Act 1992, s 220) see *Broome v DPP* [1974] 1 All ER 314, 138 JP 105. The erection of a *permanent* bollard was held to contravene this section in *Dixon v Atfield* [1975] 3 All ER 265, [1975] 1 WLR 1171. The onus is on the prosecution to prove that the defendant was obstructing the highway without lawful authority or excuse. Lawful authority includes permits and licences granted to market and street traders, and those collecting for charitable causes. Lawful excuse embraces activities otherwise lawful in themselves which may or may not be reasonable in all the circumstances (*Hirst and Agu v Chief Constable of West Yorkshire* (1986) 151 JP 304, [1987] Crim LR 330). It is not a lawful authority or excuse for a livestock smallholder to erect across a bridleway three metal gates tied to hedges with twine to prevent livestock wandering onto a nearby road (*Durham County Council v Scott* [1990] Crim LR 726). Freedom of expression is a qualified right and it is not a trump card to permit protesters to circumvent other regulations; however, it is a significant consideration to take into account when determining reasonableness (*Westminster City Council v Haw* (2002) 166 JPN 823).
2. If anybody by the exercise of free will does something which causes an obstruction an offence is committed (*Arrowsmith v Jenkins* [1963] 2 QB 561, [1963] 2 All ER 210, 127 JP 289). A man who marched into a "Bull Ring" and there addressed a crowd who had gathered round him was rightly convicted notwithstanding that there was free space for traffic outside the crowd; his action in assembling the crowd was to render the highway less convenient and commodious (*Homer v Cadman* (1886) 50 JP 454). Exposing goods for sale on land dedicated as a footway is an obstruction unless the practice prevailed before the dedication (*Spice v Peacock* (1875) 39 JP 581). Posts erected on a footpath to prevent undesirable vehicular traffic may be an obstruction (*A-G v Wilcox* [1938] Ch 934, [1938] 2 All ER 367). In *Dixon v Atfield* [1975] 3 All ER 265, [1975] 1 WLR 1171 it was stated that the broad interpretation of "reasonable excuse" applied in the case of a temporary obstruction did not apply to a permanent obstruction. An offence may be committed by a shopkeeper in respect of a "queue" forming outside his shop if the facts disclose that he is carrying on his business not in an ordinary way, ie, by serving his customers through the window (*Fabbri v Morris* [1947] 1 All ER 315, 111 JP 97); otherwise if he is carrying on business in his shop in the ordinary way (*Dwyer v Mansfield* [1946] KB 437, [1946] 2 All ER 247). Encroachment on to a highway may be found to be minimal; best endeavours to prevent encroachment of a queue may not be a defence, but is relevant to considerations of lawful authority or reasonable excuse; situation of a stall in the same place for several years is relevant but not conclusive; payment of rates does not imply lawful authority (*Pugh v Pigden and Powley* (1987) 151 JP 664). The fact that neither the police nor local authority prosecute in respect of an alleged obstruction over a period of years does not give the defendant a licence to perform an unlawful act of obstruction (*Redbridge London Borough v Jacques* [1971] 1 All ER 260, 135 JP 98). A driver of a motor car, travelling slowly and holding the crown of the road so that faster cars may pass only at favourable moments, may be convicted of obstruction, if not of dangerous driving (*Norton v Lees* (1921) 85 JP Jo 500; on appeal (1923) 87 JP Jo 675). For a case where the obstruction was to access way of a public market, held to be dedicated as a highway under s 31(1) of this Act, ante, see *Brandon v Barnes* [1966] 3 All ER 296, 130 JP 389. In *Armstrong v Whitfield* [1974] QB 16, [1973] 2 All ER 546, 137 JP 554 a prior decision by quarter sessions under s 31 of the National Parks and Access to the Countryside Act 1949 as to a right of way was binding on justices hearing a case of wilful obstruction.
This offence is punishable summarily in accordance with s 310, post. Consequently, the jurisdiction of a magistrates' court cannot be ousted by any claim of right (*R v Ogden, ex p Long Ashton RDC* [1963] 1 All ER 574, 127 JP 206).
3. The test of whether a particular use of a highway, eg, by a vehicle, amounts to an obstruction is whether such use is

unreasonable having regard to all the circumstances including its duration, position and purpose, and whether it causes an actual, as opposed to a potential, obstruction (*Nagy v Weston* [1965] 1 All ER 78, 129 JP 104). Although the *de minimis* principle applies to obstruction cases, the principle is reserved for cases of fractional obstructions (*Torbay Borough Council v Cross* (1995) 159 JP 682—displays of goods on the pavement outside a shop projecting by no more than 5% of the total width of the pavement held to be an obstruction which did not satisfy the *de minimis* principle). A defendant selling hot dogs from a van parked in a line of parked vehicles in a busy street was properly convicted; as soon as his van turned itself into a shop it ceased to make a reasonable use of the road (*Pitcher v Lockett* [1966] Crim LR 283); applied in *Waltham Forest London Borough Council v Mills* [1980] RTR 201, [1980] Crim LR 243, where it was held that the selling of refreshments from a mobile snack bar on the highway was an unreasonable user. The placing of shopping trolleys in three parallel rows outside a supermarket was held to constitute an unreasonable user because of the performance of the obstruction, the substantial nature of it, and its denial to the public of free access over the whole of the highway (*Devon County Council v Gateway Foodmarkets Ltd* (1990) 154 JP 557, DC). Where a club tout approached groups of pedestrians on four occasions and on each of those occasions the free passage of other people using the highway was obstructed to an extent that members of the public passing were forced to step into the roadway, it was held that it was such an unreasonable use of the highway as to amount to an obstruction (*Cooper v Metropolitan Police Comr* (1985) 82 Cr App Rep 238). An unauthorised encroachment restricting access to any part of the highway is such an obstruction and the prosecution is not obliged to allege or prove that any particular person was incommoded: see *Wolverton UDC v Willis* [1962] 1 All ER 243, 126 JP 84. Similarly, the display for sale of garden produce on a grass verge adjacent to a footpath, which formed part of the highway, was held to be an unreasonable user and, therefore, an obstruction, notwithstanding that the display did not encroach on the footpath itself and there was no evidence of anyone being inconvenienced (*Hertfordshire County Council v Bolden* (1986) 151 JP 252). In *Bunting v British Railways Board* (18 November 1981, unreported), it was held, on the facts of that case, that a railway line did not constitute an obstruction of a footpath, which it crossed, since the public were still at liberty to walk over the area of the footpath. If stopping on a highway is merely part and parcel of reasonably passing and repassing, it is not obstruction; to stand juggling with lighted firesticks is not part and parcel of one's right to pass and repass nor is it a user ancillary to that right (*Waite v Taylor* (1985) 149 JP 551).

4. For meaning of "highway" and "carriageway", see ss 328 and 329 respectively, post.

7–6009A   137ZA. Power to order offender to remove obstruction.   (1) Where a person is convicted of an offence under section 137 above in respect of the obstruction of a highway and it appears to the court that—

(a)   the obstruction is continuing, and

(b)   it is in that person's power to remove the cause of the obstruction,

the court may, in addition to or instead of imposing any punishment, order him to take, within such reasonable period as may be fixed by the order, such steps as may be specified in the order for removing the cause of the obstruction.

(2)   The time fixed by an order under subsection (1) above may be extended or further extended by order of the court on an application made before the end of the time as originally fixed or as extended under this subsection, as the case may be.

(3)   If a person fails without reasonable excuse to comply with an order under subsection (1) above, he is guilty of an offence and liable to a fine not exceeding level 5 on the standard scale; and if the offence is continued after conviction he is guilty of a further offence and liable to a fine not exceeding one-twentieth of that level for each day on which the offence is so continued.

(4)   Where, after a person is convicted of an offence under subsection (3) above, the highway authority for the highway concerned exercise any power to remove the cause of the obstruction, they may recover from that person the amount of any expenses reasonably incurred by them in, or in connection with, doing so.

(5)   A person against whom an order is made under subsection (1) above is not liable under section 137 above in respect of the obstruction concerned—

(a)   during the period fixed under that subsection or any extension under subsection (2) above, or

(b)   during any period fixed under section 311(1) below by a court before whom he is convicted of an offence under subsection (3) above in respect of the order.

[Highways Act 1980, s 137ZA as inserted by the Countryside and Rights of Way Act 2000, s 64(1).]

7–6010   137A. Interference by crops.   (1) Where a crop other than grass has been sown or planted on any agricultural land the occupier of the land shall from time to time take such steps as may be necessary—

(*a*)   to ensure that the line on the ground of any relevant highway on the land is so indicated to not less than its minimum width as to be apparent to members of the public wishing to use the highway; and

(*b*)   to prevent the crop from so encroaching on any relevant highway, whether passing over that or adjoining land, as to render it inconvenient for the exercise of the public right of way.

(2)   for the purposes of subsection (1) above, a crop shall be treated as encroaching on a highway if, and only if, any part of the crop grows on, or otherwise extends onto or over, the highway in such a way as to reduce the apparent width of the highway to less than its minimum width.

(3)   For the purposes of the application of subsection (1) above in the case of a particular crop, the crop shall be treated as grass if, and only if—

(*a*)   it is of a variety or mixture commonly used for pasture, silage or haymaking, whether or not it is intended for such a use in that case; and

(*b*)   it is not a cereal crop.

(4) If the occupier fails to comply with the duty imposed by subsection (1) above he is guilty of an offence and liable to a fine not exceeding **level 3** on the standard scale.

(5) Without prejudice to section 130 (protection of public rights) above, it is the duty of the highway authority to enforce the provisions of this section.

(6) In this section—

"minimum width", in relation to a highway, has the same meaning as in Schedule 12A to this Act; and

"relevant highway" means—

(*a*) a footpath,

(*b*) a bridleway, or

(*c*) any other highway which consists of or comprises a carriageway other than a made-up carriageway.

[Highways Act 1980, s 137A as inserted by the Rights of Way Act 1990, s 1.]

7–6011   138. Penalty for erecting building, etc, in highway. If a person, without lawful authority or excuse, erects a building or fence, or plants a hedge, in a highway[1] which consists of or comprises a carriageway[1] he is guilty of an offence and liable to a fine not exceeding **level 3** on the standard scale.

[Highways Act 1980, s 138 as amended by the Criminal Justice Act 1982, ss 38 and 46.]

---

1. For meaning of "highway" and "carriageway", see ss 328 and 329 respectively, post.

7–6012   139. Control of builders' skips. (1) A builder's skip shall not be deposited[1] on a highway without the permission[2] of the highway authority for the highway.

(2) A permission under this section shall be a permission for a person to whom it is granted to deposit, or cause to be deposited, a skip on the highway specified in the permission, and a highway authority may grant such permission either unconditionally or subject to such conditions as may be specified in the permission including, in particular, conditions relating to—

(*a*) the siting of the skip;

(*b*) its dimensions;

(*c*) the manner in which it is to be coated with paint and other material for the purpose of making it immediately visible to oncoming traffic;

(*d*) the care and disposal of its contents;

(*e*) the manner in which it is to be lighted or guarded;

(*f*) its removal at the end of the period of permission.

(3) If a builder's skip is deposited on a highway without a permission granted under this section, the owner of the skip is, subject to subsection (6) below, guilty of an offence and liable to a fine not exceeding **level 3** on the standard scale.

(4) Where a builder's skip has been deposited on a highway in accordance with a permission granted under this section, the owner[3] of the skip shall secure—

(*a*) that the skip is properly lighted during the hours of darkness and, where regulations made by the Secretary of State under this section require it to be marked in accordance with the regulations[4] (whether with reflecting or fluorescent material or otherwise), that it is so marked;

(*b*) that the skip is clearly and indelibly marked with the owner's name and with his telephone number or address;

(*c*) that the skip is removed as soon as practicable after it has been filled;

(*d*) that each of the conditions subject to which that permission was granted is complied with;

and, if he fails to do so, he is, subject to subsection (6) below, guilty of an offence and liable to a fine not exceeding **level 3** on the standard scale.

(5) Where the commission by any person of an offence under this section is due to the act or default[5] of some other person, that other person is guilty of the offence, and a person may be charged with and convicted of the offence by virtue of this subsection whether or not proceedings are taken against the first-mentioned person.

(6) In any proceedings for an offence under this section it is a defence, subject to subsection (7) below, for the person charged to prove that the commission of the offence was due to the act or default of another person[6] and that he took all reasonable precautions and exercised all due diligence to avoid the commission of such an offence by himself or any person under his control.

(7) A person charged with an offence under this section is not, without leave of the court, entitled to rely on the defence provided by subsection (6) above unless, within a period ending 7 clear days before the hearing, he has served on the prosecutor a notice in writing giving such information identifying or assisting in the identification of that other person as was then in his possession.

(8) Where any person is charged with an offence under any other enactment for failing to secure that a builder's skip which has been deposited on a highway in accordance with a permission granted under this section was properly lighted during the hours of darkness, it is a defence for the person charged to prove that the commission of the offence was due to the act or default of another person

and that he took all reasonable precautions and exercised all due diligence to avoid the commission of such an offence by himself or any person under his control.

(9) Where a person is charged with obstructing, or interrupting any user of, a highway by depositing a builder's skip on it, it is a defence for the person charged to prove that the skip was deposited on it in accordance with a permission granted under this section and either—

(a) that each of the requirements of subsection (4) above had been complied with; or

(b) that the commission of any offence under that subsection was due to the act or default of another person and that he took all reasonable precautions and exercised all due diligence to avoid the commission of such an offence by himself or any person under his control.

(10) Nothing in this section is to be taken as authorising the creation of a nuisance or of a danger to users of a highway or as imposing on a highway authority by whom a permission has been granted under this section any liability for any injury, damage or loss resulting from the presence on a highway of the skip to which the permission relates.

(11) In this section, section 140 and section 140A* below—

"builder's skip" means a container designed to be carried on a road vehicle and to be placed on a highway or other land for the storage of builders' materials, or for the removal and disposal of builders' rubble, waste, household and other rubbish or earth; and

"owner", in relation to a builder's skip which is the subject of a hiring agreement, being an agreement for a hiring of not less than one month, or a hire purchase agreement, means the person in possession of the skip under that agreement.

[Highways Act 1980, s 139 as amended by the Criminal Justice Act 1982, ss 38 and 46, the Transport Act 1982, s 65 and the New Roads and Street Works Act 1991, Sch 8.]

---

*Words substituted by the Traffic Management Act 2004, s 70 from a date to be appointed.

1. "Deposited" means more than merely putting down, placing or delivering, and includes the sense of leaving or remaining (*Craddock v Green* [1983] RTR 479).

2. Permission must be in writing; s 320, post. The Act does not contemplate "blanket" permits: see *York City Council v Poller* [1976] RTR 37.

3. Note defence under sub-s (6), post (successfully used in *Lambeth London Borough Council v Saunders Transport Ltd* [1974] Crim LR 311 and *Barnet London Borough Council v S & W Transport Ltd* (1975) 119 Sol Jo 99). See also *York City Council v Poller* [1976] RTR 37.

4. The Builders' Skips (Markings) Regulations 1984, SI 1984/1933, have been made.

5. In *York City Council v Poller* [1976] RTR 37 the Divisional Court derived assistance in construing this sub-division by reference to the use of the phrase "act or default" in other local government and administrative legislation.

6. It is a defence to prove that the commission of the offence was due to the act or default of a person other than the person charged, whether or not that other person is identified (*PGM Building Co Ltd v Kensington and Chelsea (Royal) London Borough Council* [1982] RTR 107).

7–6013   140. Removal of builders' skips.   (1) The following provisions of this section have effect in relation to a builder's skip deposited on a highway notwithstanding that it was deposited on it in accordance with a permission granted under section 139 above.

(2) The highway authority for the highway or a constable in uniform[1] may require the owner of the skip to remove or reposition it or cause it to be removed or repositioned.

(3) A person required to remove or reposition, or cause to be removed or repositioned, a skip under a requirement made by virtue of subsection (2) above shall comply with the requirement as soon as practicable, and if he fails to do so he is guilty of an offence and liable to a fine not exceeding **level 3** on the standard scale.

(4) The highway authority for the highway or a constable in uniform may themselves remove or reposition the skip or cause it to be removed or repositioned.

(5) Where a skip is removed under subsection (4) above, the highway authority or, as the case may be, the chief officer of police shall, where practicable, notify the owner of its removal, but if the owner cannot be traced, or if after a reasonable period of time after being so notified he has not recovered the skip, the highway authority or chief officer of police may dispose of the skip and its contents.

(6) Any expenses reasonably incurred by a highway authority or chief officer of police in the removal or repositioning of a skip under subsection (4) above or the disposal of a skip under subsection (5) above may be recovered from the owner of the skip in any court of competent jurisdiction or summarily as a civil debt.

(7) Any proceeds of the disposal of a skip under subsection (5) above shall be used in the first place to meet the expenses reasonably incurred in the removal and disposal of the skip and thereafter any surplus shall be given to the person entitled to it if he can be traced and if not may be retained by the highway authority or the chief officer of police, as the case may be; and any surplus so retained by a chief officer of police shall be paid into the police fund.

(8) References in this section to expenses incurred in the removal of a skip include references to expenses incurred in storing the skip until it is recovered by the owner or, as the case may be, disposed of.

(9) The owner of a skip is not guilty of an offence under section 139(4) above of failing to secure that a condition relating to the siting of the skip was complied with if the failure resulted from the repositioning of the skip under subsection (3) or (4) above.

[Highways Act 1980, s 140 as amended by the Criminal Justice Act 1982, ss 38 and 46.]

1. The communication of the requirement must be made face to face and not, for example, by telephone (*R v Worthing Justices, ex p Waste Management Ltd* (1988) 152 JP 362, [1989] RTR 131, DC).

7–6013A   140A–140C. *Builders' skips: charge for occupation of highway*

7–6014   141. Restriction on planting of trees etc in or near carriageway.   (1) Subject to sections 64 and 96 above and section 142 below, no tree or shrub shall be planted in a made-up carriageway, or within 15 feet from the centre of a made-up carriageway.

(2) If a tree or shrub is planted in contravention of this section the highway authority for the highway or, in the case of a highway maintainable by reason of tenure, enclosure or prescription, the person liable to maintain the highway, may by notice given either to the owner or to the occupier of the land in which the tree or shrub is planted require him to remove it within 21 days from the date of service of the notice.

(3) If a person fails to comply with a notice under subsection (2) above he is guilty of an offence and liable to a fine not exceeding **level 1** on the standard scale and if the offence is continued after conviction he is guilty of a further offence and liable to a fine not exceeding **50p** for each day on which the offence is so continued.
[Highways Act 1980, s 141 as amended by the Criminal Justice Act 1982, s 46.]

7–6015   142. Licence to plant trees, shrubs, etc, in a highway.   (1) The highway authority for a highway may by a licence granted under this section permit the occupier or the owner of any premises adjoining the highway to plant and maintain, or to retain and maintain, trees, shrubs, plants or grass in such part of the highway as may be specified in the licence.

(2)–(8), (10) *Miscellaneous provisions with respect to the grant of licences.*

(9) If any person plants a tree or shrub in a highway otherwise than in pursuance of a licence granted under this section, the tree or shrub is to be deemed, for the purposes of section 141 above, to have been planted in contravention of that section.
[Highways Act 1980, s 142 amended by the Telecommunications Act 1984, Sch 4, the Water Act 1989, Sch 27 and the Road Traffic (Driver Licensing and Information Systems) Act 1989, Sch 4.]

7–6016   143. Power to remove structures from highways.   (1) Where a structure[1] has been erected or set up on a highway otherwise than under a provision of this Act or some other enactment, a competent authority may by notice require the person having control or possession of the structure to remove it within such time as may be specified in the notice.

For the purposes of this section the following are competent authorities—

(*a*)   in the case of a highway which is for the time being maintained by a non-metropolitan district council by virtue of section 42 or 50 above, that council and also the highway authority, and

(*b*)   in the case of any other highway, the highway authority.

(2) If a structure in respect of which a notice is served under this section is not removed within the time specified in the notice, the competent authority serving the notice may, subject to subsection (3) below, remove the structure and recover the expenses[2] reasonably incurred by them in so doing from the person having control or possession of the structure.

(3) The authority shall not exercise their power under subsection (2) above until the expiration of one month from the date of service of the notice.

(4) In this section "structure"[1] includes any machine, pump, post or other object of such a nature as to be capable of causing obstruction, and a structure may be treated for the purposes of this section as having been erected or set up notwithstanding that it is on wheels.
[Highways Act 1980, s 143 as amended by the Local Government Act 1985, Sch 4.]

1. A caravan is capable of being a "structure" for the purposes of this section (*R v Welwyn and Hatfield District Council, ex p Brinkley* (1982) 80 LGR 727, [1982] LS Gaz R 954).
2. For recovery of expenses, see s 305, post.

7–6017   144. Power to erect flagpoles etc on highways.   (1) Subject to subsection (2) below, a local authority may—

(*a*)   erect flagpoles, pylons and other structures on any highway in their area for the purpose of displaying decorations;

(*b*)   make slots in such a highway for the purpose of erecting the structures; and

(*c*)   remove any structure erected or slot made by the authority in pursuance of paragraph (*a*) or (*b*) above;

and any structures or slots which may be erected or made by virtue of this subsection are hereafter in this section referred to as "relevant works".

(2) A local authority are not entitled to exercise the powers conferred on them by subsection (1) above in respect of a highway for which they are not the highway authority except with the consent in writing of the highway authority for the highway, and are not entitled to exercise those powers in respect of so much of a highway as—

(a) is carried by a bridge which a body other than the local authority and the highway authority has a duty to maintain; or

(b) forms part of the approaches to such a bridge and is supported or protected by works or materials which a body other than the local authority and the highway authority has a duty to maintain,

except with the consent in writing of that body.

In this subsection "bridge" includes a structure which carries a highway superimposed over a cutting.

(3) A highway authority or other body may give their consent in pursuance of subsection (2) above on such terms as they think fit (including in particular, without prejudice to the generality of the preceding provisions of this subsection, terms providing for the highway authority or body to remove any of the relevant works and reinstate the highway and to recover the reasonable cost of doing so from the local authority to whom the consent was given).

(4) It is the duty of an authority by whom relevant works are erected or made by virtue of the preceding provisions of this section—

(a) to ensure that the works are erected or made so as to obstruct the highway in question as little as is reasonably possible, so as not to obscure or conflict with traffic signs connected with the highway and so as to interfere as little as is reasonably possible with the enjoyment of premises adjacent to the highway and with, and with access to, any apparatus in or on the highway which belongs to or is used or maintained by statutory undertakers; and

(b) to ensure that while the works are retained they are properly maintained and, so far as it is necessary to light them to avoid danger to users of the highway, are properly lit; and

(c) if the authority are not the highway authority for the highway, to indemnify the highway authority against any payments falling to be made by the highway authority in consequence of the works.

(5) A person who without lawful authority interferes with or removes any relevant works is guilty of an offence and liable to a fine not exceeding **level 3** on the standard scale.

(6) In this section—

"local authority" means any of the following, namely, the council of a county, district or London borough, the Common Council, the Council of the Isles of Scilly and a parish or community council; and

"statutory undertakers" means any of the following, namely, any body which is a statutory undertaker within the meaning provided by section 329(1) below, any universal service provider in connection with the provision of a universal postal service, any licensee under a street works licence and the operator of a telecommunications code system★ or a driver information system.

[Highways Act 1980, s 144 as amended by the Criminal Justice Act 1982, ss 35, 38 and 46, the Telecommunications Act 1984, Schs 4 and 7, the Local Government Act 1985, Sch 17, the Water Act 1989, Sch 27, the Road Traffic (Driver Licensing and Information Systems) Act 1989, Sch 4, the New Roads and Street Works Act 1991, Sch 8 and SI 2001/1149.]

★**Words substituted by the Communications Act 2003, Sch 17, from a date to be appointed.**

7–6018 **145. Powers as to gates across highways.**   (1) Where there is a gate of less than the minimum width across so much of a highway as consists of a carriageway, or across a highway that is a bridleway, the highway authority for the highway may by notice to the owner of the gate require him to enlarge the gate to that width or remove it.

In this subsection "the minimum width" means, in relation to a gate across so much of a highway as consists of a carriageway, 10 feet and, in relation to a gate across a bridleway, 5 feet, measured in either case between the posts of the gate.

(2) If a person on whom a notice under subsection (1) above is served fails to comply, within 21 days from the date of service of the notice on him, with a requirement of the notice, he is guilty of an offence and liable to a fine not exceeding **50p** for each day during which the failure continues.

[Highways Act 1980, s 145.]

7–6019 **146. Duty to maintain stiles etc on footpaths and bridleways.**   (1) Any stile, gate or other similar structure across a footpath or bridleway shall be maintained by the owner of the land in a safe condition, and to the standard of repair required to prevent unreasonable interference with the rights of the persons using the footpath or bridleway.

(2) If it appears to the appropriate authority that the duty imposed by subsection (1) above is not being complied with, they may, after giving to the owner and occupier not less than 14 days' notice of their intention, take all necessary steps for repairing and making good the stile, gate or other works.

For the purposes of this section the appropriate authority is—

(a) in the case of a footpath or bridleway which is for the time being maintained by a non-metropolitan district council by virtue of section 42 or 50 above, that council, and

(b) in the case of any other footpath or bridleway, the highway authority.

(3) The appropriate authority may recover from the owner of the land the amount of any

expenses[1] reasonably incurred by the authority in and in connection with the exercise of their powers under subsection (2) above, or such part of those expenses as the authority think fit.

(4) The appropriate authority shall contribute not less than a quarter of any expenses shown to their satisfaction to have been reasonably incurred in compliance with subsection (1) above, and may make further contributions of such amount in each case as, having regard to all the circumstances, they consider reasonable.

(5) Subsection (1) above does not apply to any structure—

(a) if any conditions for the maintenance of the structure are for the time being in force under section 147 below, or

(b) if and so long as, under an agreement in writing with any other person, there is a liability to maintain the structure on the part of the appropriate authority or, where the appropriate authority are a non-metropolitan district council, on the part of either the appropriate authority or the highway authority.

[Highways Act 1980, s 146 as amended by the Local Government Act 1985, Sch 4.]

---

1. For recovery of expenses, see s 305, post.

7–6020   147A. Road-side sales. (1) Subject to subsection (4) below, no person shall, for the purpose of selling anything, or offering or exposing anything for sale, use any stall or similar structure or any container or vehicle, kept or placed on—

(a) the verge of a trunk road or a principal road;

(b) a lay-by on any such road; or

(c) unenclosed land within 15 metres of any part of any such road,

where its presence or its use for that purpose causes or is likely to cause danger on the road or interrupts or is likely to interrupt any user of the road.

(2) Any person who contravenes this section shall be guilty of an offence and liable on summary conviction to a fine not exceeding **level 3** on the standard scale.

(3) It shall be a defence for a person charged with an offence under this section to prove that he took all reasonable precautions and exercised all due diligence to avoid commission of the offence.

(4) This section does not apply—

(a) to the sale or offer or exposure for sale of things from or on a vehicle which is used only for the purposes of itinerant trading with the occupiers of premises, or is used only for that purpose and for purposes other than trading;

(b) to the sale or offer or exposure for sale of newspapers;

(c) to anything done at a market in respect of which tolls, stallages or rents are payable; or

(d) to the sale or offer or exposure for sale of anything by way of street trading which has been authorised under Schedule 4 to the Local Government (Miscellaneous Provisions) Act 1982 or under any local enactment which makes provision similar to that made by that Schedule, either by the person so authorised or by a person acting as assistant to the person so authorised.

[Highways Act 1980, s 147A, as inserted by the Local Government (Miscellaneous Provisions) Act 1982, s 23 as amended by the Criminal Justice Act 1982, s 46.]

7–6021   148. Penalty for depositing things or pitching booths etc on highway. If, without lawful authority or excuse[1]—

(a) a person deposits[2] on a made-up carriageway[3] any dung, compost or other material for dressing land, or any rubbish, or

(b) a person deposits[2] on any highway[4] that consists of or comprises a made-up carriageway any dung, compost or other material for dressing land, or any rubbish, within 15 feet from the centre of that carriageway, or

(c) a person deposits[5] any thing whatsoever on a highway[4] to the interruption[1] of any user of the highway, or

(d) a hawker or other itinerant trader pitches[6] a booth, stall or stand, or encamps[7], on a highway,

he is guilty of an offence and liable to a fine not exceeding **level 3** on the standard scale.

[Highways Act 1980, s 148 as amended by the Criminal Justice Act 1982, ss 38 and 46.]

---

1. To show lawful excuse the defendant must show (i) that he honestly, but mistakenly, believed on reasonable grounds that the facts were of a certain order and (ii) that if those facts were of that order his conduct would have been lawful (*Cambridgeshire County Council v Rust* [1972] 2 QB 426, [1972] 3 All ER 232, 136 JP 702). "Excuse" imports the concept of reasonableness as a question of fact; therefore, so far as s 148(*c*) is concerned, justices must be satisfied that the interruption of any user, in all the circumstances, was an unreasonable interruption (*Putnam v Colvin* [1984] RTR 150).

2. See also PART VII title LITTER, DUMPING ETC, post.

3. For meaning of "made-up carriageway", see s 329, post.

4. For meaning of "highway", see s 328, post.

5. For an offence to be committed there must be a conscious and deliberate depositing of something on the highway (*Remet Co Ltd v Newham London Borough Council* [1981] RTR 502).

6. The driver of a vehicle who stops on a highway and sells from his vehicle, eg ice cream, does not thereby "pitch a stall" (*Divito v Stickings* [1948] 1 All ER 207, 112 JP 166); but a mobile snack bar which can be detached from its towing

vehicle is a "stall" and can be "pitched" for the purposes of this section (*Waltham Forest London Borough Council v Mills* [1980] RTR 201, [1980] Crim LR 243).

7. "Encamps" means the actual setting up of a camp and not the continuation of it. Thus there can be no conviction under this section in respect of a date after the camp has been established (*Smith v Wood* (1971) 135 JP 257).

7–6022   149. Removal of things so deposited on highways as to be a nuisance etc.   (1) If any thing is so deposited on a highway as to constitute a nuisance, the highway authority for the highway may by notice require the person who deposited[1] it there to remove it forthwith and if he fails to comply with the notice the authority may make a complaint to a magistrates' court for a removal and disposal order under this section.

(2) If the highway authority for any highway have reasonable grounds for considering—

(a)   that any thing unlawfully deposited[1] on the highway constitutes a danger (including a danger caused by obstructing the view) to users of the highway, and

(b)   that the thing in question ought to be removed without the delay involved in giving notice or obtaining a removal and disposal order from a magistrates' court under this section,

the authority may remove the thing forthwith.

(3) The highway authority by whom a thing is removed in pursuance of subsection (2) above may either—

(a)   recover from the person by whom it was deposited on the highway, or from any person claiming to be entitled to it, any expenses reasonably incurred by the authority in removing it, or

(b)   make a complaint to a magistrates' court for a disposal order under this section.

(4) A magistrates' court may, on a complaint made under this section, make an order authorising the complainant authority—

(a)   either to remove the thing in question and dispose of it or, as the case may be, to dispose of the thing in question, and

(b)   after payment out of any proceeds arising from the disposal of the expenses incurred in the removal and disposal, to apply the balance, if any, of the proceeds to the maintenance of highways maintainable at the public expense by them.

(5) If the thing in question is not of sufficient value to defray the expenses of removing it, the complainant authority may recover from the person who deposited it on the highway the expenses, or the balance of the expenses, reasonably incurred by them in removing it.

(6) A magistrates' court composed of a single justice may hear a complaint under this section.
[Highways Act 1980, s 149.]

1. "Deposit" should be given a broad meaning and could include the siting of braziers for roasting chestnuts on barrows with attendants selling from them (*Scott v Westminster City Council* [1995] RTR 327, CA).

7–6023   150. Duty to remove snow soil etc from highway.   (1) If an obstruction arises in a highway from accumulation of snow or from the falling down of banks on the side of the highway, or from any other cause, the highway authority shall remove the obstruction.

(2) If a highway authority fail to remove an obstruction which it is their duty under this section to remove, a magistrates' court may, on a complaint made by any person, by order require the authority to remove the obstruction within such period (not being less than 24 hours) from the making of the order as the court thinks reasonable, having regard to all the circumstances of the case.

(3) In considering whether to make an order under this section and, if so, what period to allow for the removal of the obstruction, the court shall in particular have regard to—

(a)   the character of the highway to which the complaint relates, and the nature and amount of the traffic by which it is ordinarily used,

(b)   the nature and extent of the obstruction, and

(c)   the resources of manpower, vehicles and equipment for the time being available to the highway authority for work on highways and the extent to which those resources are being, or need to be, employed elsewhere by that authority on such work.

(4) Where they are under a duty to remove an obstruction under subsection (1) above, a highway authority may—

(a)   take any reasonable steps (including the placing of lights, signs and fences on the highway) for warning users of the highway of the obstruction;

(b)   sell any thing removed in carrying out the duty, unless the thing is claimed by its owner before the expiration of 7 days from the date of its removal;

(c)   recover from the owner of the thing which caused or contributed to the obstruction, or where the thing has been sold under paragraph (b) above, from its previous owner, the expenses reasonably incurred as respects the obstruction in carrying out the duty and in exercising any powers conferred by this subsection, but so that no such expenses are recoverable from a person who proves that he took reasonable care to secure that the thing in question did not cause or contribute to the obstruction.

(5) Where a highway authority sell any thing in exercise of their powers under subsection (4) above, then—

  (a) if any expenses are recoverable under that subsection by the authority from the previous owner of the thing, they may set off the expenses against the proceeds of sale (without prejudice to the recovery of any balance of the expenses from the previous owner) and shall pay over any balance of the proceeds to the previous owner; and

  (b) if no expenses are so recoverable, they shall pay over the whole of the proceeds of sale to the previous owner.

(6) The foregoing provisions of this section apply to a person liable to maintain a highway by reason of tenure, enclosure or prescription as they apply to the highway authority for that highway, and references in those provisions to a highway authority are to be construed accordingly.
[Highways Act 1980, s 150.]

7–6024   151. Prevention of soil etc being washed on to street.   (1) A competent authority may, by notice to the owner or occupier of any land adjoining a street which is a highway maintainable at the public expense, require him, within 28 days from the date of service of the notice, to execute such works as will prevent soil or refuse from that land from falling, or being washed or carried, on to the street or into any sewer or gully in it in such quantities as to obstruct the street or choke the sewer or gully.

For the purposes of this section the following are competent authorities—

  (a) in relation to a street outside Greater London, the highway authority for the street and also, if the street is situated in a non-metropolitan district, the council of that district; and

  (b) in relation to a street within Greater London, the council of the London borough in which the street is situated or, if it is situated in the City of London, the Common Council.

(1A) In relation to a street in Wales, the competent authorities for the purposes of this section are the highway authority for the street, and if different, the Welsh council in whose area the street is situated.

(2) A person aggrieved by a requirement under this section may appeal to a magistrates' court.

(3) Subject to any order made on appeal, if a person on whom a notice is served under this section fails to comply with it within the period specified in subsection (1) above, he is guilty of an offence[1] and liable to a fine not exceeding **level 3** on the standard scale; and if the offence is continued after conviction, he is guilty of a further offence and liable to a fine not exceeding £1 for each day on which the offence is so continued.
[Highways Act 1980, s 151 as amended by the Criminal Justice Act 1982, ss 35, 38 and 46, the Local Government Act 1985, Schs 4 and 17 and the Local Government (Wales) Act 1994, Sch 7.]

---

1. For restriction on the institution of proceedings, see s 312 and Sch 22, post.

7–6025   152. Powers as to removal of projections from buildings.   (1) A competent authority may by notice to the occupier of any building require him to remove or alter any porch, shed, projecting window, step, cellar, cellar door, cellar window, sign, signpost, sign iron, showboard, window shutter, wall, gate, fence or other obstruction or projection which has been erected or placed against or in front of the building and is an obstruction to safe or convenient passage along a street.

(2) A notice under subsection (1) above may, at the option of the authority, be served on the owner of the building instead of on the occupier or may be served on both the owner and the occupier.

(3) A person aggrieved by a requirement under subsection (1) above may appeal to a magistrates' court.

(4) Subject to any order made on appeal, if a person on whom a notice under subsection (1) above is served fails to comply, within 14 days from the date of service of the notice on him, with a requirement of the notice, he is guilty of an offence[1] and liable to a fine not exceeding **level 1** on the standard scale.

(5) Where an authority serve a notice under subsection (1) above on any person and he is guilty of an offence by reason of his failure to comply with a requirement of the notice within the time specified in subsection (4) above then, whether or not proceedings are taken against him in respect of the offence, the authority may remove the obstruction or projection to which the notice relates and may recover the expenses reasonably incurred by them in so doing from the owner or occupier of the building if, in either case, he is a person on whom the notice was served.

(6) In a case where a requirement under subsection (1) above is made in connection with an obstruction or projection not erected or placed by the occupier of the relevant building Schedule 13 to this Act applies in relation to any sum paid by the occupier in complying with a requirement under that subsection, or, where the requirement is not complied with, in reimbursing the relevant authority for expenses reasonably incurred by them under subsection (5) above.

(7) Subsection (1) above does not apply in respect of any such obstruction or projection as is there mentioned if it was erected or placed before the date when section 69 of the Towns Improvement Clauses Act 1847 first applied in the area in which the building in question is situated.

(8) If any such obstruction or projection was erected or placed before that date against or in front of a building in a street, a competent authority may, on the expiration of 30 days from the date of service on either the owner or the occupier of the building of a notice of their intention, remove or alter the obstruction or projection as they think fit, and, if the obstruction or projection was lawfully erected or placed, the authority shall pay reasonable compensation to every person who suffers damage by reason of its removal or alteration.

(9) For the purposes of this section—

(a) the competent authorities are the local authority in whose area the street is situated and also, where the street is a highway, the highway authority for it;

(b) a projection which is erected or placed against or in front of a building, and which by reason of its being insecurely fixed or of defective construction or otherwise is a source of danger to persons lawfully using a street, is to be deemed to be an obstruction to safe or convenient passage along the street.

[Highways Act 1980, s 152 as amended by the Criminal Justice Act 1982, s 46.]

1. For restriction on the institution of proceedings, see s 312 and Sch 22, post.

7–6026   153. Doors etc in streets not to open outwards.   (1) A door, gate or bar which is put up on any premises and opens on a street shall be so put up as not to open outwards unless, in the case of a door, gate or bar put up on a public building, the local authority for the area in which the building is situated and also, if the street is a highway, the highway authority consent to its being otherwise put up.

(2) Where a door, gate or bar is put up on any premises in contravention of subsection (1) above the local authority for the area in which the premises are situated or alternatively, if the street concerned is a highway, the highway authority may, by notice to the occupier, require him to alter, so as not to open outwards, the door, gate or bar.

(3) A notice under subsection (2) above may, at the option of the highway authority or local authority, be served on the owner of the premises instead of on the occupier or may be served on both the owner and the occupier of the premises.

(4) A person aggrieved by the refusal of a consent under subsection (1) above or by a requirement under subsection (2) above may appeal to a magistrates' court.

(5) Subject to any order made on appeal, if a person on whom a notice under subsection (2) above is served fails to comply, within 8 days from the date of service of the notice on him, with a requirement of the notice, he is guilty of an offence[1] and liable to a fine not exceeding **level 1** on the standard scale.

(6) Where a highway authority or local authority serve a notice under subsection (2) above on any person and he is guilty of an offence by reason of his failure to comply with a requirement of the notice within the time specified in subsection (5) above, then, whether or not proceedings are taken against him in respect of the offence, the authority may do the work required by the notice and recover the expenses reasonably incurred by them in so doing from the owner or occupier of the premises if, in either case, he is a person on whom the notice was served.

(7) Where a requirement under subsection (2) above is made in connection with a door, gate or bar not put up by the occupier of the premises Schedule 13 to this Act applies in relation to any sum paid by the occupier in complying with a requirement under subsection (2) above or, where the requirement is not complied with, in reimbursing the authority for expenses reasonably incurred by them under subsection (6) above.

[Highways Act 1980, s 153 as amended by the Criminal Justice Act 1982, s 46.]

1. For restriction on the institution of proceedings, see s 312 and Sch 22, post.

7–6027   154. Cutting or felling etc trees etc that overhang or are a danger to roads or footpaths.   (1) Where a hedge, tree or shrub overhangs a highway or any other road or footpath to which the public has access so as to endanger or obstruct the passage of vehicles or pedestrians, or obstructs or interferes with the view of drivers of vehicles or the light from a public lamp, or overhangs a highway so as to endanger or obstruct the passage of horse-riders, a competent authority may, by notice either to the owner of the hedge, tree or shrub or to the occupier of the land on which it is growing, require him within 14 days from the date of service of the notice so to lop or cut it as to remove the cause of the danger, obstruction or interference.

For the purposes of this section the following are competent authorities—

(a) in relation to a highway for which the Minister is the highway authority and which is in a district or London borough, the Minister and also the council of the district or, as the case may be, borough;

(b) in relation to a highway for which a local highway authority are the highway authority, that authority and also, if the highway is situated in a non-metropolitan district, the council of that district;

(c) in relation to a road or footpath that is not a highway, the local authority in whose area the road or footpath is situated;

and "hedge, tree or shrub" includes vegetation of any description.

(1A) In subsection (1)(*a*) above, any reference to a district includes a reference to a Welsh county or county borough.

(2) Where it appears to a competent authority for any highway, or for any other road or footpath to which the public has access—

(*a*) that any hedge, tree or shrub is dead, diseased, damaged or insecurely rooted, and

(*b*) that by reason of its condition it, or part of it, is likely to cause danger by falling on the highway, road or footpath,

the authority may, by notice either to the owner of the hedge, tree or shrub or to the occupier of the land on which it is situated, require him within 14 days from the date of service of the notice so to cut or fell it as to remove the likelihood of danger.

(3) A person aggrieved by a requirement under subsection (1) or (2) above may appeal to a magistrates' court.

(4) Subject to any order made on appeal, if a person on whom a notice is served under subsection (1) or (2) above fails to comply with it within the period specified in those subsections, the authority who served the notice may carry out the work[1] required by the notice and recover the expenses reasonably incurred by them in so doing from the person in default.

[Highways Act 1980, s 154 as amended by the Local Government Act 1985, Sch 4, the Local Government (Wales) Act 1994, Sch 7 and the Countryside and Rights of Way Act 2000, s 65.]

---

1. We suggest that this power should not be exercised until after 21 days, the period allowed by s 316, post, for appeal.

7–6028   155. Penalties in connection with straying animals.   (1) If any horses[1], cattle, sheep, goats or swine are at any time found[2] straying or lying on or at the side of a highway[3] their keeper is guilty of an offence; but this subsection does not apply in relation to a part of a highway passing over[4] any common, waste or unenclosed ground.

In this section "keeper", in relation to any animals, means a person in whose possession they are.

(2) A person guilty of an offence under this section is liable to a fine not exceeding **level 3** on the standard scale.

(3) A person guilty of an offence under this section is also liable to pay the reasonable expenses of removing any animal so found straying or lying to the premises of their keeper, or to the common pound, or to such other place as may have been provided for the purpose, and any person who incurs such expenses is entitled to recover them summarily as a civil debt[5].

For the purposes of this subsection "expenses", in a case where an animal has been removed to the common pound, includes the usual fees and charges of the authorised keeper of the pound.

(4) If a person, without lawful authority or excuse, releases any animal seized for the purpose of being impounded under this section from the pound or other place where it is impounded, or on the way to or from any such place, or damages any such place, he is guilty of an offence and liable to a fine not exceeding **level 2** on the standard scale.

(5) Nothing in this section prejudices or affects any right of pasture on the side of a highway.

[Highways Act 1980, s 155 as amended by the Criminal Justice Act 1982, ss 35, 38 and 46.]

---

1. "Horse" includes pony, ass and mule (s 329, post).
2. The offence is complete when an animal is "found straying or lying on or at the side of a highway", whether with or without a keeper (*Lawrence v King* (1868) LR 3 QB 345, 32 JP 310, and *Golding v Stocking* (1869) LR 4 QB 516, 33 JP 566). It will not, however, be an offence if the keeper is *bona fide* driving sheep along a road, and merely stopping for a short time for them or him to take a rest (*Horwood v Goodall* (1872) 36 JP 486; *Horwood v Hill* (1872) 36 JP 486; *Morris v Jeffries* (1866) LR 1 QB 261, 30 JP 198). Where sheep owned by the renter of the herbage and depastured on the side of a barrier drainage bank were found on the metalled part of a highway a conviction was sustained (*Bothamley v Danby* (1871) 36 JP 135).
3. For meaning of "highway", see s 328, post.
4. See *Rees v Morgan* [1976] Crim LR 252.
5. See Magistrates' Courts Act 1980 s 58, in PART I: MAGISTRATES' COURTS, PROCEDURE, ante.

Danger or annoyance to users of highways and streets

7–6030   161. Penalties for causing certain kinds of danger or annoyance.   (1) If a person, without lawful authority or excuse, deposits[1] any thing whatsoever on a highway in consequence of which a user of the highway is injured or endangered[2], that person is guilty of an offence and liable to a fine not exceeding **level 3** on the standard scale.

(2) If a person without lawful authority or excuse—

(*a*) lights any fire on or over a highway which consists of or comprises a carriageway[3]; or

(*b*) discharges any firearm or firework within 50 feet of the centre of such a highway,

and in consequence a user of the highway is injured, interrupted or endangered, that person is guilty of an offence and liable to a fine not exceeding **level 3** on the standard scale.

(3) If a person plays at football or any other game[4] on a highway to the annoyance of a user of the highway he is guilty of an offence and liable to a fine not exceeding **level 1** on the standard scale.

(4) If a person, without lawful authority or excuse, allows any filth, dirt, lime or other offensive

matter or thing to run or flow[5] on to a highway from any adjoining premises, he is guilty of an offence and liable to a fine not exceeding **level 1** on the standard scale.
[Highways Act 1980, s 161 as amended by the Criminal Justice Act 1982, ss 35, 38 and 46 and the Highways (Amendment) Act 1986, s 1.]

1. For offences relating to the throwing down, etc, of litter, see Environmental Protection Act 1990, s 87 in PART VII: title PUBLIC HEALTH, ante.
2. It is up to the prosecution to prove that the injury or danger is caused by the thing deposited (*Gatland v Metropolitan Police Comr* [1968] 2 QB 279, [1968] 2 All ER 100, 132 JP 323).
3. For meaning of "carriageway", see s 329, post.
4. A mock hunt, with fancy dresses and trumpets, after a man dressed like a stag, is a game (*Pappin v Maynard* (1863) 27 JP 745).
5. The flow of rainwater from the eaves of a house is not an offensive thing within the meaning of this section (*Crossdill v Ratcliff* (1862) 26 JP 165); but see s 163, post.

7–6031   161A. Danger or annoyance caused by fires lit otherwise than on highways.   (1) If a person—

    (*a*)   lights a fire on any land not forming part of a highway which consists of or comprises a carriageway; or

    (*b*)   directs or permits a fire to be lit on any such land,

and in consequence a user of any highway which consists of or comprises a carriageway is injured, interrupted or endangered by, or by smoke from, that fire or any other fire caused by that fire, that person is guilty of an offence and liable to a fine not exceeding **level 5** on the standard scale.

(2)   In any proceedings for an offence under this section it shall be a defence for the accused to prove—

    (*a*)   that at the time the fire was lit he was satisfied on reasonable grounds that it was unlikely that users of any highway consisting of or comprising a carriageway would be injured, interrupted or endangered by, or by smoke from, that fire or any other fire caused by that fire; and

    (*b*)   either—

        (i)   that both before and after the fire was lit he did all he reasonably could to prevent users of any such highway from being so injured, interrupted or endangered, or

        (ii)   that he had a reasonable excuse for not doing so.

[Highways Act 1980, s 161A, as inserted by the Highways (Amendment) Act 1986, s 1.]

7–6032   162. Penalty for placing rope, etc across highway.   A person who for any purpose places any rope, wire or other apparatus[1] across a highway in such a manner as to be likely to cause danger to persons using the highway is, unless he proves that he had taken all necessary means to give adequate warning of the danger, guilty of an offence and liable to a fine not exceeding **level 3** on the standard scale.
[Highways Act 1980, s 162 as amended by the Criminal Justice Act 1982, ss 38 and 46.]

1. "Apparatus" includes any structure constructed for the lodging therein of apparatus (see s 329, post).

7–6033   163. Prevention of water falling on or flowing on to highway.   (1) A competent authority may, by notice[1] to the occupier of premises adjoining a highway, require him within 28 days[2] from the date of service of the notice to construct or erect and thereafter to maintain such channels, gutters or downpipes as may be necessary to prevent—

    (*a*)   water from the roof or any other part of the premises falling upon persons using the highway, or

    (*b*)   so far as is reasonably practicable, surface water from the premises flowing on to, or over, the footway[3] of the highway.

For the purposes of this section the competent authorities, in relation to any highway, are the highway authority and also (where they are not the highway authority) the local authority for the area in which the highway is situated.

(2)   A notice under subsection (1) above may, at the option of the authority, be served on the owner[3] of the premises[3] in question instead of on the occupier or may be served on both the owner and the occupier of the premises.

(3)   A person aggrieved by a requirement under this section may appeal[4] to a magistrates' court.

(4)   Subject to any order made on appeal, if a person on whom a notice is served under this section fails[5] to comply with the requirement of the notice within the period specified in subsection (1) above he is guilty of an offence and liable to a fine not exceeding **level 1** on the standard scale; and if the offence is continued after conviction he is guilty of a further offence and liable to a fine not exceeding £2 for each day on which the offence is so continued.
[Highways Act 1980, s 163 as amended by the Criminal Justice Act 1982, ss 38 and 46.]

1. For form of notice and its authentication and service, see ss 320–322, post.
2. For rule governing the reckoning of periods, see s 323, post.

3. For meaning of "footway", "owner", "premises", see s 329, post.
4. Procedure on appeal is by way of complaint for an order: s 316, post. Notice must be given to a prospective appellant of this right of appeal: see s 315, post.
5. Proceedings for an offence shall not, without the written consent of the Attorney-General, be taken by any person other than a person aggrieved, or a highway authority or council having an interest in the enforcement of the provision (s 312, post; Sch 22, post).

7–6034 164. Power to require removal of barbed wire. (1) Where on land adjoining a highway there is a fence made with barbed wire, or having barbed wire in or on it, and the wire is a nuisance to the highway, a competent authority may by notice served on the occupier of the land require him to abate the nuisance within such time, not being less than one month nor more than 6 months from the date of service of the notice, as may be specified in it.
For the purposes of this section—

(a) the competent authorities, in relation to any highway, are the highway authority and also (where they are not the highway authority) the local authority for the area in which the highway is situated;
(b) "barbed wire" means wire with spikes or jagged projections, and barbed wire is to be deemed to be a nuisance to a highway if it is likely to be injurious to persons or animals lawfully using the highway.

(2) If at the expiration of the time specified in the notice the occupier has failed to comply with the notice, a magistrates' court, if satisfied on complaint made by the authority that the wire is a nuisance to the highway, may order the occupier to abate the nuisance and, if he fails to comply with the order within a reasonable time, the authority may do whatever may be necessary in execution of the order and recover from him the expenses reasonably incurred by them in so doing.
(3) If the local authority who are a competent authority in relation to the highway concerned are the occupiers of the land in question proceedings under this section may be taken against them by any ratepayer within the area of that local authority and the foregoing provisions apply accordingly in relation to him and to the authority as they apply in relation to an authority and to an occupier of land.
[Highways Act 1980, s 164.]

7–6035 165. Dangerous land adjoining street. (1) If, in or on any land adjoining a street, there is an unfenced or inadequately fenced source of danger[1] to persons using the street, the local authority in whose area the street is situated may, by notice to the owner or occupier of that land, require him within such time as may be specified in the notice to execute such works of repair, protection, removal or enclosure as will obviate the danger.
(2) A person aggrieved by a requirement under subsection (1) above may appeal to a magistrates' court.
(3) Subject to any order made on appeal, if a person on whom a notice is served under this section fails to comply with the notice within the time specified in it, the authority by whom the notice was served may execute such works as are necessary to comply with the notice and may recover the expenses reasonably incurred by them in so doing from that person.
(4) Where the power conferred by subsection (1) above is exercisable in relation to land adjoining a street and has not been exercised by the local authority empowered to exercise it, then, if that authority are not the highway authority for the street, the highway authority for the street may request the local authority to exercise the power.
(5) If the local authority refuse to comply with a request made under subsection (4) above or fail within a reasonable time after the request is made to them to do so, the highway authority may exercise the power (and where they do so subsections (2) and (3) above apply accordingly).
[Highways Act 1980, s 165.]

---

1. The expression "source of danger" does not include that which arises because of the difference of levels between land and the footpath adjoining the road (*Myers v Harrow Corpn* [1962] 2 QB 442, [1962] 1 All ER 876, 126 JP 266).

7–6036 166. Forecourt abutting on streets. (1) If it appears to a competent authority that the forecourt of premises abutting on a street, or any steps or projection or goods (whether for sale or not) placed in such a forecourt, is or are a source of danger, obstruction or inconvenience to the public, the authority may by notice require the owner or occupier of the forecourt to fence the forecourt from the street or, at his election, to take such other steps as may be specified in the notice to obviate the danger, obstruction or inconvenience to the public.
For the purposes of this section the following are competent authorities—

(a) in the case of a street outside Greater London which is a highway, a local authority and also the highway authority;
(b) in the case of any other street, a local authority.

(2) If it appears to a competent authority that a stall or other erection on a forecourt of premises abutting on a street is by reason of its character injurious to the amenities of the street, the authority may by notice require the owner or occupier of the forecourt to make such alterations in the stall or

other erection as may be necessary to prevent its being injurious to the amenities of the street or, at his election, to remove it.

This subsection does not apply to any erection which has been in position in the forecourt of any premises at all times since 10th November 1960.

(3) A competent authority does not have power under subsection (1) or (2) above to give a notice applying to any advertisement as defined in section 336(1) of the Town and Country Planning Act 1990, or under subsection (2) above to give a notice applying to anything erected in conformity with planning permission granted on an application under Part III of that Act.

(4) The provisions of Part XII of the Public Health Act 1936 with respect to appeals against, and the enforcement of, notices requiring the execution of works apply in relation to any notice under this section as if this section were contained in that Act (and as if the references to the local authority included references to the highway authority); and section 290(6) of that Act shall authorise the authority at their election to take either of the courses which were open to the person on whom the notice was served in order to comply with it.

(5) In this section, "local authority" means any of the following, namely, the council of a district or London borough, the Common Council, the sub-treasurer of the Inner Temple, the under-treasurer of the Middle Temple a Welsh Council, and the Council of the Isles of Scilly and the Local Government (Wales) Act 1994, Sch 7.

[Highways Act 1980, s 166 as amended by the Planning (Consequential Provisions) Act 1990, Sch 2 and the Local Government (Wales) Act 1994, Sch 7.]

7–6037 167. Powers relating to retaining walls near streets. (1) This section applies to any length of a retaining wall, being a length—

(a) any cross-section of which is wholly or partly within 4 yards of a street; and

(b) which is at any point of a greater height than 4 feet 6 inches above the level of the ground at the boundary of the street nearest that point;

but does not apply to any length of a retaining wall erected on land belonging to any transport undertakers so long as that land is used by them primarily for the purpose of their undertaking or to any length of a retaining wall for the maintenance of which a highway authority are responsible.

(2) No length of retaining wall, being a length which when erected will be a length of retaining wall to which this section applies, shall be erected otherwise than in accordance with plans, sections and specifications approved by the local authority in whose area the street is situated; and before giving such approval that authority, if they are not the highway authority for the street, shall consult the highway authority.

(3) Any person aggrieved by the refusal of a local authority to approve any plans, sections and specifications submitted to them under this section may appeal to a magistrates' court.

(4) If a person erects a length of retaining wall in contravention of this section, he is guilty of an offence[1] and liable to a fine not exceeding **level 3** on the standard scale.

(5) If a length of retaining wall to which this section applies is in such condition (whether for want of repair or some other reason) as to be liable to endanger persons using the street, the local authority in whose area the street is situated may, by notice served on the owner or occupier of the land on which that length of wall is, require him to execute such works as will obviate the danger.

(6) Where the power conferred by subsection (5) above is exercisable in relation to a length of wall and has not been exercised by the local authority empowered to exercise it, then, if that authority are not the highway authority for the street in question, the highway authority may request the local authority to exercise the power; and if the local authority refuse to comply with the request or fail within a reasonable time after the request is made to them to do so, the highway authority may exercise the power.

(7) Subsections (2) to (7) of section 290 of the Public Health Act 1936 (appeals against and the enforcement of, certain notices under that Act) apply to any notice served under subsection (5) above as they apply to such notices as are mentioned in subsection (1) of that section, but subject to the following modifications—

(a) references to the local authority are to be construed as including references to the highway authority;

(b) for paragraph (f) of subsection (3) there is substituted the following paragraph—

"(f) that some other person ought to contribute towards the expense of executing any works required by the notice".

(8) Sections 300 to 302 of the Public Health Act 1936 (supplementary provisions relating to appeals under the said section 290) apply, with the necessary modifications, to appeals brought by virtue of subsection (7) above.

(9) In this section "retaining wall" means a wall, not forming part of a permanent building, which serves, or is intended to serve, as a support for earth or other material on one side only.

[Highways Act 1980, s 167 as amended by the Criminal Justice Act 1982, ss 38 and 46.]

---

1. Proceedings for an offence shall not, without the written consent of the Attorney-General, be taken by any person other than a person aggrieved, or a highway authority or council having an interest in the enforcement of the provision (s 312, post; Sch 22, post).

Precautions to be taken in doing certain works in or near streets or highways

7-6038   168. Building operations affecting public safety.   (1) If in the course of the carrying out of any building operation in or near a street there occurs an accident which—

    (*a*) gives rise to the risk of serious bodily injury to a person in the street, whether or not the death or disablement of any person is caused thereby; or

    (*b*) would have given rise to such risk but for the fact that a local authority or highway authority had in the exercise of their powers under section 78 of the Building Act 1984 (emergency measures to deal with dangerous buildings) or any other enactment taken steps to ensure that if an accident occurred it would not give rise to such risk,

then, subject to the provisions of this section, the owner of the land or building on which the building operation is being carried out is, without prejudice to any liability to which he or any other person may be subject apart from this section, guilty of an offence and liable to a fine not exceeding **level 5** on the standard scale.

(2) Where the commission by any person of an offence under this section is due to the act or default of some other person, that other person is guilty of the offence, and a person may be charged with and convicted of the offence by virtue of this subsection whether or not proceedings are taken against the first-mentioned person.

(3) In any proceedings for an offence under this section it is a defence, subject to subsection (4) below, for the person charged to prove—

    (*a*) that he took all reasonable precautions to secure that the building operation was so carried out as to avoid causing danger to persons in a street; or

    (*b*) that the commission of the offence was due to the act or default of another person and that he took all reasonable precautions and exercised all due diligence to avoid the commission of such an offence by himself or any person under his control.

(4) A person charged with an offence under this section is not, without leave of the court, entitled to rely on the defence provided by subsection (3)(*b*) above unless, within a period ending 7 clear days before the hearing, he has served on the prosecutor a notice in writing giving such information identifying or assisting in the identification of that other person as was then in his possession.

(5) In this section "building operation" means the construction, structural alteration, repair or maintenance of a building (including re-pointing, external re-decoration and external cleaning), the demolition of a building, the preparation for, and laying the foundations of, an intended building and the erection or dismantling of cranes or scaffolding.

[Highways Act 1980, s 168 as amended by the Criminal Justice Act 1982, ss 38 and 46 and the Building Act 1984, Sch 6.]

7-6039   169. Control of scaffolding on highways.   (1) Subject to subsection (6) below no person shall, in connection with any building or demolition work or the alteration, repair, maintenance or cleaning of any building, erect or retain on or over a highway any scaffolding or other structure which obstructs the highway (hereafter in this section referred to as a "relevant structure") unless he is authorised to do so by a licence in writing issued for the purposes of this section by the highway authority (hereafter in this section referred to as "a licence") and complies with the terms of the licence; and a licence may contain such terms as the authority issuing it thinks fit.

(2) If a person applies to a highway authority for a licence in respect of any relevant structure and furnishes the authority with such particulars in connection with the structure as the authority reasonably demand, it is the duty of the authority to issue a licence to him in respect of the structure unless the authority consider—

    (*a*) that the structure would cause unreasonable obstruction of a highway; or

    (*b*) that a relevant structure erected otherwise than as proposed by the applicant would cause less obstruction of a highway than the structure proposed by him and could conveniently be used for the work in question.

(3) If on an application for a licence in connection with a highway the highway authority refuse to issue a licence or issue a licence containing terms to which the applicant objects, the applicant may appeal to a magistrates' court against the refusal or terms; and on such an appeal the court may—

    (*a*) in the case of an appeal against a refusal, direct the highway authority to issue a licence in pursuance of the application;

    (*b*) in the case of an appeal against the terms of the licence, alter the terms.

(4) Subject to subsection (6) below, it is the duty of a person to whom a licence is issued by a highway authority in respect of a relevant structure—

    (*a*) to ensure that the structure is adequately lit at all times between half an hour after sunset and half an hour before sunrise;

    (*b*) to comply with any directions given to him in writing by the authority with respect to the erection and maintenance of traffic signs in connection with the structure;

    (*c*) to do such things in connection with the structure as any statutory undertakers reasonably request him to do for the purpose of protecting or giving access to any apparatus belonging to or used or maintained by the undertakers.

In this subsection and in section 171(2) below "statutory undertakers" means any of the following, namely, any body who are statutory undertakers within the meaning provided by section 329(1) below, any universal service provider in connection with the provision of a universal postal service, any licensee under a street works licence and the operator of a telecommunications code system* or a driver information system.

(5) A person who contravenes the provisions of subsection (1) above otherwise than by failing to comply with the terms of a licence or who fails without reasonable excuse to comply with the terms of a licence or to perform a duty imposed on him by subsection (4) above, is guilty of an offence and liable to a fine not exceeding **level 5** on the standard scale.

(6) Nothing in the preceding provisions of this section applies to a relevant structure erected before 14 February 1977 or erected or retained by the British Railways Board, the British Waterways Board or Transport for London or any of its subsidiaries (within the meaning of the Greater London Authority Act 1999) in the exercise of powers conferred on the body in question by any enactment; and nothing in paragraph (*a*) or (*b*) of subsection (4) above applies to a relevant structure if no part of it is less than 18 inches in a horizontal direction from a carriageway of the relevant highway and no part of it over a footway of the relevant highway is less than 8 feet in a vertical direction above the footway.

(7) No civil or criminal proceedings lie in respect of any obstruction of a highway which is caused by a relevant structure if the structure is on or over the highway in accordance with a licence and the person to whom the licence is issued performs the duties imposed on him in respect of the structure by subsection (4) above; and a highway authority by whom a licence is issued do not incur any liability by reason of the issue of the licence.

[Highways Act 1980, s 169 as amended by the Criminal Justice Act 1982, ss 38 and 46, the London Regional Transport Act 1984, Sch 6, the Telecommunications Act 1984 Schs 4 and 7, the Water Act 1989, Sch 27, the Road Traffic (Driver Licensing and Information Systems) Act 1989, Sch 4, the New Roads and Street Works Act 1991, Sch 8, SI 2001/1149 and SI 2003/1615.]

*Words substituted by the Communications Act 2003, Sch 17, from a date to be appointed.

7–6040 170. Control of mixing of mortar etc on highways. (1) subject to subsection (2) below, a person who mixes or deposits on a highway any mortar or cement or any other substance which is likely to stick to the surface of the highway or which, if it enters drains or sewers connected with the highway, is likely to solidify in the drains or sewers is guilty of an offence and liable to a fine not exceeding **level 4** on the standard scale.

(2) Nothing in subsection (1) above applies to any mixing or deposit—

(*a*) in a receptacle or on a plate which prevents the substance in question from coming into contact with the highway and from entering any drains and sewers connected with the highway;

(*b*) by the highway authority or a local authority in connection with the maintenance or alteration of the highway or a bridge over which or a tunnel through which the highway passes;

(*c*) by a body having a duty under an enactment to maintain—

(i) a bridge over which or a tunnel through which the highway passes, or

(ii) works or materials supporting or protecting the highway where it forms part of the approaches to such a bridge or tunnel,

if the mixing or deposit is in connection with the maintenance or alteration of the bridge, tunnel, works or materials;

(*d*) by statutory undertakers in connection with apparatus in or the placing of apparatus in the highway;

(*e*) by a person any licensee under a street works licence if the mixing or deposit cannot reasonably be done elsewhere than on the highway.

(3) In subsection (2) above—

"local authority" means any of the following, namely, the council of a county, district or London borough, the Common Council and the Council of the Isles of Scilly; and

"statutory undertakers" means any of the following, namely, any body who are statutory undertakers within the meaning provided by section 329(1) below, any universal service provider in connection with the provision of a universal postal service, and the operator of a telecommunications code system* or a driver information systems.

[Highways Act 1980, s 170 as amended by Criminal Justice Act 1982, ss 38 and 46, the Telecommunications Act 1984 Schs 4 and 7, the Local Government Act 1985, Sch 17, the Water Act 1989, Sch 27, the Road Traffic (Driver Licensing and Information Systems) Act 1989, Sch 4, the New Roads and Street Works Act 1991, Sch 8 and SI 2001/1149.]

*Words substituted by the Communications Act 2003, Sch 17, from a date to be appointed.

7–6041 171. Control of deposit of building materials and making of excavations in streets.
(1) A person may, with the consent of the highway authority for a street that is a highway

maintainable at the public expense, temporarily deposit building materials, rubbish or other things in the street or make a temporary excavation in it.

(2) A highway authority may give their consent under subsection (1) above subject to such conditions as they think fit including in particular, without prejudice to the generality of the foregoing, conditions for preventing damage or ensuring access to apparatus of statutory undertakers.

In this section "statutory undertakers" has the meaning provided by section 169(4) above.

(3) A person aggrieved by the refusal of consent under subsection (1) above, and a person to whom such a consent is given subject to conditions, may appeal to a magistrates' court against the refusal or, as the case may be, the conditions.

(4) It is the duty of a person who makes such a deposit or excavation as is mentioned in subsection (1) above to comply with any directions given to him in writing by the highway authority with respect to the erection and maintenance of traffic signs in connection with the deposit or excavation.

(5) Where a person places any building materials, rubbish or other thing in, or makes an excavation in, a street he shall—

(a) cause the obstruction or excavation to be properly fenced and during the hours of darkness to be properly lighted, and

(b) if required so to do by the highway authority for the street or, in the case of a street that is not a highway, by the local authority in whose area the street is situated, remove the obstruction or, as the case may be, fill in the excavation;

and in any case he shall not allow the obstruction or excavation to remain in the street longer than is necessary.

(6) A person who—

(a) without reasonable excuse contravenes any condition subject to which a consent is given to him under subsection (1) above, or

(b) without reasonable excuse fails to perform the duty imposed on him by subsection (4) above, or

(c) fails to perform a duty imposed on him by subsection (5) above,

is guilty of an offence[1] and liable to a fine not exceeding £10 in respect of each day on which the contravention or failure occurs.

The liability of any person to a fine under this subsection by virtue of paragraph (b) or (c) above is without prejudice to any other liability to which he may be subject apart from this subsection.

(7) Where an offence under this section by virtue of subsection (6)(c) above is committed in a street, the highway authority for the street or, in the case of a street that is not a highway, the local authority in whose area the street is situated, may remove the obstruction or, as the case may be, fill in the excavation and recover the expenses reasonably incurred by them in so doing from the person convicted of the offence.

[Highways Act 1980, s 171.]

---

1. For restriction on the institution of proceedings, see s 312 and Sch 22, post.

7–6041A 171A–171C. *Scaffolding, building materials and excavations: charge for occupation of highway*

7–6042 172. Hoardings to be set up during building etc. (1) Subject to subsection (2) below, a person proposing to erect or take down a building in a street or court, or to alter or repair the outside of a building in a street or court, shall, before beginning the work, erect a close boarded hoarding or fence to the satisfaction of the appropriate authority so as to separate the building from the street or court.

For the purposes of this section the appropriate authority, in relation to any street or court, is the council of the county, metropolitan district or London borough in which it is situated or, if it is situated in the City, the Common Council.

(2) The obligation to erect a hoarding or fence imposed by subsection (1) above may be dispensed with if the appropriate authority so consent.

(3) Where a person has erected a hoarding or fence in compliance with subsection (1) above, he shall—

(a) if the appropriate authority so require, make a convenient covered platform and handrail to serve as a footway for pedestrians outside the hoarding or fence;

(b) maintain the hoarding or fence and any such platform and handrail in good condition to the satisfaction of the authority during such time as the authority may require;

(c) if the authority so require, sufficiently light the hoarding or fence and any such platform and handrail during the hours of darkness; and

(d) remove the hoarding or fence and any such platform and handrail when required by the authority.

(4) A person aggrieved by the refusal of a consent under subsection (2) above or by a requirement under subsection (3) above may appeal to a magistrates' court.

(5) Subject to any order made on appeal, if a person contravenes this section he is guilty of an

offence[1] and liable to a fine not exceeding **level 3** on the standard scale; and if the offence is continued after conviction he is guilty of a further offence and liable to a fine not exceeding £2 for each day on which the offence is so continued.

[Highways Act 1980, s 172 as amended by the Criminal Justice Act 1982, ss 38 and 46 and the Local Government Act 1985, Sch 4.]

---

1. For restriction on the institution of proceedings, see s 312 and Sch 22, post.

7–6043 173. Hoardings to be securely erected. (1) No person shall use for any purpose a hoarding or similar structure that is in, or adjoins, any street unless it is securely fixed to the satisfaction of the council who, in relation to that street, are the appropriate authority for the purposes of section 172 above.

(2) If a person contravenes this section he is guilty of an offence[1] and liable to a fine not exceeding **level 1** on the standard scale; and if the offence is continued after conviction he is guilty of a further offence and liable to a fine not exceeding £1 for each day on which the offence is so continued.

[Highways Act 1980, s 173 as amended by the Criminal Justice Act 1982, s 46.]

---

1. For restriction on the institution of proceedings, see s 312 and Sch 22, post.

7–6044 174. Precautions to be taken by persons executing works in streets. (1) Where a person is executing works of any description in a street (other than street works within the meaning of Part III of the New Roads and Street Works Act 1991), he

(a) shall erect such barriers and traffic signs for preventing danger to traffic, for regulating traffic, and for warning traffic of danger, as may be necessary and remove them as soon as they cease to be needed for any of those purposes;

(b) shall cause the works to be properly guarded and lighted during the hours of darkness; and

(c) where the nature of the works so requires, shall cause any building adjoining the street to be shored up or otherwise protected.*

(2) Subject to subsection (3) below, if any person fails to satisfy an obligation to which he is subject by virtue of subsection (1) above he is guilty of an offence[1] and, without prejudice to any other liability to which he may be subject apart from this subsection, is liable to a fine not exceeding £10 in respect of each day of such failure.

(3) Where a person is subject to the same obligation by virtue of subsection (1) above and by virtue of some other enactment, then, without prejudice to section 18 of the Interpretation Act 1978 (offences under two or more laws), if a failure by him to satisfy that obligation is an offence under an enactment other than subsection (2) above, subsection (2) above does not apply in relation to a failure by him to satisfy that obligation.

(4) If a person, without lawful authority or excuse—

(a) takes down, alters or removes any barrier, traffic sign, support or light erected or placed in pursuance of subsection (1) above or any fence, barrier, traffic sign or light erected or placed on or near a street in pursuance of any other enactment for the purpose of warning users of the street of any obstruction, whether caused by the execution of works in or near the street or otherwise, or of protecting them from danger arising out of such an obstruction, or

(b) extinguishes any light so placed,

he is guilty of an offence[1] and liable to a fine not exceeding **level 3** on the standard scale.

(5) For the purposes of section 312 below in its application to an offence under this section statutory undertakers a universal service provider in connection with the provision of a universal postal service are each to be deemed to be a person aggrieved.

[Highways Act 1980, s 174 as amended by the Criminal Justice Act 1982, ss 38 and 46, the New Roads and Street Works Act 1991, Sch 8 and SI 2001/1149.]

---

*New sub-ss (1A)–(1C) inserted by the **Traffic Management Act 2004, s 71 from a date to be apppointed.**
1. For restriction on the institution of proceedings, see s 312 and Sch 22, post.

7–6045 175. Liability of certain persons in respect of materials left on highway. If—

(a) any officer or servant of the highway authority for a highway, or

(b) any officer or servant of a non-metropolitan district council maintaining a highway by virtue of section 42 or 50 above, or

(c) a person liable to maintain a highway by reason of tenure, enclosure or prescription,

causes any heap of materials or any other object to be laid on the highway, he is, if he allows it to remain there at night to the danger of traffic without taking all reasonable precautions for the prevention of accidents, guilty of an offence and liable to a fine not exceeding **level 1** on the standard scale.

[Highways Act 1980, s 175 as amended by the Criminal Justice Act 1982, s 46 and the Local Government Act 1985, Sch 4.]

Miscellaneous

7–6046   176. Restriction on construction of bridges over highways.   (1) The highway authority for a highway may grant to the owner or occupier of any premises adjoining the highway a licence to construct a bridge over the highway on such terms and conditions, and to use it for such period and on such terms and conditions, as the authority think fit.

(2) No fine, rent or other sum of money, except a reasonable sum in respect of legal or other expenses, is payable in respect of a licence under this section.

(3) A licence under this section shall not authorise any interference with the convenience of persons using the highway, or affect the rights of owners of premises adjoining the highway, or the rights of tramway, railway, dock, harbour or electricity undertakers[1].

(4) It shall be a condition of every licence under this section that the person to whom it is granted is, at his own expense, to remove the bridge or alter it in such manner as the authority may require, if at any time they consider the removal or alteration necessary or desirable in connection with the carrying out of improvements to the highway.

The decision of the authority that the removal or alteration is necessary or desirable in that connection shall be final, and the condition shall be enforceable by the authority against the owner for the time being of the premises.

(5) Subject to subsection (6) below, a person aggrieved by the refusal of an authority to grant a licence under this section or by the period for which the licence is granted or by a term or condition of the licence (other than the condition mentioned in subsection (4) above) may appeal to the Crown Court.

(6) No appeal lies under subsection (5) above against any term or condition of a licence granted by the Minister under this section if he declares the term or condition to be necessary for the purpose of securing the safety of persons using the highway or of preventing interference with traffic on it.

(7) If a person, except in the exercise of statutory powers—

(a)   constructs a bridge over a highway without a licence under this section, or

(b)   constructs or uses a bridge otherwise than in accordance with the terms and conditions of such a licence, or

(c)   fails to remove or alter a bridge when required to do so in accordance with any condition of the licence or within one month from the date of the expiration of the licence,

he is guilty of an offence[2] and is liable to a fine not exceeding **level 2** on the standard scale, and if the offence is continued after conviction he is guilty of a further offence and is liable to a fine not exceeding £5 for each day on which the offence is so continued.

(8) In this section "bridge" means a structure the sole purpose of which is to provide a way over a highway.

[Highways Act 1980, s 176 as amended by the Criminal Justice Act 1982, s 46.]

---

1. The reference to "electricity undertaker" in this section shall be construed as a reference to the holder of a licence under s 6 of the Electricity Act 1989 who is entitled to exercise any power conferred by para 1 of Sch 4 to the Act (street works etc) (Electricity Act 1989, Sch 16, para 2(5)).

2. For restriction on the institution of proceedings, see s 312 and Sch 22, post.

7–6047   177. Restriction on construction of buildings over highways.   (1) No person shall—

(a)   except in the exercise of statutory powers, construct a building over any part of a highway maintainable at the public expense (whether it is intended to span the highway or not), or alter a building so constructed, without a licence granted under this section by the highway authority for that highway or otherwise than in accordance with the terms and conditions of a licence so granted;

(b)   use a building so constructed or altered in pursuance of a licence so granted otherwise than in accordance with the terms and conditions thereof;

and any person who contravenes any provision of this subsection is guilty of an offence[1] and liable to a fine not exceeding **level 5** on the standard scale; and if the offence is continued after conviction, he is guilty of a further offence and liable to a fine not exceeding £50 for each day on which the offence is so continued.

(2) Subject to subsections (3) and (4) below, a licence under this section may contain such terms and conditions, including terms and conditions with respect to the construction (including the headway over the highway), maintenance, lighting and use of the building, as the highway authority think fit; and, any such term of condition is binding on the successor in title to every owner, and every lessee and occupier, of the building.

(3) No fine, rent or other sum of money is payable in respect of a licence granted under this section except—

(a)   a reasonable sum in respect of legal or other expenses incurred in connection with the grant of the licence; and

(b)   an annual charge of a reasonable amount for administering the licence;

and any sum payable by virtue of paragraph (a) above is recoverable from the applicant for the licence and any sum payable by virtue of paragraph (*b*) above is recoverable from the owner of the building.

(4) No such licence shall authorise any interference with the convenience of persons using the highway, or affect the rights of the owners of premises adjoining the highway, or the rights of statutory undertakers or the operator of a telecommunications code system* or a driver information system.

(5) Where a licence under this section makes provision for the execution of any works or the provision of any facilities which in the opinion of the highway authority require to be executed or provided by them in connection with the building or its construction or alteration, the authority may execute those works or, as the case may be, provide those facilities and may recover the expenses reasonably incurred by them in so doing from the licensee or from the owner of the building.

(6) A person aggrieved by the refusal of a highway authority to grant a licence under this section or by a term or condition of the licence may appeal to the Crown Court, except that no such appeal lies—

(*a*) if the land on which the highway in question is situated is owned by the highway authority, or

(*b*) against any term or condition which the highway authority declare to be necessary for the purpose of securing the safety of persons using the highway or of preventing interference with traffic thereon.

(7) Where a person has constructed or altered a building for the construction, or, as the case may be, alteration, of which a licence is required by this section without such a licence or otherwise than in accordance with the terms and conditions of the licence, the highway authority may by notice served on the licensee or the owner of the building require him to demolish the building within such time as may be specified in the notice or, as the case may be, to make such alterations therein and within such times as may be so specified.

(8) Where there has been a failure to comply with any terms or conditions of a licence under this section with respect to the maintenance or use of a building, the highway authority may by notice served on the licensee or the owner of the building require him to execute such works or take such steps as are necessary to secure compliance with those terms or conditions within such time as may be specified in the notice.

(9) If a person on whom a notice is served under subsection (7) or (8) above fails to comply with the notice within the time specified in it, the highway authority may demolish the building or, as the case may be, execute such works or take such steps as are necessary to comply with the notice and may recover the expenses reasonably incurred by them in so doing from that person.

(10) Where by virtue of subsection (9) above a highway authority demolish a building, they may dispose of the materials resulting from the demolition.

(11) In relation to any prohibition or restriction on the use of a building imposed by the Minister by virtue of any term or condition contained in a licence granted by him under this section, section 1(1)(*c*) of the Local Land Charges Act 1975 has effect as if the references to the date of the commencement of that Act were references to 1st November 1971.

(12) Paragraph 23 of the telecommunications code* (which provides a procedure for certain cases where works involve the alteration of telecommunication apparatus*) shall apply, for the purposes of works authorised or required by a licence under this section to be executed, to the licensee.

(13) This section does not apply to a building which constitutes a bridge within the meaning of section 176 above, but subject to that in this section "building" includes any structure and any part of a building.

(14) Where the land on which a highway is situated is owned by the highway authority, nothing in subsection (3) above is to be taken as affecting the rights of that authority as the owner of that land to sell or lease the air-space above the surface of that land or grant any rights in relation to it.

[Highways Act 1980, s 177 as amended by the Criminal Justice Act 1982, ss 38 and 46, the Telecommunications Act 1984, Sch 4 and the Road Traffic (Driver Licensing and Information Systems) Act 1989, Sch 4.]

---

*Words substituted by the Communications Act 2003, Sch 17, from a date to be appointed.
1. For restriction on the institution of proceedings, see s 312 and Sch 22, post.

7–6048 178. Restriction on placing rails, beams etc over highways. (1) No person shall fix or place any overhead beam, rail, pipe, cable, wire or other similar apparatus over, along or across a highway without the consent of the highway authority for the highway, and the highway authority may attach to their consent such reasonable terms and conditions as they think fit.

(2) Subject to subsection (3) below, a person aggrieved by the refusal of a consent under subsection (1) above, or by any terms or conditions attached to such a consent, may appeal to a magistrates' court.

(3) No appeal lies under subsection (2) above against any term or condition attached by the Minister to a consent given by him under this section if he declares the term or condition to be necessary for the purpose of securing the safety of persons using the highway to which the consent relates or of preventing interference with traffic on it.

(4) If a person contravenes subsection (1) above, or the terms or conditions of any consent given under that subsection, he is guilty of an offence[1] and liable to a fine not exceeding **level 1** on the standard scale; and if the offence is continued after conviction he is guilty of a further offence and liable to a fine not exceeding £1 for each day on which the offence is so continued.

(5) This section does not apply to any works or apparatus belonging to any statutory undertakers, and for this purpose the Civil Aviation Authority, a person who holds a licence under Chapter I part I of the Transport Act 2000 (to the extent that the person is carrying out activities authorised by the licence), and a universal service provider in connection with the provision of a universal postal service and the operator of a <u>telecommunications code system</u>* or a driver information system are to be deemed to be statutory undertakers.
[Highways Act 1980, s 178 as amended by the Criminal Justice Act 1982, s 46, the Telecommunications Act 1984, Sch 4, the Road Traffic (Driver Licensing and Information Systems) Act 1989, Sch 4, SI 2001/1149 and SI 2001/4050.]

---

*Words substituted by the Communications Act 2003, Sch 17, from a date to be appointed.
1. For restriction on the institution of proceedings, see s 312 and Sch 22, post.

7–6049   179. Control of construction of cellars etc under street.   (1) No person shall construct works to which this section applies under any part of a street without the consent of the appropriate authority, and the authority may by notice served on a person who has constructed such works in contravention of this section require him to remove them, or to alter or deal with them in such a manner as may be specified in the notice.

For the purposes of this section the appropriate authority is—

(i)   in relation to a street outside Greater London which is a highway, the highway authority for the street; and

(ii) in relation to any other street, the local authority in whose area the street is situated.

(2) A person aggrieved by the refusal of a consent, or by a requirement of a notice, under subsection (1) above may appeal to a magistrates' court.

(3) A person who constructs works to which this section applies in contravention of this section is guilty of an offence[1] and is liable to a fine not exceeding **level 1** on the standard scale; and, subject to any order made on appeal, if he fails to comply with a requirement of a notice served on him under subsection (1) above he is guilty of a further offence and is liable to a fine not exceeding £2 for each day during which the failure continues.

(4) The appropriate authority may also cause works to which this section applies constructed in contravention of this section to be removed, altered or otherwise dealt with as they think fit, and may recover the expenses reasonably incurred by them in so doing from the offender.

(5) As soon as may be after an authority consent to the construction of works to which this section applies under a street they shall give notice of their consent to any public utility undertakers having any apparatus under the street.

(6) Subject to subsection (7) below, the works to which this section applies are—

(*a*) any part of a building; and

(*b*) without prejudice to the generality of paragraph (*a*) above, a vault, arch or cellar, whether forming part of a building or not.

(7) This section does not apply to street works within the meaning of Part III of the New Roads and Street Works Act 1991.
[Highways Act 1980, s 179 as amended by the Local Government (Miscellaneous Provisions) Act 1982, s 22, the Criminal Justice Act 1982, s 46 and the New Roads and Street Works Act 1991, Sch 8.]

---

1. For restriction on the institution of proceedings, see s 312 and Sch 22, post.

7–6050   180. Control of openings into cellars etc under streets, and pavement lights and ventilators.   (1) No person shall make an opening in the footway of a street as an entrance to a cellar or vault thereunder without the consent of the appropriate authority, and where an authority give consent under this subsection they shall require the person to whom the consent is given to provide a door or covering constructed in such manner and of such materials as they direct.

For the purposes of this section the appropriate authority is the same as for the purposes of section 179 above.

(2) No person shall carry out any works in a street to provide means for the admission of air or light to premises situated under, or abutting on, the street without the consent of the local authority, and the local authority in giving any consent under this subsection may impose any requirement as to the construction of the works.

(3) A person aggrieved by the refusal of a consent, or by a requirement, under subsection (1) above may appeal to a magistrates' court and a person who applies for consent under subsection (2) above may appeal to such a court against a refusal of consent, or a requirement, under subsection (2).

(4) Subject to any order made on appeal—

(*a*) a person who—

(i)   makes an opening in the footway of a street in contravention of subsection (1) above, or

(ii) fails to comply with a requirement made to him under that subsection, is guilty of an offence[1] and, without prejudice to any other liability to which he may be subject, liable to a fine not exceeding **level 1** on the standard scale;

(b) a person who—

(i) carries out any works in contravention of subsection (2) above, or

(ii) fails to comply with a requirement made to him under that subsection,

is guilty of an offence and, without prejudice to any other liability to which he may be subject, liable to a fine not exceeding **level 1** on the standard scale.

(5) As soon as may be after an authority give consent under either subsection (1) or subsection (2) above they shall give notice thereof to any public utility undertakers having any apparatus under the street.

(6) The following, namely—

(a) every vault, arch and cellar under a street,

(b) every opening in the surface of any street into any such vault, arch or cellar,

(c) every door or covering to any such opening,

(d) every cellar-head, grating, light and coal hole in the surface of a street, and

(e) all landings, flags or stones of the street by which any of the above are supported,

shall be kept in good condition and repair by the owner or occupier of the vault, arch or cellar, or of the premises to which it belongs.

(7) If default is made in complying with subsection (6) above, the appropriate authority may, after the expiration of 24 hours from the service of a notice of their intention to do so on any person in default, cause any thing as respects which there has been such a default to be repaired or put into good condition, and may recover the expenses reasonably incurred by them in so doing from the owner or occupier thereof or of the premises to which it belongs.

[Highways Act 1980, s 180 as amended by the Criminal Justice Act 1982, ss 38 and 46.]

---

1. For restriction on the institution of proceedings, see s 312 and Sch 22, post.

7–6053 184. Vehicle crossings over footways and verges.   (1) Where the occupier of any premises adjoining or having access to a highway maintainable at the public expense habitually takes or permits to be taken a mechanically propelled vehicle across a kerbed footway or a verge in the highway to or from those premises, the highway authority for the highway may, subject to subsection (2) below, serve a notice on the owner and the occupier of the premises—

(a) stating that they propose to execute such works for the construction of a vehicle crossing over the footway or verge as may be specified in the notice; or

(b) imposing such reasonable conditions on the use of the footway or verge as a crossing as may be so specified.

(2) A highway authority is not entitled by virtue of subsection (1) above to construct a vehicle crossing on, or on any part of, the site of a made-up vehicle crossing which has been constructed either under this section or under section 40 of the Highways Act 1971 (which this section replaces) or before the commencement of the said section 40, or to impose conditions on the use of such a crossing.

(3) Where any land is being, or is to be, developed in accordance with a planning permission granted, or deemed to have been granted, under the Town and Country Planning Act 1990, and it appears to the highway authority for a highway maintainable at the public expense that the development makes it necessary—

(a) to construct a crossing over a kerbed footway or a verge in the highway so as to provide an access for mechanically propelled vehicles to or from the carriageway of the highway from or to premises adjoining or having access to the highway; or

(b) to improve or otherwise alter a made-up vehicle crossing that provides such an access as is mentioned in paragraph (a) above (whenever constructed),

that authority may serve on the owner and the occupier of the premises a notice stating that they propose to execute such works for the construction or, as the case may be, alteration of the crossing as may be specified in the notice.

(4) Unless the development giving rise to a notice under subsection (3) above consists solely of the provision of a new means of access to or from a highway from or to premises, there may be specified in a notice under that subsection works for the construction as part of the whole vehicle crossing proposed to be constructed or altered, as the case may be, of acceleration and deceleration lanes.

(5) In determining whether to exercise their powers under subsection (1) or (3) above, a highway authority shall have regard to the need to prevent damage to a footway or verge, and in determining the works to be specified in a notice under subsection (1)(a) or (3) an authority shall have regard to that and the following other matters, namely—

(a) the need to ensure, so far as practicable, safe access to and egress from premises; and

(b) the need to facilitate, so far as practicable, the passage of vehicular traffic in highways.

(6)　Schedule 14 to this Act has effect with respect to the making of objections to a notice under subsection (1) or (3) above and to the date on which such a notice becomes effective.

(7)　Where a notice under subsection (1)(*a*) or (3) above has become effective, the highway authority by whom the notice was served may execute such works as are specified in the notice, subject to such modifications (if any) as may have been made by the Minister, and may recover the expenses reasonably incurred by them in so doing from the owner or occupier of the premises in question.

(8)　A notice under subsection (1) or (3) above shall inform the person on whom it is served of his right to object to the notice and (except in the case of a notice under subsection (1)(*b*)) shall state the effect of subsection (7) above.

(9)　Where a person who is carrying out, or proposes to carry out, such a development as is referred to in subsection (3) above offers to execute the works specified in a notice under that subsection, the highway authority by whom the notice was served may authorise him to execute those works in accordance with plans approved by them.

(10)　If a person authorised under subsection (9) above to execute any works fails to execute them to the satisfaction of the highway authority before the development is completed, the authority may execute the works or alter the works executed by that person and recover the expenses reasonably incurred by them in so doing from him.

(11)　Any person may request the highway authority for a highway maintainable at the public expense to execute such works as are specified in the request for constructing a vehicle crossing over a footway or verge in the highway, and the authority may approve the request with or without modification, or may propose alternative works or reject the request; and in determining how to exercise their powers under this subsection an authority shall have regard to the matters mentioned in subsection (5) above.

(12)　An authority to whom a request under subsection (11) above is made shall notify the person making the request of their decision and if they approve, with or without modification, the works proposed in the request or propose alternative works, they shall supply him with a quotation of the cost of the works as approved or proposed by them, and he may, on depositing with them the amount quoted, require them to execute those works.

(13)　As soon as practicable after such a deposit has been made with an authority the authority shall execute the works as approved or proposed by them.

(14)　(*Repealed*).

(15)　The expenses recoverable under subsection (7) or (10) above and the cost of the works for the purposes of subsection (12) above include the cost of any measures needing to be taken in relation to undertaker's apparatus to be executed in consequence of the construction of the crossing.

(16)　Nothing in this section imposes on any person other than a highway authority any obligation to maintain a vehicle crossing.

(17)　If a person knowingly uses a footway or verge as a crossing in contravention of any condition imposed under subsection (1)(*b*) above, or knowingly permits it to be so used, he is guilty of an offence and liable to a fine not exceeding **level 3** on the standard scale.

[Highways Act 1980, s 184 as amended by the Criminal Justice Act 1982, ss 35, 38 and 46, the Planning (Consequential Provisions) Act 1990, Sch 2 and the New Roads and Street Works Act 1991, Sch 8.]

PART XI[1]
MAKING UP OF PRIVATE STREETS

Introductory

7–6066　203. Interpretation of Part XI.　(1)　In this Part of this Act (and elsewhere in this Act) "the private street works code" means sections 205 to 218 below; and "the advance payments code" means sections 219 to 225 below.

(2)　In this Part of this Act "private street" means a street that is not a highway maintainable at the public expense, and—

(*a*)　includes any land that is deemed to be a private street by virtue of a declaration made under section 232 below, and

(*b*)　for the purpose of the application of the advance payments code or section 229 below in relation to any building, includes—

(i)　any land shown as a proposed street on plans deposited with respect to that building either under building regulations or on an application for planning permission under the Town and Country Planning Act 1990, and

(ii)　(*Repealed*); or

but the fact that a part of a street is a highway maintainable at the public expense does not prevent any other part of it from being a part of a private street for the purposes of this Part of this Act.

(3)　In this Part of this Act—

"contributory place" has the same meaning as in section 343 of the Public Health Act 1936;

"fronting" includes adjoining, and "front" is to be construed accordingly;

"industrial premises" means premises used or designed or suitable for use for the carrying on of any such process or research as is specified in section 66(1) of the Town and Country Planning

Act 1971, and includes premises used for purposes ancillary to the carrying on of any such process or research;

"local Act" includes a provisional order confirmed by Parliament and the confirming Act so far as it relates to that order;

"paving, metalling and flagging" includes all methods of making a carriageway or footway;

"place of public religious worship" means a place of public religious worship which belongs to the Church of England or to the Church in Wales (within the meaning of the Welsh Church Act 1914), or which is for the time being certified as required by law as a place of religious worship;

"street works" means any works for the sewering, levelling, paving, metalling, flagging, channelling and making good of a street, and includes the provision of proper means for lighting a street;

"street works authority" means—

(a) as respects a street outside Greater London, the council of the county or metropolitan district in which the street is situated;

(b) as respects a street in a London borough, the council of the borough, and

(c) as respects a street in the City, the Common Council.

(4) For the purposes of the advance payments code and of section 229 below, the frontage of a building or proposed building on a street shall be deemed to be the frontage that the building itself and any land occupied or, as the case may be, proposed to be occupied, with the building and for the purposes of it has or will have on the street.

(5) In ascertaining a majority in number of owners for the purposes of any provision of this Part of this Act, joint owners are to be treated as one owner.

[Highways Act 1980, s 203 as amended by the Local Government Act 1985, Sch 4 and the Planning (Consequential Provisions) Act 1990, Sch 2.]

---

1. Part XI contains ss 203–237.

7–6067   204. Purposes and application of private street works code and advance payments code.   (1) The private street works code has effect for securing the execution of street works in private streets anywhere in England or Wales.

(2) The advance payments code has effect for securing payment of the expenses of the execution of street works in private streets adjacent to new buildings, and applies—

(a) in all outer London boroughs;

(b) in all areas in counties in which the advance payments code in the Highways Act 1959 (which is replaced by the advance payments code in this Act) was in force immediately before 1st April 1974; and

(c) in any parish or community in which the advance payments code in the Highways Act 1959 was, after 1st April 1974, adopted in accordance with Schedule 14 to that Act, or in which the advance payments code is adopted in accordance with Schedule 15 to this Act.

(3) The areas in which the advance payments code applies by virtue of subsection (2)(b) above shall be taken to include any area in Wales—

(a) which is, or is in, a county borough; and

(b) in which the code applied immediately before 1st April 1996 by virtue of that subsection.

[Highways Act 1980, s 204 amended by the Local Government (Wales) Act 1994, Sch 7.]

The private street works code[1]

7–6068   205. Street works in private streets.   (1) Where a private street is not, to the satisfaction of the street works authority, sewered, levelled, paved, metalled, flagged, channelled, made good and lighted, the authority may from time to time resolve with respect to the street to execute street works and, subject to the private street works code, the expenses incurred by the authority in executing those works shall be apportioned between the premises fronting[2] the street.

(2) Where the authority resolve to execute street works with respect to a part only of the street[3] (other than a part extending for the whole of the length of the street), the expenses incurred by them in executing the works shall be apportioned only between the premises fronting the length of the street which constitutes or comprises that part.

(3) Where an authority have passed a resolution under subsection (1) above, the proper officer of the council shall prepare—

(a) a specification of the street works referred to in the resolution, with any necessary plans and sections,

(b) an estimate of the probable expenses of the works, and

(c) a provisional apportionment apportioning the estimated expenses between the premises liable to be charged with them under the private street works code;

and the specification, plans, sections, estimate and provisional apportionment shall comprise the particulars specified in paragraphs 1 to 4 of Schedule 16[4] to this Act and shall be submitted to the authority, who may by a further resolution (hereafter in the private street works code referred to as "the resolution of approval") approve them with or without modification or addition as they think fit.

(4) If, in the case of a street outside Greater London, the street works referred to in the resolution under subsection (1) above include the sewering of the street, the proper officer of the county council shall, when preparing the specification required by subsection (3) above, consult the council of the district in which the street works are to be carried out.

(4A) In the case of a street in Wales—

(*a*) subsection (4) above does not apply; but

(*b*) if the street works referred to in the resolution under subsection (1) above—

(i) are to be carried out in a part of the street which is treated as being in the area of a street works authority other than the local Welsh council for it; and

(ii) include the sewering of the street,

the proper officer of the council which are the street works authority shall, when preparing the specification required by subsection (3) above, consult the local Welsh council for it,

and, in the case of any part of a street in Wales which is treated as being in the area of a street works authority which are not the local Welsh council for it, at the offices of the Local Welsh council.

(5A) For the purposes of this section, the local Welsh council for a street in Wales are the council of the county or county borough in which it is situated.

(5) After the resolution of approval has been passed, a notice containing the particulars specified in paragraph 5 of Schedule 16 to this Act shall—

(*a*) be published once in each of 2 successive weeks in a local newspaper circulating in the area of the street works authority, and

(*b*) be posted in a prominent position in or near to the street to which the resolution relates once at least in each of 3 successive weeks, and

(*c*) within 7 days from the date of the first publication under paragraph (*a*) above, be served on the owners of the premises shown in the provisional apportionment as liable to be charged;

and during one month from the said date a copy of the resolution of approval, and the approved documents or copies of them certified by the proper officer of the council, shall be kept deposited and open to inspection free of charge at all reasonable hours at the offices of the street works authority and, in the case of a street situated in a non-metropolitan district, at the offices of the council of that district.

(6) Where a notice is served on an owner of premises under subsection (5)(*c*) above it shall be accompanied by a statement of the sum apportioned on those premises by the provisional apportionment.

[Highways Act 1980, s 205 as amended by the Local Government Act 1985, Sch 4 and the Local Government (Wales) Act 1994, Sch 7.]

---

1. Previously known as "The Code of 1892". The code re-enacts provisions formerly contained in the (repealed) Private Street Works Act 1892. The Code shall have effect for the purpose of securing the execution of street works in private streets, and shall apply in all counties in England and Wales.

2. An upper flat, separated from a street by a garden in the ownership of the occupier of a lower flat does not "front" the street (*Buckinghamshire County Council v Trigg* [1963] 1 All ER 403, 127 JP 171).

3. The question whether a path is a street cannot be raised at all if not on an objection arising out of this section; see *Woodford UDC v Henwood* (1900) 64 JP 118.

4. Post.

7–6069   206. Incidental works.   A street works authority may include in street works to be executed under the private street works code with respect to a street any works which they think necessary for bringing the street, as regards sewerage, drainage, level, or other matters, into conformity with any other streets, whether maintainable at the public expense or not, including the provision of separate sewers for the reception of sewage and of surface water respectively.

[Highways Act 1980, s 206.]

7–6070   207. Provisional apportionment of expenses.   (1) In a provisional apportionment of expenses of street works under the private street works code, the apportionment of expenses between the premises liable to be charged with them shall, subject to the provisions of this section, be made according to the frontage[1] of the respective premises.

(2) The street works authority may, if they think just, resolve that in settling the apportionment regard shall be had to the following considerations[2]:—

(*a*) the greater or less degree of benefit to be derived by any premises[3] from the street works;

(*b*) the amount and value of any work already done by the owners or occupiers of any premises.

(3) The authority may—

(*a*) if they think just, include in the apportionment any premises which do not front the street, but have access to it through a court, passage, or otherwise[4], and which will, in the opinion of the authority, be benefited by the works, and (*b*) fix, by reference to the degree of benefit to be derived by those premises, the amount to be apportioned on them.

[Highways Act 1980, s 207.]

1. Different premises belonging to one owner should not be lumped together (*Croydon RDC v Betts* [1914] 1 Ch 870; *Pontypridd UDC v Jones* (1911) 75 JP 345). Frontage is an overriding consideration (*Parkstone Primrose Laundry Ltd v Poole Corpn* (1950) 114 JP 354). All the adjoining premises must be included, including those *extra commercium* which have no "owner" (*Herne Bay UDC v Payne and Wood* [1907] 2 KB 130, 71 JP 282).

2. The authority, after passing a resolution under (*a*), may abandon that resolution and pass another under (*b*) which will operate as fresh instructions to their surveyor to prepare a provisional apportionment, etc, on the new basis: see *Wilson v Wrexham Corpn* [1959] 3 All ER 674, 124 JP 41.

3. Where the street works authority have not so resolved, a magistrates' court has no jurisdiction to make an order relating to degree of benefit (*Hornchurch UDC v Webber* [1938] 1 KB 698, [1938] 1 All ER 309, 102 JP 167).

4. "Court, passage or otherwise" includes anything which gives access to the premises in the same manner as a court or passage, but do not include a public street or a road made for a purpose other than that of giving access to the street (*Newquay UDC v Rickeard* [1911] 2 KB 846, 75 JP 382; *Chatterton v Glanford RDC* [1915] 3 KB 707, 79 JP 441). "Passage" means something in the nature of a feeder of the street to be made up, but need not be the only means of approach (*Oakley v Merthyr Tydfil Corpn* [1922] 1 KB 409, 86 JP 1).

7–6071 208. Objections to proposed works. (1) Within one month[1] from the date of the first publication of a notice under section 205(5)(*a*) above, an owner of premises shown in a provisional apportionment of expenses as liable to be charged with any part of the expenses of executing street works with respect to a private street or a part of a private street may, by notice to the street works authority, object to their proposals on any of the following grounds:—

(*a*) that the alleged private street[2] is not a private street or, as the case may be, that the alleged part of a private street is not a part of a private street;

(*b*) that there has been some material informality, defect or error in, or in respect of, the resolution, notice, plans, sections or estimate;

(*c*) that the proposed works are insufficient[3] or unreasonable[4];

(*d*) that the estimated expenses of the proposed works are excessive;

(*e*) that any premises ought to be excluded from or inserted in the provisional apportionment;

(*f*) that the provisional apportionment is incorrect in respect of some matter of fact[5] to be specified in the objection or, where the provisional apportionment is made with regard to other considerations than frontage[6], in respect of the degree of benefit to be derived by any premises, or of the amount or value of any work already done by the owner or occupier of premises.

(2) Where premises are owned jointly by 2 or more persons, a notice under subsection (1) above may be given on behalf of those persons by one of their number, if he is authorised in writing by a majority[7] of them to do so.

[Highways Act 1980, s 208.]

1. For rule governing the reckoning of periods, see s 323, post.

2. See *Margate Corpn v Roach* [1960] 3 All ER 774, 125 JP 34; *Ware UDC v Gaunt* [1960] 3 All ER 778, 125 JP 55; *Alsager UDC v Barratt* [1965] 2 QB 343, [1965] 1 All ER 889, 129 JP 218.

3. "Insufficient" points exclusively to a comparison of the thing ordered and the means of effecting it: this provision ought not to be read as meaning "having regard to some matter which might make a better scheme for the neighbourhood in general". If a magistrates' court finds that works ought not to be executed, and the scheme is unreasonable, it may quash the resolution approving the plans, but it has no power to find the scheme unreasonable based on an opinion that the authority ought to have widened the street (*Mansfield Corpn v Butterworth* [1898] 2 QB 274, 62 JP 500). "Unreasonable" is a word of very wide import: for instance it may be unreasonable that the works shall be done at all, or at a particular time (*Southgate Corpn v Park Estates (Southgate) Ltd* [1953] 2 All ER 1008, 117 JP 541; affd [1954] 1 QB 359, [1954] 1 All ER 520, 118 JP 207, CA).

4. Works may be "unreasonable" because plans adopted by the second resolution are insufficient to carry out the original resolution; also that it is proposed to carry out in two stages the whole work mentioned in the original resolution (*Bognor Regis UDC v Boldero* [1962] 2 QB 448, [1962] 2 All ER 673, 126 JP 379).

5. If a magistrates' court finds that a person is not the owner, it should amend by substituting another name, and then adjourn to enable the other to be served, so that he may object: otherwise the street works authority must begin *de novo*.

6. Thus, where apportionment is based on frontage, objections in respect of degree of benefit may not be heard: see *Wilson v Wrexham Corpn* [1959] 3 All ER 674, 124 JP 41.

7. In ascertaining a majority, joint owners shall be treated as one owner (s 203(5), ante).

7–6072 209. Hearing and determination of objections. (1) If an objection is made under section 208 above within the period there specified, and is not withdrawn, the street works authority may, after the expiration of that period, apply to a magistrates' court to appoint a time for hearing and determining all objections[1] so made within that period, and shall serve on the objectors notice of the time and place so appointed.

(2) At the hearing the court shall hear and determine the objections in the same manner as nearly as may be as if the authority were proceeding summarily against the objectors to enforce payment of a sum of money summarily recoverable.

The court may quash in whole or in part or may amend[2] the resolution of approval, specification, plans, sections, estimate and provisional apportionment, or any of them, on the application either of an objector or of the authority, and may also, if it thinks fit, adjourn the hearing and direct further notices to be given.

(3) The costs of any proceedings before a magistrates' court in relation to objections under the private street works code are in the discretion of the court, and the court may, if it thinks fit, direct that the whole or a part of any costs ordered to be paid by an objector or objectors are to be paid in the first instance by the authority, and charged as part of the expenses of the works on the premises of the objector, or, as the case may be, on the premises of the objectors in such proportions as may appear just.
[Highways Act 1980, s 209.]

---

1. The street works authority must apply to a magistrates' court to determine the objections before the work is done (*Faulkner v Hythe Corpn* [1927] 1 KB 532, 91 JP 22). The burden of proof is on the authority (*Vyner v Wirral RDC* (1909) 73 JP 242; *Huyton-with-Roby UDC v Hunter* [1955] 2 All ER 398, 119 JP 407). Appeal against a decision of magistrates' court lies to the Crown Court (*Pearce v Maidenhead Corpn* [1907] 2 KB 96, 71 JP 230).

2. An amendment must be founded on evidence (*Birmingham Corpn v Mother-General of Convent of Sisters of Charity of St Paul* (1927) 91 JP 186). In support of an objection to that effect, an owner may bring evidence to show that the street is a highway maintainable at the public expense (*Carey v Bexhill Corpn* [1904] 1 KB 142, 68 JP 78). On proof that part of the street is a highway maintainable at the public expense, a magistrates' court may amend the documents by limiting them to the remaining portion of the street, and may adjourn the hearing and direct the service of further notices (*Twickenham Urban Council v Munton* [1899] 2 Ch 603).

7–6073　210. Power to amend specification, apportionment, etc.　(1) Subject to the provisions of this section, the street works authority may from time to time amend the specification, plans, sections, estimate and provisional apportionment for any street works proposed under section 205 above.

(2) If the street works authority propose to amend the estimate so as to increase the amount of it, then, before the amendment is made, a notice containing the particulars specified in paragraph 6 of Schedule 16 to this Act shall—

(*a*) be published once in each of 2 successive weeks in a local newspaper circulating in the area of the street works authority, and

(*b*) be posted in a prominent position in or near to the street to which the resolution of approval relates once at least in each of 3 successive weeks, and

(*c*) within 7 days from the date of the first publication under paragraph (*a*) above, be served on the owners of the premises shown in the provisional apportionment as liable to be charged;

and, during one month from the said date, a document certified by the proper officer of the council giving details of the amendment of the estimate and of the consequential amendment of the provisional apportionment shall be kept deposited and open to inspection free of charge at all reasonable hours at the offices of the street works authority and also, in the case of a street situated in a non-metropolitan district, at the offices of the council of that district and, in the case of any part of a street in Wales, the Welsh council for the county, or county borough in which it is situated, if different from the street works authority in whose area it is treated as situated.

(3) Where a notice is served on an owner of premises under subsection (2)(*c*) above it shall be accompanied by a statement of the sum apportioned on those premises by the provisional apportionment as proposed to be amended.

(4) Within one month from the date of the first publication of a notice under subsection (2)(*a*) above, objections may be made and, if made, shall be heard and determined in like manner, and subject to the like provisions with respect to the persons entitled to be heard and otherwise, as objections under section 208 above.
[Highways Act 1980, s 210 as amended by the Local Government Act 1985, Sch 4 and the Local Government (Wales) Act 1994, Sch 7.]

7–6074　211. Final apportionment and objections to it.　(1) When any street works to be executed under the private street works code have been completed, and the expenses of them ascertained, the proper officer of the council shall make a final apportionment by dividing the expenses in the same proportions as those in which the estimated expenses were divided in the original or amended provisional apportionment, as the case may be, and notice of the final apportionment shall be served on the owners of the premises affected by it.

(2) Within one month from the date on which notice of the final apportionment is served on him, the owner of any premises shown in the apportionment as liable to be charged may, by notice to the authority, object to the apportionment on the following grounds, or any of them:—

(*a*) that there has been an unreasonable departure from the specification, plans and sections;

(*b*) that the actual expenses have without sufficient reason exceeded the estimated expenses by more than 15 per cent;

(*c*) that the apportionment has not been made in accordance with this section.

Objections under this section shall be determined in the like manner, and subject to the like provisions with respect to the persons entitled to be heard and otherwise, as objections to the provisional apportionment.

(3) The final apportionment, subject to any amendment made to it by a court on the hearing of objections to it under this section, is conclusive for all purposes.
[Highways Act 1980, s 211.]

7–6075 212. Recovery of expenses and charge thereof on premises. (1) A street works authority may from time to time recover[1] from the owner for the time being of any premises in respect of which any sum is due for expenses of street works the whole or any portion of that sum together with interest at such reasonable rates as the authority may determine from the date of the final apportionment.

(2) The sum apportioned on any premises by the final apportionment or, as the case may be, by that apportionment as amended by a court, together with interest from the date of the final apportionment is, until recovered, a charge on the premises and on all estates and interests therein.

(3) A street works authority, for the purpose of enforcing a charge under subsection (2) above before it is registered under the Local Land Charges Act 1975, have the same powers and remedies under the Law of Property Act 1925 and otherwise as if they were mortgagees by deed having powers of sale and lease and of appointing a receiver.

(4) A street works authority may by order declare the expenses apportioned on any premises by a final apportionment made by the proper officer of the council or, as the case may be, by that apportionment as amended by a court, to be payable by annual instalments within a period not exceeding 30 years, together with interest from the date of the final apportionment; and any such instalment and interest, or any part thereof, may be recovered from the owner or occupier for the time being of the premises.

Schedule 13 to this Act applies in relation to any sum paid by an occupier of premises under this subsection.
[Highways Act 1980, s 212.]

---

1. For recovery of expenses, see s 305, post; for limitation of time for summary proceedings therefor, see s 306, post; for power to include several sums in one complaint, see s 313, post.

7–6076 213–214. *Power for limited owners to borrow for expenses; financial provisions.*

7–6077 215. Exemption for place of public religious worship. (1) The incumbent or minister, or trustee, of a place of public religious worship is not liable to expenses of street works under the private street works code as the owner of that place, or of a churchyard or burial ground attached to it, and the proportion of expenses in respect of which an exemption is allowed under this section shall be borne by the street works authority.

(2) No such expenses as aforesaid are to be deemed—

(a) to be a charge on such a place, or churchyard or burial ground, or

(b) to subject such a place, or churchyard or burial ground, to distress, execution or other legal process.
[Highways Act 1980, s 215.]

7–6078 216. *Certain railways and canals not to be chargeable with expenses.*

7–6079 217. Objections only to be made as provided by private street works code. No objections which could be made under any provision of the private street works code shall be made in any proceeding or manner otherwise than as provided by that code.

7–6080 218. *Saving for Thames Water Authority and Port of London Authority.*

The advance payments code

7–6081 219. Payments to be made by owners of new buildings in respect of street works. (1) Subject to the provisions of this section, where—

(a) it is proposed to erect a building for which plans are required to be deposited with the local authority in accordance with building regulations, and

(b) the building will have a frontage on a private street in which the street works authority have power under the private street works code to require works to be executed or to execute works,

no work shall be done in or for the purpose of erecting the building unless the owner of the land on which it is to be erected or a previous owner thereof has paid to the street works authority, or secured to the satisfaction of that authority the payment to them of, such sum as may be required under section 220 below in respect of the cost of street works in that street.

(2) If work is done in contravention of subsection (1) above, the owner of the land on which the building is to be erected and, if he is a different person, the person undertaking the erection of the building is guilty of an offence and liable to a fine not exceeding **level 3** on the standard scale, and any further contravention in respect of the same building constitutes a new offence and may be punished accordingly.

Proceedings under this subsection shall not be taken by any person other than the street works authority.

(3) Where the person undertaking the erection of the building is not the owner of the land on

which it is to be erected and is charged with an offence under subsection (2) above, it shall be a defence for him to prove that he had reasonable grounds for believing that the sum required under section 220 below had been paid or secured by the owner of the land in accordance with subsection (1) above.

(4) This section does not apply—

(a) where the owner of the land on which the building is to be erected will be exempt, by virtue of a provision in the private street works code, from liability to expenses incurred in respect of street works in the private street in question;

(b) where the building proposed to be erected will be situated in the curtilage of, and be appurtenant to, an existing building;

(c) where the building is proposed to be erected in a parish or community and plans for the building were deposited with the district council or, according to the date of deposit, the rural district council before the date on which the New Streets Act 1951, or the advance payments code (either in this Act or in the Highways Act 1959) was applied in the parish or community or, as the case may require, in the part of the parish or community in which the building is to be erected;

(d) where an agreement has been made by any person with the street works authority under section 38 above providing for the carrying out at the expense of that person of street works in the whole of the street or a part of the street comprising the whole of the part on which the frontage of the building will be, and for securing that the street or the part thereof, on completion of the works, will become a highway maintainable at the public expense;

(e) where the street works authority, being satisfied that the whole of the street or such a part thereof as aforesaid is not, and is not likely within a reasonable time to be, substantially built-up or in so unsatisfactory a condition as to justify the use of powers under the private street works code for securing the carrying out of street works in the street or part thereof, by notice exempt the building from this section;

(f) where the street works authority, being satisfied that the street is not, and is not likely within a reasonable time to become, joined to a highway maintainable at the public expense, by notice exempt the building from this section;

(g) where the whole street, being less than 100 yards in length, or a part of the street not less than 100 yards in length and comprising the whole of the part on which the frontage of the building will be, was on the material date built-up to such an extent that the aggregate length of the frontages of the buildings on both sides of the street or part constituted at least one half of the aggregate length of all the frontages on both sides of the street or part;

(h) where (in a case not falling within paragraph (g) above) the street works authority, being satisfied that the whole of the street was on the material date substantially built-up, by notice exempt the building from this section;

(i) Where the building is proposed to be erected on land belonging to, or in the possession of—

     (i) the British Railways Board, the British Waterways Board, Transport for London, any wholly-owned subsidiary (within the meaning of the Transport Act 1968) or joint subsidiary (within the meaning of section 51(5) of that Act) of any of those bodies other than Transport for London, or any of its subsidiaries (within the meaning of the Greater London Authority Act 1999);

     (ii) the council of a county, district or London borough, or the Common Council;

     (iii) the Commission for the New Towns or a new town development corporation;

(j) where the building is to be erected by a company the objects of which include the provision of industrial premises for use by persons other than the company, being a company the constitution of which prohibits the distribution of the profits of the company to its members, and the cost of the building is to be defrayed wholly or mainly by a government department;

(k) where the street works authority, being satisfied—

     (i) that more than three-quarters of the aggregate length of all the frontages on both sides of the street, or of a part of the street not less than 100 yards in length and comprising the whole of the part on which the frontage of the building will be, consists, or is at some future time likely to consist, of the frontages of industrial premises, and

     (ii) that their powers under the private street works code are not likely to be exercised in relation to the street, or to that part of it, as the case may be, within a reasonable time,

by resolution exempt the street, or that part of it, from this section.

(4A) In subsection (4)(c) above, "district council" is to be read in relation to plans deposited on or after 1st April 1996 for a building to be erected in Wales as "Welsh Council".

(5) Where a sum has been paid or secured under this section by the owner of the land in relation to a building proposed to be erected on it, and thereafter a notice is served under subsection (4) above exempting the building from this section, or a resolution is passed under paragraph (k) of that subsection exempting the street or part of a street on which the building will have a frontage from this section, the street works authority shall refund that sum to the person who is for the time being owner of the land or shall release the security, as the case may be.

Where the said sum was paid, and after the payment but before the service of the said notice or the passing of the said resolution, as the case may be, the land in respect of which it was paid was divided into 2 or more parts each having a frontage on the private street in question, the sum is to be treated for the purposes of this subsection as apportioned between the owners of the land according to their respective frontages.

(6) For the purposes of this section "the material date" is—

(a) in relation to a building proposed to be erected in an area which before 1st April 1974 was a rural district or a contributory place within a rural district, the date on which the New Streets Act 1951 or the advance payments code (either in this Act or in the Highways Act 1959) was applied in that area;

(b) in relation to a building proposed to be erected anywhere else, 1st October 1951.

[Highways Act 1980, s 219 as amended by the Criminal Justice Act 1982, ss 38 and 46, the London Regional Transport Act 1984, Schs 6 and 7, the Local Government Act 1985, Sch 17, the Statute Law (Repeals) Act 1989, Sch 1, the Local Government (Wales) Act 1994, Sch 7 and SI 2003/1615.]

7–6082   220. Determination of liability for, and amount of, payments.   In a case to which section 219 applies the street works authority shall, within six weeks from the passing of any required plans relating to the erection of a building deposited with them, serve a notice on the person by or on whose behalf the plans were deposited requiring the payment or the securing under section 219 of a sum specified in the notice.

[Highways Act 1980, s 220 amended by the Local Government Act 1985, Sch 4—summarised.]

General

7–6083   228. Adoption of private street after execution of street works.   (1) When any street works have been executed in a private street, the street works authority may, by notice displayed in a prominent position in the street, declare the street to be a highway which for the purposes of this Act is a highway maintainable at the public expense, and on the expiration of one month from the day on which the notice was first so displayed the street shall, subject to subsections (2) to (4) below, become such a highway.

(2) A street shall not become a highway maintainable at the public expense by virtue of subsection (1) above if, within the period there mentioned, the owner of the street, or, if more than one, the majority in number of the owners of the street, by notice to the authority object; but within 2 months from the expiration of that period the street works authority may apply to a magistrates' court for an order overruling the objection.

(3) If an order overruling an objection under subsection (2) above is made pursuant to an application under that subsection and no appeal against the order is brought within the time limited for such an appeal, the street or part in question shall become a highway maintainable at the public expense on the expiration of that time.

(4) Where such an order is made or refused and an appeal, or an appeal arising out of that appeal, is brought against or rises out of the order or refusal, then—

(a) if the final determination of the matter is in favour of the authority, or

(b) the appeal is abandoned by the objectors,

the street shall become a highway maintainable at the public expense on that final determination or, as the case may be, on the abandonment of the appeal.

(5) Notwithstanding anything in any other enactment or provision, for the purposes of this section the time for bringing or seeking leave for any appeal (including an application for certiorari) is 2 months from the date of the decision or of the conclusion of the proceedings appealed against, unless apart from this subsection the time is less than that period; and no power however worded, to enlarge any such time is exercisable for the purposes of this section.

(6) Where street works have been executed in a part only of a street (other than a part extending for the whole of the length of the street), subsections (1) to (4) above have effect as if for references in those subsections to the street there were substituted references to the length of the street which constitutes or comprises that part.

(7) If all street works (whether or not including lighting) have been executed in a private street to the satisfaction of the street works authority, then, on the application of the majority in rateable value of the owners of premises in the street, the street works authority shall, within the period of 3 months from the date of the application, by notice displayed in a prominent position in the street, declare the street to be a highway which for the purposes of this Act is a highway maintainable at the public expense and thereupon the street shall become such a highway.

In this subsection a reference to a street does not include a reference to a part of a street.

[Highways Act 1980, s 228.]

7–6084   229.   *Power of majority of frontagers to require adoption where advance payment made.*

7–6085   230. Urgent repairs to private streets.   (1) Where repairs are needed to obviate danger to traffic[1] in a private street the street works authority may by notice[2] require the owners[1] of the premises[1] fronting the street to execute, within such time as may be specified in the notice, such repairs as may be so specified.

(2) Where such repairs as are mentioned in subsection (1) above are needed in a part only of the street (other than a part extending for the whole of the length of the street), a requirement under that subsection shall be made only of the owners of the premises fronting the length of the street which constitutes or comprises that part.

(3) A person aggrieved by a requirement of a street works authority under this section may appeal[3] to a magistrates' court.

(4) Subject to any order made on appeal and to subsection (5) below, if, within the time specified in a notice served under subsection (1) above, the repairs required thereby have not been executed, the authority may execute the repairs, and may recover the expenses reasonably incurred by them in so doing from the owners in default, the expenses being apportioned between those owners according to the extent to which their respective premises front the street.

(5) If, within the time so specified, the majority in number or rateable value of owners of premises in the street by notice require the street works authority to proceed in relation to the street under the private street works code, the street works authority shall so proceed, and on the completion of the necessary works shall forthwith declare the street to be a highway which for the purposes of this Act is a highway maintainable at the public expense; and thereupon the street shall become such a highway.

(6) Where a requirement under subsection (1) above has been made in respect of a part only of a street (other than a part extending for the whole of the length of the street), subsection (5) above has effect as if for references therein to the street there were substituted references to the length of the street which constitutes or comprises that part.

(7) Without prejudice to the foregoing provisions of this section or to any other enactment for the time being in force relating to private street works, the street works authority and also, in the cases mentioned below, the district council may, in any street that is not a highway maintainable at the public expense, execute such repairs as are in their opinion urgently required to prevent or remove danger to persons or vehicles in the street.

The cases in which the district council may act under this subsection are those in which the street concerned is situated in a non-metropolitan district and is a footpath, bridleway or any such road as is mentioned in section 42(2)(c) above (urban roads).

(8) The power of a district council under subsection (7) above is subject to Part I of Schedule 7 to this Act.

[Highways Act 1980, s 230 as amended by the Local Government Act 1985, Sch 4.]

1. For meaning of "traffic", "owner", "premises", see s 329, post.
2. For form of notice and its authentication and service, see ss 320–322, post.
3. Procedure on appeal is by way of complaint for an order; see s 316, post. Notice must be given to a prospective appellant of this right of appeal; see s 315, post. Without prejudice to this section, the authority may itself execute urgent repairs to prevent or remove danger (Public Health Act 1961, s 47).

7–6086   233. Appeal to Minister under private street works code.   (1) Subject to section 217 above, a person aggrieved by a decision of a street works authority in a case where the authority are empowered by section 212 above to recover any expenses incurred by them may appeal to the Minister, who may make such decision as to him seems equitable; and the decision shall be final and binding on all parties.

(2) The time within which an appeal may be brought under subsection (1) above is 21 days from the date on which a demand for the payment of the expenses, or any part of them, was first served on the person wishing to appeal.

(3) A person appealing under subsection (1) above shall in his appeal state the grounds thereof, and shall serve a copy of his appeal on the street works authority; and any proceedings commenced for the recovery of any such expenses as aforesaid by the street works authority shall, on the service on them of the copy of the appeal, be stayed.

(4) The Minister may, if he thinks fit, by his decision direct the authority to pay to the person so proceeded against such sum as he may consider to be a just compensation for the loss or damage sustained by that person by reason of the proceedings.

[Highways Act 1980, s 233.]

7–6087   234. Provisions as to private street in area of more than one street works authority.
(1) In a case where a part only of a private street is within the area of a street works authority, the authority may, with the consent of the street works authority in whose area any other part of the street is situated, and subject to subsection (3) below, resolve to treat that other part for the purposes of this Part of this Act as if it were within their own area.

(2) Where the authority so resolve, then, without prejudice to the operation of any enactment not contained in this Part of this Act, this Part of this Act applies in relation to that other part of the street as if it, together with the premises fronting it, were within the area of the authority passing the resolution.

(3) A street works authority shall not resolve under subsection (1) above to treat a part of a street as if it were within their own area if that part comprises a length of the street wholly outside that area.

(4) In a case where a private street is within the area of a street works authority but premises fronting the street are wholly or partly outside that area, then, without prejudice to the operation of any enactment not contained in this Part of this Act, this Part of this Act applies in relation to that street as if those premises were wholly within the area of the authority.

In this subsection a reference to a street includes a reference to a length of the street but does not include a reference to any other part of it.

(5) A resolution passed by a street works authority under subsection (1) above shall be published by advertisement in one or more local newspapers circulating within the area in which the street is situated and otherwise in such manner as the authority think sufficient for giving notice to all persons interested.

[Highways Act 1980, s 234.]

7–6088 235. Evasion of private street works expenses by owners. (1) Where a street works authority are empowered by section 212 above to recover any sum from the owner of any premises, and the authority are unable by the exercise of their powers (other than powers conferred by this section) to recover that sum, then if—

(a) the said premises were previously transferred by a person ("the transferor") who at the time of the transfer was the owner of other premises adjoining those premises, and

(b) a magistrates' court is satisfied that the transfer was intended for the purpose of evading the payment of expenses of street works,

the court may make an order under this section.

(2) An order under this section shall provide that, to such extent as the court making the order may determine, the street works authority may recover the said sum, and, where that sum is payable under an order made under section 212(4) above or section 305(2) below, any further sums which may fall due under that order, from the transferor.

(3) In this section "transfer" includes any disposal of land whether by way of sale, lease, exchange, gift or otherwise.

[Highways Act 1980, s 235.]

7–6089 236. Contribution by street works authority to expenses of street works. (1) A street works authority may at any time resolve to bear the whole or a portion of the expenses of any street works in their area under the private street works code and where an authority so resolve the liabilities of the owners of premises in respect of those expenses are to be treated as discharged or as proportionately reduced, accordingly.

(2) Without prejudice to their powers under subsection (1) above, a street works authority may at any time resolve to bear the whole or a portion of the expenses of any street works in their area under the private street works code which would otherwise be apportioned on, or to the owner of, any premises of which the rear or a flank fronts the street; and where an authority so resolve the liability of the owner of those premises in respect of those expenses is to be treated as discharged or reduced accordingly.

[Highways Act 1980, s 236.]

7–6090 237. Power of street works authority to grant charging order. (1) Where a person has paid, or advanced money for, expenses which by section 212 above a street works authority are empowered to recover, that person may apply to the authority for a charging order, and the authority, on being satisfied as to the amount of the expenditure on private street works, and, in the case of an advance, as to the sum advanced, may make an order accordingly charging on the premises in respect of which the expenses are recoverable, and on all estates and interests therein, an annuity to repay the sum expended or advanced.

(2) The annuity charged shall be such sum as the street works authority may determine in respect of every £100 of the amount of the expenditure and so in proportion in respect of any fraction of that amount, and shall commence from the date of the order and be payable by equal half-yearly payments for a term of 30 years to the person named in the order, his executors, administrators or assigns.

(3) A person aggrieved by an order of a street works authority under subsection (1) above, or by the refusal of the authority to make an order under that subsection, may appeal to a magistrates' court.

(4) Schedule 13 to this Act applies in relation to any sum paid by an occupier of premises in respect of an annuity charged on those premises under this section.

[Highways Act 1980, s 237.]

7–6091

PART XII[1]

ACQUISITION, VESTING AND TRANSFER OF LAND ETC

---

1. Part XII contains ss 238–271.

7–6092

PART XIII[1]
FINANCIAL PROVISIONS

---

1. Part XIII contains ss 272–281.

PART XIV[1]
MISCELLANEOUS AND SUPPLEMENTARY PROVISIONS
Miscellaneous powers etc of highway authorities and local authorities

7–6093   286. Power to require angles of new buildings at corners of streets to be rounded off.   (1) A local authority or, if there is a local highway authority for either of the two streets in question, that highway authority, may require the corner of a building intended to be erected at the corner of two streets in the area of the local authority to be rounded or splayed off to the height of the first storey or to the full height of the building, and to such extent otherwise as they may determine.

(2) A person aggrieved by a requirement of a local authority or local highway authority under this section may appeal[2] to a magistrates' court.

(3) A local authority or local highway authority shall pay compensation for any loss which may be sustained through the exercise by them of their powers under this section.

(4) This section does not apply to a building, other than a dwelling-house, belonging to any of the following undertakers and used by them for the following purposes respectively—

  (*a*)   railway undertakers, for purposes of a railway comprised in the railway undertaking;
  (*b*)   canal undertakers, for purposes of a canal comprised in the canal undertaking;
  (*c*)   inland navigation undertakers, for purposes of a navigation comprised in the inland navigation undertaking;
  (*d*)   dock undertakers, for purposes of a dock comprised in the dock undertaking;
  (*e*)   harbour undertakers, for purposes of a harbour comprised in the harbour undertaking;
  (*f*)   pier undertakers for purposes of a pier comprised in the pier undertaking.

[Highways Act 1980, s 286.]

---

1. Part XIV contains ss 282–345.
2. Procedure on appeal is by way of complaint for an order; see s 316, post. Notice must be given to a prospective appellant of this right of appeal; see s 315, post.

7–6094   287. Power to erect barriers in streets in cases of emergency etc.   (1) Subject to the provisions of this section, for the purpose of securing public order or public safety or preventing congestion of traffic a competent authority may, in any case of emergency or on any occasion on which it is likely by reason of some special attraction that any street will be thronged or obstructed, cause barriers to be erected in any street and kept in position for so long as may be necessary for that purpose.

For the purposes of this section the following are competent authorities—

  (*a*)   in the case of a street outside Greater London which is a highway, a local authority and also the highway authority;
  (*b*)   in the case of any other street, a local authority.

(2) For the purpose of erecting barriers in a street under this section a competent authority may provide and maintain sockets or slots in or under the surface of the street.

(3) A competent authority shall not exercise the powers conferred by this section in such a way as to deprive pedestrians of reasonable access to any premises.

(4) Schedule 8 to this Act applies to the powers conferred on competent authorities by this section.

(5) If a person wilfully removes a barrier, socket or slot erected or provided under this section, he is guilty of an offence and liable to a fine not exceeding **level 1** on the standard scale.

(6) In this section "local authority" means any of the following, namely, the council of a district or London borough, the Common Council and the Council of the Isles of Scilly but, in relation to Wales, means a Welsh council.

[Highways Act 1980, s 287 as amended by the Criminal Justice Act 1982, ss 38 and 46 and the Local Government Act 1985, Sch 17 and the Local Government (Wales) Act 1994, Sch 7.]

7–6095   289. Powers of entry of highway authority for the purpose of survey.   (1) A person duly authorised in writing by a highway authority may at any reasonable time enter on any land for the purpose of surveying that or any other land in connection with the exercise by that authority, in their capacity as a highway authority, of any of their functions.

(2) The power conferred by this section to enter on land includes power to place and leave on or in the land any apparatus for use in connection with any survey of that or any other land (whether from the air or on the ground) and to remove such apparatus.

(3) The power conferred by this section to survey land includes power to search and bore for the purpose of ascertaining—

(a) the nature of the subsoil or the presence of minerals in it;

(b) whether any damage to a highway maintainable at the public expense for which the authority are the highway authority is being caused or is likely to be caused by mining operations or other activities taking place under the highway or in or under land adjoining, or in the vicinity of the highway.

[Highways Act 1980, s 289.]

7–6096 290. Supplementary provisions as to powers of entry for the purpose of survey. (1) A person authorised under section 289 above to enter on any land shall, if so required, produce evidence of his authority before or after entering on that land.

(2) A person so authorised may take with him on to the land in question such other persons, and such vehicles and equipment, as he may consider necessary.

(3) Subject to subsection (6) below, a person shall not under section 289 above demand admission as of right to any land which is occupied unless at least 7 days' notice of the intended entry has been given to the occupier.

(4) Subject to subsection (6) below, a person shall not, in the exercise of a power conferred by section 289 above, place or leave any apparatus on or in any land or remove any apparatus therefrom unless notice of his intention to do so has been included in the notice required by subsection (3) above and a like notice has been given to the owner of the land.

(5) A person shall not execute any works authorised by section 289(3) above unless notice of his intention to do so was included in the notices required by subsections (3) and (4) above and, where the interests of the Coal Authority, of any licensed operator (within the meaning of the Coal Industry Act 1994) or of any statutory undertakers are liable to be affected by the proposed works, a like notice has been given to that Authority or, as the case may be, to the licensed operator or statutory undertakers concerned.

(6) Where a highway authority intend to place and leave apparatus on or in a highway or to remove apparatus therefrom, or to execute in relation thereto such works as are authorised by section 289(3) above, no notice need be given to the occupier or owner of the land over which the highway subsists; but if the highway authority are not the highway authority for the highway, they shall give to that authority such notice as is required by subsections (4) and (5) above to be given to the owner.

(7) If the British Coal Corporation, or any statutory undertakers to whom notice is given under subsection (5) above object to the proposed works on the ground that the execution thereof would be seriously detrimental to the carrying on of their undertaking, the works shall not be executed except with the authority of the appropriate Minister.

(8) Where in the exercise of a power conferred by section 289 above works authorised by subsection (3) of that section are to be executed in a street—

(a) section 55 of the New Roads and Street Works Act 1991 (notice of starting date of works), so far as it requires notice to be given to a person having apparatus in the street which is likely to be affected by the works,

(b) section 69 of that Act (requirements to be complied with where works likely to affect another person's apparatus in the street), and

(c) section 82 of that Act (liability for damage or loss caused),

have effect in relation to the works as if they were street works within the meaning of Part III of that Act.

(9) A universal service provider in connection with the provision of a universal postal service, the Civil Aviation Authority and a person who holds a licence under Chapter I of Part I of the Transport Act 2000 (to the extent that the person is carrying out activities authorised by the licence) are to be deemed to be statutory undertakers and their respective undertakings statutory undertakings for the purposes of the foregoing provisions of this section.

(9A) For the purposes of subsection (9) above, the undertaking of a universal service provider shall be taken to be his undertaking so far as it relates to the provision of a universal postal service.

(9B) For the purposes of subsection (9) above, the undertaking of a person who holds a licence under Chapter I of Part I of the Transport Act 2000 shall not be considered to be a statutory undertaking except to the extent that it is the person's undertaking as licence holder.

(10) In this section "the appropriate Minister" means—

(a) (Repealed);

(b) in relation to statutory undertakers carrying on any railway, tramway, road transport, dock, harbour or pier undertaking, the Minister of Transport; and

(c) in all other cases, the Secretary of State.

[Highways Act 1980, s 290, as amended by the Coal Industry Act 1987, Sch 1, the Water Act 1989, Sch 27, the New Roads and Street Works Act 1991, Sch 8, the Coal Industry Act 1994, Schs 9 and 11, SI 2001/1149 and SI 2002/4050.]

7–6097 291. Powers of entry of highway authority for purpose of maintaining, etc certain structures and works. (1) Where a highway authority have power or a right to maintain, alter or remove any structure or work which is situated on, over or under any land, and that land neither belongs to the highway authority nor forms part of a highway for which they are the highway authority, then, if for the purpose of exercising that power or that right it is necessary for a person to enter on that land or any other land, a person duly authorised in writing by that authority may at any reasonable time enter on that land or any other land for that purpose.

(2) Subsections (1), (2) and (3) of section 290 above have effect in relation to a person authorised under this section to enter on any land as they have effect in relation to a person authorised under section 289 above to enter on any land.

(3) In relation to a bridge to which section 118 of the Transport Act 1968 (duty of highway authorities, etc as respects bridges over railways or inland waterways) applies, and which belongs to a highway authority, subsections (1) and (2) above have effect subject to the provisions of that section.

(4) In this section—

"structure" includes a bridge, fence, barrier or post;
"work" includes a tunnel, ditch, gutter, watercourse, culvert, drain, soak-away or pipe.

(5) Nothing in this section affects the powers of a highway authority under section 100 above.

(6) Nothing in this section affects any agreement for the time being in force between a highway authority having power or a right to maintain, alter or remove a structure or work and any person having an interest in the land on, over or under which it is situated, being an agreement relating to the maintenance of or other dealing with the structure or work.
[Highways Act 1980, s 291.]

7–6098   292. Compensation for damage resulting from, and offences connected with, exercise of powers of entry etc under section 289 or 291.   (1) Where, in the exercise of a power conferred by section 289 or 291 above to enter, or to do anything, on any land, any damage is caused to that land or to any chattels on it, any person interested in that land or those chattels may, subject to subsection (2) below, recover compensation in respect of that damage from the highway authority by whom or on whose behalf the power was exercised; and where in consequence of the exercise of such a power any person interested in the land or in any chattels on it is disturbed in his enjoyment thereof, he may recover from that authority compensation in respect of the disturbance.

(2) Where any person is entitled under section 82 of the New Roads and Street Works Act 1991, as applied by section 290(8) above, to compensation in respect of any matter, he is not entitled to recover compensation under subsection (1) above in respect of the same matter.

(3) A person who wilfully obstructs a person acting in the exercise of a power conferred by section 289 or 291 above, or who removes or otherwise interferes with any apparatus placed or left on or in any land in exercise of a power conferred by section 289 above, is guilty of an offence and liable to a fine not exceeding **level 3** on the standard scale.

(4) If a person who, in compliance with the provisions of section 289 or 291 above, is admitted into a factory, workshop or workplace discloses to any person any information obtained by him therein as to any manufacturing process or trade secret, then, unless the disclosure is made in the course of performing his duty in connection with the purposes for which he was authorised to enter the land, he is guilty of an offence and liable[1]—

(a)   on summary conviction to a fine not exceeding **the prescribed sum** within the meaning of section 32(9) of the Magistrates' Courts Act 1980 (£1,000 or such other sum as may be fixed by order under section 143(1) of that Act); or

(b)   on conviction on indictment to imprisonment for a term not exceeding **2 years** or to a **fine**, or **both**.

[Highways Act 1980, s 292 as amended by the Criminal Justice Act 1982, ss 38 and 46 and the New Roads and Street Works Act 1991, Sch 8.]

---

1. For procedure in respect of this offence triable either way, see the Magistrates' Courts Act 1980, ss 17A–21, in PART I: MAGISTRATES' COURTS, PROCEDURE, *ante*.

7–6099   293. Powers of entry for purposes connected with certain orders relating to footpaths and bridleways.   (1) A person duly authorised in writing by the Secretary of State or other authority having power under this Act to make a public path creation order, a public path extinguishment order a rail crossing extinguishment order, a special extinguishment order, a public path diversion order, a rail crossing diversion order, a special diversion order or an SSSI diversion order may enter upon any land for the purpose of surveying it in connection with the making of the order.*

(2) For the purpose of surveying land, or of estimating its value, in connection with a claim for compensation payable by an authority in respect of that or any other land under section 28 above, or under that section as applied by section 121(2) above, a person who is an officer of the Valuation Office or who has been duly authorised in writing by the authority from whom the compensation is claimed may enter upon the land.

(3) A person authorised under this section to enter upon any land shall, if so required, produce evidence of his authority before entering; and a person shall not under this section demand admission as of right to any land which is occupied unless at least 7 days' notice in writing of the intended entry has been given to the occupier.

(4) A person who wilfully obstructs a person acting in the exercise of his powers under this section is guilty of an offence and liable to a fine not exceeding **level 3** on the standard scale.
[Highways Act 1980, s 293 as amended by the Criminal Justice Act 1982, ss 38 and 46, the Transport and Works Act 1992, Sch 2 and the Countryside and Rights of Way Act 2000, Sch 6.]

---

*Reproduced as amended by the Countryside and Rights of Way Act 2000, Sch 6, in force in relation to England, except in relation to an SSSI order, 12 February 2003, for certain purposes in Wales 15 July 2005. In force in relation to remaining purposes in England and Wales, from a date to be appointed.

7–6100   294. Entry, etc of premises by highway authority or council for certain purposes.

(1) If, in the discharge of functions conferred or imposed on an authority, being a highway authority or council, by a provision of this Act to which this section applies, it becomes necessary for an authorised officer of the authority to enter, examine or lay open any premises for the purpose of—

  (a) surveying,
  (b) making plans,
  (c) executing, maintaining or examining works,
  (d) ascertaining the course of sewers or drains,
  (e) ascertaining or fixing boundaries, or
  (f) ascertaining whether any hedge, tree or shrub is dead, diseased, damaged or insecurely rooted,

and the owner or occupier of the premises refuses to permit the premises to be entered, examined or laid open for any such purpose, the authority, after giving notice to the owner or occupier of their intention to do so, may make a complaint to a magistrates' court for an order authorising the authority by any authorised officer to enter, examine and lay open the premises for any such purpose.

(2) If on the hearing of the complaint no sufficient cause is shown against the making of the order for which the complaint is made, the court may make the order, and thereupon any authorised officer of the complainant authority may, subject to subsection (3) below, at all reasonable times between the hours of 9 am and 6 pm, enter, examine or lay open the premises described in the order for such of the purposes mentioned in subsection (1) above as are specified in the order.

(3) Except in a case of emergency, no entry shall be made on any premises, and no works shall be begun therein, under subsection (2) above unless at least 7 days' notice of the intended entry, and of the object thereof, has been given to the occupier of the premises.

(4) Where, in the course of an entry on or examination or laying open of premises authorised by an order under this section, damage is caused to land or to chattels, any person interested in the land or chattels may recover compensation in respect of that damage from the authority on whose complaint the order was made; and where by reason of any such entry, examination or laying open any person is disturbed in his enjoyment of land or chattels, he may recover from that authority compensation in respect of the disturbance.

(5) This section applies to sections 101 and 154(2) above and to the other provisions of this Act specified in Schedule 22 to this Act.
[Highways Act 1980, s 294.]

7–6101   295. Power of councils to dispose of certain materials.

(1) The council of a county or a council who are a local authority may remove, appropriate, or use, sell or otherwise dispose of all old materials existing in any street other than a highway maintainable at the public expense at the time of the execution by the council of any works in the street, unless those materials are removed by the owners of premises in the street within 3 days from the date of service of a notice from the proper officer of the council requiring the owners of those premises to remove the materials.

(2) Where a council remove, appropriate, or use, sell or otherwise dispose of any materials in a street under subsection (1) above, they shall, on demand, pay or allow to the owner of any premises in the street such proportion of the reasonable value of the material as is attributable to those premises, and the amount thereof shall be settled, in case of dispute, by arbitration, or, if the amount claimed does not exceed £50 and either party so requires, by a magistrates' court.
[Highways Act 1980, s 295.]

7–6102   297. Power of highway authority or council to require information as to ownership of land.

(1) A highway authority or a council may, for the purpose of enabling them to discharge or exercise any of their functions under this Act, require the occupier of any premises and any person who, either directly or indirectly, receives rent in respect of any premises, to state in writing the nature of his own interest therein and the name and address of any other person known to him as having an interest therein, whether as freeholder, mortgagee, lessee or otherwise.

(2) Any person who, having been required in pursuance of this section to give any information, fails to give that information is guilty of an offence and liable to a fine not exceeding **level 3** on the standard scale.

(3) Any person who, having been so required to give any information, knowingly makes any mis-statement in respect thereof is guilty of an offence[1] and liable[2]—

(a) on summary conviction to a fine not exceeding **the prescribed sum** within the meaning of section 32(9) of the Magistrates' Courts Act 1980 (£1,000 or such other sum as may be fixed by order under section 143(1) of that Act); or

(b) on conviction on indictment to imprisonment for a term not exceeding **2 years** or to a **fine**, or **both**.

[Highways Act 1980, s 297 as amended by the Criminal Justice Act 1982, ss 38 and 46.]

1. For restriction on the institution of proceedings, see s 312 and Sch 22, post.

2. For procedure in respect of this offence triable either way, see the Magistrates' Courts Act 1980, ss 17A–21, in Part I: Magistrates' Courts, Procedure, ante.

Obstruction of persons executing Act

7–6103   303. Penalty for obstructing execution of Act.   A person who wilfully obstructs any person acting in the execution of this Act or any byelaw or order made under it is, in any case for which no other provision is made by this Act, guilty of an offence[1] and liable to a fine not exceeding **level 1** on the standard scale; and if the offence is continued after conviction, he is guilty of a further offence and liable to a fine not exceeding £5 for each day on which the offence is so continued.

[Highways Act 1980, s 303 as amended by the Criminal Justice Act 1982, s 46.]

1. For restriction on the institution of proceedings, see s 312 and Sch 22, post.

7–6104   304. Power to require occupier to permit works to be executed by owner.   If on a complaint[1] made by the owner of any premises, it appears to a magistrates' court that the occupier of the premises prevents the owner from executing any work which he is by this Act required to execute, the court may order the occupier to permit the execution of the work.

[Highways Act 1980, s 304.]

1. See Magistrates' Courts Act 1980, s 51, ante; for penalty for disobedience of order, see Magistrates' Courts Act 1980, s 63, in Part I: Magistrates' Courts, Procedure, ante.

Recovery of expenses

7–6105   305. Recovery of expenses by councils and highway authorities.   (1) Where a council or a highway authority have incurred expenses for the repayment of which the owner of the premises in respect of which the expenses were incurred is liable—

(a) under any of the provisions of this Act to which this section applies, or

(b) by agreement with the council or highway authority,

those expenses, together with interest at such reasonable rate as the council may determine from the date of service of a demand for the expenses, may be recovered by the council or the highway authority from the owner for the time being of the premises; and as from the date of the completion of the works the expenses and interest accrued due thereon are, until recovered, a charge on the premises and on all estates and interests therein.

(2) A council or highway authority may by order declare any expenses and interest recoverable by them under this section to be payable by annual instalments within a period not exceeding 30 years, together with interest on them at such reasonable rate as the authority may determine; and any such instalment and interest, or any part thereof, may be recovered from the owner or occupier for the time being of the premises in respect of which the expenses were incurred.

(3) A person aggrieved by an order of a council or highway authority under subsection (2) above, or by the refusal of a council or highway authority to make such an order, may, except in a case where an appeal lies to the Minister under section 233 above, appeal[1] to a magistrates' court.

(4) Schedule 13 to this Act applies in relation to any sum paid by an occupier of premises under the foregoing provisions of this section.

(5) Any sum which a council or highway authority are entitled to recover under this section or any other provision of this Act, and with respect to the mode of recovery of which provision is not made by any other section of this Act, may be recovered either summarily as a civil debt or in any court of competent jurisdiction.

(6) Any charge acquired by the Minister by virtue of subsection (1) above is (without prejudice to the operation of section 1 of the Local Land Charges Act 1975 as regards any charge acquired by a council by virtue of that subsection) a local land charge.

(7) This section applies to the following provisions of this Act, namely, sections 152, 153, 165, 167, 177, 180, 184 and 230, except 230(7).

[Highways Act 1980, s 305.]

1. Procedure on appeal is by way of complaint for an order; see s 316, post. Notice must be given to a prospective appellant of this right of appeal; see s 315, post.

7–6106   306. Time-limit for summary proceedings for recovery of expenses. The time within which summary proceedings may be taken for the recovery of any sum which a highway authority or council are entitled to recover under this Act shall be reckoned—

(*a*)   in all cases except the one mentioned in paragraph (*b*) below, from the date of the service of a demand for the sum; and

(*b*)   in a case in which an appeal has been made to the Minister under section 233 above, from the date on which the decision on the appeal is notified to the appellant or the appeal is withdrawn, as the case may be.

[Highways Act 1980, s 306.]

Prosecutions, appeals, etc

7–6107   310. Summary proceedings for offences. All offences under this Act or under byelaws made under it are, except as provided by sections 292(4) and 297(3) above, punishable on summary conviction[1].

[Highways Act 1980, s 310.]

---

1. This mandatory provision prevails over any claim of right in any case which may only be dealt with summarily (*R v Ogden, ex p Long Ashton RDC* [1963] 1 All ER 574, 127 JP 206).

7–6108   311. Continuing offences. (1) Where by virtue of any provision of this Act, or of byelaws made under it, a person convicted of an offence is, if the offence in respect of which he was convicted is continued after conviction, guilty of a further offence and liable to a fine for each day on which the offence is so continued, the court before whom the person is convicted of the original offence may fix a reasonable period from the date of conviction for compliance by the defendant with any directions given by the court.

(2) Where a court fixes such a period the defendant is not liable to a fine in respect of the further offence for any day before the expiration of that period.

[Highways Act 1980, s 311.]

7–6109   312. Restriction on institution of proceedings. (1) Subject to subsection (3) below, proceedings for an offence under any provision of this Act to which this section applies or under byelaws made under any such provision shall not, without the written consent of the Attorney General[1], be taken by any person other than the person aggrieved, or a highway authority or council having an interest in the enforcement of the provision or byelaws in question.

(2) This section applies to sections 167 and 177 above and to the provisions of this Act specified in Schedule 22[2] to this Act.

(3) A constable may take proceedings—

(*a*)   for an offence under paragraph (*b*) of section 171(6) above; or

(*b*)   for an offence under paragraph (*c*) of that subsection consisting of failure to perform a duty imposed by section 171(5)(*a*) above; or

(*c*)   for an offence under section 174 above,

without the consent of the Attorney General.

[Highways Act 1980, s 312 as amended by the Local Government (Miscellaneous Provisions) Act 1982, s 21.]

---

1. Any function of the Attorney-General may be discharged by the Solicitor-General if (a) the office of Attorney-General is vacant, or (b) he is unable to act owing to absence or illness, or (c) he authorises the Solicitor-General to act in any particular case (Law Officers Act 1944, s 1). The justice who issues the summons (or his clerk) should satisfy himself as to the authority (*Price v Humphries* [1958] 2 QB 353, [1958] 2 All ER 725, 122 JP 423).

2. Post.

7–6110   313. *Repealed.*

7–6111   314. Offences by body corporate. (1) Where an offence under any provision of this Act to which this section applies is committed by a body corporate and it is proved to have been committed with the consent or connivance of, or to be attributable to any neglect on the part of, any director, manager, secretary or other similar officer of the body corporate or any person who was purporting to act in any such capacity, he as well as the body corporate is guilty of that offence and liable to be proceeded against and punished accordingly.

(2) Where the affairs of a body corporate are managed by its members, subsection (1) above applies in relation to the acts and defaults of a member in connection with his functions of management as if he were a director of the body corporate.

(3) This section applies to sections 137, 137ZA, 139, 140, 167, 168 and 177 above.

[Highways Act 1980, s 314 as amended by the New Roads and Street Works Act 1991, Sch 8 and the Highways (Obstruction by Body Corporate) Act 2004, s 1.]

7–6112   315. Notice to be given of right of appeal. Where an appeal lies under this Act to the Crown Court or a magistrates' court against a requirement, order, refusal or other decision of a

highway authority or a council, the notice given by the authority or council to the person concerned of the making of the requirement or order or of the refusal or other decision against which such an appeal lies shall state the right of appeal to the Crown Court or a magistrates' court, as the case may be, and the time within which such an appeal may be brought.
[Highways Act 1980, s 315.]

7–6113   316. Appeals and applications to magistrates' courts.   (1) Where any provision of this Act provides—

     (*a*)   for an appeal to a magistrates' court against a requirement, order, refusal or other decision of a highway authority or a council, or

     (*b*)   for any other matter to be determined by, or an application in respect of any matter to be made to, a magistrates' court,

the procedure shall be by way of complaint for an order.

   (2) The time within which an appeal such as is mentioned in subsection (1)(*a*) above may be brought is 21 days from the date on which notice of the decision of the highway authority or council is served on the person wishing to appeal, and for the purpose of this subsection the making of the complaint is to be deemed to be the bringing of the appeal.
[Highways Act 1980, s 316.]

7–6114   317. Appeals to the Crown Court from decisions of magistrates' courts.   (1) Where a person aggrieved[1] by an order, determination or other decision of a magistrates' court under this Act is not by any other enactment authorised to appeal to the Crown Court he may appeal to that court.

   (2) The applicant for an order under section 116[2] above or any person who was entitled under subsection (7) of that section to be, and was, or claimed to be, heard on the application may appeal to the Crown Court against the decision made by the magistrates' court on the application.
[Highways Act 1980, s 317.]

---

   1. A local authority, being the street works authority and the highway authority, may be a person aggrieved by the quashing of an order for making up a street under s 205, ante (*Phillips v Berkshire County Council* [1967] 2 QB 991, [1967] 2 All ER 675, 131 JP 382).
   2. See this section, ante; it relates to the power of a magistrates' court to authorise the stopping up or diversion of a highway.

7–6115   318. Effect of decision of court upon an appeal.   Where on an appeal under this Act a court varies or reverses a decision of a highway authority or of a council it shall be the duty of the authority or the council to give effect to the order of the court and, in particular, to grant or issue any necessary consent, certificate or other document, and to make any necessary entry in any register.
[Highways Act 1980, s 318.]

7–6116   319. Judges and justices not to be disqualified by liability to rates.   The judge of any court or a justice of the peace is not disqualified for acting in cases arising under this Act by reason only of his being as one of several ratepayers, or as one of any other class of persons, liable in common with the others to contribute to, or to be benefited by, any rate or fund out of which any expenses of a council are to be defrayed.
[Highways Act 1980, s 319.]

Notices, etc

7–6117   320. Form of notices etc.   All notices, consents, approvals, orders, demands, licences, certificates and other documents authorised or required by or under this Act to be given, made or issued by, or on behalf of, a highway authority or a council, and all notices, consents, requests and applications authorised or required by or under this Act to be given or made to a highway authority or a council, shall be in writing.
[Highways Act 1980, s 320.]

7–6118   321. Authentication of documents etc.   (1) Any notice, consent, approval, order, demand, licence, certificate or other document which a council (whether as a highway authority or in any other capacity) are authorised or required by or under this Act to give, make or issue may be signed on behalf of the council—

     (*a*)   by the proper officer of the council, or

     (*b*)   by any officer of the council authorised by them in writing to sign documents of a particular kind or, as the case may be, the particular document.

   (2) Any document purporting to bear the signature of the proper officer of the council, or of an officer expressed to be duly authorised by the council to sign such a document or the particular document, shall for the purposes of this Act, and of any byelaws, regulations and orders made under it, be deemed, until the contrary is proved, to have been duly given, made or issued by the council.

In this subsection "signature" includes a facsimile of a signature by whatever process reproduced.
[Highways Act 1980, s 321.]

7–6119   322. Service of notices etc.   (1) Any notice, consent, approval, order, demand, licence, certificate or other document required or authorised by or under this Act to be given or served on a corporation is duly given or served if it is given to or served on the secretary or clerk of the corporation.

(2) Subject to the provisions of this section, any notice, consent, approval, order, demand, licence, certificate or other document required or authorised by or under this Act to be given or served on any person may be given or served either—

(a)   by delivering it to that person, or
(b)   by leaving it at his proper address, or
(c)   by post;

so, however, that where any such document is sent by post otherwise than in a registered letter, or by the recorded delivery service, it shall be deemed not to have been given or served if it is proved that it was not received by the person to whom it was addressed.

(3) For the purposes of this section, and of section 7 of the Interpretation Act 1978 in its application to this section, the proper address of any person to or on whom any such document is to be given or served—

(a)   where the person has furnished an address for service in accordance with arrangements agreed to in that behalf, is the address furnished;
(b)   where the person has not furnished an address as provided by paragraph (a) above, is

(i)   in the case of the secretary or clerk of a corporation, that of the registered or principal office of the corporation, and
(ii)   in any other case, the person's usual or last known place of abode.

(4) If the name or the address of any owner, lessee or occupier of premises to or on whom any such document is to be given or served cannot after reasonable inquiry be ascertained by the person seeking to give or serve the document, the document may be given or served by—

(a)   addressing it to the person to whom it is to be given or on whom it is to be served by the description of "owner", "lessee", or "occupier" of the premises (describing them) to which the document relates, and
(b)   delivering it to some responsible person resident or appearing to be resident on the premises or if there is no such person to whom it can be delivered, affixing it or a copy of it to some conspicuous part of the premises.

(5) The foregoing provisions of this section do not apply to the service of—

(a)   a notice required or authorised to be served under Part II of, or Schedule 1 to, the Acquisition of Land Act 1981 as applied by this Act, or★
(b)   a summons.
[Highways Act 1980, s 322 as amended by the Acquisition of Land Act 1981, Sch 4.]

★**New sub-para (5)(ab) inserted by the Traffic Management Act 2004, s 64 from a a date to be appointed.**

7–6120   323. Reckoning of periods.   (1) For the purposes of this Act—

(a)   in reckoning any period which is therein expressed to be a period from or before a given date, that date is to be excluded; and
(b)   in reckoning any period therein mentioned of 8 days or less which apart from this provision would include a Sunday, Christmas Day, Good Friday or a bank holiday, that day is to be excluded.

(2) In this section "bank holiday" means a day which is a bank holiday under the Banking and Financial Dealings Act 1971.
[Highways Act 1980, s 323.]

Interpretation

7–6121   328. Meaning of "highway".   (1) In this Act, except where the context otherwise requires, "highway" means the whole or a part of a highway other than a ferry or waterway.

(2) Where a highway passes over a bridge or through a tunnel, that bridge or tunnel is to be taken for the purposes of this Act to be a part of the highway.

(3) In this Act, "highway maintainable at the public expense" and any other expression defined by reference to a highway is to be construed in accordance with the foregoing provisions of this section.
[Highways Act 1980, s 328.]

7–6122   329. Further provision as to interpretation.   (1) In this Act, except where the context otherwise requires—

"Act of 1965" means the Compulsory Purchase Act 1965;

"adjoining" includes abutting on, and "adjoins" is to be construed accordingly;

"advance payments code" has the meaning provided by section 203(1) above;

"agriculture" includes horticulture, fruit growing, seed growing, dairy farming, the breeding and keeping of livestock (including any creature kept for the production of food, wool, skins or fur, or for the purpose of its use in the farming of land), the use of land as grazing land, meadow land, osier land, market gardens and nursery grounds, and the use of land for woodlands where that use is ancillary to the farming of land for other agricultural purposes, and "agricultural" is to be construed accordingly;

"apparatus" includes any structure constructed for the lodging therein of apparatus;

"approach", in relation to a bridge or tunnel, means the highway giving access thereto, that is to say, the surface of that highway together with any embankment, retaining wall or other work or substance supporting or protecting the surface;

"bridge" does not include a culvert, but, save as aforesaid, means a bridge or viaduct which is part of a highway, and includes the abutments and any other part of a bridge but not the highway carried thereby;

"bridleway" means a highway over which the public have the following, but not other, rights of way, that is to say, a right of way on foot and a right of way on horseback or leading a horse, with or without a right to drive animals of any description along the highway[1];

"by-pass" has the meaning provided by section 82(6) above;

"canal undertakers" means persons authorised by any enactment to carry on a canal undertaking;

"carriageway" means a way constituting or comprised in a highway, being a way (other than a cycle track) over which the public have a right of way for the passage of vehicles;

"cattle-grid" has the meaning provided by section 82(6) above;

"City" means the City of London;

"classified road" means a highway or proposed highway which is a classified road in accordance with section 12 above;

"Common Council" means the Common Council of the City of London;

"contravention" in relation to a condition, restriction or requirement, includes failure to comply with that condition, restriction or requirement, and "contravene" is to be construed accordingly;

"council" means a county council or a local authority;

"cycle track" means a way constituting or comprised in a highway, being a way over which the public have the following, but no other, rights of way, that is to say, a right of way on pedal cycles (other than pedal cycles which are motor vehicles within the meaning of the Road Traffic Act 1988) with or without a right of way on foot[2];

"definitive map and statement" has the same meaning as in Part III of the Wildlife and Countryside Act 1981;*

"dock undertakers" means persons authorised by any enactments to carry on a dock undertaking;

"drainage authority" means the Environment Agency or an internal drainage board;

"driver information system" has the same meaning as in Part II of the Road Traffic (Driver Licensing and Information Systems) Act 1989, and references to an "operator" of a driver information system are references to an operator licensed under that Part of that Act;

"enactment" includes an enactment in a local or private Act of Parliament and a provision of an order, scheme, regulations or other instrument made under or confirmed by a public general, local or private Act of Parliament;

"field-edge path" means a footpath or bridleway that follows the sides or headlands of a field or enclosure;

"financial year" means a year ending on 31 March;

"footpath" means a highway over which the public have a right of way on foot only, not being a footway;

"footway" means a way comprised in a highway which also comprises a carriageway, being a way over which the public have a right of way on foot only;

"functions" includes powers and duties;

"GLA road" shall be construed in accordance with section 14D(1) above;

"harbour undertakers" means persons authorised by any enactment to carry on a harbour undertaking;

"highway land acquisition powers" has the meaning provided by section 250(1) above;

"highway maintainable at the public expense" means a highway which by virtue of section 36 above or of any other enactment (whether contained in this Act or not) is a highway which for the purposes of this Act is a highway maintainable at the public expense;

"horse" includes pony, ass and mule, and "horseback" is to be construed accordingly;

"hours of darkness" means the time between half an hour after sunset and half an hour before sunrise;

"improvement" means the doing of any act under powers conferred by Part V of this Act and includes the erection, maintenance, alteration and removal of traffic signs, and the freeing of a highway or road-ferry from tolls;

"inland navigation undertakers" means persons authorised by any enactment to carry on an inland navigation undertaking;

"land" includes land covered by water and any interest or right in, over or under land;

"lease" includes an underlease and an agreement for a lease or underlease, but does not include an option to take a lease or mortgage, and "lessee" is to be construed accordingly;

"lighting authority" means a council or other body authorised to provide lighting under section 161 of the Public Health Act 1875 or under section 3 of the Parish Councils Act 1957 or any corresponding local enactment;

"local authority" means the council of a district or London borough or the Common Council but, in relation to Wales, means a Welsh Council;

"local highway authority" means a highway authority other than the Minister;

"local planning authority" has the same meaning as in the Town and Country Planning Act 1990;

"lorry area" means an area provided under section 115 above;

"made-up carriageway" means a carriageway, or a part thereof, which has been metalled or in any other way provided with a surface suitable for the passage of vehicles;

"maintenance" includes repair, and "maintain" and "maintainable" are to be construed accordingly;

"maintenance compound" means an area of land (with or without buildings) used or to be used in connection with the maintenance of highways, or a particular highway;

"the Minister", subject to subsection (5) below, means as respects England, the Minister of Transport and as respects Wales, the Secretary of State; and in section 258 of, and paragraphs 7, 8(1) and (3), 14, 15(1) and (3), 18(2), 19 and 21 of Schedule 1 to, this Act, references to the Minister and the Secretary of State acting jointly are to be construed, as respects Wales, as references to the Secretary of State acting alone;

"navigation authority" means persons authorised by any enactment to work, maintain, conserve, improve or control any canal or other inland navigation, navigable river, estuary, harbour or dock;

"owner", in relation to any premises, means a person, other than a mortgagee not in possession, who, whether in his own right or as trustee or agent for any other person, is entitled to receive the rack rent of the premises or, where the premises are not let at a rack rent, would be so entitled if the premises were so let;

"pier undertakers" means persons authorised by any enactment to carry on a pier undertaking;

"premises" includes land and buildings;

"private street works code" has the meaning provided by section 203(1) above;

"proposed highway" means land on which, in accordance with plans made by a highway authority, that authority are for the time being constructing or intending to construct a highway shown in the plans;

"proprietor", in relation to a school, has the same meaning as in the Education Act 1996;★

"public general enactment" means an enactment in an Act treated as a public general Act under the system of division of Acts adopted in the regnal year 38 George 3, other than an Act for confirming a provisional order;

"public path creation agreement" means an agreement under section 25 above;

"public path creation order" means an order under section 26 above;

"public path diversion order" means an order under section 119 above;

"public path extinguishment order" means an order under section 118 above;

"public utility undertakers" means persons authorised by any enactment to carry on any of the following undertakings, that is to say, an undertaking for the supply of gas or hydraulic power;

"rack rent", in relation to any premises, means a rent which is not less than two-thirds of the rent at which the premises might reasonably be expected to let from year to year, free from all usual tenant's rates and taxes, and deducting therefrom the probable average annual cost of the repairs, insurance and other expenses (if any) necessary to maintain the same in a state to command such rent;

"rail crossing diversion order" means an order under section 119A above;

"rail crossing extinguishment order" means an order under section 118A above;

"railway" includes a light railway;

"railway undertakers" means person authorised by any enactment to carry on a railway undertaking;

"reconstruction", in relation to a bridge, includes the construction of a new bridge and approaches thereto in substitution for the existing bridge and the approaches thereto;

"restricted byway" has the same meaning as in Part II of the Countryside and Rights of Way Act 2000;★★

"road-ferry" means a ferry connecting the termination of a highway which is, or is to become, a highway maintainable at the public expense with the termination of another highway which is, or is to become, such a highway;

"road hump" has the meaning provided by section 90F(1);

"school" has the same meaning as in the Education Act 1996;★

"service area" means an area of land adjoining, or in the vicinity of, a special road, being an area in which there are, or are to be, provided service stations or other buildings or facilities to be used in connection with the use of the special road;

"special diversion order" means an order under section 119B(4) above;★

"special enactment" means any enactment other than a public general enactment;

"special extinguishment order" means an order under section 118B(4) above;★

"special road"[3] means a highway, or a proposed highway, which is a special road in accordance with section 16 above;

"SSSI diversion order" means an order under section 119D above;★

"special road authority" has the meaning provided by section 16(4) above;

"statutory undertakers" means persons authorised by any enactment to carry on any of the following undertakings—

(*a*) a railway, tramway, road transport, water transport, canal, inland navigation, dock, harbour, pier or lighthouse undertaking, or

(*b*) an undertaking for the supply of hydraulic[4] power,

and "statutory undertaking" is to be construed accordingly;

"street" has the same meaning as in Part III of the New Roads and Street Works Act 1991;

"street works licence" means a licence under section 50 of the New Roads and Street Works Act 1991, and a "licensee" in relation to such a licence, has the meaning given by subsection (3) of that section;

"swing bridge" includes any opening bridge operated by mechanical means;

"traffic" includes pedestrians and animals;

"traffic calming works", in relation to a highway, means works affecting the movement of vehicular and other traffic for the purpose of—

(*a*) promoting safety (including avaoiding or reducing, or reducing the likelihood of, danger connected with terrorism within the meaning of section 1 of the Terrorism Act 2000 (c 11)) or

(*b*) preserving or improving the environment through which the highway runs;

"traffic sign" has the same meaning as in section 64 of the Road Traffic Regulation Act 1984;

"tramway undertakers" means persons authorised by any enactment to carry on a tramway undertaking;

"transport undertakers" means persons authorised by any enactment to carry on any of the following undertakings, that is to say, a railway, canal, inland navigation, dock, harbour or pier undertaking, and "transport undertaking" is to be construed accordingly;

"trunk road" means a highway, or a proposed highway, which is a trunk road by virtue of section 10(1) or section 19 above or by virtue of an order or direction under section 10 above or under any other enactment;

"trunk road picnic area" has the meaning provided by section 112(1) above;

"universal service provider" has the same meaning as in the Postal Services Act 2000; and references to the provision of a universal postal service shall be construed in accordance with that Act;

"water undertakers" means the Environment Agency or a water undertaker;

"Welsh Council" means the council of a Welsh county or county borough.

(2) A highway at the side of a river, canal or other inland navigation is not excluded from the definition in subsection (1) above of either "bridleway" or "footpath",★★★ by reason only that the public have a right to use the highway for purposes of navigation, if the highway would fall within that definition if the public had no such right thereover.

(2A) In this Act—

(*a*) any reference to a county shall be construed in relation to Wales as including a reference to a county borough;

(*b*) any reference to a county council shall be construed in relation to Wales as including a reference to a county borough council; and

(*c*) section 17(4) and (5) of the Local Government (Wales) Act 1994 (references to counties and districts to be construed generally in relation to Wales as references to counties and county boroughs) shall not apply.

(3) In a case where two or more parishes are grouped under a common parish council, references in this Act to a parish are to be construed as references to those parishes.

(3A) In a case where two or more communities are grouped under a common community council, references in this Act to a community are to be construed as references to those communities.

(4) Any reference in this Act to property of railway undertakers, canal undertakers, inland navigation undertakers, dock undertakers, harbour undertakers or pier undertakers is, where the undertakers are a body to which this subsection applies, to be taken as a reference to property of that body held or used by them wholly or mainly for the purposes of so much of their undertaking as consists of the carrying on of a railway undertaking or, as the case may be, of a canal undertaking, an inland navigation undertaking, a dock undertaking, a harbour undertaking or a pier undertaking.

This subsection applies to the following bodies, namely, the British Railways Board, the British Transport Docks Board, the British Waterways Board, Transport for London, any wholly-owned subsidiary (within the meaning of the Transport Act 1968) or joint subsidiary (within the meaning of section 51(5) of that Act) of any of those bodies other than Transport for London, or any of its subsidiaries (within the meaning of the Greater London Authority Act 1999).

(4A) Any reference in this Act to apparatus belonging to, or used or maintained by the operator of an electronic communications code network shall have effect as a reference to electronic communications apparatus kept installed for the purposes of that network.

(5) In relation to that part of the road constructed by the Minister of Transport along the line described in Schedule 1 to the North of Almondsbury—South of Haysgate Trunk Road Order 1947 and referred to in that Order as "the new road" which lies to the east of the most easterly point before reaching the River Wye at which eastbound traffic of Classes I and II (as specified in Schedule 4 to this Act) can leave that road by another special road, the functions of the Minister under this Act shall be exercisable by the Minister of Transport and not by the Secretary of State.

[Highways Act 1980, s 329 as amended by the Acquisition of Land Act 1981, Sch 6, the Road Traffic Regulation Act 1984, Sch 13, the Cycle Tracks Act 1984, s 1, the Telecommunications Act 1984, Sch 4, the London Regional Transport Act 1984, Schs 6 and 7, the Local Government Act 1985, Sch 17, the Gas Act 1986, Sch 9, the Road Traffic (Consequential Provisions) Act 1988, Sch 3 the Water Act 1989, Sch 25, the Electricity Act 1989, Sch 18, the Road Traffic (Driver Licensing and Information Systems) Act 1989, Sch 4, the Statute Law (Repeals) Act 1989, Sch 1, the Rights of Way Act 1990, s 2, the Planning (Consequential Provisions) Act 1990, Sch 2, the New Roads and Street Works Act 1991, Sch 8, the Transport and Works Act 1992, Sch 2, the Statute Law (Repeals) Act 1993, Sch 1, the Local Government (Wales) Act 1994, Sch 7, the Countryside and Rights of Way Act 2000, Sch 6, SI 2003/1615 and the Civil Contigencies Act 2004, Sch 2.]

---

*New definitions inserted by the Countryside and Rights of Way Act 2000, Sch 6, in force in relation to England 12 February 2003. In force in Wales for cerratin purposes 15 July 2005, date for remaining purposes to be appointed.

**New definition inserted by the Countryside and Rights of Way Act 2000, Sch 5, from a date to be appointed.

***Amended by the Countryside and Rights of Way Act 2000, Sch 5, from a date to be appointed.

1. Subject to any orders made by a local authority and to any byelaws, the public have, as a right of way, the right to ride a pedal cycle on any bridleway but cyclists must give way to pedestrians and persons on horseback; see the Countryside Act 1968, s 30.

2. For a prohibition of driving or parking on cycle tracks, see the Road Traffic Act 1988, s 21, post.

3. For restriction on the grant of a justices' licence for the sale of intoxicating liquor for premises on special roads, see the Licensing Act 1964, s 9(3).

4. The National Rivers Authority, (see now the Environment Agency) every water undertaker and every sewerage undertaker is deemed to be a statutory undertaker for the purposes of this Act (Water Act 1989, Sch 25, para 1).

7–6123 **344.** *Application to Isles of Scilly.*

SCHEDULES

Sections 67, 287.   SCHEDULE 8
Consents Required for Execution of Certain Works in Streets

7–6124 **1.** In this Schedule "the authority" means the highway authority or local authority (within the meaning of section 67 or section 287 of this Act) having power to carry out the works to which this Schedule applies.

2. The authority shall not carry out any works to which this Schedule applies in any such situation or position as is described in the first column of the following Table except with the consent of the person described in relation thereto in the second column of that Table.

In any street which is a highway for which there is a highway authority other than the authority carrying out the works.	The highway authority.
In any street belonging to and repairable by any railway, dock, harbour, canal, inland navigation or passenger road transport undertakers and forming the approach to any station, dock, wharf or depot of those undertakers.	The undertakers.
On any bridge not vested in the authority carrying out the works or on the approaches to any such bridge.	The authority or other person in whom the bridge is vested.
On any bridge carrying a street over any railway, canal or inland navigation, or on the approaches to any such bridge, or under any bridge carrying a railway, canal or inland navigation over a street.	The railway, canal or inland navigation undertakers concerned.
In the case of works under section 67 of this Act, in a position obstructing or interfering with any existing access to any land or premises abutting upon a street.	The owner and the occupier of the land or premises.

3. A consent required by this Schedule in respect of any works shall not unreasonably be withheld but may be given subject to any reasonable conditions, including a condition that the authority shall remove the works either at any time or at or after the expiration of a period if reasonably required so to do by the person giving the consent.

4. Where the consent of the Minister is required under this Schedule, any dispute between the Minister whose consent is required and the authority as to whether the Minister's consent is unreasonably withheld or is given subject to reasonable conditions, or whether the removal of anything to the provision of which the consent relates in accordance with any condition of the consent is reasonably required shall be referred to and determined by an arbitrator to be appointed in default of agreement by the President of the Institution of Civil Engineers.

Section 116, 256   SCHEDULE 12
PROVISIONS AS TO ORDERS UNDER SECTION 116 AND CONVEYANCES UNDER SECTION 256

(*As amended by the Local Government Act 1985, Sch 4 and the Local Government (Wales) Act 1994, Sch 7.*)

PART I
NOTICES TO BE GIVEN BY APPLICANT FOR ORDER UNDER SECTION 116

7–6125 **1.** At least 28 days before the day on which an application for an order under section 116 of this Act is made in relation to a highway the applicant authority shall give notice of their intention to apply for the order, specifying the time and place at which the application is to be made and the terms of the order applied for (embodying a plan showing what will be the effect thereof)—

    (*a*) to the owners and occupiers of all lands adjoining the highway;
    (*b*) to any statutory undertakers having apparatus under, in, upon, over, along or across the highway;
    (*c*) if the highway is a classified road, to the Minister;
    (*d*) if the highway is a classified road in a non-metropolitan district, to the district council if the highway is a classified road in a Welsh county or county borough and the council of that county or county borough is not the highway authority, to the council of that county or county borough, and if the highway is a classified road in, or partly in, a parish or community which has a separate parish council or community council, to the parish or community council, as the case may require or, in the case of a parish which does not have a separate parish council, to the chairman of the parish meeting.

    2. Not later than 28 days before the day on which the application is made the applicant authority shall cause a copy of the said notice to be displayed in a prominent position at the ends of the highway.
    3. At least 28 days before the day on which the application is made the applicant authority shall publish in the London Gazette and in at least one local newspaper circulating in the area in which the highway is situated a notice containing the particulars specified in paragraph 1 above, except that there may be substituted for the plan a statement of a place in the said area where the plan may be inspected free of charge at all reasonable hours.

PART II

7–6126 **4–10.** *Apparatus of Statutory Undertakers.*

Section 160A   SCHEDULE 12A
FURTHER POWERS OF HIGHWAY AUTHORITIES AND COUNCILS IN RELATION TO INTERFERENCE WITH HIGHWAYS

(*Added by the Rights of Way Act 1990, s 4.*)

Interpretation

7–6127 **1.** (1) For the purposes of this Schedule the "minimum width" and "maximum width" of a highway shall be determined in accordance with sub-paragraphs (2) and (3) below.
    (2) In any case where the width of the highway is proved, that width is both the "minimum width" and the "maximum width".
    (3) In any other case—

    (*a*) the "minimum width" is—

        (i) as respects a footpath which is not a field-edge path, 1 metre,
        (ii) as respects a footpath which is a field-edge path, 1.5 metres,
        (iii) as respects a bridleway which is not a field-edge path, 2 metres, or
        (iv) as respects any other highway, 3 metres; and

    (*b*) the "maximum width" is—

        (i) as respects a footpath, 1.8 metres,
        (ii) as respects a bridleway, 3 metres, or
        (iii) as respects any other highway, 5 metres.

The rest of this Schedule deals with the power of competent authorities to carry out work in default.

Section 184   SCHEDULE 14
PROVISIONS WITH RESPECT TO NOTICES UNDER SECTION 184

7–6128 **1.** A person on whom a notice under section 184(1) or (3) of this Act is served may within 28 days from the date of his being served therewith object to the notice on any of the following grounds which are appropriate in the circumstances of the particular case:—

    (*a*) that the notice is not justified by the terms of section 184(1) or (3);
    (*b*) that there has been some defect or error in, or in connection with, the notice;
    (*c*) that the proposed works are unreasonable in character or extent, or are unnecessary;
    (*d*) that the conditions imposed by the notice are unreasonable;
    (*e*) that some other person having an interest in the premises also habitually takes or permits to be taken a mechanically propelled vehicle across the footway or verge and should be required to defray part of the expenses of executing the proposed works;

   (*f*) that the authority are not entitled to serve the notice by reason of section 184(2);

   (*g*) that a person carrying out or proposing to carry out such a development as is referred to in section 184(3) offers to execute the works himself.

  2. An objection under paragraph 1 above shall be made by notice to the highway authority, and the notice shall state the grounds of objection.

  3. Where objection is made to a notice given by a local highway authority under section 184(1) or (3), that authority shall send a copy of the notice and of the notice of objection to the Minister.

  4. If objection is made to such a notice and the objection is not withdrawn the notice does not become effective until it has been confirmed by the Minister, and the Minister after considering the objection may confirm the notice without modification or subject to such modifications as he thinks fit.

  5. Subject to paragraph 4 above, such a notice becomes effective at the expiration of the period during which the person served therewith may object to it.

Section 204

SCHEDULE 15

APPLICATION OF ADVANCE PAYMENTS CODE

(As amended by the Local Government Act 1985, Sch 4.)

7–6129 **1.** Where the advance payments code does not apply in a parish or community or any part of a parish or community, the council of the county or metropolitan district in which the parish or community is situated may, subject to the provisions of this Schedule, by resolution adopt that code for the parish or community or, as the case may be, for that part at a meeting of which not less than one month's notice has been duly given to all the members of the council specifying the intention to propose the resolution.

  2. The resolution shall come into operation at such time, not being less than one month from the date of the first publication of an advertisement under paragraph 3(*a*) below, as the council may by the resolution fix, and upon its coming into operation the advance payments code shall apply in the parish or community, or part of the parish or community specified in the resolution.

  3. When it has been passed, the resolution shall be published—

   (*a*) by advertisement in at least one local newspaper circulating in the parish or community concerned or, as the case may be, the part of the parish or community concerned, and

   (*b*) by notice thereof fixed to the principal doors of every church and chapel in the parish or community concerned or, as the case may be, the part of the parish or community concerned, in the place to which notices are usually fixed, and

   (*c*) otherwise in such manner as the council think sufficient for giving notice thereof to all persons interested,

and a copy of the resolution shall be sent to the Minister.

  4. A copy of the advertisement of the resolution published under paragraph 3(*a*) above is sufficient evidence of the passing of the resolution unless the contrary is shown, and, on the expiration of 3 months from the date of the first publication of that advertisement, an objection to the resolution on the ground—

   (*a*) that notice to propose it was not duly given, or

   (*b*) that the resolution was not sufficiently published,

is of no effect.

  5. For the purposes of this Schedule a notice is to be deemed to have been duly given to a member of a council if—

   (*a*) it is given in the mode in which notices to attend meetings of the council are usually given, or

   (*b*) where there is no such mode, it is signed by the proper officer of the council and delivered to the member or left at this usual or last known place of abode in England and Wales, or sent by post in a prepaid registered letter, or letter sent by the recorded delivery service, addressed to the member at his usual or last-known place of abode in England or Wales.

Sections 205, 210.

SCHEDULE 16

PARTICULARS TO BE STATED IN SPECIFICATIONS, NOTICES, ETC, UNDER THE PRIVATE STREET WORKS CODE

7–6130 **1.** The specification shall describe generally the works and things to be done, and, in the case of structural works, shall specify so far as may be practicable the foundation, form, material and dimensions thereof.

  2. The plans and sections shall show the constructional character of the works, the connections (if any) with existing streets, sewers or other works, and the lines and levels of the works, subject to such limits of deviation (if any) as may be indicated on the plans and sections respectively.

  3. The estimate shall show the particulars of the probable cost of the whole works, including any additional charge in respect of surveys, superintendence and notices.

  4. The provisional apportionment shall state the amounts charged on the respective premises and the names of the respective owners, or reputed owners, and shall also state whether the apportionment is made according to the frontage of the respective premises or not, and the measurements of the frontages, and the other considerations (if any) on which the apportionment is based.

  5. The notice under section 205 of this Act shall contain the following particulars—

   (*a*) a statement that the street works authority have resolved to execute street works in the private street in question;

   (*b*) the address of the offices of the authority at which a copy of the resolution of approval, and the approved documents or copies of them certified by the proper officer, may be inspected, and the times at which, and the period during which, they may be inspected; and

   (*c*) a statement that an owner of premises liable to be charged with any part of the expenses of executing the street works may object to the proposal to execute the works, giving the period during which such objection may be made.

  6. The notice under section 210 of this Act shall contain the following particulars—

(a) a statement that the street works authority propose to amend the estimate so as to increase the amount of it, specifying the former amount and the amount to which it is to be increased;

(b) the address of the offices of the authority at which a document certified by the proper officer giving details of the proposed amendment and of the proposed consequential amendment of the provisional apportionment may be inspected, and the times at which, and the period during which, it may be inspected; and

(c) a statement that an owner of premises liable to be charged with any part of the expenses of executing the street works may object to the proposed amendments, giving the period during which such objection may be made.

Sections 288, 294, 312, 338, 339, 341.   SCHEDULE 22
PROVISIONS OF THIS ACT TO WHICH SECTIONS 288, 294, 312, 338, 339 AND 341 OF THIS ACT APPLY

7–6131 **1.** *Provisions contained in Part IV*
Section 36(6) and (7) and section 38.
2. *Provisions contained in Part V*
Section 66(2) to (8), sections 73 and 77 and section 96(4) and (5).
3. *Provisions contained in Part IX*
Sections 133, and 151 to 153, section 154(1), and 154(4) so far as relating to a notice under 154(1), sections 163 and 165, sections 171 to 174, 176, 178 and 179, section 180 other than subsection (2) and subsection (4) so far as relating to subsection (2), and section 185.
4. *Provisions contained in Part X*
Sections 186 to 188, 190 to 197, 200 and 201.
5. *Provisions contained in Part XI*
The private street works code, sections 226 and 228, section 230(1) to (6), and sections 231, 233, 236 and 237.
6. *Provisions contained in Part XII*
Section 239(6) and section 241.
7. *Provisions contained in Part XIV*
Sections 286, 295, 297, 303, 304 and 305.

Cycle Tracks Act 1984
(1984 c 38)

7–6132 **1. Amendment of definition of "cycle track".** *Amendment of Highways Act 1980, s 329.*

7–6133 **2.** *(Repealed).*

7–6134 **3. Conversion of footpaths into cycle tracks.** (1) A local highway authority may in the case of any footpath for which they are the highway authority by order made by them and either—
(a) submitted to and confirmed by the Secretary of State[1], or
(b) confirmed by them as an unopposed order,
designate the footpath or any part of it as a cycle track, with the effect that, on such date as the order takes effect in accordance with the following provisions of this section, the footpath or part of the footpath to which the order relates shall become a highway which for the purposes of the 1980 Act is a highway maintainable at the public expense and over which the public have a right of way on pedal cycles (other than pedal cycles which are motor vehicles) and a right of way on foot.
(2)–(11) *Procedure for the making of an order under this section.*
[Cycle Tracks Act 1984, s 3 amended by the Agricultural Holdings Act 1986, Sch 14 and the Planning (Consequential Provisions) Act 1990, Sch 2.]

1. Functions of the Minister, so far as exercisable in relation to Wales, have been transferred to the National Assembly for Wales, by the National Assembly for Wales (Transfer of Functions) Order 1999, SI 1999/672, art 2, Sch 1.

7–6135 **8. Interpretation.** (1) In this Act—
"the 1980 Act" means the Highways Act 1980; and
"motor vehicle" means a motor vehicle within the meaning of the Road Traffic Act 1988.

(2) Except where the context otherwise requires, any expression used in this Act which is also used in the 1980 Act has the same meaning as in that Act.
[Cycle Tracks Act 1984, s 8 amended by the Road Traffic (Consequential Provisions) Act 1988.]

7–6135A **9.** *Short title, commencement[1] and extent.*

1. This Act came into force on the 12 September 1984.

New Roads and Street Works Act 1991[1]
(1991 c 22)

PART I[2]
NEW ROADS IN ENGLAND AND WALES
Further provisions with respect to tolls

7–6136 **14. Collection of tolls.** (1) The Secretary of State may make provision by regulations with respect to the collection of tolls in pursuance of a toll order.

(2) Different provision may be made for different types of road or different types of toll, or for particular roads or particular tolls.

(3) Regulations may, in particular, impose requirements with respect to—

(a) the displaying of lists of tolls, and

(b) the manner of implementing changes in the amount of tolls;

and where any such requirements are imposed, a toll may not be demanded unless they are, or as the case may be have been, complied with.

(4) A person who in respect of the use of a road to which a toll order relates demands a toll—

(a) which he is not authorised to charge, or

(b) which by virtue of subsection (3) may not be demanded,

commits an offence and is liable on summary conviction to a fine not exceeding **level 3** on the standard scale.

(5) Regulations under this section shall be made by statutory instrument which shall be subject to annulment in pursuance of a resolution of either House of Parliament.

[New Roads and Street Works Act 1991, s 14.]

---

1. The parts of this Act printed here are now in force with the exceptions of ss 79 and 80 see the following commencement orders: (No 1) SI 1991/2288; (No 3) SI 1992/1686; (No 5 and Transitional Provisions) SI 1992/1686 (other orders relate to Scotland); (No 1) (Wales) SI 2004/1780 (s 79 with the exception of sub-s (1)(c) on 23 July 2004).

2. Part I contains ss 1–26.

7–6137   **15. Refusal or failure to pay tolls.**   (1) A person who without reasonable excuse refuses or fails to pay, or who attempts to evade payment of, a toll which he is liable to pay by virtue of a toll order commits an offence and is liable on summary conviction to a fine not exceeding **level 3** on the standard scale.

(2) If it appears to a person employed for the purpose of collecting tolls that a person has, without reasonable excuse, refused or failed to pay a toll which he is liable to pay by virtue of a toll order, he may—

(a) refuse to permit him to pass, or prevent him from passing, through any place at which tolls are payable, and

(b) require him to remove his vehicle from any such place by a particular route, and if he does not comply with such a requirement cause the vehicle to be so removed;

and for the purpose of exercising the powers conferred by this subsection, a person employed for the purpose of the collection of tolls may call upon such assistance as he thinks necessary.

(3) Where a person does not comply with a requirement under subsection (2)(b) as to the removal of his vehicle, he is liable to pay a prescribed charge in respect of the removal of the vehicle.

(4) Where there remains unpaid—

(a) a toll which a person is liable to pay by virtue of a toll order, or

(b) a prescribed charge which he is liable to pay by virtue of subsection (3),

the person authorised to charge tolls may recover from the person liable the amount of the toll or charge together with a reasonable sum to cover administrative expenses.

(5) In this section a "prescribed charge" means such charge as may be specified in, or calculated in accordance with, regulations made by the Secretary of State.

The regulations may provide for the amount of the charge, or any amount used for the purpose of calculating the charge, to be varied in accordance with a formula specified in the regulations.

(6) Regulations under this section shall be made by statutory instrument which shall be subject to annulment in pursuance of a resolution of either House of Parliament.

[New Roads and Street Works Act 1991, s 15.]

General

7–6138   **25. Application of provisions of the Highways Act 1980, etc.**   (1) The following provisions of the Highways Act 1980 apply for the purposes of this Part as if it were a part of that Act—

section 302 (inquiries),

section 303 (penalty for obstructing execution of Act),

section 312 (restriction on institution of proceedings for offence),

section 319 (judges and justices not to be disqualified by liability to rates),

sections 320 to 322 (provisions as to notices), and

section 323 (reckoning of periods).

(2) Nothing in this Part shall be construed as restricting the powers of a highway authority with respect to a road subject to a concession—

(a) as to the matters which may be provided for in the concession agreement or as to the making of agreements of any other description for any purpose connected with the special road; or (*b*) as to the acquisition, by agreement or compulsorily, of any land which in the opinion of the authority is required, in connection with the road, for any purpose for which the authority may acquire land under Part XII of the Highways Act 1980.

(3) Nothing in a concession agreement shall be construed as affecting the status of the road subject to the concession as a highway maintainable at the public expense.

[New Roads and Street Works Act 1991, s 25.]

PART III[1]

STREET WORKS IN ENGLAND AND WALES

Introductory provisions

7–6139 48. Streets, street works and undertakers. (1) In this Part a "street" means the whole or any part of any of the following, irrespective of whether it is a thoroughfare—

(*a*) any highway, road, lane, footway, alley or passage,

(*b*) any square or court, and

(*c*) any land laid out as a way whether it is for the time being formed as a way or not.

Where a street passes over a bridge or through a tunnel, references in this Part to the street include that bridge or tunnel.

(2) The provisions of this Part apply to a street which is not a maintainable highway subject to such exceptions and adaptations as may be prescribed[2].

(3) In this Part "street works" means works of any of the following kinds (other than works for road purposes) executed in a street in pursuance of a statutory right or a street works licence—

(*a*) placing apparatus, or

(*b*) inspecting, maintaining, adjusting, repairing, altering or renewing apparatus, changing the position of apparatus or removing it,

or works required for or incidental to any such works (including, in particular, breaking up or opening the street, or any sewer, drain or tunnel under it, or tunnelling or boring under the street).

(4) In this Part "undertaker" in relation to street works means the person by whom the relevant statutory right is exercisable (in the capacity in which it is exercisable by him) or the licensee under the relevant street works licence, as the case may be.

(5) References in this Part to the undertaker in relation to apparatus in a street are to the person entitled, by virtue of a statutory right or a street works licence, to carry out in relation to the apparatus such works as are mentioned in subsection (3); and references to an undertaker having apparatus in the street, or to the undertaker to whom apparatus belongs, shall be construed accordingly.

[New Roads and Street Works Act 1991, s 48.]

---

1. Part III contains ss 47–106.

2. See the Street Works (Registers, Notices, Directions and Designations) Regulations 1992, SI 1992/2985 amended by SI 1999/1049.

7–6140 49. The street authority and other relevant authorities. (1) In this Part "the street authority" in relation to a street means, subject to the following provisions—

(*a*) if the street is a maintainable highway, the highway authority, and

(*b*) if the street is not a maintainable highway, the street managers.

(2) In the case of a highway for which the Secretary of State is the highway authority but in relation to which a local highway authority acts as his agent under section 6 of the Highways Act 1980, the local highway authority shall be regarded as the street authority for the purposes of section 53 (the street works register) and sections 54 to 60 (advance notice and co-ordination of works).

(3) Subsection (1)(*b*) has effect subject to section 87 as regards the application of this Part to prospectively maintainable highways.

(4) In this Part the expression "street managers", used in relation to a street which is not a maintainable highway, means the authority, body or person liable to the public to maintain or repair the street or, if there is none, any authority, body or person having the management or control of the street.

(5) The Secretary of State may by regulations[1] make provision for exempting street managers from provisions of this Part which would otherwise apply to them as the street authority in relation to a street.

(6) References in this Part to the relevant authorities in relation to any works in a street are to the street authority and also—

(*a*) where the works include the breaking up or opening of a public sewer in the street, the sewer authority;

(*b*) where the street is carried or crossed by a bridge vested in a transport authority, or crosses or is crossed by any other property held or used for the purposes of a transport authority, that authority; and

(*c*)   where in any other case the street is carried or crossed by a bridge, the bridge authority.
[New Roads and Street Works Act 1991, s 49.]

---

1. See the Street Works (Registers, Notices, Directions and Designations) Regulations 1992, SI 1992/2985 amended by SI 1999/1049.

7–6141   50. Street works licences.   *The street authority may grant a street works licence.*
[New Roads and Street Works Act 1991, s 50—summarised.]

7–6142   51. Prohibition of unauthorised street works.   (1) It is an offence for a person other than the street authority—

(*a*)   to place apparatus in a street, or

(*b*)   to break up or open a street, or a sewer, drain or tunnel under it, or to tunnel or bore under a street, for the purpose of placing, inspecting, maintaining, adjusting, repairing, altering or renewing apparatus, or of changing the position of apparatus or removing it,

otherwise than in pursuance of a statutory right or a street works licence.

(2) A person committing an offence under this section is liable on summary conviction to a fine not exceeding **level 5★** on the standard scale.

(3) This section does not apply to works for road purposes or to emergency works of any description.

(4) If a person commits an offence under this section, the street authority may—

(*a*)   in the case of an offence under subsection (1)(*a*), direct him to remove the apparatus in respect of which the offence was committed, and

(*b*)   in any case, direct him to take such steps as appear to them necessary to reinstate the street or any sewer, drain or tunnel under it.

If he fails to comply with the direction, the authority may remove the apparatus or, as the case may be, carry out the necessary works and recover from him the costs reasonably incurred by them in doing so.
[New Roads and Street Works Act 1991, s 51 as amended by the Traffic Management Act 2004, Sch 1.]

★Reproduced as amended by the Traffic Management Act 2004, Sch 1. In force in relation to England, in Wales from a date to be appointed.

7–6143   52. Emergency works.   (1) In this Part "emergency works" means works whose execution at the time when they are executed is required in order to put an end to, or to prevent the occurrence of, circumstances then existing or imminent (or which the person responsible for the works believes on reasonable grounds to be existing or imminent) which are likely to cause danger to persons or property.

(2) Where works comprise items some of which fall within the preceding definition, the expression "emergency works" shall be taken to include such of the items as do not fall within that definition as cannot reasonably be severed from those that do.

(3) Where in any civil or criminal proceedings brought by virtue of any provision of this Part the question arises whether works were emergency works, it is for the person alleging that they were to prove it.
[New Roads and Street Works Act 1991, s 52.]

The street works register

7–6144   53. The street works register.   *A street authority shall keep a register showing with respect to each street for which they are responsible such information as may be prescribed and make it available for inspection.*
[New Roads and Street Works Act 1991, s 53—summarised.]

7–6144A   53A. Duty to inspect records.   *Regulations may require an undertaker to inspect statutory records before commencing street works and create a summary offence in respect of contraventions.*
[New Roads and Street Works Act 1991, s 53A—summarised.]

Notice and co-ordination of works

7–6145   54. Advance notice of certain works.   (1) In such cases as may be prescribed[1] an undertaker proposing to execute street works shall give the prescribed[1] advance notice of the works to the street authority.

(2) Different periods of notice may be prescribed[1] for different descriptions of works.

(3) The notice shall contain such★ information as may be prescribed[1].

(4) After giving advance notice under this section an undertaker shall comply with such requirements as may be prescribed[1], or imposed by the street authority, as to the providing of information and other procedural steps to be taken for the purpose of co-ordinating the proposed works with other works of any description proposed to be executed in the street.★

(5) An undertaker who fails to comply with his duties under this section commits an offence and is liable on summary conviction to a fine not exceeding **level 3★** on the standard scale.
[New Roads and Street Works Act 1991, s 54.]

★New sub-ss (4A)–(4C) inserted and sub-ss (3) and (9) amended by the Traffic Management Act 2004, s 49 and Sch 1 from a date to be appointed.
1. See the Street Works (Registers, Notices, Directions and Designations) Regulations 1992, SI 1992/2985 amended by SI 1999/1049.

7–6146   **55. Notice of starting date of works.**   (1) An undertaker proposing to begin to execute street works involving—

     (a)   breaking up or opening the street, or any sewer, drain or tunnel under it, or

     (b)   tunnelling or boring under the street,

shall give not less than 7 working days' notice (or such other notice as may be prescribed[1]) to the street authority, to any other relevant authority and to any other person having apparatus in the street which is likely to be affected by the works.

(2) Different periods of notice may be prescribed[1] for different descriptions of works,★ and cases may be prescribed[1] in which no notice is required.

(3) The notice shall state the date on which it is proposed to begin the works and shall contain such other information as may be prescribed[1].

(4) Where notice is required to be given under this section, the works shall not be begun without notice or before the end of the notice period, except with the consent of those to whom notice is required to be given.

(5) An undertaker who begins to execute any works in contravention of this section commits an offence and is liable on summary conviction to a fine not exceeding level 4★★ on the standard scale.

(6) In proceedings against a person for such an offence it is a defence for him to show that the contravention was attributable—

     (a)   to his not knowing the position, or not knowing of the existence, of another person's apparatus, or

     (b)   to his not knowing the identity or address of—

         (i)   a relevant authority, or

         (ii)   the person to whom any apparatus belongs,

and that his ignorance was not due to any negligence on his part or to any failure to make inquiries which he ought reasonably to have made.

(7) A notice under this section shall cease to have effect if the works to which it relates are not substantially begun before the end of the period of 7 working days (or such other period as may be prescribed[1]) beginning with the starting date specified in the notice, or such further period as may be allowed by those to whom notice is required to be given.★
[New Roads and Street Works Act 1991, s 55 as amended by the Traffic Management Act 2004, s 40.]

★New sub-ss (8) and (9) inserted and sub-ss (2) amended by the Traffic Management Act 2004, s 49 and Sch 1 from a date to be appointed.
★★Reproduced as amended by the Traffic Management Act 2004, Sch 1. In force in relation to England, in Wales from a date to be appointed.
1. See the Street Works (Registers, Notices, Directions and Designations) Regulations 1992, SI 1992/2985 amended by SI 1999/1049.

7–6147   **56. Power to give directions as to timing of street works.**   (1) If it appears to the street authority—

     (a)   that proposed street works are likely to cause serious disruption to traffic, and

     (b)   that the disruption would be avoided or reduced if the works were carried out only at certain times or on certain days (or at certain times on certain days),

the authority may give the undertaker such directions as may be appropriate as to the times or days (or both) when the works may or may not be carried out.★

(2) The procedure for giving a direction shall be prescribed[1] by the Secretary of State.

(3) An undertaker who executes works in contravention of a direction under this section commits an offence and is liable on summary conviction to a fine not exceeding **level 5** on the standard scale.

(3A) An undertaker shall be taken not to have failed to fulfil any statutory duty to afford a supply or service if, or to the extent that, this failure is attributable to a direction under this section.

(4) The Secretary of State may issue or approve for the purposes of this section a code of practice giving practical guidance as to the exercise by street authorities of the power conferred by this section; and in exercising that power a street authority shall have regard to the code of practice.★
[New Roads and Street Works Act 1991, s 56 as amended by the Traffic Management Act 2004, s 43.]

★Section reproduced as amended by the Traffic Management Act 2004, s 43. In force in relation to England, and in Wales from a date to be appointed. New s 56A inserted by the Traffic Management Act 2004, s 44 from a date to be appointed.

1. See the Street Works (Registers, Notices, Directions and Designations) Regulations 1992, SI 1992/2985 amended by SI 1999/1049.

7–6148 57. Notice of emergency works. (1) Nothing in section 54 (advance notice), section 55 (notice of starting date) or section 56 (directions as to timing of works) affects the right of an undertaker to execute emergency works.*

(2) An undertaker executing emergency works shall, if the works are of a kind in respect of which notice is required by section 55, give notice as soon as reasonably practicable, and in any event within two hours (or such other period as may be prescribed[1]) of the works being begun, to the persons to whom notice would be required to be given under that section.*

(3) The notice shall state his intention or, as the case may be, the fact that he has begun to execute the works and shall contain such other information as may be prescribed[1].

(4) An undertaker who fails to give notice in accordance with this section commits an offence and is liable on summary conviction to a fine not exceeding **level 4**on the standard scale.**

(5) In proceedings against a person for such an offence it is a defence for him to show that the contravention was attributable—

(a) to his not knowing the position, or not knowing of the existence, of another person's apparatus, or

(b) to his not knowing the identity or address of—

(i)   a relevant authority, or
(ii) the person to whom any apparatus belongs,

and that his ignorance was not due to any negligence on his part or to any failure to make inquiries which he ought reasonably to have made.
[New Roads and Street Works Act 1991, s 57 as amended by the Traffic Management Act 2004, s 40.]

***Amended by the Traffic Management Act 2004, s 99 from a date to be appointed.**
****Sub-section reproduced as amended by the Traffic Management Act 2004, s 40. In force in relation to England, and in Wales from a date to be appointed.**
1. See the Street Works (Registers, Notices, Directions and Designations) Regulations 1992, SI 1992/2985 amended by SI 1999/1049.

7–6149 58. Restriction on works following substantial road works. (1) Where it is proposed to carry out substantial road works in a highway, the street authority may by notice in accordance with this section restrict the execution of street works during the twelve months following the completion of those works.

For this purpose substantial road works means works for road purposes, or such works together with other works, of such description as may be prescribed[1].

(2) The notice shall be published in the prescribed[1] manner and shall specify the nature and location of the proposed works, the date (not being less than three months after the notice is published, or first published) on which it is proposed to begin the works, and the extent of the restriction.

(3) A copy of the notice shall be given to each of the following—

(a) where there is a public sewer in the part of the highway to which the restriction relates, to the sewer authority,

(b) where the part of the highway to which the restriction relates is carried or crossed by a bridge vested in a transport authority, or crosses or is crossed by any other property held or used for the purposes of a transport authority, to that authority,

(c) where in any other case the part of the highway to which the restriction relates is carried or crossed by a bridge, to the bridge authority,

(d) any person who has given notice under section 54 (advance notice of certain works) of his intention to execute street works in the part of the highway to which the restriction relates, and

(e) any other person having apparatus in the part of the highway to which the restriction relates;

but a failure to do so does not affect the validity of the restriction imposed by the notice.

(4) A notice ceases to be effective if the works to which it relates are not substantially begun—

(a) on or within one month from the date specified in the notice, or

(b) where street works are in progress on that date in the part of the highway to which the restriction relates, within one month from the completion of those works.

(5) An undertaker shall not in contravention of a restriction imposed by a notice under this section break up or open the part of the highway to which the restriction relates, except—

(a) to execute emergency works,
(b) with the consent of the street authority, or
(c) in such other cases as may be prescribed[1].

(6) If he does—

(*a*) he commits an offence and is liable on summary conviction to a fine not exceeding **level 5** on the standard scale, and

(*b*) he is liable to reimburse the street authority any costs reasonably incurred by them in reinstating the highway.★

(7) The consent of the street authority under subsection (5)(*b*) shall not be unreasonably withheld; and any question whether the withholding of consent is unreasonable shall be settled by arbitration.

(8) An undertaker shall be taken not to have failed to fulfil any statutory duty to afford a supply or service if, or to the extent that, his failure is attributable to a restriction imposed by a notice under this section.★★

[New Roads and Street Works Act 1991, s 58 as amended by the Traffic Management Act 2004, s 40.]

★**Sub-section reproduced as amended by the Traffic Management Act 2004, s 40. In force in relation to England, and in Wales from a date to be appointed.**

★★**New s 58A inserted and s 58 amended by the Traffic Management Act 2004, ss 52 and 99 from a date to be appointed.**

1. See the Street Works (Registers, Notices, Directions and Designations) Regulations 1992, SI 1992/2985 amended by SI 1999/1049.

7–6150   59.   *General duty of street authority to co-ordinate works.*

7–6151   60.   General duty of undertakers to co-operate.   (1) An undertaker shall as regards the execution of street works use his best endeavours to co-operate with the street authority and with other undertakers—

(*a*) in the interests of safety,

(*b*) to minimise the inconvenience to persons using the street (having regard, in particular, to the needs of people with a disability), and

(*c*) to protect the structure of the street and the integrity of apparatus in it.

(2) The Secretary of State shall issue or approve for the purposes of this section codes of practice giving practical guidance as to the matters mentioned in subsection (1); and—

(*a*) so far as an undertaker complies with such a code of practice he shall be taken to comply with his duty under that subsection, and

(*b*) a failure in any respect to comply with any such code is evidence of failure in that respect to comply with that duty.

(3) An undertaker who fails to comply with his duty under subsection (1) commits an offence and is liable on summary conviction to a fine not exceeding **level 5** on the standard scale.★

[New Roads and Street Works Act 1991, s 60 as amended by the Traffic Management Act 2004, s 40.]

★**Reproduced as amended by the Traffic Management Act 2004, s 40. In force in relation to England, and in Wales from a date to be appointed.**

Streets subject to special controls

7–6152   61.   *Protected streets.*

7–6153   62.   *Supplementary provisions as to designation of protected streets.*

7–6154   63.   *Streets with special engineering difficulties.*

7–6155   64.   *Traffic-sensitive streets.*

General requirements as to execution of street works

7–6156   65.   Safety measures.   (1) An undertaker executing street works shall secure—

(*a*) that any part of the street which is broken up or open, or is obstructed by plant or materials used or deposited in connection with the works, is adequately guarded and lit, and

(*b*) that such traffic signs are placed and maintained, and where necessary operated, as are reasonably required for the guidance or direction of persons using the street,

having regard, in particular, to the needs of people with a disability.

(2) In discharging in relation to a highway his duty with respect to the placing, maintenance or operation of traffic signs, an undertaker shall comply with any directions given by the traffic authority.

The power of the traffic authority to give directions under this subsection is exercisable subject to any directions given by the Secretary of State under section 65 of the Road Traffic Regulation Act 1984.

(3) The Secretary of State may issue or approve for the purposes of this section codes of practice giving practical guidance as to the matters mentioned in subsection (1); and—

(*a*) so far as an undertaker complies with such a code of practice he shall be taken to comply with that subsection; and (*b*) a failure in any respect to comply with any such code is evidence of failure in that respect to comply with that subsection.

(4) An undertaker who fails to comply with subsection (1) or (2) commits an offence and is liable on summary conviction to a fine not exceeding **level 5** on the standard scale.

(5) If it appears to the street authority that an undertaker has failed to comply with subsection (1) or (2), they may take such steps as appear to them necessary and may recover from the undertaker the costs reasonably incurred by them in doing so.

(6) If a person without lawful authority or excuse—

(*a*) takes down, alters or removes any fence, barrier, traffic sign or light erected or placed in pursuance of subsection (1) or (2) above, or

(*b*) extinguishes a light so placed,

he commits an offence and is liable on summary conviction to a fine not exceeding **level 5** on the standard scale.*

[New Roads and Street Works Act 1991, s 65 as amended by the Traffic Management Act 2004, s 40.]

---

*Reproduced as amended by the Traffic Management Act 2004, s 40. In force in relation to England, and in Wales from a date to be appointed.

7–6157 **66. Avoidance of unnecessary delay or obstruction.** (1) An undertaker executing street works which involve—

(*a*) breaking up or opening the street, or any sewer, drain or tunnel under it, or

(*b*) tunnelling or boring under the street,

shall carry on and complete the works with all such dispatch as is reasonably practicable.

(2) An undertaker who fails to do so commits an offence and is liable on summary conviction to a fine not exceeding **level 5** on the standard scale.

(3) Where an undertaker executing any street works creates an obstruction in a street to a greater extent or for a longer period than is reasonably necessary, the street authority may by notice require him to take such reasonable steps as are specified in the notice to mitigate or discontinue the obstruction.

(4) If the undertaker fails to comply with such a notice within 24 hours of receiving it, or any longer period specified in the notice, the authority may take the necessary steps and recover from him the costs reasonably incurred by them in doing so.*

[New Roads and Street Works Act 1991, s 66 as amended by the Traffic Management Act 2004, s 40.]

---

*Reproduced as amended by the Traffic Management Act 2004, s 40. In force in relation to England, and in Wales from a date to be appointed.

7–6158 **67. Qualifications of supervisors and operatives.** (1) It is the duty of an undertaker executing street works involving—

(*a*) breaking up the street, or any sewer, drain or tunnel under it, or

(*b*) tunnelling or boring under the street,

to secure that, except in such cases as may be prescribed, the execution of the works is supervised by a person having a prescribed[1] qualification as a supervisor.

(2) It is the duty of an undertaker executing street works involving—

(*a*) breaking up or opening the street, or any sewer, drain or tunnel under it, or

(*b*) tunnelling or boring under the street,

to secure that, except in such cases as may be prescribed, there is on site at all times when any such works are in progress at least one person having a prescribed qualification as a trained operative.

(3) An undertaker who fails to comply with his duty under subsection (1) or (2) commits an offence and is liable on summary conviction to a fine not exceeding **level 5** on the standard scale.*

(4) *Regulations made by the Secretary of State.***

[New Roads and Street Works Act 1991, s 67.]

---

*Sub-section reproduced as amended by the Traffic Management Act 2004, s 40. In force in relation to England, and in Wales from a date to be appointed.
**New sub-ss (1A), (2A)–(2C) inserted and sub-ss (3) and (4) amended by the Traffic Management Act 2004, s 50 from a date to be appointed.
. See the Street Works (Qualifications of Supervisors and Operatives) Regulations 1992, SI 1992/1687.

7–6159 **68. Facilities to be afforded to street authority.** (1) An undertaker executing street works shall afford the street authority reasonable facilities for ascertaining whether he is complying with his duties under this Part.

(2) An undertaker who fails to afford the street authority such facilities commits an offence in

respect of each failure and is liable on summary conviction to a fine not exceeding **level 4** on the standard scale.★
[New Roads and Street Works Act 1991, s 68 as amended by the Traffic Management Act 2004, s 40.]

★**Reproduced as amended by the Traffic Management Act 2004, s 40. In force in relation to England, and in Wales from a date to be appointed.**

7–6160   69. Works likely to affect other apparatus in the street.   (1) Where street works are likely to affect another person's apparatus in the street, the undertaker executing the works shall take all reasonably practicable steps—

(*a*) to give the person to whom the apparatus belongs reasonable facilities for monitoring the execution of the works, and

(*b*) to comply with any requirement made by him which is reasonably necessary for the protection of the apparatus or for securing access to it.

(2) An undertaker who fails to comply with subsection (1) commits an offence in respect of each failure and is liable on summary conviction to a fine not exceeding **level 4** on the standard scale.

(3) In proceedings against a person for such an offence it is a defence for him to show that the failure was attributable—

(*a*) to his not knowing the position, or not knowing of the existence, of another person's apparatus, or

(*b*) to his not knowing the identity or address of the person to whom any apparatus belongs,

and that his ignorance was not due to any negligence on his part or to any failure to make inquiries which he ought reasonably to have made.★
[New Roads and Street Works Act 1991, s 69 as amended by the Traffic Management Act 2004, s 40.]

★**Reproduced as amended by the Traffic Management Act 2004, s 40. In force in relation to England, and in Wales from a date to be appointed.**

Reinstatement

7–6161   70. Duty of undertaker to reinstate.   (1) It is the duty of the undertaker by whom street works are executed to reinstate the street.

(2) He shall begin the reinstatement as soon after the completion of any part of the street works as is reasonably practicable and shall carry on and complete the reinstatement with all such dispatch as is reasonably practicable.

(3) He shall before the end of the next working day after the day on which the reinstatement is completed inform the street authority that he has completed the reinstatement of the street, stating whether the reinstatement is permanent or interim.

(4) If it is interim, he shall complete the permanent reinstatement of the street as soon as reasonably practicable and in any event within six months (or such other period as may be prescribed[1]) from the date on which the interim reinstatement was completed; and he shall notify the street authority when he has done so.

(5) The permanent reinstatement of the street shall include, in particular, the reinstatement of features designed to assist people with a disability.

(6) An undertaker who fails to comply with any provision of this section commits an offence[2] and is liable on summary conviction

(*a*) in the case of an offence consisting of a failure to comply with subsection (3), to a fine not exceeding level 4 on the standard scale; and

(*b*) in any other case, to a fine not exceeding level 5 on that scale.★

(7) In proceedings against a person for an offence of failing to comply with subsection (2) it is a defence for him to show that any delay in reinstating the street was in order to avoid hindering the execution of other works, or other parts of the same works, to be undertaken immediately or shortly thereafter.★★
[New Roads and Street Works Act 1991, s 70 as amended by the Traffic Management Act 2004, s 40.]

★**Sub-section (6) reproduced as amended by the Traffic Management Act 2004, s 40. In force in relation to England, and in Wales from a date to be appointed.**
★★**Sub-sections (3) and (4) substituted, new sub-ss (1A), (4A) and (4B) inserted and sub-s (6) further amended by the Traffic Management Act 2004, s 54 from a date to be appointed.**
  1. See the Street Works (Reinstatement) Regulations 1992, SI 1992/1689 amended by SI 1992/3110.
  2. An offence under s 70 is a continuing offence, see note to s 71, post.

7–6162   71. Materials, workmanship and standard of reinstatement.   (1) An undertaker executing street works shall in reinstating the street comply with such requirements as may be prescribed[1] as to the specification of materials to be used and the standards of workmanship to be observed.

(2) He shall also ensure that the reinstatement conforms to such performance standards as may be prescribed[1]—

(a) in the case of interim reinstatement, until permanent reinstatement is effected, and

(b) in the case of permanent reinstatement, for the prescribed period after the completion of the reinstatement.

This obligation is extended in certain cases and restricted in others by the provisions of section 73 as to cases where a reinstatement is affected by subsequent works.

(3) Regulations made for the purposes of this section may make different provision in relation to different classes of excavation and different descriptions of street, and in relation to interim and permanent reinstatement.

(4) The Secretary of State may issue or approve for the purposes of this section codes of practice giving practical guidance as to the matters mentioned in subsections (1) and (2); and regulations made for the purposes of this section may provide that—

(a) so far as an undertaker complies with such a code of practice he shall be taken to comply with his duties under this section; and

(b) a failure in any respect to comply with any such code is evidence of failure in that respect to comply with those duties.

(5) An undertaker who fails to comply with his duties under this section commits an offence[2] and is liable on summary conviction to a fine not exceeding **level 5** on the standard scale.★

[New Roads and Street Works Act 1991, s 71 as amended by the Traffic Management Act 2004, s 40.]

★**Reproduced as amended by the Traffic Management Act 2004, s 40. In force in relation to England, and in Wales from a date to be appointed.**

1. See the Street Works (Reinstatement) Regulations 1992, SI 1992/1689 amended by SI 1992/3110 and SI 2002/1487 (England).

2. Failure to reinstate in accordance with the Act and the prescribed standards and specification is a continuing offence which may be the subject of prosecution unless and until the time comes when the reinstatement is properly carried out (*British Telecommunication plc v Nottingham County Council* [1999] Crim LR 217, DC).

7–6163   72. *Powers of street authority in relation to reinstatement.*

7–6164   73. *Reinstatement affected by subsequent works.*

7–6164A   73A

***Power to require undertaker to re-surface street.*7–6164B   73B.** *Power to specify timing etc of re-surfacing.*

7–6164C   73C. *Materials, workmanship and standard of re-surfacing.*

7–6164D   73D. *Re-surfacing: regulations*

7–6164E   73E. *Re-surfacing: guidance*

7–6164F   73F. *Guidance about street authority inspections*

Duties and liabilities of undertakers with respect to apparatus

7–6165   79. Records of location of apparatus.   (1) An undertaker shall, except in such cases as may be prescribed[1], record the location of every item of apparatus belonging to him as soon as reasonably practicable after—

(a) placing it in the street or altering its position,

(b) locating it in the street in the course of executing any other works, or

(c) being informed of its location under section 80 below,

stating the nature of the apparatus and (if known) whether it is for the time being in use.

(2) The records shall be kept up to date and shall be kept in such form and manner as may be prescribed.

(3) An undertaker shall make his records available for inspection, at all reasonable hours and free of charge, by any person having authority to execute works of any description in the street or otherwise appearing to the undertaker to have a sufficient interest.

(4) If an undertaker fails to comply with his duties under this section—

(a) he commits an offence and is liable on summary conviction to a fine not exceeding **level 5** on the standard scale; and★

(b) he is liable to compensate any person in respect of damage or loss incurred by him in consequence of the failure.

(5) In criminal or civil proceedings arising out of any such failure it is a defence for the undertaker

to show that all reasonable care was taken by him, and by his contractors and by persons in his employ or that of his contractors, to secure that no such failure occurred.

(6) *Provision as to order.***

[New Roads and Street Works Act 1991, s 79 as amended by the Traffic Management Act 2004, s 40.]

---

*Sub-section reproduced as amended by the Traffic Management Act 2004, s 40. In force in relation to England, and in Wales from a date to be appointed.

**New sub-ss (1A), (2A) and (3A) inserted by the Traffic Management Act 2004, s 46 from a date to be appointed.

1. See the Street Works (Records) (England) Regulations 2002, SI 2002/3217 and the Street Works (Records) (Wales) Regulations 2005, SI 2005/1812.

7–6166   80. Duty to inform undertakers of location of apparatus.   (1) A person executing works of any description in the street who finds apparatus belonging to an undertaker which is not marked, or is wrongly marked, on the records made available by the undertaker, shall take such steps as are reasonably practicable to inform the undertaker to whom the apparatus belongs of its location and (so far as appears from external inspection) its nature and whether it is in use.

(2) Where a person executing works of any description in the street finds apparatus which does not belong to him and is unable, after taking such steps as are reasonably practicable, to ascertain to whom the apparatus belongs, he shall—

(a) if he is an undertaker, note on the records kept by him under section 79(1) (in such manner as may be prescribed) the location of the apparatus he has found and its general description; and

(b) in any other case, inform the street authority of the location and general description of the apparatus he has found.

(3) Subsections (1) and (2) have effect subject to such exceptions as may be prescribed.

(4) A person who fails to comply with subsection (1) or (2) commits an offence and is liable on summary conviction to a fine not exceeding **level 4** on the standard scale.* **

[New Roads and Street Works Act 1991, s 80 as amended by the Traffic Management Act 2004, s 40.]

---

*Reproduced as amended by the Traffic Management Act 2004, s 40. In force in relation to England, and in Wales from a date to be appointed.

**New sub-ss (1A), (2A), (5) and (6) inserted, sub-ss (2) and (3) substituted and sub-s (1) amended and sub-s (4) further amended by the Traffic Management Act 2004, s 47.

7–6167   81. *Duty to maintain apparatus.*

7–6168   82. *Liability for damage or loss caused.*

Apparatus affected by highway, bridge or transport works

7–6169   83. Works for road purposes likely to affect apparatus in the street.   (1) This section applies to works for road purposes other than major highway works (as to which see section 84 below).

(2) Where works to which this section applies are likely to affect apparatus in the street, the authority executing the works shall take all reasonably practicable steps—

(a) to give the person to whom the apparatus belongs reasonable facilities for monitoring the execution of the works, and

(b) to comply with any requirement made by him which is reasonably necessary for the protection of the apparatus or for securing access to it.

(3) An authority who fail to comply with subsection (2) commit an offence in respect of each failure and are liable on summary conviction to a fine not exceeding **level 4** on the standard scale.*

(4) In proceedings against an authority for such an offence it is a defence for them to show that the failure was attributable—

(a) to their not knowing the position, or not knowing of the existence, of a person's apparatus, or

(b) to their not knowing the identity or address of the person to whom any apparatus belongs,

and that their ignorance was not due to any negligence on their part or to any failure to make inquiries which they ought reasonably to have made.

[New Roads and Street Works Act 1991, s 83.]

---

*Reproduced as amended by the Traffic Management Act 2004, s 40. In force in relation to England, and in Wales from a date to be appointed.

Provisions with respect to particular authorities and undertakings

7–6170   86. Highway authorities, highways and related matters.   (1) In this Part—

"highway authority" and "local highway authority" have the same meaning as in the Highways Act 1980; and "maintainable highway" means a highway which for the purposes of that Act is maintainable at the public expense.

(2) In this Part "works for road purposes" means works of any of the following descriptions executed in relation to a highway—

(a) works for the maintenance of the highway,

(b) any works under powers conferred by Part V of the Highways Act 1980 (improvement),

(c) the erection, maintenance, alteration or removal of traffic signs on or near the highway, or

(d) the construction of a crossing for vehicles across a footway or grass verge or the strengthening or adaptation of a footway for use as a crossing for vehicles,

or works of any corresponding description executed in relation to a street which is not a highway.

(3) In this Part "major highway works" means works of any of the following descriptions executed by the highway authority in relation to a highway which consists of or includes a carriageway—

(a) reconstruction or widening of the highway,

(b) works carried out in exercise of the powers conferred by section 64 of the Highways Act 1980 (dual carriageways and roundabouts),

(c) substantial alteration of the level of the highway,

(d) provision, alteration of the position or width, or substantial alteration in the level of a carriageway, footway or cycle track in the highway,

(e) the construction or removal of a road hump within the meaning of section 90F of the Highways Act 1980,

(f) works carried out in exercise of the powers conferred by section 184 of the Highways Act 1980 (vehicle crossings over footways and verges),

(g) provision of a cattle-grid in the highway or works ancillary thereto, or

(h) tunnelling or boring under the highway.

(4) Works executed under section 184(9) of the Highways Act 1980 by a person other than the highway authority shall also be treated for the purposes of this Part as major highway works; and in relation to such works the references in sections 84 and 85 to the highway authority shall be construed as references to him.

[New Roads and Street Works Act 1991, s 86.]

7–6171 **87.** *Prospectively maintainable highways.*

7–6172 **88. Bridges, bridge authorities and related matters.** (1) In this Part—

(a) references to a bridge include so much of any street as gives access to the bridge and any embankment, retaining wall or other work or substance supporting or protecting that part of the street; and

(b) "bridge authority" means the authority, body or person in whom a bridge is vested.

(2) In this Part "major bridge works" means works for the replacement, reconstruction or substantial alteration of a bridge.

(3) Where a street is carried or crossed by a bridge, any statutory right to place apparatus in the street includes the right to place apparatus in, and attach apparatus to, the structure of the bridge; and other rights to execute works in relation to the apparatus extend accordingly.

References in this Part to apparatus in the street include apparatus so placed or attached.

(4) An undertaker proposing to execute street works affecting the structure of a bridge shall consult the bridge authority before giving notice under section 55 (notice of starting date) in relation to the works.*

(5) An undertaker executing such works shall take all reasonably practicable steps—

(a) to give the bridge authority reasonable facilities for monitoring the execution of the works, and

(b) to comply with any requirement made by them which is reasonably necessary for the protection of the bridge or for securing access to it.

(6) An undertaker who fails to comply with subsection (4) or (5) commits an offence in respect of each failure and is liable on summary conviction

(a) in the case of an offence consisting of a failure to take all reasonably practicable steps to comply with subsection (5)(a), to a fine not exceeding level 4 on the standard scale; and

(b) in any other case, to a fine not exceeding level 5 on that scale.**

(7) Subsections (4) to (6) do not apply to works in relation to which Schedule 4 applies (works in streets with special engineering difficulties).

[New Roads and Street Works Act 1991, s 88 as amended by the Traffic Management Act 2004, s 40.]

---

*Amended by the Traffic Management Act 2004, s 52 from a date to be appointed.

**Reproduced as amended by the Traffic Management Act 2004, s 40. In force in relation to England, and in Wales from a date to be appointed.

7–6173 92. Special precautions as to displaying of lights. (1) An undertaker executing street works in a street which crosses, or is crossed by, or is in the vicinity of, a railway, tramway, dock, harbour, pier, canal or inland navigation, shall comply with any reasonable requirements imposed by the transport authority concerned with respect to the displaying of lights so as to avoid any risk of their—

(a) being mistaken for any signal light or other light used for controlling, directing or securing the safety of traffic thereon, or

(b) being a hindrance to the ready interpretation of any such signal or other light.

(2) An undertaker who fails to comply with any such requirement commits an offence and is liable on summary conviction to a fine not exceeding **level 5** on the standard scale.⋆

(3) In proceedings for such an offence it is a defence for the undertaker to show that all reasonable care was taken by him, and by his contractors and by persons in his employ or that of his contractors, to secure that no such failure occurred.

[New Roads and Street Works Act 1991, s 92.]

⋆**Reproduced as amended by the Traffic Management Act 2004, s 40. In force in relation to England, and in Wales from a date to be appointed.**

7–6174 93. Works affecting level crossings or tramways. (1) This section applies to street works at a crossing of a railway on the level or which affect a tramway.

In this section "the relevant transport authority" means the authority having the management of the railway or tramway undertaking concerned.

(2) An undertaker proposing to begin to execute works to which this section applies shall give the prescribed notice to the relevant transport authority notwithstanding that such notice is not required under section 55 (notice of starting date).

The provisions of subsections (2) to (7)⋆ of that section (contents of notice, when works may be begun, &c) apply in relation to the notice required by this subsection as in relation to a notice under subsection (1) of that section.

(3) An undertaker executing works to which this section applies shall comply with any reasonable requirements made by the relevant transport authority—

(a) for securing the safety of persons employed in connection with the works, or

(b) for securing that interference with traffic on the railway or tramway caused by the execution of the works is reduced so far as is practicable;

and, except where submission of a plan and section is required, he shall defer beginning the works for such further period as the relevant transport authority may reasonably request as needed for formulating their requirements under this subsection or making their traffic arrangements.

(4) Nothing in subsection (2) or (3) affects the right of an undertaker to execute emergency works.

(5) An undertaker executing emergency works shall give notice to the relevant transport authority as soon as reasonably practicable of his intention or, as the case may be, of his having begun to do so notwithstanding that such notice is not required by section 57 (notice of emergency works).

The provisions of subsections (3) and (4) of that section (contents of notice and penalty for failure to give notice) apply in relation to the notice required by this subsection as in relation to a notice under subsection (2) of that section.

[New Roads and Street Works Act 1991, s 93.]

⋆**Substituted by the Traffic Management Act 2004, s 49 from a date to be appointed.**

Supplementary provisions

7–6175 95. Offences. (1) Any provision of this Part imposing criminal liability in respect of any matter is without prejudice to any civil liability in respect of the same matter.

(2) Where a failure to comply with a duty imposed by this Part is continued after conviction, the person in default commits a further offence.⋆

[New Roads and Street Works Act 1991, s 95.]

⋆**New s 95A inserted by the Traffic Management Act 2004, s 41 from a date to be appointed.**

7–6176 97. Service of notices and other documents. (1) Notices required or authorised to be given for the purposes of this Part shall be given in the prescribed[1] form.

(2) The Secretary of State may make provision by regulations[1] as to the manner of service of notices and other documents required or authorised to be served for the purposes of this Part.⋆

[New Roads and Street Works Act 1991, s 97.]

⋆**New sub-s (3) inserted by the Traffic Management Act 2004, s 64 from a date to be appointed.**

1. See the Street Works (Registers, Notices, Directions and Designations) Regulations 1992, SI 1992/2985 amended by SI 1999/1049.

7–6177 98. Reckoning of periods. (1) In reckoning for the purposes of this Part a period expressed as a period from or before a given date, that date shall be excluded.

(2) For the purposes of this Part a working day means a day other than a Saturday, Sunday, Christmas Day, Good Friday or a bank holiday; and a notice given after 4.30 p.m. on a working day shall be treated as given on the next working day.

(3) In subsection (2) a "bank holiday" means a day which is a bank holiday under the Banking and Financial Dealings Act 1971 in the locality in which the street in question is situated.
[New Roads and Street Works Act 1991, s 98.]

7–6178 105. Minor definitions. (1) In this Part—

"apparatus" includes any structure for the lodging therein of apparatus or for gaining access to apparatus;

"carriageway" and "footway" have the same meaning as in the Highways Act 1980;

"enactment" includes an enactment contained in subordinate legislation within the meaning of the Interpretation Act 1978;

"in", in a context referring to works, apparatus or other property in a street or other place includes a reference to works, apparatus or other property under, over, across, along or upon it;

"railway" includes a light railway other than one in the nature of a tramway (see the definition of "tramway" below);

"reinstatement" includes making good;

"special enactment" means an enactment which is not a public general enactment, and includes—

(a) any Act for confirming a provisional order,

(b) any provision of a public general Act in relation to the passing of which any of the Standing Orders of the House of Lords or the House of Commons relating to Private Business applied, and

(c) any enactment to the extent that it is incorporated or applied for the purposes of a special enactment;

"statutory right" means a right (whether expressed as a right, a power or otherwise) conferred by an enactment (whenever passed or made), other than a right exercisable by virtue of a street works licence;

"traffic" includes pedestrians and animals;

"traffic authority" and "traffic sign" have the same meaning as in the Road Traffic Regulation Act 1984;

"tramway" means a system, mainly or exclusively for the carriage of passengers, using vehicles guided, or powered by energy transmitted, by rails or other fixed apparatus installed exclusively or mainly in a street.

(2) A right to execute works which extends both to a street and to other land is included in references in this Part to a right to execute works in a street in so far as it extends to the street.

(3) A right to execute works which extends to part of the street but not the whole is included in references in this Part to a right to execute works in a street; and in relation to such a right references in this Part to the street in which it is exercisable shall be construed as references to the part to which the right extends.

(4) For the purposes of this Part apparatus shall be regarded as affected by works if the effect of the works is to prevent or restrict access to the apparatus (for example, by laying other apparatus above or adjacent to it).

(5) Section 28 of the Chronically Sick and Disabled Persons Act 1970 (power to define "disability" and other expressions) applies in relation to the provisions of this Part as to the provisions of that Act.
[New Roads and Street Works Act 1991, s 105.]

7–6179 106. Index of defined expressions. The expressions listed below are defined or otherwise fall to be construed for the purposes of this Part in accordance with the provisions indicated—

affected by (in relation to apparatus and works)	section 105(4)
apparatus	sections 89(3) and 105(1)
arbitration	section 99
bridge	section 88(1)(a)
bridge authority	section 88(1)(b)
carriageway	section 105(1)
costs	section 96
disability	(see section 105(5))
emergency works	section 52
enactment	section 105(1)
expenses	section 96
footway	section 105(1)
highway authority	section 86(1)

in (in a context referring to works, apparatus or other property in a street)	section 105(1)
licensee (in relation to a street works licence)	section 50(3)
local highway authority	section 86(1)
maintainable highway	section 86(1)
major bridge works	section 88(2)
major highway works	section 86(3)
major transport works	section 91(2)
notice	section 97
prescribed	section 104
public sewer	section 89(1)(*a*)
railway	section 105(1)
reinstatement	section 105(1) (and see sections 70(5) and 90(1))
relevant authority (in relation to street works)	section 49(6) (and see section 91(3))
sewer	section 89(1)(*a*)
sewer authority	section 89(1)(*b*)
special enactment	section 105(1)
statutory right	section 105(1)
street	section 48(1)
street authority	section 49(1)
street managers	section 49(4)
street works	section 48(3) (and see section 105(2) and (3))
street works licence	section 50(1)
traffic	section 105(1)
traffic authority	section 105(1)
traffic sign	section 105(1)
tramway	section 105(1)
transport authority	section 91(1)(*a*)
transport undertaking	section 91(1)(*b*)
undertaker (in relation to street works or apparatus)	sections 48(4) and (5) and 89(4)
working day	section 98(2)
works for road purposes	section 86(2).★

[New Roads and Street Works Act 1991, s 106.]

★New definitions "fixed penalty offence", "re-surfacing notice", "re-surfacing works" and "surface" inserted by the Traffic Management Act 2004, ss 41 and 55 from a date to be appointed.

MERCHANT SHIPPING

Preliminary Note

7–6180   This title contains references to the following statutes—

7–6183	Harbours, Docks and Piers Clauses Act 1847
7–6185	Marine Insurance (Gambling Policies) Act 1909
7–6190	Ferries (Acquisition By Local Authorities) Act 1919
7–6200	Dangerous Vessels Act 1985
7–6220	Pilotage Act 1987
7–6225	Aviation and Maritime Security Act 1990
7–6300	Merchant Shipping Act 1995
7–6560	Shipping and Trading Interests (Protection) Act 1995
7–6600	Merchant Shipping and Maritime Security Act 1997
7–6601	Railways and Transport Safety Act 2003

7–6180A   Application of shipping legislation to structures, craft, etc.   The Secretary of State may, in accordance with s 112 of the Railways and Transport Safety Act 2003, provide by order made by statutory instrument for legislation which applies to ships, vessels or boats to apply in relation to specified things which are used, navigated or situated wholly or partly in or on water.

7–6181   European Communities Act 1972: regulations.   Within the scope of the title MERCHANT SHIPPING would logically fall the subject matter of a number of regulations made under the very wide enabling powers provided in s 2(2) of the European Communities Act 1972. Where such regulations create offences they are noted below—

Tankers (EEC Requirements) Regulations, 1981, SI 1981/1077 amended by SI 1982/1637;

Minimum Standards of Safety Communication Regulations 1997, SI 1997/529 amended by SI 1999/1704, SI 2004/1266 and SI 2006/89;

Statistical Returns (Carriage of Goods and Passengers by Sea) 1997, SI 1997/2330;

ISM Code (Ro-Ro Passenger Ferries) Regulations 1997, SI 1997/3022 amended by SI 2001/3209;

Merchant Shipping and Fishing Vessels (Health and Safety at Work)(Employment of Young Persons) Regulations 1998, SI 1998/2411 amended by SI 2001/54;

Fishing Vessels (EC Directive on Harmonised Safety Regime) Regulations 1999, SI 1999/2998 amended by SI 1999/3210 and SI 2003/1112;

Merchant Shipping and Fishing Vessels (Safety Signs and Signals) Regulations 2001, SI 2001/3444;

Ship and Port Facility (Security) Regulations 2004, SI 2004/1495 amended by SI 2005/1434.

Harbours, Docks and Piers Clauses Act 1847

(10 & 11 Vict c 47)

7–6183   The owner of every vessel or float of timber is liable for any[1] damage done by such vessel, etc, or by any person employed about the same, to a harbour, dock or pier, or the quays or works connected therewith, and the master or person having charge of such vessel, etc, through whose wilful act or negligence such damage is done, is also liable therefor (s 74). Damage not exceeding £50 recoverable before two justices, who may cause vessel, etc, to be distrained and kept, and if damage and costs are not paid within seven days, to be sold (s 75). Owner may recover before two justices damage paid by him from person who actually did same (s 76).

Harbour master may remove unserviceable vessels and recover charges on summary complaint before a justice of the peace (s 57).

Various offences include unjustified claims for exemption from harbour rates (s 28); master's failure to report arrival of vessel (s 35), to produce certificate of registry (s 36), to give proper account of cargo unshipped (s 38)—likewise the shipper (s 39)—to comply with harbour master's directions (s 53). Other offences involve bribes (s 55), dismantling (s 59), sails (s 60), hawsers (s 61), moorings (s 62), position near harbour entrance (s 63), harbour repairs (s 64), removal after discharge of cargo (s 66), fires, firearms, combustible and explosive matter (s 71), obstruction of harbour master (s 72), ballast (s 73). Failure to remove combustible matter from quays (s 69) carries an hourly penalty of £50. There is an additional daily penalty of £20 for offences under ss 53 and 63. All offences carry a maximum penalty not exceeding level 3 on the standard scale (British Transport Docks Act 1981, s 17 and Sch 1 as amended by the Criminal Justice Act 1982, s 46).

Section 83 enables the making of byelaws by the undertakers, and s 84 empowers the imposition of penalties for breach of the byelaws. The majority of maximum fines for offences against byelaws have been raised to level 3 on the standard scale by the British Transport Docks Act 1981 (British Transport Docks Act 1981, s 17 and Sch 1[2] as amended by the Criminal Justice Act 1982, s 46).

---

1. Where damage was caused by a vessel through violence of wind and waves at a time when master and crew had been compelled to abandon vessel and had consequently no control over it, owners were held not liable (*Wear River Comrs v Adamson* (1877) 2 App Cas 743, 42 JP 244), but where the vessel is under that control, the owners are liable for the damage without proof of negligence (*Great Western Rly Co v Mostyn (Owners)* [1928] AC 57, 92 JP 18; *Dee Conservancy Board v McConnell* [1928] 2 KB 159, 92 JP 54). Compulsory pilotage is no defence (Pilotage Act 1983, s 35).

2. There have been numerous British Transport Docks Acts. Sections 52 and 54 of the 1964 Act (1964 c xxxviii) enable the making of further byelaws and their enforcement by a fine not exceeding a figure, raised to £50 by the 1981 Act (1981, c xxxi) for some, and £200 for others. In addition there are byelaws in existence which have been made under local Acts and which generally carry a maximum fine of £50.

Marine Insurance (Gambling Policies) Act 1909

(9 Edw 7 c 12)

The object of this Act is to prohibit gambling on loss by maritime perils.

7–6185   1. Gambling policies.   (1) If—

(a) Any person effects a contract of marine insurance without having any *bona fide* interest, direct or indirect, either in the safe arrival of the ship in relation to which the contract is made or in the safety or preservation of the subject-matter insured, or a *bona fide* expectation of acquiring such an interest, or

(b) Any person in the employment of the owner of a ship, not being a part owner of the ship, effects a contract of marine insurance in relation to the ship, and the contract is made "interest or no interest", or "without further proof of interest than the policy itself", or "without benefit of salvage to the insurer", or subject to any other like term, the contract shall be deemed to be a contract by way of gambling on loss by maritime perils, and the person effecting it shall be guilty of an offence—*Imprisonment*, not exceeding **six months**, or *Fine*, and in either case forfeiture to Crown of any money he may receive under the contract.

(2) Any broker or other person through whom and any insurer with whom any such contract is

effected shall be liable to same punishment if he acted knowing that contract was by way of gambling within meaning of Act.

Proceedings not to be instituted without consent of Attorney-General[1] (sub-s (3)). Proceedings not to be instituted against person (other than person in employment of owner of ship) until opportunity has been afforded him of showing that contract was not a gambling contract as aforesaid and information given by that person not to be admissible as evidence against him in any prosecution under Act. [Marine Insurance (Gambling Policies) Act 1909, s 1(4)]. Onus of proof (sub-s (5)). Proceedings may be instituted where offence committed or in place where offender may be (sub-s (6)). Appeal to the Crown Court (sub-s (7)). "Owner" includes charterer (sub-s (8)).

[Marine Insurance (Gambling Policies) Act 1909, s 1, as amended by the Criminal Law Act 1977, s 32—summarised.]

---

1. See PART I: MAGISTRATES' COURTS, PROCEDURE, para 1–410 **Criminal prosecutions**, ante.

Ferries (Acquisition by Local Authorities) Act 1919
(9 & 10 Geo 5 c 75)

7–6190 This Act enables local authorities to acquire existing ferries by agreement (s 1(1), (2), (3)). "Existing ferry" means any ferry legally established by Act of Parliament or otherwise at the date of the purchase or transfer, and includes all boats and other vessels, landing stages, approaches, apparatus, plant and other property used in connection with the ferry (s 1(4)). Provision is made for the protection of Crown rights (s 3).

The following sections relate to offences punishable summarily:

7–6191 2. Protection of general public. In the case of every ferry acquired under this Act, regulations with regard to the working shall be made by the local authority for the protection from injury of passengers and the general public: Provided that no such regulation shall have any force or validity until the same have been confirmed by the Minister of Transport with or without amendment. Offenders against such regulations shall be liable on summary conviction to such penalties, not exceeding **level 1** on the standard scale, as may be thereby prescribed.
[Ferries (Acquisition by Local Authorities) Act 1919, s 2, as amended by the Criminal Law Act 1977, s 31 and the Criminal Justice Act 1982, s 46.]

7–6192 4. Exemption from tolls in case of persons in service of Crown, etc. Without prejudice to any existing right of Her Majesty, nothing in this Act shall extend to authorise any tolls to be demanded or received from any person when on duty in the service[1] of the Crown, or for any animal, vehicle, or goods the property[1] of, or when being used in the service of, the Crown, or returning after being so used, or from any police officer acting in the execution of his duty, or for any mail bag as defined by (what is now) the[2] Post Office Act 1953.
[Ferries (Acquisition by Local Authorities) Act 1919, s 4, as amended by Criminal Justice Act 1967, 3rd Sch and the Theft Act 1968, 3rd Sch.]

---

1. References to the service of the Crown and to the property of the Crown shall include respectively references to the service of a visiting force or of a headquarters of an international organisation and to the property of such a force or headquarters (Visiting Forces and International Headquarters (Application of Law) Order 1965, SI 1965/1536, art 12, Sch 3, amended by SI 1987/928).
2. See Post Office Act 1953, s 87.

Dangerous Vessels Act 1985
(1985 c 22)

7–6200 1. Directions by harbour master concerning dangerous vessels etc. (1) Subject to section 3 below and without prejudice to any other power already conferred upon him, a harbour master may give directions prohibiting the entry into, or requiring the removal from, the harbour for which he is harbour master of any vessel if in his opinion the condition of that vessel or the nature or condition of anything it contains is such that its presence in the harbour might involve—

(a) grave and imminent danger to the safety of any person or property; or
(b) grave and imminent risk that the vessel may, by sinking or foundering in the harbour, prevent or seriously prejudice the use of the harbour by other vessels.

(2) The directions referred to in subsection (1) above may be given as respects the vessel in question—

(a) to the owner of the vessel, or to any person in possession of the vessel;
(b) to the master of the vessel; or

(c) to any salvor in possession of the vessel, or to any person who is the servant or agent of any salvor in possession of the vessel, and who is in charge of the salvage operation;

and in paragraph (b) of this subsection, "master" means the person having command or charge of the vessel, but does not include a pilot (that is to say, a person not belonging to the vessel who has the conduct of it).

(3) In determining whether to give any directions under subsection (1) above in any particular case, a harbour master shall have regard to all the circumstances of that case and, in particular, he shall have regard to the safety of any person or vessel (whether that person or vessel is in or outside the harbour and including the vessel in question in that case).

(4) Directions may be given under subsection (1) above in any such reasonable manner as the harbour master may think fit.

(5) At the time any directions under subsection (1) above are given to any person, the harbour master giving the directions shall inform that person of the grounds for giving them.

[Dangerous Vessels Act 1985, s 1.]

7–6201 **2.** *Application of Merchant Shipping (Liability of Shipowners and Others) Act 1900.*

7–6202 **3. Further directions by Secretary of State.** (1) Where a harbour master has given directions under section 1 above as respects any vessel, the Secretary of State may, for the purpose of securing the safety of any person or vessel (including the vessel to which those directions relate), give directions under this section to that harbour master requiring him—

(a) to permit the vessel to which the directions given under section 1 relate to enter and remain, or (as the case may be) to remain, in the harbour in question; and

(b) to take such action (if any) as may be specified in the directions given under this section, for the purpose of enabling the vessel to do so or for any connected purpose;

and the directions under section 1 shall thereupon cease to have effect.

(2) A harbour master to whom any directions are given under this section shall give notice of those directions as respects the vessel in question to the person to whom the directions under section 1 were given or failing that, to any of the other persons mentioned in section 1(2) above, in any such reasonable manner as the harbour master may think fit; and it shall be the duty—

(a) of the harbour master to take any action in relation to that vessel specified in those directions; and

(b) of the harbour master and the harbour authority to take all such further action as may be reasonably necessary to enable that vessel to enter and remain, or to remain, in the harbour.

[Dangerous Vessels Act 1985, s 3.]

7–6203 **5. Offences.** (1) A person who without reasonable excuse contravenes or fails to comply with any directions given under section 1 above shall be guilty of an offence and shall be liable[1] on summary conviction to a fine not exceeding **£25,000** and on conviction on indictment to a fine.

(2) It shall be a defence for a person charged under this section to show that he took all reasonable precautions and exercised all due diligence to avoid the commission of the offence.

[Dangerous Vessels Act 1985, s 5.]

---

1. For procedure in respect of an offence triable either way, see the Magistrates' Courts Act 1980, ss 17–21, in PART I: MAGISTRATES' COURTS, PROCEDURE, ante.

7–6204 **6. Saving for certain vessels.** No directions under section 1 of this Act shall apply in relation to—

(a) any vessel belonging to Her Majesty, or employed in the service of the Crown for any purpose, including any such vessel in the possession of a salvor; or

(b) any vessel which is a pleasure boat of 24 metres or less in length.

[Dangerous Vessels Act 1985, s 6.]

7–6204A **6A. Saving for safety directions.** Directions under section 1 of this Act shall have no effect in so far as they—

(a) are inconsistent with the exercise by or on behalf of the Secretary of State of a power under Schedule 3A to the Merchant Shipping Act 1995 (c 21) (safety directions)[1],

(b) would interfere with a person's compliance with a direction under that Schedule, or

(c) would interfere with action taken by virtue of that Schedule.

[Dangerous Vessels Act 1985, s 6A inserted by the Marine Safety Act 2003, Sch 2.]

---

1. In this PART, post.

7–6205　7. Interpretation.　In this Act—

"harbour" and "harbour authority" have the respective meanings given to them by section 57 of the Harbours Act 1964;

"harbour master" includes any dock master or pier master who is not a subordinate of a harbour master and any deputy or assistant of a harbour master or of such a dock master or pier master;

"vessel" includes—

    (*a*)　a ship or boat, or any other description of craft used in navigation;

    (*b*)　a rig, raft or floating platform, or any other moveable thing constructed or adapted for floating on, or partial or total submersion in, water; and

    (*c*)　a seaplane, a hovercraft within the meaning of the Hovercraft Act 1968 or any other amphibious vehicle.

[Dangerous Vessels Act 1985, s 7.]

7–6206　8. *Short title, commencement and extent.*

Pilotage Act 1987
(1987 c 21)

7–6220　This Act makes new provision in respect of pilotage. Provisions relevant to magistrates' courts are as follows. Person not authorised pilot for area holds himself out or indicates himself to be such—Penalty level 5 (s 3). Master of ship not under pilotage where such compulsory and pilot has offered to take charge—Penalty level 5; master navigating where pilotage compulsory without notifying harbour authority—Penalty level 2 (s 15). Master navigates under pilotage of unauthorised person without notifying harbour authority—Penalty level 2; unauthorised person pilots knowing authorised pilot has offered to pilot, or master knowingly employs unauthorised person after authorised pilot has offered to pilot—Penalty level 4 (s 17). Master refuses to provide information to pilot or makes false statement about ship or without reasonable excuse does not inform pilot of matters affecting ship's navigation—Penalty false statement level 5, otherwise level 4 (s 18). Master taking pilot out of his area—Penalty level 5 (s 19). Master not facilitating pilot boarding and leaving ship—Penalty level 4 (s 20). Misconduct of pilot endangering ship or persons on board—Penalty on summary conviction 6 months imprisonment and/or fine not exceeding statutory maximum, on indictment imprisonment not exceeding 2 years and/or fine (s 21).

Aviation and Maritime Security Act 1990
(1990 c 31)

PART I[1]
AVIATION SECURITY
Endangering safety at aerodromes

7–6225　1. Endangering safety at aerodromes.　(1) It is an offence for any person by means of any device, substance or weapon intentionally to commit at an aerodrome serving international civil aviation any act of violence which—

    (*a*)　causes or is likely to cause death or serious personal injury, and

    (*b*)　endangers or is likely to endanger the safe operation of the aerodrome or the safety of persons at the aerodrome.

(2) It is also, subject to subsection (4) below, an offence for any person by means of any device, substance or weapon unlawfully and intentionally—

    (*a*)　to destroy or seriously to damage—

        (i)　property used for the provision of any facilities at an aerodrome serving international civil aviation (including any apparatus or equipment so used), or

        (ii)　any aircraft which is at such an aerodrome but is not in service, or

    (*b*)　to disrupt the services of such an aerodrome,

in such a way as to endanger or be likely to endanger the safe operation of the aerodrome or the safety of persons at the aerodrome.

(3) Except as provided by subsection (4) below, subsections (1) and (2) above apply whether any such act as is referred to in those subsections is committed in the United Kingdom or elsewhere and whatever the nationality of the person committing the act.

(4) Subsection (2)(*a*)(ii) above does not apply to any act committed in relation to an aircraft used in military, customs or police service unless—

    (*a*)　the act is committed in the United Kingdom, or

(b) where the act is committed outside the United Kingdom, the person committing it is a United Kingdom national.

(5) A person who commits an offence under this section is liable on conviction on indictment to imprisonment for **life**.

(6) Sections 38(3)(b) (period during which aircraft in service) and 38(4) (territorial waters) of the Aviation Security Act 1982 apply for the purposes of this section as they apply for the purposes of that Act; and the references in section 38(7) of that Act (other proceedings) to Part I of that Act and to that Act include references to this section.

(7) Proceedings for an offence under this section shall not be instituted—

(a) in England and Wales, except by, or with the consent of, the Attorney General, and

(b) *Northern Ireland.*

(8) *Scotland.*

(9) In this section—

"act of violence" means—

(a) any act done in the United Kingdom which constitutes the offence of murder, attempted murder, manslaughter, culpable homicide or assault or an offence under section 18, 20, 21, 22, 23, 24, 28 or 29 of the Offences against the Person Act 1861 or under section 2 of the Explosive Substances Act 1883, and

(b) any act done outside the United Kingdom which, if done in the United Kingdom, would constitute such an offence as is mentioned in paragraph (a) above;

"aerodrome" has the same meaning as in the Civil Aviation Act 1982;

"military service" and "United Kingdom national" have the same meaning as in the Aviation Security Act 1982; and

"unlawfully"—

(a) in relation to the commission of an act in the United Kingdom, means so as (apart from this section) to constitute an offence under the law of the part of the United Kingdom in which the act is committed, and

(b) in relation to the commission of an act outside the United Kingdom, means so that the commission of the act would (apart from this section) have been an offence under the law of England and Wales if it had been committed in England and Wales or of Scotland if it had been committed in Scotland.

[Aviation and Maritime Security Act 1990, s 1.]

---

1. Part I contains ss 1–8. For other provisions relating to aviation security, see the Aviation Security Act 1982, this PART, title AVIATION, ante.

PART II[1]
OFFENCES AGAINST THE SAFETY OF SHIPS AND FIXED PLATFORMS

7–6226 9. Hijacking of ships. (1) A person who unlawfully, by the use of force or by threats of any kind, seizes a ship or exercises control of it, commits the offence of hijacking a ship, whatever his nationality and whether the ship is in the United Kingdom or elsewhere, but subject to subsection (2) below.

(2) Subsection (1) above does not apply in relation to a warship or any other ship used as a naval auxiliary or in customs or police service unless—

(a) the person seizing or exercising control of the ship is a United Kingdom national, or

(b) his act is committed in the United Kingdom, or

(c) the ship is used in the naval or customs service of the United Kingdom or in the service of any police force in the United Kingdom.

(3) A person guilty of the offence of hijacking a ship is liable on conviction on indictment to imprisonment for **life**.

[Aviation and Maritime Security Act 1990, s 9.]

---

1. Part II contains ss 9–17.

7–6227 10. Seizing or exercising control of fixed platforms. (1) A person who unlawfully, by the use of force or by threats of any kind, seizes a fixed platform or exercises control of it, commits an offence, whatever his nationality and whether the fixed platform is in the United Kingdom or elsewhere.

(2) A person guilty of an offence under this section is liable on conviction on indictment to imprisonment for life.

[Aviation and Maritime Security Act 1990, s 10.]

7–6228 11. Destroying ships or fixed platforms or endangering their safety. (1) Subject to subsection (5) below, a person commits an offence if he unlawfully and intentionally—

(a)   destroys a ship or a fixed platform,

(b)   damages a ship, its cargo or a fixed platform so as to endanger, or to be likely to endanger, the safe navigation of the ship, or as the case may be, the safety of the platform, or

(c)   commits on board a ship or on a fixed platform an act of violence which is likely to endanger the safe navigation of the ship, or as the case may be, the safety of the platform.

(2)   Subject to subsection (5) below, a person commits an offence if he unlawfully and intentionally places, or causes to be placed, on a ship or fixed platform any device or substance which—

(a)   in the case of a ship, is likely to destroy the ship or is likely so to damage it or its cargo as to endanger its safe navigation, or

(b)   in the case of a fixed platform, is likely to destroy the fixed platform or so to damage it as to endanger its safety.

(3)   Nothing in subsection (2) above is to be construed as limiting the circumstances in which the commission of any act—

(a)   may constitute an offence under subsection (1) above, or

(b)   may constitute attempting or conspiring to commit, or aiding, abetting, counselling, procuring or inciting, or being art and part in, the commission of such an offence.

(4)   Except as provided by subsection (5) below, subsections (1) and (2) above apply whether any such act as is mentioned in those subsections is committed in the United Kingdom or elsewhere and whatever the nationality of the person committing the act.

(5)   Subsections (1) and (2) above do not apply in relation to any act committed in relation to a warship or any other ship used as a naval auxiliary or in customs or police service unless—

(a)   the person committing the act is a United Kingdom national, or

(b)   his act is committed in the United Kingdom, or

(c)   the ship is used in the naval or customs service of the United Kingdom or in the service of any police force in the United Kingdom.

(6)   A person guilty of an offence under this section is liable on conviction on indictment to imprisonment for life.

(7)   In this section—

"act of violence" means—

(a)   any act done in the United Kingdom which constitutes the offence of murder, attempted murder, manslaughter, culpable homicide or assault or an offence under section 18, 20, 21, 22, 23, 24, 28 or 29 of the Offences against the Person Act 1861 or under section 2 of the Explosive Substances Act 1883, and

(b)   any act done outside the United Kingdom which, if done in the United Kingdom, would constitute such an offence as is mentioned in paragraph (a) above, and

"unlawfully"—

(a)   in relation to the commission of an act in the United Kingdom, means so as (apart from this Act) to constitute an offence under the law of the part of the United Kingdom in which the act is committed, and

(b)   in relation to the commission of an act outside the United Kingdom, means so that the commission of the act would (apart from this Act) have been an offence under the law of England and Wales if it had been committed in England and Wales or of Scotland if it had been committed in Scotland.

[Aviation and Maritime Security Act 1990, s 11.]

7-6229   12. Other acts endangering or likely to endanger safe navigation.   (1) Subject to subsection (6) below, it is an offence for any person unlawfully and intentionally—

(a)   to destroy or damage any property to which this subsection applies, or

(b)   seriously to interfere with the operation of any such property,

where the destruction, damage or interference is likely to endanger the safe navigation of any ship.

(2)   Subsection (1) above applies to any property used for the provision of maritime navigation facilities, including any land, building or ship so used, and including any apparatus or equipment so used, whether it is on board a ship or elsewhere.

(3)   Subject to subsection (6) below, it is also an offence for any person intentionally to communicate any information which he knows to be false in a material particular, where the communication of the information endangers the safe navigation of any ship.

(4)   It is a defence for a person charged with an offence under subsection (3) above to prove that, when he communicated the information, he was lawfully employed to perform duties which consisted of or included the communication of information and that he communicated the information in good faith in performance of those duties.

(5)   Except as provided by subsection (6) below, subsections (1) and (3) above apply whether any such act as is mentioned in those subsections is committed in the United Kingdom or elsewhere and whatever the nationality of the person committing the act.

(6) For the purposes of subsections (1) and (3) above any danger, or likelihood of danger, to the safe navigation of a warship or any other ship used as a naval auxiliary or in customs or police service is to be disregarded unless—

(a) the person committing the act is a United Kingdom national, or
(b) his act is committed in the United Kingdom, or
(c) the ship is used in the naval or customs service of the United Kingdom or in the service of any police force in the United Kingdom.

(7) A person guilty of an offence under this section is liable on conviction on indictment to imprisonment for life.

(8) In this section "unlawfully" has the same meaning as in section 11 of this Act.
[Aviation and Maritime Security Act 1990, s 12.]

7–6230   13. Offences involving threats.   (1) A person commits an offence if—

(a) in order to compel any other person to do or abstain from doing any act, he threatens that he or some other person will do in relation to any ship or fixed platform an act which is an offence by virtue of section 11(1) of this Act, and
(b) the making of that threat is likely to endanger the safe navigation of the ship or, as the case may be, the safety of the fixed platform.

(2) Subject to subsection (4) below, a person commits an offence if—

(a) in order to compel any other person to do or abstain from doing any act, he threatens that he or some other person will do an act which is an offence by virtue of section 12(1) of this Act, and
(b) the making of that threat is likely to endanger the safe navigation of any ship.

(3) Except as provided by subsection (4) below, subsections (1) and (2) above apply whether any such act as is mentioned in those subsections is committed in the United Kingdom or elsewhere and whatever the nationality of the person committing the act.

(4) Section 12(6) of this Act applies for the purposes of subsection (2)(b) above as it applies for the purposes of section 12(1) and (3) of this Act.

(5) A person guilty of an offence under this section is liable on conviction on indictment to imprisonment for life.
[Aviation and Maritime Security Act 1990, s 13.]

7–6231   14. Ancillary offences.   (1) Where a person (of whatever nationality) does outside the United Kingdom any act which, if done in the United Kingdom, would constitute an offence falling within subsection (2) below, his act shall constitute that offence if it is done in connection with an offence under section 9, 10, 11 or 12 of this Act committed or attempted by him.

(2) The offences falling within this subsection are murder, attempted murder, manslaughter, culpable homicide and assault and offences under sections 18, 20, 21, 22, 23, 28 and 29 of the Offences against the Person Act 1861 and section 2 of the Explosive Substances Act 1883.

(3) Subsection (1) above has effect without prejudice to section 281 or 282 of the Merchant Shipping Act 1995 (offences committed on board British ships or by British seamen) or section 10 of the Petroleum Act 1998 (application of criminal law to offshore installations).

(4) It is an offence for any person in the United Kingdom to induce or assist the commission outside the United Kingdom of any act which—

(a) would, but for subsection (2) of section 9 of this Act, be an offence under that section, or
(b) would, but for subsection (5) of section 11 of this Act, be an offence under that section, or
(c) would, but for subsection (6) of section 12 of this Act, be an offence under that section, or
(d) would, but for subsection (4) of section 13 of this Act, be an offence under that section.

(5) A person who commits an offence under subsection (4) above is liable on conviction on indictment to imprisonment for life.

(6) Subsection (4) above has effect without prejudice to the operation, in relation to any offence under section 9, 11, 12 or 13 of this Act—

(a) in England and Wales, or in Northern Ireland, of section 8 of the Accessories and Abettors Act 1861, or
(b) in Scotland, of any rule of law relating to art and part guilt.
[Aviation and Maritime Security Act 1990, s 14 as amended by the Merchant Shipping Act 1995, Sch 13.]

7–6232   15. Master's power of delivery.   (1) The provisions of this section shall have effect for the purposes of any proceedings before any court in the United Kingdom.

(2) If the master of a ship, wherever that ship may be, and whatever the State (if any) in which it may be registered, has reasonable grounds to believe that any person on board the ship has—

(a) committed any offence under section 9, 11, 12 or 13 of this Act,
(b) attempted to commit such an offence, or

(c) aided, abetted, counselled, procured or incited, or been art and part in, the commission of such an offence,

in relation to any ship other than a warship or other ship used as a naval auxiliary or in customs or police service, he may deliver that person to an appropriate officer in the United Kingdom or any other Convention country.

(3) Where the master of a ship intends to deliver any person in the United Kingdom or any other Convention country in accordance with subsection (2) above he shall give notification to an appropriate officer in that country—

(a) of his intention to deliver that person to an appropriate officer in that country; and
(b) of his reasons for intending to do so.

(4) Any notification under subsection (3) above must be given—

(a) before the ship in question has entered the territorial sea of the country concerned; or
(b) if in the circumstances it is not reasonably practicable to comply with paragraph (a) above, as soon as reasonably practicable after the ship has entered that territorial sea.

(5) Where the master of a ship delivers any person to an appropriate officer in any country under subsection (2) above he shall—

(a) make to an appropriate officer in that country such oral or written statements relating to the alleged offence as that officer may reasonably require; and
(b) deliver to an appropriate officer in that country such other evidence relating to the alleged offence as is in the master's possession.

(6) The master of a ship who without reasonable excuse fails to comply with subsection (3) or (5) above is guilty of an offence and liable on summary conviction to a fine not exceeding **level 3** on the standard scale.

(7) It is a defence for a master of a ship charged with an offence under subsection (6) above of failing to comply with subsection (3) above to show that he believed on reasonable grounds that the giving of the notification required by subsection (3) above would endanger the safety of the ship and, except where the country concerned is the United Kingdom, that either—

(a) he notified some other competent authority in the country concerned within the time required by subsection (4) above, or
(b) he believed on reasonable grounds that the giving of notification to any competent authority in that country would endanger the safety of the ship.

(8) In this section—

"appropriate officer" means—

(a) in relation to the United Kingdom, a constable or immigration officer, and
(b) in relation to any other Convention country, an officer having functions corresponding to the functions in the United Kingdom either of a constable or of an immigration officer,

"Convention country" means a country in which the Convention for the Suppression of Unlawful Acts against the Safety of Maritime Navigation, which was signed at Rome on 10th March 1988, is for the time being in force; and Her Majesty may by Order in Council certify that any country specified in the Order is for the time being a Convention country and any such Order in Council for the time being in force shall be conclusive evidence that the country in question is for the time being a Convention country, and

"master" has the same meaning as in the Merchant Shipping Act 1995.

[Aviation and Maritime Security Act 1990, s 15 as amended by the Merchant Shipping Act 1995, Sch 13.]

7–6233   16. Prosecution of offences and proceedings.   (1) Proceedings for an offence under any provision of this Part of this Act shall not be instituted—

(a) in England and Wales, except by, or with the consent of, the Attorney General, and
(b) in Northern Ireland, except by, or with the consent of, the Attorney General for Northern Ireland.

(2) As respects Scotland, for the purpose of conferring on the sheriff jurisdiction to entertain proceedings for an offence under or by virtue of this Part of this Act, any such offence shall, without prejudice to any jurisdiction exercisable apart from this subsection, be deemed to have been committed in any place in Scotland where the offender may for the time being be.

[Aviation and Maritime Security Act 1990, s 16.]

7–6234   17. Interpretation of Part II.   (1) In this Part of this Act—

"fixed platform" means—

(a) any offshore installation, within the meaning of the Mineral Workings (Offshore Installations) Act 1971, which is not a ship, and
(b) any other artificial island, installation or structure which—

(i) permanently rests on, or is permanently attached to, the seabed,
(ii) is maintained for the purposes of the exploration or exploitation of resources or for other economic purposes, and
(iii) is not connected with dry land by a permanent structure providing access at all times and for all purposes;

"naval service" includes military and air force service;

"ship" means any vessel (including hovercraft, submersible craft and other floating craft) other than one which—

(a) permanently rests on, or is permanently attached to, the seabed, or
(b) has been withdrawn from navigation or laid up; and

"United Kingdom national" means an individual who is—

(a) a British citizen, a British overseas territories citizen, a British National (Overseas) or a British Overseas citizen,
(b) a person who under the British Nationality Act 1981 is a British subject, or
(c) a British protected person (within the meaning of that Act).

(2) For the purposes of this Part of this Act the territorial waters adjacent to any part of the United Kingdom shall be treated as included in that part of the United Kingdom.

[Aviation and Maritime Security Act 1990, s 17, as amended by the British Overseas Territories Act 2002, s 2(3).]

PART III
PROTECTION OF SHIPS AND HARBOUR AREAS AGAINST ACTS OF VIOLENCE

General purposes

7–6235 18. Purposes to which Part III applies. (1) The purposes to which this Part of this Act applies are the protection against acts of violence—

(a) of ships, and of persons or property on board ships, and
(b) of harbour areas, of such persons as are at any time present in any part of a harbour area and of such property as forms part of a harbour area or is at any time (whether permanently or temporarily) in any part of a harbour area.

(2) In this Part of this Act "act of violence" means any act (whether actual or potential, and whether done or to be done in the United Kingdom or elsewhere) which either—

(a) being an act done in Great Britain, constitutes, or
(b) if done in Great Britain would constitute,

the offence of murder, attempted murder, manslaughter, culpable homicide or assault, or an offence under section 18, 20, 21, 22, 23, 24, 28 or 29 of the Offences against the Person Act 1861, under section 2 of the Explosive Substances Act 1883 or under section 1 of the Criminal Damage Act 1971 or, in Scotland, the offence of malicious mischief.

(3) In this Part of this Act "harbour area" means—

(a) the aggregate of—

(i) any harbour in the United Kingdom in respect of which there is a harbour authority within the meaning of the Merchant Shipping Act 1995, and
(ii) any land which is adjacent to such a harbour and which is either land occupied by the harbour authority or land in respect of which the harbour authority or land in respect of which the harbour authority has functions of improvement, maintenance or management, or

(b) any hoverport which does not form part of any area which falls within paragraph (a)(i) or (ii) above.

[Aviation and Maritime Security Act 1990, s 18 as amended by the Merchant Shipping and Maritime Security Act 1997, Sch 4.]

Powers of Secretary of State

7–6236 19. Power of Secretary of State to require information. (1) The Secretary of State may, by notice in writing served on any of the following persons—

(a) the owner, charterer, manager or master of—

(i) a British ship, or
(ii) any other ship which is in, or appears to the Secretary of State to be likely to enter, a harbour area,

(b) a harbour authority,
(c) any person who carries on harbour operations in a harbour area, and
(d) any person who is permitted to have access to a restricted zone of a harbour area for the purposes of the activities of a business carried on by him,

require that person to provide the Secretary of State with such information specified in the notice as the Secretary of State may require in connection with the exercise by the Secretary of State of his functions under this Part of this Act.

(2) A notice under subsection (1) above shall specify a date (not being earlier than seven days from the date on which the notice is served) before which the information required by the notice in accordance with subsection (1) above is to be furnished to the Secretary of State.

(3) Any such notice may also require the person on whom it is served, after he has furnished to the Secretary of State the information required by the notice in accordance with subsection (1) above, to inform the Secretary of State if at any time the information previously furnished to the Secretary of State (including any information furnished in pursuance of a requirement imposed by virtue of this subsection) is rendered inaccurate by any change of circumstances (including the taking of any further measures for purposes to which this Part of this Act applies or the alteration or discontinuance of any measures already being taken).

(4) In so far as such a notice requires further information to be furnished to the Secretary of State in accordance with subsection (3) above, it shall require that information to be furnished to him before the end of such period (not being less than seven days from the date on which the change of circumstances occurs) as is specified in the notice for the purposes of this subsection.

(5) Any person who—

(*a*) without reasonable excuse, fails to comply with a requirement imposed on him by a notice under this section, or

(*b*) in furnishing any information so required, makes a statement which he knows to be false in a material particular, or recklessly makes a statement which is false in a material particular,

commits an offence.

(6) A person guilty of an offence under subsection (5) above is liable[1]—

(*a*) on summary conviction, to a fine not exceeding the **statutory maximum**;

(*b*) on conviction on indictment, to a **fine** or to imprisonment for a term not exceeding **two years** or to **both**.

(7) A notice served on a person under subsection (1) above may at any time—

(*a*) be revoked by a notice in writing served on him by the Secretary of State, or

(*b*) be varied by a further notice under subsection (1) above.

[Aviation and Maritime Security Act 1990, s 19.]

---

1. For procedure in respect of an offence which is triable either way, see the Magistrates' Courts Act 1980, ss 17A–21 in PART I: MAGISTRATES' COURTS, PROCEDURE, *ante.*

7–6237   20. Designation of restricted zones of harbour areas.   (1) A harbour authority may, and shall if so requested in writing by the Secretary of State, apply to the Secretary of State for the designation of the whole or any part of the harbour area as a restricted zone for the purposes of this Part of this Act.

(1A) A harbour operator may, and shall if so requested in writing by the Secretary of State, apply to the Secretary of State for the designation of the whole or any part of the operating area as a restricted zone for the purposes of this Part of this Act.

(2) An application under subsection (1) or (1A) above shall be in such form, and accompanied by such plans, as the Secretary of State may require.

(3) If the Secretary of State approves an application under subsection (1) or (1A) above with or without modifications, he shall designate the restricted zone accordingly.

(4) Before approving an application with modifications, the Secretary of State shall consult the applicant.

(5) If a person is requested in writing by the Secretary of State to make an application under subsection (1) or (1A) above within a specified period but fails to do so within that period, the Secretary of State may designate the whole or any part of the harbour area or, as the case may be, of the operating area as a restricted zone.

(6) The whole or any part of a harbour area may be designated as a restricted zone, or part of a restricted zone, for specified days or times of day only.

(7) The Secretary of State shall give notice to the person who made, or was requested to make, the application of any designation under this section and the designation of the restricted zone shall take effect on the giving of the notice.

(8) Where the whole or any part of a harbour area or, as the case may be, of an operating area has been designated under this section as a restricted zone—

(*a*) subsections (1) to (7) above also have effect in relation to any variation of the designation, and

(*b*) the designation may at any time be revoked by the Secretary of State.

(9) In this Part of this Act "harbour operator" means a person who—

(*a*) carries on harbour operations in a harbour area, and

(*b*) is designated for the purposes of this Part by an order made by the Secretary of State;

and "operating area" means, in relation to that person, so much of the harbour area as is under his control.

(10) An order under subsection (9) above may be revoked by a subsequent order.

[Aviation and Maritime Security Act 1990, s 20 as amended by the Merchant Shipping and Maritime Security Act 1997, Sch 4.]

7–6238 21. Power to impose restrictions in relation to ships. (1) For purposes to which this Part of this Act applies, the Secretary of State may give a direction in writing to a harbour authority or to the owner, charterer, manager or master of a British ship, or of any other ship which is in a harbour area requiring that person—

(*a*) not to cause or permit persons or property to go or be taken on board any ship to which the direction relates, or to come or be brought into proximity to any such ship, unless such searches of those persons or that property as are specified in the direction have been carried out by constables or by other persons of a description specified in the direction, or

(*b*) not to cause or permit any such ship to go to sea unless such searches of the ship as are specified in the direction have been carried out by constables or by other persons of a description so specified.

(2) For purposes to which this Part of this Act applies, the Secretary of State may give a direction in writing to the owner, charterer, manager or master of—

(*a*) a British ship, or

(*b*) any other ship which is in a harbour area,

requiring him not to cause or permit the ship to go to sea unless such modifications or alterations of the ship, or of apparatus or equipment installed in or carried on board the ship, as are specified in the direction have first been carried out, or such additional apparatus or equipment as is so specified is first installed in or carried on board the ship.

(3) In giving any direction under subsection (2) above, the Secretary of State shall allow, and shall specify in the direction, such period as appears to him to be reasonably required for carrying out the modifications or alterations or installing or obtaining the additional apparatus or equipment in question; and the direction shall not take effect before the end of the period so specified.

(4) Subject to the following provisions of this Part of this Act, a direction given to an owner, charterer or manager of a ship under subsection (1) or (2) above may be given so as to relate either to all the ships falling within that subsection of which at the time when the direction is given or at any subsequent time he is the owner, charterer or manager or only to one or more such ships specified in the direction; and a direction given to a harbour authority under subsection (1) above may be given so as to relate either to all ships which at the time when the direction is given or at any subsequent time are in any part of the harbour area, or to a class of such ships specified in the direction.

(5) Subject to the following provisions of this Part of this Act, a direction under subsection (1) above may be given so as to relate—

(*a*) either to all persons or only to one or more persons, or persons of one or more descriptions, specified in the direction, and

(*b*) either to property of every description or only to particular property, or property of one or more descriptions, so specified.

(6) Subject to the following provisions of this Part of this Act, any direction given under this section to any person not to cause or permit anything to be done shall be construed as requiring him to take all such steps as in any particular circumstances are practicable and necessary to prevent that thing from being done.

(7) A direction may be given under this section to a person appearing to the Secretary of State to be about to become such a person as is mentioned in subsection (1) or (2) above, but a direction given to a person by virtue of this subsection shall not take effect until he becomes a person so mentioned and, in relation to a direction so given, the preceding provisions of this section shall apply with the necessary modifications.

(8) Any person who, without reasonable excuse, fails to comply with a direction given to him under this section is guilty of an offence and liable[1]—

(*a*) on summary conviction, to a fine not exceeding the **statutory maximum**;

(*b*) on conviction on indictment, to a **fine** or to imprisonment for a term not exceeding **two years** or to **both**.

(9) Where a person is convicted of an offence under subsection (8) above, then, if without reasonable excuse the failure in respect of which he was convicted is continued after the conviction, he is guilty of a further offence and liable on summary conviction to a fine not exceeding one-tenth of level 5 on the standard scale for each day on which the failure continues.

[Aviation and Maritime Security Act 1990, s 21.]

---

1. For procedure in respect of an offence which is triable either way, see the Magistrates' Courts Act 1980, ss 17A–21 in Part I: Magistrates' Courts, Procedure, ante.

7–6239   22. Power to require harbour authorities to promote searches in harbour areas.
(1) For purposes to which this Part of this Act applies, the Secretary of State may give a direction in writing to—

    (*a*) a harbour authority, or
    (*b*) a harbour operator

requiring that person to use his best endeavours to secure that such searches to which this section applies as are specified in the direction are carried out by constables or by other persons of a description specified in the direction.
(2) The searches to which this section applies, in relation to a harbour area, are searches—

    (*a*) of the harbour area or any part of it,
    (*b*) of any ship which at the time when the direction is given or at any subsequent time is in the harbour area, and
    (*c*) of persons and property (other than ships) which may at any time be in the harbour area.

(2A) The searches to which this section applies, in relation to an operating area, are searches—

    (*a*) of the operating area or any part of it,
    (*b*) of any ship which at the time when the direction is given or at any subsequent time is in the harbour area, and
    (*c*) of persons and property (other than ships) which may at any time be in the operating area.

(3) Where a direction under this section to a harbour authority is for the time being in force, then subject to subsections (4) and (5) below, if a constable or any other person specified in the direction in accordance with this section, has reasonable cause to suspect that an article to which this subsection applies is in, or may be brought into, any part of the harbour area, he may, by virtue of this subsection and without a warrant, search any part of the harbour area or any ship, vehicle, goods or other moveable property of any description which, or any person who, is for the time being in any part of the harbour area, and for that purpose—

    (*a*) may enter any building or works in the harbour area, or enter upon any land in the harbour area, if need be by force,
    (*b*) may go on board any such ship and inspect the ship,
    (*c*) may stop any such ship and, for so long as may be necessary for that purpose, prevent it from being moved, and
    (*d*) may stop any such vehicle, goods, property or person and detain it or him for so long as may be necessary for that purpose.

(3A) Subsection (3) above applies in relation to a direction under this section to a harbour operator as it applies in relation to a direction to a harbour authority, but as if the references to the harbour area (or to any part of the harbour area) were references to the operating are (or any part of the operating area).
(4) In the case of premises used only as a private dwelling any power to search or enter conferred by subsection (3) above may not be exercised except—

    (*a*) under the authority of a warrant issued by a justice of the peace; and
    (*b*) by a constable—

        (i) who is a member of a body of constables maintained in England, Scotland or Wales by a policy authority or an authority which has entered into an agreement with the Police Complaints Authority under section 96(1) of the Police and Criminal Evidence Act 1984;* or
        (ii) who is a member of a body of constables maintained in Northern Ireland, by the Police Authority for Northern Ireland or an authority which has entered into an agreement with the Independent Commission for Police Complaints for Northern Ireland under Article 16 of the Police (Northern Ireland) Order 1987, or
        (iii) who is a member of the National Criminal Intelligence Service within section 9(1)(*a*) or (*b*) of the Police Act 1997 or a member of the National Crime Squad within section 55(1)(*a*) or (*b*) of that Act

(5) If, on an application made by a constable, a justice of the peace is satisfied that there are reasonable grounds for suspecting that an article to which subsection (3) above applies is in any premises used only as a private dwelling, he may issue a warrant authorising a constable to enter and search the premises.
(6) Subsection (3) above applies to the following articles—

    (*a*) any firearm, or any article having the appearance of being a firearm, whether capable of being discharged or not,
    (*b*) any explosive, any article manufactured or adapted (whether in the form of a bomb, grenade or otherwise) so as to have the appearance of being an explosive, whether it is capable of producing a practical effect by explosion or not, or any article marked or labelled so as to indicate that it is or contains an explosive, and

(*c*) any article (not falling within either of the preceding paragraphs) made or adapted for use for causing injury to or incapacitating a person or for destroying or damaging property, or intended by the person having it with him for such use, whether by him or by any other person.

(7) Any person who—

(*a*) without reasonable excuse, fails to comply with a direction given to him under this section, or
(*b*) intentionally obstructs a person acting in the exercise of a power conferred on him by subsection (3) above,

commits an offence.

(8) A person guilty of an offence under subsection (7) above is liable[1]—

(*a*) on summary conviction, to a fine not exceeding the **statutory maximum**;
(*b*) on conviction on indictment, to a fine or to imprisonment for a term not exceeding **two years** or to **both**.

(9) Where a person is convicted of an offence under subsection (7)(*a*) above, then, if without reasonable excuse the failure in respect of which he was convicted is continued after the conviction, he is guilty of a further offence and liable on summary conviction to a fine not exceeding **one-tenth of level 5** on the standard scale for each day on which the failure continues.

(10) Subsection (3) above has effect without prejudice to the operation, in relation to any offence under this Act—

(*a*) in England and Wales, of sections 17, 24 and 25 of the Police and Criminal Evidence Act 1984 (which confer power to arrest without warrant and to enter premises for the purpose of making an arrest) or of section 3 of the Criminal Law Act 1967 (use of force in making arrest etc), or
(*b*) in Scotland, of any rule of law relating to the power to arrest without warrant, or
(*c*) in Northern Ireland, of Articles 19, 26 and 27 of the Police and Criminal Evidence (Northern Ireland) Order 1989 or of section 3 of the Criminal Law Act (Northern Ireland) 1967.

[Aviation and Maritime Security Act 1990, s 22 as amended by the Merchant Shipping and Maritime Security Act 1997, Sch 4 and the Police Act 1997, Sch 9.]

---

*Amended by the Police Reform Act 2002, Sch 7 when in force, to substitute a reference to s 26 of the Police Reform Act 2002.

1. For procedure in respect of an offence which is triable either way, see the Magistrates' Courts Act 1980, ss 17A–21, in Part I: Magistrates' Courts, Procedure, ante.

7–6240 23. Power to require other persons to promote searches. (1) For purposes to which this Part of this Act applies, the Secretary of State may give a direction in writing to any person who—

(*a*) carries on harbour operations in a harbour area, or
(*b*) is permitted to have access to a restricted zone of a harbour area for the purposes of the activities of a business carried on by him,

requiring him to use his best endeavours to secure that such searches to which this section applies as are specified in the direction are carried out by constables or by other persons of a description specified in the direction.

(1A) A direction may not be given under this section to—

(*a*) a harbour authority, or
(*b*) a harbour operator.

(2) The searches to which this section applies are—

(*a*) in relation to a person falling within subsection (1)(*a*) above, searches—

(i) of any land which he occupies within the harbour area, and
(ii) of persons or property which may at any time be on that land; and

(*b*) in relation to a person falling within subsection (1)(*b*) above, searches—

(i) of any land which he occupies outside the harbour area for the purposes of his business, and
(ii) of persons or property which may at any time be on that land.

(3) Any person who, without reasonable excuse, fails to comply with a direction given to him under this section is guilty of an offence and liable[1]—

(*a*) on summary conviction, to a fine not exceeding the **statutory maximum**;
(*b*) on conviction on indictment, to a fine or to imprisonment for a term not exceeding **two years** or to **both**.

(4) Where a person is convicted of an offence under subsection (3) above, then, if without reasonable excuse the failure in respect of which he was convicted is continued after the conviction, he is guilty of a further offence and liable on summary conviction to a fine not exceeding **one-tenth of level 5** on the standard scale for each day on which the failure continues.

[Aviation and Maritime Security Act 1990, s 23 as amended by the Merchant Shipping and Maritime Security Act 1997, Sch 4.]

---

1. For procedure in respect of an offence which is triable either way, see the Magistrates' Courts Act 1980, ss 17A–21, in PART I: MAGISTRATES' COURTS, PROCEDURE, ante.

7–6241 24. General power to direct measures to be taken for purposes to which Part III applies. (1) Subsection (2) below applies to—

(a) any person who is the owner, charterer or manager of one or more ships which—

    (i) are British ships, or

    (ii) are in a harbour area,

(b) any harbour authority,

(c) any person other than a harbour authority who carries on harbour operations in a harbour area, and

(d) any person who is permitted to have access to a restricted zone of a harbour area for the purposes of the activities of a business carried on by him.

(2) Subject to the following provisions of this section, the Secretary of State may give a direction in writing to any person to whom this subsection applies requiring him to take such measures for purposes to which this Part of this Act applies as are specified in the direction—

(a) in the case of a direction given to a person as the owner, charterer or manager of a ship, in respect of all the ships falling within subsection (1)(a) above of which (at the time when the direction is given or at any subsequent time) he is the owner, charterer or manager, or in respect of any such ships specified in the direction,

(b) in the case of a direction given to a harbour authority, in respect of the harbour area,

(c) in the case of a direction given to a person as a person falling within subsection (1)(c) above, in respect of the harbour operations carried on by him, and

(d) in the case of a direction given to a person as a person who is permitted to have access to a restricted zone as mentioned in subsection (1)(d) above, in respect of such activities carried on by that person in that zone as are specified in the direction.

(3) Without prejudice to the generality of subsection (2) above, the measures to be specified in a direction given under this section to any person to whom that subsection applies may include the provision by that person of persons charged with the duty (at such times as may be specified in the direction)—

(a) where the direction is given to a person as the owner, charterer or manager of ships, of guarding the ships against acts of violence,

(b) where the direction is given to a harbour authority, of guarding the harbour area, or persons or property (including ships) in any part of the harbour area, against acts of violence,

(c) where the direction is given to a person as falling within subsection (1)(c) above, of guarding against acts of violence any ship in the harbour area which is for the time being under his control, or

(d) where the direction is given to a person as falling within subsection (1)(d) above, of guarding—

    (i) any land outside the harbour area occupied by him for the purposes of his business, any vehicles or equipment used for those purposes and any goods which are in his possession for those purposes, and

    (ii) any ship which is for the time being under his control,

for purposes to which this Part of this Act applies.

(4) A direction given under this section may be either of a general or of a specific character, and may require any measures specified in the direction to be taken at such time or within such period as may be so specified.

(5) A direction under this section—

(a) shall not require any search (whether of persons or of property), and

(b) shall not require the modification or alteration of any ship, or of any of its apparatus or equipment, or the installation or carriage of additional apparatus or equipment, or prohibit any ship from being caused or permitted to go to sea without some modification or alteration of the ship or its apparatus or equipment or the installation or carriage of additional apparatus or equipment.

(6) A direction may be given under this section to a person appearing to the Secretary of State to be about to become a person to whom subsection (2) above applies, but a direction given to a person by virtue of this subsection shall not take effect until he becomes a person to whom subsection (2) above applies and, in relation to a direction so given, the preceding provisions of this section shall apply with the necessary modifications.

(7) Any person who—

(a) without reasonable excuse, fails to comply with a direction given to him under this section, or (*b*) intentionally interferes with any building constructed or works executed on any land in compliance with a direction under this section or with anything installed on, under, over or across any land in compliance with such a direction,

commits an offence.

(8) A person guilty of an offence under subsection (7) above is liable[1]—

(*a*) on summary conviction, to a fine not exceeding the **statutory maximum**;
(*b*) on conviction on indictment, to a fine or to imprisonment for a term not exceeding **two years** or to **both**.

(9) Where a person is convicted of an offence under subsection (7)(*a*) above, then, if without reasonable excuse the failure in respect of which he was convicted is continued after the conviction, he is guilty of a further offence and liable on summary conviction to a fine not exceeding **one-tenth of level 5** on the standard scale for each day on which the failure continues.

(10) The ownership of any property shall not be affected by reason only that it is placed on or under, or affixed to, any land in compliance with a direction under this section.

[Aviation and Maritime Security Act 1990, s 24.]

---

1. For procedure in respect of an offence which is triable either way, see the Magistrates' Courts Act 1980, ss 17A–21, in PART I: MAGISTRATES' COURTS, PROCEDURE, ante.

Supplemental provisions with respect to directions

7–6242 **25. Matters which may be included in directions under sections 21 to 24.** (1) A direction under subsection (1) of section 21 or under section 22 or 23 of this Act may specify the minimum number of persons by whom any search to which the direction relates is to be carried out, the qualifications which persons carrying out any such search are to have, the manner in which any such search is to be carried out, and any apparatus, equipment or other aids to be used for the purpose of carrying out any such search.

(2) A direction under subsection (2) of section 21 of this Act may specify the qualifications required to be had by persons carrying out any modifications or alterations, or the installation of any additional apparatus or equipment, to which the direction relates.

(3) A direction under section 24 of this Act may specify—

(*a*) the minimum number of persons to be employed for the purposes of any measures required by the direction to be taken by the person to whom it is given, and the qualifications which persons employed for those purposes are to have, and
(*b*) any apparatus, equipment or other aids to be used for those purposes.

(4) Where a direction under any of the preceding provisions of this Part of this Act requires searches to be carried out, or other measures to be taken, by constables, the direction may require the person to whom it is given to inform the chief officer of police for the police area in which the searches are to be carried out or the other measures taken that the Secretary of State considers it appropriate that constables should be duly authorised to carry, and should carry, firearms when carrying out the searches or taking the measures in question.

(5) Nothing in subsections (1) to (4) above shall be construed as limiting the generality of any of the preceding provisions of this Part of this Act.

(6) In this section "qualifications" includes training and experience.

(7) *Northern Ireland.*

[Aviation and Maritime Security Act 1990, s 25.]

7–6243 **26. Limitations on scope of directions under sections 21 to 24.** (1) Without prejudice to section 25(4) of this Act, a direction shall not require or authorise any person to carry a firearm except to the extent necessary for the purpose of removing any firearm found pursuant to a search under section 22 of this Act from the restricted zone and delivering the firearm to a person authorised to carry it.

(2) A direction shall not have effect in relation to any ship used in naval, customs or police service.

(3) A direction shall not have effect in relation to any ship which is registered outside the United Kingdom and of which the owner is the Government of a country outside the United Kingdom, or is a department or agency of such a Government, except at a time when any such ship is being used for commercial purposes or is for the time being allocated by that Government, department or agency for such use.

(4) A direction (except in so far as it requires any building or other works to be constructed, executed, altered, demolished or removed) shall not be construed as requiring or authorising the person to whom the direction was given, or any person acting as his employee or agent, to do anything which, apart from the direction, would constitute an act of violence; but nothing in this subsection shall restrict the use of such force as is reasonable in the circumstances (whether at the instance of the person to whom the direction was given or otherwise) by a constable, or its use by any other person in the exercise of a power conferred by section 22(3) of this Act.

(5) In so far as a direction requires anything to be done or not done at a place outside the United Kingdom—

(a) it shall not have effect except in relation to British ships, and

(b) it shall not have effect so as to require anything to be done or not done in contravention of any provision of the law (whether civil or criminal) in force at that place, other than any such provision relating to breach of contract.

(6) In so far as a direction given to a harbour authority or to any person mentioned in section 24(1)(c) or (d) of this Act requires a building or other works to be constructed, executed, altered, demolished or removed on land outside the harbour area, or requires any other measures to be taken on such land, the direction shall not confer on the person to whom it is given any rights as against a person having—

(a) an interest in that land, or

(b) a right to occupy that land, or

(c) a right restrictive of its use;

and accordingly, the direction shall not be construed as requiring the person to whom it is given to do anything which would be actionable at the suit or instance of a person having such interest or right in his capacity as a person having that interest or right.

(7) Nothing in this section shall be construed as derogating from any exemption or immunity of the Crown in relation to the provisions of this Part of this Act.

(8) In this section "direction" means a direction under section 21, 22, 23 or 24 of this Act.

[Aviation and Maritime Security Act 1990, s 26 as amended by the Merchant Shipping and Maritime Security Act 1997, Sch 4.]

7–6244   27. General or urgent directions under sections 21 to 24.   (1) A direction given to any person under section 21, 22, 23 or 24 of this Act need not be addressed to that particular person, but may be framed in general terms applicable to all persons to whom such a direction may be given or to any class of such persons to which that particular person belongs.

(2) If it appears to the Secretary of State that an exception from any direction given under any of those sections is required as a matter of urgency in any particular case he may, by a notification given (otherwise than in writing) to the person for the time being subject to the direction, authorise that person to disregard the requirements of the direction—

(a) in relation to such ships or class of ships, in relation to such harbour area or part of a harbour area, in relation to such land outside a harbour area, in relation to such activities or in relation to such persons or property or such description of persons or property, and

(b) on such occasion or series of occasions, or for such period,

as he may specify; and the direction shall have effect in that case subject to any exceptions so specified.

(3) Any notification given to any person under subsection (2) above with respect to any direction shall cease to have effect (if it has not already done so)—

(a) if a direction in writing is subsequently given to that person varying or revoking the original direction, or

(b) if no such direction in writing is given within the period of thirty days beginning with the date on which the notification was given, at the end of that period.

(4) Any notification given under subsection (2) above shall be regarded as given to the person to whom it is directed if it is given—

(a) to any person authorised by that person to receive any such direction or notification,

(b) where that person is a body corporate, to the secretary, clerk or similar officer of the body corporate, and

(c) in any other case, to anyone holding a comparable office or position in that person's employment.

[Aviation and Maritime Security Act 1990, s 27.]

7–6245   28. Objections to certain directions under section 24.   (1) This section applies to any direction given under section 24 of this Act which—

(a) requires a person to take measures consisting of or including the construction, execution, alteration, demolition or removal of a building or other works, and

(b) does not contain a statement that the measures are urgently required and that accordingly the direction is to take effect immediately.

(2) At any time before the end of the period of thirty days beginning with the date on which a direction to which this section applies is given, the person to whom the direction is given may serve on the Secretary of State a notice in writing objecting to the direction, on the grounds that the measures specified in the direction, in so far as they relate to the construction, execution, alteration, demolition or removal of a building or other works—

(a) are unnecessary and should be dispensed with, or

(*b*) are excessively onerous or inconvenient and should be modified in a manner specified in the notice.

(3) Where the person to whom such a direction is given serves a notice under subsection (2) above objecting to the direction, the Secretary of State shall consider the grounds of the objection and, if so required by the objector, shall afford to him an opportunity of appearing before and being heard by a person appointed by the Secretary of State for the purpose, and shall then serve on the objector a notice in writing either—

(*a*) confirming the direction as originally given, or
(*b*) confirming it subject to one or more modifications specified in the notice under this subsection, or
(*c*) withdrawing the direction;

and the direction shall not take effect until it has been confirmed (with or without modification) by a notice served under this subsection.
[Aviation and Maritime Security Act 1990, s 28.]

7–6246 29. Enforcement notices.   (1) Where an authorised person is of the opinion that any person has failed to comply with any general requirement of a direction given to him under section 21, 22, 23 or 24 of this Act, the authorised person may serve on that person a notice (in this Part of this Act referred to as an "enforcement notice")—

(*a*) specifying those general requirements of the direction with which he has, in the opinion of the authorised person, failed to comply, and
(*b*) specifying, subject to section 30 of this Act, the measures that ought to be taken in order to comply with those requirements.

(2) For the purposes of this section a requirement of a direction given by the Secretary of State under section 21, 22, 23 or 24 of this Act is a "general requirement" if the provision imposing the requirement—

(*a*) has been included in two or more directions given to different persons (whether or not at the same time), and
(*b*) is framed in general terms applicable to all the persons to whom those directions are given.

(3) If an enforcement notice is served under this section on the owner, charterer or manager of a ship, then (whether or not that service is effected by virtue of section 45(8) of this Act) an authorised person may serve on the master of the ship—

(*a*) a copy of the enforcement notice and of the direction to which it relates, and
(*b*) a notice stating that the master is required to comply with the enforcement notice,

and, if he does so, sections 31, 32 and 33 of this Act shall have effect as if the enforcement notice had been served on him as well as on the owner, charterer or manager of the ship.
[Aviation and Maritime Security Act 1990, s 29.]

7–6247 30. Contents of enforcement notice.   (1) An enforcement notice may specify in greater detail measures which are described in general terms in those provisions of the direction to which it relates which impose general requirements, but may not impose any requirement which could not have been imposed by a direction given by the Secretary of State under the provision under which the direction was given.

(2) An enforcement notice may be framed so as to afford the person on whom it is served a choice between different ways of complying with the specified general requirements of the direction.

(3) Subject to subsection (4) below, an enforcement notice which relates to a direction given under section 21 of this Act must require the person to whom the direction was given not to cause or permit things to be done as mentioned in subsection (1)(*a*) or (*b*) or (2) of that section, as the case requires, until the specified measures have been taken.

(4) In serving an enforcement notice which relates to a direction under section 21(2) of this Act, the authorised person shall allow, and shall specify in the notice, such period as appears to him to be reasonably required for taking the measures specified in the notice; and the notice shall not take effect before the end of the period so specified.

(5) An enforcement notice which relates to a direction given under section 22, 23 or 24 of this Act must either—

(*a*) require the person to whom the direction was given to take the specified measures within a specified period which—

  (i) where the measures consist of or include the construction, execution, alteration, demolition or removal of a building or other works, must not be less than thirty days beginning with the date of service of the notice, and
  (ii) in any other case, must not be less than seven days beginning with that date; or

(*b*) require him not to do specified things or cause or permit specified things to be done, until the specified measures have been taken.

(6) Subject to section 33(2) of this Act, an enforcement notice requiring a person not to cause or permit anything to be done shall be construed as requiring him to take all such steps as in any particular circumstances are practicable and necessary to prevent that thing from being done.
[Aviation and Maritime Security Act 1990, s 30.]

7–6248 31. Offences relating to enforcement notices. (1) Any person who, without reasonable excuse, fails to comply with an enforcement notice served on him is guilty of an offence and liable[1]—

    (a) on summary conviction, to a fine not exceeding **the statutory maximum**;
    (b) on conviction on indictment, to a **fine**.

(2) Where a person is convicted of an offence under subsection (1) above, then, if without reasonable excuse the failure in respect of which he was convicted is continued after the conviction, he is guilty of a further offence and liable on summary conviction to a fine not exceeding **one-tenth of level 5** on the standard scale for each day on which the failure continues.

(3) Any person who intentionally interferes with any building constructed or works executed on any land in compliance with an enforcement notice or with anything installed on, under, over or across any land in compliance with such a notice is guilty of an offence and liable[1]—

    (a) on summary conviction, to a fine not exceeding **the statutory maximum**;
    (b) on conviction on indictment, to a **fine**.
[Aviation and Maritime Security Act 1990, s 31.]

---

    1. For procedure in respect of an offence which is triable either way, see the Magistrates' Courts Act 1980, ss 17A–21, in PART I: MAGISTRATES' COURTS, PROCEDURE, ante.

7–6249 32. Objections to enforcement notices. (1) The person on whom an enforcement notice is served may serve on the Secretary of State a notice in writing of his objection to the enforcement notice, specifying the grounds of the objection.

(2) Any notice of objection under subsection (1) above must be served—

    (a) where the enforcement notice specifies measures falling within section 30(5)(a)(i) of this Act, before the end of the period of thirty days beginning with the date on which the enforcement notice was served, or
    (b) in any other case, before the end of the period of seven days beginning with that date.

(3) The grounds of objection to an enforcement notice are—

    (a) that the general requirements of the direction which are specified in the notice for the purposes of section 29(1)(a) of this Act have been complied with,
    (b) that the notice purports to impose a requirement which could not have been imposed by a direction given under the provision under which the direction to which the notice relates was given, or
    (c) that any requirement of the notice—

        (i) is unnecessary for complying with the general requirements specified as mentioned in paragraph (a) above and should be dispensed with, or
        (ii) having regard to the terms of those general requirements, is excessively onerous or inconvenient and should be modified in a manner specified in the notice of objection under subsection (1) above.

(4) Where the person on whom an enforcement notice is served serves a notice under subsection (1) above objecting to the enforcement notice, the Secretary of State shall consider the grounds of the objection and, if so required by the objector, shall afford to him an opportunity of appearing before and being heard by a person appointed by the Secretary of State for the purpose, and shall then serve on the objector a notice in writing either—

    (a) confirming the enforcement notice as originally served, or
    (b) confirming it subject to one or more modifications specified in the notice under this subsection, or
    (c) cancelling the enforcement notice.

(5) An enforcement notice to which an objection has been made under subsection (1) above—

    (a) if it contains such a requirement as is mentioned in section 30(3) or (5)(b) of this Act, shall continue to have effect as originally served until it has been cancelled, or it has been confirmed subject to modification by a notice under subsection (4) above, and
    (b) in any other case, shall not take effect until it has been confirmed (with or without modification) by a notice under subsection (4) above.
[Aviation and Maritime Security Act 1990, s 32.]

7–6250 33. Enforcement notices: supplementary. (1) An enforcement notice served on any person—

    (a) may be revoked by a notice served on him by an authorised person, and
    (b) may be varied by a further enforcement notice.

(2) Sections 25 and 26 of this Act apply to an enforcement notice as they apply to the direction to which the notice relates.

(3) The ownership of any property shall not be affected by reason only that it is placed on or under or affixed to, any land in compliance with an enforcement notice.

(4) Where an authorised person has served an enforcement notice specifying the general requirements of a direction with which the person on whom it is served has, in the opinion of the authorised person, failed to comply, the person on whom the notice is served shall not be taken, for the purposes of section 21(8), 22(7), 23(3) or 24(7) of this Act, to have failed to comply with the direction by reason of the matters specified in the notice.

(5) Subsection (4) above does not apply in relation to any proceedings commenced before the service of the enforcement notice.

(6) Where an enforcement notice has been served in relation to a direction, the fact that the notice specifies certain general requirements of the direction as those with which the person on whom the notice is served has, in the opinion of the authorised person, failed to comply shall not in any proceedings be evidence that any other requirement of the direction has been complied with.

(7) In this section "direction" means a direction under section 21, 22, 23 or 24 of this Act.

[Aviation and Maritime Security Act 1990, s 33.]

7–6251 34. Operation of directions under Part III in relation to rights and duties under other laws.   (1) In subsections (2) to (4) below references to a direction are references to a direction under section 21, 22, 23 or 24 of this Act as the direction has effect subject to any limitation imposed on its operation—

(a) by section 26 of this Act, or
(b) by any exemption or immunity of the Crown;

and any reference in those subsections to compliance with a direction is a reference to compliance with it subject to any limitation so imposed.

(2) In so far as a direction requires anything to be done or not done in the United Kingdom, the direction shall have effect notwithstanding anything contained in any contract (whether a United Kingdom contract or not) or contained in, or having effect by virtue of, any other Act or any rule of law; and accordingly no proceedings (whether civil or criminal) shall lie against any person in any United Kingdom court by reason of anything done or not done by him or on his behalf in compliance with a direction.

(3) In so far as a direction requires anything to be done or not done at a place outside the United Kingdom, the direction shall have effect notwithstanding anything contained in any contract (whether a United Kingdom contract or not); and accordingly, where a direction is inconsistent with anything in such a contract, it shall (without prejudice to any proceedings in a court other than a United Kingdom court) be construed as requiring compliance with the direction notwithstanding that compliance would be in breach of that contract.

(4) No proceedings for breach of contract shall lie against any person in a United Kingdom court by reason of anything done or not done by him or on his behalf at a place outside the United Kingdom in compliance with a direction, if the contract in question is a United Kingdom contract.

(5) Subsections (1) to (4) above have effect in relation to an enforcement notice as they have effect in relation to a direction under section 21, 22, 23 or 24 of this Act.

(6) In this section "United Kingdom court" means a court exercising jurisdiction in any part of the United Kingdom under the law of the United Kingdom or of part of the United Kingdom, and "United Kingdom contract" means a contract which is either expressed to have effect in accordance with the law of the United Kingdom or of part of the United Kingdom or (not being so expressed) is a contract the law applicable to which is the law of the United Kingdom or of part of the United Kingdom.

[Aviation and Maritime Security Act 1990, s 34.]

7–6252 35. Detention of ships.   (1) Where an authorised person is satisfied that the owner, charterer, manager or master of a ship has failed to comply with—

(a) a direction given to him under section 21 or 24 of this Act in respect of that ship, or
(b) an enforcement notice which has been served on him in respect of that ship and which relates to such a direction,

and the authorised person certifies in writing to that effect, stating particulars of the non-compliance, the ship may be detained until the authorised person otherwise directs.

(2) Where the authorised person does not himself detain the ship, he shall deliver the certificate to the officer detaining the ship.

(3) On detaining the ship, the authorised person or other officer shall deliver to the master of the ship a copy of the certificate.

(4) Section 284 of the Merchant Shipping Act 1995 (enforcement of detention of ships) applies in the case of detention under this section as if it were authorised or ordered under that Act.

[Aviation and Maritime Security Act 1990, s 35 as amended by the Merchant Shipping Act 1995, Sch 13.]

7–6253   36. Inspection of ships and harbour areas.   (1) For the purpose of enabling the Secretary of State to determine whether to give a direction to any person under any of sections 21 to 24 of this Act, or of ascertaining whether any such direction or any enforcement notice is being or has been complied with, an authorised person shall have power, on production (if required) of his credentials, to inspect—

(*a*)   any British ship,

(*b*)   any other ship while in a harbour area,

(*c*)   any part of any harbour area, or

(*d*)   any land outside a harbour area which is occupied for the purposes of a business by a person who—

     (i)   carries on (or appears to the authorised person to be about to carry on) harbour operations in a harbour area for the purposes of that business, or

     (ii)   is permitted (or appears to the authorised person to be about to be permitted) to have access to a restricted zone of a harbour area for the purposes of the activities of that business.

(2) An authorised person inspecting a ship or any part of a harbour area or any land outside a harbour area under subsection (1) above shall have power—

(*a*)   to subject any property found by him on the ship (but not the ship itself or any apparatus or equipment installed in it) or, as the case may be, to subject that part of the harbour area or any property found by him there or on that land, to such tests,

(*b*)   to take such steps—

     (i)   to ascertain what practices or procedures are being followed in relation to security, or

     (ii)   to test the effectiveness of any practice or procedure relating to security, or

(*c*)   to require the owner, charterer, manager or master of the ship, the harbour authority the occupier of the land or any harbour operator to furnish to him such information,

as the authorised person may consider necessary for the purpose for which the inspection is carried out.

(3) Subject to subsection (4) below, an authorised person, for the purpose of exercising any power conferred on him by subsection (1) or (2) above in relation to a ship, in relation to a harbour area or in relation to any land outside a harbour area, shall have power—

(*a*)   for the purpose of inspecting a ship, to go on board it and to take all such steps as are necessary to ensure that it is not moved, or

(*b*)   for the purpose of inspecting any part of a harbour area, to enter any building or works in the harbour area or enter upon any land in the harbour area, or

(*c*)   for the purpose of inspecting any land outside a harbour area, to enter upon the land and to enter any building or works on the land.

(4) The powers conferred by subsection (3) above shall not include power for an authorised person to use force for the purpose of going on board any ship, entering any building or works or entering upon any land.

(5) Any person who—

(*a*)   without reasonable excuse, fails to comply with a requirement imposed on him under subsection (2)(*c*) above, or

(*b*)   in furnishing any information so required, makes a statement which he knows to be false in a material particular, or recklessly makes a statement which is false in a material particular,

commits an offence.

(6) A person guilty of an offence under subsection (5) above is liable[1]—

(*a*)   on summary conviction, to a fine not exceeding the **statutory maximum**;

(*b*)   on conviction on indictment, to a fine or to imprisonment for a term not exceeding **two years** or to **both**.

[Aviation and Maritime Security Act 1990, s 36 as amended by the Merchant Shipping and Maritime Security Act 1997, Sch 4.]

---

   1.   For procedure in respect of an offence which is triable either way, see the Magistrates' Courts Act 1980, ss 17A–21, in PART I: MAGISTRATES' COURTS, PROCEDURE, ante.

7–6253A   36A. Maritime security services approved providers.   *Regulations may provide for the Secretary of State to maintain a list of approved providers of maritime security services.*

Offences relating to security of ships and harbour areas

7–6254   37. False statements relating to baggage, cargo etc.   (1) Subject to subsection (3) below, a person commits an offence if, in answer to a question which—

(*a*)   relates to any baggage, cargo or stores (whether belonging to him or to another) that is or are intended for carriage by sea—

    (i) by a British ship, or

    (ii) by any other ship to or from the United Kingdom, and

  (b) is put to him for purposes to which this Part of this Act applies—

    (i) by any of the persons mentioned in subsection (2) below,

    (ii) by any employee or agent of such a person in his capacity as employee or agent, or

    (iii) by a constable,

he makes a statement which he knows to be false in a material particular, or recklessly makes a statement which is false in a material particular.

  (2) The persons referred to in subsection (1)(b) above are—

  (a) a harbour authority,

  (aa) a harbour operator,

  (b) the owner, charterer or manager of any ship, and

  (c) any person who—

    (i) is permitted to have access to a restricted zone of a harbour area for the purposes of the activities of a business carried on by him, and

    (ii) has control in that restricted zone over the baggage, cargo or stores to which the question relates.

  (3) Subsection (1) above does not apply in relation to any statement made by an authorised person in the exercise of the power conferred by section 36(2)(b) of this Act.

  (4) A person guilty of an offence under subsection (1) above is liable on summary conviction to a fine not exceeding **level 5** on the standard scale.

  (5) In this section—

    "cargo" includes mail;

    "ship" does not include a ship used in naval, customs or police service; and

    "stores" means any goods intended for sale or use in a ship, including fuel and spare parts and other articles of equipment, whether or not for immediate fitting.

[Aviation and Maritime Security Act 1990, s 37 as amended by the Merchant Shipping and Maritime Security Act 1997, Sch 4.]

7–6255 38. False statements in connection with identity documents. (1) Subject to subsection (4) below, a person commits an offence if—

  (a) for the purpose of, or in connection with, an application made by him or another for the issue of an identity document to which this subsection applies, or

  (b) in connection with the continued holding by him or another of any such document which has already been issued,

he makes to any of the persons specified in subsection (3) below, to any employee or agent of such a person or to a constable, a statement which he knows to be false in a material particular, or recklessly makes to any of those persons, to any such employee or agent or to a constable, a statement which is false in a material particular.

  (2) Subsection (1) above applies to any identity document which is to be or has been issued by any of the persons specified in subsection (3) below in accordance with arrangements the maintenance of which is required by a direction given by the Secretary of State under section 24 of this Act.

  (3) The persons referred to in subsection (1) above are—

  (a) a harbour authority,

  (aa) a harbour operator,

  (b) the owner, charterer or manager of any ship, and

  (c) any person who is permitted to have access to a restricted zone of a harbour area for the purposes of the activities of a business carried on by him.

  (4) Subsection (1) above does not apply in relation to any statement made by an authorised person in the exercise of the power conferred by section 36(2)(b) of this Act.

  (5) A person guilty of an offence under subsection (1) above is liable on summary conviction to a fine not exceeding **level 5** on the standard scale.

[Aviation and Maritime Security Act 1990, s 38 as amended by the Merchant Shipping and Maritime Security Act 1997, Sch 4.]

7–6256 39. Unauthorised presence in restricted zone. (1) A person shall not—

  (a) go, with or without a vehicle or vessel, onto or into any part of a restricted zone of a harbour area except with the permission of the competent authority, or a person acting on behalf of that authority and in accordance with any conditions subject to which that permission is for the time being granted, or

  (b) remain in any part of such a restricted zone after being requested to leave by the competent authority, or a person acting on behalf of that authority.

  (2) *Power to extend provisions to Isle of Man, Channel Islands and any colony by Order in Council.*

(2A) A constable or any person acting on behalf of the competent authority may use such force as is reasonable in the circumstances to remove from a restricted zone a person remaining in it in contravention of subsection (1)(*b*) above.

(2B) For the purposes of this section the competent authority in relation to a restricted zone is—

(*a*) if the zone was designated on the application of a harbour authority, that authority; and

(*b*) if the zone was designated on the application of a harbour operator, that operator.

(3) A person who contravenes subsection (1) above without lawful authority or reasonable excuse is guilty of an offence and liable on summary conviction to a fine not exceeding **level 5** on the standard scale.

[Aviation and Maritime Security Act 1990, s 39 as amended by the Merchant Shipping and Maritime Security Act 1997, Sch 4.]

7–6257   40. Offences relating to authorised persons.   (1) A person who—

(*a*) intentionally obstructs an authorised person acting in the exercise of a power conferred on him by or under this Part of this Act, or

(*b*) falsely pretends to be an authorised person,

commits an offence.

(2) A person guilty of an offence under subsection (1)(*a*) above is liable[1]—

(*a*) on summary conviction, to a fine not exceeding the **statutory maximum**;

(*b*) on conviction on indictment, to a **fine** or to imprisonment for a term not exceeding **two years** or to **both**.

(3) A person guilty of an offence under subsection (1)(*b*) above is liable on summary conviction to a fine not exceeding **level 5** on the standard scale.

[Aviation and Maritime Security Act 1990, s 40.]

---

1. For procedure in respect of an offence which is triable either way, see the Magistrates' Courts Act 1980, ss 17A–21, in PART I: MAGISTRATES' COURTS, PROCEDURE, ante.

Sea cargo agents

7–6258   41. Sea cargo agents.   (1) The Secretary of State may by regulations made by statutory instrument make provision, for purposes to which this Part of this Act applies, in relation to persons (in this section referred to as "sea cargo agents") who carry on a business of handling cargo which is to be delivered (whether by them or any other person) to the owner, charterer or manager of any ship for carriage by sea from any harbour area.

(2)–(5) *Supplementary provisions as to regulations.*

(6) In this section—

"cargo" includes stores and mail;

"carriage by sea" does not include carriage by any ship used in naval, customs or police service; and

"stores" means any goods intended for sale or use in a ship, including fuel and spare parts and other articles of equipment, whether or not for immediate fitting.

[Aviation and Maritime Security Act 1990, s 41.]

Reporting of certain occurrences

7–6259   42. Duty to report certain occurrences.   (1) For purposes to which this Part of this Act applies, the Secretary of State may by regulations made by statutory instrument require such persons as are specified in the regulations to make a report to him, in such manner and within such period as are so specified, of any occurrence of a description so specified.

(2) Before making any regulations under this section, the Secretary of State shall consult organisations appearing to him to represent persons affected by the proposed regulations.

(3) Regulations under this section may—

(*a*) provide that any person who, in making a report required by the regulations, makes a statement which he knows to be false in a material particular, or recklessly makes a statement which is false in a material particular, is to be guilty of an offence and liable[1]—

(i) on summary conviction, to a fine not exceeding the **statutory maximum**;

(ii) on conviction on indictment, to a fine or to imprisonment for a term not exceeding two years or to both; and

(*b*) provide for persons to be guilty of an offence in such other circumstances as may be specified in the regulations and to be liable on summary conviction to a fine not exceeding **level 5** on the standard scale.

(4) Regulations under this section may require the reporting of occurrences taking place outside the United Kingdom only if those occurrences relate to British ships.

(5) Any statutory instrument containing regulations under this section shall be subject to annulment in pursuance of a resolution of either House of Parliament.
[Aviation and Maritime Security Act 1990, s 42.]

---

1. For procedure in respect of an offence which is triable either way, see the Magistrates' Courts Act 1980, ss 17A–21, in PART I: MAGISTRATES' COURTS, PROCEDURE, ante.

General supplemental provisions

7–6260   **43.** *Compensation in respect of certain measures taken under Part III.*

7–6261   **45. Service of documents.**   (1) This section has effect in relation to any notice, any document containing a direction and any other document authorised or required by any provision of this Part of this Act to be served on or given to any person.

(2) Any such document may be given to or served on any person—

(*a*) by delivering it to him, or
(*b*) by leaving it at his proper address, or
(*c*) by sending it by post to him at that address, or
(*d*) by sending it to him at that address by telex or other similar means which produce a document containing the text of the communication.

(3) Any such document may, in the case of a body corporate, be given to or served on the secretary, clerk or similar officer of that body.

(4) For the purposes of this section and section 7 of the Interpretation Act 1978 (service of documents by post) in its application to this section, the proper address of any person to whom or on whom any document is to be given or served is his usual or last known address or place of business (whether in the United Kingdom or elsewhere), except that in the case of a body corporate or its secretary, clerk, or similar officer it shall be the address of the registered or principal office of that body in the United Kingdom (or, if it has no office in the United Kingdom, of its principal office, wherever it may be).

(5) In the case of a person registered under any of the United Kingdom registration provisions as the owner of any ship so registered, the address for the time being recorded in relation to him in the register in which the ship is registered shall also be treated for the purposes of this section and section 7 of the Interpretation Act 1978 as his proper address.

(6) If the person to or on whom any document mentioned in subsection (1) above is to be given or served has notified the Secretary of State of an address within the United Kingdom, other than an address determined under subsection (4) or (5) above, as the one at which he or someone else on his behalf will accept documents of the same description as that document, that address shall also be treated for the purposes of this section and section 7 of the Interpretation Act 1978 as his proper address.

(7) Any document mentioned in subsection (1) above shall, where there are two or more owners registered under any of the United Kingdom registration provisions, be treated as duly served on each of those owners—

(*a*) in the case of a ship in relation to which a managing owner is for the time being registered under registration regulations, if served on that managing owner, and
(*b*) in the case of any other ship, if served on any one of the registered owners.

(8) Where an enforcement notice is to be served under section 29 of this Act on the owner, charterer or manager of a ship, it shall be treated as duly served on him if it is served on the master of the ship in question, but (except as provided by section 29(3) of this Act) the master shall not be obliged by virtue of this subsection to comply with the notice.

(9) Where any document mentioned in subsection (1) above is to be served (for the purposes of subsection (8) above or otherwise) on the master of a ship, it shall be treated as duly served if it is left on board that ship with the person being or appearing to be in command or charge of the ship.

(10) In this section "the United Kingdom registration provisions" mean Part II of the Merchant Shipping Act 1995, or any Order in Council under section 1 of the Hovercraft Act 1968.
[Aviation and Maritime Security Act 1990, s 45 as amended by the Merchant Shipping Act 1995, Sch 13.]

7–6262   **46. Interpretation of Part III.**   (1) In this Part of this Act, except in so far as the context otherwise requires—

"act of violence" shall be construed in accordance with section 18(2) of this Act,
"article" includes any substance, whether in solid or liquid form or in the form of a gas or vapour,
"authorised person" means a person authorised in writing by the Secretary of State for the purposes of this Part of this Act,
"British ship" means a ship which—

(*a*) is registered in the United Kingdom under Part II of the Merchant Shipping Act 1995 or any Order in Council under section 1 of the Hovercraft Act 1968, or

(b) is not registered under the law of any country and is entitled to be registered in the United Kingdom under Part II of the Merchant Shipping Act 1995,

"constable" includes any person having the powers and privileges of a constable,

"employee", in relation to a body corporate, includes officer,

"enforcement notice" has the meaning given by section 29(1) of this Act,

"explosive" means any article manufactured for the purpose of producing a practical effect by explosion, or intended for that purpose by a person having the article with him,

"firearm" includes an airgun or air pistol,

"harbour" has the same meaning as in the Merchant Shipping Act 1995;

"harbour area" has the meaning given by section 18(3) of this Act,

"harbour authority" means—

(a) a harbour authority within the meaning of the Merchant Shipping Act 1995;

(b) the manager of any hoverport which does not form part of an area mentioned in section 18(13)(a)(i) or (ii) of this Act,

"harbour" operations means—

(a) the marking or lighting of a harbour or any part of it,

(b) the berthing or dry docking of a ship or the towing or moving of a ship into or out of or within the harbour area,

(c) the transportation, handling or warehousing of goods within the harbour area, or

(d) the embarking, disembarking or movement of passengers within the harbour area;

"harbour operator" has the meaning given by section 20(9) of this Act;

"hoverport" has the same meaning as in the Hovercraft Act 1968,

"manager", in relation to a hoverport, means the person by whom the hoverport is managed,

"master" has the same meaning as in the Merchant Shipping Act 1995,

"measures" (without prejudice to the generality of that expression) includes the construction, execution, alteration, demolition or removal of any building or other works (whether on dry land or on the seabed or other land covered by water), and also includes the institution or modification, and the supervision and enforcement, of any practice or procedure,

"naval service" includes military and air force service,

"operating area" has the meaning given by section 20(9) of this Act;

"owner", in relation to a ship registered in the United Kingdom or in any other country, means registered owner,

"property" includes any land, buildings or works, any ship or vehicle and any baggage, cargo or other article of any description, and

"ship" includes hovercraft and every other description of vessel used in navigation.

(2) Any power to give a direction under any provision of this Part of this Act includes power to revoke or vary any such direction by a further direction.

(2A) In this Part of this Act "restricted zones" means an area designated under section 20 of this Act; and references to a restricted zone of a harbour area include references to a restricted zone which is or is part of an operating area.

(3) For the purposes of this Part of this Act a person is permitted to have access to a restricted zone of a harbour area if he is permitted to enter that zone or if arrangements exist for permitting any of his employees or agents to enter that zone.

[Aviation and Maritime Security Act 1990, s 46 as amended by the Merchant Shipping Act 1995, Sch 13 and the Merchant Shipping and Maritime Security Act 1997, Sch 4.]

PART IV[1]

MISCELLANEOUS AND GENERAL

Miscellaneous

7–6263   48. Powers in relation to certain aircraft.   (1) Except as provided by subsection (2) below, this section applies to any aircraft which—

(a) is registered in, or owned by, any State which appears to the Secretary of State to be contravening any international agreement relating to civil aviation to which that State and the United Kingdom are parties—

(i) by prohibiting any one or more aircraft registered in the United Kingdom from flying over its territory, or

(ii) by prohibiting any one or more such aircraft from landing in its territory, or

(b) is being operated under the direction of nationals of such a State.

(2) This section does not apply to any aircraft by reason only of any prohibition which affects only aircraft belonging to or exclusively employed in the service of the Crown.

(3) For the purposes of this section a State which has taken steps to prevent certain aircraft from flying over or landing in its territory is to be taken to prohibit them from doing so.

(4) Subsection (5) below applies where an aircraft to which this section applies—

(a) has landed in the United Kingdom and is situated at an aerodrome,

(b) has landed on any land in the United Kingdom outside an aerodrome, with the consent of the occupier of that land, and is situated on that land, or

(c) has landed in the United Kingdom and is situated on land outside an aerodrome to which it has been moved with the consent of the occupier of that land,

but that subsection does not apply where the aircraft has landed in the United Kingdom in accordance with permission granted by the Secretary of State under any enactment.

(5) Where this subsection applies, the Secretary of State may give a direction, in a case falling within subsection (4)(a) above to the manager of the aerodrome or in a case falling within subsection (4)(b) or (c) above to the occupier of the land, requiring him to take all such steps as may be reasonably practicable to prevent any person, other than a constable, from gaining access to the aircraft unless—

(a) it is necessary for that person to do so for the purpose of preparing the aircraft for a flight out of the United Kingdom (either directly or following an intermediate stop elsewhere in the United Kingdom for non-traffic purposes),

(b) that person is acting—

(i) with the permission of a constable, or

(ii) in the exercise of powers conferred by subsection (7) below or by or under any other enactment, or

(c) that person is a person specified in the direction acting in circumstances so specified.

(6) A direction under subsection (5) above may also prohibit the person to whom it is given from gaining access to the aircraft except in such circumstances as may be specified in the direction.

(7) Where a direction has been given under subsection (5) above, a constable or any other person specified for the purposes of this subsection in the direction—

(a) may, for the purpose of ascertaining whether the direction is being complied with or, if the direction so provides, for the purpose of moving the aircraft as mentioned in paragraph (b) below or causing it to be so moved—

(i) enter any part of the aerodrome or other land concerned (including any building or works in that aerodrome or on that land), and

(ii) go into or onto the aircraft, if need be by force,

(b) may, if the direction so provides, move the aircraft or cause it to be moved—

(i) in a case falling within subsection (4)(a) above, to such other part of the aerodrome concerned as is specified in the direction, for the purpose of preventing any interference with the functioning of the aerodrome, or

(ii) in a case falling within subsection (4)(b) or (c) above, to any aerodrome specified in the direction, for the purpose of facilitating the preparation of the aircraft for a flight out of the United Kingdom,

(c) may require—

(i) the commander of the aircraft, or

(ii) in the absence of the commander, any other person who the person making the requirement has reason to believe has in his possession documents relating to the aircraft,

to produce any such documents, and

(d) may remove and detain any such documents.

(8) Subject to subsection (9) below, a direction under subsection (5) above shall have effect notwithstanding anything contained in any contract (whether a United Kingdom contract or not) or contained in, or having effect by virtue of, any other enactment or rule of law; and accordingly no proceedings (whether civil or criminal) shall lie against any person in any United Kingdom court by reason of anything done or not done by him or on his behalf in compliance with a direction.

(9) The giving of a direction under subsection (5) above does not affect—

(a) any liability to pay airport charges incurred in respect of the aircraft to which the direction relates, or

(b) the exercise of any power arising under section 88 of the Civil Aviation Act 1982 (detention and sale of aircraft for unpaid airport charges).

(10) If a person who has removed and detained any documents under subsection (7)(d) above is satisfied that the aircraft is being prepared for a flight out of the United Kingdom (either directly or following an intermediate stop elsewhere in the United Kingdom for non-traffic purposes), he shall return them to the commander of the aircraft.

(11) A person commits an offence if—

(a) without reasonable excuse, he fails to comply with a direction given to him under subsection (5) above,

(b) he intentionally obstructs a person acting in the exercise of a power conferred by subsection (7) above, or

(c) knowing that a direction under subsection (5) above has effect in relation to an aircraft, he gains access to the aircraft without lawful authority or reasonable excuse and otherwise than in accordance with the direction.

(12) A person guilty of an offence under subsection (11) above is liable[2]—

(a) on summary conviction, to a fine not exceeding the **statutory maximum**;

(b) on conviction on indictment, to a **fine** or to imprisonment for a term not exceeding **two years** or to **both**.

(13) In this section—

"aerodrome" has the same meaning as in the Civil Aviation Act 1982,

"airport charges" has the same meaning as in section 88 of the Civil Aviation Act 1982,

"commander", in relation to an aircraft, has the same meaning as in section 94 of the Civil Aviation Act 1982,

"manager", in relation to an aerodrome, has the same meaning as in the Aviation Security Act 1982,

"reward" has the same meaning as in the Civil Aviation Act 1982,

"stop for non-traffic purposes" means a landing for any purpose other than the taking on board or discharging of passengers carried for reward or of cargo so carried, and

"United Kingdom court" and "United Kingdom contract" have the same meaning as in section 19 of the Aviation Security Act 1982;

and for the purposes of this section a person gains access to an aircraft if, and only if, he goes into or onto the aircraft, carries out any work on the aircraft or delivers anything to the aircraft or to persons on board the aircraft.

[Aviation and Maritime Security Act 1990, s 48.]

---

1. Part IV contains ss 47–54.
2. For procedure in respect of an offence which is triable either way, see the Magistrates' Courts Act 1980, ss 17A–21, in Part I: Magistrates' Courts, Procedure, ante.

General

7–6264　49. Extradition by virtue of Orders in Council under section 2 of Extradition Act 1870.　The offences to which an Order in Council under section 2 of the Extradition Act 1870 can apply shall include—

(a) offences under sections 1, 9, 10, 11, 12 and 13 of this Act, and

(b) attempts to commit such offences.

[Aviation and Maritime Security Act 1990, s 49.]

7–6265　50. Offences by bodies corporate.　(1) Where an offence under this Act (including any provision of Part III as applied by regulations made under section 41 of this Act) or under regulations made under section 42 of this Act has been committed by a body corporate and is proved to have been committed with the consent or connivance of, or to be attributable to any neglect on the part of, any director, manager, secretary or other similar officer of the body corporate, or any person who was purporting to act in any such capacity, he as well as the body corporate shall be guilty of that offence and shall be liable to be proceeded against and punished accordingly.

(2) Where the affairs of a body corporate are managed by its members, subsection (1) above shall apply in relation to the acts and defaults of a member in connection with his functions of management as if he were a director of the body corporate.

[Aviation and Maritime Security Act 1990, s 50.]

7–6266　51. *Extension of Act outside the United Kingdom.*

7–6267　54. *Short title, commencement and extent.*

Merchant Shipping Act 1995[1]
(1995 c 21)

Part I[2]
British ships

7–6300　1. British ships and United Kingdom ships.　(1) A ship is a British ship if—

(a) the ship is registered in the United Kingdom under Part II; or

(b) the ship is, as a Government ship, registered in the United Kingdom in pursuance of an Order in Council under section 308; or

(c) the ship is registered under the law of a relevant British possession; or

(d) the ship is a small ship other than a fishing vessel and—

    (i) is not registered under Part II, but

    (ii) is wholly owned by qualified owners, and

    (iii) is not registered under the law of a country outside the United Kingdom.

  (2) For the purposes of subsection (1)(*d*) above—

"qualified owners" means persons of such description qualified to own British ships as is prescribed
    by regulations made by the Secretary of State for the purposes of that paragraph; and

"small ship" means a ship less than 24 metres in length ("length" having the same meaning as in
    the tonnage regulations).

  (3) A ship is a "United Kingdom ship" for the purposes of this Act (except section 85 and 144(3))
if the ship is registered in the United Kingdom under Part II (and in Part V "United Kingdom fishing
vessel" has a corresponding meaning).

[Merchant Shipping Act 1995, s 1.]

---

  1. The Act is amended by the Marine Safety Act 2003 (c 16).

  2. Part I contains ss 1–7.

7–6301 2. British flag. (1) The flag which every British ship is entitled to fly is the red ensign
(without any defacement or modification) and, subject to subsections (2) and (3) below, no other
colours.

  (2) Subsection (1) above does not apply to Government ships.

  (3) The following are also proper national colours, that is to say—

  (*a*) any colours allowed to be worn in pursuance of a warrant from Her Majesty or from the
    Secretary of State;

  (*b*) in the case of British ships registered in a relevant British possession, any colours consisting of
    the red ensign defaced or modified whose adoption for ships registered in that possession is
    authorised or confirmed by Her Majesty by Order in Council[1].

  (4) Any Order under subsection (3)(*b*) above shall be laid before Parliament after being made.

[Merchant Shipping Act 1995, s 2.]

---

  1. The Merchant Shipping (Gibraltar Colours) Order 1996, SI 1996/281 and the Merchant Shipping (Falkland Islands
Colours) Order 1998, SI 1998/3147 have been made.

7–6302 3. Offences relating to British character of ship. (1) If the master or owner of a ship
which is not a British ship does anything, or permits anything to be done, for the purpose of causing
the ship to appear to be a British ship then, except as provided by subsections (2) and (3) below, the
ship shall be liable to forfeiture and the master, the owner and any charterer shall each be guilty of an
offence.

  (2) No liability arises under subsection (1) above where the assumption of British nationality has
been made for the purpose of escaping capture by an enemy or by a foreign ship of war in the exercise
of some belligerent right.

  (3) Where the registration of any ship has terminated by virtue of any provision of registration
regulations, any marks prescribed by registration regulations displayed on the ship within the period
of 14 days beginning with the date of termination of that registration shall be disregarded for the
purposes of subsection (1) above.

  (4) If the master or owner of a British ship does anything, or permits anything to be done, for the
purpose of concealing the nationality of the ship, the ship shall be liable to forfeiture and the master,
the owner and any charterer of the ship shall each be guilty of an offence.

  (5) Without prejudice to the generality of subsections (1) and (4) above, those subsections apply
in particular to acts or deliberate omissions as respects—

  (*a*) the flying of a national flag;

  (*b*) the carrying or production of certificates of registration or other documents relating to the
    nationality of the ship; and

  (*c*) the display of marks required by the law of any country.

  (6) Any person guilty of an offence under this section shall be liable[1]—

  (*a*) on summary conviction, to a fine not exceeding £50,000;

  (*b*) on conviction on indictment, to imprisonment for a term not exceeding **two years** or a **fine**,
    or **both**.

  (7) This section applies to things done outside, as well as to things done within, the United
Kingdom.

[Merchant Shipping Act 1995, s 3.]

---

  1. For procedure in respect of an offence triable either way, see the Magistrates' Courts Act 1980, ss 17A–21, in PART
I: MAGISTRATES' COURTS, PROCEDURE, *ante*.

7–6303 4. Penalty for carrying improper colours. (1) If any of the following colours, namely—

   (*a*) any distinctive national colours except—

      (i) the red ensign,

      (ii) the Union flag (commonly known as the Union Jack) with a white border, or

      (iii) any colours authorised or confirmed under section 2(3)(*b*); or

   (*b*) any colours usually worn by Her Majesty's ships or resembling those of Her Majesty, or

   (*c*) the pendant usually carried by Her Majesty's ships or any pendant resembling that pendant,

are hoisted on board any British ship without warrant from Her Majesty or from the Secretary of State, the master of the ship, or the owner of the ship (if on board), and every other person hoisting them shall be guilty of an offence.

   (2) A person guilty of an offence under subsection (1) above shall be liable[1]—

   (*a*) on summary conviction, to a fine not exceeding the **statutory maximum**;

   (*b*) on conviction on indictment, to a **fine**

   (3) If any colours are hoisted on board a ship in contravention of subsection (1) above, any of the following, namely—

   (*a*) any commissioned naval or military officer,

   (*b*) any officer of customs and excise, and

   (*c*) any British consular officer,

may board the ship and seize and take away the colours.

   (4) Any colours seized under subsection (3) above shall be forfeited to Her Majesty.

   (5) In this section "colours" includes any pendant.

[Merchant Shipping Act 1995, s 4.]

---

   1. For procedure in respect of an offence triable either way, see the Magistrates' Courts Act 1980, ss 17A–21, in PART I: MAGISTRATES' COURTS, PROCEDURE, ante.

7–6304 5. Duty to show British flag. (1) Subject to subsection (2) below, a British ship, other than a fishing vessel, shall hoist the red ensign or other proper national colours—

   (*a*) on a signal being made to the ship by one of Her Majesty's ships (including any ship under the command of a commissioned naval officer); and

   (*b*) on entering or leaving any foreign port; and

   (*c*) in the case of ships of 50 or more tons gross tonnage, on entering or leaving any British port.

   (2) Subsection (1)(*c*) above does not apply to a small ship (as defined in section 1(2)) registered under Part II.

[Merchant Shipping Act 1995, s 5.]

7–6305 6. Duty to declare national character of ship. (1) An officer of customs and excise shall not grant a clearance or transire for any ship until the master of such ship has declared to the officer the name of the nation to which he claims that the ship belongs, and that officer shall thereupon enter that name on the clearance or transire.

   (2) If a ship attempts to proceed to sea without such clearance or transire, the ship may be detained until the declaration is made.

[Merchant Shipping Act 1995, s 6.]

7–6306 7. Proceedings on forfeiture of a ship. *Power, in proceedings before the High Court, to adjudge a ship and her equipment to be forfeited to Her Majesty.*

PART II[1]

REGISTRATION

General

7–6311 14. Offences relating to a ship's British connection. (1) Any person who in relation to any matter relevant to the British connection of a ship—

   (*a*) makes to the registrar a statement which he knows to be false or recklessly makes a statement which is false; or

   (*b*) furnishes to the registrar information which is false,

shall be guilty of an offence.

   (2) If at any time there occurs, in relation to a registered ship, any change affecting the British connection of the ship the owner of the ship shall, as soon as practicable after the change occurs, notify the registrar of that change; and if he fails to do so he shall be guilty of an offence.

   (3) Any person who intentionally alters, suppresses, conceals or destroys a document which contains information relating to the British connection of a ship and which he has been required to produce to the registrar in pursuance of registration regulations shall be guilty of an offence.

   (4) A person guilty of an offence under this section shall be liable[2]—

   (*a*) on summary conviction, to a fine not exceeding the **statutory maximum**;

(b) on conviction on indictment, to imprisonment for a term not exceeding **two years** or a **fine**, or **both**.

(5) This section applies to things done outside, as well as to things done within, the United Kingdom.
[Merchant Shipping Act 1995, s 14.]

---

1. Part II contains ss 8–23.
2. For procedure in respect of an offence triable either way, see the Magistrates' Courts Act 1980, ss 17A–21, in PART I: MAGISTRATES' COURTS, PROCEDURE, ante.

7–6312 15. Supplementary provisions as respects fishing vessels.   (1) Subject to subsection (2) below, if a fishing vessel which—

(a) is either—

(i)   entitled to be registered, or,
(ii) wholly owned by persons qualified to be owners of British ships, but

(b) is registered neither under this Act in the part of the register relating to fishing vessels nor under the law of any country outside the United Kingdom,

fishes for profit the vessel shall be liable to forfeiture and the skipper, the owner and the charterer of the vessel shall each be guilty of an offence.

(2) Subsection (1) above does not apply to fishing vessels of such classes or descriptions or in such circumstances as may be specified in regulations made by the Secretary of State.

(3) If the skipper or owner of a fishing vessel which is not registered in the United Kingdom does anything, or permits anything to be done, for the purpose of causing the vessel to appear to be a vessel registered in the United Kingdom, then, subject to subsection (4) below, the vessel shall be liable to forfeiture and the skipper, the owner and any charterer of the vessel shall each be guilty of an offence.

(4) Where the registration of a fishing vessel has terminated by virtue of any provision of registration regulations, any marks prescribed by registration regulations displayed on the fishing vessel within the period of 14 days beginning with the date of termination of that registration shall be disregarded for the purposes of subsection (3) above.

(5) Any person guilty of an offence under this section shall be liable—

(a) on summary conviction, to a fine not exceeding **£50,000;**
(b) on conviction on indictment, to imprisonment for a term not exceeding **two years** or a **fine**, or both[1].

(6) Proceedings for an offence under this section shall not be instituted—

(a) in England and Wales, except by or with the consent of the Attorney General or the Secretary of State; or
(b) *Northern Ireland.*

(7) In subsection (6) above "the Minister"—

(a) *repealed;*
(b) *Northern Ireland.*

(8) This section applies to things done outside, as well as to things done within, the United Kingdom.

(9) Sections 8 and 9 of the Sea Fisheries Act 1968 (general powers of British sea-fishery officers and powers of sea-fishery officers to enforce conventions) shall apply in relation to any provision of this section or of registration regulations in their application to fishing vessels or fishing vessels of any class or description as they apply in relation to any order mentioned in section 8 of that Act and in relation to any convention mentioned in section 9 of that Act respectively; and sections 10 to 12 and 14 of that Act (offences and supplemental proceedings to legal proceedings) shall apply accordingly.
[Merchant Shipping Act 1995, s 15, as amended by SI 2002/794.]

Supplemental

7–6313 19. Tonnage regulations.   (1) The tonnage of any ship to be registered under this Part shall be ascertained in accordance with regulations[1] made by the Secretary of State ("tonnage regulations").

(2) Tonnage regulations[1]—

(a) may make different provisions for different descriptions of ships or for the same description of ships in different circumstances;
(b) may make any regulation dependent on compliance with such conditions, to be evidenced in such manner, as may be specified in the regulations;
(c) may prohibit or restrict the carriage of goods or stores in spaces not included in the registered tonnage and may provide for making the master and the owner each liable to a fine not exceeding level 3 on the standard scale where such a prohibition or restriction is contravened.

(3)–(5) Further provisions as to regulations.

(6) Regulations requiring the delivery up of any certificate may make a failure to comply with the requirement an offence punishable on summary conviction with a fine not exceeding **level 3** on the standard scale.

[Merchant Shipping Act 1995, s 19.]

---

1. See the Merchant Shipping (Tonnage) Regulations 1997, SI 1997/1510 amended by SI 1998/1916 and SI 1999/3206 and the Merchant Shipping (Fishing Vessels-Tonnage) Regulations 1988, SI 1988/1909 amended by 1998/1916, SI 1999/3206 and SI 2005/2114.

7–6314   23. Interpretation.   (1) In this Part[1]—

"British connection" and "declaration of British connection" have the meaning given in section 9(9);

"the private law provisions for registered ships" has the meaning given in section 16;

"the register" means the register of British ships maintained for the United Kingdom under section 8 and "registered" (except with reference to the law of another country) is to be construed accordingly; and

"the registrar" means the Registrar General of Shipping and Seamen in his capacity as registrar or, as respects functions of his being discharged by another authority or person, that authority or person.

(2) Where, for the purposes of any enactment the question arises whether a ship is owned by persons qualified to own British ships, the question shall be determined by reference to registration regulations made under section 9(2)(*a*).

[Merchant Shipping Act 1995, s 23.]

---

1. Ie ss 8–23.

PART III[1]

MASTERS AND SEAMEN

Application of Part

7–6319   24. Application of this Part.   (1) With the exceptions specified in subsection (2) below, this Part applies only to ships which are sea-going ships[2] and masters and seamen employed in sea-going ships[2].

(2) Those exceptions are sections 43, 46 to 52, 54, 55, 58, 61 to 68 and 69.

(3) This Part, in its application to fishing vessels and persons serving in them, has effect subject to the modifications made by Part V and in particular sections 110 and 112 apply to the exclusion of sections 30 and 31.

[Merchant Shipping Act 1995, s 24.]

---

1. Part III contains ss 24–84.

2. It was held under the repealed Merchant Shipping Act 1854 that a ship engaged in carrying cargo on rivers and their estuaries, although it was capable of going to sea, was not a "sea-going ship" within s 109 of that Act (*Salt Union Ltd v Wood* [1893] 1 QB 370, 57 JP 201).

Engagement and discharge of crews

7–6320   25. Crew agreements.   (1) Except as provided under subsection (5) below, an agreement in writing shall be made between each person employed as a seaman in a United Kingdom ship and the persons employing him and shall be signed both by him and by or on behalf of them.

(2) The agreements made under this section with the several persons employed in a ship shall be contained in one document (in this Part referred to as a crew agreement) except that in such cases as the Secretary of State may approve—

(*a*) the agreements to be made under this section with the persons employed in a ship may be contained in more than one crew agreement; and

(*b*) one crew agreement may relate to more than one ship.

(3) The provisions and form of a crew agreement must be of a kind approved by the Secretary of State; and different provisions and forms may be so approved for different circumstances.

(4) Subject to the following provisions of this section, a crew agreement shall be carried in the ship to which it relates whenever the ship goes to sea.

(5) The Secretary of State may make regulations[1] providing for exemptions from the requirements of this section—

(*a*) with respect to such descriptions of ship as may be specified in the regulations or with respect to voyages in such areas or such description of voyages as may be so specified; or

(*b*) with respect to such descriptions of seamen as may be specified in the regulations;

and the Secretary of State may grant other exemptions from those requirements (whether with respect to particular seamen or with respect to seamen employed by a specified person or in a specified ship or in the ships of a specified person) in cases where the Secretary of State is satisfied that the seamen to be employed otherwise than under a crew agreement will be adequately protected.

(6) Where, but for an exemption granted by the Secretary of State, a crew agreement would be required to be carried in a ship or a crew agreement carried in the ship would be required to contain an agreement with a person employed in a ship, the ship shall carry such document evidencing the exemption as the Secretary of State may direct.

(7) Regulations under this section may enable ships required under this section to carry a crew agreement to comply with the requirement by carrying a copy thereof, certified in such manner as may be provided by the regulations.

(8) If a ship goes to sea or attempts to go to sea in contravention of the requirements of this section the master or the person employing the crew shall be liable on summary conviction to a fine not exceeding **level 4** on the standard scale and the ship, if in the United Kingdom, may be detained.
[Merchant Shipping Act 1995, s 25.]

---

1. The Merchant Shipping (Crew Agreements, Lists of Crew and Discharge of Seamen) Regulations 1991, SI 1991/2144 as amended, and Merchant Shipping (Crew Agreements, Lists of Crew and Discharge of Seamen) (Fishing Vessels) Regulations 1972, SI 1972/919 as amended have been made. For amendment of penalties prescribed by the above Regulations, see SI 1979/1519.

7–6321   26. Regulations relating to crew agreements. (1) The Secretary of State may make regulations[1]—

(*a*) requiring such notice as may be specified in the regulations to be given to a superintendent or proper officer, except in such circumstances as may be so specified, before a crew agreement is made or an agreement with any person is added to those contained in a crew agreement;

(*b*) providing for the delivery to a superintendent or proper officer or the Registrar General of Shipping and Seamen of crew agreements and agreements added to those contained in a crew agreement and of copies of crew agreements and of agreements so added;

(*c*) requiring the posting in ships of copies of or extracts from crew agreements;

(*d*) requiring copies of or extracts from crew agreements to be supplied to members of the crew demanding them and requiring copies of or extracts from documents referred to in crew agreements to be made available, in such circumstances as may be specified in the regulations, for inspection by members of the crew; and

(*e*) requiring any documents carried in a ship in pursuance of section 25 to be produced on demand to an officer of customs and excise.

(2) Regulations under this section may make a contravention of any provision thereof an offence punishable, on summary conviction, with a fine not exceeding **level 3** on the standard scale or such less amount as may be specified in the regulations.
[Merchant Shipping Act 1995, s 26.]

---

1. See note to s 25, ante.

7–6322   27. Discharge of seamen. (1) The Secretary may make regulations[1] prescribing the procedure to be followed in connection with the discharge of seamen from United Kingdom ships.

(2) Without prejudice to the generality of subsection (1) above, regulations under this section may make provision—

(*a*) requiring notice of such a discharge to be given at such time as may be specified in the regulations to the superintendent or proper officer at a place specified in or determined under the regulations;

(*b*) requiring such a discharge to be recorded, whether by entries in the crew agreement and discharge book or otherwise, and requiring copies of any such entry to be given to a superintendent or proper officer or the Registrar General of Shipping and Seamen.

(3) Regulations under this section may provide that in such cases as may be specified in the regulations, or except in such cases as may be specified in or determined under the regulations, a seaman shall not be discharged outside the United Kingdom from a United Kingdom ship without the consent of the proper officer.

(4) Regulations under this section may make a contravention of any provision thereof an offence punishable, on summary conviction, with a fine not exceeding level 3 on the standard scale or such less amount as may be specified in the regulations.
[Merchant Shipping Act 1995, s 27.]

---

1. See note to s 25, ante.

Wages etc

7–6323   30. Payment of seamen's wages. (1) Where a seaman employed under a crew agreement relating to a United Kingdom ship leaves the ship on being discharged from it, then, except as provided by or under this Part or any other enactment, the wages due to the seaman under the agreement shall either—

(a) be paid to him in full at the time when he so leaves the ship (in this section and in section 31 referred to as the time of discharge), or

(b) be paid to him in accordance with subsections (4) and (5) below.

(2) If the amount shown in the account delivered to a seaman under section 31(1) as being the amount payable to him under subsection (1)(a) above is replaced by an increased amount shown in a further account delivered to him under section 31(3), the balance shall be paid to him within seven days of the time of discharge; and if the amount so shown in the account delivered to him under section 31(1) exceeds £50 and it is not practicable to pay the whole of it at the time of discharge, not less than £50 nor less than one-quarter of the amount so shown shall be paid to him at that time.

(3) If any amount which, under subsection (1)(a) or (2) above is payable to a seaman is not paid at the time at which it is so payable the seaman shall be entitled to wages at the rate last payable under the crew agreement for every day on which it remains unpaid during the period of 56 days following the time of discharge; and if any such amount or any amount payable by virtue of this subsection remains unpaid after the end of that period it shall carry interest at the rate of 20 per cent per annum.

(4) Where the crew agreement referred to in subsection (1) above provides for the seaman's basic wages to be payable up-to-date at specified intervals not exceeding one month, and for any additional amounts of wages to be payable within the pay cycle following that to which they relate, any amount of wages due to the seaman under the agreement shall (subject to subsection (5) below) be paid to him not later than the date on which the next payment of his basic wages following the time of discharge would have fallen due if his employment under the agreement had continued.

(5) If it is not practicable, in the case of any amount due to the seaman by way of wages additional to his basic wages, to pay that amount by the date mentioned in subsection (4) above, that amount shall be paid to him not later than what would have been the last day of the pay cycle immediately following that date if his employment under the crew agreement had continued.

(6) If any amount which, under subsection (4) or (5) above, is payable to a seaman is not paid at the time at which it is so payable, it shall carry interest at the rate of 20 per cent per annum.

(7) The provisions of subsection (3) or (6) above shall not apply if the failure to pay was due to—

(a) a mistake,

(b) a reasonable dispute as to liability,

(c) the act or default of the seaman, or

(d) any other cause, not being the wrongful act or default of the persons liable to pay his wages or of their servants or agents;

and so much of those provisions as relates to interest on the amount due shall not apply if a court in proceedings for its recovery so directs.

(8) Where a seaman is employed under a crew agreement relating to more than one ship the preceding provisions of this section shall have effect, in relation to wages due to him under the agreement, as if for any reference to the time of discharge there were substituted a reference to the termination of his employment under the crew agreement.

(9) Where a seaman, in pursuance of section 29, is discharged from a ship outside the United Kingdom but returns to the United Kingdom under arrangements made by the persons who employed him, the preceding provisions of this section shall have effect, in relation to the wages due to him under a crew agreement relating to the ship, as if for the references in subsections (1) to (4) above to the time of discharge there were substituted references to the time of his return to the United Kingdom, and subsection (8) above were omitted.

(10) For the purposes of this section any amount of wages shall, if not paid to him in cash, be taken to have been paid to a seaman—

(a) on the date when a cheque, or a money or postal order issued by the Post Office company (within the meaning of Part IV of the Postal Services Act 2000), for that amount was despatched by the recorded delivery service to the seaman's last known address, or

(b) on the date when any account kept by the seaman with a bank or other institution was credited with that amount.

[Merchant Shipping Act 1995, s 30, as amended by SI 2001/1149.]

7–6324   31. Account of seaman's wages.   (1) Subject to subsections (4) and (5) below and to regulations[1] made under section 32 or 73, the master of every United Kingdom ship shall deliver to every seaman employed in the ship under a crew agreement an account of the wages[2] due to him under that crew agreement and of the deductions subject to which the wages are payable.

(2) The account shall indicate that the amounts stated therein are subject to any later adjustment that may be found necessary and shall be delivered not later than 24 hours before the time of discharge or, if the seaman is discharged without notice or at less than 24 hours' notice, at the time of discharge.

(3) If the amounts stated in the account require adjustment the persons who employed the seaman shall deliver to him a further account stating the adjusted amounts; and that account shall be delivered not later than the time at which the balance of wages is payable to the seaman.

(4) Where section 30(4) or (5) applies to the payment of any amount of wages due to a seaman under a crew agreement—

(a) the persons who employed the seaman shall deliver to him an account of the wages payable to him under that subsection and of the deductions subject to which the wages are payable; and

(b) any such account shall be so delivered at the time when the wages are paid to him; and

(c) subsections (1) to (3) above shall not apply;

and section 30(10) shall apply for the purposes of this subsection as it applies for the purposes of that section.

(5) Where a seaman is employed under a crew agreement relating to more than one ship any account which under the preceding provisions of this section would be required to be delivered to him by the master shall instead be delivered to him by the persons employing him and shall be so delivered on or before the termination of his employment under the crew agreement.

(6) If a person fails without reasonable excuse to comply with the preceding provisions of this section he shall be liable, on summary conviction, to a fine not exceeding **level 2** on the standard scale.

[Merchant Shipping Act 1995, s 31.]

---

1. The Merchant Shipping (Seaman's Wages and Accounts) Regulations 1972, SI 1972/1700 amended by SI 1978/1757, SI 1985/340, SI 1994/791 and SI 1999/3360 have been made. See also the Merchant Shipping (Seamen's Wages and Accounts) (Fishing Vessels) Regulations 1972, SI 1972/1701 amended by SI 1988/2064 and SI 1999/3360 and extended to unregistered fishing vessels by the Merchant Shipping (Unregistered Fishing Vessels) Regulations 1991, SI 1991/1365.

2. It was held under previous corresponding provisions that to be recoverable as wages all sums payable to seamen must appear in the agreement (*Thompson v Nelson Ltd* [1913] 2 KB 523).

7–6325 **32.** *Regulations relating to wages and accounts.*

7–6326 **34. Restriction on assignment of and charge upon wages.** (1) As respects the wages due or accruing to a seaman employed in a United Kingdom ship—

(a) the wages shall not be subject to attachment;

(b) *Scotland*;

(c) an assignment thereof before they have accrued shall not bind the seaman and the payment of the wages to the seaman shall be valid notwithstanding any previous assignment or charge; and

(d) a power of attorney or authority for the receipt of the wages shall not be irrevocable.

(2) Nothing in this section shall affect the provisions of this Part with respect to allotment notes.

(3) Nothing in this section applies to any disposition relating to the application of wages—

(a) in the payment of contributions to a fund declared by regulations made by the Secretary of State to be a fund to which this section applies; or

(b) in the payment of contributions in respect of the membership of a body declared by regulations made by the Secretary of State to be a body to which this section applies;

or to anything done or to be done for giving effect to such a disposition.

(4) Subsection (1)(a) above is subject, in relation to England and Wales, to the Attachment of Earnings Act 1971.

(5) Subsection (1)(a) above is subject to any provision made by or under—

(a) section 31 or 33 of the Child Support Act 1991 (deductions from earnings orders); or

(b) Article 31 or 32 of the Child Support (Northern Ireland) Order 1991 (deductions from earnings orders).

[Merchant Shipping Act 1995, s 34.]

7–6327 **40. Claims against seaman's wages for maintenance, etc of dependants.** (1) Where, during a seaman's employment in a ship, expenses are incurred by a responsible authority for the benefit of any dependant of his and the expenses are of a kind specified in regulations under this section[1] and such further conditions, if any, as may be so specified are satisfied, the authority may by notice in writing complying with the regulations require the persons employing the seaman—

(a) to retain for a period specified in the notice such proportion of his net wages as may be so specified; and

(b) to give to the responsible authority as soon as may be notice in writing of the seaman's discharge from the ship;

and the persons employing the seaman shall comply with the notice (subject to subsection (3) below) and give notice in writing of its contents to the seaman.

(2) For the purposes of this section—

(a) the following persons, and no others, shall be taken to be a seaman's dependants, that is to say, his spouse and any person under the age of 19 whom he is liable, for the purposes of any enactment in any part of the United Kingdom, to maintain or in respect of whom he is liable under any such enactment to make contributions to a local authority; and (*b*) expenses incurred for the benefit of any person include (in addition to any payments made to him or on his behalf) expenses incurred for providing him with accommodation or care or for exercising supervision over him;

but no expenses shall be specified in regulations under this section unless they are such that a magistrates' court has power under any enactment in force in any part of the United Kingdom to order the making of payments in respect thereof.

(3) Not more than the following proportion of a seaman's net wages shall be retained under subsection (1) above (whether in pursuance of one or more notices)—

(*a*) one-half if the notice or notices relate to one dependant only;
(*b*) two-thirds if the notice or notices relate to two or more dependants.

(4) Where a responsible authority have served a notice under this section on the persons employing a seaman a magistrates' court may, on the application of the authority, make an order for the payment to the authority of such sum, not exceeding the proportion of the seaman's wages which those persons were required by virtue of this section to retain, as the court, having regard to the expenses incurred by the authority and the seaman's means, thinks fit.

(5) Any sums paid out of a seaman's wages in pursuance of an order under this section shall be deemed to be paid to him in respect of his wages; and the service, on the persons who employed the seaman, of such an order or of an order dismissing an application for such an order shall terminate the period for which they were required to retain the wages.

(6) An application for an order under this section for the payment of any sum by the persons who employed a seaman shall be deemed, for the purposes of any proceedings, to be an application for an order against the seaman; but the order, when served on those persons, shall have effect as an order against them and may be enforced accordingly.

(7) Parts I and III of the Maintenance Orders Act 1950 shall have effect as if an order under this section were included among those referred to in sections 4(1) and (2), 9(1) and (2), and 12(1) and (2) of that Act; and any sum payable by any persons under an order made under this section in any part of the United Kingdom may, in any other part of the United Kingdom, be recovered from them as a debt due to the authority on whose application the order was made.

(8) Any notice or order under this section may be served by registered post or recorded delivery service.

(9) *Power to make regulations.*

(10) In this section "responsibility authority" means the Secretary of State, the Department of Health and Social Services for Northern Ireland, a Health and Social Services Board acting on behalf of that Department, or (except in Northern Ireland) any local authority.

(11) *Northern Ireland.*

(12) *Scotland, Northern Ireland.*

[Merchant Shipping Act 1995, s 40.]

---

1. See the Merchant Shipping (Maintenance of Seamen's Dependants) Regulations 1972 (SI 1972/1635, amended by SI 1972/1875 and SI 1988/479). The expenses specified include (i) benefit under the Supplementary Benefits Act 1976 (see now the Social Security Contributions and Benefits Act 1992), (ii) accommodation under Part III of the National Assistance Act 1948 (see now the Children Act 1989, s 20), and (iii) expenses of a local authority in respect of a child under 16 received into care under s 1 of the Children Act 1948 or committed to care under the Children and Young Persons Act 1969 (see now the Children Act 1989, Pts III and IV in PART VI: FAMILY LAW, ante).

Safety, health and welfare

7–6328   **43. Crew accommodation.**   (1) The Secretary of State may make regulations[1] with respect to the crew accommodation to be provided in United Kingdom ships.

(2) Without prejudice to the generality of subsection (1) above, regulations made under this section may, in particular—

(*a*) prescribe the minimum space per man which must be provided by way of sleeping accommodation for seamen and the maximum number of persons by whom a specified part of such sleeping accommodation may be used;
(*b*) regulate the position in the ship in which the crew accommodation or any part thereof may be located and the standards to be observed in the construction, equipment and furnishing of any such accommodation;
(*c*) require the submission to a surveyor of ships of plans and specifications of any works proposed to be carried out for the purpose of the provision or alteration of any such accommodation and authorise the surveyor to inspect any such works; and
(*d*) provide for the maintenance and repair of any such accommodation and prohibit or restrict the use of any such accommodation for purposes other than those for which it is designed.

(3) Regulations under this section may make different provision with respect to different descriptions of ship or with respect to ships which were registered in the United Kingdom at different dates or the construction of which was begun at different dates and with respect to crew accommodation provided for seamen of different descriptions.

(4) Regulations under this section may exempt ships of any description from any requirements of

the regulations and the Secretary of State may grant other exemptions from any such requirement with respect to any ship.

(5) Regulations under this section may require the master of a ship or any officer authorised by him for the purpose to carry out such inspections of the crew accommodation as may be prescribed by the regulations.

(6) If the provisions of any regulations under this section are contravened in the case of a ship the owner or master shall be liable, on summary conviction, to a fine not exceeding **level 5** on the standard scale and the ship, if in the United Kingdom, may be detained.

(7) In this section "crew accommodation" includes sleeping rooms, mess rooms, sanitary accommodation, hospital accommodation, recreation accommodation, store rooms and catering accommodation provided for the use of seamen but does not include any accommodation which is also used by or provided for the use of passengers.

[Merchant Shipping Act 1995, s 43.]

---

1. The Merchant Shipping (Crew Accommodation) Regulations 1997, SI 1997/1508 amended by SI 2005/2114 and the Merchant Shipping (Crew Accommodation) (Fishing Vessels) Regulations 1975, SI 1975/2220, amended by SI 1998/929 and SI 2002/2201, have been made.

7–6329 44. Complaints about provisions or water. (1) If three or more seamen employed in a United Kingdom ship consider that the provisions or water provided for the seamen employed in that ship are not in accordance with safety regulations containing requirements as to the provisions and water to be provided on ships (whether because of bad quality, unfitness for use or deficiency in quantity) they may complain to the master, who shall investigate the complaint.

(2) If the seamen are dissatisfied with the action taken by the master as a result of his investigation or by his failure to take any action they may state their dissatisfaction to him and may claim to complain to a superintendent or proper officer; and thereupon the master shall make adequate arrangements to enable the seamen to do so as soon as the service of the ship permits.

(3) the superintendent or proper officer to whom a complaint has been made under this section shall investigate the complaint and may examine the provisions or water or cause them to be examined.

(4) If the master fails without reasonable excuse to comply with the provisions of subsection (2) above he shall be liable on summary conviction to a fine not exceeding **level 3** on the standard scale and if he has been notified in writing by the person making an examination under subsection (3) above that any provisions or water are found to be unfit for use or not of the quality required by the regulations, then—

(a) if they are not replaced within a reasonable time the master or owner shall be liable on summary conviction to a fine not exceeding **level 4** on the standard scale unless he proves that the failure to replace them was not due to his neglect or default; or

(b) if the master, without reasonable excuse, permits them to be used he shall be liable on summary conviction to a fine not exceeding **level 4** on the standard scale.

[Merchant Shipping Act 1995, s 44.]

Manning, qualifications, training and uniform

7–6330 46. Application of sections 47 to 51. (1) Sections 47 to 51 apply to every United Kingdom ship and also to any ship registered under the law of a country outside the United Kingdom which carries passengers—

(a) between places in the United Kingdom or between the United Kingdom and the Isle of Man or any of the Channel Islands; or

(b) on a voyage which begins and ends at the same place in the United Kingdom and on which the ship calls at no place outside the United Kingdom.

[Merchant Shipping Act 1995, s 46.]

7–6331 47. Manning. (1)–(4) *Power of Secretary of State to make regulations*[1] *with regard to the manning of ships.*

(5) If a person makes a statement which he knows to be false or recklessly makes a statement which is false in a material particular for the purpose of obtaining for himself or another person a certificate or other document which may be issued under this section he shall be liable on summary conviction to a fine not exceeding **level 5** on the standard scale.

[Merchant Shipping Act 1995, s 47.]

---

1. The Merchant Shipping (Certification of Ships' Cooks) Regulations 1981, SI 1981/1076; the Fishing Vessels (Certification of Deck Officers and Engineer Officers and Engineering Officers) Regulations 1984, SI 1984/1115 amended by SI 1995/1428 and SI 1998/1013; the Merchant Shipping (Local Passenger Vessels) (Masters' Licences and Hours, Manning and Training) Regulations 1993, SI 1993/1213 amended by SI 2002/2125 and SI 2003/3049; the Merchant Shipping (Ships' Doctors) Regulations 1995, SI 1995/1803; the Merchant Shipping (Officer Nationality) Regulations 1995, SI 1995/1427; and the Merchant Shipping (Training and Certificate) Regulations 1997, SI 1997/348 amended by SI 1997/1911, SI 2000/836 and SI 2006/89 have been made.

7–6332   48. Power to exempt from manning requirements. (1) The Secretary of State may exempt any ship or description of ship from any requirements of regulations made under section 47.

(2) An exemption given under this section may be confined to a particular period or to one or more particular voyages.

[Merchant Shipping Act 1995, s 48.]

7–6333   49. Prohibition of going to sea undermanned. (1) Subject to section 48, if a ship to which this section applies goes to sea or attempts to go to sea without carrying such officers and other seamen as it is required to carry under section 47, the owner or master shall be liable[1]—

(*a*) on summary conviction, to a fine not exceeding the **statutory maximum;**

(*b*) on conviction on indictment, to a **fine**;

and the ship, if in the United Kingdom, may be detained.

(2) This section shall, in its application to ships which are not sea-going ships, have effect as if for the words "goes to sea or attempts to go to sea" there were substituted the words "goes on a voyage or excursion or attempts to do so" and the words "if in the United Kingdom" were omitted.

[Merchant Shipping Act 1995, s 49.]

---

1. For procedure in respect of an offence triable either way, see the Magistrates' Courts Act 1980, ss 17A–21, in PART I: MAGISTRATES' COURTS, PROCEDURE, ante.

7–6334   50. Production of certificates and other documents of qualification. (1) Any person serving or engaged to serve in any ship to which this section applies and holding any certificate or other document which is evidence that he is qualified for the purposes of section 47 shall on demand produce it to any superintendent, surveyor of ships or proper officer and (if he is not himself the master) to the master of the ship.

(2) If, without reasonable excuse, a person fails to comply with subsection (1) above he shall be liable on summary conviction to a fine not exceeding **level 3** on the standard scale.

[Merchant Shipping Act 1995, s 50.]

7–6335   51. Crew's knowledge of English. (1) Where in the opinion of a superintendent or proper officer the crew of a ship to which this section applies consists of or includes persons who may not understand orders given to them in the course of their duty because of their insufficient knowledge of English and the absence of adequate arrangements for transmitting the orders in a language of which they have sufficient knowledge, then—

(*a*) if the superintendent or proper officer has informed the master of that opinion, the ship shall not go to sea; and

(*b*) if the ship is in the United Kingdom, it may be detained.

(2) If a ship goes to sea or attempts to go to sea in contravention of this section the owner or master shall be liable on summary conviction to a fine not exceeding **level 5** on the standard scale.

[Merchant Shipping Act 1995, s 51.]

7–6336   52. Unqualified persons going to sea as qualified officers or seamen. (1) If a person goes to sea as a qualified officer or seaman of any description without being such a qualified officer or seaman he shall be liable—

(*a*) on summary conviction, to a fine not exceeding the statutory maximum,

(*b*) on conviction on indictment, to a fine.

(2) In this section "qualified" means qualified for the purposes of section 47.

[Merchant Shipping Act 1995, s 52.]

7–6337   54. Special certificates of competence. (1) The Secretary of State may issue and record documents certifying the attainment of any standard of competence relating to ships or their operation, notwithstanding that the standard is not among those prescribed or specified under section 47(1)(*b*); and may, in relation thereto, make regulations for purposes corresponding to those mentioned in section 47(4).

(2) If a person makes a statement which he knows to be false or recklessly makes a statement which is false in a material particular for the purpose of obtaining for himself or another person a document which may be issued under this section he shall be liable on summary conviction to a fine not exceeding **level 5** on the standard scale.

[Merchant Shipping Act 1995, s 54.]

7–6338   55. Young persons. (1) Subject to subsection (1A), a person under school-leaving age shall not be employed in any United Kingdom ship except as permitted by regulations[1] under this section.

(1A) A person under 16 years of age shall not be employed in any sea-going United Kingdom ship.

(2)–(3) *Further provisions relating to regulations.*

(4) If any person is employed in a ship in contravention of this section or if any condition subject to which a person may be employed under regulations made for the purposes of this section is not complied with, the owner or master shall be liable on summary conviction to a fine not exceeding **level 3** on the standard scale.

(5) For the purposes of this section a person employed in a ship shall be deemed to be over school-leaving age if he has, and under school-leaving age if he has not, attained the age which is the upper limit of compulsory school age (in Scotland school age) under the enactments relating to education in the part of the United Kingdom in which he entered into the agreement under which he is so employed or, if he entered into that agreement outside the United Kingdom or is employed otherwise than under an agreement, under the enactments relating to education in England and Wales; and if he is treated for the purposes of those enactments as not having attained that age he shall be so treated also for the purposes of this section.

[Merchant Shipping Act 1995, s 55 as amended by SI 2002/2125.]

---

1. The Merchant Shipping and Fishing Vessels (Health and Safety at Work) (Employment of Young Persons) Regulations 1998, SI 1998/2411 amended by SI 2002/2125 have been made.

7–6339 57. Uniform. (1) Subject to subsection (3), if any person, not being entitled to wear the merchant navy uniform[1], wears that uniform or any part thereof, or any dress having the appearance or bearing any of the distinctive marks of that uniform, he shall be guilty of an offence.

(2) A person guilty of an offence under subsection (1) above shall be liable, on summary conviction,—

(a) except in a case falling within paragraph (b) below, to a fine not exceeding **level 1** on the standard scale;

(b) if he wears it in such a manner or under such circumstances as to be likely to bring contempt on the uniform, to a fine not exceeding **level 1** on the standard scale or to imprisonment for a term not exceeding **one month**.

(3) Subsection (1) above shall not prevent any person from wearing any uniform or dress in the course or for the purposes of a stage play or representation, or a music-hall or circus performance if the uniform is not worn in such a manner or under such circumstances as to bring it into contempt.

(4) If any person entitled to wear the merchant navy uniform when aboard a ship in port or on shore appears dressed partly in uniform and partly not in uniform under such circumstances as to be likely to bring contempt on the uniform, or, being entitled to wear the uniform appropriate to a particular rank or position, wears the uniform appropriate to some higher rank or position, he shall be liable on summary conviction to a fine not exceeding **level 1** on the standard scale.

[Merchant Shipping Act 1995, s 57.]

---

1. This uniform is prescribed by Order in Council dated 13 December 1921.

Offences by seamen, etc

7–6340 58. Conduct endangering ships, structures or individuals. (1) This section applies—

(a) to the master of, or any seaman employed in, a United Kingdom ship; and

(b) to the master of, or any seaman employed in, a ship which—

(i) is registered under the law of any country outside the United Kingdom; and

(ii) is in a port in the United Kingdom or within United Kingdom waters while proceeding to or from any such port.

(2) If a person to whom this section applies, while on board his ship or in its immediate vicinity—

(a) does any act which causes or is likely to cause—

(i) the loss or destruction of or serious damage to his ship or its machinery, navigational equipment or safety equipment, or

(ii) the loss or destruction of or serious damage to any other ship or any structure, or

(iii) the death of or serious injury to any person, or

(b) omits to do anything required—

(i) to preserve his ship or its machinery, navigational equipment or safety equipment from being lost, destroyed or seriously damaged, or

(ii) to preserve any person on board his ship from death or serous injury, or

(iii) to prevent his ship from causing the loss or destruction of or serious damage to any other ship or any structure, or the death of or serious injury to any person not on board his ship,

and either of the conditions specified in subsection (3) below is satisfied with respect to that act or omission, he shall (subject to subsections (6) and (7) below) be guilty of an offence.

(3) Those conditions are—

(a) that the act or omission was deliberate or amounted to a breach or neglect of duty[1];

(b) that the master or seaman in question was under the influence of drink or a drug at the time of the act or omission.

(4) If a person to whom this section applies—

(a) discharges any of his duties, or performs any other function in relation to the operation of his ship or its machinery or equipment, in such a manner as to cause, or to be likely to cause, any such loss, destruction, death or injury as is mentioned in subsection (2)(a) above, or

(b) fails to discharge any of his duties, or to perform any such function, properly to such an extent as to cause, or to be likely to cause, any of those things,

he shall (subject to subsection (6) and (7) below) be guilty of an offence.

(5) A person guilty of an offence under this section shall be liable[2]—

(a) on summary conviction, to a fine not exceeding the **statutory maximum**;

(b) on conviction on indictment, to imprisonment for a term not exceeding **two years** or a **fine**, or **both**.

(6) In proceedings for an offence under this section it shall be a defence to prove—

(a) in the case of an offence under subsection (2) above where the act or omission alleged against the accused constituted a breach or neglect of duty, that the accused took all reasonable steps to discharge that duty;

(b) in the case of an offence under subsection (2) above, that at the time of the act or omission alleged against the accused he was under the influence of a drug taken by him for medical purposes and either that he took it on medical advice and complied with any directions given as part of that advice or that he had no reason to believe that the drug might have the influence it had;

(c) in the case of an offence under subsection (4) above that the accused took all reasonable precautions and exercised all due diligence to avoid committing the offence; or

(d) in the case of an offence under either of those subsections—

(i) that he could have avoided committing the offence only by disobeying a lawful command, or

(ii) that in all the circumstances the loss, destruction, damage, death or injury in question, or (as the case may be) the likelihood of its being caused, either could not reasonably have been foreseen by the accused or could not reasonably have been avoided by him.

(7) In the application of this section to any person falling within subsection (1)(b) above, subsections (2) and (4) above shall have effect as if subsection (2)(a)(i) and (b)(i) above were omitted; and no proceedings for any offence under this section shall be instituted against any such person—

(a) in England and Wales, except by or with the consent of the Secretary of State or the Director of Public Prosecutions;

(b) *Northern Ireland.*

(8) In this section—

"breach or neglect of duty", except in relation to a master, includes any disobedience to a lawful command;

"duty"—

(a) in relation to a master or seaman, means any duty falling to be discharged by him in his capacity as such; and

(b) in relation to a master, includes his duty with respect to the good management of his ship and his duty with respect to the safety of operation of his ship, its machinery and equipment; and

"structure" means any fixed or movable structure (of whatever description) other than a ship.
[Merchant Shipping Act 1995, s 58.]

---

1. Failure of the master of a ship to display a forward anchor light has been held to be an omission amounting to a neglect of duty (*Hodge v Higgins* [1980] 2 Lloyd's Rep 589).
2. For procedure in respect of an offence triable either way, see the Magistrates' Courts Act 1980, ss 17A–22 in PART I: MAGISTRATES' COURTS: PROCEDURE, *ante*.

7–6341　59. Concerted disobedience and neglect of duty[1]. (1) If a seaman employed in a United Kingdom ship combines with other seamen employed in that ship—

(a) to disobey lawful commands which are required to be obeyed at a time while the ship is at sea;

(b) to neglect any duty which is required to be discharged at such a time; or

(c) to impede, at such a time, the progress of a voyage or the navigation of the ship,

he shall be liable[2]—

(i) on summary conviction, to a fine not exceeding the **statutory maximum**;

(ii) on conviction on indictment, to imprisonment for a term not exceeding **two years** or a **fine** or **both**.

(2) For the purposes of this section a ship shall be treated as being at sea at any time when it is not securely moored in a safe berth.
[Merchant Shipping Act 1995, s 59.]

---

1. In exceptional conditions, eg exposure to the risk of capture, seamen may be entitled to decline to voyage (*Robson v Sykes* [1938] 2 All ER 612). Similar cases are reviewed at 108 LJ (1958), p 403.
2. For procedure in respect of an offence triable either way, see the Magistrates' Courts Act 1980, ss 17A–21, in PART I: MAGISTRATES' COURTS, PROCEDURE, ante.

Disqualification of seamen and inquiries

7–6342 66. Failure to deliver cancelled or suspended certificate. If a person fails to deliver a certificate as required under section 61, 62 or 63[1] he shall be liable on summary conviction to a fine not exceeding **level 3** on the standard scale.
[Merchant Shipping Act 1995, s 66.]

---

1. Section 61 empowers the Secretary of State to require an officer to deliver to them any certificate issued to the officer in pursuance of s 47, ante, if it appears that he is unfit to discharge his duties or has been seriously negligent in the discharge of his duties. Section 62 requires a person whose certificate under s 47 or s 4 has been suspended or cancelled to deliver the certificate to the Board of Trade not later than the date specified (the Merchant Shipping (Disqualification of Holder of Seaman's Certificates) Regulations 1997, SI 1997/346 have been made). Where such a certificate is cancelled or suspended following an inquiry into fitness or conduct of a seaman other than an officer, the person concerned is required by s 63 to deliver the certificate forthwith to the persons holding the inquiry or to the Secretary of State. The conduct of inquiries is provided for by the Merchant Shipping (Section 63 Inquiries) Rules 1997, SI 1997/347. If after holding a formal investigation into a shipping casualty under s 268, a wreck commissioner cancels or suspends any certificate issued to an officer under s 47, ante, the officer shall deliver the certificate forthwith to the wreck commissioner or to the Secretary of State.

7–6343 68. Power to summon witness to inquiry into fitness or conduct of officer or other seaman. (1) The persons holding an inquiry under section 61 or 63 may—

(a) by summons require any person to attend, at a time and place stated in the summons, to give evidence or to produce any documents in his custody or under this control which relate to any matter in question at the inquiry; and

(b) take evidence on oath (and for that purpose administer oaths) or, instead of administering an oath, require the person examined to make a solemn affirmation.

(2) In on the failure of a person to attend such an inquiry in answer to a summons under this section—

(a) the persons holding the inquiry are satisfied by evidence on oath—

(i) that the person in question is likely to be able to give material evidence or produce any document which relates to any matter in question at the inquiry.

(ii) that he has been duly served with the summons, and

(iii) that a reasonable sum has been paid or tendered to him for costs and expenses, and

(b) it appears to them that there is no just excuse for the failure,

they may issue a warrant to arrest him and bring him before the inquiry at a time and place specified in the warrant.

(3) If any person attending or brought before such an inquiry refuses without just excuse to be sworn or give evidence, or to produce any document, the persons holding the inquiry may—

(a) commit him to custody until the end of such period not exceeding one month as may be specified in the warrant or until he gives evidence or produces the document (whichever occurs first), or

(b) impose on him a fine not exceeding £1,000,

or both.

(4) A fine imposed under subsection (3)(b) above shall be treated for the purposes of its collection, enforcement and remission as having been imposed by the magistrates' court for the area in which the inquiry in question was held, and the persons holding the inquiry shall, as soon as practicable after imposing the fine, give particulars of it to the proper officer of that court.

(4A) In subsection (4) above "proper officer" means—

(a) in relation to a magistrates' court in England and Wales, the designated officer for the court, and

(b) in relation to a magistrates' court in Northern Ireland, the clerk of the court.

(5) This section does not apply to Scotland.
[Merchant Shipping Act 1995, s 68, as amended by the Access to Justice Act 1999, Sch 13.]

Relief and repatriation and relief costs

7–6344 73. Relief and return of seamen etc left behind and shipwrecked. (1) Where—

(a) a person employed as a seaman in a United Kingdom ship is left behind in any country outside the United Kingdom or is taken to such a country on being shipwrecked; or

(b) a person who became so employed under an agreement entered into outside the United Kingdom is left behind in the United Kingdom or is taken to the United Kingdom on being shipwrecked;

the person who last employed him as a seaman shall make such provision for his return and for his relief and maintenance until his return and such other provisions as may be required by regulations[1] made by the Secretary of State.

(2) The provisions to be so made may include the repayment of expenses incurred in bringing a shipwrecked seaman ashore and maintaining him until he is brought ashore and the payment of the expenses of the burial or cremation of a seaman who dies before he can be returned.

(3)–(5) *Regulations.*

(6) Regulations under this section may make a contravention of any provision thereof an offence punishable on summary conviction with a fine not exceeding **level 3** on the standard scale or such less amount as may be specified in the regulations.

(7) This section applies to a person left behind on being discharged in pursuance of section 29, whether or not at a time he is left behind the ship is still a United Kingdom ship.

(8) This section applies to the master of a ship as it applies to a seaman and sections 74 and 75 shall have effect accordingly.

[Merchant Shipping Act 1995, s 73, as amended by the British Overseas Territories Act 2002, s 2(3).]

---

1. The Merchant Shipping (Repatriation) Regulations 1979, SI 1979/97, amended by SI 1979/1519, have been made.

Documentation

7–6345 77. Official log books. (1) Except as provided by regulations under this section an official log book in a form approved by the Secretary of State shall be kept in every United Kingdom ship.

(2) The Secretary of State may make regulations[1] prescribing the particulars to be entered in official log books, the persons by whom such entries are to be made, signed or witnessed, and the procedure to be followed in the making of such entries and in their amendment or cancellation.

(3) The regulations may require the production or delivery of official log books to such persons, in such circumstances and within such times as may be specified therein.

(4) Regulations under this section may exempt ships of any description from any requirements thereof, either generally or in such circumstances as may be specified in the regulations.

(5) Regulations under this section may make a contravention of any provision thereof an offence punishable on summary conviction with a fine not exceeding **level 2** on the standard scale or not exceeding a lesser amount.

(6) If a person intentionally destroys or mutilates or renders illegible any entry in an official log book he shall be liable on summary conviction to a fine not exceeding **level 4** on the standard scale.

[Merchant Shipping Act 1995, s 77.]

---

1. The Merchant Shipping (Official Log Books) Regulations 1981, SI 1981/569, amended by SI 1983/1801, SI 1985/1828, SI 1991/2145, SI 1997/1511 and SI 2002/1473, the Merchant Shipping (Official Log Books) (Fishing Vessels) Regulations 1981, SI 1981/570, amended by SI 1983/1801, SI 1997/1511 and SI 2002/1473 have been made. See also the Merchant Shipping (Repatriation) Regulations 1979, SI 1979/97, amended by SI 1979/1519.

7–6346 78. Lists of crew. (1) Except as provided by regulations made under this section, the master of every United Kingdom ship shall make and maintain a list of the crew containing such particulars as may be required by the regulations.

(2)–(4) *Regulations.*

(5) Regulations under this section may make a contravention of any provision thereof an offence punishable on summary conviction with a fine not exceeding **level 2** on the standard scale or not exceeding a lesser amount.

[Merchant Shipping Act 1995, s 78.]

7–6347 79. British seamen's cards. (1) The Secretary of State may make regulations[1] providing—

(a) for the issue to British seamen of cards (in this section referred to as "British seamen's cards") in such form and containing such particulars with respect to the holders thereof and such other particulars (if any) as may be prescribed by the regulations, and for requiring British seamen to apply for such cards;

(b) for requiring the holders of British seamen's cards to produce them to such persons and in such circumstances as may be prescribed by the regulations;

(c) for the surrender of British seamen's cards in such circumstances as may be prescribed by the regulations;

(*d*) for any incidental or supplementary matters for which the Secretary of State thinks it expedient for the purposes of the regulations to provide;

and any provision of the regulations having effect by virtue of paragraph[1] above may be so framed as to apply to all British seamen or any description of them and as to have effect subject to any exemptions for which provision may be made by the regulations.

(2) Regulations under this section may make a contravention of any provision thereof an offence punishable on summary conviction with a fine not exceeding **level 2** on the standard scale or not exceeding a lesser amount.

(3) In this section "British seamen" means persons who are not aliens within the meaning of the British Nationality Act 1981 and are employed, or ordinarily employed, as masters or seamen.

(4) If a person makes a statement which he knows to be false or recklessly makes a statement which is false in a material particular for the purpose of obtaining for himself or another person a British seaman's card he shall be liable on summary conviction to a fine not exceeding level 4 on the standard scale.

[Merchant Shipping Act 1995, s 79.]

---

1. See the Merchant Shipping (Seaman's Documents) Regulations 1987, SI 1987/408, as amended by SI 1995/1900.

7–6348   80. Discharge books.   (1)–(2) *Secretary of State may make regulations[1] in respect of the issue, production and surrender of discharge books and for cessation of entitlement to such a book.*

(3) Regulations under this section may make a contravention of any provision thereof an offence punishable on summary conviction with a fine not exceeding **level 2** on the standard scale or not exceeding a lesser amount.

(4) A person who, in the United Kingdom or elsewhere—

(*a*) obtains employment as a seaman on board a United Kingdom ship and does so when he is disentitled to a discharge book by virtue of regulations made under subsection (2)(*a*) above; or

(*b*) employs as such a seaman a person who he knows or has reason to suspect is disentitled as aforesaid,

shall be liable[2] on summary conviction to a fine not exceeding the **statutory maximum** or, on conviction on indictment, to imprisonment for a term not exceeding **two years** or a **fine** or **both**.

[Merchant Shipping Act 1995, s 80 as amended by the Merchant Shipping and Maritime Security Act 1997, s 18.]

---

1. The Merchant Shipping (Seamen's Documents) Regulations 1987, SI 1987/408 amended by SI 1999/3281, have been made.

2. For procedure in respect of an offence triable either way, see the Magistrates' Courts Act 1980, ss 17A–21, in PART I: MAGISTRATES' COURTS, PROCEDURE, ante.

7–6349   81. Handing over of documents by master.   (1) If a person ceases to be the master of a United Kingdom ship during a voyage of the ship he shall deliver to his successor the documents relating to the ship or its crew which are in his custody.

(2) If, without reasonable excuse, the master of such a ship fails to comply with subsection (1) above, he shall be liable on summary conviction to a fine not exceeding **level 3** on the standard scale.

[Merchant Shipping Act 1995, s 81.]

Merchant Navy Reserve

7–6350   82. Maintenance of Merchant Navy Reserve.   (1) The Secretary of State may maintain the body of persons known as the Merchant Navy Reserve whose members may, in such circumstances and for such periods as the Secretary of State may determine, be required by him to serve in ships belonging to or employed in the service of Her Majesty.

(2) The Merchant Navy Reserve shall consist of such number of persons as the Secretary of State may determine who voluntarily undertake to become members of the Reserve and are accepted as members of it.

(3) The Secretary of State may determine the procedure by which, and the conditions under which, persons may become, or (subject to any regulations made by him under this section) may cease to be, members of the Merchant Navy Reserve.

(4) The Secretary of State may make regulations[1] with respect to the calling into and discharge from, service of members of the Merchant Navy Reserve and with respect to other matters relating to the service of members of the Reserve.

(5) Any such regulations may, in particular, make provision—

(*a*) for call-out notices to be served on members of the Reserve;
(*b*) for the requirements to be complied with by persons on whom such notices have been served;
(*c*) as to the uniform and equipment with which members of the Reserve are to be provided;
(*d*) for regulating the conduct and discipline of members of the Reserve who have entered into service, and for securing their attendance at their places of duty;

(*e*) for the imposition of fines, or the forfeiture of pay or other amounts, for misconduct or breaches of discipline or for contravention of provisions of the regulations.

(6) Without prejudice to the operation of subsection (5)(*e*) above, regulations under this section may provide that a contravention of the regulations shall be an offence punishable on summary conviction by a fine not exceeding **level 3** on the standard scale or such lower amount as is prescribed by the regulations.

(7) Regulations under this section may make different provision for different circumstances.
[Merchant Shipping Act 1995, s 82.]

---

1. The Merchant Shipping (Merchant Navy Reserve) Regulations 1989, SI 1989/662 were made and a Merchant Navy Reserve formed. However, the regulations were revoked and the Reserve disbanded as from 15 December 2003 by the Merchant Shipping (Merchant Navy Reserve) (Revocation) Regulations 2003, SI 2003/2861.

Interpretation

7–6351   84. Interpretation.   (1) In this Part[1]—

"crew agreement" has the meaning given to it by section 25(2);
"relief and maintenance" includes the provision of surgical or medical treatment and such dental and optical treatment (including the repair or replacement of any appliance) as cannot be postponed without impairing efficiency; and
"ship's boat" includes a life-raft.

(2) References in this Part to going to sea include references to going to sea from any country outside the United Kingdom.

(3) For the purposes of this Part a seaman is discharged from a ship when his employment in that ship is terminated.

(4) For the purposes of this Part a seaman discharged from a ship in any country and left there shall be deemed to be left behind in that country notwithstanding that the ship also remains there.

(5) Any power conferred by this Part to provide for or grant an exemption includes power to provide for or grant the exemptions subject to conditions.
[Merchant Shipping Act 1995, s 84.]

---

1. Ie ss 24–84.

PART IV[1]
SAFETY

Safety and health on ships

7–6356   85–86. Safety and health on ships (summarised)[2].   *Power of the Secretary of State[3] to make safety regulations[4] for the purpose of securing the safety of ships and sea planes and persons on them and for protecting the health of persons on ships.*
[Merchant Shipping Act 1995, ss 85, 86—summarised.]

---

1. Part IV contains ss 85–108.
2. The Hovercraft (Application of Enactments) Order 1989, SI 1989/1350, applies the safety regulations made under ss 21, 22 to hovercraft.
Regulations have been made both under s 85 and s 2 of the European Communities Act 1972. These are listed at the beginning of this title. Regulations made under the following repealed provisions continue to have effect until superseded by regulations made under s 85 of the 1995 Act (Merchant Shipping Act 1995, Sch 14):

    Merchant Shipping Act 1894, s 427;
    Merchant Shipping (Safety Convention) Act 1949, ss 3 and 21;
    Merchant Shipping Act 1964, s 2;
    Anchors and Chain Cables Act 1967, s 1;
    Merchant Shipping (Safety Conventions) Act 1977, s 2;
3. The Merchant Shipping (Delegation of Type Approval) Regulations 1996, SI 1996/147 provide that certain bodies specified in a Merchant Shipping Notice may give type approval of safety equipment and arrangements for ships in connection with the provisions of the Safety of Life at Sea Convention 1974, the International Regulations for Preventing Collisions at Sea 1972 or the International Convention for the Prevention of Pollution from Ships 1973.
4. Regulations as to the manning and certification of crew (although made partly under these sections) are also listed under s 47. Regulations have been made under s 21 of the Merchant Shipping Act 1979 (now s 85 of the 1995 Act) dealing with the following:
    Cargo Ship Safety Equipment Survey, SI 1981/573 amended by SI 1985/211 and SI 1995/1210;
    Fishing Vessels (Certification of Deck Officers and Engineers), SI 1984/1115;
    Closing of Openings in Hulls and in Watertight Bulkheads, SI 1987/1298;
    Fishing Vessels (Life Saving Appliances), SI 1988/38 amended by SI 1998/927, SI 1999/2998 and 3210, SI 2001/9 and SI 2002/2201;
    Weighing of Goods Vehicles and Other Cargo, SI 1988/1275 amended by SI 1989/270;
    Fishing Vessels (Medical Stores), SI 1988/1547;
    Guarding of Machinery and Safety of Electrical Equipment, SI 1988/1636 amended by SI 1988/2274 and SI 1993/1072;

Means of Access, SI 1988/1637 amended by SI 1988/2274, SI 1993/1072 and SI 2005/2114;
Entry into Dangerous Spaces, SI 1988/1638 amended by SI 1988/2274, SI 1993/1072 and SI 2005/2114;
Hatches and Lifting Plant, SI 1988/1639 amended by SI 1988/2274 and SI 1993/1072;
Safe Movement On Board Ship, SI 1988/1641 amended by SI 1988/2274, SI 1993/1072, SI 2001/3444 and SI 2005/2114;
Emergency Equipment Lockers for Ro/Ro Passenger Ships, SI 1988/2272;
Safety at Work Regulations (Non-UK Ships), SI 1988/2274;
Provisions and Water, SI 1989/102 amended by SI 1993/1072;
Fishing Vessels (Safety Training) Regulations 1989, SI 1989/126 amended by SI 2004/2169;
Weighing of Goods Vehicles and Other Cargo (Application to Non-UK Ships) Regulations 1989, SI 1989/568;
Emergency Information for Passengers Regulations 1990, SI 1990/660;
Radio and Radio Navigational Equipment Survey Regulations 1991, SI 1991/1341 amended by SI 1995/1210;
Accident Reporting and Investigation Regulations 1994, SI 1994/2013;
Gas Carriers Regulations 1994, SI 1994/2464 amended by SI 2004/929;
Survey and Certification Regulations 1995, SI 1995/1210 amended by SI 1996/2418 and 3188, SI 2000/1334 and 2687, SI 2002/1473, SI 2003/771, SI 2004/302, 1107 and 2883 and SI 2005/2114;
Medical Stores Regulations 1995, SI 1995/1802 amended by SI 1996/2821;
Reporting Requirements for Ships Carrying Dangerous or Polluting Goods Regulations 1995, SI 1995/2498 amended by SI 1999/2121, SI 2001/1638, SI 2004/2110 and SI 2005/1092;
Port State Control Regulations 1995, SI 1995/3128 amended by SI 1998/1433, SI 2001/2349 and SI 2003/1636;

The following regulations have been made under s 85 of the Merchant Shipping Act 1995:
Distress Signals and Prevention of Collisions Regulations 1996, SI 1996/75 amended by 2004/302;
Ship Inspection And Survey Organizations Regulations 1996, SI 1996/2908 amended by SI 2004/1266;
Dangerous or Noxious Liquid Substances in Bulk Regulations 1996, SI 1996/3010 amended by SI 1998/1153 and SI 2004/930;
Training and Certification Regulations 1997, SI 1997/348 amended by SI 1997/1911, SI 2004/302; and SI 2006/89
Safe Manning, Hours of Work and Watchkeeping Regulations 1997, SI 1997/1320 amended by SI 1997/1911, SI 2000/484 and SI 2002/2125;
Cargo Ship Construction Regulations 1997, SI 1997/1509 amended by SI 1999/643, SI 2004/302 and SI 2005/2114;
Dangerous Goods and Marine Pollutants Regulations 1997, SI 1997/2367 amended by SI 2004/2110;
Health and Safety at Work Regulations 1997, SI 1997/2962 amended by SI 1998/2411 and SI 2001/54;
Load Line Regulations 1998, SI 1998/241, amended by SI 2000/1335 and SI 2005/2114;
Fire Protection: Small Ships Regulations 1998, SI 1998/1011 amended by SI 1999/992, SI 2000/2687, SI 2003/2951, SI 2004/302 and SI 2005/2114;
Fire Protection: Large Ships Regulations 1998, SI 1998/1012 amended by SI 1999/992, SI 2000/2687, SI 2001/1638, SI 2003/2950 and 2951, SI 2004/302 and SI 2005/2114;
International Safety Management (ISM Code) Regulations 1998, SI 1998/1561 amended by SI 2001/3209;
Small Workboats and Pilot Boats Regulations 1998, SI 1998/1609;
Distress Messages Regulations 1998, SI 1998/1691 amended by SI 2002/1473;
Code of Safe Working Practices for Merchant Seamen Regulations, SI 1998/1838;
Radio Installation Regulations 1998, SI 1998/2070 amended by SI 2000/2687, SI 2001/1638, SI 2004/302 and SI 2005/2114;
Passenger Ship Construction: Ships of Classes I, II and II (a) Regulations 1998, SI 1998/2514 amended by SI 2000/2687, SI 2001/1638, SI 2002/1650 and SI 2004/302;
Passenger Ship Construction: Ships of Classes III to VI (A) Regulations 1998, SI 1998/2515 amended by SI 2000/2687, SI 2001/1638, SI 2002/1650 and SI 2004/302 and 2844;
Vessels in Commercial Use for Sport or Pleasure Regulations 1998, SI 1998/2771 amended by SI 2000/482, SI 2002/1473 and SI 2005/2114;
Carriage of Cargoes Regulations 1999, SI 1999/336;
Additional Safety Measures for Bulk Carriers Regulations 1999, SI 1999/1644 amended by SI 2004/2151
Counting and Registration of Persons on Board Passenger Ships Regulations 1999, SI 1999/1869;
Marine Equipment Regulations 1999, SI 1999/1957 amended by SI 2001/1638 and SI 2004/302 and 1266;
Personal Protective Equipment Regulations 1999, SI 1999/2205;
Life-Saving Appliances for Ships Other Than Ships of Classes III to VI (A) Regulations 1999, SI 1999/2721 amended by SI 2000/2558 and 2687, SI 2001/2642, SI 2002/1473, SI 2004/2259 and SI 2005/2114;
Musters, Training and Decision Support System Regulations 1999, SI 1999/2722 amended by SI 2004/302 and SI 2005/2114;
Life-Saving Appliances for Passenger Ships of Classes III to VI (A) Regulations 1999, SI 1999/2723 amended by SI 2000/2687;
Radio (Fishing Vessels) Regulations 1999, SI 1999/3210 and SI 2002/2201;
EPIRB Registration Regulations 2000, SI 2000/1850;
Passenger Ships on Domestic Voyages Regulations 2000, SI 2000/2687 amended by SI 2002/1473, SI 2003/771 and SI 2004/302, 1107 and 2883;
Carriage of Packaged Irradiated Nuclear Fuel etc) (INF Code) Regulations 2000, SI 2000/3216;
Fishing Vessels (Code of Practice for the Safety of Small Fishing Vessels) Regulations 2001, SI 2001/9 amended by SI 2002/2201;
Domestic Passenger Ships (Safety Management Code) Regulations 2001, SI 2001/3209 amended by SI 2004/302;
Safety of Navigation Regulations 2002, SI 2002/1473 amended by SI 2004/302 and 2110 and SI 2005/2114;
Medical Examination Regulations 2002, SI 2002/2055 amended by SI 2003/3049, SI 2004/1713 and SI 2005/1919 and 2114;
Hours of Work Regulations 2002, SI 2002/2125 amended by SI 2003/3049, SI 2004/1469 and 1713 and SI 2005/2114;
Fishing Vessels (Safety of 15–24 Metre Vessels) Regulations 2002, SI 2002/2201;
Safe Loading and Unloading of Bulk Carriers Regulations 2003, SI 2003/2002;
Fire Protection Regulations 2003, SI 2003/2950 and SI 2005/2114;
Working Time: Inland Waterways Regulations 2003, SI 2003/3049;
High Speed Craft Regulations 2004, SI 2004/302 amended by SI 2004/2883 and SI 2005/2114;
Fishing Vessels (Working Time: Sea-Fishermen) Regulations 2004, SI 2004/1713;
Vessel Traffic (Monitoring and Reporting Requirements) Regulations 2004, SI 2004/2110 amended by SI 2005/1092;
Ro-Ro Passenger Ships (Stability) Regulations 2004, SI 2004/2884;
Bridge Visibility (Small Passenger Ships) Regulations 2005, SI 2005/2286.

7–6357   88. Safety of submersible and supporting apparatus.   (1) This section applies to any submersible or supporting apparatus—

   (*a*)   operated within United Kingdom waters, or
   (*b*)   launched or operated from, or comprising, a United Kingdom ship.

  (2)   The Secretary of State may make regulations[1]—

   (*a*)   for the safety of submersible and supporting apparatus;
   (*b*)   for the prevention of accidents in or near submersible or supporting apparatus;
   (*c*)   for the safety, health and welfare of persons on or in submersible and supporting apparatus;
   (*d*)   for prohibiting or otherwise restricting the operation of any submersible apparatus except in accordance with the conditions of a licence granted under the regulations; and
   (*e*)   for the registration of submersible apparatus.

  (3)   Schedule 2 shall have effect for supplementing the provisions of this section.
  (4)   In this section—

"apparatus" includes any vessel, vehicle or hovercraft, any structure, any diving plant or equipment and any other form of equipment;

"specified" means specified in regulations made by the Secretary of State for the purposes of this section;

"submersible apparatus" means any apparatus used, or designed for use, in supporting human life on or under the bed of any waters or elsewhere under the surface of any waters; and

"supporting apparatus" means any apparatus used, or designed for use, in connection with the operation of any submersible apparatus.

[Merchant Shipping Act 1995, s 88.]

---

1. See the Merchant Shipping (Registration of Submersible Craft) Regulations 1976, SI 1976/940 as amended by SI 1979/1519 and SI 1987/306, the Merchant Shipping (Submersible Craft Construction and Survey) Regulations 1981, SI 1981/1098 amended by SI 1987/306, the Merchant Shipping (Submersible Craft Operations) Regulations 1987, SI 1987/311, amended by SI 1987/1603 and the Merchant Shipping (Diving Safety) Regulations 2002, SI 2002/1587. Regulations in respect of fees under this section are continued in force by SI 1993/3137.

Special provisions

7–6358   90. Charts and other information.   *Repealed by SI 1998/2647.*

7–6359   91. Report of dangers to navigation.   (1)–(4) *Repealed.*

  (5)   Every person in charge of a controlled station for wireless telegraphy shall, on receiving the signal prescribed under safety regulations relating to dangers to navigation, which indicates that a message is about to be sent under those regulations, refrain from sending messages for a time sufficient to allow other stations to receive the message, and, if so required by the Secretary of State, shall transmit the message in such manner as may be required by the Secretary of State.

  (6)   Compliance with subsection (5) above shall be deemed to be a condition of every wireless telegraphy licence.

  (7)   In this section—

"controlled station for wireless telegraphy" means such a station controlled by the Secretary of State★; and "controlled" includes controlled by means of a licence granted by him★;

"wireless telegraphy licence" and "station for wireless telegraphy" have the same meaning as in the Wireless Telegraphy Act 1949.

[Merchant Shipping Act 1995, s 91, as amended by SI 2002/1473.]

★**Amended by the Communications Act 2003, Sch 17, from a date to be appointed.**

Assistance at sea

7–6360   92. Duty of ship to assist the other in case of collision.   (1) In every case of collision between two ships, it shall be the duty of the master of each ship, if and so far as he can do so without danger to his own ship, crew and passengers (if any)—

   (*a*)   to render to the other ship, its master, crew and passengers (if any) such assistance as may be practicable, and may be necessary to save them from any danger caused by the collision, and to stay by the other ship until he has ascertained that it has no need of further assistance; and
   (*b*)   to give to the master of the other ship the name of his own ship and also the names of the ports from which it comes and to which it is bound.

  (2)   The duties imposed on the master of a ship by subsection (1) above apply to the masters of United Kingdom ships and to the masters of foreign ships when in United Kingdom waters.

  (3)   The failure of the master of a ship to comply with the provisions of this section shall not raise any presumption of law that the collision was caused by his wrongful act, neglect, or default.

  (4)   If the master fails without reasonable excuse to comply with this section, he shall—

   (*a*)   in the case of a failure to comply with subsection (1)(*a*) above, be liable[1]—

    (i) on summary conviction, to a fine not exceeding **£50,000** or imprisonment for a term not exceeding **six months** or both;

    (ii) on conviction on indictment, to a **fine** or imprisonment for a term not exceeding **two years** or both; and

  (b) in the case of a failure to comply with subsection (1)(*b*) above, be liable[1]—

    (i) on summary conviction, to a fine not exceeding the **statutory maximum**;

    (ii) on conviction on indictment, to a **fine**;

and in either case if he is a certified officer, an inquiry into his conduct may be held, and his certificate cancelled or suspended.

[Merchant Shipping Act 1995, s 92.]

---

1. For procedure in respect of an offence triable either way, see the Magistrates' Courts Act 1980, ss 17A–21, in Part I: Magistrates' Courts, Procedure, ante.

7–6361 93. Duty to assist aircraft in distress. (1) The master of a ship, on receiving at sea a signal of distress from an aircraft or information from any source that an aircraft is in distress, shall proceed with all speed to the assistance of the persons in distress (informing them if possible that he is doing so) unless he is unable, or in the special circumstances of the case considers it unreasonable or unnecessary, to do so, or unless he is released from this duty under subsection (4) or (5) below.

  (2) *Repealed.*

  (3) The duties imposed on the master of a ship by subsections (1) above apply to the masters of United Kingdom ships and to the masters of foreign ships when in United Kingdom waters.

  (4) *Repealed.*

  (5) A master shall be released from the duty imposed by subsection (1) above, if he is informed by the persons in distress, or by the master of any ship that has reached the persons in distress, that assistance is no longer required.

  (6) If a master fails to comply with the preceding provisions of this section he shall be liable[1]—

  (a) on summary conviction, to imprisonment for a term not exceeding **six months** or to a fine not exceeding the **statutory maximum**, or **both**;

  (b) on conviction on indictment, to imprisonment for a term not exceeding **two years** or to a **fine**, or **both**.

  (7) Compliance by the master of a ship with the provisions of this section shall not affect his right, or the right of any other person, to salvage.

[Merchant Shipping Act 1995, s 93 and the Merchant Shipping (Distress Messages Regulations 1998, SI 1998/1691.]

---

1. For procedure in respect of an offence triable either way, see the Magistrates' Courts Act 1980, ss 17A–21, in Part I: Magistrates' Courts, Procedure, ante.

Unsafe ships

7–6362 94. Meaning of "dangerously unsafe ship". (1) For the purposes of sections 95, 96, 97[1] and 98 a ship in port is "dangerously unsafe" if, having regard to the nature of the service for which it is intended, the ship is, by reason of the matters mentioned in subsection (2) below, unfit to go to sea without serious danger to human life.

  (1A) For the purposes of those sections a ship at sea is "dangerously unsafe" if, having regard to the nature of the service for which it is being used or is intended, the ship is, by reason of the matters mentioned in subsection (2) below, either—

  (a) unfit to remain at sea without serious danger to human life, or

  (b) unfit to go on a voyage without serious danger to human life.

  (2) those matters are—

  (a) the condition, or the unsuitability for its purpose, of—

    (i) the ship or its machinery or equipment, or

    (ii) any part of the ship or its machinery or equipment;

  (b) undermanning;

  (c) overloading or unsafe or improper loading;

  (d) any other matter relevant to the safety of the ship;

and are referred to in those sections, in relation to any ship, as "the matters relevant to its safety".

  (3) Any reference in those sections to "going to sea" shall, in a case where the service for which the ship is intended consists of going on voyages or excursions that do not involve going to sea, be construed as a reference to going on such a voyage or excursion.

[Merchant Shipping Act 1995, s 94 as amended by the Merchant Shipping and Maritime Security Act 1997, Sch 1.]

1. Section 95 confers power on a "relevant inspector" (defined in s 258) to detain a dangerously unsafe ship; ss 96 and 97 provide for any dispute about a detention notice to be referred to arbitration on request by a master or ship owner and for the payment of compensation for the invalid detention of a ship.

7–6363   **98.**—(1) If a ship[1] which—

   (a)   is in a port in the United Kingdom, or

   (b)   is a United Kingdom ship and is in any other port,

is dangerously unsafe, then, subject to subsections (4) and (5) below, the master and the owner of the ship shall each be guilty of an offence.

(2) Where, at the time when a ship is dangerously unsafe, any responsibilities of the owner with respect to the matters relevant to its safety have been assumed (whether wholly or in part) by any person or persons other than the owner, and have been so assumed by that person or (as the case may be) by each of those persons either—

   (a)   directly, under the terms of a charter-party or management agreement made with the owner, or

   (b)   indirectly, under the terms of a series of charter-parties or management agreements,

the reference to the owner in subsection (1) above shall be construed as a reference to that other person or (as the case may be) to each of those other persons.

(3) A person guilty of an offence under this sections shall be liable[2]—

   (a)   on summary conviction, to a fine not exceeding **£50,000**;

   (b)   on conviction on indictment, to imprisonment for a term not exceeding **two years** or a **fine**, or **both**.

(4) It shall be a defence in proceedings for an offence under this section to prove that at the time of the alleged offence—

   (a)   arrangements had been made which were appropriate to ensure that before the ship went to sea it was made fit to do so without serious danger to human life by reason of the matters relevant to its safety which are specified in the charge (or, in Scotland, which are libelled in the complaint, petition or indictment); or

   (b)   it was reasonable for such arrangements not to have been made.

(5) It shall also be a defence in proceedings for an offence under this section to prove—

   (a)   that, under the terms of one or more charter-parties or management agreements entered into by the accused, the relevant responsibilities, namely—

      (i)   where the accused is the owner, his responsibilities with respect to the matters relevant to the ship's safety, or

      (ii)   where the accused is liable to proceedings under this section by virtue of subsection (2) above, so much of those responsibilities as had been assumed by him as mentioned in that subsection,

had at the time of the alleged offence been wholly assumed by some other person or persons party thereto; and

   (b)   that in all the circumstances of the case the accused had taken such steps as it was reasonable for him to take, and exercised such diligence as it was reasonable for him to exercise, to secure the proper discharge of the relevant responsibilities during the period during which they had been assumed by some other person or persons as mentioned in paragraph (a) above;

and, in determining whether the accused had done so, regard shall be had in particular to the matters mentioned in subsection (6) below.

(6) Those matters are—

   (a)   whether prior to the time of the alleged offence the accused was, or in all the circumstances ought reasonable to have been, aware of any deficiency in the discharge of the relevant responsibilities; and

   (b)   the extent to which the accused was or was not able, under the terms of any such charter-party or management agreement as is mentioned in subsection (5)(a) above—

      (i)   to terminate it, or

      (ii)   to intervene in the management of the ship,

in the event of any such deficiency, and whether it was reasonable for the accused to place himself in that position.

(7) No proceedings for an offence under this section shall be instituted—

   (a)   in England and Wales, except by or with the consent of the Secretary of State or the Director of Public Prosecutions;

   (b)   *Northern Ireland.*

(8) In this section—

"management agreement", in relation to a ship, means any agreement (other than a charter-party or a contract of employment) under which the ship is managed, either wholly or in part, by a person other than the owner (whether on behalf of the owner or on behalf of some other person); and

"relevant responsibilities" shall be construed in accordance with subsection (5) above.

(9) References in this section to responsibilities being assumed by a person under the terms of a charter-party or management agreement are references to their being so assumed by him whether or not he has entered into a further charter-party or management agreement providing for them to be assumed by some other person.

[Merchant Shipping Act 1995, s 98.]

---

1. This section has been extended to certain unregistered ships; see the Merchant Shipping Act 1988 (Unregistered Ships) Regulations 1991, SI 1991/1367.

2. For procedure in respect of an offence triable either way, see ss 17A–22 of the Magistrates' Courts Act 1980 in PART I: MAGISTRATES' COURTS, PROCEDURE, ante.

7–6364   99. Use of unsafe lighters, etc. (1) If any person uses or causes or permits to be used in navigation any lighter, barge or like vessel when, because of—

(a) the defective condition of its hull or equipment,

(b) overloading or improper loading, or

(c) undermanning,

it is so unsafe that human life is thereby endangered, he shall be liable[1]—

(i) on summary conviction, to a fine not exceeding the **statutory maximum**;

(ii) on conviction on indictment, to a **fine**.

(2) Proceedings for an offence under this section shall not be instituted—

(a) in England and Wales, except by or with the consent of the Secretary of State; or

(b) *Northern Ireland*.

(3) this section does not affect the liability of the owners of any lighter, barge or like vessel in respect of loss of life or personal injury caused to any person carried in the vessel.

[Merchant Shipping Act 1995, s 99.]

---

1. For procedure in respect of an offence triable either way, see the Magistrates' Courts Act 1980, ss 17A–21, in PART I: MAGISTRATES' COURTS, PROCEDURE, ante.

7–6365   100. Owner liable for unsafe operation of ship[1]. (1) It shall be the duty of the owner of a ship to which this section applies to take all reasonable steps to secure that the ship is operated in a safe manner.

(2) This section applies to—

(a) any United Kingdom ship; and

(b) any ship which—

(i) is registered under the law of any country outside the United Kingdom, and

(ii) is within United Kingdom waters while proceeding to or from a port in the United Kingdom,

unless the ship would not be so proceeding but for weather conditions or any other unavoidable circumstances.

(3) If the owner[2] of a ship to which this section applies fails to discharge the duty imposed on him by subsection (1) above, he shall be liable[3]—

(a) on summary conviction, to a fine not exceeding £50,000;

(b) on conviction on indictment, to imprisonment for a term not exceeding **two years** or a **fine**, or **both**.

(4) Where any such ship—

(a) is chartered by demise, or

(b) is managed, either wholly or in part, by a person other than the owner under the terms of a management agreement within the meaning of section 98,

any reference to the owner of the ship in subsection (1) or (3) above shall be construed as including a reference—

(i) to the charterer under the charter by demise, or

(ii) to any such manager as is referred to in paragraph (b) above, or

(iii) (if the ship is both chartered and managed as mentioned above) to both the charterer and any such manager,

and accordingly the reference in subsection (1) above to the taking of all reasonable steps shall, in relation to the owner, the charterer or any such manager, be construed as a reference to the taking of all such steps as it is reasonable for him to take in the circumstances of the case.

(5) No proceedings for an offence under this section shall be instituted—

(a) in England and Wales, except by or with the consent of the Secretary of State or the Director of Public Prosecutions;

(b) in Northern Ireland, except by or with the consent of the Secretary of State or the Director of Public Prosecutions for Northern Ireland.

[Merchant Shipping Act 1995, s 100.]

---

1. This section has been extended to certain unregistered ships; see the Merchant Shipping Act 1988 (Unregistered Ships) Regulations 1991, SI 1991/1367.

2. The owner, charterer or manager is criminally liable if he fails personally in the duty imposed by s 31, but is not criminally liable for the acts or omissions of his subordinate employees if he has himself taken all such reasonable steps (*Seaboard Offshore Ltd v Secretary of State for Transport* [1994] 2 All ER 99, HL).

3. For procedure in respect of an offence triable either way, see the Magistrates' Courts Act 1980, ss 17A–22 in PART I: MAGISTRATES' COURTS, PROCEDURE, ante.

Temporary exclusion zones

7–6365A   100A. The Secretary of State may, wherever he is satisfied that significant harm may result from a ship or other structure being wrecked, damaged or in distress, or that a restriction on access to the area would prevent or reduce such harm, identify a temporary exclusion zone.

[Merchant Shipping Act 1995, s 100A as inserted by the Merchant Shipping and Maritime Security Act 1997, s 1—summarised.]

7–6365B   100B. Temporary exclusion zones: offences.   (1) If a direction establishing a temporary exclusion zone contains a statement of a description mentioned in subsection (2) below, then, subject to subsection (4) below, no ship shall enter or remain in the zone.

(2) The statement is one to the effect that the direction is given for the purpose of preventing or reducing significant pollution, or the risk of significant pollution, in the United Kingdom, in United Kingdom waters or in a part of the sea specified by virtue of section 129(2)(b).

(3) If a direction establishing a temporary exclusion zone does not contain a statement of a description mentioned in subsection (2) above, then, subject to subsection (4) and (5) below—

(a) no ship shall enter or remain in any part of the zone that is in United Kingdom waters; and

(b) no United Kingdom ship shall enter or remain in any part of the zone that is in a part of the sea specified by virtue of section 129(2)(b).

(4) A ship may enter or remain in a temporary exclusion zone or a part of such a zone if it does so—

(a) in accordance with the direction establishing the zone;

(b) with the consent of the Secretary of State; or

(c) in accordance with regulations made by the Secretary of State for the purposes of this section.

(5) A qualifying foreign ship may enter a temporary exclusion zone or a part of such a zone if in doing so it is exercising the right of transit passage through straits used for international navigation.

(6) If a ship enters or remains in a temporary exclusion zone or a part of such a zone in contravention of subsection (1) or (3) above then, subject to subsection (7) below, its owner and its master shall each be guilty of an offence and liable[1]—

(a) on summary conviction, to a fine not exceeding **£50,000**;

(b) on conviction on indictment, to imprisonment for a term not exceeding two years or to a **fine** or to **both**.

(7) It shall be a defence for a person charged with an offence under this section to prove that the existence or area of the temporary exclusion zone was not, and would not on reasonable enquiry have become, known to the master.

[Merchant Shipping Act 1995, s 100B as inserted by the Merchant Shipping and Maritime Security Act 1997, s 1.]

---

1. For procedure in respect of this offence which is triable either way, see the Magistrates' Courts Act 1980, ss 17A–21, in PART I: MAGISTRATES' COURTS, PROCEDURE, ante.

7–6365C   100C–100E

Repealed by the Marine Safety Act 1995, Sch 2.

7–6365F   100F. Requirements to be met by ships in respect of which trans-shipment licences in force.   (1) In this section and section 100G "trans-shipment licence" means a licence under section 4A of the Sea Fish Conservation Act 1967 (prohibition of trans-shipment of fish unless authorised by a licence).

(2)–(5) *Regulations.*

[Merchant Shipping Act 1995, s 100F as inserted by the Merchant Shipping and Maritime Security Act 1997, s 11.]

7–6365G 100G. Failure to comply with prescribed standards in respect of ship in respect of which trans-shipment licence is in force. (1) If it appears to the Secretary of State that any requirement of regulations under section 100F(2) or regulations under section 192A is being contravened in respect of a ship in respect of which a trans-shipment licence is in force, he may serve on the master a notice under subsection (2) below.

(2) A notice under this subsection must specify the contravention by reason of which it is given and must—

(a) prohibit the receiving by the ship of fish trans-shipped from another ship.
(b) prohibit the process of fish on the ship, or
(c) prohibit both such receiving and such processing.

(3) The Secretary of State shall revoke a notice under subsection (2) above if he is satisfied that the contravention specified in it has been remedied.

(4) If a trans-shipment licence ceases to be in force in respect of a ship to which a notice under subsection (2) above relates, the notice is revoked by virtue of this subsection.

(5) If without reasonable excuse the master of a ship causes or permits any prohibition imposed by a notice under subsection (2) above to be contravened in respect of the ship, he shall be liable[1]—

(a) on summary conviction, to a fine not exceeding **£50,000**;
(b) on conviction on indictment, to imprisonment for a term not exceeding **two years** or a **fine** or **both**.

(6) The obligation imposed by regulations under section 100F(2) shall not be enforceable except in accordance with this section, but this subsection does not limit the powers conferred by section 258.

[Merchant Shipping Act 1995, s 100G as inserted by the Merchant Shipping and Maritime Security Act 1997, s 11.]

---

1. For procedure in respect of this offence which is triable either way, see the Magistrates' Courts Act 1980, ss 17A–21 in PART I: MAGISTRATES' COURTS, PROCEDURE, ante.

Control of, and returns as to, persons on ships

7–6366 101. Offences in connection with passenger ships. (1) A person commits an offence if, in relation to a ship to which this section applies, he does any of the following things, that is to say—

(a) if, being drunk or disorderly, he has been on that account refused admission to the ship by the owner or any person in his employment, and, after having the amount of his fare (if he has paid it) returned or tendered to him, nevertheless persists in attempting to enter the ship;
(b) if, being drunk or disorderly on board the ship, he is requested by the owner or any person in his employment to leave the ship at any place in the United Kingdom at which he can conveniently do so, and, after having the amount of his fare (if he has paid it) returned or tendered to him, does not comply with the request;
(c) if, on board the ship, after warning by the master or other officer thereof, he molests or continues to molest any passenger;
(d) if, after having been refused admission to the ship by the owner or any person in his employment on account of the ship being full, and having had the amount of his fare (if he has paid it) returned or tendered to him, he nevertheless persists in attempting to enter the ship;
(e) if, having gone on board the ship at any place, and being requested, on account of the ship being full, by the owner or any person in his employment to leave the ship before it has left that place, and having had the amount of his fare (if he has paid it) returned or tendered to him, he does not comply with that request;
(f) if, on arriving in the ship at a point to which he has paid his fare, he knowingly and intentionally refuses or neglects to leave the ship; and
(g) if, on board the ship he fails, when requested by the master or other officer thereof, either to pay his fare or show such ticket or other receipt, if any, showing the payment of his fare, as is usually given to persons travelling by and paying their fare for the ship;

but his liability in respect of any such offence shall not prejudice the recovery of any fare payable by him.

(2) A person commits an offence if, on board any ship to which this section applies he intentionally does or causes to be done anything in such a manner as to—

(a) obstruct or damage any part of the machinery or equipment of the ship, or
(b) obstruct, impede or molest the crew, or any of them, in the navigation or management of the ship, or otherwise in the execution of their duty on or about the ship.

(3) The master or other officer of any ship to which this section applies, and all persons called by him to his assistance, may, without any warrant, detain any person who commits any offence against subsection (1) or (2) above and whose name and address are unknown to the master or officer, and deliver that person to a constable.

(4) A person guilty of an offence against subsection (1) or (2) above shall be liable, on summary conviction, to a fine not exceeding **level 2** on the standard scale.

(5) If any person commits an offence against subsection (1) or (2) above and on the application of the master of the ship, or any other person in the employment of the owner thereof, refuses to give his name and address, or gives a false name or address, that person shall be liable, on summary conviction, to a fine not exceeding **level 2** on the standard scale.

(6) This section applies to a ship for which there is in force a Passenger Ship Safety Certificate or Passenger Certificate, as the case may be, issued under or recognised by safety regulations.
[Merchant Shipping Act 1995, s 101.]

7–6367   **102. Power to exclude drunken passengers from certain passenger ships.**   (1) The master of any ship to which this section applies may refuse to receive on board any person who by reason of drunkenness or otherwise is in such a state, or misconducts himself in such a manner, as to cause annoyance or injury to passengers on board, and if any such person is on board, may put him on shore at any convenient place.

(2) A person so refused admittance or put on shore shall not be entitled to the return of any fare he has paid.

(3) This section applies to a ship (whether or not a United Kingdom ship) carrying more than 12 passengers and employed in carrying passengers between places in the limited European trading area as for the time being defined in regulations made under section 47 by the Secretary of State.
[Merchant Shipping Act 1995, s 102.]

7–6368   **103. Stowaways.**   (1) If a person, without the consent of the master or of any other person authorised to give it, goes to sea[1] or attempts to go to sea in a United Kingdom ship, he shall be liable on summary conviction to a fine not exceeding **level 3** on the standard scale[2].

(2) Nothing in section 281 shall be taken to limit the jurisdiction of any court in the United Kingdom to deal with an offence under this section which has been committed in a country outside the United Kingdom by a person who is not a British citizen.
[Merchant Shipping Act 1995, s 103.]

---

1. This is a compound continuing offence, and an English court has jurisdiction to try an alien who stows away and goes to sea in a British ship from a foreign port (*Robey v Vladinier* (1935) 99 JP 428).

2. A stowaway is also subject to the provisions of this Act as to discipline as if he were a seaman employed in the ship (s 106, post).

7–6369   **104. Unauthorised presence on board ship.**   (1) Where a United Kingdom ship or a ship registered in any other country is in a port in the United Kingdom and a person who is neither in Her Majesty's service nor authorised by law to do so—

(*a*)   goes on board the ship without the consent of the master or of any other persons authorised to give it; or

(*b*)   remains on board the ship after being requested to leave by the master, a constable, an officer authorised by the Secretary of State or an officer of customs and excise,

he shall be liable on summary conviction to a fine not exceeding **level 5** on the standard scale.
[Merchant Shipping Act 1995, s 104.]

7–6370   **105. Master's power of arrest.**   (1) The master of any United Kingdom ship may cause any person on board the ship to be put under restraint if and for so long as it appears to him necessary or expedient in the interest of safety or for the preservation of good order or discipline on board the ship.
[Merchant Shipping Act 1995, s 105.]

7–6371   **106. Unauthorised persons: offences relating to safety.**   (1) Where a person goes to sea in a ship without the consent of the master or of any other person authorised to give it or is conveyed in a ship in pursuance of section 73(5)(*b*), sections 58 and 59 shall apply as if he were a seaman employed in the ship.

(2) Subsection (1) above shall, in its application to section 58 so far as that section applies to ships which are not sea-going ships have effect—

(*a*)   with the omission of the words "goes to sea in a ship"; and

(*b*)   with the insertion, after the words "to give it", of the words "is on board a ship while it is on a voyage or excursion".

(3) This section does not apply to fishing vessels.
[Merchant Shipping Act 1995, s 106.]

7–6372   **107. Return to be furnished by masters of ships as to passengers[1].**   (1) The master of every ship, whether or not a United Kingdom ship, which carries any passenger to a place in the United Kingdom from any place out of the United Kingdom, or from any place in the United Kingdom to any place out of the United Kingdom, shall furnish to such person and in such manner as the Secretary of State directs a return giving the total number of any passengers so carried, distinguishing, if so directed by the Secretary of State, the total number of any class of passengers so carried, and giving, if the Secretary of State so directs, such particulars with respect to passengers as may be for the time being required by the Secretary of State.

(2) Any passenger shall furnish the master of the ship with any information required by him for the purpose of the return.

(3) If—

(a) the master of a ship fails to make a return as required by this section, or makes a false return,

(b) any passenger refuses to give any information required by the master of the ship for the purpose of the return required by this section, or, for that purpose, gives to the master information which he knows to be false or recklessly gives to him information which is false,

the master or (as the case may be) passenger shall be liable on summary conviction to a fine not exceeding **level 2** on the standard scale in the case of a failure or refusal and **level 3** on the standard scale in the case of a false return or false information.

[Merchant Shipping Act 1995, s 107.]

---

1. The Merchant Shipping (Passenger Returns) Regulations 1960, SI 1960/1477 have been made and deal with matters to be directed or specified by the (now defunct) Board of Trade.

7–6373   108. Returns of births and deaths in ships, etc.   (1) The Secretary of State may make regulations[1] under the following provisions of this section in relation to births and deaths in the circumstances specified in those provisions.

(2) Regulations under this section may require the master of any United Kingdom ship to make a return to a superintendent or proper officer of—

(a) the birth or death of any person occurring in the ship; and

(b) the death of any person employed in the ship, wherever occurring outside the United Kingdom;

and to notify any such death to such person (if any) as the deceased may have named to him as his next of kin.

(3) Regulations under this section may require the master of any ship not registered in the United Kingdom which calls at a port in the United Kingdom in the course of or at the end of a voyage to make a return to a superintendent of any birth or death of a British citizen, a British overseas territories citizen or a British Overseas citizen which has occurred in the ship during the voyage.

(4) The returns referred to in subsections (2) and (3) above shall be for transmission to the Registrar General of Shipping and Seamen.

(5) Regulations under this section may require the Registrar General of Shipping and Seamen to record such information as may be specified in the regulations about such a death as is referred to in subsection (2) above in a case where—

(a) it appears to him that the master of the ship cannot perform his duty under that subsection because he has himself died or is incapacitated or missing; and

(b) any of the circumstances specified in subsection (6) below exist.

(6) Those circumstances are that—

(a) the death in question has been the subject of—

(i) an inquest held by a coroner,

(ii) an inquiry held in pursuance of section 271, or

(iii) an inquiry held in pursuance of the Fatal Accidents and Sudden Deaths Inquiry (Scotland) Act 1976;

and the findings of the inquest or inquiry include a finding that the death occurred;

(b) the deceased's body has been the subject of—

(i) a post-mortem examination in England and Wales, or

(ii) *Northern Ireland*;

and in consequence the coroner is satisfied that an inquest is unnecessary; or

(c) *Scotland.*

(7) Regulations under this section may require the Registrar General of Shipping and Seamen to send a certified copy of any return or record made thereunder to the Registrar General for England and Wales, the Registrar General of Births, Deaths and Marriages for Scotland or the Registrar General for Northern Ireland, as the case may require.

(8) The Registrar General to whom any such certified copies are sent—

(a) shall record the information contained therein in the marine register; and

(b) may record in the marine register such additional information as appears to him desirable for the purpose of ensuring the completeness and correctness of the register;

and the enactments relating to the registration of births and deaths in England, Scotland and Northern

Ireland shall have effect as if the marine register were a register of births (other than stillbirths) or deaths or certified copies of entries in such a register had been transmitted to the Registrar General in accordance with those enactments.

(9) Regulations under this section may make a contravention of any provision thereof an offence punishable on summary conviction with a fine not exceeding **level 2** on the standard scale or not exceeding a lesser amount.

(10) Regulations under this section may contain provisions authorising the registration of the following births and deaths occurring outside the United Kingdom in circumstances where no return is required to be made under the preceding provisions of this section—

(*a*) any birth or death of a British citizen, a British overseas territories citizen or a British Overseas citizen which occurs in a ship not registered in the United Kingdom;

(*b*) any death of any such citizen who has been employed in a ship not registered in the United Kingdom which occurs elsewhere than in the ship; and

(*c*) any death of a person who has been employed in a United Kingdom ship which occurs elsewhere than in the ship.

(11) References in this section to deaths occurring in a ship include references to deaths occurring in a ship's boat.

[Merchant Shipping Act 1995, s 108, as amended by the British Overseas Territories Act 2002, s 2(3).]

---

1. The Merchant Shipping (Returns of Births and Deaths) Regulations 1979, SI 1979/1577, have been made.

7–6373A 108A. Safety directions. (1) Schedule 3A (safety directions) shall have effect.

(2) A provision made by or by virtue of this Act (including one which creates an offence) shall have no effect in so far as it—

(*a*) is inconsistent with the exercise by or on behalf of the Secretary of State of a power under Schedule 3A (safety directions),

(*b*) would interfere with a person's compliance with a direction under that Schedule, or

(*c*) would interfere with action taken by virtue of that Schedule.

[Merchant Shipping Act 1995, s 108A, inserted by the Marine Safety Act 2003, s 1.]

PART V[1]
FISHING VESSELS

CHAPTER I
SKIPPER AND SEAMEN

Engagement and discharge of crews

7–6378 109. Regulations relating to crew agreements. (1) The Secretary of State may make regulations prescribing the procedure to be followed in connection with the making of crew agreements between persons employed in United Kingdom fishing vessels and persons employing them and prescribing the places where such crew agreements are to be made or where an agreement with any person may be added to those contained in such a crew agreement.

(2) Regulations under this section may make a contravention of any provision thereof an offence punishable on summary conviction with a fine not exceeding **level 3** on the standard scale or such less amount as may be specified in the regulations.

[Merchant Shipping Act 1995, s 109.]

---

1. Part V contains ss 109–127.

Wages

7–6379 112. Accounts of wages and catch. (1) Subject to regulations[1] made under section 32 or 73, the persons employing any seaman under a crew agreement relating to a United Kingdom fishing vessel shall deliver to him at a time prescribed by regulations under this section an account of the wages[1] due to him under that crew agreement and of the deductions subject to which the wages are payable.

(2) Where the wages of any person employed in a United Kingdom fishing vessel are in any manner related to the catch the persons employing him shall at a time prescribed by regulations under this section deliver to the master an account (or, if the master is the person employing him, make out an account) showing how those wages (or any part thereof related to the catch) are arrived at and shall make the account available to the crew in such manner as may be prescribed by the regulations.

(3) Where there is a partnership between the master and any members of the crew of a United Kingdom fishing vessel the owner of the vessel shall at a time prescribed by regulations under this section make out an account showing the sums due to each partner in respect of his share and shall make the account available to the partners.

(4) The Secretary of State may make regulations prescribing the time at which any account

required by this section is to be delivered or made out and the manner in which the account required by subsections (2) and (3) above is to be made available.

(5) If a person fails without reasonable excuse to comply with the preceding provisions of this section he shall be liable on summary conviction to a fine not exceeding **level 2** on the standard scale. [Merchant Shipping Act 1995, s 112.]

---

1. See notes to s 31, ante.

7–6380 113. Restriction on assignment of and charge upon wages. (1) Nothing in section 34 shall affect the operation of—

(a) the Attachment of Earnings Act 1971, or
(b) *Northern Ireland,*

in relation to wages due to a person employed in a fishing vessel.

(2) *Northern Ireland.*
[Merchant Shipping Act 1995, s 113.]

Safety, health and welfare

7–6381 115. Hours of work. (1) The Secretary of State may make regulations prescribing maximum periods of duty and minimum periods of rest for seamen employed in United Kingdom fishing vessels, and such regulations may make different provision for different descriptions of fishing vessels or seamen employed in them or for fishing vessels and seamen of the same description in different circumstances.

(2) If any provision of regulations made under this section is contravened in the case of any seaman employed in a fishing vessel the persons employing him and the master shall each be liable on summary conviction to a fine not exceeding **level 4** on the standard scale.
[Merchant Shipping Act 1995, s 115.]

Manning and qualifications

7–6382 116. Production of crew certificates and other documents of qualification[1]. (1) Any person serving or engaged to serve in a United Kingdom fishing vessel and holding any certificate or other document which is evidence that he is qualified for the purposes of section 47 shall on demand produce it to any person who is a British sea-fishery officer for the purposes of the Sea Fisheries Acts.

(2) If a person fails without reasonable excuse to produce on demand any such certificate or other document he shall be liable on summary conviction to a fine not exceeding **level 3** on the standard scale.

(3) In this section the "Sea Fisheries Acts" means any enactment for the time being in force relating to sea fishing, including any enactment relating to fishing for shellfish, salmon or migratory trout.
[Merchant Shipping Act 1995, s 116.]

---

1 The Merchant Shipping Act 1995 (Appointed Day No 2) Order 1997, SI 1997/3107 made under the Merchant Shipping Act 1995, Sch 14 provides that 1 February 1998 is the day appointed for the coming into force of this section.

Offences by seamen

7–6383 117. Drunkenness on duty. *Repealed by the Railways and Transport Safety Act 2003, Sch 8.*

7–6384 118. Unauthorised liquor. (1) A person who, in the United Kingdom or elsewhere—

(a) takes any unauthorised liquor on board a United Kingdom fishing vessel;
(b) has any unauthorised liquor in his possession on board such a vessel;
(c) permits another person to take on board such a vessel, or to have in his possession on board such a vessel, any unauthorised liquor; or
(d) intentionally obstructs another person in the exercise of powers conferred on the other person by subsection (5) below,

shall, subject to subsections (3) and (4) below, be guilty of an offence.

(2) A person guilty of an offence under subsection (1) above shall be liable—

(a) on summary conviction, to a fine not exceeding the **statutory maximum**;
(b) on conviction on indictment, to imprisonment for a term not exceeding **two years** or a **fine** or **both**[1].

(3) It shall be a defence in proceedings for an offence under subsection (1)(a) or (b) above to prove—

(a) that the accused believed that the liquor in question was not unauthorised liquor in relation to the vessel in question and that he had reasonable grounds for the belief; or
(b) that the accused did not know that the liquor in question was in his possession.

(4) It shall be a defence in proceedings for an offence under subsection (1)(*c*) above to prove that the accused believed that the liquor in question was not unauthorised liquor in relation to the vessel in question and that he had reasonable grounds for the belief.

(5) If an authorised person has reason to believe that an offence under subsection (1)(*a*) or (*b*) above has been committed by another person in connection with a fishing vessel, the authorised person—

(*a*)   may go on board the vessel and search it and any property on it and may, if the other person is on board the vessel, search him there in an authorised manner; and

(*b*)   may take possession of any liquor which he finds on the vessel and has reason to believe is unauthorised liquor and may detain the liquor for the period needed to ensure that the liquor is available as evidence in proceedings for the offence.

(6) In this section—

"an authorised manner" means a manner authorised by regulations made by the Secretary of State;
"authorised person", in relation to a vessel, means—

(*a*)   a superintendent;
(*b*)   a proper officer;
(*c*)   a person appointed in pursuance of section 258(1)(*c*);
(*d*)   the master of the vessel in question;
(*e*)   the owner of the vessel in question;
(*f*)   any person instructed by the master or owner to prevent the commission of offences under subsection (1) above in relation to the vessel;

"liquor" means spirits, wine, beer, cider, perry and any other fermented, distilled or spirituous liquor; and
"unauthorised liquor" means, in relation to a vessel, liquor as to which permission to take it on board the vessel has been given neither by the master nor the owner of the vessel nor by a person authorised by the owner of the vessel to give such permission.

(7) Any reference in subsection (6) above to the owner of a vessel shall be construed—

(*a*)   as excluding any member of the crew of the vessel; and
(*b*)   subject to that, as a reference to the person or all the persons who, in the certificate of registration of the vessel, is or are stated to be the registered owner or owners of the vessel.

[Merchant Shipping Act 1995, s 118.]

---

1. For procedure in respect of an offence triable either way, see the Magistrates' Courts Act 1980, ss 17A–21, in PART I: MAGISTRATES' COURTS, PROCEDURE, ante.

7–6385   119. Disciplinary offences.   (1) Section 59(1)(*a*) and (*b*) shall not apply to fishing vessels and persons serving in them.

(2) In relation to United Kingdom fishing vessels, section 60 shall have effect with the substitution for subsection (2) of the following—

"(2) Regulations may provide for the hearing on shore in the United Kingdom, by a disciplinary body, of a complaint by the master or owner of such a fishing vessel against a seaman alleging that during his employment in the vessel, the seaman contravened a local industrial agreement relating to his employment on the vessel and for requiring the disciplinary body to have regard to the agreement in determining whether the allegation is proved."

The alleged contravention may be one on or off the ship and in the United Kingdom or elsewhere.

(3) Regulations under section 60 may include provision authorising persons to determine, for the purposes of that section in its application to United Kingdom fishing vessels what agreements are or were local industrial agreements and which local industrial agreement relates or related to a person's employment in a particular vessel.

[Merchant Shipping Act 1995, s 119.]

Exemptions

7–6386   120. Power to grant exemptions from this Chapter.   (1) The Secretary of State may grant exemptions from any requirements of Part III or this Chapter or of any regulations made thereunder—

(*a*)   with respect to any fishing vessel or to a fishing vessel of any description; or
(*b*)   with respect to any person or a person of any description serving in a fishing vessel or in a fishing vessel of any description;

and nothing in any other provision of Part III or this Chapter conferring a power to provide for or grant exemptions shall be taken to restrict the power conferred by this section.

[Merchant Shipping Act 1995, s 120.]

CHAPTER II
SAFETY

7–6387   121. Fishing vessel construction rules.   (1) The Secretary of State may make rules[1] (in this Chapter referred to as "fishing vessel construction rules") prescribing requirements for the hull, equipment and machinery of United Kingdom fishing vessels of any description (including any description framed by reference to the areas in which the vessels operate or the dates on which they were first registered in the United Kingdom or on which their construction was begun).

(2) The Secretary of State may exempt any fishing vessel or description of fishing vessel from any requirement of the fishing vessel construction rules.

(3) He may do so generally or for a specified time or with respect to a specified voyage or to voyages in a specified area, and may do so subject to any specified conditions.

(4) A surveyor of ships may inspect any fishing vessel for the purpose of seeing that it complies with the fishing vessel construction rules.

(5) If—

(a) the fishing vessel construction rules are contravened with respect to any vessel; or

(b) a vessel is, under subsection (2) above, exempted from any requirement subject to a condition and the condition is not complied with;

the owner or master of the vessel shall be liable[2]—

(i) on summary conviction, to a fine not exceeding the **statutory maximum**;

(ii) on conviction on indictment, to a **fine**.

[Merchant Shipping Act 1995, s 121.]

---

1. The Fishing Vessels (Safety Provisions) Rules 1975, SI 1975/330 amended by SI 1975/471, SI 1976/432, SIs 1977/313 and 498, SIs 1978/1598 and 1873, SI 1981/567, SI 1991/1342, SI 1996/2419, SI 1998/928 and 2647, SI 1999/2998, SI 2001/9 and SI 2002/2201 and the Merchant Shipping (Crew Accommodation) (Fishing Vessels) Regulations 1975, SI 1975/2220 amended by SI 1998/929 have been made.

2. For procedure in respect of an offence triable either way, see the Magistrates' Courts Act 1980, ss 17A–21, in PART I: MAGISTRATES' COURTS, PROCEDURE, ante.

7–6388 124. Provisions supplementary to section 123.   (1) The Secretary of State may require a fishing vessel certificate which has expired or been cancelled, to be delivered up as he directs.

(2) If the owner or skipper of the fishing vessel fails without reasonable excuse to comply with a requirement made under subsection (1) above, he shall be liable on summary conviction to a fine not exceeding **level 2** on the standard scale.

(3) The owner or skipper of a fishing vessel to whom a fishing vessel certificate is issued shall forthwith, on the receipt of the certificate by him (or his agent), cause a copy of it to be put up in some conspicuous place on board the vessel, so as to be legible to all persons on board, and to be kept so put up and legible while the certificate remains in force and the vessel is in use.

(4) If the owner or skipper of a fishing vessel fails without reasonable excuse to comply with subsection (3) above, he shall be liable, on summary conviction, to a fine not exceeding **level 2** on the standard scale.

(5) If any person intentionally makes, or assists in making, or procures to be made, a false or fraudulent fishing vessel certificate he shall be liable—

(a) on summary conviction, to a fine not exceeding the **statutory maximum** or to imprisonment for a term not exceeding **six months** or both;

(b) on conviction on indictment, to imprisonment for a term not exceeding **two years** or a **fine** or both[1].

(6) *Scotland.*

(7) A fishing vessel certificate shall be admissible in evidence.

[Merchant Shipping Act 1995, s 124.]

---

1. For procedure in respect of an offence triable either way, see the Magistrates' Courts Act 1980, ss 18–21, in PART I: MAGISTRATES' COURTS, PROCEDURE, ante.

7–6389 125. Prohibition on going to sea without appropriate certificate.   (1) No fishing vessel required to be surveyed under the fishing vessel survey rules shall go to sea unless there are in force fishing vessel certificates showing that the vessel complies with such of the requirements of the fishing vessel construction and equipment provisions as are applicable to the vessel.

(2) If a fishing vessel goes to sea in contravention of subsection (1) above the owner or skipper of the vessel shall be liable[1]—

(a) on summary conviction, to a fine not exceeding the **statutory maximum**;

(b) on conviction on indictment, to a **fine**.

(3) The skipper of any United Kingdom fishing vessel shall on demand produce to any officer of customs and excise or of the Secretary of State any certificate required by this Chapter; and the fishing vessel, if in United Kingdom waters, may be detained until the certificate is so produced.

[Merchant Shipping Act 1995, s 125 as amended by the Merchant Shipping and Maritime Security Act 1997, Sch 1.]

---

1. For procedure in respect of an offence triable either way, see the Magistrates' Courts Act 1980, ss 17A–21, in PART I: MAGISTRATES' COURTS, PROCEDURE, ante.

7–6390   126. Notice of alterations.   (1) Where a fishing vessel certificate is in force in respect of a fishing vessel and—

(a) the certificate shows compliance with requirements of the fishing vessel construction rules[1] and an alteration is made in the vessel's hull, equipment or machinery which affects the efficiency thereof or the seaworthiness of the vessel; or

(b) the certificate show compliance with requirements of the fishing vessel equipment provisions and an alteration is made affecting the efficiency or completeness of the appliance or equipment which the vessel is required to carry by the fishing vessel equipment provisions;

the owner or skipper shall, as soon as possible after the alteration is made, give written notice containing full particulars of it to the Secretary of State or, if the certificate was issued by another person, to that person.

(2) If the notice required by subsection (1) above is not given as required by that subsection the owner or skipper shall be liable on summary conviction to a fine not exceeding **level 3** on the standard scale.

In this section—

"alteration" in relation to anything includes the renewal of any part of it and

"the fishing vessel equipment provisions" means the provisions of the fishing vessel construction and equipment provisions other than the fishing vessel construction rules.

[Merchant Shipping Act 1995, s 126.]

---

1. See note 1 to s 121, ante.

Training

7–6391   127. Training in safety matters.   (1) The Secretary of State may make regulations for securing that the skipper of and every seaman employed or engaged in a United Kingdom fishing vessel is trained in safety matters.

(2) The regulations may provide that if a person goes to sea on a fishing vessel in contravention of a requirement of the regulations—

(a) he commits an offence and is liable on summary conviction to a fine not exceeding **level 2**, or if he is the skipper or an owner of the vessel **level 5**, on the standard scale; and

(b) the skipper and each owner of the vessel is (except in respect of a contravention by himself) liable on summary conviction to a fine not exceeding **level 5** on the standard scale.

(3) Regulations under this section may make different provision for different cases, or descriptions of case, including different provisions for different descriptions of vessel or according to the circumstances of operation of a vessel.

[Merchant Shipping Act 1995, s 127.]

PART VI[1]
PREVENTION OF POLLUTION

CHAPTER I
POLLUTION GENERALLY

7–6396   128. Prevention of pollution from ships etc.   (1) *Her Majesty may by Order[2] in Council make provision for the purpose of giving effect to the International Convention for the Prevention of Pollution from Ships, certain protocols and any international agreement relating to the prevention of pollution of the sea.*

[Merchant Shipping Act 1995, s 128—summarised.]

---

1. Part VI contains ss 128–182.

2. The Merchant Shipping (Prevention of Oil Pollution) Order 1983, SI 1983/1106, as amended by SI 1985/2002, SI 1991/2885, SI 1992/98 and SI 1993/1580, enables effect to be given to the International Convention for the Prevention of Pollution from Ships 1973. The Order empowers the Secretary of State to make regulations for the purpose of giving effect to the Convention and Protocol, and in particular with respect to the carrying out of surveys, the issue of certificates, the application of the regulations to the Crown, the imposition of penalties and the detention of ships for that purpose. The Merchant Shipping (Prevention of Oil Pollution) Regulations 1996, SI 1996/2154 amended by SI 2000/2688, SI 2004/303 and 2110 and SI 2005/1916 have been made.

The Merchant Shipping (Prevention and Control of Pollution) Order 1987, SI 1987/470 amended by SI 1990/2595, SI 1997/2569 and SI 1998/254 made under this section and giving effect to international convention enables the Secretary of State to make regulations to prevent pollution, in particular pollution by noxious liquid substances, require the reporting of incidents and apply provisions of the convention. The Merchant Shipping (Reporting of Pollution Incidents) SI 1987/586, requires the reporting of incidents and specifies particulars to be recorded. The Merchant Shipping (Dangerous Goods and Marine Pollutants) Regulations 1990, SI 1990/2605 bring certain goods within the ambit of international codes and in particular require shipowners to retain marine pollutant manifests and stowage plans ashore until goods have been discharged from the ship. The Merchant Shipping Act (Dangerous or Noxious Liquid Substances in Bulk) Regulations 1996, SI 1996/3010 amended by SI 1998/1153 apply to all ships carrying in bulk noxious liquid substances or unassessed liquid substances, all chemical tankers carrying dangerous substances in bulk and all oil tankers carrying pollution hazard substances in bulk and make provision in relation to the construction, equipment and operation of every ship; discharge, loading and carriage; procedures and records; surveys and certificates; responsibilities of the owner and master; exemptions; inspection and detention. Each of the regulations creates offences punishable either summarily with a maximum fine of **level 4** on the standard scale or, on indictment by a fine; for procedure in respect of an offence triable either way, see Magistrates' Courts Act 1980, ss 17A–22 in PART I: MAGISTRATES' COURTS, PROCEDURE. Each set of regulations provides a defence to persons who can establish that they took all reasonable steps to ensure compliance with the regulation.

The Merchant Shipping (Prevention of Pollution by Garbage) Order 1988, SI 1988/2252 amended by SI 1993/1581, SI 1997/2569 and SI 1998/254, enables the Secretary of State to regulate pollution by garbage as required by international convention. The Merchant Shipping (Reception Facilities for Garbage) Regulations 1988, SI 1988/2293 and the Merchant Shipping (Prevention of Pollution by Garbage) Regulations 1998, SI 1998/1377 have been made.

The Merchant Shipping (Prevention of Pollution) (Law of The Sea Convention) Order 1996, SI 1996/282, enables regulations to be made implementing provisions in the United Nations Convention on the Law of the Sea 1982, which relates to the protection and preservation of the marine environment from pollution from ships caused beyond the territorial sea of the United Kingdom. The Merchant Shipping (Prevention of Pollution) (Limits) Regulations 1996, SI 1996/2128 amended by SI 1997/506 and the Merchant Shipping (Prevention of Oil Pollution) Regulations 1996, SI 1996/2154 amended by SI 1997/1910, SI 2000/2688, SI 2004/303 and 2110 and SI 2005/1916 have been made.

The Merchant Shipping (Oil Pollution Preparedness, Response and Co-operation Convention) Order 1997, SI 1997/2567 has been made which enables the Secretary of State to make regulations to give effect to the International Convention on Oil Pollution Preparedness, Response and Co-operation 1990. The Merchant Shipping (Oil Pollution Preparedness, Response and Co-operation Convention) Regulations 1998, SI 1998/1056 amended by SI 2001/1639 have been made.

The Merchant Shipping (Control of Pollution) (SOLAS) Order 1998, SI 1998/1500 has been made which enables the Secretary of State to make regulations to give effect to the International Convention for the Safety of Life at Sea Convention 1974 in so far as it relates to the prevention, reduction or control of pollution of the sea or other waters by waste matter from ships. The Merchant Shipping (International Safety Management (ISM Code) Regulations 1998, SI 1998/1561 have been made.

The Merchant Shipping (Prevention of Pollution) (Drilling Rigs and Other Platforms) Order 2005, SI 2005/74 made under the Railways and Transport Safety Act 2003, s 112(7)(c) provides that s 128(1)(e) of the Merchant Shipping Act 1995 applies in relation to drilling rigs and other platforms which are used, navigated or situated wholly or partly in or on water, as it applies in relation to ships.

7–6397   129. Further provision for prevention of pollution from ships.   (1) *Her Majesty may by Order in Council make provision for the purpose of giving effect to any provision of the United Nations Convention on the Law on the Sea 1982 for the protection and preservation of the marine environment from pollution by matter from ships.*
[Merchant Shipping Act 1995, s 129—summarised.]

7–6398   130. Regulation of transfers between ships in territorial waters.   (1) *Regulations may be made to prevent pollution, danger to health or navigation or hazards to the environment or natural resources with penalties for contravention.*
[Merchant Shipping Act 1995, s 130—summarised.]

CHAPTER IA
WASTE RECEPTION FACILITIES AT HARBOURS

7–6398A   130A–130E.   *Powers of Secretary of State to make regulations[1] in relation to the provision of facilities at harbours for the reception of waste from ships. A harbour authority may levy charges for use of waste reception facilities. Breach of regulations may be an offence friable either way, maximum penalty on summary conviction a fine not exceeding the* **statutory maximum** *and on indictment imprisonment for a term not exceeding* **two years** *or a* **fine** *or* **both.**

---

1. The Merchant Shipping (Port Waste Reception Facilities) Regulations 1997, SI 1997/3018 amended by SI 2003/1809 have been made.

CHAPTER II
OIL POLLUTION

General provisions for preventing pollution

7–6399   131. Discharge of oil from ships into certain United Kingdom waters.   (1) If any oil or mixture containing oil is discharged as mentioned in the following paragraphs into United Kingdom national waters which are navigable by sea-going ships, then, subject to the following provisions of this Chapter, the following shall be guilty of an offence[1], that is to say—

(a) if the discharge is from a ship, the owner or master of the ship, unless he proves[2] that the discharge took place and was caused as mentioned in paragraph (b) below;

(b) if the discharge is from a ship but takes place in the course of a transfer of oil to or from another ship or a place on land and is caused by the act or omission of any person in charge of any apparatus in that other ship or that place, the owner or master of that other ship or, as the case may be, the occupier of that place.

(2) Subsection (1) above does not apply to any discharge which—

(a) is made into the sea; and

(b) is a kind or is made in circumstances for the time being prescribed by regulations made by the Secretary of State.

(3) A person guilty of an offence under this section shall be liable[3]—

    (*a*) on summary conviction, to a fine not exceeding £250,000[4];

    (*b*) on conviction on indictment, to a **fine**.

(4) In this section "sea" includes any estuary or arm of the sea.

(5) In this section "place on land" includes anything resting on the bed or shore of the sea, or of any other waters included in United Kingdom national waters, and also includes anything afloat (other than a ship) if it is anchored or attached to the bed or shore of the sea or any such waters.

(6) In this section "occupier", in relation to any such thing as is mentioned in subsection (5) above, if it has no occupier, means the owner thereof.

[Merchant Shipping Act 1995, s 131 as amended by the Merchant Shipping and Maritime Security Act 1997, s 7.]

---

    1. See special defences in ss 132–134, post, provisions relating to the prosecution of offences in s 143 post, and enforcement and application of fines (which can be used to pay expenses and make good damage) in s 146, post.

    2. On a preponderance of probabilities: *R v Carr-Briant* [1943] 2 All ER 156, 107 JP 167.

    3. For procedure in respect of an offence triable either way, see the Magistrates' Courts Act 1980, ss 17A–21, in Part I: Magistrates' Courts, Procedure, ante.

    4. Increased from £50,000 in respect of offences committed after 17 July 1997, the commencement of s 7(1) of the Merchant Shipping and Maritime Security Act 1997.

7–6400   132. Defences of owner or master charged with offence under section 131. (1) Where a person is charged with an offence under section 131 as the owner or master of a ship, it shall be a defence to prove that the oil or mixture was discharged for the purpose of—

    (*a*) securing the safety of any ship;

    (*b*) preventing damage to any ship or cargo, or

    (*c*) saving life,

unless the court is satisfied that the discharge of the oil or mixture was not necessary for that purpose or was not a reasonable step to take in the circumstances,

(2) Where a person is charged with an offence under section 131 as the owner or master of a ship, it shall also be a defence to prove—

    (*a*) that the oil or mixture escaped in consequence of damage to the ship, and that as soon as practicable after the damage occurred all reasonable steps were taken for preventing, or (if it could not be prevented) for stopping or reducing, the escape of the oil or mixture; or

    (*b*) that the oil or mixture escaped by reason of leakage, that neither the leakage nor any delay in discovering it was due to any want of reasonable care, and that as soon as practicable after the escape was discovered all reasonable steps were taken for stopping or reducing it.

[Merchant Shipping Act 1995, s 132.]

7–6401   133. Defences of occupier charged with offence under section 131. (1) Where a person is charged, in respect of the escape of any oil or mixture containing oil, with an offence under section 131 as the occupier of a place on land, it shall be a defence to prove that neither the escape nor any delay in discovering it was due to any want of reasonable care and that as soon as practicable after it was discovered all reasonable steps were taken for stopping or reducing it.

[Merchant Shipping Act 1995, s 133.]

7–6402   134. Protection for acts done in exercise of certain powers of harbour authorities, etc. (1) Where any oil, or mixture containing oil, is discharged in consequence of—

    (*a*) the exercise of any power conferred by section 252 or 253; or

    (*b*) the exercise, for the purpose of preventing obstruction or danger to navigation, of any power to dispose of sunk, stranded or abandoned ships which is exercisable by a harbour authority under any local enactment;

and apart from this subsection the authority exercising the power, or a person employed by or acting on behalf of the authority, would be guilty of an offence under section 131 in respect of that discharge, the authority or person shall not be convicted unless it is shown that they or he failed to take such steps (if any) as were reasonable in the circumstances for preventing, stopping or reducing the discharge.

(2) Subsection (1) above shall apply to the exercise of any power conferred by section 13 of the Dockyard Ports Regulation Act 1865 (removal of obstructions to dockyard ports) as it applies to the exercise of the powers under sections 252 and 253, and shall, as so applying, have effect as if references to the authority exercising the power were references to the Queen's harbour master for the port in question.

[Merchant Shipping Act 1995, s 134.]

7–6403   135. Restrictions on transfer of oil at night. (1) No oil shall be transferred between sunset and sunrise to or from a ship in any harbour in the United Kingdom unless the requisite notice has been given in accordance with this section or the transfer is for the purposes of a fire and rescue authority or other employer of fire-fighters.

(2) A general notice may be given to the harbour master of a harbour that transfers of oil between sunset and sunrise will be frequently carried out at a place in the harbour within such period, not ending later than twelve months after the date on which the notice is given, as is specified in the notice; and if such a notice is given it shall be the requisite notice for the purposes of this section as regards transfers of oil at that place within the period specified in the notice.

(3) Subject to subsection (2) above, the requisite notice for the purposes of this section shall be a notice given to the harbour master not less than three hours nor more than 96 hours before the transfer of oil begins.

(4) In the case of a harbour which has no harbour master, references in this section to the harbour master shall be construed as references to the harbour authority.

(5) If any oil is transferred to or from a ship in contravention of this section, the master of the ship, and, if the oil is transferred from or to a place on land, the occupier of that place, shall be liable on summary conviction to a fine not exceeding **level 3** on the standard scale.

[Merchant Shipping Act 1995, s 135 as amended by the Fire and Rescue Services Act 2004, Sch 1.]

7–6404 136. Duty to report discharge of oil into waters of harbours. (1) If any oil or mixture containing oil—

    (*a*) is discharged from a ship into the waters of a harbour in the United Kingdom; or

    (*b*) is found to be escaping or to have escaped from a ship into any such waters;

the owner or master of the ship shall forthwith report the occurrence to the harbour master, or, if the harbour has no harbour master, to the harbour authority.

(2) A report made under subsection (1) above shall state whether the occurrence falls within subsection (1)(*a*) or (*b*) above.

(3) If a person fails to make a report as required by this section he shall be liable on summary conviction to a fine not exceeding **level 5** on the standard scale.

[Merchant Shipping Act 1995, s 136.]

7–6404A 136A. Discharges etc authorised under other enactments. The provisions of sections 131(1) and 136(1) shall not apply to any discharge which is made under, and the provisions of section 136(1) shall not apply to any escape which is authorised by, an authorisation granted under Part I of the Environmental Protection Act 1990 or a permit granted under regulations under section 2 of the Pollution Prevention and Control Act 1999.★

[Merchant Shipping Act 1995, s 136A as prospectively inserted by the Pollution Prevention and Control Act 1999, Sch 2, s 13 and prospectively amended by the Pollution Prevention and Control Act 1999, Sch 3.]

★**Repealed by the Pollution Prevention and Control Act 1999, s 6 and Sch 3, when in force.**

Shipping casualties

7–6405 137–141. *Repealed by the Marine Safety Act 2003, Sch 2.*

Enforcement

7–6410 142. Oil records. (1)–(5) *Regulations may require oil record books to be carried in ships to record the discharge and transfer of oil from ships*[1].

(6) If any ship fails to carry such an oil record book as it is required to carry under this section the owner or master shall be liable on summary conviction to a fine not exceeding **level 5** on the standard scale.

(7) If any person fails to comply with any requirements imposed on him by or under this section, he shall be liable on summary conviction to a fine not exceeding **level 5** on the standard scale.

(8) If any person makes an entry in any oil record book carried or record kept under this section which is to his knowledge false or misleading in any material particular, he shall be liable[2]—

    (*a*) on summary conviction, to a fine not exceeding the **statutory maximum**, or imprisonment for a term not exceeding **six months**, or **both**;

    (*b*) on conviction on indictment, to a **fine** or to imprisonment for a term not exceeding **two years**, or **both**.

(9) In any proceedings under this Chapter—

    (*a*) any oil record book carried or record kept in pursuance of regulations made under this section shall be admissible as evidence, and in Scotland shall be sufficient evidence, of the facts stated in it;

    (*b*) any copy of an entry in such an oil record book or record which is certified by the master of the ship in which the book is carried or by the person by whom the record is required to be kept to be a true copy of the entry shall be admissible as evidence, and in Scotland shall be sufficient evidence, of the facts stated in the entry;

(c) any document purporting to be an oil record book carried or record kept in pursuance of regulations made under this section, or purporting to be such a certified copy as is mentioned in paragraph[2] above, shall, unless the contrary is proved, be presumed to be such a book, record or copy, as the case may be.

(10) In this section "barge" includes a lighter and any similar vessel.
[Merchant Shipping Act 1995, s 142.]

1. The Oil in Navigable Waters (Transfer Records) Regulations 1957, SI 1957/358, and the Oil in Navigable Waters (Transfer Records) Regulations 1972, SI 1972/1929 have been made.

2. For procedure in respect of an offence triable either way, see the Magistrates' Courts Act 1980, ss 17A–21, in PART I: MAGISTRATES' COURTS, PROCEDURE, ante.

7–6411 143. Prosecutions and enforcement of fines. (1) Proceedings for an offence under this Chapter may, in England and Wales be brought only—

(a) by or with the consent of the Attorney General[1], or

(b) if the offence is one to which subsection (4) below applies, by the harbour authority, or

(c) unless the offence is one mentioned in subsection (4)(b) or (c) below, by the Secretary of State or a person authorised by any general or special direction of the Secretary of State.

(2) Subject to subsection (3) below, proceedings for an offence under this Chapter may, in Northern Ireland, be brought only—

(a) by or with the consent of the Attorney General for Northern Ireland,

(b) if the offence is one to which subsection (4) below applies, by a harbour authority, or

(c) unless the offence is one mentioned in subsection (4)(b) or (c) below, by the Secretary of State or a person authorised by any general or special direction of the Secretary of State.

(3) Subsection (2) above shall have effect in relation to proceedings for an offence under section 131 relating to the discharge of oil or a mixture containing oil from a ship in a harbour in Northern Ireland as if the references in paragraph (c) to the Secretary of State were references to the Secretary of State or the Department of the Environment for Northern Ireland.

(4) This subsection applies to the following offences—

(a) any offence under section 131 which is alleged to have been committed by the discharge of oil, or a mixture containing oil, into the waters of a harbour in the United Kingdom;

(b) any offence in relation to a harbour in the United Kingdom under section 135 or 136; and

(c) any offence under section 142 relating to the keeping of records of the transfer of oil within such a harbour.

(5) The preceding provisions of this section shall apply in relation to any part of a dockyard port within the meaning of the Dockyard Ports Regulation Act 1865 as follows—

(a) if that part is comprised in a harbour in the United Kingdom, the reference to the harbour authority shall be construed as including a reference to the Queen's harbour master for the port;

(b) if that part is not comprised in a harbour in the United Kingdom, the references to such a harbour shall be construed as references to such a dockyard port and the reference to the harbour authority as a reference to the Queen's harbour master for the port.

(6) Any document required or authorised, by virtue of any statutory provision, to be served on a foreign company for the purposes of the institution of, or otherwise in connection with, proceedings for an offence under section 131 alleged to have been committed by the company as the owner of the ship shall be treated as duly served on that company if the document is served on the master of the ship.

In this subsection "foreign company" means a company or body which is not one to which any of sections 695 and 725 of the Companies Act 1985 and Articles 645 and 673 of the Companies (Northern Ireland) Order 1986 applies so as to authorise the service of the document in question under any of those provisions.

(7) Any person authorised to serve any document for the purposes of the institution of, or otherwise in connection with, proceedings for an offence under this Chapter shall, for that purpose, have the right to go on board the ship in question.
[Merchant Shipping Act 1995, s 143.]

1. See PART I: MAGISTRATES' COURTS, PROCEDURE, para **1–410 Criminal prosecutions**, ante.

7–6412 144. Power to detain ships for section 131 offences. (1) Where a harbour master has reason to believe that the master or owner of a ship has committed an offence under section 131 by the discharge from the ship of oil, or a mixture containing oil, into the waters of the harbour, the harbour master may detain the ship.

(2) Section 284, in its application to the detention of a ship under this section, shall have effect with the omission of subsections (1), (6) and (7) and as if—

(a) in subsection (2), the reference to competent authority were a reference to the harbour authority; and

(b) in subsection (4), the persons in relation to whom that subsection applies were the harbour master or any person acting on his behalf.

(3) Where a harbour master detains a ship other than a United Kingdom ship under this section he shall immediately notify the Secretary of State, who shall then inform the consul or diplomatic representative of the State whose flag the ship is entitled to fly or the appropriate maritime authorities of that State.

In this subsection "United Kingdom ship" has the same meaning as in section 85.

(4) A harbour master who detains a ship under this section shall immediately release the ship—

(a) if no proceedings for the offence are instituted within the period of seven days beginning with the day on which the ship is detained;

(b) if proceedings for the offence, having been instituted within that period, are concluded without the master or owner being convicted;

(c) if either—

    (i) the sum of £255,000 is paid to the harbour authority by way of security, or

    (ii) security which, in the opinion of the harbour authority, is satisfactory and is for an amount not less than £255,000 is given to the harbour authority,

    by or on behalf of the master or owner; or

(d) where the master or owner is convicted of the offence, if any costs or expenses ordered to be paid by him, and any fine imposed on him, have been paid.

(5) The harbour authority shall repay any sum paid in pursuance of subsection (4)(c) above or release any security so given—

(a) if no proceedings for the offence are instituted within the period of seven days beginning with the day on which the sum is paid; or

(b) if proceedings for the offence, having been instituted within that period, are concluded without the master or owner being convicted.

(6) Where a sum has been paid, or security has been given, by any person in pursuance of subsection (4)(c) above and the master or owner is convicted of the offence, the sum so paid or the amount made available under the security shall be applied as follows—

(a) first payment of any costs or expenses ordered by the court to be paid by the master or owner; and

(b) next in payment of any fine imposed by the court;

and any balance shall be repaid to the first-mentioned person.

(7) Any reference in this section to a harbour master or a harbour authority shall, where the harbour in question consists of or includes the whole or any part of a dockyard port within the meaning of the Dockyard Ports Regulation Act 1865, be construed as including a reference to the Queen's harbour master for the port.

(8) This section does not apply in relation to a ship of Her Majesty's navy or any Government ship.

[Merchant Shipping Act 1995, s 144 as amended by the Merchant Shipping and Maritime Security Act 1997, s 7.]

7–6413 145. Interpretation of section 144. (1) This section has effect for the interpretation of the references in section 144 to the institution of proceedings or their conclusion without the master or owner of a ship being convicted of an offence under section 131.

(2) For the purposes of section 144 in its application to England and Wales—

(a) proceedings for an offence under section 131 are instituted—

    (i) when a justice of the peace issues a summons or warrant under section 1 of the Magistrates' Courts Act 1980 in respect of the offence;

    (ii) when a person is charged with the offence after being taken into custody without a warrant;

    (iii) when a bill of indictment is preferred under section 2(2)(b) of the Administration of Justice (Miscellaneous Provisions) Act 1933; and

(b) proceedings for the offence are concluded without the master or owner being convicted on the occurrence of one of the following events—

    (i) the discontinuance of the proceedings;

    (ii) the acquittal of the master or owner;

    (iii) the quashing of the master's or owner's conviction of the offence;

    (iv) the grant of Her Majesty's pardon in respect of the master's or owner's conviction of the offence.

(3) *Northern Ireland.*

(4) Where the application of subsection (2)(*a*) or (3)(*a*) above would result in there being more than one time for the institution of proceedings, they shall be taken to have been instituted at the earliest of those times.

(5) *Scotland.*

[Merchant Shipping Act 1995, s 145.]

7–6414   146. Enforcement and application of fines.   (1) Where a fine imposed by a court in proceedings against the owner or master of a ship for an offence under this Chapter is not paid, or any costs or expenses ordered to be paid by him are not paid, at the time ordered by the court, the court shall, in addition to any other powers of enforcing payment, have power—

(*a*)   except in Scotland, to direct the amount remaining unpaid to be levied by distress,

(*b*)   in Scotland, to grant warrant authorising the arrestment and sale,

of the ship and its equipment.

(2) Where a person is convicted of an offence under section 131, and the court imposes a fine in respect of the offence, then, if it appears to the court that any person has incurred, or will incur, expenses in removing any pollution, or making good any damage, which is attributable to the offence, the court may order the whole or part of the fine to be paid to that person for or towards defraying those expenses.

[Merchant Shipping Act 1995, s 146.]

7–6415   147. Enforcement of Conventions relating to oil pollution.   Provision may be made by Order in Council[1] for this purpose.

[Merchant Shipping Act 1995, s 147—summarised.]

---

1. The Prevention of Oil Pollution (Convention Countries) Order 1981, SI 1981/612 lists those countries which have accepted the International Convention for the Prevention of Pollution of the Sea by Oil 1954, and those territories to which it extends.

Miscellaneous and supplementary

7–6416   148. Power of Secretary of State to grant exemptions.   The Secretary of State may exempt from any of the provisions of this Chapter or of any regulations made thereunder, either absolutely or subject to such conditions as he thinks fit—

(*a*)   any ship or classes of ships;

(*b*)   any discharge of, or of a mixture containing, oil.

[Merchant Shipping Act 1995, s 148.]

7–6417   149. Application to Government ships.   (1) This Chapter does not apply to ships of Her Majesty's navy, nor to Government ships in the service of the Secretary of State while employed for the purposes of Her Majesty's navy.

(2) Subject to subsection (1) above and to section 141(4) and section 144(8)—

(*a*)   provisions of this Chapter which are expressed to apply only to United Kingdom ships apply to government ships registered in the United Kingdom and also to Government ships not so registered but held for the purposes of Her Majesty's Government in the United Kingdom;

(*b*)   provisions of this Chapter which are expressed to apply to ships generally apply to Government ships.

[Merchant Shipping Act 1995, s 149.]

7–6418   150. Annual Report.   *Report by the Secretary of State on the exercise and performance of his functions under this Chapter.*

[Merchant Shipping Act 1995, s 150.]

7–6419   151. Interpretation.   (1) In this Chapter—

"harbour authority" means a person or body of persons empowered by an enactment to make charges in respect of ships entering a harbour in the United Kingdom or using facilities therein;

"harbour in the United Kingdom" means a port, estuary, haven, dock or other place the waters of which are within United Kingdom national waters and in respect of entry into or the use of which by ships a person or body of persons is empowered by an enactment (including a local enactment) to make any charges other than charges in respect of navigational aids or pilotage;

"harbour master" includes a dock master or pier master, and any person specially appointed by a harbour authority for the purpose of enforcing the provisions of this Chapter in relation to the harbour;

"local enactment" means a local or private Act, or an order confirmed by Parliament or brought into operation in accordance with special Parliamentary procedure;

"oil" means oil of any description and includes spirit produced from oil of any description, and also includes coal tar;

"oil residues" means any waste consisting of, or arising from, oil or a mixture containing oil;

"place on land" has the meaning given in section 131;

"transfer", in relation to oil, means transfer in bulk.

(2) For the purposes of the definition of "harbour in the United Kingdom" "charges in respect of navigational aids" means general light dues, local light dues and any other charges payable in respect of lighthouses, buoys or beacons.

(3) Any reference in any provision of this Chapter to a mixture containing oil shall be construed as a reference to any mixture of oil (or, as the case may be, of oil of a description referred to in that provision) with water or with any other substance.

(4) Any reference in this Chapter, other than in section 136, to the discharge of oil or a mixture containing oil, or to its being discharged, from a ship, place or thing, except where the reference is to its being discharged for a specific purpose, includes a reference to the escape of oil or mixture, or (as the case may be) to its escaping, from that ship, place or thing.

(5) For the purposes of any provision of this Chapter relating to the discharge of oil or a mixture containing oil from a ship, any floating craft (other than a ship) which is attached to a ship shall be treated as part of the ship.

(6) Any power conferred by section 259 in its application to this Chapter to test any equipment on board a ship shall be construed as including a power to require persons on board the ship to carry out such work as may be requisite for the purpose of testing the equipment; and any provision of that section as to submitting equipment for testing shall be construed accordingly.

(7) Subject to section 18 of the Interpretation Act 1978 (offence under two or more laws) nothing in this Chapter shall—

    (a)   affect any restriction imposed by or under any other enactment, whether contained in a public general Act or a local or private Act; or

    (b)   derogate from any right of action or other remedy (whether civil or criminal) in proceedings instituted otherwise than under this Chapter.

[Merchant Shipping Act 1995, s 151.]

CHAPTER III[1]
LIABILITY FOR OIL POLLUTION

Compulsory insurance

7-6420   **163. Compulsory insurance against liability for pollution.**   (1) Subject to the provisions of this Chapter relating to Government ships, subsection (2) below shall apply to any ship carrying in bulk a cargo of more than 2,000 tons of oil of a description specified in regulations made by the Secretary of State.

(2) The ship shall not enter or leave a port in the United Kingdom or arrive at or leave a terminal in the territorial sea of the United Kingdom nor, if the ship is a United Kingdom ship, a port in any other country or a terminal in the territorial sea of any other country, unless there is in force a certificate[2] complying with the provisions of subsection (3) below and showing that there is in force in respect of the ship a contract of insurance or other security satisfying the requirements of Article VII of the Liability Convention (cover for owner's liability).

(3) The certificate must be—

    (a)   if the ship is a United Kingdom ship, a certificate issued by the Secretary of State;

    (b)   if the ship is registered in a Liability Convention country other than the United Kingdom, a certificate issued by or under the authority of the government of the other Liability Convention country; and

    (c)   if the ship is registered in a country which is not a Liability Convention country, a certificate issued by the Secretary of State or by or under the authority of the government of any Liability Convention country other than the United Kingdom.

(4) Any certificate required by this section to be in force in respect of a ship shall be carried in the ship and shall, on demand, be produced by the master to any officer of customs and excise or of the Secretary of State and, if the ship is a United Kingdom ship, to any proper officer.

(5) If a ship enters or leaves, or attempts to enter or leave, a port or arrives at or leaves, or attempts to arrive at or leave, a terminal in contravention of subsection (2) above, the master or owner shall be liable[3] on conviction on indictment to a **fine**, or on summary conviction to a fine not exceeding **£50,000**.

(6) If a ship fails to carry, or the master of a ship fails to produce, a certificate as required by subsection (4) above, the master shall be liable on summary conviction to a fine not exceeding **level 4** on the standard scale.

(7) If a ship attempts to leave a port in the United Kingdom in contravention of this section the ship may be detained.

[Merchant Shipping Act 1995, s 163.]

---

1. The main purpose of these provisions is to enable the United Kingdom to give effect to the International Convention on Civil Liability for Oil Pollution Damage agreed at Brussels in November 1969 (Cmnd 4403). The act imposes strict liability on a shipowner for oil pollution damage in the United Kingdom (and for the cost of measures taken to prevent or minimise such damage) resulting from the escape of oil from a ship carrying persistent oil in bulk as cargo. There are,

however, certain exceptions from this liability. For the commencement of this section and transitory provisions, see s 171, post.

Sections 163 and 164, post, deal with the arrangements for the compulsory insurance aspects of the Convention. They provide that ships, other than Government ships carrying cargo of more than 2,000 tons of persistent oil in bulk, are not to enter or leave United Kingdom ports or terminals without having in their possession a certificate of insurance or other financial security, and that ships registered in the United Kingdom must carry a certificate wherever they dock throughout the world.

See also the Prevention of Oil Pollution Act 1971 in PART VIII: PUBLIC HEALTH, post.

2. The Oil Pollution (Compulsory Insurance) Regulations 1977, SI 1997/1820, make provision with respect to certificates of insurance and define "persistent oil".

3. For procedure in respect of an offence triable either way, see the Magistrates' Courts Act 1989, ss 17A–21, in PART I: MAGISTRATES' COURTS, PROCEDURE, ante.

7–6421   **164. Issue of certificate by Secretary of State[1].** (1) Subject to subsection (2) below, if the Secretary of State is satisfied, on the application for such a certificate as is mentioned in section 163 in respect of a United Kingdom ship or a ship registered in any country which is not a Liability Convention country, that there will be in force in respect of the ship, throughout the period for which the certificate is to be issued, a contract of insurance or other security satisfying the requirements of Article VII of the Liability Convention, the Secretary of State shall issue such a certificate to the owner.

(2) If the Secretary of State is of opinion that there is a doubt whether the person providing the insurance or other security will be able to meet his obligations thereunder, or whether the insurance or other security will cover the owner's liability under section 153 in all circumstances, he may refuse the certificate.

(3) The Secretary of State may make regulations[2] providing for the cancellation and delivery up of a certificate under this section in such circumstances as may be prescribed by the regulations.

(4) If a person required by regulations under subsection (3) above to deliver up a certificate fails to do so he shall be liable on summary conviction to a fine not exceeding **level 4** on the standard scale.

(5) The Secretary of State shall send a copy of any certificate issued by him under this section in respect of a United Kingdom ship to the Registrar General of Shipping and Seamen, and the Registrar shall make the copy available for public inspection.

[Merchant Shipping Act 1995, s 164.]

---

1. For the commencement of this section and transitory provisions, s 171, post.
2. The Oil Pollution (Compulsory Insurance) Regulations 1997, SI 1997/1820, make provision with respect to certificates of insurance and define "persistent oil".

7–6422   **170. Interpretation[1].** (1) In this Chapter—

"the court" means the High Court or, in Scotland, the Court of Session;

"damage" includes loss;

"oil" means persistent hydrocarbon mineral oil;

"owner" means the person or persons registered as the owner of the ship or, in the absence of registration, the person or persons owning the ship, except that, in relation to a ship owned by a State which is operated by a person registered as the ship's operator, it means the person registered as its operator;

"relevant threat of contamination" shall be construed in accordance with section 153(2) or 154(2); and

"ship" (subject to section 154(5)) means any sea-going vessel or seaborne craft of any type whatsoever.

(2) In relation to any damage or cost resulting from the discharge or escape of any oil from a ship, or from a relevant threat of contamination, references in this Chapter to the owner of the ship are references to the owner at the time of the occurrence or first of the occurrences resulting in the discharge or escape or (as the case may be) in the threat of contamination.

(3) *Scotland.*

(4) References in this Chapter to the territory of any country include the territorial sea of that country and—

(a) in the case of the United Kingdom, any area specified by virtue of section 129(2)(b); and

(b) in the case of any other Liability Convention country, the exclusive economic zone of that country established in accordance with international law, or, if such a zone has not been established, such area adjacent to the territorial sea of that country and extending not more than 200 nautical miles from the baselines from which the breadth of that sea is measured as may have been determined by that State in question in accordance with international law.

[Merchant Shipping Act 1995, s 170 as amended by the Merchant Shipping and Maritime Security Act 1997, Sch 6.]

---

1. For the commencement of this section and transitory provisions, see s 171, post.

7–6423 171. Transitory text of this Chapter and power to make transitional provisions.
(1) Until such day as the Secretary of State may by order[1] appoint the provisions set out in Schedule 4 as Chapter III shall have effect instead of the foregoing provisions of this Chapter; and references in that Schedule to a section whose number is included in that Schedule is a reference to the section so included.

(2) Notwithstanding subsection (1) above, Her Majesty may by Order in Council[2] make such provision as appears to Her Majesty to be appropriate in connection with the implementation of any transitional provisions contained in the 1992 Protocol or the Conventions which they amend; and any such Order may in particular provide, in relation to occurrences of any description specified in the Order—

(a) for specified provisions of this Chapter, whether as contained in this Chapter or in the Chapter III set out in Schedule 4, to have effect;
(b) for any such provisions to have effect subject to specified modifications.

(3) In subsection (2) above—

"the 1992 Protocol" means the Protocol of 1992 to amend the International Convention for Oil Pollution Damage 1969 signed in London on 27th November 1992; and
"specified" means specified in the Order.
[Merchant Shipping Act 1995, s 171.]

---

1. 30 May 1996 was appointed by the Merchant Shipping (Appointed Day No 1) Order 1996, SI 1996/1210.
2. The Merchant Shipping (Liability and Compensation for Oil Pollution Damage) (Transitional Provisions) Order 1996, SI 1996/1143 was made under this provision but was revoked by SI 1997/2566 in consequence of the United Kingdom ceasing to be a party to the International Convention on Civil Liability for Oil Pollution Damage 1969.

CHAPTER IV[1]
INTERNATIONAL OIL POLLUTION
COMPENSATION FUND

Preliminary

7–6424 172. Meaning of the "Liability Convention", "the Fund Convention" and related expressions. (1) In this Chapter—

(a) "the Liability Convention" has the same meaning as in Chapter III of this Part;
(b) "the Fund Convention" means the International Convention on the Establishment of an International Fund for Compensation for Oil Pollution Damage 1992;
(c) "the Fund" means the International Fund established by the Fund Convention; and
(d) "Fund Convention country" means a country in respect of which the Fund Convention is in force.

(2) If Her Majesty by Order in Council declares that any State specified in the Order is a party to the Fund Convention in respect of any country so specified, the Order shall, while in force, be conclusive evidence that the State is a party to that Convention in respect of that country.
[Merchant Shipping Act 1995, s 172.]

---

1. For the commencement of this section and transitory provisions, see s 182, post.

Contributions to Fund

7–6425 173. Contributions by importers of oil and others. *Provides for contributions to be made to an International Fund which Fund is to be liable for pollution damage. The Secretary of State may make regulations imposing on persons who are or may be liable to make contributions obligations to give security for payment and the regulations may impose penalties for contravention of the regulations punishable on summary conviction by a fine not exceeding* **level 5** *on the standard scale or such lower limit as may be specified by the regulations.*

7–6426 174. Power to obtain information[1]. (1)–(4) *Power of the Secretary of State to require persons to obtain information.*
(5) If a person discloses any information which has been furnished to or obtained by him under this section, or in connection with the execution of this section, then, unless the disclosure is made—

(a) with the consent of the person from whom the information was obtained, or
(b) in connection with the execution of this section, or
(c) for the purposes of any legal proceedings arising out of this section or of any report of such proceedings,

he shall be liable on summary conviction to a fine not exceeding **level 5** on the standard scale.
(6) A person who—

(a) refuses or wilfully neglects to comply with a notice under this section, or

(b) in furnishing any information in compliance with a notice under this section makes any statement which he knows to be false in a material particular, or recklessly makes any statement which is false in a material particular,

shall be liable[2]—

(i) on summary conviction, to a fine not exceeding **level 4** on the standard scale in the case of an offence under paragraph (a) above and not exceeding the **statutory maximum** in the case of an offence under paragraph (b) above, and

(ii) on conviction on indictment, to a **fine**, or to imprisonment for a term not exceeding **twelve months**, or to **both**.

[Merchant Shipping Act 1995, s 174.]

---

1. For the commencement of this section and transitory provisions, see s 182, post.
2. For procedure in respect of an offence triable either way, see the Magistrates' Courts Act 1989, ss 17A–21, in PART I: MAGISTRATES' COURTS, PROCEDURE, ante.

7–6427   181. Interpretation[1]**.** (1) In this Chapter, unless the context otherwise requires—

"damage" includes loss;

"discharge or escape", in relation to pollution damage, means the discharge or escape of oil from the ship;

"guarantor" means any person providing insurance or other financial security to cover the owner's liability of the kind described in section 163;

"incident" means any occurrence, or series of occurrences having the same origin, resulting in a discharge or escape of oil from a ship or in a relevant threat of contamination;

"oil", except in section 173 and 174, means persistent hydrocarbon mineral oil;

"owner" means the person or persons registered as the owner of the ship or in the absence of registration, the person or persons owning the ship, except that, in relation to a ship owned by a State which is operated by a person registered as the ship's operator, it means the person registered as its operator;

"pollution damage" means—

(a) damage caused outside a ship by contamination resulting from a discharge or escape of oil from the ship,

(b) the cost of preventive measures,

(c) further damage caused by preventive measures,

but does not include any damage attributable to any impairment of the environment except to the extent that any such damage consists of—

(i) any loss of profits, or

(ii) the cost of any reasonable measures of reinstatement actually taken or to be taken;

"preventive measures" means any reasonable measures taken by any person to prevent or minimise pollution damage, being measures taken—

(a) after an incident has occurred, or

(b) in the case of an incident consisting of a series of occurrences, after the first of those occurrences;

"relevant threat of contamination" means a grave and imminent threat of damage being caused outside a ship by contamination resulting from a discharge or escape of oil from the ship; and

"ship" means any ship (within the meaning of Chapter III of this Part) to which section 153 applies.

(2) For the purposes of this Chapter—

(a) references to a discharge or escape of oil from a ship are references to such a discharge or escape wherever it may occur, and whether it is of oil carried in a cargo tank or of oil carried in a bunker fuel tank; and

(b) where more than one discharge or escape results from the same occurrence or from a series of occurrences having the same origin, they shall be treated as one.

(3) References in this Chapter to the territory of any country shall be construed in accordance with section 170(4) reading the reference to a Liability Convention country as a reference to a Fund Convention country.

[Merchant Shipping Act 1995, s 181.]

---

1. For the commencement of this section and transitory provisions, see s 182, post.

7–6428   182. Transitory text of this Chapter and power to make transitional provisions.
(1) Until such day as the Secretary of State may by order[1] appoint the provisions set out in Schedule 4 as Chapter IV shall have effect instead of the foregoing provisions of this Chapter; and references in that Schedule to a section whose number is included in that Schedule is a reference to the section so included.

(2) Notwithstanding subsection (1) above, Her Majesty may by Order in Council[2] make such provision as appears to Her Majesty to be appropriate in connection with the implementation of any transitional provisions contained in the 1992 Protocol or the Conventions which they amend; and any such Order may in particular provide, in relation to occurrences of any description specified in the Order—

(a) for specified provisions of this Chapter, whether as contained in this Chapter or in the Chapter IV set out in Schedule 4, to have effect;

(b) for any such provisions to have effect subject to specified modifications.

(3) In subsection (2) above—

"the 1992 Protocol" means the Protocol of 1992 to amend the International Convention on the Establishment of an International Fund for Compensation for Oil Pollution Damage 1971 signed in London on 27th November 1992; and

"specified" means specified in the Order.

[Merchant Shipping Act 1995, s 182.]

1. 30 May 1996 was appointed by the Merchant Shipping (Appointed Day No 1) Order 1996, SI 1996/1210.
2. The Merchant Shipping (Liability and Compensation for Oil Pollution Damage) (Transitional Provisions) Order 1996, SI 1996/1143 was made under this provision but was revoked by SI 1997/2566 in consequence of the United Kingdom ceasing to be a party to the International Convention on Civil Liability for Oil Pollution Damage 1969.

CHAPTER V
CARRIAGE OF HAZARDOUS AND NOXIOUS SUBSTANCES

7–6428A 182A. Introductory. *Convention on Liability and Compensation for Damage in Connection with the Carriage of Hazardous and Noxious Substances by Sea 1996[1].*
[Merchant Shipping Act 1995, s 182A as inserted by the Merchant Shipping and Maritime Security Act 1997, s 14—summarised.]

1. The text of the Convention is set out in Sch 5A to the Act which is not reproduced in this work.

7–6428B 182B–C. *Provides for effect to be given to the Convention by Order in Council and for the Secretary of State to modify these provisions by order.*

PART VIII[1]
LIGHTHOUSES

Offences in connection with lighthouses, buoys, beacons, etc

7–6438 219. Damage etc to lighthouses etc. (1) A person who, without lawful authority—

(a) intentionally or recklessly damages—

(i) any lighthouse or the lights exhibited in it, or
(ii) any lightship, buoy or beacon;

(b) removes, casts adrift or sinks any lightship, buoy or beacon; or
(c) conceals or obscures any lighthouse, buoy or beacon;

commits an offence.

(2) A person who, without reasonable excuse,—

(a) rides by,
(b) makes fast to, or
(c) runs foul of,

any lightship, buoy or beacon commits an offence.

(3) A person who is guilty of an offence under this section shall, in addition to being liable for the expenses of making good any damage so occasioned, be liable, on summary conviction, to a fine not exceeding **level 4** on the standard scale.

[Merchant Shipping Act 1995, s 219.]

1. Part VIII contains ss 193–223.

7–6439 220. Prevention of false lights. (1) Whenever any light is exhibited at such place or in such manner as to be liable to be mistaken for a light proceeding from a lighthouse, the general lighthouse authority within whose area the place is situated, may serve a notice ("a prevention notice") upon the owner of the place where the light is exhibited or upon the person having the charge of the light.

(2) A prevention notice is a notice directing the person to whom it is addressed to take, within a reasonable time specified in the notice, effectual means for extinguishing or effectually screening the light and for preventing for the future any similar light.

(3) A prevention notice may, in addition to any other mode of service authorised by this Act, be served by affixing the notice in some conspicuous spot near to the light to which it relates.

(4) If a person on whom a prevention notice is served fails, without reasonable excuse, to comply with the directions contained in the notice, he shall be liable, on summary conviction, to a fine not exceeding **level 5** on the standard scale.

(5) If a person on whom a prevention notice is served neglects for a period of seven days to extinguish or effectually screen the light mentioned in the notice, the general lighthouse authority may enter the place where the light is and forthwith extinguish it, doing no unnecessary damage.

(6) Where a general lighthouse authority incur any expenses in exercising their powers under subsection (5) above they may recover the expenses form the person on whom the prevention notice was served.

(7) Any such expenses may, in England and Wales and Northern Ireland, be recovered summarily as a civil debt.

(8) *Scotland.*

[Merchant Shipping Act 1995, s 220.]

Supplemental

7–6440   223. Interpretation, etc.   (1) In this Part—

"buoys and beacons" includes all other marks and signs of the sea;

"the Commissioners of Irish Lights" means the body incorporated by that name under the local Act of the session held in the 30th and 31st years of the reign of Queen Victoria intituled "An Act to alter the constitution of the Corporation for preserving and improving the port of Dublin and for other purposes connected with that body and with the Port of Dublin Corporation";

"general light dues" has the meaning given in section 205(1);

"lighthouse" includes any floating and other light exhibited for the guidance of ships, and also any sirens and any other description of fog signals, and also any addition to a lighthouse of any improved light, or any siren, or any description of fog signal;

"the Trinity House" means the master, wardens and assistants of the guild, fraternity or brotherhood of the most glorious and undivided Trinity and of St Clement in the parish of Deptford Strond in the county of Kent, commonly called the corporation of the Trinity House of Deptford Strond;

"the 1894 Act" means the Merchant Shipping Act 1894.

(2) Any reference in this Part to a lighthouse, buoy or beacon includes its appurtenances.

(3) The Secretary of State may by order provide that references or a particular reference to a buoy or beacon in this Part shall be construed as including, in such circumstances as are specified in the order[1], equipment of a kind so specified which is intended as an aid in the navigation of ships.

(4) No order shall be made under subsection (3) above unless a draft of the order has been laid before and approved by resolution of each House of Parliament.

[Merchant Shipping Act 1995, s 223.]

---

1. The General Lighthouse Authorities (Beacons: Maritime Differential Correction Systems) Order 1997, SI 1997/3016 has been made.

PART IX[1]
SALVAGE AND WRECK

CHAPTER II
WRECK

Vessels in distress

7–6445   231. Application of, and discharge of functions under, sections 232, 233, 234 and 235.   (1) Sections 232, 233, 234 and 235 apply in circumstances where a United Kingdom or foreign vessel is wrecked, stranded, or in distress at any place on or near the coasts of the United Kingdom or any tidal water within United Kingdom waters.

(2) Where any function is conferred on the receiver by any of those sections that function may be discharged by any officer of customs and excise or any principal officer of the coastguard.

(3) An officer discharging any such functions of the receiver shall, with respect to any goods or articles belonging to a vessel the delivery of which to the receiver is required by any provision of this Chapter, be treated as the agent of the receiver.

(4) However, an officer discharging such functions shall not—

(a) be entitled to any fees payable to receivers, or

(b) be deprived of any right to salvage to which he would otherwise be entitled.

(5) In any of those sections "shipwrecked persons", in relation to a vessel, means persons belonging to the vessel.

[Merchant Shipping Act 1995, s 231.]

1. Part IX contains ss 224–255.

7–6446   232. Duty of receiver where vessel in distress.   (1) In circumstances in which this section applies by virtue of section 231 in relation to any vessel the receiver shall, on being informed of the circumstances, discharge the following functions.

(2) Subject to subsection (3) below, the receiver shall—

(a)   forthwith proceed to the place where the vessel is;

(b)   take command of all persons present; and

(c)   assign such duties and give such directions to each person as he thinks fit for the preservation of the vessel and of the lives of the shipwrecked persons.

(3) The receiver shall not interfere between the master and crew of the vessel in reference to the management of the vessel unless he is requested to do so by the master.

(4) Subject to subsection (3) above, if any person intentionally disobeys the direction of the receiver he shall be liable, on summary conviction, to a fine not exceeding **level 3** on the standard scale.

[Merchant Shipping Act 1995, s 232 as amended by the Merchant Shipping and Maritime Security Act 1997, Sch 6.]

7–6447   233. Powers of receiver in case of vessel in distress.   (1) In circumstances where this section applies by virtue of section 231 in relation to any vessel the receiver may, for the purpose of the preservation of shipwrecked persons or of the vessel, cargo and equipment—

(a)   require such persons as he thinks necessary to assist him;

(b)   require the master, or other person having the charge, of any vessel near at hand to give such assistance with his men, or vessel, as may be in his power; and

(c)   require the use of any vehicle that may be near at hand.

(1A) The receiver may not under section (1) above impose any requirement on the master or other person having the charge of a vessel owned or operated by the Royal National Lifeboat Institution.

(2) If any person refuses, without reasonable excuse, to comply with any requirement made under subsection (1) above he shall be liable, on summary conviction, to a fine not exceeding **level 3** on the standard scale.

[Merchant Shipping Act 1995, s 233 as amended by the Merchant Shipping and Maritime Security Act 1997, s 21.]

7–6448   234. Power to pass over adjoining land.   (1) In circumstances where this section applies by virtue of section 231 in relation to any vessel, all persons may, subject to subsections (3) and (4) below, for the purpose of—

(a)   rendering assistance to the vessel,

(b)   saving the lives of shipwrecked persons, or

(c)   saving the cargo or equipment of the vessel,

pass and repass over any adjoining land without being subject to interruption by the owner or occupier and deposit on the land any cargo or other article recovered from the vessel.

(2) The right of passage conferred by subsection (1) above is a right of passage with or without vehicles.

(3) No right of passage is conferred by subsection (1) above where there is some public road equally convenient.

(4) The rights conferred by subsection (1) above shall be so exercised as to do as little damage as possible.

(5) Any damage sustained by an owner or occupier of land in consequence of the exercise of the rights conferred by this section shall be a charge on the vessel, cargo or articles in respect of or by which the damage is caused.

(6) Any amount payable in respect of such damage shall, in case of dispute, be determined and shall, in default of payment, be recoverable in the same manner as the amount of salvage is determined and recoverable under this Part.

(7) If the owner or occupier of any land—

(a)   impedes or hinders any person in the exercise of the rights conferred by this section;

(b)   impedes or hinders the deposit on the land of any cargo or other article recovered from the vessel; or

(c)   prevents or attempts to prevent any cargo or other article recovered from the vessel from remaining deposited on the land for a reasonable time until it can be removed to a safe place of public deposit;

he shall be liable, on summary conviction, to a fine not exceeding **level 3** on the standard scale.

[Merchant Shipping Act 1995, s 234.]

7–6449   235. *Liability for damage in case of plundered vessel.*

Dealing with wreck

7–6450　236. Duties of finder etc of wreck.　(1) If any person finds or takes possession of any wreck in United Kingdom waters or finds or takes possession of any wreck outside United Kingdom waters and brings it within those waters he shall—

(a) if he is the owner of it, give notice to the receiver stating that he has found or taken possession of it and describing the marks by which it may be recognised;

(b) if he is not the owner of it, give notice to the receiver that he has found or taken possession of it and, as directed by the receiver, either hold it to the receiver's order or deliver it to the receiver.

(2) If any person fails, without reasonable excuse, to comply with subsection (1) above he shall be liable, on summary conviction, to a fine not exceeding **level 4** on the standard scale and if he is not the owner of the wreck he shall also—

(a) forfeit any claim to salvage; and

(b) be liable to pay twice the value of the wreck—

　(i) if it is claimed, to the owner of it; or

　(ii) if it is unclaimed, to the person entitled to the wreck.

(3) Any sum payable under subsection (2)(b) above to the owner of the wreck or to the persons entitled to the wreck may, in England and Wales and Northern Ireland, be recovered summarily as a civil debt.

(4) *Scotland.*

[Merchant Shipping Act 1995, s 236.]

7–6451　237. Provisions as respects cargo, etc.　(1) Where a vessel is wrecked, stranded, or in distress at any place on or near the coasts of the United Kingdom or any tidal water within United Kingdom waters, any cargo or other articles belonging to or separated from the vessel which are washed on shore or otherwise lost or taken from the vessel shall be delivered to the receiver.

(2) If any person (whether the owner or not)—

(a) conceals or keeps possession of any such cargo or article, or

(b) refuses to deliver any such cargo or article to the receiver or to any person authorised by the receiver to require delivery,

he shall be liable, on summary conviction, to a fine not exceeding **level 4** on the standard scale.

(3) The receiver or any person authorised by him may take any such cargo or article (if necessary by force) from any person who refuses to deliver it.

[Merchant Shipping Act 1995, s 237.]

Offences in respect of wreck

7–6452　245. Taking wreck to foreign port.　(1) A person commits an offence if he takes into any foreign port and sells—

(a) any vessel stranded, derelict or otherwise in distress found on or near the coasts of the United Kingdom or any tidal water within United Kingdom waters;

(b) any part of the cargo or equipment of, or anything belonging to, such a vessel; or

(c) any wreck found within those waters.

(2) A person who is guilty of an offence under this section shall be liable, on conviction on indictment, to imprisonment for a term not exceeding **five years**.

[Merchant Shipping Act 1995, s 245.]

7–6453　246. Interfering with wrecked vessel or wreck.　(1) Subject to subsection (2) below, a person commits an offence if, without the permission of the master, he boards or attempts to board any vessel which is wrecked, stranded or in distress.

(2) No offence is committed under subsection (1) above if the person is the receiver or a person lawfully acting as the receiver or if he acts by command of the receiver or a person so acting.

(3) A person commits an offence if—

(a) he impedes or hinders or attempts to impede or hinder the saving of—

　(i) any vessel stranded or in danger of being stranded, or otherwise in distress, on or near any coast or tidal water; or

　(ii) any part of the cargo or equipment of any such vessel; or

　(iii) any wreck;

(b) he conceals any wreck;

(c) he defaces or obliterates any mark on a vessel; or

(d) he wrongfully carries away or removes—

　(i) any part of any vessel stranded or in danger of being stranded, or otherwise in distress, on or near any coast or tidal water;

(ii) any part of the cargo or equipment of any such vessel; or

(iii) any wreck.

(4) The master of a vessel may forcibly repel any person committing or attempting to commit an offence under subsection (1) above.

(5) A person who is guilty of an offence under this section shall be liable, on summary conviction—

(*a*) in the case of an offence under subsection (1) above, to a fine not exceeding **level 3** on the standard scale;

(*b*) in the case of an offence under subsection (3) above, to a fine not exceeding **level 4** on the standard scale.

[Merchant Shipping Act 1995, s 246.]

7–6454   247. Powers of entry etc.   (1) Where the receiver has reason to believe that—

(*a*) any wreck is being concealed by or is in the possession of some person who is not the owner of it; or

(*b*) any wreck is being otherwise improperly dealt with,

he may apply to a justice of the peace for a search warrant.

(2) Where a search warrant is granted under subsection (1) above to the receiver, the receiver may, by virtue of the warrant—

(*a*) enter any house, or other place (wherever situated) or any vessel; and

(*b*) search for, seize and detain any wreck found there.

(3) If any seizure of wreck is made under this section in consequence of information given by any person to the receiver, the person giving the information shall be entitled, by way of salvage, to such sum, not exceeding £100, as the receiver may allow.

[Merchant Shipping Act 1995, s 247.]

CHAPTER III
SUPPLEMENTAL

Interpretation

7–6455   255. Interpretation.   (1) In this Part—

"receiver" means a receiver of wreck appointed under section 248;

"salvage" includes, subject to the Salvage Convention, all expenses properly incurred by the salvor in the performance of the salvage services;

"the Salvage Convention" has the meaning given by section 224(1);

"salvor" means, in the case of salvage services rendered by the officers or crew or part of the crew of any ship belonging to Her Majesty, the person in command of the ship;

"tidal water" means any part of the sea and any part of a river within the ebb and flow of the tide at ordinary spring tides, and not being a harbour;

"vessel" includes any ship or boat, or any other description of vessel used in navigation; and

"wreck" includes jetsam, flotsam, lagan and derelict found in or on the shores of the sea or any tidal water.

(2) Fishing boats or fishing gear lost or abandoned at sea and either—

(*a*) found or taken possession of within United Kingdom waters; or

(*b*) found or taken possession of beyond those waters and brought within those waters;

shall be treated as wreck for the purposes of this Part.

(3) *Scotland.*

[Merchant Shipping Act 1995, s 255.]

PART X[1]
ENFORCEMENT OFFICERS AND POWERS

Inspection etc powers

7–6460   257. Powers to require production of ships documents.   (1) The powers conferred by this section are conferred in relation to United Kingdom ships and are available to any of the following officers, namely—

(*a*) any Departmental officer,

(*b*) any commissioned naval officer,

(*c*) any British consular officer,

(*d*) the Registrar General of Shipping and Seamen or any person discharging his functions,

(*e*) any chief officer of customs and excise,

(*f*) any superintendent,

whenever the officer has reason to suspect that this Act or any law for the time being in force relating to merchant seamen or navigation is not complied with.

(2) Those powers are—

(a) to require the owner, master, or any of the crew to produce any official log-books or other documents relating to the crew or any member of the crew in their possession or control;

(b) to require the master to produce a list of all persons on board his ship, and take copies of or extracts from the official log-books or other such documents;

(c) to muster the crew; and

(d) to require the master to appear and give any explanation concerning the ship or her crew or the official log-books or documents produced or required to be produced.

(3) If any person, on being duly required by an officer under this section to produce a log-book or any document, fails without reasonable excuse to produce the log-book or document, he shall be liable on summary conviction to a fine not exceeding **level 3** on the standard scale.

(4) If any person, on being duly required by any officer under this section—

(a) to produce a log-book or document, refuses to allow the log-book or document to be inspected or copied;

(b) to muster the crew, impedes the muster; or

(c) to give any explanation, refuses or neglects to give the explanation or knowingly misleads or deceives the officer;

he shall be liable on summary conviction to a fine not exceeding **level 5** on the standard scale.
[Merchant Shipping Act 1995, s 257.]

---

1. Part X contains ss 256–266.

7–6461   258. Powers to inspect ships and their equipment, etc.   (1) For the purposes of seeing that the provisions of this Act other than sections 131 to 141 and sections 143 to 151 and the provisions of regulations and rules made under this Act (other than those sections) are complied with or that the terms of any approval, licence, consent, direction or exemption given by virtue of such regulations are duly complied with, the following persons, namely—

(a) a surveyor of ships,

(b) a superintendent,

(c) any person appointed by the Secretary of State, either generally or in a particular case, to exercise powers under this section,

may at all reasonable times go on board a ship in the United Kingdom or in United Kingdom waters and inspect the ship and its equipment or any part thereof, any articles on board and any document carried in the ship in pursuance of this Act or in pursuance of regulations or rules under this Act.

(1A) The powers conferred by subsection (1) above are not exercisable in relation to a qualifying foreign ship while the ship is exercising—

(a) the right of innocent passage, or

(b) the right of transit passage through straits used for international navigation.

(2) The powers conferred by subsection (1) above are, if the ship is a United Kingdom ship, also exercisable outside United Kingdom waters and may be so exercised by a proper officer as well as the persons mentioned in that subsection.

(3) A person exercising powers under this section shall not unnecessarily detain or delay a ship but may, if he considers it necessary in consequence of an accident or for any other reason, require a ship to be taken into dock for a survey of its hull or machinery.

(4) Where any such person as is mentioned in subsection (1) above has reasonable grounds for believing that there are on any premises provisions or water intended for supply to a United Kingdom ship which, if provided on the ship, would not be in accordance with safety regulations containing requirements as to provisions and water to be provided on ships he may enter the premises and inspect the provisions or water for the purpose of ascertaining whether they would be in accordance with the regulations.

(5) If any person obstructs a person in the exercise of his powers under this section, or fails to comply with a requirement made under subsection (3) above, he shall be liable, on summary conviction, to a fine not exceeding **level 5** on the standard scale.
[Merchant Shipping Act 1995, s 258 as amended by the Merchant Shipping and Maritime Security Act 1997, Sch 1.]

7–6462   259. Powers of inspectors in relation to premises and ships.   (1) The powers conferred by this section are conferred in relation to—

(a) any premises in the United Kingdom; or

(b) any United Kingdom ship wherever it may be and any other ship which is present in the United Kingdom or in United Kingdom waters;

and are available to any Departmental inspector, or any inspector appointed under section 256(6), for the purpose of performing his functions.

(2) Such an inspector—

(a) may at any reasonable time (or, in a situation which in his opinion is or may be dangerous, at any time)—

    (i)   enter any premises, or
    (ii) board any ship,

    if he has reason to believe that it is necessary for him to do so;

(b) may, on entering any premises by virtue of paragraph (a) above or on boarding a ship by virtue of that paragraph, take with him any other person authorised for the purpose by the Secretary of State and any equipment or materials he requires;

(c) may make such examination and investigation as he considers necessary;

(d) may give a direction requiring that the premises or ship or any part of the premises or ship or any thing in the premises or ship or such a part shall be left undisturbed (whether generally or in particular respects) for so long as is reasonably necessary for the purposes of any examination or investigation under paragraph (c) above;

(e) may take such measurements and photographs and make such recordings as he considers necessary for the purpose of any examination or investigation under paragraph (c) above;

(f) may take samples of any articles or substances found in the premises or ship and of the atmosphere in or in the vicinity of the premises or ship;

(g) may, in the case of any article or substance which he finds in the premises or ship and which appears to him to have caused or to be likely to cause danger to health or safety, cause it to be dismantled or subjected to any process or test (but not so as to damage or destroy it unless that is in the circumstances necessary);

(h) may, in the case of any such article or substance as is mentioned in paragraph (g) above, take possession of it and detain it for so long as is necessary for all or any of the following purposes, namely—

    (i)   to examine it and do to it anything which he has power to do under that paragraph,
    (ii) to ensure that it is not tampered with before his examination of it is completed,
    (iii) to ensure that it is available for use as evidence in any proceedings for an offence under this Act or any instrument made under it;

(i) may require any person who he has reasonable cause to believe is able to give any information relevant to any examination or investigation under paragraph (c) above—

    (i)   to attend at a place and time specified by the inspector, and
    (ii) to answer (in the absence of persons other than any persons whom the inspector may allow to be present and a person nominated to be present by the person on whom the requirement is imposed) such questions as the inspector thinks fit to ask, and
    (iii) to sign a declaration of the truth of his answers;

(j) may require the production of, and inspect and take copies of or of any entry in,—

    (i)   any books or documents which by virtue of any provision of this Act are required to be kept; and
    (ii) any other books or documents which he considers it necessary for him to see for the purposes of any examination or investigation under paragraph (c) above;

(k) may require any person to afford him such facilities and assistance with respect to any matters or things within that person's control or in relation to which that person has responsibilities as the inspector considers are necessary to enable him to exercise any of the powers conferred on him by this subsection.

(3) The powers conferred by subsection (2) above to require the production of any document and copy it include, in relation to oil record books required to be carried under section 142, power to require the master to certify the copy as a true copy.

(4) The powers conferred by subsection (2) above to inspect premises shall also be exercisable, for the purpose of Chapter II of Part VI, in relation to any apparatus used for transferring oil.

(5) The powers of entry and inspection of premises conferred by subsection (2) and (4) above for the purposes of Chapter II of Part VI shall not be exercisable by Departmental inspectors (or surveyors of ships in their capacity as Departmental inspectors) in relation to places on land in Northern Ireland and apparatus located in Northern Ireland otherwise than on board ships; but persons appointed by the Department of the Environment for Northern Ireland shall have the like powers; and those subsections shall have effect accordingly in relation to persons so appointed.

(6) The powers conferred by subsection (2)(a), (c) and (j) above shall also be exercisable, in relation to a ship in a harbour in the United Kingdom, by the harbour master or other persons appointed by the Secretary of State for the purpose, for the purpose of ascertaining the circumstances relating to an alleged discharge of oil or a mixture containing oil from the ship into the harbour.

(7) It is hereby declared that nothing in the preceding provisions of this section authorises a person unnecessarily to prevent a ship from proceeding on a voyage.

(8) The Secretary of State may by regulations make provision as to the procedure to be followed in connection with the taking of samples under subsection (2)(f) above and subsection (11) below and provision as to the way in which samples that have been so taken are to be dealt with.

(9) Where an inspector proposes to exercise the power conferred by subsection (2)(*g*) above in the case of an article or substance found in any premises or ship, he shall, if so requested by a person who at the time is present in and has responsibilities in relation to their premises or ship, cause anything which is to be done by virtue of that power to be done in the presence of that person unless the inspector considers that its being done in that person's presence would be prejudicial to the safety of that person.

(10) Before exercising the power conferred by subsection (2)(*g*) above, an inspector shall consult such persons as appear to him appropriate for the purpose of ascertaining what dangers, if any, there may be in doing anything which he proposes to do under that power.

(11) Where under the power conferred by subsection (2)(*h*) above an inspector takes possession of any article or substance found in any premises or ship, he shall leave there, either with a responsible person or, if that is impracticable, fixed in a conspicuous position, a notice giving particulars of that article or substance sufficient to identify it and stating that he has taken possession of it under that power; and before taking possession of any such substance under that power an inspector shall, if it is practicable for him to do so, take a sample of the substance and give to a responsible person at the premises or on board the ship a portion of the sample marked in a manner sufficient to identify it.

(12) No answer given by a person in pursuance of a requirement imposed under subsection (2)(*i*) above shall be admissible in evidence against that person or the husband or wife of that person in any proceedings except proceedings in pursuance of subsection (1)(*c*) of section 260 in respect of a statement in or a declaration relating to the answer; and a person nominated as mentioned in the said subsection (2)(*i*) shall be entitled, on the occasion on which the questions there mentioned are asked, to make representations to the inspector on behalf of the person who nominated him.
[Merchant Shipping Act 1995, s 259.]

7–6463 260. Provisions supplementary to section 259. (1) A person who—

(*a*) intentionally obstructs an inspector in the exercise of any power available to him under section 259; or

(*b*) without reasonable excuse, does not comply with a requirement imposed in pursuance of section 259 or prevents another person from complying with such a requirement; or

(*c*) without prejudice to the generality of paragraph (*b*) above, makes a statement or signs a declaration which he knows is false, or recklessly makes a statement or signs a declaration which is false, in purported compliance with a requirement made in pursuance of subsection (2)(*i*) of section 259,

shall be liable[1]—

(i) on summary conviction, to a fine not exceeding the **statutory maximum**;

(ii) on conviction on indictment, to imprisonment for a term not exceeding **two years**, or a **fine** or **both**.

(2) Nothing in section 259 shall be taken to compel the production by any person of a document of which he would on grounds of legal professional privilege be entitled to withhold production on an order for discovery in an action in the High Court or, as the case may be, on an order for the production of documents in an action in the Court of Session.

(3) A person who complies with a requirement imposed on him in pursuance of paragraph (*i*)(i) or (*k*) of subsection (2) of section 259 shall be entitled to recover from the person who imposed the requirement such sums in respect of the expenses incurred in complying with the requirement as are prescribed by regulations made by the Secretary of State.

(4) Regulations under subsection (3) above may make different provision for different circumstances.

(5) Any payments under subsection (3) above shall be made out of money provided by Parliament.
[Merchant Shipping Act 1995, s 260.]

---

1. For procedure in respect of an offence triable either way, see the Magistrates' Courts Act 1980, ss 17A–21, in PART I: MAGISTRATES' COURTS, PROCEDURE, *ante*.

Improvement notices and prohibition notices

7–6464 261. *Improvement notices.*

7–6465 262. *Prohibition notices.*

7–6466 263. *Provisions supplementary to section s 261 and 262.*

7–6467 264. *References of notices to arbitration.*

7–6468 265. *Compensation in connection with invalid prohibition notices.*

7–6469 266. Offences. (1) Any person who contravenes any requirement imposed by an improvement notice shall be liable[1]—

(*a*) on summary conviction, to a fine not exceeding the **statutory maximum**;

(*b*) on conviction on indictment, to a **fine**.

(2) Any person who contravenes any prohibition imposed by a prohibition notice shall be liable—

(*a*) on summary conviction, to a fine not exceeding the **statutory maximum**;

(*b*) on conviction on indictment, to imprisonment for a term not exceeding **two years** or a **fine** or **both**.

(3) It shall be a defence for a person charged with an offence under this section to prove[2] that he exercised all due diligence to avoid a contravention of the requirement or prohibition in question.

(4) In this section any reference to an improvement notice or a prohibition notice includes a reference to any such notice as modified under section 264(3).

[Merchant Shipping Act 1995, s 266.]

---

1. For procedure in respect of an offence triable either way, see the Magistrates' Courts Act 1980, ss 17A–21, in PART I: MAGISTRATES' COURTS, PROCEDURE, ante.

2. On the balance of probabilities: *R v Carr-Briant* [1943] KB 607, [1943] 2 All ER 156, 107 JP 167.

PART XI[1]

ACCIDENT INVESTIGATIONS AND INQUIRIES

Marine accident investigations

7–6474 268. Formal investigation into marine accidents. (1)–(4) *Conduct of formal investigations[2]*.

(5) If as a result of the investigation the wreck commissioner or sheriff is satisfied, with respect to any officer, of any of the matters mentioned in paragraphs (*a*) to (*c*) of section 61(1) and, if it is a matter mentioned in paragraph (*a*) or (*b*) of that section, is further satisfied that it caused or contributed to the accident, he may cancel or suspend any certificate issued to the officer under section 47 or censure him; and if he cancels or suspends the certificate the officer shall deliver it forthwith to him or to the Secretary of State.

(6) If a person fails to deliver a certificate as required under subsection (5) above he shall be liable on summary conviction to a fine not exceeding **level 3** on the standard scale

(7)–(11) *Reissue of a certificate, compensation and costs.*

[Merchant Shipping Act 1995, s 268.]

---

1. Part XI contains ss 267–273.

2. The Merchant Shipping (Accident Reporting and Investigation) Regulations 1999, SI 1999/2567 amended by SI 2001/152 and SI 2004/1266 have been made under s 267 which create penalties for failure to comply with the requirements imposed by the regulations.

PART XII[1]

LEGAL PROCEEDINGS

Prosecution of offences

7–6479 274. Time limit for summary offences. (1) Subject to subsections (2) and (3) below, no person shall be convicted of an offence under this Act in summary proceedings unless—

(*a*) the proceedings were commenced within six months beginning with the date on which the offence was committed; or

(*b*) in a case where the accused happens during that period to be out of the United Kingdom, the proceedings were commenced within two months after he first happens to arrive within the United Kingdom and before the expiration of three years beginning with the date on which the offence was committed.

(2) Nothing in subsection (1) above shall apply in relation to any indictable offence.

(3) Subsection (1) above shall not prevent a conviction for an offence in summary proceedings begun before the expiration of three years beginning with the date on which the offence was committed and before—

(*a*) the expiration of the period of six months beginning with the day when evidence which the Secretary of State considers is sufficient to justify a prosecution for the offence came to his knowledge; or

(*b*) the expiration of two months beginning with the day when the accused was first present in the United Kingdom after the expiration of the period mentioned in paragraph (*a*) above if throughout that period the accused was absent from the United Kingdom.

(4) For the purpose of subsection (3) above—

(*a*) a certificate of the Secretary of State stating that evidence came to his knowledge on a particular day shall be conclusive evidence of that fact; and

(b) a document purporting to be a certificate of the Secretary of State and to be signed on his behalf shall be presumed to be such a certificate unless the contrary is proved.

(5) *Scotland.*
[Merchant Shipping Act 1995, s 274.]

---

1. Part XII contains ss 274–291.

7–6480   275. Time limit for summary orders. No order for the payment of money shall be made under this Act in proceedings before a magistrates' court unless—

(a) the proceedings were commenced within six months beginning with the date on which the matter of complaint arose; or

(b) in a case where both or either of the parties to the proceedings happen during that period to be out of the United Kingdom, the proceedings were commenced within six months after they both first happen to arrive, or to be at one time, within the United Kingdom.
[Merchant Shipping Act 1995, s 275.]

7–6481   276. *Scotland.*

7–6482   277. Offences by officers of bodies corporate. (1) Where a body corporate is guilty of an offence under this Act or any instrument made under it, and that offence is proved to have been committed with the consent or connivance of, or to be attributable to any neglect on the part of, a director, manager, secretary or other similar officer of the body corporate or any person who was purporting to act in such a capacity, he as well as the body corporate shall be guilty of that offence and shall be liable to be proceeded against and punished accordingly.

(2) Where the affairs of a body corporate are managed by its members, subsection (1) above shall apply in relation to the acts and defaults of a member in connection with his functions of management as if he were a director of the body corporate.
[Merchant Shipping Act 1995, s 277.]

7–6483   278. *Scotland.*

Jurisdiction

7–6484   279. Jurisdiction in relation to offences. (1) For the purpose of conferring jurisdiction, any offence under this Act shall be deemed to have been committed in any place in the United Kingdom where the offender may for the time being be.

(2) For the same purpose, any matter of complaint under this Act shall be deemed to have arisen in any place in the United Kingdom where the person complained against may for the time being be.

(3) The jurisdiction under subsections (1) and (2) above shall be in addition to and not in derogation of any jurisdiction or power of a court under any other enactment.
[Merchant Shipping Act 1995, s 279.]

7–6485   280. Jurisdiction over ships lying off coasts. (1) Where the area within which a court in any part of the United Kingdom has jurisdiction is situated on the coast of any sea or abuts on or projects into any bay, channel, lake, river or other navigable water the court shall have jurisdiction as respects offences under this Act over any vessel being on, or lying or passing off, that coast or being in or near that bay, channel, lake, river or navigable water and over all persons on board that vessel or for the time being belonging to it.

(2) The jurisdiction under subsection (1) above shall be in addition to and not in derogation of any jurisdiction or power of a court under the Magistrates' Courts Act 1980 or the Magistrates' Courts (Northern Ireland) Order 1981.
[Merchant Shipping Act 1995, s 280.]

7–6486   281. Jurisdiction in case of offences on board ship. Where any person is charged with having committed any offence under this Act then—

(a) if he is a British citizen and is charged with having committed it—

(i) on board any United Kingdom ship on the high seas[1].
(ii) in any foreign port or harbour, or
(iii) on board any foreign ship[2] to which he does not belong[3]; or

(b) if he is not a British citizen and is charged with having committed it on board any United Kingdom ship on the high seas;

and he is found[4] within the jurisdiction of any court in any part of the United Kingdom which would have had jurisdiction in relation to the offence if it had been committed on board a United Kingdom ship within the limits of its ordinary jurisdiction to try the offence that court shall have jurisdiction to try the offence as if it had been so committed.
[Merchant Shipping Act 1995, s 281.]

1. This means all oceans, seas, bays, channels, rivers, creeks and waters below low-water mark, and "where great ships can go", except only such parts of such oceans, etc as lie within the body of some country (*R v Liverpool Justices, ex p Molyneux* [1972] 2 QB 384, [1972] 2 All ER 471, 136 JP 477).

2. The fact that a foreign ship is berthed in a foreign port with the gang plank in place, does not deprive an English court of jurisdiction; the position might be different if the ship is dry-docked or hauled up on to the shore (*R v Cumberworth* [1989] Crim LR 591).

3. Persons "belong to" a vessel if they are members of the crew; accordingly, passengers on a passenger ferry were held not to belong to the ship (*R v Kelly* [1981] QB 174, [1981] 2 All ER 1098).

4. This section is divided into two parts (*Robey v Vladinier* (1935) 99 JP 428). He may be so found even if he has been illegally arrested and brought there (*R v Lopez, R v Settler* (1858) 22 JP 84).

7–6487 282. Offences committed by British seamen. (1) Any act in relation to property or person done in or at any place (ashore or afloat) outside the United Kingdom by any master or seaman who at the time is employed in a United Kingdom ship, which, if done in any part of the United Kingdom, would be an offence under the law of any part of the United Kingdom, shall—

(*a*) be an offence under that law, and

(*b*) be treated for the purposes of jurisdiction and trial, as if it had been done within the jurisdiction of the Admiralty of England.

(2) Subsection (1) above also applies in relation to a person who had been so employed within the period of three months expiring with the time when the act was done.

(3) Subsection (1) and (2) above apply to omissions as they apply to acts.

[Merchant Shipping Act 1995, s 282.]

Return of offenders

7–6488 283. Return of offenders. (1) The powers conferred on a British consular officer by subsection (2) below are exercisable in the event of any complaint being made to him—

(*a*) that any offence against property or persons has been committed at any place (ashore or afloat) outside the United Kingdom by any master or seaman who at the time when the offence was committed, or within three months before that time, was employed in a United Kingdom ship; or

(*b*) that any offence on the high seas has been committed by any master or seaman belonging to any United Kingdom ship.

(2) Those powers are—

(*a*) to inquire into the case upon oath, and

(*b*) if the case so requires, to take any steps in his power for the purpose of placing the offender under the necessary restraint and sending him by United Kingdom ship as soon as practicable in safe custody to the United Kingdom for proceedings to be taken against him.

(3) The consular officer may, subject to subsections (4) and (5) below, order the master of any United Kingdom ship bound for the United Kingdom to receive and carry the offender and the witnesses to the United Kingdom; and the officer shall endorse upon the agreement of the ship such particulars with respect to them as the Secretary of State requires.

(4) A consular officer shall not exercise the power conferred by subsection (3) above unless no more convenient means of transport is available or it is available only at disproportionate expense.

(5) No master of a ship may be required under subsection (3) above to receive more than one offender for every 100 tons of his ship's registered tonnage, or more than one witness for every 50 tons of his ship's registered tonnage.

(6) The master of any ship to whose charge an offender has been committed under subsection (3) above shall, on his ship's arrival in the United Kingdom, give the offender into the custody of some police officer or constable.

(7) If any master of a ship, when required under subsection (3) above to receive and carry any offender or witness in his ship—

(*a*) fails to do so; or

(*b*) in the case of an offender, fails to deliver him as required by subsection (6) above;

he shall be liable on summary conviction to a fine not exceeding **level 5** on the standard scale.

(8) The expense of imprisoning any such offender and of carrying him and witnesses to the United Kingdom otherwise than in the ship to which they respectively belong shall be paid out of money provided by Parliament.

(9) References in this section to carrying a person in a ship include affording him subsistence during the voyage.

[Merchant Shipping Act 1995, s 283.]

Detention of ship and distress on ship

7–6489 284. Enforcing detention of ship. (1) Where under this Act a ship is to be or may be detained any of the following officers may detain the ship—

(*a*) any commissioned naval or military officer,

(b) any officer of a Minister of the Crown or Northern Ireland department who is authorised by the Secretary of State, either generally or in a particular case, to exercise powers under this section,

(c) any officer of customs and excise, and

(d) any British consular officer.

(1A) A notice of detention may—

(a) include a direction that the ship—

(i) must remain in a particular place, or

(ii) must be moved to a particular anchorage or berth, and

(b) if it includes such a direction, may specify circumstances relating to safety or the prevention of pollution in which the master may move his ship from that place, anchorage or berth.

(2) If a ship as respects which notice of detention has been served on the master proceeds to sea, otherwise than in accordance with such a notice, before it is released by a competent authority, the master of the ship shall be guilty of an offence.

(2A) If a ship as respects which notice of detention has been served on the master fails to comply with a direction given under subsection (1A)(a) above, the master of the ship shall be guilty of an offence.

(2B) A person guilty of an offence under subsection (2) or (2A) above shall be liable[1]—

(a) on summary conviction, to a fine not exceeding £50,000;

(b) on conviction on indictment, to a **fine**.

(3) The owner of a ship, and any person who sends to sea a ship, as respects which an offence is committed under subsection (2) or (2A) above shall, if party or privy to the offence, also be guilty of an offence under that subsection and liable accordingly.

(4) Where a ship proceeding to sea in contravention of subsection (2) above or failing to comply with a direction given under subsection (1A)(a) above carries away without his consent any of the following who is on board the ship in the execution of his duty, namely—

(a) any officer authorised by subsection (1) above to detain the ship, or

(b) any surveyor of ships,

the owner and master of the ship shall each—

(i) be liable to pay all expenses of and incidental to the officer or surveyor being so carried away; and

(ii) be guilty of an offence.

(5) A person guilty of an offence under subsection (4) above shall be liable[1]—

(a) on summary conviction, to a fine not exceeding the **statutory maximum**;

(b) on conviction on indictment, to a **fine**.

(6) Where under this Act a ship is to be detained an officer of customs and excise shall, and where under this Act a ship may be detained an officer of customs and excise may, refuse to clear the ship outwards or grant a transire to the ship.

(7) When any provision of this Act provides that a ship may be detained until any document is produced to the proper officer of customs and excise the officer able to grant a clearance or transire of the ship is (unless the context otherwise requires) that officer.

(8) Any reference in this section to proceeding to sea includes a reference to going on a voyage or excursion that does not involve going to sea, and references to sending or taking to sea shall be construed accordingly.

[Merchant Shipping Act 1995, s 284 as amended by the Merchant Shipping and Maritime Security Act 1997, Sch 1.]

---

1. For procedure in respect of an offence triable either way, see the Magistrates' Courts Act 1980, ss 17A–21, in PART I: MAGISTRATES' COURTS, PROCEDURE, ante.

7–6490   285. Sums ordered to be paid leviable by distress on the ship.   (1) Where any court has power to make an order directing payment to be made of any seaman's wages, fines or other sums of money, then, if the person directed to pay is the master or owner of the ship and the money directed to be paid is not paid in accordance with the order, the court who made the order may—

(a) except in Scotland, direct the amount remaining unpaid to be levied by distress,

(b) Scotland.

(2) The remedy made available by this section is in addition to any other powers for compelling the payment of money ordered to be paid.

[Merchant Shipping Act 1995, s 285.]

Special evidential provisions

7–6491   286. Depositions of persons abroad admissible.   (1) If the evidence of any person is required in the course of any legal proceeding before a judge or magistrate in relation to the subject matter of the proceeding and it is proved that that person cannot be found in the United Kingdom, any deposition that he may have previously made at a place outside the United Kingdom in relation to the same subject matter shall, subject to subsection (2) below, be admissible in evidence in those proceedings.

(2) For a deposition to be admissible under subsection (1) above in any proceedings, the deposition—

(a)   must have been taken on oath;

(b)   must have been taken before a justice or magistrate in any colony or a British consular officer in any other place;

(c)   must be authenticated by the signature of the justice, magistrate or officer taking it; and

(d)   must, if the proceedings are criminal proceedings, have been taken in the presence of the accused;

and, in a case falling within paragraph (d) above, the deposition shall be certified by the justice, magistrate or officer taking it to have been taken in the presence of the accused.

(3) No proof need be given of the signature or official character of the person appearing to have signed any such deposition and, in any criminal proceedings, a certificate stating that the deposition was taken in the presence of the accused shall, unless the contrary is proved, be evidence (and in Scotland sufficient evidence) of that fact.

(4) This section also applies to proceedings before any person authorised by law or consent of the parties to receive evidence.

(5) Nothing in this section affects the admissibility in evidence of depositions under any other enactment or the practice of any court.

[Merchant Shipping Act 1995, s 286.]

7–6492   287. Admissibility in evidence and inspection of certain documents.   (1) The following documents shall be admissible in evidence and, when in the custody of the Registrar General of Shipping and Seamen, shall be open to public inspection—

(a)   documents purporting to be submissions to or decisions by superintendents or proper officers under section 33;

(b)   the official log book of any ship kept under section 77 and, without prejudice to section 288(2), any document purporting to be a copy of an entry therein and to be certified as a true copy by the master of the ship;

(c)   crew agreements, lists of crews made under section 78 and notices given under Part III of additions to or changes in crew agreements and lists of crews;

(d)   returns or reports under section 108;

(e)   documents transmitted to the Registrar General of Shipping and Seamen under section 298.

(2) A certificate issued under section 47 shall be admissible in evidence.

[Merchant Shipping Act 1995, s 287.]

7–6493   288. Admissibility of documents in evidence.   (1) Where a document is by this Act declared to be admissible in evidence the document shall, on its production from proper custody—

(a)   be admissible in evidence in any court or before any person having by law or consent of parties authority to receive evidence; and

(b)   subject to all just exceptions, be evidence (or in Scotland sufficient evidence) of the matters stated in the document.

(2) A copy of, or extract from, any document so made admissible in evidence shall, subject to subsection (3) below, also be admissible in evidence and evidence (and in Scotland sufficient evidence) of the matters stated in the document.

(3) A copy of, or extract from, a document shall not be admissible by virtue of subsection (2) above unless—

(a)   it is proved to be an examined copy or extract; or

(b)   it purports to be signed and certified as a true copy or extract by the officer to whose custody the original document was entrusted;

and that officer shall furnish the certified copy or extract to any person who applies for it at a reasonable time and pays such reasonable price as the Secretary of State determines.

(4) A person shall, on payment of such reasonable price as the Secretary of State determines, be entitled to have a certified copy of any declaration or document a copy of which is made evidence by this Act.

(5) If any officer having duties of certification under subsection (3) above in relation to any document intentionally certifies any document as being a true copy or extract he shall be liable[1]—

(a)   on summary conviction, to imprisonment for a term not exceeding **six months** or a fine not exceeding the **statutory maximum**;

(b)   on conviction on indictment, to imprisonment for a term not exceeding **two years** or a **fine** or **both**.

(6)–(8) *Scotland.*
[Merchant Shipping Act 1995, s 288.]

---

1. For procedure in respect of an offence triable either way, see the Magistrates' Courts Act 1980, ss 17A–21, in PART I: MAGISTRATES' COURTS, PROCEDURE, ante.

7–6494 289. Inspection and admissibility in evidence of copies of certain documents.
(1) Where under any enactment a document is open to public inspection when in the custody of the Registrar General of Shipping and Seamen—

(*a*) there may be supplied for public inspection a copy or other reproduction of the document instead of the original; but

(*b*) the original shall nevertheless be made available for public inspection if the copy or other reproduction is illegible.

(2) Where the Registrar General of Shipping and Seamen destroys any document which has been sent to him under or by virtue of any enactment, and keeps a copy or other reproduction of that document, then—

(*a*) any enactment providing for that document to be admissible in evidence or open to public inspection, and

(*b*) in the case of a document falling within subsection (1) above, that subsection,

shall apply to the copy or other reproduction as if it were the original.

(3) For the purposes of this section, and of section 288(2) in its application to documents in the custody of the Registrar General of Shipping and Seamen, a copy is to be taken to be the copy of a document notwithstanding that it is taken from a copy or other reproduction of the original.
[Merchant Shipping Act 1995, s 289.]

7–6495 290. Proof, etc of exemptions. (1) Where any exception, exemption, excuse or qualification applies in relation to an offence under this Act—

(*a*) it may be proved by the defendant, but

(*b*) need not be specified or negatived in any information or complaint;

and, if so specified or negatived, shall not require to be proved by the informant or complainant.

(2) This section applies in relation to an offence whether or not the exception, exemption, excuse or qualification is contained in the section creating the offence.

(3) This section does not apply to Scotland.
[Merchant Shipping Act 1995, s 290.]

Service of documents

7–6496 291. Service of documents. (1) Any document authorised or required to be served on any person may be served on that person—

(*a*) by delivering it to him;

(*b*) by leaving it at his proper address; or

(*c*) by sending it by post to him at his proper address.

(2) any such document required to be served on the master of a ship may be served—

(*a*) where there is a master, by leaving it for him on board the ship with the person appearing to be in command or charge of the ship;

(*b*) where there is no master, on—

(i) the managing owner of the ship; or

(ii) if there is no managing owner, on any agent of the owner; or

(iii) where no such agent is known or can be found, by leaving a copy of the document fixed to the mast of the ship.

(3) Any document authorised or required to be served on any person may—

(*a*) in the case of a body corporate, be served on the secretary or clerk of that body;

(*b*) in the case of a partnership, be served on a partner or a person having the control or management of the partnership business or, in Scotland, on the firm.

(4) Any notice authorised or required by or under Part II to be served on the Secretary of State may be served by post.

(5) Any notice authorised by section 261, 262, 263 or 264 to be given to an inspector may be given by delivering it to him or by leaving it at, or sending it by post to, his office.

(6) Any document authorised or required by or under any enactment to be served on the registered owner of a United Kingdom ship shall be treated as duly served on him if served on such persons, in such circumstances and by such method, as may be specified in registration regulations.

(7) For the purposes of this section and of section 7 of the Interpretation Act 1978 (service of documents by post) in its application to this section, the proper address of any person on whom any document is to be served shall be his last known address, except that—

(*a*) in the case of a body corporate or their secretary or clerk it shall be the address of the registered or principal office of that body;

(*b*) in the case of a partnership or a person having the control or management of the partnership business, it shall be the principal office of the partnership;

and for the purposes of this subsection the principal office of a company registered outside the United Kingdom or of a partnership carrying on business outside the United Kingdom shall be their principal office in the United Kingdom.

(8) If the person to be served with any notice has (whether in pursuance of registration regulations or otherwise) specified an address in the United Kingdom other than his proper address within the meaning of subsection (7) above as the one at which he or someone on his behalf will accept notices of the same description as that notice, that address shall also be treated for the purposes of this section and section 7 of the Interpretation Act 1978 as his proper address.

(9) For the purposes of the said section 7 a letter containing—

(*a*) a notice to be served on any person in pursuance of subsection (6) above, or

(*b*) a notice authorised or required to be served under registration regulations on a representative person (within the meaning of those regulations),

shall be deemed to be properly addressed if it is addressed to that person at the address for the time being recorded in relation to him in the register; and a letter containing any other notice under registration regulations shall be deemed to be properly addressed if it is addressed to the last known address of the person to be served (whether of his residence or of a place where he carries on business).

[Merchant Shipping Act 1995, s 291.]

PART XIII[1]
SUPPLEMENTAL

Application of Act to certain descriptions of ships, etc

7–6501 307. Application of Act to non-United Kingdom ships. (1) The Secretary of State may make regulations specifying any description of non-United Kingdom ships and directing that such of the provisions of this Act and of instruments under this Act as may be specified in the regulations—

(*a*) shall extend to non-United Kingdom ships of that description and to masters and seamen employed in them, or

(*b*) shall so extend in such circumstances as may be so specified, with such modifications (if any) as may be so specified.

(2) Regulations under this section may contain such transitional, supplementary and consequential provisions as appear to the Secretary of State to be expedient.

(3) In this section "non-United Kingdom ships" means ships which are not registered in the United Kingdom.

[Merchant Shipping Act 1995, s 307.]

---

1. Part XIII contains ss 292–316.

7–6502 308. Application of Act to government ships. (1) Subject to any other provision of it, this Act shall not apply to ships belonging to Her Majesty.

(2) Her Majesty may by Order in Council make regulations with respect to the manner in which Government ships may be registered as British ships under Part II; and this Act, subject to any exceptions and modifications which may be made by Order in Council, either generally or as respects any special class of Government ships, shall apply to government ships registered in accordance with the Order as if they were registered in accordance with Part II.

(3) Any Order in Council under subsection (2) above shall be laid before Parliament after being made.

(4) In this section "Government ships" means ships not forming part of Her Majesty's Navy which belong to Her Majesty, or are held by any person on behalf of or for the benefit of the Crown (and for that reason cannot be registered under Part II).

[Merchant Shipping Act 1995, s 308.]

7–6503 309. *Application of Act to ships chartered by demise to the Crown*

7–6504 310. Application of Act to hovercraft. The enactments and instruments with respect to which provision may be made by Order in Council under section 1(1)(*h*) of the Hovercraft Act 1968 shall include this Act (except Parts I and II) and any instrument made thereunder.

[Merchant Shipping Act 1995, s 310.]

7–6505 311. Application of Act to certain structures, etc. *Repealed by the Railways and Transport Safety Act 2003, Sch 8.*

Final provisions

7–6506 313. Definitions. (1) In this Act, unless the context otherwise requires—

"British connection" has the meaning given in section 9(9);

"British citizen", "British overseas territories citizen", "British Overseas citizen" and "Commonwealth citizen" have the same meaning as in the British Nationality Act 1981;

"British ship" has the meaning given in section 1(1);

"commissioned military officer" means a commissioned officer in Her Majesty's land forces on full pay;

"commissioned naval officer" means a commissioned officer of Her Majesty's Navy on full pay;

"conservancy authority" includes all persons entrusted with the function of conserving, maintaining or improving the navigation of a tidal water (as defined in section 255);

"consular officer", in relation to a foreign country, means the officer recognised by Her Majesty as a consular officer of that foreign country;

"contravention" includes failure to comply (and "failure" includes refusal);

"Departmental inspector" and "Departmental officer" have the meanings given in section 256(9);

"fishing vessel" means a vessel for the time being used (or, in the context of an application for registration, intended to be used) for, or in connection with fishing for sea fish other than a vessel used (or intended to be used) for fishing otherwise than for profit; and for the purposes of this definition "sea fish" includes shellfish, salmon and migratory trout (as defined by section 44 of the Fisheries Act 1981);

"foreign", in relation to a ship, means that it is neither a United Kingdom ship nor a small ship (as defined in section 1(2)) which is a British ship;

"Government ship" has the meaning given in section 308;

"harbour" includes estuaries, navigable rivers, piers, jetties and other works in or at which ships can obtain shelter or ship and unship goods or passengers;

"harbour authority" means, in relation to a harbour—

    (*a*) the person who is the statutory harbour authority for the harbour, or

    (*b*) if there is no statutory harbour authority for the harbour, the person (if any) who is the proprietor of the harbour or who is entrusted with the function of managing, maintaining or improving the harbour;

"master" includes every person (except a pilot) having command or charge of a ship and, in relation to a fishing vessel, means the skipper;

"Minister of the Crown" has the same meaning as in the Ministers of the Crown Act 1975;

"port" includes place;

"proper officer" means a consular officer appointed by Her Majesty's Government in the United Kingdom and, in relation to a port in a country outside the United Kingdom which is not a foreign country, also any officer exercising in that port functions similar to those of a superintendent;

"qualifying foreign ship" has the meaning given in section 313A;

"the register" and "registered" have the meaning given in section 23(1);

"the registrar", in relation to the registration of ships, has the meaning given in section 8;

"registration regulations" means regulations under section 10;

"relevant British possession" means—

    (*a*) the Isle of Man;

    (*b*) any of the Channel Islands; and

    (*c*) any colony;

"safety regulations" means regulations under section 85;

"seaman" includes every person (except masters and pilots) employed or engaged in any capacity on board any ship;

"ship" includes every description of vessel used in navigation;

"statutory harbour authority" means—

    (*a*) in relation to Great Britain, a harbour authority within the meaning of the Harbours Act 1964; and

    (*b*) in relation to Northern Ireland, a harbour authority within the meaning of the Harbours Act (Northern Ireland) 1970.

"superintendent" means a mercantile marine superintendent appointed under section 296;

"surveyor of ships" has the meaning given in section 256(9);

"the tonnage regulations" means regulations under section 19;

"United Kingdom ship" (and in Part V "United Kingdom fishing vessel") has the meaning given in section 1(3) except in the contexts there mentioned; and

"wages" includes emoluments.

(2) In this Act—

(*a*) "United Kingdom waters" means the sea or other waters within the seaward limits of the territorial sea of the United Kingdom; and

(b) "national waters", in relation to the United Kingdom, means United Kingdom waters landward of the baselines for measuring the breadth of its territorial sea.

(2A) In this Act "right of innocent passage", "right of transit passage" and "straits used for international navigation" shall be construed in accordance with the United Nations Convention on the Law of the Sea 1982.

(3) A vessel for the time being used (or intended to be used) wholly for the purpose of conveying persons wishing to fish for pleasure is not a fishing vessel.
[Merchant Shipping Act 1995, s 313 as amended by the Merchant Shipping and Maritime Security Act 1997, Sch 6 and the British Overseas Territories Act 2002, s 2(3).]

7–6506A 313A. Meaning of "qualifying foreign ship". In this Act "qualifying foreign ship" means any ship other than—

(a) a British ship, or
(b) a ship which is not registered under Part II and which (although not by virtue of section 1(1)(a) a British ship)—

   (i) is wholly owned by persons falling within subsection (2) below, and
   (ii) is not registered under the law of a country outside the United Kingdom.

(2) The following persons fall within this subsection, namely—

(a) British citizens,
(b) British overseas territories citizens,
(c) British Overseas citizens,
(d) persons who under the British Nationality Act 1981 are British subjects,
(e) British Nationals (Overseas) (within the meaning of that Act),
(f) British protected persons (within the meaning of that Act), or
(g) bodies corporate incorporated in the United Kingdom or in any relevant British possession and having their principal place of business in the United Kingdom or in any relevant British possession.
[Merchant Shipping Act 1995, s 313A as inserted by the Merchant Shipping and Maritime Security Act 1997, Sch 6 and amended by the British Overseas Territories Act 2002, s 2(3).]

7–6507 314. *Repeals, consequential amendments and transitional provisions.*

7–6508 315. Extent and application. (1) Except for sections 18 and 193(5), this Act extends to England and Wales, Scotland and Northern Ireland.
(2)–(5) *Provisions of the Act may, by Order in Council[1] be extended to any relevant British possession.*
[Merchant Shipping Act 1995, s 315.]

---

1. See the Merchant Shipping (Confirmation of Legislation and Repeals) (Jersey) Order 2004, SI 2004/1284; the Merchant Shipping (Oil Pollution and General Provisions) (Isle of Man) Order 2004, SI 2004/3041; the Merchant Shipping (Oil Pollution) (Gibraltar) Order 2004, SI 2004/3042.

7–6509 316. *Short title and commencement.*

Section 88   SCHEDULE 2
REGULATIONS RELATING TO SUBMERSIBLE AND SUPPORTING APPARATUS

7–6514 1. (1) In this Schedule "regulations" means regulations made under section 88 and "prescribed" means prescribed by regulations.
(2) Nothing in this Schedule shall be taken to prejudice the generality of section 88.

Offences

7–6515 3. (1) Subject to sub-paragraph (2) below, regulations—

(a) may provide for the creation of offences and for their punishment on summary conviction or on conviction on indictment, and
(b) may afford, in respect of any description of offence created by the regulations, such defence (if any) as may be prescribed.

(2) The punishment for an offence created by regulations shall be—

(a) on summary conviction, a fine not exceeding the **statutory maximum,**
(b) on conviction on indictment, imprisonment for a term not exceeding **two years**, or a **fine**, or both[1],

but without prejudice to any further restriction contained in the regulations on the punishments which can be awarded and without prejudice to the exclusion by the regulations of proceedings on indictment.

---

1. For procedure in respect of an offence triable either way, see the Magistrates' Courts Act 1980, ss 17A–21, in PART I: MAGISTRATES' COURTS, PROCEDURE, ante.

SCHEDULE 3

(Repealed by the Merchant Shipping (Load Line) Regulations 1998, SI 1998/2241.)

SCHEDULE 3A
SAFETY DIRECTIONS

(Inserted by the Marine Safety Act 2003, s 1(2), Sch 1 and SI 2004/2110.)

7–6516   *Direction following accident: person in control of ship*
    1–4. *Power of Secretary of State to give directions following an accident to persons in control of ship, in control of land and other directions and actions in lieu of directions.*
    Enforcement
    5. A person to whom a direction is given under this Schedule—

    (a)   must comply with the direction, and
    (b)   must try to comply with the direction in a manner which avoids risk to human life.

    6. (1) A person commits an offence if he contravenes paragraph 5*(a)*.
    (2) It is a defence for a person charged with an offence under sub-paragraph (1) to prove—

    (a)   that he tried as hard as he could to comply with the relevant direction, or
    (b)   that he reasonably believed that compliance with the direction would involve a serious risk to human life.

    7. A person commits an offence if he intentionally obstructs a person who is—

    (a)   acting on behalf of the Secretary of State in connection with the giving of a direction under this Schedule,
    (b)   complying with a direction under this Schedule, or
    (c)   acting by virtue of paragraph 4.

    8. A person guilty of an offence under paragraph 6 or 7 shall be liable—

    (a)   on summary conviction, to a fine not exceeding **£50,000**, or
    (b)   on conviction on indictment, to a **fine**.

    9. (1) Proceedings for an offence under paragraph 6 or 7 may be brought in England and Wales only—

    (a)   by or with the consent of the Attorney General, or
    (b)   by or with the authority of the Secretary of State.

    (2) Proceedings for an offence under paragraph 6 or 7 may be brought in Northern Ireland only—

    (a)   by or with the consent of the Attorney General for Northern Ireland, or
    (b)   by or with the authority of the Secretary of State.

    10–16. *Variation and revocation of directions, procedure, compensation payable by Secretary of State for unreasonable loss and damage, recovery of expenses, jurisdiction of High Court in respect of claims.*
    Ships to which Schedule applies
    17. A direction under paragraph 1 or 2, in so far as it relates to a risk of pollution, may have effect in respect of a ship only if it—

    (a)   is a United Kingdom ship, or
    (b)   is in United Kingdom waters or an area of the sea specified under section 129(2)(b).

    18. *Designation of other ships by Order in Council.*
    19. A direction under paragraph 1 or 2, in so far as it relates to a risk to safety, may have effect in respect of a ship only if it is in United Kingdom waters and—

    (a)   it is not a qualifying foreign ship, or
    (b)   it is a qualifying foreign ship which in the Secretary of State's opinion is exercising neither the right of innocent passage nor the right of transit passage through straits used for international navigation.

    20. (1) A direction under paragraph 3 may have effect in respect of a ship only if it is in United Kingdom waters and—

    (a)   it is not a qualifying foreign ship, or
    (b)   it is a qualifying foreign ship which in the Secretary of State's opinion is exercising neither the right of innocent passage nor the right of transit passage through straits used for international navigation.

    (2) A direction may not be given under paragraph 3(3)(d) in respect of a United Kingdom ship.
    21. *Provisions not to apply to Navy and Government ships.*
    Interpretation
    22. (1) In this Schedule—
    "accident" means a collision of ships, a stranding, another incident of navigation or another event (whether on board a ship or not) which results in material damage to a ship or its cargo or in an imminent threat of material damage to a ship or its cargo,
    "action" includes omission,
    "enactment" includes an enactment comprised in, or in an instrument made under, an Act of the Scottish Parliament,
    "harbour authority" has the meaning given by section 151(1),
    "harbour master" includes a dock master or pier master, and any person specially appointed by a harbour authority for the purpose of enforcing the provisions of this Schedule in relation to the harbour,
    "hazardous substance" has the meaning given by sub-paragraph (2),
    "owner", in relation to the ship to or in which an accident has occurred, includes its owner at the time of the accident,

"pilot" means a person who does not belong to a ship but who has the conduct of it,

"pollution" means significant pollution in the United Kingdom, United Kingdom waters or an area of the sea specified under section 129(2)(b), and

"risk to safety" means a risk to the safety of persons, property or anything navigating in or using United Kingdom waters.

(2) In this Schedule "hazardous substance" means—

(a) oil (within the meaning given by section 151(1)),

(b) any other substance which creates a hazard to human health, harms living resources or marine life, damages amenities or interferes with lawful use of the sea, and

(c) any substance prescribed by order of the Secretary of State.

23, 24. *Savings, contempt of court and civil proceedings.*

SCHEDULE 11
INTERNATIONAL CONVENTION ON SALVAGE 1989
PART I
TEXT OF CONVENTION
CHAPTER II — PERFORMANCE OF SALVAGE OPERATIONS

Article 10

Duty to render assistance

7–6551   **1.** Every master is bound, so far as he can do so without serious danger to his vessel and persons thereon, to render assistance to any person in danger of being lost at sea.

2. The States Parties shall adopt the measures necessary to enforce the duty set out in paragraph 1.

3. The owner of the vessel shall incur no liability for a breach of the duty of the master under paragraph 1.

PART II
PROVISIONS HAVING EFFECT IN CONNECTION WITH CONVENTION

Interpretation

7–6552   **1.** In this Part of this Schedule "the Convention" means the Convention as set out in Part I of this Schedule and any reference to a numbered article is a reference to the article of the Convention which is so numbered.

Assistance to persons in danger at sea

7–6553   **3.** (1) The master of a vessel who fails to comply with the duty imposed on him by article 10, paragraph 1 commits an offence and shall be liable[1]—

(a) on summary conviction, to imprisonment for a term not exceeding **six months** or a fine not exceeding the **statutory maximum** or **both;**

(b) on conviction on indictment, to imprisonment for a term not exceeding **two years** or a **fine**, or **both**.

(2) Compliance by the master of a vessel with that duty shall not affect his right or the right of any other person to a payment under the Convention or under any contract.

---

1. For procedure in respect of an offence triable either way, see the Magistrates' Courts Act 1980, ss 17A–21, in PART I: MAGISTRATES' COURTS, PROCEDURE, ante.

Shipping and Trading Interests (Protection) Act 1995
(1995 c 22)

7–6560   **1. Power to regulate provision of shipping services, etc in event of foreign action.**

(1)–(8) *Power of Secretary of State to make orders requiring information and regulating shipping.*

[Shipping and Trading Interests (Protection) Act 1995, s 1.]

7–6561   **2.** *Special provisions for orders under section 1 imposing taxation etc.*

7–6562   **3. Enforcement of section 1.**   (1)–(3) *Enforcement of orders made under section 1 by Customs and Excise.*

(4) If a person discloses any information which has been furnished to or obtained by him under section 1 or 2, or in connection with the execution of section 1 or 2, he shall, unless the disclosure is made—

(a) with the consent of the person from whom the information was obtained, or

(b) in connection with the execution of section 1 or 2, or

(c) for the purposes of any legal proceedings arising out of this section or of any report of such proceedings, or

(d) in pursuance of a Community obligation to a Community institution,

be liable, on summary conviction, to a fine not exceeding **level 5** on the standard scale.

(5) A person who—

(*a*) refuses or intentionally neglects to furnish any information which he is required to furnish under section 1 or 2, or

(*b*) in furnishing any such information makes any statement which he knows to be false in a material particular, or recklessly makes any statement which is false in a material particular,

shall be liable, on summary conviction, to a fine not exceeding **level 4** on the standard scale in the case of an offence under paragraph (*a*) above and not exceeding **level 5** on the standard scale in the case of an offence under paragraph (*b*) above.

(6) A person who intentionally contravenes or fails to comply with any provision of an order or direction made or given pursuant to section 1 or 2, other than a provision requiring him to give any information, shall be liable[1]—

(*a*) on summary conviction, to a fine of not more than **£5,000**;

(*b*) on conviction on indictment, to a **fine**.

and where the order or direction requires anything to be done, or not to be done, by, to or on a ship, and the requirement is not complied with, the owner and master of the ship are each to be regarded as intentionally failing to comply, without prejudice to the liability of anyone else.

(7) A person shall not be guilty of an offence against any provision contained in or having effect under section 1 or 2 by reason only of something done by that person wholly outside the territory of the United Kingdom unless that person is a Commonwealth citizen under the British Nationality Act 1981 or a company incorporated under the law of any part of the United Kingdom.

[Shipping and Trading Interests (Protection) Act 1995, s 3.]

_____

1. For procedure in respect of an offence triable either way, see the Magistrates' Courts Act 1980, ss 17A–21 in PART I: MAGISTRATES' COURTS, PROCEDURE, ante.

7–6563 5. Power to prohibit provision of coastal shipping services which are not British based. Order may prohibit shipping services except from one or more permanent places of business maintained in the British Islands.

[Shipping and Trading Interests (Protection) Act 1995, s 5—summarised.]

7–6564 6. Enforcement of section 5. (1) Where—

(*a*) any ship is used in the course of the provision of any shipping services to which section 5 applies, or

(*b*) anything is done on board a ship with a view to its being used to provide such services,

and the provision of those services is prohibited by virtue of subsection (1) of that section and is not sanctioned by any licence issued by virtue of subsection (3)(*b*) of that section, then (subject to subsections (6) and (7) below), the master and the owner of the ship shall each be guilty of an offence[1].

(2) Where the ship—

(*a*) is chartered by demise, or

(*b*) is managed, either wholly or in part, by a person other than the owner under the terms of a management agreement,

the reference in subsection (1) above to the owner of the ship shall be construed as including a reference—

(i) to the charterer under the charter by demise, or

(ii) to any such manager as is referred to in paragraph (*b*) above, or

(iii) (if the ship is both chartered and managed as mentioned above) to both the charterer and any such manager.

(3) Any person who—

(*a*) in connection with an application for such a licence as is mentioned in section 5(3)(*b*), or

(*b*) in purported compliance with the requirements of any notice served on him by virtue of section 5(3)(*e*),

knowingly or recklessly furnishes information which is false in a material particular shall be guilty of an offence[1].

(4) Any person who—

(*a*) without reasonable excuse (the proof of which lies on him) fails to comply with the requirements of any such notice, or

(*b*) intentionally alters, suppresses, conceals or destroys a document which he has been required to produce in pursuance of section 5(3)(*e*),

shall be guilty of an offence[1].

(5) Any person guilty of an offence under this section shall be liable[2]—

(*a*) on summary conviction, to a fine not exceeding **£50,000**;

(*b*) on conviction on indictment, to imprisonment for a term not exceeding **two years** or a **fine**, or **both**.

(6) It shall be a defence in proceedings under subsection (1) above against the master of a ship to prove—

(a) that he did not know and had no reason to suspect that, in the circumstances of the case, the provision of the shipping services referred to in paragraph (a) or (as the case may be) paragraph (b) of that subsection was prohibited by virtue of section 5(1), or

(b) that he had reasonable grounds for believing that the provision of those services was sanctioned by a licence issued by virtue of section 5(3)(b).

(7) It shall be a defence in proceedings brought under subsection (1) above against a person other than the master of a ship to prove that, under the terms of one or more charter-parties or management agreements entered into by the defendant, the right to determine the purpose for which the ship in question was being used at the time of the alleged offence was wholly vested in some other person or persons party thereto (whether or not any such other person or persons had entered into a further charter-party or management agreement providing for that right to be vested in some other person).

(8) Subsections (1), (3) and (4) above apply to offences falling within those subsections wherever committed.

(9) In this section "management agreement", in relation to a ship, means any agreement (other than a charter-party or a contract of employment) under which the ship is managed, either wholly or in part, by a person other than the owner (whether on behalf of the owner or on behalf of some other person).

[Shipping and Trading Interests (Protection) Act 1995, s 6.]

---

1. Proceedings for an offence under this section shall not be instituted without the consent of the Attorney General or Secretary of State (s 7, post).

2. For procedure in respect of an offence triable either way, see the Magistrates' Courts Act 1980, ss 17A–21 in Part I: MAGISTRATES' COURTS, PROCEDURE, ante.

Supplementary

7–6565 7. Supplementary. (1) Part XII of the Merchant Shipping Act 1995 (which makes provision in relation to legal proceedings and related matters) shall apply for the purposes of this Act as it applies for the purposes of that Act.

(2) Proceedings for an offence under section 6 shall not be instituted—

(a) in England and Wales, except by or with the consent of the Attorney General or the Secretary of State; or

(b) *Northern Ireland.*

(3) Without prejudice to section 291 of the Merchant Shipping Act 1995 in its application to this Act, any document required or authorised by or under any enactment to be served for the purpose of the institution of, or otherwise in connection with, proceedings for an offence under section 6(1) shall, where it is to be served on a person who was, at the time of the alleged offence—

(a) the owner of the ship in question, or

(b) such a charterer by demise or manager of that ship as is mentioned in subsection (2) of that section,

be treated as duly served on that person if—

(i) sent to him by post at his last-known address (whether of his residence or of a place where he carries on business), or

(ii) left for him at that address,

or if the document is served on the master of the ship in question.

[Shipping and Trading Interests (Protection) Act 1995, s 7.]

7–6566 9. Short title, interpretation, citation, commencement and extent. (2) In this Act "protective order" has the meaning given by section 1(3) and, subject to this Act, other expressions used in this Act and in the Merchant Shipping Act 1995 shall have the same meaning in this Act as in that Act.

[Shipping and Trading Interests (Protection) Act 1995, s 9.]

Merchant Shipping and Maritime Security Act 1997[1]

(1997 c 28)

7–6600 24. Implementation of international agreements relating to protection of wrecks[1].
*(1)–(2) Secretary of State may make provision by order to give effect to any international agreement which relates to the protection of wrecks outside United Kingdom waters. Contravention punishable summarily by a fine not exceeding the **statutory maximum** or on indictment by a **fine**[2].*

(3) No person shall be guilty of an offence under an order under subsection (1) unless—

(a)   the acts or omissions which constitute the offence are committed in the United Kingdom, in United Kingdom waters or on board a United Kingdom ship, or

(b)   in a case where those acts or omissions are committed in international waters but not on board a United Kingdom ship, that person is—

     (i)   a British citizen, a British overseas territories citizen or a British Overseas citizen,

     (ii)   a person who under the British Nationality Act 1981 is a British subject,

     (iii)   a British National (Overseas) (within the meaning of that Act),

     (iv)   a British protected person (within the meaning of that Act), or

     (v)   a company within the meaning of the Companies Act 1985 or the Companies (Northern Ireland) Order 1986.

(4)   In subsection (3), "United Kingdom ship" means a ship which—

(a)   is registered in the United Kingdom; or

(b)   is not registered under the law of any country but is wholly owned by persons each of whom is a person mentioned in paragraph (b)(i) to (v) of that subsection.

(5)   Subject to subsection (3), any offence under an order under subsection (1) shall, for the purpose only of conferring jurisdiction on any court, be deemed to have been committed in any place where the offender may for the time being be.

(6)   No proceedings for an offence under any order under subsection (1) shall be instituted—

(a)   in England and Wales, except by or with the consent of the Director of Public Prosecutions;

(b)   in Northern Ireland, except by or with the consent of the Director of Public Prosecutions for Northern Ireland.

(7)   A statutory instrument containing an order under subsection (1) shall be subject to annulment in pursuance of a resolution of either House of Parliament.

(8)   In this section—

"international waters" means any part of the sea outside the seaward limits of the territorial sea of any country or territory;

"ship" includes any description of vessel used in navigation;

"United Kingdom waters" means the sea or other waters within the seaward limits of the territorial sea of the United Kingdom;

"wreck" means the wreck of any ship other than a ship which, at the time it sank or was stranded, was in service with, or used for the purposes of, any of the armed forces of the United Kingdom or any other country or territory.

[Merchant Shipping and Maritime Security Act 1997, s 24, as amended by the British Overseas Territories Act 2002, s 2(3).]

---

1.   This Act is to be brought into force in accordance with the provisions of section 31 and orders made thereunder. Sections 5, 8, 11–13, 16, 24, 28, 30 and 31, Sch 2 and Sch 6 (part) came into effect on Royal Assent, 19 March 1997. In addition, the following commencement orders have been made: Commencement Order (No 1) 1997, SI 1997/1082 and Commencement Order (No 2) 1997, SI 1997/1539.

2.   For procedure in respect of this offence which is triable either way, see the Magistrates' Courts Act 1980, ss 17A–21, in PART I: MAGISTRATES' COURTS, PROCEDURE, ante.

Railways and Transport Safety Act 2003[1]
2003 c 20

PART 4[2]
SHIPPING: ALCOHOL AND DRUGS

Offences

7–6601   78. Professional staff on duty.   (1) This section applies to—

(a)   a professional master of a ship,

(b)   a professional pilot of a ship, and

(c)   a professional seaman in a ship while on duty.

(2)   A person to whom this section applies commits an offence if his ability to carry out his duties is impaired because of drink or drugs.

(3)   A person to whom this section applies commits an offence if the proportion of alcohol in his breath, blood or urine exceeds the prescribed limit.

(4)   For the purposes of this section a master, pilot or seaman is professional if (and only if) he acts as master, pilot or seaman in the course of a business or employment.

(5)   Where a person is charged with an offence under this section in respect of the effect of a drug on his ability to carry out duties on a fishing vessel, it is a defence for him to show that—

(a)   he took the drug for a medicinal purpose on, and in accordance with, medical advice, or

(b) he took the drug for a medicinal purpose and had no reason to believe that it would impair his ability to carry out his duties.

[Railways and Transport Safety Act 2003, s 78.]

1. This Act makes provision about railways, including tramways and transport safety. Reproduced in this title are those provisions relating to shipping, alcohol and drugs, Part 1 relating to railways is reproduced in PART VII: TRANSPORT, title RAILWAYS, Part 3 relating to the British Transport Police is reproduced in PART VIII, title POLICE and Part 5 relating to aviation, alcohol and drugs is reproduced in PART VII: TRANSPORT, title AVIATION.

Sections 104 and 114 came into force on the passing of the Act (10 July 2003) and ss 105 and 112 came into force on 10 September 2003. The remaining provisions come into force in accordance with orders made under s 120. At the date of going to press the following commencement orders had been made: (No 1) SI 2003/2681 which brought into force on 31 October 2003, ss 111 and 115; (No 2) SI 2004/827; (No 3) SI 2004/1572; (No 4) SI 2004/2759. Part 4 was brought into force on 30 March 2004, except s 83 (in force 29 March 2004 for certain purposes) and s 80(1)–(3).

2. Part 4 comprises ss 78–91.

7–6602   79. Professional staff off duty.   (1) This section applies to a professional seaman in a ship at a time when—

(a) he is not on duty, but

(b) in the event of an emergency he would or might be required by the nature or terms of his engagement or employment to take action to protect the safety of passengers.

(2) A person to whom this section applies commits an offence if his ability to take the action mentioned in subsection (1)(b) is impaired because of drink or drugs.

(3) A person to whom this section applies commits an offence if the proportion of alcohol in his breath, blood or urine exceeds the prescribed limit.

(4) For the purposes of this section a seaman is professional if (and only if) he acts as seaman in the course of a business or employment.

(5) Where a person is charged with an offence under this section in respect of the effect of a drug on his ability to take action it is a defence for him to show that—

(a) he took the drug for a medicinal purpose on, and in accordance with, medical advice, or

(b) he took the drug for a medicinal purpose and had no reason to believe that it would impair his ability to take the action.

[Railways and Transport Safety Act 2003, s 79.]

7–6603   80. Non-professionals.   (1) This section applies to a person who—

(a) is on board a ship which is under way,

(b) is exercising, or purporting or attempting to exercise, a function in connection with the navigation of the ship, and

(c) is not a person to whom section 78 or 79 applies.

(2) A person to whom this section applies commits an offence if his ability to exercise the function mentioned in subsection (1)(b) is impaired because of drink or drugs.

(3) A person to whom this section applies commits an offence if the proportion of alcohol in his breath, blood or urine exceeds the prescribed limit.

(4) The Secretary of State may make regulations providing for subsection (3) not to apply in specified circumstances.

(5) Regulations under subsection (4) may make provision by reference, in particular—

(a) to the power of a motor;

(b) to the size of a ship;

(c) to location.

[Railways and Transport Safety Act 2003, s 80.]

7–6604   81. Prescribed limit.   (1) The prescribed limit of alcohol for the purposes of this Part is—

(a) in the case of breath, 35 microgrammes of alcohol in 100 millilitres,

(b) in the case of blood, 80 milligrammes of alcohol in 100 millilitres, and

(c) in the case of urine, 107 milligrammes of alcohol in 100 millilitres.

(2) The Secretary of State may make regulations amending subsection (1).

[Railways and Transport Safety Act 2003, s 81.]

Enforcement

7–6605   82. Penalty.   A person guilty of an offence under this Part shall be liable—

(a) on conviction on indictment, to imprisonment for a term not exceeding two years, to a fine or to both, or

(b) on summary conviction, to a fine not exceeding the statutory maximum.

[Railways and Transport Safety Act 2003, s 82.]

7–6606　83. Specimens, &c. (1) The provisions specified in the first column of the table below, with the modifications specified in the third column and any other necessary modifications, shall have effect in relation to an offence under this Part.

Provision	Description	Modification
Road Traffic Act 1988[1] (c 52)		
Section 6	Power to administer preliminary tests	In place of subsections (2) to (5) the power to require a person to co-operate with a preliminary test shall apply where— (a) a constable in uniform reasonably suspects that the person is committing an offence under section 78, 79 or 80, (b) a constable in uniform reasonably suspects that the person has committed an offence under section 78, 79 or 80 and still has alcohol or a drug in his body or is still under the influence of a drug, or (c) an accident occurs owing to the presence of a ship in a public place and a constable reasonably suspects that the person was at the time of the accident a person to whom section 78, 79 or 80 applied.
Sections 6A to 6E	Preliminary breath test, impairment test, and drug test	In place of sections 6A(2) and (3), 6B(4) and 6C(2), a preliminary breath test, preliminary impairment test or preliminary drug test may be administered by a constable— (a) at or near the place where the requirement to co-operate with the test is imposed, or (b) at a police station specified by the constable. In section 6B(3) a reference to unfitness to drive shall be treated as a reference to having an impaired ability, because of drink or drugs, to do anything specified in section 78(2), 79(2) or 80(2).
Section 7	Provision of specimen	In subsection (1) the reference to an offence under section 3A, 4 or 5 of the 1988 Act shall be treated as a reference to an offence under section 78, 79 or 80 of this Act. In subsection (3)(c) the reference to an offence under section 3A or 4 of the 1988 Act shall be treated as a reference to an offence under section 78(2), 79(2) or 80(2) of this Act.
Section 7A	Specimen of blood taken from person incapable of consenting	
Section 8	Choice of specimen of breath	
Section 9	Protection for hospital patient	
Section 10	Detention of person affected by alcohol or drug	In subsection (1)— (a) the reference to driving or attempting to drive a mechanically propelled vehicle on a road shall be treated as a reference to exercising a function in connection with the navigation of a ship, and (b) the reference to an offence under section 4 or 5 of the 1988 Act shall be treated as a reference to an offence under section 78, 79 or 80 of this Act.

Provision	Description	Modification
		In subsection (2) the reference to driving a mechanically propelled vehicle shall be treated as a reference to exercising a function in connection with the navigation of a ship. In subsection (3) the reference to driving properly shall be treated as a reference to exercising a function in connection with the navigation of a ship.
Section 11	Interpretation	For the definition of "the prescribed limit" there shall be substituted the definition given in this Part.

Road Traffic Offenders Act 1988[1] (c 53)

Section 15	Use of specimens	In subsection (1), the reference to an offence under section 3A, 4 or 5 of the Road Traffic Act 1988 shall be treated as a reference to an offence under section 78, 79 or 80 of this Act. The relevant time for the consumption of alcohol for the purpose of subsection (3)(a) shall be before providing the specimen and after the time of the alleged offence. In subsection (3)(b) the reference to driving shall be treated as a reference to exercising a function in connection with the navigation of a ship.
Section 16	Documentary evidence	

(2) The Secretary of State may by regulations amend the table in subsection (1) so as—

(*a*) to add a provision relating to an offence which concerns alcohol or drugs in relation to road traffic;

(*b*) to add, remove or amend a modification (whether or not in connection with an amendment of a provision specified in the table).

(3) For the purpose of the application by subsection (1) of a provision listed in the table in that subsection—

(*a*) the provision shall extend to the whole of the United Kingdom, and

(*b*) a reference to the provision shall be treated, unless the context otherwise requires, as including a reference to the provision as applied.

[Railways and Transport Safety Act 2003, s 83.]

---

1. In this PART, ante.

7–6607 84. Detention pending arrival of police. (1) A marine official may detain a ship if he reasonably suspects that a person who is or may be on board the ship—

(*a*) is committing an offence under section 78, 79 or 80, or

(*b*) has committed an offence under section 78, 79 or 80.

(2) The power of detention under subsection (1)—

(*a*) is conditional upon the marine official making a request, either before the detention or as soon as possible after its commencement, for a constable in uniform to attend, and

(*b*) lapses when a constable in uniform has decided whether or not to exercise a power by virtue of section 83 and has informed the marine official of his decision.

(3) In this section "marine official" means—

(*a*) a harbour master, or an assistant of a harbour master, appointed by a harbour authority,

(*b*) a person listed in section 284(1)(a) to (d) of the Merchant Shipping Act 1995 (c 21) (detention of ship), and

(*c*) a person falling within a class designated by order of the Secretary of State.

(4) In construing section 284(1)(b) of the Merchant Shipping Act 1995 (detention by person authorised by Secretary of State) for the purpose of subsection (3)(b) above, the reference to authorisation to exercise powers under that section shall be taken as a reference—

(*a*) to general authorisation to exercise powers under that section, and

(*b*) to general or particular authorisation to exercise powers under this section.

[Railways and Transport Safety Act 2003, s 84.]

7–6608   85. Arrest without warrant.   (1) A constable may arrest a person without a warrant if the constable reasonably suspects that the person—

(*a*)   is committing an offence under section 78(2), 79(2) or 80(2), or

(*b*)   has committed one of those offences and is still under the influence of drink or drugs.

(2) But a person may not be arrested under this section while he is at a hospital as a patient.

(3) In subsection (2) "hospital" means an institution which—

(*a*)   provides medical or surgical treatment for in-patients or out-patients, and

(*b*)   is not on a ship.

(4) Arrest under this section shall be treated as arrest for an offence for the purposes of—

(*a*)   Part IV of the Police and Criminal Evidence Act 1984 (c 60) (detention), and

(*b*)   Part V of the Police and Criminal Evidence (Northern Ireland) Order 1989 (SI 1989/1341 (NI 12)) (detention).

[Railways and Transport Safety Act 2003, s 85.]

7–6609   86. Right of entry.   (1) A constable in uniform may board a ship if he reasonably suspects that he may wish to exercise a power by virtue of section 83 or under section 85 in respect of a person who is or may be on the ship.

(2) A constable in uniform may enter any place if he reasonably suspects that he may wish to exercise a power by virtue of section 83 or under section 85 in respect of a person who is or may be in that place.

(3) For the purposes of boarding a ship or entering a place under this section a constable—

(*a*)   may use reasonable force;

(*b*)   may be accompanied by one or more persons.

[Railways and Transport Safety Act 2003, s 86.]

General

7–6610   87.   (*Repeals s 117 of the Merchant Shipping Act 1995.*)

7–6611   88. *Orders and regulations*

7–6612   89. Interpretation.   (1) In this Part—

(*a*)   "ship" includes every description of vessel used in navigation, and

(*b*)   a reference to the navigation of a vessel includes a reference to the control or direction, or participation in the control or direction, of the course of a vessel.

(2) Section 313 of the Merchant Shipping Act 1995 (c 21) (interpretation) shall apply to the following expressions used in this Part—

(*a*)   fishing vessel,

(*b*)   foreign ship,

(*c*)   harbour authority,

(*d*)   master,

(*e*)   registered,

(*f*)   seaman,

(*g*)   United Kingdom ship, and

(*h*)   United Kingdom waters.

(3) In this Part "pilot" has the meaning given by section 31(1) of the Pilotage Act 1987 (c 21) (interpretation).

(4) Regulations under section 267(4)(a) of the Merchant Shipping Act 1995 (power to define "accident" for the purposes of provisions about marine accident investigations) shall, so far as is practicable, apply to the word "accident" as used in relation to this Part.

(5) In this Part "drug" includes any intoxicant other than alcohol.

[Railways and Transport Safety Act 2003, s 89.]

7–6613   90. Crown application, &c.   (1) This Part shall not apply to a member of Her Majesty's naval forces, military forces or air forces, within the meaning given by section 225(1) of the Army Act 1955 (c 18), while acting in the course of his duties.

(2) Subject to subsection (1), this Part shall apply to a person in the service of the Crown.

(3) But section 84 shall not have effect in relation to a ship which—

(*a*)   is being used for a purpose of Her Majesty's forces, or

(*b*)   forms part of the Royal Fleet Auxiliary Service.

(4) This Part shall not apply to—

(a)   a member of a visiting force, within the meaning which that expression has in section 3 of the Visiting Forces Act 1952 (c 67) by virtue of section 12(1) of that Act, while acting in the course of his duties, or

(b)   a member of a civilian component of a visiting force, within that meaning, while acting in the course of his duties.

[Railways and Transport Safety Act 2003, s 90.]

7–6614   91. Territorial application.   (1) This Part shall have effect in relation to—

(a)   United Kingdom ships,

(b)   foreign ships in United Kingdom waters, and

(c)   un-registered ships in United Kingdom waters.

(2) Section 86 shall not extend to Scotland.

(3) Subsection (2) does not affect any rule of law or enactment concerning the right of a constable in Scotland to board a ship or enter any place for any purpose.

[Railways and Transport Safety Act 2003, s 91.]

RAILWAYS AND TRAMWAYS

7–6969   This title contains relevant parts of the following statutes—

7–6979	Railway Regulation Act 1840
7–6990	Railway Regulation Act 1842
7–7000	Railways Clauses Consolidation Act 1845
7–7020	Malicious Damage Act 1861
7–7037	Offences Against the Person Act 1861
7–7040	Regulation of Railways Act 1868
7–7043	Regulation of Railways Act 1889
7–7043A	British Transport Commission Act 1949
7–7078	Transport and Works Act 1992
7–7098A	Railways Act 1993
7–7108Q	Railways and Transport Safety Act 2003
7–7108ZA	Railways Act 2005

and the following material—

7–7110	Framework Railway Byelaws
7–7245	Carriage of Goods (Prohibition of Discrimination) Regulations 1977
7–7254	Railways (Penalty Fares) Regulations 1994

Other relevant provisions are contained in the Offices, Shops and Railway Premises Act 1963, in PART VIII; title HEALTH AND SAFETY, post. See also statutory provisions regarding British Transport Police in PART VIII, title POLICE, post. A good many other regulatory and penal provisions exist, but as they are unlikely to be invoked, they are not printed here.

7–6970   European Communities Act 1972: regulations.   The following regulations have been made—

    Cableway Installations Regulations 2004, SI 2004/129 amended by SI 2004/1230;

    Railways Infrastructure (Access and Management) Regulations 2005, SI 2005/3049;

    Railways (Licensing of Railway Undertakings) Regulations 2005, SI 2005/3050.

Railway Regulation Act 1840[1]

(3 & 4 Vict c 97)

7–6979   16. Punishment of persons obstructing the officers of any railway company, or trespassing upon any railway.   If any person shall wilfully obstruct or impede any officer or agent of any railway company[2] in the execution of his duty upon any railway, or upon or in any of the stations or other works or premises connected therewith, or if any person shall wilfully trespass[3] upon any railway, or any of the stations or other works or premises connected therewith, and shall refuse to quit the same upon request to him made by any officer or agent of the said company, every such person so offending, and all others aiding or assisting therein, shall, upon conviction by a magistrates' court, at the discretion of the court, be imprisoned[4] for a term not exceeding **one month** or forfeit to her Majesty any sum not exceeding **level 3** on the standard scale and in default of payment thereof shall or may be imprisoned[5].

[Railway Regulation Act 1840, s 16, as amended by the Summary Jurisdiction Act 1884, s 4, the Statute Law Revision (No 2) Act 1888, the Statute Law Revision Act 1892, the Magistrates' Courts Act 1952, Sch 6, the

British Railways Act 1965, s 35(1), the London Transport Act 1965, s 34(1), the British Railways Act 1977, Sch 1, the Criminal Justice Act 1982, s 46 and the Police and Criminal Evidence Act 1984, Sch 6.]

1. This Act is to be construed as one with the Railway Regulation Act 1842, and the Regulation of Railways Acts 1868, 1871, 1873 (s 2 of the 1842 Act, s 1 of the 1871 Act and the 1873 Act).
2. In the Regulation of Railways Acts 1840 to 1873, the word "railway" extends to all railways constructed under the powers of any Act of Parliament and intended for the conveyance of passengers in or upon carriages drawn or impelled by the power of steam or by any other mechanical power; "company" includes the proprietors for the time being of any such railway (s 21 of the 1840 Act).
3. A railway company can exclude anyone not wishing to use the railway, or admit subject to conditions (*Perth General Station Committee v Ross* [1897] AC 479, [1895–9] All ER Rep 1267). Additional powers are contained in the Regulation of Railways Act 1868, s 23 and the British Transport Commission Act 1949, s 55, as amended, post.
4. The discretion must nowadays be exercised within the restrictions of ss 79 et seq of the Powers of Criminal Courts (Sentencing) Act 2000, ante.
5. See Magistrates' Courts Act 1980, s 76, ante.

Railway Regulation Act 1842
(5 & 6 Vict c 55)

7–6990   17. Punishment of persons employed on railways guilty of misconduct. It shall be lawful for any officer or agent of any railway company[1], and all such persons as they may call to their assistance, to seize and detain[2] any engine driver, waggon driver, guard, porter, servant, or other person employed by the said or by any other railway company or by any other company or person, in conducting traffic upon the railway belonging to the said company, or in repairing and maintaining the works of the said railway, who shall commit any offence against any of the byelaws, rules, or regulations of the said company, or who shall wilfully, maliciously, or negligently do or omit to do any act whereby the life or limb of any person passing along or being upon such railway or the works thereof respectively shall be or might be injured or endangered, or whereby the passage of any engines, carriages, or trains shall be or might be obstructed or impeded, and to convey such engine driver, guard, porter, servant, or other person so offending, or any person counselling, aiding, or assisting in such offence, with all convenient despatch[3], before some justice of the peace for the place within which such offence shall be committed without any other warrant or authority than this Act; and every such person so offending, and every person counselling, aiding, or assisting therein, as aforesaid, shall, when convicted upon the oath of one or more credible witness or witnesses before such justice[4] as aforesaid (who is hereby authorised and required, upon complaint to him made . . ., without information in writing, to take cognisance thereof, and to act summarily in the premises), in the discretion of such justice, be imprisoned[5] . . ., for any term not exceeding **three calendar months** or, in the like discretion of such justice, shall for every such offence forfeit to her Majesty any sum not exceeding **level 3** on the standard scale and in default of payment thereof shall be imprisoned, . . . as aforesaid, for such period not exceeding two calendar months as such justice shall appoint, such commitment to be determined on payment of the amount of the penalty[6].
[Railway Regulation Act 1842, s 17, as amended by the SLR (No 2) Act 1890, the Criminal Justice Act 1948, s 1(2), the Magistrates' Courts Act 1952, Sch 6, the British Railways Act 1965, s 35, the British Railways Act 1977, s 13(2) and Sch 1, the Criminal Justice Act 1982, s 46, the Police and Criminal Evidence Act 1984, Sch 7 and the Transport and Works Act 1992, s 40.]

1. In the Regulation of Railways Acts 1840 to 1873, the word "railway" extends to all railways constructed under the powers of any Act of Parliament and intended for the conveyance of passengers in or upon carriages drawn or impelled by the power of steam or by any other mechanical power; "company" includes the proprietors for the time being of any such railway (s 21 of the 1840 Act).
2. Note the restricted power of search and arrest under the British Transport Commission Act 1949, s 54; see also Magistrates' Courts Act 1980, s 43 (bail on arrest) and note the provisions of the Police and Criminal Evidence Act 1984, ante in PART I: MAGISTRATES' COURTS, PROCEDURE: in particular s 30 (person taken into custody by a constable after arrest for an offence by a person other than a constable), ss 37, 38 (bail before or after charge), s 47 (bail after arrest).
3. See Magistrates' Courts Act 1980, s 43 (bail on arrest) and note the provisions of the Police and Criminal Evidence Act indicated in note 2 above.
4. If convicted before one justice, the imprisonment must not exceed fourteen days and the fine must not exceed £1 (Magistrates' Courts Act 1980, s 121, ante).
5. The discretion must nowadays be exercised within the restrictions of ss 79 et seq of the Powers of Criminal Courts (Sentencing) Act 2000, ante.
6. See Magistrates' Courts Act 1980, s 76, ante.

Railways Clauses Consolidation Act 1845[1]
(8 & 9 Vict c 20)

7–7000   75. Penalty on persons omitting to fasten gates. If any person[2] omit to shut and fasten any gate or to lower any barrier set up at either side of the railway for the accommodation of the owners or occupiers of the adjoining lands as soon as he and the carriage, cattle, or other animals

under his care have passed through the same, he shall forfeit for every such offence any sum not exceeding **level 3** on the standard scale.
[Railways Clauses Consolidation Act 1845, s 75, as amended by the British Railways Act 1965, s 35, the British Railways Act 1977, Sch 1, the Criminal Justice Act 1982, s 46 and the Transport and Works Act 1992, s 49.]

1. This Act is to be incorporated with any Act for the construction of a railway, and is to be construed therewith (ss 1, 2).
2. The time for ascertaining obligations under this Act was when the railway was constructed; the subsequent creation of a public highway from what was originally an accommodation crossing did not alter the responsibility of the user under this section (*Copps v Payne* [1950] 1 KB 611, [1950] 1 All ER 246, 114 JP 118).

7–7001 103. Penalty on passengers refusing to quit carriage at destination. If any person knowingly and wilfully refuse or neglect, on arriving at the point to which he has paid his fare, to quit such carriage, every such person shall for every such offence[1] forfeit . . . a sum not exceeding **level 2** on the standard scale.
[Railways Clauses Consolidation Act 1845, s 103, as amended by the Statute Law Revision Act 1892, the Justices of the Peace Act 1949, Sch 7, the Criminal Law Act 1977, s 31 the British Railways Act 1980, Sch 3 and the Criminal Justice Act 1982, s 46.]

1. A person committing or attempting an offence against this section may be arrested and detained until he can be brought before the court (s 104). For offence of avoiding payment of fare, see the Regulation of Railways Act 1889, s 5, post.

7–7002 105. Carriage of dangerous goods on railway. No person shall be entitled to carry, or to require the company to carry, upon the railway, any aquafortis, oil of vitriol, gunpowder, lucifer matches, or any other goods which in the judgment of the company may be of a dangerous nature; and if any person send[1] by the railway any such goods without distinctly marking their nature on the outside of the package containing the same, or otherwise giving notice in writing to the book-keeper or other servant of the company with whom the same are left, at the time of so sending, he shall forfeit . . . **level 2** on the standard scale for every such offence; and it shall be lawful for the company to refuse to take any parcel that they may suspect to contain goods of a dangerous nature, or require the same to be opened to ascertain the fact.
[Railways Clauses Consolidation Act 1845, s 105, as amended by the Justices of the Peace Act 1949, Sch 7, the Criminal Law Act 1977, s 31 and the Criminal Justice Act 1982, s 46.]

1. Guilty knowledge must be proved (*Hearne v Garton* (1859) 2 E & E 66, 23 JP 693).

7–7003 144. Penalty for defacing boards. If any person pull down or injure any board put up or affixed for the purpose of publishing any byelaw[1] of the company or any penalty imposed by this or the special Act[2], or shall obliterate any of the letters or figures thereon, he shall forfeit for every such offence a sum not exceeding **level 1** on the standard scale, and shall defray the expenses attending the restoration of such board.
[Railways Clauses Consolidation Act 1845, s 144, as amended by the Transport Act 1962, s 84(4), the Criminal Law Act 1977, s 31 and the Criminal Justice Act 1982, s 46.]

1. See now s 219 of the Transport Act 2000.
2. The "special Act" is any Act passed after this Act authorising the construction of a railway (s 2).

Malicious Damage Act 1861
(24 & 25 Vict c 97)

7–7020 35. Placing wood, etc, on railway, taking up rails, etc turning points, showing or hiding signals, etc, with intent to obstruct or overthrow any engine, etc. Whosoever shall unlawfully and maliciously[1] put, place, cast, or throw upon or across any railway[2] any wood, stone, or other matter or thing[3], or shall unlawfully and maliciously take up, remove, or displace any rail, sleeper, or other matter or thing belonging to any railway, or shall unlawfully and maliciously turn, move, or divert any points or other machinery belonging to any railway, or shall unlawfully and maliciously make or show, hide or remove, any signal or light upon or near to any railway, or shall unlawfully and maliciously do or cause to be done any other matter or thing, with intent, in any of the cases aforesaid, to obstruct, upset, overthrow, injure, or destroy any engine, tender, carriage, or truck using such railway, shall be guilty of [an offence], and being convicted thereof shall be liable to [imprisonment for life].
[Malicious Damage Act 1861, s 35, as amended by the Statute Law Revision Act 1892, and the Criminal Justice Act 1948, Sch 10.]

1. The word "maliciously" can extend to acts done in sport and mischievously with a view to obstruct (*R v Upton and Gutteridge* (1851) 5 Cox CC 298, 15 JP 612).
2. This includes a private railway not constructed under an Act of Parliament (*O'Gorman v Sweet* (1890) 54 JP 663).

3. Stone-throwing is variously covered by the Malicious Damage Act 1861, s 35, the Offences Against the Person Act 1861, ss 32, 33, and the British Transport Commission Act 1949, s 56.

7–7021   **36. Obstructing engines or carriages on railways.**   Whosoever, by any unlawful act[1], or by any wilful omission or neglect[2], shall obstruct or cause to be obstructed any engine or carriage using any railway[3] or shall aid or assist therein, shall be guilty of [an offence][4] and being convicted thereof shall be liable, at the discretion of the court, to be imprisoned for any term not exceeding **two years**.

[Malicious Damage Act 1861, s 36, as amended by the Criminal Justice Act 1948, s 1(2).]

---

1. Including acts described in s 35 (*R v Hardy* (1871) LR 1 CCR 278, 35 JP 198).
2. In order to be guilty of wilful neglect, it must be proved that the defendant knew that his conduct involved the risk of an obstruction to the railway unless he took reasonable care and that he deliberately fell short of exercising care (*R v Gittins* [1982] RTR 363, [1982] Crim LR 584).
3. This includes a private railway not constructed under an Act of Parliament (*O'Gorman v Sweet* (1890) 54 JP 663).
4. Triable either way; see the Magistrates' Courts Act 1980, s 17 and Sch 1, also ss 18–21 (procedure) and s 32 (penalty).

Offences Against the Person Act 1861
(24 & 25 Vict c 100)

7–7037   **32. Placing wood, etc, on railway, taking up rails, turning points, showing or hiding signals, etc, with intent to endanger passengers.**   Whosoever shall unlawfully and maliciously[1] put or throw upon or across any railway any wood, stone, or other matter or thing[2], or shall unlawfully and maliciously[1] take up, remove, or displace any rail, sleeper, or other matter or thing belonging to any railway, or shall unlawfully and maliciously[1] turn, move or divert any points or other machinery belonging to any railway, or shall unlawfully and maliciously[1] make or show, hide or remove, any signal or light upon or near to any railway, or shall unlawfully and maliciously[1] do or cause to be done any other matter or thing, with intent, in any of the cases aforesaid, to endanger the safety of any person travelling or being upon such railway, shall be guilty of [an offence], and being convicted thereof shall be liable, at the discretion of the court, to be [imprisoned for life].

[Offences Against the Person Act 1861, s 32, as amended by the Statute Law Revision Act 1892; and the Criminal Justice Act 1948, ss 1(1), 83(3) and Sch 10.]

---

1. The word "maliciously" can extend to acts done in sport and mischievously with a view to obstruct (*R v Upton and Gutteridge* (1851) 5 Cox CC 298, 15 JP 612).
2. Stone-throwing is variously covered by the Malicious Damage Act 1861, s 35, the Offences Against the Person Act 1861 ss 32, 33, and the British Transport Commission Act 1949, s 56.

7–7038   **33. Casting stone, etc, upon a railway carriage, with intent to endanger the safety of any person therein, or in any part of the same train.**   Whosoever shall unlawfully and maliciously[1] throw, or cause to fall or strike, at, against, into, or upon any engine, tender, carriage, or truck used upon any railway, any wood, stone, or other matter or thing[2], with intent to injure or endanger the safety of any person being in or upon such engine, tender, carriage, or truck, or in or upon any other engine, tender, carriage, or truck of any train of which such first-mentioned engine, tender, carriage, or truck shall form part, shall be guilty of [an offence], and being convicted shall be liable . . . to be [imprisoned for life].

[Offences Against the Person Act 1861, s 33, as amended by the Statute Law Revision Act 1892 and the Criminal Justice Act 1948, s 1(1).]

---

1. The word "maliciously" can extend to acts done in sport and mischievously with a view to obstruct (*R v Upton and Gutteridge* (1851) 5 Cox CC 298, 15 JP 612).
2. Stone-throwing is variously covered by the Malicious Damage Act 1861, s 35, the Offences Against the Person Act 1861, ss 32, 33, and the British Transport Commission Act 1949, s 56.

7–7039   **34. Doing or omitting anything so as to endanger passengers by railway.**   Whosoever, by any unlawful act, or by any wilful omission or neglect, shall endanger or cause to be endangered[1] the safety of any person conveyed or being in or upon a railway, or shall aid or assist therein, shall be guilty of [an offence][2], and being convicted thereof shall be liable, at the discretion of the court, to be imprisoned for any term not exceeding **two years**.

[Offences Against the Person Act 1861, s 34, as amended by the Criminal Justice Act 1948, s 1(2).]

---

1. This will include potential danger, even if obviated by the act of a third party (*R v Pearce* [1967] 1 QB 150, [1966] 3 All ER 618).
2. For procedure in respect of this offence which is triable either way, see the Magistrates' Courts Act 1980, ss 17A–21 and for penalty on summary conviction, s 32, in PART I: MAGISTRATES' COURTS, PROCEDURE, ante.

Regulation of Railways Act 1868[1]

(31 & 32 Vict c 119)

III.—Provisions for Safety of Passengers

7–7040   22. Means of communication between passengers and the company's servants to be provided. *Repealed.*

---

1. As to construction of this Act, see the Railway Regulation Act 1840, ante.

7–7041   23. Penalty for trespassing on railways. If any person shall be or pass upon any railway[1], except for the purpose of crossing the same at any authorised crossing[2], after having once received warning by the company which works such railway, or by any of their agents or servants, not to go or pass thereon, every person so offending shall forfeit and pay any sum not exceeding **level 1** on the standard scale for every such offence.
[Regulation of Railways Act 1868, s 23, as amended by the Regulation of Railways Act 1871, s 14, the Criminal Law Act 1977, s 31 and the Criminal Justice Act 1982, s 46.]

---

1. A railway station platform is not part of a railway within this section, consequently proceedings thereunder for trespass on the platform do not lie (*Thomson v Great North of Scotland Rly Co* (1829) 64 JP 178).
2. If a claim of right is set up to cross the railway at a point where there had been a public footway previous to the statute authorising the railway, and the right of way has not been extinguished by the statute, the jurisdiction of justices to determine the case is ousted (*Cole v Miles* (1888) 53 JP 228). See also *Arnold v Morgan* [1911] 2 KB 314, 75 JP 105.

7–7042   24. Removal of trees dangerous to railways. If any tree standing near to a railway shall be in danger of falling on the railway so as to obstruct the traffic, it shall be lawful for any two justices, on the complaint of the company which works such railway, to cause such tree to be removed or otherwise dealt with as such justices may order, and the justices making such order may award compensation[1] to be paid by the company making such complaint to the owner of the tree so ordered to be removed or otherwise dealt with as such justices shall think proper. . . .
[Regulation of Railways Act 1868, s 24.]

---

1. As to provisions of the Railway Clauses Consolidation Act 1845, which also apply here, see note to the British Transport Commission Act 1949, s 55, post.

Regulation of Railways Act 1889[1]

(52 & 53 Vict c 57)

7–7043   5. Penalty for avoiding payment of fare. (1) Every passenger[2] by a railway shall, on request by an officer[3] or servant of a railway company, either produce, and if so requested deliver up, a ticket[4] showing that his fare is paid, or pay his fare from the place whence he started[5], or give the officer or servant his name and address; and in case of default shall be liable on summary conviction to a fine not exceeding **level 2** on the standard scale[6].

(2) If a passenger having failed either to produce[7] or if requested to deliver up a ticket showing that his fare is paid, or to pay his fare, refuses or fails, on request by an officer or servant of a railway company, to give his name and address, any officer of the company may detain[8] him until he can be conveniently brought before some justice or otherwise discharged by due course of law.

(3) If any person—

(*a*) travels or attempts to travel on a railway without having previously paid his fare and with intent to avoid payment thereof[9]; or

(*b*) having paid his fare for a certain distance, knowingly and wilfully proceeds by train beyond that distance[10] without previously paying the additional fare for the additional distance, and with intent to avoid payment thereof; or

(*c*) having failed to pay his fare, gives in reply to a request by an officer of a railway company a false name or address,

he shall be liable on summary conviction to a fine not exceeding **level 3** on the standard scale, or in the discretion of the court to imprisonment for a term not exceeding **three months**.

(4) The liability of an offender to punishment under this section shall not prejudice the recovery of any fare payable by him.

(5) In this section—

(*a*) "railway company" includes an operator of a train, and

(*b*) "operator", in relation to a train, means the person having the management of that train for the time being.

[Regulation of Railways Act 1889, s 5, as amended by the Transport Act 1962, ss 84(2) and 93(1), the British Railways Act 1965, s 35(5), the British Railways Act 1970, s 18, the British Railways Act 1977, Sch 1, the Criminal Justice Act 1982, ss 35 and 46, the Police and Criminal Evidence Act 1984, Sch 7 and SI 1994/857.]

1. This Act and the Regulation of Railways Act 1840 to 1871 may be cited collectively as the Regulation of Railways Acts 1849 to 1889.

2. Holders of annual tickets are bound to produce them as much as ordinary passengers (*Woodard v Eastern Counties Rly Co* (1861) 25 JP 310).

3. A leading railwayman who was employed by the railway company to collect and inspect tickets was held to be an "officer" for this purpose and, therefore, had the power of detention under sub-s (2) (*Moberly v Allsop* (1991) 156 JP 514).

4. For other ticket offences, see bye-laws 17 to 22 of the Framework Railway Board Bye-laws in this PART, post.

5. This means the full fare less any amount that he has already paid (*Covington v Wright* [1963] 2 QB 469, [1963] 2 All ER 212).

6. See note 2 to the Railways Regulation Act 1840, s 16, ante, as to London.

7. It is a question of fact whether a passenger who has mislaid his ticket has failed to produce it (*Brotherton v Metropolitan and District Joint Committee* (1893) 9 TLR 645).

8. The company are not authorised under this section to detain a passenger pending an inquiry whether the name and address given by him are correct when the name and address turn out upon inquiry to have been correctly given (*Knights v London, Chatham and Dover Rly Co* (1893) 62 LJQB 378). See also *Ormiston v Great Western Rly Co* [1917] 1 KB 598. If the passenger gives his name and address it would seem the company have no power to eject him from the carriage (*Butler v Manchester, Sheffield and Lincolnshire Rly Co* (1888) 21 QBD 207, 52 JP 612). But see bye-law No 2(3) of the British Railways Board Bye-laws in this PART, post.

9. A person travelling with a return ticket of another person may be rightly convicted for travelling without having paid his fare, and with intent to avoid payment (*Langdon v Howells* (1879) 4 QBD 337, 43 JP 717; *London, Midland and Scottish Rly Co v Greaver* [1937] 1 KB 367, [1936] 3 All ER 333, 100 JP 511). Payment of fare means payment to the railway company, or to their servant or agent. The intent to avoid payment thereof is proved by travelling on a non-transferable ticket issued to someone else. It is not necessary to show that the offender knew the ticket was non-transferable. The transferor is guilty of aiding and abetting him in the commission of the offence (*Reynolds v Beasley* [1919] 1 KB 215, 83 JP 35).

Proof of intent to defraud is not required; there need only be proof of intent to avoid payment (*Browning v Floyd* [1946] KB 597, [1946] 2 All ER 367, 110 JP 308). A dishonest intention is not necessarily imported and an offence is committed if a passenger travels or attempts to travel intending not to pay what, in fact, turns out to be the proper fare; see *Covington v Wright* [1963] 2 QB 469, [1963] 2 All ER 212. But there must be proof of intent to avoid payment and the burden of proof remains throughout on the prosecution (*R v Steane* [1947] KB 997, [1947] 1 All ER 813, 111 JP 387). "His fare" means the fare by the train and for the class of carriage in which the passenger travels; so a person travelling in a first-class carriage with a second-class ticket, and fraudulently intending to avoid payment of first-class fare, may be convicted for travelling "without having previously paid his fare" (*Gillingham v Walker* (1881) 45 JP 470). In such circumstances, the passenger may be convicted on proof that he declined to pay the excess fare demanded (*Noble v Killick* (1891) 60 LJMC 61).

The intent to avoid payment refers in point of time to the period of travel and this continues at least until the traveller reaches the ticket barrier (*Bremme v Dubery* [1964] 1 All ER 193, 128 JP 148; *Murphy v Verati* [1967] 1 All ER 861). There is no reason for importing the adverb "permanently" into s 5(3)(*a*)—an intention not to pay the proper fare unless and until he was tracked down and payment requested is sufficient to constitute an intent to avoid payment (*Corbyn v Saunders* [1978] 2 All ER 697, 142 JP 458).

10. The case of *R v Frere* (1855) 4 E & B 598 dealt with the case where the fare for the greater distance was *less* than that for the shorter distance. But see byelaw 5 in this PART, post.

British Transport Commission Act 1949

(12 & 13 Geo 6 c xxix)

7–7043A 53. **Appointment of railway constables.** *Appointment and jurisdiction*[1].

1. Section 53 which makes provision in relation to transport police, including jurisidiction, is printed in PART VIII: title POLICE, post.

7–7044 54. **Powers of police as to search and arrest**[1]. (1) Any person in the employment or employed upon the property of any of the Boards[2] and the Hotel Company who is found upon or in the immediate vicinity of any railway harbour dock inland waterway station or other premises now or hereafter belonging or leased to or worked by any of the Boards[3] and the Hotel Company and used for the conveyance handling or storage of goods or upon any vessel in any such harbour dock or inland waterway and who may be reasonably suspected of having in his possession or conveying in any manner anything stolen or unlawfully obtained on or from any such premises or any such vessel may be stopped searched and taken into custody without a warrant by any constable to be dealt with according to law and any constable may stop search and detain any vessel cart or carriage in any such premises as aforesaid in or upon which there shall be reason to suspect that anything stolen or unlawfully obtained may be found.
[British Transport Commission Act 1949, s 54, as amended by the Transport Act 1962, Sch 2 and the Transport Act 1968, Sch 16.]

1. Section 54(3) contained an expiry provision it is suggested that anyone seeking to rely on these provisions in court should be prepared to satisfy the court of the continuing application of these powers.

2. The Boards are the British Railways Board, the British Transport Docks Board, the British Waterways Board, the Freight Corpn and any wholly-owned subsidiary of the Freight Corpn, and (by virtue of the London Regional Transport Act 1984, s 67) London Regional Transport. By virtue of the Railways Act 1993 (Consequential Modifications) (No 2) Order 1999, SI 1999/1998, art 3, references in the 1949 Act to any of the Boards and to any wholly owned subsidiary of any of the Boards shall include references to any successor of the British Railways Board (but not to a subsidiary of such a successor unless it is itself such a successor). The reference to persons in the employment or employed upon the property

of any successor of the British Railways Board (or a subsidiary of such a successor if it is itself a successor) has effect as a reference to persons so employed in connection with a relevant undertaking,

3. The Railways Clauses Consolidation Act 1845, s 140 provides that in the case of dispute over damages, costs or expenses, the amount shall be ascertained and determined by two justices, and if it is not paid within seven days after demand, shall be recovered by distress. Section 142 provides for proceedings to be commenced by summons, for the court to hear and determine in the absence of parties on proof of due service, to receive evidence on oath, and to have a complete discretion as to costs. Penalties are summarily recoverable before two justices (s 145).

7-7045 55. For better prevention of trespass on railways, etc. (1) Any person, who shall trespass upon any of the lines of railway or sidings or in any tunnel or upon any railway embankment cutting or similar work now or hereafter belonging or leased to or worked by any of the Boards[1] or who shall trespass upon any other lands of any of the Boards[1] in dangerous proximity to any such lines of railway or other works or to any electrical apparatus used for or in connection with the working of the railway shall on summary conviction be liable to a penalty not exceeding **level 3** on the standard scale[2].

(2) The provisions of the Railways Clauses Consolidation Act 1845[3] with respect to the recovery of damages not specially provided for and of penalties and to the determination of any other matter referred to justices shall apply to this section.

(3) No person shall be subject to any penalty under this section unless it shall be proved to the satisfaction of the court before which complaint is laid that public warning has been given to persons not to trespass upon the railway by notice clearly exhibited and that such notice has been affixed at the station on the railway nearest to the place where such offence is alleged to have been committed and such notice shall be renewed as often as the same shall be obliterated or destroyed and no penalty shall be recoverable unless such notice is so placed and renewed.

(4) A notice shall not be invalid for the purposes of this section by reason only that it refers to an enactment other than this Act.

[British Transport Commission Act 1949, s 55 as amended by the Transport Act 1962, Sch 2, the British Railways Act 1965, s 35(6), the Transport Act 1968, Sch 16, the British Railways Act 1977, Sch 1 and the Criminal Justice Act 1982, s 46.]

---

1. The Boards are the British Railways Board, the British Transport Docks Board, the British Waterways Board, the Freight Corpn and any wholly-owned subsidiary of Freight Corpn, and (by virtue of the London Regional Transport Act 1984, s 67) London Regional Transport. By virtue of the Railways Act 1993 (Consequential Modifications) (No 2) Order 1999, SI 1999/1998, art 3, references in the 1949 Act to any of the Boards and to any wholly owned subsidiary of any of the Boards shall include references to any successor of the British Railways Board (but not to a subsidiary of such a successor unless it is itself such a successor).

2. See note 2 to the Railways Regulation Act 1840, s 16 ante, as to London.

3. The Railways Clauses Consolidation Act 1845, s 140 provides that in the case of dispute over damages, costs or expenses, the amount shall be ascertained and determined by two justices, and if it is not paid within seven days after demand, shall be recovered by distress. Section 142 provides for proceedings to be commenced by summons, for the court to hear and determine in the absence of parties on proof of due service, to receive evidence on oath, and to have a complete discretion as to costs. Penalties are summarily recoverable before two justices (s 145), any overplus arising from the sale of goods and chattels after meeting the amount and cost of distress, shall be returned to the person whose goods have been distrained (s 148). Distress is not rendered unlawful by any want of form (s 149). Damage is to be made good in addition to a penalty, the amount to be settled if in dispute by the justices, and levied by distress if not paid on demand (s 152). Although these provisions remain in force, magistrates will now follow the provisions of the Magistrates' Courts Act 1980, Part III (s 75 et seq) as to satisfaction and enforcement, and s 130 of the Powers of Criminal Courts (Sentencing) Act 2000 as to compensation orders.

7-7046 56. Stone throwing on railway. (1) Any person who shall unlawfully throw or cause to fall or strike at against into or upon any engine tender motor carriage or truck used upon or any works or apparatus upon any railway or siding now or hereafter belonging or leased to or worked by any of the Boards[1] any stone matter or thing[2] likely to cause damage or injury to persons or property shall on conviction be liable to a penalty not exceeding **level 3** on the standard scale[3] and the provisions of the Railways Clauses Consolidation Act 1845[4] with respect to the recovery of damages not specially provided for and of penalties and to the determination of any other matter referred to justices shall apply to this section.

[British Transport Commission Act 1949, s 56, as amended by the Transport Act 1962, Sch 2, the Transport Act 1968, Sch 16 the British Railways Act 1977, Sch 1 and the Criminal Justice Act 1982, s 46.]

---

1. The Boards are the British Railways Board, the British Transport Docks Board, the British Waterways Board, the Freight Corpn and any wholly-owned subsidiary of the Freight Corpn, and (by virtue of the London Regional Transport Act 1984, s 67) London Regional Transport. By virtue of the Railways Act 1993 (Consequential Modifications) (No 2) Order 1999, SI 1999/1998, art 3, references in the 1949 Act to any of the Boards and to any wholly owned subsidiary of any of the Boards shall include references to any successor of the British Railways Board (but not to a subsidiary of such a successor unless it is itself such a successor).

2. Stone-throwing is variously covered by the Malicious Damage Act 1861, s 35, the Offences Against the Person Act 1861, ss 32, 33, and the British Transport Commission Act 1949, s 56.

3. See note 2 to the Railway Regulations Act 1840, s 16, ante, as to London.

4. The Railways Clauses Consolidation Act, 1845, s 140 provides that in the case of dispute over damages, costs or expenses, the amount shall be ascertained and determined by two justices, and if it is not paid within seven days after demand, shall be recovered by distress. Section 142 provides for proceedings to be commenced by summons, for the court to hear and determine in the absence of parties on proof of due service, to receive evidence on oath, and to have a complete discretion as to costs. Penalties are summarily recoverable before two justices (s 145), any overplus arising from the sale of

goods and chattels after meeting the amount and cost of distress, shall be returned to the person whose goods have been distrained (s 148). Distress is not rendered unlawful by any want of form (s 149). Damage is to be made good in addition to a penalty, the amount to be settled if in dispute by the justices, and levied by distress if not paid on demand (s 152). Although these provisions remain in force, magistrates will now follow the provisions of the Magistrates' Courts Act 1980, Part III (s 75 et seq) as to satisfaction and enforcement, and s 130 of the Powers of Criminal Courts (Sentencing) Act 2000 as to compensation orders.

Transport and Works Act 1992[1]
(1992 c 42)

PART II[2]
SAFETY OF RAILWAYS ETC

CHAPTER I
OFFENCES INVOLVING DRINK OR DRUGS

Preliminary

7–7078   26. Transport systems to which Chapter I applies.   (1) This Chapter[3] applies to transport systems of any of the following kinds—

   (*a*) a railway;
   (*b*) a tramway;
   (*c*) a system which uses another mode of guided transport and is specified for the purposes of this Chapter by an order made by the Secretary of State.

  (2) This Chapter shall not apply to a transport system unless it is used, or is intended to be used, wholly or partly for the carriage of members of the public.

  (3) The power to make orders under this section shall be exercisable by statutory instrument, which shall be subject to annulment in pursuance of a resolution of either House of Parliament.
[Transport and Works Act 1992, s 26.]

---

  1. This Act is to come into force on days appointed by order of the Secretary of State (s 70). All the sections printed in this work have been brought into force, as follows: ss 45, 46, 58, 59, 67 (SI 1992/1347); ss 26–38 (SI 1992/2043); ss 41 and 42 (SI 1992/3114); ss 55 and 56 (SI 1996/1609).
  2. Part II comprises ss 26–59.
  3. Chapter I of Part II comprises ss 26–40.

Principal offences

7–7079   27. Offences involving drink or drugs on transport systems.   (1) If a person works on a transport system to which this Chapter applies—

   (*a*) as a driver, guard, conductor or signalman or in any other capacity in which he can control or affect the movement of a vehicle, or
   (*b*) in a maintenance capacity or as a supervisor of, or look-out for, persons working in a maintenance capacity,

when he is unfit to carry out that work through drink or drugs, he shall be guilty of an offence.

  (2) If a person works on a transport system to which this Chapter applies—

   (*a*) as a driver, guard, conductor or signalman or in any other capacity in which he can control or affect the movement of a vehicle, or
   (*b*) in a maintenance capacity or as a supervisor of, or look-out for, persons working in a maintenance capacity,

after consuming so much alcohol that the proportion of it in his breath, blood or urine exceeds the prescribed limit, he shall be guilty of an offence.

  (3) For the purposes of this section, a person works on a transport system in a maintenance capacity if his work on the system involves maintenance, repair or alteration of—

   (*a*) the permanent way or other means of guiding or supporting vehicles,
   (*b*) signals or any other means of controlling the movement of vehicles, or
   (*c*) any means of supplying electricity to vehicles or to the means of guiding or supporting vehicles,

or involves coupling or uncoupling vehicles or checking that they are working properly before they are used on any occasion.

  (4) For the purposes of subsection (1) above, a person shall be taken to be unfit to carry out any work if his ability to carry out that work properly is for the time being impaired.
[Transport and Works Act 1992, s 27.]

7–7080   28. Offences by operators of transport systems.   (1) If a person commits an offence under section 27 above, the responsible operator shall also be guilty of an offence.
  (2) In this section "the responsible operator" means—

(a) in a case where the transport system on which the offence under section 27 above is committed has only one operator, that operator;

(b) in a case where the transport system on which the offence under section 27 above is committed has more than one operator, whichever of them is responsible for the work giving rise to the offence.

(3) No offence is committed under subsection (1) above if the responsible operator has exercised all due diligence to prevent the commission on the transport system of any offence under section 27 above.

(4) If a person commits an offence under section 27 above in the course of his employment with a person other than the responsible operator, his employer shall (without prejudice to any liability of that operator under subsection (1) above) also be guilty of an offence.

(5) No offence is committed under subsection (4) above if the employer has exercised all due diligence to prevent the commission on the transport system by any of his employees of any offence under section 27 above.

[Transport and Works Act 1992, s 28.]

Police powers etc

7–7081   29. Breath tests.   (1) Where a constable in uniform has reasonable cause to suspect—

(a) that a person working on a transport system to which this Chapter applies in any capacity mentioned in section 27(1) and (2) above has alcohol in his body, or

(b) that a person has been working on a transport system to which this Chapter applies in any capacity mentioned in section 27(1) and (2) above with alcohol in his body and still has alcohol in his body,

he may require that person to provide a specimen of breath for a breath test.

(2) Where an accident or dangerous incident occurs on a transport system to which this Chapter applies, a constable in uniform may require a person to provide a specimen of breath for a breath test if he has reasonable cause to suspect that—

(a) at the time of the accident or incident that person was working on the transport system in a capacity mentioned in section 27(1) and (2) above, and

(b) an act or omission of that person while he was so working may have been a cause of the accident or incident.

(3) In subsection (2) above "dangerous incident" means an incident which in the constable's opinion involved a danger of death or personal injury.

(4) A person may be required under subsection (1) or subsection (2) above to provide a specimen either at or near the place where the requirement is made or, if the requirement is made under subsection (2) above and the constable making the requirement thinks fit, at a police station specified by the constable.

(5) A person who, without reasonable excuse, fails to provide a specimen of breath when required to do so in pursuance of this section shall be guilty of an offence.

[Transport and Works Act 1992, s 29.]

7–7082   30. Powers of arrest and entry.   (1) A constable may arrest a person without warrant if he has reasonable cause to suspect that that person is or has been committing an offence under section 27(1) above.

(2) A constable may arrest a person without warrant if—

(a) as a result of a breath test under section 29 above he has reasonable cause to suspect that the proportion of alcohol in that person's breath or blood exceeds the prescribed limit, or

(b) that person has failed to provide a specimen of breath for a breath test when required to do so in pursuance of section 29 above and the constable has reasonable cause to suspect that he has alcohol in his body.

(3) For the purpose of arresting a person under subsection (1) above, a constable may enter (if need be by force) any place where that person is or where the constable, with reasonable cause, suspects him to be.

(4) A constable may, for the purpose of—

(a) requiring a person to provide a specimen of breath under section 29(2) above in the case of an accident which the constable has reasonable cause to suspect involved the death of or injury to, another person, or

(b) arresting a person in such a case under subsection (2) above,

enter (if need be by force) any place where that person is or where the constable, with reasonable cause, suspects him to be.

[Transport and Works Act 1992, s 30.]

7–7083   31. Provision of specimens for analysis.   (1) In the course of an investigation into whether a person has committed an offence under section 27 above, a constable may require him—

(*a*) to provide two specimens of breath for analysis by means of a device of a type approved[1] by the Secretary of State, or

(*b*) to provide a specimen of blood or urine for a laboratory test.

(2) A requirement under this section to provide specimens of breath shall only be made at a police station.

(3) A requirement under this section to provide a specimen of blood or urine shall only be made at a police station or at a hospital; and it shall not be made at a police station unless subsection (4) below applies.

(4) This subsection applies if—

(*a*) the constable making the requirement has reasonable cause to believe that for medical reasons a specimen of breath cannot be provided or should not be required,

(*b*) at the time the requirement is made, either a device (or reliable device) of the type mentioned in subsection (1)(*a*) above is not available at the police station or it is for any other reason not practicable to use such a device there,

(*bb*) a device of the type mentioned in subsection (1)(*a*) above has been used at the police station but the constable who required the specimens of breath has reasonable cause to believe that the device has not produced a reliable indication of the proportion of alcohol in the breath of the person concerned, or

(*c*) the suspected offence is one under section 27(1) above and the constable making the requirement has been advised by a medical practitioner that the condition of the person required to provide the specimen might be due to a drug.

(5) A person may be required to provide a specimen of blood or urine in pursuance of this section notwithstanding that he has already provided or been required to provide two specimens of breath.

(6) If the provision of a specimen other than a specimen of breath may be required in pursuance of this section, the question whether it is to be a specimen of blood or a specimen of urine and, in the case of a specimen of blood, the question who is to be asked to take it shall be decided (subject to subsection (6A)) by the constable making the requirement.

(6A) Where a constable decides for the purposes of subsection (6) to require the provision of a specimen of blood, there shall be no requirement to provide such a specimen if—

(*a*) the medical practitioner who is asked to take the specimen is of the opinion that, for medical reasons, it cannot or should not be taken; or

(*b*) the registered health care professional who is asked to take it is of that opinion and there is no contrary opinion from a medical practitioner,

and, where by virtue of this subsection there can be no requirement to provide a specimen of blood, the constable may require a specimen of urine instead.

(7) A specimen of urine shall be provided within one hour of the requirement for its provision being made and after the provision of a previous specimen of urine.

(8) A person who, without reasonable excuse, fails to provide a specimen when required to do so in pursuance of this section shall be guilty of an offence.

(9) A constable shall, on requiring a person to provide a specimen in pursuance of this section, warn him that a failure to provide it may render him liable to prosecution.

(9A) In this section "health care professional" means a person (other than a medical practitioner) who is—

(*a*) a registered nurse; or

(*b*) a registered member of a health care profession which is designated for the purposes of this paragraph by an order[2] made by the Secretary of State.

(9B) A health care professional is any profession mentioned in section 60(2) of the Health Act 1999 (c 8) other than the profession of practising medicine and the profession of nursing.

(9C) An order under subsection (9A)(*b*) shall be made by statutory instrument; and any such statutory instrument shall be subject to annulment in pursuance of a resolution of either House of Parliament.

[Transport and Works Act 1992, s 31 as amended by the Criminal Procedure and Investigations Act 1996, s 63 and Sch 5, and the Police Reform Act 2002, s 58.]

---

1. The following approvals have been given:

Transport and Works Act 1992: Breath Analysis Devices Approval 1998 as from 1 March 1998 the device known as the **Camic Datamaster**, manufactured by Camic (Car and Medical Instrument Company) Ltd, composed of the Camic Datamaster, the Camic Gas System and software version 31-10-95; the device known as the **Lion Intoxilyzer 6000UK**, manufactured by Lion Laboratories plc, composed of the Lion Intoxilyzer 6000UK, the Lion Intoxilyzer 6000UK Gas Delivery System Type A or Type C and software version 2.33.

Transport and Works Act 1992: Breath Analysis Devices (No 2) Approval 1998 as from 1 March 1998 The device known as the **Intoximeter EC/IR**, manufactured by Intoximeters Inc. of Saint Louis Missouri, composed of the Intoximeter EC/IR, the Intoximeter EC/IR Gas Delivery System and software version EC/IR – UK 5.23.

Transport and Works Act 1992: Breath Analysis Devices Approval 1999 as from 2 November 1999 the **Lion Intoxilyzer 6000UK**, manufactured by Lion Laboratories plc, composed of the Lion Intoxilyzer 6000UK, the Lion Intoxilyzer 6000UK Gas Delivery System Type A, B and C software version 2.34.

2. The Registered Health Care Profession (Designation No 2) Order 2003, SI 2003/2462 has been made which designates the profession of paramedics.

7–7083A   **31A. Specimens of blood taken from persons incapable of consenting.**   (1) A constable may make a request to a medical practitioner for him to take a specimen of blood from a person ("the person concerned") irrespective of whether that person consents if—

(a) that person is a person from whom the constable would (in the absence of any incapacity of that person and of any objection under section 33) be entitled under section 31 to require the provision of a specimen of blood for a laboratory test;

(b) it appears to the constable that that person has been involved in—

    (i) an accident that constitutes or is comprised in the matter that is under investigation or the circumstances of that matter; or

    (ii) a dangerous incident (within the meaning given by section 29(3)) that constitutes or is comprised in that matter or those circumstances;

(c) it appears to the constable that that person is or may be incapable (whether or not he has purported to do so) of giving a valid consent to the taking of a specimen of blood; and

(d) it appears to that constable that that person's incapacity is attributable to medical reasons.

(2) A request under this section—

(a) shall not be made to a medical practitioner who for the time being has any responsibility (apart from the request) for the clinical care of the person concerned; and

(b) shall not be made to a medical practitioner other than a police medical practitioner unless—

    (i) it is not reasonably practicable for the request to be made to a police medical practitioner; or

    (ii) it is not reasonably practicable for such a medical practitioner (assuming him to be willing to do so) to take the specimen.

(3) It shall be lawful for a medical practitioner to whom a request is made under this section, if he thinks fit—

(a) to take a specimen of blood from the person concerned irrespective of whether that person consents; and

(b) to provide the sample to a constable.

(4) If a specimen is taken in pursuance of a request under this section, the specimen shall not be subjected to a laboratory test unless the person from whom it was taken—

(a) has been informed that it was taken; and

(b) has been required by a constable to give his permission for a laboratory test of the specimen; and

(c) has given his permission.

(5) A constable must, on requiring a person to give his permission for the purposes of this section for a laboratory test of a specimen, warn that person that a failure to give the permission, may render him liable to prosecution.

(6) A person who, without reasonable excuse, fails to give his permission for a laboratory test of a specimen of blood taken from him under this section is guilty of an offence.

(7) In this section "police medical practitioner" means a medical practitioner who is engaged under any agreement to provide medical services for purposes connected with the activities of a police force.

[Transport and Works Act 1992, s 31A as inserted by the Police Reform Act 2002, s 58.]

7–7084   **32. Choice of specimens of breath.**   (1) Of any two specimens of breath provided by a person in pursuance of section 31 above, the one with the lower proportion of alcohol in the breath shall be used and the other shall be disregarded.

(2) But if the specimen with the lower proportion of alcohol contains no more than 50 microgrammes of alcohol in 100 millilitres of breath, the person who provided it may claim that it should be replaced by such specimen as may be required under section 31(6) above and, if he then provides such a specimen, neither specimen of breath shall be used.

(3) The Secretary of State may by regulations substitute another proportion of alcohol in the breath for that specified in subsection (2) above.

(4) The power to make regulations under this section shall be exercisable by statutory instrument; and no such regulations shall be made unless a draft of the instrument containing them has been laid before, and approved by a resolution of, each House of Parliament.

[Transport and Works Act 1992, s 32.]

7–7085   **33. Protection for hospital patients.**   (1) While a person is at a hospital as a patient, he shall not be required to provide a specimen of breath for a breath test or to provide a specimen for a laboratory test unless the medical practitioner in immediate charge of his case has been notified of the proposal to make the requirement; and—

(*a*) if the requirement is then made, it shall be for the provision of a specimen at the hospital, but
(*b*) if the medical practitioner objects on the ground specified in subsection (2) below, the requirement shall not be made.

(1A) While a person is at a hospital as a patient, no specimen of blood shall be taken from him under section 31A of this Act and he shall not be required to give his permission for a laboratory test of a specimen taken under that section unless the medical practitioner in immediate charge of his case—

(*a*) has been notified of the proposal to take the specimen or to make the requirement; and
(*b*) has not objected on the ground specified in subsection (2).

(2) The ground on which the medical practitioner may object is—

(*a*) in a case falling withing subsection (1), that the requirement or the provision of a specimen or (if one is required) the warning required under section 31(9) of this Act would be prejudicial to the proper care and treatment of the patient; and
(*b*) in a case falling within subsection (1A), that the taking of the specimen, the requirement or the warning required by section 31A(5) of this Act would be so prejudicial.

(3) A person shall not be arrested under section 30(2) above while he is at a hospital as a patient.
[Transport and Works Act 1992, s 33 as amended by the Police Reform Act 2002, s 58.]

Evidence in proceedings for offences under section 27

7–7086   34. Use of specimens in proceedings.   (1) In proceedings for any offence under section 27 above—

(*a*) evidence of the proportion of alcohol or any drug in a specimen of breath, blood or urine provided by or taken from the accused shall be taken into account, and
(*b*) it shall be assumed that the proportion of alcohol in the accused's breath, blood or urine at the time of the alleged offence was not less than in the specimen.

(2) That assumption shall not be made if the accused proves—

(*a*) that he consumed alcohol before he provided the specimen or had it taken from him and after he had stopped work on the occasion of the alleged offence, and
(*b*) that, had he not done so, the proportion of alcohol in his breath, blood or urine would not have exceeded the prescribed limit and, where the offence alleged is an offence of being unfit to carry out the work in question through drink, would not have been such as to impair his ability to carry out that work properly.

(3) Where, at the time a specimen of blood or urine was provided by the accused, he asked to be provided with such a specimen, evidence of the proportion of alcohol or any drug found in the specimen shall not be admissible in the proceedings on behalf of the prosecution unless—

(*a*) the specimen in which the alcohol or drug was found is one of two parts into which the specimen provided by the accused was divided at the time it was provided, and
(*b*) the other part was supplied to the accused.

(3A) Where the specimen of blood was taken from the accused under section 31A, evidence of the proportion of alcohol or any drug found in the specimen is not admissible on behalf of the prosecution in the proceedings unless—

(*a*) the specimen in which the alcohol or drug was found is one of two parts into which the specimen taken from the accused was divided at the time it was taken; and
(*b*) any request to be supplied with the other part which was made by the accused at the time when he gave his permission for a laboratory test of the specimen was complied with.
[Transport and Works Act 1992, s 34 as amended by the Police Reform Act 2002, s 58.]

7–7087   35. Documentary evidence as to specimens.   (1) In proceedings for any offence under section 27 above, evidence of the proportion of alcohol in a specimen of breath may be given by the production of a document (or documents) purporting to be—

(*a*) a statement automatically produced by the device by which the proportion of alcohol in the specimen was measured, and
(*b*) a certificate signed by a constable (which may but need not be contained in the same document as the statement) that the specimen was provided by the accused at the date and time shown in the statement.

(2) In such proceedings, evidence of the proportion of alcohol or a drug in a specimen of blood or urine may be given by the production of a document purporting to be a certificate signed by an authorised analyst identifying the specimen and stating the proportion of alcohol or drug found in it.

(3) In such proceedings, evidence that a specimen of blood was taken from the accused with his consent by a medical practitioner* may be given by the production of a document purporting to be a certificate to that effect signed by the practitioner*.

(4) A document such as is mentioned in subsection (1) above shall be admissible in evidence on

behalf of the prosecution in pursuance of this section only if a copy of it either was handed to the accused when the document was produced or was served on him not later than seven days before the hearing.

(5) A document such as is mentioned in subsection (2) or (3) above shall be admissible in evidence on behalf of the prosecution in pursuance of this section only if a copy of it was served on the accused not later than seven days before the hearing.

(6) A document purporting to be a certificate (or so much of a document as purports to be a certificate) shall not be admissible in evidence on behalf of the prosecution in pursuance of this section if the accused, not later than three days before the hearing or within such further time as the court may in special circumstances allow, has served notice on the prosecutor requiring the attendance at the hearing of the person by whom the document purports to be signed.

(7) In this section "served" means served personally or sent by registered post or recorded delivery service.

(8) In subsection (2) above "authorised analyst" means—

(a) any person possessing the qualifications prescribed by regulations made under section 76 of the Food Act 1984 or section 27 of the Food and Drugs (Scotland) Act 1956 as qualifying persons for appointment as public analysts under those Acts, or

(b) any other person authorised by the Secretary of State to make analyses for the purposes of this section.

[Transport and Works Act 1992, s 35.]

---

*Sub-section (3) amended, with the insertion of the words "or a registered health care professional", by the Police Reform Act 2002, s 58, from a date to be appointed.

Penalties

7–7088   36. Penalties.   (1) A person guilty of any offence under this Chapter other than an offence under section 29(5) above shall be liable on summary conviction to imprisonment for a term not exceeding **six months**, to a fine not exceeding **level 5** on the standard scale or to **both**.

(2) A person guilty of an offence under section 29(5) above shall be liable on summary conviction to a fine not exceeding **level 3** on the standard scale.

[Transport and Works Act 1992, s 36.]

Miscellaneous and supplementary

7–7089   38. Interpretation of Chapter I.   (1) In this Chapter—

"breath test" means a preliminary test for the purpose of obtaining, by means of a device of a type approved[1] by the Secretary of State, an indication whether the proportion of alcohol in a person's breath or blood is likely to exceed the prescribed limit;

"drug" includes any intoxicant other than alcohol;

"fail" includes refuse;

"hospital" means an institution which provides medical or surgical treatment for in-patients or out-patients.

(2) In this Chapter "the prescribed limit" means, as the case may require—

(a)   35 microgrammes of alcohol in 100 millilitres of breath,

(b)   80 milligrammes of alcohol in 100 millilitres of blood, or

(c)   107 milligrammes of alcohol in 100 millilitres of urine,

or such other proportion as may be prescribed by regulations made by the Secretary of State.

(2A) In this Chapter "registered health care professional" means a person (other than a medical practitioner) who is—

(a)   a registered nurse; or

(b)   a registered member of a health care profession which is designated for the purposes of this paragraph by an order[1] made by the Secretary of State.

(2B) A health care profession is any profession mentioned in section 60(2) of the Health Act 1999 (c 8) other than the profession of practising medicine and the profession of nursing.

(2C) An order under subsection (2A)(b) shall be made by statutory instrument; and any such statutory instrument shall be subject to annulment in pursuance of a resolution of either House of Parliament.

(3) For the purposes of this Chapter, it is immaterial whether a person who works on a transport system does so in the course of his employment, under a contract for services, voluntarily or otherwise.

(4) For the purposes of this Chapter, a person does not provide a specimen of breath for a breath test or for analysis unless the specimen—

(a)   is sufficient to enable the test or the analysis to be carried out, and

(b)   is provided in such a way as to enable the objective of the test or analysis to be satisfactorily achieved.

(5) For the purposes of this Chapter, a person provides a specimen of blood if and only if—

(a) he consents to the taking of such a specimen from him; and

(b) the specimen is taken from him by a medical practitioner or, if it is taken in a police station, either by a medical practitioner or by a registered health care professional.

(6) *Making regulations*[2].

[Transport and Works Act 1992, s 38, as amended by the Police Reform Act 2002, s 58.]

---

1. The following approvals have been given:

Breath Test Device Approval 1999 as from 15th October 1999 the type of device known as the **Alcosensor IV UK** manufactured by Intoximeters UK.

Breath Test Device Approval 2000 as from 25th February 2000 the type of device known as the **Lion Alcolmeter SL-400A (indicating display form),** manufactured by Lion Laboratories plc.

Breath Test Device Approval (No 2) 2002 as from 12 December 2002 the type of device known as the **Lion Alcolmeter SL-400B** manufactured by Lion Laboratories.

2. The Registered Health Care Profession (Designation No 2) Order 2003, SI 2003/2462 has been made which designates the profession of paramedics.

CHAPTER II[1]
OTHER SAFETY PROVISIONS

General

7–7090　41. Approval of works, plant and equipment.　*Secretary of State*[2] *may make regulations*[3]; person guilty of offence under this section liable to fine not exceeding **level 5**.

[Transport and Works Act 1992, s 41—summarised.]

---

1. Chapter II of Part II comprises ss 41–56.

2. Any reference to the Secretary of State in s 41 (other than sub-s (1)) is to have effect as if it were a reference to the Health and Safety Executive (Railway Safety (Miscellaneous Provisions) Regulations 1997, SI 1997/553, reg 10).

3. The Railways and Other Transport Systems (Approval of Works, Plant and Equipment) Regulations 1994, SI 1994/157 have been made.

7–7092　45. Directions limiting speeds and loads.　*Secretary of State may give directions: contravention is a summary offence punishable by a fine not exceeding* **level 5**.

[Transport and Works Act 1992, s 45—summarised.]

7–7093　46. Directions requiring insurance.　*Secretary of State may give directions about insurance against death or personal injury liability: contravention is a summary offence punishable by a fine not exceeding* **level 5**.

[Transport and Works Act 1992, s 46—summarised.]

7–7094　55. Offence of failing to comply with sign.　(1) A person who fails to comply with any requirement, restriction or prohibition conveyed by a crossing sign lawfully placed on or near a private road or path near a place where it crosses a railway or tramway shall be guilty of an offence.

(2) In any proceedings for an offence under this section, a crossing sign on or near a private road or path near a place where it crosses a railway or tramway shall be taken to have been lawfully placed there unless the contrary is proved.

(3) A person guilty of an offence under this section shall be liable on summary conviction to a fine not exceeding **level 3** on the standard scale.

[Transport and Works Act 1992, s 55.]

7–7095　56. Interpretation of sections 52 to 55.　(1) In sections 52 to 55 above (and this section)—

"barrier" includes gate;

"cross" means cross otherwise than by tunnel or bridge;

"crossing sign", in relation to a private road or path and any place where it crosses a railway or tramway, means—

(a) any object or device (whether fixed or portable), or

(b) any line or mark on the road or path,

for conveying to users of the road or path warnings, information, requirements, restrictions or prohibitions relating to the crossing;

"fail" includes refuse;

"lawfully placed" means placed in accordance with sections 52 to 54 above;

"maintain" includes repair and replace;

"place" includes erect and (in relation to a sign) display;

"private road or path" means any length of road or path to which the public does not have access.

(2) In the case of a railway or tramway which has more than one operator, the powers conferred by sections 52 to 54 above shall only be exercisable by or in relation to the operator carrying on the undertaking which includes maintaining the permanent way.

[Transport and Works Act 1992, s 56.]

Chapter III[1]
Supplementary

7–7096   58. Prosecutions.   No proceedings shall be instituted in England and Wales in respect of an offence under this Part, other than an offence under section 41 or 43 above except by or with the consent of the Secretary of State or the Director of Public Prosecutions.
[Transport and Works Act 1992, s 58 amended by the Railways Act 1993, s 117.]

---

1. Chapter III of Pt II contains ss 57–59.

7–7097   59. Offences by bodies corporate etc.   (1) Where an offence under this Part committed by a body corporate is committed with the consent or connivance of, or is attributable to any neglect on the part of, a director, manager, secretary or other similar officer of the body, or a person purporting to act in such a capacity, he as well as the body corporate shall be guilty of the offence.

(2) In subsection (1) above "director", in relation to a body corporate whose affairs are managed by its members, means a member of the body corporate.

(3) Where, in Scotland, an offence under this Part committed by a partnership or by an unincorporated association other than a partnership is committed with the consent or connivance of, or is attributable to any neglect on the part of, a partner in the partnership or (as the case may be) a person concerned in the management or control of the association, he, as well as the partnership or association, shall be guilty of the offence.
[Transport and Works Act 1992, s 59.]

Part III[1]
Miscellaneous and General

7–7098   67. Interpretation.   (1) In this Act, except where the context otherwise requires—

"carriageway" has the same meaning as in the Highways Act 1980, or in Scotland the Roads (Scotland) Act 1984;

"guided transport" means transport by vehicles guided by means external to the vehicles (whether or not the vehicles are also capable of being operated in some other way);

"inland waterway" includes both natural and artificial waterways, and waterways within parts of the sea that are in Great Britain, but not any waterway managed or maintained by a person who is a harbour authority (within the meaning of the Harbours Act 1964) in relation to the waterway;

"operator", in relation to a transport system, means any person carrying on an undertaking which includes the system or any part of it or the provision of transport services on the system;

"railway" means a system of transport employing parallel rails which—

    (*a*)   provide support and guidance for vehicles carried on flanged wheels, and

    (*b*)   form a track which either is of a gauge of at least 350 millimetres or crosses a carriageway (whether or not on the same level),

but does not include a tramway;

"street" means—

    (*a*)   in England and Wales, a street within the meaning of section 48 of the New Roads and Street Works Act 1991, together with land on the verge of a street or between two carriageways;

    (*b*)   in Scotland, a road within the meaning of section 107 of the New Roads and Street Works Act 1991, together with land on the verge of a road or between two carriageways;

"tramway" means a system of transport used wholly or mainly for the carriage of passengers and employing parallel rails which—

    (*a*)   provide support and guidance for vehicles carried on flanged wheels, and

    (*b*)   are laid wholly or mainly along a street or in any other place to which the public has access (including a place to which the public has access only on making a payment);

"trolley vehicle system" means a system of transport by vehicles constructed or adapted for use on roads without rails under electric power transmitted to them by overhead wires (whether or not there is in addition a source of power on board the vehicles);

"vehicle" includes mobile traction unit.

(2) References in this Act to rights over land include references to rights to do, or to place and maintain, anything in, on or under land or in the air-space above its surface.
[Transport and Works Act 1992, s 67.]

---

1. Part III contains ss 60–72.

Railways Act 1993[1]

(1993 c 43)

7-7098A

PART I[2]
THE PROVISION OF RAILWAY SERVICES

---

1. At the time of going to press five commencement orders have been made under s 154 of the Act: SI 1993/3237 and SIs 1994/202, 447, 571 and 1648. The whole Act is in force except ss 132(8) (partially), 134 (1) (partially), 152 (partially), Schs 10 (partially) 12 (partially) and 14 (partially).
2. Part I consists of ss 1–83.

7-7098B

PART II[1]
RE-ORGANISATION OF THE RAILWAYS

---

1. Part II consists of ss 84–116.

PART III[1]
MISCELLANEOUS, GENERAL AND SUPPLEMENTAL PROVISIONS

Safety, emergencies, security etc

7-7099   **117. Safety of railways and other guided transport systems.**   (1) Part I of the Health and Safety at Work etc Act 1974 ("the 1974 Act") shall have effect as if the provisions mentioned in subsection (4) below (which relate to the proper construction and safe operation of certain transport systems, and of the vehicles used on those systems, and the protection of railway employees or the general public from personal injury and other risks arising therefrom)—

(a) were existing statutory provisions, within the meaning of that Part; and
(b) in the case of the enactments mentioned in paragraphs (a) to (m) of that subsection, were specified in the third column of Schedule 1 to that Act.

(2) If to any extent they would not do so apart from this subsection, the general purposes of Part I of the 1974 Act shall include—

(a) securing the proper construction and safe operation of transport systems to which this section applies, and of any locomotives, rolling stock or other vehicles used, or to be used, on those systems; and
(b) protecting the public (whether passengers or not) from personal injury and other risks arising from the construction and operation of transport systems to which this section applies.

(3) Without prejudice to the generality of subsection (1) of section 15 of the 1974 Act (health and safety regulations), regulations under that section may—

(a) repeal or modify any of the provisions mentioned in subsection (4) below; and
(b) make any provision which, but for any such repeal or modification, could be made by regulations or orders made under any enactment there mentioned.

(4) The provisions referred to in subsections (1) and (3) above are—

(a) the Highway (Railway Crossings) Act 1839;
(b) sections 9 and 10 of the Railway Regulation Act 1842;
(c) section 22 of the Regulation of Railways Act 1868;
(d) the Regulation of Railways Act 1871;
(e) sections 1 and 4 of the Regulation of Railways Act 1889;
(f) the Railway Employment (Prevention of Accidents) Act 1900;
(g) section 42 of the Road and Rail Traffic Act 1933;
(h) section 40 of the British Transport Commission Act 1954;
(j) section 66 of the British Transport Commission Act 1957;
(k) sections 124 and 125 of the Transport Act 1968;
(l) the Level Crossings Act 1983;
(m) sections 41 to 45 of the Transport and Works Act 1992;
(n) any regulations made under section 2 of the European Communities Act 1972 for the purpose of implementing the Council Directive of 29th July 1991 on the development of the Community's railways, so far as the regulations are made for safety purposes.

(5) *Amendment of Transport and Works Act 1992.*
(6) This section applies to the following transport systems, that is to say—

(a) any railway, tramway or trolley vehicle system; or
(b) any transport system using any other mode of guided transport.

(7) The definitions of "guided transport", "railway", "tramway", "trolley vehicle system" and

"vehicle" in section 67(1) of the Transport and Works Act 1992 shall have effect for the purposes of this section as they have effect for the purposes of that Act, but disregarding for the purposes of this section paragraph (*b*) of the definition of "railway" (which includes a condition as to the minimum gauge of the track).

[Railways Act 1993, s 117.]

---

1. Part III contains ss 117–154.

7–7100　118. Control of railways in time of hostilities, severe international tension or great national emergency.　(1)–(6)　*Directions by the Secretary of State.*

(7) Any person who, without reasonable excuse, contravenes or fails to comply with a direction given to him under this section is guilty of an offence and shall be liable[1]—

- (*a*)　on summary conviction, to a fine not exceeding the **statutory maximum**; or
- (*b*)　on conviction on indictment, to a **fine** or imprisonment for a term not exceeding **two years** or **both**.

(8) No proceedings shall be instituted in England and Wales in respect of an offence under this section except by or with the consent of the Secretary of State or the Director of Public Prosecutions.

(9), (10)　*Financial arrangements.*

(11) In this section—

"great national emergency" means any natural disaster or other emergency which, in the opinion of the Secretary of State, is or may be likely to give rise to such disruption of the means of transport that the population, or a substantial part of the population, of Great Britain is or may be likely to be deprived of essential goods or services;
"operator", in relation to a relevant asset, means the person having the management of the relevant asset for the time being;
"owner", in relation to a relevant asset, means any person—

- (*a*)　who is the owner of, or who has any right over or interest in, the relevant asset; and
- (*b*)　whose consent is needed to the use of the relevant asset by any other person;

"relevant asset" means a network, a station, a light maintenance depot or any track or rolling stock;

and, subject to that, expressions used in this section and in Part I above have the same meaning in this section as they have in that Part with "railway" having its wider meaning for the purposes of this section.

(12)　*Repealed.*

[Railways Act 1993, s 118 as amended by the Transport Act 2000, Sch 31 and the Railways Act 2005, s 54.]

---

1. For procedure in respect of an offence triable either way, see the Magistrates' Courts Act 1980, ss 17A–21 in PART I: MAGISTRATES' COURTS, PROCEDURE, ante.

7–7101　119. Security: power of Secretary of State to give instructions.　(1)–(7)　*Instructions by the Secretary of State to protect relevant assets against acts of violence.*

(8) A person who is the owner or operator of a relevant asset or who provides railway services shall be under a duty to comply with an instruction given to him under this section, notwithstanding the requirements of any other enactment or instrument relating to him or to—

- (*a*)　the use of, or the exercise of rights over, the relevant asset,
- (*b*)　the management of the relevant asset, or
- (*c*)　the railway services,

as the case may be, and notwithstanding any other duty or obligation to which he may be subject.

(9) A person who without reasonable excuse fails to do anything required of him by an instruction is guilty of an offence and shall be liable[1]—

- (*a*)　on summary conviction, to a fine not exceeding the **statutory maximum**; or
- (*b*)　on conviction on indictment, to a **fine** or to a term of imprisonment not exceeding **two years**, or to **both**.

(10) No proceedings shall be instituted in England and Wales in respect of an offence under subsection (9) above except by or with the consent of the Secretary of State or the Director of Public Prosecutions.

(11) In this section—

"act of violence" means—

- (*a*)　any act which constitutes, or
- (*b*)　any potential act which, if carried out, would constitute,

the offence of murder, attempted murder, manslaughter, culpable homicide, assault, real injury or malicious mischief, or an offence undersection 18, 20, 21, 22, 23, 24, 28 or 29 of the Offences against the Person Act 1861, under section 2 of the Explosive Substances Act 1883 or under section 1 of the Criminal Damage Act 1971;

"designated" means specified in an instruction, or of a class or description so specified;

"instruction" means an instruction given under this section, and any reference to an instruction includes a reference to an instruction as varied under subsection (6)(c) above;

"operator" and "owner" have the same meaning as in section 118 above;

"relevant asset" has the same meaning as in section 118 above, and any reference to such an asset includes a reference to any part of any such asset;

"specified" means specified in an instruction;

"terrorism" has the same meaning as in the Terrorism Act 2000 (c 110 (see section 1 of that Act); and, subject to that, expressions used in this section and in Part I above have the same meaning in this section as they have in that Part with "railway" having its wider meaning for the purposes of this section.

[Railways Act 1993, s 119 as amended by the Railways Act 2005, s 54.]

---

1. For procedure in respect of an offence triable either way, see the Magistrates' Courts Act 1980, ss 17A–21 in PART I: MAGISTRATES' COURTS, PROCEDURE, ante.

7–7102   120. Security: enforcement notices.   (1) Where it appears to the Secretary of State that a person upon whom an instruction has been served has failed, is failing or is likely to fail to comply with that instruction, he may serve on that person a notice (in this section referred to as an "enforcement notice") containing such provision as the Secretary of State may consider requisite for the purpose of ensuring that the person complies with the instruction and specifying, in particular—

(a)   the things, or the description of things, which the person is required to do, or refrain from doing, in order to comply with the instruction;

(b)   the time within which, or after which, the person must do, or refrain from doing, those things; and

(c)   the period during which the person is to do, or refrain from doing, those things.

(2) The Secretary of State may vary or revoke an enforcement notice, and any reference in this section to an enforcement notice includes a reference to such a notice as varied under this subsection.

(3) Where the Secretary of State varies or revokes an enforcement notice under subsection (2) above he shall serve notice of the variation or revocation on the person on whom the enforcement notice in question was served.

(4) A person who without reasonable excuse fails to do anything required of him by an enforcement notice is guilty of an offence and shall be liable[1]—

(a)   on summary conviction, to a fine not exceeding the **statutory maximum**; or

(b)   on conviction on indictment, to a **fine** or to a term of imprisonment not exceeding **two years**, or to **both**.

(5) No proceedings shall be instituted in England and Wales in respect of an offence under subsection (4) above except by or with the consent of the Secretary of State or the Director of Public Prosecutions.

(6) Section 119(8) above shall have effect in relation to an enforcement notice as it has effect in relation to an instruction.

(7) Expressions used in this section and in section 119 above have the same meaning in this section as they have in that section.

[Railways Act 1993, s 120.]

---

1. For procedure in respect of an offence triable either way, see the Magistrates' Courts Act 1980, ss 17A–21 in PART I: MAGISTRATES' COURTS, PROCEDURE, ante.

7–7103   121. Security: inspections.   (1) For the purpose of enabling the Secretary of State to determine whether to give an instruction to any person, or of ascertaining whether any instruction or enforcement notice is being or has been complied with, a person authorised for the purpose by the Secretary of State in writing (in this section referred to as "an authorised person") shall have power, on production (if required) of his credentials, to inspect any relevant asset.

(2) An authorised person inspecting a relevant asset under subsection (1) above shall have power—

(a)   to subject any property found by him on or in the relevant asset, or any apparatus or equipment installed in the relevant asset, to such tests as he considers necessary for the purpose for which the inspection is carried out;

(b)   to take such steps as he considers necessary for that purpose—

(i)   to ascertain what practices or procedures are being followed in relation to security; or

(ii)   to test the effectiveness of any practice or procedure relating to security; or

(c)   to require the owner or operator of the relevant asset to furnish to him such information as the authorised person considers necessary for that purpose;

but nothing in paragraph (a) above shall entitle an authorised person to subject any rolling stock, or any part of any rolling stock, to any test.

(3) An authorised person, for the purpose of exercising any power conferred on him by subsection (1) or (2) above in relation to any relevant asset, shall have power—

(a) to board any rolling stock and to take all such steps as are necessary to ensure that it is not moved; or

(b) to enter any land or other property comprised either in any track or in a network, station or light maintenance depot;

but nothing in this subsection authorises any use of force.

(4) A person is guilty of an offence if he—

(a) intentionally obstructs an authorised person acting in the exercise of any power conferred on him by this section;

(b) fails, without reasonable excuse, to comply with a requirement imposed on him under paragraph (c) of subsection (2) above to furnish information to an authorised person; or

(c) in furnishing any information required under that paragraph, makes a statement which he knows to be false in a material particular, or recklessly makes a statement which is false in a material particular.

(5) A person guilty of an offence under subsection (4) above shall be liable[1]—

(a) on summary conviction, to a fine not exceeding the **statutory maximum**;

(b) on conviction on indictment, to a **fine** or to imprisonment for a term not exceeding **two years**, or to **both**.

(6) No proceedings shall be instituted in England and Wales in respect of an offence under subsection (4) above except by or with the consent of the Secretary of State or the Director of Public Prosecutions.

(7) Expressions used in this section and in section 119 or 120 above have the same meaning in this section as they have in that section.

[Railways Act 1993, s 121.]

---

1. For procedure in respect of an offence triable either way, see the Magistrates' Courts Act 1980, ss 17A–21 in PART I: MAGISTRATES' COURTS, PROCEDURE, ante.

7–7103A 121A. Railway security: approved providers. *Regulations may provide for the Secretary of State to maintain a list of approved providers of railway security services.*

7–7105 130. Penalty fares. (1)–(6) *Regulations.*

(7) Regulations[1] may provide that where information is required to be furnished pursuant to the regulations—

(a) a refusal to furnish any such information, or

(b) the furnishing of information which is false in a material particular,

shall, in prescribed circumstances, be an offence punishable on summary conviction by a fine not exceeding **level 2** on the standard scale.

(8) Apart from subsection (7) above, nothing in this section creates, or authorises the creation of, any offence.

(9)–(12) *Regulations and interpretation.*

[Railways Act 1993, s 130 amended by the Greater London Authority Act 1999, s 206 and the Railways Act 2005, s 47.]

---

1. The Railways (Penalty Fares) Regulations 1994, this PART, post, have been made. By reg 12 a person charged a penalty pursuant to reg 4 shall give his name and address to the authorised collector when so required. Failure to do so is an offence punishable on summary conviction by a fine not exceeding **level 2** on the standard scale.

7–7106 145. General restrictions on disclosure of information. (1) Subject to the following provisions of this section, no information with respect to any particular business which—

(a) has been obtained under or by virtue of any of the provisions of this Act; and

(b) relates to the affairs of any individual or to any particular business,

shall during the lifetime of that individual or so long as that business continues to be carried on, be disclosed without the consent of that individual or the person for the time being carrying on that business.

(2) Subsection (1) above does not apply to any disclosure of information which is made—

(a) for the purpose of facilitating the carrying out by the Secretary of State, the Scottish Ministers, the Regulator, the Authority or the Competition Commission of any of his or, as the case may be, their functions under this Act, the Transport Act 2000 or the Railways Act 2005;

(aa) for the purpose of facilitating the carrying out or carrying on by the Secretary of State or the Scottish Ministers of any other functions or activities of his or theirs in relation to railways or railway services;

(b) for the purpose of facilitating the carrying out by—

    (i)   any Minister of the Crown,

    (ii) the Director General of Fair Trading,

    (iii) the Competition Commission,

    (iv) the Office of Communications,

    (v) the Gas and Electricity Markets Authority,

    (vi) the Director General of Water Supply,

    (vii) *repealed*

    (viii)the Civil Aviation Authority,

    (ix) the Insolvency Practitioners Tribunal, or

    (x) a local weights and measures authority in Great Britain,

of any of his or, as the case may be, their functions under any of the enactments or instruments specified in subsection (3) below;

(c) for the purpose of enabling or assisting the Secretary of State, the Treasury or the Financial Services Authority to exercise any powers conferred by or under the Financial Services and Markets Act 2000 or by the enactments relating to companies or insolvency;

(ca) for the purpose of enabling or assisting any inspector appointed under enactments relating to companies to carry out his functions;

(d) for the purpose of enabling or assisting an official receiver to carry out his functions under the enactments relating to insolvency or for the purpose of enabling or assisting a recognised professional body for the purposes of section 391 of the Insolvency Act 1986 to carry out its functions as such;

(e) for the purpose of facilitating the carrying out by the Health and Safety Commission or the Health and Safety Executive of any of its functions under any enactment or of facilitating the carrying out by any enforcing authority, within the meaning of Part I of the Health and Safety at Work etc Act 1974, of any functions under a relevant statutory provision, within the meaning of that Act;

(f) for the purpose of facilitating the carrying out by the Comptroller and Auditor General of any of his functions under any enactment;

(g) *repealed*;

(ga) for the purpose of facilitating the carrying out by the Office of Rail Regulation of any of its functions under any instrument made for the purpose of implementing Council Directive 95/18/EC dated 19th June 1995 on the licensing of railway undertakings, as amended by Directive 2001/13/EC dated 26th February 2001 and Directive 2004/49/EC dated 29th April 2004, both of the European Parliament and of the Council;

(gb) for the purpose of facilitating the carrying out by the Office of Rail Regulation of any of its functions under any instrument made for the purpose of implementing Council Directive 91/440/EEC dated 29 July 1991 on the development of the Community's railways, as amended by Directive 2001/12/EC dated 26 February 2001 and Directive 2004/51/EC dated 29 April 2004, both of the European Parliament and of the Council, and Directive 2001/14/EC dated 26 February 2001 on the allocation of railway infrastructure capacity and the levying of charges for the use of railway infrastructure, as amended by Directive 2004/49/EC dated 29 April 2004 on safety on the Community's railways, both of the European Parliament and of the Council;

(h) in connection with the investigation of any criminal offence or for the purposes of any criminal proceedings;

(j) for the purposes of any civil proceedings brought under or by virtue of this Act or any of the enactments or instruments specified in subsection (3) below; or

(k) in pursuance of a Community obligation.

(3) The enactments and instruments referred to in subsection (2) above are—

(a) the Trade Descriptions Act 1968;

(b) the Fair Trading Act 1973;

(c) the Consumer Credit Act 1974;

(d) *Repealed*

(e) *Repealed*

(f) the Estate Agents Act 1979;

(g) the Competition Act 1980;

(h) the Telecommunications Act 1984;

(j) the Airports Act 1986;

(k) the Gas Act 1986;

(l) the Insolvency Act 1986;

(m) the Consumer Protection Act 1987;

(n) the Electricity Act 1989;

(o) the Property Misdescriptions Act 1991;

(p) the Water Industry Act 1991;

(q) the Water Resources Act 1991;

(qq) the Competition Act 1998;

(*qr*) Part I of the Transport Act 2000;

(*qs*) the Enterprise Act 2002;

(*qt*) the Communications Act 2003;

(*r*) any subordinate legislation made for the purpose of securing compliance with the Directive of the Council of the European Communities dated 10th September 1984 on the approximation of the laws, regulations and administrative provisions of the member States concerning misleading advertising.

(4) The Secretary of State may by order provide that subsections (2) and (3) above shall have effect subject to such modifications as are specified in the order.

(5) Nothing in subsection (1) above shall be construed—

(*a*) as limiting the matters which may be published under section 71 above or may be included in, or made public as part of, a report of the Office of Rail Regulation, the Authority*, the Competition Commission, or the Rail Passengers' Council under any provision of Part I above;

(*b*) as applying to any information—

(i) which has been so published or has been made public as part of such a report; or

(ii) which has otherwise been made available to the public by virtue of being disclosed in any circumstances in which, or for any purpose for which, disclosure is not precluded by this section.

(5A) Subsection (1) above does not prevent the transfer of receords in accordance with section 3(4) of the Public Records Act 1958.

(6) Any person who discloses any information in contravention of this section is guilty of an offence and shall be liable[1]—

(*a*) on summary conviction, to a fine not exceeding the **statutory maximum**;

(*b*) on conviction on indictment, to imprisonment for a term not exceeding **two years** or to a **fine** or to **both**.

(6A) Information obtained by the Office of Rail Regulation in the exercise of functions which are exercisable concurrently with the Office of Fair Trading under Part I of the Competition Act 1998 is subject to Part 9 of the Enterprise Act 2002 (Information) and not to subsections (1) to (6) of this section.

(7) *Repealed.*

[Railways Act 1993, s 145 amended by SI 1998/1340 and the Competition Act 1998, Schs 10 and 14, the Greater London Authority Act 1999, Sch 19, the Utilities Act 2000, s 3, SI 2001/3649 and 4050, the Railways and Transport Safety Act 2003, Sch 2, the Enterprise Act 2002, Sch 25, the Railways Act 2005, Schs 11 and 13, SI 2005/3049 and 3050.]

---

*. Repealed by the Railways Act 2005, Sch 13 from a date to be apppointed.

1. For procedure in respect of an offence triable either way, see the Magistrates' Courts Act 1980, ss 17A–21 in Part I: Magistrates' Courts, Procedure, *ante*.

7–7107 146. Making of false statements etc. (1) If any person, in giving any information or making any application under or for the purposes of any provision of this Act, or of any regulations made under this Act, makes any statement which he knows to be false in a material particular, or recklessly makes any statement which is false in a material particular, he is guilty of an offence and shall be liable[1]—

(*a*) on summary conviction, to a fine not exceeding the **statutory maximum**;

(*b*) on conviction on indictment, to a fine.

(2) No proceedings shall be instituted in England and Wales in respect of an offence under this section except by or with the consent of the Secretary of State or the Director of Public Prosecutions.

[Railways Act 1993, s 146.]

---

1. For procedure in respect of an offence triable either way, see the Magistrates' Courts Act 1980, ss 17A–21 in Part I: Magistrates' Courts, Procedure, *ante*.

7–7108 147. Offences by bodies corporate or Scottish partnerships. (1) Where a body corporate is guilty of an offence under this Act and that offence is proved to have been committed with the consent or connivance of, or to be attributable to any neglect on the part of, any director, manager, secretary or other similar officer of the body corporate or any person who was purporting to act in any such capacity he, as well as the body corporate, shall be guilty of that offence and shall be liable to be proceeded against and punished accordingly.

(2) Where the affairs of a body corporate are managed by its members, subsection (1) above shall apply in relation to the acts and defaults of a member in connection with his functions of management as if he were a director of the body corporate.

(3) *Scotland.*

[Railways Act 1993, s 147.]

Railways and Transport Safety Act 2003[1]

(2003 c 20)

PART 1[2]
INVESTIGATION OF RAILWAY ACCIDENTS

Introduction

7–7108Q 1. Meaning of "railway" and "railway property". (1) In this Part—

"railway" means a railway or tramway within the meaning given by section 67 of the Transport and Works Act 1992 (c 42), and

"railway property" means anything which falls within the definition of "light maintenance depot", "network", "rolling stock", "station" or "track" in section 83 of the Railways Act 1993 (c 43), or which falls within the equivalent of any those definitions in relation to a tramway.

(2) The Secretary of State may by regulations amend this section.

(3) This section is subject to section 14(2).

[Railways and Transport Safety Act 2003, s 1.]

---

1. This Act makes provision about railways, including tramways and transport safety. Reproduced in this title are those provisions relating to railways, Part 3 of the Act relating to the British Transport Police is reproduced in PART VIII, title POLICE, Part 4 relating to shipping, alcohol and drugs is reproduced in this PART, title MERCHANT SHIPPING and Part 5 relating to aviation, alcohol and drugs is reproduced in this PART, title AVIATION.

Sections 104 and 114 came into force on the passing of the Act (10 July 2003) and ss 105 and 112 came into force on 10 September 2003. The remaining provisions come into force in accordance with orders made under s 120. At the date of going to press the following commencement orders had been made: (No 1) SI 2003/2681 which brought into force on 31 October 2003 ss 111 and 115; (No 2) SI 2004/827; (No 3) SI 2004/1572; (No 4) SI 2004/2759; (No 5) 2005/1991. Part 1 was brought into force on 17 October 2005.

2. Part 1 comprises ss 1–14.

7–7108R 2. Meaning of "railway accident" and "railway incident". (1) In this Part a reference to a railway accident or railway incident is a reference to an accident or incident which occurs on railway property in so far as it is or may be relevant to the operation of the railway.

(2)–(4) *Regulations.*

[Railways and Transport Safety Act 2003, s 2.]

The Rail Accident Investigation Branch

7–7108S 3. *Establishment of Rail Accident Investigation Branch and appointment of inspectors and Chief Inspector.*

[Railways and Transport Safety Act 2003, s 3.]

7–7108T 4–6. *General aim of Inspectorate to improve the safety of railways, and to prevent railway accidents and railway incidents. The Inspectorate may assist any person with or without charge and must produce an Annual Report.*

Investigation by Branch

7–7108U 7. Investigations. (1) The Rail Accident Investigation Branch—

(a) shall investigate any serious railway accident,

(b) may investigate a non-serious railway accident or a railway incident, and

(c) shall investigate a non-serious railway accident or a railway incident if required to do so by or in accordance with regulations[1] made by the Secretary of State.

(2) For the purposes of subsection (1)(a) a tramway shall not be treated as a railway (despite section 1(1)).

(3) In investigating an accident or incident the Branch shall try to determine what caused it.

(4) On completion of an investigation the Branch shall report to the Secretary of State.

(5) In performing a function in relation to an accident or incident the Branch—

(a) shall not consider or determine blame or liability, but

(b) may determine and report on a cause of an accident or incident whether or not blame or liability is likely to be inferred from the determination or report.

(6) The Branch may conduct an investigation and report whether or not civil or criminal proceedings are in progress or may be instituted (but this subsection is without prejudice to the operation of the law of contempt of court).

(7) The Chief Inspector of Rail Accidents may apply to the High Court or the Crown Court for a declaration that the making of a report in connection with a specified accident or incident will not amount to a contempt of court in relation to civil or criminal proceedings which have been or may be instituted in connection with the accident or incident.

(8) The Chief Inspector of Rail Accidents may reopen an investigation if he believes that significant new evidence may be available.
[Railways and Transport Safety Act 2003, s 7.]

---

1. The Railways (Accident Investigation and Reporting) Regulations 2005, SI 2005/1992 amended by SI 2005/3261 have been made.

7–7108V 8. Investigator's powers. (1) For the purpose of conducting an investigation by virtue of section 7 an inspector of rail accidents may, provided that he produces evidence of his identity if asked to do so—

(a) enter railway property;

(b) enter land (which may include a dwelling-house) which adjoins or abuts railway property;

(c) enter a vehicle or structure which is on railway property or which is on land which could be entered under paragraph (b);

(d) enter land which does not fall within paragraph (a), (b) or (c) if—

    (i) it is used wholly or partly for the purposes of or in connection with anything done on or with railway property, or

    (ii) the inspector reasonably believes that it may contain evidence relating to an accident or incident;

(e) in entering anything under paragraph (a), (b), (c) or (d), be accompanied by one or more persons authorised by the Chief Inspector of Rail Accidents for that purpose (whether generally or specifically);

(f) in entering anything under paragraph (a), (b), (c) or (d), make arrangements to have with him equipment or materials.

(2) For the purpose of conducting an investigation by virtue of section 7 an inspector of rail accidents may—

(a) make a written, electronic, photographic or other record;

(b) remove and retain samples;

(c) arrange for anything to be removed and retained for the purpose of analysis or other examination or for the purpose of preserving evidence;

(d) require access to a record or to recording equipment;

(e) require a person to answer a question;

(f) require a person to provide information;

(g) require a person to disclose a record;

(h) require a person to provide a copy of a record;

(i) require disclosure of the result of an examination of a person, body or thing;

(j) require a person to certify the truth, accuracy or authenticity of a statement made, of information or a document provided or of a record disclosed.

(3) A person commits an offence if without reasonable excuse he—

(a) fails to comply with a requirement imposed by an inspector of rail accidents for the purpose of an investigation by virtue of section 7,

(b) makes a statement for the purpose of an investigation by virtue of section 7 knowing or suspecting that the statement is inaccurate or misleading,

(c) provides information or a record for the purpose of an investigation by virtue of section 7 knowing or suspecting that the information or record is inaccurate or misleading,

(d) obstructs an inspector of rail accidents in the course of his conduct of an investigation by virtue of section 7,

(e) obstructs a person accompanying an inspector of rail accidents under subsection (1)(e), or

(f) obstructs a person exercising a power of an inspector by virtue of regulations under section 9(1)(d).

(4) A person who is guilty of an offence under subsection (3) shall be liable on summary conviction to—

(a) imprisonment for a term not exceeding 51 weeks,

(b) a fine not exceeding level 5 on the standard scale, or

(c) both.

(5) Subsection (6) applies where—

(a) the Rail Accident Investigation Branch is conducting an investigation by virtue of section 7 in respect of an accident or incident, and

(b) a question arises as to the desirability of action which any other person proposes to take for the purpose of investigating the accident or incident.

(6) The question may be determined by—

(a) the Chief Inspector of Rail Accidents, or

(b) an inspector of rail accidents acting on behalf of the Chief Inspector.

[Railways and Transport Safety Act 2003, s 8.]

7–7108W 9. Regulations. *Secretary of State may make regulations[1] about the conduct of investigations, the form, content and publication of an accident report and the use, disclosure and destruction of information acquired by the Branch. Regulations may create offences punishable by imprisonment.*

---

1. The Railways (Accident Investigation and Reporting) Regulations 2005, SI 2005/1992 amended by SI 2005/3261 have been made.

Investigation by industry

7–7108X 10. Requirement to investigate. (1) The Chief Inspector of Rail Accidents may direct that any railway accident or railway incident of a specified kind or which occurs in specified circumstances shall be investigated by each person who manages or controls, or participates in managing or controlling, all or any part of railway property—

(a) on which the accident or incident takes place, or
(b) which is involved in the accident or incident.

(2) A direction—

(a) shall specify the manner in which the investigation is to be conducted, and
(b) may make provision for a case where more than one person would be required to conduct an investigation, whether by requiring a joint investigation or by requiring or enabling one or more persons to conduct an investigation on behalf of others.

(3) A person to whom a direction under subsection (1) applies commits an offence if he fails to comply with it.

(4) A person guilty of an offence under subsection (3) shall be liable[1]—

(a) on summary conviction, to a fine not exceeding the **statutory maximum**, or
(b) on conviction on indictment, to a **fine**.

(5) The Chief Inspector shall publish a direction issued by him under subsection (1) in a manner which he considers will bring it to the attention of each person who is likely to be required to comply with it.

(6) But in proceedings against a person for an offence under subsection (3) of failing to comply with a direction it shall not be necessary to prove that he was aware of the direction.

(7) A direction under subsection (1)—

(a) may make provision which applies generally or only in specified circumstances,
(b) may make different provision for different cases or circumstances, and
(c) may be varied or revoked by a further direction.

[Railways and Transport Safety Act 2003, s 10.]

---

1. For procedure in respect of this offence which is triable either way, see the Magistrates' Courts Act 1980, ss 17A–21, in PART I: MAGISTRATES' COURTS, PROCEDURE, ante.

Accident regulations

7–7108Y 11. Accident regulations. *Secretary of State may make regulations[1] in connection with the investigation of railway accidents and railway incidents.*

---

1. The Railways (Accident Investigation and Reporting) Regulations 2005, SI 2005/1992 amended by SI 2005/3261 have been made.

General

7–7108Z 12. Crown application

13. Regulations

14. Extent

Railways Act 2005[1]
(2005 c 14)

7–7108ZA 46. Bye-laws. (1) A railway operator may make bye-laws regulating one or more of the following—

(a) the use and working of a relevant asset;
(b) travel on or by means of a relevant asset;
(c) the maintenance of order on relevant assets;
(d) the conduct of persons while on relevant assets.

(2) Those bye-laws may include, in particular—

(*a*) bye-laws with respect to tickets issued for entry on relevant assets or for travel by railway or with respect to evasion of the payment of fares or other charges;

(*b*) bye-laws with respect to the obstruction of a railway;

(*c*) bye-laws with respect to any other interference with the working of a railway, with a relevant asset or with the provision of a railway service;

(*d*) bye-laws prohibiting or restricting smoking in railway carriages and elsewhere;

(*e*) bye-laws for the prevention of nuisance;

(*f*) bye-laws with respect to the receipt and delivery of goods; and

(*g*) bye-laws for regulating the passage of bicycles and other vehicles on footways and other premises controlled by the railway operator in question and intended to be used by those on foot.

(3) Schedule 9 (which makes provisions about bye-laws under this section) has effect.

(4) Bye-laws which—

(*a*) were made by the Strategic Rail Authority under section 219 of the 2000 Act, and

(*b*) are in force immediately before the repeal of that section by this Act,

shall continue to have effect after the coming into force of that repeal as if every reference in those bye-laws to that Authority were a reference to the Secretary of State.

(5) The Secretary of State may by order revoke or amend—

(*a*) any bye-laws having effect in accordance with subsection (4); or

(*b*) any bye-laws saved by the 2000 Act.

(6) In subsection (5), "bye-laws saved by the 2000 Act" means bye-laws which—

(*a*) were made (or have effect as if they were made) under section 67 of the Transport Act 1962 (c 46) or section 129 of the 1993 Act;

(*b*) were continued in force by paragraph 5(2) of Schedule 28 to the 2000 Act; and

(*c*) are in force immediately before the commencement of this section.

(7) In this section "railway operator" means an operator of a railway asset who is—

(*a*) authorised to be the operator of that asset by a licence granted under section 8 of the 1993 Act; or

(*b*) exempt by virtue of section 7 of that Act or any other enactment from the requirement to be so authorised.

(8) In this section "relevant asset", in relation to a railway operator, means—

(*a*) a railway asset of which he is the operator; or

(*b*) any rolling stock not falling within paragraph (a) of which he has the management for the time being.

---

1. This Act is to be brought into force by commencement orders made under s 60. At the date of going to press the following orders had been made: (No 1) 2005, SI 2005/1444; (No 2) 2005, SI 2005/1909; (No 3) 2005, SI 2005/2252; (No 4) 2005, SI 2005/2812; (No 5) SI 2006/266. Section 46 and Sch 9 came fully into force on 16 October 2005.

7–7108ZB

Section 46

SCHEDULE 9[1]
BYE-LAWS BY RAILWAY OPERATORS

Introductory

1. (1) In this Schedule—

"appropriate national authority", in relation to any bye-laws, means—

(*a*) where the relevant assets by reference to which the bye-laws are or were made are all Scottish assets, the Scottish Ministers;

(*b*) where some but not all of those assets are Scottish assets or include assets that are used partly in Scotland and partly elsewhere, the Secretary of State and the Scottish Ministers; and

(*c*) in any other case, the Secretary of State;

"bye-laws" means bye-laws under section 46; and
"railway operator" has the same meaning as in that section.

(2) In sub-paragraph (1) "Scottish asset" means—

(*a*) an asset that is permanently situated in Scotland; or

(*b*) an asset that is used only in Scotland.

(3) In the case of bye-laws in relation to which both the Secretary of State and the Scottish Ministers are the appropriate national authority—

(*a*) anything that must be done under this Schedule in relation to those bye-laws by the appropriate national authority must be done by them both, acting jointly;

(*b*) anything that may be done under this Schedule in relation to those bye-laws by the appropriate national authority may be done only by them both, acting jointly; and

(c) any requirement of this Schedule in relation to those bye-laws to send something to the appropriate national authority is complied with only if that thing is sent both to the Secretary of State and to the Scottish Ministers.

1. Framework byelaws have been agreed by the Association of Train Operating Companies for the guidance of TOCs, see this title, post.

Penalties

2. Bye-laws may provide that a person contravening them is guilty of an offence and liable, on summary conviction, to a fine not exceeding—

(a) level 3 on the standard scale; or
(b) such lower amount as is specified in the bye-laws.

Confirmation

3. Bye-laws do not come into force until they have been confirmed by the appropriate national authority.

4. (1) A railway operator who proposes to make bye-laws must publish a notice stating—

(a) that he proposes to make bye-laws;
(b) the manner in which a copy of the proposed bye-laws will be open to public inspection; and
(c) that any person affected by the proposed bye-laws may make representations about them to the appropriate national authority within the period specified in the notice.

(2) The publication of the notice must be in the manner approved by the appropriate national authority.

(3) The period specified for the purposes of sub-paragraph (1)(c) must be the period of 28 days beginning with the day after that on which the railway operator's notice is published, or a longer period.

(4) At the end of the period so specified the appropriate national authority must forward any representations that have been made to it to the railway operator.

(5) The railway operator must not submit the bye-laws for confirmation unless he has considered the representations forwarded by the appropriate national authority.

5. (1) The appropriate national authority may—

(a) confirm (with or without modifications) any bye-laws submitted to it for confirmation; or
(b) refuse to confirm them.

(2) The appropriate national authority may fix the date of the coming into force of any bye-laws confirmed by it.

(3) If the appropriate national authority confirms bye-laws without fixing the date on which they come into force, they come into force at the end of the period of 28 days beginning with the day after that on which they are confirmed.

Publicity for confirmed bye-laws

6. If the appropriate national authority has confirmed bye-laws—

(a) copies of the bye-laws must be printed;
(b) at least one copy must be kept at the principal offices of the railway operator who made them;
(c) the railway operator must send one copy to the appropriate national authority; and
(d) the railway operator must supply one copy (free of charge) to every person who applies for a copy or for more than one copy.

Evidence

7. (1) The production of a printed copy of bye-laws which is indorsed with a certificate—

(a) stating one or more matters specified in sub-paragraph (2), and
(b) purporting to be signed by an officer of the railway operator by whom the bye-laws purport to have been made,

is evidence of what is stated.

(2) Those matters are—

(a) that the bye-laws were made by the railway operator in question;
(b) that the copy is a true copy of the bye-laws;
(c) that the bye-laws were confirmed by the appropriate national authority on the date specified in the certificate;
(d) the date of the coming into force of the bye-laws.

Power to amend or vary

8. (1) The power to make bye-laws includes the power to make bye-laws amending or revoking bye-laws.

(2) The appropriate national authority may by order revoke bye-laws.

FRAMEWORK RAILWAY BYELAWS[1]

7–7110

CONDUCT AND BEHAVIOUR

1. QUEUEING

(1) The Operator or an authorised person may require any person to queue in order to regulate order or safety on or near the railway.

(2) Any person directed by a notice to queue or when asked to queue by an authorised person, shall join the rear of the queue and obey the reasonable instructions of any authorised person regulating the queue.

---

1. The provisions of the Railways Act 1993 (see now the Railways Act 2005, s 46 and Sch 9) enabled individual railway operators and Network Rail to make byelaws covering the railway assets which they operate. In order to avoid each operator making its own byelaws, agreed Framework Railway Byelaws have been proposed by the railway industry to be adopted by individual operators. The Secretary of State on 19 December 2000 confirmed the new byelaws for each individual operator which came into force on 18 February 2001. The corresponding byelaws for London Transport are made under s 67 of the Transport Act 1962 as amended by s 37 of the Transport Act 1981 and para 2 of Schedule 4 to the London Regional Transport Act 1984 by London Regional Transport.

2. POTENTIALLY DANGEROUS ITEMS

7–7111   (1) Except with written permission from the Operator or an authorised person, no person shall bring with him or allow to remain on the railway any item which, in the opinion of an authorised person, may threaten, annoy, soil or damage any person or any property. For the avoidance of doubt, the Operator may ban, amongst other things, carriage of the following items

(i)   a loaded weapon of any kind;
(ii) any inflammable, explosive or corrosive substance;
(iii) any item which is or may become dangerous.

(2) If any person in charge of an item in breach of Byelaw 2(1) is asked by an authorised person to remove it and fails to do so immediately, then it may be removed by or under the direction of an authorised person.

3. NO SMOKING

7–7112   No person shall smoke or carry a lighted pipe, cigar, cigarette, match, lighter or other lighted item on any part of the railway on or near which there is a notice indicating that smoking is not allowed[1].

---

1. In relation to byelaws made under s 67(1) of the Transport Act 1962 it was held that the banning by a railway company of all smoking in its trains is a form of regulating the railway, or travel on the railway, there is nothing unlawful in a byelaw which bans all smoking in all carriages of trains (*Boddington v British Transport Police* [1998] 2 All ER 203, 162 JP 455).

4. INTOXICATION AND POSSESSION OF INTOXICATING LIQUOR

7–7113   (1) No person in a state of intoxication shall enter or remain on the railway.

(2) Where reasonable notice is, or has been given prohibiting intoxicating liquor on any train service, no person shall have any intoxicating liquor with him on it, or attempt to enter such train with intoxicating liquor with him.

(3) Where an authorised person reasonably believes that any person is in a state of intoxication or has with him intoxicating liquor contrary to this Byelaw, the authorised person may:

(i) require him to leave the railway; and
(ii) prevent him entering or remaining on the railway until the authorised person is satisfied that he has no intoxicating liquor with him.

5. UNFIT TO BE ON THE RAILWAY

7–7114   No person shall enter or remain on the railway if, in the reasonable opinion of an authorised person, he is in an unfit or improper condition or his clothing may soil or damage any part of the railway or the clothing of any person.

6. UNACCEPTABLE BEHAVIOUR

7–7115   (1) No person shall use any threatening, abusive, obscene or offensive language.
(2) No person shall behave in a disorderly, indecent or offensive manner.
(3) No person shall write, draw, paint or fix anything on the property of the railway.
(4) No person shall soil any part of the railway.
(5) No person shall damage or detach any property on the railway.
(6) No person shall spit.
(7) No person shall drop litter or dump waste.
(8) No person shall molest or wilfully interfere with the comfort or convenience of any person on the railway.

7. MUSIC, SOUND, ADVERTISING AND CARRYING ON A TRADE

7–7116   (1) Except with written permission from the Operator no person on the railway shall, to the annoyance of any person:

(i) sing; or
(ii) use any instrument, article or equipment for the production or reproduction of sound.

(2) Except with written permission from the Operator no person on the railway shall:

(i)   display anything for the purpose of advertising or publicity, or distribute anything; or

(ii)   sell or expose or offer anything for sale; or

(iii) tout for, or solicit money, reward, custom or employment of any kind.

(3) A person shall have the written permission referred to in this Byelaw 7 with him when undertaking the activities referred to in Byelaw 7(1) or 7(2)(iii) on the railway and shall hand it over for inspection when asked by an authorised person. A person shall comply with any conditions attached to the written permission.

8. UNAUTHORISED GAMBLING

7–7117   No person shall gamble on any part of the railway except lawful gambling on premises authorised by the Operator for that purpose.

EQUIPMENT AND SAFETY

9. STATIONS AND RAILWAY PREMISES

7–7118   (1) No person shall use any escalator except by standing or walking on it in the direction intended for travel.

(2) Where the entrance to or exit from any platform or station is via an automatic ticket barrier no person shall enter or leave the station, except with permission from an authorised person, without passing through the barrier in the correct manner.

(3) No person shall open a barrier or any other gate on the railway except where there is a notice indicating that it may be used by him or with permission from an authorised person.

(4) Where there is a notice by an entrance or exit on any part of the railway indicating that it shall be used for entrance or exit only, no person shall enter by the exit or leave by the entrance. No person shall enter or leave by an emergency exit except in an emergency or when directed to do so by an authorised person.

(5) No person shall move, operate or stop any lift or escalator except:

(i)   in an emergency by means of equipment on or near which is a notice indicating that it is intended to be used in an emergency; or

(ii)   in case of a lift, by means of any of the controls intended for the use of passengers.

10. TRAINS

7–7119   (1) No person shall enter through any train door until any person leaving by that door has passed through.

(2) No person shall be in or on any train except on the parts of it intended for the use of that person.

(3) No person shall open a train door, or enter or leave any train, while it is in motion or between stations.

(4) No person shall enter or leave a train except by proper use of a train door.

(5) In the case of automatic closing train doors, no person shall enter or leave by the door when it is closing.

11. GENERAL SAFETY

7–7120   (1) No person shall move, operate, obstruct, stop or in any other way interfere with any automatic closing train door, train, or any other equipment on the railway except:

(i)   in an emergency, by means of any equipment on or near which is a notice indicating that it is intended to be used in an emergency; or

(ii)   any equipment intended for the use of passengers in that way in normal operating circumstances.

(2) No person shall place, throw, drop or trail anything capable of injuring, damaging or endangering any person or any property on the railway.

12. SAFETY INSTRUCTIONS

7–7121   (1) The Operator may issue to any person reasonable instructions relating to safety on any part of the railway by means of a notice on or near that part of the railway. No person, without good cause, shall disobey such notice.

(2) An authorised person may, in an emergency or in other circumstances in which he believes he should act in the interest of safety, issue instructions to any person on any part of the railway. No person, without good cause, shall disobey such instruction.

(3) No offence is committed under these Byelaws where a person proves he was acting in accordance with the instructions or notice given under this Byelaw.

CONTROL OF PREMISES

13. UNAUTHORISED ACCESS AND LOITERING

7–7122   (1) No person shall enter or remain on any part of the railway where there is a notice:

(i)　prohibiting access; or

(ii)　indicating that it is reserved or provided for a specified category of person only, except where he belongs to that specified category.

(2)　No person shall loiter on the railway if asked to leave by an authorised person.

14. TRAFFIC SIGNS, CAUSING OBSTRUCTIONS AND PARKING

7–7123　(1)　No person in charge of any motor vehicle, bicycle or other conveyance shall use it on any part of the railway in contravention of any traffic sign.

(2)　No person in charge of any motor vehicle, bicycle or other conveyance shall leave or place it on any part of the railway:

(i)　in any manner or place where it may cause an obstruction or hindrance to the Operator or any person using the railway; or

(ii)　otherwise than in accordance with any instructions of the Operator (or other person on its behalf) or directions from an authorised person.

(3)　No person in charge of any motor vehicle, bicycle or other conveyance shall park where charges are made for parking by the Operator (or other person on its behalf) without paying the appropriate charge at the appropriate time in accordance with instructions given by the Operator (or other person on its behalf) at that place.

(4)　England and Wales

(i)　Any motor vehicle, bicycle or other conveyance used, left or placed in breach of these Byelaws may be clamped, removed, and stored, by or under the direction of an authorised person.

(ii)　The owner of the motor vehicle, bicycle or other conveyance shall be liable to the Operator (or other person on its behalf) for the costs incurred in clamping, removing, storing and/or disposing of it from any area provided that there is in that area or the nearest station, a notice advising that any vehicle parked contrary to these Byelaws may be clamped, removed, stored and/or disposed of by the Operator (or other person on its behalf) and that the costs incurred by the Operator (or other person on its behalf) for this may be recovered from the vehicle's owner.

(iii)　The power of clamping referred to in sub-paragraph (i) above shall not be exercisable in any area where passenger parking is permitted unless there is on display in that area a notice advising that any vehicle parked contrary to these Byelaws may be clamped by the Operator (or other person on its behalf).

(2)　Scotland

(i)　Any motor vehicle, bicycle or other conveyance used, left or placed in breach of this Byelaw in Scotland may be removed by or under the direction of a constable.

15. PEDESTRIAN-ONLY AREAS

7–7124　(1)　Any person who enters or is on any part of the railway to which the public have access must be on foot, except

(i)　where there is a notice permitting access to that part of the railway to those with specified conveyances; or

(ii)　where the Operator or an authorised person has given permission, and in either case he shall obey any instructions given.

(2)　No person shall be in breach of this Byelaw for properly using a baby carriage or wheelchair, except where there is a notice or instructions given by an authorised person to the contrary.

16. CONTROL OF ANIMALS

7–7125　(1)　The Operator may refuse carriage or entry to any animal.

(2)　No person shall bring an animal on to the railway without a valid ticket for that animal, if the Operator requires him to have a valid ticket for the carriage of such an animal.

(3)　Except with permission from the Operator or an authorised person, no person shall bring an animal on to the railway, which, in the opinion of an authorised person, may threaten, annoy, soil or damage any person or any property.

(4)　If any person in charge of an animal in breach of Byelaw 16(1), (2) or (3) is asked by an authorised person to remove it and fails to do so immediately, then it may be removed by or under the direction of an authorised person.

(5)　No person in charge of an animal shall allow it to foul or damage any part of the railway.

(6)　Any person in charge of an animal shall carry it when on an escalator that is in motion.

(7)　No person in charge of any animal shall leave or place it unattended on any part of the railway (except in a place provided for that purpose by the Operator and only for as long as is absolutely necessary and in accordance with any direction of the Operator or an authorised person).

(8)　Any animal left or placed in breach of Byelaw 16(7) may be removed and/or stored by or under the direction of an authorised person. The person in charge of the animal shall be liable to the Operator for the cost incurred by the Operator (or other person on its behalf) in removing and storing it.

(9) Any person in charge of an animal that has soiled or caused damage to any part of the railway shall be liable to the Operator for the cost of putting the property soiled or damaged back into its proper condition.

(10) Any liability to the Operator under Byelaw 16(8) or (9) is in addition to any penalty for the breach of Byelaw 16.

TRAVEL AND FARES
17. COMPULSORY TICKET AREAS

7–7126 (1) No person shall enter a compulsory ticket[1] area unless he has with him a valid ticket.

(2) A person shall hand over his ticket for inspection when asked to do so by an authorised person.

---

1. See note to byelaw 18, post.

18. TICKETLESS TRAVEL IN NON - COMPULSORY TICKET AREAS

7–7127 (1) In any area not designated as a compulsory ticket area, no person shall enter any train for the purpose of travelling unless he has with him a valid ticket entitling him to travel[1].

(2) A person shall hand over this ticket for inspection when asked to do so by an authorised person.

(3) No person shall be in breach of this Byelaw 18 if:

    (i)   there were no facilities for the issue of tickets available at the time when and the station where he began his journey; or

    (ii) there was a notice at the station where he began his journey indicating that he may travel without a valid ticket; or

    (iii) an authorised person gave him permission to travel without a valid ticket.

---

1. It is reasonable to insist on payment of the fare before allowing a passenger to travel (per BRAMWELL LJ, in *London and Brighton Rly Co v Watson* (1879) 4 CPD 118, 43 JP 301). A passenger is not entitled to refuse payment till the end of the journey in contravention of a bye-law requiring payment on demand (*Egginton v Pearl* (1875) 40 JP 56). The right of expulsion where no ticket is taken is reasonable (per COCKBURN LCJ, in *Saunders v South Eastern Rly Co* (1880) 5 QBD 456, 44 JP 781); and also the case of a passenger being in a carriage in which he is not entitled to be (*Lowe v Great Northern Rly Co* (1893) 62 LJQB 524). The right to expulsion from the company's premises for non-production of a ticket is confined to the case where no ticket is taken (see *Butler v Manchester, Sheffield and Lincolnshire Rly Co* (1888) 21 QBD 207, 52 JP 612).

19. CLASSES OF ACCOMMODATION, RESERVED SEATS AND SLEEPING BERTHS

7–7128 Except with permission of an authorised person, no person shall remain in any seat, berth or any part of a train where a notice indicates that it is reserved for a specified ticket holder or holders of tickets of a specific class, except the holder of a valid ticket entitling him to be in that particular place.

20. ALTERING TICKETS AND USE OF ALTERED TICKETS

7–7129 (1) No person shall alter any ticket in any way with the intent that the Operator or any other railway Operator shall be defrauded or prejudiced.

(2) No person shall knowingly use any ticket which has been altered in any way in breach of Byelaw 20(1).

21. UNAUTHORISED BUYING OR SELLING OF TICKETS

7–7130 (1) Subject to Byelaw 21(4), no person shall sell or buy any ticket.

(2) Subject to Byelaw 21(4), no person shall transfer or receive any unused or partly used ticket, intending that any person shall use it for travelling.

(3) Subject to Byelaw 21(4) no person shall knowingly use any ticket which has been obtained in breach of this Byelaw.

(4) The sale or transfer by, or the purchase or receipt from, an authorised person in the course of his duties or from an authorised ticket machine is excepted from the provisions of this Byelaw.

22. FARES OFFENCES COMMITTED ON BEHALF OF ANOTHER PERSON

7–7131 (1) No person shall buy a ticket on behalf of another intending to enable that other person to travel without having paid the correct fare.

(2) No person shall transfer or produce a ticket on behalf of another intending to enable that other person to travel without having paid the correct fare.

ENFORCEMENT AND INTERPRETATION
23. NAME AND ADDRESS

7–7132 (1) Any person reasonably suspected by an authorised person of breaching or attempting to breach any of these Byelaws shall give his name and address when asked by an authorised person.

(2) The authorised person shall state the nature of the breach of any of these Byelaws in general terms.

24. ENFORCEMENT

7-7133   (1) Offence and level of fines

Any person who breaches any of these Byelaws, except Byelaw 17, commits an offence and shall be liable for each such offence to a penalty not exceeding **level 3** on the standard scale.

(2) Removal of persons

(i)   Any person who is reasonably believed by an authorised person to be in breach of any of these Byelaws shall leave the railway immediately if asked to do so by an authorised person.

(ii)   Any person who is reasonably believed by an authorised person to be in breach of any of these Byelaws and who fails to desist or leave when asked to do so by an authorised person may be removed from the railway by an authorised person using reasonable force. This right of removal is in addition to the imposition of any penalty for the breach of these Byelaws.

(iii)   No person shall fail to carry out the instructions of an authorised person acting in accordance with powers given by these Byelaws or any other enactment.

(iv)   In Byelaws 24(2)(i) and 24(2)(ii) the authorised person shall state the nature of the breach of any of these Byelaws in general terms.

(3) Identification of authorised persons

An authorised person, who is exercising any power conferred on him by any of these Byelaws, shall produce a form of identification when requested to do so and such identification shall state the name of his employer and shall contain a means of identifying the authorised person.

(4) Notices

No person shall be subject to any penalty for breach of any of the Byelaws by disobeying a notice unless it is proved to the satisfaction of the Court before whom the complaint is laid that the notice referred to in the particular Byelaw was displayed.

(5) Attempts

Any person who attempts to breach any of the Byelaws numbered 9, 10, 11, 13(1), 20(2) and 21 shall be liable to the same penalty as given above for breach of that Byelaw.

(6) Breaches by authorised persons

An authorised person acting in the course of his duties shall not be liable for breach of any of the Byelaws numbered 2, 4(2), 6(3) and (5), 7, 9, 10, 11(1), 13, 14, 15, 17, 18, 19 and 20(1).

25. INTERPRETATION

7-7134   (1) Definitions

In these Byelaws the following expressions have the following meanings:
"authorised person" means;

(i)   a person acting in the course of his duties, who is an employee or agent of or any other person authorised by the Operator or authorised by a person operating any railway assets, and

(ii)   any constable, acting in the execution of his duties upon or in connection with the railway;

"compulsory ticket area" means any part of the railway identified by a notice stating that no person may enter there without being in possession of a valid ticket;

"escalator" includes travelator or similar device;

"intoxication" means being under the influence of intoxicating liquor, drugs or other substances;

"intoxicating liquor" has the meaning in England and Wales given to it the Licensing Act 1964 (as amended or replaced from time to time) and in Scotland means "alcoholic liquor" as that term is defined in the Licensing (Scotland) Act 1976 (as amended or replaced from time to time).

"notice" means a notice given by or on behalf of the Operator;

"Operator" means [company name & company number];

"previous byelaws" means the byelaws previously made in relation to the railway by the British Railways Board under the provisions of Section 67 of the Transport Act 1962 on 6th August, 1965 and confirmed by the Minister of Transport on 1st September 1965 and amendments thereto confirmed by the Minister of Transport on 12th August, 1980; by the Secretary of State for Transport on 16th November, 1981; 9th July 1986; 26th October 1990; and transferred to the Operator by virtue of Section 129 of the Railways Act 1993;

"railway" means the relevant assets of the Operator, and includes railways, railway premises, trains or any other vehicle upon the railway;

"railway assets" means any train, station, depot, track or associated equipment of any person;

"relevant assets" means any train, station, depot, track or associated equipment under the management of the Operator;

"standard scale" means:

> in relation to England & Wales the meaning given by section 37 of the Criminal Justice Act 1982, and
>
> in relation to Scotland the meaning given by section 225(1) of the Criminal Procedure (Scotland) Act 1995,

and any replacement, modification or amendment thereto;

"ticket" includes

> (i) a ticket (including one issued by another railway undertaking) authorising the person for whom it is issued to make the journey covered by the fare paid on a train provided by the Operator (whether or not it also authorises that person to make a journey on a train provided by another railway undertaking);
>
> (ii) any permit authorising the person to whom it is issued to travel on a train provided by the Operator (whether or not it also authorises that person to make a journey on a train provided by another railway undertaking);
>
> (iii) an authority to travel on a train provided by the Operator subject to a condition that payment of the correct fare for the person using that authority on which it is used is made during or at the end of that journey or otherwise as provided by the terms applicable to its use;
>
> (iv) a ticket authorising a person to enter a compulsory ticket area but not to make a train journey;
>
> any type of free pass, privilege ticket, or any warrant, identity card, voucher or other similar authority accepted by the Operator as authority to travel, or in exchange for or on production of which a ticket for travel may be issued;
>
> any identity card, reservation or other document required by the Operator to be held or produced for use with other travel documents; and
>
> any other ticket or document issued for the purpose of travel of any animal or article on the railway accepted by the Operator.

"traffic sign" means an object or device for conveying, to traffic or any specified class or traffic, warnings, information, requirements, restrictions or prohibitions of any kind;

"train" means any railway train and includes any carriage or compartment of a train;

"valid ticket" means a current ticket (including any associated photo/identity card and/or other travel document) lawfully obtained by or on behalf of the person using or attempting to use it and entitling that person to use the particular railway service he is using or attempting to use. Where the terms attaching to the ticket require validation of the ticket such ticket shall not be considered to be a valid ticket for the purposes of these Byelaws unless and until the ticket has been properly validated.

(2) Preamble*, table of contents* and headings

The preamble, table of contents and headings used in these Byelaws are for assistance only and are not to be considered as part of these Byelaws for the purpose of interpretation.

(3) Plural

Unless the context requires to the contrary, words importing the singular shall include the plural and vice versa.

(4) Gender

Unless the context requires to the contrary, words importing one gender shall include the other gender.

---

*. Not reproduced here.

26. Coming into Operation of these Byelaws and Revocation of Previous Byelaws

7–7135   These Byelaws will come into operation in accordance with the provisions of [Section 129 of the Railways Act 1993/Section 67 of the Transport Act 1962].

When these Byelaws come into effect, the previous byelaws shall be revoked. This revocation is without prejudice to the validity of anything done under the previous byelaws or to any liability incurred in respect of any act or omission before the date of the coming into operation of these Byelaws.

The Common Seal of [name of the Operator] was here affixed
in the presence of [Secretary/Director etc]
on [date of fixing the seal]

The Secretary of State for the Environment, Transport and Regions confirms the above Byelaws and fixes 18 February 2001 as the date the Byelaws shall come into operation.

Signed by authority of Secretary of State for the Environment, Transport and Regions on 19 December 2000.

[signature]

Peter Thomas
Head of Division, Railways International and General

Department of Environment, Transport and the Regions

27. CERTIFICATE OF AUTHENTICITY

7–7136   It is hereby certified that

(1)   the above Byelaws were made by [name of the Operator];

(2)   this is a true copy of the Byelaws;

(3)   on 19 December 2000 the Byelaws were confirmed by the Secretary of State for the Environment, Transport and Regions; and

(4)   the Byelaws came into operation on 18 February 2001. .... Secretary of [name of the Operator].

Published 19 December 2000.

Carriage of Goods (Prohibition of Discrimination) Regulations 1977[1]
(SI 1977/276)

7–7245   **2.** (1) In these Regulations, unless the context otherwise requires—

"driver", where a separate person acts as steersman of a motor vehicle, includes that person as well as any other person engaged in the driving of it and any reference to the driver of a vehicle shall, in relation to a trailer, be construed as a reference to the driver of the motor vehicle by which the trailer is drawn;

"examiner" means an examiner appointed under section [68(1)] of the Road Traffic Act [1988];

"goods vehicle" means a motor vehicle constructed or adapted for use by the carriage or haulage by road of goods or burden of any description, or a trailer so constructed or adapted;

"goods" means any goods other than goods listed in Annexes I and III to the ECSC Treaty;

"the principal Regulation" means Council Regulation (EEC) No 11 concerning the abolition of discrimination in transport rates and conditions, in implementation of Article 79(3) of the Treaty establishing the European Economic Community;

"transport undertaking" means any undertaking whose business includes the carriage of goods for hire or reward whether by rail, road or inland waterway, being carriage to which these Regulations apply.

(2) References in these Regulations to a numbered article shall, unless the reference specifies the instrument containing that article, be construed as references to the article bearing that number in the principal Regulation.

(3) The Interpretation Act [1978] shall apply for the interpretation of these Regulations as it applies for the interpretation of an Act of Parliament.

(4) These Regulations apply to the carriage in Great Britain of all goods by rail, road or inland waterway being carriage to which by virtue of Articles 1 to 3 inclusive the principal Regulation applies.

---

1.   Made under s 2(2) of the European Communities Act 1972.

7–7246   **3.** (1) Any person who carries on a transport undertaking shall be guilty of an offence under this Regulation if that person fails, without reasonable excuse, to notify the Secretary of State, in accordance with paragraph (2) of this Regulation, of any measure of the kind referred to in Article 5(2) (that is to say, any tariff, or formal or other agreement on transport rates and conditions whereby the rates and conditions for carrying the same goods over the same transport links vary according to the country of origin or of destination of the goods in question) being such a measure presently in force or subsequently introduced.

(2) The notification referred to in paragraph (1) above shall be given in the case of a measure presently in force, within one month of the coming into operation of these Regulations, and, in the case of a measure subsequently introduced, within one month of its introduction.

(3) A person guilty of an offence under this Regulation shall be liable on summary conviction to a fine not exceeding **£200** and if the offence in respect of which he is convicted under this Regulation is continued after the conviction, he shall be guilty of a further offence and be liable in respect thereof on summary conviction to a fine not exceeding **£5** for each day on which the offence is so continued.

7–7247   **4.** (1) Except where by virtue of Article 8 or 9 the provisions of Article 6 (concerning transport documents) do not apply to the carriage of goods to which these Regulations apply, and subject to the provisions of the next following paragraph, any person who, in relation to any consignment of goods within the Economic Community, is the carrier of those goods within Great Britain, whether by rail, road or inland waterway, shall be guilty of an offence under this Regulation if—

(a)   no transport document giving the details specified in Article 6(1) has at the time when the carriage within Great Britain of the goods so consigned first commences, been properly prepared in duplicate and numbered as required by Article 6, or

(b)   one copy of such document does not accompany the goods, to which it relates, or

(c) the other copy thereof is not retained by the carrier for the period, in the manner and showing the charges and other particulars required by Article 6(2).

(2) The provisions of paragraph (1) of this Regulation do not apply to any person where existing documents give all the details specified in Article 6(1) and, in conjunction with that person's recording and accounting systems, enable a full check to be made of transport rates and conditions so as to abolish or avoid certain forms of discrimination as mentioned in Article 6(3).

(3) A person guilty of an offence under sub-paragraph (a), or (b) or (c) of the said paragraph (1), shall be liable, on summary conviction to a fine not exceeding **£200** for each such offence.

7–7248 5. (1) Paragraph (2) of this Regulation applies to undertakings concerned with the carriage within Great Britain of goods by road whether as carriers or as such agents or providers of services as are mentioned in Article 13, and paragraph (3) of this Regulation applies to undertakings concerned with the carriage within Great Britain of goods by rail and by inland waterway whether as carriers or as such agents or providers as aforesaid.

(2) An examiner, on production if so required of his authority, may—

(a) at any time require the driver of a goods vehicle belonging to an undertaking to which this paragraph applies, to produce and permit him to inspect and copy any consignment note or other transport document (including a document which is an existing document within the meaning of Article 6(3)) or any copy thereof which accompanies any goods on or carried by that vehicle, and

(b) at any time which is reasonable having regard to the circumstances of the case, enter any premises occupied by a person carrying on an undertaking to which this paragraph applies and on which he has reason to believe that such a vehicle is kept or that there are to be found—

(i) any consignment notes or other transport documents (including the said existing documents and any recording or accounting systems associated therewith) relating to goods carried or to be carried by that person or any copies of such notes or documents or

(ii) any document containing particulars which relate to any measure which falls to be notified by that person to the Secretary of State under Article 5(2) or which has been so notified by him, or which relates to information which falls to be sent or furnished to the Secretary of State by that person or has been so sent or furnished by him in accordance with either of the two next following Regulations or any copy of a document containing such particulars,
and inspect any such vehicle and inspect and copy any such notes, documents or copies or any recording or accounting systems which he finds there.

(3)

(a) The Secretary of State may appoint any one or more persons for the purpose of checking compliance with the obligations imposed by the principal Regulation in relation to the carriage of goods by rail or by inland waterway and any person so appointed (in this Regulation called "an inspector") may exercise the powers conferred on an inspector by the next following sub-paragraph.

(b) An inspector, on production if so required of his authority in that behalf, may at any time which is reasonable having regard to the circumstances of the case, enter any premises occupied by a person carrying on an undertaking to which this paragraph applies and on which he has reason to believe that there are to be found in connection with the carriage of goods by rail or inland waterway:—

(i) any consignment notes or other transport documents (including the said existing documents and any recording or accounting systems associated therewith) relating to goods carried or to be carried by that person or any copies of such notes or documents or

(ii) any document containing particulars which relate to any measure which falls to be notified by that person to the Secretary of State under Article 5(2) or which has been so notified by him, or which relate to information which falls to be sent or furnished to the Secretary of State by that person or has been so sent or furnished by him in accordance with either of the two next following Regulations or any copy of a document containing such particulars,
and inspect and copy any such notes, documents or copies or any recording or accounting systems which he finds there.

(4) It shall be the duty of any person who has in his power or custody on premises entered pursuant to paragraph (2) or (3) of this Regulation any such note, document or copy thereof as is described in sub-paragraph (b)(i) and (ii) of either of the said paragraphs or who is in charge of, or employed in connection with, any recording or accounting system which operates there to produce to the examiner or, as the case may be, to the inspector the said note, document or copy for his inspection, and any books, documents or material used in connection with the said system and otherwise to give to the examiner or inspector all assistance in connection with the inspection which that person is reasonably able to give.

(5) An examiner in the exercise of his powers under paragraph (2) of this Regulation may detain the vehicle in question during such time as is required for the exercise of those powers.

(6) Any person who—

(a) fails to comply with any requirement under paragraph 2 (a) of this Regulation or to carry out his duty under paragraph (4) of this Regulation, or

(b) wilfully obstructs an examiner or an inspector in the exercise of his powers under paragraph 2(b), 3(b) or (5) of this Regulation shall be liable on summary conviction to a fine not exceeding **£100**.

7–7249   6. (1) This Regulation applies to any person—

(a) who carries on a transport undertaking,

(b) who is a forwarding or other agent concerned with the carriage of goods by rail, road or inland waterway, or

(c) who is a direct provider of services ancillary to such carriage in any case specified in Article 13(2).

(2) In this Regulation references to information are references to any additional information which in the terms of Article 11(1) may be needed concerning any tariff, or formal or other agreement on transport rates and conditions and to all information relevant to the services provided, and to the rates and conditions applied by the persons mentioned in paragraph (1)(b) and (c) above.

(3) Where the Commission of the European Communities has requested a person to whom this Regulation applies to supply information, that person shall first before supplying it obtain the approval of the Secretary of State to the disclosure of any facts involved in the information proposed to be supplied which approval shall not be refused unless the said information involves the disclosure of any facts which the Secretary of State considers would be contrary to the essential interests of the security of the United Kingdom; and for this purpose a statement in writing of such information shall be sent to the Secretary of State so as to reach him not less than 2 weeks before the time limit (if any) set under Article 11(2) or if no such limit has been set, before the information will be so supplied.

(4) A person shall be guilty of an offence under this Regulation if he contravenes or fails to comply with the provisions of paragraph (3) of this Regulation and shall be liable on summary conviction to a fine of **£200**.

7–7250   7. (1) For the purpose of obtaining any information which the Secretary of State may need to have in order to enable him to discharge or to secure the discharge of any Community obligation arising in relation to the principal Regulation and, without prejudice to the generality of the foregoing, in particular the obligation to supply certain information to the said Commission the Secretary of State may, by notice in writing served on any person on whom any obligation is imposed by or under the principal Regulation or these Regulations, require that person to furnish, in such form and manner and within such time as may be specified in the notice such information and particulars as may be requested in the notice, being information and particulars relating to tariffs, to any agreement or arrangement on transport rates and conditions or to the services provided and the rates and conditions applied to them.

(2) The said notice shall state that it is served under this Regulation and generally the purpose for which the information is required.

(3) If any person required to furnish information under this Regulation fails without reasonable excuse to do so as required, he shall be liable on summary conviction to a fine not exceeding **£200** and if the failure in respect of which a person is convicted under the foregoing provisions is continued after the conviction, he shall be guilty of a further offence and liable in respect thereof on summary conviction to a fine not exceeding **£5** for each day on which the offence is so continued.

7–7251   8. (1) A person shall be guilty of an offence under this Regulation who in supplying or furnishing any information or particulars to the Secretary of State, in notifying him of any measure, sending any statement to him or in preparing or producing any transport document (including any such other existing document as aforesaid or the recording or accounting systems associated therewith) in accordance with any of these Regulations or the principal Regulation makes a statement which he knows to be false in a material particular, or produces, furnishes, sends, prepares, notifies, supplies or otherwise makes use of a document which he knows to be false in a material particular.

(2) A person guilty of an offence under paragraph (1) of this Regulation shall be liable[1] on summary conviction to a fine not exceeding **£400**, or on conviction on indictment to imprisonment for a term not exceeding **2 years** or a fine or both.

---

1. For procedure in respect of this offence which is triable either way, see the Magistrates' Courts Act 1980, ss 17A–21, in PART I: MAGISTRATES' COURTS, PROCEDURE, ante.

7–7252   9. (1) Without prejudice to Article 22, where a body corporate is guilty of an offence under these Regulations and the offence is proved to have been committed with the consent or connivance of, or to be attributable to neglect on the part of a director, manager, secretary or other similar officer of the body corporate, or a person who was purporting to act in any such capacity, he as well as the body corporate, shall be guilty of that offence and liable to be proceeded against and punished accordingly.

(2) Subject and without prejudice to any decision to the contrary under Article 15(2), no information with respect to any particular transport undertaking or transport agency or business which has been obtained under or by virtue of these Regulations or of the principal Regulation shall be disclosed without the consent of the person for the time being carrying on the undertaking, agency or business, unless the disclosure is for the purpose of or in connection with the implementation, or securing or facilitating the implementation of the principal Regulation or is for the purpose of, or connected with any proceedings before the European Court or any other legal proceedings whether civil or criminal under or arising out of the carrying into effect of these Regulations or the principal Regulations.

(3) Any person (except one who is otherwise obliged to observe professional secrecy in accordance with Article 214 of the EEC Treaty) who discloses any information in contravention of paragraph (2) of this Regulation shall be guilty of an offence, and shall be liable on summary conviction to a fine not exceeding **£200**.

7-7253   **10.** Any notice, notification, statement or other communication of information authorised or required by these Regulations or the principal Regulation to be given, sent or supplied to the Secretary of State or to any other person may be given, sent or supplied by delivering it to him or by leaving it at his proper address, or without prejudice to section 26 of the Interpretation Act 1889[1] by sending it to him by post.

---

1. See now the 1978 Act, s 7, in PART II: EVIDENCE, ante.

Railways (Penalty Fares) Regulations 1994[1]

(SI 1994/576 amended by SI 2005/1095)

7-7254   **1.** *Citation and commencement.*

---

1. Made by the Secretary of State under ss 130, 143(3) and 143(4) of the Railways Act 1993 and which continue to have effect as if made by the Strategic Rail Authority (Sch 28 to the Transport Act 2000).

7-7255   **2. Interpretation.** In these Regulations—

"authorised collector" means a person authorised to be a collector by or under rules;

"compulsory ticket area" means any area at a station identified by a notice which indicates that person may not enter that area without being able to produce a ticket or other authority authorising travel on a train arriving at or departing form the area or otherwise authorising entry in that area;

"operator" in relation to any train, means the person having the management of that train for the time being and, in relation to any station, means the person having the management of that station for the time being, and "operated" shall be construed accordingly;

"preceding train" means a train

    (a) by which a person travelled before changing to the train by which he is travelling, on which he is present or which he is leaving for the purposes of these Regulations; and

    (b) which was operated by the operator of the train to which that person changed; "rules" means rules made by the Regulator under regulation 11; "section 130" means section 130 of the Railways Act 1993.

(2) In these Regulations any reference to a person leaving a train includes a person present in or leaving a compulsory ticket area having left a train arriving at that compulsory ticket area.

(3) Where the terms on which a ticket or other authority is issued require the holder to produce on request any other document when using that ticket or other authority, any reference in these Regulations to a ticket or other authority includes such a document.

(4) In these Regulations, where the context so admits, any reference to a ticket or other authority includes a ticket or other authority valid for the class of travel used or being used by the holder of that ticket or other authority.

(5) In these Regulations, any reference to a numbered regulation shall mean the regulation bearing that number in these Regulations and any reference in a regulation to a numbered paragraph is a reference to the paragraph bearing that number in that regulation.

7-7256   **3. Requirement to produce a ticket.** (1) Subject to the provisions of these Regulations and to rules, any person present travelling by, present on or leaving a train shall, if required to do so by or on behalf of the operator of that train in accordance with these Regulations and with rules, produce a ticket or other authority authorising his travelling by or his being present on that train, as the case may be.

(2) Subject to the provisions of these Regulations and to rules, any person present in or leaving a compulsory ticket area, other than a person leaving a train, shall, if required to do so by or on behalf of the operator of a train in accordance with these Regulations and with rules, produce a ticket or other authority authorising him to be present in or leave that compulsory ticket area.

(3) Any requirement imposed pursuant to this regulation shall be imposed by an authorised collector in the manner specified in rules.

7–7257   4. Charge to a penalty fare.   (1) Subject to the provisions of these Regulations and to rules, where a person fails to produce a ticket or other authority when required to do so by or on behalf of an operator pursuant to regulation 3, that operator, or any person acting on behalf of that operator, may charge that person a penalty fare.

(2) Nothing in these Regulations or in rules shall authorise the operator of a train or a person acting on behalf of him to charge a penalty fare in respect of:

(*a*)   travel by, presence on or leaving a train other than a train operated by that operator; or

(*b*)   presence in or leaving a compulsory ticket area unless it is a compulsory ticket area at which a train operated by that operator has arrived or from which such a train will depart.

(3) Any charge made pursuant to this regulation shall be imposed by an authorised collector in the manner specified in rules.

(4) The amount of any penalty fare charged in accordance with these Regulations shall be paid in the manner and within the period specified in rules.

7–7258   5. Amount of a penalty fare.   (1) Subject to paragraph (5), the amount of any penalty fare which may be charged under regulation 4 is £20.00 or twice the amount of the full single fare applicable in the case whichever is the greater.

(2) The full single fare applicable in the case of a person charged a penalty fare while travelling by, being present on or leaving a train, having travelled on or having been present on a preceding train, is the full single fare in respect of a journey from the station (in this regulation referred to as "the first boarding station"), at which that person boarded the preceding train, to the next station at which the train by which he is travelling or on which he is present is scheduled to stop, or, where that person is leaving the train at a station, that station.

(3) The full single fare applicable in the case of a person, other than a person referred to in paragraph (2), charged a penalty fare while travelling by, being present on or leaving a train is the full single fare in respect of a journey from the station (in this regulation referred to as "the boarding station"), at which that person boarded the train, to the next station at which the train by which he is travelling or on which he is present is scheduled to stop, or, where that person is leaving the train at a station, that station.

(4) Where the first boarding station or, as the case may be, the boarding station is not known to the authorised collector, the full single fare applicable in the case of a person charged a penalty fare while travelling by, being present on or leaving a train is the full single fare in respect of a journey from the station at which the train last made a scheduled stop, to the next station at which the train by which he is travelling or on which he is present is scheduled to stop, or, or where that person is leaving the train at a station, that station.

(5) The amount of any penalty fare which may be charged under regulation 4 to a person present in or leaving a compulsory ticket area, other than a person leaving a train, is £20.00.

7–7259   6. Circumstances in which a penalty fare is not to be charged where a person is travelling on a train.   (1) Subject to the provisions of paragraph (3), in the case of a person travelling by, being present on or leaving a train (in this regulation referred to as "the relevant train"), no person shall be charged a penalty fare in the circumstances to which this regulation applies.

(2) The circumstances to which this regulation applies are that, at the time when and at the station where the person in question boarded the relevant train, or, in the case where a person has boarded the relevant train after travelling on a preceding train, that, at the time when and at the station where the person in question boarded that preceding train,

(*a*)   there were no facilities in operation for the sale of the appropriate ticket or other authority to make the journey being or having been made by that person;

(*b*)   the requirements of rules in respect of the display of notices were not satisfied;

(*c*)   a notice was displayed indicating that the person in question was, or persons generally were, permitted to travel by or be present on the relevant train or, as the case may be, the preceding train without having a ticket or other authority; or

(*d*)   a person acting or purporting to act on behalf of

(i)   the operator of the relevant train, or

(ii)   the operator of the station in question,

indicated that the person in question was, or persons generally were, permitted to travel by or be present on the relevant train or, as the case may be, any preceding train without having a ticket or other authority

(3) Paragraphs (1) and (2) of this regulation shall not prevent a person from being charged a penalty fare where he had been invited by anybody acting on behalf of the operator of the relevant train or any preceding train to obtain a ticket or other authority while travelling on or present on the relevant train or that preceding train.

7–7260   7. Circumstances in which a penalty fare is not to be charged where a person is in a compulsory ticket area.   (1) No person present in or leaving a compulsory ticket area, but who is not leaving a train, shall be charged a penalty fare in the circumstances to which this regulation applies.

(2) The circumstances to which this regulation applies are that

(a) there were no facilities in operation at the station (in this regulation referred to as "the relevant station") of which the compulsory ticket area formed part for the sale of the appropriate ticket or other authority to be present in that compulsory ticket area;

(b) the requirements of rules with respect of the display of notices were not satisfied in relation to that compulsory ticket area;

(c) a notice was displayed at the relevant station indicating that the person in question was, or persons generally were, permitted to be present in that compulsory ticket area without having a ticket or other authority; or

(d) a person acting or purporting to act on behalf of

(i) the operator of the train departing from that compulsory ticket area, or
(ii) the operator of the relevant station

indicated that the person in question was, or persons in general were, permitted to be present in that compulsory ticket area without having a ticket or other authority

7–7261 8. Recovery of a penalty fare as a civil debt.   The amount of any penalty fare charged in accordance with these Regulations and rules and not paid within the period specified in rules in accordance with regulation 4(4) may be recovered from the person charged as a civil debt.

7–7262 9. Relevant statement.   (1) Where a person charged a penalty fare has in due time provided the operator by or on whose behalf the penalty fare was charged with a relevant statement, in any proceedings for the recovery of that penalty fare, it shall be for that operator to show that any of the facts described in the relevant statement is not true.

(2) A relevant statement is a statement in writing informing the operator in question—

(a) in the case of a person charged a penalty fare in circumstances where he was travelling by, present on or leaving a train—

(i) of the train and of any preceding train by which he was travelling or had travelled or on which he was present or had been present;

(ii) of the station and the time at which he boarded that train and any preceding train and, other than in the case of his leaving a train at a station, the station at which he intended to leave that train;

(iii) whether any of the circumstances described in regulation 6(2) arose in relation to the station at which he boarded the train and any preceding train, and, if so, which:

(b) in the case of a person charged a penalty fare in circumstances where he was present in or leaving a compulsory ticket area but was not leaving a train—

(i) whether he was proposing to travel by train, and if so, by which train and to which station, and if not so proposing to travel, the reason for his presence in the compulsory ticket area;

(ii) whether any of the circumstances described in regulation 7(2) arose in relation to the station of which the compulsory ticket area formed part and, if so, which.

(3) For the purpose of paragraph (1) a relevant statement is provided in due time if it is provided at any time within the period of 21 days commencing with the day on which the person was charged a penalty fare.

7–7263 10. Exclusion of double liability.   (1) Where a person has been charged a penalty fare in respect of his failure to produce a ticket or other authority when required to do so pursuant to regulation 3, and, arising from that failure, proceedings are brought against that person in respect of any of the offences specified in paragraph (2), that person shall cease to be liable to pay the penalty fare which he has been charged, and, if he has paid it, the operator by or on whose behalf the penalty fare was charged shall be liable to repay to him an amount equal to that amount of that penalty fare.

(2) The offences mentioned in paragraph (1) are an offence under section 5(3)(a) or (b) of the Regulation of Railways Act 1889, or an offence under any byelaw made under section 67 of the Transport Act 1962[1] or section 129 of the Railways Act 1993 or section 219 of the Transport Act 2000 in respect of:

(a) his travelling by, or his presence on, a train without having previously paid his fare, or, having paid his fare for a certain distance, his travelling beyond that distance without previously paying the additional fare for the additional distance;

(b) his travelling by, or his presence on, a train without a ticket or other authority entitling him to travel by or be present on a train;

(c) his presence in part of a station without a ticket or other authority authorising him to be present there.

---

1. See the British Railways Board Byelaws in this PART, ante.

7–7264 11. Power for the Regulator to make rules.   (1) Subject to the provisions of these Regulations, the Regulator may make rules to make provision for and in connection with—

(*a*)   the imposition of requirements on persons travelling by, being present on or leaving trains or being present in or leaving compulsory ticket areas to produce a ticket or other authority authorising them to travel by, or be present on or leave the train in question or to be present in or leave the compulsory ticket area in question; and

(*b*)   the charging of persons in breach of such requirements to penalty fares;

and, subject to paragraph (2), with respect to any of the matters referred to in subsections (2) and (4) of section 130.

(2)   Nothing in these Regulations shall confer on the Regulator power to make rules to make provision for or with respect to any matter specified in paragraph (*d*), (*l*) and (*o*) of subsection (2), or subsection (7), of section 130.

(3)   Rules made pursuant to this regulation shall have effect as if they were regulations.

7–7265   12. Requirement for a person to give his name and address.   (1) A person charged a penalty fare pursuant to regulation 4 shall give his name and address to the authorised collector when so required.

(2)   Any person who fails to give his name and address in accordance with paragraph (1) shall be guilty of an offence and liable on summary conviction to a fine not exceeding **level 2** on the standard scale.

PART VIII
MISCELLANEOUS OFFENCES AND CIVIL PROCEEDINGS

AGRICULTURE

8–1   This title contains the following statutes which may conveniently be grouped together—

The following statutes which are relevant to this title are NOT reproduced in this Manual—

8–2   European Communities Act 1972: regulations.   Within the scope of the title Agriculture there also falls the subject matter of a number of regulations made under the very wide enabling power provided in section 2(2) of the European Communities Act 1972. In respect of those regulations listed in Sch 1 to the National Assembly for Wales (Transfer of Functions) Order 2000, SI 2000/253, the functions of the Secretary of State, so far as exercisable in relation to Wales, have been transferred to the National Assembly for Wales. Where such regulations create offences they are noted below in chronological order:

Dairy Herd Conversion Premium Regulations SI 1973/1642;

Non-marketing of Milk and Milk Products and the Dairy Herd Premiums Regulations SI 1977/1304 amended by SI 1980/124 and 1394;

Hops Certification Regulations SI 1979/1095 amended by SI 1991/2198;

Agricultural and Horticultural Development Regulations SI 1980/1298 amended by SI 1981/1708, SI 1983/508 and 1763, SI 1984/618 and 1922 and SI 1985/1025;

Sheep Variable Premium (Protection of Payments) Regulations SI 1980/1811;

Milk Marketing Boards (Special Conditions) Regulations SI 1981/322;

Farm and Horticultural Development Regulations SI 1981/1707 amended by SI 1983/507, 925 and 1762, SI 1984/620 and 1924, SI 1985/1266 and SI 1986/1295;

Suckler Cow Premium Regulations SI 1982/1683;

Butter Subsidy (Protection of Community Arrangements) Regulations SI 1984/1739;

Agricultural Improvement Regulations SI 1985/1266 amended by SI 1987/1950 and SI 1988/1201, 1982 and 2065, SI 1989/219 and SI 1991/1630;

Cereals Co-responsibility Levy Regulations SI 1988/1001 amended by SI 1989/576 and 1823;

Set-aside Regulations 1988, SI 1988/1352 amended by SI 1989/1042 and SI 1991/1993;

Farm and Conservation Grant Regulations SI 1989/219, amended by SI 1990/1125, SI 1991/1630 and SI 1993/2900;

Sludge (Use in Agriculture) Regulations 1989, SI 1989/1263 amended by SI 1990/880, SI 1994/3003 and SI 2000/656;

Farm and Conservation Grant Regulations 1991, SI 1991/1630 amended by SI 1992/3174;

Agriculture, Fishery and Aquaculture Products (Improvement Grant) Regulations 1991, SI 1991/777;

Temporary Set-Aside Regulations 1991, SI 1991/1847;

Beef Carcase (Classification) Regulations 1991, SI 1991/2242 amended by SI 1994/2853 and SI 1998/12 (revoked in relation to England by SI 2004/1317);

Suckler Cow Premium Regulations 1991, SI 1991/2632 amended by SI 1992/270, 1210 and 2918;

Common Agricultural Policy (Protection of Community Arrangements) Regulations 1992, SI 1992/314 amended by SI 2001/3198 and 3686;

Oilseed Producers (Support System) Regulations 1992, SI 1992/695;

Zoo Technical Standards Regulations 1992, SI 1992/2370;

Habitat (Water Fringe) Regulations 1994, SI 1994/1291 amended by SI 1996/1480 and 3106 and SI 1999/3160;

Habitat (Former Set-aside Land) Regulations 1994 SI 1994/1292 amended by SI 1996/1478 and 3107;

Habitat (Salt-Marsh) Regulations 1994, SI 1994/1293 amended by SI 1996/1479 and 3108, and SI 1999/3161;

Organic Farming (Aid) Regulations 1994, SI 1994/1721 amended by SI 1996/3109, SI 1998/1606 and SI 2001/340;

Nitrate Sensitive Areas Regulations 1994, SI 1994/1729 amended by SI 1995/1708 and 2095, SI 1996/3105, SI 1997/990, SI 1998/79 and 2138 and SI 2002/744;

Pig Carcase (Grading) Regulations 1994, SI 1994/2155 amended by SI 2003/2949 and SI 2004/106 (W) and 1505 (E);

Countryside Access Regulations 1994, SI 1994/2349 amended by SI 1999/1174 and 2197;

Habitat (Broadleaved Woodland) (Wales) Regulations 1994, SI 1994/3099 amended by SI 1996/3075;

Surplus Food Regulations 1995, SI 1995/184 amended by SI 2001/3686;

Moorland (Livestock Extensification) Regulations 1995, SI 1995/904 amended by SI 1996/2393 and 3110 and SI 1999/2361;

Moorland (Livestock Extensification) (Wales) Regulations 1995, SI 1995/1159 amended by SI 1996/2449 and 3076;

Rural Development Grants (Agriculture) (No 2) Regulations 1995, SI 1995/2202 amended by SI 1996/2394;

Marketing of Vegetable Plant Material Regulations 1995, SI 1995/2652;

Marketing of Fruit Plant Material Regulations 1995, SI 1995/2653 amended by SI 2004/2603 and SI 2005/1155 (W);

Sheep Annual Premium and Suckler Cow Premium Quotas (Re-assessment of Eligibility) Regulations 1996, SI 1996/48;

Beef (Marketing Payment) Regulations 1996, SI 1996/2005 amended by SI 1996/2561 and 2999 and SI 1997/195;

Bovine Products (Despatch to other Member States) Regulations 1996, SI 1996/2265 amended by SI 1996/3000;

Products of Animal Origin (Import and Export) Regulations 1996, SI 1996/3124 amended by SI 1997/3023, SI 1998/994, SI 1999/683, SI 2000/225, 656, 1885 (Wales), 2215 and 2257 (Wales), SI 2001/1553 (England), 1640 (England), 1660 (Wales), 2198 (Wales) and 2253 (Wales), SI 2002/1227 (England) and 1387 (Wales), SI 2003/1736, 3003 (E), 3229 (W) and 3177, SI 2004/82 and 1430 (W) and SI 2005/209 (E);

Bovine Products (Production and Despatch) Regulations 1997, SI 1997/389;

Bovine Hides Regulations 1997, SI 1997/813;

Veal (Marketing Payment) Regulations 1997, SI 1997/1986;

Plant Breeders Rights (Information Notices) (Extension to European Community Plant Variety Rights) Regulations 1998, SI 1998/1023;

Feedingstuffs (Zootechnical Products) Regulations 1998, SI 1998/1047.

Apple and Pear Orchard Grubbing Up Regulations 1998, SI 1998/1131;

Bovines and Bovine Products (Trade) Regulations 1999, SI 1999/1103, amended by SI 1999/1554, SI 2000/656 and 1667 (England) and SI 2002/1174 (Wales), 2325 (Wales) and 2357 (England);

Land in Care Scheme (Tir Gofal) (Wales) Regulations 1999, SI 1999/1176 amended by SI 1999/3337, SI 2001/423 and SI 2003/529;

Marketing of Ornamental Plant Material Regulations 1999, SI 1999/1801;

Environmental Impact Assessment (Forestry) (England and Wales) Regulations 1999, SI 1999/2228;

Organic Farming (Wales) Regulations 1999, SI 1999/2611 amended by SI 1999/3337 and SI 2001/430 and 432;

Hill Livestock (Compensatory Allowances) (Enforcement) Regulations 1999, SI 1999/3315;

Hill Livestock (Compensatory Allowances) Regulations 1999, SI 1999/3316;

Pesticides (Maximum Residue Levels in Crops, Food and Feeding Stuffs) (England and Wales) Regulations 1999, (SI 1999/3483 amended by SI 2001/1113, 2420 and 3834 and SI 2003/661 and 2591;

Energy Crops Regulations 2000, SI 2000/3042 amended by SI 2001/3900 (England);

Rural Enterprise Regulations 2000, SI 2000/3043 amended by SI 2001/3900;

England Rural Development Programme (Enforcement) Regulations 2000, SI 2000/3044 amended by SI 2001/431 and SI 2002/271, SI 2005/154 and 621 and SI 2006/225;

Vocational Training Grants (Agriculture and Forestry) Regulations 2000, SI 2000/3045 amended by SI 2001/3900 (England);

Agricultural Processing and Marketing Grants Regulations 2000, SI 2000/3046 amended by SI 2001/3897;

Organic Farming Scheme (Wales) Regulations 2001, SI 2001/424 amended by SI 2004/105;

Organic Products Regulations 2001, SI 2001/460;

Hill Farm Allowance Regulations 2001, SI 2001/476 amended by SI 2004/145;

Tir Mynydd (Wales) Regulations 2001, SI 2001/496 amended by SI 2002/1806 and SI 2005/1269;

Common Agricultural Policy (Wine) (England and Northern Ireland) Regulations 2001, SI 2001/686 amended by SI 2003/114, SI 2004/1046 and SI 2005/2992;

Common Agricultural Policy (Wine) (Wales) Regulations 2001, SI 2001/2193 amended by SI 2003/1776 and SI 2004/2599;

Foot-and-Mouth Disease (Prohibition of Vaccination) (Wales) Regulations 2001, SI 2001/2374;

Agricultural Processing and Marketing Grant (Wales) Regulations 2001, SI 2001/2446.

Beef Special Premium Regulations 2001, SI 2001/2503 amended by SI 2005/219;

Seeds (National Lists of Varieties) Regulations 2001, SI 2001/3510 amended by SI 2004/2949;

Farm Enterprise and Farm Improvement Grant (Wales) Regulations 2001, SI 2001/3806;

Rural Development (Local Communities) Regulations 2001, SI 2001/3899;

Patents and Plant Variety Rights Compulsory Licensing) Regulations 2002, SI 2002/247;

Hill Farm Allowance Regulations 2002, SI 2002/271 amended by SI 2003/289;

Dairy Produce Quotas (General Provisions) Regulations 2002, SI 2002/458 amended by SI 2005/466;

Hemp (Third Country Imports) Regulations 2002, SI 2002/787 amended by SI 2002/1924;

TSE (Wales) Regulations 2002, SI 2002/1416 amended by SI 2003/2756, SI 2004/2735 and SI 2005/1392 and 2902;

Environmental Impact Assessment (Uncultivated Land and Semi-Natural Areas) (Wales) Regulations 2002, SI 2002/2127;

Forest Reproductive Material (Great Britain) Regulations 2002, SI 2002/3026;

Olive Oil (Marketing Standards) Regulations 2003, SI 2003/2577 amended by SI 2004/2661;

Organic Products (Imports from Third Countries) Regulations 2003, SI 2003/2821;

Potatoes Originating in Egypt (England) Regulations 2004, SI 2004/1165;

Beef Carcase (Classification) Regulations 2004, SI 2004/1317;

Organic Products Regulations 2004, SI 2004/1604 amended by SI 2005/2003;

Potatoes Originating in Egypt (Wales) Regulations 2004, SI 2004/2245;

Genetically Modified Animal Feed (England) Regulations 2004, SI 2004/2334 amended by SI 2005/1265 and 1323;

Genetically Modified Animal Feed (Wales) Regulations 2004, SI 2004/3221;

Common Agricultural Policy Single Payment and Support Schemes (Cross Compliance) (Wales) Regulations 2004, SI 2004/3280 amended by SI 2005/3367;

Products of Animal Origin (Third Country Imports) (England) (No 4) Regulations 2004, SI 2004/3388 amended by SI 2005/3386;

Hill Farm Allowance Regulations 2005, SI 2005/154;

Common Agricultural Policy Single Payment and Support Schemes (Integrated Administration and Control System) Regulations 2005, SI 2005/218;

Common Agricultural Policy Single Payment and Support Schemes Regulations 2005, SI 2005/219 amended by SI 2005/1087 and SI 2006/239 and 301;

Common Agricultural Policy Single Payment and Support Schemes (Wales) Regulations 2005, SI 2005/360 amended by SI 2006/357;

Dairy Produce Quotas Regulations 2005, SI 2005/465 amended by SI 2006/120;

Dairy Produce Quotas (Wales) Regulations 2005, SI 2005/537;

Environmental Stewardship (England) Regulations 2005, SI 2005/621 amended by SI 2005/2003;

Products of Animal Origin (Third Country Imports) (Wales) Regulations 2005, SI 2005/666 amended by SI 2005/3395;

Feed (Corn Gluten Feed and Brewers Grains) (Emergency Control) (England) Regulations 2005, SI 2005/1265;

Feed (Corn Gluten Feed and Brewers Grains) (Emergency Control) (Wales) Regulations 2005, SI 2005/1323;

Reporting of Prices Milk Products (England) Regulations 2005, SI 2005/1441;

Plant Protection Products Regulations 2005, SI 2005/1435 amended by SI 2005/3197;

Reporting of Prices of Milk Products (Wales) Regulations 2005, SI 2005/2907;

Official Feed and Food Controls (Wales) Regulations 2005, SI 2005/3254;

Feed (Hygiene and Enforcement) (England) Regulations 2005, SI 2005/3280 amended by SI 2006/15;

Pesticides (Maximum Residue Levels in Crops, Food and Feeding Stuffs) (England and Wales) Regulations 2005, SI 2005/3286;

Common Agricultural Policy Single Payment and Support Schemes (Cross-compliance) (England) Regulations 2005, SI 2005/3459;

Older Cattle (Disposal) (England) Regulations 2005, SI 2005/3522;

Feed (Hygiene and Enforcement) (Wales) Regulations 2005, SI 2005/3368;

Official Feed and Food Controls (England) Regulations 2006, SI 2006/15;

Older Cattle (Disposal) (Wales) Regulations 2006, SI 2006/62;

Hill Farm Allowance Regulations 2006, SI 2006/225.

Corn Returns Act 1882

(1882 c 37)

8–3   **Corn Returns.**   The Corn Returns Act 1882, amended by Corn Sales Act 1921, requires return of all purchases of British corn, in *such areas as may from time to time be prescribed*[1] (s 4), from "buyers of corn", ie dealers in British corn, corn factors, millers, maltsters, brewers, or distillers; also every person who is the owner or part owner of any carriage carrying goods or passengers for hire; also every person who, as a merchant, clerk, agent, or otherwise, purchases British corn for sale, or for the sale of meal, flour, malt, or bread made or to be made thereof.

Penalty, for failure to make the return, not exceeding **level 2** on the standard scale (s 11, as amended by the Criminal Law Act 1977, s 31 and the Criminal Justice Act 1982, s 46).

Making a fraudulent statement is a misdemeanour (s 12).

---

1. The words in italics are substituted by the Agriculture (Miscellaneous Provisions) Act 1943, s 18, Sch 3, as amended by the Agriculture Act 1970, s 108(3). See the Corn Returns Regulations 1997, SI 1997/1873.

Horticultural Produce (Sales on Commission) Act 1926
(16 & 17 Geo 5 c 39)
Not reproduced in this Manual.

8–12

Agricultural Produce (Grading and Marking) Act 1928
(18 & 19 Geo 5 c 19)
Not reproduced in this Manual.

8–16

Agricultural Credits Act 1928
(18 & 19 Geo 5 c 43)
Not reproduced in this Manual.

8–18

Agricultural Produce (Grading and Marking) Amendment Act 1931
(21 & 22 Geo 5 c 40)
Not reproduced in this Manual.

Hill Farming Act 1946
(9 & 10 Geo 6 c 73)

8–19 **18.** The Minister[1] of Agriculture and Fisheries is empowered to make regulations for controlling the keeping of rams and uncastrated ram lambs on land in England and Wales.
[Hill Farming Act 1946, s 18, summarised, and Livestock Rearing Act 1951, s 7.]

---

1. The appropriate Minister is the Minister of Agriculture, Fisheries and Food (SI 1999/3141). The functions of the Minister, so far as exercisable in relation to Wales, have been transferred to the National Assembly for Wales, by the National Assembly for Wales (Transfer of Functions) Order 1999, SI 1999/672, art 2, Sch 1.

Control of Rams (England and Wales)

8–20 **19. Penalties for offences in connection with control of rams.** (1) If any person permits a ram or lamb to be on any land in contravention of regulations made under the last preceding section, he shall be guilty of an offence and liable on summary conviction to a fine not exceeding **level 1** on the standard scale, and, if any such contravention in respect of which a person has been convicted continues after the conviction, he shall be guilty of a further offence and liable on summary conviction to a fine not exceeding £5 for each day on which the contravention so continues.

(2) If any person with intent to deceive—

(*a*) uses, or lends to or allows to be used by another person, a licence granted under regulations made under the last preceding section; or

(*b*) makes or has in his possession a document so closely resembling such a licence as to be calculated to deceive; or

(*c*) alters or defaces a mark placed on a ram or lamb in pursuance of regulations so made;

he shall be guilty of an offence and liable on summary conviction to a fine not exceeding **level 2** on the standard scale or to imprisonment for a term not exceeding **three months**, or to both such fine and such imprisonment.

(3) If any person—

(*a*) places on a ram or lamb, otherwise than in pursuance of regulations made under the last preceding section, a mark prescribed by regulations so made; or

(*b*) places on a ram or lamb a mark so closely resembling a mark so prescribed as to be calculated to deceive;

he shall be guilty of an offence and liable on summary conviction to a fine not exceeding **level 2** on the standard scale or to imprisonment for a term not exceeding **three months**, or to both such fine and such imprisonment.

(4) If a person on whom a requisition for the slaughter or castration of a ram or lamb has been duly served under regulations made under the last preceding section fails to comply with the requisition, he shall be liable on summary conviction to a fine not exceeding **level 2** on the standard scale, and, if any such failure in respect of which a person has been convicted continues after the conviction, he shall be guilty of a further offence and liable on summary conviction to a further fine not exceeding £5 for every day during which the failure so continues.

(5) If any person, without the permission of the Minister of Agriculture and Fisheries, at any time after any such requisition as aforesaid has been duly served on him under regulations made under the last preceding section removes (otherwise than to a slaughter-house for the purpose of slaughter) the ram or lamb to which the requisition relates, he shall be guilty of an offence and liable on summary conviction to a fine not exceeding **level 2** on the standard scale.

(6) If any person obstructs or impedes any person in the exercise of any power conferred upon him by virtue of the last preceding section, he shall be liable on summary conviction to a fine not exceeding **level 2** on the standard scale.

[Hill Farming Act 1946, s 19, as amended by the Criminal Law Act 1977, s 31, Forgery and Counterfeiting Act 1981, Sch and Criminal Justice Act 1982, ss 35 and 46.]

Burning of Heather and Grass (England and Wales)

8–21 **20. Power to regulate heather and grass burning in England and Wales.** (1) The Minister of Agriculture and Fisheries may by regulation[1] make provision for regulating or prohibiting the burning of heather, grass, bracken, gorse and vaccinium on land in England or Wales, and any such regulations may be made so as to extend to the whole of England or Wales or to any specified area therein, may regulate or prohibit the burning of heather, grass, bracken, gorse and vaccinium at all times or during such period as may be specified in the regulations and may contain different provisions with respect to land in different parts of England and Wales and to different periods.

(2) If any person contravenes any provision of regulations made under this section, he shall be liable on summary conviction to a fine not exceeding **level 3** on the standard scale.

[Hill Farming Act 1946, s 20, as amended by the Wildlife and Countryside Act 1981, s 72(2), the Criminal Justice Act 1982, s 46 and the Hill Farming Act 1985, s 1.]

---

1. See the Heather and Grass Burning (England and Wales) Regulations 1986, SI 1986/428, amended by SI 1987/1208.

General

8–22 **34. Power to enter on and inspect land.** (1) For the purposes of this Act, an officer of the appropriate Minister[1] authorised in that behalf by general or special directions given by him shall, on producing, if so required written evidence of his authority, have power at all reasonable times to enter on and inspect—

(*a*) any land which he has reason to believe to be used, or to be capable of being used, for livestock rearing purposes; and

(*b*) any land which he has reason to believe to be used in connection with the use for livestock rearing purposes of other land:

Provided that admission to any land shall not be demanded as of right unless twenty-four hours' notice of the intended entry has been given to the occupier.

(2) If any person obstructs or impedes an officer of the appropriate Minister authorised as aforesaid in the exercise of his powers under the preceding subsection, he shall be guilty of an offence and liable on summary conviction to a fine not exceeding **level 2** on the standard scale.

[Hill Farming Act 1946, s 34, as amended by Livestock Rearing Act 1951, s 1, the Agriculture (Miscellaneous Provisions) Act 1972, Sch 6, the Criminal Law Act 1977, s 31 and the Criminal Justice Act 1982, ss 35 and 46.]

---

1. As to the appropriate Minister, see footnote to s 18(1), ante.

8–23 **35. Recovery of sums by Ministers.** Any sum recoverable under this Act by the Ministers[1] or either of them may be recovered as a debt due to the Crown or summarily as a civil debt[2], and a complaint made for the purposes of recovering any such sum summarily as a civil debt may be made at any time within twelve months[3] from the time when the matter of the complaint arose.

[Hill Farming Act 1946, s 35.]

---

1. As to the appropriate Minister, see footnote to s 18(1), ante.
2. See Magistrates' Courts Act 1980, s 58, in PART I: MAGISTRATES' COURTS, PROCEDURE, ante.
3. An enlargement of the limitation imposed by Magistrates' Courts Act 1980, s 127.

Agriculture Act 1947
(10 & 11 Geo 6 c 48)

8–25 **98. Prevention of damage by pests.** The Minister[1] may serve notice in writing requiring any person to take such steps as may be necessary for the killing, taking or destruction on land specified in the notice of animals and birds to which this section applies or the eggs of such birds. The animals to which this section applies are rabbits, hares and other rodents, deer, foxes and moles, and the birds to which this section applies are wild birds other than those included in the First Schedule to the Protection of Birds Act 1954[2]. The section shall apply to such other animals as may be prescribed. The Minister may serve notice in writing on the occupier of land (or, in the case of unoccupied land, the person entitled to occupy it) requiring him to take on the land such steps as are specified to destroy or reduce the breeding places or cover for rabbits or to exclude rabbits therefrom, or to prevent the rabbits living in any place on the land or spreading to or doing damage in any other place.

[Agriculture Act 1947, s 98, as amended by Protection of Birds Act 1954, 5th Sch, and the Pests Act 1954, s 2(1)—summarised.]

No notice shall require any person to take any steps which he could have been required to take under s 4 of the Prevention of Damage by Pests Act 1949 (qv s 20).

_____

1. The functions of the Minister, so far as exercisable in relation to Wales, have been transferred to the National Assembly for Wales, by the National Assembly for Wales (Transfer of Functions) Order 1999, SI 1999/672, art 2, Sch 1.
2. See now the Wildlife and Countryside Act 1981, ss 4 and 10.

8–26   99. Prevention of escape of captive animals.   The Minister may serve notice in writing on the occupier of land requiring him to take steps to prevent the escape of animals from land on which they are kept in captivity.
[Agriculture Act 1947, s 99—summarised.]

8–27   100. Penalty for failing to comply with requirement under ss 98 and 99.   (1) If any person fails to comply with a requirement imposed under either of the two last foregoing sections he shall be liable on summary conviction to a fine not exceeding **level 2** on the standard scale, and to a further fine not exceeding £5 for each day after conviction on which the failure continues.
[Agriculture Act 1947, s 100(1), as amended by the Criminal Law Act 1977, s 31 and the Criminal Justice Act 1982, s 46.]

(2) Where this requirement is not complied with, any person authorised by the Minister may at any time enter on the land and take such steps as the Minister may direct to secure compliance.
[Agriculture Act 1947, s 100(2).]

8–28   106. Provisions as to entry and inspection.   (1) Any person authorised by the Minister in that behalf shall have power at all reasonable times to enter on and inspect any land for the purpose of determining whether, and if so in what manner, any of the powers conferred by this Act are to be exercised in relation to the land, or whether, and if so in what manner, any direction given under any such power has been complied with.

(2) Any person authorised by the Minister who proposes to exercise any power of entry or inspection conferred by this Act shall if so required produce some duly authenticated document showing his authority to exercise the power.

(3) Admission to any land shall not be demanded as of right in the exercise of any such power as aforesaid—

(*a*)   if the power is being exercised for determining whether the land is to be acquired under Part IV[1] of this Act or this Part[2] thereof; or

(*b*)   if the land is being used for residential purposes;

unless twenty-four hours' notice of the intended entry has been given to the occupier[3] of the land.

(4) Save as provided by the last foregoing subsection, admission to any land shall not be demanded as of right in the exercise of any such power as aforesaid unless notice has been given to the occupier of the land that it is proposed to enter during a period, specified in the notice, not exceeding fourteen days and beginning at least twenty-four hours after the giving of the notice, and the entry is made on the land during the period specified in the notice: Provided that where the power of entry is being exercised for the purpose of taking measures to secure compliance with a direction or requirement under the foregoing provisions of this Part of this Act, and notice is given in accordance with this subsection on the first occasion on which the power is exercised, no further notice shall be required before entering on the land on a subsequent occasion in connection with the taking of the measures.

(5) Where notice is served[4] in a case falling within the proviso to the last foregoing subsection, and the person to whom the direction therein referred to was given, or on whom the requirement therein referred to was imposed, is not the occupier of the land, a like notice shall be served[5] on that person.

(6) Any notice served in pursuance of the last foregoing subsection or the proviso therein referred to may be served in like manner as the notice giving the said direction or imposing the said requirement.

(7) Any person who, in any case for which no penalty is provided by the foregoing provisions of this Act, obstructs the exercise of any such power as aforesaid or of any other power conferred by s 100(2) of this Act shall be guilty of an offence and liable on summary conviction to a fine not exceeding **level 2** on the standard scale.
[Agriculture Act 1947, s 106, as amended by Pests Act 1954, s 5(1), Agriculture Act 1958, Sch 2 (repealed), Agriculture Act 1970, Sch 5 the Criminal Law Act 1977, s 31 and the Criminal Justice Act 1982, ss 35 and 46.]

1. Part IV includes ss 58 and 59, and 67—"Smallholdings", amended by the Agriculture Act 1970.
2. Part V includes ss 73–111—"Administrative and General", amended by the Agriculture Act 1970.
3. "Occupier", in relation to unoccupied land, means the person entitled to occupy the land (Pests Act 1954, s 1(13)).
4. For mode of service, see s 107.

8–29

Agricultural Wages Act 1948
(11 & 12 Geo 6 c 47)
Not reproduced in this Manual.

Agriculture (Poisonous Substances) Act 1952
(15 & 16 Geo 6 & 1 Eliz 2 c 60)

8–46   This Act provides that regulations shall be made protecting workers against risks of poisoning by substances to which the Act applies[1] arising from their working (a) in connection with the use in agriculture[2] of such substances, or (b) on land on which such substances are being or have been used in agriculture.
[Agriculture (Poisonous Substances) Act 1952, s 1—summarised.]

1. These substances are specified in s 9 and may include other substances specified by an Order made by the Minister for Agriculture, Fisheries and Food, and the Secretary of State for Scotland. The functions of the Minister, so far as exercisable in relation to Wales, have been transferred to the National Assembly for Wales, by the National Assembly for Wales (Transfer of Functions) Order 1999, SI 1999/672, art 2, Sch 1.
2. "Agriculture" is defined in s 10(1).

8–47   2. Duties of employees.   (1) No worker employed to work as mentioned in subsection (1) of section one of this Act shall—

(a) wilfully interfere with or misuse any appliance, clothing, equipment, facilities or other thing provided in pursuance of regulations under this Act; or
(b) wilfully and without reasonable cause do anything likely to cause risk of poisoning, by a substance to which this Act applies, to himself or others.

(2) Nothing in this section shall be taken as limiting the power conferred by section one of this Act to make by regulations any such provision as is therein mentioned, including further provision as to matters which are the subject of this section.
[Agriculture (Poisonous Substances) Act 1952, s 2.]

8–48   4. Offences and punishment therefor.   (1) If a person—

(a) contravenes[1] any provision of regulations under this Act;
(b) contravenes[1] any provision of section two of this Act;
(c) obstructs an inspector appointed under this Act[2] in the execution of his powers[3] or duties under this Act or regulations thereunder; or
(d) wilfully makes a false entry in a register, record, return or other document kept or furnished in pursuance of regulations under this Act, or wilfully makes use of such a false entry, or wilfully makes or signs as being a declaration required by an inspector in pursuance of this Act a declaration which is false;

he shall be guilty of an offence against this Act.

(2) A person found guilty of an offence against this Act shall be liable on summary conviction to a fine not exceeding **level 4** on the standard scale, and, if a contravention of a provision of this Act or of regulations thereunder in respect of which a person had been convicted is continued by him after his conviction, he shall be guilty of a further offence and liable in respect thereof to a fine not exceeding £10 for each day on which the contravention is so continued.

(3) Where a contravention of a provision of regulations under this Act consists in a failure to do anything at or within a time specified in the regulations, and the regulations provide that this subsection shall apply to a failure so to do it, the contravention shall be deemed to continue until that thing is done.

(4) Where an offence against this Act which has been committed by a body corporate is proved to have been committed with the consent or connivance of, or to be attributable to any neglect on the part of, any director, manager, secretary or other similar officer of the body corporate, or any person purporting to act in any such capacity, he as well as the body corporate shall be deemed to be guilty of that offence and shall be liable to be proceeded against and punished accordingly.
In this subsection, the expression "director", in relation to any body corporate which is established by or under any enactment for the purpose of carrying on under national ownership any industry or

part of an industry or undertaking and whose affairs are managed by the members thereof, means a member of that body.

[Agriculture (Poisonous Substances) Act 1952, s 4, as amended by the Agriculture (Miscellaneous Provisions) Act 1972, s 14 and the Criminal Justice Act 1982, ss 38 and 46.]

---

1. This includes a failure to comply with such provision (s 10(2)).
2. In accordance with s 3.
3. Delaying an inspector, failing to comply with his requirement or concealing or preventing a person from appearing before him is a form of obstruction (s 3(4) (*summarised*)).

8–49 5. Defence available in certain circumstances to person charged where some other person is responsible.   (1) A person against whom proceedings are brought under this Act shall, upon information duly laid by him and on giving to the prosecution not less than three clear days' notice of his intention, be entitled to have brought before the court in the proceedings any person to whose act or default he alleges that the contravention of the provision in question was due, and, if after the contravention has been proved the original defendant proves that the contravention was due to the act or default of that other person, that other person may be convicted of the offence, and, if the original defendant further proves—

(*a*) that he has used all due diligence to secure that the provision in question was complied with, and
(*b*) that the said other person's act or default was without his consent, connivance or wilful default.

he shall be acquitted of the offence.

(2) Where a defendant seeks to avail himself of the preceding subsection—

(*a*) the prosecution, as well as the person whom the defendant charges with the offence, shall have the right to cross-examine the defendant, if he gives evidence, and any witness called by him in support of his pleas, and to call rebutting evidence;
(*b*) the court may make any such order as it thinks fit for the payment of costs by any party to the proceedings to any other party thereto.

(3) Where it appears to the Health and Safety Executive that an offence has been committed in respect of which proceedings might be taken under this Act against some person and the said Minister is reasonably satisfied that the offence of which the complaint is made was due to an act or default of some other person and that the first-mentioned person could establish a defence under subsection (1) of this section, he may cause proceedings to be taken against that other person without first causing proceedings to be taken against the first-mentioned person.

In any such proceedings the defendant may be charged with, and, on proof that the contravention was due to his act or default, be convicted of, the offence with which the first-mentioned person might have been charged.

[Agriculture (Poisonous Substances) Act 1952, s 5.]

8–50 6. Provisions as to samples.   (1) An inspector appointed under this Act may take for analysis a sample of any substance or thing which in his opinion may be or contain a substance to which this Act applies, and which he finds on, or has reasonable cause to believe to be in transit to or from, such land or premises as are mentioned in subsection (2) of section three of this Act.

(2) An inspector taking a sample under the preceding subsection with the intention of having it analysed shall, if practicable, forthwith after taking it give information of his intention to the employer of any person then working as mentioned in subsection (1) of section one of this Act on the land or premises in question, and shall then and there divide the sample into parts, each part to be marked, and sealed or fastened up, in such manner as its nature will permit, and shall—

(*a*) if required so to do by an employer so informed, deliver one part to him;
(*b*) retain one part for future comparison; and
(*c*) if the inspector thinks fit to have an analysis made, submit one part to an analyst approved by the Health and Safety Executive for the purposes of this Act.

(3) Where it is not practicable for the inspector to give information of his intention as mentioned in the last preceding subsection to an employer, the inspector shall, if he intends to have the sample analysed and if he can ascertain the name and address of the employer, forward one part of the sample to him by registered post or otherwise, together with a notice informing him that he intends to have the sample analysed.

(4) A document purporting to be a certificate by an analyst approved by the Health and Safety Executive for the purposes of this Act as to the result of an analysis of a sample shall in proceedings under this Act be admissible as evidence of the matters stated therein, but either party may require the person by whom the analysis was made to be called as a witness.

(5) In any proceedings under this Act in which the prosecutor intends to rely on evidence relating to a sample taken under this section, the summons shall not be made returnable less than fourteen days from the day on which it is served, and a copy of any certificate of analysis obtained on behalf of the prosecutor shall be served with the summons.

(6) In any proceedings under this Act in which the prosecutor relies on evidence relating to a

sample taken under this section, the part of the sample retained by the inspector for future comparison shall be produced at the hearing.

(7) The court before which any proceedings are taken under this Act may, if it thinks fit, and upon the request of either party shall, cause the part of any sample produced before the court under the last preceding subsection to be sent to the Government Chemist who shall make an analysis, and transmit to the court a certificate of the result thereof, and the cost of the analysis shall be paid by the prosecutor or the defendant as the court may order.

If, in a case where an appeal is brought, no action has been taken under the preceding provisions of this subsection, those provisions shall apply also in relation to the court by which the appeal is heard.
[Agriculture (Poisonous Substances) Act 1952, s 6, as amended by SI 1976/1247.]

Agricultural Land (Removal of Surface Soil) Act 1953
(1 & 2 Eliz 2 c 10)

8–51 1. Removal of surface soil without planning permission to be an offence against this Act. (1) If—

(*a*) a person removes surface soil from agricultural[1] land with a view to the sale of that soil, and

(*b*) the removal of that soil constitutes development[2] within the meaning of the Town and Country Planning Act 1990, and is carried out without the grant of permission required in that behalf under Part III of that Act, and

(*c*) the quality of soil so removed in any period of three months amounts to more than five cubic yards,

he shall be guilty of an offence against this Act.

(2) Subsection (1) of this section shall not apply to the cutting of peat or to the removal of so much surface soil as it is reasonably necessary to remove in the course of cutting turf.

(3) The reference in subsection (1) of this section to agricultural[1] land shall include a reference to land the use of which for agriculture[1] has been discontinued in consequence of the intention to remove surface soil from that land.
[Agricultural Land (Removal of Surface Soil) Act 1953, s 1 as amended by the Planning (Consequential Provisions) Act 1990, Sch 2.]

---

1. "Agriculture" and "agricultural" are now defined in s 336 of the Town and Country Planning Act 1990, post.
2. "Development" is defined in s 55 of the Town and Country Planning Act 1990, post.

8–52 2. Punishment of offences against this Act. (1) A person guilty of an offence against this Act shall be liable on summary conviction[1] to a fine not exceeding **level 3** on the standard scale:

Provided that where a person is convicted of an offence against this Act and it is shown to the satisfaction of the court that the offence was substantially a repetition or continuation of an earlier offence by him after he had been convicted of the earlier offence, he shall be liable—

(*a*) to imprisonment for a term not exceeding **three months**[2]; or

(*b*) to a fine not exceeding £50 for every day on which the earlier offence has been so repeated or continued by him or £200 (whichever is the greater),

or to both.

(2) Where an offence against this Act which has been committed by a body corporate is proved to have been committed with the consent or connivance of, or to be attributable to any neglect on the part of, any director, manager, secretary or other similar officer of that body corporate, or any person purporting to act in any such capacity, he as well as the body corporate shall be guilty of that offence and shall be liable to be proceeded against and punished accordingly.

In this subsection the expression "director", in relation to any body corporate established by or under any enactment for the purpose of carrying on under national ownership any industry or part of an industry or undertaking, being a body corporate whose affairs are managed by members thereof, means a member of that body.

(3) In proceedings under this Act it shall be a defence to show that, before the carrying out of the operations in respect of which the proceedings are brought, it was determined or decided under section 64 of the Town and Country Planning Act 1990, that those particular operations would not fall within paragraph (*b*) of subsection (1) of the foregoing section[3]; but a determination or decision under the said section seventeen shall not in other circumstances be treated as conclusive for the purpose of this Act.
[Agricultural Land (Removal of Surface Soil) Act 1953, s 2 as amended by the Criminal Justice Act 1982, ss 38 and 46 and the Planning (Consequential Provisions) Act 1990, Sch 2.]

---

1. Prosecution in England and Wales requires the consent of the Attorney-General or the Director of Public Prosecutions (s 3).
2. It would seem, by virtue of the Criminal Justice Act 1982, s 35, in PART III: SENTENCING, ante, that an offender is now liable to imprisonment on a first conviction.
3. That is, would not constitute development.

Agriculture (Miscellaneous Provisions) Act 1954
(2 & 3 Eliz 2 c 39)

8–53   9. Collection of kitchen waste, etc for animal feeding stuffs.   (1) and (2) A local authority may collect kitchen or other waste in their area for use as animal feeding stuffs (*summarised*).

(3) *Repealed.*

(4) A local authority collecting waste under this section may provide receptacles in which the waste may be deposited for collection, and may place any receptacles so provided in any street or public place.

(5) If a person wilfully deposits in any receptacle provided under the last foregoing subsection, or otherwise used for the deposit of waste to be collected under this section, anything which he knows or has reasonable cause to believe to be unsuitable for use as animal feeding stuffs, he shall be liable on summary conviction to a fine not exceeding **level 1** on the standard scale; and if any person (other than a person employed in connection with the local authority's collection of the waste) removes the whole or part of the contents of any such receptacle when placed in a street or public place or set out for the purpose of its contents being removed under this section, he shall be liable on summary conviction to a fine not exceeding **level 1** on the standard scale.

(6) A local authority may make bye-laws regulating the collection, etc of kitchen or other waste (*summarised*).

(7) Proceedings in respect of an offence created by or under this section shall not be taken by any person other than the local authority in whose area the offence is alleged to have been committed, unless taken by or with the consent of the Director of Public Prosecutions: Provided that, where a local authority collects waste under this section outside their area, they may without the consent of the Director of Public Prosecutions take proceedings in respect of an offence under subsection (5) of this section alleged to have been committed at any place within the limits of their collection.

[Agriculture (Miscellaneous Provisions) Act 1954, s 9 as amended by the Local Government Act 1972, s 272(1), Sch 30.and the Criminal Justice Act 1982, ss 35, 38 and 46.]

Pests Act 1954
(2 & 3 Eliz 2 c 68)

8–54   This Act makes provision with respect to the destruction or control of rabbits and other animals and birds, and to the use of spring traps for killing or taking animals. The Minister[1] for Agriculture and Fisheries may make rabbit clearance orders designating rabbit clearance areas to be freed, so far as practicable, of wild rabbits, and the occupier of any land in such a district shall take necessary steps for the killing or taking of wild rabbits and for the prevention of damage by those rabbits and shall comply with directions contained in the rabbit clearance order.

[Pests Act 1954, s 1—summarised.]

---

1. Sections 100 and 106(2)–(7) of the Agriculture Act 1947, ante, have been applied to the provisions of this section (Pests Act 1954, s 1(9)). The functions of the Minister, so far as exercisable in relation to Wales, have been transferred to the National Assembly for Wales, by the National Assembly for Wales (Transfer of Functions) Order 1999, SI 1999/672, art 2, Sch 1.

8–55   4. Provisions for facilitating giving of notices.   The Minister may require any person who is the occupier of any land, or who appears to the Minister or Secretary of State to have an interest in any land, or who directly or indirectly receives rent in respect of any land, to state in writing the nature of his own interest in the land, and the name and address of any other person known to him as having an interest in it, or as having the right to kill on the land any animals or birds to which s 98[1] of the Agriculture Act 1947, applies: Penalty for failing to give required information, or knowingly making any misstatement in respect of it, on summary conviction, fine not exceeding **level 1** on the standard scale.

[Pests Act 1954, s 4 as amended by the Criminal Justice Act 1982, ss 38 and 46—summarised.]

---

1. See ante.

PART II
AMENDMENT OF LAW AS TO USE OF SPRING TRAPS AND AS TO SPREADING MYXOMATOSIS

8–56   8. Restriction on type of trap in England and Wales.   Subject to the provisions of this section, a person shall be guilty of an offence under this subsection if either—

(a) for the purpose of killing or taking animals, he uses, or knowingly permits the use of, any spring trap other than an approved trap, or uses, or knowingly permits the use of, an approved trap for animals or in circumstances for which it is not approved; or

(b) he sells, or exposes or offers for sale, any spring trap other than an approved trap with a view to its being used for a purpose which is unlawful under the foregoing paragraph; or (*c*) he has any spring trap in his possession for a purpose which is unlawful under this subsection.

(2) A person guilty of an offence under the foregoing subsection shall be liable on summary conviction to a fine not exceeding **level 3** on the standard scale.

(3) In subsection (1) of this section any reference to an approved trap refers to a trap of a type and make for the time being specified by order of the Minister of Agriculture and Fisheries as approved by him either generally or subject to conditions as to the animals for which or the circumstances in which it may be used, and any reference to the animals or circumstances for which a trap is approved shall be construed accordingly[1].

(4) Paragraph (*a*) of subsection (1) of this section shall not render unlawful the experimental use of a spring trap under and in accordance with a licence or authority given by the Minister of Agriculture and Fisheries to enable a trap to be developed or tested with a view to its being approved under the last foregoing subsection.

(5) Subsection (1) of this section shall not apply to traps of any description specified by order of the Minister of Agriculture and Fisheries as being adapted solely for the destruction of rats, mice or other small ground vermin.

(6) *Repealed.*

(7) Any order under this section (other than an order made under the last foregoing subsection) may be varied or revoked by a subsequent order of the Minister of Agriculture and Fisheries.

(8) The power of the Minister of Agriculture and Fisheries to make orders under this section shall be exercisable by statutory instrument which, in the case of an order made under subsection (5) or varying or revoking an order so made, shall be subject to annulment by resolution of either House of Parliament.

(9) This section applies to England and Wales, but not to Scotland.

[Pests Act 1954, s 8, as amended by the Statute Law (Repeals) Act 1973, Sch 1, the Criminal Law Act 1977, Sch 6 and the Criminal Justice Act 1982, s 46.]

---

1. The Spring Traps Approval Order 1995, SI 1995/2427 has been made.

8–57   9. Open trapping of hares and rabbits in England and Wales.   (1) Subject to the provisions of this section, a person shall be guilty of an offence under this subsection if, for the purpose of killing or taking hares or rabbits, he uses, or knowingly permits the use of a spring trap elsewhere than in a rabbit hole.

(2) A person guilty of an offence under the foregoing subsection shall be liable on summary conviction to a fine not exceeding **level 3** on the standard scale.

(3) Subsection (1) of this section shall not render unlawful the use of spring traps in such circumstances and subject to such conditions as may be prescribed by regulations made by statutory instrument by the Minister of Agriculture and Fisheries, or their use under and in accordance with a licence given by him—

(4) A licence under this section—

(*a*)   may be embodied in a rabbit clearance order under this Act, or in a notice given under section ninety-eight[1] of the Agriculture Act 1947; and

(*b*)   whether so embodied or not, may be revoked by the Minister (in whole or in part) by giving notice of the revocation in such manner as he thinks sufficient to inform the persons concerned.

(5) This section applies to England and Wales, but not to Scotland.

[Pests Act 1954, s 9, as amended by the Criminal Law Act 1977, Sch 6 and the Criminal Justice Act 1982, s 46.]

---

1. See ante.

8–58   12. Spreading of myxomatosis.   A person shall be guilty of an offence if he knowingly uses or permits the use of a rabbit infected with myxomatosis to spread the disease among uninfected rabbits and shall be liable on summary conviction to a fine not exceeding **level 3** on the standard scale. Provided that this section shall not render unlawful any procedure duly authorised under the Animals (Scientific Procedures) Act 1986[1].

[Pests Act 1954, s 12, as amended by the Criminal Law Act 1977, Sch 6, the Criminal Justice Act 1982, s 46 and the Animals (Scientific Procedures) Act 1986, Sch 3.]

---

1. See title ANIMALS, post.

Agriculture (Safety, Health and Welfare Provisions) Act 1956

(4 & 5 Eliz 2 c 49)

8–59   NOTE.—This Act is amended by the Agriculture (Safety, Health and Welfare Provisions) Act 1956 (Repeals and Modifications) Regulations 1975, SI 1975/46, the Health and Safety (Enforcing Authority) Regulations 1977, SI 1977/746 and the Manual Handling Operations Regulations 1992,

SI 1992/2793 and the Workplace (Health, Safety and Welfare) Regulations 1992, in this PART, HEALTH AND SAFETY, post, consequent upon the enactment of the Health and Safety at Work etc Act 1974.

Safety, Health and Welfare of Employees

8–60   1. Regulations for securing safety and health of employees.   (1)–(5) *Power to make regulations—repealed*[1].

(6) A person who contravenes any provision of regulations under this section shall be guilty of an offence[2].

[Agriculture (Safety, Health and Welfare Provisions) Act 1956, s 1, as amended by SI 1965/46.]

---

1. The following regulations have been made:

Agriculture (Ladders) Regulations 1957, SI 1957/1385 amended by SI 1981/1414;

Agriculture (Circular Saws) Regulations 1959, SI 1959/427 amended by SI 1976/1247, SI 1981/1414, SI 1989/2311 and SI 1992/2932;

Agriculture (Safeguarding of Workplaces) Regulations 1959, SI 1959/428 amended by SI 1976/1247 and SI 1981/1414;

Agriculture (Threshers and Bailers) Regulations 1960, SI 1960/1199 amended by SI 1976/1247, SI 1981/1414, SI 1989/2311 and SI 1992/2932;

Agriculture (Field Machinery) Regulations 1962, SI 1962/1472 amended by SI 1976/1247, SI 1981/1414, SI 1989/2311 and SI 1992/2932;

Agriculture (Tractor Cabs) Regulations 1974, SI 1974/2034 amended by SI 1976/1247, SI 1981/1414, SI 1990/1075.

The enabling provision having been repealed, the above regulations are saved by SI 1975/46, reg 5(3).

2. For penalty, see Health and Safety at Work etc Act 1974, s 33 title HEALTH AND SAFETY, post.

Measures for Avoiding Accidents to Children

8–74   7. Power to prohibit children from riding on or driving vehicles, machinery or implements used in agriculture.   (1)–(2) *Power to make regulations—repealed.*

(3) A person who causes or permits a child, in contravention of the provisions of regulations under this section, to ride on or drive a vehicle or machine or, as the case may be, to ride on an agricultural implement, shall be guilty of an offence[1].

[Agricultural (Safety, Health and Welfare Provisions) Act 1956, s 7, as amended by SI 1975/46.]

---

1. For penalty, see the Health and Safety at Work etc Act 1974, s 33.

Notification and Investigation of Accidents and Diseases

8–75   9. Inquest in case of death by accident.   Duties are placed on a coroner who holds an inquest on the body of a person whose death may have been caused by an accident occurring in the course of agricultural operations.

[Agriculture (Safety, Health and Welfare Provisions) Act 1956, s 9—summarised.]

Supplementary Provisions

8–76   16. Defence available to persons charged with offences.   It shall be a defence of a person charged with a contravention of a provision of this Act or of regulations thereunder to prove that he used all due diligence[1] to secure compliance with that provision.

[Agriculture (Safety, Health and Welfare Provisions) Act 1956, s 16.]

---

1. This is a question of fact, not of law: there is no legal standard of diligence (*RC Hammett Ltd v Crabb*; *RC Hammett v Beldam* (1931) 95 JP 180).

8–77   24. Interpretation.   (1) In this Act, unless the context otherwise requires, the following expressions have the meanings hereby assigned to them respectively, that is to say:

"agriculture" includes dairy-farming, the production of any consumable produce which is grown for sale or for consumption or other use for the purposes of a trade or business or of any other undertaking (whether carried on for profit or not), and the use of land as grazing, meadow or pasture land or orchard or osier land or woodland or for market gardens or nursery grounds, and "agricultural" shall be construed accordingly;

"agricultural holding", "fixed equipment" and "landlord" have the same meanings as in the Agricultural Holdings Act 1986;

"agricultural unit" means land which is occupied as a unit for agricultural purposes;

"consumable produce" means produce grown for consumption or for other use after severance from the land on which it is grown;

"inspector" means an inspector appointed by the Health and Safety Executive under section 19 of the Health and Safety at Work etc Act 1974;

"worker" means a person employed under a contract of service or apprenticeship and "employer" and "employed" have corresponding meanings;

"young person" means a person who is over compulsory school age (construed in accordance with section 8 of the Education Act 1996), but has not attained the age of eighteen.

(2) Any reference in this Act to a contravention of any provision shall include a reference to a failure to comply with that provision.

(3) *Repealed.*

(4) Any reference in this Act to any other enactment shall be construed as a reference to that enactment as amended by any subsequent enactment.

[Agriculture (Safety, Health and Welfare Provisions) Act 1956, s 24, as amended by the Local Government Act 1972, Sch 30, SI 1975/46, SI 1976/1247, SI 1977/746, the Agricultural Holdings Act 1986, Sch 14 and the Education Act 1996, Sch 37.]

Agriculture Act 1957
(5 & 6 Eliz 2 c 57)

8–78 The Agriculture Act 1957, ss 5 and 6, read with s 6 of the European Communities Act 1972, empower the Minister for Agriculture, Fisheries and Food[1] to make orders by statutory instrument providing for the protection of guaranteed prices or assured markets for producers of produce and containing special provisions relating to the importation of livestock.

---

1. See the Transfer of Functions (Agriculture and Food) Order 1999, SI 1999/3141. The functions of the Minister, so far as exercisable in relation to Wales, have been transferred to the National Assembly for Wales, by the National Assembly for Wales (Transfer of Functions) Order 1999, SI 1999/672, art 2, Sch 1.

8–79 7. Penalties. (1) If any person contravenes or fails to comply with any provision of an order under section five or section six of this Act, or knowingly has in his possession or control any livestock[1] imported, removed or brought into the United Kingdom in contravention of an order under the said section six, he shall be liable on summary conviction to a fine not exceeding **level 3** on the standard scale or imprisonment for a term not exceeding **three months★** or both.

(2) If any person wilfully obstructs an authorised officer or other person in the exercise of powers conferred on him by an order under section five or section six of this Act, he shall be liable on summary conviction to imprisonment for a term not exceeding **one month★** or to a fine not exceeding **level 3** on the standard scale or both.

(3) If any person—

(a) knowingly or recklessly makes any false statement for the purpose of obtaining for himself or any other person any sum payable in pursuance of an order under this Part[2] of this Act;

(b) with intent to deceive[3], alters, conceals or defaces any mark applied to produce in pursuance of any such order;

(c) applies to produce, without due authority and with intent to deceive[3], any mark prescribed by or under any such order or applies to produce a mark so closely resembling a prescribed mark as to be calculated to deceive; or

(d) wilfully makes a false entry in any book, account or record which is required to be produced in pursuance of any such order or, with intent to deceive[3], makes use of any such entry which he knows to be false;

he shall be liable[4] on summary conviction to a fine not exceeding **the statutory maximum** or to imprisonment for a term not exceeding **three months** or both, or on conviction on indictment to a fine or to imprisonment for a term not exceeding **two years** or both.

(4) Where an offence under this section which has been committed by a body corporate is proved to have been committed with the consent or connivance of, or to be attributable to any neglect on the part of, any director, manager, secretary or other similar officer, of the body corporate, or any person who was purporting to act in any such capacity, he as well as the body corporate shall be deemed to be guilty of that offence and shall be liable to be proceeded against and punished accordingly.

[Agriculture Act 1957, s 7, as amended by the Criminal Law Act 1977, ss 28 and 32 and the Criminal Justice Act 1982, ss 35, 38, 40 and 46.]

★**"51 weeks" substituted by the Criminal Justice Act 2003, Sch 26, from a date to be appointed.**

1. "Livestock" includes the carcases of livestock (Agriculture Act 1957, s 6(6)).

2. Part I—Guaranteed Prices and Assured Markets—includes ss 1–11.

3. To deceive is by falsehood to induce a state of mind; to defraud is by deceit to induce a course of action (*Re London and Globe Finance Corpn Ltd* [1903] 1 Ch 728, 82 JP 447; *R v Wines* [1953] 2 All ER 1497, 118 JP 49).

4. For procedure in respect of this offence which is triable either way, see Magistrates' Courts Act 1980, ss 17A–21 in PART I: MAGISTRATES' COURTS, PROCEDURE, ante.

Agricultural Marketing Act 1958
(1958 c 47)

8–80 Under this Act, persons who are substantially representative of the producers[1] may submit a scheme regulating the marketing of an agricultural product[2] by the producers thereof in a defined area. The draft of the scheme, with or without modifications, will be laid before each House of Parliament and after they have resolved that the scheme shall be approved, the Minister[3] shall make an order[4] approving the scheme. Every scheme shall provide for the registration of producers and shall constitute a board[5] to administer the scheme. Every scheme except a substitutional scheme[6] shall require a poll of the registered producers[7] to be taken on the question whether the scheme shall remain in force. It shall provide for the manner in which polls are to be taken and may impose penalties for furnishing false information relating to the regulated product[8] which is to be furnished by every registered producer before or at the time of voting. The Minister must cause a list of producers to be compiled. The scheme may provide for the regulation of marketing and encouragement of co-operation, education, and research. The scheme shall provide, *inter alia*—(*a*) for requiring that no sale of the regulated product shall be made by any producer who is not either a registered producer or a person exempted from registration by or under the provisions of the scheme; and (*b*) for requiring the disciplinary committee[9] to impose on, and recover from, any registered producer, such monetary penalties as may be specified, so, however, that no such penalty may be imposed in respect of a contravention[10] of a scheme which constitutes an offence under any other Act.

1. "Producer" means, in relation to any scheme, any person who produces the regulated product (s 52(1)). For the purposes of a scheme regulating the marketing of live stock of any kind, every person whose business it is to keep live stock of any kind for the purpose of breeding from it or selling it in an improved condition shall (except in so far as the scheme otherwise provides) be deemed to produce it (s 51(3)).

2. "Agricultural product" includes any product of agriculture or horticulture and any article of food or drink wholly or partly manufactured or derived from any such product, and fleeces and the skins of animals (s 52(1)). Schemes relating to fresh horticultural produce must conform with regulations made under Part III of the Agriculture and Horticulture Act 1964 (Agriculture and Horticulture Act 1964, s 22(3)), post.

3. "Minister" is defined extensively in s 52(1) of the Act: generally it is the Minister for Agriculture, Fisheries and Food. See the Transfer of Functions (Agriculture and Food) Order 1999, SI 1999/3141. The functions of the Minister, so far as exercisable in relation to Wales, have been transferred to the National Assembly for Wales, by the National Assembly for Wales (Transfer of Functions) Order 1999, SI 1999/672, art 2, Sch 1. Residual functions of the Secretary of State and the Secretary of State for Wales were transferred to the Minister of Agriculture, Fisheries and Food by the Transfer of Functions (Agriculture and Fisheries) Order 2000, SI 2000/1812.

4. The making of the order shall be conclusive evidence that the requirements of the Act have been complied with and that the order and the scheme approved thereby have been duly made and approved and are within the powers conferred by this Act (s 2(11)).

5. "Board" means a board administering a scheme, and in relation to any scheme means the board administering that scheme (s 52(1)).

6. "Substitutional scheme" means a scheme which revokes one or more existing schemes, and is such that at the time when it comes into force—(*a*) every person is entitled to be registered as a producer thereunder who was entitled to be registered as a producer under the existing scheme or one or more of the existing schemes; and (*b*) no person is entitled to be registered as a producer thereunder who was not entitled to be registered as a producer under the existing scheme or any of the existing schemes (s 52(1)). A declaration by the Minister, contained in an order approving a scheme, that the scheme is a substitutional scheme shall be conclusive evidence of that fact (s 52(2)).

7. "Registered producer" means, in relation to any scheme, a producer registered under that scheme (s 52(1)).

8. "Regulated product" means, in relation to any scheme, any product the marketing of which is regulated by the scheme, but does not (except in the expression "consumers of the regulated product") include any product in so far as it is produced outside the area to which the scheme is applicable (s 52(1)).

9. The scheme shall provide for a committee of the board, known as the disciplinary committee, to be set up, and for the regulation of the proceedings of such a committee. The disciplinary committee will carry out the disciplinary duties of the board under this paragraph (s 9).

10. "Contravention" includes, in relation to a provision of this Act or of a scheme, a failure to comply with the provision, and the expression "contravenes" shall be construed accordingly (s 52(1)).

8–81 6. Penalty for selling in contravention of scheme. Any producer who sells the regulated produce in contravention of the provisions of the scheme made in pursuance of sub-s (1) of this section shall for each offence be liable[1] on summary conviction to a fine not exceeding **the statutory maximum**, or on conviction on indictment to a fine, and in either case to an additional fine not exceeding half the price at which the product was sold: Provided that the fines imposed on summary conviction for any offence under this subsection shall not exceed in the aggregate **the statutory maximum**[2].
[Agricultural Marketing Act 1958, s 6(6), as amended by Criminal Justice Act 1967, 3rd Sch and Criminal Law Act 1977, ss 28 and 32.]

1. For procedure in respect of this offence which is triable either way, see Magistrates' Courts Act 1980, ss 17A–21, in PART I: MAGISTRATES' COURTS, PROCEDURE, ante.

2. There is no liability to penalty if the defendant proves that the contravention was necessary for the performance of a contract which, by reason of s 17(1), (2), was not, at the time of the contravention, void or unenforceable (s 17(5)).

8–82 47. Restrictions on disclosing certain information obtained under the Act. (1) No information with respect to any particular undertaking (other than the undertaking of a board) shall, without the consent of the owner of that undertaking, be included in any report laid before Parliament in pursuance of this Act or in any recommendations of an Agricultural Marketing Reorganisation Commission published in pursuance of this Act.

(2) No information obtained by any person in the exercise of any power conferred on him relating to polls, or in the exercise of any power conferred on any board, consumers' committee, committee

of investigation or Agricultural Marketing Reorganisation Commission, shall be disclosed by him (*summarised*).

Provided that nothing in this subsection shall restrict the disclosure of information—

(*a*) made by a board in compliance with a requirement of the Minister of Agriculture, Fisheries and Food or the Secretary of State under section seventy-two of the Diseases of Animals Act 1950;

(*aa*) made to the Competition Commission or to any member, of that Commission or to any of the staff of that commission, or to the Director General of Fair Trading or any of the staff appointed by that Director General, if it is made for the purpose of enabling the Commission or the Director General to perform any functions of theirs or his under the Fair Trading Act 1973 or the Competition Act 1980;

(*b*) made for the purposes of legal proceedings (including arbitrations) under this Act or any scheme, or for the purpose of any report of such proceedings;

(*c*) if, and in so far as, the disclosure is required or authorised by this Act or any scheme.

(3) Any person who discloses any information[1] in contravention of the last foregoing subsection shall be liable[2] on summary conviction to imprisonment for a term not exceeding **three months** or to a fine not exceeding **the statutory maximum**, or both such imprisonment and such fine, or on conviction on indictment to imprisonment for a term not exceeding **two years**, or a fine, or to both such imprisonment and fine.

[Agricultural Marketing Act 1958, s 47 as amended by Criminal Law Act 1977, ss 28, and 32, the Competition Act 1980, s 19 and SI 1999/506.]

---

1. This prohibition does not include giving evidence under legal process in court (*Rowell v Pratt* [1938] AC 101, [1937] 3 All ER 660).

2. For procedure in respect of this offence which is triable either way, see Magistrates' Courts Act 1980, ss 17A–21, in Part I: Magistrates' Court, Procedure, ante.

8–83 48. Offences committed by bodies corporate. Where an offence under this Act committed by a body corporate is proved to have been committed with the consent or approval of any director[1], manager, secretary or other officer of the body corporate he, as well as the body corporate, shall be deemed to be guilty of the offence and shall be liable to be proceeded against and punished accordingly.

[Agricultural Marketing Act 1958, s 48.]

---

1. See *Dean v Hiesler* [1942] 2 All ER 340, 106 JP 282.

Weeds Act 1959
(7 & 8 Eliz 2 c 54)

8–84 The Minister of Agriculture, Fisheries and Food (and the Secretary of State for Wales; SI 1978/272), if satisfied that injurious weeds to which this Act applies[1] are growing upon any land[2], may serve upon the occupier[3] thereof a written notice requiring him, within a specified time, to take necessary action to prevent the weeds from spreading (s 1). The Minister may make a code of practice for the purpose of providing guidance on how to prevent the spread of ragwort. If the code appears to a court to be relevant to any question arising in proceedings it is to be taken into account in determining that question (s 1A as inserted by the Ragwort Control Act 2003). Unreasonable failure to comply is a summary offence[4]: Penalty, fine, not exceeding **level 3** on the standard scale (s 2 amended by the Criminal Justice Act 1982, ss 35, 38 and 46). Proceedings may be taken only by the Minister, but he may delegate his powers to the council of a county or metropolitan district (s 5, amended by the Local Government Act 1985, Sch 8).

Authorised persons have a power of entry upon and inspection of land after notice to the occupier. Obstruction of such persons is a summary offence: Penalty, fine not exceeding **level 3** on the standard scale (s 4 amended by the Criminal Justice Act 1982, ss 35, 38 and 46).

Provision is made regarding the service of notices and where any notice is served on a tenant a copy must be served on the landlord (s 6).

[Weeds Act 1959—summarised.]

---

1. These are spear thistle, creeping or field thistle, curled dock, broad-leaved dock, and ragwort, and such additional injurious weeds as the Minister may prescribe (s 1 (2)).

2. From the definition of "occupier", infra, it is evident that "land" may include a road.

3. "Occupier" means, in the case of any public road, the authority by whom the road is being maintained, and, in the case of unoccupied land, the person entitled to the occupation thereof (s 11(2)). It is apparent that this definition is not comprehensive.

4. If a failure in respect of which a person is convicted is not remedied within 14 days thereafter, he is thereby guilty of a further offence and liable to a further penalty (s 2(2)).

Plant Varieties and Seeds Act 1964
(1964 c 14)

PART II
SEED AND SEED POTATOES
Regulations of sales

8–87   16. Seeds regulations.   The Minister of Agriculture, Fisheries and Food may make regulations for the purpose of carrying this Part of the Act into effect (s 16(1)–(6) (*summarised*)). References in this Act to seeds refer to seeds for sowing (s 38(2)).
(7) If any person—

(a) in a statutory statement[1] includes anything which is false in a material particular, or
(b) contravenes any provisions contained in seed regulations he shall be liable on summary conviction to a fine not exceeding **level 5** on the standard scale[2].

(8) The Ministers acting jointly may make seeds regulations[3] for the whole of Great Britain.
[Plant Varieties and Seeds Act 1964, s 16, as amended by the European Communities Act 1972, Sch 4, and SI 1977/1112, the Criminal Justice Act 1982, ss 40 and 46 and the Agriculture Act 1986, s 2.]

---

1. Prescribed by regulations made under s 16.
2. For provisions relating to the prosecution of offences, including the venue thereof, see s 35, post.
3. The Seeds (National Lists of Varieties) Regulations 2001, SI 2001/3510 made under s 2 of the European Communities Act 1972 and listed ante, regulate the marketing of agricultural and vegetable seeds: contravention of regs 11 or 18 is punishable on summary conviction with a fine not exceeding the **statutory maximum** or imprisonment not exceeding **three months** or **both** or on conviction on indictment with a **fine** or imprisonment not exceeding **two years** or **both**. The Seeds (Registration, Licensing and Enforcement) Regulations 2002, SI 2002/3176 amended by SI 2004/2390 and SI 2005/2676 and the Seed (Registration, Licensing and Enforcement) (Wales) Regulations 2005, SI 2005/3038 provide for the registration of all seed merchants, seed packers and seed processors, and for the prohibition of marketing of particular seeds by a person whose seeds have failed to satisfy the requirements of regulations. Provision is also made for the licensing of seed testing stations, crop inspectors and seed samplers.

    The following regulations apply to specific varieties:
    Forest Reproductive Materials, SI 1977/891 amended by SI 1977/1264 and SI 1992/3078;
    Seed Potatoes, SI 1991/2206 amended by SI 1992/1031, SI 1993/1878, SI 2000/1788 (England), and SI 2001/3510 and 3666 (Wales);
    Beet Seed (England) Regulations 2002, SI 2002/3171 amended by SI 2004/2385 and SI 2005/2671;
    Fodder Plant Seed (England) Regulations 2002, SI 2002/3172 amended by SI 2004/2386 and SI 2005/2673;
    Cereal Seed (England) Regulations 2002, SI 2002/3173 amended by SI 2004/2387 and SI 2005/2672;
    Oil and Fibre Plant Seed (England) Regulations 2002, SI 2002/3174 amended by SI 2003/3101, SI 2004/2388 and SI 2005/2674;
    Vegetable Seed (England) Regulations 2002, SI 2002/3175 amended by SI 2004/2389 and SI 2005/2675;
    Oil and Fibre Plant Seed (Wales) Regulations 2004, SI 2004/2881;
    Fodder Plant Seed (Wales) Regulations 2005, SI 2005/1207;
    Vegetable Seed (Wales) Regulations 2005, SI 20053035;
    Cereal Seed (Wales) Regulations 2005, SI 2005/3036;
    Beet Seed (Wales) Regulations 2005, SI 2005/3037.

8–88   18. Defences in proceedings for offences against seeds regulations.   (1) If and so far as seeds regulations for the purposes of this section prescribe limits of variation in relation to the particulars in a statutory statement[1], it shall be a defence to proceedings under this Act for including in a statutory statement any false particulars to prove that the mis-statements in the particulars alleged to be false do not exceed the limits of variation so prescribed.
(2) Subject to the provisions of this section, it shall be a defence—

(a) to proceedings under this Part of this Act for including false particulars in a statutory statement,
(b) to proceedings under this Part of this Act for any other offence,

to prove—

(i) that the accused took all reasonable precautions against committing an offence of the kind alleged and had not at the time of the alleged offence any reason to suspect that an offence was being committed by him, and
(ii) where the accused obtained the seeds to which the alleged offence relates from some other person, that on demand by or on behalf of the prosecutor the accused gave all the information in his power with respect to the name and address of that other person, and with respect to any statutory statement or other document in his possession or power relating to the seeds, and the contract of sale.

(3) If in any proceedings as are mentioned in subsection (2)(a) of this section any of the particulars alleged to be false are particulars which, by seeds regulations, are to be particulars ascertained by means of a test made in accordance with the regulations, the defence under subsection (2) of this section shall not be available unless it is proved—

(a) that those particulars were ascertained on such a test and that the test was made not earlier than the date, if any, prescribed by seeds regulations for the purpose, or

(b) that—

    (i) the accused purchased the seeds from another person who, in connection with the sale, duly delivered to the accused a statutory statement giving particulars of the seeds which were the same as the particulars alleged to be false, and

    (ii) the accused had no reason to believe that paragraph (a) of this subsection did not apply in relation to those particulars.

[Plant Varieties and Seeds Act 1964, s 18, as amended by the European Communities Act 1972, Sch 4.]

---

1. Prescribed by regulations made under section 16.

8–89 19. Presumption as respects statutory statements under seeds regulations. For the purposes of this Part of this Act and of any seed regulations, any statutory statement made as respects seeds which are in distinct portions shall be presumed to be made both as respects the seeds as a whole and also as respects each portion taken separately.
[Plant Varieties and Seeds Act 1964, s 19.]

Official testing stations

8–90 24. Official testing stations and certificates of test. Provision is made for the establishment and maintenance of seed testing stations (sub-ss (1)–(5) (*summarised*)).

(6) A certificate of the result of a test at an official seed testing station of a sample taken for the purposes of this Act, and purporting to be issued by an officer of an official seed testing station—

(a) if the sample was taken by an authorised officer, shall, if a copy of the certificate has been served on the accused with the summons or complaint, be sufficient evidence of the facts stated in the certificate in any proceedings for an offence under this Part of this Act, and

(b) if the sample was taken by a person other than an authorised officer in order to obtain the test for the purposes of section 17(3) of this Act, shall be sufficient evidence of the facts stated in the certificate in any such legal proceedings as are mentioned in that subsection,

unless, in either case, either party to the proceedings requires that the person under whose direction the test was made be called as a witness; and in that event (*applies to Scotland*).

(7) In any proceedings for an offence under this Part of this Act in which a copy of a certificate of the result of a test has been served with the summons or complaint in pursuance of paragraph (a) of the last foregoing subsection, the accused, unless the court otherwise directs, shall not be entitled to require that the person under whose direction the test was made be called as a witness unless he has, at least three clear days before the day on which the summons is returnable or, in Scotland, the case proceeds to trial, given notice to the prosecutor that he intends to do so.
[Plant Varieties and Seeds Act 1964, s 24.]

Supplemental

8–91 25. Powers of entry. (1) The powers of entry conferred by subsections (3) and (4) of this section may be exercised for the purpose of exercising—

(a) the further powers conferred by subsections (5) and (6) of this section, or

(b) any powers of calling for, inspecting or taking copies of records or other documents conferred by seeds regulations,

or for the purpose of ascertaining whether there is, or has been, on or in connection with the premises (including any vehicle or vessel) any contravention of any provision contained in this Part of this Act or in seeds regulations.

(2) This section shall not authorise entry into any premises which are used exclusively as a private dwelling.

(3) Any person duly authorised by the Minister in that behalf may, on production if so required of his authority, at all reasonable hours enter any premises which he has reasonable cause to believe to be used for any purpose of a business in the course of which seeds are sold, whether the sale is by wholesale or retail, and whether the person conducting it acts as principal or agent.

(4) Any person duly authorised by the Minister in that behalf may, on production if so required of his authority, at all reasonable hours enter any premises on which he has reasonable cause to believe that there are any seed potatoes.[1]

(5) A person may, on any premises (including any vehicle or vessel) which he has power under this section to enter for the purpose of exercising the powers conferred by this subsection, examine any seeds which he finds there and may without payment take samples of any seeds so found.

(6) The owner of any seeds which are offered or exposed for sale, or are stored for purposes of sale, or any person authorised to sell those seeds, may be required by a person duly authorised by the Minister in that behalf to deliver to him such a statement, if any, as the person selling them would by seeds regulations be obliged to deliver to a purchaser of those seeds, and to deliver it within the time prescribed for such a statement.

(7) If any person fails to comply with a requirement under subsection (6) of this section he shall be liable on summary conviction to a fine not exceeding **level 5** on the standard scale and references in this Part of this Act to a statutory statement shall include references to a statement delivered under subsection (6) of this section.

(8) This section shall apply as respects—

(a) all kinds of seeds in respect of which an offence may under any circumstances be committed under seeds regulations as for the time being in force,

(b) *Repealed.*

(9) A person who obstructs or impedes any person acting in the exercise of the powers conferred by this section shall be liable on summary conviction to a fine not exceeding **level 3** on the standard scale.

[Plant Varieties and Seeds Act 1964, s 25, as amended by the European Communities Act 1972, Schs 3 and 4, the Criminal Justice Act 1982, ss 38, 39 and 46 and Sch 3 and SI 1991/2206.]

---

1. Further modified, in relation to seed potatoes in Scotland by SI 2000/201.

8–92 26. Use of samples in criminal proceedings. (1) Evidence shall not be adduced in proceedings for an offence under this Part of this Act respecting a sample taken by an authorised officer unless the sample was taken in the manner prescribed by seeds regulations[1].

(2) Seeds regulations[1] shall provide for the sample being divided into at least two parts, and for one of the parts being given to the owner of the seeds or to such other person as may be prescribed by seeds regulations, and shall provide for a third part of the sample to be retained for production in all cases where use of it may be made by the court under this section.

(3) A certificate in the form prescribed by seeds regulations[1] purporting to be issued by an authorised officer and stating that a sample was taken in the prescribed manner shall be sufficient evidence of the facts stated in the certificate.

(4) If part of a sample taken by an authorised officer is sent to the chief officer of an official testing station, it shall be so sent as soon as practicable after the sample is taken, and the person to whom any other part of the sample is given shall be informed before the first-mentioned part is sent.

(5) A copy of a certificate issued by an official testing station stating the result of a test of part of a sample taken by an authorised officer shall be sent to the person to whom any other part of the sample is given.

(6) In any proceedings for an offence under this Part of this Act in respect of seeds which have been sampled by an authorised officer, the summons shall not be made returnable, and, in Scotland[2], the case shall not proceed to trial, less than fourteen days from the day on which the summons or complaint is served, and a copy of any certificate of an official testing station which the prosecutor intends to adduce as evidence shall be served with the summons or complaint.

(7) In proceedings for including in a statutory statement false particulars concerning matters which are under seeds regulations[1] to be ascertained, for the purpose of the statement, by a test of seeds, if any sample of the seeds has been taken by an authorised officer, the third part of that sample required by seeds regulations[1] to be retained as mentioned in subsection (2) of this section shall be produced at the hearing.

(8) The court may, if it thinks fit, on the request of either party, cause the part so produced to be sent to the chief officer of an official testing station, who shall transmit to the court a certificate of the result of a test of that part of the sample.

(9) If, in a case where an appeal is brought, no action has been taken under the last foregoing subsection the provisions of that subsection shall apply also to the court by which the appeal is heard.

(10) A sample taken before the coming into force of this Part of this Act in accordance with section 4 of the Seeds Act 1920, shall be regarded as taken in the prescribed manner for the purposes of subsection (1) of this section.

[Plant Varieties and Seeds Act 1964, s 26.]

---

1. These are listed in a footnote to s 16(8), ante.
2. Further modified, in relation to seed potatoes in Scotland by SI 2000/201.

8–93 27. Tampering with samples. (1) If any person—

(a) tampers with any seeds so as to procure that a sample taken in the manner prescribed by seeds regulations for any purpose does not correctly represent the bulk of the seeds, or

(b) tampers with any sample so taken, or

(c) with intent to deceive sends, or causes or allows to be sent to any official testing station or licensed testing establishment, to be tested for any purpose, a sample of seeds which to his knowledge does not correctly represent the bulk of the seeds,

he shall be liable on summary conviction to a fine not exceeding **level 5** on the standard scale or to imprisonment for a term not exceeding **three months***, or to both.

(2) In this section "licensed testing establishment" means an establishment licensed under seeds regulations for the testing of seeds.

[Plant Varieties and Seeds Act 1964, s 27 as amended by the Criminal Justice Act 1982, ss 39 and 46 and Sch 3.]

*"51 weeks" substituted by the Criminal Justice Act 2003, Sch 26, from a date to be appointed.

8–94   28. Institution of criminal proceedings.   (1) Notwithstanding anything in section 127(1) of the Magistrates' Courts Act 1980, or section 23 of the Summary Jurisdiction (Scotland) Act 1954 (time limit for proceedings), where a part of a sample has been tested at an official testing station proceedings for including in a statutory statement false particulars concerning the matters which are under seeds regulations to be ascertained, for the purposes of the statement, by a test of the seeds, being proceedings relating to the seeds from which the sample was taken, may be brought at any time not more than six months from the time when the sample was taken.

(2) If at any time before a test is begun at an official testing station to ascertain whether a part of a sample of seeds is of a specified variety or type, and not more than six months after the sample was taken, the person to whom any other part of the sample was given, or any other person, is notified in writing by an authorised officer that it is intended so to test the seeds and that, after the test, proceedings may be brought against that person for including in a statutory statement a false statement that seeds were of a specified variety or type, then notwithstanding anything in the said section 127(1) or 23, any such proceedings relating to the seeds from which the sample was taken may be brought against the person so notified at any time not more than two years from the time when the sample was taken.

A certificate purporting to be issued by an authorised officer and stating that a person was so notified shall be sufficient evidence of that fact.

(2A) Notwithstanding anything in section 127(1) of the Magistrates' Courts Act 1980 or section 136 of the Criminal Procedure (Scotland) Act 1995, proceedings for contravening a provision contained in seeds regulations may be brought at any time not more than one year from the time when the contravention occurred.

(3) Proceedings for an offence under this Part of this Act relating to a statutory statement which has been delivered to a purchaser of seeds, or relating to seeds which have been sold and delivered to the purchaser may be brought before a court having jurisdiction at the place of delivery of the statement or seeds.

[Plant Varieties and Seeds Act 1964, s 28 as amended by the Magistrates' Courts Act 1980, Sch 7 and the Plant Varieties Act 1997, s 47.]

8–95   29. Application of Part II to seed potatoes, etc.   (1) This part of this Act applies to seed potatoes, to any other vegetative propagating material and to silvicultural planting material as it applies to seeds, and accordingly, except where the context otherwise requires, references in this Part of this Act to seeds includes references to seed potatoes, to any other vegetative propagating material and to silvicultural planting material.

(2) The Forestry Commissioners may establish and maintain an official seed testing station for silvicultural propagating and planting material and seeds regulations may confer on those Commissioners any functions the regulations may confer on a Minister, and the Commissioners may charge or authorise the charging of fees for services given at any such station or in connection with any such functions; and accordingly—

(a)   references in this Part of this Act to an authorised officer shall include an officer of those Commissioners; and

(b)   in section 25 above the references in subsections (3), (4) and (6) to a person duly authorised by the Minister shall include a person duly authorised by the Commissioners.

Any expenses incurred or fees received by the Commissioners by virtue of this subsection shall be defrayed, or as the case may be treated, in accordance with section 41 of the Forestry Act 1967.

(3) In relation to matters concerning silvicultural propagating or planting material or concerning the Forestry Commissioners, "the Minister" shall in this Part of this Act mean, in relation to Wales and Monmouthshire, the Secretary of State, and the reference in section 16(8) to the Ministers shall be construed accordingly.

[Plant Varieties and Seeds Act 1964, s 29, as amended by the European Communities Act 1972, Sch 4 and SI 2000/746.]

8–96   30. Interpretation of Part II.   (1) In this Part of this Act, unless the context otherwise requires—

"authorised officer" means an officer of the Minister or a person authorised by the Minister to execute this Part of this Act;

"official testing station" means an official seed testing station maintained under this Part of this Act;

"seeds" includes agricultural and horticultural seeds, vegetable seeds, flower seeds, seeds of grasses, whether used for agricultural purposes or other purposes, and seeds of trees;

"statutory statement" means a statement given in pursuance of seeds regulations, whether the statement be in the form of a notice or other document, or in the form of particulars given on any label or container or package, or in any other form, and includes a statement delivered under section 25(6) of this Act.

(2) In this Part of this Act references to a contravention of any provision contained in this Act or in seeds regulations include references to a failure to comply with such a provision, and references to a contravention of any provision contained in seeds regulations include references to anything which, by the regulations, is expressed to be an offence against a provision contained in the regulations and also include references to any failure to comply with a condition subject to which an exemption is granted by or under seeds regulations.

(3) In this Part of this Act any reference to an offence under this Part of this Act includes, unless the context otherwise requires, a reference to a contravention of any provision contained in seeds regulations.

[Plant Varieties and Seeds Act 1964, s 30, as amended by the European Communities Act 1972, Sch 4.]

PART III
CONTROL OF IMPORTS AND PREVENTION OF CROSS-POLLINATION

8–97 **33. Measures to prevent injurious cross-pollination affecting crops of seeds.** (1) This section shall have effect for the purpose of maintaining the purity of seed of any types and varieties of plants of any species of the genus Allium, Beta or Brassica.

(2) The Minister may by order bring this section into force in an area in any part of Great Britain in which persons are engaged in growing crops of seeds of any type or variety of plant mentioned in subsection (1) of this section if he is satisfied that in that area satisfactory arrangements (whether legally enforceable or not) have been made for locating such crops so as to isolate them from crops or plants which might cause injurious cross-pollination.

(3) An order under this section—

(a) shall be made after consultation with the persons responsible for the arrangements mentioned in subsection (2) of this section, and with persons representative of such other interests as appear to the Minister to be concerned, and

(b) shall be made by statutory instrument and may be varied or revoked by a subsequent order so made.

(4) An order under this section—

(a) shall state which of the types and varieties of plants mentioned in subsection (1) of this section are protected by the order, and

(b) shall specify the kinds of crops and plants which are to be controlled in the area to which the order relates, and

(c) may relate to more than one area and, if so, may make different provision under paragraphs (a) and (b) of this subsection in respect of the different areas to which it relates;

and in this section, in relation to an area to which an order under this section relates—

(i) "protected crop" means a crop of a type or variety of plant which is protected by the order in that area, being a crop grown for the purpose of producing seeds, and

(ii) "controlled crops of plants" means crops, grown for any purpose, of the types or varieties of plants which are protected by the order in that area, and such additional kinds of crops or plants, whether grown or self-sown and whether of those or any other types or varieties, as may be specified in the order for the purposes of this definition in that area.

(5) If in an area where this section is in force controlled crops or plants are growing and, on an application made in accordance with Schedule 7 to this Act, the Minister is satisfied—

(a) that they are causing or may cause injurious cross-pollination in a protected crop which is being grown in the area, and

(b) in the case of controlled crops or plants which are not self-sown, that the person growing them did not give to the persons responsible for the arrangements mentioned in subsection (2) of this section such notice of his intention to grow those crops or plants to the flowering stage as would have enabled them to take any appropriate steps for altering the arrangements,

the Minister may serve a notice on the occupier of the land where the controlled crops or plants are growing requiring him to take such steps as may be specified in the notice for the purpose of preventing any of the controlled crops or plants from causing or continuing to cause injurious cross-pollination in the protected crop.

(6) If the person served with a notice under this section does not comply with any requirement in the notice, the Minister may enter and do what that person has failed to do or, if in the opinion of the Minister that would no longer serve the purpose for which the notice was served, may take such other action as appears to the Minister appropriate for that purpose; and where, when the default occurs, further obligations remain under the notice, the Minister may also take such action as appears to him appropriate to meet the purposes for which those further obligations were imposed.

The Minister may recover from the person on whom the notice was served a sum equal to the reasonable cost incurred by the Minister in taking any action under this subsection.

(7) Without prejudice to the power of proceeding under the last foregoing subsection, a person who unreasonably fails to comply with any requirement in a notice under this section shall be liable on summary conviction to a fine not exceeding **level 3** on the standard scale.

(8) A person duly authorised by the Minister may, on production if so required of his authority, at all reasonable hours enter on any land (but not into any dwelling-house) in an area where this section is in force for the purpose of ascertaining whether controlled crops or plants are growing on the land or of inspecting and taking samples of any controlled crops or plants growing on the land.

(9) A notice under this section or Schedule 7 to this Act may be served by leaving it at, or sending it by post addressed to, the last known address of the person on whom it is to be served, and if it is not practicable after reasonable inquiry to ascertain his name and address, the notice may be served by addressing it to him as "the occupier" of the land and affixing it or a copy of it to some conspicuous object on the land.

(10) A person who obstructs or impedes a person acting in the exercise of the powers conferred by subsection (6) or subsection (8) of this section shall be liable on summary conviction to a fine not exceeding **level 1** on the standard scale.

(11) In this section, and in the said Schedule—

"the occupier" means, in the case of unoccupied land, the person entitled to occupy the land;
"protected crop" and "controlled crops or plants" have the meanings respectively assigned by subsection (4) of this section.

[Plant Varieties and Seeds Act 1964, s 33 as amended by the Criminal Justice Act 1982, ss 35, 38 and 46.]

PART IV
GENERAL

8–98 34. The gazette. (1) The Ministers shall from time to time publish a gazette (in this Act referred to as "the gazette"), and shall use the gazette as one of the means of publishing notice of matters to be published under this Act or Part I of the Plant Varieties Act 1997.

(2) It shall be no defence in civil or criminal proceedings to show that at any time a person did not know of an entry in the register under section 18 of the Plant Varieties Act 1997, if before that time notice of that entry or fact had been published in the gazette.

[Plant Varieties and Seeds Act 1964, s 34 as amended by the European Communities Act 1972, Sch 3 and the Plant Varieties Act 1997, s 51.]

8–99 35. General provisions as to offences. (1) Where an offence punishable under this Act committed by a body corporate is proved to have been committed with the consent or connivance of, or to be attributable to any neglect on the part of, any director, manager, secretary or other similar officer of the body corporate, or any person who was purporting to act in any such capacity, he, as well as the body corporate, shall be guilty of that offence and shall be liable to be proceeded against and punished accordingly.

(2) Proceedings for any offence punishable under this Act may (without prejudice to any jurisdiction exercisable apart from this subsection) be taken against a person before the appropriate court in Great Britain having jurisdiction in the place where that person is for the time being.

[Plant Varieties and Seeds Act 1964, s 35.]

Agriculture and Horticulture Act 1964[1]
(1964 c 28)

PART III
GRADING AND TRANSPORT OF FRESH HORTICULTURAL PRODUCE

Grading of produce

8–100 11. Power to prescribe grades. (1) The Ministers[1] may in relation to any description of fresh horticultural produce[2] by regulations designate and define grades of quality, and prescribe for each grade the form of a label[3] for indicating that produce in connection with which the label is used falls within that grade.

(2) Regulations under subsection (1) above may provide that a label recognised under the law of any country outside Great Britain as indicating that produce in connection with which it is used is of a quality not inferior to that required for a grade prescribed under that subsection shall be treated for the purposes of this Part of this Act as if it were in the form so prescribed for that grade.

(3) Regulations under subsection (1) above shall not apply to produce of any description for the time being subject to Community grading rules; but in relation to any such produce the Ministers may by regulations[4]—

(a) make additional provision as to the form of any label required for the purpose of those rules or as to the inclusion in any such label of additional particulars (not effecting the grading of the produce);

(b) provide for the application, subject to any modifications specified in the regulations, of all or any of the following provisions of this Part of this Act as if the produce were regulated produce and as if the standards of quality established by those rules were prescribed grades.

[Agriculture and Horticulture Act 1964, s 11, as amended by the European Communities Act 1972, Sch 4.]

1. The Minister for Agriculture, Fisheries and Food. Any expenses incurred or fees received by the Commissioners by virtue of this subsection shall be defrayed, or as the case may be treated, in accordance with section 41 of the Forestry Act 1967.

2. Defined in s 24, post.

3. The expression "label" includes such a device as is described in s 24, post.

4. See the Grading of Horticulture Produce (Amendment) Regulations 1973, SI 1973/22, and SI 1983/1053, which provide for the application, subject to modifications specified therein, of ss 13–20 and 22–24 of this Act as if produce of any description for the time being subject to Community grading rules were regulated produce and as if the standards of quality established by those rules were prescribed grades.

8–101 12. Duties as to grading of produce. (1) Except in such circumstances as are mentioned in subsection (2) below, a person shall not sell any fresh horticultural produce[1] of a description in relation to which grades of quality are designated and defined under s 11(1) above (in this Part of this Act referred to as "regulated produce") unless the produce falls within a prescribed grade and is packed in a container[2] to which is affixed a label[3] in the form prescribed for that or any lower grade or, if not packed in a container, has affixed to it such a label.

(2) The circumstances referred to in subsection (1) above are as follows:

(a) a sale of the produce by retail;

(b) a sale where the produce is to be transported to a country outside the United Kingdom by, or to the order of, the buyer;

(c) a sale where the produce is to be used by the buyer in manufacturing or producing any commodity for sale or other disposal by him;

(d) a direct sale[4] by the producer of any produce to a person who undertakes—

(i) that before any sale by him of any of the produce, not being a sale such as is mentioned in paragraph (b) or (c) above, the produce will be sorted into the prescribed grades and produce the quality of which is inferior to that required for the lowest prescribed grade will be separated from other produce, and

(ii) that on any sale by him of any of the produce falling within a prescribed grade, not being a sale such as is mentioned in paragraph (b) or (c) above, the produce will be packed in a container to which is affixed a label in the form prescribed for that or any lower grade or, if not packed in a container, will have affixed to it such a label; or

(e) a direct sale[4] by the producer of any produce where the produce is, or is to be, delivered at premises, or at any stall or vehicle, from which it is to be sold by retail.

(3) The Ministers may if they think fit by order provide that subsection (2) above have effect, in relation to such sales as are described in the order, as if paragraph (e) were omitted; and an order made under this subsection may be varied or revoked by a subsequent order made by the Ministers.

(4) In this section "direct sale" means a sale where negotiations on behalf of the vendor are not conducted by any agent other than a person employed by him under a contract of service.

[Agriculture and Horticulture Act 1964, s 12.]

1. Defined in s 24, post.

2. The expression "container" is defined in s 24, post.

3. See the Grading of Horticulture Produce (Amendment) Regulations 1973, SI 1973/22, and SI 1983/1053, which provide for the application, subject to modifications specified therein, of ss 13–20 and 22–24 of this Act as if produce of any description for the time being subject to Community grading rules were regulated produce and as if the standards of quality established by those rules were prescribed grades.

4. As defined by sub-s (4), post.

8–102 13. Powers as to entry of premises and regrading of produce[1]. (1) A person authorised in that behalf either by the Minister[2] or the Secretary of State (in this Part of this Act referred to as an "authorised officer"), on producing, if so required, a duly authenticated document showing his authority, shall have a right—

(a) to enter, at any reasonable time, any premises (other than a building used only as a private dwelling-house) which he has reasonable cause to believe to be premises where regulated produce[3] is grown for sale, graded or packed, or on which regulated produce is displayed or offered for sale, sold, delivered or marketed in any other manner or on which regulated produce intended for sale is to be found, and

(b) to inspect and take samples of any regulated produce found on the premises and to seize and detain any certificate or label (together with any container accompanied by a certificate or to which a label is affixed) used in connection with such produce.

(2) Where on premises which he has a right to enter under the foregoing subsection, an authorised officer finds any regulated produce—

(a) which has affixed to it a label or which is accompanied by a certificate indicating in either case a standard of quality or is in a container to which such a label is affixed or which is accompanied by such a certificate, but

(b) which he has reasonable cause to believe to be of a quality inferior to the quality required for that standard or which is of a standard not marketable under Community grading rules, he may amend or cancel that label or certificate and may affix to the regulated produce, or, as the case may be, the container a label in such form as may be prescribed[4], by regulations made by the Ministers, indicating what appears to the authorised officer to be the correct standard or, where it appears to him that the produce is of a standard not marketable under Community grading rules, indicating that fact.

(3) If a justice of the peace, on sworn information in writing, is satisfied—

(a) that an authorised officer has been refused admission to any premises which he has a right to enter under subsection (1) above, or that such a refusal is apprehended, and that notice of the intention to apply for a warrant has been given to the occupier; or

(b) that an application for admission to the premises, or the giving of such a notice, would defeat the object of the entry, or that the premises are unoccupied or the occupier temporarily absent;

the justice may by warrant under his hand, which shall continue in force for a period of one month, give authority to an authorised officer to enter the premises by force if need be.

(*Application to Scotland*).

(4) An authorised officer entering any premises by virtue of this section may take with him such other persons and such equipment as may appear to him necessary.

(5) On leaving any premises which he has entered by virtue of this section, being premises which are unoccupied or the occupier of which is temporarily absent, an authorised officer shall leave them as effectively secured against unauthorised entry as he found them.

(6) If any authorised officer or other person who enters any workplace by virtue of this section discloses to any person any information obtained by him in the work-place with regard to any manufacturing process or trade secret, he shall, unless the disclosure was made in the performance of this duty, be guilty of an offence[5].

(7) The foregoing provisions of this section shall apply in relation to any land, stall, vehicle, vessel, aircraft or hovercraft as they apply in relation to premises.

[Agriculture and Horticulture Act 1964, s 13, as amended by SI 1973/22.]

---

1. An authorised officer who inspects produce in accordance with this section may prohibit its movement if he is satisfied that a grading offence, within the meaning of s 14(1), post, is being committed in respect of it; see the Horticultural Produce Act 1986, s 1, post.

2. That is, the Minister for Agriculture, Fisheries and Food (s 26(2)) see also para **8–100** note 1 above.

3. This means any fresh horticultural produce of a description in relation to which grades of quality are designated and defined under s 11(1) (s 12(1), ante).

4. The Grading of Horticultural Produce (Form of Labels) Regulations 1982, SI 1982/387, have been made.

5. The penalty for an offence is prescribed by s 20(2), post. Proceedings may be instituted only by or with the consent of the Minister or with the consent of the Attorney-General (s 20(3), post).

In relation to offences under s 14(1), (2) or (3), proceedings may be taken against any person whose act or default led to the commission of the offence (s 16, post) and s 18 provides special defences in respect of such offences. A warranty may be pleaded in relation to an offence under s 14(1) or (2) (s 17, post). Section 19, post, makes special provision regarding offences by corporate bodies.

8–103 14. Offences in connection with grading. (1) A person shall be guilty of an offence if he displays or offers for sale, sells, delivers or markets in any other manner regulated produce in contravention of Community grading rules applying thereto or with intent to sell, offer for sale, deliver or so market in circumstances such that the display or offer for sale, delivery or marketing of the produce would contravene those rules, he—

(a) exposes the produce for sale, or

(b) not being the producer thereof, has the produce in his possession for sale, or

(c) being the producer thereof, consigns the produce for sale.

(2) A person shall be guilty of an offence[1] if, on behalf of the owner of any regulated produce—

(a) he carries out a sale of the regulated produce in circumstances such that the sale contravenes Community grading rules applying thereto, or

(b) with intent to carry out a sale of the regulated produce in such circumstances, he displays or offers it for sale, delivers or markets it with a view to sale or has it in his possession for sale.

(3) A person shall be guilty of an offence[1] if having given an undertaking or having been responsible for the giving of an undertaking on his behalf by another person as to any re-sorting, regrading or labelling of regulated produce found not to conform to Community grading rules, he fails to comply with the undertaking.

(4) A person shall be guilty of an offence[1] if—

(a) he knowingly gives in relation to regulated produce whether by affixing an incorrect label or in any other manner a description of the produce which does not comply with the requirements of Community grading rules, or

(b) without lawful authority he affixes to the container of any regulated produce, or to the produce itself or to the certificate accompanying the produce, a label in a form prescribed for the purposes of s 13(2) above or for the purposes of any corresponding provision of an enactment of the Parliament of Northern Ireland for the time being in force, or

(c) where under the said s 13(2) or any such corresponding provision a label has been affixed to the container of any regulated produce, or to the produce itself or the said produce or container[2], as the case may be, is accompanied by a certificate, he, with intent to deceive, removes, alters, defaces or conceals the label or certificate, or

(d) he offers regulated produce of a description included in Chapter 6 of the Common Customs Tariff of the European Communities, as amended or replaced from time to time, for which there is a prescribed grade and in relation to which a price has been quoted in any advertisement, catalogue or price list without giving particulars required by Community grading rules relating thereto, or

(e) he dispatches any consignment of regulated produce weighing 4 metric tons or more from one dispatching area, as specified from time to time in Community grading rules, to another such dispatching area or exports any consignment of regulated produce to any place outside the European Economic Community without any certificate accompanying the produce as required by Community grading rules.

[Agriculture and Horticulture Act 1964, s 14, as amended by SI 1973/22.]

---

1. The Grading of Horticultural Produce (Form of Labels) Regulations 1982, SI 1982/387, have been made.
2. "Label" and "container" are defined in s 24, post.

8–104   15. Obstruction.   (1) A person shall be guilty of an offence[1] if—

(a) he wilfully obstructs an authorised officer acting in the execution of this Part of this Act or in the execution of Community grading rules, or

(b) without reasonable cause he fails to give to any authorised officer acting as aforesaid any assistance or information which the authorised officer may reasonably require of him for the purposes of the performance by the authorised officer of his functions under this Part of this Act or under Community grading rules, or

(c) he fails to make any request for inspection or give any notice or information required by Community grading rules.

(2) A person shall be guilty of an offence if, in giving to an authorised officer any such information as is mentioned in the foregoing subsection, he gives any information which he knows to be false[2].

(3) Nothing in this section shall be construed as requiring a person to answer any question or give any information if to do so might incriminate him.

[Agriculture and Horticulture Act 1964, s 15, as amended by SI 1973/22.]

---

1. Punishable in accordance with s 20(1), post. Proceedings may be instituted only by or with the consent of the Minister or with the consent of the Attorney-General (s 20(3)).
2. Punishable in accordance with s 20(2), post. See note 5, in para **8–102**, ante.

8–105   16. Penalty for act or default leading to commission of offence by another.   Where the commission by any person of an offence under s 14 (1), (2) or (3) above was due to an act or default of another person then, whether proceedings are taken against the first-mentioned person or not, that other person may be charged with and convicted of the offence, and shall on conviction be liable to the same punishment as that to which the first-mentioned person is, on conviction, liable.

[Agriculture and Horticulture Act 1964, s 16, as amended by SI 1973/22.]

8–106   17. Pleading of warranty as defence.   (1) Subject to the provisions of this section, where in proceedings for an offence in relation to any produce under s 14(1) or (2) above it would have been a defence for the person charged to prove that the produce conformed to a standard of quality permitted to be displayed or offered for sale, sold, delivered or marketed in accordance with community grading rules, it shall be a defence for him to prove—

(a) that he bought or took delivery of the produce as being of a quality falling within that standard of quality, and with a written warranty to that effect; and

(b) that at the time of the commission of the offence he had no reason to believe the statement contained in the warranty to be inaccurate, that he then did believe in its accuracy and that he had taken such steps (if any) as were reasonably practicable to check its accuracy; and

(c) that he took all reasonable steps to ensure that the quality of the produce was the same at the time of the commission of the offence as when it left the possession of the person by whom the warranty was given.

(2) Where the proceedings are in respect of an offence committed by the person charged in the course of his employment, it shall be a defence for him to prove—

(a) that if his employer had been charged the employer would have had a defence under subsection (1) above in respect of a warranty, and

(b) that at the time of the commission of the offence the person charged had no reason to believe the statement contained in the warranty to be inaccurate.

(3) Where the person charged intends to set up a defence under this section he shall, not later than three days before the date of the hearing—

    (*a*) send to the prosecutor a copy of the warranty with a notice stating that he intends to rely on it and specifying the name and address of the person by whom it is alleged to have been given, and

    (*b*) send to the last-mentioned person a notice giving the date and place of the hearing and stating that he intends to rely on the warranty.

(4) The person by whom the warranty is alleged to have been given shall be entitled to appear at the hearing and give evidence.

(5) If the person charged in any such proceedings as aforesaid wilfully attributes to any produce a warranty given in relation to any goods not including that produce, he shall be guilty of an offence[1].

(6) For the purposes of this section any standard of quality entered in an invoice or certificate relating to any produce or indicated by a label affixed to the produce or to the container thereof shall be deemed to be a written warranty that the produce conforms to the standard of quality so entered or indicated.

[Agriculture and Horticulture Act 1964, s 17, as amended by SI 1973/22.]

---

    1. Punishable in accordance with s 20(2), post. See note 5 in para **8–102**, ante.

8–107 **18. Pleading of mistake, act of third party, etc as defence.** In proceedings for an offence in respect of any produce under s 14(1), (2) or (3) above it shall be a defence of the person charged to prove—

    (*a*) that the commission of the offence was due to the act or default of some other person, or to a mistake, or to an accident or some other cause beyond his control; and

    (*b*) that he took all reasonable precautions and exercised all due diligence to avoid the commission of such an offence in respect of that produce by himself or any person under his control.

[Agriculture and Horticulture Act 1964, s 18.]

8–108 **19. Offences by corporations.** (1) Where an offence under any of the provisions of this Part of this Act which has been committed by a body corporate is proved to have been committed with the consent or connivance of, or to be attributable to any neglect on the part of, any director, manager, secretary or other similar officer of the body corporate or any person who was purporting to act in any such capacity, he as well as the body corporate shall be deemed to be guilty of that offence and shall be liable to be proceeded against and punished accordingly.

(2) In the foregoing subsection, "director", in relation to any board established under the Agricultural Marketing Act 1958, or any body corporate established by or under any enactment for the purpose of carrying on under national ownership any industry or part of an industry or undertaking, being a body corporate whose affairs are managed by the members thereof, means a member of that board or body corporate.

[Agriculture and Horticulture Act 1964, s 19 as amended by the Horticultural Produce Act 1986, s 7.]

8–109 **20. Punishment of offences.** (1) A person guilty of an offence under s 15(1) of this Act shall be liable on summary conviction to a fine not exceeding **level 3** on the standard scale.

(2) A person guilty of an offence under any of the foregoing provisions of this Part of this Act other than s 15(1) shall be liable on summary conviction to a fine not exceeding **level 5** on the standard scale, or to imprisonment for a term not exceeding **three months**, or to **both**.

(3) Proceedings in England or Wales for an offence under any of the provisions of this Part of this Act may be instituted only by or with the consent of the Minister[1] or with the consent of the Attorney General.

[Agriculture and Horticulture Act 1964, s 20, as amended by SI 1973/22, the Criminal Justice Act 1982, ss 35, 39 and 46 and Sch 3 and the Horticultural Produce Act 1986, s 7.]

---

    1. That is, the Minister for Agriculture, Fisheries and Food (s 26(2)). The functions of the Minister, so far as exercisable in relation to Wales, have been transferred to the National Assembly for Wales, by the National Assembly for Wales (Transfer of Functions) Order 1999, SI 1999/672, art 2, Sch 1.

Transport of produce

8–110 **21. Power to require use of prescribed containers etc.** (1) With a view to reducing the risk of deterioration of or damage to produce while in transit or promoting efficiency in the transport and handling of produce, the Ministers[1] may make regulations imposing a duty on any person carrying on a horticultural production business to secure that such containers, pallets and other articles as may be prescribed by the regulations are used for the transport of fresh horticultural produce from premises where that business is carried on to any such market or other premises as may be so prescribed.

(2) Regulations under this section may confer powers of entry, inspection and sampling, may provide for the punishment of offences against the regulations and may contain such other provisions as the Ministers consider expedient for the purposes of the regulations:

Provided that—

(*a*) the regulations shall not confer power to enter any building used only as a private dwelling-house or to stop any vehicle on a highway, and in relation to any power of entry conferred thereby shall include provisions to the like effect as s 13(5) and (6) of this Act; and

(*b*) the penalty for an offence under the regulations shall be limited to a fine not exceeding **level 3** on the standard scale.

(3) In this section "horticultural production business" has the same meaning as in Part I of the Horticulture Act 1960.
[Agriculture and Horticulture Act 1964, s 21 as amended by the Criminal Justice Act 1982, ss 36, 40 and 46.]

1. The Minister for Agriculture, Fisheries and Food and the Secretary of State for Scotland acting jointly (s 26(2)). The functions of the Minister, so far as exercisable in relation to Wales, have been transferred to the National Assembly for Wales, by the National Assembly for Wales (Transfer of Functions) Order 1999, SI 1999/672, art 2, Sch 1.

8–111   24. Interpretation of Part III—In this Part of this Act—

"authorised officer" has the meaning assigned to it by s 13(1) of this Act;

"certificate" includes any document, other than a label, which accompanies any produce and which contains information relating to the standard of quality of that produce;

"Community grading rules" means any directly applicable Community provisions establishing standards of quality for fresh horticultural produce;

"container" includes any basket, pail, tray, package or receptacle of any kind, whether open or closed;

"label" includes any device for conveying information by written characters or other symbols, and any characters or symbols stamped or otherwise placed directly on to any produce or container, and references to the affixing of a label shall be construed accordingly;

"standard of quality" means, in relation to produce, a common standard imposed by Community grading rules relating to quality, size, packaging, presentation and marking.
[Agriculture and Horticulture Act 1964, s 24, as amended by the European Communities Act 1972, Sch 4 and SI 1973/22.]

Cereals Marketing Act 1965
(1965 c 14)

8–112   This Act establishes a Home-Grown Cereals Authority which is empowered to submit to the Minister for Agriculture, Fisheries and Food[1] a scheme for imposing a levy upon growers, etc of home-grown cereals. For this purpose, the Authority may require growers, etc to be registered, to furnish returns and other information, to keep records and produce them for examination.
[Cereals Marketing Act 1965, s 16, amended by the Agriculture Act 1986, s 5 and Sch 3—summarised.]

1. See the Transfer of Functions (Agriculture and Food) Order 1999, SI 1999/3141. The functions of the Minister, so far as exercisable in relation to Wales, have been transferred to the National Assembly for Wales, by the National Assembly for Wales (Transfer of Functions) Order 1999, SI 1999/672, art 2, Sch 1.

8–113   17. Offences in relation to scheme under s 16.   (1) Any person who fails to comply with a requirement imposed by or under a scheme in accordance with subsection (2) of the last preceding section shall be guilty of an offence and liable[1] on summary conviction to a fine not exceeding **level 3** on the standard scale or to imprisonment for a term not exceeding **three months** or both.

(2) Returns or other information furnished to or obtained by any person in pursuance of such a requirement shall not be disclosed except (*a*) with the written consent of the person by whom the information was furnished, or (*b*) to a member, officer or servant of the Authority, or (*c*) to any of the three Ministers mentioned in section 24(1) of this Act or an officer or servant appointed by one of those Ministers, or (*d*) in the form of a summary of similar returns or information furnished by or obtained from a number of persons, being a summary so framed as not to enable particulars relating to any one person or business to be ascertained from it, or (*e*) for the purposes of any proceedings pursuant to this Act or of any criminal proceedings which may be taken, whether pursuant to this Act or otherwise, or for the purposes of a report of any such proceedings.

(3) Any person who—

(*a*) in furnishing any information for the purposes of a scheme under the last preceding section, makes a statement which he knows to be false in a material particular, or recklessly makes a statement which is false in a material particular, or

(*b*) wilfully makes a false entry in any document which is required to be produced in pursuance of any such scheme, or

(*c*) disclose any information in contravention of subsection (2) of this subsection,

shall be liable[1] on summary conviction to a fine not exceeding **the statutory maximum** or to imprisonment for a term not exceeding **three months** or both, or on conviction on indictment[2] to a fine or to imprisonment for a term not exceeding **two years** or both.

[Cereals Marketing Act 1965, s 17, as amended by the Criminal Law Act 1977, s 28 and the Criminal Justice Act 1982, ss 38 and 46.]

1. No proceedings shall be instituted except by the Home-Grown Cereals Authority or by, or with the consent of, the Director of Public Prosecutions (s 22 (1)): for liability of a director, etc of a body corporate, see s 22(3).
2. For procedure in respect of this offence which is triable either way, see Magistrates' Courts Act 1980, ss 17A–21, in PART I: MAGISTRATES' COURTS, PROCEDURE, ante.

Plant Health Act 1967
(1976 c 8)

8–114　This Act is designed to control pests and diseases injurious to agricultural or horticultural crops, trees or bushes. The Minister for Agriculture, Fisheries and Food, (or as regards forest trees and timber, the Forestry Comrs) may make orders[1] to effect such control, and contraventions are punishable on summary conviction by a fine not exceeding **level 5**[2] on the standard scale (s 3(4) as substituted by the Criminal Justice Act 1982, s 42).

Offences under the Act have a limitation period of 12 months.

A local authority may be given the responsibility of carrying an Order into effect.

The numerous Orders do not appear in this Manual.

See also the Plant Varieties and Seeds Act 1964, ante.

1. The Plant Health (Great Britain) Order 1993, SI 1993/1320 amended by SI 1993/3213, SI 1994/3094, SI 1995/1358 and 2929, SI 1996/25, 1165 and 3242, SI 1997/1145 and 2907, SI 1998/349, 1121 and 2245, SI 1999/2126 (England), SI 2001/2342 (England), 2500 (Wales), 2641 (Wales), 2726 (England) and 3761 (Wales) and SI 2002/1067 (England) and 1805 (Wales) SI 2003/1157 (E) and 1851 (W), SI 2004/2365 and SI 2005/70 (W) has been made but has now been revoked in relation to England by SI 2005/2530; Article 33 creates offences in relation to failing to comply with the Order, the making of false etc statements and obstruction, and fixes a maximum fine not exceeding **level 5** on the standard scale. The Potatoes Originating in Germany (Notification) (England) Order 2001, SI 2001/3194, the Potatoes Originating in Germany (Notification) (Wales) Order 2001, SI 2001/3541, the Plant Health (Phytophthora ramorum) (Wales) (No 2) Order 2002, SI 2002/2762; the Polish Potatoes (Notification) (England) Order 2004, SI 2004/1452, the Plant Health (Export Certification) (England) Order 2004, SI 2004/1404 amended by SI 2005/3480; the Plant Health (Export Certification) (Forestry) (Great Britain) Order 2004, SI 2004/1684; the Plant Health (Phytophthora ramorum) (England) Order 2004, SI 2004/2590; the Polish Potatoes (Notification) (Wales) Order 2004, SI 2004/2697; the Plant Health (Forestry) (Phyophthora ramorum) (Great Britain) Order 2004, SI 2004/3213; the Plant Health (Phytophthora kernovii Management Zone) (England) Order 2004, SI 2004/3367; the Dutch Potatoes (Notification) (England) Order 2005, SI 2005/279; the Dutch Potatoes (Notification) (Wales) Order 2005, SI 2005/1162; the Plant Health (Forestry) Order 2005, SI 2005/2517; the Plant Health (England) Order 2005, SI 2005/2530 have also been made. The functions of the Minister, so far as exercisable in relation to Wales, have been transferred to the National Assembly for Wales, by the National Assembly for Wales (Transfer of Functions) Order 1999, SI 1999/672, art 2, Sch 1.
2. A person landing a plant or plant product in contravention of an order under s 3 of this Act may be guilty of an offence under the Customs and Excise Management Act 1979, s 50(2) and liable to the higher penalties there prescribed for an offence triable either way. The provisions of the Plant Health (Great Britain) Order 1987 are specifically stated to apply without prejudice to the Customs Act: Article 43 of the said Order.

Forestry Act 1967
(1967 c 10)

8–115　This Act re-constitutes the Forestry Commission and charges the Commission with duties of promoting the interests of forestry, the development of afforestation, the production and supply of timber, and the establishment and maintenance of adequate reserves of growing trees.

The Commissioners may authorise the killing and taking of rabbits, hares or vermin (which includes squirrels), for the protection of trees or tree plants, and is empowered to recover summarily as a civil debt from the occupier of land the net cost of so doing; the person entitled to kill rabbits, hares or vermin on any common land shall be deemed to be the occupier. Obstruction of a person so authorised in writing is a summary offence.—*Penalty*, not exceeding **level 2** on the standard scale (s 7, as amended by the Criminal Law Act 1977, s 31 and the Criminal Justice Act 1982, s 46—*summarised*).

The Commissioners are given large powers to control the felling of growing trees: the expression "felling" includes wilfully destroying by any means (s 35). Subject to extensive exceptions[1] contained in s 9(2) of the Act, a licence is required for the felling of any growing tree (s 9(1)).

1. Further exceptions are contained in the Forestry (Exceptions from Restrictions of Felling) Regulations 1998, SI 1998/603.

8–116　17. Penalty for felling without licence.　(1) Anyone[1] who fells a tree without the authority of a felling licence[2], the case being one in which section 9(1) of this Act applies so as to require such a licence, shall be guilty of an offence[3] and liable on summary conviction to a fine not exceeding **level 4** on the standard scale or twice the sum which appears to the court to be the value of the tree, whichever is the higher.

(2) Proceedings for an offence under this section may be instituted within six months from the first discovery of the offence by the person taking the proceedings, provided that no proceedings shall be instituted more than two years after the date of the offence.
[Forestry Act 1967, s 17, amended by Civic Amenities Act 1967, s 15 and the Criminal Justice Act 1982, ss 38 and 46.]

1. "Anyone" is to be construed as meaning, in its ordinary sense, "any person"; it is not confined to persons with an estate or interest in the land in question who are entitled to apply for a licence under s 10 of the Act (*Forestry Commission v Frost and Thompson* (1989) 154 JP 14).
2. The procedure for applying for a felling licence is prescribed by the Forestry (Felling of Trees) Regulations 1979, SI 1979/791 amended by SI 1987/632, SI 2002/226 and SI 2003/2155.
3. An information which alleged the felling of 90 trees over a period of 3 days was held not to be bad for duplicity (*Cullen v Jardine* [1985] Crim LR 668).
Once the prosecution has proved that the defendant felled a tree, the burden shifts to the defendant to prove on a balance of probabilities that the circumstances fell within one of the exceptions provided by the Act; mens rea is not an essential element of the offence: *R (on the application of Grundy & Co Excavations Ltd) v Halton Division Magistrates' Court* [2003] EWHC 272 (Admin), (2002) 167 JP 387.

8–117   17A–17C. *Power of Forestry Commissioners to require the restocking of land with trees after a person is convicted of an offence of unauthorised felling under s 17; appeal against restocking notice; enforcement of restocking notice.*

8–118   24. Notice to require compliance with conditions or directions.   The Commissioners are empowered to give felling directions requiring the owner of growing trees to fell them within a specified period[1]; failure to comply with the directions, or with the conditions of a felling licence, is an offence: Penalty not exceeding **level 5** on the standard scale (s 24 amended by the Criminal Justice Act 1982, ss 39 and 46, and Sch 3—*summarised*).

1. The period specified shall not be less than three months (Forestry (Felling of Trees) Regulations 1979, SI 1979/791, amended by SI 1987/632, reg 13, SI 2002/226 and SI 2003/2155).

8–119   30. Service of documents.   (1) to (4)   prescribe methods of serving documents under the Act.
(5) The Commissioners may, for the purposes of enabling them to serve or give any document or direction under this Part[1] of this Act, require the occupier of any land and any person who, either directly or indirectly, receives rent in respect of any land, to state in writing the nature of his interest therein and the name and address of any other person known to him as having an interest therein, whether as a freeholder or owner, mortgagee or creditor in a heritable security, lessee or otherwise; and anyone who, having been required in pursuance of this subsection to give any information, fails to give it, or knowingly makes any misstatement in respect thereof, shall be liable on summary conviction to a fine not exceeding **level 1** on the standard scale.
[Forestry Act 1967, s 30, as amended by Criminal Justice Act 1967, 3rd Sch and the Criminal Justice Act 1982, ss 38 and 46.]

1. Part II—Commissioners' powers to control felling of trees.

8–120   46. Commissioners power to make byelaws.   (1) to (4)   empower the Commissioners to make byelaws[1] with respect to land under their management or control to which the public have, or may be permitted to have, access (*summarised*).
(4A) A draft of any statutory instrument containing byelaws made under this section with respect to land in Scotland shall be laid before the Scottish Parliament.
(4B) The Statutory Instruments Act 1946 shall apply to any statutory instrument containing byelaws made under this section with respect to land in Scotland as it applies to any statutory instrument made by the Scottish Ministers.
(5) If anyone fails to comply with, or acts in contravention of, any byelaw made under this section he shall be guilty of an offence and be liable on summary conviction to a fine not exceeding **level 2** on the standard scale and in the case of a continuing offence he shall be liable to a further fine not exceeding **50p**, for each day upon which the offence continues.
[Forestry Act 1967, s 46, as amended by Criminal Justice Act 1967, Schs 3 and 4, the Criminal Justice Act 1972, Sch 6 and the Criminal Justice Act 1982, ss 39 and 46, and Sch 3.]

1. See the Forestry Commission Byelaws 1982, SI 1982/648.

8–121   48. Powers of entry and enforcement.   (1) An officer of the Commissioners or any other person authorised by them in that behalf may (on production, if so required, of his authority) enter on and survey any land for the purpose of ascertaining whether it is suitable for afforestation or for the purpose of inspecting any timber thereon, or for any other purpose in connection with the exercise of the powers and performance of the duties of the Commissioners under this Act of the Plant Health Act 1967.

(2) The Commissioners may authorise an officer or servant appointed or employed by them to exercise and perform on their behalf such powers and duties as they may consider necessary for the enforcement of byelaws under section 46 of this Act, and in particular to remove or exclude, after due warning, from any land to which the byelaws relate a person who commits, or whom he reasonably suspects of committing, an offence against the said section or against the Vagrancy Act 1824.

(3) Anyone who obstructs an officer or servant appointed or employed by the Commissioners in the due exercise or performance of his powers or duties under the foregoing subsection shall be guilty of an offence and be liable on summary conviction to a fine not exceeding **level 3** on the standard scale.

[Forestry Act 1967, s 48, as amended by Criminal Justice Act 1967, 3rd Sch, the Criminal Justice Act 1982, ss 39 and 46, and Sch 3 and SI 1999/1747, Sch 12.]

Agriculture Act 1967
(1967 c 22)

8–122   6. Compulsory use of systems of classification of carcases.   (1) to (3) General power of the Minister of Agriculture, Fisheries and Food jointly to make provision by order for the marking of carcases (*summarised*)[1].

(4) If any person contravenes or fails to comply with any provision of an order under this section he shall be liable on summary conviction to a fine not exceeding **level 3** on the standard scale or imprisonment for a term not exceeding **three months*** or both: Provided that if in proceedings against any person for an offence under this subsection it is proved—

(*a*)   that the commission of the offence was due to an act or default of some other person, and

(*b*)   that the person charged took all reasonable precautions and exercised all due diligence to avoid the commission of the offence by him or any person under his control,

then, subject to the next following subsection, the person charged shall be acquitted of the offence.

(5) A person charged with an offence under the last foregoing subsection shall not be entitled to be acquitted by virtue of the proviso thereto unless, not less than fourteen clear[2] days before the hearing, he has given notice in writing to the prosecutor of his intention to rely on that proviso, specifying the name and address of the person to whose act or default he alleges the commission of the offence was due, and has sent a like notice to that person; and that person shall be entitled to appear at the hearing and to give evidence. This subsection shall not apply to Scotland.

(6) Where the commission by any person of an offence under subsection (4) above is due to an act or default of some other person, that other person shall be guilty of the offence; and a person may be charged with and convicted of the offence by virtue of this subsection whether or not proceedings are taken against the first-mentioned person.

(7) If any person wilfully obstructs an authorised officer of the Commission[4] or other person in the performance of his duty in connection with the operation of a system in pursuance of an order under this section he shall be liable on summary conviction to a fine not exceeding **level 1** on the standard scale.

(8) If any person—

(*a*)   with intent to deceive, removes, alters, conceals or defaces any mark applied in the course of the operation by the Commission[3] of a system compiled under the last foregoing section[4] (whether or not operated in pursuance of an order under this section), or

(*b*)   applies to any carcase, without due authority and with intent to deceive, any mark prescribed by a system so compiled and operated, or applies to any carcase a mark so closely resembling a prescribed mark as to be calculated to deceive, or

(*c*)   wilfully makes a false entry in any record which is required to be kept in pursuance of an order under this section or, with intent to deceive, make use of any such entry which he knows to be false,

he shall be liable[5] on summary conviction to a fine not exceeding **the statutory maximum** or to imprisonment for a term not exceeding **three months** or both, or on conviction on indictment to a fine or to imprisonment for a term not exceeding **two years** or both.

(9) For the purpose of ascertaining whether an offence has been committed under this subsection an authorised officer of the Commission may, on producing if so required a duly authenticated document showing his authority, require a person carrying on or managing a slaughterhouse or other undertaking for the slaughter of livestock, or an undertaking for the storage, processing, grading, classification, packing or cutting of carcases, or for the sale of carcases by wholesale, to produce any books, accounts or records relating to the conduct of the undertaking which the officer may require to inspect, and may take a copy or extract from any such book, account or record produced to him.

If a person fails to comply with the requirement under this subsection he shall be liable on summary conviction to a fine not exceeding **level 3** on the standard scale or to imprisonment for a term not exceeding **three months** or both.

(10) and (11) Orders to be made by statutory instrument (*summarised*).

[Agriculture Act 1967, s 6, as amended by the Criminal Law Act 1977, s 28 and the Criminal Justice Act 1982, ss, 38, 40 and 46.]

---

*"51 weeks" substituted by the Criminal Justice Act 2003, Sch 26, from a date to be appointed.

13. The Meat and Livestock commission may make a levy on persons engaged in the production, etc of livestock and livestock products and having the control of slaughterhouses to meet the Commission's expenses.

[Agriculture Act 1967, s 13 amended by the Animal Health Act 1981, Sch 5—summarised.]

---

1. See the Transfer of Functions (Agriculture and Food) Order 1999, SI 1999/3141. The Functions of the Minister, so far as exercisable in relation to Wales, have been transferred to the National Assembly for Wales, by the National Assembly for Wales (Transfer of Functions) Order 1999, SI 1999/672, art 2, Sch 1. Order making functions under this section: the Scotland Act 1998 (Cross-Border Public Authorities) (Adaptation of Functions etc) Order 1999, SI 1999/1747, art 3, Sch 16, Pt II, para 3 provides that the Secretary of State for Scotland shall no longer have the power to make orders under this section.
2. I.e. 16 days.
3. I.e. the Meat and Livestock Commission.
4. Section 5 empowers the Commission to compile systems of classifying meat and marking and labelling it and standard codes of practice for the way in which meat is cut for sale by retail.
5. For procedure in respect of this offence which is triable either way, see Magistrates' Courts Act 1980, ss 17A–21, in PART I: MAGISTRATES' COURTS, PROCEDURE, ante.

8-123 14. Levy: registration, returns and records. (1) A levy scheme may, so far as is necessary for determining the liability of persons to charges thereunder, confer on the Commission power to require persons on whom charges may be imposed by a levy scheme (*a*) to be registered in a register kept for the purpose by the Commission, (*b*) to furnish returns and other information, and to produce for examination on behalf of the Commission, books and other documents in their custody or under their control, and (*c*) to keep records and to produce them for examination as aforesaid.

(2) Any person who fails to comply with a requirement made under a levy scheme by virtue of subsection (1) above shall be liable on summary conviction to a fine not exceeding **level 3** on the standard scale or to imprisonment for a term not exceeding **three months** or both.

(3) Any person who—

(*a*) in furnishing any information for the purposes of a levy scheme, knowingly or recklessly makes a statement which is false in a material particular, or

(*b*) wilfully makes a false entry in any document which is required to be produced in pursuance of a levy scheme,

shall be liable[1] on summary conviction to a fine not exceeding **the statutory maximum** or to imprisonment for a term not exceeding **three months** or both, or on conviction on indictment to a fine or to imprisonment for a term not exceeding **two years** or both.

[Agriculture Act 1967, s 14, as amended by the Criminal Law Act 1977, s 28 and the Criminal Justice Act 1982, ss 38 and 46.]

---

1. For procedure in respect of this offence which is triable either way, see Magistrates' Courts Act 1980, ss 17A–21, in PART I: MAGISTRATES' COURTS, PROCEDURE, ante.

8-124 21. Inquiries by Commission. (1) to (10) The Meat and Livestock Commission may conduct inquiries, and may require by summons any person to give evidence (subject to that person having a right of appeal to the High Court against the requirement): if the witness is required to travel more than 10 miles from his place of residence his necessary expenses must be paid or tendered to him (*summarised*).

(11) A person who—

(*a*) refuses or wilfully neglects to attend in obedience to a summons under this section, or to give evidence as required by such a summons, or

(*b*) wilfully alters, suppresses, conceals, destroys or refuses to produce any book or other document which he may be required to produce for the purposes of this section,

shall be liable on summary conviction to a fine not exceeding **level 3** on the standard scale or to imprisonment for a term not exceeding **three months**★ or to both.

[Agriculture Act 1967, s 21, as amended by the Administration of Justice Act 1977, Sch 5 and the Criminal Justice Act 1982, ss 38 and 46.]

---

*"51 weeks" substituted by the Criminal Justice Act 2003, Sch 26, from a date to be appointed.

8-125 24. Disclosure of information. (1) and (2) Information obtained in connection with a levy scheme or other information with respect to any particular undertaking having reference to livestock and meat marketing shall not be disclosed except with the consent of the person from whom it was obtained or for specified official purposes (*summarised*).

(3) Any person who discloses any information in contravention of this section shall be liable[1] on

summary conviction to a fine not exceeding **the statutory maximum** or to imprisonment for a term not exceeding **three months** or both, or on conviction on indictment to a fine or to imprisonment for a term not exceeding **two years** or both.
[Agriculture Act 1967, s 24, as amended by the Criminal Law Act 1977, s 28.]

---

1. For procedure in respect of this offence which is triable either way, see Magistrates' Courts Act 1980, ss 17A–21, in PART I: MAGISTRATES' COURTS, PROCEDURE, ante.

8–126 52. Control of afforestation.   (1) Subject to this section, no person shall plant land in the area of a Rural Development Board[1] with trees except under the authority of a licence granted by the Board.

(2) to (7) Deal with exemptions from the provisions of sub-s (1) and with the procedure for the granting of licences and for appeal (*summarised*).

(8) A person who contravenes subsection (1) of this section, or any condition subject to which a licence is granted under this section, shall be liable on summary conviction to a fine not exceeding **level 3** on the standard scale.

(9) Where a person is convicted of an offence under the last foregoing subsection the court may, in addition to or instead of inflicting a fine, order him, within the time specified in the order, to take such steps as may be so specified for remedying the matters in respect of which the contravention occurred, and may on application enlarge the time so specified; and if the order is not complied with that person shall be liable on summary conviction to a fine not exceeding £10 for each day on which the non-compliance continues.

(10) Proceedings in respect of an offence under subsection (8) of this section may be instituted within six months of the first discovery of the offence by the person taking the proceedings, so, however, that no proceedings shall be instituted in respect of such an offence more than two years after the date of the offence.
[Agriculture Act 1967, s 52(1)–(10), as amended by SI 1978/244, the Criminal Justice Act 1982, ss 38 and 46 and the Planning (Consequential Provisions) Act 1990, Sch 2.]

---

1. The Rural Development Board may be established by the Minister of Agriculture, Fisheries and Food in pursuance of s 45 of the Act.

8–127 55. Powers of entry and of obtaining information.   (1) A person duly authorised in writing by a Rural Development Board may, on producing if so required a duly authenticated document showing his authority, enter on any land in the Board's area for the purpose of determining whether, and in what way, any of the functions of the Board should be exercised in relation to the land.

The right of entry under this subsection may be exercised at any reasonable time, but a person shall not demand admission as of right to any land which is occupied unless at least forty-eight hours' notice, or in the case of land occupied for residential purposes at least seven days' notice, of the intended entry has been given to the occupier.

A person who obstructs any person acting in the exercise of his powers under this subsection shall be liable on summary conviction to a fine not exceeding **level 1** on the standard scale.

(2) A person leaving any land which he has entered by virtue of the foregoing subsection shall, if the land is unoccupied or the occupier is temporarily absent, leave it as effectively secured against trespassers as he found it.

(3) A Board may by notice served on the owner or occupier of any land in their area, require him to furnish them with such information as may be specified in the notice with regard to the land as the Board may reasonably require for the discharge of such of their functions in relation to the land as may be specified in the notice.

A person who fails without reasonable cause, or neglects, to furnish to the Board within three months after service of the notice the information specified in the notice shall be liable on summary conviction to a fine not exceeding **level 3** on the standard scale.

(4) Information obtained under this section shall not be disclosed except—

(*a*) with the consent of the person by whom the information was furnished, or
(*b*) to a member, officer or servant of the Board or to any person exercising functions on behalf of the Board, or
(*c*) to any Minister or to an officer or servant or other person appointed by the exercising functions on behalf of any Minister, or
(*d*) for the purpose of any proceedings pursuant to this Part[1] of this Act, or of any criminal proceedings which may be taken whether pursuant to this Act or otherwise, or for the purpose of a report of any such proceedings.

and a person who discloses information in contravention of this subsection shall be liable[2] on summary conviction to a fine not exceeding **the statutory maximum** or imprisonment for a term not exceeding **three months** or both, or on conviction on indictment to a fine or imprisonment for a term not exceeding **two years**, or both.

[Agriculture Act 1967, s 55, as amended by the Criminal Law Act 1977, s 28 and the Criminal Justice Act 1982, ss 38 and 46.]

---

1. I.e., Part III—Hill Land.
2. For procedure in respect of this offence which is triable either way, see Magistrates' Courts Act 1980, ss 17A–21, in PART I: MAGISTRATES' COURTS, PROCEDURE, ante.

8–128 71. Offences by bodies corporate. Where a body corporate is guilty of an offence under this Act, and that offence is proved to have been committed with the consent or connivance of, or to be attributable to any neglect on the part of, any director, manager, secretary or other similar officer of the body corporate, or any person who was purporting to act in any such capacity, he, as well as the body corporate, shall be guilty of that offence and shall be liable to be proceeded against and punished accordingly.

In this section "director", in relation to a body corporate established by or under any enactment for the purpose of carrying on under national ownership any industry or part of an industry or undertaking, being a body corporate whose affairs are managed by its members, means a member of that body corporate.

[Agriculture Act 1967, s 71.]

Farm and Garden Chemicals Act 1967
(1967 c 50)

8–129 1. *Regulations as to labelling and marking of farm and garden chemicals*[1]

---

1. The Farm and Garden Chemicals Regulations 1967, SI 1971/729, have been made.

8–130 2. Substances to which this Act applies. This Act applies to any substance (whether organic or inorganic) having any of the following properties:

  (*a*) destroying or repelling any insect, mite, mollusc, nematode, fungus, bacterial organism, virus, or other pest capable of destroying or damaging plants;
  (*b*) directly or indirectly controlling the activity of, or preventing or mitigating the harmful effect on plants of, any such pest;
  (*c*) destroying weeds;
  (*d*) acting as a bird or animal repellant, plant growth regulator, defoliant, desiccant or agent for thinning fruit or for preventing the premature fall of fruit.

[Farm and Garden Chemicals Act 1967, s 2.]

8–131 3. Transactions in unlabelled products. (1) Subject to the provisions of this section, no person shall (whether personally or by another, and whether on his own behalf or as servant or agent for another)—

  (*a*) sell, or offer or expose for sale, for use in agriculture[1] or gardening[2] for protecting, or controlling the growth of, plants[3] or for destroying weeds, any product required by regulations under this Act to be labelled or accompanied by a label; or
  (*b*) consign or deliver any such product with a view to or in connection with its sale for such use;

unless the requirements of the regulations under this Act which are applicable to the transaction in question are complied with, and, if he does so, he shall be guilty of an offence.

(2) Subject as aforesaid, any person who causes or permits another person to contravene the provisions of the foregoing subsection shall be guilty of an offence.

(3) Any person guilty of an offence under this section shall be liable on summary conviction to a fine not exceeding **level 4** on the standard scale.

(4) A person shall not be guilty of an offence under this section consisting of consigning or delivering, or causing or permitting the consignment or delivery of, a product by reason only that he was a carrier of the product for another person, whether for reward or otherwise.

(5) It shall be a defence for a person charged with an offence under this section to prove that he used all due diligence to secure compliance with this section.

(6) Where a contravention of subsection (1) or (2) of this section by a person was due to an act or default of another person, then, whether proceedings are or are not taken against the first-mentioned person, that other person may be charged with, and convicted of, the contravention and shall, on conviction, be liable to the punishment prescribed by subsection (3) of this section.

(7) For the purposes of this section, any product commonly used in agriculture or gardening for protecting, or controlling the growth of, plants or for destroying weeds shall, if sold or offered or exposed for sale, or consigned or delivered with a view to or in connection with its sale, be presumed, until the contrary is proved, to have been sold or, as the case may be, to have been or to be intended for sale for such use.

[Farm and Garden Chemicals Act 1967, s 3 as amended by the Criminal Justice Act 1982, ss 35, 38 and 46.]

1. "Agriculture" has the same meaning as in the Agriculture Act 1947 (s 5), ante.
2. "Gardening" includes destroying weeds in drives, paths and court yards (s 5).
3. "Plants" includes trees, bushes and seeds (s 5).

8–132   4. Evidence of analysis of products.   (1) In proceedings for an offence under this Act the prosecutor shall not call evidence of the results of any analysis of the product in relation to which the offence is alleged to have been committed unless the following provisions of this subsection are complied with, that is to say—

(*a*)   the summons for the offence shall be served on the defendant not less than eighteen days before the date of the hearing and shall be accompanied by a notice in writing that the prosecutor proposes to rely on such evidence, together with a statement or a summary of the results of the analysis;

(*b*)   the prosecutor shall, not less than eighteen days before the date of the hearing, give the defendant a sample of the product in sufficient quantity to make a proper analysis of the sample, or shall include in the notice given under the foregoing paragraph a statement that the defendant may at any time not later than eleven days before that date request the prosecutor to give him such a sample;

(*c*)   the prosecutor shall, where so required in response to a statement under the last foregoing paragraph, give the defendant such a sample not later than seven days before the date of the hearing;

(*d*)   the prosecutor shall retain another sample and produce it at the hearing.

(2) The requirement imposed by the foregoing subsection to give a sample of a product may be satisfied in the case of a product contained in unopened containers[1] by giving a container purchased at the same time as that product and sold as containing, or appearing from the appearance of the container, or from any label attached to, written on or supplied with it, to contain, the identical product.

(3) A document purporting to be a certificate by an analyst possessing the requisite qualifications for appointment as a public analyst under section 27 of the Food Safety Act 1990[2] as to the result of an analysis of a sample shall in proceedings for an offence under this Act be admissible as evidence of the matters stated therein, provided, in the case of a certificate tendered by the prosecutor, that a copy of the certificate has been given to the defendant together with the notice under subsection (1) of this section; but either party may require the person by whom the analysis was made to be called as a witness.

(4) If in proceedings for an offence under this Act evidence is given of the results of an analysis of the product in relation to which the offence is alleged to have been committed, the court may, if it thinks fit, and upon the request of either party shall, cause the sample to be produced before the court under subsection (1) of this section to be sent to the Government Chemist who shall make an analysis and transmit to the court a certificate of the result thereof, and the cost of the analysis shall be paid by the prosecutor or the defendant as the court may order.

(5) If, in a case where an appeal is brought, no action has been taken under the last foregoing subsection, that subsection shall apply also in relation to the court by which the appeal is heard.

(6) Any sample required to be given to the defendant under this section may be given to him either—

(*a*)   by delivering it to him; or

(*b*)   in the case of an individual, by leaving it, or sending it by registered post or the recorded delivery service addressed to him, at his usual or last known residence; or

(*c*)   in the case of an incorporated company or body, by delivering it to their secretary or clerk at their registered or principle office, or by sending it by registered post or the recorded delivery service addressed to him at that office.

(7) *Applies to Scotland.*

[Farm and Garden Chemicals Act 1967, s 4 as amended by the Food Act 1984, Sch 10 and the Food Safety Act 1990, Sch 3.]

---

1. "Container" includes any form of packaging of goods for sale as a single item whether by way of wholly or partly enclosing the goods or by way of attaching the goods to, or winding the goods round, some other article, and in particular includes a wrapper or confining band (s 5).
2. Post.

Agriculture Act 1970

(1970 c 40)

PART II
CAPITAL AND OTHER GRANTS

8–133   29. Farm Capital Grants.   (1)–(4) *Power to make capital grants.*

(5) If any person, for the purpose of obtaining for himself or any other person any grant under

such a scheme[1], knowingly or recklessly makes a false statement[2], he shall be liable on summary conviction to a fine not exceeding **level 5** on the standard scale.

(6), (7) *Repeals.*

[Agriculture Act 1970, s 29, as amended by the Agriculture (Miscellaneous Provisions) Act 1976, s 15 and the Criminal Justice Act 1982, ss 38 and 46.]

---

1. See the Agriculture Improvement Scheme 1985, SI 1985/1029, amended by SI 1988/1056, 1983 and 2066, and SI 1989/128 amended by SI 1994/1302 and 3002, the Farm Diversification Grant Scheme 1987, SI 1987/1949 amended by SI 1988/1398 and SI 1991/2 and 1339, the Farm and Conservation Grant Scheme 1989, SI 1989/128, amended by SI 1990/1126, SI 1991/1338, SI 1993/2901, SI 1994/1302 and 3002 and SI 1996/230, the Pig Industry Restructuring (Capital Grant) Scheme 2001, SI 2001/251 amended by SI 2001/3649, the Pig Industry Restructuring (Non Capital Grant) Scheme 2001, SI 2001/252 amended by SI 2001/3649, the Farm Waste Grant (Nitrate Vulnerable Zones) (Wales) Scheme 2001, SI 2001/3709 amended by SI 2004/1606 and the Farm Waste Grant (Nitrate Vulnerable Zones) (England) Scheme 2003, SI 2003/562.

2. The offence is committed when the false statement is received by the appropriate authority (*Lawrence v Ministry of Agriculture, Fisheries and Food* (1992) Times, 26 February).

PART IV
FERTILISERS AND FEEDING STUFFS
Preliminary

8–134 **66. Interpretation of Part IV.** (1) In this Part of this Act—

"agricultural analyst" means an agricultural analyst appointed under section 67 of this Act and, unless the context otherwise requires, includes a deputy agricultural analyst so appointed for the same area;

"analysis" includes any process for determining any fact as to the nature, substance or quality of any material;

"animal" includes any bird, insect or fish;

"enforcement authority" has the meaning assigned by section 67(3) of this Act;

"feeding stuff" means—

(a) a product of vegetable or animal origin in its natural state (whether fresh or preserved);
(b) a product derived from the industrial processing of such a product; or
(c) an organic or inorganic substance, used singly or in a mixture (and whether or not containing additives);

for oral feeding to pet animals and such descriptions of animals as may be prescribed, being animals which, or kinds of which, are commonly kept for the production of food, wool, skins or fur or for the purpose of their use in the farming of land;

"fertiliser" means a fertiliser used for the cultivation of crops or plants of any description, including trees;

"fish" includes shellfish;

"inspector" means an inspector appointed under section 67 of this Act;

"the Minister" means, in relation to England and Wales, the Minister for Agriculture, Fisheries and Food and, in relation to Scotland, the Secretary of State[1];

"the Ministers" means the Minister for Agriculture, Fisheries and Food and the Secretary of State for Scotland and the Secretary of State for Wales acting jointly[1a];

"pet animal" means any animal belonging to a species normally kept and nourished but not consumed by man, not being an animal which has been or may be prescribed for the purpose of the definition of "feeding stuff";

"premixture" means a mixture of additives, or a mixture of additives with substances used as carriers, intended for the manufacture of feeding stuffs;

"prescribed" means prescribed by regulations;

"prescribed metric substitution", in relation to a quantity specified in any provision of this Part of this Act in terms of tons, pounds or gallons, means any quantity expressed in terms of metric units of measurement which regulations may direct to be substituted in that provision, either generally or in prescribed circumstances, for the quantity so specified, being a quantity so expressed appearing to the Ministers appropriate to be so substituted having regard to the convenience of persons likely to be affected and with a view to the effective execution of this Part of this Act;

"Regulation (EC) No 178/2002" means Regulation (EC) No 178/2002 of the European Parliament and of the Council laying down the general principles and requirements of food law, establishing the European Food Safety Authority and laying down procedures in matters of food safety;

"regulations" means regulations made as provided in section 84 of this Act;

"sampled portion", in relation to any material, means a prescribed amount[2] of that material from which a sample has been taken by an inspector in the prescribed manner[4], being an amount—

(a) consisting either—

(i)   entirely of material packed in one or more containers; or

(ii)   entirely of material not so packed; and

(b)   not exceeding, in the case of an amount consisting of material so packed, the requisite quantity, that is to say, five tons or 1,000 gallons or the prescribed[3] metric substitution, except where—

(i)   it consists of material packed in a single container; or

(ii)   it consists of material packed in two or more containers each of which holds less than the requisite quantity, in which case the prescribed amount may be the contents of the lowest number of those containers which together hold the requisite quantity;

"statutory statement" has the meaning assigned by section 68(1) of this Act.

(2)   For the purposes of this Act—

(a)   material shall be treated as sold for use as a fertiliser whether it is sold to be so used by itself or as an ingredient in something which is to be so used;

(b)   material shall be treated—

(i)   as imported or sold for use as a feeding stuff whether it is imported or, as the case may be, sold to be so used by itself or as an ingredient or additive in something which is to be so used; and

(ii)   as used as a feeding stuff whether it is so used by itself or as an ingredient or additive in something which is to be so used.

(3)   Any material consigned to a purchaser shall not for the purposes of this Part of the Act be deemed to be delivered to him until it arrives at the place to which it is consigned whether the consignment is by direction of the seller or the purchaser.

(4)   Where any material is delivered to a purchaser in two or more consignments this Part of this Act shall apply to each consignment.

(5)   For the purposes of this Part of this Act, the appropriation of any material by one person for use—

(a)   in the performance for hire or reward of services to another person in pursuance of a contract in that behalf; or

(b)   under arrangements with another person not constituting a sale of the material to that other person, being arrangements which are intended to benefit both the person appropriating the material and that other person but under which the probability or extent of any benefit to that other person may be affected by the quality of the material,

shall be treated as a sale of that material to that other person by the person so appropriating it, and references to sale or purchase and cognate expressions shall be construed accordingly.
[Agriculture Act 1970, s 66 as amended by SI 1978/1108, SI 1978/272, SI 1981/10, SI 1982/980 and 1144, SI 1988/396, SI 1995/1412, SI 1999/1663, SI 2000/2481 and SI 2004/3254.]

---

1.   Now the the Secretary of State for Environment, Food and Rural Affairs (Ministry of Agriculture, Fisheries and Food (Dissolution) Order 2002, SI 2002/794) alone, see the Transfer of Functions (Agriculture and Food) Order 1999, SI 1999/3141. The functions of the Minister, so far as exercisable in relation to Wales, have been transferred to the National Assembly for Wales, by the National Assembly for Wales (Transfer of Functions) Order 1999, SI 1999/672, art 2, Sch 1.

2.   The prescribed amount for the purposes of this definition, so far as it relates to feedingstuffs, is determined in accordance with the Feedingstuffs (Sampling and Analysis) Regulations 1999, SI 1999/1663, reg 2.

3.   See the Feedingstuffs (Sampling and Analysis) Regulations 1999, SI 1999/1663 amended by SI 1999/1871, SI 2000/2481 (England), SI 2001/343 (Wales), 541 (England), 2253 (Wales) and 3389 (England), SI 2002/892 and 1797 (Wales), SI 2003/1296 (E), 1503 (E), 1677 (W), 1850 (W), 2912 (E) and 3119 (W), SI 2004/1301 (E), 1749 (W), 2146 (E), 2734 (W), 2688 (E) and 3091 (W), SI 2005/3281 (E) and SI 2006/113 (E) and 116 (W); the Feeding Stuffs (England) Regulations 2005, SI 2005/3281 amended by SI 2006/113; the Feeding Stuffs (Wales) Regulations 2006, SI 2006/116.

4.   For the purposes of its application to feedingstuffs the words 'five tonnes or 5,000 litres' have been substituted for 'five tons or 1,000 gallons' by SI 1999/1663, reg 9.

8–135   67. Enforcement authorities and appointment of inspectors and analysts.   (1)   In England it shall be the duty of the council of a county, metropolitan district[1], or London borough and of the Common Council of the City of London to enforce this Part of this Act within their respective areas; and the health authority of the Port of London shall have the like duty as respects the district of the Port of London, which shall accordingly be treated for the purposes of this subsection as not forming part of the area of any of those councils.

(1A)   In Wales it shall be the duty of each county council and each county borough council to enforce this Part of this Act within its area.

(2)   *Scotland.*

(3)   For the purpose of performing their duty under the foregoing provisions of this section each of the bodies there mentioned (in this Part of this Act referred to as an enforcement authority) shall appoint—

(a)   such inspectors as may be necessary; and

(b) an agricultural analyst and, if they think fit, one or more deputy agricultural analysts.

(4) An inspector shall not exercise his powers under this Part of this Act in respect of any premises outside the area for which he is appointed except with the consent of the enforcement authority for the area in which those premises are situated.

(5) A person shall not be appointed as agricultural analyst or deputy agricultural analyst unless he has the prescribed[2] qualifications.

(6)–(9) *Further provisions as to appointments and functions of enforcement authorities.*
[Agriculture Act 1970, s 67, as amended by the Local Government Act 1972, Sch 30, the Local Government, Planning and Land Act 1980, Sch 34, the Local Government Act 1985, Sch 8 and the Local Government (Wales) Act 1994, Sch 16.]

---

1. For the purpose of enforcing this Part of this Act councils of the districts in a metropolitan county shall establish a joint committee of members of those councils whose duty it shall be from the 1st April 1986 to co-ordinate—

  (a) the exercise by those councils of the enforcement functions conferred on them with a view to securing uniformity in the exercise of those functions throughout the county; and
  (b) the employment, provision or use by those councils for the purposes of those functions of staff, property and facilities.

If after the 1st April 1986 it appears to the Secretary of State to be necessary or expedient to do so he may, after consultation with the councils of the districts in a metropolitan county, by order establish a single authority for the county to discharge from a date specified in the order the functions conferred on the councils by virtue of s 67 of the Act (Local Government Act 1985, Sch 8, para 15(4) and (6)).

2. See the Fertilisers (Sampling and Analysis) Regulations 1996, SI 1996/1342 and the Feeding Stuffs (Sampling and Analysis) Regulations 1999, SI 1999/1663 amended by SI 1999/1871, SI 2000/2481 (England), SI 2001/343 (Wales), 541 (England), 2253 (Wales) and 3389 (England), SI 2002/892 and 1797 (Wales), SI 2003/1296 (E), 1503 (E), 1677 (W), 1850 (W), 2912 (E) and 3119 (W), SI 2004/1301 (E), 1749 (W), 2146 (E), 2734 (W), 2688 (E) and 3091 (W), SI 2005/3281 (E) and SI 2006/113 (E) and 116 (W).

Obligations relating to material sold and prepared for sale

8–136 68. Duty of seller to give statutory statement.   (1) Subject to the provisions of this section, a person who sells material of a prescribed[1] description for use as a fertiliser[2] or feeding stuff[2] shall give to the purchaser a statement in writing (in this Part of this Act referred to as a statutory statement) in such form, if any, as may be prescribed containing—

(a) such particulars as may be prescribed of the nature, substance or quantity of the material; and
(b) such information or instructions as to the storage, handling or use of the material as may be prescribed[3].

(1A) A person selling material for use as feeding stuff may, in conjunction with the matters required by virtue of subsection (1) of this section, include in the statutory statement given under the said subsection (1) only such additional particulars, information or instructions as may be prescribed, and any such seller giving a statutory statement including additional particulars, information or instructions other than those prescribed shall be liable on summary conviction to a fine not exceeding **level 2** on the standard scale.

(2) Subsection (1) of this section shall not apply—

(a) to sales of two or more materials which are mixed at the request of the purchaser before delivery to him; or
(b) to sales of small quantities (that is to say, sales in quantities of not more than fifty-six pounds or the prescribed metric substitution) if the material sold is taken in the presence of the purchaser from a parcel bearing a conspicuous label on which are marked in the prescribed manner the matters which would, apart from this subsection, be required to be contained in a statutory statement on the sale of the material.

(3) Any statutory statement required to be given on the sale of any material shall be given not later than the time when the material is delivered to the purchaser and, if given before that time, shall be deemed to have been given at that time; but regulations may permit the statutory statement to be given later in such cases and subject to compliance with such conditions, if any, as may be specified in the regulations.

(4) Any person who—

(a) fails to give a statutory statement within the time or in the form required by or under this section, or gives a statutory statement which does not require all or any of the information or instructions required to be contained in it by virtue of subsection (1)(b) of this section; or
(b) gives a statutory statement which, as respects a sampled portion of the material—

  (i) does not contain all or any of the particulars required to be contained in the statement by virtue of subsection (1)(a) of this section; or
  (ii) contains any such particulars or, in the case of feeding stuffs, any of the additional particulars permitted to be contained in the statutory statement by virtue of subsection (1A) of this section, which are false to the prejudice of purchaser.

(c) sells or exposes for sale material from a parcel purporting to be labelled as mentioned in subsection (2)(b) of this section in a case where the label does not contain all or any of the said particulars or contains any such particulars which are false as aforesaid, shall be liable on summary conviction to a fine not exceeding **level 5** on the standard scale or imprisonment for a term not exceeding **three months*** or both.

(5) In proceedings for an offence under paragraph (*b*) of subsection (4) of this section the fact that any particulars ought to have been included or are false shall be proved by evidence of the result of an analysis of the sample taken from the portion in question; and in proceedings for an offence under paragraph (*c*) of that subsection the fact that any particulars ought to have been included or are false shall be proved by evidence of the result of an analysis of a sample taken by an inspector in the prescribed manner from the material sold or, where the alleged offence is exposing for sale, from the parcel bearing the label.

(6) Failure to comply with this section shall not invalidate a contract of sale; and a statutory statement shall, notwithstanding any contract or notice to the contrary, have effect as a warranty by the person who gives it that the particulars contained in it are correct; but in Scotland a contract of sale may not be treated as repudiated by reason only of a breach of that warranty.

[Agriculture Act 1970, s 68 as amended by the Agriculture Act 1970 Amendment Regulations 1982, SI 1982/980 and the Criminal Justice Act 1982, ss 35, 38 and 46.]

***"51 weeks" substituted by the Criminal Justice Act 2003, Sch 26, from a date to be appointed.**

1. See the Fertiliser Regulations 1991, SI 1991/2197, amended by SI 1995/16, SI 1997/1543, SI 1998/2024 and SI 2001/2253 (Wales) and the Feedingstuffs Regulations 2000, SI 2000/2481 amended SI 2001/2253 (Wales) and 3389 (England), SI 2002/892, SI 2003/1026, 1503 (E) and 2912 (E) and SI 2004/1301 (E), 2688 (E) and 3091 (W); the Feeding Stuffs (England) Regulations 2005, SI 2005/3281 amended by SI 2006/113; the Feeding Stuffs (Wales) Regulations 2006, SI 2006/116.

2. "Fertiliser" and "feeding stuff" are defined in s 66, ante.

3. For the purposes of its application to feedingstuffs, the words "the sales in quantities of not more than 25 kilograms" shall be substituted for the words "to sales of small quantities (that is to say, sales in quantities of not more than fifty six pounds or the prescribed metric substitution)" by SI 1999/1663, reg 9.

8–137 69. Marking of material prepared for sale. (1) Subject to the provisions of this section, a person who has material of a prescribed[1] description on his premises for the purpose of selling it in the course of trade for use as a fertiliser or feeding stuff shall—

(*a*) as soon as practicable after it is made ready for sale; or
(*b*) if it is ready for sale when it comes on to the premises and is not then already marked as required by this section, as soon as practicable after it comes on to the premises,

mark it in such manner, if any, as may be prescribed with the matters required to be contained in a statutory statement relating to that material, and shall secure that the material continues to be so marked until it leaves the premises.

(2) For the purposes of the foregoing subsection material which is normally packed before being delivered to a purchaser shall not be treated as ready for sale until it is so packed if the packing takes place on the premises where the material is manufactured but, if the packing takes place elsewhere, shall be treated as ready for sale when it is ready for packing.

(3) In the case of material which has been imported, subsections (1) and (2) of this section shall have effect subject to such modifications as may be prescribed.

(4) Where, at a time when subsection (1) of this section applies to any person, that person has on his premises for the purposes of selling it as mentioned in that subsection any material to which that subsection applies which is ready for sale and which—

(*a*) is not marked in the manner required by or under this section; or
(*b*) is not marked with all the information or instructions referred to in section 68(1)(*b*) of this Act with which it is required by this section to be marked; or
(*c*) is marked with a mark which, as respects a sampled portion of the material—

   (i) does not contain all the particulars referred to in section 68(1)(*a*) of this Act with which the material is required by this section to be marked; or
   (ii) contains any such particulars which are false to the prejudice of a purchaser,

that person shall be liable on summary conviction to a fine not exceeding **level 5** on the standard scale or imprisonment for a term not exceeding **three months*** or both; but, except where the time in question is the time of the removal of the material from the premises, it shall be a defence for a person charged with an offence under this subsection to show that it was not practicable for the material to be marked in accordance with the requirements of this section by the time in question.

(5) In proceedings for an offence under subsection (4)(*c*) of this section the fact that any particulars ought to have been included or are false shall be proved by evidence of the result of an analysis of the sample taken from the portion in question.

(6) Regulations may provide for enabling the matters required by this section to be marked on any material to be denoted by a mark whose meaning can be ascertained by reference to a register kept in such manner and form as may be specified in the regulations; and any material marked in accordance with the regulations shall be treated for the purposes of this Part of this Act as marked with the matters which the mark denotes.

(7) A person keeping a register pursuant to regulations under subsection (6) of this section shall preserve the register for such period as may be prescribed and a person who has such a register in his

possession or under his control shall on demand by an inspector produce it for his inspection and allow him to take copies of it; and any person who fails to comply with this subsection shall be liable on summary conviction to a fine not exceeding **level 3** on the standard scale.

[Agriculture Act 1970, s 69 as amended by the Criminal Justice Act 1982, ss 35, 38 and 46 and SI 2000/2481.]

---

*"51 weeks" substituted by the Criminal Justice Act 2003, Sch 26, from a date to be appointed.

1. See the Fertiliser Regulations 1991, SI 1991/2197, amended by SI 1995/16, SI 1997/1543, SI 1998/2024 and SI 2001/2253 (Wales) and the Feedingstuffs Regulations 2000, SI 2000/2481 amended SI 2001/2253 (Wales) and 3389 (England), SI 2002/892, SI 2003/1026, 1503 (E) and 2912 (E) and SI 2004/1301 (E) and 2688 (E); the Feeding Stuffs (England) Regulations 2005, SI 2005/3281 amended by SI 2006/113; the Feeding Stuffs (Wales) Regulations 2006, SI 2006/116.

8–138   70. Use of names or expressions with prescribed meanings.   (1) Subject to the provisions of this section, where a person sells for use as a fertiliser or feeding stuff any material—

(*a*) which he describes, in a statutory statement or any document given by him to the purchaser in connection with the sale, by a name or expression to which a meaning has been assigned by regulations[1] made for the purposes of this section; or

(*b*) which is marked with such a name or expression as aforesaid,

there shall, notwithstanding any contract or notice to the contrary, be implied a warranty by the seller that the material accords with that meaning; but in Scotland a contract of sale may not be treated as repudiated by reason only of a breach of that warranty.

(2) Subject to the provisions of this section, where a person—

(*a*) sells for use as a fertiliser or feeding stuff any material—

(i)   which he describes, in such a statement or document as is mentioned in subsection (1) of this section, by such a name or expression as is there mentioned; or

(ii) which is marked with such a name or expression as aforesaid; or

(*b*) has on his premises for the purposes of selling it in the course of trade for such use any material which is ready for sale and marked as aforesaid,

then, if a sampled portion of the material fails, to the prejudice of a purchase, to accord with the meaning which has been assigned to that name or expression, he shall be liable on summary conviction to a fine not exceeding **level 5** on the standard scale or imprisonment for a term not exceeding **three months*** or both.

(3) In the case of any material which has been imported subsections (1) and (2) of this section shall have effect subject to such modifications as may be prescribed.

(4) In proceedings for an offence under subsection (2) of this section the fact that a sampled portion of any material fails to accord with the meaning in question shall be proved by evidence of the result of an analysis of the sample taken from that portion.

(5) For the purposes of this section material shall be treated as marked whether the mark is on the material itself, on a label attached to the material, on a package or container enclosing the material or, in a case within subsection (2)(*b*) of this section, in such a place on the premises in question that it is likely to be taken as referring to the material.

[Agriculture Act 1970, s 70 as amended by the Criminal Justice Act 1982, ss 35, 38 and 46.]

---

*"51 weeks" substituted by the Criminal Justice Act 2003, Sch 26, from a date to be appointed.

1. See the Fertiliser Regulations 1991, SI 1991/2197, amended by SI 1995/16, SI 1997/1543, SI 1998/2024 and SI 2001/2253 (Wales) and the Feedingstuffs Regulations 2000, SI 2000/2481 amended SI 2001/2253 (Wales) and 3389 (England), SI 2002/892, SI 2003/1026, 1503 (E) and 2912 (E) and SI 2004/1301 (E) and 2688 (E); the Feeding Stuffs (England) Regulations 2005, SI 2005/3281 amended by SI 2006/113; the Feeding Stuffs (Wales) Regulations 2006, SI 2006/116.

8–139   71. Particulars to be given of certain attributes if claimed to be present.   (1) A person shall not—

(*a*) sell for use as a fertiliser or feeding stuff any material—

(i)   which he describes, in a statutory statement or any document given by him to the purchaser in connection with the sale, as having any attribute prescribed for the purposes of this section (not being an attribute of which particulars are required to be contained in the statutory statement); or

(ii) which is marked with a statement that it has any such attribute; or

(*b*) have on his premises for the purpose of selling it in the course of trade for such use any material which is ready for sale and marked as aforesaid,

unless the statement, document or mark, as the case may be, also states such particulars of that attribute as may be prescribed.

(2) Any person who—

(*a*) fails to comply with subsection (1) of this section; or

(b) in purported compliance with that subsection describes or marks any material with particulars which, as respects a sampled portion of that material, are false to the prejudice of a purchaser,

shall be liable on summary conviction to a fine not exceeding **level 5** on the standard scale or imprisonment for a term not exceeding **three months*** or both.

(3) In proceedings for an offence under subsection (2)(b) of this section the fact that any particulars are false as respects a sampled portion of any material shall be proved by evidence of the result of an analysis of the sample taken from that portion.

(4) Failure to comply with subsection (1) of this section shall not invalidate a contract of sale; and on the sale of any material in relation to which particulars are or purport to be stated as required by that subsection there shall, notwithstanding any contract or notice to the contrary, be implied a warranty by the seller that the particulars are correct; but in Scotland a contract of sale may not be treated as repudiated by reason only of a breach of that warranty.

(5) For the purposes of this section material shall be treated as marked whether the mark is on the material itself, on a label attached to the material, on a package or container enclosing the material or, in a case within subsection (1)(b) of this section, in such a place on the premises in question that it is likely to be taken as referring to the material.

[Agriculture Act 1970, s 71 as amended by the Criminal Justice Act 1982, ss 35, 38 and 46.]

---

*"51 weeks" substituted by the Criminal Justice Act 2003, Sch 26, from a date to be appointed.

8–140   72. Warranty of fitness of feeding stuff.   (1) On the sale of any material for use as a feeding stuff there shall be implied a warranty by the seller that the material is suitable to be used as such; but—

(a) if the material is sold as suitable only for animals of a particular description, no warranty shall be implied by virtue of this subsection that the material is suitable for other animals; and

(b) if the material is sold to be used as a feeding stuff only after being mixed with something else, no warranty shall be implied as aforesaid that the material is suitable to be so used without being so mixed.

(2) On the sale of any material of a prescribed description for use as a feeding stuff there shall be implied a warranty by the seller that the material does not, except as stated in the statutory statement, contain any ingredient prescribed for the purposes of this subsection.

(3) This section shall have effect notwithstanding any contract or notice to the contrary; but in Scotland a contract of sale may not be treated as repudiated by reason only of a breach of such a warranty as is referred to in subsection (1) or (2) of this section.

[Agriculture Act 1970, s 72.]

8–141   73. Deleterious ingredients in feeding stuff.   (1) Subject to the provisions of this section, any person who—

(a) sells any material for use as a feeding stuff; or

(b) has on his premises for the purpose of selling it in the course of trade for such use any material which is ready for sale,

shall be guilty of an offence if a sampled portion of the material is shown by an analysis of the sample taken from it to contain any ingredient which is deleterious any farmed creatures or deleterious to pet animals or, through the consumption of products of an animal fed with the material, deleterious to human beings.

(2) If in proceedings for an offence under subsection (1) of this section the person charged proves that he sold the material in question or, in a case under paragraph (b) of that subsection that he intended to sell it, as suitable only for animals of a specified kind, then—

(a) in the case of proceedings for an offence of selling, or having for sale, material which is deleterious to animals he shall not be convicted by reason of the fact that a sampled portion of the material contains an ingredient which is deleterious only to animals of a kind different from that specified;

(b) in the case of proceedings for an offence of selling, or having for sale, material which is deleterious to human beings, he shall not be convicted by reason of the fact that a sampled portion of the material contains an ingredient which is deleterious to human beings only if fed to animals of a kind different from that specified; and

(2A) If in proceedings for an offence under subsection (1) of this section the person charged proves that he sold the material in question or, in a case under paragraph (b) of that subsection that he intended to sell it, for use in accordance with written instructions given by him to the purchaser he shall not be convicted by reason of the fact that the sampled portion of the material contains an ingredient which is deleterious only if used otherwise than in accordance with those instructions.

(3) For the purposes of this section it shall be presumed, until the contrary is proved—

(a) that any substance prescribed for the purposes of this subsection; or

(b) in such cases as may be so prescribed, that any substance so prescribed if present in a sampled portion of any material to an amount exceeding such quantity as may be so prescribed, is an ingredient which is deleterious to animals of any such description as aforesaid in relation to which that substance is so prescribed.

(4) Person guilty of an offence under subsection (1) of this section shall be liable on summary conviction to a fine not exceeding **level 5** on the standard scale or imprisonment for a term not exceeding **three months*** or both.

(5) Nothing in this section applies to any person to whom Article 15.1 of Regulation (EC) No 178/2002 applies.

[Agriculture Act 1970, s 73 as amended by the Agriculture Act 1970 Amendment Regulations 1982, SI 1982/980 and the Criminal Justice Act 1982, ss 35, 38 and 46, SI 2000/2481 and SI 2004/3254.]

---

*"51 weeks" substituted by the Criminal Justice Act 2003, Sch 26, from a date to be appointed.

8–142   **73A.** (1) Subject to the provisions of this section, any person who—

(*a*)   sells any material for use as a feeding stuff, or
(*b*)   has on his premises, for the purpose of selling it in the course of trade for such use, any material which is ready for sale,

shall be guilty of an offence if the material is found, or if a sampled portion of the material is shown by an analysis of the sample taken from it, to be unwholesome for or to be dangerous to any farmed creatures, or to be unwholesome for or to be dangerous to, pet animals or, through the consumption of the products of an animal fed with the material, dangerous to human beings.

(2) If in proceedings for an offence under subsection (1) of this section the person charged proves that he sold the material in question or, in a case under paragraph (*b*) of that subsection, that he intended to sell it, as suitable only for animals of a specified kind, then—

(*a*)   in the case of proceedings for an offence of selling, or having for sale, material which is unwholesome for, or dangerous to animals he shall not be convicted by reason of the fact that the material is found, or a sampled portion of it is shown, to be unwholesome only for or, as the case may be, dangerous only to animals of a kind different from that specified;
(*b*)   in the case of proceedings for an offence of selling, or having for sale, material dangerous to human beings, he shall not be convicted by reason of the fact that the material is found, or the sampled portion of it is shown, to be dangerous to human beings only if fed to animals of a kind different from that specified.

(3) If in proceedings for an offence under subsection (1) of this section the person charged proves that he sold the material or, in a case under paragraph (*b*) of that subsection, that he intended to sell it for use in accordance with written instructions given by him to the purchaser he shall not be convicted by reason of the fact that the material is found, or the sampled portion of it is shown, to be unwholesome or, as the case may be, dangerous only if used otherwise than in accordance with the instructions given.

(4) A person guilty of an offence under subsection (1) of this section shall be liable on summary conviction to a fine not exceeding **£400** or imprisonment for a term not exceeding **three months*** or both.

(5) Nothing in this section applies to any person to whom Article 15.1 of Regulation (EC) No 178/2002 applies.

[Agriculture Act 1970, s 73A, as inserted by the Agriculture Act 1970 Amendment Regulations 1982, SI 1982/980 and SI 2004/3254.]

---

*"51 weeks" substituted by the Criminal Justice Act 2003, Sch 26, from a date to be appointed.

8–143   **74. Limits of variation.**   (1) No action shall lie on any warranty arising under the foregoing provisions of this Part of this Act for any mis-statement as to the nature, substance or quality of any material if the mis-statement does not exceed any limits of variation prescribed in relation thereto for the purposes of this section; but if the mis-statement exceeds any such limits the purchaser's rights under the warranty shall not be affected by the limits.

(2) Particulars with respect to any material which are contained in a statutory statement or in any document, or which are marked on, or denoted by a mark on, the material, shall not for the purposes of this Part of this Act be treated as false by reason of any mis-statement therein as to the nature, substance or quality of the material if the mis-statement does not exceed the said limits of variation.

[Agriculture Act 1970, s 74.]

8–144   **74A.** (1), (2) and (4) *Power to make regulations*[1] *regarding fertilisers and feeding stuffs.*

(3) Any person who contravenes any prohibition or restriction imposed by any provision specified in regulation 25(2) of the Feeding Stuffs Regulations 2000 shall be liable on summary conviction to a fine not exceeding **level 5** on the standard scale or to imprisonment for a term not exceeding **three months***, or to both.

[Agriculture Act 1970, s 74A, added by the European Communities Act 1972, Sch 4, para 6 and amended by the Criminal Justice Act 1982, ss 35, 40 and 46.]

*"51 weeks" substituted by the Criminal Justice Act 2003, Sch 26, from a date to be appointed.

1. See the Fertilisers (Sampling and Analysis) Regulations 1996, SI 1996/1342, the Feeding Stuffs (Sampling and Analysis) Regulations 1999, SI 1999/1663 amended by SI 1999/1871, SI 2000/2481 (England), SI 2001/343 (Wales), 541 (England), 2253 (Wales) and 3389 (England), SI 2002/892 and 1797 (Wales), SI 2003/1296 (E), 1503 (E), 1677 (W), 1850 (W), 2912 (E) and 3119 (W), SI 2004/1301 (E), 1749 (W) , 2146 (E), 2734 (W), 2688 (E) and 3091 (W), SI 2005/3281 (E) and SI 2006/113 (E) and 116 (W), the Fertiliser Regulations 1991, SI 1991/2197, amended by SI 1995/16, SI 1997/1543 and SI 1998/2024, the Feedingstuffs Regulations 2000, SI 2000/2481 amended by SI 2001/2253 (Wales), 3389 (E), and SI 2002/892, SI 2003/2912 (E) and SI 2004/1301 (E) and 2688 (E); the Feeding Stuffs (England) Regulations 2005, SI 2005/3281 amended by SI 2006/113; the Feeding Stuffs (Wales) Regulations 2006, SI 2006/116.

Sampling and analysis

8–145   75. *Purchaser's right to have sample taken and analysed.*

8–146   76. Inspector's power to enter premises and take samples. (1) An inspector[1] may at all reasonable times enter—

(a) any premises on which he has reasonable cause to believe that there is any fertiliser or feeding stuff which is kept there for the purpose of being sold in the course of trade and is ready for sale;

(b) any premises (not being premises used only as a dwelling) on which he has reasonable cause to believe that there is any fertiliser or feeding stuff which the occupier of the premises has purchased;

and the inspector may take a sample in the prescribed[2] manner on those premises of any material on the premises (including any material in a vehicle) which he has reasonable cause to believe to be such a fertiliser or feeding stuff as aforesaid.

(2) An inspector may require a person who has purchased any fertiliser or feeding stuff—

(a) to tell him the name and address of the seller; and

(b) to produce, and allow him to take copies of—

(i) any statutory statement received from the seller;

(ii) where the fertiliser or feeding stuff was described or marked as mentioned in section 70(1) or 71(1) of this Act, the document or mark in question;

and any person who without reasonable excuse fails to comply with such a requirement shall be liable on summary conviction to a fine not exceeding **level 3** on the standard scale.

(3) An inspector entering any premises by virtue of this section may take with him such other persons and such equipment as may appear to him to be necessary.

(4) Without prejudice to his powers and duties as to the taking of samples in the prescribed manner, an inspector may for the purposes of this Part of this Act take a sample in a manner other than that prescribed of any material which has been sold for use as a fertiliser or feeding stuff or which he has reasonable cause to believe to be intended for sale as such.

(5) Where for the purpose of taking a sample of any material an inspector takes some of it from each of one or more parcels of the material which are exposed for sale by retail and none of which weighs more than fourteen pounds or the prescribed metric substitution the owner of the parcel or parcels may require the inspector to purchase the parcel or parcels on behalf of the authority for whom he acts.

[Agriculture Act 1970, s 76, as amended by the Criminal Justice Act 1982, ss 38 and 46.]

1. "Inspector" means a person appointed under s 67 (s 66, ante).
2. See the Fertilisers (Sampling and Analysis) Regulation 1996, SI 1996/1342 and the Feeding Stuffs (Sampling and Analysis) Regulations 1999, SI 1999/1663 amended by SI 1999/1871, SI 2000/2481 (England), SI 2001/343 (Wales), 541 (England), 2253 (Wales) and 3389 (England), SI 2002/892 and 1797 (Wales), SI 2003/1296 (E), 1503 (E), 1677 (W), 1850 (W), 2912 (E) and 3119 (W), SI 2004/1301 (E), 1749 (W) , 2146 (E), 2734 (W), 2688 (E) and 3091 (W), SI 2005/3281 (E) and SI 2006/113 (E) and 116 (W); the Feeding Stuffs (England) Regulations 2005, SI 2005/3281 amended by SI 2006/113; the Feeding Stuffs (Wales) Regulations 2006, SI 2006/116.

8–147   77. Division of samples and analysis by agricultural analyst. (1) Where a sample has been taken by an inspector in the prescribed[1] manner, then, subject to subsection (2) of this section, he shall divide it into three parts of as near as may be equal size and cause each part to be marked, sealed and fastened up in the prescribed manner; and the inspector—

(a) shall send one part to the agricultural analyst for the inspector's area;

(b) shall send another part—

(i) where the sample was taken pursuant to the request of a purchaser under section 75 of this Act, to the seller or his agent;

(ii) in any other case, if the person on whose premises the sample was taken purchased the material in question for use and not for resale, to the seller or his agent and otherwise to the person on whose premises the sample was taken; and

(c) subject to section 78 of this Act, shall retain the remaining part for nine months.

(2) If the person who manufactured any material of which an inspector has taken a sample in the

prescribed manner is not a person to whom a part of the sample is required to be sent under subsection (1) of this section, that subsection shall have effect as if for the reference to three parts there were substituted a reference to four parts, and the inspector shall send the fourth part to the manufacturer unless he does not know the manufacturer's name, or any address or the manufacturer in the United Kingdom, and is unable after making reasonable inquiries to ascertain that name, or, as the case may be, any such address before the expiration of fourteen days from the date when the sample was taken.

(3) There shall be sent with the part of a sample sent to the agricultural analyst—

(*a*) a statement signed by the inspector that the sample was taken in the prescribed manner;

(*b*) a copy of any statutory statement relating to the material sampled, a copy of any matters with which that material had been marked pursuant to this Part of this Act and, where the material sampled was described or marked as mentioned in section 70(1) or 71(1) of this Act, a copy of the document or the matters stated by the mark in question.

(4) The agricultural analyst shall analyse the part of a sample which is sent to him under subsection (1)(*a*) of this section in such manner, if any, as may be prescribed[2] and send a certificate of analysis in the prescribed form to the inspector who shall send a copy of it—

(*a*) where the sample was taken pursuant to the request of a purchaser under section 75 of this Act, to the purchaser and to the seller or his agent;

(*b*) in any other case, to the person to whom a part of the sample has been sent under subsection (1)(*b*)(ii) of this section;

and, in either case, to any person to whom he has sent a part of the sample under subsection (2) of this section.

(5) If the agricultural analyst to whom a sample is sent for analysis determines that for any reason an effective analysis of the sample cannot be made by him or under his direction he shall send it to the agricultural analyst for another area together with any documents received by him with the sample; and thereupon the foregoing provisions of this section shall apply as if that other analyst were the agricultural analyst for the inspector's area and the sample had originally been sent to him. [Agriculture Act 1970, s 77.]

---

1. See the Fertilisers (Sampling and Analysis) Regulations 1996, SI 1996/1342.
2. See the Feeding Stuffs (Sampling and Analysis) Regulations 1999, SI 1999/1663 amended by SI 1999/1871, SI 2000/2481, SI 2001/343 (Wales), 541 (England), 2253 (Wales) and 3389 (England), SI 2002/892 (Wales) and 1797 (Wales), SI 2003/1296 (E), 1503 (E), 1677 (W), 1850 (W), 2912 (E) and 3119 (W), SI 2004/1301 (E), 1749 (W) , 2146 (E), 2734 (W), 2688 (E) and 3091(W), SI 2005/3281 (E) and SI 2006/113 (E) and 116 (W); the Feeding Stuffs (England) Regulations 2005, SI 2005/3281 amended by SI 2006/113; the Feeding Stuffs (Wales) Regulations 2006, SI 2006/116.

8–148   78. Further analysis by Government Chemist.   (1) Where a sample of any material has been taken pursuant to the request of a purchaser under section 75 of this Act, any of the following persons, that is to say, the purchaser, the person who sold the material to him and any other person against whom a cause of action may lie in respect of the sale of that material, shall be entitled to require the inspector—

(*a*) to send the part retained by the inspector under section 77(1)(*c*) of this Act (hereafter in this section referred to as "the remaining part") for analysis to the Government Chemist;

(*b*) to supply the person making the request with a copy of the Government Chemist's certificate of analysis of that remaining part, whether that part was sent to the Government Chemist for analysis in pursuance of the request of that person or otherwise.

(2) Where a sample of any material has been taken by an inspector in the prescribed manner and it is intended to institute proceedings against any person for an offence under this Part of this Act and to adduce on behalf of the prosecution evidence of the result of an analysis of the sample—

(*a*) the prosecutor, if a person other than the inspector, shall be entitled to require the inspector—

(i) to send the remaining part of the sample for analysis to the Government Chemist;

(ii) to supply the prosecutor with a copy of the Government Chemist's certificate of analysis of that remaining part, whether that part was sent to the Government Chemist for analysis in pursuance of the request of the prosecutor or otherwise;

(*b*) the inspector, if he is the prosecutor, shall be entitled himself so to send that remaining part.

(3) Where a prosecutor avails himself of his rights under subsection (2) of this section he shall cause to be served with the summons a copy of the agricultural analyst's certificate of analysis and a copy of the Government Chemist's certificate of analysis; and where a prosecutor does not avail himself of his rights under that subsection he shall, not less than fourteen days before the service of the summons, cause to be served on the person charged a copy of the agricultural analyst's certificate of analysis and a notice of intended prosecution, and if, within the period of fourteen days beginning with the service of the notice, that person sends the prosecutor a written request to that effect accompanied by the amount of the fee payable by the prosecutor for the purpose under subsection (8) of this section (which shall be refunded to that person by the prosecutor if the prosecution is not brought) the prosecutor shall exercise his rights under subsection (2) of this section and the

proceedings shall not be instituted until he has sent that person a copy of the Government Chemist's certificate of analysis.

(4) Where proceedings are brought against any person for an offence under this Part of this Act and evidence is given or sought to be given of the result of an analysis of a sample of any material taken by an inspector in the prescribed[1] manner but it appears that the sample has not been analysed by the Government Chemist, the court may, of its own motion or on the application of either party, order the remaining part of the sample to be sent for analysis to the Government Chemist.

(5) Where under this section a part of a sample is sent for analysis to the Government Chemist there shall be sent with it—

(a) a copy of any document which was sent with the part of the sample sent to the agricultural analyst; and

(b) if the part is sent to the Government Chemist under subsection (2) or (4) of this section, a statement of the particulars on which the proceedings or intended proceedings are based.

(6) The Government Chemist shall analyse in such manner, if any, as may be prescribed[2] any part of a sample sent to him under this section but, where the part is accompanied by a statement such as is mentioned in subsection (5)(b) of this section, the analysis shall be made only with respect to the particulars in the statement unless the person or court requesting or ordering the analysis requires it to extend also to other matters.

(7) A certificate of any analysis under this section shall be sent by the Government Chemist—

(a) if the material analysed was sent to him in pursuance of subsection (1) or (2) of this section, to the inspector;

(b) if it was sent to him in pursuance of an order of the court under subsection (4) of this section, to the court.

(8) A request for an analysis under subsection (1) or (2) of this section shall be of no effect unless accompanied by the appropriate fee; and the appropriate fee for any analysis by the court under subsection (4) of this section shall be paid by such party to the proceedings as the court may direct.

(9) *Scotland.*

(10) In subsection (8) of this section "the appropriate fee" means such fee as may be fixed by the Minister of Technology with the approval of the Treasury, and different fees may be fixed for different materials and for different analyses of the same material.

[Agriculture Act 1970, s 78.]

---

1. See the Fertilisers (Sampling and Analysis) Regulations 1996, SI 1996/1342.

2. See the Fertilisers (Sampling and Analysis) Regulations 1996, SI 1996/1342 and the Feeding Stuffs (Sampling and Analysis) Regulations 1999, SI 1999/1663 amended by SI 1999/1871, SI 2000/2481 (England), SI 2001/343 (Wales), 541 (England), 2253 (Wales) and 3389 (England), SI 2002/892 and 1797 (Wales), SI 2003/1296 (E), 1503 (E), 1677 (W), 1850 (W), 2912 (E) and 3119 (W), SI 2004/1301 (E), 1749 (W) , 2146 (E), 2734 (W), 2688 (E) and 3091(W), SI 2005/3281 (E) and SI 2006/113 (E) and 116 (W); the Feeding Stuffs (England) Regulations 2005, SI 2005/3281 amended by SI 2006/113; the Feeding Stuffs (Wales) Regulations 2006, SI 2006/116.

8–149 79. Supplementary provisions relating to samples and analysis. (1) The regulations[1] with respect to the taking of samples under this Part of this Act may include provision requiring an inspector who proposes to take such a sample, in such circumstances as may be specified in the regulations, to satisfy himself as to such matters affecting the state of the material to be sampled as may be so specified.

(2) Regulations[1] may make provision with respect to the handling and storage of the parts into which samples are divided and with respect to the period within which analyses are to be carried out.

(3) Where the method of analysis for determining any fact as to the nature, substance or quality of any material is prescribed, any statement of that fact—

(a) in a statutory statement or in, or denoted by, a mark applied to any material in pursuance of this Part of this Act; or

(b) in any document or in, or denoted by, any mark, being a document or mark which is not a statutory statement but which gives rise to a warranty by virtue of this Part of this Act,

shall be taken to be a statement of that fact as determined by analysis in accordance with the method prescribed.

(4) Any analysis required to be made by an agricultural analyst or the Government Chemist may be made by any person acting under his directions.

(5) A certificate of analysis by an analyst appointed under section 67(3)(b) of this Act shall be signed by that analyst or another analyst so appointed for the same area, and a certificate of analysis by the Government Chemist shall be signed by him or a person authorised by him to sign the certificate.

(6) A certificate of analysis by an agricultural analyst or the Government Chemist shall, in any legal proceedings, be received as evidence of the facts stated therein if the party against whom it is to be given in evidence has been served with a copy of it not less than twenty-one days before the hearing and has not, before the seventh day preceding the hearing, served on the other part a notice requiring the attendance of the person who made the analysis.

(7) *Scotland.*

(8) Any document purporting to be a certificate of the kind mentioned in the foregoing provisions of this section shall be deemed to be such a certificate unless the contrary is proved.

(9) Any part of a sample, notice, certificate or other document required to be sent to or served on any person under this section or section 77 or 78 of this Act shall be sent or served in such manner, if any, as may be prescribed[1].

(10) Any person who—

(*a*) tampers with any material so as to procure that any sample of it taken or submitted for analysis under this Part of this Act does not correctly represent the material; or

(*b*) tampers or interferes with any sample taken or submitted for analysis under this Part of this Act,

shall be liable on summary conviction to a fine not exceeding **level 5** on the standard scale or imprisonment for a term not exceeding **three months★** or both.

[Agriculture Act 1970, s 79 as amended by the Criminal Justice Act 1982, ss 35, 38 and 46.]

★"51 weeks" substituted by the Criminal Justice Act 2003, Sch 26, from a date to be appointed.
1. See the Fertilisers (Sampling and Analysis) Regulations 1996, SI 1996/1342 and the Feeding Stuffs (Sampling and Analysis) Regulations 1999, SI 1999/1663 amended by SI 1999/1871, SI 2000/2481 (England), SI 2001/343 (Wales), 541 (England), 2253 (Wales) and 3389 (England), SI 2002/892 and 1797 (Wales), SI 2003/1296 (E), 1503 (E), 1677 (W), 1850 (W), 2912 (E) and 3119 (W), SI 2004/1301 (E), 1749 (W) , 2146 (E), 2734 (W), 2688 (E) and 3091(W), SI 2005/3281 (E) and SI 2006/113 (E) and 116 (W); the Feeding Stuffs (England) Regulations 2005, SI 2005/3281 amended by SI 2006/113; the Feeding Stuffs (Wales) Regulations 2006, SI 2006/116.

Prosecutions under Part IV

8–150 80. Institution of prosecutions.   (1) Without prejudice to any other enactment relating to the place where proceedings may be taken, proceedings for an offence under this Part of this Act may be taken in the place where the person charged resides or carries on business.

(2)–(4) *Repealed.*

[Agriculture Act 1970, s 80 as amended by the Local Government, Planning and Land Act 1980, Sch 34.]

8–151 81. Offences due to fault of other person.   Where the commission by any person of an offence under this Part of this Act is due to the act or default of some other person that other person shall be guilty of the offence, and a person may be charged with and convicted of the offence by virtue of this section whether or not proceedings are taken against the first-mentioned person.

[Agriculture Act 1970, s 81.]

8–152 82. Defence of mistake, accident, etc.   (1) In any proceedings for an offence under any of the following provisions of this Act, namely, sections 68(1A), (4)(*b*) and (*c*), 69(4)(*c*), 70(2), 71(2)(*b*), 73, 73A and 74A, it shall, subject to subsection (2) of this section, be a defence for the person charged to prove—

(*a*) that the commission of the offence was due to a mistake, or to reliance on information supplied to him, or to the act or default of another person, or to an accident or some other cause beyond his control; and

(*b*) that he took all reasonable precautions and exercised all due diligence to avoid the commission of such an offence by himself or any person under his control.

(2) If in any case the defence provided by the foregoing subsection involves the allegation that the commission of the offence was due to the act or default of another person or to reliance on information supplied by another person, the person charged shall not, without leave of the court, be entitled to rely on that defence unless, within a period ending seven clear days before the hearing, he has served on the prosecutor a notice in writing giving such information identifying or assisting in the identification of that other person as was then in his possession.

[Agriculture Act 1970, s 82 as amended by SI 1981/10 and SI 1995/1412.]

Supplementary provisions

8–153 83. Exercise of powers by inspectors.   (1) An inspector exercising his powers under this Part of this Act shall, if so required, produce written evidence of his authority.

(2) Any person who wilfully obstructs an inspector in the exercise of his powers under this Part of this Act shall be liable on summary conviction to a fine not exceeding **level 3** on the standard scale.

(3) Any person who, not being an inspector, purports to act as such under this Part of this Act shall be liable on summary conviction to a fine not exceeding **level 3** on the standard scale or on a second or subsequent conviction under this subsection, to a fine not exceeding **level 4** on the standard scale or imprisonment for a term not exceeding **three months★** or both.

(4) Subject to subsection (5) of this section, if any person discloses to any other person—

(*a*) any information with respect to any manufacturing process or trade secret obtained by him in premises which he has entered by virtue of this Part of this Act; or

(*b*) any information obtained by him in pursuance of this Part of this Act, then, unless the disclosure was made in and for the purpose of the performance by him or any other person of functions under this Part of this Act, he shall be liable on summary conviction to a fine not exceeding **level 5** on the standard scale.

(5) Subsection (4) of this section shall not prevent an inspector who has taken a sample of any material under section 76(4) of this Act from disclosing to the manufacturer or to the last seller of the material information as to the place where and the person from whom the sample was taken or from disclosing to that manufacturer or last seller or to any person who had the material on his premises for the purpose of sale information as to the results of any analysis of that sample.

[Agriculture Act 1970, s 83 as amended by the Criminal Justice Act 1982, ss 35, 38 and 46.]

---

*"51 weeks" substituted by the Criminal Justice Act 2003, Sch 26, from a date to be appointed.

8–154   85. Exemption for certain sales.   This Part of this Act shall not apply—

(a)–(b) *Repealed*

(c)   to the sale of any material in the exercise of a statutory power to enforce a right or to satisfy a claim or lien[1]; or

(d)   where the sale is made by a sheriff, bailiff or other officer to satisfy a writ of execution or warrant or decree of any court, or a distress for rent or warrant of distress.

[Agriculture Act 1970, s 85 as amended by SI 2000/2841.]

---

1. Where the sale is to satisfy a lien, the operation of the Act is to be excluded only where that sale is in the exercise of a statutory power (*G C Dobell & Co Ltd v Barber and Garratt* [1931] 1 KB 219).

PART VII
MISCELLANEOUS PROVISIONS

8–155   106. Eradication of brucellosis.   (1), (2) *Power to make grants in connection with the eradication of brucellosis.*

(4) Any person who offers for sale, otherwise than for slaughter, any animal known to him to be a reactor to brucella abortus shall be guilty of an offence and liable on summary conviction to a fine not exceeding **level 5** on the standard scale, or, if the offence is committed with respect to more than ten animals, to a fine not exceeding **level 3** on the standard scale for each animal.

(7) Any person who knowingly or recklessly makes any false statement for the purpose of obtaining for himself or any other person any payment under a scheme under subsection (1) or (2) of this section shall be liable on summary conviction to a fine not exceeding **level 3** on the standard scale or imprisonment for a term not exceeding **three months*** or both.

(8) Any of the following officers—

(a)   in England and Wales, any officer of the Minister of Agriculture, Fisheries and Food authorised in writing by that Minister to exercise the powers conferred by this subsection;

(b)   *Scotland*;

(c)   *Northern Ireland*;

may, for the purpose of obtaining any information which he may consider necessary in connection with a scheme under subsection (1) or (2) of this section, enter upon any land or premises and there inspect any animal, apply any test or take any sample, and examine and take copies of or extracts from any document.

The right of entry under this subsection may be exercised at any reasonable time, but only after production of the officer's authority if so required; and any person who obstructs or impedes an officer acting in the exercise of his powers under this subsection shall be liable on summary conviction to a fine not exceeding **level 3** on the standard scale or imprisonment for a term not exceeding **one month** or both.

(9), (10) *Interpretation of subsections* (1) *and* (2).

[Agriculture Act 1970, s 106, amended by the Animal Health Act 1981, Schs 5 and 6 and the Criminal Justice Act 1982, ss 35, 38 and 46.]

---

*"51 weeks" substituted by the Criminal Justice Act 2003, Sch 26, from a date to be appointed.

8–156   108. Corn Returns.   (1) *Power of Minister to authorise[1] the Home Grown Cereals Authority to discharge specified functions, including the receiving of returns, under the Corn Returns Act 1882.*

(2) The contents of any return furnished to the Authority aforesaid by virtue of any functions of the Minister under the said Act of 1882 which they are required and authorised to discharge by an order under subsection (1) of this section shall not without the consent of the person furnishing the return be published or otherwise disclosed except—

(a)   to a member of the Authority appointed by virtue of section 1(2)(a) of the said Act of 1965 or to an officer of the Authority duly authorised in that behalf; or

(b)   to, or to an officer of, the Minister[2]; or

(c) in the form of a summary of similar returns furnished by or obtained from a number of persons, being a summary so framed as not to enable particulars relating to any one person or undertaking to be ascertained from it; or

(d) with a view to the institution of, or otherwise for the purposes of, any criminal proceedings pursuant to or arising out of the said Act of 1882;

and any person who publishes or otherwise discloses the contents of any return in contravention of this subsection shall be liable on summary conviction to a fine not exceeding **the statutory maximum** or on conviction on indictment to a fine or to imprisonment for a term not exceeding **two years** or to both.

(3)–(5) *Amendments, definition of "Minister" and application to Scotland.*
[Agriculture Act 1970, s 108, as amended by the Criminal Law Act 1977, s 28.]

---

1. See the Corn Returns (Delegation of Functions) Order 1981, SI 1981/142.
2. The functions of the Minister, so far as exercisable in relation to Wales, have been transferred to the National Assembly for Wales, by the National Assembly for Wales (Transfer of Functions) Order 1999, SI 1999/672, art 2, Sch 1.

PART VIII
GENERAL

8–157 110. Offences by bodies corporate. (1) Where a body corporate is guilty of an offence under this Act or any order or scheme made thereunder and that offence is proved to have been committed with the consent or connivance of, or to be attributable to any neglect on the part of, any director, manager, secretary or other similar officer of the body corporate, or any person who was purporting to act in any such capacity, he, as well as the body corporate, shall be guilty of that offence and shall be liable to be proceeded against and punished accordingly.

(2) Where the affairs of a body corporate are managed by its members, the foregoing subsection shall apply in relation to the acts and defaults of a member in connection with his functions of management as if he were a director of the body corporate.
[Agriculture Act 1970, s 110.]

Agriculture (Miscellaneous Provisions) Act 1972
(1972 c 62)

8–158 19. Use of poison against grey squirrels and coypus. (1) The relevant Minister[1] may, by an order made for the purposes of this section and applying either to the whole of Great Britain or to any specified part or area thereof, specify a poison for use for the purpose of destroying grey squirrels[2] or coypus and the manner of its use for that purpose; and it shall be a defence in proceedings for an offence against any of the enactments mentioned in subsection (2) of this section to show that—

(a) the act alleged to constitute the offence was done for the purpose of destroying grey squirrels or coypus and was done at a time when, and in a place where, such an order had effect; and

(b) the poison used and manner of its use were such as to comply with the provisions of the order.

(2) The said enactments are section 8(b) of the Protection of Animals Act 1911, section 7(b) of the Protection of Animals (Scotland) Act 1912 (which restrict the placing on land of poison and poisoned substances) and so much of section 5(1)(a) of the Protection of Birds Act 1954[3] as relates to poisoned or poisonous substances.

(3) The relevant Minister shall not make an order for the purposes of this section except after such consultation as he considers appropriate with such organisations as appear to him to represent the interests concerned and unless a draft of the order has been laid before, and approved by a resolution of, each House of Parliament.

(4) Any order made for the purposes of this section may make different provision in relation to grey squirrels and in relation to coypus; and the power to make orders for the purposes of this section shall be exercisable by statutory instrument and shall include power to vary or revoke a previous order.

(5) In this section "the relevant Minister" means—

(a) in the case of an order which does not apply outside England, the Minister;

(b) in the case of an order which does not apply outside Scotland, the Secretary of State for Scotland;

(c) in the case of an order which applies both in England and in Scotland but not in Wales, the Minister and the Secretary of State for Scotland acting jointly;

(d) in the case of an order which applies in Wales or both in England and Wales but not (in either case) in Scotland, the Minister and the Secretary of State for Wales acting jointly; and

(e) in the case of an order which applies in England, Scotland and Wales, the Minister and those Secretaries of State acting jointly.

For the purposes of this subsection Monmouthshire shall be treated as part of Wales and not of England.

(6) This section is without prejudice to any defence available apart from this section in proceedings for any such offence as is mentioned in subsection (1) of this section; and nothing in this section shall be construed as conferring any exemption from any provision contained in or having effect under any enactment not mentioned in subsection (2) of this section.

[Agriculture (Miscellaneous Provisions) Act 1972, s 19.]

---

1. The Minister of Agriculture, Fisheries and Food, see the Transfer of Functions (Agriculture and Food) Order 1999, SI 1999/3141. The functions of the Minister, so far as exercisable in relation to Wales, have been transferred to the National Assembly for Wales, by the National Assembly for Wales (Transfer of Functions) Order 1999, SI 1999/672, art 2, Sch 1.

2. The Grey Squirrels (Warfarin) Order 1973, SI 1973/744 has been made.

3. Repealed and replaced by the Wildlife and Countryside Act 1981, s 5(1)(*a*), title CONSERVATION, post.

Horticulture (Special Payments) Act 1974

(1974 c 5)

8–159 **1.** *Power of Minister to make payments under a scheme to assist commercial growers.*

8–160 **3. False statements to obtain payments.**   If any person for the purpose of obtaining for himself or any other person any payment under such a scheme knowingly or recklessly makes a false statement he shall be liable on summary conviction to a fine not exceeding **level 5** on the standard scale.

[Horticulture (Special Payments) Act 1974, s 3 as amended by the Criminal Justice Act 1982, ss 38 and 46.]

8–161 **4. Powers of entry.**   (1) For the purposes of this Act an authorised officer shall on producing if so required written evidence of his authority have power to enter land (other than a dwelling house) at all reasonable times for the purpose of ascertaining whether any requirement of a scheme or any condition subject to which payment may be or has been made under a scheme is being, or has been, complied with.

(2) If any person wilfully obstructs or impedes an authorised officer in the exercise of his powers under the preceding subsection he shall be liable on summary conviction to a fine not exceeding **level 5** on the standard scale.

(3) In this section "authorised officer" means—

   (*a*)   in relation to England or Wales an authorised officer of the Minister[1];
   (*b*)   in relation to Scotland an authorised officer of the Secretary of State; and
   (*c*)   in relation to Northern Ireland an authorised officer of the Minister or of the Ministry of Agriculture for Northern Ireland.

[Horticulture (Special Payments) Act 1974, s 4 as amended by the Criminal Justice Act 1982, ss 38 and 46.]

---

1. The functions of the Minister, so far as exercisable in relation to Wales, have been transferred to the National Assembly for Wales, by the National Assembly for Wales (Transfer of Functions) Order 1999, SI 1999/672, art 2, Sch 1.

Agriculture (Miscellaneous Provisions) Act 1976

(1976 c 55)

8–162 **Measures to restrict the growing of male hop plants.**   The Minister of Agriculture, Fisheries and Food, for the purpose of facilitating the production of seedless hops, may by order bring this section into force in any area in England. If male hops are growing on land within an area where this section is in force, the Minister may serve notice on the occupier requiring him within a specified time to take steps for the removal of such plants. Failure, without reasonable excuse, to comply with such a notice is a summary offence: penalty, fine not exceeding **level 3** on the standard scale. Intentional obstruction of a person exercising power to enter land and do what a person served with a notice has failed to do, or to enter land for the purpose of inspection is a summary offence: penalty, fine not exceeding **level 3** on the standard scale.

[Agriculture (Miscellaneous Provisions) Act 1976, s 5 as amended by the Criminal Justice Act 1982, ss 38 and 46—summarised.]

Agricultural Statistics Act 1979

(1979 c 13)

8–163 **1. Power to obtain agricultural statistics.**   (1) Where it appears to the appropriate Minister[1] expedient so to do for the purpose of obtaining statistical information relating to agriculture, he may serve on any owners or occupiers of land used for agriculture, or of land which he has reason to believe may be so used, notices requiring them to furnish in writing, in such form and manner and to such person as may be specified in the notice, and within such time and with respect to such date or dates or such period or periods as may be so specified, the information referred to in the notice (including, as respects paragraphs (*d*) to (*f*) of this subsection, the information referred to in the notice as to quantities, values, expenditure and receipts) relating to—

  (*a*) the situation, area and description of relevant land owned or occupied by them, the date of acquisition of the land, and the date at which so much of it as is comprised in any agricultural unit became comprised in that unit, and the rates payable in respect of the land,

  (*b*) any person who is an owner or occupier of the land or any part of it and the terms on which, and arrangements under which, the land or any part of it is owned, occupied, managed or farmed by any person;

  (*c*) *repealed*;

  (*d*) the character and use of different parts of the land, the time at which any use of such parts was begun or will become fully effective, and their produce at any time during the period beginning one year before, and ending one year after, the time at which the information is required to be furnished,

  (*e*) fixed and other equipment, livestock, and the stocks of agricultural produce and requisites held in respect of the land, and the provision and maintenance of such equipment, livestock and requisites and the provision of agricultural services for the benefit of the land,

  (*f*) the methods and operations used on the land, the marketing or other disposal of its produce, any payments received under any enactment in respect of such produce, and the provision of agricultural services otherwise than for the benefit of the land,

  (*g*) the number and description of persons employed on the land, or employed by the occupier in disposing of its produce, and the remuneration paid to, and hours worked by, persons so employed or such persons of different descriptions.

(2) For the purpose of obtaining statistical information relating to agriculture, any person authorised by the appropriate Minister in that behalf may, after giving not less than 24 hours notice and on producing if so required evidence of his authority to act for the purposes of this subsection, orally require the owner or occupier of land to furnish to him within a reasonable time, and either orally or in writing as the said owner or occupier may elect, such information, whether or not specified in the notice, as the said person authorised by the appropriate Minister may require, being information which the owner or occupier, as the case may be, could have been required to furnish under subsection (1) above.

(3) References in subsections (1) and (2) above to the owner of land include references to a person exercising, as servant or agent of the owner, functions of estate management in relation to the land, and references in those subsections to the occupier of land include references to a person responsible for the control of the farming of the land as servant or agent of the occupier of the land.

(4) No person shall be required under this section to furnish any balance sheet or profit and loss account, but this subsection shall not prevent the requiring of information by reason only that it is or might be contained as an item in such a balance sheet or account.

(5) *Repealed.*

[Agricultural Statistics Act 1979, s 1 as amended by the Agriculture (Amendment) Act 1984, s 2.]

---

1. The functions of the Minister, so far as exercisable in relation to Wales, have been transferred to the National Assembly for Wales, by the National Assembly for Wales (Transfer of Functions) Order 1999, SI 1999/672, art 2, Sch 1.

8–165   **3. Restriction on disclosure of information.**   (1) Subject to subsection (2) below, no information relating to any particular land or business which has been obtained under section 1 or 2 above shall be published or otherwise disclosed without the previous consent in writing of the person by whom the information was furnished and every other person who is an owner or the occupier of the land and whose interests may in the opinion of the appropriate Minister be affected by the disclosure.

(2) Nothing in subsection (1) above shall restrict the disclosure of information—

  (*a*) to the Minister in charge of any Government department, to the Scottish Ministers, to any authority acting under an enactment for regulating the marketing of any agricultural produce, or to any person exercising functions on behalf of any such Minister, the Scottish Ministers or authority for the purpose of the exercise of those functions;

  (*b*) to an authority having power under any enactment to give permission for the development of land, for the purpose of assisting that authority in the preparation of proposals relating to such development or in considering whether or not to give such permission;

  (*c*) if the disclosure is confined to situation, extent, number and kind of livestock, character of land, and name and address of owner and occupier, to any person to whom the appropriate Minister considers that the disclosure is required in the public interest;

  (*d*) to any person for the purposes of any criminal proceedings under section 4 below or for the purposes of any report of such proceedings;

  (*e*) to the Agricultural Training Board under section 2B of the Industrial Training Act 1964; or

  (*f*) to an institution of the European Communities under section 12 of the European Communities Act 1972, (*g*) to the Food Standards Agency for purposes connected with the carrying out of any of its functions,

or the use of information in any manner which the appropriate Minister thinks necessary or expedient in connection with the maintenance of the supply of food in the United Kingdom.
[Agricultural Statistics Act 1979, s 3 as amended by SI 1999/1820 and the Food Standards Act 1999, Sch 5.]

8–166 4. Penalties. (1) Any person who without reasonable excuse fails to furnish information in compliance with a requirement under section 1 or 2 above shall be liable on summary conviction to a fine not exceeding **level 3** on the standard scale.

(2) If any person—

(*a*) in purported compliance with a requirement imposed under section 1 or 2 above knowingly or recklessly furnishes any information which is false in any material particular, or

(*b*) publishes or otherwise discloses any information in contravention of section 3 above,

he shall be liable[1] on summary conviction to imprisonment for a term not exceeding **3 months** or to a fine not exceeding the prescribed sum or to both, or on conviction on indictment to imprisonment for a term not exceeding **2 years** or to a fine or to both.
[Agricultural Statistics Act 1979, s 4 as amended by the Criminal Justice Act 1982, ss 38 and 46.]

---

1. For procedure in respect of this offence which is triable either way, see the Magistrates' Courts Act 1980, ss 17A–21, in PART I: MAGISTRATES' COURTS, PROCEDURE, ante.

8–167 5. Service of notices. (1) Any notice authorised by this Act to be served on any person shall be duly served if it is delivered to him, or left at his proper address or sent to him by post in a registered letter.

(2) Any such notice authorised to be served on an incorporated company or body shall be duly served if served on the secretary or clerk of the company or body.

(3) For the purposes of this section and of section 7 of the Interpretation Act 1978, the proper address of any person on whom any such notice is to be served shall, in the case of the secretary or clerk of any incorporated company or body be that of the registered or principal office of the company or body, and in any other case be the last known address of the person in question.

(4) Where any such notice is to be served on a person as being the person having any interest in land, and it is not practicable after reasonable inquiry to ascertain his name or address, the notice may be served by addressing it to him by the description of the person having that interest in the land (naming it), and delivering the notice to some responsible person on the land or by affixing it, or a copy of it, to some conspicuous object on the land.

(5) Where any such notice is to be served on any person as being the owner of the land and the land belongs to an ecclesiastical benefice a copy shall be served on the Church Commissioners.

(6) Without prejudice to subsections (1) to (5) above, any notice under this Act to be served on an occupier shall be deemed to be duly served if it is addressed to him by the description of "the occupier" of the land in question and sent by post to, or delivered to some person on, the land.
[Agricultural Statistics Act 1979, s 5.]

8–168 6. Interpretation. (1) In this Act—

"the appropriate Minister" means, in relation to England, the Secretary of State and, in relation to Wales, the Secretary of State;

"land" includes messuages, tenements and hereditaments, houses and buildings of any tenure;

"livestock" includes creatures kept for any purpose;

"owner" means, in relation to land, a person, other than a mortgagee not in possession, who is for the time being entitled to dispose of the fee simple of the land, and includes also a person holding, or entitled to the rents and profits of, the land under a lease or agreement;

"the prescribed sum" means the prescribed sum within the meaning of section 32 of the Magistrates' Courts Act 1980 (£1,000 or other sum substituted by order under section 143(1) of that Act); and

"relevant land" in the case of any owner or occupier of land used for agriculture, means the aggregate of—

(*a*) the land owned or occupied by him which is comprised in any agricultural unit; and

(*b*) any other land owned or occupied by him which is either—

(i) used for forestry; or

(ii) not used for any purpose, but capable of use for agriculture or forestry,

but which, if used as agricultural land by the occupier of that agricultural unit, would be comprised in that unit.

(2) Section 109 of the Agriculture Act 1947 (interpretation) shall have effect for the purposes of this Act as it has effect for the purposes of that Act except that the definition of "livestock" shall be omitted from subsection (3).
[Agricultural Statistics Act 1979, s 6, as amended by the Magistrates' Courts Act 1980, Sch 7 and SI 2002/794.]

Bees Act 1980
(1980 c 12)

8–169 1. Control of pests and diseases affecting bees. (1) The Minister for Agriculture, Fisheries and Food[1], the Secretary of State for Scotland and the Secretary of State for Wales, acting jointly, may by order[2] make such provision as they think fit for the purpose of preventing the introduction into or spreading within Great Britain of pests or diseases affecting bees.

(2) Without prejudice to the generality of subsection (1) above, for the purpose there mentioned an order[2] under this section—

(a) may prohibit or regulate the importation into or movement within Great Britain of bees and combs, bee products, hives, containers and other appliances used in connection with keeping or transporting bees, and of any other thing which has or may have been exposed to infection with any pest or disease to which the order applies;

(b) may make provision with respect to any of the matters specified in the Schedule to this Act; and

(c) may make different provision for different cases or different areas.

(3) Any authorised person may examine any bees or other things subject to control under an order under this section, and may take samples of them, in order to see if they are free from infection.

(4) Where any bees or other things subject to control under any such order are found to be infected, or to have been exposed to infection, with any pest or disease to which the order applies, any authorised person may destroy them by such means as he thinks fit, or cause them to be so destroyed.

(5) Without prejudice to subsection (4) above, where any bees or other things are imported into Great Britain in contravention of an order under this section, any authorised person may destroy them by such means as he thinks fit, or cause them to be so destroyed, and may do so with or without first allowing an opportunity for them to be re-exported.

(6) No compensation shall be payable in respect of any exercise of the powers conferred by subsections (3) and (5) above.

(7) Any person who—

(a) imports any bees or other things into Great Britain in contravention of an order under this section;

(b) moves any bees or other things within Great Britain in contravention of any such order; or

(c) otherwise contravenes or fails to comply with the provisions of any such order or with any condition imposed by any licence issued under any such order;

shall be liable on summary conviction to a fine not exceeding **level 5** on the standard scale.

(8) Any expenses incurred by any of the Ministers mentioned in subsection (1) above under this section (or under any order made under this section) shall be defrayed out of moneys provided by Parliament.

(9) The power to make an order under this section shall be exercisable by statutory instrument, which shall be subject to annulment by resolution of either House of Parliament.

[Bees Act 1980, s 1 as amended by the Criminal Justice Act 1982, s 46.]

---

1. See the Transfer of Functions (Agriculture and Food) Order 1999, SI 1999/3141. The functions of the Minister, so far as exercisable in relation to Wales, have been transferred to the National Assembly for Wales, by the National Assembly for Wales (Transfer of Functions) Order 1999, SI 1999/672, art 2, Sch 1 and SI 2004/3044, art 2 and Sch 1.

2. The Bee Diseases and Pests Control (England) Order 2006, SI 2006/342 has been made. As regards Wales the Bee Diseases Control Order 1982, SI 1982/107 and the Importation of Bees Order 1997, SI 1997/310 have been made.

8–170 2. Power of entry. (1) For the purpose of exercising any power conferred on him by or under section 1 of this Act an authorised person may at any time enter—

(a) any premises or other place; or

(b) any vessel, boat, hovercraft, aircraft or vehicle of any other description;

on or in which he has reasonable grounds for supposing there are or have been any bees or other things subject to control under an order under that section.

(2) A person seeking to enter any premises or other place, or any vessel, boat, hovercraft, aircraft or other vehicle in exercise of the power of entry under this section, shall, if so required by or on behalf of the owner or occupier or person in charge, produce evidence of his authority before entering.

(3) Any person who intentionally obstructs a person acting in exercise of the power of entry under this section shall be liable on summary conviction, or, in Scotland, on conviction by a court of summary jurisdiction, to a fine not exceeding **level 3** on the standard scale.

[Bees Act 1980, s 2 as amended by the Criminal Justice Act 1982, s 46.]

8–171 3. Interpretation. In this Act—

"authorised person" means a person generally or specially authorised in writing by the responsible Minister;

"bees" includes bees in any stage of their life cycle;

"bee product" means any natural product of the activities of bees (such as, for example, honey or beeswax) in its natural state; and

"the responsible Minister" means—

(a) in relation to England, the Minister of Agriculture, Fisheries and Food; and
(b) in relation to Scotland and Wales, the Secretary of State[1].

[Bees Act 1980, s 3.]

1. The functions of the Minister, so far as exercisable in relation to Wales, have been transferred to the National Assembly for Wales, by the National Assembly for Wales (Transfer of Functions) Order 1999, SI 1999/672, art 2, Sch 1.

8–172   SCHEDULE

Specific Matters with respect to which Provision may be made by Orders under section 1

Horticultural Produce Act 1986

(1986 c 20)

8–173 1. Power to control the movement of produce. (1) Where an authorised officer inspects any produce which he is entitled to inspect under section 13 of the Act of 1964, he may prohibit its movement if he is satisfied that a grading offence is being committed in respect of it.

(2) An officer who exercises the power conferred by subsection (1) above shall, without delay, give to the person who appears to him to be in charge of the produce concerned notice in writing—

(a) specifying the produce in relation to which the power has been exercised; and
(b) stating that the produce may not be moved without the written consent of an authorised officer.

(3) If the person to whom the officer gives the notice does not appear to him to be the owner of the produce or an agent or employee of the owner, the officer shall use his best endeavours to bring the contents of the notice to the attention of such a person as soon as practicable.

(4) An authorised officer may affix to any produce in relation to which the power conferred by subsection (1) above has been exercised, or to any container in which the produce is packed, labels warning of the exercise of the power.

[Horticultural Produce Act 1986, s 1.]

8–174 2. Consents to the movement of controlled produce. (1) An authorised officer may, at any time, give written consent to the movement of controlled produce.

(2) An authorised officer shall, upon request, give written consent to the movement of controlled produce if—

(a) he is satisfied that no grading offence would be committed in respect of the produce if it were sold in circumstances in which grading rules apply; or
(b) he, or another authorised officer, has been given a written undertaking that the produce will be disposed of in a specified manner, he is satisfied that if the produce is disposed of in that manner no grading offence will be committed in respect of it and he has no reason to doubt that the terms of the undertaking will be met.

(3) An authorised officer shall, upon request, give written consent to the movement of controlled produce if—

(a) he, or another authorised officer, has been given a written undertaking to the effect that—

(i) the produce will be moved to a place approved by an authorised officer;
(ii) there will be taken there the steps required to ensure that the produce may be sold in circumstances in which grading rules apply without a grading offence being committed in respect of it; and
(iii) the produce will not be moved from that place without the written consent of an authorised officer; and

(b) he has no reason to doubt that the terms of the undertaking will be met.

(4) A consent given by an authorised officer under this section shall—

(a) specify the produce to which it relates; and
(b) where the consent is given under subsection (3) above, state that the produce continues to be controlled.

[Horticultural Produce Act 1986, s 2.]

8–175 3. Power to change the circumstances in which consent must be given. The Ministers may by order made by statutory instrument make such amendments of this Act as they think fit for the purpose of changing the circumstances in which an authorised officer is required to give written consent to the movement of produce.
[Horticultural Produce Act 1986, s 3—summarised.]

8–176 4. Offences. (1) Any person who, knowing produce to be controlled, knowingly—

(*a*) moves it, or
(*b*) causes it to be moved,

without the written consent of an authorised officer shall be guilty of an offence.
(2) Any person who, knowing produce to be controlled, knowingly—

(*a*) removes from it, or
(*b*) causes to be removed from it,

a label which has been affixed under section 1(4) of this Act shall be guilty of an offence.
(3) Any person who fails to comply with an undertaking given by him for the purposes of section 2 of this Act shall be guilty of an offence.
(4) It shall be a defence—

(*a*) for a person charged with any offence under this section, to prove that, when the power conferred by section 1(1) of this Act was exercised, no grading offence was being committed in respect of the produce concerned;
(*b*) for a person charged with an offence under subsection (1) or (2) above, to prove that there was a reasonable excuse for the act or omission in respect of which he is charged; and
(*c*) for a person charged with an offence under subsection (3) above, to prove that he took all reasonable precautions and exercised all due diligence to avoid the commission of such an offence.

(5) A person guilty of an offence under this section shall be liable, on summary conviction, to a fine not exceeding **level 5** on the standard scale.
[Horticultural Produce Act 1986, s 4.]

8–177 5. Extension of the Act of 1964. The following provisions of the Act of 1964 shall have effect as if the provisions of this Act were contained in Part III of that Act—

(*a*) section 15 (which penalises the obstruction of an authorised officer acting under that Part);
(*b*) section 19 (which applies in relation to the commission by corporations of offences under that Part); and
(*c*) section 20(3) (which provides that proceedings in England and Wales for an offence under that Part may only be instituted with the consent of the Attorney General or, in England, the Minister of Agriculture, Fisheries and Food and, in Wales, the Secretary of State[1]).
[Horticultural Produce Act 1986, s 5.]

_____

1. Now the Minister of Agriculture, Fisheries and Food alone, see the Transfer of Functions (Agriculture and Food) Order 1999, SI 1999/3141. The functions of the Minister, so far as exercisable in relation to Wales, have been transferred to the National Assembly for Wales, by the National Assembly for Wales (Transfer of Functions) Order 1999, SI 1999/672, art 2, Sch 1.

8–178 6. Interpretation. In this Act—

"the Act of 1964" means the Agriculture and Horticulture Act 1964;
"authorised officer" means a person who is an authorised officer for the purposes of Part III of the Act of 1964 (grading of fresh horticultural produce);
"controlled", in relation to produce, means that the power conferred by section 1(1) of this Act has been exercised in relation to it and that no consent to its movement has been given under section 2(1) or (2) of this Act;
"grading offence" means an offence under section 14(1) or (2) of the Act of 1964;
"grading rules" means the rules enforced under Part III of the Act of 1964.
[Horticultural Produce Act 1986, s 6.]

8–179 7. *Short title, repeals, commencement and extent*

Agriculture and Forestry (Financial Provisions) Act 1991
(1991 c 33)

8–180 2. Recovery of cost of supervising Community livestock carcase grading procedures.
(1) The Minister may require the occupiers of slaughterhouses at which livestock carcases are required to be graded in pursuance of any Community obligation to pay to him in respect of the

supervision of the grading by his officers such fees as he may with the approval of the Treasury specify.

(2) The fees shall be such as to secure, so far as practicable, that the amounts payable are sufficient, taking one year with another, to cover the cost of the supervision referred to in subsection (1) above.

(3) Different fees may be specified in relation to slaughterhouses of different classes or descriptions but this section shall not be construed as requiring the fees payable in the case of any particular slaughterhouse to be related to the cost of supervision at that slaughterhouse or as precluding exceptions from the liability to pay fees.

(4) Before making any decision as to the total fees to be recovered under this section or the method of apportioning them between the persons liable to pay them the Minister shall consult with such organisations as appear to him to be representative of those persons.

(5) The Minister may permit payment of any fees under this section by instalments and arrange for the refund, adjustment, set-off, waiver or reduction of the whole or part of any such fee in such cases as he may determine.

(6) The Minister may require the occupiers of slaughterhouses to keep and preserve such records, to make such annual or other returns and to provide him with such other information as he may reasonably require for the purpose of determining whether any and, if so, what fees are payable by them under this section.

(7) For the purpose of determining whether any and, if so, what fees are payable under this section by the occupier of any slaughterhouse any officer of the Minister may, on producing if required written evidence of his authority—

(a) enter and inspect that slaughterhouse and any carcase in it; and

(b) require the occupier to produce for inspection, and allow the officer to make a copy of, or extracts from, any records relevant for that purpose and remove any such record for a reasonable period.

(8) Any person who—

(a) without reasonable excuse fails to comply with a requirement imposed under subsection (6) or (7)(b) above; or

(b) intentionally obstructs any officer in the exercise of his powers under subsection (7)(a) above,

is guilty of an offence and liable on summary conviction to a fine not exceeding **level 3** on the standard scale.

(9) Any person who, for the purpose of avoiding payment, or payment in full, of any fee for which he is liable under this section, makes a statement which he knows to be false in a material particular or recklessly makes a statement which is false in a material particular is guilty of an offence and liable on summary conviction to a fine not exceeding **level 5** on the standard scale.

(10) Fees received by the Minister by virtue of this section shall be paid into the Consolidated Fund.

(11) In this section—

"the Minister" means, in relation to England, the Minister of Agriculture, Fisheries and Food and, in relation to Wales or Scotland, the Secretary of State concerned with agriculture in those parts of the United Kingdom but arrangements may be made for any function of any of those Ministers or of the officers of any of those Ministers to be discharged by another of those Ministers or, as the case may be, the officers of another of those Ministers[1];

"slaughterhouse" has, in England and Wales, the meaning given in section 34 of the Slaughterhouses Act 1974 and, in Scotland, the meaning given by section 22 of the Slaughter of Animals (Scotland) Act 1980;

"livestock" means cattle, sheep and pigs;

"grading" includes weighing and marking.

[Agriculture and Forestry (Financial Provisions) Act 1991, s 2.]

---

1. The functions of the Minister, so far as exercisable in relation to Wales, have been transferred to the National Assembly for Wales, by the National Assembly for Wales (Transfer of Functions) Order 1999, SI 1999/672, art 2, Sch 1.

Agriculture Act 1993[1]

(1993 c 37)

PART III[2]
GRANTS FOR MARKETING

8–181 50. Grants. (1) The Ministers may, by a scheme[3] made with the approval of the Treasury, make provision for the payment by the appropriate Minister of grants towards expenditure which has been, or is to be, incurred in carrying out proposals to which this section applies.

(2) This section applies to proposals for the organisation, promotion, encouragement, development, co-ordination or facilitation of the marketing in Great Britain or elsewhere of—

(a) the produce of agriculture (including horticulture),

(b) the produce of fish farming,

(c) the produce of an activity specified[4] for the purposes of this subsection by order made by the Ministers, or

(d) anything derived from produce falling within any of paragraphs (a) to (c) above.

(3) Without prejudice to the generality of subsection (1) above, a scheme under this section may—

(a) provide for the payment of grant by reference to proposals which have been approved by the appropriate Minister after submission to and recommendation by such person as may be specified in the scheme;

(b) authorise the approval of proposals to be varied or withdrawn with the written consent of the person making the proposals;

(c) authorise the reduction or withholding of grant where assistance in respect of expenditure for which the grant is made is given under any enactment other than this section;

(d) confer a discretion on the appropriate Minister as to the payment of grant, as to the manner and timing of payment of grant and as to the amount of grant;

(e) make the payment of grant subject to such conditions as may be specified in or determined under the scheme;

(f) provide for functions in connection with the administration of the scheme to be carried out, subject to such conditions as may be specified in the scheme, by such person as may be so specified;

(g) provide for any discretion conferred by or under the scheme to be exercisable in such circumstances and by reference to such matters as may be specified in or determined under the scheme;

(h) contain such supplementary and consequential provision as the Ministers think fit; and

(i) make different provision for different cases (including different provision for different areas).

(4) A scheme under this section may, in relation to any discretion under the scheme, include provision for such person as may be specified in the scheme to be, to such extent and subject to such conditions as may be so specified, the delegate of the appropriate Minister.

(5) If at any time after the approval of proposals under a scheme under this section (and whether before or after the proposals have been fully carried out) it appears to the appropriate Minister—

(a) that any condition imposed under the scheme in relation to the proposals has not been complied with, or

(b) that in connection with the submission of the proposals the person submitting them gave information on any matter which was false or misleading in a material respect,

he may, subject to subsection (6) below, on demand recover any grant or any part of a grant paid with reference to the proposals, and may revoke the approval in whole or in part.

(6) The appropriate Minister may not make a demand or revoke an approval under subsection (5) above unless he has given at least 30 days' written notice of the reasons for the proposed action to any person to whom any payment by way of a grant in relation to the proposals would be payable, or from whom any such payment would be recoverable.

(7) Where a scheme under this section provides for functions under the scheme to be carried out by any body created by a statutory provision, the Ministers may, after consultation with the body, by regulations modify or add to its constitution or powers for the purpose of enabling it to carry them out.

(8) The power to make a scheme under this section shall be exercisable by statutory instrument subject to annulment in pursuance of a resolution of either House of Parliament.

(9) In this section—

"agriculture"—

(a) in relation to England and Wales, has the same meaning as in the Agriculture Act 1947, and

(b) in relation to Scotland, has the same meaning as in the Agriculture (Scotland) Act 1948;

"the appropriate Minister" means—

(a) in relation to England, the Minister of Agriculture, Fisheries and Food, and

(b) in relation to Scotland or Wales, the Secretary of State[5];

"fish farming" means the breeding, rearing or cultivating of fish (including shellfish) whether or not for the purpose of producing food for human consumption;

"the Ministers" means the Minister of Agriculture, Fisheries and Food, the Secretary of State for Scotland and the Secretary of State for Wales acting jointly;

"shellfish" includes crustaceans and molluscs of any kind.

[Agriculture Act 1993, s 50.]

---

1. This Act makes provision about milk marketing and potato marketing, and provides for the payment of grants in connection with the marketing of certain commodities. The Act contains a number of offences and only those relating to grants for marketing are contained in this work. Residual functions of the Secretary of State and the Secretary of State for

Wales were transferred to the Minister of Agriculture, Fisheries and Food by the Transfer of Functions (Agriculture and Fisheries) Order 2000, SI 2000/1812.

    2. Part III contains ss 50–53.

    3. The Marketing Development Scheme 1994, SI 1994/1403 amended by SI 1996/2629, and the Food Industry Development Scheme 1997, SI 1997/2673 amended by SI 2001/3339 (England) have been made.

    4. See the Marketing Development Scheme (Specification of Activities) Order 1994, SI 1994/1404.

    5. Now the Minister of Agriculture Fisheries and Food alone see the Transfer of Functions (Agriculture and Food) Order 1999, SI 1999/3141. The functions of the Minister, so far as exercisable in relation to Wales, have been transferred to the National Assembly for Wales, by the National Assembly for Wales (Transfer of Functions) Order 1999, SI 1999/672, art 2, Sch 1.

8–182   51. False statements to obtain payments.   Any person who, for the purpose of obtaining a payment under a scheme under section 50 above for himself or another, knowingly or recklessly makes a statement which is false or misleading in a material respect shall be guilty of an offence and liable on summary conviction to a fine not exceeding **level 5** on the standard scale or to imprisonment for a term not exceeding **six months** or to **both**.

[Agriculture Act 1993, s 51.]

8–183   52. Time limit for prosecutions.   (1) Notwithstanding anything in any other enactment, proceedings for an offence under this Part of this Act may, subject to subsection (2) below, be commenced within the period of six months from the date on which evidence sufficient in the opinion of the prosecutor to warrant the proceedings came to his knowledge.

    (2) No such proceedings shall be commenced by virtue of this section more than three years after the commission of the offence.

    (3) For the purposes of this section, a certificate signed by or on behalf of the prosecutor and stating the date on which evidence sufficient in his opinion to warrant the proceedings came to his knowledge shall be conclusive evidence of that fact.

    (4) A certificate stating that matter and purporting to be so signed shall be deemed to be so signed unless the contrary is proved.

    (5) *Scotland.*

[Agriculture Act 1993, s 52.]

PART IV[1]
MISCELLANEOUS AND SUPPLEMENTARY

Supplementary

8–184   61. Offences by bodies corporate.   (1) Where a body corporate is guilty of an offence under this Act, and that offence is proved to have been committed with the consent or connivance of, or to be attributable to any neglect on the part of—

    (*a*) any director, manager, secretary or other similar officer of the body corporate, or

    (*b*) any person who was purporting to act in any such capacity,

he, as well as the body corporate, shall be guilty of the offence and be liable to be proceeded against and punished accordingly.

    (2) For the purposes of subsection (1) above, "director", in relation to a body corporate whose affairs are managed by its members, means a member of the body corporate.

    (3) *Scotland.*

[Agriculture Act 1993, s 61.]

    1. Part IV contains ss 54–65.

8–185   62. *Orders and regulations.*

8–186   65. Short title, commencement and extent.   (1) This Act may be cited as the Agriculture Act 1993.

    (2)–(5) *Commencement and extent.*

[Agriculture Act 1993, s 65.]

Plant Varieties Act 1997
(1997 c 66)

PART I
PLANT VARIETIES

8–200   Part I of this Act (ss 1–41) makes provision for rights in relation to plant varieties and repeals Part I of the Plant Varieties and Seeds Act 1964. The Controller of the Plant Variety Rights Office may grant "plant breeders' rights" in respect of varieties of all plant genera and species provided specified conditions are met (ss 1–5). Subject to exceptions for non commercial or experimental purposes or farm saved seed[1], the reproduction or dealing in a protected variety may be prevented by the owner of plant breeders' rights (ss 8–9)[2]. Provision is made for the duration of licences and civil remedies for infringement (ss 1–16)[3]. The Controller may intervene where the holder of plant breeders' rights unreasonably refuses to grant a licence to another (s 17).

1. See the Plant Breeders' Rights (Farm Saved Seed) (Specification of Species and Groups) Order 1998, SI 1998/1025 and the Plant Breeders' Rights (Farm Saved Seed) (Specified Information) Regulations 1998, SI 1998/1024.
2. The following Order has been made under s 9: Plant Breeders' Rights (Discontinuation of Prior Use Exemption) Order 2005, SI 2005/2726.
3. The following regulations have been made under section 14: the Plant Breeders' Rights (Information Notices) Regulations 1998, SI 1998/1024.

Naming of protected varieties

8–201 18. Selection and registration of names. *Regulations[1] may provide for the selection of names for varieties which are the subject of applications for the grant of plant breeder' rights and for the keeping of a register of such names.*

1. See the Plant Breeders' Rights Regulations 1998, SI 1998/1027.

8–202 19. Duty to use registered name. (1) Where a name is registered under section 18 above in respect of a variety, a person may not use any other name in selling, offering for sale or otherwise marketing propagating material of the variety.

(2) Subsection (1) above shall have effect in relation to any variety from the date on which plant breeders' rights in respect of that variety are granted, and shall continue to apply after the period for which the grant of those rights has effect.

(3) Subsection (1) above shall not preclude the use of any trade mark or trade name (whether registered under the Trade Marks Act 1994 or not) if—

(*a*) that mark or name and the registered name are juxtaposed, and
(*b*) the registered name is easily recognisable.

(4) A person who contravenes subsection (1) above shall be liable on summary conviction to a fine not exceeding **level 3** on the standard scale.

(5) In any proceedings for an offence under subsection (4) above, it shall be a defence to prove that the accused took all reasonable precautions against committing the offence and had not at the time of the offence any reason to suspect that he was committing an offence.
[Plant Varieties Act 1997, s 19.]

8–203 20. Improper use of registered name. *Civil remedies.*

False information and representations as to rights

8–204 31. False information. (1) If any information to which this section applies is false in a material particular and the person giving the information knows that it is false or gives it recklessly, he shall be guilty of an offence and liable on summary conviction to a fine not exceeding **level 3** on the standard scale.

(2) The information to which this section applies is—

(*a*) information given in an application to the Controller for a decision against which an appeal lies to the Tribunal,
(*b*) information given by or on behalf of the applicant in connection with such an application, and
(*c*) information given in pursuance of a request under section 16(2) above.
[Plant Varieties Act 1997, s 31.]

8–205 32. False representations as to rights. (1) If, in relation to any variety, a person falsely represents that he is entitled to exercise plant breeders' rights, or any rights derived from such rights, and he knows that the representation is false, or makes it recklessly, he shall be guilty of an offence and liable on summary conviction to a fine not exceeding **level 3** on the standard scale.

(2) It is immaterial for the purposes of subsection (1) above whether or not the variety to which the representation relates is the subject of plant breeders' rights.
[Plant Varieties Act 1997, s 32.]

General

8–206 36. Offences by bodies corporate, etc. (1) Where an offence under this Part of this Act committed by a body corporate is proved to have been committed with the consent or connivance of, or to be attributable to any neglect on the part of, any director, manager, secretary or other similar officer of the body corporate, or any person who was purporting to act in any such capacity, he, as well as the body corporate, shall be guilty of the offence and liable to be proceeded against and punished accordingly.

(2) Where an offence under this Part of this Act committed by a Scottish partnership is proved to have been committed with the consent or connivance of, or to be attributable to any neglect on the

part of, a partner, he, as well as the partnership, shall be guilty of the offence and liable to be proceeded against and punished accordingly.
[Plant Varieties Act 1997, s 36.]

8–207 37. Jurisdiction in relation to offences. (1) Proceedings for an offence under this Part of this Act may be taken against a person before the appropriate court in the United Kingdom having jurisdiction in the place where that person is for the time being.

(2) Subsection (1) above is without prejudice to any jurisdiction exercisable apart from that subsection.
[Plant Varieties Act 1997, s 37.]

PART II
THE PLANT VARIETIES AND SEEDS TRIBUNAL

8–208 42–46. *Plant Varieties and Seeds Tribunal*

ANCIENT MONUMENTS, HERITAGE AND CULTURAL OBJECTS

8–640 This title contains the following statutes—

Ancient Monuments and Archaeological Areas Act 1979[1]
(1979 c 46)

PART I[2]
ANCIENT MONUMENTS

Protection of scheduled monuments

8–658 1. Schedule of monuments. (1) The Secretary of State[3] shall compile[4] and maintain for the purposes of this Act (in such form as he thinks fit) a schedule of monuments[5] (referred to below in this Act as "the Schedule").

(2)–(6A) *Supplementary provisions as to compilation of the Schedule.*

(7) Subject to subsection (7A) below the Secretary of State shall from time to time publish a list of all the monuments which are for the time being included in the Schedule, whether as a single list or in sections containing the monuments situated in particular areas; but in the case of a list published in sections, all sections of the list need not be published simultaneously.

(7A) Subsection (7) above shall not apply as regards monuments situated in England, but the Secretary of State shall from time to time supply the Commission with a list of all the monuments which are so situated and are for the time being included in the Schedule, whether as a single list or in sections containing the monuments situated in particular areas; but in the case of a list supplied in sections, all sections of the list need not be supplied simultaneously.

(8) The Secretary of State may from time to time publish amendments of any list published under subsection (7) above, and any such list (as amended) shall be evidence of the inclusion in the Schedule for the time being—

(*a*) of the monuments listed; and

(*b*) of any matters purporting to be reproduced in the list from the entries in the Schedule relating to the monuments listed.

(8A) The Secretary of State shall from time to time supply the Commission with amendments of any list supplied under subsection (7A) above.

(9)–(10) *Entries in Schedule to be a local land charge; Scotland.*

(11) In this Act "scheduled monument" means any monument which is for the time being included in the Schedule.
[Ancient Monuments and Archaeological Areas Act 1979, s 1 as amended by the National Heritage Act 1983, Sch 4.]

---

1. For the purposes of this Act, the holder of a licence under s 6(1) of the Electricity Act 1989 shall be deemed to be a statutory undertaker and his undertaking a statutory undertaking (Electricity Act 1989, Sch 16, para 1).
2. Part I contains ss 1–32.
3. The functions of the Minister, so far as exercisable in relation to Wales, have been transferred to the National Assembly for Wales, by the National Assembly for Wales (Transfer of Functions) Order 1999, SI 1999/672, art 2, Sch 1.

4. The Secretary of State shall consult the Historic Buildings and Monuments Commission for England (in the Act referred to as "the Commission") before he includes in the Schedule a monument situated in England (s 1(3)).

5. For meaning of "monument", "works", "flooding operations", "tipping operations" and "land", see s 61, post.

8–659   1A. Commission's functions as to informing and publishing.   (1) As soon as may be after the Commission[1]—

(a)   have been informed as mentioned in section 1(6A) of this Act, and

(b)   in a case falling within section 1(6)(a) or (b) of this Act, have received a copy of the entry or (as the case may be) of the amended entry from the Secretary of State,

the Commission shall inform the owner and (if the owner is not the occupier) the occupier of the monument, and any local authority in whose area the monument is situated, of the inclusion, amendment or exclusion and, in a case falling within section 1(6)(a) or (b), shall also send to him or them a copy of the entry or (as the case may be) of the amended entry in the Schedule relating to that monument.

(2)   As soon as may be after the Commission receive a list or a section in pursuance of section 1(7A) of this Act, they shall publish the list or section (as the case may be).

(3)   The Commission shall from time to time publish amendments of any list published under subsection (2) above, and any such list (as amended) shall be evidence of the inclusion in the Schedule for the time being—

(a)   of the monuments listed; and

(b)   of any matters purporting to be reproduced in the list from the entries in the Schedule relating to monuments listed.

[Ancient Monuments and Archaeological Areas Act 1979, s 1A, as inserted by the National Heritage Act 1983, Sch 4.]

---

1. "The Commission" means the Historic Buildings and Monuments Commission for England (s 61, post).

8–660   2. Control of works affecting scheduled monuments.   (1) If any person executes or causes or permits to be executed any works to which this section applies he shall be guilty of an offence unless the works are authorised under this Part of this Act.

(2)   This section applies to any of the following works, that is to say—

(a)   any works[1] resulting in the demolition or destruction of or any damage to a scheduled monument[2];

(b)   any works for the purpose of removing or repairing a scheduled monument or any part of it or of making any alterations or additions thereto; and

(c)   any flooding[1] or tipping operations[1] on land[1] in, on or under which there is a scheduled monument.

(3)   Without prejudice to any other authority to execute works[1] conferred under this Part of this Act, works to which this section applies are authorised under this Part of this Act if—

(a)   the Secretary of State has granted written consent (referred to below in this Act as "scheduled monument consent") for the execution of the works; and

(b)   the works are executed in accordance with the terms of the consent and of any conditions attached to the consent.

(4)   Scheduled monument consent may be granted either unconditionally or subject to conditions (whether with respect to the manner in which or the persons by whom the works or any of the works are to be executed or otherwise).

(5)   Without prejudice to the generality of subsection (4) above, a condition attached to a scheduled monument consent may require that—

(a)   a person authorised by the Commission (in a case where the monument in question is situated in England), or

(b)   the Secretary of State or a person authorised by the Secretary of State (in any other case)

be afforded an opportunity, before any works to which the consent relates are begun, to examine the monument and its site and carry out such excavations therein as appear to the Secretary of State to be desirable for the purpose of archaeological investigation.

(6)   Without prejudice to subsection (1) above, if a person executing or causing or permitting to be executed any works to which a scheduled monument consent relates fails to comply with any condition attached to the consent he shall be guilty of an offence, unless he proves that he took all reasonable precautions and exercised all due diligence to avoid contravening the condition.

(7)   In any proceedings for an offence under this section in relation to works within subsection (2)(a) above it shall be a defence for the accused to prove that he took all reasonable precautions and exercised all due diligence to avoid or prevent damage to the monument.

(8)   In any proceedings for an offence under this section in relation to works within subsection (2)(a) or (c) above it shall be a defence for the accused to prove that he did not know and had no reason to believe that the monument was within the area affected by the works or (as the case may be) that it was a scheduled monument.

(9) In any proceedings for an offence under this section it shall be a defence to prove that the works were urgently necessary in the interests of safety or health and that notice in writing of the need for the works was given to the Secretary of State as soon as reasonably practicable.

(10) A person guilty of an offence under this section shall be liable[3]—

(a) on summary conviction or, in Scotland, on conviction before a court of summary jurisdiction, to a fine not exceeding **the statutory maximum**[4]; or

(b) on conviction on indictment to a fine.

(11) Part I of Schedule 1 to this Act shall have effect with respect to applications for, and the effect of, scheduled monument consent[5].

[Ancient Monuments and Archaeological Areas Act 1979, s 2 as amended by the National Heritage Act 1983, Sch 4.]

---

1. For meaning of "monument", "works", "flooding operations", "tipping operations" and "land", see s 61, post.
2. For meaning of "scheduled monument", see s 1(11) ante.
3. For procedure in respect of this offence which is triable either way, see the Magistrates' Courts Act 1980, ss 17A–21, in PART I: MAGISTRATES' COURTS, PROCEDURE, ante.
4. For meaning of "the statutory maximum", see s 61, post.
5. The Ancient Monuments (Applications for Scheduled Monument Consent) Regulations 1981, SI 1981/1301, amended by SI 1994/2567, and the Ancient Monuments (Class Consents) Order 1994, SI 1994/1381 have been made. See also the Transport and Works Applications (Listed Buildings, Conservation Areas and Ancient Monuments Procedure) Regulations 1992, SI 1992/3138.

Public access to monuments under public control

8–661   19. Public access to monuments under public control.   (1) Subject to the following provisions of this section, the public shall have access to any monument under the ownership or guardianship of the Secretary of State or the Commission or any local authority by virtue of this Act.

(2) The Secretary of State and the Commission and any local authority may nevertheless control the times of normal public access to any monument under their ownership or guardianship by virtue of this Act and may also, if they consider it necessary or expedient to do so in the interests of safety or for the maintenance or preservation of the monument, entirely exclude the public from access to any such monument or to any part of it, for such period as they think fit:

Provided that—

(a) the power of a local authority under this subsection to control the times of normal public access to any monument shall only be exercisable by regulations under this section; and

(b) the power of a local authority under this subsection entirely to exclude the public from access to any monument with a view to its preservation shall only be exercisable with the consent of the Secretary of State.

(3) The Secretary of State and any local authority may by regulations under this subsection regulate public access to any monument, or to all or any of the monuments, under their ownership or guardianship by virtue of this Act and any such regulations made by the Secretary of State may also apply to any monument, or to all or any of the monuments, under his control or management for any other reason.

The Secretary of State shall consult with the Commission before he makes any regulations under this subsection in relation only to monuments situated in England.

(4) Without prejudice to the generality of subsection (3) above, regulations made by the Secretary of State or a local authority under that subsection may prescribe the times when the public are to have access to monuments to which the regulations apply and may make such provision as appears to the Secretary of State or to the local authority in question to be necessary for—

(a) the preservation of any such monument and its amenities or of any property of the Secretary of State or local authority; and

(b) prohibiting or regulating any act or thing which would tend to injure or disfigure any such monument or its amenities or to disturb the public in their enjoyment of it;

and may prescribe charges for the admission of the public to any such monument or to any class or description of monuments to which the regulations apply.

(4A) The Secretary of State may by regulations under this subsection make such provision as appears to him necessary for prohibiting or regulating any act or thing which would tend to injure or disfigure any monument under the ownership or guardianship of the Commission by virtue of this Act or the monument's amenities or to disturb the public in their enjoyment of it.

(4B) The Secretary of State shall consult with the Commission before he makes any regulations under subsection (4A) above.

(5) Without prejudice to subsections (3) and (4) above, the Secretary of State and the Commission and any local authority shall have power to make such charges as they may from time to time determine for the admission of the public to any monument under their ownership or guardianship by virtue of this Act or (in the case of the Secretary of State) to any monument otherwise under his control or management.

(6) Notwithstanding subsection (1) above, any person authorised in that behalf by the Secretary of State or by the Commission or by a local authority may refuse admission—

(a) to any monument under the ownership or guardianship of the Secretary of State or the Commission or that local authority (as the case may be) by virtue of this Act; or

(b) (in the case of the Secretary of State) to any monument otherwise under his control or management;

to any person he has reasonable cause to believe is likely to do anything which would tend to injure or disfigure the monument or its amenities or to disturb the public in their enjoyment of it.

(7) If any person contravenes or fails to comply with any provision of any regulations under this section, he shall be liable on summary conviction or, in Scotland, on conviction before a court of summary jurisdiction, to a fine not exceeding **level 2** on the standard scale.

(8) Regulations made by a local authority under this section shall not take effect unless they are submitted to and confirmed by the Secretary of State, and the Secretary of State may confirm any such regulations either with or without modifications.

(9) In relation to any monument under guardianship, subsection (1) above is subject to any provision to the contrary in the guardianship deed.

[Ancient Monuments and Archaeological Areas Act 1979, s 19 as amended by the Criminal Justice Act 1982, s 46 and the National Heritage Act 1983, Sch 4.]

8–662 28. Offence of damaging certain ancient monuments. (1) A person who without lawful excuse destroys or damages any protected monument—

(a) knowing that it is a protected monument; and

(b) intending to destroy or damage the monument or being reckless as to whether the monument would be destroyed or damaged;

shall be guilty of an offence.

(2) This section applies to anything done by or under the authority of the owner of the monument, other than an act for the execution of excepted works, as it applies to anything done by any other person.

In this subsection "excepted works" means works for which scheduled monument consent has been given under this Act (including any consent granted by order under section 3).

(3) In this section "protected monument" means any scheduled monument[1] and any monument under the ownership or guardianship of the Secretary of State or the Commission or a local authority by virtue of this Act.

(4) A person guilty of an offence under this section shall be liable[2]—

(a) on summary conviction, to a fine not exceeding **the statutory maximum**[3] or to imprisonment for a term not exceeding **six months** or both; or

(b) on conviction on indictment, to a fine or to imprisonment for a term not exceeding **two years** or both.

[Ancient Monuments and Archaeological Areas Act 1979, s 28 as amended by the National Heritage Act 1983, Sch 4.]

1. For meaning of "scheduled monument", see s 1(11), ante.
2. For procedure in respect of this offence which is triable either way, see the Magistrates' Courts Act 1980, ss 17A–21, in PART I: MAGISTRATES' COURTS, PROCEDURE, ante.
3. For meaning of "the statutory maximum" and "monument", see s 61, post.

8–663 29. Compensation orders for damage to monuments under guardianship in England and Wales. Where the owner or any other person is convicted of an offence involving damage to a monument[1] situated in England or Wales which was at the time of the offence under the guardianship[2] of the Secretary of State or the Commission or any local authority[3] by virtue of this Act, any compensation order made under section 130 of the Powers of Criminal Courts (Sentencing) Act 2000 (compensation orders against convicted persons) in respect of that damage shall be made in favour of the Secretary of State or the Commission or the local authority in question (as the case may require).

[Ancient Monuments and Archaeological Areas Act 1979, s 29 as amended by the National Heritage Act 1983, Sch 4 and the Powers of Criminal Courts (Sentencing) Act 2000, Sch 9.]

1. For meaning of "monument", see s 61, post.
2. For guardianship of ancient monuments, see ss 12–14. The Secretary of State and any local authority are under a duty to maintain any monument which is under their guardianship by virtue of this Act, and have full control and management of such a monument (s 13).
3. Anything which on 1 April 1986 was in process of being done by or in relation to the Greater London Council or a metropolitan county council in connection with the guardianship of a monument under this Act may be continued by the Historic Buildings and Monuments Commission for England or the council of a metropolitan district respectively (Local Government Reorganisation (Transitional Provisions) Order 1985, SI 1985/1781).

PART II[1]
ARCHAEOLOGICAL AREAS

8–664 33. Designation of areas of archaeological importance. (1) The Secretary of State may from time to time by order designate as an area of archaeological importance any area which appears to him to merit treatment as such for the purposes of this Act; but, where the area in question is situated in England, he shall consult with the Commission before doing so.

(2) A local authority may from time to time by order designate as an area of archaeological importance any area within the area of that local authority which appears to them to merit treatment as such for the purposes of this Act; but, where the area in question is situated in England, the authority shall first notify the Commission of their intention to do so.

(2A) The Commission may from time to time by order designate as an area of archaeological importance any area in Greater London which appears to them to merit treatment as such for the purposes of this Act.

(3) An order under this section designating an area as an area of archaeological importance (whether made by the Secretary of State or by a local authority or by the Commission) is referred to below in this Act as a designation order.

(4) The Secretary of State may at any time by order vary or revoke a designation order, but his power to vary such an order is confined to reducing the area designated by the order.

The Secretary of State shall consult with the Commission before varying or revoking an order relating to an area situated in England.

(5) A designation order relating to an area in England and Wales shall be a local land charge.

(6) Schedule 2 to this Act shall have effect with respect to the making, and with respect to the variation and revocation, of designation orders.

[Ancient Monuments and Archaeological Areas Act 1979, s 33 as amended by the National Heritage Act 1983, Sch 4 and the Local Government Act 1985, Sch 2.]

---

1. Part II contains ss 33–41.

8–665   35. Notice required of operations in areas of archaeological importance. (1) Subject to section 37 of this Act, if any person carries out, or causes or permits to be carried out, on land in an area of archaeological importance any operations to which this section applies—

(*a*) without having first served a notice relating to those operations which complies with subsections (4) and (5) below; or

(*b*) within six weeks of serving such a notice;

he shall be guilty of an offence.

(2) Subject to section 37 of this Act, this section applies to any of the following operations, that is to say—

(*a*) operations which disturb the ground;

(*b*) flooding operations[1]; and

(*c*) tipping operations[1].

(3) In this Part of this Act the person carrying out or proposing to carry out any operations is referred to, in relation to those operations, as "the developer", and a notice complying with subsections (4) and (5) below is referred to as an "operations notice".

(4) A notice required for the purposes of this section—

(*a*) shall specify the operations to which it relates, the site on which they are to be carried out, the date on which it is proposed to begin them and, where the operations are to be carried out after clearance of the site, the developer's estimated date for completion of the clearance operations;

(*b*) shall be accompanied by a certificate in the prescribed form which satisfies the requirements of section 36 of this Act; and

(*c*) shall be in the prescribed form.

(5) A notice required for the purposes of this section shall be served by the developer—

(*a*) in the case of land in England, on the district council or London borough council or (as the case may be) on each district council or London borough council in whose area the site of the operations is wholly or partly situated;

(*aa*) in the case of land in Wales on the council of each county or county borough in which the site of the operations is wholly or partially situated;

(*b*) *Scotland*; or

(*c*) in a case where the developer is any such council or local authority, on the Secretary of State.

(6) Regulations made by the Secretary of State may prescribe the steps to be taken by any council or local authority on whom an operations notice is served in accordance with subsection (5) above.

(7) Where an operations notice is served with respect to operations which are to be carried out after clearance of any site, the developer shall notify the investigating authority for the area of archaeological importance in question of the clearance of the site immediately on completion of the clearance operations.

(8) If in a case falling within subsection (7) above the developer carries out, or causes or permits to be carried out, any of the operations to which the operations notice relates without having first notified the investigating authority of the clearance of the site in accordance with that subsection, this section shall have effect in relation to those operations as if the operations notice had not been served.

(9) A person guilty of an offence under this section shall be liable[2]—

(a)   on summary conviction or, in Scotland, on conviction before a court of summary jurisdiction, to a fine not exceeding **the statutory maximum**[3]; or

(b)   on conviction on indictment to a fine.

(10) *Power of local authority to take proceedings in the High Court.*

(11) This section shall have effect, in relation to any land within the Broads (as defined by the Norfolk and Suffolk Broads Act 1988), as if the Broads Authority were the district council (to the exclusion of the authority which is otherwise the district council for the area in question) and the Broads were its local authority area.

[Ancient Monuments and Archaeological Areas Act 1979, s 35 as amended by the Norfolk and Suffolk Broads Act 1988, Sch 3 and the Local Government (Wales) Act 1994, Sch 16.]

1. For meaning of "flooding operations" and "tipping operations", see s 61, post.
2. For procedure in respect of this offence which is triable either way, see the Magistrates' Courts Act 1980 ss 17A–21, in PART I: MAGISTRATES' COURTS, PROCEDURE, ante.
3. For meaning of "the statutory maximum", see s 61, post.

8–666   36. Certificate to accompany operations notice under section 35.   (1) A person is qualified to issue a certificate for the purposes of section 35(4)(b) of this Act if he either—

(a)   has an interest in the site of the operations which (apart from any restrictions imposed by law) entitles him to carry out the operations in question; or

(b)   has a right to enter on and take possession of that site under section 11(1) or (2) of the Compulsory Purchase Act 1965 (powers of entry on land subject to compulsory purchase) or, in the case of a site in Scotland, under paragraph 3(1) of Schedule 2 to the Acquisition of Land (Authorisation Procedure) (Scotland) Act 1947.

(2) Statutory undertakers are qualified to issue a certificate for the purposes of section 35(4)(b) of this Act if they are entitled by or under any enactment to carry out the operations in question.

(3) Any such certificate—

(a)   shall be signed by or on behalf of a person or persons qualified in accordance with subsection (1) or (2) above to issue it;

(b)   shall state that the person issuing the certificate has an interest within paragraph (a) or (as the case may be) a right within paragraph (b) of subsection (1) above or, in the case of a certificate issued by statutory undertakers, shall state that it is so issued and specify the enactment by or under which they are entitled to carry out the operations in question; and

(c)   if the person issuing the certificate is not the developer, shall state that he has authorised the developer to carry out the operations.

(4) If any person issues a certificate which purports to comply with the requirements of this section and which contains a statement which he knows to be false or misleading in a material particular, or recklessly issues a certificate which purports to comply with those requirements and which contains a statement which is false or misleading in a material particular, he shall be guilty of an offence and liable on summary conviction or, in Scotland, on conviction before a court of summary jurisdiction, to a fine not exceeding **level 3** on the standard scale.

[Ancient Monuments and Archaeological Areas Act 1979, s 36 as amended by the Criminal Justice Act 1982, s 46.]

8–667   37. Exemptions from offence under section 35.   (1) Section 35 of this Act does not apply to any operations carried out with the consent of the investigating authority for the area of archaeological importance in question.

(2) The Secretary of State may by order direct that section 35 shall not apply to the carrying out, or to the carrying out by any class or description of persons specified in the order, of operations of any class or description so specified; and an exemption conferred by an order under this subsection may be either unconditional or subject to any conditions specified in the order.

(3) The Secretary of State may direct that any exemption conferred by an order under subsection (2) above shall not apply to the carrying out on any land specified in the direction, or to the carrying out on any land so specified by any class or description of persons so specified, of operations of any class or description so specified, and may withdraw any direction given under this subsection.

The Secretary of State shall consult with the Commission before giving or withdrawing a direction under this subsection in relation to land situated in England.

(4) A direction under subsection (3) above shall not take effect until notice of it has been served on the occupier or (if there is no occupier) on the owner of the land in question.

(5) In any proceedings for an offence under section 35 consisting in carrying out, or causing or permitting to be carried out, any operations which disturb the ground, it shall be a defence for the accused to prove that he took all reasonable precautions and exercised all due diligence to avoid or prevent disturbance of the ground.

(6) In any proceedings for an offence under section 35 it shall be a defence for the accused to prove either—

(a) that he did not know and had no reason to believe that the site of the operations was within an area of archaeological importance;

(b) that the operations were urgently necessary in the interests of safety or health and that notice in writing of the need for the operations was given to the Secretary of State as soon as reasonably practicable.

[Ancient Monuments and Archaeological Areas Act 1979, s 37 as amended by the National Heritage Act 1983, Sch 4.]

8–668 41. Interpretation of Part II. (1) In this Part of this Act—

(a) "the developer" and "operations notice" have the meanings respectively given by section 35(3) of this Act;

(b) references to a London borough council include references to the Common Council of the City of London;

(c) references to operations on any land include references to operations in, under or over the land in question;

(d) references to the clearance of any site are references to the demolition and removal of any existing building or other structure on the site and the removal of any other materials thereon so as to clear the surface of the land (but do not include the levelling of the surface or the removal of materials from below the surface); and

(e) references to clearance operations are references to operations undertaken for the purpose of or in connection with the clearance of any site.

(2) For the purposes of this Part of this Act, the investigating authority for an area of archaeological importance is the person for the time being holding appointment as such under section 34 of this Act or (if there is no such person) the Commission (in a case where the area is situated in England) or the Secretary of State (in any other case).

[Ancient Monuments and Archaeological Areas Act 1979, s 41 as amended by the National Heritage Act 1983, Sch 4.]

PART III[1]
MISCELLANEOUS AND SUPPLEMENTAL

Restrictions on use of metal detectors

8–669 42. Restrictions on use of metal detectors. (1) If a person uses a metal detector in a protected place without the written consent of the Commission (in the case of a place situated in England) or of the Secretary of State (in any other case) he shall be guilty of an offence and liable on summary conviction or, in Scotland, on conviction before a court of summary jurisdiction, to a fine not exceeding **level 3** on the standard scale.

(2) In this section—

"metal detector" means any device designed or adapted for detecting or locating any metal or mineral in the ground; and

"protected place" means any place which is either—

(a) the site of a scheduled monument or of any monument under the ownership or guardianship of the Secretary of State or the Commission or a local authority by virtue of this Act; or

(b) situated in an area of archaeological importance.

(3) If a person without written consent removes any object of archaeological or historical interest which he has discovered by the use of a metal detector in a protected place he shall be guilty of an offence and liable[2] on summary conviction to a fine not exceeding **the statutory maximum**[3] or on conviction on indictment to a fine.

The reference in this subsection to written consent is to that of the Commission (where the place in question is situated in England) or of the Secretary of State (in any other case).

(4) A consent granted by the Secretary of State or the Commission for the purposes of this section may be granted either unconditionally or subject to conditions.

(5) If any person—

(a) in using a metal detector in a protected place in accordance with any consent granted by the Secretary of State or the Commission for the purposes of this section; or

(b) in removing or otherwise dealing with any object which he has discovered by the use of a metal detector in a protected place in accordance with any such consent,

fails to comply with any condition attached to the consent, he shall be guilty of an offence and liable, in a case falling within paragraph (a) above, to the penalty provided by subsection (1) above, and in a case falling within paragraph (b) above, to the penalty provided by subsection (3) above.

(6) In any proceedings for an offence under subsection (1) above, it shall be a defence for the accused to prove that he used the metal detector for a purpose other than detecting or locating objects of archaeological or historical interest.

(7) In any proceedings for an offence under subsection (1) or (3) above, it shall be a defence for

the accused to prove that he had taken all reasonable precautions to find out whether the place where he used the metal detector was a protected place and did not believe that it was.
[Ancient Monuments and Archaeological Areas Act 1979, s 42 as amended by the Criminal Justice Act 1982, s 46 and the National Heritage Act 1983, Sch 4.]

1. Part III contains ss 42–65.
2. For procedure in respect of this offence which is triable either way, see the Magistrates' Courts Act 1980, ss 17A–21, in PART I: MAGISTRATES' COURTS, PROCEDURE, ante.
3. For meaning of "the statutory maximum", see s 61, post.

Powers of entry

8–670   43. Power of entry for survey and valuation.   (1) Any person authorised under this section may at any reasonable time enter any land for the purpose of surveying it, or estimating its value, in connection with any proposal to acquire that or any other land under this Act or in connection with any claim for compensation under this Act in respect of any such acquisition or for any damage to that or any other land.

(2) A person is authorised under this section if he is an officer of the Valuation Office of the Inland Revenue Department or a person duly authorised in writing by the Secretary of State or other authority proposing to make the acquisition which is the occasion of the survey or valuation or (as the case may be) from whom in accordance with this Act compensation in respect of the damage is recoverable.

(3) Subject to section 44(9) of this Act, the power to survey land conferred by this section shall be construed as including power to search and bore for the purposes of ascertaining the nature of the subsoil or the presence of minerals therein.
[Ancient Monuments and Archaeological Areas Act 1979, s 43.]

8–671   44. Supplementary provisions with respect to powers of entry.   (1) A person may not in the exercise of any power of entry under this Act, other than that conferred by section 43, enter any building or part of a building occupied as a dwelling house without the consent of the occupier.

(2) Subject to the following provisions of this subsection a person may not in the exercise of any power of entry under this Act demand admission as of right to any land which is occupied unless prior notice of the intended entry has been given to the occupier—

(a)   where the purpose of the entry is to carry out any works on the land (other than excavations in exercise of the power under section 26 or 38 of this Act), not less than fourteen days before the day on which admission is demanded; or

(b)   in any other case, not less than twenty-four hours before admission is demanded.

This subsection does not apply in relation to the power of entry under section 5 of this Act.

(3) A person seeking to enter any land in exercise of any power of entry under this Act shall, if so required by or on behalf of the owner or occupier thereof, produce evidence of his authority before entering.

(4) Any power of entry under this Act shall be construed as including power for any person entering any land in exercise of the power of entry to take with him any assistance or equipment reasonably required for the purpose to which his entry relates and to do there anything reasonably necessary for carrying out that purpose.

(5) Without prejudice to subsection (4) above, where a person enters any land in exercise of any power of entry under this Act for the purpose of carrying out any archaeological investigation or examination of the land, he may take and remove such samples of any description as appear to him to be reasonably required for the purpose of archaeological analysis.

(6) Subject to subsection (7) below, where any works are being carried out on any land in relation to which any power of entry under this Act is exercisable, a person acting in the exercise of that power shall comply with any reasonable requirements or conditions imposed by the person by whom the works are being carried out for the purpose of preventing interference with or delay to the works.

(7) Any requirements or conditions imposed by a person by whom any works are being carried out shall not be regarded as reasonable for the purposes of subsection (6) above if compliance therewith would in effect frustrate the exercise of the power of entry or the purpose of the entry; and that subsection does not apply where the works in question are being carried out in contravention of section 2(1) or (6) or 35 of this Act.

(8) Any person who intentionally obstructs a person acting in the exercise of any power of entry under this Act shall be guilty of an offence and liable on summary conviction or, in Scotland, on conviction before a court of summary jurisdiction, to a fine not exceeding **level 3** on the standard scale.

(9) Where under section 43 of this Act a person proposes to carry out any works authorised by virtue of subsection (3) of that section—

(a)   he shall not carry out those works unless notice of his intention to do so was included in the notice required by subsection (2)(a) above; and

(b)   if the land in question is held by statutory undertakers, and those undertakers object to the proposed works on the grounds that the carrying out thereof would be seriously detrimental

to the carrying on of their undertaking, the works shall not be carried out except with the authority of the Secretary of State.
[Ancient Monuments and Archaeological Areas Act 1979, s 44 as amended by the Criminal Justice Act 1982, s 46.]

Application to special cases

8–671A   50–53. *Application to Crown land; Ecclesiastical property; the Isles of Scilly; the Broads, and Monuments in territorial waters.*

Supplemental

8–672   56. *Service of documents.*

8–673   57. Power to require information as to interests in land.   (1) For the purpose of enabling the Secretary of State or the Commission or a local authority to exercise any function under this Act, the Secretary of State or the Commission or the local authority may require the occupier of any land[1] and any person who, either directly or indirectly, receives rent in respect of any land to state in writing the nature of his interest therein, and the name and address of any other person known to him as having an interest therein, whether as a freeholder, owner of the dominium utile*, mortgagee, lessee, or otherwise.

(2) Any person who, having been required under this section to give any information, fails without reasonable excuse to give that information, shall be guilty of an offence and liable on summary conviction or, in Scotland, on conviction before a court of summary jurisdiction, to a fine not exceeding **level 3** on the standard scale.

(3) Any person who, having been so required to give any information, knowingly makes any mis-statement in respect of it, shall be guilty of an offence and liable[2]—

   (*a*)   on summary conviction or, in Scotland, on conviction before a court of summary jurisdiction, to a fine not exceeding **the statutory maximum**[3]; or
   (*b*)   on conviction on indictment to a fine.

[Ancient Monuments and Archaeological Areas Act 1979, s 57 as amended by the Criminal Justice Act 1982, s 46 and the National Heritage Act 1983, Sch 4.]

---

*Repealed in relation to Scotland by the Abolition of Feudal Tenure etc (Scotland) Act 2000, Schs 12 and 13.

  1. For meaning of "land", see s 61, post.
  2. For procedure in respect of this offence which is triable either way, see the Magistrates' Courts Act 1980, ss 17A–21, in PART I: MAGISTRATES' COURTS, PROCEDURE, ante.
  3. For the meaning of "the statutory maximum", see s 61, post.

8–674   58. Offences by corporations.   (1) Where an offence under this Act which has been committed by a body corporate is proved to have been committed with the consent or connivance of, or to be attributable to any neglect on the part of, a director, manager, secretary or other similar officer of the body corporate, or any person who was purporting to act in any such capacity, he, as well as the body corporate, shall be guilty of that offence and be liable to be proceeded against accordingly.

(2) In subsection (1) above the expression "director", in relation to any body corporate established by or under an enactment for the purpose of carrying on under national ownership an industry or part of an industry or undertaking, being a body corporate whose affairs are managed by the members thereof, means a member of that body corporate.
[Ancient Monuments and Archaeological Areas Act 1979, s 58.]

8–675   61. Interpretation.   (1) In this Act—

   "ancient monument" has the meaning given by subsection (12) below;
   "area of archaeological importance" means an area designated as such under section 33 of this Act;
   "the Commission" means the Historic Buildings and Monuments Commission for England;
   "designation order" means an order under that section;
   "enactment" includes an enactment in any local or private Act of Parliament, and an order, rule, regulation, bye-law or scheme made under an Act of Parliament;
   "flooding operations" means covering land with water or any other liquid or partially liquid substance;
   "functions" includes powers and duties;
   "guardianship deed" has the meaning given by section 12(6) of this Act;
   "land" means—

   (*a*)   in England and Wales, any corporeal hereditament;
   (*b*)   in Scotland, any heritable property;

including a building or a monument and, in relation to any acquisition of land, includes any interest in or right over land;

"local authority"[1] means—

(a) in England, the council of a county or district, the council of a London borough, and the Common Council of the City of London;

(aa) in Wales, the council of a county or county borough; and

(b) *Scotland*;

"monument" has the meaning given by subsection (7) below;

"owner", in relation to any land in England and Wales means (except for the purposes of paragraph 2(1) of Schedule 1 to this Act and any regulations made for the purposes of that paragraph) a person, other than a mortgagee not in possession, who, whether in his own right or as trustee for any other person, is entitled to receive the rack rent of the land, or where the land is not let at a rack rent, would be so entitled if it were so let;

"possession" includes receipt of rents and profits or the right to receive rents and profits (if any);

"prescribed" means prescribed by regulations made by the Secretary of State;

"the Schedule" has the meaning given by section 1(1) of this Act;

"scheduled monument" has the meaning given by section 1(11) of this Act and references to "scheduled monument consent" shall be construed in accordance with section 2(3) and 3(5) of this Act;

"tipping operations" means tipping soil or spoil or depositing building or other materials or matter (including waste materials or refuse) on any land; and

"universal postal service provider" means a universal service provider within the meaning of the Postal Services Act 2000; and references to the provision of a universal postal service shall be construed in accordance with that Act;

"works" includes operations of any description and, in particular (but without prejudice to the generality of the preceding provision) flooding or tipping operations and any operations undertaken for purposes of agriculture (within the meaning of the Town and Country Planning Act 1990 or, as regards Scotland, the Town and Country Planning (Scotland) Act 1972) or forestry (including afforestation).

(2) In this Act "statutory undertakers" means—

(a) persons authorised by any enactment to carry on any railway, light railway, tramway, road transport, water transport, canal, inland navigation, dock, harbour, pier or lighthouse undertaking, or any undertaking for the supply of hydraulic power;

(b) the Civil Aviation Authority, a universal postal service provide in connection with the provision pf a universal postal service and any other authority, body or undertakers which by virtue of any enactment are to be treated as statutory undertakers for any of the purposes of the Town and Country Planning Act 1990 or of the Town and Country Planning (Scotland) Act 1972; and

(c) any other authority, body or undertakers specified in an order made by the Secretary of State under this paragraph.

(2A) The undertaking of a universal postal service provider so far as relating to the provision of a universal postal service shall be taken to be his statutory undertaking for the purposes of this Act; and references in this Act to his undertaking shall be construed accordingly.

(3) For the purposes of sections 14(1) and 21(2) of this Act and paragraph 6(1)(b) and (2)(b) of Schedule 3 to this Act a person shall be taken to be immediately affected by the operation of a guardianship deed relating to any land if he is bound by that deed and is in possession or occupation of the land.

(4) For the purposes of this Act "archaeological investigation" means any investigation of any land, objects or other material for the purpose of obtaining and recording any information of archaeological or historical interest and (without prejudice to the generality of the preceding provision) includes in the case of an archaeological investigation of any land—

(a) any investigation for the purpose of discovering and revealing and (where appropriate) recovering and removing any objects or other material of archaeological or historical interest situated in, on or under the land; and

(b) examining, testing, treating, recording and preserving any such objects or material discovered during the course of any excavations or inspections carried out for the purposes of any such investigation.

(5) For the purposes of this Act, an archaeological examination of any land means any examination or inspection of the land (including any buildings or other structures thereon) for the purpose of obtaining and recording any information of archaeological or historical interest.

(6) In this Act references to land associated with any monument (or to associated land) shall be construed in accordance with section 15(6) of this Act.

(7) "Monument" means (subject to subsection (8) below)—

(a) any building, structure or work, whether above or below the surface of the land, and any cave or excavation;

(b) any site comprising the remains of any such building, structure or work or of any cave or excavation; and

(c) any site comprising, or comprising the remains of, any vehicle, vessel, aircraft or other movable structure or part thereof which neither constitutes nor forms part of any work which is a monument within paragraph (a) above;

and any machinery attached to a monument shall be regarded as part of the monument if it could not be detached without being dismantled.

(8) Subsection (7)(a) above does not apply to any ecclesiastical building for the time being used for ecclesiastical purposes, and subsection (7)(c) above does not apply—

(a) to a site comprising any object or its remains unless the situation of that object or its remains in that particular site is a matter of public interest;

(b) to a site comprising, or comprising the remains of, any vessel which is protected by an order under section 1 of the Protection of Wrecks Act 1973 designating an area round the site as a restricted area.

(9) For the purposes of this Act, the site of a monument includes not only the land in or on which it is situated but also any land comprising or adjoining it which appears to the Secretary of State or the Commission or a local authority, in the exercise in relation to that monument of any of their functions under this Act, to be essential for the monument's support and preservation.

(10) References in this Act to a monument include references—

(a) to the site of the monument in question; and

(b) to a group of monuments or any part of a monument or group of monuments.

(11) References in this Act to the site of a monument—

(a) are references to the monument itself where it consists of a site; and

(b) in any other case include references to the monument itself.

(12) "Ancient monument" means—

(a) any scheduled monument; and

(b) any other monument which in the opinion of the Secretary of State is of public interest by reason of the historic, architectural, traditional, artistic or archaeological interest attaching to it.

(13) In this section "remains" includes any trace or sign of the previous existence of the thing in question.

[Ancient Monuments and Archaeological Areas Act 1979, s 61 as amended by the Magistrates' Courts Act 1980, Sch 7, the National Heritage Act 1983, Sch 4, the Local Government Act 1985, Sch 17, the Airports Act 1986, Sch 6, the Gas Act 1986, Sch 9, the Coal Industry Act 1987, Sch 1, the Water Act 1989, Sch 25, the Electricity Act 1989, Sch 18, the Planning (Consequential Provisions) Act 1990, Sch 2, the Statute Law (Repeals) Act 1993, Sch 1, the Coal Industry Act 1994, Schs 9 and 11, the Local Government (Wales) Act 1994, Sch 16 and SI 2001/149.]

---

1. This Act (except Part II) has effect, in relation to Scotland, as if references to a local authority and the authority's area included references to a National Park authority and the National Park, by virtue of the National Parks (Scotland) Act 2000, Sch 5.

National Heritage Act 1983

(1983 c 47)

Historic Buildings and Monuments Commission for England

8–780 32. Establishment of Commission. (1) There shall be a body known as the Historic Buildings and Monuments Commission for England.

(2) Schedule 3 shall have effect with respect to the Commission.

[National Heritage Act 1983, s 32.]

8–781 33. The Commission's general functions[1]. (1) It shall be the duty of the Commission (so far as practicable)—

(a) to secure the preservation of ancient monuments and historic buildings situated in England,

(b) to promote the preservation and enhancement of the character and appearance of conservation areas situated in England, and

(c) to promote the public's enjoyment of, and advance their knowledge of, ancient monuments and historic buildings situated in England and their preservation, in exercising the functions conferred on them by virtue of sub-sections (2) to (4) and section 34; but in the event of a conflict between those functions and that duty those functions shall prevail.

(2) The Commission—

(a) shall (so far as practicable) provide educational facilities and services, instruction and information to the public in relation to ancient monuments and historic buildings, with particular reference to those in England, and in relation to conservation areas situated in England;

(b) may give advice to any person in relation to ancient monuments, historic buildings and conservation areas situated in England, whether or not they have been consulted;

(c) may, for the purpose of exercising their functions, carry out or defray or contribute towards the cost of, research in relation to ancient monuments, historic buildings and conservation areas situated in England;

(d) may, for the purpose of exercising their functions, make and maintain records in relation to ancient monuments and historic buildings situated in England.

(e) may produce souvenirs relating to ancient monuments or historic buildings situated in England and sell souvenirs;]

(f) may defray or contribute to the cost of any activity undertaken by another person if the activity—

(i)   relates to ancient monuments or historic buildings, and

(ii) is of a kind which the Commission may itself undertake.

(2A) In relation to England, the Commission may—

(a)   prosecute any offence under Part I of the Ancient Monuments and Archaeological Areas Act 1979 or under the Planning (Listed Buildings and Conservation Areas) Act 1990, or

(b)   institute in their own name proceedings for an injunction to restrain any contravention of any provision of that Part or of that Act of 1990.

(2B) In relation to England, the Commission may make, or join in the making of, applications under section 73(1) of the Leasehold Reform, Housing and Urban Development Act 1993, and may exercise, or participate in the exercise of, any rights or powers conferred by a scheme approved under section 70 of that Act.

(3) *Consequential amendments in Schedule 4.*

(4) Without prejudice to the generality of subsection (2)(b), the Commission may advise the Secretary of State with regard to the exercise of functions exercisable by him in relation to England under the Historic Buildings and Ancient Monuments Act 1953 and the Ancient Monuments and Archaeological Areas Act 1979, whether or not they have been consulted.

(5) For the purpose of exercising their functions the Commission may, subject to the provisions of this and any other Act—

(a)   enter into contracts and other agreements;

(b)   acquire and dispose of property other than land;

(c)   with the consent of the Secretary of State, acquire land for providing the Commission with office or other accommodation and dispose of the land when no longer required for such accommodation;

(d)   do such other things as the Commission think necessary or expedient.

(6)–(7) *Charges and financial provisions.*

(8) In subsections (1) and (2)—

"ancient monument" means any structure, work, site (including any site comprising, or comprising the remains of, any vehicle, vessel, aircraft or other movable structure or part thereof), garden or area which in the Commission's opinion is of historic, architectural, traditional, artistic or archaeological interest;

"conservation area" means an area designated as a conservation area under section 69 of the Planning (Listed Buildings and Conservation Areas) Act 1990;

"historic building" means any building which in the Commission's opinion is of historic or architectural interest.

(9) In this section references to ancient monuments in England include ancient monuments in, on or under the seabed within the seaward limits of the United Kingdom territorial waters adjacent to England.

(10) For this purpose the Secretary of State may, by order², determine (or make provision for determining) any boundary between—

(a)   the parts of the United Kingdom territorial waters which are to be treated as adjacent to England, and

(b)   those which are not.

(11) The power to make an order under subsection (10) shall be exercisable by statutory instrument which shall be subject to annulment in pursuance of a resolution of either House of Parliament.

[National Heritage Act 1983, s 33 as amended by the Planning (Consequential Provisions) Act 1990, Sch 2, the

Planning and Compensation Act 1991, s 29, the Leasehold Reform, Housing and Urban Development Act 1993, Sch 21 and the National Heritage Act 2002, ss 1, 4 and 7.]

---

1. For further functions of the Commission, see the Local Government Act 1985, Sch 2.
2. The National Heritage (Territorial Waters Adjacent to England) Order 2002, SI 2002/2427 has been made.

8–781A   33A–33C . *Functions in relation to foreign monuments and buildings, exploiting intangible assets and assistance in relation to protected wrecks.*

8–782   34–35. *Power of Commission to exercise certain ministerial functions, and power to form companies.*

8–783   36. Records: powers of entry.   (1) Any person duly authorised in writing by the Commission may at any reasonable time enter any land in England for the purpose of inspecting it with a view to obtaining information for inclusion in the Commission's records made under section 33(2)(*d*); and the following provisions of this section shall apply to any such power of entry.

(2)   The power includes power for any person entering any land in exercise of the power to take with him any assistance or equipment reasonably required for the purpose to which the entry relates and to do there anything reasonably necessary for carrying out the purpose.

(3)   The Commission may not authorise the power to be exercised in relation to any land unless they know or have reason to believe there is in, on or under the land an ancient monument or historic building; and in this subsection "ancient monument" and "historic building" have the meanings given by section 33(8).

(4)   A person may not in the exercise of the power—

(*a*)   enter any building or part of a building occupied as a dwelling-house without the consent of the occupier;

(*b*)   demand admission as of right to any land which is occupied unless prior notice of the intended entry has been given to the occupier not less than 24 hours before admission is demanded.

(5)   A person seeking to enter any land in exercise of the power shall, if so required by or on behalf of the owner or occupier of the land, produce evidence of his authority before entering.

(6)   Where any works are being carried out on any land in relation to which the power is exercisable, a person acting in the exercise of the power shall comply with any reasonable requirements or conditions imposed by the person by whom the works are being carried out for the purpose of preventing interference with or delay to the works; but any requirements or conditions so imposed shall not be regarded as reasonable for the purposes of this subsection if compliance with them would in effect frustrate the exercise of the power or the purpose of the entry.

(7)   Any person who intentionally obstructs a person acting in the exercise of the power shall be guilty of an offence and liable on summary conviction to a fine not exceeding **level 3** on the standard scale.

(8)   Where in the exercise of the power damage has been caused to land or chattels on land, any person interested in the land or chattels may recover compensation in respect of the damage from the Commission.

(9)–(10)   *Supplementary provisions as to compensation under subsection (8).*
[National Heritage Act 1983, s 36 as amended by the Statute Law (Repeals) Act 1993, Sch 1.]

8–784   37. Monuments etc partly situated in England.   (1)   The Secretary of State may by order provide that the Commission shall have such functions as—

(*a*)   he thinks appropriate (having regard to their functions in relation to monuments, buildings, gardens, areas or sites situated in England), and

(*b*)   are specified in the order,

in relation to the parts situated in England of any monuments, buildings, gardens, areas or sites which are only partly so situated and which are specified in the order.

(2)   For the purpose of making such provision, any such order may contain—

(*a*)   amendments of section 33 or 34, and

(*b*)   amendments of any section or Schedule amended by Schedule 4 (including consequential amendments relating to the parts of monuments, buildings, gardens, areas or sites not situated in England).

(3)   Any such order shall have effect subject to such supplementary provisions (which may include savings and transitionals) as may be specified in the order.

(4)   Nothing in this section permits the Commission to be given a function of making regulations or other instruments of a legislative character.

(5)   The power to make an order under this section shall be exercisable by statutory instrument, and no such order shall be made unless a draft of the order has been laid before and approved by resolution of each House of Parliament.
[National Heritage Act 1983, s 37.]

Treasure Act 1996
(1996 c 24)

Meaning of "treasure"

8–785 1. Meaning of "treasure". (1) Treasure is—

(a) any object at least 300 years old when found which—

    (i) is not a coin but has metallic content of which at least 10 per cent by weight is precious metal;

    (ii) when found, is one of at least two coins in the same find which are at least 300 years old at that time and have that percentage of precious metal; or

    (iii) when found, is one of at least ten coins in the same find which are at least 300 years old at that time;

(b) any object at least 200 years old when found which belongs to a class designated under section 2(1);

(c) any object which would have been treasure trove if found before the commencement of section 4;

(d) any object which, when found, is part of the same find as—

    (i) an object within paragraph (a), (b) or (c) found at the same time or earlier; or

    (ii) an object found earlier which would be within paragraph (a) or (b) if it had been found at the same time.

(2) Treasure does not include objects which are—

(a) unworked natural objects, or

(b) minerals as extracted from a natural deposit,

or which belong to a class designated under section 2(2).
[Treasure Act 1996, s 1.]

8–786 2. Power to alter meaning. (1) The Secretary of State may by order[1], for the purposes of section 1(1)(b), designate any class of object which he considers to be of outstanding historical, archaeological or cultural importance.

(2) The Secretary of State may by order, for the purposes of section 1(2), designate any class of object which (apart from the order) would be treasure.

(3) An order under this section shall be made by statutory instrument.

(4) No order is to be made under this section unless a draft of the order has been laid before Parliament and approved by a resolution of each House.
[Treasure Act 1996, s 2.]

---

1. The Treasure (Designation) Order 2002, SI 2002/2666 has been made which designates (a) any object (other than a coin), any part of which is base metal, which, when found is one of at least two base metal objects in the same find which are of prehistoric date; and (b) any object, (other than a coin) which is of prehistoric date, and any part of which is gold or silver. The Order applies only in relation to objects found on or after 1 January 2003.

8–787 3. Supplementary. (1) This section supplements section 1.

(2) "Coin" includes any metal token which was, or can reasonably be assumed to have been, used or intended for use as or instead of money.

(3) "Precious metal" means gold or silver.

(4) When an object is found, it is part of the same find as another object if—

(a) they are found together,

(b) the other object was found earlier in the same place where they had been left together,

(c) the other object was found earlier in a different place, but they had been left together and had become separated before being found.

(5) If the circumstances in which objects are found can reasonably be taken to indicate that they were together at some time before being found, the objects are to be presumed to have been left together, unless shown not to have been.

(6) An object which can reasonably be taken to be at least a particular age is to be presumed to be at least that age, unless shown not to be.

(7) An object is not treasure if it is wreck within the meaning of Part IX of the Merchant Shipping Act 1995[1].
[Treasure Act 1996, s 3.]

---

1. See the Merchant Shipping Act 1995, s 255 in PART VII, MERCHANT SHIPPING, ante.

Ownership of treasure

8–788 4. *Ownership of treasure which is found.*

8–789 8. Duty of finder to notify coroner.   (1) A person who finds an object which he believes or has reasonable grounds for believing is treasure must notify the coroner for the district in which the object was found before the end of the notice period.

(2) The notice period is fourteen days beginning with—

(a) the day after the find; or

(b) if later, the day on which the finder first believes or has reason to believe the object is treasure.

(3) Any person who fails to comply with subsection (1) is guilty of an offence and liable on summary conviction to—

(a) imprisonment for a term not exceeding three months;

(b) a fine of an amount not exceeding **level 5** on the standard scale; or

(c) both.

(4) In proceedings for an offence under this section, it is a defence for the defendant to show that he had, and has continued to have, a reasonable excuse for failing to notify the coroner.

(5) If the office of coroner for a district is vacant, the person acting as coroner for that district is the coroner for the purposes of subsection (1).

[Treasure Act 1996, s 8.]

Miscellaneous

8–790 15. Short title, commencement and extent.   (1) This Act may be cited as the Treasure Act 1996.

(2) This Act comes into force on such day as the Secretary of State may by order[1] made by statutory instrument appoint; and different days may be appointed for different purposes.

(3) This Act does not extend to Scotland.

[Treasure Act 1996, s 15.]

---

1. This Act was brought fully into force by the following Orders: Commencement No 1 Order 1997, SI 1997/760 and Commencement No 2 Order 1997, SI 1997/1977.

Dealing in Cultural Objects (Offences) Act 2003[1]
(2003 c 27)

8–791 1. Offence of dealing in tainted cultural objects.   (1) A person is guilty of an offence if he dishonestly deals in a cultural object that is tainted, knowing or believing that the object is tainted.

(2) It is immaterial whether he knows or believes that the object is a cultural object.

(3) A person guilty of the offence is liable—

(a) on conviction on indictment, to imprisonment for a term not exceeding seven years or a fine (or both),

(b) on summary conviction, to imprisonment for a term not exceeding six months or a fine not exceeding the statutory maximum (or both)[2].

[Dealing in Cultural Objects (Offences) Act 2003, s 1.]

---

1. This Act provides for an offence of acquiring, disposing or, importing or exporting tainted cultural objects, or agreeing or arranging to do so.
2. For procedure in respect of offences triable either way see the Magistrates' Courts' Act 1980, s 17A–21 in PART 1: MAGISTRATES' COURTS, PROCEDURE, ante.

8–792 2. Meaning of "tainted cultural object".   (1) "Cultural object" means an object of historical, architectural or archaeological interest.

(2) A cultural object is tainted if, after the commencement of this Act—

(a) a person removes the object in a case falling within subsection (4) or he excavates the object, and

(b) the removal or excavation constitutes an offence.

(3) It is immaterial whether—

(a) the removal or excavation was done in the United Kingdom or elsewhere,

(b) the offence is committed under the law of a part of the United Kingdom or under the law of any other country or territory.

(4) An object is removed in a case falling within this subsection if—

(a) it is removed from a building or structure of historical, architectural or archaeological interest where the object has at any time formed part of the building or structure, or

(b) it is removed from a monument of such interest.

(5) "Monument" means—

(a) any work, cave or excavation,

(b)   any site comprising the remains of any building or structure or of any work, cave or excavation,

(c)   any site comprising, or comprising the remains of, any vehicle, vessel, aircraft or other movable structure, or part of any such thing.

(6)   "Remains" includes any trace or sign of the previous existence of the thing in question.

(7)   It is immaterial whether—

(a)   a building, structure or work is above or below the surface of the land,

(b)   a site is above or below water.

(8)   This section has effect for the purposes of section 1.

[Dealing in Cultural Objects (Offences) Act 2003, s 2.]

8–793   3. Meaning of "deals in".   (1)   A person deals in an object if (and only if) he—

(a)   acquires, disposes of, imports or exports it,

(b)   agrees with another to do an act mentioned in paragraph (a), or

(c)   makes arrangements under which another person does such an act or under which another person agrees with a third person to do such an act.

(2)   "Acquires" means buys, hires, borrows or accepts.

(3)   "Disposes of" means sells, lets on hire, lends or gives.

(4)   In relation to agreeing or arranging to do an act, it is immaterial whether the act is agreed or arranged to take place in the United Kingdom or elsewhere.

(5)   This section has effect for the purposes of section 1.

[Dealing in Cultural Objects (Offences) Act 2003, s 3.]

8–794   4. Customs and Excise prosecutions.   (1)   Proceedings for an offence relating to the dealing in a tainted cultural object may be instituted by order of the Commissioners of Customs and Excise if it appears to them that the offence has involved the importation or exportation of such an object.

(2)   An offence relates to the dealing in a tainted cultural object if it is—

(a)   an offence under section 1, or

(b)   an offence of inciting the commission of, or attempting or conspiring to commit, such an offence.

(3)   Proceedings for an offence which are instituted under subsection (1) are to be commenced in the name of an officer, but may be continued by another officer.

(4)   Where the Commissioners of Customs and Excise investigate, or propose to investigate, any matter with a view to determining—

(a)   whether there are grounds for believing that a person has committed an offence which relates to the dealing in a tainted cultural object and which involves the importation or exportation of such an object, or

(b)   whether a person should be prosecuted for such an offence,

the matter is to be treated as an assigned matter within the meaning of the Customs and Excise Management Act 1979 (c 2).

(5)   Nothing in this section affects any powers of any person (including any officer) apart from this section.

(6)   "Officer" means a person commissioned by the Commissioners of Customs and Excise under section 6(3) of the Customs and Excise Management Act 1979.

[Dealing in Cultural Objects (Offences) Act 2003, s 4.]

8–795   5. Offences by bodies corporate.   (1)   If an offence under section 1 committed by a body corporate is proved—

(a)   to have been committed with the consent or connivance of an officer, or

(b)   to be attributable to any neglect on his part,

he (as well as the body corporate) is guilty of the offence and liable to be proceeded against and punished accordingly.

(2)   "Officer", in relation to a body corporate, means—

(a)   a director, manager, secretary or other similar officer of the body,

(b)   a person purporting to act in any such capacity.

(3)   If the affairs of a body corporate are managed by its members, subsection (1) applies in relation to the acts and defaults of a member in connection with his functions of management as if he were a director of the body.

[Dealing in Cultural Objects (Offences) Act 2003, s 5.]

8–796   6. Short title, commencement and extent.   (1)   This Act may be cited as the Dealing in Cultural Objects (Offences) Act 2003.

(2) This Act comes into force at the end of the period of two months[1] beginning with the day on which it is passed.

(3) This Act does not extend to Scotland.

[Dealing in Cultural Objects (Offences) Act 2003, s 6.]

1. The Act received the Royal Assent on 30 October 2003.

ANIMALS

8–800 This title contains the following statutes—

and the following statutory instruments—

Other Acts concerning animals which appear elsewhere in this work are:

Other titles in this work which may be relevant are GAME and FISHERIES.

8–810 European Communities Act 1972: regulations. Within the scope of the title Animals there falls the subject matter of a number of regulations made under the very wide enabling power provided in section 2(2) of the European Communities Act 1972. In respect of those regulations listed in Sch 1 to the National Assembly for Wales (Transfer of Functions) Order 2000, SI 2000/253, the functions of the Secretary of State, so far as exercisable in relation to Wales, have been transferred to the National Assembly for Wales. Where such regulations create offences they are noted below in chronological order:

Sheep and Goats (Removal to Northern Ireland), SI 1983/1158;

Control of Trade in Endangered Species (Designation of Ports of Entry), SI 1985/1154;

Zootechnical Standards, SI 1992/2370;

Horses (Free Access to Competition), SI 1992/3044;

Horses (Zootechnical Standards), SI 1992/3045;

Fish Health, SI 1992/3300 amended by SI 1993/2255, SI 1994/1448, SI 1995/886 and SI 1996/3124;

Welfare of Livestock, SI 1994/2126 amended by SI 1998/1709 and revoked in so far as they apply to England by SI 2000/1870;

Welfare of Animals During Transport, SI 1994/3249[1];

Welfare of Animals (Slaughter or Killing), SI 1995/731 amended by SI 1999/400, SI 2000/656, SI 2001/770 (England), 3352 (Wales) and 3830 and SI 2003/3272 (E);

Import of Seal Skins Regulations 1996, SI 1996/2686;

Selective Cull (Enforcement of Community Compensation Conditions) Regulations 1996, SI 1996/3186;

Cattle Identification Regulations 1998, SI 1998/871 amended by 1796, SI 1998/2969, SI 1999/1179 and 1339 and SI 2001/1644 (England), 2360 (Wales) and 3960 (England);

Cattle Database Regulations 1998, SI 1998/1796 amended by SI 2002/94 (England) and 304 (Wales);

Miscellaneous Products of Animal Origin (Import Conditions) Regulations 1999, SI 1999/157 (revoked in relation to Wales by SI 2004/1430);

Sheep and Goats Identification (Wales) Regulations 2000, SI 2000/2335;

Cattle (Identification of Older Animals) Regulations 2000, SI 2000/2976 amended by SI 2001/1644 (England), 2376 and 3960 (England) and SI 2002/95 and 273 (Wales);

Slaughter Premium Regulations 2000, SI 2000/3126;

Cattle (Identification of Older Animals) (Wales) Regulations 2000, SI 2000/3339;

Restriction on Pithing (Wales) Regulations 2001, SI 2001/1303 amended by SI 2002/1416;

Gelatine (Intra-Community Trade) (England) Regulations 2001, SI 2001/1553;

BSE Monitoring (England) Regulations 2001, SI 2001/1644 amended by SI 2001/3960;

BSE Monitoring (Wales) Regulations 2001, SI 2001/2360 amended by SI 2001/4048 and SI 2002/1416;

Animal By-products (Wales) Regulations 2003, SI 2003/2756;

Registration of Establishments (Laying Hens) (England) Regulations 2003, SI 2003/3100;

Registration of Establishments (Laying Hens) (Wales) Regulations 2004, SI 2004/1432;

Horse Passports (England) Regulations 2004, in this title, post;

Non Commercial Movement of Pet Animals (England) Regulations 2004, in this title, post;

Horse Passports (Wales) Regulations 2005, SI 2005/231;

Salmonella in Laying Flocks (Survey Powers) Regulations 2005, SI 2005/359;

Salmonella in Laying Flocks (Survey Powers) (Wales) Regulations 2005, SI 2005/586;

Animals and Animal Products (Import and Export) (Wales) Regulations 2005, SI 2005/1158;

Animals and Animal Products (Import and Export) (England) Regulations 2005, SI 2005/2002;

Animal By-Products Regulations 2005, SI 2005/2347;

Salmonella in Broiler Flocks (Survey Powers) (England) Regulations 2005, SI 2005/2927;

Avian Influenza (Preventive Measures) (Wales) (No 2) Regulations 2005, SI 2005/3384;

Avian Influenza (Preventive Measures in Zoos) (Wales) (No 2) Regulations 2005, SI 2005/3385;

Avian Influenza (Preventive Measures) (No 2) Regulations 2005, SI 2005/3394;

Transmissible Spongiform Encephalopathies Regulations 2006, SI 2006/68;

Foot-and Mouth Disease (Control of Vaccination) (England) Regulations 2006, SI 2006/183.

---

1. See *Ken Lane Transport Ltd v North Yorkshire County Council* [1995] 1 WLR 1416, 160 JP 91, [1996] RTR 335, (decided under the revoked Welfare of Animals During Transport Order 1992, SI 1992/3304).

Protection of Animals Act 1911

(1 & 2 Geo 5 c 27)

8–811 1. Cruelty. (1)[1] If any person—

(a) shall cruelly[2] beat, kick[3], ill-treat[4], over-ride, over-drive, over-load, torture, infuriate, or terrify any animal, or shall cause or procure, or, being the owner, permit any animal to be so used, or shall, by wantonly or unreasonably[5] doing or omitting to do any act, or causing or procuring the commission or omission of any act, cause any unnecessary[6] suffering, or, being the owner, permit any unnecessary suffering to be so caused to any animal; or

(b) shall convey or carry, or cause or procure, or, being the owner, permit to be conveyed or carried, any animal in such manner or position as to cause that animal any unnecessary suffering; or

(c) shall cause, procure, or assist at the fighting or[7] baiting of any animal[8]; or shall keep, use, manage, or act or assist in the management of, any premises or place for the purpose, or partly for the purpose, of fighting or baiting any animal, or shall permit any premises or place to be so kept, managed, or used, or shall receive, or cause or procure any person to receive, money for the admission of any person to such premises or place; or

(d) shall wilfully, without any reasonable cause or excuse, administer, or cause or procure, or being the owner permit, such administration of, any poisonous or injurious drug or substance to any animal, or shall wilfully, without any reasonable cause or excuse, cause any such substance to be taken by any animal; or (*e*)   shall[9] subject, or cause or procure, or being the owner permit, to be subjected, any animal to any operation which is performed without due care and humanity[10]; or

(*f*)   shall tether any horse, ass or mule under such conditions or in such manner as to cause that animal unnecessary suffering;

such person shall be guilty of an offence of cruelty within the meaning of this Act and shall be liable[11] on summary conviction to imprisonment for a term not exceeding **six months** or to a fine not exceeding **level 5** on the standard scale, or both.

(2) For the purposes of this section, an owner shall be[12] deemed to have permitted cruelty within the meaning of this Act if he shall have failed to exercise reasonable care and supervision in respect of the protection of the animal therefrom:

Provided that, where an owner is convicted of permitting cruelty within the meaning of this Act by reason only of his having failed to exercise such care and supervision, he shall not be liable to imprisonment without the option of a fine.

(3) Nothing in this section shall render illegal any act lawfully done under the Animals (Scientific Procedures) Act 1986[13], or shall apply—

(*a*)   to the commission or omission of any act in the course of the destruction, or the preparation for destruction, of any animal as food for mankind, unless such destruction or such preparation was accompanied by the infliction of unnecessary suffering; or

(*b*)   to the coursing or hunting[14] of any captive animal, unless such animal is[15] liberated in an injured, mutilated, or exhausted condition; but a captive animal shall not, for the purposes of this section, be deemed to be coursed or hunted before it is liberated for the purpose of being coursed or hunted, or after it has been recaptured, or if it is[16] under control and a captive animal shall not be deemed to be coursed or hunted within the meaning of this subsection if it is coursed or hunted in an enclosed space from which it has no reasonable chance of escape.

[Protection of Animals Act 1911, s 1; amended by Protection of Animals Act (1911) Amendment Act 1912, s 1, the Protection of Animals (1911) Amendment Act 1921, s 1, the Criminal Law Act 1977, Sch 617, the Criminal Justice Act 1982, s 46, the Animals (Scientific Procedures) Act 1986, Sch 3, the Protection of Animals (Penalties) Act 1987, s 1, and the Protection Against Cruel Tethering Act 1988, s 1.]

---

1. For cruelty arising from the abandonment of an animal, see Abandonment of Animals Act 1960, this title, post. For provisions on the care, disposal or slaughter of animals kept for commercial purposes in respect of which proceedings have been brought under this section and are not yet concluded, see the Protection of Animals (Amendment) Act 2000, in this title, post.

2. These words create separate offences (*Johnson v Needham* [1909] 1 KB 626, 73 JP 117). Where the charge is in connection with several animals, one summons may charge the offence in respect of all the animals (*R v Cable, ex p O'Shea* [1906] 1 KB 719, 70 JP 246); in such case there should not be a conviction in respect of each animal (*R v Rawson* [1909] 2 KB 748, 73 JP 483); there would obviously be separate convictions where the defendant was originally separately charged in respect of each animal. Guilty knowledge was held to be an essential ingredient of the offence of unlawfully causing to be cruelly ill-treated, abused and tortured, under the 1849 Act (*Greenwood v Backhouse* (1902) 66 JP 519). The offence does not depend upon any concept of recklessness (*Peterssen v RSPCA* [1993] Crim LR 852).

A person charged with an offence under s 1 is entitled to know what act or omission is alleged to have caused the unnecessary suffering, and if a charge is specified in this way problems of duplicity will often fall away since it will be obvious whether separate acts or omissions constituting separate offences are being charged; however, the absence of such particularity does not render the proceedings a nullity or a conviction unsafe provided the requisite information is given to the defendant in good time for him/her to be able fairly to meet the case against him/her: *Nash v Birmingham Crown Court* [2005] EWHC Admin 338, (2005) 169 JP 157.

3. The Queen's Bench Division held in *Ford v Wiley* (1889) 23 QBD 203, 53 JP 485, that the mere infliction of pain for a necessary purpose is not cruelty, but that unnecessary and unreasonable abuse of the animal is an offence.

4. Cruelty means "causing unnecessary suffering", and a defendant will be convicted if he was doing something which it was not reasonably necessary to do and which he was not justified in doing, such as shooting at a trespassing dog where there was no evidence of it worrying sheep or fowls (*Barnard v Evans* [1925] 2 KB 794, 89 JP 165; considered in *Isted v DPP* (1997) 162 JP 513, [1998] Crim LR 194). Whether any particular countryside activity amounts to ill-treatment in particular circumstances, whether or not it is unnecessary and whether or not any suffering which has been suffered by the animal has been caused by a human, is a question of fact for the magistrates. The higher the risk of injury to which the human has exposed the animal, the more likely there is to be a finding of causation by the magistrates; if the risk of injury is very low then a finding of no causation is very likely *Bandeira and Brannigan v Royal Society for the Prevention of Cruelty to Animals* (2000) 164 JP 307, DC).

5. The question is one of fact for the justices to decide (*Dee v Yorke* (1914) 78 JP 359). Comparison with civil law concepts of negligence are not helpful (*Peterssen v RSPCA* [1993] Crim LR 852).

6. The suffering becomes unnecessary when it is not inevitable, in that it can be terminated or alleviated by some reasonably practicable measure (*Royal Society for the Prevention of Cruelty to Animals v Isaacs* [1994] Crim LR 517). The fact that a trap, a *Larsen* trap, was being lawfully used in accordance with a licence granted under s 16 of the Wildlife and Countryside Act 1981 so that an offence under s 8 of the 1981 Act was not committed, does not mean that an offence under this section cannot be made out (*R (RSPCA) v Shinton* [2003] EWHC 1696 (Admin), 167 JP 513). If a dog which was worrying livestock is killed outright in circumstances where it does not suffer unnecessarily, no offence under s 1(1) is committed; see *Isted v DPP* (1997) 162 JP 513, [1998] Crim LR 194.

7. Coursing rabbits with dogs, in an enclosure from which they cannot escape, is not baiting (*Pitts v Millar* (1874) LR 9 QB 380, 38 JP 615). Town Police Clauses Act 1847, post, contains provisions as to cock-fighting in places where that Act is in force. See also Cockfighting Act 1952, this title, post.

8. "Animal" means a domestic or captive animal (*Crown Prosecution Service v Barry* (1989) 153 JP 557, [1989] Crim LR 645).

9. Note the exception in sub-s (3) as to acts lawfully done under the Animals (Scientific Procedures) Act 1986, post.

10. Certain operations are deemed to be performed without due care and humanity; see Protection of Animals (Anaesthetics) Act 1954, s 1, post.

11. He may also be disqualified from keeping a pet shop (Pet Animals Act 1951, s 5, this title, post), a boarding establishment for animals (Animal Boarding Establishments Act 1963, s 3, this title, post), a riding establishment (Riding Establishments Act 1964, s 4(3), this title, post), or any dangerous wild animal (Dangerous Wild Animals Act 1976, s 6(2), this title, post), or, for keeping any animal (Protection of Animals (Amendment) Act 1954, s 1, this title, post). A magistrates' court shall not in a person's absence impose any disqualification on him, except after an adjournment after conviction and before sentencing him; see Magistrates' Courts Act 1980, s 11(4), ante. If the defendant is registered under the Performing Animals (Regulation) Act 1925, post, an order may be made that his name be removed from the register, and that he be disqualified from being registered.

12. Where respondent, knowing the condition of a horse when bought was poor, omitted to take steps to prevent its being worked in that condition, there is *prima facie* evidence of permitting cruelty (*Whiting v Ivens* (1915) 79 JP 457).

13. See this title, post.

14. As to what constitutes "hunting", see *Rodgers v Pickersgill* (1910) 74 JP 324.

15. This means liberated from the receptacle in which the animal has been confined (*Waters v Meakin* [1916] 2 KB 111, 80 JP 276). Where a rabbit was dangled near to and in front of greyhounds before being thrown to the ground and subsequently worried by them, a conviction was ordered (*Jenkins v Ash* (1929) 93 JP 229).

16. This is a question of fact. See *Waters v Meakin*, supra.

17. This Act now makes an offence the "coursing" described in *Waters v Meakin*, supra.

8–812   2. Destruction of animal.

Where the owner of an animal is convicted of an offence of cruelty within the meaning of this Act, it shall be lawful for the court, if the court is satisfied that it would be cruel to keep the animal alive, to direct that the animal be destroyed, and to assign the animal to any suitable person for that purpose[1]; and the person to whom such animal is so assigned shall, as soon as possible, destroy such animal, or cause or procure such animal to be destroyed, in his presence without unnecessary suffering. Any reasonable expenses incurred in destroying the animal may be ordered by the court to be paid by the owner, and thereupon shall be recoverable summarily as a civil debt:

Provided that, unless the owner assent, no order shall be made under this section except upon the evidence of a duly registered veterinary surgeon.
[Protection of Animals Act 1911, s 2.]

1. There is no right of appeal against this order (s 14, post, and the Magistrates' Courts Act 1980, s 108, ante).

8–813   3. Deprivation of ownership.

If the owner of any animal shall be guilty of cruelty within the meaning of this Act to the animal, the court, upon his conviction thereof, may, if they think fit, in addition to any other punishment, deprive[1] such person of the ownership of the animal, and may make such order as to the disposal of the animal as they think fit under the circumstances:

Provided that no order shall be made under this section, unless it is shown by evidence as to a previous conviction, or as to the character of the owner, or otherwise, that the animal, if left with the owner, is likely to be exposed to further cruelty.
[Protection of Animals Act 1911, s 3.]

1. In addition, the court may disqualify for having custody of any animal; see Protection of Animals (Amendment) Act 1954, s 1, this title, post. Where the defendant is not present, note the requirements of the Magistrates' Courts Act 1980, s 11 in PART I: MAGISTRATES' COURTS, PROCEDURE, ante.

8–814   5. Entry by constable.

Any constable shall have a right to enter any knacker's yard at any hour by day, or at any hour when business is or apparently is in progress or is usually carried on therein, for the purpose of examining whether there is or has been any contravention of or non-compliance with the provisions of this Act. Any person refusing to permit any constable to enter any premises which he is entitled to enter under this section, or obstructing or impeding him in the execution of his duty under this section—Penalty, upon summary conviction, not exceeding **level 1** on the standard scale.
[Protection of Animals Act 1911, s 5(2), as amended by the Criminal Law Act 1977, s 31 and the Criminal Justice Act 1982, s 46.]

8–815   5A. Attendance at animal fights.

A person who, without reasonable excuse, is present when animals are placed together for the purpose of their fighting each other shall be liable on summary conviction to a fine not exceeding **level 4** on the standard scale.
[Protection of Animals Act 1911, s 5A added by the Protection of Animals (Amendment) Act 1988, s 2.]

8–816   5B. Advertising of animal fights.

If a person who publishes or causes to be published an advertisement for a fight between animals knows that it is such an advertisement he shall be liable on summary conviction to a fine not exceeding **level 4** on the standard scale.
[Protection of Animals Act 1911, s 5B added by the Protection of Animals (Amendment) Act 1988, s 2.]

8–817   7. Animals in pounds.

Any person who impounds[1] or confines, or causes to be impounded or confined, any animal in any pound failing, while the animal is so impounded or confined, to supply[2] it with a sufficient quantity of wholesome and suitable food and water—Penalty, upon summary conviction, not exceeding **level 1** on the standard scale.
[Protection of Animals Act 1911, s 7(1), as amended by the Criminal Law Act 1977, s 31 and the Criminal Justice Act 1982, s 46.]

1. It is not the keeper of the pound, but the party who delivered the animal to the keeper, who is liable for the penalty (*Dargan v Davies* (1877) 2 QBD 118, 41 JP 468); but the pound keeper may be liable if he undertook to supply food (*Mason v Newland and Rosier* (1840) 9 C & P 575).

2. If any animal is without sufficient food or water for six successive hours, or longer, any person may enter the pound for the purpose of supplying it therewith (s 7(2)). The reasonable cost of food and water supplied may be recovered summarily from the owner of the animal as a civil debt (s 7(3)).

8–818 8. Poisoned grain and flesh, etc. Any person—

(a) selling or offering or exposing for sale[1], or giving away, or causing or procuring any person to sell or offer or expose for sale or give away, or knowingly being a party to the sale or offering or exposing for sale or giving away of any grain or seed which has been rendered poisonous except for *bona fide* use in agriculture; or

(b) knowingly putting or placing or causing or procuring any person to put or place, or knowingly being a party to the putting or placing, in or upon any land or building any[2] poison, or any fluid or edible matter (not being sown seed or grain) which has been rendered poisonous.

Penalty, upon summary conviction, not exceeding **level 4** on the standard scale.

Provided that, in any proceedings under paragraph (b) of this section, it shall be a defence[3] that the poison was placed by the accused for the purpose of destroying insects and other invertebrates, rats, mice, or other small ground vermin, where such is found to be necessary in the interests of public health, agriculture, or the preservation of other animals, domestic or wild, or for the purpose of manuring the land, and that he took all reasonable precautions to prevent injury thereby to dogs, cats, fowls, or other domestic animals and wild birds.

[Protection of Animals Act 1911, s 8, with proviso substituted by Protection of Animals (Amendment) Act 1927, s 1, and as amended by the Criminal Law Act 1977, s 31 and the Criminal Justice Act 1982, ss 39 and 46, and Sch 3.]

1. Cf *Keating v Horwood* (1926) 90 JP 141.

2. As to putting poison to destroy or injure game, see Game Act 1831, s 3, title GAME, post, and Ground Game Act 1880, s 6, post. See also Agriculture (Miscellaneous Provisions) Act 1972, s 19, title AGRICULTURE, ante (for defence when specified poison is used for the destruction of grey squirrels or coypus).

A person shall not be guilty of an offence under this section by reason only that he uses poisonous gas in a rabbit hole, or places in a rabbit hole a substance which, by evaporation or in contact with moisture, generates poisonous gas. (Prevention of Damage by Rabbits Act 1939, s 4.)

3. For exceptions to this statutory defence where prohibited poison is used, see Animals (Cruel Poisons) Act 1962:

Exception to statutory defence where prohibited poison used.—(1) Where the use of any poison for the purpose of destroying any animal has been prohibited or restricted by regulations under this Act—

(a) the fact that the poison was used as mentioned in the proviso to s 8 of the Protection of Animals Act 1911 . . . shall not be a defence in proceedings under paragraph (b) of that section if the poison was used in contravention of the regulations; and

(b) any person convicted in such proceedings of an offence committed by or in connection with the use of the poison in contravention of the regulations shall be liable to a fine not exceeding **level 3** on the standard scale or to imprisonment for a term not exceeding **three months** or to both. (Animals (Cruel Poisons) Act 1962, s 1, as amended by the Criminal Law Act 1977, Sch 6 and the Criminal Justice Act 1982, s 46.)

"Animal" in s 1(1) above means any mammal (Animals (Cruel Poisons) Act 1962, s 3).

The Animals (Cruel Poisons) Regulations 1963, SI 1963/1278, have been made.

8–819 9. Using dogs for draught. Any person using, or causing or procuring, or being the owner permitting, to be used, any dog for the purpose of drawing or helping to draw any cart, carriage, truck, or barrow, on any public highway—Penalty, upon summary conviction, not exceeding **level 1** on the standard scale.

[Protection of Animals Act 1911, s 9, as amended by the Criminal Law Act 1977, s 31 and the Criminal Justice Act 1982, ss 35 and 46.]

8–820 10. Traps. Any person who sets, or causes or procures to be set, any spring trap for the purpose of catching any hare or rabbit, or which is so placed as to be likely to catch any hare or rabbit, failing to inspect, or cause some competent person to inspect, the trap at reasonable intervals of time and at least once every day between sunrise and sunset—Penalty, upon summary conviction, not exceeding **level 1** on the standard scale.

[Protection of Animals Act 1911, s 10, as amended by the Criminal Law Act 1977, s 31 and the Criminal Justice Act 1982, s 46.]

8–821 11. Injured animals. (1) If a police constable finds any animal so diseased or so severely injured or in such a physical condition that, in his opinion, having regard to the means available for removing the animal, there is no possibility of removing it without cruelty, he shall, if the owner is absent or refuses to consent to the destruction of the animal, at once summon a duly registered veterinary surgeon, if any such veterinary surgeon resides within a reasonable distance, and, if it appears by the certificate of such veterinary surgeon that the animal is mortally injured, or so severely injured, or so diseased, or in such physical condition, that it is cruel to keep it alive, it shall be lawful for the police constable, without the consent of the owner, to slaughter the animal, or cause or procure it to be slaughtered, with such instruments or appliances, and with such precautions, and in such manner, as to inflict as little suffering as practicable, and, if the slaughter takes place on any public highway, to remove the carcase or cause or procure it to be removed therefrom.

(2) If any veterinary surgeon summoned under this section certifies that the injured animal can without cruelty be removed, it shall be the duty of the person in charge of the animal to cause it forthwith to be removed with as little suffering as possible, and, if that person fail so to do, the police constable may, without the consent of that person, cause the animal forthwith to be so removed.

(3) Any expense which may be reasonably incurred by any constable in carrying out the provisions of this section (including the expenses of any veterinary surgeon summoned by the constable, and whether the animal is slaughtered under this section or not) may be recovered from the owner summarily as a civil debt, and, subject thereto, any such expense shall be defrayed out of the fund from which the expenses of the police are payable in the area in which the animal is found.

(4) For the purposes of this section, the expression "animal" means any horse, mule, ass, bull, sheep, goat, or pig.
[Protection of Animals Act 1911, s 11.]

8–822 12. Powers of constables. (1) A police[1] constable may apprehend without warrant[2] any person who he has reason to believe is guilty of an offence under this Act which is punishable by imprisonment without the option of a fine, whether upon his own view thereof or upon the complaint and information of any other person who shall declare his name and place of abode to such constable.

(2) Where a person having charge of a vehicle or animal is apprehended by a police constable for an offence under this Act, it shall be lawful for that or any other constable to take charge of such vehicle or animal, and to deposit the same in some place of safe custody until the termination of the proceedings or until the court shall direct such vehicle or animal to be delivered to the person charged or the owner, and the reasonable costs of such detention, including the reasonable costs of veterinary treatment where such treatment is required, shall, in the event of a conviction in respect of the said animal, be recoverable from the owner summarily as a civil debt, or, where the owner himself is convicted, shall be part of the costs of the case.
[Protection of Animals Act 1911, s 12.]

---

1. An officer of the Royal Society for Prevention of Cruelty to Animals has no right to give offenders into custody; he should complain to a constable (*Line v Royal Society for Prevention of Cruelty to Animals* (1902) 18 TLR 634).
2. This power of arrest is preserved by the Police and Criminal Evidence Act 1984, s 26 and Sch 2.

8–823 13. Production of drivers or animals. (1) Where proceedings are instituted under this Act against the driver or conductor of any vehicle, it shall be lawful for the court to issue a summons directed to the employer of the driver or conductor, as the case may be, requiring him, if it is in his power so to do, to produce the driver or conductor at the hearing of the case.

(2) Where proceedings are instituted under this Act, it shall be lawful for the court to issue a summons directed to the owner of the animal requiring him to produce either at, or at any time before, the hearing of the case, as may be stated in the summons, the animal for the inspection of the court, if such production is possible without cruelty.

(3) Where a summons is issued under either of the foregoing subsections of this section, owner or employer, as the case may be, failing to comply therewith without satisfactory excuse—Penalty, upon summary conviction, not exceeding **level 1** on the standard scale for the first occasion, and not exceeding **level 1** on the standard scale for the second or any subsequent occasion, on which he so fails, and may be required to pay the costs of any adjournment rendered necessary by his failure.
[Protection of Animals Act 1911, s 13, as amended by the Criminal Law Act 1977, s 31 and the Criminal Justice Act 1982, s 46.]

8–824 14. Appeal. (1) An appeal shall lie from any conviction or order (other than an order for the destruction of an animal) by a court of summary jurisdiction under this Act to the Crown Court.

(2) Where there is an appeal by the owner of an animal from any conviction or order by a court of summary jurisdiction under this Act, the court may order him not to sell or part with the animal until the appeal is determined or abandoned, and to produce it on the hearing of the appeal if such production is possible without cruelty and a person who fails to comply with an order under this section without satisfactory excuse shall be liable on summary conviction to a fine not exceeding **level 1** on the standard scale.
[Protection of Animals Act 1911, s 14, as amended by Criminal Justice Act 1948, 10th Sch, the Courts Act 1971, Sch 9, the Criminal Law Act 1977, s 31 and the Criminal Justice Act 1982, s 46.]

8–825 15. Definitions. Except the context otherwise requires, or it is otherwise expressly provided—

    (*a*) the expression "animal" means any domestic or captive animal;

    (*b*) the expression[1] "domestic animal" means any horse, ass, mule, bull, sheep, pig, goat, dog, cat, or fowl, or any other animal of whatsoever kind or species, and whether a quadruped or not which is tame or which has been or is being sufficiently tamed to serve some purpose for the use of man;

    (*c*) the expression "captive animal" means any animal (not being a domestic animal) of whatsoever kind or species and whether a quadruped or not, including any bird, fish, or reptile, which is in^2 captivity, or confinement, or which is maimed, pinioned, or subjected to any appliance or contrivance for the purpose of hindering or preventing its escape from captivity or confinement;

    (*d*)   the expression "horse" includes any mare, gelding, pony, foal, colt, filly, or stallion; "bull" includes any cow, bullock, heifer, calf, steer, or ox; "sheep" includes any lamb, ewe, or ram; "pig" includes any boar, hog, or sow; "goat" includes a kid; "dog" includes any bitch, sapling, or puppy; "cat" includes a kitten; "fowl" includes any cock, hen, chicken, capon, turkey, goose, gander, duck, drake, guinea-fowl, peacock, peahen, swan, or pigeon;

    (*e*)   the expression "knacker" means a person whose trade or business it is to kill any cattle not killed for the purpose of the flesh being used as butcher's meat, and the expression "knacker's yard" means any building or place used for the purpose, or partly for the purpose, of such trade or business, and the expression "cattle" includes any horse, ass, mule, bull, sheep, goat, or pig;

    (*f*)   the expression "pound", used in relation to the impounding or confining of animals, includes any receptacle of a like nature.

[Protection of Animals Act 1911, s 15.]

---

1. The following decisions are under s 3 of the repealed Cruelty to Animals Act 1854: a fighting cock is a "domestic animal" (*Budge v Parsons* (1863) 27 JP 231). Wild birds kept in confinement and trained as decoy birds for bird-catching are domestic animals (*Colam v Pagett* (1883) 12 QBD 66, 48 JP 263); but young parrots newly imported are not (*Swan v Saunders* (1881) 45 JP 522), nor are wild rabbits caught in nets, and confined in boxes, and fed five or six days before they are liberated, and coursed (*Aplin v Porritt* [1893] 2 QB 57, 57 JP 456).

2. It was held, under the repealed Wild Animals in Captivity Protection Act 1900, that a stranded whale unable to escape for a time, but which would have floated off with the incoming tide, was not "in captivity or close confinement" (*Steele v Rogers* (1912) 76 JP 150); applied in *Rowley v Murphy* [1964] 2 QB 43, [1964] 1 All ER 50, 128 JP 88, where it was held that a hunted stag, temporarily unable to escape, is not "in captivity" even though it is then taken and killed by its pursuers.

Performing Animals (Regulation) Act 1925

(15 & 16 Geo 5 c 38)

8–1060   1. Restriction on exhibition and training of performing animals.   (1) No person shall exhibit^1 or train^1 any performing animal^2 unless he is registered^3 in accordance with this Act.

    (2)–(8) *Provisions as to registration.*

[Performing Animals (Regulation) Act 1925, s 1, amended by the Local Government Act 1974, Schs 6 and 8.]

---

1. For the purposes of this Act "exhibit" means exhibit at any entertainment to which the public are admitted, whether on payment or otherwise and "train" means train for the purpose of any such exhibition, and "exhibitor" and "trainer" have respectively the corresponding meanings (s 5(1)). See general exemption in s 7, post.

2. For the purposes of this Act, "animal" does not include invertebrates (s 5(1)).

3. The local authority will keep the register, and give to every person entered therein a certificate of registration containing the particulars entered in the register, and transmit a copy of every certificate to the Secretary of State. The register will be open for inspection and extracts can be made therefrom and appropriate fees charged (s 1(2)–(8), as amended by the Local Government Act 1974, Sch 6). See also the Performing Animals Rules 1925, S R & O, 1925/1219, amended by SI 1968/1464.

8–1061   2. Power of courts to prohibit or restrict exhibition and training of performing animals.   (1) Where it is proved to the satisfaction of a court of summary jurisdiction on a complaint made by a constable or an officer of a local authority that the training or exhibition of any performing animal has been accompanied by cruelty and should be prohibited or allowed only subject to conditions, the court may make an order^1 against the person in respect of whom the complaint is made prohibiting the training or exhibition or imposing such conditions thereon as may be specified by the order.

    (2) If any person is aggrieved by the making of such an order or a refusal to make such an order, he may appeal to the Crown Court . . .

    (3) An order made under this Act shall not come into force until seven days after it is made, or, if an appeal has been entered within that period, until the determination of the appeal.

    (4) Any court by which an order is made under this section shall cause a copy of the order to be sent as soon as may be after the order comes into force to the local authority by which the person against whom the order is made is registered and to the Secretary of State, and shall cause the particulars of the order to be endorsed upon the certificate held by that person, and that person shall produce his certificate on being so required by the court for the purposes of endorsement. A local authority to which a copy of an order is sent under this section shall enter the particulars of the order on the register.

[Performing Animals (Regulation) Act 1925, s 2, as amended by the Courts Act 1971, Sch 9, and the Crown Court Rules 1971, SI 1971/1292, r 24, Sch 3.]

---

1. To obviate the necessity for a second sitting of the court that made the order, we advise that a conditional order as to endorsement on and production of the certificate be made at the original hearing.

8–1062　3. Power to enter premises.　(1) Any officer of a local authority duly authorised in that behalf by the local authority and any constable may (*a*) enter at all reasonable times and inspect any premises in which any performing animals are being trained or exhibited or kept for training or exhibition, and any animals found thereon; and (*b*) require any person who he has reason to believe is a trainer or exhibitor of performing animals to produce his certificate.

(2) No constable or such officer as aforesaid shall be entitled under this section to go on or behind the stage during a public performance of performing animals.
[Performing Animals (Regulation) Act 1925, s 3.]

8–1063　4. Offences and legal proceedings.　(1) If any person (*a*) not being registered under this Act exhibits or trains any performing animal; or (*b*) being registered under this Act exhibits or trains any performing animal with respect to which or in a manner with respect to which he is not registered; or (*c*) being a person against whom an order by a court of summary jurisdiction has been made on complaint under this Act, contravenes or fails to comply with the order in any part of Great Britain, whether within or without the area of jurisdiction of that court; or (*d*) obstructs or wilfully delays any constable or officer of a local authority in the execution of his powers under this Act as to entry or inspection; or (*e*) conceals any animal with a view to avoiding such inspection; or (*f*) being a person registered under this Act, on being required in pursuance of this Act to produce his certificate under this Act fails without reasonable excuse so to do; or (*g*) applies to be registered under this Act when prohibited from being so registered; he shall be guilty of an offence against this Act, and shall be liable on summary conviction upon a complaint made by a constable or an officer of a local authority to a fine not exceeding **level 3** on the standard scale.

(2) Where a person is convicted of an offence against this Act, or against the Protection of Animals Act 1911[1], as amended by any subsequent enactment, the court before which he is convicted may in addition to or in lieu of imposing any other penalty (*a*) if such person is registered under this Act order that his name be removed from the register; (*b*) order that such person shall either permanently or for such time as may be specified in the order be disqualified for being registered under this Act; and where such an order is made, the provisions of subsections (2), (3) and (4) of s 2 of this Act shall apply to the order as they apply to an order made under that section.
[Performing Animals (Regulation) Act 1925, s 4, as amended by the Criminal Justice Act 1982, ss 38 and 46.]

---

1. *Ante.*

8–1064　5. Interpretation, rules, and expenses.　(1) For the purposes of this Act—

The expression "animal" does not include invertebrates;

The expression "exhibit" means exhibit at any entertainment to which the public are admitted, whether on payment of money or otherwise, and the expression "train" means train for the purpose of any such exhibition, and the expressions "exhibitor" and "trainer" have respectively the corresponding meanings;

The expression "local authority" means—

As respects the City of London, the common council;

As respects any London borough, the council of the borough;

As respects any county or metropolitan district, the council of the county or district;

The expression "prescribed" means prescribed by rules made by the Secretary of State.

(2)–(3) *Rules; expenses.*
[Performing Animals (Regulation) Act 1925, s 5, as amended by the London Government Order 1966, SI 1966/1305, the Local Government Act 1974, Sch 8, and the Local Government Act 1985, Sch 8.]

8–1065　7. Exemptions.　This Act shall not apply to the training of animals for *bona fide* military, police, agricultural or sporting purposes, or the exhibition of any animals so trained.
[Performing Animals (Regulation) Act 1925, s 7.]

Destructive Imported Animals Act 1932
(22 & 23 Geo 5 c 12)

8–1066　1. Power to prohibit or control the importation or keeping of musk rats.　(1) It shall be lawful for the Minister of [Agriculture, Fisheries and Food][1] and the Secretary of State for Scotland (in this Act referred to as the "Minister" and "the Secretary of State" respectively), acting jointly, to prohibit by order[2], either absolutely[3] or except under a licence granted under this Act, the importation[4] into and keeping within Great Britain[5] of any animal of the species designated *Fiber Zibethicus* or *Ondatra Zithethica*, and commonly known as the musk rat, or musquash. An order made under this subsection may prohibit absolutely the importation of musk rats, notwithstanding that the keeping of them is not prohibited absolutely.
[Destructive Imported Animals Act 1932, s 1.]

1. Now the Minister of Agriculture, Fisheries and Food alone see the Transfer of Functions (Agriculture and Food) Order 1999, SI 1999/3141. The functions of the Minister, so far as exercisable in relation to Wales, have been transferred to the National Assembly for Wales, by the National Assembly for Wales (Transfer of Functions) Order 1999, SI 1999/672, art 2, Sch 1.

2. Every order shall be laid before Parliament, and if either House within the next 28 days resolves that the order shall be annulled, the order shall be void (sub-s (2)). The Musk Rats (Prohibition of Importation and Keeping) Order 1933, SR & O 1933/106 has been made. As to power to extend this section to other destructive non-indigenous animals, see s 10, post.

3. A special licence can be granted under s 8, post, notwithstanding a prohibition order absolute. As to compensation for musk rats kept for profit, and for structures and equipment which are destroyed in consequence of an order prohibiting absolutely the keeping of musk rats, see s 7.

4. Any reference to importation into Great Britain does not include a reference to importation from a member state (Destructive Imported Animals Act 1932 (Amendment) Regulations 1992, SI 1992/3302).

5. This Act shall not extend to Northern Ireland, and for the purposes of the Government of Ireland Act 1920, 10 & 11 Geo 5, c 67, the enactment of legislation for purposes similar to the purposes of this Act, shall not be deemed to be beyond the powers of the Parliament of Northern Ireland by reason only of the restrictions on those powers contained in s 4 of the said Act (s 12(2)).

8–1067   2. Power to make regulations and prescribe form of licences.   For the purpose of enabling effect to be given to orders made under the last preceding section, the Minister and the Secretary of State, acting jointly, may—(*a*) make regulations[1] with respect to the ports at which musk rats may be imported under a licence, the form of container to be used for their transport from place to place, the nature of the premises upon which, and the manner in which, they may be kept under a licence, and the precautions to be taken against their escape; (*b*) prescribe the forms of licences to be used under this Act, the duration of such licences, and the terms and conditions to be attached thereto; and (*c*) with the approval of the Treasury prescribe the fees to be charged in respect of the grant or renewal of such licences.
[Destructive Imported Animals Act 1932, s 2.]

1. For penalty for breach of regulations, see s 6(1)(*e*), post. Regulations have been made in respect of Mink (SI 1987/2225) and Coypus (SI 1987/2224).

8–1068   3. Grant and revocation of licences.   The appropriate department[1] may at their discretion—(*a*) upon payment by an applicant of the prescribed fee, grant to him a licence in the prescribed form authorising him to import and keep, or to keep, musk rats in accordance with the terms of the licence and with the regulations, and from time to time renew any licence so granted; and (*b*) revoke any such licence, if it is shown to their satisfaction that the holder thereof has failed to comply with any term of the licence or with any of the regulations, or has been convicted of an offence under this Act.
[Destructive Imported Animals Act 1932, s 3.]

1. In this Act "the appropriate department" means, as respects England, the Minister, and, as respects Scotland, the Department of Agriculture for Scotland (s 11), but as to ss 3–8, note the Transfer of Functions (Wales) (No 1) Order 1978, SI 1978/272.

8–1069   5. Provisions as to musk rats found at large.   (1) The following provisions of this section shall have effect with respect to musk rats found at large at any time while an order under section 1 of this Act is in force. (2) The occupier[1] of any land who knows that musk rats, not being musk rats kept by him under a licence, are to be found thereon, shall forthwith give notice to the appropriate department. (3) The appropriate department so soon as they become aware that musk rats, not being musk rats kept under a licence, are to be found on any land, may take such steps as they consider necessary for their destruction, and it shall be the duty of the occupier[1] of the land to afford all such facilities as it is in his power to afford to any persons employed by, or on behalf of, that department for that purpose. (5) No action for damages[2] shall lie in respect of the killing or wounding of any musk rat which is found at large.
[Destructive Imported Animals Act 1932, s 5.]

1. In this Act the expression "occupier" means, in the case of and not occupied by any tenant or other person, the owner of the land (s 11).

2. If an order is made under s 10, post, extending the provisions of the Act to other destructive non-indigenous animals, it will not apply to any species which was at the date mentioned in s 10(2) commonly kept in Great Britain in a domesticated state (s 10(2), post).

8–1070   6. Offences and power to seize.   (1) Any person who—(*a*) at a time when the importation of musk rats is prohibited absolutely, imports, or attempts to import, any musk rat into Great Britain, or at a time when such importation is prohibited under a licence, imports, or attempts to import, any musk rat into Great Britain without having in force a licence authorising him to do so; or (*b*) at a time when the keeping of musk rats if prohibited absolutely, keeps any musk rat in Great Britain, or at a time when the keeping of musk rats is prohibited except under a licence, keeps any musk rat in Great Britain without having in force a licence authorising him to do so; or (*c*) being the holder of a licence granted to him under this Act, acts in contravention of or fails to comply with any regulation made

under this Act, or any term of his licence; or (*d*) turns loose any musk rat, or wilfully allows any musk rat to escape; or (*e*) obstructs any officer of, or person authorised by or employed by or on behalf of, the appropriate department in the execution of his duty under this Act; or (*f*) fails to give a notice which he is required by subsection (2) of the last preceding section to give, shall be guilty of an offence under this Act, and shall on summary conviction be liable, in the case of an offence under para (*a*), para (*b*), or para (*d*) of this subsection, to a penalty of **level 2** on the standard scale, or, if the offence was committed in respect of more than four animals, to a penalty of **level 1** on the standard scale in respect of each animal; in the case of an offence under para (*c*), to a penalty of **level 1** on the standard scale, and to a further penalty of £2 for every day on which the offence continues after conviction therefor; in the case of an offence under para (*e*), to a penalty of **level 2** on the standard scale; and in the case of an offence under para (*f*), to a penalty of **level 1** on the standard scale; and the court before which any person is convicted of an offence under para (*a*), para (*b*), or para (*c*) of this subsection may order any musk rats in respect of which the offence was committed to be forfeited and destroyed. (2) Any officer of police and any person duly authorised by the appropriate department may seize any musk rats with respect to which he has reason to believe[1] that an offence under para (*a*) of the last preceding subsection has been committed, and may detain them pending the determination of any proceedings to be instituted under that subsection, or until the appropriate department are satisfied that no such proceedings are likely to be instituted.
[Destructive Imported Animals Act 1932, s 6, as amended by the Criminal Law Act 1977, s 31 and the Criminal Justice Act 1982, s 46.]

---

1. Cf *Trebeck v Croudace* [1918] 1 KB 158, 82 JP 69; *Isaacs v Keech* [1925] 2 KB 354, 89 JP 189; and *Ledwith v Roberts* [1937] 1 KB 232, [1936] 3 All ER 570, 101 JP 23.

8–1071   8. Saving in respect of animals kept for exhibition, etc. (1) A person who desires to keep musk rats for exhibition, or for purposes of scientific research or other exceptional purposes, may apply to the appropriate department, and the department at their discretion may grant to him a special licence (which may be revoked by them at any time) authorising him to import and keep such limited number of musk rats, in such manner and upon such conditions as may be specified in the licence. (2) A special licence may be granted under this section, and shall have effect according to its tenor, notwithstanding that the acts authorised by it are for the time being prohibited by an order made under section 1 of this Act.
[Destructive Imported Animals Act 1932, s 8.]

8–1072   10. Power to extend provisions of Act to other destructive non-indigenous animals. (1) If at any time the Minister[1] and the Secretary of State[1] are satisfied with respect to animals of any non-indigenous mammalian species that by reason of their destructive habits it is desirable to prohibit or control the importation or keeping of them, and to destroy any which may be at large, they may make with respect to animals of that species any such order[2] as they are empowered by subsection (1) of section 1 of this Act to make with respect to musk rats, and thereupon all the provisions of this Act shall apply in relation to animals of that species as they apply in relation to musk rats, subject, however, to the modification that in subsection (1) of section 7[3] of this Act the words "and on the 24th day of June, 1932," shall be omitted, and subject also to such exceptions and modifications, if any, as may be specified in the order: Provided that, notwithstanding anything in subsection (2) of section 1 of this Act, an order made under this section shall be of no effect until a resolution approving it has been passed by each House of Parliament. (2) In this section the expression "non-indigenous mammalian species" means a mammalian species which at the date of the commencement[4] of this Act was not established in a wild state in Great Britain, or had only become so established during the preceding fifty years: Provided that nothing in this section shall apply to any species which was at the said date commonly kept in Great Britain in a domesticated state.
[Destructive Imported Animals Act 1932, s 10.]

---

1. For definitions, see s 1, ante.
2. The following are the subject of Orders under this section: Grey Squirrels (SI 1937/478); Non-Indigenous Rabbits (SI 1954/927); Coypus (SI 1987/2195). See also the Mink Keeping (England) Order 2004, SI 2004/100.
3. This section relates to compensation.
4. 17 March 1932, when the Act was passed.

Protection of Animals Act 1934
(24 & 25 Geo 5 c 21)

8–1080   1. Prohibition of certain contests, performances and exhibitions with animals. (1) No person shall promote, or cause or knowingly permit to take place any public performance[1] which includes any episode consisting or involving—(*a*) throwing or casting, with ropes or other appliances, any unbroken horse[2] or untrained bull[2], or (*b*) wrestling, fighting or struggling with any untrained bull; or (*c*) riding, or attempting to ride, any horse or bull which by the use of any appliance or treatment involving cruelty is, or has been, stimulated with the intention of making it buck during the performance; and no person shall in any public performance take part in any such episode as aforesaid.

(2) For the purposes of proceedings under paragraph (*a*) or paragraph (*b*) of the preceding subsection, if an animal appears or is represented to spectators to be unbroken or untrained, it shall be on the defendant to prove that the animal is in fact broken or trained.

In proceedings under paragraph (*c*) of the subsection in respect of the use of any such appliance or treatment as is therein mentioned upon a horse before or during a performance, it shall be a defence for the defendant to prove that he did not know, and could not reasonably be expected to know that the appliance or treatment was to be or was used.

[Protection of Animals Act 1934, s 1.]

----

1. The expression "public performance" does not include a performance presented to the public by means of the cinematograph (sub-s (3)).
2. The expressions "horse" and "bull" have, respectively, the same meanings as in the Protection of Animals Act 1911 (sub-s (3)). See s 15 thereof, ante.

8–1081   2. Penalties.   If any person contravenes any of the provisions of the foregoing section, he shall be liable upon summary conviction to a fine not exceeding **level 4** on the standard scale, or, alternatively or in addition thereto, to be imprisoned for any term not exceeding **three months**.

[Protection of Animals Act 1934, s 2, as amended by the Criminal Law Act 1977, Sch 6 and the Criminal Justice Act 1982, s 46.]

Docking and Nicking of Horses Act 1949
(12, 13 & 14 Geo 6 c 70)

8–1100   1. Prohibition of docking and nicking except in certain cases.   (1) Save as hereinafter provided, the docking[1] or nicking[2] of horses[3] is prohibited.

(2) The operation of docking or nicking may be performed in any case in which a member of the Royal College of Veterinary Surgeons, after examination of the horse, has certified in writing that the operation is in his opinion necessary for the health of the horse because of disease or injury to the tail.

(3) Any person who performs such an operation as aforesaid in contravention of the provisions of this section or who causes or permits such an operation to be so performed, shall be liable upon summary conviction to a fine not exceeding **level 3** on the standard scale or to imprisonment for a term not exceeding **three months★** or to both such fine and such imprisonment.

[Docking and Nicking of Horses Act 1949, s 1, as amended by the Criminal Law Act 1977, Sch 6 and the Criminal Justice Act 1982, s 46.]

★Words substituted by the Criminal Justice Act 2003, Sch 26, from a date to be appointed.
1. "Docking" means the deliberate removal of any bone or any part of a bone from the tail of a horse, and the expression "docked" shall be construed accordingly (s 3).
2. "Nicking" means the deliberate severing of any tendon or muscle in the tail of a horse, and the expression "nicked" shall be construed accordingly (s 3).
3. "Horse" includes stallion, gelding, colt, mare, filly, pony, mule, and hinny (s 3).

8–1101   2. Restrictions on landing, docked horses.   *This section relates to the landing from a ship or aircraft of a docked horse, and matters incidental thereto.*

Pet Animals Act 1951
(14 & 15 Geo 6 c 35)

8–1120   1. Licensing of pet shops.   (1) No person shall keep a pet shop except under the authority of a licence granted in accordance with the provisions of this Act.

(2) Every local authority may, on application being made to them for that purpose by a person who is not for the time being disqualified[1] from keeping a pet shop, and on payment of such fee as may be determined by the local authority, grant a licence to that person to keep a pet shop at such premises in their area as may be specified in the application and subject to compliance with such conditions as may be specified in the licence.

(3) In determining whether to grant a licence for the keeping of a pet shop by any person at any premises, a local authority shall in particular (but without prejudice to their discretion to withhold a licence on other grounds) have regard to the need for securing—

(*a*) that animals will at all times be kept in accommodation suitable as respects size, temperature, lighting, ventilation and cleanliness;

(*b*) that animals will be adequately supplied with suitable food and drink and (so far as necessary) visited at suitable intervals;

(*c*) that animals, being mammals, will not be sold at too early an age;

(*d*) that all reasonable precautions will be taken to prevent the spread among animals of infectious diseases;

(*e*) that appropriate steps will be taken in case of fire or other emergency;

and shall specify such conditions in the licence, if granted by them, as appear to the local authority necessary or expedient in the particular case for securing all or any of the objects specified in paragraphs (*a*) to (*e*) of this subsection.

(3A) No condition may be specified under subsection (3) of this section in so far as it relates to any matter in relation to which requirements or prohibitions are or could be imposed by or under the Regulatory Reform (Fire Safety) Order 2005.

(4) Any person aggrieved by the refusal of a local authority to grant such a licence, or by any condition subject to which such a licence is proposed to be granted, may appeal[2] to a court of summary jurisdiction having jurisdiction in the place in which the premises are situated; and the court may on such an appeal give such directions with respect to the issue of a licence or, as the case may be, with respect to the conditions subject to which a licence is to be granted as they think proper.

(5) Any such licence shall (according to the applicant's requirements) relate to the year in which it is granted or to the next following year. In the former case, the licence shall come into force at the beginning of the day on which it is granted, and in the latter case it shall come into force at the beginning of the next following year.

(6) Subject to the provisions hereinafter contained with respect to cancellation[3], any such licence shall remain in force until the end of the year to which it relates and shall then expire.

(7) Any person who contravenes the provisions of subsection (1) of this section shall be guilty[4] of an offence; and if any condition subject to which a licence is granted in accordance with the provisions of this Act is contravened or not complied with the person to whom the licence was granted shall be guilty[4] of an offence.

(8) *Application to Scotland.*

[Pet Animals Act 1951, s 1, as amended by the Local Government Act 1974, Sch 8 and SI 2005/1541.]

---

1. Disqualified on conviction for certain offences under s 5, post.

2. For method of appeal, see Magistrates' Courts Rules 1981, r 34, in PART I: MAGISTRATES' COURTS, PROCEDURE, ante.

3. Cancelled on conviction, see s 5, post.

4. For penalty, see s 5(1), post.

8–1121 2. Pets not to be sold in streets, etc.   If any person carries on a business of selling animals as pets in any part of a street or public place, or at a stall or barrow in a market, he shall be guilty[1] of an offence.

[Pet Animals Act 1951, s 2 as amended by the Pet Animals Act 1951 (Amendment) Act 1983, s 1.]

---

1. For penalty, see s 5, post.

8–1122 3. Pets not to be sold to children under twelve years of age.   If any person[1] sells an animal as a pet to a person who he has reasonable cause to believe to be under the age of twelve years, the seller shall be guilty[2] of an offence.

[Pet Animals Act 1951, s 3.]

---

1. Note that this section is wide enough to cover a single transaction: the defendant need not be "carrying on a business of selling animals as pets" as the preceding section requires.

2. For penalty, see s 5, post.

8–1123 4. Inspection of pet shops.   (1) A local authority may authorise in writing any of its officers or any veterinary surgeon or veterinary practitioner to inspect (subject to compliance with such precautions as the authority may specify to prevent the spread among animals of infectious diseases) any premises in their area as respects which a licence granted in accordance with the provisions of this Act is for the time being in force, and any person authorised under this section may, on producing his authority if so required, enter any such premises at all reasonable times and inspect them and any animals found thereon or any thing therein, for the purpose of ascertaining whether an offence has been committed against this Act.

(2) Any person who wilfully obstructs or delays any person in the exercise of his powers of entry or inspection under this section shall be guilty[1] of an offence.

[Pet Animals Act 1951, s 4.]

---

1. For penalty, see s 5(2), post.

8–1124 5. Offences and disqualifications.   (1) Any person guilty of an offence under any provision of this Act other than the last foregoing section shall be liable on summary conviction to a fine not exceeding **level 2** on the standard scale or to imprisonment for a term not exceeding **three months** or to both such fine and such imprisonment.

(2) Any person guilty of an offence under the last foregoing section shall be liable on summary conviction to a fine not exceeding **level 2** on the standard scale.

(3) Where a person is convicted of any offence under this Act or of any offence under the Protection of Animals Act 1911[1], or the Protection of Animals (Scotland) Act 1912, the court by which he is convicted may cancel any licence held by him under this Act, and may, whether or not he is a holder of such a licence, disqualify him from keeping a pet shop for such a period as the court thinks fit[2].

(4) A court which has ordered the cancellation of a person's licence, or his disqualification, in pursuance of the last foregoing section may, if it thinks fit, suspend the operation of the order pending an appeal.

[Pet Animals Act 1951, s 5 as amended by the Criminal Justice Act 1982, ss 38 and 46.]

---

1. Ante.

2. He may also be disqualified from keeping a boarding establishment for animals (Animal Boarding Establishments Act 1963, s 3(3), this title, post), a riding establishment (Riding Establishments Act 1964, s 4(3), post), or any dangerous wild animal (Dangerous Wild Animals Act 1976, s 6(2), post). A magistrates' court may not in a person's absence impose any disqualification on him, except after an adjournment after convicting and before sentencing him; see Magistrates' Courts Act 1980, s 11(4), in PART I: MAGISTRATES' COURTS, PROCEDURE, ante.

8–1125   6. Power of local authority to prosecute.   A local authority in England or Wales may[1] prosecute proceedings for any offence under this Act committed in the area of the authority.
[Pet Animals Act 1951, s 6.]

---

1. This section does not give a local authority an exclusive power to prosecute. For appearance of local authority in legal proceedings, see Local Government Act 1972, s 223, in title LOCAL GOVERNMENT, post.

8–1126   7. Interpretation.   (1) References in this Act to the keeping of a pet shop shall, subject to the following provisions of this section, be construed as references to the carrying on at premises of any nature (including a private dwelling) of a business of selling animals as pets, and as including references to the keeping of animals in any such premises as aforesaid with a view to their being sold in the course of such a business, whether by the keeper thereof or by any other person:

Provided that—

(a) a person shall not be deemed to keep a pet shop by reason only of his keeping or selling pedigree animals bred by him, or the offspring of an animal kept by him as a pet;

(b) where a person carries on a business of selling animals as pets in conjunction with a business of breeding pedigree animals, and the local authority are satisfied that the animals so sold by him (in so far as they are not pedigree animals bred by him) are animals which were acquired by him with a view to being used, if suitable, for breeding or show purposes but have subsequently been found by him not to be suitable or required for such use, the local authority may if they think fit direct that the said person shall not be deemed to keep a pet shop by reason only of his carrying on the first-mentioned business.

(2) References in this Act to the selling or keeping of animals as pets shall be construed in accordance with the following provisions, that is to say—

(a) as respects cats and dogs, such references shall be construed as including references to selling or keeping, as the case may be, wholly or mainly for domestic purposes; and

(b) as respects any animal, such references shall be construed as including references to selling or keeping, as the case may be, for ornamental purposes.

(3) In this Act, unless the context otherwise requires, the following expressions have the meanings hereby respectively assigned to them, that is to say—

"animal" includes any description of vertebrate;

"local authority" means the council of any county district, the council of a borough or the Common Council of the City of London and in Scotland means the council of any county or burgh;

"pedigree animal" means an animal of any description which is by its breeding eligible for registration with a recognised club or society keeping a register of animals of that description;

"veterinary surgeon" means a person who is for the time being registered in the Register of Veterinary Surgeons;

"veterinary practitioner" means a person who is for the time being registered in the Supplementary Veterinary Register.

[Pet Animals Act 1951, s 7 amended by the Local Government Act 1972, Sch 30 and the Pet Animals Act 1951 (Amendment) Act 1983, s 1.]

Cockfighting Act 1952

(15 & 16 Geo 6 & 1 Eliz 2 c 59)

8–1140   1. Possession of appliances for use in fighting of domestic fowl rendered unlawful.
(1) If any person has in his possession any instrument or appliance designed or adapted for use in

connection with the fighting of any domestic fowl, he shall, if the court is satisfied that he had it in his possession for the purposes of using it or permitting it to be used as aforesaid, be guilty of an offence under this section and shall be liable, on summary conviction, to imprisonment for a term not exceeding **three months**, or to a fine not exceeding **level 3** on the standard scale, or to both such imprisonment and such fine.

(2) Where any person is convicted of an offence under this section, the court may order any instrument or appliance in respect of which the offence was committed to be destroyed or dealt with in such manner as may be specified in the order: Provided that such an order shall not take effect until the expiration of the period of 21 days within which notice of appeal may be given by virtue of [the Crown Court Rules 1971] and if notice of appeal is given within that period, the order shall not take effect unless and until the appeal is dismissed or withdrawn.

[Cockfighting Act 1952, s 1, as amended by the Criminal Law Act 1977, Sch 6 and the Criminal Justice Act 1982, s 46.]

Protection of Animals (Amendment) Act 1954
(2 & 3 Eliz 2 c 40)

8–1150　1. Power to disqualify persons convicted of cruelty to animals.　(1) Where a person has been convicted under the Protection of Animals Act 1911 or the Protection of Animals (Scotland) Act 1912 of an offence of cruelty to any animal the court by which he is convicted may, if it thinks fit, in addition to or in substitution for any other punishment, order him to be disqualified[1], for such period as it thinks fit, for having custody of any animal or any animal of a kind specified[2] in the order.

(2) A court which has ordered the disqualification of a person in pursuance of this section may, if it thinks fit, suspend the operation of the order—

(*a*)　for such period as the court thinks necessary for enabling arrangements to be made for the custody of any animal or animals to which the disqualification relates; or

(*b*)　pending an appeal.

(3) A person who is disqualified by virtue of an order under this section may, at any time after the expiration of twelve months from the date of the order, and from time to time apply[3] to the court by which the order was made to remove the disqualification, and on any such application the court may, as it thinks proper, having regard to the character of the applicant and his conduct subsequent to the order, the nature of the offence of which he was convicted, and any other circumstances of the case, either—

(*a*)　direct that, as from such date as may be specified in the direction, the disqualification be removed or the order be so varied as to apply only to animals of a kind specified in the direction; or

(*b*)　refuse the application:

Provided that where on an application under this section the court directs the variation of the order or refuses the application, a further application thereunder shall not be entertained if made within twelve months after the date of the direction or, as the case may be, the refusal.

[Protection of Animals (Amendment) Act 1954, s 1, as amended by the Protection of Animals (Amendment) Act 1988, s 1.]

1.　A magistrates' court shall not in a person's absence impose any disqualification on him, except after an adjournment after convicting and before sentencing him; see Magistrates' Courts Act 1980, s 11(4), in PART I: MAGISTRATES' COURTS, PROCEDURE, ante.

2.　An order disqualifying a person from keeping cattle will disqualify him from keeping "cattle" as defined in the Protection of Animals Act 1911, s 15(*e*) (*Wastie v Phillips* [1972] 3 All ER 302, 136 JP 780).

3.　No procedure is laid down for the making of such an application to a magistrates' court, and therefore, it seems, the court may regulate its own procedure; we suggest a procedure corresponding *mutatis mutandis*, with that of the Criminal Procedure Rules 2005, r 55.2 in PART I: MAGISTRATES' COURTS, PROCEDURE, ante.

8–1151　2. Breach of disqualification order[1].　If a person has custody[2] of any animal in contravention of an order made under this Act, he shall be liable on summary conviction to a fine not exceeding **level 3** on the standard scale or to imprisonment for a term not exceeding **three months★** or to both such fine and imprisonment.

[Protection of Animals (Amendment) Act 1954, s 2, as amended by the Criminal Justice Act 1982, ss 38 and 46.]

★"51 weeks" substituted by the Criminal Justice Act 2003, Sch 26, from a date to be appointed.

1.　A civil court does not have the power to grant a local authority an injunction to enter land and remove animals kept there in breach of a disqualification in circumstances where there is a lacuna in the criminal law (*Worcestershire County Council v Tongue* [2004] EWCA Civ 140, [2004] 2 WLR 140, 168 JP 548). Although, in relation to animals, there is no such obvious distinction between the words "keeping" and "having custody of" so as to invalidate an order drafted in terms to prohibit "keeping" an animal, steps should be taken to ensure that the court order uses the statutory form of words: *R (Arthur) v RSPCA* [2005] EWHC 2616 (Admin), 169 JP 676.

2.　Whether a defendant has custody in any particular case will be a finding of fact dependent upon the circumstances, on which the tribunal of fact will make its own decision. The essence of custody is control or the power to control. A person with sole physical control even for a short time has custody, but where physical control is shared and the person with actual physical control is subject to the direction, supervision or control of another, eg the owner, the one with actual physical control may or may not have custody depending on the degree of direction, supervision or control exercised by the other person (*RSPCA v Miller* [1994] Crim LR 516 cited in *Taylor and Taylor v RSPCA* [2001] EWHC Admin 103, [2001] 2 Cr App Rep 24, 165 JP 567).

Protection of Animals (Anaesthetics) Act 1954

(2 & 3 Eliz 2 c 46)

8–1170   1. Use of anaesthetic in operations on animals.   (1) If any operation to which this section applies is performed on any animal without the use of an anaesthetic so administered as to prevent any pain during the operation, that operation shall be deemed for the purposes[1] of the Protection of Animals Act 1911, as amended by or under any other enactment, to be an operation which is performed without due care and humanity.

(2) This section applies to any operation with or without the use of instruments which involves interference with the sensitive tissues or the bone structure of an animal, other than (*a*) the making of injections or extractions by means of a hollow needle; or (*b*) an operation included in the First Schedule to this Act.

(3) Empowers the Minister of Agriculture and Fisheries to make orders (*summarised*).

(4) this Act shall be construed[2] as one with the Protection of Animals Act 1911, as amended by or under any other enactment, so, however, that in this Act the expression "animal" shall not include a fowl or other bird, fish or reptile.

[Protection of Animals (Anaesthetics) Act 1954, s 1, as amended by SI 1978/272.]

1. See, in particular, the Protection of Animals Act 1911, s 1(1)(*e*), ante.
2. Where two or more acts are to be construed as one, every part of each of them must be construed as if it had been contained on one Act, unless there is some manifest discrepancy (*Hart v Hudson Bros Ltd* [1928] 2 KB 629, 92 JP 170).

8–1171   FIRST SCHEDULE

(As amended by the Protection of Animals (Anaesthetics) Act 1964, s 1, the Protection of Animals (Anaesthetics) Act 1954 (Amendment) Order 1982, SI 1982/1626, the Animals (Scientific Procedures) Act 1986, Sch 3, the Welfare of Livestock Regulations 1994, SI 1994/2126 and SI 2003/1328 (E) and 1844 (W).)

Excepted Operations

1. Any procedure duly authorised under the Animals (Scientific Procedures) Act 1986[1].
2. The rendering in emergency of first aid for the purpose of saving life or relieving pain.
3. The docking of the tail of a dog before its eyes are open.
4. The amputation of the dew claws of a dog before its eyes are open.
5. *Repealed.*
6. The castration of a male animal specified in the following table before it has reached the age so specified[2], that is to say—bull 2 months; sheep 3 months; goat 2 months; pig, in Wales, 8 days; and in England, 8 days.

6A. The foregoing paragraph shall not apply to the castration of an animal by using a rubber ring or other device to constrict the flow of blood to the scrotum unless the device is applied within the first week of life.

7. Any minor operation performed by a veterinary surgeon or veterinary practitioner, being an operation which, by reason of its quickness or painlessness, is customarily so performed without the use of an anæsthetic[3].

8. Any minor operation, whether performed by a veterinary surgeon or veterinary practitioner or by some other person, being an operation which is not customarily performed only by such a surgeon or practitioner[3].

1. See this title, post.
2. Any of the specified ages may be varied by order under s 1(3), ante.
3. Paragraphs 7 and 8 shall not in any circumstances permit—(*a*) the castration of a male animal (but without prejudice to the circumstances in which castration is permitted by para 6); (*b*) the de-horning of cattle; (*c*) the dis-budding of calves, except by means of chemical cauterisation applied within the first week of life; or (*d*) the docking of lambs' tails by using a rubber ring or other device to constrict the flow of blood to the tail, unless the device is applied within the first week of life. "Cattle" means bulls, cows, bullocks, heifers, calves, steers or oxen (Protection of Animals (Anaesthetics) Act 1964, s 1(4) (5)). The appropriate Ministers may further remove from the exemptions in paras 7 and 8 such operations as may be specified (Agriculture (Miscellaneous Provisions) Act 1968, s 5).

Abandonment of Animals Act 1960

(8 & 9 Eliz 2 c 43)

8–1190   1. Penalties for abandonment of animals.   If any person being the owner or having charge or control of any animal[1] shall without reasonable cause or excuse abandon[2] it, whether permanently or not, in circumstances likely to cause the animal any unnecessary suffering, or cause or procure or, being the owner, permit it to be so abandoned, he shall be guilty of an offence of cruelty within the meaning of the principal Act[3] and liable to the penalties prescribed by s 1(1) of that Act, and the provisions of the Protection of Animals Acts[3] shall apply to an offence under this section as they apply to an offence under the said subsection (1).

[Abandonment of Animals Act 1960, s 1.]

1. "Animal" has the same meaning as in the Protection of Animals Act 1911, see s 15 thereof, ante (Abandonment of Animals Act 1960, s 2).

2. "Abandon" implies something more than merely "left or leaving unattended". There must be a physical leaving unattended of the animal in circumstances where suffering was likely and where there was sufficient evidence to prove that the defendant had relinquished, wholly disregarded or given up his duty to care for the animal (*Hunt v Duckering* [1993] Crim LR 678).

3. This means, in relation to England and Wales, the Protection of Animals Act 1911, as amended by or under any other enactment, and the Protection of Animals Act 1911 to 1954, ante (Abandonment of Animals Act 1960, s 2).

Animal Boarding Establishments Act 1963
(1963 c 43)

8–1200   1. Licensing of boarding establishments for animals.   (1) No person shall keep a boarding establishment for animals[1] except under the authority of a licence granted in accordance with the provisions of this Act.

(2) Every local authority[2] may, on application being made to them for that purpose by a person who is not for the time being disqualified—

(a)   under this Act[3], from keeping a boarding establishment for animals; or
(b)   under the Pet Animals Act 1951[4], from keeping a pet shop; or
(c), (d) *repealed*;
(d)   under the Protection of Animals (Cruelty to Dogs) (Scotland) Act 1934, from keeping a dog; or
(e)   under the Protection of Animals (Amendment) Act 1954[6], from having the custody of animals,

and on payment of such fee as may be determined by the local authority, grant a licence to that person to keep a boarding establishment for animals at such premises in their area as may be specified in the application and subject to compliance with such conditions as may be specified in the licence.

(3) In determining whether to grant a licence for the keeping of a boarding establishment for animals by any person at any premises, a local authority shall in particular (but without prejudice to their discretion to withhold a licence on other grounds) have regard to the need for securing—

(a)   that animals will at all times be kept in accommodation suitable as respects construction, size of quarters, number of occupants, exercising facilities, temperature, lighting, ventilation and cleanliness;
(b)   that animals will be adequately supplied with suitable food, drink and bedding material, adequately exercised, and (so far as necessary) visited at suitable intervals;
(c)   that all reasonable precautions will be taken to prevent and control the spread among animals of infectious or contagious diseases, including the provision of adequate isolation facilities;
(d)   that appropriate steps will be taken for the protection of the animals in case of fire or other emergency;
(e)   that a register be kept containing a description of any animals received into the establishment, date of arrival and departure, and the name and address of the owner, such register to be available for inspection at all times by an officer of the local authority[2], veterinary surgeon[2] or veterinary practitioner[2] authorised under section 2(1) of this Act;

and shall specify such conditions in the licence, if granted by them, as appear to the local authority necessary or expedient in the particular case for securing all the objects specified in paragraphs (a) to (e) of this subsection.

(4) Any person aggrieved by the refusal of a local authority to grant such a licence, or by any condition subject to which such a licence is proposed to be granted, may appeal[7] to a magistrates' court; and the court may on such an appeal give such directions with respect to the issue of a licence or, as the case may be, with respect to the conditions subject to which a licence is to be granted as it thinks proper.

(5) Any such licence shall (according to the applicant's requirements) relate to the year in which it is granted or to the next following year. In the former case, the licence shall come into force at the beginning of the day on which it is granted, and in the latter case it shall come into force at the beginning of the next following year.

(6) Subject to the provisions[8] hereinafter contained with respect to cancellation, any such licence shall remain in force until the end of the year to which it relates and shall then expire.

(7) In the event of the death of a person who is keeping a boarding establishment for animals at any premises under the authority of a licence granted under this Act, that licence shall be deemed to have been granted to his personal representatives in respect of those premises and shall, notwithstanding subsection (6) of this section (but subject to the provisions hereinafter contained with respect to cancellation), remain in force until the end of the period of three months beginning with the death and shall then expire:

Provided that the local authority by whom the licence was granted may from time to time, on the application of those representatives extend or further extend the said period of three months if the authority are satisfied that the extension is necessary for the purpose of winding up the deceased's estate and that no other circumstances make it undesirable.

(8) Any person who contravenes the provisions of subsection (1) of this section shall be guilty of an offence[9]; and if any condition subject to which a licence is granted in accordance with the provisions of this Act is contravened or not complied with, the person to whom the licence was granted shall be guilty of an offence[9].

(9) *Application to Scotland.*

[Animal Boarding Establishments Act 1963, s 1, amended by the Local Government Act 1974, Sch 8 and the Protection of Animals (Amendment) Act 1988, Sch.]

1. "Animal" means any dog or cat (s 5(2), post).
2. For meaning of "local authority", "veterinary practitioner", "veterinary Surgeon", see s 5(2), post.
3. See s 3(3), post.
4. See Pet Animals Act 1951, s 5(3), ante.
6. See Protection of Animals (Amendment) Act 1954, s 1, ante.
7. Appeal will be by way of complaint for an order: see Magistrates' Courts Rules 1981, r 34, in PART I: MAGISTRATES' COURTS, PROCEDURE, ante.
8. See s 3(3), post.
9. For penalty, power to cancel licence, and to disqualify person convicted, see s 3(1), (3), post.

8–1201   2. Inspection of boarding establishments for animals.   (1) A local authority[1] may authorise in writing any of its officers or any veterinary Surgeon[1] or veterinary Practitioner[1] to inspect (subject to compliance with such precautions as the authority may specify to prevent the spread among animals[1] of infectious or contagious diseases) any premises in their area as respects which a licence granted in accordance with the provisions of this Act is for the time being in force, and any person authorised under this section may, on producing his authority if so required, enter any such premises at all reasonable times and inspect them and any animals found thereon or any thing therein, for the purpose of ascertaining whether an offence has been or is being committed against this Act.

(2) Any person who wilfully obstructs or delays any person in the exercise of his powers of entry or inspection under this section shall be guilty of an offence[2].

[Animal Boarding Establishments Act 1963, s 2.]

1. For meaning of "animal", "local authority", "veterinary practitioner", "veterinary surgeon", see s 5(2), post.
2. For penalty, power to cancel licence, and to disqualify person convicted, see s 3(1), (3), post.

8–1202   3. Offences and disqualifications.   (1) Any person guilty of an offence under any provision of this Act other than the last foregoing section shall be liable on summary conviction to a fine not exceeding **level 2** on the standard scale or to imprisonment for a term not exceeding **three months** or to both such fine and such imprisonment.

(2) Any person guilty of an offence under the last foregoing section shall be liable on summary conviction to a fine not exceeding **level 2** on the standard scale.

(3) Where a person is convicted of any offence under this Act or of any offence under the Protection of Animals Act 1911 of the Protection of Animals (Scotland) Act 1912 or the Pet Animals Act 1951, the court by which he is convicted may cancel any licence held by him under this Act, and may, whether or not he is the holder of such a licence, disqualify[1] him from keeping a boarding establishment for animals for such period as the court thinks fit.

(4) A court which has ordered the cancellation of a person's licence, or his disqualification, in pursuance of the last foregoing subsection may, if it thinks fit, suspend the operation of the order pending an appeal.

[Animal Boarding Establishments Act 1963, s 3 as amended by the Criminal Justice Act 1982, ss 38 and 46.]

1. Similarly he may be disqualified from keeping a riding establishment (Riding Establishments Act 1964, s 4(3), post), or any dangerous wild animal (Dangerous Wild Animals Act 1976, s 6(2), post). A magistrates' court shall not in a person's absence impose any disqualification on him, except after an adjournment after convicting and before sentencing him; see Magistrates' Courts Act 1980, s 11(4), in PART I: MAGISTRATES' COURTS, PROCEDURE, ante.

8–1203   4. Power of local authorities to prosecute.   A local authority in England or Wales may[1] prosecute proceedings for any offence under this Act committed in the area of the authority.

[Animal Boarding Establishments Act 1963, s 4.]

1. This section does not give a local authority an exclusive power to prosecute. For appearance of local authority in legal proceedings, see Local Government Act 1972, s 223, title LOCAL GOVERNMENT, post.

8–1204   5. Interpretation.   (1) References in this Act to the keeping by any person of a boarding establishment for animals shall, subject to the following provisions of this section, be construed as references to the carrying on by him at premises of any nature (including a private dwelling) of a business of providing accommodation for other people's animals:

Provided that—

(a) a person shall not be deemed to keep a boarding establishment for animals by reason only of his providing accommodation for other people's animals in connection with a business of which the provision of such accommodation is not the main activity; and

(b) nothing in this Act shall apply to the keeping of an animal at any premises in pursuance of a requirement imposed under, or having effect by virtue of, the Animal Health Act 1981.

(2) In this Act, unless the context otherwise requires, the following expressions have the meanings hereby respectively assigned to them, that is to say—

"animal" means any dog or cat;

"local authority" means the council of any county district, the council of a borough or the Common Council of the City of London . . .;

"veterinary practitioner" means a person who is for the time being registered in the Supplementary Veterinary Register;

"veterinary surgeon" means a person who is for the time being registered in the Register of Veterinary Surgeons.

[Animal Boarding Establishments Act 1963, s 5, as amended by the Local Government Act 1972, Sch 30 and the Animal Health Act 1981, Sch 5.]

Riding Establishments Act 1964[1]
(1964 c 70)

8–1205 1. Licensing of riding establishments. (1) No person shall keep a riding establishment[1] except under the authority of a licence granted in accordance with the provisions of this Act.

(2) Every local authority[2] may, on application being made to them for that purpose by a person who is an individual over the age of eighteen years or a body corporate, being a person who is not for the time being disqualified—

(a) under this Act from keeping a riding establishment; or

(b), (c) *repealed*;

(d) under the Pet Animals Act 1951[3]; from keeping a pet shop; or

(e) under the Protection of Animals (Amendment) Act 1954[3], from having the custody of animals; or

(f) under the Animal Boarding Establishments Act 1963[3], from keeping a boarding establishment for animals;

grant, on payment of such fee as may be determined by the local authority, a licence to that person to keep a riding establishment at such premises[4] in their area as may be specified in the application and subject to compliance with such conditions as may be specified in the licence.

(3) Where an application for the grant of a licence for the keeping of a riding establishment at any premises is made to a local authority, they shall not proceed to a decision in the matter unless they have received and considered a report by a veterinary surgeon or veterinary practitioner[5] authorised by them to carry out inspections under the next following section of an inspection of the premises carried out by him within the period of twelve months immediately preceding the date on which the application is received by the local authority or on or after that date on which the application is received by the local authority or on or after that date, being a report containing such particulars as in their view enable them to determine whether the premises are suitable for the keeping thereat of a riding establishment, and describing the condition of the premises and of any horses found thereon or anything thereat.

(4) In determining whether to grant a licence for the keeping of a riding establishment by any person at any premises a local authority shall in particular (but without prejudice to their discretion to withhold a licence on any grounds) have regard to—

(a) whether that person appears to them to be suitable and qualified either by experience in the management of horses or by being the holder of an approved certificate or by employing in the management of the riding establishment a person so qualified, to be the holder of such a licence; and

(b) the need for securing—

(i) that paramount consideration will be given to the condition of horses and that they will be maintained in good health, and in all respects physically fit and that, in the case of a horse kept for the purpose of its being let out on hire for riding or a horse kept for the purposes of its being used in providing instruction in riding, the horse will be suitable for the purpose for which it is kept;

(ii) that the feet of all animals are properly trimmed and that, if shod, their shoes are properly fitted and in good condition;

(iii) that there will be available at all times, accommodation for horses suitable as respects construction, size, number of occupants, lighting, ventilation, drainage and cleanliness and that these requirements be complied with not only in the case of new buildings but also in the case of buildings converted for use as stabling;

(iv) that in the case of horses maintained at grass there will be available for them at all times during which they are so maintained adequate pasture and shelter and water and that supplementary feeds will be provided as and when required;

(v) that horses will be adequately supplied with suitable food, drink and (except in the case of horses maintained at grass, so long as they are so maintained) bedding material, and will be adequately exercised, groomed and rested and visited at suitable intervals;

(vi) that all reasonable precautions will be taken to prevent and control the spread among horses of infectious or contagious diseases and that veterinary first aid equipment and medicines shall be provided and maintained in the premises;

(vii) that appropriate steps will be taken for the protection and extrication of horses in case of fire and, in particular, that the name, address and telephone number of the licence holder or some other responsible person will be kept displayed in a prominent position on the outside of the premises and that instructions as to action to be taken in the event of fire, with particular regard to the extrication of horses, will be kept displayed in a prominent position on the outside of the premises;

(viii) that adequate accommodation will be provided for forage, bedding, stable equipment and saddlery;

and shall specify such conditions in the licence, if granted by them, as appear to the local authority necessary or expedient in the particular case for securing all the objects specified in sub-paragraphs (i) to (viii) of paragraph (*b*) of this subsection.

(4A) Without prejudice to the provisions of subsection (2) or (4) of this section, every licence granted under this Act after 31st December, 1970 shall be subject to the following conditions (whether they are specified in the licence or not), namely—

(*a*) a horse found on inspection of the premises by an authorised officer to be in need of veterinary attention shall not be returned to work until the holder of the licence has obtained at his own expense and has lodged with the local authority a veterinary certificate that the horse is fit for work;

(*b*) no horse will be let out on hire for riding or used for providing instruction in riding without supervision by a responsible person of the age of 16 years or over unless (in the case of a horse let out for hire for riding) the holder of the licence is satisfied that the hirer of the horse is competent to ride without supervision;

(*c*) the carrying on of the business of a riding establishment shall at no time be left in the charge of any person under 16 years of age;

(*d*) the licence holder shall hold a current insurance policy which insures him against liability for any injury sustained by those who hire a horse from him for riding and those who use a horse in the course of receiving from him, in return for payment, instruction in riding and arising out of the hire or use of a horse as aforesaid and which also insures such persons in respect of any liability which may be incurred by them in respect of injury to any person caused by, or arising out of, the hire or use of a horse as aforesaid;

(*e*) a register shall be kept by the licence holder of all horses in his possession aged three years and under and usually kept on the premises which shall be available for inspection by an authorised officer at all reasonable times.

(5) Any person aggrieved by the refusal of a local authority to grant such a licence, or by any condition subject to which such a licence is proposed to be granted (not being one of the conditions set out in subsection (4A) of this section), may appeal to a magistrates' court[6]; and the court may on such an appeal give such directions with respect to the issue of a licence or, as the case may be, to the conditions subject to which a licence is to be granted as it thinks proper.

(6) Any such licence shall (according to the applicant's requirements) relate to the year in which it is granted or to the next following year. In the former case, the licence shall come into force at the beginning of the day on which it is granted, and in the latter case it shall come into force at the beginning of the next following year.

(7) Subject to the provisions hereinafter contained with respect to cancellation, any such licence shall remain in force for one year beginning with the day on which it comes into force and shall then expire.

(8) (*Provision for continuance on death of licence holder.*)

(9) Any person who contravenes the provisions of subsection (1) of this section shall be guilty of an offence[7]; and if any condition to which a licence under this Act is subject (whether by virtue of subsection (4A) of this subsection or otherwise) is contravened or not complied with, the person to whom the licence was granted shall be guilty of an offence[8].

(10) (*Application to Scotland.*)

[Riding Establishments Act 1964, s 1, amended by the Riding Establishments Act 1970, s 2, the Local Government Act 1974, Sch 6 and the Protection of Animals (Amendment) Act 1988, Sch.]

---

1. A "riding establishment" to which the Act applies is defined in s 6 (1)–(3), *post*.

2. "Local authority" means the council of a district, the council of a London borough or the Common Council of the City of London (s 6(4)).

3. See *ante*.

4. "Premises" includes land (s 6(4)).

5. "Veterinary surgeon" means a person who is for the time being registered in the Register of Veterinary Surgeons in pursuance of the Veterinary Surgeons Act 1966. "Veterinary practitioner" means a person who is for the time being registered in the Supplementary Veterinary Register in pursuance of the Veterinary Surgeons Act 1966 (s 6(4)).

6. Appeal will be by way of complaint. See Magistrates' Courts Rules 1981, r 34, in PART I: MAGISTRATES' COURTS, PROCEDURE, ante.

7. For penalty, see s 4(1), post. Proceedings for an offence under s 1(9) may be taken only by the local authority (see note 2 ante) (s 5(2), post).

8. See note 7, supra. The local authority shall receive and consider a report from a veterinary surgeon or veterinary practitioner before instituting proceedings for contravention of or failure to comply with a condition subject to which a licence was granted (s 5(2), post).

8–1206 2. Inspection of riding establishments. (1) A local authority may, subject to the provisions of this section, authorise in writing any such person as the following, namely, an officer of theirs, an officer of any other local authority, a veterinary surgeon and a veterinary practitioner[1] to inspect any such premises[2] in their area as the following, that is to say—

(a) any premises where they have reason to believe a person is keeping a riding establishment;

(b) any premises as respects which a licence granted in accordance with the provisions of this Act is for the time being in force; and

(c) any premises as respects which a licence has been applied for under this Act.

(2) Any person authorised under this section may, on producing his authority if so required, enter at all reasonable times any premises which he is authorised under this section to enter and inspect them and any horses[3] found thereon or any thing therein for the purpose (except in the case of any such premises as are mentioned in paragraph (a) of the foregoing subsection) of making a report to the local authority for the purposes of s 1(3) of this Act or for the purpose of ascertaining whether an offence has been or is being committed against this Act.

(3) A local authority shall not authorise a veterinary surgeon or veterinary practitioner to inspect any premises under this section except one chosen by them from a list of such persons drawn up jointly by the Royal College of Veterinary Surgeons and the British Veterinary Association.

(4) Any person who wilfully obstructs or delays any person in the exercise of his powers of entry or inspection conferred by subsection (2) above shall be guilty of an offence[4].
[Riding Establishments Act 1964, s 2.]

1. See note 5 to s 1, ante.
2. "Premises" includes land (s 6(4)).
3. "Horse" includes any mare, gelding, pony, foal, colt, filly or stallion and also any ass, mule or jennet (s 6(4)).
4. For penalty see s 4(2), post.

8–1207 3. Offences. (1) If any person—

(a) at a time when a horse[1] is in such a condition, that its riding would be likely to cause suffering to the horse, lets out the horse on hire or uses it for the purpose of providing, in return for payment, instruction in riding or for the purpose of demonstrating riding;

(aa) lets out on hire for riding or uses for the purpose of providing, in return for payment, instruction in riding or for the purpose of demonstrating riding any horse aged three years or under or any mare heavy with foal or any mare within three months after foaling;

(b) supplies for a horse[1] which is let out on hire by him for riding equipment which is used in the course of the hiring and suffers, at the time when it is supplied, from a defect of such a nature as to be apparent on inspection and as to be likely to cause suffering to the horse or an accident to the rider;

(c) fails to provide such curative care as may be suitable, if any, for a sick or injured horse[1] which is kept by him with a view to its being let out on hire or used for a purpose mentioned in paragraph (a) of this subsection;

(d) in keeping a riding establishment knowingly permits any person, who is for the time being disqualified under this Act from keeping a riding establishment, to have control or management of the keeping of the establishment; or

(e) with intent to avoid inspection under s 2 of this Act, conceals, or causes to be concealed, any horse[1] maintained by the riding establishment;

he shall be guilty of an offence under this Act[2].

(2) A person who for the purpose of obtaining the grant of a licence under this Act gives any information which he knows to be false in a material particular or makes a statement which he knows to be so false or recklessly gives any information which is so false or recklessly makes any statement which is so false shall be guilty of an offence under this Act[2].
[Riding Establishments Act 1964, s 3 and the Riding Establishments Act 1970, s 2.]

1. "Horse" includes any mare, gelding, pony, foal, colt, filly or stallion and also any ass, mule or jennet (s 6(4)).
2. For penalty, see s 4(1), post.

8–1208 4. Penalties and disqualifications. (1) Any person guilty of an offence under any provision of this Act other than s 2(4) thereof shall be liable on summary conviction to a fine not exceeding **level 3** on the standard scale or to imprisonment for a term not exceeding **three months** or to both such fine and such imprisonment.

(2) Any person guilty of an offence under s 2(4) of this Act shall be liable on summary conviction to a fine not exceeding **level 2** on the standard scale.

(3) Where a person is convicted of any offence under this Act or of any offence under the Protection of Animals Act 1911[1], or the Protection of Animals (Scotland) Act 1912, or the Pet Animals Act 1951[1], or the Animal Boarding Establishments Act 1963[1] the court by which he is convicted may cancel any licence held by him under this Act and may, whether or not he is the holder of such a licence, disqualify[2] him from keeping a riding establishment for such period as the court thinks fit.

(4) A court which has ordered the cancellation of a person's licence, or his disqualification in pursuance of the last foregoing subsection may, if it thinks fit, suspend the operation of the order pending an appeal.

[Riding Establishments Act 1964, s 4 as amended by the Criminal Justice Act 1982, ss 38 and 46.]

1. See ante.
2. He may also be disqualified from keeping any dangerous wild animal (Dangerous Wild Animals Act 1976, s 6(2), post). A magistrates' court shall not in a person's absence impose any disqualification on him, except after an adjournment after convicting and before sentencing him, see the Magistrates' Courts Act 1980, s 11(4), in PART I: MAGISTRATES' COURTS, PROCEDURE, ante.

8–1209 5. Power of local authorities to prosecute. (1) A local authority[1] in England or Wales may subject to the provisions of this section prosecute proceedings for any offence under this Act committed in the area of the authority.

(2) In England and Wales no proceedings for an offence under section 1(9) of this Act in respect of a contravention of or failure to comply with a condition subject to which a licence is granted in accordance with the provisions of this Act shall be instituted except by a local authority, and a local authority shall not institute any such proceedings except after receiving and considering a report by a veterinary surgeon or veterinary practitioner authorised by them to carry out inspections under section 2 of this Act being a report which in their opinion indicates that such an offence has been committed.

[Riding Establishments Act 1964, s 5.]

1. See note 2 to s 1, ante.

8–1210 6. Interpretation. (1) References in this Act to the keeping of a riding establishment shall, subject to the provisions of this section be construed as references to the carrying on of a business of keeping horses[1] for either or both of the following purposes, that is to say, the purpose of their being let out on hire for riding or the purpose of their being used in providing, in return for payment, instruction in riding, but as not including a reference to the carrying on of such a business—

(a) in a case where the premises where the horses employed for the purposes of the business are kept are occupied by or under the management of the Secretary of State for Defence; or
(b) solely for police purposes; or
(c) by the Zoological Society of London; or
(d) by the Royal Zoological Society of Scotland.

(2) Where a university provides courses of study and examinations leading to a veterinary degree to which relates an order made under section [3 of the Veterinary Surgeons Act 1966] (which section enables the Privy Council, where a university provides such courses and it appears to the Privy Council that the courses are of the standard therein mentioned, to direct that a holder of the degree to which the courses lead shall be qualified to be a member of the Royal College of Veterinary Surgeons), horses kept by the university for use in the instruction of students undergoing such courses shall, during the continuance in force of the order, be deemed for the purposes of the foregoing subsection not to be kept as mentioned in that subsection.

(3) For the purposes of this Act a person keeping a riding establishment shall be taken to keep it at the premises where the horses[1] employed for the purposes of the business concerned are kept.

[Riding Establishments Act 1964, s 6 (1)–(3).]

1. For meaning of "horses", see note 1 to s 3, ante.

Veterinary Surgeons Act 1966
(1966 c 36)

Restrictions of practise of veterinary surgery

8–1211 19. Restriction of practise of veterinary surgery by unqualified persons. (1) Subject to the following provisions of this section, no individual shall practise, or hold himself out as practising or as being prepared to practise, veterinary surgery[1] unless he is registered[2] in the register of veterinary surgeons or the supplementary veterinary register, and an individual who acts in contravention of this subsection shall be liable[3]—

    (*a*)   on summary conviction to a fine not exceeding **the statutory maximum**;

    (*b*)   on conviction on indictment to a fine.

(2) *Repealed.*

(3) The Council may make regulations[4] exempting from subsection (1) of this section the carrying out or performance of any veterinary treatment, test or operation prescribed by the regulations, subject to compliance with prescribed conditions, by students of veterinary surgery of any prescribed class.

(4) Subsection (1) of this section shall not prohibit—

    (*a*)   the carrying out of any procedure authorised under the Animals (Scientific Procedures) Act 1986[5];

    (*b*)   the doing of anything specified in Part I of Schedule 3 to this Act[6] and not excluded by Part II of that Schedule;

    (*c*)   the performance by a registered medical practitioner of an operation on an animal for the purpose of removing an organ or tissue for use in the treatment of human beings;

    (*d*)   the carrying out or performance of any treatment, test or operation by a registered medical practitioner or a registered dentist at the request of a person registered in the register of veterinary surgeons or the supplementary veterinary register;

    (*e*)   the carrying out or performance of any minor treatment, test or operation specified in an order[7] made by the Ministers[8] after consultation with the Council, so long as any conditions so specified are complied with.

(5) The Ministers may, after consultation with the Council and with persons appearing to the Ministers to represent interests so appearing to be substantially affected, by order[9] amend the provisions of Schedule 3 to this Act.

(6) Any order under subsection (4) or (5) of this section may be varied or revoked by a subsequent order of the Ministers under that subsection made after the like consultation.

[Veterinary Surgeons Act 1966, s 19, as amended by the Criminal Law Act 1977, s 28 and Sch 13 and the Animals (Scientific Procedures) Act 1986, Sch 3.]

---

1. "Veterinary surgery" shall be taken to include: (*a*) the diagnosis of diseases in, and injuries to, animals including tests performed on animals for diagnostic purposes; (*a*) the giving of advice based upon such diagnosis; (*c*) the medical or surgical treatment of animals and (*d*) the performance of surgical operations on animals (s 27(1)).

2. The Veterinary Surgeons' Qualifications (European Recognition) Order 2003, SI 2003/2919 implements the provisions of Directive 2001/19/EC and extends them to all states in the EEA and to Switzerland. It also provides for all veterinary qualifications, training and experience acquired by applicants for registration who are EEA or Swiss nationals to be taken into account. See also the Veterinary Surgeons and Veterinary Practitioners (Registration) Regulations Order of Council 2005, SI 2005/3517.

3. For procedure in respect of this offence which is triable either way, see the Magistrates' Courts Act 1980, ss 17A–21 in PART I: MAGISTRATES' COURTS, PROCEDURE, ante.

4. The Veterinary Surgeons (Practice by Students) Regulations 1981, SI 1981/988 amended by SI 1995/2397 prescribes the class of students who have attained the age of 18 years, are attending full-time courses at a university or veterinary school in the United Kingdom or elsewhere, leading to a veterinary qualification, and have entered upon that part of the curriculum which deals with clinical studies as being enabled to (*a*) examine animals; (*b*) carry out tests upon animals under the direction of a registered veterinary surgeon; (*c*) administer treatment (other than by way of surgical operations) to animals under the supervision of a registered veterinary surgeon; and (*d*) perform surgical operations upon animals in accordance with the directions and under the direct and continuous personal supervision of a registered veterinary surgeon.

5. See post.

6. This Schedule is not included in this work. It includes treatment by the owner or his servant, treatment in an emergency, treatment or minor surgery by veterinary nurse or a student veterinary nurse in specified circumstances and certain routine operations on young animals.

7. The following orders have been made under this provision: Veterinary Surgery (Blood Sampling) Order 1983, SI 1983/6 amended by SI 1988/1090 and SI 1990/2217; Veterinary Surgery (Epidural Anaesthesia) Order 1992, SI 1992/696; Veterinary Surgery (Rectal Ultrasound Scanning of Bovines) Order 2002, SI 2002/2584; Veterinary Surgery (Artificial Insemination of Mares) Order 2004, SI 2004/1504; Veterinary Surgery (Vaccination Against Foot-and-Mouth Disease) Order 2004, SI 2004/2780; Veterinary Surgery (Testing for Tuberculosis in Bovines) Order 2005, SI 2005/2015.

8. "The Ministers" Secretary of State for Environment, Food and Rural Affairs (SI 2002/794), the Secretary of State and the Minister of Agriculture for N Ireland, acting jointly; also the Secretary of State for Wales (SI 1978/272).

By the Veterinary Surgeons (Exemption) Order 1962, SI 1962/2557 amended by SI 1982/1627, the expression "veterinary surgery" does not include the minor treatments, tests and operations therein specified.

9. Schedule 3, Pt II specifies operations which can be performed only by a veterinary surgeon: it has been amended by SI 1982/1885.

8–1212   **20. Prohibition of use of practitioners' titles by unqualified persons.** (1) If a person not registered in the register takes or uses the title of veterinary surgeon or any name, title, addition or description implying that he is so registered[1], he shall be guilty of an offence.

(2) If any person not registered in the register of veterinary surgeons or the supplementary veterinary register takes or uses the title of veterinary practitioner or any name, addition or description implying that he is a practitioner of, or qualified to practise, veterinary surgery to any greater extent than is authorised by or under subsection (3) of the last foregoing section, he shall be guilty of an offence.

(3) Without prejudice to the foregoing provisions of this section, if any person uses, in connection with any business carried on by him or at any premises at which such a business is carried on, a description implying that he or any person acting for the purposes of the business possesses veterinary qualifications which he does not in fact possess he shall be guilty of an offence.

(4) A person guilty of an offence under this section shall be liable[2]—

(a) on summary conviction to a fine not exceeding **the statutory maximum**;

(b) on conviction on indictment to a fine.

(5) Where an offence by a body corporate under this section is proved to have been committed with the consent or connivance of, or be attributable to any neglect on the part of, any director, manager, secretary or other similar officer of the body corporate, or a person purporting to act in any such capacity, he, as well as the body corporate shall be deemed to be guilty of that offence and shall be liable to be proceeded against and punished accordingly.

[Veterinary Surgeons Act 1966, s 20, as amended by the Criminal Law Act 1977, s 28 and Sch 13.]

---

1. The following cases decided under repealed statutes may be helpful: An unqualified person who displayed over the door of his forge and on his billheads "J. Robinson, Veterinary Forge", was held guilty of an offence (*Royal College of Veterinary Surgeons v Robinson* [1892] 1 QB 557, 56 JP 313). And so was an unqualified person who exhibited over his residence a board with the words, "Canine Specialists, Dogs and Cats treated for all Deseases" (*Royal College of Veterinary Surgeons v Collinson* [1908] 2 KB 248, 72 JP 267); or "Churchill's Veterinary Sanatorium, Limited. Dogs and Cats Boarded. Jas. Churchill, MD, USA, Specialist, Managing Director" (*A-G v Churchill's Veterinary Sanatorium Ltd* [1910] 2 Ch 401, 74 JP 397).

2. For procedure in respect of this offence which is triable either way, see the Magistrates' Courts Act 1980, ss 17A–21 in PART I: MAGISTRATES' COURTS, PROCEDURE, ante.

Slaughter of Poultry Act 1967
(1967 c 24)

8–1213 1–2. *Repealed.*

8–1215 3. *Regulations[1] for securing humane conditions of slaughter.*

---

1. See now the Welfare of Animals (Slaughter or Killing) Regulations 1995, SI 1995/731, made under s 2(2) of the European Communities Act 1972.

Regulations may provide for any functions exercisable by local authorities to be transferred to the Minister of Agriculture, Fisheries and Food (in England) or the Secretary of State (in Scotland or Wales): Deregulation and Contracting Out Act 1994, s 31 and Sch 9.

8–1216 3A. Codes of practice. (1) The Ministers may from time to time after consultation with such persons or bodies as seem to them representative of the interests concerned—

(a) prepare and issue codes of practice for the purpose of providing practical guidance in respect of any provision of this Act or regulations under it; and

(b) revise any such code by revoking, varying, amending or adding to the provisions of the code.

(2) A code prepared in pursuance of this section and any alterations proposed to be made on a revision of such a code shall be laid before both Houses of Parliament, and the Ministers shall not issue the code or revised code, as the case may be, until after the end of the period of 40 days beginning with the day on which the code or the proposed alterations were so laid.

(3) If, within the period mentioned in subsection (2) of this section, either House resolves that the code be not issued or the proposed alterations be not made, as the case may be, the Ministers shall not issue the code or revised code (without prejudice to their power under that subsection to lay further codes or proposed alterations before Parliament).

(4) For the purposes of subsection (2) of this section—

(a) where a code or proposed alterations are laid before each House of Parliament on different days, the later day shall be taken to be the day on which the code or the proposed alterations, as the case may be, were laid before both Houses; and

(b) in reckoning any period of 40 days, no account shall be taken of any time during which Parliament is dissolved or prorogued or during which both Houses are adjourned for more than four days.

(5) The Ministers shall cause any code issued or revised under this section to be printed and distributed, and may make such arrangements as they think fit for its distribution, including causing copies of it to be put on sale to the public at such reasonable price as the Ministers may determine.

(6) A failure on the part of any person to follow any guidance contained in a code issued under this section shall not of itself render that person liable to proceedings of any kind.

(7) If, in proceedings against any person for an offence consisting of the contravention of any provision of this Act or of regulations under it, it is shown that, at any material time, he failed to follow any guidance contained in a code issued under this section, being guidance which was relevant

to the provision concerned, that failure may be relied on by the prosecution as tending to establish his guilt.
[Slaughter of Poultry Act 1967, s 3A, as inserted by the Animal Health and Welfare Act 1984, s 7.]

8–1217   4. Power of entry[1].   (1) Where the power conferred by this subsection is exercisable in relation to any premises to which regulations under section 3 of this Act apply, a person authorised in that behalf by the Minister of Agriculture, Fisheries and Food or the Secretary of State or by the local authority[2] within whose area the premises are situated may enter the premises for the purpose of ascertaining whether there is, or has been, on those premises any contravention of any provision of this Act or of any regulations made or code of practice issued under it.

(2) Where it is, or appears to the person so authorised to be, the case that the slaughter of birds to which this Act applies is in progress on the premises, the power conferred by subsection (1) of this section is exercisable at any time.

(3) Where it is, or appears to the person so authorised to be, the case that—

(a)   the slaughter of such birds has within 48 hours been in progress on the premises, or

(b)   such birds are on the premises for the purpose of their being slaughtered,

the power conferred by subsection (1) of this section is exercisable at all reasonable hours.

(4) A person who intentionally obstructs a person in the exercise of his powers under subsection (1) of this section shall be guilty of an offence and liable on summary conviction to a fine not exceeding **level 2** on the standard scale.
[Slaughter of Poultry Act 1967, s 4, as substituted by the Animal Health and Welfare Act 1983, s 8 and amended by the Deregulation and Contracting Out Act 1994, s 31 and Sch 9.]

---

1. Regulations may provide for any functions exercisable by local authorities to be transferred to the Minister of Agriculture, Fisheries and Food (in England) or the Secretary of State (in Scotland or Wales): Deregulation and Contracting Out Act 1994, s 31 and Sch 9.
2. "Local authority" means the council of a London borough or a county district or the Common council of the City of London (s 8).

8–1218   5. Offences by corporations.   Where a body corporate is guilty of an offence under this Act and the offence is proved to have been committed with the consent or connivance of, or to be attributable to any neglect on the part of, a director, manager, secretary or other similar officer of the body corporate or any person who was purporting to act in any such capacity, he, as well as the body corporate, shall be guilty of that offence and shall be liable to be proceeded against and punished accordingly.
[Slaughter of Poultry Act 1967, s 5.]

8–1219   6. Execution and enforcement[1].   (1) Every local authority[2] shall execute and enforce in their area the provisions of this Act and of regulations under section 3 of this Act.

(2) In particular, every local authority shall, for the purpose of securing the execution of those provisions, make arrangements for the supervision by persons having such qualifications as may be specified in the regulations of any premises in their area to which the regulations apply.

(3) Arrangements under subsection (2) of this section shall comply with such directions as the Ministers may give from time to time.

(4) This section does not authorise a local authority in Scotland to institute proceedings for any offence.
[Slaughter of Poultry Act 1967, s 6, as substituted by the Animal Health and Welfare Act 1984, s 9 and amended by the Deregulation and Contracting Out Act 1994, s 31 and Sch 9.]

---

1. Regulations may provide for any functions exercisable by local authorities to be transferred to the Minister of Agriculture, Fisheries and Food (in England) or the Secretary of State (in Scotland or Wales): Deregulation and Contracting Out Act 1994, s 31 and Sch 9.
2. "Local authority" means the council of a London borough or a county district or the Common Council of the City of London (s 8).

8–1220   7. Power to extend Act to birds.   (1) The Ministers may, after consultation with such persons or bodies as seem to them representative of the interests concerned, by order extend this Act (subject to such, if any, exceptions, adaptations and modifications as may be specified in the order) to the slaughter of birds of any kind kept in captivity.

(2) An order under this section may be varied or revoked by a subsequent order thereunder made by the Ministers.

(3) The powers conferred by this section shall be exercisable by statutory instrument, and no order shall be made under this section unless a draft thereof has been laid before Parliament and has been approved by resolution of each House of Parliament.
[Slaughter of Poultry Act 1967, s 7, as amended by the Animal Health and Welfare Act 1984, Schs 1 and 2.]

8–1221   8. Interpretation.   (1) In this Act—

"contravention" includes failure to comply;

"local authority" means, as respects England, the council of a London borough or a county district or the Common Council of the City of London, as respects Wales, the council of a county or county borough and, as respects Scotland, a county council or a town council;

"the Ministers" means the Minister of Agriculture, Fisheries and Food and the Secretary of State for Scotland and the Secretary of State for Wales acting jointly[1];

"the standard scale" has the meaning given by section 75 of the Criminal Justice Act 1982.

(2) This act applies to turkeys kept in captivity and domestic fowls, guinea fowls, ducks, geese and quails so kept; and references in this Act to birds to which this Act applies shall be construed in accordance with this subsection and any order under section 7 above.

[Slaughter of Poultry Act 1967, s 8, as amended by the Local Government Act 1972, s 272 and Sch 30, the Transfer of Functions (Wales) (No 1) Order 1978, SI 1978/272, the Animal Health and Welfare Act 1984, Sch 1 and the Local Government (Wales) Act 1994, Sch 16.]

---

1. Now the Minister of Agriculture, Fisheries and Food alone see the Transfer of Functions (Agriculture and Food) Order 1999, SI 1999/3141. The functions of the Minister, so far as exercisable in relation to Wales, have been transferred to the National Assembly for Wales, by the National Assembly for Wales (Transfer of Functions) Order 1999, SI 1999/672, art 2, Sch 1.

Agriculture (Miscellaneous Provisions) Act 1968

(1968 c 34)

PART I
WELFARE OF LIVESTOCK

8–1222 1. Prevention of unnecessary pain and distress for livestock. (1) Any person who causes unnecessary pain or unnecessary distress to any livestock[1] for the time being situated on agricultural land[1] and under his control or permits any such livestock to suffer any such pain or distress of which he knows or may reasonably be expected to know shall be guilty of an offence[2] under this section.

(2) Nothing in the foregoing subsection shall apply to any act lawfully done under the Animals (Scientific Procedures) Act 1986 or to any thing done or omitted by or under the direction of any person in accordance with the terms of a licence issued by the Minister for the purpose of enabling that person to undertake scientific research.

[Agriculture (Miscellaneous Provisions) Act 1968, s 1 as amended by the Animals (Scientific Procedures) Act 1986, Sch 3.]

---

1. Defined in s 8(1), post.
2. Triable summarily; for penalty see s 7(1), post.

8–1223 2–3. Regulations and Codes of recommendation[1][Agriculture (Miscellaneous Provisions) Act 1968, ss 2 and 3.]

---

1. The following regulations have been made:

Welfare of Livestock (Prohibited Operations) Regulations 1982, SI 1982/1884 amended by SI 1987/114;

Welfare of Farmed Animals (England) Regulations 2000, SI 2000/1870 amended by SI 2002/1646 and 1898 and SI 2003/299;

Welfare of Farmed Animals (Wales) Regulations 2001, SI 2001/2682 amended by SI 2003/1726.

Penalty for contravention of a regulation is set out in s 7(1), post.

8–1224 5. Extension of classes of operations in which anaesthetics must be used. Minister may by Order[1] prevent exemptions in the Protection of Animals (Anaesthetics) Act 1954 from applying to particular operations.

[Agriculture (Miscellaneous Provisions) Act 1968, s 5—summarised].

---

1. See the Docking of Pigs (Use of Anaesthetics) Order 1974, SI 1974/798; the Removal of Antlers in Velvet (Anaesthetics) Order 1980, SI 1980/685.

8–1225 6. Powers of entry, etc. (1) A person duly authorised in writing by the Minister may at any reasonable time enter upon any land, other than premises used wholly or mainly as a dwelling, for the purpose of ascertaining whether an offence under this part of this Act has been committed on the land.

(2) A person duly authorised in writing by a local authority may at any reasonable time enter upon any land, other than such premises as aforesaid, for the purpose of ascertaining whether an offence under this Part of this Act has been committed on the land, being an offence consisting of a contravention of or failure to comply with provisions or regulations made in pursuance of section 2(1)(*b*) of this Act.

(3) A person authorised as mentioned in the foregoing provisions of this section to enter upon any land—

(a) shall if so required produce evidence of his authority before entering and while present on the land; and

(b) may take with him on to the land such other persons as he considers necessary.

(4) Any person authorised as aforesaid may take for analysis a sample of any substance which he finds on the land and which appears to him to be intended for use as food for livestock;

(5) Any veterinary surgeon or veterinary practitioner authorised as mentioned in subsection (1) of this section to enter upon any land may examine any livestock which he finds on the land and apply to and take from the livestock such tests and samples as he considers appropriate; and a person by whom a sample is taken from livestock in pursuance of this subsection shall, if before the sample is taken he is requested to do so by any person appearing to him to have the custody of the livestock, deliver a part of the sample or a similar sample to the person who made the request.

(6) If a person entitled to enter upon any land in pursuance of this section requests any person present on the land, being the occupier or a servant of the occupier of the land or a person having the custody of any livestock present on the land—

(a) to indicate to the person so entitled the places on the land used for the accommodation of livestock or for the storage or treatment of any substance intended for use as food for livestock; or

(b) to facilitate the access of the person so entitled to any such place, it shall be the duty of the person to whom the request is addressed to comply with the request so far as he is able to do so.

(7) A person who fails to perform his duty under subsection (6) of this section or otherwise wilfully obstructs a person entitled as aforesaid in the execution of that person's powers under this section shall be guilty of an offence[1] under this section.

[Agriculture (Miscellaneous Provisions) Act 1968, s 6 as amended by the Statute Law (Repeals) Act 2004.]

---

1. For penalty, see s 7(2), post.

8–1226   7. Punishment of offences under Part I.   (1) A person guilty of an offence under section 1 or section 2 of this Act shall be liable on summary conviction to imprisonment for a term not exceeding **three months*** or a fine not exceeding **level 4** on the standard scale or both.

(2) A person guilty of an offence under section 6 of this Act shall be liable on summary conviction to a fine not exceeding **level 3** on the standard scale.

(3) In England and Wales a local authority shall, without prejudice to the powers of any other person to institute proceedings for an offence under this Part of this Act, have power to institute proceedings for such an offence as is mentioned in section 6(2) of this Act which is alleged to have been committed in their area.

[Agriculture (Miscellaneous Provisions) Act 1968, s 7, as amended by the Criminal Law Act 1977, Sch 6 and the Criminal Justice Act 1982, ss 39 and 46, and Sch 3.]

---

*Words substituted by the Criminal Justice Act 2003, Sch 26, from a date to be appointed.

8–1227   8. Interpretation, etc, of Part I.   (1) In this Part of this Act—

"agricultural land" means land used for agriculture (within the meaning of the Agriculture Act 1947 or, in Scotland, the Agriculture (Scotland) Act 1948) which is so used for the purposes of a trade or business; and

"livestock" means any creature kept for the production of food, wool, skin or fur or for use in the farming of land or for such purpose as the Minister may by order[1] specify.

(2) Subsections (2) and (3) of section 50 of the Animal Health Act 1981 (which define the expression "local authority") shall have effect for the purposes of this Part of this Act as if for references to that Act there were substituted references to this Part of this Act and as if paragraph (b)(ii) were omitted from subsection (2).

(3) This Part of this Act applies to officers and servants of the Crown, and references to land in this Part of this Act include references to land belonging to Her Majesty in right of the Crown or the Duchy of Lancaster, land belonging to the Duchy of Cornwall and land held on behalf of Her Majesty for the purposes of any Government department; and in relation to any such land occupied by or on behalf of Her Majesty or the Duchy of Cornwall section 6 of this Act shall have the effect as if subsection 2 were omitted.

(5) Nothing in this Part of this Act shall be construed as prejudicing any provision of the Protection of Animals Acts 1911 to 1964 or the Protection of Animals (Scotland) Acts 1912 to 1964.

[Agriculture (Miscellaneous Provisions) Act 1968, s 8 as amended by the Animal Health Act 1981, Sch 5.]

---

1. By the Welfare of Livestock (Deer) Order 1980, SI 1980/593 deer kept for the production of antlers in velvet are brought within the definition of "livestock".

8–1228   50. Interpretation, etc—general.   (1)   Subject to subsection (7) of section 45 of this Act, in this Act—

"the Minister" means, except in the application of this Act to Scotland, the Minister of Agriculture, Fisheries and Food and, in the application of this Act to Scotland, the Secretary of State[1];

"the Ministers" means the Minister of Agriculture, Fisheries and Food and the Secretary of State acting jointly[1]; and

"notice" means notice in writing.

(2) *Repealed.*

(3) Any reference in this Act to any enactment is a reference to it as amended, and includes a reference to it as applied, by or under any other enactment including an enactment in this Act

(4) Where an offence under this Act committed by a body corporate is proved to have been committed with the consent or connivance of, or to be attributable to any neglect on the part of, any director, manager, secretary or other similar officer of the body corporate or any person who was purporting to act in any such capacity, he as well as the body corporate shall be guilty of that offence and shall be liable to be proceeded against and punished accordingly.

In this subsection "director", in relation to a body corporate established by or under any enactment for the purpose of carrying on under national ownership any industry or undertaking or part of an industry or undertaking or part of an industry or undertaking, being a body corporate whose affairs are managed by its members, means a member of that body corporate.

[Agriculture (Miscellaneous Provisions) Act 1968, s 50 as amended by the Water Act 1973, s 40(3), Sch 9.]

---

1. The functions of the Minister, so far as exercisable in relation to Wales, have been transferred to the National Assembly for Wales, by the National Assembly for Wales (Transfer of Functions) Order 1999, SI 1999/672, art 2, Sch 1.

Conservation of Seals Act 1970
(1970 c 30)

8–1240   1. Prohibited methods of killing seals.   (1)   Subject to section 9(2) and section 10 of this Act, if any person—

(*a*)   uses for the purposes of killing or taking any seal any poisonous substance; or

(*b*)   uses for the purpose of killing, injuring or taking any seal any firearm[1] other than a rifle using ammunition[1] having a muzzle energy of not less than 600 footpounds and a bullet weighing not less than 45 grains,

he shall be guilty of an offence.

(2)   the Secretary of State[2] may by order amend paragraph (*b*) of subsection (1) of this section by adding any firearm or ammunition[1] to, or by altering the description of, or by substituting any other firearm or ammunition for, the firearm or ammunition mentioned in that subsection.

[Conservation of Seals Act 1970, s 1.]

---

1. "Firearm" and "ammunition" have the same meaning as in the Firearms Act 1968 (s 15).

2. The functions of the Minister, so far as exercisable in relation to Wales, have been transferred to the National Assembly for Wales, by the National Assembly for Wales (Transfer of Functions) Order 1999, SI 1999/672, art 2, Sch 1.

8–1241   2. Close seasons for seals.   (1)   There shall be an annual close season for grey seals, that is to say seals of the species known as Halichoerus grypus, extending from 1st September to 31st December both inclusive and an annual close season for common seals, that is to say seals of the species known as Phoca vitulina, extending from 1st June to 31st August both inclusive.

(2)   Subject to sections 9 and 10 of this Act, if any person wilfully kills, injures or takes a seal during the close season prescribed by subsection (1) of this section for seals of the species so killed, injured or taken he shall be guilty of an offence.

[Conservation of Seals Act 1970, s 2.]

8–1242   3. Orders prohibiting killing seals.   (1)   Where, after consultation with the Council[1], it appears to the Secretary of State necessary for the proper conservation of seals he may by order[2] prohibit with respect to any area specified in the order the killing, injuring or taking of the seals of both or either of the species mentioned in section 2 of this Act.

(2)   Subject to sections 9 and 10 of this Act, if any person wilfully kills, injures or takes a seal in contravention of an order made under subsection (1) of this section he shall be guilty of an offence.

[Conservation of Seals Act 1970, s 3.]

---

1. "Council" means the National Environment Research Council (s 15).

2. The Conservation of Seals (England) Order 1999, SI 1999/3052, which has effect for a period of three years from 19 December 1999, has been made.

8–1243   4. Apprehension of offenders and powers to search and seizure.   (1) A constable may stop any person he suspects with reasonable cause of committing an offence under this Act and may—

    (*a*)   *repealed;*
    (*b*)   without warrant search any vehicle or boat which that person may be using at that time; and
    (*c*)   seize any seal, seal skin, firearm, ammunition or poisonous substance which is liable to be forfeited under s 6 of this Act.

(2) A constable may sell or otherwise dispose of any seal seized under this section and the net proceeds of any sale shall be liable to forfeiture in the same manner as the seal sold:

Provided that no constable shall be subjected to any liability on account of his neglect or failure in the exercise of the powers conferred on him by this subsection.

[Conservation of Seals Act 1970, s 4 as amended by the Police and Criminal Evidence Act 1984, Sch 7.]

8–1244   5. Penalties.   (1) Any person guilty of an offence under section 11(7) of this Act shall be liable on summary conviction to a fine not exceeding **level 3** on the standard scale.

(2) Any person guilty of any other offence under this Act shall be liable on summary conviction to a fine not exceeding **level 4** on the standard scale.

[Conservation of Seals Act 1970, s 5, as amended by the Criminal Law Act 1977, Sch 6 and the Criminal Justice Act 1982, ss 38 and 46.]

8–1245   6. Forfeitures.   The court by which a person is convicted of an offence under this Act may order the forfeiture of any seal or seal skin in respect of which that offence was committed or of any seal, seal skin, firearm, ammunition or poisonous substance in his possession at the time of the offence.

[Conservation of Seals Act 1970, s 6.]

8–1246   7. Jurisdiction of courts.   Where any offence under this Act is committed at some place on the sea coast or at sea outside the area of any commission of the peace, the place of the commission of the offence shall, for the purposes of the jurisdiction of any court, be deemed to be any place where the offender is found or to which he is first brought after the commission of the offence[1].

[Conservation of Seals Act 1970, s 7.]

---

1. But nothing done outside the seaward limits of the territorial waters adjacent to Great Britain shall constitute an offence under this Act (s 17).

8–1247   8. Attempt to commit offence.   (1) Any person who attempts to commit an offence under this Act shall be guilty of an offence.

(2) Any person who, for the purpose of committing an offence under this Act, has in his possession any poisonous substance or any firearm or ammunition the use of which is prohibited by section 1(1)(*b*) of this Act shall be guilty of an offence.

[Conservation of Seals Act 1970, s 8.]

8–1248   9. General exceptions.   (1) A person shall not be guilty of an offence under section 2 or 3 of this Act by reason only of—

    (*a*)   the taking or attempted taking of any seal which had been disabled otherwise than by his act and was taken or to be taken solely for the purpose of tending it and releasing it when no longer disabled;
    (*b*)   the unavoidable killing or injuring of any seal as an incidental result of a lawful action;
    (*c*)   the killing or attempted killing of any seal to prevent it from causing damage to a fishing net or fishing tackle in his possession or in the possession of a person at whose request he killed or attempted to kill the seal, or to any fish for the time being in such fishing net, provided that at the time the seal was in the vicinity of such net or tackle.

(2) A person shall not be guilty of an offence under section 1, 2 or 3 of this Act by reason only of the killing of any seal which had been so seriously disabled otherwise than by his act that there was no reasonable chance of its recovering.

[Conservation of Seals Act 1970, s 9.]

8–1249   10. (1) and (3) *Power to grant licences to kill or take seals.*

(2) A licence granted under this section may be revoked at any time by the Secretary of State and, without prejudice to any other liability to a penalty which he may have incurred under this or any other Act, any person who contravenes or fails to comply with any condition imposed on the grant of a licence under this section shall be guilty of an offence.

(4) *Application of sub-ss* (1) *and* (3).

(5) *Meaning of "the Nature Conservancy Council".*

[Conservation of Seals Act 1970, s 10 as amended by the Wildlife and Countryside Act 1981, Schs 7 and 17, the Environmental Protection Act 1990, Sch 9 and the Countryside and Rights of Way Act 2000, Sch 16.]

8–1250 11. (1)–(6) and (8) *Power to authorise entry upon land to obtain information about seals or to kill or take seals.*

(7) If any person wilfully obstructs any person authorised by the Secretary of State exercising a power of entry under this section, he shall be guilty of an offence.
[Conservation of Seals Act 1970, s 11.]

8–1251 12. Giving of notice. (1) Any notice required by this Act to be given to any person shall be duly given if it is delivered to him, or left at his proper address, or sent to him by post.

(2) Any such notice required to be given to an incorporated company or body shall be duly given to the secretary or clerk of the company or body.

(3) For the purposes of this section and of section 26 of the Interpretation Act 1889[1] the proper address of any person to whom any such notice is to be given shall, in the case of the secretary or clerk of any incorporated company or body, be that of the registered or principal office of the company or body, and in any other case be the last-known address of the person in question.

(4) Where such notice is to given to a person as being the person having interest in land, and it is not practicable after reasonable enquiry to ascertain his name or address, the notice may be given by addressing it to him by the description of the person having that interest in the land (naming it), and delivering the notice to some responsible person on the land or by affixing it, or a copy of it, to some conspicuous object on the land.
[Conservation of Seals Act 1970, s 12.]

---

1. Now s 7 of the Interpretation Act 1978.

Slaughterhouses Act 1974[1]
(1974 c 3)

PART I
SLAUGHTERHOUSES AND KNACKERS' YARDS
Licensing of private slaughterhouses and knackers' yards

8–1279 1. Slaughterhouses and knackers' yards to be licensed. (1) It shall be an offence[2]—

(a) for the occupier of any premises to use them as a knacker's yard[3] or to permit them to be so used, unless he holds a licence under this section authorising him to keep those premises as a knacker's yard, or

(b) for any person other than the occupier to use any premises as a knacker's yard, unless the occupier holds such a licence in respect of those premises.

(2) Licences[4] under this section (in this Part of this Act referred to as "licences") shall be granted by the local authority, subject to and in accordance with the provisions of this Part.

(3) Where any premises used or to be used for the confinement of animals awaiting slaughter in a slaughterhouse or knacker's yard are situated outside the curtilage of the premises used or to be used for the slaughter, separate licences may be granted authorising the use of those premises for the purposes of the confinement and the slaughter respectively.

(4) In relation to the use of any premises for or in connection with the slaughter of horses[5] a licence shall be of no effect unless it expressly authorises the use of the premises for that purpose.★
[Slaughterhouses Act 1974, s 1, as amended by SI 1996/2235.]

★**Repealed in relation to England by SI 2005/2347 from 28 September 2005.**
1. This Act is to be executed and enforced by every local authority in their district except where a duty under Part 1 is expressly or by necessary implication imposed on some other authority (ss 19 and 41; see also s 22). Sections 19 and 41 were further extended by the Welfare of Animals at Slaughter Act 1991 which also enabled the issue of Codes of Practice. An Order in Council made by statutory instrument under s 33 may apply certain provisions of Part I, as well as regulations under it, to the Crown. The following provisions of the Public Health Act 1936 are deemed (by s 32) to be incorporated in Part I; s 283 (forms of notices), s 284 (authentication of documents), s 285 (service of notices), s 304 (judges and justices not disqualified by rates liability), s 317 (power to repeal and alter local Acts), ss 322–325 (default powers) and s 328 (powers of Act to be cumulative).
The Act does not apply to Scotland or Northern Ireland (s 48).
2. For penalty, see s 23, post. For procedure where it is alleged that the contravention is due to the default of some other person, see s 25, post.
3. For definition of "knacker's yard", see s 34, post. On the definition of "slaughterhouse" formerly contained in a repealed enactment, it was held that the use on one occasion of premises not regularly used as a slaughterhouse was no offence (*Perrins v Smith* [1946] KB 90, [1945] 2 All ER 706, 110 JP 91); this decision no longer applies in the case of building alleged to be a slaughterhouse (*East Retford District Council v Horne* [1955] Crim LR 310), but probably it is still good law in the case of a knacker's yard.
4. A licence remains in force for a period not exceeding 13 months fixed by the local authority, and may be renewed from time to time for periods each not exceeding 13 months (s 9). Provision is made by s 10 for temporary continuance of licence on death.
5. "Horse" includes ass and mule (s 34, post).

8–1280 2. Slaughterhouse licences and application for such licences. *Repealed.*

8–1281   3. Certain applications for slaughterhouse licence to be refused forthwith.   *Repealed.*

8–1282   4. Knacker's yard licences and applications for such licences.   (1) Where a local authority receive from the occupier of, or a person proposing to occupy, any premises an application for the grant or renewal of a licence authorising him to occupy those premises as a knacker's yard, then, subject to subsections (3) and (4) below, the authority may grant or, as the case may be, renew the licence.

(2) Without prejudice to subsection (1) above and subject to section 6 below, a local authority may refuse to grant or, as the case may be, renew a knacker's yard licence in respect of any premises if they are not satisfied that the requirements relating to knacker's yards—

  (a)   of regulations under section 16 of the Food Safety Act 1990, or
  (b)   of byelaws, if any, made by the authority under section 12 below, are complied with in respect of those premises, or will be complied with before the date on which the licence or renewed licence comes into force.

(3)   Subject to section 6 below, a local authority shall refuse to grant or, as the case may be, renew a knacker's yard licence in respect of any premises unless they are satisfied that the requirements relating to knacker's yards of construction regulations are complied with in respect of those premises, or will be complied with before the date on which the licence or renewed licence comes into force.

(4)   A local authority shall not grant or renew a knacker's yard licence until an officer of the authority has inspected the premises named in the application and has made a report on those premises.

(5)   A local authority may require a person who applies for the grant or renewal of a knacker's yard licence to give to them, before his application is considered, information as to any other licence which he has held in respect of a slaughterhouse or which he holds or has held in respect of a knacker's yard, either in their district or in the district of another local authority, or as to any slaughterhouse licence which he holds or held, and if an applicant who is so required gives the authority any information which is false in a material respect, he shall be guilty of an offence[1].

(6)   In subsection (5) above, "slaughterhouse licence" means a licence issued under regulations made by virtue of section 19(1)(b) of the Food Safety Act 1990 for the use of any premises as a slaughterhouse.★
[Slaughterhouses Act 1974, s 4 as amended by the Food Act 1984, Sch 10, the Food Safety Act 1990, Sch 3, SI 1995/731 and SI 1996/2235.]

  ★**Repealed in relation to England by SI 2005/2347 from 28 September 2005.**
  1. For penalty, see s 23, post. For procedure where it is alleged that the contravention is due to the default of some other person, see s 25, post.

8–1283   5. Notification of refusal of licence.   (1) If a local authority refuse to grant or renew a licence they shall forthwith give notice to the applicant of their decision in the matter, and a statement of the grounds on which that decision was based shall—

  (a)   in the case of a refusal of a slaughterhouse licence under section 3 above, be included in the notice;
  (b)   in any other case, if so required by the applicant within 14 days from the date of the decision, be given to him by the authority not later than 48 hours after they receive the requirement.

(2)   Every notice under subsection (1) above shall state the right of appeal to a magistrates' court for which provision is made by section 6(1) below and the time within which such an appeal may be brought.

(3)   For the purposes of this section and sections 6 and 7 below, a refusal by a local authority—

  (a)   to grant a licence with an authorisation in respect of horses under section 1(4) above, or
  (b)   to renew a licence with such an authorisation,

shall be treated as a refusal to grant or, as the case may be, as a refusal to renew a licence.★
[Slaughterhouses Act 1974, s 5.]

  ★**Repealed in relation to England by SI 2005/2347 from 28 September 2005.**

8–1284   6. Appeals against refusal of licence.   (1) A person aggrieved by the refusal of a local authority to grant or renew a licence may appeal to a magistrates' court, and that court may—

  (a)   in the case of a refusal of a slaughterhouse licence under section 3 above, if satisfied that the authority acted unreasonably in refusing the application on the grounds stated in the notice, declare the refusal to be of no effect;
  (b)   in any other case, vary or reverse the authority's decision[1].

(2)   The procedure on an appeal to a magistrates' court under subsection (1) above shall be by way of complaint for an order, and the Magistrates' Courts Act 1980 shall apply to the proceedings[2].
(3)   The time within which such an appeal may be brought shall be 21 days from the date on which

notice of the authority's refusal was served upon the person desiring to appeal, and for the purpose of this subsection the making of the complaint shall be deemed to be the bringing of the appeal.

(4) A person aggrieved by an order, determination or other decision of a magistrates' court under subsection (1) above may appeal to the Crown Court.*

[Slaughterhouses Act 1974, s 6, as amended by the Magistrates' Courts Act 1980, Sch 7.]

---

*Repealed in relation to England by SI 2005/2347 from 28 September 2005.

1. Where an appeal (or further appeal to the Crown Court under sub-s (4)) is allowed, the local authority is required by s 8 to give effect to the order of the court. Where a person has been lawfully using the premises up to the date of the local authority decision, he may so continue until expiry of time, for appeal, or until the appeal is finally disposed of, abandoned, or fails for want of prosecution (s 7).

As to duration of licence, see footnote to s 1(2), supra.

2. See Magistrates' Courts Rules 1981, r 34, in PART I: MAGISTRATES' COURTS, PROCEDURE, ante. A right of appeal to a judicial tribunal on a question of fact is a right to have a rehearing of the whole matter (*per* HUMPHREYS, J, in *Fulham Metropolitan Borough Council v Santilli* [1933] 2 KB 357, 97 JP 174).

Regulation or private slaughterhouses and knackers' yards

8–1285   11. Restriction of dwellings in slaughterhouses.   *Repealed.*

8–1286   12. Byelaws about knackers' yards.   (1) A local authority may make byelaws—

(*a*)   for securing that knackers' yards are kept in a sanitary condition and are properly managed, and

(*b*)   requiring a person to keep a knacker's yard to keep, and to produce when required, records of animals brought into the yard and of the manner in which those animals and the different parts thereof were disposed of.

(2) Nothing in Part II of this Act shall be construed as restricting any power to make byelaws under paragraph (*a*) of subsection (1) above; but, in so far as any byelaws under that subsection conflict with regulations under section 16 of the Food Safety Act 1990, the regulations shall prevail.

(3) The confirming authority in respect of any byelaws under this section shall be the Minister.

(4) If a person convicted of an offence against any byelaw made under this section holds a licence in respect of the premises where the act was committed, the court may, in addition to any other punishment, cancel the licence[1].*

[Slaughterhouses Act 1974, s 12, as amended by the Local Government, Planning and Land Act 1980, Sch 34, the Food Act 1984, Sch 10 and the Food Safety Act 1990, Sch 3.]

---

*Repealed in relation to England by SI 2005/2347 from 28 September 2005.

1. Appeal from such an order lies to the Crown Court (s 26, post).

Enforcement and legal proceedings

8–1288   20. Powers of entry.   (1) Subject to the provisions of this section, an authorised officer of a council shall, on producing, if so required, some duly authenticated document showing his authority, have a right to enter any premises at all reasonable hours—

(*a*)   for the purpose of ascertaining whether there is or has been on, or in connection with, the premises any contravention of the provisions of this Part of this Act or of any byelaws made under it, being provisions which the council are required or empowered to enforce, and

(*b*)   generally for the purpose of the performance by the council of their functions under this Part of this Act or under any such byelaws;

but admission to any premises used only as a private dwellinghouse shall not be demanded as of right unless 24 hours' notice of the intended entry has been given to the occupier.

(2) If a justice of the peace, on sworn information in writing,—

(*a*)   is satisfied that there is reasonable ground for entry into any premises for any such purpose as mentioned in subsection (1) above, and

(*b*)   is also satisfied either—

(i)   that admission to the premises has been refused, or a refusal is apprehended and that notice of the intention to apply for a warrant has been given to the occupier, or

(ii)   that an application for admission, or the giving of such a notice, would defeat the object of the entry, or that the case is one of urgency, or that the premises are unoccupied or the occupier temporarily absent,

the justice may by warrant under his hand, which shall continue in force for a period of one month, authorise the council by any authorised officer to enter the premises, if need be by force.

(3) An authorised officer entering any premises by virtue of this section, or of a warrant issued it, may take with him such other persons as may be necessary, and on leaving any unoccupied premises which he has entered by virtue of such a warrant shall leave them as effectively secured against trespassers as he found them.

(4) If any person who, in compliance with the provisions of this section, or of a warrant issued under it, is admitted into a factory or workplace discloses to any person any information obtained by

him in the factory or workplace with regard to any manufacturing process or trade secret, he shall, unless the disclosure was made in the performance of his duty, be liable to a fine not exceeding **level 3** on the standard scale or to imprisonment for a term not exceeding **three months★**.

(5) Nothing in this section shall authorise any person, except with the permission of the local authority under the Animal Health Act 1981, to enter any cowshed or other place in which an animal affected with any disease to which that Act applies is kept and which is situated in a place declared under that Act to be infected with such a disease.

(6) In this section "authorised officer", in relation to a council, means an officer of the council authorised by them in writing, either generally or specially, to act in matters of any specified kind or in any specified manner.★★

[Slaughterhouses Act 1974, s 20, as amended by the Animal Health Act 1981, Sch 5 and the Criminal Justice Act 1982, ss 38 and 46.]

★Words substituted by the Criminal Justice Act 2003, Sch 26, from a date to be appointed.
★★Repealed in relation to England by SI 2005/2347 from 28 September 2005.

8–1289 21. Obstruction. (1) A person who wilfully obstructs any person acting in the execution of this Part of this Act, or of any byelaw or warrant made or issued under it, shall be liable—

(*a*) if the court is satisfied that he committed the offence with intent to prevent the discovery of some other offence under this Part of this Act, or if he has within the previous 12 months been convicted of an offence under this subsection, to a fine not exceeding **level 3** on the standard scale or to imprisonment for a term not exceeding **one month★**;

(*b*) in any other case, to a fine not exceeding **level 1** on the standard scale.

(2) A person who—

(*a*) fails to give to any person acting in the execution of this Part of this Act, or of any byelaw or warrant made or issued under it, any assistance which that person may reasonably request him to give;

(*b*) fails to give to any such person any information which that person is expressly authorised by this Part of this Act to call for or may reasonably require; or

(*c*) when required to give any such information, knowingly makes any misstatement in respect thereof,

shall be liable to a fine not exceeding **level 1** on the standard scale; but nothing in this subsection shall be construed as requiring a person to answer any question or give any information, if to do so might incriminate him.★★

[Slaughterhouses Act 1974, s 21, as amended by the Criminal Justice Act 1982, ss 38 and 46.]

★Words substituted by the Criminal Justice Act 2003, Sch 26, from a date to be appointed.
★★Repealed in relation to England by SI 2005/2347 from 28 September 2005.

8–1290 22. Institution of proceedings by local authorities. A local authority may institute proceedings under any section of this Part of this Act if, and only if, they are the authority charged with its execution and enforcement.★

[Slaughterhouses Act 1974, s 22.]

★Repealed in relation to England by SI 2005/2347 from 28 September 2005.

8–1291 23. Prosecution and punishment of offences. (1) All offences under this Part of this Act and byelaws made under it, shall be punishable on summary conviction.

(2) A person guilty of an offence under this Part of this Act shall, unless a special punishment for that offence is provided by this Part, be liable—

(*a*) to a fine not exceeding **level 3** on the standard scale or to imprisonment for a term not exceeding **three months★** or to both, and

(*b*) in the case of a continuing offence, to further fine not exceeding £5 for each day during which the offence continues after conviction.★★

[Slaughterhouses Act 1974, s 23, as amended by the Criminal Justice Act 1982, ss 38 and 46.]

★Words substituted by the Criminal Justice Act 2003, Sch 26, from a date to be appointed.
★★Repealed in relation to England by SI 2005/2347 from 28 September 2005.

8–1292 24. Offences by corporations. (1) Where an offence under this Part of this Act which has been committed by a body corporate is proved to have been committed with the consent or connivance of, or to be attributable to any neglect on the part of, any director, manager, secretary or other similar officer of the body corporate, or any person who was purporting to act in any such capacity, he as well as the body corporate shall be deemed to be guilty of that offence and shall be liable to be proceeded against and punished accordingly.

(2) In subsection (1) above "director", in relation to any body corporate established by or under

any enactment for the purpose of carrying on under national ownership any industry or part of an industry or undertaking, being a body corporate whose affairs are managed by the members thereof, means a member of that body corporate.★
[Slaughterhouses Act 1974, s 24.]

★Repealed in relation to England by SI 2005/2347 from 28 September 2005.

8–1293 25. Contravention due to default of some other person.   (1) A person against whom proceedings are brought under this Part of this Act shall, upon information duly laid by him and on giving to the prosecution not less than three clear days' notice of his intention, be entitled to have any person to whose act or default he alleges that the contravention of the provisions in question was due brought before the court in the proceedings; and if, after the contravention has been proved,—

(a) the original defendant proves that the contravention was due to the act or default of that other person, that other person may be convicted of the offence;

(b) the original defendant further proves that he has used all due diligence to secure that the provisions in question were complied with, he shall be acquitted of the offence.

(2) Where a defendant seeks to avail himself of the provisions of subsection (1) above—

(a) the prosecution, as well as the person whom the defendant charges with the offence, shall have the right to cross-examine him, if he gives evidence, and any witness called by him in support of his pleas, and to call rebutting evidence;

(b) the court may make such order as it thinks fit for the payment of costs by any party to the proceedings to any other party thereto.

(3) Where it appears to the authority concerned that an offence has been committed in respect of which proceedings might be taken under this Part of this Act against some person and the authority are reasonably satisfied that the offence of which complaint is made was due to an act or default of some other person and that the first-mentioned person could establish a defence under subsection (1) above, they may cause proceedings to be taken against that other person without first causing proceedings to be taken against the first-mentioned person.

(4) In any proceedings taken by virtue of subsection (3) above the defendant may be charged with, and, on proof that the contravention was due to his act or default, be convicted of, the offence with which the person first mentioned in that subsection might have been charged.★
[Slaughterhouses Act 1974, s 25.]

★Repealed in relation to England by SI 2005/2347 from 28 September 2005.

8–1294 26. Appeals to Crown Court.   Where a person aggrieved by an order, determination or other decision of a magistrates' court under this Part of this Act is not by any other enactment authorised to appeal to the Crown Court, he may appeal to that court.★
[Slaughterhouses Act 1974, s 26.]

★Repealed in relation to England by SI 2005/2347 from 28 September 2005.

Miscellaneous and supplemental

8–1295 27. Local authorities for purposes of Part I.   In this Part of this Act "local authority"[1] means—

(a) as respects the City of London, the Common Council;

(b) as respects any London borough, the council of the borough;

(c) as respects any district in England, the council of the district; and

(d) as respects any county or county borough in Wales, the council of the county or county borough.

[Slaughterhouses Act 1974, s 27, as amended by the Local Government (Wales) Act 1994, Sch 16.]

---

1. The Secretary of State may make orders under s 3 of the Public Health (Control of Diseases) Act 1984 assigning to a port health authority any of the functions, rights and liabilities of a local authority under Part I, or under the Control of Pollution Act 1974, or constituting a united district (s 28).

8–1296 34. Interpretation of Part I.   In this Part of this Act, unless the context otherwise requires,—

"animal" does not include bird or fish;

"construction regulations" means regulations with respect to the construction, lay-out or equipment of premises used as a slaughterhouse or knacker's yard;★

"council" includes a port health authority;

"district", in relation to the local authority of a London borough or the City of London, and in relation to the officers of such an authority, means the borough or the City, as the case may be and in relation to (*a*) a local authority who are the council of a Welsh county or county borough, and

    (*b*) the officers of such an authority, means that county or county borough;

"functions" includes powers and duties;

"horse" includes ass and mule;★

"knacker's yard" means any premises used in connection with the business of slaughtering, flaying or cutting up animals whose flesh is not intended for human consumption;★

"licence" means a licence under section 1 above authorising the use of any premises as a slaughterhouse or knacker's yard, and "knacker's yard licence" shall be construed accordingly;★

"local authority" has the meaning assigned to it by section 27 above and, in relation to any premises or to an application in respect of any premises, means the local authority within whose district the premises are situated;

"the Minister" means the Minister of Agriculture, Fisheries and Food[1];

"officer" includes servant;

"slaughterhouse" means a place for slaughtering animals whose flesh is intended for sale for human consumption, and includes any place available in connection therewith for the confinement of animals while awaiting slaughter there or for keeping or subjecting to any treatment or process, products of the slaughtering of animals there.

[Slaughterhouses Act 1974, s 34, as amended by the Local Government (Wales) Act 1994, Sch 16 and SI 1996/2235.]

★Definitions repealed in relation to England by SI 2005/2347 from 28 September 2005.

1. Also the Secretary of State for Wales (SI 1978/272). The functions of the Minister, so far as exercisable in relation to Wales, have been transferred to the National Assembly for Wales, by the National Assembly for Wales (Transfer of Functions) Order 1999, SI 1999/672, art 2, Sch 1 and SI 2004/3044, art 2 and Sch 1.

8–1297 35. Saving for port slaughterhouses and knackers' yards. Nothing in this Part of this Act shall apply to any slaughterhouse or knacker's yard forming part of an imported animals' wharf or landing place approved by the Minister under the Animal Health Act 1981 for the purpose of the landing of imported animals.

[Slaughterhouses Act 1974, s 35, as amended by the Animal Health Act 1981, Sch 5.]

PART II

SLAUGHTER OF ANIMALS

Provisions as to slaughter

8–1298 36–37. (*Repealed*).

8–1300 38. Regulations for securing humane conditions of slaughter in slaughterhouses and knackers' yards[1]. (1) The Minister may, after consultation with such organisations as appear to him to represent the interests concerned, make such regulations[2] as appear to him to be expedient for securing humane conditions and practices in connection with the slaughter, in slaughterhouses and knackers' yards, of horses, cattle, sheep, swine or goats; and such regulations may in particular—

    (*a*) prescribe requirements as to the construction, lay-out and equipment of premises used as slaughterhouses or knackers' yards;

    (*b*) prescribe conditions to be observed in connection with the confinement and treatment of horses, cattle, sheep, swine or goats while awaiting slaughter in such premises, and in connection with the slaughter there of such animals.

(2) Regulations under this section may make different provision in relation to different kinds of animals and in relation to premises used for different purposes in connection with the slaughter of animals and may—

    (*a*) so far as they are made for the purposes mentioned in subsection (1) (*a*) above, be made to apply subject to exceptions or modifications in relation to premises constructed or adapted for use before the date on which the regulations come into force;

    (*b*) in any case be made without applying, or applying subject to exceptions or modifications, in relation to slaughterhouses forming part of an imported animals' wharf or approved landing place for the purposes of the Animal Health Act 1981, or applying (with or without exceptions or modifications) only in relation to any such slaughterhouse of that description as may be specified in the regulations;

    (*c*) provide, subject to such limitations and safeguards, if any, as may be specified in the regulations, for the appropriate authority to grant in relation to particular premises, either unconditionally or subject to conditions, exemption from the operation of specific provisions of those regulations where it appears to the authority that compliance with those provisions cannot for the time being reasonably be required with respect to the premises or any activities carried on there;

    (*d*) provide for the regulations to come into force on different days fixed by, or by an order to be made by statutory instrument under, the regulations in respect of different classes or descriptions of premises and different areas, and for different provisions to come into force on different days;

and in paragraph (c) above "appropriate authority", except in relation to a slaughterhouse provided by a local authority, means a local authority, and in relation to a slaughterhouse so provided means the Minister.

(3) Regulations under this section may make provision corresponding (with or without modifications) with any of the provisions in force immediately before the commencement of the Slaughter of Animals (Amendment) Act 1954, under section 5(1) of the Protection of Animals Act 1911, section 4 of the Slaughter of Animals Act 1933 or section 1 of the Slaughter of Animals (Amendment) Act 1954.

(4) (*Repealed*).

(5) Regulations under this section may prescribe penalties for offences against the regulations, not exceeding a fine of **level 3** on the standard scale or imprisonment for a term of **three months** or both*, and may impose on the occupiers of premises to which the regulations apply responsibility for compliance with any of the provisions of the regulations.

(5A) Regulations under this section may require occupiers of premises used as slaughterhouses or knackers' yards to secure that the provisions of regulations under this section are complied with on the premises.

(6) Where a person convicted of any offence against regulations under this section (including a person so convicted by virtue of section 44[3] of the Magistrates' Courts Act 1980) is the holder of a licence under section 1 above in respect of the premises where the offence was committed, the court may, in addition to any other punishment, cancel the licence.

[Slaughterhouses Act 1974, s 38 as amended by the Magistrates' Courts Act 1980, Sch 7, the Animal Health Act 1981, Sch 5, the Criminal Justice Act 1982, ss 40 and 46, the Welfare of Animals at Slaughter Act 1991, s 1, the Deregulation and Contracting Out Act 1994, s 31 and Sch 9 and SI 1995/731.]

---

*Words repealed by the Criminal Justice Act 2003, Sch 27, from a date to be appointed.

1. Regulations may provide for any functions exercisable by local authorities to be transferred to the Minister of Agriculture, Fisheries and Food (in England) or the Secretary of State (in Scotland or Wales): Deregulation and Contracting Out Act 1994, s 31 and Sch 9.

2. See now the Welfare of Animals (Slaughter or Killing) Regulations 1995, SI 1995/731, made under s 2(2) of the European Communities Act 1972.

3. Aiders and abettors; see PART I: MAGISTRATES' COURTS, PROCEDURE, ante.

Licensing of slaughtermen

8–1301   **39–40.** (*Repealed*).

Enforcement and legal proceedings

8–1303   **42. Powers of entry[1].** (1) Subject to subsection (3) below, at any time when business is, or appears to be, in progress, or is usually carried on, in a slaughterhouse or knacker's yard, any officer of the Minister, or an officer appointed for the purpose by the local authority within whose district the slaughterhouse or knacker's yard is situate, may enter it for the purpose of ascertaining[2] whether there is or has been any contravention of this Part of this Act or of any regulations made under it.

(2) Any person who obstructs a person in the exercise of his powers under subsection (1) above shall be guilty of an offence and liable to a fine not exceeding **level 1** on the standard scale.

(3) Subsection (1) above shall not authorise entry into a slaughterhouse or knacker's yard which for the time being is, or is comprised in, an infected place within the meaning of the Animal Health Act 1981.

[Slaughterhouses Act 1974, s 42, as amended by the Animal Health Act 1981, Sch 5, the Criminal Justice Act 1982, ss 38 and 46 and the Deregulation and Contracting Out Act 1994, s 31 and Sch 9.]

---

1. Regulations may provide for any functions exercisable by local authorities to be transferred to the Minister of Agriculture, Fisheries and Food (in England) or the Secretary of State (in Scotland or Wales): Deregulation and Contracting Out Act 1994, s 31 and Sch 9.

2. Cf *R v Dobbins* (1883) 48 JP 182; *Duncan v Dowding* [1897] 1 QB 575, 61 JP 280.

8–1304   **43. Prosecutions and punishment of offences.** (1) All offences under this Part of this Act and regulations made under it shall be punishable on summary conviction.

(2)–(3) (*Repealed*).

[Slaughterhouses Act 1974, s 43 as amended by the Magistrates' Courts Act 1980, Sch 7, the Criminal Justice Act 1982, ss 38 and 46 and SI 1995/731.]

8–1305   **45. Interpretation of Part II.** In this Part of this Act, unless the context otherwise requires,—

"contravention" in relation to a provision of this Part of this Act or of any regulations made under it, includes a failure to comply with that provision;

"district", in relation to a local authority who are the council of a Welsh county or county borough, means that county or county borough;

"horse" includes ass and mule;

"knacker's yard" means any building, premises or place used in connection with the business of killing animals whose flesh is not intended for sale for human consumption;

"local authority" means the council of a Welsh county or county borough, of a district or London borough or the Common Council of the City of London;

"the Minister" means the Minister of Agriculture, Fisheries and Food[1];

"slaughterhouse" means any building, premises or place used in connection with the business of killing animals whose flesh is intended for sale for human consumption.

[Slaughterhouses Act 1974, s 45 amended by the Local Government (Wales) Act 1994, Sch 16.]

---

1. Also the Secretary of State for Wales (SI 1978/272). The functions of the Minister, so far as exercisable in relation to Wales, have been transferred to the National Assembly for Wales, by the National Assembly for Wales (Transfer of Functions) Order 1999, SI 1999/672, art 2, Sch 1.

Farriers (Registration) Act 1975
(1975 c 36)

8–1307   This Act, as amended by the Farriers (Registration) (Amendment) Act 1977 and the European Communities (Recognition of Qualifications and Experience) (Third General System) Regulations 2002, SI 2002/1597, provides for the registration of farriers, the control of their training and qualification, and maintenance of standards.

It is an offence under s 5 for a person wilfully to procure or attempt to procure the entry of his name in the register by a false or fraudulent representation or declaration.

Offences under s 16 comprise an unregistered person carrying out farriery, or adopting the description of "farrier" or "shoeing smith".

Offences under s 5 or 16 are punishable on summary conviction by a fine not exceeding level 3 on the standard scale.

There are savings in s 16 for apprentices, trainees, veterinary surgeons or veterinary practitioners, or persons rendering first aid in case of emergency to a horse. Provision is made for equal liability for employers failing to take all reasonable steps to prevent offences by employees, and for officers of a body corporate as well as the body corporate itself.

Dangerous Wild Animals Act 1976
(1976 c 38)

8–1308   **1. Licences.**   (1) Subject to section 5 of this Act, no person shall keep any dangerous wild animals[1] except under the authority of a licence granted in accordance with the provisions of this Act by a local authority[2].

(2) A local authority shall not grant a licence under this Act unless an application for it—

(*a*) specifies the species (whether one or more) of animal, and the number of animals of each species, proposed to be kept under the authority of the licence;

(*b*) specifies the premises[2] where any animal concerned will normally be held;

(*c*) is made to the local authority in whose area those premises are situated;

(*d*) is made by a person who is neither under the age of 18 nor disqualified under this Act from keeping any dangerous wild animal; and

(*e*) is accompanied by such fee as the authority may stipulate (being a fee which is in the authority's opinion sufficient to meet the direct and indirect costs which it may incur as a result of the application).

(3) A local authority shall not grant a licence under this Act unless it is satisfied that—

(*a*) it is not contrary to the public interest on the grounds of safety, nuisance or otherwise to grant the licence;

(*b*) the applicant for the licence is a suitable person to hold a licence under this Act;

(*c*) any animal concerned will at all times of its being kept only under the authority of the licence—

     (i) be held in accommodation which secures that the animal will not escape, which is suitable as regards construction, size, temperature, lighting, ventilation, drainage and cleanliness and which is suitable for the number of animals proposed to be held in the accommodation, and

     (ii) be supplied with adequate and suitable food, drink and bedding material and be visited at suitable intervals;

(*d*) appropriate steps will at all such times be taken for the protection of any animal concerned in case of fire or other emergency;

(*e*) all reasonable precautions will be taken at all such times to prevent and control the spread of infectious diseases;

(f) while any animal concerned is at the premises where it will normally be held, its accommodation is such that it can take adequate exercise.

(4) A local authority shall not grant a licence under this Act unless the application for it is made by a person who both owns and possesses, or proposes both to own or to possess, any animal concerned, except where the circumstances are in the authority's opinion exceptional.

(5) A local authority shall not grant a licence under this Act unless a veterinary surgeon[3] or veterinary practitioner[3] authorised by the authority to do so under section 3 of this Act has inspected the premises where any animal will normally be held in pursuance of the licence and the authority has received and considered a report by the surgeon or practitioner, containing such particulars as in the authority's opinion enable it to decide whether the premises are such that any animal proposed to be kept under the authority of the licence may suitably be held there, and describing the condition of the premises and of any animal or other thing found there.

(6) Subject to subsections (2) to (5) of this section, a local authority may grant or refuse a licence under this Act as it thinks fit, but where it decides to grant such a licence it shall specify as conditions of the licence—

(a) conditions that, while any animal concerned is being kept only under the authority of the licence,—

 (i) the animal shall be kept by no person other than such person or persons as is or are specified (whether by name or description) in the licence;
 (ii) the animal shall normally be held at such premises as are specified in the licence;
 (iii) the animal shall not be moved from those premises or shall only be moved from them in such circumstances as are specified in the licence;
 (iv) the person to whom the licence is granted shall hold a current insurance policy which insures him and any other person entitled to keep the animal under the authority of the licence against liability for any damage[4] which may be caused by the animal; and
 (v) the terms of any such policy shall be satisfactory in the opinion of the authority;

(b) conditions restricting the species (whether one or more) of animal, and number of animals of each species, which may be kept under the authority of the licence;

(c) a condition that the person to whom the licence is granted shall at all reasonable times make available a copy of the licence to any person entitled to keep any animal under the authority of the licence;

(d) such other conditions as in the opinion of the authority are necessary or desirable for the purpose of securing the objects specified in paragraphs (c) to (f) of subsection (3) of this section.

(7) Subject to subsection (6) of this section, a local authority may, in granting a licence under this Act, specify such conditions of the licence as it thinks fit.

(8) Where a local authority proposes to insert in a licence under this Act a provision permitting any animal to be, for any continuous period exceeding 72 hours, at premises outside the area of the authority, the authority shall consult the local authority in whose area those premises are situated.

(9) A local authority which grants a licence under this Act may at any time vary the licence by specifying any new condition of the licence or varying or revoking any condition of it (including any condition specified, or previously varied, under this subsection); but any condition of a licence specified by virtue of subsection (6) of this section may not be revoked and any condition specified by virtue of paragraph (a)(ii) of that subsection may not be varied.

(10) Where a local authority varies a licence under subsection (9) of this section, then—

(a) if the variation was requested by the person to whom the licence was granted, the variation shall take effect immediately after the authority decides to make it;

(b) in any other case, the variation shall not take effect until the person to whom the licence was granted has become aware of the variation and had a reasonable time to comply with it.

[Dangerous Wild Animals Act 1976, s 1.]

---

1. For meaning of "dangerous wild animal" see s 7(4) and the Schedule to this Act, post.
2. For meaning of "local authority" and "premises" see s 7(4), post.
3. For meaning of "veterinary surgeon" and "veterinary practitioner" see s 7(4), post.
4. For meaning of "damage" see s 7(4), post.

8–1309 2. Provisions supplementary to section 1. (1) Where—

(a) a person is aggrieved by the refusal of a local authority to grant a licence under this Act, or

(b) a person to whom such a licence had been granted is aggrieved by a condition of the licence (whether specified at the time the licence is granted or later) or by the variation or revocation of any condition of the licence,

he may appeal[1] to a magistrates' court; and the court may on such appeal give such directions with respect to the grant of a licence or, as the case may be, with respect to the conditions of the licence as it thinks proper, having regard to the provisions of this Act.

(2) Any licence under this Act shall (according to the applicant's requirements) relate to the calendar year in which it is granted or to the next following year.

In the former case, the licence shall come into force at the beginning of the day on which it is granted, and in the latter case it shall come into force at the beginning of the next following year.

(3) Subject to the provisions hereinafter contained with respect to cancellation, any licence under this Act shall remain in force until the end of the year to which it relates and shall then expire:

Provided that if application is made for a further licence before the said date of expiry the licence shall be deemed to be still in force pending the grant or refusal of the said application, and if it is granted the new licence shall commence from the date of the expiry of the last licence.

(4) In the event of the death of anyone to whom a licence had been granted under this Act the said licence shall continue in force for a period of twenty-eight days as if it had been granted to the personal representatives of the deceased and if application is made for a new licence within the said period the said licence shall be deemed to be still in force pending the grant or refusal of that application.

(5) Any person who contravenes the provisions of section 1(1) of this Act shall be guilty of an offence[2].

(6) If any condition of a licence under this Act is contravened or not complied with, then,—

(*a*) the person to whom the licence was granted, and

(*b*) any other person who is entitled to keep any animal under the authority of the licence and who was primarily responsible for the contravention or failure to comply,

shall, subject to subsection (7) of this section, be guilty of an offence[2].

(7) In any proceedings for an offence under subsection (6) of this section, it shall be a defence for the person charged to prove that he took all reasonable precautions and exercised all due diligence to avoid the commission of such an offence.

(8) *Scotland.*

[Dangerous Wild Animals Act 1976, s 2.]

---

1. Appeal will be by complaint (Magistrates' Courts Rules 1981, r 34, in PART I: MAGISTRATES' COURTS, PROCEDURE, ante).

2. For penalty see s 6, post.

8–1310 3. Inspection by local authority. (1) Subject to subsection (2) of this section, a local authority to which an application has been made for a licence under this Act, or which has granted such a licence, may authorise in writing any veterinary surgeon or veterinary practitioner or such other person as it may deem competent to do so to inspect any premises where any animal is proposed to be held in pursuance of a licence for which an application had been made under this Act, or where any animal is or may be held in pursuance of a licence which has been granted under this Act; and any person authorised under this section may, on producing their authority if so required, enter any such premises at all reasonable times and inspect them and any animal or other thing found there, for the purpose of ascertaining whether or not a licence should be granted or varied or whether an offence has been or is being committed against this Act.

(2) A local authority shall not give an authority under subsection (1) of this section to inspect premises situated outside its area unless it had obtained the approval of the local authority in whose area those premises are situated.

(3) The local authority may require the person who has applied for a licence under this Act or, as the case may be, to whom the licence concerned has been granted under this Act to pay the local authority the reasonable costs of the inspection.

(4) Any person who wilfully obstructs or delays any person in the exercise of his power of entry or inspection under this section shall be guilty of an offence[1].

[Dangerous Wild Animals Act 1976, s 3.]

---

1. For penalty, see s 6, post.

8–1311 4. Power to seize and to dispose of animals without compensation. (1) Where—

(*a*) an animal is being kept contrary to section 1(1) of this Act, or

(*b*) any condition of a licence under this Act is contravened or not complied with,

the local authority in whose area any animal concerned is for the time being may seize the animal, and either retain it in the authority's possession or destroy or otherwise dispose of it, and shall not be liable to pay compensation to any person in respect of the exercise of its powers under this subsection.

(2) A local authority which incurs any expenditure in exercising its powers under subsection (1)(*a*) of this section shall be entitled to recover the amount of the expenditure summarily as a civil debt[1] from any person who was at the time of the seizure a keeper of the animal concerned.

(3) A local authority which incurs any expenditure in exercising its powers under subsection (1)(*b*) of this section shall be entitled to recover the amount or the expenditure summarily as a civil debt[1] from the person to whom the licence concerned was granted.

[Dangerous Wild Animals Act 1976, s 4.]

1. See Magistrates' Courts Act 1980, s 58, in PART I: MAGISTRATES' COURTS, PROCEDURE, ante, for procedure to obtain order for payment of a civil debt, and ibid, s 96 for the enforcement of such order.

8–1312 5. Exemptions. The provisions of this Act shall not apply to any dangerous wild animal kept in—

(1) a zoo within the meaning of the Zoo Licensing Act 1981 for which a licence is in force (or is not for the time being required) under that Act[1];

(2) a circus[2];

(3) premises licensed as a pet shop under the Pet Animals Act 1951[3];

(4) a place which is a designated establishment within the meaning of the Animals (Scientific Procedures) Act 1986.

[Dangerous Wild Animals Act 1976, s 5, as amended by the Zoo Licensing Act 1981, s 22 and the Animals (Scientific Procedures) Act 1986, Sch 3.]

1. For the purpose of the said Act an animal shall be treated as kept in a zoo when it is elsewhere in the personal possession of the operator of the zoo, or of competent persons acting on his behalf (Zoo Licensing Act 1981 s 22(2)).

2. For meaning of "circus" see s 7(4) post.

3. Ante.

8–1313 6. Penalties. (1) Any person guilty of an offence under any provision of this Act shall be liable on summary conviction to a fine not exceeding **level 5** on the standard scale.

(2) Where a person is convicted of any offence under this Act or of any offence under the Protection of Animals Acts 1911 to 1964[1], the Protection of Animals (Scotland) Acts 1912 to 1964, the Pet Animals Act 1951[1], the Animal Boarding Establishments Act 1963[1], the Riding Establishments Acts 1964 and 1970[2], or the Breeding of Dogs Act 1973[3], the court by which he is convicted may cancel any licence held by him under this Act, and may, whether or not he is the holder of such a licence, disqualify[4] him from keeping any dangerous wild animal for such period as the court thinks fit.

(3) A court which has ordered the cancellation of a person's licence, or his disqualification, in pursuance of the last foregoing subsection may, if it thinks fit, suspend the operation of the order pending an appeal.

[Dangerous Wild Animals Act 1976, s 6, as amended by the Criminal Justice Act 1982, ss 38 and 46.]

1. Ante.

2. See ante.

3. See title DOGS, post.

4. A magistrates' court shall not in a person's absence impose any disqualification on him, except after an adjournment after convicting and before sentencing him (Magistrates' Courts Act 1980, s 11(4), in PART I: MAGISTRATES' COURTS, PROCEDURE, ante).

8–1314 7. Interpretation. (1) Subject to subsection (2) of this section, for the purposes of this Act a person is a keeper of an animal if he has it in his possession; and if at any time an animal ceases to be in the possession of a person, any person who immediately before that time was a keeper thereof by virtue of the preceding provisions of this subsection continues to be a keeper of the animal until another person becomes a keeper thereof by virtue of those provisions.

(2) Where an animal is in the possession of any person for the purpose of—

(a) preventing it from causing damage,

(b) restoring it to its owner,

(c) undergoing veterinary treatment, or

(d) being transported on behalf of another person,

the person having such possession shall not by virtue only of that possession be treated for the purposes of this Act as a keeper of the animal.

(3) In this Act expressions cognate with "keeper" shall be construed in accordance with subsections (1) and (2) of this section.

(4) In this Act, unless the context otherwise requires, the following expressions have the meanings hereby respectively assigned to them, that is to say—

"circus" includes any place where animals are kept or introduced wholly or mainly for the purpose of performing tricks or manœuvres[1];

"damage" includes the death of, or injury to, any person;

"dangerous wild animal" means any animal of a kind for the time being specified in the first column of the Schedule to this Act;

"local authority" means in relation to England a district council, a London borough council or the Common Council of the City of London, in relation to Wales, a county council or county borough council, and, in relation to Scotland, an islands council or a district council;

"premises" includes any place;

"veterinary practitioner" means a person who is for the time being registered in the supplementary veterinary register;

"veterinary surgeon" means a person who is for the time being registered in the register of veterinary surgeons;

(5) The second column of the Schedule to this Act is included by way of explanation only; in the event of any dispute or proceedings, only the first column is to be taken into account.
[Dangerous Wild Animals Act 1976, s 7, as amended by the Zoo Licensing Act 1981, s 22 and the Local Government (Wales) Act 1994, Sch 16.]

1. 'Circus' encompasses a travelling circus's winter quarters for which no licence is therefore required (*South Kesteven District Council v Mackie* [2000] 1 All ER 497, [2000] 1 WLR 1461, CA).

8–1315 8. *Power of Secretary of State to modify the Schedule.*

Section 7   SCHEDULE
                            KINDS OF DANGEROUS WILD ANIMALS

(As substituted by SI 1984/1111.)

8–1316   Note: see section 7(5) of this Act for the effect of the second column of this Schedule.

Scientific name of kind	*Common name or names*

MAMMALS
Marsupials

Dasyuridae of the species Sarcophilus harrisi	The Tasmanian devil
Macropodidae of the species Macropus fuliginosus, Macropus giganteus, Macropus robustus and Macropus rufus	Grey kangaroos, the euro, the wallaroo and the red kangaroo

Primates

Callitrichidae of the species of the genera Leontophithecus and Saguinus	Tamarins
Cebidae	New-world monkeys (including capuchin, howler, saki, spider, squirrel, titi, uakari and woolly monkeys and the night monkey (otherwise known as the douroucouli))
Cercopithecidae	Old-world monkeys (including baboons, the drill, colobus monkeys, the gelada, guenons, langurs, leaf monkeys, macaques, the mandrill, mangabeys, the patas and proboscis monkeys and the talapoin)
Indriidae	Leaping lemurs (including the indri, sifakas and the woolly lemur)
Lemuridae, except the species of the genus Hapalemur	Large lemurs (the broad-nosed gentle lemur and the grey gentle lemur are excepted)
Pongidae	Anthropoid apes (including chimpanzees, gibbons, the gorilla and the orang-utan)

Edentates

Bradypodidae	Sloths
Dasypodidae of the species Priodontes giganteus (otherwise known as Priodontes maximus)	The giant armadillo
Myrmecophagidae of the species Myrmecophaga tridactyla	The giant anteater

Rodents

Erithizontidae of the species Erithizon dorsatum	The North American porcupine
Hydrochoeridae	The capybara
Hystricidae of the species of the genus Hystrix	Crested porcupines

Carnivores

Ailuropodidae (Ailuridae)	The giant panda and the red panda
Canidae, except the species of the genera Alopex, Dusicyon, Otocyon, Nyctereutes and Vulpes and the species Canis familiaris	Jackals, wild dogs, wolves and the coyote (foxes, the raccoon-dog and the domestic dog are excepted)
Felidae, except the species Felis catus	The bobcat, caracal, cheetah, jaguar, lion, lynx, ocelot, puma, serval, tiger and all other cats (the domestic cat is excepted)
Hyaenidae except the species Proteles cristatus	Hyaenas (except the aardwolf)
Mustelidae of the species of the genera Arctonyx, Aonyx, Enhdra, Lutra (except Lutra lutra), Melogale, Mydaus, Pteronura and Taxidea and of the species Eira barbara, Gulo gulo, Martes pennanti and Mellivora capensis	Badgers (except the Eurasian badger), otters (except the European otter), and the tayra, wolverine, fisher and ratel (otherwise known as the honey badger)
Procyonidae	Cacomistles, raccoons, coatis, olingos, the little coatimundi and the kinkajou

Ursidae	Bears
Viverridae of the species of the genus Viverra and of the species Arctictis binturong and Cryptoprocta ferox	The African, large-spotted, Malay and large Indian civets, the binturong and the fossa

Pinnipedes

Odobenidae, Otariidae and Phocidae, except Phoca vitulina and Halichoerus grypus	The walrus, eared seals, and sealions and earless seals (the common and grey seals are excepted)

Elephants

Elephantidae	Elephants

Odd-toed ungulates

Equidae, except the species Equus asinus, Equus caballus and Equus asinus x Equus caballus	Asses, horses and zebras (the donkey, domestic horse and domestic hybrids are excepted)
Rhinocerotidae	Rhinoceroses
Tapiridae	Tapirs

Hyraxes

Procaviidae	Tree and rock hyraxes (otherwise known as dassies)

Aardvark

Orycteropidae	The aardvark

Even-toed ungulates

Antilocapridae	The Pronghorn
Bovidae, except any domestic form of the genera Bos and Bubalus, of the species Capra aegagrus (hircus) and the species Ovis aries	Antelopes, bison, buffalo, cattle, gazelles, goats and sheep (domestic cattle, goats and sheep are excepted)
Camelidae except the species Lama glama and Lama pacos	Camels, the guanaco and the vicugna (the domestic llama and alpaca are excepted)
Cervidae of the species Alces alces and Rangifer tarandus, except any domestic form of the species Rangifer tarandus	The moose or elk and the caribou or reindeer (the domestic reindeer is excepted)
Giraffidae	The giraffe and the okapi
Hippopotamidae	The hippopotamus and the pygmy hippopotamus
Suidae, except any domestic form of the species Sus scrofa	Old-world pigs (including the wild boar and the wart hog) (the domestic pig is excepted)
Tayassuidae	New-world pigs (otherwise known as peccaries)
Any hybrid of a kind of animal specified in the foregoing provisions of this column where one parent is, or both parents are, of a kind so specified	Mammalian hybrids with a parent (or parents) of a specified kind

BIRDS

Cassowaries and emu

Casuariidae	Cassowaries
Dromaiidae	The emu

Ostrich

Struthionidae	The ostrich

REPTILES

Crocodilians

Alligatoridae	Alligators and caimans
Crocodylidae	Crocodiles and the false gharial
Gavialidae	The gharial (otherwise known as the gavial)

Lizards and snakes

Colubridae of the species of the genera Atractaspis, Malpolon, Psammophis and Thelatornis and of the species Boiga dendrophila, Dispholidus typus, Rhabdophis subminiatus and Rhabdophis tigrinus	Mole vipers and certain rear-fanged venomous snakes (including the moila and montpellier snakes, sand snakes, twig snakes, the mangrove (otherwise known as the yellow-ringed catsnake), the boomslang, the red-necked keelback and the yamakagashi (otherwise known as the Japanese tiger-snake))
Elapidae	Certain front-fanged venomous snakes (including cobras, coral snakes, the desert black snake, kraits, mambas, sea snakes and all Australian poisonous snakes (including the death adders))
Helodermatidae	The gila monster and the (Mexican) beaded lizard
Viperidae	Certain front-fanged venomous snakes (including adders, the barba amarilla, the bushmaster, the copperhead, the fer-de-lance, moccasins, rattlesnakes and vipers)

INVERTEBRATES
Spiders

Ctenidae of the species of the genus Phoneutria	Wandering spiders
Dipluridae of the species of the genus Atrax	The Sydney funnel-web spider and its close relatives
Lycosidae of the species Lycosa raptoria	The Brazilian wolf spider
Sicariidae of the species of the genus Loxosceles	Brown recluse spiders (otherwise known as violin spiders)
Theridiidae of the species of the genus Latrodectus	The black widow spider (otherwise known as redback spider) and its close relatives

Scorpions

Buthidae	Buthid scorpions

Animal Health Act 1981[1]
(1981 c 22)

PART I[2]
GENERAL

General powers of Ministers to make orders and to authorise regulations

8–1317   1. General powers of Ministers[3] to make orders[4]. The Ministers may make such orders[4] as they think fit—

(a) generally for the better execution of this Act, or for the purpose of in any manner preventing the spreading of disease[5]; and

(b) in particular for the several purposes set out in this Act, and for prescribing and regulating the payment and recovery of expenses in respect of animals[6].

[Animal Health Act 1981, s 1.]

---

1. This Act consolidates the Diseases of Animals Act 1935, the Diseases of Animals Act 1950, the Ponies Act 1969, the Rabies Act 1974 and the Diseases of Animals Act 1975.

The Animal Health Act 2002 makes various amendments to the Animal Health Act 1981 principally as to slaughter, disease control, powers of entry and inspection, the preparation of biosecurity guidance, the annual review of import controls and the making of a national contingency plan. The 2002 Act also inserts a new offence in the 1981 Act in relation to causing specified diseases.

Sections 19–22 of the Act came into force on Royal Assent. Sections 1–15, 17 and Sch 1 came into force on 14 January 2003; s 18 came into force on 24 March, 2003, and s 16 came into force on 1 July 2003: Animal Health Act 2002 (Commencement) Order 2002, SI 2002/3044.

2. Part I contains ss 1–14.

3. The functions of the Minister, so far as exercisable in relation to Wales, have been transferred to the National Assembly for Wales, by the National Assembly for Wales (Transfer of Functions) Order 1999, SI 1999/672, art 2, Sch 1 and SI 2004/3044, art 2 and Sch 1.

4. Section 95 contains saving provisions for existing orders. The Control of Dogs Order 1992 is contained in title DOGS, post and the Rabies (Importation of Dogs, Cats and Other Mammals) Order 1974 is contained in this title, post.

The following orders, similarly saved, have effect:

Foot and Mouth Disease (Packing Materials), SR & O 1925/1178 amended by SR & O 1926/42;
Miscellaneous Provisions, SR & O 1927/290 amended by SR & O 1938/197, SI 1976/919 and SI 1992/1361;
Pleuro-Pneumonia, SR & O 1928/205 amended by SR & O 1938/195, SI 1977/944;
Cattle Plague, SR & O 1928/206 amended by SR & O 1938/194 and SI 1977/944;
Miscellaneous Provisions, SR & O 1938/197;
Psittacosis or Ornithosis, SI 1953/38;
Markets (Protection of Animals), SI 1964/1055 amended by SI 1965/1981;
Seizure of Carcases, etc, SI 1964/1255 amended by SI 1972/2041 and SI 1983/346;
Hares (Control of Importation), SI 1965/2040 amended by SI 1990/2371;
Export of Horses (Veterinary Examination), SI 1966/507 amended by SI 1995/2922;
Export of Horses (Excepted Cases), SI 1969/1742;
Export of Horses (Protection), SI 1969/1784;
Foot and Mouth Disease (Infected Areas) (Vaccination), SI 1972/1509 (revoked in relation to England by SI 2006/182);
Rabies (Control), SI 1974/2212 amended by SI 1994/1716, SI 1995/2922 and SI 2002/882 (Wales);
Transit of Animals (Road and Rail), SI 1975/1024 amended by SI 1988/815, SI 1993/3304, SI 1994/3249, SI 1995/11, SI 1997/1480, SI 2000/1618 (England) and SI 2001/2662 (Wales);
Importation of Animals, SI 1977/944 amended by SI 1990/2371, SI 1992/1361 and 3159, SI 1995/1760 and 2922, SI 2000/1618 (England) and SI 2001/2662 (Wales);
Approved Disinfectants, SI 1978/32 as amended by SI 1993/3086, SI 1997/2347, SI 2001/641(W), SI 2003/1428 (England), SI 2004/2891(E), SI 2005/583 (W) and 1908 (E) and SI 2006/182 (E);
Importation of Equine Animals, SI 1979/1701 amended by SI 1990/2371;
Importation of Birds, Poultry and Hatching Eggs, SI 1979/1702 amended by SI 1990/2371;
Importation of Hay and Straw, SI 1979/1703 amended by SI 1990/2371;
Importation of Embryos, Ova and Semen, SI 1980/12 amended by SI 1984/1326 and SI 1994/2920;
Importation of Animal Products and Poultry Products, SI 1980/14 amended by SI 1980/1934, SI 1981/1238, SI 1982/948, SI 1990/2371, SI 1993/1331 and SI 1994/2920;
Importation of Animal Pathogens, SI 1980/1212 amended by SI 1993/3250;
Importation of Processed Animal Protein, SI 1981/677 amended by SI 1982/459 and SI 1990/2371.
The following orders have been made under section 1—

Export of Animals (Protection), SI 1981/1051;

Warble Fly, SI 1982/234 amended by SI 1985/328, SI 1987/1601 and SI 1989/244;

Aujesky's Disease, SI 1983/344 amended by SI 1994/3141, SI 1995/11 and SI 1995/2922;

Foot and Mouth Disease, SI 1983/1950 amended by SI 1993/3119 and SI 2001/571 (England), 572 (Wales), 658 (Wales), 680 (England), 968 (Wales), 974 (England), 1033 (amended by 1034) (Wales), 1078 (England) (amended by 1241) 1406 (Wales) 1407 (England) 1509 (Wales) 1514 (England), 1862 (England), 1874 (Wales), 2238 (England), 2735 (England), 2981 (Wales), 2813 (Wales), 2814 (England), 2994 (England), 3140 (England), 3145 (Wales), 3686 and 4029 (England) (revoked in relation to England by SI 2006/182);

Tuberculosis, SI 1984/1943 amended by SI 1990/1869 and SI 1995/2922 (revoked in relation to England by SI 2005/3446);

Warble Fly (Infected Areas), SI 1985/1542;

Importation of Salmonid Viscera, SI 1986/2265;

Zoonoses, SI 1988/2264 amended by SI 1988/2299, SI 1989/2326 and SI 1997/2964;

Zoonoses, SI 1989/284;

Poultry (Seizure of Hatching Eggs) 1990, SI 1990/232;

Welfare of Horses at Markets (and Other Places of Sale) 1990, SI 1990/2627;

Anthrax 1991, SI 1991/2841 amended by SI 1995/1855 and SI 1995/2922;

Specified Diseases (Notification and Slaughter) 1992, SI 1992/3159, SI 1994/2627, SI 1995/2922 and SI 2003/130 and 326;

Shellfish and Specified Fish (Third Country Imports) 1993, SI 1993/3301;

Poultry Breeding Flocks and Hatcheries 1993, SI 1993/1898;

Bovine Animals (Records, Identification and Movement) 1995, SI 1995/12 amended by SI 1995/1686, 2922, SI 1997/1901 and SI 1998/871;

Equine Viral Arteritis 1995, SI 1995/1755 amended by SI 1995/2922;

Animals (Post Import Control) Regulations 1995, SI 1995/2439;

Specified Bovine Offal 1995, SI 1995/1928 amended by SI 1995/3246;

Sheep and Goats (Records, Identification and Movement) Order 1996, SI 1996/28 (revoked in so far as it applies to England by SI 2000/2027);

Specified Diseases (Notification) 1996, SI 1996/2628 amended by SI 2003/130 and 326;

Enzootic Bovine Leukosis 1997, SI 1997/757 (revoked in so far as it applies to England by SI 2000/2056);

Brucellosis 1997, SI 1997/758 (revoked in so far as it applies to England by SI 2000/2055);

Welfare of Animals (Transport) 1997, SI 1997/1480 amended by SI 1998/2537, SI 1999/1622, SI 2000/1618 (England) and SI 2001/2662 (Wales),

Specified Animal Pathogens 1998, SI 1998/463;

Welfare of Animals (Staging points) Order 1998, SI 1998/2537;

Animal By-products 1999, SI 1999/646 amended by SI 2001/1704 (England), and 1735 (Wales) and SI 2003/2756 (Wales);

Welfare of Animals (Transport) (Electronic Route Plans Pilot Schemes) (England) Order 2000, SI 2000/646;

Sheep and Goats Identification (England) 2000, SI 2000/2027 amended by SI 2001/281;

Brucellosis (England) 2000, SI 2000/2055;

Enzootic Bovine Leukosis (England) 2000, SI 2000/2056;

Movement of Animals (Restrictions) 2002, SI 2002/3229;

Bluetongue 2003, SI 2003/130;

Bluetongue (Wales) 2003, SI 2003/326;

Movement of Animals (Restrictions) (Wales) 2003, SI 2003/399;

Diseases of Poultry (England) 2003, SI 2003/1078;

Diseases of Poultry (Wales) 2003, SI 2003/1079;

Disease Control (England) 2003, SI 2003/1729 amended by SI 2005/3100 and SI 2006/182;

Transport of Animals (Cleansing and Disinfection) (England) (No 3) 2003, SI 2003/1724;

Disease Control (Wales) 2003, SI 2003/1966;

Transport of Animals (Cleansing and Disinfection) (Wales) (No 3) 2003, SI 2003/1968;

Classical Swine Fever (England) Order 2003, SI 2003/2329;

Classical Swine Fever (Wales) 2003, SI 2003/2456;

Pigs (Records, Identification and Movement) 2003, SI 2003/2632;

African Swine Fever 2003, SI 2003/2913;

African Swine Fever (Wales) Order 2003, SI 2003/3273;

Pigs (Records, Identification and Movement) (Wales), SI 2004/996;

Animal Gatherings (England), SI 2004/1202;

Animal Gatherings (Wales), SI 2004/1803;

Sheep and Goats (Records, Identification and Movement) (England) Order 2005, SI 2005/3100;

Tuberculosis (England) Order 2005, SI 2005/3446 amended by SI 2006/140;

Foot-and Mouth Disease (England) Order 2006, SI 2006/182.

5. For the meaning of "disease", see s 88, post.

6. For the meaning of "animals", see s 87, post.

8–1318   2. Local authority regulations.   The Ministers may make such orders as they think fit for authorising a local authority to make regulations for any of the purposes—

  (a) of this Act, or

  (b) of an order of the Minister,

subject to such conditions, if any, as the Ministers for the purpose of securing uniformity and the due execution of this Act, think fit to prescribe.

[Animal Health Act 1981, s 2.]

Eradication and prevention of disease

8–1319   3. Expenditure for eradication.   (1) The Ministers may, with the Treasury's approval, expend such sums as they think fit with the object of eradicating as far as practicable diseases of animals (including horses) in Great Britain.

In this subsection "disease" is not restricted by its definition in this Act.

(2) To obtain information required for the purposes of subsection (1) above the Ministers may authorise in writing any veterinary inspector or other officer of the Ministry to inspect animals (including horses).

(3) A person so authorised may, for the purpose of any inspection to be carried out by him—

(*a*) at all reasonable times, and
(*b*) upon production of his authority on demand,

enter on any land or premises and apply such tests and take such samples as he considers necessary.

(4) No payment may be made under subsection (1) which was capable of being made under section 3 of the Diseases of Animals Act 1950 (payments for the eradication of bovine tuberculosis) before the expiry of that section.
[Animal Health Act 1981, s 3.]

8–1320 4. Offences as to s 3. (1) A person who knowingly or recklessly makes any false statement for the purpose of obtaining for himself or any other person any sum payable under section 3 above shall (unless in the case of an indictable offence he is indicted for the offence) be liable on summary conviction[1]—

(*a*) to a fine not exceeding **level 3** on the standard scale; or
(*b*) to imprisonment for a term not exceeding **3 months**; or
(*c*) to both such imprisonment and fine.

(2) A person who obstructs or impedes any person duly authorised under subsection (2) of section 3 to make any inspection shall be liable on summary conviction[1]—

(i) to a fine not exceeding **level 3** on the standard scale, or
(ii) to imprisonment for a term not exceeding **one month**; or
(iii) to both such imprisonment and fine.
[Animal Health Act 1981, s 4, as amended by the Criminal Justice Act 1982, ss 35, 38 and 46.]

---

1. Appeal to the Crown Court under this section may be taken by the person convicted in accordance with the Magistrates' Courts Act 1980, s 108, in PART I: MAGISTRATES' COURTS, PROCEDURE, *ante*. No appeal under this section lies in accordance with s 78, *post*.

8–1321 5. *Veterinary services and therapeutic substances.*

8–1322 6. Eradication areas and attested areas. *Power of the Ministers to make orders declaring areas to be eradication areas or attested areas, and regulating the movement of cattle*

8–1322A 6A. *Biosecurity guidance.*

8–1322B 6B. *Biosecurity compliance.*

Cleansing and movement

8–1323 7. Cleansing and disinfection. *Power of the Ministers to make orders[1] regulating cleansing and disinfection.*

---

1. A number of the orders made, or deemed to be made, under s 1 and listed in the notes thereto were also made under this section, see particularly: SI 1978/32 amended by SI 1991/631 and SI 2006/182 (E) (Approved Disinfectants).

8–1324 8. Movement generally. (1) The Ministers may make such orders[1] as they think fit—

(*a*) for prescribing and regulating the marking of animals;
(*b*) for prohibiting or regulating the movement of animals, and the removal of carcases, fodder, litter, dung and other things, and for prescribing and regulating the isolation of animals newly purchased;
(*c*) for prescribing and regulating the issue and production of licences respecting movement and removal of animals and things;
(*d*) for prohibiting, absolutely or conditionally, the use, for the carrying of animals or for any connected purpose, of a vessel, aircraft, vehicle, or pen or other place in respect of which or the use of which a penalty has been recovered from any person for an offence against this Act;
(*e*) for prohibiting or regulating the holding of markets, fairs, exhibitions and sales of animals.

(2) A person is guilty of an offence[2] against this Act if, where an order of the Minister absolutely or conditionally prohibits the use of a vessel, aircraft, vehicle or pen, or other place, for the carrying of animals or for any connected purpose, he, without lawful authority or excuse, proof of which shall lie on him, does anything so prohibited.
[Animal Health Act 1981, s 8.]

1. A number of the orders made, or deemed to be made, under s 1 and listed in the notes thereto were also made under this section, see particularly: SI 1952/1291 amended by SI 1958/1272 (Horses (Sea-Transport)); SI 1975/1024 amended by SI 1988/815, SI 1993/3304, SI 1994/3429, SI 1995/11 and 1997/1480, (Transit of Animals (Road and Rail)); SI 1981/1051 (Export of Animals (Protection)); SI 1990/760 amended by SI 1991/1155 (Movement of Animals (Restrictions)) and SI 1996/28 (Sheep and Goats (Records, Identification and Movement)). In addition various Interim Measures Orders are made from time to time.

2. For penalty, see s 75, post.

Transport by sea and air

8–1325   9. Prohibition in specific cases.   The Ministers may make such orders as they think fit for prohibiting the conveyance of animals by any specified vessel or aircraft to or from any port or aerodrome in the United Kingdom or by any specified vehicle through the tunnel system as defined in the Channel Tunnel Act 1987 for such time as the Ministers may consider expedient.
[Animal Health Act 1981, s 9, as amended by SI 1990/2371.]

8–1326   10. Importation.   (1) The Ministers[1] may by orders[2] make such provision as they think fit for the purpose of preventing the introduction or spreading of disease into or within Great Britain through the importation of—

(*a*)   animals and carcases;

(*b*)   carcases of poultry and eggs; and

(*c*)   other things, whether animate or inanimate, by or by means of which it appears to them that any disease might be carried or transmitted.

(2)–(8)   *Supplementary provisions with respect to orders under this section.*
[Animal Health Act 1981, s 10, as amended by SI 1993/1813.]

1. Regulations have also been made under s 2(2) of the European Communities Act 1972.

The Pet Travel Scheme (Pilot Arrangements) (England) Order 1999, SI 1999/3443 amended by SI 2000/1298 and 1641, SI 2001/6, SI 2002/1011 and 2850 and SI 2004/828 (all the preceding regulations have been revoked in relation to England by the Non Commercial Movement of Pet Animals (England) Regulations 2004, SI 2004/2363) makes provision for an exemption from the requirements for pet cats and pet dogs imported into England to be placed into quarantine under the Rabies (Inportation of Dogs, Cats and Other Mammals) Order 1974, SI 1974/2211.

2. A number of the orders made, or deemed to be made, under s 1 and listed in the notes thereto were also made under this section, see particularly: SI 1965/2040 amended by SI 1990/2371 (Hares); SI 1977/944 amended by SI 1990/2371, SI 1992/1361 and 3159, SI 1995/1760 and 2922 (Importation of Animals); SI 1979/1701 amended by SI 1990/2371 (Equine Animals); SI 1979/1702 amended by SI 1990/2371 (Birds, Poultry and Hatching Eggs); SI 1979/1703 amended by SI 1990/2371 (Hay and Straw); SI 1980/12 amended by SI 1984/1326, SI 1990/2371 and SI 1994/2920 (Embryos, Ova and Semen); SI 1980/14 amended by SI 1980/1934, 1981/1238, 1982/948, SI 1990/2371, SI 1993/1331 and SI 1994/2920 (Animal Products and Poultry Products); SI 1980/1212 amended by SI 1993/3250 (Animal Pathogens); SI 1981/677 amended by SI 1982/459 and SI 1990/2371 (Processed Animal Protein); SI 1986/2285 (Salmonid Viscera); SI 1993/14 (Post Import Control); SI 1993/3301 (Shellfish and Specified Fish).

The Rabies Virus Order 1979, SI 1979/135, provides for control of rabies virus. Contravention of, or non-compliance with, any provision of the Order or of any licence or notice served under the Order (or causing or permitting such contravention or non-compliance) is punishable on summary conviction by a maximum fine of £1,000. See also the Rabies (Importation of Dogs, Cats and other Mammals) Order 1974, post.

8–1326A   10A. Annual review of import controls.   (1) The Ministers shall prepare a report during each financial year which will—

(*a*)   review all activities of government departments, the Food Standards Agency, local authorities, customs, police authorities and other relevant public agencies directed to the prevention of the introduction of disease into or within England and Wales through the importation of animal products and matter, whether animate or inanimate, and other things;

(*b*)   identify the nature, origin and quantity of such animal products and matter and stating whether the product or matter was destined for personal or commercial consumption;

(*c*)   assess the making of any orders under section 10 of this Act;

(*d*)   assess the effectiveness of any action taken under an order made under section 10 of this Act; and

(*e*)   propose such further action as may, on the basis of advice given to the Ministers by suitably qualified individuals appointed as scientific advisers to the Ministers, be required to further reduce the risk of disease being imported.

(2)   The Ministers shall lay their report before Parliament and the National Assembly for Wales at the end of each financial year.
[Animal Health Act 1981, s 10A, as inserted by the Animal Health Act 2002, s 17.]

8–1327   11. Export to member States.   The Minister may by order[1] make provision in the interests of animal health or of human health, for regulating the exportation from Great Britain to a member State of animals or animal or poultry carcases, and in particular—

(*a*)   for prohibiting exportation without such certificate or licence as may be prescribed by the order, and

(*b*) as to the circumstances in which and conditions on which a certificate or licence may be obtained.
[Animal Health Act 1981, s 11.]

1. Orders have been made under s 2(2) of the European Communities Act 1972, see para **8–810**.

8–1328 **12.** *Export quarantine stations.*

Control of dogs, and preventive treatment of sheep

8–1329 **13. Orders as to dogs.** (1) The Minister may make such orders[1] as he thinks fit for prescribing and regulating—

(*a*) the muzzling of dogs, and the keeping of dogs under control; and
(*b*) so far as is supplemental to paragraph (*a*) above—

   (i) the seizure, detention, and disposal (including slaughter) of stray dogs and of dogs not muzzled, and of dogs not being kept under control; and
   (ii) the recovery from the owners of dogs of the expenses incurred in respect of their detention.

(2) The appropriate Minister may make such orders as he thinks fit—

(*a*) for prescribing and regulating the wearing by dogs, while in a highway or in a place of public resort, of a collar with the name and address of the owner inscribed on the collar or on a plate or a badge attached to it;
(*b*) with a view to the prevention of worrying of animals (including horses), for preventing dogs or any class of dogs from straying during all or any of the hours between sunset and sunrise;
(*c*) for providing that any dog in respect of which an offence is being committed against provisions made under either paragraph (*a*) or (*b*) above, may be seized and treated as a stray dog under the enactments relating to dogs;
(*d*) for prescribing and regulating

   (i) the seizure, detention and disposal (including slaughter) of stray dogs and of dogs not muzzled; and
   (ii) the recovery from the owners of dogs of the expenses incurred in respect of their detention.

(3) An order under subsection (2)(*a*) above may include provision for the execution and enforcement of the order by the officers of local authorities (and not by the police force for any area).
(4) In subsection (3) above "local authority" and "officer" have the same meaning as in section 149 of the Environmental Protection Act 1990.
[Animal Health Act 1981, s 13, as amended by the Environmental Protection Act 1990, s 151.]

1. See the Control of Dogs Order, 1992, title DOGS, post.

8–1330 **14. Prevention of sheep scab.** (1) The Ministers may make such orders[1] as they think fit for prescribing, regulating and securing the periodical treatment of all sheep by effective dipping or by the use of some other remedy for sheep scab.
(2) An inspector of the Minister and, if so authorised by order of the Minister, an inspector of the local authority, may—

(*a*) subject to the directions of the authority by which he was appointed, and
(*b*) for the purposes of any order or regulation under subsection (1) above,

enter any premises and examine any sheep on those premises.
(3) The owner and the person in charge of any sheep shall comply with all reasonable requirements of the inspector as to the collection and penning of the sheep and afford all other reasonable facilities for the examination of the sheep by the inspector.
[Animal Health Act 1981, s 14.]

1. See the Sheep Scab Order 1992, SI 1992/45, the Sheep Scab Order 1997, SI 1997/968, and the Sheep Scab (National Dip) Order 1990, SI 1990/1557 amended by SI 1991/1879.

PART II[1]
DISEASE

Outbreak

8–1330A **14A. National contingency plan.** (1) The appropriate authority must prepare a document (the national contingency plan) indicating the arrangements the authority intends to put in place for the purpose of dealing with any occurrence of—

(*a*) foot-and-mouth disease;
(*b*) such other disease as the authority by order specifies.

(2) After preparing a draft of the national contingency plan the appropriate authority—

(a) must send a copy of the draft to such persons and organisations as the authority thinks are representative of those having an interest in the arrangements;

(b) must consider any representations made to the authority about the draft by such persons and organisations;

(c) may amend the draft accordingly.

(3) After the appropriate authority has proceeded under subsection (2) the authority must—

(a) lay the plan before Parliament (unless subsection (9) applies);

(b) publish it in such manner as the authority thinks likely to bring it to the attention of persons who may be affected by the arrangements.

(4) The appropriate authority must from time to time (but not less frequently than at intervals of one year) review the plan and if the authority thinks it appropriate revise the plan.

(5) Subsections (2) and (3) apply to a revision of the plan as they apply to its preparation.

(6) The power to make an order[1] must be exercised by statutory instrument.

(7) The instrument is subject to annulment in pursuance of a resolution of either House of Parliament (unless subsection (9) applies).

(8) The appropriate authority is—

(a) the Secretary of State in relation to England;

(b) the Secretary of State and the National Assembly for Wales acting jointly in relation to Wales (except for the purposes of subsection (1)(b));

(c) the National Assembly for Wales in relation to Wales for the purposes of subsection (1)(b).

(9) This subsection applies to a plan prepared in relation to Wales.

(10) It is immaterial that anything done for the purposes of subsections (1) to (3) (except the making of an order under subsection (1)(b)) is done before the passing of the Animal Health Act 2002.

[Animal Health Act 1981, s 14A as inserted by the Animal Health Act 2002, s 18.]

---

1. The Avian Influenza and Newcastle Disease (Contingency Planning) (England) Order 2003, SI 2003/2036 and the Avian Influenza and Newcastle Disease (Contingency Planning) (Wales) Order 2005, SI 2005/2840 have been made.

8–1330B 14B. Duty to consider vaccination. (1) In relation to any occurrence of foot-and-mouth disease the Secretary of State must consider what is the most appropriate means of preventing the spread of the disease.

(2) In particular he must consider whether in relation to the occurrence treating animals with serum or vaccine is more appropriate than any other means of preventing the spread of the disease.

[Animal Health Act 1981, s 14B as inserted by the Animal Health Act 2002, s 15.]

8–1331 15. Separation and notice. (1) Any person having in his possession or under his charge an animal[2] affected with disease[2] shall—

(a) as far as practicable keep that animal separate from animals not so affected; and

(b) with all practicable speed give notice of the fact of the animal being so affected to a constable of the police force for the police area in which the animal is so affected[3].

(2) Any person who knows or suspects that an animal (whether in captivity or not) is affected with rabies shall give notice of that fact to a constable unless—

(a) he believes on reasonable grounds that another person has given notice under this section in respect of that animal, or

(b) he is exempted from doing so by an order under section 1 above,

and, if the animal is in his possession or under his charge, shall as far as practicable keep the animal separate from other animals.

(3) The constable to whom notice is given shall forthwith give information of it to such person or authority as the Ministers by order direct.

(4) *Power of the Ministers to make orders[4] as to notices.*

(5) Subsections (1) to (4) above do not have effect in relation to poultry, but the Ministers may by order prescribe and regulate—

(a) the separation of diseased poultry from poultry not affected with disease; and

(b) the notification of disease in, or illness of, poultry.

(6) *Fees.*

(7) A person is guilty of an offence[5] against this Act who, without lawful authority or excuse, proof of which shall lie on him, fails where required by this Act or by an order of the Minister—

(a) to keep an animal separate so far as practicable; or

(b) to give notice of disease with all practicable speed.

[Animal Health Act 1981, s 15.]

1. Part II contains ss 15–36.
2. For meaning of "animals" and "disease", see ss 87 and 88, respectively, *post*.
3. Contravention of this section is an offence (s 15(7), *post*). For penalty, see s 75, *post*.
4. The Orders listed to s 1, *ante* include Orders made under this section.
5. For penalty, see s 75, *post*.

8–1332   16. Treatment after exposure to infection.   (1) For the purpose of preventing the spread of disease, the Ministers may cause to be treated with serum or vaccine, or with both serum and vaccine, any animal or bird—

(*a*) which has been in contact with a diseased animal or bird, or
(*b*) which appears to the Ministers to be or to have been in any way exposed to the infection of disease; or
(*c*) which is in an infected area.

(2) The powers conferred by this section shall be construed as extending to the taking of any action—

(*a*) which is requisite for enabling the appropriate treatment to be administered, or
(*b*) which is otherwise required in connection with that treatment,

and for the purpose of exercising those powers any inspector may, subject to production of his authority on demand, enter any land or premises.

(3) If a justice of the peace is satisfied on sworn information in writing that the first condition is satisfied and that the second or third condition is satisfied he may issue a warrant authorising an inspector to enter any land or premises, if necessary using reasonable force, for the purpose mentioned in subsection (2).

(4) The information must include—

(*a*) a statement as to whether any representations have been made by the occupier of the land or premises to an inspector concerning the purpose for which the warrant is sought;
(*b*) a summary of any such representations.

(5) The first condition is that there are reasonable grounds for an inspector to enter the land or premises for that purpose.

(6) The second condition is that each of the following applies to the occupier of the premises—

(*a*) he has been informed of the decision to seek entry to the premises and of the reasons for that decision;
(*b*) he has failed to allow entry to the premises on being requested to do so by an inspector;
(*c*) he has been informed of the decision to apply for the warrant.

(7) The third condition is that—

(*a*) the premises are unoccupied or the occupier is absent and (in either case) notice of intention to apply for the warrant has been left in a conspicuous place on the premises, or
(*b*) an application for admission to the premises or the giving of notice of intention to apply for the warrant would defeat the object of entering the premises.

(8) Subsections (9) to (12) apply to an inspector who enters any land or premises by virtue of subsection (2) or under a warrant issued under subsection (3).

(9) The inspector may take with him—

(*a*) such other persons as he thinks necessary to give him such assistance as he thinks necessary;
(*b*) such equipment as he thinks necessary.

(10) The inspector may require any person on the land or premises who falls within subsection (11) to give him such assistance as he may reasonably require for the purpose mentioned in subsection (2).

(11) The following persons fall within this subsection—

(*a*) the occupier of the premises;
(*b*) a person appearing to the inspector to have charge of animals on the premises;
(*c*) a person appearing to the inspector to be under the direction or control of a person mentioned in paragraph (*a*) or (*b*).

(12) If the inspector enters any unoccupied premises he must leave them as effectively secured against entry as he found them.

(13) If the inspector enters any premises by virtue of a warrant issued under subsection (3) he must at the time of entry—

(*a*) serve a copy of the warrant on the occupier of the premises, or (if the occupier is not on the premises)
(*b*) leave a copy of the warrant in a conspicuous place on the premises.

(14) A warrant issued under subsection (3) remains in force for one month starting with the date of its approval by the justice of the peace, which date shall be clearly visible on the warrant.

(15) A warrant issued under subsection (3) must be executed only at a reasonable hour unless the inspector thinks that the case is one of urgency.

(16) In relation to any premises to which entry is obtained by virtue of a warrant under this section the Secretary of State must retain for a period of not less than 12 months beginning with the day after entry—

(a) a copy of the warrant;
(b) a copy of any record of the steps taken to effect entry to the premises and the actions taken on the premises by the inspector and any other person entering the premises with him.

(17) A person commits an offence if—

(a) he is required to give assistance under subsection (10), and
(b) he fails to give it.

[Animal Health Act 1981, s 16, as amended by the Animal Health Act 2002, s 7.]

8–1332A 16A. Slaughter of vaccinated animals. (1) This section applies to any animal which has been treated with vaccine for the purpose of preventing the spread of foot-and-mouth disease or such other disease as the Secretary of State may by order[1] specify.

(2) The Secretary of State may cause to be slaughtered any animal to which this section applies.

(3) The power conferred by this section extends to taking any action—

(a) which is required to enable any such animal to be slaughtered, or
(b) which is otherwise required in connection with the slaughter.

(4) For any animal slaughtered under this section the Secretary of State must pay compensation in accordance with subsections (5) and (6).

(5) In the case of an animal treated with vaccine for the purpose of preventing the spread of foot-and-mouth disease—

(a) if the animal was affected with foot-and-mouth disease the compensation is the value of the animal immediately before it became so affected;
(b) in any other case the compensation is the value of the animal immediately before it was slaughtered.

(6) In the case of an animal treated with vaccine for the purpose of preventing the spread of a disease specified by order under subsection (1) the compensation is of such an amount as may be prescribed by order of the Secretary of State.

(7) In arriving at a value under subsection (5) above no account is to be taken of the fact that the animal had been treated with vaccine as mentioned in that subsection.

(8) No order may be made under subsection (1) unless a draft of the order has been laid before Parliament and approved by a resolution of each House.

(9) A statutory instrument containing an order under subsection (6) is subject to annulment in pursuance of a resolution of either House of Parliament.

[Animal Health Act 1981, s 16A as inserted by the Animal Health Act 2002, s 5.]

---

1. The Avian Influenza and Newcastle Disease (England and Wales) Order 2003, SI 2003/1734 has been made.

Infection

8–1333 17. Powers as to infected place and areas. (1) The Ministers may make such orders[1] as they think fit for prescribing the cases in which places and areas are to be declared to be infected with a disease and the authority, mode, and conditions by, in, and on which declarations in that behalf are to be made, and their effect and consequences, and their duration and discontinuance, and other connected matters.

(2) Every place or area so declared infected shall be an infected place or area for the purposes of this Act.

(3) A notice served in pursuance of directions of the Minister or of a local authority by virtue of an order made under this section shall be conclusive evidence to all intents of the existence or past existence or cessation of the disease, or of the error, and of any other matter on which the notice proceeds.

(4) (*Repealed*).

[Animal Health Act 1981, s 17, as amended by the Animal Health and Welfare Act 1984, s 4 and Sch 2.]

---

1. The Orders listed to s 1 include orders made under this section. Other orders made under this section include: Diseases of Poultry Declaratory (Infected Areas) (England) (No 2) Order 2005, SI 2005/2116.

8–1334 18. *Other provisions as to infected places and areas.*

8–1335 19. Destruction of foxes etc on rabies infection. (1) An order[1] under section 17 above prescribing the cases in which areas are to be declared to be infected with rabies may include provision for the destruction in an area declared to be so infected, by persons authorised in accordance with the order, of foxes and such other wild mammals as may be prescribed by the order (not in either case being animals held in captivity).

(2)–(3) *Supplementary provisions as to orders under this section.*
[Animal Health Act 1981, s 19.]

---

1. See the Rabies (Control) Order 1974, SI 1974/2212.

8–1336   **20.** *Additional provisions under section 17 on rabies infection.*

8–1337   **21. Destruction of wild life on infection other than rabies.**   (1) This section—

(a)   applies to any disease other than rabies which is for the time being a disease for the purposes of section 1(*a*) above; and

(b)   is without prejudice to any powers conferred by other provisions of this Act on the Minister, the appropriate Minister and the Ministers.

(2) The Minister, if satisfied in the case of any area—

(a)   that there exists among the wild members of one or more species in the area a disease to which this section applies which has been or is being transmitted from members of that or those species to animals of any kind in the area, and

(b)   that destruction of wild members of that or those species in that area is necessary in order to eliminate, or substantially reduce the incidence of, that disease in animals of any kind in the area,

may, subject to the following provisions of this section, by order provide for the destruction of wild members of that or those species in that area.

(3) Before making an order under his section the Minister shall consult with the Nature Conservancy Council for the area to which it will apply, and every order so made shall specify—

(a)   the area to which it applies
(b)   the disease to which it applies; and
(c)   the one or more species to which it relates.

(4) An order under this section providing for the destruction of wild members of one or more species in any area may provide for authorising the use for that purpose of one or more methods of destruction that would otherwise be unlawful.

The order shall not authorise such use unless the Minister is satisfied that use of the method or methods in question is the most appropriate way of carrying out that destruction, having regard to all relevant considerations and, in particular, the need to avoid causing unnecessary suffering to wild members of the species in question.

(5) An order under this section may include provision—

(a)   for ensuring that destruction of wild members of any species to which the order relates is properly and effectively carried out, and in particular—

   (i)   for preventing persons from taking into captivity harbouring, concealing or otherwise protecting wild members of any such species with intent to prevent their destruction, or

   (ii)   in any other way obstructing or interfering with anything which has been, is being or is to be done or used in connection with that destruction

(b)   for regulating the ownership and disposal of the carcases of members of any such species destroyed in the area to which the order relates.

(6) Before commencing the destruction of wild members of a species on any land within an area to which an order under this section applies the Minister shall take all reasonable steps to inform—

(a)   the occupier of the land, and
(b)   any other person who may be there,

of his intention to carry out that destruction and of the methods of destruction to be used.

It shall be the Minister's duty to ensure that destruction is carried out on any such land in as safe a manner as is possible in all the circumstances.

(7) Where an order under this section is in force, the Minister shall have power to take such measures (including the erection of fences or other obstacles) as he considers appropriate—

(a)   for preventing the movement of living creatures into or out of the area or any part of the area to which the order applies while destruction of wild members of any species to which the order relates is being carried out in the area; and

(b)   where destruction of wild members of any such species has been or is to be carried out in any part of that area, for preventing the recolonisation of that part by members of that species for as long as he considers necessary to prevent reappearance among them of the disease to which the order applies.

(8) As soon as may be after the Minister is satisfied, in the case of any land, that any measures affecting that land which have been taken in connection with an order under this section are no longer necessary, he shall—

(a) remove from the land anything placed or erected on it; and
(b) take such other steps as are reasonably practicable to reinstate the land.

(9) In this section and section 22 below—

"animals" includes horses,
"Nature Conservancy Council" means English Nature, Scottish Natural Heritage or the Countryside Council for Wales,
"species" means any species of bird or mammal, except man,

and references to wild members of any species in an area are references to members of the species in the area that are neither domesticated nor held in captivity.

(10) A statutory instrument containing an order under this section shall be subject to annulment in pursuance of a resolution of either House of Parliament.
[Animal Health Act 1981, s 21, as amended by the Environmental Protection Act 1990, Sch 9 and the Countryside and Rights of Way Act 2000, Sch 8.]

8–1338 22. Powers of entry etc for section 21. (1) In relation to any disease to which section 21 above applies the following persons are authorised officers for the purposes of this section—

(a) an officer of the appropriate Minister,
(b) a veterinary inspector, and
(c) any person who, not being such an officer or inspector, is authorised by the appropriate Minister to exercise the powers conferred by this section,

and subsection (9) of section 21 applies to this section.

(2) Where an authorised officer has reasonable grounds for suspecting, in the case of any area, that there exists among the wild members of any species in the area a disease to which section 21 applies, he may enter any land in the area and—

(a) take samples of the wild members of that species, or of their excreta, or of any materials (whether or not forming part of the land) with which wild members of that species may have been in contact;
(b) carry out any other investigations which he considers necessary for the purpose of determining, as regards that species and that disease, whether an order under section 21 should be made in respect of the whole or part of the area in question.

(3) An authorised officer may at any time enter any land in the area to which an order under section 21 applies for any of the following purposes—

(a) to carry out the destruction of any wild members of a species to which the order relates that may be on that land;
(b) to take any such measures as are mentioned in subsection (7) of that section;
(c) to ascertain, as regards any wild members of a species to which the order relates, whether destruction has been effectively carried out.

(4) Where in pursuance of an order under section 21 destruction of wild members of any species to which the order relates has been carried out on any land in the area to which the order applies, then, for the purpose of ascertaining—

(a) whether the land has been or is being recolonised by wild members of that species, and, if so,
(b) whether there exists among them the disease to which the order applies (or, if the order has been revoked, to which it previously applied),

an authorised officer may enter the land and take such samples of or relating to that species as are mentioned in paragraph (a) of subsection (2) above; but the powers conferred by this subsection shall not be exercisable at any time more than 2 years after the revocation of the order in question.

(5) Nothing in this section authorises any person to enter a dwellinghouse.

(6) A person entering any land in the exercise of powers conferred on him by this section shall, if so required by the owner or occupier or person in charge of the land—

(a) produce to him some duly authenticated document showing his authority; and
(b) state in writing his reasons for entering.

(7) Without prejudice to subsection (6) above, an authorised officer—

(a) shall not demand admission as of right to any land forming part of a nature reserve (within the meaning of section 15 of the National Parks and Access to the Countryside Act 1949) maintained or managed by a Nature Conservancy Council under section 132 of the Environmental Protection Act 1990 unless 7 days' notice of the intended entry has been given to the Council; and
(b) in exercising any of his powers under subsection (2), (3) or (4) above on any such land shall, as far as possible, do so in accordance with such reasonable requirements for minimising damage to flora, fauna or geological or physiographical features within the reserve as may have been notified by the Council to the appropriate Minister.

(8) The preceding provisions of this section are without prejudice to any powers conferred on inspectors or others by or by virtue of any other provision of this Act.
[Animal Health Act 1981, s 22, as amended by the Environmental Protection Act 1990, Sch 9.]

8–1339   23. *Orders as to infected places and areas*[1]

---

1. The Orders listed to s 1 include orders made under this section.

8–1340   25. Movement of diseased or suspected animals. *Power of the Ministers to make orders*[1] *with respect to diseased or suspected animals.*

---

1. The Orders listed to s 1, ante include Orders made under this section. The Transit of Animals (General) Order 1973, SI 1973/1377, is designed to prevent injury and unnecessary suffering to animals during loading, carriage and unloading. See also the Transit of Animals (Road and Rail) Order 1975, SI 1975/1024, amended by SI 1979/1013; a contravention or non-compliance is an offence against this Act; for penalty, see s 75, post.

8–1341   26. Pleuro-pneumonia or foot-and-mouth disease found in transit. *Power of the Ministers to make orders*[1] *respecting animals found to be affected with pleuro-pneumonia or foot-and-mouth disease.*

---

1. The Pleuro-Pneumonia Order 1928, SR & O 1928/205 amended by SR & O 1938/195 and SI 1977/944 has been made.

8–1342   27. Exclusion of strangers. (1) A person owning or having charge of any animals in a place or area declared infected with any disease may affix, at or near the entrance to a building or enclosure in which the animals are, a notice forbidding persons to enter the building or enclosure without the permission mentioned in the notice.
(2) Thereupon it shall not be lawful for any person, not having by law a right of entry or way into, on, or over that building or enclosure, to enter or go into, on, or over the building or enclosure without that permission.
[Animal Health Act 1981, s 27.]

8–1343   28. Seizure of diseased or suspected animals. The Ministers may make such orders[1] as they think fit—

(a) for prescribing and regulating the seizure, detention and disposal of a diseased or suspected animal exposed, carried, kept or otherwise dealt with in contravention of an order of the Minister; and

(b) for prescribing and regulating the liability of the owner or consignor or consignee of such animal to the expenses connected with its seizure, detention and disposal.
[Animal Health Act 1981, s 28.]

---

1. See the Brucellosis Order 1981, SI 1981/1455 and the Warble Fly Order 1982, SI 1982/234 amended by SI 1985/328.

8–1343A   28A. Deliberate infection. (1) A person commits an offence if without lawful authority or excuse (proof of which shall lie on him) he knowingly does anything which causes or is intended to cause an animal to be infected with a disease specified in Schedule 2A.
(2) A person guilty of an offence under subsection (1) is liable—

(a) on summary conviction, to imprisonment for a term not exceeding six months or to a fine not exceeding the statutory maximum or to both;

(b) on conviction on indictment, to imprisonment for a term not exceeding two years or to a fine or to both.

(3) The Secretary of State may by order amend Schedule 2A.
(4) A statutory instrument containing an order under subsection (3) is subject to annulment in pursuance of a resolution of either House of Parliament.
[Animal Health Act 1981, s 28A as inserted by the Animal Health Act 2002, s 12(1).]

8–1343B   28B. Deliberate infection: disqualification. (1) If a person is convicted of an offence under section 28A the court may by order disqualify him, for such period as it thinks fit, from keeping or dealing in—

(a) any animals, or
(b) any animals of a specified kind.

(2) The court may suspend the operation of the order—

(a) for such period as it thinks necessary to enable arrangements to be made for the keeping of any animals to which the disqualification relates;
(b) pending an appeal.

(3) A person who is disqualified under subsection (1) may from time to time apply to the court which imposed the disqualification to remove it or vary it.

(4) On an application under subsection (3) the court may by order—

(*a*) refuse the application,

(*b*) remove the disqualification, or

(*c*) vary the disqualification to apply it only to such animals or kind of animals as it specifies.

(5) In considering an application under subsection (3) the court may have regard to—

(*a*) the nature of the offence in respect of which the disqualification was imposed;

(*b*) the character of the applicant;

(*c*) his conduct since the disqualification was imposed.

(6) The first application under subsection (3) must not be made before the end of the period of one year starting with the date the disqualification starts.

(7) A further application must not be made before the end of the period of one year starting with the date of the court's last order.

(8) For the purposes of this section keeping or dealing in an animal includes—

(*a*) having custody or control of an animal;

(*b*) being concerned in the management or control of a body (whether or not incorporated) whose activities include keeping or dealing in animals.

[Animal Health Act 1981, s 28B as inserted by the Animal Health Act 2002, s 12(1).]

Risk to human health

8–1344   29. Control of zoonoses.   (1) This section shall have effect with a view to reducing the risk to human health from any disease of, or organism carried in, animals; and the Ministers may by order[1] designate any such disease or organism which in their opinion constitutes such a risk as is mentioned in this subsection.

In this section "disease" is not restricted by its definition in this Act.

(2) Where any disease or organism is for the time being designated under this section, the Ministers may by order—

(*a*) provide for any provision of this Act which has effect in relation to the disease to have that effect in relation to the disease so designated subject to such modifications as may be specified in the order;

(*b*) apply any provision if this Act, subject to any modifications so specified, in relation to the presence of the organism in an animal as if the presence of the organism were a disease to which this Act applied.

(3) The Ministers may by order make provision for requiring a person who, in such circumstances as are specified by the order, knows or has reason to suspect that an animal of such description as is specified in the order is or was—

(*a*) affected with a disease designated under this section, or

(*b*) a carrier of an organism so designated,

to furnish to such person and in such form and within such period as are specified in the order such information relating to the animal as is so specified.

[Animal Health Act 1981, s 29.]

---

1. See the Zoonoses Order 1975, SI 1975/1030.

8–1345   30. Provisions supplemental to section 29.   (1) If it appears to the appropriate Minister that a person may have information relating to—

(*a*) an animal affected with a disease designated under section 29 above, or

(*b*) an animal which is a carrier of an organism so designated,

that Minister may by notice in writing require him to furnish to such person and in such form and within such period as are specified in the notice such information relating to the animal as he possesses and is so specified.

In this section "disease" is not restricted by its definition in this Act.

(2) Where a veterinary inspector has reason to believe that an animal such as is mentioned in subsection (1) above is or has been on any land he may, on producing if so required evidence of his authority—

(*a*) enter the land and make such tests and take such samples of any animal, feeding stuff, litter, dung, vessel, pen, vehicle or other thing whatsoever which is on or forms part of the land as he thinks appropriate for the purpose of ascertaining whether such an animal is or has been on the land; and

(*b*) require the owner or person having charge of any animals on the land to take such reasonable steps as the inspector may specify for the purpose of collecting or restraining them so as to facilitate the exercise in relation to them of the powers conferred on the inspector by paragraph (*a*) above.

(3) A person is guilty of an offence[1] against this Act who—

(*a*) fails to comply with a requirement imposed on him by virtue of section 29 and this section; or

(*b*) in purported compliance with a requirement to furnish information which is imposed on him by virtue of section 29 and this section, knowingly or recklessly furnishes information which is false in a material particular.

[Animal Health Act 1981, s 30.]

---

1. For penalty, see s 75, post.

Slaughter

8–1346   31. Slaughter in certain diseases.   Schedule 3 to this Act has effect as to the slaughter of animals in relation to—

(*a*) cattle plague;
(*b*) pleuro-pneumonia;
(*c*) foot-and-mouth disease;
(*d*) swine-fever; and
(*e*) diseases of poultry.

[Animal Health Act 1981, s 31.]

8–1347   32. Slaughter in other diseases.   The Minister[1] may cause to be slaughtered any animal which—

(*a*) is affected or suspected of being affected with any disease to which this section applies; or
(*b*) has been exposed to the infection of any such disease.

[Animal Health Act 1981, s 32—summarised.]

---

1. The Minister may make orders; the orders listed to s 1, ante include orders made under this section.

8–1347A   32A. Slaughter to prevent disease.   (1) The Secretary of State may by order amend Schedule 3 for the purpose of—

(*a*) authorising or requiring the slaughter of animals to be caused with a view to preventing the spread of disease other than foot-and-mouth disease;

(*b*) requiring the payment of compensation in respect of animals slaughtered by virtue of the order[1].

(2) An order under this section may include—

(*a*) amendments corresponding to those made by section 1 of the Animal Health Act 2002;

(*b*) amendments as to slaughter in relation to any disease not referred to in Schedule 3 (apart from the order);

(*c*) supplementary or incidental provisions (including amendments of provisions other than Schedule 3).

(3) No order may be made under this section unless a draft of the order has been laid before Parliament and approved by a resolution of each House.

[Animal Health Act 1981, s 32A as inserted by the Animal Health Act 2002, s 2(1).]

---

1. The Avian Influenza and Newcastle Disease (England and Wales) Order 2003, SI 2003/1734 has been made.

8–1347B   32B. Disease control (slaughter) protocol.   (1) This section applies to a power exercisable by the Secretary of State under—

(*a*) paragraph 3(1)(*c*) of Schedule 3;

(*b*) such other provision of that Schedule (as amended by an order[1] under section 32A(1)(*a*)) as the Secretary of State by order specifies;

(*c*) such other provisions of this Act relating to the control of disease as the Secretary of State by order[1] specifies.

(2) The Secretary of State must prepare a document (the disease control (slaughter) protocol) indicating—

(*a*) the purposes for which any power to which this section applies will be exercised;

(*b*) the principal factors to be taken into account in deciding whether to exercise the power;

(*c*) the procedure to be followed in deciding whether in any circumstances or description of circumstances the power is to be exercised, which shall include the application of such methods of detecting disease in animals as may be available;

(*d*) the procedure to be followed by persons who have functions in relation to the exercise of the power;

(e) the means by which a particular decision to exercise the power may be reviewed.

(3) After preparing a draft of the disease control (slaughter) protocol the Secretary of State—

(a) must send a copy of the draft to such persons and organisations as he thinks are representative of those having an interest in the exercise of the power;

(b) must consider any representations made to him about the draft by such persons and organisations;

(c) may amend the draft accordingly.

(4) After the Secretary of State has proceeded under subsection (3) he must publish the protocol in such manner as he thinks appropriate.

(5) The Secretary of State must from time to time review the protocol and if he thinks it appropriate revise the protocol.

(6) Subsections (2) to (4) apply to a revision of the protocol as they apply to its preparation.

(7) The power to make an order must be exercised by statutory instrument subject to annulment in pursuance of a resolution of either House of Parliament.

(8) It is immaterial that anything done for the purposes of subsections (2) to (4) is done before the passing of the Animal Health Act 2002.

[Animal Health Act 1981, s 32B as inserted by the Animal Health Act 2002, s 3.]

---

1. The Avian Influenza and Newcastle Disease (Biosecurity Guidance and Disease control (Slaughter) Protocol) (England and Wales) Order 2003, SI 2003/2035 has been made.

8–1347C 32C. Protocol: exercise of powers. (1) A power to which section 32B applies must not be exercised unless the protocol mentioned in that section has been published and has not been withdrawn.

(2) Any act which is done in contravention of subsection (1) is done without lawful authority.

(3) If a person who has any function in relation to the exercise of a power to which section 32B applies fails to act in accordance with the protocol he is not by reason only of that failure liable in any civil or criminal proceedings.

(4) But the protocol is admissible in evidence in such proceedings and a court may take account of any failure to act in accordance with it in deciding any question in the proceedings.

[Animal Health Act 1981, s 32C as inserted by the Animal Health Act 2002, s 3.]

8–1347D 32D. Explanation of preventive slaughter. (1) This section applies to a power exercisable by the Secretary of State under—

(a) paragraph 3(1)(c) of Schedule 3;

(b) any other provision of that Schedule as amended by an order under section 32A(1)(a).

(2) The Secretary of State must not exercise a power to which this section applies unless before he first exercises the power in relation to any description of circumstances he publishes his reasons in relation to the circumstances of that description—

(a) for the exercise of the power;

(b) for not exercising his power under section 16 to cause animals to be treated with serum or vaccine.

(3) If the Secretary of State does not comply with subsection (2) in relation to any description of circumstances anything done in connection with the exercise of the power in such circumstances must be taken to have been done without lawful authority.

[Animal Health Act 1981, s 32D as inserted by the Animal Health Act 2002, s 4.]

8–1348 33–34. *Additional staff expenses; slaughter and compensation generally.*

Carcases etc liable to spread disease

8–1349 35. Seizure and disposal of carcases etc. (1) The Ministers may by order make such provision[1]—

(a) for the seizure of anything, whether animate or inanimate, by or by means of which it appears to them that any disease to which this subsection applies might be carried or transmitted, and

(b) for the destruction, burial, disposal or treatment of anything seized under the order,

as they may think expedient for preventing the spread of any such disease.

(1A) Subsection (1) above does not authorise provision for the seizure of any animal; but such an order may provide for the seizure of carcases and of anything obtained from or produced by an animal.

In this subsection, "animal" includes anything that may, by virtue of an order under section 87 below, be included for any of the purposes of this Act in the definition of animals or of poultry contained in that section, and "carcases" is to be construed accordingly.

(2) Subsection (1) above applies to the diseases in the case of which powers of slaughter are exercisable under this Act, that is to say—

(*a*)　to cattle plague, pleuro-pneumonia, foot-and-mouth disease, swine fever and transmissible spongiform encephalopthies, and any disease within the meaning of section 32 above to which that section for the time being applies and any disease in respect of which an order under section 32A is in force; and

(*b*)　to any disease as defined in relation to poultry by or under section 88 below.

(3)　The Ministers may make such orders as they think fit—

(*a*)　for prescribing and regulating the destruction, burial, disposal or treatment of carcases of animals dying while diseased or suspected;

(*b*)　for prescribing and regulating the destruction, burial or disposal of anything seized under subsection (1);

(*c*)　for prohibiting or regulating the digging up of carcases which have been buried.

(4)　A person is guilty of an offence[2] against this Act who, without lawful authority or excuse, proof of which shall lie on him—

(*a*)　throws or places, or causes or suffers to be thrown or placed, into any river, stream, canal, navigation, or other water, or into the sea within 4.8 kilometres of the shore, the carcase of an animal which has died of disease, or been slaughtered as diseased or suspected; or

(*b*)　digs up, or causes to be dug up, a carcase buried under the direction of the Minister or of a local authority or of a receiver of wreck.

[Animal Health Act 1981, s 35 as amended by the Animal Health and Welfare Act 1984, s 1 and the Animal Health Act 2002, s 2.]

1.　See article 15 of the Animals (Miscellaneous Provisions) Order 1927, SR & O 1927/290 amended by SR & O 1938/197, SI 1959/1335, 1974/1185 and 1976/919 and the Diseases of Animals (Seizure) Order 1993, SI 1993/1685.

2.　For penalty, see s 75, post.

PART III[1]

WELFARE AND EXPORT

Care

8–1350　37. Prevention of suffering.　(1)　The Ministers may make such orders[2] as they think fit for the purpose of protecting animals from unnecessary suffering—

(*a*)　during inland transit[3], including transit by an aircraft on a flight beginning and ending in Great Britain; or

(*b*)　while exposed for sale; or

(*c*)　while awaiting removal after being exposed for sale.

(2)　The Ministers may make such orders as they think fit—

(*a*)　for ensuring for animals carried by sea or by air proper ventilation during the passage and on landing; and

(*b*)　for protecting them from unnecessary suffering during the passage and on landing.

[Animal Health Act 1981, s 37.]

1.　Part III contains ss 37–49.

2.　A number of the orders made, or deemed to be made, under s 1 and listed in the notes thereto were also made under this section; see also the Poultry (Exposure for Sale) Order 1937, SR & O 1937/554 amended by SI 1988/851 and the Welfare of Poultry (Transport) Order 1988, SI 1988/851.

3.　This section refers only to the carriage of animals while in United Kingdom territorial waters or airspace; as to how this affects extra-territorial conduct, and cases where some animals die in transit, see *Air-India v Wiggins* [1980] 2 All ER 593, [1980] 1 WLR 815 (relating to the Transit of Animals (General) Order 1973, art 5(2)).

8–1351　38. Food and water.　(1)　The Ministers may make such orders[1] as they think fit for ensuring for animals a proper supply of food and water—

(*a*)　for any period in which the animals are detained; and

(*b*)　during their passage by sea or by air and on landing.

(2)　The following bodies—

(*a*)　The Boards established by the Transport Act 1962,

(*b*)　Transport for London, and

(*c*)　every railway company,

shall to the satisfaction of the appropriate Minister provide food and water, or either of them, at such railway stations as the appropriate Minister by general or specific description directs, for animals carried, or about to be or having been carried, on the railway of any of those bodies, and the additional provisions of Schedule 4 to this Act have effect accordingly.

In this subsection and in Schedule 4—

(i)　references to the bodies mentioned in paragraphs (*a*) and (*b*) include in the case of those mentioned in paragraph (*a*) wholly-owned subsidiaries of those bodies and in the case of

Transport for London, any of its subsidiaries (within the meaning of the Greater London Authority Act 1999);

(ii) "railway company" includes a person working a railway under lease or otherwise.

[Animal Health Act 1981, s 38 as amended by the London Regional Transport Act 1984, Sch 6 and amended by SI 2003/1615.]

---

1. A number of the orders made, or deemed to be made, under s 1 and listed in the notes thereto were also made under this section.

Export

8–1352 39. Export of animals; generally. (1) The Ministers may by order[1] provide in the interests of animal welfare for regulating the exportation from Great Britain of animals, and in particular—

(a) for prohibiting exportation without such certificate or licence as may be prescribed by the order; and

(b) as to the circumstances in which and conditions on which a certificate or licence may be obtained.

(2) Without prejudice to the generality of subsection (1) above, an order under this section may include provision for requiring persons proposing to export animals from Great Britain to furnish information about—

(a) the intended ultimate destination of the animals;

(b) the arrangements for conveying them to that destination; and

(c) any other matters which may be specified in the order.

[Animal Health Act 1981, s 39.]

---

1. The Export of Animals (Protection) Order 1981, SI 1981/1051, has been made.

Export of horses other than those defined as ponies

8–1353 40. Restriction on export of horses. (1) It is an offence against this Act to ship or attempt to ship any horse (which for the purpose of this section does not include a horse defined by this Act to be a pony) in any vessel or aircraft from any port or aerodrome in Great Britain to any port or aerodrome outside the British Islands unless the horse—

(a) immediately before shipment has been examined by a veterinary inspector appointed by the Minister for the purpose of conducting examinations under this section, and

(b) has been certified in writing by the inspector to comply with the conditions mentioned in subsection (2) below,

but this subsection shall not apply in such cases as may be prescribed by order[1] of the Ministers.

A statutory instrument containing an order under this subsection shall be subject to annulment in pursuance of a resolution of either House of Parliament.

(2) The conditions referred to in subsection (1) above are that the horse—

(a) is capable of being conveyed to the port or aerodrome outside the British Islands and disembarked without cruelty; and

(b) is capable of being worked without suffering.

(3) Where the inspector is satisfied that the horse is of one of the categories set out in the first column of the following table the conditions to be complied with shall include the condition that in the inspector's opinion the horse—

(a) is not more than 8 years of age; and

(b) is of not less value than the amount specified in respect of it in the second column of that table, or such other amount as may be prescribed by order of the Ministers.

TABLE

	£
A heavy draft horse	715
A vanner, mule or jennet	495
An ass	220

(4) Subsection (3) above shall not apply in the case of any horse where the inspector is satisfied—

(a) that it is intended to use the horse as a performing animal; or

(b) that the horse is registered in the stud book of a society for the encouragement of horse-breeding recognised by the Ministers, and is intended to be used for breeding or exhibition; or

(*c*) that the horse is a foal at foot accompanying such a horse as is referred to in paragraph (*b*) above.
[Animal Health Act 1981, s 40.]

---

1. See the Export of Horses (Excepted Cases) Order 1969, SI 1969/1742.

Export of horses defined as ponies

8–1354   41. Restriction on export of ponies.   (1) It is an offence[1] against this Act to ship or attempt to ship any pony in any vessel or aircraft from any port or aerodrome in Great Britain to any port or aerodrome outside the British Islands unless—

(*a*) the appropriate Minister is satisfied that the pony is intended for breeding, riding or exhibition and—

   (i)   it is not of less value than £300, or

   (ii) in the case of a pony not exceeding 122 centimetres in height other than a pony of the Shetland breed not exceeding 107 centimetres in height, it is not of less value than £220, or

   (iii) in the case of such a pony of the Shetland breed, it is not of less value than £145, or

   (iv) such other value in any of those cases as may be prescribed by order of the Ministers; and

(*b*) immediately before shipment the pony has been individually inspected by a veterinary inspector and has been certified in writing by the inspector to be capable of being conveyed to the port or aerodrome to which it is to be shipped, and disembarked, without unnecessary suffering.

(2) Without prejudice to paragraph (*b*) of subsection (1) above, a veterinary inspector shall not certify a pony to be capable of being conveyed and disembarked as described in that subsection if—

(*a*) being a mare, it is in his opinion heavy in foal, showing fullness of udder or too old to travel; or

(*b*) being a foal, it is in his opinion too young to travel.
[Animal Health Act 1981, s 41.]

---

1. For penalty, see s 75, post.

8–1355   42. Restriction on export of registered ponies.   It is an offence[1] against this Act to ship or attempt to ship a registered pony in any vessel or aircraft from any port or aerodrome in Great Britain to any port or aerodrome outside the British Islands unless there has first been obtained from the secretary of a society in whose stud book the pony is registered a certificate ("the export certificate") that the pony is registered with that society.

For the purposes of this section the expression "registered pony" means a pony registered in—

(*a*) the Arab Horse Society Stud Book,

(*b*) the National Pony Society Stud Book,

(*c*) the British Palomino Society Stud Book, or

(*d*) the British Spotted Horse and Pony Society Stud Book, or in the stud book of any of the following native breed societies, namely, English Connemara, Dales, Dartmoor, Exmoor, Fell, Highland, New Forest, Shetland and Welsh.
[Animal Health Act 1981, s 42.]

---

1. For penalty, see s 75, post.

8–1356   43. Regulation of export of ponies.   The Ministers shall by order[1] make such provision as they think necessary or expedient for the following purposes—

(*a*) for prohibiting the export of ponies by sea or air from any place in Great Britain to any place outside the British Islands unless such ponies are rested immediately before being loaded in the vessel or aircraft in which they are to be carried;

(*b*) for regulating and prescribing the premises at which and the periods during which ponies are to be so rested;

(*c*) for prescribing and regulating the cleansing and supervision of such premises and the provision at them of clean and sufficient bedding and adequate supplies of fodder and water.
[Animal Health Act 1981, s 43.]

---

1. See art 13 of the Export of Horses (Protection) Order 1969, SI 1969/1784.

Other provisions as to export of horses

8–1357   44. Slaughter on examination or inspection.   If any horse examined under section 40(1) above or inspected under section 41(1) above is found by the veterinary inspector—

(*a*) to be in such a physical condition that it is cruel to keep it alive, or

(b)   to be permanently incapable of being worked without suffering,

the inspector shall forthwith slaughter it (or cause it to be slaughtered) with a mechanically operated instrument suitable and sufficient for the purpose, and no compensation shall be made to the owner of that animal.
[Animal Health Act 1981, s 44.]

8–1358   45. Marking of horses certified for export.   (1) A veterinary inspector may, for the purposes of identification, mark a horse certified by him under section 40(1) above or section 41(1) above in such manner as the Ministers may by order prescribe.

(2) A person who, with a view to evading the provisions of section 40 above or section 41 above, marks a horse—

(a)   with the prescribed mark, or
(b)   with any mark so nearly resembling it as to be calculated to deceive,

is guilty of an offence[1] against this Act.
[Animal Health Act 1981, s 45.]

---

1. For penalty, see s 75, post.

8–1359   46. Slaughter of injured horses.   (1) If any horse shipped from any port in Great Britain to any port outside the British Isles has a limb broken or is otherwise seriously injured while on board so as to be incapable of being disembarked without cruelty—

(a)   the master of the vessel shall forthwith cause the animal to be slaughtered; and
(b)   every vessel on which a horse is so shipped shall carry a proper killing instrument, to be approved by the Ministers for that purpose.

(2) It is the duty of the owner and master of every such vessel to see that the vessel is provided with such an instrument, and the master, if so required by an inspector, shall produce the instrument for his inspection.
[Animal Health Act 1981, s 46.]

8–1360   47. Exemption of thoroughbreds in transit.   Sections 40 and 41 and 46 above shall not apply in the case of shipment of any thoroughbred horse certified in writing by a steward or the secretary of the Jockey Club—

(a)   to have arrived in Great Britain not more than one month before the date of shipment for the purpose of being run in a race; or
(b)   to be shipped for the purpose of being run in a race; or
(c)   to be shipped in order to be used for breeding purposes.
[Animal Health Act 1981, s 47.]

8–1361   48. Certificates.   Where—

(a)   a certificate is given under section 40(1), section 41(1) or section 47 above, or
(b)   an export certificate is given under section 42 above,

that certificate shall be delivered at the time of shipment to the master of the vessel or the pilot of the aircraft on which the animal is shipped, who shall—

(i)   on demand produce the certificate to any constable or any inspector or other officer of the appropriate Minister or the local authority; and
(ii)   allow such constable, inspector or other officer to take a copy of or extract from the certificate.
[Animal Health Act 1981, s 48.]

8–1362   49. Enforcement and interpretation.   (1) An inspector may enter any vessel or aircraft for the purpose of ascertaining whether the provisions—

(a)   of sections 40 to 42 and 44 to 48 above (in this section described as "the relevant sections"), or
(b)   of any order under this Act relating to the exportation or shipment of horses,

are being complied with.

(2) Every local authority shall, if and so far as the Ministers by order so direct, execute and enforce the relevant sections.

(3) If—

(a)   a person does anything or omits to do anything in contravention of the provisions of the relevant sections, or
(b)   the master of a vessel or the pilot of an aircraft permits a horse to be shipped in a vessel or aircraft in contravention of those provisions,

he shall be guilty of an offence[1] against this Act, and the provisions of this Act relating to offences and legal proceedings shall apply accordingly as if the expression "animal" in those provisions included horses.

(4) In this section and the relevant sections—

(*a*) "master", "owner" and "port" have the same meanings as in the Merchant Shipping Act 1995, and "vessel" has the same meaning as "ship" in the Merchant Shipping Act 1995; and

(*b*) "pilot of an aircraft" includes any other person having the command or charge of the aircraft.

[Animal Health Act 1981, s 49, as amended by the Merchant Shipping Act 1995, Sch 13.]

---

1. For penalty, see s 75, post.

Part IV[1]

Local Authorities

8–1363　50. Local authorities for purposes of this Act.　(1) In this Act "local authority" has the meaning given by subsections (2) and (3) below, but subject to subsection (4) below and to section 13(3) above.

(2) In the application of this Act to England and Wales "local authority" means—

(*a*) as respects a London borough, the borough council,

(*b*) as respects a non-metropolitan county, the county council,

(*bb*) as respects a county borough, the county borough council,

(*c*) as respects a metropolitan district, the district council,

and the Common Council of the City of London shall be the local authority—

(i) for the City of London, and

(ii) in and for the whole of Greater London for the purpose of the provisions of this Act relating to imported animals.

(3) In the application of this Act to Scotland "local authority" means a regional or islands council.

(4) Where the district or part of a district of a local authority is or comprises, or is comprised in—

(*a*) a port or part of a port, or

(*b*) an aerodrome or part of an aerodrome,

the appropriate Minister may, if he thinks fit, in relation to either paragraph (*a*) or paragraph (*b*) above by order make any body, other than the local authority under subsection (2) or subsection (3) above, the local authority for the purposes of the provisions of this Act relating to imported animals.

(5) A local authority shall execute and enforce this Act and every order of the Minister so far as they are to be executed and enforced by local authorities.

[Animal Health Act 1981, s 50, as amended by the Local Government Act 1985, Sch 8, the Environmental Protection Act 1990, s 151 and the Local Government (Wales) Act 1994, Sch 16.]

---

1. Part IV contains ss 50–59.

8–1364　51. Local authorities and their districts.　(1) The provisions of this Act conferring powers on, or otherwise relating to, a local authority, or their inspectors or officers shall, unless otherwise expressed, be read as having reference to the district of the local authority.

(2) The powers so conferred shall, unless it is otherwise expressed, be exercisable and shall operate within and in relation to that district only.

[Animal Health Act 1981, s 51.]

8–1365　52. Inspectors and other officers.　(1) Every local authority shall appoint as many inspectors and other officers as the local authority think necessary for the execution and enforcement of this Act.

(2) Every local authority shall assign to those inspectors and officers such duties, and salaries or allowances, and may delegate to any of them such authorities and discretion, as to the local authority seem fit, and may at any time revoke any appointment so made.

[Animal Health Act 1981, s 52.]

8–1366　58. Regulations.　(1) A regulation of a local authority may be proved—

(*a*) by the production of a newspaper purporting to contain the regulation as an advertisement; or

(*b*) by the production of a copy of the regulation purporting to be certified by the clerk of the local authority as a true copy.

(2) A regulation so proved shall be taken to have been duly made, unless and until the contrary is proved.

(3) A regulation of a local authority authorised by this Act or by an order of the Minister shall alone be deemed for the purposes of this Act a regulation of a local authority.

[Animal Health Act 1981, s 58.]

8–1367　59. Default.　(1) Where a local authority fail to execute or enforce any of the provisions of this Act, or of an order of the Minister, the appropriate Minister may by order empower a person named in that order—

(*a*)　to execute and enforce those provisions; or

(*b*)　to procure their execution and enforcement.

(2)–(4)　*Expenses, etc.*

[Animal Health Act 1981, s 59.]

PART V[1]

ENFORCEMENT, OFFENCES AND PROCEEDINGS

Enforcement

8–1368　60. Duties and authorities of constables.　(1) The police force of each police area shall execute and enforce this Act and every order of the Minister but subject, in the case of orders under section 13, to any provision made under subsection (3) of that section.

(2) Where a person is seen or found committing, or is reasonably suspected of being engaged in committing, an offence against this Act, a constable may, without warrant, stop and detain him.

(3) (*Repealed*).

(4) The constable may, whether so stopping or detaining the person or not—

(*a*)　stop, detain and examine any animal, vehicle, boat or thing to which the offence or suspected offence relates; and

(*b*)　require it to be forthwith taken back to or into any place or district from which or out of which it was unlawfully removed and execute and enforce that requisition.

(5) If a person obstructs or impedes or assists in obstructing or impeding an inspector[2] in the execution—

(*a*)　of this Act, or

(*b*)　of an order of the Minister, or

(*c*)　of a regulation of a local authority,

the inspector or a constable may without warrant apprehend[3] the offender.

(6) A person apprehended under this section—

(*a*)　shall be taken with all practicable speed before a justice, or, in Scotland, a sheriff or district court; and

(*b*)　shall not be detained without a warrant longer than is necessary for that purpose.

(7) All enactments relating to the release of persons on bail by an officer of police or a constable shall apply in the case of a person apprehended under this section.

(8) The foregoing provisions of this section respecting a constable extend and apply to any person called by a constable to his assistance.

(9) A constable shall forthwith make a report in writing to his superior officer of every case in which he stops any person, animal, vehicle, boat, or thing under this section, and of his proceedings in consequence.

(10) Nothing in this section shall take away or abridge any power or authority that a constable would have had if this section had not been enacted.

[Animal Health Act 1981, s 60, as amended by the Police and Criminal Evidence Act 1984, Schs 6 and 7, the Environmental Protection Act 1990, s 151 and the Animal Health Act 2002, s 11.]

1.　Part V contains ss 60–79.

2.　Obstruction of a constable is an offence under s 89(2) of the Police Act 1996 title: POLICE, post; as to police powers of arrest see the Police and Criminal Evidence Act 1984, s 25 in PART I: MAGISTRATES' COURTS, PROCEDURE, ante.

3.　This power of arrest is preserved by the Police and Criminal Evidence Act 1984, s 26 and Sch 2.

8–1369　61. Powers of arrest as to rabies.　(1) Without prejudice to the powers of arrest conferred by section 60 above or otherwise, a constable may arrest[1] without warrant any person whom he, with reasonable cause, suspects to be in the act of committing or to have committed an offence to which this section applies.

(2) The offences to which this section applies are offences against this Act consisting of—

(*a*)　the landing or attempted landing of any animal or importation or attempted importation through the tunnel system as defined in the Channel Tunnel Act 1987 of any animal in contravention of an order made under this Act and expressed to be made for the purpose of preventing the introduction of rabies into Great Britain; or

(*b*)　the failure by the person having the charge or control of any vessel or boat to discharge any obligation imposed on him in that capacity by such an order; or

(*c*)　the movement, in contravention of an order under section 17 or section 23 above, of any animal into, within or out of a place or area declared to be infected with rabies.

[Animal Health Act 1981, s 61, as amended by SI 1990/2371.]

1. This power of arrest is preserved by the Police and Criminal Evidence Act 1984, s 26 and Sch 2.

8–1370   62. Entry and search under section 61.   (1) For the purpose of arresting a person under the power conferred by section 61 above a constable may enter (if need be, by force) and search any vessel, boat, aircraft or vehicle of any other description in which that person is or in which the constable, with reasonable cause, suspects him to be.

(2) For the purpose of exercising any power to seize an animal or cause an animal to be seized, and—

(*a*) where that power is conferred on constables by an order made under this Act, and

(*b*) where that power is expressed to be made for the purpose of preventing the introduction of rabies into Great Britain,

a constable may enter (if need be, by force) and search any vessel, boat, aircraft or vehicle of any other description in which there is, or in which he, with reasonable cause, suspects that there is, an animal to which that power applies.

[Animal Health Act 1981, s 62.]

8–1370A   62A. Slaughter: power of entry.   (1) An inspector may at any time enter any premises for the purpose of—

(*a*) ascertaining whether a power conferred by or under this Act to cause an animal to be slaughtered should be exercised, or

(*b*) doing anything in pursuance of the exercise of that power.

(2) In this section and sections 62B and 62C premises includes any land, building or other place.

[Animal Health Act 1981, s 62A as inserted by the Animal Health Act 2002, s 8(1).]

8–1370B   62B. Slaughter: warrants.   (1) If a justice of the peace is satisfied on sworn information in writing that the first condition is satisfied and that the second or third condition is satisfied he may issue a warrant authorising an inspector to enter any premises, if necessary using reasonable force, for the purpose mentioned in section 62A.

(2) The information must include—

(*a*) a statement as to whether any representations have been made by the occupier of the land or premises to an inspector concerning the purpose for which the warrant is sought;

(*b*) a summary of any such representations.

(3) The first condition is that there are reasonable grounds for an inspector to enter the premises for that purpose.

(4) The second condition is that each of the following applies to the occupier of the premises—

(*a*) he has been informed of the decision to seek entry to the premises and of the reasons for that decision;

(*b*) he has failed to allow entry to the premises on being requested to do so by an inspector;

(*c*) he has been informed of the decision to apply for the warrant.

(5) The third condition is that—

(*a*) the premises are unoccupied or the occupier is absent and (in either case) notice of intention to apply for the warrant has been left in a conspicuous place on the premises, or

(*b*) an application for admission to the premises or the giving of notice of intention to apply for the warrant would defeat the object of entering the premises.

(6) A warrant issued under this section remains in force for one month starting with the date of its approval by the justice of the peace, which date shall be clearly visible on the warrant.

(7) A warrant issued under this section must be executed only at a reasonable hour unless the inspector thinks that the case is one of urgency.

(8) In relation to any premises to which entry is obtained by virtue of a warrant under this section the Secretary of State must retain for a period of not less than 12 months beginning with the day after entry—

(*a*) a copy of the warrant;

(*b*) a copy of any record of the steps taken to effect entry to the premises and the actions taken on the premises by the inspector and any other person entering the premises with him.

[Animal Health Act 1981, s 62B as inserted by the Animal Health Act 2002, s 8(1).]

8–1370C   62C. Slaughter: supplementary.   (1) This section applies to an inspector who enters any premises by virtue of section 62A or under a warrant issued under section 62B.

(2) The inspector may take with him—

(*a*) such other persons as he thinks necessary to give him such assistance as he thinks necessary;

(*b*) such equipment as he thinks necessary.

(3) The inspector may require any person on the premises who falls within subsection (4) to give him such assistance as he may reasonably require for the purpose mentioned in section 62A.

(4) The following persons fall within this subsection—

(*a*) the occupier of the premises;

(*b*) a person appearing to the inspector to have charge of animals on the premises;

(*c*) a person appearing to the inspector to be under the direction or control of a person mentioned in paragraph (*a*) or (*b*).

(5) If the inspector enters any premises by virtue of a warrant issued under section 62B he must at the time of entry—

(*a*) serve a copy of the warrant on the occupier of the premises, or (if the occupier is not on the premises)

(*b*) leave a copy of the warrant in a conspicuous place on the premises.

(6) If the inspector enters any unoccupied premises he must leave them as effectively secured against entry as he found them.

[Animal Health Act 1981, s 62C as inserted by the Animal Health Act 2002, s 8(1).]

8–1370D   62D. Tests and samples: power of entry.   (1) A veterinary inspector may at any time enter any premises for the purpose of ascertaining—

(*a*) whether disease anti-bodies exist in animals on the premises;

(*b*) whether any animal on the premises or which was kept there at any time is, or was at that time, infected with disease;

(*c*) whether any causative agent of disease is present on the premises.

(2) Disease is foot-and-mouth disease and such other disease as the Secretary of State may by order[1] specify.

(3) No order may be made under subsection (2) unless a draft of the order has been laid before Parliament and approved by a resolution of each House.

(4) Causative agent includes any virus, bacterium and any other organism or infectious substance which may cause or transmit disease.

(5) In this section and sections 62E and 62F premises includes any land, building or other place.

[Animal Health Act 1981, s 62D, as inserted by the Animal Health Act 2002, s 9.]

---

1. The Avian Influenza and Newcastle Disease (England and Wales) Order 2003, SI 2003/1734 has been made.

8–1370E   62E. Tests and samples: warrants.   (1) If a justice of the peace is satisfied on sworn information in writing that the first condition is satisfied and that the second or third condition is satisfied he may issue a warrant authorising a veterinary inspector to enter any premises, if necessary using reasonable force, for the purpose mentioned in section 62D.

(2) The information must include—

(*a*) a statement as to whether any representations have been made by the occupier of the land or premises to an inspector concerning the purpose for which the warrant is sought;

(*b*) a summary of any such representations.

(3) The first condition is that there are reasonable grounds for a veterinary inspector to enter the premises for that purpose.

(4) The second condition is that each of the following applies to the occupier of the premises—

(*a*) he has been informed of the decision to seek entry to the premises and of the reasons for that decision;

(*b*) he has failed to allow entry to the premises on being requested to do so by an inspector;

(*c*) he has been informed of the decision to apply for the warrant.

(5) The third condition is that—

(*a*) the premises are unoccupied or the occupier is absent and (in either case) notice of intention to apply for the warrant has been left in a conspicuous place on the premises, or

(*b*) an application for admission to the premises or the giving of notice of intention to apply for the warrant would defeat the object of entering the premises.

(6) A warrant issued under this section remains in force for one month starting with the date of its approval by the justice of the peace, which date shall be clearly visible on the warrant.

(7) A warrant issued under this section must be executed only at a reasonable hour unless the inspector thinks that the case is one of urgency.

(8) In relation to any premises to which entry is obtained by virtue of a warrant under this section the Secretary of State must retain for a period of not less than 12 months beginning with the day after entry—

(*a*) a copy of the warrant;

(*b*) a copy of any record of the steps taken to effect entry to the premises and the actions taken on the premises by the inspector and any other person entering the premises with him.

[Animal Health Act 1981, s 62E as inserted by the Animal Health Act 2002, s 9.]

8–1370F **62F. Tests and samples: supplementary.** (1) This section applies to a veterinary inspector who enters any premises by virtue of section 62D or under a warrant issued under section 62E.

(2) The inspector may take with him—

(*a*) such other persons as he thinks necessary to give him such assistance as he thinks necessary;
(*b*) such equipment as he thinks necessary.

(3) The inspector may take such samples (including samples from any animal on the premises) and carry out such tests as he thinks are necessary for the purpose mentioned in section 62D(1).

(4) The inspector may require any person on the premises who falls within subsection (5) to give him such assistance as he may reasonably require for the purpose mentioned in section 62D(1).

(5) The following persons fall within this subsection—

(*a*) the occupier of the premises;
(*b*) a person appearing to the inspector to have charge of animals on the premises;
(*c*) a person appearing to the inspector to be under the direction or control of a person mentioned in paragraph (*a*) or (*b*).

(6) If the inspector enters any unoccupied premises he must leave them as effectively secured against entry as he found them.

(7) If the inspector enters any premises by virtue of a warrant issued under section 62E he must at the time of entry—

(*a*) serve a copy of the warrant on the occupier of the premises, or (if the occupier is not on the premises)
(*b*) leave a copy of the warrant in a conspicuous place on the premises.

(8) A person commits an offence if—

(*a*) he is required to give assistance under subsection (4), and
(*b*) he fails to give it.

[Animal Health Act 1981, s 62F as inserted by the Animal Health Act 2002, s 9.]

8–1371 **63. General powers of inspectors.** (1) An inspector has—

(*a*) for the purposes of this Act, but
(*b*) with the exception of the powers conferred by sections 61 and 62 above,

all the powers which a constable has, under this Act or otherwise, in the place where the inspector is acting.

(2) An inspector may at any time enter any land or shed to which this Act applies, or other building or place where he has reasonable grounds for supposing—

(*a*) that disease exists or has within 56 days existed; or
(*b*) that the carcase of a diseased or suspected animal is or has been kept, or has been buried, destroyed, or otherwise disposed of; or
(*c*) that there is to be found any pen, place, vehicle, or thing in respect of which any person has on any occasion failed to comply with the provisions of this Act, or of an order of the Minister, or of a regulation of a local authority; or
(*d*) that this Act or an order of the Minister or a regulation of a local authority has not been or is not being complied with.

(3) An inspector may at any time enter any pen, vehicle, vessel, boat or aircraft in which or in respect of which he has reasonable grounds for supposing that this Act or an order of the Minister or a regulation of a local authority has not been or is not being complied with.

(4) An inspector entering as authorised by the foregoing provisions of this section shall, if required by the owner, or occupier, or person in charge of the land, building, place, pen, vehicle, vessel, boat or aircraft state in writing his reasons for entering.

(5) For the purpose of ascertaining whether the provisions of any order under section 10 above or the conditions of any licence issued in accordance with any such order are being complied with, an inspector may at any time enter—

(*a*) any vessel, boat, aircraft or vehicle of any other description which is for the time being within the limits of a port, within the meaning of the Customs and Excise Management Act 1979, or at a customs and excise airport, within the meaning of that Act; or
(*b*) any vessel, boat or aircraft which does not fall within paragraph (*a*) above but which he has reasonable grounds for supposing has recently been brought into Great Britain.

(6) Without prejudice to subsection (5) above, an inspector may at any time enter—

(*a*) any land, building or other place, or
(*b*) any vessel, boat, aircraft or vehicle of any other description,

on or in which he has reasonable grounds for supposing that there is being or has been kept any animal or other thing which has been imported and the importation of which is for the time being prohibited or regulated by an order under section 10; and in this subsection "animals" and "imported" have the same meaning as in that section.

(7) A certificate of a veterinary inspector to the effect that an animal is or was affected with a disease specified in the certificate shall, for the purposes of this Act, be conclusive evidence in all courts of justice of the matter certified.

(8) An inspector of the Minister has all the powers of an inspector throughout Great Britain or that part for which he is appointed.

(9) In addition to the powers conferred by this section upon inspectors, an inspector of the Minister may at any time, enter any land, building or other place, on or in which he has reasonable grounds for supposing that animals[1] are or have been kept, for the purpose of ascertaining whether any disease[1] exists there or has within 56 days existed there.

This subsection does not have effect in relation to poultry.
[Animal Health Act 1981, s 63, as amended by the Animal Health and Welfare Act 1984, s 2 and Sch 1.]

---

1. For the purposes of s 63(9) the definition of "animals" in s 87(1), post, and the definition of "disease" in s 88(1), post, is extended by the Diseases of Animals (Ascertainment of Disease) Order 1985, SI 1985/1765, amended by SI 1992/3159; see notes to ss 87 and 88 respectively, post.

8–1372   64. Powers of inspectors as to poultry.   (1) An inspector of the Ministry and, if so authorised by an order of the Minister, an inspector of a local authority, may at any time enter any pen, shed, land or other place in which he has reasonable grounds for supposing that poultry are or have been kept, for the purpose of ascertaining whether disease exists or has existed in or on them.

(2) For the purpose of enforcing any order for protecting poultry from unnecessary suffering, an inspector may examine—

(*a*)   poultry in any circumstances to which the order relates, and

(*b*)   any receptacle or vehicle used for their conveyance or exposure for sale,

and he may enter any premises, vessel or aircraft in which he has reasonable ground for supposing that there are poultry—

(i)   exposed for sale; or

(ii)   in course of conveyance; or

(iii)   packed for conveyance or exposure for sale.
[Animal Health Act 1981, s 64.]

8–1372A   64A. Powers of inspectors relating to Community obligations.   In addition to the powers conferred by sections 63 and 64, an inspector (on producing, if required to do so, some duly authenticated document showing his authority) may at all reasonable hours—

(*a*)   enter—

(i)   any land, building, or other place, or

(ii)   any vessel, boat, aircraft, hovercraft or vehicle of any other description,

for the purpose of ascertaining whether the provisions of any order made under this Act in implementation of any Community obligation have been or are being complied with, and

(*b*)   carry out such inspections (including inspection of documents) as may be necessary for that purpose.
[Animal Health Act 1981, s 64A inserted by the Animal Health Act 1981 (Amendment) Regulations 1992, SI 1992/3293.]

8–1373   65. Power to detain vessels and aircraft.   (1) Where an inspector of the Minister is satisfied that this Act or an order of the Minister or a regulation of a local authority has not been or is not being complied with on board a vessel in port, then, on the inspector's representation in writing to that effect, stating particulars of non-compliance, the vessel may be detained until the appropriate Minister otherwise directs.

(2) The officer detaining the vessel shall forthwith deliver to the master or person in charge of the vessel a copy of the representation.

(3) Section 284 of the Merchant Shipping Act 1995 shall apply in the case of such detention as if it were authorised or ordered under that Act.

(4) In relation to aircraft the Ministers may—

(*a*)   by an order under this Act adapt that section of the 1995 Act as applied in the case of the detention of a vessel under this section; or

(*b*)   make such other provision instead of it as they think expedient.
[Animal Health Act 1981, s 65, as amended by the Merchant Shipping Act 1995, Sch 13.]

8–1373A   65A. Inspection of vehicles.   (1) If each of the conditions in subsection (2) is satisfied, an inspector may stop, detain and inspect any vehicle to ascertain whether the provisions of any of the following are being complied with—

(*a*)   this Act;

(b)   an order made under this Act;

(c)   a regulation of a local authority made in pursuance of such an order.

(2)   The conditions are—

(a)   that the vehicle is in a designated area in a designated period;

(b)   that the inspector is accompanied by a constable in uniform.

(3)   In subsection (2) "designated" means designated by an order made by the Secretary of State.

(4)   A vehicle includes—

(a)   a trailer, semi-trailer or other thing which is designed or adapted to be towed by another vehicle;

(b)   anything on a vehicle;

(c)   a detachable part of a vehicle;

(d)   a container or other structure designed or adapted to be carried by or on a vehicle.

[Animal Health Act 1981, s 65A as inserted by the Animal Health Act 2002, s 10.]

8–1374   66. Refusal and obstruction.   A person is guilty of an offence[1] against this Act who, without lawful authority or excuse, proof of which shall lie on him—

(a)   refuses to an inspector or other officer, acting in execution of this Act, or of an order of the Minister, or of a regulation of a local authority, admission to any land, building, place, pen, vessel, boat, aircraft or vehicle of any other description which the inspector or officer is entitled to enter or examine; or

(b)   obstructs or impedes him in so entering or examining; or

(c)   otherwise in any respect obstructs or impedes an inspector or constable or other officer in the execution of his duty, or assists in any such obstructing or impeding.

[Animal Health Act 1981, s 66.]

_____

1. For penalty, see s 75, post.

8–1374A   66A. Refusal and obstruction of inspector.   (1) A person commits an offence if without lawful authority or excuse (proof of which shall lie on him) he—

(a)   refuses admission to any premises to a person acting under section 62A above,

(b)   obstructs or impedes him in so acting, or

(c)   assists in any such obstruction or impeding.

(2)   A person commits an offence if—

(a)   he is required to give assistance under section 62C(3), and

(b)   he fails to give it.

[Animal Health Act 1981, s 66A as inserted by the Animal Health Act 2002, s 8(2).]

Offences as to licences, declarations, certificates and instruments

8–1375   67. Issue of false licences, etc.   A person is guilty of an offence[1] against this Act—

(a)   who grants or issues a licence, certificate or instrument made or issued, or purporting to be made or issued under or for any purpose of this Act, or of an order of the Minister, or of a regulation of a local authority, which is false in any date or other material particular, unless he shows to the court's satisfaction that he did not know of that falsity, and that he could not with reasonable diligence have obtained knowledge of it; or

(b)   who grants or issues such a licence, certificate or instrument not having, and knowing that he has not, lawful authority to grant or issue it.

[Animal Health Act 1981, s 67.]

_____

1. For penalty, see s 75, post.

8–1376   68. Issue of licences, etc in blank.   A person is guilty of an offence[1] against this Act—

(a)   who, with intent unlawfully to evade or defeat this Act, or an order of the Minister, or a regulation of a local authority, grants or issues an instrument being in form a licence, certificate or instrument made or issued under this Act, or such an order or regulation, for permitting or regulating the movement of a particular animal, or the doing of any other particular thing, but being issued in blank, that is to say, not being before its issue so filled up as to specify any particular animal or thing;

(b)   who uses or offers or attempts to use for any purpose of this Act, or such an order or regulation, an instrument so issued in blank, unless he shows to the court's satisfaction that he did not know of it having been so issued in blank, and that he could not with reasonable diligence have obtained knowledge of it.

[Animal Health Act 1981, s 68.]

_____

1. For penalty see s 75, post.

8–1377   69. Falsely obtaining licences, etc.   A person is guilty of an offence[1] against this Act—

(a)   who for the purpose of obtaining a licence, certificate or instrument makes a declaration or statement false in any material particular, or

(b)   who obtains or endeavours to obtain a licence, certificate or instrument by means of a false pretence,

unless he shows to the court's satisfaction that he did not know of that falsity, and that he could not with reasonable diligence have obtained knowledge of it.

[Animal Health Act 1981, s 69.]

---

1. For penalty, see s 75, post.

8–1378   70. (*Repealed*).

8–1379   71. Other offences as to licences.   A person is guilty of an offence[1] against this Act—

(a)   who, with intent unlawfully to evade this Act, or an order of the Minister, or a regulation of a local authority, does anything for which a licence is requisite under this Act, or such an order or regulation, without having obtained a licence; or

(b)   who, where a licence is so requisite, having obtained a licence, with the like intent does the thing licensed after the licence has expired; or

(c)   who uses or offers or attempts to use as such a licence—

(i)   an instrument not being a complete licence, or

(ii)   an instrument untruly purporting or appearing to be a licence,

unless he shows to the court's satisfaction that he did not know of that incompleteness or untruth, and that he could not with reasonable diligence have obtained knowledge of it.

[Animal Health Act 1981, s 71.]

---

1. For penalty, see s 75, post.

Offences generally

8–1379A   71A. Prosecutions: time limit.   (1) Despite anything in section 127(1) of the Magistrates' Courts Act 1980 an information relating to an offence under this Act which is triable by a magistrates' court in England and Wales may be so tried if it is laid at any time—

(a)   within the period of three years starting with the date of the commission of the offence, and

(b)   within the period of six months starting with the day on which evidence which the prosecutor thinks is sufficient to justify the proceedings comes to his knowledge.

(2)   A certificate by the prosecutor as to the date on which such evidence came to his knowledge is conclusive evidence of that fact.

[Animal Health Act 1981, s 71A as inserted by the Animal Health Act 2002, s 14.]

8–1380   72. Offences made and declared by and under this Act.   A person is guilty of an offence[1] against this Act who, without lawful authority or excuse, proof of which shall lie on him—

(a)   does or omits anything the doing or omission of which is declared by this Act or by an order of the minister to be an offence by that person against this Act; or

(b)   does anything which by this Act or such an order is made or declared to be not lawful.

[Animal Health Act 1981, s 72.]

---

1. For penalty, see s 75, post.

8–1381   73. General offences.   A person is guilty of an offence[1] against this Act who, without lawful authority or excuse[2], proof of which shall lie on him—

(a)   does anything in contravention of this Act, or of an order of the Minister, or of a regulation of a local authority; or

(b)   fails to give, produce, observe or do any notice, licence, rule or thing which by this Act or such an order or regulation he is required to give, produce, observe or do.

[Animal Health Act 1981, s 73.]

---

1. For penalty, see s 75, post.

2. For the defendant to have a lawful excuse for what he did he must honestly believe on reasonable grounds that that the facts are of a certain order and, if they were of that order, his conduct would be lawful: *Corporation of London v Eurostar (UK) Ltd* [2004] EWHC Admin 187, (2005) 169 JP 263.

Further provisions as to punishment of offences

8–1382   74. Liability under the customs and excise Acts.   A person who—

(*a*)   lands or ships or attempts to land or ship or brings or attempts to bring through the tunnel system as defined in the Channel Tunnel Act 1987 an animal or thing, and

(*b*)   by so doing is in contravention of this Act or of an order of the Minister,

is liable under and according to the customs and excise Acts[1] to the penalties imposed on persons importing or exporting or attempting to import or export goods the importation or exportation of which is prohibited.

This section is without prejudice to any proceeding under this Act against such a person for an offence against this Act.

[Animal Health Act 1981, s 74 amended by SI 1990/2371.]

---

1. See ss 50 and 68 of the Customs and Excise Management Act 1979, title CUSTOMS AND EXCISE, post.

8–1383   75. Penalties for certain summary offences.   (1) This section applies to any offence under this Act for which no penalty is specified.

(2) A person guilty of an offence to which this section applies is liable on summary conviction to imprisonment for a term not exceeding six months or to a fine not exceeding level 5 on the standard scale or to both.

[Animal Health Act 1981, s 75, as substituted by th Animal Health Act 2002, s 13.]

8–1384   76. Certain importation offences triable either summarily or on indictment. (1) Where—

(*a*)   an offence against this Act which is declared to be such by an order under section 10 above, and

(*b*)   that order is expressed to be made for the purpose of preventing the introduction of rabies into Great Britain,

that offence may be tried either summarily or on indictment.

(2) For an offence triable under subsection (1) above a person shall be liable[1]—

(*a*)   on summary conviction to a fine not exceeding **the statutory maximum**;

(*b*)   on conviction on indictment to a fine or to imprisonment for a term not exceeding **12 months** or to both.

(3) Where an order under section 10 declares that this subsection applies to an offence which consists of—

(*a*)   a contravention of, or failure to comply with, any provision of that order, or

(*b*)   a failure to observe any conditions to which a licence issued in accordance with that order is subject,

that offence may be tried either summarily or on indictment, and a person convicted of such an offence shall be liable as provided in paragraphs (*a*) and (*b*) of subsection (2) above.

(4) (*Repealed*).

[Animal Health Act 1981, s 76 amended by the Statute Law (Repeals) Act 1993, Sch 1.]

---

1. For procedure in respect of this offence which is triable either way, see the Magistrates' Courts Act 1980, ss 17A–21, in PART I: MAGISTRATES' COURTS, PROCEDURE, ante.

Proceedings

8–1385   77. Money recoverable summarily.   Any money by this Act or an order of the Minister made recoverable summarily may be so recovered as a civil debt, and in England and Wales this shall be in accordance with the Magistrates' Courts Act 1980.

[Animal Health Act 1981, s 77 as amended by the Statute Law (Repeals) Act 2004.]

8–1386   78. Appeal.   If any person thinks himself aggrieved—

(*a*)   by the dismissal of a complaint by, or

(*b*)   by any determination or adjudication of,

a magistrates' court in England and Wales under this Act, he may appeal to the Crown Court.

Nothing in this section applies in relation to an offence punishable under section 4 above.

[Animal Health Act 1981, s 78.]

8–1387   79. Evidence and procedure.   (1) In any proceeding under this Act no proof shall be required of the appointment or handwriting of an inspector or other officer of the Minister or of the clerk or an inspector or other officer of a local authority.

(2) Where the owner or person in charge of an animal is charged with an offence against this Act relative to disease or to any illness of the animal, he shall be presumed to have known of the existence of the disease or illness unless and until he shows to the court's satisfaction that—

(*a*)   he had not knowledge of the existence of that disease or illness, and

(*b*)   he could not with reasonable diligence have obtained that knowledge.

(3) Where a person—

(*a*) is charged with an offence against this Act in not having duly cleansed or disinfected any place, vessel, aircraft, vehicle or thing belonging to him or under his charge, and

(*b*) a presumption against him on the part of the prosecution is raised,

it shall lie on him to prove that due cleansing and disinfection mentioned in paragraph (*a*).

(4) Every offence against this Act shall be deemed to have been committed, and every cause of complaint or matter for summary proceeding under this Act or an order of the Minister or regulation of a local authority shall be deemed[1] to have arisen, either in any place—

(*a*) where it actually was committed or arose; or

(*b*) where the person charged or complained of or proceeded against happens to be at the time of the institution or commencement of the charge, complaint or proceeding.

(5) Nothing in subsections (2) to (4) above applies in relation to an offence under section 4 above. [Animal Health Act 1981, s 79.]

---

1. The provisions of this section would seem to refer to ascertaining which court has jurisdiction over an offence committed in England and Wales. Whether there was an offence committed which was triable in England under the Welfare of Animals During Transport Order 1992, SI 1992/3304 (now replaced by the similarly entitled SI 1994/3249), where the acts and omissions constituting the offence were not committed within the jurisdiction of the Crown was left unresolved in *Ken Lane Transport Ltd v North Yorkshire County Council* [1995] 1 WLR 1416, 160 JP 91, [1996] Crim LR 189.

PART VI[1]
SUPPLEMENTAL

Notices, fees, and exemption from stamp duty

8–1388 83. Form and service of instruments. (1) Every notice under this Act or under any order or regulation made under this Act must be in writing.

(2) The Ministers may make such orders[2] as they think fit for prescribing and regulating the form and mode of service or delivery of notices and other instruments.

(3) Any notice or other instrument under this Act or under an order of the Minister or a regulation of a local authority may be served on the person to be affected by it, either—

(*a*) by its delivery to him personally; or

(*b*) by the leaving of it for him at his last known place of abode or business; or

(*c*) by the sending of it through the post in a letter addressed to him at his last known place of abode or business.

(4) A notice or other instrument—

(*a*) to be served on the occupier of any building, land or place, may, except when sent by post, be addressed to him by the designation of the occupier of that building, land or place, without naming or further describing him; and

(*b*) where it is to be served on the several occupiers of several buildings, lands, or places, may, except when sent by post, be addressed to them collectively by the designation of the occupiers of those several buildings, lands or places, without further naming or describing them, but separate copies of it being served on them severally.

[Animal Health Act 1981, s 83.]

---

1. Part VI contains ss 80–97.
2. The Orders listed to s 1, ante include Orders made under this section.

Interpretation, functions, and orders etc

8–1389 86. Ministers and their functions. (1) In this Act—

(*a*) "the Minister" means, in relation to the whole of Great Britain, the Minister of Agriculture, Fisheries and Food, and "Ministry" shall be construed accordingly[1].

(*b*) "the appropriate Minister" means, in relation to England, the Minister of Agriculture, Fisheries and Food, and in relation to Scotland or to Wales, the Secretary of State[1],

(*c*) "the Ministers" means, in relation to the whole of Great Britain, the Minister of Agriculture, Fisheries and Food, the Secretary of State for Scotland and the Secretary of State for Wales, acting jointly[1],

but in the case of any function under the following provisions of this Act—

(i) section 21, so far as it is applicable in relation to brucellosis, tuberculosis, dourine or infestation with maggot of the warble fly,

(ii) any other provision so far as it is applicable in relation to brucellosis, brucellosis melitensis, tuberculosis or infestation of cattle with the maggot of the warble fly.

that function, notwithstanding that it is expressed to be exercisable by the Minister or the Ministers, shall be exercisable only by the appropriate Minister.

(2) The powers and duties conferred and imposed by this Act on the Minister shall be executed and discharged by the Minister in manner provided by this Act.

[Animal Health Act 1981, s 86, as amended by SI 2002/794.]

1. The functions of the Secretaries of State for Wales and Scotland (except for s 57) have been transferred to the Minister for Agriculture, Fisheries and Food see the Transfer of Functions (Agriculture and Food) Order 1999, SI 1999/3141.The functions of the Minister, so far as exercisable in relation to Wales, have been transferred to the National Assembly for Wales, by the National Assembly for Wales (Transfer of Functions) Order 1999, SI 1999/672, art 2, Sch 1. The functions of the Minister for Agriculture, Fisheries and Food have been transferred to the Secretary of State for Environment, Food and Rural Affairs, see the Ministry of Agriculture, Fisheries and Food (Dissolution) Order 2002, SI 2002/794.

8–1390   **87. Meaning of "animals" and "poultry".**   (1) In this Act, unless the context otherwise requires, "animals"[1] means—

    (a)   cattle, sheep and goats, and
    (b)   all other ruminating animals and swine,

subject to subsections (2) and (3) below.

(2) The Ministers may by order[2] for all or any of the purposes of this Act extend the definition of "animals" in subsection (1) above so that it shall for those or any of those purposes comprise—

    (a)   any kind of mammal except man; and
    (b)   any kind of four-footed beast which is not a mammal.

(3) The Ministers may by order for all or any of the purposes of this Act (except so far as it relates to disease) extend the definition of "animals" in subsection (1) so that it shall for those or any of those purposes comprise—

    (a)   fish, reptiles, crustaceans, or
    (b)   other cold-blooded creatures of any species,

not being creatures in respect of which an order can be made under subsection (2) above.

(4) In this Act, subject to subsection (5) below and unless the context otherwise requires, "poultry" means birds of the following species—

    (a)   domestic fowls, turkeys, geese, ducks, guinea-fowls and pigeons, and
    (b)   pheasants and partridges,

and subject to the provisions mentioned below, this Act has effect in relation to poultry as it has effect in relation to animals.

The provisions of this Act referred to above are section 15(5), 32(4), and 63(9).

(5) The Ministers may by order[3] for all or any of the purposes of this Act, in so far as it applies to poultry—

    (a)   extend the definition of "poultry" in subsection (4) above so that it shall for those or any of those purposes comprise any other species of bird; or
    (b)   restrict that definition so that it shall for those or any of those purposes exclude any of the species of bird mentioned in paragraph (b) of subsection (4).

[Animal Health Act 1981, s 87 as amended by the Animal Health and Welfare Act 1984, s 2.]

1. For the purposes of s 63(9), ante, this definition of "animals" is extended so as to comprise any animal (except man) belonging to any of the orders of mammals except animals of the orders of Cetacea (whales, dolphins and porpoises), Pinnipedia (seals) and Sirenia (dugongs and manatees), (Diseases of Animals (Ascertainment of Disease) Order 1985, SI 1985/1765).
2. The Orders listed to s 1, ante include Orders made under this section.
3. The Diseases of Poultry Order 1994, SI 1994/3141, extends the definition of "poultry" in s 87(4) to include all birds for the purposes of the Order (Diseases of Poultry Order 1994, SI 1994/3141, reg 2).

8–1391   **88. Meaning of "disease".**   (1) In this Act, unless the context otherwise requires, "disease"[1] means cattle plague, pleuro-pneumonia, foot-and-mouth disease, sheep-pox, sheep scab, or swine fever, subject to subsection (2) below.

(2) The Ministers may by order for all or any of the purposes of this Act extend the definition of "disease" in subsection (1) above so that it shall for those or any of those purposes comprise any other disease of animals[2].

(3) In this Act, in so far as it applies to poultry, and unless the context otherwise requires, "disease" means—

    (a)   fowl pest in any of its forms, including Newcastle disease and fowl plague; and
    (b)   fowl cholera, infectious bronchitis, infectious laryngotracheitis, pullorum disease, fowl typhoid, fowl pox and fowl paralysis,

subject to subsection (4) below.

(4) The Ministers may by order for all or any of the purposes of this Act—

    (a)   extend the definition of "disease" in subsection (3) above so that it shall for those or any of those purposes comprise any other disease of birds[3]; or

(*b*) restrict that definition so that it shall for those or any of those purposes exclude any of the diseases mentioned in paragraph (*b*) of subsection (3).
[Animal Health Act 1981, s 88.]

1. For the purposes of s 63(9), ante, this definition of "disease" is extended so as to comprise African horse sickness, Aujeszky's disease, Brucellosis caused by Brucella melitensis, contagious agalactia, contagious epidydimitis, dourine, enzootic bovine leukosis, equine infectious anaemia, equine encephalomyelitis, rabies and Teschen diseases, (Diseases of Animals (Ascertainment of Disease) Order 1985, SI 1985/1765), and the warble fly (SI 1985/1766). Sheep scab is now for practical purposes deregulated by the Sheep Scab (Revocation) Order 1992, SI 1992/1361 and foot-and-mouth disease is controlled by the Foot and Mouth Disease Order (England) Order 2006, SI 2006/182.

2. The definition of disease has been extended by orders to include: anthrax (SR & O 1938/204); brucellosis suis and tularaemia (SI 1965/2040); brucellosis (SI 1971/531); swine vesicular disease (SI 1972/1980); rabies (SI 1974/2212); bovine leukosis (SI 1980/79); African Swine fever (SI 1980/145); warble fly (SI 1982/234); Aujeszky's disease (SI 1983/344); tuberculosis (SI 1984/1943); infectious diseases of horses (SI 1987/790) and equine viral arteritis (SI 1995/1755).

3. For the purposes of the Diseases of Poultry Order 1994, SI 1994/3141, the definition of "disease" in s 88(3) is extended to include paramyxovirus 1 in pigeons and restricted so as to exclude the diseases mentioned in paragraph (*b*) of s 88(3) of the Act (Diseases of Poultry Order 1994, SI 1994/3141, reg 2).

8–1392 89. Other interpretation provisions.   (1) In this Act, unless the context otherwise requires—

"aerodrome" means any area of land or water designed, equipped, set apart or commonly used for affording facilities for the landing and departure of aircraft;

"carcase" means the carcase of an animal and includes part of a carcase, and the meat, bones, hide, skin, hooves, offal or other part of an animal, separately or otherwise, or any portion thereof;

"cattle" means bulls, cows, steers, heifers, and calves;

"cattle plague'" means rinderpest or the disease commonly called cattle plague;

"the customs and excise Acts" has the meaning given by the Customs and Excise Management Act 1979;

"diseased" means affected with disease;

"district", when used with reference to a local authority, means the area for which the local authority exercises powers under this Act;

"export quarantine station" has the meaning given by section 12(1) above;

"fodder" means hay or other substance commonly used for food of animals;

"horse" includes ass and mule;

"imported" means brought to Great Britain from a country out of Great Britain;

"inspector" means a person appointed to be an inspector for the purposes of this Act by the Minister or by a local authority, and, when used in relation to an officer of the Ministry, includes a veterinary inspector;

"justice" means justice of the peace;

"litter" means straw or other substance commonly used for bedding or otherwise for or about animals;

"local authority" has the meaning given by section 50 above;

"order of the Minister" means an order under this Act of the Minister, the appropriate Minister, or the Ministers, as the case may be;

"pleuro-pneumonia" means contagious pleuro-pneumonia of cattle;

"pony" means any horse not more than 147 centimetres in height, except a foal travelling with its dam if the dam is over 147 centimetres;

"suspected" means suspected of being diseased;

"swine-fever" means the disease known as typhoid fever of swine, soldier purples, red disease, hog cholera or swine-plague;

"veterinary inspector" means a veterinary inspector appointed by the Minister.

(2) In the computation of time for the purposes of this Act, a period reckoned by days from the happening of an event or the doing of an act or thing shall be deemed to be exclusive of the day on which the event happened or the act or thing is done.
[Animal Health Act 1981, s 89.]

8–1393 90. Application to hovercraft.   The enactments and instruments with respect to which provision may be made by Order in Council in pursuance of section 1(1)(*h*) of the Hovercraft Act 1968 include this Act and any instrument made or having effect as if made under it.

This section is without prejudice to section 17 of the Interpretation Act 1978 (repeal and re-enactment).
[Animal Health Act 1981, s 90.]

8–1394

SCHEDULES

Section 5(2)   SCHEDULE 1
REGULATION OF MANUFACTURE OF AND OTHER MATTERS CONNECTED WITH VETERINARY THERAPEUTIC
SUBSTANCES

(As amended by the Criminal Justice Act 1982, ss 35, 38 and 46 and the Animal Health Act 2002, s 12.)

Offences under this Schedule

8–1395   **6.** A person who—

    (*a*)   contravenes or fails to comply with any condition subject to which any such licence as is mentioned in this Schedule is issued,

    (*b*)   sells or offers for sale or has in his possession for sale any substance to which this Schedule applies knowing it to have been manufactured or imported in contravention of an order in force for any of the purposes of paragraph 2 above,

    (*c*)   contravenes or fails to comply with the provisions of any such order as is mentioned above,

is liable on summary conviction to a fine not exceeding **level 3** on the standard scale or imprisonment for a term not exceeding **2 months**, and in either case to forfeit any goods in connection with which the offence was committed, and without prejudice, if the offender is the holder of a licence, to the power of the appropriate Minister to revoke or suspend the licence.

8–1395A

Section 28A

SCHEDULE 2A
SPECIFIED DISEASES

Foot-and-mouth disease
Swine vesicular disease
Peste des petits ruminants
Lumpy skin disease
Bluetongue
African horse sickness
Classical swine fever
Newcastle disease
Vesicular stomatitis
Rinderpest
Contagious bovine pleuropneumonia
Rift Valley fever
Sheep pox and goat pox
African swine fever
Highly pathogenic avian influenza.

Section 38(2)

SCHEDULE 4
ADDITIONAL PROVISIONS AS TO FOOD AND WATER AT RAILWAY STATIONS

8–1396   **1.** The food and water, or either of them, provided under section 38(2) above shall be supplied to the animal by the body carrying the animal on the request—

    (*a*)   of the consignor; or

    (*b*)   of any person in charge of the animal.

  2. As regards water, if, in the case of any animal, such a request is not made, so that the animal remains without a supply of water for 24 consecutive hours—

    (*a*)   the consignor and the person in charge of the animal shall each be guilty of an offence against this Act; and

    (*b*)   it shall lie on the person charged to prove such a request and the time within which the animal had a supply of water.

  3. The Ministers may, if they think fit, by order prescribe any other period, not less than 12 hours instead of the period of 24 hours mentioned above, either generally, or in respect of any particular kind of animals.

  4. The body supplying food or water under section 38(2) may make in respect of that supply such reasonable charges (if any) as the Ministers by order approve, in addition to such charges as they are for the time being authorised to make in respect of the carriage of animals.

  5. The amount of those additional charges accrued due in respect of any animal shall be a debt from the consignor and from the consignee of the animal to the body concerned, and shall be recoverable by the body concerned, with costs, by proceedings in any court of competent jurisdiction.

  6. The body concerned shall have a lien for the amount of that debt on the animal in respect of which the debt accrued due, and on any other animal at any time consigned by or to the same consignor or consignee to be carried by that body.

Zoo Licensing Act 1981
(1981 c 37)

Licences

8–1397   **1. Licensing of zoos by local authorities.**   (1) Subject to this section it is unlawful to operate a zoo to which this Act applies except under the authority of a licence issued under this Act by the local authority for the area within which the whole or the major part of the zoo is situated.

    (2) In this Act "zoo" means an establishment where wild animals (as defined by section 21) are kept for exhibition to the public otherwise than for purposes of a circus (as so defined) and otherwise than in a pet shop (as so defined).

    (2A) This Act applies to any zoo to which members of the public have access, with or without charge for admission, on seven days or more in any period of twelve consecutive months.

    (2B) This Act also applies in accordance with its terms to any zoo to which members of the public do not have such access if a licence is in force in respect of it or as otherwise provided (in particular, in sections 13 and 16C to 16G).

(2C) In this Act—

(*a*) a section of a zoo means—

(i) a particular part of the zoo premises;
(ii) animals of a particular description in the zoo; or
(iii) animals of a particular description which are kept in a particular part of the zoo premises; and

(*b*) references to the closure of a section of a zoo to the public mean—

(i) the closure to the public of a particular part of the zoo premises;
(ii) ceasing to exhibit animals of a particular description to the public; or
(iii) ceasing to exhibit animals of a particular description to the public in a particular part of the zoo premises.

(3) The local authorities for the purposes of this Act are—

(*a*) in England, the district councils, the councils of London boroughs and the Common Council of the City of London;
(*aa*) in Wales, the councils of counties and county boroughs;
(*b*) in Scotland, the councils constituted under section 2 of the Local Government etc (Scotland) Act 1994.

(4) *Repealed.*

[Zoo Licensing Act 1981, s 1 amended by the Local Government (Wales) Act 1994, Sch 16 and SI 2002/3080 (England), SSI 2003/174 (Scotland), SI 2003/992 (Wales) and the Statute Law (Repeals) Act 2004.]

8–1397AA   1A. Conservation measures for zoos. The following are conservation measures to be implemented in zoos in accordance with this Act—

(*a*) participating in at least one of the following—

(i) research from which conservation benefits accrue to species of wild animals;
(ii) training in relevant conservation skills;
(iii) the exchange of information relating to the conservation of species of wild animals;
(iv) where appropriate, breeding of wild animals in captivity; and
(v) where appropriate, the repopulation of an area with, or the reintroduction into the wild of, wild animals;

(*b*) promoting public education and awareness in relation to the conservation of biodiversity, in particular by providing information about the species of wild animals kept in the zoo and their natural habitats;
(*c*) accommodating their animals under conditions which aim to satisfy the biological and conservation requirements of the species to which they belong, including—

(i) providing each animal with an environment well adapted to meet the physical, psychological and social needs of the species to which it belongs; and
(ii) providing a high standard of animal husbandry with a developed programme of preventative and curative veterinary care and nutrition;

(*d*) preventing the escape of animals and putting in place measures to be taken in the event of any escape or unauthorised release of animals;
(*e*) preventing the intrusion of pests and vermin into the zoo premises; and
(*f*) keeping up-to-date records of the zoo's collection, including records of—

(i) the numbers of different animals;
(ii) acquisitions, births, deaths, disposals and escapes of animals;
(iii) the causes of any such deaths; and
(iv) the health of the animals.

[Zoo Licensing Act 1981, s 1A inserted by SI 2002/3080 (England), SSI 2003/174 (Scotland) and SI 2003/992 (Wales).]

Sections 2–17 make detailed provision for licensing, inspection etc.

8–1397A   16E. Welfare of animals following closure of zoo. (1) Subsections (2) to (7) apply to a zoo to which this section applies unless the local authority are satisfied, after reasonable enquiries have been made, that the operator of the zoo cannot be found.

(2) As soon as reasonably practicable after the date from which this section applies, the operator shall give to the authority a plan of the arrangements he proposes to make in relation to the animals kept in the zoo—

(*a*) for their future care; or
(*b*) for their disposal and for their care until they are disposed of.

(3) The operator shall supply the authority with any information they request about the care or disposal of animals kept in the zoo.

(4) Where the authority notify the operator that they approve a plan prepared under subsection (2), he shall implement it under the supervision of the authority.

(5) Except with the agreement of the authority, the operator shall not—

(a) dispose of any animal kept in the zoo before a plan prepared under subsection (2) has been approved by the authority; or

(b) dispose of any animal kept in the zoo otherwise than in accordance with a plan so approved.

(6) Where—

(a) the authority are not satisfied with a plan prepared under subsection (2);

(b) the authority are not satisfied with the way in which such a plan is being implemented;

(c) the operator of the zoo has not prepared such a plan within a reasonable period after the date from which this section applies; or

(d) the authority consider that urgent steps need to be taken by the operator to safeguard the welfare of animals kept in the zoo,

the authority may, after giving the operator an opportunity to be heard, make a direction in such terms as they see fit as to the future care of the animals kept in the zoo, or for their disposal and for their care until they are disposed of.

(7) Where—

(a) the zoo operator has not complied with a direction under subsection (6) to the satisfaction of the authority; or

(b) the authority consider that urgent steps need to be taken by them to safeguard the welfare of animals kept in the zoo,

the authority shall, after giving the operator an opportunity to be heard, make arrangements for the future care of the animals kept in the zoo, or for their disposal and for their care until they are disposed of.

(8) Where the authority are satisfied, after reasonable enquiries have been made, that the operator of the zoo cannot be found, they shall make arrangements for the future care of the animals kept in the zoo, or for their disposal and for their care until they are disposed of.

(9) Subject to section 16G, for the purpose of giving effect to arrangements under subsection (7) or (8) the authority may—

(a) care for any animal on the premises of the zoo; or

(b) remove any animal found on the premises of the zoo and either retain it in the authority's possession or dispose of it.

(10) Arrangements for the care or disposal of animals under this section shall not be prejudicial to the protection of wild animals and the conservation of biodiversity.

(11) The authority may make a direction varying or revoking a direction under subsection (6) (including such a direction as varied by a direction under this subsection), but, unless they are satisfied, after reasonable enquiries have been made, that the operator cannot be found, they shall not do so without first giving him an opportunity to be heard.

(12) Where this section applies by virtue of section 16D(3), references in this section to a zoo shall be read as references to that section of the zoo which is closed permanently to the public.

[Zoo Licensing Act 1981, s 16E inserted by SI 2002/3080.]

8–1397B   16G. Powers of entry.   (1) For the purpose of giving effect to arrangements under section 16E(7) or (8), a person duly authorised by the authority for the purposes of this subsection may, on producing his authority if so required, enter the premises of the zoo for the purposes of—

(a) inspecting any animal found there to which the arrangements relate;

(b) inspecting the accommodation of any such animal;

(c) caring for any such animal; or

(d) removing any such animal.

(2) Subsection (1) shall not authorise entry into any part of the premises of the zoo which is used as a private dwelling.

(3) If a justice of the peace is satisfied by sworn information in writing that—

(a) it is necessary or desirable for the purpose of giving effect to arrangements under section 16E(7) or (8) for a person duly authorised by the authority for the purposes of this subsection to enter the premises of the zoo for any of the purposes mentioned in subsection (1); and

(b) either—

(i) any part of the premises to which admission for any of those purposes is sought is used as a private dwelling; or

(ii) admission to the premises or any part of the premises for any of those purposes has been refused,

he may grant a warrant authorising that person to enter the premises, or (as the case may be) the part of the premises used as a private dwelling or to which admission has been refused, for all or any of those purposes, with or without constables and any other persons who may be necessary, and if need be by reasonable force.

(4) A warrant granted under subsection (3) shall also specify—

(*a*) the length of time for which it is valid; and

(*b*) the times at which entry may be effected,

and may contain such restrictions as the justice thinks fit.

(5) A person duly authorised for the purposes of subsection (3) shall, if so required, produce his authority and warrant before entering the premises of the zoo or part of the premises to which the warrant relates (as the case may be).

[Zoo Licensing Act 1981, s 16G inserted by SI 2002/3080.]

8–1398 18. Appeals. (1) A person aggrieved by the refusal to grant a licence, by any condition attached to a licence, by any variation or cancellation of a condition or by the revocation of a licence may appeal—

(*a*) in England and Wales, to a magistrates' court acting for the petty sessions area in which the zoo is situated;

(*b*) in Scotland, by summary application to the sheriff.

(2) Any such appeal shall be brought within twenty-one days from the date on which the person wishing to appeal receives written notification of the authority's decision to refuse to grant a licence, to revoke a licence, to attach a condition (whether on the grant of the licence or later) or to vary or cancel a condition, as the case may be; but an appeal may be brought under this section whether or not the authority's decision was made in pursuance of a direction of the Secretary of State under this Act.

(3) On an appeal under this section to a magistrates' court, the court may confirm, vary or reverse the local authority's decision and generally give such directions as it thinks proper, having regard to the provisions of this Act.

(4) On an appeal under this section to the sheriff, he shall have power (without prejudice to any other power which he may have) to confirm, vary or reverse the local authority's decision and to award such expenses as he thinks fit.

(5) The procedure on an appeal to a magistrates' court under this section shall be by way of complaint for an order, and the Magistrates' Courts Act 1980 shall apply to the proceedings.

(6) The decision of the sheriff on an appeal under this section shall be final.

(7) In so far as a condition attached to a licence (whether on its grant or later), or the variation of a condition, imposes a requirement on the holder of the licence to carry out works he would not otherwise be required to carry out, the condition or the variation shall not have effect—

(*a*) during the period within which the holder is entitled to appeal against the attachment or variation, or

(*b*) where such an appeal is brought within that period, during the period before the appeal is determined or abandoned.

(8) A licence revoked under section 17 shall be deemed to continue in force—

(*a*) if no appeal is brought under this section within the time mentioned in subsection (2), until the expiration of the period of six months commencing with the expiration of that time; or

(*b*) if an appeal is so brought, until the determination or abandonment of the appeal (but without prejudice to the licence continuing in force further by virtue of the court's or sheriff's decision or of subsection (9)).

(9) If, on an appeal brought under this section, the court or the sheriff confirms a revocation under section 17, the licence shall be deemed to continue in force for a further period of six months commencing with the date of the confirmation.

[Zoo Licensing Act 1981, s 18.]

8–1399 19. Offences and penalties. (1) If a zoo is operated without a licence in contravention of this Act, the operator is guilty of an offence.

(2) If the operator of a zoo fails without reasonable excuse to comply with any condition for the time being attached to a licence for the zoo granted under this Act and held by him, he is guilty of an offence.

(3) Any person who intentionally obstructs an inspector acting pursuant to this Act is guilty of an offence.

(4) A person guilty of an offence under this section is liable on summary conviction to a fine not exceeding **level 4** on the standard scale for an offence under subsection (1) or (2) and **level 3** on the standard scale for an offence under subsection (3).

(5) Where an offence under this section committed by a body corporate is proved to have been committed with the consent or connivance of, or to have been attributed to any neglect on the part of, any director, manager, secretary or any other similar officer of the body corporate, or any person

who was purporting to act in any such capacity, he, as well as the body corporate, is guilty of that offence and liable to be proceeded against and punished accordingly.
[Zoo Licensing Act 1981, s 19 as amended by the Criminal Justice Act 1982, s 46.]

8–1400   20. *Repealed.*

8–1400A   21. Interpretation.   (1) In this Act—

"animals" means animals of the classes Mammalia, Aves, Reptilia, Amphibia, Pisces and Insecta and any other multi cellular organism that is not a plant or a fungus and "wild animals" means animals not normally domesticated in Great Britain;

"circus" means a place where animals are kept or introduced wholly or mainly for the purpose of performing tricks or manoeuvres at that place;

"keeper" includes any person employed under the directions of a keeper;

"the list" means the list compiled by the Secretary of State under section 8;

"pet shop" means premises for whose keeping as a pet shop a licence is in force, or is required, under the Pet Animals Act 1951;

"taxonomic category" means a group or assemblage of species recognised as an entity in scientific classification;

"zoo" has the meaning assigned by section 1(2).

(2) Nothing in this Act and nothing done under it shall prejudice or affect the operation of any of the relevant statutory provisions (whenever made) as defined in Part I of the Health and Safety at Work etc Act 1974.
[Zoo Licensing Act 1981, s 21.]

Animal Health and Welfare Act 1984
(1984 c 40)

Animal Health Act 1981

8–1401   3. Exercise of certain powers in territorial zone.   Where, apart from this section, any power to make provision by an order under the Animal Health Act 1981 does not include power to provide for its operation in or over territorial waters of the United Kingdom adjacent to Great Britain[1], it shall be treated as including such a power unless the context otherwise requires.
[Animal Health and Welfare Act 1984, s 3.]

---

1.   UK territorial waters extend to 12 miles; see the Territorial Waters Jurisdiction Act 1878 and the Territorial Sea Act 1987.

Controls over Breeding of Livestock

8–1402   10. Artificial breeding of livestock.   (1) The appropriate Minister may make regulations[1] for controlling the practice of artificial breeding of livestock.

In this section "artificial breeding" includes artificial insemination and transfer of ova or embryos.

(2) Regulations under this section–

(a) may, for the purpose of controlling the use for artificial breeding of any specified kind of livestock or of semen, ova or embryos of such livestock, prohibit the carrying on of any specified activity in connection with such livestock or with such semen, ova or embryos except under the authority of a licence or approval issued under the regulations;

(b) may, for the purpose of controlling their use for artificial breeding, prohibit the importation of semen, ova or embryos of any specified kind of livestock except under the authority of such a licence;

and, accordingly, the regulations may make such provision as appears to the appropriate Minister to be expedient in respect of the issue, modification, suspension and revocation of licences or approvals under the regulations including the conditions subject to which they may be issued.

(3) Regulations under this section may include provision—

(a) in respect of advertisements in connection with artificial breeding;

(b) for the seizure and detention of anything imported in contravention of any provision of the regulations or any conditions of any licence under them or anything which appears to any person authorised in that behalf to have been so imported and for dealing with anything so imported (whether by requiring it to be destroyed or taken out of Great Britain or otherwise);

(c) for the payment of fees in connection with—

(i) the issue of licences or approvals under the regulations, and

(ii) tests or examinations carried out for the purposes of the regulations,

and, where the regulations provide for an appeal against a refusal to issue any such licence or approval, in connection with such an appeal, being (in all cases) fees determined with the approval of the Treasury;

but subsection (2) above and this subsection are without prejudice to the generality of subsection (1) above.

(4) For the purpose of ascertaining whether the provisions of regulations under this section or the conditions of any licence or approval under them are being or have been contravened, a person authorised in writing in that behalf by the appropriate Minister may, on producing his authority, enter at all reasonable times—

(a) any premises used by the holder of a licence or approval under the regulations, being premises used for or in connection with any of the purposes authorised by the licence or approval; and

(b) any premises on which he has reasonable grounds for suspecting that an offence under this section is being or has been committed;

and may inspect the premises and any livestock or articles on them and carry out such test or other investigation as he thinks fit.

(5) For the purposes of any test or investigation under subsection (4) above, the person so authorised may require any person on the premises to give such information as it is in his power to give.

(6) A person who—

(a) contravenes any provision of regulations under this section or any conditions of a licence or approval under such regulations;

(b) intentionally obstructs any person in the exercise of the powers conferred on him by or under this section; or

(c) refuses to give any such person any information which he is required to give under subsection (5) above;

is guilty of an offence and liable on summary conviction to imprisonment for a term not exceeding **three months*** or to a fine not exceeding **level 3** on the standard scale, or both.

(7) It is a defence to a charge of committing an offence under subsection (6)(a) above to prove that the accused took all reasonable steps and exercised all due diligence to avoid committing the offence.

(8) In this section—

"appropriate Minister" means, in relation to England, the Minister of Agriculture, Fisheries and Food and, in relation to Scotland or to Wales, the Secretary of State[2];

"contravention" includes failure to comply and "contravene" is to be construed accordingly;

"livestock" includes any animal or bird not in the wild state;

"premises" includes any description of vehicle;

"specified" means specified in regulations under this section;

and anything brought to Great Britain from a country out of Great Britain and landed here or brought here through the tunnel system as defined in the Channel Tunnel Act 1987 is imported for the purposes of this section.

[Animal Health and Welfare Act 1984, s 10 amended by SI 1990/2371 and the Statute Law (Repeals) Act 1993, Sch 1.]

---

*Words substituted by the Criminal Justice Act 2003, Sch 26, from a date to be appointed.

1. The Artificial Insemination of Pigs (England and Wales) Regulations 1964, SI 1964/1172 has effect under this section. The Artificial Insemination of Pigs (EEC) Regulations 1992, SI 1992/3161 regulate exports to EEC states and approval of semen collection centres which engage in intra-Community trade are regulated and the following orders have been made: the Importation of Bovine Semen Regulations 1984, SI 1984/1325 amended by SI 1993/1966; the Artificial Insemination of Cattle (Animal Health) (England and Wales) Regulations 1985, SI 1985/1861 amended by SI 1987/904, SI 1995/2549, SI 2001/380 (England) and1539 (Wales), SI 2002/824 (England) and 1131 (Wales) and SI 2004/3231 (E); the Artificial Insemination of Cattle (Advertising Controls etc) (Great Britain) Regulations 1987, SI 1987/904; the Bovine Embryo (Collection, Production and Transfer) Regulations 1995, SI 1995/2478; the Artificial Insemination of Cattle (Emergency Licences) (Wales) Regulations 2001, SI 2001/1539.

The Artificial Breeding of Sheep and Goats Regulations 1993, SI 1993/3248, implement EEC Council Directive 92/65 in relation to the production for intra Community trade of the semen, ova and embryos of sheep and goats and provide for the approval of semen collection centres and embryo collection teams.

2. The functions of the Minister, so far as exercisable in relation to Wales, have been transferred to the National Assembly for Wales, by the National Assembly for Wales (Transfer of Functions) Order 1999, SI 1999/672, art 2, Sch 1.

8–1403 11. Provisions supplementary to section 10. (1) Where an offence committed by a body corporate under section 10 of this Act is proved to have been committed with the consent or connivance of, or to be attributable to any neglect on the part of, any director, manager, secretary or other similar officer of the body corporate, or any person who was purporting to act in any such capacity, he as well as the body corporate shall be guilty of the offence, and shall be liable to be proceeded against and punished accordingly.

(2) Where the affairs of a body corporate are managed by its members, subsection (1) above shall apply in relation to the acts and defaults of a member in connection with his functions of management as if he were a director of the body corporate.

(3) *Repeal.*

(4) The power conferred by section 10 of this Act to make regulations shall be exercisable by statutory instrument which shall be subject to annulment in pursuance of a resolution of either House of Parliament.
[Animal Health and Welfare Act 1984, s 11.]

Supplementary

8–1404 16. Minor and consequential amendments and repeals. (1) Schedule 1 to this Act (which contains minor and consequential amendments) shall have effect.

(2) The enactments mentioned in Schedule 2 to this Act are repealed to the extent specified in the third column of that Schedule and the Slaughter of Poultry Act 1967 Extension Order 1978 is revoked.
[Animal Health and Welfare Act 1984, s 16.]

8–1405 17. Short title commencement and extent. (1) This Act may be cited as the Animal Health and Welfare Act 1984.

(2)–(4) *Repealed.*

(5) *Northern Ireland.*
[Animal Health and Welfare Act 1984, s 17, as amended by SI 1995/731 and the Statute Law (Repeals) Act 2004.]

Animals (Scientific Procedures) Act 1986[1]

(1986 c 14)

Preliminary

8–1406 1. Protected animals. (1) Subject to the provisions of this section, "a protected animal" for the purposes of this Act means any living vertebrate other than man.

(2) Any such vertebrate in its foetal, larval or embryonic form is a protected animal only from the stage of its development when—

(*a*) in the case of a mammal, bird or reptile, half the gestation or incubation period for the relevant species has elapsed; and

(*b*) in any other case, it becomes capable of independent feeding.

(3) The Secretary of State may by order—

(*a*) extend the definition of protected animal so as to include invertebrates of any description[2];

(*b*) alter the stage of development specified in subsection (2) above;

(*c*) make provision in lieu of subsection (2) above as respects any animal which becomes a protected animal by virtue of an order under paragraph (*a*) above.

(4) For the purposes of this section an animal shall be regarded as continuing to live until the permanent cessation of circulation or the destruction of its brain.

(5) In this section "vertebrate" means any animal of the Sub-phylum Vertebrata of the Phylum Chordata and "invertebrate" means any animal not of that Sub-phylum.
[Animals (Scientific Procedures) Act 1986, s 1.]

---

1. This Act makes new provision for the protection of animals used for experimental or other scientific purposes
2. "Protected animal" includes any invertebrate of the species Octopus vulgaris from the stage of its development when it becomes capable of independent feeding, SI 1993/2103.

8–1407 2. Regulated procedures. (1) Subject to the provisions of this section, "a regulated procedure" for the purposes of this Act means any experimental or other scientific procedure applied to a protected animal which may have the effect of causing that animal pain, suffering, distress or lasting harm.

(2) An experimental or other scientific procedure applied to an animal is also a regulated procedure if—

(*a*) it is part of a series or combination of such procedures (whether the same or different) applied to the same animal; and

(*b*) the series or combination may have the effect mentioned in subsection (1) above; and

(*c*) the animal is a protected animal throughout the series or combination or in the course of it attains the stage of its development when it becomes such an animal.

(3) Anything done for the purpose of, or liable to result in, the birth or hatching of a protected animal is also a regulated procedure if it may as respects that animal have the effect mentioned in subsection (1) above.

(4) In determining whether any procedure may have the effect mentioned in subsection (1) above the use of an anaesthetic or analgesic, decerebration and any other procedure for rendering an animal insentient shall be disregarded; and the administration of an anaesthetic or analgesic to a protected

animal, or decerebration or any other such procedure applied to such an animal, for the purposes of any experimental or other scientific procedure shall itself be a regulated procedure.

(5) The ringing, tagging or marking of an animal, or the application of any other humane procedure for the sole purpose of enabling an animal to be identified, is not a regulated procedure if it causes only momentary pain or distress and no lasting harm.

(6) The administration of any substance or article to an animal by way of a medicinal test on animals as defined in subsection (6) of section 32 of the Medicines Act 1968 is not a regulated procedure if the substance or article is administered in accordance with the provisions of subsection (4) of that section or of an order under section 35(8)(*b*) of that Act.

(7) Killing a protected animal is a regulated procedure only if it is killed for experimental or other scientific use, the place where it is killed is a designated establishment and the method employed is not one appropriate to the animal under Schedule 1 to this Act.

(8) In this section references to a scientific procedure do not include references to any recognised veterinary, agricultural or animal husbandry practice.

(9) Schedule 1 to this Act may be amended by orders made by the Secretary of State.

[Animals (Scientific Procedures) Act 1986, s 2.]

Personal and project licences

8–1408   3. Prohibition of unlicensed procedures.   No person shall apply a regulated procedure to an animal unless—

(*a*) he holds a personal licence qualifying him to apply a regulated procedure of that description to an animal of that description;

(*b*) the procedure is applied as part of a programme of work specified in a project licence authorising the application, as part of that programme, of a regulated procedure of that description to an animal of that description; and

(*c*) the place where the procedure is carried out is a place specified in the personal licence and the project licence.

[Animals (Scientific Procedures) Act 1986, s 3.]

8–1409   4. Personal licences.   (1) A personal licence is a licence granted by the Secretary of State qualifying the holder to apply specified regulated procedures to animals of specified descriptions at a specified place or specified places.

(2) An application for a personal licence shall be made to the Secretary of State in such form and shall be supported by such information as he may reasonably require.

(3) Except where the Secretary of State dispenses with the requirements of this subsection any such application shall be endorsed by a person who—

(*a*) is himself the holder of a personal licence or a licence treated as such a licence by virtue of Schedule 4 to this Act; and

(*b*) has knowledge of the biological or other relevant qualifications and of the training, experience and character of the applicant;

and the person endorsing an application shall, if practicable, be a person occupying a position of authority at a place where the applicant is to be authorised by the licence to carry out the procedures specified in it.

(4) No personal licence shall be granted to a person under the age of eighteen.

(5) A personal licence shall continue in force until revoked but the Secretary of State shall review each personal licence granted by him at intervals not exceeding five years and may for that purpose require the holder to furnish him with such information as he may reasonably require.

(4A) The Secretary of State shall not grant a personal licence to a person unless he is satisfied that the person—

(*a*) has appropriate education and training (including instruction in a relevant scientific discipline) for the purpose of applying the regulated procedures to be specified in the licence; and

(*b*) is competent to apply those procedures in accordance with the conditions which are to be included in the licence and to handle and take care of laboratory animals.

[Animals (Scientific Procedures) Act 1986, s 4 as amended by SI 1998/1974.]

8–1410   5. Project licences.   (1) A project licence is a licence granted by the Secretary of State specifying a programme of work and authorising the application, as part of that programme, of specified regulated procedures to animals of specified descriptions at a specified place or specified places.

(2) A project licence shall not be granted except to a person who undertakes overall responsibility for the programme to be specified in the licence.

(3) A project licence shall not be granted for any programme unless the Secretary of State is satisfied that it is undertaken for one or more of the following purposes—

(*a*) the prevention (whether by the testing of any product or otherwise) or the diagnosis or treatment of disease, ill-health or abnormality, or their effects, in man, animals or plants;

(b)   the assessment, detection, regulation or modification of physiological conditions in man, animals or plants;

(c)   the protection of the natural environment in the interests of the health or welfare of man or animals;

(d)   the advancement of knowledge in biological or behavioural sciences;

(e)   education or training otherwise than in primary or secondary schools;

(f)   forensic enquiries;

(g)   the breeding of animals for experimental or other scientific use.

(4)   In determining whether and on what terms to grant a project licence the Secretary of State shall weigh the likely adverse effects on the animals concerned against the benefit likely to accrue as a result of the programme to be specified in the licence.

(5)   The Secretary of State shall not grant a project licence unless he is satisfied—

(a)   that the purpose of the programme to be specified in the licence cannot be achieved satisfactorily by any other reasonably practicable method not entailing the use of protected animals; and

(b)   that the regulated procedures to be used are those which use the minimum number of animals, involve animals with the lowest degree of neurophysiological sensitivity, cause the least pain, suffering, distress or lasting harm, and are most likely to produce satisfactory results.

(6)   The Secretary of State shall not grant a project licence authorising the use of cats, dogs, primates or equidae unless he is satisfied that animals of no other species are suitable for the purposes of the programme to be specified in the licence or that it is not practicable to obtain animals of any other species that are suitable for those purposes.

(7)   Unless revoked and subject to subsection (8) below, a project licence shall continue in force for such period as is specified in the licence and may be renewed for further periods but (without prejudice to the grant of a new licence in respect of the programme in question) no such licence shall be in force for more than five years in all.

(8)   A project licence shall terminate on the death of the holder but if—

(a)   the holder of a certificate under section 6 below in respect of a place specified in the licence; or

(b)   where by virtue of subsection (2) of that section the licence does not specify a place in respect of which there is such a certificate, the holder of a personal licence engaged on the programme in question,

notifies the Secretary of State of the holder's death within seven days of its coming to his knowledge the licence shall, unless the Secretary of State otherwise directs, continue in force until the end of the period of twenty-eight days beginning with the date of the notification.

[Animals (Scientific Procedures) Act 1986, s 5 as amended by SI 1998/1974.]

Designated establishments

8–1411   6. Scientific procedure establishments.   (1) Subject to subsection (2) below, no place shall be specified in a project licence unless it is a place designated by a certificate issued by the Secretary of State under this section as a scientific procedure establishment.

(2)   Subsection (1) above shall not apply in any case in which it appears to the Secretary of State that the programme or procedures authorised by the licence require him to specify a different place.

(3)   An application for a certificate in respect of a scientific procedure establishment shall be made to the Secretary of State in such form and shall be supported by such information as he may reasonably require.

(4)   A certificate shall not be issued under this section—

(a)   except to a person occupying a position of authority at the establishment in question; and

(b)   unless the application nominates for inclusion in the certificate pursuant to subsection (5) below a person or persons appearing to the Secretary of State to be suitable for that purpose.

(5)   A certificate under this section shall specify—

(a)   a person to be responsible for the day-to-day care of the protected animals kept for experimental or other scientific purposes at the establishment; and

(b)   a veterinary surgeon or other suitably qualified person to provide advice on their health and welfare;

and the same person may, if the Secretary of State thinks fit, be specified under both paragraphs of this subsection.

(6)   If it appears to any person specified in a certificate pursuant to subsection (5) above that the health or welfare of any such animal as is mentioned in that subsection gives rise to concern he shall—

(a)   notify the person holding a personal licence who is in charge of the animal; or

(b)   if there is no such person or it is not practicable to notify him, take steps to ensure that the animal is cared for and, if it is necessary for it to be killed, that it is killed by a method which is appropriate under Schedule 1 to this Act or approved by the Secretary of State.

(7) In any case to which subsection (6) above applies the person specified in the certificate pursuant to paragraph (*a*) of subsection (5) above may also notify the person (if different) specified pursuant to paragraph (*b*) of that subsection; and the person specified pursuant to either paragraph of that subsection may also notify one of the inspectors appointed under this Act.

(8) A certificate under this section shall continue in force until revoked.

[Animals (Scientific Procedures) Act 1986, s 6.]

8–1412 7. Breeding and supplying establishments. (1) A person shall not at any place breed for use in regulated procedures (whether there or elsewhere) protected animals of a description specified in Schedule 2 to this Act unless that place is designated by a certificate issued by the Secretary of State under this section as a breeding establishment.

(2) A person shall not any place keep any such protected animals which have not been bred there but are to be supplied for use elsewhere in regulated procedures unless that place is designated by a certificate issued by the Secretary of State under this section as a supplying establishment.

(3) An application for a certificate in respect of a breeding or supplying establishment shall be made to the Secretary of State in such form and shall be supported by such information as he may reasonably require.

(4) A certificate shall not be issued under this section unless the application nominates for inclusion in the certificate pursuant to subsection (5) below a person or persons appearing to the Secretary of State to be suitable for that purpose.

(5) A certificate under this section shall specify—

(*a*) a person to be responsible for the day-to-day care of the animals bred or kept for breeding at the establishment or, as the case may be, kept there for the purpose of being supplied for use in regulated procedures; and

(*b*) a veterinary surgeon or other suitably qualified person to provide advice on their health and welfare;

and the same person may, if the Secretary of State thinks fit, be specified under both paragraphs of this subsection.

(6) If it appears to any person specified in a certificate pursuant to subsection (5) above that the health or welfare of any such animal as is mentioned in that subsection gives rise to concern he shall take steps to ensure that it is cared for and, if it is necessary for it to be killed, that it is killed by a method appropriate under Schedule 1 to this Act or approved by the Secretary of State.

(7) In any case to which subsection (6) above applies the person specified in the certificate pursuant to paragraph (*a*) of subsection (5) above may also notify the person (if different) specified pursuant to paragraph (*b*) of that subsection; and the person specified pursuant to either paragraph of that subsection may also notify one of the inspectors appointed under this Act.

(8) A certificate under this section shall continue in force until revoked.

(9) Schedule 2 to this Act may be amended by orders made by the Secretary of State.

[Animals (Scientific Procedures) Act 1986, s 7.]

8–1412A 8. *Fees.*

8–1413 9–13. *Licences and designation certificates: general provisions.*

Additional controls

8–1414 14. Re-use of protected animals. (1) Where—

(*a*) a protected animal has been subjected to a series of regulated procedures for a particular purpose; and

(*b*) any of those procedures has caused severe pain or distress to that animal,

that animal shall not be used for any further regulated procedures which will entail severe pain or distress.

(2) Where a protected animal has been subjected to a series of regulated procedures for a particular purpose and has been given a general anaesthetic for any of those procedures and been allowed to recover consciousness, that animal shall not be used for any further regulated procedures unless the Secretary of State has given his consent to such further use and—

(*a*) the procedure, or each procedure, for which the anaesthetic was given consisted only of surgical preparation essential for a subsequent procedure; or

(*b*) the anaesthetic was administered solely to immobilise the animal; or

(*c*) the animal will be under general anaesthesia throughout the further procedures and will not be allowed to recover consciousness.

(3) Without prejudice to subsections (1) and (2) above, where a protected animal has been subjected to a series of regulated procedures for a particular purpose it shall not be used for any further regulated procedures except with the consent of the Secretary of State.

(4) Any consent for the purposes of this section may relate to a specified animal or to animals used in specified procedures or specified circumstances.
[Animals (Scientific Procedures) Act 1986, s 14.]

8–1415   15. Killing animals at conclusion of regulated procedures.   (1) Where a protected animal—

(*a*) has been subjected to a series of regulated procedures for a particular purpose; and

(*b*) at the conclusion of the series is suffering or likely to suffer adverse effects,

the person who applied those procedures, or the last of them, shall cause the animal to be immediately killed by a method appropriate to the animal under Schedule 1 to this Act or by such other method as may be authorised by the personal licence of the person by whom the animal is killed.

(2) Subsection (1) above is without prejudice to any condition of a project licence requiring an animal to be killed at the conclusion of a regulated procedure in circumstances other than those mentioned in that subsection.
[Animals (Scientific Procedures) Act 1986, s 15.]

8–1416   16. Prohibition of public displays.   (1) No person shall carry out any regulated procedure as an exhibition to the general public or carry out any such procedure which is shown live on television for general reception.

(2) No person shall publish a notice or advertisement announcing the carrying out of any regulated procedure in a manner that would contravene subsection (1) above.
[Animals (Scientific Procedures) Act 1986, s 16.]

8–1417   17. Neuromuscular blocking agents.   No person shall in the course of a regulated procedure—

(*a*) use any neuromuscular blocking agent unless expressly authorised to do so by the personal and project licences under which the procedure is carried out; or

(*b*) use any such agent instead of an anaesthetic.
[Animals (Scientific Procedures) Act 1986, s 17.]

The inspectorate and the committee

8–1418   18. Inspectors.   (1) The Secretary of State shall, with the consent of the Treasury as to numbers and remuneration, appoint as inspectors for the purposes of this Act persons having such medical or veterinary qualifications as he thinks requisite.

(2) It shall be the duty of an inspector—

(*a*) to advise the Secretary of State on applications for personal and project licences, on requests for their variation or revocation and on their periodical review;

(*b*) to advise him on applications for certificates under this Act and on requests for their variation or revocation;

(*c*) to visit places where regulated procedures are carried out for the purpose of determining whether those procedures are authorised by the requisite licences and whether the conditions of those licences are being complied with;

(*d*) to visit designated establishments for the purpose of determining whether the conditions of the certificates in respect of those establishments are being complied with;

(*e*) to report to the Secretary of State any case in which any provision of this Act or any condition of a licence or certificate under this Act has not been or is not being complied with and to advise him on the action to be taken in any such case.

(3) If an inspector considers that a protected animal is undergoing excessive suffering he may require it to be immediately killed by a method appropriate to the animal under Schedule 1 to this Act or by such other method as may be authorised by any personal licence held by the person to whom the requirement is addressed.
[Animals (Scientific Procedures) Act 1986, s 18.]

8–1419   19–20.   *The Animal Procedures Committee; functions of the Committee.*

Miscellaneous and supplementary

8–1420   21. Guidance, codes of practice and statistics.   (1) The Secretary of State shall publish information to serve as guidance with respect to the manner in which he proposes to exercise his power to grant licences and certificates under this Act and with respect to the conditions which he proposes to include in such licences and certificates.

(2) The Secretary of State shall issue codes of practice as to the care of protected animals and their use for regulated procedures and may approve such codes issued by other persons.

(3) The Secretary of State shall consult the Animal Procedures Committee before publishing or altering any information under subsection (1) above or issuing, approving, altering or approving any alteration in any code issued or approved under subsection (2) above.

(4) A failure on the part of any person to comply with any provision of a code issued or approved under subsection (2) above shall not of itself render that person liable to criminal or civil proceedings but—

    (*a*)   any such code shall be admissible in evidence in any such proceedings; and

    (*b*)   if any of its provisions appears to the court conducting the proceedings to be relevant to any question arising in the proceedings it shall be taken into account in determining that question.

(5)–(7) *Secretary of State to lay before Parliament copies of any information published or code issued, and to report annually to Parliament with respect to the use of protected animals.*
[Animals (Scientific Procedures) Act 1986, s 21.]

8–1421   22. Penalties for contraventions.   (1) Any person who contravenes section 3 above shall be guilty of an offence and liable[1]—

    (*a*)   on conviction on indictment, to imprisonment for a term not exceeding **two years** or to a **fine** or to both;

    (*b*)   on summary conviction, to imprisonment for a term not exceeding **six months** or to a fine not exceeding **the statutory maximum** or to both.

(2) Any person who, being the holder of a project licence—

    (*a*)   procures or knowingly permits a person under his control to carry out a regulated procedure otherwise than as part of the programme specified in the licence; or

    (*b*)   procures or knowingly permits a person under his control to carry out a regulated procedure otherwise than in accordance with that person's personal licence,

shall be guilty of an offence and liable to the penalties specified in subsection (1) above.

(3) Any person who—

    (*a*)   contravenes section 7(1) or (2), 14, 15, 16 or 17 above; or

    (*b*)   fails to comply with a requirement imposed on him under section 18(3) above,

shall be guilty of an offence and liable on summary conviction to imprisonment for a term not exceeding **three months** or to a fine not exceeding **the fourth level** on the standard scale or to both.

(4) A person shall not be guilty of an offence under section 3 or 17(*a*) above by reason only that he acted without the authority of a project licence if he shows that he reasonably believed, after making due enquiry, that he had such authority.

(5) A person guilty of an offence under section 1 of the Protection of Animals Act 1911 or section 1 of the Protection of Animals (Scotland) Act 1912 in respect of an animal at a designated establishment shall be liable to the penalties specified in subsection (1) above.
[Animals (Scientific Procedures) Act 1986, s 22.]

---

1. For procedure in respect of this offence which is triable either way, see the Magistrates Courts Act 1980, ss 17A–21, in Part I: Magistrates' Courts, Procedure, ante.

8–1422   23. False statements.   (1) A person is guilty of an offence if for the purpose of obtaining or assisting another person to obtain a licence or certificate under this Act he furnishes information which he knows to be false or misleading in a material particular or recklessly furnishes information which is false or misleading in a material particular.

(2) A person guilty of an offence under this section shall be liable on summary conviction to imprisonment for a term not exceeding **three months** or to a fine not exceeding **the fourth level** on the standard scale or to both.
[Animals (Scientific Procedures) Act 1986, s 23.]

8–1423   24. Protection of confidential information.   (1) A person is guilty of an offence if otherwise than for the purpose of discharging his functions under this Act he discloses any information which has been obtained by him in the exercise of those functions and which he knows or has reasonable grounds for believing to have been given in confidence.

(2) A person guilty of an offence under this section shall be liable[1]—

    (*a*)   on conviction on indictment, to imprisonment for a term not exceeding **two years** or to a **fine** or to both;

    (*b*)   on summary conviction, to imprisonment for a term not exceeding six months or to a fine not exceeding the statutory maximum or to both.
[Animals (Scientific Procedures) Act 1986, s 24.]

---

1. For procedure in respect of this offence which is triable either way, see the Magistrates Courts Act 1980, ss 17A–21, in Part I: Magistrates' Courts, Procedure, ante.

8–1424   25. Powers of entry.   (1) If a justice of the peace or in Scotland a sheriff is satisfied by information on oath that there are reasonable grounds for believing that an offence under this Act has been or is being committed at any place, he may issue a warrant authorising a constable to enter that place if need be by such force as is reasonably necessary, to search it and to require any person found there to give his name and address.

(2) A warrant under this section may authorise a constable to be accompanied by an inspector appointed under this Act and shall require him to be accompanied by such an inspector if the place in question is a designated establishment.

(3) Any person who—

(*a*) intentionally obstructs a constable or inspector in the exercise of his powers under this section; or

(*b*) refuses on demand to give his name and address or gives a false name or address,

shall be guilty of an offence and liable on summary conviction to imprisonment for a term not exceeding **three months** or to a fine not exceeding **the fourth level** on the standard scale or to both.

[Animals (Scientific Procedures) Act 1986, s 25.]

8–1425   26. Prosecutions.   (1) No proceedings for—

(*a*)   an offence under this Act; or

(*b*)   an offence under section 1 of the Protection of Animals Act 1911 which is alleged to have been committed in respect of an animal at a designated establishment,

shall be brought in England and Wales except by or with the consent of the Director of Public Prosecutions.

(2) Summary proceedings for an offence under this Act may (without prejudice to any jurisdiction exercisable apart from this subsection) be taken against any person at any place at which he is for the time being.

(3) Notwithstanding anything in section 127(1) of the Magistrates' Courts Act 1980, an information relating to an offence under this Act which is triable by a magistrates' court in England and Wales may be so tried if it is laid at any time within three years after the commission of the offence and within six months after the date on which evidence sufficient in the opinion of the Director of Public Prosecutions to justify the proceedings comes to his knowledge.

(4) *Scotland.*

(5) For the purposes of subsections (3) and (4) above a certificate of the Director of Public Prosecutions or, as the case may be, the Lord Advocate as to the date on which such evidence as is there mentioned came to his knowledge shall be conclusive evidence of that fact.

[Animals (Scientific Procedures) Act 1986, s 26.]

8–1426   27. *Repeal, consequential amendments and transitional provisions.*

8–1427   28. Orders.   (1) Any power of the Secretary of State to make an order under this Act shall be exercisable by statutory instrument.

(2) A statutory instrument containing an order under any of the foregoing provisions of this Act shall be subject to annulment in pursuance of a resolution of either House of Parliament.

[Animals (Scientific Procedures) Act 1986, s 28.]

8–1428   29. *Application to Northern Ireland.*

8–1429   30. Short title, interpretation and commencement.   (1) This Act may be cited as the Animals (Scientific Procedures) Act 1986.

(2) In this Act—

"designated", in relation to an establishment, means designated by a certificate under section 6 or 7 above;

"personal licence" means a licence granted under section 4 above;

"place" includes any place within the seaward limits of the territorial waters of the United Kingdom, including any vessel other than a ship which is not a British ship;

"project licence" means a licence granted under section 5 above;

"protected animal" has the meaning given in section 1 above but subject to any order under subsection (3) of that section;

"regulated procedure" has the meaning given in section 2 above.

(3) This Act shall come into force on such date as the Secretary of State may by order[1] appoint; and different dates may be appointed for different provisions or different purposes.

[Animals (Scientific Procedures) Act 1986, s 30.]

---

1. See the Animals (Scientific Procedures) Act (Commencement) Order 1986, SI 1986/2088.

SCHEDULES

     SCHEDULE 1
APPROPRIATE METHODS OF HUMANE KILLING

(As inserted by SI 1996/3278.)

1. Subject to paragraph 2 below, the methods of humane killing listed in Tables A and B below are appropriate for the animals listed in the corresponding entries in those tables only if the process of killing is completed by one of the methods listed in sub-paragraphs (*a*) to (*f*) below:

(*a*)   confirmation of permanent cessation of the circulation
(*b*)   destruction of the brain
(*c*)   dislocation of the neck
(*d*)   exsanguination
(*e*)   confirming the onset of *rigor mortis*
(*f*)   instantaneous destruction of the body in a macerator.

2. Paragraph 1 above does not apply in those cases where Table A specifies one of the methods listed in that paragraph as an appropriate method of humane killing.

A **Methods for animals other than foetal, larval and embryonic forms**	**Animals for which appropriate**
1 Overdose of an anaesthetic using a route and an anaesthetic agent appropriate for the size and species of animal	All animals
2 Exposure to carbon dioxide gas in a rising concentration	Rodents, Rabbits and Birds up to 1.5 kg
3 Dislocation of the neck	Rodents up to 500g Rabbits up to 1 kg Birds up to 3 kg
4 Concussion of the brain by striking the cranium	Rodents and Rabbits up to 1kg Birds up to 250g Amphibians and reptiles (with destruction of the brain before the return of consciousness) up to 1 kg Fishes (with destruction of the brain before the return of consciousness)
5 One of the recognised methods of slaughter set out below which is appropriate to the animal and is performed by a registered veterinary surgeon, or, in the case of the methods described in paragraph (ii) below, performed by the holder of a current licence granted under the Welfare of Animals (Slaughter or Killing) Regulations 1995 (i) Destruction of the brain by free bullet, or (ii) captive bolt, percussion or electrical stunning followed by destruction of the brain or exsanguination before return of consciousness	Ungulates
B **Methods for foetal, larval and embryonic forms**	**Animals for which appropriate**
1 Overdose of an anaesthetic using a route and anaesthetic agent appropriate for the size, stage of development and species of animal	All animals
2 Refrigeration, or disruption of membranes, or maceration in apparatus approved under appropriate slaughter legislation, or exposure to carbon dioxide in near 100% concentration until they are dead	Birds, Reptiles
3 Cooling of foetuses followed by immersion in cold tissue fixative	Mice, Rats and Rabbits
4 Decapitation	Mammals and Birds up to 50g.

     SCHEDULE 2
ANIMALS TO BE OBTAINED ONLY FROM DESIGNATED BREEDING OR SUPPLYING ESTABLISHMENTS

(Amended by SI 1993/2103 and SI 1998/1674.)

Mouse
Rat
Guinea-pig
Hamster
Rabbit
Dog
Cat
Primate
Any bird of the species Coturnix coturnix (quail)
Ferret
Gerbil

Pig, if genetically modified
Sheep, if genetically modified

Section 10(2A)
SCHEDULE 2A
(*Inserted by SI 1998/1974*)
ARTICLE 8 OF COUNCIL DIRECTIVE NO 86/609/EEC

1. All experiments shall be carried out under general or local anaesthesia.

2. Paragraph 1 above does not apply when:

(*a*) anaesthesia is judged to be more traumatic to the animal than the experiment itself;

(*b*) anaesthesia is incompatible with the object of the experiment. In such cases appropriate legislative and/or administrative measures shall be taken to ensure that no such experiment is carried out unnecessarily. Anaesthesia should be used in the case of serious injuries which may cause severe pain.

3. If anaesthesia is not possible, analgesics or other appropriate methods should be used in order to ensure as far as possible that pain, suffering, distress or harm are limited and that in any event the animal is not subject to severe pain, distress or suffering.

4. Provided such action is compatible with the object of the experiment, an anaesthetised animal, which suffers considerable pain once anaesthesia has worn off, shall be treated in good time with pain-relieving means or, if this is not possible, shall be immediately killed by a humane method.

Horses (Protective Headgear for Young Riders) Act 1990

(1990 c 25)

8–1431   **1. Causing or permitting child under 14 to ride on road without protective headgear.**
(1) Except as provided by regulations, it is an offence for any person to whom this subsection applies to cause or permit a child under the age of 14 years to ride a horse on a road unless the child is wearing protective headgear, of such description as may be specified in regulations, in such manner as may be so specified.

(2) Subsection (1) above applies to the following persons—

(*a*) any person who—

(i) for the purposes of Part I of the Children and Young Persons Act 1933, has responsibility for the child; or

(ii) for the purposes of Part II of the Children and Young Persons (Scotland) Act 1937, has parental responsibilities (within the meaning given by section 1(3) of the Children (Scotland) Act 1995) in relation to, or has charge or care of the child;

(*b*) any owner of the horse;

(*c*) any person other than its owner who has custody of or is in possession of the horse immediately before the child rides it; and

(*d*) where the child is employed, his employer and any other person to whose orders the child is subject in the course of his employment.

(3) A person guilty of an offence under subsection (1) above is liable on summary conviction to a fine not exceeding **level 1** on the standard scale.

(4) Until the coming into force of paragraph 5 of Schedule 13 to the Children Act 1989, subsection (2)(*a*)(i) above shall have effect as if for "responsibility for the child" there were substituted "custody, charge or care of the child".

[Horses (Protective Headgear for Young Riders) Act 1990, s 1, as amended by the Children (Scotland) Act 1995, Sch 4.]

8–1432   **2. Regulations.**   (1) The Secretary of State may by regulations[1] made by statutory instrument—

(*a*) provide that section 1 of this Act shall not apply in relation to children of any prescribed description, or in relation to the riding of horses in such circumstances as may be prescribed;

(*b*) prescribe for the purposes of that section (by reference to shape, construction or any other quality) the descriptions of protective headgear to be worn by children of any prescribed description in prescribed circumstances; and

(*c*) prescribe for those purposes the manner in which such headgear is to be worn.

(2) Before making any regulations under this section the Secretary of State shall consult such representative organisations as he thinks fit.

(3) Any statutory instrument containing regulations under this section shall be subject to annulment in pursuance of a resolution of either House of Parliament.

[Horses (Protective Headgear for Young Riders) Act 1990, s 2.]

---

1. The Horses (Protective Headgear for Young Riders) Regulations 1992, SI 1992/1201, have been made.

8–1433   **3. Interpretation.**   (1) In this Act—

"horse" includes pony, mule, donkey or other equine animal;

"regulations" means regulations under section 2 of this Act; and

"road" does not include a footpath or bridleway but, subject to that, has—

    (a) in England and Wales the meaning given by section 192(1) of the Road Traffic Act 1988; and

    (b) in Scotland the meaning given by section 151(1) of the Roads (Scotland) Act 1984.

(2) For the purposes of the definition of "road" in subsection (1) above—

    (a) "footpath" means a way—

        (i) over which the public have a right of way or, in Scotland, of passage on foot only; and

        (ii) which is not associated with a carriageway; and

    (b) "bridleway" means a way over which the public have the following, but no other, rights of way; a right of way on foot and a right of way on horseback or leading a horse, with or without a right to drive animals of any description along the way.

[Horses (Protective Headgear for Young Riders) Act 1990, s 3.]

8–1434   **4.** *Corresponding provision for Northern Ireland.*

8–1435   **5.** *Short title, commencement and extent.*

Protection of Badgers Act 1992
(1992 c 51)

Offences

8–1501   **1. Taking, injuring or killing badgers.**   (1) A person is guilty of an offence if, except as permitted by or under this Act, he wilfully kills, injures or takes, or attempts to kill, injure or take,★ a badger.

(2) If, in any proceedings for an offence under subsection (1) above consisting of attempting to kill, injure or take a badger, there is evidence from which it could reasonably be concluded that at the material time the accused was attempting to kill, injure or take a badger, he shall be presumed to have been attempting to kill, injure or take a badger unless the contrary is shown.★

(3) A person is guilty of an offence if, except as permitted by or under this Act, he has in his possession or under his control any dead badger or any part of, or anything derived from, a dead badger.

(4) A person is not guilty of an offence under subsection (3) above if he shows that—

    (a) the badger had not been killed, or had been killed otherwise than in contravention of the provisions of this Act or of the Badgers Act 1973; or

    (b) the badger or other thing in his possession or control had been sold (whether to him or any other person) and, at the time of the purchase, the purchaser had had no reason to believe that the badger had been killed in contravention of any of those provisions.

(5) If a person is found committing an offence under this section on any land it shall be lawful for the owner or occupier of the land, or any servant of the owner or occupier, or any constable, to require that person forthwith to quit the land and also to give his name and address; and if that person on being so required wilfully remains on the land or refuses to give his full name or address he is guilty of an offence.

[Protection of Badgers Act 1992, s 1.]

★Words in sub-s (1) and sub-s (2) **repealed by the Nature Conservation (Scotland) Act 2004, Sch 6 as from 1 October 2004.**

8–1502   **2. Cruelty.**   (1) A person is guilty of an offence if—

    (a) he cruelly ill-treats a badger;

    (b) he uses any badger tongs in the course of killing or taking, or attempting to kill or take, a badger;

    (c) except as permitted by or under this Act, he digs for a badger; or

    (d) he uses for the purpose of killing or taking a badger any firearm other than a smooth bore weapon of not less than 20 bore or a rifle using ammunition having a muzzle energy not less than 160 footpounds and a bullet weighing not less than 38 grains.

(2) If in any proceedings for an offence under subsection (1)(c) above there is evidence from which it could reasonably be concluded that at the material time the accused was digging for a badger he shall be presumed to have been digging for a badger unless the contrary is shown.

[Protection of Badgers Act 1992, s 2.]

8–1503   **3. Interfering with badger setts.**   A person is guilty of an offence if, except as permitted by or under this Act, he interferes[1] with a badger sett[2] by doing any of the following things—

(a)   damaging a badger sett or any part of it;
(b)   destroying a badger sett;
(c)   obstructing access to, or any entrance of, a badger sett;
(d)   causing a dog to enter a badger sett; or
(e)   disturbing a badger when it is occupying a badger sett,

intending to do any of those things or being reckless as to whether his actions would have any of those consequences.★
[Protection of Badgers Act 1992, s 3.]

★Amended in relation to Scotland by the Nature Conservation (Scotland) Act 2004, Sch 6.
    1. Interference will only be established if, on the evidence, it appears that the system of the tunnels and chambers has been destabilised, or otherwise damaged, or compromised by the digging activity which was being carried on in the vicinity; see *DPP v Green* [2001] 1 WLR 505, 164 JP 477, DC.
    2. For the meaning of "badger sett", see s 14, post.

8–1504   4. Selling and possession of live badgers.   A person is guilty of an offence if, except as permitted by or under this Act, he sells a live badger or offers one for sale or has a live badger in his possession or under his control.
[Protection of Badgers Act 1992, s 4.]

8–1505   5. Marking and ringing.   A person is guilty of an offence if, except as authorised by a licence under section 10 below, he marks, or attaches any ring, tag or other marking device to, a badger other than one which is lawfully in his possession by virtue of such a licence.
[Protection of Badgers Act 1992, s 5.]

Exceptions and licences

8–1506   6. General exceptions.   A person is not guilty of an offence under this Act by reason only of—

(a)   taking or attempting to take a badger which has been disabled otherwise than by his act and is taken or to be taken solely for the purpose of tending it;
(b)   killing or attempting to kill a badger which appears to be so seriously injured or in such a condition that to kill it would be an act of mercy;
(c)   unavoidably killing or injuring a badger as an incidental result of a lawful action;
(d)   doing anything which is authorised under the Animals (Scientific Procedures) Act 1986.★
[Protection of Badgers Act 1992, s 6.]

★Amended in relation to Scotland by the Nature Conservation (Scotland) Act 2004, Sch 6.

8–1507   7. Exceptions from s. 1.   (1) Subject to subsection (2) below, a person is not guilty of an offence under section 1(1) above by reason of—

(a)   killing or taking, or attempting to kill or take, a badger; or
(b)   injuring a badger in the course of taking it or attempting to kill or take it,

if he shows that his action was necessary for the purpose of preventing serious damage to land, crops, poultry or any other form of property.
    (2) The defence provided by subsection (1) above does not apply in relation to any action taken at any time if it had become apparent, before that time, that the action would prove necessary for the purpose there mentioned and either—

(a)   a licence under section 10 below authorising that action had not been applied for as soon as reasonably practicable after that fact had become apparent; or
(b)   an application for such a licence had been determined.
[Protection of Badgers Act 1992, s 7.]

8–1508   8. Exceptions from section 3.   (1) Subject to subsection (2) below, a person is not guilty of an offence under section 3 above if he shows that his action was necessary for the purpose of preventing serious damage to land, crops, poultry or any other form of property.★
    (2) Subsection (2) of section 7 above applies to the defence in subsection (1) above as it applies to the defence in subsection (1) of that section.
    (3) A person is not guilty of an offence under section 3(a), (c) or (e) above if he shows that his action was the incidental result of a lawful operation and could not reasonably have been avoided.★
    (4)–(9) *Repealed.*
[Protection of Badgers Act 1992, s 8 as amended by the Protection of Wild Mammals (Scotland) Act 2002, s 11 and the Hunting Act 2004, s 13.]

★Amended in relation to Scotland by the Nature Conservation (Scotland) Act 2004, Sch 6.
    1. "Loose soil", following the four other materials referred to in s 8(5)(a), is properly to be construed *ejusdem generis* with them. What is contemplated is something readily removable and of an obstructive character which is not permanent. If clay is used to block up a sett, it must be sufficiently broken up so it does not form a compacted structure before it can

qualify for the description "loose soil"; spit sized or near spit sized lumps of clay do not fall within the description. What is properly to be described as "loose" is a question of fact and degree in each case (*Lovett v Bussey* (1998) 162 JP 423).

8–1509 9. Exceptions from section 4. A person is not guilty of an offence under section 4 above by reason of having a live badger in his possession or under his control if—

(a) it is in his possession or under his control, as the case may be, in the course of his business as a carrier; or

(b) it has been disabled otherwise than by his act and taken by him solely for the purpose of tending it and it is necessary for that purpose for it to remain in his possession or under his control, as the case may be.★

[Protection of Badgers Act 1992, s 9.]

★**Amended in relation to Scotland by the Nature Conservation (Scotland) Act 2004, Sch 6.**

8–1510 10. Licences. (1) A licence may be granted to any person by the appropriate Conservancy Council authorising him, notwithstanding anything in the foregoing provisions of this Act, but subject to compliance with any conditions specified in the licence—

(a) for scientific or educational purposes or for the conservation of badgers—

(i) to kill or take, within an area specified in the licence by any means so specified, or to sell, or to have in his possession, any number of badgers so specified; or

(ii) to interfere with any badger sett within an area specified in the licence by any means so specified;

(b) for the purpose of any zoological gardens or collection specified in the licence, to take within an area specified in the licence by any means so specified, or to sell, or to have in his possession, any number of badgers so specified;

(c) for the purpose of ringing and marking, to take badgers within an area specified in the licence, to mark such badgers or to attach to them any ring, tag or other marking device as specified in the licence;

(d) for the purpose of any development as defined in section 55(1) of the Town and Country Planning Act 1990 or, as respects Scotland, section 19(1) of the Town and Country Planning (Scotland) Act 1972, to interfere with a badger sett within an area specified in the licence by any means so specified;

(e) for the purpose of the preservation, or archaeological investigation, of a monument scheduled under section 1 of the Ancient Monuments and Archaeological Areas Act 1979, to interfere with a badger sett within an area specified in the licence by any means so specified;

(f) for the purpose of investigating whether any offence has been committed or gathering evidence in connection with proceedings before any court, to interfere with a badger sett within an area specified in the licence by any means so specified.

(2) A licence may be granted to any person by the appropriate Minister authorising him, notwithstanding anything in the foregoing provisions of this Act, but subject to compliance with any conditions specified in the licence—

(a) for the purpose of preventing the spread of disease, to kill or take badgers, or to interfere with a badger sett, within an area specified in the licence by any means so specified;

(b) for the purpose of preventing serious damage to land, crops, poultry or any other form of property, to kill or take badgers, or to interfere with a badger sett, within an area specified in the licence by any means so specified;

(c) for the purpose of any agricultural or forestry operation, to interfere with a badger sett within an area specified in the licence by any means so specified;

(d) for the purpose of any operation (whether by virtue of the Land Drainage Act 1991 or otherwise) to maintain or improve any existing watercourse or drainage works, or to construct new works required for the drainage of any land, including works for the purpose of defence against sea water or tidal water, to interfere with a badger sett within an area specified in the licence by any means so specified.

(3) A licence may be granted to any person either by the appropriate Conservancy Council or the appropriate Minister authorising that person, notwithstanding anything in the foregoing provisions of this Act, but subject to compliance with any conditions specified in the licence, to interfere with a badger sett within an area specified in the licence by any means so specified for the purpose of controlling foxes in order to protect livestock, game or wild life.

(4) In this section "the appropriate Conservancy Council" means, in relation to a licence for an area—

(a) in England, English Nature;

(b) in Wales, the Countryside Council for Wales; and

(c) in Scotland, Scottish Natural Heritage.

(5) In this section "the appropriate Minister" means in relation to a licence for an area—

(*a*) in England, the Secretary of State; and

(*b*) in Wales or in Scotland, the Secretary of State.

(6) The appropriate Minister shall from time to time consult with the appropriate Conservancy Council as to the exercise of his functions under subsection (2)(*b*), (*c*) or (*d*) above and shall not grant a licence of any description unless he has been advised by the appropriate Conservancy Council as to the circumstances in which, in that Council's opinion, licences of that description should be granted.

(7) In relation to Scottish Natural Heritage subsection (6) above shall have effect with the omission of the reference to subsection (2)(*c*) and (*d*).

(8) A licence granted under this section may be revoked at any time by the authority by whom it was granted, and without prejudice to any other liability to a penalty which he may have incurred under this or any other Act, a person who contravenes or fails to comply with any condition imposed on the grant of a licence under this section is guilty of an offence.

(9) A licence under this section shall not be unreasonably withheld or revoked.

(10) It shall be a defence in proceedings for an offence under section 8(*b*) of the Protection of Animals Act 1911 or section 7(*b*) of the Protection of Animals (Scotland) Act 1912 (each of which restricts the placing on land of poison and poisonous substances) to show that—

(*a*) the act alleged to constitute the offence was done under the authority of a licence granted under subsection (2)(*a*) above; and

(*b*) any conditions specified in the licence were complied with.

[Protection of Badgers Act 1992, s 10, as amended by the Countryside and Rights of Way Act 2000, Sch 8 and SI 2002/794.]

Enforcement and penalties

8–1511   11. Powers of constables. Where a constable has reasonable grounds for suspecting that a person is committing an offence under the foregoing provisions of this Act, or has committed an offence under those provisions or those of the Badgers Act 1973 and that evidence of the commission of the offence is to be found on that person or any vehicle or article he may have with him, the constable may—

(*a*) without warrant stop and search that person and any vehicle or article he may have with him;

(*b*) seize and detain for the purposes of proceedings under any of those provisions anything which may be evidence of the commission of the offence or may be liable to be forfeited under section 12(4) below;

(*c*) Scotland.*

[Protection of Badgers Act 1992, s 11.]

----

*Section amended and new s 11A inserted in relation to Scotland by the **Nature Conservation (Scotland) Act 2004, Sch 6.**

8–1512   12. Penalties and forfeiture. (1) A person guilty of an offence under section 1(1) or (3), 2 or 3 above is liable on summary conviction to imprisonment for a term not exceeding **six months** or a fine not exceeding **level 5** on the standard scale or both; and a person guilty of an offence under section 4, 5 or 10(8) above or 13(7) below is liable on summary conviction to a fine not exceeding **that level**.*

(2) Where an offence was committed in respect of more than one badger the maximum fine which may be imposed under subsection (1) above shall be determined as if the person convicted had been convicted of a separate offence in respect of each badger.*

(3) A person guilty of an offence under section 1(5) above is liable on summary conviction to a fine not exceeding **level 3** on the standard scale.

(4) The court by which a person is convicted of an offence under this Act shall order the forfeiture of any badger or badger skin in respect of which the offence was committed and may, if they think fit, order the forfeiture of any weapon or article in respect of or by means of which the offence was committed.

[Protection of Badgers Act 1992, s 12.]

----

*Amended in relation to Scotland and new ss 12A and 12B inserted by the **Nature Conservation (Scotland) Act 2004, Sch 6.**

8–1513   13. Powers of court where dog used or present at commission of offence. (1) Where a dog has been used in or was present at the commission of an offence under sections 1(1), 2 or 3* above, the court, on convicting the offender, may, in addition to or in substitution for any other punishment, make either or both of the following orders—

(*a*) an order for the destruction or other disposal of the dog;

(*b*) an order disqualifying the offender, for such period as it thinks fit, for having custody of a dog.

(2) Where the court makes an order under subsection (1)(*a*) above, it may—

(a) appoint a person to undertake the destruction or other disposal of the dog and require any person having custody of the dog to deliver it up for that purpose; and

(b) order the offender to pay such sum as the court may determine to be the reasonable expenses of destroying or otherwise disposing of the dog and of keeping it pending its destruction or disposal.

(3) Where an order under subsection (1)(*a*) above is made in relation to a dog owned by a person other than the offender, the owner of the dog may appeal to the Crown Court against the order.

(4) A dog shall not be destroyed pursuant to an order under subsection (1)(*a*) above—

(a) until the end of the period within which notice of appeal to the Crown Court against the order can be given; and

(b) if notice of appeal is given in that period, until the appeal is determined or withdrawn,

unless the owner of the dog gives notice to the court which made the order that he does not intend to appeal against it.

(5) A person who is disqualified for having custody of a dog by virtue of an order made under subsection (1)(*b*) above may, at any time after the end of the period of one year beginning with the date of the order, apply to the court that made it (or any magistrates' court acting for the same petty sessions area as that court) for a direction terminating the disqualification.

(6) On an application under subsection (5) above the court may—

(a) having regard to the applicant's character, his conduct since the disqualification was imposed and any other circumstances of the case, grant or refuse the application; and

(b) order the applicant to pay all or any part of the costs of the application;

and where an application in respect of an order is refused no further application in respect of that order shall be entertained if made before the end of the period of one year beginning with the date of the refusal.

(7) Any person who—

(a) has custody of a dog in contravention of an order under subsection (1)(*b*) above; or

(b) fails to comply with a requirement imposed on him under subsection (2)(*a*) above,

is guilty of an offence.

(8) A sum ordered to be paid by an order under subsection (2)(*b*) above shall be recoverable summarily as a civil debt.

(9) *Scotland.*

[Protection of Badgers Act 1992, s 13.]

---

*Amended in relation to Scotland by the Nature Conservation (Scotland) Act 2004, Sch 6.

8–1514 14. Interpretation. In this Act—

 "ammunition" has the same meaning as in the Firearms Act 1968;

 "badger" means any animal of the species *Meles meles*;

 "badger sett" means any structure or place which displays signs indicating current use by a badger[1];

 "firearm" has the same meaning as in the Firearms Act 1968;

 "sale" includes hire, barter and exchange and cognate expressions shall be construed accordingly.

[Protection of Badgers Act 1992, s 14.]

---

1. The phrase "badger sett" refers to the tunnels and chambers constructed by badgers and the entrance holes to those tunnels and chambers. It may also apply to other structures, where badgers, for example, occupy culverts or disused sheds as their shelter or refuge. The phrase "badger sett" does not, however, apply to tunnels or chambers constructed by badgers which are no longer in current use (*Crown Prosecution Service v Green* [2001] 1 WLR 505, (2000) 164 JP 477).

8–1515 15. *Short title, repeals, commencement and extent.*

Wild Mammals (Protection) Act 1996

(1996 c 3)

8–1520 1. Offences. If, save as permitted by this Act, any person mutilates, kicks, beats, nails or otherwise impales, stabs, burns, stones, crushes, drowns, drags or asphyxiates any wild mammal with intent to inflict unnecessary suffering he shall be guilty of an offence.

[Wild Mammals (Protection) Act 1996, s 1.]

8–1521 2. Exceptions from offence under the Act. A person shall not be guilty of an offence under this Act by reason of—

(*a*) the attempted killing of any such wild mammal as an act of mercy if he shows that the mammal had been so seriously disabled otherwise than by his unlawful act that there was no reasonable chance of its recovering;

(*b*) the killing in a reasonably swift and humane manner of any such wild mammal if he shows that the wild mammal had been injured or taken in the course of either lawful shooting, hunting, coursing or *lawful** pest control activity;

(*c*) doing anything which is authorised by or under any enactment;

(*d*) any act made unlawful by section 1 if the act was done by means of any snare, trap, dog, or bird lawfully used for the purpose of killing or taking any wild mammal; or

(*e*) the lawful use of any poisonous or noxious substance on any wild mammal.

[Wild Mammals (Protection) Act 1996, s 2.]

---

*Word in italics relates to Scotland only by virtue of the Protection of Wild Mammals (Scotland) Act 2002, s 11.

8–1522　3. Interpretation.　In this Act "wild mammal" means any mammal which is not a domestic or captive animal within the meaning of the Protection of Animals Act 1911[1] or the Protection of Animals (Scotland) Act 1912.

[Wild Mammals (Protection) Act 1996, s 3.]

---

1. This PART, ante.

8–1523　4. Powers of constable.　Where a constable has reasonable grounds for suspecting that a person has committed an offence under the provisions of this Act and that evidence of the commission of the offence may be found on that person or in or on any vehicle he may have with him, the constable may—

(*a*) without warrant, stop and search that person and any vehicle or article he may have with him: and

(*b*) seize and detain for the purposes of proceedings under any of those provisions anything which may be evidence of the commission of the offence or may be liable to be confiscated under section 6 of this Act

[Wild Mammals (Protection) Act 1996, s 4.]

8–1524　5. Penalties.　(1) A person guilty of an offence under this Act shall be liable on summary conviction to a fine not exceeding **level 5** on the standard scale, or a term of imprisonment not exceeding **six months**, or **both**.

(2) Provided that where the offence was committed in respect of more than one wild mammal, the maximum fine which may be imposed shall be determined as if the person had been convicted of a separate offence in respect of each such wild mammal.

[Wild Mammals (Protection) Act 1996, s 5.]

8–1525　6. Court powers of confiscation &c.　(1) The court before whom any person is convicted under this Act may, in addition to any other punishment, order the confiscation of any vehicle or equipment used in the commission of the offence.

(2) The Secretary of State may, by regulations made by statutory instrument and subject to annulment in pursuance of a resolution of either House of Parliament, make provision for the disposal or destruction in prescribed circumstances of any vehicle or equipment confiscated under this section.

[Wild Mammals (Protection) Act 1996, s 6.]

8–1526　7. Citation, commencement and extent.　(1) This Act my be cited as the Wild Mammals (Protection) Act 1996.

(2) This Act shall come into force with the expiration of the period of two months beginning with its passing.

(3) This Act shall not apply to Northern Ireland.

(4) Section 6 of this Act shall not apply to Scotland, and so much of section 4 as refers to that section shall also not apply there.

[Wild Mammals (Protection) Act 1996, s 7.]

Fur Farming (Prohibition) Act 2000[1]

(2000 c 33)

8–1530　1. Offences relating to fur farming.　(1) A person is guilty of an offence if he keeps animals solely or primarily—

(*a*) for slaughter (whether by himself or another) for the value of their fur, or

(*b*) for breeding progeny for such slaughter.

(2) A person is guilty of an offence if he knowingly causes or permits another person to keep animals as mentioned in subsection (1).

(3) The references in this section to keeping animals for slaughter or to breeding progeny for slaughter include keeping or (as the case may be) breeding them for sale for slaughter.

(4) A person who is guilty of an offence under subsection (1) or subsection (2) is liable on summary conviction to a fine not exceeding £20,000.

[Fur Farming (Prohibition) Act 2000, s 1.]

---

1. This Act prohibits the keeping of animals solely or primarily for slaughter for the value of their fur. The Act is to come into force in accordance with s 7, below.

8–1531   2. Forfeiture orders.   (1) If a person is convicted of an offence under section 1(1) in respect of animals of a particular description, the court may make a forfeiture order in respect of any animals of that description which are kept by that person when the order is made or which come into his keeping during the relevant period.

(2) If a person is convicted of an offence under section 1(2) in respect of animals of a particular description kept by another person, the court may make a forfeiture order in respect of any animals of that description which are kept by that other person when the order is made or which come into his keeping during the relevant period.

(3) For the purposes of this Act, a forfeiture order is an order for the forfeiture and destruction or other disposal of the animals to which the order applies (including any subsequent progeny of those animals).

(4) The court may make a forfeiture order whether or not it also deals with the offender in respect of the offence in any other way.

(5) Where—

(*a*) the court proposes to make a forfeiture order, and

(*b*) a person claiming to have an interest in the animals concerned applies to be heard by the court,

the court shall not make the order unless that person has been given an opportunity to show cause why the order should not be made.

(6) In this section"relevant period" means the period beginning with the making of the forfeiture order and ending with the destruction or other disposal of the animals in pursuance of the order.

[Fur Farming (Prohibition) Act 2000, s 2.]

8–1532   3. Effect of forfeiture orders.   (1) A forfeiture order operates in relation to the forfeiture of animals so as to deprive any person of his rights in those animals.

(2) Any person claiming to have an interest in the animals concerned may appeal against a forfeiture order to the Crown Court.

(3) Where the court makes a forfeiture order, it may in particular—

(*a*) appoint a person to carry out the order,

(*b*) impose requirements on any person in relation to the keeping of the animals concerned pending their destruction or other disposal,

(*c*) order the offender to pay such sum as the court may determine in respect of the reasonable expenses of carrying out the order and, where he does not keep the animals himself, of keeping them pending their destruction or other disposal,

(*d*) make such provision as the court considers appropriate in relation to the operation of the order pending the making or determination of any appeal or application relevant to the order.

(4) Any sum ordered to be paid under subsection (3)(*c*) shall be treated for the purposes of enforcement as if it were a fine imposed on conviction.

[Fur Farming (Prohibition) Act 2000, s 3.]

8–1533   4. Powers of entry and enforcement.   (1) A person authorised in writing by the appropriate authority (whether generally or in a particular case) may at any reasonable time enter any premises on which he has reasonable grounds for suspecting that an offence under section 1(1) has been or is being committed and may inspect the premises and any animals or things found there.

(2) A person appointed by the court under section 3(3)(*a*) to carry out a forfeiture order may at any reasonable time enter any premises on which he has reasonable grounds for suspecting that animals to which the order applies are being kept, and carry out the order.

(3) A person seeking to enter any premises in the exercise of his powers under subsection (1) or (2) shall, if required by or on behalf of the owner or occupier or person in charge of the premises, produce evidence of his identity, and of his authority or (as the case may be) appointment, before entering.

(4) A person who has entered any premises in the exercise of his powers under subsection (1) or (2) shall, if required as mentioned in subsection (3), state in writing his reasons for entering.

(5) A person is guilty of an offence if he intentionally obstructs or delays any person in the exercise of his powers under subsection (1) or (2).

(6) A person who is guilty of an offence under subsection (5) is liable on summary conviction to a fine not exceeding level 3 on the standard scale.

(7) In this section—

"premises" includes any place but not any private dwelling, and

"private dwelling" means any premises for the time being used as a private dwelling excluding any garage, outhouse or other structure (whether or not forming part of the same building as the premises) which belongs to or is usually enjoyed with the premises.

[Fur Farming (Prohibition) Act 2000, s 4.]

8–1534   5. *Compensation for existing businesses*[1]

1. The Fur Farming (Compensation Scheme) (England) Order 2004, SI 2004/1964has been made.

8–1535   6. Interpretation.   In this Act "the appropriate authority" means—

(a) in relation to England, the Minister of Agriculture, Fisheries and Food, and

(b) in relation to Wales, the National Assembly for Wales.

[Fur Farming (Prohibition) Act 2000, s 6 amended by SI 2002/794.]

8–1536   7. Short title, commencement and extent.   (1) This Act may be cited as the Fur Farming (Prohibition) Act 2000.

(2) Sections 1 to 4 shall come into force on such day as the Minister of Agriculture, Fisheries and Food may by order[1] made by statutory instrument appoint; but no day before 1st January 2003 shall be appointed.

(3) Section 5 shall come into force at the end of the period of two months beginning with the day on which this Act is passed.

(4) This Act extends to England and Wales only.

[Fur Farming (Prohibition) Act 2000, s 7 amended by SI 2002/794.]

1. At the date of going to press, no order had been made.

Protection of Animals (Amendment) Act 2000
(2000 c 40)

8–1540   1. Application of Act.   (1) Sections 2 to 4 apply where—

(a) a person who is mentioned in subsection (3) (referred to in this Act as "the prosecutor") has brought proceedings for an offence under section 1 of the Protection of Animals Act 1911[1] (referred to in this Act as "the 1911 Act") against the owner of the animals to which the offence relates; and

(b) the proceedings have not been discontinued or otherwise disposed of.

(2) But those sections only apply in relation to an animal which the owner keeps or has kept for commercial purposes.

(3) The persons referred to in subsection (1) are—

(a) the Director of Public Prosecutions;

(b) a Crown Prosecutor;

(c) a government department;

(d) a local authority;

(e) in relation to a prosecution in England, a person who, at the request of the Secretary of State, has entered into a written agreement under which he may perform the functions conferred on a prosecutor by virtue of this Act;

(f) in relation to a prosecution in Wales, a person who, at the request of the National Assembly for Wales, has entered into a written agreement under which he may perform the functions conferred on a prosecutor by virtue of this Act.

[Protection of Animals (Amendment) Act 2000, s 1 amended by SI 2002/794.]

1. In this title, ante.

8–1541   2. Orders for the care, disposal or slaughter of animals.   (1) If, on the application of the prosecutor, it appears to the court from evidence given by a veterinary surgeon that it is necessary in the interests of the welfare of the animals in question[1] for the prosecutor to do one or more of the things mentioned in subsection (2), the court may make an order authorising him to do so.

(2) Those things are—

(a) taking charge of the animals and caring for them, or causing or procuring them to be cared for, on the premises on which they are kept or at some other place;

(b) selling the animals at a fair price;
(c) disposing of the animals otherwise than by way of sale;
(d) slaughtering the animals, or causing or procuring them to be slaughtered.

(3) In determining what to authorise by the order, the court must have regard to all the circumstances, including the desirability of protecting the owner's interest in the value of the animals and avoiding increasing his costs.

(4) An order under this section ceases to have effect on the discontinuance or other disposal of the proceedings under section 1 of the 1911 Act; but this is without prejudice to anything done before, or done in pursuance of a contract entered into before, the order ceases to have effect.
[Protection of Animals (Amendment) Act 2000, s 2.]

1. This means the animals to which the offence relates; therefore, an application cannot seek an order in respect of animals not identified in the information against the defendant: *Cornwall County Council v Baker* [2003] EWHC 374 (Admin), [2003] 2 ALL ER 178, [2003] 1 WLR 1813, (2003) 167 JP 198.

8–1542   3. Powers of entry, etc.   (1) Where—

(a) the prosecutor has given notice to the court of his intention to apply for an order under section 2; and
(b) he is of the opinion that the animals need to be marked for identification purposes,

the prosecutor, or a person authorised by him, may enter the premises on which the animals are kept and mark them for those purposes.

(2) Where an order is made under section 2, the prosecutor, or a person authorised by him, may—

(a) enter the premises on which the animals are kept for the purpose of exercising the powers conferred by the order;
(b) mark the animals (whether by the application of an ear tag or by any other means); and
(c) in the case of an order making any provision mentioned in section 2(2)(a), make use for that purpose of any equipment on the premises.

(3) Any person who obstructs the prosecutor, or a person authorised by him, in the exercise of powers conferred by subsection (1) or (2) or an order under section 2 is guilty of an offence and liable on summary conviction to a fine not exceeding level 3 on the standard scale.

(4) Nothing in this section authorises a person to enter a dwellinghouse.

(5) A person entering any premises in the exercise of powers conferred on him by this section must, if so required by the owner or occupier or person in charge of the premises—

(a) produce to him some duly authenticated document showing that he is, or is a person authorised by, the prosecutor; and
(b) state in writing his reasons for entering.
[Protection of Animals (Amendment) Act 2000, s 3.]

8–1543   4. Other supplementary provisions.   (1) Where an order is made under section 2—

(a) the prosecutor is entitled to be reimbursed for any reasonable expenses incurred by him in the exercise of the powers conferred by virtue of the order; and
(b) subject to that, in the case of an order making any provision mentioned in subsection (2)(b), (c) or (d) of that section, the prosecutor must pay to the owner the proceeds of any disposal or slaughter of the animals.

(2) Any amount for which the prosecutor is entitled to be reimbursed under subsection (1) may be recovered by him from the owner summarily as a civil debt[1].

(3) Where—

(a) an order under section 2 makes any provision mentioned in subsection (2)(b), (c) or (d) of that section; and
(b) the owner has in his possession or under his control documents—

(i) without which the animals cannot be slaughtered for human consumption; or
(ii) which are otherwise relevant to the condition or value of the animals,

the owner must, as soon as practicable and in any event within 10 days of the making of the order, deliver those documents to the prosecutor.

(4) If the owner without reasonable excuse fails to deliver any documents as required by subsection (3), he is guilty of an offence and liable on summary conviction to a fine not exceeding level 3 on the standard scale.

(5) The prosecutor may, if the owner fails to deliver as required by subsection (3) any documents within paragraph (b)(i), apply to the person by whom the documents were issued for replacement documents to be issued and that person must, if he has sufficient information to do so, issue replacement documents to the prosecutor.

(6) An application under subsection (5) is to be accompanied by—

(a) a copy of the order under section 2; and
(b) such reasonable fee (if any) as is determined by the person to whom the application is made.

(7) In this section, "owner" means the owner against whom the proceedings were brought.
[Protection of Animals (Amendment) Act 2000, s 4.]

---

1. For collection of sums recoverable summarily as a civil debt, see the Magistrates' Courts Act 1980, Part III, in PART I: MAGISTRATES' COURTS PROCEDURE, ante.

8–1544   5. Short title, interpretation, commencement and extent.   (1) This Act may be cited as the Protection of Animals (Amendment) Act 2000.

(2) In this Act—

"the 1911 Act" means the Protection of Animals Act 1911;
"local authority"—

    (a) in relation to England, means a county council, a district council, a London borough council, the Common Council of the City of London or the Council of the Isles of Scilly;
    (b) in relation to Wales, means a county council or a county borough council;

"prosecutor" has the meaning given by section 1(3);
"veterinary surgeon" means a person registered in the register of veterinary surgeons, or the supplementary veterinary register, kept under the Veterinary Surgeons Act 1966;

and expressions which are used in the 1911 Act have the same meanings as in that Act.

(3) This Act comes into force at the end of the period of two months beginning with the day on which it is passed.

(4) This Act extends to England and Wales only.
[Protection of Animals (Amendment) Act 2000, s 5.]

Hunting Act 2004[1]
(2004 c 37)

PART 1[2]
OFFENCES

8–1550   1. Hunting wild mammals with dogs.   A person commits an offence if he hunts a wild mammal with a dog, unless his hunting is exempt.
[Hunting Act 2004, s 1.]

---

1. This Act outlaws hunting with dogs (with exemptions), assisting non-exempt hunting with dogs, and participating in and facilitating hare coursing. The Act is in 3 Parts and contains 3 Schedules.
2. Part 1 contains ss 1–5.

8–1551   2. Exempt hunting.   (1) Hunting is exempt if it is within a class specified in Schedule 1.

(2) The Secretary of State may by order amend Schedule 1 so as to vary a class of exempt hunting.
[Hunting Act 2004, s 2.]

8–1552   3. Hunting: assistance.   (1) A person commits an offence if he knowingly permits land which belongs to him to be entered or used in the course of the commission of an offence under section 1.

(2) A person commits an offence if he knowingly permits a dog which belongs to him to be used in the course of the commission of an offence under section 1.
[Hunting Act 2004, s 3.]

8–1553   4. Hunting: defence.   It is a defence for a person charged with an offence under section 1 in respect of hunting to show that he reasonably believed that the hunting was exempt.
[Hunting Act 2004, s 4.]

8–1554   5. Hare coursing.   (1) A person commits an offence if he—

    (a) participates in a hare coursing event,
    (b) attends a hare coursing event,
    (c) knowingly facilitates a hare coursing event, or
    (d) permits land which belongs to him to be used for the purposes of a hare coursing event.

(2) Each of the following persons commits an offence if a dog participates in a hare coursing event—

    (a) any person who enters the dog for the event,
    (b) any person who permits the dog to be entered, and
    (c) any person who controls or handles the dog in the course of or for the purposes of the event.

(3) A "hare coursing event" is a competition in which dogs are, by the use of live hares, assessed as to skill in hunting hares.
[Hunting Act 2004, s 5.]

PART 2[1]
ENFORCEMENT

8–1555   6. Penalty.   A person guilty of an offence under this Act shall be liable on summary conviction to a fine not exceeding level 5 on the standard scale.
[Hunting Act 2004, s 6.]

---

1. Part 2 contains ss 6–10.

8–1556   7. Arrest.   A constable without a warrant may arrest a person whom he reasonably suspects—

(*a*)   to have committed an offence under section 1 or 5(1)(*a*), (*b*) or (2),
(*b*)   to be committing an offence under any of those provisions, or
(*c*)   to be about to commit an offence under any of those provisions.
[Hunting Act 2004, s 7.]

8–1557   8. Search and seizure.   (1) This section applies where a constable reasonably suspects that a person ("the suspect") is committing or has committed an offence under Part 1 of this Act.

(2) If the constable reasonably believes that evidence of the offence is likely to be found on the suspect, the constable may stop the suspect and search him.

(3) If the constable reasonably believes that evidence of the offence is likely to be found on or in a vehicle, animal or other thing of which the suspect appears to be in possession or control, the constable may stop and search the vehicle, animal or other thing.

(4) A constable may seize and detain a vehicle, animal or other thing if he reasonably believes that—

(*a*)   it may be used as evidence in criminal proceedings for an offence under Part 1 of this Act, or
(*b*)   it may be made the subject of an order under section 9.

(5) For the purposes of exercising a power under this section a constable may enter—

(*a*)   land;
(*b*)   premises other than a dwelling;
(*c*)   a vehicle.

(6) The exercise of a power under this section does not require a warrant.
[Hunting Act 2004, s 8.]

8–1558   9. Forfeiture.   (1) A court which convicts a person of an offence under Part 1 of this Act may order the forfeiture of any dog or hunting article which—

(*a*)   was used in the commission of the offence, or
(*b*)   was in the possession of the person convicted at the time of his arrest.

(2) A court which convicts a person of an offence under Part 1 of this Act may order the forfeiture of any vehicle which was used in the commission of the offence.

(3) In subsection (1) "hunting article" means anything designed or adapted for use in connection with—

(*a*)   hunting a wild mammal, or
(*b*)   hare coursing.

(4) A forfeiture order—

(*a*)   may include such provision about the treatment of the dog, vehicle or article forfeited as the court thinks appropriate, and
(*b*)   subject to provision made under paragraph (a), shall be treated as requiring any person who is in possession of the dog, vehicle or article to surrender it to a constable as soon as is reasonably practicable.

(5) Where a forfeited dog, vehicle or article is retained by or surrendered to a constable, the police force of which the constable is a member shall ensure that such arrangements are made for its destruction or disposal—

(*a*)   as are specified in the forfeiture order, or
(*b*)   where no arrangements are specified in the order, as seem to the police force to be appropriate.

(6) The court which makes a forfeiture order may order the return of the forfeited dog, vehicle or article on an application made—

(*a*)   by a person who claims to have an interest in the dog, vehicle or article (other than the person on whose conviction the order was made), and
(*b*)   before the dog, vehicle or article has been destroyed or finally disposed of under subsection (5).

(7) A person commits an offence if he fails to—

(*a*)   comply with a forfeiture order, or

(*b*) co-operate with a step taken for the purpose of giving effect to a forfeiture order.
[Hunting Act 2004, s 9.]

8–1559 10. Offence by body corporate. (1) This section applies where an offence under this Act is committed by a body corporate with the consent or connivance of an officer of the body.

(2) The officer, as well as the body, shall be guilty of the offence.

(3) In subsection (1) a reference to an officer of a body corporate includes a reference to—

(*a*) a director, manager or secretary,

(*b*) a person purporting to act as a director, manager or secretary, and

(*c*) if the affairs of the body are managed by its members, a member.
[Hunting Act 2004, s 10.]

PART 3[1]
GENERAL

8–1560 11. Interpretation. (1) In this Act "wild mammal" includes, in particular—

(*a*) a wild mammal which has been bred or tamed for any purpose,

(*b*) a wild mammal which is in captivity or confinement,

(*c*) a wild mammal which has escaped or been released from captivity or confinement, and

(*d*) any mammal which is living wild.

(2) For the purposes of this Act a reference to a person hunting a wild mammal with a dog includes, in particular, any case where—

(*a*) a person engages or participates in the pursuit of a wild mammal, and

(*b*) one or more dogs are employed in that pursuit (whether or not by him and whether or not under his control or direction).

(3) For the purposes of this Act land belongs to a person if he—

(*a*) owns an interest in it,

(*b*) manages or controls it, or

(*c*) occupies it.

(4) For the purposes of this Act a dog belongs to a person if he—

(*a*) owns it,

(*b*) is in charge of it, or

(*c*) has control of it.
[Hunting Act 2004, s 11.]

---

1. Part 3 contains ss 11–17.

8–1561 12. Crown application. This Act—

(*a*) binds the Crown, and

(*b*) applies to anything done on or in respect of land irrespective of whether it belongs to or is used for the purposes of the Crown or a Duchy.
[Hunting Act 2004, s 12.]

8–1562 13. Amendments and repeals. (1) Schedule 2 (consequential amendments) shall have effect.

(2) The enactments listed in Schedule 3 are hereby repealed to the extent specified.
[Hunting Act 2004, s 13.]

8–1563 14. Subordinate legislation. An order of the Secretary of State under this Act—

(*a*) shall be made by statutory instrument,

(*b*) may not be made unless a draft has been laid before and approved by resolution of each House of Parliament,

(*c*) may make provision which applies generally or only in specified circumstances or for specified purposes,

(*d*) may make different provision for different circumstances or purposes, and

(*e*) may make transitional, consequential and incidental provision.
[Hunting Act 2004, s 14.]

8–1564 15. Commencement. This Act shall come into force at the end of the period of three months beginning with the date on which it is passed.
[Hunting Act 2004, s 15.]

8–1565 16. Short title. This Act may be cited as the Hunting Act 2004.
[Hunting Act 2004, s 16.]

17. Extent.   This Act shall extend only to England and Wales.
[Hunting Act 2004, s 17.]

8–1567

Section 2   SCHEDULE 1
                                  EXEMPT HUNTING

Stalking and flushing out

1. (1) Stalking a wild mammal, or flushing it out of cover, is exempt hunting if the conditions in this paragraph
are satisfied.

(2) The first condition is that the stalking or flushing out is undertaken for the purpose of—

(*a*) preventing or reducing serious damage which the wild mammal would otherwise cause—

   (i)   to livestock,
   (ii) to game birds or wild birds (within the meaning of section 27 of the Wildlife and Countryside Act 1981
         (c 69)),
   (iii) to food for livestock,
   (iv) to crops (including vegetables and fruit),
   (v)   to growing timber,
   (vi) to fisheries,
   (vii) to other property, or
   (viii)to the biological diversity of an area (within the meaning of the United Nations Environmental
         Programme Convention on Biological Diversity of 1992),

(*b*) obtaining meat to be used for human or animal consumption, or
(*c*) participation in a field trial.

(3) In subparagraph (2)(*c*) "field trial" means a competition (other than a hare coursing event within the
meaning of section 5) in which dogs—

(*a*) flush animals out of cover or retrieve animals that have been shot (or both), and
(*b*) are assessed as to their likely usefulness in connection with shooting.

(4) The second condition is that the stalking or flushing out takes place on land—

(*a*) which belongs to the person doing the stalking or flushing out, or
(*b*) which he has been given permission to use for the purpose by the occupier or, in the case of unoccupied
       land, by a person to whom it belongs.

(5) The third condition is that the stalking or flushing out does not involve the use of more than two dogs.

(6) The fourth condition is that the stalking or flushing out does not involve the use of a dog below ground
otherwise than in accordance with paragraph 2 below.

(7) The fifth condition is that—

(*a*) reasonable steps are taken for the purpose of ensuring that as soon as possible after being found or flushed
       out the wild mammal is shot dead by a competent person, and
(*b*) in particular, each dog used in the stalking or flushing out is kept under sufficiently close control to ensure
       that it does not prevent or obstruct achievement of the objective in paragraph (*a*).

Use of dogs below ground to protect birds for shooting

2. (1) The use of a dog below ground in the course of stalking or flushing out is in accordance with this
paragraph if the conditions in this paragraph are satisfied.

(2) The first condition is that the stalking or flushing out is undertaken for the purpose of preventing or reducing
serious damage to game birds or wild birds (within the meaning of section 27 of the Wildlife and Countryside Act
1981 (c 69)) which a person is keeping or preserving for the purpose of their being shot.

(3) The second condition is that the person doing the stalking or flushing out—

(*a*) has with him written evidence—

   (i)   that the land on which the stalking or flushing out takes place belongs to him, or
   (ii) that he has been given permission to use that land for the purpose by the occupier or, in the case of
         unoccupied land, by a person to whom it belongs, and

(*b*) makes the evidence immediately available for inspection by a constable who asks to see it.

(4) The third condition is that the stalking or flushing out does not involve the use of more than one dog below
ground at any one time.

(5) In so far as stalking or flushing out is undertaken with the use of a dog below ground in accordance with this
paragraph, paragraph 1 shall have effect as if for the condition in paragraph 1(7) there were substituted the
condition that—

(*a*) reasonable steps are taken for the purpose of ensuring that as soon as possible after being found the wild
       mammal is flushed out from below ground,
(*b*) reasonable steps are taken for the purpose of ensuring that as soon as possible after being flushed out from
       below ground the wild mammal is shot dead by a competent person,
(*c*) in particular, the dog is brought under sufficiently close control to ensure that it does not prevent or obstruct
       achievement of the objective in paragraph (b),
(*d*) reasonable steps are taken for the purpose of preventing injury to the dog, and
(*e*) the manner in which the dog is used complies with any code of practice which is issued or approved for the
       purpose of this paragraph by the Secretary of State.

Rats

3. The hunting of rats is exempt if it takes place on land—

(*a*) which belongs to the hunter, or

(*b*) which he has been given permission to use for the purpose by the occupier or, in the case of unoccupied land, by a person to whom it belongs.

Rabbits

4. The hunting of rabbits is exempt if it takes place on land—

(*a*) which belongs to the hunter, or

(*b*) which he has been given permission to use for the purpose by the occupier or, in the case of unoccupied land, by a person to whom it belongs.

Retrieval of hares

5. The hunting of a hare which has been shot is exempt if it takes place on land—

(*a*) which belongs to the hunter, or

(*b*) which he has been given permission to use for the purpose of hunting hares by the occupier or, in the case of unoccupied land, by a person to whom it belongs.

Falconry

6. Flushing a wild mammal from cover is exempt hunting if undertaken—

(*a*) for the purpose of enabling a bird of prey to hunt the wild mammal, and

(*b*) on land which belongs to the hunter or which he has been given permission to use for the purpose by the occupier or, in the case of unoccupied land, by a person to whom it belongs.

Recapture of wild mammal

7. (1) The hunting of a wild mammal which has escaped or been released from captivity or confinement is exempt if the conditions in this paragraph are satisfied.

(2) The first condition is that the hunting takes place—

(*a*) on land which belongs to the hunter,

(*b*) on land which he has been given permission to use for the purpose by the occupier or, in the case of unoccupied land, by a person to whom it belongs, or

(*c*) with the authority of a constable.

(3) The second condition is that—

(*a*) reasonable steps are taken for the purpose of ensuring that as soon as possible after being found the wild mammal is recaptured or shot dead by a competent person, and

(*b*) in particular, each dog used in the hunt is kept under sufficiently close control to ensure that it does not prevent or obstruct achievement of the objective in paragraph (*a*).

(4) The third condition is that the wild mammal—

(*a*) was not released for the purpose of being hunted, and

(*b*) was not, for that purpose, permitted to escape.

Rescue of wild mammal

8. (1) The hunting of a wild mammal is exempt if the conditions in this paragraph are satisfied.

(2) The first condition is that the hunter reasonably believes that the wild mammal is or may be injured.

(3) The second condition is that the hunting is undertaken for the purpose of relieving the wild mammal's suffering.

(4) The third condition is that the hunting does not involve the use of more than two dogs.

(5) The fourth condition is that the hunting does not involve the use of a dog below ground.

(6) The fifth condition is that the hunting takes place—

(*a*) on land which belongs to the hunter,

(*b*) on land which he has been given permission to use for the purpose by the occupier or, in the case of unoccupied land, by a person to whom it belongs, or

(*c*) with the authority of a constable.

(7) The sixth condition is that—

(*a*) reasonable steps are taken for the purpose of ensuring that as soon as possible after the wild mammal is found appropriate action (if any) is taken to relieve its suffering, and

(*b*) in particular, each dog used in the hunt is kept under sufficiently close control to ensure that it does not prevent or obstruct achievement of the objective in paragraph (*a*).

(8) The seventh condition is that the wild mammal was not harmed for the purpose of enabling it to be hunted in reliance upon this paragraph.

Research and observation

9. (1) The hunting of a wild mammal is exempt if the conditions in this paragraph are satisfied.

(2) The first condition is that the hunting is undertaken for the purpose of or in connection with the observation or study of the wild mammal.

(3) The second condition is that the hunting does not involve the use of more than two dogs.

(4) The third condition is that the hunting does not involve the use of a dog below ground.

(5) The fourth condition is that the hunting takes place on land—

(a) which belongs to the hunter, or

(b) which he has been given permission to use for the purpose by the occupier or, in the case of unoccupied land, by a person to whom it belongs.

(6) The fifth condition is that each dog used in the hunt is kept under sufficiently close control to ensure that it does not injure the wild mammal.

SCHEDULE 2[1]
CONSEQUENTIAL AMENDMENTS

1. These are shown in the legislation concerned.

SCHEDULE 3
REPEALS

Rabies (Importation of Dogs, Cats and Other Mammals) Order 1974[1]

(SI 1974/2211 amended by SI 1977/361, SI 1984/1182, SI 1986/2062, SI 1990/2371, SI 1993/1813, SI 1994/1405, SI 1994/1716, SI 1995/2922, SI 1999/3443, SI 2000/1298, SI 2001/6 and SI 2004/828, 2363 (E) and 2364 (E))

Citation, extent and commencement

8–1790 **1.** This order, which may be cited as the Rabies (Importation of Dogs, Cats and Other Mammals) Order 1974, shall apply throughout Great Britain, and shall come into operation on 5th February 1975.

1. This order now has effect under the Animal Health Act 1981 ss 1, 10, 24 and 87. Summary offences are created by art 16 and indictable offences by art 17; summary offences are subject to a fine not exceeding **level 5** on the standard scale: s 75 of the Act.

Interpretation

8–1791 **2.** (1) In this order, unless the context otherwise requires—

"the Act" means the Diseases of Animals Act 1950[1], as amended or extended by any subsequent enactment;

"animal" means an animal (other than man) belonging to any of the orders of mammals specified in Part I and Part II of Schedule 1 to this order;

"authorised carrying agent" means a person authorised by the Minister under Article 10 of this order to carry animals;

"authorised quarantine premises" means premises authorised by the Minister under Article 9 of this order for use for the detention and isolation of animals in quarantine;

"cat" means an animal belonging to the species Felis catus of the order of mammals Carnivora;

"contact animal" means an animal belonging to any of the orders of mammals specified in Part III of Schedule 1 to this order;

"dog" means an animal belonging to the species Canis familiaris of the order of mammals Carnivora;

"harbour" means any harbour, whether natural or artificial, and any port, haven, estuary, tidal or other river or inland waterway, and includes a dock, a wharf, any place at which hovercraft are loaded or unloaded and, in Scotland, a boatslip being a marine work within the meaning of section 57 of the Harbours Act 1964;

"inspector" means a person appointed to be an inspector for the purposes of the Act by the Minister of Agriculture, Fisheries and Food or by a local authority, and, when used in relation to an inspector of the said Minister, includes a veterinary inspector;

"licence" means a licence granted under this order, and includes any permit, approval or other form of authorisation;

"the Minister" and "the Ministry" mean respectively, in the application of this order to England and Wales, the Minister and the Ministry of Agriculture, Fisheries and Food, and, in its corresponding application to Scotland, the Secretary of State and the Department of Agriculture and Fisheries for Scotland[2];

"registered medical practitioner" means a person included in the Medical Register maintained by the General Medical Council;

"research premises" means premises at which animals which have been brought to Great Britain from a place outside Great Britain are used in connection with scientific research;

"vessel" includes hovercraft;

"veterinary inspector" means a veterinary inspector appointed by the Minister of Agriculture, Fisheries and Food;

"veterinary surgeon" means a veterinary surgeon entered in a register maintained under section 2 of the Veterinary Surgeons Act 1966.

(1A) In this Order "control zone" includes a control zone within the meaning of the Channel

Tunnel (International Arrangements) Order 1993 and a control zone within the meaning of the Channel Tunnel (Miscellaneous Provisions) Order 1994.

(2) For the purposes of this order, an animal shall be deemed[3] to have been landed in Great Britain immediately it is unloaded or taken out of, or in any other manner leaves or escapes from, a vessel, or aircraft or immediately it is brought into a control zone in France or Belgium, and "land" and "landing" are to be construed accordingly:

Provided that this paragraph shall not apply in respect of an animal which is, under the authority of an inspector, transported by water directly from one vessel to another, without the boat in which the animal is carried touching land, or the animal being put on land.

(3) The Animals (Importation) Order of 1930[4] shall not apply to animals brought to Great Britain under this order.

(4) The Interpretation Act 1889 applies to the interpretation of this order as it applies to the interpretation of an Act of Parliament, and as if this order and the orders hereby revoked were Acts of Parliament.

---

1. See now the Animal Health Act 1981, ante.

2. The functions of the Minister, so far as exercisable in relation to Wales, have been transferred to the National Assembly for Wales, by the National Assembly for Wales (Transfer of Functions) Order 1999, SI 1999/672, art 2, Sch 1.

3. This is a deeming provision which in no way detracts from the legislation relating to actual landing in Great Britain; it merely provides an additional location in which UK frontier controls may be exercised and does not purport to exclude the operation of the legislation on the mainland itself or limit the generality of art 4(1): *Corporation of London v Eurostar (UK) Ltd* [2004] EWHC Admin 187, (2005) 169 JP 263.

4. See now the Importation of Animals Order 1977, SI 1977/944.

Extension of the definition of "animals" for the purposes of the Act in its application to rabies

8–1792   3. For the purposes of the Act (other than section 25 thereof) in its application to rabies, the definition of "animals" contained in section 84(1) of the Act is hereby extended so as to comprise all animals (other than man) belonging to the orders of mammals specified in Parts I, II and III of Schedule I to this order.

Prohibition on landing of animals in Great Britain

8–1793   4. (1) Subject to the provisions of this order, the landing in Great Britain of an animal brought from a place outside Great Britain is hereby prohibited.

(2) The prohibition on landing contained in paragraph (1) above shall not apply to an animal brought to Great Britain from a place in Northern Ireland, the Republic of Ireland, the Channel Islands or the Isle of Man:

Provided that, where an animal has been brought to that place from a place outside those countries (other than a place in Great Britain), the said prohibition shall apply to that animal unless

(a) where landing in England, it is an animal which was imported into one of those countries from another member State or Norway subject to and in accordance with Council Directive 92/65/EEC, or*

(b) in any other case it has been detained and isolated in quarantine for a period of at least six calendar months before being landed in Great Britain."

(2A) The prohibition on landing contained in paragraph (1) shall not apply to an animal brought into England from Northern Ireland, the Republic of Ireland, the Channel Islands or the Isle of Man if—

(a) it has been admitted into one of those countries or territories in accordance with Regulation (EC) No 998/2003, and

(b) in the case of a dog, cat or ferret, not less than 24 and not more than 48 hours before embarkation for that country or territory it has been treated against *Echinococcus multilocularis* and ticks by a veterinary surgeon entitled to practise medicine in the country or territory in which the treatment is administered. The treatment shall be with a veterinary medicine with a marketing authorisation in the country or territory in which it is administered and shall be at an appropriate dosage. In the case of *Echinococcus multilocularis*, the treatment shall contain praziquantel as the active ingredient and in the case of ticks the treatment shall not be by means of a collar impregnated by acaricide.*

(2B) *Revoked.*

(3) The prohibition on landing contained in paragraph (1) above shall not apply when the landing is under the authority of a licence previously granted by the Minister, and in accordance with the terms and conditions subject to which it was granted.

(4) The ports and airports which alone may be used for the landing of animals in Great Britain are the ports and airports respectively specified in Part I and Part II of Schedule 2 to this order:

Provided that nothing in this paragraph shall be construed as precluding the Minister, on his being satisfied that exceptional circumstances exist in connection with the bringing to Great Britain of a particular animal, from granting a licence for the landing of that animal at a port or airport other than a port or airport specified in that Schedule.

(4A) Paragraph (4) above shall not have effect in relation to the landing in Great Britain of an animal to which paragraph (2) above applies unless that animal is one referred to in the proviso to that paragraph.

(4B) Notwithstanding the provisions of paragraph (4) above and Schedule 2 to this Order, animals may also be brought into England at Cheriton through the Channel Tunnel.

(5) Nothing in paragraph (4) above shall render it unlawful (subject to the authority of an inspector first having been obtained) for an animal to which this order applies to be landed at a place in Great Britain other than the port or airport at which the animal is licensed to be landed to which the vessel or, as the case may be, the aircraft which is bringing the animal to Great Britain is ordered to be diverted in the interest of safety, or in the light of other exceptional circumstances.

(6) Notwithstanding the provisions of paragraph (2) above, if at any time the Minister has reason to believe that there is an outbreak of rabies in one of the countries referred to in that paragraph, and it appears to him to be necessary to act as a matter of urgency for the purpose of preventing the introduction of that disease into Great Britain, he may direct that the provisions of paragraph (1) above shall apply to animals brought to Great Britain from that country and any such direction shall remain in force for a period of 28 days unless revoked by a subsequent direction before the end of that period.

(7) Where the Minister makes a direction under paragraph (6) above, he shall take all reasonable steps to bring it to the notice of any person who is likely to be affected by it, and in any proceedings for an offence arising by virtue only of the direction, it shall be a defence that at the time when the offence was committed the accused had no reason to believe that the direction was in existence.

(8) For the purposes of this order, an animal which—

(a) is taken from a place in Great Britain, Northern Ireland, the Republic of Ireland, the Channel Islands or the Isle of Man to a place outside those countries (whether or not it is landed at that place, or comes into contact with any other animal while there, or during the journey thereto or therefrom), or

(b) while outside Great Britain, comes into contact with an animal to which, if it were brought to Great Britain, the prohibition on landing contained in paragraph (1) above would apply,

shall be deemed to be an animal brought from a place outside Great Britain when landed in Great Britain.

(9) Subject to paragraph (10) below, where an animal landed in Great Britain is brought into Great Britain from a place other than a country outside Great Britain, the prohibition on landing contained in paragraph (1) above shall apply to that animal if while outside Great Britain it has been or may have been in contact with an animal to which, if it were brought into Great Britain, the prohibition on landing contained in paragraph (1) above would apply.

(10) The prohibition on the landing of an animal brought into Great Britain from a place other than a country outside Great Britain contained in paragraph (9) above shall not apply to a dog belonging to the police, Her Majesty's Customs and Excise or Her Majesty's Forces which is kept under the constant control of a trained handler while outside Great Britain.

*Para (2)(a) and sub-s (2A) reproduced as substituted in relation to England by SI 2004/2364.

8–1793A

Importation of animals from a member State other than the Republic of Ireland

4A. The prohibition and restrictions on landing contained in paragraphs (1) and (4) respectively of article 4 above shall not apply in the case of importation into England from another member State (other than the Republic of Ireland) of animals to which Council Directive 92/65/EEC and the Animal and Animal Products (Import and Export) Regulations 2004 apply and which are imported in accordance with those Regulations.*

*Reproduced as substituted in relation to England by SI 2004/2364.

Disapplication in relation to pet animals complying with Regulation (EC) No 998/2003 and the Non Commercial Movement of Pet Animals (England) Regulations 2004

8–1793B 4B. The provisions of this Order shall not apply in relation to animals brought into England in accordance with the provisions of Regulation (EC) No 998/2003 and the Non Commercial Movement of Pet Animals (England) Regulations 2004.

*Inserted in relation to the importation of pet cats and pet dogs into England by SI 1999/3443, art 13(1), (3) (with effect from 17 January 2000); substituted by SI 2004/2364, art 2(1), (4).

Detention and isolation in quarantine

8–1794 5. (1) Where an animal specified in Part I of Schedule 1 to this order is landed in Great Britain in accordance with a licence granted under Article 4 above, it shall, after being so landed, be immediately detained and isolated in quarantine at its owner's expense for the rest of its life, at such premises and subject to such conditions as may be specified in the licence; and in the event of such an animal being born in Great Britain (whether or not its parents or any one of them was brought from a place outside Great Britain) it shall, for the purposes of this order, be deemed to be an animal brought from a place outside Great Britain, and the foregoing provisions of this paragraph with regard to detention and isolation in quarantine for life shall apply to that animal.

(2) Where an animal specified in Part II of Schedule 1 to this order is landed in Great Britain in accordance with a licence granted under Article 4 above, it shall, after being so landed, be immediately detained and isolated in quarantine at its owner's expense—

(a) for a period of six calendar months, or

(b) in the case of an animal brought to Great Britain from Northern Ireland, the Republic of Ireland, the Channel Islands or the Isle of Man before the end of a period of detention and isolation in quarantine in that country, for such period as the Minister may specify as will ensure that the animal is detained and isolated in quarantine for an aggregate period of not less than six calendar months from the date of its landing in that country,

at such premises and subject to such conditions as may be specified in the licence; and in the event of any offspring being born to any such animal during the period of its detention and isolation in quarantine, such offspring shall be similarly detained and isolated at its owner's expense for the remainder of the period applying in respect of its dam, or for such shorter period, and at such premises and subject to such conditions, as the Minister may in any particular case direct.

(2A) Paragraph (2) shall not apply to any animal of the Order Rodentia or Lagomorpha where a licence granted under article 4(3) states that it is being brought into England—

(a) for use at research premises in connection with scientific research; or

(b) to an establishment licensed as a zoo under section 1 of the Zoo Licensing Act 1981.*

(3) The Minister may by licence permit two or more animals required to be detained under the foregoing provisions of this Article to be kept together in quarantine, subject to such conditions as may be specified in the licence:

Provided that, where the licence is granted in respect of two or more animals to which paragraph (2) above applies, the period of quarantine referred to in that paragraph shall, unless the Minister otherwise directs, be computed in respect of all the animals to which the licence relates by reference to the latest date on which any such animal was landed in Great Britain.

(4) Where the Minister is satisfied that exceptional circumstances exist, he may by licence permit other animals to be kept with animals being detained in quarantine under the foregoing provisions of this Article, subject to compliance with such conditions as may be specified in the licence; and where an animal to which such a licence relates has been in contact with an animal detained under the foregoing provisions of this Article, it shall remain in quarantine at its owner's expense for the remainder of the period applying in respect of the animal with which it has been in contact, or for such shorter period as the Minister may in any particular case direct, and shall be treated for the purposes of this order as an animal which has been brought to Great Britain from a place outside Great Britain.

(5) Notwithstanding the foregoing provisions of this Article, where an outbreak of rabies occurs at authorised quarantine premises, or where the Minister has reason to suspect that an animal detained or previously detained at such premises may be or may have been affected with that disease, he may (without prejudice to the operation of the provisions of the Rabies Order of 1938[1], or of any order amending, extending or replacing that order), by notice in writing served on the veterinary surgeon or registered medical practitioner supervising the premises, and (where practicable) on the owner of any animal detained thereat, require that any such animal be detained and isolated at its owner's expense for such longer period as may be specified in the notice, and subject to such conditions as may be so specified.

---

*Sub-section (2A) inserted in relation to England by SI 2004/2364.
1. See now the Rabies (Control) Order 1974, SI 1974/2212.

Release from quarantine

8–1794A **5A.** If a pet dog, cat or ferret is in quarantine in England, the Secretary of State may grant a licence releasing it if she is satisfied that—

(a) it has been identified and vaccinated (including any revaccination where required) in accordance with the requirements of Regulation (EC) No 998/2003 and the Non Commercial Movement of Pet Animals (England) Regulations 2004;

(b) at least 24 hours before release it has been treated by a veterinary surgeon against *Echinococcus multilocularis* and ticks (and in the case of treatment against *Echinococcus multilocularis* the treatment contains praziquantel as the active ingredient);

(c) a neutralising antibody titration has been carried out on a blood sample from it in accordance with the requirements of Regulation (EC) No 998/2003 and the Non Commercial Movement of Pet Animals (England) Regulations 2004 and the result is in accordance with the requirements of those instruments;

(d) the waiting period before entry to England required by Regulation (EC) No 998/2003 and the Non Commercial Movement of Pet Animals (England) Regulations 2004 has elapsed; and

(e) it has not been outside the countries and territories in Annex II of Regulation (EC) No 998/2003 in the six months prior to its import to England.*

*Article inserted in relation to the importation of pet cats and pet dogs into England only by SI 1999/3443; substituted by SI 2004/2364.

Release from quarantine in Wales

8–1794B 5B. If a cat or dog is in quarantine in Wales, the National Assembly for Wales may grant a licence releasing the animal if it is satisfied that—

(a) the animal has been microchipped, vaccinated and blood tested in accordance with the Pet Travel Scheme (Pilot Arrangements) (England) Order 1999;

(b) a sample of blood was taken from the animal at least six months before the release date and tested in accordance with the 1999 Order;

(c) at least twenty four hours before release the animal has been treated by a veterinary surgeon against *Echinococcus multilocularis* and ticks, using a veterinary medicine with a marketing authorisation in the UK at an appropriate dosage (in the case of treatment against *Echinococcus multilocularis* the medicine must contain praziquantel as the active ingredient), and in the case of an animal which has been in Cyprus, Malta or one of the countries or territories in Schedule 6 to the 1999 Order the treatment against ticks must contain fipronil as the active ingredient;]

(d) the animal has not been outside the countries or territories in Schedules 2 or 6 to the 1999 Order in the six months prior to the release date; and

(e) in the case of an animal from a country or territory in Schedule 6 to the 1999 Order, it arrived in Great Britain in a sealed container with the seal intact. The container must have been sealed by an official authorised by the competent authority of the exporting country, who must have written the number on the seal on the import licence granted by the Minister under article 4(3) and stamped the licence with his official stamp. The number on the seal must be the same as the number on the licence, but if the National Assembly for Wales is satisfied that the animal was not exposed to risk of infection with rabies during its journey, it may release the animal from quarantine if the provisions relating to sealing are not complied with.

Vaccination of animals in quarantine*

8–1795 6. (1) During the period of its detention and isolation in quarantine under the provisions of Article 5(2) above, every dog and cat shall, at its owner's expense, be vaccinated against rabies with a vaccine approved for the purpose by the Minister, in such manner, and on such number of occasions and at such intervals, as the Minister may require either generally, or in relation to a particular case.

(2) Where the Minister is satisfied that a dog or cat has been brought to Great Britain for use at research premises in connection with scientific research, and that the vaccination of the dog or cat might interfere with the kind of research in connection with which it is intended to be used, he may direct that the provisions of paragraph (1) above shall not apply in respect of that animal.

(3) The requirement to vaccinate against rabies in paragraph (1) above shall not apply in any case where the Secretary of State is satisfied that—

(a) the animal has been vaccinated in accordance with Regulation (EC) No 998/2003 and the period of cover of the vaccination has not expired; and

(b) a neutralising antibody titration has been carried out on a blood sample from the animal in accordance with Regulation (EC) No 998/2003 and the Non Commercial Movement of Pet Animals (England) Regulations 2004 and the result is in accordance with the requirements of those instruments.*

*Para (3) (inserted in relation to the importation of pet cats and pet dogs into England only by SI 1999/3443) and provision heading substituted by SI 2004/2364.

Control of movement of animals after landing

8–1796 7. (1) Where an animal is landed in Great Britain in accordance with a licence granted under Article 4 above (other than an animal brought into England which is exempted from quarantine by article 5(2A), it shall be the duty of the person in charge of the animal at the time of landing to ensure that it is either—

(a) immediately handed over to the authorised carrying agent named in the licence, who shall forthwith remove the animal to the authorised quarantine premises specified in the licence at which it is to be kept for the remainder of the period of its detention and isolation in quarantine; or

(b) immediately removed by an authorised carrying agent to premises within or in the vicinity of the port or airport which have been approved by the Minister for the temporary accommodation of animals to which this order applies.

(2) Where an animal is moved under paragraph (1)(b) above to approved premises within or in the vicinity of the port or airport, it shall be detained and isolated there pending its removal without avoidable delay (and in any case, not more than 48 hours after its landing) by an authorised carrying agent to the authorised quarantine premises specified in the licence at which it is to be kept for the remainder of the period of its detention and isolation in quarantine.

(3) During the period of its detention and isolation in quarantine at the authorised quarantine premises specified in the licence, an animal shall not be moved from those premises except to other authorised quarantine premises, or to a vessel or aircraft for exportation, and in either case only by an authorised carrying agent, and in accordance with the terms and conditions of a further licence granted by the Minister.

(4) Notwithstanding the provisions of paragraph (3) above, where a veterinary inspector is satisfied that an animal to which they apply is in urgent need of veterinary treatment of a kind which cannot be administered at the authorised quarantine premises at which the animal is detained and isolated in quarantine, he may authorise the movement of the animal by an authorised carrying agent to a place at which such treatment can be administered, subject to compliance with such conditions as he may consider appropriate; and it shall be the duty of the veterinary surgeon or registered medical practitioner supervising the authorised quarantine premises at which the animal is being detained to ensure that all such conditions are complied with.

(5) Where, in accordance with Article 4(5) above, an animal is landed at a place in Great Britain other than the port or airport at which it is licensed to be landed, a veterinary inspector may authorise the movement of such animal by a person other than an authorised carrying agent, subject to compliance with such conditions as he may consider appropriate.

Control of animals passing through Great Britain

8–1797 **8.** (1) Subject to paragraph (7) below, the provisions of Articles 4(1) and (3), 5, 6 and 7 above shall not apply to an animal landed at a port or airport in Great Britain in circumstances where satisfactory arrangements have previously been made for the exportation of that animal from that port or airport within a period of 48 hours after its landing; and it shall be for the person who purports to land an animal under the foregoing provisions of this paragraph to prove to the satisfaction of an inspector if required so to do that the arrangements referred to in those provisions have been made in respect of that animal.

(2) It shall be the duty of the person for the time being in charge of an animal to which paragraph (1) above applies—

(*a*) to ensure that the animal is exported from the port or airport within a period of 48 hours after its landing;

(*b*) subject to sub-paragraph (*d*) below, to ensure that the animal does not in any circumstances leave the port or airport before it is exported;

(*c*) in the case of an animal which is at the port or airport for a period not exceeding four hours, to ensure that it is securely confined throughout that period, and kept isolated from any other animal or any contact animal (other than an animal or contact animal with it which it is being transported);

(*d*) in the case of an animal which is at the port or airport for a period exceeding four hours, to ensure that it is detained throughout that period, and isolated from any other animal or any contact animal (other than an animal or contact animal with which it is being transported) at premises within or in the vicinity of the port or airport which have been approved by the Minister for the temporary accommodation of animals to which this order applies;

(*e*) to ensure that the animal is only moved during its stay at the port or airport by an authorised carrying agent; and

(*f*) immediately to report the loss of the animal to an inspector, a constable or an officer of Customs and Excise.

(3) Subject to paragraph (7) below, the provisions of Articles 4(1), 5, 6 and 7 above shall not apply to an animal landed in Great Britain in compliance with the terms and conditions of a licence (which may be general or specific) previously granted by the Minister authorising the landing of the animal, and its subsequent transit through Great Britain to a port or airport for exportation.

(4) The conditions subject to which a licence referred to in paragraph (3) above shall be granted shall include a condition that the animal to which the licence relates shall only be moved in Great Britain by an authorised carrying agent, and it shall be the duty of the person for the time being in charge of the animal—

(*a*) to comply with the conditions subject to which the licence was granted;

(*b*) to ensure that the animal does not come into contact with any other animal or with any contact animal (other than an animal or contact animal with which it has been transported to Great Britain); and

(*c*) immediately to report the loss of the animal to an inspector, a constable or an officer of Customs and Excise.

(5) If an animal to which this Article applies is involved while in Great Britain in an incident whereby rabies virus could, if present in that animal, be transmitted to a human being, or to another animal or a contact animal (other than an animal or contact animal with which it is permitted to come into contact under the foregoing provisions of this Article), the person for the time being in charge of the animal shall forthwith give notice of the incident to an inspector; and on receipt of such notice, the inspector may, if he considers it expedient so to do, require that the animal shall not leave Great Britain until after it has undergone detention and isolation in

quarantine at its owner's expense, at such premises, and for such period (not exceeding six calendar months) and subject to such conditions, as the inspector may direct.

(6) Where an inspector considers that anything connected with an animal to which this Article applies, or connected with the detention, isolation or movement of such an animal, may give rise to the risk of the introduction of rabies into Great Britain, he may by written or oral notice given to the person for the time being in charge of the animal, impose such further conditions with regard to the animal, or with regard to its detention, isolation or movement, as he may consider necessary for the purpose of reducing that risk, and it shall be the duty of the person to whom such notice is given to comply with the requirements thereof.

(7) Where an animal to which the foregoing provisions of this Article apply is not detained and isolated in accordance with those provisions, or is in any other respect the subject of a contravention thereof, that animal shall be deemed to have been illegally landed in Great Britain for the purposes of this order, and the provisions of Articles 13 and 14 below shall accordingly apply thereto.

Authorised quarantine premises

8–1798 **9.** (1) No premises shall be used for the detention and isolation in quarantine of an animal to which this order applies unless they have been authorised for use for the purpose by a licence granted by the Minister.

(2) A licence shall not be granted under paragraph (1) above unless the Minister is satisfied that the premises to which it relates are under the supervision of a veterinary surgeon or (in the case of research premises only) a registered medical practitioner who has been authorised in writing by him to act in that behalf, and any such authorisation may be issued for such period as may be specified therein, and given subject to such conditions as may be so specified.

(3) A licence granted under paragraph (1) above shall remain in force for such period as may be specified therein, and shall be granted subject to such terms and conditions as may be so specified.

(4) Nothing in the foregoing provisions of this Article shall be construed as precluding the Minister at any time from withdrawing an authorisation given or revoking a licence granted thereunder, or from varying the terms or conditions subject to which it was given or granted, but without prejudice to anything lawfully done pursuant thereto before such withdrawal, revocation or variation takes effect.

Authorised carrying agents

8–1799 **10.** (1) The Minister may authorise in writing any person to act as an authorised carrying agent in connection with the movement of animals to which this order applies, and any such authorisation may be issued for such period as may be specified therein, and given subject to such terms and conditions as may be so specified.

(2) An authorisation issued by the Minister under paragraph (1) above may relate generally to the movement of animals to which this order applies, or to any class or species of such animals, or to the movement of a specified animal or specified animals on an occasion or on occasions so specified.

(3) Where the Minister has, in accordance with the foregoing provisions of this Article, authorised a person to act as an authorised carrying agent, he may at any time withdraw such authorisation, or vary the terms and conditions subject to which it was given, but without prejudice to anything lawfully done pursuant thereto before such withdrawal or variation takes effect.

Records

8–1800 **11.** (1) The person in charge of authorised quarantine premises shall adopt such system for the identification of animals received at such premises, and shall keep such records in relation to their receipt, treatment and subsequent release (or death) and other matters, as may be required by the Minister, either generally or in relation to a particular case.

(2) Every entry in such a record shall be made in a permanent and legible form within 36 hours of the event which is required by this Article to be recorded.

(3) Every entry in such a record shall be retained by the person whose duty it is to keep such records for a period of at least 12 months from such event, and shall be produced by him for inspection at all reasonable times on demand to an inspector or a constable, who shall be entitled to take a copy of such entry.

(4) A local authority may supply forms of record for the purposes of this Article to any person in the district of the local authority.

Detention of animals on board vessels in harbour

8–1801 **12.** (1) Paragraph (2) below shall apply to an animal which has, within the preceding 6 calendar months, been in a place outside Great Britain, Northern Ireland, the Republic of Ireland, the Channel Islands and the Isle of Man.

(2) Subject to paragraph (3) below, it shall be the duty of the person having charge or control of a vessel in harbour in Great Britain to ensure that an animal to which this paragraph applies which is on board that vessel—

(a) is at all times restrained, and kept securely confined within a totally enclosed part of the vessel from which it cannot escape;

(b) does not come into contact with any other animal or any contact animal (other than an animal or contact animal with which it has been transported to Great Britain); and

(c) is in no circumstances permitted to land.

(3) Paragraph (2)(c) above shall not apply to an animal which is landed—

(a) in accordance with a licence granted under Article 4 above; or

(b) in the circumstances referred to in Article 8 above.

(4) If an animal to which paragraph (2) above applies is lost from a vessel in harbour in Great Britain, the person having charge or control of that vessel shall forthwith give notice of the loss to an inspector, a constable or an officer of Customs and Excise.

(5) If an animal to which paragraph (2) above applies is involved in an incident whereby rabies virus could, if present in that animal, be transmitted to a human being, or to another animal or a contact animal (other than an animal or contact animal with which it has been transported to Great Britain), the person for the time being in charge of the animal shall forthwith give notice of the incident to an inspector; and on receipt of such notice, the inspector may, if he considers it expedient so to do, require (in the case of an animal which would otherwise not be permitted to land under this Article) that the animal shall not leave Great Britain until after it has undergone detention and isolation in quarantine at its owner's expense, at such premises, for such period (not exceeding six calendar months) and subject to such conditions, as the inspector may direct.

(6) Subject to paragraph (7) below, no person shall cause or permit a native animal or a native contact animal to go on board a vessel in harbour in Great Britain on which there is an animal to which paragraph (2) above applies; and for the purposes of this paragraph and paragraph (8) below—

(a) "native animal" means an animal to which paragraph (2) above does not apply; and

(b) "native contact animal" means a contact animal which is ashore in Great Britain, whether or not it has been landed from a vessel.

(7) Paragraph (6) above shall not apply to—

(a) the use on board a vessel in harbour in Great Britain of dogs belonging to the police, Her Majesty's Customs and Excise or Her Majesty's Forces, so long as such dogs are kept under constant control of a trained handler while on board; or

(b) the loading on board a vessel in harbour in Great Britain of any animal or contact animal intended for exportation from Great Britain on that vessel.

(8) An inspector or a constable may seize or cause to be seized—

(a) any animal to which paragraph (2) above applies in relation to which there has been a contravention of or failure to comply with any provision of that paragraph; and

(b) any native animal or native contact animal in relation to which there has been a contravention of or failure to comply with the provisions of paragraph (6) above;

and where an animal or contact animal has been seized in accordance with the foregoing provisions of this paragraph, an inspector or a constable may—

(i) destroy it or cause it to be destroyed;

(ii) move it or cause it to be moved to authorised quarantine premises for the purposes of detention and isolation in quarantine at its owner's expense for a period of six calendar months, or for such shorter period as an inspector may direct; or

(iii) in the case of an animal to which paragraph (2) above applies, export it from Great Britain or cause it to be so exported:

and provided that, where an animal or a contact animal to which this paragraph applies has been seized by a constable, it shall only be dealt with in accordance with sub-paragraph (ii) or sub-paragraph (iii) above with the agreement of an inspector.

(9) The reasonable expenses incurred by an inspector or a constable in exercising the powers conferred on him by paragraph (8) above shall be recoverable on demand by the Minister, the local authority or, as the case may be, the police authority as a civil debt from the owner of the animal or contact animal.

Action in case of illegal landing or breach of quarantine

8–1802 **13.** (1) Without prejudice to Article 14 below, where—

(a) an animal which is required to be detained and isolated in quarantine under any of the provisions of this order, or under the provisions of a licence granted or notice served hereunder, is not so detained and isolated, or

(b) there is reason to believe that an animal has been landed in Great Britain in contravention of this order or of a licence granted hereunder,

an inspector may by written or oral notice served on the person appearing to him to be in charge of the animal, require that person, at the expense of the owner of the animal or of the person on whom the notice is served, immediately to detain and isolate the animal, and, within the time specified in the notice, to ensure that it is moved in such manner, and in compliance with such conditions, as may be so specified—

    (i)   to a vessel, vehicle or aircraft for exportation; or

    (ii) to authorised quarantine premises for the purpose of detention and isolation in quarantine at its owner's expense for a period of six calendar months from the date of the notice, or for such shorter period as may be specified therein.

(2) If any person on whom a notice is served under paragraph (1) above fails to comply with the requirements thereof, an inspector or a constable, may, without prejudice to any proceedings for an offence arising from such default, or arising in connection with any other contravention of this order or of a licence granted or notice served hereunder, seize or cause to be seized the animal to which the notice relates, and arrange for the notice to be complied with; and the person on whom the notice was served, and the owner of the animal and any other person having charge thereof, shall render all reasonable assistance to an inspector or a constable to enable him to exercise the power conferred by the foregoing provisions of this paragraph, and the reasonable expenses incurred in the exercise of that power shall be recoverable on demand by the Minister the local authority or, as the case may be, the police authority as a civil debt from the owner of the animal, or from the person on whom the notice was served.

(3) The operation of a notice served under paragraph (1) above may be terminated by notice to that effect given by an inspector to the owner or person in charge of the animal on proof to the satisfaction of the inspector that the animal was not landed in Great Britain in contravention of this order, or of a licence granted hereunder, or that six calendar months have expired since the date of the landing of the animal.

(4) Without prejudice to Article 14 below, where in respect of an animal to which paragraph (1) above applies an inspector—

    (a) has reasonable grounds for believing that the animal does not have an owner, or

    (b) is unable, after reasonable inquiry, to trace the owner of the animal, or any person otherwise having charge of it, or

    (c) has reason to believe that the service of a notice under paragraph (1) above would result in an unreasonable delay in dealing with the animal,

he may seize the animal, or cause it to be seized, and arrange for its exportation or detention and isolation in quarantine at authorised quarantine premises:

Provided that he shall (where the identity of the owner of the animal is known or subsequently becomes known to him), as soon as practicable, inform that person in writing of the action he has taken.

(5) The reasonable expenses incurred in the exercise of the power conferred on an inspector by paragraph (4) above shall, without prejudice to any proceedings arising in connection with any contravention of this order, or of a licence granted hereunder, be recoverable on demand by the Minister or, as the case may be, the local authority as a civil debt from the owner of the animal.

(6) Nothing in this Article shall affect the powers of the Commissioners of Customs and Excise to seize or detain as liable to forfeiture under the Customs and Excise Acts an animal which is landed in Great Britain in contravention of this order, or of a licence granted hereunder, or to institute legal proceedings under those Acts in respect of such contravention.

Power to destroy imported animals

8–1803   **14.** An inspector or a constable may seize or cause to be seized, and thereafter destroy or cause to be destroyed any animal landed in Great Britain in contravention of this order, or of a licence granted hereunder, or any animal in respect of which there is, after it has been landed, a contravention of any such licence, and the reasonable expenses incurred in the exercise of the power conferred by the foregoing provisions of this paragraph shall, without prejudice to any proceedings arising in connection with a contravention of this order, or of a licence granted hereunder, be recoverable on demand by the Minister, the local authority or, as the case may be, the police authority as a civil debt from the owner of the animal.

Contact Animals

8–1804   **15.** (1) Except as provided for in the foregoing provisions of this order, where an animal or contact animal comes into contact with an animal—

    (a) which is being or should be detained and isolated in quarantine under the provisions of this order, or which has escaped from such detention and isolation, or

    (b) which is awaiting exportation from a port or airport, or which is in the course of transit through Great Britain, under the provisions of Article 8 above, or

    (c) which is on board a vessel in any harbour in Great Britain in circumstances to which Article 12 above applies, or

    (d) which has been or which is suspected of having been landed in Great Britain in contravention of the provisions of this order, or of a licence granted hereunder,

an inspector may, by notice in writing served on the owner or other person appearing to him to have the control or custody of the said animal or contact animal, apply such of the provisions of this order thereto as he may consider expedient, with such modifications or variations as may be specified in the notice, and it shall be the duty of the person on whom such a notice is served to comply with the requirements thereof.

(2) A notice served under paragraph (1) above shall remain in force for such period as may be specified therein, unless withdrawn by a further notice served in like manner.

Summary offences

8–1805   16. (1) No person shall land or attempt to land an animal in Great Britain the landing of which is prohibited under Article 4(1) above, or cause or permit the landing or attempted landing of any such animal[1].

(2) It shall be unlawful to contravene any provision of this order, or of a licence granted or notice served hereunder, or to fail to comply with any such provision, or to cause or permit any such contravention or non-compliance.

---

1. The offence under art 16(1) of landing animals prohibited by art 4(1) is one of strict liability, and the extended meaning given to the term "landing" makes plain that liability is not confined to the party engaged in unloading an animal and carriers are liable to be convicted as principals in such circumstances: *Corporation of London v Eurostar (UK) Ltd* [2004] EWHC Admin 187, (2005) 169 JP 263.

Indictable offences

8–1806   17. Without prejudice to section 80 of the Act (summary proceedings), any person who knowingly, and with intent to evade any provision of this order, or any provision of a licence granted hereunder;—

(*a*) lands or attempts to land an animal in Great Britain the landing of which is prohibited by Article 4(1) above, or causes or permits the landing or attempted landing of any such animal, or

(*b*) lands or attempts to land an animal in Great Britain in contravention of any provision of this order, or of a licence granted hereunder, or in respect of the landing of an animal in Great Britain, fails to comply with any such provision, or causes or permits any such contravention or non-compliance, or

(*c*) with respect to an animal which has been landed in Great Britain, does or omits to do anything relating to the detention and isolation in quarantine of the animal in contravention of any provision of this order, or of a licence granted hereunder,

commits an offence against the Act, and shall be liable to prosecution on indictment.

Local authority to enforce order

8–1807   18. This order shall, except where otherwise provided, be executed and enforced by the local authority.

8–1808

SCHEDULE 1
ANIMALS TO WHICH THE ORDER APPLIES

PART I
ANIMALS SUBJECT TO QUARANTINE FOR LIFE

Order		*Common names of some species* (see note below)
Chiroptera	Desmodontidae only	Vampire bats

PART II
ANIMALS SUBJECT TO 6 MONTHS' QUARANTINE

Order		*Common names of some species* (see note below)
Carnivora	All families and species	Dogs, cats, jackals, foxes, wolves, bears, racoons, coatis, pandas, otters, weasels, martens, polecats, badgers, skunks, mink, ratels, genets, civets, linsangs, mongooses, hyaenas, ocelets, pumas, cheetahs, lions, tigers, leopards.
Chiroptera	All families except Desmodontidae	Bats, flying foxes
Dermoptera		Flying lemurs
Edentata		Anteaters, sloths, armadillos
Hyracoidea		Hyraxes
Insectivora		Solenodons, tenrecs, otter shrews, golden moles, hedgehogs, elephant shrews, shrews, moles, desmans
Lagomorpha		Pikas, rabbits, hare
Marsupialia		Opossums, marsupial mice, dasyures, marsupial moles, marsupial anteaters, bandicoots, rat opossums, cuscuses, phalangers, koalas, wombats, wallabies, kangaroos

| Primates | All families except Homini- dae (Man) | Tree-shrews, lemurs, indrises, sifakas, aye-ayes, lorises, bushbabies, tarsiers, titis, uakaris, sakis, howlers, capuchins, squirrel monkeys, marmosets, tamarins, macaques, mangabeys, baboons, langurs, gibbons, great apes |
| Rodentia | | Gophers, squirrels, chipmunks, marmots, scaly-tailed squirrels, pocket mice, kangaroo-rats, beavers, mountain beavers, springhaas, mice, rats, hamsters, lemmings, voles, gerbils, water rats, dormice, jumping mice, jerboas, porcupines, cavies (including guinea-pigs), capybaras, chinchillas, spiny rats, gundis. |

SCHEDULE 2

8–1809 Ports and airports at which authorised landings of animals may take place:

PART I
PORTS

Dover, Eastern Docks
Harwich and Parkeston Quay
Hull
Portsmouth
Southampton

PART II
AIRPORTS

Birmingham
Edinburgh
Gatwick
Glasgow
Heathrow
Leeds
Manchester
Prestwick

Horse Passports (England) Regulations 2004[1]
(SI 2004/1397)

8–1810 **1. Title, application and commencement.** These Regulations may be cited as the Horse Passports (England) Regulations 2004; they apply in England, and shall come into force on 10 June 2004.

1. Made by the Secretary of State, being designated for the purposes of section 2(2) of the European Communities Act 1972 in relation to the common agricultural policy of the European Community, in exercise of the powers conferred on her by that section.

8–1811 **2. Interpretation.** In these Regulations—

"horse" means an animal of the equine or asinine species or crossbreeds of those species, but does not include zebras;

"keeper" means a person appointed by the owner to have day to day charge of the horse;

"local authority" means—

(a) in any part of England where there is, within the meaning of the Local Government Changes for England Regulations 1994, a unitary authority for that local government area, that authority;

(b) where there is not a unitary authority—

(i) in a metropolitan district, the council of that district;
(ii) in a non-metropolitan county, the council of that county; or
(iii) in each London borough, the council of that borough;

(c) in the City of London, the Common Council;

"passport" means—

(a) an identification document for a horse issued by a passport-issuing organisation containing all the information required by regulation 8(2) or 8(3); or

(b) in the case of such an identification document issued before the coming into force of these Regulations but which does not contain the pages in Section IX of the passport, that document with the Section IX pages attached in accordance with regulation 9,

and "Section IX pages" means those pages;

"passport-issuing organisation" has the meaning assigned in regulation 3;

"sell" includes any transfer of ownership.

8–1812 **3. Organisations authorised to issue passports.** (1) The following organisations (referred to in these Regulations as "passport-issuing organisations") are authorised to issue passports—

(a) organisations authorised in writing by the Secretary of State under these Regulations to issue passports;

(b) organisations that maintain or establish stud-books for registered horses and are recognised by the Secretary of State under regulation 3 of the Horses (Zootechnical Standards) Regulations 1992;

(c) organisations recognised in another part of the United Kingdom or another Member State under legislation that implements either—

(i) Commission Decision 92/353/EEC (laying down the criteria for approval or recognition of organisations and associations which maintain or establish stud-books for registered equidae); or

(ii) Commission Decision 2000/68/EC (amending Commission Decision 93/623/EEC and establishing the identification of equidae for breeding and production); and

(d) international associations or organisations that manage or regulate horses for competition or racing and are registered with the Secretary of State to issue passports.

(2) The Secretary of State may by notice in writing withdraw authorisation under paragraph (1)(a) or registration under paragraph (1)(d) if she is satisfied on reasonable grounds that an association or organisation is not complying with the provisions of these Regulations.

(3) No person shall issue a document which falsely purports to be a passport.

8–1813 **4. Powers and duties of passport-issuing organisations.** (1) The passport-issuing organisation is "the competent authority" for the purposes of the passport.

(2) A passport-issuing organisation may cancel a passport issued by it if it is satisfied on reasonable grounds that—

(a) the provisions of these Regulations have not been or are not being complied with; or

(b) the passport has not been properly completed or has been falsified in any way.

(3) When a passport is returned because a horse has died, the passport-issuing organisation shall mark the passport accordingly but may then return it to the owner if permitted by its rules.

8–1814 **5. Records.** (1) A passport-issuing organisation shall maintain a record of—

(a) information contained in applications for passports and Section IX pages;

(b) any change of ownership of a horse; and

(c) the death of a horse.

(2) It shall keep this record until three years after the death of the horse.

(3) A passport-issuing organisation shall supply to the Secretary of State information from its records in such form and at such intervals as she may require by notice in writing.

8–1815 **6. Application for a passport.** (1) An application for a passport shall—

(a) be made by the owner of the horse;

(b) be made in writing to a passport-issuing organisation; and

(c) be in the format specified by that organisation.

(2) No person shall—

(a) apply for more than one passport for a horse; or

(b) apply for a second passport (other than a replacement passport) for a horse.

8–1816 **7. Time limits for obtaining a passport.** (1) The owner of a horse that was born on or before 30th November 2003 who does not already have a passport for that horse shall apply for a passport for it before 1st July 2004.

(2) The owner of a horse that was born after 30th November 2003 shall obtain a passport for it on or before 31st December of the year of its birth, or by six months after its birth, whichever is the later.

8–1817 **8. Issue of a passport.** (1) On application, provided all its requirements are complied with, the passport-issuing organisation shall issue a passport duly completed in the format set out in Schedule 1.

(2) In the case of a horse either registered or eligible for entry in a stud-book of a recognised organisation in accordance with Article 2(c) of Council Directive 90/426/EEC on animal health conditions governing the movement and import from third countries of equidae, the passport shall contain all the Sections specified in Schedule 1.

(3) In any other case the passport shall contain at least Sections I to IV and IX but may contain more Sections or all the Sections.

8–1818 **9. Section IX pages for existing passports.** (1) In the case of a horse born before these Regulations come into force that already has an identification document issued by a passport-issuing organisation containing all the information required by regulation 8(2) or 8(3) except for the Section IX pages, a passport may consist of that identification document together with the

Section IX pages obtained by the owner from a passport-issuing organisation, provided that the applicant—

(a) applies for them before 1st July 2004, and
(b) attaches them to the identification document.

(2) Regulation 6 applies to an application for Section IX pages as it applies to an application for a passport.
(3) The Section IX pages shall contain the same number or alphanumeric code as in Section II of the original identification document.

8–1819   10. Identification.   (1) The passport-issuing organisation when issuing a passport shall identify the horse with a number or alphanumeric code not previously used by that organisation.
(2) It shall record the number or alphanumeric code in Section II of the passport.

8–1820   11. Language of passports.   (1) Sections I to VIII of passports issued in England shall be in English and French.
(2) Section IX shall be in English.
(3) A passport or any part of it may also be in an additional language.

8–1821   12. Horses entering England.   (1) The owner (or, in the case of an owner living outside England, the keeper) of a horse brought into England without a passport (or with a document that would be a passport but for the fact that it does not contain Section IX) shall apply for a passport or the Section IX pages within 30 days of the horse being brought into England.
(2) A passport or Section IX pages issued following an application made under paragraph (1) shall state that the horse is not intended for slaughter for human consumption.
(3) This regulation shall not apply in relation to a horse that remains in England for less than 30 days.

8–1822   13. Horses in the New Forest or Dartmoor.   Schedule 2 (special arrangements for the New Forest and Dartmoor) shall have effect.

8–1823   14. Declaration concerning slaughter for human consumption.   (1) Subject to the following provisions of this regulation, an owner may at any time sign the declaration in Section IX concerning whether or not the animal is intended for slaughter for human consumption, or may choose not to sign it.
(2) An owner must sign the declaration before any veterinary medicinal product containing a substance specified in Annex IV to Council Regulation (EEC) No 2377/90 (laying down a Community procedure for the establishment of maximum residue limits of veterinary medicinal products in foodstuffs of animal origin) is administered to a horse and must indicate that the horse is not intended for slaughter for human consumption (unless the declaration has already been so signed).
(3) An owner must sign the declaration before the horse is consigned for slaughter for human consumption (in which case the declaration must state that the horse is intended for slaughter for human consumption).
(4) An owner must sign the declaration and ensure that it is countersigned by a passport-issuing organisation or the Secretary of State before the horse is sent outside the United Kingdom.

8–1824   15. Prohibitions.   (1) No person shall—

(a) destroy or deface a passport;
(b) alter any entry made in Section I of the passport;
(c) alter any of the details in Section II or III of the passport unless authorised in writing to do so by a passport-issuing organisation;
(d) make an entry in Section IV of the passport except in accordance with the rules and regulations of a passport-issuing organisation, and no person shall alter any entry;
(e) alter any details in Section V, VI, VII, VIII or IX of the passport; or
(f) change a declaration in section IX that a horse is not intended for slaughter for human consumption (but if the declaration shows that the horse is intended for slaughter for human consumption, an owner may subsequently declare that the horse is not intended for slaughter for human consumption, in which case the horse will not be intended for slaughter for human consumption).

(2) No person shall be in possession of a document which falsely purports to be a passport.
(3) In proceedings against a person for an offence of failing to comply with paragraph (2) it is a defence for him to prove that he was not aware that the document was not a passport.

8–1825   16. Replacement of a lost or damaged passport.   (1) Where a passport has been lost or damaged the owner of the horse shall, within 30 days of the loss or damage being discovered, apply for a replacement passport for that horse—

(a) where the passport-issuing organisation of issue is known to him, to that organisation; or

(b) where the passport-issuing organisation of issue is not known, to any passport-issuing organisation.

(2) The passport-issuing organisation applied to in accordance with paragraph (1) shall issue a replacement passport marked with the word "Duplicate".

(3) If all the original information in Section IX is legible the replacement passport shall repeat that information.

(4) If any information in Section IX is illegible the passport issuing organisation shall indicate in the replacement passport that the horse is not intended for slaughter for human consumption by completing Part II of that Section.

8–1826　17. Restrictions on the use of horses without passports.　If a passport should have been issued for a horse, after 28th February 2005 no person shall—

(a) use it for the purposes of competition or breeding;
(b) move it out of the United Kingdom; or
(c) move it on to the premises of a new keeper,

unless the horse is accompanied by its passport.

8–1827　18. Requirements on persons administering veterinary medicinal products.　(1) Where a veterinary medicinal product is to be administered to a horse, the person in possession of its passport shall make it available to the veterinary surgeon or other person administering the product.

(2) The veterinary surgeon or other person administering the veterinary medicinal product shall—

(a) satisfy himself that the horse is the one described in the passport;
(b) if the passport contains Sections V and VI, record in the appropriate section any vaccine given, and if it contains Section VII, record the results of any laboratory health tests carried out for transmissible diseases;
(c) if the passport shows that the horse is intended for slaughter for human consumption, or if the declaration relating to slaughter for human consumption has not yet been completed, complete Part IIIB of Section IX of the passport if the product administered contains a substance not included in Annexes I, II, III or IV to Council Regulation (EEC) No 2377/90 for administration to horses; and
(d) if the product contains any substance listed in Annex IV to Council Regulation (EEC) No 2377/90, indicate on the passport that the horse is not intended for human consumption.

(3) In the case of a horse in relation to which a passport has not yet been obtained or is unavailable for any reason, or in relation to which the veterinary surgeon or other person administering the veterinary medicinal product is not satisfied that the horse is the one described in the passport, the veterinary surgeon or other person administering the veterinary medicinal product shall give to the keeper—

(a) a written record of the treatment of any product containing a substance not included in Annexes I, II, III or IV to Council Regulation (EEC) No 2377/90 for administration to horses, and written notification that these must be recorded in the passport; and
(b) if the product administered contains a substance specified in Annex IV to that Council Regulation, written notification to that effect and that the horse may not be slaughtered for human consumption,

and the keeper shall give the information to the owner.

(4) Following receipt of a written record or notice by the keeper of treatment under paragraph (3), the owner shall, as soon as the passport becomes available—

(a) enter any information received under paragraph (3)(a) in the passport unless he immediately signs the declaration in the passport that the horse is not intended for slaughter for human consumption; and
(b) if a product containing a substance specified in Annex IV to Council Regulation (EEC) No 2377/90 has been administered, sign the declaration in the passport that the horse is not intended for slaughter for human consumption.

8–1828　19. Duties on owners.　(1) After 28th February 2005 no person shall sell a horse without a passport.

(2) On the sale of a horse, the seller shall give the passport to the buyer or, at auction sales, the auctioneer shall give the passport to the buyer.

(3) The new owner or his representative shall, within 30 days of purchase send to the passport-issuing organisation that issued the passport—

(a) the name and address of the new owner; and
(b) the name and identification number or alphanumeric code of the horse as entered in Section II of the passport,

and shall complete Section I of the passport in accordance with the rules of the passport-issuing organisation.

(4) A person in possession of a passport shall produce it on reasonable demand to the

passport-issuing organisation that issued it, and shall surrender it on reasonable demand to that organisation.

(5) An owner of a horse that dies or is slaughtered shall send the passport to the passport-issuing authority within 30 days of the death.

8–1829   20. Slaughter for human consumption.   After 28th February 2005 no person shall slaughter a horse for human consumption or consign it for such slaughter unless it is accompanied by its passport and the declaration in Section IX does not show that the animal is not intended for slaughter for human consumption.

8–1830   21. Powers of entry.   (1) An inspector shall, on producing a duly authenticated document showing his authority, have a right at all reasonable hours, to enter any premises (excluding any premises not containing any horse and used only as a dwelling) for the purpose of administering and enforcing these Regulations; and in this regulation "premises" includes any vehicle or container.

(2) An inspector may—

(a)   require the production of a passport;
(b)   carry out any inquiries;
(c)   have access to, and inspect and copy any records (in whatever form they are held) kept under these Regulations;
(d)   remove such records to enable them to be copied;
(e)   have access to, inspect and check the operation of any computer and any associated apparatus or material that is or has been in use in connection with the records; and for this purpose may require any person having charge of, or otherwise concerned with the operation of, the computer, apparatus or material to afford him such assistance as he may reasonably require and, where a record is kept by means of a computer, may require the records to be produced in a form in which they may be taken away;
(f)   mark any animal or other thing for identification purposes; and
(g)   take with him—

(i)   such other persons as he considers necessary; and
(ii)   any representative of the European Commission properly interested in the administration of these Regulations.

(3) No person shall deface, obliterate or remove any mark applied under paragraph (2) except under the written authority of an inspector.

(4) If an inspector enters any unoccupied premises he shall leave them as effectively secured against unauthorised entry as he found them.

(5) In this regulation "inspector" means a person appointed as such by a local authority or the Secretary of State for the enforcement of these Regulations.

8–1831   22. Obstruction.   No person shall—

(a)   intentionally obstruct any person acting in the execution of these Regulations;
(b)   without reasonable cause, fail to give to any person acting in the execution of these Regulations any assistance or information that that person may reasonably require of him for the performance of his functions under these Regulations;
(c)   furnish to any person acting in the execution of these Regulations any information that he knows to be false or misleading; or
(d)   fail to produce a record when required to do so to any person acting in the execution of these Regulations.

8–1832   23. Offences.   (1) It shall be an offence for any person or organisation to fail to comply with—

(a)   regulation 3(3) (issue of a document purporting to be a passport);
(b)   regulation 6(2) (applying for more than one passport for a horse);
(c)   regulation 7 (time limits for obtaining a passport);
(d)   regulation 12(1) (bringing a horse into England);
(e)   regulation 14(2),14(3), or 14(4) (signing the declaration relating to slaughter for human consumption);
(f)   regulation 15(1) (alteration of a passport) or 15(2) (possession of a document purporting to be a passport);
(g)   regulation 16(1) (application for a replacement passport);
(h)   regulation 17 (restrictions on the use of a horse without a passport);
(i)   regulation 18 (administration of veterinary medicinal products);
(j)   regulation 19 (duties on owners);
(k)   regulation 20 (slaughter for human consumption);
(l)   regulation 22 (obstruction).

(2) Where a body corporate is guilty of an offence under these Regulations, and that offence is proved to have been committed with the consent or connivance of, or to have been attributable to any neglect on the part of—

(a) any director, manager, secretary or other similar person of the body corporate, or

(b) any person who was purporting to act in any such capacity,

he, as well as the body corporate, shall be guilty of the offence and shall be liable to be proceeded against and punished accordingly.

(3) For the purposes of paragraph (2), "director", in relation to a body corporate whose affairs are managed by its members, means a member of the body corporate.

(4) Where an organisation that is not a body corporate is guilty of an offence under these Regulations, and that offence is proved to have been committed with the consent or connivance of, or to have been attributable to any neglect on the part of any officer of that organisation, he, as well as the organisation, shall be guilty of the offence and shall be liable to be proceeded against and punished accordingly.

8–1833 24. Penalties. (1) A person guilty of an offence of failing to comply with regulation 3(3) (issue of a document purporting to be a passport), regulation 18(2)(c), 18(2)(d) or 18(4) (completion of the passport following administration of a veterinary medicinal product) or regulation 20 (slaughter for human consumption) shall be liable—

(a) on summary conviction, to a fine not exceeding the statutory maximum or to imprisonment for a term not exceeding three months or both; or

(b) on conviction on indictment, to a fine or to imprisonment for a term not exceeding two years or both.

(2) A person guilty of any other offence under these Regulations shall be liable on summary conviction to a fine not exceeding level 5 on the standard scale.

8–1834 25. Enforcement. (1) These Regulations shall be enforced by the local authority.

(2) The Secretary of State may direct, in relation to cases of a particular description or any particular case, that an enforcement duty imposed on a local authority by this regulation shall be discharged by the Secretary of State and not by the local authority.

8–1835 26. Revocation. The Horse Passports (England) Regulations 2003 are revoked.

8–1836

Regulation 8   SCHEDULE 1
                              IDENTIFICATION DOCUMENT FOR REGISTERED EQUIDAE

                                            PASSPORT

8–1837

Regulation 13   SCHEDULE 2
                       SPECIAL ARRANGEMENTS FOR THE NEW FOREST AND DARTMOOR

Exemption for listed New Forest and Dartmoor horses
1. (1) Where a horse is individually identified in the lists kept by the New Forest Verderers, or Dartmoor Commoners Council, an owner shall not be required to apply for a passport provided that the horse is not moved from the area regulated by one of those bodies, other than temporarily for welfare reasons.

(2) In the case of a horse born before the coming into force of these Regulations, this exemption shall only apply if the horse is identified in the lists before 1st July 2004.

(3) In the case of a horse born after the coming into force of these Regulations, this exemption shall only apply if the horse is identified in the lists by 31st December of the year of its birth; or by six months after its birth, whichever is the later.

Information recorded in a passport
2. If the owner of a horse that has been identified in the lists kept by the New Forest Verderers, or Dartmoor Commoners Council applies for a passport, the passport-issuing organisation shall record in the passport all the information kept in those lists for that horse.

Exemption from the prohibition on sale without a passport
3. (1) Notwithstanding regulation 19, an owner may sell a foal without a passport if the provisions of this paragraph are complied with.

(2) The foal must be sold in its year of birth through the Beaulieu Road Pony Sales held in the New Forest at Beaulieu, Brockenhurst, Hampshire SO42 7YQ.

(3) The foal must have been born in the crown lands of the New Forest out of a mare which—

(a) has been lawfully depastured on those lands, and

(b) in relation to which the marking fees have been paid to the verderers.

(4) The owner must provide to the auctioneer at the sale a completed passport application for a passport addressed to the New Forest Pony Breeding and Cattle Society including a silhouette of the horse, and the passport fee charged by that society.

(5) The auctioneer must—

(a) stamp the original application form with the lot number and photocopy it;

(b) give the photocopy to the buyer; and

(c) immediately submit the application form and the fee to the New Forest Pony Breeding and Cattle Society.

(6) If the conditions of this paragraph are complied with the buyer may move the foal out of the New Forest using the photocopied application form instead of a passport, but may not sell the horse, slaughter it for human consumption or use it for any of the purposes in regulation 17 until he receives the passport.

Non Commercial Movement of Pet Animals (England) Regulations 2004[1]

(SI 2004/2363)

PART 1
INTRODUCTION

8–1838   1. Title, application and commencement. These Regulations may be cited as the Non Commercial Movement of Pet Animals (England) Regulations 2004; they apply only to England and come into force on 1st October 2004.

---

1. Made by the Secretary of State, being a Minister designated for the purposes of section 2(2) of the European Communities Act 1972 in relation to the common agricultural policy of the European Community and in relation to measures in the veterinary and phytosanitary fields for the protection of public health, exercising the powers conferred upon her by that section.

8–1839   2. Interpretation. (1) In these Regulations—

"airport" means the aggregate of the buildings and works comprised in an aerodrome within the meaning of the Civil Aviation Act 1982;

"carrier" means any undertaking carrying goods or passengers for hire by land, sea or air;

"the Community Regulation" means Regulation (EC) No 998/2003 of the European Parliament and of the Council of 26 May 2003 on the animal health requirements applicable to the non-commercial movement of pet animals and amending Council Directive 92/65/EC as amended by Commission Regulation (EC) No 592/2004 and as read with Commission Decisions—

   (a) 2003/803/EC of 26 November 2003 establishing a model passport for the intra-Community movement of dogs, cats and ferrets,

   (b) 2004/203/EC of 18 February 2004 establishing a model health certificate for non-commercial movements from third countries of dogs, cats and ferrets,

   (c) 2004/301/EC of 30 March 2004 derogating from Decisions 2003/803/EC and 2004/203/EC as regards the format for certificates and passports for the non-commercial movement of dogs, cats and ferrets and amending Decision 2004/203/EC, and

   (d) 2004/539/EC of 1 July 2004 establishing a transitional measure for the implementation of Regulation (EC) No 998/2003 on the animal health requirements applicable to the non-commercial movement of pet animals;

"Hendra certificate" means the certificate described in regulation 5(c);

"inspector" means a person appointed by the Secretary of State or a local authority to be an inspector for the purposes of these Regulations and a person appointed as an inspector or a veterinary inspector for the purposes of the Animal Health Act 1981 shall be an inspector for the purposes of these Regulations;

"local authority" means—

   (a) in any part of England where there is, within the meaning of the Local Government Changes for England Regulations 1994, a unitary authority for that local government area, that authority;

   (b) where there is not a unitary authority—

      (i) in a metropolitan district, the council of that district;

      (ii) in a non-metropolitan county, the council of that county; or

      (iii) in each London borough, the council of that borough;

   (c) in the City of London, the Common Council;

"microchip" means the electronic identification system (transponder) specified in article 4(1) of the Community Regulation;

"PETS certification" means either the official health certificate relating to rabies required by article 7 of the Pet Travel Scheme (Pilot Arrangements) (England) Order 1999 or the official health certificate required by paragraph 4(a) of Schedule 6 to that Order;

"third country health certificate" means a health certificate complying with Commission Decision 2004/203/EC and the supporting documentation (or a certified copy of that documentation) referred to in article 3 of that Decision.

(2) Expressions defined in the Community Regulation have the same meaning in these Regulations.

8–1840   3. Approvals. Approvals issued under these Regulations shall be in writing, may be made subject to such conditions as the Secretary of State considers necessary to—

   (a) ensure that the provisions of the Community Regulation and these Regulations are complied with; and

   (b) protect public or animal health

and may be amended, suspended or revoked by notice in writing at any time; in particular approvals granted under regulation 8 may be suspended or revoked if the Secretary of State is reasonably of the opinion that the written procedures and contingency plans produced under Schedule 1 have not been complied with.

8–1841 4. Exemption from the provisions of the Rabies (Importation of Dogs, Cats and Other Mammals) Order 1974. (1) A person may bring a pet animal into England without complying with the provisions of the Rabies (Importation of Dogs, Cats and Other Mammals) Order 1974 provided the movement complies with the Community Regulation and these Regulations.

(2) Nothing in these Regulations shall apply in relation to an animal brought into England directly from other parts of the British Islands or the Republic of Ireland.

8–1842 5. Exceptions. These Regulations shall not apply to the movement to England of—

(a) more than five pet animals if they—

    (i) are travelling together; and

    (ii) come from a third country other than one listed in Section 2 of Part B of Annex II to the Community Regulation;

(b) prairie dogs originating in or travelling from the United States of America; or

(c) cats travelling from Australia unless accompanied by a certificate which—

    (i) is signed by a representative of the Australian government veterinary services;

    (ii) states the number of the microchip implanted in the cat; and

    (iii) certifies that the cat has not been on a holding where Hendra disease has been confirmed during the 60 days prior to departure from Australia,

and a cat in transit through Australia by air shall not be treated as travelling from Australia if it does not leave the airport.

PART 2

IDENTIFICATION AND BLOOD-TESTING OF PET ANIMALS

8–1843 6. Identification of pet dogs, cats and ferrets. For the purposes of article 4 of the Community Regulation, pet dogs, cats and ferrets shall be identified by microchip.

8–1844 7. Waiting period after satisfactory blood test. The neutralising antibody titration at least equal to 0.5 IU/ml referred to in article 6(1) of the Community Regulation shall be carried out on a blood sample taken at least six months before the pet animal is brought into England.

PART 3

CARRIERS, CERTIFICATION AND CHECKING ARRANGEMENTS

8–1845 8. Carriers. (1) Pet dogs, cats and ferrets shall be brought into England under the Community Regulation using a carrier approved to transport them under this regulation.

(2) The Secretary of State may approve a carrier under this regulation if she is satisfied that—

(a) the carrier complies with the requirements in Schedule 1;

(b) the written procedures and contingency plans required in that Schedule are adequate; and

(c) the carrier will comply with the Community Regulation and these Regulations, the written procedures required in Schedule 1 and any conditions of the approval.

(3) The approval shall specify—

(a) where checks must be carried out;

(b) the routes to be used by the approved carrier to bring a pet dog, cat or ferret into England; and

(c) any other conditions the Secretary of State considers appropriate.

(4) The carrier shall provide such information to the Secretary of State as she shall reasonably require.

(5) Every carrier shall comply with the terms and conditions of its approval.

8–1846 9. Treatment and certification in respect of *Echinococcus multilocularis* and ticks. (1) This regulation shall apply to pet dogs, cats and ferrets during the transitional period specified in article 16 of the Community Regulation.

(2) Not less than 24 and not more than 48 hours before embarkation for England the pet dog, cat or ferret shall have been treated by a veterinary surgeon entitled to practise medicine in the country in which the treatment is administered against *Echinococcus multilocularis* and ticks.

(3) The treatment shall be with a veterinary medicine with a marketing authorisation in the country in which the treatment is administered, shall be at an appropriate dosage, and—

(a) in the case of treatment against *Echinococcus multilocularis* shall contain praziquantel as the active ingredient; and

(b) in the case of treatment against ticks shall not be by means of a collar impregnated with acaricide.

(4) In addition to the certification required by the Community Regulation, the passport or third country health certificate accompanying each pet dog, cat and ferret shall—

(a) specify the manufacturer of each treatment administered in respect of *Echinococcus multilocularis* and ticks, the product used for each treatment, and the date and time of such administration; and

(b) be signed and stamped in respect of those treatments by the veterinary surgeon who administered them.

8–1847   10. Duties on carriers.   (1) A carrier shall check—

(a) the microchip, and

(b) either the passport or the third country health certificate

of every pet dog, cat or ferret it brings into England under the Community Regulation.

(2) A carrier shall check the Hendra certificate of every cat it brings into England from Australia.

(3) The checks shall be performed in the place and in the manner specified in the carrier's approval.

(4) The carrier shall satisfy itself that—

(a) the animal has been implanted with a microchip,

(b) the number of the microchip corresponds with the number of the microchip recorded in the passport or the third country health certificate (and such number must appear on both the health certificate and its supporting documentation) and, for a cat travelling from Australia, the Hendra certificate,

(c) the passport or third country health certificate shows that—

(i) it is current;

(ii) the animal has been vaccinated against rabies (and revaccinated where required) in accordance with the Community Regulation;

(iii) a neutralising antibody titration has been carried out on a blood sample from the animal in accordance with the Community Regulation and these Regulations and with a result in accordance with that required by the Community Regulation; and

(iv) the animal has been treated against *Echinococcus multilocularis* and ticks in accordance with these Regulations and those treatments have been certified in accordance with regulation 9(4),

(d) any Hendra certificate shows that the cat has not been on a holding where Hendra disease has been confirmed during the 60 days prior to departure from Australia, and

(e) there is no indication that the passport, third country health certificate or Hendra certificate has been falsified or unlawfully altered.

(5) If the passport or third country health certificate of a pet dog or cat shows that it was vaccinated or its blood sample was taken before its microchip was inserted it shall not fail either of the checks in paragraphs (4)(c)(ii) and (4)(c)(iii) for that reason if—

(a) the animal was vaccinated in a country or territory where the competent authority (or a body authorised by that authority) operates a mandatory identification system under which that species is required to be registered and identified by tattoo or microchip, or by tattoo only,

(b) the number of the animal's tattoo corresponds with the number of the tattoo recorded in the passport or third country health certificate (and such number must appear on both the health certificate and its supporting documentation), and

(c) the passport or third country health certificate shows that the animal was vaccinated after it was tattooed and before the blood sample was taken.

(6) If, after carrying out the checks, the carrier is not satisfied that the pet dog, cat or ferret may be brought into England under the Community Regulation and these Regulations—

(a) where the checks were performed outside England (other than during transport directly to England), the carrier shall not bring the animal into England under the Community Regulation;

(b) where the checks were performed in England or during transport directly to England, the carrier shall ensure that the animal is transferred to quarantine facilities in accordance with the Rabies (Importation of Dogs, Cats and Other Mammals) Order 1974 or is otherwise dealt with under the provisions of that Order and compliance with this sub-paragraph shall be a defence to a breach of article 4(1) of that Order.

(7) If, after carrying out the checks, the carrier is satisfied that the pet dog, cat or ferret may be brought into England under the Community Regulations and these Regulations it shall—

(a) issue a certificate to the person in charge of the animal which—

(i) is signed and dated by a representative of the carrier,

(ii) states that the animal complies with the provisions of the Community Regulation and these Regulations, and

(iii) states the date of importation to England; and

(b) if the animal is brought into England in a motor vehicle, give the person in charge a sticker or hanger for display on the vehicle stating that it is carrying a pet animal which has been checked and found to comply with the provisions of the Community Regulation and these Regulations.

8–1848   11. Duties at the port of arrival.   (1) A person bringing a pet dog, cat or ferret into England in a vehicle under the Community Regulation and these Regulations shall display the sticker or hanger given by the carrier in a prominent position in the windscreen until the vehicle leaves the port of arrival or, in the case of the Channel Tunnel, the Folkestone Terminal at Cheriton.

(2) A person bringing a pet dog, cat or ferret into England under the Community Regulation and these Regulations shall produce on demand by an inspector—

(a)   in the case of arrival by sea, in the port area,

(b)   in the case of transport through the Channel Tunnel, in the Tunnel System as defined in section 1(7) of the Channel Tunnel Act 1987 or the Folkestone Terminal at Cheriton, except that an inspector of a local authority shall only have powers in England,

(c)   in the case of air transport, in the airport,

the passport or third country health certificate, any Hendra certificate, and the certificate of entry given by the carrier under regulation 10(7)(a) and shall make the animal available for checking.

PART 4

ADMINISTRATION AND ENFORCEMENT

8–1849   12. Designation of competent authority.   (1) The Secretary of State shall be the competent authority for the purposes of—

(a)   approving veterinarians in accordance with articles 5(1) and 6(1) of the Community Regulation, and

(b)   granting derogations in relation to animals under three months old in accordance with article 6(2) of the Community Regulation and each such derogation shall be granted by an approval under these Regulations.

(2) Every person granted an approval under this regulation shall comply with its terms and conditions.

8–1850   13. Powers of inspectors.   (1) An inspector shall, on producing if required to do so, some duly authenticated document showing his authority, have a right at all reasonable hours to enter any land or premises (other than premises used exclusively as a dwellinghouse) for the purpose of administering and enforcing these Regulations and the Community Regulation; and in this regulation "premises" includes any vessel, boat, aircraft or vehicle of any other description.

(2) Such an inspector shall have powers to carry out all checks, searches and examinations which may be necessary to ascertain whether the Community Regulation and these Regulations are being complied with and in particular may examine and copy documentary or data processing material.

8–1851   14. Obstruction.   (1) No person shall—

(a)   intentionally obstruct any person acting in the execution of the Community Regulation and these Regulations;

(b)   without reasonable cause, fail to give any person acting in the execution of the Community Regulation and these Regulations any assistance or information which that person may reasonably require for the purposes of his functions under these Regulations; or

(c)   furnish to any person acting in the execution of the Community Regulations and these Regulations any information which he knows to be false or misleading.

8–1852   15. Falsification of documents.   (1) No person, other than a duly approved veterinary surgeon or a person acting at his direction, shall alter—

(a)   any part of a passport save for Section I,

(b)   any part of a third country health certificate, or

(c)   any part of a Hendra certificate.

(2) No person shall knowingly be in possession of—

(a)   a passport, third country health certificate or Hendra certificate which has been unlawfully altered, or

(b)   a document which falsely purports to be a passport, third country health certificate or Hendra certificate.

8–1853   16. Offences.   (1) It shall be an offence for any person to fail to comply with—

(a)   regulation 8(5) (failure by a carrier to comply with the terms and conditions of its approval);

(b)   regulation 10 (duties on carriers);

(c)   regulation 11 (duties at the port of arrival);

(d)   regulation 12(2) (failure by a veterinarian or a person importing animals under three months old to comply with the terms and conditions of their approval);

(e)   regulation 14 (obstruction);

(f)   regulation 15 (falsification of documents).

(2) Where a body corporate is guilty of an offence under these Regulations, and that offence is proved to have been committed with the consent or connivance of, or to have been attributable to any neglect on the part of—

(*a*)   any director, manager, secretary or similar officer of the body corporate, or
(*b*)   any person who was purporting to act in such a capacity,

he as well as the body corporate shall be guilty of an offence and be liable to be proceeded against and punished accordingly.
(3) For the purposes of paragraph (2), "director" in relation to a body corporate whose affairs are managed by its members, means a member of the body corporate.

8–1854   17. Penalties.   A person guilty of an offence under these Regulations shall be liable on summary conviction to imprisonment for a term not exceeding six months or to a fine not exceeding level 5 on the standard scale or to both.

8–1855   18. Enforcement.   (1) The provisions of these Regulations shall be enforced by the local authority.
(2) The Secretary of State may direct, in relation to cases of a particular description or a particular case, that any duty imposed on a local authority under paragraph (1) shall be discharged by the Secretary of State and not by the local authority.

PART 5
AMENDMENT, TRANSITIONAL PROVISIONS, SAVINGS AND REVOCATIONS

8–1856

Regulation 8(2)   SCHEDULE 1
CONDITIONS OF APPROVAL FOR CARRIERS

1. Staff having contact with passengers who may be travelling with pet dogs, cats or ferrets or staff who may be involved in checking pet dogs, cats or ferrets under these Regulations shall be appropriately trained.
2. The carrier shall set out in writing procedures to ensure that a pet dog, cat or ferret presented for travel under the Community Regulation is—

(*a*)   directed to an appropriate checking point;
(*b*)   checked under these Regulations; and
(*c*)   transported in an appropriate part of the vessel, train or aircraft in appropriate conditions.

3. The carrier shall set out in writing procedures on what it will do if a pet dog, cat or ferret presented for travel fails to comply with the Community Regulation or these Regulations, or if a pet dog, cat or ferret is discovered that the carrier reasonably suspects is intended to be transported to England without being presented to the carrier for checking.
4. The carrier shall set out in writing contingency plans for dealing with emergencies, including plans for vessels being diverted to another place of landing.
5. Adequate facilities for checking pet dogs, cats and ferrets under these Regulations shall be provided. They shall be adequately equipped, manned and maintained.
6. The carrier shall make arrangements for veterinary assistance to be provided where necessary.

Regulation 22   SCHEDULE 2
ORDERS REVOKED

ARCHITECTS

8–2019   This title contains the following statute—

8–2020   ARCHITECTS ACT 1997

Architects Act 1997[1]
(1997 c 22)

PART I[2]
THE ARCHITECTS REGISTRATION BOARD

8–2020   1. The Board.   (1) There shall continue to be a body corporate known as the Architects Registration Board.
(2)–(6). *Further provisions with respect to the Board.*
[Architects Act 1997, s 1.]

---

1. This Act consolidates the enactments relating to architects.
2. Part I contains s 1.

PART II[1]
REGISTRATION ETC.

The Registrar and the Register

8–2021   2. The Registrar.   (1) The Board shall appoint a person to be known as the Registrar of Architects.

(2)–(4) *Further provisions with respect to the Registrar.*
[Architects Act 1997, s 2.]

---

1. Part II contains ss 2 to 12.

8–2022 3. The Register. (1) The Registrar shall maintain the Register of Architects in which there shall be entered the name of every person entitled to be registered under this Act.

(2) The Register shall show the regular business address of each registered person.

(3) The Registrar shall make any necessary alterations to the Register and, in particular, shall remove from the Register the name of any registered person who has died or has applied in the prescribed manner requesting the removal of his name.

(4) The Board shall publish the current version of the Register annually and a copy of the most recently published version shall be provided to any person who requests one on payment of a reasonable charge decided by the Board.

(5) A copy of the Register purporting to be published by the Board shall be evidence (and, in Scotland, sufficient evidence) of any matter mentioned in it.

(6) A certificate purporting to be signed by the Registrar which states that a person—

(a) is registered;
(b) is not registered;
(c) was registered on a specified date or during a specified period;
(d) was not registered on a specified date or during a specified period; or
(e) has never been registered,

shall be evidence (and, in Scotland, sufficient evidence) of any matter stated.
[Architects Act 1997, s 3.]

Registration

8–2023 4. Registration: general. (1) A person who has applied to the Registrar in the prescribed manner for registration in pursuance of this section is entitled to be registered if—

(a) he holds such qualifications and has gained such practical experience as may be prescribed; or
(b) he has a standard of competence which, in the opinion of the Board, is equivalent to that demonstrated by satisfying paragraph (a).

(2) The Board may require a person who applies for registration on the ground that he satisfies subsection (1)(b) to pass a prescribed examination in architecture.

(2A) Subsection (2B) applies where it appears to the Board that the applicant is a national of an EEA State who—

(a) holds a qualification recognised in an EEA State, other than the United Kingdom, as equivalent to a recognised EEA qualification, an established EEA qualification or a relevant EEA certificate (within the meaning of section 5); or
(b) has undergone significant training or has gained significant experience in an EEA State, other than the United Kingdom.

(2B) Where this subsection applies the Board, in determining the standard of competence of the applicant under subsection (1)(b)—

(a) shall take into account the qualification, training or experience; and
(b) may not require the applicant to pass a prescribed examination in architecture unless the Board considers it appropriate in the circumstances of the applicant's case.

(3)–(6) Board to consult before prescribing qualifications; powers of the Registrar.
[Architects Act 1997, s 4 as amended by SI 2002/2842.]

8–2024 5. Registration: EEA qualifications. (1) A national of an EEA State who has applied to the Registrar in the prescribed manner for registration in pursuance of this section is entitled to be registered if he holds—

(a) a recognised EEA qualification;
(b) an established EEA qualification; or
(c) a relevant EEA certificate.

(2)–(7) Further provisions with respect to EEA qualifications and certificates.
[Architects Act 1997, s 5.]

8–2025 7. Penalty for obtaining registration by false representation. (1) A person commits an offence if he intentionally becomes or attempts to become registered under this Act by making or producing, or causing to be made or produced, any false or fraudulent representation or declaration (whether oral or written).

(2) A person guilty of an offence under this section is liable on summary conviction to a fine not exceeding **level 3** on the standard scale.
[Architects Act 1997, s 7.]

Removal from Register etc.[1]

8–2026 8–11. *Retention of name in Register; competence to practise; disqualification in an EEA State; failure to notify change of address*[2]

1. The Professional Conduct Committee may make a disciplinary order in relation to a registered person if— (*a*) it is satisfied, after considering his case, that he is guilty of unacceptable professional conduct or serious professional incompetence; or (*b*) he has been convicted of a criminal offence other than an offence which has no material relevance to his fitness to practise as an architect. A "disciplinary order" means a reprimand; a penalty order; a suspension order; or an erasure order (s 15(1) and (2)).

2. A name may be removed from the Register after a failure to pay, after written demand, a retention fee; if the fee is paid before the end of the calendar year for which the fee is payable the Board may allow the name to be re-entered in the Register and treated as having been re-entered on the date on which it was removed (s 8). A name may be removed from the Register if it was entered in the Register in pursuance of s 5 at a time when there was a disqualifying decision in another EEA State in force in respect of the person and at the time the Board was unaware of that fact (s 10). A name may be removed from the Register for failure to notify a change of address (s 11).

PART IV[1]
USE OF TITLE "ARCHITECT"

8–2027 20. Use of title "architect". (1) A person shall not practise[2] or carry on business under any name, style or title containing the word "architect" unless he is a person registered under this Act.

(2) Subsection (1) does not prevent any use of the designation "naval architect", "landscape architect" or "golf-course architect".

(3) Subsection (1) does not prevent a body corporate, firm or partnership from carrying on business under a name, style or title containing the word "architect" if—

(*a*) the business of the body corporate, firm or partnership so far as it relates to architecture is under the control and management of a registered person who does not act at the same time in a similar capacity for any other body corporate, firm or partnership; and

(*b*) in all premises where its business relating to architecture is carried on it is carried on by or under the supervision of a registered person.

(4) The Board may by rules provide that subsection (3) shall not apply in relation to a body corporate, firm or partnership unless it has provided to the Board such information necessary for determining whether that subsection applies as may be prescribed.

(5) A person enrolled on the list of visiting EEA architects may practise or carry on business under a name, style or title containing the word "architect" while visiting the United Kingdom without being a person registered under this Act during the period, and in respect of the services, for which his enrolment is effective.

(6) For the purposes of this section a person is not treated as not practising by reason only of his being in the employment of another person.

(7) In this section "business" includes any undertaking which is carried on for gain or reward or in the course of which services are provided otherwise than free of charge.

(8) Nothing in this section affects the validity of any building contract in customary form.
[Architects Act 1997, s 20.]

1. Part IV contains ss 20 and 21.
2. Whether he has so practised appears to be a question of fact (cf *Brown v Whitlock* (1903) 67 JP 451). This section does not forbid any one practising as an architect, or advertising his own personal accomplishments or skill (cf *Bellerby v Heyworth* [1910] AC 377, 74 JP 257). As to the meaning of "practising as an architect", see *R v Architects' Registration Tribunal, ex p Jaggar* [1945] 2 All ER 131, where it was held that the following test had been properly adopted by the tribunal for the purpose of deciding whether a person was practising as an architect within the meaning of the Act:

"An 'architect' is one who possesses, with due regard to aesthetic as well as practical considerations, adequate skill and knowledge to enable him (i) to originate, (ii) to design and plan, (iii) to arrange for and supervise the erection of such buildings or other works calling for skill in design and planning as he might, in the course of his business, reasonably be asked to carry out or in respect of which he offers his services as a specialist. 'Practising' in this context means: Holding out for reward to act in a professional capacity in activities which form at least a material part of his business. A man is not practising who operates incidentally, occasionally, in an administrative capacity only, or in pursuit of a hobby."

8–2028 21. Offence. (1) If any person contravenes section 20(1) he commits an offence and is liable on summary conviction to a fine not exceeding **level 4** on the standard scale.

(2) A person is not guilty of an offence by reason of contravening section 20(1) on any particular date if—

(*a*) the contravention is occasioned by the fact that an application on his part for registration under this Act has not been granted; and

(b) notice of the decision not to grant the application had not been duly served under this Act before that date.

(3) A person is not guilty of an offence by reason of contravening section 20(1) on any particular date if the contravention is occasioned by the removal of his name from the Register in circumstances in which notice is required to be served on him and—

(a) the notice had not been duly served before that date;

(b) the time for bringing an appeal against the removal had not expired at that date; or

(c) such an appeal had been duly brought, but had not been determined, before that date.

(4) In relation to an offence under subsection (1)—

(a) section 127(1) of the Magistrates' Courts Act 1980 (information to be laid within six months of offence);

(b) (*Northern Ireland*); and

(c) (*Scotland*).

shall have effect as if for the references in them to six months there were substituted references to two years.

[Architects Act 1997, s 21.]

PART V[1]
GENERAL AND SUPPLEMENTARY

General

8–2029   24. Service of documents.   (1) Any notice or document required to be served by or for the purposes of this Act may be sent by post, and when sent to any registered person shall be deemed to be properly addressed if addressed to him at his address in the Register.

(2) Any notice relating to the refusal to register any person or required to be served by section 9(2), 10(2), 11(*a*), 14(4)(*a*) or 15(3) shall be sent by post as a registered letter.

[Architects Act 1997, s 24.]

---

1. Part V contains ss 22 to 28.

Supplementary

8–2030   25. Interpretation[1].   (1) In this Act—

"the Board" means the Architects Registration Board;

"competent authority", in relation to an EEA State, means an authority or body designated by the State in accordance with the Directive;

"disciplinary order" has the meaning given by section 15;

"disqualifying decision in another EEA State", in relation to any person, means a decision made by a competent authority of an EEA State other than the United Kingdom which—

(a) is expressed to be made on the ground that he has committed a criminal offence or has misconducted himself in a professional respect; and

(b) has the effect in that State that he is no longer registered or otherwise officially recognised as an architect or that he is prohibited from practising as an architect there;

"EEA State" means any State which is a Contracting Party to the Agreement on the European Economic Area signed at Oporto on 2nd May 1992, as adjusted by the Protocol signed at Brussels on 17th March 1993, or Switzerland;

"erasure order" shall be construed in accordance with section 18;

"penalty order" shall be construed in accordance with section 16;

"prescribed" means prescribed by rules made by the Board and "prescribe" means prescribed by rules;

"the Register" means the Register of Architects;

"registered person" means a person whose name is in the Register;

"the Registrar" means the Registrar of Architects;

"suspension order" shall be construed in accordance with section 17; and

"unacceptable professional conduct" has the meaning given by section 14.

(2) Any person who is not a national of an EEA State, but who is, by virtue of a right conferred by Article 11 of Council Regulation (EEC) No 1612/68 or any other enforceable Community right, entitled to be treated, for the purposes of access to the profession of architecture, no less favourably than a national of such a State, shall be treated for the purposes of this Act as if he were such a national.

[Architects Act 1997, s 25 as amended by SI 2002/2842.]

---

1. This section is printed in an abridged form and contains only those definitions which are relevant to the provisions of the Act that are contained in this Manual.

8–2031   28. *Short title, commencement and extent*

ARMED FORCES

8–2060   This title contains the following statutes—

8–2070	Seamen's and Soldiers' False Characters Act 1906
8–2072	Incitement to Disaffection Act 1934
8–2075	Naval Forces (Enforcement of Maintenance Liabilities) Act 1947
8–2076	Visiting Forces Act 1952
8–2190	Army and Air Force Acts 1955
8–2251	Naval Discipline Act 1957
8–2282	Manoeuvres Act 1958
8–2327	Reserve Forces (Safeguard of Employment) Act 1985
8–2328	Arms Control and Disarmament (Inspections) Act 1991
8–2340	Reserve Forces Act 1996

This title contains the following statutory instrument—

8–2380	Visiting Forces and International Headquarters (Application of Law) Order 1999

Seamen's and Soldiers' False Characters Act 1906
(6 Edw 7 c 5)

8–2070   **1. Forging, etc sailors' and soldiers' certificates.**   Any person personating the holder of a certificate of service or discharge—*Penalty*, on summary conviction, but exceeding **level 2** on the standard scale, or imprisonment for term not exceeding **three months**.
[Seamen's and Soldiers' False Characters Act 1906, s 1(1), as amended by the Criminal Law Act 1977, s 31, the Forgery and Counterfeiting Act 1981, Sch and the Criminal Justice Act 1982, ss 35 and 46.]

8–2071   **2. False statements on enlistment.**   If any man when entering or enlisting or offering himself for entry or enlistment in Her Majesty's naval, military, or marine forces makes use of any statement as to his character or previous employment, which to his knowledge is false in any material particular, and if the person makes a written statement as to the character or previous employment of any man which he knows to be false in any material particular, and which he allows or intends to be used for the purpose of the entry or enlistment of that man in Her Majesty's said forces, he shall be liable on summary conviction to a fine not exceeding **level 2** on the standard scale.
[Seaman's and Soldiers' False Characters Act 1906, s 2, extended to the Air Force by Order in Council, SR & O 1918/548 and amended by the Criminal Law Act 1977, s 31, the Forgery and Counterfeiting Act 1981, Sch and the Criminal Justice Act 1982, s 46.]

Incitement to Disaffection Act 1934
(24 & 25 Geo 5 c 56)

8–2072   **1. Penalty on persons endeavouring to seduce members of Her Majesty's forces from their duty or allegiance.**   If any person maliciously and advisedly endeavours to seduce[1] any member of Her Majesty's forces from his duty or allegiance to Her Majesty, he shall be guilty of an offence under this Act.
[Incitement to Disaffection Act 1934, s 1.]

---

1. See *R v Arrowsmith* [1975] QB 678, [1975] All ER 463, 139 JP 221.

8–2073   **2. Provisions for the prevention and detection of offences under this Act.**   (1) If any person, with intent to commit or to aid, abet, counsel, or procure[1] the commission of an offence under section 1 of this Act, has in his possession or[2] under his control any document of such a nature that the dissemination of copies thereof among members of Her Majesty's forces would constitute such an offence, he shall be guilty of an offence under this Act.
   (2) Search warrant in respect of a suspected offence within past three months may be granted by a Judge of the High Court on reasonable grounds of suspicion, on the application of a police officer not lower than that of inspector, authorising any such officer together with any other officers and any other named persons to search within one month premises or place and persons found therein and to seize anything suspected to be evidence. Occupier to be notified of search and he is to be supplied with a list of documents or other objects removed and any other person from whom documents have been removed (*summarised*).

(3) No woman to be searched except by a woman (*summarised*).

(4) Anything seized under this section may be retained for a period not exceeding one month, or if within that period proceedings are commenced for an offence under this Act until the conclusion of those proceedings, and, in relation to property which has come into the possession of the police under this section, the Police (Property) Act 1897[3] (which makes provisions with regard to the disposal of property in the possession of the police) shall have effect subject to the foregoing provisions of this subsection and to the provisions of this Act conferring powers on courts dealing with offences.

[Incitement to Disaffection Act 1934, s 2, as amended by the Criminal Justice Act 1972, Sch 5.]

---

1. See para **1–301, Criminal Responsibility—Aid, abet counsel or procure**, in PART I: MAGISTRATES' COURTS, PROCEDURE, ante.

2. See *R v Arrowsmith* [1975] QB 678, [1975] All ER 463, 139 JP 221.

3. See title POLICE, post, and cf, *Elias v Pasmore* [1934] 2 KB 164, 98 JP 92.

8–2074　3. Provisions as to punishment of offences.　(1) A person guilty of an offence under this Act shall be liable[1], on conviction on indictment to imprisonment for a term not exceeding **two months** or to a fine, or on summary conviction to imprisonment for a term not exceeding **four months** or to a fine not exceeding **the statutory maximum**, or (whether on conviction on indictment or on summary conviction) to both such imprisonment and fine.

(2) No prosecution in England under this Act shall take place without the consent of the Director of Public Prosecutions.

(3) Where a prosecution under this Act is being carried on by the Director of Public Prosecutions, a court of summary jurisdiction shall not deal with the case summarily without the consent of the Director.

(4) Where any person is convicted of an offence under this Act, the court dealing with the case may order any documents[2] connected with the offence to be destroyed or dealt with in such other manner as may be specified in the order, but no documents shall be destroyed before the expiration of the period within which an appeal may be lodged, and if an appeal is lodged no document shall be destroyed until after the appeal has been heard and decided.

[Incitement to Disaffection Act 1934, s 3 amended by the Criminal Law Act 1977, ss 28 and 32.]

---

1. For procedure in respect of this offence which is triable either way, see Magistrates' Courts Act 1980, ss 17A–21, in PART I: MAGISTRATES' COURTS, PROCEDURE, ante.

2. The search warrant will authorise the seizure of anything suspected to be evidence of the offence.

Naval Forces (Enforcement of Maintenance Liabilities) Act 1947

(10 & 11 Geo 6 c 24)

8–2075　1. Deduction from pay in respect of liabilities for maintenance, etc[1].　(1) Section three of the Naval and Marine Pay and Pensions Act 1865 (which provides that pay, pensions and certain other moneys payable in respect of service in His Majesty's naval or marine force shall be paid in such manner and subject to such restrictions, conditions and provisions as are from time to time directed by Order in Council) shall have effect as if the expression "restrictions", in relation to the pay of a person being an officer, seaman or marine, included deductions for the purpose of providing, to such an extent and in such circumstances as may be specified in the Order in Council,—

(*a*)　for the maintenance[2] of the wife or civil partner of that person;

(*aa*)　for the maintenance of any child of that person or his wife or civil partner or of any other child who has been treated by them both as a child of their family;

(*aaa*)　for the payment of interest (by virtue of regulations made under section 41(3) of the Child Support Act 1991) with respect to arrears of child support maintenance payable in accordance with any maintenance assessment made under that Act;*

(*b*)　for the payment of any sum[2] adjudged as costs, or awarded as expenses, incurred in obtaining against that person an order or decree of any court in His Majesty's dominions in respect of the maintenance of his wife or civil partner or any such child as is mentioned in paragraph (*aa*) above;

(*c*)　for the payment of any sum adjudged as costs, or awarded as expenses, incurred in proceedings on appeal against, or for the variation, revocation or revival of, any such order or decree.

(2) No deduction from pay shall be made under the last foregoing subsection in liquidation of a sum adjudged to be paid by an order or decree of any court unless such authority as may be specified by Order in Council under section three of the said Act of 1865 is satisfied that the person against whom the order or decree was made has had a reasonable opportunity of appearing himself, or has appeared by a duly authorised legal representative, to defend the case before the court by which the order or decree was made; and a certificate purporting to be a certificate of the commanding officer of the ship in which he was or is serving, or on the books of which he was or is borne, that the person

has been prevented by the requirements of the service from attending at a hearing of any such case shall be evidence of the fact unless the contrary is proved[3].

(2A) For the purposes of this section—

(*a*) if, in proceedings in connection with the dissolution or annulment of a marriage, an order has been made for the payment of any periodical or other sum in respect of the maintenance of the person who, if the marriage had subsisted, would have been the wife of any such person as is mentioned in subsection (1) above, references in this section to that person's wife include references to the person in whose favour the order was made;

(*aa*) if, in proceedings in connection with the dissolution or annulment of a civil partnership, an order has been made for the payment of any periodical or other sum in respect of the maintenance of the person who, if the civil partnership had subsisted, would have been the civil partner of any such person as is mentioned in subsection (1) above, references in this section to that person's civil partner include references to the person in whose favour the order was made; and

(*b*) any reference to an order or decree of any court in Her Majesty's dominions includes a reference to an order registered in a court in the United Kingdom under Part I of the Maintenance Orders (Reciprocal Enforcement) Act 1972 or under Council Regulation (EC) No 44/2001 of 22nd December 2000 on jurisdiction and the recognition and enforcement of judgments in civil and commercial matters or registered under Part I of the Civil Jurisdiction and Judgments Act 1982 in a court in any territory to which that Act for the time being extends; and

(*c*) without prejudice to any enactment or rule of law relating to adoption or legitimation, references to a child of a person or his wife shall be construed without regard to whether or not the father and mother of the child have or had been married to each other at any time.

(2B) In relation to women members of Her Majesty's naval forces, within the meaning of the Naval Discipline Act 1957, references in this section to a wife shall be construed as references to a husband.

(3)–(5) *Repealed.*

[Naval Forces (Enforcement of Maintenance Liabilities) Act 1947, s 1, as amended by the Naval Discipline Act 1957, Sch 6, the Administration of Justice Act 1970, s 43(6), the Armed Forces Act 1971, Sch 4, the Armed Forces Act 1991, s 15 and Sch 3, SI 1993/785, SI 2001/3929 and the Civil Partnership Act 2004, Sch 26.]

---

*Section 1(1)(aaa) isrepealed by the Child Support, Pensions and Social Security Act 2000, Sch 9, from a date to be appointed.

1. The provisions of sub-ss (1) and (2) also apply to prescribed members of the reserve naval and marine forces (Reserve Forces Act 1996, s 7(3)).

2. For a limit on the amount of such deductions, see s 128E (3) of the Naval Discipline Act 1957, post. See also Home Office Circular No 251/1970, dated 18 November, 1970.

3. For service of process in proceedings for a maintenance order, see s 101 of the Naval Discipline Act 1957, post.

Visiting Forces Act 1952[1]
(15 & 16 Geo 6 & 1 Eliz 2 c 67)

PART I
VISITING FORCES

8–2076 1. Countries to which Act applies. (1) References in this Act to a country to which a provision of this Act applies are references to—

(*a*) Canada, Australia, New Zealand, South Africa, India, Pakistan, Ceylon, Ghana, Malaysia, the Republic of Cyprus, Nigeria, Sierra Leone, Tanganyika or Jamaica, or Trinidad and Tobago, or Uganda, or Kenya, or Zanzibar, or Malawi, or Zambia, or Malta, or The Gambia, or Guyana, or Botswana , or Lesotho, or Singapore, or Barbados, or Mauritius, or Swaziland, or Tonga, or Fiji, or the Bahamas, or Bangladesh, or Grenada, or Seychelles, or Solomon Island, or Tuvalu, or Dominica, or Saint Lucia, or Kiribati, or Saint Vincent and the Grenadines, Papua New Guinea, Western Samoa or Nauru, or Zimbabwe, or the New Hebrides, or Belize, or Antigua and Barbuda, or Saint Christopher and Nevis, or Brunei or Maldives, or Namibia, or Cameroon or Mozambique, or

(*b*) any country designated for the purposes of that provision by Order in Council under the next following subsection.

(2) Where it appears to Her Majesty, as respects any country not mentioned in paragraph (*a*) of the foregoing subsection, that having regard to any arrangements for common defence to which Her Majesty's Government in the United Kingdom and the Government of that country are for the time being parties it is expedient that the following provisions of this Act, or any of those provisions, should have effect in relation to that country, Her Majesty may by Order[2] in Council designate that country for the purposes of the provisions in question.

(3) Her Majesty may by Order in Council provide that in so far as this Act has effect in relation to

any country designated under the last foregoing subsection, it shall have effect subject to such limitations, adaptations or modifications as may be specified in the Order.

(4) No recommendation shall be made to Her Majesty in Council to make an Order under the last foregoing subsection unless a draft thereof has been laid before Parliament and approved by resolution of each House of Parliament.

[Visiting Forces Act 1952, s 1, as amended by the Ghana Independence Act 1957, s 4 and Sch 2, the Federation of Malaya Independence Act 1957, s 2 and Sch 1, the Cyprus Act 1960, s 3, Schedule; the Nigeria Independence Act 1960, s 3 and Sch 2; the Sierra Leone Independence Act 1961, s 3 and Sch 3; the Tanganyika Independence Act 1961, s 3 and Sch 2; the South Africa Act 1962, s 2 and Sch 5; the Jamaica Independence Act 1962, s 3 and Sch 2; the Trinidad and Tobago Independence Act 1962, s 3 and Sch 2; the Uganda Independence Act 1962, s 3 and Sch 3; the Kenya Independence Act 1963, s 4 and Sch 2; the Zanzibar Act 1963, s 1 and Sch 1; the Malawi Independence Act 1964, s 4 and Sch 2; the Zambia Independence Act 1964, s 2 and Sch 1; the Malta Independence Act 1964, s 4 and Sch 2; the Gambia Independence Act 1964, s 4 and Sch 2; the Guyana Independence Act 1966, s 5 and Sch 2; the Botswana Independence Act 1966, s 2 and Schedule; the Lesotho Independence Act 1966, s 2 and Schedule; the Singapore Act 1966, s 1 and Schedule; the Barbados Independence Act 1966, s 4 and Sch 2; the Mauritius Independence Act 1968 s 4 and Sch 2; the Swaziland Independence Act 1968, s 2 and Schedule; the Tonga Act 1970, s 1 and Sch; the Fiji Independence Act 1970, s 4 and Sch 2; the Bahamas Independence Act 1973, s 4 and Sch 2; the Pakistan Act 1973, s 4 and Sch 4; the Bangladesh Act 1973, s 1 and Schedule; SI 1973/2156; the Seychelles Act 1976, s 7 and Schedule; the Solomon Islands Act 1978, s 7 and Schedule; the Tuvalu Act 1978, s 4 and Sch 2; SI 1978/1030 and 1899; the Kiribati Act 1979, s 3 and Schedule; SI 1979/917; the Papua New Guinea, Western Samoa and Nauru (Miscellaneous Provisions) Act 1980, s 3 and Schedule; SI 1980/701; the New Hebrides Act 1980, s 2 and Sch 1; the Belize Act 1981, s 3 and Sch 2; SI 1981/1105; SI 1983/882; the Brunei and Maldives Act 1985, s 1 and Schedule; the Pakistan Act 1990, s 1 and Schedule; the Namibia Act 1991, s 1 and Schedule; the South Africa Act 1995, s 1 and Schedule and the Commonwealth Act 2002, s 2.]

---

1. This Act makes provision with respect to naval, military and air forces visiting the United Kingdom from certain other countries. Only those provisions of the Act that are relevant to the work of magistrates' courts are set out in this Manual. Further provision with respect to visiting forces is made by the Visiting Forces and International Headquarters (Application of Law) Order 1999, this title, post.

2. For the countries that have been designated under s 1(2), see Part II of Schedule 1 to the Visiting forces and International Headquarters (Application of Law) Order 1999, this title post. The Act also applies to the headquarters specified in Schedule 2 to the above Order.

8–2077 2. Exercise of powers by service courts and authorities of countries sending visiting forces. (1) The service courts and service authorities of a country to which this section applies may within the United Kingdom, or on board any of Her Majesty's ships or aircraft, exercise over persons subject to their jurisdiction in accordance with this section all such powers as are exercisable by them according to the law of that country.

(2) The persons subject to the jurisdiction of the service courts and service authorities of a country in accordance with this section are the following, that is to say—

(a) members[2] of any visiting force of that country; and

(b) all other[3] persons who, being neither citizens of the United Kingdom, are for the time being subject to the service law of that country otherwise than as members of that country's forces:

Provided that for the purposes of this subsection a person shall not be treated as a member of a visiting force of a country if he became (or last became) a member of that country's forces at a time when he was in the United Kingdom unless it is shown that he then became a member of those forces with his consent.

(3) Where any sentence has, whether within or outside the United Kingdom, been passed by a service court of a country to which this section applies upon a person who immediately before the sentence was passed was subject to the jurisdiction of that court in accordance with this section, then for the purposes of any proceedings in a United Kingdom court the said service court shall be deemed to have been properly constituted, and the sentence shall be deemed to be within the jurisdiction of that court and in accordance with the law of that country, and if executed according to the tenor of the sentence shall be deemed to have been lawfully executed.

(4) Notwithstanding anything in the foregoing provisions of this section, a sentence of death passed by a service court of a country to which this section applies shall not be carried out in the United Kingdom unless under United Kingdom law a sentence of death could have been passed in a similar case.

(5) Any person who—

(a) is detained in custody in pursuance of a sentence as respects which subsection (3) of this section has effect, or

(b) being subject in accordance with this section to the jurisdiction of the service courts of a country to which this section applies, is detained in custody pending or during the trial by such a court of a charge brought against him,

shall for the purposes of any proceedings in any United Kingdom court be deemed to be in legal custody.

(6) For the purpose of enabling the service courts and service authorities of a country to which this section applies to exercise more effectively the powers referred to in subsection (1) of this section,

[the Defence Council], if so requested by the appropriate authority of that country, may from time to time by general or special orders direct members of the home forces to arrest any person, being a member of a visiting force of that country, who is alleged to be guilty of an offence punishable under the law of that country and to hand him over to such service authority of that country as may be designated by or under the orders.

[Visiting Forces Act 1952, s 2, as amended by the Defence (Transfer of Functions) (No 1) Order 1964, SI 1964/488.]

---

1. This section does not exclude the jurisdiction of United Kingdom courts in respect of offences against United Kingdom law. There is therefore a concurrent jurisdiction in respect of offences which are offences against both the law of the United Kingdom and the law of the sending country. The Secretary of State understands that under the law of both Canada and the United States of America any offence against United Kingdom law committed in this country by a person subject to the jurisdiction of Canadian or United States service courts can be dealt with by those courts (Home Office Circular 116/54, dated 1 June, 1954; 118 JPN 579).

2. Membership may be proved, if necessary, by a certificate issued by or on behalf of the appropriate authority of a country under s 11(1) of the Act, post.

3. These are (i) members of civilian component of a visiting force, defined in s 10 (1) as a person for the time being fulfilling the following conditions, that is to say—

    (*a*) that he holds a passport issued in respect of him by a Government, not being a passport issued by the passport authorities of the United Kingdom or any colony;

    (*b*) that the passport contains an uncancelled entry made by or on behalf of the appropriate authority of the sending country stating that he is a member of a civilian component of a visiting force of that country; and

    (*c*) that the passport contains a note of recognition of that entry by or on behalf of the Secretary of State which has not been cancelled and as respects which no notification in writing has been given by or on behalf of the Secretary of State to the appropriate authority of the sending country stating that the recognition is withdrawn,

and (ii) dependants of members of a visiting force or of members of a civilian component, defined in s 12(4) in relation to a person as (a) the wife or husband of that person; and (b) any other person wholly or mainly maintained by him or in his custody, charge or care.

Where a person, who is a member of a visiting force or a military member of a headquarters, has been sentenced to imprisonment or any other form of custody, he may be detained in any naval, military or air-force establishment in which a person sentenced to detention by a court martial under the Naval Discipline Act 1957, the Army Act 1955 or the Air Force Act 1955 may be detained (Visiting Forces and International Headquarters (Application of Law) Order 1999, SI 1999/1736, Sch 8).

8–2078   3. Restriction, as respects certain offences, of trial by United Kingdom courts of offenders connected with visiting force.   (1) Subject to the provisions of this section, a person charged with an offence against United Kingdom law shall not be liable[1] to be tried for that offence by a United Kingdom court if at the time when the offence is alleged to have been committed he was a member of a visiting force or a member of a civilian component of such a force and—

    (*a*) the alleged offence, if committed by him, arose out of and in the course of his duty[2] as a member of that force or component, as the case may be; or

    (*b*) the alleged offence is an offence against the person[3], and the person or, if more than one, each of the persons in relation to whom it is alleged to have been committed had at the time thereof a relevant association[4] either with that force or with another visiting force of the same country; or

    (*c*) the alleged offence is an offence against property[5], and the whole of the property in relation to which it is alleged to have been committed (or, in a case where different parts of that property were differently owned, each part of the property) was at the time thereof the property either of the sending country or of an authority of that country or of a person having such an association as aforesaid[6]; or

    (*d*) the alleged offence is the offence of hijacking on board a military aircraft in the service of that force or consists of inducing or assisting, in relation to such an aircraft, the commission of any such act as is mentioned in section 6(2) (*a*) of the Aviation Security Act 1982; or

    (*e*) the alleged offence is an offence under section 2 or section 3 of that Act, or consists of inducing or assisting the commission of any such act as is mentioned in section 6(2) (*b*) and (*c*) of that Act, where (in either case) one or more such aircraft was or were the only aircraft alleged to have been, or to have been likely to be, thereby destroyed or damaged or whose safety is alleged to have been, or to have been likely to be, thereby endangered; or

    (*f*) the alleged offence is an offence under section 1(2) (*a*) (ii) of the Aviation and Maritime Security Act 1990, where one or more such aircraft was or were the only aircraft alleged to have been thereby destroyed or seriously damaged; or

    (*g*) the alleged offence is the offence of hijacking a warship in the service of that force or any other ship used as a naval auxiliary in that service or consists of inducing or assisting, in relation to any such warship or other ship, the commission of any such act as is mentioned in section 14(4) (*a*) of the Aviation and Maritime Security Act 1990; or

    (*h*) the alleged offence is an offence under section 11, 12 or 13 of that Act in relation to a ship, or consists of inducing or assisting the commission of any such act as is mentioned in section 14(4) (*b*), (*c*) or (*d*) of that Act in relation to a ship, where (in either case) one or more warships in the service of that force or other ships used as naval auxiliaries in that service were the only ships alleged to have been, or to have been likely to be, thereby destroyed or damaged or whose save navigation is alleged to have been, or to have been likely to be, thereby endangered.

Provided that this subsection shall not apply if at the time when the offence is alleged to have been committed the alleged offender was a person not subject to the jurisdiction of the service courts of the country in question in accordance with the last foregoing section.

(2) In relation to the trial of a person who was a member of a civilian component of a visiting force at the time when the offence is alleged to have been committed, the last foregoing subsection shall not have effect unless it is shown[7] that the case can be dealt with under the law of the sending country.

(3) Nothing in subsection (1) of this section—

(a) shall prevent a person from being tried by a United Kingdom court in a case where the Director of Public Prosecutions (in the case of a court in England or Wales), . . . certifies, either before or in the course of the trial, that the appropriate authority of the sending country has notified him that it is not proposed to deal with the case under the law of that country; or

(b) shall affect anything done or omitted in the course of a trial unless in the course thereof objection has already been made that by reason of that subsection the court is not competent to deal with the case; or

(c) shall, after the conclusion of a trial, be treated as having affected the validity thereof if no such objection was made in the proceedings at any stage before the conclusion of the trial.

(4) In relation to cases where the charge (by whatever words expressed) is a charge of attempting or conspiring to commit an offence, or of aiding, abetting, procuring or being accessory to, or of being art and part in, the commission of an offence, paragraphs (b), (c) and (f) of subsection (1) of this section and (except in so far as they relate to inducing or assisting the commission of any act) paragraphs (d), (e), (g) and (h) of that subsection shall have effect as if references in those paragraphs to the alleged offence were references to the offence which the person charged is alleged to have attempted or conspired to commit or, as the case may be, the offence as respects which it is alleged that he aided, abetted, procured or was accessory to, or was art and part in, the commission thereof; and references in paragraphs (b) and (c) of that subsection to persons in relation to whom, or property in relation to which, the offence is alleged to have been committed shall be construed accordingly.

(5) Nothing in this section shall be construed as derogating from the provisions of any other enactment restricting the prosecution of any proceedings or requiring the consent of any authority to the prosecution thereof.

(6) For the purposes of this section the expressions "offence against the person" and "offence against property" shall be construed in accordance with the provisions of the Schedule to this Act.
[Visiting Forces Act 1952, s 3; as amended by the Protection of Aircraft Act 1973, the Aviation Security Act 1982, Sch 2 and the Aviation and Maritime Security Act 1990, Sch 3.]

1. This relates to the primary right to exercise jurisdiction where concurrent jurisdiction exists. This is done by removing from the jurisdiction of United Kingdom courts, subject to a power of waiver, any offence committed by a member of a visiting force or of a civilian component, but not by a dependant of such a person (Home Office Circular 116/54, dated 1 June, 1954; 118 JPN 579).

2. That an offence arose out of and in the course of duty may be proved by a certificate issued by or on behalf of an appropriate authority of a sending country under s 11(4), post; this certificate shall be sufficient evidence of the fact unless the contrary is proved.

3. For "offence against the person" see the Schedule to this Act, post.

4. "A person having a relevant association with a visiting force" is defined in s 12 (2) as (a) a member of that visiting force or a member of a civilian component of that force, or (b) a person, not being a citizen of the United Kingdom and Colonies or ordinarily resident in the United Kingdom, but being a dependant of a member of that visiting force or of a civilian component of that force.

5. For "offence against property" see the Schedule to this Act, post.

6. A United Kingdom court has the primary right to exercise jurisdiction in respect of all offences against United Kingdom law, except those mentioned in paras (a), (b) and (c). Chief officers of police have been advised that in all other cases the offender should be dealt with so far as they are concerned in the same way as any other offender, except that they have been informed that the Secretary of State is of opinion that an exception may reasonably be made when an offence is trivial from the point of view of the criminal law, but is a serious breach of military discipline (Home Office Circular, No 116/54, dated 1 June 1954; 118 JPN 579.)

7. This may be proved by a certificate issued by or on behalf of the appropriate authority of a country: such a certificate shall be conclusive evidence of the fact stated (s 11(8), post).

8–2079 4. United Kingdom courts not to try offenders tried by service courts of visiting forces. (1) Without prejudice to the last foregoing section, where a person has been tried by a service court of a country to which this section applies in the exercise of the powers referred to in subsection (1) of section two of this Act, he shall not be tried for the same crime by a United Kingdom court.

(2) Where a person who has been convicted by a service court of such a country in the exercise of the said powers is convicted by a United Kingdom court for a different crime, but it appears to that court that the conviction by the service court was wholly or partly in respect of acts or omissions in respect of which he is convicted by the United Kingdom court, that court shall have regard to the sentence of the service court.
[Visiting Forces Act 1952, s 4.]

8–2080   5. Arrest, custody, etc of offenders against United Kingdom law.   (1) Neither of the two last foregoing sections shall affect—

(*a*)   any powers of arrest, search, entry, seizure or custody exercisable under United Kingdom law with respect to offences committed or believed to have been committed against that law; or

(*b*)   any obligation of any person in respect of a recognisance or bail bond entered into a consequence of his arrest, or the arrest of any other person, for such an offence; or

(*c*)   any power of any court to remand (whether on bail or in custody) a person brought before the court in connection with such an offence.

(2) Where a person has been taken into custody by a constable without a warrant for such an offence as aforesaid, and there is reasonable ground for believing that in accordance with section two of this Act he is subject to the jurisdiction of the service courts of a country to which this section applies, then, with a view to its being determined whether he is to be dealt with for that offence under United Kingdom law or dealt with by the courts of that country for an offence under the law thereof, he may notwithstanding anything in Part IV of the Police and Criminal Evidence Act 1984[1], be detained in custody for a period not exceeding three days without being brought before a court of summary jurisdiction; but if within that period he is not delivered into the custody of an authority of that country he shall, in accordance with the said section thirty-eight, be released on bail or brought before a court of summary jurisdiction as soon as practicable after the expiration of that period.

(3)–(4) *Scotland; Northern Ireland.*
[Visiting Forces Act 1952, s 5 as amended by the Criminal Justice Act 1988, Sch 15.]

---

1. See PART I: MAGISTRATES' COURTS, PROCEDURE, ante.

8–2081   7. Provisions as to coroners' inquests and as to removal of bodies of deceased persons.   No inquest shall be held, or, if an inquest has been begun but not completed, it shall not be resumed, except by the direction of the Secretary of State, where the coroner is satisfied that the deceased person at the time of his death had a relevant association with a visiting force; and, generally, the body of such a person may be removed from England without notice to the coroner.
[Visiting Forces Act 1952, s 7—summarised.]

8–2082   11. Evidence for purposes of Part I.   (1) For the purposes of this Part of this Act a certificate issued by or on behalf of the appropriate authority of a country, stating that at a time specified in the certificate a person so specified either was or was not a member of a visiting force of that country, shall in any proceedings in any United Kingdom court be sufficient evidence of the fact so stated unless the contrary is proved.

(2) For the purposes of this Part of this Act a certificate issued by or on behalf of the appropriate authority of a country, stating, as respects a person specified in the certificate,—

(*a*)   that on a date so specified he was sentenced by a service court of that country to such punishment as is specified in the certificate, or

(*b*)   that he is, or was at a time so specified, detained in custody in pursuance of a sentence passed upon him by a service court of that country or pending or during the trial by such a court of a charge brought against him, or

(*c*)   that he has been tried, at a time and place specified in the certificate, by a service court of that country for a crime so specified,

shall in any proceedings in any United Kingdom court be conclusive evidence of the facts so stated.

(3) For the purposes of subsection (2) of section three of this Act a certificate issued by or on behalf of the appropriate authority of a country, stating in connection with any charge against a person of an offence against United Kingdom law, being a charge specified in the certificate, that his case can be dealt with under the law of that country, shall in any such proceedings as aforesaid be conclusive evidence of the fact so stated.

(4) Where a person is charged with an offence against United Kingdom law and at the time when the offence is alleged to have been committed he was a member of a visiting force or a member of a civilian component of such a force, a certificate issued by or on behalf of the appropriate authority of the sending country, stating that the alleged offence, if committed by him, arose out of and in the course of his duty as a member of that force or component, as the case may be, shall in any such proceedings as aforesaid be sufficient evidence of that fact unless the contrary is proved.
[Visiting Forces Act 1952, s 11.]

8–2083   12. Interpretation of Part I.   (1) In this Part of this Act, unless the context otherwise requires, the following expressions have the meanings hereby assigned to them respectively, that is to say:—

"court" includes a service court;

"Her Majesty's ships or aircraft" does not include ships or aircraft belonging to Her Majesty otherwise than in right of Her Majesty's Government in the United Kingdom;

"the home forces" means any of the forces of Her Majesty raised in the United Kingdom and for the time being serving in the United Kingdom;

"member", in relation to a visiting force, means a member of the forces of the sending country, being one of the members thereof for the time being appointed to serve with that visiting force;

"the sending country", in relation to a visiting force, means the country to whose forces the visiting force belongs;

"service authorities" means naval, military or air force authorities;

"service court" means a court established under service law and includes any authority of a country who under the law thereof is empowered to review the proceedings of such a court or to try or investigate charges brought against persons subject to the service law of that country; and references to trial by, or to sentences passed by, service courts of a country shall be construed respectively as including references to trial by, and to punishment imposed by, such an authority in the exercise of such powers;

"service law", in relation to a country, means the law governing all or any of the forces of that country; and

"visiting force" means, for the purposes of any provision in this Part of this Act, any body, contingent or detachment of the forces of a country to which that provision applies, being a body, contingent or detachment for the time being present in the United Kingdom (including United Kingdom territorial waters), or in any place to which subsection (1A) below applies, on the invitation of Her Majesty's Government in the United Kingdom.

(1A) This subsection applies to any place on, under or above an installation in a designated area within the meaning of section 1(7) of the Continental Shelf Act 1964 or any waters within 500 metres of such an installation.

(2) References in this Part of this Act to a person's having at any time a relevant association with a visiting force are references to his being at that time a person of one or other of the following descriptions, that is to say—

(a) a member of that visiting force or a member of a civilian component of that force;

(b) a person, not being a citizen of the United Kingdom and Colonies or ordinarily resident in the United Kingdom, but being a dependant of a member of that visiting force or of a civilian component of that force.

(3) In determining for the purposes of any provision in this Part of this Act whether a person is, or was at any time, ordinarily resident in the United Kingdom, no account shall be taken of any period during which he has been or intends to be present in the United Kingdom while being a member of a visiting force or of a civilian component of such a force, or while being a dependant of a member of a visiting force or of such a civilian component.

(4) In this section the expression "dependant", in relation to a person, means any of the following, that is to say,—

(a) the wife or husband of that person; and

(b) any other person wholly or mainly maintained by him or in his custody, charge or care.

[Visiting Forces Act 1952, s 12, as amended by the Criminal Justice Act 1988, Sch 15.]

PART II
DESERTERS AND ABSENTEES WITHOUT LEAVE

8–2084   13. Apprehension and disposal of deserters and absentees without leave. (1) Subject to the provisions of this section, sections 186 to 188 and 190[1] of the Army Act 1955 (which relate to the apprehension, custody and delivery into military custody of deserters and absentees without leave from the regular forces) shall within the United Kingdom apply in relation to deserters[2] and absentees without leave from the forces[3] of any country to which this section applies as they apply in relation to deserters and absentees without leave from the regular forces.

(2) The powers conferred by the said sections 186 and 188, as applied by the last foregoing subsection, shall not be exercised in relation to a person except in compliance with a request[4] (whether specific or general) of the appropriate authority of the country to which he belongs.

(3) In sections 187, 188 and 190 of the Army Act 1955, as applied by subsection (1) of this section, references to the delivery of a person into military custody shall be construed as references to the handing over of that person to such authority of the country to which he belongs, at such place in the United Kingdom, as may be designated by the appropriate authority of that country.

(6) In this section references to the country to which a person belongs are references to the country from whose forces he is suspected of being, or (where he has surrendered himself) appears from his confession to be, a deserter or absentee without leave.

[Visiting Forces Act 1952, s 13: amended by Revision of the Army and Air Force Acts (Transitional Provisions) Act 1955, Schs 2 and 4.]

---

1. See these sections, post. The power of arrest is preserved by the Police and Criminal Evidence Act 1984, s 26 and Sch 2.

2. The section applied to a deserter from the forces of the United States even though he had deserted in Germany (*R v Thames Justices, ex p Brindle* [1975] 3 All ER 71, [1975] 1 WLR 1400).

3. Section 192 of the Army Act 1955, ante (punishment for procuring and assisting desertion or absence without leave) shall have effect as if any reference therein to a member of the regular forces included a reference to a member of a visiting

force or of a headquarters of an international organisation (Visiting Forces and International Headquarters (Application of Law) Order 1965, SI 1965/1536, art 14).

4. So far general requests have been made by the appropriate authorities of Canada, Australia, New Zealand, South Africa, and the United States of America (see Home Office Circular No 49/1960, dated 17 March 1960); Pakistan (see Home Office Circular No 149/57, dated 14 August 1957): Ghana (see Home Office Circular No 150/1963, dated 9 July 1963); India and Nigeria (see Home Office Circular No 31/1976); Kenya (see Home Office Circular No 80/1979).

8–2085   14. Evidence for purposes of Part II.   A document purporting to be a certificate under the hand of the Secretary of the Defence Council, stating that a request has been made for deserters or absentees without leave so to be dealt with, or under the hand of the officer commanding a detachment or unit of a visiting force stating that the person named is a deserter or absentee without leave, is sufficient evidence, unless the contrary is proved, of the facts certified in the document. [Visiting Forces Act 1952, s 14—summarised.]

Section 3   SCHEDULE

(As amended by the Sexual Offences Act 1956, s 51 and Sch 4, the Suicide Act 1961, s 2(3) and Sch 1, the Theft Act 1968, s 33(2) and Sch 2, the Criminal Damage Act 1971, s 11(6), the Criminal Damage (Northern Ireland) Order 1977, SI 1997/426, the Protection of Children Act 1978, s 1(7), the Protection of Children (Northern Ireland) Order 1978, SI 1978/1047, the Theft Act 1978, s 5(4), the Theft (Northern Ireland) Order 1978, SI 1978/1407, the Internationally Protected Persons Act 1978, s 2(4), the Nuclear Materials (Offences) Act 1983, s 4(2), the Child Abduction Act 1984, s 11(1) and the United Nations Personnel Act 1997, Schedule.)

Offences referred to in s 3

8–2086   1. In the application of section 3 of this Act to England and Wales and to Northern Ireland, the expression "offence against the person" means any of the following offences, that is to say*—

(a) murder, manslaughter, rape*, torture, buggery*, robbery and assault and any offence of aiding, abetting, counselling or procuring suicide or an attempt to commit suicide;

(b) any offence not falling within the foregoing sub-paragraph, being an offence punishable under any of the following enactments—

(i)   the Offences against the Person Act 1861, except section 57 thereof (which relates to bigamy);

(ii)–(iii) *(Repealed)*;

(iv) section 89 of the Mental Health Act (Northern Ireland) 1948 (which relate respectively to certain offences against mentally defective females);

(v) *(Repealed)*;

(vi) sections 1 to 5 and section 11 of the Children and Young Persons Act 1933, and sections 11, 12, 14, 15, 16 and 21 of the Children and Young Persons Act (Northern Ireland) 1950;

(vii) the Infanticide Act 1938 and the Infanticide Act (Northern Ireland), 1939;

(vii)(A) Article 3(1)(a) of the Protection of Children (Northern Ireland) Order 1978;

(viii) sections 2 to 28 of the Sexual Offences Act 1956*;

(ix) section 1(1)(a) of the Protection of Children Act 1978;

(x) the Child Abduction Act 1984;

(xi) section 1 of the Prohibition of Female Circumcision Act 1985**.

(c) an offence of making such a threat as is mentioned in section 1(3)(a) of the Internationally Protected Persons Act 1978 and any of the following offences against a protected person within the meaning of that section, namely, an offence of kidnapping, an offence of false imprisonment and an offence under section 2 of the Explosive Substances Act 1883 of causing an explosion likely to endanger life;

(d) an offence under section 2 of the Nuclear Material (Offences) Act 1983, where the circumstances are that—

(i)   in the case of a contravention of subsection (2), the act falling within paragraph (a) or (b) of that subsection would, had it been done, have constituted an offence falling within sub-paragraph (a) or (b) of this paragraph, or

(ii) in the case of a contravention of subsection (3) or (4), the act threatened would, had it been done, have constituted such an offence;

(e) an offence of making such a threat as is mentioned in section 3 of the United Nations Personnel Act 1997 and any of the following offences against a UN worker within the meaning of that Act—

(i)   an offence of kidnapping;

(ii) an offence of false imprisonment;

(iii) an offence under section 2 of the Explosive Substances Act 1883 of causing an explosion likely to endanger life.

---

*Paragraph 1 amended by the Sexual Offences Act 2003, Sch 6, from a date to be appointed.
**Sub-paragraph (b)(xi) substituted by the Female Genital Mutilation Act 2003, s 7, from a date to be appointed.

2. *Scotland.*
3. In the application of the said section 3 to England and Wales and to Northern Ireland, the expression "offence against property" means any offence punishable under any of the following enactments, that is to say—

(a) *Repealed*;
(b) the Malicious Damage Act 1861;
(c) section 13 of the Debtors Act 1869, and section 13 of the Debtors Act (Ireland) 1872 (which relate respectively to the obtaining of credit by false pretences and to certain frauds on creditors);
(d), (e) *Repealed*;
(f) section 28 of the Road Traffic Act 1930, and section 4 of the Motor Vehicles and Road Traffic Act (Northern Ireland) 1930 (which relate respectively to the taking of a motor vehicle without the owner's consent);
(g) the Theft Act 1968, except section 8 (robbery);
(h) the Criminal Damage Act 1971 and the Criminal Damage (Northern Ireland) Order 1977;
(i) an offence under section 2 of the Explosive Substances Act 1883 of causing an explosion likely to cause serious injury to property in connection with such an attack as is mentioned in section 1(1)(b) of the Internationally Protected Persons Act 1978;
(j) the Theft Act 1978 and the Theft (Northern Ireland) Order 1978;
(k) an offence under section 2 of the Nuclear Material (Offences) Act 1983, where the circumstances are that—

    (i) in the case of a contravention of subsection (2), the act falling within paragraph (a) or (b) of that subsection would, had it been done, have constituted an offence falling within the foregoing sub-paragraphs, or
    (ii) in the case of a contravention of subsection (3) or (4), the act threatened would, had it been done, have constituted such an offence;

(l) an offence under section 2 of the Explosive Substances Act 1883 of causing an explosion likely to cause serious injury to property in connection with such an attack as is mentioned in section 2(1) of the United Nations Personnel Act 1997.

Army Act 1955
(3 & 4 Eliz 2 c 18)

Air Force Act 1955
(3 & 4 Eliz 2 c 19)

8–2190 These Acts contain parallel provisions with respect to the army and the air force. Such provisions as are important to magistrates' courts are set out hereunder in sections of the Army Act: they apply similarly in every case to the Air Force Act, subject to the substitution of "air force" for "army", "airman" for "soldier" and other consequential verbal changes of a like kind.

Forces of certain other countries present in the United Kingdom at the invitation of Her Majesty's Government are subject to the Visiting Forces Act 1952 (15 & 16 Geo 6 & 1 Eliz 2 c 67), ante. The Army Act 1955, and the Air Force Act 1955, apply in modified form to certain Commonwealth personnel attached to home forces (Visiting Forces (Royal Australian Air Force) Order 1960, SI 1960 No 1053; Visiting Forces (Canadian Military and Air Forces) Order 1960, SI 1960 No 1956).

Provisions, in many respects similar to those of the Army Act 1955, and the Air Force Act 1955, are contained in the Naval Discipline Act 1957 (5 & 6 Eliz 2 c 53), post.

The Armed Services Act 2001 (not reproduced in this work) established procedures, similar to those in the Police and Criminal Evidence Act 1984, for the exercise by Service police and commanding officers of powers of entry and seizure in the course of investigations into offences under the Service discipline Acts. Procedures for the trial and punishment of offences were also modified in various respects, partly to achieve consistency with the civilian criminal justice system. The Act further empowers the Secretary of State to make orders applying changes in civilian criminal justice legislation to the armed forces.

By virtue of the Defence (Transfer of Functions) Act 1964, c 15, and Orders made thereunder, the office of Secretary of State for Defence was established. Functions of the Minister of Defence, the Secretaries of State for War and for Air and the Admiralty were transferred to the new Minister or to the Defence Council. Functions of the Army Council and the Air Council were transferred to the newly formed Defence Council. The text of this title has been amended accordingly.

The Armed Forces Act 2001, s 1, provides that both Acts, instead of expiring on 31 August 2001, shall continue in force until 31 August 2002, and shall then expire unless continued in force by Order in Council. The Acts have been continued in force for periods of 12 months beyond 31 August in each year by the following Army, Air Force and Naval Discipline Acts (Continuation) Orders: 2002, SI 2002/1820, 2003, SI 2003/1869, 2004, SI 2004/1496, 2005, SI 2005/2021.

PART I
ENLISTMENT AND TERMS OF SERVICE

8–2191 **19. False answers in attestation paper.** (1) If a person appearing before a recruiting officer[1] for the purpose of being attested knowingly makes a false answer to any question contained in the attestation paper and put to him by or by the direction of the recruiting officer, he shall be liable[2] on summary conviction to imprisonment for a term not exceeding **three months** or to a fine not exceeding **level 1** on the standard scale.

(2) For the avoidance of doubt it is hereby declared that a person may be proceeded against under this section notwithstanding that he has since become subject to military law.

[The Army Act 1955, the Air Force Act 1955 and the Naval Discipline Act 1957 (collectively known as the 'Service Discipline Acts') have a finite life and Parliament must be asked to renew them every 5 years. This is achieved by the enactment of 5-yearly Armed Forces Acts, which are also used as the principal means of amending the Service Discipline Acts. The Armed Forces Act 2001, s 1, continues the life of the Service Discipline Acts until 31 August, 2002, when they will expire unless continued in force by Order in Council for up to one year at a time until no later than 2006.]

---

1. "Recruiting officers" are specified in s 1; the procedure on attestation is set out in the 1st Sch.

2. Proceedings must be taken within six months from the date of attestation (Magistrates' Courts Act 1980, s 127, ante). Corresponding provisions appear in the Reserve Forces Act 1980, Sch 3, para 4, post as regards reserve and territorial and auxiliary air force personnel; see also s 47 thereof as regards naval and marine reserves.

A magistrates' court in England and Wales having jurisdiction in the place where the offender is for the time being has jurisdiction to try him for this offence, notwithstanding that the offence was committed in England and Wales outside the jurisdiction of that court (Army Act 1955, s 220; Air Force Act 1955, s 218).

PART II
RELATIONS BETWEEN MILITARY LAW AND CIVIL COURTS

8–2192   133.   Jurisdiction of civil courts.   (1) Where a person subject to military law—

(a) has been tried for an offence by a court-martial[1] or has had an offence committed by him taken into consideration by a court-martial in sentencing him, or

(b) has been charged with an offence under this Act and has had the charge dealt with summarily by his commanding officer or the appropriate superior authority,

a civil court[2] shall be debarred from trying him subsequently for the same, or substantially the same offence; but except as aforesaid nothing in this Act shall be construed as restricting the jurisdiction of any civil court to try a person subject to this Act for an offence.

(2) For the purposes of this section

(a) *repealed*;

(b) a person shall not be deemed to have had an offence taken into consideration by a court-martial in sentencing him if the sentence is quashed (as well as in a case where the taking into consideration of the offence has been annulled by the reviewing authority);

(c) a case shall be deemed to have been dealt with summarily by the commanding officer or appropriate superior authority notwithstanding that the finding or award of that officer or authority has been quashed on review or quashed or varied by the summary appeal court.

[Army Act 1955, s 133; Air Force Act 1955, s 133, as substituted by Armed Forces Act 1966, s 25 and amended by the Armed Forces Act 1981, s 5, the Armed Forces Act 1991, Sch 2, the Armed Forces Act 1996, Sch 7 and the Armed Forces Discipline Act 2000, Sch 3.]

---

1. This may be proved by certificate (see Army Act 1955, s 200; Air Force Act 1955, s 200). For the purposes of this section "court-martial" includes a reference to a Standing Civilian Court (Armed Forces Act 1976, Sch 3, para 16).

2. "Civil court" means a court of ordinary criminal jurisdiction but does not, except where otherwise expressly provided, include any such court outside Her Majesty's dominions (Army Act 1955, s 225(1); Air Force Act 1955, s 223(1)).

8–2193   133A.   Financial penalty enforcement orders.   (1) If—

(a) a financial penalty has been awarded against any person under this Act, and

(b) the penalty was—

(i) a fine awarded in respect of a qualifying offence (or in respect of such an offence together with other offences) on the conviction of a qualifying offence either of that person or of the person as whose parent or guardian that person is to pay the penalty; or

(ii) stoppages or a compensation order awarded in respect of a qualifying offence, (whether on the conviction of any person of the offence or on a request by any person for the offence to be taken into consideration); and

(c) no term of imprisonment was imposed in default of payment, and

(d) no appeal is outstanding and the time provided for the giving of notice of appeal against the award has expired, and

(e) the whole or any part of the penalty remains unpaid or unrecovered, and

(f) the person against whom the award was made is a person to whom this section applies,

the Defence Council or an officer authorised by them may make an order (in this section referred to as a "financial penalty enforcement order") for the registration of the penalty by the relevant court.

(2) This section applies to a person who

(a) is, or would be but for section 131 above, neither subject to service law nor a civilian to whom Part II of this Act is applied by section 209 below, Part II of the Air Force Act 1955 is applied by section 209 of that Act or Parts I and II of the Naval Discipline Act 1957 are applied by section 118 of that Act; or (*b*) is subject to service law because he is a special member of a reserve force within the meaning of the Reserved Forces Act 1996.

(3) In this section "qualifying offence" means

(*a*) an offence under section 36 above committed outside the United Kingdom and consisting of or including acts or omissions that would constitute a comparable foreign offence or a local road traffic offence;

(*b*) an offence under section 70 above;

(*c*) an offence under any provision of this Act other than section 70 above consisting of or including acts or omissions which would also constitute an offence under section 70 above;

and for the purposes of this definition—

"comparable foreign offence" means an offence under the civil law of any place outside the United Kingdom which is comparable to an offence under the law of England and Wales; and

"local road traffic offence" means an offence under the civil law of any place outside the United Kingdom relating to road traffic.

(4) A financial penalty enforcement order shall contain a certificate issued on behalf of the Defence Council or by an officer authorised by them and stating—

(*a*) that a financial penalty has been awarded against the person named in the order;

(*b*) that the conditions specified in paragraphs (*b*) to (*f*) of subsection (1) above are satisfied;

(*c*) the nature and amount of the penalty;

(*d*) the date on which and the offence or offences in respect of which it was awarded;

(*e*) if it was awarded against the person named in the order as the parent or guardian of some other person, the fact that it was so awarded and the name of that other person;

(*f*) sufficient particulars of the case (including particulars of any offences taken into consideration at the trial);

(*g*) the date of any payment or recovery of a sum on account of the penalty;

(*h*) the sum outstanding; and

(*j*) the authority to whom and address to which any stoppages or compensation included in the penalty will fall, on recovery, to be remitted under subsection (7) below.

(5) A document purporting to be a financial penalty enforcement order and to be signed on behalf of the Defence Council or by an officer authorised by them shall be deemed to be such an order unless the contrary is proved, and a certificate under subsection (4) above shall be evidence of the matters stated.

(6) Subject to subsection (7) below, upon registration of a financial penalty enforcement order—

(*a*) service enforcement procedures shall cease to be available for the recovery of the sum certified as outstanding, and

(*b*) that sum shall be treated for all purposes as if it had been a fine imposed upon a conviction by the relevant court.

(7) Stoppages or compensation recovered under this section shall be remitted to the authority at the address specified in the certificate under subsection (4) above.

(8) Where it appears from a financial penalty enforcement order that the penalty was imposed in respect of more than one offence, it shall be deemed for the purposes of enforcement to be a single penalty only.

(9) Where—

(*a*) a financial penalty enforcement order has been made against any person, and

(*b*) he ceases to be a person to whom this section applies at a time when the whole or any part of the certified sum is still outstanding,

service enforcement procedures shall apply to the amount outstanding as if it were a sum payable by way of a fine imposed by a civil court.

(10) In this section—

"financial penalty" means—

(*a*) a fine, including a fine imposed by virtue of paragraph 13 of Schedule 5A below;

(*b*) stoppages;

(*c*) a compensation order imposed by virtue of paragraph 11 or 13 of Schedule 5A below;

"the relevant court" means—

(*a*) the magistrates' court in England or Wales,

(*b*) the sheriff court in Scotland, or

(*c*) the court of summary jurisdiction in Northern Ireland,

within whose jurisdiction the person against whom a financial penalty enforcement order is made appears to the Defence Council or an officer authorised by them to reside or to be likely to reside;

"service enforcement procedures" means any procedure available by virtue of any of the following enactments, namely—

(a) sections 144, 146 and 209(4) and (4A) below and sections 144, 146 and 209(4) and (4A) of the Air Force Act 1955, and

(b) sections 128A and 128B of the Naval Discipline Act 1957; and

"stoppages" does not include sums awarded by virtue of section 147 or 148 below."

(11) Where a fine has been awarded together with stoppages or a compensation order, this section shall have effect in relation to the fine and to the stoppages or compensation order as if they were separate penalties.

[Army Act 1955, s 133A; Air Force Act 1955, s 133A, as inserted by Armed Forces Act 1976, Sch 8 and amended by the Armed Forces Act 1986, Schs 1 and 2 and SI 1998/3086.]

PART III
FORFEITURES AND DEDUCTIONS AND ENFORCEMENT OF MAINTENANCE LIABILITIES

8–2194 144. Forfeiture and deductions: general provisions. (5) Notwithstanding any deduction from the pay of an officer, warrant officer, non-commissioned officer or soldier of the regular forces he shall (subject to any forfeiture) remain in receipt of pay at not less than such minimum rate as may be prescribed by order of [the Defence Council][1].

[Army Act 1955, s 144; Air Force Act 1955, s 144.]

1. By the Minimum Rates of Pay (Army) Order 1982 it is provided that a person serving in the regular forces other than the Royal Marines shall remain in receipt, notwithstanding any deduction, of a minimum rate of pay equal to one-half of his relevant net emoluments (as defined in the Order), or three-quarters of such emoluments if he is married, or, whether married or not, he maintains in relation to a former marriage of his a dependent child of the family.

8–2195 146. Deductions for payment of civil penalties. Where a person sentenced or ordered by a civil court[1] (whether within or without Her Majesty's dominions) to pay a sum by way of fine, penalty, damages, compensation or costs in consequence of being charged before the court with an offence is at the time of the sentence or order, or subsequently becomes, a member of the regular forces[2], then if the whole or any part of that sum is met by a payment made by or on behalf of any military authority, the amount of the payment may be deducted from his pay.

[Army Act 1955, s 146; Air Force Act 1955, s 146, as substituted by Army and Air Force Act 1961, s 27.]

1. "Civil court" means a court of ordinary criminal jurisdiction but does not, except where otherwise expressly provided, include any such court outside Her Majesty's dominions (Army Act 1955, s 225(1): Air Force Act 1955, s 223(1)).

2. "Regular forces" means any of Her Majesty's military forces other than the army reserve, the territorial army and the Home Guard, and other than forces raised under the law of a colony (Army Act 1955, s 225(1); and see Air Force Act 1955, s 223(1)). The section is adapted to the Royal Marines by the Army Act 1955, Sch 7, Pt II, para 16. A corresponding provision relating to the navy is added to the Naval Discipline Act 1957 by s 61 of the Armed Forces Act 1971.

8–2196 150. Enforcement of maintenance and affiliation orders by deduction from pay[1].
(1) Where any court in the United Kingdom has made an order against any person (hereinafter referred to as "the defendant") for the payment of any periodical or other sum specified in the order for or in respect of—

(a) the maintenance of his wife[2]; or★

(aa) the maintenance of any child of his or his wife or of any other child who has been treated by them both as a child of their family; or★

(b) any costs incurred in obtaining the order; or

(c) any costs incurred in proceedings on appeal against, or for the variation, revocation or revival of, any such order,

and the defendant is an officer, warrant officer, non-commissioned officer or soldier of the regular forces[3], then (whether or not he was a member of those forces when the said order was made) the Army Council or an officer authorised by them may order such sum to be deducted from the pay of the defendant and appropriated in or towards satisfaction of the payment due under the order of the court as the Defence Council or officer think fit.

(1A) Without prejudice to any enactment or rule of law relating to adoption or legitimation, in subsection (1)(aa) above any reference to a child of the defendant or his wife shall be construed without regard to whether or not the father and mother of the child have or had been married to each other at any time.

(2) Where to the knowledge of the court making any such order as aforesaid, or an order varying, revoking or reviving any such order, the defendant is an officer, warrant officer, non-commissioned officer or soldier of the regular forces the court shall send a copy of the order to the Defence Council[4] or an officer authorised by them.

(3) *Relates to an order made by a court in Her Majesty's dominions outside the United Kingdom.*

(4) The Defence Council or an officer authorised by them may by order vary or revoke any order previously made under this section, and may treat any order made under this section as being in suspense at any time while the person against whom the order was made is absent as mentioned in paragraph (a) of subsection (1)[5] of section one hundred and forty-five of this Act,

(5) In this section—

references to an order made by a court in the United Kingdom include references to an order registered in or confirmed by such a court under the provisions of the Maintenance Orders (Facilities for Enforcement) Act 1920 and to an order registered in such a court under Part I of the Maintenance Orders (Reciprocal Enforcement) Act 1972[6] or Part I of the Civil Jurisdiction and Judgments Act 1982 or Council regulation (EC) No 44/2001 of 22nd December 2000 on jurisdiction and the recognition and enforcement of judgments in civil and commercial matters; references to a wife include, in relation to an order made in proceedings in connection with the dissolution or annulment of a marriage, references to a person who would have been the wife of the defendant if the marriage had subsisted.*

[Army Act 1955, s 150; Air Force Act 1955, s 150, as amended by Army and Air Force Act 1961, s 29, Defence (Transfer of Functions) (No 1) Order 1964, Administration of Justice Act 1970, s 43, Armed Forces Act 1971, s 59, the Maintenance Orders (Reciprocal Enforcement) Act 1972, Schedule, the Children Act 1975, Sch 4, the Civil Jurisdiction and Judgments Act 1982, Sch 12, the Family Law Reform Act 1987, Sch 4, the Armed Forces Act 1991, s 14 and Sch 3 and SI 2001/3929.]

---

*Sub-sections (1) and (5) amended by the Civil Partnership Act 2004, ss 257 and 263 from a date to be appointed.

1. Guidance in the making of an order against a member of Her Majesty's forces is given in Home Office Circular No 251/1970, dated 18 November, 1970. For orders against members of the Royal Navy and the Royal Marines, see Home Office Circular No 12/1982, dated 10 February 1982.

2. In relation to women members of the regular forces, this reference to a wife shall be construed as a reference to a husband (Army Act 1955, s 213; Air Force Act 1955, s 211).

3. "Regular forces" means any of Her Majesty's military forces other than the army reserve, the territorial army and the Home Guard, and other than forces raised under the law of a colony (Army Act 1955, s 225(1); and see Air Force Act 1955, s 223(1)). The section is adapted to the Royal Marines by the Army Act 1955, Sch 7, Pt II, para 16. A corresponding provision relating to the navy is added to the Naval Discipline Act 1957 by s 61 of the Armed Forces Act 1971.

4. The copy of the order should be sent to the appropriate service authority as detailed in Home Office Circular No 251/1970.

5. Section 145(1) (*a*) authorises forfeiture of pay during periods of absence from duty.

6. See PART VI: FAMILY LAW, ante. In relation to an order made in the Isle of Man this refers to an Act of Tynwald entitled the Maintenance Orders (Facilities for Enforcement) Act 1920 (Army Act 1955, s 216(4); Air Force Act 1955, s 214(4)).

7. This section does not apply to officers, non-commissioned officers and men of the Royal Marines, the Royal Marine Forces Volunteer Reserve or the Royal Fleet Reserve (Army Act 1955, 7th Sch, Part II, para 19). See Naval Forces (Enforcement of Maintenance Liabilities) Act 1947, s 1.

8–2196A   150A. *Enforcement of maintenance calculation by deductions from pay*

8–2197   151. Deductions from pay for maintenance of wife or child. (1) Where the Defence Council or an officer authorised by them are satisfied that an officer, warrant officer, non-commissioned officer or soldier of the regular forces[1] is neglecting, without reasonable cause, to maintain his wife[2] or civil partner or any child of his under the age of seventeen, or that such a child of his is in care, the Defence Council or officer may order such sum to be deducted from his pay and appropriated towards the maintenance of his wife[2], civil partner or child as the Defence Council or officer think fit.

(1A) A child is in care for the purposes of this section at any time when by virtue of any enactment (including an enactment of the Parliament of Northern Ireland or a Measure of the Northern Ireland Assembly)—

(*a*)   he is being looked after by a local authority in England or Wales (within the meaning of the Children Act 1989); or

(*b*)   *Scotland*;

(*c*)   *Northern Ireland*.

(2) On an application made to the Defence Council or an officer authorised by them for an order under subsection (1) of this section the Defence Council or officer, if satisfied that a prima facie case has been made out for the making of such an order, may make an interim order for such deduction and appropriation as is mentioned in the last foregoing subsection to take effect pending the further examination of the case.

(3) Where an order is in force under subsection (1) of subsection (3) of the last foregoing section for the making of deductions in favour of any person from the pay of an officer, warrant officer, non-commissioned officer or soldier of the regular forces[1], no deductions from his pay in favour of the same person shall be ordered under the foregoing provisions of this section unless the officer, warrant officer, non-commissioned officer or soldier is in a place where process cannot be served on him in connection with proceedings for the variation of the order of the court in consequence of which the order under the last foregoing section was made.

(3A) Where an order is in force under section 150A of this Act for deductions to be made from the pay of any member of the regular forces with respect to the maintenance of a child of his, no order may be made under this section for the deductions of any sums from the pay of that person with respect to the maintenance of that child.

(3AA) *Northern Ireland*.

(4) The Defence Council or an officer authorised by them may by order vary or revoke any order

previously made under this section, and may treat any order made under this section as being in suspense at any time while the person against whom the order was made is absent as mentioned in paragraph (*a*) of subsection (1)[3] of section one hundred and forty-five of this Act.

(5) The power to make an order under this section for the deduction of any sum and its appropriation towards the maintenance of a child shall include power—

(*a*) subject to the provisions of subsection (3) of this section, to make such an order after the child has attained the age of seventeen, if an order in favour of the child is in force under subsection (1) or subsection (3) of the last foregoing section; or

(*b*) to make such an order after the child has attained the age of seventeen if—

(i) such an order of the court as is mentioned in subsection (1) of the last foregoing section was in force in favour of the child at the time when the child attained that age, and

(ii) the person from whose pay the deductions are ordered is in such a place as is mentioned in subsection (3) of this section, and

(iii) the child is for the time being engaged in a course of education or training; or

(*c*) to continue such an order from time to time after the child has attained the age of seventeen, if the child is for the time being engaged in a course of education or training;

but no order so made or continued shall remain in force after the child attains the age of twenty-one or shall, unless continued under paragraph (*c*) of this subsection, remain in force for more than two years.

(6) Without prejudice to any enactment or rule of law relating to adoption or legitimation, references in this section to a child of any person shall be construed without regard to whether the father and mother of the child have or had been married to each other at any time.

[Army Act 1955, s 1514; Air Force Act 1955, s 151: amended by Defence (Transfer of Functions) (No 1) Order 1964, the Armed Forces Act 1976, s 18, the Armed Forces Act 1981, Sch 2, the Children Act 1989, Sch 12, the Armed Forces Act 1991, s 14, SI 1993/785, SI 1995/756 and the Civil Partnership Act 2004, s 257.]

---

1. See note 2 to s 146, ante.

2. In relation to women members of the regular forces, this reference to a wife shall be construed as a reference to a husband (Army Act 1955, s 213; Air Force Act 1955, s 211).

3. Section 145(1)(*a*) authorises forfeiture of pay during periods of absence from duty.

4. This section does not apply to officers, non-commissioned officers and men of the Royal Marines, the Royal Marine Forces Volunteer Reserve or the Royal Fleet Reserve (Army Act 1955, Sch 7, Part II, para 19). See Naval Forces (Enforcement of Maintenance Liabilities) Act 1947, s 1.

8–2198 151A. Deductions from pay in respect of judgment debts etc.

(1) Where by any judgment or order enforceable by a court in the United Kingdom any sum is required to be paid by a person who is a member of the regular forces, the Defence Council or an officer authorised by them may, whether or not that person was a member of the regular forces at the time when the judgment or order was given or made, order such amount or amounts as the Council or officer think fit to be deducted from the pay of that person, and appropriated in or towards satisfaction of that sum:

Provided that this subsection shall not apply to any such sum as is mentioned in section 146 of this Act, to any sum in respect of which deductions may be ordered under section 150 of this Act, or to any sum in respect of which deductions may be made by virtue of section 32(2)(*b*) of the Courts-Martial (Appeals) Act 1968.

(2) The Defence Council or an officer authorised by them may by order vary or revoke any order previously made under this section, and may treat any order made under this section as being in suspense at any time while the person against whom the order was made is absent as mentioned in section 145(1)(*a*) of this Act.

[Army Act 1955, s 151A; Air Force Act 1955, s 151A; as added by the Armed Forces Act 1971, s 59.]

8–2199 152. Limit of deductions under sections 150 and 151 and effect on forfeiture[1].

(1) The sums deducted from a person's pay under sections 150, 151 and 151A above shall not together exceed such proportion of his pay as the Defence Council may determine[2].

(2) Where any deductions have been ordered under section 150, 151 or 151A above from a person's pay and (whether before or after the deductions have been ordered) he incurs a forfeiture of pay in consequence of the finding or sentence of a court-martial or the finding or award of the appropriate superior authority or his commanding officer, it shall apply only to so much of his pay as remains after the deductions have been made.

[Army Act 1955, s 1523; Air Force Act 1955, s 152; as amended by the Armed Forces Act 1971, s 59 and Sch 4.]

---

1. This section is amended by s 59 of the Armed Forces Act 1971.

2. The amount deducted may be only *towards satisfaction* of the payment due under the order of the court (see s 150, ante): any balance due must be paid out of resources other than army pay.

3. This section does not apply to officers, non-commissioned officers and men of the Royal Marines, the Royal Marine Forces Volunteer Reserve or the Royal Fleet Reserve Army (Army Act 1955, Sch 7, Pt II, para 19). See Naval Forces (Enforcement of Maintenance Liabilities) Act 1947, s 1.

8–2200 153. Service of process in maintenance proceedings[1].

(1) Any process to be served on an officer, warrant officer, non-commissioned officer or soldier of the regular forces[2] (hereinafter

referred to as "the defendant") in connection with proceedings for any such order[3] of a court in the United Kingdom as is mentioned in subsection (1) of section one hundred and fifty of this Act, or for the variation, revocation or revival of such an order, shall be deemed to be duly served on him if served on his commanding officer, and may, without prejudice to any other method of service, be so served by registered post[4].

(3) Where any such process as is mentioned in subsection (1) of this section is served in the United Kingdom and the defendant will be required to appear in person at the hearing, the service of the process shall be of no effect if his commanding officer certifies to the court by which the process was issued that the defendant is under orders for active service out of the United Kingdom and that in the commanding officer's opinion it would not be possible for the defendant to attend the hearing and return in time to embark for that service.

(3A) Where any such process as is mentioned in subsection (1) of this section is to be served in the United Kingdom or elsewhere and the defendant will be required to appear in person at the hearing, the service of the process shall be of no effect if his commanding officer certifies to the court by which the process was issued that the defendant is absent without leave or has deserted and remains in desertion.

(4) Nothing in this section shall be construed as enabling process to be served in connection with proceedings in a court of summary jurisdiction unless the defendant is within the United Kingdom. [Army Act 1955, s 153; Air Force Act 1955, s 153; as amended by the Armed Forces Act 1971, s 62 and the Armed Forces Act 1981, s 18 and Sch 5.]

---

1. For a similar provision in relation to the naval forces, see Naval Discipline Act 1957, s 101, post.

2. "Regular forces" means any of Her Majesty's military forces other than the army reserve, the territorial army and the Home Guard, and other than forces raised under the law of a colony (Army Act 1955, s 225(1); and see Air Force Act 1955, s 223(1)). The section is adapted to the Royal Marines by the Army Act 1955, Sch 7, Pt II, para 16. A corresponding provision relating to the navy is added to the Naval Discipline Act 1957 by s 61 of the Armed Forces Act 1971.

3. In *Smith v Chuter* [1988] FCR 171, [1989] 1 FLR 93, it was held that this provision and s 150, ante, when read together, apply to proceedings for an order for maintenance and are not confined to proceedings for the enforcement of such an order; accordingly, an originating summons for an affiliation order was effectively served on a serving soldier by delivering it to his commanding officer.

4. This provision seems to supersede in relation to the army and air force the exception contained in the Magistrates' Courts Rules 1981, r 99(6)(b): the section does not require that service by registered post shall be supplemented by proof that the summons came to the defendant's knowledge. The recorded delivery service may be used (Recorded Delivery Service Act 1962, s 1).

PART IV[1]
BILLETING AND REQUISITIONING OF VEHICLES

Billeting

8–2201   154. Billeting requisitions.   At any time when this section is in operation any general or field officer commanding any part of the regular forces in the United Kingdom may issue a billeting requisition requiring the chief officer of police for any area in the United Kingdom specified in the requisition to provide billets at such places in that area, for such numbers of members[2] of Her Majesty's forces and, if the requisition so provides, for such number of vehicles in use for the purpose of Her Majesty's forces, being vehicles of any class specified in the requisition, as may be so specified. [Army Act 1955, s 154; Air Force Act 1955, s 154[3].]

---

1. For application of this Part of the Act to naval billeting, see Naval Billeting &c Act 1914, and the Revision of the Army and Air Force Acts (Transitional Provisions) Act 1955, Sch 2, para 6.

2. Regulations may be made applying the provisions as to billeting to civilians employed with the forces (s 162).

3. To be brought into operation by order of the Secretary of State when it appears to him that the public interest so requires (s 174).

8–2202   155. Premises in which billets may be provided.   (1) Billets, other than for vehicles, may be provided in pursuance of a billeting requisition—

(a) in any inn or hotel (whether licensed or not) or in any other premises occupied for the purposes of a business consisting of or including the provision of sleeping accommodation for reward;

(b) in any building not falling within the last foregoing paragraph, being a building to which the public habitually have access, whether on payment or otherwise, or which is wholly or partly provided or maintained out of rates;

(c) in any dwelling, outhouse, warehouse, barn or stables;

but not in any other premises.

(2) Billets for vehicles may be provided as aforesaid in any building or on any land. [Army Act 1955, s 155; Air Force Act 1955, s 155.]

8–2203   156. Provision of billets.   (1) Where a billeting requisition has been produced to the chief officer of police for the area specified in the requisition he shall, on the demand of the officer commanding any portion of the regular forces, or on the demand of an officer or soldier authorised in writing by such an officer commanding, billet on the occupiers of premises falling within the last foregoing section, being premises at such place in that area as may be specified by the officer or soldier by whom the demand is made, such number of persons or vehicles as may be required by the officer or soldier by whom the demand is made, not exceeding the number specified in the requisition.

(2) Without prejudice to the provisions of the next following section, a chief officer of police shall exercise his functions under this section in such manner as in his opinion will cause least hardship to persons on whom billeting may take place.

(3) A chief officer of police may to such extent and subject to such restrictions as he thinks proper authorise any constable, or constables of any class, to exercise his said functions on his behalf, and the foregoing provisions of this section shall apply accordingly.

[Army Act 1955, s 156; Air Force Act 1955, s 156.]

8–2204   157. Billeting schemes. (1) A local authority[1] may make a scheme for the provision of billets in their area in pursuance of billeting requisition; and where such a scheme is in force the chief officer of police shall so far as the scheme extends exercise his functions under the last foregoing section in accordance with the scheme.

(2) Any scheme under this section may be revoked by the local authority by whom it was made, or may be varied by that authority by a subsequent scheme under this section.

(3) Where a local authority make a scheme under this section they shall furnish the chief officer of police for the area to which the scheme relates with a copy of the scheme.

(4) A scheme under this section shall not come into force until approved by the Minister of Housing and Local Government; and that Minister may require the local authority to revoke any scheme in force under this section and in substitution therefor to submit for his approval a further scheme under this section.

[Army Act 1955, s 157; Air Force Act 1955, s 157.]

---

1. The local authority shall be the council of a county borough, county district or metropolitan borough or the Common Council of the City of London (s 163).

8–2205   158. Accommodation to be provided and payment therefor

8–2206   159. Appeals against billeting. (1) Any person who—

    (*a*)   is aggrieved by having an undue number of persons billeted upon him in pursuance of a billeting requisition, or

    (*b*)   claims that by reason of special circumstances he should be exempted from having persons so billeted on him, either generally or on a particular occasion,

may apply to a person or persons appointed on behalf of the local authority in accordance with arrangements made by the Minister of Housing and Local Government.

(2) On any application on the grounds mentioned in paragraph (*a*) of the last foregoing subsection the person or persons to whom the application is made may direct the billeting elsewhere of such number of the persons billeted as may seem just or may dismiss the application.

(3) On any application on the grounds mentioned in paragraph (*b*) of subsection (1) of this section the person or persons to whom the application is made may grant such exemption as may seem just or may dismiss the application.

(4) An application under this section shall not affect billeting pending the determination of the application.

[Army Act 1955, s 159; Air Force Act 1955, s 159.]

8–2207   160. *Compensation for damage*

8–2208   161. Refusal to receive persons billeted, etc. Any person who—

    (*a*)   refuses to receive any person billeted upon him in pursuance of a billeting requisition[1] or without reasonable excuse fails to furnish him with the accommodation properly required for him, or

    (*b*)   gives or agrees to give to any person billeted upon him in pursuance of a billeting requisition any money or reward in lieu of receiving any person or vehicle or of furnishing accommodation properly required for him, or

    (*c*)   obstructs the billeting in his building or on his land of any vehicle,

shall be liable[2] on summary conviction to a fine not exceeding £50, or to imprisonment for a term not exceeding **three months**, or to both such a fine and such imprisonment.

[Army Act 1955, s 161; Air Force Act 1955, s 161.]

---

1. The requisition should be produced at the hearing of the case (*Lightfoot v McCrone* (1941) 85 Sol Jo 190).

2. A magistrates' court in England and Wales having jurisdiction in the place where the offender is for the time being has jurisdiction to try him for this offence, notwithstanding that the offence was committed in England and Wales outside the jurisdiction of that court (Army Act 1955, s 220; Air Force Act 1955, s 218).

Requisitioning of vehicles

8–2209 Sections 165[1]–176 and the fourth Schedule deal with the issuing of requisitioning orders requiring persons to furnish mechanically propelled and other vehicles, horses and mules, food, forage and stores. The chief officer of police for any area specified in a requisitioning order shall, on a request to that effect made by or on behalf of the officer to whom the order is issued, give instructions for securing that so far as practicable constables will be available, if required, for accompanying officers or soldiers requisitioning vehicles, etc, in pursuance of the order.

1. To be brought into operation by order of the Secretary of State when it appears to him that the public interest so requires (s 174).

8–2220   170. Record and inspection of mechanically propelled vehicles. The Defence Council may by regulations require persons having in their possession in the United Kingdom mechanically-propelled vehicles[1], or trailers normally drawn by mechanically propelled vehicles, if required so to do by such authority or person as may be specified in the regulations—

(*a*) to furnish to such authority or person as may be so specified a return containing such particulars as to the vehicles as may be required by or under the regulations, and

(*b*) to afford all reasonable facilities for enabling any such vehicles in his possession to be inspected and examined, at such times as may be specified by or under the regulations, by such authority or person as may be so specified.

[Army Act 1955, s 170; Air Force Act 1955, s 170: amended by Defence (Transfer of Functions) (No 1) Order 1964.]

1. This section applies in relation to horses and mules as it applies in relation to mechanically-propelled vehicles (s 172(4)).

8–2221   171. Enforcement of provisions as to requisitioning. (1) If any person—

(*a*) fails to furnish any vehicle which he is directed to furnish in pursuance of a requisitioning order, or fails to furnish any such vehicle at the time and place at which he is directed to furnish it, or

(*b*) fails to comply with any regulations of the Defence Council under the last foregoing section, or

(*c*) obstructs any officer or other person in the exercise of his functions under this Part of this Act in relation to the inspection or requisitioning of vehicles,

he shall be guilty of an offence and liable[1] on summary conviction to a fine not exceeding **level 3** on the standard scale, or to imprisonment for a term not exceeding **three months**, or to both such a fine and such imprisonment.

(2) Without prejudice to any penalty under the last foregoing subsection, if any person is obstructed in the exercise of powers of inspection conferred on him by regulations under the last foregoing section, a justice of the peace may, if satisfied by information on oath that the person has been so obstructed, issue a search warrant authorising a constable named therein, accompanied by the said person, to enter the premises in respect of which the obstruction took place at any time between six o'clock in the morning and nine o'clock in the evening and to inspect any vehicles which may be found therein.

[Army Act 1955, s 171; Air Force Act 1955, s 171: amended by Defence (Transfer of Functions) (No 1) Order 1964 and the Criminal Justice Act 1982, ss 38 and 46.]

1. A magistrates' court in England and Wales having jurisdiction in the place where the offender is for the time being has jurisdiction to try him for this offence, notwithstanding that the offence was committed in England and Wales outside the jurisdiction of that court (Army Act 1955, s 220; Air Force Act 1955, s 218).

PART V

GENERAL PROVISIONS

8–2222   185. Exemption from taking in execution of property used for military purposes[1].
No judgment or order given or made against a member of any of Her Majesty's military forces by any court in the United Kingdom or a colony shall be enforced by the levying of execution on any property of the person against whom it is given or made, being arms, ammunition, equipment, instruments or clothing used by him for military purposes.

[Army Act 1955, s 185; Air Force Act 1955, s 185.]

1. A similarly worded provision relating to a member of Her Majesty's naval forces is contained in the Naval Discipline Act 1957, s 102.

Provisions relating to deserters and absentees without leave

8–2223   186. Arrest of deserters and absentees without leave[1]. (1) A constable may arrest[2] any person whom he has reasonable cause to suspect of being an officer, warrant officer, non-commissioned officer or soldier of the regular forces[3] who has deserted or is absent without leave.

(2) Where no constable is available, any officer, warrant officer, non-commissioned officer or soldier of the regular forces, or any other person, may arrest any person whom he has reasonable cause to suspect as aforesaid.

(3) Any person having authority to issue a warrant for the arrest of a person charged with crime, if satisfied by evidence on oath that there is, or is reasonably suspected of being, within his jurisdiction an officer, warrant officer, non-commissioned officer or soldier of the regular forces who has deserted or is absent without leave or is reasonably suspected of having deserted or of being absent without leave, may issue a warrant authorising his arrest.

(4) Any person in custody in pursuance of this section shall as soon as practicable be brought before a court of summary jurisdiction.

(4A) A person shall also be brought before a court of summary jurisdiction if, having been brought before such a court by virtue of subsection (4) above and discharged by that court by virtue of section 187(3) below—

(a) he is subsequently arrested as an alleged or suspected deserter or absentee without leave under section 74 of this Act, or under a warrant issued under section 190A thereof, and

(b) the question whether he is in fact in desertion or absent without leave raises any issue which was investigated by the court discharging him, and

(c) he does not admit that he is in desertion or absent without leave to the person arresting him under the said section 74 or, as the case may be, to the person into whose custody he is delivered pursuant to the said section 190A.

(5) This section shall have effect in the United Kingdom and in any colony.
[Army Act 1955, s 186; Air Force Act 1955, s 186, as amended by the Armed Forces Act 1971, s 56.]

---

1. For corresponding provision relating to the navy, see Naval Discipline Act 1957, s 105, post.
2. This power of arrest is preserved by the Police and Criminal Evidence Act 1984, s 26 and Sch 2.
3. Section 13 of the Visiting Forces Act 1952 (ante) applies this section to members of visiting forces. See Home Office Circular No 28/1956, dated 11 September 1956. For modified application to visiting Commonwealth forces, see Introductory Note to this title.

8–2224 187. Proceedings before a civil court where persons suspected of illegal absence[1].
(1) Where a person who is brought before a court of summary jurisdiction is alleged to be an officer, warrant officer, non-commissioned officer or soldier of the regular[2] forces who has deserted or is absent without leave, the following provisions shall have effect.

(2)[3] If he admits that he is illegally absent from the regular forces and the court is satisfied of the truth of the admission, then—

(a) unless he is in custody for some other cause the court shall, and
(b) notwithstanding that he is in custody for some other cause, the court may,

forthwith either cause him to be delivered into military custody in such manner as the court may think fit or, where it is unable to do so, adjourn the proceedings and remand him for such time as appears reasonably necessary for the purpose of arranging for him to be delivered into military custody.

Any time specified by the court may be extended by the court from time to time if it appears to the court reasonably necessary so to do for the purpose aforesaid.

(3) If he does not admit that he is illegally absent as aforesaid, or the court is not satisfied of the truth of the admission, the court shall consider the evidence[4] and any statement of the accused, and if satisfied that he is subject to military law and if of opinion that there is sufficient evidence to justify his being tried under this Act for an offence of desertion or absence without leave then, unless he is in custody for some other cause, the court shall cause him to be delivered into military custody or, where it is unable to do so, adjourn the proceedings and remand him for such time as appears reasonably necessary for the purpose of arranging for him to be delivered into military custody, but otherwise shall discharge him:

Provided that if he is in custody for some other cause the court shall have power, but shall not be required, to act in accordance with this subsection.

(4) The following provisions of the Magistrates' Courts Act 1980, or any corresponding enactment in force as respects the court in question, that is to say the provisions relating to the constitution and procedure of courts of summary jurisdiction acting as examining justices[5] and conferring powers of adjournment and remand on such courts so acting, and the provisions as to evidence and the issue and enforcement of summonses or warrants to secure the attendance of witnesses[6], shall apply to any proceedings under this section.

(4A) For the purposes of any proceedings under this section, a certificate which states that a person is a member of, and illegally absent from, the regular forces, and purports to be signed by an officer who, if that person were charged with an offence, would be either his commanding officer or authorised to act as his appropriate superior authority, shall be evidence of the matters so stated.

(5) This section shall have effect in the United Kingdom and in any colony.
[Army Act 1955, s 187; Air Force Act 1955, s 187; as amended by the Armed Forces Act 1971, s 56, the Magistrates' Courts Act 1980, Sch 7 and the Armed Forces Discipline Act 2000, s 9.]

1. For corresponding provision in relation to the navy, see Naval Discipline Act 1957, s 109, post.
2. This section also applies to members of visiting forces (Visiting Forces Act 1952, s 13, ante). See Home Office Circular (No 28/1956) dated 11 September 1956. For procedure arranged in relation to absentees without leave from the women's corps and services attached to the army and the air force, see Home Office letter, 7 August 1941, to chief constables.
3. This subsection is adapted to the Royal Marines, by the Army Act 1955, 7th Sch, Part II, para 16.
4. See *R v Tottenham Magistrates' Court, ex p Williams* [1982] 2 All ER 705.
5. See Magistrates' Courts Act 1980, ss 4–6, in Part I: Magistrates' Courts, Procedure, ante. One justice may act alone (*Walder v Turner* [1917] 1 KB 39, 80 JP 405). If a person raises the issue that he is not a deserter or an absentee, the court should take depositions and commit him to military custody for the purpose of trial by military law, just as a civilian prisoner would be committed to the Crown Court (see, generally, remarks of Goddard, LJ, in *R v Secretary of State for Home Affairs, ex p Amand* [1942] 2 KB 26, [1942] 1 All ER 480).
6. See Magistrates' Courts Act 1980, s 97, in Part I: Magistrates' Courts, Procedure, ante.

8–2225   188. Deserters and absentees without leave surrendering to police[1].   (1) Where in the United Kingdom or any colony a person surrenders himself to a constable as being illegally absent from the regular forces[2], the constable shall (unless he surrenders himself at a police station) bring him to a police station.

(2) The officer of police in charge of a police station at which a person has surrendered himself as aforesaid, or to which a person who has so surrendered himself is brought, shall forthwith inquire into the case, and if it appears to that officer that the said person is illegally absent as aforesaid he may cause him to be delivered into military custody without bringing him before a court of summary jurisdiction or may bring him before such a court.
[Army Act 1955, s 188; Air Force Act 1955, s 188.]

1. For corresponding provision in relation to the navy, see Naval Discipline Act 1957, s 108, post.
2. This section is adapted to the Royal Marines by the Army Act 1955, Sch 7, Pt II, para 16, and to members of visiting forces (Visiting Forces Act 1952, s 13, post): see Home Office Circular (No 28/1956) dated 11 September 1956.

8–2226   189. Certificates of arrest or surrender of deserters and absentees[1].   (1) Where a court of summary jurisdiction in pursuance of section one hundred and eighty-seven of this Act deals with a person as illegally absent, then when that person is delivered into military custody there shall be handed over with him a certificate in the prescribed[2] form, signed by a justice of the peace (*Northern Ireland*) or the proper officer of the court[3], containing the prescribed particulars as to his arrest or surrender and the proceedings before the court; and for any such certificate there shall be payable to the proper officer of the court, by such person as the Defence Council may direct, such fee[2] (if any) as may be prescribed.

(2) Where under the last foregoing section a person is delivered into military custody without being brought before a court, there shall be handed over with him a certificate in the prescribed[2] form, signed by the officer of police who causes him to be delivered into military custody, containing the prescribed particulars relating to his surrender.★

(3) In any proceedings for an offence under section thirty-seven or thirty-eight of this Act—

(a) a document purporting to be a certificate under either of the two last foregoing subsections and to be signed as thereby required, shall be evidence of the matters stated in the document;

(aa) where the proceedings are against a person who has surrendered himself to a consular officer, a certificate purporting to be signed by that officer and stating the fact, date, time and place of surrender shall be evidence of the matters stated in the certificate;

(b) where the proceedings are against a person who has been taken into military, naval or air-force custody on arrest or surrender, a certificate purporting to be signed by a provost officer, or any corresponding officer of a Commonwealth force or a force raised under the law of a colony, or by any other officer in charge of the guardroom or other place where that person was confined on being taken into custody, stating the fact, date, time and place of arrest or surrender shall be evidence of the matters stated in the certificate.

(3A) In subsection (1) of this section "proper officer" means—

(a) in relation to a court of summary jurisdiction in England and Wales, the designated officer for the court; and

(b) in relation to a court of summary jurisdiction elsewhere, the clerk of the court.★

(4) In this section the expression "prescribed" means prescribed by regulations made by a Secretary of State by statutory instrument.
[Army Act 1955, s 189; Air Force Act 1955, s 189: amended by Defence (Transfer of Functions) (No 1) Order 1964 and the Armed Forces Act 1971, s 56, the Access to Justice Act 1999, Sch 13 and the Courts Act 2003, Sch 8.]

1. For corresponding provision in relation to the navy, see Naval Discipline Act 1957, s 110, post.
2. This certificate is prescribed in the Certificate of Arrest and Surrender (Army) Regulations 1972, SI 1972/318 and the Certificates of Arrest and Surrender (Air Force) Regulations 1972, SI 1972/1286.
3. The reference to the clerk of the court was inserted by Army and Air Force Act 1961, s 30.

8–2227 190. Duties of governors of prisons and others to receive deserters and absentees[1].
(1) It shall be the duty of the governor of a civil prison in the United Kingdom or of the superintendent or other person in charge of a civil prison in a colony to receive any person duly committed to that prison by a court of summary jurisdiction as illegally absent from the regular forces[2] and to detain him until in accordance with the directions[3] of the court he is delivered into military custody.

(2) The last foregoing subsection shall apply to the person having charge of any police station or other place (not being a prison) provided for the confinement of persons in custody, whether in the United Kingdom or in a colony, as it applies to the governor or superintendent of a prison.
[Army Act 1955, s 190; Air Force Act 1955, s 190.]

1. For corresponding provision in relation to the navy, see Naval Discipline Act 1957, s 107.
2. This section is applied to visiting forces by s 13 of the Visiting Forces Act 1952, ante. A similar provision is contained in the Naval Discipline Act 1957, s 107(1)(c).
3. It is desirable that an escort shall be present when a suspected deserter or absentee is dealt with, in order that he may be handed over forthwith and not be committed to prison. If the police have reason to expect that an escort will arrive before the court rises, it is suggested that the case should be put back until later in the day. If the escort is expected to attend on the following day, it may be possible to avoid committal to prison by remanding the man for one day to a police station. If it is necessary to commit to prison or some other place to await the arrival of an escort, some care should be taken that the warrant of commitment specifies the number of days during which the man may be detained (Secretary of State's letter, 7 April, 1941). Section 13(4) of the Visiting Forces Act 1952, applies this provision to deserters and absentees from visiting forces dealt with in that Act.

Offences[1] relating to military matters punishable by civil courts

8–2228 191. Punishment for pretending to be a deserter[2]. Any person who in the United Kingdom or any colony falsely represents himself to any military, naval, air-force or civil authority to be a deserter from the regular forces shall be liable on summary conviction to a fine not exceeding **level 3** on the standard scale or to imprisonment for a term not exceeding **three months** or to both such a fine and such imprisonment.
[Army Act 1955, s 191; Air Force Act 1955, s 191 as amended by the Criminal Justice Act 1982, ss 38 and 46.]

1. A magistrates' court in England and Wales having jurisdiction in the place where the offender is for the time being has jurisdiction to try him for offences appearing under this heading (ss 191–197), notwithstanding that the offence was committed in England and Wales outside the jurisdiction of that court (Army Act 1955, s 220; Air Force Act 1955, s 218).
2. For a similar section relating to pretending to be a deserter or absentee without leave from the navy, see Naval Discipline Act 1957, s 96, post.

8–2229 192. Punishment for procuring and assisting desertion[1]. (1) Any person who, whether within or without Her Majesty's dominions—

(a) procures or persuades any officer, warrant officer, non-commissioned officer or soldier of the regular forces to desert or to absent himself without leave; or

(b) knowing that any such officer, warrant officer, non-commissioned officer or soldier is about to desert or absent himself without leave, assist him in so doing; or

(c) knowing any person to be a deserter or absentee without leave from the regular forces, procures or persuades or assists him to remain such a deserter or absentee, or assists in his rescue from custody,

shall be guilty of an offence against this section.

(2) Any person guilty of an offence against this section shall be liable[2] on summary conviction to a fine not exceeding **the statutory maximum** or to imprisonment for a term not exceeding **three months**, or to both such a fine and such imprisonment, or on conviction on indictment to a fine or to imprisonment for a term not exceeding **two years** or to both such a fine and such imprisonment.
[Army Act 1955, s 192; Air Force Act 1955, s 192, as amended by Armed Forces Act 1966, s 18 and Criminal Law Act 1977, ss 28 and 32.]

1. For a similar section relating to procuring or assisting desertion or absence without leave from the navy, see Naval Discipline Act 1957, s 97, post.
2. For procedure in respect of this offence which is triable either way, see Magistrates' Courts Act 1980, ss 17A–21, in PART I: MAGISTRATES' COURTS, PROCEDURE, ante.

8–2230 193. Punishment for obstructing members of regular forces in execution of duty.
Any person who, in the United Kingdom or any colony, wilfully obstructs or otherwise interferes with any officer, warrant officer, non-commissioned officer or soldier of the regular forces acting in the execution of his duty shall be liable on summary conviction to a fine not exceeding **level 3** on the standard scale or to imprisonment for a term not exceeding **three months** or to both such a fine and such imprisonment.
[Army Act 1955, s 193; Air Force Act 1955, s 193 as amended by the Criminal Justice Act 1982, ss 38 and 46.]

8–2231 194. Punishment for aiding malingering. Any person who, whether within or without Her Majesty's dominions—

(a) produces in an officer, warrant officer, non-commissioned officer or soldier of the regular forces any sickness or disability; or

(b) supplies to or for him any drug or preparation calculated or likely to render him, or lead to the belief that he is, permanently or temporarily unfit for service,

with a view to enabling him to avoid military service, whether permanently or temporarily, shall be liable[1] on summary conviction to a fine not exceeding **the statutory maximum** or to imprisonment for a term not exceeding **three months** or to both such a fine and such imprisonment, or on conviction on indictment to a fine or to imprisonment for a term not exceeding **two years** or to both such a fine and such imprisonment.

[Army Act 1955, s 194; Air Force Act 1955, s 194, as amended by the Criminal Law Act 1977, ss 28 and 32.]

---

1. For procedure in respect of this offence which is triable either way, see Magistrates' Courts Act 1980, ss 17A–21, in Part I: Magistrates' Courts, Procedure, ante.

8–2232　195. Unlawful purchase, etc, of military stores[1]. (1) Any person who, whether within or without Her Majesty's dominions, acquires any military stores or solicits or procures any person to dispose of any military stores, or acts for any person in the disposing of any military stores, shall be guilty of an offence against this section unless he proves either—

(a) that he did not know, and could not reasonably be expected to know, that the chattels in question were military stores, or

(b) that those chattels had (by the transaction with which he is charged or some earlier transaction) been disposed of by order or with the consent of the Defence Council or of some person or authority who had, or whom he had reasonable cause to believe to have, power to give the order or consent, or

(c) that those chattels had become the property of an officer who had retired or ceased to be an officer, or of a warrant officer, non-commissioned officer or soldier who had been discharged, or of the personal representatives of a person who had died.

(2) Any person guilty of an offence against this section shall be liable[2] on summary conviction to a fine not exceeding **the statutory maximum** or to imprisonment for a term not exceeding **three months** or to both such a fine and such imprisonment, or on conviction on indictment to a fine or imprisonment for a term not exceeding **two years** or to both such a fine and such imprisonment.

(3) A constable may seize any property which he has reasonable grounds for suspecting of having been the subject of an offence against this section.

(4) Any person having authority to issue a warrant for the arrest of a person charged with crime may, if satisfied by evidence on oath that a person within his jurisdiction has, or is reasonably suspected of having, in his possession any property which has been the subject of an offence against this section, grant a warrant to search for such property as in the case of stolen goods[3]; and any property suspected of having been the subject of such an offence which is found on such a search shall be seized by the officer charged with the execution of the warrant, and that officer shall bring the person in whose possession or keeping the property is found before a court of summary jurisdiction.

(5) In this section—

the expression "acquire" means buy, take in exchange, take in pawn[4] or otherwise receive (whether apart from this section the receiving is lawful or not);

the expression "dispose" means sell, give in exchange, pledge or otherwise hand over (whether apart from this section the handing over is lawful or not);

the expression "military stores" means any chattel of any description belonging to Her Majesty, which has been issued for use for military purposes or is held in store for the purpose of being so issued when required, and includes any chattel which had belonged, and had been issued or held, as aforesaid at some past time.

(6) For the purposes of subsection (4) of this section property shall be deemed to be in the possession of a person if he has it under his control, and whether he has it for his own use or benefit or for the use or benefit of another.

[Army Act 1955, s 195; Air Force Act 1955, s 195 as amended by the Defence (Transfer of Functions) (No 1) Order 1964, the Criminal Law Act 1977, ss 28 and 32 and the Police and Criminal Evidence Act 1984, Sch 6.]

---

1. For a similar section relating to the unlawful purchase of naval property, see Naval Discipline Act 1957, s 98, post.
2. For procedure in respect of this offence which is triable either way, see Magistrates' Courts Act 1980, ss 17A–21, in Part I: Magistrates' Courts, Procedure, ante.
3. See the Theft Act 1968, s 26, post.
4. It is unnecessary to prove personal knowledge of the pawnbroker that the stores were in his possession: he is liable for the acts of his servants (*O'Brien v Macgregor* (1904) 5 F 74).

8–2233　196. Illegal dealings in documents relating to pay, pensions, mobilisation, etc.

(1) Any person who—

(a) as a pledge or a security for a debt, or

(*b*) with a view to obtaining payment from the person entitled thereto of a debt due either to himself or to any other person,

receives, detains or has in his possession any official document issued in connection with the payment to any person of any pay, pension, allowance, gratuity or other payment payable in respect of his or any other person's military[1] service shall be guilty of an offence against this section.

(2) Any person who has in his possession without lawful authority or excuse (the proof whereof shall lie on him) any such document as aforesaid, or any official document issued in connection with the mobilisation or demobilisation of any of Her Majesty's military forces or any member thereof, shall be guilty of an offence against this section.

(3) Any person guilty of an offence against this section shall be liable on summary conviction to a fine not exceeding **level 3** on the standard scale or to imprisonment for a term not exceeding **three months** or to both such a fine and such imprisonment.

(4) For the purposes of this section a document shall be deemed to be in the possession of a person if he has it under his control and whether he has it for his own use or benefit or for the use or benefit of another.

(5) This section shall have effect in the United Kingdom and in any colony.

[Army Act 1955, s 196; Air Force Act 1955, s 196, as amended by the Criminal Justice Act 1982, ss 38 and 46.]

---

1. For a similar section relating to illegal dealings in official documents relating to the navy, see Naval Discipline Act 1957, s 99, post.

8–2234 197. Unauthorised use of and dealing in decorations, etc. (1) Any person who, in the United Kingdom or in any colony—

(*a*) without authority uses or wears any military decoration[1], or any badge, wound stripe or emblem supplied or authorised by the Defence Council, or

(*b*) uses or wears any decoration[1], badge, wound stripe, or emblem so nearly resembling any military decoration, or any such badge, stripe or emblem as aforesaid, as to be calculated to deceive, or

(*c*) falsely represents himself to be a person who is or has been entitled to use or wear any such decoration[1], badge, stripe or emblem as is mentioned in paragraph (*a*) of this subsection,

shall be guilty of an offence against this section:
Provided that nothing in this subsection shall prohibit the use or wearing of ordinary regimental badges or of brooches or ornaments representing them.

(2) Any person who purchases or takes in pawn any naval, military or air-force decoration awarded to any member of Her Majesty's military forces, or solicits or procures any person to sell or pledge any such decoration, or acts for any person in the sale or pledging thereof, shall be guilty of an offence against this section unless he proves that at the time of the alleged offence the person to whom the decoration was awarded was dead or had ceased to be a member of those forces.

(3) Any person guilty of an offence against this section shall be liable on summary conviction to a fine not exceeding **level 3** on the standard scale or to imprisonment for a term not exceeding **three months** or to both such a fine and such imprisonment.

[Army Act 1955, s 197; Air Force Act 1955, s 197 as amended by the Defence (Transfer of Functions) (No 1) Order, 1964 and the Criminal Justice Act 1982, ss 38 and 46.]

---

1. "Decoration" includes medal, medal ribbon, clasp and good conduct badge (Army Act 1955, s 225; Air Force Act 1955, s 223).

Provisions as to evidence

8–2235 198. General provisions as to evidence. (1) The following provisions shall have effect with respect to evidence, in proceedings under this Act, whether before a court-martial, a civil court or otherwise.

(2) A document purporting to be a copy of the attestation paper signed by any person and to be certified to be a true copy by a person stated in the certificate to have the custody of the attestation paper shall be evidence of the enlistment of the person attested.

(3) The attestation paper purporting to be signed by a person on his enlistment shall be evidence of his having given the answers to questions which he is therein recorded as having given.

(4) A letter, return or other document stating that any person—

(*a*) was or was not serving at any specified time or during any specified period in any part of Her Majesty's forces or was discharged from any part of those forces at or before any specified time, or

(*b*) held or did not hold at any specified time any specified rank or appointment in any of those forces, or had at or before any specified time been attached, posted or transferred to any part of those forces, or at any specified time or during any specified period was or was not serving or held or did not hold any rank or appointment in any particular country or place, or

(*c*) was or was not at any specified time authorised to use or wear any decoration, badge, wound stripe or emblem, shall, if purporting to be issued by or on behalf of the Defence Council, or by a person authorised by any of them, be evidence of the matters stated in the document.

(5) A record made in any service book or other document prescribed by Queen's Regulations for the purposes of this subsection, being a record made in pursuance of any Act or of Queen's Regulations, or otherwise in pursuance of military duty, and purporting to be signed by the commanding officer or by any person whose duty it was to make the record, shall be evidence of the facts stated therein; and a copy of a record (including the signature thereto) in any such book or other document as aforesaid, purporting to be certified to be a true copy by a person stated in the certificate to have the custody of the book or other document, shall be evidence of the record.

(6) A document purporting to be issued by order of the Defence Council and to contain instructions or regulations given or made by the Defence Council shall be evidence of the giving of the instructions or making of the regulations and of their contents.

(7) A certificate purporting to be issued by or on behalf of the Defence Council, or by a person authorised by any of them, and stating—

   (*a*)　that a decoration of a description specified in or annexed to the certificate is a military, naval or air-force decoration, or

   (*b*)　that a badge, wound stripe or emblem of a description specified in or annexed to the certificate is one supplied or authorised by the Defence Council,

shall be evidence of the matters stated in the certificate.

(8) A certificate purporting to be signed by a person's commanding officer or any officer authorised by him to give the certificate, and stating the contents of, or of any part of, standing orders or other routine orders of a continuing nature made for—

   (*a*)　any formation or unit or body or troops, or

   (*b*)　any command or other area, garrison or place, or

   (*c*)　any ship, train or aircraft,

shall in proceedings against the said person be evidence of the matters stated in the certificate.

(9) Any document which would be evidence in any proceedings under the Air Force Act 1955, by virtue of section 198 of that Act, or in any proceedings under the Naval Discipline Act 1957, by virtue of section 64C of that Act, shall in like manner, subject to the like conditions, and for the like purpose be evidence in the like proceedings under this Act.

[Army Act 1955, s 198; Air Force Act 1955, s 198, as amended by the Army and Air Force Act 1961, Sch 2, the Defence (Transfer of Functions) (No 1) Order 1964, the Armed Forces Act 1981, s 9, the Police and Criminal Evidence Act 1984, Sch 7 and the Armed Forces Act 1996, Sch 1.]

8–2236　199. Proof of outcome of civil trial.　(1) Where a person subject to military law has been tried before a civil court (whether at the time of the trial he was subject to military law or not), a certificate signed by the proper officer of the court and stating all or any of the following matters—

   (*a*)　that the said person has been tried before the court for an offence specified in the certificate,

   (*b*)　the result of the trial,

   (*c*)　what judgment or order was given or made by the court,

   (*d*)　that other offences specified in the certificate were taken into consideration at the trial,

shall for the purposes of this Act be evidence of the matters stated in the certificate.

(2) The proper officer of the court shall, if required by the commanding officer of the person in question or any other officer, furnish a certificate under this section and shall be paid such fee as may be prescribed by regulations made by a Secretary of State.

(3) A document purporting to be a certificate under this section and to be signed by the proper officer of the court shall, unless the contrary is shown, be deemed to be such a certificate.

(4) In this section "proper officer" means—

   (a)　in relation to a court of summary jurisdiction in England and Wales, the designated officer for the court; and

   (b)　in relation to any other court, the clerk of the court, his deputy or any other person having custody of the records of the court.

[Army Act 1955, s 199: Air Force Act 1955, s 199, as amended by the Access to Justice Act 1999, Sch 13 and the Courts Act 2003, Sch 8.]

8–2237　200A. False statements in computer record certificates.　*Repealed.*

8–2238　202. Temporary reception in civil custody of persons under escort.　(1) Where a person is in military custody when charged with, or with a view to his being charged with, an offence against Part II of this Act, it shall be the duty of the governor, superintendent or other person in charge of a prison (not being a military prison), or of the person having charge of any police station or other place in which prisoners may be lawfully detained, upon delivery to him of a written order purporting to be signed by the commanding officer of the person in custody to receive him into his custody for a period not exceeding seven days.

(2) This section shall have effect in the United Kingdom and in any colony.

[Army Act 1955, s 202; Air Force Act 1955, s 202.]

8–2239 203. Avoidance of assignment of or charge on military pay, pensions, etc. (1) Every assignment of or charge on, and every agreement to assign or charge, any pay, military award, grant, pension or allowance payable to any person in respect of his or any other person's service in Her Majesty's military forces shall be void[1].

(2) Save as expressly provided by this Act, no order[2] shall be made by any court the effect of which would be to restrain any person from receiving anything which by virtue of this section he is precluded from assigning and to direct payment thereof to another person.

(3) Nothing in this section shall prejudice any enactment providing for the payment of any sum to a bankrupt's trustee in bankruptcy for distribution among creditors.

(4) This section shall have effect in the United Kingdom and in any colony.
[Army Act 1955, s 203; Air Force Act 1955, s 203.]

1. It has been held that s 203(1) does not inhibit a court ordering an ex-serviceman to make a lump sum payment to his former wife out of a gratuity which he has already received (*Happé v Happé* [1991] 4 All ER 527, [1990] 1 WLR 1282, [1990] 2 FLR 212, CA).
2. There is no similar restriction on the court with respect to a naval rating or marine by virtue of the Naval and Marine Pay and Pensions Act 1865, ss 4, 5 (*Cotgrave v Cotgrave* [1992] Fam 33, [1991] 4 All ER 537, [1991] FCR 838, CA).

Naval Discipline Act 1957[1]
(5 & 6 Eliz 2 c 53)

Offences punishable by civil courts

8–2251 96. False pretence of desertion or absence without leave[2]. Every person who, whether within or without the United Kingdom, falsely represents himself to any naval, military, air force, or civil authority to be a person who is illegally absent from any of Her Majesty's naval forces shall be liable on summary conviction to a fine not exceeding **level 3** on the standard scale or to imprisonment for a term not exceeding **three months** or to both such a fine and such imprisonment.
[Naval Discipline Act 1957, s 96, as amended by the Armed Forces Act 1976, s 15 and the Criminal Justice Act 1982, ss 38 and 46.]

1. The Armed Forces Act 2001, s 1, provides that this Act, instead of expiring on 31 August 2001, shall continue in force until 31 August 2002, and shall then expire unless continued in force by Order in Council. The Acts have been continued in force for periods of 12 months beyond 31 August in each year by the following Army, Air Force and Naval Discipline Acts (Continuation) Orders: 2002, SI 2002/1820, 2003, SI 2003/1869, 2004, SI 2004/1496, 2005, SI 2005/2021.
2. For corresponding provision relating to the army or air force, see Army Act 1955, s 191; Air Force Act 1955, s 191, ante.

8–2252 97. Procuring or assisting desertion or absence without leave[1]. (1) Every person who, whether within or without the United Kingdom,

(*a*) procures or persuades any person subject to this Act to commit an offence of desertion, of absenting himself without leave or of improperly leaving his ship or place of duty; or

(*b*) knowing that any such person is about to commit such an offence as aforesaid, assists him in so doing; or

(*c*) knowing any such person to have committed such an offence, procures or persuades or assists him to remain a deserter, absentee without leave or improperly absent from his ship or place of duty, or assists in his rescue from custody,

shall be guilty of an offence against this section.

(2) A person guilty of an offence against this section shall be liable[2] on summary conviction to a fine not exceeding **the statutory maximum** or to imprisonment for a term not exceeding **three months**, or to both such a fine and such imprisonment, or on conviction on indictment to a fine or to imprisonment for a term not exceeding **two years**, or to both such a fine and such imprisonment.
[Naval Discipline Act 1957, s 97, as amended by the Armed Forces Act 1966, s 18, the Armed Forces Act 1976, s 15 and the Criminal Law Act 1977, ss 28 and 32.]

1. For corresponding provision relating to the army or air force, see Army Act 1955, s 192; Air Force Act 1955, s 192, ante.
2. For procedure in respect of this offence which is triable either way, see Magistrates' Courts Act 1980, ss 17A–21, in PART I: MAGISTRATES' COURTS, PROCEDURE, ante.

8–2253 98. Unlawful purchase of naval property[1]. (1) Every person who whether within or without the United Kingdom, acquires any naval property, or solicits or procures any person to dispose of any naval property, or acts for any person in the disposing of any naval property, shall be guilty of an offence against this section unless he proves either—

(*a*) that he did not know, and could not reasonably be expected to know, that the chattels in question were naval property; or

(*b*) that those chattels had (by the transaction with which he is charged or some earlier transaction) been disposed of by order of or with the consent of the Defence Council or of some person in authority who had, or whom he had reasonable cause to believe to have, power to give the order or consent; or

(c) that those chattels had become the property of an officer who had retired or ceased to be an officer, or of a rating who had been discharged, or of the personal representatives of a person who had died.

(2) A person guilty of an offence against this section shall be liable[2] on summary conviction to a fine not exceeding **the statutory maximum** or to imprisonment for a term not exceeding **three months**, or to both such a fine and such imprisonment, or on conviction on indictment to a fine or imprisonment for a term not exceeding **two years**, or to both such a fine and such imprisonment.

(3) In this section the following expressions have the meanings hereby respectively assigned to them—

"acquire" means, buy, take in exchange, take in pawn or otherwise receive (whether apart from this section the receiving is lawful or not);

"dispose" means, sell, give in exchange, pledge or otherwise hand over (whether apart from this section the handing over is lawful or not);

"naval property" means any chattel of any description belonging to Her Majesty, which has been issued for use for naval purposes or is held in store for the purpose of being so issued when required, and includes any chattel which had belonged, and had been issued or held, as aforesaid at some past time.

[Naval Discipline Act 1957, s 98, as amended by the Defence (Transfer of Functions) (No 1) Order 1964, the Armed Forces Act 1976, s 15 and the Criminal Law Act 1977, ss 28 and 32.]

---

1. For corresponding provision relating to the army or air force, see Army Act 1955, s 195; Air Force Act 1955, s 195, ante.

2. For procedure in respect of this offence which is triable either way, see Magistrates' Courts Act 1980, ss 17A–21, in PART I: MAGISTRATES' COURTS, PROCEDURE, ante. For power of seizure of property, and for issue of search warrant, see s 106, post.

8–2254   99. Illegal dealings in official documents[1]. (1) Every person who receives, detains or has in his possession—

(a) as a pledge or as security for a debt; or

(b) with a view to obtaining payment from the person entitled thereto of a debt due either to himself or to any other person,

any official document issued in connection with the payment to any person of any pay, pension, allowance, gratuity or other payment payable in respect of his or any other person's service in Her Majesty's naval forces shall be guilty of an offence against this section.

(2) Every person who has in his possession without lawful authority or excuse (the proof whereof shall lie on him) any such document as aforesaid, or any official document issued in connection with the mobilisation or demobilisation of any of Her Majesty's naval forces or any member thereof, shall be guilty of an offence against this section.

(3) A person guilty of an offence against this section shall be liable on summary conviction to a fine not exceeding **level 3** on the standard scale or to imprisonment for a term not exceeding **three months**, or to both such a fine and such imprisonment.

(4) For the purpose of this section a document shall be deemed to be in the possession of a person if he has it under his control, and whether he has it for his own use or benefit or for the use or benefit of another.

(5) References in this section to Her Majesty's naval forces include references to the naval forces of any Commonwealth country or raised under the law of any colony.

[Naval Discipline Act 1957, s 99, as amended by the Criminal Justice Act 1982, ss 38 and 46.]

---

1. For corresponding provision relating to the army or air force, see Army Act 1955, s 196; Air Force Act 1955, s 196, ante.

8–2255   100. Jurisdiction and application of summary fines. (1) A person alleged to have committed an offence under the provisions of sections 96 to 99 of this Act may, subject to the provisions of this section, be tried by a civil court having jurisdiction in the place where he is for the time being, notwithstanding that the offence was committed outside the jurisdiction of that court.

[Naval Discipline Act 1957, s 100, as amended by the Criminal Justice Act 1972, Sch 6.]

Process and execution in certain civil proceedings

8–2256   101. Service of proceedings for maintenance, etc[1]. (1) Any process to be served on an officer or rating who is subject to this Act (in this section referred to as "the defendant") in connection with proceedings for a maintenance order as defined by this section, or for the variation, revocation or revival of such an order, shall be deemed to be duly served on the defendant if served on the commanding officer of the ship or establishment in which the defendant is serving or on the books of which he is borne, and may, without prejudice to any other method of service, be so served within the United Kingdom by registered post[2].

(2), (3) *Repealed.*

(4) Where any such process is served in the United Kingdom and the defendant will be required to appear in person at the hearing, the service of the process shall be of no effect if his commanding officer certifies to the court by which the process was issued that the defendant is under orders for service on a foreign station and that in the commanding officer's opinion it would not be possible for the defendant to attend the hearing and return in time to embark for that service.

(4A) Where any such process is to be served in the United Kingdom or elsewhere and the defendant will be required to appear in person at the hearing, the service of that process shall be of no effect if his commanding officer certifies to the court by which the process was issued that the defendant is absent without leave or has deserted and remains in desertion.

(5) In this section the expression "maintenance order"[3] means an order made by a court in the United Kingdom or registered in or confirmed by such a court under the provisions of the Maintenance Orders (Facilities for Enforcement) Act 1920 or registered in such a court under Part I of the Maintenance Orders (Reciprocal Enforcement) Act 1972[4] or or Part I of the Civil Jurisdiction and Judgments Act 1982 or Council Regulation (EC) No 44/2001 of 22nd Decmeber 2000 on jurisdiction and the recognition and enforcement of judgments in civil and commerical matters, being an order for the payment of any periodical or other sum specified therein for or in respect of—

(a)　the maintenance of the wife or civil partner of the person against whom the order is made; or
(b)　the maintenance of any child of that person or his wife or civil partner or of any other child who has been treated by them both as a child of their family; or
(c)　any costs incurred in obtaining the order; or
(d)　any costs incurred in proceedings on appeal against or for the variation, revocation or revival of any such order.

(5A) In subsection (5) above—

(a)　references to the wife of a person include, in relation to an order made in proceedings in connection with the dissolution or annulment of a marriage, references to a person who would have been his wife if the marriage had subsisted; and
(aa)　references to the civil partner of a person include, in relation to an order made in proceedings in connection with the dissolution or annulment of a civil partnership, references to a person who would have been his civil partner if the civil partnership had subsisted; and
(b)　without prejudice to any enactment or rule of law relating to adoption or legitimation, references to a child of a person or his wife shall be construed without regard to whether or not the father and mother of the child have or had been married to each other at any time.

(5B) In relation to women members of Her Majesty's naval forces, references in this section to a wife shall be construed as references to a husband.

(6) Nothing in this section shall be construed as enabling process to be served in connection with proceedings in a court of summary jurisdiction unless the defendant is within the United Kingdom or is serving in a ship on a home station or a naval establishment within the United Kingdom.

[Naval Discipline Act 1957, s 101, as amended by the Defence (Transfer of Functions) (No 1) Order 1964, the Armed Forces Act 1971, s 62, the Maintenance Order (Reciprocal Enforcement) Act 1972, Schedule, the Armed Forces Act 1981, s 18 and Sch 5, the Civil Jurisdiction and Judgments Act 1982, Sch 12, the Family Law Reform Act 1987, Sch 4, the Armed Forces Act 1991, s 15, SI 2001/3929 and the Civil Partnership Act 2004, Sch 26.]

---

1. For corresponding provisions relating to the army or air force, see Army Act 1955, s 153; Air Force Act 1955, s 153, ante; and see notes to these sections. A copy of any maintenance order that is made should be sent to the appropriate service authority as detailed in Home Office Circular No 251/1970, dated 18 November 1970.

2. The recorded delivery service may be used. (Recorded Delivery Service Act 1962, s 1.)

3. Deductions from pay in respect of liabilities for maintenance will be made by virtue of the Naval Forces (Enforcement of Maintenance Liabilities) Act 1947, ante; and see Home Office Circular No 251/1970, dated 18 November 1970.

4. See PART VI: FAMILY LAW, ante.

Arrest and detention of offenders by civil authorities

8–2257　103. Arrest under warrants of naval authorities. (1) A warrant for the arrest of any person suspected of any offence under Part I[1] of this Act may be issued by any Commander-in-Chief, by the senior naval officer present at any port, by any officer in command of any of Her Majesty's ships or naval establishments, or by any officer who by virtue of regulations under section 52E(2)(a) above may exercise the powers of that person's commanding officer.

(2) A warrant issued under this section shall be addressed to an officer or officers of police, and shall specify the name of the person for whose arrest it is issued and the offence which he is alleged to have committed; and any such warrant may be issued in respect of two or more persons alleged to have committed the same offence or offences of the same class.

(3) A person arrested under a warrant issued under this section shall as soon as practicable be delivered into naval custody; and there shall be handed over with him a certificate signed by the officer of police who causes him to be delivered into naval custody stating the fact, date, time and place of arrest, and whether or not the person arrested was at the time of arrest wearing the uniform of any of Her Majesty's naval forces.

[Naval Discipline Act 1957, s 103, as amended by the Armed Forces Act 1996, Sch 1.]

1. These are offences against naval discipline punishable by court-martial.

8–2258 104. Arrest of persons unlawfully at large. (1) A constable may arrest[1] without warrant any person who, having been sentenced under Part II[2] of this Act to imprisonment or detention, is unlawfully at large during the currency of the sentence, and may take him to any place in which he may be required in accordance with law to be detained.

(2) The provisions of s 88(2), (3)[3] of this Act shall have effect for the purpose of the foregoing subsection as they have effect for the purposes of that section.

[Naval Discipline Act 1957, s 104.]

1. This power of arrest is preserved by the Police and Criminal Evidence Act 1984, s 26 and Sch 2.
2. This relates to sentences imposed by naval courts.
3. These subsections relate to a person temporarily released from custody being treated as a person unlawfully at large if he fails to return at the expiration of the period, or to comply with any condition, of his release.

8–2259 105. Arrest of deserters and absentees[1]. (1) A constable may arrest[2] without warrant any person whom he has reasonable cause to suspect of being an officer or rating of any of Her Majesty's naval forces who has deserted or is absent without leave.

(2) Where no constable is available, any officer or rating who is subject to this Act, or any other person, may arrest any person whom he has reasonable cause to suspect as aforesaid.

(3) Any person having authority to issue a warrant for the arrest of a person charged with crime, if satisfied by evidence on oath that there is, or is reasonably suspected of being, within his jurisdiction an officer or rating of any of Her Majesty's naval forces who has deserted or is absent without leave, or is reasonably suspected of having deserted or being absent without leave, may issue a warrant authorising his arrest.

(4) Any person taken into custody in pursuance of this section shall as soon as practicable be brought before a court of summary jurisdiction.

(4A) A person shall also be brought before a court of summary jurisdiction if, having been brought before such a court by virtue of subsection (4) above and discharged by that court by virtue of section 109 (3)(*b*) below—

(*a*) he is subsequently arrested as an alleged or suspected deserter or absentee without leave under section 45 of this Act, or under a warrant issued under section 103 thereof, and

(*b*) the question whether he is in fact in desertion or absent without leave raises any issue which was investigated by the court discharging him, and

(*c*) he does not admit that he is in desertion or absent without leave to the person arresting him under the said section 45 or, as the case may be, to the person into whose custody he is delivered pursuant to the said section 103;

[Naval Discipline Act 1957, s 105, as amended by the Armed Forces Act 1971.]

1. For corresponding provision relating to the army and air force, see Army Act 1955, s 186; Air Force Act 1955, s 186, ante. As to deserters or absentees without leave from visiting forces, see Visiting Forces Act 1952, ss 13, 17, which apply provisions of ss 186, 187, 188, 190 of the Army Act 1955 to all members of visiting forces, whether naval, military or air force. The provisions of the Naval Discipline Act 1957, relating to desertion and absence without leave are applied to the Royal Navies of Australia and Ceylon (now Sri Lanka) and to the Ghana, Pakistan and Indian Navies (Naval Discipline (Commonwealth Navies) Order 1959, SI 1959/1972, as amended).
2. This power of arrest is preserved by the Police and Criminal Evidence Act 1984, s 26 and Sch 2.

8–2260 106. Arrest of any persons suspected of offences punishable by civil courts. (1) A constable may seize any property which he has reasonable grounds for suspecting of having been the subject of an offence against section 98[1] of this Act.

(2) Any person having authority to issue a warrant for the arrest of a person charged with crime may, if satisfied by evidence on oath that a person within his jurisdiction has, or is reasonably suspected of having, in his possession any property which has been the subject of an offence against the said section 98[1], grant a warrant to search for such property as in the case of stolen goods[2]; and any property suspected of having been the subject of such an offence which is found on such a search shall be seized by the officer charged with the execution of the warrant, and that officer shall bring the person in whose possession or keeping the property is found before a court of summary jurisdiction.

(3) For the purposes of this section property shall be deemed to be in the possession of a person if he has it under his control, and whether he has it for his own use or benefit or for the use or benefit of another.

[Naval Discipline Act 1957, s 106, as amended by the Police and Criminal Evidence Act 1984, Sch 7.]

1. See this section, ante: unlawful purchase of naval property.
2. See Theft Act 1968, s 26, post.

Power of civil courts and authorities as to deserters and absentees[1]

8–2261 108. Deserters and absentees surrendering to police[2]. (1) Where a person surrenders himself to a constable as being a person who is illegally absent from any of Her Majesty's naval forces, the constable shall, unless that person surrenders himself at a police station, bring him to a police station.

(2) The officer of police in charge of a police station at which a person has surrendered himself as aforesaid, or to which a person who has so surrendered himself is brought, shall forthwith inquire into the case; and if it appears to that officer that the said person is illegally absent as aforesaid he may cause him to be delivered into naval custody without bringing him before a court of summary jurisdiction or may bring him before such a court.

[Naval Discipline Act 1957, s 108.]

---

1. See Naval Discipline (Commonwealth Navies) Order 1959, SI 1959/1972 (as amended by SI 1961/568), which applies these provisions to the naval forces of Australia, Ceylon (now Sri Lanka), Ghana, Pakistan and India.

2. For corresponding provision relating to the army or air force, see Army Act 1955, s 188; Air Force Act 1955, s 188, ante.

8–2262 **109. Proceedings before summary courts**[1]. (1) Where a person who is brought before a court of summary jurisdiction as being illegally absent from any of Her Majesty's naval forces admits that he is so absent and the court is satisfied of the truth of the admission, the court may in any case, and shall unless he is in custody for some other cause, forthwith either—

(a) cause him to be delivered into naval custody in such manner as the court may think fit; or
(b) where it is unable to do so, adjourn the proceedings and remand him for such time as appears reasonably necessary for the purpose of arranging for him to be delivered into naval custody.

(2) *Repealed.*

(3) Where a person who is brought as aforesaid does not admit that he is illegally absent as aforesaid, or does so admit but the court is not satisfied of the truth of the admission, the court shall consider the evidence and any statement of the accused, and thereupon—

(a) if the court is satisfied that he is subject to this Act[2] and is of opinion that there is sufficient evidence to justify his being tried under Part II of this Act[3] for an offence of desertion, absence without leave or improperly leaving his ship, the court may in any case, and shall unless he is in custody for some other cause, either cause him to be delivered into naval custody or, where it is unable to do so, adjourn the proceedings and remand him for such time as appears reasonably necessary for the purpose of arranging for him to be delivered into naval custody;
(b) in any other case the court shall unless he is in custody for some other cause, discharge him.

(4) The following provisions of the Magistrates' Courts Act 1952[4], that is to say the provisions relating to the constitution and procedure of courts of summary jurisdiction acting as examining justices and conferring powers of adjournment and remand on such courts so acting, and the provisions as to evidence and the issue and enforcement of summonses or warrants to secure the attendance of witnesses, shall apply to any proceedings under this section; and for the purposes of any such proceedings, a certificate purporting to be signed by the officer in command of any of Her Majesty's ships or naval establishments and stating that a person is subject to this Act and is illegally absent as aforesaid shall be evidence of the matters so stated.

[Naval Discipline Act 1957, s 109, as amended by the Armed Forces Act 1971, Sch 7 and the Armed Forces Discipline Act 2000, s 9 and Sch 4.]

---

1. For corresponding provision relating to the army or air force, see Army Act 1955, s 187; Air Force Act 1955, s 187, ante; and see notes to these sections.

2. Evidence of this may be given by certificate, see sub-s (4), infra.

3. Ie, by court-martial or other naval court.

4. Now the Magistrates' Courts Act 1980, in PART I: MAGISTRATES' COURTS, PROCEDURE, ante.

8–2263 **110. Certificates of arrest or surrender**[1]. (1) Where an officer of police causes any person to be delivered into naval custody under section 108 of this Act without being brought before a court of summary jurisdiction, there shall be handed over to that person a certificate in the prescribed form[2] signed by the officer of police, containing a statement of the fact, date, time and place of surrender and whether or not the said person was at the time of surrender wearing the uniform of any of Her Majesty's naval forces.

(2) Where a court of summary jurisdiction causes any person to be delivered into naval custody under section 109 of this Act, or any person is so delivered after having been committed under that section, there shall be handed over with him a certificate in the prescribed form[3], signed by a justice of the peace*, containing—

(a) a statement of the fact, date, time and place of arrest or surrender, and whether or not the said person was, at the time of arrest or surrender, wearing the uniform of any of Her Majesty's naval forces; and
(b) such particulars of the proceedings before the court as may be prescribed[3]; and for any such certificate there shall be payable to the proper officer of the court, by such person as the Defence Council may direct, such fee (if any) as may be prescribed[3].

(2A) In subsection (2) of this section "proper officer" means—

(a) in relation to a court of summary jurisdiction in England and Wales, the justices' chief executive for the court; and

(b) in relation to a court of summary jurisdiction elsewhere, the clerk of the court.

(3) In this section "prescribed" means prescribed by regulations made by the Secretary of State by statutory instrument.
[Naval Discipline Act 1957, s 110, as amended by the Defence (Transfer of Functions) (No 1) Order 1964 and the Access to Justice Act 1999, Sch 13.]

---

*Sub-section (2) amended by the Justice (Northern Ireland) Act 2002, s 10(6) from a date to be appointed.
1. For corresponding provision relating to the army or air force, see Army Act 1955, s 189; Air Force Act 1955, s 189, ante.
2. See Certificates of Arrest and Surrender (Royal Navy) Regulations 1972, SI 1972/430.
3. See note 2, ante. The certificate may be signed either by a justice of the peace or the clerk of the court (Armed Forces Act 1966, s 33).

8–2264   128B. Deductions for payment of civil penalties. Where a person sentenced or ordered by a civil court (whether within or without Her Majesty's dominions) to pay a sum by way of fine, penalty, damages, compensation or costs in consequence of his being charged before the court with an offence is at the time of the sentence or order, or subsequently becomes, a person subject to this Act, then, if the whole or any part of that sum is met by a payment made by or on behalf of any naval authority, the amount of the payment may be deducted from his pay.
[Naval Discipline Act 1957, s 128B added by the Armed Forces Act 1971, s 61.]

8–2265   128E. Deductions in respect of judgment debts etc. (1) Where by any judgment or order enforceable by a court in the United Kingdom any sum is required to be paid by a person who is subject to this Act, the Defence Council or an officer authorised by them may, whether or not that person was subject to this Act at the time when the judgment or order was given or made, order such amount or amounts as the Council or officer think fit to be deducted from the pay of that person, and appropriated in or towards satisfaction of that sum:
Provided that this subsection shall not apply to any such sum as is mentioned in section 128B of this Act, or to any sum in respect of which deductions may be authorised by virtue of section 1(1) of the Naval Forces (Enforcement of Maintenance Liabilities) Act 1947 or made by virtue of section 32(2)(b) of the Courts-Martial (Appeals) Act 1968.
(2) The Defence Council or an officer authorised by them may by order vary or revoke any order previously made under this section.
(3) The sums deducted from a person's pay by virtue of this section and section 1(1) of the Naval Forces (Enforcement of Maintenance Liabilities) Act 1947 shall not together exceed such proportion of his pay as the Defence Council may determine.
[Naval Discipline Act 1957, s 128E added by the Armed Forces Act 1971, s 61.]

8–2266   128F. Financial penalty enforcement orders. (1) If—

(a) a financial penalty has been awarded against any person under this Act, and
(b) the penalty was—

   (i) a fine awarded in respect of a qualifying offence (or in respect of such an offence together with other offences) on the conviction of a qualifying offence either of that person or of the person as whose parent or guardian that person is to pay the penalty; or
   (ii) stoppages or a compensation order awarded in respect of a qualifying offence, (whether on the conviction of any person of the offence or on a request by any person for the offence to be taken into consideration); and

(c) no term of imprisonment was imposed in default of payment, and
(d) no appeal is outstanding and the time provided for the giving of notice of appeal against the award has expired, and
(e) the whole or any part of the penalty remains unpaid or unrecovered, and
(f) the person against whom the award was made is a person to whom this section applies,

the Defence Council or an officer authorised by them may make an order (in this section referred to as a "financial penalty enforcement order") for the registration of the penalty by the relevant court.
(2) This section applies to a person who

(a) is, or would be but for section 119 above, neither subject to service law nor a civilian to whom Parts I and II of this Act are applied by section 118 above, Part II of the Army Act 1955 is applied by section 209 of that Act or Part II of the Air Force Act 1955 is applied by section 209 of that Act; or
(b) is subject to service law because he is a special member of a reserve force within the meaning of the Reserve Forces Act 1996.

(3) In this section "qualifying offence" means—

(*a*) an offence under section 14A above committed outside the United Kingdom and consisting of or including acts or omissions that would constitute a comparable foreign offence or a local traffic offence;

(*b*) an offence under section 42 above;

(*c*) an offence under any provision of this Act other than section 42 above consisting of or including acts or omissions which would also constitute an offence under section 42 above;

and for the purposes of this definition—

"comparable foreign offence" means an offence under the civil law of any place outside the United Kingdom which is comparable to an offence under the law of England and Wales; and

"local road traffic offence" means an offence under the civil law of any place outside the United Kingdom relating to road traffic.

(4) A financial penalty enforcement order shall contain a certificate issued on behalf of the Defence Council or by an officer authorised by them and stating—

(*a*) that a financial penalty has been awarded against the person named in the order;

(*b*) that the conditions specified in paragraphs (*b*) to (*f*) of subsection (1) above are satisfied;

(*c*) the nature and amount of the penalty;

(*d*) the date on which and the offence or offences in respect of which it was awarded;

(*e*) if it was awarded against the person named in the order as the parent or guardian of some other person, the fact that it was so awarded and the name of that other person;

(*f*) sufficient particulars of the case (including particulars of any offences taken into consideration at the trial);

(*g*) the date of any payment or recovery of a sum on account of the penalty;

(*h*) the sum outstanding; and

(*j*) the authority to whom and address to which any stoppages or compensation included in the penalty will fall, on recovery, to be remitted under subsection (7) below.

(5) A document purporting to be a financial penalty enforcement order and to be signed on behalf of the Defence Council or by an officer authorised by them shall be deemed to be such an order unless the contrary is proved, and a certificate under subsection (4) above shall be evidence of the matters stated.

(6) Subject to subsection (7) below, upon registration of a financial penalty enforcement order—

(*a*) service enforcement procedures shall cease to be available for the recovery of the sum certified as outstanding, and

(*b*) that sum shall be treated for all purposes as if it had been a fine imposed upon a conviction by the relevant court.

(7) Stoppages or compensation recovered under this section shall be remitted to the authority at the address specified in the certificate under subsection (4) above.

(8) Where it appears from a financial penalty enforcement order that the penalty was imposed in respect of more than one offence, it shall be deemed for the purposes of enforcement to be a single penalty only.

(9) Where—

(*a*) a financial penalty enforcement order has been made against any person, and

(*b*) he ceases to be a person to whom this section applies at a time when the whole or any part of the certified sum is still outstanding,

service enforcement procedures shall apply to the amount outstanding as if it were a sum payable by way of a fine imposed by a civil court.

(10) In this section—

"financial penalty" means—

(*a*) a fine, including a fine imposed by virtue of paragraph 13 of Schedule 4A below;

(*b*) stoppages;

(*c*) a compensation order imposed by virtue of paragraph 11 or 13 of Schedule 4A below;

"the relevant court" means—

(*a*) the magistrates' court in England or Wales,

(*b*) the sheriff court in Scotland, or

(*c*) the court of summary jurisdiction in Northern Ireland,

within whose jurisdiction the person against whom a financial penalty enforcement order is made appears to the Defence Council or an officer authorised by them to reside or to be likely to reside;

"service enforcement procedures" means any procedure available by virtue of any of the following enactments, namely—

(*a*) section 128A and section 128B above; and

(*b*) sections 144, 146 and 209(4) and (4A) of the Army Act 1955 and the Air Force Act 1955;

"stoppages" has the meaning assigned to it by section 43(1) (*l*) above except that it does not include sums awarded by virtue of section 128C above.

(11) Where a fine has been awarded together with stoppages or a compensation order, this section shall have effect in relation to the fine and to the stoppages or compensation order as if they were separate penalties.
[Naval Discipline Act 1957, s 128F, as inserted by the Armed Forces Act 1976, Sch 8 and amended by the Armed Forces Act 1986, Schs 1 and 2 and SI 1998/3086.]

8–2267　128G. Avoidance of assignment of or charge on naval pay and pensions etc.
(1) Every assignment of or charge on, and every agreement to assign or charge, any pay, pensions, bounty, grants or other allowances in the nature thereof payable to any person in respect of his or any other person's service in Her Majesty's naval forces shall be void.

(2) Save as expressly provided by this Act, no order shall be made by any court the effect of which would be to restrain any person from receiving anything which by virtue of this section he is precluded from assigning and to direct payment thereof to another person.

(3) Nothing in this section—

(*a*) shall apply to the making or variation of attachment of earnings orders; or
(*b*) shall prejudice any enactment providing for the payment of any sum to a bankrupt's trustee in bankruptcy for distribution among creditors.

(4) *Northern Ireland.*
[Naval Discipline Act 1957, s 128G, as inserted by the Armed Forces Act 1991, s 16.]

8–2268　129. Jurisdiction of civil courts.
(1) Where a person subject to this Act is acquitted or convicted of an offence on trial by a court-martial, or on summary trial under s 52D of this Act or has had an offence committed by him taken into consideration by a court-martial in sentencing him, a civil court shall be debarred from trying him subsequently for the same, or substantially the same, offence; but except as aforesaid nothing in this Act shall be construed as restricting the jurisdiction of any civil court to try a person subject to this Act for any offence.

(2) Where a person subject to this Act is acquitted or convicted of an offence on trial by a civil court wherever situated or has had an offence committed by him taken into consideration when being sentenced by a civil court in the United Kingdom, he shall not subsequently be tried under this Act for the same, or substantially the same, offence . . .
[Naval Discipline Act 1957, s 129, as amended by Armed Forces Act 1966, s 35, the Armed Forces Act 1971, s 55, the Armed Forces Act 1991, Sch 3, the Armed Forces Act 1996, Sch 1 and the Armed Forces Act 2001, s 38.]

8–2269　129B. Proof of outcome of civil trial.
(1) Where a person subject to this Act has been tried before a civil court (whether at the time of the trial he was subject to this Act or not), a certificate signed by the proper officer of the court stating all or any of the following matters—

(*a*) that the said person has been tried before the court for the offences specified in that certificate,
(*b*) the result of the trial,
(*c*) what judgment or order was given or made by the court,
(*d*) that other offences specified in the certificate were taken into consideration at the trial,

shall for the purposes of this Act be evidence of the matters stated in the certificate.

(2) The proper officer of the court shall, if required by the commanding officer of the person in question or any other officer, furnish a certificate under this section, and shall be paid such fee as may be prescribed by regulations made by a Secretary of State.

(3) A document purporting to be a certificate under this section and to be signed by the proper officer of the court shall, unless the contrary is shown, be deemed to be such a certificate.

(4) In this section "proper officer" means—

(*a*) in relation to a court of summary jurisdiction in England and Wales, the justices' chief executive for the court; and
(*b*) in relation to any other court, the clerk of the court, his deputy or any other person having the custody of the records of the court.
[Naval Discipline Act 1957, s 129B, as added by the Armed Forces Act 1971, s 57 and amended by the Access to Justice Act 1999, Sch 13.]

Manœuvres Act 1958
(7 Eliz 2 c 7)

8–2282　3. Powers to close highways.
(1) Where, in the case of, or of any part of, any highway which is a trunk road or a special road within the meaning of the Special Roads Act 1949[1], or which is repairable by the inhabitants at large, being a highway or part situated within the manœuvres area[2], an application for the purpose is made by a person authorised in that behalf by the Secretary of State, and not less than seven days' notice of the intention to make the application has been published in

one or more newspapers circulating generally in the district in question, two or more justices of the peace sitting in petty sessions in the petty sessions area within which that highway or part of a highway is situated may, if they think fit, by order—

   (a)   subject to such terms and conditions as may be required by the justices for the protection of individuals or of the public or of public bodies, suspend for any part of the manœuvres period[3] not exceeding twelve hours, or

   (b)   authorise any officer in command of the authorised forces[4], or any part thereof, being a general or field officer or an officer of corresponding naval or air force rank, to make an order suspending for a time not exceeding six hours in any one day of the said period,

any right of way over that highway or that part of a highway.

   (2) In the case of any other highway or part of a highway, being a highway or part situated within the manœuvres area[2], two justices of the peace[5] may, if they think fit, on the application of a person authorised in that behalf by the Secretary of State, by order—

   (a)   suspend for any part of the manœuvres period[5] not exceeding forty-eight hours, or

   (b)   authorise any such officer as aforesaid to make an order suspending for a time not exceeding six hours in any one day of the said period,

any right of way over that highway or part of a highway, being a highway or part within the jurisdiction of those justices.

   (3) The officer directing the manœuvres shall cause such public notice of any order made under paragraph (a) of either of the two foregoing subsections as the justices may require to be given not less than twelve hours before the order comes into force, and provide for the giving of all reasonable facilities for traffic whilst the order is in force; and any officer making an order by virtue of paragraph (b) of either of the two foregoing subsections shall take such steps as in the circumstances he may consider practicable for giving publicity to his intention to make that order and shall give all reasonable facilities for traffic whilst that order is in force.

   (4) The justices acting for the purposes of this section shall not be persons belonging to the authorised forces.

   (5) *Application to Scotland.*

[Manœuvres Act 1958, s 3.]

---

   1. Repealed by the Statute Law (Repeals) Act 1989, Sch 1.
   2. A "manœuvres area" is authorised by Order in Council made in accordance with s 1 of the Act.
   3. A "manœuvres period" shall not exceed three months as specified in an Order in Council made under s 1 of the Act.
   4. "Authorised forces" means persons taking part with the authority of Her Majesty in the manœuvres authorised by Order in Council made in accordance with s 1 of the Act.
   5. This apparently does not require that the justices shall be sitting in petty sessions: cf. the reference to justices of the peace in sub-s (1), supra.
   5. See note 2, ante.

8–2283   8. Offences.   (1) If, within a manœuvres area and during a manœuvres period, any person—(a) wilfully and unlawfully obstructs or interferes with the execution of the manœuvres; or (b) without due authority enters or remains in any camp, he shall be liable on summary conviction to a fine not exceeding **level 1** on the standard scale, and he and any animal or vehicle or other property under his charge may be removed by any constable, or by, or by order of, any commissioned officer of the authorised forces.

   (2) If, within the area and during the period aforesaid, any person—(a) without due authority moves any flag or other mark distinguishing for the purpose of the manœuvres any lands; or (b) maliciously cuts or damages any telegraph wire laid down by or for the use of the authorised forces, or (c) erects or displays any notice or mark on or relating to any land or source of water within the manœuvres area representing or implying that the use of that land or source is not authorised, other than a notice or mark indicating a restriction imposed by or under this Act, he shall be liable on summary conviction to a fine not exceeding **level 1** on the standard scale.

[Manœuvres Act 1958, s 8, as amended by the Criminal Law Act 1977, s 31 and the Criminal Justice Act 1982, s 46.]

Reserve Forces (Safeguard of Employment) Act 1985

(1985 c 17)

8–2327   This Act provides that where a person returns to civil employment after a period of whole-time service as a member of reserve or auxiliary forces, he shall be reinstated; an application may be made to a Reinstatement Committee if he is not; failure to obey an order of a Committee is punishable on summary conviction by a fine not exceeding level 3 on the standard scale together with compensation not exceeding the amount of the remuneration which the person would have been entitled to receive from his former employer if there had been compliance with the order and the obligation as to subsequent employment (summarised).

Arms Control and Disarmament (Inspections) Act 1991

(1991 c 41)

Preliminary

8–2328 1. Interpretation etc.   (1) In this Act "the Protocol" means the Protocol on Inspection incorporated in the Treaty on Conventional Armed Forces in Europe signed in Paris on 19th November 1990.★

(2) In this Act—

(a) "challenge inspection" means an inspection conducted pursuant to Section VIII of the Protocol (challenge inspections within specified areas);★

(b) "inspector" has the meaning given by Section I of the Protocol (definitions); and

(c) (subject to subsection (3) below) "escort team", "inspection team" and "specified area" shall be construed, in relation to any challenge inspection★, in accordance with that Section.

(3) In this Act—

(a) any reference to an escort team includes a reference to an escort team in which any liaison officer is included pursuant to paragraph 2 of Section V of the Protocol (procedures upon arrival at point of entry and exit); and

(b) any reference to an inspection team includes a reference to an inspection team in which any inspector is included pursuant to paragraph 1 of★ Section VI of the Protocol (general rules for conducting inspections).

(4) For ease of reference the following provisions[1] of the Protocol are set out in the Schedule to this Act, namely—

(a)   certain definitions contained in Section I; and

(b)   Section VI.★

[Arms Control and Disarmament (Inspections) Act 1991, s 1.]

★Subsections (1) and (4), and words in sub-ss (2) and (3) substituted by the Arms Control and Disarmament (Inspections) Act 2003, Sch 1, from a date to be appointed.
  1. These provisions of the Protocol are not printed in this work.

Challenge inspections

8–2329 2. Rights of entry etc for purposes of challenge inspections under★ the Protocol.
(1) Where a request to conduct a challenge inspection within any specified area★ in the United Kingdom—

(a)   has been made under the Protocol, and

(b)   has been granted by Her Majesty's Government in the United Kingdom,

the Secretary of State may issue an authorisation under this section in respect of that inspection.★

(2) An authorisation under this section shall contain a description of the specified area★ and state the names of the members of the inspection team by whom the inspection is to be carried out.

(3) Such an authorisation shall have the effect of authorising the inspection team—

(a)   to exercise within the specified area★ such rights of access, entry and unobstructed inspection as are conferred on them by Section VI[1] of the Protocol, and

(b)   to do such other things within that area in connection with the conduct of the inspection as they are entitled to do by virtue of that Section.

(4) Such an authorisation shall in addition have the effect of—

(a)   authorising an escort team to accompany the inspection team at all times, and

(b)   authorising any constable to give such assistance as the person in command of the escort team may request for the purpose of facilitating the conduct of the inspection in accordance with Section VI[1] of the Protocol;

and the name of the person in command of the escort team shall be stated in the authorisation.

(5) Where the inspection team is divided into sub-teams in accordance with paragraph 2★ of Section VI of the Protocol—

(a)   subsection (3) shall apply to each of the sub-teams as it applies to the inspection team as a whole, and

(b)   subsection (4)(a) shall be construed as authorising members of the escort team to accompany each of the sub-teams.

(6) Any constable giving assistance in accordance with subsection (4)(b) may use such reasonable force as he considers necessary for the purpose mentioned in that provision.

(7) The occupier of any premises—

(a)   in relation to which it is proposed to exercise a right of entry in reliance on an authorisation under this section, or

(b)   on which an inspection is being carried out in reliance on such an authorisation, or a person acting on behalf of the occupier of any such premises, shall be entitled to require a copy of the authorisation to be shown to him by a member of the escort team.

(8) The validity of any authorisation purporting to be issued under this section in respect of any challenge* inspection shall not be called in question in any court of law at any time before the conclusion of that inspection; and accordingly no proceedings (of whatever nature) shall be brought at any time before the conclusion of any challenge inspection if they would, if successful, have the effect of preventing, delaying or otherwise affecting the carrying out of any such inspection.

(9) If in any proceedings any question arises whether a person at any time was or was not, in relation to any challenge* inspection, a member of the inspection team or (as the case may be) a member of the escort team, a certificate issued by or under the authority of the Secretary of State stating any fact relating to that question shall be conclusive evidence of that fact.

[Arms Control and Disarmament (Inspections) Act 1991, s 2.]

---

*New sub-s (1A) inserted, words in sub-ss (1), (2), (3) and (5) substituted and words in (8) and (9) repealed by the Arms Control and Disarmament (Inspections) Act 2003, Sch 1, from a date to be appointed.

1. These provisions of the Protocol are not printed in this work.

8–2330   3. Offences.   (1) Where an authorisation has been issued under section 2 in respect of any challenge* inspection, any person who—

(*a*)   refuses to comply with any request made by any constable for the purpose of facilitating the conduct of that inspection in accordance with Section VI[1] of the Protocol, or

(*b*)   wilfully obstructs any member of the inspection team or of the escort team in the conduct of that inspection in accordance with that Section,

shall be guilty of an offence and liable on summary conviction to a fine not exceeding the **third level** on the standard scale.

(2) Where an offence under this section is committed by a body corporate and is proved to have been committed with the consent or connivance of any director, manager, secretary or other similar officer of the body corporate, or any person who was purporting to act in any such capacity, he as well as the body corporate shall be guilty of that offence and shall be liable to be proceeded against and punished accordingly.

In relation to a body corporate whose affairs are managed by its members, "director" means a member of the body corporate.

(3) *Scotland.*

[Arms Control and Disarmament (Inspections) Act 1991, s 3.]

---

*Word repealed by the Arms Control and Disarmament (Inspections) Act 2003, Sch 1, from a date to be appointed.

1. These provisions of the Protocol are not printed in this work.

8–2331   4. Exercise of powers in relation to Crown land in private occupation.   (1) The powers exercisable in the case of any authorisation by virtue of section 2 shall be exercisable in relation to any Crown land only to the extent that it is land which any person is entitled to occupy by virtue of a private interest (whether it is an interest in land or arises under a licence).

(2) In subsection (1)—

"Crown land" means land in which there is a Crown interest or a Duchy interest; and

"private interest" means an interest which is neither a Crown interest nor a Duchy interest;

and for this purpose—

"Crown interest" means in interest—

(*a*)   belonging to Her Majesty in right of the Crown (including the Crown in right of Her Majesty's Government in Northern Ireland), or

(*b*)   belonging to a government department or Northern Ireland department,

or an interest held in trust for Her Majesty for the purposes of any such department; and

"Duchy interest" means an interest belonging to Her Majesty in right of the Duchy of Lancaster or belonging to the Duchy of Cornwall.

[Arms Control and Disarmament (Inspections) Act 1991, s 4.]

Privileges and immunities

8–2332   5. *Privileges and immunities of inspectors and transport crew members in connection with inspections under the Protocol.*

Supplementary

8–2333   6. Short title, commencement and extent.   (1) This Act may be cited as the Arms Control and Disarmament (Inspections) Act 1991.

(2) Except for this section, this Act shall come into force on such day as the Secretary of State may appoint by order[1] made by statutory instrument.

(3) This Act extends to Northern Ireland.

(4) Her Majesty may by Order in Council provide for this Act to extend to any of the following territories, namely—

(a) the Isle of Man,
(b) any of the Channel Islands,
(c) Gibraltar, or
(d) the Sovereign Base Areas of Akrotiri and Dhekelia (that is to say, the areas mentioned in section 2(1) of the Cyprus Act 1960),

with such modifications as appear to Her Majesty to be appropriate.

[Arms Control and Disarmament (Inspections) Act 1991, s 6.]

---

1. Sections 1–5 of this Act were brought into force on 17 July 1992 (SI 1992/1750).

Reserve Forces Act 1996
(1996 c 14)

PART I[1]
THE RESERVE FORCES
Regulation and organisation

8–2340   **4.** *Orders and regulations concerning the reserve forces*

---

1. Part I comprises ss 1–8.

PART VIII[1]
SCHEMES FOR EXEMPTIONS AND FINANCIAL ASSISTANCE
Individual exemptions etc. from call out or recall

8–2341   **78. Individual exemptions etc from call out.**   (1) The Secretary of State may by regulations[2] make provision enabling a person liable to be called out, or any employer of such a person, to apply for any deferral, revocation, entitlement to release or exemption which, under the regulations, may be granted to the person by or in respect of whom such an application is made.

(2)–(4) *Further provisions as to regulations.*

[Reserve Forces Act 1996, s 78.]

---

1. Part VIII comprises s 78–87.
2. The Reserve Forces (Call-out and Recall) (Exemptions etc) Regulations 1997, SI 1997/307 have been made.

8–2342   **79. Individual exemptions etc from recall.**   (1) The Secretary of State may by regulations[2] make provision enabling any person liable to be recalled, or any employer of such a person, to apply for any deferral, revocation, entitlement to release or discharge or exemption which, under the regulations, may be granted to the person by or in respect of whom such an application is made.

(2)–(5) *Further provisions as to regulations.*

[Reserve Forces Act 1996, s 79.]

---

1. The Reserve Forces (Call-out and Recall) (Exemptions etc) Regulations 1997, SI 1997/307 have been made.

8–2343   **82. Offences in connection with regulations under s 78 or 79.**   (1) Any person who fails without reasonable excuse to provide information in connection with the lapse of a deferral, entitlement to be released or discharged or an exemption, which he is required to provide under regulations under section 78 or 79 is guilty of an offence and liable, on summary conviction, to imprisonment for a term not exceeding **3 months** or a fine not exceeding **level 4** on the standard scale (**or both**).

(2) Any person who—

(a) in connection with an application under regulations under section 78 or 79 or
(b) in connection with the lapse of a deferral, determination of entitlement to release or discharge or an exemption granted under those regulations,

knowingly or recklessly provides information which is false or misleading in a material particular is guilty of an offence and liable, on summary conviction, to imprisonment for a term not exceeding **6 months** or a fine not exceeding **level 5** on the standard scale (**or both**).

[Reserve Forces Act 1996, s 82.]

PART IX[1]
RESERVE FORCES APPEAL TRIBUNALS

8–2344 **88–89.** *Reserve Forces Appeal Tribunals may hear appeals in respect of determinations under regulations under ss 78, 79, 83 or 84.*

---

1. Part IX comprises ss 88–94.

8–2345 **94. Offences in connection with appeals.** (1) Any person who, in connection with an appeal to an appeal tribunal, knowingly or recklessly provides information which is false or misleading in a material particular is guilty of an offence.

(2) Any person who without reasonable excuse—

(a) fails to provide information in connection with an appeal to an appeal tribunal which he is required to provide by rules under section 93; or

(b) fails to attend an appeal tribunal when required to do so by rules under that section,

is guilty of an offence.

(3) Any person guilty of an offence under this section is liable on summary conviction to imprisonment for a term not exceeding **6 months** or a fine not exceeding **level 5** on the standard scale (**or both**).

[Reserve Forces Act 1996, s 94.]

PART X[1]
GENERAL OFFENCES
Offences against good order and discipline

8–2346 **95. Offences against orders and regulations under s 4.** (1) A member of a reserve force who—

(a) when required by or in pursuance of orders or regulations under section 4 to attend at any place, fails without reasonable excuse to attend in accordance with the requirement;

(b) uses threatening or insulting language or behaves in an insubordinate manner to any officer, warrant officer, non-commissioned officer or petty officer who in pursuance of orders or regulations under section 4 is acting in the execution of his office, and who would be the superior officer of the offender if he were subject to service law;

(c) by any fraudulent means obtains or is an accessory to the obtaining of any pay or other sum contrary to orders or regulations under section 4;

(d) knowingly or recklessly makes a statement false in any material particular in giving any information required by orders or regulations under section 4; or

(e) fails without reasonable excuse to comply with orders or regulations under section 4,

is guilty of an offence triable by court-martial or summarily by a civil court.

(2) A person guilty of an offence under this section is liable—

(a) on conviction by court-martial to suffer imprisonment, or such less punishment provided for by service law;

(b) on summary conviction by a civil court—

(i) in the case of an offence under subsection (1)(a), (b), or (e), to a fine not exceeding **level 3** on the standard scale; and

(ii) in the case of an offence under subsection (1)(c) or (d), to imprisonment for a term not exceeding **6 months** or a fine not exceeding **level 5** on the standard scale (**or both**).

(3) A person convicted of an offence under this section is liable, if sentenced to a term of imprisonment or if such a term is imposed in default of payment of any fine, to be taken into military custody, air-force custody or naval custody (as the case may be).

[Reserve Forces Act 1996, s 95.]

---

1. Part X comprises ss 95–109.

Desertion and absence without leave from service, duty or training

8–2347 **96. Failure to attend for service on call out or recall.** (1) A member of a reserve force served with a call-out notice under any provision of this Act who, without leave lawfully granted or reasonable excuse—

(a) fails to present himself for service at the time and place specified in the call-out notice under section 32(3)(b), 43(4)(b) or 58(3)(c) (as the case may be);

(b) having so presented himself, fails to remain there until accepted into service or informed that he is not to be accepted into service in pursuance of that notice; or

(c) where he has for any reason failed to present himself at the time and place so specified or to remain there, fails—

    (i) to present himself to a person specified in the call-out notice or to any other authorised officer; or

    (ii) having so presented himself, to remain until accepted into service or informed that he is not to be accepted into service in pursuance of that notice,

is guilty, according to the circumstances, of desertion or absence without leave.

    (2) Subsection (1) applies to a person liable to recall as it applies to a member of a reserve force—

    (*a*) with the substitution for references to a call-out notice of references to a recall notice; and

    (*b*) as if paragraph (*a*) of that subsection referred to the time and place specified in the recall notice under section 70(3)(*c*).

    (3) An offence under this section is triable by court-martial or summarily by a civil court.

[Reserve Forces Act 1996, s 96.]

8–2348 97. Failure to attend for duty or training. (1) A member of a reserve force who has entered into a full-time service commitment or an additional duties commitment and, without leave lawfully granted or reasonable excuse, fails to appear at the time and place at which he is required to attend—

    (*a*) in the case of a full-time service commitment, to begin the period of full-time service contemplated by the commitment;

    (*b*) in the case of an additional duties commitment, to begin a period of service under the commitment,

is guilty, according to the circumstances, of desertion or absence without leave.

    (2) A member of a reserve force who—

    (*a*) is required to undergo a period of training in accordance with section 22, a special agreement or an employee agreement (or any other requirement applicable to special members), and

    (*b*) fails, without leave lawfully granted or reasonable excuse, to appear at any time and place at which he is required to attend,

is guilty of absence without leave.

    (3) An offence under this section is triable by court-martial or summarily by a civil court.

[Reserve Forces Act 1996, s 97.]

8–2349 98. Punishment etc of offences of desertion or absence without leave. (1) An offence under section 37 or 38 of the Army Act 1955 or the Air Force Act 1955 or section 16 or 17 of the Naval Discipline Act 1957 (offences under service law of desertion or absence without leave) committed by a member of a reserve force is triable summarily by a civil court as well as by court-martial.

    (2) A member of a reserve force convicted by court-martial of an offence under section 96(1) or 97(1) is punishable as for an offence under service law of desertion or absence without leave (as the case may be).

    (3) A member of a reserve force convicted by a civil court of—

    (*a*) an offence under section 96(1) or 97(1), or

    (*b*) an offence under service law of desertion or absence without leave,

is liable to imprisonment for a term not exceeding **6 months** or a fine not exceeding **level 5** on the standard scale (**or both**).

    (4) A person convicted of an offence under section 97(2) is liable—

    (*a*) if convicted by court-martial, to the same punishment as for an offence under service law of absence without leave;

    (*b*) if convicted by a civil court, to imprisonment for a term not exceeding **6 months** or a fine not exceeding **level 5** on the standard scale (**or both**).

    (5) A person convicted by a civil court of an offence mentioned in this section, if sentenced to a term of imprisonment or if such a term is imposed in default of payment of any fine, is liable to be taken into military, air-force or naval custody (as the case may require).

    (6) Where a member of a reserve force or a person liable to recall is convicted of an offence of desertion, the time which elapsed between the time of his desertion and the time of his apprehension or voluntary surrender shall not be taken into account in reckoning his service for the purpose of release from permanent service or discharge.

[Reserve Forces Act 1996, s 98.]

8–2350 99. False pretence of illegal absence. (1) Any person who falsely represents himself to be a deserter or absentee without leave from any reserve force is guilty of an offence and liable on summary conviction to imprisonment for a term not exceeding **3 months** or a fine not exceeding **level 4** on the standard scale (**or both**).

[Reserve Forces Act 1996, s 99.]

8–2351   **100. Treatment of deserters etc.**   (1) Schedule 2 (arrest and subsequent treatment of suspected deserters or absentees without leave from the reserve forces) shall have effect.

(2) Schedule 2 shall apply to a person liable to recall who is a suspected deserter or absentee without leave by virtue of this Part and is not otherwise subject to service law as it applies to a member of a reserve force.

(3) The delivery under that Schedule of a member of a reserve force or a person liable to recall into military, air-force or naval custody, or the committal of any such person for the purpose of being so delivered, shall not prevent his subsequently being tried summarily in accordance with this Part.

[Reserve Forces Act 1996, s 100.]

8–2352   **101. Inducing a person to desert or absent himself.**   (1) A person who, in the United Kingdom or elsewhere, by any means—

(a)   procures or persuades, or attempts to procure or persuade, a member of a reserve force to commit an offence of desertion or absence without leave;

(b)   knowing that a member of a reserve force is about to commit such an offence, aids or assists him in so doing; or

(c)   knowing a member of a reserve force to be a deserter or an absentee without leave, procures or persuades or assists him to remain a deserter or absentee, or assists in his rescue from custody,

is guilty of an offence.

(2) A person who—

(a)   procures or persuades, or attempts to procure or persuade, a person liable to recall to commit an offence of desertion or absence without leave;

(b)   knowing that such a person is about to commit such an offence, aids or assists him in so doing; or

(c)   knowing a person liable to recall to be a deserter or absentee without leave, procures or persuades or assists him to remain a deserter or absentee, or assists in his rescue from custody,

is guilty of an offence.

(3) A person guilty of an offence under subsection (1) or (2) is liable on summary conviction—

(a)   in the case of an offence involving an offence of desertion or a deserter, to imprisonment for a term not exceeding **6 months** or a fine not exceeding **level 5** on the standard scale (**or both**) and

(b)   in the case of an offence of absence without leave or an absentee without leave, to a fine not exceeding **level 5** on the standard scale.

[Reserve Forces Act 1980, s 101.]

8–2353   **102.** *Record of illegal absence.*

General

8–2354   **103.** *Trial of offences as offences under service law.*

8–2355   **104. Jurisdiction of civil courts.**   (1) A civil court in the United Kingdom with jurisdiction in the place where a person is for the time being shall have jurisdiction to try him for any offence under this Part which is triable by such a court.

(2) Subsection (1) applies notwithstanding that the alleged offence was committed outside the jurisdiction of the court, except that where it was committed in any part of the United Kingdom it shall be triable only by a court in that part of the United Kingdom.

(3) Every fine imposed under this Part by a court-martial shall be paid to such authority as may be prescribed.

[Reserve Forces Act 1996, s 104.]

8–2356   **105. Trial of offences by civil court.**   (1) Any offence to which this section applies which is triable by a court-martial is also triable summarily by a civil court and punishable with imprisonment for a term not exceeding **3 months** or a fine not exceeding **level 4** on the standard scale (**or both**).

(2) Nothing in this section affects the liability of a person charged with an offence to which this section applies to be taken into military, air-force or naval custody.

(3) This section applies to an offence under service law (other than an offence of desertion or absence without leave) committed by a member of a reserve force when not in permanent service under Part IV or Part V or under a call-out order.

[Reserve Forces Act 1996, s 105.]

8–2357   **106. Offences triable by court-martial or civil court.**   (1) A person charged with an offence which under this Part is triable both by a court-martial and by a civil court may be tried either by a court-martial (or by an officer having power to deal summarily with the case) or by a civil court but not by both of them.

(2) It is immaterial, for the purposes of any provision of this Part making an offence triable by court-martial, whether the person concerned is otherwise subject to service law.
[Reserve Forces Act 1996, s 106.]

8–2358 107. Time for institution of proceedings. (1) Proceedings against a person before either—

(a) a court-martial or an officer having power to deal with the case summarily; or
(b) a civil court,

in respect of an offence under this Act or under service law and alleged to have been committed by him during his period of service in a reserve force may be instituted whether or not he has ceased to be a member of that reserve force.

(2) Such proceedings may, notwithstanding anything in any other enactment, be instituted at any time within 2 months after—

(a) the time at which the offence becomes known to his commanding officer; or
(b) the time at which he is apprehended.

whichever is later.
[Reserve Forces Act 1996, s 107.]

8–2359 108. Evidence. (1) Schedule 3 (evidence) shall have effect in relation to proceedings under this Part and any other proceedings for an offence under any other Part of this Act.

(2) Paragraphs 2 to 8 of that Schedule apply to a member of a reserve force who is tried by a civil court, whether or not he is at the time of the trial subject to service law.

(3) Where by virtue of any provision of this Act a document is admissible in evidence or is evidence of any matter stated in it in proceedings before a civil court in England and Wales, it shall be sufficient evidence of the matter so stated in such proceedings in Scotland.
[Reserve Forces Act 1980, s 108.]

8–2360 109. Meaning of "civil court". In this Part a reference to a civil court shall be construed as a reference—

(a) in England and Wales, to a magistrates' court;
(b) Scotland;
(c) Northern Ireland.
[Reserve Forces Act 1996, s 109.]

PART XII[1]
MISCELLANEOUS AND GENERAL

Miscellaneous

8–2361 125. Absence for voting. No member of a reserve force shall be liable, when not in permanent service, to any penalty or punishment on account of his absence from duty in the United Kingdom for voting at—

(a) any election of a Member of Parliament, a Member of the Scottish Parliament, a Member of the National Assembly for Wales, a Member of the Northern Ireland Assembly or a Member of the European Parliament, or
(b) any local election,

or going to or returning from such voting.
[Reserve Forces Act 1996, s 125, as amended by SI 1999/787 and the Armed Forces Act 2001, Sch 6.]

---

1. Part XII comprises ss 120–132.

General

8–2362 127. Interpretation. (1) In this Act—

"additional duties commitment" means a commitment under section 25;
"call-out order" has the meaning given by section 64;
"the ex-regular reserve forces" has the meaning given by section 2(2);
"full-time service commitment" means a commitment under section 24;
"man" (except in Part VII) has the meaning given by section 2(4);
"prescribed" means (except in Part VII) prescribed by orders or regulations under section 4;
"recall" and "recall order" have the meanings given by section 77;
"regular air force" has the same meaning as in the Air Force Act 1955;
"regular army" means the regular forces within the meaning of the Army Act 1955 (but does not include the Royal Marines);
"regular services" means the Royal Navy, the Royal Marines, the regular army or the regular air force;

"the reserve forces", "the reserve naval and marine forces", "the reserve land forces" and "the reserve air forces" have the meaning given by section 1(2);

"reserve marine force" means the Royal Marines Reserve;

"service law" means military law, air-force law or the Naval Discipline Act 1957 (as the case may require);

"special member" means a member of a reserve force who is, by virtue of Part V, a special member of that force;

"term of compulsory service" has the meaning given by section 13(7);

"the volunteer reserve forces" has the meaning given by section 2(3).

(2) Any reference in this Act to a member of a reserve force or a member of the reserve forces is to an officer in, or a man of, that force or any of those forces, as the case may be.
[Reserve Forces Act 1996, s 127.]

8–2363   **128.** *Transitory provisions.*

8–2364   **129.** *Application of Act to persons currently serving in the reserve forces or regular services.*

8–2365   **130.** *Power to make transitional, consequential etc. provisions.*

8–2366   **131.** *Consequential amendments and repeals.*

8–2367   **132. Short title, extent and commencement.**   (1) This Act may be cited as the Reserve Forces Act 1996.

(2) This Act extends to Northern Ireland.

(3) Her Majesty may by Order in Council direct that any of the provisions of this Act shall extend, with such exceptions and modifications as appear to Her Majesty to be appropriate, to the Channel Islands and the Isle of Man.

(4) This Act shall come into force on such day as the Secretary of State may by order made by statutory instrument appoint; and different days may be appointed for different purposes.[1]
[Reserve Forces Act 1996, s 132, as amended by SI 1998/3086.]

---

1. The entire Act was brought into force (with the exception of repeals of the Reserve Forces Act 1980 in Sch 11) by the Reserve Forces Act 1996 (Commencement No 1) Order 1997, SI 1997/305.

SCHEDULES
SCHEDULE 1
ENLISTMENT

False answers in attestation papers

8–2368   **5.** (1) Any person appearing before an enlisting officer for the purpose of being attested who knowingly or recklessly makes a false answer to any question contained in the attestation paper and put to him by or by the direction of the enlisting officer is guilty of an offence.

(2) A person guilty of an offence under sub-paragraph (1) is liable on summary conviction to imprisonment for a term not exceeding **3 months** or a fine not exceeding **level 4** on the standard scale (**or both**); and he may be proceeded against summarily notwithstanding that he has since become subject to service law.

(3) A person guilty of an offence under sub-paragraph (1) who has since become and remains subject to service law is liable on conviction by court-martial to imprisonment for a term not exceeding 3 months or to any less punishment provided by service law.

Evidence as to attestation papers

8–2369   **6.** (1) With respect to evidence in proceedings under Part X, whether before a court-martial, a civil court or otherwise—

(a) a document purporting—

(i) to be a copy of the attestation paper signed by any person; and

(ii) to be certified to be a true copy by a person stated in the certificate to have the custody of the attestation paper,

shall be evidence of the enlistment of the person attested; and

(b) the attestation paper purporting to be signed by a person on his enlistment shall be evidence of his having given the answers to questions which he is recorded in that paper as having given.

(2) In this paragraph "civil court" has the same meaning as in Part X.

Meaning of "appropriate minimum age"

8–2370   **7.** In this Schedule "appropriate minimum age" means the age of 17 years and 6 months, except that in such classes of case as may be prescribed it means the age of 17 years.

Section 100

SCHEDULE 2
Deserters and Absentees Without Leave

(As amended by the Armed Forces Discipline Act 2000, s 9).

Preliminary

8–2371   **1.** (1) This Schedule applies in relation to anyone who is, or is suspected of being, a deserter or absentee without leave from a reserve force.

(2) *Scotland and Northern Ireland.*

Arrest

8–2372   **2.** (1) Where a constable has reasonable grounds for suspecting that a person is a member of a reserve force who has deserted or is absent without leave, he may arrest that person without a warrant.

(2) Where no constable is available, any person may arrest a person he has reasonable grounds for suspecting is a member of a reserve force who has deserted or is absent without leave.

(3) Any person having authority to issue a warrant for the arrest of a person charged with a criminal offence, if satisfied by evidence on oath that there is, or is reasonably suspected of being, within his jurisdiction a member of a reserve force who—

(*a*)   has deserted or is absent without leave; or

(*b*)   is reasonably suspected of having deserted or being absent without leave,

may issue a warrant authorising his arrest.

(4) Any person arrested as a deserter or absentee without leave from a reserve force shall as soon as practicable be brought before a magistrates' court.

Proceedings before a civil court where persons suspected of illegal absence

8–2373   **3.** (1) Paragraphs 4 and 5 apply in the case of a person ("the accused") who is brought before a magistrates' court and alleged to be a member of a reserve force who has deserted or is absent without leave.

(2) The provisions of the Magistrates' Courts Act 1980—

(*a*)   relating to the constitution and procedure of magistrates' courts acting as examining justices and conferring powers of adjournment and remand on such courts so acting; and

(*b*)   as to evidence and the issue and enforcement of summonses or warrants to secure the attendance of witnesses,

shall apply to proceedings to which paragraph 4 or 5 applies.

(3) In the application of this Schedule to Scotland and Northern Ireland, the reference in sub-paragraph (2) to provisions of the Magistrates' Courts Act 1980 shall be construed as a reference to any corresponding enactment in force as respects courts of summary jurisdiction.

4. (1) This paragraph applies where the accused admits that he is illegally absent from a reserve force and the court is satisfied of the truth of the admission.

(2) If the accused is not in custody for some cause other than illegal absence from his reserve force, the court shall—

(*a*)   cause him to be delivered into military, air-force or naval custody (as the case may require) in such manner as the court may think fit; or

(*b*)   where it is unable to do so, adjourn the proceedings and remand him for such time as appears reasonably necessary for the purpose of arranging for him to be delivered into such custody.

(3) If the accused is in custody for some other cause, the court may act as mentioned in sub-paragraph (2).

(4) Any period specified as mentioned in sub-paragraph (2)(*b*)—

(*a*)   shall not exceed such time as appears to the court reasonably necessary to enable the accused to be delivered into military, air-force or naval custody; and

(*b*)   may be extended by the court from time to time if it appears to the court reasonably necessary to do so for that purpose.

5. (1) This paragraph applies where—

(*a*)   the accused does not admit that he is illegally absent from a reserve force; or

(*b*)   the court is not satisfied of the truth of any such admission.

(2) The court shall consider the evidence with a view to determining whether there is sufficient evidence to justify his being tried under this Act for an offence of desertion or absence without leave.

(3) Where the court considers that there is sufficient evidence to justify his being tried under this Act for an offence of desertion or absence without leave, the court shall (unless he is in custody for some other cause) cause him to be delivered into military, air-force or naval custody (as the case may require) or where it is unable to do so, adjourn the proceedings and remand him for such time as appears reasonably necessary for the purpose of arranging for him to be delivered into such custody.

If the accused is in custody for some other cause, the court may act as mentioned in this paragraph.

(4) If the court does not consider that there is sufficient evidence to justify the trial of the accused for an offence of desertion or absence without leave, he shall be discharged.

Surrender to police

8–2374   **6.** (1) Where a person surrenders himself to a constable as being illegally absent from a reserve force—

(*a*)   the constable shall, unless the person concerned surrenders himself at a police station, bring him to a police station; and

(b) the police officer in charge of the police station to which that person is brought, or at which he surrendered himself, shall forthwith inquire into his case.

(2) If it appears to that police officer that the person concerned is illegally absent from a reserve force, he may—

(a) cause him to be delivered into military, air-force or naval custody (as the case may require) without bringing him before a magistrates' court; or

(b) bring him before a magistrates' court.

Certificates of arrest or surrender

8–2375   7. (1) Where a person is delivered into military, air-force or naval custody under this Schedule, there shall be handed over with him a certificate in such form as may be prescribed signed by a justice of the peace.

(2) The certificate shall contain such particulars as may be prescribed as to the arrest or surrender of the person concerned and the proceedings before the court.

(3) For any such certificate there shall be payable to the proper officer of the court, by such person as the Defence Council may direct, such fee (if any) as may be prescribed.

(3A) In sub-paragraph (3) "proper officer" means—

(a) in relation to a magistrates' court in England and Wales, the justices' chief executive for the court; and

(b) in relation to any other court, the clerk of the court.

(4) In this paragraph and paragraph 8, "prescribed" means prescribed by regulations made by the Secretary of State by statutory instrument under section 189 of the Army Act 1955 (for a person delivered into military custody), section 189 of the Air Force Act 1955 (for a person delivered into air-force custody) or section 110 of the Naval Discipline Act 1957 (for a person delivered into naval custody).

8. (1) Where a person is delivered into military, air force or naval custody under this Schedule without being brought before a court, there shall be handed over with him a certificate in such form as may be prescribed signed by the police officer who caused him to be delivered into custody.

(2) The certificate shall contain such particulars as may be prescribed relating to the surrender of the person concerned.

9. (1) In proceedings for an offence under section 96 a document purporting to be a duly signed certificate under paragraph 7 or 8 shall be evidence of the matters stated in the document.

(2) In proceedings for such an offence against a person who was taken into military, air-force or naval custody on arrest or surrender, a certificate—

(a) purporting to be signed by a provost officer or by any other officer in charge of the guardroom or other place where that person was confined on being taken into custody; and

(b) stating the fact, date, time and place of arrest or surrender,

shall be evidence of the matters stated in the certificate.

Duties of governors of prisons and others to receive deserters and absentees

8–2376   10. (1) It shall be the duty of the governor of a civil prison—

(a) to receive any person duly committed to that prison by a magistrates' court as being illegally absent from a reserve force; and

(b) to detain him until (in accordance with the directions of the court) he is delivered into military, air-force or naval custody.

(2) Sub-paragraph (1) shall apply to the person having charge of any police station or other place (not being a prison) provided for the confinement of persons in custody as it applies to the governor of a prison.

Section 108   SCHEDULE 3
                             EVIDENCE

General provisions as to evidence

8–2377   1. This Schedule has effect with respect to evidence in proceedings under Part X and proceedings for an offence under any other Part of this Act, whether before a court-martial, a civil court or otherwise.

2. A letter, return or other document stating that any person—

(a) was or was not serving at any specified time or during any specified period in any part of Her Majesty's forces or was discharged from any part of those forces at or before any specified time;

(b) held or did not hold at any specified time any specified rank or appointment in any of those forces, or had at or before any specified time been attached, posted or transferred to any part of those forces;

(c) at any specified time or during any specified period was or was not serving or held or did not hold any rank or appointment in any particular country or place; or

(d) was or was not at any specified time authorised to use or wear any decoration, badge, wound stripe or emblem,

shall, if it purports to be issued by or on behalf of the Defence Council or by a person authorised by them, be evidence of the matters stated in the document.

3. (1) A record made in any service book or other document prescribed by Queen's Regulations for the purposes of this paragraph, being a record—

(a) made in pursuance of any Act or of Queen's Regulations, or otherwise in pursuance of military, air-force or naval duty, as the case may be; and

(b) purporting to be signed by the commanding officer or by any person whose duty it was to make the record,

shall be evidence of the facts stated therein.

(2) A copy of a record (including the signature thereto) in any book or other document to which sub-paragraph (1) applies, if it purports to be certified to be a true copy by a person stated in the certificate to have the custody of the book or other document, shall be evidence of the record.

4. A document purporting to be issued by order of the Defence Council and to contain instructions or regulations given or made by the Defence Council shall be evidence of the giving of the instructions or making of the regulations and of their contents.

5. A certificate purporting to be issued by or on behalf of the Defence Council or by a person authorised by them, and stating—

(a) that a decoration of a description specified in or annexed to the certificate is or is not a military, naval or air-force decoration; or

(b) that a badge, wound stripe or emblem of a description specified in or annexed to the certificate is or is not one supplied or authorised by the Defence Council,

shall be evidence of the matters stated in the certificate.

6. A certificate purporting to be signed by a person's commanding officer or any officer authorised by him to give the certificate, and stating the contents of, or of any part of, standing orders or other routine orders of a continuing nature made for—

(a) any formation, unit or body of—

(i) the regular army or any reserve land force;
(ii) the Royal Marines or the Royal Marines Reserve; or
(iii) the regular air force or any reserve air force;

(b) any division, class or other body of the Royal Navy, the Royal Fleet Reserve or the Royal Naval Reserve;
(c) any command or other area, garrison or place; or
(d) any ship, submarine, train or aircraft,

shall in proceedings against the person concerned be evidence of the matters stated in the certificate.

7. Where, in relation to one reserve force, any document would be evidence in any proceedings under Part X by virtue of this Schedule, or paragraph 6 of Schedule 1, that document shall in like manner, subject to the same conditions and for the like purpose be evidence in the like proceedings in relation to any other reserve force.

Proceedings for offences under section 95

8–2378 8. Where a man of any reserve force is required by or in pursuance of orders or regulations under section 4 to attend at any place, a certificate—

(a) purporting to be signed by any officer or person who is mentioned in it as being appointed to be present at that place for the purpose of inspecting men of the force in question or for any other purpose connected with that force; and

(b) stating that the man failed to attend in accordance with that requirement,

shall without proof of the signature or appointment of the officer or person be evidence of the failure in any proceedings relating to such a failure under section 95.

Proof of outcome of civil trial

8–2379 9. (1) Where a person subject to service law has been tried before a civil court (whether at the time of the trial he was or was not subject to service law), a certificate signed by the proper officer of the court and stating all or any of the following matters—

(a) that the person concerned was tried before the court for an offence specified in the certificate;
(b) the result of the trial;
(c) what judgment or order was given or made by the court; and
(d) that other offences specified in the certificate were taken into consideration at the trial,

shall be evidence of the matters stated in the certificate.

(2) The proper officer of the court shall, if required by the commanding officer of the person in question or any other officer, furnish a certificate under this paragraph and shall be paid such fee as may be prescribed by regulations made by the Secretary of State under section 199 of the Army Act 1955, section 199 of the Air Force Act 1955 or section 129B of the Naval Discipline Act 1957, as the case may be.

(3) A document purporting to be a certificate under this paragraph and to be signed by the proper officer of the court shall, unless the contrary is shown, be deemed to be such a certificate.

"(4) In this paragraph "proper officer" means—

(a) in relation to a court of summary jurisdiction in England and Wales, the justices' chief executive for the court; and

(b) in relation to any other court, the clerk of the court, his deputy or any other person having the custody of the records of the court."

Visiting Forces and International Headquarters (Application of Law) Order 1999[1]

(1999/1736 amended by SI 2001/1149)

8–2380 **1. Citation and commencement.** This Order may be cited as the Visiting Forces and International Headquarters (Application of Law) Order 1999 and shall come into force on the day after the date on which it is made.

---

1. Made by Her Majesty in pursuance of s 8 of the Visiting Forces Act 1952 and paragraph 7 of the Schedule to the International Headquarters and Defence Organisations Act 1964.

8–2381   **2. Interpretation.** In this Order—

"military member of a headquarters" shall be construed in accordance with paragraph 1 of the Schedule to the International Headquarters and Defence Organisations Act 1964; and

"service court" means a service court of a country in respect of which section 8 of the Visiting Forces Act 1952 has effect.

8–2382   **3. Visiting forces and headquarters to which the Order applies.**   (1) This Order applies to a visiting force of—

(a)   any country specified in Part I of Schedule 1, or

(b)   any country specified in Part II of that Schedule, where that country has been designated by Order in Council under section 1(2) of the Visiting Forces Act 1952 for the purposes of giving effect to section 8 of that Act with respect to that country.

(2) This Order applies to the headquarters specified in Schedule 2.

8–2383   **4.** *Provision of supplies*

8–2384   **5.** *Exercise of powers by the Secretary of State in relation to land*

8–2385   **6.** *Use of intellectual property rights*

8–2386   **7. Wireless telegraphy, postal service and telecommunication systems.**   (1) The establishment or use of a station for wireless telegraphy, and the installation or use of any apparatus for wireless telegraphy, by—

(a)   a member of a visiting force or any person working in support of such a force, or

(b)   a member of a headquarters,

if done in the course of his duties as such, shall be exempt from the operation of Part I of the Wireless Telegraphy Act 1949 (which provides for the licensing etc of wireless telegraphy).

(2) Section 10 of the Wireless Telegraphy Act 1949 (which is concerned with regulating the radiation of electromagnetic energy from apparatus), and any regulations made thereunder, shall not apply to the use of any apparatus by a member of a visiting force or headquarters, if done in the course of his duties as such.

(3) Section 6 of the Postal Services Act 2000 (which prohibits the conveyance of letteres by a person unless he is the holder of a licence authorising him to convey letters) shall not have effect to prohibit a visiting force or headquarters from conveying letters from one place to another in the United Kingdom, or from performing the incidental services of receiving, collecting and delivering letters in the United Kingdom.

(4) The running of a telecommunications system by a visiting force or headquarters for service purposes shall be exempt from the operation of Part II of the Telecommunications Act 1984 (which provides for the licensing etc of telecommunications systems).

(5) The provisions of this article shall only have effect in relation to a visiting force or headquarters, or a member of such a force or headquarters, or a person working in support of such a force, to the extent provided by an agreement for the time being in force made by or on behalf of Her Majesty's Government in the United Kingdom with (as the case may be)—

(a)   the Government or the service authorities of the country to which the visiting force belongs, or

(b)   the headquarters.

(6) Where a provision of this article has effect by virtue of such an agreement, it shall be subject to such conditions and restrictions as may be specified in the agreement.

(7) In this article, "service purposes" means naval, military or air force purposes.

8–2387   **8. Road vehicles.**   (1) Subject to paragraphs (6) and (7)—

(a)   Part VI of the Transport Act 1968 (which is concerned with the regulation of drivers' hours), and

(b)   the provisions of the Road Traffic Regulation Act 1984 ("the 1984 Act") and the Road Traffic Act 1988 ("the 1988 Act") specified in paragraph (2),

shall not apply to a person or vehicle in the service of a visiting force or headquarters.

(2) The provisions referred to in paragraph (1)(b) are—

(a)   sections 6 to 8, 19, 20, 102 and 103 of the 1984 Act; and

(b)   sections 68 to 74, 123 to 162, 165, 170(5) to (7) and 171 of the 1988 Act.

(3) Section 130(3) of the 1984 Act (which enables the Secretary of State to vary in relation to certain vehicles provisions imposing speed limits) shall have effect in relation to vehicles used for the purposes of a visiting force or headquarters, while being driven by a person subject to the orders of a member of such a force or headquarters, as it has effect in relation to vehicles used for naval, military or air force purposes, while being driven as mentioned in that subsection.

(4) Neither section 97(3) nor section 98(3) of the 1988 Act, in so far as they prevent such a licence as is there mentioned from authorising a person to drive certain motor cycles, shall apply in the case of motor cycles in the service of a visiting force.

(5) Subject to any regulations made under section 101(2) of the 1988 Act, that section (in so far as it prohibits persons under 21 from holding or obtaining a licence to drive motor vehicles or persons under 18 from holding or obtaining a licence to drive medium-sized goods vehicles) shall not apply in the case of vehicles in the service of a visiting force.

(6) Section 165 of the 1988 Act, in so far as it provides for the production of test certificates and the giving of names and addresses, shall apply to a person in connection with a vehicle to which section 47 of the 1988 Act applies notwithstanding that he or the driver is or was at any material time a person in the service of a visiting force or headquarters.

(7) Section 165(1) of the 1988 Act, in so far as it provides for the production of any certificate mentioned in subsection (2)(*c*) of that section, shall apply to a person in connection with a goods vehicle so mentioned notwithstanding that he or the driver is or was at any time a person in the service of a visiting force or headquarters.

(8) No vehicle excise duty shall be charged under the Vehicle Excise and Registration Act 1994 in respect of any vehicle in the service of a visiting force.

(9) In this article and in article 9—

(a) any reference to a person in the service of a visiting force or headquarters is a reference to—

(i) a member of a visiting force or headquarters, or
(ii) a person employed in the service of such a force,

when acting in the course of his duties as such; and

(b) any reference to a vehicle in the service of a visiting force or headquarters is a reference to a vehicle (including a motorcycle)—

(i) which belongs to a visiting force or headquarters and is used for the purposes of that force or headquarters, or
(ii) which is used for the purposes of a visiting force or headquarters, while being driven by a person for the time being subject to the orders of a member of a visiting force or headquarters.

8–2388   9. *Road vehicles (Northern Ireland)*

8–2389   10. *Exemption from harbour dues*

8–2390   11. Town and country planning.   (1) The Town and Country Planning Act 1990, the Planning (Listed Buildings and Conservation Areas) Act 1990 and the Planning (Hazardous Substances) Act 1990 (referred to collectively below as "the Planning Acts") shall apply to land—

(*a*) in which an interest is held by or on behalf of a visiting force or headquarters, and
(*b*) which is used for the purposes of that force or headquarters,

to the extent that it applies to Crown land within the meaning of respectively section 293(1) of the Town and Country Planning Act 1990, section 83(5) of the Planning (Listed Buildings and Conservation Areas) Act 1990, and section 31(3) of the Planning (Hazardous Substances) Act 1990.

(2) In their application to land such as is mentioned in paragraph (1), the Planning Acts shall have effect as if in those Acts—

(*a*) any reference to Crown land included a reference to such land;
(*b*) any reference to the Crown included a reference to the visiting force or headquarters; and
(*c*) any reference to the appropriate authority was a reference to the Ministry of Defence.

(3) *Scotland*
(4) *Northern Ireland*

8–2391   12. Miscellaneous exemptions, immunities and privileges.   (1) A visiting force or headquarters, members of such a force or headquarters, persons employed in the service of such a force, and property used for the purposes of such a force or headquarters shall be exempt from the operation of the enactments specified in Schedule 5 to the extent that, by virtue of the rule of law whereby enactments do not bind the Crown, such a force or headquarters, such members, such persons, or such property, would be so exempt if the force or headquarters were a part of any of the home forces.

(2) The enactments specified in the left hand column of Schedule 6 shall have effect subject to the modifications set out in the right hand column of that Schedule (being modifications which have the effect of conferring on a visiting force or headquarters, members of such a force or headquarters, persons employed in the service of such a force, or property used for the purposes of such a force or headquarters, the same exemptions, privileges and immunities which they would enjoy under those enactments if the force or headquarters formed a part of any of the home forces).

8–2392   13. Application of Factories Acts.   (1) For the purposes of the Factories Act 1961 ("the 1961 Act") and the Factories Act (Northern Ireland) 1965 ("the 1965 Act")—

(*a*) any premises in the occupation of a visiting force or headquarters shall not be deemed not to be a factory, and

(b)   any building operations or works of engineering construction undertaken by or on behalf of a visiting force or headquarters shall not be excluded from the operation of those Acts,

by reason only that the work carried on there is not carried on by way of trade or for the purposes of gain.

(2) The power under section 173(1) of the 1961 Act, or under section 173(1) of the 1965 Act, to exempt by order certain factories, building operations or works of engineering construction shall apply to—

(a)   a factory belonging to, and in the occupation of, a visiting force as it applies to a factory belonging to the Crown; and

(b)   any building operations or works of engineering construction undertaken by or on behalf of a visiting force or headquarters as it applies to any such operations or works where undertaken by or on behalf of the Crown.

8–2393   14. Notification of diseases.   Any reference—

(a)   in section 11 of the Public Health (Control of Disease) Act 1984 (which requires cases of notifiable diseases and food poisoning to be reported) to a registered medical practitioner, or

(b)   in section 2 of the Public Health Act (Northern Ireland) 1967 (which specifies the duties of a medical practitioner on diagnosis of notifiable diseases) to a medical practitioner,

shall include a reference to a person who holds an appointment as a medical officer in the service of a visiting force or headquarters.

8–2394   15. Application of Clean Air legislation.   The Clean Air Act 1993 (except Parts IV and V) and the Clean Air (Northern Ireland) Order 1981 shall have effect in relation to premises occupied for the purposes of a headquarters as if the premises were occupied for the public service of the Crown and were under the control of the government department by arrangement with whom the premises are occupied.

8–2395   16. *Attendance of witnesses before service courts*

8–2396   17. *Temporary detention of persons sentenced by service courts*

8–2397   18. Punishment for inducing or assisting desertion.   Section 192 of the Army Act 1955[1] (punishment for procuring and assisting desertion or absence without leave) shall have effect as if any reference to a member of any of Her Majesty's regular military forces included a reference to a member of a visiting force or a military member of a headquarters.

---

1. Ante.

8–2398   19. *Revocations*

BANKS AND BANKING

Bank of England Act 1998

(1998 c 11)

Note

8–2500

The Bank of England Act 1998, which is not printed in this work, makes provision about the constitution, regulation, financial arrangements and functions of the Bank of England, including provision for the transfer of supervisory functions. The Act also amends the Banking Act 1987 in relation to the provision and disclosure of information.

A person who fails without reasonable excuse to comply with any requirement imposed on him under the Act to provide information to the Bank shall be guilty of an offence and liable on summary conviction to a fine not exceeding **level 4** on the standard scale (**s 38(1)**).

A person who in purported compliance with such a requirement provides information which he knows to be false or misleading in a material particular, or recklessly provides information which is false or misleading in a material particular, shall be guilty of an offence which is triable either way, punishable on summary conviction by imprisonment for a term not exceeding **3 months** or to a fine not exceeding **the statutory minimum**, or to both (**s 38(3)**).

The Act was brought into force on 1 June 1998 (SI 1998/1120).

BIRTHS AND DEATHS[1]

8–2620   This title contains the following statutes—

8–2639   BIRTHS AND DEATHS REGISTRATION ACT 1874
8–2660   BIRTHS AND DEATHS REGISTRATION ACT 1926
8–2680   BIRTHS AND DEATHS REGISTRATION ACT 1953

---

1. For provisions as to births and deaths at sea and in the air, see the Merchant Shipping Act 1995, s 108, in PART VII: TRANSPORT, title MERCHANT SHIPPING, ante, and the Civil Aviation Act 1982, s 83, in PART VII: TRANSPORT, title AVIATION, ante, respectively.

Births and Deaths Registration Act 1874
(37 & 38 Vict c 88)

Registration of Deaths

8–2639   **18. Burial of deceased children as still-born.**   A person shall not wilfully bury or procure to be buried the body of any deceased child as if it were still-born.

A person who has control over or ordinarily buries bodies in any burial ground shall not permit to be buried in such burial ground the body of any deceased child as if it were still-born.

Any person who acts in contravention of this section shall be liable on summary conviction to a fine not exceeding **level 1** on the standard scale.

[Births and Deaths Registration Act 1874, s 18, as amended by the Births and Deaths Registration Act 1926, s 13 and Sch 2, the Criminal Law Act 1977, s 31, the Criminal Justice Act 1982, s 46 and the Statute Law (Repeals) Act 1993, Sch 2.]

8–2640   **19. Notice where coffin contains more than one body.**   Where there is in the coffin in which any deceased person is brought for burial the body of any other deceased person, or the body of any still-born child, the undertaker or other person who has charge of the funeral shall deliver to the person who buries or performs any funeral or religious service for the burial of such body or bodies notice in writing signed by such undertaker or other person, and stating to the best of his knowledge and belief with respect to each such body the following particulars:

(a)   If the body is the body of a deceased person, the name, sex, and place of abode of the said deceased person;

(b)   If the body has been found exposed, and the name and place of abode are unknown, the fact of the body having been so found and of the said particulars being unknown; and

(c)   If the body is that of a deceased child without a name, or a still-born child, the name and place of abode of the father, or, if it is illegitimate, of the mother of such child.

Every person who fails to comply with this section shall be liable on summary conviction to a fine not exceeding **level 1** on the standard scale.

[Births and Deaths Registration Act 1874, s 19, as amended by the Criminal Law Act 1977, s 31, the Criminal Justice Act 1982, s 46 and the Statute Law (Repeals) Act 1993, Sch 2.]

Births and Deaths Registration Act 1926
(16 & 17 Geo 5 c 48)

8–2660   **1. Prohibition of disposal except on registrar's certificate or coroner's order.**   (1) Subject as hereinafter provided, the body of a deceased person shall not be disposed of[1] before a certificate of the registrar given in pursuance of this Act or an order of the coroner has been delivered to the person effecting the disposal[1]:

Provided that it shall be lawful for the person effecting the disposal by burial of the body of any deceased person, if satisfied by a written declaration in the prescribed[2] form by the person procuring the disposal that a certificate of the registrar or order of the coroner has been issued in respect of the deceased, to proceed with the burial notwithstanding that the certificate or order has not been previously delivered to him.

(2) Any person contravening the provisions of this section shall be liable on summary conviction to a fine not exceeding **level 1** on the standard scale.

[Births and Deaths Registration Act 1926, s 1, as amended by the Criminal Justice Act 1967, Sch 3, and the Criminal Justice Act 1982, ss 38 and 46.]

---

1. For meaning of "disposal", "disposed of", and "person effecting the disposal", see s 12, post.
2. See the Registration of Births, Deaths and Marriages Regulations 1987, SI 1987/2088, as amended.

8–2661 3. Notification of disposal to registrar. (1) The person effecting the disposal[1] of the body of any deceased person shall, within ninety-six hours of the disposal, deliver to the registrar in the prescribed[2] manner a notification as to the date, place and means of disposal of the body.

(2) *Repealed.*

[Births and Deaths Registration Act 1926, s 3, as amended by the Births and Deaths Registration Act 1953, s 43 and Sch 2.]

---

1. For meaning of "disposal", "disposed of", and "person effecting the disposal", see s 12, post.
2. See the Registration of Births, Deaths and Marriages Regulations 1987, SI 1987/2088, as amended.

8–2662 4. Prohibition of removal of body out of England without notice[1]. The body of a deceased person shall not be removed out of England until the expiration of the prescribed period after notice of the removal has been given to the coroner within whose jurisdiction the body is lying or otherwise than in accordance with such procedure as may be prescribed, and any person contravening the provisions of this section shall be liable on summary conviction to a fine not exceeding **level 3** on the standard scale.

[Births and Deaths Registration Act 1926, s 4, as amended by the Criminal Justice Act 1967, Sch 3, and the Criminal Justice Act 1982, ss 38 and 46.]

---

1. Except where it is directed by the Secretary of State that an inquest shall be held or resumed, this section does not apply to the body of a person who at the time of his death had a relevant association with a visiting force (Visiting Forces Act 1952, s 7, title ARMED FORCES, ante).

8–2663 5. Burial of still-born children. It shall not be lawful for a person who has control over or who ordinarily buries bodies in any burial ground to permit to be buried or to bury in such burial ground a still-born[1] child before there is delivered to him either a certificate given by the registrar under the provisions of this Act[2] relating to still-births[1] or, if there has been an inquest, an order of the coroner.

[Births and Deaths Registration Act 1926, s 5.]

---

1. For meaning of "still-born" and "still-birth", see s 12, post.
2. Now s 11(2) or (3) of the Births and Deaths Registration Act 1953 (Births and Deaths Registration Act 1953, s 43 and Sch 1).

8–2664 9. Regulations. *Power of Secretary of State to make regulations[1].*

---

1. See the Removal of Bodies Regulations 1954, SI 1954/448, amended by SI 1971/1354.

8–2665 10. Application to cremation. The power to make regulations under section seven of the Cremation Act, 1902[1], shall include a power to make regulations for the purpose of applying the provisions of this Act to cases where human remains are disposed of by cremation, and except as may be provided by any such regulations this Act shall not apply to cremation.

[Births and Death Registration Act 1926, s 10.]

---

1. See title BURIAL AND CREMATION, post.

8–2666 11. Penalties. Any person contravening any of the provisions of this Act in respect of which no penalty is expressly imposed shall be liable on summary conviction to a fine not exceeding **level 1** on the standard scale.

[Births and Deaths Registration Act 1926, s 11, as amended by the Criminal Justice Act 1967, Sch 3, and the Criminal Justice Act 1982, ss 38 and 46.]

8–2667 12. Definitions. In this Act, unless the context otherwise requires—

"Prescribed"[1] means prescribed by the Registrar-General with the concurrence of the Chancellor of the Exchequer;

"Registrar" means, with respect to any death or birth the registrar who is the registrar for the sub-district in which the death or birth takes place;

"disposal" means disposal by burial, cremation or any other means, and "disposed of" has a corresponding meaning;

"person effecting the disposal" means the person by whom or whose officer the register of burials in which the disposal is to be registered is kept, except that in the case of a burial under the Burial Laws Amendment Act, 1880, in the churchyard or graveyard of a parish or ecclesiastical district the expression "person effecting the disposal" shall be construed as referring to the relative, friend, or legal representative having charge of or being responsible for the burial of the deceased person;

"still-born" and "still-birth" shall apply to any child which has issued forth from its mother after the twenty-eighth week of pregnancy and which did not at any time after being completely expelled from its mother, breathe or show any other signs of life.

[Births and Deaths Registration Act 1926, s 12, as amended by SI 1996/273.]

1. See the Registration of Births, Deaths and Marriages Regulations 1987, SI 1987/2088, as amended.

Births and Deaths Registration Act 1953[1]

(1 & 2 Eliz 2 c 20)

PART I[2]
REGISTRATION OF BIRTHS[3]

8–2680 1. Particulars of births to be registered.   (1) Subject to the provisions of this Part of this Act, the birth of every child born in England or Wales shall be registered by the registrar of births and deaths for the sub-district in which the child was born by entering in a register kept for that sub-district such particulars concerning the birth as may be prescribed[4]; and different registers shall be kept and different particulars may be prescribed for live-births and still-births respectively:

Provided that, where a still-born child is found exposed and no information as to the place of birth is available, the birth shall be registered by the registrar of births and deaths for the sub-district in which the child is found.

(2) The following persons shall be qualified to give information concerning a birth, that is to say—

(a)   the father and mother of the child;
(b)   the occupier of the house in which the child was to the knowledge of that occupier born;
(c)   any person present at the birth;
(d)   any person having charge of the child;
(e)   in the case of a still-born child found exposed, the person who found the child.

[Births and Deaths Registration Act 1953, s 1, as amended by the Children Act 1975, Sch 3.]

1. This Act consolidated the enactments relating to the registration of births and deaths in England and Wales. For the unrepealed provisions of the Births and Deaths Registration Act 1874 and the Births and Deaths Registration Act 1926, see this title, ante. See also the title BURIAL AND CREMATION, post.
   Provisions regarding the re-registration of legitimated children are contained in the Legitimacy Act 1976, s 9, in PART VI: FAMILY LAW, ante, and the registration of adopted children is governed by the Adoption and Children Act 2002, in PART VI: FAMILY LAW, ante.
2. Part I contains ss 1–14.
3. The registration system and the appointment of registrars of births and deaths is governed by the Registration Service Act 1953.
4. See the Registration of Births, Deaths and Marriages Regulations 1987, SI 1987/2088, as amended, which have been made by the Registrar General in exercise of powers conferred upon him by s 39, post, and s 20 of the Registration Service Act 1953.

8–2681 2. Information concerning birth to be given to registrar within forty-two days.   In the case of every birth it shall be the duty—

(a)   of the father and mother of the child; and
(b)   in the case of the death or inability of the father and mother, of each other qualified informant,

to give to the registrar, before the expiration of a period of forty-two days from the date of the birth, information of the particulars required to be registered concerning the birth, and in the presence of the registrar to sign the register:

Provided that—

(i)   the giving of information and the signing of the register by any one qualified informant shall act as a discharge of any duty under this section of every other qualified informant;
(ii) this section shall cease to apply if, before the expiration of the said period and before the birth has been registered, an inquest is held at which the child is found to have been still-born.

[Births and Deaths Registration Act 1953, s 2.]

8–2682 3. Information concerning finding of new-born child to be given to registrar within forty-two days.   Where any still-born child is found exposed, it shall be the duty of the person finding the child, to give to the best of his knowledge and belief to the registrar, before the expiration of forty-two days from the date on which the child was found, such information of the particulars required to be registered concerning the birth of the child as the informant possesses, and in the presence of the registrar to sign the register.

[Births and Deaths Registration Act 1953, s 3, as amended by the Children Act 1975, Schs 3 and 4.]

8–2683 3A. Registration of births of abandoned children.   (1) Where the place and date of birth of a child who was abandoned are unknown to, and cannot be ascertained by, the person who has charge of the child, that person may apply to the Registrar General for the child's birth to be registered under this section.

(2) On an application under this section the Registrar General shall enter in a register maintained at the General Register Office—

(a) as the child's place of birth, if the child was found by the applicant or by any person from whom (directly or indirectly) the applicant took charge of the child, the registration district and sub-district where the child was found, or, in any other case, where the child was abandoned;

(b) as the child's date of birth, the date which, having regard to such evidence as is produced to him, appears to him to be the most likely date of birth of the child, and

(c) such other particulars as may be prescribed.

(3) The Registrar General shall not register a child's birth under this section if—

(a) he is satisfied that the child was not born in England or Wales;

(b) the child has been adopted in pursuance of a court order made in the United Kingdom, the Isle of Man or the Channel Islands; or

(c) subject to subsection (5) below, the child's birth is known to have been previously registered under this Act.

(4) If no entry can be traced in any register of births relating to a person who has attained the age of 18 and has not been adopted as aforesaid, that person may apply to the Registrar General for his birth to be registered under this section.

(5) On the application of—

(a) a person having the charge of a child whose birth had been registered under this Act by virtue of the proviso to section 1 of this Act (as originally enacted), or

(b) any such child who has attained the age of 18 years,

the Registrar General shall re-register the birth of the child under this section, and shall direct the officer having custody of the register of births in which the entry relating to the child was previously made to enter in the margin of the register a reference to the re-registration of the birth.

[Births and Deaths Registration Act 1953, s 3A, as inserted by the Children Act 1975, s 92.]

8–2684 4. Registrar's power to require information concerning birth. Where, after the expiration of forty-two days from the date of the birth of any child or from the date when any still-born child is found exposed, the birth of the child has, owing to the default of the persons required to give information concerning it, not been registered, the registrar may by notice in writing require any qualified informant—

(a) to attend personally at the registrar's office, or at some other place appointed by the registrar within his sub-district, before such date (being not less than seven days after the receipt of the notice nor more than three months after the date of the birth or finding) as may be specified in the notice; and

(b) to give information to the best of that person's knowledge and belief of the particulars required to be registered concerning the birth; and

(c) to sign the register in the presence of the registrar:

Provided that any such requirement shall cease to have effect if, before the date specified in the notice and before the person to whom the notice is given complies with it, the birth is duly registered.

[Births and Deaths Registration Act 1953, s 4, as amended by the Children Act 1975, Sch 3.]

8–2685 5. *Registration of births free of charge.*

8–2686 6. Registration between three and twelve months from date of birth. (1) Where, after the expiration of three months from the date of the birth of any child, the birth of the child has not been registered, the registrar may by notice in writing require any qualified informant—

(a) to attend personally at the district register office before such date (being not less than seven days after the receipt of the notice nor more than twelve months after the date of the birth) as may be specified in the notice; and

(b) to make before the superintendent registrar a declaration according to the best of the declarant's knowledge and belief of the particulars required to be registered concerning the birth; and

(c) to sign the register in the presence of the registrar and the superintendent registrar.

(2) Upon any qualified informant attending before the registrar and superintendent registrar, whether in pursuance of a requirement or not, and making such a declaration as aforesaid and giving information concerning the birth, the registrar shall then and there in the presence of the superintendent registrar register the birth according to the information of the declarant, and the superintendent registrar before whom the declaration is made, the registrar and the declarant shall each sign the entry of the birth.

(3) *Repealed.*

(4) This section shall not apply in the case of a still-birth.

[Births and Deaths Registration Act 1953, s 6, as amended by the Registration of Births, Deaths and Marriages (Fees) Order 1968, SI 1968/1242, and the Children Act 1975, Sch 4.]

8–2687 7. Registration after twelve months from date of birth.   Where, after the expiration of twelve months from the date of the birth of any child, the birth of the child has not been registered, the birth shall not be registered except with the written authority of the Registrar General and in such manner and subject to such conditions as may be prescribed, and the fact that the authority of the Registrar General has been obtained shall be entered in the register.

(2) *Repealed.*

(3) This section shall not apply in the case of a still-birth.

[Births and Deaths Registration Act 1953, s 7, as amended by the Registration of Births, Deaths and Marriages (Fees) Order 1968, SI 1968/1242, and the Children Act 1975, Sch 4.]

8–2688 8. Penalty for improper registration after three months from date of birth.   Save as provided in the two last foregoing sections, a registrar shall not register the birth of any child after the expiration of three months from the date of birth, and any person who registers any birth, or causes any birth to be registered, in contravention of this section shall be liable on summary conviction to a fine not exceeding **level 1** on the standard scale.

[Births and Deaths Registration Act 1953, s 8, as amended by the Children Act 1975, Sch 4, the Criminal Law Act 1977, s 31, and the Criminal Justice Act 1982, s 46.]

8–2689 10. Registration of father where parents not married.   (1) Notwithstanding anything in the foregoing provisions of this Act and subject to section 10ZA of this Act, in the case of a child whose father and mother were not married to each other at the time of his birth, no person shall as father of the child be required to give information concerning the birth of the child, and the registrar shall not enter in the register the name of any person as father of the child except—

(*a*)   at the joint request of the mother and the person stating himself to be the father of the child (in which case that person shall sign the register together with the mother); or

(*b*)   at the request of the mother on production of—

    (i)   a declaration in the prescribed form made by the mother stating that that person is the father of the child; and

    (ii)   a statutory declaration made by that person stating himself to be the father of the child; or

(*c*)   at the request of that person on production of—

    (i)   a declaration in the prescribed form by that person stating himself to be the father of the child; and

    (ii)   a statutory declaration made by the mother stating that that person is the father of the child; or

(*d*)   at the request of the mother or that person on production of—

    (i)   a copy of any agreement made between them under section 4(1)(*b*) of the Children Act 1989 in relation to the child; and

    (ii)   a declaration in the prescribed form by the person making the request stating that the agreement was made in compliance with section 4 of that Act and has not been brought to an end by an order of a court; or

(*e*)   at the request of the mother or that person on production of—

    (i)   a certified copy of an order under section 4 of the Children Act 1989 giving that person parental responsibility for the child; and

    (ii)   a declaration in the prescribed form by the person making the request stating that the order has not been brought to an end by an order of a court; or

(*f*)   at the request of the mother or that person on production of—

    (i)   a certified copy of an order under paragraph 1 of Schedule 1 to the Children Act 1989 which requires that person to make any financial provision for the child and which is not an order falling within paragraph 4(3) of that Schedule; and

    (ii)   a declaration in the prescribed form by the person making the request stating that the order has not been discharged by an order of a court; or

(*g*)   at the request of the mother or that person on production of—

    (i)   a certified copy of any of the orders which are mentioned in subsection (1A) of this section which has been made in relation to the child; and

    (ii)   a declaration in the prescribed form by the person making the request stating that the order has not been brought to an end or discharged by an order of a court.

(1A) The orders are—

(a) an order under section 4 of the Family Law Reform Act 1987 that that person shall have all the parental rights and duties with respect to the child;

(b) an order that that person shall have custody or care and control or legal custody of the child made under section 9 of the Guardianship of Minors Act 1971 at a time when such an order could only be made in favour of a parent;

(c) an order under section 9 or 11B of that Act which requires that person to make any financial provision in relation to the child;

(d) an order under section 4 of the Affiliation Proceedings Act 1957 naming that person as putative father of the child.

(2) Where, in the case of a child whose father and mother were not married to each other at the time of his birth, a person stating himself to be the father of the child makes a request to the registrar in accordance with paragraph (c) or (g) subsection (1) of this section—

(a) he shall be treated as a qualified informant concerning the birth of the child for the purposes of this Act; and

(b) the giving of information concerning the birth of the child by that person and the signing of the register by him in the presence of the registrar shall act as a discharge of any duty of any other qualified informant under section 2 of this Act.

(3) In this section and section 10A of this Act references to a child whose father and mother were not married to each other at the time of his birth shall be construed in accordance with section 1 of the Family Law Reform Act 1987 and "parental responsibility agreement" has the same meaning as in the Children Act 1989.

[Births and Deaths Registration Act 1953, s 10, as substituted by the Family Law Reform Act 1987, s 24 and amended by the Children Act 1989, Sch 12, the Human Fertilisation and Embryology (Deceased Fathers) Act 2003, Schedule and the Adoption and Children Act 2002, Sch 3.]

8–2689A 10ZA. Registration of father by virtue of certain provisions of the Human Fertilisation and Embryology Act 1990. (1) Notwithstanding anything in the foregoing provisions of this Act, the registrar shall not enter in the register as the father of a child the name of a man who is to be treated for that purpose as the father of the child by virtue of section 28(5A), (5B), (5C) or (5D) of the Human Fertilisation and Embryology Act 1990 (circumstances in which man to be treated as father of child for purposes of registration of birth where fertility treatment undertaken after his death) unless the condition in subsection (2) below is satisfied.

(2) The condition in this subsection is satisfied if—

(a) the mother requests the registrar to make such an entry in the register and produces the relevant documents; or

(b) in the case of the death or inability of the mother, the relevant documents are produced by some other person who is a qualified informant.

(3) In this section "the relevant documents" means—

(a) the consent in writing and election mentioned in section 28(5A), (5B), (5C) or (as the case may be) (5D) of the Act of 1990;

(b) a certificate of a registered medical practitioner as to the medical facts concerned; and

(c) such other documentary evidence (if any) as the registrar considers appropriate.

[Births and Deaths Registration Act 1953, s 10ZA, as inserted by the Human Fertilisation and Embryology (Deceased Fathers) Act 2003, Schedule.]

8–2690 10A. Re-registration where parents not married[1]. (1) Where there has been registered under this Act the birth of a child whose father and mother were not married to each other at the time of the birth, but no person has been registered as the father of the child, the registrar shall re-register the birth so as to show a person as the father—

(a) at the joint request of the mother and that person; or

(b) at the request of the mother on production of—

(i) a declaration in the prescribed form made by the mother stating that that person is the father of the child; and

(ii) a statutory declaration made by that person stating himself to be the father of the child; or

(c) at the request of that person on production of—

(i) a declaration in the prescribed form by that person stating himself to be the father of the child; and

(ii) a statutory declaration made by the mother stating that that person is the father of the child; or

(d) at the request of the mother or that person on production of—

(i) a copy of any agreement made between them under section 4(1)(b) of the Children Act 1989 in relation to the child; and

    (ii) a declaration in the prescribed form by the person making the request stating that the agreement was made in compliance with section 4 of that Act and has not been brought to an end by an order of a court; or

(e) at the request of the mother or that person on production of—

    (i) a certified copy of an order under section 4 of the Children Act 1989 giving that person parental responsibility for the child; and

    (ii) a declaration in the prescribed form by the person making the request stating that the order has not been brought to an end by an order of a court; or

(f) at the request of the mother or that person on production of—

    (i) a certified copy of an order under paragraph 1 of Schedule 1 to the Children Act 1989 which requires that person to make any financial provision for the child and which is not an order falling within paragraph 4(3) of that Schedule; and

    (ii) a declaration in the prescribed form by the person making the request stating that the order has not been discharged by an order of a court; or

(ff) in a case of a man who is to be treated as the father of the child by virtue of section 28(5A), (5B), (5C) or (5D) of the Human Fertilisation and Embryology Act 1990, if the condition set in section 10ZA(2) of this Act is satisfied; or

(g) at the request of the mother or that person on production of—

    (i) a certified copy of any of the orders which are mentioned in subsection (1A) of this section which has been made in relation to the child; and

    (ii) a declaration in the prescribed form by the person making the request stating that the order has not been brought to an end or discharged by an order of a court.

(1A) The orders are—

(a) an order under section 4 of the Family Law Reform Act 1987 that that person shall have all the parental rights and duties with respect to the child;

(b) an order that that person shall have custody or care and control or legal custody of the child made under section 9 of the Guardianship of Minors Act 1971 at a time when such an order could only be made in favour of a parent;

(c) an order under section 9 or 11B of that Act which requires that person to make any financial provision in relation to the child;

(d) an order under section 4 of the Affiliation Proceedings Act 1957 naming that person as putative father of the child.

(2) On the re-registration of a birth under this section—

(a) the registrar shall sign the register;

(b) in the case of a request under paragraph (a) or (c) of subsection (1) of this section, or a request under any of paragraphs (d) to (g) of that subsection made by the mother of the child, the mother shall also sign the register;

(bb) in a case within paragraph (ff) of that subsection, the mother or (as the case may be) the qualified informant shall also sign the register;

(c) in the case of a request under paragraph (d) or (g) of that subsection, or a request made under any of paragraphs (d) to (g) of that subsection by the person requesting to be registered as the father of the child, that person shall also sign the register; and

(d) if the re-registration takes place more than three months after the birth, the superintendent registrar shall also sign the register.

[Births and Deaths Registration Act 1953, s 10A, as inserted by the Children Act 1975, s 93, and substituted by the Family Law Reform Act 1987, s 25 and amended by the Children Act 1989, Sch 12, the Human Fertilisation and Embryology (Deceased Fathers) Act 2003, Schedule and the Adoption and Children Act 2002, Sch 3.]

---

    1. For the re-registration of birth of legitimated persons, see s 14, post, and the Legitimacy Act 1976, s 9, in PART VI: FAMILY LAW ante.

8–2691 12. Certificate of registration of birth. At the time of registering the birth of any child, the registrar shall, if so required by the informant of the birth . . . give to the informant a certificate under his hand in the prescribed form that he has registered the birth.

[Births and Deaths Registration Act 1953, s 12, as amended by the Registration of Births, Deaths and Marriage (Fees) Order 1968, SI 1968/1242.]

8–2692 13. Registration of name of child or of alteration of name. (1) Where, before the expiration of twelve months from the date of the registration of the birth of any child, the name by which it was registered is altered or, if it was registered without a name, a name is given to the child, the registrar or superintendent registrar having the custody of the register in which the birth was registered, upon delivery to him at any time of a certificate in the prescribed form signed—

(a) if the name was altered or given in baptism, either by the person who performed the rite of baptism or by the person who has the custody of the register, if any, in which the baptism is recorded, or

(b) if a name has not been given to the child in baptism, by the father, mother or guardian of the child or other person procuring the name of the child to be altered or given,

shall, without any erasure of the original entry, forthwith enter in the register the name mentioned in the certificate as having been given to the child, and, after stating upon the certificate the fact that the entry has been made, shall forthwith send the certificate to the Registrar General together with a certified copy of the entry of the birth with the name added under this subsection.

(2) Where the name of a child is altered or given in baptism, the person who performed the rite of baptism or who has the custody of any register in which the baptism is recorded shall issue the certificate required under this section on payment of a fee not exceeding £1·00.

(3) *Repealed.*

(4) This section shall not apply in relation to a still-born child.

[Births and Deaths Registration Act 1953, s 13, as amended by the Registration of Births, Deaths and Marriage (Fees) Order 1968, SI 1968/1242, the Merchant Shipping Act 1970, Sch 5, SI 1995/3162, SI 1997/2939 and SI 1999/3311.]

8–2693 14. Re-registration of births of legitimated persons[1]. (1) Where, in the case of any person whose birth has been registered in England or Wales, evidence is produced to the Registrar General which appears to him to be satisfactory that that person has become a legitimated person . . . the Registrar General may authorise at any time the re-registration of that person's birth, and the re-registration shall be effected in such manner and at such place as may be prescribed:

Provided that, except where—

(a) the name of a person stating himself to be the father of the legitimated person has been entered in the register in pursuance of section ten or 10A of this Act; or

(b) the paternity of the legitimated person has been established by a decree of a court of competent jurisdiction; or

(c) a declaration of the legitimacy of the legitimated person has been made under section seventeen of the Matrimonial Causes Act, 1950, or section 56 of the Family Law Reform Act 1987,

the Registrar General shall not authorise the re-registration unless information with a view to obtaining it is furnished by both parents.

(2) Where the Registrar General believes any person to have become a legitimated person . . . on the marriage of his parents, and the parents or either of them fail to furnish within a period of three months from the date of the marriage such information, if any, as may be necessary to enable the Registrar General to authorise the re-registration of that person's birth, the Registrar General may at any time after the expiration of the said period require the parents or either of them to give him such information concerning the matter as he may consider necessary, verified in such manner as he may direct, and for that purpose to attend personally either at a registrar's office or at any other place appointed by him within such time, not being less than seven days after the receipt of the notice, as may be specified in the notice.

(3) *Repealed.*

(4) This section shall apply with the prescribed modifications in relation to births at sea of which a return is sent to the Registrar General.

(5) This section shall apply and be deemed always to have applied in relation to all persons recognised by the law of England and Wales as having been legitimated by the subsequent marriage of their parents whether or not their legitimation or the recognition thereof was effected under any enactment.

[Births and Deaths Registration Act 1953, s 14, as amended by the Legitimation (Re-registration of Birth) Act 1957, s 1, the Registration of Births, Deaths and Marriage (Fees) Order 1968, SI 1968/1242, the Children Act 1975, Sch 3, the Legitimacy Act 1976, Sch 1 and the Family Law Reform Act 1987, Sch 2.]

---

1. See also the Legitimacy Act 1976, s 9, in PART VI: FAMILY LAW ante.

8–2694 14A. Re-registration after declaration of parentage. (1) Where, in the case of a person whose birth has been registered in England and Wales—

(a) the Registrar General receives, by virtue of section 55A(7) or 56(4) of the Family Law Act 1986, a notification of the making of a declaration of parentage in respect of that person; and

(b) it appears to him that the birth of that person should be re-registered,

he shall authorise the re-registration of that person's birth, and the re-registration shall be effected in such manner and at such place as may be prescribed.

(2) This section shall apply with the prescribed modifications in relation to births at sea of which a return is sent to the Registrar General.

[Births and Deaths Registration Act 1953, s 14A, as inserted by the Family Law Reform Act 1987, s 26 and amended by the Child Support, Pensions and Social Security Act 2000, Sch 8.]

8–2695 15. Particulars of deaths to be registered.   Subject to the provisions of this Part of this Act, the death of every person dying in England or Wales and the cause thereof shall be registered by the registrar of births and deaths for the sub-district in which the death occurred by entering in a register kept for that sub-district such particulars concerning the death as may be prescribed:

Provided that where a dead body is found and no information as to the place of death is available, the death shall be registered by the registrar of births and deaths for the sub-district in which the body is found.

[Births and Deaths Registration Act 1953, s 15.]

---

1. Part II contains ss 15–24.

8–2696 16. Information concerning death in a house.   (1) The following provisions of this section shall have effect where a person dies in a house.

(2) The following persons shall be qualified to give information concerning the death, that is to say—

(*a*)   any relative of the deceased person present at the death or in attendance during his last illness;
(*b*)   any other relative of the deceased residing or being in the sub-district where the death occurred;
(*c*)   any person present at the death;
(*d*)   the occupier of the house if he knew of the happening of the death;
(*e*)   any inmate of the house who knew of the happening of the death;
(*f*)   the person causing the disposal of the body.

(3) It shall be the duty—

(*a*)   of the nearest relative such as is mentioned in paragraph (*a*) of the last foregoing subsection; or
(*b*)   if there is no such relative, of each such relative as is mentioned in paragraph (*b*) of that subsection; or
(*c*)   if there are no such relatives, of each such person as is mentioned in paragraph (*c*) or (*d*) of that subsection; or
(*d*)   if there are no such relatives or persons as aforesaid, of each such person as is mentioned in paragraph (*e*) or (*f*) of that subsection,

to give to the registrar, before the expiration of five days from the date of the death, information to the best of his knowledge and belief of the particulars required to be registered concerning the death, and in the presence of the registrar to sign the register:

Provided that—

(i)   the giving of information and the signing of the register by any one qualified informant shall act as a discharge of any duty under this subsection of every other qualified informant;
(ii)   this subsection shall not have effect if an inquest is held touching the death of the deceased person.

[Births and Deaths Registration Act 1953, s 16, as amended by the Coroners Act 1980, Sch 2.]

8–2697 17. Information concerning other deaths.   (1) The following provisions of this section shall have effect where a person dies elsewhere than in a house or where a dead body is found and no information as to the place of death is available.

(2) The following persons shall be qualified to give information concerning the death, that is to say—

(*a*)   any relative of the deceased who has knowledge of any of the particulars required to be registered concerning the death;
(*b*)   any person present at the death;
(*c*)   any person finding or taking charge of the body;
(*d*)   any person causing the disposal of the body.

(3) It shall be the duty—

(*a*)   of each such relative as is mentioned in paragraph (*a*) of the last foregoing subsection; or
(*b*)   if there are no such relatives, of each other qualified informant,

to give to the registrar, before the expiration of five days from the date of the death or of the finding of the body, such information of the particulars required to be registered concerning the death as the informant possesses, and in the presence of the registrar to sign the register:

Provided that—

(i)   the giving of information and the signing of the register by any one qualified informant shall act as a discharge of any duty under this subsection of every other qualified informant;

(ii) this subsection shall not have effect if an inquest is held touching the death of the deceased person.
[Births and Deaths Registration Act 1953, s 17, as amended by the Coroners Act 1980, Sch 2.]

8–2698 18. Notice preliminary to information of death. If, before the expiration of five days from the date of the death or of the finding of the dead body of any person, a qualified informant of that person's death sends to the registrar a written notice of the occurrence of the death or of the finding of the body accompanied by a notice given under subsection (2) of section twenty-two of this Act of the signing of a certificate of the cause of death, the information of the particulars required to be registered concerning the death need not be given before the expiration of the said five days, but shall, notwithstanding the notice, be given before the expiration of fourteen days from the date aforesaid by the person giving the notice or by some other qualified informant.
[Births and Deaths Registration Act 1953, s 18.]

8–2699 19. Registrar's power to require information concerning death. (1) Where, after the expiration of the relevant period from the date of the death or finding of the dead body of any person, the death of that person has, owing to the default of the persons required to give information concerning it, not been registered, the registrar may by notice in writing require any qualified informant—

(*a*) to attend personally at the registrar's office, or at some other place appointed by the registrar within his sub-district, before such date (being not less than seven days after the receipt of the notice nor more than twelve months from the date of the death or of the finding of the body) as may be specified in the notice; and

(*b*) to give information to the best of the informant's knowledge and belief of the particulars required to be registered concerning the death; and

(*c*) to sign the register in the presence of the registrar:

Provided that any such requirement shall cease to have effect if, before the date specified in the notice and before the person to whom the notice is given complies with it, either—

(i) the death is duly registered; or
(ii) an inquest is held touching the death of the deceased person.

(2) In this section, the expression "the relevant period" means—

(*a*) where notice has been duly given to the registrar in accordance with the last foregoing section, fourteen days;

(*b*) in any other case, five days.
[Births and Deaths Registration Act 1953, s 19, as amended by the Coroners Act 1980, Sch 2.]

8–2710 21. Registration of death after twelve months. (1) After the expiration of twelve months from the date of the death or finding of the dead body of any person, the death of that person shall not be registered except with the written authority of the Registrar General and in such manner and subject to such conditions as may be prescribed, and the fact that the authority of the Registrar General has been obtained shall be entered in the register.

(2) (*Repealed*).

(3) Any person who registers any death, or causes any death to be registered, in contravention of this section shall be liable on summary conviction to a fine not exceeding **level 1** on the standard scale.
[Births and Deaths Registration Act 1953, s 21, as amended by the Registration of Births, Deaths and Marriage (Fees) Order 1968, SI 1968/1242, the Criminal Law Act 1977, s 31, and the Criminal Justice Act 1982, s 46.]

8–2711 22. Certificates of cause of death. In the case of the death of any person who has been attended during his last illness by a registered medical practitioner, that practitioner shall sign a certificate in the prescribed form stating to the best of his knowledge and belief the cause of death and shall forthwith deliver that certificate to the registrar.
[Births and Deaths Registration Act 1953, s 22, as amended by the Coroners Act 1980, Sch 2 and the Coroners Act 1988, Sch 3—summarised.]

8–2712 24. Certificates as to registration of death. The registrar, upon registering any death, shall forthwith give to the person giving information concerning the death a certificate under his hand that he has registered the death; but may, before registering the death and subject to such conditions as may be prescribed, upon receiving written notice of the occurrence of a death in respect of which he has received a certificate under section twenty-two of this Act, give to the person sending the notice, if required to do so, a certificate under his hand that he has received notice of the death; and any certificate given under this subsection shall be given without fee:

Provided that the registrar shall not issue any such certificate in any case in which he is satisfied that a coroner's order has been issued authorising the disposal of the body.
[Births and Deaths Registration Act 1953, s 24, amended by the Registration of Births, Deaths and Marriage (Fees) Order 1968, SI 1968/1242—summarised.]

PART III[1]
GENERAL

Registers, certified copies, etc

8–2713   25. Provision of registers, etc, by Registrar General.   Registers of live-births, still-births and deaths shall be in such form as may be respectively prescribed, and the Registrar General shall provide any such registers, and any of the forms hereafter mentioned for making certified copies of entries in registers, which may be required for the purposes of this Act.
[Births and Deaths Registration Act 1953, s 25.]

1. Part III contains ss 25–44.

8–2714   26–32.   *Returns by registrars; correction of errors in registers, and searches in registers.*

8–2715   33. Short certificate of births.   (1) Any person shall, on payment of a fee of £2·00[1] and on furnishing the prescribed particulars, be entitled to obtain from the Registrar General, a superintendent registrar or a registrar a short certificate of the birth of any person.
   (2) Any such certificate shall be in the prescribed form and shall be compiled in the prescribed manner from the records and registers in the custody of the Registrar General, or from the registers in the custody of the superintendent registrar or registrar, as the case may be, and shall contain such particulars as may be prescribed:
   Provided that any particulars prescribed in addition to name, surname, sex and date of birth shall not include any particulars relating to parentage or adoption contained in any such records or registers.
[Births and Deaths Registration Act 1953, s 33, as amended by the Registration of Births, Deaths and Marriage (Fees) Order 1994, SI 1995/3162, SI 1997/2939 and SI 1999/3311.]

1. No fee is payable for a short certificate of birth, (or if more than one is obtained the first such certificate), obtained at the time of registration; a fee of £3·50 is payable for any other short certificate of birth obtained from a registrar; a fee of £5.50 is payable for a short certificate obtained from a superintendent registrar, a fee of £7.00 is payable for a short certificate of birth obtained from the Registrar General where that certificate is compiled from a certified copy of an entry in the register of live births, and a fee of £5.50 is payable for a short certificate of birth obtained from the Registrar General where that certificate is compiled from any other records and registers in the custody of the Registrar General (Registration of Births, Deaths and Marriages (Fees) Order 2002, SI 2002/3076 amended by SI 2005/1997).

8–2716   34. Entry in register as evidence of birth or death[1].   (1) The following provisions of this section shall have effect in relation to entries in registers under this Act or any enactment repealed by this Act.
   (2) An entry or a certified copy of an entry of a birth or death in a register, or in a certified copy of a register, shall not be evidence of the birth or death unless the entry purports to be signed by some person professing to be the informant and to be such a person as might be required or permitted by law at the date of the entry to give to the registrar information concerning that birth or death:
   Provided that this subsection shall not apply—

   (*a*)   in relation to an entry of a birth which, not being an entry signed by a person professing to be a superintendent registrar, purports to have been made with the authority of the Registrar General; or
   (*b*)   in relation to an entry of a death which purports to have been made upon a certificate from a coroner; or
   (*c*)   in relation to an entry of a birth or death which purports to have been made in pursuance of the enactments with respect to the registration of births and deaths at sea,
   (*d*)   in relation to the re-registration of a birth under section 9(5) of this Act.

   (3) Where more than three months have intervened between the date of the birth of any child or the date when any living new-born child or still-born child was found exposed and the date of the registration of the birth of that child, the entry or a certified copy of the entry of the birth of the child in the register, or in a certified copy of the register, shall not be evidence of the birth unless—

   (*a*)   if it appears that not more than twelve months have so intervened, the entry purports either to be signed by the superintendent registrar as well as by the registrar or to have been made with the authority of the Registrar General;
   (*b*)   if more than twelve months have so intervened, the entry purports to have been made with the authority of the Registrar General:

   Provided that this subsection shall not apply in any case where the original entry in the register was made before the first day of January, eighteen hundred and seventy-five.
   (4) Where more than twelve months have intervened between the date of the death or of the finding of the dead body of any person and the date of the registration of that person's death, the entry or a certified copy of the entry of the death in the register, or in a certified copy of the register, shall not be evidence of the death unless the entry purports to have been made with the authority of the Registrar General:

Provided that this subsection shall not apply in any case where the original entry in the register was made before the first day of January, eighteen hundred and seventy-five.

(5) A certified copy of an entry in a register or in a certified copy of a register shall be deemed to be a true copy notwithstanding that it is made on a form different from that on which the original entry was made if any differences in the column headings under which the particulars appear in the original entry and the copy respectively are differences of form only and not of substance.

(6) The Registrar General shall cause any certified copy of an entry given in the General Register Office to be sealed or stamped with the seal of that Office; and, subject to the foregoing provisions of this section, any certified copy of an entry purporting to be sealed or stamped with the said seal shall be received as evidence of the birth or death to which it relates without any further or other proof of the entry, and no certified copy purporting to have been given in the said Office shall be of any force or effect unless it is sealed or stamped as aforesaid.

[Births and Deaths Registration Act 1953, s 34, as amended by the Children Act 1975, Sch 3 and the Family Law Reform Act 1987, Sch 2.]

---

1. Entries in certain consular registers and certified copies thereof may be admissible as evidence; see the Evidence (Foreign, Dominion and Colonial Documents) Act 1933, in PART II: EVIDENCE, ante.

Offences

8–2717 35. Offences relating to registers. If any person commits any of the following offences, that is to say—

(a) if, being a registrar, he refuses or without reasonable cause omits to register any birth or death or particulars concerning which information has been tendered to him by a qualified informant and which he is required by or under this Act to register; or

(b) if, being a person having the custody of any register of births or register of deaths, he carelessly loses or injures the register or allows the register to be injured,

he shall be liable on summary conviction to a fine not exceeding **level 3** on the standard scale.

[Births and Deaths Registration Act 1953, s 35, as amended by the Criminal Justice Act 1982, ss 38 and 46.]

8–2718 36. Penalties for failure to give information, etc. If any person commits any of the following offences, that is to say—

(a) if, being required by or under this Act to give information concerning any birth or death or any dead body, he wilfully refuses to answer any question put to him by the registrar relating to the particulars required to be registered concerning the birth or death, or save as provided in this Act, fails to comply with any requirement of the registrar made thereunder;

(b) if he refuses or fails without reasonable excuse to give, deliver or send any certificate which he is required by this Act to give, deliver or send;

(c) if, being a parent and save as provided in this Act, he fails to give information concerning the birth of his child as required by this Act; or

(d) if, being a parent of a legitimated person . . . he fails to comply with any requirement of the Registrar General made under or by virtue of section fourteen of this Act; or

(e) if, being a person upon whom a duty to give information concerning a death is imposed by paragraph (a) of subsection (3) of section sixteen or seventeen of this Act, he fails to give that information and that information is not given,

he shall be liable on summary conviction to a fine not exceeding **level 1** on the standard scale for each offence.

[Births and Deaths Registration Act 1953, s 36, as amended by the Legitimation (Re-registration of Birth) Act 1957, the Criminal Justice Act 1967, Sch 3, the Children Act 1975, Sch 4, and the Criminal Justice Act 1982, ss 38 and 46.]

8–2719 37. Penalty for forging certificate, etc. If any person falsifies any certificate, declaration or order under this Act, or knowingly uses, or gives or sends to any person, as genuine any false certificate, declaration or order for the purposes of this Act, he shall be liable on summary conviction to a fine not exceeding **level 1** on the standard scale.

[Births and Deaths Registration Act 1953, s 37, as amended by the Criminal Law Act 1977, s 31, the Forgery and Counterfeiting Act 1981, Sch, and the Criminal Justice Act 1982, s 46.]

8–2720 38. Prosecution of offences and application of fines. (1) Subject as may be prescribed, a superintendent registrar may prosecute[1] any person for an offence under this Act committed within his district, and any costs incurred by him in any such prosecution, being costs which are not otherwise provided for, shall be defrayed out of moneys provided by Parliament.

(2) *Repealed.*

[Births and Deaths Registration Act 1953, s 38, as amended by the Criminal Justice Act 1972, Sch 6.]

---

1. But see reg 72 of the Registration of Births and Deaths Regulations 1987, SI 1987/2088, as amended, which prohibits a superintendent registrar commencing proceedings under this Act without the consent of the Registrar General.

8-2721 39. Regulations. *Power of the Registrar General, with the approval of the Minister, by statutory instrument to make regulations*[1].

1. See the Registration of Births, and Deaths Regulations 1987, SI 1987/2088, amended by SI 1988/638, SI 1989/497, SI 1991/2275, SI 1992/2753, SI 1994/1948 and SI 1997/844, 1533 and SI 2005/3177 and the Registration of Births and Deaths (Welsh Language) Regulations 1987, SI 1987/2089 amended by SI 2005/3177.

8-2722 41. Interpretation. In this Act, except where the context otherwise requires, the following expressions have the meanings hereby respectively assigned to them, that is to say—

"birth" includes a live-birth and a still-birth;

"disposal", in relation to a dead body, means disposal by burial, cremation or any other means, and cognate expressions shall be construed accordingly;

"father", in relation to an adopted child, means the child's natural father;

"general search" means a search conducted during any number of successive hours not exceeding six, without the object of the search being specified;

"house" includes a public institution;

"live-birth" means the birth of a child born alive;

"the Minister" means the Chancellor of the Exchequer;

"mother", in relation to an adopted child, means the child's natural mother;

"occupier" in relation to a public institution, includes the governor, keeper, master, matron, superintendent, or other chief resident officer, and, in relation to a house let in separate apartments or lodgings, includes any person residing in the house who is the person under whom the lodgings or separate apartments are immediately held, or his agent;

"particular search" means a search of the indexes covering a period not exceeding five years for a specified entry;

"public institution" means a prison, lock-up or hospital, and such other public or charitable institution as may be prescribed;

"prescribed" means prescribed by regulations made under section thirty-nine of this Act;

"qualified informant", in relation to any birth or death, means a person who is by this Act or, in the case of a birth or death occurring before the commencement of this Act, by any enactment repealed by this Act required, or stated to be qualified, to give information concerning that birth or death;

"registrar" in relation to any birth or death, means the registrar of births and deaths for the sub-district in which the birth or death takes place, or where any still-born child is found exposed or any dead body is found and no information as to the place of birth or death is available, for the sub-district in which the child or the dead body is found;

"relative" includes a relative by marriage or civil partnership;

"still-born child" means a child which has issued forth from its mother after the twenty-fourth week of pregnancy and which did not at any time after being completely expelled from its mother breathe or show any other signs of life, and the expression "still-birth" shall be construed accordingly;

"superintendent registrar" in relation to any registrar, means the superintendent registrar of births, deaths and marriages for the district in which that registrar's sub-district is situate.

[Births and Deaths Registration Act 1953, s 41, as amended by the Children Act 1975, Schs 3 and 4, the Still-Birth (Definition) Act 1992, s 1, SI 1996/273 and the Civil Partnership Act 2004, Sch 27.]

BLASPHEMY

8-2830 General rules. "Serious arguments" (observes Paley) "are fair on all sides. Christianity is but ill defended by refusing audience or toleration to the objection of unbelievers. But whilst we would have freedom of inquiry restrained by no laws but those of decency, we are entitled to demand on behalf of a religion which holds forth to mankind assurances of immortality, that its credit be assailed by no other weapons than those of sober discussion and legitimate reasoning." Our law has adopted this as the rule; sober argument you may answer, but indecent reviling you cannot, and therefore the law steps in and punishes it (*per* Lord ERSKINE). Assuming the correctness of this proposition, it may be laid down that no prosecution could be sustained at the present day for calmly and dispassionately discussing, or even calling in question, the truth of Christianity; and that the offence of blasphemy consists in attacking it by ribaldry, profanity, or indecency, and not in endeavouring by legitimate argument to prove its falsity. On March 5th, 1883, in a prosecution against the *Freethinker*, NORTH J, defined the legal meaning of blasphemy as being a contumelious reproach or profane scoffing against the Christian religion or the Holy Scriptures, and any act exposing the Holy Scriptures and the Christian religion to ridicule, contempt, or derision (*R v Foote* (1883) 10 QBD 378, CA. In the case of *R v Ramsay and Foote* (1883) 48 LT 733, Lord COLERIDGE directed the jury that the mere denial of the truths of Christianity does not amount to blasphemy; but a wilful intention to pervert, insult, and mislead others by means of licentious and contumelious abuse applied to sacred subjects, or by wilful misrepresentations or artful sophistry calculated to mislead the ignorant and unwary, is the criterion and test of guilt; and supposing that the decencies of controversy were observed, even the fundamentals of religion might be attacked; this was approved by PHILLIMORE J, in *R v Boulter* (1908) 72 JP 188. The offence may be committed by written matter as well as by spoken words (*R v Gott* (1922) 16 Cr App Rep 87). In *R v Lemon* [1979] 1 All ER 898, 143 JP 315, the House of Lords, after reviewing earlier authorities on the law of blasphemy, held (1) that blasphemous libel was the publication of any matter that insulted, offended or vilified the Deity or Christ or the Christian religion; that it was the publication of an offensive nature, or in offensive terms, to the Christian religion that constituted the offence; and (2) that provided there was an intention to publish the material the absence of an intention to be blasphemous was irrelevant.

Under the European Convention of Human Rights there is a tension between the protection of religion under Article 9 and freedom of expression under Article 10. Blasphemy laws can be justified[1], but only if–

1. restrictions apply only to the *manner* in which information or ideas are conveyed
2. a high profanity threshold is applied and
3. there are effective safeguards against the over-broad application of any such restrictions[2].

The law of blasphemy does not extend to religions other than Christianity (*R v Chief Metropolitan Stipendiary Magistrate, ex p Choudhury* [1991] 1 QB 429, [1991] 1 All ER 306, 91 Cr App Rep 363, DC.

The crime of blasphemy is triable on indictment. It is punishable by fine or imprisonment, or both.

---

1. *Otto-Preminger Institute v Austria* (1994) 19 EHRR 34 and *Wingrove v United Kingdom* (1996) 24 EHRR 1. The prohibition on discrimination in Article 14 of the European Convention on Human Rights includes discrimination based on disability: *Malone v United Kingdom* (1996) EHRLR 440.
2. *Wingrove v United Kingdom* (1996) 24 EHRR 1.

BRIBERY AND CORRUPTION

8–2839 This title contains the following statutes—

Public Bodies Corrupt Practices Act 1889[1]
(52 & 53 Vict c 69)

8–2840 **1. Corruption in office a misdemeanour.** (1) Every person who shall by himself or by or in conjunction with any other person, corruptly[2] solicit or receive, or agree to receive, for himself, or for any other person, any gift, loan, fee, reward[3], or advantage whatever as an inducement to, or reward for, or otherwise on account of any member, officer, or servant of a public body as in this Act defined, doing or forbearing to do[4] anything in respect of any matter or transaction whatsoever, actual or proposed, in which the said public body is concerned, shall be guilty of a misdemeanour[6].

(2) Every person[5] who shall by himself or by or in conjunction with any other person corruptly[5] give, promise, or offer any gift, loan, fee, reward, or advantage whatsoever to any person, whether for the benefit of that person or of another person, as an inducement to or reward for or otherwise on account of any member, officer, or servant of any public body as in this Act defined, doing or forbearing to do anything in respect of any matter or transaction whatsoever, actual or proposed, in which such public body as aforesaid is concerned, shall be guilty of a misdemeanour[6].
[Public Bodies Corrupt Practices Act 1889, s 1.]

---

1. As to corrupt practices at elections, see the Representation of the People Act 1983, title ELECTIONS, post.
2. See Prevention of Corruption Act 1916, s 2, post. The word "corruptly" denotes that the person making the offer does so deliberately and with the intention that the person to whom it is addressed should enter into a corrupt bargain (*R v Smith* [1960] 2 QB 423, [1960] 1 All ER 256, 124 JP 137).
3. "Reward" covers receipt of money for a past favour without any antecedent agreement, see *R v Sporle* [1972] 1 WLR 118; the offence lies not in showing favour to an application but in accepting a reward for doing so; *R v Parker* (1985) 82 Cr App Rep 69.
4. The words "doing or forbearing to do" are equally applicable to past conduct as to future conduct (*R v Andrews Weatherfoil Ltd* [1972] 1 All ER 65, 136 JP 128).
5. An attempt to induce a shopman by a bribe to sell fraudulently his master's goods at less than the selling price, has been held to be an attempt to incite the shopman to conspire to defraud his master. This case is a common law offence, and is not within the statute, which only applies to servants of public bodies (*R v De Kromme* (1892) 56 JP 682). E tried to obtain money on the pretext that he would forbear himself, or induce someone else to forbear from giving evidence on an application for a music hall licence. E had been in the employ of the London County Council and had given evidence on a previous application—*Held*, it was not necessary to prove he was an officer of the Council at the time of the commission of the offences (*R v Edwards* (1895) 59 JP 88).

6. The distinctions between felony and misdemeanour have been abolished, and the law and practice applying in relation to misdemeanour have in general been made applicable to all offences (Criminal Law Act 1967, s 1, in PART I: MAGISTRATES' COURTS, PROCEDURE, ante).

8–2850   **2. Penalty for offences.**   Any person on conviction for offending as aforesaid shall, at the discretion of the court before which he is convicted—

(a)   be liable[1]—

     (i)   on summary conviction, to imprisonment for a term not exceeding **6 months** or to a fine not exceeding **the statutory maximum,** or to **both**; and

     (ii)   on conviction on indictment, to imprisonment for a term not exceeding 7 **years** or to a **fine**, or to **both**; and

(b)   in addition be liable to be ordered to pay to such body, and in such manner as the court directs, the amount or value of any gift, loan fee, or reward received by him or any part thereof; and

(c)   be liable to be adjudged incapable of being elected or appointed to any public office for five years from the date of his conviction, and to forfeit any such office held by him at the time of his conviction; and

(d)   in the event of a second conviction for a like offence he shall, in addition to the foregoing penalties, be liable to be adjudged to be for ever incapable of holding any public office, and to be incapable for five years of being registered as an elector, or voting at an election either of members to serve in Parliament or of members of any public body, and the enactments for preventing the voting and registration of persons declared by reason of corrupt practices to be incapable of voting shall apply to a person adjudged in pursuance of this section to be incapable of voting; and

(e)   if such person is an officer or servant in the employ of any public body upon such conviction he shall, at the discretion of the court, be liable to forfeit his right and claim to any compensation or pension to which he would otherwise have been entitled.

[Public Bodies Corrupt Practices Act 1889, s 2, as amended by the Representation of the People Act 1948, s 52, the Criminal Justice Act 1948, s 1, the Criminal Justice Act 1967, s 92 and the Criminal Justice Act 1988, s 47.]

---

1. For procedure in respect of this offence which is triable either way, see the Magistrates' Courts Act 1980, ss 17A–21, in PART I: MAGISTRATES' COURTS, PROCEDURE, ante.

8–2851   **3. Savings.**   (1) (*Repealed*).

(2) A person shall not be exempt from punishment under this Act by reason of the invalidity of the appointment or election of a person to a public office.

[Public Bodies Corrupt Practices Act 1889, s 3, as amended by the Statute Law Revision Act 1908.]

8–2852   **4. Restriction on prosecution.**   (1) A prosecution for an offence under this Act shall not be instituted except by or with the consent of the Attorney-General.

(2) In this section the expression "Attorney-General" means the Attorney General for England, and as respects Scotland means the Lord Advocate.

[Public Bodies Corrupt Practices Act 1889, s 4, as amended by the Statute Law Revision Act (Northern Ireland) 1954 and the Law Officers Act 1997, Schedule.]

8–2853   **7. Interpretation.**   In this Act—

The expression "public body"[1] means any council of a county or county of a city or town, any council of a municipal borough, also any board, commissioners, select vestry, or other body which has power to act under and for the purposes of any Act relating to local government, or the public health, or to poor law or otherwise to administer money raised by rates in pursuance of any public general Act, and includes any body which exists in a country or territory outside the United Kingdom and is equivalent to any body described above:

The expression "public office" means any office or employment of a person as a member, officer, or servant of such public body:

The expression "person" includes a body of persons, corporate or unincorporate:

The expression "advantage" includes any office or dignity, and any forbearance to demand any money or money's worth or valuable thing, and includes any aid, vote, consent, or influence, or pretended aid, vote, consent, or influence, and also includes any promise or procurement of or agreement or endeavour to procure, or the holding out of any expectation of any gift, loan, fee, reward, or advantage, as before defined.

[Public Bodies Corrupt Practices Act 1889, s 7, as amended by the Anti-terrorism, Crime and Security Act 2001, s 108(3).]

---

1. This expression is extended to local and public authorities of all descriptions by the Prevention of Corruption Act 1916, s 4(2), post, and to the Civil Aviation Authority by the Civil Aviation Act 1982, s 19.

Prevention of Corruption Act 1906
(6 Edw 7 c 34)

8–2870 1. Punishment of corrupt transactions with agents. (1) If any agent corruptly[1] accepts or obtains, or agrees to accept or attempts to obtain, from any person, for himself or for any other person, any gift or consideration as an inducement[2] or reward for doing or forbearing to do, or for having after the passing of this Act done or forborne to do, any act in relation to his principal's affairs[3] or business, or for showing of forbearing to show favour or disfavour to any person in relation to his principal's affairs or business; or

If any person corruptly gives or agrees to give or offers any gift or consideration to any agent[4] as an inducement or reward for doing or forbearing to do, or for having after the passing of this Act done or forborne to do, any act in relation to his principal's affairs or business, or for showing or forbearing to show favour or disfavour to any person in relation to his principal's affairs or business; or

If any person knowingly[5] gives to any agent, or if any agent knowingly uses with intent to deceive his principal, any receipt, account, or other document[6] in respect of which the principal is interested, and which contains any statement which is false or erroneous or defective in any material particular, and which to his knowledge is intended to mislead the principal;
he shall be guilty of a misdemeanor[7], and shall be liable[8]—

(a) on summary conviction, to imprisonment for a term not exceeding **6 months** or to a fine not exceeding **the statutory maximum**, or to **both**; and

(b) on conviction on indictment, to imprisonment for a term not exceeding **7 years** or to a **fine**, or to **both**.

(2) For the purposes of this Act the expression "consideration"[11] includes valuable consideration of any kind; the expression "agent"[12] includes any person employed by or acting for another; and the expression "principal" includes an employer.

(3) A person serving under the Crown[13] or under any corporation or any borough, county, or district council, or any board of guardians, is an agent within the meaning of this Act.

(4) For the purposes of this Act it is immaterial if—

(a) the principal's affairs or business have no connection with the United Kingdom and are conducted in a country or territory outside the United Kingdom;

(b) the agent's functions have no connection with the United Kingdom and are carried out in a country or territory outside the United Kingdom.

[Prevention of Corruption Act 1906, s 1, as amended by the Criminal Justice Act 1948, s 1, the Criminal Justice Act 1967, s 92 and Sch 3, the Local Authorities etc (Miscellaneous Provisions) (No 2) Order 1974, SI 1974/595, Sch 1, Part I, the Criminal Law Act 1977, s 28, the Criminal Justice Act 1988, s 47 and the Anti-terrorism, Crime and Security Act 2001, s 108(2).]

---

1. See Prevention of Corruption Act 1916, s 2, post. "Corruptly" means purposely doing an act which the law forbids as tending to corrupt (*R v Welburn, Nurdin, Randel* (1979) 69 Cr App Rep 254). It is unnecessary under s 1(1) to prove dishonesty, even where a private organisation as opposed to a public body is involved: *R v Godden-Wood* [2001] Crim LR 810, CA.

2. An inducement to show favour does not require to be completed by proof that in fact favour was shown (*R v Carr* [1956] 3 All ER 979n, 121 JP 58).

3. These words fall to be construed widely and the defendant need not be acting in direct relation to his principal's affairs (*Morgan v DPP* [1970] 3 All ER 1053, 135 JP 86).

4. The Scottish courts have held on a complaint charging an attempt to bribe a police constable whilst in the execution of his duty and acting for his employer, the chief constable, that the police constable was an agent within the section (*Graham v Hart* 1908 SC (J) 26).

5. An intention to corrupt the agent is not an essential ingredient in this offence (*Sage v Eichols* [1919] 2 KB 171, 83 JP 170).

6. The words "receipt, account" refer to documents passing between *parties*, that is between principal and a third party, and the words "other documents" should be construed similarly; thus the third paragraph of s 1(1) does not apply to a false document knowingly used by an employee with intent to deceive or mislead his employers (*R v Tweedie* [1984] QB 729, [1984] 2 All ER 136, 148 JP 716, CA).

7. The contract is also void. The Bankruptcy Court will go behind a judgment founded on it (*Re A Debtor (No 229 of 1927)* [1927] 2 Ch 367).

8. For the procedure in respect of this offence which is triable either way, see the Magistrates' Courts Act 1980, ss 17A–21, in PART I: MAGISTRATES' COURTS, PROCEDURE, ante.

11. "Consideration" connotes the existence of something in the shape of a contract or bargain between the parties (*R v Braithwaite* [1983] 2 All ER 87, [1983] 1 WLR 385, 147 JP 301).

12. See Prevention of Corruption Act 1916, s 4(2), post.

13. An additional superintendent registrar appointed by a local authority under the Registration Service Act 1953 was held to be a person serving under the Crown (*R v Barrett* [1976] 3 All ER 895, 141 JP 46).

8–2871 2. Prosecution of offences. (1) A prosecution for an offence under this Act shall not be instituted without the consent, in England of the Attorney-General.

(2) (*Repealed*).

(3) Every information for any offence under this Act shall be upon oath[1].

(4),(5) (*Repealed*).

(6) Any person aggrieved by a summary conviction under this Act may appeal to the Crown Court.

[Prevention of Corruption Act 1906, s 2, as amended by the Costs in Criminal Cases Act 1908, s 10 and Sch, the Administration of Justice (Miscellaneous Provisions) Act 1933, s 10 and Sch 3, the Criminal Law Act 1967, s 10 and Sch 3, the Courts Act 1971, Sch 8 and the Law Officers Act 1997, Schedule.]

---

1. This provision was not repealed by the Magistrates' Courts Act 1952.

Prevention of Corruption Act 1916
(6 & 7 Geo 5 c 64)

8–2890   1. (*Repealed*).

8–2891   2. Presumption of corruption in certain cases.   Where in any proceedings against a person for an offence under the Prevention of Corruption Act 1906, or the Public Bodies Corrupt Practices Act 1889, it is proved that any money, gift, or other consideration has been paid or given to or received[1] by a person in the employment of Her Majesty or any Government Department or a public body by or from a person, or agent of a person, holding or seeking to obtain a contract from Her Majesty or any Government Department or public body, the money, gift, or consideration shall be deemed to have been paid or given and received corruptly as such inducement or reward as is mentioned in such Act unless the contrary is proved[2].

[Prevention of Corruption Act 1916, s 2.]

---

1. When the payment, etc, of the money has been proved, the onus is on the defendant (*R v Jenkins, R v Evans-Jones* (1923) 87 JP 115).
2. As to the evidence required to rebut this presumption, see *R v Carr-Briant* [1943] KB 607, [1943] 2 All ER 156, 107 JP 167. The presumption in s 2 does not apply to a statutory conspiracy to corrupt contrary to s 1(1) of the Criminal Law Act 1977 (*R v A–G, ex p Rockall* [1999] 4 All ER 312).

8–2892   3. (*Repealed*).

8–2893   4. Short title and Interpretation.   (1) This Act may be cited as the Prevention of Corruption Act, 1916, and the Public Bodies Corrupt Practices Act 1889, the Prevention of Corruption Act, 1906, and this Act may be cited together as the Prevention of Corruption Acts, 1889 to 1916.

(2) In this Act and in the Public Bodies Corrupt Practices Act 1889, the expression "public body" includes, in addition to the bodies mentioned in the last-mentioned Act, local and public authorities of all descriptions[1] (including authorities existing in a country or territory outside the United Kingdom) and companies which, in accordance with Part V of the Local Government and Housing Act 1989, are under the control of one or more local authorities.

(3) A person serving under any such public body is an agent within the meaning of the Prevention of Corruption Act 1906, and the expressions "agent" and "consideration" in this Act have the same[2] meaning as in the Prevention of Corruption Act 1906, as amended by this Act.

[Prevention of Corruption Act 1916, s 4, as amended by the Anti-terrorism, Crime and Security Act 2001, s 108(4).]

---

1. The expression "public body" includes the Civil Aviation Authority: Civil Aviation Act 1982, s 19. The expression refers also to any body which has public or statutory duties to perform and which perform those duties and carry out their transactions for the benefit of the public and not for private profit (*DPP v Manners* [1977] 1 All ER 316, 141 JP 143) but the term does not extend to the Crown or a government department. The appropriate statutory provision relating to civil servants is s s 1 of the Prevention of Corruption Act 1906 (*R v Natji* [2002] EWCA Crim 271, [2002] 1 WLR 2337, [2002] 2 Cr App Rep 20, [2002] Crim LR 580).
2. Prevention of Corruption Act 1906, s 1(2), (3), ante.

Honours (Prevention of Abuses) Act 1925
(15 & 16 Geo 5 c 72)

8–2910   1. Punishment of abuses in connection with the grant of honours.   (1) If any person accepts or obtains or agrees to accept or attempts to obtain from any person, for himself or for any other person, or for any purpose, any gift, money, or valuable consideration as an inducement or reward for procuring or assisting or endeavouring to procure the grant of a dignity or title of honour to any person, or otherwise in connection with such a grant, he shall be guilty of a misdemeanour.

(2) If any person gives or agrees or proposes to give, or offers to any person any gift, money or valuable consideration as an inducement or reward for procuring or assisting or endeavouring to procure the grant of a dignity or title of honour to any person, or otherwise in connection with such a grant, he shall be guilty of a misdemeanour.

(3) Any person guilty of a misdemeanour under this Act shall be liable[1] on conviction on indictment to imprisonment for a term not exceeding **two years**, or to a fine, or to both such imprisonment and such fine, or on summary conviction to imprisonment for a term not exceeding **three months** or to a fine not exceeding **the statutory maximum**, or to both such imprisonment and such fine, and where the person convicted (whether on indictment or summarily) received any such gift, money or consideration as aforesaid which is capable of forfeiture, he shall in addition to any other punishment be liable to forfeit the same to Her Majesty.

[Honours (Prevention of Abuses) Act 1925, s 1 amended by the Criminal Law Act 1977, ss 28 and 32.]

---

1. For procedure in respect of this offence which is triable either way, see the Magistrates' Courts Act 1980, ss 17A–21, in PART I: MAGISTRATES' COURTS, PROCEDURE, ante.

BUILDING SOCIETIES

Building Societies Act 1986
(1986 c 53)

Note

8–2920   The Building Societies Act 1986 is not printed in this work. The Act makes fresh provision with respect to building societies giving them expanded powers to lend money and provide other services to their members. The Act establishes the Building Societies Commission, makes provision for the constitution of building societies, the protection of investors, and gives powers to the Commission to protect the interests of building society shareholders and depositors. Societies are required to maintain appropriate accounting records and control systems. The societies' auditors must report to the members on the annual accounts which are to be laid before each society's annual general meeting and each year report to the Commission on whether the accounting requirements have been complied with.

The Act creates many offences and makes special provision as to time limits for commencing proceedings (s 111), liability of officers and defence of due diligence (s 112), and evidence of documents (s 113).

Subject to specified exceptions, all provisions of the Act were brought into force over a period beginning with 25 September 1986 and finishing on 1 January 1988 (s 126 and the Building Societies Act 1986 (Commencement No 1) Order 1986, SI 1986/1560). Further provisions were brought into force on 17 July 1989 by the Building Societies Act 1986 (Commencement No 2) Order 1989, SI 1989/1083. At the date of going to press, s 35 (prohibition on linking services); and s 124 and Sch 21 (recognition of institutions and practitioners for provision of conveyancing services) had not been brought into force; however these provisions are prospectively repealed by the Courts and Legal Services Act 1990, s 125 and Sch 20.

The Building Societies Act 1986 has been extensively amended. The Building Societies Act 1997 makes numerous amendments to the 1986 Act and, in particular, makes provision for amalgamating the Building Societies Investor Protection Board and the Deposit Protection Board into a single board. This Act is to be brought into force on such days as the Treasury may order and at the date of going to press the Building Societies Act 1997 (Commencement No 1) Order 1997, SI 1997/1307, and (Commencement No 2) Order 1997, SI 1997/1427, had been made. The Building Societies (Distribution) Act 1997 amends the law in respect of distribution of assets on the take over or conversion of a building society, and the Act applies in relation to a transfer of a business of a building society where the decision of the board of directors of the society to enter into the transfer in question was made public after 22 January 1997.

For the full text of the Acts, see *Halsbury's Statutes*, Fourth Edition, Vol 5 BUILDING SOCIETIES.

BURIAL AND CREMATION

8–2930   This title contains the following statutes—

Cemeteries Clauses Act 1847
(10 & 11 Vict c 65)

8–2949   1. Incorporation with special Act.   This Act shall extend only to such cemeteries as shall be authorized by any Act of Parliament hereafter to be passed which shall declare that this Act shall

be incorporated therewith; and all the clauses of this Act, save so far as they shall be expressly varied or excepted in any such Act, shall apply to the cemetery authorized thereby, so far as they are applicable to such cemetery, and shall, with the clauses of every other Act incorporated therewith, form part of such Act, and be construed therewith as forming one Act.
[Cemeteries Clauses Act 1847, as amended by the Statute Law Revision Act 1891.]

Interpretation

8–2950   And with respect to the construction of this Act, and any Act incorporated therewith, be it enacted as follows:

8–2951   2.   *"The special Act"*[1].—The expression "the special Act" used in this Act shall be construed to mean any Act which shall be hereafter passed authorizing the making of a cemetery, and with which this Act shall be incorporated; and

"Prescribed."—The word "prescribed" used in this Act in reference to any matter herein stated shall be construed to refer to such matter as the same shall be prescribed or provided for in the special Act, and the sentence in which such word occurs shall be construed as if instead of the word "prescribed" the expression "prescribed for that purpose in the special Act" had been used; and

"The lands."—The expression "the lands" shall mean the lands which shall by the special Act be authorized to be taken or used for the purposes thereof; and

"The company."—The expression "the company" shall mean the person by the special Act authorized to construct the cemetery.
[Cemeteries Clauses Act 1847, s 2.]

---

1. If a cemetery is provided by a local authority under the Public Health (Interments) Act 1879, the "special Act" mentioned in this section is that Act and the "company" is the local authority.

8–2952   3.   Interpretations in this and the special Act.   The following words and expressions in both this and the special Act, and any Act incorporated therewith, shall have the meanings hereby assigned to them, unless there be something in the subject or context repugnant to such construction; (that is to say,)

Number.—Words importing the singular number shall include the plural number, and words importing the plural number only shall include also the singular number:
Gender.—Words importing the masculine gender shall include females:
"Person."—The word "person" shall include a corporation, whether aggregate or sole:
"Lands."—The word "lands" shall include messuages, lands, and hereditaments, of any tenure:
"The cemetery."—The expression "the cemetery" shall mean the cemetery or burial ground, and the works connected therewith, by the special Act authorized to be constructed:
"Month".—The word "month" shall mean calendar month:
"Superior courts."—The expression "superior courts" shall mean her Majesty's superior courts at Westminster or Dublin, as the case may require
"Established Church."—The expression "Established Church" shall mean the United Church of England and Ireland as by law established:
"Justice"—"Two justices."—The word "justice" shall mean justice of the peace acting for the place where the matter requiring the cognizance of any such justice arises, and if such matter arise in respect of lands situated not wholly in one jurisdiction shall mean a justice acting for the place where any part of such lands shall be situated; and where any matter is authorized or required to be done by "two justices", the expression "two justices" shall be understood to mean two or more justices met and acting together:*
[Cemeteries Clauses Act 1847, s 3, as amended by the Statute Law Revision Act, 1891, and the Statute Law (Repeals) Act 1981, Sch 1.]

---

*Words in definition repealed in relation to England and Wales by the Courts Act 2003, Sch 8, from a date to be appointed.

Citing the Act

And with respect to citing this Act or any part thereof, be it enacted as follows:

8–2954   4.   Short title.   In citing this Act in other Acts of Parliament, and in legal instruments, it shall be sufficient to use the expression, "The Cemeteries Clauses Act, 1847."
[Cemeteries Clauses Act 1847, s 4.]

Protection of cemetery

And with respect to the protection of the cemetery, be it enacted as follows:

8–2956   59.   Disturbances and nuisances in cemetery.   Every person who shall play at any game or sport, or discharge firearms, save at a military funeral, in the cemetery, or who shall wilfully and

unlawfully disturb any persons assembled in the cemetery for the purpose of burying any body therein, or who shall commit any nuisance within the cemetery, shall forfeit . . . for every such offence a sum not exceeding **level 1** on the standard scale.
[Cemeteries Clauses Act 1847, s 59, as amended by the Justices of the Peace Act 1949, s 46 and Sch 7, the Criminal Justice Act 1967, Sch 3, and the Criminal Justice Act 1982, ss 38 and 46.]

Recovery of damages and penalties
And with respect to the recovery of damages not specially provided for, and of penalties, and to the determination of any other matter referred to justices, be it enacted as follows:

8–2958 62. Railways Clauses Consolidation Act, 8 & 9 Vict c 20, incorporated as to damages, etc. The clauses of the Railways Clauses Consolidation Act, 1845, with respect to the recovery of damages not specially provided for, and of penalties, and to the determination of any other matter referred to justices, shall be incorporated with this and the special Act; and such clauses shall apply to the cemetery and to the company respectively.
[Cemeteries Clauses Act 1847, s 62.]

8–2959 67. Penalty on company failing to keep or deposit such copies. If the company fail to keep or deposit any of the said copies of the special Act as herein-before mentioned[1], they shall forfeit a penalty not exceeding **level 2** on the standard scale for every such offence, and also **five pounds** for every day afterwards during which such copy shall be not so kept or deposited.
[Cemeteries Clauses Act 1847, s 67, as amended by the Criminal Law Act 1977, s 31, and the Criminal Justice Act 1982, s 46.]

---

1. Section 66 requires the company at all times to keep copies of the special Act open to inspection.

Burial Act 1855
(18 & 19 Vict c 128)

8–2980 2. Penalty of persons burying contrary to the provisions of Orders in Council. If any person, after the time mentioned in any Order in Council under the said Acts or any of them, or this Act, for the discontinuance of burials, shall knowingly and wilfully bury any body or in anywise act or assist in the burial of any body in any church, chapel, churchyard, burial ground, or place of burial, or (as the case may be) within the limits in which burials have by such Orders been ordered to be discontinued, in violation of the provisions of any such Order, every person so offending shall, upon summary conviction before two justices of the peace, forfeit a sum not exceeding **level 1** on the standard scale.
[Burial Act 1855, s 2, as amended by the Criminal Law Act 1977, s 31, and the Criminal Justice Act 1982, s 46.]

Burial Act 1857
(20 & 21 Vict c 81)

8–2990 15. Persons wilfully destroying, etc, register book of burials, guilty of an offence. Every person who shall wilfully destroy or injure, or cause to be destroyed or injured, any register book of burials, kept according to the provisions of this Act, or any part or certified copy of any part of such register . . . or shall wilfully insert or cause to be inserted in any registry book or certified copy thereof any false entry of any burial, or shall wilfully give any false certificate, or shall certify any writing to be a copy or extract of any such register book, knowing the same to be false in any part thereof . . . shall be guilty of an offence[1].
[Burial Act 1857, s 15, as amended by the Forgery Act 1913, s 20 and Sch, the Criminal Law Act 1967, ss 1 and 12.]

---

1. This offence is triable only on indictment.

8–2991 25. Bodies not to be removed[1] from burial grounds, save under faculty, without licence of Secretary of State[2]. Except in the cases where a body is removed from one consecrated place of burial to another by faculty granted by the ordinary for that purpose, it shall not be lawful to remove any body, or the remains of any body, which may have been interred in any place of burial, without licence under the hand of one of Her Majesty's Principal Secretaries of State[3], and with such precautions as such Secretary of State may prescribe as the condition of such licence; and any person who shall remove any such body or remains, contrary to this enactment, or who shall neglect to observe the precautions prescribed as the condition of the licence for removal, shall, on summary conviction before any two justices of the peace, forfeit and pay for every such offence a sum not exceeding **level 1** on the standard scale.
[Burial Act 1857, s 25, as amended by the Criminal Law Act 1977, s 31, and the Criminal Justice Act 1982, s 46.]

1. It is also an indictable offence to remove a dead body from the grave (*R v Lynn* (1788) 2 Term Rep 733; *R v Sharpe* (1857) Dears & B 160, 21 JP 86). The executors have the right to possession of the body, and it is their duty to bury it (*Williams v Williams* (1882) 20 Ch D 659, 46 JP 726).

2. This section does not apply to a removal carried out in accordance with the provisions of the Schedule to the Disused Burial Grounds (Amendment) Act 1981.

3. The functions of the Minister, so far as exercisable in relation to Wales, have been transferred to the National Assembly for Wales, by the National Assembly for Wales (Transfer of Functions) Order 1999, SI 1999/672, art 2, Sch 1.

Registration of Burials Act 1864
(27 & 28 Vict c 97)

8–3010   **1. All burials in burial grounds in England not now required to be registered shall be registered.**   All burials in any burial ground in England which are not now by law required to be registered shall be registered in register books to be provided for each such burial ground by the company, body, or persons to whom the same belongs, and to be kept for that purpose according to the laws in force by which registers are required to be kept by rectors, vicars, or curates of parishes or ecclesiastical districts in England.
[Registration of Burials Act 1864, s 1.]

8–3011   **2. Officers by whom books shall be kept.**   Such register books shall be so kept for every such burial ground by some officer or person to be appointed to that duty by the company, body, or persons to whom such burial ground belongs.
[Registration of Burials Act 1864, s 2.]

8–3012   **3.**   (*Repealed*).

8–3013   **4. Penalty for failure to comply with Act.**   If any such company, body, or persons, or any such officer or person as aforesaid wilfully fail to comply with any of the provisions of this Act, they or he shall be guilty of an offence against this Act, and on summary conviction thereof before a justice of the peace shall be liable for every such offence to a penalty not exceeding **level 1** on the standard scale.
[Registration of Burials Act 1864, s 4, as amended by the Criminal Law Act 1977, s 31, and the Criminal Justice Act 1982, s 46.]

8–3014   **5. Registers and copies, etc, to be evidence.**   The register books kept under this Act, or copies thereof or extracts therefrom, shall be received in all courts as evidence of the burials entered therein.
[Registration of Burials Act 1864, s 5.]

8–3015   **6.**   *Searches*

8–3016   **7. As to "burial ground".**   In this Act the term "burial ground" includes a vault or other place where any body is buried.
[Registration of Burials Act 1864, s 7.]

Burial Laws Amendment Act 1880
(43 & 44 Vict c 41)

8–3030   **7. Burials to be conducted in a decent and orderly manner and without obstruction.** All burials under this Act, whether with or without a religious service, shall be conducted in a decent and orderly manner; and every person guilty of any riotous, violent, or indecent behaviour at any burial under this Act, or wilfully obstructing such burial or any such service as aforesaid thereat, or who shall, in any such churchyard or graveyard as aforesaid, deliver any address, not being part of or incidental to a religious service permitted by this Act, and not otherwise permitted by any lawful authority, or who shall, under colour of any religious service or otherwise, in any such churchyard or graveyard, wilfully endeavour to bring into contempt or obloquy the Christian religion, or the belief or worship of any church or denomination of Christians, or the members or any minister of any such church or denomination, or any other person, shall be guilty of an offence[1].
[Burial Laws Amendment Act 1880, s 7, as amended by the Criminal Law Act 1967, s 1.]

1. This offence is triable only on indictment.

8–3031   **8. Powers for prevention of disorder.**   All powers and authorities now existing by law for the preservation of order, and for the prevention and punishment of disorderly behaviour in any churchyard or graveyard, may be exercised in any case of burial under this Act in the same manner

and by the same persons as if the same had been a burial according to the rites of the Church of England[1].
[Burial Laws Amendment Act 1880, s 8.]

---

1. See in particular the Ecclesiastical Courts Jurisdiction Act 1860. The Cemeteries Clauses Act 1847, s 59, ante, contains provisions against disorderly conduct in cemeteries.

8–3032   10. Burials under Act to be registered.   When any burial has taken place under this Act the person so having the charge of or being responsible for such burial as aforesaid shall, on the day thereof, or the next day thereafter, transmit a certificate of such burial, in the form or to the effect of Schedule (B) annexed to this Act, to the rector, vicar, incumbent, or other officiating minister in charge of the parish or district in which the churchyard or graveyard is situate or to which it belongs, or in the case of any burial ground or cemetery vested in any burial board to the person required by law to keep the register of burials in such burial ground or cemetery, who shall thereupon enter such burial in the register of burials of such parish or district, or of such burial ground or cemetery, and such entry shall form part thereof. Such entry, instead of stating by whom the ceremony of burial was performed, shall state by whom the same has been certified under this Act . . . any rector, vicar, or minister, or other such person as aforesaid, receiving such certificate, who shall refuse or neglect duly to enter such burial in such register as aforesaid, shall be guilty of an offence[1].
[Burial Laws Amendment Act 1880, s 10, as amended by the Perjury Act, 1911, s 17 and Sch, the Criminal Law Act 1967, s 1, and the Local Authorities' Cemeteries Order 1974, SI 1974/628.]

---

1. This offence is triable only on indictment.

Cremation Act 1902
(2 Edw 7 c 8)

8–3050   1. Short title.   This Act may be cited as the Cremation Act, 1902.
[Cremation Act 1902, s 1.]

8–3051   2. Definitions.   In this Act—

   The expression "burial authority"[1] shall mean any burial board, any council, committee or other local authority having the powers and duties of a burial board, and any local authority maintaining a cemetery under the Public Health (Interments) Act, 1879, or under any local Act;
   The expression "crematorium" shall mean any building fitted with appliances for the purpose of burning human remains, and shall include everything incidental or ancillary thereto.
[Cremation Act 1902, s 2.]

8–3052   4. Burial authority may provide for cremation.   The powers of a burial authority to provide and maintain burial grounds or cemeteries, or anything essential, ancillary or incidental thereto, shall be deemed to extend to and include the provision and maintenance of crematoria.
[Cremation Act 1902, s 4, as amended by the Cremation Act 1952, s 1.]

---

1. For the purpose of this Act and the Cremation Act 1952, the expression "burial authority" shall be deemed to include any council having power to provide a cemetery under the Public Health (Interments) Act 1879 (Cremation Act 1952, s 4(1)).

8–3053   5. Site of crematorium[1].   No crematorium shall be constructed nearer to any dwelling-house than two hundred yards, except with the consent, in writing, of the owner, lessee and occupier of such house, nor within fifty yards of any public highway, nor in the consecrated part of the burial ground of any burial authority.
[Cremation Act 1902, s 5.]

---

1. New crematoria may not be used for the burning of human remains unless the site and plans have been approved by the Secretary of State for the Environment and it has been certified to the Secretary of State that the premises have been completed and are properly equipped (Cremation Act 1952, s 1).

8–3054   7. Regulations as to burning.   The Secretary of State shall make regulations[1] as to the maintenance and inspection of crematoria, and prescribing in what cases and under what conditions the burning of any human remains may take place, and directing the disposition or interment of the ashes, and prescribing the forms of the notices, certificates and [applications] to be given or made before any such burning is permitted to take place, . . . and also regulations as to the registration of such burnings as have taken place. [Each such application shall be verified in such manner as the Secretary of State may by such regulations prescribe.] . . . . All statutory provisions relating to the destruction and falsification of registers of burials, and the admissibility of extracts therefrom as evidence in courts and otherwise, shall apply to the register of burnings directed by such regulations to be kept. . . .

[Cremation Act 1902, s 7, as amended by the Finance Act 1949, s 52 and Sch 11, and the Cremation Act 1952, s 2.]

---

1. This includes power to make regulations applying the provisions of the Births and Deaths Registration Act 1926 (Births and Deaths Registration Act 1926, s 10, title BIRTHS AND DEATHS, ante). See the Regulations as to Cremation 1930, SR & O No 1016, as amended by SI 1952/1568; SI 1965/1146, SI 1979/1138, SI 1985/153 and SI 2000/58.

8-3055   8. Penalties for breach of regulations, etc.   (1) Every person who shall contravene any such regulation[1] as aforesaid, or shall knowingly carry out or procure or take part in the burning of any human remains except in accordance with such regulations and the provisions of this Act, shall (in addition to any liability or penalty which he may otherwise incur) be liable, on summary conviction, to a penalty not exceeding **level 3** on the standard scale.

(2) Every person who shall wilfully make any false . . . representation, or sign or utter any false certificate, with a view to procuring the burning of any human remains, shall (in addition to any penalty or liability which he may otherwise incur) be liable[2] to imprisonment, not exceeding **two years**.

[Cremation Act 1902, s 8, as amended by the Perjury Act 1911, s 17 and Sch, the Criminal Law Act 1967, s 10 and Sch 3, the Courts Act 1971, Sch 8, the Criminal Justice Act 1982, ss 38 and 46 and the Statute Law (Repeals) Act 1993, Sch 1.]

---

1. This includes power to make regulations applying the provisions of the Births and Deaths Registration Act 1926 (Births and Deaths Registration Act 1926, s 10, title BIRTHS AND DEATHS, ante). See the Regulations as to Cremation 1930, SR & O No 1016, as amended by SI 1952/1568; SI 1965/1146, SI 1979/1138 and SI 1985/153.
2. This offence is triable either way (Magistrates' Courts Act 1980, Sch 1, in PART I, ante). For procedure see the Magistrates' Courts Act 1980, ss 17A–21, in PART I: MAGISTRATES' COURTS, PROCEDURE, ante.

8-3056   13. Application of 10 & 11 Vict, c 65, ss 52 and 57.   Sections fifty-two and fifty-seven of the Cemeteries Clauses Act, 1847, and any similar provisions in any local and personal Act authorising the making of a cemetery, shall apply to the disposition or interment of the ashes of a cremated body, as if it were the burial of a body.

[Cremation Act 1902, s 13.]

CENSUS OF POPULATION

8-3057   This title contains the following statutes—

Census Act 1920[1]
(10 & 11 Geo 5 c 41)

8-3058   1. Power to direct taking of census.   *Power of Her Majesty by Order[2] in Council from time to time to direct that a census shall be taken for Great Britain or any part thereof.*

---

1. The Census Regulations 2000, SI 2000/1473, make provision for the conduct of the Census directed to be taken by the Census Order 2000, SI 2000/744 on 29 April 2001.
2. The Census Order 2000, SI 2000/744, appointed the 29 April 2001 as a census day.

8-3059   2. Duty of Registrar-General to carry out census, and provision for expenses.   (1) It shall be the duty of the Registrar-General to make such arrangements and do all such things as are necessary for the taking of a census in accordance with the provisions of this Act and of any Order in Council or regulations made thereunder, and for that purpose to make arrangements for the preparation and issue of the necessary forms and instructions and for the collection of the forms when filled up.

(2) The Registrar-General in the exercise of his powers and in the performance of his duties under this Act or under any Order in Council or regulations made thereunder, shall be subject to the control of, and comply with any directions given by, the Chancellor of the Exchequer.

(3) *Expenses.*

[Census Act 1920, s 2, as amended by SI 1968/1699 and SI 1996/273.]

8-3060   3. Regulations with respect to proceedings for taking census.   *Power of the Secretary of State to make regulations[1] for the purpose of enabling any Order in Council directing a census to be taken to be carried into effect.*

8–3061   6. *Provision with respect to local census.*

8–3062   8. Penalties.   (1) If any person—

(a)   refuses or neglects to comply with or acts in contravention of any of the provisions of this Act or any Order in Council or regulations made under this Act; or

(b)   being a person required under this Act to make a statutory declaration with respect to the performance of his duties, makes a false declaration; or

(c)   being a person required by an Order in Council or regulations made under this Act to make, sign, or deliver any document, makes, signs, or delivers, or causes to be made, signed, or delivered a false document; or

(d)   being a person required in pursuance of any such Order in Council or regulations to answer any question, refuses[1] to answer or gives a false answer to that question;

he shall for each offence be liable on summary conviction to a fine not exceeding **level 3** on the standard scale.

(1A) But no person shall be liable to a penalty under subsection (1) for refusing or neglecting to state any particulars in respect of religion.

(2) If the Registrar-General for England and Wales or the Registrar-General for Scotland ("the Registrars") or any person who is—

(a)   under the control of either of the Registrars; or

(b)   a supplier of any services to either of them,

discloses any personal census information to another person, without lawful authority, he shall be guilty of an offence.

(3) If any person discloses to another person any personal census information which he knows has been disclosed in contravention of this Act, he shall be guilty of an offence.

(4) It shall be a defence for a person charged with an offence under subsection (2) or (3) to prove—

(a)   that at the time of the alleged offence he believed—

(i)   that he was acting with lawful authority; or

(ii) that the information in question was not personal census information; and

(b)   that he had no reasonable cause to believe otherwise.

(5) A person guilty of an offence under subsection (2) or (3) shall be liable[2]—

(a)   on summary conviction, to imprisonment for a term not exceeding **six months** or to a fine not exceeding **the statutory maximum** or to both;

(b)   on conviction on indictment, to imprisonment for a term not exceeding **two years** or to a **fine** or to both.

(6) For the purposes of this section—

(a)   references to a Registrar include, where he is also the holder of a designated office, references to him in his capacity as the holder of that office;

(b)   a person is to be treated as under the control of one of the Registrars if he is, or has been—

(i)   employed by that Registrar (whether or not on a full-time basis); or

(ii) otherwise employed, or acting (whether or not on a full-time basis) as part of that Registrar's staff for purposes of this Act;

(c)   a person is to be treated as a supplier of services to a Registrar if he—

(i)   supplies, or has supplied, any services to that Registrar in connection with the discharge by that Registrar of any of his functions; or

(ii) is, or has been, employed by such a supplier.

(7) In this section—

"census information" means any information which is—

(i)   acquired by any person mentioned in subsection (2) above in the course of any work done by him in connection with the discharge of functions under section 2 or 4 of this Act;

(ii) acquired by any such person in the course of working, for purposes of section 5 of this Act, with any information acquired as mentioned in sub-paragraph (i) above; or

(iii) derived from any information so acquired;

"designated office", in relation to a Registrar, means any office for the time being designated by him in writing for the purposes of this section; and

"personal census information" means any census information which relates to an identifiable person or household.*

[Census Act 1920, s 8, as amended by the Criminal Justice Act 1948, s 1(2), the Criminal Justice Act 1967, Sch 3, the Criminal Justice Act 1982, ss 38 and 46, the Census (Confidentiality) Act 1991, s 1, the Census (Amendment) (Scotland) Act 2000, s 1 and the Census (Amendment) Act 2000, s 1.]

---

*Amended in relation to Scotland by the Freedom of Information (Scotland) Act 2002.
1. See *Turner v Midgley* [1967] 3 All ER 601.
2. This offence is triable either way; for procedure see the Magistrates' Courts Act 1980, ss 17A–21, in PART I: MAGISTRATES' COURTS, PROCEDURE, ante.

Population (Statistics) Act 1938 [1]

(1 & 2 Geo 6 c 12)

8–3063   1. Power to direct information to be furnished.   With a view to the compilation of statistical information with respect to the social and civil condition of the population of Great Britain, every person giving information in accordance with the Registration Acts[2], upon the registration, on or after the first day of July nineteen hundred and thirty-eight, of any birth, still-birth, or death, shall furnish to the registration officer such of the particulars specified in the Schedule to this Act as are appropriate to the registration and are within the knowledge of the person giving the information.
[Population (Statistics) Act 1938, s 1.]

---

1. This Act, enacted so as to be of temporary duration, was given permanent effect by the Population (Statistics) Act 1960, s 1. Prosecutions under this Act may not be commenced by superintendent registrars except with the consent of the Registrar General: reg 72 of the Registration of Births and Deaths Regulations 1987, SI 1987/2088 as amended.
2. For the meaning of the "Registration Acts", see s 7(2), post, and note thereto.

8–3064   2. Duty of Registrar-General to collect information, and provision for expenses. (1) It shall be the duty of the Registrar-General to make such arrangements and to do all such things as are necessary for the collection and collation of all particulars furnished to registration officers pursuant to this Act, and for that purpose to make arrangements for the preparation and issue of any necessary forms and instructions.
   (2) The Registrar-General in the performance of his functions under this Act shall be subject to the control of, and shall comply with any directions given by, the Chancellor of the Exchequer.
   (3) *Expenses.*
[Population (Statistics) Act 1938, s 2, as amended by SI 1996/273.]

8–3065   4. Penalties. (1) If any person—
   (a) refuses or neglects to furnish in accordance with this Act any information which he is required by this Act to furnish; or
   (b) in furnishing any such information makes any statement which, to his knowledge, is false in a material particular;
he shall be liable on summary conviction to a fine not exceeding **level 1** on the standard scale.
   (2) No information obtained by virtue of this Act with respect to any particular person shall be disclosed except so far as may be necessary—
   (a) for the performance by any person of his functions under this Act in connection with the furnishing, collection or collation of such information; or
   (b) for the performance by the Registrar-General of his functions under section five of the Census Act, 1920;
and if any person discloses any such information in contravention of this subsection, he shall be liable[1] on summary conviction to imprisonment for a term not exceeding **three months** or to a fine not exceeding **the statutory maximum**, or to both such imprisonment and such fine, or, on conviction on indictment, to imprisonment for a term not exceeding **two years** or to a fine, or to both such imprisonment and such fine:
   Provided that nothing in this subsection shall apply to any disclosure of information made for the purposes of any proceedings which may be taken in respect of an offence under this section, or for the purposes of any report of such proceedings.
[Population (Statistics) Act 1938, s 4, as amended by the Criminal Law Act 1977, ss 28, 31 and 32 and the Criminal Justice Act 1982, s 46.]

---

1. For procedure in respect of this offence triable either way, see the Magistrates' Courts Act 1980, ss 17A–21, in PART I, ante.

8–3066   5. Saving for Registration Acts.   Nothing in this Act requiring particulars to be furnished for the purposes of this Act shall affect any provision of the Registration Acts[1] requiring information to be given for the purposes of those Acts.
[Population (Statistics) Act 1938, s 5.]

---

1. For the meaning of the "Registration Acts", see s 7(2), post, and note thereto.

8–3067   **7. Short title, interpretation and extent.**   (1) This Act may be cited as the Population (Statistics) Act, 1938.

(2) In this Act the expression "Registration Acts"[1] means the Births and Deaths Registration Acts, 1836 to 1929, and the expression "registration officer" means any superintendent registrar and registrar of births and deaths.

(3) This Act shall not extend to Northern Ireland.

[Population (Statistics) Act 1938, s 7.]

---

1. See now the Births and Deaths Registration Act 1953, and in particular s 42(5), for saving provision with respect to the Population (Statistics) Act 1938. The Act of 1953 has been amended as to the registration of still-births by the Population (Statistics) Act 1960, s 2.

SCHEDULE

PARTICULARS WHICH MAY BE REQUIRED

(*As substituted by the Population (Statistics) Act 1960, s 1(2) and amended by the Civil Partnership Act 2004, Sch 7.*)

8–3068   **1.**   *On registration of a birth (including a still-birth)*

   (*a*) in all cases the age of the mother;

   (*b*) where the name of any person is to be entered in the register of births as father of the child, the age of that person;

   (*c*) except where the birth is of an illegitimate child—

      (i) the date of the parents' marriage;

      (ii) whether the mother had been married before her marriage to the father of the child;

      (iii) the number of children of the mother by her present husband and by any former husband, and how many of them were born alive or were still-born.

   2.   *On registration of death*

   (*a*) whether the deceased was single, married, widowed, divorced, a civil partner or former civil partner, and, if a former civil partner, whether the civil partnership ended on death or dissolution;

   (*b*) the age of the surviving spouse or civil partner, if any, of the deceased.

CHARITIES

8–3069   This title contains references to the following statutes—

    8–3070   CHARITIES ACT 1992
    8–3089   CHARITIES ACT 1993

The statute law governing charities has been consolidated and is contained now primarily in the Charities Act 1993.

The Charities Act 1992 regulates fund-raising activities carried on in connection with charities and other institutions, and makes fresh provision with respect to public charitable collections. The Charities Act 1992 (when fully in force) repeals the Police, Factories, etc (Miscellaneous Provisions) Act 1916[1], the House to House Collections Act 1939[1] and the War Charities Act 1940.

The Charities Acts 1992 and 1993 create a number of offences which are punishable on summary conviction; only those provisions which are thought more likely to be the subject of prosecutions are contained in this work.

---

1. See this PART, title STREET AND HOUSE TO HOUSE COLLECTIONS, post. At the date of going to press the repeal of these Acts had not taken effect.

Charities Act 1992[1]
(1992 c 41)

---

1. This Act shall come into force on such day or days as may be appointed by order of the Secretary of State (s 79(2), post). At the date of going to press on 1 January 1995, the Charities Act (Commencement No 1 and Transitional Provisions) Order 1992, SI 1992/1900 and the Charities Act 1992 (Commencement No 2) Order 1994, SI 1994/3023, had been made. Of the provisions printed in this work, the following had not been brought fully into force:

PART II[1]

CONTROL OF FUND-RAISING FOR CHARITABLE INSTITUTIONS

Preliminary

8–3070   **58. Interpretation of Part II.**   (1) In this Part—

"charitable contributions", in relation to any representation made by any commercial participator or other person, means—

   (*a*) the whole or part of—

    (i)   the consideration given for goods or services sold or supplied by him, or

    (ii) any proceeds (other than such consideration) of a promotional venture undertaken by him, or

  (b)   sums given by him by way of donation in connection with the sale or supply of any such goods or services (whether the amount of such sums is determined by reference to the value of any such goods or services or otherwise);

"charitable institution" means a charity or an institution (other than a charity) which is established for charitable, benevolent or philanthropic purposes;

"charity" means a charity within the meaning of the Charities Act 1993;

"commercial participator", in relation to any charitable institution, means any person (apart from a company connected with the institution) who—

  (a)   carries on for gain a business other than a fund-raising business, but

  (b)   in the course of that business, engages in any promotional venture in the course of which it is represented that charitable contributions are to be given to or applied for the benefit of the institution;

"company" has the meaning given by section 97 of the Charities Act 1993;

"the court" means the High Court or a county court;

"credit card" means a card which is a credit-token within the meaning of the Consumer Credit Act 1974;

"debit card" means a card the use of which by its holder to make a payment results in a current account of his at a bank, or at any other institution providing banking services, being debited with the payment;

"fund-raising business" means any business carried on for gain and wholly or primarily engaged in soliciting or otherwise procuring money or other property for charitable, benevolent or philanthropic purposes;

"institution" includes any trust or undertaking;

"professional fund-raiser" means—

  (a)   any person (apart from a charitable institution or a company connected with such an institution) who carries on a fund-raising business, or

  (b)   any other person (apart from a person excluded by virtue of subsection (2) or (3)) who for reward solicits money or other property for the benefit of a charitable institution, if he does so otherwise than in the course of any fund-raising venture undertaken by a person falling within paragraph (a) above;

"promotional venture" means any advertising or sales campaign or any other venture undertaken for promotional purposes;

"radio or television programme" includes any item included in a programme service within the meaning of the Broadcasting Act 1990.

(2) In subsection (1), paragraph (b) of the definition of "professional fund-raiser" does not apply to any of the following, namely—

  (a)   any charitable institution or any company connected with any such institution;

  (b)   any officer or employee of any such institution or company, or any trustee of any such institution, acting (in each case) in his capacity as such;

  (c)   any person acting as a collector in respect of a public charitable collection (apart from a person who is to be treated as a promoter of such a collection by virtue of section 65(3));

  (d)   any person who in the course of a relevant programme, that is to say a radio or television programme in the course of which a fund-raising venture is undertaken by—

    (i)   a charitable institution, or

    (ii) a company connected with such an institution,

makes any solicitation at the instance of that institution or company; or

  (e)   any commercial participator;

and for this purpose "collector" and "public charitable collection" have the same meaning as in Part III of this Act.

(3) In addition, paragraph (b) of the definition of "professional fund-raiser" does not apply to a person if he does not receive—

  (a)   more than—

    (i)   £5 per day, or

    (ii) £500 per year,

by way of remuneration in connection with soliciting money or other property for the benefit of the charitable institution referred to in that paragraph; or

  (b)   more than £500 by way of remuneration in connection with any fund-raising venture in the course of which he solicits money or other property for the benefit of that institution.

(4) In this Part any reference to charitable purposes, where occurring in the context of a reference

to charitable, benevolent or philanthropic purposes, is a reference to charitable purposes whether or not the purposes are charitable within the meaning of any rule of law.

(5) For the purposes of this Part a company is connected with a charitable institution if—

(a) the institution, or

(b) the institution and one or more other charitable institutions, taken together,

is or are entitled (whether directly or through one or more nominees) to exercise, or control the exercise of, the whole of the voting power at any general meeting of the company.

(6) In this Part—

(a) "represent" and "solicit" mean respectively represent and solicit in any manner whatever, whether expressly or impliedly and whether done—

(i) by speaking directly to the person or persons to whom the representation or solicitation is addressed (whether when in his or their presence or not), or

(ii) by means of a statement published in any newspaper, film or radio or television programme,

or otherwise, and references to a representation or solicitation shall be construed accordingly; and

(b) any reference to soliciting or otherwise procuring money or other property is a reference to soliciting or otherwise procuring money or other property whether any consideration is, or is to be, given in return for the money or other property or not.

(7) Where—

(a) any solicitation of money or other property for the benefit of a charitable institution is made in accordance with arrangements between any person and that institution, and

(b) under those arrangements that person will be responsible for receiving on behalf of the institution money or other property given in response to the solicitation,

then (if he would not be so regarded apart from this subsection) that person shall be regarded for the purposes of this Part as soliciting money or other property for the benefit of the institution.

(8) Where any fund-raising venture is undertaken by a professional fund-raiser in the course of a radio or television programme, any solicitation which is made by a person in the course of the programme at the instance of the fund-raiser shall be regarded for the purposes of this Part as made by the fund-raiser and not by that person (and shall be so regarded whether or not the solicitation is made by that person for any reward).

(9) In this Part "services" includes facilities, and in particular—

(a) access to any premises or event;

(b) membership of any organisation;

(c) the provision of advertising space; and

(d) the provision of any financial facilities;

and references to the supply of services shall be construed accordingly.

(10) The Secretary of State may by order amend subsection (3) by substituting a different sum for any sum for the time being specified there.

[Charities Act 1992, s 58 as amended by the Charities Act 1993, Sch 6 and the Deregulation and Contracting Out Act 1994, s 25.]

---

1. Part II contains ss 58–64.

Control of fund-raising

8–3071 60. Professional fund-raisers etc required to indicate institutions benefiting and arrangements for remuneration. (1) Where a professional fund-raiser solicits money or other property for the benefit of one or more particular charitable institutions, the solicitation shall be accompanied by a statement clearly indicating—

(a) the name or names of the institution or institutions concerned;

(b) if there is more than one institution concerned, the proportions in which the institutions are respectively to benefit; and

(c) (in general terms) the method by which the fund-raiser's remuneration in connection with the appeal is to be determined.

(2) Where a professional fund-raiser solicits money or other property for charitable, benevolent or philanthropic purposes of any description (rather than for the benefit of one or more particular charitable institutions), the solicitation shall be accompanied by a statement clearly indicating—

(a) the fact that he is soliciting money or other property for those purposes and not for the benefit of any particular charitable institution or institutions;

(b) the method by which it is to be determined how the proceeds of the appeal are to be distributed between different charitable institutions; and

(c) (in general terms) the method by which his remuneration in connection with the appeal is to be determined.

(3) Where any representation is made by a commercial participator to the effect that charitable contributions are to be given to or applied for the benefit of one or more particular charitable institutions, the representation shall be accompanied by a statement clearly indicating—

(a) the name or names of the institution or institutions concerned;

(b) if there is more than one institution concerned, the proportions in which the institutions are respectively to benefit; and

(c) (in general terms) the method by which it is to be determined—

(i) what proportion of the consideration given for goods or services sold or supplied by him, or of any other proceeds of a promotional venture undertaken by him, is to be given to or applied for the benefit of the institution or institutions concerned, or

(ii) what sums by way of donations by him in connection with the sale or supply of any such goods or services are to be so given or applied,

as the case may require.

(4) If any such solicitation or representation as is mentioned in any of subsections (1) to (3) is made—

(a) in the course of a radio or television programme, and

(b) in association with an announcement to the effect that payment may be made, in response to the solicitation or representation, by means of a credit or debit card,

the statement required by virtue of subsection (1), (2) or (3) (as the case may be) shall include full details of the right to have refunded under section 61(1) any payment of £50 or more which is so made.

(5) If any such solicitation or representation as is mentioned in any of subsections (1) to (3) is made orally but is not made—

(a) by speaking directly to the particular person or persons to whom it is addressed and in his or their presence, or

(b) in the course of any radio or television programme,

the professional fund-raiser or commercial participator concerned shall, within seven days of any payment of £50 or more being made to him in response to the solicitation or representation, give to the person making the payment a written statement—

(i) of the matters specified in paragraphs (a) to (c) of that subsection; and

(ii) including full details of the right to cancel under section 61(2) an agreement made in response to the solicitation or representation, and the right to have refunded under section 61(2) or (3) any payment of £50 or more made in response thereto.

(6) In subsection (5) above the reference to the making of a payment is a reference to the making of a payment of whatever nature and by whatever means, including a payment made by means of a credit card or a debit card; and for the purposes of that subsection—

(a) where the person making any such payment makes it in person, it shall be regarded as made at the time when it is so made;

(b) where the person making any such payment sends it by post, it shall be regarded as made at the time when it is posted; and

(c) where the person making any such payment makes it by giving, by telephone or by means of any other telecommunication apparatus⋆, authority for an account to be debited with the payment, it shall be regarded as made at the time when any such authority is given.

(7) Where any requirement of subsections (1) to (5) is not complied with in relation to any solicitation or representation, the professional fund-raiser or commercial participator concerned shall be guilty of an offence and liable on summary conviction to a fine not exceeding the **fifth level** on the standard scale.

(8) It shall be a defence for a person charged with any such offence to prove that he took all reasonable precautions and exercised all due diligence to avoid the commission of the offence.

(9) Where the commission by any person of an offence under subsection (7) is due to the act or default of some other person, that other person shall be guilty of the offence; and a person may be charged with and convicted of the offence by virtue of this subsection whether or not proceedings are taken against the first-mentioned person.

(10) In this section—

"the appeal", in relation to any solicitation by a professional fund-raiser, means the campaign or other fund-raising venture in the course of which the solicitation is made;

"telecommunication apparatus" has the same meaning as in the Telecommunications Act 1984.⋆

[Charities Act 1992, s 60.]

⋆**Words in subs (6) and definition substituted by the Communications Act 2003, Sch 17, from a date to be appointed.**

8–3072   63. False statements relating to institutions which are not registered charities.
(1) Where—

(*a*)   a person solicits money or other property for the benefit of an institution in association with a representation that the institution is a registered charity, and

(*b*)   the institution is not such a charity,

he shall be guilty of an offence and liable on summary conviction to a fine not exceeding the **fifth level** on the standard scale.

(1A)   In any proceedings for an offence under subsection (1), it shall be a defence for the accused to prove that he believed on reasonable grounds that the institution was a registered charity.

(2)   In this section "registered charity" means a charity which is for the time being registered in the register of charities kept under section 3 of the Charities Act 1993.

[Charities Act 1992, s 63 as amended by the Charities Act 1993, Sch 6 and the Deregulation and Contracting Out Act 1994, s 26.]

Supplementary

8–3073   64. Regulations about fund-raising.   (1) The Secretary of State may make such regulations[1] as appear to him to be necessary or desirable for any purposes connected with any of the preceding provisions of this Part.

(2)   Without prejudice to the generality of subsection (1), any such regulations may—

(*a*)   prescribe the form and content of—

     (i)   agreements made for the purposes of section 59, and

     (ii)   notices served under section 62(3);

(*b*)   require professional fund-raisers or commercial participators who are parties to such agreements with charitable institutions to make available to the institutions books, documents or other records (however kept) which relate to the institutions;

(*c*)   specify the manner in which money or other property acquired by professional fund-raisers or commercial participators for the benefit of, or otherwise falling to be given to or applied by such persons for the benefit of, charitable institutions is to be transmitted to such institutions;

(*d*)   provide for any provisions of section 60 or 61 having effect in relation to solicitations or representations made in the course of radio or television programmes to have effect, subject to any modifications specified in the regulations, in relation to solicitations or representations made in the course of such programmes—

     (i)   by charitable institutions, or

     (ii)   by companies connected with such institutions,

and, in that connection, provide for any other provisions of this Part to have effect for the purposes of the regulations subject to any modifications so specified;

(*e*)   make other provision regulating the raising of funds for charitable, benevolent or philanthropic purposes (whether by professional fund-raisers or commercial participators or otherwise).

(3)   In subsection (2)(*c*) the reference to such money or other property as is there mentioned includes a reference to money or other property which, in the case of a professional fund-raiser or commercial participator—

(*a*)   has been acquired by him otherwise than in accordance with an agreement with a charitable institution, but

(*b*)   by reason of any solicitation or representation in consequence of which it has been acquired, is held by him on trust for such an institution.

(4)   Regulations under this section may provide that any failure to comply with a specified provision of the regulations shall be an offence punishable on summary conviction by a fine not exceeding the **second level** on the standard scale.

[Charities Act 1992, s 64.]

---

1. The Charitable Institutions (Fund Raising) Regulations 1994, SI 1994/3024 amended by SI 1998/1129 have been made.

PART III[1]
PUBLIC CHARITABLE COLLECTIONS
Preliminary

8–3074   65. Interpretation of Part III.   (1) In this Part—

(*a*)   "public charitable collection" means (subject to subsection (2)) a charitable appeal which is made—

     (i)   in any public place, or

     (ii)   by means of visits from house to house; and

(b) "charitable appeal" means an appeal to members of the public to give money or other property (whether for consideration or otherwise) which is made in association with a representation that the whole or any part of its proceeds is to be applied for charitable, benevolent or philanthropic purposes.

(2) Subsection (1)(*a*) does not apply to a charitable appeal which—

(a) is made in the course of a public meeting; or

(b) is made—

    (i) on land within a churchyard or burial ground contiguous or adjacent to a place of public worship, or

    (ii) on other land occupied for the purposes of a place of public worship and contiguous or adjacent to it,

being (in each case) land which is enclosed or substantially enclosed (whether by any wall or building or otherwise); or

(c) is an appeal to members of the public to give money or other property by placing it in an unattended receptacle;

and for the purposes of paragraph (*c*) above a receptacle is unattended if it is not in the possession or custody of a person acting as a collector.

(3) In this Part, in relation to a public charitable collection—

(a) "promoter" means a person who (whether alone or with others and whether for remuneration or otherwise) organises or controls the conduct of the charitable appeal in question, and associated expressions shall be construed accordingly; and

(b) "collector" means any person by whom that appeal is made (whether made by him alone or with others and whether made by him for remuneration or otherwise);

but where no person acts in the manner mentioned in paragraph (*a*) above in respect of a public charitable collection, any person who acts as a collector in respect of it shall for the purposes of this Part be treated as a promoter of it as well.

(4) In this Part—

"local authority" means the council of a Welsh county or county borough, of a district or of a London borough, the Common Council of the City of London, or the Council of the Isles of Scilly; and

"proceeds", in relation to a public charitable collection, means all money or other property given (whether for consideration or otherwise) in response to the charitable appeal in question.

(5) In this Part any reference to charitable purposes, where occurring in the context of a reference to charitable, benevolent or philanthropic purposes, is a reference to charitable purposes whether or not the purposes are charitable within the meaning of any rule of law.

(6) The functions exercisable under this Part by a local authority shall be exercisable—

(a) as respects the Inner Temple, by its Sub-Treasurer, and

(b) as respects the Middle Temple, by its Under Treasurer;

and references in this Part to a local authority or to the area of a local authority shall be construed accordingly.

(7) It is hereby declared that an appeal to members of the public (other than one falling within subsection (2)) is a public charitable collection for the purposes of this Part if—

(a) it consists in or includes the making of an offer to sell goods or to supply services, or the exposing of goods for sale, to members of the public, and

(b) it is made as mentioned in sub-paragraph (i) or (ii) of subsection (1)(*a*) and in association with a representation that the whole or any part of its proceeds is to be applied for charitable, benevolent or philanthropic purposes.

This subsection shall not be taken as prejudicing the generality of subsection (1)(*b*).

(8) In this section—

"house" includes any part of a building constituting a separate dwelling;

"public place", in relation to a charitable appeal, means—

(a) any highway, and

(b) (subject to subsection (9)) any other place to which, at any time when the appeal is made, members of the public have or are permitted to have access and which either—

    (i) is not within a building, or

    (ii) if within a building, is a public area within any station, airport or shopping precinct or any other similar public area.

(9) In subsection (8), paragraph (*b*) of the definition of "public place" does not apply to—

(a) any place to which members of the public are permitted to have access only if any payment or ticket required as a condition of access has been made or purchased; or

(*b*) any place to which members of the public are permitted to have access only by virtue of permission given for the purposes of the appeal in question.
[Charities Act 1992, s 65 amended by the Local Government (Wales) Act 1994, Sch 16.]

---

1. Part III contains ss 65–74. At the date of going to press, ss 65–74 had not been brought into force.

Prohibition on conducting unauthorised collections

8–3075   66. Prohibition on conducting public charitable collections without authorisation.
(1) No public charitable collection shall be conducted in the area of any local authority except in accordance with—

(*a*) a permit issued by the authority under section 68; or

(*b*) an order made by the Charity Commissioners under section 72.

(2) Where a public charitable collection is conducted in contravention of subsection (1), any promoter of that collection shall be guilty of an offence and liable on summary conviction to a fine not exceeding the fourth level on the standard scale.
[Charities Act 1992, s 66.]

Permits

8–3076   67. Applications for permits to conduct public charitable collections.   (1) An application for a permit to conduct a public charitable collection in the area of a local authority shall be made to the authority by the person or persons proposing to promote that collection.

(2) Any such application—

(*a*) shall specify the period for which it is desired that the permit, if issued, should have effect, being a period not exceeding 12 months; and

(*b*) shall contain such information as may be prescribed by regulations under section 73.

(3) Any such application—

(*a*) shall be made at least one month before the relevant day or before such later date as the local authority may in the case of that application allow,

(*b*) (*Repealed*),

and for this purpose "the relevant day" means the day on which the collection is to be conducted or, where it is to be conducted on more than one day, the first of those days.

(4) Before determining any application duly made to them under this section, a local authority shall consult the chief officer of police for the police area which comprises or includes their area and may make such other inquiries as they think fit.
[Charities Act 1992, s 67 and the Deregulation and Contracting Out Act 1994, s 27.]

8–3077   68. Determination of applications and issue of permits.   (1) Where an application for a permit is duly made to a local authority under section 67 in respect of a public charitable collection, the authority shall either—

(*a*) issue a permit in respect of the collection, or

(*b*) refuse the application on one or more of the grounds specified in section 69,

and, where they issue such a permit, it shall (subject to section 70) have effect for the period specified in the application in accordance with section 67(2)(*a*).

(2) A local authority may, at the time of issuing a permit under this section, attach to it such conditions as they think fit, having regard to the local circumstances of the collection; but the authority shall secure that the terms of any such conditions are consistent with the provisions of any regulations under section 73.

(3) Without prejudice to the generality of subsection (2), a local authority may attach conditions—

(*a*) specifying the day of the week, date, time or frequency of the collection;

(*b*) specifying the locality or localities within their area in which the collection may be conducted;

(*c*) regulating the manner in which the collection is to be conducted.

(4) Where a local authority—

(*a*) refuse to issue a permit, or

(*b*) attach any condition to a permit under subsection (2),

they shall serve on the applicant written notice of their decision to do so and of the reasons for their decision; and that notice shall also state the right of appeal conferred by section 71(1) or (as the case may be) section 71(2), and the time within which such an appeal must be brought.
[Charities Act 1992, s 68.]

8–3078   69. Refusal of permits.   (1) A local authority may refuse to issue a permit to conduct a public charitable collection on any of the following grounds, namely—

(a)   that it appears to them that the collection would cause undue inconvenience to members of the public by reason of—

  (i)   the day of the week or date on which,
  (ii)   the time at which,
  (iii)   the frequency with which, or
  (iv)   the locality or localities in which,

  it is proposed to be conducted;

(b)   that the collection is proposed to be conducted on a day on which another public charitable collection is already authorised (whether under section 68 or otherwise) to be conducted in the authority's area, or on the day falling immediately before, or immediately after, any such day;

(c)   that it appears to them that the amount likely to be applied for charitable, benevolent or philanthropic purposes in consequence of the collection would be inadequate, having regard to the likely amount of the proceeds of the collection;

(d)   that it appears to them that the applicant or any other person would be likely to receive an excessive amount by way of remuneration in connection with the collection;

(e)   that the applicant has been convicted—

  (i)   of an offence under section 5 of the 1916 Act, under the 1939 Act, under section 119 of the 1982 Act or regulations made under it, or under this Part or regulations made under section 73 below, or
  (ii)   of any offence involving dishonesty or of a kind the commission of which would in their opinion be likely to be facilitated by the issuing to him of a permit under section 68 above;

(f)   where the applicant is a person other than a charitable, benevolent or philanthropic institution for whose benefit the collection is proposed to be conducted, that they are not satisfied that the applicant is authorised (whether by any such institution or by any person acting on behalf of any such institution) to promote the collection; or

(g)   that it appears to them that the applicant, in promoting any other collection authorised under this Part or under section 119 of the 1982 Act, failed to exercise due diligence—

  (i)   to secure that persons authorised by him to act as collectors for the purposes of the collection were fit and proper persons;
  (ii)   to secure that such persons complied with the provisions of regulations under section 73 below or (as the case may be) section 119 of the 1982 Act; or
  (iii)   to prevent badges or certificates of authority being obtained by persons other than those he had so authorised.

(2)   A local authority shall not, however, refuse to issue such a permit on the ground mentioned in subsection (1)(b) if it appears to them—

(a)   that the collection would be conducted only in one location, which is on land to which members of the public would have access only by virtue of the express or implied permission of the occupier of the land; and

(b)   that the occupier of the land consents to the collection being conducted there;

and for this purpose "the occupier", in relation to unoccupied land, means the person entitled to occupy it.

(3)   In subsection (1)—

(a)   in the case of a collection in relation to which there is more than one applicant, any reference to the applicant shall be construed as a reference to any of the applicants; and

(b)   (subject to subsection (4)) the reference in paragraph (g)(iii) to badges or certificates of authority is a reference to badges or certificates of authority in a form prescribed by regulations under section 73 below or (as the case may be) under section 119 of the 1982 Act.

(4)   Subsection (1)(g) applies to the conduct of the applicant (or any of the applicants) in relation to any public charitable collection authorised under regulations made under section 5 of the 1916 Act (collection of money or sale of articles in a street or other public place), or authorised under the 1939 Act (collection of money or other property by means of visits from house to house), as it applies to his conduct in relation to a collection authorised under this Part, subject to the following modifications, namely—

(a)   in the case of a collection authorised under regulations made under the 1916 Act—

  (i)   the reference in sub-paragraph (ii) to regulations under section 73 below shall be construed as a reference to the regulations under which the collection in question was authorised, and
  (ii)   the reference in sub-paragraph (iii) to badges or certificates of authority shall be construed as a reference to any written authority provided to a collector pursuant to those regulations; and

(b)   in the case of a collection authorised under the 1939 Act—

(i)   the reference in sub-paragraph (ii) to regulations under section 73 below shall be construed as a reference to regulations under section 4 of that Act, and

(ii) the reference in sub-paragraph (iii) to badges or certificates of authority shall be construed as a reference to badges or certificates of authority in a form prescribed by such regulations.

(5) In this section—

"the 1916 Act" means the Police, Factories, &c. (Miscellaneous Provisions) Act 1916;

"the 1939 Act" means the House to House Collections Act 1939; and

"the 1982 Act" means the Civic Government (Scotland) Act 1982.

[Charities Act 1992, s 69.]

8–3079   70. Withdrawal etc of permits.   (1) Where a local authority who have issued a permit under section 68—

(a) have reason to believe that there has been a change in the circumstances which prevailed at the time when they issued the permit, and are of the opinion that, if the application for the permit had been made in the new circumstances of the case, the permit would not have been issued by them, or

(b) have reason to believe that any information furnished to them by the promoter (or, in the case of a collection in relation to which there is more than one promoter, by any of them) for the purposes of the application for the permit was false in a material particular,

then (subject to subsection (2)) they may—

(i)   withdraw the permit;

(ii) attach any condition to the permit; or

(iii) vary any existing condition of the permit.

(2) Any condition imposed by the local authority under subsection (1) (whether by attaching a new condition to the permit or by varying an existing condition) must be one that could have been attached to the permit under section 68(2) at the time when it was issued, assuming for this purpose—

(a) that the new circumstances of the case had prevailed at that time, or

(b) (in a case falling within paragraph (b) of subsection (1) above) that the authority had been aware of the true circumstances of the case at that time.

(3) Where a local authority who have issued a permit under section 68 have reason to believe that there has been or is likely to be a breach of any condition of it, or that a breach of such a condition is continuing, they may withdraw the permit.

(4) Where under this section a local authority withdraw, attach any condition to, or vary an existing condition of, a permit, they shall serve on the promoter written notice of their decision to do so and of the reasons for their decision; and that notice shall also state the right of appeal conferred by section 71(2) and the time within which such an appeal must be brought.

(5) Where a local authority so withdraw, attach any condition to, or vary an existing condition of, a permit, the permit shall nevertheless continue to have effect as if it had not been withdrawn or (as the case may be) as if the condition had not been attached or the variation had not been made—

(a) until the time for bringing an appeal under section 71(2) has expired, or

(b) if such an appeal is duly brought, until the determination or abandonment of the appeal.

[Charities Act 1992, s 70.]

8–3080   71. Appeals.   (1) A person who has duly applied to a local authority under section 67 for a permit to conduct a public charitable collection in the authority's area may appeal to a magistrates' court against a decision of the authority to refuse to issue a permit to him.

(2) A person to whom a permit has been issued under section 68 may appeal to a magistrates' court against—

(a) a decision of the local authority under that section or section 70 to attach any condition to the permit; or

(b) a decision of the local authority under section 70 to vary any condition so attached or to withdraw the permit.

(3) An appeal under subsection (1) or (2) shall be by way of complaint for an order, and the Magistrates' Courts Act 1980 shall apply to the proceedings; and references in this section to a magistrates' court are to a magistrates' court acting for the petty sessions area in which is situated the office or principal office of the local authority against whose decision the appeal is brought.

(4) Any such appeal shall be brought within 14 days of the date of service on the person in question of the relevant notice under section 68(4) or (as the case may be) section 70(4); and for the purposes of this subsection an appeal shall be taken to be brought when the complaint is made.

(5) An appeal against the decision of a magistrates' court on an appeal under subsection (1) or (2) may be brought to the Crown Court.

(6) On an appeal to a magistrates' court or the Crown Court under this section, the court may

confirm, vary or reverse the local authority's decision and generally give such directions as it thinks fit, having regard to the provisions of this Part and of regulations under section 73.

(7) It shall be the duty of the local authority to comply with any directions given by the court under subsection (6); but the authority need not comply with any directions given by a magistrates' court—

(a)   until the time for bringing an appeal under subsection (5) has expired, or

(b)   if such an appeal is duly brought, until the determination or abandonment of the appeal.
[Charities Act 1992, s 71.]

Orders made by Charity Commissioners

8–3081   72. Orders made by Charity Commissioners.   (1) Where the Charity Commissioners are satisfied, on the application of any charity, that that charity proposes—

(a)   to promote public charitable collections—

(i)   throughout England and Wales, or

(ii)   throughout a substantial part of England and Wales,

in connection with any charitable purposes pursued by the charity, or

(b)   to authorise other persons to promote public charitable collections as mentioned in paragraph (a),

the Commissioners may make an order under this subsection in respect of the charity.

(2) Such an order shall have the effect of authorising public charitable collections which—

(a)   are promoted by the charity in respect of which the order is made, or by persons authorised by the charity, and

(b)   are so promoted in connection with the charitable purposes mentioned in subsection (1),

to be conducted in such area or areas as may be specified in the order.

(3) An order under subsection (1) may—

(a)   include such conditions as the Commissioners think fit;

(b)   be expressed (without prejudice to paragraph (c)) to have effect without limit of time, or for a specified period only;

(c)   be revoked or varied by a further order of the Commissioners.

(4) Where the Commissioners, having made an order under subsection (1) in respect of a charity, make any further order revoking or varying that order, they shall serve on the charity written notice of their reasons for making the further order, unless it appears to them that the interests of the charity would not be prejudiced by the further order.

(5) Section 89(1), (2) and (4) of the Charities Act 1993 (provisions as to orders made by the Commissioners) shall apply to an order made by them under this section as it applies to an order made by them under that Act.

(6) In this section "charity" and "charitable purposes" have the same meaning as in that Act.
[Charities Act 1992, s 72 as amended by the Charities Act 1993, Sch 6.]

Supplementary

8–3082   73. Regulations.   (1) The Secretary of State may make regulations—

(a)   prescribing the information which is to be contained in applications made under section 67;

(b)   for the purpose of regulating the conduct of public charitable collections authorised under—

(i)   permits issued under section 68; or

(ii)   orders made by the Charity Commissioners under section 72.

(2) Regulations under subsection (1)(b) may, without prejudice to the generality of that provision, make provision—

(a)   about the keeping and publication of accounts;

(b)   for the prevention of annoyance to members of the public;

(c)   with respect to the use by collectors of badges and certificates of authority, or badges incorporating such certificates, and to other matters relating to such badges and certificates, including, in particular, provision—

(i)   prescribing the form of such badges and certificates;

(ii)   requiring a collector, on request, to permit his badge, or any certificate of authority held by him for the purposes of the collection, to be inspected by a constable or a duly authorised officer of a local authority, or by an occupier of any premises visited by him in the course of the collection;

(d) for prohibiting persons under a prescribed age from acting as collectors, and prohibiting others from causing them so to act.

(3) Regulations under this section may provide that any failure to comply with a specified provision of the regulations shall be an offence punishable on summary conviction by a fine not exceeding the **second** level on the standard scale.
[Charities Act 1992, s 73.]

8–3083 74. Offences. (1) A person shall be guilty of an offence if, in connection with any charitable appeal, he displays or uses—

(a) a prescribed badge or a prescribed certificate of authority which is not for the time being held by him for the purposes of the appeal pursuant to regulations under section 73, or

(b) any badge or article, or any certificate or other document, so nearly resembling a prescribed badge or (as the case may be) a prescribed certificate of authority as to be likely to deceive a member of the public.

(2) A person guilty of an offence under subsection (1) shall be liable on summary conviction to a fine not exceeding the **fourth level** on the standard scale.

(3) Any person who, for the purposes of an application made under section 67, knowingly or recklessly furnishes any information which is false in a material particular shall be guilty of an offence and liable on summary conviction to a fine not exceeding the **fourth level** on the standard scale.

(3A) Any person who knowingly or recklessly provides the Commissioners with information which is false or misleading in a material particular shall be guilty of an offence if the information is provided in circumstances in which he intends, or could reasonably be expected to know, that it would be used by them for the purpose of discharging their functions under section 72.

(3B) A person guilty of an offence under subsection (3A) shall be liable[1]—

(a) on summary conviction, to a fine not exceeding **the statutory maximum**;

(b) on conviction or indictment, to imprisonment for a term not exceeding **two years** or to a **fine**, or **both**.

(4) In subsection (1) "prescribed badge" and "prescribed certificate of authority" mean respectively a badge and a certificate of authority in such form as may be prescribed by regulations under section 73.
[Charities Act 1992, s 74 as amended by the Charities Act 1993, Sch 6.]

---

1. For procedure in respect of this offence which is triable either way, see the Magistrates' Courts Act 1980, ss 17A–21, in PART I: MAGISTRATES' COURTS, PROCEDURE, ante.

PART IV[1]
GENERAL

8–3084 75. Offences by bodies corporate. Where any offence—

(a) under this Act or any regulations made under it, or

(b) (Repealed);

is committed by a body corporate and is proved to have been committed with the consent or connivance of, or to be attributable to any neglect on the part of, any director, manager, secretary or other similar officer of the body corporate, or any person who was purporting to act in any such capacity, he as well as the body corporate shall be guilty of that offence and shall be liable to be proceeded against and punished accordingly.

In relation to a body corporate whose affairs are managed by its members, "director" means a member of the body corporate.
[Charities Act 1992, s 75 as amended by the Charities Act 1993, Sch 7.]

---

1. Part IV contains ss 75–79.

8–3085 76. Service of documents. (1) This section applies to—

(a) (Repealed);

(b) any notice or other document required or authorised to be given or served under Part II of this Act; and

(c) any notice required to be served under Part III of this Act.

(2) A document to which this section applies may be served on or given to a person (other than a body corporate)—

(a) by delivering it to that person;

(b) by leaving it at his last known address in the United Kingdom; or

(c) by sending it by post to him at that address.

(3) A document to which this section applies may be served on or given to a body corporate by delivering it or sending it by post—

(*a*)   to the registered or principal office of the body in the United Kingdom, or

(*b*)   if it has no such office in the United Kingdom, to any place in the United Kingdom where it carries on business or conducts its activities (as the case may be).

(4) Any such document may also be served on or given to a person (including a body corporate) by sending it by post to that person at an address notified by that person for the purposes of this subsection to the person or persons by whom it is required or authorised to be served or given.

[Charities Act 1992, s 76 as amended by the Charities Act 1993, Sch 7.]

8–3086   77. Regulations and orders.   (1) Any regulations or order of the Secretary of State under this Act—

(*a*)   shall be made by statutory instrument; and

(*b*)   (subject to subsection (2)) shall be subject to annulment in pursuance of a resolution of either House of Parliament.

(2) Subsection (1)(b) does not apply—

(*a*)–(*c*)   (*Repealed*);

(*d*)   to an order under section 79(2).

(3) Any regulations or order of the Secretary of State under this Act may make—

(*a*)   different provision for different cases; and

(*b*)   such supplemental, incidental, consequential or transitional provision or savings as the Secretary of State considers appropriate.

(4) Before making any regulations under section 64 or 73 the Secretary of State shall consult such persons or bodies of persons as he considers appropriate.

[Charities Act 1992, s 77 as amended by the Charities Act 1993, Sch 7.]

8–3087   78. Minor and consequential amendments and repeals.   (1) The enactments mentioned in Schedule 6 to this Act shall have effect subject to the amendments there specified (which are either minor amendments or amendments consequential on the provisions of this Act).

(2) The enactments mentioned in Schedule 7 to this Act (which include some that are already spent or are no longer of practical utility) are hereby repealed to the extent specified in the third column of that Schedule.

[Charities Act 1992, s 78.]

8–3088   79. Short title, commencement and extent.   (1) This Act may be cited as the Charities Act 1992.

(2) This Act shall come into force on such day as the Secretary of State may by order[1] appoint; and different days may be so appointed for different provisions or for different purposes.

(3) Subject to subsections (4) to (6) below, this Act extends only to England and Wales.

(4)–(5) (*Repealed*).

(6) The amendments in Schedule 6, and (subject to subsection (7)) the repeals in Schedule 7, have the same extent as the enactments to which they refer, and section 78 extends accordingly.

(7) The repeal in Schedule 7 of the Police, Factories, &c. (Miscellaneous Provisions) Act 1916 does not extend to Northern Ireland.

[Charities Act 1992, s 79 as amended by the Charities Act 1993, Sch 7.]

---

1. At the date of going to press the Charities Act 1992 (Commencement No 1 and Transitional Provisions) Order 1992, SI 1992/1900 and the Charities Act 1992 (Commencement No 2) Order 1994, SI 1994/3023, had been made.

Charities Act 1993[1]

(1993 c 10)

PART I[2]
THE CHARITY COMMISSIONERS AND THE OFFICIAL CUSTODIAN FOR CHARITIES

8–3089   1.   *The Charity Commissioners*

---

1. This Act consolidates the Charitable Trustees Incorporation Act 1872, the Charities Act 1960 and Pt I of the Charities Act 1992.

2. Part I contains ss 1–2.

PART II[1]
REGISTRATION AND NAMES OF CHARITIES
Registration of charities

8–3090   **3. The register of charities.**   *The Commissioners shall continue to keep a register of charities, which shall be kept by them in such manner as they think fit.*

---

1. Part II contains ss 3–7.

8–3091   **5. Status of registered charity (other than small charity) to appear on official publications etc.**   (1) This section applies to a registered charity if its gross income in its last financial year exceeded £10,000[1].

(2) Where this section applies to a registered charity, the fact that it is a registered charity shall be stated in legible characters—

(*a*)   in all notices, advertisements and other documents issued by or on behalf of the charity and soliciting money or other property for the benefit of the charity;

(*b*)   in all bills of exchange, promissory notes, endorsements, cheques and orders for money or goods purporting to be signed on behalf of the charity; and

(*c*)   in all bills rendered by it and in all its invoices, receipts and letters of credit.

(2A)   The statement required by subsection (2) above shall be in English, except that, in the case of a document which is otherwise wholly in Welsh, the statement may be in Welsh if it consists of or includes the words "elusen cofrestredig" (the Welsh equivalent of "registered charity").

(3)   Subsection (2)(*a*) above has effect whether the solicitation is express or implied, and whether the money or other property is to be given for any consideration or not.

(4)   If, in the case of a registered charity to which this section applies, any person issues or authorises the issue of any document falling within paragraph (*a*) or (*c*) of subsection (2) above which does not contain the statement required by that subsection, he shall be guilty of an offence and liable on summary conviction to a fine not exceeding **level 3** on the standard scale.

(5)   If, in the case of any such registered charity, any person signs any document falling within paragraph (*b*) of subsection (2) above which does not contain the statement required by that subsection, he shall be guilty of an offence and liable on summary conviction to a fine not exceeding **level 3** on the standard scale.

(6)   The Secretary of State may by order amend subsection (1) above by substituting a different sum for the sum for the time being specified there.

[Charities Act 1993, s 5 as amended by the Welsh Language Act 1993, s 32 and SI 1995/2696.]

---

1. As substituted by the Charities Act 1993 (Substitution of Sums) Order 1995, SI 1995/2696.

PART III[1]
COMMISSIONERS' INFORMATION POWERS

8–3092   **8–10.**   *General power to institute inquiries; power to call for documents and search records; disclosure of information to and by Commissioners.*

---

1. Part III contains ss 8–12.

8–3093   **11. Supply of false or misleading information to Commissioners, etc.**   (1) Any person who knowingly or recklessly provides the Commissioners with information which is false or misleading in a material particular shall be guilty of an offence if the information—

(*a*)   is provided in purported compliance with a requirement imposed by or under this Act; or

(*b*)   is provided otherwise than as mentioned in paragraph (*a*) above but in circumstances in which the person providing the information intends, or could reasonably be expected to know, that it would be used by the Commissioners for the purpose of discharging their functions under this Act.

(2)   Any person who wilfully alters, suppresses, conceals or destroys any document which he is or is liable to be required, by or under this Act, to produce to the Commissioners shall be guilty of an offence.

(3)   Any person guilty of an offence under this section shall be liable[1]—

(*a*)   on summary conviction, to a fine not exceeding **the statutory maximum**;

(*b*)   on conviction on indictment, to imprisonment for a term not exceeding **two years** or to a **fine**, or **both**.

(4)   In this section references to the Commissioners include references to any person conducting an inquiry under section 8 above.

[Charities Act 1993, s 11.]

1. For procedure in respect of this offence which is triable either way, see the Magistrates' Courts Act 1980, ss 17A–21, in PART I: MAGISTRATES' COURTS, PROCEDURE, ante.

8–3094   12. Data protection.   *Repealed.*

PART IV[1]

APPLICATION OF PROPERTY CY-PRÈS AND ASSISTANCE AND SUPERVISION OF CHARITIES BY COURT AND COMMISSIONERS

Powers of Commissioners to make schemes and act for protection of charities etc

8–3095   16.   *Concurrent jurisdiction with High Court for certain purposes*

1. Part IV contains ss 13–35.

8–3096   18. Power to act for protection of charities.   (1) Where, at any time after they have instituted an inquiry under section 8 above with respect to any charity, the Commissioners are satisfied—

(*a*) that there is or has been any misconduct or mismanagement in the administration of the charity; or

(*b*) that it is necessary or desirable to act for the purpose of protecting the property of the charity or securing a proper application for the purposes of the charity of that property or of property coming to the charity,

the Commissioners may of their own motion do one or more of the following things—

(i) by order suspend any trustee, charity trustee, officer, agent or employee of the charity from the exercise of his office or employment pending consideration being given to his removal (whether under this section or otherwise);

(ii) by order appoint such number of additional charity trustees as they consider necessary for the proper administration of the charity;

(iii) by order vest any property held by or in trust for the charity in the official custodian, or require the persons in whom any such property is vested to transfer it to him, or appoint any person to transfer any such property to him;

(iv) order any person who holds any property on behalf of the charity, or of any trustee for it, not to part with the property without the approval of the Commissioners;

(v) order any debtor of the charity not to make any payment in or towards the discharge of his liability to the charity without the approval of the Commissioners;

(vi) by order restrict (notwithstanding anything in the trusts of the charity) the transactions which may be entered into, or the nature or amount of the payments which may be made, in the administration of the charity without the approval of the Commissioners;

(vii) by order appoint (in accordance with section 19 below) a receiver and manager in respect of the property and affairs of the charity.

(2) Where, at any time after they have instituted an inquiry under section 8 above with respect to any charity, the Commissioners are satisfied—

(*a*) that there is or has been any misconduct or mismanagement in the administration of the charity; and

(*b*) that it is necessary or desirable to act for the purpose of protecting the property of the charity or securing a proper application for the purposes of the charity of that property or of property coming to the charity,

the Commissioners may of their own motion do either or both of the following things—

(i) by order remove any trustee, charity trustee, officer, agent or employee of the charity who has been responsible for or privy to the misconduct or mismanagement or has by his conduct contributed to it or facilitated it;

(ii) by order establish a scheme for the administration of the charity.

(3) The references in subsection (1) or (2) above to misconduct or mismanagement shall (notwithstanding anything in the trusts of the charity) extend to the employment for the remuneration or reward of persons acting in the affairs of the charity, or for other administrative purposes, of sums which are excessive in relation to the property which is or is likely to be applied or applicable for the purposes of the charity.

(4)–(10) *Powers of the Commissioners to appoint or remove a charity trustee by order made of their own motion; application of certain provisions of s 16 to orders under this section; supplementary provisions.*

(11) The power of the Commissioners to make an order under subsection (1)(i) above shall not be exercisable so as to suspend any person from the exercise of his office or employment for a period of more than twelve months; but (without prejudice to the generality of section 89(1) below), any such order made in the case of any person may make provision as respects the period of his suspension for matters arising out of it, and in particular for enabling any person to execute any

instrument in his name or otherwise act for him and, in the case of a charity trustee, for adjusting any rules governing the proceedings of the charity trustees to take account of the reduction in the number capable of acting.

(12) Before exercising any jurisdiction under this section otherwise than by virtue of subsection (1) above, the Commissioners shall give notice of their intention to do so to each of the charity trustees, except any that cannot be found or has no known address in the United Kingdom; and any such notice may be given by post and, if given by post, may be addressed to the recipient's last known address in the United Kingdom.

(13) The Commissioners shall, at such intervals as they think fit, review any order made by them under paragraph (i), or any of paragraphs (iii) to (vii), of subsection (1) above; and, if on any such review it appears to them that it would be appropriate to discharge the order in whole or in part, they shall so discharge it (whether subject to any savings or other transitional provisions or not).

(14) If any person contravenes an order under subsection (1)(iv), (v) or (vi) above, he shall be guilty of an offence and liable on summary conviction to a fine not exceeding **level 5** on the standard scale.

(15) Subsection (14) above shall not be taken to preclude the bringing of proceedings for breach of trust against any charity trustee or trustee for a charity in respect of a contravention of an order under subsection (1)(iv) or (vi) above (whether proceedings in respect of the contravention are brought against him under subsection (14) above or not).

(16) This section shall not apply to an exempt charity.

[Charities Act 1993, s 18.]

PART VI[1]
CHARITY ACCOUNTS, REPORTS AND RETURNS

8–3097   45. Annual reports. (1) The charity trustees of a charity shall prepare in respect of each financial year of the charity an annual report containing—

(a) such a report by the trustees on the activities of the charity during that year, and

(b) such other information relating to the charity or to its trustees or officers,

as may be prescribed by regulations[2] made by the Secretary of State.

(2) Without prejudice to the generality of subsection (1) above, regulations under that subsection may make provision—

(a) for any such report as is mentioned in paragraph (a) of that subsection to be prepared in accordance with such principles as are specified or referred to in the regulations;

(b) enabling the Commissioners to dispense with any requirement prescribed by virtue of subsection (1)(b) above in the case of a particular charity or a particular class of charities, or in the case of a particular financial year of a charity or of any class of charities.

(3) Where in any financial year of a charity its gross income or total expenditure exceeds £10,000, the annual report required to be prepared under this section in respect of that year shall be transmitted to the Commissioners by the charity trustees—

(a) within ten months from the end of that year, or

(b) within such longer period as the Commissioners may for any special reason allow in the case of that report.

(3A) Where in any financial year of a charity neither its gross income nor its total expenditure exceeds £10,000, the annual report required to be prepared under this section in respect of that year shall, if the Commissioners so request, be transmitted to them by the charity trustees—

(a) in the case of a request made before the end of seven months from the end of the financial year to which the report relates, within ten months from the end of that year, and

(b) in the case of a request not so made, within three months from the date of the request,

or, in either case, within such longer period as the Commissioners may for any special reason allow in the case of that report.

(4) Subject to subsection (5) below, any annual report transmitted to the Commissioners under this section shall have attached to it the statement of accounts prepared for the financial year in question under section 42(1) above or (as the case may be) the account and statement so prepared under section 42(3) above, together with—

(a) where the accounts of the charity for that year have been audited under section 43 above, a copy of the report made by the auditor on that statement of accounts or (as the case may be) on that account and statement;

(b) where the accounts of the charity for that year have been examined under section 43 above, a copy of the report made by the independent examiner in respect of the examination carried out by him under that section.

(5) Subsection (4) above does not apply to a charity which is a company, and any annual report transmitted by the charity trustees of such a charity under this section shall instead have attached to it a copy of the charity's annual accounts prepared for the financial year in question under Part VII

of the Companies Act 1985, together with a copy of any auditors' report or report made for the purposes of section 249A(2) of that Act on those accounts.

(6) Any annual report transmitted to the Commissioners under this section, together with the documents attached to it, shall be kept by the Commissioners for such period as they think fit.

(7) The charity trustees of a charity shall preserve, for at least six years from the end of the financial year to which it relates, any annual report prepared by them under subsection (1) above which they have not been required to transmit to the Commissioners.

(8) Subsection (4) of section 41 above shall apply in relation to the preservation of any such annual report as it applies in relation to the preservation of any accounting records (the references in subsection (3) of that section being read as references to subsection (7) above).

(9) The Secretary of State may by order amend subsection (3) or (3A) above by substituting a different sum for the sum for the time being specified there.

[Charities Act 1993, s 45 amended by the Deregulation and Contracting Out Act 1994, s 29 and SI 1994/1935.]

---

1. Part VI contains 41–49.

2. The Charities (Accounts and Reports) Regulations 1995, SI 1995/2724 amended by SI 1998/1129 and SI 2000/2868, have been made.

8–3098　46. Special provision as respects accounts and annual reports of exempt and other excepted charities.

(1) Nothing in sections 41 to 45 above applies to any exempt charity; but the charity trustees of an exempt charity shall keep proper books of account with respect to the affairs of the charity, and if not required by or under the authority of any other Act to prepare periodical statements of account shall prepare consecutive statements of account consisting on each occasion of an income and expenditure account relating to a period of not more than fifteen months and a balance sheet relating to the end of that period.

(2) The books of accounts and statements of account relating to an exempt charity shall be preserved for a period of six years at least unless the charity ceases to exist and the Commissioners consent in writing to their being destroyed or otherwise disposed of.

(3) Nothing in sections 43 to 45 above applies to any charity which—

(a) falls within section 3(5)(c) above, and
(b) is not registered.

(4) Except in accordance with subsection (7) below, nothing in section 45 above applies to any charity (other than an exempt charity or a charity which falls within section 3(5)(c) above) which—

(a) is excepted by section 3(5) above, and
(b) is not registered.

(5) If requested to do so by the Commissioners, the charity trustees of any such charity as is mentioned in subsection (4) above shall prepare an annual report in respect of such financial year of the charity as is specified in the Commissioners' request.

(6) Any report prepared under subsection (5) above shall contain—

(a) such a report by the charity trustees on the activities of the charity during the year in question, and
(b) such other information relating to the charity or to its trustees or officers,

as may be prescribed by regulations made under section 45(1) above in relation to annual reports prepared under that provision.

(7) Subsections (3) to (6) of section 45 (as originally enacted) above shall apply to any report required to be prepared under subsection (5) above as if it were an annual report required to be prepared under subsection (1) of that section.

(8) Any reference in this section to a charity which falls within section 3(5)(c) above includes a reference to a charity which falls within that provision but is also excepted from registration by section 3(5)(b) above.

[Charities Act 1993, s 46 amended by the Deregulation and Contracting Out Act 1994, s 29.]

8–3099　47. Public inspection of annual reports etc.

(1) Any annual report or other document kept by the Commissioners in pursuance of section 45(6) above shall be open to public inspection at all reasonable times—

(a) during the period for which it is so kept; or
(b) if the Commissioners so determine, during such lesser period as they may specify.

(2) Where any person—

(a) requests the charity trustees of a charity in writing to provide him with a copy of the charity's most recent accounts, and
(b) pays them such reasonable fee (if any) as they may require in respect of the costs of complying with the request,

those trustees shall comply with the request within the period of two months beginning with the date on which it is made.

(3) In subsection (2) above the reference to a charity's most recent accounts is—

(a) *(Repealed)*;

(b) in the case of a charity other than one falling within paragraph (c) or (d) below, a reference to the statement of accounts or account and statement prepared in pursuance of section 42(1) or (3) above in respect of the last financial year of the charity in respect of which a statement of accounts or account and statement has or have been so prepared;

(c) in the case of a charity which is a company, a reference to the most recent annual accounts of the company prepared under Part VII of the Companies Act 1985 in relation to which any of the following conditions is satisfied—

   (i) they have been audited;

   (ii) a report required for the purposes of section 249A(2) of that Act has been made in respect of them; or

   (iii) they relate to a year in respect of which the company is exempt from audit by virtue of section 249A(1) of that Act; and

(d) in the case of an exempt charity, a reference to the accounts of the charity most recently audited in pursuance of any statutory or other requirement or, if its accounts are not required to be audited, the accounts most recently prepared in respect of the charity.

[Charities Act 1993, s 47 amended by SI 1994/1935 and the Deregulation and Contracting Out Act 1994, s 39 and Sch 11.]

8–3100 **48. Annual returns by registered charities.** (1) Subject to subsection (1A) below every registered charity shall prepare in respect of each of its financial years an annual return in such form, and containing such information, as may be prescribed by regulations made by the Commissioners.

(1A) Subsection (1) above shall not apply in relation to any financial year of a charity in which neither the gross income nor the total expenditure of the charity exceeds £10,000.

(2) Any such return shall be transmitted to the Commissioners by the date by which the charity trustees are, by virtue of section 45(3) above, required to transmit to them the annual report required to be prepared in respect of the financial year in question.

(3) The Commissioners may dispense with the requirements of subsection (1) above in the case of a particular charity or a particular class of charities, or in the case of a particular financial year of a charity or of any class of charities.

(4) The Secretary of State may by order amend subsection (1A) above by substituting a different sum for the sum for the time being specified there.

[Charities Act 1993, s 48 amended by the Deregulation and Contracting Out Act 1994, s 30.]

8–3101 **49. Offences.** Any person who, without reasonable excuse, is persistently in default in relation to any requirement imposed—

(a) by section 45(3) or (3A) above (taken with section 45(4) or (5), as the case may require), or

(b) by section 47(2) or 48(2) above,

shall be guilty of an offence and liable on summary conviction to a fine not exceeding **level 4** on the standard scale.

[Charities Act 1993, s 49 amended by the Deregulation and Contracting Out Act 1994, s 29.]

PART IX[1]

MISCELLANEOUS

Disqualification for acting as charity trustee

8–3102 **72. Persons disqualified for being trustees of a charity.** (1) Subject to the following provisions of this section, a person shall be disqualified for being a charity trustee or trustee for a charity if—

(a) he has been convicted of any offence involving dishonesty or deception;

(b) he has been adjudged bankrupt or sequestration of his estate has been awarded and (in either case) he has not been discharged;

(c) he has made a composition or arrangement with, or granted a trust deed for, his creditors and has not been discharged in respect of it;

(d) he has been removed from the office of charity trustee or trustee for a charity by an order made—

   (i) by the Commissioners under section 18(2)(i) above, or

   (ii) by the Commissioners under section 20(1A)(i) of the Charities Act 1960 (power to act for protection of charities) or under section 20(1)(i) of that Act (as in force before the commencement of section 8 of the Charities Act 1992), or

   (iii) by the High Court,

on the grounds of any misconduct or mismanagement in the administration of the charity for which he was responsible or to which he was privy, or which he by his conduct contributed to or facilitated;

(e) he has been removed, under section 7 of the Law Reform (Miscellaneous Provisions) (Scotland) Act 1990 (powers of Court of Session to deal with management of charities), from being concerned in the management or control of any body;

(f) he is subject to a disqualification order under the Company Directors Disqualification Act 1986* or to an order made under section 429(2)(b) of the Insolvency Act 1986 (failure to pay under county court administration order).

(2) In subsection (1) above—

(a) paragraph (a) applies whether the conviction occurred before or after the commencement of that subsection, but does not apply in relation to any conviction which is a spent conviction for the purposes of the Rehabilitation of Offenders Act 1974;

(b) paragraph (b) applies whether the adjudication of bankruptcy or the sequestration occurred before or after the commencement of that subsection;

(c) paragraph (c) applies whether the composition or arrangement was made, or the trust deed was granted, before or after the commencement of that subsection; and

(d) paragraphs (d) to (f) apply in relation to orders made and removals effected before or after the commencement of that subsection.

(3) Where (apart from this subsection) a person is disqualified under subsection (1)(b) above for being a charity trustee or trustee for any charity which is a company, he shall not be so disqualified if leave has been granted under section 11 of the Company Directors Disqualification Act 1986 (undischarged bankrupts) for him to act as director of the charity; and similarly a person shall not be disqualified under subsection (1)(f) above for being a charity trustee or trustee for such a charity if—

(a) in the case of a person subject to a disqualification order, leave under the order has been granted for him to act as director of the charity, or

(b) in the case of a person subject to an order under section 429(2)(b) of the Insolvency Act 1986, leave has been granted by the court which made the order for him to so act.

(4) The Commissioners may, on the application of any person disqualified under subsection (1) above, waive his disqualification either generally or in relation to a particular charity or a particular class of charities; but no such waiver may be granted in relation to any charity which is a company if—

(a) the person concerned is for the time being prohibited, by virtue of—

(i) a disqualification order under the Company Directors Disqualification Act 1986*, or

(ii) section 11(1) or 12(2) of that Act (undischarged bankrupts; failure to pay under county court administration order),

from acting as director of the charity; and

(b) leave has not been granted for him to act as director of any other company.

(5) Any waiver under subsection (4) above shall be notified in writing to the person concerned.

(6) For the purposes of this section the Commissioners shall keep, in such manner as they think fit, a register of all persons who have been removed from office as mentioned in subsection (1)(d) above either—

(a) by an order of the Commissioners made before or after the commencement of subsection (1) above, or

(b) by an order of the High Court made after the commencement of section 45(1) of the Charities Act 1992;

and, where any person is so removed from office by an order of the High Court, the court shall notify the Commissioners of his removal.

(7) The entries in the register kept under subsection (6) above shall be available for public inspection in legible form at all reasonable times.
[Charities Act 1993, s 72.]

---

*Amended in relation to Northern Ireland by SI 2004/1941.
1. Part IX contains ss 70–83.

8–3103   73. Person acting as charity trustee while disqualified.   (1) Subject to subsection (2) below, any person who acts as a charity trustee or trustee for a charity while he is disqualified for being such a trustee by virtue of section 72 above shall be guilty of an offence and liable[1]—

(a) on summary conviction, to imprisonment for a term not exceeding **six months** or to a fine not exceeding **the statutory maximum**, or **both**;

(b) on conviction on indictment, to imprisonment for a term not exceeding **two years** or to a **fine**, or **both**.

(2) Subsection (1) above shall not apply where—

(a) the charity concerned is a company; and

(b) the disqualified person is disqualified by virtue only of paragraph (b) or (f) of section 72(1) above.

(3) Any acts done as charity trustee or trustee for a charity by a person disqualified for being such a trustee by virtue of section 72 above shall not be invalid by reason only of that disqualification.

(4) Where the Commissioners are satisfied—

(*a*) that any person has acted as charity trustee or trustee for a charity (other than an exempt charity) while disqualified for being such a trustee by virtue of section 72 above, and

(*b*) that, while so acting, he has received from the charity any sums by way of remuneration or expenses, or any benefit in kind, in connection with his acting as charity trustee or trustee for the charity,

they may by order direct him to repay to the charity the whole or part of any such sums, or (as the case may be) to pay to the charity the whole or part of the monetary value (as determined by them) of any such benefit.

(5) Subsection (4) above does not apply to any sums received by way of remuneration or expenses in respect of any time when the person concerned was not disqualified for being a charity trustee or trustee for the charity.

[Charities Act 1993, s 73.]

---

1. For procedure in respect of this offence which is triable either way, see the Magistrates' Courts Act 1980, ss 17A–21, in PART I: MAGISTRATES' COURTS, PROCEDURE, ante.

PART X[1]
SUPPLEMENTARY

8–3104 **94. Restriction on institution of proceedings for certain offences.** (1) No proceedings for an offence under this Act to which this section applies shall be instituted except by or with the consent of the Director of Public Prosecutions.

(2) This section applies to any offence under—

(*a*) section 5;
(*b*) section 11;
(*c*) section 18(14);
(*d*) section 49; or
(*e*) section 73(1).

[Charities Act 1993, s 94.]

---

1. Part X contains ss 84–100.

8–3105 **95. Offences by bodies corporate.** Where any offence under this Act is committed by a body corporate and is proved to have been committed with the consent or connivance of, or to be attributable to any neglect on the part of, any director, manager, secretary or other similar officer of the body corporate, or any person who was purporting to act in any such capacity, he as well as the body corporate shall be guilty of that offence and shall be liable to be proceeded against and punished accordingly.

In relation to a body corporate whose affairs are managed by its members, "director" means a member of the body corporate.

[Charities Act 1993, s 95.]

8–3106 **96. Construction of references to a "charity" or to particular classes of charity.**

(1) In this Act, except in so far as the context otherwise requires—

"charity" means any institution, corporate or not, which is established for charitable purposes and is subject to the control of the High Court in the exercise of the court's jurisdiction with respect to charities;

"ecclesiastical charity" has the same meaning as in the Local Government Act 1894;

"exempt charity" means (subject to section 24(8) above) a charity comprised in Schedule 2 to this Act[1];

"local charity" means, in relation to any area, a charity established for purposes which are by their nature or by the trusts of the charity directed wholly or mainly to the benefit of that area or of part of it;

"parochial charity" means, in relation to any parish or (in Wales) community, a charity the benefits of which are, or the separate distribution of the benefits of which is, confined to inhabitants of the parish or community, or of a single ancient ecclesiastical parish which included that parish or community or part of it, or of an area consisting of that parish or community with not more than four neighbouring parishes or communities.

(2) The expression "charity" is not in this Act applicable—

(*a*) to any ecclesiastical corporation (that is to say, any corporation in the Church of England, whether sole or aggregate, which is established for spiritual purposes) in respect of the corporate property of the corporation, except to a corporation aggregate having some purposes which are not ecclesiastical in respect of its corporate property held for those purposes; or

(b)   to any Diocesan Board of Finance within the meaning of the Endowments and Glebe Measure 1976 for any diocese in respect of the diocesan glebe land of that diocese within the meaning of that Measure; or

(c)   to any trust of property for purposes for which the property has been consecrated.

(3) A charity shall be deemed for the purposes of this Act to have a permanent endowment unless all property held for the purposes of the charity may be expended for those purposes without distinction between capital and income, and in this Act "permanent endowment" means, in relation to any charity, property held subject to a restriction on its being expended for the purposes of the charity.

(4) References in this Act to a charity whose income from all sources does not in aggregate amount to more than a specified amount shall be construed—

(a)   by reference to the gross revenues of the charity, or

(b)   if the Commissioners so determine, by reference to the amount which they estimate to be the likely amount of those revenues,

but without (in either case) bringing into account anything for the yearly value of land occupied by the charity apart from the pecuniary income (if any) received from that land; and any question as to the application of any such reference to a charity shall be determined by the Commissioners, whose decision shall be final.

(5) The Commissioners may direct that for all or any of the purposes of this Act an institution established for any special purposes of or in connection with a charity (being charitable purposes) shall be treated as forming part of that charity or as forming a distinct charity.

(6) The Commissioners may direct that for all or any of the purposes of this Act two or more charities having the same charity trustees shall be treated as a single charity.★

[Charities Act 1993, s 96 as amended by the Charities (Amendment) Act 1995, s 1.]

★Section 96(2)(b) is amended by the Church of England (Miscellaneous Provisions) Measure 2000, s 11, when in force.

1. The Exempt Charities Order 1993, SI 1993/2359 has been made under para (c) of Sch 2.

8–3107   97. General interpretation.   (1) In this Act, except in so far as the context otherwise requires—

"charitable purposes" means purposes which are exclusively charitable according to the law of England and Wales;

"charity trustees" means the persons having the general control and management of the administration of a charity;

"the Commissioners" means the Charity Commissioners for England and Wales;

"company" means a company formed and registered under the Companies Act 1985 or to which the provisions of that Act apply as they apply to such a company;

"the court" means the High Court and, within the limits of its jurisdiction, any other court in England and Wales having a jurisdiction in respect of charities concurrent (within any limit of area or amount) with that of the High Court, and includes any judge or officer of the court exercising the jurisdiction of the court;

"financial year"—

(a)   in relation to a charity which is a company, shall be construed in accordance with section 223 of the Companies Act 1985; and

(b)   in relation to any other charity, shall be construed in accordance with regulations made by virtue of section 42(2) above;

but this definition is subject to the transitional provisions in section 99(4) below and Part II of Schedule 8 to this Act;

"gross income", in relation to charity, means its gross recorded income from all sources including special trusts;

"independent examiner", in relation to a charity, means such a person as is mentioned in section 43(3)(a) above;

"institution" includes any trust or undertaking;

"the official custodian" means the official custodian for charities;

"permanent endowment" shall be construed in accordance with section 96(3) above;

"the register" means the register of charities kept under section 3 above and "registered" shall be construed accordingly;

"special trust" means property which is held and administered by or on behalf of a charity for any special purposes of the charity, and is so held and administered on separate trusts relating only to that property but a special trust shall not, by itself, constitute a charity for the purposes of Part VI of this Act;

"trusts" in relation to a charity, means the provisions establishing it as a charity and regulating its purposes and administration, whether those provisions take effect by way of trust or not, and in relation to other institutions has a corresponding meaning.

(2) In this Act, except in so far as the context otherwise requires, "document" includes information recorded in any form, and, in relation to information recorded otherwise than in legible form—

 (*a*) any reference to its production shall be construed as a reference to the furnishing of a copy of it in legible form; and

 (*b*) any reference to the furnishing of a copy of, or extract from, it shall accordingly be construed as a reference to the furnishing of a copy of, or extract from, it in legible form.

(3) No vesting or transfer of any property in pursuance of any provision of Part IV or IX of this Act shall operate as a breach of a covenant or condition against alienation or give rise to a forfeiture.
[Charities Act 1993, s 97.]

8–3108 **99. Commencement and transitional provisions.** *Repealed.*

8–3109 **100.** *Short title and extent.*

CIVIL RIGHTS

8–3110 This title contains the following statutes—

 8–3111 Disability Discrimination Act 1995
 8–3116C Disability Rights Commission Act 1999
 8–3117 Freedom of Information Act 2000

and the following statutory instrument—

 8–3122 Disability Discrimination (Meaning of Disability) Regulations 1996
 8–3122F Freedom of Information and Data Protection (Appropriate Limit and Fees) Regulations 2004

8–3110A **European Communities Act 1972: regulations.** Within the scope of the title Civil Rights there also falls the subject matter of regulations made under the very wide enabling power provided in section 2(2) of the European Communities Act 1972. As such regulations create offences they are noted below:

 Environmental Information Regulations 2004, SI 2004/3391.

Disability Discrimination Act 1995[1]

(1995 c 50)

PART I[2]
DISABILITY

8–3111 **1. Meaning of "disability" and "disabled person".** (1) Subject to the provisions of Schedule 1, a person has a disability for the purposes of this Act and Part III of the 2005 Order if he has a physical or mental impairment which has a substantial and long-term adverse effect on his ability to carry out normal day-to-day activities.

(2) In this Act and Part III of the 2005 Order "disabled person" means a person who has a disability.
[Disability Discrimination Act 1995, s 1.]

---

 1. This Act makes it unlawful to discriminate against disabled persons in connection with employment, the provision of goods, facilities and services or the disposal or management of premises; makes provision about the employment of disabled persons and establishes a National Disability Council. Only those provisions of the Act, relating mainly to Public Transport, which are relevant to the work of magistrates' courts are included in this Manual.

 The Act is to be brought into force in accordance with the provisions of s 70, post. At the date of going to press, of the provisions in Part V Public Transport printed below, ss 37, 38 and 40 to 48 had been brought into force.

 2. Part I contains ss 1 to 3.

8–3111A **2. Past disabilities.** (1) The provisions of this Part and Parts II to 4 and 5A and Part III of the 2005 Order apply in relation to a person who has had a disability as they apply in relation to a person who has that disability.

(2) Those provisions are subject to the modifications made by Schedule 2.

(3) Any regulations or order made under this Act by the Secretary of State, the Scottish Ministers or the National Assembly for Wales or Part III of the 2005 Order may include provision with respect to persons who have had a disability.

(4) In any proceedings under Part II, 3 or 4★ of this Act or Part III of the 2005 Order, the question whether a person had a disability at a particular time ('the relevant time") shall be determined, for the purposes of this section, as if the provisions of, or made under, this Act or Part III of the 2005 Order in force when the act complained of was done had been in force at the relevant time.

(5) The relevant time may be a time before the passing of this Act or (as the case may be) the maiking of the 2005 Order.

[Disability Discrimination Act 1995, s 2 as amended by the Special Educational Needs and Disability Act 2001, s 38 and the Disability Discrimination Act 2005, Sch 1.]

---

*"2, 3, 4 or 5A" substituted by the Disability Discrimination Act 2005, Sch 1 from 4 December 2006.

8–3111B 3. Guidance. (A1) The Secretary of State may issue guidance about matters to be taken into account in determining whether a person is a disabled person.

(1) Without prejudice to the generality of subsection (A1), the Secretary of State may, in particular, issue guidance about the matters to be taken into account in determining—

(*a*) whether an impairment has a substantial adverse effect on a person's ability to carry out normal day-to-day activities; or

(*b*) whether such an impairment has a long-term effect.

(2) Without prejudice to the generality of subsection (A1), guidance about the matters mentioned in subsection (1) may, among other things, give examples of—

(*a*) effects which it would be reasonable, in relation to particular activities, to regard for purposes of this Act as substantial adverse effects;

(*b*) effects which it would not be reasonable, in relation to particular activities, to regard for such purposes as substantial adverse effects;

(*c*) substantial adverse effects which it would be reasonable to regard, for such purposes, as long-term;

(*d*) substantial adverse effects which it would not be reasonable to regard, for such purposes, as long-term.

(3) An adjudicating body determining, for any purpose of this Act or Part III of the 2005 Order, whether a person is a disabled person, shall take into account any guidance which appears to it to be relevant.

(3A) "Adjudicating body" means—

(*a*) a court;

(*b*) a tribunal; and

(*c*) any other person who, or body which, may decide a claim under Part 4.

(4) In preparing a draft of any guidance, the Secretary of State shall consult such persons as he considers appropriate.

(5) Where the Secretary of State proposes to issue any guidance, he shall publish a draft of it, consider any representations that are made to him about the draft and, if he thinks it appropriate, modify his proposals in the light of any of those representations.

(6) If the Secretary of State decides to proceed with any proposed guidance, he shall lay a draft of it before each House of Parliament.

(7) If, within the 40-day period, either House resolves not to approve the draft, the Secretary of State shall take no further steps in relation to the proposed guidance.

(8) If no such resolution is made within the 40-day period, the Secretary of State shall issue the guidance in the form of his draft.

(9) The guidance shall come into force on such date as the Secretary of State may appoint by order.

(10) Subsection (7) does not prevent a new draft of the proposed guidance from being laid before Parliament.

(11) The Secretary of State may—

(*a*) from time to time revise the whole or part of any guidance and re-issue it;

(*b*) by order revoke any guidance.

(12) In this section—

"40-day period", in relation to the draft of any proposed guidance, means—

(*a*) if the draft is laid before one House on a day later than the day on which it is laid before the other House, the period of 40 days beginning with the later of the two days, and

(*b*) in any other case, the period of 40 days beginning with the day on which the draft is laid before each House,

no account being taken of any period during which Parliament is dissolved or prorogued or during which both Houses are adjourned for more than 4 days; and

"guidance" means guidance issued by the Secretary of State under this section and includes guidance which has been revised and re-issued.

[Disability Discrimination Act 1995, s 3 as amended by the Special Educational Needs and Disability Act 2001, s 38 and the Disability Discrimination Act 2005, Sch 1.]

8–3111BZA 3A. Meaning of "discrimination". (1) For the purposes of this Part, a person discriminates against a disabled person if—

(a) for a reason which relates to the disabled person's disability, he treats him less favourably than he treats or would treat others to whom that reason does not or would not apply, and

(b) he cannot show that the treatment in question is justified.

(2) For the purposes of this Part, a person also discriminates against a disabled person if he fails to comply with a duty to make reasonable adjustments imposed on him in relation to the disabled person.

(3) Treatment is justified for the purposes of subsection (1)(b) if, but only if, the reason for it is both material to the circumstances of the particular case and substantial.

(4) But treatment of a disabled person cannot be justified under subsection (3) if it amounts to direct discrimination falling within subsection (5).

(5) A person directly discriminates against a disabled person if, on the ground of the disabled person's disability, he treats the disabled person less favourably than he treats or would treat a person not having that particular disability whose relevant circumstances, including his abilities, are the same as, or not materially different from, those of the disabled person.

(6) If, in a case falling within subsection (1), a person is under a duty to make reasonable adjustments in relation to a disabled person but fails to comply with that duty, his treatment of that person cannot be justified under subsection (3) unless it would have been justified even if he had complied with that duty.

[Disability Discrimination Act 1995, s 3A as inserted by SI 2003/1673.]

8–3111BZB 3B. Meaning of "harassment". (1) For the purposes of this Part, a person subjects a disabled person to harassment where, for a reason which relates to the disabled person's disability, he engages in unwanted conduct which has the purpose or effect of—

(a) violating the disabled person's dignity, or

(b) creating an intimidating, hostile, degrading, humiliating or offensive environment for him.

(2) Conduct shall be regarded as having the effect referred to in paragraph (a) or (b) of subsection (1) only if, having regard to all the circumstances, including in particular the perception of the disabled person, it should reasonably be considered as having that effect.

[Disability Discrimination Act 1995, s 3B as inserted by SI 2003/1673.]

8–3111BA

PART II[1]

THE EMPLOYMENT FIELD

PART III[2]

DISCRIMINATION IN OTHER AREAS

PART IV[3]

EDUCATION

---

1. Part II, which contains ss 4 to 18D, is not reproduced in this Manual.
2. Part III, which contains ss 19 to 28 and makes provision with respect to discrimination in relation to goods, facilities and services and in relation to premises, is not reproduced in this Manual.
3. Part IV, which contains ss 29 to 31, is not reproduced in this Manual.

PART V[4]

PUBLIC TRANSPORT

Taxis

8–3111C 32. Taxi accessibility regulations. (1) The Secretary of State may make regulations ("taxi accessibility regulations") for the purpose of securing that it is possible—

(a) for disabled persons—

(i) to get into and out of taxis in safety;

(ii) to be carried in taxis in safety and in reasonable comfort; and

(b) for disabled persons in wheelchairs—

(i) to be conveyed in safety into and out of taxis while remaining in their wheelchairs; and

(ii) to be carried in taxis in safety and in reasonable comfort while remaining in their wheelchairs.

(2) Taxi accessibility regulations may, in particular—

(a) require any regulated taxi to conform with provisions of the regulations as to—

(i) the size of any door opening which is for the use of passengers;

(ii) the floor area of the passenger compartment;

(iii) the amount of headroom in the passenger compartment;

  (iv) the fitting of restraining devices designed to ensure the stability of a wheelchair while the taxi is moving;

 (*b*) require the driver of any regulated taxi which is plying for hire, or which has been hired, to comply with provisions of the regulations as to the carrying of ramps or other devices designed to facilitate the loading and unloading of wheelchairs;

 (*c*) require the driver of any regulated taxi in which a disabled person who is in a wheelchair is being carried (while remaining in his wheelchair) to comply with provisions of the regulations as to the position in which the wheelchair is to be secured.

(3) The driver of a regulated taxi which is plying for hire, or which has been hired, is guilty of an offence if—

 (*a*) he fails to comply with any requirement imposed on him by the regulations; or

 (*b*) the taxi fails to conform with any provision of the regulations with which it is required to conform.

(4) A person who is guilty of such an offence is liable, on summary conviction, to a fine not exceeding **level 3** on the standard scale.

(5) In this section—

"passenger compartment" has such meaning as may be prescribed;

"regulated taxi" means any taxi to which the regulations are expressed to apply;

"taxi" means a vehicle licensed under—

 (*a*) section 37 of the Town Police Clauses Act 1847, or

 (*b*) section 6 of the Metropolitan Public Carriage Act 1869,

but does not include a taxi which is drawn by a horse or other animal.
[Disability Discrimination Act 1995, s 32.]

---

 1. Part V contains ss 32 to 49. At the date of going to press, of the provisions in Part V Public Transport printed below, only ss 37, 38 and 40 to 48 had been brought into force

8–3111D 33. Designated transport facilities. (1) In this section "a franchise agreement" means a contract entered into by the operator of a designated transport facility for the provision by the other party to the contract of hire car services—

 (*a*) for members of the public using any part of the transport facility; and

 (*b*) which involve vehicles entering any part of that facility.

(2) The appropriate national authority may by regulations provide for the application of any taxi provision in relation to—

 (*a*) vehicles used for the provision of services under a franchise agreement; or

 (*b*) the drivers of such vehicles.

(3) Any regulations under subsection (2) may apply any taxi provision with such modifications as the authority making the regulations considers appropriate.

(4) In this section—

"appropriate national authority" means—

 (*a*) in relation to transport facilities in England and Wales, the Secretary of State, and

 (*b*) in relation to transport facilities in Scotland, the Scottish Ministers (but see subsection (5));

"designated" means designated for the purposes of this section by an order made by the appropriate national authority;

"hire car" has such meaning as may be specified by regulations made by the appropriate national authority;

"operator", in relation to a transport facility, means any person who is concerned with the management or operation of the facility;

"tax provision" means any provision of—

 (*a*) this Act, or

 (*b*) regulations made in pursuance of section 20(2A) of the Civic Government (Scotland) Act 1982,

which applies in relation to taxis or the drivers of taxis; and

"transport facility" means any premises which form part of any port, airport, railway station or bus station.

(5) The Secretary of State may, for the purposes mentioned in section 2(2) of the European Communities Act 1972 (implementation of Community obligations etc of the United Kingdom), exercise the powers conferred by this section on the Scottish Ministers.
[Disability Discrimination Act 1995, s 33 as amended by the Disability Discrimination Act 2005, Sch 1.]

8–3112 **34. New licences conditional on compliance with taxi accessibility regulations.**
(1) No licensing authority shall grant a licence for a taxi to ply for hire unless the vehicle conforms with those provisions of the taxi accessibility regulations with which it will be required to conform if licensed.

(2) Subsection (1) does not apply if such a licence was in force with respect to the vehicle at any time during the period of 28 days immediately before the day on which the licence is granted.

(3) The Secretary of State may by order provide for subsection (2) to cease to have effect on such date as may be specified in the order.

(4) Separate orders may be made under subsection (3) with respect to different areas or localities.
[Disability Discrimination Act 1995, s 34.]

8–3112A **35. Exemption from taxi accessibility regulations.** (1) The Secretary of State may make regulations ("exemption regulations") for the purpose of enabling any relevant licensing authority to apply to him for an order (an "exemption order") exempting the authority from the requirements of section 34.

(2) Exemption regulations may, in particular, make provision requiring a licensing authority proposing to apply for an exemption order—

(a) to carry out such consultations as may be prescribed;
(b) to publish the proposal in the prescribed manner;
(c) to consider any representations made to it about the proposal, before applying for the order;
(d) to make its application in the prescribed form.

(3) A licensing authority may apply for an exemption order only if it is satisfied—

(a) that, having regard to the circumstances prevailing in its area, it would be inappropriate for the requirements of section 34 to apply; and
(b) that the application of section 34 would result in an unacceptable reduction in the number of taxis in its area.

(4) After considering any application for an exemption order and consulting the Disabled Persons Transport Advisory Committee and such other persons as he considers appropriate, the Secretary of State may—

(a) make an exemption order in the terms of the application;
(b) make an exemption order in such other terms as he considers appropriate; or
(c) refuse to make an exemption order.

(5) The Secretary of State may by regulations ("swivel seat regulations") make provision requiring any exempt taxi plying for hire in an area in respect of which an exemption order is in force to conform with provisions of the regulations as to the fitting and use of swivel seats.

(6) The Secretary of State may by regulations make provision with respect to swivel seat regulations similar to that made by section 34 with respect to taxi accessibility regulations.

(7) In this section—

"exempt taxi" means a taxi in relation to which section 34(1) would apply if the exemption order were not in force;

"relevant licensing authority" means a licensing authority responsible for licensing taxis in any area of England and Wales other than the area to which the Metropolitan Public Carriage Act 1869 applies; and

"swivel seats" has such meaning as may be prescribed.
[Disability Discrimination Act 1995, s 35.]

8–3112B **36. Carrying of passengers in wheelchairs.** (1) This section imposes duties on the driver of a regulated taxi which has been hired—

(a) by or for a disabled person who is in a wheelchair; or
(b) by a person who wishes such a disabled person to accompany him in the taxi.

(2) In this section—

"carry" means carry in the taxi concerned; and
"the passenger" means the disabled person concerned.

(3) The duties are—

(a) to carry the passenger while he remains in his wheelchair;
(b) not to make any additional charge for doing so;
(c) if the passenger chooses to sit in a passenger seat, to carry the wheelchair;
(d) to take such steps as are necessary to ensure that the passenger is carried in safety and in reasonable comfort;
(e) to give such assistance as may be reasonably required—

(i) to enable the passenger to get into or out of the taxi;
(ii) if the passenger wishes to remain in his wheelchair, to enable him to be conveyed into and out of the taxi while in his wheelchair;

(iii) to load the passenger's luggage into or out of the taxi;

(iv) if the passenger does not wish to remain in his wheelchair, to load the wheelchair into or out of the taxi.

(4) Nothing in this section is to be taken to require the driver of any taxi—

(a) except in the case of a taxi of a prescribed description, to carry more than one person in a wheelchair, or more than one wheelchair, on any one journey; or

(b) to carry any person in circumstances in which it would otherwise be lawful for him to refuse to carry that person.

(5) A driver of a regulated taxi who fails to comply with any duty imposed on him by this section is guilty of an offence and liable, on summary conviction, to a fine not exceeding **level 3** on the standard scale.

(6) In any proceedings for an offence under this section, it is a defence for the accused to show that, even though at the time of the alleged offence the taxi conformed with those provisions of the taxi accessibility regulations with which it was required to conform, it would not have been possible for the wheelchair in question to be carried in safety in the taxi.

(7) If the licensing authority is satisfied that it is appropriate to exempt a person from the duties imposed by this section—

(a) on medical grounds, or

(b) on the ground that his physical condition makes it impossible or unreasonably difficult for him to comply with the duties imposed on drivers by this section,

it shall issue him with a certificate of exemption.

(8) A certificate of exemption shall be issued for such period as may be specified in the certificate.

(9) The driver of a regulated taxi is exempt from the duties imposed by this section if—

(a) a certificate of exemption issued to him under this section is in force; and

(b) the prescribed notice of his exemption is exhibited on the taxi in the prescribed manner.

[Disability Discrimination Act 1995, s 36.]

8–3112C 37. Carrying of guide dogs and hearing dogs.   (1) This section imposes duties on the driver of a taxi which has been hired—

(a) by or for a disabled person who is accompanied by his guide dog or hearing dog, or

(b) by a person who wishes such a disabled person to accompany him in the taxi.

(2) The disabled person is referred to in this section as "the passenger".

(3) The duties are—

(a) to carry the passenger's dog and allow it to remain with the passenger; and

(b) not to make any additional charge for doing so.

(4) A driver of a taxi who fails to comply with any duty imposed on him by this section is guilty of an offence and liable, on summary conviction, to a fine not exceeding **level 3** on the standard scale.

(5) If the licensing authority is satisfied that it is appropriate on medical grounds to exempt a person from the duties imposed by this section, it shall issue him with a certificate of exemption.

(6) In determining whether to issue a certificate of exemption, the licensing authority shall, in particular, have regard to the physical characteristics of the taxi which the applicant drives or those of any kind of taxi in relation to which he requires the certificate.

(7) A certificate of exemption shall be issued—

(a) with respect to a specified taxi or a specified kind of taxi; and

(b) for such period as may be specified in the certificate.

(8) The driver of a taxi is exempt from the duties imposed by this section if—

(a) a certificate of exemption issued to him under this section is in force with respect to the taxi; and

(b) the prescribed[1] notice of his exemption is exhibited on the taxi in the prescribed[1] manner.

(9) The Secretary of State may, for the purposes of this section, prescribe[1] any other category of dog trained to assist a disabled person who has a disability of a prescribed[1] kind.

(10) This section applies in relation to any such prescribed category of dog as it applies in relation to guide dogs.

(11) In this section—

"guide dog" means a dog which has been trained to guide a blind person; and

"hearing dog" means a dog which has been trained to assist a deaf person.

[Disability Discrimination Act 1995, s 37.]

---

1. See the Disability Discrimination Act 1995 (Taxis) (Carrying of Guide Dogs etc) (England and Wales) Regulations 2000, SI 2000/2990.

8–3112D 37A. Carrying of assistance dogs in private hire vehicles.   (1) It is an offence for the operator of a private hire vehicle to fail or refuse to accept a booking for a private hire vehicle—

(a) if the booking is requested by or on behalf of a disabled person, or a person who wishes a disabled person to accompany him; and

(b) the reason for the failure or refusal is that the disabled person will be accompanied by his assistance dog.

(2) It is an offence for the operator of a private hire vehicle to make an additional charge for carrying an assistance dog which is accompanying a disabled person.

(3) It is an offence for the driver of a private hire vehicle to fail or refuse to carry out a booking accepted by the operator of the vehicle—

(a) if the booking was made by or on behalf of a disabled person, or a person who wishes a disabled person to accompany him; and

(b) the reason for the failure or refusal is that the disabled person is accompanied by his assistance dog.

(4) A person who is guilty of an offence under this section is liable on summary conviction to a fine not exceeding level 3 on the standard scale.

(5) If the licensing authority is satisfied that it is appropriate on medical grounds to issue a certificate of exemption to a driver in respect of subsection (3) it must do so.

(6) In determining whether to issue a certificate of exemption, the licensing authority shall, in particular, have regard to the physical characteristics of the private hire vehicle which the applicant drives or those of any kind of private hire vehicle in relation to which he requires the certificate.

(7) A certificate of exemption shall be issued—

(a) with respect to a specified private hire vehicle or a specified kind of private hire vehicle; and

(b) for such period as may be specified in the certificate.

(8) No offence is committed by a driver under subsection (3) if—

(a) a certificate of exemption issued to him under this section is in force with respect to the private hire vehicle; and

(b) the prescribed[1] notice is exhibited on the private hire vehicle in the prescribed[1] manner.

(9) In this section—

"assistance dog" means a dog which—

(a) has been trained to guide a blind person;

(b) has been trained to assist a deaf person;

(c) has been trained by a prescribed[1] charity to assist a disabled person who has a disability which—

(i) consists of epilepsy; or

(ii) otherwise affects his mobility, manual dexterity, physical co-ordination or ability to lift, carry or otherwise move everyday objects;

"driver" means a person who holds a licence granted under—

(a) section 13 of the Private Hire Vehicles (London) Act 1998 (c 34) ("the 1998 Act");

(b) section 51 of the Local Government (Miscellaneous Provisions) Act 1976 (c 57) ("the 1976 Act"); or

(c) an equivalent provision of a local enactment;

"licensing authority", in relation to any area of England and Wales, means the authority responsible for licensing private hire vehicles in that area;

"operator" means a person who holds a licence granted under—

(a) section 3 of the 1998 Act;

(b) section 55 of the 1976 Act; or

(c) an equivalent provision of a local enactment;

"private hire vehicle" means a vehicle licensed under—

(a) section 6 of the 1998 Act;

(b) section 48 of the 1976 Act; or

(c) an equivalent provision of a local enactment.

[Disability Discrimination Act 1995, s 37A as inserted by the Private Hire Vehicles (Carriage of Guide Dogs etc) Act 2002, s 1(1).]

---

1. See the Disability Discrimination Act 1995 (Private Hire Vehicles) (Carriage of Guide Dogs, etc.) (England and Wales) Regulations 2003, SI 2003/3122.

8–3112E 38. Appeal against refusal of exemption certificate. (1) Any person who is aggrieved by the refusal of a licensing authority to issue an exemption certificate under section 36, 37 or 37A may appeal to the appropriate court before the end of the period of 28 days beginning with the date of the refusal.

(2) On an appeal to it under this section, the court may direct the licensing authority concerned

to issue the appropriate certificate of exemption to have effect for such period as may be specified in the direction.

(3) "Appropriate court" means the magistrates' court for the petty sessions area in which the licensing authority has its principal office.

[Disability Discrimination Act 1995, s 38, as amended by the Private Hire Vehicles (Carriage of Guide Dogs etc) Act 2002, s 3.]

Public service vehicles

8–3113   40. PSV accessibility regulations.   (1) The Secretary of State may make regulations[1] ("PSV accessibility regulations") for the purpose of securing that it is possible for disabled persons—

(a)   to get on to and off regulated public service vehicles in safety and without unreasonable difficulty (and, in the case of disabled persons in wheelchairs, to do so while remaining in their wheelchairs); and

(b)   to be carried in such vehicles in safety and in reasonable comfort.

(2) PSV accessibility regulations[1] may, in particular, make provision as to the construction, use and maintenance of regulated public service vehicles including provision as to—

(a)   the fitting of equipment to vehicles;
(b)   equipment to be carried by vehicles;
(c)   the design of equipment to be fitted to, or carried by, vehicles;
(d)   the fitting and use of restraining devices designed to ensure the stability of wheelchairs while vehicles are moving;
(e)   the position in which wheelchairs are to be secured while vehicles are moving.

(3) Any person who—

(a)   contravenes or fails to comply with any provision of the PSV accessibility regulations,
(b)   uses on a road a regulated public service vehicle which does not conform with any provision of the regulations with which it is required to conform, or
(c)   causes or permits to be used on a road such a regulated public service vehicle,

is guilty of an offence.

(4) A person who is guilty of such an offence is liable, on summary conviction, to a fine not exceeding **level 4** on the standard scale.

(5) In this section—

"public service vehicle" means a vehicle which is—

(a)   adapted to carry more than eight passengers; and
(b)   a public service vehicle for the purposes of the Public Passenger Vehicles Act 1981;

"regulated public service vehicle" means any public service vehicle to which the PSV accessibility regulations are expressed to apply.

(6) Different provision may be made in regulations[1] under this section—

(a)   as respects different classes or descriptions of vehicle;
(b)   as respects the same class or description of vehicle in different circumstances.

(7) Before making any regulations under this section or section 41 or 42 the Secretary of State shall consult the Disabled Persons Transport Advisory Committee and such other representative organisations as he thinks fit.

[Disability Discrimination Act 1995, s 40.]

─────────────

1. The Public Service Vehicles Accessibility Regulations 2000, SI 2000/1970 amended by SI 2000/3318, SI 2002/2981.SI 2003/1818,SI 2004/1881 and SI 2005/2988 have been made.

8–3113A   41. Accessibility certificates.   (1) A regulated public service vehicle shall not be used on a road unless—

(a)   a vehicle examiner has issued a certificate (an "accessibility certificate") that such provisions of the PSV accessibility regulations as may be prescribed are satisfied in respect of the vehicle; or

(b)   an approval certificate has been issued under section 42 in respect of the vehicle.

(2) The Secretary of State may make regulations[1]—

(a)   with respect to applications for, and the issue of, accessibility certificates;
(b)   providing for the examination of vehicles in respect of which applications have been made;
(c)   with respect to the issue of copies of accessibility certificates in place of certificates which have been lost or destroyed.

(3) If a regulated public service vehicle is used in contravention of this section, the operator of the vehicle is guilty of an offence and liable on summary conviction to a fine not exceeding **level 4** on the standard scale.

(4) In this section "operator" has the same meaning as in the Public Passenger Vehicles Act 1981.
[Disability Discrimination Act 1995, s 41.]

---

1. The Public Service Vehicles Accessibility Regulations 2000, SI 2000/1970 amended by SI 2000/3318, SI 2002/2981, SI 2003/1818, SI 2004/1881 and SI 2005/2988 have been made.

8–3113B 42. Approval certificates. (1) Where the Secretary of State is satisfied that such provisions of the PSV accessibility regulations as may be prescribed for the purposes of section 41 are satisfied in respect of a particular vehicle he may approve the vehicle for the purposes of this section.

(2) A vehicle which has been so approved is referred to in this section as a "type vehicle".

(3) Subsection (4) applies where a declaration in the prescribed form has been made by an authorised person that a particular vehicle conforms in design, construction and equipment with a type vehicle.

(4) A vehicle examiner may, after examining (if he thinks fit) the vehicle to which the declaration applies, issue a certificate in the prescribed form ("an approval certificate") that it conforms to the type vehicle.

(5) The Secretary of State may make regulations[1]—

(a) with respect to applications for, and grants of, approval under subsection (1);
(b) with respect to applications for, and the issue of, approval certificates;
(c) providing for the examination of vehicles in respect of which applications have been made;
(d) with respect to the issue of copies of approval certificates in place of certificates which have been lost or destroyed.

(6) The Secretary of State may at any time withdraw his approval of a type vehicle.

(7) Where an approval is withdrawn—

(a) no further approval certificates shall be issued by reference to the type vehicle; but
(b) any approval certificate issued by reference to the type vehicle before the withdrawal shall continue to have effect for the purposes of section 41.

(8) In subsection (3) "authorised person" means a person authorised by the Secretary of State for the purposes of that subsection.
[Disability Discrimination Act 1995, s 42.]

---

1. The Public Service Vehicles Accessibility Regulations 2000, SI 2000/1970 amended by SI 2000/3318, SI 2002/2981, SI 2003/1818, SI 2004/1881 and SI 2005/2988 have been made.

8–3113C 43. Special authorisations. (1) The Secretary of State may by order authorise the use on roads of—

(a) any regulated public service vehicle of a class or description specified by the order, or
(b) any regulated public service vehicle which is so specified,

and nothing in section 40, 41 or 42 prevents the use of any vehicle in accordance with the order.

(2) Any such authorisation may be given subject to such restrictions and conditions as may be specified by or under the order.

(3) The Secretary of State may by order make provision for the purpose of securing that, subject to such restrictions and conditions as may be specified by or under the order, provisions of the PSV accessibility regulations apply to regulated public service vehicles of a description specified by the order subject to such modifications or exceptions as may be specified by the order.
[Disability Discrimination Act 1995, s 43.]

Rail vehicles

8–3114 46. Rail vehicle accessibility regulations[1]. (1) The Secretary of State may make regulations ("rail vehicle accessibility regulations") for the purpose of securing that it is possible—

(a) for disabled persons—

(i) to get on to and off regulated rail vehicles in safety and without unreasonable difficulty;
(ii) to be carried in such vehicles in safety and in reasonable comfort; and

(b) for disabled persons in wheelchairs—

(i) to get on to and off such vehicles in safety and without unreasonable difficulty while remaining in their wheelchairs, and
(ii) to be carried in such vehicles in safety and in reasonable comfort while remaining in their wheelchairs.

(2) Rail vehicle accessibility regulations may, in particular, make provision as to the construction, use and maintenance of regulated rail vehicles including provision as to—

(a) the fitting of equipment to vehicles;
(b) equipment to be carried by vehicles;

(c)   the design of equipment to be fitted to, or carried by, vehicles;

(d)   the use of equipment fitted to, or carried by, vehicles;

(e)   the toilet facilities to be provided in vehicles;

(f)   the location and floor area of the wheelchair accommodation to be provided in vehicles;

(g)   assistance to be given to disabled persons.

(3) If a regulated rail vehicle which does not conform with any provision of the rail vehicle accessibility regulations with which it is required to conform is used for carriage, the operator of the vehicle is guilty of an offence.

(4) A person who is guilty of such an offence is liable, on summary conviction, to a fine not exceeding **level 4** on the standard scale.

(5) Different provision may be made in rail vehicle accessibility regulations—

(a)   as respects different classes or descriptions of rail vehicle;

(b)   as respects the same class or description of rail vehicle in different circumstances;

(c)   as respects different networks.

(6) In this section—

"network" means any permanent way or other means of guiding or supporting rail vehicles or any section of it;

"operator", in relation to any rail vehicle, means the person having the management of that vehicle;

"rail vehicle" means a vehicle—

(a)   constructed or adapted to carry passengers on any railway, tramway or prescribed system; and

(b)   first brought into use, or belonging to a class of vehicle first brought into use, after 31 December 1998;

"regulated rail vehicle" means any rail vehicle to which the rail vehicle accessibility regulations are expressed to apply; and

"wheelchair accommodation" has such meaning as may be prescribed.

(7) In subsection (6)—

"prescribed system" means a system using a prescribed mode of guided transport ("guided transport" having the same meaning as in the Transport and Works Act 1992); and

"railway" and "tramway" have the same meaning as in that Act.

(8) The Secretary of State may by regulations make provision as to the time when a rail vehicle, or a class of rail vehicle, is to be treated, for the purposes of this section, as first brought into use.

(9) Regulations under subsection (8) may include provision for disregarding periods of testing and other prescribed periods of use.

(10) For the purposes of this section and section 47, a person uses a vehicle for carriage if he uses it for the carriage of members of the public for hire or reward at separate fares.

(11) Before making any regulations under subsection (1) or section 47 the Secretary of State shall consult the Disabled Persons Transport Advisory Committee and such other representative organisations as he thinks fit.

[Disability Discrimination Act 1995, s 46.]

---

1. The Rail Vehicle Accessibility Regulations 1998, SI 1998/2456 amended by SI 2000/3215 have been made.

8–3114A   47. Exemption from rail vehicle accessibility regulations[1]. (1) The Secretary of State may by order (an "exemption order")—

(a)   authorise the use for carriage of a regulated rail vehicle even though the vehicle does not conform with the provisions of rail vehicle accessibility regulations with which it is required to conform;

(b)   authorise a regulated rail vehicle to be used for carriage otherwise than in conformity with the provisions of rail vehicle accessibility regulations with which use of the vehicle is required to conform.

(1A) Authority under subsection (1)(a) or (b) may be for—

(a)   any regulated rail vehicle that is specified or is of a specified description; or

(b)   use in specified circumstances of—

    (i)   any regulated rail vehicle, or

    (ii)   any regulated rail vehicle that is specified or is of a specified description.

(2) Regulations may make provision with respect to exemption orders including, in particular, provision as to—

(a)   the persons by whom applications for exemption orders may be made;

(b)   the form in which such applications are to be made;

(c)   information to be supplied in connection with such applications;

(d)   the period for which exemption orders are to continue in force;

(*e*) the revocation of exemption orders.

(3) After considering any application for an exemption order and consulting the Disabled Persons Transport Advisory Committee and such other persons as he considers appropriate, the Secretary of State may—

(*a*) make an exemption order in the terms of the application;
(*b*) make an exemption order in such other terms as he considers appropriate;
(*c*) refuse to make an exemption order.

(4) An exemption order may be made subject to such restrictions and conditions as may be specified.

(5) In this section "specified" means specified in an exemption order.

[Disability Discrimination Act 1995, s 47 as amended by the Disability Discrimination Act 2005, Sch 1.]

1. The Rail Vehicle (Exemption Applications) Regulations 1998, SI 1998/2457 have been made and numerous Rail Vehicle Accessibility Exemption Orders which exempt various classes of trains or individual carriages from the requirements of the legislation.

Supplemental

8–3114B 48. Offences by bodies corporate etc. (1) Where an offence under section 40 or 46 committed by a body corporate is committed with the consent or connivance of, or is attributable to any neglect on the part of, a director, manager, secretary or other similar officer of the body, or a person purporting to act in such a capacity, he as well as the body corporate is guilty of the offence.

(2) In subsection (1) "director", in relation to a body corporate whose affairs are managed by its members, means a member of the body corporate.

(3) Where, in Scotland, an offence under section 40 or 46 committed by a partnership or by an unincorporated association other than a partnership is committed with the consent or connivance of, or is attributable to any neglect on the part of, a partner in the partnership or (as the case may be) a person concerned in the management or control of the association, he, as well as the partnership or association, is guilty of the offence.

[Disability Discrimination Act 1995, s 48.]

8–3114C 49. Forgery and false statements. (1) In this section "relevant document" means—

(*a*) a certificate of exemption issued under section 36, 37 or 37A;
(*b*) a notice of a kind mentioned in section 36(9)(*b*), 37(8)(*b*) or 37A(8)(*b*);
(*c*) an accessibility certificate; or
(*d*) an approval certificate.

(2) A person is guilty of an offence if, with intent to deceive, he—

(*a*) forges, alters or uses a relevant document;
(*b*) lends a relevant document to any other person;
(*c*) allows a relevant document to be used by any other person; or
(*d*) makes or has in his possession any document which closely resembles a relevant document.

(3) A person who is guilty of an offence under subsection (2) is liable[1]—

(*a*) on summary conviction, to a fine not exceeding **the statutory maximum;**
(*b*) on conviction on indictment, to imprisonment for a term not exceeding **two years** or to a **fine** or both.

(4) a person who knowingly makes a false statement for the purpose of obtaining an accessibility certificate or an approval certificate is guilty of an offence and liable on summary conviction to a fine not exceeding **level 4** on the standard scale.

[Disability Discrimination Act 1995, s 49, as amended by the Private Hire Vehicles (Carriage of Guide Dogs etc) Act 2002, s 6(2).]

1. For procedure in respect of this offence which is triable either way, see the Magistrates' Courts Act 1980, ss 17A–21, in PART I: MAGISTRATES' COURTS, PROCEDURE, ante.

8–3114CA 49A. General duty[1]. (1) Every public authority shall in carrying out its functions have due regard to—

(*a*) the need to eliminate discrimination that is unlawful under this Act;
(*b*) the need to eliminate harassment of disabled persons that is related to their disabilities;
(*c*) the need to promote equality of opportunity between disabled persons and other persons;
(*d*) the need to take steps to take account of disabled persons' disabilities, even where that involves treating disabled persons more favourably than other persons;
(*e*) the need to promote positive attitudes towards disabled persons; and
(*f*) the need to encourage participation by disabled persons in public life.

(2) Subsection (1) is without prejudice to any obligation of a public authority to comply with any other provision of this Act.*

[Disability Discrimination Act 1995, s 49A, as inserted by Disability Discrimination Act 2005, s 3).]

---

*In force (in so far as it relates to sub-s (1) for certain purposes) 5 December 2005, for remaining purposes 4 December 2006.

1. The Disability Discrimination (Public Authorities) (Statutory Duties) Regulations 2005, SI 2005/2966 have been made which require the bodies listed in Schedule 1 to the regulations to publish, implement and report on a Disability Equality Scheme. Different duties apply to the Secretary of State and to the National Assembly for Wales who are required, in relation to public authorities which operate in policy spheres for which they are responsible.

PART VII[1]
SUPPLEMENTAL

8–3114D 57. Aiding unlawful acts. (1) A person who knowingly aids another person to do an unlawful act is to be treated for the purposes of this Act as himself doing the same kind of unlawful act.

(2) For the purposes of subsection (1), an employee or agent for whose act the employer or principal is liable under section 58 (or would be so liable but for section 58(5)) shall be taken to have aided the employer or principal to do the act.

(3) For the purposes of this section, a person does not knowingly aid another to do an unlawful act if—

(a) he acts in reliance on a statement made to him by that other person that, because of any provision of this Act, the act would not be unlawful; and

(b) it is reasonable for him to rely on the statement.

(4) A person who knowingly or recklessly makes such a statement which is false or misleading in a material respect is guilty of an offence.

(5) Any person guilty of an offence under subsection (4) shall be liable on summary conviction to a fine not exceeding **level 5** on the standard scale.

(6) "Unlawful act" means an act made unlawful by any provision of this Act other than a provision contained in Chapter 1 of Part 4.

[Disability Discrimination Act 1995, s 57 as amended by the Special Educational Needs and Disability Act 2001, s 38.]

---

1. Part VII contains ss 53 to 59.
2. This will include an act made unlawful by s 4 (discrimination against applicants and employees), s 19 (discrimination in relation to goods, facilities and services) and s 22 (discrimination in relation to premises), being provisions of the Act which are not reproduced in this Manual.

8–3115 58. Liability of employers and principals. (1) Anything done by a person in the course of his employment shall be treated for the purposes of this Act as also done by his employer, whether or not it was done with the employer's knowledge or approval.

(2) Anything done by a person as agent for another person with the authority of that other person shall be treated for the purposes of this Act as also done by that other person.

(3) Subsection (2) applies whether the authority was—

(a) express or implied; or

(b) given before or after the act in question was done.

(4) Subsections (1) and (2) do not apply in relation to an offence under section 57(4).

(5) In proceedings under this Act against any person in respect of an act alleged to have been done by an employee of his, it shall be a defence for that person to prove that he took such steps as were reasonably practicable to prevent the employee from—

(a) doing that act; or

(b) doing, in the course of his employment, acts of that description.

[Disability Discrimination Act 1995, s 58.]

8–3115A 59. Statutory authority and national security etc. (1) Nothing in this Act makes unlawful any act done—

(a) in pursuance of any enactment; or

(b) in pursuance of any instrument made under any enactment by—

(i) a Minister of the Crown,

(ii) a member of the Scottish Executive, or

(iii) the National Assembly for Wales; or

(c) to comply with any condition or requirement—

(i) imposed by a Minister of the Crown (whether before or after the passing of this Act) by virtue of any enactment,

(ii) imposed by a member of the Scottish Executive (whether before or after the coming into force of this sub-paragraph) by virtue of any enactment, or

(iii) imposed by the National Assembly for Wales (whether before or after the coming into force of this sub-paragraph) by virtue of any enactment.

(2) In subsection (1) "enactment" includes one passed or made after the date on which this Act is passed and "instrument" includes one made after that date.

(2A) Nothing in—

(*a*) Part 2 of this Act, or

(*b*) Part 3 of this Act to the extent that it relates to the provision of employment services,

makes unlawful any act done for the purpose of safeguarding national security if the doing of the act was justified by that purpose.

(3) Nothing in any other provision of this Act makes unlawful any act done for the purpose of safeguarding national security.

[Disability Discrimination Act 1995, s 59 as amended by SI 2003/1673 and the Disability Discrimination Act 2005, Sch 1.]

PART VIII[1]
MISCELLANEOUS

8–3115B   **64. Application to Crown etc.**   (A1) The following provisions bind the Crown—

(*a*) sections 21B to 21E and Part 5A, and

(*b*) the other provisions of this Act so far as applying for the purposes of provisions mentioned in paragraph (*a*);

and sections 57 and 58 shall apply for purposes of provisions mentioned in paragraph (*a*) as if service as a Crown servant were employment by the Crown.]

(1) This Act, other than the provisions mentioned in paragraphs (*a*) and (*b*) of subsection (A1), applies—

(*a*) to an act done by or for purposes of a Minister of the Crown or government department, or

(*b*) to an act done on behalf of the Crown by a statutory body, or a person holding a statutory office,

as it applies to an act done by a private person.

(2) Part II applies to service—

(*a*) for purposes of a Minister of the Crown or government department, other than service of a person holding a statutory office, or

(*b*) on behalf of the Crown for purposes of a person holding a statutory office or purposes of a statutory body,

as it applies to employment by a private person.

(2A) Subsections (1) and (A1) to (2) have effect subject to section 64A.

(3) The provisions of Parts II to IV of the 1947 Act apply to proceedings against the Crown under this Act as they apply to Crown proceedings in England and Wales.

(4) The provisions of Part V of the 1947 Act apply to proceedings against the Crown under this Act as they apply to proceedings in Scotland which by virtue of that Part are treated as civil proceedings by or against the Crown; but the proviso to section 44 of that Act (removal of proceedings from the sheriff court to the Court of Session) does not apply.

(5), (6) *Repealed.*

(7) Part II does not apply to service in any of the naval, military or air forces of the Crown.

(8) In this section—

"the 1947 Act" means the Crown Proceedings Act 1947;

"Crown proceedings" means proceedings which, by virtue of section 23 of the 1947 Act, are treated for the purposes of Part II of that Act as civil proceedings by or against the Crown;

"service for purposes of a Minister of the Crown or government department" does not include service in any office for the time being mentioned in Schedule 2 (Ministerial offices) to the House of Commons Disqualification Act 1975;

"statutory body" means a body set up by or under an enactment;

"statutory office" means an office so set up.★

[Disability Discrimination Act 1995, s 64, as amended by SI 2003/1673, SI 2005/2712 and the Disability Discrimination Act 2005, Sch 1.]

★Section reproduced as in force for certain pupuses; in force for remaining purposes 4 December 2005.
1. Part VIII contains ss 60 to 70.

64A. *Police*

8–3115C   **67.** *Regulations and orders.*

8–3115D   68. Interpretation.   (1) In this Act—

"the 2005 Order" means the Special Educational Needs and Disability (Nortrhern Ireland) Order 2005;

"accessibility certificate" means a certificate issued under section 41(1)(*a*);

"act" includes a deliberate omission;

"approval certificate" means a certificate issued under section 42(4);

"conciliation officer" means a person designated under section 211 of the Trade Union and Labour Relations (Consolidation) Act 1992;★

"employment" means, subject to any prescribed provision, employment under a contract of service or of apprenticeship or a contract personally to do any work, and related expressions are to be construed accordingly;

"employment at an establishment in Great Britain" is to be construed in accordance with subsections (2) to (4A);

"employment services" has the meaning given in section 21A(1);

"enactment" includes subordinate legislation and any Order in Council, and (except in section 56(5)) includes an enactment comprised in, or in an instrument made under, an Act of the Scottish Parliament;

"Great Britain" includes such of the territorial waters of the United Kingdom as are adjacent to Great Britain;

"group insurance arrangement" means an arrangement between an employer and another for the provision by the other of facilities by way of insurance to the employer's employees or to any class of those employees;

"licensing authority", except in 37A, means—

     (*a*)   in relation to the area to which the Metropolitan Public Carriage Act 1869 applies, the Secretary of State or the holder of any office for the time being designated by the Secretary of State; or

     (*b*)   in relation to any other area in England and Wales, the authority responsible for licensing taxis in that area;

"mental impairment" does not have the same meaning as in the Mental Health Act 1983 but the fact that an impairment would be a mental impairment for the purposes of either of that Act does not prevent it from being a mental impairment for the purposes of this Act;

"Minister of the Crown" includes the Treasury and the Defence Council;

"occupational pension scheme" has the same meaning as in the Pension Schemes Act 1993;

"premises" includes land of any description;

"prescribed" means prescribed by regulations, except in section 28D (where it has the meaning given by section 28D(17));

"profession" includes any vocation or occupation;

"provider of services" has the meaning given in section 19(2)(*b*);★

"public service vehicle" and "regulated public service vehicle" have the meaning given in section 40;

"PSV accessibility regulations" means regulations made under section 40(1);

"rail vehicle" and "regulated rail vehicle" have the meaning given in section 46;★

"rail vehicle accessibility regulations" means regulations made under section 46(1);

"regulations" means regulations made by the Secretary of State, except in sections 2(3), 28D, 28L(6), 28Q(7), 33, 49D to 49F and 67 (provisions where the meaning of "regulations" is apparent);

"section 21 duty" means any duty imposed by or under section 21;

"subordinate legislation" has the same meaning as in section 21 of the Interpretation Act 1978;

"taxi" and "regulated taxi" have the meaning given in section 32;

"taxi accessibility regulations" means regulations made under section 32(1);

"trade" includes any business;

"trade organisation" has the meaning given in section 13;

"vehicle examiner" means an examiner appointed under section 66A of the Road Traffic Act 1988.★

(2) Employment (including employment on board a ship to which subsection (2B) applies or on an aircraft or hovercraft to which subsection (2C) applies) is to be regarded as being employment at an establishment in Great Britain if the employee—

     (*a*)   does his work wholly or partly in Great Britain; or

     (*b*)   does his work wholly outside Great Britain and subsection (2A) applies.

(2A) This subsection applies if—

     (*a*)   the employer has a place of business at an establishment in Great Britain;

     (*b*)   the work is for the purposes of the business carried on at the establishment; and

     (*c*)   the employee is ordinarily resident in Great Britain—

         (i)   at the time when he applies for or is offered the employment, or

         (ii)   at any time during the course of the employment.

(2B) This subsection applies to a ship if—

(*a*) it is registered at a port of registry in Great Britain; or
(*b*) it belongs to or is possessed by Her Majesty in right of the Government of the United Kingdom.

(2C) This subsection applies to an aircraft or hovercraft if—

(*a*) it is—
    (i) registered in the United Kingdom, and
    (ii) operated by a person who has his principal place of business, or is ordinarily resident, in Great Britain; or
(*b*) it belongs to or is possessed by Her Majesty in right of the Government of the United Kingdom.

(2D) The following are not to be regarded as being employment at an establishment in Great Britain—

(*a*) employment on board a ship to which subsection (2B) does not apply;
(*b*) employment on an aircraft or hovercraft to which subsection (2C) does not apply.

(4) Employment of a prescribed kind, or in prescribed circumstances, is to be regarded as not being employment at an establishment in Great Britain.

(4A) For the purposes of determining if employment concerned with the exploration of the sea bed or sub-soil or the exploitation of their natural resources is outside Great Britain, subsections (2)(*a*) and (*b*), (2A) and (2C) of this section each have effect as if "Great Britain" had the same meaning as that given to the last reference to Great Britain in section 10(1) of the Sex Discrimination Act 1975 by section 10(5) of that Act read with the Sex Discrimination and Equal Pay (Offshore Employment) Order 1987.

(5) *Repealed.*

[Disability Discrimination Act 1995, s 68 as amended by SI 2000/2040, the Private Hire Vehicles (Carriage of Guide Dogs etc) Act 2002, s 5, SI 2003/1673, SI 2005/1117 and the Disability Discrimination Act 2005, Sch 1.]

---

*Definitions inserted by the Disability Discrimination Act 2005, Sch 1 from 4 December 2006.

8–3116 **70. Short title, commencement, extent etc.** (1) This Act may be cited as the Disability Discrimination Act 1995.

(2) This section (apart from subsections (4), (5) and (7)) comes into force on the passing of this Act.

(3) The other provisions of this Act come into force on such day as the Secretary of State may by order[1] appoint and different days may be appointed for different purposes.

(4) Schedule 6 makes consequential amendments.

(5) The repeals set out in Schedule 7 shall have effect.

(5A) Sections 7A and 7B extend to England and Wales only.*

(5B) Sections 7C and 7D extend to Scotland only.

(6) Subject to subsections (5A) and (5B), this Act extends to England and Wales, Scotland and Northern Ireland; but in their application to Northern Ireland the provisions of this Act mentioned in Schedule 8 shall have effect subject to the modifications set out in that Schedule.

(7) *Repealed.*

(8) Consultations which are required by any provision of this Act to be held by the Secretary of State may be held by him before the coming into force of that provision.

[Disability Discrimination Act 1995, s 70 as amended by the Disability Rights Commission Act 1999, Sch 5 and SI 2003/1673.]

---

*Amended by the Disability Discrimination Act 2005, Sch 1 from 4 December 2006.
1. At the date of going to press, the following orders had been made: Disability Discrimination Act 1995 (Commencement No 1) Order 1995, SI 1995/3330; Disability Discrimination Act 1995 (Commencement No 2) Order 1996, SI 1996/1336; Disability Discrimination Act 1995 (Commencement No 3 and Saving and Transitional Provisions) Order 1996, SI 1996/1474; Disability Discrimination Act 1995 (Commencement No 4) Order 1996, SI 1996/3003, the Disability Discrimination Act 1995 (Commencement No 5) Order 1998, SI 1998/1282, the Disability Discrimination Act 1995 (Commencement Order No 6) Order 1999, SI 1999/1190, the Disability Discrimination Act 1995 (Commencement No 7) Order 2000, SI 2000/1969 and the Disability Discrimination Act 1995 (Commencement No 8) Order 2000, SI 2000/2989.

SCHEDULES

Section 1(1)   SCHEDULE 1
PROVISIONS SUPPLEMENTING SECTION 1

(*Amended by the Disability Discrimination Act 2005, Sch 2.*)

Impairment

8–3116A **1.** (1) *Repealed.*

(2) Regulations[1] may make provision, for the purposes of this Act—

(*a*) for conditions of a prescribed description to be treated as amounting to impairments;
(*b*) for conditions of a prescribed description to be treated as not amounting to impairments.

(3) Regulations made under sub-paragraph (2) may make provision as to the meaning of "condition" for the purposes of those regulations.

Long-term effects

2. (1) The effect of an impairment is a long-term effect if—

(a) it has lasted at least 12 months;
(b) the period for which it lasts is likely to be at least 12 months; or
(c) it is likely to last for the rest of the life of the person affected.

(2) Where an impairment ceases to have a substantial adverse effect on a person's ability to carry out normal day-to-day activities, it is to be treated as continuing to have that effect if that effect is likely to recur.

(3) For the purposes of sub-paragraph (2), the likelihood of an effect recurring shall be disregarded in prescribed circumstances.

(4) Regulations[1] may prescribe circumstances in which, for the purposes of this Act—

(a) an effect which would not otherwise be a long-term effect is to be treated as such an effect; or
(b) an effect which would otherwise be a long-term effect is to be treated as not being such an effect.

Severe disfigurement

3. (1) An impairment which consists of a severe disfigurement is to be treated as having a substantial adverse effect on the ability of the person concerned to carry out normal day-to-day activities.

(2) Regulations[1] may provide that in prescribed circumstances a severe disfigurement is not to be treated as having that effect.

(3) Regulations[1] under sub-paragraph (2) may, in particular, make provision with respect to deliberately acquired disfigurements.

Normal day-to-day activities

4. (1) An impairment is to be taken to affect the ability of the person concerned to carry out normal day-to-day activities only if it affects one of the following—

(a) mobility;
(b) manual dexterity;
(c) physical co-ordination;
(d) continence;
(e) ability to lift, carry or otherwise move everyday objects;
(f) speech, hearing or eyesight;
(g) memory or ability to concentrate, learn or understand; or
(h) perception of the risk of physical danger.

(2) Regulations[1] may prescribe—

(a) circumstances in which an impairment which does not have an effect falling within sub-paragraph (1) is to be taken to affect the ability of the person concerned to carry out normal day-to-day activities;
(b) circumstances in which an impairment which has an effect falling within sub-paragraph (1) is to be taken not to affect the ability of the person concerned to carry out normal day-to-day activities.

Substantial adverse effects

5. Regulations[1] may make provision for the purposes of this Act—

(a) for an effect of a prescribed kind on the ability of a person to carry out normal day-to-day activities to be treated as a substantial adverse effect;
(b) for an effect of a prescribed kind on the ability of a person to carry out normal day-to-day activities to be treated as not being a substantial adverse effect.

Effect of medical treatment

6. (1) An impairment which would be likely to have a substantial adverse effect on the ability of the person concerned to carry out normal day-to-day activities, but for the fact that measures are being taken to treat or correct it, is to be treated as having that effect.

(2) In sub-paragraph (1) "measures" includes, in particular, medical treatment and the use of a prosthesis or other aid.

(3) Sub-paragraph (1) does not apply—

(a) in relation to the impairment of a person's sight, to the extent that the impairment is, in his case, correctable by spectacles or contact lenses or in such other ways as may be prescribed; or
(b) in relation to such other impairments as may be prescribed, in such circumstances as may be prescribed.

6A. (1) Subject to sub-paragraph (2), a person who has cancer, HIV infection or multiple sclerosis is to be deemed to have a disability, and hence to be a disabled person.

(2) Regulations may provide for sub-paragraph (1) not to apply in the case of a person who has cancer if he has cancer of a prescribed description.

(3) A description of cancer prescribed under sub-paragraph (2) may (in particular) be framed by reference to consequences for a person of his having it.

Persons deemed to be disabled

7. (1) Sub-paragraph (2) applies to any person whose name is, both on 12th January 1995 and on the date when this paragraph comes into force, in the register of disabled persons maintained under section 6 of the Disabled Persons (Employment) Act 1944.

(2) That person is to be deemed—

(a) during the initial period, to have a disability, and hence to be a disabled person; and

(b) afterwards, to have had a disability and hence to have been a disabled person during that period.

(3) A certificate of registration shall be conclusive evidence, in relation to the person with respect to whom it was issued, of the matters certified.

(4) Unless the contrary is shown, any document purporting to be a certificate of registration shall be taken to be such a certificate and to have been validly issued.

(5) Regulations[1] may provide for prescribed descriptions of person to be deemed to have disabilities, and hence to be disabled persons, for the purposes of this Act.

(5A) The generality of sub-paragraph (5) shall not be taken to be prejudiced by the other provisions of this Schedule.

(6) Regulations may prescribe circumstances in which a person who has been deemed to be a disabled person by the provisions of sub-paragraph (1) or regulations made under sub-paragraph (5) is to be treated as no longer being deemed to be such a person.

(7) In this paragraph—

"certificate of registration" means a certificate issued under regulations made under section 6 of the Act of 1944; and

"initial period" means the period of three years beginning with the date on which this paragraph comes into force.

---

1. The Disability Discrimination (Blind and Partially Sighted Persons) Regulations 2003, SI 2003/712 have been made.

Progressive conditions

8. Where—

(a) a person has a progressive condition (such as cancer, multiple sclerosis or muscular dystrophy or HIV infection),

(b) as a result of that condition, he has an impairment which has (or had) an effect on his ability to carry out normal day-to-day activities, but

(c) that effect is not (or was not) a substantial adverse effect,

he shall be taken to have an impairment which has such a substantial adverse effect if the condition is likely to result in his having such an impairment.

(2) Regulations may make provision, for the purposes of this paragraph—

(a) for conditions of a prescribed description to be treated as being progressive;

(b) for conditions of a prescribed description to be treated as not being progressive.

Progressive conditions

9. In this Schedule "HIV infection" means infection by a virus capable of causing the Acquired Immune Deficiency Syndrome.

---

1. See the Disability Discrimination (Meaning of Disability) Regulations 1996, this title, post.

Section 2(2)   SCHEDULE 2
                         PAST DISABILITIES

(Amended by the Special Educational Needs and Disability Act 2001, s 38(1), SI 2003/1673 and 2770, the Disability Discrimination Act 2005, Sch 1 and SI 2005/1117.)

8–3116B   **1.** The modifications referred to in section 2 and 5A and Part III of the 2005 Order are as follows.

2. References in Parts II to 4 to a disabled person are to be read as references to a person who has had a disability.

2A. References in Chapter 1 of Part 4 to a disabled pupil are to be read as references to a pupil who has had a disability.

2B. References in Chapter 2 of Part 4 to a disabled student are to be read as references to a student who has had a disability.

2C. In section 3A(5), after "not having that particular disability" insert "and who has not had that particular disability".★

3. In sections 4A(1), 4B(4), 4E(1), 4H(1), 6B(1), 7B(1), 7D(1), 14(1), 14B(1), 14D(1) and 16A(4), section 21A(4)(a) (in the words to be read as section 19(1)(aa)) and section 21A(6)(a) (in the words to be substituted in section 21(1)), after "not disabled" (in each place it occurs) insert "and who have not had a disability".★

4. In sections 4A(3)(b), 4E(3)(b), 4H(3)(b), 6B(3)(b), 7B(4)(b), 7D(3)(b), 14(3)(b), 14B(3)(b), 14D(3)(b) and 16A(6), for "has" (in each place it occurs) substitute "has had".★

4A. In section 28B(3)(a) and (4), after "disabled" insert "or that he had had a disability".

4B. In section 28C(1), in paragraphs (a) and (b), after "not disabled" insert "and who have not had a disability".

4C. In section 28S(3)(a) and (4), after "disabled" insert "or that he had had a disability".

4D. In subsection (1) of section 28T, after "not disabled" insert "and who have not had a disability".

4E. In that subsection as substituted by paragraphs 2 and 6 of Schedule 4C, after "not disabled" insert "and who have not had a disability".

5. For paragraph 2(1) to (3) of Schedule 1, substitute—

"(1) The effect of an impairment is a long-term effect if it has lasted for at least 12 months.

(2) Where an impairment ceases to have a substantial adverse effect on a person's ability to carry out normal day-to-day activities, it is to be treated as continuing to have that effect if that effect recurs.

(3) For the purposes of sub-paragraph (2), the recurrence of an effect shall be disregarded in prescribed circumstances."

6–13. *Northern Ireland.*

---

*Paragraphs 3 and 4 amended and new paras 4ZA and 4ZB inserted by the Disability Discrimination Act 2005, Sch 1 from 4 December 2006.

Disability Rights Commission Act 1999[1]
(1999 c 17)

8–3116C 1. The Disability Rights Commission.   (1) There shall be a body known as the Disability Rights Commission (referred to in this Act as "the Commission").

(2) The Secretary of State shall pay to the Commission such sums as he thinks fit to enable it to meet its expenses.

(3) Schedule 1[2] (the Commission's constitution and related matters) has effect.

(4) *Repealed.*

[Disability Rights Commission Act 1999, s 1 as amended by the Statute Law (Repeals) Act 2004.]

---

1. The Disability Rights Commission Act 1999 establishes a Disability Rights Commission and makes provision as to its functions. Only those provisions of the Act which are likely to be of relevance to the work of magistrates' courts are set out below.

   For commencement provisions, see s 16, post.

2. Schedule 1 is not reproduced in this work.

8–3116D 2. General functions.   (1) The Commission shall have the following duties—

 (*a*) to work towards the elimination of discrimination against and harassment of disabled persons;
 (*b*) to promote the equalisation of opportunities for disabled persons;
 (*c*) to take such steps as it considers appropriate with a view to encouraging good practice in the treatment of disabled persons; and
 (*d*) to keep under review the working of the Disability Discrimination Act 1995 (referred to in this Act as "the 1995 Act") and this Act.

(2) The Commission may, for any purpose connected with the performance of its functions—

 (*a*) make proposals or give other advice to any Minister of the Crown as to any aspect of the law or a proposed change to the law;
 (*b*) make proposals or give other advice to any Government agency or other public authority as to the practical application of any law;
 (*c*) undertake, or arrange for or support (whether financially or otherwise), the carrying out of research or the provision of advice or information.

Nothing in this subsection is to be regarded as limiting the Commission's powers.

(3) The Commission shall make proposals or give other advice under subsection (2)(*a*) on any matter specified in a request from a Minister of the Crown.

(4) The Commission may make charges for facilities or services made available by it for any purpose.

(5) In this section—

"disabled persons" includes persons who have had a disability;

"discrimination" means anything which is discrimination for the purposes of any provision of Part II, Part 3 or Chapter 1 or 2 of Part 4* of the 1995 Act; and

"harassment" means anything which is harassment for the purposes of any provision of Part 2 or 3* of the 1995 Act;

"the law" includes Community law and the international obligations of the United Kingdom.

[Disability Rights Commission Act 1999, s 2, as amended by the Special Educational Needs and Disability Act 2001, s 35 and SI 2003/1673.]

---

*Substituted by the Disability Discrimination Act 2005, Sch 1 from 4 December 2006.

8–3116E 3. Formal investigations.   (1) The Commission may decide to conduct a formal investigation for any purpose connected with the performance of its duties under section 2(1).

(2) The Commission shall conduct a formal investigation if directed to do so by the Secretary of State for any such purpose.

(3) The Commission may at any time decide to stop or to suspend the conduct of a formal investigation; but any such decision requires the approval of the Secretary of State if the investigation is being conducted in pursuance of a direction under subsection (2).

(4) The Commission may, as respects any formal investigation which it has decided or been directed to conduct—

(*a*) nominate one or more commissioners, with or without one or more additional commissioners appointed for the purposes of the investigation, to conduct the investigation on its behalf; and

(*b*) authorise those persons to exercise such of its functions in relation to the investigation (which may include drawing up or revising terms of reference) as it may determine.

(5) Schedule 2[1] (appointment and tenure of office of additional commissioners) and Schedule 3[2] (so far as relating to the conduct of formal investigations) have effect.
[Disability Rights Commission Act 1999, s 3.]

_____

1. Schedule 2 is not reproduced in the work.
2. Only those provisions of Schedule 3 which are likely to be of relevance to magistrates' courts are set out below.

8–3116F 4. Non-discrimination notices. (1) If in the course of a formal investigation the Commission is satisfied that a person has committed or is committing an unlawful act, it may serve on him a notice (referred to in this Act as a non-discrimination notice) which—

(*a*) gives details of the unlawful act which the Commission has found that he has committed or is committing; and

(*b*) requires him not to commit any further unlawful acts of the same kind (and, if the finding is that he is committing an unlawful act, to cease doing so).

(2) The notice may include recommendations to the person concerned as to action which the Commission considers he could reasonably be expected to take with a view to complying with the requirement mentioned in subsection (1)(*b*).

(3) The notice may require the person concerned—

(*a*) to propose an adequate action plan (subject to and in accordance with Part III of Schedule 3) with a view to securing compliance with the requirement mentioned in subsection (1)(*b*); and

(*b*) once an action plan proposed by him has become final, to take any action which—

(i) is specified in the plan; and
(ii) he has not already taken,

at the time or times specified in the plan.

(4) For the purposes of subsection (3)—

(*a*) an action plan is a document drawn up by the person concerned specifying action (including action he has already taken) intended to change anything in his practices, policies, procedures or other arrangements which—

(i) caused or contributed to the commission of the unlawful act concerned; or
(ii) is liable to cause or contribute to a failure to comply with the requirement mentioned in subsection (1)(*b*); and

(*b*) an action plan is adequate if the action specified in it would be sufficient to ensure, within a reasonable time, that he is not prevented from complying with that requirement by anything in his practices, policies, procedures or other arrangements;

and the action specified in an action plan may include ceasing an activity or taking continuing action over a period.

(5) In this section "unlawful act" means an act which is unlawful for the purposes of any provision of Part II, Part 3 or Chapter 1 or 2 of Part 4* of the 1995 Act or any other unlawful act of a description prescribed for the purposes of this section.

(6) Schedule 3[1] (so far as relating to non-discrimination notices and action plans) has effect.
[Disability Rights Commission Act 1999, s 4, as amended by the Special Educational Needs and Disability Act 2001, s 35 and SI 2003/1673.]

_____

*Substituted by the Disability Discrimination Act 2005, Sch 1 from 4 December 2006.
1. Only those provisions of Schedule 3 which are likely to be of relevance to magistrates' courts are set out below.

8–3116G 5. Agreements in lieu of enforcement action. (1) If the Commission has reason to believe that a person has committed or is committing an unlawful act, it may (subject to section 3(3)) enter into an agreement in writing under this section with that person on the assumption that that belief is well founded (whether or not that person admits that he committed or is committing the act in question).

(2) An agreement under this section is one by which—

(*a*) the Commission undertakes not to take any relevant enforcement action in relation to the unlawful act in question; and

(*b*) the person concerned undertakes—

(i) not to commit any further unlawful acts of the same kind (and, where appropriate, to cease committing the unlawful act in question); and
(ii) to take such action (which may include ceasing an activity or taking continuing action over any period) as may be specified in the agreement.

(3) Those undertakings are binding on the parties to the agreement; but undertakings under subsection (2)(*b*) are enforceable by the Commission only as provided by subsection (8).

(4) For the purposes of subsection (2)(*a*), "relevant enforcement action" means—

(*a*)   beginning a formal investigation into the commission by the person concerned of the unlawful act in question;

(*b*)   if such an investigation has begun (whether or not the investigation is confined to that matter), taking any further steps in the investigation of that matter; and

(*c*)   taking any steps, or further steps, with a view to the issue of a non-discrimination notice based on the commission of the unlawful act in question.

(5) The action specified in an undertaking under subsection (2)(*b*)(ii) must be action intended to change anything in the practices, policies, procedures or other arrangements of the person concerned which—

(*a*)   caused or contributed to the commission of the unlawful act in question; or

(*b*)   is liable to cause or contribute to a failure to comply with his undertaking under subsection (2)(*b*)(i).

(6) An agreement under this section—

(*a*)   may include terms providing for incidental or supplementary matters (including the termination of the agreement, or the right of either party to terminate it, in certain circumstances); and

(*b*)   may be varied or revoked by agreement of the parties.

(7) An agreement under this section may not include any provisions other than terms mentioned in subsections (2) and (6)(*a*) unless their inclusion is authorised by regulations made by the Secretary of State for the purposes of this section; but any provisions so authorised are not enforceable by the Commission under subsection (8).

(8) The Commission may apply to a county court or by summary application to the sheriff for an order under this subsection if—

(*a*)   the other party to an agreement under this section has failed to comply with any undertaking under subsection (2)(*b*); or

(*b*)   the Commission has reasonable cause to believe that he intends not to comply with any such undertaking.

(9) An order under subsection (8) is an order requiring the other party to comply with the undertaking or with such directions for the same purpose as are contained in the order.

(10) Nothing in this section affects the Commission's powers to settle or compromise legal proceedings of any description.

(11) In this section "unlawful act" means an act which is unlawful for the purposes of any provision of Part II, Part 3 or Chapter 1 or 2 of Part 4* of the 1995 Act or any other unlawful act of a description prescribed for the purposes of this section.

(12) Schedule 3[1] (so far as relating to agreements under this section) has effect.

[Disability Rights Commission Act 1999, s 5, as amended by the Special Educational Needs and Disability Act 2001, s 35 and SI 2003/1673.]

---

*Substituted by the Disability Discrimination Act 2005, Sch 1 from 4 December 2006.

1. Only those provisions of Schedule 3 which are likely to be of relevance to magistrates' courts are set out below.

8–3116H   13. Interpretation.   (1) In this Act—

"Commission" means the Disability Rights Commission;

"final", in relation to a non-discrimination notice, has the meaning given by paragraph 11 of Schedule 3;

"formal investigation" means an investigation under section 3;

"non-discrimination notice" means a notice under section 4;

"notice" means notice in writing;

"prescribed" means prescribed in regulations made by the Secretary of State; and

"the 1995 Act" means the Disability Discrimination Act 1995.

(2) Expressions used in this Act which are defined for the purposes of the 1995 Act have the same meaning in this Act as in that Act.

[Disability Rights Commission Act 1999, s 13.]

8–3116I   14. *Consequential amendments and repeals*

8–3116J   15. Crown application.   This Act binds the Crown (but does not affect Her Majesty in her private capacity or in right of Her Duchy of Lancaster or the Duke of Cornwall).

[Disability Rights Commission Act 1999, s 15.]

8–3116K   16. Short title, commencement and extent.   (1) This Act may be cited as the Disability Rights Commission Act 1999.

(2) This Act (apart from this section) shall come into force on such day as the Secretary of State may by order[1] made by statutory instrument appoint; and different days may be appointed for different purposes.

(3) An order under subsection (2) may contain transitional provisions and savings relating to the provisions brought into force by the order.★

(4) *Northern Ireland.*

(5) Except as mentioned in subsection (4), this Act does not extend to Northern Ireland.

[Disability Rights Commission Act 1999, s 16.]

★**New subs (3A) inserted by the Disability Discrimination Act 2005, Sch 1 from 4 December 2006.**

1. At the date of going to press, the Disability Rights Commission Act 1999 (Commencement No 1 and Transitional Provision) Order 1999, SI 1999/2210 and the Disability Rights Commission Act 1999 (Commencement No 2 and Transitional Provision) Order 2000, SI 2000/880, had been made. All the provisions of the Act that are set out in this work had been brought into force.

SCHEDULES

SCHEDULE 3

FORMAL INVESTIGATIONS AND NON-DISCRIMINATION NOTICES

(*Amended by the Special Educational Needs and Disability Act 2001, s 35 and SI 2003/1673.*)

Sections 3(5), 4(6) and 5(12)   PART I
                          CONDUCT OF FORMAL INVESTIGATIONS

Introductory

8–3116L   1. (1) This Part of this Schedule applies to a formal investigation which the Commission has decided or has been directed to conduct.

(2) Any subsequent action required or authorised by this Part of this Schedule (or by Part IV of this Schedule) to be taken by the Commission in relation to the conduct of a formal investigation may be taken, so far as they are authorised to do so, by persons nominated under section 3(4) for the purposes of the investigation.

Power to obtain information

4. (1) For the purposes of a formal investigation the Commission may serve a notice on any person requiring him—

(*a*)   to give such written information as may be described in the notice; or

(*b*)   to attend and give oral information about any matter specified in the notice, and to produce all documents in his possession or control relating to any such matter.

(2) A notice under this paragraph may only be served on the written authority of the Secretary of State unless the terms of reference confine the investigation to the activities of one or more named persons and the person being served is one of those persons.

(3) A person may not be required by a notice under this paragraph—

(*a*)   to give information, or produce a document, which he could not be compelled to give in evidence, or produce, in civil proceedings before the High Court or the Court of Session; or

(*b*)   to attend at any place unless the necessary expenses of his journey to and from that place are paid or tendered to him.

5. (1) The Commission may apply to a county court or by summary application to the sheriff for an order under this paragraph if—

(*a*)   a person has been served with a notice under paragraph 4; and

(*b*)   he fails to comply with it or the Commission has reasonable cause to believe that he intends not to comply with it.

(2) An order under this paragraph is an order requiring the person concerned to comply with the notice or with such directions for the same purpose as may be contained in the order.

PART III

ACTION PLANS

Introductory

8–3116M   14. (1) This Part of this Schedule applies where a person ("P") has been served with a non-discrimination notice which has become final and includes a requirement for him to propose an action plan.

(2) In this Part "adequate" in relation to a proposed action plan means adequate (as defined in section 4(4)(*b*)) for the purposes of the requirement mentioned in section 4(1)(*b*).

Power to obtain information

21. (1) For the purposes of determining whether—

(*a*)   an action plan proposed by P is an adequate action plan; or

(*b*)   P has complied or is complying with the requirement to take the action specified in an action plan which has become final, the Commission may serve a notice on any person requiring him to give such information in writing, or copies of documents in his possession or control, relating to those matters as may be described in the notice.

(2) A person may not be required by a notice under this paragraph to give information, or produce a document, which he could not be compelled to give in evidence or produce in civil proceedings before the High Court or the Court of Session.

(3) The Commission may apply to a county court or by summary application to the sheriff for an order under this sub-paragraph if a person has been served with a notice under this paragraph and fails to comply with it.

(4) An order under sub-paragraph (3) is an order requiring the person concerned to comply with the notice or with such directions for the same purpose as may be contained in the order.

PART IV
SUPPLEMENTARY
Restriction on disclosure of information

8–3116N   **22.** (1) No information given to the Commission by any person ("the informant") in connection with—

(a) a formal investigation; or

(b) the exercise of any of its functions in relation to non-discrimination notices, action plans and agreements under section 5,

shall be disclosed by the Commission or by any person who is or has been a commissioner, an additional commissioner or an employee of the Commission.

(2) Sub-paragraph (1) does not apply to any disclosure made—

(a) on the order of a court,

(b) with the informant's consent,

(c) in the form of a summary or other general statement published by the Commission which does not identify the informant or any other person to whom the information relates,

(d) in a report of the investigation published by the Commission,

(e) to a commissioner, an additional commissioner or an employee of the Commission, or, so far as is necessary for the proper performance of the Commission's functions, to other persons, or

(f) for the purpose of any civil proceedings to which the Commission is a party, or of any criminal proceedings.

(3) A person who discloses information contrary to sub-paragraph (1) is guilty of an offence and liable on summary conviction to a fine not exceeding **level 5** on the standard scale.

Offences

24. (1) A person who—

(a) deliberately alters, suppresses, conceals or destroys a document to which a notice under paragraph 4 or 21, or an order under paragraph 5 or 21(3), relates; or

(b) in complying with—

    (i) a notice under paragraph 4 or 21;

    (ii) a non-discrimination notice;

    (iii) an agreement under section 5; or

    (iv) an order of a court under section 5(8) or under any provision of this Schedule,

makes any statement which he knows to be false or misleading in a material particular or recklessly makes a statement which is false or misleading in a material particular,

is guilty of an offence and liable on summary conviction to a fine not exceeding level 5 on the standard scale.

(2) Proceedings for an offence under this paragraph may (without prejudice to any jurisdiction exercisable apart from this sub-paragraph) be instituted—

(a) against any person at any place at which he has an office or other place of business;

(b) against an individual at any place where he resides, or at which he is for the time being.

Service of notices

25. (1) Any notice required or authorised by any provision of this Schedule to be served on a person may be served by delivering it to him, by leaving it at his proper address or by sending it by post to him at that address.

(2) Any such notice may—

(a) in the case of a body corporate, be served on the secretary or clerk of that body;

(b) in the case of a partnership, be served on any partner or a person having control or management of the partnership business;

(c) in the case of an unincorporated association (other than a partnership), may be served on any member of its governing body.

(3) For the purposes of this paragraph and section 7 of the Interpretation Act 1978 (service of documents) in its application to this paragraph, the proper address of any person is—

(a) in the case of a body corporate, its secretary or clerk, the address of its registered or principal office in the United Kingdom;

(b) in the case of an unincorporated association (other than a partnership) or a member of its governing body, its principal office in the United Kingdom;

(c) in any other case, his usual or last-known address (whether of his residence or of a place where he carries on business or is employed).

Freedom of Information Act 2000[1]

(2000 c 36)

PART I[2]

ACCESS TO INFORMATION HELD BY PUBLIC AUTHORITIES

Right to information

8–3117   **1. General right of access to information held by public authorities.**   (1) Any person making a request for information to a public authority is entitled—

(*a*) to be informed in writing by the public authority whether it holds information of the description specified in the request, and

(*b*) if that is the case, to have that information communicated to him.

(2) Subsection (1) has effect subject to the following provisions of this section and to the provisions of sections 2, 9, 12 and 14.

(3) Where a public authority—

(*a*) reasonably requires further information in order to identify and locate the information requested, and

(*b*) has informed the applicant of that requirement,

the authority is not obliged to comply with subsection (1) unless it is supplied with that further information.

(4) The information—

(*a*) in respect of which the applicant is to be informed under subsection (1)(*a*), or

(*b*) which is to be communicated under subsection (1)(*b*),

is the information in question held at the time when the request is received, except that account may be taken of any amendment or deletion made between that time and the time when the information is to be communicated under subsection (1)(*b*), being an amendment or deletion that would have been made regardless of the receipt of the request.

(5) A public authority is to be taken to have complied with subsection (1)(*a*) in relation to any information if it has communicated the information to the applicant in accordance with subsection (1)(*b*).

(6) In this Act, the duty of a public authority to comply with subsection (1)(*a*) is referred to as "the duty to confirm or deny".

[Freedom of Information Act 2000, s 1.]

---

1. The Freedom of Information Act 2000 makes provision for the disclosure of information held by public authorities or by persons providing services for them and amends the Data Protection Act 1998 and the Public Records Act 1958.

Only those provisions of the Act which are likely to be of relevance to the work of practitioners in the magistrates' courts are included in this work.

The Act is to be brought into force in accordance with s 87 below.

2. Part I comprises ss 1 to 20.

8–3118   **2. Effect of the exemptions in Part II.**   (1) Where any provision of Part II states that the duty to confirm or deny does not arise in relation to any information, the effect of the provision is that where either—

(*a*) the provision confers absolute exemption, or

(*b*) in all the circumstances of the case, the public interest in maintaining the exclusion of the duty to confirm or deny outweighs the public interest in disclosing whether the public authority holds the information,

section 1(1)(*a*) does not apply.

(2) In respect of any information which is exempt information by virtue of any provision of Part II, section 1(1)(*b*) does not apply if or to the extent that—

(*a*) the information is exempt information by virtue of a provision conferring absolute exemption, or

(*b*) in all the circumstances of the case, the public interest in maintaining the exemption outweighs the public interest in disclosing the information.

(3) For the purposes of this section, the following provisions of Part II (and no others) are to be regarded as conferring absolute exemption—

(*a*) section 21,

(*b*) section 23,

(*c*) section 32,

(*d*) section 34,

(*e*) section 36 so far as relating to information held by the House of Commons or the House of Lords,

(*f*) in section 40—

(i) subsection (1), and
(ii) subsection (2) so far as relating to cases where the first condition referred to in that subsection is satisfied by virtue of subsection (3)(*a*)(i) or (*b*) of that section,

(*g*) section 41, and
(*h*) section 44.

[Freedom of Information Act 2000, s 2.]

8–3119 3. Public authorities. (1) In this Act "public authority" means—

(*a*) subject to section 4(4), any body which, any other person who, or the holder of any office which—

(i) is listed in Schedule 1, or
(ii) is designated by order under section 5, or

(*b*) a publicly-owned company as defined by section 6.

(2) For the purposes of this Act, information is held by a public authority if—

(*a*) it is held by the authority, otherwise than on behalf of another person, or
(*b*) it is held by another person on behalf of the authority.

[Freedom of Information Act 2000, s 3.]

8–3120 4. Amendment of Schedule 1. The Secretary of State may by order amend Schedule 1 by adding to that Schedule a reference to any body or the holder of any office which (in either case) is not for the time being listed in that Schedule but as respects which both the first and the second conditions specified are satisfied.

[Freedom of Information Act 2000, s 4.]

8–3121 5. *Further power to designate public authorities.*

8–3121A 6. Publicly-owned companies. (1) A company is a "publicly-owned company" for the purposes of section 3(1)(*b*) if—

(*a*) it is wholly owned by the Crown, or
(*b*) it is wholly owned by any public authority listed in Schedule 1 other than—

(i) a government department, or
(ii) any authority which is listed only in relation to particular information.

(2) For the purposes of this section—

(*a*) a company is wholly owned by the Crown if it has no members except—

(i) Ministers of the Crown, government departments or companies wholly owned by the Crown, or
(ii) persons acting on behalf of Ministers of the Crown, government departments or companies wholly owned by the Crown, and

(*b*) a company is wholly owned by a public authority other than a government department if it has no members except—

(i) that public authority or companies wholly owned by that public authority, or
(ii) persons acting on behalf of that public authority or of companies wholly owned by that public authority.

(3) In this section—

"company" includes any body corporate;
"Minister of the Crown" includes a Northern Ireland Minister.

[Freedom of Information Act 2000, s 6.]

8–3121B 7. Public authorities to which Act has limited application. (1) Where a public authority is listed in Schedule 1 only in relation to information of a specified description, nothing in Parts I to V of this Act applies to any other information held by the authority.

(2) An order under section 4(1) may, in adding an entry to Schedule 1, list the public authority only in relation to information of a specified description.

(3) The Lord Chancellor may by order amend Schedule 1—

(*a*) by limiting to information of a specified description the entry relating to any public authority, or
(*b*) by removing or amending any limitation to information of a specified description which is for the time being contained in any entry.

(4) Before making an order under subsection (3), the Lord Chancellor shall—

(*a*) if the order relates to the National Assembly for Wales or a Welsh public authority, consult the National Assembly for Wales, (*b*) if the order relates to the Northern Ireland Assembly, consult the Presiding Officer of that Assembly, and

(*c*) if the order relates to a Northern Ireland department or a Northern Ireland public authority, consult the First Minister and deputy First Minister in Northern Ireland.

(5) An order under section 5(1)(*a*) must specify the functions of the public authority designated by the order with respect to which the designation is to have effect; and nothing in Parts I to V of this Act applies to information which is held by the authority but does not relate to the exercise of those functions.

(6) An order under section 5(1)(*b*) must specify the services provided under contract with respect to which the designation is to have effect; and nothing in Parts I to V of this Act applies to information which is held by the public authority designated by the order but does not relate to the provision of those services.

(7) Nothing in Parts I to V of this Act applies in relation to any information held by a publicly-owned company which is excluded information in relation to that company.

(8) In subsection (7) "excluded information", in relation to a publicly-owned company, means information which is of a description specified in relation to that company in an order made by the Lord Chancellor for the purposes of this subsection.

(9) In this section "publicly-owned company" has the meaning given by section 6.

[Freedom of Information Act 2000, s 7, as amended by SI 2001/3500.]

8–3121C 8. Request for information. (1) In this Act any reference to a "request for information" is a reference to such a request which—

(*a*) is in writing,

(*b*) states the name of the applicant and an address for correspondence, and

(*c*) describes the information requested.

(2) For the purposes of subsection (1)(*a*), a request is to be treated as made in writing where the text of the request—

(*a*) is transmitted by electronic means,

(*b*) is received in legible form, and

(*c*) is capable of being used for subsequent reference.

[Freedom of Information Act 2000, s 8.]

8–3121D 9. Fees. (1) A public authority to whom a request for information is made may, within the period for complying with section 1(1), give the applicant a notice in writing (in this Act referred to as a "fees notice") stating that a fee of an amount specified in the notice is to be charged by the authority for complying with section 1(1).

(2) Where a fees notice has been given to the applicant, the public authority is not obliged to comply with section 1(1) unless the fee is paid within the period of three months beginning with the day on which the fees notice is given to the applicant.

(3) Subject to subsection (5), any fee under this section must be determined by the public authority in accordance with regulations[1] made by the Lord Chancellor.

(4) Regulations under subsection (3) may, in particular, provide—

(*a*) that no fee is to be payable in prescribed cases,

(*b*) that any fee is not to exceed such maximum as may be specified in, or determined in accordance with, the regulations, and

(*c*) that any fee is to be calculated in such manner as may be prescribed by the regulations

(5) Subsection (3) does not apply where provision is made by or under any enactment as to the fee that may be charged by the public authority for the disclosure of the information.

[Freedom of Information Act 2000, s 9, as amended by SI 2001/3500.]

---

1. See the Freedom of Information and Data Protection (Appropriate Limit and Fees) Regulations 2004, SI 2004/3244, in this title, post.

8–3121E 10. Time for compliance with request. (1) Subject to subsections (2) and (3), a public authority must comply with section 1(1) promptly and in any event not later than the twentieth working day following the date of receipt.

(2) Where the authority has given a fees notice to the applicant and the fee is paid in accordance with section 9(2), the working days in the period beginning with the day on which the fees notice is given to the applicant and ending with the day on which the fee is received by the authority are to be disregarded in calculating for the purposes of subsection (1) the twentieth working day following the date of receipt.

(3) If, and to the extent that—

(*a*) section 1(1)(*a*) would not apply if the condition in section 2(1)(*b*) were satisfied, or

(*b*) section 1(1)(*b*) would not apply if the condition in section 2(2)(*b*) were satisfied,

the public authority need not comply with section 1(1)(*a*) or (*b*) until such time as is reasonable in the circumstances; but this subsection does not affect the time by which any notice under section 17(1) must be given.

(4) The Lord Chancellor may by regulations provide that subsections (1) and (2) are to have effect as if any reference to the twentieth working day following the date of receipt were a reference to such other day, not later than the sixtieth working day following the date of receipt, as may be specified in, or determined in accordance with, the regulations[1].

(5) Regulations under subsection (4) may—

(a) prescribe different days in relation to different cases, and

(b) confer a discretion on the Commissioner.

(6) In this section—

"the date of receipt" means—

(a) the day on which the public authority receives the request for information, or

(b) if later, the day on which it receives the information referred to in section 1(3);

"working day" means any day other than a Saturday, a Sunday, Christmas Day, Good Friday or a day which is a bank holiday under the Banking and Financial Dealings Act 1971 in any part of the United Kingdom.

[Freedom of Information Act 2000, s 10, as amended by SI 2001/3500.]

---

1. The Freedom of Information (Time for Compliance with Request) Regulations 2004, SI 2004/3364 have been made which make provision in respect of Governing bodies of maintained schools or maintained nursery schools and schools maintained by the Secretary of State for Defence; archives held under the Public Records Act 1958; situations where a public authority cannot comply with s 1(1) of the Act without obtaining information (whether or not recorded) from any individual (whether or not a member of the armed forces of the Crown) who is actively involved in an operation of the armed forces of the Crown, or in the preparations for such an operation; also where information held outside the United Kingdom.

8–3121F **11. Means by which communication to be made.** (1) Where, on making his request for information, the applicant expresses a preference for communication by any one or more of the following means, namely—

(a) the provision to the applicant of a copy of the information in permanent form or in another form acceptable to the applicant,

(b) the provision to the applicant of a reasonable opportunity to inspect a record containing the information, and

(c) the provision to the applicant of a digest or summary of the information in permanent form or in another form acceptable to the applicant,

the public authority shall so far as reasonably practicable give effect to that preference.

(2) In determining for the purposes of this section whether it is reasonably practicable to communicate information by particular means, the public authority may have regard to all the circumstances, including the cost of doing so.

(3) Where the public authority determines that it is not reasonably practicable to comply with any preference expressed by the applicant in making his request, the authority shall notify the applicant of the reasons for its determination.

(4) Subject to subsection (1), a public authority may comply with a request by communicating information by any means which are reasonable in the circumstances.

[Freedom of Information Act 2000, s 11.]

8–3121G **12. Exemption where cost of compliance exceeds appropriate limit.** (1) Section 1(1) does not oblige a public authority to comply with a request for information if the authority estimates that the cost of complying with the request would exceed the appropriate limit.

(2) Subsection (1) does not exempt the public authority from its obligation to comply with paragraph (a) of section 1(1) unless the estimated cost of complying with that paragraph alone would exceed the appropriate limit.

(3) In subsections (1) and (2) "the appropriate limit" means such amount as may be prescribed, and different amounts may be prescribed[1] in relation to different cases

(4) The Lord Chancellor may by regulations[1] provide that, in such circumstances as may be prescribed, where two or more requests for information are made to a public authority—

(a) by one person, or

(b) by different persons who appear to the public authority to be acting in concert or in pursuance of a campaign,

the estimated cost of complying with any of the requests is to be taken to be the estimated total cost of complying with all of them.

(5) The Lord Chancellor may by regulations make provision for the purposes of this section as to the costs to be estimated and as to the manner in which they are to be estimated.

[Freedom of Information Act 2000, s 12, as amended by SI 2001/2500.]

1. See the Freedom of Information and Data Protection (Appropriate Limit and Fees) Regulations 2004, SI 2004/3244, in this title, post.

8–3121H   13. Fees for disclosure where cost of compliance exceeds appropriate limit.   (1) A public authority may charge for the communication of any information whose communication—

(a)   is not required by section 1(1) because the cost of complying with the request for information exceeds the amount which is the appropriate limit for the purposes of section 12(1) and (2), and

(b)   is not otherwise required by law,

such fee as may be determined by the public authority in accordance with regulations[1] made by the Lord Chancellor.

(2) Regulations under this section may, in particular, provide—

(a)   that any fee is not to exceed such maximum as may be specified in, or determined in accordance with, the regulations, and

(b)   that any fee is to be calculated in such manner as may be prescribed by the regulations

(3) Subsection (1) does not apply where provision is made by or under any enactment as to the fee that may be charged by the public authority for the disclosure of the information.
[Freedom of Information Act 2000, s 13, as amended by SI 2001/3500.]

1. See the Freedom of Information and Data Protection (Appropriate Limit and Fees) Regulations 2004, SI 2004/3244, in this title, post.

8–3121I   14. Vexatious or repeated requests.   (1) Section 1(1) does not oblige a public authority to comply with a request for information if the request is vexatious

(2) Where a public authority has previously complied with a request for information which was made by any person, it is not obliged to comply with a subsequent identical or substantially similar request from that person unless a reasonable interval has elapsed between compliance with the previous request and the making of the current request.
[Freedom of Information Act 2000, s 14.]

8–3121J   15. *Special provisions relating to public records transferred to Public Record Office, etc*

8–3121K   16. Duty to provide advice and assistance.   (1) It shall be the duty of a public authority to provide advice and assistance, so far as it would be reasonable to expect the authority to do so, to persons who propose to make, or have made, requests for information to it.

(2) Any public authority which, in relation to the provision of advice or assistance in any case, conforms with the code of practice under section 45 is to be taken to comply with the duty imposed by subsection (1) in relation to that case.
[Freedom of Information Act 2000, s 16.]

Refusal of request

8–3121L   17. Refusal of request.   (1) A public authority which, in relation to any request for information, is to any extent relying on a claim that any provision of Part II relating to the duty to confirm or deny is relevant to the request or on a claim that information is exempt information must, within the time for complying with section 1(1), give the applicant a notice which—

(a)   states that fact,

(b)   specifies the exemption in question, and

(c)   states (if that would not otherwise be apparent) why the exemption applies

(2) Where—

(a)   in relation to any request for information, a public authority is, as respects any information, relying on a claim—

(i)   that any provision of Part II which relates to the duty to confirm or deny and is not specified in section 2(3) is relevant to the request, or

(ii)   that the information is exempt information only by virtue of a provision not specified in section 2(3), and

(b)   at the time when the notice under subsection (1) is given to the applicant, the public authority (or, in a case falling within section 66(3) or (4), the responsible authority) has not yet reached a decision as to the application of subsection (1)(b) or (2)(b) of section 2,

the notice under subsection (1) must indicate that no decision as to the application of that provision has yet been reached and must contain an estimate of the date by which the authority expects that such a decision will have been reached.

(3) A public authority which, in relation to any request for information, is to any extent relying on a claim that subsection (1)(b) or (2)(b) of section 2 applies must, either in the notice under subsection

(1) or in a separate notice given within such time as is reasonable in the circumstances, state the reasons for claiming—

(a)   that, in all the circumstances of the case, the public interest in maintaining the exclusion of the duty to confirm or deny outweighs the public interest in disclosing whether the authority holds the information, or

(b)   that, in all the circumstances of the case, the public interest in maintaining the exemption outweighs the public interest in disclosing the information.

(4) A public authority is not obliged to make a statement under subsection (1)(c) or (3) if, or to the extent that, the statement would involve the disclosure of information which would itself be exempt information.

(5) A public authority which, in relation to any request for information, is relying on a claim that section 12 or 14 applies must, within the time for complying with section 1(1), give the applicant a notice stating that fact.

(6) Subsection (5) does not apply where—

(a)   the public authority is relying on a claim that section 14 applies,

(b)   the authority has given the applicant a notice, in relation to a previous request for information, stating that it is relying on such a claim, and

(c)   it would in all the circumstances be unreasonable to expect the authority to serve a further notice under subsection (5) in relation to the current request.

(7) A notice under subsection (1), (3) or (5) must—

(a)   contain particulars of any procedure provided by the public authority for dealing with complaints about the handling of requests for information or state that the authority does not provide such a procedure, and

(b)   contain particulars of the right conferred by section 50.

[Freedom of Information Act 2000, s 17.]

The Information Commissioner and the Information Tribunal

8–3121M   18. The Information Commissioner and the Information Tribunal.   (1) The Data Protection Commissioner shall be known instead as the Information Commissioner.

(2) The Data Protection Tribunal shall be known instead as the Information Tribunal.

(3) In this Act—

(a)   the Information Commissioner is referred to as "the Commissioner", and

(b)   the Information Tribunal is referred to as "the Tribunal".

(4) Schedule 2 (which makes provision consequential on subsections (1) and (2) and amendments of the Data Protection Act 1998 relating to the extension by this Act of the functions of the Commissioner and the Tribunal) has effect.

(5) If the person who held office as Data Protection Commissioner immediately before the day on which this Act is passed remains in office as Information Commissioner at the end of the period of two years beginning with that day, he shall vacate his office at the end of that period.

(6) Subsection (5) does not prevent the re-appointment of a person whose appointment is terminated by that subsection.

(7) In the application of paragraph 2(4)(b) and (5) of Schedule 5 to the Data Protection Act 1998 (Commissioner not to serve for more than fifteen years and not to be appointed, except in special circumstances, for a third or subsequent term) to anything done after the passing of this Act, there shall be left out of account any term of office served by virtue of an appointment made before the passing of this Act.

[Freedom of Information Act 2000, s 18.]

Publication schemes

8–3121N   19. Publication schemes.   (1) It shall be the duty of every public authority—

(a)   to adopt and maintain a scheme which relates to the publication of information by the authority and is approved by the Commissioner (in this Act referred to as a "publication scheme"),

(b)   to publish information in accordance with its publication scheme, and

(c)   from time to time to review its publication scheme.

(2) A publication scheme must—

(a)   specify classes of information which the public authority publishes or intends to publish,

(b)   specify the manner in which information of each class is, or is intended to be, published, and

(c)   specify whether the material is, or is intended to be, available to the public free of charge or on payment.

(3) In adopting or reviewing a publication scheme, a public authority shall have regard to the public interest—

(a)   in allowing public access to information held by the authority, and (*b*) in the publication of reasons for decisions made by the authority.

(4) A public authority shall publish its publication scheme in such manner as it thinks fit.

(5) The Commissioner may, when approving a scheme, provide that his approval is to expire at the end of a specified period.

(6) Where the Commissioner has approved the publication scheme of any public authority, he may at any time give notice to the public authority revoking his approval of the scheme as from the end of the period of six months beginning with the day on which the notice is given.

(7) Where the Commissioner—

(*a*) refuses to approve a proposed publication scheme, or

(*b*) revokes his approval of a publication scheme,

he must give the public authority a statement of his reasons for doing so.
[Freedom of Information Act 2000, s 19.]

8–3121O 20. Model publication schemes. (1) The Commissioner may from time to time approve, in relation to public authorities falling within particular classes, model publication schemes prepared by him or by other persons

(2) Where a public authority falling within the class to which an approved model scheme relates adopts such a scheme without modification, no further approval of the Commissioner is required so long as the model scheme remains approved; and where such an authority adopts such a scheme with modifications, the approval of the Commissioner is required only in relation to the modifications

(3) The Commissioner may, when approving a model publication scheme, provide that his approval is to expire at the end of a specified period.

(4) Where the Commissioner has approved a model publication scheme, he may at any time publish, in such manner as he thinks fit, a notice revoking his approval of the scheme as from the end of the period of six months beginning with the day on which the notice is published.

(5) Where the Commissioner refuses to approve a proposed model publication scheme on the application of any person, he must give the person who applied for approval of the scheme a statement of the reasons for his refusal.

(6) Where the Commissioner refuses to approve any modifications under subsection (2), he must give the public authority a statement of the reasons for his refusal.

(7) Where the Commissioner revokes his approval of a model publication scheme, he must include in the notice under subsection (4) a statement of his reasons for doing so.
[Freedom of Information Act 2000, s 20.]

PART II[1]
EXEMPT INFORMATION

8–3121P 21. Information accessible to applicant by other means. (1) Information which is reasonably accessible to the applicant otherwise than under section 1 is exempt information.

(2) For the purposes of subsection (1)—

(*a*) information may be reasonably accessible to the applicant even though it is accessible only on payment, and

(*b*) information is to be taken to be reasonably accessible to the applicant if it is information which the public authority or any other person is obliged by or under any enactment to communicate (otherwise than by making the information available for inspection) to members of the public on request, whether free of charge or on payment.

(3) For the purposes of subsection (1), information which is held by a public authority and does not fall within subsection (2)(*b*) is not to be regarded as reasonably accessible to the applicant merely because the information is available from the public authority itself on request, unless the information is made available in accordance with the authority's publication scheme and any payment required is specified in, or determined in accordance with, the scheme.
[Freedom of Information Act 2000, s 21.]

---

1. Part II comprises ss 21 to 44.

8–3121Q 22. Information intended for future publication. (1) Information is exempt information if—

(*a*) the information is held by the public authority with a view to its publication, by the authority or any other person, at some future date (whether determined or not),

(*b*) the information was already held with a view to such publication at the time when the request for information was made, and

(*c*) it is reasonable in all the circumstances that the information should be withheld from disclosure until the date referred to in paragraph (*a*).

(2) The duty to confirm or deny does not arise if, or to the extent that, compliance with section

$1(1)(a)$ would involve the disclosure of any information (whether or not already recorded) which falls within subsection (1).

[Freedom of Information Act 2000, s 22.]

8–3121R 28. Relations within the United Kingdom. (1) Information is exempt information if its disclosure under this Act would, or would be likely to, prejudice relations between any administration in the United Kingdom and any other such administration.

(2) In subsection (1) "administration in the United Kingdom" means—

(a) the government of the United Kingdom,
(b) the Scottish Administration,
(c) the Executive Committee of the Northern Ireland Assembly, or
(d) the National Assembly for Wales

(3) The duty to confirm or deny does not arise if, or to the extent that, compliance with section $1(1)(a)$ would, or would be likely to, prejudice any of the matters mentioned in subsection (1).

[Freedom of Information Act 2000, s 28.]

8–3121S 30. Investigations and proceedings conducted by public authorities. (1) Information held by a public authority is exempt information if it has at any time been held by the authority for the purposes of—

(a) any investigation which the public authority has a duty to conduct with a view to it being ascertained—

(i) whether a person should be charged with an offence, or
(ii) whether a person charged with an offence is guilty of it,

(b) any investigation which is conducted by the authority and in the circumstances may lead to a decision by the authority to institute criminal proceedings which the authority has power to conduct, or
(c) any criminal proceedings which the authority has power to conduct.

(2) Information held by a public authority is exempt information if—

(a) it was obtained or recorded by the authority for the purposes of its functions relating to—

(i) investigations falling within subsection $(1)(a)$ or (b),
(ii) criminal proceedings which the authority has power to conduct,
(iii) investigations (other than investigations falling within subsection $(1)(a)$ or (b)) which are conducted by the authority for any of the purposes specified in section 31(2) and either by virtue of Her Majesty's prerogative or by virtue of powers conferred by or under any enactment, or
(iv) civil proceedings which are brought by or on behalf of the authority and arise out of such investigations, and

(b) it relates to the obtaining of information from confidential sources.

(3) The duty to confirm or deny does not arise in relation to information which is (or if it were held by the public authority would be) exempt information by virtue of subsection (1) or (2).

(4) In relation to the institution or conduct of criminal proceedings or the power to conduct them, references in subsection $(1)(b)$ or (c) and subsection $(2)(a)$ to the public authority include references—

(a) to any officer of the authority,
(b) in the case of a government department other than a Northern Ireland department, to the Minister of the Crown in charge of the department, and
(c) in the case of a Northern Ireland department, to the Northern Ireland Minister in charge of the department.

(5) In this section—

"criminal proceedings" includes—

(a) proceedings before a court-martial constituted under the Army Act 1955, the Air Force Act 1955 or the Naval Discipline Act 1957,
(b) proceedings on dealing summarily with a charge under the Army Act 1955 or the Air Force Act 1955 or on summary trial under the Naval Discipline Act 1957,
(c) proceedings before a court established by section 83ZA of the Army Act 1955, section 83ZA of the Air Force Act 1955 or section 52FF of the Naval Discipline Act 1957 (summary appeal courts),
(d) proceedings before the Courts-Martial Appeal Court, and
(e) proceedings before a Standing Civilian Court;

"offence" includes any offence under the Army Act 1955, the Air Force Act 1955 or the Naval Discipline Act 1957.

(6) *Scotland.*
[Freedom of Information Act 2000, s 30, as amended by the Armed Forces Act 2001, s 38.]

8–3121T   31. Law enforcement.   (1) Information which is not exempt information by virtue of section 30 is exempt information if its disclosure under this Act would, or would be likely to, prejudice—

- (a) the prevention or detection of crime,
- (b) the apprehension or prosecution of offenders,
- (c) the administration of justice,
- (d) the assessment or collection of any tax or duty or of any imposition of a similar nature,
- (e) the operation of the immigration controls,
- (f) the maintenance of security and good order in prisons or in other institutions where persons are lawfully detained,
- (g) the exercise by any public authority of its functions for any of the purposes specified in subsection (2),
- (h) any civil proceedings which are brought by or on behalf of a public authority and arise out of an investigation conducted, for any of the purposes specified in subsection (2), by or on behalf of the authority by virtue of Her Majesty's prerogative or by virtue of powers conferred by or under an enactment, or
- (i) any inquiry held under the Fatal Accidents and Sudden Deaths Inquiries (Scotland) Act 1976 to the extent that the inquiry arises out of an investigation conducted, for any of the purposes specified in subsection (2), by or on behalf of the authority by virtue of Her Majesty's prerogative or by virtue of powers conferred by or under an enactment.

(2) The purposes referred to in subsection (1)(g) to (i) are—

- (a) the purpose of ascertaining whether any person has failed to comply with the law,
- (b) the purpose of ascertaining whether any person is responsible for any conduct which is improper,
- (c) the purpose of ascertaining whether circumstances which would justify regulatory action in pursuance of any enactment exist or may arise,
- (d) the purpose of ascertaining a person's fitness or competence in relation to the management of bodies corporate or in relation to any profession or other activity which he is, or seeks to become, authorised to carry on,
- (e) the purpose of ascertaining the cause of an accident,
- (f) the purpose of protecting charities against misconduct or mismanagement (whether by trustees or other persons) in their administration,
- (g) the purpose of protecting the property of charities from loss or misapplication,
- (h) the purpose of recovering the property of charities,
- (i) the purpose of securing the health, safety and welfare of persons at work, and
- (j) the purpose of protecting persons other than persons at work against risk to health or safety arising out of or in connection with the actions of persons at work.

(3) The duty to confirm or deny does not arise if, or to the extent that, compliance with section 1(1)(a) would, or would be likely to, prejudice any of the matters mentioned in subsection (1).
[Freedom of Information Act 2000, s 31.]

8–3121U   32. Court records, etc.   (1) Information held by a public authority is exempt information if it is held only by virtue of being contained in—

- (a) any document filed with, or otherwise placed in the custody of, a court for the purposes of proceedings in a particular cause or matter,
- (b) any document served upon, or by, a public authority for the purposes of proceedings in a particular cause or matter, or
- (c) any document created by—
  - (i) a court, or
  - (ii) a member of the administrative staff of a court,

  for the purposes of proceedings in a particular cause or matter.

(2) Information held by a public authority is exempt information if it is held only by virtue of being contained in—

- (a) any document placed in the custody of a person conducting an inquiry or arbitration, for the purposes of the inquiry or arbitration, or
- (b) any document created by a person conducting an inquiry or arbitration, for the purposes of the inquiry or arbitration.

(3) The duty to confirm or deny does not arise in relation to information which is (or if it were held by the public authority would be) exempt information by virtue of this section.

(4) In this section—

- (a) "court" includes any tribunal or body exercising the judicial power of the State, (*b*) "proceedings in a particular cause or matter" includes any inquest or post-mortem examination,

(*c*) "inquiry" means any inquiry or hearing held under any provision contained in, or made under, an enactment, and

(*d*) except in relation to Scotland, "arbitration" means any arbitration to which Part I of the Arbitration Act 1996 applies

[Freedom of Information Act 2000, s 32.]

8–3121V   33. Audit functions.   (1) This section applies to any public authority which has functions in relation to—

(*a*)   the audit of the accounts of other public authorities, or

(*b*)   the examination of the economy, efficiency and effectiveness with which other public authorities use their resources in discharging their functions

(2) Information held by a public authority to which this section applies is exempt information if its disclosure would, or would be likely to, prejudice the exercise of any of the authority's functions in relation to any of the matters referred to in subsection (1).

(3) The duty to confirm or deny does not arise in relation to a public authority to which this section applies if, or to the extent that, compliance with section 1(1)(*a*) would, or would be likely to, prejudice the exercise of any of the authority's functions in relation to any of the matters referred to in subsection (1).

[Freedom of Information Act 2000, s 33.]

8–3121W   34. *Parliamentary privilege*

8–3121X   35. Formulation of government policy, etc.   (1) Information held by a government department or by the National Assembly for Wales is exempt information if it relates to—

(*a*)   the formulation or development of government policy,

(*b*)   Ministerial communications,

(*c*)   the provision of advice by any of the Law Officers or any request for the provision of such advice, or

(*d*)   the operation of any Ministerial private office.

[Freedom of Information Act 2000, s 35.]

8–3121Y   37. *Communications with Her Majesty, etc and honours*

8–3121Z   38. Health and safety.   (1) Information is exempt information if its disclosure under this Act would, or would be likely to—

(*a*)   endanger the physical or mental health of any individual, or

(*b*)   endanger the safety of any individual.

(2) The duty to confirm or deny does not arise if, or to the extent that, compliance with section 1(1)(*a*) would, or would be likely to, have either of the effects mentioned in subsection (1).

[Freedom of Information Act 2000, s 38.]

8–3121ZA   39. Environmental information.   (1) Information is exempt information if the public authority holding it—

(*a*)   is obliged by environmental information regulations to make the information available to the public in accordance with the regulations, or

(*b*)   would be so obliged but for any exemption contained in the regulations

(1A)   In subsection (1) "environmental information regulations" means—

(*a*)   regulations made under section 74. or

(*b*)   regulations made under section 2(2) of the European Communities Act 1972 for the purpose of implementing any Community obligation relating to public access to, and the dissemination of, information on the environment.

(2) The duty to confirm or deny does not arise in relation to information which is (or if it were held by the public authority would be) exempt information by virtue of subsection (1).

(3) Subsection (1)(*a*) does not limit the generality of section 21(1).

[Freedom of Information Act 2000, s 39 as amended by SI 2004/3391.]

8–3121ZB   40. Personal information.   (1) Any information to which a request for information relates is exempt information if it constitutes personal data of which the applicant is the data subject.

(2) Any information to which a request for information relates is also exempt information if—

(*a*)   it constitutes personal data which do not fall within subsection (1), and

(*b*)   either the first or the second condition below is satisfied.

(3) The first condition is—

(*a*) in a case where the information falls within any of paragraphs (*a*) to (*d*) of the definition of "data" in section 1(1) of the Data Protection Act 1998, that the disclosure of the information to a member of the public otherwise than under this Act would contravene—

    (i) any of the data protection principles, or

    (ii) section 10 of that Act (right to prevent processing likely to cause damage or distress), and

(*b*) in any other case, that the disclosure of the information to a member of the public otherwise than under this Act would contravene any of the data protection principles if the exemptions in section 33A(1) of the Data Protection Act 1998 (which relate to manual data held by public authorities) were disregarded.

(4) The second condition is that by virtue of any provision of Part IV of the Data Protection Act 1998 the information is exempt from section 7(1)(*c*) of that Act (data subject's right of access to personal data).

(5) The duty to confirm or deny—

(*a*) does not arise in relation to information which is (or if it were held by the public authority would be) exempt information by virtue of subsection (1), and

(*b*) does not arise in relation to other information if or to the extent that either—

    (i) the giving to a member of the public of the confirmation or denial that would have to be given to comply with section 1(1)(*a*) would (apart from this Act) contravene any of the data protection principles or section 10 of the Data Protection Act 1998 or would do so if the exemptions in section 33A(1) of that Act were disregarded, or

    (ii) by virtue of any provision of Part IV of the Data Protection Act 1998 the information is exempt from section 7(1)(*a*) of that Act (data subject's right to be informed whether personal data being processed).

(6) In determining for the purposes of this section whether anything done before 24th October 2007 would contravene any of the data protection principles, the exemptions in Part III of Schedule 8 to the Data Protection Act 1998 shall be disregarded.

(7) In this section—

"the data protection principles" means the principles set out in Part I of Schedule 1 to the Data Protection Act 1998, as read subject to Part II of that Schedule and section 27(1) of that Act;

"data subject" has the same meaning as in section 1(1) of that Act;

"personal data" has the same meaning as in section 1(1) of that Act.

[Freedom of Information Act 2000, s 40.]

8–3121ZC   41. Information provided in confidence.   (1) Information is exempt information if—

(*a*) it was obtained by the public authority from any other person (including another public authority), and

(*b*) the disclosure of the information to the public (otherwise than under this Act) by the public authority holding it would constitute a breach of confidence actionable by that or any other person.

(2) The duty to confirm or deny does not arise if, or to the extent that, the confirmation or denial that would have to be given to comply with section 1(1)(*a*) would (apart from this Act) constitute an actionable breach of confidence.

[Freedom of Information Act 2000, s 41.]

8–3121ZD   42. Legal professional privilege.   (1) Information in respect of which a claim to legal professional privilege or, in Scotland, to confidentiality of communications could be maintained in legal proceedings is exempt information.

(2) The duty to confirm or deny does not arise if, or to the extent that, compliance with section 1(1)(*a*) would involve the disclosure of any information (whether or not already recorded) in respect of which such a claim could be maintained in legal proceedings

[Freedom of Information Act 2000, s 42.]

8–3121ZE   43. Commercial interests.   (1) Information is exempt information if it constitutes a trade secret.

(2) Information is exempt information if its disclosure under this Act would, or would be likely to, prejudice the commercial interests of any person (including the public authority holding it).

(3) The duty to confirm or deny does not arise if, or to the extent that, compliance with section 1(1)(*a*) would, or would be likely to, prejudice the interests mentioned in subsection (2).

[Freedom of Information Act 2000, s 43.]

8–3121ZF   44. Prohibitions on disclosure.   (1) Information is exempt information if its disclosure (otherwise than under this Act) by the public authority holding it—

(*a*) is prohibited by or under any enactment,

(*b*) is incompatible with any Community obligation, or

(c)   would constitute or be punishable as a contempt of court.

(2)   The duty to confirm or deny does not arise if the confirmation or denial that would have to be given to comply with section 1(1)(*a*) would (apart from this Act) fall within any of paragraphs (*a*) to (*c*) of subsection (1).

[Freedom of Information Act 2000, s 44.]

PART III[1]
GENERAL FUNCTIONS OF SECRETARY OF STATE, LORD CHANCELLOR AND INFORMATION COMMISSIONER

8–3121ZG   45. Issue of code of practice by Lord Chancellor.   (1) The Lord Chancellor shall issue, and may from time to time revise, a code of practice providing guidance to public authorities as to the practice which it would, in his opinion, be desirable for them to follow in connection with the discharge of the authorities' functions under Part I.

(2)   The code of practice must, in particular, include provision relating to—

(a)   the provision of advice and assistance by public authorities to persons who propose to make, or have made, requests for information to them,
(b)   the transfer of requests by one public authority to another public authority by which the information requested is or may be held,
(c)   consultation with persons to whom the information requested relates or persons whose interests are likely to be affected by the disclosure of information,
(d)   the inclusion in contracts entered into by public authorities of terms relating to the disclosure of information, and
(e)   the provision by public authorities of procedures for dealing with complaints about the handling by them of requests for information.

(3)   The code may make different provision for different public authorities

(4)   Before issuing or revising any code under this section, the Lord Chancellor shall consult the Commissioner.

(5)   The Lord Chancellor shall lay before each House of Parliament any code or revised code made under this section.

[Freedom of Information Act 2000, s 45, as amended by SI 2001/3500.]

---

1. Part III comprises ss 45 to 49.

8–3121ZH   46. Issue of code of practice by Lord Chancellor.   (1) The Lord Chancellor shall issue, and may from time to time revise, a code of practice providing guidance to relevant authorities as to the practice which it would, in his opinion, be desirable for them to follow in connection with the keeping, management and destruction of their records

(2)   For the purpose of facilitating the performance by the Public Record Office, the Public Record Office of Northern Ireland and other public authorities of their functions under this Act in relation to records which are public records for the purposes of the Public Records Act 1958 or the Public Records Act (Northern Ireland) 1923, the code may also include guidance as to—

(a)   the practice to be adopted in relation to the transfer of records under section 3(4) of the Public Records Act 1958 or section 3 of the Public Records Act (Northern Ireland) 1923, and
(b)   the practice of reviewing records before they are transferred under those provisions

(3)   In exercising his functions under this section, the Lord Chancellor shall have regard to the public interest in allowing public access to information held by relevant authorities

(4)   The code may make different provision for different relevant authorities

(5)   Before issuing or revising any code under this section the Lord Chancellor shall consult—

(a)   the Secretary of State,
(b)   the Commissioner, and
(c)   in relation to Northern Ireland, the appropriate Northern Ireland Minister.

(6)   The Lord Chancellor shall lay before each House of Parliament any code or revised code made under this section.

(7)   In this section "relevant authority" means—

(a)   any public authority, and
(b)   any office or body which is not a public authority but whose administrative and departmental records are public records for the purposes of the Public Records Act 1958 or the Public Records Act (Northern Ireland) 1923.

[Freedom of Information Act 2000, s 46.]

8–3121ZI   47. General functions of Commissioner.   (1) It shall be the duty of the Commissioner to promote the following of good practice by public authorities and, in particular, so to perform his functions under this Act as to promote the observance by public authorities of—

(a)   the requirements of this Act, and

(*b*)   the provisions of the codes of practice under sections 45 and 46.

(2)   The Commissioner shall arrange for the dissemination in such form and manner as he considers appropriate of such information as it may appear to him expedient to give to the public—

(*a*)   about the operation of this Act,

(*b*)   about good practice, and

(*c*)   about other matters within the scope of his functions under this Act,

and may give advice to any person as to any of those matters

(3)   The Commissioner may, with the consent of any public authority, assess whether that authority is following good practice.

(4)   The Commissioner may charge such sums as he may with the consent of the Lord Chancellor determine for any services provided by the Commissioner under this section.

(5)   The Commissioner shall from time to time as he considers appropriate—

(*a*)   consult the Keeper of Public Records about the promotion by the Commissioner of the observance by public authorities of the provisions of the code of practice under section 46 in relation to records which are public records for the purposes of the Public Records Act 1958, and

(*b*)   consult the Deputy Keeper of the Records of Northern Ireland about the promotion by the Commissioner of the observance by public authorities of those provisions in relation to records which are public records for the purposes of the Public Records Act (Northern Ireland) 1923.

(6)   In this section "good practice", in relation to a public authority, means such practice in the discharge of its functions under this Act as appears to the Commissioner to be desirable, and includes (but is not limited to) compliance with the requirements of this Act and the provisions of the codes of practice under sections 45 and 46.

[Freedom of Information Act 2000, s 47, as amended by SI 2001/3500.]

8–3121ZJ   48. Recommendations as to good practice.   (1)   If it appears to the Commissioner that the practice of a public authority in relation to the exercise of its functions under this Act does not conform with that proposed in the codes of practice under sections 45 and 46, he may give to the authority a recommendation (in this section referred to as a "practice recommendation") specifying the steps which ought in his opinion to be taken for promoting such conformity.

(2)   A practice recommendation must be given in writing and must refer to the particular provisions of the code of practice with which, in the Commissioner's opinion, the public authority's practice does not conform.

(3)   Before giving to a public authority other than the Public Record Office a practice recommendation which relates to conformity with the code of practice under section 46 in respect of records which are public records for the purposes of the Public Records Act 1958, the Commissioner shall consult the Keeper of Public Records

(4)   Before giving to a public authority other than the Public Record Office of Northern Ireland a practice recommendation which relates to conformity with the code of practice under section 46 in respect of records which are public records for the purposes of the Public Records Act (Northern Ireland) 1923, the Commissioner shall consult the Deputy Keeper of the Records of Northern Ireland.

[Freedom of Information Act 2000, s 48.]

8–3121ZK   49.   *Reports to be laid before Parliament*

PART IV[1]

ENFORCEMENT

8–3121ZL   50. Application for decision by Commissioner.   (1)   Any person (in this section referred to as "the complainant") may apply to the Commissioner for a decision whether, in any specified respect, a request for information made by the complainant to a public authority has been dealt with in accordance with the requirements of Part I.

(2)   On receiving an application under this section, the Commissioner shall make a decision unless it appears to him—

(*a*)   that the complainant has not exhausted any complaints procedure which is provided by the public authority in conformity with the code of practice under section 45,

(*b*)   that there has been undue delay in making the application,

(*c*)   that the application is frivolous or vexatious, or

(*d*)   that the application has been withdrawn or abandoned.

(3)   Where the Commissioner has received an application under this section, he shall either—

(*a*)   notify the complainant that he has not made any decision under this section as a result of the application and of his grounds for not doing so, or

(*b*)   serve notice of his decision (in this Act referred to as a "decision notice") on the complainant and the public authority.

(4) Where the Commissioner decides that a public authority—

(a) has failed to communicate information, or to provide confirmation or denial, in a case where it is required to do so by section 1(1), or

(b) has failed to comply with any of the requirements of sections 11 and 17,

the decision notice must specify the steps which must be taken by the authority for complying with that requirement and the period within which they must be taken.

(5) A decision notice must contain particulars of the right of appeal conferred by section 57.

(6) Where a decision notice requires steps to be taken by the public authority within a specified period, the time specified in the notice must not expire before the end of the period within which an appeal can be brought against the notice and, if such an appeal is brought, no step which is affected by the appeal need be taken pending the determination or withdrawal of the appeal.

(7) This section has effect subject to section 53.

[Freedom of Information Act 2000, s 50.]

---

1. Part IV comprises ss 50 to 56.

8–3121ZM 51. Information notices. (1) If the Commissioner—

(a) has received an application under section 50, or

(b) reasonably requires any information—

(i) for the purpose of determining whether a public authority has complied or is complying with any of the requirements of Part I, or

(ii) for the purpose of determining whether the practice of a public authority in relation to the exercise of its functions under this Act conforms with that proposed in the codes of practice under sections 45 and 46,

he may serve the authority with a notice (in this Act referred to as "an information notice") requiring it, within such time as is specified in the notice, to furnish the Commissioner, in such form as may be so specified, with such information relating to the application, to compliance with Part I or to conformity with the code of practice as is so specified.

(2) An information notice must contain—

(a) in a case falling within subsection (1)(a), a statement that the Commissioner has received an application under section 50, or

(b) in a case falling within subsection (1)(b), a statement—

(i) that the Commissioner regards the specified information as relevant for either of the purposes referred to in subsection (1)(b), and

(ii) of his reasons for regarding that information as relevant for that purpose.

(3) An information notice must also contain particulars of the right of appeal conferred by section 57.

(4) The time specified in an information notice must not expire before the end of the period within which an appeal can be brought against the notice and, if such an appeal is brought, the information need not be furnished pending the determination or withdrawal of the appeal.

(5) An authority shall not be required by virtue of this section to furnish the Commissioner with any information in respect of—

(a) any communication between a professional legal adviser and his client in connection with the giving of legal advice to the client with respect to his obligations, liabilities or rights under this Act, or

(b) any communication between a professional legal adviser and his client, or between such an adviser or his client and any other person, made in connection with or in contemplation of proceedings under or arising out of this Act (including proceedings before the Tribunal) and for the purposes of such proceedings

(6) In subsection (5) references to the client of a professional legal adviser include references to any person representing such a client.

(7) The Commissioner may cancel an information notice by written notice to the authority on which it was served.

(8) In this section "information" includes unrecorded information.

[Freedom of Information Act 2000, s 51.]

8–3121ZN 52. Enforcement notices. (1) If the Commissioner is satisfied that a public authority has failed to comply with any of the requirements of Part I, the Commissioner may serve the authority with a notice (in this Act referred to as "an enforcement notice") requiring the authority to take, within such time as may be specified in the notice, such steps as may be so specified for complying with those requirements

(2) An enforcement notice must contain—

(*a*) a statement of the requirement or requirements of Part I with which the Commissioner is satisfied that the public authority has failed to comply and his reasons for reaching that conclusion, and

(*b*) particulars of the right of appeal conferred by section 57.

(3) An enforcement notice must not require any of the provisions of the notice to be complied with before the end of the period within which an appeal can be brought against the notice and, if such an appeal is brought, the notice need not be complied with pending the determination or withdrawal of the appeal.

(4) The Commissioner may cancel an enforcement notice by written notice to the authority on which it was served.

(5) This section has effect subject to section 53.

[Freedom of Information Act 2000, s 52.]

8–3121ZO   53. Exception from duty to comply with decision notice or enforcement notice.

(1) This section applies to a decision notice or enforcement notice which—

(*a*) is served on—

    (i) a government department,

    (ii) the National Assembly for Wales, or

    (iii) any public authority designated for the purposes of this section by an order made by the Lord Chancellor, and

(*b*) relates to a failure, in respect of one or more requests for information—

    (i) to comply with section 1(1)(*a*) in respect of information which falls within any provision of Part II stating that the duty to confirm or deny does not arise, or

    (ii) to comply with section 1(1)(*b*) in respect of exempt information.

(2) A decision notice or enforcement notice to which this section applies shall cease to have effect if, not later than the twentieth working day following the effective date, the accountable person in relation to that authority gives the Commissioner a certificate signed by him stating that he has on reasonable grounds formed the opinion that, in respect of the request or requests concerned, there was no failure falling within subsection (1)(*b*).

(3) Where the accountable person gives a certificate to the Commissioner under subsection (2) he shall as soon as practicable thereafter lay a copy of the certificate before—

(*a*) each House of Parliament,

(*b*) the Northern Ireland Assembly, in any case where the certificate relates to a decision notice or enforcement notice which has been served on a Northern Ireland department or any Northern Ireland public authority, or

(*c*) the National Assembly for Wales, in any case where the certificate relates to a decision notice or enforcement notice which has been served on the National Assembly for Wales or any Welsh public authority.

(4) In subsection (2) "the effective date", in relation to a decision notice or enforcement notice, means—

(*a*) the day on which the notice was given to the public authority, or

(*b*) where an appeal under section 57 is brought, the day on which that appeal (or any further appeal arising out of it) is determined or withdrawn.

(5) Before making an order under subsection (1)(*a*)(iii), the Lord Chancellor shall—

(*a*) if the order relates to a Welsh public authority, consult the National Assembly for Wales,

(*b*) if the order relates to the Northern Ireland Assembly, consult the Presiding Officer of that Assembly, and

(*c*) if the order relates to a Northern Ireland public authority, consult the First Minister and deputy First Minister in Northern Ireland.

(6) Where the accountable person gives a certificate to the Commissioner under subsection (2) in relation to a decision notice, the accountable person shall, on doing so or as soon as reasonably practicable after doing so, inform the person who is the complainant for the purposes of section 50 of the reasons for his opinion.

(7) The accountable person is not obliged to provide information under subsection (6) if, or to the extent that, compliance with that subsection would involve the disclosure of exempt information.

(8) In this section "the accountable person"—

(*a*) in relation to a Northern Ireland department or any Northern Ireland public authority, means the First Minister and deputy First Minister in Northern Ireland acting jointly,

(*b*) in relation to the National Assembly for Wales or any Welsh public authority, means the Assembly First Secretary, and

(*c*) in relation to any other public authority, means—

    (i) a Minister of the Crown who is a member of the Cabinet, or

(ii) the Attorney General, the Advocate General for Scotland or the Attorney General for Northern Ireland.

(9) In this section "working day" has the same meaning as in section 10.
[Freedom of Information Act 2000, s 53, as amended by SI 2001/3500.]

8–3121ZP 54. Failure to comply with notice.   (1) If a public authority has failed to comply with—

(a) so much of a decision notice as requires steps to be taken,
(b) an information notice, or
(c) an enforcement notice,

the Commissioner may certify in writing to the court that the public authority has failed to comply with that notice.

(2) For the purposes of this section, a public authority which, in purported compliance with an information notice—

(a) makes a statement which it knows to be false in a material respect, or
(b) recklessly makes a statement which is false in a material respect,

is to be taken to have failed to comply with the notice.

(3) Where a failure to comply is certified under subsection (1), the court may inquire into the matter and, after hearing any witness who may be produced against or on behalf of the public authority, and after hearing any statement that may be offered in defence, deal with the authority as if it had committed a contempt of court.

(4) In this section "the court" means the High Court or, in Scotland, the Court of Session.
[Freedom of Information Act 2000, s 54.]

8–3121ZQ 55. Powers of entry and inspection.   Schedule 3 (powers of entry and inspection) has effect.
[Freedom of Information Act 2000, s 55.]

8–3121ZR 56. No action against public authority.   (1) This Act does not confer any right of action in civil proceedings in respect of any failure to comply with any duty imposed by or under this Act.

(2) Subsection (1) does not affect the powers of the Commissioner under section 54.
[Freedom of Information Act 2000, s 56.]

PART V[1]
APPEALS

8–3121ZS 57. Appeal against notices served under Part IV.   (1) Where a decision notice has been served, the complainant or the public authority may appeal to the Tribunal against the notice.

(2) A public authority on which an information notice or an enforcement notice has been served by the Commissioner may appeal to the Tribunal against the notice.

(3) In relation to a decision notice or enforcement notice which relates—

(a) to information to which section 66 applies, and
(b) to a matter which by virtue of subsection (3) or (4) of that section falls to be determined by the responsible authority instead of the appropriate records authority,

subsections (1) and (2) shall have effect as if the reference to the public authority were a reference to the public authority or the responsible authority.
[Freedom of Information Act 2000, s 57.]

---

1. Part V comprises ss 57 to 61.

8–3121ZT 58. Determination of appeals.   (1) If on an appeal under section 57 the Tribunal considers—

(a) that the notice against which the appeal is brought is not in accordance with the law, or
(b) to the extent that the notice involved an exercise of discretion by the Commissioner, that he ought to have exercised his discretion differently,

the Tribunal shall allow the appeal or substitute such other notice as could have been served by the Commissioner; and in any other case the Tribunal shall dismiss the appeal.

(2) On such an appeal, the Tribunal may review any finding of fact on which the notice in question was based.
[Freedom of Information Act 2000, s 58.]

8–3121ZU 59. *Appeals from decision of tribunal*

PART VIII[1]

MISCELLANEOUS AND SUPPLEMENTAL

8–3121ZV   75. Power to amend or repeal enactments prohibiting disclosure of information.
(1) If, with respect to any enactment which prohibits the disclosure of information held by a public authority, it appears to the Lord Chancellor that by virtue of section 44(1)(a) the enactment is capable of preventing the disclosure of information under section 1, he may by order repeal or amend the enactment for the purpose of removing or relaxing the prohibition.

(2) In subsection (1)—

"enactment" means—

    (a) any enactment contained in an Act passed before or in the same Session as this Act, or

    (b) any enactment contained in Northern Ireland legislation or subordinate legislation passed or made before the passing of this Act;

"information" includes unrecorded information.

(3) An order under this section may do all or any of the following—

    (a) make such modifications of enactments as, in the opinion of the Lord Chancellor, are consequential upon, or incidental to, the amendment or repeal of the enactment containing the prohibition;

    (b) contain such transitional provisions and savings as appear to the Lord Chancellor to be appropriate;

    (c) make different provision for different cases.

[Freedom of Information Act 2000, s 75, as amended by SI 2001/3500.]

---

1. Part VIII comprises ss 74 to 88.

8–3121ZW   77. Offence of altering etc records with intent to prevent disclosure.
(1) Where—

    (a) a request for information has been made to a public authority, and

    (b) under section 1 of this Act or section 7 of the Data Protection Act 1998, the applicant would have been entitled (subject to payment of any fee) to communication of any information in accordance with that section,

any person to whom this subsection applies is guilty of an offence if he alters, defaces, blocks, erases, destroys or conceals any record held by the public authority, with the intention of preventing the disclosure by that authority of all, or any part, of the information to the communication of which the applicant would have been entitled.

(2) Subsection (1) applies to the public authority and to any person who is employed by, is an officer of, or is subject to the direction of, the public authority.

(3) A person guilty of an offence under this section is liable on summary conviction to a fine not exceeding level 5 on the standard scale.

(4) No proceedings for an offence under this section shall be instituted—

    (a) in England or Wales, except by the Commissioner or by or with the consent of the Director of Public Prosecutions;

    (b) in Northern Ireland, except by the Commissioner or by or with the consent of the Director of Public Prosecutions for Northern Ireland.

[Freedom of Information Act 2000, s 77.]

8–3121ZX   78. Saving for existing powers.   Nothing in this Act is to be taken to limit the powers of a public authority to disclose information held by it.
[Freedom of Information Act 2000, s 78.]

8–3121ZY   79. Defamation.   Where any information communicated by a public authority to a person ("the applicant") under section 1 was supplied to the public authority by a third person, the publication to the applicant of any defamatory matter contained in the information shall be privileged unless the publication is shown to have been made with malice.
[Freedom of Information Act 2000, s 79.]

8–3121ZZ   81.   *Application to government departments, etc*

8–3121ZZA   82.   *Orders and regulations*

8–3121ZZB   83. Meaning of "Welsh public authority".   (1) In this Act "Welsh public authority" means—

    (a) any public authority which is listed in Part II, III, IV or VI of Schedule 1 and whose functions are exercisable only or mainly in or as regards Wales, other than an excluded authority, or (*b*) any public authority which is an Assembly subsidiary as defined by section 99(4) of the Government of Wales Act 1998.

(2) In paragraph (*a*) of subsection (1) "excluded authority" means a public authority which is designated by the Lord Chancellor by order[1] as an excluded authority for the purposes of that paragraph.

(3) Before making an order under subsection (2), the Lord Chancellor shall consult the National Assembly for Wales

[Freedom of Information Act 2000, s 83, as amended by SI 2001/3500.]

---

1. The Freedom of Information (Excluded Welsh Authorities) Order 2002, SI 2002/2832 has been made which specifies inter alia Welsh magistrates' courts committees and Lord Chancellor's Advisory Committees on appointments of Justices of the Peace.

8–3121ZZC 84. Interpretation. In this Act, unless the context otherwise requires—

"applicant", in relation to a request for information, means the person who made the request;

"appropriate Northern Ireland Minister" means the Northern Ireland Minister in charge of the Department of Culture, Arts and Leisure in Northern Ireland;

"appropriate records authority", in relation to a transferred public record, has the meaning given by section 15(5);

"body" includes an unincorporated association;

"the Commissioner" means the Information Commissioner;

"decision notice" has the meaning given by section 50;

"the duty to confirm or deny" has the meaning given by section 1(6);

"enactment" includes an enactment contained in Northern Ireland legislation;

"enforcement notice" has the meaning given by section 52;

"executive committee", in relation to the National Assembly for Wales, has the same meaning as in the Government of Wales Act 1998;

"exempt information" means information which is exempt information by virtue of any provision of Part II;

"fees notice" has the meaning given by section 9(1);

"government department" includes a Northern Ireland department, the Northern Ireland Court Service and any other body or authority exercising statutory functions on behalf of the Crown, but does not include—

    (*a*) any of the bodies specified in section 80(2),

    (*b*) the Security Service, the Secret Intelligence Service or the Government Communications Headquarters, or

    (*c*) the National Assembly for Wales;

"information" (subject to sections 51(8) and 75(2)) means information recorded in any form;

"information notice" has the meaning given by section 51;

"Minister of the Crown" has the same meaning as in the Ministers of the Crown Act 1975;

"Northern Ireland Minister" includes the First Minister and deputy First Minister in Northern Ireland;

"Northern Ireland public authority" means any public authority, other than the Northern Ireland Assembly or a Northern Ireland department, whose functions are exercisable only or mainly in or as regards Northern Ireland and relate only or mainly to transferred matters;

"prescribed" means prescribed by regulations made by the Lord Chancellor;

"public authority" has the meaning given by section 3(1);

"public record" means a public record within the meaning of the Public Records Act 1958 or a public record to which the Public Records Act (Northern Ireland) 1923 applies;

"publication scheme" has the meaning given by section 19;

"request for information" has the meaning given by section 8;

"responsible authority", in relation to a transferred public record, has the meaning given by section 15(5);

"the special forces" means those units of the armed forces of the Crown the maintenance of whose capabilities is the responsibility of the Director of Special Forces or which are for the time being subject to the operational command of that Director;

"subordinate legislation" has the meaning given by subsection (1) of section 21 of the Interpretation Act 1978, except that the definition of that term in that subsection shall have effect as if "Act" included Northern Ireland legislation;

"transferred matter", in relation to Northern Ireland, has the meaning given by section 4(1) of the Northern Ireland Act 1998;

"transferred public record" has the meaning given by section 15(4);

"the Tribunal" means the Information Tribunal;

"Welsh public authority" has the meaning given by section 83.

[Freedom of Information Act 2000, s 84, as amended by SI 2001/3500.]

8–3121ZZD 86. *Repeals*

8–3121ZZE 87. Commencement. (1) The following provisions of this Act shall come into force on the day on which this Act is passed—

(a) sections 3 to 8 and Schedule 1,

(b) section 19 so far as relating to the approval of publication schemes,

(c) section 20 so far as relating to the approval and preparation by the Commissioner of model publication schemes,

(d) section 47(2) to (6),

(e) section 49,

(f) section 74,

(g) section 75,

(h) sections 78 to 85 and this section,

(i) paragraphs 2 and 17 to 22 of Schedule 2 (and section 18(4) so far as relating to those paragraphs),

(j) paragraph 4 of Schedule 5 (and section 67 so far as relating to that paragraph),

(k) paragraph 8 of Schedule 6 (and section 73 so far as relating to that paragraph),

(l) Part I of Schedule 8 (and section 86 so far as relating to that Part), and

(m) so much of any other provision of this Act as confers power to make any order, regulations or code of practice.

(2) The following provisions of this Act shall come into force at the end of the period of two months beginning with the day on which this Act is passed—

(a) section 18(1),

(b) section 76 and Schedule 7,

(c) paragraphs 1(1), 3(1), 4, 6, 7, 8(2), 9(2), 10(a), 13(1) and (2), 14(a) and 15(1) and (2) of Schedule 2 (and section 18(4) so far as relating to those provisions), and

(d) Part II of Schedule 8 (and section 86 so far as relating to that Part).

(3) Except as provided by subsections (1) and (2), this Act shall come into force at the end of the period of five years beginning with the day on which this Act is passed or on such day before the end of that period as the Lord Chancellor may by order appoint; and different days may be appointed for different purposes[1].

(4) An order under subsection (3) may contain such transitional provisions and savings (including provisions capable of having effect after the end of the period referred to in that subsection) as the Lord Chancellor considers appropriate.

(5) During the twelve months beginning with the day on which this Act is passed, and during each subsequent complete period of twelve months in the period beginning with that day and ending with the first day on which all the provisions of this Act are fully in force, the Lord Chancellor shall—

(a) prepare a report on his proposals for bringing fully into force those provisions of this Act which are not yet fully in force, and

(b) lay a copy of the report before each House of Parliament.

[Freedom of Information Act 2000, s 87, as amended by SI 2001/3500.]

---

1. The Freedom of Information Act 2000 (Commencement No 1) Order 2001, SI 2001/1637; Freedom of Information Act 2000 (Commencement No 2) Order 2002, SI 2002/2812; Freedom of Information Act 2000 (Commencement No 3) Order 2003, SI 2003/2603; Freedom of Information Act 2000 (Commencement No 4) Order 2004, SI 2004/1909; and Freedom of Information Act 2000 (Commencement No 5) Order 2004, SI 2004/3122 have been made. All the Act's provisions are now in force.

8–3121ZZF 88. Short title and extent. (1) This Act may be cited as the Freedom of Information Act 2000.

(2) Subject to subsection (3), this Act extends to Northern Ireland.

(3) The amendment or repeal of any enactment by this Act has the same extent as that enactment.

[Freedom of Information Act 2000, s 88.]

SCHEDULE 1
PUBLIC AUTHORITIES

(Amended by SI 2002/2623, SI 2003/1882 and 1883, the Fire and Rescue Services Act 2004, Sch 1 and SI 2004/938, 1641 and 1870, the Courts Act 2003, Sch 8, the Energy Act 2004, Sch 10, the Gangmasters (Licensing) Act 2004, Sch 1, the Human Tissue Act 2004, Sch 2, the Civil Contigencies Act 2004, Sch 2 and SI 2005/3593 and 3594.)

Section 3(1)(a)(i)

PART I
GENERAL

8–3121ZZG 1. Any government department.

2. The House of Commons

3. The House of Lords

4. The Northern Ireland Assembly.

5. The National Assembly for Wales

6. The armed forces of the Crown, except—

   (*a*) the special forces, and

   (*b*) any unit or part of a unit which is for the time being required by the Secretary of State to assist the Government Communications Headquarters in the exercise of its functions.

PART II
LOCAL GOVERNMENT

England and Wales

8–3121ZZH   **7.** A local authority within the meaning of the Local Government Act 1972, namely—

   (*a*) in England, a county council, a London borough council, a district council or a parish council,

   (*b*) in Wales, a county council, a county borough council or a community council.

8. The Greater London Authority.

9. The Common Council of the City of London, in respect of information held in its capacity as a local authority, police authority or port health authority.

10. The Sub-Treasurer of the Inner Temple or the Under-Treasurer of the Middle Temple, in respect of information held in his capacity as a local authority.

11. The Council of the Isles of Scilly.

12. A parish meeting constituted under section 13 of the Local Government Act 1972.

13. Any charter trustees constituted under section 246 of the Local Government Act 1972.

14. A fire and rescue authority constituted by a scheme under section 2 of the Fire and Rescue Services Act 2004 or a scheme to which section 4 of that Act applies.

15. A waste disposal authority established by virtue of an order under section 10(1) of the Local Government Act 1985.

16. A port health authority constituted by an order under section 2 of the Public Health (Control of Disease) Act 1984.

17. A licensing planning committee constituted under section 119 of the Licensing Act 1964.

18. An internal drainage board which is continued in being by virtue of section 1 of the Land Drainage Act 1991.

19. A joint authority established under Part IV of the Local Government Act 1985 (fire and rescue servicesand transport).

20. The London Fire and Emergency Planning Authority.

21. A joint fire authority established by virtue of an order under section 42(2) of the Local Government Act 1985 (reorganisation of functions).

22. A body corporate established pursuant to an order under section 67 of the Local Government Act 1985 (transfer of functions to successors of residuary bodies, etc).

23. A body corporate established pursuant to an order under section 22 of the Local Government Act 1992 (residuary bodies).

24. The Broads Authority established by section 1 of the Norfolk and Suffolk Broads Act 1988.

25. A joint committee constituted in accordance with section 102(1)(*b*) of the Local Government Act 1972.

26. A joint board which is continued in being by virtue of section 263(1) of the Local Government Act 1972.

27. A joint authority established under section 21 of the Local Government Act 1992.

28. A Passenger Transport Executive for a passenger transport area within the meaning of Part II of the Transport Act 1968.

29. Transport for London.

30. The London Transport Users Committee.

31. A joint board the constituent members of which consist of any of the public authorities described in paragraphs 8, 9, 10, 12, 15, 16, 20 to 31, 57 and 58.

32. A National Park authority established by an order under section 63 of the Environment Act 1995.

33. A joint planning board constituted for an area in Wales outside a National Park by an order under section 2(1B) of the Town and Country Planning Act 1990.

34. *Repealed.*

35. The London Development Agency.

35A. A local fisheries committee for a sea fisheries district established under section 1 of the Sea Fisheries Regulation Act 1966.

Northern Ireland

36. *Northern Ireland*

8–3121ZZI

PART III
THE NATIONAL HEALTH SERVICE

8–3121ZZJ

PART IV
MAINTAINED SCHOOLS AND OTHER EDUCATIONAL INSTITUTIONS

PART V
POLICE

England and Wales

8–3121ZZJA   **57.** A police authority established under section 3 of the Police Act 1996.

58. The Metropolitan Police Authority established under section 5B of the Police Act 1996.

59. A chief officer of police of a police force in England or Wales

Northern Ireland

60–61. *Northern Ireland*

Miscellaneous

62. The British Transport Police.
63. The Ministry of Defence Police established by section 1 of the Ministry of Defence Police Act 1987.
63A   The Civil Nuclear Police Authority.63B. The chief constable of the Civil Nuclear Police Authority.
64. Any person who—

    (a)   by virtue of any enactment has the function of nominating individuals who may be appointed as special constables by justices of the peace, and

    (b)   is not a public authority by virtue of any other provision of this Act,

in respect of information relating to the exercise by any person appointed on his nomination of the functions of a special constable.

8–3121ZZK

PART VI

OTHER PUBLIC BODIES AND OFFICES: GENERAL[1]

1. The list of other public bodies and offices is too long to be reproduced in this work. However, users of the work may find it of interest to note that the list includes the following public bodies:

The Advisory Board on Family Law;
An Advisory Committee on Justices of the Peace in England and Wales;
The Advisory Committee on Statute Law
The Advisory Council on the Misuse of Drugs;
Any Board of Visitors established under s 6(2) of the Prison Act 1952;
The British Transport Police Authority.
The Children and Family Court Advisory and Support Service;
The Children's Commissioner.
The Criminal Cases Review Commission;
The Criminal Justice Consultative Council;
The Criminal Procedure Rule Committee.
The Crown Court Rule Committee;
The Family Justice Council.
The Family Procedure Rule Committee.
The Gaming Board for Great Britain;
Gangmasters Licensing Authority;
The Health and Safety Executive;
The Human Tissue Authority;
The Legal Services Complaints Commisssioner
A local probation board established under s 4 of the Criminal Justice and Court Services Act 2000;
The Magistrates' Courts Rules Committee;
Her Majesty's Commissioner for Judicial Appointments
The Parole Board;
The Police Advisory Board for England and Wales
The Police Complaints Authority;
The Registrar General for England and Wales.
The Sentencing Advisory Panel;
The Sentencing Guidelines Council.
The Youth Justice Board for England and Wales.

Section 55

SCHEDULE 3

POWERS OF ENTRY AND INSPECTION

Issue of warrants

8–3121ZZL   **1.** (1) If a circuit judge is satisfied by information on oath supplied by the Commissioner that there are reasonable grounds for suspecting—

    (a)   that a public authority has failed or is failing to comply with—

        (i)   any of the requirements of Part I of this Act,

        (ii)   so much of a decision notice as requires steps to be taken, or

        (iii)   an information notice or an enforcement notice, or

    (b)   that an offence under section 77 has been or is being committed,

and that evidence of such a failure to comply or of the commission of the offence is to be found on any premises specified in the information, he may, subject to paragraph 2, grant a warrant to the Commissioner.

    (2) A warrant issued under sub-paragraph (1) shall authorise the Commissioner or any of his officers or staff at any time within seven days of the date of the warrant—

    (a)   to enter and search the premises,

    (b)   to inspect and seize any documents or other material found there which may be such evidence as is mentioned in that sub-paragraph, and

    (c)   to inspect, examine, operate and test any equipment found there in which information held by the public authority may be recorded.

    2. (1) A judge shall not issue a warrant under this Schedule unless he is satisfied—

(a) that the Commissioner has given seven days' notice in writing to the occupier of the premises in question demanding access to the premises, and

(b) that either—

    (i) access was demanded at a reasonable hour and was unreasonably refused, or

    (ii) although entry to the premises was granted, the occupier unreasonably refused to comply with a request by the Commissioner or any of the Commissioner's officers or staff to permit the Commissioner or the officer or member of staff to do any of the things referred to in paragraph 1(2), and

(c) that the occupier, has, after the refusal, been notified by the Commissioner of the application for the warrant and has had an opportunity of being heard by the judge on the question whether or not it should be issued.

(2) Sub-paragraph (1) shall not apply if the judge is satisfied that the case is one of urgency or that compliance with those provisions would defeat the object of the entry.

3. A judge who issues a warrant under this Schedule shall also issue two copies of it and certify them clearly as copies

Execution of warrants

4. A person executing a warrant issued under this Schedule may use such reasonable force as may be necessary.

5. A warrant issued under this Schedule shall be executed at a reasonable hour unless it appears to the person executing it that there are grounds for suspecting that the evidence in question would not be found if it were so executed.

6. (1) If the premises in respect of which a warrant is issued under this Schedule are occupied by a public authority and any officer or employee of the authority is present when the warrant is executed, he shall be shown the warrant and supplied with a copy of it; and if no such officer or employee is present a copy of the warrant shall be left in a prominent place on the premises

(2) If the premises in respect of which a warrant is issued under this Schedule are occupied by a person other than a public authority and he is present when the warrant is executed, he shall be shown the warrant and supplied with a copy of it; and if that person is not present a copy of the warrant shall be left in a prominent place on the premises

7. (1) A person seizing anything in pursuance of a warrant under this Schedule shall give a receipt for it if asked to do so.

(2) Anything so seized may be retained for so long as is necessary in all the circumstances but the person in occupation of the premises in question shall be given a copy of anything that is seized if he so requests and the person executing the warrant considers that it can be done without undue delay[1].

---

1. These provisions confer, by ss 50 and 51, additional powers of seizure of property in relation to searches carried out under existing powers. However, s 57 (retention of seized items) does not authorise the retention of any property which could not be retained under the provisions listed in s 57(1), which include para 7(2) of Sch 3 to the Freedom of Information Act 2000, if the property was seized under the new powers (ie those conferred by ss 50 and 51) in reliance on one of those powers (ie those conferred by the provisions listed in s 57(1)). Section 57(4) further provides that nothing in any of the provisions listed in s 57(1) authorises the retention of anything after an obligation to return it has arisen under Part 2.

Matters exempt from inspection and seizure

8. The powers of inspection and seizure conferred by a warrant issued under this Schedule shall not be exercisable in respect of information which is exempt information by virtue of section 23(1) or 24(1).

9. (1) Subject to the provisions of this paragraph, the powers of inspection and seizure conferred by a warrant issued under this Schedule shall not be exercisable in respect of—

(a) any communication between a professional legal adviser and his client in connection with the giving of legal advice to the client with respect to his obligations, liabilities or rights under this Act, or

(b) any communication between a professional legal adviser and his client, or between such an adviser or his client and any other person, made in connection with or in contemplation of proceedings under or arising out of this Act (including proceedings before the Tribunal) and for the purposes of such proceedings

(2) Sub-paragraph (1) applies also to—

(a) any copy or other record of any such communication as is there mentioned, and

(b) any document or article enclosed with or referred to in any such communication if made in connection with the giving of any advice or, as the case may be, in connection with or in contemplation of and for the purposes of such proceedings as are there mentioned.

(3) This paragraph does not apply to anything in the possession of any person other than the professional legal adviser or his client or to anything held with the intention of furthering a criminal purpose.

(4) In this paragraph references to the client of a professional legal adviser include references to any person representing such a client.

10. If the person in occupation of any premises in respect of which a warrant is issued under this Schedule objects to the inspection or seizure under the warrant of any material on the grounds that it consists partly of matters in respect of which those powers are not exercisable, he shall, if the person executing the warrant so requests, furnish that person with a copy of so much of the material in relation to which the powers are exercisable.

Return of warrants

11. A warrant issued under this Schedule shall be returned to the court from which it was issued—

(a) after being executed, or

(b) if not executed within the time authorised for its execution;

and the person by whom any such warrant is executed shall make an endorsement on it stating what powers have been exercised by him under the warrant.

Offences

12. Any person who—

(*a*) intentionally obstructs a person in the execution of a warrant issued under this Schedule, or

(*b*) fails without reasonable excuse to give any person executing such a warrant such assistance as he may reasonably require for the execution of the warrant,

is guilty of an offence.

Vessels, vehicles etc

13. In this Schedule "premises" includes any vessel, vehicle, aircraft or hovercraft, and references to the occupier of any premises include references to the person in charge of any vessel, vehicle, aircraft or hovercraft.

Scotland and Northern Ireland

14–15. *Scotland and Northern Ireland*

Disability Discrimination (Meaning of Disability) Regulations 1996[1]
(SI 1996/1455)

8–3122   1. *Citation and commencement*

1. Made by the Secretary of State in exercise of powers conferred by paras 1(2), 2(4), 3(2) and (3), 4(2)(a) and 5(a) of Sch 1 to the Disability Discrimination Act 1995.

8–3122A   2. Interpretation.   In these Regulations—

"the Act" means the Disability Discrimination Act 1995; and
"addiction" includes a dependency.

8–3122B   3. Addictions.   (1) Subject to paragraph (2) below, addiction to alcohol, nicotine or any other substance is to be treated as not amounting to an impairment for the purposes of the Act.

(2) Paragraph (1) above does not apply to addiction which was originally the result of administration of medically prescribed drugs or other medical treatment.

8–3122C   4. Other conditions not to be treated as impairments.   (1) For the purposes of the Act the following conditions are to be treated as not amounting to impairments:

(*a*)   a tendency to set fires,
(*b*)   a tendency to steal,
(*c*)   a tendency to physical or sexual abuse of other persons,
(*d*)   exhibitionism, and
(*e*)   voyeurism.

(2) Subject to paragraph (3) below for the purposes of the Act the conditions known as seasonal allergic rhinitis shall be treated as not amounting to an impairment.

(3) Paragraph (2) above shall not prevent that condition from being taken into account for the purposes of the Act where it aggravates the effect of another condition.

8–3122D   5. Tattoos and piercings.   For the purposes of paragraph 3 of Schedule 1 to the Act a severe disfigurement is not to be treated as having a substantial adverse effect on the ability of the person concerned to carry out normal day-to-day activities if it consists of—

(*a*)   a tattoo (which has not been removed) or,
(*b*)   a piercing of the body for decorative or other non-medical purposes, including any object attached through the piercing for such purposes.

8–3122E   6. Babies and young children.   For the purposes of the Act where a child under six years of age has an impairment which does not have an effect falling within paragraph 4(1) of Schedule 1 to the Act that impairment is to be taken to have a substantial and long-term adverse effect on the ability of that child to carry out normal day-to-day activities where it would normally have a substantial and long-term adverse effect on the ability of a person aged 6 years or over to carry out normal day-to-day activities.

Freedom of Information and Data Protection (Appropriate Limit and Fees) Regulations 2004[1]
(SI 2004/3244)

8–3122F   1. Citation and commencement.   These Regulations may be cited as the Freedom of Information and Data Protection (Appropriate Limit and Fees) Regulations 2004 and come into force on 1st January 2005.

1. Made by the Secretary of State, in exercise of the powers conferred upon him by sections 9(3) and (4), 12(3), (4) and (5), and 13(1) and (2) of the Freedom of Information Act 2000, and by sections 9A(5) and 67(2) of the Data Protection Act 1998.

8–3122G   2. Interpretation.   In these Regulations—

"the 2000 Act" means the Freedom of Information Act 2000;

"the 1998 Act" means the Data Protection Act 1998; and

"the appropriate limit" is to be construed in accordance with the provision made in regulation 3.

8–3122H   3. The appropriate limit.   (1) This regulation has effect to prescribe the appropriate limit referred to in section 9A(3) and (4) of the 1998 Act and the appropriate limit referred to in section 12(1) and (2) of the 2000 Act.

(2) In the case of a public authority which is listed in Part I of Schedule 1 to the 2000 Act, the appropriate limit is £600.

(3) In the case of any other public authority, the appropriate limit is £450.

8–3122I   4. Estimating the cost of complying with a request – general.   (1) This regulation has effect in any case in which a public authority proposes to estimate whether the cost of complying with a relevant request would exceed the appropriate limit.

(2) A relevant request is any request to the extent that it is a request—

(a) for unstructured personal data within the meaning of section 9A(1) of the 1998 Act, and to which section 7(1) of that Act would, apart from the appropriate limit, to any extent apply, or

(b) information to which section 1(1) of the 2000 Act would, apart from the appropriate limit, to any extent apply.

(3) In a case in which this regulation has effect, a public authority may, for the purpose of its estimate, take account only of the costs it reasonably expects to incur in relation to the request in—

(a) determining whether it holds the information,
(b) locating the information, or a document which may contain the information,
(c) retrieving the information, or a document which may contain the information, and
(d) extracting the information from a document containing it.

(4) To the extent to which any of the costs which a public authority takes into account are attributable to the time which persons undertaking any of the activities mentioned in paragraph (3) on behalf of the authority are expected to spend on those activities, those costs are to be estimated at a rate of £25 per person per hour.

8–3122J   5. Estimating the cost of complying with a request – aggregation of related requests.
(1) In circumstances in which this regulation applies, where two or more requests for information to which section 1(1) of the 2000 Act would, apart from the appropriate limit, to any extent apply, are made to a public authority—

(a) by one person, or
(b) by different persons who appear to the public authority to be acting in concert or in pursuance of a campaign,

the estimated cost of complying with any of the requests is to be taken to be the total costs which may be taken into account by the authority, under regulation 4, of complying with all of them.

(2) This regulation applies in circumstances in which—

(a) the two or more requests referred to in paragraph (1) relate, to any extent, to the same or similar information, and

(b) those requests are received by the public authority within any period of sixty consecutive working days.

(3) In this regulation, "working day" means any day other than a Saturday, a Sunday, Christmas Day, Good Friday or a day which is a bank holiday under the Banking and Financial Dealings Act 1971 in any part of the United Kingdom.

8–3122K   6. Maximum fee for complying with section 1(1) of the 2000 Act.   (1) Any fee to be charged under section 9 of the 2000 Act by a public authority to whom a request for information is made is not to exceed the maximum determined by the public authority in accordance with this regulation.

(2) Subject to paragraph (4), the maximum fee is a sum equivalent to the total costs the public authority reasonably expects to incur in relation to the request in—

(a) informing the person making the request whether it holds the information, and
(b) communicating the information to the person making the request.

(3) Costs which may be taken into account by a public authority for the purposes of this regulation include, but are not limited to, the costs of—

(a) complying with any obligation under section 11(1) of the 2000 Act as to the means or form of communicating the information,

(b) reproducing any document containing the information, and

(c) postage and other forms of transmitting the information.

(4) But a public authority may not take into account for the purposes of this regulation any costs which are attributable to the time which persons undertaking activities mentioned in paragraph (2) on behalf of the authority are expected to spend on those activities.

8–3122L 7. Maximum fee for communication of information under section 13 of the 2000 Act.
(1) Any fee to be charged under section 13 of the 2000 Act by a public authority to whom a request for information is made is not to exceed the maximum determined by a public authority in accordance with this regulation.

(2) The maximum fee is a sum equivalent to the total of—

(a) the costs which the public authority may take into account under regulation 4 in relation to that request, and

(b) the costs it reasonably expects to incur in relation to the request in—

(i) informing the person making the request whether it holds the information, and

(ii) communicating the information to the person making the request.

(3) But a public authority is to disregard, for the purposes of paragraph(2)(a), any costs which it may take into account under regulation 4 solely by virtue of the provision made by regulation 5.

(4) Costs which may be taken into account by a public authority for the purposes of paragraph (2)(b) include, but are not limited to, the costs of—

(a) giving effect to any preference expressed by the person making the request as to the means or form of communicating the information,

(b) reproducing any document containing the information, and

(c) postage and other forms of transmitting the information.

(5) For the purposes of this regulation, the provision for the estimation of costs made by regulation 4(4) is to be taken to apply to the costs mentioned in paragraph (2)(b) as it does to the costs mentioned in regulation 4(3).

COAST PROTECTION

8–3123   The Coast Protection Act 1949 (12, 13 & 14 Geo 6, c 74), amended by the Territorial Sea Act 1987 Sch 1, contains the law relating to the protection of the coast of Great Britain against erosion and encroachment by the sea, and provides for the restriction and removal of works detrimental to navigation. Coast protection authorities are constituted. Offences: Excavating or removal of materials[1] (other than minerals more than 50 feet below the surface) on, under or forming part of any portion of the seashore[2] without licence (s 18); Obstructing authorised person in his powers of entry and inspection (s 25); Carrying out works so that obstruction or danger to navigation is caused (s 34 as amended by the Criminal Justice Act 1982, ss 35, 38 and 46)—*Penalty* on summary conviction: fine not exceeding **level 3** on the standard scale.

1. "Materials" includes minerals and growing seaweed, but does not include seaweed. "Minerals" includes coal and stone and any metallic or other mineral substance (s 49).
2. "Seashore" means the bed and shore of the sea and of every channel, creek, bay or estuary, and of every river so far up that river as the tide flows, and any cliff, bank, barrier, dune, beach, flat or other land adjacent to the shore (s 49).

COMMONS AND WASTE LANDS

8–3124   This title contains the following statutes—

Commons Act 1908
(8 Edw 7 c 44)

8–3125   1. Power of making regulations as to the turning out of entire animals on commons.
(1) The persons for the time being entitled to turn out animals on a common[1] at a meeting convened in manner provided by the Act may by resolution make, alter or revoke regulations for determining the times, if any, at which and the conditions under which entire animals, as specified, may be upon

the common; but no such regulations and no alteration or revocation thereof shall take effect unless and until they have been confirmed by the Secretary of State (*SUMMARISED*).

(2) The owner of any animal which is found on any common in contravention of a regulation made under this Act, and any person who obstructs any officer appointed under this Act in the execution or enforcement of a regulation, shall be liable on summary conviction to a fine not exceeding **level 1 on the standard scale**, or in the case of a continuing offence not exceeding **50p** for every day during which the offence continues.

(3)–(4) *Meetings for purposes of Act.*

(5) If any question arises as to whether a resolution has been passed by the required majority, the question shall be settled by the Board of Agriculture and Fisheries[2], whose decision shall be final for the purposes of this Act, but such decision shall not otherwise affect or prejudice any right or claim in respect of the common.

(6) No regulation approved by the Board of Agriculture and Fisheries shall be questioned on the ground of informality, and the Documentary Evidence Acts 1868 to 1895, shall apply to regulations so approved as if they were regulations issued by the Board.

(7) For the purposes of this Act two or more adjoining commons may, by order of the Board of Agriculture and Fisheries, be declared to be one common, and shall be treated as such accordingly.

(8) This Act shall apply to a common[1] notwithstanding that the soil of the common is vested in His Majesty by right of His Crown or His Duchy of Lancaster or forms part of the possessions of the Duchy of Cornwall, but shall not apply to the New Forest or to any common in respect of which the conservators or other body appointed by or under any Act of Parliament to regulate the common have powers of making byelaws in respect of matters for which regulations may be made under this Act.

(9) In this Act the expression "animals" means horses, asses, cattle, sheep, goats and swine, and the expression "common" includes any commonable land.

[Commons Act 1908, s 1, as amended by the Justices of the Peace Act 1949, s 46 and Sch 7, Criminal Justice Act 1967, Sch 3, Criminal Justice Act 1982, ss 38 and 46, the Local Government Act 1985, Sch 8 and the Local Government (Wales) Act 1994, Sch 16.]

---

1. Proof that land is common land may depend upon registration thereof in accordance with the Commons Registration Act 1965 (1965, c 64).

2. Now the Secretary of State (Board of Agriculture and Fisheries Act 1903, s 10, the Ministry of Agriculture and Fisheries Act 1919, s 1, and the Secretary of State for the Environment Order 1970, SI 1970/1681). Functions of the Minister, so far as exercisable in relation to Wales, have been transferred to the National Assembly for Wales, by the National Assembly for Wales (Transfer of Functions) Order 1999, SI 1999/672, art 2, Sch 1.

8–3126   2. *Application of Act to Dartmoor.*

Law of Property Act 1925
(15 & 16 Geo 5 c 20)

8–3127   **193. Rights of the public over common and waste lands**[1].   (1) Members of the public shall, subject as hereinafter provided, have rights of access for air and exercise[2] to any land which is a metropolitan common within the meaning of the Metropolitan Commons Acts 1866 to 1898, or manorial waste, or a common, which is wholly or partly situated within a borough or urban district, and to any land which at the commencement of this Act is subject to rights of common and to which this section may be applied:

Provided that—

(a) such rights of access shall be subject to any Act, scheme, or provisional order for the regulation of the land, and to any byelaw, regulation or order made thereunder or under any other statutory authority; and

(b) the Minister[3] shall, on the application of any person entitled as lord of the manor or otherwise to the soil of the land, or any commonable rights, impose such limitations on and conditions as to the exercise of the rights which, in the opinion of the Minister, are necessary or desirable; and

(c) such rights of access shall not include any right to draw or drive upon the land a carriage, cart, caravan, truck, or other vehicle, or to camp or light any fire thereon; and

(d) the rights of access shall cease to apply when the commonable rights are extinguished under any statutory provision or if the council for the county or metropolitan district in which the land is situated by resolution assent to its exclusion from the operation of this section, and the resolution is approved by the Minister[2] (*summarised*).

(2) The lord of the manor or other person entitled to the soil of any land subject to rights of common may by deed, revocable or irrevocable, declare that this section shall apply to the land, and upon such deed being deposited with the Minister the land shall, so long as the deed remains operative, be land to which this section applies.*

(3) Where limitations or conditions are imposed by the Minister under this section, they shall be published by such person and in such manner as the Minister may direct.

(4) Any person who, without lawful authority, draws or drives upon any land to which this section applies any carriage, cart, caravan, truck, or other vehicle, or camps or lights any fire thereon, or who fails to observe any limitation or condition imposed by the Minister under this section in respect of any such land, shall be liable on summary conviction to a fine not exceeding **level 1** on the standard scale for each offence[4].

(5) Nothing in this section shall prejudice or affect the right of any person to get and remove mines or minerals or to let down the surface of the manorial waste or common.

(6) This section does not apply to any common or manorial waste which is for the time being held for Naval, Military or Air Force purposes and in respect of which rights of common have been extinguished or cannot be exercised.

[Law of Property Act 1925, s 193, as amended by the Criminal Justice Act 1967, Sch 3, the Local Government Act 1972, ss 189 and 272 and Sch 30, the Criminal Justice Act 1982, ss 38 and 46, the Local Government Act 1985, Sch 8 and the Local Government (Wales) Act 1994, Sch 16.]

---

*Repealed by the Countryside and Rights of Way Act 2000, Sch 16. Inforce in reltion to Wales 21 June 2004, in England to be appointed.
1. This section binds the Crown (s 208(3)).
2. Rights of access to commons are not confined to access on foot but extend to access on horseback (*R v Secretary of State for the Environment, ex p Billson* [1998] 2 All ER 587, DC.
3. Ie the Minister of Agriculture, Fisheries and Food (s 205 (xv)); now the Secretary of State and the Secretary of State for Wales (see the Secretary of State for the Environment Order 1970, SI 1970/1681).
4. See also Road Traffic Act 1988, s 34, post, prohibiting the driving of motor vehicles on any common land or moor land.

COMPANIES

8–3128   This title contains the following statutes—

This title contains the following statutory instrument—

8–3128A   Companies Acts: The law relating to companies and business names, previously contained in the Companies Acts 1948 to 1983, was consolidated by the Companies Act 1985, the Business Names Act 1985, the Company Securities (Insider Dealing) Act 1985 and the Companies Consolidation (Consequential Provisions) Act 1985. The latter Act made provision for transitional matters and savings, repeals and consequential amendments of other Acts. In particular, reference should be made to s 31 of the Companies Consolidation (Consequential Provisions) Act 1985, post, which made provision as to continuity of law, including transitional provisions relating to the prosecution of offences. These consolidation Acts came into force on the 1st July 1985.

The Companies Act 1985 contains over two hundred offences and it is not practicable in a Manual of this kind to set out fully all the penal provisions of the Act. However, we have included in this title sections of the Act containing offences which experience has shown are most likely to be the subject of prosecutions, together with procedural and evidential provisions relevant to criminal trials. The punishment of offences under the Companies Act 1985 is provided for by Schedule 24 which is printed in an abridged form so as to correspond to the substantive provisions of the Act contained in the Manual. The powers of courts to make disqualification orders against directors, including disqualification on summary conviction, have been further consolidated by the Company Directors Disqualification Act 1986, relevant provisions of which appear under this title.

The Companies Act 1985 has been substantially amended by the Companies Act 1989. Part II of that Act (see para **8–3894**, et seq, post) also makes new provision with respect to the persons eligible for appointment as company auditors. The Company Securities (Insider Dealing) Act 1985 was repealed by the Criminal Justice Act 1993, Sch 6, and the law relating to insider dealing is now contained in Part V of the Criminal Justice Act 1993 (see para **8–3915**, et seq, post).

European Communities Act 1972: regulations.   Within the scope of the title Companies there falls the subject matter of regulations made under the very wide enabling powers provided in section 2(2) of the European Communities Act 1972. The following regulations create offences:

Insurance Companies (Legal Expense Insurance) Regulations 1990, SI 1990/1159;
Insurance Companies (Credit Insurance) Regulations 1990, SI 1990/1181;

Companies Act 1985[1]

(1985 c 6)

PART I[2]
FORMATION AND REGISTRATION OF COMPANIES; JURIDICAL STATUS AND MEMBERSHIP

CHAPTER I
COMPANY FORMATION

Memorandum of association

8–3300   1. Mode of forming incorporated company.   (1) Any two or more persons associated for a lawful purpose may, by subscribing their names to a memorandum of association and otherwise complying with the requirements of this Act in respect of registration, form an incorporated company, with or without limited liability.

(2) A company so formed may be either—

(a)   a company having the liability of its members limited by the memorandum to the amount, if any, unpaid on the shares respectively held by them ("a company limited by shares");

(b)   a company having the liability of its members limited by the memorandum to such amount as the members may respectively thereby undertake to contribute to the assets of the company in the event of its being wound up ("a company limited by guarantee"); or

(c)   a company not having any limit on the liability of its members ("an unlimited company").

(3) A "public company" is a company limited by shares or limited by guarantee and having a share capital, being a company—

(a)   the memorandum of which states that it is to be a public company, and

(b)   in relation to which the provisions of this Act or the former Companies Acts as to the registration or re-registration of a company as a public company have been complied with on or after 22nd December 1980;

and a "private company" is a company that is not a public company.

(4) With effect from 22nd December 1980, a company cannot be formed as, or become, a company limited by guarantee with a share capital.
[Companies Act 1985, s 1.]

---

1. This Act consolidates the greater part of the law relating to companies previously contained in the Companies Acts 1948–1983. See also the Business Names Act 1985 and the Companies Consolidation (Consequential Provisions) Act 1985, post.

The Companies Act 1985 creates many offences and only those offences which are more often likely to be the subject of prosecutions are included in this Manual. For mode of trial and punishment of offences under this Act, see s 730 and Sch 24, post. See also the preliminary note to this title in para **8–3128**, ante.

2. Part I contains: Chapter I, ss 1–24, Chapter II, ss 25–34, and Chapter III, ss 35–42.

8–3301   2. Requirements with respect to memorandum.   The memorandum of every company must state—(a) the name of the company; (b) whether the registered office of the company is to be situated in England and Wales, or in Scotland; (c) the objects of the company. The memorandum of a company limited by shares or by guarantee must also state that the liability of its members is limited. A company may not alter the conditions contained in its memorandum except in the cases, in the mode and to the extent, for which express provision is made by the Act.
[Companies Act 1985, s 2—summarised.]

CHAPTER II
COMPANY NAMES

8–3302   25. Name as stated in memorandum.   (1) The name of a public company must end with the words "public limited company" or, if the memorandum states that the company's registered office is to be situated in Wales, those words or their equivalent in Welsh ("cwmni cyfyngedig cyhoeddus"); and those words or that equivalent may not be preceded by the word "limited" or its equivalent in Welsh ("cyfyngedig").

(2) In the case of a company limited by shares or by guarantee (not being a public company), the name must have "limited" as its last word, except that—

(a)   this is subject to section 30 (exempting, in certain circumstances, a company from the requirement to have "limited" as part of the name), and

(b)   if the company is to be registered with a memorandum stating that its registered office is to be situated in Wales, the name may have "cyfyngedig" as its last word.
[Companies Act 1985, s 25.]

8–3303   26–27. *Prohibition on registration of certain names; alternatives of statutory designations.*

8–3304   28. Change of name.   (1) A company may by special resolution change its name (but subject to section 31 in the case of a company which has received a direction under subsection (2) of that section from the Secretary of State).

(2) Where a company has been registered by a name which—

(a) is the same as or, in the opinion of the Secretary of State, too like a name appearing at the time of the registration in the registrar's index of company names, or

(b) is the same as or, in the opinion of the Secretary of State, too like a name which should have appeared in that index at that time,

the Secretary of State may within 12 months of that time, in writing, direct the company to change its name within such period as he may specify.

Section 26(3) applies in determining under this subsection whether a name is the same as or too like another.

(3) If it appears to the Secretary of State that misleading information has been given for the purpose of a company's registration with a particular name, or that undertakings or assurances have been given for that purpose and have not been fulfilled, he may within 5 years of the date of its registration with that name in writing direct the company to change its name within such period as he may specify.

(4) Where a direction has been given under subsection (2) or (3), the Secretary of State may by a further direction in writing extend the period within which the company is to change its name, at any time before the end of that period.

(5) A company which fails to comply with a direction under this section, and any officer of it who is in default, is liable[1] to a fine and, for continued contravention, to a daily default fine.

(6) Where a company changes its name under this section, the registrar of companies shall (subject to section 26) enter the new name on the register in place of the former name, and shall issue a certificate of incorporation altered to meet the circumstances of the case; and the change of name has effect from the date on which the altered certificate is issued.

(7) A change of name by a company under this section does not affect any rights or obligations of the company or render defective any legal proceedings by or against it; and any legal proceedings that might have been continued or commenced against it by its former name may be continued or commenced against it by its new name.

[Companies Act 1985, s 28.]

---

1. For mode of trial and punishment, see Sch 24, post.

8–3305   29. Regulations about names.   *Power of the Secretary of State by regulations to specify words or expressions for which approval is required.*

8–3306   30. Exemption from requirement of "limited" as part of the name.   (1) Certain companies are exempt from requirements of this Act relating to the use of "limited" as part of the company name.

(2) A private company limited by guarantee is exempt from those requirements, and so too is a company which on 25th February 1982 was a private company limited by shares with a name which, by virtue of a licence under section 19 of the Companies Act 1948, did not include "limited"; but in either case the company must, to have the exemption, comply with the requirements of the following subsection.

(3) Those requirements are that—

(a) the objects of the company are (or, in the case of a company about to be registered, are to be) the promotion of commerce, art, science, education, religion, charity or any profession, and anything incidental or conducive to any of those objects; and

(b) the company's memorandum or articles—

(i) require its profits (if any) or other income to be applied in promoting its objects,

(ii) prohibit the payment of dividends to its members, and

(iii) require all the assets which would otherwise be available to its members generally to be transferred on its winding up either to another body with objects similar to its own or to another body the objects of which are the promotion of charity and anything incidental or conducive thereto (whether or not the body is a member of the company).

(4) Subject to subsection (5A), a statutory declaration that a company complies with the requirements of sub- section (3) may be delivered to the registrar of companies, who may accept the declaration as sufficient evidence of the matters stated in it.

(5) The statutory declaration must be in the prescribed form and be made—

(a) in the case of a company to be formed, by a solicitor engaged in its formation or by a person named as director or secretary in the statement delivered under section 10(2);

(b) in the case of a company to be registered in pursuance of section 680, by two or more directors or other principal officers of the company; and

(c) in the case of a company proposing to change its name so that it ceases to have the word "limited" as part of its name, by a director or secretary of the company.

(5A) In place of the statutory declaration referred to in subsection (4), there may be delivered to the registrar of companies using electronic communications a statement made by a person falling within the applicable paragraph of subsection (5) stating that the company complies with the requirements of subsection (3); and the registrar may accept such a statement as sufficient evidence of the matters stated in it.

(5B) The registrar may refuse to register a company by a name which does not include the word "limited" unless a statutory declaration under subsection (4) or statement under subsection (5A) has been delivered to him.

(5C) Any person who makes a false statement under subsection (5A) which he knows to be false or does not believe to be true is liable to imprisonment or a fine, or both.

(6) References in this section to the word "limited" include (in an appropriate case) its Welsh equivalent ("cyfyngedig"), and the appropriate alternative ("ltd" or "cyf", as the case may be).

(7) A company which under this section is exempt from requirements relating to the use of "limited" and does not include that word as part of its name, is also exempt from the requirements of this Act relating to the publication of its name and the sending of lists of members to the registrar of companies.

[Companies Act 1985, s 30 as amended by SI 2000/3373 and the Companies (Audit, Investigations and Community Enterprise) Act 2004, Sch 6.]

8–3307 31. Provisions applying to company exempt under s 30.   (1) A company which is exempt under section 30 and whose name does not include "limited" shall not alter its memorandum or articles of association so that it ceases to comply with the requirements of subsection (3) of that section.

(2) If it appears to the Secretary of State that such a company—

(a) has carried on any business other than the promotion of any of the objects mentioned in that subsection, or

(b) has applied any of its profits or other income otherwise than in promoting such objects, or

(c) has paid a dividend to any of its members,

he may, in writing, direct the company to change its name by resolution of the directors within such period as may be specified in the direction, so that its name ends with "limited".

A resolution passed by the directors in compliance with a direction under this subsection is subject to section 380 of this Act (copy to be forwarded to the registrar of companies within 15 days).

(3) A company which has received a direction under subsection (2) shall not thereafter be registered by a name which does not include "limited", without the approval of the Secretary of State.

(4) References in this section to the word "limited" include (in an appropriate case) its Welsh equivalent ("cyfyngedig"), and the appropriate alternative ("ltd" or "cyf", as the case may be).

(5) A company which contravenes subsection (1), and any officer of it who is in default, is liable[1] to a fine and, for continued contravention, to a daily default fine.

(6) A company which fails to comply with a direction by the Secretary of State under subsection (2), and any officer of the company who is in default, is liable[1] to a fine and, for continued contravention, to a daily default fine.

[Companies Act 1985, s 31.]

---

1. For mode of trial and punishment, see Sch 24, post.

8–3308 32. Power to require company to abandon misleading name.   (1) If in the Secretary of State's opinion the name by which a company is registered gives so misleading an indication of the nature of its activities as to be likely to cause harm to the public, he may direct it to change its name.

(2) The direction must, if not duly made the subject of an application to the court under the following subsection, be complied with within a period of 6 weeks from the date of the direction or such longer period as the Secretary of State may think fit to allow.

(3) The company may, within a period of 3 weeks from the date of the direction, apply to the court to set it aside; and the court may set the direction aside or confirm it and, if it confirms the direction, shall specify a period within which it must be complied with.

(4) If a company makes default in complying with a direction under this section, it is liable[1] to a fine and, for continued contravention, to a daily default fine.

(5) Where a company changes its name under this section, the registrar shall (subject to section 26) enter the new name on the register in place of the former name, and shall issue a certificate of incorporation altered to meet the circumstances of the case; and the change of name has effect from the date on which the altered certificate is issued.

(6) A change of name by a company under this section does not affect any of the rights or obligations of the company, or render defective any legal proceedings by or against it; and any legal proceedings that might have been continued or commenced against it by its former name may be continued or commenced against it by its new name.

[Companies Act 1985, s 32.]

1. For mode of trial and punishment, see Sch 24, post.

8–3309 33. Prohibition on trading under misleading name. (1) A person who is not a public company is guilty of an offence if he carries on any trade, profession or business under a name which includes, as its last part, the words "public limited company" or their equivalent in Welsh ("cwmni cyfyngedig cyhoeddus"); and a community interest company which is not a public company is guilty of an offence if it does so under a name which includes, as its last part, the words "cwmni buddiant cymunedol cyhoeddus cyfyngedig.

(2) A public company is guilty of an offence if, in circumstances in which the fact that it is a public company is likely to be material to any person, it uses a name which may reasonably be expected to give the impression that it is a private company.

(3) A person guilty of an offence under subsection (1) or (2) and, if that person is a company, any officer of the company who is in default, is liable[1] to a fine and, for continued contravention, to a daily default fine.

[Companies Act 1985, s 33 as amended by the Companies (Audit, Investigations and Community Enterprise) Act 2004, Sch 6.]

1. For mode of trial and punishment, see Sch 24, post.

8–3310 34. Penalty for improper use of "limited" or "cyfyngedig". If any person trades or carries on business under a name or title of which "limited" or "cyfyngedig", or any contraction or imitation of either of those words, is the last word, that person, unless duly incorporated with limited liability, is liable[1] to a fine and, for continued contravention, to a daily default fine.

[Companies Act 1985, s 34.]

1. For mode of trial and punishment, see Sch 24, post.

PART VII[1]
ACCOUNTS AND AUDIT

CHAPTER I
PROVISIONS APPLYING TO COMPANIES GENERALLY

Accounting records

8–3311 221. Duty to keep accounting records. (1) Every company shall keep accounting records[2] which are sufficient to show and explain the company's transactions and are such as to—

(*a*) disclose with reasonable accuracy, at any time, the financial position of the company at that time, and

(*b*) enable the directors to ensure that any accounts required to be prepared under this part comply with the requirements of this Act (and, where applicable, of Article 4 of the IAS Regulation).

(2) The accounting records shall in particular contain—

(*a*) entries from day to day of all sums of money received and expended by the company, and the matters in respect of which the receipt and expenditure takes place, and

(*b*) a record of assets and liabilities of the company.

(3) If the company's business involves dealing in goods, the accounting records shall contain—

(*a*) statements of stock held by the company at the end of each financial year of the company,

(*b*) all statements of stocktakings from which any such statement of stock as is mentioned in paragraph (*a*) has been or is to be prepared, and

(*c*) except in the case of goods sold by way of ordinary retail trade, statements of all goods sold and purchased, showing the goods and the buyers and sellers in sufficient detail to enable all these to be identified.

(4) A parent company which has a subsidiary undertaking in relation to which the above requirements do not apply shall take reasonable steps to secure that the undertaking keeps such accounting records as to enable the directors of the parent company to ensure that any accounts required to be prepared under this part comply with the requirements of this Act (and, where applicable, of Article 4 of the IAS Regulation).

(5) If a company fails to comply with any provision of this section, every officer of the company who is in default is guilty of an offence unless he shows that he acted honestly and that in the circumstances in which the company's business was carried on the default was excusable.

(6) A person guilty of an offence under this section is liable[3] to imprisonment or a fine or both.★

[Companies Act 1985, s 221, as substituted by the Companies Act 1989, s 2 and amended by SI 2004/2947.]

★**Section reproduced as amended has effect in relation to companies' financial years beginning on or after 1 January 2005.**

1. Part VII contains Chapter I, ss 221–245C, Chapter II, ss 246–255D, and Chapter III, ss 256–262A. See also the Partnerships and Unlimited Companies (Accounts) Regulations 1993, SI 1993/1820 implementing EC Council Directive

90/605/EEC imposing requirements to prepare accounts and a directors' report and obtain an auditors' report on such accounts in respect of partnerships, limited partnerships and unlimited companies all of whose members having unlimited liability are limited companies.

2. "It is not enough that there should be books with entries in them which would require a prolonged examination by a skilled accountant in order to ascertain the result of them. That is not keeping proper books. The books shall be properly kept and balanced from time to time so that at any moment the real state of the trader's affairs may at once appear"; per Lord Esher MR in *ex p Reed and Bowen* [1886] 17 QBD 244; followed in *R v Garvey* [2001] EWCA Crim 1365.

3. For mode of trial and punishment, see Sch 24, post.

8–3312 222. Where and for how long records to be kept. (1) A company's accounting records shall be kept at its registered office or such other place as the directors think fit, and shall at all times be open to inspection by the company's officers.

(2) If accounting records are kept at a place outside Great Britain, accounts and returns with respect to the business dealt with in the accounting records so kept shall be sent to, and kept at, a place in Great Britain, and shall at all times be open to such inspection.

(3) The accounts and returns to be sent to Great Britain shall be such as to—

(a) disclose with reasonable accuracy the financial position of the business in question at intervals of not more than six months, and

(b) enable the directors to ensure that the accounts required to be prepared under this part comply with the requirements of this Act (and, where applicable, of Article 4 of the IAS Regulation).

(4) If a company fails to comply with any provision of subsections (1) to (3), every officer of the company who is in default is guilty of an offence, and liable to imprisonment or a fine or both, unless he shows that he acted honestly and that in the circumstances in which the company's business was carried on the default was excusable.

(5) Accounting records which a company is required by section 221 to keep shall be preserved by it—

(a) in the case of a private company, for three years from the date on which they are made, and

(b) in the case of a public company, for six years from the date on which they are made.

This is subject to any provision contained in rules made under section 411 of the Insolvency Act 1986 (company insolvency rules).

(6) An officer of a company is guilty of an offence, and liable[1] to imprisonment or a fine or both, if he fails to take all reasonable steps for securing compliance by the company with subsection (5) or intentionally causes any default by the company under that subsection.*

[Companies Act 1985, s 222, as substituted by the Companies Act 1989, s 2 and amended by SI 2004/2947.]

---

*Section reproduced as amended has effect in relation to companies' financial years beginning on or after 1 January 2005.

1. For mode of trial and punishment, see Sch 24, post.

8–3313 223–232. *A company's financial year and accounting reference periods; Annual accounts.*

Approval and signing of accounts

8–3314 233. Approval and signing of accounts. (1) A company's annual accounts shall be approved by the board of directors and signed on behalf of the board by a director of the company.

(2) The signature shall be on the company's balance sheet.

(3) Every copy of the balance sheet which is laid before the company in general meeting, or which is otherwise circulated, published or issued, shall state the name of the person who signed the balance sheet on behalf of the board.

(4) The copy of the company's balance sheet which is delivered to the registrar shall be signed on behalf of the board by a director of the company.

(5) If annual accounts are approved which do not comply with the requirements of this Act (or, where applicable, of Article 4 of the IAS Regulation), every director of the company who is party to their approval and who knows that they do not comply or is reckless as to whether they comply is guilty of an offence and liable[1] to a fine.

For this purpose every director of the company at the time the accounts are approved shall be taken to be a party to their approval unless he shows that he took all reasonable steps to prevent their being approved.

(6) If a copy of the balance sheet—

(a) is laid before the company, or otherwise circulated, published or issued, without the balance sheet having been signed as required by this section or without the required statement of the signatory's name being included, or

(b) is delivered to the registrar without being signed as required by this section,

the company and every officer of it who is in default is guilty of an offence and liable[2] to a fine.*

[Companies Act 1985, s 233, as substituted by the Companies Act 1989, s 7 and amended by SI 2004/2947.]

---

*Section reproduced as amended has effect in relation to companies' financial years beginning on or after 1 January 2005.

1. For mode of trial and punishment, see Sch 24, post.

Directors' report

8–3315   234. Duty to prepare directors' report.   (1) The directors of a company shall for each financial year prepare a report (a "directors' report") complying with the general requirements of section 234ZZA and containing—

(a)   the business review specified in section 234ZZB, and

(b)   if section 234ZA applies to the report, the statement as to disclosure of information to auditors required by that section.

(2) For a financial year in which—

(a)   the company is a parent company, and

(b)   the directors of the company prepare group accounts,

the directors' report must be a consolidated report (a "group directors' report") relating, to the extent specified in the following provisions of this Part, to the company and its subsidiary undertakings included in the consolidation.

(3) A group directors' report may, where appropriate, give greater emphasis to the matters that are significant to the company and its subsidiary undertakings included in the consolidation, taken as a whole.

(4) *Repealed.*

(5) If a directors' report does not comply with the provisions of this Part relating to the preparation and contents of the report, every director of the company who—

(a)   knew that it did not comply or was reckless as to whether it complied, and

(b)   failed to take all reasonable steps to secure compliance with the provision in question,

is guilty of an offence and liable[1] to a fine.

[Companies Act 1985, s 234, as substituted by SI 2005/1011 and amended by SI 2005/3442.]

---

1. For mode of trial and punishment, see Sch 24, post.

8–3315ZZA   234ZZA. Directors' report: general requirements.   (1) The directors' report for a financial year must state—

(a)   the names of the persons who, at any time during the financial year, were directors of the company,

(b)   the principal activities of the company in the course of the year, and

(c)   the amount (if any) that the directors recommend should be paid by way of dividend.

(2) In relation to a group directors' report subsection (1)(b) has effect as if the reference to the company was a reference to the company and its subsidiary undertakings included in the consolidation.

(3) The report must also comply with Schedule 7 as regards the disclosure of the matters mentioned there.

(4) In Schedule 7[1]—

Part 1 relates to matters of a general nature, including changes in asset values, directors' shareholdings and other interests and contributions for political and charitable purposes;

Part 2 relates to the acquisition by a company of its own shares or a charge on them;

Part 3 relates to the employment, training and advancement of disabled persons;

Part 5 relates to the involvement of employees in the affairs, policy and performance of the company;

Part 6 relates to the company's policy and practice on the payment of creditors.

[Companies Act 1985, s 234ZZA, inserted by SI 2005/1011.]

---

1. Schedule 7 is not reproduced in this work.

8–3315ZZB   234ZZB. Directors' report: business review.   (1) The directors' report for a financial year must contain—

(a)   a fair review of the business of the company, and

(b)   a description of the principal risks and uncertainties facing the company.

(2) The review required is a balanced and comprehensive analysis of—

(a)   the development and performance of the business of the company during the financial year, and

(b)   the position of the company at the end of that year,

consistent with the size and complexity of the business.

(3) The review must, to the extent necessary for an understanding of the development, performance or position of the business of the company, include—

(a)   analysis using financial key performance indicators, and

(b) where appropriate, analysis using other key performance indicators, including information relating to environmental matters and employee matters.

(4) The review must, where appropriate, include references to, and additional explanations of, amounts included in the annual accounts of the company.

(5) In this section, "key performance indicators" means factors by reference to which the development, performance or position of the business of the company can be measured effectively.

(6) In relation to a group directors' report this section has effect as if the references to the company were references to the company and its subsidiary undertakings included in the consolidation.

[Companies Act 1985, s 234ZZB, inserted by SI 2005/1011.]

8–3315A   234ZA. Statement as to disclosure of information to auditors.   (1) This section applies to a directors' report unless the directors have taken advantage of the exemption conferred by section 249A(1) or 249AA(1).

(2) The report must contain a statement to the effect that, in the case of each of the persons who are directors at the time when the report is approved under section 234A, the following applies—

(a) so far as the director is aware, there is no relevant audit information of which the company's auditors are unaware, and

(b) he has taken all the steps that he ought to have taken as a director in order to make himself aware of any relevant audit information and to establish that the company's auditors are aware of that information.

(3) In subsection (2) "relevant audit information" means information needed by the company's auditors in connection with preparing their report.

(4) For the purposes of subsection (2) a director has taken all the steps that he ought to have taken as a director in order to do the things mentioned in paragraph (b) of that subsection if he has—

(a) made such enquiries of his fellow directors and of the company's auditors for that purpose, and

(b) taken such other steps (if any) for that purpose,

as were required by his duty as a director of the company to exercise due care, skill and diligence.

(5) In determining for the purposes of subsection (2) the extent of that duty in the case of a particular director, the following considerations (in particular) are relevant—

(a) the knowledge, skill and experience that may reasonably be expected of a person carrying out the same functions as are carried out by the director in relation to the company, and

(b) (so far as they exceed what may reasonably be so expected) the knowledge, skill and experience that the director in fact has.

(6) Where a directors' report containing the statement required by subsection (2) is approved under section 234A but the statement is false, every director of the company who—

(a) knew that the statement was false, or was reckless as to whether it was false, and

(b) failed to take reasonable steps to prevent the report from being approved,

is guilty of an offence and liable to imprisonment or a fine, or both.

[Companies Act 1985, s 234ZA, as inserted by the Companies (Audit, Investigations and Community Enterprise) Act 2004, s 9.]

8–3316   234A. Approval and signing of directors' report.   (1) The directors' report shall be approved by the board of directors and signed on behalf of the board by a director or the secretary of the company.

(2) Every copy of the directors' report which is laid before the company in general meeting, or which is otherwise circulated, published or issued, shall state the name of the person who signed it on behalf of the board.

(3) The copy of the directors' report which is delivered to the registrar shall be signed on behalf of the board by a director or the secretary of the company.

(4) If a copy of the directors' report—

(a) is laid before the company, or otherwise circulated, published or issued, without the report having been signed as required by this section or without the required statement of the signatory's name being included, or

(b) is delivered to the registrar without being signed as required by this section,

the company and every officer of it who is in default is guilty of an offence and liable to a fine.

[Companies Act 1985, s 234A, as substituted by the Companies Act 1989, s 8.]

---

1. For mode of trial and punishment, see Sch 24, post.

Quoted companies: directors' remuneration report

8–3316A   234B. Duty to prepare directors' remuneration report.   (1) The directors of a quoted company shall for each financial year prepare a directors' remuneration report which shall contain the information specified in Schedule 7A and comply with any requirement of that Schedule as to how information is to be set out in the report.

(2) In Schedule 7A—

Part 1 is introductory,

Part 2 relates to information about remuneration committees, performance related remuneration and liabilities in respect of directors' contracts,

Part 3 relates to detailed information about directors' remuneration (information included under Part 3 is required to be reported on by the auditors, see section 235), and

Part 4 contains interpretative and supplementary provisions.

(3) In the case of any failure to comply with the provisions of this Part as to the preparation of a directors' remuneration report and the contents of the report, every person who was a director of the quoted company immediately before the end of the period for laying and delivering accounts and reports for the financial year in question is guilty of an offence and liable to a fine.

(4) In proceedings against a person for an offence under subsection (3) it is a defence for him to prove that he took all reasonable steps for securing compliance with the requirements in question.

(5) It is the duty of any director of a company, and any person who has at any time in the preceding five years been a director of the company, to give notice to the company of such matters relating to himself as may be necessary for the purposes of Parts 2 and 3 of Schedule 7A.

(6) A person who makes default in complying with subsection (5) commits an offence and is liable to a fine.*

[Companies Act 1985, s 234B, as inserted by SI 2002/1986, reg 3.]

---

*This section has effect in relation to companies' financial years ending on or after 31 December 2002.

8–3316B   234C. Approval and signing of directors' remuneration report.   (1) The directors' remuneration report shall be approved by the board of directors and signed on behalf of the board by a director or the secretary of the company.

(2) Every copy of the directors' remuneration report which is laid before the company in general meeting, or which is otherwise circulated, published or issued, shall state the name of the person who signed it on behalf of the board.

(3) The copy of the directors' remuneration report which is delivered to the registrar shall be signed on behalf of the board by a director or the secretary of the company.

(4) If a copy of the directors' remuneration report—

(a) is laid before the company, or otherwise circulated, published or issued, without the report having been signed as required by this section or without the required statement of the signatory's name being included, or

(b) is delivered to the registrar without being signed as required by this section,

the company and every officer of it who is in default is guilty of an offence and liable to a fine.

[Companies Act 1985, s 234C, as inserted by SI 2002/1986, reg 3.]

---

*This section has effect in relation to companies' financial years ending on or after 31 December 2002.

Auditors' report

8–3317   235. Auditors' report.   (1) A company's auditors shall make a report to the company's members on all annual accounts of the company of which copies are to be laid before the company in general meeting during their tenure of office.

(1A) The auditors' report must include—

(a) an introduction identifying the annual accounts that are the subject of the audit and the financial reporting framework that has been applied in their preparation;

(b) a description of the scope of the audit identifying the auditing standards in accordance with which the audit was conducted.

(1B) The report must state clearly whether in the auditors' opinion the annual accounts have been properly prepared in accordance with the requirements of this Act (and, where applicable, Article 4 of the IAS Regulation).

(2) The report must state in particular whether the annual accounts give a true and fair view, in accordance with the relevant financial reporting framework—

(a) in the case of an individual balance sheet, of the state of affairs of the company as at the end of the financial year,

(b) in the case of an individual profit and loss account, of the profit or loss of the company for the financial year,

(c) in the case of group accounts, of the state of affairs as at the end of the financial year and of the profit or loss for the financial year, of the undertakings included in the consolidation as a whole, so far as concerns members of the company.

(2A) The auditors' report—

(a) must be either unqualified or qualified, and
(b) must include a reference to any matters to which the auditors wish to draw attention by way of emphasis without qualifying the report.★

(3) The auditors shall consider whether the information given in the directors' report for the financial year for which the annual accounts are prepared is consistent with those accounts; and if they are of opinion that it is not they shall state that fact in their report.

(4) If a directors' remuneration report is prepared for the financial year for which the annual accounts are prepared the auditors shall in their report

(a) report to the company's members on the auditable part of the directors' remuneration report, and
(b) state whether in their opinion that part of the directors' remuneration report has been properly prepared in accordance with this Act.★

(5) For the purposes of this Part, "the auditable part" of a directors' remuneration report is the part containing the information required by Part 3 of Schedule 7A.★★
[Companies Act 1985, s 235, as substituted by the Companies Act 1989, s 9 and amended by SI 2002/1986 and SI 2004/2947.]

★**Sub-sections (1A), (1B), (2), (2A) substituted, for sub-s (2) as originally enacted, by SI 2004/2947 with effect in relation to companies' financial years beginning on or after 1 January 2005.**
★★**Sub-sections (4) and (5) inserted by SI 2002/1986, reg 4 and have effect in relation to companies' financial years ending on or after 31 December 2002.**

8–3318   236. Signature of auditors' report.   (1) The auditors' report shall state the names of the auditors and be signed and dated by them.
(2) Every copy of the auditors' report which is laid before the company in general meeting, or which is otherwise circulated, published or issued, shall state the names of the auditors.
(3) The copy of the auditors' report which is delivered to the registrar shall state the names of the auditors and be signed by them.
(4) If a copy of the auditors' report—

(a) is laid before the company, or otherwise circulated, published or issued, without the required statement of the auditors' names, or
(b) is delivered to the registrar without the required statement of the auditors' names or without being signed as required by this section,

the company and every officer of it who is in default is guilty of an offence and liable[1] to a fine.
(5) References in this section to signature by the auditors are, where the office of auditor is held by a body corporate or partnership, to signature in the name of the body corporate or partnership by a person authorised to sign on its behalf.★
[Companies Act 1985, s 236, as substituted by the Companies Act 1989, s 9 and amended by SI 2004/2947.]

★**Section reproduced as amended has effect in relation to companies' financial years beginning on or after 1 January 2005.**
   1. For mode of trial and punishment, see Sch 24, post.

8–3319   237. *Duties of auditors.*

Publication of accounts and reports

8–3320   238. Persons entitled to receive copies of accounts and reports.   (1) A copy of each of the documents mentioned in subsection (1A) shall be sent to—

(a) every member of the company,
(b) every holder of the company's debentures, and
(c) every person who is entitled to receive notice of general meetings,

not less than 21 days before the date of the meeting at which copies of those documents are to be laid in accordance with section 241.
(1A) Those documents are—

(a) the company's annual accounts for the financial year,
(b) the directors' report for that financial year,
(c) (in the case of a quoted company) the directors' remuneration report for that financial year, and
(d) the auditors' report on those accounts or (in the case of a quoted company) on those accounts and the auditable part of the directors' remuneration report.

(2) Copies need not be sent—

(a) to a person who is not entitled to receive notices of general meetings and of whose address the company is unaware, or (*b*) to more than one of the joint holders of shares or debentures none of whom is entitled to receive such notices, or

(*c*) in the case of joint holders of shares or debentures some of whom are, and some not, entitled to receive such notices, to those who are not so entitled.

(3) In the case of a company not having a share capital, copies need not be sent to anyone who is not entitled to receive notices of general meetings of the company.

(4) If copies are sent less than 21 days before the date of the meeting, they shall, notwithstanding that fact, be deemed to have been duly sent if it is so agreed by all the members entitled to attend and vote at the meeting.

(4A) References in this section to sending to any person copies of copies of the documents mentioned in subsection (1A) include references to using electronic communications for sending copies of those documents to such address as may for the time being be notified to the company by that person for that purpose.

(4B) For the purposes of this section copies of those documents are also to be treated as sent to a person where—

(*a*) the company and that person have agreed to his having access to the documents on a web site (instead of their being sent to him);

(*b*) the documents are documents to which that agreement applies; and

(*c*) that person is notified, in a manner for the time being agreed for the purpose between him and the company, of—

(i) the publication of the documents on a web site;

(ii) the address of that web site; and

(iii) the place on that web site where the documents may be accessed, and how they may be accessed.

(4C) For the purposes of this section documents treated in accordance with subsection (4B) as sent to any person are to be treated as sent to him not less than 21 days before the date of a meeting if, and only if—

(*a*) the documents are published on the web site throughout a period beginning at least 21 days before the date of the meeting and ending with the conclusion of the meeting; and

(*b*) the notification given for the purposes of paragraph (c) of that subsection is given not less than 21 days before the date of the meeting.

(4D) Nothing in subsection (4C) shall invalidate the proceedings of a meeting where—

(*a*) any documents that are required to be published as mentioned in paragraph (*a*) of that subsection are published for a part, but not all, of the period mentioned in that paragraph; and

(*b*) the failure to publish those documents throughout that period is wholly attributable to circumstances which it would not be reasonable to have expected the company to prevent or avoid.

(4E) A company may, notwithstanding any provision to the contrary in its articles, take advantage of any of subsections (4A) to (4D).

(5) If default is made in complying with this section, the company and every officer of it who is in default is guilty of an offence and liable[1] to a fine.

(6) Where copies are sent out under this section over a period of days, references elsewhere in this Act to the day on which copies are sent out shall be construed as references to the last day of that period.

[Companies Act 1985, s 238, as substituted by the Companies Act 1989, s 10 and amended by SI 2000/3373 and SI 2002/1986.]

---

1. For mode of trial and punishment, see Sch 24, post.

8–3321 239. Right to demand copies of accounts and reports. (1) Any member of a company and any holder of a company's debentures is entitled to be furnished, on demand and without charge, with a copy of—

(*a*) the company's last annual accounts,

(*b*) the last directors' report,

(*c*) (in the case of a quoted company) the last directors' remuneration report, and

(*d*) the auditors' report on those accounts or (in the case of a quoted company) on those accounts and the auditable part of the directors' remuneration report for the financial year for which those accounts are prepared.*

(2) The entitlement under this section is to a single copy of those documents, but that is in addition to any copy to which a person may be entitled under section 238.

(2A) Any obligation by virtue of subsection (1) to furnish a person with a document may be complied with by using electronic communications for sending that document to such address as may for the time being be notified to the company by that person for that purpose.

(2B) A company may, notwithstanding any provision to the contrary in its articles, take advantage of subsection (2A).

(3) If a demand under this section is not complied with within seven days, the company and every officer of it who is in default is guilty of an offence and liable[1] to a fine and, for continued contravention, to a daily default fine.

(4) If in proceedings for such an offence the issue arises whether a person had already been furnished with a copy of the relevant document under this section, it is for the defendant to prove that he had.

[Companies Act 1985, s 239, as substituted by the Companies Act 1989, s 10 and amended by SI 2000/3373 and SI 2002/1986.]

---

*Sub-section (1) amended by SI 2002/1986 with effect in relation to companies' financial years ending on or after 31 December 2002.

1. For mode of trial and punishment, see Sch 24, post.

8–3322   240. Requirements in connection with publication of accounts.   (1) If a company publishes any of its statutory accounts, they must be accompanied by the relevant auditors' report under section 235 or, as the case may be, the relevant report made for the purposes of section 249A(2).

(2) A company which is required to prepare group accounts for a financial year shall not publish its statutory individual accounts for that year without also publishing with them its statutory group accounts.

(3) If a company publishes non-statutory accounts, it shall publish with them a statement indicating—

(a) that they are not the company's statutory accounts,
(b) whether statutory accounts dealing with any financial year with which the non-statutory accounts purport to deal have been delivered to the registrar,
(c) whether the company's auditors have made a report under section 235 on the statutory accounts for any such financial year and, if no such report has been made, whether the company's reporting accountant has made a report for the purposes of section 249A(2) on the statutory accounts for any such financial year,
(d) whether any such auditors' report—

  (i)   was qualified or unqualified, or included a reference to any matters to which the auditors drew attention by way of emphasis without qualifying the report, or
  (ii) contained a statement under section 237(2) or (3) (accounting records or returns inadequate, accounts not agreeing with records and returns or failure to obtain necessary information and explanations); and*

(e) whether any report made for the purposes of section 249A(2) was qualified;*

and it shall not publish with the non-statutory accounts any auditors' report under section 235 or any report made for the purposes of section 249A(2).

(4) For the purposes of this section a company shall be regarded as publishing a document if it publishes, issues or circulates it or otherwise makes it available for public inspection in a manner calculated to invite members of the public generally, or any class of members of the public, to read it.

(5) References in this section to a company's statutory accounts are to its individual or group accounts for a financial year as required to be delivered to the registrar under section 242; and references to the publication by a company of "non-statutory accounts" are to the publication of—

(a) any balance sheet or profit and loss account relating to, or purporting to deal with, a financial year of the company, or
(b) an account in any form purporting to be a balance sheet or profit and loss account for the group consisting of the company and its subsidiary undertakings relating to, or purporting to deal with, a financial year of the company,

otherwise than as part of the company's statutory accounts.

(6) A company which contravenes any provision of this section, and any officer of it who is in default, is guilty of an offence and liable[1] to a fine.*

[Companies Act 1985, s 240, as substituted by the Companies Act 1989, s 10 and amended by SI 1994/1935 and SI 2004/2947.]

---

*Sub-section (3) "and" preceding para (d) repealed and para (d) substituted, by subsequent paras (d), (e), by SI 2004/2947 with effect in relation to companies' financial years beginning on or after 1 January 2005.

1. For mode of trial and punishment, see Sch 24, post.

Laying and delivering of accounts and reports

8–3323   241. Accounts and reports to be laid before company in general meeting.   (1) The directors of a company shall in respect of each financial year lay before the company in general meeting copies of copies of—

(a) the company's annual accounts,

(b) the directors' report,

(c) (in the case of a quoted company) the directors' remuneration report, and

(d) the auditors' report on those accounts or (in the case of a quoted company) on those accounts and the auditable part of the directors' remuneration report.★

(2) If the requirements of subsection (1) are not complied with before the end of the period allowed for laying and delivering accounts and reports, every person who immediately before the end of that period was a director of the company is guilty of an offence and liable[1] to a fine and, for continued contravention, to a daily default fine.

(3) It is a defence for a person charged with such an offence to prove that he took all reasonable steps for securing that those requirements would be complied with before the end of that period.

(4) This section applies to a shadow director as to a director.

(5) This section is not to be taken as penalising a person who buys a right to subscribe for shares in, or debentures of, a body corporate or buys debentures of a body corporate that confer upon the holder of them a right to subscribe for, or to convert the debentures (in whole or in part) into, shares of that body.

(6) This section is not to be taken as penalising a director of a company who buys a right to call for delivery at a specified price within a specified time of a specified number of shares held as treasury shares by the company or by a relevant company which is that company's subsidiary or holding company or a subsidiary of that company's holding company.

(7) For the purposes of subsection (6)—

(a) "relevant company" means a company listed in Article 1 of Council Directive 77/91/EEC; and

(b) shares of a relevant company (other than a company within the meaning of section 735(1)) are held as treasury shares if—

(i) they fall within section 162(4)(a) to (d) (qualifying shares); and

(ii) they are held by the relevant company in accordance with provisions of the law of a member State implementing Articles 19 to 22 of that Directive.

[Companies Act 1985, s 241, as substituted by the Companies Act 1989, s 11 and amended by SI 2002/1986 and SI 2003/3031.]

★**Sub-section (1) printed as amended by SI 2002/1986, with effect in relation to companies' financial years ending on or after 31 December 2002.**

1. For mode of trial and punishment, see Sch 24, post.

8–3323A 241A. Members' approval of directors' remuneration report. (1) This section applies to every company that is a quoted company immediately before the end of a financial year.

(2) In this section "the meeting" means the general meeting of the company before which the company's annual accounts for the financial year are to be laid.

(3) The company must, prior to the meeting, give to the members of the company entitled to be sent notice of the meeting notice of the intention to move at the meeting, as an ordinary resolution, a resolution approving the directors' remuneration report for the financial year.

(4) Notice under subsection (3) shall be given to each such member in any manner permitted for the service on him of notice of the meeting.

(5) The business that may be dealt with at the meeting includes the resolution.

(6) The existing directors must ensure that the resolution is put to the vote of the meeting.

(7) Subsection (5) has effect notwithstanding—

(a) any default in complying with subsections (3) and (4);

(b) anything in the company's articles.

(8) No entitlement of a person to remuneration is made conditional on the resolution being passed by reason only of the provision made by this section.

(9) In the event of default in complying with the requirements of subsections (3) and (4), every officer of the company who is in default is liable to a fine.

(10) If the resolution is not put to the vote of the meeting, each existing director is guilty of an offence and liable to a fine.

(11) If an existing director is charged with an offence under subsection (10), it is a defence for him to prove that he took all reasonable steps for securing that the resolution was put to the vote of the meeting.

(12) In this section "existing director" means a person who, immediately before the meeting, is a director of the company.★

[Companies Act 1985, s 241A, as inserted by SI 2002/1986.]

★**Section 241A has effect in relation to companies' financial years ending on or after 31 December 2002.**

8–3324 242. Accounts and reports to be delivered to the registrar. (1) The directors of a company shall in respect of each financial year deliver to the registrar a copy of a copy of—

   (*a*)   the company's annual accounts,
   (*b*)   the directors' report,
   (*c*)   (in the case of a quoted company) the directors' remuneration report, and
   (*d*)   the auditors' report on those accounts or (in the case of a quoted company) on those accounts and the auditable part of the directors' remuneration report.★

If any document comprised in those accounts or reports is in a language other than English then, subject to section 710B(6) (delivery of certain Welsh documents without a translation), the directors shall annex to the copy of that document delivered a translation of it into English, certified in the prescribed manner to be a correct translation.

(2) If the requirements of subsection (1) are not complied with before the end of the period allowed for laying and delivering accounts and reports, every person who immediately before the end of that period was a director of the company is guilty of an offence and liable[1] to a fine and, for continued contravention, to a daily default fine.

(3) Further, if the directors of the company fail to make good the default within 14 days after the service of a notice on them requiring compliance, the court may on the application of any member or creditor of the company or of the registrar, make an order directing the directors (or any of them) to make good the default within such time as may be specified in the order.
The court's order may provide that all costs of and incidental to the application shall be borne by the directors.

(4) It is a defence for a person charged with an offence under this section to prove that he took all reasonable steps for securing that the requirements of subsection (1) would be complied with before the end of the period allowed for laying and delivering accounts and reports.

(5) It is not a defence in any proceedings under this section to prove that the documents in question were not in fact prepared as required by this Part.
[Companies Act 1985, s 242, as substituted by the Companies Act 1989, s 11 and amended by SI 1992/1083, the Welsh Language Act 1993, s 30 and Sch 2 and SI 2002/1986.]

★**Sub-section (1) printed as amended by SI 2002/1986, with effect in relation to companies' financial years ending on or after 31 December 2002.**
  1. For mode of trial and punishment, see Sch 24, post.

8–3325   242A. *Civil penalty for failure to deliver accounts.*

8–3326   243. **Accounts of subsidiary undertakings to be appended in certain cases.** *Repealed by SI 2004/2947 with effect in relation to companies' financial years beginning on or after 1 January 2005.*

8–3327   244. **Period allowed for laying and delivering accounts and reports.** (1) The period allowed for laying and delivering accounts and reports is—

   (*a*)   for a private company, 10 months after the end of the relevant accounting reference period, and
   (*b*)   for a public company, 7 months after the end of that period.

This is subject to the following provisions of this section.

(2) If the relevant accounting reference period is the company's first and is a period of more than 12 months, the period allowed is—

   (*a*)   10 months or 7 months, as the case may be, from the first anniversary of the incorporation of the company, or
   (*b*)   3 months from the end of the accounting reference period,

whichever last expires.

(3) *Repealed.*

(4) If the relevant accounting period is treated as shortened by virtue of a notice given by the company under section 225 (alteration of accounting reference date), the period allowed for laying and delivering accounts is that applicable in accordance with the above provisions or 3 months from the date of the notice under that section, whichever last expires.

(5) If for any special reason the Secretary of State thinks fit he may, on an application made before the expiry of the period otherwise allowed, by notice in writing to a company extend that period by such further period as may be specified in the notice.

(6) In this section "the relevant accounting reference period" means the accounting reference period by reference to which the financial year for the accounts in question was determined.★
[Companies Act 1985, s 244, as substituted by the Companies Act 1989, s 11 and amended by SI 2004/2947.]

★**Sub-section (3) repealed by SI 2004/2947; section reproduced as amended has effect in relation to companies' financial years beginning on or after 1 January 2005.**

8–3328   **245. Voluntary revision of annual accounts or directors' report.**   (1) If it appears to the directors of a company that any annual accounts [or summary financial statement of the company, or any directors' report or directors' remuneration report, did not comply with the requirements of this Act (or, where applicable, of Article 4 of the IAS Regulation), they may prepare revised accounts or a [revised statement or report.

(2) Where copies of the previous accounts or report have been laid before the company in general meeting or delivered to the registrar, the revisions shall be confined to—

   (a)   the correction of those respects in which the previous accounts or report did not comply with the requirements of this Act (or, where applicable, of Article 4 of the IAS Regulation), and

   (b)   the making of any necessary consequential alterations.

(3) The Secretary of State may make provision by regulations as to the application of the provisions of this Act in relation to revised annual accounts or a revised summary financial statement or a revised directors' report [or a revised directors' remuneration report.

(4) The regulations may, in particular—

   (a)   make different provision according to whether the previous accounts, statement or report are replaced or are supplemented by a document indicating the corrections to be made;

   (b)   make provision with respect to the functions of the company's auditors or reporting accountant] in relation to the revised accounts, statement or report;

   (c)   require the directors to take such steps as may be specified in the regulations where the previous accounts or report have been—

      (i)   sent out to members and others under section 238(1),

      (ii)   laid before the company in general meeting, or

      (iii)   delivered to the registrar,

      or where a summary financial statement based on the previous accounts or report has been sent to members under section 251;

   (d)   apply the provisions of this Act (including those creating criminal offences) subject to such additions, exceptions and modifications as are specified in the regulations.

(5) Regulations under this section shall be made by statutory instrument which shall be subject to annulment in pursuance of a resolution of either House of Parliament.★
[Companies Act 1985, s 245, as amended by SI 2004/2947 and the Companies (Audit, Investigations and Community Enterprise) Act 2004, s 64, Sch 8.]

★Section reproduced as amended has effect in relation to companies' financial years beginning on or after 1 January 2005.

8–3328A   **245A. Secretary of State's notice in respect of annual accounts.**   (1) Where copies of a company's annual accounts have been sent out under section 238, or a copy of a company's annual accounts has been laid before the company in general meeting or delivered to the registrar, and it appears to the Secretary of State that there is, or may be, a question whether the accounts comply with the requirements of this Act (or, where applicable, of Article 4 of the IAS Regulation), he may give notice to the directors of the company indicating the respects in which it appears to him that such a question arises, or may arise.

(2) The notice shall specify a period of not less than one month for the directors to give him an explanation of the accounts or prepare revised accounts.

(3) If at the end of the specified period, or such longer period as he may allow, it appears to the Secretary of State that no satisfactory explanation of the accounts has been given and that the accounts have not been revised so as to comply with the requirements of this Act, he may if he thinks fit apply to the court.

(4) The provisions of this section apply equally to revised annual accounts, in which case the references to revised accounts shall be read as references to further revised accounts.★
[Companies Act 1985, s 245A, as inserted by the Companies Act 1989, s 12 and amended by SI 2004/2947.]

★Section reproduced as amended has effect in relation to companies' financial years beginning on or after 1 January 2005.

8–3328B   **245B. Application to court in respect of defective accounts.**   (1) An application may be made to the court—

   (a)   by the Secretary of State, after having complied with section 245A, or

   (b)   by a person authorised by the Secretary of State for the purposes of this section,

for a declaration or declarator that the annual accounts of a company do not comply with the requirements of this Act (or, where applicable, of Article 4 of the IAS Regulation)] and for an order requiring the directors of the company to prepare revised accounts.

(2) Notice of the application, together with a general statement of the matters at issue in the proceedings, shall be given by the applicant to the registrar for registration.

(3) If the court orders the preparation of revised accounts, it may give directions with respect to—

(a) the auditing of the accounts,

(b) the revision of any directors' report[, directors' remuneration report] or summary financial statement, and

(c) the taking of steps by the directors to bring the making of the order to the notice of persons likely to rely on the previous accounts,

and such other matters as the court thinks fit.

(4) If the court finds that the accounts did not comply with the requirements of this Act (or, where applicable, of Article 4 of the IAS Regulation) it may order that all or part of—

(a) the costs (or in Scotland expenses) of and incidental to the application, and

(b) any reasonable expenses incurred by the company in connection with or in consequence of the preparation of revised accounts,

shall be borne by such of the directors as were party to the approval of the defective accounts.

For this purpose every director of the company at the time the accounts were approved shall be taken to have been a party to their approval unless he shows that he took all reasonable steps to prevent their being approved.

(5) Where the court makes an order under subsection (4) it shall have regard to whether the directors party to the approval of the defective accounts knew or ought to have known that the accounts did not comply with the requirements of this Act (or, where applicable, of Article 4 of the IAS Regulation), and it may exclude one or more directors from the order or order the payment of different amounts by different directors.

(6) On the conclusion of proceedings on an application under this section, the applicant shall give to the registrar for registration an office copy of the court order or, as the case may be, notice that the application has failed or been withdrawn.

(7) The provisions of this section apply equally to revised annual accounts, in which case the references to revised accounts shall be read as references to further revised accounts.★

[Companies Act 1985, s 245B, as inserted by the Companies Act 1989, s 12 and amended by SI 2004/2947.]

★Section reproduced as amended has effect in relation to companies' financial years beginning on or after 1 January 2005.

8–3328C 245C. Other persons authorised to apply to court. (1) The Secretary of State may authorise for the purposes of section 245B any person appearing to him—

(a) to have an interest in, and to have satisfactory procedures directed to securing, compliance by companies with the accounting requirements of this Act [(or, where applicable, of Article 4 of the IAS Regulation)],

(b) to have satisfactory procedures for receiving and investigating complaints about the annual accounts of companies, and

(c) otherwise to be a fit and proper person to be authorised.

(1A) But where the order giving authorisation (see subsection (4)) is to contain any requirements or other provisions specified under subsection (4A), the Secretary of State may not authorise a person unless, in addition, it appears to him that the person would, if authorised, exercise his functions as an authorised person in accordance with any such requirements or provisions.

(2) A person may be authorised generally or in respect of particular classes of case, and different persons may be authorised in respect of different classes of case.

(3) The Secretary of State may refuse to authorise a person if he considers that his authorisation is unnecessary having regard to the fact that there are one or more other persons who have been or are likely to be authorised.

(4) Authorisation shall be by order made by statutory instrument which shall be subject to annulment in pursuance of a resolution of either House of Parliament.

(4A) An order under subsection (4) may contain such requirements or other provisions relating to the exercise of functions by the authorised person as appear to the Secretary of State to be appropriate.

(4B) If the authorised person is an unincorporated association, any relevant proceedings may be brought by or against that association in the name of any body corporate whose constitution provides for the establishment of the association.

For this purpose "relevant proceedings" means proceedings brought in, or in connection with, the exercise of any function by the association as an authorised person.]

(5) Where authorisation is revoked, the revoking order may make such provision as the Secretary of State thinks fit with respect to pending proceedings.

(6) *Repealed.*★

[Companies Act 1985, s 245C, as inserted by the Companies Act 1989, s 12 and amended by SI 2004/2947 and the Companies (Audit, Investigations and Community Enterprise) Act 2004, s 10.]

*Section reproduced as amended has effect in relation to companies' financial years beginning on or after 1 January 2005.

245D. Disclosure of information held by Inland Revenue to persons authorised to apply to court. (1) Information which is held by or on behalf of the Commissioners of Inland Revenue may be disclosed to a person who is authorised under section 245C of this Act, or under Article 253C of the Companies (Northern Ireland) Order 1986 (SI 1986/1032 (NI 6)), if the disclosure—

(*a*) is made for a permitted purpose, and

(*b*) is made by the Commissioners or is authorised by them.

(2) Such information—

(*a*) may be so disclosed despite any other restriction on the disclosure of information whether imposed by any statutory provision or otherwise, but

(*b*) in the case of personal data (within the meaning of the Data Protection Act 1998), may not be disclosed in contravention of that Act.

(3) For the purposes of subsection (1), a disclosure is made for a permitted purpose if it is made for the purpose of facilitating—

(*a*) the taking of steps by the authorised person to discover whether there are grounds for an application to the court under section 245B of this Act or Article 253B of the Companies (Northern Ireland) Order 1986; or

(*b*) a determination by the authorised person as to whether or not to make such an application.

(4) The power of the Commissioners to authorise a disclosure under subsection (1)(b) may be delegated (either generally or for a specified purpose) to an officer of the Board of Inland Revenue.

245E. Restrictions on use and further disclosure of information disclosed under section 245D. (1) Information that is disclosed to an authorised person under section 245D may not be used except in or in connection with—

(*a*) taking steps to discover whether there are grounds for an application to the court as mentioned in section 245D(3)(*a*);

(*b*) determining whether or not to make such an application; or

(*c*) proceedings on any such application.

(2) Information that is disclosed to an authorised person under section 245D may not be further disclosed except—

(*a*) to the person to whom the information relates; or

(*b*) in or in connection with proceedings on any such application to the court.

(3) A person who contravenes subsection (1) or (2) is guilty of an offence and liable to imprisonment or a fine, or both.

(4) It is a defence for a person charged with an offence under subsection (3) to prove—

(*a*) that he did not know, and had no reason to suspect, that the information had been disclosed under section 245D; or

(*b*) that he took all reasonable steps and exercised all due diligence to avoid the commission of the offence.

(5) Sections 732 (restriction on prosecutions), 733(2) and (3) (liability of individuals for corporate default) and 734 (criminal proceedings against unincorporated bodies) apply to offences under this section.

245F. Power of authorised persons to require documents, information and explanations. (1) This section applies where it appears to a person who is authorised under section 245C of this Act that there is, or may be, a question whether the annual accounts of a company comply with the requirements of this Act.

(2) The authorised person may require any of the persons mentioned in subsection (3) to produce any document, or to provide him with any information or explanations, that he may reasonably require for the purpose of—

(*a*) discovering whether there are grounds for an application to the court under section 245B; or

(*b*) determining whether or not to make such an application.

(3) Those persons are—

(*a*) the company;

(*b*) any officer, employee, or auditor of the company;

(*c*) any persons who fell within paragraph (*b*) at a time to which the document or information required by the authorised person relates.

(4) If a person fails to comply with a requirement under subsection (2), the authorised person may apply to the court for an order under subsection (5).

(5) If on such an application the court decides that the person has failed to comply with the

requirement under subsection (2), it may order the person to take such steps as it directs for securing that the documents are produced or the information or explanations are provided.

(6)   A statement made by a person in response to a requirement under subsection (2) or an order under subsection (5) may not be used in evidence against him in any criminal proceedings.

(7)   Nothing in this section compels any person to disclose documents or information in respect of which in an action in the High Court a claim to legal professional privilege, or in an action in the Court of Session a claim to confidentiality of communications, could be maintained.

(8)   In this section "document" includes information recorded in any form.

245G.   Restrictions on further disclosure of information obtained under section 245F.
(1)   This section applies to information (in whatever form) which—

(a)   has been obtained in pursuance of a requirement or order under section 245F, and
(b)   relates to the private affairs of an individual or to any particular business.

(2)   No such information may, during the lifetime of that individual or so long as that business continues to be carried on, be disclosed without the consent of that individual or the person for the time being carrying on that business.

(3)   Subsection (2) does not apply to any disclosure of information which—

(a)   is made for the purpose of facilitating the carrying out by a person authorised under section 245C of his functions under section 245B;
(b)   is made to a person specified in Part 1 of Schedule 7B;
(c)   is of a description specified in Part 2 of that Schedule; or
(d)   is made in accordance with Part 3 of that Schedule.

(4)   The Secretary of State may by order amend Schedule 7B.
(5)   An order under subsection (4) must not—

(a)   amend Part 1 of Schedule 7B by specifying a person unless the person exercises functions of a public nature (whether or not he exercises any other function);
(b)   amend Part 2 of Schedule 7B by adding or modifying a description of disclosure unless the purpose for which the disclosure is permitted is likely to facilitate the exercise of a function of a public nature;
(c)   amend Part 3 of Schedule 7B so as to have the effect of permitting disclosures to be made to a body other than one that exercises functions of a public nature in a country or territory outside the United Kingdom.

(6)   An order under subsection (4) shall be made by statutory instrument which shall be subject to annulment in pursuance of a resolution of either House of Parliament.

(7)   A person who discloses any information in contravention of this section—

(a)   is guilty of an offence, and
(b)   is liable on conviction to imprisonment or a fine, or both.

(8)   However, it is a defence for a person charged with an offence under subsection (7) to prove—

(a)   that he did not know, and had no reason to suspect, that the information had been disclosed under section 245F; or
(b)   that he took all reasonable steps and exercised all due diligence to avoid the commission of the offence.

(9)   Sections 732 (restriction on prosecutions), 733 (liability of individuals for corporate default) and 734 (criminal proceedings against unincorporated bodies) apply to offences under this section.

(10)   This section does not prohibit the disclosure of information if the information is or has been available to the public from any other source.

(11)   Nothing in this section authorises the making of a disclosure in contravention of the Data Protection Act 1998.

CHAPTER II
EXEMPTIONS, EXCEPTIONS AND SPECIAL PROVISIONS

8–3329   246–249AA.   *Small and medium-sized companies and groups; dormant companies.*

Listed public companies

8–3330   251.   Provision of summary financial statement to shareholders.   (1)   A company whose shares or debentures, or any class of whose shares or debentures, are listed need not, in such cases as may be specified by regulations¹ made by the Secretary of State, and provided any conditions so specified are complied with, send copies of the documents referred to in section 238(1) to entitled persons, but may instead send them a summary financial statement.
In this section—

"entitled persons", in relation to a company, means such of the persons specified in paragraphs (a) to (c) of subsection (1) of section 238 as are or would apart from this section be entitled to be sent copies of those documents relating to the company which are referred to in that subsection;

(*repealed*).★

(2) Copies of the documents referred to in section 238(1) shall, however, be sent to any entitled person who wishes to receive them; and the Secretary of State may by regulations make provision as to the manner in which it is to be ascertained an entitled person (whether before or after he becomes an entitled person) whether a member of the company wishes to receive them.

(2A) References in this section to sending a summary financial statement to an entitled person include references to using electronic communications for sending the statement to such address as may for the time being be notified to the company by that person for that purpose.

(2B) For the purposes of this section a summary financial statement is also to be treated as sent to an entitled person where—

(*a*) the company and that person have agreed to his having access to summary financial statements on a web site (instead of their being sent to him);

(*b*) the statement is a statement to which that agreement applies; and

(*c*) that person is notified, in a manner for the time being agreed for the purpose between him and the company, of—

(i) the publication of the statement on a web site;

(ii) the address of that web site; and

(iii) the place on that web site where the statement may be accessed, and how it may be accessed.

(2C) For the purposes of this section a statement treated in accordance with subsection (2B) as sent to an entitled person is to be treated as sent to him if, and only if—

(*a*) the statement is published on the web site throughout a period beginning at least 21 days before the date of the meeting at which the accounts and directors' report from which the statement is derived are to be laid and ending with the conclusion of that meeting; and

(*b*) the notification given for the purposes of paragraph (*c*) of that subsection is given not less than 21 days before the date of the meeting.

(2D) Nothing in subsection (2C) shall invalidate the proceedings of a meeting where—

(*a*) any statement that is required to be published as mentioned in paragraph (*a*) of that subsection is published for a part, but not all, of the period mentioned in that paragraph; and

(*b*) the failure to publish that statement throughout that period is wholly attributable to circumstances which it would not be reasonable to have expected the company to prevent or avoid.

(2E) A company may, notwithstanding any provision to the contrary in its articles, take advantage of any of subsections (2A) to (2D).

(3) The summary financial statement—

(*a*) shall be derived from the company's annual accounts, the directors' report and (in the case of a quoted company) the directors' remuneration report, and

(*b*) shall be in such form and contain such information as may be specified by regulations made by the Secretary of State.★★

(4) Every summary financial statement shall—

(*a*) state that it is only a summary of information in the company's annual accounts, the directors' report and (in the case of a quoted company) the directors' remuneration report;

(*b*) contain a statement by the company's auditors of their opinion as to whether the summary financial statement is consistent with those accounts and those reports and complies with the requirements of this section and regulations made under it;

(*c*) state whether the auditors' report on the annual accounts, or on the annual accounts and the auditable part of the directors' remuneration report, was unqualified or qualified, and if it was qualified set out the report in full together with any further material needed to understand the qualification;

(*d*) state whether that auditors' report contained a statement under—

(i) section 237(2) (accounting records or returns inadequate or accounts or directors' remuneration report not agreeing with records and returns); or

(ii) section 237(3) (failure to obtain necessary information and explanations),

and if so, set out the statement in full.★★

(5) Regulations under this section shall be made by statutory instrument which shall be subject to annulment in pursuance of a resolution of either House of Parliament.

(6) If default is made in complying with this section or regulations made under it, the company and every officer of it who is in default is guilty of an offence and liable[2] to a fine.

(7) Section 240 (requirements in connection with publication of accounts) does not apply in relation to the provision to entitled persons of a summary financial statement in accordance with this section.

[Companies Act 1985, s 251, as substituted by the Companies Act 1989, s 15 and amended by SI 1992/3003, SI 2000/3373, SI 2001/3649, SI 2002/1986 and SI 2004/2947.]

---

*Sub-section (1) reproduced as amended by SI 2004/2947, with effect in relation to companies' financial years ending on or after 1 January 2005.
**Sub-sections (3) and (4) reproduced as amended by SI 2002/1986, with effect in relation to companies' financial years ending on or after 31 December 2002.
   1. See the Companies (Summary Financial Statement) Regulations 1992, SI 1992/3075 amended by SI 2002/1780 and SI 2005/2281.
   2. For mode of trial and punishment, see Sch 24, post.

8–3331   **252–255D.** *Private companies; unlimited companies; banking and insurance companies and groups.*

CHAPTER III
SUPPLEMENTARY PROVISIONS
Accounting standards

8–3332   **256. Accounting standards.**   (1) In this Part "accounting standards" means statements of standard accounting practice issued by such body or bodies as may be prescribed by regulations.

   (2) References in this Part to accounting standards applicable to a company's annual accounts are to such standards as are, in accordance with their terms, relevant to the company's circumstances and to the accounts.

   (3) *Repealed.*

   (4) *Powers of Secretary of State to make regulations.*
[Companies Act 1985, s 256, as substituted by the Companies Act 1989, s 19 and amended by the Companies (Audit, Investigations and Community Enterprise) Act 2004, Sch 8.]

Other interpretation provisions

8–3333   **259. Meaning of "undertaking" and related expressions.**   (1) In this Part "undertaking" means—

   (*a*) a body corporate or partnership, or
   (*b*) an unincorporated association carrying on a trade or business, with or without a view to profit.

   (2) In this Part references to shares—

   (*a*) in relation to an undertaking with a share capital, are to allotted shares;
   (*b*) in relation to an undertaking with capital but no share capital, are to rights to share in the capital of the undertaking; and
   (*c*) in relation to an undertaking without capital, are to interests—

      (i) conferring any right to share in the profits or liability to contribute to the losses of the undertaking, or
      (ii) giving rise to an obligation to contribute to the debts or expenses of the undertaking in the event of a winding up.

   (3) Other expressions appropriate to companies shall be construed, in relation to an undertaking which is not a company, as references to the corresponding persons, officers, documents or organs, as the case may be, appropriate to undertakings of that description.
This is subject to provision in any specific context providing for the translation of such expressions.

   (4) References in this Part to "fellow subsidiary undertakings" are to undertakings which are subsidiary undertakings of the same parent undertaking but are not parent undertakings or subsidiary undertakings of each other.

   (5) In this Part "group undertaking", in relation to an undertaking, means an undertaking which is—

   (*a*) a parent undertaking or subsidiary undertaking of that undertaking, or
   (*b*) a subsidiary undertaking of any parent undertaking of that undertaking.
[Companies Act 1985, s 259, as substituted by the Companies Act 1989, s 22.]

8–3334   **260.** *Participating interests.—Meaning of "participating interest".*

8–3335   **261. Notes to the accounts.**   (1) Information required by this Part to be given in notes to a company's annual accounts may be contained in the accounts or in a separate document annexed to the accounts.

   (2) References in this Part to a company's annual accounts, or to a balance sheet or profit and loss account, include notes to the accounts giving information which is required by any provision of this Act or international accounting standards, and required or allowed by any such provision to be given in a note to company accounts.
[Companies Act 1985, s 261, as substituted by the Companies Act 1989, s 22 and amended by SI 2004/2947.]

*Sub-section (2) reproduced as amended by SI 2004/2947, with effect in relation to companies' financial years ending on or after 1 January 2005.

8–3336   **262. Minor definitions.**   (1) In this Part—

"address", except in section 228, in relation to electronic communications, includes any number or address used for the purposes of such communications;

"annual accounts" means—

     (a)   the individual accounts required by section 226, and

     (b)   any group accounts required by section 227,

     (but see also section 230 (treatment of individual profit and loss account where group accounts prepared));

"annual report", in relation to a company, means the directors' report required by section 234;

"balance sheet date" means the date as at which the balance sheet was made up;

"capitalisation", in relation to work or costs, means treating that work or those costs as a fixed asset;

"Companies Act accounts" means Companies Act individual accounts or Companies Act group accounts;★★

"credit institution" means a credit institution as defined in article 1(1)(a) of Directive 2000/12/EC of the European Parliament and of the Council of 20 March 2000 relating to the taking up and pursuit of the business of credit institutions, that is to say an undertaking whose business is to receive deposits or other repayable funds from the public and to grant credits for its own account;

"fixed assets" means assets of a company which are intended for use on a continuing basis in the company's activities, and "current assets" means assets not intended for such use;

"group" means a parent undertaking and its subsidiary undertakings;

"IAS" accounts" means IAS indidivual accounts or IAS group accounts;★★

"IAS Regulation" means EC Regulation No 1606/2002 of the European Parliament and of the Council of 19th July 2002 on the application of international accounting standards;★★

"included in the consolidation", in relation to group accounts, or "included in consolidated group accounts", means that the undertaking is included in the accounts by the method of full (and not proportional) consolidation, and references to an undertaking excluded from consolidation shall be construed accordingly;

"international accounting standards" means the international accounting standards, within the meaning of the IAS Regulation, adopted from time to time by the European Commisssion in accordance with that Regulation;★★

"profit and loss acccount", in relation to a company that prepares IAS accounts, includes an income statement or other equivalent financial statement to be prepared by international accounting standards;★★

"purchase price", in relation to an asset of a company or any raw materials or consumables used in the production of such an asset, includes any consideration (whether in cash or otherwise) given by the company in respect of that asset or those materials or consumables, as the case may be;

"qualified" in relation to an auditors' report, means that the report does not state the auditors' unqualified opinion that the accounts have been properly prepared in accordance with this Act or, in the case of an undertaking not required to prepare accounts in accordance with this Act, under any corresponding legislation under which it is required to prepare accounts;

"quoted company" means a company whose equity share capital—

     (a)   has been included in the official list in accordance with the provisions of Part VI of the Financial Services and Markets Act 2000; or

     (b)   is officially listed in an EEA State; or

     (c)   is admitted to dealing on either the New York Stock Exchange or the exchange known as Nasdaq;

     and in paragraph (a) "the official list" shall have the meaning given it by section 103(1) of the Financial Services and Markets Act 2000;★

"true and fair view" refers—

     (a)   in the case of individual accounts, to the requirement of section 226(2), and

     (b)   in the case of group accounts, to the requirement of section 227(3);★★

"turnover, in relation to a company, means the amounts derived from the provision of goods and services falling within the company's ordinary activities, after deduction of—

     (i)   trade discounts,

     (ii)   value added tax, and

     (iii)   any other taxes based on the amounts so derived.

(2) In the case of an undertaking not trading for profit, any reference in this Part to a profit and

loss account is to an income and expenditure account; and references to profit and loss and, in relation to group accounts, to a consolidated profit and loss account shall be construed accordingly.

(2A) References in this Part to accounts giving a "true and fair view" are references—

(a) in the case of Companies Act individual accounts, to the requirement under section 226A that such accounts give a true and fair view;

(b) in the case of Companies Act group accounts, to the requirement under section 227A that such accounts give a true and fair view;

(c) in the case of IAS accounts, to the requirement under international accounting standards that such accounts achieve a fair presentation.**

(3) References in this Part to "realised profits" and "realised losses", in relation to a company's accounts, are to such profits or losses of the company as fall to be treated as realised in accordance with principles generally accepted, at the time when the accounts are prepared, with respect to the determination for accounting purposes of realised profits or losses.
This is without prejudice to—

(a) the construction of any other expression (where appropriate) by reference to accepted accounting principles or practice, or

(b) any specific provision for the treatment of profits or losses of any description as realised.

[Companies Act 1985, s 262, as substituted by the Companies Act 1989, s 22 and as amended by SI 1992/3178, SI 2000/2952, SI 2000/3373, SI 2002/765, 1986 and SI 2004/2947.]

---

*Sub-section (1), definition "quoted company" reproduced as inserted by SI 2002/1986, with effect in relation to companies' financial years ending on or after 31 December 2002.
**Definitions "Companies Act accounts", "IAS accounts", "IAS Regulation", "international accounting standards" and "profit and loss account" and new sub-s (2A) reproduced as inserted, and definition "true and fair view" repealed by SI 2004/2947, with effect in relation to companies' financial years ending on or after 1 January 2005.

8–3337 262A. *Index of defined expressions.*

PART IX[1]
A COMPANY'S MANAGEMENT; DIRECTORS AND SECRETARIES; THEIR QUALIFICATIONS, DUTIES AND RESPONSIBILITIES

Officers and registered office

8–3338 282. Directors.   (1) Every company registered on or after 1st November 1929 (other than a private company) shall have at least two directors.

(2) Every company registered before that date (other than a private company) shall have at least one director.

(3) Every private company shall have at least one director.

[Companies Act 1985, s 282.]

---

1. Part IX contains ss 282–310.

8–3339 283. Secretary.   (1) Every company shall have a secretary.

(2) A sole director shall not also be secretary.

(3) Anything required or authorised to be done by or to the secretary may, if the office is vacant or there is for any other reason no secretary capable of acting, be done by or to any assistant or deputy secretary or, if there is no assistant or deputy secretary capable of acting, by or to any officer of the company authorised generally or specially in that behalf by the directors.

(4) No company shall—

(a) have as secretary to the company a corporation the sole director of which is a sole director of the company;

(b) have as sole director of the company a corporation the sole director of which is secretary to the company.

[Companies Act 1985, s 283.]

8–3340 287. Registered office.   (1) A company shall at all times have a registered office to which all communications and notices may be addressed.

(2) On incorporation the situation of the company's registered office is that specified in the statement sent to the registrar under section 10.

(3) The company may change the situation of its registered office from time to time by giving notice in the prescribed form[1] to the registrar.

(4) The change takes effect upon the notice being registered by the registrar, but until the end of the period of 14 days beginning with the date on which it is registered a person may validly serve any document on the company at its previous registered office.

(5) For the purposes of any duty of a company—

(a)   to keep at its registered office, or make available for public inspection there, any register, index or other document, or

(b)   to mention the address of its registered office in any document,

a company which has given notice to the registrar of a change in the situation of its registered office may act on the change as from such date, not more than 14 days after the notice is given, as it may determine.

(6)   Where a company unavoidably ceases to perform at its registered office any such duty as is mentioned in subsection (5)(a) in circumstances in which it was not practicable to give prior notice to the registrar of a change in the situation of its registered office, but—

(a)   resumes performance of that duty at other premises as soon as practicable, and

(b)   gives notice accordingly to the registrar of a change in the situation of its registered office within 14 days of doing so,

it shall not be treated as having failed to comply with that duty.

(7)   In proceedings for an offence of failing to comply with any such duty as is mentioned in subsection (5), it is for the person charged to show that by reason of the matters referred to in that subsection or subsection (6) no offence was committed.

[Companies Act 1985, s 287, as substituted by the Companies Act 1989, s 136.]

---

1. See the Companies (Forms) Regulations 1985, SI 1985/854 amended by SI 1986/2097, SI 1987/752 amended by SI 1999/1820, SI 1998/1359, SI 1990/572 and 1766, SI 1992/3006 and SI 1995/736. Further forms are prescribed by SI 1987/752, SI 1988/1359 amended by SI 1999/2356, SI 1990/572 and 1766, SI 1991/879, SI 1992/3006, SI 1995/1479, SI 1996/594, SI 1998/1702, SI 1999/1820 and 2356 and SI 2002/691.

8–3341   288. Register of directors and secretaries.   (1) Every company shall keep at its registered office a register of its directors and secretaries; and the register shall, with respect to the particulars to be contained in it of those persons, comply with sections 289 and 290 below.

(2)   The company shall, within the period of 14 days from the occurrence of—

(a)   any change among its directors or in its secretary, or

(b)   any change in the particulars contained in the register,

send to the registrar of companies a notification in the prescribed form[1] of the change and of the date on which it occurred; and a notification of a person having become a director or secretary, or one of joint secretaries, of the company shall contain a consent, signed by that person, to act in the relevant capacity.

(3)   The register shall be open to the inspection of any member of the company without charge and of any other person on payment of such fee as may be prescribed.

(4)   If an inspection required under this section is refused, or if default is made in complying with subsection (1) or (2), the company and every officer of it who is in default is liable[2] to a fine and, for continued contravention, to a daily default fine.

(5)   In the case of a refusal of inspection of the register, the court may by order compel an immediate inspection of it.

(5A)   Where a confidentiality order made under section 723B is in force in respect of a director or secretary of a company, subsections (3) and (5) shall not apply in relation to that part of the register of the company as contains particulars of the usual residential address of that individual.

(6)   For purposes of this and the next section, a shadow director of a company is deemed a director and officer of it.

[Companies Act 1985, s 288 as amended by the Companies Act 1989, s 143 and Sch 24, the Criminal Justice and Police Act 2001, s 45(1), (3) and SI 2002/912.]

---

1. See the Companies (Forms) (Amendment) Regulations 1998, SI 1998/1702 and the Companies (Welsh Language Forms) Regulations 2003, SI 2003/62.

2. For mode of trial and punishment, see Sch 24, post.

Provisions governing appointment of directors

8–3342   291. Share qualification of directors.   (1) It is the duty of every director who is by the company's articles required to hold a specified share qualification, and who is not already qualified, to obtain his qualification within 2 months after his appointment, or such shorter time as may be fixed by the articles.

(2)   For the purpose of any provision of the articles requiring a director or manager to hold any specified share qualification, the bearer of a share warrant is not deemed the holder of the shares specified in the warrant.

(3)   The office of director of a company is vacated if the director does not within 2 months from the date of his appointment (or within such shorter time as may be fixed by the articles) obtain his qualification, or if after the expiration of that period or shorter time he ceases at any time to hold his qualification.

(4)   A person vacating office under this section is incapable of being reappointed to be a director of the company until he has obtained his qualification.

(5) If after the expiration of that period or shorter time any unqualified person acts as a director of the company, he is liable[1] to a fine and, for continued contravention, to a daily default fine. [Companies Act 1985, s 291.]

---

1. For mode of trial and punishment, see Sch 24, post.

8–3343   **292.** *Appointment of directors to be voted on individually.*

8–3344   **293. Age limit for directors.**   (1) A company is subject to this section if—

(*a*)   it is a public company, or

(*b*)   being a private company, it is a subsidiary of a public company or of a body corporate registered under the law relating to companies for the time being in force in Northern Ireland as a public company.

(2) No person is capable of being appointed a director of a company which is subject to this section if at the time of his appointment he has attained the age of 70.

(3) A director of such a company shall vacate his office at the conclusion of the annual general meeting commencing next after he attains the age of 70; but acts done by a person as director are valid notwithstanding that it is afterwards discovered that his appointment had terminated under this subsection.

(4) Where a person retires under subsection (3), no provision for the automatic reappointment of retiring directors in default of another appointment applies; and if at the meeting at which he retires the vacancy is not filled, it may be filled as a casual vacancy.

(5) Nothing in subsections (2) to (4) prevents the appointment of a director at any age, or requires a director to retire at any time, if his appointment is or was made or approved by the company in general meeting; but special notice is required of a resolution appointing or approving the appointment of a director for it to have effect under this subsection, and the notice of the resolution given to the company, and by the company to its members, must state, or have stated, the age of the person to whom it relates.

(6) A person reappointed director on retiring under subsection (3), or appointed in place of a director so retiring, is to be treated, for the purpose of determining the time at which he or any other director is to retire, as if he had become director on the day on which the retiring director was last appointed before his retirement.

Subject to this, the retirement of a director out of turn under subsection (3) is to be disregarded in determining when any other directors are to retire.

(7) In the case of a company first registered after the beginning of 1947, this section has effect subject to the provisions of the company's articles; and in the case of a company first registered before the beginning of that year—

(*a*)   this section has effect subject to any alterations of the company's articles made after the beginning of that year; and

(*b*)   if at the beginning of that year the company's articles contained provision for retirement of directors under an age limit, or for preventing or restricting appointments of directors over a given age, this section does not apply to directors to whom that provision applies.

[Companies Act 1985, s 293.]

8–3345   **294. Duty of director to disclose his age.**   (1) A person who is appointed or to his knowledge proposed to be appointed director of a company subject to section 293 at a time when he has attained any retiring age applicable to him under that section or under the company's articles shall give notice of his age to the company.

(2) For purposes of this section, a company is deemed subject to section 293 notwithstanding that all or any of the section's provisions are excluded or modified by the company's articles.

(3) Subsection (1) does not apply in relation to a person's reappointment on the termination of a previous appointment as director of the company.

(4) A person who—

(*a*)   fails to give notice of his age as required by this section; or

(*b*)   acts as director under any appointment which is invalid or has terminated by reason of his age,

is liable[1] to a fine and, for continued contravention, to a daily default fine.

(5) For purposes of subsection (4), a person who has acted as director under an appointment which is invalid or has terminated is deemed to have continued so to act throughout the period from the invalid appointment or the date on which the appointment terminated (as the case may be), until the last day on which he is shown to have acted thereunder.

[Companies Act 1985, s 294.]

---

1. For mode of trial and punishment, see Sch 24, post.

Other provisions about directors and officers

8–3346 305. Directors' names on company correspondence, etc. (1) A company to which this section applies shall not state, in any form, the name of any of its directors (otherwise than in the text or as a signatory) on any business letter on which the company's name appears unless it states on the letter in legible characters the name of every director of the company.

(2) This section applies to—

(a) every company registered under this Act or under the former Companies Acts (except a company registered before 23rd November 1916); and

(b) every company incorporated outside Great Britain which has an established place of business within Great Britain, unless it had established such a place of business before that date.

(3) If a company makes default in complying with this section, every officer of the company who is in default is liable[1] for each offence to a fine; and for this purpose, where a corporation is an officer of the company, any officer of the corporation is deemed an officer of the company.

(4) For purposes of the obligation under subsection (1) to state the name of every director of the company, a person's "name" means—

(a) in the case of an individual, his Christian name (or other forename) and surname; and

(b) in the case of a corporation or Scottish firm, its corporate or firm name.

(5) The initial or a recognised abbreviation of a person's Christian name or other forename may be stated instead of the full Christian name or other forename.

(6) In the case of a peer, or an individual usually known by a title, the title may be stated instead of his Christian name (or other forename) and surname or in addition to either or both of them.

(7) In this section "director" includes a shadow director and the reference in subsection (3) to an "officer" shall be construed accordingly.

[Companies Act 1985, s 305 as amended by the Companies Act 1989, Sch 19.]

---

1. For mode of trial and punishment, see Sch 24, post.

PART X[1]
ENFORCEMENT OF FAIR DEALING BY DIRECTORS
Share dealings by directors and their families

8–3347 323. Prohibition on directors dealing in share options. (1) It is an offence for a director of a company to buy—

(a) a right to call for delivery at a specified price and within a specified time of a specified number of relevant shares or a specified amount of relevant debentures; or

(b) a right to make delivery at a specified price and within a specified time of a specified number of relevant shares or a specified amount of relevant debentures; or

(c) a right (as he may elect) to call for delivery at a specified price and within a specified time or to make delivery at a specified price and within a specified time of a specified number of relevant shares or a specified amount of relevant debentures.

(2) A person guilty of an offence under subsection (1) is liable[2] to imprisonment or a fine, or both.

(3) In subsection (1)—

(a) "relevant shares", in relation to a director of a company, means shares in the company or in any other body corporate, being the company's subsidiary or holding company, or a subsidiary of the company's holding company, being shares as respects which there has been granted a listing on a stock exchange (whether in Great Britain or elsewhere);

(b) "relevant debentures", in relation to a director of a company, means debentures of the company or of any other body corporate, being the company's subsidiary or holding company or a subsidiary of the company's holding company, being debentures as respects which there has been granted such a listing; and

(c) "price" includes any consideration other than money.

(4) This section applies to a shadow director as to a director.

(5) This section is not to be taken as penalising a person who buys a right to subscribe for shares in, or debentures of, a body corporate or buys debentures of a body corporate that confer upon the holder of them a right to subscribe for, or to convert the debentures (in whole or in part) into, shares of that body.

[Companies Act 1985, s 323.]

---

1. Part X contains ss 311–347.
2. For mode of trial and punishment, see Sch 24, post.

8–3348 324. Duty of director to disclose shareholdings in own company. (1) A person who becomes a director of a company and at the time when he does so is interested in shares in, or debentures of, the company or any other body corporate, being the company's subsidiary or holding company or a subsidiary of the company's holding company, is under obligation to notify the company in writing—

(a) of the subsistence of his interests at that time; and

(b) of the number of shares of each class in, and the amount of debentures of each class of, the company or other such body corporate in which each interest of his subsists at that time.

(2) A director of a company is under obligation to notify the company in writing of the occurrence, while he is a director, of any of the following events—

(a) any event in consequence of whose occurrence he becomes, or ceases to be, interested in shares in, or debentures of, the company or any other body corporate, being the company's subsidiary or holding company or a subsidiary of the company's holding company;

(b) the entering into by him of a contract to sell any such shares or debentures;

(c) the assignment by him of a right granted to him by the company to subscribe for shares in, or debentures of, the company; and

(d) the grant to him by another body corporate, being the company's subsidiary or holding company or a subsidiary of the company's holding company, of a right to subscribe for shares in, or debentures of, that other body corporate, the exercise of such a right granted to him and the assignment by him of such a right so granted;

and notification to the company must state the number or amount, and class, of shares or debentures involved.

(3) Schedule 13 has effect in connection with subsections (1) and (2) above; and of that Schedule—

(a) Part I contains rules for the interpretation of, and otherwise in relation to, those subsections and applies in determining, for purposes of those subsections, whether a person has an interest in shares or debentures;

(b) Part II applies with respect to the periods within which obligations imposed by the subsections must be fulfilled; and

(c) Part III specifies certain circumstances in which obligations arising from subsection (2) are to be treated as not discharged;

and subsections (1) and (2) are subject to any exceptions for which provision may be made by regulations[1] made by the Secretary of State by statutory instrument.

(4) Subsection (2) does not require the notification by a person of the occurrence of an event whose occurrence comes to his knowledge after he has ceased to be a director.

(5) An obligation imposed by this section is treated as not discharged unless the notice by means of which it purports to be discharged is expressed to be given in fulfilment of that obligation.

(6) This section applies to shadow directors as to directors; but nothing in it operates so as to impose an obligation with respect to shares in a body corporate which is the wholly-owned subsidiary of another body corporate.

(7) A person who—

(a) fails to discharge, within the proper period, an obligation to which he is subject under subsection (1) or (2), or

(b) in purported discharge of an obligation to which he is so subject, makes to the company a statement which he knows to be false, or recklessly makes to it a statement which is false,

is guilty of an offence and liable[2] to imprisonment or a fine, or both.

(8) Section 732 (restriction on prosecutions) applies to an offence under this section.
[Companies Act 1985, s 324.]

---

1. See the Companies (Disclosure of Directors' Interests) (Exceptions) Regulations 1985, SI 1985/802.
2. For mode of trial and punishment, see Sch 24, post.

8–3349 325. Register of directors' interests notified under s 324.   (1) Every company shall keep a register for the purposes of section 324.

(2) Whenever a company receives information from a director given in fulfilment of an obligation imposed on him by that section, it is under obligation to enter in the register, against the director's name, the information received and the date of the entry.

(3) The company is also under obligation, whenever it grants to a director a right to subscribe for shares in, or debentures of, the company to enter in the register against his name—

(a) the date on which the right is granted,

(b) the period during which, or time at which, it is exercisable,

(c) the consideration for the grant (or, if there is no consideration, that fact), and

(d) the description of shares or debentures involved and the number or amount of them, and the price to be paid for them (or the consideration, if otherwise than in money).

(4) Whenever such a right as is mentioned above is exercised by a director, the company is under obligation to enter in the register against his name that fact (identifying the right), the number or amount of shares or debentures in respect of which it is exercised and, if they were registered in his

name, that fact and, if not, the name or names of the person or persons in whose name or names they were registered, together (if they were registered in the names of two persons or more) with the number or amount of the shares or debentures registered in the name of each of them.

(5) Part IV of Schedule 13 has effect with respect to the register to be kept under this section, to the way in which entries in it are to be made, to the right of inspection, and generally.

(6) For the purposes of this section, a shadow director is deemed a director.

[Companies Act 1985, s 325.]

8–3360 326. Sanctions for non-compliance. (1) The following applies with respect to defaults in complying with, and to contraventions of, section 325 and Part IV of Schedule 13.

(2) If default is made in complying with any of the following provisions—

   (*a*) section 325(1), (2), (3) or (4), or
   (*b*) Schedule 13, paragraph 21, 22 or 28,

the company and every officer of it who is in default is liable[1] to a fine and, for continued contravention, to a daily default fine.

(3) If an inspection of the register required under paragraph 25 of the Schedule is refused, or a copy required under paragraph 26 is not sent within the proper period, the company and every officer of it who is in default is liable[1] to a fine and, for continued contravention, to a daily default fine.

(4) If default is made for 14 days in complying with paragraph 27 of the Schedule (notice to registrar of where register is kept), the company and every officer of it who is in default is liable[1] to a fine and, for continued contravention, to a daily default fine.

(5) If default is made in complying with paragraph 29 of the Schedule (register to be produced at annual general meeting), the company and every officer of it who is in default is liable[1] to a fine.

(6) In the case of a refusal of an inspection of the register required under paragraph 25 of the Schedule, the court may by order compel an immediate inspection of it; and in the case of failure to send within the proper period a copy required under paragraph 26, the court may by order direct that the copy be sent to the person requiring it.

[Companies Act 1985, s 326.]

---

1. For mode of trial and punishment, see Sch 24, post.

8–3361 327. Extension of s 323 to spouses* and children. (1) Section 323 applies to—

   (*a*) the wife or husband* of a director of a company (not being herself or himself a director of it), and
   (*b*) an infant son or infant daughter of a director (not being himself or herself a director of the company),

as it applies to the director; but it is a defence for a person charged by virtue of this section with an offence under section 323 to prove that he (she) had no reason to believe that his (her) spouse or, as the case may be,* parent was a director of the company in question.

(2) For purposes of this section—

   (*a*) "son" includes step-son, and "daughter" includes step-daughter ("parent" being construed accordingly),
   (*b*) "infant" means, in relation to Scotland, pupil or minor, and
   (*c*) a shadow director of a company is deemed a director of it.

[Companies Act 1985, s 327.]

---

*Words inserted by the Civil Partnership Act 2004, Sch 27 from a date to be appointed.

8–3362 328. Extension of s 324 to spouses* and children. (1) For the purposes of section 324—

   (*a*) an interest of the wife or husband* of a director of a company (not being herself or himself a director of it) in shares or debentures is to be treated as the director's interest; and
   (*b*) the same applies to an interest of an infant son or infant daughter of a director of a company (not being himself or herself a director of it) in shares or debentures.

(2) For those purposes—

   (*a*) a contract, assignment or right of subscription entered into, exercised or made by, or a grant made to, the wife or husband* of a director of a company (not being herself or himself a director of it) is to be treated as having been entered into, exercised or made by, or (as the case may be) as having been made to, the director; and
   (*b*) the same applies to a contract, assignment or right of subscription entered into, exercised or made by, or grant made to, an infant son or infant daughter of a director of a company (not being himself or herself a director of it).

(3) A director of a company is under obligation to notify the company in writing of the occurrence while he or she is a director, of either of the following events, namely—

(a)   the grant by the company to his (her) spouse*, or to his or her infant son or infant daughter, of a right to subscribe for shares in, or debentures of, the company; and

(b)   the exercise by his (her) spouse* or by his or her infant son or infant daughter of such a right granted by the company to the wife, husband, * son or daughter.

(4)   In a notice given to the company under subsection (3) there shall be stated—

(a)   in the case of the grant of a right, the like information as is required by section 324 to be stated by the director on the grant to him by another body corporate of a right to subscribe for shares in, or debentures of, that other body corporate; and

(b)   in the case of the exercise of a right, the like information as is required by that section to be stated by the director on the exercise of a right granted to him by another body corporate to subscribe for shares in, or debentures of, that other body corporate.

(5)   An obligation imposed by subsection (3) on a director must be fulfilled by him before the end of 5 days beginning with the day following that on which the occurrence of the event giving rise to it comes to his knowledge; but in reckoning that period of days there is disregarded any Saturday or Sunday, and any day which is a bank holiday in any part of Great Britain.

(6)   A person who—

(a)   fails to fulfil, within the proper period, an obligation to which he is subject under subsection (3), or

(b)   in purported fulfilment of such an obligation, makes to a company a statement which he knows to be false, or recklessly makes to a company a statement which is false,

is guilty of an offence and liable[1] to imprisonment or a fine, or both.

(7)   The rules set out in Part I of Schedule 13 have effect for the interpretation of, and otherwise in relation to, subsections (1) and (2); and subsections (5), (6) and (8) of section 324 apply with any requisite modification.

(8)   In this section, "son" includes step-son, "daughter" includes step-daughter, and "infant" means, in relation to Scotland, pupil or minor.

(9)   For purposes of section 325, an obligation imposed on a director by this section is to be treated as if imposed by section 324.

[Companies Act 1985, s 328.]

---

*Words inserted by the Civil Partnership Act 2004, Sch 27 from a date to be appointed.

1. For mode of trial and punishment, see Sch 24, post.

8–3363   329. Duty to notify stock exchange of matters notified under preceding sections.
(1)   Whenever a company whose shares or debentures are listed on a [recognised investment exchange other than an overseas investment exchange is notified of any matter by a director in consequence of the fulfilment of an obligation imposed by section 324 or 328, and that matter relates to shares or debentures so listed, the company is under obligation to notify that investment exchange of that matter; and the investment exchange may publish, in such manner as it may determine, any information received by it under this subsection.

(2)   An obligation imposed by subsection (1) must be fulfilled before the end of the day next following that on which it arises; but there is disregarded for this purpose a day which is a Saturday or a Sunday or a bank holiday in any part of Great Britain.

(3)   If default is made in complying with this section, the company and every officer of it who is in default is guilty of an offence and liable[1] to a fine and, for continued contravention, to a daily default fine.

Section 732 (restriction on prosecutions) applies to an offence under this section.

(4)   In subsection (1) "recognised investment exchange" and "overseas investment exchange" have the same meaning as in Part 18 of the Financial Services and Markets Act 2000.

[Companies Act 1985, s 329 as amended by the Financial Services Act 1986, Sch 16 and SI 2001/3649.]

---

1. For mode of trial and punishment, see Sch 24, post.

PART XI[1]
COMPANY ADMINISTRATION AND PROCEDURE

CHAPTER I
COMPANY IDENTIFICATION

8–3364   348. Company name to appear outside place of business.   (1)   Every company shall paint or affix, and keep painted or affixed, its name on the outside of every office or place in which its business is carried on, in a conspicuous position and in letters easily legible.

(2)   If a company does not paint or affix its name as required above, the company and every officer of it who is in default is liable to a fine; and if a company does not keep its name painted or affixed as

so required, the company and every officer of it who is in default is liable[2] to a fine and, for continued contravention, to a daily default fine.
[Companies Act 1985, s 348.]

---

1. Part XI contains Chapter I, ss 348–351, Chapter II, ss 352–362, Chapter III, ss 363–365, Chapter IV, ss 366–383, Chapter V, ss 384–394.
2. For mode of trial and punishment, see Sch 24, post.

8–3365 **349. Company's name to appear in its correspondence, etc.** (1) Every company shall have its name mentioned in legible characters—

(a) in all business letters of the company,
(b) in all its notices and other official publications,
(c) in all bills of exchange, promissory notes, endorsements, cheques and orders for money or goods purporting to be signed by or on behalf of the company, and
(d) in all its bills of parcels, invoices, receipts and letters of credit.

(2) If a company fails to comply with subsection (1) it is liable[1] to a fine.
(3) If an officer of a company or a person on its behalf—

(a) issues or authorises the issue of any business letter of the company, or any notice or other official publication of the company, in which the company's name is not mentioned as required by subsection (1), or
(b) issues or authorises the issue of any bill of parcels, invoice, receipt or letter of credit of the company in which its name is not so mentioned,

he is liable[1] to a fine.
(4) If an officer of a company or a person on its behalf signs or authorises to be signed on behalf of the company any bill of exchange, promissory note, endorsement, cheque or order for money or goods in which the company's name is not mentioned as required by subsection (1), he is liable[1] to a fine; and he is further personally liable to the holder of the bill of exchange, promissory note, cheque or order for money or goods for the amount of it (unless it is duly paid by the company).
[Companies Act 1985, s 349.]

---

1. For mode of trial and punishment, see Sch 24, post.

8–3366 **350. Company seal.** (1) A company which has a common seal shall have its name engraved in legible characters on the seal; and if it fails to comply with this subsection it is liable[1] to a fine.
(2) If an officer of a company or a person on its behalf uses or authorises the use of any seal purporting to be a seal of the company on which its name is not engraved as required by subsection (1), he is liable[1] to a fine.
[Companies Act 1985, s 350 as amended by the Companies Act 1989, Sch 17.]

---

1. For mode of trial and punishment, see Sch 24, post.

8–3367 **351. Particulars in correspondence etc.** (1) Every company shall have the following particulars mentioned in legible characters in all business letters and order forms of the company, that is to say—

(a) the company's place of registration and the number with which it is registered,
(b) the address of its registered office,
(c) in the case of an investment company (as defined in section 266), the fact that it is such a company, and
(d) in the case of a limited company exempt from the obligation to use the word "limited" as part of its name★, the fact that it is a limited company.

(2) If in the case of a company having a share capital there is on the stationery used for any such letters, or on the company's order forms, a reference to the amount of share capital, the reference must be to paid-up share capital.
(3)–(4) (*Repealed*).
(5) As to contraventions of this section, the following applies—

(a) if a company fails to comply with subsection (1) or (2), it is liable[1] to a fine,
(b) if an officer of a company or a person on its behalf issues or authorises the issue of any business letter or order form not complying with those subsections, he is liable[1] to a fine.
[Companies Act 1985, s 351 as amended by the Welsh Language Act 1993, s 31 and Sch 2.]

★**Words "under section 30 or a community interest company which is not a public company" inserted by the Companies (Audit, Investigations and Community Enterprise) Act 2004, Sch 6 from 1 July 2005.**
1. For mode of trial and punishment, see Sch 24, post.

CHAPTER III
ANNUAL RETURN

8–3368   363. Duty to deliver annual returns.   (1) Every company shall deliver to the registrar successive annual returns each of which is made up to a date not later than the date which is from time to time the company's "return date", that is—

(*a*)   the anniversary of the company's incorporation, or

(*b*)   if the company's last return delivered in accordance with this Chapter was made up to a different date, the anniversary of that date.

(2) Each return shall—

(*a*)   be in the prescribed form,

(*b*)   contain the information required by or under the following provisions of this Chapter, and

(*c*)   be signed by a director or the secretary of the company;

and it shall be delivered to the registrar within 28 days after the date to which it is made up.

(3) If a company fails to deliver an annual return in accordance with this Chapter before the end of the period of 28 days after a return date, the company is guilty of an offence and liable[1] to a fine and, in the case of continued contravention, to a daily default fine.

The contravention continues until such time as an annual return made up to that return date and complying with the requirements of subsection (2) (except as to date of delivery) is delivered by the company to the registrar.

(4) Where a company is guilty of an offence under subsection (3), every director or secretary of the company is similarly liable unless he shows that he took all reasonable steps to avoid the commission or continuation of the offence.

(5) The references in this section to a return being delivered "in accordance with this Chapter" are—

(*a*)   in relation to a return made after the commencement of section 139 of the Companies Act 1989, to a return with respect to which all the requirements of subsection (2) are complied with;

(*b*)   in relation to a return made before that commencement, to a return with respect to which the formal and substantive requirements of this Chapter as it then had effect were complied with, whether or not the return was delivered in time.

[Companies Act 1985, s 363, as substituted by the Companies Act 1989, s 139.]

---

1. For mode of trial and punishment, see Sch 24, post.

8–3369   364. Contents of annual return: general.   (1) Every annual return shall state the date to which it is made up and shall contain the following information—

(*a*)   the address of the company's registered office;

(*b*)   the type of company it is and its principal business activities;

(*c*)   the name and address of the company secretary;

(*d*)   the name and address of every director of the company;

(*e*)   in the case of each individual director his nationality, date of birth and business occupation;

(*f*)   *Repealed.*

(*g*)   if the register of members is not kept at the company's registered office, the address of the place where it is kept;

(*h*)   if any register of debenture holders (or a duplicate of any such register or a part of it) is not kept at the company's registered office, the address of the place where it is kept;

(*i*)   *Repealed.*

(2) The information as to the company's type shall be given by reference to the classification scheme prescribed for the purposes of this section.

(3) The information as to the company's principal business activities may be given by reference to one or more categories of any prescribed system of classifying business activities.

(4) A person's "name" and "address" mean, respectively—

(*a*)   in the case of an individual, his Christian name (or other forename) and surname and his usual residential address;

(*b*)   in the case of a corporation or Scottish firm, its corporate or firm name and its registered or principal office.

(5) In the case of a peer, or an individual usually known by a title, the title may be stated instead of his Christian name (or other forename) and surname or in addition to either or both of them.

(6) Where all the partners in a firm are joint secretaries, the name and principal office of the firm may be stated instead of the names and addresses of the partners.

[Companies Act 1985, s 364, as substituted by the Companies Act 1989 s 139 and as amended SI 1999/2322, reg 2.]

8–3370   364A. Contents of annual return: particulars of share capital and shareholders.
(1) The annual return of a company having a share capital shall contain the following information with respect to its share capital and members.

(2) The return shall state the total number of issued shares of the company at the date to which the return is made up and the aggregate nominal value of those shares.

(3) The return shall state with respect to each class of shares in the company—

(a) the nature of the class, and

(b) the total number and aggregate nominal value of issued shares of that class at the date to which the return is made up.

(4) The return shall contain a list of the names and addresses of every person who—

(a) is a member of the company on the date to which the return is made up, or

(b) has ceased to be a member of the company since the date to which the last return was made up (or, in the case of the first return, since the incorporation of the company);

and if the names are not arranged in alphabetical order the return shall have annexed to it an index sufficient to enable the name of any person in the list to be easily found.

(5) The return shall also state—

(a) the number of shares of each class held by each member of the company at the date to which the return is made up, and

(b) the number of shares of each class transferred since the date to which the last return was made up (or, in the case of the first return, since the incorporation of the company) by each member or person who has ceased to be a member, and the dates of registration of the transfers.

(6) The return may, if either of the two immediately preceding returns has given the full particulars required by subsections (4) and (5), give only such particulars as relate to persons ceasing to be or becoming members since the date of the last return and to shares transferred since that date.

(7) Subsections (4) and (5) do not require the inclusion of particulars entered in an overseas branch register if copies of those entries have not been received at the company's registered office by the date to which the return is made up.

Those particulars shall be included in the company's next annual return after they are received.

(8) Where the company has converted any of its shares into stock, the return shall give the corresponding information in relation to that stock, stating the amount of stock instead of the number or nominal value of shares.

[Companies Act 1985, s 364A, as inserted by the Companies Act 1989, s 139.]

8–3371   365. Supplementary provisions: regulations and interpretation.   (1) The Secretary of State may by regulations make further provision as to the information to be given in a company's annual return, which may amend or repeal the provisions of sections 364 and 364A.

(2) Regulations under this section shall be made by statutory instrument which shall be subject to annulment in pursuance of a resolution of either House of Parliament.

(3) For the purposes of this Chapter, except section 363(2)(c) (signature of annual return), a shadow director shall be deemed to be a director.

[Companies Act 1985, s 365, as substituted by the Companies Act 1989, s 139.]

CHAPTER V
AUDITORS

Rights of auditors

8–3372   389A. Rights to information.   (1) An auditor of a company—

(a) has a right of access at all times to the company's books, accounts and vouchers (in whatever form they are held), and

(b) may require any of the persons mentioned in subsection (2) to provide him with such information or explanations as he thinks necessary for the performance of his duties as auditor.

(2) Those persons are—

(a) any officer or employee of the company;

(b) any person holding or accountable for any of the company's books, accounts or vouchers;

(c) any subsidiary undertaking of the company which is a body corporate incorporated in Great Britain;

(d) any officer, employee or auditor of any such subsidiary undertaking or any person holding or accountable for any books, accounts or vouchers of any such subsidiary undertaking;

(e) any person who fell within any of paragraphs (a) to (d) at a time to which the information or explanations required by the auditor relates or relate.

(3) Where a parent company has a subsidiary undertaking which is not a body corporate incorporated in Great Britain, the auditor of the parent company may require it to obtain from any of the persons mentioned in subsection (4) such information or explanations as he may reasonably require for the purposes of his duties as auditor.

(4) Those persons are—

(a) the undertaking;

(b) any officer, employee or auditor of the undertaking;

(c) any person holding or accountable for any of the undertaking's books, accounts or vouchers;

(d) any person who fell within paragraph (b) or (c) at a time to which the information or explanations relates or relate.

(5) If so required, the parent company must take all such steps as are reasonably open to it to obtain the information or explanations from the person within subsection (4) from whom the auditor has required the company to obtain the information or explanations.

(6) A statement made by a person in response to a requirement under subsection (1)(b) or (3) may not be used in evidence against him in any criminal proceedings except proceedings for an offence under section 389B.

(7) Nothing in this section or section 389B compels any person to disclose information in respect of which in an action in the High Court a claim to legal professional privilege, or in an action in the Court of Session a claim to confidentiality of communications, could be maintained.

[Companies Act 1985, s 389A, as substituted by the Companies Act 1989, s 120 and further substituted by the Companies (Audit, Investigations and Community Enterprise) Act 2004, s 8.]

---

1. For mode of trial and punishment, see Sch 24, post.

8–3373   390. *Right to attend company meetings, etc.*

Removal, resignation, etc of auditors

8–3374   391. Removal of auditors. (1) A company may by ordinary resolution at any time remove an auditor from office, notwithstanding anything in any agreement between it and him.

(2) Where a resolution removing an auditor is passed at a general meeting of a company, the company shall within 14 days give notice of that fact in the prescribed form to the registrar.

If a company fails to give notice required by this subsection, the company and every officer of it who is in default is guilty of an offence and liable[1] to a fine and, for continued contravention, to a daily default fine.

(3) Nothing in this section shall be taken as depriving a person removed under it of compensation or damages payable to him in respect of the termination of his appointment as auditor or of any appointment terminating with that as auditor.

(4) An auditor of a company who has been removed has, notwithstanding his removal, the rights conferred by section 390 in relation to any general meeting of the company—

(a) at which his term of office would otherwise have expired, or

(b) at which it is proposed to fill the vacancy caused by his removal.

In such a case the references in that section to matters concerning the auditors as auditors shall be construed as references to matters concerning him as a former auditor.

[Companies Act 1985, s 391, as substituted by the Companies Act 1989, s 122.]

---

1. For mode of trial and punishment, see Sch 24, post.

8–3375   391A. *Rights of auditors who are removed or not re-appointed.*

8–3376   392. Resignation of auditors. (1) An auditor of a company may resign his office by depositing a notice in writing to that effect at the company's registered office.

The notice is not effective unless it is accompanied by the statement required by section 394.

(2) An effective notice of resignation operates to bring the auditor's term of office to an end as of the date on which the notice is deposited or on such later date as may be specified in it.

(3) The company shall within 14 days of the deposit of a notice of resignation send a copy of the notice to the registrar of companies.

If default is made in complying with this subsection, the company and every officer of it who is in default is guilty of an offence and liable[1] to a fine and, for continued contravention, a daily default fine.

[Companies Act 1985, s 392, as substituted by the Companies Act 1989, s 122.]

---

1. For mode of trial and punishment, see Sch 24, post.

8–3377   392A. Rights of resigning auditors. (1) This section applies where an auditor's notice of resignation is accompanied by a statement of circumstances which he considers should be brought to the attention of members or creditors of the company.

(2) He may deposit with the notice a signed requisition calling on the directors of the company forthwith duly to convene an extraordinary general meeting of the company for the purpose of receiving and considering such explanation of the circumstances connected with his resignation as he may wish to place before the meeting.

(3) He may request the company to circulate to its members—

(a) before the meeting convened on his requisition, or

(*b*) before any general meeting at which his term of office would otherwise have expired or at which it is proposed to fill the vacancy caused by his resignation,

a statement in writing (not exceeding a reasonable length) of the circumstances connected with his resignation.

(4) The company shall (unless the statement is received too late for it to comply)—

(*a*) in any notice of the meeting given to members of the company, state the fact of the statement having been made, and

(*b*) send a copy of the statement to every member of the company to whom notice of the meeting is or has been sent.

(5) If the directors do not within 21 days from the date of the deposit of a requisition under this section proceed duly to convene a meeting for a day not more than 28 days after the date on which the notice convening the meeting is given, every director who failed to take all reasonable steps to secure that a meeting was convened as mentioned above is guilty of an offence and liable[1] to a fine.

(6) If a copy of the statement mentioned above is not sent out as required because received too late or because of the company's default, the auditor may (without prejudice to his right to be heard orally) require that the statement be read out at the meeting.

(7) Copies of a statement need not be sent out and the statement need not be read out at the meeting if, on the application either of the company or of any other person who claims to be aggrieved, the court is satisfied that the rights conferred by this section are being abused to secure needless publicity for defamatory matter; and the court may order the company's costs on such an application to be paid in whole or in part by the auditor, notwithstanding that he is not a party to the application.

(8) An auditor who has resigned has, notwithstanding his resignation, the rights conferred by section 390 in relation to any such general meeting of the company as is mentioned in subsection (3)(*a*) or (*b*).

In such a case the references in that section to matters concerning the auditors as auditors shall be construed as references to matters concerning him as a former auditor.

[Companies Act 1985, s 392A, as substituted by the Companies Act 1989, s 122.]

---

1. For mode of trial and punishment, see Sch 24, post.

8–3378   393. *Termination of appointment of auditors not appointed annually.*

8–3379   394. Statement by person ceasing to hold office as auditor. (1) Where an auditor ceases for any reason to hold office, he shall deposit at the company's registered office a statement of any circumstances connected with his ceasing to hold office which he considers should be brought to the attention of the members or creditors of the company or, if he considers that there are no such circumstances, a statement that there are none.

(2) In the case of resignation, the statement shall be deposited along with the notice of resignation; in the case of failure to seek re-appointment, the statement shall be deposited not less than 14 days before the end of the time allowed for next appointing auditors; in any other case, the statement shall be deposited not later than the end of the period of 14 days beginning with the date on which he ceases to hold office.

(3) If the statement is of circumstances which the auditor considers should be brought to the attention of the members or creditors of the company, the company shall within 14 days of the deposit of the statement either—

(*a*) send a copy of it to every person who under section 238 is entitled to be sent copies of the accounts, or

(*b*) apply to the court.

(4) The company shall if it applies to the court notify the auditor of the application.

(5) Unless the auditor receives notice of such an application before the end of the period of 21 days beginning with the day on which he deposited the statement, he shall within a further seven days send a copy of the statement to the registrar.

(6) If the court is satisfied that the auditor is using the statement to secure needless publicity for defamatory matter—

(*a*) it shall direct that copies of the statement need not be sent out, and

(*b*) it may further order the company's costs on the application to be paid in whole or in part by the auditor, notwithstanding that he is not a party to the application;

and the company shall within 14 days of the court's decision send to the persons mentioned in subsection (3)(*a*) a statement setting out the effect of the order.

(7) If the court is not so satisfied, the company shall within 14 days of the court's decision—

(*a*) send copies of the statement to the persons mentioned in subsection (3)(*a*), and

(*b*) notify the auditor of the court's decision;

and the auditor shall within seven days of receiving such notice send a copy of the statement to the registrar.

[Companies Act 1985, s 394, as substituted by the Companies Act 1989, s 123.]

8–3380   394A. Offences of failing to comply with section 394.   (1) If a person ceasing to hold office as auditor fails to comply with section 394 he is guilty of an offence and liable[1] to a fine.

(2) In proceedings for an offence under subsection (1) it is a defence for the person charged to show that he took all reasonable steps and exercised all due diligence to avoid the commission of the offence.

(3) Sections 733 (liability of individuals for corporate default) and 734 (criminal proceedings against unincorporated bodies) apply to an offence under subsection (1).

(4) If a company makes default in complying with section 394, the company and every officer of it who is in default is guilty of an offence and liable[1] to a fine and, for continued contravention, to a daily default fine.

[Companies Act 1985, s 394A, as inserted by the Companies Act 1989, s 123.]

---

1. For mode of trial and punishment, see Sch 24, post.

PART XIV[1]
INVESTIGATION OF COMPANIES AND THEIR AFFAIRS; REQUISITION OF DOCUMENTS
Requisition and seizure of books and papers

8–3381   447. Secretary of State's power to require production of documents.   (1) *Repealed.*

(2) The Secretary of State may at any time, if he thinks there is good reason to do so, give directions to a company requiring it, at such time and place as may be specified in the directions, to produce such documents as may be so specified.

(3) The Secretary of State may at any time, if he thinks there is good reason to do so, authorise an officer of his or any other competent person, on producing (if so required) evidence of his authority, to require a company to produce to him (the officer or other person) forthwith any documents which he (the officer or other person) may specify.

(4) Where by virtue of subsection (2) or (3) the Secretary of State or an officer of his or other person has power to require the production of documents from a company, he or the officer or other person has the like power to require production of those documents from any person who appears to him or the officer or other person to be in possession of them; but where any such person claims a lien on documents produced by him, the production is without prejudice to the lien.

(5) The power under this section to require a company or other person to produce documents includes power—

(a) if the documents are produced—

   (i) to take copies of them or extracts from them, and
   (ii) to require that person, or any other person who is a present or past officer of, or is or was at any time employed by, the company in question, to provide an explanation of any of them;

(b) if the documents are not produced, to require the person who was required to produce them to state, to the best of his knowledge and belief, where they are[2].

(6) If the requirement to produce documents or provide an explanation or make a statement is not complied with, the company or other person on whom the requirement was so imposed is guilty of an offence and liable[3] to a fine.
Sections 732 (restriction on prosecutions), 733 (liability of individuals for corporate default) and 734 (criminal proceedings against unincorporated bodies) apply to this offence.

(7) However, where a person is charged with an offence under subsection (6) in respect of a requirement to produce any books or papers, it is a defence to prove that they were not in his possession or under his control and that it was not reasonably practicable for him to comply with the requirement.

(8) A statement made by a person in compliance with such a requirement may be used in evidence against him.

(8A) However, in criminal proceedings in which that person is charged with an offence to which this subsection applies—

(a) no evidence relating to the statement may be adduced, and
(b) no question relating to it may be asked,

by or on behalf of the prosecution, unless evidence relating to it is adduced, or a question relating to it is asked, in the proceedings by or on behalf of that person.

(8B) Subsection (8A) applies to any offence other than—

(a) an offence under subsection (6) or section 451;
(b) an offence under section 5 of the Perjury Act 1911 (false statements made otherwise than on oath); or

(c) an offence under section 44(2) of the Criminal Law (Consolidation) (Scotland) Act 1995 (false statements made otherwise than on oath).

(9) In this section "documents" includes information recorded in any form; and, in relation to information recorded otherwise than in legible form, the power to require its production includes power to require the production of a copy of it in legible form, or in a form from which it can readily be produced in visible and legible form.

[Companies Act 1985, s 447 as amended by the Companies Act 1989, s 63, the Youth Justice and Criminal Evidence Act 1999, Sch 3 and the Criminal Justice and Police Act 2001, Sch 2.]

---

1. Part XIV contains ss 431–453.

2. See the Criminal Justice and Police Act 2001, Part 2 (PART I, ante). These provisions (summarised at para **1–180**, ante) confer, by ss 50 and 51, additional powers of seizure of property in relation to searches carried out under existing powers. However, s 57 (retention of seized items) does not authorise the retention of any property which could not be retained under the provisions listed in s 57(1), which include s 199(5) of the Financial Services Act 1986, if the property was seized under the new powers (ie those conferred by ss 50 and 51) in reliance on one of those powers (ie those conferred by the provisions listed in s 57(1)). Section 57(4) further provides that nothing in any of the provisions listed in s 57(1) authorises the retention of anything after an obligation to return it has arisen under Part 2.

3. For mode of trial and punishment, see Sch 24, post.

8–3382   448. Entry and search of premises.   (1) A justice of the peace may issue a warrant under this section if satisfied on information on oath given by or on behalf of the Secretary of State, or by a person appointed or authorised to exercise powers under this Part, that there are reasonable grounds for believing that there are on any premises documents whose production has been required under this Part and which have not been produced in compliance with the requirement.

(2) A justice of the peace may also issue a warrant under this section if satisfied on information on oath given by or on behalf of the Secretary of State, or by a person appointed or authorised to exercise powers under this Part—

(a) that there are reasonable grounds for believing that an offence has been committed for which the penalty on conviction on indictment is imprisonment for a term of not less than two years and that there are on any premises documents relating to whether the offence has been committed,

(b) that the Secretary of State, or the person so appointed or authorised, has power to require the production of the documents under this Part, and

(c) that there are reasonable grounds for believing that if production was so required the documents would not be produced but would be removed from the premises, hidden, tampered with or destroyed.

(3) A warrant under this section shall authorise a constable, together with any other person named in it and any other constables—

(a) to enter the premises specified in the information, using such force as is reasonably necessary for the purpose;

(b) to search the premises and take possession of any documents appearing to be such documents as are mentioned in subsection (1) or (2), as the case may be, or to take, in relation to any such documents, any other steps which may appear to be necessary for preserving them or preventing interference with them;

(c) to take copies of any such documents; and

(d) to require any person named in the warrant to provide an explanation of them or to state where they may be found.

(4) If in the case of a warrant under subsection (2) the justice of the peace is satisfied on information on oath that there are reasonable grounds for believing that there are also on the premises other documents relevant to the investigation, the warrant shall also authorise the actions mentioned in subsection (3) to be taken in relation to such documents.

(5) A warrant under this section shall continue in force until the end of the period of one month beginning with the day on which it is issued.

(6) Any documents of which possession is taken under this section may be retained—

(a) for a period of three months; or

(b) if within that period proceedings to which the documents are relevant are commenced against any person for any criminal offence, until the conclusion of those proceedings[1].

(7) Any person who intentionally obstructs the exercise of any rights conferred by a warrant issued under this section or fails without reasonable excuse to comply with any requirement imposed in accordance with subsection (3)(d) is guilty of an offence and liable[2] to a fine.

Sections 732 (restriction on prosecutions), 733 (liability of individuals for corporate default) and 734 (criminal proceedings against unincorporated bodies) apply to this offence.

(8) For the purposes of sections 449 and 451A (provision for security of information) documents obtained under this section shall be treated as if they had been obtained under the provision of this Part under which their production was or, as the case may be, could have been required.

(9) *Scotland.*

(10) In this section "document" includes information recorded in any form.

[Companies Act 1985, s 448, as substituted by the Companies Act 1989, s 64.]

---

1. See the Criminal Justice and Police Act 2001, Part 2 (Part I, ante). These provisions (summarised at para **1–205**, ante) confer, by ss 50 and 51, additional powers of seizure of property in relation to searches carried out under existing powers. However, s 57 (retention of seized items) does not authorise the retention of any property which could not be retained under the provisions listed in s 57(1), which include s 448(6) of the Companies Act 1985, if the property was seized under the new powers (ie those conferred by ss 50 and 51) in reliance on one of those powers (i.e. those conferred by the provisions listed in s 57(1)). Section 57(4) further provides that nothing in any of the provisions listed in s 57(1) authorises the retention of anything after an obligation to return it has arisen under Part 2.

1. For mode of trial and punishment, see Sch 24, post.

8–3382A   448A. Protection in relation to certain disclosures: information provided to Secretary of State.   (1) A person who makes a relevant disclosure is not liable by reason only of that disclosure in any proceedings relating to a breach of an obligation of confidence.

(2) A relevant disclosure is a disclosure which satisfies each of the following conditions—

(a)   it is made to the Secretary of State otherwise than in compliance with a requirement under this Part;

(b)   it is of a kind that the person making the disclosure could be required to make in pursuance of this Part;

(c)   the person who makes the disclosure does so in good faith and in the reasonable belief that the disclosure is capable of assisting the Secretary of State for the purposes of the exercise of his functions under this Part;

(d)   the information disclosed is not more than is reasonably necessary for the purpose of assisting the Secretary of State for the purposes of the exercise of those functions;

(e)   the disclosure is not one falling within subsection (3) or (4).

(3) A disclosure falls within this subsection if the disclosure is prohibited by virtue of any enactment.

(4) A disclosure falls within this subsection if—

(a)   it is made by a person carrying on the business of banking or by a lawyer, and

(b)   it involves the disclosure of information in respect of which he owes an obligation of confidence in that capacity.

(5) An enactment includes an enactment—

(a)   comprised in, or in an instrument made under, an Act of the Scottish Parliament;

(b)   comprised in subordinate legislation (within the meaning of the Interpretation Act 1978);

(c)   whenever passed or made.

[Companies Act 1985, s 448A, as inserted by the Companies (Audit, Investigations and Community Enterprise) Act 2004, s 22.]

8–3383   449. Provision for security of information obtained.   (1) This section applies to information[1] (in whatever form) obtained—

(a)   in pursuance of a requirement imposed under section 447;

(b)   by means of a relevant disclosure within the meaning of section 448A(2);

(c)   by an investigator in consequence of the exercise of his powers under section 453A.

(2) Such information must not be disclosed unless the disclosure—

(a)   is made to a person specified in Schedule 15C, or

(b)   is of a description specified in Schedule 15D.

(3) The Secretary of State may by order[2] amend Schedules 15C and 15D.

(4) An order under subsection (3) must not—

(a)   amend Schedule 15C by specifying a person unless the person exercises functions of a public nature (whether or not he exercises any other function);

(b)   amend Schedule 15D by adding or modifying a description of disclosure unless the purpose for which the disclosure is permitted is likely to facilitate the exercise of a function of a public nature.

(5) An order under subsection (3) must be made by statutory instrument subject to annulment in pursuance of a resolution of either House of Parliament.

(6) A person who discloses any information in contravention of this section—

(a)   is guilty of an offence, and

(b)   is liable[3] on conviction to imprisonment or a fine or to both.

(7) Sections 732 (restriction on prosecutions), 733 (liability of individuals for corporate default) and 734 (criminal proceedings against unincorporated bodies) apply to the offence under subsection (6).

(8) Any information which may by virtue of this section be disclosed to a person specified in Schedule 15C may be disclosed to any officer or employee of the person.

(9) This section does not prohibit the disclosure of information if the information is or has been available to the public from any other source.

(10) For the purposes of this section, information obtained by an investigator in consequence of the exercise of his powers under section 453A includes information obtained by a person accompanying the investigator in pursuance of subsection (4) of that section in consequence of that person's accompanying the investigator.

(11) Nothing in this section authorises the making of a disclosure in contravention of the Data Protection Act 1998.

[Companies Act 1985, s 449, as substituted by the Companies (Audit, Investigations and Community Enterprise) Act 2004, s 25.]

---

1. Information disclosed to the Bank of England under s 449(1) for the purpose of enabling or assisting it to discharge its functions under the Banking Act 1987 or in its capacity as a competent authority under s 449(3) may be disclosed—

    (*a*) with the consent of the Secretary of State, in any case in which information to which section 82 of the Banking Act 1987 applies could be disclosed by virtue of section 84(1) or (2) of the 1987 Act; and

    (*b*) in any case in which information to which the said section 82 applies could be disclosed by virtue of any of the other provisions of Part V of the Banking Act 1987.

    (Banking Act 1987, s 87).

2. See the Financial Services (Disclosure of Information) (Designated Authorities) Orders, SI 1986/2046, SI 1987/859 and 1141, SI 1988/1058, SI 1989/940 and 2009, SI 1993/1826 and SI 1994/340, and the Companies (Disclosure of Information) (Designated Authorities) Order 1988, SI 1988/1334 amended by SI 2002/1889 and SI 2003/1398.

3. For mode of trial and punishment, see Sch 24, post.

8–3384   450. Punishment for destroying, mutilating etc company documents.   (1) An officer of a company who—

    (*a*) destroys, mutilates or falsifies, or is privy to the destruction, mutilation or falsification of a document affecting or relating to the company's property or affairs, or

    (*b*) makes, or is privy to the making of, a false entry in such a document,

is guilty of an offence, unless he proves that he had no intention to conceal the state of affairs of the company or to defeat the law.

(1A) Subsection (1) applies to an officer of an authorised insurance company which is not a body corporate as it applies to an officer of a company.

(2) Such a person as above mentioned who fraudulently either parts with, alters or makes an omission in any such document or is privy to fraudulent parting with, fraudulent altering or fraudulent making of an omission in, any such document, is guilty of an offence.

(3) A person guilty of an offence under this section is liable[1] to imprisonment or a fine, or both.

(4) Sections 732 (restriction on prosecutions), 733 (liability of individuals for corporate default) and 734 (criminal proceedings against unincorporated bodies) apply to an offence under this section.

(5) In this section "document" includes information recorded in any form.

[Companies Act 1985, s 450 as amended by the Companies Act 1989, s 66 and SI 2001/3649.]

---

1. For mode of trial and punishment, see Sch 24, post.

8–3385   451. Punishment for furnishing false information.   (1) A person commits an offence if in purported compliance with a requirement under section 447 to provide information—

    (*a*) he provides information which he knows to be false in a material particular;

    (*b*) he recklessly provides information which is false in a material particular.

(2) A person guilty of an offence under this section is liable on conviction to imprisonment or a fine or to both.

(3) Sections 732 (restriction on prosecutions), 733 (liability of individuals for corporate default) and 734 (criminal proceedings against unincorporated bodies) apply to an offence under this section.

[Companies Act 1985, s 451 as substituted by the Companies (Audit, Investigations and Community Enterprise) Act 2004, s 25.]

---

1. For mode of trial and punishment, see Sch 24, post.

8–3386   451A. Disclosure of information by Secretary of State or inspector.   (1) This section applies to information obtained—

    (*a*) under sections 434 to 446;

    (*b*) by an inspector in consequence of the exercise of his powers under section 453A.

(2) The Secretary of State may, if he thinks fit—

    (*a*) disclose any information to which this section applies to any person to whom, or for any purpose for which, disclosure is permitted under section 449, or

    (*b*) authorise or require an inspector appointed under this Part to disclose such information to any such person or for any such purpose.

(3) Information to which this section applies may also be disclosed by an inspector appointed under this Part to—

(*a*) another inspector appointed under this Part;

(*b*) a person appointed under—

  (i)   section 167 of the Financial Services and Markets Act 2000 (general investigations),
  (ii) section 168 of that Act (investigations in particular cases),
  (iii) section 169(1)(*b*) of that Act (investigation in support of overseas regulator);
  (iv) section 284 of that Act (investigations into affairs of certain collective investment schemes), or
  (v)   regulations made as a result of section 262(2)(*k*) of that Act (investigations into open-ended investment companies),

  to conduct an investigation; or

(*c*) a person authorised to exercise powers under—

  (i)   section 447 of this Act; or
  (ii) section 84 of the Companies Act 1989 (exercise of powers to assist overseas regulatory authority).

(4) Any information which may by virtue of subsection (3) be disclosed to any person may be disclosed to any officer or servant of that person.

(5) The Secretary of State may, if he thinks fit, disclose any information obtained under section 444 to—

(*a*) the company whose ownership was the subject of the investigation,

(*b*) any member of the company,

(*c*) any person whose conduct was investigated in the course of the investigation,

(*d*) the auditors of the company, or

(*e*) any person whose financial interests appear to the Secretary of State to be affected by matters covered by the investigation.

(6) For the purposes of this section, information obtained by an inspector in consequence of the exercise of his powers under section 453A includes information obtained by a person accompanying the inspector in pursuance of subsection (4) of that section in consequence of that person's accompanying the inspector.

(7) The reference to an inspector in subsection (2)(*b*) above includes a reference to a person accompanying an inspector in pursuance of section 453A(4).

[Companies Act 1985, s 451A as inserted by the Financial Services Act 1986, Sch 13, substituted by the Companies Act 1989, s 68 and amended by the Insurance Companies (Third Insurance Directives) Regulations 1994, SI 1994/1696, SI 2001/3649 and the Companies (Audit, Investigations and Community Enterprise) Act 2004, s 25.]

Supplementary

8–3387 452. Privileged information.   (1) Nothing in sections 431 to 446 compels the disclosure by any person to the Secretary of State or to an inspector appointed by him of information in respect of which in an action in the High Court a claim to legal professional privilege, or in an action in the Court of Session a claim to confidentiality of communications, could be maintained.

(1A) Nothing in section 434, 443 or 446 requires a person (except as mentioned in subsection (1B) below) to disclose information or produce documents in respect of which he owes an obligation of confidence by virtue of carrying on the business of banking unless—

(*a*) the person to whom the obligation of confidence is owed is the company or other body corporate under investigation,

(*b*) the person to whom the obligation of confidence is owed consents to the disclosure or production, or

(*c*) the making of the requirement is authorised by the Secretary of State.

(1B) Subsection (1A) does not apply where the person owing the obligation of confidence is the company or other body corporate under investigation under section 431, 432 or 433.

(2) Nothing in sections 447 to 451—

(*a*) compels the production by any person of a document or the disclosure by any person of information in respect of which in an action in the High Court a claim to legal professional privilege, or in an action in the Court of Session a claim to confidentiality of communications, could be maintained;

(*b*) authorises the taking of possession of any such document which is in the person's possession.

(3) The Secretary of State must not under section 447 require, or authorise a person to require—

(*a*) the production by a person carrying on the business of banking of a document relating to the affairs of a customer of his, or

(*b*) the disclosure by him of information relating to those affairs,

unless one of the conditions in subsection (4) is met.

(4) The conditions are—

(a) the Secretary of State thinks it is necessary to do so for the purpose of investigating the affairs of the person carrying on the business of banking;

(b) the customer is a person on whom a requirement has been imposed under section 447;

(c) the customer is a person on whom a requirement to produce information or documents has been imposed by an investigator appointed by the Secretary of State in pursuance of section 171 or 173 of the Financial Services and Markets Act 2000 (powers of persons appointed under section 167 or as a result of section 168(2) to conduct an investigation).

(5) Despite subsections (1) and (2) a person who is a lawyer may be compelled to disclose the name and address of his client.

[Companies Act 1985, s 452 as amended by the Companies Act 1989, s 69 and Sch 24, SI 1994/1696, SI 2001/3649 and the Companies (Audit, Investigations and Community Enterprise) Act 2004, s 25.]

PART XVI[1]
FRAUDULENT TRADING BY A COMPANY

8–3388 458. Punishment for fraudulent trading.   If any business of a company is carried on with intent to defraud[2] creditors[3] of the company or creditors of any other person, or for any fraudulent purpose, every person who was knowingly a party to the carrying on of the business[4] in that manner is liable[5] to imprisonment or a fine, or both.

This applies whether or not the company has been, or is in the course of being, wound up.

[Companies Act 1985, s 458.]

---

1. Part XVI contains only s 458.

2. A charge of fraudulent trading with intent which particularises the methods by which the trading was carried out is not void for duplicity (*R v Inman* [1967] 1 QB 140, [1966] 3 All ER 414). A company carrying on business and incurring debts when to the knowledge of the directors there is no reasonable prospect of the debts being paid may in general be properly inferred to be carrying on business "with intent to defraud creditors" (*Re William C Leitch Bros Ltd* [1932] 2 Ch 71). On a prosecution under this section, it is not necessary to prove that the defendant knew at the time the debts were incurred that there was no reasonable prospect of the creditors ever receiving payment but it is sufficient to prove an intention dishonestly to prejudice the creditors in receiving payment; see *R v Grantham* [1984] QB 675, [1984] 3 All ER 166, CA.

3. "Creditors" includes persons to whom money would be owed at a future date; it is immaterial that the debt cannot presently be sued for (*R v Smith (Wallace Duncan)* [1996] Crim LR 329).

4. Circumstances will vary widely, but the section is designed to include those who exercise a controlling or managerial function or who are "running the business" (*R v Miles* [1992] Crim LR 657).

5. For mode of trial and punishment, see Sch 24, post.

PART XXIV[1]

8–3389 709. Inspection, etc of records kept by the registrar.   (1) Subject to section 723B, any person may inspect any records kept by the registrar for the purposes of the Companies Acts and may require—

(a) a copy, in such form as the registrar considers appropriate, of any information contained in those records, or

(b) a certified copy of, or extract from, any such record.

(2) The right of inspection extends to the originals of documents delivered to the registrar in legible form only where the record kept by the registrar of the contents of the document is illegible or unavailable.

(3) A copy of or extract from a record kept at any of the offices for the registration of companies in England and Wales or Scotland, certified in writing by the registrar (whose official position it is unnecessary to prove) to be an accurate record of the contents of any document delivered to him under the Companies Acts, is in all legal proceedings admissible in evidence as of equal validity with the original document and as evidence of any fact stated therein of which direct oral evidence would be admissible.

(4) Copies of or extracts from records furnished by the registrar may, instead of being certified by him in writing to be an accurate record, be sealed with his official seal.

(5) No process for compelling the production of a record kept by the registrar shall issue from any court except with the leave of the court; and any such process shall bear on it a statement that it is issued with the leave of the court.

[Companies Act 1985, s 709, as substituted by the Companies Act 1989, s 126 and as amended by the Civil Evidence Act 1995, Sch 1, the Youth Justice and Criminal Evidence Act 1999, Sch 6 and the Criminal Justice and Police Act 2001, s 45(1), (4).]

---

1. Part XXIV contains ss 704–715A.

8–3390 710. Certificate of incorporation.   Any person may require a certificate of the incorporation of a company, signed by the registrar or authenticated by his official seal.

[Companies Act 1985, s 710, as substituted by the Companies Act 1989, s 126 and as amended by the Civil Evidence Act 1995, Sch 1.]

8–3391　710A. Provision and authentication by registrar of documents in non-legible form.
(1) Any requirement of the Companies Acts as to the supply by the registrar of a document may, if the registrar thinks fit, be satisfied by the communication by the registrar of the requisite information in any non-legible form prescribed for the purposes of this section by regulations or approved by him.

(2) Where the document is required to be signed by him or sealed with his official seal, it shall instead be authenticated in such manner as may be prescribed by regulations or approved by the registrar.

[Companies Act 1985, s 710A, as inserted by the Companies Act 1989, s 126.]

8–3391A　710B. Documents relating to Welsh companies.　(1) This section applies to any document which—

　(*a*)　is delivered to the registrar under this Act, the Insolvency Act 1986 or Part 2 of the Companies (Audit, Investigations and Community Enterprise) Act 2004, and
　(*b*)　relates to a company (whether already registered or to be registered) whose memorandum states that its registered office is to be situated in Wales.

(2) A document to which this section applies may be in Welsh but, subject to subsection (3), shall on delivery to the registrar be accompanied by a certified translation into English.

(3) The requirement for a translation imposed by subsection (2) shall not apply—

　(*a*)　to documents of such descriptions as may be prescribed[1] for the purposes of this paragraph, or
　(*b*)　to documents in a form prescribed in Welsh (or partly in Welsh and partly in English) by virtue of section 26 of the Welsh Language Act 1993.

(4) Where by virtue of subsection (3) the registrar receives a document in Welsh without a certified translation into English, he shall, if that document is to be available for inspection, himself obtain such a translation; and that translation shall be treated as delivered to him in accordance with the same provision as the original.

(5) A company whose memorandum states that its registered office is to be situated in Wales may deliver to the registrar a certified translation into Welsh of any document in English which relates to the company and which is or has been delivered to the registrar.

(6) The provisions within subsection (7) (which require certified translations into English of certain documents delivered to the registrar) shall not apply where a translation is required by subsection (2) or would be required but for subsection (3).

(7) The provisions within this subsection are section 228(2)(*f*), the second sentence of section 242(1), sections 243(4), 272(5) and 273(7) and paragraph 7(3) of Part II of Schedule 9.

(8) In this section "certified translation" means a translation certified in the prescribed manner to be a correct translation.

[Companies Act 1985, s 710B, as inserted by the Welsh Language Act 1993, s 30 and amended by SI 2005/1788.]

---

1. See the Companies (Welsh Language Forms and Documents) Regulations 1994, SI 1994/117, amended by SI 1994/727 and SI 2000/2413.

8–3392　715A. Interpretation.　(1) In this Part—

"document" includes information recorded in any form; and
"legible", in the context of documents in legible or non-legible form, means capable of being read with the naked eye.

(2) References in this Part to delivering a document include sending, forwarding, producing or (in the case of a notice) giving it.

(3) References in this Part to the Companies Acts include Part 2 of the Companies (Audit, Investigations and Community Enterprise) Act 2004

[Companies Act 1985, s 715A, as inserted by the Companies Act 1989, s 127 as amended by SI 2005/1788.]

PART XXV[1]
MISCELLANEOUS AND SUPPLEMENTARY PROVISIONS

8–3393　721. Production and inspection of books where offence suspected.　(1) The following applies if on an application made—

　(*a*)　in England and Wales, to a judge of the High Court by the Director of Public Prosecutions, the Secretary of State or a chief officer of police, or
　(*b*)　in Scotland, to one of the Lords Commissioners of Justiciary by the Lord Advocate,

there is shown to be reasonable cause to believe that any person has, while an officer of a company, committed an offence in connection with the management of the company's affairs and that evidence of the commission of the offence is to be found in any books or papers of or under the control of the company.

(2) An order may be made—

(a) authorising any person named in it to inspect the books or papers in question, or any of them, for the purpose of investigating and obtaining evidence of the offence, or

(b) requiring the secretary of the company or such other officer of it as may be named in the order to produce the books or papers (or any of them) to a person named in the order at a place so named.

(3) The above applies also in relation to any books or papers of a person carrying on the business of banking so far as they relate to the company's affairs, as it applies to any books or papers of or under the control of the company, except that no such order as is referred to in subsection (2)(b) shall be made by virtue of this subsection.

(4) The decision of a judge of the High Court or of any of the Lords Commissioners of Justiciary on an application under this section is not appealable.

[Companies Act 1985, s 721.]

---

1. Part XXV contains ss 716–734.

8–3394   722. Form of company registers, etc.   (1) Any register, index, minute book or accounting records required by the Companies Acts to be kept by a company may be kept either by making entries in bound books or by recording the matters in question in any other manner.

(2) Where any such register, index, minute book or accounting record is not kept by making entries in a bound book, but by some other means, adequate precautions shall be taken for guarding against falsification and facilitating its discovery.

(3) If default is made in complying with subsection (2), the company and every officer of it who is in default is liable[1] to a fine and, for continued contravention, to a daily default fine.

[Companies Act 1985, s 722.]

---

1. For mode of trial and punishment, see Sch 24, post.

8–3395   723. Use of computers for company records.   (1) The power conferred on companies by section 722(1) to keep a register or other record by recording the matters in question otherwise than by making entries in bound books includes power to record those matters otherwise than in a legible form, so long as the record is capable of being reproduced in a legible form.

(2) Any provision of an instrument made by a company before 12th February 1979 which requires a register of holders of the company's debentures to be kept in a legible form is to be read as requiring the register to be kept in a legible or non-legible form

(3) If any such register or record is kept by a company otherwise than in a legible form, the duty imposed on the company by s 722(1) to allow inspection of, or to furnish a copy of the register, is to be treated as a duty to allow inspection of, or to furnish, a reproduction of the recording in a legible form.

(4) The Secretary of State may make regulations[1] in connection with registers or records referred to in subsection (3).

[Companies Act 1985, s 723.]

---

1. See the Companies (Registers and other Records) Regulations 1985, SI 1985/724.

8–3396   723A. Obligations of company as to inspection of registers etc.   *Power of Secretary of State to make regulations.*

8–3396A   723B. Confidentiality orders[1].   (1) Subject to the provisions of this section, an individual may make an application under this section to the Secretary of State where the condition in subsection (2) is satisfied.

(2) That condition is that the individual—

(a) is or proposes to become a director, secretary or permanent representative of a relevant company; and

(b) considers that the availability for inspection by members of the public of particulars of his usual residential address creates, or (if an order is not made under this section) is likely to create, a serious risk that he or a person who lives with him will be subjected to violence or intimidation.

(3) Where, on an application made by an individual under this section, the Secretary of State is satisfied that the availability for inspection by members of the public of particulars of the individual's usual residential address creates, or (if an order is not made under this section) is likely to create, a serious risk that the individual, or a person who lives with him, will be subjected to violence or intimidation, he shall make an order under this section ('a confidentiality order') in relation to him.

(4) Otherwise, he shall dismiss the application.

(5) An application under this section shall specify, in relation to each company of which the individual is a director, secretary or permanent representative, an address satisfying such conditions as may be prescribed[2].

(6) The Secretary of State shall give the applicant notice of his decision under subsection (3) or (4); and a notice under this subsection shall be given within the prescribed[2] period after the making of the decision and contain such information as may be prescribed.

(7) Regulations[2] may make provision about applications for confidentiality orders; and the regulations may in particular—

   (a) require the payment, on the making of an application, of such fees as may be specified in the regulations;

   (b) make provision about the form and manner in which applications are to be made;

   (c) provide that applications shall contain such information, and be accompanied by such evidence, as the Secretary of State may from time to time direct.

(8) Regulations[2] may make provision—

   (a) about the manner in which determinations are to be made under subsection (3) or (4);

   (b) for questions to be referred to such persons as the Secretary of State thinks fit for the purposes of such determinations;

   (c) about the review of such determinations;

   (d) about the period for which confidentiality orders shall remain in force and the renewal of confidentiality orders.

(9) The Secretary of State may at any time revoke a confidentiality order if he is satisfied that such conditions as may be prescribed[2] are satisfied.

(10) Regulations may make provision about the manner in which a determination under subsection (9) is to be made and notified to the individual concerned.

[Companies Act 1985, s 723B as inserted by the Criminal Justice and Police Act 2001, s 45(1), (2).]

---

1. Sections 723B–E were inserted by the Criminal Justice and Police Act 2001, s 45. These provisions allow an existing or prospective company director, secretary or permanent representative to apply for a confidentiality order, the effect of which is to disapply the requirement that his usual residential address shall be available for inspection on the public record. S 723E enables the making of regulations to provide that false statements in applications for confidentiality orders under s 723B, and disclosure of information in contravention of regulations made under 723C(4), shall be offences and that any person guilty of such an offence shall be liable – on conviction on indictment, to imprisonment for a term not exceeding 2 years, or to a fine, or to both; and on summary conviction, to imprisonment for a term not exceeding 6 months, or to a fine not exceeding the statutory maximum, or to both.

2. See the Companies (Particulars of Usual Residential Address) (Confidentiality Orders) Regulations 2002, SI 2002/912.

8–3396B 723C. Effect of confidentiality orders. (1) At any time when a confidentiality order is in force in relation to an individual—

   (a) section 709(1) shall not apply to so much of any record kept by the registrar as contains information which is recorded as particulars of the individual's usual residential address that were contained in a document delivered to the registrar after the order came into force;

   (b) section 364 shall have effect in relation to each affected company of which the individual is a director or secretary as if the reference in subsection (4)(a) of that section to the individual's usual residential address were a reference to the address for the time being specified by the individual in relation to that company under section 723B(5) or subsection (7) below.

(2) Regulations may make provision about the inspection and copying of confidential records, and such provision may include—

   (a) provision as to the persons by whom, and the circumstances in which, confidential records may be inspected or copies taken of such records;

   (b) provision under which the registrar may be required to provide certified copies of, or of extracts from, such records.

(3) Provision under subsection (2) may include provision—

   (a) for persons of a prescribed[1] description to be entitled to apply to the court for authority to inspect or take copies of confidential records;

   (b) as to the criteria to be used by the court in determining whether an authorisation should be given.

(4) Regulations may make provision for restricting the persons to whom, and the purposes for which, relevant information may be disclosed.

(5) In subsection (4) 'relevant information' means information, relating to the usual residential address of an individual in relation to whom a confidentiality order is in force, which has been obtained in prescribed[1] circumstances.

(6) Regulations may—

   (a) provide that, where a confidentiality order is in force in relation to an individual who is a director or secretary of a company, subsections (3) and (5) of section 288 shall not apply in relation to so much of the register kept by the company under that section as contains particulars of the usual residential address of that individual ('the protected part of the register'); and

(b)   make provision as to the persons by whom the protected part of the register may be inspected and the conditions (which may include conditions as to the payment of a fee) on which they may inspect it.

(7)   Regulations may make provision—

(a)   requiring any individual in relation to whom a confidentiality order is in force to specify in the prescribed manner, in relation to each company of which he becomes a director, secretary or permanent representative at a time when the order is in force, an address satisfying such conditions as may be prescribed;

(b)   as to the manner in which the address specified in relation to a company under section 723B(5) or this subsection may be changed.

(8)   A company is an affected company for the purposes of subsection (1) if—

(a)   it is required to deliver annual returns in accordance with section 363; and

(b)   the individual has specified an address in relation to it under section 723B(5) or subsection (7) above.

[Companies Act 1985, s 723C as inserted by the Criminal Justice and Police Act 2001, s 45(1), (2).]

---

1. See the Companies (Particulars of Usual Residential Address) (Confidentiality Orders) Regulations 2002, SI 2002/912.

8–3396C   723D. Construction of sections 723B and 723C.   (1) In section 723B 'relevant company' means—

(a)   a company formed and registered under this Act or an existing company; or

(b)   an overseas company.

(2)   For the purposes of sections 723B and 723C, an individual is a permanent representative of a company if—

(a)   the company is a company to which section 690A applies; and

(b)   he is authorised to represent the company as a permanent representative of the company for the business of one or more of its branches in Great Britain.

(3)   In section 723C 'confidential records' means so much of any records kept by the registrar for the purposes of the Companies Acts as contains information—

(a)   which relates to an individual in relation to whom a confidentiality order is in force; and

(b)   is recorded as particulars of the individual's usual residential address that were contained in a document delivered to the registrar after the order came into force.

(4)   In sections 723B and 723C—

"confidentiality order" means an order under section 723B;

"the court" means such court as may be specified in regulations;

"director" and "secretary", in relation to an overseas company, have the same meanings as in Chapter 1 of Part 23 of this Act;

"document" has the same meaning as in Part 24 of this Act;

"prescribed" means prescribed by regulations.

(5)   Section 715A(2) applies in relation to sections 723B and 723C as it applies in relation to Part 24 of this Act.

(6)   Regulations[1] may provide that in determining for the purposes of sections 723B and 723C whether a document has been delivered after the coming into force of a confidentiality order, any document delivered to the registrar after the latest time permitted for the delivery of that document shall be deemed to have been delivered at that time.

(7)   For the purposes of section 723B(2)(a) and subsection (2) above it is immaterial whether or not the company in question has already been incorporated or become a relevant company or a company to which section 690A applies at the time of the application under section 723B.

(8)   For the purposes of section 723C(1) and subsection (3) above, it is immaterial whether the record in question consists in the original document concerned.]

[Companies Act 1985, s 723D as inserted by the Criminal Justice and Police Act 2001, s 45(1), (2).]

---

1. See the Companies (Particulars of Usual Residential Address) (Confidentiality Orders) Regulations 2002, SI 2002/912.

8–3396D   723E. Sections 723B and 723C: offences.   (1) Regulations[1] may provide—

(a)   that any person who in an application under section 723B makes a statement which he knows to be false in a material particular, or recklessly makes a statement which is false in a material particular, shall be guilty of an offence;

(b)   that any person who discloses information in contravention of regulations under section 723C(4) shall be guilty of an offence.

(2) Regulations[1] may provide that a person guilty of an offence under subsection (1) shall be liable—

(a) on conviction on indictment, to imprisonment for a term not exceeding two years, or to a fine, or to both; and

(b) on summary conviction, to imprisonment for a term not exceeding six months, or to a fine not exceeding the statutory maximum, or to both.]

[Companies Act 1985, s 723E as inserted by the Criminal Justice and Police Act 2001, s 45(1), (2).]

---

1. See the Companies (Particulars of Usual Residential Address) (Confidentiality Orders) Regulations 2002, SI 2002/912.

8–3396E 723F. Regulations under sections 723B to 723E.   (1) In sections 723B to 723E 'regulations[1]' means regulations made by the Secretary of State.

(2) Any power of the Secretary of State to make regulations under any of those sections shall be exercisable by statutory instrument.

(3) Regulations[1] under sections 723B to 723E—

(a) may make different provision for different cases;

(b) may contain such incidental, supplemental, consequential and transitional provision, as the Secretary of State thinks fit.

(4) The provision that may be made by virtue of subsection (3)(b) includes provision repealing or modifying any enactment.

(5) No regulations shall be made under any of sections 723B to 723E unless a draft of the instrument containing them has been laid before Parliament and approved by a resolution of each House.

[Companies Act 1985, s 723F as inserted by the Criminal Justice and Police Act 2001, s 45(1), (2).]

---

1. See the Companies (Particulars of Usual Residential Address) (Confidentiality Orders) Regulations 2002, SI 2002/912.

8–3397 725. Service of documents.   (1) A document[1] may be served on a company by leaving it at, or sending it by post[2] to, the company's registered office.

(2) Where a company registered in Scotland carries on business in England and Wales, the process of any court in England and Wales may be served on the company by leaving it at, or sending it by post to, the company's principal place of business in England and Wales, addressed to the manager or other head officer in England and Wales of the company.

(3) Where process is served on a company under subsection (2), the person issuing out the process shall send a copy of it by post to the company's registered office.

[Companies Act 1985, s 725.]

---

1. For meaning of "document", see s 744, post.
2. See presumption of due delivery in s 7 of the Interpretation Act 1978, in PART II: EVIDENCE, ante.

8–3398 730. Punishment of offences.   (1) Schedule 24[1] to this Act has effect with respect to the way in which offences under this Act are punishable on conviction.

(2) In relation to an offence under a provision of this Act specified in the first column of the Schedule (the general nature of the offence being described in the second column), the third column shows whether the offence is punishable on conviction on indictment, or on summary conviction, or either in the one way or the other.

(3) The fourth column of the Schedule shows, in relation to an offence, the maximum punishment by way of fine or imprisonment under this Act which may be imposed on a person convicted of the offence in the way specified in relation to it in the third column (that is to say, on indictment or summarily), a reference to a period of years or months being to a term of imprisonment of that duration.

(4) The fifth column shows (in relation to an offence for which there is an entry in that column) that a person convicted of the offence after continued contravention is liable to a daily default fine; that is to say, he is liable on a second or subsequent summary conviction of the offence to the fine specified in that column for each day on which the contravention is continued (instead of the penalty specified for the offence in the fourth column of the Schedule).

(5) For the purpose of any enactment in the Companies Acts which provides that an officer of a company or other body who is in default is liable to a fine or penalty, the expression "officer who is in default" means any officer of the company or other body who knowingly and wilfully authorises or permits the default, refusal or contravention mentioned in the enactment.

[Companies Act 1985, s 730 as amended by the Companies Act 1989, Sch 19.]

---

1. See post.

8–3399   731. Summary proceedings.   (1) Summary proceedings for any offence under the Companies Acts may (without prejudice to any jurisdiction exercisable apart from this subsection) be taken against a body corporate at any place at which the body has a place of business, and against any other person at any place at which he is for the time being.

(2) Notwithstanding anything in section 127(1) of the Magistrates' Courts Act 1980, an information relating to an offence[1] under the Companies Acts which is triable by a magistrates' court in England and Wales may be so tried if it is laid at any time within 3 years after the commission of the offence and within 12 months after the date on which evidence sufficient in the opinion of the Director of Public Prosecutions or the Secretary of State (as the case may be) to justify the proceedings comes to his knowledge.

(3) *Scotland.*

(4) For purposes of this section, a certificate of the Director of Public Prosecutions, the Lord Advocate or the Secretary of State (as the case may be) as to the date on which such evidence as is referred to above came to his knowledge is conclusive evidence.

---

1. This subsection must be read with s 127 of the Magistrates' Courts Act 1980 in Part I: Magistrates' Courts, Procedure, ante, subsection (2) of which provides that the time limits for summary offences in s 127(1) do not apply to indictable offences which includes offences triable either way. Accordingly, the time limits in s 371(2) do not apply to offences under the Companies Act 1985 which are triable either way (*R v Thames Metropolitan Stipendiary Magistrate, ex p Horgan* [1998] QB 719, [1998] 1 All ER 559, [1998] 2 Cr App Rep 47, DC.

[Companies Act 1985, s 731.]

8–3400   732. Prosecution by public authorities.   (1) In respect of an offence under any of sections 210, 245E, 245G, 324, 329, 448, 449 to 451, 453A and 455, proceedings shall not, in England and Wales, be instituted except by or with the consent of the appropriate authority.

(2) That authority is—

(*a*)   for an offence under any of sections 210, 245E, 245G, 324 and 329, the Secretary of State or the Director of Public Prosecutions,

(*b*)   for an offence under any of sections 448, 449 to 451, 453A, either one of those two persons or the Industrial Assurance Commissioner, and

(*c*)   for an offence under section 455, the Secretary of State.

(3) Where proceedings are instituted under the Companies Acts against any person by the Director of Public Prosecutions or by or on behalf of the Secretary of State or the Lord Advocate, nothing in those Acts is to be taken to require any person to disclose any information which he is entitled to refuse to disclose on grounds of legal professional privilege or, in Scotland, confidentiality of communications.

[Companies Act 1985, s 732 as amended by the Companies (Audit, Investigations and Community Enterprise) Act 2004, Sch 2.]

8–3401   733. Offences by bodies corporate.   (1) The following applies to offences under any of sections 210, 216(3), 245E(3), 245G(7), 394A(1) and 448, 449 to 451 and 453A.

(2) Where a body corporate is guilty of such an offence and it is proved that the offence occurred with the consent or connivance of, or was attributable to any neglect on the part of any director, manager, secretary or other similar officer of the body, or any person who was purporting to act in any such capacity, he as well as the body corporate is guilty of that offence and is liable to be proceeded against and punished accordingly.

(3) Where the affairs of a body corporate are managed by its members, subsection (2) above applies in relation to the acts and defaults of a member in connection with his functions of management as if he were a director of the body corporate.

(4) In this section "director", in relation to an offence under any of sections 448, 449 to 451 and 453A, includes a shadow director.

[Companies Act 1985, s 733 as amended by the Insolvency Act 1985, Sch 6, the Insolvency Act 1986, Sch 13 and the Companies Act 1989, s 123 and Sch 24 and the Companies (Audit, Investigations and Community Enterprise) Act 2004, Sch 2.]

8–3402   734. Criminal proceedings against unincorporated bodies.   (1) Proceedings for an offence alleged to have been committed under section 245E(3), 245G(7), section 394A(1) or any of sections 448, 449 to 451 and 453Aby an unincorporated body shall be brought in the name of that body (and not in that of any of its members), and for the purposes of any such proceedings, any rules of court relating to the service of documents apply as if that body were a corporation.

(2) A fine imposed on an unincorporated body on its conviction of such an offence shall be paid out of the funds of that body.

(3) In a case in which an unincorporated body is charged in England and Wales with such an offence, section 33 of the Criminal Justice Act 1925 and Schedule 3 to the Magistrates' Courts Act 1980 (procedure on charge of an offence against a corporation) have effect in like manner as in the case of a corporation so charged.

(4) *Scotland.*

(5) Where such an offence committed by a partnership is proved to have been committed with

the consent or connivance of, or to be attributable to any neglect on the part of, a partner, he as well as the partnership is guilty of the offence and liable to be proceeded against and punished accordingly.

(6) Where such an offence committed by an unincorporated body (other than a partnership) is proved to have been committed with the consent or connivance of, or to be attributable to any neglect on the part of, any officer of the body or any member of its governing body, he as well as the body is guilty of the offence and liable to be proceeded against and punished accordingly.

[Companies Act 1985, s 734 as amended by the Companies Act 1989, ss 120 and 123 and Sch 19 and the Companies (Audit, Investigations and Community Enterprise) Act 2004, Sch 2.]

PART XXVI[1]
INTERPRETATION

8–3403   735. "Company", etc.   (1) In this Act—

(a) "company" means a company formed and registered under this Act, or an existing company;

(b) "existing company" means a company formed and registered under the former Companies Acts, but does not include a company registered under the Joint Stock Companies Acts, the Companies Act 1862 or the Companies (Consolidation) Act 1908 in what was then Ireland;

(c) "the former Companies Acts" means the Joint Stock Companies Acts, the Companies Act 1862, the Companies (Consolidation) Act 1908, the Companies Act 1929 and the Companies Acts 1948 to 1983.

(2) "Public company" and "private company" have the meanings given by section 1(3).

(3) "The Joint Stock Companies Acts" means the Joint Stock Companies Act 1856, the Joint Stock Companies Acts 1856, 1857, the Joint Stock Banking Companies Act 1857 and the Act to enable Joint Stock Banking Companies to be formed on the principle of limited liability, or any one or more of those Acts (as the case may require), but does not include the Joint Stock Companies Act 1844.

(4) The definitions in this section apply unless the contrary intention appears.

[Companies Act 1985, s 735.]

---

1. Part XXVI contains ss 735–744.

8–3404   735A. Relationship of this Act to Insolvency Act.   (1) In this Act "the Insolvency Act" means the Insolvency Act 1986; and in the following provisions of this Act, namely, sections 375(1)(b), 425(6)(a), 460(2), 675, 676, 677, 699(1), 728 and Schedule 21, paragraph 6(1), the words "this Act" are to be read as including Parts I to VII of that Act, sections 411, 413, 414, 416 and 417 in Part XV of that Act, and also the Company Directors Disqualification Act 1986.

(2) In sections 704(5), 706(1), 707(1), 707A(1), 708(1)(a) and (4), 709(1) and (3), 710A, 713(1), 729 and 732(3) references to the Companies Acts include Parts I to VII of the Insolvency Act, sections 411, 413, 414, 416 and 417 in Part XV of that Act, and also the Company Directors Disqualification Act 1986.

(3) Subsections (1) and (2) apply unless the contrary intention appears.

[Companies Act 1985, s 735A, as inserted by the Insolvency Act 1986, Sch 13, Part II and amended by the Companies Act 1989, s 127 and Sch 24.]

8–3405   735B. Relationship of this Act to Parts IV and V of the Financial Services Act 1986.
In sections 704(5), 706(1), 707(1), 707A(1), 708(1)(a) and (4), 709(1) and (3), 710A and 713(1) references to the Companies Acts include Parts IV and V of the Financial Services Act 1986.

[Companies Act 1985, s 735B, as inserted by the Companies Act 1989, s 127.]

8–3406   736. "Subsidiary", "holding company" and "wholly-owned subsidiary".   (1) A company is a "subsidiary" of another company, its "holding company", if that other company—

(a) holds a majority of the voting rights in it, or

(b) is a member of it and has the right to appoint or remove a majority of its board of directors, or

(c) is a member of it and controls alone, pursuant to an agreement with other shareholders or members, a majority of the voting rights in it,

or if it is a subsidiary of a company which is itself a subsidiary of that other company.

(2) A company is a "wholly-owned subsidiary" of another company if it has no members except that other and that other's wholly-owned subsidiaries or persons acting on behalf of that other or its wholly-owned subsidiaries.

(3) In this section "company" includes any body corporate.

[Companies Act 1985, s 736, as substituted by the Companies Act 1989, s 144.]

8–3407   736A. Provisions supplementing s 736.   (1) The provisions of this section explain expressions used in section 736 and otherwise supplement that section.

(2) In section 736(1)(a) and (c) the references to the voting rights in a company are to the rights

conferred on shareholders in respect of their shares or, in the case of a company not having a share capital, on members, to vote at general meetings of the company on all, or substantially all, matters.

(3) In section 736(1)(*b*) the reference to the right to appoint or remove a majority of the board of directors is to the right to appoint or remove directors holding a majority of the voting rights at meetings of the board on all, or substantially all, matters; and for the purposes of that provision—

    (*a*) a company shall be treated as having the right to appoint to a directorship if—

        (i) a person's appointment to it follows necessarily from his appointment as director of the company, or

        (ii) the directorship is held by the company itself; and

    (*b*) a right to appoint or remove which is exercisable only with the consent or concurrence of another person shall be left out of account unless no other person has a right to appoint or, as the case may be, remove in relation to that directorship.

(4) Rights which are exercisable only in certain circumstances shall be taken into account only—

    (*a*) when the circumstances have arisen, and for so long as they continue to obtain, or
    (*b*) when the circumstances are within the control of the person having the rights;

and rights which are normally exercisable but are temporarily incapable of exercise shall continue to be taken into account.

(5) Rights held by a person in a fiduciary capacity shall be treated as not held by him.

(6) Rights held by a person as nominee for another shall be treated as held by the other; and rights shall be regarded as held as nominee for another if they are exercisable only on his instructions or with his consent or concurrence.

(7) Rights attached to shares held by way of security shall be treated as held by the person providing the security—

    (*a*) where apart from the right to exercise them for the purpose of preserving the value of the security, or of realising it, the rights are exercisable only in accordance with his instructions;

    (*b*) where the shares are held in connection with the granting of loans as part of normal business activities and apart from the right to exercise them for the purpose of preserving the value of the security, or of realising it, the rights are exercisable only in his interests.

(8) Rights shall be treated as held by a company if they are held by any of its subsidiaries; and nothing in subsection (6) or (7) shall be construed as requiring rights held by a company to be treated as held by any of its subsidiaries.

(9) For the purposes of subsection (7) rights shall be treated as being exercisable in accordance with the instructions or in the interests of a company if they are exercisable in accordance with the instructions of or, as the case may be, in the interests of—

    (*a*) any subsidiary or holding company of that company, or
    (*b*) any subsidiary of a holding company of that company.

(10) The voting rights in a company shall be reduced by any rights held by the company itself.

(11) References in any provision of subsections (5) to (10) to rights held by a person include rights falling to be treated as held by him by virtue of any other provision of those subsections but not rights which by virtue of any such provision are to be treated as not held by him.

(12) In this section "company" includes any body corporate.

[Companies Act 1985, s 736A, as inserted by the Companies Act 1989, s 144.]

8–3408　736B. Power to amend ss 736 and 736A.　(1) The Secretary of State may by regulations amend sections 736 and 736A so as to alter the meaning of the expressions "holding company", "subsidiary" or "wholly-owned subsidiary".

(2) The regulations may make different provision for different cases or classes of case and may contain such incidental and supplementary provisions as the Secretary of State thinks fit.

(3) Regulations under this section shall be made by statutory instrument which shall be subject to annulment in pursuance of a resolution of either House of Parliament.

(4) Any amendment made by regulations under this section does not apply for the purposes of enactments outside the Companies Acts unless the regulations so provide.

(5) So much of section 23(3) of the Interpretation Act 1978 as applies section 17(2)(*a*) of that Act (effect of repeal and re-enactment) to deeds, instruments and documents other than enactments shall not apply in relation to any repeal and re-enactment effected by regulations made under this section.

[Companies Act 1985, s 736B, as inserted by the Companies Act 1989, s 144.]

8–3409　737. "Called-up share capital".　(1) In this Act, "called-up share capital", in relation to a company, means so much of its share capital as equals the aggregate amount of the calls made on its shares (whether or not those calls have been paid), together with any share capital paid up without being called and any share capital to be paid on a specified future date under the articles, the terms of allotment of the relevant shares or any other arrangements for payment of those shares.

(2) "Uncalled share capital" is to be construed accordingly.

(3) The definitions in this section apply unless the contrary intention appears.
[Companies Act 1985, s 737.]

8–3410   738. "Allotment" and "paid up".   (1) In relation to an allotment of shares in a company, the shares are to be taken for the purposes of this Act to be allotted when a person acquires the unconditional right to be included in the company's register of members in respect of those shares.

(2) For purposes of this Act, a share in a company is deemed paid up (as to its nominal value or any premium on it) in cash, or allotted for cash, if the consideration for the allotment or payment up is cash received by the company, or is a cheque received by it in good faith which the directors have no reason for suspecting will not be paid, or is a release of a liability of the company for a liquidated sum, or is an undertaking to pay cash to the company at a future date.

(3) In relation to the allotment or payment up of any shares in a company, references in this Act (except sections 89 to 94) to consideration other than cash and to the payment up of shares and premiums on shares otherwise than in cash include the payment of, or any undertaking to pay, cash to any person other than the company.

(4) For the purpose of determining whether a share is or is to be allotted for cash, or paid up in cash, "cash" includes foreign currency.
[Companies Act 1985, s 738.]

8–3411   739. "Non-cash asset".   (1) In this Act "non-cash asset" means any property or interest in property other than cash; and for this purpose "cash" includes foreign currency.

(2) A reference to the transfer or acquisition of a non-cash asset includes the creation or extinction of an estate or interest in, or a right over, any property and also the discharge of any person's liability, other than a liability for a liquidated sum.
[Companies Act 1985, s 739.]

8–3412   740. "Body corporate" and "corporation".   References in this Act to a body corporate or to a corporation do not include a corporation sole, but include a company incorporated elsewhere than in Great Britain.
Such references to a body corporate do not include a Scottish firm.
[Companies Act 1985, s 740.]

8–3413   741. "Director" and "shadow director".   (1) In this Act, "director" includes any person occupying the position of director, by whatever name called.

(2) In relation to a company, "shadow director" means a person in accordance with whose directions or instructions the directors of the company are accustomed to act.
However, a person is not deemed a shadow director by reason only that the directors act on advice given by him in a professional capacity.

(3) For the purposes of the following provisions of this Act, namely—

section 309 (directors' duty to have regard to interests of employees),
section 319 (directors' long-term contracts of employment),
sections 320 to 322 (substantial property transactions involving directors), and
sections 330 to 346 (general restrictions on power of companies to make loans, etc, to directors and others connected with them),

(being provisions under which shadow directors are treated as directors), a body corporate is not to be treated as a shadow director of any of its subsidiary companies by reason only that the directors of the subsidiary are accustomed to act in accordance with its directions or instructions.
[Companies Act 1985, s 741.]

8–3414   742. Expressions used in connection with accounts.   (1) In this Act, unless a contrary intention appears, the following expressions have the same meaning as in Part VII (accounts)—

"annual accounts",
"accounting reference date" and "accounting reference period",
"balance sheet" and "balance sheet date",
"Companies Act accounts",
"Companies Act individual accounts";
"current assets",
"financial year", in relation to a company,
"fixed assets",
"IAS accounts",
"IAS individual accounts",
"parent company" and "parent undertaking",
"profit and loss account", and
"subsidiary undertaking".

(2) References in this Act to "realised profits" and "realised losses", in relation to a company's accounts, shall be construed in accordance with section 262(3).
[Companies Act 1985, s 742, as substituted by the Companies Act 1989, s 10 and amended by SI 2004/2947.]

8–3414A **742A. Meaning of "offer to the public".** (1) Any reference in Part IV (allotment of shares and debentures), Part 7 (accounts) or section 744 (general interpretation) to offering shares or debentures to the public is to be read as including a reference to offering them to any section of the public, however selected.

(2) This section does not require an offer to be treated as made to the public if it can properly be regarded, in all the circumstances—

(*a*) as not being calculated to result, directly or indirectly, in the shares or debentures becoming available for subscription or purchase by persons other than those receiving the offer; or

(*b*) as being a domestic concern of the persons receiving and making it.

(3) An offer of shares in or debentures of a private company (other than an offer to which subsection (5) applies) is to be regarded (unless the contrary is proved) as being a domestic concern of the persons making and receiving it if—

(*a*) it is made to—

   (i) an existing member of the company making the offer;

   (ii) an existing employee of that company;

   (iii) the widow or widower or surviving civil partner of a person who was a member or employee of that company;

   (iv) a member of the family of a person who is or was a member of that company; or

   (v) an existing debenture holder; or

(*b*) it is an offer to subscribe for shares or debentures to be held under an employee's share scheme.

(4) Subsection (5) applies to an offer—

(*a*) which falls within paragraph (*a*) or (*b*) of subsection (3); but

(*b*) which is made on terms which permit the person to whom it is made to renounce his right to the allotment of shares or issue of debentures.

(5) The offer is to be regarded (unless the contrary is proved) as being a domestic concern of the persons making and receiving it if the terms are such that the right may be renounced only in favour—

(*a*) of any person mentioned in subsection (3)(*a*), or

(*b*) in the case of an employee's share scheme, of a person entitled to hold shares or debentures under the scheme.

(6) For the purposes of subsection (3)(*a*)(iv), the members of a person's family are—

(*a*) the person's spouse or civil partner and children (including step-children) and their descendants, and

(*b*) any trustee (acting in his capacity as such) of a trust the principal beneficiary of which is the person him or herself or of any of those relatives.

(7) Where an application has been made to the competent authority in any EEA State for the admission of any securities to official listing, then an offer of those securities for subscription or sale to a person whose ordinary business it is to buy or sell shares or debentures (whether as principal or agent) is not to be regarded as an offer to the public for the purposes of this Part.

(8) For the purposes of subsection (7)—

(*a*) "competent authority" means a competent authority appointed for the purposes of the Council Directive of 28 May 2001 on the admission of securities to official stock exchange listing and on information to be published on those securities; and

(*b*) "official listing" means official listing pursuant to that directive.

[Companies Act 1985, s 742A, as inserted by the Financial Services and Markets Act (Consequential Amendments and Repeals) Order 2001, SI 2001/3949 and the Civil Partnership Act 2004, Sch 27.]

8–3414B **742B. Meaning of "banking company".** (1) Subject to subsection (2), "banking company" means a person who has permission under Part 4 of the Financial Services and Markets Act 2000 to accept deposits.

(2) A banking company does not include—

(*a*) a person who is not a company, and

(*b*) a person who has permission to accept deposits only for the purpose of carrying on another regulated activity in accordance with that permission.

(3) This section must be read with—

(*a*) section 22 of the Financial Services and Markets Act 2000;

(*b*) any relevant order under that section; and

(*c*) Schedule 2 to that Act.

[Companies Act 1985, s 742B, as inserted by the Financial Services and Markets Act (Consequential Amendments and Repeals) Order 2001, SI 2001/3949.]

8–3414C 742C. Meaning of "insurance company" and "authorised insurance company".
(1) For the purposes of this Act, "insurance company" has the meaning given in subsection (2) and "authorised insurance company" has the meaning given in subsection (3).

(2) Subject to subsection (3), "insurance company" means a person (whether incorporated or not)—

(*a*) who has permission under Part 4 of the Financial Services and Markets Act 2000 to effect or carry out contracts of insurance; or

(*b*) who carries on insurance market activity, or

(*c*) who may effect or carry out contracts of insurance under which the benefits provided by that person are exclusively or primarily benefits in kind in the event of accident to or breakdown of a vehicle, and does not fall within paragraph (a).

(3) An insurance company does not include a friendly society, within the meaning of section 116 of the Friendly Societies Act 1992.

(4) An "authorised insurance company" means a person falling within paragraph (*a*) of subsection (2).

(5) References in this section to contracts of insurance and the effecting or carrying out of such contracts must be read with—

(*a*) section 22 of the Financial Services and Markets Act 2000;

(*b*) any relevant order under that section; and

(*c*) Schedule 2 to that Act.

[Companies Act 1985, s 742C, as inserted by the Financial Services and Markets Act (Consequential Amendments and Repeals) Order 2001, SI 2001/3949.]

8–3420 743. "Employees' share scheme". For purposes of this Act, an employees' share scheme is a scheme for encouraging or facilitating the holding of shares or debentures in a company by or for the benefit of—

(*a*) the bona fide employees or former employees of the company, the company's subsidiary or holding company or a subsidiary of the company's holding company, or

(*b*) the spouses, civil partners, surviving spouses, surviving civil partners or children or step-children under the age of 18 of such employees or former employees.

[Companies Act 1985, s 743 as amended by SI 2005/3542.]

8–3421 744. Expressions used generally in this Act. In this Act, unless the contrary intention appears, the following definitions apply—

"agent" does not include a person's counsel acting as such;

"articles" means, in relation to a company, its articles of association, as originally framed or as altered by resolution, including (so far as applicable to the company) regulations contained in or annexed to any enactment relating to companies passed before this Act, as altered by or under any such enactment;

"authorised minimum" has the meaning given by section 118;

"bank holiday" means a holiday under the Banking and Financial Dealings Act 1971;

"books and papers" and "books or papers" include accounts, deeds, writings and documents;

"communication" means the same as in the Electronic Communications Act 2000;

"the Companies Acts" means this Act, the Insider Dealing Act and the Consequential Provisions Act;

"the Consequential Provisions Act" means the Companies Consolidation (Consequential Provisions) Act 1985;

"the court", in relation to a company, means the court having jurisdiction to wind up the company;

"debenture" includes debenture stock, bonds and any other securities of a company, whether constituting a charge on the assets of the company or not;

"document" includes summons, notice, order, and other legal process, and registers;

"EEA State" means a State which is a Contracting Party to the Agreement on the European Economic Area signed at Oporto on 2 May 1992 as adjusted by the Protocol signed at Brussels on 17 March 1993;

"electronic communication" means the same as in the Electronic Communications Act 2000;

"equity share capital" means, in relation to a company, its issued share capital excluding any part of that capital which, neither as respects dividends nor as respects capital, carries any right to participate beyond a specified amount in a distribution;

"expert" has the meaning given by section 62;

"floating charge" includes a floating charge within the meaning given by section 462;

"the Gazette" means, as respects companies registered in England and Wales, the London Gazette and, as respects companies registered in Scotland, the Edinburgh Gazette;

"hire-purchase agreement" has the same meaning as in the Consumer Credit Act 1974;

"the insider dealing legislation" means Part V of the Criminal Justice Act 1993 (insider dealing);

"insurance market activity" has the meaning given in section 316(3) of the Financial Services and Markets Act 2000;

"joint stock company" has the meaning given by section 683;

"memorandum", in relation to a company, means its memorandum of association, as originally framed or as altered in pursuance of any enactment;

"number", in relation to shares, includes amount, where the context admits of the reference to shares being construed to include stock;

"officer", in relation to a body corporate, includes a director, manager or secretary;

"official seal", in relation to the registrar of companies, means a seal prepared under section 704(4) for the authentication of documents required for or in connection with the registration of companies;

"overseas company" means—

    (*a*) a company incorporated elsewhere than in Great Britain which, after the commencement of this Act, establishes a place of business in Great Britain, and

    (*b*) a company so incorporated which has, before that commencement, established a place of business and continues to have an established place of business in Great Britain at that commencement;

"place of business" includes a share transfer or share registration office;

"prescribed" means—

    (*a*) as respects provisions of this Act relating to winding up, prescribed by general rules, and

    (*b*) otherwise, prescribed by statutory instrument made by the Secretary of State;

"prospectus" means any prospectus, notice, circular, advertisement, or other invitation, offering to the public for subscription or purchase any shares in or debentures of a company;

"regulated activity" has the meaning given in section 22 of the Financial Services and Markets Act 2000;

"the registrar of companies" and "the registrar" mean the registrar or other officer performing under this Act the duty of registration of companies in England and Wales or in Scotland, as the case may require;

"share" means share in the share capital of a company, and includes stock (except where a distinction between shares and stock is express or implied); and

"undistributable reserves" has the meaning given by section 264(3).★

[Companies Act 1985, s 744 as amended by the Insolvency Act 1985, Sch 10, the Banking Act 1987, Schs 6 and 7, and the Financial Services Act 1986, Sch 17, the Companies Act 1989, Schs 10 and 24, the Criminal Justice Act 1993, Sch 5, SI 1997/2306, SI 2000/3373 and SI 2001/3649.]

★**Amended by the Companies Act 1989, Sch 24, when in force**.

8–3422   744A. Index of defined expressions.   The following Table shows provisions defining or otherwise explaining expressions for the purposes of this Act generally—

accounting reference date, accounting reference period	sections 224 and 742(1)
acquisition (in relation to a non-cash asset)	section 739(2)
Agent	section 744
allotment (and related expressions)	section 738
annual accounts	sections 261(2), 262(1) and 742(1)
annual general meeting	section 366
annual return	section 363
Articles	section 744
authorised insurance company	section 742C
authorised minimum	section 118
balance sheet and balance sheet date	sections 261(2), 262(1) and 742(1)
bank holiday	section 744
banking company	section 742B
body corporate	section 740
books and papers, books or papers	section 744
called-up share capital	section 737(1)
capital redemption reserve	section 170(1)
the Companies Acts	section 744
Companies Act accounts	sections 262(1) and 742(1)
Companies Act individual accounts	sections 226(2), 255(4A) and 742(1)
companies charges register	section 397
communication	section 744
Company	section 735(1)
the Consequential Provisions Act	section 744
Corporation	section 740
the court (in relation to a company)	section 744
current assets	sections 262(1) and 742(1)
debenture	section 744
director	section 741(1)
document	section 744
EEA State	section 744
elective resolution	section 379A

electronic communication	section 744
employees' share scheme	section 743
equity share capital	section 744
existing company	section 735(1)
extraordinary general meeting	section 368
extraordinary resolution	section 378(1)
financial year (of a company)	sections 223 and 742(1)
fixed assets	sections 262(1) and 742(1)
floating charge (in Scotland)	section 462
the former Companies Acts	section 735(1)
the Gazette	section 744
hire-purchase agreement	section 744
holding company	section 736
IAS accounts	sections 262(1) and 742(1)
IAS individual accounts	sectons 226(2) and 742(1)
the insider dealing legislation	section 744
the Insolvency Act	section 735A(1)
insurance company	section 742C
insurance market activity	rection 744
the Joint Stock Companies Acts	section 735(3)
limited company	section 1(2)
member (of a company)	section 22
memorandum (in relation to a company)	section 744
non-cash asset	section 739(1)
number (in relation to shares)	section 744
office copy (in relation to a court order in Scotland)	section 743A
officer (in relation to a body corporate)	section 744
official seal (in relation to the registrar of companies)	section 744
overseas company	section 744
overseas branch register	section 362
paid up (and related expressions)	section 738
parent company and parent undertaking	sections 258 and 742(1)
place of business	section 744
prescribed	section 744
private company	section 1(3)
profit and loss account	sections 261(2), 262(1) and (2) and 742(1)
prospectus	section 744
public company	section 1(3)
realised profits or losses	sections 262(3) and 742(2)
registered number (of a company)	section 705(1)
registered office (of a company)	section 287
registrar and registrar of companies	section 744
regulated activity	section 744
resolution for reducing share capital	section 135(3)
shadow director	section 741(2) and (3)
share	section 744
share premium account	section 130(1)
share warrant	section 188
special notice (in relation to a resolution)	section 379
special resolution	section 378(2)
subsidiary	section 736
subsidiary undertaking	sections 258 and 742(1)
transfer (in relation to a non-cash asset)	section 739(2)
uncalled share capital	section 737(2)
undistributable reserves	section 264(3)
unlimited company	section 1(2)
unregistered company	section 718
wholly-owned subsidiary	section 736(2)

[Companies Act 1985, s 744A, as inserted by the Companies Act 1989, Sch 19 and amended by SI 1997/2306, SI 2000/3373, SI 2001/3649 and SI 2004/2947.]

---

*Entries "Companies Act accounts", "Companies Act individual accounts", "IAS accounts", "IAS individual accounts" and "profit and loss acccount" reproduced as inserted or amended by SI 2004/2947, with effect in relation to companies' financial years ending on or after 1 January 2005.

PART XXVII[1]
FINAL PROVISIONS

8–3423   746. *Commencement.*

---

1. Part XXVII contains ss 745–747.

8–3424   747. Citation. This Act may be cited as the Companies Act 1985.
[Companies Act 1985, s 747.]

8–3424A   Section 730

SCHEDULE 24[1]

PUNISHMENT OF OFFENCES UNDER THIS ACT

(As amended by the Insolvency Act 1986, Sch 12, the Company Directors Disqualification Act 1986, Schs 16 and 17, the Financial Services Act 1986, Sch 4, the Companies Act 1989, ss 63, 64, 119, 120, 122, 123, 139, and Schs 10, 16 and 24, the Statute Law (Repeals) Act 1993, Sch 1, SI 2000/3373 and SI 2002/1986) (abridged)

1. Schedule 24 is reproduced in an abridged form and contains references only to those offences in respect of which the substantive provisions creating the offences are printed in this Manual.

Section of Act creating offence	General nature of offence[2]	Mode of prosecution[2]	Punishment	Daily default fine (where applicable)
28(5)	Company failing to change name on direction of Secretary of State.	Summary.	One-fifth of the statutory maximum.	One-fiftieth of the statutory maximum.
30(5C)	Person making false statement under section 30(5)A which he knows to be false or does not believe to be true	1. On indictment. 2. On Summary.	2 years or a fine or both. 6 months or the statutory maximum, or both.	
31(5)	Company altering its memorandum or articles, so ceasing to be exempt from having "limited" as part of its name.	Summary.	The statutory maximum.	One-tenth of the maximum.
31(6)	Company failing to change name, on Secretary of State's direction, so as to have "limited" (or Welsh equivalent) at the end.	Summary.	One-fifth of the statutory maximum.	One-fiftieth of the maximum.
32(4)	Company failing to comply with Secretary of State's direction to change its name, on grounds that the name is misleading.	Summary.	One-fifth of the statutory maximum.	One-fiftieth of the maximum.
33	Trading under misleading name (use of "public limited company" or Welsh equivalent when not so entitled); purporting to be a private company.	Summary.	One-fifth of the statutory maximum.	One-fiftieth of the maximum.
34	Trading or carrying on business with improper use of "limited" or "cyfyngedig".	Summary.	One-fifth of the statutory maximum.	One-fiftieth of the maximum.
221(5) or 222(4)	Company failing to keep accounting records (liability of officers).	1. On indictment. 2. Summary.	2 years or a fine; or both. 6 months or the statutory maximum; or both.	
222(6)	Officer of company failing to secure compliance with, or intentionally causing default under section 222(5) (preservation of accounting records for requisite number of years).	1. On indictment. 2. Summary.	2 years or a fine; or both. 6 months or the statutory maximum; or both.	
233(5)	Approving defective accounts.	1. On indictment. 2. Summary.	A fine. The statutory maximum.	
233(6)	Laying or delivery of unsigned balance sheet; circulating copies of balance sheet without signature.	Summary.	One-fifth of the statutory maximum.	
234(5)	Non-compliance with Part VII, as to directors' report and its content; directors individually liable.	1. On indictment. 2. Summary.	A fine. The statutory maximum.	

Section of Act creating offence	General nature of offence	Mode of prosecution[1]	Punishment	Daily default fine (where applicable)
234A(4)	Laying, circulating or delivering directors' report without required signature.	Summary.	One-fifth of the statutory maximum.	
234B(3)	Non-compliance with requirements as to preparation and content of directors' remuneration report.	Summary.	One-fifth of the statutory maximum.	
234B(6)	Default in complying with section 234B(5)	Summary.	One-fifth of the statutory maximum.	
236(4)	Laying, circulating or delivering auditors' report without required signature.	Summary.	One-fifth of the statutory maximum.	
238(5)	Failing to send company's annual accounts, directors' report and auditors' report to those entitled to receive them.	1. On indictment. 2. Summary.	A fine. The statutory maximum.	
239(3)	Company failing to supply copy of accounts and reports to shareholder on demand.	Summary.	One-fifth of the statutory maximum.	One-fiftieth of the statutory maximum.
240(6)	Failure to comply with requirements in connection with publication of accounts.	Summary.	One-fifth of the statutory maximum.	
241(2) or 242(2)	Director in default as regards duty to lay and deliver company's annual accounts, director's report and auditor's report.	Summary.	The statutory maximum.	One-tenth of the statutory maximum.
241A(9)	Default in complying with the requirements of section 241A(3) and (4).	Summary.	One-fifth of the statutory maximum.	One-fifth of the statutory maximum.
241A(10)	Failure to put resolution to vote of meeting.	Summary.	One-fifth of the statutory maximum.	One-fifth of the statutory maximum.
251(6)	Failure to comply with requirements in relation to summary financial statements	Summary.	One-fifth of the statutory maximum.	
288(4)	Default in complying with section 288 (keeping register of directors and secretaries, refusal of inspection).	Summary.	The statutory maximum.	One-tenth of the statutory maximum.
291(5)	Acting as director of a company without having the requisite share qualification.	Summary.	One-fifth of the statutory maximum.	One-fiftieth of the statutory maximum.
294(3)	Director failing to give notice of his attaining retirement age; acting as director under appointment invalid due to his attaining it	Summary.	One-fifth of the statutory maximum.	One-fiftieth of the statutory maximum.
323(2)	Director dealing in options to buy or sell company's listed shares or debentures.	1. On indictment. 2. Summary.	2 years or a fine; or both. 6 months or the statutory maximum; or both.	
324(7)	Director failing to notify interest in company's shares; making false statement in purported notification.	1. On indictment. 2. Summary.	2 years or a fine; or both. 6 months or the statutory maximum; or both.	

Section of Act creating offence	General nature of offence	Mode of prosecution[1]	Punishment	Daily default fine (where applicable)
326(2), (3), (4), (5).	Various defaults in connection with company register of directors' interests.	Summary.	One-fifth of the statutory maximum.	Except in the case of section 326(5), one-fiftieth of the statutory maximum.
328(6)	Director failing to notify company that members of his family have, or have exercised, options to buy shares or debentures; making false statement in purported notification.	1. On indictment. 2. Summary.	2 years or a fine; or both. 6 months or the statutory maximum; or both.	
329(3)	Company failing to notify investment exchange of acquisition of its securities by a director.	Summary. 2. Summary.	One-fifth of the statutory maximum. The statutory maximum.	One-fiftieth of the statutory maximum.
348(2)	Company failing to paint or affix name; failing to keep it painted or affixed.	Summary.	One-fifth of the statutory maximum.	In the case of failure to keep the name painted or affixed, one-fiftieth of the statutory maximum.
349(2)	Company failing to have name on business correspondence, invoices, etc.	Summary.	One-fifth of the statutory maximum.	
349(3)	Officer of company issuing business letter or document not bearing company's name.	Summary.	One-fifth of the statutory maximum.	
349(4)	Officer of company signing cheque, bill of exchange, etc on which company's name not mentioned.	Summary.	One-fifth of the statutory maximum.	
350(1)	Company failing to have its name engraved on company seal.	Summary.	One-fifth of the statutory maximum.	
350(2)	Officer of company, etc, using company seal without name engraved on it.	Summary.	One-fifth of the statutory maximum.	
351(5)(a)	Company failing to comply with section 351(1) or (2) (matters to be stated on business correspondence, etc)	Summary.	One-fifth of the statutory maximum.	
351(5)(b)	Officer or agent of company issuing or authorising issue of, business document not complying with those subsections.	Summary.	One-fifth of the statutory maximum.	
351(5)(c)	Contravention of section 351(3) or (4) (information in English to be stated on Welsh company's business correspondence, etc).	Summary.	One-fifth of the statutory maximum.	For contravention of section 351(3), one-fiftieth of the statutory maximum.
363(3)	Company with share capital failing to make annual return.	Summary.	The statutory maximum.	One-tenth of the statutory maximum.
364(4)	Company without share capital failing to complete and register annual return in due time.	Summary.	The statutory maximum.	One-tenth of the statutory maximum.
389A(2)	Officer of company making false, misleading or deceptive statement to auditors.	1. On indictment. 2. Summary.	2 years or a fine; or both. 6 months or the statutory maximum; or both.	

Section of Act creating offence	General nature of offence	Mode of prosecution[1]	Punishment	Daily default fine (where applicable)
389A(3)	Subsidiary undertaking or its auditor failing to give information to auditors of parent company.	Summary.	One-fifth of the statutory maximum.	One-fifth of the statutory maximum.
389A(4)	Parent company failing to obtain from subsidiary undertaking information for purposes of audit.	Summary.	One-fifth of the statutory maximum.	
391(2)	Failing to give notice to registrar of removal of auditor.	Summary.	One-fifth of the statutory maximum.	One-fiftieth of the statutory maximum.
392(3)	Company failing to forward notice of auditor's resignation to registrar.	1. On indictment. 2. Summary.	A fine. The statutory maximum.	One-tenth of the statutory maximum.
392A(5)	Directors failing to convene meeting requisitioned by resigning auditor.	1. On indictment. 2. Summary.	A fine. The statutory maximum.	
394A(1)	Person ceasing to hold office as auditor failing to deposit statement as to circumstances.	1. On indictment. 2. Summary.	A fine. The statutory maximum.	
394A(4)	Company failing to comply with requirements as to statement of person ceasing to hold office as auditor.	1. On indictment. 2. Summary.	A fine. The statutory maximum.	One-tenth of the statutory maximum.
447(6)	Failure to comply with requirement to produce documents imposed by Secretary of State under section 447.	1. On indictment. 2. Summary.	A fine. The statutory maximum.	
448(7)	Obstructing the exercise of any rights conferred by a warrant or failing to comply with a requirement imposed under subsection (3)(d).	1. On indictment. 2. Summary.	A fine. The statutory maximum.	
449(2)	Wrongful disclosure of information or document obtained under section 447 or 448.	1. On indictment. 2. Summary.	2 years, or a fine; or both. 6 months or the statutory maximum; or both.	
450	Destroying or mutilating company documents; falsifying such documents or making false entries; parting with such documents or altering them or making omissions.	1. On indictment. 2. Summary.	7 years, or a fine; or both. 6 months, or the statutory maximum; or both.	
451	Making false statement or explanation in purported compliance with section 447.	1. On indictment. 2. Summary.	2 years, or a fine; or both. 6 months, or the statutory maximum; or both.	
458	Being a party to carrying on company's business with intent to defraud creditors, or for any fraudulent purpose.	1. On indictment. 2. Summary.	7 years or a fine; or both. 6 months or the statutory maximum; or both.	
722(3)	Company failing to comply with section 722(2), as regards the manner of keeping registers, minute books and accounting records.	Summary.	One-fifth of the statutory maximum.	One fiftieth of the statutory maximum.

2. For procedure in respect of an offence triable either way, see the Magistrates' Courts Act 1980, ss 17A–21, in PART I: MAGISTRATES COURTS, PROCEDURE, ante.

Business Names Act 1985[1]
(1985 c 7)

8–3530   1. Persons subject to this Act.   (1) This Act applies to any person who has a place of business in Great Britain and who carries on business in Great Britain under a name which—

(a)   in the case of a partnership, does not consist of the surnames of all partners who are individuals and the corporate names of all partners who are bodies corporate without any addition other than an addition permitted by this Act;

(b)   in the case of an individual, does not consist of his surname without any addition other than one so permitted;

(c)   in the case of a company, being a company which is capable of being wound up under the Companies Act 1985[2], does not consist of its corporate name without any addition other than one so permitted;

(d)   in the case of a limited liability partnership, does not consist of its corporate name without any addition other than one so permitted.

(2)   The following are permitted additions for the purposes of subsection (1)—

(a)   in the case of a partnership, the forenames of individual partners or the initials of those forenames or, where two or more individual partners have the same surname, the addition of "s" at the end of that surname; or

(b)   in the case of an individual, his forename or its initial;

(c)   in any case, any addition merely indicating that the business is carried on in succession to a former owner of the business.

[Business Names Act 1985, s 1, as amended by SI 2001/1090.]

---

1.   This Act consolidates enactments relating to the names under which persons may carry on business in Great Britain.
2.   This includes a company which would be capable of being wound up but for s 25 of the Water Industry Act 1991).

8–3531   2. Prohibition of use of certain business names.   (1) Subject to the following subsections, a person to whom this Act applies shall not, without the written approval of the Secretary of State, carry on business in Great Britain under a name which—

(a)   would be likely to give the impression that the business is connected with Her Majesty's Government with any part of the Scottish Administration, or with any local authority; or

(b)   includes any word or expression for the time being specified in regulations made under this Act.

(2)   Subsection (1) does not apply to the carrying on of a business by a person—

(a)   to whom the business has been transferred on or after 26th February 1982; and

(b)   who carries on the business under the name which was its lawful business name immediately before that transfer,

during the period of 12 months beginning with the date of that transfer.

(3)   Subsection (1) does not apply to the carrying on of a business by a person who—

(a)   carried on that business immediately before 26th February 1982; and

(b)   continues to carry it on under the name which immediately before that date was its lawful business name.

(4)   A person who contravenes subsection (1) is guilty of an offence[1].

[Business Names Act 1985, s 2.]

---

1.   For penalty, see s 7, post.

8–3532   3. Words and expressions requiring Secretary of State's approval.   (1) The Secretary of State may by regulations[1]—

(a)   specify words or expressions for the use of which as or as part of a business name his approval is required by section 2(1)(b); and

(b)   in relation to any such word or expression, specify a Government department or other body as the relevant body for purposes of the following subsection.

(2)   Where a person to whom this Act applies proposes to carry on a business under a name which is or includes any such word or expression, and a Government department or other body is specified under subsection (1)(b) in relation to that word or expression, that person shall—

(a)   request (in writing) the relevant body to indicate whether (and if so why) it has any objections to the proposal; and

(b)   submit to the Secretary of State a statement that such a request has been made and a copy of any response received from the relevant body.

[Business Names Act 1985, s 3.]

1. See the Company and Business Names Regulations 1981, SI 1981/1685, amended by SI 1982/1653, SI 1992/1196, SI 1995/3022, SI 2002/1397 and SI 2004/1771.

8–3533   4. Disclosure required of persons using business names.   (1) A person to whom this Act applies shall—

    (*a*)   subject to subsections (3) and (3A), state in legible characters on all business letters, written orders for goods or services to be supplied to the business, invoices and receipts issued in the course of the business and written demands for payment of debts arising in the course of the business—

         (i)   in the case of a partnership, the name of each partner,

         (ii)   in the case of an individual, his name,

         (iii)   in the case of a company, its corporate name,

         (iiia) In the case of a limited liability partnership, its corporate name and the name of each member, and

         (iv)   in relation to each person so named, an address in Great Britain at which service of any document relating in any way to the business will be effective; and

    (*b*)   in any premises where the business is carried on and to which the customers of the business or suppliers of any goods or services to the business have access, display in a prominent position so that it may easily be read by such customers or suppliers a notice containing such names and addresses.

(2) A person to whom this Act applies shall secure that the names and addresses required by subsection (1)(*a*) to be stated on his business letters, or which would have been so required but for subsection (3) or (3A), are immediately given, by written notice to any person with whom anything is done or discussed in the course of the business and who asks for such names and addresses.

(3) Subsection (1)(*a*) does not apply in relation to any document issued by a partnership of more than 20 persons which maintains at its principal place of business a list of the names of all the partners if—

    (*a*)   none of the names of the partners appears in the document otherwise than in the text or as a signatory; and

    (*b*)   the document states in legible characters the address of the partnership's principal place of business and that the list of the partners' names is open to inspection at that place.

(3A) Subsection (1)(a) does not apply in relation to any document issued by a limited liability partnership with more than 20 members which maintains at its principal place of business a list of the names of all the members if—

    (a)   none of the names of the members appears in the document otherwise than in the text or as a signatory; and

    (b)   the document states in legible characters the address of the principal place of business of the limited liability partnership and that the list of the members' names is open to inspection at that place.

(4) Where a partnership maintains a list of the partners' names for purposes of subsection (3), any person may inspect the list during office hours.

(4A) Where a limited liability partnership maintains a list of the members' names for the purposes of subsection (3A), any person may inspect the list during office hours.

(5) The Secretary of State may by regulations require notices under subsection (1)(*b*) or (2) to be displayed or given in a specified form.

(6) A person who without reasonable excuse contravenes subsection (1) or (2), or any regulations made under subsection (5), is guilty of an offence[1].

(7) Where an inspection required by a person in accordance with subsection (4) or (4A) is refused, any partner of the partnership concerned, or any member of the limited liability partnership concerned, who without reasonable excuse refused that inspection, or permitted it to be refused, is guilty of an offence[1].

[Business Names Act 1985, s 4, as amended by SI 2001/1090.]

1. For penalty, see s 7, post.

8–3534   5.   *Civil remedies for breach of section 4.*

8–3535   6. Regulations.   *Power of Secretary of State to make regulations under sections 3 and 4.*

8–3536   7. Offences.   (1) Offences under this Act are punishable on summary conviction.

(2) A person guilty of an offence under this Act is liable to a fine not exceeding **one-fifth of the statutory maximum**.

(3) If after a person has been convicted summarily of an offence under section 2 or 4(6) the original contravention is continued, he is liable on a second or subsequent summary conviction of the

offence to a fine not exceeding **one-fiftieth of the statutory maximum** for each day on which the contravention is continued (instead of to the penalty which may be imposed on the first conviction of the offence).

(4) Where an offence under section 2 or 4(6) or (7) committed by a body corporate is proved to have been committed with the consent or connivance of, or to be attributable to any neglect on the part of, any director, manager, secretary or other similar officer of the body corporate, or any person who was purporting to act in any such capacity, he as well as the body corporate is guilty of the offence and liable to be proceeded against and punished accordingly.

(5) Where the affairs of a body corporate are managed by its members, subsection (4) applies in relation to the acts and defaults of a member in connection with his functions of management as if he were a director of the body corporate.

(6) For purposes of the following provisions of the Companies Act 1985—

(a)   section 731 (summary proceedings under the Companies Acts), and
(b)   section 732(3) (legal professional privilege),

this Act is to be treated as included in those Acts.
[Business Names Act 1985, s 7.]

8–3537   8. Interpretation.   (1) The following definitions apply for purposes of this Act—

"business" includes a profession;
"initial" includes any recognised abbreviation of a name;
"lawful business name", in relation to a business, means a name under which the business was carried on without contravening section 2(1) of this Act or section 2 of the Registration of Business Names Act 1916;
"local authority" means any local authority within the meaning of the Local Government Act 1972 or the Local Government (Scotland) Act 1973, the Common Council of the City of London or the Council of the Isles of Scilly;
"partnership" includes a foreign partnership;

and "surname", in relation to a peer or person usually known by a British title different from his surname, means the title by which he is known.

(2) Any expression used in this Act and also in the Companies Act 1985 has the same meaning in this Act as in that.
[Business Names Act 1985, s 8 as amended by the Statute Law (Repeals) Act 1993, Sch 1.]

8–3538   9.   *Northern Ireland.*

8–3539   10. Commencement.   This Act came into force on 1st July 1985.
[Business Names Act 1985, s 10.]

8–3540   11. Citation.   This Act may be cited as the Business Names Act 1985.
[Business Names Act 1985, s 11.]

Companies Consolidation (Consequential Provisions) Act 1985[1]
(1985 c 9)

Repeals, etc consequential on Companies Acts consolidation; continuity of law

8–3670   31. Continuity of law.   (1) In this section—

(a)   "the new Acts" means the principal Act, the Company Securities (Insider Dealing) Act 1985, the Business Names Act 1985 and this Act;
(b)   "the old Acts" means the Companies Acts 1948 to 1983 and any other enactment which is repealed by this Act and replaced by a corresponding provision in the new Acts; and
(c)   "the commencement date" means 1st July 1985.

(2) So far as anything done or treated as done under or for the purposes of any provision of the old Acts could have been done under or for the purposes of the corresponding provision of the new Acts, it is not invalidated by the repeal of that provision but has effect as if done under or for the purposes of the corresponding provision; and any order, regulation or other instrument made or having effect under any provision of the old Acts shall, in so far as its effect is preserved by this subsection, be treated for all purposes as made and having effect under the corresponding provision.

(3) Where any period of time specified in a provision of the old Acts is current immediately before the commencement date, the new Acts have effect as if the corresponding provision had been in force when the period began to run; and (without prejudice to the foregoing) any period of time so specified and current is deemed for the purposes of the new Acts—

(a)   to run from the date or event from which it was running immediately before the commencement date, and (*b*)   to expire (subject to any provision of the new Acts for its extension) whenever it would have expired if the new Acts had not been passed;

and any rights, priorities, liabilities, reliefs, obligations, requirements, powers, duties or exemptions dependent on the beginning, duration or end of such a period as above mentioned shall be under the new Acts as they were or would have been under the old.

(4)   Where in any provision of the new Acts there is a reference to another provision of those Acts, and the first-mentioned provision operates, or is capable of operating, in relation to things done or omitted, or events occurring or not occurring, in the past (including in particular past acts of compliance with any enactment, failures of compliance, contraventions, offences and convictions of offences), the reference to that other provision is to be read as including a reference to the corresponding provision of the old Acts.

(5)   A contravention of any provision of the old Acts committed before the commencement date shall not be visited with any severer punishment under or by virtue of the new Acts than would have been applicable under that provision at the time of the contravention; but—

(*a*)   where an offence for the continuance of which a penalty was provided has been committed under any provision of the old Acts, proceedings may be taken under the new Acts in respect of the continuance of the offence after the commencement date in the like manner as if the offence had been committed under the corresponding provision of the new Acts; and

(*b*)   the repeal of any transitory provision of the old Acts (not replaced by any corresponding provision of the new Acts) requiring a thing to be done within a certain time does not affect a person's continued liability to be prosecuted and punished in respect of the failure, or continued failure, to do that thing.

(6)   A reference in any enactment, instrument or document (whether express or implied, and in whatever phraseology) to a provision (whether first in force before or after the Act of 1948 or contained in that Act) which is replaced by a corresponding provision of the new Acts is to be read, where necessary to retain for the enactment, instrument or document the same force and effect as it would have had but for the passing of the new Acts, as, or as including, a reference to that corresponding provision.

(7)   The generality of subsection (6) is not affected by any specific conversion of references made by this Act, nor by the inclusion in any provision of the new Acts of a reference (whether express or implied, and in whatever phraseology) to the provision of the old Acts corresponding to that provision, or to a provision of the old Acts which is replaced by a corresponding provision of the new.

(8)   Nothing in the new Acts affects—

(*a*)   the registration or re-registration of any company under the former Companies Acts, or the continued existence of any company by virtue of such registration or re-registration; or

(*b*)   the application of—

(i)   Table B in the Joint Stock Companies Act 1856, or

(ii)   Table A in the Companies Act 1862, the Companies (Consolidation) Act 1908, the Companies Act 1929 or the Companies Act 1948,

to any company existing immediately before the commencement date; or

(*c*)   the operation of any enactment providing for any partnership, association or company being wound up, or being wound up as a company or as an unregistered company under any of the former Companies Acts.

(9)   Anything saved from repeal by section 459 of the Act of 1948 and still in force immediately before the commencement date remains in force notwithstanding the repeal of the whole of that Act.

(10)   Where any provision of the new Acts was, immediately before the commencement date, contained in or given effect by a statutory instrument (whether or not made under a power in any of the old Acts), then—

(*a*)   the foregoing provisions of this section have effect as if that provision was contained in the old Acts, and

(*b*)   insofar as the provision was, immediately before that date, subject to a power (whether or not under the old Acts) of variation or revocation, nothing in the new Acts is to be taken as prejudicing any future exercise of the power.

(11)   The provisions of this section are without prejudice to the operation of sections 16 and 17 of the Interpretation Act 1978 (savings from, and effect of, repeals); and for the purposes of section 17(2) of that Act (construction of references to enactments repealed and replaced; continuity of powers preserved in repealing enactment), any provision of the old Acts which is replaced by a provision of the principal Act, the Company Securities (Insider Dealing) Act 1985 or the Business Names Act 1985 is deemed to have been repealed and re-enacted by that one of the new Acts and not by this Act.

[Companies Consolidation (Consequential Provisions) Act 1985, s 31.]

---

1. This Act makes provision for transitional matters and savings, repeals and consequential amendments of other Acts, in connection with the consolidation of the Companies Acts 1948 to 1983 and other enactments relating to companies. Only those provisions of the Act relating to continuity of law are printed in this Manual.

General

8–3671　32. Interpretation.　In this Act—

"the Act of 1948" means the Companies Act 1948,
"the Act of 1980" means the Companies Act 1980,
"the Act of 1981" means the Companies Act 1981, and
"the principal Act" means the Companies Act 1985;

and expressions used in this Act and also in the principal Act have the same meanings in this Act as in that (the provisions of Part XXVI of that Act to apply accordingly).
[Companies Consolidation (Consequential Provisions) Act 1985, s 32.]

8–3672　34. *Commencement.*

8–3673　35. *Citation.*

Company Directors Disqualification Act 1986[1]
(1986 c 46)

Preliminary

8–3690　1. Disqualification orders: general.　(1) In the circumstances specified below in this Act a court may, and under sections 6 and 9A shall, make against a person a disqualification order, that is to say an order that for a period specified in the order—

(*a*)　he shall not be a director of a company, act as receiver of a company's property or in any way, whether directly or indirectly, be concerned or take part in the promotion, formation or management of a company unless (in each case) he has the leave of the court, and

(*b*)　he shall not act as an insolvency practitioner.

(2) In each section of this Act which gives to a court power or, as the case may be, imposes on it the duty to make a disqualification order there is specified the maximum (and, in section 6, the minimum) period of disqualification which may or (as the case may be) must be imposed by means of the order and, unless the court otherwise orders, the period of disqualification so imposed shall begin at the end of the period of 21 days beginning with the date of the order.

(3) Where a disqualification order is made against a person who is already subject to such an order, the periods specified in those orders shall run concurrently.

(4) A disqualification order may be made on grounds which are or include matters other than criminal convictions, notwithstanding that the person in respect of whom it is to be made may be criminally liable in respect of those matters.
[Company Directors Disqualification Act 1986, s 1, as amended by the Insolvency Act 2000, s 5 and the Enterprise Act 2002, s 204.]

---

1. This Act consolidates enactments previously contained in the Companies Act 1985 and the Insolvency Act 1985 relating to the disqualification of persons from being directors of companies, and from being otherwise concerned with a company's affairs. Only those provisions of the Act which are relevant to the work of magistrates' court are included in this manual.

This Act came into force simultaneously with the Insolvency Act 1986 (s 25). The Insolvency Act 1986 was brought into force on the 29 December 1986 in accordance with s 443 of that Act and by virtue of SI 1986/1924.

8–3690A　1A. *Disqualification undertakings: general*

Disqualification for general misconduct in connection with companies

8–3691　2. Disqualification for general misconduct in connection with companies.　(1) The court may make a disqualification order against a person where he is convicted of an indictable offence (whether on indictment or summarily) in connection with the promotion, formation, management[1], liquidation or striking off of a company, or with the receivership of a company's property or with his being an administrative receiver of a company.

(2) "The court" for this purpose means—

(*a*)　any court having jurisdiction to wind up the company in relation to which the offence was committed, or

(*b*)　the court by or before which the person is convicted of the offence, or

(*c*)　in the case of a summary conviction in[2] England and Wales, any other magistrates' court acting for the same petty sessions area;

and for the purposes of this section the definition of "indictable offence" in Schedule 1 to the Interpretation Act 1978 applies for Scotland as it does for England and Wales.

(3) The maximum period of disqualification under this section is—

(*a*)　where the disqualification order is made by a court of summary jurisdiction, 5 years, and

(*b*) in any other case, 15 years.
[Company Directors Disqualification Act 1986, s 2 amended by the Deregulation and Contracting Out Act 1994, s 39 and Sch 11 and the Insolvency Act 2000, Sch 4.]

---

1. The words "in connection with the management of a company" are not limited to offences related to the internal management of the company, but have been held to apply to the carrying on of an insurance business without authorisation; see *R v Georgiou* (1988) 87 Cr App Rep 207, [1988] Crim LR 472, CA. It is sufficient if the offence has some relevant factual connection with the management of a company; therefore, an offence of insider dealing will render the offender liable to disqualification (*R v Goodman* [1993] 2 All ER 789, [1992] Crim LR 676).

The rationale behind disqualification from being a company director is to protect the public from the activities of persons who whether for reasons of dishonesty, or of naivety or incompetence, use or abuse their role and status as a company director to the detriment of the public. Periods of disqualification for over 10 years should be reserved for particularly serious cases, which may include cases where a director has already had one period of disqualification. The lower bracket of 2 to 5 years disqualification should be reserved for cases which are relatively not very serious, and the bracket of 6 to 10 years should apply to serious cases which do not merit the top bracket (*R v Edwards* [1998] Crim LR 298).

2. On summary conviction the clerk to the justices is required to furnish the Secretary of State with particulars of any disqualification order; see s 18 and note 1 thereto, post.

8-3692   3-4. *Disqualification for persistent breaches of companies legislation; disqualification for fraud, etc, in winding up.*

8-3693   5. Disqualification on summary conviction. (1) An offence counting for the purposes of this section is one of which a person is convicted (either on indictment or summarily) in consequence of a contravention of, or failure to comply with, any provision of the companies legislation requiring a return, account or other document to be filed with, delivered or sent, or notice of any matter to be given, to the registrar of companies (whether the contravention or failure is on the person's own part or on the part of any company).

(2) Where a person is convicted of a summary offence counting for those purposes, the court by which he is convicted (or, in England and Wales, any other magistrates' court acting for the same petty sessions area) may make a disqualification order against him if the circumstances specified in the next subsection are present.

(3) Those circumstances are that, during the 5 years ending with the date of the conviction, the person has had made against him, or has been convicted of, in total not less than 3 default orders and offences counting for the purposes of this section; and those offences may include that of which he is convicted as mentioned in subsection (2) and any other offence of which he is convicted on the same occasion.

(4) For the purposes of this section—

(*a*) the definition of "summary offence" in Schedule 1 to the Interpretation Act 1978 applies for Scotland as for England and Wales, and

(*b*) "default order" means the same as in section 3(3)(*b*).

(5) The maximum period of disqualification under this section is 5 years.
[Company Directors Disqualification Act 1986, s 5.]

8-3694   6-9. *Disqualification for unfitness.*

Other cases of disqualification

8-3695   10. *Participation in wrongful trading.*

8-3696   11. Undischarged bankrupts. (1) It is an offence[1] for a person to act as director of a company or directly or indirectly to take part in or be concerned in the promotion, formation or management of a company, without the leave of the court, at a time when—

(*a*) he is an undischarged bankrupt, or
(*b*) a bankruptcy restrictions order is in force in respect of him[2].

(2) "The court" for this purpose is the court by which the person was adjudged bankrupt or, in Scotland, sequestration of his estates was awarded.

(3) In England and Wales, the leave of the court shall not be given unless notice of intention to apply for it has been served on the official receiver; and it is the latter's duty, if he is of opinion that it is contrary to the public interest that the application should be granted, to attend on the hearing of the application and oppose it.
[Company Directors Disqualification Act 1986, s 11.]

---

1. This is an absolute offence (*R v Brockley* [1994] Crim LR 671; confirmed in *R v Doring* [2002] EWCA Crim 1695, [2003] 1 Cr App R 9, [2002] Crim LR 817). For penalty, see s 13, post.

2. Subsection (1) reproduced as substituted in relation to England and Wales by the Enterprise Act 2002, Sch 21, from 1 April 2004.

8–3697   12. Failure to pay under county court administration order.   (1) The following has effect where a court under section 429 of the Insolvency Act revokes an administration order under Part VI of the County Courts Act 1984.

(2) A person to whom that section applies by virtue of the order under section 429(2)(b) shall not, except with the leave of the court which made the order, act as director or liquidator of, or directly or indirectly take part or be concerned in the promotion, formation or management of, a company.

[Company Directors Disqualification Act 1986, s 12.]

8–3697A   12A. Northern Irish disqualification orders.   *Northern Ireland.*

8–3697B   12B. Northern Irish disqualification undertakings.   *Northern Ireland.*

Consequences of contravention

8–3698   13. Criminal penalties.   If a person acts in contravention of a disqualification order or of section 12(2), 12A or 12B* or is guilty of an offence under section 11, he is liable[1]—

    (a)   on conviction on indictment, to imprisonment for not more than **2 years** or a **fine**, or **both**; and

    (b)   on summary conviction, to imprisonment for not more than **6 months** or a fine not exceeding **the statutory maximum**, or both.

[Company Directors Disqualification Act 1986, s 13 as amended by SI 2004/1941.]

---

*", 12A or 12B" inserted in relation to Northern Ireland by SI 2004/1941.
1. For procedure in respect of this offence which is triable either way, see the Magistrates' Courts Act 1980, ss 17A–21, in PART I: MAGISTRATES' COURTS, PROCEDURE, ante.

8–3699   14. Offences by body corporate.   (1) Where a body corporate is guilty of an offence of acting in contravention of a disqualification order or disqualification undertaking or in contravention of section 12A*, and it is proved that the offence occurred with the consent or connivance of, or was attributable to any neglect on the part of any director, manager, secretary or other similar officer of the body corporate, or any person who was purporting to act in any such capacity he, as well as the body corporate, is guilty of the offence and liable to be proceeded against and punished accordingly.

(2) Where the affairs of a body corporate are managed by its members, subsection (1) applies in relation to the acts and defaults of a member in connection with his functions of managements as if he were a director of the body corporate.

[Company Directors Disqualification Act 1986, s 14, as amended by the Insolvency Act 2000, Sch 4.]

---

*"or 12B" inserted in relation to Northern Ireland by SI 2004/1941.

8–3700   15.   *Personal liability for company's debts where person acts while disqualified.*

Supplementary provisions

8–3701   16. Application for disqualification order.   *Application to a court with jurisdiction to wind up a company.*

8–3702   17. Application for leave under an order or undertaking*.   (1) Where a person is subject to a disqualification order made by a court having jurisdiction to wind up companies, any application for leave for the purposes of section 1(1)(a) shall be made to that court.

(2) Where—

    (a)   a person is subject to a disqualification order made under section 2 by a court other than a court having jurisdiction to wind up companies, or

    (b)   a person is subject to a disqualification order made under section 5,

any application for leave for the purposes of section 1(1)(a) shall be made to any court which, when the order was made, had jurisdiction to wind up the company (or, if there is more than one such company, any of the companies) to which the offence (or any of the offences) in question related.

(3) Where a person is subject to a disqualification undertaking accepted at any time under section 7 or 8, any application for leave for the purposes of section 1A(1)(a) shall be made to any court to which, if the Secretary of State had applied for a disqualification order under the section in question at that time, his application could have been made.

(3A) Where a person is subject to a disqualification undertaking accepted at any time under section 9B any application for leave for the purposes of section 9B(4) must be made to the High Court or (in Scotland) the Court of Session.

(4) But where a person is subject to two or more disqualification orders or undertakings (or to one or more disqualification orders and to one or more disqualification undertakings), any application for leave for the purposes of section 1(1)(a), 1A(1)(a) or 9B(4) shall be made to any court to which any

such application relating to the latest order to be made, or undertaking to be accepted, could be made.

(5) On the hearing of an application for leave for the purposes of section 1(1)(*a*) or 1A(1)(*a*), the Secretary of State shall appear and call the attention of the court to any matters which seem to him to be relevant, and may himself give evidence or call witnesses.

(6) Subsection (5) does not apply to an application for leave for the purposes of section 1(1)(a) if the application for the disqualification order was made under section 9A.

(7) In such a case and in the case of an application for leave for the purposes of section 9B(4) on the hearing of the application whichever of the OFT or a specified regulator (within the meaning of section 9E) applied for the order or accepted the undertaking (as the case may be)—

(*a*) must appear and draw the attention of the court to any matters which appear to it or him (as the case may be) to be relevant;
(*b*) may give evidence or call witnesses.

[Company Directors Disqualification Act 1986, s 17, as substituted by the Insolvency Act 2000, Sch 4 and amended by the Enterprise Act 2002, s 204.]

8–3703   18. Register of disqualification orders and undertakings.   (1) The Secretary of State may make regulations[1] requiring officers of courts to furnish him with such particulars as the regulations may specify of cases in which—

(*a*) a disqualification order is made, or
(*b*) any action is taken by a court in consequence of which such an order or a disqualification undertaking is varied or ceases to be in force, or
(*c*) leave is granted by a court for a person subject to such an order to do any thing which otherwise the order prohibits him from doing; or
(*d*) leave is granted by a court for a person subject to such an undertaking to do anything which otherwise the undertaking prohibits him from doing;

and the regulations may specify the time within which, and the form and manner in which, such particulars are to be furnished.

(2) The Secretary of State shall, from the particulars so furnished, continue to maintain the register of orders, and of cases in which leave has been granted as mentioned in subsection (1)(*c*), which was set up by him under section 29 of the Companies Act 1976 and continued under section 301 of the Companies Act 1985.

(2A) The Secretary of State must include in the register such particulars as he considers appropriate of—

(*a*) disqualification undertakings accepted by him under section 7 or 8;
(*b*) disqualification undertakings accepted by the OFT or a specified regulator under section 9B;
(*c*) of cases in which leave has been granted as mentioned in subsection (1)(d).

(3) When an order or undertaking of which entry is made in the register ceases to be in force, the Secretary of State shall delete the entry from the register and all particulars relating to it which have been furnished to him under this section or any previous corresponding provision and, in the case of a disqualification undertaking, any other particulars he has included in the register.

(4) The register shall be open to inspection on payment of such fee as may be specified by the Secretary of State in regulations.

(4A) Regulations under this section may extend the preceding provisions of this section, to such extent and with such modifications as may be specified in the regulations, to disqualification orders made under Part II of the Companies (Northern Ireland) Order 1989.

(5) Regulations under this section shall be made by statutory instrument subject to annulment in pursuance of a resolution of either House of Parliament.

[Company Directors Disqualification Act 1986, s 18, as amended by the Insolvency Act 2000, Sch 4, the Enterprise Act 2002, Sch 4 and SI 2004/1941.]

---

1. Where a disqualification order is made by a magistrates' court, the clerk to the justices is required to furnish to the Secretary of State particulars of the disqualification (Companies (Disqualification Orders) Regulations 2001, post). For guidance on the notification of particulars of disqualification orders to the Secretary of State, see Home Office Circulars Nos 52/1982, 46/1985 and 97/1986.

Miscellaneous and general

8–3704   22. Interpretation.   (1) This section has effect with respect to the meaning of expressions used in this Act, and applies unless the context otherwise requires.

(2) The expression "company"—

(*a*) in section 11, includes an unregistered company and a company incorporated outside Great Britain which has an established place of business in Great Britain, and
(*b*) elsewhere, includes any company which may be wound up under Part V of the Insolvency Act.

(3) Section 247 in Part VII of the Insolvency Act (interpretation for the first Group of Parts of

that Act) applies as regards references to a company's insolvency and to its going into liquidation; and "administrative receiver" has the meaning given by section 251 of that Act and references to acting as an insolvency practitioner are to be read in accordance with section 388 of that Act.

(4) "Director" includes any person occupying the position of director, by whatever name called, and in sections 6 to 9 includes a shadow director.

(5) "Shadow director", in relation to a company, means a person in accordance with whose directions or instructions the directors of the company are accustomed to Act (but so that a person is not deemed a shadow director by reason only that the directors act on advice given by him in a professional capacity).

(6) Section 740 of the Companies Act applies as regards the meaning of "body corporate"; and "officer" has the meaning given by section 744 of that Act.

(7) In references to legislation other than this Act—

"the Companies Act" means the Companies Act 1985;
"the Companies Acts" has the meaning given by section 744 of that Act; and
"the Insolvency Act" means the Insolvency Act 1986;

and in section 3(1) and 5(1) of this Act "the companies legislation" means the Companies Acts (except the Insider Dealing Act), Parts I to VII of the Insolvency Act and, in Part XV of that Act, sections 411, 413, 414, 416 and 417.

(8) Any reference to provisions, or a particular provision, of the Companies Acts or the Insolvency Act includes the corresponding provisions or provision of the former Companies Acts (as defined by section 735(1)(c) of the Companies Act, but including also that Act itself) or, as the case may be, the Insolvency Act 1985.

(9) Any expression for whose interpretation provision is made by Part XXVI of the Companies Act (and not by subsections (3) to (8) above) is to be construed in accordance with that provision.

(10) Any reference to acting as receiver—

(a) includes acting as manager or as both receiver and manager, but
(b) does not include acting as administrative receiver;

and "receivership" is to be read accordingly.
[Company Directors Disqualification Act 1986, s 22, as amended by the Insolvency Act 2000, Sch 4.]

8–3705   22A.   *Application of Act to building societies.*

8–3706   22B. Application of Act to incorporated friendly societies.   (1) This Act applies to incorporated friendly societies as it applies to companies.

(2) References in this Act to a company, or to a director or an officer of a company include, respectively, references to an incorporated friendly society within the meaning of the Friendly Societies Act 1992 or to a member of the committee of management or officer, within the meaning of that Act, of an incorporated friendly society.

(3) In relation to an incorporated friendly society every reference to a shadow director shall be omitted.

(4) In the application of Schedule 1 to the members of the committee of management of an incorporated friendly society, references to provisions of the Insolvency Act or the Companies Act include references to the corresponding provisions of the Friendly Societies Act 1992.
[Company Directors Disqualification Act 1986, s 22B, as inserted by the Friendly Societies Act 1992, Sch 21.]

8–3706A   22C. Application of Act to NHS foundation trusts.   (1) This Act applies to NHS foundation trusts as it applies to companies within the meaning of this Act.

(2) References in this Act to a company, or to a director or officer of a company, include, respectively, references to an NHS foundation trust or to a director or officer of the trust; but references to shadow directors are omitted.

(3) In the application of Schedule 1 to the directors of an NHS foundation trust, references to the provisions of the Insolvency Act or the Companies Act include references to the corresponding provisions of Part 1 of the Health and Social Care (Community Health and Standards) Act 2003.
[Company Directors Disqualification Act 1986, s 22C, as inserted by the Health and Social Care (Community Health and Standards) Act 2003, Sch 4.]

8–3707   23.   *Transitional provisions, savings, repeals.*

8–3708   24.   *Extent.*

8–3709   25.   *Commencement.*

8–3710   26.   *Citation.*

8–3711

SCHEDULES

Section 1   SCHEDULE 1
MATTERS FOR DETERMINING UNFITNESS OF DIRECTORS

8–3712

Section 19   SCHEDULE 2
SAVINGS FROM COMPANIES ACT 1981 SS 93, 94, AND INSOLVENCY ACT 1985 SCHEDULE 9

8–3713   SCHEDULE 3
TRANSITIONAL PROVISIONS AND SAVINGS.

Companies Act 1989
(1989 c 40)

PART II[1]
ELIGIBILITY FOR APPOINTMENT AS COMPANY AUDITOR

Introduction

8–3894   24. Introduction.   (1) The main purposes of this Part are to secure that only persons who are properly supervised and appropriately qualified are appointed company auditors, and that audits by persons so appointed are carried out properly and with integrity and with a proper degree of independence.

(2) A "company auditor" means a person appointed as auditor under Chapter V of Part XI of the Companies Act 1985; and the expressions "company audit" and "company audit work" shall be construed accordingly.
[Companies Act 1989, s 24.]

---

1. Part II contains ss 24–54. At the date of going to press all the provisions of Part II of this Act, except s 46 and Sch 13, s 47(2) to (6), and s 48(3), had been brought into force by the Companies Act 1989 (Commencement No 2) Order 1990, SI 1990/142 and the Companies Act 1989 (Commencement No 12 and Transitional Provision) Order 1991, SI 1991/1996).

Eligibility for appointment

8–3895   25. Eligibility for appointment.   (1) A person is eligible for appointment as a company auditor only if he—

(a) is a member of a recognised supervisory body, and
(b) is eligible for the appointment under the rules of that body.

(2) An individual or a firm may be appointed a company auditor.

(3) In the cases to which section 34 applies (individuals retaining only 1967 Act authorisation) a person's eligibility for appointment as a company auditor is restricted as mentioned in that section.
[Companies Act 1989, s 25.]

8–3896   26. Effect of appointment of partnership.   (1) The following provisions apply to the appointment as company auditor of a partnership constituted under the law of England and Wales or Northern Ireland, or under the law of any other country or territory in which a partnership is not a legal person.

(2) The appointment is (unless a contrary intention appears) an appointment of the partnership as such and not of the partners.

(3) Where the partnership ceases, the appointment shall be treated as extending to—

(a) any partnership which succeeds to the practice of that partnership and is eligible for the appointment, and
(b) any person who succeeds to that practice having previously carried it on in partnership and is eligible for the appointment.

(4) For this purpose a partnership shall be regarded as succeeding to the practice of another partnership only if the members of the successor partnership are substantially the same as those of the former partnership; and a partnership or other person shall be regarded as succeeding to the practice of a partnership only if it or he succeeds to the whole or substantially the whole of the business of the former partnership.

(5) Where the partnership ceases and no person succeeds to the appointment under subsection (3), the appointment may with the consent of the company be treated as extending to a partnership or other person eligible for the appointment who succeeds to the business of the former partnership or to such part of it as is agreed by the company shall be treated as comprising the appointment.
[Companies Act 1989, s 26.]

8–3897 27. Ineligibility on ground of lack of independence. (1) A person is ineligible for appointment as company auditor of a company if he is—

    (*a*) an officer or employee of the company, or

    (*b*) a partner or employee of such a person, or a partnership of which such a person is a partner,

or if he is ineligible by virtue of paragraph (*a*) or (*b*) for appointment as company auditor of any associated undertaking of the company.

For this purpose an auditor of a company shall not be regarded as an officer or employee of the company.

(2) A person is also ineligible for appointment as company auditor of a company if there exists between him or any associate of his and the company or any associated undertaking a connection of any such description as may be specified by regulations made by the Secretary of State.

The regulations may make different provisions for different cases.

(3) In this section "associated undertaking", in relation to a company, means—

    (*a*) a parent undertaking or subsidiary undertaking of the company, or

    (*b*) a subsidiary undertaking of any parent undertaking of the company.

(4) Regulations under this section shall be made by statutory instrument which shall be subject to annulment in pursuance of a resolution of either House of Parliament.
[Companies Act 1989, s 27.]

8–3898 28. Effect of ineligibility. (1) No person shall act as a company auditor if he is ineligible for appointment to the office.

(2) If during his term of office a company auditor becomes ineligible for appointment to the office, he shall thereupon vacate office and shall forthwith give notice in writing to the company concerned that he has vacated it by reason of ineligibility.

(3) A person who acts as company auditor in contravention of subsection (1), or fails to give notice of vacating his office as required by subsection (2), is guilty of an offence and liable[1]—

    (*a*) on conviction on indictment, to a **fine**, and

    (*b*) on summary conviction, to a fine not exceeding **the statutory maximum**.

(4) In the case of continued contravention he is liable on a second or subsequent summary conviction (instead of the fine mentioned in subsection (3)(*b*)) to a fine not exceeding **one-tenth of the statutory maximum** in respect of each day on which the contravention is continued.

(5) In proceedings against a person for an offence under this section it is a defence for him to show that he did not know and had no reason to believe that he was, or had become, ineligible for appointment.
[Companies Act 1989, s 28.]

---

1. For procedure in respect of this offence which is triable either way, see the Magistrates' Courts Act 1980, ss 17A–21, in PART I: MAGISTRATES' COURTS, PROCEDURE, ante.

8–3899 29. Power of Secretary of State to require second audit. (1) Where a person appointed company auditor was, for any part of the period during which the audit was conducted, ineligible for appointment to that office, the Secretary of State may direct the company concerned to retain a person eligible for appointment as auditor of the company—

    (*a*) to audit the relevant accounts again, or

    (*b*) to review the first audit and to report (giving his reasons) whether a second audit is needed;

and the company shall comply with such a direction within 21 days of its being given.

(2) If a second audit is recommended the company shall forthwith take such steps as are necessary to comply with the recommendation.

(3) Where a direction is given under this section, the Secretary of State shall send a copy of the direction to the registrar of companies; and the company shall within 21 days of receiving any report under subsection (1)(*b*) send a copy of it to the registrar of companies.

The provisions of the Companies Act 1985 relating to the delivery of documents to the registrar apply for the purposes of this subsection.

(4) Any statutory or other provisions applying in relation to the first audit shall apply, so far as practicable, in relation to a second audit under this section.

(5) If a company fails to comply with the requirements of this section, it is guilty of an offence and liable on summary conviction to a fine not exceeding **the statutory maximum**; and in the case of continued contravention it is liable on a second or subsequent summary conviction (instead of the fine mentioned above) to a fine not exceeding **one-tenth of the statutory maximum** in respect of each day on which the contravention is continued.

(6) *Scotland.*

(7) If a person accepts an appointment, or continues to act, as company auditor at a time when he knows he is ineligible, the company concerned may recover from him any costs incurred by it in complying with the requirements of this section.
[Companies Act 1989, s 29.]

8–3900   30. Supervisory bodies.   In this Part a "supervisory body" means a body established in the United Kingdom (whether a body corporate or an unincorporated association) which maintains and enforces rules as to—

 (*a*) the eligibility of persons to seek appointment as company auditors, and
 (*b*) the conduct of company audit work,

which are binding on persons seeking appointment or acting as company auditors either because they are members of that body or because they are otherwise subject to its control.
[Companies Act 1989, s 30—summarised.]

8–3901   31. *Meaning of "appropriate qualification".*

Duties of recognised bodies

8–3902   35. The register of auditors.   The Secretary of State shall make regulations[1] requiring the keeping of a register of—

 (*a*) the individuals and firms eligible for appointment as company auditor, and
 (*b*) the individuals holding an appropriate qualification who are responsible for company audit work on behalf of such firms.
[Companies Act 1989, s 35—summarised.]

---

   1. See the Companies Act 1989 (Register of Auditors and Information about Audit Firms) Regulations 1991, SI 1991/1566.

8–3903   36. Information about firms to be available to public.   The Secretary of State shall make regulations[1] requiring recognised supervisory bodies to keep and make available to the public information with respect to the firms eligible under their rules for appointment as a company auditor.
[Companies Act 1989, s 36—summarised.]

---

   1. See the Companies Act 1989 (Register of Auditors and Information about Audit Firms) Regulations 1991, SI 1991/1566.

8–3904   37. Matters to be notified to the Secretary of State.   (1) The Secretary of State may require a recognised supervisory or qualifying body—

 (*a*) to notify him forthwith of the occurrence of such events as he may specify in writing and to give him such information in respect of those events as is so specified;
 (*b*) to give him, at such times or in respect of such periods as he may specify in writing, such information as is so specified.

 (2) The notices and information required to be given shall be such as the Secretary of State may reasonably require for the exercise of his functions under this Part.
 (3) The Secretary of State may require information given under this section to be given in a specified form or verified in a specified manner.
 (4) Any notice or information required to be given under this section shall be given in writing unless the Secretary of State specifies or approves some other manner.
[Companies Act 1989, s 37.]

8–3905   38. Power to call for information.   (1) The Secretary of State may by notice in writing require a recognised supervisory or qualifying body to give him such information as he may reasonably require for the exercise of his functions under this Part.
 (2) The Secretary of State may require that any information which he requires under this section shall be given within such reasonable time and verified in such manner as he may specify.
[Companies Act 1989, s 38.]

Offences

8–3906   41. False and misleading statements.   (1) A person commits an offence if—

 (*a*) for the purposes of or in connection with any application under this Part, or
 (*b*) in purported compliance with any requirement imposed on him by or under this Part,

he furnishes information which he knows to be false or misleading in a material particular or recklessly furnishes information which is false or misleading in a material particular.
 (2) It is an offence for a person whose name does not appear on the register of auditors kept under regulations under section 35 to describe himself as a registered auditor or so to hold himself out as to indicate, or be reasonably understood to indicate, that he is a registered auditor.
 (3) It is an offence for a body which is not a recognised supervisory or qualifying body to describe itself as so recognised or so to describe itself or hold itself out as to indicate, or be reasonably understood to indicate, that it is so recognised.

(4) A person guilty of an offence under subsection (1) is liable[1]—

(a) on conviction on indictment, to imprisonment for a term not exceeding **two years** or to a **fine** or both;

(b) on summary conviction, to imprisonment for a term not exceeding **six months** or to a fine not exceeding **the statutory maximum** or both.

(5) A person guilty of an offence under subsection (2) or (3) is liable on summary conviction to imprisonment for a term not exceeding **six months** or to a fine not exceeding **level 5** on the standard scale or both.

Where a contravention of subsection (2) or (3) involves a public display of the offending description, the maximum fine that may be imposed is (in place of that mentioned above) an amount equal to level 5 on the standard scale multiplied by the number of days for which the display has continued.

(6) It is a defence for a person charged with an offence under subsection (2) or (3) to show that he took all reasonable precautions and exercised all due diligence to avoid the commission of the offence.

[Companies Act 1989, s 41.]

---

1. For procedure in respect of this offence which is triable either way, see the Magistrates' Courts Act 1980, ss 17A–21, in PART I: MAGISTRATES' COURTS, PROCEDURE, ante.

8–3907 42. Offences by bodies corporate, partnerships and unincorporated associations.
(1) Where an offence under this Part committed by a body corporate is proved to have been committed with the consent or connivance of, or to be attributable to any neglect on the part of, a director, manager, secretary or other similar officer of the body, or a person purporting to act in any such capacity, he as well as the body corporate is guilty of the offence and liable to be proceeded against and punished accordingly.

(2) Where the affairs of a body corporate are managed by its members, subsection (1) applies in relation to the acts and defaults of a member in connection with his functions of management as to a director of a body corporate.

(3) Where an offence under this Part committed by a partnership is proved to have been committed with the consent or connivance of, or to be attributable to any neglect on the part of, a partner, he as well as the partnership is guilty of the offence and liable to be proceeded against and punished accordingly.

(4) Where an offence under this Part committed by an unincorporated association (other than a partnership) is proved to have been committed with the consent or connivance of, or to be attributable to any neglect on the part of, any officer of the association or any member of its governing body, he as well as the association is guilty of the offence and liable to be proceeded against and punished accordingly.

[Companies Act 1989, s 42.]

8–3908 43. Time limits for prosecution of offences.   (1) An information relating to an offence under this Part which is triable by a magistrates' court in England and Wales may be so tried on an information laid at any time within twelve months after the date on which evidence sufficient in the opinion of the Director of Public Prosecutions or the Secretary of State to justify the proceedings comes to his knowledge.

(2) *Scotland.*

(3) Subsection (1) does not authorise the trial of an information laid, and subsection (2) does not authorise the commencement of proceedings, more than three years after the commission of the offence.

(4) For the purposes of this section a certificate of the Director of Public Prosecutions, the Lord Advocate or the Secretary of State as to the date on which such evidence as is referred to above came to his knowledge is conclusive evidence.

(5) Nothing in this section affects proceedings within the time limits prescribed by section 127(1) of the Magistrates' Courts Act 1980 or section 331 of the Criminal Procedure (Scotland) Act 1975 (the usual time limits for criminal proceedings).

[Companies Act 1989, s 43.]

8–3909 44. Jurisdiction and procedure in respect of offences.   (1) Summary proceedings for an offence under this Part may, without prejudice to any jurisdiction exercisable apart from this section, be taken against a body corporate or unincorporated association at any place at which it has a place of business and against an individual at any place where he is for the time being.

(2) Proceedings for an offence alleged to have been committed under this Part by an unincorporated association shall be brought in the name of the association (and not in that of any of its members), and for the purposes of any such proceedings any rules of court relating to the service of documents apply as in relation to a body corporate.

(3) Section 33 of the Criminal Justice Act 1925 and Schedule 3 to the Magistrates' Courts Act 1980 (procedure on charge of offence against a corporation) apply in a case in which an

unincorporated association is charged in England and Wales with an offence under this Part as they apply in the case of a corporation.

(4) *Scotland.*

(5) A fine imposed on an unincorporated association on its conviction of such an offence shall be paid out of the funds of the association.
[Companies Act 1989, s 44.]

Supplementary provisions

8–3910 46. Delegation of functions of Secretary of State. The Secretary of State may by order[1] (a "delegation order") establish a body corporate or un incorprorated association to exercise his functions under this Part.
[Companies Act 1989, s 46—summarised.]

---

1. The Companies Act 1989 (Delegation) Order 2005, SI 2005/2337 has been made which transfers the majority of the functions of the Secretary of State under Part 2 of the Companies Act 1989 (eligibility for appointment as company auditor) to the Professional Oversight Board for Accountancy.

8–3910A 46A. Circumstances in which Secretary of State may delegate functions to existing body

8–3911 49. Service of notices. (1) This section has effect in relation to any notice, direction or other document required or authorised by or under this Part to be given to or served on any person other than the Secretary of State.

(2) Any such document may be given to or served on the person in question—

(a) by delivering it to him,
(b) by leaving it at his proper address, or
(c) by sending it by post to him at that address.

(3) Any such document may—

(a) in the case of a body corporate, be given to or served on the secretary or clerk of that body;
(b) in the case of a partnership, be given to or served on any partner;
(c) in the case of an unincorporated association other than a partnership, be given to or served on any member of the governing body of the association.

(4) For the purposes of this section and section 7 of the Interpretation Act 1978 (service of documents by post) in its application to this section, the proper address of any person is his last known address (whether of his residence or of a place where he carries on business or is employed) and also—

(a) in the case of a person who is eligible under the rules of a recognised supervisory body for appointment as company auditor and who does not have a place of business in the United Kingdom, the address of that body;
(b) in the case of a body corporate, its secretary or its clerk, the address of its registered or principal office in the United Kingdom;
(c) in the case of an unincorporated association (other than a partnership) or a member of its governing body, its principal office in the United Kingdom.
[Companies Act 1989, s 49.]

8–3912 52. Meaning of "associate". (1) In this Part "associate", in relation to a person, shall be construed as follows.

(2) In relation to an individual "associate" means—

(a) that individual's spouse or civil partner or minor child or step-child,
(b) any body corporate of which that individual is a director, and
(c) any employee or partner of that individual.

(3) In relation to a body corporate "associate" means—

(a) any body corporate of which that body is a director,
(b) any body corporate in the same group as that body, and
(c) any employee or partner of that body or of any body corporate in the same group.

(4) In relation to a Scottish firm, or a partnership constituted under the law of any other country or territory in which a partnership is a legal person, "associate" means—

(a) any body corporate of which the firm is a director,
(b) any employee of or partner in the firm, and
(c) any person who is an associate of a partner in the firm.

(5) In relation to a partnership constituted under the law of England and Wales or Northern Ireland, or the law of any other country or territory in which a partnership is not a legal person, "associate" means any person who is an associate of any of the partners.
[Companies Act 1989, s 52 as amended by the Civil Partnership Act 2004, Sch 27.]

8–3913   53. Minor definitions.   (1) In this Part—

"address" means—

   (*a*) in relation to an individual, his usual residential or business address, and
   (*b*) in relation to a firm, its registered or principal office in Great Britain;

"company" means any company or other body to which section 384 of the Companies Act 1985 (duty to appoint auditors) applies;

"director", in relation to a body corporate, includes any person occupying in relation to it the position of a director (by whatever name called) and any person in accordance with whose directions or instructions (not being advice given in a professional capacity) the directors of the body are accustomed to act;

"enactment" includes an enactment contained in subordinate legislation within the meaning of the Interpretation Act 1978;

"firm" means a body corporate or a partnership;

"group", in relation to a body corporate, means the body corporate, any other body corporate which is its holding company or subsidiary and any other body corporate which is a subsidiary of that holding company; and

"holding company" and "subsidiary" have the meaning given by section 736 of the Companies Act 1985;

"parent undertaking" and "subsidiary undertaking" have the same meaning as in Part VII of the Companies Act 1985.

(2) For the purposes of this Part a body shall be regarded as "established in the United Kingdom" if and only if—

   (*a*) it is incorporated or formed under the law of the United Kingdom or a part of the United Kingdom, or
   (*b*) its central management and control is exercised in the United Kingdom;

and any reference to a qualification "obtained in the United Kingdom" is to a qualification obtained from such a body.
[Companies Act 1989, s 53.]

8–3914   54. Index of defined expressions.   The following Table shows provisions defining or otherwise explaining expressions used in this Part (other than provisions defining or explaining an expression used only in the same section)—

address	section 53(1)
appropriate qualification	section 31
associate	section 52
company	section 53(1)
company auditor, company audit and company audit work	section 24(2)
delegation order	section 46
director (of a body corporate)	section 53(1)
Director (in Schedule 14)	paragraph 1(1) of that Schedule
enactment	section 53(1)
established in the United Kingdom	section 53(2)
firm	section 53(1)
group (in relation to a body corporate)	section 53(1)
guidance	
—of a qualifying body	section 32(3)
—of a supervisory body	section 30(4)
holding company	section 53(1)
member (of a supervisory body)	section 30(2)
obtained in the United Kingdom	section 53(2)
parent undertaking	section 53(1)
purposes of this Part	section 24(1)
qualifying body	section 32(1)
recognised	
—in relation to a professional qualification	section 32(4) and Schedule 12
—in relation to a qualifying body	paragraph 2(1) of Schedule 12
—in relation to a supervisory body	section 30(5) and Schedule 11
rules	
—of a qualifying body	section 32(2)
—of a supervisory body	section 30(3)
subsidiary and subsidiary undertaking	section 53(1)
supervisory body	section 30(1)

[Companies Act 1989, s 54.]

Criminal Justice Act 1993[1]

(1993 c 36)

PART V[2]
INSIDER DEALING

The offence of insider dealing

8–3915   52. The offence.   (1) An individual who has information as an insider is guilty of insider dealing if, in the circumstances mentioned in subsection (3), he deals in securities that are price-affected securities in relation to the information.

(2) An individual who has information as an insider is also guilty of insider dealing if—

(a) he encourages another person to deal in securities that are (whether or not that other knows it) price-affected securities in relation to the information, knowing or having reasonable cause to believe that the dealing would take place in the circumstances mentioned in subsection (3); or

(b) he discloses the information, otherwise than in the proper performance of the functions of his employment, office or profession, to another person.

(3) The circumstances referred to above are that the acquisition or disposal in question occurs on a regulated market, or that the person dealing relies on a professional intermediary or is himself acting as a professional intermediary.

(4) This section has effect subject to section 53.

[Criminal Justice Act 1993, s 52.]

---

1. Other provisions of the Criminal Justice Act 1993 may be found in PART I: MAGISTRATES' COURTS, PROCEDURE, ante.

2. Part V contains ss 52 to 64.

8–3916   53. Defences.   (1) An individual is not guilty of insider dealing by virtue of dealing in securities if he shows—

(a) that he did not at the time expect the dealing to result in a profit attributable to the fact that the information in question was price-sensitive information in relation to the securities, or

(b) that at the time he believed on reasonable grounds that the information had been disclosed widely enough to ensure that none of those taking part in the dealing would be prejudiced by not having the information, or

(c) that he would have done what he did even if he had not had the information.

(2) An individual is not guilty of insider dealing by virtue of encouraging another person to deal in securities if he shows—

(a) that he did not at the time expect the dealing to result in a profit attributable to the fact that the information in question was price-sensitive information in relation to the securities, or

(b) that at the time he believed on reasonable grounds that the information had been or would be disclosed widely enough to ensure that none of those taking part in the dealing would be prejudiced by not having the information, or

(c) that he would have done what he did even if he had not had the information.

(3) An individual is not guilty of insider dealing by virtue of a disclosure of information if he shows—

(a) that he did not at the time expect any person, because of the disclosure, to deal in securities in the circumstances mentioned in subsection (3) of section 52; or

(b) that, although he had such an expectation at the time, he did not expect the dealing to result in a profit attributable to the fact that the information was price-sensitive information in relation to the securities.

(4) Schedule 1[1] (special defences) shall have effect.

(5) The Treasury may by order amend Schedule 1.

(6) In this section references to a profit include references to the avoidance of a loss.

[Criminal Justice Act 1993, s 53.]

---

1. See, post.

Interpretation

8–3917   54. Securities to which Part V applies.   (1) This Part applies to any security which—

(a) falls within any paragraph of Schedule 2; and

(b) satisfies any conditions applying to it under an order[1] made by the Treasury for the purposes of this subsection;

and in the provisions of this Part (other than that Schedule) any reference to a security is a reference to a security to which this Part applies.

(2) The Treasury may by order amend Schedule 2[2].

[Criminal Justice Act 1993, s 54.]

---

1. The Insider Dealing (Securities and Regulated Markets) Order 1994, SI 1994/187 has been made.
2. See, post.

8–3918 55. "Dealing" in securities. (1) For the purposes of this Part, a person deals in securities if—

(a) he acquires or disposes of the securities (whether as principal or agent); or

(b) he procures, directly or indirectly, an acquisition or disposal of the securities by any other person.

(2) For the purposes of this Part, "acquire", in relation to a security, includes—

(a) agreeing to acquire the security; and

(b) entering into a contract which creates the security.

(3) For the purposes of this Part, "dispose", in relation to a security, includes—

(a) agreeing to dispose of the security; and

(b) bringing to an end a contract which created the security.

(4) For the purposes of subsection (1), a person procures an acquisition or disposal of a security if the security is acquired or disposed of by a person who is—

(a) his agent,

(b) his nominee, or

(c) a person who is acting at his direction,

in relation to the acquisition or disposal.

(5) Subsection (4) is not exhaustive as to the circumstances in which one person may be regarded as procuring an acquisition or disposal of securities by another.

[Criminal Justice Act 1993, s 55.]

8–3919 56. "Inside information", etc. (1) For the purposes of this section and section 57, "inside information" means information which—

(a) relates to particular securities or to a particular issuer of securities or to particular issuers of securities and not to securities generally or to issuers of securities generally;

(b) is specific or precise;

(c) has not been made public; and

(d) if it were made public would be likely to have a significant effect on the price of any securities.

(2) For the purposes of this Part, securities are "price-affected securities" in relation to inside information, and inside information is "price-sensitive information" in relation to securities, if and only if the information would, if made public, be likely to have a significant effect on the price of the securities.

(3) For the purposes of this section "price" includes value.

[Criminal Justice Act 1993, s 56.]

8–3920 57. "Insiders". (1) For the purposes of this Part, a person has information as an insider if and only if—

(a) it is, and he knows that it is, inside information, and

(b) he has it, and knows that he has it, from an inside source.

(2) For the purposes of subsection (1), a person has information from an inside source if and only if—

(a) he has it through—

(i) being a director, employee or shareholder of an issuer of securities; or

(ii) having access to the information by virtue of his employment, office or profession; or

(b) the direct or indirect source of his information is a person within paragraph (a).

[Criminal Justice Act 1993, s 57.]

8–3921 58. Information "made public". (1) For the purposes of section 56, "made public", in relation to information, shall be construed in accordance with the following provisions of this section; but those provisions are not exhaustive as to the meaning of that expression.

(2) Information is made public if—

(a) it is published in accordance with the rules of a regulated market for the purpose of informing investors and their professional advisers;

(*b*) it is contained in records which by virtue of any enactment are open to inspection by the public;

(*c*) it can be readily acquired by those likely to deal in any securities—

    (i) to which the information relates, or

    (ii) of an issuer to which the information relates; or

(*d*) it is derived from information which has been made public.

(3) Information may be treated as made public even though—

(*a*) it can be acquired only by persons exercising diligence or expertise;

(*b*) it is communicated to a section of the public and not to the public at large;

(*c*) it can be acquired only by observation;

(*d*) it is communicated only on payment of a fee; or

(*e*) it is published only outside the United Kingdom.

[Criminal Justice Act 1993, s 58.]

8–3922   59. "Professional intermediary".   (1) For the purposes of this Part, a "professional intermediary" is a person—

(*a*) who carries on a business consisting of an activity mentioned in subsection (2) and who holds himself out to the public or any section of the public (including a section of the public constituted by persons such as himself) as willing to engage in any such business; or

(*b*) who is employed by a person falling within paragraph (a) to carry out any such activity.

(2) The activities referred to in subsection (1) are—

(*a*) acquiring or disposing of securities (whether as principal or agent); or

(*b*) acting as an intermediary between persons taking part in any dealing in securities.

(3) A person is not to be treated as carrying on a business consisting of an activity mentioned in subsection (2)—

(*a*) if the activity in question is merely incidental to some other activity not falling within subsection (2); or

(*b*) merely because he occasionally conducts one of those activities.

(4) For the purposes of section 52, a person dealing in securities relies on a professional intermediary if and only if a person who is acting as a professional intermediary carries out an activity mentioned in subsection (2) in relation to that dealing.

[Criminal Justice Act 1993, s 59.]

8–3923   60. Other interpretation provisions.   (1) For the purposes of this Part, "regulated market" means any market, however operated, which, by an order[1] made by the Treasury, is identified (whether by name or by reference to criteria prescribed by the order) as a regulated market for the purposes of this Part.

(2) For the purposes of this Part an "issuer", in relation to any securities, means any company, public sector body or individual by which or by whom the securities have been or are to be issued.

(3) For the purposes of this Part—

(*a*) "company" means any body (whether or not incorporated and wherever incorporated or constituted) which is not a public sector body; and

(*b*) "public sector body" means—

    (i) the government of the United Kingdom, of Northern Ireland or of any country or territory outside the United Kingdom;

    (ii) a local authority in the United Kingdom or elsewhere;

    (iii) any international organisation the members of which include the United Kingdom or another member state;

    (iv) the Bank of England; or

    (v) the central bank of any sovereign State.

(4) For the purposes of this Part, information shall be treated as relating to an issuer of securities which is a company not only where it is about the company but also where it may affect the company's business prospects.

[Criminal Justice Act 1993, s 60.]

---

1. The Insider Dealing (Securities and Regulated Markets) Order 1994, SI 1994/187 amended by SI 1996/1561, SI 2000/1923 and SI 2002/1874 has been made.

Miscellaneous

8–3924   61. Penalties and prosecution.   (1) An individual guilty of insider dealing shall be liable[1]—

(*a*) on summary conviction, to a fine not exceeding **the statutory maximum** or imprisonment for a term not exceeding **six months** or to **both**; or

(b) on conviction on indictment, to a **fine** or imprisonment for a term not exceeding **seven years** or to **both**.

(2) Proceedings for offences under this Part shall not be instituted in England and Wales except by or with the consent of—

(a) the Secretary of State; or
(b) the Director of Public Prosecutions.

(3) *Northern Ireland.*
[Criminal Justice Act 1993, s 61.]

---

1. For procedure in respect of this offence which is triable either way, see the Magistrates' Courts Act 1980, ss 17A–21, in PART I: MAGISTRATES' COURTS, PROCEDURE, ante.

8–3925 62. Territorial scope of offence of insider dealing. (1) An individual is not guilty of an offence falling within subsection (1) of section 52 unless—

(a) he was within the United Kingdom at the time when he is alleged to have done any act constituting or forming part of the alleged dealing;
(b) the regulated market on which the dealing is alleged to have occurred is one which, by an order[1] made by the Treasury, is identified (whether by name or by reference to criteria prescribed by the order) as being, for the purposes of this Part, regulated in the United Kingdom; or
(c) the professional intermediary was within the United Kingdom at the time when he is alleged to have done anything by means of which the offence is alleged to have been committed.

(2) An individual is not guilty of an offence falling within subsection (2) of section 52 unless—

(a) he was within the United Kingdom at the time when he is alleged to have disclosed the information or encouraged the dealing; or
(b) the alleged recipient of the information or encouragement was within the United Kingdom at the time when he is alleged to have received the information or encouragement.

[Criminal Justice Act 1993, s 62.]

---

1. The Insider Dealing (Securities and Regulated Markets) Order 1994, SI 1994/187 amended by SI 1996/1561 and SI 2000/1923 has been made.

8–3926 63. Limits on section 52. (1) Section 52 does not apply to anything done by an individual acting on behalf of a public sector body in pursuit of monetary policies or policies with respect to exchange rates or the management of public debt or foreign exchange reserves.

(2) No contract shall be void or unenforceable by reason only of section 52.
[Criminal Justice Act 1993, s 63.]

8–3927 64. Orders. (1) Any power under this Part to make an order shall be exercisable by statutory instrument.

(2) No order shall be made under this Part unless a draft of it has been laid before and approved by a resolution of each House of Parliament.

(3) An order under this Part—

(a) may make different provision for different cases; and
(b) may contain such incidental, supplemental and transitional provisions as the Treasury consider expedient.

[Criminal Justice Act 1993, s 64.]

8–3928

SCHEDULES

Section 53(4)

SCHEDULE 1
SPECIAL DEFENCES

(As amended by SI 2001/3649 and SI 2005/381)

Market makers

1. (1) An individual is not guilty of insider dealing by virtue of dealing in securities or encouraging another person to deal if he shows that he acted in good faith in the course of—

(a) his business as a market maker, or
(b) his employment in the business of a market maker.

(2) A market maker is a person who—

(a) holds himself out at all normal times in compliance with the rules of a regulated market or an approved organisation as willing to acquire or dispose of securities; and

(b) is recognised as doing so under those rules.

(3) In this paragraph "approved organisation" means an international securities self-regulating organisation approved under paragraph 25B of Schedule 1 to the Financial Services Act 1986.

Market information

2. (1) An individual is not guilty of insider dealing by virtue of dealing in securities or encouraging another person to deal if he shows that—

(a) the information which he had as an insider was market information; and

(b) it was reasonable for an individual in his position to have acted as he did despite having that information as an insider at the time.

(2) In determining whether it is reasonable for an individual to do any act despite having market information at the time, there shall, in particular, be taken into account—

(a) the content of the information;

(b) the circumstances in which he first had the information and in what capacity; and

(c) the capacity in which he now acts.

3. An individual is not guilty of insider dealing by virtue of dealing in securities or encouraging another person to deal if he shows—

(a) that he acted—

(i) in connection with an acquisition or disposal which was under consideration or the subject of negotiation, or in the course of a series of such acquisitions or disposals; and

(ii) with a view to facilitating the accomplishment of the acquisition or disposal or the series of acquisitions or disposals; and

(b) that the information which he had as an insider was market information arising directly out of his involvement in the acquisition or disposal or series of acquisitions or disposals.

4. For the purposes of paragraphs 2 and 3 market information is information consisting of one or more of the following facts—

(a) that securities of a particular kind have been or are to be acquired or disposed of, or that their acquisition or disposal is under consideration or the subject of negotiation;

(b) that securities of a particular kind have not been or are not to be acquired or disposed of;

(c) the number of securities acquired or disposed of or to be acquired or disposed of or whose acquisition or disposal is under consideration or the subject of negotiation;

(d) the price (or range of prices) at which securities have been or are to be acquired or disposed of or the price (or range of prices) at which securities whose acquisition or disposal is under consideration or the subject of negotiation may be acquired or disposed of;

(e) the identity of the persons involved or likely to be involved in any capacity in an acquisition or disposal.

Price stabilisation

5. (1) An individual is not guilty of insider dealing by virtue of dealing in securities or encouraging another person to deal if he shows that he acted in conformity with the price stabilisation rules or with the relevant provisions of Commission Regulation (EC) No 2273/2003 of 22 December 2003 implementing Directive 2003/6/EC of the European Parliament and of the Council as regards exemptions for buy-back programmes and stabilisation of financial instruments.

(2) "Price stabilisation rules" means rules made under section 144(1) of the Financial Services and Markets Act 2000.

8–3929

Section 54   SCHEDULE 2
                           SECURITIES

Shares

1. Shares and stock in the share capital of a company ("shares").

Debt securities

2. Any instrument creating or acknowledging indebtedness which is issued by a company or public sector body, including, in particular, debentures, debenture stock, loan stock, bonds and certificates of deposit ("debt securities").

Warrants

3. Any right (whether conferred by warrant or otherwise) to subscribe for shares or debt securities ("warrants").

Depositary receipts

4. (1) The rights under any depositary receipt.

(2) For the purposes of sub-paragraph (1) a "depositary receipt" means a certificate or other record (whether or not in the form of a document)—

(a) which is issued by or on behalf of a person who holds any relevant securities of a particular issuer; and

(b) which acknowledges that another person is entitled to rights in relation to the relevant securities or relevant securities of the same kind.

(3) In sub-paragraph (2) "relevant securities" means shares, debt securities and warrants.

Options

5. Any option to acquire or dispose of any security falling within any other paragraph of this Schedule.

Futures

6. (1) Rights under a contract for the acquisition or disposal of relevant securities under which delivery is to be made at a future date and at a price agreed when the contract is made.

(2) In sub-paragraph (1)—

(*a*) the references to a future date and to a price agreed when the contract is made include references to a date and a price determined in accordance with terms of the contract; and

(*b*) "relevant securities" means any security falling within any other paragraph of this Schedule.

Contracts for differences

7. (1) Rights under a contract which does not provide for the delivery of securities but whose purpose or pretended purpose is to secure a profit or avoid a loss by reference to fluctuations in—

(*a*) a share index or other similar factor connected with relevant securities;

(*b*) the price of particular relevant securities; or

(*c*) the interest rate offered on money placed on deposit.

(2) In sub-paragraph (1) "relevant securities" means any security falling within any other paragraph of this Schedule.

Limited Liability Partnerships Act 2000[1]
(2000 c 12)

8–3929A   There is a new form of legal entity known as a limited liability partnership which is a body corporate (with legal personality separate from that of its members) which is formed by being incorporated under this Act. Except as otherwise provided by this Act or any other enactment, the law relating to partnerships does not apply (**s 1**). A limited liability partnership is incorporated by an incorporation document which must be in a form approved by the registrar which must state that two or more persons associated for carrying on a lawful business with a view to profit have subscribed their names to the incorporation document. A person who makes a false statement to this effect which he knows to be false or does not believe to be true commits an offence triable either way which is punishable on summary conviction by 6 months imprisonment or a **fine** not exceeding the **statutory maximum** or **both** or on indictment by **two years imprisonment** or a **fine** or **both** (**s 2**). Provision is made for membership (ss **3–8**) and the registrar must be notified of membership changes. If the limited liability membership fails to notify changes, it and every designated member commits an offence punishable by a fine not exceeding **level 5** but it is a defence for a designated member to prove that he took all reasonable steps to secure that the notification requirements were complied with (**s 9**).

---

1. This Act, with the exception of s 19, which came into force on Royal Assent, was brought into force on 6 April 2001 by the Limited Liability Partnerships Act 2000 (Commencement) Order 2000, SI 2000/3316.

Companies (Audit, Investigations and Community Enterprise) Act 2004
(2004 c 27)

8–3930

PART 1[1]
AUDITORS, ACCOUNTS, DIRECTORS' LIABILITIES AND INVESTIGATIONS
CHAPTER 2[2]
Accounts and Reports

---

1. Part 1 contains ss 1–25.
2. Chapter 2 contains ss 8–18.

Auditing of accounts

8–3930A   **8. Auditors' rights to information.**   For section 389A of the Companies Act 1985 (c 6) substitute—

"**389A. Rights to information.**   (1) An auditor of a company—

(*a*) has a right of access at all times to the company's books, accounts and vouchers (in whatever form they are held), and

(b) may require any of the persons mentioned in subsection (2) to provide him with such information or explanations as he thinks necessary for the performance of his duties as auditor.

(2) Those persons are—

(a) any officer or employee of the company;

(b) any person holding or accountable for any of the company's books, accounts or vouchers;

(c) any subsidiary undertaking of the company which is a body corporate incorporated in Great Britain;

(d) any officer, employee or auditor of any such subsidiary undertaking or any person holding or accountable for any books, accounts or vouchers of any such subsidiary undertaking;

(e) any person who fell within any of paragraphs (a) to (d) at a time to which the information or explanations required by the auditor relates or relate.

(3) Where a parent company has a subsidiary undertaking which is not a body corporate incorporated in Great Britain, the auditor of the parent company may require it to obtain from any of the persons mentioned in subsection (4) such information or explanations as he may reasonably require for the purposes of his duties as auditor.

(4) Those persons are—

(a) the undertaking;

(b) any officer, employee or auditor of the undertaking;

(c) any person holding or accountable for any of the undertaking's books, accounts or vouchers;

(d) any person who fell within paragraph (b) or (c) at a time to which the information or explanations relates or relate.

(5) If so required, the parent company must take all such steps as are reasonably open to it to obtain the information or explanations from the person within subsection (4) from whom the auditor has required the company to obtain the information or explanations.

(6) A statement made by a person in response to a requirement under subsection (1)(b) or (3) may not be used in evidence against him in any criminal proceedings except proceedings for an offence under section 389B.

(7) Nothing in this section or section 389B compels any person to disclose information in respect of which in an action in the High Court a claim to legal professional privilege, or in an action in the Court of Session a claim to confidentiality of communications, could be maintained.

389B. Offences relating to the provision of information to auditors.   (1) If a person knowingly or recklessly makes to an auditor of a company a statement (oral or written) that—

(a) conveys or purports to convey any information or explanations which the auditor requires, or is entitled to require, under section 389A(1)(b), and

(b) is misleading, false or deceptive in a material particular,

the person is guilty of an offence and liable to imprisonment or a fine, or both.

(2) A person who fails to comply with a requirement under section 389A(1)(b) without delay is guilty of an offence and is liable to a fine.

(3) However, it is a defence for a person charged with an offence under subsection (2) to prove that it was not reasonably practicable for him to provide the required information or explanations.

(4) If a company fails to comply with section 389A(5), the company and every officer of it who is in default is guilty of an offence and liable to a fine.

(5) Nothing in this section affects any right of an auditor to apply for an injunction to enforce any of his rights under section 389A."

[Companies (Audit, Investigations and Community Enterprise) Act 2004, s 8.]

8–3930B   9. Statement in directors' report as to disclosure of information to auditors.

(1) Part 7 of the Companies Act 1985 (c 6) (accounts and audit) is amended as follows.

(2) In section 234 (duty to prepare directors' report), after subsection (2) insert—

"(2A) If section 234ZA applies to the report, it shall contain the statement required by subsection (2) of that section."

(3) After section 234 insert—

"234ZA. Statement as to disclosure of information to auditors.   (1) This section applies to a directors' report unless the directors have taken advantage of the exemption conferred by section 249A(1) or 249AA(1).

(2) The report must contain a statement to the effect that, in the case of each of the persons who are directors at the time when the report is approved under section 234A, the following applies—

(a) so far as the director is aware, there is no relevant audit information of which the company's auditors are unaware, and

(b) he has taken all the steps that he ought to have taken as a director in order to make himself aware of any relevant audit information and to establish that the company's auditors are aware of that information.

(3) In subsection (2) "relevant audit information" means information needed by the company's auditors in connection with preparing their report.

(4) For the purposes of subsection (2) a director has taken all the steps that he ought to have taken as a director in order to do the things mentioned in paragraph (b) of that subsection if he has—

(a) made such enquiries of his fellow directors and of the company's auditors for that purpose, and

(b) taken such other steps (if any) for that purpose,

as were required by his duty as a director of the company to exercise due care, skill and diligence.

(5) In determining for the purposes of subsection (2) the extent of that duty in the case of a particular director, the following considerations (in particular) are relevant—

(a) the knowledge, skill and experience that may reasonably be expected of a person carrying out the same functions as are carried out by the director in relation to the company, and

(b) (so far as they exceed what may reasonably be so expected) the knowledge, skill and experience that the director in fact has.

(6) Where a directors' report containing the statement required by subsection (2) is approved under section 234A but the statement is false, every director of the company who—

(a) knew that the statement was false, or was reckless as to whether it was false, and

(b) failed to take reasonable steps to prevent the report from being approved,

is guilty of an offence and liable to imprisonment or a fine, or both."

[Companies (Audit, Investigations and Community Enterprise) Act 2004, s 9.]

Defective accounts

8–3930C 10. Persons authorised to apply to court in connection with defective accounts. *Amends s 245C of the Companies Act 1985.*

11. Disclosure of tax information by Inland Revenue to facilitate application for declaration that accounts are defective. (1) *Inserts ss 245D and E into the Companies Act 1985.*

(2) *Northern Ireland.*

[Companies (Audit, Investigations and Community Enterprise) Act 2004, s 11.]

12. Power of person authorised to require documents, information and explanations. (1) *Inserts ss 245F and G into the Companies Act 1985.*

(2) Schedule 1 (which inserts Schedule 7B in the Companies Act 1985 (c 6)) has effect.

[Companies (Audit, Investigations and Community Enterprise) Act 2004, s 12.]

Supervision of accounts and reports

8–3930D 15. Application of provisions inserted by sections 11 and 12 to bodies appointed under section 14. (1) The following provisions apply, in accordance with this section, in relation to prescribed bodies and their functions under section 14 of this Act—

(a) sections 245D and 245E of the Companies Act 1985 (c 6) (as inserted by section 11(1) of this Act),

(b) Articles 253D and 253E of the Companies (Northern Ireland) Order 1986 (SI 1986/1032 (NI 6)) (as inserted by section 11(2) of this Act), and

(c) sections 245F and 245G of and Schedule 7B to the Companies Act 1985 (as inserted by section 12(1) of this Act).

(2) Sections 245D and 245E apply in relation to prescribed bodies and their functions as they apply in relation to persons authorised under section 245C of that Act and persons authorised under Article 253C of the Companies (Northern Ireland) Order 1986 and the functions of such persons mentioned in sections 245D(3) and 245E(1).

But section 245E so applies as if subsection (2)(b) of that section were omitted.

(3) Articles 253D and 253E apply in relation to prescribed bodies and their functions as they apply in relation to persons authorised under Article 253C of that Order and persons authorised under section 245C of the Companies Act 1985 and the functions of such persons mentioned in Articles 253D(3) and 253E(1).

But Article 253E so applies as if paragraph (2)(b) of that Article were omitted.

(4) Sections 245F and 245G and Schedule 7B apply in relation to prescribed bodies and their functions as they apply in relation to persons authorised under section 245C of that Act and the functions of such persons mentioned in section 245F(2), section 245G(3)(a) and paragraph 16 of Schedule 7B.

(5) But section 245F so applies as if—

(a) subsection (1) of that section provided that the section applies where it appears to a prescribed body that there is, or may be, a question whether any relevant accounts or reports produced by an issuer of listed securities comply with any accounting requirements imposed by listing rules;

(b) the references in section 245F(3)(a) and (b) to "the company" were references to that issuer; and

(c) the references in section 245F(4) and (5) to "the court" were to the High Court or, in Scotland, the Court of Session.

(6) In subsection (5)—

(a) "relevant accounts or reports" means accounts or reports in relation to which the prescribed body has functions under section 14; and

(b) "issuer", "listing rules" and "security" have the same meanings as in section 14.

(7) In this section "prescribed body" has the same meaning as in section 14.

[Companies (Audit, Investigations and Community Enterprise) Act 2004, s 15.]

CHAPTER 4[1]
Investigations

8–3930E   21. Power to require documents and information.   For section 447 of the Companies Act 1985 (c 6) substitute—

"447. Power to require documents and information.   (1) The Secretary of State may act under subsections (2) and (3) in relation to a company.

(2) The Secretary of State may give directions to the company requiring it—

(a) to produce such documents (or documents of such description) as may be specified in the directions;

(b) to provide such information (or information of such description) as may be so specified.

(3) The Secretary of State may authorise a person (an investigator) to require the company or any other person—

(a) to produce such documents (or documents of such description) as the investigator may specify;

(b) to provide such information (or information of such description) as the investigator may specify.

(4) A person on whom a requirement under subsection (3) is imposed may require the investigator to produce evidence of his authority.

(5) A requirement under subsection (2) or (3) must be complied with at such time and place as may be specified in the directions or by the investigator (as the case may be).

(6) The production of a document in pursuance of this section does not affect any lien which a person has on the document.

(7) The Secretary of State or the investigator (as the case may be) may take copies of or extracts from a document produced in pursuance of this section.

(8) A "document" includes information recorded in any form.

(9) In relation to information recorded otherwise than in legible form, the power to require production of it includes power to require the production of a copy of it in legible form or in a form from which it can readily be produced in visible and legible form."

---

1. Chapter 4 contains ss 21–24.

8–3930F   22. Protection in relation to certain disclosures.   After section 448 of the Companies Act 1985 (c 6) insert—

"448A. Protection in relation to certain disclosures: information provided to Secretary of State.   (1) A person who makes a relevant disclosure is not liable by reason only of that disclosure in any proceedings relating to a breach of an obligation of confidence.

(2) A relevant disclosure is a disclosure which satisfies each of the following conditions—

(a) it is made to the Secretary of State otherwise than in compliance with a requirement under this Part;

(b) it is of a kind that the person making the disclosure could be required to make in pursuance of this Part;

(c) the person who makes the disclosure does so in good faith and in the reasonable belief that the disclosure is capable of assisting the Secretary of State for the purposes of the exercise of his functions under this Part;

(d) the information disclosed is not more than is reasonably necessary for the purpose of assisting the Secretary of State for the purposes of the exercise of those functions;

(*e*)   the disclosure is not one falling within subsection (3) or (4).

(3)   A disclosure falls within this subsection if the disclosure is prohibited by virtue of any enactment.

(4)   A disclosure falls within this subsection if—

(*a*)   it is made by a person carrying on the business of banking or by a lawyer, and

(*b*)   it involves the disclosure of information in respect of which he owes an obligation of confidence in that capacity.

(5)   An enactment includes an enactment—

(*a*)   comprised in, or in an instrument made under, an Act of the Scottish Parliament;

(*b*)   comprised in subordinate legislation (within the meaning of the Interpretation Act 1978);

(*c*)   whenever passed or made."

[Companies (Audit, Investigations and Community Enterprise) Act 2004, s 22.]

8–3930G   23. Power to enter and remain on premises.   *Inserts new ss 435A and 435B in the Companies Act 1985.*

8–3930H   24. Failure to comply with certain requirements.   *Inserts new s 435C in the Companies Act 1985.*

CHAPTER 5[1]
Supplementary

8–3930I   25. Minor and consequential amendments.   (1)   Schedule 2 (minor and consequential amendments relating to Part 1) has effect.

(2)   That Schedule has effect subject to the modifications set out in subsection (3)—

(*a*)   in relation to England and Wales, in the case of an offence committed before section 154(1) of the Criminal Justice Act 2003 (c 44) comes into force, and

(*b*)   in relation to Scotland.

(3)   The modifications are—

(*a*)   the amendment in paragraph 10(2) has effect as if for "12 months" there were substituted "6 months";

(*b*)   the amendment in paragraph 10(3) has effect as if for "12 months", in both places where it occurs, there were substituted "3 months";

(*c*)   the amendment in paragraph 10(4) has effect as if for "12 months" there were substituted "6 months";

(*d*)   the amendment in paragraph 26(2) has effect as if for "12 months" there were substituted "6 months"; and

(*e*)   the amendment in paragraph 26(3) has effect as if for "12 months" there were substituted "6 months".

[Companies (Audit, Investigations and Community Enterprise) Act 2004, s 25.]

---

1.   Chapter 5 contains s 25.

PART 2
COMMUNITY INTEREST COMPANIES[1]

Introductory

8–3930J   26. Community interest companies.   (1)   There is to be a new type of company to be known as the community interest company.

(2)   In accordance with this Part—

(*a*)   a company limited by shares or a company limited by guarantee and not having a share capital may be formed as or become a community interest company, and

(*b*)   a company limited by guarantee and having a share capital may become a community interest company.

(3)   A community interest company established for charitable purposes is to be treated as not being so established and accordingly—

(*a*)   is not a charity, and

(*b*)   must not be given such intimation as is mentioned in section 1(7) of the Law Reform (Miscellaneous Provisions) (Scotland) Act 1990 (c 40) (Scottish charities).

[Companies (Audit, Investigations and Community Enterprise) Act 2004, s 26.]

---

1.   Part 2 contains ss 26–62.

8–3930K   27. Regulator.   (1)   There is to be an officer known as the Regulator of Community Interest Companies (referred to in this Part as "the Regulator").

(2) The Secretary of State must appoint a person to be the Regulator.

(3) The Regulator has such functions relating to community interest companies as are conferred or imposed by or by virtue of this Act or any other enactment.

(4) The Regulator must adopt an approach to the discharge of those functions which is based on good regulatory practice, that is an approach adopted having regard to—

(a) the likely impact on those who may be affected by the discharge of those functions,

(b) the outcome of consultations with, and with organisations representing, community interest companies and others with relevant experience, and

(c) the desirability of using the Regulator's resources in the most efficient and economic way.

(5) The Regulator may issue guidance, or otherwise provide assistance, about any matter relating to community interest companies.

(6) The Secretary of State may require the Regulator to issue guidance or otherwise provide assistance about any matter relating to community interest companies which is specified by the Secretary of State.

(7) Any guidance issued under this section must be such that it is readily accessible to, and capable of being easily understood by, those at whom it is aimed; and any other assistance provided under this section must be provided in the manner which the Regulator considers is most likely to be helpful to those to whom it is provided.

(8) Schedule 3 (further provisions about the Regulator) has effect.

[Companies (Audit, Investigations and Community Enterprise) Act 2004, s 27.]

8–3930L   28. Appeal Officer.   (1) There is to be an officer known as the Appeal Officer for Community Interest Companies (referred to in this Part as "the Appeal Officer").

(2) The Secretary of State must appoint a person to be the Appeal Officer.

(3) The Appeal Officer has the function of determining appeals against decisions and orders of the Regulator which under or by virtue of this Act or any other enactment lie to the Appeal Officer.

(4) An appeal to the Appeal Officer against a decision or order of the Regulator may be brought on the ground that the Regulator made a material error of law or fact.

(5) On such an appeal the Appeal Officer must—

(a) dismiss the appeal,

(b) allow the appeal, or

(c) remit the case to the Regulator.

(6) Where a case is remitted the Regulator must reconsider it in accordance with any rulings of law and findings of fact made by the Appeal Officer.

(7) Schedule 4 (further provisions about the Appeal Officer) has effect.

[Companies (Audit, Investigations and Community Enterprise) Act 2004, s 28.]

8–3930M   29. Official Property Holder.   (1) There is to be an officer known as the Official Property Holder for Community Interest Companies (referred to in this Part as "the Official Property Holder").

(2) The Regulator must appoint a member of the Regulator's staff to be the Official Property Holder.

(3) The Official Property Holder has such functions relating to property of community interest companies as are conferred or imposed by or by virtue of this Act or any other enactment.

(4) Schedule 5 (further provisions about the Official Property Holder) has effect.

[Companies (Audit, Investigations and Community Enterprise) Act 2004, s 29.]

Supervision by Regulator

8–3930N   45. Appointment of director.   (1) The Regulator may by order appoint a director of a community interest company.

(2) The person appointed may be anyone whom the Regulator thinks appropriate, other than a member of the Regulator's staff.

(3) A person may be appointed as a director of a company under this section—

(a) whether or not the person is a member of the company, and

(b) irrespective of any provision made by the memorandum or articles of the company or a resolution of the company in general meeting.

(4) An order appointing a person to be a director of a company under this section must specify the terms on which the director is to hold office; and those terms have effect as if contained in a contract between the director and the company.

(5) The terms specified must include the period for which the director is to hold office, and may include terms as to the remuneration of the director by the company.

(6) A director appointed under this section has all the powers of the directors appointed by the company (including powers exercisable only by a particular director or class of directors).

(7) A director appointed under this section may not be removed by the company, but may be removed by the Regulator at any time.

(8) Where—

(*a*)   a person is appointed to be a director of the company under this section, or

(*b*)   a person so appointed ceases to be a director of the company,

the obligation which would otherwise be imposed on the company under section 288(2) of the Companies Act 1985 (c 6) (requirement that company notify change among directors to registrar) is instead an obligation of the Regulator.

(9)   But if subsection (10) applies, section 288(2) applies as if the period within which the Regulator must send a notification to the registrar of companies is 14 days from the date on which the Regulator receives notification under that subsection.

(10)   Where a person appointed to be a director of the company under this section ceases to be a director of the company (otherwise than by removal under subsection (7)), the company must give notification of that fact to the Regulator in a form approved by the Regulator before the end of the period of 14 days beginning with the date on which the person ceases to be a director.

(11)   If the company fails to comply with subsection (10) it commits an offence.

(12)   A person guilty of an offence under subsection (11) is liable on summary conviction to a fine not exceeding level 5 on the standard scale.

(13)   The company may appeal to the Appeal Officer against an order under this section.

[Companies (Audit, Investigations and Community Enterprise) Act 2004, s 45.]

8–3930P   48. Property.   (1)   The Regulator may by order—

(*a*)   vest in the Official Property Holder any property held by or in trust for a community interest company, or

(*b*)   require persons in whom such property is vested to transfer it to the Official Property Holder.

(2)   The Regulator—

(*a*)   may order a person who holds property on behalf of a community interest company, or on behalf of a trustee of a community interest company, not to part with the property without the Regulator's consent, and

(*b*)   may order any debtor of a community interest company not to make any payment in respect of the debtor's liability to the company without the Regulator's consent.

(3)   The Regulator may by order restrict—

(*a*)   the transactions which may be entered into by a community interest company, or

(*b*)   the nature or amount of the payments that a community interest company may make,

and the order may in particular provide that transactions may not be entered into or payments made without the Regulator's consent.

(4)   The vesting or transfer of property under subsection (1) does not constitute a breach of a covenant or condition against alienation, and no right listed in subsection (5) operates or becomes exercisable as a result of the vesting or transfer.

(5)   The rights are—

(*a*)   a right of reverter (or, in Scotland, the right of the fiar on the termination of a liferent),

(*b*)   a right of pre-emption,

(*c*)   a right of forfeiture,

(*d*)   a right of re-entry,

(*e*)   a right of irritancy,

(*f*)   an option, and

(*g*)   any right similar to those listed in paragraphs (*a*) to (*f*).

(6)   The Regulator must from time to time review any order under this section and, if it is appropriate to do so, discharge the order in whole or in part.

(7)   On discharging an order under subsection (1) the Regulator may make any order as to the vesting or transfer of the property, and give any directions, which he considers appropriate.

(8)   If a person fails to comply with an order under subsection (1)(*b*), the Regulator may certify that fact in writing to the court.

(9)   If, after hearing—

(*a*)   any witnesses who may be produced against or on behalf of the alleged offender, and

(*b*)   any statement which may be offered in defence,

the court is satisfied that the offender failed without reasonable excuse to comply with the order, it may deal with him as if he had been guilty of contempt of the court.

(10)   A person who contravenes an order under subsection (2) or (3) commits an offence, but a prosecution may be instituted in England and Wales only with the consent of the Regulator or the Director of Public Prosecutions.

(11)   A person guilty of an offence under subsection (10) is liable on summary conviction to a fine not exceeding level 5 on the standard scale.

(12)   Subsections (8) to (10) do not prevent the bringing of civil proceedings in respect of a contravention of an order under subsection (1)(*b*), (2) or (3).

(13) The company and any person to whom the order is directed may appeal to the Appeal Officer against an order under subsection (1) or (2).

(14) The company may appeal to the Appeal Officer against an order under subsection (3).

[Companies (Audit, Investigations and Community Enterprise) Act 2004, s 48.]

Supplementary

8–3930Q   **59. Information.**   (1) Regulations may require the registrar of companies—

(*a*) to notify the Regulator of matters specified in the regulations, and

(*b*) to provide the Regulator with copies of documents specified in the regulations.

(2) *Amends s 71 of the Bankruptcy (Scotland) Act 1985.*

(3) In section 31(2) of the Data Protection Act 1998 (c 29) (restricted access to data processed for specified purposes)—

(*a*) in paragraphs (*b*), (*c*) and (*d*), after "charities" insert "or community interest companies", and

(*b*) in paragraph (*b*), after "trustees" insert ", directors".

(4) A public authority may disclose to the Regulator, for any purpose connected with the exercise of the Regulator's functions, information received by the authority in connection with its functions.

(5) The Regulator may disclose to a public authority any information received by the Regulator in connection with the functions of the Regulator—

(*a*) for a purpose connected with the exercise of those functions, or

(*b*) for a purpose connected with the exercise by the authority of its functions.

(6) In deciding whether to disclose information to a public authority in a country or territory outside the United Kingdom the Regulator must have regard to the considerations listed in section 243(6) of the Enterprise Act 2002 (c 40) (overseas disclosures), but as if the reference to information of a kind to which section 237 of that Act applies were to information of the kind the Regulator is considering disclosing.

(7) The powers to disclose information in subsections (4) and (5) are subject to—

(*a*) any restriction on disclosure imposed by or by virtue of an enactment, and

(*b*) any express restriction on disclosure subject to which information was supplied.

(8) Information may be disclosed under subsection (4) or (5) subject to a restriction on its further disclosure.

(9) A person who discloses information in contravention of a restriction imposed under subsection (8) is guilty of an offence, but a prosecution may be instituted in England or Wales only with the consent of the Regulator or the Director of Public Prosecutions.

(10) A person guilty of an offence under subsection (9) is liable on summary conviction to a fine not exceeding level 3 on the standard scale.

(11) "Public authority" means a person or body having functions of a public nature.

[Companies (Audit, Investigations and Community Enterprise) Act 2004, s 59.]

8–3930R   **60. Offences.**   (1) If an offence under this Part committed by a body corporate is proved—

(*a*) to have been committed with the consent or connivance of an officer, or

(*b*) to be attributable to any neglect on the part of an officer,

the officer as well as the body corporate is guilty of the offence and liable to be proceeded against and punished accordingly.

(2) "Officer" means a director, manager, secretary or other similar officer of the body corporate, or a person purporting to act in any such capacity.

(3) "Director"—

(*a*) includes a shadow director, and

(*b*) if the affairs of a body corporate are managed by its members, means a member of the body.

[Companies (Audit, Investigations and Community Enterprise) Act 2004, s 60.]

8–3930S   **61. Orders made by Regulator.**   (1) An order made by the Regulator under this Part must be given to the community interest company in relation to which it is made and—

(*a*) if the order is under section 46(1) or (3), to the director removed or suspended,

(*b*) if the order is under section 48(1)(*b*) or (2), to the person to whom the order is directed,

(*c*) if the order is under section 49(1), to the persons from and to whom shares are transferred,

(*d*) if the order is under section 49(2), to the person whose interest is extinguished and any person appointed in his place.

(2) Orders made by the Regulator under or by virtue of this Part may contain any incidental or supplementary provisions the Regulator considers expedient.

(3) When discharging an order made under or by virtue of this Part, the Regulator may make savings and transitional provisions.

(4) A document certified by the Regulator to be a true copy of an order made by the Regulator is

evidence of the order without further proof; and a document purporting to be so certified shall, unless the contrary is proved, be taken to be so certified.

(5) Where the Regulator makes an order or decision against which an appeal lies under or by virtue of this Part, the Regulator must give reasons for the order or decision to the persons entitled to appeal against it.

[Companies (Audit, Investigations and Community Enterprise) Act 2004, s 61.]

PART 3[1]
SUPPLEMENTARY

8–3930T   64. Repeals and revocations.   Schedule 8 (repeals and revocations) has effect.

[Companies (Audit, Investigations and Community Enterprise) Act 2004, s 64.]

---

1. Part 3 contains ss 64–67.

8–3930U   65. Commencement etc.   (1) This Act (apart from this section and sections 66 and 67) does not come into force until such day as the Secretary of State may by order made by statutory instrument appoint; and different days may be appointed for different provisions or otherwise for different purposes.

(2) The Secretary of State may by order[1] made by statutory instrument make any transitional provisions or savings which appear appropriate in connection with the commencement of any provision of this Act.

[Companies (Audit, Investigations and Community Enterprise) Act 2004, s 65.]

---

1. At the time of going to press the following commencement orders had been made: Companies (Audit, Investigations and Community Enterprise) Act 2004 (Commencement) and Companies Act 1989 (Commencement No 18) Order 2004, SI 2004/3322, bringing the whole of the Act into force.

SCHEDULE 2
MINOR AND CONSEQUENTIAL AMENDMENTS RELATING TO PART 1[1]

---

1. Where these amendments concern provisions reproduced in this work they will be shown when they take effect.

8–3930V

Section 42

SCHEDULE 7
COMMUNITY INTEREST COMPANIES: INVESTIGATIONS

Power to require documents and information

1. (1) The investigator of a community interest company may require the company or any other person—

(*a*) to produce such documents (or documents of such description) as the investigator may specify;

(*b*) to provide such information (or information of such description) as the investigator may specify.

(2) A person on whom a requirement is imposed under sub-paragraph (1) may require the investigator to produce evidence of his authority.

(3) A requirement under sub-paragraph (1) must be complied with at such time and place as may be specified by the investigator.

(4) The production of a document in pursuance of this paragraph does not affect any lien which a person has on the document.

(5) The investigator may take copies of or extracts from a document produced in pursuance of this paragraph.

(6) In relation to information recorded otherwise than in legible form, the power to require production of it includes power to require the production of a copy of it in legible form or in a form from which it can readily be produced in visible and legible form.

(7) In this Schedule—

(*a*) "the investigator of a community interest company" means a person investigating the company's affairs under section 42, and

(*b*) "document" includes information recorded in any form.

Privileged information

2. (1) Nothing in paragraph 1 requires a person to produce a document or provide information in respect of which a claim could be maintained—

(*a*) in an action in the High Court, to legal professional privilege, or

(*b*) in an action in the Court of Session, to confidentiality of communications,

but a person who is a lawyer may be required to provide the name and address of his client.

(2) Nothing in paragraph 1 requires a person carrying on the business of banking to produce a document, or provide information, relating to the affairs of a customer unless a requirement to produce the document, or provide the information, has been imposed on the customer under that paragraph.

Use of information as evidence

3. (1) A statement made by a person in compliance with a requirement imposed under paragraph 1 may be used in evidence against the person.

(2) But in criminal proceedings—

(*a*) no evidence relating to the statement may be adduced by or on behalf of the prosecution, and
(*b*) no question relating to it may be asked by or on behalf of the prosecution,

unless evidence relating to it is adduced or a question relating to it is asked in the proceedings by or on behalf of that person.

(3) However, sub-paragraph (2) does not apply to proceedings in which a person is charged with an offence under—

(*a*) paragraph 5,
(*b*) section 5 of the Perjury Act 1911 (c 6) (false statement made otherwise than on oath), or
(*c*) section 44(2) of the Criminal Law (Consolidation) (Scotland) Act 1995 (c 39) (false statement made otherwise than on oath).

Failure to comply with requirement

4. (1) This paragraph applies if a person fails to comply with a requirement imposed under paragraph 1.
(2) The investigator may certify that fact in writing to the court.
(3) If, after hearing—

(*a*) any witnesses who may be produced against or on behalf of the alleged offender, and
(*b*) any statement which may be offered in defence,

the court is satisfied that the offender failed without reasonable excuse to comply with the requirement, it may deal with him as if he had been guilty of contempt of the court.

False information

5. (1) A person commits an offence if in purported compliance with a requirement under paragraph 1 to provide information, the person—

(*a*) provides information which the person knows to be false in a material particular, or
(*b*) recklessly provides information which is false in a material particular,

but a prosecution may be instituted in England and Wales only with the consent of the Director of Public Prosecutions.

(2) A person guilty of an offence under sub-paragraph (1) is liable—

(*a*) on conviction on indictment to imprisonment for a term not exceeding two years or a fine or to both,
(*b*) on summary conviction in England and Wales, to imprisonment for a term not exceeding twelve months or a fine of an amount not exceeding the statutory maximum or to both, and
(*c*) on summary conviction in Scotland, to imprisonment for a term not exceeding six months or a fine of an amount not exceeding the statutory maximum or to both.

(3) In relation to an offence committed before section 154(1) of the Criminal Justice Act 2003 (c 44) comes into force, sub-paragraph (2)(*b*) has effect as if for "twelve" there were substituted "six".

SCHEDULE 8
REPEALS AND REVOCATIONS[1]

1. Where these repeals and revocations concern provisions reproduced in this work they will be shown when they take effect.

Companies (Disqualification Orders) Regulations 2001[1]
(SI 2001/967 amended by SI 2002/1834 and SI 2004/1940)

8–3940 1. Citation and commencement. These Regulations may be cited as the Companies (Disqualification Orders) Regulations 2001 and shall come into force on 6th April 2001.

1. Made by the Secretary of State in exercise of powers under s 18 of the Company Directors Disqualification Act 1986.

8–3941 2. Definitions. In these Regulations:

"the Act" means the Company Directors Disqualification Act 1986;
"disqualification order" means an order of the court under any of sections 2 to 6, 8, and 10 of the Act;
"disqualification undertaking" means an undertaking accepted by the Secretary of State under section 7 or 8 of the Act;
"grant of leave" means a grant by the court of leave under section 17 of the Act to any person in relation to a disqualification order or a disqualification undertaking.

8–3942 3. Revocation. The Companies (Disqualification Orders) Regulations 1986 are hereby revoked.

8–3943 4. Transitional provisions. Other than regulation 9, these regulations apply in relation to:

(a) a disqualification order made after the coming into force of these Regulations; and
(b)

      (i)   a grant of leave made after the coming into force of these Regulations; or

      (ii)   any action taken by a court after the coming into force of these Regulations in consequence of which a disqualification order or a disqualification undertaking is varied or ceases to be in force,

whether the disqualification order or disqualification undertaking to which, as the case may be, the grant of leave or the action relates was made by the court or accepted by the Secretary of State before or after the coming into force of these Regulations.

8–3944   5.   Regulation 9 applies to particulars of orders made and leave granted under Part II of the Companies (Northern Ireland) Order 1989 received by the Secretary of State after the coming into force of these Regulations other than particulars of orders made and leave granted under that Order which relate to disqualification orders made by the courts of Northern Ireland before 2 April 2001.

8–3945   6. Particulars to be furnished by officers of the court.   (1) The following officers of the court shall furnish to the Secretary of State the particulars specified in Regulation 7(a) to (c) below in the form and manner there specified:

    (a)   where a disqualification order is made by the Crown Court, the Court Manager;

    (b)   where a disqualification order or grant of leave is made by the High Court, the Court Manager;

    (c)   where a disqualification order or grant of leave is made by a County Court, the Court Manager;

    (d)   where a disqualification order is made by a Magistrates' Court, the Chief Executive to the Justices;

    (e)   where a disqualification order is made by the High Court of Justiciary, the Deputy Principal Clerk of Justiciary;

    (f)   where a disqualification order or grant of leave is made by a Sheriff Court, the Sheriff Clerk;

    (g)   where a disqualification order or grant of leave is made by the Court of Session, the Deputy Principal Clerk of Session;

    (h)   where a disqualification order or grant of leave is made by the Court of Appeal, the Court Manager; and

    (i)   where a disqualification order or grant of leave is made by the House of Lords, the Judicial Clerk.

(2) Where a disqualification order has been made by any of the courts mentioned in paragraph (1) above or a disqualification undertaking has been accepted by the Secretary of State, and subsequently any action is taken by a court in consequence of which, as the case may be, that order or that undertaking is varied or ceases to be in force, the officer specified in paragraph (1) above of the court which takes such action shall furnish to the Secretary of State the particulars specified in Regulation 7(d) below in the form and manner there specified.

8–3946   7.   The form in which the particulars are to be furnished is:

    (a)   that set out in Schedule 1 to these Regulations with such variations as circumstances require when the person against whom the disqualification order is made is an individual, and the particulars contained therein are the particulars specified for that purpose;

    (b)   that set out in Schedule 2 to these Regulations with such variations as circumstances require when the person against whom the disqualification order is made is a body corporate, and the particulars contained therein are the particulars specified for that purpose;

    (c)   that set out in Schedule 3 to these Regulations with such variations as circumstances require when a grant of leave is made by the court, and the particulars contained therein are the particulars specified for that purpose;

    (d)   that set out in Schedule 4 to these Regulations with such variations as circumstances require when any action is taken by a court in consequence of which a disqualification order or a disqualification undertaking is varied or ceases to be in force, and the particulars contained therein are the particulars specified for that purpose.

8–3946A   8.   The time within which the officer specified in regulation 6(1) is to furnish the Secretary of State with the said particulars shall be a period of fourteen days beginning with the day on which the disqualification order or grant of leave is made, or any action is taken by a court in consequence of which the disqualification order or disqualification undertaking is varied or ceases to be in force, as the case may be.

8–3947   9. Extension of certain of the provisions of section 18 of the Act to orders made and leave granted in Northern Ireland.   (1) Section 18(2) of the Act is hereby extended to the particulars furnished to the Secretary of State of orders made and leave granted under Part II of the Companies (Northern Ireland) Order 1989.

(1A) Section 18(2A) is hereby extended to the particulars of disqualification undertakings accepted under and orders made and leave granted in relation to disqualification undertakings under the Company Directors Disqualification (Northern Ireland) Order 2002.*

(2) Section 18(3) of the Act is hereby extended to all entries in the register and particulars relating to them furnished to the Secretary of State in respect of orders made under Part II of the Companies (Northern Ireland) Order 1989 or disqualification undertakings accepted under the Company Directors Disqualification (Northern Ireland) Order 2002.

---

*Sub-section (1A) and in sub-s (2) words after " . . . Order 1989" as inserted by SI 2004/1940 apply only to particulars of undertakings accepted and orders made and leave granted relating to those undertakings under the Company Directors Disqualification (Northern Ireland) Order 2002 on or after the date on which these Regulations come into force.

SCHEDULE 1

DO1

DISQUALIFICATION ORDER AGAINST AN INDIVIDUAL

DO1

Disqualification order against an individual

To be completed in typescript or bold black capitals by a member of the court staff who should then sign it

CHWP007

Particulars required by the Companies (Disqualification Orders) Regulations 1986:

Section of the Company Directors Disqualification Act 1986 under which the order was made

S2	S3	S4	S5	S6	S8	S10

Please tick the appropriate box

Name of the individual against whom the order was made

❶ "Surname" in the case of a peer or person usually known by a title different from his surname means that title

Style / Title	
Forename(s)	
Surname ❶	

Date of birth   Day   Month   Year

Usual residential address

Post town

County / Region   Postcode

Country   Nationality

Date on which the order was made   Day   Month   Year

Period of disqualification specified in the order

Company(ies) named (if any) in relation to conduct leading to disqualification

Case number

Signed   **Date**

Name   **Court**

Companies House receipt date barcode

When you have completed the form please send it to
The Secretary of State,
The Subpoena Clerk,
Companies House,
Crown Way,
Cardiff, CF14 3UZ   DX 33050 Cardiff

Form revised June 1998

8–3949
Regulation 7(b)

SCHEDULE 2

DO2
DISQUALIFICATION ORDER AGAINST A BODY CORPORATE

DO2

Disqualification order against a body corporate

To be completed in typescript or bold black capitals by a member of the court staff who should then sign it.

CHWP007

Particulars required by the Companies (Disqualification Orders) Regulations 1986:

Section of the Company Directors Disqualification Act 1986 under which the order was made:

S2	S3	S4	S5	S6	S8	S10

Please tick the appropriate box

Particulars of the body corporate against whom the order was made

Corporate Name

Registered Number (if any)

Address of registered or principal office in Great Britain of the body corporate at the date of the order

Post town

County / Region   Postcode

Country

Date on which the order was made
Day Month Year

Period of disqualification specified in the order

Company(ies) named (if any) in relation to conduct leading to disqualification

Case number

Signed   **Date**

Name   **Court**

Companies House receipt date barcode

When you have completed the form please send it to
The Secretary of State,
The Subpoena Clerk,
Companies House,
Crown Way,
Cardiff, CF14 3UZ DX 33050 Cardiff

Form revised June 1998

SCHEDULE 3

DO3

GRANT OF LEAVE IN RELATION TO A DISQUALIFICATION ORDER OR DISQUALIFICATION UNDERTAKING

DO3

To be completed in typescript or bold black capitals by a member of the court staff who should then sign it.

CHWP007

Grant of leave in relation to a disqualification order

Particulars required by the Companies (Disqualification Orders) Regulations 1986:

	Day	Month	Year

Date of disqualification order in relation to which leave was granted

Court which made the disqualification order in relation to which leave was granted

Name of person to whom leave was granted **if an individual,**   Style / Title   Forename(s)

Surname

if a body corporate,   Corporate Name

Registered Number (if any)

If the name in which the disqualification order was made was different from that above, the name in which that order was made

if an individual,   Style / Title   Forename(s)

Surname

if a body corporate,   Corporate Name

Registered Number (if any)

Name of the company in respect of which
leave was granted, or in the case of leave
to promote or form a company, the
proposed name of the company where it is
available, or if not, a brief description of
the activities of the company

Date on which leave was granted   Day   Month   Year

Please tick the appropriate box(es) to indicate the activity for which leave was granted

Promotion   Formation   Directorship or other participation in management

Liquidation or administration   Receivership or management of the property of the company

Signed   **Date**

Name   **Court**

Companies House receipt date barcode

When you have completed the form please send it to
The Secretary of State,
The Subpoena Clerk,
Companies House,
Crown Way,   DX 33050 Cardiff
Cardiff, CF14 3UZ

Form revised June 1998

SCHEDULE 4

DO4

VARIATION OR CESSATION OF A DISQUALIFICATION ORDER OR DISQUALIFICATION UNDERTAKING

DO4

Variation or cessation of a disqualification order

To be completed in typescript or bold black capitals by a member of the court staff who should then sign it.

CHWP007

Particulars required by the Companies (Disqualification Orders) Regulations 1986

	Day	Month	Year

Date on which disqualification order was made by this court

Name of person against whom disqualification order was made:

if an individual,   Style / Title   Forename(s)

❶ "Surname" in the case of a peer or person usually known by a title different from his surname means that title

Surname ❶

if a body corporate,   Corporate Name

Registered Number (if any)

Name of court by which action was taken whereby the above order was varied or ceased to be in force

Case Number

Result of such action
Please tick appropriate box   (a) Order ceased to be in force   (b) Order varied

If (b), please state period of disqualification now specified in the order (to run from the date on which the order was originally made)

Signed   **Date**

Name   **Court**

Companies House receipt date barcode

When you have completed the form please send it to
The Secretary of State,
The Subpoena Clerk,
Companies House,
Crown Way,
Cardiff, CF14 3UZ   DX 33050 Cardiff

Form revised June 1998

COMPOUNDING OFFENCES

Criminal Law Act 1967[1]

(1967 c 58)

8–4010   4. Penalties for assisting offenders.   (1) Where a person has committed an arrestable offence, any other person who, knowing or believing him[2] to be guilty of the offence or of some other arrestable offence, does without lawful authority or reasonable excuse[3] any act with intent to impede his apprehension or prosecution shall be guilty of an offence[4].

(1A) In this section and section 5 below "arrestable offence" has the meaning assigned to it by section 24 of the Police and Criminal Evidence Act 1984.

(2) On a trial on indictment an accused not guilty of an arrestable offence as charged may be found guilty of an offence under subsection (1) above (*SUMMARISED*).

(3) A person committing an offence under subsection (1) above with intent to impede another person's apprehension or prosecution shall on conviction on indictment be liable to imprisonment according to the gravity of the other person's offence, as follows: (*a*) if that offence is one for which the sentence is fixed by law, he shall be liable to imprisonment for not more than **ten years**; (*b*) if it is one for which a person (not previously convicted) may be sentenced to imprisonment for a term of **fourteen years**, he shall be liable to imprisonment for not more than **seven years**; (*c*) if it is not one included above but is one for which a person (not previously convicted) may be sentenced to imprisonment for a term of **ten years**, he shall be liable to imprisonment for not more than **five years**; (*d*) in any other case, he shall be liable to imprisonment for not more than **three years**.

(4) No proceedings shall be instituted for an offence under subsection (1) above except by or with the consent of the Director of Public Prosecutions.

(5) *Repealed.*

(6) *Repealed.*

(7) *Repealed.*

[Criminal Law Act 1967, s 4, as amended by the Theft Act 1968, the Criminal Jurisdiction Act 1975, Sch 6, the Criminal Law Act 1977, Sch 13, the Police and Criminal Evidence Act 1984, Sch 6 and the Extradition Act 1989, Sch 2.]

---

1. For ss 1, 3 and 9 of this Act see PART I: MAGISTRATES' COURTS, PROCEDURE, ante. These cover the abolition of the distinction between felony and misdemeanour, the power of arrest without warrant, and use of force in making arrest. Sections 4 and 5, printed here, provide statutory offences in place of the abolished common law crime of compounding a felony.

2. It is not necessary for the prosecution to prove that a person accused under this section knew the identity of the person who had committed the principal offence (*R v Brindley, R v Long* [1971] 2 QB 300, [1971] 2 All ER 698, 135 JP 357). For wording of charge under this subsection, see *R v Morgan* [1972] 1 QB 436 at 438, [1972] 1 All ER 348 at 352, 136 JP 160 at 162.

3. Note that it is not here enacted (as is usual: cf Prevention of Crime Act 1953, s. 1; Firearms Act 1965, ss 3, 4) that proof of lawful authority or reasonable excuse shall lie on the accused.

4. This offence is triable either way (Magistrates' Courts Act 1980, Sch 1, in PART I: MAGISTRATES' COURTS, PROCEDURE, ante). For procedure see *ibid.*, ss 17A–21, ante.

Despite the possible perils of such a prosecution, it is not necessary that there should be a prior conviction of the principal offender before convicting a person of assisting that offender under s 4(1) of this Act (*R v Donald* (1986) 83 Cr App Rep 49).

8–4011   5. Penalties for concealing offences or giving false information.   (1) Where a person has committed an arrestable offence, any other person who, knowing or believing that the offence or some other arrestable offence has been committed, and that he has information which might be of material assistance in securing the prosecution or conviction of an offender for it, accepts or agrees to accept for not disclosing that information any consideration other than the making good of loss or injury caused by the offence, or the making of reasonable compensation for that loss or injury, shall be liable on conviction on indictment[1] to imprisonment for not more than two years.

(2) Where a person causes any wasteful employment[2] of the police by knowingly making to any person a false report tending to show that an offence has been committed, or to give rise to apprehension for the safety of any persons or property, or tending to show that he has information material to any police inquiry, he shall be liable on summary conviction to imprisonment for not more than **six months** or to a fine of not more than **level 4** on the standard scale or to both.

(3) No proceedings shall be instituted for an offence under this section except by or with the consent of the Director of Public Prosecutions.

(4) *Repealed.*

(5) The compounding of an offence other than treason shall not be an offence otherwise than under this section.

[Criminal Law Act 1967, s 5, as amended by the Criminal Law Act 1977, Sch 13 and the Criminal Justice Act 1982, ss 38 and 46.]

---

1. This offence is triable either way where the offence to which it relates is triable either way (Sch 1, in PART I: MAGISTRATES' COURTS, PROCEDURE, ante). For procedure see Magistrates' Courts Act 1980, ss 17A–21, ante.

2. This subsection is designed to cover, *inter alia*, the conduct that in *R v Manley* [1933] 1 KB 529, 97 JP 6, was prosecuted as a common law offence of effecting a public mischief. Despite the fact that *DPP v Withers* [1975] AC 842, [1974] 3 All ER 984, 139 JP 94 appeared to decide that there was no offence of effecting a public mischief, it was held in *R v Rowell* [1978] 1 All ER 665, 142 JP 181, that conduct tending to pervert the course of justice is an offence known to law.

CONSERVATION

8–4012   This title contains the following statutes—

> 8–4030   ENDANGERED SPECIES (IMPORT AND EXPORT) ACT 1976
> 8–4140   WILDLIFE AND COUNTRYSIDE ACT 1981
> 8–4206   COUNTRYSIDE AND RIGHTS OF WAY ACT 2000

and the following statutory instrument—

> 8–4298   Control of Trade in Endangered Species (Enforcement) Regulations 1997

8–4013   European Communities Act 1972: regulations.   Within the scope of the title Conservation there falls the subject matter of regulations made under the very wide enabling powers provided in s 2(2) of the European Communities Act 1972. The following regulations create offences:

> Conservation (Natural Habitats, etc) Regulations 1994, SI 1994/2716 amended by the Environment Act 1995, Sch 22, SI 1996/525, SI 1997/3055, SI 2000/192 and 1973, SI 2003/2155 and SI 2005/3389;
> Protection of Water against Agricultural Nitrate Pollution (England and Wales) Regulations 1996, SI 1996/888 amended by SI 1998/1202 and SI 2002/2614 (England);
> Import of Seal Skins Regulations 1996, SI 1996/2686;
> Control of Trade in Endangered Species (Enforcement) Regulations 1997[1], in this title, post;
> Action Programme for Nitrate Vulnerable Zones (England and Wales) Regulations 1998, SI 1998/1202 amended by SI 2002/2614 (England);
> Offshore Petroleum Activities (Conservation of Habitats) Regulations 2001, SI 2001/1754;
> Environmental Impact Assessment (Uncultivated Land and Semi- natural Areas) (England) Regulations 2001, SI 2001/3966 amended by SI 2005/1430.

---

1. For procedure for issuing a search warrant under these provisions, see *R v Marylebone Magistrates' Court, ex p Amdrell Ltd* (1998) 162 JP 719, DC.

8–4013A   In addition there are Council Regulations which are directly applicable within member states and which constitute 'enactments' contravention of which may incur criminal liability under domestic legislation such as s 170 of the Customs and Excise Management Act 1979 (fraudulent evasion of duty or prohibition or restriction on goods). Such regulations include Council Regulation (EEC) 3626/82 which implements the Convention on the international trade in endangered species (3 March 1973) and Council Regulation 338/97. See generally *R v Sissen* [2001] 1 WLR 902, [2001] Crim LR 232, CA. Under Council Regulations (EC) No 338/97 for which criminal sanctions are provided by SI 1997/1372, an importing authority is entitled to rely on an export permit issued by the exporting state unless and until it is unilaterally revoked or cancelled by the authority which issued it or set aside by agreement or a court order (*R (Greenpeace Ltd) v Secretary of State for the Environment, Food and Rural Affairs* [2002] EWCA Civ 1036, [2002] 1 WLR 3304).

Endangered Species (Import and Export) Act 1976[1]
(1976 c 72)

8–4030   1. Restriction of importation and exportation of certain animals and plants.
(1) Subject to subsection (2) below, the importation and the exportation of the following things are hereby prohibited[2], namely—

> (*a*)   a live or dead animal[3] of any of the kinds to which Schedule 1 to this Act for the time being applies;
> (*b*)   a live or dead plant[4] of any of the kinds to which Schedule 2 to this Act for the time being applies;
> (*c*)   an item to which Schedule 3 to this Act for the time being applies.

(2) Subsection (1) above does not apply to the importation or exportation of anything under and in accordance with the terms of a licence issued by the Secretary of State.
(3) *Secretary of State to submit any application for a licence to a scientific authority.*
(3A) *Exception from sub-s (3).*
(3B) *Secretary of State may issue licence to facilitate importation or exportation of item.*
(4) A licence issued under subsection (2) or (3B) above—
> (*a*)   may be, to any degree, general or specific,

(*aa*) may be issued either to all persons, to persons of a class or to a particular person;

(*ab*) may be subject to compliance with any specified conditions;

(*b*) may be modified or revoked at any time by the Secretary of State, and

(*c*) subject to paragraph (*b*) above, shall be valid for such period as is stated in the licence.

(5) *Power of Secretary of State to charge for the issue of a licence.*

(6) A person who, for the purpose of obtaining, whether for himself or another, the issue of a licence under subsection (2) or (3B) above—

(*a*) makes a statement or representation which he knows to be false in a material particular,

(*b*) furnishes a document or information which he knows to be false in a material particular,

(*c*) recklessly makes a statement or representation which is false in a material particular, or

(*d*) recklessly furnishes a document or information which is false in a material particular,

shall be liable[5] on summary conviction to a fine not exceeding **the statutory maximum** or on conviction on indictment to imprisonment for a term not exceeding **two years** or a fine, or both.

(7) Where a licence is issued under subsection (2) or (3B) above and, for the purpose of obtaining its issue, a person commits an offence under subsection (6) above, the licence shall be void.

(8) Where—

(*a*) any live or dead animal or plant, or

(*b*) an item to which Schedule 3 to this Act for the time being applies,

is being imported or exported or has been imported or brought to any place for the purpose of being exported, a person commissioned by the Comrs of Customs and Excise or a person authorised by them may require any person possessing or having control of the animal, plant or item to furnish proof that its importation or exportation is or was not unlawful by virtue of this section; and if such proof is not furnished to the satisfaction of the said Comrs the animal, plant or item shall be liable to forfeiture under the Customs and Excise Management Act 1979.

(9) *Recovery of expenses with regard to forfeited live animal or plant.*

(10) Any person duly authorised in writing by the Secretary of State may, at any reasonable time and (if required to do so) upon producing evidence that he is so authorised, enter any premises where animals of any of the kinds to which Schedule 1 or plants of any of the kinds to which Schedule 2 to this Act for the time being applies are kept (whether temporarily or permanently) in order to ascertain whether any of the animals or plants kept there have been imported contrary to this section.

(11) Any person who wilfully obstructs a person acting under subsection (10) above shall be liable on summary conviction to a fine not exceeding **level 3** on the standard scale.

[Endangered Species (Import and Export) Act 1976, s 1, as amended by the Criminal Law Act 1977, s 28, the Customs and Excise Management Act 1979, Sch 4, the Wildlife and Countryside Act 1981, Sch 10, and the Criminal Justice Act 1982, s 46.]

---

1. This Act contains powers to implement the Convention on International Trade in endangered Species of Wild Fauna and Flora signed on behalf of the United Kingdom in 1973.

2. For offences under the Customs and Excise Management Act 1979 in respect of goods imported or exported contrary to statutory prohibition see, in particular, ss 50 and 170 of that Act, title CUSTOMS AND EXCISE, post. For restrictions on the institution of proceedings, see s 145 of that Act.

3. For the purposes of this Act an individual of the family *Hominidae* (man) is not an animal. A "dead animal" of any particular kind includes the body of an animal of that kind—(a) which is frozen, dried or preserved by chemicals, or (b) which, although not complete (whether because it has been eviscerated or because it has had the whole of its inside removed and has been stuffed, or for any other reason), is substantially complete and externally substantially resembles the complete body of an animal of the kind concerned (s 12(1) and (2)).

4. A "dead plant" of any particular kind includes a plant of that kind—(a) which is frozen, dried or preserved by chemicals, or (b) which, although for any reason not complete, is substantially complete and externally substantially resembles a complete dead plant of the kind concerned (s 12(3)).

5. For procedure in respect of this offence which is triable either way, see the Magistrates' Courts Act 1980, ss 17A–21, in PART I: MAGISTRATES' COURTS, PROCEDURE, ante.

8–4031   **2.** *Establishment of scientific authorities to advise the Secretary of State.*

8–4032   **3.** *Power of Secretary of State to modify the Schedules to this Act.*

8–4033   **4. Offence to sell etc things imported contrary to section 1 or their derivatives.**

(1) Subject to subsections (1B) and (2) below, a person who sells, offers or exposes for sale, has in his possession or transports for the purpose of sale, or displays to the public—

(*a*) anything which has been imported contrary to section 1 above, or

(*b*) anything which is made wholly or partly from anything referred to in paragraph (*a*) above and which at the time of the alleged offence (though not necessarily at the time of importation) constitutes an item to which Schedule 3 to this Act for the time being applies,

shall be guilty of an offence.

(1A) Subject to subsections (1B) and (2) below, a person who sells, offers or exposes for sale, or has in his possession or transports for the purpose of sale—

(*a*) a live or dead animal of any of the kinds to which Schedule 4 to this Act for the time being applies or an egg or other immature stage of such an animal;

(*b*) a live or dead plant of any of the kinds to which Schedule 5 to this Act for the time being applies; or

(*c*) any part of or anything which derives from or is made wholly or partly from anything referred to in paragraph (*a*) or (*b*) above,

shall be guilty of an offence; but nothing in this subsection shall apply in relation to anything falling within subsection (1) above or anything which has been imported, or is a part of or derives from or is made wholly or partly from anything which has been imported, before the passing of the Wildlife and Countryside Act 1981.

(1B) Subsections (1) and (1A) above do not apply to anything done under and in accordance with the terms of a licence issued by the Secretary of State; and subsections (4) to (7) of section 1 above shall apply in relation to a licence issued under this subsection as they apply in relation to a licence issued under subsection (2) of that section.

(1C) In the following provisions of this section "restricted article" means anything falling within subsection (1) or (1A) above.

(2) A person shall not be guilty of an offence under subsection (1) or (1A) above with respect to a restricted article if he proves to the satisfaction of the court—

(*a*) that at the time when it first came into his possession he made such enquiries (if any) as in the circumstances were reasonable in order to ascertain whether it was a restricted article, and

(*b*) that, at the time the alleged offence was committed, he had no reason to believe that it was a restricted article.

(3) Without prejudice to the generality of subsection (2)(*a*) above, a person shall be taken to have made such enquiries as are there mentioned if he produces to the court a certificate which was furnished by the person from whom the accused obtained possession of the restricted article (the supplier), which was signed by the supplier or by a person authorised by him, and which states that—

(*a*) the supplier made enquiries at the time the restricted article came into his possession in order to ascertain whether it was a restricted article, and

(*b*) the supplier had no reason to believe at the time he relinquished possession of the restricted article to the accused that the article was at that time a restricted article.

(4) A person who furnishes for the purposes of subsection (3) above a certificate which he knows to be false in a material particular, or recklessly furnishes for those purposes a certificate which is false in a material particular, shall be guilty of an offence.

(5) A person guilty of an offence under subsection (1), (1A) or (4) above shall be liable[1]—

(*a*) on summary conviction, to a fine not exceeding **the statutory maximum**;

(*b*) on conviction on indictment, to imprisonment for a term not exceeding **two years** or a fine, or both.

(6) In this section any reference to sale includes references to hire, barter and exchange.

(7) For the purposes of this section a restricted article is displayed to the public if it is displayed to the public generally or any section of it, and (in either case) whether in return for money or otherwise.

(8) For the purposes of any proceedings under section 50 or 170 of the Customs and Excise Management Act 1979[2] (penalties for improper importation and evasion of restriction on importation) for an offence in connection with the importation of anything contrary to section 1 above, this section shall not be taken expressly to provide a penalty for that offence.

[Endangered Species (Import and Export) Act 1976, s 4, as amended by the Criminal Law Act 1977, s 28, the Customs and Excise Management Act 1979, Sch 4 and the Wildlife and Countryside Act 1981, Sch 10.]

---

1. For procedure in respect of this offence which is triable either way, see the Magistrates' Courts Act 1980, ss 17A–21, in PART I: MAGISTRATES' COURTS, PROCEDURE, *ante*.

2. See title CUSTOMS AND EXCISE, *post*.

8–4034   5. *Power of Secretary of State by order to restrict places at which live animals may be imported.*

8–4035   6. Restriction of movement of certain live animals after importation.   (1) Where a licence under section 1(2) above has been issued or applied for in respect of the importation of a live animal of any of the kinds to which Schedule 1 to this Act for the time being applies and, after consulting one or more of the scientific authorities, the Secretary of State considers that it is desirable to do so, he may give a direction under this section in relation to the animal.

(2) Where a direction has been given under this section in relation to an animal, and has not been revoked by the Secretary of State, the animal shall, immediately after the relevant event, be taken to and subsequently kept at the specified premises until such time as the Secretary of State may require or permit the animal to be moved to other specified premises or revoke the direction.

(3) Where a direction has been given under this section in relation to an animal, and has not been revoked by the Secretary of State, any person who knows or ought to know that a direction has been so given and who—

   (*a*)   knowingly takes the animal, or knowingly permits it to be taken, at any time after the relevant event to premises which he knows or ought to know are not at the time of the taking the specified premises; or

   (*b*)   knowingly moves the animal, or knowingly permits it to be moved, at any time after the relevant event, the circumstances of the removal being that—

      (i)   it is made from premises which he knows or ought to know are at the time of the removal the specified premises, and

      (ii)   he knows or ought to know that the removal is made in the absence of, or otherwise than in accordance with any condition attached to, such a requirement or permission as is referred to in subsection (2) above; or

   (*c*)   knowingly keeps the animal at any time after the relevant event at premises which are occupied by him and which he knows or ought to know are not at the time of the keeping the specified premises,

shall be liable on summary conviction to a fine not exceeding **level 4** on the standard scale.

(4) In this section "relevant event" means, in relation to an animal, whichever of the following occurs later—

   (*a*)   the completion by the animal of any period of detention (whether in quarantine or otherwise) in accordance with any provision made by or under any enactment, being detention connected with the importation in respect of which the direction concerned was given;

   (*b*)   the departure of the animal from any premises connected with the importation in respect of which the direction concerned was given.

(5) In this section "specified premises" means, in relation to an animal, such premises as are for the time being (and in whatever manner) specified in relation to that animal by the Secretary of State for the purposes of this section.

(6) Proceedings for an offence under subsection (3) above may be brought within a period of six months from the date on which evidence sufficient in the opinion of the prosecutor to warrant the proceedings came to his knowledge; but no such proceedings shall be brought by virtue of this section more than three years after the commission of the offence.

(7) For the purposes of subsection (6) above—

   (*a*)   a certificate signed by or on behalf of the prosecutor and stating the date on which such evidence as aforesaid came to his knowledge shall be conclusive evidence of that fact; and

   (*b*)   a certificate stating that matter and purporting to be so signed shall be deemed to be so signed unless the contrary is proved.

(8) *Scotland.*

[Endangered Species (Import and Export) Act 1976, s 6 as amended by the Criminal Justice Act 1982, ss 38 and 46.]

8–4036   7. Provisions supplementary to section 6.   (1) Before he specifies any premises for the purposes of section 6 above or revokes a direction given under that section, the Secretary of State shall consult one or more of the scientific authorities[1].

(2) The Secretary of State shall not specify any premises for those purposes unless they are such that in his opinion the animal in relation to which he proposes to give, or has given, a direction under section 6 above may suitably be kept there.

(3) Any person duly authorised in writing by the Secretary of State may, at any reasonable time and (if required to do so) upon producing evidence that he is so authorised, enter any premises which are for the time being specified in relation to any animal for the purposes of section 6 above for one or both of the following purposes—

   (*a*)   in order to enable the Secretary of State to decide whether the premises remain such that in his opinion the animal may suitably be kept there;

   (*b*)   in order to ascertain whether the animal is being kept on the premises.

(4) Any person who wilfully obstructs a person acting under subsection (3) above shall be liable on summary conviction to a fine not exceeding **level 5** on the standard scale.

[Endangered Species (Import and Export) Act 1976, s 7 as amended by the Criminal Justice Act 1982, ss 38 and 46.]

---

1. This means a scientific authority for the purposes of s 2 of this Act (s 2(3)).

8–4037   8. Offences by corporations.   Where an offence under this Act which has been committed by a body corporate is proved to have been committed with the consent or connivance of, or to be attributable to any neglect on the part of, a director, manager, secretary or other similar officer of the body corporate, or any person who was purporting to act in any such capacity, he, as well as the body corporate, shall be guilty of that offence and shall be liable to be proceeded against and punished accordingly.

In this section "director", in relation to a body corporate established by or under any enactment for the purpose of carrying on under public ownership any industry or part of an industry or undertaking, being a body corporate whose affairs are managed by its members, means a member of that body corporate.

[Endangered Species (Import and Export) Act 1976, s 8.]

8–4038   SCHEDULES[1]

Schedule 1   Animals the importation and exportation of which are restricted.
Schedule 2   Plants the importation and exportation of which are restricted.
Schedule 3   Items the importation and exportation of which are restricted.
Schedule 4   Animals the sale etc of which is restricted.
Schedule 5   Plants the sale etc of which is restricted.

---

1. These Schedules have been modified by the Endangered Species (Import and Export) Act 1976 (Amendment) Regulations 1996, SI 1996/2684. Schedules 4 and 5 were added by the Wildlife and Countryside Act 1981, Sch 10.

Wildlife and Countryside Act 1981
(1981 c 69)

PART I[1]
WILDLIFE

Protection of birds

8–4140   **1. Protection of wild birds, their nests and eggs.**   (1) Subject to the provisions of this Part, if any person intentionally—

(a)   kills, injures or takes[2] any wild bird[3];
(b)   takes, damages or destroys the nest of any wild bird while that nest is in use or being built; or
(c)   takes or destroys an egg of any wild bird,

he shall be guilty of an offence.★

(2) Subject to the provisions of this Part, if any person has in his possession[4] or control—

(a)   any live or dead wild bird[5] or any part of, or anything derived from, such a bird; or
(b)   an egg of a wild bird or any part of such an egg,

he shall be guilty of an offence.

(3) A person shall not be guilty of an offence under subsection (2) if he shows that—

(a)   the bird or egg had not been killed or taken, or had been killed or taken otherwise than in contravention of the relevant provisions; or
(b)   the bird, egg or other thing in his possession or control had been sold (whether to him or any other person) otherwise than in contravention of those provisions;

and in this subsection "the relevant provisions" means the provisions of this Part and of orders made under it and, in the case of a bird or other thing falling within subsection (2)(a), the provisions of the Protection of Birds Acts 1954 to 1967 and of orders made under those Acts.★

(3A) In subsection (3) "lawfully" means without any contravention of—

(a)   this Part and orders made under it,
(b)   the Protection of Birds Acts 1954 to 1967 and orders made under those Acts,
(c)   any other legislation which implements Council Directive 79/409/EEC on the conservation of wild birds and extends to any part of the United Kingdom, to any area designated in accordance with section 1(7) of the Continental Shelf Act 1964, or to any area to which British fishery limits extend in accordance with section 1 of the Fishery Limits Act 1976, and
(d)   the provisions of the law of any member State (other than the United Kingdom) implementing the Council Directive referred to in paragraph (c).

(4) *Repealed.*

(5) Subject to the provisions of this Part, if any person intentionally or recklessly—

(a)   disturbs any wild bird included in Schedule 1 while it is building a nest or is in, on or near a nest containing eggs or young; or
(b)   disturbs dependent young of such a bird,

he shall be guilty of an offence.★

(6) In this section "wild bird" does not include any bird which is shown[6] to have been bred in captivity.

(7) Any reference in this Part to any bird included in Schedule 1 is a reference to any bird included in Part I and, during the close season[7] for the bird in question, any bird included in Part II of that Schedule.

[Wildlife and Countryside Act 1981, s 1, as amended by the Countryside and Rights of Way Act 2000, Sch 12 and SI 2004/1487.]

*Amended and new sub-ss (5A)–(5C) inserted in relation to Scotland by the Nature Conservation (Scotland) Act 2004, Sch 6.

1. Part I comprises ss 1–27.

2. "Takes" means "captures"; see *Robinson v Everett and W & FC Bonham & Son Ltd* [1988] Crim LR 699.

3. Defined by s 27, post.

4. This is an offence of strict liability (*Kirkland v Robinson* (1986) 151 JP 377).

5. It has been held that a golden eagle remained a "dead wild bird" within the meaning of this section even after it had been stuffed and mounted (*Robinson v Everett and W & FC Bonham & Son Ltd* [1988] Crim LR 699).

6. The burden of proving that a wild bird was born in captivity rests on the defendant, and this burden is not incompatible with art 6 of the Convention (*Hughes v DPP* [2003] EWHC Admin 2470, (2003) 167 JP 589).

7. See s 2(4), post.

8–4141   2. Exceptions to section 1.   (1) Subject to the provisions of this section, a person shall not be guilty of an offence under section 1 by reason of the killing or taking of a bird included in Part I of Schedule 2 outside the close season for that bird, or the injuring of such a bird outside that season in the course of an attempt to kill it.

(2) Subject to the provisions of this section, an authorised person[1] shall not be guilty of an offence under section 1 by reason of—

(*a*)   the killing or taking of a bird included in Part II of Schedule 2, or the injuring of such a bird in the course of an attempt to kill it;

(*b*)   the taking, damaging or destruction of a nest of such a bird; or

(*c*)   the taking or destruction of an egg of such a bird.*

(3) Subsections (1) and (2) shall not apply in Scotland on Sundays or on Christmas Day; and subsection (1) shall not apply on Sundays in any area of England and Wales which the Secretary of State may by order prescribe for the purposes of that subsection.*

(4) In this section and section 1 "close season" means—

(*a*)   in the case of capercaillie and** (except in Scotland) woodcock, the period in any year commencing with 1st February and ending with 30th September;

(*b*)   in the case of snipe, the period in any year commencing with 1st February and ending with 11th August;

(*c*)   in the case of wild duck and wild geese in or over any area below high-water mark of ordinary spring tides, the period in any year commencing with 21st February and ending with 31st August;

(*d*)   in any other case, subject to the provisions of this Part, the period in any year commencing with 1st February and ending with 31st August.

(5) The Secretary of State may by order made with respect to the whole or any specified part of Great Britain vary the close season for any wild bird specified in the order.

(6) If it appears to the Secretary of State expedient that any wild birds included in Part II of Schedule 1 or Part I of Schedule 2 should be protected during any period outside the close season for those birds, he may by order made with respect to the whole or any specified part of Great Britain declare any period (which shall not in the case of any order exceed fourteen days) as a period of special protection for those birds; and this section and section 1 shall have effect as if any period of special protection declared under this subsection for any birds formed part of the close season for those birds.

(7) Before making an order under subsection (6) the Secretary of State shall consult a person appearing to him to be a representative of persons interested in the shooting of birds of the kind proposed to be protected by the order.

[Wildlife and Countryside Act 1981 s 2, as amended by SSI 2001/337.]

*Sub-section (2) repealed and sub-s (3) amended in relation to Scotland by the Nature Conservation (Scotland) Act 2004, Sch 6.

**Repealed in relation to Scotland by SSI 2001/337, reg 2.

1. Defined by s 27, post.

8–4142   3. Areas of special protection.   (1) The Secretary of State may by order[1] make provision with respect to any area specified in the order providing for all or any of the following matters, that is to say—

(*a*)   that any person who, within that area or any part of it specified in the order, at any time or during any period so specified, intentionally*—

(i)   kills, injures or takes any wild bird[2] or any wild bird so specified;

(ii)   takes, damages, or destroys the nest of such a bird while that nest is in use or being built;

(iii)   takes or destroys an egg of such a bird;

(iv)   disturbs such a bird while it is building a nest or is in, on or near a nest containing eggs or young; or

(v)   disturbs dependent young of such a bird,

shall be guilty of an offence under this section;

(b) that any person who, except as may be provided in the order, enters into that area or any part of it specified in the order at any time or during any period so specified shall be guilty of an offence under this section;

(c) that where any offence under this Part, or any such offence under this Part as may be specified in the order, is committed within that area, the offence shall be treated as falling within section 7(3A).**

(2) An authorised person shall not by virtue of any such order be guilty of an offence by reason of—

(a) the killing or taking of a bird included in Part II of Schedule 2, or the injuring of such a bird in the course of an attempt to kill it;

(b) the taking, damaging or destruction of the nest of such a bird;

(c) the taking or destruction of an egg of such a bird; or

(d) the disturbance of such a bird or dependent young of such a bird.*

(3) The making of any order under this section with respect to any area shall not affect the exercise by any person of any right vested in him, whether as owner, lessee or occupier of any land in that area or by virtue of a licence or agreement.

(4) Before making any order under this section the Secretary of State shall give particulars of the intended order either by notice in writing to every owner and every occupier of any land included in the area with respect to which the order is to be made or, where the giving of such a notice is in his opinion impracticable, by advertisement in a newspaper circulating in the locality in which that area is situated.

(5) The Secretary of State shall not make an order under this section unless—

(a) all the owners and occupiers aforesaid have consented thereto;

(b) no objections thereto have been made by any of those owners or occupiers before the expiration of a period of three months from the date of the giving of the notice or the publication of the advertisement; or

(c) any such objections so made have been withdrawn.

[Wildlife and Countryside Act 1981, s 3 amended by the Local Government (Wales) Act 1994, Sch 16 and the Countryside and Rights of Way Act 2000, Sch 12.]

---

*Amended and sub-s (2) repealed in relation to Scotland by the Nature Conservation (Scotland) Act 2004, Sch 6.

** Repealed in relation to Scotland by the Criminal Justice (Scotland) Act 2003, Sch 5.

1. A number of orders have been made which are not listed herein: the full list may be found in Halsbury's Statutory Instruments, Volume 2.

2. Defined by s 27, post.

8–4143   **4. Exceptions to sections 1 and 3.**   (1) Nothing in section 1 or in any order made under section 3 shall make unlawful—

(a) anything done in pursuance of a requirement by the Minister of Agriculture, Fisheries and Food or the Secretary of State under section 98 of the Agriculture Act 1947, or by the Secretary of State under section 39 of the Agriculture (Scotland) Act 1948;

(b) anything done under, or in pursuance of an order made under, section 21 or 22 of the Animal Health Act 1981; or

(c) except in the case of a wild bird included in Schedule 1 or the nest or egg of such a bird, anything done under, or in pursuance of an order made under, any other provision of the said Act of 1981.

(2) Notwithstanding anything in the provisions of section 1 or any order made under section 3, a person shall not be guilty of an offence by reason of—

(a) the taking of any wild bird if he shows that the bird had been disabled otherwise than by his unlawful act and was taken solely for the purpose of tending it and releasing it when no longer disabled;

(b) the killing of any wild bird if he shows that the bird had been so seriously disabled otherwise than by his unlawful act that there was no reasonable chance of its recovering; or

(c) any act made unlawful by those provisions if he shows that the act was the incidental result of a lawful operation and could not reasonably have been avoided*.

(3) Notwithstanding anything in the provisions of section 1 or any order made under section 3, an authorised person shall not be guilty of an offence by reason of the killing or injuring of any wild bird, other than a bird included in Schedule 1, if he shows that his action was necessary for the purpose of—

(a) preserving public health or public or air safety;

(b) preventing the spread of disease; or

(c) preventing serious damage to livestock, foodstuffs for livestock, crops, vegetables, fruit, growing timber, fisheries or inland waters.

(4) An authorised person shall not be regarded as showing that any action of his was necessary for

a purpose mentioned in subsection (3)(c)* unless he shows that as regards that purpose, there was no other satisfactory solution.

(5) An authorised person shall not be entitled to rely on the defence provided by subsection (3)(c)* as respects any action taken at any time for any purpose mentioned in that paragraph* if it had become apparent, before that time, that that action would prove necessary for that purpose and either—

(a) a licence under section 16 authorising that action had not been applied for by him as soon as reasonably practicable after that fact had become apparent; or

(b) an application by him for such a licence had been determined.

(6) An authorised person shall not be entitled to rely on the defence provided by subsection (3)(c)* as respects any action taken at any time unless he notified the agriculture Minister as soon as reasonably practicable after that time that he had taken the action.

[Wildlife and Countryside Act 1981, s 4 as amended by SI 1995/2825.]

---

*Words substituted and new sub-s (2A) inserted in relation to Scotland by the Nature Conservation (Scotland) Act 2004, Sch 6.

8–4144   5. Prohibition of certain methods of killing or taking wild birds[1]. (1) Subject to the provisions of this Part, if any person—

(a) sets in position any of the following articles, being an article which is of such a nature and is so placed as to be calculated* to cause bodily injury to any wild bird coming into contact therewith, that is to say, any springe, trap, gin, snare, hook and line, any electrical device for killing, stunning or frightening or any poisonous, poisoned or stupefying substance[2];

(b) uses for the purpose of killing or taking any wild bird any such article as aforesaid, whether or not of such a nature and so placed as aforesaid, or any net, baited board, bird-lime or substance of a like nature to bird-lime;

(c) uses for the purpose of killing or taking any wild bird—

   (i)   any bow or crossbow;

   (ii)   any explosive other than ammunition for a firearm;

   (iii)   any automatic or semi-automatic weapon;

   (iv)   any shot-gun of which the barrel has an internal diameter at the muzzle of more than one and three-quarter inches;

   (v)   any device for illuminating a target or any sighting device for night shooting;

   (vi)   any form of artificial lighting or any mirror or other dazzling device;

   (vii) any gas or smoke not falling within paragraphs (a) and (b); or

   (viii)any chemical wetting agent;

(d) uses as a decoy, for the purpose of killing or taking any wild bird, any sound recording or any live bird or other animal whatever which is tethered, or which is secured by means of braces or other similar appliances, or which is blind, maimed[3] or injured;

(e) uses any mechanically propelled vehicle in immediate pursuit of a wild bird for the purpose of killing or taking that bird; or

(f) knowingly causes or permits to be done an act which is mentioned in the foregoing provisions of this subsection and which is not lawful under subsection (5),

he shall be guilty of an offence.

(2) Subject to subsection (3), the Secretary of State may by order, either generally or in relation to any kind of wild bird specified in the order, amend subsection (1) by adding any method of killing or taking wild birds or by omitting any such method which is mentioned in that subsection.

(3) The power conferred by subsection (2) shall not be exercisable, except for the purpose of complying with an international obligation, in relation to any method of killing or taking wild birds which involves the use of a firearm.

(4) In any proceedings under subsection (1)(a) it shall be a defence to show that the article was set in position for the purpose of killing or taking, in the interests of public health, agriculture, forestry, fisheries or nature conservation, any wild animals which could be lawfully killed or taken by those means and that he took all reasonable precautions to prevent injury thereby to wild birds.

(4A) In any proceedings under subsection (1)(f) relating to an act which is mentioned in subsection (1)(a) it shall be a defence to show that the article was set in position for the purpose of killing or taking, in the interests of public health, agriculture, forestry, fisheries or nature conservation, any wild animals which could be lawfully killed or taken by those means and that he took or caused to be taken all reasonable precautions to prevent injury thereby to wild birds.

(5) Nothing in subsection (1) shall make unlawful—

(a) the use of a cage-trap or net by an authorised person for the purpose of taking a bird included in Part II of Schedule 2;*

(b) the use of nets for the purpose of taking wild duck in a duck decoy which is shown to have been in use immediately before the passing of the Protection of Birds Act 1954; or*

(c) the use of a cage-trap or net for the purpose of taking any game bird if it is shown that the taking of the bird is solely for the purpose of breeding;

but nothing in this subsection shall make lawful the use of any net for taking birds in flight or the use for taking birds on the ground of any net which is projected or propelled otherwise than by hand.
[Wildlife and Countryside Act 1981, s 5 as amended by the Wildlife and Countryside (Amendment) Act 1991, s 1 and the Countryside and Rights of Way Act 2000, Schs 12 and 16.]

---

*Words substituted and paras (5)(a) and (b) repealed in relation to Scotland by the Nature Conservation (Scotland) Act 2004, Sch 6.

1. Defined by s 27, post.

2. This section distinguishes between a substance poisonous *per se*, a substance with which poison had been mixed (so that it became a poisoned substance) and a substance which was intended to and had the effect of stupefying; if there is doubt about which of these categories applies to a substance, separate informations should be laid; see *Robinson v Hughes* [1987] Crim LR 644.

3. "Maim" denotes permanent deprivation of a member or mutilation or crippling, therefore jackdaws who had their primary wing feathers clipped but which would grow back at the moulting stage were not "maimed" within the meaning of the act (*Holden v Lancaster Justices* (1998) 162 JP 789, DC).

8–4145   6. Sale etc of live or dead wild birds, eggs etc.   (1) Subject to the provisions of this Part, if any person—

(a) sells, offers or exposes for sale, or has in his possession or transports for the purpose of sale[1], any live wild bird[1] other than a bird included in Part I of Schedule 3, or an egg of a wild bird or any part of such an egg; or

(b) publishes or causes to be published any advertisement likely to be understood as conveying that he buys or sells, or intends to buy or sell, any of those things,

he shall be guilty of an offence.

(2) Subject to the provisions of this Part, if any person—

(a) sells, offers or exposes for sale, or has in his possession or transports for the purpose of sale, any dead wild bird other than a bird included in Part II or III of Schedule 3, or any part of, or anything derived from, such a wild bird; or

(b) publishes or causes to be published any advertisement likely to be understood as conveying that he buys or sells, or intends to buy or sell, any of those things,

he shall be guilty of an offence.

(3) Subject to the provisions of this Part, if any person shows or causes or permits to be shown for the purposes of any competition or in any premises in which a competition is being held—

(a) any live wild bird other than a bird included in Part I of Schedule 3; or

(b) any live bird one of whose parents was such a wild bird,

he shall be guilty of an offence.

(4) *Repealed.*

(5) Any reference in this section to any bird included in Part I of Schedule 3 is a reference to any bird included in that Part which was bred in captivity and has been ringed or marked in accordance with regulations made by the Secretary of State; and regulations so made may make different provision for different birds or different provisions of this section.

(6) Any reference in this section to any bird included in Part II or III of Schedule 3 is a reference to any bird included in Part II and, during the period commencing with 1st September in any year and ending with 28th February of the following year, any bird included in Part III of that Schedule.

(7)–(10) *Repealed.*
[Wildlife and Countryside Act 1981, s 6 as amended by the Birds (Registration Charges) Act 1997, s 1 and the Countryside and Rights of Way Act 2000, Sch 12.]

---

1. Defined by s 27, post.

8–4146   7. Registration etc of certain captive birds.   (1) If any person keeps or has in his possession or under his control any bird included in Schedule 4 which has not been registered and ringed or marked in accordance with regulations[1] made by the Secretary of State, he shall be guilty of an offence.

(2) The power of the Secretary of State to make regulations[1] under subsection (1) shall include power—

(a) to impose requirements which must be satisfied in relation to a bird included in Schedule 4 before it can be registered in accordance with the regulations; and

(b) to make different provision for different birds or different descriptions of birds.

(2A) *Power of Secretary of State to impose a charge for registration under subsection (1).*

(3) If any person keeps or has in his possession or under his control any bird included in Schedule 4—

(a) within five years of his having been convicted of an offence under this Part which falls within subsection (3A); or*

(b) within three years of his having been convicted of any other offence under this Part so far as it relates to the protection of birds or other animals or any offence involving their ill-treatment,*

he shall be guilty of an offence.

(3A) The offences falling within this subsection are—

(a) any offence under section 1(1) or (2) in respect of—

(i) a bird included in Schedule 1 or any part of, or anything derived from, such a bird,

(ii) the nest of such a bird, or

(iii) an egg of such a bird or any part of such an egg;

(b) any offence under section 1(5) or 5;

(c) any offence under section 6 in respect of—

(i) a bird included in Schedule 1 or any part of, or anything derived from, such a bird, or

(ii) an egg of such a bird or any part of such an egg

(d) any offence under section 8.

(4) If any person knowingly disposes of or offers to dispose of any bird included in Schedule 4 to any person—

(a) within five years of that person's having been convicted of such an offence as is mentioned in paragraph (a) of subsection (3); or*

(b) within three years of that person's having been convicted of such an offence as is mentioned in paragraph (b) of that subsection,*

he shall be guilty of an offence.

(5) No account shall be taken for the purposes of subsections (3) and (4) of any conviction which has become spent for the purpose of the Rehabilitation of Offenders Act 1974.

(6)–(7) *Repealed.*

[Wildlife and Countryside Act 1981, s 7 as amended by the Birds (Registration Charges) Act 1997, s 1 and the Countryside and Rights of Way Act 2000, Sch 12.]

---

*Sub-sections (3) and (4), paras (a) and (b) substituted in relation to Scotland by the Criminal Justice (Scotland) Act 2003, Sch 3 and para (c) inserted by the Nature Conservation (Scotland) Act 2004, Sch 6.

1. The Wildlife and Countryside (Registration and Ringing of Certain Captive Birds) Regulations 1982, SI 1982/1221 amended by SI 1991/478, SI 1994/1152 and SI 2004/640 (revoked in relation to Wales by SI 2003/3235), have been made.

8–4147 8. Protection of captive birds. (1) If any person keeps or confines any bird whatever in any cage or other receptacle which is not sufficient in height, length or breadth to permit the bird to stretch its wings freely, he shall be guilty of an offence.

(2) Subsection (1) does not apply to poultry, or to the keeping or confining of any bird—

(a) while that bird is in the course of conveyance, by whatever means;

(b) while that bird is being shown for the purposes of any public exhibition or competition if the time during which the bird is kept or confined for those purposes does not in the aggregate exceed 72 hours; or

(c) while that bird is undergoing examination or treatment by a veterinary surgeon or veterinary practitioner.

(3) Every person who—

(a) promotes, arranges, conducts, assists in, receives money for, or takes part in, any event whatever at or in the course of which captive birds are liberated by hand or by any other means whatever for the purpose of being shot immediately after their liberation; or

(b) being the owner or occupier of any land, permits that land to be used for the purposes of such an event.

shall be guilty of an offence.

[Wildlife and Countryside Act 1981, s 8, as amended by the Countryside and Rights of Way Act 2000, Sch 16.]

Protection of other animals

8–4148 9. Protection of certain wild animals. (1) Subject to the provisions of this Part, if any person intentionally kills, injures or takes any wild animal included in Schedule 5, he shall be guilty of an offence.*

(2) Subject to the provisions of this Part, if any person has in his possession or control any live or dead wild animals included in Schedule 5 or any part of, or anything derived from, such an animal, he shall be guilty of an offence.

(3) A person shall not be guilty of an offence under subsection (2) if he shows that—

(a) the animal had not been killed or taken, or had been killed or taken otherwise than in contravention of the relevant provisions; or*

(b) the animal or other thing in his possession or control had been sold (whether to him or to any other person) otherwise than in contravention of those provisions;*

and in this subsection "the relevant provisions" means the provisions of this Part of the Conservation of Wild Creatures and Wild Plants Act 1975.

(4) Subject to the provisions of this Part, if any person intentionally or recklessly—

(a) damages or destroys, or obstructs access to, any structure or place which any wild animal included in Schedule 5 uses for shelter or protection; or

(b) disturbs any such animal while it is occupying a structure or place which it uses for that purpose,

he shall be guilty of an offence.

(4A) Subject to the provisions of this Part, if any person intentionally or recklessly disturbs any wild animal included in Schedule 5 as—

(a) a dolphin or whale (cetacea), or

(b) a basking shark (cetorhinus maximus),

he shall be guilty of an offence.

(5) Subject to the provisions of this Part, if any person—

(a) sells, offers or exposes for sale, or has in his possession or transports for the purpose of sale, any live or dead wild animal included in Schedule 5, or any part of, or anything derived from, such an animal; or

(b) publishes or causes to be published any advertisement likely to be understood as conveying that he buys or sells, or intends to buy or sell, any of those things,

he shall be guilty of an offence.★

(6) In any proceedings for an offence under subsection (1), (2) or (5) (a), the animal in question shall be presumed to have been a wild animal unless the contrary is shown.

[Wildlife and Countryside Act 1981, s 9, as amended by the Countryside and Rights of Way Act 2000, Sch 12.]

★**Sub-sections (1), (3)(a), (b) and (6) amended and new para (3)(c) and sub-ss (3A) and (5A) inserted in relation to Scotland by the Nature Conservation (Scotland) Act 2004, Sch 6.**

8–4149　10. Exceptions to s 9.　(1) Nothing in section 9 shall make unlawful—

(a) anything done in pursuance of a requirement by the Minister of Agriculture, Fisheries and Food or the Secretary of State under section 98 of the Agriculture Act 1947, or by the Secretary of State under section 39 of the Agriculture (Scotland) Act 1948; or

(b) anything done under, or in pursuance of an order made under, the Animal Health Act 1981.

(2) Nothing in subsection (4) of section 9 shall make unlawful anything done within a dwelling-house.

(3) Notwithstanding anything in section 9, a person shall not be guilty of an offence by reason of—

(a) the taking of any such animal if he shows that the animal had been disabled otherwise than by his unlawful act and was taken solely for the purpose of tending it and releasing it when no longer disabled;

(b) the killing of any such animal if he shows that the animal had been so seriously disabled otherwise than by his unlawful act that there was no reasonable chance of its recovering; or

(c) any act made unlawful by that section if he shows that the act was the incidental result of a lawful operation and could not reasonably have been avoided.★

(4) Notwithstanding anything in section 9, an authorised person shall not be guilty of an offence by reason of the killing or injuring of a wild animal included in Schedule 5 if he shows that his action was necessary for the purpose of preventing serious damage to livestock, foodstuffs for livestock, crops, vegetables, fruit, growing timber or any other form of property or to fisheries.

(5) A person shall not be entitled to rely on the defence provided by subsection (2) or (3)(c) as respects anything done in relation to a bat otherwise than in the living area of a dwelling house unless he had notified the Nature Conservancy Council for the area in which the house is situated or, as the case may be, the act is to take place, of the proposed action or operation and allowed them a reasonable time to advise him as to whether it should be carried out and, if so, the method to be used.

(6) An authorised person shall not be entitled to rely on the defence provided by subsection (4) as respects any action taken at any time if it had become apparent, before that time, that that action would prove necessary for the purpose mentioned in that subsection and either—

(a) a licence under section 16 authorising that action had not been applied for as soon as reasonably practicable after that fact had become apparent; or

(b) an application for such a licence had been determined.★

[Wildlife and Countryside Act 1981, s 10 as amended by the Environmental Protection Act 1990, Sch 9.]

★**Sub-section (3)(c) amended and new sub-ss (3A) and (6A) inserted in relation to Scotland by the Nature Conservation (Scotland) Act 2004, Sch 6.**

8–4150　11. Prohibition of certain methods of killing or taking wild animals.　(1) Subject to the provisions of this Part, if any person—

(a) sets in position any self-locking snare which is of such a nature and so placed as to be calculated to cause bodily injury to any wild animal coming into contact therewith;★

(b) uses for the purpose of killing or taking any wild animal any self-locking snare, whether or not of such a nature or so placed as aforesaid, any bow or cross-bow or any explosive other than ammunition for a firearm;★

(c) uses as a decoy, for the purpose of killing or taking any wild animal, any live mammal or bird whatever; or

(d) knowingly causes or permits to be done an act which is mentioned in the foregoing provisions of this section,

he shall be guilty of an offence.

(2) Subject to the provisions of this Part, if any person—

(a) sets in position any of the following articles, being an article which is of such a nature and so placed as to be calculated to cause bodily injury to any wild animal included in Schedule 6 which comes into contact therewith, that is to say, any trap or snare, any electrical device for killing or stunning or any poisonous, poisoned or stupefying substance;

(b) uses for the purpose of killing or taking any such wild animal any such article as aforesaid, whether or not of such a nature and so placed as aforesaid, or any net;

(c) uses for the purpose of killing or taking any such wild animal—

    (i) any automatic or semi-automatic weapon;
    (ii) any device for illuminating a target or sighting device for night shooting;
    (iii) any form of artificial light or any mirror or other dazzling device; or
    (iv) any gas or smoke not falling within paragraphs (a) and (b);

(d) uses as a decoy, for the purpose of killing or taking any such wild animal, any sound recording;

(e) uses any mechanically propelled vehicle in immediate pursuit of any such wild animal for the purpose of driving, killing or taking that animal; or

(f) knowingly causes or permits to be done an act which is mentioned in the foregoing provisions of this subsection,

he shall be guilty of an offence.

(3) Subject to the provisions of this Part, if any person—

(a) sets in position or knowingly causes or permits to be set in position any snare which is of such a nature and so placed as to be calculated to cause bodily injury to any wild animal coming into contact therewith; and

(b) while the snare remains in position fails, without reasonable excuse, to inspect it, or cause it to be inspected, at least once every day,

he shall be guilty of an offence.★

(4) The Secretary of State may, for the purpose of complying with an international obligation, by order, either generally or in relation to any kind of wild animal specified in the order, amend subsection (1) or (2) by adding any method of killing or taking wild animals or by omitting any such method as is mentioned in that subsection.★

(5) In any proceedings for an offence under subsection (1)(b) or (c) or (2)(b), (c), (d) or (e) and in any proceedings for an offence under subsection (1)(d) or (2)(f) relating to an act which is mentioned in any of those paragraphs, the animal in question shall be presumed to have been a wild animal unless the contrary is shown.

(6) In any proceedings for an offence under subsection (2)(a) it shall be a defence to show that the article was set in position by the accused for the purpose of killing or taking, in the interests of public health, agriculture, forestry, fisheries or nature conservation, any wild animals which could be lawfully killed or taken by those means and that he took all reasonable precautions to prevent injury thereby to any wild animals included in Schedule 6.

(7) In any proceedings for an offence under subsection (2)(f) relating to an act which is mentioned in subsection (2)(a) it shall be a defence to show that the article was set in position for the purpose of killing or taking, in the interests of public health, agriculture, forestry, fisheries or nature conservation, any wild animals which could be lawfully killed or taken by those means and that he took or caused to be taken all reasonable precautions to prevent injury thereby to any wild animals included in Schedule 6.

[Wildlife and Countryside Act 1981, s 11 as amended by the Wildlife and Countryside (Amendment) Act 1991, s 2.]

★**Paragraphs (1)(a), (b) and (2)(a) amended, sub-s (3) substituted and new sub-ss (3A)–(3D) and (4A) inserted in relation to Scotland by the Nature Conservation (Scotland) Act 2004, Sch 6.**

Protection of plants

8–4151 13. Protection of wild plants. (1) Subject to the provisions of this Part, if any person—

(a) intentionally picks, uproots or destroys any wild plant included in Schedule 8; or (*b*) not being an authorised person, intentionally uproots any wild plant not included in that Schedule,

he shall be guilty of an offence.★

(2) Subject to the provisions of this Part, if any person—

(*a*) sells, offers or exposes for sale, or has in his possession or transports for the purpose of sale, any live or dead wild plant included in Schedule 8, or any part of, or anything derived from, such a plant; or

(*b*) publishes or causes to be published any advertisement likely to be understood as conveying that he buys or sells, or intends to buy or sell, any of those things,

he shall be guilty of an offence[1].

(3) Notwithstanding anything in subsection (1), a person shall not be guilty of an offence by reason of any act made unlawful by that subsection if he shows that the act was an incidental result of a lawful operation and could not reasonably have been avoided.★

(4) In any proceedings for an offence under subsection (2)(*a*), the plant in question shall be presumed to have been a wild plant unless the contrary is shown.★

[Wildlife and Countryside Act 1981, s 13.]

★Sub-sections (1), (3) and (4) amended and new sub-s (3A) inserted in relation to Scotland by the Nature Conservation (Scotland) Act 2004, Sch 6.

Miscellaneous

8–4152 14. Introduction of new species etc. (1) Subject to the provisions of this Part, if any person releases or allows to escape into the wild any animal which—

(*a*) is of a kind which is not ordinarily resident in and is not a regular visitor to Great Britain in a wild state; or

(*b*) is included in Part I of Schedule 9,

he shall be guilty of an offence.★

(2) Subject to the provisions of this Part, if any person plants or otherwise causes to grow in the wild any plant which is included in Part II of Schedule 9, he shall be guilty of an offence.★

(3) Subject to subsection (4), it shall be a defence to a charge of committing an offence under subsection (1) or (2) to prove that the accused took all reasonable steps and exercised all due diligence to avoid committing the offence.

(4) Where the defence provided by subsection (3) involves an allegation that the commission of the offence was due to the act or default of another person, the person charged shall not, without leave of the court, be entitled to rely on the defence unless, within a period ending seven clear days before the hearing, he has served on the prosecutor a notice giving such information identifying or assisting in the identification of the other person as was then in his possession.

(5)–(6) (*Repealed*)★

[Wildlife and Countryside Act 1981, s 14, as amended by the Countryside and Rights of Way Act 2000, Sch 12.]

★Sub-sections (1)(*b*) and (2) amended, new sub-s (1A) and new ss 14A, 14B and 15A inserted in relation to Scotland by the Nature Conservation (Scotland) Act 2004, Sch 6.

Supplemental

8–4153 16. Power to grant licences[1]. (1) Sections 1, 5, 6(3), 7 and 8 and orders under section 3 do not apply to anything done—

(*a*) for scientific, research or educational purposes;

(*b*) for the purpose of ringing or marking, or examining any ring or mark on, wild birds;

(*c*) for the purpose of conserving wild birds[2];

(*ca*) for the purposes of the re-population of an area with, or the re-introduction into an area of, wild birds, including any breeding necessary for those purposes;

(*cb*) for the purpose of conserving flora or fauna;]

(*d*) for the purpose of protecting any collection of wild birds;

(*e*) for the purposes of falconry or aviculture;

(*f*) for the purposes of any public exhibition or competition;

(*g*) for the purposes of taxidermy;

(*h*) for the purpose of photography;

(*i*) for the purposes of preserving public health or public or air safety;

(*j*) for the purpose of preventing the spread of disease; or

(*k*) for the purposes of preventing serious damage to livestock, foodstuffs for livestock, crops, vegetables, fruit, growing timber[, fisheries or inland waters],

if it is done under and in accordance with the terms of a licence granted by the appropriate authority.

(1A) The appropriate authority—

(a) shall not grant a licence for any purpose mentioned in subsection (1) unless it is satisfied that, as regards that purpose, there is no other satisfactory solution; and

(b) shall not grant a licence for any purpose mentioned in paragraphs (e) to (h) of that subsection otherwise than on a selective basis and in respect of a small number of birds.]

(2) Section 1 and orders under section 3 do not apply to anything done for the purpose of providing food for human consumption in relation to—

(a) a gannet on the island of Sula Sgeir; or

(b) a gull's egg or, at any time before 15th April in any year, a lapwing's egg,★

if it is done under and in accordance with the terms of a licence granted by the appropriate authority.

(3) Sections 9(1), (2), (4) and (4A), 11(1) and (2) and 13(1) do not apply to anything done★—

(a) for scientific or educational purposes;★

(b) for the purpose of ringing or marking, or examining any ring or mark on, wild animals;

(c) for the purpose of conserving wild animals or wild plants or introducing them to particular areas;★

(d) for the purpose of protecting any zoological or botanical collection;

(e) for the purpose of photography;

(f) for the purpose of preserving public health or public safety;

(g) for the purpose of preventing the spread of disease; or

(h) for the purpose of preventing serious damage to livestock, foodstuffs for livestock, crops, vegetables, fruit, growing timber or any other form of property or to fisheries,

if it is done under and in accordance with the terms of a licence granted by the appropriate authority.

(4) The following provisions, namely—

(a) section 6(1) and (2);

(b) sections 9(5) and 13(2); and

(c) section 14,★

do not apply to anything done under and in accordance with the terms of a licence granted by the appropriate authority.★

(5) Subject to subsections (5A) and (6), a licence under the foregoing provisions of this section—

(a) may be, to any degree, general or specific;

(b) may be granted either to persons of a class or to a particular person;

(c) may be subject to compliance with any specified conditions;

(d) may be modified or revoked at any time by the appropriate authority; and

(e) subject to paragraph (d), shall be valid for the period stated in the licence;

and the appropriate authority may charge therefor such reasonable sum (if any) as they may determine.

(5A) A licence under subsection (1) which authorises any action in respect of wild birds—

(a) shall specify the species of wild birds in respect of which, the circumstances in which, and the conditions subject to which, the action may be taken;

(b) shall specify the methods, means or arrangements which are authorised or required for the taking of the action; and

(c) subject to subsection (5)(d), shall be valid for the period, not exceeding two years, stated in the licence.

(6) A licence under subsection (2) or (3) which authorises any person to kill wild birds or wild animals—

(a) shall specify the area within which, and the methods by which the wild birds or wild animals may be killed; and

(b) subject to subsection (5)(d), shall be valid for the period, not exceeding two years, stated in the licence.

(7) It shall be a defence in proceedings for an offence under section 8(b) of the Protection of Animals Act 1911 or section 7(b) of the Protection of Animals (Scotland) Act 1912 (which restrict the placing on land of poison and poisonous substances) to show that—

(a) the act alleged to constitute the offence was done under and in accordance with the terms of a licence issued under subsection (1) or (3); and

(b) any conditions specified in the licence were complied with.

(8) For the purposes of a licence granted under the foregoing provisions of this section, the definition of a class of persons may be framed by reference to any circumstances whatever including, in particular, their being authorised by any other person.

(9) In this section "the appropriate authority" means—

(a) in the case of a licence under any of paragraphs (a) to (cb) of subsection (1), either the Secretary of State after consultation with whichever one of the advisory bodies he considers is best able to advise him as to whether the licence should be granted, or the [relevant] Nature Conservancy Council;

(b) in the case of a licence under any of paragraphs (d) to (g) of subsection (1), subsection (2) or paragraph (a) or (b) of subsection (4), the Secretary of State after such consultation as aforesaid;

(c) in the case of a licence under paragraph (h) of subsection (1) or any of paragraphs (a) to (e) of subsection (3), the relevant Nature Conservancy Council;

(d) in the case of a licence under paragraph (i), (j) or (k) of subsection (1) or paragraph (f), (g) or (h) of subsection (3) or a licence under paragraph (c) of subsection (4) which authorises anything to be done in relation to fish or shellfish, the agriculture Minister; and

(e) in the case of any other licence under paragraph (c) of subsection (4), the Secretary of State.

(9A) In this section "re-population" and "re-introduction", in relation to wild birds, have the same meaning as in the Directive of the Council of the European Communities dated 2nd April 1979 (No 79/409/EEC) on the conservation of wild birds.

(10) The Agricultural Minister—

(a) shall from time to time consult with each of the Nature Conservancy Councils as to the exercise in the area of that Council of his functions under this section; and

(b) shall not grant a licence of any description unless he has been advised by the relevant Nature Conservancy Council as to the circumstances in which, in their opinion, licences of that description should be granted.

(11) For the purposes of this section a reference to a relevant Nature Conservancy Council is a reference to the Nature Conservancy Council for the area in which it is proposed to carry on the activity requiring a licence.

[Wildlife and Countryside Act 1981, s 16 as amended by the Environmental Protection Act 1990, Sch 9, SI 1995/2825 and the Countryside and Rights of Way Act 2000, Sch 13.]

---

*Sub-sections (2)(b), (3) and (4) amended and new para (3)(ca) and sub-s (4A) inserted in relation to Scotland by the Nature Conservation (Scotland) Act 2004, Sch 6.

1. A licence issued under 16 will not assist a person carrying out an act covered by the licence if the act is not for one of the purposes listed in sub-s (1) (*RSPCA v Cundey* [2001] EWHC Admin 906, (2002) 166 JP 125.

2. It is sufficient defence to a charge of unlawfully confining a bird, contrary to s 8, ante, if the occupier can demonstrate that the use of the trap was for the purpose identified in the licence (*R (RSPCA) v Shinton* [2003] EWHC 1696 (Admin), 167 JP 513) (although the court left open the question whether the terms of the licence might not be breached if it could be shown that the trap used could not fulfil the purposes stated in the licence and the occupier knew this).

8–4154   17. False statements made for obtaining registration or licence etc.   A person who, for the purposes of obtaining, whether for himself or another, a registration in accordance with regulations made under section 7(1) or the grant of a licence under section 16—

(a) makes a statement or representation, or furnishes a document or information, which he knows to be false in a material particular; or

(b) recklessly makes a statement or representation, or furnishes a document or information, which is false in a material particular,

shall be guilty of an offence.

[Wildlife and Countryside Act 1981, s 17, as amended by the Countryside and Rights of Way Act 2000, Sch 13.]

8–4155   18. Attempts to commit offences etc.   (1) Any person who attempts to commit an offence under the foregoing provisions of this Part shall be guilty of an offence and shall be punishable in like manner as for the said offence.

(2) Any person who for the purposes of committing an offence under the foregoing provisions of this Part, has in his possession anything capable of being used for committing the offence shall be guilty of an offence and shall be punishable in like manner as for the said offence.

[Wildlife and Countryside Act 1981, s 18.]

8–4156   19. Enforcement.   (1) If a constable suspects with reasonable cause that any person is committing or has committed an offence under this Part, the constable may without warrant—

(a) stop and search that person if the constable suspects with reasonable cause that evidence of the commission of the offence is to be found on that person;

(b) search or examine any thing which that person may then be using or have in his possession if the constable suspects with reasonable cause that evidence of the commission of the offence is to be found on that thing;★

(c) (repealed);

(d) seize and detain for the purposes of proceedings under this Part any thing which may be evidence of the commission of the offence or may be liable to be forfeited under section 21.

(2) If a constable suspects with reasonable cause that any person is committing an offence under this Part, he may, for the purpose of exercising the powers conferred by subsection (1) or arresting a person, in accordance with section 25 of the Police and Criminal Evidence Act 1984, for such an offence, enter any land other than a dwelling-house.★

(3) If a justice of the peace is satisfied by information on oath that there are reasonable grounds

for suspecting that an offence under this Part has been committed and that evidence of the offence may be found on any premises, he may grant a warrant to any constable (with or without other persons) to enter upon and search those premises for the purpose of obtaining that evidence.

In the application of this subsection to Scotland, the reference to a justice of the peace includes a reference to the sheriff.*

[Wildlife and Countryside Act, 1981, s 19 as amended by the Police and Criminal Evidence Act 1984, Schs 6 and 7 and the Countryside and Rights of Way Act 2000, Sch 12.]

---

*Sub-sections (1)–(3) amended, sub-s (4) substituted and new sub-ss (5)–(8) inserted in relation to Scotland by the Nature Conservation (Scotland) Act 2004, Sch 6.

8–4156A   19ZA. Enforcement: wildlife inspectors.   (1) In this Part, "wildlife inspector" means a person authorised in writing by the Secretary of State under this subsection.

(2) An authorisation under subsection (1) is subject to any conditions or limitations specified in it.

(3) A wildlife inspector may, at any reasonable time and (if required to do so) upon producing evidence that he is authorised—

(*a*) enter and inspect any premises for the purpose of ascertaining whether an offence under section 6, 9(5) or 13(2) is being, or has been, committed on those premises;

(*b*) enter and inspect any premises where he has reasonable cause to believe that any birds included in Schedule 4 are kept, for the purpose of ascertaining whether an offence under section 7 is being, or has been, committed on those premises;

(*c*) enter any premises for the purpose of ascertaining whether an offence under section 14 is being, or has been, committed on those premises;

(*d*) enter and inspect any premises for the purpose of verifying any statement or representation which has been made by an occupier, or any document or information which has been furnished by him, and which he made or furnished—

(i) for the purposes of obtaining (whether for himself or another) a relevant registration or licence, or

(ii) in connection with a relevant registration or licence held by him.

(4) In subsection (3)—

(*a*) paragraphs (*a*) and (*b*) do not confer power to enter a dwelling except for purposes connected with—

(i) a relevant registration or licence held by an occupier of the dwelling, or

(ii) an application by an occupier of the dwelling for a relevant registration or licence; and

(*b*) paragraph (*c*) does not confer any power to enter a dwelling.

(5) A wildlife inspector may, for the purpose of ascertaining whether an offence under section 6, 7, 9(5), 13(2) or 14 is being, or has been, committed in respect of any specimen, require any person who has the specimen in his possession or control to make it available for examination by the inspector.

(6) Any person who has in his possession or control any live bird or other animal shall give any wildlife inspector acting in the exercise of powers conferred by this section such assistance as the inspector may reasonably require for the purpose of examining the bird or other animal.

(7) Any person who—

(*a*) intentionally obstructs a wildlife inspector acting in the exercise of powers conferred by subsection (3) or (5), or

(*b*) fails without reasonable excuse to give any assistance reasonably required under subsection (6),

shall be guilty of an offence.

(8) Any person who, with intent to deceive, falsely pretends to be a wildlife inspector shall be guilty of an offence.

(9) In this section—

"relevant registration or licence" means—

(*a*) a registration in accordance with regulations under section 7(1), or

(*b*) a licence under section 16 authorising anything which would otherwise be an offence under section 6, 7, 9(5), 13(2) or 14; and

"specimen" means any bird, other animal or plant or any part of, or anything derived from, a bird, other animal or plant.

[Wildlife and Countryside Act 1981, s 19ZA inserted by the Countryside and Rights of Way Act 2000, Sch 12.]

8–4156B   19ZB. Power to take samples.   (1) A constable who suspects with reasonable cause that a specimen found by him in the exercise of powers conferred by section 19 is one in respect of which an offence under this Part is being or has been committed may require the taking from it of a sample of blood or tissue in order to determine its identity or ancestry.

(2) A constable who suspects with reasonable cause that an offence under this Part is being or has been committed in respect of any specimen ("the relevant specimen") may require any person to make available for the taking of a sample of blood or tissue any specimen (other than the relevant specimen) in that person's possession or control which is alleged to be, or which the constable suspects with reasonable cause to be, a specimen a sample from which will tend to establish the identity or ancestry of the relevant specimen.

(3) A wildlife inspector may, for the purpose of ascertaining whether an offence under section 6, 7, 9(5), 13(2) or 14 is being or has been committed, require the taking of a sample of blood or tissue from a specimen found by him in the exercise of powers conferred by section 19ZA(3)(a) to (c) in order to determine its identity or ancestry.

(4) A wildlife inspector may, for the purpose of ascertaining whether an offence under section 6, 7, 9(5), 13(2) or 14 is being or has been committed in respect of any specimen ("the relevant specimen"), require any person to make available for the taking of a sample of blood or tissue any specimen (other than the relevant specimen) in that person's possession or control which is alleged to be, or which the wildlife inspector suspects with reasonable cause to be, a specimen a sample from which will tend to establish the identity or ancestry of the relevant specimen.

(5) No sample from a live bird, other animal or plant shall be taken pursuant to a requirement under this section unless the person taking it is satisfied on reasonable grounds that taking the sample will not cause lasting harm to the specimen.

(6) No sample from a live bird or other animal shall be taken pursuant to such a requirement except by a veterinary surgeon.

(7) Where a sample from a live bird or other animal is to be taken pursuant to such a requirement, any person who has possession or control of the specimen shall give the person taking the sample such assistance as he may reasonably require for that purpose.

(8) A constable entering premises under section 19(2), and any wildlife inspector entering premises under section 19ZA(3), may take with him a veterinary surgeon if he has reasonable grounds for believing that such a person will be required for the exercise on the premises of powers under subsections (1) to (4).

(9) Any person who—

(a) intentionally obstructs a wildlife inspector acting in the exercise of the power conferred by subsection (3),

(b) fails without reasonable excuse to make available any specimen in accordance with a requirement under subsection (2) or (4), or

(c) fails without reasonable excuse to give any assistance reasonably required under subsection (7),

shall be guilty of an offence.

(10) In this section—

(a) "specimen" has the same meaning as in section 19ZA, and

(b) in relation to a specimen which is a part of, or is derived from, a bird, other animal or plant, references to determining its identity or ancestry are to determining the identity or ancestry of the bird, other animal or plant.*

[Wildlife and Countryside Act 1981, s 19ZB inserted by the Countryside and Rights of Way Act 2000, Sch 12.]

---

*New ss 19ZC and D inserted in relation to Scotland by the Nature Conservation (Scotland) Act 2004, Sch 6.

8–4157   20. Summary prosecutions. (1) *Repealed.*

(2) Summary proceedings for an offence under this Part may be brought within a period of six months from the date on which evidence sufficient in the opinion of the prosecutor to warrant the proceedings came to his knowledge; but no such proceedings shall be brought by virtue of this section more than two years after the commission of the offence.*

(3) For the purpose of this section a certificate signed by or on behalf of the prosecutor and stating the date on which such evidence as aforesaid came to his knowledge shall be conclusive evidence of that fact; and a certificate stating that matter and purporting to be so signed shall be deemed to be so signed unless the contrary is proved.

[Wildlife and Countryside Act 1981, s 20, as amended by the Countryside and Rights of Way Act 2000, Sch 12.]

---

*Sub-section (2) amended in relation to Scotland by the Nature Conservation (Scotland) Act 2004, Sch 6.

8–4158   21. Penalties, forfeitures etc. (1) Subject to subsection (5), a person guilty of an offence under any of sections 1 to 13 or section 17 shall be liable on summary conviction to imprisonment for a term not exceeding six months or to a fine not exceeding level 5 on the standard scale, or to both.*

(2)–(3) (*Repealed*)

(4) A person guilty of an offence under section 14 shall be liable[1]—

(*a*) on summary conviction, to imprisonment for a term not exceeding six months or to a fine not exceeding the **statutory maximum**, or to both;

(*b*) on conviction on indictment, to imprisonment for a term not exceeding two years or to a fine, or to both.*

(4A) Except in a case falling within subsection (4B), a person guilty of an offence under section 19ZA(7) shall be liable on summary conviction to a fine not exceeding level 5 on the standard scale.

(4B) A person guilty of an offence under subsection (7) of section 19ZA in relation to a wildlife inspector acting in the exercise of the power conferred by subsection (3)(c) of that section shall be liable—

(a) on summary conviction, to a fine not exceeding the statutory maximum;

(b) on conviction on indictment, to a fine.

(4C) A person guilty of an offence under section 19ZA(8) shall be liable—

(a) on summary conviction, to imprisonment for a term not exceeding six months or a fine not exceeding the statutory maximum, or to both;

(b) on conviction on indictment, to imprisonment for a term not exceeding two years or to a fine, or to both.

(4D) A person guilty of an offence under section 19ZB(9) shall be liable on summary conviction to a fine not exceeding level 5 on the standard scale.

(5) Where an offence to which subsection (1) applies was committed in respect of more than one bird, nest, egg, other animal, plant or other thing, the maximum fine which may be imposed under that subsection shall be determined as if the person convicted had been convicted of a separate offence in respect of each bird, nest, egg, animal, plant or thing.

(6) The court by which any person is convicted of an offence under this Part—

(*a*) shall order the forfeiture of any bird, nest, egg, other animal, plant or other thing in respect of which the offence was committed; and

(*b*) may order the forfeiture of any vehicle, animal, weapon or other thing which was used to commit the offence and, in the case of an offence under section 14, any animal or plant which is of the same kind as that in respect of which the offence was committed and was found in his possession.*

(7) Any offence under this Part shall, for the purpose of conferring jurisdiction[2], be deemed to have been committed in any place where the offender is found or to which he is first brought after the commission of the offence.

[Wildlife and Countryside Act 1981, s 21 as amended by the Criminal Justice Act 1982, s 46 and the Countryside and Rights of Way Act 2000, Sch 12.]

---

*Sub-sections (1), (4) and (6) amended relation to Scotland by the Nature Conservation (Scotland) Act 2004, Sch 6.

1. For procedure in respect of this offence which is triable either way, see Magistrates' Courts Act 1980, ss 17A–21 in PART I: MAGISTRATES' COURTS, PROCEDURE, *ante*.

2. Section 25(2), provides that a local authority in England and Wales may institute proceedings for any offence under Part I of this Act or any order made under it which is committed within their area.

8–4159   22.   *Power to vary Schedules.*

8–4160   27. Interpretation of Part I.   (1)   In this Part, unless the context otherwise requires—

"advertisement" includes a catalogue, a circular and a price list;

"advisory body" has the meaning given by section 23;

"agriculture Minister" means the Minister of Agriculture, Fisheries and Food or the Secretary of State;

"authorised person" means—

(*a*) the owner or occupier, or any person authorised by the owner or occupier, of the land on which the action authorised is taken;

(*b*) any person authorised in writing by the local authority for the area within which the action authorised is taken;

(*c*) as respects anything done in relation to wild birds, any person authorised in writing by any of the following bodies, that is to say, any of the Nature Conservancy Councils, a district board for a fishery district within the meaning of the Salmon Fisheries (Scotland) Act 1862 or a local fisheries committee constituted under the Sea Fisheries Regulation Act 1966;

(*d*) any person authorised in writing by the Environment Agency, a water undertakers or a sewerage undertaker;

so, however, that the authorisation of any person for the purposes of this definition shall not confer any right of entry upon any land;

"automatic weapon" and "semi-automatic weapon" do not include any weapon the magazine of which is incapable of holding more than two rounds;

"aviculture" means the breeding and rearing of birds in captivity;

"destroy", in relation to an egg, includes doing anything to the egg which is calculated to prevent it from hatching, and "destruction" shall be construed accordingly;

"domestic duck" means any domestic form of duck;

"domestic goose" means any domestic form of goose;

"firearm" has the same meaning as in the Firearms Act 1968;

"game bird" means any pheasant, partridge, grouse (or moor game), black (or heath) game or ptarmigan;

"inland waters" means—

    (*a*) inland waters within the meaning of the Water Resources Act 1991;

    (*b*) any waters not falling within paragraph (*a*) above which are within the seaward limits of the territorial sea;

    (*c*) controlled waters within the meaning of Part II of the Control of Pollution Act 1974 other than ground waters as defined in section 30A(1)(*d*) of that Act.

"livestock" includes any animal which is kept—

    (*a*) for the provision of food, wool, skins or fur;

    (*b*) for the purpose of its use in the carrying on of any agricultural activity; or

    (*c*) for the provision or improvement of shooting or fishing;

"local authority" means—

    (*a*) in relation to England, a county, district or London borough council;

    (*aa*) in relation to Wales, a county council or county borough council;

    (*b*) in relation to Scotland, a council constituted under section 2 of the Local Government etc (Scotland) Act 1994;

"occupier", in relation to any land other than the foreshore, includes any person having any right of hunting, shooting, fishing or taking game or fish;

"pick", in relation to a plant, means gather or pluck any part of the plant without uprooting it;

"poultry" means domestic fowls, geese, ducks, guinea-fowls, pigeons and quails, and turkeys;★

"sale" includes hire, barter and exchange and cognate expressions shall be construed accordingly;

"uproot", in relation to a plant, means dig up or otherwise remove the plant from the land on which it is growing;

"vehicle" includes aircraft, hovercraft and boat;

"wild animal" means any animal (other than a bird) which is or (before it was killed or taken) was living wild;

"wild bird" means any bird of a species which is ordinarily resident in or is a visitor to the European territory of any member State in a wild state but does not include poultry or, except in sections 5 and 16, any game bird[2];★

"wild plant" means any plant which is or (before it was picked, uprooted or destroyed) was growing wild and is of a kind which ordinarily grows in Great Britain in a wild state★

"wildlife inspector" has the meaning given by section 19ZA(1).

(2) A bird shall not be treated as bred in captivity for the purposes of this Part unless its parents were lawfully in captivity when the egg was laid.★

(3) Any reference in this Part to an animal of any kind includes, unless the context otherwise requires, a reference to an egg, larva, pupa, or other immature stage of an animal of that kind.★

(3A) Any reference in this Part to the Nature Conservancy Councils is a reference to English Nature, Scottish Natural Heritage and the Countryside Council for Wales.

(4) This Part shall apply to the Isles of Scilly as if the Isles were a county and as if the Council of the Isles were a county council.

(5) This Part extends to the territorial waters adjacent to Great Britain, and for the purposes of this Part any part of Great Britain which is bounded by territorial waters shall be taken to include the territorial waters adjacent to that part.

[Wildlife and Countryside Act 1981, s 27 as amended by the Local Government Act 1985, Sch 17, the Water Act 1989, Schs 25 and 27, the Environmental Protection Act 1990, Sch 9, the Local Government (Wales) Act 1994, Sch 16, SI 1995/2825 and the Water Industry (Scotland) Act 2002, s 71(2).]

★**Definitions amended and new sub-ss (2A) and (3ZA) inserted in relation to Scotland by the Nature Conservation (Scotland) Act 2004, Sch 6.**

1. To be construed as the Environment Agency (The Environment Act 1955 (Consequential Amendments) Regulations 1995, SI 1995/593).

2. Justices may use, and should be encouraged to use, their common sense and local and general knowledge, and are entitled to take judicial notice that birds as common as goldfinches are "ordinarily resident in or visitors to Great Britain" (*Hughes v DPP* [2003] EWHC Admin 2470, (2003) 167 JP 167).

8–4160A 27ZA. Application of Part 1 to England and Wales. (1) The amendments made to this Part of the Act by the 2004 Regulations have effect in relation to England only, and accordingly, in the application of this Act in relation to Wales, this Part continues to have effect without the amendments made by the 2004 Regulations.

This subsection is subject to any regulations which may be made under section 2(2) of the European Communities Act 1972 by the National Assembly for Wales.

(2) In this section "the 2004 Regulations" means the Wildlife and Countryside Act 1981 (England and Wales) (Amendment) Regulations 2004.*

[Wildlife and Countryside Act 1981, s 27ZA as inserted by SI 2004/1487.]

---

*By virtue of SI 2004/1733 this section ceases to have effect, so that the amendments to Part 1 of the Act which were made by regulations 3 and 4 of SI 2004/1487 and which are contained in the Schedule to these Regulations apply also in relation to Wales.

PART II[1]
NATURE CONSERVATION, COUNTRYSIDE AND NATIONAL PARKS

Nature conservation

8–4161 27A. Construction of references to Nature Conservancy Council. In this Part references to "the Nature Conservancy Council" are, unless the contrary intention appears, references—

    (a) in relation to land in, or land covered by waters adjacent to, England, to English Nature;
    (b) in relation to land in, or land covered by waters adjacent to, Scotland, to the Nature Conservancy Council for Scotland; and
    (c) in relation to land in, or land covered by waters adjacent to, Wales, to the Countryside Council for Wales;

and references to "the Council" shall be construed accordingly.

[Wildlife and Countryside Act 1981, s 27A, as inserted by the Environmental Protection Act 1990, Sch 9 and the Countryside and Rights of Way Act 2000, Sch 12.]

---

1. Part II contains ss 28–52.

8–4171 28. Sites of special scientific interest. (1) Where the Nature Conservancy Council are of the opinion that any area of land is of special interest by reason of any of its flora, fauna, or geological or physiographical features, it shall be the duty[1] of the Council to notify that fact—

    (a) to the local planning authority in whose area the land is situated;
    (b) to every owner and occupier of any of that land; and
    (c) to the Secretary of State.

(2) The Council shall also publish a notification of that fact in at least one local newspaper circulating in the area in which the land is situated.

(3) A notification under subsection (1) shall specify the time (not being less than three months from the date of the giving of the notification) within which, and the manner in which, representations or objections with respect to it may be made; and the Council shall consider any representation or objection duly made.

(4) A notification under subsection (1)(b) shall also specify—

    (a) the flora, fauna, or geological or physiographical features by reason of which the land is of special interest, and
    (b) any operations appearing to the Council to be likely to damage that flora or fauna or those features,

and shall contain a statement of the Council's views about the management of the land (including any views the Council may have about the conservation and enhancement of that flora or fauna or those features).

(5) Where a notification under subsection (1) has been given, the Council may[2] within the period of nine months beginning with the date on which the notification was served on the Secretary of State either—

    (a) give notice to the persons mentioned in subsection (1) withdrawing the notification; or
    (b) give notice to those persons confirming the notification (with or without modifications).

(6) A notification shall cease to have effect—

    (a) on the giving of notice of its withdrawal under subsection (5)(a) to any of the persons mentioned in subsection (1); or
    (b) if not withdrawn or confirmed by notice under subsection (5) within the period of nine months referred to there, at the end of that period.

(7) The Council's power under subsection (5)(b) to confirm a notification under subsection (1) with modifications shall not be exercised so as to add to the operations specified in the notification or extend the area to which it applies.

(8) As from the time when there is served on the owner or occupier of any land which has been notified under subsection (1)(b) a notice under subsection (5)(b) confirming the notification with

modifications, the notification shall have effect in its modified form in relation to so much (if any) of that land as remains subject to it.

(9) A notification under subsection (1)(*b*) of land in England and Wales shall be a local land charge.

(10) For the purposes of this section and sections 28A to 28D, "local planning authority", in relation to land within the Broads, includes the Broads Authority.

[Wildlife and Countryside Act 1981, s 28 as substituted by the Countryside and Rights of Way Act 2000, Sch 9.]

---

1. Section 28 of the Wildlife and Countryside Act 1981 requires English Nature to exercise its judgment but confers no discretion; thus, if it judges that the statutory criteria are satisfied it has no discretion to decline to notify or confirm a site of special scientific interest by reason of a preference for the application of some other statutory or non-statutory scheme or because it considers that voluntary agreements with landowners or classification as a special protection area will protect the special interest more: *R (Fisher) v English Nature* [2004] EWCA Civ 663, [2004] 4 ALL ER 861, [2005] 1 WLR 147.

2. As to the exercise of powers under s 28 see *R (Fisher) v English Nature* [2004] EWCA Civ 663, [2004] 4 ALL ER 861, [2005] 1 WLR 147.

8–4171A   28A. Variation of notification under section 28.   (1) At any time after notice has been given under section 28(5)(*b*) confirming a notification (with or without modifications), the Nature Conservancy Council may by notice vary the matters specified or stated in the confirmed notification (whether by adding to them, changing them, or removing matter from them).

(2) The area of land cannot be varied under this section.

(3) The Council shall give notice setting out the variation to—

(*a*)   the local planning authority in whose area the land is situated,

(*b*)   every owner and occupier of any of the land who in the opinion of the Council may be affected by the variation, and

(*c*)   the Secretary of State,

and after service of a notice under paragraph (*b*) the notification under section 28(1)(*b*) shall have effect in its varied form.

(4) Section 28(3) shall apply to such a notice as it applies to a notification under section 28(1).

(5) Where a notice under subsection (3) has been given, the Council may within the period of nine months beginning with the date the last of the owners and occupiers referred to in subsection (3)(*b*) was served with the notice either—

(*a*)   give notice to the persons mentioned in subsection (3) withdrawing the notice; or

(*b*)   give notice to them confirming the notice (with or without modifications).

(6) A notice under subsection (3) shall cease to have effect—

(*a*)   on the giving of notice of its withdrawal under subsection (5)(*a*) to any of the persons mentioned in subsection (3); or

(*b*)   if not withdrawn or confirmed by notice under subsection (5) within the period of nine months referred to in that subsection, at the end of that period.

(7) As from the time when there is served on the owner or occupier of any land a notice under subsection (5)(*b*) confirming a notice of variation with modifications, the notification under section 28(1)(*b*) shall have effect as so varied.

(8) A local land charge existing by virtue of section 28(9) shall be varied in accordance with a notice under subsection (3) or (5)(*b*).

[Wildlife and Countryside Act 1981, s 28A as inserted by the Countryside and Rights of Way Act 2000, s 75(1), Sch 9.]

8–4171B   28B. Notification of additional land.   (1) Where the Nature Conservancy Council are of the opinion that if land adjacent to a site of special scientific interest ("the extra land") were combined with the site of special scientific interest ("the SSSI"), the combined area of land would be of special interest by reason of any of its flora, fauna, or geological or physiographical features, the Council may decide to notify that fact.

(2) If they do so decide, the persons whom they must notify are—

(*a*)   the local planning authority in whose area the extra land is situated;

(*b*)   every owner and occupier of any of that extra land; and

(*c*)   the Secretary of State.

(3) No such notification may be given until after notice has been given under section 28(5)(*b*) confirming (with or without modifications) the notification under section 28(1) relating to the SSSI.

(4) Subsections (2) and (3) of section 28 shall apply for the purposes of this section as they apply for the purposes of that section.

(5) A notification under subsection (2)(*b*) shall also specify—

(*a*)   the area of land constituting the SSSI;

(*b*)   what (as at the date of the notification under subsection (2)(*b*)) is specified or contained in the notification under section 28(1)(*b*) relating to the SSSI by virtue of section 28(4); and

(*c*)   the reasons why the Council is of the opinion referred to in subsection (1).

(6) In addition, the notification under subsection (2)(*b*) shall include a statement—

(*a*) saying whether or not anything among the matters specified in the notification by virtue of subsection (5)(*c*) is particularly relevant to the extra land; and

(*b*) if any such thing is of particular relevance, specifying which.

(7) Subsections (5) to (7) of section 28 apply in relation to a notification under subsection (2) of this section as they apply in relation to a notification under subsection (1) of that section, as if references to "subsection (1)" in section 28(5) to (7) were references to subsection (2) of this section.

(8) As from the time when a notification under subsection (2)(*b*) is served on the owner or occupier of any land, the notification under section 28(1)(*b*) shall have effect as if it included the notification under subsection (2)(*b*).

(9) As from the time when there is served on the owner or occupier of any land which has been notified under subsection (2)(*b*) a notice under section 28(5)(*b*) (as applied by subsection (7) of this section) confirming the notification under subsection (2)(*b*) with modifications, the notification under section 28(1)(*b*) (as extended by virtue of subsection (8) of this section) shall have effect in its modified form.

(10) A local land charge existing by virtue of section 28(9) shall be varied in accordance with a notification under subsection (2) or under section 28(5)(*b*) as applied by subsection (7) of this section.

[Wildlife and Countryside Act 1981, s 28B as inserted by the Countryside and Rights of Way Act 2000, s 75(1), Sch 9.]

8–4171C   28C. Enlargement of SSSI.   (1) Where the Nature Conservancy Council are of the opinion that any area of land which includes, but also extends beyond, a site of special scientific interest ("the SSSI") is of special interest by reason of any of its flora, fauna, or geological or physiographical features, the Council may decide to notify that fact.

(2) If they do so decide, the persons whom they must notify are—

(*a*) the local planning authority in whose area the land (including the SSSI) is situated;

(*b*) every owner and occupier of any of that land (including the SSSI); and

(*c*) the Secretary of State.

(3) Subsections (2) to (8) of section 28 apply to a notification under subsection (2) of this section as they apply to a notification under subsection (1) of that section, as if references to "subsection (1)" and "subsection (1)(*b*)" in section 28(2) to (8) were references to subsection (2) and subsection (2)(*b*) of this section respectively.

(4) No notification may be given under subsection (2) until after notice has been given under section 28(5)(*b*) (or section 28(5)(*b*) as applied by subsection (3)) confirming (with or without modifications) the notifications under section 28(1) (or subsection (2)) relating to the SSSI.

(5) As from the time when a notification under subsection (2) is served on the owner or occupier of any land included in the SSSI, the notification in relation to that land which had effect immediately before the service of the notification under subsection (2) shall cease to have effect.

(6) A notification under subsection (2)(*b*) of land in England and Wales shall be a local land charge; and, to the extent that any such land was the subject of a local land charge by virtue of section 28(9), that local land charge shall be discharged.

(7) A notice under section 28E(1)(*a*) and a consent under section 28E(3)(*a*) given before a notification under subsection (2)(*b*) continue to have effect.

(8) The enlargement of a site of special scientific interest under this section does not affect anything done under section 28J to 28L.

(9) Any reference to—

(*a*) a notification under section 28(1) (or any of its paragraphs) shall be construed as including the corresponding notification under subsection (2);

(*b*) a notification under section 28(5)(*b*) shall be construed as including a notification under that provision as applied by subsection (3); and

(*c*) a local land charge existing by virtue of section 28(9) shall be treated as including one existing by virtue of subsection (6).

[Wildlife and Countryside Act 1981, s 28C as inserted by the Countryside and Rights of Way Act 2000, s 75(1), Sch 9.]

8–4171D   28D. Denotification.   (1) Where the Nature Conservancy Council are of the opinion that all or part of a site of special scientific interest is no longer of special interest by reason of any of the matters mentioned in section 28(1), they may decide to notify that fact.

(2) If they do so decide, the persons whom they must notify are—

(*a*) the local planning authority in whose area the land which the Council no longer consider to be of special interest is situated;

(*b*) every owner and occupier of any of that land;

(*c*) the Secretary of State;

(*d*) the Environment Agency; and

(*e*)   every relevant undertaker (within the meaning of section 4(1) of the Water Industry Act 1991) and every internal drainage board (within the meaning of section 61C(1) of the Land Drainage Act 1991) whose works, operations or activities may affect the land.

(3)   The Council shall also publish a notification of that fact in at least one local newspaper circulating in the area in which the land referred to in subsection (2)(*a*) is situated.

(4)   Section 28(3) shall apply to a notification under subsection (2) or (3) as it applies to a notification under section 28(1).

(5)   Where a notification under subsection (2) has been given, the Council may within the period of nine months beginning with the date on which the notification was served on the Secretary of State either—

(*a*)   give notice to the persons mentioned in subsection (2) withdrawing the notification, or

(*b*)   give notice to those persons confirming the notification, or confirming it in relation to an area of land specified in the notice which is smaller than that specified in the notification under subsection (2),

but if they do neither the notification shall cease to have effect.

(6)   A notification under subsection (2) shall have effect in relation to any land as from the time a notice under subsection (5)(*b*) is served on its owner or occupier, and from that time a notification under section 28(1)(*b*) in relation to that land shall cease to have effect.

(7)   A local land charge existing by virtue of section 28(9) shall be discharged in relation to land which is the subject of a notice under subsection (5)(*b*).

[Wildlife and Countryside Act 1981, s 28D as inserted by the Countryside and Rights of Way Act 2000, s 75(1), Sch 9.]

8–4171E   28E. Duties in relation to sites of special scientific interest.   (1) The owner or occupier of any land included in a site of special scientific interest shall not while the notification under section 28(1)(*b*) remains in force carry out, or cause or permit to be carried out, on that land any operation specified in the notification unless—

(*a*)   one of them has, after service of the notification, given the Nature Conservancy Council notice of a proposal to carry out the operation specifying its nature and the land on which it is proposed to carry it out; and

(*b*)   one of the conditions specified in subsection (3) is fulfilled.

(2)   Subsection (1) does not apply to an owner or occupier being an authority to which section 28G applies acting in the exercise of its functions.

(3)   The conditions are—

(*a*)   that the operation is carried out with the Council's written consent;

(*b*)   that the operation is carried out in accordance with the terms of an agreement under section 16 of the 1949 Act or section 15 of the 1968 Act;

(*c*)   that the operation is carried out in accordance with a management scheme under section 28J or a management notice under section 28K.

(4)   A consent under subsection (3)(*a*) may be given—

(*a*)   subject to conditions, and

(*b*)   for a limited period,

as specified in the consent.

(5)   If the Council do not consent, they shall give notice saying so to the person who gave the notice under subsection (1).

(6)   The Council may, by notice given to every owner and occupier of any of the land included in the site of special scientific interest, or the part of it to which the consent relates—

(*a*)   withdraw the consent; or

(*b*)   modify it (or further modify it) in any way.

(7)   The following—

(*a*)   a consent under subsection (3)(*a*) granting consent subject to conditions or for a limited period, and

(*b*)   a notice under subsection (5) or (6),

must include a notice of the Council's reasons for imposing the conditions, for the limitation of the period, for refusing consent, or for withdrawing or modifying the consent, and also a notice of the matters set out in subsection (8).

(8)   The matters referred to in subsection (7) are—

(*a*)   the rights of appeal under section 28F;

(*b*)   the effect of subsection (9); and

(*c*)   in the case of a notice under subsection (6), the effect of section 28M.

(9)   A withdrawal or modification of a consent is not to take effect until—

(*a*)   the expiry of the period for appealing against it; or

(b) if an appeal is brought, its withdrawal or final determination.

(10) The Council shall have power to enforce the provisions of this section.
[Wildlife and Countryside Act 1981, s 28E as inserted by the Countryside and Rights of Way Act 2000, s 75(1), Sch 9.]

8–4171F **28F. Appeals in connection with consents.** (1) The following persons—

(a) an owner or occupier who has been refused a consent under section 28E(3)(*a*),
(b) an owner or occupier who has been granted such a consent but who is aggrieved by conditions attached to it, or by the fact that it is for a limited period, or by the length of that period,
(c) an owner or occupier who is aggrieved by the modification of a consent;
(d) an owner or occupier who is aggrieved by the withdrawal of a consent,

may by notice appeal to the Secretary of State against the relevant decision.

(2) If the Nature Conservancy Council neither give consent nor refuse it within the period of four months beginning with the date on which the notice referred to in section 28E(1)(*a*) was sent, the person who gave that notice may for the purposes of subsection (1) treat the Council as having refused consent (and his appeal is to be determined on that basis).

(3) Notice of an appeal must reach the Secretary of State—

(a) except in a case falling within subsection (2), within the period of two months beginning with the date of the notice giving consent or the notice under section 28E(5) or (6), or
(b) in a case falling within subsection (2), within the period of two months beginning immediately after the expiry of the four-month period referred to there,

or, in either case, within such longer period as is agreed in writing between the Council and the appellant.

(4) Before determining an appeal, the Secretary of State may, if he thinks fit—

(a) cause the appeal to take, or continue in, the form of a hearing (which may be held wholly or partly in private if the appellant so requests and the person hearing the appeal agrees), or
(b) cause a local inquiry to be held,

and he must act as mentioned in paragraph (*a*) or (*b*) if either party to the appeal asks to be heard in connection with the appeal.

(5) On determining an appeal against a decision, the Secretary of State may—

(a) affirm the decision,
(b) where the decision was a refusal of consent, direct the Council to give consent,
(c) where the decision was as to the terms of a consent (whether the original or a modified one), quash all or any of those terms,
(d) where the decision was a withdrawal or modification of consent, quash the decision,

and where he exercises any of the powers in paragraphs (*b*), (*c*) or (*d*) he may give directions to the Council as to the terms on which they are to give consent.

(6) The Secretary of State may by regulations[1] made by statutory instrument make provision about appeals under this section, and in particular about—

(a) notices of appeal and supporting documentation required, and
(b) how appeals are to be brought and considered,

and any such regulations may make different provision for different cases and circumstances.

(7) A statutory instrument containing regulations under subsection (6) shall be subject to annulment in pursuance of a resolution of either House of Parliament.

(8) The Secretary of State may appoint any person to exercise on his behalf, with or without payment, his function of determining an appeal under this section or any matter involved in such an appeal.

(9) Schedule 10A shall have effect with respect to appointments under subsection (8).

(10) Subsections (2) to (5) of section 250 of the Local Government Act 1972 (local inquiries: evidence and costs) apply in relation to hearings or local inquiries under this section as they apply in relation to local inquiries under that section, but as if the reference there—

(a) to the person appointed to hold the inquiry were a reference to the Secretary of State or to the person appointed to conduct the hearing or hold the inquiry under this section; and
(b) to the Minister causing an inquiry to be held were to the Secretary of State.

(11) Section 322A of the Town and Country Planning Act 1990 (orders as to costs where no hearing or inquiry takes place) applies in relation to a hearing or local inquiry under this section as it applies in relation to a hearing or local inquiry referred to in that section.
[Wildlife and Countryside Act 1981, s 28F as inserted by the Countryside and Rights of Way Act 2000, s 75(1), Sch 9.]

---

1. The Wildlife and Countryside (Sites of Special Scientific Interest, Appeals) (Wales) Regulations 2002, SI 2002/1772 have been made.

8–4171G   28G.   Statutory undertakers, etc: general duty.   (1) An authority to which this section applies (referred to in this section and in sections 28H and 28I as "a section 28G authority") shall have the duty set out in subsection (2) in exercising its functions so far as their exercise is likely to affect the flora, fauna or geological or physiographical features by reason of which a site of special scientific interest is of special interest.

(2) The duty is to take reasonable steps, consistent with the proper exercise of the authority's functions, to further the conservation and enhancement of the flora, fauna or geological or physiographical features by reason of which the site is of special scientific interest.

(3) The following are section 28G authorities—

(*a*)   a Minister of the Crown (within the meaning of the Ministers of the Crown Act 1975) or a Government department;
(*b*)   the National Assembly for Wales;
(*c*)   a local authority;
(*d*)   a person holding an office—

    (i)   under the Crown,
    (ii)   created or continued in existence by a public general Act of Parliament, or
    (iii)   the remuneration in respect of which is paid out of money provided by Parliament;

(*e*)   a statutory undertaker (meaning the persons referred to in section 262(1), (3) and (6) of the Town and Country Planning Act 1990); and
(*f*)   any other public body of any description.

[Wildlife and Countryside Act 1981, s 28G as inserted by the Countryside and Rights of Way Act 2000, s 75(1), Sch 9.]

8–4171H   28H.   Statutory undertakers, etc: duty in relation to carrying out operations.
(1) A section 28G authority shall give notice to the Nature Conservancy Council before carrying out, in the exercise of its functions, operations likely to damage any of the flora, fauna or geological or physiographical features by reason of which a site of special scientific interest is of special interest.

(2) Subsection (1) applies even if the operations would not take place on land included in a site of special scientific interest.

(3) In response to the notice referred to in subsection (1), the Council may send a notice—

(*a*)   saying that they do not assent to the proposed operations, or
(*b*)   assenting to them (with or without conditions),

but if they do not send a notice under paragraph (*b*) within the period of 28 days beginning with the date of the notice under subsection (1) they shall be treated as having declined to assent.

(4) If the Council do not assent, or if the authority proposes to carry out the operations otherwise than in accordance with the terms of the Council's assent, the authority—

(*a*)   shall not carry out the operations unless the condition set out in subsection (5) is satisfied, and
(*b*)   shall comply with the requirements set out in subsection (6) when carrying them out.

(5) The condition is that the authority has, after the expiry of the period of 28 days beginning with the date of the notice under subsection (1), notified the Council of—

(*a*)   the date on which it proposes to start the operations (which must be after the expiry of the period of 28 days beginning with the date of the notification under this paragraph), and
(*b*)   how (if at all) it has taken account of any written advice it received from the Council, before the date of the notification under this paragraph, in response to the notice under subsection (1).

(6) The requirements are—

(*a*)   that the authority carry out the operations in such a way as to give rise to as little damage as is reasonably practicable in all the circumstances to the flora, fauna or geological or physiographical features by reason of which the site is of special interest (taking account, in particular, of any such advice as is referred to in subsection (5)(*b*)); and
(*b*)   that the authority restore the site to its former condition, so far as is reasonably practicable, if any such damage does occur.

[Wildlife and Countryside Act 1981, s 28H as inserted by the Countryside and Rights of Way Act 2000, s 75(1), Sch 9.]

8–4171I   28I.   Statutory undertakers, etc: duty in relation to authorising operations.
(1) This section applies where the permission of a section 28G authority is needed before operations may be carried out.

(2) Before permitting the carrying out of operations likely to damage any of the flora, fauna or geological or physiographical features by reason of which a site of special scientific interest is of special interest, a section 28G authority shall give notice of the proposed operations to the Nature Conservancy Council.

(3) Subsection (2) applies even if the operations would not take place on land included in a site of special scientific interest.

(4) The authority shall wait until the expiry of the period of 28 days beginning with the date of the notice under subsection (2) before deciding whether to give its permission, unless the Nature Conservancy Council have notified the authority that it need not wait until then.

(5) The authority shall take any advice received from the Council into account—

(a) in deciding whether or not to permit the proposed operations, and

(b) if it does decide to do so, in deciding what (if any) conditions are to be attached to the permission.

(6) If the Council advise against permitting the operations, or advise that certain conditions should be attached, but the section 28G authority does not follow that advice, the authority—

(a) shall give notice of the permission, and of its terms, to the Council, the notice to include a statement of how (if at all) the authority has taken account of the Council's advice, and

(b) shall not grant a permission which would allow the operations to start before the end of the period of 21 days beginning with the date of that notice.

(7) In this section "permission", in relation to any operations, includes authorisation, consent, and any other type of permission (and "permit" and "permitting" are to be construed accordingly).
[Wildlife and Countryside Act 1981, s 28I as inserted by the Countryside and Rights of Way Act 2000, s 75(1), Sch 9.]

8–4171J   28J. Management schemes.   (1) The Nature Conservancy Council may formulate a management scheme for all or part of a site of special scientific interest.

(2) A management scheme is a scheme for—

(a) conserving the flora, fauna, or geological or physiographical features by reason of which the land (or the part of it to which the scheme relates) is of special interest; or

(b) restoring them; or

(c) both.

(3) The Council shall serve notice of a proposed management scheme on every owner and occupier of any of the land (or the part of it to which the scheme would relate); but it may be served on them only after they have been consulted about the proposed management scheme.

(4) The notice may be served with the notification referred to in section 28(1)(b) or afterwards.

(5) The owners and occupiers upon whom the notice must be served (referred to in this section as "the relevant owners and occupiers") are—

(a) if it is served with the notification under section 28(1)(b), or later but before the notification referred to in section 28(5)(b), the owners and occupiers referred to in section 28(1)(b);

(b) if it is served with the notification under section 28(5)(b) or later, the owners and occupiers of such of the land as remains subject to the notification.

(6) The notice of a proposed management scheme must include a copy of the proposed scheme.

(7) The notice must specify the time (not being less than three months from the date of the giving of the notice) within which, and the manner in which, representations or objections with respect to the proposed management scheme may be made; and the Council shall consider any representation or objection duly made.

(8) Where a notice under subsection (3) has been given, the Council may within the period of nine months beginning with the date on which the notice was served on the last of the relevant owners and occupiers either—

(a) give notice to the relevant owners and occupiers withdrawing the notice, or

(b) give notice to them confirming the management scheme (with or without modifications),

and if notice under paragraph (b) is given, the management scheme shall have effect from the time the notice is served on all of the relevant owners or occupiers.

(9) A notice under subsection (3) shall cease to have effect—

(a) on the giving of a notice of withdrawal under subsection (8)(a) to any of the relevant owners and occupiers; or

(b) if not withdrawn or confirmed by notice under subsection (8) within the period of nine months referred to there, at the end of that period.

(10) The Council's power under subsection (8)(b) to confirm a management scheme with modifications shall not be exercised so as to make complying with it more onerous.

(11) The Council may at any time cancel or propose the modification of a management scheme.

(12) In relation to—

(a) the cancellation of a management scheme, subsections (3) to (5) apply, and

(b) a proposal to modify a management scheme, subsections (3) to (10) apply,

as they apply in relation to a proposal for a management scheme.

(13) An agreement under section 16 of the 1949 Act or section 15 of the 1968 Act relating to a

site of special scientific interest may provide for any matter for which a management scheme relating to that site provides (or could provide).
[Wildlife and Countryside Act 1981, s 28J as inserted by the Countryside and Rights of Way Act 2000, s 75(1), Sch 9.]

8–4171K   28K. Management notices.   (1) Where it appears to the Nature Conservancy Council that—

(*a*)   an owner or occupier of land is not giving effect to a provision of a management scheme, and

(*b*)   as a result any flora, fauna or geological or physiographical features by reason of which the land is of special interest are being inadequately conserved or restored,

they may if they think fit serve a notice on him (a "management notice").

(2) They may not serve a management notice unless they are satisfied that they are unable to conclude, on reasonable terms, an agreement with the owner or occupier as to the management of the land in accordance with the management scheme.

(3) A management notice is a notice requiring the owner or occupier to—

(*a*)   carry out such work on the land, and

(*b*)   do such other things with respect to it,

as are specified in the notice, and to do so before the dates or within the periods so specified.

(4) The work and other things specified in the notice must appear to the Council to be measures which it is reasonable to require in order to ensure that the land is managed in accordance with the management scheme.

(5) The management notice must explain the effect of subsection (7) and (8) and of sections 28L and 28M(2) to (4).

(6) A copy of the management notice must be served on every other owner and occupier of the land.

(7) If any of the work or other things required by a management notice have not been done within the period or by the date specified in it, the Council may—

(*a*)   enter the land, and any other land, and carry out the work, or do the other things; and

(*b*)   recover from the owner or occupier upon whom the notice was served any expenses reasonably incurred by them in carrying out the work or doing the other things.

(8) If an appeal is brought against the management notice, and upon the final determination of the appeal the notice is affirmed (with or without modifications), subsection (7) applies as if the references there to the management notice were to the notice as affirmed.
[Wildlife and Countryside Act 1981, s 28K as inserted by the Countryside and Rights of Way Act 2000, s 75(1), Sch 9.]

8–4171L   28L. *Appeals against management notices*

8–4171M   28M. Payments.   (1) Where the Council, under section 28E(6), modify or withdraw a consent, they shall make a payment to any owner or occupier of the land who suffers loss because of the modification or withdrawal.

(2) The Council may, if they think fit, make one or more payments to any owner or occupier of land in relation to which a management scheme under section 28J is in force.

(3) The amount of a payment under this section is to be determined by the Council in accordance with guidance given and published by the Ministers.

(4) Section 50(3) applies to the determination of the amount of payments under this section as it applies to the determination of the amount of payments under that section.
[Wildlife and Countryside Act 1981, s 28M as inserted by the Countryside and Rights of Way Act 2000, s 75(1), Sch 9.]

8–4171N   28N. *Compulsory purchase*

8–4171O   28P. Offences.   (1) A person who, without reasonable excuse, contravenes section 28E(1) is guilty of an offence and is liable on summary conviction to a fine not exceeding £20,000 or on conviction on indictment to a fine.

(2) A section 28G authority which, in the exercise of its functions, carries out an operation which damages any of the flora, fauna or geological or physiographical features by reason of which a site of special scientific interest is of special interest—

(*a*)   without first complying with section 28H(1), or

(*b*)   (if it has complied with section 28H(1)) without first complying with section 28H(4)(*a*),

is, unless there was a reasonable excuse for carrying out the operation without complying, guilty of an offence and is liable on summary conviction to a fine not exceeding £20,000 or on conviction on indictment to a fine.

(3) A section 28G authority acting in the exercise of its functions which, having complied with section 28H(1), fails without reasonable excuse to comply with section 28H(4)(*b*) is guilty of an

offence and is liable on summary conviction to a fine not exceeding £20,000 or on conviction on indictment to a fine.

(4) For the purposes of subsections (1), (2) and (3), it is a reasonable excuse in any event for a person to carry out an operation (or to fail to comply with a requirement to send a notice about it) if—

(a) subject to subsection (5), the operation in question was authorised by a planning permission granted on an application under Part III of the Town and Country Planning Act 1990 or permitted by a section 28G authority which has acted in accordance with section 28I; or

(b) the operation in question was an emergency operation particulars of which (including details of the emergency) were notified to the Nature Conservancy Council as soon as practicable after the commencement of the operation.

(5) If an operation needs both a planning permission and the permission of a section 28G authority, subsection (4)(a) does not provide reasonable excuse unless both have been obtained.

(6) A person (other than a section 28G authority acting in the exercise of its functions) who without reasonable excuse—

(a) intentionally or recklessly destroys or damages any of the flora, fauna, or geological or physiographical features by reason of which land is of special interest, or intentionally or recklessly disturbs any of those fauna, and

(b) knew that what he destroyed, damaged or disturbed was within a site of special scientific interest,

is guilty of an offence and is liable on summary conviction to a fine not exceeding £20,000 or on conviction on indictment to a fine.

(7) It is a reasonable excuse in any event for a person to do what is mentioned in subsection (6) if—

(a) paragraph (a) or (b) of subsection (4) is satisfied in relation to what was done (reading references there to an operation as references to the destruction, damage or disturbance referred to in subsection (6)), and

(b) where appropriate, subsection (5) is also satisfied, reading the reference there to an operation in the same way.

(8) A person who without reasonable excuse fails to comply with a requirement of a management notice is guilty of an offence and is liable on summary conviction to a fine not exceeding the statutory maximum or on conviction on indictment to a fine.

(9) In determining the amount of any fine to be imposed on a person convicted of an offence under this section, the court shall in particular have regard to any financial benefit which has accrued or appears likely to accrue to him in consequence of the offence.

(10) Proceedings in England and Wales for an offence under this section shall not, without the consent of the Director of Public Prosecutions, be taken by a person other than the Council.

(11) In this section, "a section 28G authority" means an authority to which section 28G applies.
[Wildlife and Countryside Act 1981, s 28P as inserted by the Countryside and Rights of Way Act 2000, s 75(1), Sch 9.]

8–4171P   28Q. Change of owner or occupier.   (1) This section applies where the owner of land included in a site of special scientific interest—

(a) disposes of any interest of his in the land; or

(b) becomes aware that it is occupied by an additional or a different occupier.

(2) If this section applies, the owner shall send a notice to the Nature Conservancy Council before the end of the period of 28 days beginning with the date on which he disposed of the interest or became aware of the change in occupation.

(3) The notice is to specify the land concerned and—

(a) in a subsection (1)(a) case, the date on which the owner disposed of the interest in the land, and the name and address of the person to whom he disposed of the interest; or

(b) in a subsection (1)(b) case, the date on which the change of occupation took place (or, if the owner does not know the exact date, an indication of when to the best of the owner's knowledge it took place), and, as far as the owner knows them, the name and address of the additional or different occupier.

(4) A person who fails without reasonable excuse to comply with the requirements of this section is guilty of an offence and is liable on summary conviction to a fine not exceeding level 1 on the standard scale.

(5) For the purposes of subsection (1), an owner "disposes of" an interest in land if he disposes of it by way of sale, exchange or lease, or by way of the creation of any easement, right or privilege, or in any other way except by way of mortgage.
[Wildlife and Countryside Act 1981, s 28Q as inserted by the Countryside and Rights of Way Act 2000, s 75(1), Sch 9.]

8–4171Q   28R. Byelaws.   (1) The Nature Conservancy Council may make byelaws for the protection of a site of special scientific interest.

(2) The following provisions of the 1949 Act apply in relation to byelaws under this section as they apply in relation to byelaws under section 20 of that Act—

(a) subsections (2) and (3) of section 20 (reading references there to nature reserves as references to sites of special scientific interest); and

(b) sections 106 and 107.

[Wildlife and Countryside Act 1981, s 28R as inserted by the Countryside and Rights of Way Act 2000, s 75(1), Sch 9.]

8–4172 29. Special protection for certain areas of special scientific interest. *Repealed.*

8–4173 31. Restoration following offence unser section 28P. (1) Where—

(a) the operation in respect of which a person is convicted of an offence under section 28P(1), (2) or (3) has destroyed or damaged any of the flora, fauna or geological or physiographical features by reason of which a site of special scientific interest is of special interest, or

(b) a person is convicted of an offence under section 28P(6),

the court by which he is convicted, in addition to dealing with him in any other way, may make an order requiring him to carry out, within such period as may be specified in the order, such operations (whether on land included in the site of special scientific interest or not) as may be so specified for the purpose of restoring the site of special scientific interest to its former condition.

(2) An order under this section made on conviction on indictment shall be treated for the purposes of sections 30 and 42(1) and (2) of the Criminal Appeal Act 1968 (effect of appeals on orders for the restitution of property) as an order for the restitution of property; and where by reason of the quashing by the Court of Appeal of a person's conviction any such order does not take effect, and on appeal to the House of Lords the conviction is restored by that House, the House may make any order under this section which could be made on his conviction by the court which convicted him.

(3) In the case of an order under this section made by a magistrates' court the period specified in the order shall not begin to run—

(a) in any case until the expiration of the period for the time being prescribed by law for the giving of notice of appeal against a decision of a magistrates' court;

(b) where notice of appeal is given within the period so prescribed, until determination of the appeal.

(4) At any time before an order under this section has been complied with or fully complied with, the court by which it was made may, on the application of the person against whom it was made, discharge or vary the order if it appears to the court that a change in circumstances has made compliance or full compliance with the order impracticable or unnecessary.

(5) If, within the period specified in an order under this section, the person against whom it was made fails, without reasonable excuse, to comply with it, he shall be liable on summary conviction—

(a) to a fine not exceeding **level 5** on the standard scale; and

(b) in the case of a continuing offence, to a further fine not exceeding **£100** for each day during which the offence continues after conviction.

(6) If, within the period specified in an order under this section, any operations specified in the order have not been carried out, the Nature Conservancy Council may enter the land and carry out those operations and recover from the person against whom the order was made any expenses reasonably incurred by them in doing so.

(7) *Scotland.*★

[Wildlife and Countryside Act 1981, s 31 as amended by the Criminal Justice Act 1982, s 46 and the Countryside and Rights of Way Act 2000, Sch 9.]

★**Repealed in relation to Scotland by the Nature Conservation (Scotland) Act 2004, Sch 7.**

8–4174 34. Limestone pavement orders. Nature Conservancy Council or the Countryside Commission may notify the local planning authority that a limestone pavement is of special interest by reason of its flora, fauna or geological or physiographical features; Secretary of State or relevant authority may make an order prohibiting the removal or disturbance of limestone on that land. It is an offence to remove or disturb limestone on designated land, punishable on summary conviction by a fine not exceeding the statutory maximum or on conviction on indictment by a fine[1]. Defence of Part III planning permission available.★

[Wildlife and Countryside Act 1981, s 34, amended by the Local Government Act 1985, Sch 3, the Planning (Consequential Provisions) Act 1990, Sch 2, the Environmental Protection Act 1990, Schs 8 and 16 and the Local Government (Wales) Act 1994, Sch 16—summarised.]

★**Repealed in relation to Scotland by the Nature Conservation (Scotland) Act 2004, Sch 7.**

1. For procedure in respect of this offence which is triable either way, see Magistrates' Courts Act 1980 ss 17A–21 in PART I: MAGISTRATES' COURTS, PROCEDURE, ante.

8-4175 37. Byelaws for protection of marine nature reserves. Nature Conservancy Council may make byelaws[1] for the protection of area designated as marine nature reserve. Nothing in byelaws shall prohibit or restrict the exercise of any right of passage by a vessel other than a pleasure boat, or prohibit except with respect to particular parts of the reserve at particular times of the year, the exercise of right of passage by a pleasure boat, nor make unlawful anything done for the purpose of securing the safety of any vessel or of preventing damage to any vessel or cargo, or of saving life, nor the discharge of any substance from a vessel, nor anything done more than 30 metres below the sea bed. Local Government Act 1972, sections 236–238 apply with any modifications made by the Secretary of State. Consent of the Director of Public Prosecutions is necessary before proceedings for an offence under byelaws are taken by anyone other than the Nature Conservancy Council.
[Wildlife and Countryside Act 1981, s 37—summarised.]

1. SI 1986/143 modifies ss 236–238 of the Local Government Act 1972 in their application to byelaws made under this section for marine nature reserves.

8-4176 42. Notification of agricultural operations on moor and heath in National Parks. Agricultural and forestry operations on moor and heath in National Parks are subject to controls[1]; contravention is an offence triable either way.
[Wildlife and Countryside Act 1981, s 42, amended by the Local Government Act 1985, Sch 3 and the Environment Act 1995, Sch 10—summarised.]

1. See the Peak District National Park Authority (Restriction of Agricultural Operations) Order 2002, SI 2002/80.

8-4177 51. Powers of entry. (1) Any person authorised in writing by the relevant authority may, at any reasonable time and (if required to do so) upon producing evidence that he is authorised, enter any land for any of the following purposes—

(a) to determine whether the land should be notified under section 28(1);

(b) to assess the condition of the flora, fauna, or geological or physiographical features by reason of which land which has been notified under section 28(1) is of special interest;

(c) to determine whether or not to offer to enter into an agreement under section 16 of the 1949 Act or section 15 of the 1968 Act in relation to the land;

(d) to ascertain whether a condition to which a consent referred to in section 28E(3)(a) was subject has been complied with in relation to the land;

(e) to ascertain whether an offence under section 28P or under byelaws made by virtue of section 28R is being, or has been, committed on or in relation to the land;

(f) to formulate a management scheme for the land or determine whether a management scheme (or a proposed management scheme) for the land should be modified;

(g) to prepare a management notice for the land;

(h) to ascertain whether the terms of an agreement under section 16 of the 1949 Act or section 15 of the 1968 Act in relation to the land, or the terms of a management scheme or the requirements of a management notice in relation to the land, have been complied with;

(i) to determine whether or not to offer to make a payment under section 28M in relation to the land;

(j) to determine any question in relation to the acquisition of the land by agreement or compulsorily;

(k) to determine any question in relation to compensation under section 20(3) of the 1949 Act as applied by section 28R of this Act;

(l) to ascertain whether an order should be made in relation to the land under section 34 or if an offence under that section is being, or has been, committed on the land;

(m) to ascertain whether an order should be made in relation to the land under section 42 or if an offence under that section is being, or has been, committed on the land;]

(n) to determine whether or not to give or vary a stop notice;

but nothing in this subsection shall authorise any person to enter a dwelling.

(1A) The power conferred by subsection (1) to enter land for any purpose includes power to enter for the same purpose any land other than that referred to in subsection (1).

(1B) More than one person may be authorised for the time being under subsection (1) to enter any land.

(2) In subsection (1) "the relevant authority" means—

(a) for the purposes of paragraphs (a) to (k)* of that subsection, the Nature Conservancy Council;

(b) for the purposes of paragraph (l) of that subsection, the Secretary of State or the relevant authority within the meaning of section 34;

(c) for the purposes of paragraph (m) of that subsection, the Ministers or the National Park authority.

(3) A person shall not demand admission as of right to any land which is occupied unless either—

(a) 24 hours notice of the intended entry has been given to the occupier; or (*b*) the purpose of the entry is to ascertain if an offence under section 28P, 34 or 42 is being, or has been, committed on or (as the case may be) in relation to that land.

(3A) A person acting in the exercise of a power conferred by subsection (1) may—

(*a*) use a vehicle or a boat to enter the land;

(*b*) take a constable with him if he reasonably believes he is likely to be obstructed;

(*c*) take with him equipment and materials needed for the purpose for which he is exercising the power of entry;

(*d*) take samples of the land and of anything on it.

(3B) If in the exercise of a power conferred by subsection (1) a person enters land which is unoccupied or from which the occupier is temporarily absent, he must on his departure leave it as effectively secured against unauthorised entry as he found it.

(4) Any person who intentionally obstructs a person acting in the exercise of any power conferred by subsection (1) shall be liable on summary conviction to a fine not exceeding **level 3** on the standard scale.

(5) It is the duty of a relevant authority to compensate any person who has sustained damage as a result of—

(*a*) the exercise of a power conferred by subsection (1) by a person authorised to do so by that relevant authority, or

(*b*) the failure of a person so authorised to perform the duty imposed on him by subsection (3B),

except where the damage is attributable to the fault of the person who sustained it; and any dispute as to a person's entitlement to compensation under this subsection or as to its amount shall be referred to an arbitrator to be appointed, in default of agreement, by the Secretary of State.*

[Wildlife and Countryside Act 1981, s 51 as amended by the Criminal Justice Act 1982, s 46, the Local Government Act 1985, Sch 3, the Environment Act 1995, Sch 10 and the Countryside and Rights of Way Act 2000, s 80.]

---

*Repealed in relation to Scotland by the Nature Conservation (Scotland) Act 2004, Sch 6.

PART III[1]
PUBLIC RIGHTS OF WAY

Miscellaneous and supplemental

8–4178   59. Prohibition on keeping bulls on land crossed by public rights of way.   (1) If, in a case not falling within subsection (2), the occupier of a field or enclosure crossed by a right of way to which this Part applies permits a bull to be at large in the field or enclosure, he shall be liable on summary conviction to a fine not exceeding **level 3** on the standard scale.

(2) Subsection (1) shall not apply to any bull which—

(*a*) does not exceed the age of ten months; or

(*b*) is not a recognised dairy breed and is at large in any field or enclosure in which cows or heifers are also at large.

(3) Nothing in any byelaws, whenever made, shall make unlawful any act which is, or but for subsection (2) would be, made unlawful by subsection (1).

(4) In this section "recognised dairy breed" means one of the following breeds, namely, Ayrshire, British Friesian, British Holstein, Dairy Shorthorn, Guernsey, Jersey and Kerry.

(5) The Secretary of State may by order add any breed to, or remove any breed from, subsection (4); and an order under this subsection shall be made by statutory instrument which shall be subject to annulment in pursuance of a resolution of either House of Parliament.

[Wildlife and Countryside Act 1981, s 59 as amended by the Criminal Justice Act, 1982, s 46.]

---

1. PART III contains ss 53–66.

8–4180   66. Interpretation of Part III.   (1) In this Part—

"bridleway" means a highway over which the public have the following, but no other, rights of way, that is to say, a right of way on foot and a right of way on horseback or leading a horse, with or without a right to drive animals of any description along the highway;

"byway open to all traffic" means a highway over which the public have a right of way for vehicular and all other kinds of traffic, but which is used by the public mainly for the purpose for which footpaths and bridleways are so used[1];

"definitive map and statement" has the meaning given by section 53(1);

"footpath" means a highway over which the public have a right of way on foot only, other than such a highway at the side of a public road;

"horse" includes a pony, ass and mule, and "horseback" shall be construed accordingly;

"public path" means a highway being either a footpath or a bridleway;

"right of way to which this Part applies" means a right of way such that the land over which the right subsists is a public path or a byway open to all traffic;

"surveying authority", in relation to any area, means the county council, county borough council, metropolitan district council or London borough council whose area includes that area.

(2) A highway at the side of a river, canal or other inland navigation shall not be excluded from any definition contained in subsection (1) by reason only that the public have a right to use the highway for purposes of navigation, if the highway would fall within that definition if the public had no such right thereover.

(3) The provisions of section 30(1) of the 1968 Act (riding of pedal cycles on bridleways) shall not affect the definition of bridleway in subsection (1) and any rights exercisable by virtue of those provisions shall be disregarded for the purposes of this Part.
[Wildlife and Countryside Act 1981, s 66 as amended by the Local Government Act 1985, Sch 3 and the Local Government (Wales) Act 1994, Sch 16.]

---

1. The intention behind this definition is to distinguish byways from ordinary roads. The definition refers to a type of highway and does not limit byways to those which are currently and actually used in the way s 66(1) describes. The purpose of Part III of the Act is to ascertain and preserve public rights of way giving access to the countryside for walkers and horseriders. The intention is that the way be shown on the definitive map so that, if no current use is being made of the way, ramblers and horseriders will come to know of its existence and start to use it, *Masters v Secretary of State for the Environment* [2000] 4 All ER 458, [2000] 3 WLR 1894, CA.

PART IV[1]
MISCELLANEOUS AND GENERAL

8–4181   67. *Application to Crown.*

---

1. PART IV contains ss 67–74.

8–4182   68. *Application to the Isles of Scilly*[1].

---

1. See also the Wildlife and Countryside (Isles of Scilly) Order 1983, SI 1983/512 amended by SI 2001/1805.

8–4183   69. Offences by bodies corporate etc.   (1) Where a body corporate is guilty of an offence under this Act and that offence is proved to have been committed with the consent or connivance of, or to be attributable to any neglect on the part of, any director, manager, secretary or other similar officer of the body corporate or any person who was purporting to act in any such capacity he, as well as the body corporate, shall be guilty of that offence and shall be liable to be proceeded against and punished accordingly.

(2) Where the affairs of a body corporate are managed by its members subsection (1) shall apply in relation to the acts and defaults of a member in connection with his functions of management as if he were a director of the body corporate.
[Wildlife and Countryside Act 1981, s 69.]

8–4184   71. General interpretation.   In this Act—

"the 1949 Act" means the National Parks and Access to the Countryside Act 1949;
"the 1968 Act" means the Countryside Act 1968;
"the Broads" has the same meaning as in the Norfolk and Suffolk Broads Act 1988;
"the commencement date", in relation to any provision of this Act and any area, means the date of the coming into force of that provision in that area;
"London borough council" includes the Common Council of the City of London;
"modifications" includes additions, alterations and omissions, and cognate expressions shall be construed accordingly;
[Wildlife and Countryside Act 1981, s 71 as amended by the Norfolk and Suffolk Broads Act 1988, Sch 3 and the Statute Law (Repeals) Act 1993, Sch 1.]

8–4185   74. Short title, commencement and extent.   (1) This Act may be cited as the Wildlife and Countryside Act 1981.

(2) The following provisions of this Act, namely—

Part II, except sections 29 to 32, 41 and 46 to 48 and Schedule 13;
sections 59 to 62 and 65 and 66; and
Part IV, except section 72(4), (6) and (14) and section 73(1) so far as relating to Part II of Schedule 17,

shall come into force on the expiration of the period of one month beginning with the passing of this Act.

(3) The remaining provisions of this Act shall come into force on such day as the Secretary of State may by order made by statutory instrument appoint and different days may be appointed under this subsection for different provisions, different purposes or different areas.

(4) An order under subsection (3) may make such transitional provision as appears to the Secretary of State to be necessary or expedient in connection with the provisions thereby brought into force.

(5) The following provisions of this Act, namely—

sections 39, 40 and 42 to 49 and Schedule 13; and Part III,

do not extend to Scotland.

(5A) *Repealed by the Nature Conservation (Scotland) Act 2004, Sch 7.*

(6) This Act, except section 15(1) and Schedule 10 and, so far as regards any enactment mentioned in Schedule 17 that so extends, section 73 and that Schedule, does not extend to Northern Ireland.

[Wildlife and Countryside Act 1981, s 74, as amended by the Countryside and Rights of Way Act 2000, Sch 10.]

8–4186

SCHEDULES*

Sections 1, 2, 4, 6, 19 and 22   SCHEDULE 1

BIRDS WHICH ARE PROTECTED BY SPECIAL PENALTIES

(Amended by SI 2001/337.)

---

*Schedules A1 and 1A inserted in relation to Scotland by the Nature Conservation (Scotland) Act 2004, Sch 6.

PART I
AT ALL TIMES

Common name	*Scientific name*
Avocet	Recurvirostra avosetta
Bee-eater	Merops apiaster
Bittern	Botaurus stellaris
Bittern, Little	Ixobrychus minutus
Bluethroat	Luscinia svecica
Brambling	Fringilla montifringilla
Bunting, Cirl	Emberiza cirlus
Bunting, Lapland	Calcarius lapponicus
Bunting, Snow	Plectrophenax nivalis
Buzzard, Honey	Pernis apivorus
Capercaillie	Tetrao urogallus
Chough	Pyrrhocorax pyrrhocorax
Corncrake	Crex crex
Crake, Spotted	Porzana porzana
Crossbills (all species)	Loxia
Curlew, Stone	Burhinus oedicnemus
Divers (all species)	Gavia
Dotterel	Charadrius morinellus
Duck, Long-tailed	Clangula hyemalis
Eagle, Golden	Aquila chrysaetos
Eagle, White-tailed	Haliaetus albicilla
Falcon, Gyr	Falco rusticolus
Fieldfare	Turdus pilaris
Firecrest	Regulus ignicapillus
Garganey	Anas querquedula
Godwit, Black-tailed	Limosa limosa
Goshawk	Accipiter gentilis
Grebe, Black-necked	Podiceps nigricollis
Grebe, Slavonian	Podiceps auritus
Greenshank	Tringa nebularia
Gull, Little	Larus minutus
Gull, Mediterranean	Larus melanocephalus
Harriers (all species)	Circus
Heron, Purple	Ardea purpurea
Hobby	Falco subbuteo
Hoopoe	Upupa epops
Kingfisher	Alcedo atthis
Kite, Red	Milvus milvus
Merlin	Falco columbarius
Oriole, Golden	Oriolus oriolus
Osprey	Pandion haliaetus
Owl, Barn	Tyto alba
Owl, Snowy	Nyctea scandiaca
Peregrine	Falco peregrinus
Petrel, Leach's	Oceanodroma leucorhoa
Phalarope, Red-necked	Phalaropus lobatus
Plover, Kentish	Charadrius alexandrinus
Plover, Little Ringed	Charadrius dubius
Quail, Common	Coturnix coturnix
Redstart, Black	Phoenicurus ochruros

Common name	Scientific name
Redwing	Turdus iliacus
Rosefinch, Scarlet	Carpodacus erythrinus
Ruff	Philomachus pugnax
Sandpiper, Green	Tringa ochropus
Sandpiper, Purple	Calidris maritima
Sandpiper, Wood	Tringa glareola
Scaup	Aythya marila
Scoter, Common	Melanitta nigra
Scoter, Velvet	Melanitta fusca
Serin	Serinus serinus
Shorelark	Eremophila alpestris
Shrike, Red-backed	Lanius collurio
Spoonbill	Platalea leucorodia
Stilt, Black-winged	Himantopus himantopus
Stint, Temminck's	Calidris temminckii
Swan, Bewick's	Cygnus bewickii
Swan, Whooper	Cygnus cygnus
Tern, Black	Chlidonias niger
Tern, Little	Sterna albifrons
Tern, Roseate	Sterna dougallii
Tit, Bearded	Panurus biarmicus
Tit, Crested	Parus cristatus
Treecreeper, Short-toed	Certhia brachydactyla
Warbler, Cetti's	Cettia cetti
Warbler, Dartford	Sylvia undata
Warbler, Marsh	Acrocephalus palustris
Warbler, Savi's	Locustella luscinioides
Whimbrel	Numenius phaeopus
Woodlark	Lullula arborea
Wryneck	Jynx torquilla
Common name	**Scientific name**

PART II
DURING THE CLOSE SEASON

Common name	Scientific name
Goldeneye	Bucephala clangula
Goose, Greylag (in Outer, Hebrides, Caithness, Sutherland and Wester	Anser anser
Ross only) Pintail	Anas acuta

NOTE. The common name or names given in the first column of this Schedule are included by way of guidance only; in the event of any dispute or proceedings, the common name or names shall not be taken into account.★

8–4187

Sections 2, 3, and 22

SCHEDULE 2
BIRDS WHICH MAY BE KILLED OR TAKEN

(Amended by SI 1992/3010.)

PART I
OUTSIDE THE CLOSE SEASON

Common name	Scientific name
Capercaillie	Tetrao urogallus★
Coot	Fulica atra
Duck, Tufted	Aythya fuligula
Gadwall	Anas strepera
Goldeneye	Bucephala clangula
Goose, Canada	Branta canadensis
Goose, Greylag	Anser anser
Goose, Pink-footed	Anser brachyrhynchus
Goose, White-fronted (in England and Wales only)	Anser albifrons
Mallard	Anas platyrhynchos
Moorhen	Gallinula chloropus
Pintail	Anas acuta
Plover, Golden	Pluvialis apricaria
Pochard	Aythya ferina
Shoveler	Anas clypeata
Snipe, Common	Gallinago gallinago
Teal	Anas crecca
Wigeon	Anas penelope
Woodcock	Scolopax rusticola

★Repealed in realation to Scotland by SSI 2001/337, reg 2.

PART II

By Authorised Persons at all Times

Repealed

NOTE. The common name or names given in the first column of this Schedule are included by way of guidance only; in the event of any dispute or proceedings, the common name or names shall not be taken into account.

8–4188

Sections 6 and 22

SCHEDULE 3

Birds which may be Sold

(*Amended by SI 1992/3010.*)

PART I

Alive at all Times if Ringed and Bred in Captivity

Common name	Scientific name
Blackbird	Turdus merula
Brambling	Fringilla montifringilla
Bullfinch	Pyrrhula pyrrhula
Bunting, Reed	Emberiza schoeniclus
Chaffinch	Fringilla coelebs
Dunnock	Prunella modularis
Goldfinch	Carduelis carduelis
Greenfinch	Carduelis chloris
Jackdaw	Corvus monedula
Jay	Garrulus glandarius
Linnet	Carduelis cannabina
Magpie	Pica pica
Owl; Barn	Tyto alba
Redpoll	Carduelis flammea
Siskin	Carduelis spinus
Starling	Sturnus vulgaris
Thrush, Song	Turdus philomelos
Twite	Carduelis flavirostris
Yellowhammer	Emberiza citrinella

PART II

Dead at all Times

Common name	Scientific name
Woodpigeon	Columba palumbus

PART III

Dead from 1st September to 28th February

Common name	Scientific name
Capercaillie	Tetrao urogallus*
Coot	Fulica atra
Duck, Tufted	Aythya fuligula
Mallard	Anas platyrhynchos
Pintail	Anas acuta
Plover, Golden	Pluvialis apricaria
Pochard	Aythya ferina
Shoveler	Anas clypeata
Snipe, Common	Gallinago gallinago
Teal	Anas crecca
Wigeon	Anas penelope
Woodcock	Scolopax rusticola

NOTE. The common name or names given in the first column of this Schedule are included by way of guidance only; in the event of any dispute or proceedings, the common name or names shall not be taken into account.

_____

*Repealed in relation to Scotland by SSI 2001/337, reg 2.

8–4189

Sections 7 and 22

SCHEDULE 4

Birds Which Must Be Registered and Ringed if Kept in Captivity

(*As amended by SI 1994/1151.*)

Common name	Scientific name
Bunting, Cirl	Emberiza cirlus
Bunting, Lapland	Calcarius lapponicus
Bunting, Snow	Plectrophenax nivalis
Buzzard, Honey	Pernis apivorus
Eagle, Adalbert's	Aquila adalberti
Eagle, Golden	Aquila chrysaetos

Common name	Scientific name
Eagle, Great Philippine	Pithecophaga jefferyi
Eagle, Imperial	Aquila heliaca
Eagle, New Guinea	Harpyopsis novaeguineae
Eagle, White-tailed	Haliaeetus albicilla
Chough	Pyrrhocorax pyrrhocorax
Crossbills (all species)	Loxia spp
Falcon, Barbary	Falco pelegrinoides
Falcon, Gyr	Falco rusticolus
Falcon, Peregrine	Falco peregrinus
Fieldfare	Turdus pilaris
Firecrest	Regulus ignicapillus
Fish-Eagle, Madagascar	Haliaeetus vociferoides
Forest-Falcon, Plumbeous	Micrastur plumbeus
Goshawk	Accipiter gentilis
Harrier, Hen	Circus cyaneus
Harrier, Marsh	Circus aeruginosus
Harrier, Montagu's	Circus pygargus
Hawk, Galapagos	Buteo galapagoensis
Hawk, Grey-backed	Leucopternis occidentalis
Hawk, Hawaiian	Buteo solitarius
Hawk, Ridgway's	Buteo ridgwayi
Hawk, White-necked	Leucopternis lacernulata
Hawk-Eagle, Wallace's	Spizaetus nanus
Hobby	Falco subbuteo
Honey-Buzzard, Black	Henicopernis infuscatus
Kestrel, Lesser	Falco naumanni
Kestrel, Mauritius	Falco punctatus
Kite, Red	Milvus milvus
Merlin	Falco columbarius
Oriole, Golden	Oriolus oriolus
Osprey	Pandion haliaetus
Redstart, Black	Phoenicurus ochruros
Redwing	Turdus iliacus
Sea-Eagle, Pallas'	Haliaeetus leucoryphus
Sea-Eagle, Steller's	Haliaeetus pelagicus
Serin	Serinus serinus
Serpent-Eagle, Andaman	Spilornis elgini
Serpent-Eagle, Madagascar	Eutriorchis astur
Serpent-Eagle, Mountain	Spilornis kinabaluensis
Shorelark	Eremophila alpestris
Shrike, Red-backed	Lanius collurio
Sparrowhawk, New Britain	Accipiter brachyurus
Sparrowhawk, Gundlach's	Accipiter gundlachi
Sparrowhawk, Imitator	Accipiter imitator
Sparrowhawk, Small	Accipiter nanus
Tit, Bearded	Panurus biarmicus
Tit, Crested	Parus cristatus
Warbler, Cetti's	Cettia cetti
Warbler, Dartford	Sylvia undata
Warbler, Marsh	Acrocephalus palustris
Warbler, Savi's	Locustella luscinioides
Woodlark	Lullula arborea
Wryneck	Jynx torquilla

Any bird one of whose parents or other lineal ancestor was a bird of a kind specified in the foregoing provisions of this Schedule.

NOTE. The common name or names given in the first column of this Schedule are included by way of guidance only; in the event of any dispute or proceedings, the common name or names shall not be taken into account.

8–4200

Sections 9, 10, 22 and 24   SCHEDULE 5
ANIMALS WHICH ARE PROTECTED

(As amended by SI 1988/288, SI 1989/906, SI 1991/367, SI 1992/2350 and SI 1998/878.)

Common name	Scientific name
Adder (in respect of section 9(1)(in part), 9(5) only)	Vipera berus
Allis shad (in respect of section 9(1) and (4)(a) only)	Alosa alosa
Atlantic Stream Crayfish (in respect of section 9(1) (in part), (5), only)	Austropotomobius pallipes
Anemone, Ivell's Sea	Edwardsia ivelli
Anemone, Startlet Sea	Nematosella vectensis
Apus	Triops cancriformis
Bats, Horseshoe (all species)	Rhinolophidae
Bats, Typical (all species)	Vespertilionidae
Beetle	Graphoderus zonatus

Common name	Scientific name
Beetle	Hypebaeus flavipes
Beetle	Paracymus aeneus
Beetle, Lesser Silver Water	Hydrochara caraboides
Beetle, Mire Pill (in respect of section 9(4)(a) only)	Curimopsis nigrita
Beetle, Rainbow Leaf	Chrysolina cerealis
Beetle, Stag (in respect of section 9(5) only)	Lucanus cervus
Beetle, Violet Click	Limoniscus violaceus
Burbot	Lota Lota
Butterfly, Heath Fritillary	Mellicta athalia (otherwise known as Melitaea athalia)
Butterfly, Large Blue	Maculinea arion
Butterfly, Swallowtail	Papilio machaon
Butterfly, Northern Brown Argus	Aricia artaxerxes
Butterfly, Adonis Blue	Lysandra bellargus
Butterfly, Chalkhill Blue	Lysandra coridon
Butterfly, Silver-studded Blue	Plebejus argus
Butterfly, Small Blue	Cupido minimus
Butterfly, Large Copper	Lycaena dispar
Butterfly, Purple Emperor	Apatura iris
Butterfly, Duke of Burgundy	Hamearis lucina
Butterfly, Glanville Fritillary	Melitaea cinxia
Butterfly, High Brown Fritillary	Argynnis adippe
Butterfly, Marsh Fritillary	Eurodryas aurinia
Butterfly, Pearl-bordered Fritillary	Boloria euphrosyne
Butterfly, Black Hairstreak	Strymonidia pruni
Butterfly, Brown Hairstreak	Thecla betulae
Butterfly, White Letter Hairstreak	Stymonida w-album
Butterfly, Large Heath	Coenonympha tullia
Butterfly, Mountain Ringlet	Erebia epiphron
Butterfly, Chequered Skipper	Carterocephalus palaemon
Butterfly, Lulworth Skipper	Thymelicus acteon
Butterfly, Silver Spotted Skipper	Hesperia comma
Butterfly, Large Tortoiseshell	Nymphalis polychloros
Butterfly, Wood White	Leptidea sinapis
Cat, Wild	Felis silvestris
Cicada, New Forest	Cicadetta montana
Cricket, Field	Gryllus campestris
Cricket, Mole	Gryllotalpa gryllotalpa
Damselfly, Southern	Coenagrion mercuriale
Dolphin, Bottle-nosed	Tursiops truncatus (otherwise known as Tursiops tursio)
Dolphin, Common	Delphinus delphis
Dolphins (all species)	Cetacea
Dormouse	Muscardinus avellanarius
Dragonfly, Norfolk Aeshna	Aeshna isosceles
Frog, Common (in respect of section 9(5) only)	Rana temporaria
Goby, Couch's	Gobius couchii
Goby, Giant	Gobius cobitis
Grasshopper, Wart-biter	Decticus verrucivorus
Hatchet Shell, Northern	Thyasira gouldi
Hydroid, Marine	Clavopsella navis
Lagoon Snail	Paludinella littorina
Lagoon Snail, De Folin's	Caecum armoricum
Lagoon Worm, Tentacled	Alkmaria romijni
Leech, Medicinal	Hirudo medicinalis
Lizard, Sand	Lacerta agilis
Lizard, Viviparous (in respect of section 9(1) (in part), (5) only)	Lacerta vivipara
Marten, Pine	Martes martes
Mat, Trembling Sea	Victorella pavida
Moth, Barberry Carpet	Pareulype berberata
Moth, Black-veined	Siona lineata (otherwise known as Idaea lineata)
Moth, Essex Emerald	Thetidia smaragdaria
Moth, Fiery Clearwing	Bembecia chrysidiformis
Moth, Fisher's Estuarine	Gortyna borelii
Moth, New Forest Burnet	Zygaena viciae
Moth, Reddish Buff	Acosmetia caliginosa
Moth, Sussex Emerald	Thalera fimbrialis
Mussel, Fan (in respect of section 9(1), (2) and (5) only)	Atrina fragilis
Mussel, Freshwater Pearl	Margaritifera margaritifera
Newt, Great Crested (otherwise known as Warty newt)	Triturus cristatus
Newt, Palmate (in respect of section 9(5) only)	Triturus helveticus
Newt, Smooth (in respect of section 9(5) only)	Triturus vulgaris
Otter, Common	Lutra lutra

Common name	Scientific name
Porpoises (all species)	Phocaena phocaena
Sandworm, Lagoon	Armandia cirrhosa
Sea Fan, Pink (in respect of section 9(1), 9(2) and 9(5) only)	Eunicella verrucosa
Sea Slug, Lagoon	Tenellia adspersa
Shad, Twaite (in respect of section 9(4)(*a*) only)	Alosa fallax
Shark, Basking	Cetorhinus maximus
Shrimp, Fairy	Chiroephalus diaphanus
Shrimp, Lagoon Sand	Gammarus insensibilis
Slow-worm (in respect of section 9(1) (in part), (5), only)	Anguis fragilis
Snail, Glutinous	Myxas glutinosa
Snail, Sandbowl	Catinella arenaria
Snake, Grass (in respect of section 9(1) (in part), (5) only)	Natrix helvetica
Snake, Smooth	Coronella austriaca
Spider, Fen Raft	Dolomedes plantarius
Spider, Ladybird	Eresus niger
Squirrel, Red	Sciurus vulgaris
Sturgeon	Acipenser sturio
Toad, Common (in respect of section 9(5) only)	Bufo bufo
Toad, Natterjack	Bufo calamita
Turtles, Marine (all species)	Dermochelyidae and Cheloniidae
Vendace	Coregonus albula
Vole, Water (in respect of section 9(4) only)	Arvicola terrestris
Walrus	Odobenus rosmarus
Whale (all species)	Cetacea
Whitefish	Coregonus lavaretus

NOTE. The common name or names given in the first column of this Schedule are included by way of guidance only; in the event of any dispute or proceedings, the common name or names shall not be taken into account.

8–4201

Sections 11 and 22   SCHEDULE 6

ANIMALS WHICH MAY NOT BE KILLED OR TAKEN BY CERTAIN METHODS

Common name	Scientific name
Badger	Meles meles
Bats, Horseshoe (all species)	Rhinolophidae
Bats, Typical (all species)	Vespertilionidae
Cat, Wild	Felis silvestris
Dolphin, Bottle-nosed	Tursiops truncatus (otherwise known as Tursiops tursio)
Dolphin, Common	Delphinus delphis
Dormice (all species)	Gliridae
Hedgehog	Erinaceus europaeus
Marten, Pine	Martes martes
Otter, Common	Lutra lutra
Polecat	Mustela putorius
Porpoise, Harbour (otherwise known as Common porpoise)	Phocaena phocaena
Shrews (all species)	Soricidae
Squirrel, Red	Sciurus vulgaris

NOTE. The common name or names given in the first column of this Schedule are included by way of guidance only; in the event of any dispute or proceedings, the common name or names shall not be taken into account.

8–4202

Sections 13, 22 and 24   SCHEDULE 8

PLANTS WHICH ARE PROTECTED

(As amended by SI 1988/288, SI 1992/2350 and SI 1998/878.)

Common name	Scientific name
Adder's-tongue, Least	Ophioglossum lusitanicum
Alison, Small	Alyssum alyssoides
Anomodon, Long-leaved	Anomodon longifolius
Beech-lichen, New Forest	Enterographa elaborata
Blackwort	Southbya nigrella
Bluebell (in respect of section 13(2) only)	Hyacinthoides non-scripta
Bolete, Royal	Boletus regius
Broomrape, Bedstraw	Orobanche caryophyllacea
Broomrape, Oxtongue	Orobanche loricata
Broomrape, Thistle	Orobanche reticulata
Cabbage, Lundy	Rhynchosinapis wrightii
Calamint, Wood	Calamintha sylvatica

Common name	Scientific name
Caloplaca, Snow	Caloplaca nivalis
Catapyrenium, Tree	Catapyrenium psoromoides
Catchfly, Alpine	Lychnis alpina
Catillaria, Laurer's	Catellaria laureri
Centaury, Slender	Centaurium tenuiflorum
Cinquefoil, Rock	Potentilla rupestris
Cladonia, Convoluted	Cladonia convoluta
Cladonia, Upright Mountain	Cladonia stricta
Clary, Meadow	Salvia pratensis
Club-rush, Triangular	Scirpus triquetrus
Colt's-foot, Purple	Homogyne alpina
Cotoneaster, Wild	Cotoneaster integerrimus
Cottongrass, Slender	Eriophorum gracile
Cow-wheat, Field	Melampyrum arvense
Crocus, Sand	Romulea columnae
Crystalwort, Lizard	Riccia bifurca
Cudweed, Broad-leaved	Filago pyramidata
Cudweed, Jersey	Gnaphalium luteoalbum
Cudweed, Red-tipped	Fiago lutesoens
Cut-grass	Leersia oryzoides
Deptford Pink (in respect of England and Wales only)	Dianthus armeria
Diapensia	Diapensia lapponica
Dock, Shore	Rumex rupestrls
Earwort, Marsh	Jamesoniella undulifolia
Eryngo, Field	Eryngium campestre
Feather-moss, Polar	Hygrohypnum polare
Fern, Dickie's Bladder	Cystopteris dickieana
Fern, Killarney	Trichomanes speciosum
Flapwort, Norfolk	Leiocolea rutheana
Fleabane, Alpine	Erigeron borealis
Fleabane, Small	Pulicaria vulgaris
Frostwort, Pointed	Gymnomitrion apiculatum
Fungus, Hedgehog	Hericium erinaceum
Galingale, Brown	Cyperus fuscus
Gentian, Alpine	Gentiana nivalis
Gentian, Dune	Gentianella uliginosa
Gentian, Early	Gentianella anglica
Gentian, Fringed	Gentianella ciliata
Gentian, Spring	Gentiana verna
Germander, Cut-leaved	Tevarium botrys
Germander, Water	Teucrium scordium
Gladiolus, Wild	Gladiolus illyricus
Goblin Lights	Catolechia wahlenbergii
Goosefoot, Stinking	Chenopodium vulvaria
Grass-poly	Lythrum hyssopifolia
Grimmia, Blunt-leaved	Grimmia unicolor
Gyalecta, Elm	Gyalecta ulmi
Hare's-ear, Sickle-leaved	Bupleurum falcatum
Hare's-ear, Small	Bupleurum baldense
Hawk's-bead, Stinking	Crepis foetida
Hawkweed, Northroe	Hieracium northroense
Hawkweed, Shetland	Hieracium zetlandicum
Hawkweed, Weak-leaved	Hieracium attenuatifolium
Heath, Blue	Phyllodoce caerulea
Helleborine, Red	Cephalanthera rubra
Helleborine, Young's	Epipactis youngiana
Horsetail, Branched	Equisetum ramosissimum
Hound's-tongue, Green	Cynoglossum germanicum
Knawel, Perennial	Scleranthus perennis
Knotgrass, Sea	Polygonum maritimum
Lady's-slipper	Cypripedium calceolus
Lecanactis, Churchyard	Lecanactis hemisphaerica
Lecanora, Tarn	Lecanora archariana
Lecidea, Copper	Lecidea inops
Leek, Round-headed	Allium sphaerocephalon
Lettuce, Least	Lactuca saligna
Lichen, Arctic Kidney	Nephroma arcticum
Lichen, Ciliate Strap	Heterodermia leucomelos
Lichen, Coralloid Rosette	Heterodermia propagulifera
Lichen, Ear-lobed Dog	Peltigera lepidophora
Lichen, Forked Hair	Bryoria furcellata
Lichen, Golden Hair	Teloschistes flavicans
Lichen, Orange Fruited Elm	Caloplaca luteoalba
Lichen, River Jelly	Collema dichotomum

Common name	Scientific name
Lichen, Scaly Breck	Squamarina lentigera
Lichen, Stary Breck	Buellia asterella
Lily, Snowdon	Lloydia serotina
Liverwort	Petallophyllum ralfsi
Liverwort, Lindenberg's Leafy	Adelanthus lindenbergianus
Marsh-mallow, Rough	Althaea hirsuta
Marshwort, Creeping	Apium repens
Milk-parsley, Cambridge	Selinum carvifolia
Moss	Drepanocladius vernicosus
Moss, Alpine Copper	Mielichoferia mielichoferi
Moss, Baltic Bog	Sphagnum balticum
Moss, Blue Dew	Saelania glaucescens
Moss, Blunt-leaved Bristle	Orthotrichum obtusifolium
Moss, Bright Green Cave	Cyclodictyon laetevirens
Moss, Cordate Beard	Barbula cordata
Moss, Cornish Path	Ditrichum cornubicum
Moss, Derbyshire Feather	Thamnobryum angustifolium
Moss, Dune Thread	Bryum mamillatum
Moss, Flamingo	Desmatodon cernuus
Moss, Glaucous Beard	Barbula glauca
Moss, Green Shield	Buxbaumia viridis
Moss, Hair Silk	Plagiothecium piliferum
Moss, Knothole	Zygodon forsteri
Moss, Large Yellow Feather	Scorpidium turgescens
Moss, Millimetre	Micromitrium tenerum
Moss, Multifruited River	Cryphaea lamyana
Moss, Nowell's Limestone	Zygodon gracilis
Moss, Rigid Apple	Bartramia stricta
Moss, Round-leaved Feather	Rhyncostegium rotundifolium
Moss, Schleicher's Thread	Bryum schleicheri
Moss, Triangular Pygmy	Acaulon triquetrum
Moss, Vaucher's Feather	Hypnum vaucheri
Mudwort, Welsh	Limosella australis
Naiad, Holly-leaved	Najas marina
Naiad, Slender	Najas flexilis
Orache, Stalked	Halimione pedunculata
Orchid, Early Spider	Ophrys sphegodes
Orchid, Fen	Liparis loeselii
Orchid, Ghost	Epipogium aphyllum
Orchid, Lapland Marsh	Dactylorhiza lapponica
Orchid, Late Spider	Ophrys fuciflora
Orchid, Lizard	Himantoglossum hircinum
Orchid, Military	Orchis militaris
Orchid, Monkey	Orchis simia
Pannaria, Caledonia	Pannaria ignobilis
Parmelia, New Forest	Parmelia minarum
Parmentaria, Oil Stain	Parmentaria chilensis
Pear, Plymouth	Pyrus cordata
Pennyroyal	Mentha pulegium
Penny-cress, Perfoliate	Thlaspi perfoliatum
Pertusaria, Alpine Moss	Pertusaria bryontha
Physcia, Southern Grey	Physcia tribacioides
Pigmyweed	Crassula aquatica
Pine, Ground	Ajuga chamaepitys
Pink, Cheddar	Dianthus gratianopolitanus
Pink, Childling	Petroraghia nanteuilii
Plantain, Floating Water	Luronium natans
Polypore, Oak	Buglossoporus pulvinus
Pseudocyphellaria, Ragged	Pseudocyphellaria lacerata
Psora, Rusty Alpine	Psora rubiformis
Puffball, Sandy Stilt	Battarraea phalloides
Ragwort, Fen	Senecio paludosus
Rampion, Spiked	Phyteuma spicatum
Ramping-fumitory, Martin's	Fumaria martinil
Restharrow, Small	Ononis reclinata
Rock-cress, Alpine	Arabis alpina
Rock-cress, Bristol	Arabis stricta
Rustworth, Western	Marsupella profunda
Sandwort, Norwegian	Arenaria norvegica
Sandwort, Teesdale	Minuartia stricta
Saxifrage, Drooping	Saxifraga cernua
Saxifrage, Marsh	Saxifraga hirulus
Saxifrage, Tufted	Saxifraga cespitosa
Solenopsora, Serpentine	Solenopsora lipinara
Solomon's-seal, Whorled	Polygonatum verticillatum

Common name	Scientific name
Sow-thistle, Alpine	Cicerbita alpina
Spearwort, Adder's-tongue	Ranunculus ophioglossifolius
Speedwell, Fingered	Veronica, triphyllas
Speedwell, Spiked	Veronica spicata
Spike-rush, Dwarf	Eleocharis parvula
Stack Fleawort, South	Tephroseris integrifolia (ssp maritima)
Star-of-Bethlehem, Early	Gagea betremica
Starfruit	Damasonium alisma
Stonewort, Bearded	Chara canescens
Stonewort, Foxtail	Lamprothamnium papulosum
Strapwort	Carrigiola litoralis
Sulphur-tresses, Alpine	Alectoria ochroleuca
Threadmoss, Long-leaved	Bryum neodamense
Turpswort	Geocalyx graveolens
Viper's-grass	Scorzonera humilis
Violet, Fen	Viola persicifolia
Water-plantain, Ribbon leaved	Alisma gramineum
Wood-sedge, Starved	Carex depauperata
Woodsia, Alpine	Woodsia alpina
Woodsia, Oblong	Woodsia ilvensis
Wormwood, Field	Artemisia campestris
Woundwort, Downy	Stachys germanica
Woundwort, Limestone	Stachys alpina
Yellow-rattle, Greater	Rhinanthus serotinus

NOTE. The common name or names given in the first column of this Schedule are included by way of guidance only; in the event of any dispute or proceedings, the common name or names shall not be taken into account.

8–4203

Sections 16 and 22

SCHEDULE 9
ANIMALS AND PLANTS TO WHICH SECTION 14 APPLIES

(*Amended by SI 1992/320, SI 1992/2674, SI 1997/226 and SI 1999/1002.*)

PART I
ANIMALS WHICH ARE ESTABLISHED IN THE WILD

8–4204

Common name	Scientific name
Bass, Large-mouthed Black	Micropterus salmoides
Bass, Rock	Ambloplites rupestris
Bitterling	Rhodeus sericeus
Budgerigar	Melopsittacus undulatus
Capercaillie	Tetrao urogallus
Coypu	Myocastor coypus
Crayfish, Noble	Astacus astacus
Crayfish, Signal	Pacifastacus leniusculus
Crayfish, Turkish	Astacus leptodactylus
Deer, any hybrid one of whose parents or other lineal ancestor was a Sika Deer	Any hybrid of Cervus nippon
With respect to the Outer Hebrides and the islands of Arran, Islay, Jura and Rum—	
(a) Deer, Cervus (all species)	Cervus
(b) Deer, any hybrid one of whose parents or other lineal ancestor was a species of Cervus Deer	Any hybrid of the genus Cervus
Deer, Muntjac	Muntiacus reevesi
Deer, Sika	Cervus nippon
Dormouse, Fat	Glis glis
Duck, Carolina Wood	Aix sponsa
Duck, Mandarin	Aix galericulata
Duck, Ruddy	Oxyura jamaicensis
Eagle, White-tailed	Haliaetus albicilla
Flatworm, New Zealand	Artiposthia triangulata
Frog, edible	Rana esculenta
Frog, European Tree (otherwise known as Common tree frog)	Hyla arborea
Frog, Marsh	Rana ridibunda
Gerbil, Mongolian	Meriones unguiculatus
Goose, Canada	Branta canadensis
Goose, Egyptian	Alopochen aegyptiacus
Heron, Night	Nycticorax nycticorax
Lizard, Common Wall	Podarcis muralis
Marmot, Prairie (otherwise known as Prairie Dog)	Cynomys
Mink, American	Mustela vison
Newt, Alpine	Triturus alpestris
Newt, Italian Crested	Triturus carnifex

Common name	Scientific name
Owl, Barn	Tyto alba
Parakeet, Ring-necked	Psittacula krameri
Partridge, Chukar	Alextoris chukar
Partridge, Rock	Alextoris graeca
Pheasant, Golden	Chrysolophus pictus
Pheasant, Lady Amherst's	Chrysolophus amherstiae
Pheasant, Reeves'	Syrmaticus reevesii
Pheasant, Silver	Lophura nycthemera
Porcupine, Crested	Hystrix cristata
Porcupine, Himalayan	Hystrix hodgsonii
Pumpkinseed (otherwise known as Sun-fish or Pond-perch)	Lepomis gibbosus
Quail, Bobwhite	Colinus virginianus
Rat, Black	Rattus rattus
Snake, Aesculapian	Elaphe longissima
Squirrel, Grey	Sciurus carolinensis
Terrapin, European Pond	Emys orbicularis
Toad, African Clawed	Xenopus laevis
Toad, Midwife	Alytes obstetricans
Toad, Yellow-bellied	Bombina variegata
Wallaby, Red-necked	Macropus rufogriseus
Wels (otherwise known as European catfish)	Silurus glanis
Zander	Stizostedion lucioperca

PART II

PLANTS

8–4205

Common name	Scientific name
Hogweed, Giant	Heracleum mantegazzianum
Kelp, Giant	Macrocystis pyrifera
Kelp, Giant	Macrocystis angustifolia
Kelp, Giant	Macrocystis integrifolia
Kelp, Giant	Macrocystis laevis
Kelp, Japanese	Laminaria japonica
Knotweed, Japanese	Polygonum cuspidatum
Seafingers, Green	Codium fragile tomentosoides
Seaweed, Californian Red	Pikea californica
Seaweed, Hooked Asparagus	Asparagopsis armata
Seaweed, Japanese	Sargassum muticum
Seaweeds, Laver (except native species)	Porphyra spp except—
	p. amethystea
	p. leucosticta
	p. linearis
	p.miniata
	p. purpurea
	p. umbilicalis
Wakame	Undaria pinnatifida.

NOTE. The common name or names given in the first column of this Schedule are included by way of guidance only; in the event of any dispute or proceedings, the common name or names shall not be taken into account.

Countryside and Rights of Way Act 2000[1]

(2000 c 37)

PART I[2]

ACCESS TO THE COUNTRYSIDE

CHAPTER I

RIGHT OF ACCESS

General

8–4206 **1. Principal definitions for Part I.** (1) In this Part "access land" means any land which—

(a) is shown as open country on a map in conclusive form issued by the appropriate countryside body for the purposes of this Part,

(b) is shown on such a map as registered common land,

(c) is registered common land in any area outside Inner London for which no such map relating to registered common land has been issued,

(d) is situated more than 600 metres above sea level in any area for which no such map relating to open country has been issued, or (*e*) is dedicated for the purposes of this Part under section 16,

but does not (in any of those cases) include excepted land or land which is treated by section 15(1) as being accessible to the public apart from this Act.

(2) In this Part—

"access authority"—

(*a*) in relation to land in a National Park, means the National Park authority, and

(*b*) in relation to any other land, means the local highway authority in whose area the land is situated;

"the appropriate countryside body" means—

(*a*) in relation to England, the Countryside Agency, and

(*b*) in relation to Wales, the Countryside Council for Wales;

"excepted land" means land which is for the time being of any of the descriptions specified in Part I of Schedule 1[3], those descriptions having effect subject to Part II of that Schedule;

"mountain" includes, subject to the following definition, any land situated more than 600 metres above sea level;

"mountain, moor, heath or down" does not include land which appears to the appropriate countryside body to consist of improved or semi-improved grassland;

"open country" means land which—

(*a*) appears to the appropriate countryside body to consist wholly or predominantly of mountain, moor, heath or down, and

(*b*) is not registered common land.

(3) In this Part "registered common land" means—

(*a*) land which is registered as common land under the Commons Registration Act 1965 (in this section referred to as "the 1965 Act") and whose registration under that Act has become final, or

(*b*) subject to subsection (4), land which fell within paragraph (*a*) on the day on which this Act is passed or at any time after that day but has subsequently ceased to be registered as common land under the 1965 Act on the register of common land in which it was included being amended by reason of the land having ceased to be common land within the meaning of that Act.

(4) Subsection (3)(*b*) does not apply where—

(*a*) the amendment of the register of common land was made in pursuance of an application made before the day on which this Act is passed, or

(*b*) the land ceased to be common land by reason of the exercise of—

(i) any power of compulsory purchase, of appropriation or of sale which is conferred by an enactment,

(ii) any power so conferred under which land may be made common land within the meaning of the 1965 Act in substitution for other land.

[Countryside and Rights of Way Act 2000, s 1.]

---

1. The Countryside and Rights of Way Act 2000 makes new provision fo public access to the countryside; amends the law relating to public rights of way; enables traffic regulation orders to be made for the purpose of conserving an area's natural beauty; makes provision with respect to the driving of mechanically-propelled vehicles elsewhere other than on roads; amends the law relating to nature conservation and the protection of wildlife, and makes further provision with respect to areas of outstanding natural beauty.

Only those provisions of the Act which are relevant to the work of magistrates' courts are included in this work. The Act is to be brought into force in accordance with s 103, below.

At the date of going to press, the following Commencement Orders had been made: Countryside and Rights of Way Act 2000 (Commencement No 1) Order 2001, SI 2001/114; Countryside and Rights of Way Act 2000 (Commencement No 1) (Wales) Order 2001, SI 2001/203; Countryside and Rights of Way Act 2000 (Commencement No 2) (Wales) Order 2001, SI 2001/1410; Countryside and Rights of Way Act 2000 (Commencement No 3) (Wales) Order 2002, SI 2002/2615; Countryside and Rights of Way Act 2000 (Commencement No 2) Order 2002, SI 2002/2833; Countryside and Rights of Way Act 2000 (Commencement No 3) Order 2003, SI 2003/272; and Countryside and Rights of Way Act 2000 (Commencement No. 4) Order 2004, SI 2004/292. However, some of the provisions reproduced below have not yet been brought into force.

2. Part II comprises ss 1 to 46.

3. See below.

8–4207 2. Rights of public in relation to access land*.   (1) Any person is entitled by virtue of this subsection to enter and remain on any access land for the purposes of open-air recreation, if and so long as—

(*a*) he does so without breaking or damaging any wall, fence, hedge, stile or gate, and

(*b*) he observes the general restrictions in Schedule 2[1] and any other restrictions imposed in relation to the land under Chapter II.

(2) Subsection (1) has effect subject to subsections (3) and (4) and to the provisions of Chapter II.

(3) Subsection (1) does not entitle a person to enter or be on any land, or do anything on any land, in contravention of any prohibition contained in or having effect under any enactment, other than an enactment contained in a local or private Act.

(4) If a person becomes a trespasser on any access land by failing to comply with—

(a) subsection (1)(a),
(b) the general restrictions in Schedule 2, or
(c) any other restrictions imposed in relation to the land under Chapter II,

he may not, within 72 hours after leaving that land, exercise his right under subsection (1) to enter that land again or to enter other land in the same ownership.

(5) In this section "owner", in relation to any land which is subject to a farm business tenancy within the meaning of the Agricultural Tenancies Act 1995 or a tenancy to which the Agricultural Holdings Act 1986 applies, means the tenant under that tenancy, and "ownership" shall be construed accordingly.

[Countryside and Rights of Way Act 2000, s 2.]

---

*At the date of going to press this section was not in force.
1. See below.

8–4208 3. Power to extend to coastal land. (1) The Secretary of State (as respects England) or the National Assembly for Wales (as respects Wales) may by order amend the definition of "open country" in section 1(2) so as to include a reference to coastal land or to coastal land of any description.

(2) An order under this section may—

(a) make consequential amendments of other provisions of this Part, and
(b) modify the provisions of this Part in their application to land which is open country merely because it is coastal land.

(3) In this section "coastal land" means—

(a) the foreshore, and
(b) land adjacent to the foreshore (including in particular any cliff, bank, barrier, dune, beach or flat which is adjacent to the foreshore).

[Countryside and Rights of Way Act 2000, s 3.]

Maps

8–4209 4. Duty to prepare maps. (1) It shall be the duty of the Countryside Agency to prepare, in respect of England outside Inner London, maps which together show—

(a) all registered common land, and
(b) all open country.

(2) It shall be the duty of the Countryside Council for Wales to prepare, in respect of Wales, maps which together show—

(a) all registered common land, and
(b) all open country.

(3) Subsections (1) and (2) have effect subject to the following provisions of this section and to the provisions of sections 5 to 9.

(4) A map prepared under this section must distinguish between open country and registered common land, but need not distinguish between different categories of open country.

(5) In preparing a map under this section, the appropriate countryside body—

(a) may determine not to show as open country areas of open country which are so small that the body consider that their inclusion would serve no useful purpose, and
(b) may determine that any boundary of an area of open country is to be treated as coinciding with a particular physical feature (whether the effect is to include other land as open country or to exclude part of an area of open country).

[Countryside and Rights of Way Act 2000, s 4.]

8–4210 5. *Publication of draft maps*

8–4211 6–7. *Appeal against map after confirmation; Appeal procedure*

8–4212 11. *Regulations relating to maps*[1]

---

1. The Access to the Countryside (Provisional and Conclusive Maps) (England) Regulations 2002, SI 2002/1710 amended by SI 2003/32, the Countryside Access (Provisional and conclusive Maps) (Wales) Regulations 2002,

SI 2002/1796 and the Countryside Access (Exclusion or Restriction of Access) (Wales) Regulations 2003, SI 2003/142 have been made.

Rights and liabilities of owners and occupiers

8–4213 14. Offence of displaying on access land notices deterring public use*. (1) If any person places or maintains—

    (a)   on or near any access land, or

    (b)   on or near a way leading to any access land,

a notice containing any false or misleading information likely to deter the public from exercising the right conferred by section 2(1), he is liable on summary conviction to a fine not exceeding **level 1** on the standard scale.

(2) The court before whom a person is convicted of an offence under subsection (1) may, in addition to or in substitution for the imposition of a fine, order him to remove the notice in respect of which he is convicted within such period, not being less than four days, as may be specified in the order.

(3) A person who fails to comply with an order under subsection (2) is guilty of a further offence and liable on summary conviction to a fine not exceeding **level 3** on the standard scale.
[Countryside and Rights of Way Act 2000, s 14.]

---

   *At the date of going to press this section was not in force.

Miscellaneous provisions relating to right of access

8–4214 17. Byelaws. (1) An access authority may, as respects access land in their area, make byelaws—

    (a)   for the preservation of order,

    (b)   for the prevention of damage to the land or anything on or in it, and

    (c)   for securing that persons exercising the right conferred by section 2(1) so behave themselves as to avoid undue interference with the enjoyment of the land by other persons.

(2) Byelaws under this section may relate to all the access land in the area of the access authority or only to particular land.

(3) Before making byelaws under this section, the access authority shall consult—

    (a)   the appropriate countryside body, and

    (b)   any local access forum established for an area to which the byelaws relate.

(4) Byelaws under this section shall not interfere—

    (a)   with the exercise of any public right of way,

    (b)   with any authority having under any enactment functions relating to the land to which the byelaws apply, or

    (c)   with the running of a telecommunications code system or the exercise of any right conferred by or in accordance with the telecommunications code on the running of any such system.*

(5) Sections 236 to 238 of the Local Government Act 1972 (which relate to the procedure for making byelaws, authorise byelaws to impose fines not exceeding level 2 on the standard scale, and provide for the proof of byelaws in legal proceedings) apply to all byelaws under this section whether or not the authority making them is a local authority within the meaning of that Act.

(6) The confirming authority in relation to byelaws made under this section is—

    (a)   as respects England, the Secretary of State, and

    (b)   as respects Wales, the National Assembly for Wales.

(7) Byelaws under this section relating to any land—

    (a)   may not be made unless the land is access land or the access authority are satisfied that it is likely to become access land, and

    (b)   may not be confirmed unless the land is access land.

(8) Any access authority having power under this section to make byelaws also have power to enforce byelaws made by them; and any county council or district or parish council may enforce byelaws made under this section by another authority as respects land in the area of the council.
[Countryside and Rights of Way Act 2000, s 17.]

---

   *Para graph 4(c) substituted by the Communications Act 2003, Sch 17, from a date to be appointed.

8–4215 18. Wardens*. (1) An access authority or a district council may appoint such number of persons as may appear to the authority making the appointment to be necessary or expedient, to act as wardens as respects access land in their area.

(2) As respects access land in an area for which there is a local access forum, an access authority

shall, before they first exercise the power under subsection (1) and thereafter from time to time, consult the local access forum about the exercise of that power.

(3) Wardens may be appointed under subsection (1) for the following purposes—

(a) to secure compliance with byelaws under section 17 and with the general restrictions in Schedule 2 and any other restrictions imposed under Chapter II,

(b) to enforce any exclusion imposed under Chapter II,

(c) in relation to the right conferred by section 2(1), to advise and assist the public and persons interested in access land,

(d) to perform such other duties (if any) in relation to access land as the authority appointing them may determine.

(4) For the purpose of exercising any function conferred on him by or under this section, a warden appointed under subsection (1) may enter upon any access land.

(5) A warden appointed under subsection (1) shall, if so required, produce evidence of his authority before entering any access land in the exercise of the power conferred by subsection (4), and shall also produce evidence of his authority while he remains on the access land, if so required by any person.

(6) Except as provided by subsection (4), this section does not authorise a warden appointed under subsection (1), on land in which any person other than the authority who appointed him has an interest, to do anything which apart from this section would be actionable at that person's suit by virtue of that interest.

[Countryside and Rights of Way Act 2000, s 18.]

---

*At the date of going to press this section was not in force.

8–4216 19. Notices indicating boundaries, etc. (1) An access authority may erect and maintain—

(a) notices indicating the boundaries of access land and excepted land, and

(b) notices informing the public of—

(i) the effect of the general restrictions in Schedule 2,

(ii) the exclusion or restriction under Chapter II of access by virtue of section 2(1) to any land, and

(iii) any other matters relating to access land or to access by virtue of section 2(1) which the access authority consider appropriate.

(2) In subsection (1)(b)(ii), the reference to the exclusion or restriction of access by virtue of section 2(1) is to be interpreted in accordance with section 21(2) and (3).

(3) Before erecting a notice on any land under subsection (1) the access authority shall, if reasonably practicable, consult the owner or occupier of the land.

(4) An access authority may also, as respects any access land in their area, defray or contribute towards, or undertake to defray or contribute towards, expenditure incurred or to be incurred in relation to the land by any person in displaying such notices as are mentioned in subsection (1)(a) and (b).

[Countryside and Rights of Way Act 2000, s 19.]

8–4217 20. Codes of conduct and other information*. (1) In relation to England, it shall be the duty of the Countryside Agency to issue, and from time to time revise, a code of conduct for the guidance of persons exercising the right conferred by section 2(1) and of persons interested in access land, and to take such other steps as appear to them expedient for securing—

(a) that the public are informed of the situation and extent of, and means of access to, access land, and

(b) that the public and persons interested in access land are informed of their respective rights and obligations—

(i) under this Part, and

(ii) with regard to public rights of way on, and nature conservation in relation to, access land.

(2) In relation to Wales, it shall be the duty of the Countryside Council for Wales to issue, and from time to time revise, a code of conduct for the guidance of persons exercising the right conferred by section 2(1) and of persons interested in access land, and to take such other steps as appear to them expedient for securing the results mentioned in paragraphs (a) and (b) of subsection (1).

(3) A code of conduct issued by the Countryside Agency or the Countryside Council for Wales may include provisions in pursuance of subsection (1) or (2) and in pursuance of section 86(1) of the National Parks and Access to the Countryside Act 1949.

(4) The powers conferred by subsections (1) and (2) include power to contribute towards expenses incurred by other persons.

[Countryside and Rights of Way Act 2000, s 20.]

---

*At the date of going to press this section was not in force.

CHAPTER II
EXCLUSION OR RESTRICTION OF ACCESS

CHAPTER III
MEANS OF ACCESS

8–4218   34. Interpretation of Chapter III.   In this Chapter—

"access land" does not include any land in relation to which the application of section 2(1) has been excluded under any provision of Chapter II either indefinitely or for a specified period of which at least six months remain unexpired;

"means of access", in relation to land, means—

   (a)   any opening in a wall, fence or hedge bounding the land (or part of the land), with or without a gate, stile or other works for regulating passage through the opening,

   (b)   any stairs or steps for enabling persons to enter on the land (or part of the land), or

   (c)   any bridge, stepping stone or other works for crossing a watercourse, ditch or bog on the land or adjoining the boundary of the land.

[Countryside and Rights of Way Act 2000, s 34.]

8–4219   35. Agreements with respect to means of access.   (1) Where, in respect of any access land, it appears to the access authority that—

   (a)   the opening-up, improvement or repair of any means of access to the land,

   (b)   the construction of any new means of access to the land,

   (c)   the maintenance of any means of access to the land, or

   (d)   the imposition of restrictions—

      (i)   on the destruction, removal, alteration or stopping-up of any means of access to the land, or

      (ii)   on the doing of any thing whereby the use of any such means of access to the land by the public would be impeded,

is necessary for giving the public reasonable access to that land in exercise of the right conferred by section 2(1), the access authority may enter into an agreement with the owner or occupier of the land as to the carrying out of the works or the imposition of the restrictions.

   (2) An agreement under this section may provide—

   (a)   for the carrying out of works by the owner or occupier or by the access authority, and

   (b)   for the making of payments by the access authority—

      (i)   as a contribution towards, or for the purpose of defraying, costs incurred by the owner or occupier in carrying out any works for which the agreement provides, or

      (ii)   in consideration of the imposition of any restriction.

[Countryside and Rights of Way Act 2000, s 35.]

8–4220   36. Failure to comply with agreement.   (1) If the owner or occupier of any access land fails to carry out within the required time any works which he is required by an agreement under section 35 to carry out, the access authority, after giving not less than twenty-one days' notice of their intention to do so, may take all necessary steps for carrying out those works.

   (2) In subsection (1) "the required time" means the time specified in, or determined in accordance with, the agreement as that within which the works must be carried out or, if there is no such time, means a reasonable time.

   (3) If the owner or occupier of any access land fails to observe any restriction which he is required by an agreement under section 35 to observe, the access authority may give him a notice requiring him within a specified period of not less than twenty-one days to carry out such works as may be specified in the notice, for the purpose of remedying the failure to observe the restriction.

   (4) A notice under subsection (3) must contain particulars of the right of appeal conferred by section 38.

   (5) If the person to whom a notice under subsection (3) is given fails to comply with the notice, the access authority may take all necessary steps for carrying out any works specified in the notice.

   (6) Where the access authority carry out any works by virtue of subsection (1), the authority may recover the amount of any expenses reasonably incurred by them in carrying out the works, reduced by their contribution under the agreement, from the person by whom under the agreement the cost (apart from the authority's contribution) of carrying out the works would fall to be borne.

   (7) Where the access authority carry out any works by virtue of subsection (5), the authority may recover the amount of any expenses reasonably incurred by them in carrying out the works from the person to whom the notice under subsection (3) was given.

[Countryside and Rights of Way Act 2000, s 36.]

8–4221   37. Provision of access by access authority in absence of agreement.   (1) Where, in respect of any access land—

(a) it appears to the access authority that—

    (i) the opening-up, improvement or repair of any means of access to the land,

    (ii) the construction of any new means of access to the land, or

    (iii) the maintenance of any means of access to the land,

is necessary for giving the public reasonable access to that land, or to other access land, in pursuance of the right conferred by section 2(1), and

(b) the access authority are satisfied that they are unable to conclude on reasonable terms an agreement under section 35 with the owner or occupier of the land for the carrying out of the works,

the access authority may, subject to subsection (3), give the owner or occupier a notice stating that, after the end of a specified period of not less than twenty-one days, the authority intend to take all necessary steps for carrying out the works specified in the notice for the opening-up, improvement, repair, construction or maintenance of the means of access.

(2) A notice under subsection (1) must contain particulars of the right of appeal conferred by section 38.

(3) Where a notice under subsection (1) is given to any person as the owner or occupier of any land, the access authority shall give a copy of the notice to every other owner or occupier of the land.

(4) An access authority exercising the power conferred by subsection (1) in relation to the provision of a means of access shall have regard to the requirements of efficient management of the land in deciding where the means of access is to be provided.

(5) If, at the end of the period specified in a notice under subsection (1), any of the works specified in the notice have not been carried out, the access authority may take all necessary steps for carrying out those works.

[Countryside and Rights of Way Act 2000, s 37.]

8–4222 38. *Appeals relating to notices; Appeal to the Secretary of State or the national Assembly for Wales*

8–4223 39. Order to remove obstruction. (1) Where at any time two or more access notices relating to a means of access have been given to any person within the preceding thirty-six months, a magistrates' court may, on the application of the access authority, order that person—

(a) within such time as may be specified in the order, to take such steps as may be so specified to remove any obstruction of that means of access, and

(b) not to obstruct that means of access at any time when the right conferred by section 2(1) is exercisable.

(2) If a person ("the person in default") fails to comply with an order under this section—

(a) he is liable on summary conviction to a fine not exceeding **level 3** on the standard scale, and

(b) the access authority may remove any obstruction of the means of access and recover from the person in default the costs reasonably incurred by them in doing so.

(3) In this section "access notice" means a notice under section 36(3) or 37(1) in respect of which the period specified in the notice has expired, other than a notice in respect of which an appeal is pending or which has been cancelled on appeal.

[Countryside and Rights of Way Act 2000, s 39.]

GENERAL

8–4224 40. Powers of entry for purposes of Part I. (1) A person who is authorised by the appropriate countryside body to do so may enter any land—

(a) for the purpose of surveying it in connection with the preparation of any map under this Part or the review of any map issued under this Part,

(b) for the purpose of determining whether any power conferred on the appropriate countryside body by Chapter II should be exercised in relation to the land,

(c) for the purpose of ascertaining whether members of the public are being permitted to exercise the right conferred by section 2(1),

(d) in connection with an appeal under any provision of this Part, or

(e) for the purpose of determining whether to apply to the Secretary of State or the National Assembly for Wales under section 58.

(2) A person who is authorised by a local highway authority to do so may enter any land—

(a) for the purpose of determining whether the local highway authority should enter into an agreement under section 35, give a notice under section 36(1) or (3) or section 37(1) or carry out works under section 36(1) or (5), section 37(5) or section 39(2)(b),

(b) for the purpose of ascertaining whether an offence under section 14 or 39 has been or is being committed, or

(c) for the purposes of erecting or maintaining notices under section 19(1).

(3) A person who is authorised by a National Park authority to do so may enter any land—

(a)   for the purpose of enabling the authority to determine whether to exercise any power under Chapter II of this Act in relation to the land,

(b)   for the purpose of determining whether members of the public are being permitted to exercise the right conferred by section 2(1),

(c)   in connection with an appeal under any provision of this Part,

(d)   for the purpose of determining whether the authority should enter into an agreement under section 35, give a notice under section 36(1) or (3) or section 37(1) or carry out works under section 36(1) or (5), section 37(5) or section 39(2)(b),

(e)   for the purpose of ascertaining whether an offence under section 14 or 39 has been or is being committed, or

(f)   for the purposes of erecting or maintaining notices under section 19(1).

(4)   A person who is authorised by the Forestry Commissioners to do so may enter any land—

(a)   for the purpose of determining whether any power conferred on the Forestry Commissioners by Chapter II should be exercised in relation to the land, or

(b)   in connection with an appeal under any provision of this Part.

(5)   A person acting in the exercise of a power conferred by this section may—

(a)   use a vehicle to enter the land;

(b)   take a constable with him if he reasonably believes he is likely to be obstructed;

(c)   take with him equipment and materials needed for the purpose for which he is exercising the power of entry;

(d)   take samples of the land and of anything on it.

(6)   If in the exercise of a power conferred by this section a person enters land which is unoccupied or from which the occupier is temporarily absent, he must on his departure leave it as effectively secured against unauthorised entry as he found it.

(7)   A person authorised under this section to enter upon any land—

(a)   shall, if so required, produce evidence of his authority before entering, and

(b)   shall produce such evidence if required to do so at any time while he remains on the land.

(8)   A person shall not under this section demand admission as of right to any occupied land, other than access land, unless—

(a)   at least twenty-four hours' notice of the intended entry has been given to the occupier, or

(b)   it is not reasonably practicable to give such notice, or

(c)   the entry is for the purpose specified in subsection (2)(b) and (3)(e).

(9)   The rights conferred by this section are not exercisable in relation to a dwelling.

(10)   A person who intentionally obstructs a person acting in the exercise of his powers under this section is guilty of an offence and liable on summary conviction to a fine not exceeding **level 2** on the standard scale.

[Countryside and Rights of Way Act 2000, s 40.]

8–4225   **41.** *Compensation relating to powers under s 40*

8–4226   **42. References to public places in existing enactments.**   (1) This section applies to any enactment which—

(a)   is contained in an Act passed before or in the same Session as this Act, and

(b)   relates to things done, or omitted to be done, in public places or places to which the public have access.

(2)   Regulations may provide that, in determining for the purposes of any specified enactment to which this section applies whether a place is a public place or a place to which the public have access, the right conferred by section 2(1), or access by virtue of that right, is to be disregarded, either generally or in prescribed cases.

[Countryside and Rights of Way Act 2000, s 42.]

8–4227   **43. Crown application of Part I.**   (1) This Part binds the Crown.

(2)   No contravention by the Crown of any provision of this Part shall make the Crown criminally liable; but the High Court may declare unlawful any act or omission of the Crown which constitutes such a contravention.

(3)   The provisions of this Part apply to persons in the public service of the Crown as they apply to other persons.

[Countryside and Rights of Way Act 2000, s 43.]

8–4228   **44.** *Orders and regulations under Part I*

8–4229   **45. Interpretation of Part I.**   (1) In this Part, unless a contrary intention appears—

"access authority" has the meaning given by section 1(2);

"access land" has the meaning given by section 1(1);

"the appropriate countryside body" has the meaning given by section 1(2);

"excepted land" has the meaning given by section 1(2);

"Inner London" means the area comprising the inner London boroughs, the City of London, the Inner Temple and the Middle Temple;

"interest", in relation to land, includes any estate in land and any right over land, whether the right is exercisable by virtue of the ownership of an estate or interest in land or by virtue of a licence or agreement, and in particular includes rights of common and sporting rights, and references to a person interested in land shall be construed accordingly;

"livestock" means cattle, sheep, goats, swine, horses or poultry, and for the purposes of this definition "cattle" means bulls, cows, oxen, heifers or calves, "horses" include asses and mules, and "poultry" means domestic fowls, turkeys, geese or ducks;

"local highway authority" has the same meaning as in the Highways Act 1980;

"local or private Act" includes an Act confirming a provisional order;

"mountain" has the meaning given by section 1(2);

"open country" has the meaning given by section 1(2);

"owner", in relation to any land, means, subject to subsection (2), any person, other than a mortgagee not in possession, who, whether in his own right or as trustee for another person, is entitled to receive the rack rent of the land, or, where the land is not let at a rack rent, would be so entitled if it were so let;

"prescribed" means prescribed by regulations;

"registered common land" has the meaning given by section 1(3);

"regulations" means regulations made by the Secretary of State (as respects England) or by the National Assembly for Wales (as respects Wales);

"rights of common" has the same meaning as in the Commons Registration Act 1965;

"telecommunications code" and "telecommunications code system" have the same meaning as in Schedule 4 to the Telecommunications Act 1984.★

(2) In relation to any land which is subject to a farm business tenancy within the meaning of the Agricultural Tenancies Act 1995 or a tenancy to which the Agricultural Holdings Act 1986 applies, the definition of "owner" in subsection (1) does not apply where it is excluded by section 2(5) or 21(4) or by paragraph 7(4) of Schedule 2.

(3) For the purposes of this Part, the Broads are to be treated as a National Park and the Broads Authority as a National Park authority.

(4) In subsection (3) "the Broads" has the same meaning as in the Norfolk and Suffolk Broads Act 1988.

[Countryside and Rights of Way Act 2000, s 45.]

★Definition repealed by the Communications Act 2003, Sch 19, from a date to be appointed.

PART II[1]
PUBLIC RIGHTS OF WAY AND ROAD TRAFFIC
Public rights of way and definitive maps and statements

8–4230 47. Redesignation of roads used as public paths★. (1) In the Wildlife and Countryside Act 1981 (in this Act referred to as "the 1981 Act"), section 54 (duty to reclassify roads used as public paths) shall cease to have effect.

(2) Every way which, immediately before the commencement of this section, is shown in any definitive map and statement as a road used as a public path shall be treated instead as shown as a restricted byway; and the expression "road used as a public path" shall not be used in any definitive map and statement to describe any way.

[Countryside and Rights of Way Act 2000, s 47.]

★At the date of going to press this section was not in force.
1. Part II comprises ss 47 to 72.

8–4231 48. Restricted byway rights★. (1) Subject to subsections (2) and (3), the public shall have restricted byway rights over any way which, immediately before the commencement of section 47, is shown in a definitive map and statement as a road used as a public path.

(2) Subsection (1) has effect subject to the operation of any enactment or instrument (whether coming into operation before or after the commencement of section 47), and to the effect of any event otherwise within section 53(3)(a) of the 1981 Act, whereby a highway—

(a) is authorised to be stopped up, diverted, widened or extended, or

(b) becomes a public path;

and subsection (1) applies accordingly to any way as so diverted, widened or extended.

(3) Subsection (1) does not apply to any way, or part of a way, over which immediately before the commencement of section 47 there was no public right of way.

(4) In this Part—

"restricted byway rights" means—

(*a*)　a right of way on foot,

(*b*)　a right of way on horseback or leading a horse, and

(*c*)　a right of way for vehicles other than mechanically propelled vehicles; and

"restricted byway" means a highway over which the public have restricted byway rights, with or without a right to drive animals of any description along the highway, but no other rights of way.

(5)　A highway at the side of a river, canal or other inland navigation is not excluded from the definition of "restricted byway" in subsection (4) merely because the public have a right to use the highway for purposes of navigation, if the highway would fall within that definition if the public had no such right over it.

(6)　Subsection (1) is without prejudice to any question whether the public have over any way, in addition to restricted byway rights, a right of way for mechanically propelled vehicles or any other right.

(7)　In subsections (4) and (6) "mechanically propelled vehicle" does not include a vehicle falling within paragraph (*c*) of section 189(1) of the Road Traffic Act 1988.

(8)　Every surveying authority shall take such steps as they consider expedient for bringing to the attention of the public the effect of section 47(2) and this section.

(9)　The powers conferred by section 103(5) must be so exercised as to secure that nothing in section 47 or this section affects the operation of section 53 or 54 of, or Schedule 14 or 15 to, the 1981 Act in relation to—

(*a*)　a relevant order made before the commencement of section 47, or

(*b*)　an application made before that commencement for a relevant order.

(10)　In subsection (9) "relevant order" means an order which relates to a way shown in a definitive map and statement as a road used as a public path and which—

(*a*)　is made under section 53 of the 1981 Act and contains modifications relating to that way by virtue of subsection (3)(*c*)(ii) of that section, or

(*b*)　is made under section 54 of the 1981 Act.

(11)　Where—

(*a*)　by virtue of an order under subsection (3) of section 103 ("the commencement order") containing such provision as is mentioned in subsection (5) of that section, an order under Part III of the 1981 Act ("the Part III order") takes effect, after the commencement of section 47, in relation to any way which, immediately before that commencement, was shown in a definitive map and statement as a road used as a public path,

(*b*)　the commencement order does not prevent subsection (1) from having effect on that commencement in relation to that way, and

(*c*)　if the Part III order had taken effect before that commencement, that way would not have fallen within subsection (1),

all rights over that way which exist only by virtue of subsection (1) shall be extinguished when the Part III order takes effect.

[Countryside and Rights of Way Act 2000, s 48.]

---

*At the date of going to press this section was not in force.

8–4232　49. Provisions supplementary to ss 47 and 48.　(1)　Every way over which the public have restricted byway rights by virtue of subsection (1) of section 48 (whether or not they also have a right of way for mechanically propelled vehicles or any other right) shall, as from the commencement of that section, be a highway maintainable at the public expense.

(2)　As from the commencement of that section, any liability, under a special enactment (within the meaning of the Highways Act 1980) or by reason of tenure, enclosure or prescription, to maintain, otherwise than as a highway maintainable at the public expense, a restricted byway to which subsection (1) applies is extinguished.

(3)　Every way which, in pursuance of—

(*a*)　paragraph 9 of Part III of Schedule 3 to the Countryside Act 1968, or

(*b*)　any order made under section 54(1) of the 1981 Act before the coming into force of section 47,

is shown in any definitive map and statement as a byway open to all traffic, a bridleway or a footpath, shall continue to be maintainable at the public expense.

(4)　Nothing in subsections (1) and (3) or in section 48(1) obliges a highway authority to provide on any way a metalled carriage-way or a carriage-way which is by any other means provided with a surface suitable for cycles or other vehicles.

(5)　Nothing in section 48, or in section 53 of the 1981 Act, limits the operation of orders under the Road Traffic Regulation Act 1984 or the operation of any byelaws.

(6) Section 67 of the 1981 Act (application to the Crown) has effect as if this section and sections 47, 48 and 50 were contained in Part III of that Act.

[Countryside and Rights of Way Act 2000, s 49.]

8–4233   50.   Private rights over restricted byways.   (1) Restricted byway rights over any way by virtue of subsection (1) of section 48 are subject to any condition or limitation to which public rights of way over that way were subject immediately before the commencement of that section.

(2) Any owner or lessee of premises adjoining or adjacent to a relevant highway shall, so far as is necessary for the reasonable enjoyment and occupation of the premises, have a right of way for vehicular and all other kinds of traffic over the relevant highway.

(3) In subsection (2), in its application to the owner of any premises, "relevant highway" means so much of any highway maintainable at the public expense by virtue of section 49(1) as was, immediately before it became so maintainable, owned by the person who then owned the premises.

(4) In subsection (2), in its application to the lessee of any premises, "relevant highway" means so much of any highway maintainable at the public expense by virtue of section 49(1) as was, immediately before it became so maintainable, included in the lease on which the premises are held.

(5) In this section—

"lease" and "lessee" have the same meaning as in the 1980 Act;

"owner", in relation to any premises, means a person, other than a mortgagee not in possession, who is for the time being entitled to dispose of the fee simple of the premises, whether in possession or in reversion, and "owned" shall be construed accordingly; and

"premises" has the same meaning as in the 1980 Act.

[Countryside and Rights of Way Act 2000, s 50.]

Creation, stopping up and diversion of highways

8–4234   57.   Creation, stopping up and diversion of highways.   The Highways Act 1980 (in this Act referred to as "the 1980 Act") has effect subject to the amendments in Part I of Schedule 6[1] (which relate to the creation, stopping up and diversion of highways); and Part II of that Schedule (which contains consequential amendments of other Acts) has effect.

[Countryside and Rights of Way Act 2000, s 57.]

---

1. See below.

8–4235   58.   *Application for path creation order for purposes of Part I*

8–4236   59.   Effect of Part I on powers to stop up or divert highways.   (1) This section applies to any power to stop up or divert a highway of any description or to make or confirm an order authorising the stopping up or diversion of a highway of any description; and in the following provisions of this section—

(a) "the relevant authority" means the person exercising the power, and

(b) "the existing highway" means the highway to be stopped up or diverted.

(2) Where the relevant authority is required (expressly or by implication) to consider—

(a) whether the existing highway is unnecessary, or is needed for public use,

(b) whether an alternative highway should be provided, or

(c) whether any public right of way should be reserved,

the relevant authority, in considering that question, is not to regard the fact that any land is access land in respect of which the right conferred by section 2(1) is exercisable as reducing the need for the existing highway, for the provision of an alternative highway or for the reservation of a public right of way.

(3) Where—

(a) the existing highway is situated on, or in the vicinity of, any access land, and

(b) the relevant authority is required (expressly or by implication) to consider the extent (if any) to which the existing highway would, apart from the exercise of the power, be likely to be used by the public,

the relevant authority, in considering that question, is to have regard, in particular, to the extent to which the highway would be likely to be used by the public at any time when the right conferred by section 2(1) is not exercisable in relation to the access land.

(4) In this section "access land" has the same meaning as in Part I.

[Countryside and Rights of Way Act 2000, s 59.]

Rights of way improvement plans

Removal of obstructions from highways

8–4237   63.   Enforcement of duty to prevent obstructions.   *Inserts new ss 130A–130D in the Highways Act 1980.*

8–4238   64. Power to order offender to remove obstruction.   *Inserts new s 137ZA in the Highways Act 1980.*

8–4239   65. Overhanging vegetation obstructing horse-riders.   In section 154 of the 1980 Act (cutting or felling etc trees etc that overhang or are a danger to roads or footpaths) in subsection (1) after "public lamp," there is inserted "or overhangs a highway so as to endanger or obstruct the passage of horse-riders,".
[Countryside and Rights of Way Act 2000, s 65.]

Miscellaneous

8–4240   66. Making of traffic regulation orders for purposes of conserving natural beauty, etc.   *Amends s 22 of the Road Traffic Regulation Act 1984 and inserts new s 22A in that Act.*

8–4241   67. Prohibition on driving mechanically propelled vehicles elsewhere than on roads.   Schedule 7[1] (which makes amendments relating to the driving of mechanically propelled vehicles elsewhere than on roads) has effect.
[Countryside and Rights of Way Act 2000, s 67.]

---

1. See below.

8–4242   68. Vehicular access across common land etc.   (1) This section applies to a way which the owner or occupier (from time to time) of any premises has used as a means of access for vehicles to the premises, if that use of the way—

   (*a*) was an offence under an enactment applying to the land crossed by the way, but
   (*b*) would otherwise have been sufficient to create on or after the prescribed date, and to keep in existence, an easement giving a right of way for vehicles.

   (2) Regulations[1] may provide, as respects a way to which this section applies, for the creation in accordance with the regulations, on the application of the owner of the premises concerned and on compliance by him with prescribed requirements, of an easement subsisting at law for the benefit of the premises and giving a right of way for vehicles over that way.

   (3) An easement created in accordance with the regulations is subject to any enactment or rule of law which would apply to such an easement granted by the owner of the land.

   (4) The regulations may in particular—

   (*a*) require that, where an application is made after the relevant use of the way has ceased, it is to be made within a specified time,
   (*b*) specify grounds on which objections may be made and the procedure to apply to the making of objections,
   (*c*) require any matter to be referred to and determined by the Lands Tribunal, and make provision as to procedure and costs,
   (*d*) make provision as to the payment of any amount by the owner of the premises concerned to any person or into court and as to the time when any payment is to be made,
   (*e*) provide for the determination of any such amount,
   (*f*) make provision as to the date on which any easement is created,
   (*g*) specify any limitation to which the easement is subject,
   (*h*) provide for the easement to include any specified right incidental to the right of way,
   (*i*) make different provision for different circumstances.

   (5) In this section—

   "enactment" includes an enactment in a local or private Act and a byelaw, regulation or other provision having effect under an enactment;
   "owner", in relation to any premises, means—

      (*a*) a person, other than a mortgagee not in possession, who is for the time being entitled to dispose of the fee simple of the premises, whether in possession or in reversion, or
      (*b*) a tenant under a long lease, within the meaning of the Landlord and Tenant Act 1987;

   "prescribed" means prescribed by regulations;
   "regulations" means regulations made, as respects England, by the Secretary of State and, as respects Wales, by the National Assembly for Wales.

   (6) Regulations under this section shall be made by statutory instrument, and no such regulations shall be made by the Secretary of State unless a draft has been laid before, and approved by a resolution of, each House of Parliament.
[Countryside and Rights of Way Act 2000, s 68.]

---

1. The Vehicular Access Across Common and Other Land (England) Regulations 2002, SI 2002/1711 and the Vehicular Access Across Common and Other Land (Wales) Regulations 2004, SI 2004/248 have been made.

8–4243   70. Minor amendments.   *Amends ss 66(3), 134 and 300 of the Highways Act 1980 and s 21(2)(b) of the Road Traffic Act 1988.*

8–4245   72. Interpretation of Part II.   (1) In this Part, unless a contrary intention appears—

    (*a*)   "restricted byway" and "restricted byway rights" have the meaning given by section 48(4);

    (*b*)   expressions which are defined for the purposes of Part III of the 1981 Act by section 66(1) of that Act have the same meaning as in that Part.

    (2) In this Part any reference to a highway includes a reference to part of a highway.

[Countryside and Rights of Way Act 2000, s 72.]

Part III[1]

Nature Conservation and Wildlife Protection

The Nature Conservancy Council for England

8–4246   73. The Nature Conservancy Council for England: change of name.   (1) The Nature Conservancy Council for England shall be known instead as English Nature.

    (2) For any reference to the Nature Conservancy Council for England—

    (*a*)   in any provision of a local Act or subordinate legislation, or

    (*b*)   in any other instrument or document,

there is substituted, as respects any time after the commencement of subsection (1), a reference to English Nature.

    (3) Any reference to English Nature in this Act (apart from this section), or in any instrument under this Act, shall be construed, in relation to any time before the commencement of subsection (1), as a reference to the Nature Conservancy Council for England.

    (4) Schedule 8 (which makes amendments consequential on subsection (1)) has effect.

[Countryside and Rights of Way Act 2000, s 73.]

---

1.   Part III comprises ss 73 to 81.

Sites of special scientific interest

8–4247   75. Sites of special scientific interest.   (1) Schedule 9 (which makes amendments of the 1981 Act to change the law relating to sites of special scientific interest, including provision as to offences) has effect.

    (2)–(4) *Amendments of the National Parks and Access to the Countryside Act 1949 and the Countryside Act 1968.*

[Countryside and Rights of Way Act 2000, s 75.]

8–4248   76. Consequential amendments, transitional provisions and savings relating to s 75.   (1) Schedule 10 (which makes amendments of the 1981 Act consequential upon the substitution or repeal as respects England and Wales of certain sections in that Act, and also makes other consequential amendments) has effect.

    (2) Schedule 11[1] (which makes transitional provisions and savings relating to the coming into force of section 75) has effect.

[Countryside and Rights of Way Act 2000, s 76.]

---

1.   See below.

Ramsar sites

8–4249   77. Ramsar sites.   *Inserts new s 37A in the Wildlife and Countryside Act 1981.*

Limestone pavement orders

8–4250   78. Limestone pavement orders: offence.   (1) In section 34(4) of the 1981 Act (which provides for an offence in connection with land designated by a limestone pavement order), for "the statutory maximum" there is substituted "£20,000".

    (2) Subsection (1) does not have effect in relation to any offence committed before the commencement of this section.

[Countryside and Rights of Way Act 2000, s 78.]

Payments under certain agreements

8–4251   79.   *Payments under agreements under s 16 of 1949 Act or s 15 of 1968 Act*

Powers of entry

8–4252   80. Powers of entry.   (1) Section 51 of the 1981 Act (powers of entry) is amended as follows.

(2) In subsection (1), for paragraphs (*a*) to (*d*) there is substituted—

"(*a*) to determine whether the land should be notified under section 28(1);

(*b*) to assess the condition of the flora, fauna, or geological or physiographical features by reason of which land which has been notified under section 28(1) is of special interest;

(*c*) to determine whether or not to offer to enter into an agreement under section 16 of the 1949 Act or section 15 of the 1968 Act in relation to the land;

(*d*) to ascertain whether a condition to which a consent referred to in section 28E(3)(*a*) was subject has been complied with in relation to the land;

(*e*) to ascertain whether an offence under section 28P or under byelaws made by virtue of section 28R is being, or has been, committed on or in relation to the land;

(*f*) to formulate a management scheme for the land or determine whether a management scheme (or a proposed management scheme) for the land should be modified;

(*g*) to prepare a management notice for the land;

(*h*) to ascertain whether the terms of an agreement under section 16 of the 1949 Act or section 15 of the 1968 Act in relation to the land, or the terms of a management scheme or the requirements of a management notice in relation to the land, have been complied with;

(*i*) to determine whether or not to offer to make a payment under section 28M in relation to the land;

(*j*) to determine any question in relation to the acquisition of the land by agreement or compulsorily;

(*k*) to determine any question in relation to compensation under section 20(3) of the 1949 Act as applied by section 28R of this Act;

(*l*) to ascertain whether an order should be made in relation to the land under section 34 or if an offence under that section is being, or has been, committed on the land;

(*m*) to ascertain whether an order should be made in relation to the land under section 42 or if an offence under that section is being, or has been, committed on the land;".

(3) After subsection (1) there is inserted—

"(1A) The power conferred by subsection (1) to enter land for any purpose includes power to enter for the same purpose any land other than that referred to in subsection (1).

(1B) More than one person may be authorised for the time being under subsection (1) to enter any land."

(4) In subsection (2)—

(*a*) in paragraph (*a*), for "paragraphs (*a*) and (*b*)" there is substituted "paragraphs (*a*) to (k)";

(*b*) in paragraph (*b*), for "paragraph (*c*)" there is substituted "paragraph (l)"; and

(*c*) in paragraph (*c*), for "paragraph (*d*)" there is substituted "paragraph (m)".

(5) For subsection (3)(*b*) there is substituted—

"(*b*) the purpose of the entry is to ascertain if an offence under section 28P, 34 or 42 is being, or has been, committed on or (as the case may be) in relation to that land."

(6) After subsection (3) there is inserted—

"(3A) A person acting in the exercise of a power conferred by subsection (1) may—

(*a*) use a vehicle or a boat to enter the land;

(*b*) take a constable with him if he reasonably believes he is likely to be obstructed;

(*c*) take with him equipment and materials needed for the purpose for which he is exercising the power of entry;

(*d*) take samples of the land and of anything on it.

(3B) If in the exercise of a power conferred by subsection (1) a person enters land which is unoccupied or from which the occupier is temporarily absent, he must on his departure leave it as effectively secured against unauthorised entry as he found it."

(7) After subsection (4) there is inserted—

"(5) It is the duty of a relevant authority to compensate any person who has sustained damage as a result of—

(*a*) the exercise of a power conferred by subsection (1) by a person authorised to do so by that relevant authority, or

(*b*) the failure of a person so authorised to perform the duty imposed on him by subsection (3B),

except where the damage is attributable to the fault of the person who sustained it; and any dispute as to a person's entitlement to compensation under this subsection or as to its amount shall be referred to an arbitrator to be appointed, in default of agreement, by the Secretary of State".

[Countryside and Rights of Way Act 2000, s 80.]

Enforcement of wildlife legislation

8–4253 81. Enforcement of wildlife legislation. (1) Schedule 12[1] to this Act (which contains amendments relating to offences and enforcement powers under Part I of the 1981 Act) has effect.

(2) In relation to England and Wales, regulations under section 2(2) of the European Communities Act 1972 ("the 1972 Act") for the purpose of implementing any of the instruments mentioned in subsection (3) may, notwithstanding paragraph 1(1)(*d*) of Schedule 2 to the 1972 Act, create offences punishable on summary conviction with imprisonment for a term not exceeding six months.

(3) Those instruments are—

(*a*) Council Directive 92/43/EEC on the conservation of natural habitats and of wild fauna and flora as amended by the Act of Accession to the European Union of Austria, Finland and Sweden and by Council Directive 97/62/EC;

(*b*) Council Regulation 338/97/EC on the protection of species of wild fauna and flora by regulating the trade therein; and

(*c*) Commission Regulation 939/97/EC on the implementation of the Council Regulation mentioned in paragraph (*b*).

[Countryside and Rights of Way Act 2000, s 81.]

---

1. See below.

8–4254

PART IV[1]
AREAS OF OUTSTANDING NATURAL BEAUTY

---

1. Part VI comprises ss 82 to 93.

PART V[1]
MISCELLANEOUS AND SUPPLEMENTARY

Supplementary

8–4255 99. Wales. (1) In Schedule 1 to the National Assembly for Wales (Transfer of Functions) Order 1999—

(*a*) the reference to the 1980 Act is to be treated as referring to that Act as amended by this Act, and

(*b*) the reference to the 1981 Act is to be treated as referring to that Act as amended by this Act.

(2) In that Schedule, at the end of the list of Public General Acts there is inserted—

"**Countryside and Rights of Way Act 2000 (c 37)** Schedule 11.".

(3) Subsection (1), and the amendment made by subsection (2), do not affect the power to make further Orders varying or omitting the references mentioned in subsection (1) or the provision inserted by subsection (2).

[Countryside and Rights of Way Act 2000, s 99.]

---

1. Part V comprises ss 94 to 104.

8–4256 100. Isles of Scilly. (1) Subject to the provisions of any order under this section, the following provisions of this Act do not apply in relation to the Isles of Scilly—

(*a*) Part I; and

(*b*) sections 58 to 61 and 71.

(2) The Secretary of State may by order made by statutory instrument provide for the application of any of the provisions mentioned in subsection (1) in relation to the Isles of Scilly, subject to such modifications as may be specified in the order.

(3) Part IV applies in relation to the Isles of Scilly subject to such modifications as may be specified in an order made by the Secretary of State by statutory instrument.

(4) Before making an order under subsection (2) or (3), the Secretary of State shall consult the Council of the Isles of Scilly.

(5) In section 344 of the 1980 Act (application to the Isles of Scilly)—

(*a*) in subsection (2)(*a*) for "121" there is substituted "121E, 130A to 130D", and

(*b*) before "146" there is inserted "137ZA(4)".

[Countryside and Rights of Way Act 2000, s 100.]

8–4257 101. *Expenses*

8–4258 102. Repeals. The enactments mentioned in Schedule 16 are repealed to the extent specified.

[Countryside and Rights of Way Act 2000, s 102.]

8–4259 103. Commencement. (1) The following provisions of this Act come into force on the day on which this Act is passed—

section 81(2) and (3),

this section, and
section 104.

(2) The following provisions of this Act come into force at the end of the period of two months beginning with the day on which this Act is passed—

section 1 and Schedule 1,
sections 3 to 11 and Schedule 3,
sections 15 to 17,
section 19,
Chapters II and III of Part I,
sections 40 to 45,
section 52,
sections 58 and 59,
sections 64 to 67 and Schedule 7 (apart from paragraphs 6 and 7 of that Schedule),
Part III (apart from section 81(2) and (3)), and Schedules 8, 9, 10, 11 and 12 and Parts III and IV
     of Schedule 16,
sections 94 and 95, and
section 98.

(3) The remaining provisions of this Act come into force on such day as the Secretary of State (as respects England) or the National Assembly for Wales (as respects Wales) may by order[1] made by statutory instrument appoint.

(4) Different days may be appointed under subsection (3) for different purposes or different areas.

(5) An order under subsection (3) may contain such transitional provisions or savings (including provisions modifying the effect of any enactment) as appear to the Secretary of State or the National Assembly for Wales (as the case may be) to be necessary or expedient in connection with any provision brought into force by the order.
[Countryside and Rights of Way Act 2000, s 103.]

---

1. At the date of going to press, the following Commencement Orders had been made: Countryside and Rights of Way Act 2000 (Commencement No 1) Order 2001, SI 2001/114; Countryside and Rights of Way Act 2000 (Commencement No 1) (Wales) Order 2001, SI 2001/203; Countryside and Rights of Way Act 2000 (Commencement No 2) (Wales) Order 2001, SI 2001/1410; Countryside and Rights of Way Act 2000 (Commencement No 3) (Wales) Order 2002, SI 2002/2615; Countryside and Rights of Way Act 2000 (Commencement No 2) Order 2002, SI 2002/2833; Countryside and Rights of Way Act 2000 (Commencement No 3) Order 2003, SI 2003/272; and Countryside and Rights of Way Act 2000 (Commencement No 4) Order 2004, SI 2004/292.

8–4260   104. Interpretation, short title and extent.   (1) In this Act—

"the 1980 Act" means the Highways Act 1980;
"the 1981 Act" means the Wildlife and Countryside Act 1981;
"local access forum" means a local access forum established under section 94.

(2) Any reference in this Act, or in any enactment amended by this Act, to the commencement of any provision of this Act is, in relation to any area, a reference to the commencement of that provision in relation to that area.

(3) This Act may be cited as the Countryside and Rights of Way Act 2000.

(4) Subject to the following provisions of this section, this Act extends to England and Wales only.

(5) The following provisions extend also to Scotland—

sections 67 and 76;
in Schedule 7, paragraphs 3 and 5 to 7;
in Schedule 10, paragraph 2.

(6) Paragraph 1 of Schedule 10 extends to Scotland only.

(7) The provisions of Schedule 8 and of so much of Part III of Schedule 16 as relates to the enactments referred to in paragraphs 2 and 3 of Schedule 8 have the same extent as the enactments which they amend or repeal.
[Countryside and Rights of Way Act 2000, s 104.]

SCHEDULE 1
EXCEPTED LAND FOR PURPOSES OF PART I

(Amended by SI 2001/4050 and the Communications Act 2003, Sch 1)

Section 1(2)

PART I
EXCEPTED LAND

8–4261   **1.** Land on which the soil is being, or has at any time within the previous twelve months been, disturbed by any ploughing or drilling undertaken for the purposes of planting or sowing crops or trees.
     2. Land covered by buildings or the curtilage of such land.
     3. Land within 20 metres of a dwelling.

4. Land used as a park or garden.

5. Land used for the getting of minerals by surface working (including quarrying).

6. Land used for the purposes of a railway (including a light railway) or tramway.

7. Land used for the purposes of a golf course, racecourse or aerodrome.

8. Land which does not fall within any of the preceding paragraphs and is covered by works used for the purposes of a statutory undertaking or an electronic communications code network, or the curtilage of any such land.

9. Land as respects which development which will result in the land becoming land falling within any of paragraphs 2 to 8 is in the course of being carried out.

10. Land within 20 metres of a building which is used for housing livestock, not being a temporary or moveable structure.

11. Land covered by pens in use for the temporary reception or detention of livestock.

12. Land habitually used for the training of racehorses.

13. Land the use of which is regulated by byelaws under section 14 of the Military Lands Act 1892 or section 2 of the Military Lands Act 1900.

PART II
SUPPLEMENTARY PROVISIONS

8–4262   **14.** In this Schedule—

"building" includes any structure or erection and any part of a building as so defined, but does not include any fence or wall, or anything which is a means of access as defined by section 34; and for this purpose "structure" includes any tent, caravan or other temporary or moveable structure;

"development" and "minerals" have the same meaning as in the Town and Country Planning Act 1990;

"ploughing" and "drilling" include respectively agricultural or forestry operations similar to ploughing and agricultural or forestry operations similar to drilling;

"statutory undertaker" means—

    (a) a person authorised by any enactment to carry on any railway, light railway, tramway, road transport, water transport, canal, inland navigation, dock, harbour, pier or lighthouse undertaking or any undertaking for the supply of hydraulic power,

    (b) any public gas transporter, within the meaning of Part I of the Gas Act 1986,

    (c) any water or sewerage undertaker,

    (d) any holder of a licence under section 6(1) of the Electricity Act 1989, or

    (e) the Environment Agency, a universal service provider (within the meaning of the Postal Services Act 2000) in connection with the provision of a universal postal service (within the meaning of that Act), the Civil Aviation Authority or a person who holds a licence under Chapter I of Part I of the Transport Act 2000 (to the extent that the person is carrying out activities authorised by the licence);

"statutory undertaking" means—

    (a) the undertaking of a statutory undertaker (which, in the case of a universal service provider (within the meaning of the Postal Services Act 2000), means his undertaking so far as relating to the provision of a universal postal service (within the meaning of that Act) and, in the case of a person who holds a licence under Chapter I of Part I of the Transport Act 2000, means that person's undertaking as licence holder), or

    (b) an airport to which Part V of the Airports Act 1986 applies.

15. (1) Land is not to be treated as excepted land by reason of any development carried out on the land, if the carrying out of the development requires planning permission under Part III of the Town and Country Planning Act 1990 and that permission has not been granted.

(2) Sub-paragraph (1) does not apply where the development is treated by section 191(2) of the Town and Country Planning Act 1990 as being lawful for the purposes of that Act.

16. The land which is excepted land by virtue of paragraph 10 does not include—

    (a) any means of access, as defined by section 34, or

    (b) any way leading to such a means of access,

if the means of access is necessary for giving the public reasonable access to access land.

17. Land which is habitually used for the training of racehorses is not to be treated by virtue of paragraph 11 as excepted land except—

    (a) between dawn and midday on any day, and

    (b) at any other time when it is in use for that purpose.

Section 2   **SCHEDULE 2★**

RESTRICTIONS TO BE OBSERVED BY PERSONS EXERCISING RIGHT OF ACCESS

General restrictions

8–4263   **1.** Section 2(1) does not entitle a person to be on any land if, in or on that land, he—

    (a) drives or rides any vehicle other than an invalid carriage as defined by section 20(2) of the Chronically Sick and Disabled Persons Act 1970, (*b*)   uses a vessel or sailboard on any non-tidal water,

(*c*)   has with him any animal other than a dog,

(*d*)   commits any criminal offence,

(*e*)   lights or tends a fire or does any act which is likely to cause a fire,

(*f*)   intentionally or recklessly takes, kills, injures or disturbs any animal, bird or fish,

(*g*)   intentionally or recklessly takes, damages or destroys any eggs or nests,

(*h*)   feeds any livestock,

(*i*)   bathes in any non-tidal water,

(*j*)   engages in any operations of or connected with hunting, shooting, fishing, trapping, snaring, taking or destroying of animals, birds or fish or has with him any engine, instrument or apparatus used for hunting, shooting, fishing, trapping, snaring, taking or destroying animals, birds or fish,

(*k*)   uses or has with him any metal detector,

(*l*)   intentionally removes, damages or destroys any plant, shrub, tree or root or any part of a plant, shrub, tree or root,

(*m*) obstructs the flow of any drain or watercourse, or opens, shuts or otherwise interferes with any sluice-gate or other apparatus,

(*n*)   without reasonable excuse, interferes with any fence, barrier or other device designed to prevent accidents to people or to enclose livestock,

(*o*)   neglects to shut any gate or to fasten it where any means of doing so is provided, except where it is reasonable to assume that a gate is intended to be left open,

(*p*)   affixes or writes any advertisement, bill, placard or notice,

(*q*)   in relation to any lawful activity which persons are engaging in or are about to engage in on that or adjoining land, does anything which is intended by him to have the effect—

    (i)   of intimidating those persons so as to deter them or any of them from engaging in that activity,
    (ii) of obstructing that activity, or
    (iii) of disrupting that activity,

(*r*)   without reasonable excuse, does anything which (whether or not intended by him to have the effect mentioned in paragraph (*q*)) disturbs, annoys or obstructs any persons engaged in a lawful activity on the land,

(*s*)   engages in any organised games, or in camping, hang-gliding or para-gliding, or

(*t*)   engages in any activity which is organised or undertaken (whether by him or another) for any commercial purpose.

2. (1) In paragraph 1(*k*), "metal detector" means any device designed or adapted for detecting or locating any metal or mineral in the ground.

(2) For the purposes of paragraph 1(*q*) and (*r*), activity on any occasion on the part of a person or persons on land is "lawful" if he or they may engage in the activity on the land on that occasion without committing an offence or trespassing on the land.

3. Regulations may amend paragraphs 1 and 2.

4. During the period beginning with 1st March and ending with 31st July in each year, section 2(1) does not entitle a person to be on any land if he takes, or allows to enter or remain, any dog which is not on a short lead.

5. Whatever the time of year, section 2(1) does not entitle a person to be on any land if he takes, or allows to enter or remain, any dog which is not on a short lead and which is in the vicinity of livestock.

6. In paragraphs 4 and 5, "short lead" means a lead of fixed length and of not more than two metres.

---

*At the date of going to press this Schedule was not in force.

Removal or relaxation of restrictions

8–4264 **7.** (1) The relevant authority may by direction, with the consent of the owner of any land, remove or relax any of the restrictions imposed by paragraphs 1, 4 and 5 in relation to that land, either indefinitely or during a specified period.

(2) In sub-paragraph (1), the reference to a specified period includes references—

(*a*)   to a specified period in every calendar year, or

(*b*)   to a period which is to be determined by the owner of the land in accordance with the direction and notified by him to the relevant authority in accordance with regulations.

(3) Regulations may make provision as to—

(*a*)   the giving or revocation of directions under this paragraph,

(*b*)   the variation of any direction given under this paragraph by a subsequent direction so given,

(*c*)   the giving or revocation of consent for the purposes of sub-paragraph (1), and

(*d*)   the steps to be taken by the relevant authority or the owner for informing the public about any direction under this paragraph or its revocation.

(4) In this paragraph—

"the relevant authority" has the meaning given by section 21;

"owner", in relation to any land which is subject to a farm business tenancy within the meaning of the Agricultural Tenancies Act 1995 or a tenancy to which the Agricultural Holdings Act 1986 applies, means the tenant under that tenancy.

Dedicated land

8–4265 **8.** In relation to land to which a dedication under section 16 relates (whether or not it would be access land apart from the dedication), the provisions of this Schedule have effect subject to the terms of the dedication.

Section 46(3)   SCHEDULE 4
MINOR AND CONSEQUENTIAL AMENDMENTS RELATING TO PART I

Law of Property Act 1925 (c 20)

8–4266   **1.** In section 193(1) of the Law of Property Act 1925 (rights of public over commons and waste lands), in paragraph (*b*) of the proviso, after "injuriously affected," there is inserted "for conserving flora, fauna or geological or physiographical features of the land,".

Forestry Act 1967 (c 10)

8–4267   **2.** In section 9 of the Forestry Act 1967 (requirement of licence for felling), in the definition of "public open space" in subsection (6), after "1949" there is inserted "or Part I of the Countryside and Rights of Way Act 2000".

Agriculture Act 1967 (c 22)

8–4268   **3.** In section 52 of the Agriculture Act 1967 (control of afforestation), in the definition of "public open space" in subsection (15), after "1949" there is inserted "or Part I of the Countryside and Rights of Way Act 2000".

     4. *Countryside Act 1968 (c 41)*
     5. *Local Government Act 1974 (c 7)*
     6. *Wildlife and Countryside Act 1981 (c 69)*

Section 51   SCHEDULE 5
DEFINITIVE MAPS AND STATEMENTS AND RESTRICTED BYWAYS

(*Only those provisions which amend enactments contained in this work are reproduced below.*)

8–4269

PART I
AMENDMENTS OF PART III OF WILDLIFE AND COUNTRYSIDE ACT 1981

PART II*
AMENDMENTS OF OTHER ACTS

National Parks and Access to the Countryside Act 1949 (c 97)

8–4270   **12.** (1) Section 51 of the National Parks and Access to the Countryside Act 1949 (general provisions as to long-distance routes) is amended as follows.
     (2) In subsection (2)(*a*), for the words from "any public path" to the end there is substituted "any highway along which the route passes and which is a public path, a restricted byway or a way shown in a definitive map and statement as a restricted byway or byway open to all traffic;".
     (3) In subsection (5), for the words from "existing public paths" to "route passes" there is substituted "existing highways falling within paragraph (*a*) of that subsection".
     (4) After that subsection there is inserted—
     "(6) In this section—

"definitive map and statement" has the same meaning as in Part III of the Wildlife and Countryside Act 1981; and
"restricted byway" has the same meaning as in Part II of the Countryside and Rights of Way Act 2000."

---

*At the date of going to press Part II was not in force.

     13. (1) Section 57 of that Act (penalty for displaying on footpaths notices deterring public use) is amended as follows.
     (2) In subsection (1), for "road used as a public path" there is substituted "restricted byway".
     (3) In subsection (3), for "or road used as a public path" there is substituted "restricted byway or byway open to all traffic".
     (4) After that subsection there is inserted—
     "(4) In this section—

"byway open to all traffic" has the same meaning as in Part III of the Wildlife and Countryside Act 1981;
"restricted byway" has the same meaning as in Part II of the Countryside and Rights of Way Act 2000."

Highways Act 1980 (c 66)

8–4271   **15.** In section 116 of the 1980 Act (power of magistrates' court to authorise stopping up or diversion of highway) in subsection (4), for "or bridleway" there is substituted ", bridleway or restricted byway".
     16. In section 329 of the 1980 Act (interpretation)—
     (*a*) in subsection (1) after the definition of "reconstruction" there is inserted—
""restricted byway" has the same meaning as in Part II of the Countryside and Rights of Way Act 2000;",
     (*b*) in subsection (2) for "either "bridleway" or "footpath" " there is substituted " "bridleway", "footpath" or "restricted byway" ".

Criminal Justice and Public Order Act 1994 (c 33)

8–4272   **17.** In section 61 of the Criminal Justice and Public Order Act 1994 (power to remove trespassers on land), in paragraph (*b*)(i) of the definition of "land" in subsection (9) for the words from "it falls" to "public path")" there is substituted "it is a footpath, bridleway or byway open to all traffic within the meaning of Part III of the Wildlife and Countryside Act 1981, is a restricted byway within the meaning of Part II of the Countryside and Rights of Way Act 2000".

8–4273   SCHEDULE 6[1]
AMENDMENTS RELATING TO CREATION, STOPPING UP AND DIVERSION OF HIGHWAYS

_____

1. Where the amendments apply to provisions reproduced in this work, they will be shown in those provisions when they come into force.

8–4274   SCHEDULE 7[1]
DRIVING OF MECHANICALLY PROPELLED VEHICLES ELSEWHERE THAN ON ROADS

_____

1. Where the amendments apply to provisions reproduced in this work, they will be shown in those provisions when they come into force.

8–4276   SCHEDULE 8[1]
AMENDMENTS CONSEQUENTIAL ON CHANGE OF NAME OF NATURE CONSERVANCY COUNCIL FOR ENGLAND

_____

1. Where the amendments apply to provisions reproduced in this work, they will be shown in those provisions when they come into force.

8–4277   SCHEDULE 9[1]
SITES OF SPECIAL SCIENTIFIC INTEREST

_____

1. Where the amendments apply to provisions reproduced in this work, they will be shown in those provisions when they come into force.

Section 76(1)   SCHEDULE 10
CONSEQUENTIAL AMENDMENTS RELATING TO SITES OF SPECIAL SCIENTIFIC INTEREST

(*Only those provisions which amend enactments contained in this work are reproduced below.*)

PART I
AMENDMENTS OF WILDLIFE AND COUNTRYSIDE ACT 1981

8–4278   1. (1) The 1981 Act is amended as follows.
(2) In section 28 (areas of special scientific interest)—

(*a*) in subsection (8)(*a*), "Part III of the Town and Country Planning Act 1990 or" is omitted; and
(*b*) subsections (10) and (11) are omitted.

(3) In section 29 (special protection for certain areas of special scientific interest), in subsection (9)(*a*), "Part III of the Town and Country Planning Act 1990 or" is omitted.
(4) In section 30 (compensation where order is made under section 29)—

(*a*) in subsection (4)(*c*), "section 10 of the Land Compensation Act 1973 (mortgages, trusts for sale and settlements) or" is omitted;
(*b*) in subsection (5), "section 5 of the Land Compensation Act 1961 or" is omitted;
(*c*) in subsection (7), "section 32 of the Land Compensation Act 1961 or" is omitted;
(*d*) in subsection (8), "the Lands Tribunal or" is omitted; and
(*e*) in subsection (9), "sections 2 and 4 of the Land Compensation Act 1961 or" is omitted.

2. In section 74 of the 1981 Act (short title, commencement and extent), after subsection (5) there is inserted—

"(5A) Sections 29 and 30 extend to Scotland only."

PART II
OTHER AMENDMENTS

Conservation of Seals Act 1970 (c 30)

8–4279   4. In section 10 of the Conservation of Seals Act 1970 (power to grant licences to kill or take seals), in subsection (4), for paragraph (*b*) there is substituted—

"(*b*) is a site of special scientific interest (within the meaning of the Wildlife and Countryside Act 1981); or".

Environmental Protection Act 1990 (c 43)

8–4280   8. In section 36 of the Environmental Protection Act 1990 (grant of waste management licences), in subsection (7), for "land which has been notified under section 28(1) of the Wildlife and Countryside Act 1981 (protection for certain areas)" there is substituted "within a site of special scientific interest (within the meaning of the Wildlife and Countryside Act 1981)".

Section 76(2)

SCHEDULE 11

TRANSITIONAL PROVISIONS AND SAVINGS RELATING TO SITES OF SPECIAL SCIENTIFIC INTEREST

Interpretation

8–4281   **1.** (1) In this Schedule—

"the Nature Conservancy Council" has the meaning given by section 27A of the 1981 Act and "stop notice" has the meaning given by paragraph 9(3) of this Schedule;

"old section 28" means section 28 of the 1981 Act as it had effect before its substitution by section 75(1) of and Schedule 9 to this Act;

"new section 28" means section 28 of the 1981 Act as substituted by section 75(1) of and Schedule 9 to this Act; and

"the substitution date" means the date on which new section 28 is substituted for old section 28,

and references to other sections are to those sections in the 1981 Act unless otherwise specified.

(2) Nothing in this Schedule prejudices the application of section 16 (general savings) or 17 (repeal and re-enactment) of the Interpretation Act 1978 to any case not provided for in this Schedule.

Notifications given under old section 28

8–4282   **2.** Except as mentioned in paragraphs 4 and 5, a notification under old section 28(1)(*a*), (*b*) or (*c*) (including one having effect in modified form by virtue of old section 28(4C)) has effect from the substitution date as if it were a notification under new section 28(1)(*a*), (*b*) or (*c*) respectively.

3. A notice under old section 28(4A)(*a*) or (*b*) has effect from the substitution date as if it were a notice under new section 28(5)(*a*) or (*b*) respectively.

Modification of operation of new section 28

8–4283   **4.** New section 28(2) does not apply to a notification taking effect as mentioned in paragraph 2.

5. The words following paragraph (*b*) in new section 28(4) do not apply to a notification taking effect as mentioned in paragraph 2, but instead paragraph 6 applies.

6. (1) The Nature Conservancy Council shall, within the period of five years beginning with the substitution date, give a notice to every owner and occupier of any land which is the subject of—

(*a*) a notification under old section 28(4A)(*b*), or

(*b*) a notice under new section 28(5)(*b*) following a notification under old section 28(1),

containing a statement of the Council's views about the matters referred to in the words following paragraph (*b*) in new section 28(4).

(2) The notice shall specify the date (not being less than three months from the date of the giving of the notice) on or before which, and the manner in which, representations or objections with respect to it may be made; and the Council shall consider any representation or objection duly made.

(3) Within the period of two months beginning immediately after the date referred to in sub-paragraph (2), the Council shall give a notice to every owner and occupier of the land confirming the statement referred to in sub-paragraph (1) or containing a revised statement.

Modification of operation of section 28A

8–4284   **7.** (1) This paragraph applies to a notification under old section 28(1) given—

(*a*) before the commencement of the Wildlife and Countryside (Amendment) Act 1985; or

(*b*) after the commencement of that Act but preceded by a notice under section 28(2) as originally enacted, given during the six months immediately preceding that commencement.

(2) In relation to a notification to which this paragraph applies, the reference in section 28A(1) to—

(*a*) notice given under section 28(5)(*b*) confirming a notification with or without modifications, and

(*b*) the confirmed notification,

shall be construed as a reference to the notification under old section 28(1).

Modification of operation of section 28E

8–4285   **8.** (1) Except as provided in paragraph 9—

(*a*) a notice given under old section 28(5)(*a*) has effect from the substitution date as if it were a notice given under section 28E(1)(*a*); and

(*b*) a consent given under old section 28(6)(*a*) has effect from that date as if it were a consent under section 28E(3)(*a*).

(2) In relation to such a consent, section 28E has effect as if for subsections (7) and (8) there were substituted—

"(7) A notice under subsection (6) must include a notice of—

(*a*) the Council's reasons for withdrawing or modifying the consent;

(*b*) the rights of appeal under section 28F;

(*c*) the effect of subsection (9); and

(*d*) the effect of section 28M."

9. (1) Subject to paragraph 10, this paragraph applies where—

(a) a notice has been given under old section 28(5)(a) before the substitution date;

(b) on the substitution date neither of the conditions set out in old section 28(6)(a) and (b) is fulfilled; and

(c) on the substitution date four months have expired since the notice under old section 28(5)(a) was given,

but even if those conditions are fulfilled, this paragraph does not apply in relation to operations specified in a notice under section 29(4)(a) on any land if immediately before the substitution date an order under section 29 was in effect in relation to that land.

(2) Where this paragraph applies, but subject to sub-paragraph (7), the prohibition in section 28E(1) on carrying out, or causing or permitting to be carried out, an operation does not apply in relation to an operation specified in the notice under old section 28(5)(a).

(3) Where this paragraph applies, the Nature Conservancy Council may, on or after the substitution date, give a notice (a "stop notice") to every owner and occupier of the land to which the stop notice is to apply.

(4) A stop notice is to specify—

(a) the date on which it is to take effect;

(b) the operations to which it applies; and

(c) the land to which it applies,

and must contain a notice of the right of the person to whom the stop notice is given to appeal against it in accordance with paragraph 11, and a notice of the effect of sub-paragraph (8).

(5) The date on which a stop notice is to take effect may not be sooner than the end of the period of three days beginning with the date the stop notice is given, unless the Council consider that there are special reasons which justify a shorter period, and a statement of those reasons is included with the stop notice.

(6) The operations to which a stop notice may apply are all or any of the operations specified in the notice under old section 28(5)(a).

(7) From the date on which the stop notice takes effect, sub-paragraph (2) of this paragraph ceases to apply in relation to the operations specified in the stop notice on the land to which the stop notice applies.

(8) Where the Council give a stop notice, they shall make a payment to any owner or occupier of the land who suffers loss because of it.

(9) The amount of a payment under sub-paragraph (8) is to be determined by the Council in accordance with guidance given and published by the Ministers (within the meaning of section 50).

(10) Section 50(3) applies to the determination of the amount of a payment under sub-paragraph (8) as it applies to the determination of the amount of payments under that section.

(11) This paragraph ceases to apply, in relation to any operation specified in the notice referred to in sub-paragraph (1)(a) except an operation to which a stop notice applies, if the operation has not begun before the end of the period of—

(a) three years beginning with the substitution date; or

(b) in a case falling within paragraph 10(2) or (3), three years beginning immediately after the expiry of the period of one month or longer referred to there.

10. (1) An agreement under old section 28(6A) in effect immediately before the substitution date has effect from the substitution date as an agreement that paragraph 9 is not to apply in relation to the operation which is the subject of the agreement; and, accordingly, paragraph 9 does not apply in relation to that operation (as regards both the owner and the occupier of the land).

(2) Where a notice has been given under old section 28(6B) before the substitution date, paragraph 9 has effect, in relation to the operation in question, as if for the period mentioned in paragraph 9(1)(c) there were substituted the period of one month from the giving of the notice or (if a longer period is specified in the notice) that longer period.

(3) If after an agreement has taken effect as mentioned in sub-paragraph (1) the relevant person (whether a party to the agreement or not) gives the Nature Conservancy Council written notice that he wishes to terminate the agreement, then as from the giving of the notice paragraph 9 has effect, in relation to the operation in question (as regards both the owner and the occupier of the land), as if for the period mentioned in paragraph 9(1)(c) there were substituted the period of one month from the giving of the notice or (if a longer period is specified in the notice) that longer period.

(4) In sub-paragraph (3), "relevant person" has the same meaning as in old section 28(6C).

11. (1) A person to whom a stop notice is given may by notice appeal against it to the Secretary of State, but meanwhile it remains in effect.

(2) Section 28F(3) to (11) shall apply in relation to such an appeal as they apply in relation to an appeal against a decision to withdraw a consent (see section 28F(1)(d)), but with the following modifications—

(a) as if, in section 28F(3), for paragraphs (a) and (b) and the following words "or, in either case," there were substituted "within the period of two months beginning with the date of the stop notice, or"; and

(b) as if, for section 28F(5), there were substituted—

"(5) On determining the appeal, the Secretary of State may quash or affirm the stop notice; and if he affirms it, he may do so either in its original form or with the removal from it of such operations as he thinks fit, or in relation to such reduced area of land as he thinks fit."

12. (1) The Nature Conservancy Council may, by notice given to every owner and occupier of land to which a stop notice applies, vary a stop notice by removing any operation to which it applies or reducing the area of land to which it applies.

(2) Where after giving a stop notice—

(a) the Council consent to an operation to which the stop notice applies;

(b) an operation to which it applies becomes one which may be carried out under the terms of an agreement under section 16 of the National Parks and Access to the Countryside Act 1949 or section 15 of the Countryside Act 1968; or

(c) an operation to which it applies becomes one which may be carried out in accordance with a management scheme under section 28J or a management notice under section 28K,

the stop notice shall be deemed to be varied accordingly by the removal from the stop notice of the operation in question in relation to the land to which the consent, agreement or management scheme or notice relates.

Modification of operation of section 28F

8–4286   13. (1) Section 28F(1)(*a*) does not apply to a refusal of a consent under old section 28(6)(*a*).

(2) Section 28F(1)(*b*) does not apply to consents taking effect as mentioned in paragraph 8(1)(*b*).

Modification of operation of section 28H

8–4287   14. Section 28H does not apply in relation to operations which have already begun on the date section 28H comes into force.

Section 29

8–4288   15. Paragraphs 16 and 17 apply where, immediately before the coming into force of paragraph 2 of Schedule 9 to this Act, there is in effect an order applying section 29(3) to any land ("the relevant land").

    16. (1) If the relevant land is not included in a site of special scientific interest, section 28E applies to it as if it were (and accordingly section 28P(1) applies also); and references in section 28E to a notification under section 28(1)(*b*) shall be construed as references to an order under section 29.

(2) Whether or not the relevant land is included in a site of special scientific interest, a notice given under section 29(4)(*a*) has effect as if it were a notice given under section 28E(1)(*a*), except as provided in paragraph 17.

(3) Whether or not the relevant land is included in a site of special scientific interest, a consent given under section 29(5)(*a*) has effect as if it were a consent given under section 28E(3)(*a*), and in relation to such a consent section 28E has effect as if for subsections (7) and (8) there were substituted—

"(7) A notice under subsection (6) must include a notice of—

    (*a*)   the Council's reasons for withdrawing or modifying the consent;
    (*b*)   the rights of appeal under section 28F;
    (*c*)   the effect of subsection (9); and
    (*d*)   the effect of section 28M."

    17. (1) This paragraph applies where—

    (*a*)   a notice has been given under section 29(4)(*a*) before the repeal of section 29 by paragraph 2 of Schedule 9 to this Act;
    (*b*)   on the date on which paragraph 2 of Schedule 9 to this Act comes into force, neither of the conditions set out in section 29(5)(*a*) and (*b*) is fulfilled; and
    (*c*)   on that date the period mentioned in paragraph (*c*) of section 29(5) (or in that paragraph as it has effect by virtue of section 29(6) or (7)) has expired.

(2) Where this paragraph applies, but subject to paragraph 9(7) as it has effect by virtue of sub-paragraph (3) of this paragraph, the prohibition in section 28E(1) on carrying out, or causing or permitting to be carried out, an operation does not apply in relation to an operation specified in the notice under section 29(4)(*a*).

(3) Paragraphs 9(3) to (11) and 11 of this Schedule apply also in relation to this paragraph, but as if—

    (*a*)   in those provisions references to a notice under old section 28(5)(*a*) were to a notice under section 29(4)(*a*); and
    (*b*)   the reference to "sub-paragraph (2)" in paragraph 9(7) were to sub-paragraph (2) of this paragraph.

    18. (1) This paragraph applies where—

    (*a*)   as a result of the coming into force of paragraph 2 of Schedule 9 to this Act, a local inquiry or a hearing (as mentioned in paragraph 4(1)(*a*) and (*b*) respectively of Schedule 11 to the 1981 Act) comes to an end, and
    (*b*)   an owner or occupier of land in relation to which an order under section 29 has been made has incurred expense in connection with opposing the order at the local inquiry or hearing.

(2) If this paragraph applies, the Nature Conservancy Council shall (subject to sub-paragraph (3)) pay a person's expenses referred to in paragraph (1)(*b*) to the extent that they are reasonable.

(3) The Council need not pay any such expenses unless the person—

    (*a*)   applies to the Council for such a payment; and
    (*b*)   satisfies the Council that he has incurred the expenses.

Compensation and grants

8–4289   19. (1) Despite its repeal by paragraph 2 of Schedule 9 to this Act, section 30 (compensation where order made under section 29) continues to apply in connection with an order made under section 29 before the coming into force of that paragraph.

(2) After the repeal of section 29 by that paragraph, section 32 (duties of agriculture Ministers with respect to areas of special scientific interest) continues to apply, in relation to an application under that section relating to land to which section 29(3) applied immediately before its repeal, as if that land were included in a site of special scientific interest.

Offences and restoration orders

8–4290   20. (1) Section 28P does not have effect in relation to an offence committed before the substitution date, but old section 28 or, as the case may be, section 29, has effect instead.

(2) In relation to an offence under section 29, section 31 as it had effect before the coming into force of paragraph 3 of Schedule 9 to this Act shall continue to apply.

Powers of entry

8–4291   21. Section 51 (powers of entry) has effect on and after the substitution date as if, in subsection (1), after paragraph (*m*) there were inserted—

"(*n*) to determine whether or not to give or vary a stop notice;",

and as if, in subsection (2)(*a*), after "paragraphs (*a*) to (*k*)" there were inserted "and paragraph (*n*)".

Service of notices

8–4292   22. Section 70A (service of notices) applies in relation to notices given under this Schedule as it applies in relation to notices and other documents required or authorised to be served or given under the 1981 Act.

Section 81(1)   SCHEDULE 12
AMENDMENTS RELATING TO PART I OF WILDLIFE AND COUNTRYSIDE ACT 1981

8–4293   1. In section 1(5) of the 1981 Act (offence of intentional disturbance of wild birds) after "intentionally" there is inserted "or recklessly".

2. In section 3 of that Act (areas of special protection) in subsection (1)(*c*) for "the offender shall be liable to a special penalty" there is substituted "the offence shall be treated as falling within section 7(3A)".

3. In section 6 of that Act (sale etc of live or dead wild birds, eggs etc), in subsection (2) the words from "who is not" to "Secretary of State" are omitted.

4. (1) In section 7 of that Act (registration etc of certain captive birds), in subsection (3)(*a*), for "for which a special penalty is provided" there is substituted "which falls within subsection (3A)".

(2) After subsection (3) of that section there is inserted—

"(3A) The offences falling within this subsection are—

(*a*) any offence under section 1(1) or (2) in respect of—

(i)   a bird included in Schedule 1 or any part of, or anything derived from, such a bird,
(ii) the nest of such a bird, or
(iii) an egg of such a bird or any part of such an egg;

(*b*) any offence under section 1(5) or 5;
(*c*) any offence under section 6 in respect of—

(i) a bird included in Schedule 1 or any part of, or anything derived from, such a bird, or
(ii) an egg of such a bird or any part of such an egg

(*d*) any offence under section 8.".

5. In section 9 of that Act (protection of certain wild animals)—

(*a*) in subsection (4) after "intentionally" there is inserted "or recklessly", and
(*b*) after that subsection there is inserted—

"(4A) Subject to the provisions of this Part, if any person intentionally or recklessly disturbs any wild animal included in Schedule 5 as—

(*a*) a dolphin or whale (cetacea), or
(*b*) a basking shark (cetorhinus maximus),

he shall be guilty of an offence."

6. In section 16(3) of that Act (power to grant licences) for "and (4)" there is substituted ", (4) and (4A)".

7. In section 19 of that Act (enforcement of Part I), in subsection (3) for the words from "suspecting that" to "has been committed" there is substituted "suspecting that an offence under this Part has been committed".

8. After that section there is inserted—

"**19ZA. Enforcement: wildlife inspectors.**   (1) In this Part, "wildlife inspector" means a person authorised in writing by the Secretary of State under this subsection.

(2) An authorisation under subsection (1) is subject to any conditions or limitations specified in it.

(3) A wildlife inspector may, at any reasonable time and (if required to do so) upon producing evidence that he is authorised—

(*a*) enter and inspect any premises for the purpose of ascertaining whether an offence under section 6, 9(5) or 13(2) is being, or has been, committed on those premises;
(*b*) enter and inspect any premises where he has reasonable cause to believe that any birds included in Schedule 4 are kept, for the purpose of ascertaining whether an offence under section 7 is being, or has been, committed on those premises;
(*c*) enter any premises for the purpose of ascertaining whether an offence under section 14 is being, or has been, committed on those premises;
(*d*) enter and inspect any premises for the purpose of verifying any statement or representation which has been made by an occupier, or any document or information which has been furnished by him, and which he made or furnished—

(i) for the purposes of obtaining (whether for himself or another) a relevant registration or licence, or
(ii) in connection with a relevant registration or licence held by him.

(4) In subsection (3)—

(*a*) paragraphs (*a*) and (*b*) do not confer power to enter a dwelling except for purposes connected with—

(i) a relevant registration or licence held by an occupier of the dwelling, or
(ii) an application by an occupier of the dwelling for a relevant registration or licence; and

(*b*) paragraph (*c*) does not confer any power to enter a dwelling.

(5) A wildlife inspector may, for the purpose of ascertaining whether an offence under section 6, 7, 9(5), 13(2) or 14 is being, or has been, committed in respect of any specimen, require any person who has the specimen in his possession or control to make it available for examination by the inspector.

(6) Any person who has in his possession or control any live bird or other animal shall give any wildlife

inspector acting in the exercise of powers conferred by this section such assistance as the inspector may reasonably require for the purpose of examining the bird or other animal.

(7) Any person who—

(*a*) intentionally obstructs a wildlife inspector acting in the exercise of powers conferred by subsection (3) or (5), or

(*b*) fails without reasonable excuse to give any assistance reasonably required under subsection (6),

shall be guilty of an offence.

(8) Any person who, with intent to deceive, falsely pretends to be a wildlife inspector shall be guilty of an offence.

(9) In this section—

"relevant registration or licence" means—

(*a*) a registration in accordance with regulations under section 7(1), or

(*b*) a licence under section 16 authorising anything which would otherwise be an offence under section 6, 7, 9(5), 13(2) or 14; and

"specimen" means any bird, other animal or plant or any part of, or anything derived from, a bird, other animal or plant.

19ZB. Power to take samples.   (1) A constable who suspects with reasonable cause that a specimen found by him in the exercise of powers conferred by section 19 is one in respect of which an offence under this Part is being or has been committed may require the taking from it of a sample of blood or tissue in order to determine its identity or ancestry.

(2) A constable who suspects with reasonable cause that an offence under this Part is being or has been committed in respect of any specimen ("the relevant specimen") may require any person to make available for the taking of a sample of blood or tissue any specimen (other than the relevant specimen) in that person's possession or control which is alleged to be, or which the constable suspects with reasonable cause to be, a specimen a sample from which will tend to establish the identity or ancestry of the relevant specimen.

(3) A wildlife inspector may, for the purpose of ascertaining whether an offence under section 6, 7, 9(5), 13(2) or 14 is being or has been committed, require the taking of a sample of blood or tissue from a specimen found by him in the exercise of powers conferred by section 19ZA(3)(*a*) to (*c*) in order to determine its identity or ancestry.

(4) A wildlife inspector may, for the purpose of ascertaining whether an offence under section 6, 7, 9(5), 13(2) or 14 is being or has been committed in respect of any specimen ("the relevant specimen"), require any person to make available for the taking of a sample of blood or tissue any specimen (other than the relevant specimen) in that person's possession or control which is alleged to be, or which the wildlife inspector suspects with reasonable cause to be, a specimen a sample from which will tend to establish the identity or ancestry of the relevant specimen.

(5) No sample from a live bird, other animal or plant shall be taken pursuant to a requirement under this section unless the person taking it is satisfied on reasonable grounds that taking the sample will not cause lasting harm to the specimen.

(6) No sample from a live bird or other animal shall be taken pursuant to such a requirement except by a veterinary surgeon.

(7) Where a sample from a live bird or other animal is to be taken pursuant to such a requirement, any person who has possession or control of the specimen shall give the person taking the sample such assistance as he may reasonably require for that purpose.

(8) A constable entering premises under section 19(2), and any wildlife inspector entering premises under section 19ZA(3), may take with him a veterinary surgeon if he has reasonable grounds for believing that such a person will be required for the exercise on the premises of powers under subsections (1) to (4).

(9) Any person who—

(*a*) intentionally obstructs a wildlife inspector acting in the exercise of the power conferred by subsection (3),

(*b*) fails without reasonable excuse to make available any specimen in accordance with a requirement under subsection (2) or (4), or

(*c*) fails without reasonable excuse to give any assistance reasonably required under subsection (7),

shall be guilty of an offence.

(10) In this section—

(*a*) "specimen" has the same meaning as in section 19ZA, and

(*b*) in relation to a specimen which is a part of, or is derived from, a bird, other animal or plant, references to determining its identity or ancestry are to determining the identity or ancestry of the bird, other animal or plant."

9. (1) In section 20 of that Act (time limit for summary prosecution of certain offences under Part I)—

(*a*) subsection (1) is omitted, and

(*b*) in subsection (2) for "an offence to which this section applies" there is substituted "an offence under this Part".

(2) Sub-paragraph (1) does not have effect in relation to any offence committed before the commencement of this paragraph.

10. (1) Section 21 of that Act (penalties, forfeitures etc for offences under Part I) is amended as follows.

(2) For subsections (1) to (3) there is substituted—

"(1) Subject to subsection (5), a person guilty of an offence under any of sections 1 to 13 or section 17 shall be liable on summary conviction to imprisonment for a term not exceeding six months or to a fine not exceeding level 5 on the standard scale, or to both."

(3) In subsection (4)—

(a) in paragraph (a) for the words from "to a fine" to the end there is substituted "to imprisonment for a term not exceeding six months or to a fine not exceeding the statutory maximum, or to both", and

(b) in paragraph (b) for "to a fine" there is substituted "to imprisonment for a term not exceeding two years or to a fine, or to both".

(4) After subsection (4) there is inserted—

"(4A) Except in a case falling within subsection (4B), a person guilty of an offence under section 19ZA(7) shall be liable on summary conviction to a fine not exceeding level 5 on the standard scale.

(4B) A person guilty of an offence under subsection (7) of section 19ZA in relation to a wildlife inspector acting in the exercise of the power conferred by subsection (3)(c) of that section shall be liable—

(a) on summary conviction, to a fine not exceeding the statutory maximum;
(b) on conviction on indictment, to a fine.

(4C) A person guilty of an offence under section 19ZA(8) shall be liable—

(a) on summary conviction, to imprisonment for a term not exceeding six months or a fine not exceeding the statutory maximum, or to both;
(b) on conviction on indictment, to imprisonment for a term not exceeding two years or to a fine, or to both.

(4D) A person guilty of an offence under section 19ZB(9) shall be liable on summary conviction to a fine not exceeding level 5 on the standard scale."

(5) In subsection (5) the words ", (2) or (3)" are omitted.

(6) Sub-paragraphs (1) to (5) and the repeal by this Act of provisions of the 1981 Act relating to special penalties do not have effect in relation to any offence committed before the commencement of this paragraph.

11. In section 24 of that Act (functions of the Nature Conservancy Councils), in subsection (4) for paragraph (c) there is substituted—

"(c) any wildlife inspector,".

12. In section 27 of that Act (interpretation of Part I), in subsection (1) after the definition of "wild plant" there is inserted—

""wildlife inspector" has the meaning given by section 19ZA(1)."

13. In section 24(2) of the Police and Criminal Evidence Act 1984 (arrestable offences), after paragraph (r) there is inserted—

"(s) an offence under section 1(1) or (2) or 6 of the Wildlife and Countryside Act 1981 (taking, possessing, selling etc of wild birds) in respect of a bird included in Schedule 1 to that Act or any part of, or anything derived from, such a bird;

(t) an offence under any of the following provisions of the Wildlife and Countryside Act 1981—

(i) section 1(5) (disturbance of wild birds),
(ii) section 9 or 13(1)(a) or (2) (taking, possessing, selling etc of wild animals or plants),
(iii) section 14 (introduction of new species etc)."

Section 102

SCHEDULE 16
REPEALS

(*Only those provisions which amend enactments contained in this work are reproduced below.*)

8–4294

PART I
ACCESS TO THE COUNTRYSIDE

Chapter	Short title	Extent of repeal
1925 c 20	The Law of Property Act 1925	Section 193(2).

8–4295

PART II
PUBLIC RIGHTS OF WAY AND ROAD TRAFFIC

Chapter	Short title	Extent of repeal
1980 c 66	The Highways Act 1980	Section 134(5).

8–4296

PART III
SITES OF SPECIAL SCIENTIFIC INTEREST

Chapter	Short title	Extent of repeal
1970 c 30	The Conservation of Seals Act 1970	Section 10(4)(c) and the following word "or".
1981 c 69	The Wildlife and Countryside Act 1981	Sections 29 and 30.

PART IV
WILDLIFE

Chapter	Short title	Extent of repeal
1981 c 69	The Wildlife and Countryside Act 1981	In section 1, subsection (4) and, in subsection (5), the words "and liable to a special penalty".
		In section 5(1), the words "and be liable to a special penalty".
		In section 6, in subsection (2) the words from "who is not" to "Secretary of State", and subsections (4) and (7) to (10).
		In section 7, in subsection (1) the words "and be liable to a special penalty", and subsections (6) and (7).
		In section 8, in subsections (1) and (3) the words "and be liable to a special penalty".
		Section 14(5) and (6).
		In section 17 the words "6(2) or".
		Section 20(1).
		In section 21(5) the words ", (2) or (3)".

Control of Trade in Endangered Species (Enforcement) Regulations 1997[1]

(SI 1997/1372 amended by SI 2005/1674)

8–4298   1. Citation and commencement.   These regulations may be cited as the Control of Trade in Endangered Species (Enforcement) Regulations 1997 and shall come into force on 1st June 1997.

---

1. Made by the Secretary of State under s 2 of the European Communities Act 1972.

8–4299   2. Interpretation.   (1) In these Regulations—

"acquired" means, in relation to a specimen, taken from the wild or the point at which it was born in captivity or artificially propagated;

"acquired unlawfully" means acquired contrary to the provisions of the Principal Regulation or the Subsidiary Regulation;

"authorised person" means a person duly authorised in writing by the Secretary of State for the purposes of these Regulations;

"import" means introduce into the Community;

"imported unlawfully" means introduced into the Community contrary to the provisions of the Principal Regulation or the Subsidiary Regulation;

"premises" includes any place, and, in particular, includes any vehicle, vessel, aircraft, hovercraft, tent or movable structure;

"Principal Regulation" means Council Regulation (EC) No 338/97 on the protection of species of wild fauna and flora by regulating trade therein;

"registered veterinary surgeon" means a person who is registered in the register of veterinary surgeons under section 2 of the Veterinary Surgeons Act 1966;

"Subsidiary Regulation" means Commission Regulation (EC) No 939/97 on the implementation of Council Regulation (EC) No 338/97 on the protection of wild species of fauna and flora by regulating trade therein.

(2) For the purposes of these Regulations references to a permit or certificate are references to any of the following—

(a) an import permit of the kind referred to in Article 4 of the Principal Regulation;

(b) an export permit or re-export certificate of the kind referred to in Article 5 of the Principal Regulation;

(c) a certificate of any of the kinds referred to in Article 10 of the Principal Regulation;

(d) a certificate of the kind referred to in Article 18 of the Subsidiary Regulation;

(e) a label of the kind referred to in Article 7(4) of the Principal Regulation;

(f) in so far as, in accordance with Article 43 of the Subsidiary Regulation, reliance may be placed on a permit or certificate issued under Council Regulation (EEC) No 3626/82 and

Commission Regulation (EEC) No 3418/83, a permit or certificate issued under those Regulations.

(3) Unless the context otherwise requires, expressions used in these Regulations, and which are also used in the Principal or Subsidiary Regulations, shall have the meaning they bear in those Regulations.

(4) Any reference in these Regulations to a numbered paragraph is a reference to the paragraph so numbered in the regulation in which the reference appears.

8–4300 3. False statements etc.   (1) A person who, for the purpose of obtaining, whether for himself or another, the issue of a permit or certificate—

(*a*) knowingly or recklessly makes a statement or representation which is false in a material particular; or

(*b*) knowingly or recklessly furnishes a document or information which is false in a material particular; or

(*c*) for any purpose in connection with the Principal Regulation or the Subsidiary Regulation, knowingly or recklessly uses or furnishes a false, falsified or invalid permit or certificate or one altered without authorisation,

shall be guilty of an offence and liable, on summary conviction, to a fine not exceeding level 5 on the standard scale or to imprisonment for a term not exceeding three months, or to both or, on conviction on indictment, to imprisonment for a term not exceeding two years or to a fine, or to both.

(2) A person who knowingly or recklessly makes an import notification which is false in a material particular shall be guilty of an offence and liable—

(*a*) on summary conviction, to a fine not exceeding level 5 on the standard scale, or to a term of imprisonment not exceeding three months, or to both; or

(*b*) on conviction on indictment, to imprisonment for a term not exceeding two years or to a fine, or to both.

(3) Without prejudice to Article 11(2)(*a*) of the Principal Regulation—

(*a*) a permit or certificate in relation to which an offence under paragraph (1) has been committed shall be void; and

(*b*) an import notification in relation to which an offence under paragraph (2) has been committed shall be void.

8–4301 4. Misuse of permits and certificates.   (1) A person who knowingly falsifies or alters any permit or certificate shall be guilty of an offence and liable—

(*a*) on summary conviction, to a fine not exceeding level 5 on the standard scale, or to a term of imprisonment not exceeding three months, or to both; or

(*b*) on conviction on indictment, to imprisonment for a term not exceeding two years or to a fine, or to both.

(2) A person who knowingly uses a permit, certificate or import notification for any specimen other than that for which it was issued shall be guilty of an offence and liable—

(*a*) on summary conviction, to a fine not exceeding level 5 on the standard scale, or to a term of imprisonment not exceeding three months, or to both; or

(*b*) on conviction on indictment, to imprisonment for a term not exceeding two years or to a fine, or to both.

(3) A person who knowingly uses a specimen of a species listed in Annex A of the Principal Regulation otherwise than in accordance with the authorisation given at the time of issue of the import permit or subsequently, shall be guilty of an offence and liable—

(*a*) on summary conviction, to a fine not exceeding level 5 on the standard scale, or to a term of imprisonment not exceeding three months, or to both; or

(*b*) on conviction on indictment, to imprisonment for a term not exceeding two years or to a fine, or to both.

8–4302 5. Proof of lawful import or export.   Where any specimen is being imported or exported or has been imported or brought to any place for the purpose of being exported, a person commissioned by the Commissioners of Customs and Excise, or a person authorised by them, may require any person possessing or having control of that specimen to furnish proof that its importation or exportation is or was not unlawful by virtue of the Principal Regulation or, as the case may be, the Subsidiary Regulation and, until such proof is furnished, the specimen shall be liable to detention under the Customs and Excise Management Act 1979 and, if such proof is not furnished to the satisfaction of the Commissioners, the specimen shall be liable to forfeiture under that Act.

8–4303 6. Compliance with permits or certificates.   Any person who knowingly contravenes any condition or requirement of a permit or certificate issued in accordance with the Principal Regulation or Subsidiary Regulation shall be guilty of an offence and liable—

(a) on summary conviction, to a fine not exceeding level 5 on the standard scale, or to a term of imprisonment not exceeding three months, or to both; or

(b) on conviction on indictment, to imprisonment for a term not exceeding two years or to a fine, or to both.

8–4304　7. Movement of live specimens.　(1) Where an import permit or any certificate issued in accordance with the Principal Regulation in respect of a live specimen of a species listed in Annex A to the Principal Regulation specifies an address at which the specimen must be kept, any person who, without reasonable excuse, and contrary to Article 9 of the Principal Regulation,

(a) causes or permits that specimen to be transferred from that address without prior written authorisation from the Secretary of State; or

(b) keeps that specimen at premises other than the specified address or location without prior written authorisation from the Secretary of State,

shall be guilty of an offence.

(2) Any person guilty of an offence under paragraph (1) shall be liable—

(a) on summary conviction, to a fine not exceeding level 5 on the standard scale, or to a term of imprisonment not exceeding three months, or to both; or

(b) on conviction on indictment, to imprisonment for a term not exceeding two years or to a fine, or to both.

8–4305　8. Purchase and sale etc.　(1) Subject to paragraphs (3) and (4), a person who, contrary to Article 8 of the Principal Regulation, purchases, offers to purchase, acquires for commercial purposes, displays to the public for commercial purposes, uses for commercial gain, sells, keeps for sale, offers for sale or transports for sale any specimen of a species listed in Annex A to the Principal Regulation shall be guilty of an offence.

(2) Subject to paragraphs (4) and (5), any person who, contrary to Article 8 of the Principal Regulation, purchases, offers to purchase, acquires for commercial purposes, sells, keeps for sale, offers for sale or transports for sale any specimen of a species listed in Annex B to the Principal Regulation which has been imported or acquired unlawfully shall be guilty of an offence.

(3) Paragraph (1) does not apply to anything done under, and in accordance with the terms of, any certificate or general derogation granted pursuant to Article 8 of the Principal Regulation.

(4) A person shall not be guilty of an offence under paragraph (1) or (2) if he proves that at the time the alleged offence was committed he had no reason to believe that the specimen was a specimen of a species listed in Annex A, or as the case may be Annex B.

(5) A person shall not be guilty of an offence under paragraph (2) if he proves—

(a) that at the time when the specimen first came into his possession he made such enquiries (if any) as in the circumstances were reasonable in order to ascertain whether it was imported or acquired unlawfully; and

(b) that at the time the alleged offence was committed, he had no reason to believe that the specimen was imported or acquired unlawfully.

(6) Without prejudice to the generality of paragraph (5) above, a person shall be taken to have made such enquiries as are mentioned there if he produces to the court a statement which was furnished by the person from whom he obtained possession of the specimen ("the supplier"), which was signed by the supplier or by a person authorised by him, and which states that—

(a) the supplier made enquiries at the time the specimen came into his possession in order to ascertain whether it was a specimen which had been imported or acquired unlawfully; and

(b) the supplier had no reason to believe at the time he relinquished possession of the specimen to the accused that the article was at that time a specimen which had been imported or acquired lawfully.

(7) A person who furnishes, for the purposes of paragraph (6) above, a statement which he knows to be false in a material particular, or recklessly furnishes for those purposes a certificate which is false in a material particular, shall be guilty of an offence.

(8) A person shall be guilty of an offence under paragraph (1) or (2) above shall be liable—

(a) on summary conviction, to a fine not exceeding level 5 on the standard scale or to a term of imprisonment not exceeding six months, or to both; and

(b) on conviction on indictment, to a term of imprisonment not exceeding five years or to a fine, or to both.

(9) A person guilty of an offence under paragraph (7) above shall be liable—

(a) on summary conviction, to a fine not exceeding level 5 on the standard scale or a term of imprisonment not exceeding six months, or to both; and

(b) on conviction on indictment, to a term of imprisonment not exceeding two years or to a fine, or to both.

8–4306　9. Powers of entry.　(1) If, on an application made by a constable, a justice of the peace or sheriff is satisfied that there are reasonable grounds for believing—

(a) that there is any unlawfully imported or acquired specimen on premises specified in the application; or

(b) that an offence under these Regulations has been or is being committed and that evidence of the offence may be found on any premises,

and that any of the conditions specified in paragraph (2) applies, he may issue a warrant authorising any constable to enter upon and search those premises; and such a warrant may authorise persons to accompany any constable who is executing it.

(2) The conditions referred to in paragraph (1) are—

(a) that admission to the premises has been refused; or
(b) that refusal is apprehended; or
(c) that the case is one of urgency; or
(d) that an application for admission to the premises would defeat the object of the entry.

(3) A constable who is, by virtue of paragraph (1), lawfully on any premises may, in order to determine the identity or ancestry of any specimen, require the taking from any specimen of a sample of blood or tissue provided that—

(a) the sample is taken by a registered veterinary surgeon; and
(b) the taking of such a sample will not cause lasting harm to the specimen.

(4) An authorised person may, at any reasonable time and (if required to do so) upon producing evidence that he is so authorised, enter and inspect for the purpose of—

(a) ascertaining whether the premises are being used for any of the following activities: purchase, offering to purchase, acquisition for commercial purposes, display to the public for commercial purposes, use for commercial gain, sale, keeping for sale, offering for sale or transporting for sale contrary to Article 8 of the Principal Regulation; or
(b) verifying information supplied by a person for the purpose of obtaining a permit or certificate; or
(c) ascertaining whether any live specimen is being kept on premises at the address specified in the import permit issued for that specimen as that at which the specimen is to be kept; or
(d) ascertaining whether any condition of a permit or certificate has been or is being observed,

any premises where he has reasonable cause to believe a specimen is being kept.

(5) An authorised person who is, by virtue of paragraph (4), lawfully on any premises may, in order to determine the identity or ancestry of any specimen for the purposes specified in that paragraph, require the taking from any specimen of a sample of blood or tissue provided that—

(a) the sample is taken by a registered veterinary surgeon; and
(b) the taking of such a sample will not cause lasting harm to the specimen.

(6) Any person who intentionally obstructs an authorised person acting in accordance with the powers conferred by this regulation shall be guilty of an offence and shall for every such obstruction be liable on summary conviction to a fine not exceeding level 3 on the standard scale.

(7) If a person, with intent to deceive, pretends to be an authorised person, he shall be guilty of an offence and liable—

(a) on summary conviction, to a fine not exceeding level 5 on the standard scale, or to a term of imprisonment not exceeding three months, or to both; or
(b) on conviction on indictment, to imprisonment for a term not exceeding two years or to a fine, or to both.

8–4307   **10. Powers of seizure.**   A constable who is, by virtue of regulation 9(1) above, lawfully on any premises may seize any thing where he has reasonable grounds for believing that such seizure is—

(a) necessary for the protection of the constable or any person accompanying him; or
(b) otherwise essential to effect seizure of the specimen referred to in that paragraph; or
(c) necessary for the conservation of evidence; or
(d) in the interests of the welfare of the specimen.

8–4308   **11. Forfeiture.**   (1) The court by which any person is convicted of an offence under these Regulations—

(a) shall order the forfeiture of any specimen or other thing in respect of which the offence was committed; and
(b) may order the forfeiture of any vehicle, equipment or other thing which was used to commit the offence.

(2) In paragraph (1)(b) "vehicle" includes aircraft, hovercraft and boat.

8–4309   **12. Offences by corporations.**   (1) Where an offence under these regulations which is committed by a body corporate is proved to have been committed with the consent or connivance of, or to be attributable to any neglect on the part of, a director, manager, secretary or other similar officer of the body corporate, or any person who was purporting to act in any such capacity, he, as well as the body corporate, shall be guilty of that offence and shall be liable to be proceeded against and punished accordingly.

(2) For this purpose "director", in relation to any body corporate whose affairs are managed by its members, means any member of the body.

(3) Where an offence under these Regulations committed by a Scottish partnership or unincorporated association (other than a partnership) is proved to have been committed with the consent or connivance of, or to be attributable to neglect on the part of, a partner in the partnership or, as the case may be, a person concerned in the management and control of the association, he (as well as the partnership) shall be guilty of the offence and liable to be proceeded against and punished accordingly.

8–4309A   13. Revocation and savings.   The Control of Trade in Endangered Species (Enforcement) Regulations 1985 are hereby revoked.

CONSPIRACY

8–4310   The offence of conspiracy at common law has, with certain exceptions, been abolished; see the Criminal Law Act 1977, s 5, post. The only remaining common law offences[1] are conspiracy to defraud[2], to corrupt public morals or to outrage public decency[3].

A charge of conspiracy to obtain property by deception can properly be laid where the deception is practised by means of contract, the terms of which contravene Art 85(1) of the EEC Treaty. Prosecution for conspiracy in such circumstances does not amount to a breach of the duty of Member States not to undermine the effectiveness of Art 85(1), nor does it reinforce or favour a breach of that Article[4].

The scope of the law of conspiracy has been extended to conspiracy, or incitement, to commit certain sexual acts outside the United Kingdom by the Sexual Offences (Conspiracy and Incitement) Act 1996, see this PART, SEXUAL OFFENCES, post.

When there are two alleged conspirators the questions to be addressed are: is there evidence of an agreement between them which involved dishonesty on both sides; whether there is evidence admissible only against one of the accused. If there is evidence of an agreement and the evidence is admissible against both then both must be convicted or acquitted; differing verdicts can only be brought where there is evidence against one defendant, such as an admission, which is not admissible against the other[5].

---

1. As to the common law offence of attempting to pervert the course of justice, see *R v Thomas* [1979] QB 326, [1979] 1 All ER 577, 143 JP 219 and *R v Selvage, R v Morgan* [1982] QB 372, [1982] 1 All ER 96, 146 JP 115. If a conspiracy involves the commission of any substantive offence the only charge that can be brought is conspiracy contrary to s 1(1) of the 1977 Act, even if some of the conduct involved in the conspiracy would not amount to a substantive offence and even though the charge might result in serious criminal conduct going unpunished (*R v Tonner, R v Evans* [1985] 1 All ER 807, [1985] 1 WLR 344, CA).

2. The offence of conspiracy to defraud is not indictable in England where the conspiracy is to be carried out abroad, even if it would injure a company or person in England by causing damage abroad (*A-G's Reference under s 36 of the Criminal Justice Act 1972 (No 1 of 1983)* (1983) 77 Cr App Rep 9). It is not necessary to prove an overt act pursuant to the conspiracy took place in England, where an agreement was made abroad to commit a crime in England (*R v Sansom, Williams, Smith, Wilkins* [1991] 2 QB 130, [1991] 2 All ER 145, 92 Cr App Rep 115). In *R v Hollinshead* [1985] AC 975, [1985] 2 All ER 769, HL, it was held that if parties agree (a) to manufacture devices whose only use is fraudulently to alter electricity meters and (b) to sell those devices to a person who intends merely to re-sell them (and not himself to use them), the agreement constitutes a common law conspiracy to defraud.

3. As to the common law offence of outraging public decency, see *R v Rowley* [1991] 4 All ER 649, [1991] 1 WLR 1020, [1991] Crim LR 785, CA. This offence requires the presence of at least two witnesses and must be committed in a place where there exists a real possibility that members of the general public might witness the outrageous act (*R v Walker* [1996] 1 Cr App Rep 111, [1995] Crim LR 826, sub nom *R v W* (1995) 159 JP 509).

4. *R v Dearlove* (1988) 88 Cr App Rep 279 (defendants who dishonestly purchased goods wholesale at a lower export price, falsely representing that the goods would be exported to Bulgaria, with the intention of selling them at a greater profit on the home market, were held to have been properly convicted of conspiracy to obtain property by deception).

5. *R v Testouri* [2003] EWCA Crim 3735, [2004] 2 Cr App R 4, [2004] Crim LR 372.

Criminal Law Act 1977
(1977 c 45)

PART I
CONSPIRACY

8–4328   1. The offence of conspiracy[1].   (1) Subject to the following provisions of this Part of this Act, if a person agrees[2] with any other person[3] or persons that a course of conduct shall be pursued which, if the agreement is carried out in accordance with their intentions, either—

(a) will necessarily amount to or involve the commission of any offence or offences[4] by one[5] or more of the parties to the agreement, or

(b) would do so but for the existence of facts which render the commission of the offence or any of the offences impossible[6], he is guilty of conspiracy to commit the offence or offences in question[7].

(1A) and (1B) *Repealed.*

(2) Where liability for any offence may be incurred without knowledge on the part of the person committing it of any particular fact or circumstance necessary for the commission of the offence, a person shall nevertheless not be guilty of conspiracy to commit that offence by virtue of subsection (1) above unless he and at least one other party to the agreement intend or know that that fact or circumstance shall or will exist at the time when the conduct constituting the offence is to take place[8].

(3) *Repealed.*

(4) In this Part of this Act "offence" means an offence triable in England and Wales[9].

(5) and (6) *Repealed.*

[Criminal Law Act 1977, s 1 as amended by the Criminal Attempts Act 1981, s 5, the Computer Misuse Act 1990, s 7, the Trade Union and Labour Relations (Consolidation) Act 1992, Sch 1 and the Criminal Justice (Terrorism and Conspiracy) Act 1998, Schs 1 and 2.]

---

1. As to charges of and penalty for conspiracy to defraud, see the Criminal Justice Act 1987, s 12, in PART I: MAGISTRATES' COURTS, PROCEDURE, ante.

2. It is sufficient, to establish guilt, to show that the accused had known that the course of conduct to be pursued would amount to or involve the commission of an offence or offences and that he had intended to play some part in the agreed course of conduct in furtherance of the criminal purpose that it had been intended to achieve (*R v Anderson* [1986] AC 27, [1985] 2 All ER 961, HL); indeed "play some part" can apparently include continuing to an activity of others, participation in a conspiracy can be active or passive in this sense, see *R v Siracusa* [1989] Crim LR 712.

3. A secret and uncommunicated intention to join in an illegal enterprise, should the occasion arise, does not amount to conspiracy (*R v Scott* (1978) 68 Cr App Rep 164, [1979] Crim LR 456).

4. There is no compelling reason why the expression "offence or offences" in s 1(1) of the Criminal Law Act 1977 should be construed conjunctively; therefore, a count alleging conspiracy as a single agreement to contravene either s 49(2) of the Drug Trafficking Act 1994 or s 93C(2) of the Criminal Justice Act 1988, contrary to s 1 of the 1977 Act is not bad for duplicity (*R v Hussain* [2002] EWCA Crim 6, [2002] 2 Cr App Rep 363). There appear to conflicting views as to whether conspiracy to deal with criminal property can be committed before that property comes to into existence. In *Harmer* (see infra) the court based its decision principally on the ground that the conspiracy was not complete unless the criminal property existed in fact because otherwise the conspirators would not be agreeing to perform a course of conduct that would necessarily constitute a crime. In *R v Ali* [2005] EWCA Crim 87, [2005] Crim LR 854, however, doubt was cast on this aspect of *Harmer*. If A and B agree to deal with property which will exist in the future, and the prosecution prove that they will know it to be criminal property at the time that the conduct constituting the substantive offence will take place, then the elements of conspiracy will be made out because s 1(2) (infra) looks to the time when the conduct constituting the substantive offence will take place; accordingly the requirements of s 1(1)(a) are satisfied.

5. Thus where only one party to an agreement can commit an offence as principal (eg a parent abducting a child contrary to the Child Abduction Act 1984, s 1) other parties to the agreement can be guilty of the offence of conspiracy (*R v Sherry, R v El Yamani* [1993] Crim LR 536).

6. This has no applicability where the substantive offence was not impossible to commit but the prosecution cannot prove it: *R v Harmer* [2005] EWCA Crim 1, [2005] 2 Cr App R 2, [2005] Crim LR 482 (no offence of conspiracy to convert or transfer money which a defendant had reasonable grounds to suspect represented another person's proceeds of crime unless there is proof that the property was the proceeds of crime).

7. Where the offence alleged was public nuisance, namely the escape of a patient from a mental hospital, the prosecution did not have to prove actual danger to the public, but only potential danger (*R v Soul* (1980) 70 Cr App Rep 295).

8. Thus, where the substantive charge required only that the defendant had reasonable grounds to suspect that the money was the proceeds of crime, he would not be guilty of conspiracy unless he and at least one other party to the agreement intended or knew that the money would be the proceeds of crime when the agreed conduct took place; if the prosecution could not prove that the money was the proceeds of crime, they could not prove that the appellant knew that it was and, accordingly, s.1(2) of the 1977 Act applied and was not satisfied: *R v Harmer* supra). The requirement to prove knowledge was affirmed in *Ali*, supra.

9. An extraterritorial conspiracy to commit a criminal offence in England and Wales, whether under this Act or at common law, is triable here notwithstanding that no overt act took place here (*R v Sansom* [1991] 2 QB 130, [1991] 2 All ER 145.

8–4329   **1A. Conspiracy to commit offences outside the United Kingdom.** (1) Where each of the following conditions is satisfied in the case of an agreement, this Part of this Act has effect in relation to the agreement as it has effect in relation to an agreement falling within section 1(1) above.

(2) The first condition is that the pursuit of the agreed course of conduct would at some stage involve—

(a) an act by one or more of the parties, or

(b) the happening of some other event,

intended to take place in a country or territory outside the United Kingdom.

(3) The second condition is that that act or other event constitutes an offence under the law in force in that country or territory.

(4) The third condition is that the agreement would fall within section 1(1) above as an agreement relating to the commission of an offence but for the fact that the offence would not be an offence triable in England and Wales if committed in accordance with the parties' intentions.

(5) The fourth condition is that—

(a) a party to the agreement, or a party's agent, did anything in England and Wales in relation to the agreement before its formation, or

(b) a party to the agreement became a party in England and Wales (by joining it either in person or through an agent), or

(c) a party to the agreement, or a party's agent, did or omitted anything in England and Wales in pursuance of the agreement.

(6) In the application of this Part of this Act to an agreement in the case of which each of the above conditions is satisfied, a reference to an offence is to be read as a reference to what would be the offence in question but for the fact that it is not an offence triable in England and Wales.

(7) Conduct punishable under the law in force in any country or territory is an offence under that law for the purposes of this section, however it is described in that law.

(8) Subject to subsection (9) below, the second condition is to be taken to be satisfied unless, not later than rules of court may provide, the defence serve on the prosecution a notice—

(a) stating that, on the facts as alleged with respect to the agreed course of conduct, the condition is not in their opinion satisfied,

(b) showing their grounds for that opinion, and

(c) requiring the prosecution to show that it is satisfied.

(9) The court may permit the defence to require the prosecution to show that the second condition is satisfied without the prior service of a notice under subsection (8) above.

(10) In the Crown Court the question whether the second condition is satisfied shall be decided by the judge alone, and shall be treated as a question of law for the purposes of—

(a) section 9(3) of the Criminal Justice Act 1987 (preparatory hearing in fraud cases), and

(b) section 31(3) of the Criminal Procedure and Investigations Act 1996 (preparatory hearing in other cases).

(11) Any act done by means of a message (however communicated) is to be treated for the purposes of the fourth condition as done in England and Wales if the message is sent or received in England and Wales.

(12) In any proceedings in respect of an offence triable by virtue of this section, it is immaterial to guilt whether or not the accused was a British citizen at the time of any act or other event proof of which is required for conviction of the offence.

(13) References in any enactment, instrument or document (except those in this Part of this Act) to an offence of conspiracy to commit an offence include an offence triable in England and Wales as such a conspiracy by virtue of this section (without prejudice to subsection (6) above).

(14) Nothing in this section—

(a) applies to an agreement entered into before the day on which the Criminal Justice (Terrorism and Conspiracy) Act 1998 was passed, or

(b) imposes criminal liability on any person acting on behalf of, or holding office under, the Crown.

[Criminal Law Act 1977, s 1A, as inserted by the Criminal Justice (Terrorism and Conspiracy) Act 1998, s 5.]

8–4330   2. Exemptions from liability for conspiracy.   (1) A person shall not by virtue of section 1 above be guilty of conspiracy to commit any offence if he is an intended victim of that offence.

(2) A person shall not by virtue of section 1 above be guilty of conspiracy to commit any offence or offences if the only other person or persons with whom he agrees are (both initially and at all times during the currency of the agreement) persons of any one or more of the following descriptions, that is to say—

(a) his spouse[1] or civil partner;

(b) a person under the age of criminal responsibility; and

(c) an intended victim of that offence or of each of those offences.

(3) A person is under the age of criminal responsibility for the purposes of subsection (2) (b) above so long as it is conclusively presumed, by virtue of section 50 of the Children and Young Persons Act 1933, that he cannot be guilty of any offence.

[Criminal Law Act 1977, s 2 as amended by Civil Partnership Act 2004, Sch 27.]

---

1. Where a defendant entered into a criminal conspiracy with her husband, knowing that he was involved with others in the conspiracy, she was thereby agreeing with all those whom she knew were the other parties to the conspiracy, and accordingly was afforded no protection by s 2(2)(a) (*R v Chrastny* [1992] 1 All ER 189, [1991] 1 WLR 1381, 155 JP 850, CA).

8–4331   3. Penalties for conspiracy.   (1) A person guilty by virtue of section 1 above of conspiracy to commit any offence or offences shall be liable on conviction on indictment—

(a) in a case falling within subsection (2) or (3) below, to imprisonment for a term related in accordance with that subsection to the gravity of the offence or offences in question (referred to below in this section as the relevant offence or offences); and

(b) in any other case, to a fine.

Paragraph (b) above shall not be taken as prejudicing the application of section 127 of the Powers of Criminal Courts (Sentencing) Act 2000 (general power of court to fine offender convicted on indictment) in a case falling within subsection (2) or (3) below.

(2) Where the relevant offence or any of the relevant offences is an offence of any of the following descriptions, that is to say—

(*a*) murder, or any other offence the sentence for which is fixed by law;

(*b*) an offence for which a sentence extending to imprisonment for life is provided; or

(*c*) an indictable offence punishable with imprisonment for which no maximum term of imprisonment is provided,

the person convicted shall be liable to imprisonment for life.

(3) Where in a case other than one to which subsection (2) above applies the relevant offence or any of the relevant offences is punishable with imprisonment, the person convicted shall be liable to imprisonment for a term not exceeding the maximum term provided for that offence or (where more than one such offence is in question) for any one of those offences (taking the longer or the longest term as the limit for the purposes of this section where the terms provided differ).

In the case of an offence triable either way[1] the references above in this subsection to the maximum term provided for that offence are references to the maximum term so provided on conviction on indictment.

[Criminal Law Act 1977, s 3 as amended by the Powers of Criminal Courts (Sentencing) Act 2000, Sch 9.]

---

1. Although offences of criminal damage where the value of the damage is small, are triable only summarily with a maximum penalty of 3 months' imprisonment (Magistrates' Courts Act 1980, s 22), conspiracy to commit such offences is an offence contrary to s 1 of the Criminal Law Act 1977 where a penalty in excess of that for the substantive offence may be appropriate (*R v Ward* (1996) 161 JP 297, CA).

8–4332 4. Restrictions on the institution of proceedings for conspiracy. (1) Subject to subsection (2) below, proceedings under section 1 above for conspiracy to commit any offence or offences shall not be instituted against any person except by or with the consent of the Director of Public Prosecutions if the offence or (as the case may be) each of the offences in question is a summary offence.

(2) In relation to the institution of proceedings under section 1 above for conspiracy to commit—

(*a*) an offence which is subject to a prohibition by or under any enactment of the institution of proceedings otherwise than by, or on behalf or with the consent of, the Attorney General, or

(*b*) two or more offences of which at least one is subject to such a prohibition,

subsection (1) above shall have effect with the substitution of a reference to the Attorney General for the reference to the Director of Public Prosecutions.

(3) Any prohibition by or under any enactment on the institution of proceedings for any offence which is not a summary offence otherwise than by, or on behalf or with the consent of, the Director of Public Prosecutions or any other person shall apply also in relation to proceedings under section 1 above for conspiracy to commit that offence.

(4) Where—

(*a*) an offence has been committed in pursuance of any agreement; and

(*b*) proceedings may not be instituted for that offence because any time limit applicable to the institution of any such proceedings has expired,

proceedings under section 1 above for conspiracy to commit that offence shall not be instituted against any person on the basis of that agreement.

(5) Subject to subsection (6) below, no proceedings for an offence triable by virtue of section 1A above may be instituted except by or with the consent of the Attorney General.

(6) The Secretary of State may by order provide that subsection (5) above shall not apply, or shall not apply to any case of a description specified in the order.

(7) An order under subsection (6) above—

(*a*) shall be made by statutory instrument, and

(*b*) shall not be made unless a draft has been laid before, and approved by resolution of, each House of Parliament.

[Criminal Law Act 1977, s 4 as amended by the Criminal Justice (Terrorism and Conspiracy) Act 1998, s 5.]

8–4333 5. Abolitions, savings, transitional provisions, consequential amendment and repeals. (1) Subject to the following provisions of this section, the offence of conspiracy at common law is hereby abolished.

(2) Subsection (1) above shall not affect the offence of conspiracy at common law so far as relates to conspiracy to defraud[1].

(3) Subsection (1) above shall not affect the offence of conspiracy at common law if and in so far as it may be committed by entering into an agreement to engage in conduct which—

(*a*) tends to corrupt public morals or outrages public decency; but

(*b*) would not amount to or involve the commission of an offence if carried out by a single person otherwise than in pursuance of an agreement.

(4) Subsection (1) above shall not affect—

(*a*) any proceedings commenced before the time when this Part of this Act comes into force;

(b)   any proceedings commenced after that time against a person charged with the same conspiracy as that charged in any proceedings commenced before that time; or

(c)   any proceedings commenced after that time in respect of a trespass committed before that time;

but a person convicted of conspiracy to trespass in any proceedings brought by virtue of paragraph (c) above shall not in respect of that conviction be liable to imprisonment for a term exceeding six months.

(5)   Sections 1 and 2 above shall apply to things done before as well as to things done after the time when this Part of this Act comes into force, but in the application of section 3 above to a case where the agreement in question was entered into before that time—

(a)   subsection (2) shall be read without the reference to murder in paragraph (a); and

(b)   any murder intended under the agreement shall be treated as an offence for which a maximum term of imprisonment of ten years is provided.

(6)   The rules laid down by sections 1 and 2 above shall apply for determining whether a person is guilty of an offence of conspiracy under any enactment other than section 1 above, but conduct which is an offence under any such other enactment shall not also be an offence under section 1 above.

(7)   Incitement to commit the offence of conspiracy (whether the conspiracy incited would be an offence at common law or under section 1 above or any other enactment) shall cease to be offences.

(8)   The fact that the person or persons who, so far as appears from the indictment on which any person has been convicted of conspiracy, were the only other parties to the agreement on which his conviction was based have been acquitted of conspiracy by reference to that agreement (whether after being tried with the person convicted or separately) shall not be a ground for quashing his conviction unless under all the circumstances of the case his conviction is inconsistent with the acquittal of the other person or persons in question.

(9)   Any rule of law or practice inconsistent with the provisions of subsection (8) above is hereby abolished.

(11)   *(Repealed).*

[Criminal Law Act 1977, s 5 as amended by the Criminal Attempts Act 1981, Sch, the Criminal Justice Act 1987, s 12 and the Trade Union and Labour Relations (Consolidation) Act 1992, Sch 1.]

---

1. As to charges of and penalty for conspiracy to defraud, see the Criminal Justice Act 1987, s 12, in PART I: MAGISTRATES' COURTS, PROCEDURE, ante. An agreement to take positive steps to conceal the making of a secret profit from a company may amount to a conspiracy to defraud (*Adams v R* [1995] 1 WLR 52, [1995] 2 Cr App Rep 295, [1995] Crim LR 561).

CONSUMER PROTECTION

8–4358   This title contains the following statutes—

and the following statutory instruments—

8–5533W Price Marking Order 2004
8–5535   General Product Safety Regulations 2005

8–4359 European Communities Act 1972: regulations. Within the scope of the title Consumer Protection would fall the subject matter of a number of regulations made under the very wide enabling power provided in section 2(2) of the European Communities Act 1972. Where such regulations were made solely under the 1972 Act and create offences they are noted below in chronological order:

Aerosol Dispensers (EEC Requirements) Regulations, 1977, SI 1977/1140 amended by SI 1980/136, SI 1981/1549, SI 1985/1279 and SI 1996/2421;

Textile Products (Indications of Fibre Content) Regulations 1986, SI 1986/26 amended by SI 1988/1350, SI 1994/450, SI 1998/1169 and SI 2005/1401;

Control of Misleading Advertisements Regulations 1988, SI 1988/915 amended by SI 1988/1340, Broadcasting Act 1990, Sch 20, SI 2000/914, SI 2001/3649, SI 2003/1400 and 3183;

Personal Protective Equipment (EC Directive) Regulations 1992, SI 1992/3139, amended by SI 1993/3074, SI 1994/2326 and SI 1996/3039, and extended by s 2(1) of the European Economic Area Act 1993;

Package Travel, Package Holidays and Package Tours Regulations 1992 in this title, post;

Boiler (Efficiency) Regulations 1993, SI 1993/3083 amended by SI 1994/3086 and SI 2006/170;

Price Indications (Resale of Tickets) Regulations 1994, SI 1994/3248;

Footwear (Indication of Composition) Labelling Regulations 1995, SI 1995/2489;

Energy Information (Washing Machines) Regulations 1996, SI 1996/600 amended by SI 1997/803, SI 2001/3142 and SI 2003/1398;

Energy Information (Tumble Driers) Regulations 1996, SI 1996/601 amended by SI 2001/3142 and SI 2003/1398;

Energy Information (Combined Washer-driers) Regulations 1997, SI 1997/1624 amended by SI 2001/3142 and SI 2003/1398;

Energy Efficiency (Refrigerators and Freezers) Regulations 1997, SI 1997/1941 amended by SI 2001/3142 and SI 2003/1398;

Timeshare Regulations 1997, SI 1997/1081 amended by SI 2003/1398 and 1922

Packaging (Essential Requirements) Regulations 1998, SI 1998/1165;

Energy Information (Lamps) Regulations 1999/1517 amended by SI 2001/3142 and SI 2003/1398;

Energy Information (Dishwashers) Regulations 1999, SI 1999/1676 amended by SI 2001/3142 and SI 2003/1398;

Passenger Car (Fuel Consumption and CO2 Emissions Information) Regulations 2001, SI 2001/3523 amended by SI 2004/1661;

Energy Information (Household Electric Ovens) Regulations 2003, SI 2003/751;

Recreational Craft Regulations 2004, SI 2004/1464 amended by SI 2004/3201;

Energy Information (Household Refrigerators and Freezers) Regulations 2004, SI 2004/1468;

Biofuel (Labelling) Regulations 2004, SI 2004/3349 amended by SI 2005/3355;

Energy Information (Household Air Conditioners) (No 2) Regulations 2005, SI 2005/1726;

General Product Safety Regulations 2005, SI 2005/1803, this title, post.

Auctions (Bidding Agreements) Act 1927
(17 & 18 Geo 5 c 12)

8–4360 1. Certain bidding agreements to be illegal. (1) If any dealer[1] agrees to give, or gives, or offers any gift or consideration to any other person as an inducement or reward for abstaining, or for having abstained, from bidding at a sale by auction either generally or for any particular lot, or if any person agrees to accept, or accepts, or attempts to obtain from any dealer any such gift or consideration as aforesaid, he shall be guilty of an offence under this Act, and shall be liable on summary conviction[2] to a fine not exceeding **the statutory maximum**, or to a term of imprisonment for any period not exceeding **six months**, or to both such fine and imprisonment: Provided that where it is proved that a dealer has previously to an auction entered into an agreement in writing with one or more persons to purchase goods at the auction *bona fide* on a joint account, and has before the goods were purchased at the auction deposited a copy of the agreement with the auctioneer, such an agreement shall not be treated as an agreement made in contravention of this section.

[Auctions (Bidding Agreements) Act 1927, s 1, as amended by Criminal Justice Act 1967, 3rd Sch.]

---

1. "Dealer" means a person who in the normal course of his business attends sales by auction for the purposes of purchasing goods with a view to reselling them (Auctions (Bidding Agreements) Act 1927 s 1(2)).

2. In England and Wales a prosecution for an offence under this section shall not be instituted without the consent of the Attorney-General (Auctions (Bidding Agreements) Act 1927 s 1(3)). See PART I, MAGISTRATES' COURTS, PROCEDURE, para **1–380**, **Criminal prosecutions**, After conviction, any auction may, as against a purchaser who has been a party to such agreement or transaction, be treated by the vendor as a sale induced by fraud, but a notice of intimation by the vendor shall not affect the obligation of the auctioneer to deliver the goods to the purchaser (id, s. 2). By s 1(1) of the Auctions (Bidding Agreements) Act 1969, offences under this section are also **triable on indictment** and the penalty on conviction on indictment is imprisonment not exceeding two years or a fine or both; for procedure in

respect of an offence triable either way, see Magistrates' Courts Act 1980, ss 17A–21, in PART I, ante. For power to order that a person convicted of an offence shall not attend or participate in auctions and for offence of contravening such an order, see s 2 of the Auctions (Bidding Agreements) Act 1969, post.

8–4361   3. Copy of Act to be exhibited at sale.   The particulars which under s 7[1] of the Auctioneers Act 1845, are required to be affixed or suspended in some conspicuous part of the room or place where the auction is held shall include a copy of this Act[2], and that section shall have effect accordingly.
[Auctions (Bidding Agreements) Act 1927, s 3.]

1. If any auctioneer . . . begins any auction or acts as auctioneer at any auction in any room or place where his name and residence is not painted, printed or written on a ticket or board affixed or suspended as required by this section. Penalty not exceeding **level 2** on the standard scale (Auctioneers Act 1845, 8 & 9 Vict c 15, s 7, as amended by the Criminal Law Act 1977, s 31 and the Criminal Justice Act 1982, s 46).
2. By s 4 of the Auctions (Bidding Agreements) Act 1969, a copy of that Act must also be displayed.

Fraudulent Mediums Act 1951
(14 & 15 Geo 6 c 33)

8–4380   1. Punishment of fraudulent mediums, etc.   (1) Subject to the provisions of this section, any person who—

    (a)   with intent to deceive purports to act as a spiritualistic medium or to exercise any powers of telepathy, clairvoyance or other similar powers[1], or

    (b)   in purporting to act as a spiritualistic medium or to exercise such powers as aforesaid, uses any fraudulent device,

shall be guilty of an offence.

(2) A person shall not be convicted of an offence under the foregoing subsection unless it is proved that he acted for reward; and for the purposes of this section a person shall be deemed to act for reward if any money is paid, or other valuable thing given, in respect of what he does, whether to him or to any other person.

(3) A person guilty of an offence under this section shall be liable on summary conviction to a fine not exceeding **the statutory maximum** or to imprisonment for a term not exceeding **four months** or to both such fine and such imprisonment, or on conviction on indictment to a fine or to imprisonment for a term not exceeding **two years** or to both such fine and such imprisonment[2].

(4) No proceedings for an offence under this section shall be brought in England or Wales except by or with the consent of the Director of Public Prosecutions.

(5) Nothing in subsection (1) of this section shall apply to anything done solely for the purpose of entertainment.
[Fraudulent Mediums Act 1951, s 1, as amended by the Criminal Law Act 1977, ss 28 and 32.]

1. In a prosecution under the Witchcraft Act 1735 (repealed by this Act) it was held that the court was entitled to reject evidence purporting to demonstrate and prove that a person was a materialisation medium and thereby to disprove the allegations made. Evidence of matters outside the period covered by the charge should be excluded (*R v Duncan* [1944] KB 713, [1944] 2 All ER 220).
2. For procedure in respect of this offence, triable either way, see the Magistrates' Courts Act 1980, ss 17A–21, in PART I, ante.

Trading Representations (Disabled Persons) Act 1958
(6 & 7 Eliz 2 c 49)

8–4390   1. Sellers of goods advertised as made by, or sold for benefit of, blind or otherwise disabled persons, to be registered.   (1) It shall not be lawful, in selling any goods or exchanging any article or thing for any other article or thing or soliciting orders for goods of any description in the course of a business carried on by any person, for any representation that, or implying that, blind or otherwise disabled persons[1], or any description of such persons—

    (a)   are employed in the production, preparation or packing of the goods, article or thing or,

    (b)   benefit (otherwise than as users of the goods, article or thing) from the sale of the goods or the exchange of the article or thing or the carrying on of the business,

to be made in the course of visits from house to house[2], or by post, or by telephone and any person who contravenes this subsection shall be liable[3]—

    (i)   on summary conviction to a fine not exceeding **the statutory maximum**;

    (ii)   on conviction on indictment to a fine or to imprisonment for a term not exceeding two years or both.

(2) The foregoing subsection shall not apply where the business is being carried on—

(a)　by a local authority[4], or

(b)　(*Repealed*);

(c)　by a company, association or body providing facilities under s 15 of the Disabled Persons (Employment) Act 1944 in pursuance of arrangements under subsection (2) of that section, or

(d)　by any body of persons exempted by the Secretary of State from the operation of the foregoing subsection, being a body appearing to the Minister to be carrying on business without profit to its members,

or where the person carrying on the business is substantially disabled[5] and all goods, articles or things with respect to which the representation is made were produced by his own labour.

(3)　In England or Wales a local authority[4] may institute proceedings for an offence under this section.

(4)　Where an offence under this section which has been committed by a body corporate is proved to have been committed with the consent or connivance of, or to be attributable to any neglect on the part of, any director, manager, secretary, or other similar officer of the body corporate, or any person purporting to act in such capacity, he as well as the body corporate shall be deemed to be guilty of that offence and shall be liable to be proceeded against and punished accordingly.

[Trading Representations (Disabled Persons) Amendment Act 1958, s 1 as amended by the Trading Description (Disabled Persons) Amendment Act 1972, s 1, the Criminal Law Act 1977, s 28, the Local Government Act 1985, Sch 17, the Charities Act 1992, Sch 7, the Local Government (Wales) Act 1994, Sch 16 and SI 2002/1397.]

1.　This means persons under any disability, whether physical or mental, attributable to illness, injury, imperfect development or congenital deformity (s 4(1)).

2.　"House" includes a place of business (sub-s (5)).

3.　For procedure in respect of this offence which is triable either way, see the Magistrates' Courts Act 1980, ss 17A–21 in PART I: MAGISTRATES' COURTS, PROCEDURE, ante.

4.　"Local authority" means (in England or Wales), the council of a county, county borough or county district or a London borough or the Common Council of the City of London (sub-s (5)).

5.　This refers to persons substantially handicapped, whether permanently or not, by any such disability as is referred to in s 4(1) (see note 1, supra) (s 4(2)).

Mock Auctions Act 1961
(9 & 10 Eliz 2, c 47)

8–4400　1.　Penalties for promoting or conducting mock auctions.　(1)　It shall be an offence to promote or conduct, or to assist in the conduct of, a mock auction at which one or more lots to which this Act applies[1] are offered for sale.

(2)　Any person guilty of an offence under this Act shall be liable—

(a)　on summary conviction[2] to a fine not exceeding **the statutory maximum**, or to imprisonment for a term not exceeding **three months**, or to both such a fine and such imprisonment;

(b)　on conviction on indictment, to a fine or to imprisonment for a term not exceeding **two years**, or to both such a fine and such imprisonment.

(3)　Subject to the following provisions of this section, for the purposes of this Act a sale of goods by way of competitive bidding[3] shall be taken to be a mock auction if, but only if, during the course of the sale—

(a)　any lot to which this Act applies is sold to a person bidding for it, and either it is sold to him at a price lower than the amount of his highest bid for that lot, or part of the price at which it is sold to him is repaid or credited to him or is stated[4] to be so repaid or credited, or

(b)　the right to bid for any lot to which this Act applies is restricted, or is stated[4] to be restricted, to persons who have bought or agreed to buy one or more articles, or

(c)　any articles are given away or offered as gifts.

(4)　A sale of goods shall not be taken to be a mock auction by virtue of paragraph (a) of the last preceding subsection, if it is proved that the reduction in price, or the repayment or credit, as the case may be—

(a)　was on account of a defect discovered after the highest bid in question had been made, being a defect of which the person conducting the sale was unaware when that bid was made, or

(b)　was on account of damage sustained after that bid was made.

[Mock Auctions Act 1961, s 1, as amended by the Criminal Law Act 1977, ss 28 and 32.]

1.　"Lot to which this Act applies" means a lot consisting of or including plate, linen, china, glass, books, pictures, furniture, jewellery, etc, as specified in s 3(2), post.

2.　For procedure in respect of this offence triable either way, see Magistrates' Courts Act 1980, ss 17A–21, in PART I: MAGISTRATES' COURTS, PROCEDURE, ante.

3.　"Sale of goods by way of competitive bidding" is defined (s 3(1), post).

4.　Ie, stated by or on behalf of the person conducting the sale (s 3(3), post).

8–4401 2. Offences by bodies corporate. Where an offence punishable under this Act which has been committed by a body corporate is proved to have been committed with the consent or connivance or to be attributable to any neglect on the part of any director, manager, secretary or other similar officer of the body corporate or any person purporting to act in such capacity, he, as well as the body corporate, shall be deemed to be guilty of that offence and shall be liable to be proceeded against and punished accordingly.
[Mock Auctions Act 1961, s 2.]

8–4402 3. Interpretation. (1) In this Act "sale of goods by way of competitive bidding" means any sale of goods at which the persons present, or some of them, are invited to buy articles by way of competitive bidding, and "competitive bidding" includes any mode of sale whereby prospective purchasers may be enabled to compete for the purchase of articles whether by way of increasing bids or by the offer of articles to be bid for at successively decreasing prices[1] or otherwise[2].

(2) In this Act "lot to which this Act applies" means a lot consisting of or including one or more prescribed articles; and "prescribed articles" means any plate, plated articles, linen, china, glass, books, pictures, prints, furniture, jewellery, articles of household or personal use or ornament or any musical or scientific instrument or apparatus.

(3) In this Act "stated", in relation to a sale of goods by way of competitive bidding, means stated by or on behalf of the person conducting the sale, by an announcement made to the persons for the time being present at the sale.

(4) For the purposes of this Act any bid stated to have been made at a sale of goods by way of competitive bidding shall be conclusively presumed to have been made, and to have been a bid of the amount stated; and any reference in this Act to the sale of a lot to a person who has made a bid for it includes a reference to a purported sale thereof to a person stated to have bid for it, whether that person exists or not.

(5) For the purposes of this Act anything done in or about the place where a sale of goods by way of competitive bidding is held, if done in connection with the sale, shall be taken to be done during the course of the sale, whether it is done at the time when any articles are being sold or offered for sale by way of competitive bidding or before or after any such time.

(6) Subject to the provisions of s 33 of the Interpretation Act 1889[3] (which relates to offences under two or more laws), nothing in this Act shall derogate from any right of action or other remedy (whether civil or criminal) in proceedings instituted otherwise than under this Act.
[Mock Auctions Act 1961, s 3.]

1. See *Lomas v Rydeheard* (1975) 119 Sol Jo 233.
2. See *Allen v Simmons* [1978] 3 All ER 662, 143 JP 105. where "competitive bidding" was held to include the selection of one of several prospective purchasers who raised their hands when one article only was available to be sold. In *Clements v Rydeheard* [1978] 3 All ER 658, 143 JP 25, "competitive bidding" was held to include selecting a limited number of prospective purchasers of goods for sale at a fraction of their value, ie "competing to bid". The words "or otherwise" must refer to a situation quite different from that referred to in the previous words; there is no scope for the *euisdem generis* rule here (*R v Pollard* (1983) 148 JP 679, CA).
3. Now s 18 of the Interpretation Act 1978.

Hire-Purchase Act 1964[1]
(1964 c 53)

PART III[2]
TITLE TO MOTOR VEHICLES ON HIRE-PURCHASE OR CONDITIONAL SALE

8–4420 27. Protection of purchasers of motor vehicles[2]. (1) This section applies where a motor vehicle has been bailed or (in Scotland) hired under a hire-purchase agreement, or has been agreed[3] to be sold under a conditional sale agreement, and, before the property in the vehicle has become vested in the debtor, he disposes of the vehicle to another person.

(2) Where the disposition referred to in subsection (1) above is to a private purchaser, and he is a purchaser of the motor vehicle in good faith without notice of the hire-purchase or conditional sale agreement (the "relevant agreement") that disposition shall have effect as if the creditor's title to the vehicle has been vested in the debtor immediately before that disposition.

(3) Where the person to whom the disposition referred to in subsection (1) above is made (the "original purchaser") is a trade or finance purchaser, then if the person who is the first private purchaser of the motor vehicle after that disposition (the "first private purchaser") is a purchaser of the vehicle in good faith without notice of the relevant agreement, the disposition of the vehicle to the first private purchaser shall have effect as if the title of the creditor to the vehicle had been vested in the debtor immediately before he disposed of it to the original purchaser.

(4) Where, in a case within subsection (3) above—

(a) the disposition by which the first private purchaser becomes a purchaser of the motor vehicle in good faith without notice of the relevant agreement is itself a bailment or hiring under a hire-purchase agreement, and

(b) the person who is the creditor in relation to that agreement disposes of the vehicle to the first private purchaser, or a person claiming under him, by transferring to him the property in the vehicle in pursuance of a provision in the agreement in that behalf,

the disposition referred to in paragraph (b) above (whether or not the person to whom it is made is a purchaser in good faith without notice of the relevant agreement) shall as well as the disposition referred to in paragraph (a) above, have effect as mentioned in subsection (3) above.

(5) The preceding provisions of this section apply—

(a) notwithstanding anything in section 21 of the Sale of Goods Act 1893 (sale of goods by a person not the owner), but

(b) without prejudice to the provisions of the Factors Acts (as defined by section 62(1) of the said Act of 1893) or of any other enactment enabling the apparent owner of goods to dispose of them as if he were the true owner.

(6) Nothing in this section shall exonerate the debtor from any liability (whether criminal or civil) to which he would be subject apart from this section; and, in a case where the debtor disposes of the motor vehicle to a trade or finance purchaser, nothing in this section shall exonerate—

(a) that trade or finance purchaser, or

(b) any other trade or finance purchaser who becomes a purchaser of the vehicle and is not a person claiming under the first private purchaser,

from any liability (whether criminal or civil) to which he would be subject apart from this section.
[Hire Purchase Act 1964, s 27, as substituted by the Consumer Credit Act 1974, Sch 4.]

---

1. With the exception of Part III below and s 37 (Short title, citation and extent), the whole of this Act has been repealed by the Consumer Credit Act 1974, Sch 5.
2. Part III contains ss 27–29. Part III is printed as substituted by the Consumer Credit Act 1974, Sch 4, and as it has effect from the 19 May 1985; see SI 1983/1551.
3. For where the car dealer in releasing the car, acted as agent of the finance company to which property in the goods had already passsed and the offer being sufficiently certain, had been accepted by delivery of the goods see *Carlyle Finance Ltd v Pallas Industrial Finance* [1999] RTR 281, CA.

8–4421   28. Presumptions relating to dealings with motor vehicles[1]. (1) Where in any proceedings (whether criminal or civil) relating to a motor vehicle it is proved—

(a) that the vehicle was bailed or (in Scotland) hired under a hire-purchase agreement, or was agreed to be sold under a conditional sale agreement and

(b) that a person (whether a party to the proceedings or not) became a private purchaser of the vehicle in good faith without notice of the hire-purchase or conditional sale agreement (the "relevant agreement"),

this section shall have effect for the purposes of the operation of section 27 of this Act in relation to those proceedings.

(2) It shall be presumed for those purposes, unless the contrary is proved, that the disposition of the vehicle to the person referred to in subsection (1)(b) above (the "relevant purchaser") was made by the debtor.

(3) If it is proved that that disposition was not made by the debtor, then it shall be presumed for those purposes, unless the contrary is proved—

(a) that the debtor disposed of the vehicle to a private purchaser purchasing in good faith without notice of the relevant agreement, and

(b) that the relevant purchaser is or was a person claiming under the person to whom the debtor so disposed of the vehicle.

(4) If it is proved that the disposition of the vehicle to the relevant purchaser was not made by the debtor, and that the person to whom the debtor disposed of the vehicle (the "original purchaser") was a trade or finance purchaser, then it shall be presumed for those purposes, unless the contrary is proved—

(a) that the person who, after the disposition of the vehicle to the original purchaser, first became a private purchaser of the vehicle was a purchaser in good faith without notice of the relevant agreement, and

(b) that the relevant purchaser is or was a person claiming under the original purchaser.

(5) Without prejudice to any other method of proof, where in any proceedings a party thereto admits a fact, that fact shall, for the purposes of this section, be taken as against him to be proved in relation to those proceedings.
[Hire Purchase Act 1964, s 28, as substituted by the Consumer Credit Act 1974, Sch 4.]

---

1. Part III contains ss 27–29. Part III is printed as substituted by the Consumer Credit Act 1974, Sch 4, and as it has effect from the 19 May 1985; see SI 1983/1551.

8–4422   29. Interpretation of Part III[1]. (1) In this Part of this Act—

"conditional sale agreement" means an agreement for the sale of goods under which the purchase price or part of it is payable by instalments, and the property in the goods is to remain in the seller (notwithstanding that the buyer is to be in possession of the goods) until such conditions as to the payment of instalments or otherwise as may be specified in the agreement are fulfilled;

"creditor" means the person by whom goods are bailed or (in Scotland) hired under a hire-purchase agreement or as the case may be, the seller under a conditional sale agreement, or the person to whom his rights and duties have passed by assignment or operation of the law;

"disposition" means any sale or contract of sale (including a conditional sale agreement), any bailment or (in Scotland) hiring under a hire-purchase agreement and any transfer of the property in goods in pursuance of a provision in that behalf contained in a hire-purchase agreement, and includes, any transaction purporting to be a disposition (as so defined), and "dispose of" shall be construed accordingly;

"hire-purchase agreement" means an agreement, other than a conditional sale agreement, under which—

(*a*) goods are bailed or (in Scotland) hired in return for periodical payments by the person to whom they are bailed or hired, and

(*b*) the property in the goods will pass to that person if the terms of the agreement are complied with and one or more of the following occurs—

(i) the exercise of an option to purchase by that person,

(ii) the doing of any other specified act by any party to the agreement,

(iii) the happening of any other specified events; and

"motor vehicle" means a mechanically propelled vehicle intended or adapted for use on roads to which the public has access.

(2) In this Part of this Act, "trade or finance purchaser" means a purchaser who, at the time of the disposition made to him, carries on a business which consists, wholly or partly—

(*a*) of purchasing motor vehicles for the purpose of offering or exposing them for sale, or

(*b*) of providing finance by purchasing motor vehicles for the purpose of bailing or (in Scotland) hiring them under hire-purchase agreements or agreeing to sell them under conditional sale agreements,

and "private purchaser" means a purchaser who, at the time of the disposition made to him, does not carry on any such business.

(3) For the purposes of this Part of this Act a person becomes a purchaser of a motor vehicle if, and at the time when, a disposition of the vehicle is made to him; and a person shall be taken to be a purchaser of a motor vehicle without notice of a hire-purchase agreement or conditional sale agreement if, at the time of the disposition made to him, he has no actual notice that the vehicle is or was the subject of any such agreement.

(4) In this Part of this Act the "debtor" in relation to a motor vehicle which has been bailed or hired under a hire-purchase agreement, or, as the case may be, agreed to be sold under a conditional sale agreement, means the person who at the material time (whether the agreement has before that time been terminated or not) is either—

(*a*) the person to whom the vehicle is bailed or hired under that agreement, or

(*b*) is, in relation to the agreement, the buyer,

including a person who at that time is, by virtue of section 130(4) of the Consumer Credit Act 1974 treated as a bailee or (in Scotland) a custodier of the vehicle.

(5) In this Part of this Act any reference to the title of the creditor to a motor vehicle which has been bailed (in Scotland) hired under a hire-purchase agreement, or agreed to be sold under a conditional sale agreement, and is disposed of by the debtor, is a reference to such title (if any) to the vehicle as, immediately before that disposition, was vested in the person who then was the creditor in relation to the agreement.

[Hire Purchase Act 1964, s 29, as substituted by the Consumer Credit Act 1974, Sch 4.]

---

1. Part III contains ss 27–29. Part III is printed as substituted by the Consumer Credit Act 1974, Sch 4, and as it has effect from the 19 May 1985; see SI 1983/1551.

Trade Descriptions Act 1968
(1968 c 29)

Prohibition of false trade descriptions

8–4447 1. Prohibition of false trade descriptions.   (1) Any person who, in the course of a trade or business[1]—

(*a*) applies[2] a false trade description[3] to any goods; or

(*b*) supplies[4] or offers to supply[5] any goods to which a false trade[6] description[3] is applied;

shall, subject to the provisions of this Act[7], be guilty of an offence[8].

(2) Sections 2 to 6 of this Act shall have effect for the purposes of this section and for the interpretation of expressions used in this section, wherever they occur in this Act.

[Trade Descriptions Act 1968, s 1.]

---

1. The term "trade or business" is apt to cover professionals as well (*Roberts v Leonard* (1995) 159 JP 711). A person, who carried out repairs and improvements to motor vehicles in his spare time and then sold them, was held to be engaging in a hobby and, therefore, his activities did not constitute a trade or business (*Blakemore v Bellamy* (1982) 147 JP 89, [1983] RTR 303). Similarly, a taxi driver who also hired out vehicles did not act in the course of a trade or business in relation to one of 4 vehicles of which he disposed, since although the sale was incidental to the carrying on of his business, the prosecution had not established that the sale of vehicles was carried on with some degree of regularity (*Devlin v Hall* [1990] RTR 320, [1990] Crim LR 879). Transactions need to have some degree of regularity so as to form part of the normal practice of a business in order to fall within s 1(1) (*Davies v Sumner* [1984] 3 All ER 831, [1984] 1 WLR 1301, 149 JP 110, HL, but the need for some degree of regularity would not necessarily exclude a one-off venture in the nature of trade, carried through with a view to profit; see *Davies v Sumner* supra and *Corfield v Sevenways Garage Ltd* (1984) 148 JP 648, [1985] RTR 109). Where a person purports to supply goods to members of a club, such supply may still be in the course of a trade or business unless there is evidence of a genuine club which distributes goods only to a restricted group of people as opposed to the general public (*Cahalne v London Borough of Croydon* (1985) 149 JP 561). The return of a motor car following its service amounts to the supply of the car on that occasion within the meaning of s 1(1)(*a*) and (*b*) of the Act (*Formula One Autocentres Ltd v Birmingham City Council* (1998) 163 JP 234, [1999] RTR 195).

2. See s 4, post. This is a strict liability offence; the prosecution do not have to prove dishonesty (*Alec Norman Garages Ltd v Phillips* (1984) 148 JP 741). The Act applies to auctioneers and to the art world (*May v Vincent* (1990) 154 JP 997).

3. See s 3, post. A false opinion given in a notification of refusal of a test certificate (under the Road Traffic Act 1972) is not a false trade description for the purpose of this section (*Wycombe Marsh Garages Ltd v Fowler* [1972] 3 All ER 248, 137 JP 138); in which case it was also held that this section does not apply to an expert who is called upon to advise and thereby express an opinion or state a fact in regard to the condition of goods. The correct test to be applied to a statement in a test certificate is to ask how the ordinary man would react on receiving a certificate in this form (*Corfield v Sevenways Garage Ltd* (1984) 148 JP 648, [1985] RTR 109; false mileage stated). See also *R v Coventry City Justices, ex p Farrand* (1987) 152 JP 26, [1988] RTR 273 (MOT certificate stating wrong year of manufacture). In *Wickens Motors (Gloucester) Ltd v Hall* [1972] 3 All ER 759, 137 JP 8, it was held that a false trade description which is not concerned with the sale or supply of goods does not amount to an offence under s 1(1)(*a*). A false reading on an odometer can be a false trade description (*Swithland Motors Ltd v Peck* [1991] Crim LR 386, DC. But the false trade description may be given by the *buyer*, eg a car dealer making statements about the condition of a car offered to him for sale (*Fletcher v Bugden* [1974] 2 All ER 1243, 138 JP 582). The court is not concerned whether or not the purchaser got good value for money (*Furniss v Scholes* [1974] RTR 133. See also *Cadbury Ltd v Halliday* [1975] 2 All ER 226, 139 JP 428). Although it will generally be a question of fact whether a description of a car as being "in excellent condition throughout" is, or is not, a false trade description, if the facts show that the car needed a substantial number of repairs if it were to be driven safely, then such facts would not justify a dismissal; it is no answer to say that the car is in as good a condition as would be expected of an unrepaired car of its age and mileage; if repairs are needed it will not be "excellent" until they are carried out: see *Chidwick v Beer* [1974] RTR 415. It cannot be said that the words "showroom condition throughout" was merely a trade puff, indiscriminate praises and not an assertion of specific verifiable facts; to apply them to a car with defects is a false trade description (*Hawkins v Smith* [1978] Crim LR 578). It can be a false trade description to advertise a motorcar as having had one owner, when in fact the vehicle had been leased to five registered keepers (*R v South Western Justices and Hallcrest Garages Ltd, ex p London Borough of Wandsworth* (1983) 147 JP 212, [1983] RTR 425.

Section 1(1)(*a*) deals with the unscrupulous trader, s 1(1)(*b*) with the careless trader; it is not open to a person charged under the former to rely on any disclaimer; and any disclaimer under the latter has to be "as bold, precise and compelling as the trade description itself" (see *R v Southwood* [1987] 3 All ER 556, [1987] 1 WLR 1361, CA and cases cited therein and *Newham London Borough v Singh and Sandhu* (1987) 152 JP 239, [1988] RTR 359; followed in *May v Vincent* (1990) 154 JP 997. Where a motor dealer who has not himself altered or replaced the odometer, knows the vehicle's true mileage and knows that the odometer materially understates it, a disclaimer in the conventional form that the reading is incorrect to the best of the dealer's knowledge and belief seriously understates his knowledge that the reading is grossly and materially incorrect and is not the sort of emphatic contradiction of the message sent by the odometer which neutralises its effect. Only disclosure of the known fact and extent of the falsity of the registered mileage figures will achieve that. As regards mileages, dealers are required to volunteer the truth in so far as they know it: *Farrand v Lazarus* [2002] EWHC 226 (Admin), [2002] 3 All ER 175, 166 JP 227. [2002] RTR 434.Where a disclaimer is insufficient to negative a false description the defendant may in some circumstances seek to rely on the defence in s 24, post.

In cases involving an odometer reading, the following propositions can be established from the authorities:

(*a*) the mileage shown on an odometer is a trade description;

(*b*) a person who alters or replaces an odometer to show an inaccurate mileage commits an offence under s 1(1)(*a*), but only if he does so within the course of a trade or business;

(*c*) an offence under s 1(1)(*a*) is committed at the time the false trade description is applied (ie at the time the odometer reading was altered);

(*d*) a person who alters an odometer reading not in the course of a trade or business, but who then sells the vehicle in the course of a trade or business is a prima facie guilty of an offence under s 1(1)(*b*);

(*e*) such a person will not be guilty of an offence if he proves (i) the false trade description was neutralised at the time of supply, or of negotiations leading to the supply, by an expressed disclaimer or contradiction of the message contained in the trade description, which was as bold, precise and compelling as the trade description, or (ii) that the supply was to another motor dealer who did not rely on the odometer reading;

(*f*) the concept of disclaimer has no relevance to an offence under s 1(1)(*a*) (*R v Shrewsbury Crown Court, ex p Venables* [1994] Crim LR 61). See also *R v Bull* [1997] RTR 123 (whether disclaimer on sales invoice part of trade description).

In the description "vegetable lard" the adjective could be taken as a disclaimer even if the prime meaning of the word "lard" was taken to be "pig-fat" (although it is probably no longer so restricted in meaning) (*Wolkind and Northcott v Pura Foods Ltd* (1987) 151 JP 492).

4. A partner of a firm may be guilty under this section even if he was in no way a party to the applying of a false trade description to goods by another partner of the firm; an offence under this section does not require an element of mens rea (*Clode v Barnes* [1974] 1 All ER 1166, 138 JP 371).

5. See s 6, post. An offer to hire goods to members of the public on payment of a fee amounts to an "offer to supply" those goods; it is not necessary to prove there has been a sale (*Cahalne v London Borough of Croydon* (1985) 149 JP 561).

Point-of-sale literature must be kept up to date so as to correspond to goods sold, otherwise an offence is committed (*Denard v Smith and Dixons Ltd* (1990) 155 JP 253, [1991] Crim LR 63).

6. See *Havering London Borough v Stevenson* [1970] 3 All ER 609, 134 JP 689.

7. For defences available, see ss 24 and 25, post.

8. For the power of the local weights and measures authority to prosecute, see s 26, post. The proper approach is to consider the matter in four stages; (1) Had a trade description been applied to the goods? (2) Was that description false in any particular? (3) If it was, was it false to a material degree? (4) If it was not, the justices should put themselves in the position of the ordinary shopper to decide if it was misleading (*Horner v Kingsley Clothing Ltd* [1989] Crim LR 911, DC).

8–4448   2. Trade description.   (1) A trade description is an indication[1] direct or indirect, and by whatever means given, of any of the following matters with respect to any goods or parts of goods, that is to say—

(*a*)   quantity[2], size or gauge;
(*b*)   method of manufacture[3], production, processing or reconditioning;
(*c*)   composition[4];
(*d*)   fitness for purpose[5], strength, performance[6], behaviour or accuracy;
(*e*)   any physical characteristics not included in the preceding paragraphs;
(*f*)   testing by any person and results thereof;
(*g*)   approval by any person or conformity with a type approved by any person;
(*h*)   place[7], or date of manufacture, productions, processing or reconditioning;
(*i*)   person by whom manufactured[8], produced, processed or reconditioned[9];
(*j*)   other history, including previous ownership or use.

(2) The matters specified in subsection (1) of this section shall be taken—

(*a*)   in relation to any animal, to include sex, breed or cross, fertility and soundness;
(*b*)   in relation to any semen, to include the identity and characteristics of the animal from which it was taken and measure of dilution.

(3) In this section "quantity" includes length, width, height, area, volume, capacity, weight, and number.

(4) Notwithstanding anything in the preceding provisions of this section, the following shall be deemed not to be trade descriptions, that is to say, any description or mark applied in pursuance of—

(*a*)   (*Repealed*);
(*b*)   section 2 of the Agricultural Produce (Grading and Marking) Act 1928 (as amended by the Agricultural Produce (Grading and Marking) Amendment Act 1931) or any corresponding enactment of the Parliament of Northern Ireland;
(*c*)   the Plant Varieties and Seeds Act 1964;
(*d*)   the Agriculture and Horticulture Act 1964 or any Community grading rules[10] within the meaning of Part III of that Act;
(*e*)   the Seeds Act (Northern Ireland) 1965;
(*f*)   the Horticulture Act (Northern Ireland) 1966;
(*g*)   the Consumer Protection Act 1987;
(*h*)   the Plant Varieties Act 1997;

any statement made in respect of, or mark applied to, any material in pursuance of Part IV of the Agriculture Act 1970, any name or expression to which a meaning has been assigned under section 70 of that Act when applied to any material in the circumstances specified in that section, any mark prescribed by a system of classification compiled under section 5 of the Agriculture Act 1967 and any designation, mark or description applied in pursuance of a scheme brought into force under section 6(1) or an order made under section 25(1) of the Agriculture Act 1970.

(5) Notwithstanding anything in the preceding provisions of this section—

(*a*)   where provision is made under the Food Safety Act 1990, the Food and Drugs Act (Northern Ireland) 1958 or the Consumer Protection Act 1987 prohibiting the application of a description except to goods in the case of which the requirements specified in that provision are complied with, that description, when applied to goods, shall be deemed not to be a trade description;
(*b*)   where by virtue of any provision made under Part V of the Medicines Act 1968 (or made under any provisions of the said Part V as applied by an order made under section 104 or section 105 of that Act) anything which, in accordance with this Act, constitutes the application of a trade description to goods is subject to any requirements or restrictions imposed by that provision, any particular description specified in that provision, when applied to goods in circumstances to which those requirements or restrictions are applicable, shall be deemed not to be a trade description.

[Trade Descriptions Act 1968, s 2, as amended by the Medicines Act 1968, Sch 5, the Agriculture Act 1970, the European Communities Act 1972, Sch 4, the Plant Varieties and Seeds Act 1964 (Repeals) (Appointed Day) Order 1978, SI 1978/1003, the Consumer Safety Act 1978 s 7, the Food Act 1984, Sch 10, the Consumer Protection Act 1987, Sch 4, the Food Safety Act 1990, Sch 3 and the Plant Varieties Act 1997, s 51(4).]

---

1. The particular words complained of must be looked at as a whole (*Evans v British Doughnut Co Ltd* [1944] 1 KB 102, [1944] 1 All ER 158, 180 JP 59) and in their context; a description of a motor car as "beautiful" or "immaculate"

may well refer not only to the outside appearance but also to the running condition: see *Robertson v Dicicco* [1972] Crim LR 592; *Kensington and Chelsea Borough Council v Riley* [1973] Crim LR 133, [1973] RTR 122; see also *Cadbury Ltd v Halliday* [1975] 2 All ER 226, 139 JP 428, where it was held that the words "extra value" are not a trade description. A description referring to a component or separate part of a piece of equipment may be held to be a description to the effect that the goods being supplied include that component (*British Gas Corpn v Lubbock* [1974] 1 All ER 188, 138 JP 198).

2. Where the indication of quantity relates to a prepackage of wine or grape must, it shall be an indication that it satisfies the requirements of reg 5 of the Prepackaging and Labelling of Wine and Grape Must (EEC Requirements) Regulations 1978, SI 1978/463.

3. Selling machine-made cigarettes with a label describing them as hand-made is a false trade description (*Kirshenboin v Salmon and Gluckstein Ltd* [1898] 2 QB 19, 62 JP 439).

4. See *Evans v British Doughnut Co Ltd*, supra, which related to a packet of "Eggstead", the contents being described as equivalent in use to 12 eggs. The word "composition" includes not only enumeration of the separate components of a package, but also the way in which those components are arranged and put together (*Queensway Discount Warehouses Ltd v Burke* (1985) 150 JP 17). Arguably, quality may come within sub-para (*e*) below.

5. It is implicit that where functional goods are concerned and they are supplied with instructions for use, that the goods are fit for use in accordance with those instructions as understood by the reasonable purchaser (*Janbo Trading Ltd v Dudley Metropolitan Borough Council* (1993) 157 JP 1056).

6. The use of the term "Formula One Master Service" in an invoice for the service of a motor vehicle was held to be an indication of performance, in the sense that to the extent of the work carried out within the scope of the Master Service option, the performance of the vehicle, in those respects, was then at least reliable, if not actually improved (*Formula One Autocentres Ltd v Birmingham City Council* (1998) 163 JP 234, [1999] RTR 195).

7. There have been a number of reported cases as a result of prosecutions under earlier legislation. Some of these decided on similar provisions of the Merchandise Marks Act are set out below for guidance.

The foundation of a margarine mixture made in France and imported as "Oleo margarine" was mixed at Southampton with a small percentage of imported Danish butter and English milk. The finished product was called "Le Dansk" and sold in England in card boxes under the description of "Le Dansk French Factory, Le Dansk, Paris". The conviction was affirmed on the ground that the words were a false trade description and the article was obviously represented as being of foreign make when it was not (*Bischop v Toler* (1895) 59 JP 807). At his establishment in Ireland, Lipton sold under the description—(1) "Lipton's prime, mild cured" and (2) "First quality smoked ham, own cure at Lipton's market", hams which had been manufactured and cured by him in America. The Queens' Bench (Ireland) held that neither of the descriptions was a false trade description within this section (*R v Lipton* (1892) 32 LR Ir 115). See also *Hooper v Riddle & Co* (1906) 70 JP 417. The word "Scotch" added to an invoice at the request of the purchaser after purchase of a ham which proved to be an American ham amounted to a false trade description (*Coppen v Moore* [1898] 2 QB 300, 62 JP 453). See also *Cameron v Wiggins* [1901] 1 KB 1. It is an offence to sell as "Fine British Tarragona Wine" a mixture of 85 per cent of wine made in England and 15 per cent of Mistella, a form of Tarragona wine used only for blending (*Holmes v Pipers Ltd* [1914] 1 KB 57, 78 JP 37). In a magistrates' court, a defendant company was convicted of having sold watches described as "English lever watches", many of the most important parts of which were made in a foreign country, whilst they were put together in England. See *Williamson v Tierney* (1900) 65 JP 70. In the case of trade descriptions which are common property and bear the name of a place or country as Bath buns, Stilton cheese, or Brussels carpets it is submitted that these words do not lead purchasers to believe that the articles were made in the places named, but the description "Scots Whisky" applied to whisky which had not been distilled wholly in Scotland may be a false trade description (*Henderson and Turnball v Adair* (1939) 103 JP Jo 533). See also the provisions of s 36, post.

8. Gunpowder manufacturers contracted to supply gunpowder under the trade mark of "RLG, No 4". Owing to an explosion they were unable to manufacture the powder, but they obtained gunpowder equal in quality from a German manufacturer, and packed it in barrels supplied by the Government, and inserted their own trade name on the labels as contractors. They sustained a loss by having to import the gunpowder, and no complaint was made by the Government, but no communication was made on delivery that the gunpowder was of German manufacture. The QB Division held justices were wrong in refusing to convict, as the description attached implied they were delivering gunpowder of their own manufacture, when, in fact, it was not such (*Starey v Chilworth Gunpowder Co* (1889) 24 QBD 90, 54 JP 436).

9. See *Donnelly v Rowlands* in note 1 to s 3, post.

10. Defined by s 24 of that Act, ante.

8–4449　3. False trade description.　　(1) A false trade description is a trade description which is false[1] to a material degree[2].

(2) A trade description which, though not false, is misleading[3], that is to say, likely to be taken for such an indication of any of the matters specified in section 2 of this Act as would be false to material degree, shall be deemed to be a false trade description.

(3) Anything which, though not a trade description, is likely to be taken for an indication of any of those matters and, as such an indication, would be false to a material degree, shall be deemed to be a false trade description[4].

(4) A false indication, or anything likely to be taken as an indication which would be false, that any goods comply with a standard specified or recognised by any person or implied by the approval of any person shall be deemed to be a false trade description, if there is no such person or no standard so specified, recognised or implied.
[Trade Descriptions Act 1968, s 3.]

---

1. In deciding whether a label on a bottle of soft drink was false, justices are entitled to read the label as a whole and in deciding whether the words are misleading the test is whether a reasonable consumer would be misled (*Northamptonshire County Council v Purity Soft Drinks Ltd* [2004] EWHC 3119 (Admin), 169 JP 84).

2. These words control the meaning of "false trade description" throughout the Act. Probably a very small addition of cotton to an article called "silk" or "wool", as it is now manufactured, may be immaterial, but if the article is "warranted all silk", or "all wool", it will be material. We think the question will be whether the description is substantially applicable to the article. The Divisional Court (ALVERSTONE LCJ, and WILLS J, DARLING J, diss) held that a description, though true chemically, may be false as a trade description (*Fowler v Cripps* [1906] 1 KB 16, 70 JP 21). The retailer of milk supplied in bottles with the correct trade description and his name and address marked on the foil caps but with the names of other persons to whom the bottles belonged embossed on the bottles was held not to be guilty of an offence under s 1 (*Donnelly v Rowlands* [1971] 1 All ER 9). An alteration of goods which causes them to tell a lie about themselves (eg the concealment of a structural weakness in a car) may be a false trade description, see *Cottee v Douglas Seaton (Used Cars) Ltd*

[1972] 3 All ER 750, 137 JP 1. For a consideration of the position when a new car is damaged, repaired, and then sold as "new", see *R v Ford Motor Co Ltd* [1974] 3 All ER 489, 138 JP 738. It is a question of fact whether a description of a previously registered motor car as "new" is a false description; the word "new" is susceptible to a variety of interpretations depending on the context (*R v Anderson* (1987) 152 JP 373, [1988] RTR 260, CA).

A false trade description attached to goods can be negatived by a limited disclaimer notice and oral statements to prospective purchasers to the effect that the articles being sold are merely copies (*Kent County Council v Price* (1993) 157 JP 1161—market trader offering to supply T-shirts with names of brand owners attached, although items were not authentic; notice stating "brand copy" displayed on stall and trader informed prospective purchaser that the garments were copies).

3. For consideration of the distinction between a trade description which is false and one which is misleading, see *Surrey County Council v Clark* (1991) 156 JP 798.

4. In *Holloway v Cross* [1981] RTR 146, an estimated mileage of a motor vehicle which was false to a material degree was held to be a false trade description within the meaning of s 3(3).

8–4450 4. Applying a trade description to goods.   (1) A person applies a trade description to goods if he—

(*a*) affixes or annexes it to or in any manner marks it on or incorporates it with—

 (i) the goods themselves, or
 (ii) anything in, on or with which the goods are supplied;

or

(*b*) places the goods in, on or with anything which the trade description has been affixed or annexed to, marked on or incorporated with, or places any such thing with the goods[1]; or
(*c*) uses the trade description in any manner likely to be taken as referring to the goods.

(2) An oral statement may amount to the use of a trade description.

(3) Where goods are supplied in pursuance of a request in which a trade description is used and the circumstances are such as to make it reasonable to infer that the goods are supplied as goods corresponding to that trade description, the person supplying the goods shall be deemed to have applied that trade description to the goods[2].
[Trade Descriptions Act 1968, s 4.]

---

1. This paragraph "means that though the defendant has not in fact applied the description to the goods, he shall be deemed to have done so if he puts the goods in a covering" (eg a bottle) "to which the description has been applied" (ALVERSTONE LCJ, in *Stone v Burn* [1911] 1 KB 927, 74 JP 456). In *Roberts v Severn Petroleum and Trading Co Ltd* [1981] RTR 312 this applied to petrol placed in tanks at a garage displaying the "Esso" brand sign, and the petrol suppliers were convicted under s 1(1) of delivering petrol which was to their knowledge not "Esso" even though it was standard commercial practice to transfer petroleum spirit from one company to another, there was no evidence of when the brand name was acquired, and the suppliers had not misled the garage.

2. Where a tender is made in response to a request (which in contractual terms is in the nature of an "invitation to treat" or "offer"), and the vendor of the goods represents to the purchaser (or proposed purchaser) at a time prior to the supply that the goods will meet certain standards or requirements, those representations continue in force at the time of supply unless the purchaser has been told otherwise. Nor for there to be a liability for a false description, is there a requirement for there to be in the delivery note a formal representation that there has been compliance with the specification and requirements. It does not matter that, at the time of the making of the representation, the goods do not exist or are to be acquired or manufactured at some time in the future. Where the goods supplied do not comply with the description applied to them owing to the default of a third party such as a sub-contractor, the defendant, to avoid liability, must rely on the defence in s 24, post, where this is available (see *Shropshire County Council v Simon Dudley Ltd* (1996) 161 JP 224, DC)

8–4451 5. Trade descriptions used in advertisements.   (1) The following provisions of this section shall have effect where in an advertisement a trade description is used in relation to any class of goods.

(2) The trade description shall be taken as referring to all goods of the class, whether or not in existence at the time the advertisement is published—

(*a*) for the purpose of determining whether an offence has been committed under paragraph (*a*) of section 1(1) of this Act; and
(*b*) where goods of the class are supplied or offered to be supplied by a person publishing or displaying the advertisement, also for the purpose of determining whether an offence has been committed under paragraph (*b*) of the said section 1(1).

(3) In determining for the purposes of this section whether any goods are of a class to which a trade description used in an advertisement relates regard shall be had not only to the form and content of the advertisement but also to the time, place, manner and frequency of its publication and all other matters making it likely or unlikely that a person to whom the goods are supplied would think of the goods as belonging to the class in relation to which the trade description is used in the advertisement.
[Trade Descriptions Act 1968, s 5.]

8–4452 6. Offer to supply.   A person exposing[1] goods for supply or having goods in his possession[2] for supply shall be deemed to offer to supply them.
[Trade Descriptions Act 1968, s 6.]

1. Cf, *Keating v Horwood* (1926) 90 JP 141, 135 LT 29. When goods are appropriated under a contract by the vendor to the purchaser and invoiced, they cannot be said to be within the vendor's possession for supply when they are merely held by him for the purpose of delivery or collection pursuant to the contract. The words "exposing goods for supply" and "in his possession for supply" are to be read in the context of an offer to supply goods, as opposed to a concluded contract (*Miller v F A Sadd & Son Ltd*; *Miller v Pickering Bull & Co Ltd* [1981] 3 All ER 265—contractor stating higher price on invoice than was contractually agreed).

2. Goods deposited with another by a trader, eg frozen poultry deposited in an independent cold store, remain in the possession of the trader (*Towers & Co Ltd v Gray* [1961] 2 QB 351, [1961] 2 All ER 68, 125 JP 391). A shoe company was convicted under s 1(1)(*b*) because the word "all" on shoes marked "all leather" (but which were not made entirely of leather) was not removed until after the shoes had been sold and presented at the cash desk (*Haringey London Borough Council v Piro Shoes Ltd* [1976] Crim LR 462).

8–4453   8. Marking orders.   (1) Where it appears to the Board of Trade necessary or expedient in the interest of persons to whom any goods are supplied that the goods should be marked with or accompanied by any information (whether or not amounting to or including a trade description) or instruction relating to the goods, the Board may, subject to the provisions of this Act, by order impose requirements for securing that the goods are so marked or accompanied, and regulate or prohibit the supply of goods with respect to which the requirements are not complied with; and the requirements may extend to the form and manner in which the information or instruction is to be given.

(2) Where an order under this section is in force with respect to goods of any description, any person who, in the course of any trade or business, supplies or offers to supply goods of that description in contravention of the order shall, subject to the provisions of this Act, be guilty of an offence.
[Trade Descriptions Act 1968, s 8.]

8–4454   9. Information, etc to be given in advertisements.   (1) Where it appears to the Board of Trade necessary or expedient in the interest of persons to whom any goods are to be supplied that any description of advertisements of the goods should contain or refer to any information (whether or not amounting to or including a trade description) relating to the goods the Board may, subject to the provisions of this Act, by order impose requirements as to the inclusion of that information, or of an indication of the means by which it may be obtained, in such description of advertisements of the goods as may be specified in the order.

(2) An order under this section may specify the form and manner in which any such information or indication is to be included in advertisements of any description and may make different provision for different circumstances.

(3) Where an advertisement of any goods to be supplied in the course of any trade or business fails to comply with any requirement imposed under this section, any person who publishes the advertisement shall, subject to the provisions of this Act, be guilty of an offence.
[Trade Descriptions Act 1968, s 9.]

Misstatements other than false trade descriptions

8–4455   12. False representations as to royal approval or award, etc.   (1) If any person, in the course of any trade or business, gives, by whatever means, any false indication, direct or indirect, that any goods or services supplied by him or any methods adopted by him are or are of a kind supplied to or approved by Her Majesty or any member of the Royal Family, he shall, subject to the provisions of this Act, be guilty of an offence.

(2) If any person, in the course of any trade or business, uses, without the authority of Her Majesty, any device or emblem signifying the Queen's Award to Industry or anything so nearly resembling such a device or emblem as to be likely to deceive, he shall, subject to the provisions of this Act, be guilty of an offence.
[Trade Descriptions Act 1968, s 12.]

8–4456   13. False representations as to supply of goods or services.   If any person, in the course of any trade or business, gives[1], by whatever means, any false indication, direct or indirect, that any goods or services supplied by him are of a kind supplied to any person he shall, subject to the provisions of this Act, be guilty of an offence[2].

1. The burden on the prosecutor is simply to establish a prima facie case, which may be inferred from the facts, that a person in trade has given a false indication as to the services offered; it is not necessary for the prosecutor to establish by evidence that the accused initiated the statement rather than that it would have been taken as an indication of the accused (*Wall v Rose and Sargent* (1997) 162 JP 38, DC).

2. For commercial offences under this section, if fines imposed are to be effective, they must be realistic (*R v Docklands Estates Ltd* (2000) 164 JP 505 – fines of up to £7,500 for each of three offences imposed on a company with a modest turnover reduced on appeal to £2,000 for each offence having regard to the seriousness of the offences and the means of the company).
[Trade Descriptions Act 1968, s 13.]

8–4457   14. False or misleading statements as to services, etc.   (1) It shall be an offence for any person[1] in the course of any trade or business[2]—

(*a*)   to make a statement[3] which he knows[4] to be false; or
(*b*)   recklessly[5] to make a statement[3] which is false[6];

as to any of the following matters[7], that is to say,—

    (i)   the provision in the course of any trade or business of any services[8], accommodation or facilities[9];
    (ii)   the nature of any services, accommodation or facilities provided in the course of any trade or business;
    (iii)   the time at which manner in which or persons by whom any services, accommodation or facilities are so provided;
    (iv)   the examination, approval or evaluation by any person of any services, accommodation or facilities so provided; or
    (v)   the location or amenities of any accommodation so provided.

(2)   For the purposes of this section—

(*a*)   anything (whether or not a statement as to any of the matters specified in the preceding subsection) likely to be taken for such a statement as to any of those matters as would be false shall be deemed to be a false statement as to that matter; and
(*b*)   a statement made regardless of whether it is true or false shall be deemed to be made recklessly, whether or not the person making it had reasons for believing that it might be false.

(3)   In relation to any services consisting of or including the application of any treatment or process or the carrying out of any repair, the matters specified in subsection (1) of this section shall be taken to include the effect of the treatment, process or repair.

(4)   In this section "false" means false to a material degree and "services" does not include anything done under a contract of service.
[Trade Descriptions Act 1968, s 14.]

---

1.   For the liability of a company vis-à-vis its employees, see para **1–309, Proceedings against a corporation** in PART I: MAGISTRATES' COURTS, PROCEDURE, ante.

2.   The Law Society does not carry on matters in the course of trade or business and does not fall within the ambit of this section (*R v Bow Street Magistrates' Court, ex p Joseph* (1986) 150 JP 650). The qualification to a statement in a holiday leaflet that it contained all that was covered, namely that the insurance certificate detailed the terms in full, was not sufficiently bold and precise as the trade description itself so as to amount to a disclaimer (*Smallshaw v PKC Associates Ltd* (1994) 159 JP 730).

3.   This section does not apply to statements relating to the supply of goods, since the words "service" or "facility" other than in exceptional circumstances, do not involve a supply of goods; nor does the section cover false statements about the price at which services or facilities are provided (*Newell v Taylor* (1983) 148 JP 308, [1984] RTR 135, DC). A statement made after a contract has been completed and the price paid may constitute an offence (*Breed v Cluett* [1970] 2 QB 459, [1970] 2 All ER 662, 134 JP 570. Where the false statement is made in a trade publication, such as a brochure, the statement may be 'made' at various stages in the chain of distribution and continues to be made so long as the publication remains in circulation without effective correction; see *Wings Ltd v Ellis* [1985] AC 272, [1984] 3 All ER 577, 149 JP 33, HL. Statements made in a ticket as to the time of a return flight have been held to be a statement of fact, notwithstanding that the time was stated in the ticket as subject to alteration (*R v Avro plc* (1993) 157 JP 759, [1993] Crim LR 709).

4.   The offence under s 14(1)(*a*) is, in regard to the actual making of the statement, an absolute offence. Accordingly, the offence is committed merely if a statement known to be false is made on the defendant's behalf in the course of his business, and it is irrelevant that the defendant did not know that the statement had been made (*Wings Ltd v Ellis* [1985] AC 272, [1984] 3 All ER 577, 149 JP 33, HL and see *Wall v Rose and Sargent* (1997) 162 JP 38, DC).

5.   See definition in sub-s (2)(*b*). "Recklessly" does not here involve dishonesty; it suffices if the prosecution can show that the defendant did not have regard to the truth or falsity of the statement even though it cannot be shown that he was deliberately closing his eyes to the truth nor that he had any kind of dishonest mind (*M F I Warehouses Ltd v Nattrass* [1973] 1 All ER 762, 137 JP 307; see also *Best Travel Co Ltd v Patterson* (1986) 151 JP 619, [1987] BTLC 119). A company may be found to have been reckless where it is proved that there has been recklessness on the part of someone who could properly be called part of the directing mind of the company even though the particular directing mind cannot be identified (*Yugotours Ltd v Wadsley* [1988] Crim LR 623 as explained in *Airtours v Shipley plc* (1994) 158 JP 835, QBD.

6.   In *Beckett v Cohen* [1973] 1 All ER 120, 137 JP 116 it was held that if, before a contract is worked out, the person who provides a service makes a promise as to what he will do, and that promise does not relate to an existing fact, nobody can say at the date when that statement is made that it is either true or false; but it may be an offence under this section to make a false statement as to what has been done at the end of the contract. See also *R v Sunair Holidays Ltd* [1973] 2 All ER 1233, 137 JP 687, confirming that s 14 does not apply to a forecast or promise not containing by implication a statement of present fact (a swimming pool in a holiday brochure). But an airline was found guilty, having adopted a policy of overbooking, resulting in a passenger not obtaining the seat he has booked (*British Airways Board v Taylor* [1976] 1 All ER 65, 140 JP 96). A second prosecution for false statements in the same brochure (about facilities at the Golden Coast Hotel, Marathon, complained about by two individual holidaymakers) was not prevented by a plea of *autrefois convict*, nor was it an abuse or oppressive, and there was no justification for a purely nominal penalty (*R v Thomson Holidays Ltd* [1974] QB 592, [1974] 1 All ER 823, 138 JP 284 followed in *North Yorkshire Trading Standards Service v Coleman* [2001] EWHC Admin 818, (2001) 166 JP 76). The correct test to employ when considering whether a statement in a brochure is misleading is to decide what effect it would have on the minds of ordinary readers (*Thompson Travel Ltd v Roberts* (1984) 148 JP 666—an area of sand retained by a concrete wall down which one gained access to the sea not a "beach").

7.   The provisions of paragraphs (i)–(iii) overlap and difficulty will be avoided if the charge is confined to identifying the statement that was made and the way in which it is alleged to be false (*R v Piper* (1995) 160 JP 116, [1995] Crim LR 827, CA).

8.   Including the identity or qualities of the person providing them, for example falsely stating that one has architectural qualifications (*R v Breeze* [1973] 2 All ER 1141, 137 JP 680) followed in also *R v Holland* [2002] EWCA Crim 2022, (2003) 167 JP 138 where a company that presented an advertising front to the public that it was of greater substance than was in fact the case and was also an organisation in which members could safely place and invest their money was making statements that could rightly be regarded as relating to "the provision of any services"); or falsely using the logo of a trade

organisation (*R v Piper* (1995) 160 JP 116, [1995] Crim LR 827, CA). As to the meaning of "services" see *Newell v Taylor* (1983) 148 JP 308, [1984] RTR 135, DC, noted below. The offer of a refund of part of the price of goods if a cheaper price was discovered elsewhere, is not an offer to provide services (*Dixons Ltd v Roberts* (1984) 148 JP 513, [1984] RTR 135, DC). The supply of a book whose greatly inflated price represented the value of a strategy for winning on football pools was the supply of a service as well as goods, and the failure to honour the money back guarantee offered incurred liability under the section (*Ashley v London Borough of Sutton* (1994) 159 JP 631, [1995] Crim LR 657).

9. The meaning of "service" and "facility" in a criminal statute must be considered in a restrictive manner; the price of services, accommodation or facilities is not covered by s 14 which therefore did not catch salesmen whose firm offered a video cassette recorder "absolutely free" with every firm order for a car, but who reduced the amount of discount or part-exchange during the period of promotion (*Newell v Taylor* (1983) 148 JP 308, [1984] RTR 135, DC). But a statement in an advertisement to the effect that one year's insurance would be given free with every moped purchased was held to constitute a statement as to the provision of a facility (*Kinchin v Ashton Park Scooters Ltd* (1984) 148 JP 540). Categorisation of a misrepresentation as to price does not necessarily exclude the characterisation of a representation as being as to facilities or services. Accordingly, in the course of the provision of a remortgage, although representations as to a cash back scheme bore a relationship to price, they were properly characterisable as being as to the provision of services or facilities within the terms of s 14 (*R v Killian* [2002] EWCA Crim 404, 166 JP 169).

Provisions as to offences

8–4458   18. Penalty for offences. A person guilty[1] of an offence under this Act for which no other penalty is specified shall be liable[2]—

   (*a*) on summary conviction, to a fine not exceeding **the statutory maximum**; and
   (*b*) on conviction on indictment, to a fine or imprisonment for a term not exceeding two years or both.
[Trade Descriptions Act 1968, s 18, as amended by the Criminal Law Act 1977, s 28.]

1. A person convicted of an offence of strict liability under this Act should not be sentenced on the basis of an inference of actual knowledge, or recklessness without being afforded the opportunity of giving evidence (*R v Lester* (1975) 63 Cr App Rep 144). See the same case for suitability of compensation orders for certain offences under this Act.
2. For procedure in respect of this offence which is triable either way, see the Magistrates' Courts Act 1980, ss 17A–21 in PART I: MAGISTRATES' COURTS, PROCEDURE, ante.

8–4459   19. Time limit for prosecutions[1]. (1) No prosecution for an offence under this Act[2] shall be commenced after the expiration of three years from the commission of the offence or one year from its discovery[3] by the prosecutor, whichever is the earlier.

(2) Notwithstanding anything in section 127(1) of the Magistrates' Courts Act 1980, a magistrates' court may try an information for an offence under this Act if the information was laid at any time within twelve months from the commission[4] of the offence.

(3) *Scotland.*

(4) Subsection (2) and (3) of this section do not apply where—

   (*a*) the offence was committed by the making of an oral statement; or
   (*b*) the offence was one of supplying goods to which a false trade description is applied, and the trade description was applied by an oral statement; or
   (*c*) the offence was one where a false trade description is deemed to have been applied to goods by virtue of section 4(3) of this Act and the goods were supplied in pursuance of an oral request[5].
[Trade Descriptions Act 1968, s 19, amended by Magistrates' Courts Act 1980, Sch 7.]

1. Read in conjunction with s 127 of the Magistrates' Courts Act 1980 and having regard to *R v Dacorum Magistrates' Court, ex p Michael Gardner Ltd* (1985) 149 JP 677, the effect of s 19 is that indictable offences under this Act are subject to the time limit set out in sub-s (1) and summary offences are subject to the time limit set out in sub-s (2). S 127 of the 1980 Act has effectively nullified sub-s (4).
2. The prosecution are prevented by this provision from amending a charge from conspiracy to defraud to conspiracy to contravene the provisions of the 1968 Act if the time limit under this section has passed (*R v Pain, R v Jory, R v Hawkins* (1985) 150 JP 65, CA).
3. "Discovery" means no more than that all the facts material to found the relevant charge are disclosed to the prosecutor, see *Newham London Borough v Co-operative Retail Services Ltd* (1984) 149 JP 421.
4. An offence of supplying goods under s 1(1)(*b*) of this Act is committed on the date of delivery of the goods not (if earlier) the date when the property in the goods passes by virtue of the Sale of Goods Act (*Rees v Munday* [1974] 3 All ER 506, 138 JP 767).
5. It would appear that the provisions of s 19(4) have been nullified by the provisions of s 127 of the Magistrates' Courts Act 1980; see *R v Dacorum Magistrates' Court, ex p Michael Gardner Ltd* (1985) 149 JP 677, DC, and footnote 1 above.

8–4460   20. Offences by corporations.   (1) Where an offence under this Act which has been committed by a body corporate is proved to have been committed with the consent and connivance of, or to be attributable to any neglect[1] on the part of, any director, manager, secretary or other similar officer of the body corporate, or any person who was purporting to act in any such capacity, he as well as the body corporate shall be guilty of that offence and shall be liable to be proceeded against and punished accordingly.

(2) In this section "director", in relation to any body corporate established by or under any enactment for the purpose of carrying on under national ownership any industry or part of an

industry or undertaking, being a body corporate whose affairs are managed by the members thereof, means a member of that body corporate.

[Trade Descriptions Act 1968, s 20.]

---

1. For consideration of "neglect" on the part of a managing director, see *Lewin v Bland* (1983) 148 JP 69, [1985] RTR 171 and *Hirschler v Birch* (1986) 151 JP 396, [1987] RTR 13.

8–4461 21. Accessories to offences committed abroad. (1) Any person who, in the United Kingdom, assists in or induces the commission in any other country of an act in respect of goods which, if the act were committed in the United Kingdom, would be an offence under section 1 of this Act shall be guilty of an offence, except as provided by subsection (2) of this section, but only if either—

(a) the false trade description concerned is an indication (or anything likely to be taken as an indication) that the goods or any part thereof were manufactured, produced, processed or reconditioned in the United Kingdom; or

(b) the false trade description concerned—

(i) consists of or comprises an expression (or anything likely to be taken as an expression) to which a meaning is assigned by an order made by virtue of section 7(b) of this Act, and

(ii) where that meaning is so assigned only in circumstances specified in the order, the trade description is used in those circumstances.

(2) A person shall not be guilty of an offence under subsection (1) of this section if, by virtue of section 32 of this Act, the act, though committed in the United Kingdom, would not be an offence under section 1 of this Act had the goods been intended for despatch to the other country.

(3) Any person who, in the United Kingdom, assists in or induces the commission outside the United Kingdom of an act which, if committed in the United Kingdom, would be an offence under section 12 of this Act shall be guilty of an offence.

[Trade Descriptions Act 1968, s 21.]

8–4462 22. Restrictions on institution of proceedings and admission of evidence. (1) Where any act or omission constitutes both an offence under this Act and an offence under any provision contained in or having effect by virtue of Part IV of the Weights and Measures Act 1985 or Part IV of the Weights and Measures Act (Northern Ireland) 1967—

(a) proceedings for the offence shall not be instituted under this Act, except by virtue of section 23 thereof, without the service of such a notice as is required by subsection (3) of section 83 of the said Act of 1985 or, as the case may be, subsection (2) of section 33 of the said Act of 1967, nor after the expiration of the period mentioned in paragraph (c) of that subsection; and

(b) sections 35, 36 and 37(1) and (2), of the said Act of 1985 or, as the case may be, of section 20 of the said Act of 1967, shall, with the necessary modifications, apply as if the offence under this Act were an offence under Part IV of that Act or any instrument made thereunder.

(2) Where any act or omission constitutes both an offence under this Act and an offence under the food and drugs laws, evidence on behalf of the prosecution concerning any sample procured for analysis shall not be admissible in proceedings for the offence under this Act unless the relevant provisions of those laws have been complied with.

(2A) In subsection (2) of this section—

"the food and drugs laws" means the Food Safety Act 1990, the Medicines Act 1968 and the Food (Northern Ireland) Order 1989 and any instrument made thereunder;

"the relevant provisions" means—

(i) in relation to the said Act of 1990, section 31 and regulations made thereunder;

(ii) in relation to the said Act of 1968, so much of Schedule 3 to that Act as is applicable to the circumstances in which the sample was procured; and

(iii) in relation to the said Order, Articles 40 and 44,

or any provisions replacing any of those provisions by virtue of section 17 of the said Act of 1990, paragraph 27 of Schedule 3 to the said Act of 1968 or Article 72 or 73 of the said Order.

(3) The Board of Trade may by order provide that in proceedings for an offence under this Act in relation to such goods as may be specified in the order (other than proceedings for an offence falling within the preceding provisions of this section) evidence on behalf of the prosecution concerning any sample procured for analysis shall not be admissible unless the sample has been dealt with in such manner as may be specified in the order.

[Trade Descriptions Act 1968, s 22, as amended by the Medicines Act 1968, Sch 5, the European Communities Act 1972, Sch 4, the Food Act 1984, Sch 10, the Weights and Measures Act 1985 Sch 12 and the Food Safety Act 1990, Schs 3 and 5.]

8–4463   23. Offences due to fault of other person.   Where the commission by any person of an offence under this Act is due to the act or default of some other person[1] that other person shall be guilty of the offence, and a person may be charged with and convicted of the offence by virtue of this section whether or not proceedings are taken against the first-mentioned person[2].
[Trade Descriptions Act 1968, s 23.]

---

   1. The conviction of "some other person" is not precluded merely because he is not a person acting in the course of a trade or business (*Olgeirsson v Kitching* [1986] 1 All ER 746, [1986] 1 WLR 304, 150 JP 117).

   2. This section applies only if the first-mentioned person commits an offence; it has no application if that person does not commit an offence even if the "other person" referred to has committed an offence under the Act (*Cottee v Douglas Seaton (Used Cars) Ltd* [1972] 3 All ER 750, 137 JP 1). The "other person" must inevitably be acquitted, where the person first referred to in s 23 has a defence without reference to s 24 (*Coupe v Guyett* [1973] 2 All ER 1058, 137 JP 694).

Defences

8–4464   24. Defence of mistake, accident, etc.   (1) In any proceedings for an offence under this Act it shall, subject to subsection (2) of this section, be a defence[1] for the person charged to prove—

   (*a*)   that the commission of the offence was due to a mistake[2] or to reliance on information[3] supplied to him or to the act or default of another person, an accident or some other cause beyond his control; and

   (*b*)   that he took all reasonable precautions and exercised all due diligence to avoid the commission of such an offence by himself or any person under his control[4].

   (2) If in any case the defence provided by the last foregoing subsection involves the allegation that the commission of the offence was due to the act or default of another person or to reliance on information supplied by another person, the person charged shall not, without leave of the court, be entitled to rely on that defence unless, within a period ending seven clear days before the hearing, he has served on the prosecutor a notice in writing giving such information identifying or assisting in the identification of that other person as was then in his possession.

   (3) In any proceedings for an offence under this Act of supplying or offering to supply goods to which a false trade description is applied it shall be a defence for the person charged to prove that he did not know, and could not with reasonable diligence[5] have ascertained, that the goods did not conform to the description or that the description had been applied to the goods.
[Trade Descriptions Act 1968, s 24.]

---

   1. Where a defence of due diligence is made out, it is not appropriate to make an inter partes costs order against the prosecutor where serious and important questions relating to diligence are properly brought before the court (*Suffolk County Council v Rexmore Wholesale Services Ltd* (1994) 159 JP 390).

   2. There must be a conviction where the facts are known to the defendant, his only mistake being in the effect of the statute (*Stone v Burn* [1911] 1 KB 927, as explained in *Allard v Selfridge & Co Ltd* [1925] 1 KB 129).

   3. As to the information supplied by a motor-car odometer see *Simmons v Potter* [1975] RTR 347, [1975] Crim LR 354.

   4. The defence of mistake, accident, or some other cause beyond his control is not available in respect of the act or default of a person under the control of the defendant (*Walkling Ltd v Robinson* [1929] All ER Rep 658, 94 JP 73; *Hall v Farmer* [1970] 1 All ER 729; *Birkenhead District Co-operative Society Ltd v Roberts* [1970] 3 All ER 391); but the defence that the offence was due to the act or default of another person is available to the defendant in respect of a person under his control (*Beckett v Kingston Bros (Butchers) Ltd* [1970] 1 QB 606, [1970] 1 All ER 715, 134 JP 270). He must prove on a balance of probabilities that he has done all that could be reasonably expected in the way of investigation as to who was in fact responsible for the default; it is not enough (for example) simply to name all the assistants at a particular shop at the relevant time; *McGuire v Sittingbourne Co-operative Society Ltd* (1976) 140 JP 306. It is not necessarily enough for the defendant to say that he relied on his supplier; he must prove (and the onus is on him) that he took all reasonable precautions; see *Naish v Gore* [1971] 3 All ER 737 and cases referred to therein, *Simmons v Potter*, supra; *Alec Norman Garages Ltd v Phillips* (1984) 148 JP 741; *Amos v Melcon (Frozen Foods) Ltd* (1985) 149 JP 712, (frozen meat misdescribed as "rump" steak on which adequate checks could not be made unless it was defrosted, which was of itself impracticable). "Due diligence" refers to the employer personally and to no-one else; so that it is not necessary for him to prove also that an employee (a person under his control) had also exercised due diligence (*Tesco Supermarkets Ltd v Nattrass* [1972] AC 153, [1971] 2 All ER 127, 135 JP 289). In *Hicks v Sullam Ltd* (1983) 147 JP 493 it was held that it was not sufficient for a defendant company to rely on the verbal assurance of a third party as to the quality of light bulbs purchased by that third party for the company, and where the company had no system of random sampling or testing of their own. In *Rotherham Metropolitan Borough Council v Raysun (UK) Ltd* (1988) 153 JP 37 it was held not to be sufficient for the defendant company to rely on Hong Kong agents without checking whether they tested the goods, nor to sample only one packet of crayons out of 7,000 to 10,000, nor to rely on the lack of adverse reports from a trade association. Where a company has a normal stated policy on checking it is incumbent upon it to take reasonable steps to ensure its employees follow the policy (*Horner v Sherwoods of Darlington Ltd* (1989) 154 JP 299). In *Hurley v Martinez & Co Ltd* (1990) 154 JP 821, where the defendant did not carry out any tests on the alcoholic strength of wine, the Divisional Court said that the question to be asked was whether a risk that an event such as happened (alcoholic content wrongly described on label) might occur, was sufficiently large to demand that a small local supplier should carry out sampling, bearing in mind the expense, nature of analysis and the vast number of lines supplied by the defendant.

   5. A dealer could be said to be put on inquiry by a surprisingly low reading on a car odometer, and in those circumstances cannot be said to have exercised reasonable diligence if he makes no inquiries at all (*Simmons v Ravenhill* (1983) 148 JP 109). The test is whether it has been proved by the defendant that having regard to the circumstances of the case, including his position as a trader, he could not by reasonable diligence have ascertained that the goods did not conform. In *Wandsworth London Borough Council v Bentley* [1980] RTR 429 a defendant who had not consulted the immediately preceding owner as to the mileage had not taken every reasonable precaution. It may be otherwise where the previous owner was unknown and the defendant had not expected he would ever get an answer (*Ealing London Borough v Taylor* (1995) 159 JP 460, [1995] Crim LR 166). Personal attributes such as intelligence, command of English, familiarity

with the trade etc are not relevant (*Denard v Abbas* (1986) 151 JP 421, [1987] Crim LR 424). The standard of care required under s 24(3) is not lower than the standard of care required by "all reasonable precautions" and "all due diligence" in s 24(1) (*Texas Homecare Ltd v Stockport Metropolitan Borough Council* (1987) 152 JP 83, [1987] BTLC 331).

8–4465   25. Innocent publication of advertisement.   In proceedings for an offence under this Act committed by the publication of an advertisement it shall be a defence for the person charged to prove that he is a person whose business it is to publish or arrange for the publication of advertisements and that he received the advertisement for publication in the ordinary course of business and did not know and had no reason to suspect that its publication would amount to an offence under this Act.
[Trade Descriptions Act 1968, s 25.]

Enforcement

8–4466   26. Enforcing authorities.   (1) It shall be the duty of every local weights and measures authority to enforce within their area the provisions of this Act and of any order made under this Act[1].
[Trade Descriptions Act 1968, s 26 amended by the Local Government, Planning and Land Act 1980, Schs 4 and 34 and the Weights and Measures Act 1985, Sch 13.]

---

1. It is not an abuse of process for a manufacturer to assist an investigation of dealing in counterfeit parts for motor vehicles by providing resources and assistance provided the decision to prosecute is taken independently by the Trading Standards Officer (*R v Milton Keynes Magistrates' Court, ex p Roberts* [1995] Crim LR 224).

8–4477   27. Power to make test purchases.   A local weights and measures authority shall have power to make, or to authorise any of their officers to make on their behalf, such purchases of goods, and to authorise any of their officers to secure the provision of such services, accommodation or facilities, as may appear expedient for the purpose of determining whether or not the provisions of this Act and any order made thereunder are being complied with.
[Trade Descriptions Act 1968, s 27.]

8–4478   28. Power to enter premises and inspect and seize goods and documents.   (1) A duly authorised officer of a local weights and measures authority or of a Government department may, at all reasonable hours and on production, if required, of his credentials, exercise the following powers, that is to say,—

    (*a*)   he may, for the purpose of ascertaining whether any offence under this Act has been committed, inspect any goods and enter any premises other than premises used only as a dwelling;

    (*b*)   if he has reasonable cause to suspect that an offence under this Act has been committed, he may, for the purpose of ascertaining whether it has been committed, require any person carrying on a trade or business or employed in connection with a trade or business to produce any books or documents relating to the trade or business and may take copies of, or of any entry in, any such book or document;

    (*c*)   if he has reasonable cause to believe that an offence under this Act has been committed, he may seize and detain any goods for the purpose of ascertaining, by testing or otherwise, whether the offence has been committed;

    (*d*)   he may seize and detain any goods or documents which he has reason to believe may be required as evidence in proceedings for an offence under this Act;

    (*e*)   he may, for the purpose of exercising his powers under this subsection to seize goods, but only if and to the extent that it is reasonably necessary in order to secure that the provisions of this Act and of any order made thereunder are duly observed, require any person having authority to do so to break open any container or open any vending machine and, if that person does not comply with the requirement, he may do so himself.

    (2) An officer seizing any goods or documents in the exercise of his powers under this section shall inform the person from whom they are seized and, in the case of goods seized from a vending machine, the person whose name and address are stated on the machine as being the proprietor's or, if no name and address are so stated, the occupier of the premises on which the machine stands or to which it is affixed.

    (3) If a justice of the peace, on sworn information in writing—

    (*a*)   is satisfied that there is reasonable ground to believe either—

        (i)   that any goods, books or documents which a duly authorised officer has power under this section to inspect are on any premises and that their inspection is likely to disclose evidence of the commission of an offence under this Act; or

        (ii)   that any offence under this Act has been, is being or is about to be committed on any premises; and

    (*b*)   is also satisfied either—

        (i)   that admission to the premises has been or is likely to be refused and that notice of intention to apply for a warrant under this subsection has been given to the occupier; or

(ii) that an application for admission, or the giving of such a notice, would defeat the object of the entry or that the premises are unoccupied or that the occupier is temporarily absent and it might defeat the object of the entry to await his return,

the justice may by warrant under his hand, which shall continue in force for a period of one month, authorise an officer of a local weights and measures authority or of a Government department to enter the premises, if need be by force.

In the application of this subsection to Scotland, "justice of the peace" shall be construed as including a sheriff and a magistrate.

(4) An officer entering any premises by virtue of this section may take with him such other persons and such equipment as may appear to him necessary; and on leaving any premises which he has entered by virtue of a warrant under the preceding subsection he shall, if the premises are unoccupied or the occupier is temporarily absent, leave them as effectively secured against trespassers as he found them.

(5), (5A) *Repealed.*

(6) If any person who is not a duly authorised officer of a local weights and measures authority or of a Government department purports, to act as such under this section he shall be guilty of an offence.

(7) Nothing in this section shall be taken to compel the production by a solicitor of a document containing a privileged communication made by or to him in that capacity or to authorise the taking of possession of any such document which is in his possession.

[Trade Descriptions Act 1968, s 28, as amended by the Consumer Credit Act 1968, Sch 4, the Consumer Protection Act 1987, Sch 4 and the Enterprise Act 2002, Sch 26.]

8–4479   29. Obstruction of authorised officers.   (1) Any person who—

(a) wilfully obstructs an officer of a local weights and measures authority or of a Government department acting in pursuance of this Act; or

(b) wilfully fails to comply with any requirement properly made to him by such an officer under section 28 of this Act; or

(c) without reasonable cause fails to give such an officer so acting any other assistance or information which he may reasonably require of him for the purpose of the performance of his functions under this Act,

shall be guilty of an offence and liable, on summary conviction, to a fine not exceeding **level 3** on the standard scale.

(2) If any person, in giving any such information as is mentioned in the preceding subsection, makes any statement which he knows to be false[1], he shall be guilty of an offence.

(3) Nothing in this section shall be construed as requiring a person to answer any question or give any information if to do so might incriminate him.

[Trade Descriptions Act 1968, s 29 as amended by the Criminal Justice Act 1982, ss 38 and 46.]

---

1. A person is not required to answer any question which may incriminate him (see sub-s (3)). However, even where he has been cautioned by an investigating officer, if he gives information which is false he is liable for prosecution under sub-s (2) (*R v Page* (1996) 161 JP 308, [1996] Crim LR 439, CA).

8–4480   30. Notice of test and intended prosecution.   Where any goods seized or purchased by an officer in pursuance of this Act are submitted to a test, then—

(a) if the goods were seized, the officer shall inform the person mentioned in section 28(2) of this Act of the result of the test;

(b) if the goods were purchased and the test leads to the institution of proceedings for an offence under this Act, the officer shall inform the person from whom the goods were purchased, or, in the case of goods sold through a vending machine, the person mentioned in section 28(2) of this Act, of the result of the test;

and shall, where as a result of the test proceedings for an offence under this Act are instituted against any person, allow him to have the goods tested on his behalf if it is reasonably practicable to do so.

[Trade Descriptions Act 1968, s 30, as amended by the Fair Trading Act 1973, Sch 13.]

8–4481   31. Evidence by certificate.   (1) The Board of Trade may by regulations provide that certificates issued by such persons as may be specified by the regulations in relation to such matters as may be so specified shall, subject to the provisions of this section, be received in evidence of those matters in any proceedings under this Act.

(2) Such a certificate shall not be received in evidence—

(a) unless the party against whom it is to be given in evidence has been served with a copy thereof not less than seven days before the hearing; or

(b) if that party has, not less than three days before the hearing, served on the other party a notice requiring the attendance of the person issuing the certificate.

(3) *Scotland.*

(4) For the purposes of this section any document purporting to be such a certificate as is mentioned in this section shall be deemed to be such a certificate unless the contrary is shown.

(5) Regulations under this section shall be made by statutory instrument which shall be subject to annulment in pursuance of a resolution of either House of Parliament.

[Trade Descriptions Act 1968, s 31.]

8–4482 34. Trade marks containing trade descriptions.   The fact that a trade description is a trade mark[1], or part of a trade mark, does not prevent it from being a false trade description when applied to any goods, except where the following conditions are satisfied, that is to say—

(*a*) that it could have been lawfully applied to the goods if this Act had not been passed; and

(*b*) that on the day this Act is passed the trade mark either is registered under Trade Marks Act 1938 or is in use to indicate a connection in the course of trade between such goods and the proprietor of the trade mark; and

(*c*) that the trade mark as applied is used to indicate such a connection between the goods and the proprietor of the trade mark or, in the case of a registered trade mark[1], a person licensed to use it; and

(*d*) that the person who is the proprietor of the trade mark is the same person as, or a successor in title of, the proprietor on the day this Act is passed.

[Trade Descriptions Act 1968, s 34 amended by the Trade Marks Act 1994, Sch 4.]

---

1. To be construed as a reference to a trade mark or registered trade mark within the meaning of the Trade Marks Act 1994, Sch 4.

8–4483 39. Interpretation.   (1) The following provisions shall have effect, in addition to sections 2 to 6 of this Act, for the interpretation in this Act of expressions used therein, that is to say,—

"advertisement" includes a catalogue, a circular and a price list;
"goods" includes ships and aircraft, things attached to land and growing crops;
"premises" includes any place and any stall, vehicle, ship or aircraft; and
"ship" includes any boat and any other description of vessel used in navigation.

(2) For the purposes of this Act, a trade description or statement published in any newspaper, book or periodical or in any film or sound or television broadcast or in any programme included in any programme service (within the meaning of the Broadcasting Act 1990) other than a sound or television broadcasting service shall not be deemed to be a trade description applied or statement made in the course of a trade or business unless it is or forms part of an advertisement.

[Trade Descriptions Act 1968, s 39 as amended by the Cable and Broadcasting Act 1984 and the Broadcasting Act 1990, Sch 20.]

Auctions (Bidding Agreements) Act 1969
(1969 c 56)

8–4590 2. Persons convicted not to attend or participate in auctions.   (1) On any such summary conviction or conviction on indictment as is mentioned in s 1 above[1], the court may order that the person so convicted or that person and any representative of him shall not (without leave of the court) for a period from the date of such conviction—

(*a*) in the case of a summary conviction, of not more than one year, or

(*b*) in the case of a conviction on indictment, of not more than three years,

enter upon any premises where goods intended for sale by auction are on display or to attend or participate in any way in any sale by auction.

(2) In the event of a contravention of an order under this section, the person who contravenes it (and, if he is the representative of another, that other also) shall be guilty of an offence and liable—

(*a*) on summary conviction, to a fine not exceeding **the statutory maximum**.

(*b*) on conviction on indictment, to imprisonment for a term not exceeding **two years** or to a fine or to both.

(3) In any proceedings against a person in respect of a contravention of an order under this section consisting in the entry upon premises where goods intended for sale by auction were on display, it shall be a defence for him to prove that he did not know, and had no reason to suspect, that goods so intended were on display on the premises, and in any proceedings against a person in respect of a contravention of such an order consisting in his having done something as the representative of another, it shall be a defence for him to prove that he did not know, and had no reason to suspect, that that other was the subject of such an order.

(4) Any person shall not be guilty of an offence under this section by reason only of his selling property by auction or causing it to be so sold.

[Auctions (Bidding Agreements) Act 1969, s 2, as amended by the Criminal Law Act 1977, s 28.]

---

1. Section 1 refers to convictions under s 1 of the Auctions (Bidding Agreements) Act 1927, this title *ante*.

Unsolicited Goods and Services Act 1971
(1971 c 30)

8–4600   1. Rights of recipient of unsolicited goods.   *Repealed.*

8–4601   2. Demands and threats regarding payment.   (1) A person who, not having reasonable cause to believe there is a right to payment, in the course of any trade or business makes a demand for payment, or asserts a present or prospective right to payment, for what he knows are unsolicited goods sent (after the commencement of this Act) to another person with a view to his acquiring them for the purposes of his trade or business, shall be guilty of an offence and on summary conviction shall be liable to a fine not exceeding **level 4** on the standard scale.

(2) A person who, not having reasonable cause to believe there is a right to payment, in the course of any trade or business and with a view to obtaining any payment for what he knows are unsolicited goods sent as aforesaid—

     (*a*)   threatens to bring any legal proceedings; or

     (*b*)   places or causes to be placed the name or any person on a list of defaulters or debtors or threatens to do so; or

     (*c*)   invokes or causes to be invoked any other collection procedure or threatens to do so,

shall be guilty of an offence and shall be liable on summary conviction to a fine not exceeding **level 5** on the standard scale.

[Unsolicited Goods and Services Act 1971, s 2 as amended by the Criminal Justice Act 1982, ss 38 and 46 and SI 2000/2334.]

8–4602   3. Directory entries[1].   (1) A person ("the purchaser") shall not be liable to make any payment, and shall be entitled to recover any payment made by him, by way of charge for including or arranging for the inclusion in a directory of an entry relating to that person or his trade or business, unless—

     (*a*)   there has been signed by the purchaser or on his behalf an order complying with this section,

     (*b*)   there has been signed by the purchaser or on his behalf a note complying with this section of his agreement to the charge and before the note was signed, a copy of it was supplied, for retention by him, to him or a person acting on his behalf, or

     (*c*)   there has been transmitted by the purchaser or a person acting on his behalf an electronic communication which includes a statement that the purchaser agrees to the charge and the relevant condition is satisfied in relation to that communication, or

     (*d*)   the charge arises under a contract in relation to which the conditions in section 3B(1) (renewed and extended contracts) are met.

(2) A person shall be guilty of an offence punishable on summary conviction[2] with a fine not exceeding **the statutory maximum** if, in a case where a payment in respect of a charge would, in the absence of an order or note of agreement to the charge complying with this section and in the absence of an electronic communication in relation to which the relevant condition is satisfied, be recoverable from him in accordance with the terms of subsection (1) above, he demands payment, or asserts a present or prospective right to payment, of the charge or any part of it, without knowing or having reasonable cause to believe that—

     (*a*)   the entry to which the charge relates was ordered in accordance with this section,

     (*b*)   a proper note of the agreement has been duly signed, or

     (*c*)   the requirements set out in subsection (1)(*c*) or (*d*) above have been met.

(3) For the purposes of this section,

     (*a*)   an order for an entry in a directory must be made by means of an order form or other stationery belonging to the purchaser, which may be sent electronically but which must bear his name and address (or one or more of his addresses); and

     (*b*)   the note of a person's agreement to a charge must—

         (i)   specify the particulars set out in Part 1 of the Schedule to the Regulatory Reform (Unsolicited Goods and Services Act 1971) (Directory Entries and Demands for Payment) Order 2005, and

         (ii)   give reasonable particulars of the entry in respect of which the charge would be payable.

(3A) In relation to an electronic communication which includes a statement that the purchaser agrees to a charge for including or arranging the inclusion in a directory of any entry, the relevant condition is that—

     (*a*)   before the electronic communication was transmitted the information referred to in subsection (3B) below was communicated to the purchaser, and

     (*b*)   the electronic communication can readily be produced and retained in a visible and legible form.

(3B) that information is—

(a) the following particulars—

    (i) the amount of the charge;

    (ii) the name of the directory or proposed directory;

    (iii) the name of the person producing the directory;

    (iv) the geographic address at which that person is established;

    (v) if the directory is or is to be available in printed form, the proposed date of publication of the directory or of the issue in which the entry is to be included;

    (vi) if the directory or the issue in which the entry is to be included is to be put on sale, the price at which it is to be offered for sale and the minimum number of copies which are to be available for sale;

    (vii) if the directory or the issue in which the entry is to be included is to be distributed free of charge (whether or not it is also to be put on sale), the minimum number of copies which are to be so distributed;

    (viii) if the directory is or is to be available in a form other than in printed form, adequate details of how it may be accessed; and

(b) reasonable particulars of the entry in respect of which the charge would be payable.

(3C) In this section "electronic communication" has the same meaning as in the Electronic Communications Act 2000.

(4) Nothing in this section shall apply to a payment due under a contract entered into before the commencement of this Act, or entered into by the acceptance of an offer made before that commencement.

[Unsolicited Goods and Services Act 1971, s 3, as amended by the Criminal Law Act 1977, s 28, SI 2001/2778 and SI 2005/55.]

---

1. Section 3 will be amended by the Unsolicited Goods and Services (Amendment) Act 1975, when in force, to require compliance with regulations made under s 3A Section 6 is in force as amended (SI 1975/731).

2. Offences committed after 19 March 1975 are also triable on indictment (for procedure in respect of an offence triable either way, see the Magistrates' Courts Act 1980, ss 17A–21 in PART I: MAGISTRATES' COURTS, PROCEDURE, ante) and are punishable by a fine (Unsolicited Goods and Services (Amendment) Act 1975, s 3).

8–4603A 3B. Renewed and extended contracts. (1) The conditions referred to in section 3(1)(d) above are met in relation to a contract ("the new contract") if—

(a) a person ("the purchaser") has entered into an earlier contract ("the earlier contract") for including or arranging for the inclusion in a particular issue or version of a directory ("the earlier directory") of an entry ("the earlier entry") relating to him or his trade or business;

(b) the purchaser was liable to make a payment by way of a charge arising under the earlier contract for including or arranging for the inclusion of the earlier entry in the earlier directory;

(c) the new contract is a contract for including or arranging for the inclusion in a later issue or version of a directory ("the later directory") of an entry ("the later entry") relating to the purchaser or his trade or business;

(d) the form, content and distribution of the later directory is materially the same as the form, content and distribution of the earlier directory;

(e) the form and content of the later entry is materially the same as the form and content of the earlier entry;

(f) if the later directory is published other than in electronic form—

    (i) the earlier directory was the last, or the last but one, issue or version of the directory to be published before the later directory, and

    (ii) the date of publication of the later directory is not more than 13 months after the date of publication of the earlier directory;

(g) if the later directory is published in electronic form, the first date on which the new contract requires the later entry to be published is not more than the relevant period after the last date on which the earlier contract required the earlier entry to be published;

(h) if it was a term of the earlier contract that the purchaser renew or extend the contract—

    (i) before the start of the new contract the relevant publisher has given notice in writing to the purchaser containing the information set out in Part 3 of the Schedule to the Regulatory Reform (Unsolicited Goods and Services Act 1971) (Directory Entries and Demands for Payment) Order 2005¹; and

    (ii) the purchaser has not written to the relevant publisher withdrawing his agreement to the renewal or extension of the earlier contract within the period of 21 days starting when he receives the notice referred to in sub-paragraph (i); and

(i) if the parties to the earlier contract and the new contract are different—

    (i) the parties to both contracts have entered into a novation agreement in respect of the earlier contract; or

    (ii) the relevant publisher has given the purchaser the information set out in Part 4 of the Schedule to the Regulatory Reform (Unsolicited Goods and Services Act 1971) (Directory Entries and Demands for Payment) Order 2005[1].

    (2) For the purposes of subsection (1)(*d*) and (*e*), the form, content or distribution of the later directory, or the form or content of the later entry, shall be taken to be materially the same as that of the earlier directory or the earlier entry (as the case may be), if a reasonable person in the position of the purchaser would—

    (*a*) view the two as being materially the same; or

    (*b*) view that of the later directory or the later entry as being an improvement on that of the earlier directory or the earlier entry.

    (3) For the purposes of subsection (1)(*g*) "the relevant period" means the period of 13 months or (if shorter) the period of time between the first and last dates on which the earlier contract required the earlier entry to be published.

    (4) For the purposes of subsection (1)(h) and (i) "the relevant publisher" is the person with whom the purchaser has entered into the new contract.

    (5) The information referred to in subsection (1)(i)(ii) must be given to the purchaser prior to the conclusion of the new contract.

[Unsolicited Goods and Services Act 1977, s 3B as inserted by SI 2005/55.]

---

  1. SI 2005/55.

8–4604 4. Unsolicited publications. (1) A person shall be guilty of an offence if he sends or causes to be sent to another person any book, magazine or leaflet (or advertising material[1] for any such publication) which he knows or ought reasonably to know is unsolicited and which describes or illustrates human sexual techniques.

    (2) A person found guilty of an offence under this section shall be liable on summary conviction to a fine not exceeding **level 5** on the standard scale.

    (3) A prosecution for an offence under this section shall not in England and Wales be instituted except by, or with the consent of, the Director of Public Prosecutions.

[Unsolicited Goods and Services Act, 1971, s 4 as amended by the Criminal Justice Act 1982, ss 35, 38 and 46.]

---

  1. This section applies to such advertising material even though it does not of itself contain a description or illustration of human sexual techniques (*DPP v Beate Uhse (UK) Ltd* [1974] QB 158, [1974] 1 All ER 753, 138 JP 247).

8–4605 5. Offences by corporations. (1) Where an offence under this Act which has been committed by a body corporate is proved to have been committed with the consent or connivance of, or to be attributable to any neglect on the part of, any director, manager, secretary, or other similar officer of the body corporate, or of any person who was purporting to act in any such capacity, he as well as the body corporate shall be guilty of that offence and shall be liable to be proceeded against and punished accordingly.

    (2) Where the affairs of a body corporate are managed by its members, this section shall apply in relation to the acts or defaults of a member in connection with his functions of management as if he were a director of the body corporate.

[Unsolicited Goods and Services Act 1971, s 5.]

8–4606 6. Interpretation. (1) In this Act, unless the context or subject matter otherwise requires—

    "acquire" includes hire;

    "send" includes deliver, and "sender" shall be construed accordingly;

    "unsolicited" means, in relation to goods sent to any person, that they are sent without any prior request made by him or on his behalf.

    (2) For the purposes of this Act, any invoice[1] or similar document stating the amount of any payment shall be regarded as asserting a right to the payment unless it complies with the conditions set out in Part 2 of the Schedule to the Regulatory Reform (Unsolicited Goods and Services Act 1971) (Directory Entries and Demands for Payment) Order 2005.

    (3) Nothing in sections 3 or 3B shall affect the rights of any consumer under the Consumer Protection (Distance Selling) Regulations 2000.

[Unsolicited Goods and Services Act 1971, s 6, as amended by the Unsolicited Goods and Services (Amendment) Act 1975, s 2 and SI 2005/55.]

---

  1. For the precise form of invoices etc see the Unsolicited Goods and Services (Invoices etc) Regulations 1975, SI 1975/732.

Fair Trading Act 1973
(1973 c 41)

PART II[1]
REFERENCES TO CONSUMER PROTECTION ADVISORY COMMITTEE

Order in pursuance of report of Advisory Committee

8–4620   **22.** *Power of Secretary of State to make orders[2] in respect of consumer trade practices.*

---

1. Part II contains ss 13–33.
2. The Mail Order Transactions (Information) Order 1976, SI 1976/1812, the Consumer Transactions (Restrictions on Statements) Order 1976, SI 1976/1813, amended by SI 1978/127, and the Business Advertisements (Disclosure) Order 1977, SI 1977/1918, have been made.

8–4621   **23. Penalties for contravention of order under s 22.**   Subject to the following provisions of this Part of this Act, any person who contravenes a prohibition imposed by an order under section 22 of this Act, or who does not comply with a requirement imposed by such an order which applies to him, shall be guilty of an offence and shall be liable[1]—

    (*a*)   on summary conviction, to a fine not exceeding **the statutory maximum**;
    (*b*)   on conviction on indictment, to a fine or to imprisonment for a term not exceeding two years or both.

[Fair Trading Act 1973, s 23, as amended by the Criminal Law Act 1977, s 28.]

---

1. For procedure in respect of this offence which is triable either way, see the Magistrates' Courts Act 1980, ss 17A–21 in PART I: MAGISTRATES' COURTS, PROCEDURE, ante.

8–4622   **24. Offences due to default of other person.**   Where the commission by any person of an offence under section 23 of this Act is due to the act or default of some other person, that other person shall be guilty of the offence, and a person may be charged with and convicted of the offence by virtue of this section whether or not proceedings are taken against the first-mentioned person.

[Fair Trading Act 1973, s 24.]

8–4623   **25. Defences in proceedings under s 23.**   (1) In any proceedings for an offence under section 23 of this Act it shall, subject to subsection (2) of this section, be a defence for the person charged to prove—

    (*a*)   that the commission of the offence was due to a mistake, or to reliance on information supplied to him, or to the act or default of another person, an accident or some other cause beyond his control, and
    (*b*)   that he took all reasonable precautions and exercised all due diligence to avoid the commission of such an offence by himself or any person under his control.

(2) If in any case the defence provided by the preceding subsection involves the allegation that the commission of the offence was due to the act or default of another person or to reliance on information supplied by another person, the person charged shall not, without leave of the court, be entitled to rely on that defence unless, within a period ending seven clear days before the hearing, he has served on the prosecutor a notice in writing, giving such information identifying or assisting in the identification of that other person as was then in his possession.
(3) In proceedings for an offence under section 23 of this Act committed by the publication of an advertisement, it shall be a defence for the person charged to prove that he is a person whose business it is to publish or arrange for the publication of advertisements, and that he received the advertisement for publication in the ordinary course of business and did not know and had no reason to suspect that its publication would amount to an offence under section 23 of this Act.

[Fair Trading Act 1973, s 25.]

8–4624   **26. Limitation of effect of orders under s 22.**   A contract for the supply of goods or services shall not be void or unenforceable by reason only of a contravention of an order made under section 22 of this Act; and, subject to the provisions of section 33 of the Interpretation Act 1889[1] (which relates to offences under two or more laws), the provisions of this Part of this Act shall not be construed as—

    (*a*)   conferring a right of action in any civil proceedings (other than proceedings for the recovery of a fine) in respect of any contravention of such an order, or
    (*b*)   affecting any restriction imposed by or under any other enactment, whether public, local or private, or
    (*c*)   derogating from any right of action or other remedy (whether civil or criminal) in proceedings instituted otherwise than under this Part of this Act.

[Fair Trading Act 1973, s 26.]

1. Now s 18 of the Interpretation Act 1978 in PART II: EVIDENCE, *ante.*

Enforcement of orders

8–4625 27. Enforcing authorities. (1) It shall be the duty of every local weights and measures authority to enforce within their area the provisions of any order made under section 22 of this Act.

(2) Nothing in subsection (1) shall be taken as authorising a local weights and measures authority in Scotland to institute proceedings for an offence.

[Fair Trading Act 1973, s 27 as amended by the Weights and Measures Act 1985, Sch 13.]

8–4626 28. Power to make test purchases. A local weights and measures authority may make, or may authorise any of their officers to make on their behalf, such purchases of goods, and may authorise any of their officers to obtain such services, as may be expedient for the purpose of determining whether or not the provisions of any order made under section 22 of this Act are being complied with.

[Fair Trading Act 1973, s 28.]

8–4627 29. Power to enter premises and inspect and seize goods and documents. (1) A duly authorised officer of a local weights and measures authority, or a person duly authorised in writing by the Secretary of State, may at all reasonable hours, and on production, if required, of his credentials, exercise the following powers, that is to say—

(*a*) he may, for the purpose of ascertaining whether any offence under section 23 of this Act has been committed, inspect any goods and enter any premises other than premises used only as a dwelling;

(*b*) if he has reasonable cause to suspect that an offence under that section has been committed, he may, for the purpose of ascertaining whether it has been committed, require any person carrying on a business or employed in connection with a business to produce any books or documents relating to the business and may take copies of, or of any entry in, any such book or document;

(*c*) if he has reasonable cause to believe that such an offence has been committed, he may seize and detain any goods for the purpose of ascertaining, by testing or otherwise, whether the offence has been committed;

(*d*) he may seize and detain any goods or documents which he has reason to believe may be required as evidence in proceedings for such an offence;

(*e*) he may, for the purpose of exercising his powers under this subsection to seize goods, but only if and to the extent that it is reasonably necessary in order to secure that the provisions of an order made under section 22 of this Act are duly observed, require any person having authority to do so to break open any container or open any vending machine and, if that person does not comply with the requirement, he may do so himself.

(2) A person seizing any goods or documents in the exercise of his powers under this section shall inform the person from whom they are seized and, in the case of goods seized from a vending machine, the person whose name and address are stated on the machine as being the proprietor's or, if no name and address are so stated, the occupier of the premises on which the machine stands or to which it is affixed.

(3) If a justice of the peace, on sworn information in writing—,

(*a*) is satisfied that there is reasonable ground to believe either—

(i) that any goods, books or documents which a person has power under this section to inspect are on any premises and that their inspection is likely to disclose evidence of the commission of an offence under section 23 of this Act, or

(ii) that any offence under section 23 has been, is being or is about to be committed on any premises, and

(*b*) is also satisfied either—

(i) that admission to the premises has been or is likely to be refused and that notice of intention to apply for a warrant under this subsection has been given to the occupier, or

(ii) that an application for admission, or the giving of such a notice, would defeat the object of the entry or that the premises are unoccupied or that the occupier is temporarily absent, and it might defeat the object of the entry to await his return.

the justice may by warrant under his hand, which shall continue in force for a period of one month, authorise any such officer or other person as is mentioned in subsection (1) of this section to enter the premises, if need be by force.

In the application of this subsection to Scotland, "justice of the peace" shall be construed as including a sheriff and a magistrate.

(4) A person entering any premises by virtue of this section may take with him such other persons and such equipment as may appear to him necessary; and on leaving any premises which he has entered by virtue of a warrant under subsection (3) of this section he shall, if the premises are

unoccupied or the occupier is temporarily absent, leave them as effectively secured against trespassers as he found them.

(5) Nothing in this section shall be taken to compel the production by a barrister, advocate or solicitor of a document containing a privileged communication made by or to him in that capacity or to authorise the taking of possession of any such document which is in his possession.
[Fair Trading Act 1973, s 29.]

8–4628 **30. Offences in connection with exercise of powers under s 29.** (1) Subject to subsection (6) of this section, any person who—

    (a) wilfully obstructs any such officer or person as is mentioned in subsection (1) of section 29 of this Act acting in the exercise of any powers conferred on him by or under that section, or

    (b) wilfully fails to comply with any requirement properly made to him by such an officer or person under that section, or

    (c) without reasonable cause fails to give such an officer or person so acting any other assistance or information which he may reasonably require of him for the purpose of the performance of his functions under this Part of this Act,

shall be guilty of an offence.

(2) If any person, in giving any such information as is mentioned in subsection (1)(c) of this section, makes any statement which he knows to be false, he shall be guilty of an offence.

(3) *Repealed.*

(4) If any person who is neither a duly authorised officer of a weights and measures authority nor a person duly authorised in that behalf by the Secretary of State purports to act as such under section 29 of this Act or under this section, he shall be guilty of an offence.

(5) Any person guilty of an offence under subsection (1) of this section shall be liable on summary conviction to a fine not exceeding **level 3** on the standard scale; and any person guilty of an offence under subsection (2) or subsection (4) of this section shall be liable[1]—

    (a) on summary conviction, to a fine not exceeding **the statutory maximum**;

    (b) on conviction on indictment, to a fine or to imprisonment for a term not exceeding two years or to both.

(6) Nothing in this section shall be construed as requiring a person to answer any question or give any information if to do so might incriminate that person or (where that person is married or a civil partner) the spouse or civil partner of that person.
[Fair Trading Act 1973, s 30, as amended by the Criminal Law Act 1977, s 28, the Criminal Justice Act 1982, ss 38 and 46, the Enterprise Act 2002, Sch 26 and the Civil Partnership Act 2004, Sch 27.]

---

1. For procedure in respect of this offence which is triable either way, see the Magistrates' Courts Act 1980, ss 17A–21 in PART I: MAGISTRATES' COURTS, PROCEDURE, ante.

8–4629 **31. Notices of test.** Where any goods seized or purchased by a person in pursuance of this Part of this Act are submitted to a test, then—

    (a) if the goods were seized, he shall inform any such person as is mentioned in section 29(2) of this Act of the result of the test;

    (b) if the goods were purchased and the test leads to the institution of proceedings for an offence under section 23 of this Act, he shall inform the person from whom the goods were purchased, or, in the case of goods sold through a vending machine, the person mentioned in relation to such goods in section 29(2) of this Act, of the result of the test;

and where, as a result of the test, proceedings for an offence under section 23 of this Act are instituted against any person, he shall allow that person to have the goods tested on his behalf if it is reasonably practicable to do so.
[Fair Trading Act 1973, s 31.]

PART IV[1]
FUNCTIONS OF DIRECTOR AND COMMISSION IN RELATION TO MONOPOLY SITUATIONS AND UNCOMPETITIVE PRACTICES

Powers for Director to require information

8–4630 **44.** *Power of Director General to Fair Trading to require information.*

---

1. Part IV contains ss 44–56.

8–4631 **46. Supplementary provisions as to requirements to furnish information.**
(1)–(3) *Repealed.*
(4) Any person who refuses or wilfully neglects to comply with a requirement imposed under section 44(2) above is guilty of an offence and liable[1]—

    (a) on summary conviction, to a fine not exceeding the prescribed sum, or (*b*) on conviction on indictment, to imprisonment for a term not exceeding two years or to a fine or to both.

(5) If a person is charged with an offence under subsection (4) in respect of a requirement to produce a document, it is a defence for him to prove—

(*a*) that the document was not in his possession or under his control; and
(*b*) that it was not reasonably practicable for him to comply with the requirement.

(6) If a person is charged with an offence under subsection (4) in respect of a requirement—

(*a*) to provide an explanation of a document, or
(*b*) to state where a document is to be found,

it is a defence for him to prove that he had a reasonable excuse for failing to comply with the requirement.

(7) A person who intentionally obstructs the Director in the exercise of his powers under section 44 is guilty of an offence and liable[1]—

(*a*) on summary conviction, to a fine not exceeding the prescribed sum;
(*b*) on conviction on indictment, to a fine.

(8) A person who wilfully alters, suppresses or destroys any document which he has been required to produce under section 44(2) is guilty of an offence and liable[1]—

(*a*) on summary conviction, to a fine not exceeding the prescribed sum;
(*b*) on conviction on indictment, to imprisonment for a term not exceeding two years or to a fine or to both.

[Fair Trading Act 1973, s 46, as amended by the Criminal Law Act 1977, s 28, the Criminal Justice Act 1982, ss 38 and 46, the Companies Act 1989, Schs 20 and 24, and the Competition Act 1998, s 67.]

---

1. For procedure in respect of an offence which is triable either way, see the Magistrates' Courts Act 1980, ss 17A–21 in PART I: MAGISTRATES' COURTS PROCEDURE, ante.

PART V[1]
MERGERS

Newspaper merger references

8–4632 58. Prohibition of certain newspaper mergers. *Repealed.*

---

1. Part V contains ss 57–77.

8–4633 62. Enforcement provisions relating to newspaper mergers. *Repealed.*

PART VIII[1]
ADDITIONAL PROVISIONS RELATING TO REFERENCES TO COMMISSION

8–4634 85. Attendance of witnesses and production of documents. *Repealed.*

---

1. Part VIII contains ss 84–93B.

8–4635 93B. False or misleading information. (1) If a person furnishes any information—

(*a*) repealed
(*b*) to the Commission in connection with the functions of the Commission under the Airports Act 1986,

and either he knows the information to be false or misleading in a material particular, or he furnishes the information recklessly and it is false or misleading in a material particular, he is guilty of an offence.

(2) A person who—

(*a*) furnishes any information to another which he knows to be false or misleading in a material particular, or
(*b*) recklessly furnishes any information to another which is false or misleading in a material particular,

knowing that the information is to be used for the purpose of furnishing information as mentioned in subsection (1)(*a*) or (*b*) of this section, is guilty of an offence.

(3) A person guilty of an offence under subsection (1) or (2) of this section is liable[2]—

(*a*) on summary conviction, to a fine not exceeding **the statutory maximum**, and
(*b*) on conviction on indictment, to imprisonment for a term not exceeding **two years** or to a **fine** or to both.

(4) Section 129(1) of this Act does not apply to an offence under this section.

(5) This section shall not have effect in relation to the furnishing of information to the Commission

in connection with its functions under any provision of the Enterprise Act 2002 as applied by virtue of section 44B of the Airports Act 1986.
[Fair Trading Act 1973, s 93B, as inserted by the Companies Act 1989, s 151 and amended by the Enterprise Act 2002, Sch 25, SI 2003/3180 and the Communications Act 2003, Sch 19.]

---

1. "Director" includes a reference to the Rail Regulator in the exercise of functions under the Deregulation and Contracting Out Act 1994, Sch 2, paras 11 and 14.

2. For procedure in respect of an offence which is triable either way see the Magistrates' Courts Act 1980, ss 17A–21 in PART I: MAGISTRATES' COURTS, PROCEDURE, ante.

PART XI[1]
PYRAMID SELLING AND SIMILAR TRADING SCHEMES

8–4636 **118. Trading schemes to which Part XI applies.** (1) This Part of this Act applies to any trading scheme if—

- (*a*) the prospect is held out to participants of receiving payments or other benefits in respect of any of the matters specified in subsection (2) of this section; and
- (*b*) (subject to subsection (7) of this section) either or both of the conditions in subsections (3) and (4) of this section are fulfilled in relation to the scheme.

(2) The matters referred to in paragraph (*a*) of subsection (1) of this section are—

- (*a*) the introduction by any person of other persons who become participants in a trading scheme;
- (*b*) the continued participation of participants in a trading scheme;
- (*c*) the promotion, transfer or other change of status of participants within a trading scheme;
- (*d*) the supply of goods or services by any person to or for other persons;
- (*e*) the acquisition of goods or services by any person.

(3) The condition in this subsection is that—

- (*a*) goods or services, or both, are to be provided by the person promoting the scheme (in this Part of this Act referred to as "the promoter") or, in the case of a scheme promoted by two or more persons acting in concert (in this Part of this Act referred to as "the promoters"), by one or more of those persons; and
- (*b*) the goods or services so provided—

  - (i) are to be supplied to or for other persons under transactions effected by participants (whether in the capacity of agents of the promoter or of one of the promoters or in any other capacity), or
  - (ii) are to be used for the purposes of the supply of goods or services to or for other persons under such transactions.

(4) The condition in this subsection is that goods or services, or both, are to be supplied by the promoter or any of the promoters to or for persons introduced to him or any of the other promoters (or an employee or agent of his or theirs) by participants.

(5) For the purposes of this Part of this Act a prospect of a kind mentioned in paragraph (*a*) of subsection (1) of this section shall be treated as being held out to a participant whether it is held out so as to confer on him a legally enforceable right or not.

(6) This Part of this Act does not apply to any trading scheme—

- (*a*) under which the promoter or any of the promoters or participants is to carry on, or to purport to carry on, a relevant regulated activity; or
- (*b*) which otherwise falls within a description prescribed by regulations[2] made by the Secretary of State by statutory instrument.

(6A) For the purposes of subsection (6)(*a*), "relevant regulated activity" means—

- (*a*) dealing in investments as principal or agent;
- (*b*) arranging deals in investments;
- (*c*) managing investments;
- (*d*) safeguarding and administering investments;
- (*e*) sending dematerialised instructions;
- (*f*) establishing etc a collective investment scheme;
- (*g*) advising on investments,

and paragraphs (*a*) to (*g*) must be read with section 22 of the Financial Services and Markets Act 2000, any relevant order under that section, and Schedule 2 to that Act.

(7) The Secretary of State may by order made by statutory instrument—

- (*a*) disapply paragraph (*b*) of subsection (1) of this section in relation to a trading scheme of a kind specified in the order; or
- (*b*) amend or repeal paragraph (*a*) of subsection (6) of this section;

and no such order, and no order varying or revoking any such order, shall be made under this subsection unless a draft of the order has been laid before Parliament and approved by a resolution of each House of Parliament.

(8) In this Part of this Act—

"goods" includes property of any description and a right to, or interest in, property;

"participant" means, in relation to a trading scheme, a person (other than the promoter or any of the promoters) participating in the scheme;

"trading scheme" includes any arrangements made in connection with the carrying on of a business, whether those arrangements are made or recorded wholly or partly in writing or not;

and any reference to the provision or supply of goods shall be construed as including a reference to the grant or transfer of a right or interest.

(9) In this section any reference to the provision or supply of goods or services by a person shall be construed as including a reference to the provision or supply of goods or services under arrangements to which that person is a party.

[Fair Trading Act 1973, s 118 as substituted by the Trading Schemes Act 1996, s 1 and amended by SI 2001/3649.]

---

1. Part XI contains ss 118 to 123.
2. The Trading Schemes (Exclusion) Regulations 1997, SI 1997/31 amended by SI 1997/1887 have been made.

8–4637   119. *Power to make regulations*[1].

---

1. The Pyramid Selling Schemes Regulations 1989, SI 1989/2195 amended by SI 1990/150 and the Trading Schemes Regulations 1997, SI 1997/30 have been made.

8–4638   120. Offences under Part XI.   (1) Subject to the next following section, any person who issues, circulates or distributes, or causes another person to issue, circulate or distribute, an advertisement, prospectus, circular or notice in contravention of any regulations made under subsection (1) of section 119 of this Act shall be guilty of an offence.

(2) Any person who contravenes any regulations made under subsection (2) of that section shall be guilty of an offence.

(3) If any person who is a participant in a trading scheme to which this Part of this Act applies, or has applied or been invited to become a participant in such a trading scheme,—

(a) makes any payment to or for the benefit of the promoter or (if there is more than one) any of the promoters, or to or for the benefit of a participant in the trading scheme, and

(b) is induced to make that payment by reason that the prospect is held out to him of receiving payments or other benefits in respect of the introduction of other persons who become participants in the trading scheme,

any person to whom or for whose benefit that payment is made shall be guilty of an offence.

(4) If the promoter or any of the promoters of a trading scheme to which this Part of this Act applies, or any other person acting in accordance with such a trading scheme, by holding out to any person such a prospect as is mentioned in subsection (3)(b) of this section, attempts to induce him—

(a) if he is already a participant in the trading scheme, to make any payment to or for the benefit of the promoter or any of the promoters or to or for the benefit of a participant in the trading scheme, or

(b) if he is not already a participant in the trading scheme, to become such a participant and to make any such payment as is mentioned in the preceding paragraph.

the person attempting to induce him to make that payment shall be guilty of an offence.

(5) In determining, for the purposes of subsection (3) or subsection (4) of this section, whether an inducement or attempt to induce is made by holding out such a prospect as is therein mentioned, it shall be sufficient if such a prospect constitutes or would constitute a substantial part of the inducement.

(6) Where the person by whom an offence[1] is committed under subsection (3) or subsection (4) of this section is not the sole promoter of the trading scheme in question, any other person who is the promoter or (as the case may be) one of the promoters of the trading scheme shall, subject to the next following section, also be guilty of that offence.

(7) Nothing in subsections (3) to (6) of this section shall be construed as limiting the circumstances in which the commission of any act may constitute an offence under subsection (1) or subsection (2) of this section.

(8) In this section any reference to the making of a payment to or for the benefit of a person shall be construed as including the making of a payment partly to or for the benefit of that person and partly to or for the benefit of one or more other persons.

[Fair Trading Act 1973, s 120 as amended by the Trading Schemes Act 1996, s 2.]

---

1. Section 3 of the Trading Schemes Act 1996 provides:

"Where a person is charged with an offence by virtue of subsection (6) of section 120 of the Fair Trading Act 1973, it is a defence for him to prove that—

(a) the trading scheme to which the charge relates was in operation before the commencement of this Act,

(b) Part XI of the Fair Trading Act 1973 did not apply to that trading scheme at any time before that commencement, and

(c) the act constituting the offence was committed without his consent or connivance."

8–4639 121. Defences in certain proceedings under Part XI. (1) Where a person is charged with an offence under subsection (1) of section 120 of this Act in respect of an advertisement, it shall be a defence for him to prove that he is a person whose business it is to publish or arrange for the publication of advertisements, and that he received the advertisement for publication in the ordinary course of business and did not know, and had no reason to suspect, that its publication would amount to an offence under that subsection.

(2) Where a person is charged with an offence by virtue of subsection (6) of section 120 of this Act, it shall be a defence for him to prove—

(*a*) that the trading scheme to which the charge relates was in operation before the commencement of this Act, and

(*b*) that the act constituting the offence was committed without his consent or connivance.

[Fair Trading Act 1973, s 121.]

8–4640 122. Penalties for offences under Part XI. A person guilty of an offence under this Part of this Act shall be liable[1]—

(*a*) on summary conviction, to a fine not exceeding **the statutory maximum** or to imprisonment for a term not exceeding **three months or to both**;

(*b*) on conviction on indictment, to a fine or to imprisonment for a term not exceeding two years or to both.

[Fair Trading Act 1973, s 122, as amended by the Criminal Law Act 1977, s 28.]

---

1. For procedure in respect of an offence triable either way, see the Magistrates' Courts Act 1980, ss 17A–21 in Part I: Magistrates' Courts, Procedure, ante.

8–4650 123. Enforcement provisions. (1) The provisions of sections 29 to 32[1] of this Act shall have effect for the purposes of this Part of this Act as if in those provisions—

(*a*) references to a weights and measures authority or a duly authorised officer of such an authority were omitted, and

(*b*) any reference to an offence under section 23 of this Act were a reference to an offence under this Part of this Act.

(2) *Northern Ireland.*

[Fair Trading Act 1973, s 123.]

---

1. Section 32, which is not quoted in this work, relates to compensation for loss in respect of goods seized under s 29.

PART XII[1]
MISCELLANEOUS AND SUPPLEMENTARY PROVISIONS

8–4651 129. Time-limit for prosecutions. (1) No prosecution for an offence under this Act shall be commenced after the expiration of three years from the commission of the offence or one year from its discovery by the prosecutor, whichever is the earlier.

(2) Notwithstanding anything in section 127(1) of the Magistrates' Courts Act 1980, a magistrates' court may try an information for an offence under this Act if the information was laid within twelve months from the commission[2] of the offence.

(3) *Scotland.*

(4) *Northern Ireland.*

[Fair Trading Act 1973, s 129, amended by the Magistrates' Courts Act 1980, Sch 7 and the Enterprise Act 2002, Sch 26.]

---

1. Part XII contains ss 124–140.

2. The Magistrates' Courts Act 1980, s 127, allows the same time limit for an indictable offence tried summarily as for one tried on indictment.

8–4652 130. Notice to Director of intended prosecution. *Repealed.*

8–4653 131. Notification of convictions and judgments to Director. *Repealed.*

8–4654 132. Offences by bodies corporate. (1) Where an offence under section 23, section 93B or Part XI of this Act, which has been committed by a body corporate, is proved to have been committed with the consent or connivance of, or to be attributable to any neglect on the part of, any director, manager, secretary or other similar officer of the body corporate, or any person who was purporting to act in any such capacity, he as well as the body corporate shall be guilty of that offence, and be liable to be proceeded against and punished accordingly.

(2) Where the affairs of a body corporate are managed by its members, subsection (1) of this section shall apply in relation to the acts and defaults of a member in connection with his functions of management as if he were a director of the body corporate.

[Fair Trading Act 1973, s 132 as amended by the Companies Act 1989, Sch 20, the Enterprise Act 2002, Sch 26 and SI 2003/3180.]

8–4655   133.   General restrictions on disclosure of information.   *Repealed.*

8–4656   137.   General interpretation provisions.   (2) Except in so far as the context otherwise requires, in this Act, the following expressions have the meanings hereby assigned to them respectively, that is to say—

"agreement" means any agreement or arrangement, in whatever way and in whatever form it is made, and whether it is, or is intended to be, legally enforceable or not;

"the Commission" means the Monopolies and Mergers Commission;

"consumer" (subject to subsection (6) of this section) means any person who is either—

(*a*)   a person to whom goods are or are sought to be supplied (whether by way of sale or otherwise) in the course of a business carried on by the person supplying or seeking to supply them, or

(*b*)   a person for whom services are or are sought to be supplied in the course of a business carried on by the person supplying or seeking to supply them,

and who does not receive or seek to receive the goods or services in the source of a business carried on by him;

"the Director" means the Director General of Fair Trading;★

"enactment" includes an enactment of the Parliament of Northern Ireland;

"goods" includes buildings and other structures, and also includes ships, aircraft and hovercraft;

"merger situation qualifying for investigation" has the meaning assigned to it by section 64(8) of this Act;

"Minister" includes a government department but shall not by virtue of this provision be taken to include the establishment consisting of the Director and his staff, and, except where the contrary is expressly provided, does not include any Minister or department of the Government of Northern Ireland;

"practice" means any practice, whether adopted in pursuance of an agreement or otherwise;

"supply", in relation to the supply of goods, includes supply by way of sale, lease, hire or hire-purchase, and, in relation to buildings or other structures, includes the construction of them by a person for another person;

(3)   In the provisions of this Act "the supply of services" does not include the rendering of any services under a contract of employment but—

(*a*)   includes an undertaking and performance for gain or reward of engagements (whether professional or other) for any matter other than the supply of goods, and

(*b*)   includes both the rendering of services to order and the provision of services by making them available to potential users; and

(*c*)   includes the making of arrangements for a person to put or keep on land a caravan (within the meaning of Part I of the Caravan Sites and Control of Development Act 1960) other than arrangements by virtue of which the person may occupy the caravan as his only or main residence;

(*d*)   includes the making of arrangements for the use by public service vehicles (within the meaning of the Public Passenger Vehicles Act 1981) of a parking place which is used as a point at which passengers on services provided by means of such vehicles may be taken up or set down;

(*e*)   includes the making of arrangements permitting use of the tunnel system (within the meaning of the Channel Tunnel Act 1987) by a person operating services for the carriage of passengers or goods by rail, and

(*f*)   includes the making of arrangements, by means of such an agreement as is mentioned in paragraph 29 of Schedule 2 to the Telecommunications Act 1984, for the sharing of the use of any electronic communications apparatus, and

(*g*)   includes the supply of network services and station services, within the meaning of Part I of the Railways Act 1993;

and any reference in those provisions to services supplied or to be supplied, or to services provided or to be provided, shall be construed accordingly.

(3A)   The Secretary of State may by order made by statutory instrument—

(*a*)   provide that "the supply of services" in the provisions of this Act is to include, or to cease to include, any activity specified in the order which consists in, or in making arrangements in connection with, permitting the use of land; and

(*b*)   for that purpose, amend or repeal any of paragraphs (*c*), (*d*), (*e*) or (*g*) of subsection (3) above.

(3B)   No order under subsection (3A) above is to be made unless a draft of the order has been laid before Parliament and approved by a resolution of each House of Parliament.

(3C) The provisions of Schedule 9 to this Act apply in the case of a draft of any such order as they apply in the case of a draft of an order to which section 91(1) above applies.

(4) *Repealed.*

(5) For the purposes of the provisions of this Act any two bodies corporate are to be treated as interconnected if one of them is any body corporate of which the other is a subsidiary (within the meaning of section 736 of the Companies Act 1985) or if both of them are subsidiaries (within the meaning of that section) of one and the same body corporate; and in those provisions "interconnected bodies corporate" shall be construed accordingly, and "group of interconnected bodies corporate" means a group consisting of two or more bodies corporate all of whom are interconnected with each other.

(6) For the purposes of the application of any provision of this Act in relation to goods or services of a particular description or to which a particular practice applies, "consumers" means persons who are consumers (as defined by subsection (2) of this section) in relation to goods or services of that description or in relation to goods or services to which that practice applies.

(7) *Northern Ireland.*

(8) Except in so far as the context otherwise requires, any reference in this Act to an enactment shall be construed as a reference to that enactment as amended or extended by or under any other enactment, including this Act.

[Fair Trading Act 1973, s 137, as amended by the Restrictive Trade Practices Act 1976, Sch 6, the Competition Act 1980, s 23, the Companies Consolidation (Consequential Provisions) Act 1985, Sch 2, Transport Act 1985, s 116, Channel Tunnel Act 1987, s 33, the Electricity Act 1989, Sch 18, the Broadcasting Act 1990, s 192, the Railways Act 1993, s 66, the Competition Act 1998, s 68, SI 1999/506, Art 14, SI 2003/3180 and the Communications Act 2003, Sch 17.]

1. The meaning of the expression "business" for the purposes of this Act was considered in *Blakemore v Bellamy* (1982) 147 JP 89, [1983] RTR 303 where it was held, on the facts of that case, not to include an activity which was pursued as a hobby.

2. This Act was repealed by the Trade Union and Labour Relations Act 1974, and a fresh (but similar) definition of "worker" provided by s 30 thereof; that definition may now be found in s 296 of the Trade Union and Labour Relations (Consolidation) Act 1992, title EMPLOYMENT, post. It would appear however that the original definition in the 1971 Act still remains incorporated here (see PART II: EVIDENCE, title INTERPRETATION OF STATUTES—*Operation of the Statute*, ante).

8–4657   138. Supplementary interpretation provisions.   (1) This section applies to the following provisions of this Act, that is to say, section 2(4), section 137(6), and the definition of "consumer" contained in section 137(2).

(2) For the purposes of any provisions to which this section applies it is immaterial whether any person supplying goods or services has a place of business in the United Kingdom or not.

(3) For the purposes of any provisions to which this section applies any goods or services supplied wholly or partly outside the United Kingdom, if they are supplied in accordance with arrangements made in the United Kingdom, whether made orally or by one or more documents delivered in the United Kingdom or by correspondence posted from and to addresses in the United Kingdom, shall be treated as goods supplied to, or services supplied for, persons in the United Kingdom.

(4) In relation to the supply of goods under a hire-purchase agreement, a credit-sale agreement or a conditional sale agreement, the person conducting any antecedent negotiations, as well as the owner or seller, shall for the purposes of any provisions to which this section applies be treated as a person supplying or seeking to supply the goods.

(5) In subsection (4) of this section, the following expressions have the meanings given by, or referred to in, section 189 of the Consumer Credit Act 1974—

"antecedent negotiations",

"conditional sale agreement",

"credit-sale agreement",

"hire-purchase agreement".

(6) In any provisions to which this section applies—

(a) any reference to a person to or for whom goods or services are supplied shall be construed as including a reference to any guarantor of such a person, and

(b) any reference to the terms or conditions on or subject to which goods or services are supplied shall be construed as including a reference to the terms or conditions on or subject to which any person undertakes to act as such a guarantor;

and in this subsection "guarantor", in relation to a person to or for whom goods or services are supplied, includes a person who undertakes to indemnify the supplier of the goods or services against any loss which he may incur in respect of the supply of the goods or services to or for that person.

(7) For the purposes of any provisions to which this section applies goods or services supplied by a person carrying on a business shall be taken to be supplied in the course of that business if payment for the supply of the goods or services is made or (whether under a contract or by virtue of an enactment or otherwise) is required to be made.

[Fair Trading Act 1973, s 138 as amended by the Consumer Credit Act 1974, Sch 4 and the Enterprise Act 2002, Sch 26.]

Prices Act 1974
(1974 c 24)

This Act authorises the payment of food subsidies, and make provision for regulating the price of food and certain other goods. The enforcement provisions are codified in the Schedule to the Act.

Section 7   SCHEDULE
                                       ENFORCEMENT

(Amended by the Criminal Law Act 1977, s 28, the Competition Act 1980, Sch 2, the Criminal Justice Act 1982, ss 38 and 46, the Statute Law (Repeals) Act 1989, Sch 1, the Entreprise Act 2002, Sch 26 and the Statute Law (Repeals) Act 2004.)

Food subsidies

8–4760   1, 2. *Repealed.*

3[1]. (1) A duly authorised officer of the Secretary of State or of the Minister of Agriculture, Fisheries and Food may, at all reasonable hours and on production, if required, of his credentials exercise the powers specified in sub-paragraph (2) below for the purpose of determining—

(*a*) whether any payment is to be, or has been, properly made under any scheme under section 1 of this Act or falls to be repaid in accordance with any conditions subject to which it was made or falls to be made to the Secretary of State by virtue of any order under subsection (7) of that section; or

(*b*) whether any condition required to be observed under paragraph 2 above has been contravened.

(2) The said powers are—

(*a*) a power to inspect and take samples of any goods and to enter any land or any premises other than premises used only as a dwelling; and

(*b*) a power to require any person carrying on a business, or employed in connection with a business, to produce any documents relating to the business, and a power of making extracts from, or making copies of, the documents.

(3) Any person who—

(*a*) wilfully obstructs an officer acting under this paragraph; or

(*b*) wilfully fails to comply with a requirement imposed under this paragraph.

shall be guilty of an offence and liable on summary conviction to a fine not exceeding **level 5** on the standard scale.

(4) Any person who, with intent to deceive, produces, in compliance with a requirement under this paragraph, a document which to his knowledge is or may be misleading, false or deceptive in a material particular shall be guilty of an offence and liable on summary conviction to a fine not exceeding **level 5** on the standard scale.

(5) Nothing in this paragraph shall be construed as compelling the production by a barrister, advocate or solicitor of a document containing a privileged communication made by or to him in that capacity.

(6) In this paragraph "premises" include any stall, vehicle or vessel.*

4. *Repealed.*

Price regulation, price marking and price range notices

5. (1) Any person who contravenes an order under section 4 of this Act shall be guilty of an offence[3] and liable—

(*a*) on conviction on indictment, to a fine;

(*b*) on summary conviction, to a fine not exceeding **the prescribed sum**.

(2) *Repealed.*

(3) Section 23 of the Trade Descriptions Act 1968 (offences due to fault of other person) and section 24(1) and (2) of that Act (defence of mistake, accident etc) shall have effect in relation to an offence in respect of an order under section 4 of this Act as they have effect in relation to an offence under that Act.

6. It shall be the duty of every local weights and measures authority to enforce within their area any such order as is mentioned in paragraph 5(1) above.

7. A local weights and measures authority may make, or may authorise any of their officers to make, any purchases of goods and any contracts for services for the purpose of determining whether any such order is being complied with.

8. (1) Proceedings for an offence under paragraph 5 above shall not be instituted except by or on behalf of a local weights and measures authority.

(2) Proceedings for any such offence shall not be instituted—

(*a*) unless there has been served on the person charged a notice in writing of the date and nature of the offence alleged, being (except where he is a street trader) a notice served before the expiration of the period of thirty days beginning with that date; or

(*b*) after the expiration of the period of three months beginning with that date.

(3) Such a notice as is mentioned in sub-paragraph (2)(*a*) above may be served on any person either by serving it on him personally or by sending it to him by post at his usual or last known residence or place of business in the United Kingdom or, in the case of a company, at the company's registered office.

(4) Sub-paragraph (1) above does not apply to Scotland.

9. (1) A duly authorised officer of a local weights and measures authority may, at all reasonable hours and on production, if required, of his credentials, exercise any of the powers specified in paragraph 3(2) above and any of the powers specified in subparagraph (2) below for the purpose of determining whether an offence under paragraph 5 above has been committed.

(2) The said powers are—

(*a*) a power to seize and detain any document or goods which the officer has reason to believe may be required as evidence in proceedings for such an offence; and

(*b*) a power to seize and detain any goods if the officer has reason to believe that their examination is likely to produce evidence of the commission of any such offence.

(3) Any person who—

(*a*) wilfully obstructs an officer acting under this paragraph; or

(*b*) wilfully fails to comply with a requirement imposed under this paragraph; or

(*c*) without reasonable cause fails to give to any officer acting under this paragraph any other assistance or information which the officer may reasonably require for the performance by the officer of his functions under this Schedule.

shall be guilty of an offence and liable on summary conviction to a fine not exceeding **level 5** on the standard scale.

(4) Any person who, with intent to deceive, produces or gives, in compliance with a requirement under this paragraph, a document or information which to his knowledge is or may be misleading, false or deceptive in a material particular shall be guilty of an offence and liable on summary conviction to a fine not exceeding **level 5** on the standard scale.

(5) Nothing in this paragraph shall be construed as requiring a person to answer any question or give any information if to do so might incriminate him or as authorising the taking of possession of any such document as is mentioned in paragraph 3(5) above which is in the possession of a barrister, advocate or solicitor.

10. Where a local weights and measures authority have made arrangements for the discharge of any of their functions as such by another local authority, the powers conferred by paragraph 9 above shall also be exercisable by a duly authorised officer of that other local authority.

11. *Repealed.*

12. *Repealed.*

Offences by bodies corporate

13. Where an offence under this Schedule committed by a body corporate is proved to have been committed with the consent or connivance of, or to be attributable to any neglect on the part of, any director, manager, secretary or other similar officer of the body corporate or any person who was purporting to act in any such capacity, he as well as the body corporate shall be guilty of the offence and shall be liable to be proceeded against and punished accordingly.

---

1. Paragraph 3 has effect only for the purposes of paragraph 9 Statute Law (Repeals) Act 1989, Sch 1.

2. The Secretary of State is enabled by s 2 to regulate the prices of food and certain other goods, by s 4 to regulate price markings and by s 5 to require information to be displayed about the range of prices. Under s 4 the following orders have been made: Indication of Prices (Beds) Order 1978, SI 1978/1716; Price Marking (Pre-packed Milk in Vending Machines) Order 1976, SI 1976/796 amended by SI 1991/1382 and SI 1994/1853; Price Marking Order 1999, Price Marking (Food and Drink Services) Order 2003, see post.

3. For procedure in respect of an offence triable either way, see the Magistrates' Courts Act 1980, ss 17A–21 in PART I: MAGISTRATES' COURTS, PROCEDURE, ante.

Consumer Credit Act 1974

(1974 c 39)

Except as provided by s 192 and Sch 3, this Act came into force on 31st July 1974.

PART I

OFFICE OF FAIR TRADING*

8–4770 1. *Duties of Office of Fair Trading.*

8–4771 7. Penalty for false information. A person who, in connection with any application or request to the OFT under this Act, or in response to any invitation or requirement of the OFT under this Act, knowingly or recklessly gives information to the OFT which, in a material particular, is false or misleading commits an offence[1].

[Consumer Credit Act 1974, s 7 as amended by the Enterprise Act 2002, Sch 25.]

---

1. For penalty, see Sch 1, post.

PART II

CREDIT AGREEMENTS, HIRE AGREEMENTS AND LINKED TRANSACTIONS

8–4772 8. Consumer credit agreements. (1) A personal credit agreement is an agreement between an individual ("the debtor") and any other person ("the creditor") by which the creditor provides the debtor with credit of any amount.

(2) A consumer credit agreement is a personal credit agreement by which the creditor provides the debtor with credit not exceeding £25,000.

(3) A consumer credit agreement is a regulated agreement within the meaning of this Act if it is not an agreement (an "exempt agreement") specified in or under section 16.

[Consumer Credit Act 1974, s 8.]

*Amended by SI 1998/996, from a date to be appointed.

8–4773   9. Meaning of credit.   (1) In this Act "credit" includes a cash loan and any other form of financial accommodation[1].

(2) Where credit is provided otherwise than in sterling it shall be treated for the purposes of this Act as provided in sterling of an equivalent amount.

(3) Without prejudice to the generality of subsection (1), the person by whom the goods are bailed or (in Scotland) hired to an individual under a hire-purchase agreement shall be taken to provide him with fixed-sum credit to finance the transaction of an amount equal to the total price of the goods less the aggregate of the deposit (if any) and the total charge for credit.

(4) For the purposes of this Act, an item[2] entering into the total charge for credit shall not be treated as credit even though time is allowed for its payment.
[Consumer Credit Act 1974, s 9.]

1. Where a plaintiff hired a car as a replacement for her car which had been damaged in an accident under an agreement which provided that she need not pay the hire charge until the conclusion of her action for damages against the other driver but which in all other cases provided that hire charges were payable on demand, she obtained credit and on the terms of the particular transaction did so under a consumer credit agreement which required to be executed according to the statutory requirements in order to be enforceable, *Dimond v Lovell* [1999] 3 All ER 1, [1999] 3 WLR 561, [1999] RTR 297, CA; affd [2002] 1 AC 384, [2000] 2 All ER 897, [2000] RTR 297, HL.
2. A "document fee" immediately payable and deducted from the amount loaned means that the correct amount to be shown as "credit" is the net sum; if this is not specified as the amount of credit, the contract is defective and therefore unenforceable (*Wilson v Robertsons (London) Ltd* [2005] EWHC 1425 (Ch), [2005] 3 All ER 873).

8–4774   10. Running-account credit and fixed-sum credit.   (1) For the purposes of this Act—

  (*a*) running-account credit is a facility under a personal credit agreement whereby the debtor is enabled to receive from time to time (whether in his own person, or by another person) from the creditor or a third party cash, goods and services (or any of them) to an amount or value such that, taking into account payments made by or to the credit of the debtor, the credit limit (if any) is not at any time exceeded; and

  (*b*) fixed-sum credit is any other facility under a personal credit agreement whereby the debtor is enabled to receive credit (whether in one amount or by instalments).

(2) In relation to running-account credit, "credit limit" means, as respects any period, the maximum debit balance which, under the credit agreement, is allowed to stand on the account during that period, disregarding any term of the agreement allowing that maximum to be exceeded merely temporarily.

(3) For the purposes of section 8(2), running-account credit shall be taken not to exceed the amount specified in that subsection ("the specified amount") if—

  (*a*) the credit limit does not exceed the specified amount; or

  (*b*) whether or not there is a credit limit, and if there is, notwithstanding that it exceeds the specified amount,—

   (i)   the debtor is not enabled to draw at any one time an amount which, so far as (having regard to section 9(4)) it represents credit, exceeds the specified amount, or

   (ii) the agreement provides that, if the debit balance raises above a given amount (not exceeding the specified amount), the rate of the total charge for credit increases or any other condition favouring the creditor or his associate comes into operation, or

   (iii) at the time the agreement is made it is probable, having regard to the terms of the agreement and any other relevant considerations, that the debit balance will not at any time rise above the specified amount.
[Consumer Credit Act 1974, s 10.]

8–4775   11. Restricted-use credit and unrestricted-use credit.   (1) A restricted-use credit agreement is a regulated consumer credit agreement—

  (*a*) to finance a transaction between the debtor and the creditor, whether forming part of that agreement or not, or

  (*b*) to finance a transaction between the debtor and a person (the "supplier") other than the creditor, or

  (*c*) to refinance any existing indebtedness of the debtor's, whether to the creditor or another person,

and "restricted-use credit" shall be construed accordingly.

(2) An unrestricted-use credit agreement is a regulated consumer credit arrangement not falling within subsection (1), and "unrestricted-use credit" shall be construed accordingly.

(3) An agreement does not fall within subsection (1) if the credit is in fact provided in such a way as to leave the debtor free to use it as he chooses, even though certain uses would contravene that or any other agreement.

(4) An agreement may fall within subsection (1)(*b*) although the identity of the supplier is unknown at the time the agreement is made.
[Consumer Credit Act 1974, s 11.]

8–4776   12. Debtor-creditor-supplier agreements.   A debtor-creditor-supplier agreement is a regulated consumer agreement being—

(*a*)   a restricted-use credit agreement which falls within section 11(1)(*a*), or

(*b*)   a restricted-use credit agreement which falls within section 11(1)(*b*) and is made by the creditor under pre-existing arrangements, or in contemplation of future arrangements, between himself and the supplier, or

(*c*)   an unrestricted-use credit agreement which is made by the creditor under pre-existing arrangements between himself and a person (the "supplier") other than the debtor in the knowledge that the credit is to be used to finance a transaction between the debtor and the supplier.
[Consumer Credit Act 1974, s 12.]

8–4777   13. Debtor-creditor agreements.   A debtor-creditor agreement is a regulated consumer credit agreement being—

(*a*)   a restricted-use credit agreement which falls within section 11(1)(*b*) but is not made by the creditor under pre-existing arrangements, or in contemplation of future arrangements, between himself and the supplier, or

(*b*)   a restricted-use credit agreement which falls within section 11(1)(*c*), or

(*c*)   an unrestricted-use credit agreement which is not made by the creditor under pre-existing arrangements between himself and a person (the "supplier") other than the debtor in the knowledge that the credit is to be used to finance a transaction between the debtor and the supplier.
[Consumer Credit Act 1974, s 13.]

8–4778   14. Credit-token agreements.   (1) A credit-token[1] is a card, check, voucher, coupon, stamp, form, booklet or other document or thing given to an individual by a person carrying on a consumer credit business, who undertakes—

(*a*)   that on production of it (whether or not some other action is also required) he will supply cash, goods and services (or any of them) on credit, or

(*b*)   that where, on the production of it to a third party (whether or not any other action is also required), the third party supplies cash, goods and services (or any of them), he will pay the third party for them (whether or not deducting any discount or commission), in return for payment to him by the individual.

(2) A credit-token agreement is a regulated agreement for the provision of credit in connection with the use of a credit-token.

(3) Without prejudice to the generality of section 9(1), the person who gives to an individual an undertaking falling within subsection (1)(*b*) shall be taken to provide him with credit drawn on whenever a third party supplies him with cash, goods or services.

(4) For the purposes of subsection (1), use of an object to operate a machine provided by the person giving the object or a third party shall be treated as the production of the object to him.
[Consumer Credit Act 1974, s 14.]

---

1. In *Elliott v Director General of Fair Trading* [1980] 1 WLR 977, [1980] ICR 629, it was held that a card which stated on its face or back that it was a credit card available for immediate use, the sole requirements being a signature, means of identification and a bank account, was a credit-token notwithstanding that those statements were not true.

8–4779   15. Consumer hire agreements.   (1) A consumer hire agreement is an agreement made by a person with an individual (the "hirer") for the bailment or (in Scotland) the hiring of goods to the hirer, being an agreement which—

(*a*)   is not a hire-purchase agreement, and

(*b*)   is capable of subsisting for more than three months, and

(*c*)   does not require the hirer to make payments exceeding £25,000.

(2) A consumer hire agreement is a regulated agreement if it is not an exempt agreement.
[Consumer Credit Act 1974, s 15.]

---

*Amended by SI 1998/996, from a date to be appointed.

8–4780   16. Exempt agreements.   (1) This Act does not regulate a consumer credit agreement where the creditor is a local authority, or a body specified, or of a description specified, in an order[1] made by the Secretary of State, being—

(*a*)   an insurer,

(*b*)   a friendly society,

(*c*)   an organisation of employers or organisation of workers,
(*d*)   a charity,
(*e*)   a land improvement company,
(*f*)   a body corporate named or specifically referred to in any public general Act,
(*ff*)   a body corporate named or specifically referred to in an order made under—

> section 156(4), 444(1)* or 447(2)(*a*) of the Housing Act 1985,
> section 156(4) of that Act as it has effect by virtue of section 17 of the Housing Act 1996 (the right to acquire), . . . (*Scotland; Northern Ireland*); or

(*g*)   a building society, or
(*h*)   a deposit-taker.

(2)   Subsection (1) applies only where the agreement is—

(*a*)   a debtor-creditor-supplier agreement financing—

> (i)   the purchase of land, or
> (ii)   the provision of dwellings on any land, and secured by a land mortgage on that land; or

(*b*)   a debtor-collector agreement secured by any land mortgage; or
(*c*)   a debtor-creditor-supplier agreement financing a transaction in relation to—

> (i)   an agreement falling within paragraph (*a*), or
> (ii)   an agreement falling within paragraph (*b*) financing—
>
> > (*aa*) the purchase of any land, or
> > (*bb*) the provision of dwellings on any land,
>
> and secured by a land mortgage on the land referred to in paragraph (*a*) or, as the case may be, the land referred to in sub-paragraph (ii).

(3)   *Secretary of State to consult specified bodies before making order.*
(4)   An order under subsection (1) relating to a body may be limited so as to apply only to agreements by that body of a description specified in the order.
(5)   The Secretary of State may by order provide that this Act shall not regulate other consumer credit agreements where—

(*a*)   the number of payments to be made by the debtor does not exceed the number specified for that purpose in the order, or
(*b*)   the rate of the total charge for credit does not exceed the rate so specified, or
(*c*)   an agreement has a connection with a country outside the United Kingdom.

(6)   The Secretary of State may by order provide that this Act shall not regulate consumer hire agreements of a description specified in the order where—

(*a*)   the owner is a body corporate authorised by or under any enactment to supply electricity, gas or water, and
(*b*)   the subject of the agreement is a meter or metering equipment,

or where the owner is a provider of a public electronic communications service who is specified in the order.
(6A)   This Act does not regulate a consumer credit agreement where the creditor is a housing authority and the agreement is secured by a land mortgage of a dwelling.
(6B)   In subsection (6A) "housing authority" means—

(*a*)   as regards England and Wales, the Housing Corporation and an authority or body within section 80(1) of the Housing Act 1985 (the landlord condition for secure tenancies), other than a housing association or a housing trust which is a charity;
(*b*)–(*c*)   *Scotland; Northern Ireland.*

(6C)   This Act does not regulate a consumer credit agreement if—

(*a*)   it is secured by a land mortgage; and
(*b*)   entering into that agreement as lender is a regulated activity for the purposes of the Financial Services and Markets Act 2000.

(6D)   But section 126, and any other provision so far as it relates to section 126, applies to an agreement which would (but for subsection (6C)) be a regulated agreement.
(6E)   Subsection (6C) must be read with—

(*a*)   section 22 of the Financial Services and Markets Act 2000 (regulated activities: power to specify classes of activity and categories of investment);
(*b*)   any order for the time being in force under that section; and
(*c*)   Schedule 2 to that Act.

(7)   Nothing in this section affects the application of sections 137–140 (extortionate credit bargains).
(8)   *Scotland.*
(9)   *Northern Ireland.*

[Consumer Credit Act 1974, s 16 amended by the Telecommunications Act 1985, Sch 4, the Housing and

Planning Act 1986, s 22, the Building Societies Act 1986, Schs 18 and 19, the Banking Act 1987, s 88, the Housing Act 1988, Sch 17, SI 1997/627, the Bank of England Act 1998, Sch 5, the Government of Wales Act 1998, Sch 18, SI 2001/544, SI 2001/3649 and the Communications Act 2003, Sch 17.]

---

*Repealed by the Housing Act 1996, Sch 19, from a date to be appointed.
1. The Consumer Credit (Exempt Agreements) Order 1989, SI 1989/869 as amended by SI 1989/1841 and 2337, SI 1991/1393, 1949 and 2844, SI 1992/3218, SI 1993/346 and 2922, SI 1994/2420, SI 1995/1250 and 2914, SI 1996/1445 and 3081, SI 1998/1944, SI 1999/1956 and SI 2001/3649 has been made.

8–4781   17. Small agreements.   (1) A small agreement is—

(*a*)   a regulated consumer credit agreement for credit not exceeding £50, other than a hire-purchase or conditional sale agreement; or

(*b*)   a regulated consumer hire agreement which does not require the hirer to make payments exceeding £50,

being an agreement which is either unsecured or secured by a guarantee or indemnity only (whether or not the guarantee or indemnity is itself secured).

(2)   Section 10(3) applies for the purposes of subsection (1) as it applies for the purposes of section 8(2).

(3)   Where—

(*a*)   two or more small agreements are made at or about the same time between the same parties, and

(*b*)   it appears probable that they would instead have been made as a single agreement but for the desire to avoid the operation of the provisions of this Act which would have applied to that single agreement but, apart from this subsection, are not applicable to the small agreements,

this Act applies to the small agreements as if they were regulated agreements other than small agreements.

(4)   If, apart from this subsection, subsection (3) does not apply to any agreements but would apply if, for any party or parties to any of the agreements, there were substituted an associate of that party, or associates of each of those parties, as the case may be, then subsection (3) shall apply to the agreements.

[Consumer Credit Act 1974, s 17 as amended by SI 1983/878.]

8–4782   18. Multiple agreements.   (1) This section applies to an agreement (a "multiple agreement") if its terms are such as—

(*a*)   to place a part of it within one category of agreement mentioned in this Act, and another part of it within a different category of agreement so mentioned, or within a category of agreement not so mentioned, or

(*b*)   to place it, or part of it, within two or more categories of agreement so mentioned.

(2)   Where a part of an agreement falls within subsection (1), that part shall be treated for the purposes of this Act as a separate agreement.

(3)   Where an agreement falls within subsection (1)(*b*), it shall be treated as an agreement in each of the categories in question, and this Act shall apply to it accordingly.

(4)   Where under subsection (2) a part of a multiple agreement is to be treated as a separate agreement, the multiple agreement shall (with any necessary modifications) be construed accordingly; and any sum payable under the multiple agreement, if not apportioned by the parties, shall for the purposes of proceedings in any court relating to the multiple agreement be apportioned by the court as may be requisite.

(5)   In the case of an agreement for running-account credit, a term of the agreement allowing the credit limit to be exceeded merely temporarily shall not be treated as a separate agreement or as providing fixed-sum credit in respect of the excess.

(6)   This Act does not apply to a multiple agreement so far as the agreement relates to goods if under the agreement payments are to be made in respect of the goods in the form of rent (other than a rent-charge) issuing out of land.

[Consumer Credit Act 1974, s 18.]

8–4783   19. Linked transactions.   (1) A transaction entered into by the debtor or hirer, or a relative of his, with any other person ("the other party"), except one for the provision of security, is a linked transaction in relation to an actual or prospective regulated agreement (the "principal agreement") of which it does not form part if—

(*a*)   the transaction is entered into on compliance with a term of the principal agreement; or

(*b*)   the principal agreement is a debtor-creditor-supplier agreement and the transaction is financed, or to be financed, by the principal agreement; or

(*c*)   the other party is a person mentioned in subsection (2), and a person so mentioned initiated the transaction by suggesting it to the debtor or hirer, of his relative, who enters into it—

(i)   to induce the creditor or owner to enter into the principal agreement, or

    (ii) for another purpose related to the principal agreement, or

    (iii) where the principal agreement is a restricted-use credit agreement, for a purpose related to a transaction financed, or to be financed, by the principal agreement.

    (2) The persons referred to in subsection (1)(c) are—

    (a) the creditor or owner, or his associate;

    (b) a person who, in the negotiation of the transaction, is represented by a credit broker who is also a negotiator in antecedent negotiations for the principal agreement;

    (c) a person who, at the time the transaction is initiated, knows that the principal agreement has been made or contemplates that it might be made.

    (3) A linked transaction entered into before the making of the principal agreement has no effect until such time (if any) as that agreement is made.

    (4) Regulations[1] may exclude linked transactions of the prescribed description from the operation of subsection (3).

[Consumer Credit Act 1974, s 19.]

---

    1. The Consumer Credit (Linked Transactions) (Exemptions) Regulations 1983, SI 1983/1560 amended by SI 2001/3649, have been made.

PART III
LICENSING OF CREDIT AND HIRE BUSINESSES
Licensing principles

8–4784   21. Businesses needing a licence.   (1) Subject to this section, a licence is required to carry on a consumer credit business or consumer hire business.

    (2) A local authority does not need a licence to carry on a business.

    (3) A body corporate empowered by a public general Act naming it to carry on a business does not need a licence to do so.

[Consumer Credit Act 1974, s 21.]

8–4785   22. Standard and group licences.   (1) A licence may be—

    (a) a standard licence, that is a licence, issued by the Director★ to a person named in the licence on an application made by him, which, during the prescribed period[1], covers such activities[2] as are described in the licence, or

    (b) a group licence, that is a licence, issued by the Director★ (whether on the application of any person or of his own motion), which during such period as the Director thinks fit or, if he★ thinks fit, indefinitely, covers such persons and activities as are described in the licence.

    (2) A licence is not assignable or, subject to section 37, transmissible on death or in any other way.

    (3) Except in the case of a partnership or an unincorporated body of persons, a standard licence shall not be issued to more than one person.

    (4) A standard licence issued to a partnership or an unincorporated body of persons shall be issued in the name of the partnership or body.

    (5)–(8) *Provisions as to group licences.*

    (9) Subsection (10) applies if a standard licence is issued to an EEA consumer credit firm.

    (10) The activities described in the licence are not to include an activity for which the firm has, or could obtain, permission under paragraph 15 of Schedule 3 to the Financial Services and Markets Act 2000.

[Consumer Credit Act 1974, s 22 amended by SI 2001/3649.]

    ★**Amended by the Enterprise Act 2002, Sch 25, from a date to be appointed.**

    1. This is a period of 5 years beginning with the date specified for the purpose in the licence, not being earlier than the date of its issue: the Consumer Credit (Period of Standard Licence) Regulations 1975, SI 1975/2124, amended by SI 1991/817.

    2. Does not cover the carrying on by a European institution or quasi-European authorised institution of any home regulated activities (the Banking Coordination (Second Council Directive) Regulations 1992, SI 1992/3218, reg 57).

8–4786   24. Control of name of business.   A standard licence authorises the licensee to carry on a business under the name or names specified in the licence, but not under any other name.

[Consumer Credit Act 1974, s 24.]

8–4787   35. The register.   (1) The OFT shall establish and maintain a register, in which it shall cause to be kept particulars[1] of—

    (a) applications not yet determined for the issue, variation or renewal of licences, or for ending the suspension of a licence;

    (b) licences which are in force, or have at any time been suspended or revoked, with details of any variation of the terms of a licence;

    (c) decisions given by it under this Act, and any appeal from those decisions; and

    (d) such other matters (if any) as it thinks fit.

(1A) The OFT shall also cause to be kept in the register any copy of any notice or other document relating to a consumer credit EEA firm which is given to the OFT by the Financial Services Authority for inclusion in the register.

(2) The OFT shall give general notices of the various matters required to be entered in the register, and of any change in them made under subsection (1)(*d*).

(3) Any person shall be entitled, on payment of the specified fee—

(*a*)　to inspect the register during ordinary office hours and take copies of any entry, or

(*b*)　to obtain from the OFT a copy, certified by the OFT to be correct, of any entry in the register.

(4) The OFT may, if it thinks fit, determine that the right conferred by subsection (3)(*a*) shall be exercisable in relation to a copy of the register instead of, or in addition to, the original.

(5) The OFT shall give general notice of the place or places where, and times when, the register or a copy of it may be inspected.

[Consumer Credit Act 1974, s 35 as amended by SI 2001/3649 and the Enterprise Act 2002, Sch 25.]

---

1. Further particulars are to be included in respect of European institutions where the Banking Coordination (Second Council Directive) Regulations 1992 apply (the Banking Coordination (Second Council Directive) Regulations 1992, SI 1992/3218, reg 60).

8–4788　36. Duty to notify changes.　(1) Within 21 working days after a change takes place in any particulars entered in the register in respect of a standard licence or the licensee under section 35(1)(*d*) (not being a change resulting from action taken by the OFT), the licensee shall give the OFT notice of the change; and the OFT shall cause any necessary amendment to be made in the register.

(2) Within 21 working days after—

(*a*)　any change takes place in the officers of—

(i)　a body corporate, or an unincorporated body of persons, which is the licensee under a standard licence, or

(ii)　a body corporate which is a controller of a body corporate which is such a licensee, or

(*b*)　a body corporate which is such a licensee becomes aware that a person has become or ceased to be a controller of the body corporate, or

(*c*)　any change takes place in the members of a partnership which is such a licensee (including a change on the amalgamation of the partnership with another firm, or a change whereby the number of partners is reduced to one),

the licensee shall give the OFT notice of the change.

(3) Within 14 days after any change takes place in the officers of a body corporate which is a controller of another body corporate which is a licensee under a standard licence, the controller shall give the licensee notice of the change.

(4) Within 14 working days after a person becomes or ceases to be a controller of a body corporate which is a licensee under a standard licence, that person shall give the licensee notice of the fact.

(5) Where a change in a partnership has the result that the business ceases to be carried on under the name, or any of the names, specified in a standard licence the licence shall cease to have effect.

(6) Where the OFT is given notice under subsection (1) or (2) of any change, and subsection (5) does not apply, the OFT may by notice require the licensee to furnish it with such information, verified in such manner, as the OFT may stipulate.

[Consumer Credit Act 1974, s 36 as amended by the Enterprise Act 2002, Sch 25.]

8–4789　37. Death, bankruptcy etc of licensee.　(1) A licence held by one individual terminates if he—

(*a*)　dies, or

(*b*)　is adjudged bankrupt, or

(*c*)　becomes a patient within the meaning of Part VIII of the Mental Health Act 1959.*

(2) In relation to a licence held by one individual, or a partnership or other unincorporated body of persons, or a body corporate, regulations[1] may specify other events relating to the licensee on the occurrence of which the licence is to terminate.

(3) Regulations[1] may—

(*a*)　provide for the termination of a licence by subsection (1), or under subsection (2), to be deferred for a period not exceeding 12 months, and

(*b*)　authorises the business of the licensee to be carried on under the licence by some other person during the period of deferment, subject to such conditions as may be prescribed.

(4) This section does not apply to group licences.

[Consumer Credit Act 1974, s 37.]

---

*Substituted by the Mental Capacity Act 2005, Sch 6 from a date to be appointed.

1. See the Consumer Credit (Termination of Licences) Regulations 1976, this PART, post.

8–4800   39. Offences against Part III.   (1) A person who engages in any activities for which a licence is required[1] when he is not a licensee under a licence covering those activities commits an offence[2].

(2) A licensee under a standard licence who carries on business under a name not specified in that licence commits an offence[2].

(3) A person who fails to give the OFT or licensee notice under section 36 within the period required commits an offence[2].

[Consumer Credit Act 1974, s 39 as amended by the Enterprise Act 2002, Sch 25.]

---

1. See eg the credit brokerage system set up in *Hicks v Walker* [1984] Crim LR 495. The provision of display boxes and credit application forms does not amount to the introduction of a person seeking credit to a consumer credit business within the terms of s 145 of this Act (*Brookes v Retail Credit Card Ltd* (1985) 150 JP 131, [1986] Crim LR 327, DC).

2. For penalty, see Sch 1, post.

PART IV

SEEKING BUSINESS

Advertising

8–4801   43. Advertisements to which Part IV applies.   (1) This Part applies to any advertisement, published for the purposes of a business carried on by the advertiser, indicating[1] that he is willing—

(a) to provide credit, or

(b) to enter into an agreement for the bailment or (in Scotland) the hiring of the goods by him.

(2) An advertisement does not fall within subsection (1) if the advertiser does not carry on—

(a) a consumer credit business or consumer hire business, or

(b) a business in the course of which he provides credit to individuals secured on land, or

(c) a business which comprises or relates to unregulated agreements where—

(i)   the law applicable to the agreement is the law of a country outside the United Kingdom, and

(ii) if the law applicable to the agreement were the law of a part of the United Kingdom it would be a regulated agreement.

(3) An advertisement does not fall within subsection (1)(a) if it indicates—

(a) that the credit must exceed £25,000, and that no security is required, or the security is to consist of property other than land, or

(b) that the credit is available only to a body corporate.

(3A) An advertisement does not fall within subsection (1)(a) in so far as it is a communication of an invitation or inducement to engage in investment activity within the meaning of section 21 of the Financial Services and Markets Act 2000, other than an exempt generic communication.

(3B) An "exempt generic communication" is a communication to which subsection (1) of section 21 of the Financial Services and Markets Act 2000 does not apply, as a result of an order under subsection (5) of that section, because it does not identify a person as providing an investment or as carrying on an activity to which the communication relates.

(4) An advertisement does not fall within subsection (1)(b) if it indicates that the advertiser is not willing to enter into a consumer hire agreement.

(5) The Secretary of State may by order provide that this Part shall not apply to other advertisements of a description specified in the order[2].

[Consumer Credit Act 1974, s 43 as amended by SI 2001/544.]

---

1. "Indicating" means "showing". The test to be applied in each case is whether the advertisement constitutes a statement of the fact that the advertiser is willing to provide credit (*Jenkins v Lombard North Central plc* [1984] 1 All ER 828, [1984] 1 WLR 307, 148 JP 280).

2. See the Consumer Credit (Exempt Advertisements) Order 1985, SI 1985/621.

8–4802   44. *Power to make regulations*[1].

---

1. The Consumer Credit (Content of Quotations), Consumer Credit (Advertisements) (Amendment) Regulations 1999, SI 1999/2725 amended by SI 2000/1797, SI 2001/544 and SI 2004/1484 and the Consumer Credit (Advertisements) Regulations 2004, SI 2004/1484 amended by SI 2004/2619 have been made.

8–4803   45. Prohibition of advertisement where goods etc not sold for cash.   If an advertisement to which this Part applies indicates that the advertiser is willing to provide credit under a restricted-use credit agreement relating to goods or services to be supplied by any person, but at the time when the advertisement is published that person is not holding himself out as prepared to sell the goods or provide the services (as the case may be) for cash, the advertiser commits an offence[1].

[Consumer Credit Act 1974, s 45.]

1. For penalty, see Sch 1, post.

8–4804 46. False or misleading advertisements. (1) If an advertisement to which this Part applies conveys information which in a material respect is false or misleading the advertiser commits an offence[1].

(2) Information stating or implying an intention on the advertiser's part which he has not got is false.
[Consumer Credit Act 1974, s 46.]

---

1. For penalty, see Sch 1, post; *Home Insulation Ltd v Wadsley* (1987) 153 JP 92, [1988] BTLC 279, deals with rebates for early settlement on a credit agreement; *Metsoja v H Norman Pitt & Co Ltd* (1989) 153 JP 485 deals with trade-in allowances differing according to whether cash or a "0% APR" finance deal was selected.

It is not duplicitious for an information to give particulars that the information was misleading in several different ways, since only a single act or activity is alleged (*Carrington Carr Ltd v Leicestershire County Council* (1993) 158 JP 570).

8–4805 47. Advertising infringements. (1) Where an advertiser commits an offence against regulations made under section 44 or against section 45 or 46, or would be taken to commit such an offence but for the defence provided by section 168, a like offence[1] is committed by—

(a) the publisher of the advertisement, and

(b) any person who, in the course of a business carried on by him, devised the advertisement, or a part of it relevant to the first-mentioned offence, and

(c) where the advertiser did not procure the publication of the advertisement, the person who did procure it.

(2) In proceedings for an offence under subsection (1)(a) it is a defence for the person charged to prove that—

(a) the advertisement was published in the course of a business carried on by him, and

(b) he received the advertisement in the course of that business, and did not know and had no reason to suspect that its publication would be an offence under this Part.
[Consumer Credit Act 1974, s 47.]

---

1. For penalty, see Sch 1, post.

Canvassing, etc

8–4806 48. Definition of canvassing off trade premises (regulated agreements). (1) An individual (the "canvasser") canvasses a regulated agreement off trade premises if he solicits the entry (as debtor or hirer) of another individual (the "consumer") into the agreement by making oral representations to the consumer, or any other individual, during a visit by the canvasser to any place (not excluded by subsection (2)) where the consumer, or that other individual, as the case may be, is, being a visit—

(a) carried out for the purpose of making such oral representations to individuals who are at that place, but

(b) not carried out in response to a request made on a previous occasion.

(2) A place is excluded from subsection (1) if it is a place where a business is carried on (whether on a permanent or temporary basis) by—

(a) the creditor or owner, or

(b) a supplier, or

(c) the canvasser, or the person whose employee or agent the canvasser is, or

(d) the consumer.
[Consumer Credit Act 1974, s 48.]

8–4807 49. Prohibition of canvassing debtor-credit agreements off trade premises. (1) It is an offence[1] to canvass debtor-creditor agreements off trade premises.

(2) It is also an offence[1] to solicit the entry of an individual (as debtor) into a debtor-creditor agreement during a visit carried out in response to a request made on a previous occasion where—

(a) the request was not in writing signed by or on behalf of the person making it, and

(b) if no request for the visit had been made, the soliciting would have constituted the canvassing of a debtor-creditor agreement off trade premises.

(3) Subsections (1) and (2) do not apply to any soliciting for an agreement enabling the debtor to overdraw on a current account of any description kept with the creditor, where—

(a) the OFT has determined that current accounts of that description kept with the creditor are excluded from subsection (1) and (2), and

(b) the debtor already keeps an account with the creditor (whether a current account or not).

(4) A determination under subsection (3)(a)—

(a) may be made subject to such conditions as the OFT thinks fit, and

(b)   shall be made only where the OFT is of the opinion that it is not against the interests of debtors.

(5) If soliciting is done in breach of a condition imposed under subsection (4)(a), the determination under subsection (3)(a) does not apply to it.

[Consumer Credit Act 1974, s 49 as amended by the Enterprise Act 2002, Sch 25.]

---

1. For penalty, see Sch 1, post.

8–4808   50.   Circulars to minors.   (1) A person commits an offence who, with a view to financial gain, sends to a minor any document inviting him to—

(a)   borrow money[1], or
(b)   obtain goods on credit or hire, or
(c)   obtain services on credit, or
(d)   apply for information or advice on borrowing money or otherwise obtaining credit, or hiring goods.

(2) In proceedings under subsection (1) in respect of the sending of a document to a minor, it is a defence for the person charged to prove that he did not know, and had no reasonable cause to suspect, that he was a minor.

(3) Where a document is received by a minor at any school or educational establishment for minors, a person sending it to him at that establishment knowing or suspecting it to be such an establishment shall be taken to have reasonable cause to suspect that he is a minor.

[Consumer Credit Act 1974, s 50.]

---

1. The prosecution must prove that not only has the defendant sent to a minor a document inviting him to borrow money, but that when so doing the defendant carried out that act with a view to financial gain (*Alliance and Leicester Building Society v Babbs* (1993) 157 JP 706—offence not proved because although an invitation was sent to a minor it was accepted that the defendants' policy in fact was not to grant loans to minors).

8–4809   51.   Prohibition of unsolicited credit-tokens.   (1) It is an offence to give a person a credit-token if he has not asked for it.

(2) To comply with subsection (1) a request must be contained in a document signed by the person making the request, unless the credit-token agreement is a small debtor-creditor-supplier agreement.

(3) Subsection (1) does not apply to the giving of a credit-token to a person—

(a)   for use under a credit-token agreement already made, or
(b)   in renewal or replacement of a credit-token previously accepted by him under a credit-token agreement which continues in force, whether or not varied.

[Consumer Credit Act 1974, s 51.]

PART V
ENTRY INTO CREDIT OR HIRE AGREEMENTS

8–4810   56.   Antecedent negotiations.   (1) In this act "antecedent negotiations" means any negotiations with the debtor or hirer—

(a)   conducted by the creditor or owner in relation to the making of any regulated agreement, or
(b)   conducted by a credit-broker in relation to goods sold or proposed to be sold by the credit-broker to the creditor before forming the subject-matter of a debtor-collector-supplier agreement within section 12(a), or
(c)   conducted by the supplier in relation to a transaction financed or proposed to be financed by a debtor-creditor-supplier agreement within section 12(b) or (c),

and "negotiator" means the person by whom negotiations are so conducted with the debtor or hirer.

(2) Negotiations with the debtor in a case falling within subsection (1)(b) or (c) shall be deemed to be conducted by the negotiator in the capacity of agent of the creditor as well as in his actual capacity.

(3) An agreement is void if, and to the extent that, it purports in relation to an actual or prospective regulated agreement—

(a)   to provide that a person acting as, or on behalf of, a negotiator is to be treated as the agent of the debtor or hirer, or
(b)   to relieve a person from liability for acts or omissions of any person acting as, or on behalf of, a negotiator.

(4) For the purposes of this Act, antecedent negotiations shall be taken to begin when the negotiator and the debtor or hirer first enter into communication (including communication by advertisement), and to include any representations made by the negotiator to the debtor or hirer and any other dealings between them.

[Consumer Credit Act 1974, s 56.]

8–4811 65. Consequences of improper execution. (1) An improperly-executed regulated agreement is enforceable against the debtor or hirer on an order of the court only.

(2) A retaking of goods or land to which a regulated agreement relates is an enforcement of the agreement.

[Consumer Credit Act 1974, s 65.]

8–4812 67. Cancellable agreements. A regulated agreement may be cancelled by the debtor or hirer in accordance with this Part if the antecedent negotiations included oral representations made when in the presence of the debtor or hirer by an individual acting as, or on behalf of, the negotiator, unless—

(a) the agreement is secured on land, or is a restricted-use credit agreement to finance the purchase of land or is an agreement for a bridging loan in connection with the purchase of land, or

(b) the unexecuted agreement is signed by the debtor or hirer at premises at which any of the following is carrying on any business (whether on a permanent or temporary basis)—

(i) the creditor or owner;
(ii) any party to a linked transaction (other than the debtor or hirer or a relative of his);
(iii) the negotiator in any antecedent negotiations.

[Consumer Credit Act 1974, s 67.]

8–4813 69. Notice of cancellation. (1) If within the period specified in section 68 the debtor or hirer under a cancellable agreement serves on—

(a) the creditor or owner, or
(b) the person specified in the notice under section 64(1), or
(c) a person who (whether by virtue of subsection (b) or otherwise) is the agent of the creditor or owner,

a notice (a "notice of cancellation") which, however expressed and whether or not conforming to the notice given under section 64(1), indicates the intention of the debtor or hirer to withdraw from the agreement, the notice shall operate—

(i) to cancel the agreement, and any linked transaction, and
(ii) to withdraw any offer by the debtor or hirer, or his relative, to enter into a linked transaction.

(2) In the case of a debtor-creditor-supplier agreement for restricted-use credit financing—

(a) the doing of work or supply of goods to meet an emergency, or
(b) the supply of goods which, before service of the notice of cancellation, had by the act of the debtor or his relative become incorporated in any land or thing not comprised in the agreement or any linked transaction,

subsection (1) shall apply with the substitution of the following for paragraph (i)—

"(i) to cancel only such provisions of the agreement and any linked transaction as—

(aa) relate to the provision of credit, or
(bb) require the debtor to pay an item in the total charge for credit, or
(cc) subject the debtor to any obligation other than to pay for the doing of the said work, or the supply of the said goods".

(3) Except so far as is otherwise provided, references in this Act to the cancellation of an agreement or transaction do not include a case within subsection (2).

(4) Except as otherwise provided by or under this Act, an agreement or transaction cancelled under subsection (1) shall be treated as if it had never been entered into.

(5) Regulations[1] may exclude linked transactions of the prescribed description from subsection (1)(i) or (ii).

(6) Each of the following shall be deemed to be the agent of the creditor or owner for the purpose of receiving a notice of cancellation—

(a) a credit-broker or supplier who is the negotiator in antecedent negotiations, and
(b) any person who in the course of a business carried on by him, acts on behalf of the debtor or hirer in any negotiations for the agreement.

(7) Whether or not it is actually received by him, a notice of cancellation sent by post shall be deemed to be served on him—

(a) in the case of a notice sent by post, at the time of posting, and
(b) in the case of a notice transmitted in the form of an electronic communication in accordance with section 176A(1), at the time of the transmission.

[Consumer Credit Act 1974, s 69 as amended by SI 2004/3236.]

---

1. The Consumer Credit (Linked Transactions) (Exemptions) Regulations 1983, SI 1983/1560 amended by SI 2001/3649, have been made.

PART VI

MATTERS ARISING DURING CURRENCY OF CREDIT OR HIRE AGREEMENTS

8–4814   77. Duty to give information to debtor under fixed-sum credit agreement.   (1) The creditor under a regulated agreement for fixed-sum credit, within the prescribed period[1] after receiving a request in writing to that effect from the debtor and payment of a fee of £1, shall give the debtor a copy of the executed agreement (if any) and of any other document referred to in it, together with a statement signed by or on behalf of the creditor showing, according to the information to which it is practicable for him to refer,—

(a)   the total sum paid under the agreement by the debtor;

(b)   the total sum which has become payable under the agreement by the debtor but remains unpaid, and the various amounts comprised in that total sum, with the date when each became due; and

(c)   the total sum which is to become payable under the agreement by the debtor, and the various amounts comprised in that total sum, with the date, or mode of determining the date, when each becomes due.

(2) If the creditor possesses insufficient information to enable him to ascertain the amounts and dates mentioned in subsection (1)(c), he shall be taken to comply with that paragraph if his statement under subsection (1) gives the basis on which, under the regulated agreement, they would fall to be ascertained.

(3) Subsection (1) does not apply to—

(a)   an agreement under which no sum is, or will, or may become, payable by the debtor, or

(b)   a request made less than one month after a previous request under that subsection relating to the same agreement was complied with.

(4) If the creditor under an agreement fails to comply with subsection (1)—

(a)   he is not entitled, while the default continues, to enforce the agreement; and

(b)   if the default continues for one month he commits an offence[2].

(5) This section does not apply to a non-commercial agreement.

[Consumer Credit Act 1974, s 77, as amended by SI 1998/997.]

---

1. The period of 12 working days has been prescribed with effect from 19 May 1985 (SI 1983/1569).
2. For penalty, see Sch 1, post.

8–4815   78. Duty to give information to debtor under running-account credit agreement.
(1) The creditor under a regulated agreement for running-account credit, within the prescribed period[1] after receiving a request in writing to that effect from the debtor and payment of a fee of £1, shall give the debtor a copy of the executed agreement (if any) and of any other document referred to in it, together with a statement signed by or on behalf of the creditor showing, according to the information to which it is practicable for him to refer,—

(a)   the state of the account, and

(b)   the amount, if any, currently payable under the agreement by the debtor to the creditor, and

(c)   the amounts and due dates of any payments which, if the debtor does not draw further on the account, will later become payable under the agreement by the debtor to the creditor.

(2) If the creditor possesses insufficient information to enable him to ascertain the amounts and dates mentioned in subsection (1)(c), he shall be taken to comply with that paragraph if his statement under subsection (1) gives the basis on which, under the regulated agreement, they would fall to be ascertained.

(3) Subsection (1) does not apply to—

(a)   an agreement under which no sum is, or will or may become, payable by the debtor, or

(b)   a request made less than one month after a previous request under that subsection relating to the same agreement was complied with.

(4) Where running-account credit is provided under a regulated agreement, the creditor shall give the debtor statements in the prescribed[3] form, and with the prescribed contents—

(a)   showing according to the information to which it is practicable for him to refer, the state of the account at regular intervals of not more than twelve months, and

(b)   where the agreement provides, in relation to specified periods, for the making of payments by the debtor, or the charging against him of interest or any other sum, showing according to the information to which it is practicable for him to refer the state of the account at the end of each of those periods during which there is any movement in the account.

(5) A statement under subsection (4) shall be given within the prescribed[2] period after the end of the period to which the statement relates.

(6) If the creditor under an agreement fails to comply with subsection (1)—

(a)   he is not entitled, while the default continues, to enforce the agreement; and

(b)   if the default continues for one month he commits an offence[3].

(7) This section does not apply to a non-commercial agreement, and subsections (4) and (5) do not apply to a small agreement.
[Consumer Credit Act 1974, s 78 as amended by SI 1998/997.]

---

1. The period of 12 working days has been prescribed with effect from 19 May 1985 (SI 1983/1569).
2. See the Consumer Credit (Running-Account Credit Information) Regulations 1983, SI 1983/1570.
3. For penalty, see Sch 1, post.

8–4816   79. Duty to give hirer information.   (1) The owner under a regulated consumer hire agreement, within the prescribed period[1] after receiving a request in writing to that effect from the hirer and payment of a fee of £1, shall give to the hirer a copy of the executed agreement and of any other document referred to in it, together with a statement signed by or on behalf of the owner showing, according to the information to which it is practicable for him to refer, the total sum which has become payable under the agreement by the hirer but remains unpaid and the various amounts comprised in that total sum, with the date when each became due.

(2) Subsection (1) does not apply to—

(a)   an agreement under which no sum is, or will or may become, payable by the hirer, or
(b)   a request made less than one month after a previous request under that subsection relating to the same agreement was complied with.

(3) If the owner under an agreement fails to comply with subsection (1)—

(a)   he is not entitled, while the default continues, to enforce the agreement; and
(b)   if the default continues for one month he commits an offence[2].

(4) This section does not apply to a non-commercial agreement.
[Consumer Credit Act 1974, s 79 as amended by SI 1998/997.]

---

1. The period of 12 working days has been prescribed with effect from 19 May 1985 (SI 1983/1569).
2. For penalty, see Sch 1, post.

8–4817   80. Debtor or hirer to give information about goods.   (1) Where a regulated agreement, other than a non-commercial agreement, requires the debtor or hirer to keep goods to which the agreement relates in his possession or control, he shall, within seven working days after he has received a request in writing to that effect from the creditor or owner, tell the creditor or owner where the goods are.

(2) If the debtor or hirer fails to comply with subsection (1) and the default continues for 14 days, he commits an offence[1].
[Consumer Credit Act 1974, s 80.]

---

1. For penalty, see Sch 1, post.

8–4818   82. Variation of agreements.   (1) Where, under a power contained in a regulated agreement, the creditor or owner varies the agreement, the variation shall not take effect before notice of it is given to the debtor or hirer in the prescribed[1] manner.

(2) Where an agreement (a "modifying agreement") varies or supplements an earlier agreement, the modifying agreement shall for the purposes of this Act be treated as—

(a)   revoking the earlier agreement, and
(b)   containing provisions reproducing the combined effect of the two agreements,

and obligations outstanding in relation to the earlier agreement shall accordingly be treated as outstanding instead in relation to the modifying agreement.

(2A) Subsection (2) does not apply if the modifying agreement is an exempt agreement as a result of section 16(6C).

(3) If the earlier agreement is a regulated agreement but (apart from this subsection) the modifying agreement is not then, unless the modifying agreement is—

(a)   for running account credit; or
(b)   an exempt agreement as a result of section 16(6C),

it shall be treated as a regulated agreement.

(4) If the earlier agreement is a regulated agreement for running-account credit, and by the modifying agreement the creditor allows the credit limit to be exceeded but intends the excess to be merely temporary, Part V (except section 56) shall not apply to the modifying agreement.

(5) If—

(a)   the earlier agreement is a cancellable agreement, and
(b)   the modifying agreement is made within the period applicable under section 68 to the earlier agreement,

then, whether or not the modifying agreement would, apart from this subsection, be a cancellable agreement, it shall be treated as a cancellable agreement, in respect of which a notice may be served under section 68 not later than the end of the period applicable under that section to the earlier agreement.

(5A)　Subsection (5) does not apply where the modifying agreement is an exempt agreement as a result of section 16(6C).

(6)　Except under subsection (5), a modifying agreement shall not be treated as a cancellable agreement.

(7)　This section does not apply to a non-commercial agreement.

[Consumer Credit Act 1974, s 82 as amended by SI 2005/2967.]

1. See the Consumer Credit (Notice of Variation of Agreements) Regulations 1977, SI 1977/328 amended by SI 1979/661 and 667.

8–4819　85. Duty on issue of new credit-tokens.　(1) Whenever, in connection with a credit-token agreement, a credit-token (other than the first) is given by the creditor to the debtor, the creditor shall give the debtor a copy of the executed agreement (if any) and of any other document referred to in it.

(2)　If the creditor fails to comply with this section—

(a)　he is not entitled, while the default continues, to enforce the agreement; and

(b)　if the default continues for one month he commits an offence[1].

(3)　This section does not apply to a small agreement.

[Consumer Credit Act 1974, s 85.]

1. For penalty, see Sch 1, post.

PART VII
DEFAULT AND TERMINATION

8–4830　97. Duty to give information.　(1) The creditor under a regulated consumer credit agreement, within the prescribed period[1] after he has received a request in writing to that effect from the debtor, shall give the debtor a statement in the prescribed form[1] indicating, according to the information to which it is practicable for him to refer, the amount of the payment required to discharge the debtor's indebtedness under the agreement, together with the prescribed particulars[1] showing how the amount is arrived at.

(2)　Subsection (1) does not apply to a request made less than one month after a previous request under that subsection relating to the same agreement was complied with.

(3)　If the creditor fails to comply with subsection (1)—

(a)　he is not entitled, while the default continues, to enforce the agreement; and

(b)　if the default continues for one month he commits an offence[2].

[Consumer Credit Act 1974, s 97.]

1. See the Consumer Credit (Settlement Information) Regulations 1983, SI 1983/1564 amended by SI 2004/1483, and *Home Insulation Ltd v Wadsley* (1987) 153 JP 92, [1988] BTLC 279, for the operation of this section and the regulations. See also the Consumer Credit (Early Settlement) Regulations 2004, SI 2004/1483 amended by SI 2004/2619.

2. For penalty, see Sch 1, post.

8–4831　103. Termination statements.　(1) If an individual (the "customer") serves on any person (the "trader") a notice—

(a)　stating that—

(i)　the customer was the debtor or hirer under a regulated agreement described in the notice, and the trader was the creditor or owner under the agreement, and

(ii)　the customer has discharged his indebtedness to the trader under the agreement, and

(iii)　the agreement has ceased to have any operation; and

(b)　requiring the trader to give the customer a notice, signed by or on behalf of the trader, confirming that those statements are correct,

the trader shall, within the prescribed period[1] after receiving the notice, either comply with it or serve on the customer a counter-notice stating that, as the case may be, he disputes the correctness of the notice or asserts that the customer is not indebted to him under the agreement.

(2)　Where the trader disputes the correctness of the notice he shall give particulars of the way in which he alleges it to be wrong.

(3)　Subsection (1) does not apply in relation to any agreement if the trader has previously complied with that subsection on the service of a notice under it with respect to that agreement.

(4)　Subsection (1) does not apply to a non-commercial agreement.

(5)　If the trader fails to comply with subsection (1), and the default continues for one month, he commits an offence[2].

[Consumer Credit Act 1974, s 103.]

1. The period of 12 working days has been prescribed with effect from 19 May 1985 (SI 1983/1569).
2. For penalty, see Sch 1, post.

PART VIII
SECURITY

8–4832   105. Form and content of securities.   (1) Any security provided in relation to a regulated agreement shall be expressed in writing.

(2) Regulations[1] may prescribe the form and content of documents ("security instruments") to be made in compliance with subsection (1).

(3) Regulations[1] under subsection (2) may in particular—

(a)   require specified information to be included in the prescribed manner in documents, and other specified material to be excluded;

(b)   contain requirements to ensure that specified information is clearly brought to the attention of the surety, and that one part of a document is not given insufficient or excessive prominence compared with another.

(4) A security instrument is not properly executed unless—

(a)   a document in the prescribed form[1], itself containing all the prescribed terms and conforming to regulations under subsection (2), is signed in the prescribed manner by or on behalf of the surety, and

(b)   the document embodies all the terms of the security, other than implied terms, and

(c)   the document, when presented or sent for the purpose of being signed by or on behalf of the surety, is in such a state that its terms are readily legible, and

(d)   when the document is presented or sent for the purposes of being signed by or on behalf of the surety there is also presented or sent a copy of the document.

(5) A security instrument is not properly executed unless—

(a)   where the security is provided after, or at the time when, the regulated agreement is made, a copy of the executed agreement, together with a copy of any other document referred to in it, is given to the surety at the time the security is provided, or

(b)   where the security is provided before the regulated agreement is made, a copy of the executed agreement, together with a copy of any other document referred to in it, is given to the surety within seven days after the regulated agreement is made.

(6) Subsection (1) does not apply to a security provided by the debtor or hirer.

(7) If—

(a)   in contravention of subsection (1) a security is not expressed in writing or

(b)   a security instrument is improperly executed,

the security, so far as provided in relation to a regulated agreement, is enforceable against the surety on an order of the court only.

(8) If an application for an order under subsection (7) is dismissed (except on technical grounds only) section 106 (ineffective securities) shall apply to the security.

(9) Regulations[2] under section 60(1) shall include provision requiring documents embodying regulated agreements also to embody any security provided in relation to a regulated agreement by the debtor or hirer.

[Consumer Credit Act 1974, s 105.]

1. See the Consumer Credit (Guarantees and Indemnities) Regulations 1983, SI 1983/1556.
2. See the Consumer Credit (Agreements) Regulations 1983, SI 1983/1553 amended by SI 1984/1600, SI 1985/666, SI 1988/2047, SI 2001/3649 and SI 2004/1482 amended by SI 2004/2619.

8–4833   107. Duty to give information to surety under fixed-sum credit agreement.   (1) The creditor under a regulated agreement for fixed-sum credit in relation to which security is provided, within the prescribed period[1] after receiving a request in writing to that effect from the surety and payment of a fee of £1, shall give to the surety (if a different person from the debtor)—

(a)   a copy of the executed agreement (if any) and of any other document referred to in it;

(b)   a copy of the security instrument (if any); and

(c)   a statement signed by or on behalf of the creditor showing, according to the information to which it is practicable for him to refer—

(i)   the total sum paid under the agreement by the debtor,

(ii)   the total sum which has become payable under the agreement by the debtor but remains unpaid, and the various amounts comprised in that total sum, with the date when each became due, and

(iii)   the total sum which is to become payable under the agreement by the debtor, and the various amounts comprised in that total sum, with the date, or mode of determining the date, when each becomes due.

(2) If the creditor possesses insufficient information to enable him to ascertain the amounts and dates mentioned in subsection (1)(c)(iii), he shall be taken to comply with that sub-paragraph if his statement under subsection (1)(c) gives the basis on which, under the regulated agreement, they would fall to be ascertained.

(3) Subsection (1) does not apply to—

(a) an agreement under which no sum is, or will or may become, payable by the debtor, or

(b) a request made less than one month after a previous request under that subsection relating to the same agreement was complied with.

(4) If the creditor under an agreement fails to comply with subsection (1)—

(a) he is not entitled, while the default continues, to enforce the security, so far as provided in relation to the agreement; and

(b) if the default continues for one month he commits an offence[2].

(5) This section does not apply to a non-commercial agreement.
[Consumer Credit Act 1974, s 107 as amended by SI 1998/997.]

---

1. The period of 12 working days has been prescribed with effect from 19 May 1985 (SI 1983/1569).
2. For penalty, see Sch 1, post.

8–4834   108. Duty to give information to surety under running-account credit agreement.
(1) The creditor under a regulated agreement for running-account credit in relation to which security is provided, within the prescribed period[1] after receiving a request in writing to that effect from the surety and payment of a fee of £1, shall give to the surety (if a different person from the debtor)—

(a) a copy of the executed agreement (if any) and of any other document referred to in it;

(b) a copy of the security instrument (if any); and

(c) a statement signed by or on behalf of the creditor showing, according to the information to which it is practicable for him to refer—

(i) the state of the account, and

(ii) the amount, if any, currently payable under the agreement by the debtor to the creditor, and

(iii) the amounts and due dates of any payments which, if the debtor does not draw further on the account, will later become payable under the agreement by the debtor to the creditor.

(2) If the creditor possesses insufficient information to enable him to ascertain the amounts and dates mentioned in subsection (1)(c)(iii), he shall be taken to comply with that sub-paragraph if his statement under subsection (1)(c) gives the basis on which, under the regulated agreement, they would fall to be ascertained.

(3) Subsection (1) does not apply to—

(a) an agreement under which no sum is, or will or may become, payable by the debtor, or

(b) a request made less than one month after a previous request under that subsection relating to the same agreement was complied with.

(4) If the creditor under an agreement fails to comply with subsection (1)—

(a) he is not entitled, while the default continues, to enforce the security, so far as provided in relation to the agreement; and

(b) if the default continues for one month he commits an offence[2].

(5) This section does not apply to a non-commercial agreement.
[Consumer Credit Act 1974, s 108 as amended by SI 1998/997.]

---

1. The period of 12 working days has been prescribed with effect from 19 May 1985 (SI 1983/1569).
2. For penalty, see Sch 1, post.

8–4835   109. Duty to give information to surety under consumer hire agreement. (1) The owner under a regulated consumer hire agreement in relation to which security is provided, within the prescribed period[1] after receiving a request in writing to that effect from the surety and payment of a fee of £1, shall give to the surety (if a different person from the hirer)—

(a) a copy of the executed agreement and of any other document referred to in it;

(b) a copy of the security instrument (if any); and

(c) a statement signed by or on behalf of the owner showing, according to the information to which it is practicable for him to refer, the total sum which has become payable under the agreement by the hirer but remains unpaid and the various amounts comprised in that total sum, with the date when each became due.

(2) Subsection (1) does not apply to—

(a) an agreement under which no sum is, or will or may become, payable by the hirer, or

(b) a request made less than one month after a previous request under that subsection relating to the same agreement was complied with.

(3) If the owner under an agreement fails to comply with subsection (1)—

(a) he is not entitled, while the default continues, to enforce the security, so far as provided in relation to the agreement; and

(b) if the default continues for one month he commits an offence[2].

(4) This section does not apply to a non-commercial agreement.
[Consumer Credit Act 1974, s 109 as amended by SI 1998/997.]

---

1. The period of 12 working days has been prescribed with effect from 19 May 1985 (SI 1983/1569).
2. For penalty, see Sch 1, post.

8–4836 110. Duty to give information to debtor or hirer. (1) The creditor or owner under a regulated agreement, within the prescribed period[1] after receiving a request in writing to that effect from the debtor or hirer and payment of a fee of £1, shall give the debtor or hirer a copy of any security instrument executed in relation to the agreement after the making of the agreement.

(2) Subsection (1) does not apply to—

(a) a non-commercial agreement, or

(b) an agreement under which no sum is, or will or may become, payable by the debtor or hirer, or

(c) a request made less than one month after a previous request under subsection (1) relating to the same agreement was complied with.

(3) If the creditor or owner under an agreement fails to comply with subsection (1)—

(a) he is not entitled, while the default continues, to enforce the security (so far as provided in relation to the agreement); and

(b) if the default continues for one month he commits an offence[2].
[Consumer Credit Act 1974, s 110 as amended by SI 1998/997.]

---

1. The period of 12 working days has been prescribed with effect from 19 May 1985 (SI 1983/1569).
2. For penalty, see Sch 1, post.

8–4837 111. Duty to give surety copy of default etc notice. (1) When a default notice or a notice under section 76(1) or 98(1) is served on a debtor or hirer, a copy of the notice shall be served by the creditor or owner on any surety (if a different person from the debtor or hirer).

(2) If the creditor or owner fails to comply with subsection (1) in the case of any surety, the security is enforceable against the surety (in respect of the breach or other matter to which the notice relates) on an order of the court only.
[Consumer Credit Act 1974, s 111.]

Pledges

8–4838 114. Pawn-receipts. (1) At the time he receives the article, a person who takes any article in pawn under a regulated agreement shall give to the person from whom he receives it a receipt in the prescribed[1] form (a "pawn-receipt").

(2) A person who takes any article in pawn from an individual whom he knows to be, or who appears to be and is, a minor commits an offence.

(3) This section and sections 115 to 122 do not apply to—

(a) a pledge of documents of title or of bearer bonds, or

(b) a non-commercial agreement.
[Consumer Credit Act 1974, s 114, as amended by the Banking Act 1979, s 38.]

---

1. See the Consumer Credit (Pawn-Receipts) Regulations 1983, SI 1983/1566.

8–4839 115. Penalty for failure to supply copies of pledge agreement, etc. If the creditor under a regulated agreement to take any article in pawn fails to observe the requirement of sections 62 to 64 or 114(1) in relation to the agreement he commits an offence.
[Consumer Credit Act 1974, s 115.]

8–4840 116. Redemption period. (1) A pawn is redeemable at any time within six months after it was taken[1].

(2) Subject to subsection (1), the period within which a pawn is redeemable shall be the same as the period fixed by the parties for the duration of the credit secured by the pledge, or such longer period as they may agree.

(3) If the pawn is not redeemed by the end of the period laid down by subsections (1) and (2) (the "redemption period"), it nevertheless remains redeemable until it is realised by the pawnee under section 121 except where under section 120(1)(a) the property in it passes to the pawnee.

(4) No special charge shall be made for redemption of a pawn after the end of the redemption period, and charges in respect of the safe keeping of that pawn shall not be at a higher rate after the end of the redemption period than before.
[Consumer Credit Act 1974, s 116.]

1. This refers to the date on which the pawn is taken by the lender under the agreement. It cannot be earlier than the date on which the agreement is entered into by the parties and therefore cannot be backdated by overlapping with an earlier agreement (*Wilson v Robertsons (London) Ltd* [2005] EWHC 1425 (Ch), [2005] 3 All ER 873).

8–4841   117. Redemption procedure.   (1) On surrender of the pawn-receipt, and payment of the amount owing, at any time when the pawn is redeemable, the pawnee shall deliver the pawn to the bearer of the pawn-receipt.

(2) Subsection (1) does not apply if the pawnee knows or has reasonable cause to suspect that the bearer of the pawn-receipt is neither the owner of the pawn nor authorised by the owner to redeem it.

(3) The pawnee is not liable to any person in tort or delict for delivering the pawn where subsection (1) applies, or refusing to deliver it where the person demanding delivery does not comply with subsection (1) or, by reason of subsection (2), subsection (1) does not apply.
[Consumer Credit Act 1974, s 117.]

8–4842   118. Loss etc of pawn-receipt.   (1) A person (the "claimant") who is not in possession of the pawn-receipt but claims to be the owner of the pawn, or to be otherwise entitled or authorised to redeem it, may do so at any time when it is redeemable by tendering to the pawnee in place of the pawn-receipt—

(a) a statutory declaration[1] made by the claimant in the prescribed form, and with the prescribed contents, or

(b) where the pawn is security for fixed-sum credit nor exceeding £75 or running-account credit on which the credit limit does not exceed £75, and the pawnee agrees, a statement in writing in the prescribed form[1], and with the prescribed contents, signed by the claimant.

(2) On compliance by the claimant with subsection (1), section 117 shall apply as if the declaration or statement were the pawn-receipt, and the pawn-receipt itself shall become inoperative for the purposes of section 117.
[Consumer Credit Act 1974, s 118 as amended by SI 1998/997.]

1. The Consumer Credit (Loss of Pawn-Receipt) Regulations 1983, SI 1983/1567, prescribe the form and contents of the statutory declaration or statement in writing which may be tendered in the case of the loss, etc, of the pawn receipt.

8–4843   119. Unreasonable refusal to deliver pawn.   (1) If a person who has taken a pawn under a regulated agreement refuses without reasonable cause to allow the pawn to be redeemed, he commits an offence[1].

(2) On the conviction in England or Wales of a pawnee under subsection (1) where the offence does not amount to theft, section 148 of the Powers of Criminal Courts (Sentencing) Act 2000 (restitution orders) shall apply as if the pawnee had been convicted of stealing the pawn.

(3) *Northern Ireland.*
[Consumer Credit Act 1974, s 119 as amended by the Powers of Criminal Courts (Sentencing) Act 2000, Sch 9.]

1. For penalty, see Sch 1, post.

8–4844   120. Consequences of failure to redeem.   (1) If at the end of the redemption period, the pawn has not been redeemed—

(a) notwithstanding anything in section 113, the property in the pawn passes to the pawnee where the redemption period is six months and the pawn is security for fixed-sum credit not exceeding £75 or running-account credit on which the credit limit does not exceed £75; or

(b) in any other case the pawn becomes realisable by the pawnee.

(2) Where the debtor or hirer is entitled to apply to the court for a time order under section 129, subsection (1) shall apply with the substitution, for "at the end of the redemption period" of "after the expiry of five days following the end of the redemption period".
[Consumer Credit Act 1974, s 120 as amended by SI 1998/997.]

8–4845   121. Realisation of pawn.   (1) When a pawn has become realisable by him, the pawnee may sell it, after giving to the pawnor (except in such cases as may be prescribed) not less than the prescribed period[1] of notice of the intention to sell, indicating in the notice the asking price and such other particulars as may be prescribed[1].

(2) Within the prescribed period[2] after the sale takes place, the pawnee shall give the pawnor the prescribed information[2] in writing as to the sale, its proceeds and expenses.

(3) Where the net proceeds of sale are not less than the sum which, if the pawn had been redeemed

on the date of the sale, would have been payable for its redemption, the debt secured by the pawn is discharged and any surplus shall be paid by the pawnee to the pawnor.

(4) Where subsection (3) does not apply, the debt shall be treated as from the date of sale as equal to the amount by which the net proceeds of sale fall short of the sum which would have been payable for the redemption of the pawn on that date.

(5) In this section the "net proceeds of sale" is the amount realised (the "gross amount") less the expenses (if any) of the sale.

(6) If the pawnee alleges that the gross amount is less than the true market value of the pawn on the date of sale, it is for the pawnee to prove that he and any agents employed by him in the sale used reasonable care to ensure that the true market value was obtained, and if he fails to do so subsections (3) and (4) shall have effect as if the reference in subsection (5) to the gross amount were a reference to the true market value.

(7) If the pawnor alleges that the expenses of the sale were unreasonably high, it is for the pawnee to prove that they were reasonable, and if he fails to do so subsections (3) and (4) shall have effect as if the reference in subsection (5) to expenses were a reference to reasonable expenses.
[Consumer Credit Act 1974, s 121.]

1. See the Consumer Credit (Realisation of Pawn) Regulations 1993, SI 1993/1568 amended by SI 1998/998, which prescribe 14 days as the minimum period of notice which must be given of the intention to sell an article taken in pawn. The Regulations also provide that, where the credit, or credit limit, is not more than £100, the requirement to give notice of intention to sell an article taken in pawn does not apply.
2. See the Consumer Credit (Realisation of Pawn) Regulations 1993, SI 1993/1568 amended by SI 1998/998, which prescribe the period of 20 working days within which information is to be given as to the sale, its proceeds and expenses.

PART X
ANCILLARY CREDIT BUSINESS

8–4846 147. Application of Part III.   (1) The provisions of Part III (except section 40) apply to an ancillary credit business as they apply to a consumer credit business.

(2) *Regulations*[1].
[Consumer Credit Act 1974, s 147.]

1. The Consumer Credit (Conduct of Business) (Credit References) Regulations 1977, SI 1977/330 and the Consumer Credit Licensing (Appeals) Regulations 1998, SI 1998/1203 amended by SI 2003/1400 have been made.

8–4847 151. Advertisements.   (1) Sections 44 to 47 apply to an advertisement published for the purposes of a business of credit brokerage carried on by any person, whether it advertises the services of that person or the services of persons to whom he effects introductions, as they apply to an advertisement to which Part IV applies.

(2) Sections 44, 46 and 47 apply to an advertisement, published for the purposes of a business carried on by the advertiser, indicating that he is willing to advise on debts, or engage in transactions concerned with the liquidation of debts, as they apply to an advertisement to which Part IV applies.*

(2A) An advertisement does not fall within subsection (1) or (2) in so far as it is a communication of an invitation or inducement to engage in investment activity within the meaning of section 21 of the Financial Services and Markets Act 2000, other than an exempt generic communication (as defined in section 43(3B)).

(3) The Secretary of State may by order provide that an advertisement published for the purposes of a business of credit brokerage, debt adjusting or debt counselling shall not fall within subsection (1) or (2) if it is of a description specified in the order.

(4) An advertisement does not fall within subsection (2) if it indicates that the advertiser is not willing to act in relation to consumer credit agreements and consumer hire agreements.

(5) In subsections (1) and (3) "credit brokerage" includes the effecting of introductions of individuals desiring to obtain credit to any person carrying on a business in the course of which he provides credit secured on land.
[Consumer Credit Act 1974, s 151 as amended by SI 2001/544.]

8–4848 153. Definition of canvassing off trade premises (agreements for ancillary credit services).   (1) An individual (the "canvasser") canvasses off trade premises the services of a person carrying on an ancillary credit business if he solicits the entry of another individual (the "consumer") into an agreement for the provision to the consumer of those services by making oral representations to the consumer, or any other individual, during a visit by the canvasser to any place (not excluded by subsection (2)) where the consumer, or that other individual as the case may be, is, being a visit—

(a) carried out for the purpose of making such oral representations to individuals who are at that place, but

(b) not carried out in response to a request made on a previous occasion.

(2) A place is excluded from subsection (1) if it is a place where (whether on a permanent or temporary basis)—

(*a*)   the ancillary credit business is carried on, or
(*b*)   any business is carried on by the canvasser or the person whose employee or agent the canvasser is, or by the consumer.
[Consumer Credit Act 1974, s 153.]

8–4849   154. Prohibition of canvassing certain ancillary credit services off trade premises.
It is an offence[1] to canvass off trade premises the services of a person carrying on a business of credit-brokerage, debt-adjusting or debt-counselling.
[Consumer Credit Act 1974, s 154.]

1. For penalty, see Sch 1, post.

8–4860   157. Duty to disclose name etc of agency.   (1) A creditor, owner or negotiator, within the prescribed[1] period after receiving a request in writing to that effect from the debtor or hirer, shall give him notice of the name and address of any credit reference agency from which the creditor, owner or negotiator has, during the antecedent negotiations, applied for information about his financial standing.
(2) Subsection (1) does not apply to a request received more than 28 days after the termination of the antecedent negotiations, whether on the making of the regulated agreement or otherwise.
(3) If the creditor, owner or negotiator fails to comply with subsection (1) he commits an offence[2].
[Consumer Credit Act 1974, s 157.]

1. See the Consumer Credit (Credit Reference Agency) Regulations 2000, SI 2000/290.
2. For penalty, see Sch 1, post.

8–4861   158. Duty of agency to disclose filed information.   (1) A credit reference agency, within the prescribed[1] period after receiving—
(*a*)   a request in writing to that effect from any partnership or other unincorporated body of persons not consisting entirely of bodies corporate (the "consumer"), and
(*b*)   such particulars as the agency may reasonably require to enable them to identify the file, and,
(*c*)   a fee of £2,
shall give the consumer a copy of the file relating to it kept by the agency.
(2) When giving a copy of the file under subsection (1), the agency shall also give the consumer a statement in the prescribed[1] form of the consumer's rights under section 159.
(3) If the agency does not keep a file relating to the consumer it shall give the consumer notice of that fact, but need not return any money paid.
(4) If the agency contravenes any provision of this section it commits an offence[2].
(5) In this Act "file", in relation to an individual, means all the information about him kept by a credit reference agency, regardless of how the information is stored and "copy of the file", as respects information not in plain English, means a transcript into reduced plain English.
[Consumer Credit Act 1974, s 158 as amended by SI 1983/1571, the Data Protection Act 1998, s 62 and SI 1998/997.]

1. See the Consumer Credit (Credit Reference Agency) Regulations 1977, SI 1977/329.
2. For penalty, see Sch 1, post.

8–4862   159. Correction of wrong information.   (1) Any individual (the "objector") given—
(*a*)   information under section 7 of the Data Protection Act 1998 by a credit reference agency, or
(*b*)   information under section 158,
who considers that an entry in his file is incorrect, and that if it is not corrected he is likely to be prejudiced, may give notice to the agency requiring it either to remove the entry from the file or amend it.
(2) Within 28 days after receiving a notice under subsection (1), the agency shall by notice inform the objector that it has—
(*a*)   removed the entry from the file, or
(*b*)   amended the entry, or
(*c*)   taken no action,
and if the notice states that the agency has amended the entry it shall include a copy of the file so far as it comprises the amended entry.
(3) Within 28 days after receiving a notice under subsection (2) or, where no such notice was given, within 28 days after the expiry of the period mentioned in subsection (2), the objector may, unless he has been informed by the agency that it has removed the entry from his file, serve a further notice on the agency requiring it to add to the file an accompanying notice of correction (not exceeding 200 words) drawn up by the objector, and include a copy of it when furnishing information included in or based on that entry.
(4) Within 28 days after receiving a notice under subsection (3), the agency, unless it intends to

apply to the relevant authority under subsection (5), shall by notice inform the objector that it has received the notice under subsection (3) and intends to comply with it.

(5) If—

(a) the objector has not received a notice under subsection (4) within the time required, or

(b) it appears to the agency that it would be improper for it to publish a notice of correction because it is incorrect, or unjustly defames any person, or is frivolous or scandalous, or is for any other reason unsuitable,

the objector or, as the case may be, the agency may, in the prescribed[1] manner and on payment of the specified fee, apply to the relevant authority, who may make such order on the application as he thinks fit.

(6) If a person to whom an order under this section is directed fails to comply with it within the period specified in the order he commits an offence[2].

(7) The Information Commissioner may vary or revoke any order made by him under this section.

(8) In this section "the relevant authority" means—

(a) where the objector is a partnership or other unincorporated body of persons, the OFT, and

(b) in any other case, the Information Commissioner.

[Consumer Credit Act 1974, s 159 as amended by the Data Protection Act 1998, s 62, the Freedom of Information Act 2000, Sch 2 and the Enterprise Act 2002, Sch 25.]

---

1. See the Consumer Credit (Credit Reference Agency) Regulations 1977, SI 1977/329.
2. For penalty, see Sch 1, post.

8–4863   160. Alternative procedure for business consumers.   (1) The OFT, on an application made by a credit reference agency, may direct that this section shall apply to the agency if it is satisfied—

(a) that compliance with section 158 in the case of consumers who carry on a business would adversely affect the service provided to its customers by the agency, and

(b) that, having regard to the methods employed by the agency and to any other relevant factors, it is probable that consumers carrying on a business would not be prejudiced by the making of the direction.

(2) Where an agency to which this section applies receives a request, particulars and a fee under section 158(1) from a consumer who carries on a business, and section 158(3) does not apply, the agency, instead of complying with section 158, may elect to deal with the matter under the following subsections.

(3) Instead of giving the consumer a copy of the file, the agency shall within the prescribed[1] period give notice to the consumer that it is proceeding under this section, and by notice give the consumer such information included in or based on entries in the file as the OFT may direct, together with a statement in the prescribed form of the consumer's rights under subsections (4) and (5).

(4) If within 28 days after receiving the information given to the consumer under subsection (3), or such longer period as the OFT may allow, the consumer—

(a) gives notice to the OFT that the consumer is dissatisfied with the information, and

(b) satisfies the OFT that the consumer has taken such steps in relation to the agency as may be reasonable with a view to removing the cause of the consumer's dissatisfaction, and

(c) pays the OFT the specified fee,

the OFT may direct the agency to give the OFT a copy of the file, and the OFT may disclose to the consumer such of the information on the file as the OFT thinks fit.

(5) Section 159 applies with any necessary modifications to information given to the consumer under this section as it applies to information given under section 158.

(6) If an agency making an election under subsection (2) fails to comply with subsection (3) or (4) it commits an offence[2].

(7) In this section "consumer" has the same meaning as in section 158.

[Consumer Credit Act 1974, s 160 as amended by the Data Protection Act 1998, s 62, SI 2000/183, art 2(2) and the Enterprise Act 2002, Sch 25.]

---

1. See the Consumer Credit (Credit Reference Agency) Regulations 1977, SI 1977/329.
2. For penalty, see Sch 1, post.

PART XI
ENFORCEMENT OF ACT

8–4864   161. Enforcement authorities.   (1) The following authorities ("enforcement authorities") have a duty to enforce this Act and regulations made under it—

(a) the Director⋆,

(b) in Great Britain, the local weights and measures authority,

(c) *Northern Ireland.*

(2)–(3) *Duty of local weights and measures authority to notify Director* of intended proceedings and to report to him generally.*
[Consumer Credit Act 1974, s 161 as amended by the Local Government, Planning and Land Act 1980, Schs 4 and 34 and the Enterprise Act 2002, Sch 25.]

8–4865 162. Powers of entry and inspection. (1) A duly authorised officer of an enforcement authority, at all reasonable hours and on production if required, of his credentials, may—

(a) in order to ascertain whether a breach of any provision of or under this Act has been committed, inspect any goods and enter any premises (other than premises used only as a dwelling);

(b) if he has reasonable cause to suspect that a breach of any provision of or under this Act has been committed, in order to ascertain whether it has been committed, require any person—

(i) carrying on, or employed in connection with, a business to produce any books or documents relating to it; or

(ii) having control of any information relating to a business recorded otherwise than in a legible form to provide a document containing a legible reproduction of the whole or any part of the information,

and take copies of, or of any entry in, the books or documents;

(c) if he has reasonable cause to believe that a breach of any provision of or under this Act has been committed, seize and detain any goods in order to ascertain (by testing or otherwise) whether such a breach has been committed;

(d) seize and detain any goods, books or documents which he has reason to believe may be required as evidence in proceedings for an offence under this Act;

(e) for the purpose of exercising his powers under this subsection to seize goods, books or documents, but only if and to the extent that it is reasonably necessary for securing that the provisions of this Act and of any regulations made under it are duly observed, require any person having authority to do so to break open any container and, if that person does not comply, break it open himself.

(2) An officer seizing goods, books or documents in exercise of his powers under this section shall not do so without informing the person he seizes them from.

(3) If a justice of the peace, on sworn information in writing, or, in Scotland, a sheriff or a magistrate or justice of the peace, on evidence on oath—

(a) is satisfied that there is reasonable ground to believe either—

(i) that any goods, books or documents which a duly authorised officer has power to inspect under this section are on any premises and their inspection is likely to disclose evidence of a breach of any provision of or under this Act; or

(ii) that a breach of any provision of or under this Act has been, is being or is about to be committed on any premises; and

(b) is also satisfied either—

(i) that admission of the premises has been or is likely to be refused and that notice of intention to apply for a warrant under this subsection has been given to the occupier; or

(ii) that an application for admission, or the giving of such a notice, would defeat the object of the entry or that the premises are unoccupied or that the occupier is temporarily absent and it might defeat the object of the entry to wait for his return,

the justice or, as the case may be, the sheriff or magistrate may by warrant under his hand, which shall continue in force for a period of one month, authorise an officer of an enforcement authority to enter the premises (by force if need be).

(4) An officer entering premises by virtue of this section may take such other persons and equipment with him as he thinks necessary; and on leaving premises entered by virtue of a warrant under subsection (3) shall, if they are unoccupied or the occupier is temporarily absent, leave them as effectively secured against trespassers as he found them.

(5) Regulations[1] may provide that, in cases described by the regulations, an officer of a local weights and measures authority is not to be taken to be duly authorised for the purposes of this section unless he is authorised by the OFT.

(6) A person who is not a duly authorised officer of an enforcement authority, but purports to act as such under this section, commits an offence[2].

(7) Nothing in this section compels a barrister, advocate or solicitor to produce a document containing a privileged communication made by or to him in that capacity or authorises the seizing of any such document in his possession.
[Consumer Credit Act 1974, s 162 as amended by the Enterprise Act 2002, Sch 25.]

---

1. See the Consumer Credit (Entry and Inspection) Regulations 1977, SI 1977/331 amended by SI 1984/1046.
2. For penalty, see Sch 1, post.

8–4866 164. Power to make test purchases etc. (1) An enforcement authority may—

(a) make, or authorise any of their officers to make on their behalf, such purchases of goods; and

(b) authorise any of their officers to procure the provision of such services or facilities or to enter into such agreements or other transactions,

as may appear to them expedient for determining whether any provisions made by or under this Act are being complied with.

(2) Any act done by an officer authorised to do it under subsection (1) shall be treated for the purposes of this Act as done by him as an individual on his own behalf.

(3) Any goods seized by an officer under this Act may be tested, and in the event of such a test he shall inform the person mentioned in section 162(2) of the test results.

(4) Where any test leads to proceedings under this Act, the enforcement authority shall—

(a) if the goods were purchased, inform the person they were purchased from of the test results, and

(b) allow any person against whom the proceedings are taken to have the goods tested on his behalf if it is reasonably practicable to do so.

[Consumer Credit Act 1974, s 164.]

8–4867 165. Obstruction of authorised officers. (1) Any person who—

(a) wilfully obstructs an officer of an enforcement authority acting in pursuance of this Act; or

(b) wilfully fails to comply with any requirement properly made to him by such an officer under section 162; or

(c) without reasonable cause fails to give such an officer (so acting) other assistance or information he may reasonably require in performing his functions under this Act,

commits an offence[1].

(2) If any person, in giving such information as is mentioned in subsection (1)(c), makes any statement which he knows to be false he commits an offence[1].

(3) Nothing in this section requires a person to answer any question or give any information if to do so might incriminate that person or (where that person is married or a civil partner) the spouse or civil partner of that person.

[Consumer Credit Act 1974, s 165 as amended by the Civil Partnership Act 2004, Sch 27.]

---

1. For penalty, see Sch 1, post.

8–4868 166. Notification of convictions and judgments to OFT. Where a person is convicted of an offence or has a judgment given against him by or before any court in the United Kingdom and it appears to the court—

(a) having regard to the functions of the OFT under this Act, that the conviction or judgment should be brought to the OFT's attention, and

(b) that it may not be brought to its attention unless arrangements for that purpose are made by the court,

the court may make such arrangements notwithstanding that the proceedings have been finally disposed of.

[Consumer Credit Act 1974, s 166 as amended by the Enterprise Act 2002, Sch 25.]

8–4869 167. Penalties. (1) An offence under a provision of this Act specified in column 1 of Schedule 1 is triable in the mode or modes indicated in column 3 and on conviction is punishable as indicated in column 4 (where a period of time indicates the maximum term of imprisonment, and a monetary amount indicates the maximum fine, for the offence in question).

(2) A person who contravenes any regulations made under section 44, 52, 53, or 112, or made under section 26 by virtue of section 54, commits an offence[1].

[Consumer Credit Act 1974, s 167.]

---

1. For penalty, see Sch 1, post.

8–4870 168. Defences. (1) In any proceedings for an offence under this Act it is a defence for the person charged to prove—

(a) that his act or omission was due to a mistake, or to reliance on information supplied[1] to him, or to an act or omission by another person, or to an accident or some other cause beyond his control, and

(b) that he took all reasonable precautions and exercised all due diligence to avoid such an act or omission by himself or any person under his control.

(2) If in any case the defence provided by subsection (1) involves the allegation that the act or omission was due to an act or omission by another person or to reliance on information supplied by another person, the person shall not, without leave of the court, be entitled to rely on that defence unless, within a period ending seven clear days before the hearing, he has served on the prosecutor a

notice giving such information identifying or assisting in the identification of that other person as was then in his possession.
[Consumer Credit Act 1974, s 168.]

---

1. "Information supplied" includes not only factual information but can extend to advice on the law (*Coventry City Council v Lazarus* (1994) 160 JP 188).

8–4871 169. Offences by bodies corporate. Where at any time a body corporate commits an offence under this Act with the consent or connivance of, or because of neglect by, any individual, the individual commits the like offence if at that time—

(*a*) he is a director, manager, secretary or similar officer of the body corporate, or
(*b*) he is purporting to act as such an officer, or
(*c*) the body corporate is managed by its members, of whom he is one.
[Consumer Credit Act 1974, s 169.]

8–4872 170. No further sanctions for breach of Act. (1) A breach of any requirement made (otherwise than by any court) by or under this Act[1] shall incur no civil or criminal sanction as being such a breach, except to the extent (if any) expressly provided by or under this Act.

(2) In exercising its functions under this Act the OFT may take account of any matter appearing to it to constitute a breach of a requirement made by or under this Act, whether or not any sanction for that breach is provided by or under this Act and, if it is so provided whether or not proceedings have been brought in respect of the breach.

(3) Subsection (1) does not prevent the grant of an injunction, or the making of an order of certiorari, mandamus or prohibition or (*Scotland*).
[Consumer Credit Act 1974, s 170 as amended by the Enterprise Act 2002, Sch 25.]

---

1. But this does not of course exclude all criminal offences; for example proceedings may still be brought for conspiracy or for any attempt (*Brookes v Retail Credit Card Ltd* (1985) 150 JP 131, [1986] Crim LR 327).

8–4873 171. Onus of proof in various proceedings. (1) If an agreement contains a term signifying that in the opinion of the parties section 10(3)(*b*)(iii) does not apply to the agreement, it shall be taken not to apply unless the contrary is proved.

(2) It shall be assumed in any proceedings, unless the contrary is proved, that when a person initiated a transaction as mentioned in section 19(1)(*c*) he knew the principal agreement had been made, or contemplated that it might be made.

(3) Regulations under section 44 or 52 may make provision as to the onus of proof in any proceedings to enforce the regulations.

(4) In proceedings brought by the creditor under a credit-token agreement—

(*a*) it is for the creditor to prove that the credit-token was lawfully supplied to the debtor, and was accepted by him, and
(*b*) if the debtor alleges that any use made of the credit was not authorised by him, it is for the creditor to prove either—

(i) that the use was so authorised, or
(ii) that the use occurred before the creditor had been given notice under section 84(3).

(5) In proceedings under section 50(1) in respect of a document received by a minor at any school or other educational establishment for minors, it is for the person sending it to him at that establishment to prove that he did not know or suspect it to be such an establishment.

(6) In proceedings under section 119(1) it is for the pawnee to prove that he had reasonable cause to refuse to allow the pawn to be redeemed.

(7) If, in proceedings referred to in section 139(1), the debtor or any surety alleges that the credit bargain is extortionate it is for the creditor to prove the contrary.
[Consumer Credit Act 1974, s 171.]

8–4874 172. Statements by creditor or owner to be binding. (1) A statement by a creditor or owner is binding on him if given under—

section 77(1),
section 78(1),
section 79(1),
section 97(1),
section 107(1)(*c*),
section 108(1)(*c*), or
section 109(1)(*c*).

(2) Where a trader—

(*a*) gives a customer a notice in compliance with section 103(1)(*b*), or
(*b*) gives a customer a notice under section 103(1) asserting that the customer is not indebted to him under an agreement.

the notice is binding on the trader.

(3) Where in proceedings before any court—

(a) it is sought to rely on a statement or notice given as mentioned in subsection (1) or (2), and

(b) the statement or notice is shown to be incorrect,

the court may direct such relief (if any) to be given to the creditor or owner from the operation of subsection (1) or (2) as appears to the court to be just.

[Consumer Credit Act 1974, s 172.]

PART XII
SUPPLEMENTAL

8–4875   174. Restrictions on disclosure of information.   *Repealed.*

8–4876   176. Service of documents.   (1) A document to be served under this Act by one person ("the server") on another person ("the subject") is to be treated as properly served on the subject if dealt with as mentioned in the following subsections.

(2) The documents may be delivered or sent by an appropriate method to the subject, or addressed to him by name and left at his proper address.

(3) For the purposes of this Act, a document sent by post to, or left at, the address last known to the server as the address of a person shall be treated as sent by post to, or left at, his proper address.

(4) Where the document is to be served on the subject as being the person having any interest in land, and it is not practicable after reasonable inquiry to ascertain the subject's name or address, the document may be served by—

(a) addressing it to the subject by the description of the person having that interest in the land (naming it), and

(b) delivering the document to some responsible person on the land or affixing it, or a copy of it, in a conspicuous position on the land.

(5) Where a document to be served on the subject as being a debtor, hirer or surety, or as having any other capacity relevant for the purposes of this Act, is served at any time on another person who—

(a) is the person last known to the server as having that capacity, but

(b) before that time had ceased to have it,

the document shall be treated as having been served at that time on the subject.

(6) Anything done to a document in relation to a person who (whether to the knowledge of the server or not) has died shall be treated for the purposes of subsection (5) as service of the documents on that person if it would have been so treated had he not died.

(7) The following enactments shall not be construed as authorising service on the Public Trustee (in England and Wales) or the Probate Judge (in Northern Ireland) of any document which is to be served under this Act—

section 9 of the Administration of Estates Act 1925;
section 3 of the Administration of Estates Act (Northern Ireland) 1955.

(8) References in the preceding subsections to the serving of a document on a person include the giving of the document to that person.

[Consumer Credit Act 1974, s 176 as amended by the Law of Property (Miscellaneous Provisions) Act 1994, Sch 1 and SI 2004/3236.]

8–4876A   176A. Electronic transmission of documents.   (1) A document is transmitted in accordance with this subsection if—

(a) the person to whom it is transmitted agrees that it may be delivered to him by being transmitted to a particular electronic address in a particular electronic form,

(b) it is transmitted to that address in that form, and

(c) the form in which the document is transmitted is such that any information in the document which is addressed to the person to whom the document is transmitted is capable of being stored for future reference for an appropriate period in a way which allows the information to be reproduced without change.

(2) A document transmitted in accordance with subsection (1) shall, unless the contrary is proved, be treated for the purposes of this Act, except section 69, as having been delivered on the working day immediately following the day on which it is transmitted.

(3) In this section, "electronic address" includes any number or address used for the purposes of receiving electronic communications.

[Consumer Credit Act 1974, s 176A as inserted by SI 2004/3236.]

8–4877   184. *Definition of "associates".*

8–4878 185. Agreement with more than one debtor or hirer. (1) Where an actual or prospective regulated agreement has two or more debtors or hirers (not being a partnership or an unincorporated body of persons)—

(*a*) anything required by or under this Act to be done to or in relation to the debtor or hirer shall be done to or in relation to each of them; and

(*b*) anything done under this Act by or on behalf of one of them shall have effect as if done by or on behalf of all of them.

(2) Notwithstanding subsection (1)(*a*), where running-account credit is provided to two or more debtors jointly, any of them may by a notice signed by him (a "dispensing notice") authorise the creditor not to comply in his case with section 78(4) (giving of periodical statement of account); and the dispensing notice shall have effect accordingly until revoked by a further notice given by the debtor to the creditor;

Provided that:

(*a*) a dispensing notice shall not take effect if previous dispensing notices are operative in the case of the other debtor, or each of the other debtors, as the case may be;

(*b*) any dispensing notices operative in relation to an agreement shall cease to have effect if any of the debtors dies;

(*c*) a dispensing notice which is operative in relation to an agreement shall be operative also in relation to any subsequent agreement which, in relation to the earlier agreement, is a modifying agreement.

(3) Subsection (1)(*b*) does not apply for the purposes of section 61(1)(*a*) or 127(3).

(4) Where a regulated agreement has two or more debtors or hirers (not being a partnership or an unincorporated body of persons), section 86 applies to the death of any of them.

(5) An agreement for the provision of credit, or the bailment or (in Scotland) the hiring of goods, to two or more persons jointly where—

(*a*) one or more of those persons is an individual, and

(*b*) one or more of them is a body corporate,

is a consumer credit agreement or consumer hire agreement if it would have been one had they all been individuals; and the body corporate or bodies corporate shall accordingly be included among the debtors or hirers under the agreement.

(6) Where subsection (5) applies, references in this Act to the signing of any document by the debtor or hirer shall be construed in relation to a body corporate as referring to a signing on behalf of the body corporate.

[Consumer Credit Act 1974, s 185, as amended by the Banking Act 1979, s 38.]

8–4879 186. Agreement with more than one creditor or owner. Where an actual or prospective regulated agreement has two or more creditors or owners, anything required by or under this Act to be done to, or in relation to, or by, the creditor or owner shall be effective if done to, or in relation to, or by, any one of them.

[Consumer Credit Act 1974, s 186.]

8–4889 188. Examples of use of new terminology. (1) Schedule 2 shall have effect for illustrating the use of terminology employed in this Act.

(2) The examples given in Schedule 2 are not exhaustive.

(3) In the case of conflict between Schedule 2 and any other provision of this Act, that other provision shall prevail.

(4) The Secretary of State may by order amend Schedule 2 by adding further examples or in any other way.

[Consumer Credit Act 1974, s 188.]

8–4890 189. Definitions. (1) In this Act, unless the context otherwise requires—

"advertisement" includes every form of advertising, whether in a publication, by television or radio, by display of notices, signs, labels, showcards or goods, by distribution of samples, circulars, catalogues, price lists or other material, by exhibition of pictures, models or films, or in any other way, and references to the publishing of advertisements shall be construed accordingly;

"advertiser" in relation to an advertisement, means any person indicated by the advertisement as willing to enter into transactions to which the advertisement relates;

"ancillary credit business" has the meaning given by section 145(1);

"antecedent negotiations" has the meaning given by section 56;

"appeal period" means the period beginning on the first day on which an appeal to the Secretary of State may be brought and ending on the last day on which it may be brought or, if it is brought, ending on its final determination, or abandonment;

"appropriate method" means—

    (*a*) post, or

    (*b*) transmission in the form of an electronic communication in accordance with section 176A(1);

"assignment", in relation to Scotland, means assignation;

"associate" shall be construed in accordance with section 184;

"bill of sale" has the meaning given by section 4 of the Bills of Sale Act 1878 or, for Northern Ireland, by section 4 of the Bills of Sale (Ireland) Act 1879;

"building society" means a building society within the meaning of the Building Societies Act 1986;

"business" includes profession or trade, and references to a business apply subject to subsection (2);

"cancellable agreement" means a regulated agreement which, by virtue of section 67, may be cancelled by the debtor or hirer;

"canvass" shall be construed in accordance with sections 48 and 153;

"cash" includes money in any form;

"charity" means as respects England and Wales a charity registered under the Charities Act 1993 or an exempt charity (within the meaning of that Act), and as respects Scotland and Northern Ireland an institution or other organisation established for charitable purposes only ("organisation" including any persons administering a trust and "charitable" being construed in the same way as if it were contained in the Income Tax Acts);

"conditional sale agreement" means an agreement for the sale of goods or land under which the purchase price or part of it is payable by instalments, and the property in the goods or land is to remain in the seller (notwithstanding that the buyer is to be in possession of the goods or land) until such conditions as to the payment of instalments or otherwise as may be specified in the agreement are fulfilled;

"consumer credit agreement" has the meaning given by section 8, and includes a consumer credit agreement which is cancelled under section 69(1), or becomes subject to section 69(2), so far as the agreement remains in force;

"consumer credit business" means any business so far as it comprises or relates to the provision of credit under regulated consumer credit agreements;

"consumer hire agreement" has the meaning given by section 15;

"consumer hire business" means any business so far as it comprises or relates to the bailment or (in Scotland) the hiring of goods under regulated consumer hire agreements;

"controller", in relation to a body corporate, means a person—

    (*a*) in accordance with whose directions or instructions the directors of the body corporate or of another body corporate which is its controller (or any of them) are accustomed to act or

    (*b*) who, either alone or with any associate or associates, is entitled to exercise or control the exercise of, one third or more of the voting power at any general meeting of the body corporate or of another body corporate which is its controller;

"copy" shall be construed in accordance with section 180;

"costs", in relation to Scotland, means expenses;

"court" means in relation to England and Wales the county court, in relation to Scotland the sheriff court and in relation to Northern Ireland the High Court or the county court;

"credit" shall be construed in accordance with section 9;

"credit-broker" means a person carrying on a business of credit brokerage;

"credit brokerage" has the meaning given by section 145(2);

"credit limit" has the meaning given by section 10(2);

"creditor" means the person providing credit under a consumer credit agreement or the person to whom his rights and duties under the agreement have passed by assignment or operation of law, and in relation to a prospective consumer credit agreement, includes the prospective creditor;

"credit reference agency" has the meaning given by section 145(8);

"credit-sale agreement" means an agreement for the sale of goods, under which the purchase price or part of it is payable by instalments, but which is not a conditional sale agreement;

"credit-token" has the meaning given by section 14(1);

"credit-token agreement" means a regulated agreement for the provision of credit in connection with the use of a credit-token;

"debt-adjusting" has the meaning given by section 145(5);

"debt-collecting" has the meaning given by section 145(7);

"debt-counselling" has the meaning given by section 145(6);

"debtor" means the individual receiving credit under a consumer credit agreement or the person to whom his rights and duties under the agreement have passed by assignment or operation of law, and in relation to a prospective consumer credit agreement includes the prospective debtor;

"debtor-creditor agreement" has the meaning given by section 13;

"debtor-creditor-supplier agreement" has the meaning given by section 12;

"default notice" has the meaning given by section 87(1);

"deposit" means (except in section 16(10) and 25(1B)) any sum payable by a debtor or hirer by way of deposit or down-payment or credited, or to be credited to him on account of any deposit or down-payment, whether the sum is to be or has been paid to the creditor or owner or any other person, or is to be or has been discharged by a payment of money or a transfer or delivery of goods or by any other means;

"electric line" has the meaning given by the Electricity Act 1989 or, for Northern Ireland, the Electricity Supply (Northern Ireland) Order 1972;

"electronic communication" means an electronic communication within the meaning of the Electronic Communications Act 2000 (c 7);

"embodies" and related words shall be construed in accordance with subsection (4);

"enforcement authority" has the meaning given by section 161(1);

"enforcement order" means an order under section 65(1), 105(7)(*a*) or (*b*), 111(2) or 124(1) or (2);

"executed agreement" means a document, signed by or on behalf of the parties, embodying the terms of a regulated agreement or, such of them as have been reduced to writing;

"exempt agreement" means an agreement specified in or under section 16;

"finance" means to finance wholly or partly, and "financed" and "refinanced" shall be construed accordingly;

"file" and "copy of the file" have the meanings given by section 158(5);

"fixed-sum credit" has the meaning given by section 10(1)(*b*);

"friendly society" means a society registered or treated as registered under the Friendly Societies Act 1974 or the Friendly Societies Act 1992;

"future arrangements" shall be construed in accordance with section 187;

"general notice" means a notice published by the Director at a time and in a manner appearing to him suitable for securing that the notice is seen within a reasonable time by persons likely to be affected by it;

"give" means, deliver or send by an appropriate method to;

"goods" has the meaning given by section 61(1) of the Sale of Goods Act 1979;

"group licence" has the meaning given by section 22(1)(*b*);

"High Court" means Her Majesty's High Court of Justice, or the Court of Session in Scotland or the High Court of Justice in Northern Ireland;

"hire-purchase agreement" means an agreement, other than a conditional sale agreement, under which—

(*a*) goods are bailed or (in Scotland) hired in return for periodical payments by the person to whom they are bailed or hired, and

(*b*) the property in the goods will pass to that person if the terms of the agreement are complied with and one or more of the following occurs—

(i) the exercise of an option to purchase by that person,

(ii) the doing of any other specified act by any party to the agreement,

(iii) the happening of any other specified event;

"hirer" means the individual to whom goods are bailed or (in Scotland) hired under a consumer hire agreement, or the person to whom his rights and duties under the agreement have passed by assignment or operation of law, and in relation to a prospective consumer hire agreement includes the prospective hirer;

"individual" includes a partnership or other unincorporated body of persons not consisting entirely of bodies corporate;

"installation" means—

(*a*) the installing of any electric line or any gas or water pipe,

(*b*) the fixing of goods to the premises where they are to be used, and the alteration of premises to enable goods to be used on them,

(*c*) where it is reasonably necessary that goods should be constructed or erected on the premises where they are to be used, any work carried out for the purpose of constructing or erecting them on those premises;

"judgment" includes an order or decree made by any court;

"land", includes an interest in land, and in relation to Scotland includes heritable subjects of whatever description;

"land improvement company" means an improvement company as defined by section 7 of the Improvement of Land Act 1899;

"land mortgage" includes any security charged on land;

"licence" means a licence under Part III (including that Part as applied to ancillary credit business by section 147);

"licensed", in relation to any act, means authorised by a licence to do the act or cause or permit another person to do it;

"licensee", in the case of a group licence, includes any person covered by the licence;

"linked transaction" has the meaning given by section 19(1);

"local authority", in relation to England, means a county council, a London borough council, a district council, the Common Council of the City of London, or the Council of the Isles of Scilly, in relation to Wales means a county council or county borough council, and in relation to Scotland, means a regional, islands or district council and, in relation to Northern Ireland, means a district council;

"minor", in relation to Scotland, includes pupil;

"modifying agreement" has the meaning given by section 82(2);

"mortgage", in relation to Scotland, includes any heritable security;

"multiple agreement" has the meaning given by section 18(1);

"negotiator" has the meaning given by section 56(1);

"non-commercial agreement" means a consumer credit agreement or a consumer hire agreement not made by the creditor or owner in the course of a business carried on by him;

"notice" means notice in writing;

"notice of cancellation" has the meaning given by section 69(1);

"OFT" means the Office of Fair Trading;

"owner" means a person who bails or (in Scotland) hires out goods under a consumer hire agreement or the person to whom his rights and duties under the agreement have passed by assignment or operation of law, and in relation to a prospective consumer hire agreement, includes the prospective bailor or person from whom the goods are to be hired;

"pawn" means any article subject to a pledge;

"pawn-receipt" has the meaning given by section 114;

"pawnee" and "pawnor" include any person to whom the rights and duties of the original pawnee or the original pawnor, as the case may be, have passed by assignment or operation of law;

"payment" includes tender;

"personal credit agreement" has the meaning given by section 8(1);

"pledge" means the pawnee's rights over an article taken in pawn;

"prescribed" means prescribed by regulations made by the Secretary of State;

"pre-existing arrangements" shall be construed in accordance with section 187;

"principal agreement" has the meaning given by section 19(1);

"protected goods" has the meaning given by section 90(7);

"quotation" has the meaning given by section 52(1)(*a*);

"redemption period" has the meaning given by section 116(3);

"register" means the register kept by the Director under section 35;

"regulated agreement" means a consumer credit agreement, or consumer hire agreement, other than an exempt agreement, and "regulated" and "unregulated" shall be construed accordingly;

"regulations" means regulations made by the Secretary of State;

"relative", except in section 484, means a person who is an associate by virtue of section 184(1);

"representation" includes any condition or warranty, and any other statement or undertaking, whether oral or in writing;

"restricted-use credit agreement" and "restricted-use credit" have the meanings given by section 11(1);

"rules of court" in relation to Northern Ireland means, in relation to the High Court, rules made under section 7 of the Northern Ireland Act 1962, and, in relation to any other court, rules made by the authority having for the time being power to make rules regulating the practice and procedure in that court;

"running-account credit" shall be construed in accordance with section 10;

"security", in relation to an actual or prospective consumer credit agreement or consumer hire agreement, or any linked transaction, means a mortgage, charge, pledge, bond, debenture, indemnity, guarantee, bill, note, or other right provided by the debtor or hirer, or at his request (express or implied), to secure the carrying out of the obligations of the debtor or hirer under the agreement;

"security instrument" has the meaning given by section 105(2);

"serve on" means deliver or send by an appropriate method to;

"signed" shall be construed in accordance with subsection (3);

"small agreement" has the meaning given by section 17(1), and "small" in relation to an agreement within any category shall be construed accordingly;

"specified fee" shall be construed in accordance with section 2(4); and (5);

"standard licence" has the meaning given by section 22(1)(*a*);

"supplier" has the meaning given by section 11(1)(*b*) or 12(*c*) or 13(*c*) or, in relation to an agreement falling within section 11(1)(*a*), means the creditor, and includes a person to whom the rights and duties of a supplier (as so defined) have passed by assignment or operation of law, or (in relation to a prospective agreement) the prospective supplier;

"surety" means the person by whom any security is provided, or the person to whom his rights and duties in relation to the security have passed by assignment or operation of law;

"technical grounds" shall be construed in accordance with subsection (5);

"time order" has the meaning given by section 129(1);

"total charge for credit" means a sum calculated in accordance with regulations under section 20(1);

"total price" means the total sum payable by the debtor under a hire-purchase agreement or a conditional sale agreement, including any sum payable on the exercise of an option to purchase, but excluding any sum payable as a penalty or as compensation or damages for a breach of the agreement;

"unexecuted agreement" means a document embodying the terms of a prospective regulated agreement, or such of them as it is intended to reduce to writing;

"unlicensed" means without a licence, but applies only in relation to acts for which a licence is required;

"unrestricted-use credit assignment" and

"unrestricted-use credit" have the meanings given by section 11(2);

"working day" means any day other than—

 (a) Saturday or Sunday,
 (b) Christmas Day or Good Friday,
 (c) a bank holiday within the meaning given by section 1 of the Banking and Financial Dealings Act 1971.

(2) A person is not to be treated as carrying on a particular type of business merely because occasionally he enters into transactions belonging to a business of that type.

(3) Any provision of this Act requiring a document to be signed is complied with by a body corporate if the document is sealed by that body.
This subsection does not apply to Scotland.

(4) A document embodies a provision if the provision is set out either in the document itself or in another document referred to in it.

(5) An application dismissed by the court or the OFT shall, if the court or the OFT (as the case may be) so certifies, be taken to be dismissed on technical grounds only.

(6) Except in so far as the context otherwise requires, any reference in this Act to an enactment shall be construed as a reference to that enactment as amended by or under any other enactment, including this Act.

(7) In this Act, except where otherwise indicated—

 (a) a reference to a numbered Part, section or Schedule is a reference to the Part or section of, or the Schedule to, this Act so numbered, and
 (b) a reference in a section to a numbered subsection is a reference to the subsection of that section so numbered, and
 (c) a reference in a section, subsection or Schedule to a numbered paragraph is a reference to the paragraph of that section, subsection or Schedule so numbered.

[Consumer Credit Act 1974, s 189 as amended by the Sale of Goods Act 1979, Sch 2, the Insurance Companies Act 1982, Sch 5, the Local Government Act 1985, Sch 17, the Building Societies Act 1986, Sch 18, the Banking Act 1987, s 88, the Electricity Act 1989, Sch 16, the Charities Act 1993, Sch 6, the Friendly Societies Act 1992, Sch 22, the Local Government (Wales) Act 1994, Sch 16, SI 2001/3649, the Enterprise Act 2002, Sch 25 and SI 2004/3236.]

---

1. Includes a European deposit-taker (Banking Coordination (Second Council Directive) Regulations 1992, SI 1992/3218, Sch 10).

8–4890A 189A. meaning of "consumer credit EEA firm". In this Act "consumer credit EEA firm" means an EEA firm falling within sub-paragraph (a), (b) or (c) of paragraph 5 of Schedule 3 to the Financial Services and Markets Act 2000 carrying on, or seeking to carry on, consumer credit business, consumer hire business or ancillary credit business for which a licence would be required under this Act but for paragraph 15(3) of Schedule 3 to the Financial Services and Markets Act 2000.

[Consumer Credit Act 1974, s 189A as inserted by the Financial Services and Markets Act 2000 (Consequential Amendments and Repeals) Order 2001, SI 2001/3649.]

8–4891 192. Transitional and commencement provisions, amendments and repeals.
(1) The provisions of Schedule 3 shall have effect for the purposes of this Act.

(2) The appointment of a day for the purposes of any provision of Schedule 3 shall be effected by an order of the Secretary of State made by statutory instrument; and any such order shall include a provision amending Schedule 3 so as to insert an express reference to the day appointed.

(3) *and* (4) *Schedules 4 and 5 to be brought into force by order*[1].

[Consumer Credit Act 1974, s 192.]

---

1. For appointed days under s 192(2), see SI 1975/2123 and SI 1977/325, 802 and 2163 (noted where appropriate in Sch 3, post), SI 1980/50, SI 1983/1551, SI 1984/436 and SI 1989/1128. For the first Commencement Order for the purposes of s 192(4), see SI 1977/802; see also SI 1979/1685, SI 1980/50, SI 1981/280 and SI 1983/1551.

8–4892

Section 167

SCHEDULE 1
Prosecution and Punishment of Offences

(As amended by the Criminal Law Act 1977, s 28, the Criminal Justice Act 1982, ss 38 and 46, the Magistrates' Courts Act 1980, s 32 and the Enterprise Act 2002, Sch 25.)

1 Section	2 Offence	3 Mode of prosecution (1)	4 Imprisonment or fine
7	Knowingly or recklessly giving false information to Director*.	(a) Summarily. (b) On indictment.	the **prescribed sum** 2 years or a fine or both.
39(1)	Engaging in activities requiring a licence when not a licensee.	(a) Summarily. (b) On indictment.	the **prescribed sum** 2 years or a fine or both.
39(2)	Carrying on business under a name not specified in licence.	(a) Summarily. (b) On indictment.	the **prescribed sum** 2 years or a fine or both.
39(3)	Failure to notify changes in registered particulars.	(a) Summarily. (b) On indictment.	the **prescribed sum** 2 years or a fine or both.
45	Advertising credit where goods etc not available for cash.	(a) Summarily. (b) On indictment.	the **prescribed sum** 2 years or a fine or both.
46(1)	False or misleading advertisements.	(a) Summarily. (b) On indictment.	the **statutory maximum.** 2 years or a fine or both.
47(1)	Advertising infringements.	(a) Summarily. (b) On indictment.	the **prescribed sum** 2 years or a fine or both.
49(1)	Canvassing debtor-creditor agreements off trade premises.	(a) Summarily. (b) On indictment.	the **prescribed sum** 1 year or a fine or both.
49(2)	Soliciting debtor-creditor agreements during visits made in response to previous oral requests.	(a) Summarily. (b) On indictment.	the **prescribed sum** 1 year or a fine or both.
50(1)	Sending circulars to minors.	(a) Summarily. (b) On indictment.	the **prescribed sum** 1 year or a fine or both.
51(1)	Supplying unsolicited credit tokens.	(a) Summarily. (b) On indictment.	the **prescribed sum** 2 years or a fine or both.
77(4)	Failure of creditor under fixed-sum credit agreement to supply copies of documents etc	Summarily.	**Level 4** on the standard scale.
78(6)	Failure of creditor under running-account credit agreement to supply copies of documents etc	Summarily.	**Level 4** on the standard scale.
79(3)	Failure of owner under consumer hire agreement to supply copies of documents etc	Summarily.	**Level 4** on the standard scale.
80(2)	Failure to tell creditor or owner whereabouts of goods.	Summarily.	**Level 3** on the standard scale.
85(2)	Failure of creditor to supply copy of credit-token agreement.	Summarily.	**Level 4** on the standard scale.
97(3)	Failure to supply debtor with statement of amount required to discharge agreement.	Summarily.	**Level 3** on the standard scale.
103(5)	Failure to deliver notice relating to discharge of agreements.	Summarily.	**Level 3** on the standard scale.
107(4)	Failure of creditor to give information to surety under fixed-sum credit agreement.	Summarily.	**Level 4** on the standard scale.
108(4)	Failure of creditor to give information to surety under running-account credit agreement.	Summarily.	**Level 4** on the standard scale.
109(3)	Failure of owner to give information to surety under consumer hire agreement.	Summarily.	**Level 4** on the standard scale.
110(3)	Failure of creditor or owner to supply a copy of any security instrument to debtor or hirer.	Summarily.	**Level 4** on the standard scale.
114(2)	Taking pledges from minors.	(a) Summarily. (b) On indictment.	the **prescribed sum** 1 year or a fine or both.
115	Failure to supply copies of a pledge agreement or pawn-receipt.	Summarily.	**Level 4** on the standard scale.
119(1)	Unreasonable refusal to allow pawn to be redeemed.	Summarily.	**Level 4** on the standard scale.
154	Canvassing ancillary credit services off trade premises.	(a) Summarily. (b) On indictment.	the **prescribed sum** 1 year or a fine or both.
157(3)	Refusal to give name etc of credit reference agency.	Summarily.	**Level 4** on the standard scale.
158(4)	Failure of credit reference agency to disclose filed information.	Summarily.	**Level 4** on the standard scale.
159(6)	Failure of credit reference agency to correct information.	Summarily.	**Level 4** on the standard scale.
160(6)	Failure of credit reference agency to comply with section 160(3) or (4).	Summarily.	**Level 4** on the standard scale.

1 *Section*	2 *Offence*	3 *Mode of prosecution* (1)	4 *Imprisonment or fine*
162(6)	Impersonation of enforcement authority officers.	(*a*)Summarily. (*b*) On indictment.	**the prescribed sum** 2 years or a fine or both.
165(1)	Obstruction of enforcement authority officers.	Summarily.	**Level 4** on the standard scale.
165(2)	Giving false information to enforcement authority officers.	(*a*) Summarily. (*b*) On indictment.	**the prescribed sum** 2 years or a fine or both.
167(2)	Contravention of regulations under section 44, 52, 53, 54 or 112.	(*a*) Summarily. (*b*) On indictment.	**the prescribed sum** 2 years or a fine or both.
174(5)	Wrongful disclosure of information.	(*a*) Summarily. (*b*) On indictment.	**the prescribed sum** 2 years or a fine or both.

1. For procedure in respect of an offence triable either way, see the Magistrates' Courts Act 1980, ss 17A–21 in PART I: MAGISTRATES' COURTS, PROCEDURE, ante.

8–4893

Section 193(1)   SCHEDULE 3
TRANSITIONAL AND COMMENCEMENT PROVISIONS

Note. Except as otherwise mentioned in this Schedule, the provisions of this Act come into operation on its passing, that is on 31st July 1974.

PART II OF ACT
CREDIT AGREEMENTS, HIRE AGREEMENTS AND LINKED TRANSACTIONS

Regulated agreements

1. (1) An agreement made before 1st April 1977[1] is not a regulated agreement within the meaning of this Act.
(2) In this Act "prospective regulated agreement" does not include a prospective agreement which, if made as expected, would be made before 1st April 1977[1].

Linked transactions

2. A transaction may be a linked transaction in relation to a regulated agreement or prospective regulated agreement even though the transaction was entered into before the day appointed for the purposes of paragraph 1.
3. Section 19(3) applies only to transactions entered into on or after 19th May 1985[2].

Total charge for credit

4. Section 20 applies to consumer credit agreements whenever made.

PART III OF ACT
LICENSING OF CREDIT AND HIRE BUSINESSES

Businesses needing a licence

5. (1) Section 21 does not apply to the carrying on of any description of consumer credit business or consumer hire business—

(*a*) before 31st July 1989 in the case of a consumer credit business, which is carried on by an individual and in the course of which only the following regulated consumer credit agreements (excluding agreements made before that date) are made, namely—

   (i) agreements for fixed-sum credit not exceeding £30, and
   (ii) agreements for running-account credit where the credit limit does not exceed that amount;

(*b*) before 1st October 1977 in the case of any other description of consumer credit business; and
(*c*) before 1st October 1977 in the case of any consumer hire business.

(2) Where the person carrying on a consumer credit business or consumer hire business applies for a licence—

(*a*) before 31st July 1989 in the case of a consumer credit business to which subparagraph (1)(*a*) above applies, or
(*b*) before 1st October 1977 in the case of any other description of consumer credit business or in the case of any consumer hire business.

he shall be deemed to have been granted on 31st July 1989 or 1st October 1977, as the case may be, a licence covering that business and continuing in force until the licence applied for is granted or, if the application is refused, until the end of the appeal period.

The register

6. Sections 35 and 36 come into operation on 2nd February 1976[3].

Enforcement of agreements made by unlicensed trader

7. Section 40 does not apply to a regulated agreement made in the course of any business before the day specified or referred to in paragraph 5(1) in relation to the description of business in question[1].

PART IV OF ACT
SEEKING BUSINESS

Advertisements

8. Part IV does not apply to any advertisement published 6th October 1980[4].

Canvassing

9. Section 49 comes into operation on 1st October 1977[5].

Circulars to minors

10. Section 50 comes into operation on 1st July 1977[6].

Unsolicited credit-tokens

11. (1) Section 51(1) does not apply to the giving of a credit-token before 1st July 1977[6].
(2) In section 51(3), "agreement" means an agreement whenever made.

PART V OF ACT
ENTRY INTO CREDIT OR HIRE AGREEMENTS

Antecedent negotiations

12. (1) Section 56 applies to negotiations in relation to an actual or prospective regulated agreement where the negotiations begin after 16th May 1977[7].
(2) In section 56(3), "agreement", where it first occurs, means an agreement whenever made.

General

13. Sections 57 to 59, 61 to 65 and 67 to 73 come into operation on 19th May 1985[8].
14. Section 66 comes into operation on 19th May 1985[8].

PART VI OF ACT
MATTERS ARISING DURING CURRENCY OF CREDIT OR HIRE AGREEMENTS

15 and 16. *Relate to ss 75 and 76 which are not quoted in this work.*

Duty to give information

17. (1) Sections 77 to 80 come into operation on 19th May 1985[8].
(2) Sections 77 to 79 apply to an agreement made before 19th May 1985[8] where the agreement would have been a regulated agreement if made on that day.
18. *Relates to s 81; not quoted in this work.*

Variation of agreements

19. Section 82 comes into operation on 1st April 1977[9].
20. *Relates to ss 83 and 84; not quoted in this work.*

Duty on issue of new credit-tokens

21. (1) Section 85 comes into operation on 19th May 1985[8].
(2) Section 85 applies to an agreement made before 19th May 1985[8] where the agreement would have been a regulated agreement if made on that day.
22. *Relates to s 86; not quoted in this work.*

PART VII OF ACT
DEFAULT AND TERMINATION

23 to 26. *Relates to ss 89 to 91 and 93; not quoted in this work.*

Early payment by debtor

27. Sections 94 to 97 come into operation on 19th May 1985[8].

Termination of agreements

28 to 32 and 34. *Relate to ss 98 to 102 and 104; not quoted in this work.*
33. Section 103 comes into operation on 19th May 1985[8].

Old agreements

35. Part VII (except sections 90, 91, 93 and 99 to 102 and 104) applies to an agreement made before 19th May 1985[8] where the agreement would have been a regulated agreement if made on that day.

PART VIII OF ACT
SECURITY

General

36. Section 105 comes into operation on 19th May 1985[8].

37. (1) Sections 107 to 110 come into operation on 19th May 1985[10].

(2) Sections 107 to 110 apply to an agreement made before 19th May 1985[10] where the agreement would have been a regulated agreement if made on that day.

38. (1) Section 111 comes into operation on 19th May 1985[10].

(2) Section 111 applies to an agreement made before 19th May 1985[10] where the agreement would have been a regulated agreement if made on that day.

Pledges

39. Sections 114 to 122 come into operation on 19th May 1985 but only in respect of articles taken in pawn under a regulated consumer credit agreement[10].

40 and 41. *Relate to ss 123 to 126; not quoted in this work.*

PART IX OF ACT

42 and 43. *Relate to provisions in Part IX which are not quoted in this work.*

PART X OF ACT
ANCILLARY CREDIT BUSINESS

Licensing

44. (1) Section 21(1) does not apply (by virtue of section 147(1)) to the carrying on of any ancillary credit business before 3rd August 1976 in the case of any business so far as it comprises or relates to—

(a) debt-adjusting,
(b) debt-counselling,
(c) debt-collecting, or
(d) the operation of a credit reference agency.

(1A) Section 21(1) does not apply (by virtue of section 147(1)) to the carrying on of any ancillary credit business before 1st July 1978 so far as it comprises or relates to credit brokerage, not being a business which is carried on by an individual and in the course of which introductions are effected only of individuals desiring to obtain credit—

(a) under debtor-creditor-supplier agreements which fall within section 12(a) and where, in the case of any such agreement—

(i) the person carrying on the business would be willing to sell the goods which are the subject of the agreement to the debtor under a transaction not financed by credit, and
(ii) the amount of credit does not exceed £30; and

(b) under debtor-creditor-supplier agreements which fall within section 12(b) or (c) and where, in the case of any such agreement—

(i) the person carrying on the business is the supplier,
(ii) the creditor is a person referred to in section 145(2)(a)(i), and
(iii) the amount of credit or, in the case of an agreement for running-account credit, the credit limit does not exceed £30.

(1B) Section 21(1) does not apply (by virtue of section 147(1)) to the carrying on of any ancillary credit business before the day appointed for the purposes of this paragraph in the case of any description of ancillary credit business in relation to which no day is appointed under the foregoing provisions of this paragraph.

(2) Where the person carrying on an ancillary credit business applies for a licence before—

(a) 3rd August 1976 in the case of an ancillary credit business of a description to which subparagraph (1) above applies;
(b) 1st July 1978 in the case of an ancillary credit business of a description to which subparagraph (1A) above applies; or
(c) the day appointed for the purposes of this paragraph in the case of an ancillary credit business to which subparagraph (1B) above applies,

he shall be deemed to have been granted on 3rd August 1976, 1st July 1978 or the day so appointed, as the case may be, a licence covering the description of ancillary credit business in question and continuing in force until the licence applied for is granted or, if the application is refused, until the end of the appeal period[11].

45 and 46. *Relate to ss 148(1) and 149; not quoted in this work.*

Advertisements

47. Subsections (1) and (2) of section 151 do not apply to any advertisement published before 6th October 1980[12].

Credit reference agencies

48. Sections 157 and 158 do not apply to a request received before 16th May 1977[13].

PART XII

SUPPLEMENTAL

Interpretation

49. (1) In the case of an agreement—

(*a*) which was made before 19th May 1985[10] and

(*b*) to which (by virtue of paragraph 17(2)) section 78(4) applies,

section 185(2) shall have effect as respects a notice given before that day in relation to the agreement (whether given before or after the passing of this Act) as it would have effect if section 78(4) had been in operation when the notice was given.

(2) Paragraph (1) applies to an agreement made on or after 19th May 1985[10] to provide credit on a current account opened before that day as it applies to an agreement made before that day.

50. In section 189, the definition of "local authority" shall have effect in relation to matters arising before 16th May 1975 as if for the words "regional, island or district council" there were substituted "a county council or town council".

---

1. Amended by SI 1977/325, and as substituted by SI 1989/1128.
2. Amended by SI 1983/1551.
3. Amended by SI 1975/2123.
4. Amended by SI 1980/50.
5. Amended by SI 1977/802.
6. Amended by SI 1977/802.
7. Amended by SI 1977/325.
8. Amended by SI 1983/1551.
9. Amended by SI 1977/325.
10. Amended by SI 1977/1551.
11. Amended by SI 1977/325 and SI 1977/2163.
12. 6 October 1980.
13. Amended by SI 1977/325.

Consumer Protection Act 1987[1]

(1987 c 43)

8–5000

PART I[2]

PRODUCT LIABILITY

---

1. This Act consolidates with amendments the Consumer Safety Act 1978 and the Consumer Safety (Amendment) Act 1986; makes provision with respect to the giving of price indications, and amends or repeals other enactments.
2. Part I which is not printed in this work contains ss 1–9.

PART II[1]

CONSUMER SAFETY

8–5001 10. The general safety requirement. *Repealed.*

---

1. Part II contains ss 10–19.
2. For "safe" see s 19, post. In determining whether goods are reasonably safe the court is not applying an absolute standard of safety but must look at all the circumstances to decide what is safe and may receive specialist or trade evidence as to the risks involved (*P & M Supplies (Essex) Ltd v Walsall Metropolitan Borough Council* [1994] Crim LR 580).

8–5002 11. Safety regulations. (1) The Secretary of State may by regulations[1] under this section ("safety regulations") make such provision as he considers appropriate for the purpose of securing—

(*a*) that goods to which this section applies are safe;

(*b*) that goods to which this section applies which are unsafe, or would be unsafe in the hands of persons of a particular description, are not made available to persons generally or, as the case may be, to persons of that description; and

(*c*) that appropriate information is, and inappropriate information is not, provided in relation to goods to which this section applies.

(2) Without prejudice to the generality of subsection (1) above, safety regulations may contain provision—

(*a*) with respect to the composition or contents, design, construction, finish or packing of goods to which this section applies, with respect to standards for such goods and with respect to other matters relating to such goods;

(*b*) with respect to the giving, refusal, alteration or cancellation of approvals of such goods, of descriptions of such goods or of standards for such goods;

(*c*) with respect to the conditions that may be attached to any approval given under the regulations;

(d) for requiring such fees as may be determined by or under the regulations to be paid on the giving or alteration of any approval under the regulations and on the making of an application for such an approval or alteration;

(e) with respect to appeals against refusals, alterations and cancellations of approvals given under the regulations and against the conditions contained in such approvals;

(f) for requiring goods to which this section applies to be approved under the regulations or to conform to the requirements of the regulations or to descriptions or standards specified in or approved by or under the regulations;

(g) with respect to the testing or inspection of goods to which this section applies (including provision for determining the standards to be applied in carrying out any test or inspection);

(h) with respect to the ways of dealing with goods of which some or all do not satisfy a test required by or under the regulations or a standard connected with a procedure so required;

(i) for requiring a mark, warning or instruction or any other information relating to goods to be put on or to accompany the goods or to be used or provided in some other manner in relation to the goods, and for securing that inappropriate information is not given in relation to goods either by means of misleading marks or otherwise;

(j) for prohibiting persons from supplying, or from offering to supply, agreeing to supply, exposing for supply or possessing for supply, goods to which this section applies and component parts and raw materials for such goods;

(k) for requiring information to be given to any such person as may be determined by or under the regulations for the purpose of enabling that person to exercise any function conferred on him by the regulations.

(3) Without prejudice as aforesaid, safety regulations may contain provision—

(a) for requiring persons on whom functions are conferred by or under section 27 below to have regard, in exercising their functions so far as relating to any provision of safety regulations, to matters specified in a direction issued by the Secretary of State with respect to that provision;

(b) for securing that a person shall not be guilty of an offence under section 12 below unless it is shown that the goods in question do not conform to a particular standard;

(c) for securing that proceedings for such an offence are not brought in England and Wales except by or with the consent of the Secretary of State or the Director of Public Prosecutions;

(d) for securing that proceedings for such an offence are not brought in Northern Ireland except by or with the consent of the Secretary of State or the Director of Public Prosecutions for Northern Ireland;

(e) for enabling a magistrates' court in England and Wales or Northern Ireland to try an information or, in Northern Ireland, a complaint in respect of such an offence if the information was laid or the complaint made within twelve months from the time when the offence was committed;

(f) for enabling summary proceedings for such an offence to be brought in Scotland at any time within twelve months from the time when the offence was committed; and

(g) for determining the persons by whom, and the manner in which, anything required to be done by or under the regulations is to be done.

(4) Safety regulations shall not provide for any contravention of the regulations to be an offence.

(5) Where the Secretary of State proposes to make safety regulations it shall be his duty before he makes them—

(a) to consult such organisations as appear to him to be representative of interests substantially affected by the proposal;

(b) to consult such other persons as he considers appropriate; and

(c) in the case of proposed regulations relating to goods suitable for use at work, to consult the Health and Safety Commission in relation to the application of the proposed regulations to Great Britain;

but the preceding provisions of this subsection shall not apply in the case of regulations which provide for the regulations to cease to have effect at the end of a period of not more than twelve months beginning with the day on which they come into force and which contain a statement that it appears to the Secretary of State that the need to protect the public requires that the regulations should be made without delay.

(6) The power to make safety regulations shall be exercisable by statutory instrument subject to annulment in pursuance of a resolution of either House of Parliament and shall include power—

(a) to make different provision for different cases; and

(b) to make such supplemental, consequential and transitional provision as the Secretary of State considers appropriate.

(7) This section applies to any goods other than—

(a) growing crops and things comprised in land by virtue of being attached to it;

(b) water, food, feeding stuff and fertiliser;

(c) gas which is, is to be or has been supplied by a person authorised to supply it by or under section 7A of the Gas Act 1986 (licensing of gas suppliers and gas shippers) or paragraph 5 of Schedule 2A to that Act (supply to very large customers an exception to prohibition on unlicensed activities)* or under Article 8(1)(c) of the Gas (Northern Ireland) Order 1996;

(d) controlled drugs and licensed medicinal products.

[Consumer Protection Act 1987, s 11 as amended by the Gas Act 1995, Sch 4 and SI 1996/275 and SI 2005/1803.]

---

*Repealed by the Utilities Act 2000, Sch 8, when in force.

1. Regulations made under the Consumer Protection Act 1961 which were in force on 1 October 1987 shall by virtue of, and subject to modification by, the Consumer Protection Act 1987 (Commencement No 1) Order 1987, SI 1987/1680, have effect as if made under this section. Such Regulations include the following:

Cooking Utensils (Safety), SI 1972/1957 amended by SI 1987/1680;
Children's Clothing (Hood Cords), SI 1976/2 amended by SI 1987/1680;
Oil Heaters (Safety), SI 1977/167 amended by SI 1987/1680.

Regulations made under s 1 of the repealed Consumer Safety Act 1978 remain in force by virtue of the general saving provided in s 17(2)(b) of the Interpretation Act 1978. Other regulations made under the 1978 Act and now having effect under s 11 are:

Filament Lamps for Vehicles (Safety), SI 1982/444;
Motor Vehicle Tyres (Safety), SI 1984/1233 amended by SI 1992/3087 and SI 1993/2877;
Gas Catalytic Heater (Safety), SI 1984/1802 amended by SI 1987/1979;
Asbestos Products (Safety), SI 1985/2042 amended by SI 1987/1979;
Nightwear (Safety), SI 1985/2043 amended by SI 1987/286;
Pushchairs (Safety), SI 1985/2047;
Child Resistant Packaging (Safety), SI 1986/758 amended by SI 1990/1736, and SI 1993/1546;
Bunk Beds (Entrapment Hazards) (Safety), SI 1987/1337.

The Approval of Safety Standards Regulations 1987, SI 1987/1911 made under s 11 creates certain presumptions of compliance with the general safety requirements of s 10 of the Act. The Furniture and Furnishings (Fire) (Safety) Regulations 1988 are contained in this PART, post; other regulations made directly under s 11 are:

Ceramic Ware (Safety), SI 1988/1324;
Gas Cooking Appliances (Safety), SI 1989/149 (disapplied with respect to certain appliances by SI 1995/1629);
Low Voltage Electrical Equipment (Safety), SI 1989/728;
Food Imitations (Safety) Regulations 1989, SI 1989/1291, this PART, post;
All-Terrain Motor Vehicles (Safety) Regulations 1989, SI 1989/2288;
Heating Appliances (Fireguards) (Safety) Regulation 1991, SI 1991/2693 (disapplied with respect to certain appliances by SI 1995/1629);
Gas Appliances (Safety) Regulations 1992, SI 1992/711 (revoked by SI 1995/1629 save that regulations continue to apply to certain appliances);
Tobacco For Oral Use (Safety) Regulations 1992, SI 1992/3134;
Imitation Dummies (Safety) Regulations 1993, SI 1993/2923;
Plugs and Sockets etc (Safety) Regulations 1994, SI 1994/1768;
Dangerous Substances and Preparations (Safety) (Consolidation) Regulations 1994, SI 1994/2844 amended by SI 1994/3247, SI 1996/2635, SI 1999/2084, SI 2000/2897, SI 2002/3010, SI 2004/1031 and 1417 and SI 2005/2750;
Motor Vehicle Tyres (Safety) Regulations 1994, in this title post;
Electrical Equipment (Safety) Regulations 1994, SI 1994/3260;
Toys (Safety) Regulations 1995[2], SI 1995/204 amended by SI 2004/1769 and SI 2005/1082;
Gas Appliances (Safety) Regulations 1995, SI 1995/1629;
N-nitrosamines and N-nitrosatable Substances in Elastomer or Rubber Teats and Dummies Regulations 1995, SI 1995/1012;
Fireworks (Safety) Regulations 1997, SI 1997/2294 amended by SI 2004/1372;
Wheeled Child Conveyances (Safety) Regulations 1997, SI 1997/2866.
Pencils and Graphic Instruments (Safety) Regulations 1998, SI 1998/2406;
Cigarette Lighter Refill (Safety) Regulations 1999, SI 1999/1844;
Road Vehicles (Brake Linings Safety) Regulations 1999, SI 1999/2978 amended by SI 2003/3314;
Dangerous Substances and Preparations (Nickel) (Safety) Regulations 2000, SI 2000/1668;
Medical Devices Regulations 2002, SI 2002/618 amended by SI 2003/1400 and 1697 and SI 2005/2759 and 2909;
Tobacco Products (Manufacture, Presentation and Sale) (Safety) Regulations 2002, SI 2002/3041;
Pedal Bicycle (Safety) Regulations 2003, SI 2003/1101;
Unlicensed Medicinal Products for Human Use (Transmissable Spongiform Encephalopathies) (Safety) Regulations 2003, SI 2003/1680 amended by SI 2005/2750;
Creosote (Prohibition on Use and Marketing) (No 2) Regulations 2003, SI 2003/1511 amended by SI 2003/2650;
Controls on Certain Azo Dyes and "Blue Colourant" Regulations 2003, SI 2003/3310 amended by SI 2004/2913;
Cosmetic Products (Safety) Regulations 2004, SI 2004/2152 amended by SI 2004/2361 and 2988 and SI 2005/1815 and 3346;
Dangerous Substances and Preparations (Nickel) (Safety) Regulations 2005, SI 2005/2001.

2. For an example of factors to be considered when determining whether an article is a "toy" within the regulations, see *In the Pink Ltd v North East Lincolnshire Council* [2005] EWHC 1111 (Admin), 169 JP 385.

8–5003 12. Offences against the safety regulations. (1) Where safety regulations prohibit a person from supplying or offering or agreeing to supply any goods or from exposing or possessing any goods for supply, that person shall be guilty of an offence[1] if he contravenes the prohibition[2].

(2) Where safety regulations require a person who makes or processes any goods in the course of carrying on a business—

(a) to carry out a particular test or use a particular procedure in connection with the making or processing of the goods with a view to ascertaining whether the goods satisfy any requirements of such regulations; or

(b) to deal or not to deal in a particular way with a quantity of the goods of which the whole or part does not satisfy such a test or does not satisfy standards connected with such a procedure, that person shall be guilty of an offence if he does not comply with the requirement.

(3) If a person contravenes a provision of safety regulations which prohibits or requires the provision, by means of a mark or otherwise, of information of a particular kind in relation to goods, he shall be guilty of an offence.

(4) Where safety regulations require any person to give information to another for the purpose of enabling that other to exercise any function, that person shall be guilty of an offence if—

(a) he fails without reasonable cause to comply with the requirement; or

(b) in giving the information which is required of him—

    (i) he makes any statement which he knows is false in a material particular; or

    (ii) he recklessly makes any statement which is false in a material particular.

(5) A person guilty of an offence under this section shall be liable on summary conviction to imprisonment for a term not exceeding **six months** or to a fine not exceeding **level 5** on the standard scale or to both.

[Consumer Protection Act 1987, s 12.]

---

1. If a landlord at a start of a tenancy provides equipment which is defective under the safety regulations, the offence under s 12(1) is committed (*Drummond-Rees v Dorset County Council* (1996) 162 JP 651).

2. Where the justices are satisfied that the prosecution has satisfied the ignitability test in the Furniture and Furnishings (Fire) (Safety) Regulations 1988, SI 1988/1324 and that there was no procedural error, they were not entitled to dismiss an information on the basis of a test conducted using different methodology by the defence (*Northumberland County Council v PR Manufacturing Ltd* [2004] EWHC 112 (Admin), 168 JP 209).

8–5004   13. Prohibition notices and notices to warn.   (1) The Secretary of State may—

(a) serve on any person a notice ("a prohibition notice") prohibiting that person, except with the consent of the Secretary of State, from supplying, or from offering to supply, agreeing to supply, exposing for supply or possessing for supply, any relevant goods which the Secretary of State considers are unsafe and which are described in the notice;

(b) serve on any person a notice ("a notice to warn") requiring that person at his own expense to publish, in a form and manner and on occasions specified in the notice, a warning about any relevant goods which the Secretary of State considers are unsafe, which that person supplies or has supplied and which are described in the notice.

(2) Schedule 2 to this Act shall have effect with respect to prohibition notices and notices to warn; and the Secretary of State may by regulations make provision specifying the manner in which information is to be given to any person under that Schedule.

(3) A consent given by the Secretary of State for the purposes of a prohibition notice may impose such conditions on the doing of anything for which the consent is required as the Secretary of State considers appropriate.

(4) A person who contravenes a prohibition notice or a notice to warn shall be guilty of an offence and liable on summary conviction to imprisonment for a term not exceeding **six months** or to a fine not exceeding **level 5** on the standard scale or to both.

(5) The power to make regulations under subsection (2) above shall be exercisable by statutory instrument subject to annulment in pursuance of a resolution of either House of Parliament and shall include power—

(a) to make different provision for different cases; and

(b) to make such supplemental, consequential and transitional provision as the Secretary of State considers appropriate.

(6) In this section "relevant goods" means—

(a) in relation to a prohibition notice, any goods to which section 11 above applies; and

(b) in relation to a notice to warn, any goods to which that section applies or any growing crops or things comprised in land by virtue of being attached to it.

(7) A notice may not be given under this section in respect of the safety of goods, or any risk or category of risk associated with goods, concerning which provision is contained in the General Product Safety Regulations 2005.

[Consumer Protection Act 1987, s 13 as amended SI 2005/1803.]

8–5005   14. Suspension notices.   (1) Where an enforcement authority[1] has reasonable grounds for suspecting that any safety provision has been contravened in relation to any goods, the authority may serve a notice ("a suspension notice") prohibiting the person on whom it is served, for such period ending not more than six months after the date of the notice as is specified therein, from doing any of the following things without the consent of the authority, that is to say, supplying the goods, offering to supply them, agreeing to supply them or exposing them for supply.

(2) A suspension notice served by an enforcement authority in respect of any goods shall—

(a) describe the goods in a manner sufficient to identify them;

(b) set out the grounds on which the authority suspects that a safety provision has been contravened in relation to the goods; and (*c*) state that, and the manner in which, the person on whom the notice is served may appeal against the notice under section 15 below.

(3) A suspension notice served by an enforcement authority for the purpose of prohibiting a person for any period from doing the things mentioned in subsection (1) above in relation to any goods may also require that person to keep the authority informed of the whereabouts throughout that period of any of those goods in which he has an interest.

(4) Where a suspension notice has been served on any person in respect of any goods, no further such notice shall be served on that person in respect of the same goods unless—

(*a*) proceedings against that person for an offence in respect of a contravention in relation to the goods of a safety provision (not being an offence under this section); or

(*b*) proceedings for the forfeiture of the goods under section 16 or 17 below,

are pending at the end of the period specified in the first-mentioned notice.

(5) A consent given by an enforcement authority for the purposes of subsection (1) above may impose such conditions on the doing of anything for which the consent is required as the authority considers appropriate.

(6) Any person who contravenes a suspension notice shall be guilty of an offence and liable on summary conviction to imprisonment for a term not exceeding **six months** or to a fine not exceeding **level 5** on the standard scale or to both.

(7) Where an enforcement authority serves a suspension notice in respect of any goods, the authority shall be liable to pay compensation to any person having an interest in the goods in respect of any loss or damage caused by reason of the service of the notice if—

(*a*) there has been no contravention in relation to the goods of any safety provision; and

(*b*) the exercise of the power is not attributable to any neglect or default by that person.

(8) Any disputed question as to the right to or the amount of any compensation payable under this section shall be determined by arbitration or, in Scotland, by a single arbiter appointed, failing agreement between the parties, by the sheriff.
[Consumer Protection Act 1987, s 14.]

---

1. An authority may issue a suspension notice which is effective outside the authority's area although its power to prosecute is confined to breaches committed within its own area. Breaches elsewhere, may be prosecuted by the authority for that area (*Brighton and Hove District Council v Woolworths plc* [2002] EWHC 2565 (Admin) 167 JP 21).

8–5006   15. Appeals against suspension notices.   (1) Any person having an interest in any goods in respect of which a suspension notice is for the time being in force may apply for an order setting aside the notice.

(2) An application[1] under this section may be made—

(*a*) to any magistrates' court in which proceedings have been brought in England and Wales or Northern Ireland—

(i) for an offence in respect of a contravention in relation to the goods of any safety provision; or

(ii) for the forfeiture of the goods under section 16 below;

(*b*) where no such proceedings have been so brought, by way of complaint to a magistrates' court; or

(*c*) in Scotland, by summary application to the sheriff.

(3) On an application under this section to a magistrates' court in England and Wales or Northern Ireland the court shall make an order setting aside the suspension notice only if the court is satisfied that there has been no contravention in relation to the goods of any safety provision.

(4) On an application under this section to the sheriff he shall make an order setting aside the suspension notice only if he is satisfied that at the date of making the order—

(*a*) proceedings for an offence in respect of a contravention in relation to the goods of any safety provision; or

(*b*) proceedings for the forfeiture of the goods under section 17 below,

have not been brought or, having been brought, have been concluded.

(5) Any person aggrieved by an order made under this section by a magistrates' court in England and Wales or Northern Ireland, or by a decision of such a court not to make such an order, may appeal against that order or decision—

(*a*) in England and Wales, to the Crown Court;

(*b*) *Northern Ireland*;

and an order so made may contain such provision as appears to the court to be appropriate for delaying the coming into force of the order pending the making and determination of any appeal (including any application under section 111 of the Magistrates' Courts Act 1980 or Article 146 of the Magistrates' Courts (Northern Ireland) Order 1981 (statement of case)).
[Consumer Protection Act 1987, s 15.]

1. An application under this section will be the appropriate course to take where the real issue is whether the goods contravened a safety provision; only exceptionally will the alternative remedy of judicial review be granted; see *R v Birmingham City Council, ex p Ferrero Ltd* [1993] 1 All ER 530, 155 JP 721, CA.

8–5007   16. Forfeiture: England and Wales and Northern Ireland.   (1) An enforcement authority in England and Wales or Northern Ireland may apply under this section for an order for the forfeiture of any goods on the grounds that there has been a contravention in relation to the goods of a safety provision.

(2) An application under this section may be made—

(a) where proceedings have been brought in a magistrates' court for an offence in respect of a contravention in relation to some or all of the goods of any safety provision, to that court;

(b) where an application with respect to some or all of the goods has been made to a magistrates' court under section 15 above or section 33 below, to that court; and

(c) where no application for the forfeiture of the goods has been made under paragraph (a) or (b) above, by way of complaint to a magistrates' court.

(3) On an application under this section the court shall make an order for the forfeiture of any goods only if it is satisfied that there has been a contravention in relation to the goods of a safety provision.

(4) For the avoidance of doubt it is declared that a court may infer for the purposes of this section that there has been a contravention in relation to any goods of a safety provision if it is satisfied that any such provision has been contravened in relation to goods which are representative of those goods (whether by reason of being of the same design or part of the same consignment or batch or otherwise).

(5) Any person aggrieved by an order made under this section by a magistrates' court, or by a decision of such a court not to make such an order, may appeal against that order or decision—

(a) in England and Wales, to the Crown Court;

(b) in Northern Ireland, to the county court;

and an order so made may contain such provision as appears to the court to be appropriate for delaying the coming into force of the order pending the making and determination of any appeal (including any application under section 111 of the Magistrates' Courts Act 1980 or Article 146 of the Magistrates' Courts (Northern Ireland) Order 1981 (statement of case)).

(6) Subject to subsection (7) below, where any goods are forfeited under this section they shall be destroyed in accordance with such directions as the court may give.

(7) On making an order under this section a magistrates' court may, if it considers it appropriate to do so, direct that the goods to which the order relates shall (instead of being destroyed) be released, to such person as the court may specify, on condition that that person—

(a) does not supply those goods to any person otherwise than as mentioned in section 46(7)(a) or (b) below; and

(b) complies with any order to pay costs or expenses (including any order under section 35 below) which has been made against that person in the proceedings for the order for forfeiture.

[Consumer Protection Act 1987, s 16.]

8–5008   17. *Forfeiture: Scotland.*

8–5009   18. Power to obtain information.   (1) If the Secretary of State considers that, for the purpose of deciding whether—

(a) to make, vary or revoke any safety regulations; or

(b) to serve, vary or revoke a prohibition notice; or

(c) to serve or revoke a notice to warn,

he requires information which another person is likely to be able to furnish, the Secretary of State may serve on the other person a notice under this section.

(2) A notice served on any person under this section may require that person—

(a) to furnish to the Secretary of State, within a period specified in the notice, such information as is so specified;

(b) to produce such records as are specified in the notice at a time and place so specified and to permit a person appointed by the Secretary of State for the purpose to take copies of the records at that time and place.

(3) A person shall be guilty of an offence if he—

(a) fails, without reasonable cause, to comply with a notice served on him under this section; or

(b) in purporting to comply with a requirement which by virtue of paragraph (a) of subsection (2) above is contained in such a notice—

(i)   furnishes information which he knows is false in a material particular; or

(ii) recklessly furnishes information which is false in a material particular.

(4) A person guilty of an offence under subsection (3) above shall—

(a) in the case of an offence under paragraph (*a*) of that subsection, be liable on summary conviction to a fine not exceeding level 5 on the standard scale; and

(b) in the case of an offence under paragraph (*b*) of that subsection be liable—

    (i) on conviction on indictment, to a **fine**;

    (ii) on summary conviction, to a fine not exceeding the **statutory maximum**.

[Consumer Protection Act 1987, s 18.]

8–5010   **19. Interpretation of Part II.**   (1) In this Part—

"controlled drug" means a controlled drug within the meaning of the Misuse of Drugs Act 1971;

"feeding stuff" and "fertiliser" have the same meanings as in Part IV of the Agriculture Act 1970;

"food" does not include anything containing tobacco but, subject to that, has the same meaning as in the Food Safety Act 1990 or, in relation to Northern Ireland, the same meaning as in the Food and Drugs Act (Northern Ireland) 1958;

"licensed medicinal product" means—

(a) any medicinal product within the meaning of the Medicines Act 1968 in respect of which a product licence within the meaning of that Act is for the time being in force; or

(b) any other article or substance in respect of which any such licence is for the time being in force in pursuance of an order under section 104 or 105 of that Act (application of Act to other articles and substances);

"safe", in relation to any goods, means such that there is no risk, or no risk apart from one reduced to a minimum, that any of the following will (whether immediately or after a definite or indefinite period) cause the death of, or any personal injury to, any person whatsoever, that is to say—

(a) the goods;

(b) the keeping, use or consumption of the goods;

(c) the assembly of any of the goods which are, or are to be, supplied unassembled;

(d) any emission or leakage from the goods or, as a result of the keeping, use or consumption of the goods, from anything else; or

(e) reliance on the accuracy of any measurement, calculation or other reading made by or by means of the goods,

and "unsafe" shall be construed accordingly;

"tobacco" includes any tobacco product within the meaning of the Tobacco Products Duty Act 1979 and any article or substance containing tobacco and intended for oral or nasal use.

(2) In the definition of "safe" in subsection (1) above, references to the keeping, use or consumption of any goods are references to—

(a) the keeping, use or consumption of the goods by the persons by whom, and in all or any of the ways or circumstances in which, they might reasonably be expected to be kept, used or consumed; and

(b) the keeping, use or consumption of the goods either alone or in conjunction with other goods in conjunction with which they might reasonably be expected to be kept, used or consumed.

[Consumer Protection Act 1987, s 19 as amended by the Food Safety Act 1990, Sch 3 and SI 2005/1803.]

PART III[1]
MISLEADING PRICE INDICATIONS

8–5011   **20. Offence of giving misleading indication.**   (1) Subject to the following provisions of this Part, a person shall be guilty of an offence if, in the course of any business of his[2], he gives (by any means whatever) to any consumers an indication[3] which is misleading[4] as to the price[5] at which any goods, services, accommodation or facilities are available (whether generally or from particular persons).

(2) Subject as aforesaid, a person shall be guilty of an offence[6] if—

(a) in the course of any business of his[2], he has given an indication to any consumers which, after it was given, has become misleading as mentioned in subsection (1) above; and

(b) some or all of those consumers might reasonably be expected to rely on the indication at a time after it has become misleading; and

(c) he fails to take all such steps as are reasonable to prevent those consumers from relying on the indication.

(3) For the purposes of this section it shall be immaterial—

(a) whether the person who gives or gave the indication is or was acting on his own behalf or on behalf of another;

(b) whether or not that person is the person, or included among the persons, from whom the goods, services, accommodation or facilities are available; and

(c) whether the indication is or has become misleading in relation to all the consumers to whom it is or was given or only in relation to some of them.

(4) A person guilty of an offence under subsection (1) or (2) above shall be liable—

(a) on conviction on indictment, to a **fine**;

(b) on summary conviction, to a fine not exceeding the **statutory maximum**.

(5) No prosecution for an offence under subsection (1) or (2) above shall be brought after whichever is the earlier of the following, that is to say—

(a) the end of the period of three years beginning with the day on which the offence was committed; and

(b) the end of the period of one year beginning with the day on which the person bringing the prosecution discovered that the offence had been committed.

(6) In this Part—

"consumer"—

(a) in relation to any goods, means any person who might wish to be supplied with the goods for his own private use or consumption[7];

(b) in relation to any services or facilities, means any person who might wish to be provided with the services or facilities otherwise than for the purposes of any business of his; and

(c) in relation to any accommodation, means any person who might wish to occupy the accommodation otherwise than for the purposes of any business of his;

"price", in relation to any goods, services, accommodation or facilities, means—

(a) the aggregate of the sums required to be paid by a consumer for or otherwise in respect of the supply of the goods or the provision of the services, accommodation or facilities; or

(b) except in section 21 below, any method which will be or has been applied for the purpose of determining that aggregate.

[Consumer Protection Act 1987, s 20.]

---

1. Part III contains ss 20–26.

2. The words "in the course of any business of his" mean any business of which the defendant is either the owner or in which he has a controlling interest; accordingly, an employed branch manager who failed to comply with a price indication, so that the same was to be regarded as misleading, was held not to be guilty of an offence under s 20(1) of the Act (*Warwickshire County Council v Johnson* [1993] 1 All ER 299, HL).

3. The relevant time for this purpose is the time at which the indication as to price is given; in the case of goods on display in a supermarket this will be the time when the item was on the shelf with the price ticket attached to it (*Toys 'R' Us v Gloucestershire County Council* (1994) 158 JP 338, [1994] Crim LR 521). It is not necessary for the prosecution to prove that the misleading price indication was given to a particular consumer who might wish to be supplied with the goods for his own private use or consumption (*MFI Furniture Centre Ltd v Hibbert* (1995) 160 JP 178). Where a misleading price indication was given on suits which were offered for sale in the defendants' store by another company operating under a concession it was held that the misleading price indication was given in the course of the defendants' business as well as that of the third party who held the concession because it was a joint business venture and every indication from the customer's point of view, pointed to the defendant giving the misleading price indication (*Surrey County Council v Burton Retail Ltd* (1997) 162 JP 545).

4. A statement, which in itself is not misleading on the face of it, may be rendered misleading by virtue of the fact that, even in the absence of evidence to show a general practice or intention to dishonour the offer contained therein, on one occasion the person making the statement declined to enter into a contract within the terms of the statement (*Warwickshire County Council v Johnson* [1993] 1 All ER 299). A transaction is the evidence by which it is possible to test whether a notice is misleading but once tested, it is established that the notice was misleading from the outset and so a notice such as a general 'price match' offer may be misleading even though it does not relate to any particular goods (*DSG Retail Ltd v Oxford County Council* [2001] EWHC Admin 253, [2001] 1 WLR 1765, 165 JP 409).

5. See sub-s (6). An indication as to 'price' includes an indication as to the Annual Percentage Rate of interest (APR) as the total amount payable under the contract is arrived at by reference to the APR (*R v Kettering Magistrates' Court, ex p MRB Insurance Brokers Ltd* [2001] 1 WLR 1479, 164 JP 585, DC).

6. The ingredients of this offence are cumulative, and so the statement must at one time not have been misleading; must then have become misleading before the consumer relies on it and enters into the contract; and between the time of its becoming misleading and it being relied on there must have been a failure to take reasonable steps to prevent reliance. It is inapt to cover the situation where a 'price match' notice is alleged to have become misleading only at the stage where a refund was sought but refused since no reliance was placed on the notice after the refund was refused. If the price match notice was misleading at the outset, proceedings should be brought under a different provision (*Link Stores v London Borough of Harrow* (2000) 165 JP 575, DC) (See for a successful prosecution under s20(1) *DSG Retail Ltd v Oxford* [2001] EWHC Admin 253, [2001] 1 WLR 1765, 165 JP 409).

7. The word "might" is significant, and there is nothing in s 20(6)(a) to preclude a trading standards officer from being a consumer (*Toys 'R' Us v Gloucestershire County Council* (1994) 158 JP 338, [1994] Crim LR 521).

8–5012   21. Meaning of "misleading".   (1) For the purposes of section 20 above an indication given to any consumers is misleading as to a price if what is conveyed by the indication, or what those consumers might reasonably be expected to infer from the indication or any omission from it, includes any of the following, that is to say—

(a) that the price is less than in fact it is;

(b) that the applicability of the price does not depend on facts or circumstances on which its applicability does in fact depend;

(c) that the price covers matters in respect of which an additional[1] charge is in fact made;

(*d*)   that a person who in fact has no such expectation—

     (i)   expects[2] the price to be increased or reduced (whether or not at a particular time or by a particular amount); or

     (ii)   expects the price, or the price as increased or reduced, to be maintained (whether or not for a particular period); or

(*e*)   that the facts or circumstances by reference to which the consumers might reasonably be expected to judge the validity of any relevant comparison made or implied by the indication are not what in fact they are[3].

(2)   For the purposes of section 20 above, an indication given to any consumers is misleading as to a method of determining a price if what is conveyed by the indication, or what those consumers might reasonably be expected to infer from the indication or any omission from it, includes any of the following, that is to say—

(*a*)   that the method is not what in fact it is;

(*b*)   that the applicability of the method does not depend on facts or circumstances on which its applicability does in fact depend;

(*c*)   that the method takes into account matters in respect of which an additional charge will in fact be made;

(*d*)   that a person who in fact has no such expectation—

     (i)   expects the method to be altered (whether or not at a particular time or in a particular respect); or

     (ii)   expects the method, or that method as altered, to remain unaltered (whether or not for a particular period); or

(*e*)   that the facts or circumstances by reference to which the consumers might reasonably be expected to judge the validity of any relevant comparison made or implied by the indication are not what in fact they are[4].

(3)   For the purposes of subsections (1)(*e*) and (2)(*e*) above a comparison is a relevant comparison in relation to a price or method of determining a price if it is made between that price or that method, or any price which has been or may be determined by that method, and—

(*a*)   any price or value which is stated or implied to be, to have been or to be likely to be attributed or attributable to the goods, services, accommodation or facilities in question or to any other goods, services, accommodation or facilities; or

(*b*)   any method, or other method, which is stated or implied to be, to have been or to be likely to be applied or applicable for the determination of the price or value of the goods, services, accommodation or facilities in question or of the price or value of any other goods, services, accommodation or facilities.

[Consumer Protection Act 1987, s 21.]

---

1.   A compulsory delivery charge is a charge for goods and is an integral part of the purchase price of a car and therefore should be included in the advertised price or made sufficiently conspicuous in relation to the price at which the car is offered (*Toyota (GB) Ltd v North Yorkshire County Council* (1998) 162 JP 794).

2.   Where a Fair Trading Charter in a holiday brochure stated that if the total price of a holiday was reduced after booking, the consumer would only be charged the reduced price, it was held that the statement in the Charter went no further than to indicate a policy which would be applied by the tour operator to the price of a holiday after the booking had been made and that it could not be interpreted as an "expectation" that there would be a reduction within the meaning of s 21(1(*d*)(i) of the Act of the Act (*Thomson Tour Operations Ltd v Birch* (1999) 163 JP 465).

3.   Subparagraph (*e*) plainly requires that it must at least be implicit that there is a comparison that can be made between the price paid for an item and what might otherwise have to be paid for the same item in different circumstances; the justices are in the best position to form a view as to what ordinary members of the public should feel, and the High Court will not interfere unless the justices reached a conclusion that was not open to them in the particular circumstances of the case (*Suffolk County Council v Hillary's Blinds Ltd* [2002] EWHC 87 (Admin), (2002) 166 JP 380.

4.   Where a watch was advertised as 'a £50 watch for £4.99' it was reasonable to interpret the advertisement as an indication that the watches were being sold elsewhere at a price approximating to their stated value, or at least that they were shortly to be on the market at that price (*MGN Ltd v Northamptonshire County Council* (1997) 161 JP 735, [1997] Crim LR 882, DC).

8–5013   **22. Application to provision of services and facilities.**   (1) Subject to the following provisions of this section, references in this Part to services or facilities are references to any services or facilities whatever including, in particular—

(*a*)   the provision of credit or of banking or insurance services and the provision of facilities incidental to the provision of such services;

(*b*)   the purchase or sale of foreign currency;

(*c*)   the supply of electricity;[1]

(*d*)   the provision of a place, other than on a highway, for the parking of a motor vehicle;

(*e*)   the making of arrangements for a person to put or keep a caravan on any land other than arrangements by virtue of which that person may occupy the caravan as his only or main residence.

(2) References in this Part to services shall not include references to services provided to an employer under a contract of employment.

(3) *Repealed.*

(4) In relation to a service consisting in the purchase or sale of foreign currency, references in this Part to the method by which the price of the service is determined shall include references to the rate of exchange.

(5) In this section—

"caravan" has the same meaning as in the Caravan Sites and Control of Development Act 1960;

"contract of employment" and "employer" have the same meanings as in the Employment Rights Act 1996;

"credit" has the same meaning as in the Consumer Credit Act 1974.

[Consumer Protection Act 1987, s 22 as amended by the Employment Rights Act 1996, Sch 1 and SI 2001/3649.]

1. The Utilities Act 2000, s 31 provides that references to the supply of electricity shall have effect, after the commencement of that section, as references to the supply of electricity, the distribution of electricity, or both the supply and distribution of electricity, according to the nature of the activities to which they referred before that time.

8–5014   23. Application to provision of accommodation etc.   (1) Subject to subsection (2) below, references in this Part to accommodation or facilities being available shall not include references to accommodation or facilities being available to be provided by means of the creation or disposal of an interest in land except where—

(a) the person who is to create or dispose of the interest will do so in the course of any business of his; and

(b) the interest to be created or disposed of is a relevant interest in a new dwelling and is to be created or disposed of for the purpose of enabling that dwelling to be occupied as a residence, or one of the residences, of the person acquiring the interest.

(2) Subsection (1) above shall not prevent the application of any provision of this Part in relation to—

(a) the supply of any goods as part of the same transaction as any creation or disposal of an interest in land; or

(b) the provision of any services or facilities for the purposes of, or in connection with, any transaction for the creation or disposal of such an interest.

(3) In this section—

"new dwelling" means any building or part of a building in Great Britain which—

(a) has been constructed or adapted to be occupied as a residence; and

(b) has not previously been so occupied or has been so occupied only with other premises or as more than one residence,

and includes any yard, garden, out-houses or appurtenances which belong to that building or part or are to be enjoyed with it;

"relevant interest"—

(a) in relation to a new dwelling in England and Wales, means the freehold estate in the dwelling or a leasehold interest in the dwelling for a term of years absolute of more than twenty-one years, not being a term of which twenty-one years or less remains unexpired;

(b) *Scotland.*

[Consumer Protection Act 1987, s 23.]

8–5015   24. Defences.   (1) In any proceedings against a person for an offence under subsection (1) or (2) of section 20 above in respect of any indication it shall be a defence for that person to show that his acts or omissions were authorised for the purposes of this subsection by regulations made under section 26 below.

(2) In proceedings against a person for an offence under subsection (1) or (2) of section 20 above in respect of an indication published in a book, newspaper, magazine or film or in a programme included in a programme service (within the meaning of the Broadcasting Act 1990), it shall be a defence for that person to show that the indication was not contained in an advertisement.

(3) In proceedings against a person for an offence under subsection (1) or (2) of section 20 above in respect of an indication published in an advertisement it shall be a defence for that person to show that—

(a) he is a person who carries on a business of publishing or arranging for the publication of advertisements;

(b) he received the advertisement for publication in the ordinary course of that business; and

(c) at the time of publication he did not know and had no grounds for suspecting that the publication would involve the commission of the offence.

(4) In any proceedings against a person for an offence under subsection (1) of section 20 above in respect of any indication, it shall be a defence for that person to show that—

(a) the indication did not relate to the availability from him of any goods, services, accommodation or facilities;

(b) a price had been recommended to every person from whom the goods, services, accommodation or facilities were indicated as being available;

(c) the indication related to that price and was misleading as to that price only by reason of a failure by any person to follow the recommendation; and

(d) it was reasonable for the person who gave the indication to assume that the recommendation was for the most part being followed.

(5) The provisions of this section are without prejudice to the provisions of section 39 below.

(6) In this section—

"advertisement" includes a catalogue, a circular and a price list.

[Consumer Protection Act 1987, s 24 as amended by the Broadcasting Act 1990, Schs 20 and 21.]

8–5016 25. Code of practice.   (1) The Secretary of State may, after consulting the Director General of Fair Trading and such other persons as the Secretary of State considers it appropriate to consult, by order[1] approve any code of practice issued (whether by the Secretary of State or another person) for the purpose of—

(a) giving practical guidance with respect to any of the requirements of section 20 above; and

(b) promoting what appear to the Secretary of State to be desirable practices as to the circumstances and manner in which any person gives an indication as to the price at which any goods, services, accommodation or facilities are available or indicates any other matter in respect of which any such indication may be misleading.

(2) A contravention of a code of practice approved under this section shall not of itself give rise to any criminal or civil liability, but in any proceedings against any person for an offence under section 20(1) or (2) above—

(a) any contravention by that person of such a code may be relied on in relation to any matter for the purpose of establishing that that person committed the offence or of negativing any defence; and

(b) compliance by that person with such a code may be relied on in relation to any matter for the purpose of showing that the commission of the offence by that person has not been established or that that person has a defence.

(3) Where the Secretary of State approves a code of practice under this section he may, after such consultation as is mentioned in subsection (1) above, at any time by order—

(a) approve any modification of the code; or

(b) withdraw his approval;

and references in subsection (2) above to a code of practice approved under this section shall be construed accordingly.

(4) The power to make an order under this section shall be exercisable by statutory instrument subject to annulment in pursuance of a resolution of either House of Parliament.

[Consumer Protection Act 1987, s 25.]

---

1. The Consumer Protection (Code of Practice for Traders on Price Indications) Approval Order 2005, SI 2005/2705 has been made.

8–5017 26. Power to make regulations.   (1) The Secretary of State may, after consulting the Director General of Fair Trading and such other persons as the Secretary of State considers it appropriate to consult, by regulations[1] make provision—

(a) for the purpose of regulating the circumstances and manner in which any person—

(i) gives any indication as to the price at which any goods, services, accommodation or facilities will be or are available or have been supplied or provided; or

(ii) indicates any other matter in respect of which any such indication may be misleading;

(b) for the purpose of facilitating the enforcement of the provisions of section 20 above or of any regulations made under this section.

(2) The Secretary of State shall not make regulations by virtue of subsection (1)(a) above except in relation to—

(a) indications given by persons in the course of business; and

(b) such indications given otherwise than in the course of business as—

(i) are given by or on behalf of persons by whom accommodation is provided to others by means of leases or licences; and

(ii) relate to goods, services or facilities supplied or provided to those others in connection with the provision of the accommodation.

(3) Without prejudice to the generality of subsection (1) above, regulations under this section may—

(a) prohibit an indication as to a price from referring to such matters as may be prescribed by the regulations;

(b) require an indication as to a price or other matter to be accompanied or supplemented by such explanation or such additional information as may be prescribed by the regulations;

(c) require information or explanations with respect to a price or other matter to be given to an officer of an enforcement authority and to authorise such an officer to require such information or explanations to be given;

(d) require any information or explanation provided for the purposes of any regulations made by virtue of paragraph (b) or (c) above to be accurate;

(e) prohibit the inclusion in indications as to a price or other matter of statements that the indications are not to be relied upon;

(f) provide that expressions used in any indication as to a price or other matter shall be construed in a particular way for the purposes of this Part;

(g) provide that a contravention of any provision of the regulations shall constitute a criminal offence punishable—

(i) on conviction on indictment, by a fine;
(ii) on summary conviction, by a fine not exceeding the statutory maximum;

(h) apply any provision of this Act which relates to a criminal offence to an offence created by virtue of paragraph (g) above.

(4) The power to make regulations under this section shall be exercisable by statutory instrument subject to annulment in pursuance of a resolution of either House of Parliament and shall include power—

(a) to make different provision for different cases; and

(b) to make such supplemental, consequential and transitional provision as the Secretary of State considers appropriate.

(5) In this section "lease" includes a sub-lease and an agreement for a lease and a statutory tenancy (within the meaning of the Landlord and Tenant Act 1985 or the Rent (Scotland) Act 1984).
[Consumer Protection Act 1987, s 26.]

---

1. The Price Indication (Method of Payment) Regulations 1991 (see post), the Price Indications (Bureaux de Change) (No 2) Regulations 1992, SI 1992/737 and the Price Indications (Resale of Tickets) Regulations 1994, this title, post, have been made.

PART IV[1]
ENFORCEMENT OF PARTS II AND III

8–5018 27. Enforcement. (1) Subject to the following provisions of this section—

(a) it shall be the duty of every weights and measures authority in Great Britain to enforce within their area the safety provisions and the provisions made by or under Part III of this Act; and

(b) it shall be the duty of every district council in Northern Ireland to enforce within their area the safety provisions.

(2) The Secretary of State may by regulations—

(a) wholly or partly transfer any duty imposed by subsection (1) above on a weights and measures authority or a district council in Northern Ireland to such other person who has agreed to the transfer as is specified in the regulations;

(b) relieve such an authority or council of any such duty so far as it is exercisable in relation to such goods as may be described in the regulations.

(3) The power to make regulations under subsection (2) above shall be exercisable by statutory instrument subject to annulment in pursuance of a resolution of either House of Parliament and shall include power—

(a) to make different provision for different cases; and

(b) to make such supplemental, consequential and transitional provision as the Secretary of State considers appropriate.

(4) Nothing in this section shall authorise any weights and measures authority, or any person on whom functions are conferred by regulations under subsection (2) above, to bring proceedings in Scotland for an offence.
[Consumer Protection Act 1987, s 27.]

---

1. Part IV contains ss 27–35.

8–5019 28. Test purchases. (1) An enforcement authority shall have power, for the purpose of ascertaining whether any safety provision or any provision made by or under Part III of this Act has been contravened in relation to any goods, services, accommodation or facilities—

(*a*)   to make, or to authorise an officer of the authority to make, any purchase of any goods; or

(*b*)   to secure, or to authorise an officer of the authority to secure, the provision of any services, accommodation or facilities.

(2)   Where—

(*a*)   any goods purchased under this section by or on behalf of an enforcement authority are submitted to a test; and

(*b*)   the test leads to—

     (i)   the bringing of proceedings for an offence in respect of a contravention in relation to the goods of any safety provision or of any provision made by or under Part III of this Act or for the forfeiture of the goods under section 16 or 17 above; or

     (ii)   the serving of a suspension notice in respect of any goods; and

(*c*)   the authority is requested to do so and it is practicable for the authority to comply with the request,

the authority shall allow the person from whom the goods were purchased or any person who is a party to the proceedings or has an interest in any goods to which the notice relates to have the goods tested.

(3)   The Secretary of State may by regulations provide that any test of goods purchased under this section by or on behalf of an enforcement authority shall—

(*a*)   be carried out at the expense of the authority in a manner and by a person prescribed by or determined under the regulations; or

(*b*)   be carried out either as mentioned in paragraph (*a*) above or by the authority in a manner prescribed by the regulations.

(4)   The power to make regulations under subsection (3) above shall be exercisable by statutory instrument subject to annulment in pursuance of a resolution of either House of Parliament and shall include power—

(*a*)   to make different provision for different cases; and

(*b*)   to make such supplemental, consequential and transitional provision as the Secretary of State considers appropriate.

(5)   Nothing in this section shall authorise the acquisition by or on behalf of an enforcement authority of any interest in land.

[Consumer Protection Act 1987, s 28.]

8–5030   **29. Powers of search etc[1].**   (1) Subject to the following provisions of this Part, a duly authorised officer of an enforcement authority may at any reasonable hour and on production, if required, of his credentials exercise any of the powers conferred by the following provisions of this section.

(2)   The officer may, for the purposes of ascertaining whether there has been any contravention of any safety provision or of any provision made by or under Part III of this Act, inspect any goods and enter any premises other than premises occupied only as a person's residence.

(3)   The officer may, for the purpose of ascertaining whether there has been any contravention of any safety provision, examine any procedure (including any arrangements for carrying out a test) connected with the production of any goods.

(4)   If the officer has reasonable grounds for suspecting that any goods are manufactured or imported goods which have not been supplied in the United Kingdom since they were manufactured or imported he may—

(*a*)   for the purpose of ascertaining whether there has been any contravention of any safety provision in relation to the goods, require any person carrying on a business, or employed in connection with a business, to produce any records relating to the business;

(*b*)   for the purpose of ascertaining (by testing or otherwise) whether there has been any such contravention, seize and detain the goods;

(*c*)   take copies of, or of any entry in, any records produced by virtue of paragraph (*a*) above.

(5)   If the officer has reasonable grounds for suspecting that there has been a contravention in relation to any goods of any safety provision or of any provision made by or under Part III of this Act, he may—

(*a*)   for the purpose of ascertaining whether there has been any such contravention, require any person carrying on a business, or employed in connection with a business, to produce any records relating to the business[2];

(*b*)   for the purpose of ascertaining (by testing or otherwise) whether there has been any such contravention, seize and detain the goods;

(*c*)   take copies of, or of any entry in, any records produced by virtue of paragraph (*a*) above.

(6)   The officer may seize and detain—

(*a*) any goods or records which he has reasonable grounds for believing may be required as evidence in proceedings for an offence in respect of a contravention of any safety provision or of any provision made by or under Part III of this Act;

(*b*) any goods which he has reasonable grounds for suspecting may be liable to be forfeited under section 16 or 17 above.

(7) If and to the extent that it is reasonably necessary to do so to prevent a contravention of any safety provision or of any provision made by or under Part III of this Act, the officer may, for the purpose of exercising his power under subsection (4), (5) or (6) above to seize any goods or records—

(*a*) require any person having authority to do so to open any container or to open any vending machine; and

(*b*) himself open or break open any such container or machine where a requirement made under paragraph (*a*) above in relation to the container or machine has not been complied with.

[Consumer Protection Act 1987, s 29.]

---

1. Code B of the Police and Criminal Evidence Act 1984 (s 66) Codes of Practice (see PART II: EVIDENCE) applies to a routine visit by a trading standards officer where it amounted to a search because he looked about (*Dudley Metropolitan Borough Council v Debenhams plc* (1994) 159 JP 18).

2. This provision may enable a trading standards officer to call for the current price list of goods displayed for sale, whether in documentary form or on computer; however, it does not authorise him to require that a till be closed down and made available for his use (*Toys 'R' Us v Gloucestershire County Council* (1994) 158 JP 338, [1994] Crim LR 521).

8–5031   30. Provisions supplemental to s 29.   (1) An officer seizing any goods or records under section 29 above shall inform the following persons that the goods or records have been so seized, that is to say—

(*a*) the person from whom they are seized; and

(*b*) in the case of imported goods seized on any premises under the control of the Commissioners of Customs and Excise, the importer of those goods (within the meaning of the Customs and Excise Management Act 1979).

(2) If a justice of the peace—

(*a*) is satisfied by any written information on oath that there are reasonable grounds for believing either—

  (i) that any goods or records which any officer has power to inspect under section 29 above are on any premises and that their inspection is likely to disclose evidence that there has been a contravention of any safety provision or of any provision made by or under Part III of this Act; or

  (ii) that such a contravention has taken place, is taking place or is about to take place on any premises; and

(*b*) is also satisfied by any such information either—

  (i) that admission to the premises has been or is likely to be refused and that notice of intention to apply for a warrant under this subsection has been given to the occupier; or

  (ii) that an application for admission, or the giving of such a notice, would defeat the object of the entry or that the premises are unoccupied or that the occupier is temporarily absent and it might defeat the object of the entry to await his return,

the justice may by warrant under this hand, which shall continue in force for a period of one month, authorise any officer of an enforcement authority to enter the premises, if need be by force.

(3) An officer entering any premises by virtue of section 29 above or a warrant under subsection (2) above may take with him such other persons and such equipment as may appear to him necessary.

(4) On leaving any premises which a person is authorised to enter by a warrant under subsection (2) above, that person shall, if the premises are unoccupied or the occupier is temporarily absent, leave the premises as effectively secured against trespassers as he found them.

(5) If any person who is not an officer of an enforcement authority purports to act as such under section 29 above or this section he shall be guilty of an offence and liable on summary conviction to a fine not exceeding **level 5** on the standard scale.

(6) Where any goods seized by an officer under section 29 above are submitted to a test, the officer shall inform the persons mentioned in subsection (1) above of the result of the test and, if—

(*a*) proceedings are brought for an offence in respect of a contravention in relation to the goods of any safety provision or of any provision made by or under Part III of this Act or for the forfeiture of the goods under section 16 or 17 above, or a suspension notice is served in respect of any goods; and

(*b*) the officer is requested to do so and it is practicable to comply with the request,

the officer shall allow any person who is a party to the proceedings or, as the case may be, has an interest in the goods to which the notice relates to have the goods tested.

(7) The Secretary of State may by regulations provide that any test of goods seized under section 29 above by an officer of an enforcement authority shall—

(a)   be carried out at the expense of the authority in a manner and by a person prescribed by or determined under the regulations; or

(b)   be carried out either as mentioned in paragraph (a) above or by the authority in a manner prescribed by the regulations.

(8)   The power to make regulations under subsection (7) above shall be exercisable by statutory instrument subject to annulment in pursuance of a resolution of either House of Parliament and shall include power—

(a)   to make different provision for different cases; and

(b)   to make such supplemental, consequential and transitional provision as the Secretary of State considers appropriate.

(9)   *Scotland.*

(10)   *Northern Ireland.*

[Consumer Protection Act 1987, s 30.]

8–5032   **31. Power of customs officer to detain goods.**   (1) A customs officer may, for the purpose of facilitating the exercise by an enforcement authority or officer of such an authority of any functions conferred on the authority or officer by or under Part II of this Act, or by or under this Part in its application for the purposes of the safety provisions, seize any imported goods and detain them for not more than two working days.

(2)   Anything seized and detained under this section shall be dealt with during the period of its detention in such manner as the Commissioners of Customs and Excise may direct.

(3)   In subsection (1) above the reference to two working days is a reference to a period of forty-eight hours calculated from the time when the goods in question are seized but disregarding so much of any period as falls on a Saturday or Sunday or on Christmas Day, Good Friday or a day which is a bank holiday under the Banking and Financial Dealings Act 1971 in the part of the United Kingdom where the goods are seized.

(4)   In this section and section 32 below "customs officer" means any officer within the meaning of the Customs and Excise Management Act 1979.

[Consumer Protection Act 1987, s 31.]

8–5033   **32. Obstruction of authorised officer.**   (1) Any person who—

(a)   intentionally obstructs any officer of an enforcement authority who is acting in pursuance of any provision of this Part or any customs officer who is so acting; or

(b)   intentionally fails to comply with any requirement made of him by any officer of an enforcement authority under any provision of this Part; or

(c)   without reasonable cause fails to give any officer of an enforcement authority who is so[1] acting any other assistance or information which the officer may reasonably require of him for the purposes of the exercise of the officer's functions under any provision of this Part,

shall be guilty of an offence and liable on summary conviction to a fine not exceeding **level 5** on the standard scale.

(2)   A person shall be guilty of an offence if, in giving any information which is required of him by virtue of subsection (1)(c) above—

(a)   he makes any statement which he knows is false in a material particular; or

(b)   he recklessly makes a statement which is false in a material particular.

(3)   A person guilty of an offence under subsection (2) above shall be liable—

(a)   on conviction on indictment, to a fine;

(b)   on summary conviction, to a fine not exceeding **the statutory maximum**.

[Consumer Protection Act 1987, s 32.]

---

1.   Instructions of a superior to an employee not to answer questions at an interview by a trading standards officer is no defence to the requirement to answer questions under this section (*R v Greater Manchester Justices, ex p Aldi GmbH & Co KG* (1994) 159 JP 717).

8–5034   **33. Appeals against detention of goods.**   (1) Any person having an interest in any goods which are for the time being detained under any provision of this Part by an enforcement authority or by an officer of such an authority may apply for an order requiring the goods to be released to him or to another person.

(2)   An application under this section may be made—

(a)   to any magistrates' court in which proceedings have been brought in England and Wales or Northern Ireland—

(i)   for an offence in respect of a contravention in relation to the goods of any safety provision or of any provision made by or under Part III of this Act; or

(ii)   for the forfeiture of the goods under section 16 above;

(b) where no such proceedings have been so brought, by way of complaint to a magistrates' court; or

(c) in Scotland, by summary application to the sheriff.

(3) On an application under this section to a magistrates' court or to the sheriff, an order requiring goods to be released shall be made only if the court or sheriff is satisfied—

(a) that proceedings—

(i) for an offence in respect of a contravention in relation to the goods of any safety provision or of any provision made by or under Part III of this Act; or

(ii) for the forfeiture of the goods under section 16 or 17 above,

have not been brought or, having been brought, have been concluded without the goods being forfeited; and

(b) where no such proceedings have been brought, that more than six months have elapsed since the goods were seized.

(4) Any person aggrieved by an order made under this section by a magistrates' court in England and Wales or Northern Ireland, or by a decision of such a court not to make such an order, may appeal against that order or decision—

(a) in England and Wales, to the Crown Court;

(b) in Northern Ireland, to the county court;

and an order so made may contain such provision as appears to the court to be appropriate for delaying the coming into force of the order pending the making and determination of any appeal (including any application under section 111 of the Magistrates' Courts Act 1980 or Article 146 of the Magistrates' Courts (Northern Ireland) Order 1981 (statement of case)).
[Consumer Protection Act 1987, s 33.]

8–5035   34. Compensation for seizure and detention. (1) Where an officer of an enforcement authority exercises any power under section 29 above to seize and detain goods, the enforcement authority shall be liable to pay compensation to any person having an interest in the goods in respect of any loss or damage caused by reason of the exercise of the power if—

(a) there has been no contravention in relation to the goods of any safety provision or of any provision made by or under Part III of this Act; and

(b) the exercise of the power is not attributable to any neglect or default by that person.

(2) Any disputed question as to the right to or the amount of any compensation payable under this section shall be determined by arbitration or, in Scotland, by a single arbiter appointed, failing agreement between the parties, by the sheriff.
[Consumer Protection Act 1987, s 34.]

8–5036   35. Recovery of expenses of enforcement. (1) This section shall apply where a court—

(a) convicts a person of an offence in respect of a contravention in relation to any goods of any safety provision or of any provision made by or under Part III of this Act; or

(b) makes an order under section 16 or 17 above for the forfeiture of any goods.

(2) The court may (in addition to any other order it may make as to costs or expenses) order the person convicted or, as the case may be, any person having an interest in the goods to reimburse an enforcement authority for any expenditure which has been or may be incurred by that authority—

(a) in connection with any seizure or detention of the goods by or on behalf of the authority; or

(b) in connection with any compliance by the authority with directions given by the court for the purposes of any order for the forfeiture of the goods.
[Consumer Protection Act 1987, s 35.]

PART V[1]
MISCELLANEOUS AND SUPPLEMENTAL

8–5037   36. Amendments of Part I of the Health and Safety at Work etc Act 1974. Part I of the Health and Safety at Work etc Act 1974 (which includes provision with respect to the safety of certain articles and substances) shall have effect with the amendments specified in Schedule 3 to this Act; and, accordingly, the general purposes of that Part of that Act shall include the purpose of protecting persons from the risks protection from which would not be afforded by virtue of that Part but for those amendments.
[Consumer Protection Act 1987, s 36.]

---

1. Part V contains ss 36–50.

8–5038   37. Power of Commissioners of Customs and Excise to disclose information. (1) If they think it appropriate to do so for the purpose of facilitating the exercise by any person to whom subsection (2) below applies of any functions conferred on that person by or under Part II of this

Act, or by or under Part IV of this Act in its application for the purposes of the safety provisions, the Commissioners of Customs and Excise may authorise the disclosure to that person of any information obtained for the purposes of the exercise by the Commissioners of their functions in relation to imported goods.

(2) This subsection applies to an enforcement authority and to any officer of an enforcement authority.

(3) A disclosure of information made to any person under subsection (1) above shall be made in such manner as may be directed by the Commissioners of Customs and Excise and may be made through such persons acting on behalf of that person as may be so directed.

(4) Information may be disclosed to a person under subsection (1) above whether or not the disclosure of the information has been requested by or on behalf of that person.

[Consumer Protection Act 1987, s 37.]

8–5039 38. Restrictions on disclosure of information. *Repealed.*

8–5040 39. Defence of due diligence. (1) Subject to the following provisions of this section, in proceedings against any person for an offence to which this section applies it shall be a defence for that person to show that he took all reasonable steps and exercised all due diligence[1] to avoid committing the offence.

(2) Where in any proceedings against any person for such an offence the defence provided by subsection (1) above involves an allegation that the commission of the offence was due—

(*a*) to the act or default of another; or

(*b*) to reliance on information given by another,

that person shall not, without the leave of the court, be entitled to rely on the defence unless, not less than seven clear days before the hearing of the proceedings, he has served a notice under subsection (3) below on the person bringing the proceedings.

(3) A notice under this subsection shall give such information identifying or assisting in the identification of the person who committed the act or default or gave the information as is in the possession of the person serving the notice at the time he serves it.

(4) It is hereby declared that a person shall not be entitled to rely on the defence provided by subsection (1) above by reason of his reliance on information supplied by another, unless he shows that it was reasonable in all the circumstances for him to have relied on the information, having regard in particular—

(*a*) to the steps which he took, and those which might reasonably have been taken, for the purpose of verifying the information; and

(*b*) to whether he had any reason to disbelieve the information.

(5) This section shall apply to an offence under section 12(1), (2) or (3), 13(4), 14(6) or 20(1) above.

[Consumer Protection Act 1987, s 39 as amended by SI 2005/1803.]

---

1. See case law in relation to the similar phrase in s 24(1) or the Trade Descriptions Act 1968, ante.

In a prosecution under s 12 of this Act, where the defendants sought to establish the statutory defence under s 39, on the basis of "in-house" testing of samples of toys taken at random, it was held, since the burden of proof was on them, that they should have adduced independent statistical evidence as to what should be done by a reasonable trader in such circumstances (*P & M Supplies (Essex) Ltd v Devon County Council* (1991) 156 JP 328, [1991] Crim LR 832, DC—out of a total of 76,690 toys imported only 378 were randomly sampled by the defendants and only 18 were sent to the public analyst). In considering whether the defendant has established the defence under s 39 the court will weigh the risk of misleading information being given against the reasonableness of the steps taken, or those which the prosecution asserts should have been taken, to avoid the risk. Therefore justices were entitled to conclude that the defence was made out where misleading information was given by a computer where the software had been extensively tested and which arose from an unexplained fault which had occurred on a single occasion (*Berkshire County Council v Olympic Holidays Ltd* (1993) 158 JP 421, [1994] Crim LR 277). A company did not act with due diligence where it relied on a certificate showing compliance with the relevant British Standard when the British Standard did not relate to all matters covered by the regulations applicable to the toy and the toy had not been examined for compliance with the regulations (*Balding v Lew-Ways Ltd* (1995) 159 JP 541, [1995] Crim LR 878).

8–5041 40. Liability of persons other than principal offender. (1) Where the commission by any person of an offence to which section 39 above applies is due to an act or default committed by some other person in the course of any business of his, the other person shall be guilty of the offence and may be proceeded against and punished by virtue of this subsection whether or not proceedings are taken against the first-mentioned person.

(2) Where a body corporate is guilty of an offence under this Act (including where it is so guilty by virtue of subsection (1) above) in respect of any act or default which is shown to have been committed with the consent or connivance of, or to be attributable to any neglect on the part of, any director, manager, secretary or other similar officer of the body corporate or any person who was

purporting to act in any such capacity he, as well as the body corporate, shall be guilty of that offence and shall be liable to be proceeded against and punished accordingly.

(3) Where the affairs of a body corporate are managed by its members, subsection (2) above shall apply in relation to the acts and defaults of a member in connection with his functions of management as if he were a director of the body corporate.

[Consumer Protection Act 1987, s 40.]

8–5042 41. *Civil proceedings.*

8–5043 42. Reports etc. (1) It shall be the duty of the Secretary of State at least once in every five years to lay before each House of Parliament a report on the exercise during the period to which the report relates of the functions which under Part II of this Act, or under Part IV of this Act in its application for the purposes of the safety provisions, are exercisable by the Secretary of State, weights and measures authorities, district councils in Northern Ireland and persons on whom functions are conferred by regulations made under section 27(2) above.

(2) The Secretary of State may from time to time prepare and lay before each House of Parliament such other reports on the exercise of those functions as he considers appropriate.

(3) Every weights and measures authority, every district council in Northern Ireland and every person on whom functions are conferred by regulations under subsection (2) of section 27 above shall, whenever the Secretary of State so directs, make a report to the Secretary of State on the exercise of the functions exercisable by that authority or council under that section or by that person by virtue of any such regulations.

(4) A report under subsection (3) above shall be in such form and shall contain such particulars as are specified in the direction of the Secretary of State.

(5) The first report under subsection (1) above shall be laid before each House of Parliament not more than five years after the laying of the last report under section 8(2) of the Consumer Safety Act 1978.

[Consumer Protection Act 1987, s 42.]

8–5044 43. *Financial provisions.*

8–5045 44. Service of documents etc. (1) Any document required or authorised by virtue of this Act to be served on a person may be so served—

(*a*) by delivering it to him or by leaving it at his proper address or by sending it by post to him at that address; or

(*b*) if the person is a body corporate, by serving it in accordance with paragraph (*a*) above on the secretary or clerk of that body; or

(*c*) if the person is a partnership, by serving it in accordance with that paragraph on a partner or on a person having control or management of the partnership business.

(2) For the purposes of subsection (1) above, and for the purposes of section 7 of the Interpretation Act 1978 (which relates to the service of documents by post) in its application to that subsection, the proper address of any person on whom a document is to be served by virtue of this Act shall be his last known address except that—

(*a*) in the case of service on a body corporate or its secretary or clerk, it shall be the address of the registered or principal office of the body corporate;

(*b*) in the case of service on a partnership or a partner or a person having the control or management of a partnership business, it shall be the principal office of the partnership;

and for the purposes of this subsection the principal officer of a company registered outside the United Kingdom or of a partnership carrying on business outside the United Kingdom is its principal office within the United Kingdom.

(3) The Secretary of State may by regulations make provision for the manner in which any information is to be given to any person under any provision of Part IV of this Act.

(4) Without prejudice to the generality of subsection (3) above regulations made by the Secretary of State may prescribe the person, or manner of determining the person, who is to be treated for the purposes of section 28(2) or 30 above as the person from whom any goods were purchased or seized where the goods were purchased or seized from a vending machine.

(5) The power to make regulations under subsection (3) or (4) above shall be exercisable by statutory instrument subject to annulment in pursuance of a resolution of either House of Parliament and shall include power—

(*a*) to make different provision for different cases; and

(*b*) to make such supplemental, consequential and transitional provision as the Secretary of State considers appropriate.

[Consumer Protection Act 1987, s 44.]

8–5046 45. Interpretation. (1) In this Act, except in so far as the context otherwise requires—

"aircraft" includes gliders, balloons and hovercraft;

"business" includes a trade or profession and the activities of a professional or trade association or of a local authority or other public authority;

"conditional sale agreement", "credit-sale agreement" and "hire-purchase agreement" have the same meanings as in the Consumer Credit Act 1974 but as if in the definitions in that Act "goods" had the same meaning as in this Act;

"contravention" includes a failure to comply and cognate expressions shall be construed accordingly;

"enforcement authority" means the Secretary of State, any other Minister of the Crown in charge of a Government department, any such department and any authority, council or other person on whom functions under this Act are conferred by or under section 27 above;

"gas" has the same meaning as in Part I of the Gas Act 1986;

"goods" includes substances, growing crops and things comprised in land by virtue of being attached to it and any ship, aircraft or vehicle;

"information" includes accounts, estimates and returns;

"magistrates' court", in relation to Northern Ireland, means a court of summary jurisdiction;

"modifications" includes additions, alterations and omissions, and cognate expressions shall be construed accordingly;

"motor vehicle" has the same meaning as in the Road Traffic Act 1988;

"notice" means a notice in writing;

"notice to warn" means a notice under section 13(1)(*b*) above;

"officer", in relation to an enforcement authority, means a person authorised in writing to assist the authority in carrying out its functions under or for the purposes of the enforcement of any of the safety provisions or of any of the provisions made by or under Part III of this Act;

"personal injury" includes any disease and any other impairment of a person's physical or mental condition;

"premises" includes any place and any ship, aircraft or vehicle;

"prohibition notice" means a notice under section 13(1)(*a*) above;

"records" includes any books or documents and any records in non-documentary form;

"safety provision" means any provision of safety regulations, a prohibition notice or a suspension notice;

"safety regulations" means regulations under section 11 above;

"ship" includes any boat and any other description of vessel used in navigation;

"subordinate legislation" has the same meaning as in the Interpretation Act 1978;

"substance" means any natural or artificial substance, whether in solid, liquid or gaseous form or in the form of a vapour, and includes substances that are comprised in or mixed with other goods;

"supply" and cognate expressions shall be construed in accordance with section 46 below;

"suspension notice" means a notice under section 14 above.

(2) Except in so far as the context otherwise requires, references in this Act to a contravention of a safety provision shall, in relation to any goods, include references to anything which would constitute such a contravention if the goods were supplied to any person.

(3) References in this Act to any goods in relation to which any safety provision has been or may have been contravened shall include references to any goods which it is not reasonably practicable to separate from any such goods.

(4) *Repealed.*

(5) (In Scotland, any reference in this Act to things comprised in land by virtue of being attached to it is a reference to moveables which have become heritable by accession to heritable property.

[Consumer Protection Act 1987, s 45 amended by the Road Traffic (Consequential Provisions) Act, Sch 3, the Trade Marks Act 1994, Sch 5 and SI 2005/1803.]

8–5047 46. Meaning of "supply". (1) Subject to the following provisions of this section, references in this Act to supplying goods shall be construed as references to doing any of the following, whether as principal or agent, that is to say—

(*a*) selling, hiring out or lending the goods[1];

(*b*) entering into a hire-purchase agreement to furnish the goods;

(*c*) the performance of any contract for work and materials to furnish the goods;

(*d*) providing the goods in exchange for any consideration other than money;

(*e*) providing the goods in or in connection with the performance of any statutory function; or

(*f*) giving the goods as a prize or otherwise making a gift of the goods;

and, in relation to gas or water, those references shall be construed as including references to providing the service by which the gas or water is made available for use.

(2) For the purposes of any reference in this Act to supplying goods, where a person ("the ostensible supplier") supplies goods to another person ("the customer") under a hire-purchase agreement, conditional sale agreement or credit-sale agreement or under an agreement for the hiring of goods (other than a hire-purchase agreement) and the ostensible supplier—

(*a*) carries on the business of financing the provision of goods for others by means of such agreements; and

(*b*) in the course of that business acquired his interest in the goods supplied to the customer as a means of financing the provision of them for the customer by a further person ("the effective supplier"),

the effective supplier and not the ostensible supplier shall be treated as supplying the goods to the customer.

(3) Subject to subsection (4) below, the performance of any contract by the erection of any building or structure on any land or by the carrying out of any other building works shall be treated for the purposes of this Act as a supply of goods in so far as, but only in so far as, it involves the provision of any goods to any person by means of their incorporation into the building, structure or works.

(4) Except for the purposes of, and in relation to, notices to warn or any provision made by or under Part III of this Act, references in this Act to supplying goods shall not include references to supplying goods comprised in land where the supply is effected by the creation or disposal of an interest in the land.

(5) Except in Part I of this Act references in this Act to a person's supplying goods shall be confined to references to that person's supplying goods in the course of a business of his, but for the purposes of this subsection it shall be immaterial whether the business is a business of dealing in the goods.

(6) For the purposes of subsection (5) above goods shall not be treated as supplied in the course of a business if they are supplied, in pursuance of an obligation arising under or in connection with the insurance of the goods, to the person with whom they were insured.

(7) Except for the purposes of, and in relation to, prohibition notices or suspension notices, references in Parts II to IV of this Act to supplying goods shall not include—

(*a*) references to supplying goods where the person supplied carries on a business of buying goods of the same description as those goods and repairing or reconditioning them;

(*b*) references to supplying goods by a sale of articles as scrap (that is to say, for the value of materials included in the articles rather than for the value of the articles themselves).

(8) Where any goods have at any time been supplied by being hired out or lent to any person, neither a continuation or renewal of the hire or loan (whether on the same or different terms) nor any transaction for the transfer after that time of any interest in the goods to the person to whom they were hired or lent shall be treated for the purposes of this Act as a further supply of the goods to that person.

(9) A ship, aircraft or motor vehicle shall not be treated for the purposes of this Act as supplied to any person by reason only that services consisting in the carriage of goods or passengers in that ship, aircraft or vehicle, or in its use for any other purpose, are provided to that person in pursuance of an agreement relating to the use of the ship, aircraft or vehicle for a particular period or for particular voyages, flights or journeys.
[Consumer Protection Act 1987, s 46 as amended by SI 2005/871.]

---

1. A landlord who provides electrical equipment for the use of a tenant renting holiday accomodation is supplying equipment for the purpose of s 46(1)(*a*) (*Drummond-Rees v Dorset County Council* (1996) 162 JP 651.

8–5048   47. Savings for certain privileges. (1) Nothing in this Act shall be taken as requiring any person to produce any records if he would be entitled to refuse to produce those records in any proceedings in any court on the grounds that they are the subject of legal professional privilege or, in Scotland, that they contain a confidential communication made by or to an advocate or solicitor in that capacity, or as authorising any person to take possession of any records which are in the possession of a person who would be so entitled.

(2) Nothing in this Act shall be construed as requiring a person to answer any question or give any information if to do so would incriminate that person or that person's spouse or civil partner.
[Consumer Protection Act 1987, s 47 as amended by the Civil Partnership Act 2004, Sch 27.]

8–5049   48. *Minor and consequential amendments and repeals.*

8–5059   49. *Northern Ireland.*

8–5060   50. *Short title, commencement and transitional provision.*

SCHEDULES

8–5061

Section 6   SCHEDULE 1

Limitation of Actions under Part I

Section 13   SCHEDULE 2

PROHIBITION NOTICES AND NOTICES TO WARN

PART I

PROHIBITION NOTICES

8–5062   1. A prohibition notice in respect of any goods shall—

(a)   state that the Secretary of State considers that the goods are unsafe;
(b)   set out the reasons why the Secretary of State considers that the goods are unsafe;
(c)   specify the day on which the notice is to come into force; and
(d)   state that the trader may at any time make representations in writing to the Secretary of State for the purpose of establishing that the goods are safe.

2. (1) If representations in writing about a prohibition notice are made by the trader to the Secretary of State, it shall be the duty of the Secretary of State to consider whether to revoke the notice and—

(a)   if he decides to revoke it, to do so;
(b)   in any other case, to appoint a person to consider those representations, any further representations made (whether in writing or orally) by the trader about the notice and the statements of any witnesses examined under this Part of this Schedule.

(2) Where the Secretary of State has appointed a person to consider representations about a prohibition notice, he shall serve a notification on the trader which—

(a)   states that the trader may make oral representations to the appointed person for the purpose of establishing that the goods to which the notice relates are safe; and
(b)   specifies the place and time at which the oral representations may be made.

(3) The time specified in a notification served under sub-paragraph (2) above shall not be before the end of the period of twenty-one days beginning with the day on which the notification is served, unless the trader otherwise agrees.

(4) A person on whom a notification has been served under sub-paragraph (2) above or his representative may, at the place and time specified in the notification—

(a)   make oral representations to the appointed person for the purpose of establishing that the goods in question are safe; and
(b)   call and examine witnesses in connection with the representations.

3. (1) Where representations in writing about a prohibition notice are made by the trader to the Secretary of State at any time after a person has been appointed to consider representations about that notice, then, whether or not the appointed person has made a report to the Secretary of State, the following provisions of this paragraph shall apply instead of paragraph 2 above.

(2) The Secretary of State shall, before the end of the period of one month beginning with the day on which he receives the representations, serve a notification on the trader which states—

(a)   that the Secretary of State has decided to revoke the notice, has decided to vary it or, as the case may be, has decided neither to revoke nor to vary it; or
(b)   that, a person having been appointed to consider representations about the notice, the trader may, at a place and time specified in the notification, make oral representations to the appointed person for the purpose of establishing that the goods to which the notice relates are safe.

(3) The time specified in a notification served for the purposes of sub-paragraph (2)(b) above shall not be before the end of the period of twenty-one days beginning with the day on which the notification is served, unless the trader otherwise agrees or the time is the time already specified for the purposes of paragraph 2(2)(b) above.

(4) A person on whom a notification has been served for the purposes of sub-paragraph (2)(b) above or his representative may, at the place and time specified in the notification—

(a)   make oral representations to the appointed person for the purpose of establishing that the goods in question are safe; and
(b)   call and examine witnesses in connection with the representations.

4. (1) Where a person is appointed to consider representations about a prohibition notice, it shall be his duty to consider—

(a)   any written representations made by the trader about the notice, other than those in respect of which a notification is served under paragraph 3(2)(a) above;
(b)   any oral representations made under paragraph 2(4) or 3(4) above; and
(c)   any statements made by witnesses in connection with the oral representations,

and, after considering any matters under this paragraph, to make a report (including recommendations) to the Secretary of State about the matters considered by him and the notice.

(2) It shall be the duty of the Secretary of State to consider any report made to him under sub-paragraph (1) above and, after considering the report, to inform the trader of his decision with respect to the prohibition notice to which the report relates.

5. (1) The Secretary of State may revoke or vary a prohibition notice by serving on the trader a notification stating that the notice is revoked or, as the case may be, is varied as specified in the notification.

(2) The Secretary of State shall not vary a prohibition notice so as to make the effect of the notice more restrictive for the trader.

(3) Without prejudice to the power conferred by section 13(2) of this Act, the service of a notification under sub-paragraph (1) above shall be sufficient to satisfy the requirement of paragraph 4(2) above that the trader shall be informed of the Secretary of State's decision.

Part II
Notices to Warn

6. (1) If the Secretary of State proposes to serve a notice to warn on any person in respect of any goods, the Secretary of State, before he serves the notice, shall serve on that person a notification which—

(*a*) contains a draft of the proposed notice;

(*b*) states that the Secretary of State proposes to serve a notice in the form of the draft on that person;

(*c*) states that the Secretary of State considers that the goods described in the draft are unsafe;

(*d*) sets out the reasons why the Secretary of State considers that those goods are unsafe; and

(*e*) states that that person may make representations to the Secretary of State for the purpose of establishing that the goods are safe if, before the end of the period of fourteen days beginning with the day on which the notification is served, he informs the Secretary of State—

    (i) of his intention to make representations; and

    (ii) whether the representations will be made only in writing or both in writing and orally.

(2) Where the Secretary of State has served a notification containing a draft of a proposed notice to warn on any person, he shall not serve a notice to warn on that person in respect of the goods to which the proposed notice relates unless—

(*a*) the period of fourteen days beginning with the day on which the notification was served expires without the Secretary of State being informed as mentioned in sub-paragraph (1)(*e*) above;

(*b*) the period of twenty-eight days beginning with that day expires without any written representations being made by that person to the Secretary of State about the proposed notice; or

(*c*) the Secretary of State has considered a report about the proposed notice by a person appointed under paragraph 7(1) below.

7. (1) Where a person on whom a notification containing a draft of a proposed notice to warn has been served—

(*a*) informs the Secretary of State as mentioned in paragraph 6(1)(*e*) above before the end of the period of fourteen days beginning with the day on which the notification was served; and

(*b*) makes written representations to the Secretary of State about the proposed notice before the end of the period of twenty-eight days beginning with that day,

the Secretary of State shall appoint a person to consider those representations, any further representations made by that person about the draft notice and the statements of any witnesses examined under this Part of this Schedule.

(2) Where—

(*a*) the Secretary of State has appointed a person to consider representations about a proposed notice to warn; and

(*b*) the person whose representations are to be considered has informed the Secretary of State for the purposes of paragraph 6(1)(*e*) above that the representations he intends to make will include oral representations,

the Secretary of State shall inform the person intending to make the representations of the place and time at which oral representations may be made to the appointed person.

(3) Where a person on whom a notification containing a draft of a proposed notice to warn has been served is informed of a time for the purposes of sub-paragraph (2) above, that time shall not be—

(*a*) before the end of the period of twenty-eight days beginning with the day on which the notification was served; or

(*b*) before the end of the period of seven days beginning with the day on which that person is informed of the time.

(4) A person who has been informed of a place and time for the purposes of sub-paragraph (2) above or his representative may, at that place and time—

(*a*) make oral representations to the appointed person for the purpose of establishing that the goods to which the proposed notice relates are safe; and

(*b*) call and examine witnesses in connection with the representations.

8. (1) Where a person is appointed to consider representations about a proposed notice to warn, it shall be his duty to consider—

(*a*) any written representations made by the person on whom it is proposed to serve the notice; and

(*b*) in a case where a place and time has been appointed under paragraph 7(2) above for oral representations to be made by that person or his representative, any representations so made and any statements made by witnesses in connection with those representations,

and, after considering those matters, to make a report (including recommendations) to the Secretary of State about the matters considered by him and the proposal to serve the notice.

(2) It shall be the duty of the Secretary of State to consider any report made to him under sub-paragraph (1) above and, after considering the report, to inform the person on whom it was proposed that a notice to warn should be served of his decision with respect to the proposal.

(3) If at any time after serving a notification on a person under paragraph 6 above the Secretary of State decides not to serve on that person either the proposed notice to warn or that notice with modifications, the Secretary of State shall inform that person of the decision; and nothing done for the purposes of any of the preceding provisions of this Part of this Schedule before that person was so informed shall—

(*a*) entitle the Secretary of State subsequently to serve the proposed notice or that notice with modifications; or

(*b*) require the Secretary of State, or any person appointed to consider representations about the proposed notice, subsequently to do anything in respect of, or in consequence of, any such representations.

(4) Where a notification containing a draft of a proposed notice to warn is served on a person in respect of any goods, a notice to warn served on him in consequence of a decision made under sub-paragraph (2) above shall either be in the form of the draft or shall be less onerous than the draft.

9. The Secretary of State may revoke a notice to warn by serving on the person on whom the notice was served a notification stating that the notice is revoked.

PART III
GENERAL

10. (1) Where in a notification served on any person under this Schedule the Secretary of State has appointed a time for the making of oral representations or the examination of witnesses, he may, by giving that person such notification as the Secretary of State considers appropriate, change that time to a later time or appoint further times at which further representations may be made or the examination of witnesses may be continued; and paragraphs 2(4), 3(4) and 7(4) above shall have effect accordingly.

(2) For the purposes of this Schedule the Secretary of State may appoint a person (instead of the appointed person) to consider any representations or statements, if the person originally appointed, or last appointed under this sub-paragraph, to consider those representations or statements has died or appears to the Secretary of State to be otherwise unable to act.

11. In this Schedule—

"the appointed person" in relation to a prohibition notice or a proposal to serve a notice to warn, means the person for the time being appointed under this Schedule to consider representations about the notice or, as the case may be, about the proposed notice;

"notification" means a notification in writing;

"trader", in relation to a prohibition notice, means the person on whom the notice is or was served.

Property Misdescriptions Act 1991
(1991 c 29)

8–5101   1. Offence of property misdescription.   (1) Where a false or misleading statement[1] about a prescribed[2] matter is made in the course of an estate agency business or a property development business, otherwise than in providing conveyancing services, the person by whom the business is carried on shall be guilty of an offence under this section.

(2) Where the making of the statement is due to the act or default of an employee the employee shall be guilty of an offence under this section; and the employee may be proceeded against and punished whether or not proceedings are also taken against his employer.

(3) A person guilty of an offence under this section shall be liable[3]—

(a)   on summary conviction, to a fine not exceeding **the statutory maximum**, and

(b)   on conviction on indictment, to a fine.

(4) No contract shall be void or unenforceable, and no right of action in civil proceedings in respect of any loss shall arise, by reason only of the commission of an offence under this section.

(5) For the purposes of this section—

(a)   "false" means false to a material degree,

(b)   a statement is misleading if (though not false) what a reasonable person may be expected to infer from it, or from any omission from it, is false,

(c)   a statement may be made by pictures or any other method of signifying meaning as well as by words and, if made by words, may be made orally or in writing,

(d)   a prescribed matter is any matter relating to land which is specified in an order made by the Secretary of State,

(e)   a statement is made in the course of an estate agency business if (but only if) the making of the statement is a thing done as mentioned in subsection (1) of section 1 of the Estate Agents Act 1979 and that Act either applies to it or would apply to it but for subsection (2)(a) of that section (exception for things done in course of profession by practising solicitor or employee),

(f)   a statement is made in the course of a property development business if (but only if) it is made—

(i)   in the course of a business (including a business in which the person making the statement is employed) concerned wholly or substantially with the development of land, and

(ii)   for the purpose of, or with a view to, disposing of an interest in land consisting of or including a building, or a part of a building, constructed or renovated in the course of the business, and

(g)   "conveyancing services" means the preparation of any transfer, conveyance, writ, contract or other document in connection with the disposal or acquisition of an interest in land, and services ancillary to that, but does not include anything done as mentioned in section 1(1)(a) of the Estate Agents Act 1979.

(6) For the purposes of this section any reference in this section or section 1 of the Estate Agents Act 1979 to disposing of or acquiring an interest in land—

(a) in England and Wales and Northern Ireland shall be construed in accordance with section 2 of that Act, and

(b) *Scotland*.

(7) Power for Secretary of State to make Order.
[Property Misdescriptions Act 1991, s 1.]

---

1. A statement does not offend against s 1(1) of the Act unless it is a statement of existing fact. However, where house builders continued to show prospective purchasers the picture of the house type in which they were interested and invited them to view the show house itself, they were making a statement as to how they proposed to build the houses. That was their present intention and as such was a statement of fact which was false, since they knew full well that they could not build those houses with the relevant characteristics because of a change in the planning permission granted in their favour (*Lewin v Barratt Homes Ltd* (1999) 164 JP 182, [2000] Crim LR 323, DC).

1. See the Property Misdescriptions (Specified Matters) Order 1992, SI 1992/2834.

2. For procedure with respect to this offence which is triable either way, see ss 17A–22 of the Magistrates' Courts Act 1980 in PART I, MAGISTRATES' COURTS, PROCEDURE, ante.

8–5102   2. Due diligence defence.   (1) In proceedings against a person for an offence under section 1 above it shall be a defence[1] for him to show that he took all reasonable steps and exercised all due diligence to avoid committing the offence.

(2) A person shall not be entitled to rely on the defence provided by subsection (1) above by reason of his reliance on information given by another unless he shows that it was reasonable in all the circumstances for him to have relied on the information, having regard in particular—

(a) to the steps which he took, and those which might reasonably have been taken, for the purpose of verifying the information, and

(b) to whether he had any reason to disbelieve the information.

(3) Where in any proceedings against a person for an offence under section 1 above the defence provided by subsection (1) above involves an allegation that the commission of the offence was due—

(a) to the act or default of another, or

(b) to reliance on information given by another,

the person shall not, without the leave of the court, be entitled to rely on the defence unless he has served a notice under subsection (4) below on the person bringing the proceedings not less than seven clear days before the hearing of the proceedings or, in Scotland, the diet of trial.

(4) A notice under this subsection shall give such information identifying or assisting in the identification of the person who committed the act or default, or gave the information, as is in the possession of the person serving the notice at the time he serves it.
[Property Misdescriptions Act 1991, s 2.]

---

1. In *London Borough of Enfield v Castles Estate Agents Ltd* (1996) 160 JP 618, where the respondents advertised for sale a semi-detached property with a "one bedroom bungalow" although in fact there was no planning consent for the property to be used as such, it was held that the justices were entitled to find that the due diligence defence had been made out because the respondents' senior negotiator had assessed the situation based on his own experience and on what he had been told by the vendors.

8–5103   3. Enforcement.   The Schedule to this Act (which makes provision about the enforcement of this Act) shall have effect.
[Property Misdescriptions Act 1991, s 3.]

8–5104   4. Bodies corporate and Scottish partnerships.   (1) Where an offence under this Act committed by a body corporate is proved to have been committed with the consent or connivance of, or to be attributable to neglect on the part of, a director, manager, secretary or other similar officer of the body corporate or a person who was purporting to act in such a capacity, he (as well as the body corporate) is guilty of the offence and liable to be proceeded against and punished accordingly.

(2) Where the affairs of a body corporate are managed by its members, subsection (1) above applies in relation to the acts and defaults of a member in connection with his functions of management as if he were a director of the body corporate.

(3) Where an offence under this Act committed in Scotland by a Scottish partnership is proved to have been committed with the consent or connivance of, or to be attributable to neglect on the part of, a partner, he (as well as the partnership) is guilty of the offence and liable to be proceeded against and punished accordingly.
[Property Misdescriptions Act 1991, s 4.]

8–5105   5. Prosecution time limit.   (1) No proceedings for an offence under section 1 above or paragraph 5(3), 6 of the Schedule to this Act shall be commenced after—

(a) the end of the period of three years beginning with the date of the commission of the offence, or

(b) the end of the period of one year beginning with the date of the discovery of the offence by the prosecutor, whichever is the earlier.

(2) For the purposes of this section a certificate signed by or on behalf of the prosecutor and stating the date on which the offence was discovered by him shall be conclusive evidence of that fact; and a certificate stating that matter and purporting to be so signed shall be treated as so signed unless the contrary is proved.

[Property Misdescriptions Act 1991, s 5, as amended by SI 2003/1400, Sch 5.]

8–5106

Section 3

SCHEDULE

ENFORCEMENT

(*As amended by the Criminal Justice and Police Act 2001, Sch 2 and the Enterprise Act 2002, Sch 24.*)

Enforcement authority

1. (1) Every local weights and measures authority in Great Britain shall be an enforcement authority for the purposes of this Act, and it shall be the duty of each such authority to enforce the provisions of this Act within their area.

(2) *Northern Ireland.*

Powers of officers of enforcement authority

3. (1) If a duly authorised officer of an enforcement authority has reasonable grounds for suspecting that an offence under section 1 of this Act has been committed, he may—

(*a*) require a person carrying on or employed in a business to produce any book or document relating to the business, and take copies of it or any entry in it, or

(*b*) require such a person to produce in a visible and legible documentary form or from which it can readily be produced in a visible and legible form any information so relating which is stored in any electronic form and take copies of it,

for the purpose of ascertaining whether such an offence has been committed.

(2) Such an officer may inspect any goods for the purpose of ascertaining whether such an offence has been committed.

(3) If such an officer has reasonable grounds for believing that any documents or goods may be required as evidence in proceedings for such an offence, he may seize and detain them.

(4) An officer seizing any documents or goods in the exercise of his power under subparagraph (3) above shall inform the person from whom they are seized.

(5) The powers of an officer under this paragraph may be exercised by him only at a reasonable hour and on production (if required) of his credentials.

(6) Nothing in this paragraph—

(*a*) requires a person to produce a document if he would be entitled to refuse to produce it in proceedings in a court on the ground that it is the subject of legal professional privilege or, in Scotland, that it contains a confidential communication made by or to an advocate or a solicitor in that capacity, or

(*b*) authorises the taking possession of a document which is in the possession of a person who would be so entitled.

4. (1) A duly authorised officer of an enforcement authority may, at a reasonable hour and on production (if required) of his credentials, enter any premises for the purpose of ascertaining whether an offence under section 1 of this Act has been committed.

(2) If a justice of the peace, or in Scotland a justice of the peace or a sheriff, is satisfied—

(*a*) that any relevant books, documents or goods are on, or that any relevant information contained in a computer is available from, any premises, and that production or inspection is likely to disclose the commission of an offence under section 1 of this Act, or

(*b*) that such an offence has been, is being or is about to be committed on any premises,

and that any of the conditions specified in sub-paragraph (3) below is met, he may by warrant under his hand authorise an officer of an enforcement authority to enter the premises, if need be by force.

(3) The conditions referred to in sub-paragraph (2) above are—

(*a*) that admission to the premises has been or is likely to be refused and that notice of intention to apply for a warrant under that sub-paragraph has been given to the occupier,

(*b*) that an application for admission, or the giving of such a notice, would defeat the object of the entry,

(*c*) that the premises are unoccupied, and

(*d*) that the occupier is temporarily absent and it might defeat the object of the entry to await his return.

(4) In sub-paragraph (2) above "relevant", in relation to books, documents, goods or information, means books, documents, goods or information which, under paragraph 3 above, a duly authorised officer may require to be produced or may inspect.

(5) A warrant under sub-paragraph (2) above may be issued only if—

(*a*) in England and Wales, the justice of the peace is satisfied as required by that sub-paragraph by written information on oath,

(*b*) *Scotland,*

(*c*) *Northern Ireland.*

(6) A warrant under sub-paragraph (2) above shall continue in force for a period of one month.

(7) An officer entering any premises by virtue of this paragraph may take with him such other persons as may appear to him necessary.

(8) On leaving premises which he has entered by virtue of a warrant under sub-paragraph (2) above, an officer

shall, if the premises are unoccupied or the occupier is temporarily absent, leave the premises as effectively secured against trespassers as he found them.

(9) In this paragraph "premises" includes any place (including any vehicle, ship or aircraft) except premises used only as a dwelling.

Obstruction of officers

5. (1) A person who—

(a) intentionally obstructs an officer of an enforcement authority acting in pursuance of this Schedule,

(b) without reasonable excuse fails to comply with a requirement made of him by such an officer under paragraph 3(1)(a) above, or

(c) without reasonable excuse fails to give an officer of an enforcement authority acting in pursuance of this Schedule any other assistance or information which the officer may reasonably require of him for the purpose of the performance of the officer's functions under this Schedule,

shall be guilty of an offence.

(2) A person guilty of an offence under sub-paragraph (1) above shall be liable on summary conviction to a fine not exceeding **level 5** on the standard scale.

(3) If a person, in giving any such information as is mentioned in sub-paragraph (1)(c) above,—

(a) makes a statement which he knows is false in a material particular, or

(b) recklessly makes a statement which is false in a material particular,

he shall be guilty of an offence.

(4) A person guilty of an offence under sub-paragraph (3) above shall be liable[1]—

(a) on summary conviction, to a fine not exceeding the **statutory maximum**, and

(b) on conviction on indictment, to a fine.

Impersonation of officers

6. (1) If a person who is not a duly authorised officer of an enforcement authority purports to act as such under this Schedule he shall be guilty of an offence.

(2) A person guilty of an offence under sub-paragraph (1) above shall be liable[1]—

(a) on summary conviction, to a fine not exceeding the **statutory maximum**, and

(b) on conviction on indictment, to a fine.

Disclosure of information

7. *Revoked.*

Privilege against self-incrimination

8. Nothing in this Schedule requires a person to answer any question or give any information if to do so might incriminate him.

---

1. For procedure with respect to an offence triable either way, see the Magistrates' Courts Act 1980, ss 17A–22 in PART I, MAGISTRATES' COURTS, PROCEDURE, ante.

Timeshare Act 1992
(1992 c 35)

8–5110   1. Application of Act.   (1) In this Act—

(a) "timeshare accommodation" means any living accommodation, in the United Kingdom or elsewhere, used or intended to be used, wholly or partly, for leisure purposes by a class of persons (referred to below in this section as "timeshare users") all of whom have rights to use, or participate in arrangements under which they may use, that accommodation, or accommodation within a pool of accommodation to which that accommodation belongs, for a specified or ascertainable period of the year, and

(b) "timeshare rights" means rights by virtue of which a person becomes or will become a timeshare user, being rights exercisable during a period of not less than three years.

(2) For the purposes of subsection (1)(a) above—

(a) "accommodation" means accommodation in a building or in a caravan (as defined in section 29(1) of the Caravan Sites and Control of Development Act 1960)

(b) *Repealed.*

(3) Subsection (1)(b) above does not apply to a person's rights—

(a) *Repealed.*

(b) under a contract of employment (within the meaning of the Employment Rights Act 1996) or a policy of insurance,

or to such rights as may be prescribed.

(3A) For the purposes of sections 1A to 1E, 2(2B) to (2E), 3(3), 5A, 5B and 6A of this Act, subsection (1) above shall be construed as if in paragraph (*b*), after "become" there were inserted ", on payment of a global price,".

(4) In this Act "timeshare agreement" means an agreement under which timeshare rights are conferred or purport to be conferred on any person and in this Act, in relation to a timeshare agreement—

(*a*)   references to the offeree are to the person on whom timeshare rights are conferred, or purport to be conferred, and

(*b*)   references to the offeror are to the other party to the agreement,

and, in relation to any time before the agreement is entered into, references in this Act to the offeree or the offeror are to the persons who become the offeree and offeror when it is entered into.

(5) In this Act "timeshare credit agreement" means an agreement, not being a timeshare agreement, under which credit which fully or partly covers the price under a timeshare agreement is granted—

(*a*)   by the offeror, or

(*b*)   by another person, under an arrangement between that person and the offeror;

and a person who grants credit under a timeshare credit agreement is in this Act referred to as "the creditor".]

(6)   *Repealed.*

(6A)   No timeshare agreement or timeshare credit agreement to which this Act applies may be cancelled under section 67 of the Consumer Credit Act 1974.

(7)   This Act applies to any timeshare agreement or timeshare credit agreement if—

(*a*)   the agreement is to any extent governed by the law of the United Kingdom or of a part of the United Kingdom, or

(*b*)   when the agreement is entered into, one or both of the parties are in the United Kingdom.

(7A)   This Act also applies to any timeshare agreement if—

(*a*)   the relevant accommodation is situated in the United Kingdom,

(*ab*)   The relevant accommodation is situated in another EEA State and the parties to the agreement are to any extent subject to the jurisdiction of any court in the United Kingdom in relation to the agreement, or

(*b*)   when the agreement is entered into, the offeree is ordinarily resident in the United Kingdom and the relevant accommodation is situated in another EEA State.

(7B)   For the purposes of subsection (7A) above, "the relevant accommodation" means—

(*a*)   the accommodation which is the subject of the agreement, or

(*b*)   some or all of the accommodation in the pool of accommodation which is the subject of the agreement,

as the case may be.

(8)   *Northern Ireland.*

[Timeshare Act 1992, s 1 as amended by the Employment Rights Act 1996, Sch 1, SI 1997/1081 and SI 2003/1922.]

8–5111   2. Obligation for timeshare agreement to contain information on cancellation rights.   (1) A person must not in the course of a business enter into a timeshare agreement to which this Act applies as offeror unless the offeree has received the agreement and it complies with the following requirements.

(2)   The agreement must state under this section must state—

(*a*)   that the offeree is entitled to give notice of cancellation of the agreement to the offeror at any time on or before the date specified in the agreement, being a day falling not less than fourteen days after the day on which the agreement is entered into, and

(*b*)   that if the offeree gives such a notice to the offeror on or before that date he will (subject to section 5(9) of this Act) have no further rights or obligations under the agreement, but will have the right to recover any sums paid under or in contemplation of the agreement.

(2A)   If the agreement includes provision for providing credit for or in respect of the offeree, it must state that, notwithstanding the giving of notice of cancellation under section 5 or 5A of this Act, so far as the agreement relates to repayment of the credit and payment of interest, it will continue to be enforceable, subject to section 7 of this Act.

(2B)   Subsection (2C) below applies if—

(*a*)   the price under the timeshare agreement is covered fully or partly by credit granted under a timeshare credit agreement to which this Act applies,

(*b*)   the offeree is an individual, and

(*c*)   the accommodation which is the subject of the timeshare agreement is accommodation in a building, or some or all of the accommodation in the pool of accommodation which is the subject of the agreement is accommodation in a building.

(2C)   The timeshare agreement must state that, if the offeree gives to the offeror a notice as mentioned in subsection (2)(*b*) above or a notice of cancellation of the agreement under section 5A of this Act which has the effect of cancelling the agreement—

(*a*) the notice will also have the effect of cancelling the timeshare credit agreement,

(*b*) so far as the timeshare credit agreement relates to repayment of credit and payment of interest, it shall have effect subject to section 7 of this Act, and

(*c*) subject to paragraph (*b*) above, the offeree will have no further rights or obligations under the timeshare credit agreement.

(2D) Subsection (2E) below applies if—

(*a*) the offeree is an individual, and

(*b*) the accommodation which is the subject of the timeshare agreement is accommodation in a building, or some or all of the accommodation in the pool of accommodation which is the subject of the agreement is accommodation in a building.

(2E) The agreement must state that the offeree may have, in addition to the rights mentioned in subsection (2) above, further rights under section 5A of this Act to cancel the timeshare agreement.

(2F) The agreement must contain a blank notice of cancellation.

(3) A person who contravenes this section is guilty of an offence and liable[1]—

(*a*) on summary conviction, to a fine not exceeding the **statutory maximum**, and

(*b*) on conviction on indictment, to a fine.

(4) *Repealed.*

[Timeshare Act 1992, s 2, as amended by SI 1997/1081 and SI 2003/1922.]

---

1. For procedure in respect of this offence which is triable either way, see the Magistrates' Courts Act 1980, ss 17A–22 in PART I: MAGISTRATES' COURTS, PROCEDURE, ante.

8–5112 8. Defence of due diligence.   (1) In proceedings against a person for an offence under section 1A(6), 1B(2), 1C(3), 1D(6), 1E(5), 2(3) or 5B(2)] of this Act it shall be a defence for that person to show that he took all reasonable steps and exercised all due diligence to avoid committing the offence[1].

(2) Where in proceedings against a person for such an offence the defence provided by subsection (1) above involves an allegation that the commission of the offence was due—

(*a*) to the act or default of another, or

(*b*) to reliance on information given by another,

that person shall not, without the leave of the court, be entitled to rely on the defence unless he has served a notice under subsection (3) below on the person bringing the proceedings not less than seven clear days before the hearing of the proceedings or, in Scotland, the diet of trial.

(3) A notice under this subsection shall give such information identifying or assisting in the identification of the person who committed the act or default or gave the information as is in the possession of the person serving the notice at the time when he serves it.

[Timeshare Act 1992, s 8 amended by SI 1997/1081.]

---

1. This defence may also include due diligence in seeking to avoid the Act by promoting a scheme which falls outside the Act as well as due diligence in complying with the Act. Thus, on the facts of the case, the defendant should rightly have been acquitted where his scheme was based on leading counsel's advice that it was not caught by the legislation (*Popely and Harris v Scott* (2000) 165 JP 742, [2001] Crim LR 417).

8–5113 9. Liability of persons other than principal offender.   (1) Where the commission by a person of an offence under section 1A(6), 1B(2), 1C(3), 1D(6), 1E(5), 2(3) or 5B(2) of this Act is due to the act or default of some other person, that other person is guilty of the offence and may be proceeded against and punished by virtue of this section whether or not proceedings are taken against the first-mentioned person.

(2) Where a body corporate is guilty of an offence under section 1A(6), 1B(2), 1C(3), 1D(6), 1E(5), 2(3) or 5B(2) of this Act (including where it is so guilty by virtue of subsection (1) above) in respect of an act or default which is shown to have been committed with the consent or connivance of, or to be attributable to neglect on the part of, a director, manager, secretary or other similar officer of the body corporate or a person who was purporting to act in such a capacity, he (as well as the body corporate) is guilty of the offence and liable to be proceeded against and punished accordingly.

(3) Where the affairs of a body corporate are managed by its members, subsection (2) above applies in relation to the acts and defaults of a member in connection with his functions of management as if he were a director of the body corporate.

(4) Where an offence under section 1A(6), 1B(2), 1C(3), 1D(6), 1E(5), 2(3) or 5B(2) of this Act committed in Scotland by a Scottish partnership is proved to have been committed with the consent or connivance of, or to be attributable to neglect on the part of, a partner, he (as well as the partnership) is guilty of the offence and liable to be proceeded against and punished accordingly.

[Timeshare Act 1992, s 9 amended by SI 1997/1081.]

SCHEDULE 2
ENFORCEMENT

(*As amended by the Criminal Justice and Police Act 2001, Sch 2 and the Enterprise Act 2002, Sch 26.*)

Enforcement authority

8–5114 **1.** (1) Every local weights and measures authority in Great Britain shall be an enforcement authority for the purposes of this Schedule, and it shall be the duty of each such authority to enforce the provisions of this Act within their area.

(2) *Northern Ireland.*

Prosecutions

2. (1) (*Repealed*).

(2) Nothing in paragraph 1 above shall authorise a local weights and measures authority to bring proceedings in Scotland for an offence.

Powers of officers of enforcement authority

3. (1) If a duly authorised officer of an enforcement authority has reasonable grounds for suspecting that an offence under section 2 of this Act has been committed, he may—

(*a*) require a person carrying on or employed in a business to produce any book or document relating to the business, and take copies of it or any entry in it, or

(*b*) require such a person to produce in a visible and legible documentary form or from which it can readily be produced in a visible and legible form any information so relating which is stored in any electronic form and take copies of it,

for the purposes of ascertaining whether such an offence has been committed.

(2) If such an officer has reasonable grounds for believing that any documents may be required as evidence in proceedings for such an offence, he may seize and detain them and shall, if he does so, inform the person from whom they are seized.

(3) The powers of an officer under this paragraph may be exercised by him only at a reasonable hour and on production (if required) of his credentials.

(4) Nothing in this paragraph requires a person to produce, or authorises the taking from a person of, a document which he could not be compelled to produce in civil proceedings before the High Court or (in Scotland) the Court of Session.

4. (1) A person who—

(*a*) intentionally obstructs an officer of an enforcement authority acting in pursuance of this Schedule,

(*b*) without reasonable excuse fails to comply with a requirement made of him by such an officer under paragraph 3(1) above, or

(*c*) without reasonable excuse fails to give an officer of an enforcement authority acting in pursuance of this Schedule any other assistance or information which the officer has reasonably required of him for the purpose of the performance of the officer's functions under this Schedule,

is guilty of an offence.

(2) A person guilty of an offence under sub-paragraph (1) above is liable on summary conviction to a fine not exceeding **level 5** on the standard scale.

(3) If a person, in giving information to an officer of an enforcement authority who is acting in pursuance of this Schedule—

(*a*) makes a statement which he knows is false in a material particular, or

(*b*) recklessly makes a statement which is false in a material particular,

he is guilty of an offence.

(4) A person guilty of an offence under sub-paragraph (3) above is liable[1]—

(*a*) on summary conviction, to a fine not exceeding the **statutory maximum**, and

(*b*) on conviction on indictment, to a fine.

5. *Repealed.*

Privilege against self-incrimination

6. Nothing in this Schedule requires a person to answer any question or give any information if to do so might incriminate him.

---

1. For procedure in respect of this offence which is triable either way, see the Magistrates' Courts Act 1980, ss 17A–22 ante in PART I: MAGISTRATES' COURTS, PROCEDURE.

Tobacco Advertising and Promotion Act 2002

(2002 c 36)

8–5120 **1. Meaning of "tobacco advertisement" and "tobacco product".** In this Act—

"tobacco advertisement" means an advertisement—

( )(*a*) whose purpose is to promote a tobacco product, or

(*b*) whose effect is to do so, and

"tobacco product" means a product consisting wholly or partly of tobacco and intended to be smoked, sniffed, sucked or chewed.
[Tobacco Advertising and Promotion Act 2002, s 1.]

---

1. As to commencement of this Act, see s 22 and commencement orders made thereunder, post.

8–5121   2. Prohibition of tobacco advertising. (1) A person who in the course of a business publishes a tobacco advertisement, or causes one to be published, in the United Kingdom is guilty of an offence.

(2) A person who in the course of a business prints, devises or distributes in the United Kingdom a tobacco advertisement which is published in the United Kingdom, or causes such a tobacco advertisement to be so printed, devised or distributed, is guilty of an offence.

(3) Distributing a tobacco advertisement includes transmitting it in electronic form, participating in doing so, and providing the means of transmission.

(4) It is not an offence under subsection (1) for a person who does not carry on business in the United Kingdom to publish or cause to be published a tobacco advertisement by means of a website which is accessed in the United Kingdom; and, in that case, devising the advertisement or causing it to be devised is not an offence under subsection (2).
[Tobacco Advertising and Promotion Act 2002, s 2.]

8–5122   3. Advertising: newspapers, periodicals etc. If a newspaper, periodical or other publication ("the publication") containing a tobacco advertisement is in the course of a business published in the United Kingdom—

(*a*) any proprietor or editor of the publication is guilty of an offence,
(*b*) any person who (directly or indirectly) procured the inclusion of the advertisement in the publication is guilty of an offence, and
(*c*) any person who sells the publication, or offers it for sale, or otherwise makes it available to the public, is guilty of an offence.
[Tobacco Advertising and Promotion Act 2002, s 3.]

8–5123   4. Advertising: exclusions. (1) No offence is committed under section 2 or 3 in relation to a tobacco advertisement—

(*a*) if it is, or is contained in, a communication made in the course of a business which is part of the tobacco trade, and for the purposes of that trade, and directed solely at persons who—

(i) are engaged in, or employed by, a business which is also part of that trade, and
(ii) fall within subsection (2),

in their capacity as such persons,

(*b*) if it is, or is contained in, the communication made in reply to a particular request by an individual for information about a tobacco product, or
(*c*) if it is contained in a publication (other than an in-flight magazine) whose principal market is not the United Kingdom (or any part of it), or if it is contained in any internet version of such a publication.

(2) A person falls within this subsection if—

(*a*) he is responsible for making decisions on behalf of the business referred to in subsection (1)(*a*)(i) about the purchase of tobacco products which are to be sold in the course of that business,
(*b*) he occupies a position in the management structure of the business in question which is equivalent in seniority to, or of greater seniority than, that of any such person, or
(*c*) he is the person who, or is a member of the board of directors or other body of persons (however described) which, is responsible for the conduct of the business in question.

(3) The appropriate Minister may provide in regulations[1] that no offence is committed under section 2 in relation to a tobacco advertisement which—

(*a*) is in a place or on a website where tobacco products are offered for sale, and
(*b*) complies with requirements specified in the regulations.

(4) The regulations[1] may, in particular, provide for the meaning of "place" in subsection (3)(*a*).
[Tobacco Advertising and Promotion Act 2002, s 4.]

---

1. The Tobacco Advertising and Promotion (Point of Sale) Regulations 2004, SI 2004/765 have been made.

8–5124   5. Advertising: defences. (1) A person does not commit an offence under section 2 or section 3(*a*) or (*b*), in connection with an advertisement whose purpose is to promote a tobacco product, if he did not know, and had no reason to suspect, that the purpose of the advertisement was to promote a tobacco product.

(2) A person does not commit such an offence in connection with an advertisement whose effect is to promote a tobacco product if he could not reasonably have foreseen that that would be the effect of the advertisement.

(3) A person does not commit an offence under section 2(2) or 3(*a*) or (*b*) if he did not know, and had no reason to suspect, that the tobacco advertisement would be published in the United Kingdom.

(4) A person does not commit an offence under section 2(2) of distributing or causing the distribution of a tobacco advertisement, otherwise than as mentioned in section 2(3), if he did not know, and had no reason to suspect, that what he distributed or caused to be distributed was, or contained, a tobacco advertisement.

(5) In relation to a tobacco advertisement which is distributed as mentioned in section 2(3), a person does not commit an offence under section 2(2) of distributing it or causing its distribution if—

(*a*) he was unaware that what he distributed or caused to be distributed was, or contained, a tobacco advertisement,

(*b*) having become aware of it, it was not reasonably practicable for him to prevent its further distribution, or

(*c*) he did not carry on business in the United Kingdom at the relevant time.

(6) A person does not commit an offence under section 3(*c*) if he did not know, and had no reason to suspect, that the publication contained a tobacco advertisement.

[Tobacco Advertising and Promotion Act 2002, s 5.]

8–5125 6. Specialist tobacconists.   (1) A person does not commit an offence under section 2 if the tobacco advertisement—

(*a*) was in, or fixed to the outside of the premises of, a specialist tobacconist,

(*b*) was not for cigarettes or hand-rolling tobacco, and

(*c*) complied with any requirements specified by the appropriate Minister in regulations[1] in relation to tobacco advertisements on the premises of specialist tobacconists.

(2) A specialist tobacconist is a shop selling tobacco products by retail (whether or not it also sells other things) more than half of whose sales on the premises in question derive from the sale of cigars, snuff, pipe tobacco and smoking accessories.

(3) The sales referred to in subsection (2) are to be measured by sale price—

(*a*) during the most recent period of twelve months for which accounts are available, or

(*b*) during the period for which the shop has been established, if it has not been established long enough for twelve months' accounts to be available.

(4) "Shop", in subsections (2) and (3), includes a self-contained part of a shop; and, in that case, "premises" in subsections (1) and (2) means that self-contained part of the shop.

[Tobacco Advertising and Promotion Act 2002, s 6.]

---

1. The Tobacco Advertising and Promotion (Specialist Tobacconists) Regulations 2004, SI 2004/1277 have been made.

8–5126 7. Developments in technology.   The Secretary of State may by order amend any provision of this Act if he considers it appropriate to do so in consequence of any developments in technology relating to publishing or distributing by electronic means.

[Tobacco Advertising and Promotion Act 2002, s 7.]

8–5127 8. Displays.   (1) A person who in the course of a business displays or causes to be displayed tobacco products or their prices in a place or on a website where tobacco products are offered for sale is guilty of an offence if the display does not comply with such requirements (if any) as may be specified by the appropriate Minister in regulations.

(2) It is not an offence under subsection (1) for a person who does not carry on business in the United Kingdom to display or cause to be displayed tobacco products or their prices by means of a website which is accessed in the United Kingdom.

(3) The regulations may, in particular, provide for the meaning of "place" in subsection (1).

(4) The regulations must make provision for a display which also amounts to an advertisement to be treated for the purpose of offences under this Act—

(*a*) as an advertisement and not as a display, or

(*b*) as a display and not as an advertisement.

[Tobacco Advertising and Promotion Act 2002, s 8.]

8–5128 9. Prohibition of free distributions.   (1) A person is guilty of an offence if in the course of a business he—

(*a*) gives any product or coupon away to the public in the United Kingdom, or

(*b*) causes or permits that to happen,

and the purpose or effect of giving the product or coupon away is to promote a tobacco product.

(2) It does not matter whether the product or coupon accompanies something else, or is given away separately.

(3) No offence is committed under subsection (1) if—

(a) the business referred to in subsection (1) is part of the tobacco trade,

(b) the product or coupon is given away for the purposes of that trade,

(c) each person to whom it is given—

(i) is engaged in, or employed by, a business which is also part of the tobacco trade, and

(ii) falls within subsection (4), and

(d) the product or coupon is given to each such person in his capacity as such a person.

(4) A person falls within this subsection if—

(a) he is responsible for making decisions on behalf of the business referred to in subsection (3)(c)(i) about the purchase of tobacco products which are to be sold in the course of that business,

(b) he occupies a position in the management structure of the business in question which is equivalent in seniority to, or of greater seniority than, that of any such person, or

(c) he is the person who, or is a member of the board of directors or other body of persons (however described) which, is responsible for the conduct of the business in question.

(5) A person does not commit an offence under this section—

(a) where it is alleged that the purpose of giving the product or coupon away was to promote a tobacco product, if he did not know and had no reason to suspect that that was its purpose, or

(b) where it is alleged that the effect of giving the product or coupon away was to promote a tobacco product, if he could not reasonably have foreseen that that would be its effect.

(6) "Coupon" means a document or other thing which (whether by itself or not) can be redeemed for a product or service or for cash or any other benefit.

(7) The Secretary of State may make regulations providing for this section to apply to making products or coupons available for a nominal sum or at a substantial discount as it applies to giving them away.

(8) If regulations under subsection (7) provide for this section to apply to making products or coupons available at a substantial discount, the regulations must provide for the meaning of "substantial discount".

(9) The regulations may provide that this section is to apply in that case with such modifications (if any) specified in the regulations as the Secretary of State considers appropriate.

[Tobacco Advertising and Promotion Act 2002, s 9.]

8–5129   10. Prohibition of sponsorship.   (1) A person who is party to a sponsorship agreement is guilty of an offence if the purpose or effect of anything done as a result of the agreement is to promote a tobacco product in the United Kingdom.

(2) A sponsorship agreement is an agreement under which, in the course of a business, a party to it makes a contribution towards something, whether the contribution is in money or takes any other form (for example, the provision of services or of contributions in kind).

(3) A person does not commit an offence under this section—

(a) where it is alleged that the purpose of what was done as a result of the agreement was to promote a tobacco product in the United Kingdom, if he did not know, and had no reason to suspect, that that was its purpose, or

(b) where it is alleged that the effect of what was done as a result of the agreement was to promote a tobacco product in the United Kingdom, if he could not reasonably have foreseen that that would be its effect.

(4) A person does not commit an offence under this section if he did not know and had no reason to suspect that the contribution referred to in subsection (2) was made in the course of a business.

[Tobacco Advertising and Promotion Act 2002, s 10.]

8–5130   11. Brandsharing.   (1) The Secretary of State may by regulations make provision prohibiting or restricting, in such circumstances and subject to such exceptions as may be specified in the regulations, the use—

(a) in connection with any service or product (other than a tobacco product), of any name, emblem or other feature of a description specified in the regulations which is the same as, or similar to, a name, emblem or other feature so specified which is connected with a tobacco product, or

(b) in connection with any tobacco product, of any name, emblem or other feature of a description specified in the regulations which is the same as, or similar to, a name, emblem or other feature so specified which is connected with any service or product other than a tobacco product.

(2) Provision made by virtue of subsection (1) may prohibit or restrict only that use whose purpose is to promote a tobacco product, or whose effect is to do so.

(3) If regulations under this section provide for a prohibition or restriction to be subject to an exception, the regulations may also make such provision as the Secretary of State considers appropriate for a corresponding exception to have effect for the purposes of offences under section 2, 3, 8, 9 or 10.

(4) A person who contravenes a prohibition or restriction contained in regulations made under this section is guilty of an offence.

[Tobacco Advertising and Promotion Act 2002, s 11.]

8–5131   12. Television and radio broadcasting.   (1) In this section "the 1990 Act" means the Broadcasting Act 1990 (c 42) and "the 1996 Act" means the Broadcasting Act 1996 (c 55).

(2) This Act does not apply in relation to anything included in a service to which any of subsections (3) to (6) apply.

(3) This subsection applies to a service which—

(a) falls within section 2(1) of the 1990 Act (television services, etc regulated under Part 1 of the 1990 Act or Part 1 of the 1996 Act), and

(b) is not an additional service within the meaning of section 48(1) of the 1990 Act other than a teletext service.*

(4) This subsection applies to a local delivery service within the meaning of section 72 of the 1990 Act.*

(5) This subsection applies to a service falling within section 84 of the 1990 Act (independent radio services regulated under Part 3 of the 1990 Act or Part 2 of the 1996 Act) other than a digital additional service within the meaning of section 63(1) of the 1996 Act.*

(6) This subsection applies to a service provided by the British Broadcasting Corporation or Sianel Pedwar Cymru (the Welsh Authority referred to in section 56 of the 1990 Act).

[Tobacco Advertising and Promotion Act 2002, s 12.]

---

*Subsections (3) and (5) substituted and sub-s (4) repealed by the Communications Act 2003, Schs 17 and 19, from a date to be appointed.

8–5132   13. Enforcement.   (1) For the purposes of this Act "enforcement authority" means—

(a) in England and Wales, a weights and measures authority,

(b) in Scotland, a local weights and measures authority, and

(c) in Northern Ireland, a district council.

(2) It is the duty of an enforcement authority to enforce within its area the provisions of this Act and regulations made under it.

(3) The appropriate Minister may direct, in relation to cases of a particular description or a particular case, that any duty imposed on an enforcement authority in England and Wales or Scotland by subsection (2) shall be discharged by the appropriate Minister and not by the enforcement authority.

(4) The Department of Health, Social Services and Public Safety may direct, in relation to cases of a particular description or a particular case, that any duty imposed on an enforcement authority in Northern Ireland by subsection (2) shall be discharged by the Department and not by the enforcement authority.

(5) The Secretary of State may take over the conduct of any proceedings instituted in England and Wales by another person under any provision of this Act or regulations made under it.

(6) The Department of Health, Social Services and Public Safety may take over the conduct of any proceedings instituted in Northern Ireland by another person under any provision of this Act or regulations made under it.

(7) For the purposes of the trying of offences under this Act or regulations made under it—

(a) any such offence committed in England or Wales may be treated as having been committed in any place in England or Wales, so that any magistrates' court in England or Wales has jurisdiction to try the offence, and

(b) any such offence committed in Northern Ireland may be treated as having been committed in any place in Northern Ireland, so that any magistrates' court in Northern Ireland has jurisdiction to hear and determine a complaint charging the offence.

[Tobacco Advertising and Promotion Act 2002, s 13.]

8–5133   14. Powers of entry, etc.   (1) A duly authorised officer of an enforcement authority has the right, on producing, if so required, his written authority—

(a) at any reasonable hour to enter any premises, other than premises used only as a private dwelling house, which he considers it is necessary for him to enter for the purpose of the proper exercise of his functions under this Act,

(b) to carry out on those premises such inspections and examinations as he considers necessary for that purpose,

(c)   where he considers it necessary for that purpose, to require the production of any book, document, data, record (in whatever form it is held) or product and inspect it, and take copies of or extracts from it,

(d)   to take possession of any book, document, data, record (in whatever form it is held) or product which is on the premises and retain it for as long as he considers necessary for that purpose,

(e)   to require any person to give him such information, or afford him such facilities and assistance, as he considers necessary for that purpose.

(2)   A duly authorised officer of an enforcement authority may make such purchases and secure the provision of such services as he considers necessary for the purpose of the proper exercise of his functions under this Act.

(3)   A person is not obliged by subsection (1) to answer any question or produce any document which he would be entitled to refuse to answer or to produce—

(a)   in or for the purposes of proceedings in a court in England and Wales, where the question is asked or the document is required by a duly authorised officer of an enforcement authority in England and Wales,

(b)   in or for the purposes of proceedings in a court in Northern Ireland, where the question is asked or the document is required by a duly authorised officer of an enforcement authority in Northern Ireland,

(c)   in or for the purposes of proceedings in a court in Scotland, where the question is asked or the document is required by a duly authorised officer of an enforcement authority in Scotland.

(4)   If a justice of the peace is satisfied by any written information on oath that for the purpose of the proper exercise of the functions of an enforcement authority under this Act there are reasonable grounds for entry into any premises, other than premises used only as a private dwelling house, and—

(a)   that admission to the premises has been or is likely to be refused and that notice of intention to apply for a warrant under this subsection has been given to the occupier, or

(b)   that an application for admission, or the giving of such notice, would defeat the object of the entry or that the premises are unoccupied or that the occupier is temporarily absent and it might defeat the object of the entry to await his return,

the justice may by warrant signed by him, which shall continue in force until the end of the period of one month beginning with the date on which he signs it, authorise any duly authorised officer of an enforcement authority to enter the premises, if need be by force.

(5)   A duly authorised officer entering any premises by virtue of subsection (1) or of a warrant under subsection (4) may take with him when he enters those premises such other persons and such equipment as he considers necessary.

(6)   On leaving any premises which a duly authorised officer is authorised to enter by a warrant under subsection (4), that officer shall, if the premises are unoccupied or the occupier is temporarily absent, leave the premises as effectively secured against trespassers as he found them.

(7)   Where by virtue of subsection (1)(d) a duly authorised officer takes possession of any item, he shall leave on the premises from which the item was removed a statement giving particulars of what he has taken and stating that he has taken possession of it.

(8)   In the application of this section to Northern Ireland, the reference in subsection (4) to any information on oath shall be construed as a reference to any complaint on oath.

(9)   In the application of this section to Scotland, the reference in subsection (4) to a justice of the peace shall be construed as a reference to a sheriff.

(10)   Where a direction of the appropriate Minister has effect under section 13(3), this section and section 15 have effect, in relation to any case or case of a description specified in the direction, as if references to a duly authorised officer of an enforcement authority were references to a person acting on behalf of the appropriate Minister.

(11)   Where a direction of the Department of Health, Social Services and Public Safety has effect under section 13(4), this section and section 15 have effect, in relation to any case or case of a description specified in the direction, as if references to a duly authorised officer of an enforcement authority were references to a person acting on behalf of the Department.

(12)   Where—

(a)   the Secretary of State takes over any proceedings by virtue of section 13(5), or

(b)   the Department of Health, Social Services and Public Safety takes over the conduct of any proceedings by virtue of section 13(6),

this section and section 15 have effect, in relation to any case which is the subject of such proceedings, as if references to a duly authorised officer of an enforcement authority were references to a person acting on behalf of the Secretary of State or (as the case may be) the Department.

[Tobacco Advertising and Promotion Act 2002, s 14.]

8–5134   15. Obstruction, etc of officers.   (1)   A person who—

(a)   intentionally obstructs a duly authorised officer of an enforcement authority who is acting in the proper exercise of his functions under this Act, or (*b*) without reasonable cause fails to comply with any requirement made of him by such an officer who is so acting,

is guilty of an offence.

(2) A person who, in giving any information which is properly required of him by a duly authorised officer of an enforcement authority, makes a statement which is false in a material particular is guilty of an offence.

(3) A person does not commit an offence under subsection (2) if—

(*a*) he did not know the material particular was false, and

(*b*) he had reasonable grounds to believe that it was true.

[Tobacco Advertising and Promotion Act 2002, s 15.]

8–5135   16. Penalties.   (1) A person guilty of an offence under section 15(1) is liable on summary conviction to a fine not exceeding level 3 on the standard scale.

(2) A person guilty of an offence under or by virtue of any other provision of this Act is liable[1]—

(*a*) on summary conviction to imprisonment for a term not exceeding six months, or a fine not exceeding level 5 on the standard scale, or both, or

(*b*) on conviction on indictment to imprisonment for a term not exceeding 2 years, or a fine, or both.

[Tobacco Advertising and Promotion Act 2002, s 16.]

---

1. For procedure in respect of this offence which is triable either way, see the Magistrates' Courts Act 1980, ss 17A–22 in PART I: MAGISTRATES' COURTS, PROCEDURE, ante.

8–5136   17. Defences: burden of proof.   (1) This section applies where a person charged with an offence under this Act relies on a defence under any of sections 5(1) to (6), 6(1), 9(5), 10(3) and (4) and 15(3).

(2) Where evidence is adduced which is sufficient to raise an issue with respect to that defence, the court or jury shall assume that the defence is satisfied unless the prosecution proves beyond reasonable doubt that it is not.

[Tobacco Advertising and Promotion Act 2002, s 17.]

8–5137   18. Offences by bodies corporate and Scottish partnerships.   (1) If an offence under any provision of this Act committed by a body corporate is proved—

(*a*) to have been committed with the consent or connivance of an officer, or

(*b*) to be attributable to any neglect on his part,

the officer as well as the body corporate is guilty of the offence and liable to be proceeded against and punished accordingly.

(2) In subsection (1) "officer", in relation to a body corporate, means a director, manager, secretary or other similar officer of the body, or a person purporting to act in any such capacity.

(3) If the affairs of a body corporate are managed by its members, subsection (1) applies in relation to the acts and defaults of a member in connection with his functions of management as if he were a director of the body corporate.

(4) If an offence under any provision of this Act committed by a partnership in Scotland is proved—

(*a*) to have been committed with the consent or connivance of a partner, or

(*b*) to be attributable to any neglect on his part,

the partner as well as the partnership is guilty of the offence and liable to be proceeded against and punished accordingly.

(5) In subsection (4) "partner" includes a person purporting to act as a partner.

[Tobacco Advertising and Promotion Act 2002, s 18.]

8–5138   19. *Regulations*

8–5139   20. *Transitional provisions: sponsorship*[1]

---

1. The Tobacco Advertising and Promotion (Sponsorship) Transitional Regulations 2003, SI 2003/77 amended by SI 2003/1415 have been made.

8–5140   21. Interpretation.   In this Act—

"appropriate Minister" means—

(*a*) in relation to England, Wales and Northern Ireland, the Secretary of State, and

(*b*) in relation to Scotland, the Scottish Ministers,

"public" means the public generally, any section of the public or individually selected members of the public, "purpose" includes one of a number of purposes, and

"tobacco advertisement" and "tobacco product" have the meaning given in section 1,

and references to publishing include any means of publishing (and include, in particular, publishing by any electronic means, for example by means of the internet).

[Tobacco Advertising and Promotion Act 2002, s 21.]

8–5141 22. Commencement, short title and extent. (1) Apart from this section, this Act comes into force on such day as the appropriate Minister may by order[1] appoint.

(2) Different days may be appointed under subsection (1) for different provisions and for different purposes.

(3) Such an order may include such transitional provisions and savings as the appropriate Minister considers appropriate.

(4) This Act may be cited as the Tobacco Advertising and Promotion Act 2002.

(5) This Act extends to Northern Ireland.

[Tobacco Advertising and Promotion Act 2002, s 22.]

---

1. This Act has been brought into force in accordance with the following commencement orders: SI 2002/2865; (No 3 Amendment and Transitional Provisions) SI 2003/258; (No 6) SI 2003/396; (No 7) SI 2004/3138 (all provisions of the Act are in force by 31 July 2005 other than s 2 for the purposes of website advertising) (remaining commencement orders apply to Scotland).

Enterprise Act 2002[1]

(2002 c 40)

---

1. This Act is divided into 11 parts and 26 Schedules.

Part 1 of the Act establishes the Office of Fair Trading (OFT), prescribes its general functions and provides for arrangements for making super-complaints to the OFT. Part 2 establishes and provides for proceedings before the Competition Appeal Tribunal (CAT). Part 3 provides for a new merger regime, including the making and determination of references to the Competition Commission (CC), powers of enforcement, undertakings and orders, and various supplementary matters. Part 4 provides for new market investigations arrangements. It sets out, inter alia, the power of the OFT and the Secretary of State to make references to the CC. Part 5 deals with the CC and provides for its rules of procedure. Part 6 creates a new cartel offence. Part 7 deals with a number of miscellaneous competition provisions, including powers to disqualify directors who engage in serious competition breaches. Part 8 deals with procedures for enforcing certain consumer legislation, and various related matters. Part 9 provides for rules to govern the disclosure of specified information held by public authorities. Part 10 reforms insolvency law by providing a new regime for company administration and restricting the future use of administrative receivership, abolishing Crown preference, establishing a new regime for personal bankruptcy, and making changes to the operation of the Insolvency Services Account. Part 11 contains supplementary provisions.

Sections 279–282 came into force on Royal Assent. Subsequently, the following commencement orders have been made: Enterprise Act 2002 (Commencement No 1) Order 2003, SI 2003/765; Enterprise Act 2002 (Commencement No 2, Transitional and Transitory Provisions) Order 2003, SI 2003/7661; Enterprise Act 2002 (Commencement No 3, Transitional and Transitory Provisions and Savings) Order 2003, SI 2003/13973; Enterprise Act 2002 (Commencement No 4 and Transitional Provisions and Savings) Order 2003, SI 2003/2093, as amended by SI 2003/2332, SI 2003/3340; Enterprise Act 2002 (Commencement No 5 and Amendment) Order 2003, SI 2003/3340; Enterprise Act 2002 (Commencement No 6) Order 2004, SI 2004/1866; and SI 2004/1866; Enterprise Act 2002 (Commencement No 7 and Transitional Provisions and Savings) Order 2004, SI 2004/3233. All the provisions reproduced in this work are in force.

PART 3[1]

MERGERS

CHAPTER 5[2]

SUPPLEMENTARY

---

1. Part 3 contains ss 22–130.
2. Chapter 5 ss 96–130.

Investigation powers

8–5150 109. Attendance of witnesses and production of documents etc. (1) The Commission may, for the purpose of any investigation on a reference made to it under this Part, give notice to any person requiring him—

(*a*) to attend at a time and place specified in the notice; and

(*b*) to give evidence to the Commission or a person nominated by the Commission for the purpose.

(2) The Commission may, for the purpose of any investigation on a reference made to it under this Part, give notice to any person requiring him—

(*a*) to produce any documents which—

(i) are specified or described in the notice, or fall within a category of document which is specified or described in the notice; and

(ii) are in that person's custody or under his control; and

(b) to produce them at a time and place so specified and to a person so specified.

(3) The Commission may, for the purpose of any investigation on a reference made to it under this Part, give notice to any person who carries on any business requiring him—

(a) to supply to the Commission such estimates, forecasts, returns or other information as may be specified or described in the notice; and

(b) to supply it at a time and place, and in a form and manner, so specified and to a person so specified.

(4) A notice under this section shall include information about the possible consequences of not complying with the notice.

(5) The Commission or any person nominated by it for the purpose may, for the purpose of any investigation on a reference made to it under this Part, take evidence on oath, and for that purpose may administer oaths.

(6) The person to whom any document is produced in accordance with a notice under this section may, for the purpose of any investigation on a reference made to the Commission under this Part, copy the document so produced.

(7) No person shall be required under this section—

(a) to give any evidence or produce any documents which he could not be compelled to give or produce in civil proceedings before the court; or

(b) to supply any information which he could not be compelled to supply in evidence in such proceedings.

(8) No person shall be required, in compliance with a notice under this section, to go more than 10 miles from his place of residence unless his necessary travelling expenses are paid or offered to him.

(9) Any reference in this section to the production of a document includes a reference to the production of a legible and intelligible copy of information recorded otherwise than in legible form.

(10) In this section "the court" means—

(a) in relation to England and Wales or Northern Ireland, the High Court; and

(b) in relation to Scotland, the Court of Session.

[Enterprise Act 2002, s 109.]

8–5151 110. Enforcement of powers under section 109: general.   (1) Where the Commission considers that a person has, without reasonable excuse, failed to comply with any requirement of a notice under section 109, it may impose a penalty in accordance with section 111.

(2) The Commission may proceed (whether at the same time or at different times) under subsection (1) and section 39(4) or (as the case may be) 51(4) (including that enactment as applied by section 65(3)) in relation to the same failure.

(3) Where the Commission considers that a person has intentionally obstructed or delayed another person in the exercise of his powers under section 109(6), it may impose a penalty in accordance with section 111.

(4) No penalty shall be imposed by virtue of subsection (1) or (3) if more than 4 weeks have passed since the publication of the report of the Commission on the reference concerned; but this subsection shall not apply in relation to any variation or substitution of the penalty which is permitted by virtue of this Part.

(5) A person, subject to subsection (6), commits an offence if he intentionally alters, suppresses or destroys any document which he has been required to produce by a notice under section 109.

(6) A person does not commit an offence under subsection (5) in relation to any act which constitutes a failure to comply with a notice under section 109 if the Commission has proceeded against that person under subsection (1) above in relation to that failure.

(7) A person who commits an offence under subsection (5) shall be liable—

(a) on summary conviction, to a fine not exceeding the statutory maximum;

(b) on conviction on indictment, to imprisonment for a term not exceeding two years or to a fine or to both.

(8) The Commission shall not proceed against a person under subsection (1) in relation to an act which constitutes an offence under subsection (5) if that person has been found guilty of that offence.

(9) In deciding whether and, if so, how to proceed under subsection (1) or (3) or section 39(4) or 51(4) (including that enactment as applied by section 65(3)), the Commission shall have regard to the statement of policy which was most recently published under section 116 at the time when the failure concerned or (as the case may be) the obstruction or delay concerned occurred.

(10) The reference in this section to the production of a document includes a reference to the production of a legible and intelligible copy of information recorded otherwise than in legible form; and the reference to suppressing a document includes a reference to destroying the means of reproducing information recorded otherwise than in legible form.

[Enterprise Act 2002, s 110.]

8–5152   **111.** *Penalties*

8–5153   **117. False or misleading information.**   (1) A person commits an offence if—

(*a*)   he supplies any information to the OFT, OFCOM, the Commission or the Secretary of State in connection with any of their functions under this Part;

(*b*)   the information is false or misleading in a material respect; and

(*c*)   he knows that it is false or misleading in a material respect or is reckless as to whether it is false or misleading in a material respect.

(2) A person commits an offence if he—

(*a*)   supplies any information to another person which he knows to be false or misleading in a material respect; or

(*b*)   recklessly supplies any information to another person which is false or misleading in a material respect;

knowing that the information is to be used for the purpose of supplying information to the OFT, OFCOM, the Commission or the Secretary of State in connection with any of their functions under this Part.

(3) A person who commits an offence under subsection (1) or (2) shall be liable—

(*a*)   on summary conviction, to a fine not exceeding the statutory maximum;

(*b*)   on conviction on indictment, to imprisonment for a term not exceeding two years or to a fine or to both.

[Enterprise Act 2002, s 117, as amended by the Communications Act 2003, Sch 16.]

Other

8–5154   **125. Offences by bodies corporate.**   (1) Where an offence under this Part committed by a body corporate is proved to have been committed with the consent or connivance of, or to be attributable to any neglect on the part of—

(*a*)   a director, manager, secretary or other similar officer of the body corporate, or

(*b*)   a person purporting to act in such a capacity,

he as well as the body corporate commits the offence and shall be liable to be proceeded against and punished accordingly.

(2) Where the affairs of a body corporate are managed by its members, subsection (1) applies in relation to the acts and defaults of a member in connection with his functions of management as if he were a director of the body corporate.

(3) Where an offence under this Part is committed by a Scottish partnership and is proved to have been committed with the consent or connivance of a partner, or to be attributable to any neglect on the part of a partner, he as well as the partnership commits the offence and shall be liable to be proceeded against and punished accordingly.

(4) In subsection (3) "partner" includes a person purporting to act as a partner.

[Enterprise Act 2002, s 125.]

PART 4[1]
MARKET INVESTIGATIONS

---

1. Part 4 contains ss 131–184.

Investigation powers

8–5155   **174. Investigation powers of OFT.**   (1) The OFT may exercise any of the powers in subsections (3) to (5) for the purpose of assisting it in deciding whether to make a reference under section 131 or to accept undertakings under section 154 instead of making such a reference.

(2) The OFT shall not exercise any of the powers in subsections (3) to (5) for the purpose of assisting it as mentioned in subsection (1) unless it already believes that it has power to make such a reference.

(3) The OFT may give notice to any person requiring him—

(*a*)   to attend at a time and place specified in the notice; and

(*b*)   to give evidence to the OFT or a person nominated by the OFT for the purpose.

(4) The OFT may give notice to any person requiring him—

(*a*)   to produce any documents which—

(i)   are specified or described in the notice, or fall within a category of document which is specified or described in the notice; and

(ii)   are in that person's custody or under his control; and

(*b*)   to produce them at a time and place so specified and to a person so specified.

(5) The OFT may give notice to any person who carries on any business requiring him—

(*a*) to supply to the OFT such estimates, forecasts, returns or other information as may be specified or described in the notice; and

(*b*) to supply it at a time and place, and in a form and manner, so specified and to a person so specified.

(6) A notice under this section shall include information about the possible consequences of not complying with the notice.

(7) The person to whom any document is produced in accordance with a notice under this section may, for the purpose mentioned in subsection (1), copy the document so produced.

(8) No person shall be required under this section—

(*a*) to give any evidence or produce any documents which he could not be compelled to give or produce in civil proceedings before the court; or

(*b*) to supply any information which he could not be compelled to supply in evidence in such proceedings.

(9) No person shall be required, in compliance with a notice under this section, to go more than 10 miles from his place of residence unless his necessary travelling expenses are paid or offered to him.

(10) Any reference in this section to the production of a document includes a reference to the production of a legible and intelligible copy of information recorded otherwise than in legible form.

(11) In this section "the court" means—

(*a*) in relation to England and Wales or Northern Ireland, the High Court; and

(*b*) in relation to Scotland, the Court of Session.

[Enterprise Act 2002, s 174.]

8–5156   175. Enforcement of powers under section 174: offences.   (1) A person commits an offence if he, intentionally and without reasonable excuse, fails to comply with any requirement of a notice under section 174.

(2) A person commits an offence if he intentionally and without reasonable excuse alters, suppresses or destroys any document which he has been required to produce by a notice under section 174.

(3) A person who commits an offence under subsection (1) or (2) shall be liable—

(*a*) on summary conviction, to a fine not exceeding the statutory maximum;

(*b*) on conviction on indictment, to imprisonment for a term not exceeding two years or to a fine or to both.

(4) A person commits an offence if he intentionally obstructs or delays—

(*a*) the OFT in the exercise of its powers under section 174; or

(*b*) any person in the exercise of his powers under subsection (7) of that section.

(5) A person who commits an offence under subsection (4) shall be liable—

(*a*) on summary conviction, to a fine not exceeding the statutory maximum;

(*b*) on conviction on indictment, to a fine.

[Enterprise Act 2002, s 175.]

8–5157   176. Investigation powers of the Commission.   (1) The following sections in Part 3 shall apply, with the modifications mentioned in subsections (2) and (3) below, for the purposes of references under this Part as they apply for the purposes of references under that Part—

(*a*) section 109 (attendance of witnesses and production of documents etc);

(*b*) section 110 (enforcement of powers under section 109: general);

(*c*) section 111 (penalties);

(*d*) section 112 (penalties: main procedural requirements);

(*e*) section 113 (payments and interest by instalments);

(*f*) section 114 (appeals in relation to penalties);

(*g*) section 115 (recovery of penalties); and

(*h*) section 116 (statement of policy).

(2) Section 110 shall, in its application by virtue of subsection (1) above, have effect as if—

(*a*) subsection (2) were omitted; and

(*b*) in subsection (9) the words from "or section" to "section 65(3))" were omitted.

(3) Section 111(5)(*b*)(ii) shall, in its application by virtue of subsection (1) above, have effect as if—

(*a*) for the words "section 50 or 65, given" there were substituted "section 142, published or given under section 143(1) or (3)"; and

(*b*) for the words "(or given)", in both places where they appear, there were substituted "(or published or given)".

[Enterprise Act 2002, s 176.]

Other

8–5158 180. Offences. (1) Sections 117 (false or misleading information) and 125 (offences by bodies corporate) shall apply, with the modifications mentioned in subsection (2) below, for the purposes of this Part as they apply for the purposes of Part 3.

(2) Section 117 shall, in its application by virtue of subsection (1) above, have effect as if references to the Secretary of State included references to the appropriate Minister so far as he is not the Secretary of State acting alone and as if the references to OFCOM were omitted.

[Enterprise Act 2002, s 180, as amended by the Communications Act 2003, Sch 16.]

PART 6[1]

CARTEL OFFENCE

---

1. Part 6 contains ss 188–202.

8–5159 188. Cartel offence. (1) An individual is guilty of an offence if he dishonestly agrees with one or more other persons to make or implement, or to cause to be made or implemented, arrangements of the following kind relating to at least two undertakings (A and B).

(2) The arrangements must be ones which, if operating as the parties to the agreement intend, would—

(a) directly or indirectly fix a price for the supply by A in the United Kingdom (otherwise than to B) of a product or service,

(b) limit or prevent supply by A in the United Kingdom of a product or service,

(c) limit or prevent production by A in the United Kingdom of a product,

(d) divide between A and B the supply in the United Kingdom of a product or service to a customer or customers,

(e) divide between A and B customers for the supply in the United Kingdom of a product or service, or

(f) be bid-rigging arrangements.

(3) Unless subsection (2)(d), (e) or (f) applies, the arrangements must also be ones which, if operating as the parties to the agreement intend, would—

(a) directly or indirectly fix a price for the supply by B in the United Kingdom (otherwise than to A) of a product or service,

(b) limit or prevent supply by B in the United Kingdom of a product or service, or

(c) limit or prevent production by B in the United Kingdom of a product.

(4) In subsections (2)(a) to (d) and (3), references to supply or production are to supply or production in the appropriate circumstances (for which see section 189).

(5) "Bid-rigging arrangements" are arrangements under which, in response to a request for bids for the supply of a product or service in the United Kingdom, or for the production of a product in the United Kingdom—

(a) A but not B may make a bid, or

(b) A and B may each make a bid but, in one case or both, only a bid arrived at in accordance with the arrangements.

(6) But arrangements are not bid-rigging arrangements if, under them, the person requesting bids would be informed of them at or before the time when a bid is made.

(7) "Undertaking" has the same meaning as in Part 1 of the 1998 Act.

[Enterprise Act 2002, s 188.]

8–5160 189. Cartel offence: supplementary. (1) For section 188(2)(a), the appropriate circumstances are that A's supply of the product or service would be at a level in the supply chain at which the product or service would at the same time be supplied by B in the United Kingdom.

(2) For section 188(2)(b), the appropriate circumstances are that A's supply of the product or service would be at a level in the supply chain—

(a) at which the product or service would at the same time be supplied by B in the United Kingdom, or

(b) at which supply by B in the United Kingdom of the product or service would be limited or prevented by the arrangements.

(3) For section 188(2)(c), the appropriate circumstances are that A's production of the product would be at a level in the production chain—

(a) at which the product would at the same time be produced by B in the United Kingdom, or

(b) at which production by B in the United Kingdom of the product would be limited or prevented by the arrangements.

(4) For section 188(2)(d), the appropriate circumstances are that A's supply of the product or service would be at the same level in the supply chain as B's.

(5) For section 188(3)(*a*), the appropriate circumstances are that B's supply of the product or service would be at a level in the supply chain at which the product or service would at the same time be supplied by A in the United Kingdom.

(6) For section 188(3)(*b*), the appropriate circumstances are that B's supply of the product or service would be at a level in the supply chain—

(*a*) at which the product or service would at the same time be supplied by A in the United Kingdom, or

(*b*) at which supply by A in the United Kingdom of the product or service would be limited or prevented by the arrangements.

(7) For section 188(3)(*c*), the appropriate circumstances are that B's production of the product would be at a level in the production chain—

(*a*) at which the product would at the same time be produced by A in the United Kingdom, or

(*b*) at which production by A in the United Kingdom of the product would be limited or prevented by the arrangements.

[Enterprise Act 2002, s 189.]

8–5161   190. Cartel offence: penalty and prosecution.   (1) A person guilty of an offence under section 188 is liable—

(*a*) on conviction on indictment, to imprisonment for a term not exceeding five years or to a fine, or to both;

(*b*) on summary conviction, to imprisonment for a term not exceeding six months or to a fine not exceeding the statutory maximum, or to both.

(2) In England and Wales and Northern Ireland, proceedings for an offence under section 188 may be instituted only—

(*a*) by the Director of the Serious Fraud Office, or

(*b*) by or with the consent of the OFT.

(3) No proceedings may be brought for an offence under section 188 in respect of an agreement outside the United Kingdom, unless it has been implemented in whole or in part in the United Kingdom.

(4) Where, for the purpose of the investigation or prosecution of offences under section 188, the OFT gives a person written notice under this subsection, no proceedings for an offence under section 188 that falls within a description specified in the notice may be brought against that person in England and Wales or Northern Ireland except in circumstances specified in the notice.

[Enterprise Act 2002, s 190.]

8–5162   191. Extradition.   The offences to which an Order in Council under section 2 of the Extradition Act 1870 (c 52) (arrangements with foreign states) can apply include—

(*a*) an offence under section 188,

(*b*) conspiracy to commit such an offence, and

(*c*) attempt to commit such an offence.★

[Enterprise Act 2002, s 191.]

★**Repealed, except in relation to any extradition made or request for extradition received by the relevant UK authority on or before 31 December 2003.**

Criminal investigations by OFT

8–5163   192. Investigation of offences under section 188.   (1) The OFT may conduct an investigation if there are reasonable grounds for suspecting that an offence under section 188 has been committed.

(2) The powers of the OFT under sections 193 and 194 are exercisable, but only for the purposes of an investigation under subsection (1), in any case where it appears to the OFT that there is good reason to exercise them for the purpose of investigating the affairs, or any aspect of the affairs, of any person ("the person under investigation").

[Enterprise Act 2002, s 192.]

8–5164   193. Powers when conducting an investigation.   (1) The OFT may by notice in writing require the person under investigation, or any other person who it has reason to believe has relevant information, to answer questions, or otherwise provide information, with respect to any matter relevant to the investigation at a specified place and either at a specified time or forthwith.

(2) The OFT may by notice in writing require the person under investigation, or any other person, to produce, at a specified place and either at a specified time or forthwith, specified documents, or documents of a specified description, which appear to the OFT to relate to any matter relevant to the investigation.

(3) If any such documents are produced, the OFT may—

(*a*) take copies or extracts from them;

(*b*) require the person producing them to provide an explanation of any of them.

(4) If any such documents are not produced, the OFT may require the person who was required to produce them to state, to the best of his knowledge and belief, where they are.

(5) A notice under subsection (1) or (2) must indicate—

(*a*) the subject matter and purpose of the investigation; and

(*b*) the nature of the offences created by section 201.

[Enterprise Act 2002, s 193.]

8–5165   194. Power to enter premises under a warrant.   (1) On an application made by the OFT to the High Court, or, in Scotland, by the procurator fiscal to the sheriff, in accordance with rules of court, a judge or the sheriff may issue a warrant if he is satisfied that there are reasonable grounds for believing—

(*a*) that there are on any premises documents which the OFT has power under section 193 to require to be produced for the purposes of an investigation; and

(*b*) that—

(i) a person has failed to comply with a requirement under that section to produce the documents;

(ii) it is not practicable to serve a notice under that section in relation to them; or

(iii) the service of such a notice in relation to them might seriously prejudice the investigation.

(2) A warrant under this section shall authorise a named officer of the OFT, and any other officers of the OFT whom the OFT has authorised in writing to accompany the named officer—

(*a*) to enter the premises, using such force as is reasonably necessary for the purpose;

(*b*) to search the premises and—

(i) take possession of any documents appearing to be of the relevant kind, or

(ii) take, in relation to any documents appearing to be of the relevant kind, any other steps which may appear to be necessary for preserving them or preventing interference with them;

(*c*) to require any person to provide an explanation of any document appearing to be of the relevant kind or to state, to the best of his knowledge and belief, where it may be found;

(*d*) to require any information which is stored in any electronic form and is accessible from the premises and which the named officer considers relates to any matter relevant to the investigation, to be produced in a form—

(i) in which it can be taken away, and

(ii) in which it is visible and legible or from which it can readily be produced in a visible and legible form.

(3) Documents are of the relevant kind if they are of a kind in respect of which the application under subsection (1) was granted.

(4) A warrant under this section may authorise persons specified in the warrant to accompany the named officer who is executing it.

(5) In Part 1 of Schedule 1 to the Criminal Justice and Police Act 2001 (c 16) (powers of seizure to which section 50 of that Act applies), after paragraph 73 there is inserted—

"**73A. Enterprise Act 2002.**   The power of seizure conferred by section 194(2) of the Enterprise Act 2002 (seizure of documents for the purposes of an investigation under section 192(1) of that Act)."

[Enterprise Act 2002, s 194.]

8–5166   195. Exercise of powers by authorised person.   (1) The OFT may authorise any competent person who is not an officer of the OFT to exercise on its behalf all or any of the powers conferred by section 193 or 194.

(2) No such authority may be granted except for the purpose of investigating the affairs, or any aspect of the affairs, of a person specified in the authority.

(3) No person is bound to comply with any requirement imposed by a person exercising powers by virtue of any authority granted under this section unless he has, if required to do so, produced evidence of his authority.

[Enterprise Act 2002, s 195.]

8–5167   196. Privileged information etc.   (1) A person may not under section 193 or 194 be required to disclose any information or produce any document which he would be entitled to refuse to disclose or produce on grounds of legal professional privilege in proceedings in the High Court, except that a lawyer may be required to provide the name and address of his client.

(2) A person may not under section 193 or 194 be required to disclose any information or produce

any document in respect of which he owes an obligation of confidence by virtue of carrying on any banking business unless—

(a) the person to whom the obligation of confidence is owed consents to the disclosure or production; or

(b) the OFT has authorised the making of the requirement.

(3) In the application of this section to Scotland, the reference in subsection (1)—

(a) to proceedings in the High Court is to be read as a reference to legal proceedings generally; and

(b) to an entitlement on grounds of legal professional privilege is to be read as a reference to an entitlement by virtue of any rule of law whereby—

(i) communications between a professional legal adviser and his client, or

(ii) communications made in connection with or in contemplation of legal proceedings and for the purposes of those proceedings,

are in such proceedings protected from disclosure on the ground of confidentiality.
[Enterprise Act 2002, s 196.]

8–5168   197. Restriction on use of statements in court.   (1) A statement by a person in response to a requirement imposed by virtue of section 193 or 194 may only be used in evidence against him—

(a) on a prosecution for an offence under section 201(2); or

(b) on a prosecution for some other offence where in giving evidence he makes a statement inconsistent with it.

(2) However, the statement may not be used against that person by virtue of paragraph (b) of subsection (1) unless evidence relating to it is adduced, or a question relating to it is asked, by or on behalf of that person in the proceedings arising out of the prosecution.
[Enterprise Act 2002, s 197.]

8–5169   201. Offences.   (1) Any person who without reasonable excuse fails to comply with a requirement imposed on him under section 193 or 194 is guilty of an offence and liable on summary conviction to imprisonment for a term not exceeding six months or to a fine not exceeding level 5 on the standard scale or to both.

(2) A person who, in purported compliance with a requirement under section 193 or 194—

(a) makes a statement which he knows to be false or misleading in a material particular; or

(b) recklessly makes a statement which is false or misleading in a material particular,

is guilty of an offence.

(3) A person guilty of an offence under subsection (2) is liable—

(a) on conviction on indictment, to imprisonment for a term not exceeding two years or to a fine or to both; and

(b) on summary conviction, to imprisonment for a term not exceeding six months or to a fine not exceeding the statutory maximum, or to both.

(4) Where any person—

(a) knows or suspects that an investigation by the Serious Fraud Office or the OFT into an offence under section 188 is being or is likely to be carried out; and

(b) falsifies, conceals, destroys or otherwise disposes of, or causes or permits the falsification, concealment, destruction or disposal of documents which he knows or suspects are or would be relevant to such an investigation,

he is guilty of an offence unless he proves that he had no intention of concealing the facts disclosed by the documents from the persons carrying out such an investigation.

(5) A person guilty of an offence under subsection (4) is liable—

(a) on conviction on indictment, to imprisonment for a term not exceeding 5 years or to a fine or to both; and

(b) on summary conviction, to imprisonment for a term not exceeding six months or to a fine not exceeding the statutory maximum, or to both.

(6) A person who intentionally obstructs a person in the exercise of his powers under a warrant issued under section 194 is guilty of an offence and liable—

(a) on conviction on indictment, to imprisonment for a term not exceeding 2 years or to a fine or to both; and

(b) on summary conviction, to a fine not exceeding the statutory maximum.
[Enterprise Act 2002, s 201.]

8–5169A   202. Interpretation of sections 192 to 201.   In sections 192 to 201—

"documents" includes information recorded in any form and, in relation to information recorded otherwise than in a form in which it is visible and legible, references to its production include references to producing it in a form in which it is visible and legible or from which it can readily be produced in a visible and legible form;

"person under investigation" has the meaning given in section 192(2).

[Enterprise Act 2002, s 202.]

PART 9[1]
INFORMATION

1. Part 9 contains ss 237–247.

Restrictions on disclosure

8–5169B   237. General restriction.   (1) This section applies to specified information which relates to—

(*a*)   the affairs of an individual;

(*b*)   any business of an undertaking.

(2)   Such information must not be disclosed—

(*a*)   during the lifetime of the individual, or

(*b*)   while the undertaking continues in existence,

unless the disclosure is permitted under this Part.

(3)   But subsection (2) does not prevent the disclosure of any information if the information has on an earlier occasion been disclosed to the public in circumstances which do not contravene—

(*a*)   that subsection;

(*b*)   any other enactment or rule of law prohibiting or restricting the disclosure of the information.

(4)   Nothing in this Part authorises a disclosure of information which contravenes the Data Protection Act 1998 (c 29).

(5)   Nothing in this Part affects the Competition Appeal Tribunal.

(6)   This Part (except section 244) does not affect any power or duty to disclose information which exists apart from this Part.

[Enterprise Act 2002, s 237.]

8–5169C   238. Information.   (1) Information is specified information if it comes to a public authority in connection with the exercise of any function it has under or by virtue of—

(*a*)   Part 1, 3, 4, 6, 7 or 8;

(*b*)   an enactment specified in Schedule 14;

(*c*)   such subordinate legislation as the Secretary of State may by order[1] specify for the purposes of this subsection.

(2)   It is immaterial whether information comes to a public authority before or after the passing of this Act.

(3)   Public authority (except in the expression "overseas public authority") must be construed in accordance with section 6 of the Human Rights Act 1998 (c 42).

(4)   In subsection (1) the reference to an enactment includes a reference to an enactment contained in—

(*a*)   an Act of the Scottish Parliament;

(*b*)   Northern Ireland legislation;

(*c*)   subordinate legislation.

(5)   The Secretary of State may by order amend Schedule 14.

(6)   The power to make an order under subsection (5) includes power to add, vary or remove a reference to any provision of—

(*a*)   an Act of the Scottish Parliament;

(*b*)   Northern Ireland legislation.

(7)   An order under this section must be made by statutory instrument subject to annulment in pursuance of a resolution of either House of Parliament.

(8)   This section applies for the purposes of this Part.

[Enterprise Act 2002, s 238.]

1.   The following orders have been made under this provision: Enterprise Act 2002 (Part 9 Restrictions on disclosure of Information) (Amendment and Specification) Order 2003, SI 2003/1400; Enterprise Act 2002 (Part 9 Restrictions on Disclosure of Information (Amendment and Specification) (No 2) Order 2003, SI 2003/2580; Enterprise Act 2002 (Part 9 Restrictions on Disclosure of Information) (Specification) Order 2004, SI 2004/693 amended by SI 2005/281 and 2748.

Permitted disclosure

8–5169D   239. Consent.   (1) This Part does not prohibit the disclosure by a public authority of information held by it to any other person if it obtains each required consent.

(2) If the information was obtained by the authority from a person who had the information lawfully and the authority knows the identity of that person the consent of that person is required.

(3) If the information relates to the affairs of an individual the consent of the individual is required.

(4) If the information relates to the business of an undertaking the consent of the person for the time being carrying on the business is required.

(5) For the purposes of subsection (4) consent may be given—

(a) in the case of a company by a director, secretary or other officer of the company;

(b) in the case of a partnership by a partner;

(c) in the case of an unincorporated body or association by a person concerned in the management or control of the body or association.

[Enterprise Act 2002, s 239.]

8–5169E   240. *Community obligations*

8–5169F   241. Statutory functions.   (1) A public authority which holds information to which section 237 applies may disclose that information for the purpose of facilitating the exercise by the authority of any function it has under or by virtue of this Act or any other enactment.

(2) If information is disclosed under subsection (1) so that it is not made available to the public it must not be further disclosed by a person to whom it is so disclosed other than with the agreement of the public authority for the purpose mentioned in that subsection.

(3) A public authority which holds information to which section 237 applies may disclose that information to any other person for the purpose of facilitating the exercise by that person of any function he has under or by virtue of—

(a) this Act;

(b) an enactment specified in Schedule 15;

(c) such subordinate legislation as the Secretary of State may by order specify for the purposes of this subsection.

(4) Information disclosed under subsection (3) must not be used by the person to whom it is disclosed for any purpose other than a purpose relating to a function mentioned in that subsection.

(5) In subsection (1) the reference to an enactment includes a reference to an enactment contained in—

(a) an Act of the Scottish Parliament;

(b) Northern Ireland legislation;

(c) subordinate legislation.

(6) The Secretary of State may by order amend Schedule 15.

(7) The power to make an order under subsection (6) includes power to add, vary or remove a reference to any provision of—

(a) an Act of the Scottish Parliament;

(b) Northern Ireland legislation.

(8) An order under this section must be made by statutory instrument subject to annulment in pursuance of a resolution of either House of Parliament.

[Enterprise Act 2002, s 241.]

8–5169G   242. Criminal proceedings.   (1) A public authority which holds information to which section 237 applies may disclose that information to any person—

(a) in connection with the investigation of any criminal offence in any part of the United Kingdom;

(b) for the purposes of any criminal proceedings there;

(c) for the purpose of any decision whether to start or bring to an end such an investigation or proceedings.

(2) Information disclosed under this section must not be used by the person to whom it is disclosed for any purpose other than that for which it is disclosed.

(3) A public authority must not make a disclosure under this section unless it is satisfied that the making of the disclosure is proportionate to what is sought to be achieved by it.

[Enterprise Act 2002, s 242.]

8–5169H   243. *Overseas disclosures*

Offences

8–5169I   245. Offences.   (1) A person commits an offence if he discloses information to which section 237 applies in contravention of section 237(2).

(2) A person commits an offence if he discloses information in contravention of a direction given under section 243(4).

(3) A person commits an offence if he uses information disclosed to him under this Part for a purpose which is not permitted under this Part.

(4) A person who commits an offence under this section is liable—

(*a*) on summary conviction to imprisonment for a term not exceeding three months or to a fine not exceeding the statutory maximum or to both;

(*b*) on conviction on indictment to imprisonment for a term not exceeding two years or to a fine or to both.

[Enterprise Act 2002, s 245.]

PART 11[1]
SUPPLEMENTARY

1. Part 11 contains ss 273–280 and Schs 1–26.

8–5169J 273. Interpretation. In this Act—

"the 1973 Act" means the Fair Trading Act 1973 (c 41);
"the 1998 Act" means the Competition Act 1998 (c 41);
"the Commission" means the Competition Commission;
"the Director" means the Director General of Fair Trading; and
"the OFT" means the Office of Fair Trading.

[Enterprise Act 2002, s 273.]

8–5169K 279. Commencement. The preceding provisions of this Act shall come into force on such day as the Secretary of State may by order made by statutory instrument appoint; and different days may be appointed for different purposes[1].

[Enterprise Act 2002, s 279.]

1. At the date of going to press the following commencement orders had been made: Enterprise Act 2002 (Commencement No 1) Order 2003, SI 2003/765; Enterprise Act 2002 (Commencement No 2, Transitional and Transitory Provisions) Order 2003, SI 2003/7661; Enterprise Act 2002 (Commencement No 3, Transitional and Transitory Provisions and Savings) Order 2003, SI 2003/13973; Enterprise Act 2002 (Commencement No 4 and Transitional Provisions and Savings) Order 2003, SI 2003/2093, as amended by SI 2003/2332, SI 2003/3340; Enterprise Act 2002 (Commencement No 5 and Amendment) Order 2003, SI 2003/3340; Enterprise Act 2002 (Commencement No 6) Order 2004, SI 2004/1866; and SI 2004/1866; Enterprise Act 2002 (Commencement No 7 and Transitional Provisions and Savings) Order 2004, SI 2004/3233.

8–5169L 280. Extent. (1) Sections 256 to 265, 267, 269 and 272 extend only to England and Wales.

(2) Sections 204, 248 to 255 and 270 extend only to England and Wales and Scotland (but subsection (3) of section 415A as inserted by section 270 extends only to England and Wales).

(3) Any other modifications by this Act of an enactment have the same extent as the enactment being modified.

(4) Otherwise, this Act extends to England and Wales, Scotland and Northern Ireland.

[Enterprise Act 2002, s 280.]

8–5169M 281. *Short title*

Consumer Credit (Termination of Licences) Regulations 1976[1]

(SI 1976/1002, as amended by SI 1981/614 and SI 2004/3236)

Citation, commencement and interpretation

8–5170 1. (1) *Citation and commencement.*

(2) In these Regulations—

"the Act" means the Consumer Credit Act 1974;
"the court" means in relation to England and Wales the High Court or any county court having jurisdiction in bankruptcy and in relation to Scotland the Court of Session or any sheriff court having jurisdiction in bankruptcy;
"licence" means a standard licence and "licensee" shall be construed accordingly;
"period of deferment" means the period specified in Regulation 3(1) or (2), as the case may be;
"terminating event" means an event on the occurrence of which a licence is to terminate by section 37(1) of the Act or regulation 2 of these Regulations;

and except the contrary intention appears, other expressions used in these Regulations have the same respective meanings as in the Act.

(3) The Interpretation Act [1978] shall apply for the interpretation of these Regulations as it applies for the interpretation of an Act of Parliament.

---

1. Made under ss 22(1) (*a*), 37(2) and (3), 147(1), 182(2), and 189(1) of the Consumer Credit Act 1974.

Events on the occurrence of which licence is to terminate

8–5171   **2.** In addition to the events specified in section 37(1) of the Act and set out in the Schedule to these Regulations, the other events specified in that Schedule shall be events relating to a licensee on the occurrence of which the licence held by him is to terminate.

Deferment of termination of licence

8–5172   **3.** (1) Except as provided in paragraph (2) below, the termination of a licence by section 37(1) of the Act or under regulation 2 of these Regulations shall be deferred for a period of twelve months beginning with the date of the terminating event.

(2) The termination of a licence on the occurrence of the event specified in paragraph 11A of the Schedule shall be deferred for a period of one month beginning with the date of that event.

(3) The period referred to in paragraph (1) or (2) above, as the case may be, is hereinafter referred to as the "period of deferment".

Extension of licence period in certain cases

8–5173   **4.** (1) In this regulation references to the prescribed period of a licence are references to the period during which the licence covers such activities as are described in it, being the period prescribed for that purpose by regulation 2 of the Consumer Credit (Period of Standard Licence) Regulations 1975.

(2) Where, in relation to a licence, the period of deferment has effect such that it would expire after the end of the prescribed period of the licence, the said regulation 2 shall apply in relation to the licence as if the period so prescribed were one which began with the date mentioned in that regulation and ended with the expiration of the period of deferment.

Persons authorised to carry on the business of a licensee

8–5174   **5.** Where there occurs—

   (a)   any terminating event; or
   (b)   any subsequent event which would be a terminating event in relation to the licence if the licence was not already to terminate by virtue of an earlier terminating event;

any person specified in the Schedule in relation to that terminating event or that subsequent event, as the case may be, shall be authorised to carry on the business of the licensee under the licence during the period of deferment but subject to the conditions prescribed in regulation 6.

Conditions of authorisation

8–5175   **6.** A person other than the licensee authorised by regulation 5 to carry on the business of the licensee shall do so subject to the following conditions, that is to say—

   (a)   that he shall, within a period of two months beginning with the date on which he becomes authorised to carry on the business of the licensee, give notice in writing to the Director of—

      (i)   his name and the address from which he is or will be carrying on the business of the licensee;
      (ii)   the name and address of the licensee as specified in the licence;
      (iii)   the terminating event by virtue of which he is or will be carrying on the business of the licensee and the date of that event; and
      (iv)   the capacity in which he is or will be carrying on that business; and

   (b)   that if he fails to comply with (a) above, he shall not be authorised to carry on the business of the licensee after the expiry of the period specified in that paragraph until such time as he has given notice in writing to the Director of all the matters specified therein.

8–5176   **7.** Where any notice to be served on the Director under paragraph 11A of the Schedule is sent to him by an appropriate method, the service shall be deemed to be effected at the time at which the notice is delivered by an appropriate method at the proper address of the Director.

8–5177

(Regulations 2 and 5)   SCHEDULE

EVENTS RELATING TO A LICENSEE ON THE OCCURRENCE OF WHICH THE LICENCE IS TO TERMINATE: PERSONS AUTHORISED TO CARRY ON THE BUSINESS OF THE LICENSEE UNDER THE LICENCE

PART I

EVENTS RELATING TO THE UNITED KINGDOM OR TO SOME PART THEREOF, NOT BEING EVENTS RELATING TO NORTHERN IRELAND ONLY

Events relating to a licensee on the occurrence of which the licence is to terminate	Persons authorised to carry on the business of the licensee under the licence
Events relating to a licensee, being one individual, on the occurrence of which the licence is to terminate by virtue of section 37(1) of the Act:—	
1. Death of the licensee	(i) Any executor, administrator, trustee, receiver, manager, judicial factor or the official assignee of or appointed in relation to the estate of the deceased licensee or that part thereof which comprises the business carried on by the licensee under the licence; (ii) in a case where there is for the time being no person falling within sub-paragraph (i) above entitled to carry on the business of the licensee, any person entitled to apply for a grant of letters of administration or, in Scotland, confirmation.
2. The adjudication of the licensee as bankrupt or, in Scotland, the sequestration of his estate.	(i) The trustee in the bankruptcy or sequestration; (ii) the official assignee.
3. The licensee becoming a patient within the meaning of Part VIII of the Mental Health Act 1959 or, in Scotland, becoming incapable of managing his own affairs.	The person authorised under section 102 or 103 of that Act for the purpose of carrying on the business of the licensee or, in Scotland, the curator bonis or judicial factor appointed for that purpose.
Other events relating to a licensee on the occurrence of which the licence is to terminate by virtue of regulation 2 of these Regulations:—	
4. The approval by the court of a coposition or scheme of arrangement under section 16 of the Bankruptcy Act 1914 proposed by the licensee, being a composition or arrangement under or in pursuance of which the property of the licensee comprising the business carried on by him under the licence is assigned to a trustee.	The trustee appointed under or in pursuance of the composition or scheme of arrangement.
5. The registration under the Deeds of Arrangement Act 1914 of a deed of arrangement executed by the licensee, being a deed under or in pursuance of which the property of the licensee comprising the business carried on by him under the licence is assigned to a trustee.	The trustee appointed under or in pursuance of the deed of arrangement.
6. In Scotland, the granting by the licensee of a voluntary trust deed for behoof of creditors, being a deed providing for the property of the licensee comprising the business carried on by the licensee under the licence being transferred to a trustee.	The trustee appointed under or in pursuance of the trust deed.
7. In Scotland, the approval by the court under section 37 of the Bankruptcy (Scotland) Act 1913 of a deed of arrangement, being an arrangement providing for the property of the licensee comprising the business carried on by the licensee under the licence being transferred to a trustee.	The trustee appointed under or in pursuance of the deed of arrangement
8. In a case where all the members of a licensee which is a partnership or other incorporated body of persons are adjudged bankrupt, the last such adjudication.	(i) The trustee in the bankruptcy; (ii) the official assignee.
9. In Scotland, the sequestration of the estate of a licensee which is a firm.	The trustee in the sequestration.
10. The approval by the court of a composition or scheme of arrangement under section 16 of the Bankruptcy Act 1914 proposed by all the members of a licensee which is a partnership or other unincorporated body of persons, being a deed under or in pursuance of which the property of the licensee comprising the business carried on by it under the licence is assigned to a trustee.	The trustee appointed under or in pursuance of the deed of arrangement.

Events relating to a licensee on the occurrence of which the licence is to terminate	Persons authorised to carry on the business of the licensee under the licence
11. The registration under the Deeds of Arrangement Act 1914 of a deed of arrangement executed by all the members of a licensee which is a partnership or other unincorporated body of persons, being a deed under or in pursuance of which the property of the licensee comprising the business carried on by it under the licence is assigned to a trustee.	The trustee appointed under or in pursuance of the deed of arrangement
11A. The relinquishment of the licence by the licensee by notice in writing served on the Director and signed by or on behalf of the licensee, which:—	
(a) identifies the licence and the licensee;	The Licensee.
(b) states that he hereby relinquishes the licence;	
(c) states that he no longer requires the licence on account of his having ceased to engage in the activities for which that licence was in the activities for which that licence was issued, or his having become covered by another licence, as the case may be; and	
(d) is accompanied by the document constituting the licence or, where he is not in possession thereof, indicates the reasons why he is not in possession of it.	

PART II
EVENTS RELATING TO NORTHERN IRELAND ONLY

Furniture and Furnishings (Fire) (Safety) Regulations 1988[1]

SI 1988/1324 amended by SI 1989/2358 and SI 1993/207)

Citation and commencement

8–5330 **1.** (1) *Citation.*

(2) These Regulations shall come into force as follows:—

(a) this regulation and regulations 3 and 4 shall come into force on 1st November 1988;

(b) subject to subparagraph (i) below, regulation 6 (insofar as it relates to foam), 11 (insofar as it relates to foam-filled furniture), 12 (insofar as it relates to foam-filled furniture) and 13 (insofar as it relates to foam-filled furniture) and 15 shall come into force as regards the duties of manufacturers and importers, on 1st November 1988;

(c) regulation 2, insofar as it relates to the revocation of that part of the Upholstered Furniture (Safety) Regulations 1980 as amended by the Upholstered Furniture (Safety) (Amendment) Regulations 1983 which imposes requirements with respect to permanent labels; for certain furniture (insofar as those requirements apply to manufacturers and importers), shall come into force on 1st November 1988;

(d) regulation 7 (insofar as it relates to foam filling materials) shall come into force on 1st November 1988 and (insofar as it is not already in force) shall come into force on 1st March 1989;

(e) regulation 2, insofar as it relates to the revocation of that part of the Upholstered Furniture (Safety) Regulations 1980 as amended by the Upholstered Furniture (Safety) (Amendment) Regulations 1983 which imposes requirements with respect to display labels for certain furniture, shall come into force on 1st March 1989;

(f) subject to subparagraph (i) below, regulations 5, 6 (insofar as it relates to non-foam fillings), 11 (insofar as it relates to furniture), 12 (insofar as it relates to furniture) 13 and 15 shall come into force as regards the duties of manufacturers and importers (insofar as they are not already so in force) on 1st March 1989;

(g) subject to subparagraph (i) below, regulations 5, 6, 10, 11 (insofar as it relates to furniture), 12 (insofar as it relates to furniture) and 15 shall come into force as regards the duties of retailers on 1st March 1989;

(h)

   (i) regulation 8 (except in relation to those products mentioned in (ii) of this subparagraph) and regulations 9, 10, 11, 12, 13 and 15 (insofar as they are not already in force) shall come into force on 1st March 1990; and

   (ii) regulation 8 shall come into force in relation to cots, including carry-cots, playpens, prams and pushchairs and any other article of a like nature and use designed to contain a baby or small child, and high-chairs on 1st September 1990.

(i) insofar as regulations 5, 6, 10, 11, 12 and 13 apply to or in respect of—

(i) furniture (whether ready-assembled or in component form) which is ordinarily intended for private use in the open air but which is also suitable for use in a dwelling;

(ii) furniture which is ordinarily intended to be affixed to and form part of a caravan;

they shall come into force on 1st March 1990;

(*j*) regulation 14(2) shall come into force on 1st March 1993; and

(*k*) otherwise, on 1st March 1990.

---

1. Made by the Secretary of State under s 11 of the Consumer Protection Act 1987.

8–5331   2. *Revocation.*

Interpretation

8–5332   3. (1) In these Regulations—

"BS 3379" means the British Standard Specification for flexible urethane foam for loadbearing applications BS 3379: 1975 published by the British Standards Institution on 30th May 1975, as amended on 28th April 1978, subject to any further amendments made thereto and approved by the Secretary of State;

"BS 5651" means the British Standard Specification for cleansing and wetting procedures for use in the assessment of the effect of cleansing and wetting on the flammability of textiles and fabric assemblies BS 5651: 1978 published by the British Standards Institution on 29th December 1978 subject to any amendments made thereto and approved by the Secretary of State;

"BS 5852: Part 1" means the British Standard for fire tests for furniture BS 5852: Part 1: 1979 published by the British Standards Institution and which came into effect on 30th November 1979 subject to any amendments made thereto and approved by the Secretary of State;

"BS 5852: Part 2" means the British Standard for fire tests for furniture BS 5852: Part 2: 1982 published by the British Standards Institution and which came into effect on 31st August 1982 subject to any amendments made thereto and approved by the Secretary of State;

"BS 6807" means the British Standard Methods of test for the ignitability of mattresses with primary and secondary sources of ignition BS 6807: 1986 published by the British Standards Institution and which came into effect on 31st December 1986 subject to any amendments made thereto and approved by the Secretary of State;

"cushions" (except in (*a*) of the definition of "relevant ignitability test" in this paragraph and in the definition of "invisible part" in relation to covers and permanent covers in this sub-paragraph) means scatter cushions and cushions of the kind commonly used on the seats of wooden chairs;

"dwelling" includes any caravan, but does not include boats or any other vessels or motor vehicles;

"filling material" means any material used for filling or stuffing the upholstered parts of furniture or for filling, bulking-out or stuffing such articles as cushions, mattresses and pillows;

"furniture" means—

(*a*) furniture of any description which is ordinarily intended for private use in a dwelling and includes beds and divans (including the bases and headboards of both), sofa-beds, children's furniture, cots (including carry-cots, playpens, prams and pushchairs and any other article of a like nature and use designed to contain a baby or small child), cushions, high-chairs, mattresses (of any size) and pillows, but does not include bedding or floor coverings (including carpets and mats);

(*b*) furniture which is ordinarily intended for private use in the open air but which is also suitable for use in a dwelling; and

(*c*) any collection of components designed or intended to be assembled into any article of furniture defined in subparagraphs (*a*) and (*b*) above;

and "furniture" includes furniture mentioned in regulation 14(1) (second-hand furniture)—
in regulations 4, 7 and 15, from 1st November 1988;
in regulations 8(4), 9 and 14, from 1st March 1990;
in regulations 5, 6 and 8(1)–(3) from 1st March 1993.

"invisible part" in relation to covers and permanent covers means—

(*a*) any part of the cover on that part of the furniture on which any back, arm or seat cushions are intended to rest;

(*b*) the underside or reverse side of any seat or back cushions which are not designed to be reversible;

(*c*) the underside of any arm cushions which are not designed to be reversible and which are secured in such a way that they cannot be displaced in normal use; and

(*d*) the dust cover on the underside of the article of furniture.

and "visible part" in relation to covers and permanent covers means any part of the cover other than an invisible part.

"relevant ignitability test" in relation to any filling which—

(a) consists solely of polyurethane foam in slab or cushion form means the test specified in Part I of Schedule 1 to these Regulations;

(b) consists solely of polyurethane foam in crumb form means the test specified in Part II of Schedule 1 to these Regulations;

(c) consists solely of latex rubber foam means the test specified in Part III of Schedule 1 to these Regulations;

(d) consists of a single filling material other than the materials mentioned in paragraph (a), (b) or (c) above means the test specified in Part I of Schedule 2 to these Regulations;

(e) consists of more than one filling material means either:—

   (i) the test specified in Part I of Schedule 2 to these Regulations for each individual filling material tested separately; or

   (ii) the appropriate test specified in Part II, III or IV of that Schedule for the filling material tested as a composite:

provided that if the filling material includes foam of any of the kinds mentioned in paragraph (a), (b) or (c) above, the relevant ignitability test for that part of the filling which consists of such foam shall be the test (or tests) specified in paragraph (a), (b) or (c), as the case may be;

"supply", where the context so admits, includes offering and agreeing to supply and exposing and possessing for supply, and cognate expressions shall be construed accordingly.

(2) For the purposes of these Regulations any references in BS 3379, BS 5651, BS 5852: Part 1, BS 5852: Part 2 or BS 6807 to any other British Standards shall be construed as references to those other British Standards as they had effect on 28th April 1978, 29th December 1978, 30th November 1979, 31st August 1982 and 31st December 1986 respectively or as they had effect on those dates respectively subject to amendments made to them by the British Standards Institution and approved by the Secretary of State.

Exclusion of goods made before 1950 and of supply of materials for re-upholstery of furniture made before that date and of goods for export

8–5333   **4.** The requirements of these Regulations do not apply—

(a) in relation to the supply of any goods manufactured before 1 January 1950;

(b) in relation to the supply of materials when the person supplying them knows or has reasonable cause to believe that they will be used for re-covering or re-upholstering furniture manufactured before 1st January 1950; or

(c) in any case where the person supplying goods to which those requirements relate knows or has reasonable cause to believe that the goods will not be used in the United Kingdom.

Upholstery

8–5334   **5.** (1) Subject to paragraph 2 below no furniture to which this regulation applies shall include upholstery which does not pass the cigarette test in Part I of Schedule 4 in these Regulations.

(2) An invisible part of the cover on any part of furniture which includes upholstery shall not be required to pass the test in paragraph (1) above if that upholstery (including such invisible part of the cover) passes the cigarette test in Part II of Schedule 4 to these Regulations.

(3) This regulation applies to all furniture (except mattresses, bed-bases, pillows and cushions).

Filling material

8–5335   **6.** (1) Subject to paragraphs (3) and (4) below, no furniture shall include any filling material which fails the relevant ignitability test.

(2) No furniture shall include as filling any foam in crumb form unless both—

(a) the foam from which the crumb is derived passes the ignitability test specified in Part I of Schedule 1 to these Regulations; and

(b) the foam in crumb form itself passes the ignitability test specified in Part II of that Schedule.

(3) A cushion may include filling material which does not pass the ignitability test specified in Part I or Part II (or both such parts) of Schedule 2 to these Regulations if the cushion has a primary cover and, with that cover, passes the ignitability test in Part III of that Schedule.

(4) A pillow may include filling material which does not pass the ignitability test specified in Part I or Part II (or both such parts) of Schedule 2 to these Regulations if the pillow, when tested with its primary cover, passes the ignitability test in Part III of that Schedule.

Loose fillings

8–5336   **7.** No person shall supply—

(a) any polyurethane foam in slab or cushion form which fails the test specified in Part I of Schedule 1 to these Regulations;

(b) any foam in crumb form which may not be included in furniture by virtue of regulation 6(2) above; or

(c) any latex rubber foam which fails the test specified in Part III of Schedule 1 to these Regulations,

in any case where he knows or has reasonable cause to believe that the material will be used—

(i) for filling a cushion or a pillow; or
(ii) for the purpose of upholstering or re-upholstering furniture.

(2) Without prejudice to paragraph (1) above, no person shall supply any other filling material which fails test (d) or (e) in the definition of relevant ignitability test in regulation 3(1) above in any case where he knows or has reasonable cause to believe that the material will be used, otherwise than in the course of business, for a purpose mentioned in sub-paragraphs (i) or (ii) of paragraph (1) above.

Permanent Covers

8–5337　8. (1) Subject to paragraph (2) below, if furniture specified in paragraph (5)(b) below which contains filling material is supplied with a cover on it (whether or not the cover is over the filling material), any visible part of the cover shall pass the match test in Part I of Schedule 5 to these Regulations and any invisible part of the cover shall pass the match test in Part III of that Schedule.

(2) Where furniture is supplied with a cover on it and there is between it and any part of the cover an interliner which passes the test in Schedule 3 to these Regulations then provided that such part of the cover is made of a relevant material it need not pass the match test which would otherwise have been applicable to it under paragraph (1) above.

(3) Subject to paragraph (4) below, no person shall supply any cover or fabric knowing or having reasonable cause to believe that it will be used to provide or replace—

(a) a visible part of the permanent cover of any furniture specified in paragraph (5)(b) below which contains filling material or
(b) an invisible part of such a permanent cover,

unless the cover or fabric passes, in the case of (a) the match test in Part I of Schedule 5 to these Regulations or, in the case of (b), the match test in Part III of that Schedule.

(4) Paragraph (3) above does not apply if the fabric or cover supplied is made of a relevant material and the person who supplies it knows or has reasonable cause to believe that it will be used to replace or provide any part (whether visible or invisible) of the permanent cover on furniture and that there is or will be between the furniture and such part an interliner which passes the test in Schedule 3 to these Regulations.

(5) In this regulation—

(a) a "relevant material" means a material containing at least 75 per cent by weight of cotton, flax, viscose, modal, silk or wool, used separately or together and not coated with polyurethane or a polyurethane preparation; and
(b) "furniture" means any furniture other than the following: mattresses, bed-bases, pillows, cushions and insulated bags designed for carrying infants under the age of six months.

Covers other than permanent covers

8–5338　9. (1) Loose covers (other than stretch covers) for any furniture specified in paragraph (3) below shall pass the match test in Part I of Schedule 5 to these Regulations.

(2) Stretch covers for any furniture specified in paragraph (3) below shall pass the match test in Part II of that Schedule.

(3) In this regulation "furniture" means any furniture other than mattresses, bed-bases, pillows and cushions.

LABELLING REQUIREMENTS

Display labels

8–5339　10. (1) There shall be attached to furniture to which Schedule 6 to these Regulations applies and which is exposed for supply by retail the appropriate display label specified in that Schedule.

(2) The label mentioned in paragraph (1) above shall be so attached to the furniture as to be clearly visible to anyone inspecting the furniture and to enable him to read both the front and the back of the label with as little inconvenience as is reasonably practicable.

Permanent labels

8–5340　11. Furniture and covers to which Schedule 7 to these Regulations applies shall bear the permanent labelling specified in Part II or Part III of Schedule 7 to these Regulations in accordance with the provisions of Part II or Part III of that Schedule, as the case may be, (and if the furniture or cover does not bear the permanent labelling specified in Part II of Schedule 7 the requirements of regulation 12 below shall also be complied with in relation to such furniture or cover).

Requirement to give information

8–5341　12. (1) This regulation applies to any person who supplies or has supplied within the period of five years (or, if shorter, so much of that period as falls after 1st November 1988) immediately prior to his being required to give the information in question any furniture or cover to which Schedule 7 to these Regulations applies in relation to which the requirements of Part III of Schedule 7 to these Regulations and not those of Part II of that Schedule are satisfied.

(2) the information which may be required by paragraph (4) below is the following information in respect of the furniture or cover specified in paragraph (1) above—

    (a) the name and the postal code of the address of the principal place of business of the manufacturer or importer who first supplied the article in the United Kingdom;

    (b) the date on which the article was manufactured or imported (in its finished form) into the United Kingdom;

    (c) the description of all the filling materials included in the article;

    (d) the description of all the covering materials included in the article.

(3) The information specified in paragraph (2) above need not be given in relation to—

    (a) cushions and pillows (except for information required by subparagraphs (a) and (c) of paragraph (2) above);

    (b) cots, carry-cots, playpens, prams and pushchairs (except for information required by subparagraphs (a), (c) and (d) of paragraph (2) above);

    (c) any other article similar in its nature and use to any article in subparagraph (b) of this paragraph and designed to carry a baby or small child (except for information required by subparagraphs (a), (c) and (d) of paragraph (2) above);

    (d) covers (except for information required by subparagraphs (a) and (d) of paragraph (2) above).

(4) Any person to whom this regulation applies shall give to an enforcement authority, or any of its officers, the information specified in paragraph (2) above on his being required to give such information at a reasonable time.

First suppliers: requirement to give information

8–5342   **13.** (1) Any person to whom paragraph (3) below applies shall give to an enforcement authority or any of its officers such information as it or he may reasonably require for the purpose of enabling the authority to enforce any of the requirements of these Regulations relating to any furniture other than mattresses, bed-bases, pillows and cushions.

(2) Without prejudice to the generality of paragraph (1) above, information may be required to be given, in accordance with that paragraph, relating to any of the following matters, that is to say—

    (a) the results of any test prescribed by these Regulations carried out on the furniture in question or any of its components;

    (b) the means by which those results are attributed to furniture or components of a particular description or batch;

    (c) the correspondence of any records with labels, batch numbers of marks appearing on or relating to any goods.

(3) This paragraph applies to any manufacturer or importer who supplies or has supplied within the period of five years (or, if shorter, so much of that period as falls after 1st November 1988) immediately prior to his being required to give the information in question any furniture specified in paragraph (1) above.

Second-hand furniture

8–5343   **14.** (1) Subject to paragraph (1A) below this regulation applies to furniture which has previously been supplied (whether before or after 1st March 1990, provided that it is not excluded by regulation 4 above, and whether in the United Kingdom or elsewhere) to any person who acquired it otherwise than for the purposes of a business of dealing in furniture.

(1A) Until 31st December 1996 paragraph (2) below does not apply to any furniture which is hired out at the same time as and in connection with the letting of accommodation if that furniture has, before being so hired out, been hired out in connection with the letting of the same accommodation.

(2) Furniture to which this regulation applies shall satisfy the requirements of regulations 5, 6 and 8(1) to (2) subject to the exceptions to those requirements for certain furniture specified in those regulations.

(3) Subject to paragraph (4) below, no person shall supply any furniture to which this regulation applies in the period before 1st March 1993 unless:—

    (a) in the case of furniture to which regulation 3(1) of the Upholstered Furniture (Safety) Regulations 1980 as amended by the Upholstered Furniture (Safety) (Amendment) Regulations 1983 applied, any visible part of any cover on the furniture passes the cigarette test in Part I of Schedule 4 to these Regulations;

    (b) there is attached to the furniture the display label specified in Schedule 8 to these Regulations so as to be clearly visible to anyone inspecting the furniture and to enable him to read both the front and the back of the label with as little difficulty as is reasonably practicable.

(4) The display label specified in Schedule 8 to these Regulations need not be attached to the

furniture if the furniture meets all the requirements of these Regulations which would have had to be met if paragraph 2 of this regulation had been in force.

Prohibition on supply

8–5344   **15.** (1) Subject to paragraph (2) below, no person shall supply any furniture or other article in respect of which any of the requirements of these Regulations is not satisfied.

(2) Paragraph (1) above does not apply where the furniture or other article is supplied as part of the fixtures and fittings of a caravan which is being supplied at the same time and which has previously been supplied (whether before or after 1st November 1988 and whether in the United Kingdom or elsewhere) to any person who acquired it otherwise than for the purposes of a business of dealing in caravans.

8–5345   SCHEDULE 1

PART I

Ignitability test for polyurethane foam in slab or cushion form

PART II

Ignitability test for polyurethane foam in crumb form

PART III

Ignitability test for latex rubber foam

8–5346   SCHEDULE 2

PART I

Ignitability test for non-foam filling materials singly

PART II

Ignitability test for composite fillings for furniture other than mattresses, bed-bases, cushions and pillows

PART III

Composite test for ignitability of pillows and cushions with primary covers

PART IV

Ignitability test for composite fillings of mattresses and bed-bases

8–5347   SCHEDULE 3

Ignition resistance test for interliner

8–5348   SCHEDULE 4

The Cigarette test

8–5349   SCHEDULE 5

The Match test

8–5350   SCHEDULE 6

Labels

8–5351   SCHEDULE 7

Permanent labelling requirements

8–5352   SCHEDULE 8

Display labels for second-hand furniture

Food Imitations (Safety) Regulations 1989[1]
(SI 1989/1291)

8–5454   **1.** *Citation and commencement.*

---

1. Made by the Secretary of State under s 11(5) of the Consumer Protection Act 1987.

8–5455   **2.** *Revocations.*

8–5456   **3.** In these Regulations—

"food" means food for human consumption and includes drink, chewing gum and other products of a like nature and use and articles and substances used as ingredients in the preparation of food or drink or of such products;

"goods" do not include those mentioned in section 11(7)(*a*) to (*d*) of the Consumer Protection Act 1987 or—

    (*a*) marbles;
    (*b*) products bona fide intended for use to represent food in a dolls' house or other model scene or setting; or
    (*c*) anything consisting entirely of articles or substances used as ingredients in the preparation of food.

8–5457   **4.** No person shall supply, offer to supply, agree to supply, expose for supply or possess for supply any manufactured goods which are ordinarily intended for private use and are not food but which—

    (*a*) have a form, odour, colour, appearance, packaging, labelling, volume or size which is likely to cause persons, in particular, children to confuse them with food and in consequence to place them in their mouths or suck them or swallow them; and
    (*b*) where such action as is mentioned in (*a*) above is taken in relation to them, may cause death or personal injury.

Price Indications (Method of Payment) Regulations 1991[1]
(SI 1991/199)

8–5460   **1.** *Citation and commencement.*

---

1. Made by the Secretary of State, in exercise of the powers conferred on him by section 26 of the Consumer Protection Act 1987.

Interpretation and application

8–5461   **2.** (1) In these Regulations—

"the Act" means the Consumer Protection Act 1987;
"goods" do not include fuel of any kind supplied for the propulsion of a vehicle intended or adapted for use on roads; and
"the indicated price" has the meaning assigned to it in regulation 3(1).

(2) Subject to paragraph (3) below, in these Regulations, in relation to any goods, services, accommodation or facilities, "price" has the meaning assigned to it in head (a) of the definition of "price" in section 20(6) of the Act (that is to say, the aggregate of the sums required to be paid by a consumer for or otherwise in respect of the supply of the goods or the provision of the services, accommodation or facilities).

(3) In the case of an indication of a price within the meaning of head (b) of the definition of "price" in section 20(6) of the Act (that is to say, any method which will be, or has been, applied for the purpose of determining the aggregate mentioned in paragraph (2) above) these regulations shall have effect as if references to a price were to the monetary amount or to all the monetary amounts included in such a method.

(4) For the purposes of these Regulations—

    (*a*) an indication of the price at which goods will be or are available by way of hire-purchase agreement, conditional sale agreement or credit-sale agreement shall not be treated as an indication of a price;
    (*b*) the entry into, or making of payments under, such an agreement shall not be treated as a method of payment, and
    (*c*) payment in a currency other than that in which a price indication is given shall not be treated as a different method of payment from payment in the currency in which the indication is given.

(5) In these Regulations, references to a method of payment do not include a method of payment which is available only to persons having a pre-existing contractual or other connection with the person indicating the price in question or with some person connected with him, being a connection which relates principally to matters other than payment in respect of transactions between that person and the consumer.

(6) These Regulations do not have effect in relation to an indication of a price which is given to a consumer in response to a specific request from him that he be informed of the price payable by a specified method for or otherwise in respect of the supply of specified goods or the provision of specified services, accommodation or facilities.

(7) These Regulations do not apply to anything done otherwise than in the course of business.

Differential price indications

8–5462   **3.** (1) Subject to paragraph (3) below and to the following provisions of these Regulations, where a person gives to consumers an indication of a price—

    (*a*) at which any goods, services, accommodation or facilities will be or are available; and
    (*b*) which is not a price applicable to all methods of payment accepted by him,

("the indicated price") he shall, before he enters into any contract under which they are to be supplied or, as the case may be, provided, make available to consumers statements of the matters to which this paragraph applies.

(2) The matters to which paragraph (1) above applies are—

(a) any method of payment (being a method of payment accepted by the person giving the indication) to which the indicated price does not apply; and

(b) the difference between the price payable by each such method and the indicated price expressed (as the case may require) as an addition to, or a deduction from, the indicated price in terms of—

(i) an amount of money, or

(ii) a percentage of the indicated price.

(3) Where a person gives to consumers more than one indicated price relating to different methods of payment in respect of the same goods, services, accommodation or facilities,—

(a) nothing in this regulation shall require a statement to be given of the difference between those prices; and

(b) all statements under paragraph (1) above may be given in relation to any one indicated price only.

Display of statements under regulation 3

8–5463 4. (1) This regulation applies to any statement under regulation 3 above (other than one given orally) which relates—

(a) to one or more items of goods (whether goods of the same description or not) which are exposed for sale at any premises or which may be available for supply to a consumer there (or for the supply of which arrangements may there be made); or

(b) to services, facilities or accommodation (whether, in each case, of the same description or not)which may be available for provision to a consumer at any premises (or for the provision of which arrangements may there be made).

(2) Except in a case to which paragraph (4) or (6) below applies, any statement to which this regulation applies shall be displayed—

(a) at each public entrance to the premises; and

(b) at each point in the premises where consumers make payment or become bound to make payment.

(3) For the purposes of paragraph (2)(a) above—

(a) where there is on or adjacent to the forecourt of a petrol-filling station to which the public has access a place used for the exposure for sale of goods or for making available goods to consumers or for the provision of services to consumers; or

(b) where a place is used for the parking of motor vehicles;

and where in each case, apart from this paragraph, the place would be comprised in larger premises, the place shall be treated as separate premises and as not comprised in those larger premises.

(4) If the place where goods are exposed for sale or may be available for supply or where services, facilities or accommodation may be provided or, in each case, where arrangements for their supply or provision may be made—

(a) is a part of larger premises which are not wholly in the occupation of the person giving the indication, and sub-paragraph (b) below does not apply, any statement to which this regulation applies shall be displayed, as the case may require, either—

(i) at each public entrance to that part; or

(ii) if that part is so arranged that there is no specific public entrance to it, at a conspicuous place at that part,

and, in any event, at each point in that part where consumers make payment or become bound to make payment; or

(b) is a kiosk, booth, stall or similar place or a vehicle at which consumers may be served without entering, any statement to which this regulation applies shall be so displayed as to be visible to a consumer at each point where consumers make payment or become bound to make payment.

(5) In relation to prices for food or drink for consumption on the premises where it is sold, any statement to which this regulation applies shall, in addition, be given on all menus.

(6) In the case of a vehicle, ship or aircraft carrying passengers between places in the United Kingdom, any statement to which this regulation applies and which relates to a fare shall be displayed at a conspicuous place on or in the vehicle, ship or aircraft so as to be visible to a consumer before or immediately after he enters it; and in this paragraph, "fare" means the price for conveyance in the vehicle, ship or aircraft, being a price which is normally payable by a consumer on the vehicle, ship or aircraft or on leaving it.

Manner of giving price indications and statements

8–5464   **5.** (1) In the case of an oral indication of the indicated price, any statement under regulation 3 above may be given in any manner, whether orally or otherwise.

(2) In the case of an indication of the indicated price which is given otherwise than orally, any statement under regulation 3 above shall be given in the same manner as the indication of the price.

(3) Any indication of the indicated price and any statement under regulation 3 above shall be clearly expressed, unambiguous and easily identifiable by a consumer as applying to the goods, services, accommodation or facilities concerned, and—

(*a*)   in the case of an oral indication or statement, shall be given audibly; and

(*b*)   in the case of a written indication or statement, shall be given clearly, prominently and legibly.

Advertisements

8–5465   **6.** (1) These Regulations apply to an indication of a price given in an advertisement if the advertisement contains an invitation (express or implied) to consumers to place orders either by post or by means of a telecommunication system for the supply of goods or for the provision of services, accommodation or facilities.

(2) In the case of an advertisement which does not include such an invitation but which includes an indication of a price—

(*a*)   at which any goods, services, accommodation or facilities will be or are available; and

(*b*)   which is not a price applicable to all methods accepted by a specified person,

it shall be sufficient compliance with regulation 3 above to state a method of payment to which the indication applies.

(3) In this regulation, "advertisement" includes a catalogue, a circular and a price list but does not include an advertisement to which regulations under section 44 of the Consumer Credit Act 1974 apply.

Accuracy and reliability

8–5466   **7.** Any information or explanation given in any indication of the indicated price or in any statement applying to it shall be accurate and no statement shall be included that the indication is not to be relied upon.

Offences and defences

8–5467   **8.** (1) Any contravention of a requirement of regulations 3 to 7 above shall constitute a criminal offence punishable[1]—

(*a*)   on conviction on indictment, by a fine; or

(*b*)   on summary conviction, by a fine not exceeding the statutory maximum.

(2) In relation to an offence under this regulation—

(*a*)   section 24(3) of the Act (defence for publishers, etc of advertisements) shall apply as it applies to an offence under subsection (1) or (2) of section 20 of the Act;

(*b*)   section 39 of the Act (defence of due diligence) shall apply as it applies to an offence mentioned in subsection (5) of that section; and

(*c*)   subsection (1) of section 40 of the Act (liability of persons other than principal offender) shall apply as it applies to an offence mentioned in section 39(5) of the Act and subsections (2) and (3) of the said section 40 shall apply as they apply to an offence under the Act.

_____

1. For procedure in respect of an offence triable either way, see Magistrates' Courts Act 1980, ss 17A–21, ante.

Package Travel, Package Holidays and Package Tours Regulations 1992[1]

(SI 1992/3288 amended by SI 1995/1648, SI 1998/1208 and SI 2003/1376 and 1400)

8–5494   **1.** *Citation and commencement*

_____

1. Made by the Secretary of State for Trade and Industry under the European Communities Act 1972, s 2(2). Only those provisions relevant to criminal proceedings are reproduced here.

8–5495   **2. Interpretation.** (1) In these Regulations—

"brochure" means any brochure in which packages are offered for sale;

"contract" means the agreement linking the consumer to the organiser or to the retailer, or to both, as the case may be;

"the Directive" means Council Directive 90/314/EEC on package travel, package holidays and package tours;

"member state" means a member state of the European Community or another state in the European Economic Area;

"offer" includes an invitation to treat whether by means of advertising or otherwise, and cognate expressions shall be construed accordingly;

"organiser" means the person who, otherwise than occasionally, organises packages and sells or offers them for sale, whether directly or through a retailer;

"the other party to the contract" means the party, other than the consumer, to the contract, that is, the organiser or the retailer, or both, as the case may be;

"package" means the pre-arranged combination of at least two of the following components when sold or offered for sale at an inclusive price and when the service covers a period of more than twenty-four hours or includes overnight accommodation—

(a) transport;
(b) accommodation;
(c) other tourist services not ancillary to transport or accommodation and accounting for a significant proportion of the package,

and

(i) the submission of separate accounts for different components shall not cause the arrangements to be other than a package;

(ii) the fact that a combination is arranged at the request of the consumer and in accordance with his specific instructions (whether modified or not) shall not of itself cause it to be treated as other than pre-arranged; and

"retailer" means the person who sells or offers for sale the package put together by the organiser.

(2) In the definition of "contract" in paragraph (1) above, "consumer" means the person who takes or agrees to take the package ("the principal contractor") and elsewhere in these Regulations "consumer" means, as the context requires, the principal contractor, any person on whose behalf the principal contractor agrees to purchase the package ("the other beneficiaries") or any person to whom the principal contractor or any of the other beneficiaries transfers the package ("the transferee").

8–5496　3. Application of Regulations.　(1) These Regulations apply to packages sold or offered for sale in the territory of the United Kingdom.

(2) Regulations 4 to 15 apply to packages so sold or offered for sale on or after 31st December 1992.

(3) Regulations 16 to 22 apply to contracts which, in whole or part, remain to be performed on 31st December 1992.

8–5497　4. Descriptive matter relating to packages must not be misleading.　(1) No organiser or retailer shall supply to a consumer any descriptive matter concerning a package, the price of a package or any other conditions applying to the contract which contains any misleading information.

(2) If an organiser or retailer is in breach of paragraph (1) he shall be liable to compensate the consumer for any loss which the consumer suffers in consequence.

8–5498　5. Requirements as to brochures.　(1) Subject to paragraph (4) below, no organiser shall make available a brochure to a possible consumer unless it indicates in a legible, comprehensible and accurate manner the price and adequate information about the matters specified in Schedule 1 to these Regulations in respect of the packages offered for sale in the brochure to the extent that those matters are relevant to the packages so offered.

(2) Subject to paragraph (4) below, no retailer shall make available to a possible consumer a brochure which he knows or has reasonable cause to believe does not comply with the requirements of paragraph (1).

(3) An organiser who contravenes paragraph (1) of this regulation and a retailer who contravenes paragraph (2) thereof shall be guilty of an offence[1] and liable—

(a) on summary conviction, to a fine not exceeding **level 5** on the standard scale; and
(b) on conviction on indictment, to a fine.

(4) Where a brochure was first made available to consumers generally before 31st December 1992 no liability shall arise under this regulation in respect of an identical brochure being made available to a consumer at any time.

---

1. For procedure in respect of this offence which is triable either way, see Magistrates' Courts Act 1980, ss 17A–21, in PART I: MAGISTRATES' COURTS, PROCEDURE, *ante*.

8–5499　6. Circumstances in which particulars in brochure are to be binding.

8–5500   7. Information to be provided before contract is concluded.   (1) Before a contract is concluded, the other party to the contract shall provide the intending consumer with the information specified in paragraph (2) below in writing or in some other appropriate form.

(2) The information referred to in paragraph (1) is—

(a)   general information about passport and visa requirements which apply to nationals of the Member State or States concerned who purchase the package in question, including information about the length of time it is likely to take to obtain the appropriate passports and visas;

(b)   information about health formalities required for the journey and the stay; and

(c)   the arrangements for security for the money paid over and (where applicable) for the repatriation of the consumer in the event of insolvency.

(3) If the intending consumer is not provided with the information required by paragraph (1) in accordance with that paragraph the other party to the contract shall be guilty of an offence[1] and liable—

(a)   on summary conviction, to a fine not exceeding **level 5** on the standard scale; and

(b)   on conviction on indictment, to a fine.

---

1. For procedure in respect of this offence which is triable either way, see Magistrates' Courts Act 1980, ss 17A–21, in PART I: MAGISTRATES' COURTS, PROCEDURE, ante.

8–5501   8. Information to be provided in good time.   (1) The other party to the contract shall in good time before the start of the journey provide the consumer with the information specified in paragraph (2) below in writing or in some other appropriate form.

(2) The information referred to in paragraph (1) is the following—

(a)   the times and places of intermediate stops and transport connections and particulars of the place to be occupied by the traveller (for example, cabin or berth on ship, sleeper compartment on train);

(b)   the name, address and telephone number—

(i)   of the representative of the other party to the contract in the locality where the consumer is to stay,

or, if there is no such representative,

(ii)   of an agency in that locality on whose assistance a consumer in difficulty would be able to call,

or, if there is no such representative or agency, a telephone number or other information which will enable the consumer to contact the other party to the contract during the stay; and

(c)   in the case of a journey or stay abroad by a child under the age of 16 on the day when the journey or stay is due to start, information enabling direct contact to be made with the child or the person responsible at the place where he is to stay; and

(d)   except where the consumer is required as a term of the contract to take out an insurance policy in order to cover the cost of cancellation by the consumer or the cost of assistance, including repatriation, in the event of accident or illness, information about an insurance policy which the consumer may, if he wishes, take out in respect of the risk of those costs being incurred.

(3) If the consumer is not provided with the information required by paragraph (1) in accordance with that paragraph the other party to the contract shall be guilty of an offence[1] and liable—

(a)   on summary conviction, to a fine not exceeding **level 5** on the standard scale; and

(b)   on conviction on indictment, to a fine.

---

1. For procedure in respect of this offence which is triable either way, see Magistrates' Courts Act 1980, ss 17A–21, in PART I: MAGISTRATES' COURTS, PROCEDURE, ante.

8–5502   9. *Contents and form of contract.*

8–5503   10. *Transfer of bookings.*

8–5504   11. *Price revision.*

8–5505   12. *Significant alterations to essential terms.*

8–5506   13. *Withdrawal by consumer pursuant to regulation 12 and cancellation by organiser.*

8–5507   14. *Significant proportion of services not provided.*

8–5508   15. *Liability of other party to the contract for proper performance of obligations under contract.*

8–5509   16. Security in event of insolvency—requirements and offences.   (1) The other party to the contract shall at all times to be able to provide sufficient evidence of security for the refund of money paid over and for the repatriation of the consumer in the event of insolvency.

(2) Without prejudice to paragraph (1) above, and subject to paragraph (4) below, save to the extent that—

(a)   the package is covered by measures adopted or retained by the member State where he is established for the purpose of implementing Article 7 of the Directive; or

(b)   the package is one in respect of which he is required to hold a licence under the Civil Aviation (Air Travel Organisers' Licensing) Regulations 1972 or the package is one that is covered by the arrangements he has entered into for the purposes of those Regulations,

the other party to the contract shall at least ensure that there are in force arrangements as described in regulations 17, 18, 19 or 20 or, if that party is acting otherwise than in the course of business, as described in any of those regulations or in regulation 21.

(3) Any person who contravenes paragraph (1) or (2) of this regulation shall be guilty of an offence[1] and liable:—

(a)   on summary conviction to a fine not exceeding level 5 on the standard scale; and

(b)   on conviction on indictment, to a fine.

(4) A person shall not be guilty of an offence under paragraph (3) above by reason only of the fact that arrangements such as are mentioned in paragraph (2) above are not in force in respect of any period before 1 April 1993 unless money paid over is not refunded when it is due or the consumer is not repatriated in the event of insolvency.

(5) For the purposes of regulations 17 to 21 below a contract shall be treated as having been fully performed if the package or, as the case may be, the part of the package has been completed irrespective of whether the obligations under the contract have been properly performed for the purposes of regulation 15.

---

1. For procedure in respect of this offence which is triable either way, see Magistrates' Courts Act 1980, ss 17A–21, in Part I: Magistrates' Courts, Procedure, ante.

8–5510   17. *Bonding*

8–5511   18. *Bonding where approved body has reserve fund or insurance*

8–5512   19. *Insurance*

8–5513   20. Monies in trust.   (1) The other party to the contract shall ensure that all monies paid over by a consumer under or in contemplation of a contract for a relevant package are held in the United Kingdom by a person as trustee for the consumer until the contract has been fully performed or any sum of money paid by the consumer in respect of the contract has been repaid to him or has been forfeited on cancellation by the consumer.

(2) The costs of administering the trust mentioned in paragraph (1) above shall be paid for by the other party to the contract.

(3) Any interest which is earned on the monies held by the trustee pursuant to paragraph (1) shall be held for the other party to the contract and shall be payable to him on demand.

(4) Where there is produced to the trustee a statement signed by the other party to the contract to the effect that—

(a)   a contract for a package the price of which is specified in that statement has been fully performed;

(b)   the other party to the contract has repaid to the consumer a sum of money specified in that statement which the consumer had paid in respect of a contract for a package; or

(c)   the consumer has on cancellation forfeited a sum of money specified in that statement which he had paid in respect of a contract for a relevant package,

the trustee shall (subject to paragraph (5) below) release to the other party to the contract the sum specified in the statement.

(5) Where the trustee considers it appropriate to do so, he may require the other party to the contract to provide further information or evidence of the matters mentioned in sub-paragraph (a), (b) or (c) of paragraph (4) above before he releases any sum to that other party pursuant to that paragraph.

(6) Subject to paragraph (7) below, in the event of the insolvency of the other party to the contract the monies held in trust by the trustee pursuant to paragraph (1) of this regulation shall be applied to meet the claims of consumers who are creditors of that other party in respect of contracts for packages in respect of which the arrangements were established and which have not been fully performed and, if there is a surplus after those claims have been met, it shall form part of the estate of that insolvent other party for the purposes of insolvency law.

(7) If the monies held in trust by the trustee pursuant to paragraph (1) of this regulation are insufficient to meet the claims of consumers as described in paragraph (6), payments to those consumers shall be made by the trustee on a pari passu basis.

8–5514   21. Monies in trust where other party to contract is acting otherwise than in the course of business.   (1) The other party to the contract shall ensure that all monies paid over by a consumer under or in contemplation of a contract for a relevant package are held in the United Kingdom by a person as trustee for the consumer for the purpose of paying for the consumer's package.

(2) The costs of administering the trust mentioned in paragraph (1) shall be paid for out of the monies held in trust and the interest earned on those monies.

(3) Where there is produced to the trustee a statement signed by the other party to the contract to the effect that—

(*a*)   the consumer has previously paid over a sum of money specified in that statement in respect of a contract for a package and that sum is required for the purpose of paying for a component (or part of a component) of the package;

(*b*)   the consumer has previously paid over a sum of money specified in that statement in respect of a contract for a package and the other party to the contract has paid that sum in respect of a component (or part of a component) of the package;

(*c*)   the consumer requires the repayment to him of a sum of money specified in that statement which was previously paid over by the consumer in respect of a contract for a package; or

(*d*)   the consumer has on cancellation forfeited a sum of money specified in that statement which he had paid in respect of a contract for a package,

the trustee shall (subject to paragraph (4) below) release to the other party to the contract the sum specified in the statement.

(4) Where the trustee considers it appropriate to do so, he may require the other party to the contract to provide further information or evidence of the matters mentioned in sub-paragraph (*a*), (*b*), (*c*) or (*d*) of paragraph (3) above before he releases to that other party any sum from the monies held in trust for the consumer.

(5) Subject to paragraph (6) below, in the event of the insolvency of the other party to the contract and of contracts for packages not being fully performed (whether before or after the insolvency) the monies held in trust by the trustee pursuant to paragraph (1) of this regulation shall be applied to meet the claims of consumers who are creditors of that other party in respect of amounts paid over by them and remaining in the trust fund after deductions have been made in respect of amounts released to that other party pursuant to paragraph (3) and, if there is a surplus after those claims have been met, it shall be divided amongst those consumers pro rata.

(6) If the monies held in trust by the trustee pursuant to paragraph (1) of this regulation are insufficient to meet the claims of consumers as described in paragraph (5) above, payments to those consumers shall be made by the trustee on a pari passu basis.

(7) Any sums remaining after all the packages in respect of which the arrangements were established have been fully performed shall be dealt with as provided in the arrangements or, in default of such provision, may be paid to the other party to the contract.

8–5515   22. Offences arising from breach of regulations 20 and 21.   (1) If the other party to the contract makes a false statement under paragraph (4) of regulation 20 or paragraph (3) of regulation 21 he shall be guilty of an offence.

(2) If the other party to the contract applies monies released to him on the basis of a statement made by him under regulation 21(3)(*a*) or (*c*) for a purpose other than that mentioned in the statement he shall be guilty of an offence.

(3) If the other party to the contract is guilty of an offence[1] under paragraph (1) or (2) of this regulation shall be liable—

(*a*)   on summary conviction to a fine not exceeding **level 5** on the standard scale; and

(*b*)   on conviction on indictment, to a fine.

---

1. For procedure in respect of this offence which is triable either way, see Magistrates' Courts Act 1980, ss 17A–21, in Part I: Magistrates' Courts, Procedure, ante.

8–5516   23. Enforcement.   Schedule 3 to these Regulations (which makes provision about the enforcement of regulations 5, 7, 8, 16 and 22 of these Regulations) shall have effect.

8–5517   24. Due diligence defence.   (1) Subject to the following provisions of this regulation, in proceedings against any person for an offence under regulations 5, 7, 8, 16 or 22 of these Regulations, it shall be a defence for that person to show that he took all reasonable steps and exercised all due diligence to avoid committing the offence.

(2) Where in any proceedings against any person for such an offence the defence provided by paragraph (1) above involves an allegation that the commission of the offence was due—

(*a*)   to the act or default of another; or

(*b*)   to reliance on information given by another,

that person shall not, without the leave of the court, be entitled to rely on the defence unless, not less than seven clear days before the hearing of the proceedings, or, in Scotland, the trial diet, he has served a notice under paragraph (3) below on the person bringing the proceedings.

(3) A notice under this paragraph shall give such information identifying or assisting in the

identification of the person who committed the act or default or gave the information as is in the possession of the person serving the notice at the time he serves it.

(4) It is hereby declared that a person shall not be entitled to rely on the defence provided by paragraph (1) above by reason of his reliance on information supplied by another, unless he shows that it was reasonable in all the circumstances for him to have relied on the information, having regard in particular—

(a) to the steps which he took, and those which might reasonably have been taken, for the purpose of verifying the information; and

(b) to whether he had any reason to disbelieve the information.

8–5518 25. Liability of persons other than principal offender. (1) Where the commission by any person of an offence under regulation 5, 7, 8, 16 or 22 of these Regulations is due to an act or default committed by some other person in the course of any business of his, the other person shall be guilty of the offence and may be proceeded against and punished by virtue of this paragraph whether or not proceedings are taken against the first-mentioned person.

(2) Where a body corporate is guilty of an offence under any of the provisions mentioned in paragraph (1) above (including where it is so guilty by virtue of the said paragraph (1)) in respect of any act or default which is shown to have been committed with the consent or connivance of, or to be attributable to any neglect on the part of, any director, manager, secretary or other similar officer of the body corporate or any person who was purporting to act in any such capacity he, as well as the body corporate, shall be guilty of that offence and shall be liable to be proceeded against and punished accordingly.

(3) Where the affairs of a body corporate are managed by its members, paragraph (2) above shall apply in relation to the acts and defaults of a member in connection with his functions of management as if he were a director of the body corporate.

(4) Where an offence under any of the provisions mentioned in paragraph (1) above committed in Scotland by a Scottish partnership is proved to have been committed with the consent or connivance of, or to be attributable to neglect on the part of, a partner, he (as well as the partnership) is guilty of the offence and liable to be proceeded against and punished accordingly.

(5) On proceedings for an offence under regulation 5 by virtue of paragraph (1) above committed by the making available of a brochure it shall be a defence for the person charged to prove that he is a person whose business it is to publish or arrange for the publication of brochures and that he received the brochure for publication in the ordinary course of business and did not know and had no reason to suspect that its publication would amount to an offence under these Regulations.

8–5519 26. Prosecution time limit. (1) No proceedings for an offence under regulations 5, 7, 8, 16 or 22 of these Regulations or under paragraphs 5(3), 6 or 7 of Schedule 3 thereto shall be commenced after—

(a) the end of the period of three years beginning within the date of the commission of the offence; or

(b) the end of the period of one year beginning with the date of the discovery of the offence by the prosecutor,

whichever is the earlier.

(2) For the purposes of this regulation a certificate signed by or on behalf of the prosecutor and stating the date on which the offence was discovered by him shall be conclusive evidence of that fact; and a certificate stating that matter and purporting to be so signed shall be treated as so signed unless the contrary is proved.

(3) (*Scotland.*)

8–5520 27. Saving for civil consequences. No contract shall be void or unenforceable, and no right of action in civil proceedings in respect of any loss shall arise, by reason only of the commission of an offence under regulations 5, 7, 8, 16 or 22 of these Regulations.

8–5521 28. *Terms implied in contract*

8–5522

Regulation 5   SCHEDULE 1

INFORMATION TO BE INCLUDED (IN ADDITION TO THE PRICE) IN BROCHURES WHERE RELEVANT TO PACKAGES OFFERED

1. The destination and the means, characteristics and categories of transport used.

2. The type of accommodation, its location, category or degree of comfort and its main features¹ and, where the accommodation is to be provided in a member State, its approval or tourist classification under the rules of that member State.

3. The meals which are included in the package.

4. The itinerary.

5. General information about passport and visa requirements which apply for nationals of the Member State or States in which the brochure is made available and health formalities required for the journey and the stay.

6. Either the monetary amount or the percentage of the price which is to be paid on account and the timetable for payment of the balance.

7. Whether a minimum number of persons is required for the package to take place and, if so, the deadline for informing the consumer in the event of cancellation.

8. The arrangements (if any) which apply if consumers are delayed at the outward or homeward points of departure.

9. The arrangements for security for money paid over and for the repatriation of the consumer in the event of insolvency.

---

1. A package which offered access by way of a wheelchair to the swimming pool and suitability of the hotel "for those with walking difficulties or who use a wheelchair" was held to refer to the "main features" of the accommodation (*Inspirations East Ltd v Dudley Metropolitan Borough Council* (1997) 162 JP 800).

8–5523

Regulation 9 SCHEDULE 2

Elements to be included in the contract if relevant to the particular package

8–5524

Regulation 23 SCHEDULE 3
Enforcement

Enforcement authority

1. (1) Every local weights and measures authority in Great Britain shall be an enforcement authority for the purposes of regulations 5, 7, 8, 16 and 22 of these Regulations ("the relevant regulations"), and it shall be the duty of each such authority to enforce those provisions within their area.

(2) The Department of Economic Development in Northern Ireland shall be an enforcement authority for the purposes of the relevant regulations, and it shall be the duty of the Department to enforce those provisions within Northern Ireland.

Prosecutions

2. (*Revoked*).

Powers of officers of enforcement authority

3. (1) If a duly authorised officer of an enforcement authority has reasonable grounds for suspecting that an offence has been committed under any of the relevant regulations, he may—

(a) require a person whom he believes on reasonable grounds to be engaged in the organisation or retailing of packages to produce any book or document relating to the activity and take copies of it or any entry in it, or

(b) require such a person to produce in a visible and legible documentary form any information so relating which is contained in a computer, and take copies of it,

for the purpose of ascertaining whether such an offence has been committed.

(2) Such an officer may inspect any goods for the purpose of ascertaining whether such an offence has been committed.

(3) If such an officer has reasonable grounds for believing that any documents or goods may be required as evidence in proceedings for such an offence, he may seize and detain them.

(4) An officer seizing any documents or goods in the exercise of his power under sub-paragraph (3) above shall inform the person from whom they are seized.

(5) The powers of an officer under this paragraph may be exercised by him only at a reasonable hour and on production (if required) of his credentials.

(6) Nothing in this paragraph—

(a) requires a person to produce a document if he would be entitled to refuse to produce it in proceedings in a court on the ground that it is the subject of legal professional privilege or, in Scotland, that it contains a confidential communication made by or to an advocate or a solicitor in that capacity; or

(b) authorises the taking possession of a document which is in the possession of a person who would be so entitled.

4. (1) A duly authorised officer of an enforcement authority may, at a reasonable hour and on production (if required) of his credentials, enter any premises for the purpose of ascertaining whether an offence under any of the relevant regulations has been committed.

(2) If a justice of the peace, or in Scotland a justice of the peace or a sheriff, is satisfied—

(a) that any relevant books, documents or goods are on, or that any relevant information contained in a computer is available from, any premises, and that production or inspection is likely to disclose the commission of an offence under the relevant regulations; or

(b) that any such an offence has been, is being or is about to be committed on any premises,

and that any of the conditions specified in sub-paragraph (3) below is met, he may by warrant under his hand authorise an officer of an enforcement authority to enter the premises, if need be by force.

(3) The conditions referred to in sub-paragraph (2) above are—

(a) that admission to the premises has been or is likely to be refused and that notice of intention to apply for a warrant under that sub-paragraph has been given to the occupier;

(b) that an application for admission, or the giving of such a notice, would defeat the object of the entry;

(c) that the premises are unoccupied; and

(d) that the occupier is temporarily absent and it might defeat the object of the entry to await his return.

(4) In sub-paragraph (2) above "relevant", in relation to books, documents, goods or information, means books, documents, goods or information which, under paragraph 3 above, a duly authorised officer may require to be produced or may inspect.

(5) A warrant under sub-paragraph (2) above may be issued only if—

(a) in England and Wales, the justice of the peace is satisfied as required by that sub-paragraph by written information on oath;

(b) in Scotland, the justice of the peace or sheriff is so satisfied by evidence on oath; or

(c) in Northern Ireland, the justice of the peace is so satisfied by complaint on oath.

(6) A warrant under sub-paragraph (2) above shall continue in force for a period of one month.

(7) An officer entering any premises by virtue of this paragraph may take with him such other persons as may appear to him necessary.

(8) On leaving premises which he has entered by virtue of a warrant under sub-paragraph (2) above, an officer shall, if the premises are unoccupied or the occupier is temporarily absent, leave the premises as effectively secured against trespassers as he found them.

(9) In this paragraph "premises" includes any place (including any vehicle, ship or aircraft) except premises used only as a dwelling.

OBSTRUCTION OF OFFICERS

5. (1) A person who—

(a) intentionally obstructs an officer of an enforcement authority acting in pursuance of this Schedule;

(b) without reasonable excuse fails to comply with a requirement made of him by such an officer under paragraph 3(1) above; or

(c) without reasonable excuse fails to give an officer of an enforcement authority acting in pursuance of this Schedule any other assistance or information which the officer may reasonably require of him for the purpose of the performance of the officer's functions under this Schedule,

shall be guilty of an offence.

(2) A person guilty of an offence under sub-paragraph (1) above shall be liable on summary conviction to a fine not exceeding level 5 on the standard scale.

(3) If a person, in giving any such information as is mentioned in sub-paragraph (1)(c) above,—

(a) makes a statement which he knows is false in a material particular; or

(b) recklessly makes a statement which is false in a material particular,

he shall be guilty of an offence.

(4) A person guilty of an offence[1] under sub-paragraph (3) above shall be liable—

(a) on summary conviction, to a fine not exceeding **level 5** on the standard scale; and

(b) on conviction on indictment, to a fine.

---

1. For procedure in respect of this offence which is triable either way, see Magistrates' Courts Act 1980, ss 17A–21, in PART I: MAGISTRATES' COURTS, PROCEDURE, ante.

IMPERSONATION OF OFFICERS

6. (1) If a person who is not a duly authorised officer of an enforcement authority purports to act as such under this Schedule he shall be guilty of an offence[1].

(2) A person guilty of an offence under sub-paragraph (1) above shall be liable—

(a) on summary conviction, to a fine not exceeding level 5 on the standard scale; and

(b) on conviction on indictment, to a fine.

---

1. For procedure in respect of an offence triable either way, see Magistrates' Courts Act 1980, ss 17A–21, ante.

DISCLOSURE OF INFORMATION

7. (*Revoked*).

---

1. For procedure in respect of this offence which is triable either way, see Magistrates' Courts Act 1980, ss 17A–21, in PART I: MAGISTRATES' COURTS, PROCEDURE, ante.

PRIVILEGE AGAINST SELF-INCRIMINATION

8. Nothing in this Schedule requires a person to answer any question or give any information if to do so might incriminate him.

Price Indications (Resale of Tickets) Regulations 1994[1]
(SI 1994/3248)

Citation and commencement

8–5525   **1.** These Regulations may be cited as the Price Indications (Resale of Tickets) Regulations 1994 and shall come into force on 20th February 1995.

---

1. Made by the Secretary of State in exercise of the powers conferred on him by s 26 of the Consumer Protection Act 1987.

Interpretation

8–5526   **2.** In these Regulations—

"ticket" means a card, badge or document giving to its holder—

(a) the right of admission to a place of entertainment; or

(b) the said right of admission to a place of entertainment and the right to use a seat or space in such a place

and the fact that those rights are subject to the condition that the holder may be refused admission to or may be removed from the place of entertainment shall not cause it to be treated as other than a ticket; and

"entertainment" includes any gathering, amusement, exhibition, performance, game, sport or trial of skill or other similar event.

Scope of application

8–5527   3. (1) Subject to paragraph (3) below, the provisions of these Regulations have effect when a person to whom paragraph (2) below applies gives to consumers, in the course of business, an indication of the price at which a ticket, or a ticket in combination with another element, is or will be available ("a price indication").

(2) This paragraph applies to any person save for the holder or promoter of the entertainment to which the ticket relates or a person acting on behalf of such holder or promoter who is prepared or may be prepared to supply a ticket by way of resale.

(3) These Regulations do not apply where a person gives a price indication in relation to a package to which the Package Travel, Package Holidays and Package Tours Regulations 1992 apply.

Price indication information

8–5528   4. Where a person gives a price indication, the following information shall be given to consumers—

(a) the price (if any) and any other detail which appears on the ticket which relates to or affects the rights conferred or to be conferred on the holder of the ticket (including the location of the seat or space) and which has been caused to be placed thereon by the holder or promoter of the entertainment to which the ticket relates; and

(b) the location of the seat or space (if any) which the holder of the ticket will have the right to use and any features of such seat or space which would adversely affect the holder's use or enjoyment of it and which are known or could reasonably be expected to be known to the person giving the price indication.

Requirements relating to price indication information

8–5529   5. (1) The information required to be given by regulation 4 above shall be given before the person who gives a price indication enters into any contract with a consumer under which the ticket is to be supplied.

(2) Except in cases where the contract to supply the ticket by way of resale is concluded by telephone, the information required to be given by regulation 4(a) above shall be given in writing.

(3) The requirement of paragraph (2) of this regulation shall be deemed to be satisfied if the consumer is shown the ticket in accordance with paragraph (1) above and in such a manner that the details appearing on the ticket are visible by and legible to the consumer.

Manner of giving price indication information

8–5530   6. The information required to be given by regulation 4 need not be given in the same manner as the price indication but—

(a) if the information is given orally, it shall be given audibly and in a manner that is comprehensible to the consumer, and

(b) if it is given in writing, it shall be given clearly, prominently and legibly

and in any case the information shall be given in such a way that it comes to the attention of the consumer before he enters into any contract under which the ticket is to be supplied to him.

Price indication information to be accurate

8–5531   7. Any information which is given pursuant to the requirements of regulation 4 above shall be accurate.

Offences and defences

8–5532   8. (1) Any contravention of a requirement of these Regulations shall constitute a criminal offence punishable—

(a) on conviction on indictment, by a fine; or

(b) on summary conviction, by a fine not exceeding the statutory maximum.

(2) In relation to an offence under this regulation—

(a) section 24(2) of the Act (defence that indication was not contained in an advertisement) shall apply as it applies to an offence under subsection (1) or (2) of section 20 of the Act;

(b) section 39 of the Act (defence of due diligence) shall apply as it applies to an offence mentioned in subsection (5) of that section; and

(c) subsection (1) of section 40 of the Act (liability of persons other than principal offender) shall apply as it applies to an offence mentioned in section 39(5) of the Act and subsections (2) and (3) of the said section 40 shall apply as they apply to an offence under the Act.

(3) In this regulation, "the Act" means the Consumer Protection Act 1987.

Motor Vehicle Tyres (Safety) Regulations 1994[1]

(SI 1994/3117 amended by SI 1996/3227 and SI 2003/1316 and 2762)

PART I
INTRODUCTION

8–5533　1. *Preliminaries*

---

1. Made by the Secretary of State for Transport in exercise of the powers conferred by s 11 of the Consumer Protection Act 1987.

8–5533A　2. Interpretation.　(1) In these Regulations—

"the Construction and Use Regulations" means the Road Vehicles (Construction and Use) Regulations 1986 as from time to time amended;

"approval mark" means a mark of a description specified in ECE Regulation 30, 30.01, 30.02, 54 or 75 or in EC Directive 92/23 which, when applied to a tyre, indicates that the tyre conforms with a type in respect of which approval has been granted pursuant to that instrument;

"BS AU 144b: 1977" means the British Standard Automobile Series: Specification for retreaded car and commercial vehicle tyres published by the British Standards Institution under reference BS AU 144b: 1977 on 29th July 1977;

"BS AU 144c: 1988" means the British Standard Automobile Series: Specification for retreaded car and commercial vehicle tyres published by the British Standards Institution under reference BS AU 144c: 1988 on 30th September 1988;

"BS AU 144d: 1988" means BS AU 144c: 1988 as amended by Amendment No 1 (reference AMD 6592) published on 31st August 1990;

"BS AU 144e: 1988" means BS AU 144c: 1988 as amended by Amendment No 1 (reference AMD 6592) published on 31st August 1990 and by Amendment No 2 (reference AMD 7506) published on 15th December 1992;

"BS AU 159e: 1990" means the British Standard Automobile Series: Specification for repairs to tyres for motor vehicles used on the public highway published by the British Standards Institution under reference BS AU 159d: 1990 as amended by Amendment No 1 (reference AMD 8216) published on 15th June 1994;

"BS AU 159f: 1997" means the British Standard Automobile Series: "Specification for Repairs to tyres for motor vehicles used on the public highway" published by the British Standards Institution under the reference BS AU 159f: 1997 on 15th December 1997;

"commercial vehicle" means a motor vehicle which is—

(a) a goods vehicle with 4 or more wheels, or
(b) a passenger vehicle with more than 8 seats in addition to the driver's seat;

"EC Directive 92/23" means Council Directive 92/23/EEC[1];

"EC Directive 97/24" means the Directive of the European Parliament and the Council 97/24/EC, Chapter 1;

"EC Directive 2002/24" means the Directive of the European Parliament and the Council 2002/24/EC;

"passenger car" means a motor vehicle which—

(a) is a passenger vehicle or dual-purpose vehicle;
(b) has no more than 8 seats in addition to the driver's seat; and
(c) has 4 or more wheels;

"tyre" means a pneumatic tyre as defined in regulation 3(2) of the Construction and Use Regulations.

(2) For the purposes of these Regulations the following expressions have the same meanings as in the Road Traffic Act 1988—

"goods vehicle";
"motor vehicle";
"trailer" (except where it appears in the expression "light trailer");
"road".

(3) A reference in these Regulations to a British Standard Specification is a reference to BS AU 144b: 1977, BS AU 144c: 1988, BS AU 144d: 1988, BS AU 144e: 1988 or BS AU 159e: 1990.

(4) In these Regulations, in relation to a retreaded tyre,—

(a) a reference to a part-worn tyre is a reference to a tyre that has been used after the tyre was retreaded; and

(b) a reference to a tyre that has been repaired is a reference to a tyre that has been repaired after it has been so used.

(5) For the purposes of these Regulations the expressions listed in the left-hand column of the Table below shall have the meanings given by the provisions of the Construction and Use Regulations listed in the right-hand column in relation to those expressions.

"agricultural motor vehicle"	regulation 3
"agricultural trailer"	regulation 3
"agricultural trailed appliance"	regulation 3
"bias-belted tyre"	regulation 26
"breadth of tread"	regulation 27
"diagonal-ply tyre"	regulation 26
"dual-purpose vehicle"	regulation 3
"light trailer"	regulation 3
"original tread pattern"	regulation 27
"passenger vehicle"	regulation 3

(6) A reference in these Regulations to the supply of a tyre includes offering to supply, agreeing to supply, exposing for supply or possessing for supply; and cognate expressions shall be construed accordingly.

(7) A reference to a tyre-size designation is a reference to a designation described in paragraph 2.18 of ECE Regulation 30 or 30.01, paragraph 2.17 of ECE Regulation 30.02, paragraph 2.17 of ECE Regulation 54 or paragraph 2.17 of Annex II to EC Directive 92/23.

(8) A reference to an ECE Regulation shall be construed in accordance with Schedule 1 to these Regulations.

(9) Unless the context otherwise requires, any reference in the following provisions of these Regulations to—

(a) a numbered regulation is a reference to the regulation bearing that number in these Regulations; and

(b) a numbered paragraph is a reference to the paragraph bearing that number in the regulation in which the reference appears.

---

1. OJ No L129, 14.5.92, p 95.

8–5533B 3. *Application to Northern Ireland*

PART II
REQUIREMENTS RELATING TO THE SUPPLY OF TYRES

8–5533C 4. Interpretation of Part II. In this Part of these Regulations—

(a) the expressions—

"low performance moped";
"moped";
"motor cycle";
"motor tricycle";
"quadricycle"; and
"three-wheel moped"

have the same meanings as in EC Directive 2002/24; and

(b) the expressions—

"carcass";
"sidewall"; and
"tread"

have the same meanings as in EC Directive 92/23.

8–5533D 5. Supply of new tyres for certain vehicles. Subject to Part III of these Regulations, no person shall supply any tyre (not being a retreaded or part-worn tyre) designed so as to be capable of being fitted to a wheel of any of the following—

(a) a passenger car,
(b) a light trailer,
(c) a moped (not being a low performance moped),
(d) a motor cycle,
(e) a motor tricycle,
(f) a three-wheel moped, or
(g) a quadricycle,

unless the tyre is marked with an approval mark in accordance with the requirements of ECE Regulation 30, 30.01, 30.02, 54 or 75 or of EC Directives 92/23 or 97/24.

8–5533E 6. Supply of retreaded tyres for certain vehicles. (1) Subject to Part III of these Regulations, no person shall supply any retreaded tyre (not being a part-worn tyre) designed so as to be capable of being fitted to a wheel of a passenger car or a commercial vehicle or a trailer unless the following requirements are met with respect to the tyre, that is to say—

(a) it must not bear any mark indicating that it complies with the requirements of ECE Regulation 30, 30.01, 30.02 or 54 or of EC Directive 92/23;

(b) in the case of supplies taking place on or before 31st December 2003, the tyre must either—

(i) be marked in accordance with paragraph 6 of BS AU 144e (and if it has been repaired during the course of retreading then it must have been properly repaired) or

(ii) conform to a type in respect of which approval has been granted pursuant to ECE Regulation 108 or 109; and

(c) in the case of a supply taking place on or after 1st January 2004, the tyre must conform to a type in respect of which approval has been granted pursuant to ECE Regulation 108 or 109.

(2) Subject to Part III of these Regulations, no person shall supply any retreaded tyre (not being a part-worn tyre) designed so as to be capable of being fitted to the wheel of a moped (not being a low performance moped), a motor cycle, a motor tricycle, a three-wheel moped or a quadricycle, on or after 1st January 2004 unless either—

(a) the tyre complies with the requirements set out in paragraph (1)(a) and (c), or

(b) the following requirements are met with respect to the tyre, that is to say—

(i) it must not bear any mark indicating that it complies with the requirements of ECE Regulation 75 or of EC Directive 97/24;

(ii) prior to being retreaded, the carcass conformed to a type of tyre in respect of which approval had been granted pursuant either to ECE Regulation 75 or to EC Directive 97/24 and it bore an "E" or "e" mark;

(iii) it must not previously have been retreaded;

(iv) the carcass which has been retreaded must be no more than 7 years old, the age being determined on the basis of the digits of the date of manufacture code which is marked on the sidewall;

(v) it is permanently marked to enable the identification (whether through the use of a code or otherwise) of the name, and either the type or trade description or model reference, of the original manufacturer of the carcass which has been retreaded;

(vi) it complies, as regards dimensions and performance, with the requirements set out either in ECE Regulation 75 or in EC Directive 97/24;

(vii) it has moulded on to, or into, at least one of its sidewalls and in letters not less than 4 millimetres high, the word "RETREAD";

(viii) it complies, as regards markings, with the requirements set out either in ECE Regulation 75, paragraph 3 (except paragraph 3.2) or in EC Directive 97/24, Annex II, paragraph 2;

(ix) if it has been repaired during the course of retreading, it must have been properly repaired; and

(x) it must not show either a higher speed symbol or a higher load index than that originally borne by the carcass which has been retreaded.

8–5533F   7. Supply of part-worn tyres for certain vehicles.   (1) Subject to Part III of these Regulations, no person shall supply any part-worn tyre or any part-worn retreaded tyre designed so as to be capable of being fitted to a wheel of any of the following—

(a) a passenger car,

(b) a commercial vehicle,

(c) a light trailer,

(d) a moped (not being a low performance moped),

(e) a motorcycle,

(f) a motor tricycle,

(g) a three-wheel moped, or

(h) a quadricycle,

unless the following requirements are met.

(2) The tyre must not have—

(a) any cut in excess of 25 millimetres or 10 per cent of the section width of the tyre (whichever is the greater) measured in any direction on the outside of the tyre and deep enough to reach the ply or cord;

(b) any internal or external lump, bulge or tear caused by the separation or partial failure of its structure;

(c) any of the ply or cord exposed internally or externally; or

(d) any penetration damage which has not been repaired.

(3) When inflated to the highest pressure at which it is designed to operate, the tyre must not exhibit any of the external defects described in paragraph (2).

(4) The grooves of the original tread pattern of the tyre must be of a depth of at least 2 millimetres across the full breadth of tread and round the entire outer circumference of the tyre.

(5) If the tyre has not been retreaded and is designed so as to be capable of being fitted to a wheel of any of the vehicles described in paragraph (1), it must bear—

(a) immediately adjacent to every approval mark borne by the tyre, a mark that meets the requirements of paragraph (10); and

(b) an approval mark, a speed category symbol and load capacity index, being marks that were moulded on to, or into, the tyre at the time that it was manufactured and that are in accordance with the requirements of ECE Regulation 30, 30.01, 30.02, 54 or 75 or of EC Directive 92/23 or EC Directive 97/24.

(6) If the tyre has been retreaded and is designed so as to be capable of being fitted to a wheel of any of the vehicles described in paragraph (1) —

(a) it must bear —

(i) the mark "BS AU 144b", "BS AU 144c", "BS AU 144d" or "BS AU 144e", or

(ii) an approval mark indicating that the tyre complies with the requirements of ECE Regulation 108 or 109, or

(iii) comply, as regards markings, with the requirements set out in paragraph (b)(v), (vii) and (viii) of regulation 6(2);

(b) the mark must have been permanently and legibly applied to the tyre at the time it was retreaded; and

(c) it must bear —

(i) in the case of a tyre bearing a mark of a description specified in sub-paragraph (a)(i) or (ii), immediately adjacent to such mark, or

(ii) in the case of a tyre marked in accordance with sub-paragraph (a)(iii), immediately adjacent to the word "RETREAD",

a mark that meets the requirements of paragraph (10).

(7) If a tyre has been retreaded and bears the mark "BS AU 144e", it must bear a speed category symbol and load-capacity index, being marks that were permanently and legibly applied to the tyre at the time it was manufactured or retreaded and that are in accordance with BS AU 144e: 1988;

(8) If the tyre has been repaired, it must have been properly repaired.

(9) Without prejudice to paragraph (8), if the tyre has been repaired, it must meet the requirements of paragraph 8 of BS AU 159f: 1997 (which include marking requirements) and the requirements of paragraphs 5, 6 and 7 of that instrument must have been met in relation to that repair.

(10) In order for a mark to meet the requirements of this paragraph, it must consist of the word "PART-WORN" in uppercase letters at least 4 millimetres high and must have been permanently and legibly applied to the tyre other than by hot branding or otherwise cutting into the tyre.

PART III

EXEMPTIONS

8–5533G 8. Interpretation of Part III. (1) For the purposes of this Part of these Regulations, an exempt tyre is a tyre which falls within any of the descriptions set out below —

(a) a bias-belted tyre or a diagonal-ply tyre, being a tyre designed for fitting to a wheel of a motor vehicle or trailer manufactured before 1st January 1949;

(b) a tyre constructed solely for use off roads and bearing words or letters which indicate that use and which were moulded on to or into the tyre at the time of manufacture;

(c) a tyre constructed solely for use on vehicles in competitions and bearing words or letters which indicate that use and which were moulded on to or into the tyre at the time of manufacture;

(d) a tyre bearing one of the following tyre-size designations namely: 185R16, 125R400, 135R400, 145R400, 155R400, 165R400, 175R400 or 185R400, being a mark that was moulded on to or into the tyre at the time of manufacture;

(e) a tyre designed primarily for fitting to a wheel of a vehicle manufactured before 1st January 1933.

(2) For the purposes of this Part of these Regulations, a tyre is supplied in exempt circumstances if —

(a) the tyre is constructed solely for use on a vehicle for the purposes of tests or trials of the tyre, and

(b) the supply is other than in the course of a retail trade or business,

or if the supply of the tyre is by a person who reasonably believes that the tyre will not be used in the United Kingdom.

8–5533H 9. Exemptions applicable to the supply of new tyres and retreaded tyres. Regulations 5 and 6 do not apply to the supply of an exempt tyre or to the supply of a tyre in exempt circumstances.

8–5533I 10. Exemptions applicable to the supply of part-worn tyres. (1) Where a complete vehicle is supplied by any person, regulation 7 does not apply to any tyre on a wheel of the vehicle or on any spare wheel supplied with the vehicle.

(2) Regulation 7(5) to (7) does not apply to the supply of an exempt tyre or to the supply of a tyre in exempt circumstances.

(3) Regulation 7(9) does not apply to—

(a) a tyre designed primarily for fitting to a wheel of a vehicle manufactured before 1st January 1933;

(b) a tyre of the limited run-flat type, or

(c) a tyre designed primarily for fitting to a wheel of an agricultural motor vehicle, agricultural trailer or agricultural trailed appliance.

8–5533J   11. Transitional exemptions.   (1) Until 1st July 1997 regulations 4 and 6 shall not apply to the supply of a tyre constructed so as to be suitable for a vehicle travelling at a speed exceeding 210 km per hour and bearing the appropriate tyre-size designation and (in the vicinity of the tyre-size designation) the letters "VR" or "ZR", both being marks that were moulded on to or into the tyre at the time of manufacture.

(2) Until 1st July 1997 these Regulations shall not apply to the supply of a bias-belted tyre or a diagonal-ply tyre.

(3) Until 1st December 1995 regulation 6(3) shall not apply to the supply of a tyre which is marked in accordance with paragraph 10 of BS AU 144b: 1977, with paragraph 6 of BS AU 144c: 1988 or with paragraph 6 of BS AU 144d: 1988.

PART IV
GENERAL PROVISIONS

8–5533K   12. Misleading marks.   (1) No person shall supply a tyre designed so as to be capable of being fitted to a wheel of a motor vehicle or trailer if it bears—

(a) an approval mark;

(b) any mark not falling within sub-paragraph (a) which is of a description specified in any standard (including a British Standard Specification), technical specification or code of practice relating (in each case) to retreaded tyres and which indicates compliance with the requirements of that instrument; or

(c) any mark referred to in regulation 8(1)(d) of these Regulations,

and any indication given by that mark taken by itself or that mark as read with any other mark on the tyre is false.

(2) Where—

(a) a person supplies a tyre (not being a retreaded tyre) which bears a mark falling within paragraph (1)(a) or supplies a retreaded tyre which bears a mark falling within paragraph (1)(b); and

(b) the tyre is not part-worn,

the indications given by the mark shall be deemed, for the purposes of this regulation only, to include an indication that the tyre complied at the time of manufacture (in the case of a tyre that is not a retreaded tyre), or at the time of retreading (in the case of a retreaded tyre), and (in either case) at the time of supply, with the requirements of the instrument to which the mark relates.

(3) Where—

(a) a person supplies a tyre (not being a retreaded tyre) which bears a mark falling within paragraph (1)(a) or supplies a retreaded tyre which bears a mark falling within paragraph (1)(b); and

(b) the tyre is part-worn and is marked in accordance with regulation 7(5)(a) or (6)(c) as the case may be,

the indications given by the mark referred to in sub-paragraph (a) shall be deemed, for the purposes of this regulation only, to include an indication that the tyre complied at the time of manufacture (in the case of a tyre that is not a retreaded tyre), or at the time of retreading (in the case of a retreaded tyre), with the requirements of the instrument to which the mark relates, but does not (in either case) necessarily so comply at the time of supply.

(4) A mark which so nearly resembles a mark falling within paragraph (1)(a), (b) or (c) as to be likely to be taken for such a mark shall be treated for the purposes of this regulation only as if it were a mark of the kind which it so resembles.

8–5533L   13. Equivalent standards.   (1) Nothing in these Regulations shall make it unlawful to supply a tyre if it would not be unlawful to supply the tyre were there substituted, for a reference in these Regulations to any provision in a British Standard Specification, a reference to an equivalent provision in a corresponding standard.

(2) In this regulation, "corresponding standard", in relation to a British Standard Specification, means—

(a) a standard or code of practice of a national standards body or equivalent body of any EEA State;

(b) any international standard recognised for use as a standard by any EEA State; or

(c) a technical specification or code of practice which, whether mandatory or not, is recognised for use as a standard by a public authority of any EEA State, where the standard, code of practice, international standard or technical specification provides, in relation to tyres, a level of safety equivalent to that provided by the British Standard Specification and contains a requirement as respects the marking of tyres equivalent to that provided by that instrument.

(3) In this regulation—

"EEA State" means a state which is a contracting Party to the EEA Agreement but, until the EEA Agreement comes into force in relation to Liechtenstein, does not include the State of Liechtenstein; and

"EEA Agreement" means the Agreement on the European Economic Area signed at Oporto on 2nd May 1992 as adjusted by the Protocol signed at Brussels on 17th March 1993.

8–5533M

Regulation 2(8)

SCHEDULE 1
ECE REGULATIONS

1. (1) In these Regulations, references to an ECE Regulation followed by a number shall have the meaning shown in the Table below.

(2) In this Schedule, "the Agreement" means the Agreement concerning the adoption of uniform conditions of approval for motor vehicle equipment and parts and reciprocal recognition thereof concluded at Geneva on 20th March 1958 as amended to which the United Kingdom is a party.

Regulations	Meaning
"ECE Regulation 30"	Regulation 30 of the Agreement
"ECE Regulation 30.01"	Regulation 30 of the Agreement as amended by Amendment 1 dated 25th September 1977.
"ECE Regulation 30.02"	Regulation 30 of the Agreement as amended by Amendment 1 dated 25th September 1977 and by Amendment 2 dated 15th March 1981.
"ECE Regulation 54"	Regulation 54 of the Agreement.
"ECE Regulation 75"	Regulation 75 of the Agreement.

8–5533N

Regulation 3

SCHEDULE 2
MODIFICATIONS IN RELATION TO NORTHERN IRELAND

Price Marking (Food and Drink Services) Order 2003[1]
(SI 2003/2253)

8–5533P **1. Citation, commencement and interpretation.** (1) This Order may be cited as the Price Marking (Food and Drink Services) Order 2003 and shall come into force on 2nd March 2004.

(2) In this Order—

"eating area" means any part of any premises specifically set aside and equipped for the consumption of food notwithstanding that some other activity may be carried on in the area in question but does not include a supply area;

"food" means food and drink for human consumption but does not include food which is supplied—

(a) at the express request of a purchaser in a case where the seller has not indicated that food of the same description is or may be for sale by him; or

(b) at a price agreed in advance pursuant to an order made before an intending purchaser enters the eating area, supply area or take-away area in question to obtain or consume the food;

"premises" includes any vehicle or vessel;

"soft drink" means any non-alcoholic drink of a kind which is served cold;

"supply area" means any part of any premises specifically set aside and equipped for the supply of food in a case where an intending purchaser pays for food for consumption on the premises where it is sold before it is consumed notwithstanding that some other activity may be carried on in the area in question;

"take-away area" means any part of any premises specifically set aside and equipped for the supply of food prepared or heated at the request of a consumer or supplied as heated meals in each case for consumption off the premises where it is sold notwithstanding in any case that some other activity may be carried on in the area in question; and

"wine" means any drink obtained from the alcoholic fermentation of fresh grapes or the must of fresh grapes other than drink fortified with spirits or flavoured with aromatic extracts.

---

1. Made by the Secretary of State in exercise of the powers under section 4 of the Prices Act 1994.

8–5533Q **2. Revocation.** The Price Marking (Food and Drink on Premises) Order 1979 is hereby revoked.

8–5533R **3. When the Order applies.** (1) This Order applies where a person indicates that food is or may be for sale by him by retail for consumption on any premises (other than premises to which paragraph (2) applies) or in a take-away area.

(2) This Order does not apply to premises on which food is ordinarily supplied—

(a) only to members of a bona fide club or their guests; or

(b) only or mainly to members of a group determined by reference to—

(i) their employment, or the employment of a partner, parent or partner of a parent of theirs, in the service of a particular person or of one of a number of particular persons;

(ii) their membership of, or regular attendance at, an educational establishment; or

(c) only to persons for whom sleeping accommodation on those premises is provided.

8–5533S 4. Obligations to indicate prices for food and other charges. (1) A person who indicates that food is or may be for sale by him shall, subject to the other provisions of this Order, give an indication of—

(a) the price for the sale of that food (except where it is sold by reference to quantity or weight);

(b) the price for the sale of each quantity or weight where the food is sold by reference to quantity or weight, subject to paragraph (2) below;

(c) any charge which is payable in addition to the price of any food (expressed either as an amount or as a percentage of the price); and

(d) any minimum price or charge which is payable in respect of any food sold or service provided relating to the supply of food.

(2) A single indication of price is required by paragraph (1)(b) above where a food is sold in more than one quantity or weight if the quantity or weight to which that price applies is indicated and the prices of other quantities or weights are proportionate to the indicated price.

(3) Where foods of different descriptions are or may be for sale together (other than foods supplied as a fixed price meal) and the total price for the foods is the sum of the prices of the individual foods, only an indication of the price of the individual foods is required.

(4) An indication of the price of food or of a charge payable in addition to the price of any food which is subject to value added tax shall be inclusive of the tax.

5. (1) Indications of the price of food are required to be given in accordance with the table set out below:

Descriptions of food which are or may be for sale	Indications of price required
Not more than thirty descriptions of food (other than wine)	For all
More than thirty descriptions of food (other than wine)	For thirty which must, if soft drinks are or may be for sale, include five soft drinks or the actual number if less than five
More than thirty descriptions of food (other than wine) divided in any way into categories	For a minimum of thirty which must include five per category or the actual number in a category if less than five. If soft drinks are or may be for sale indications must be given for five or the actual number if less than five
Wine for consumption with other foods in an eating or supply area	For five or the actual number if less than five
Foods of different descriptions for sale together as a fixed price meal	For each fixed price meal. The preceding rules in this table shall not apply to the foods contained in the meal unless they are or may be available separately

8–5533T 6. (1) Where an indication is given that food of a particular description is or may be for sale generally (as opposed to only in an indicated period of a day) an indication of the price of that food shall be withdrawn as soon as is reasonably practicable if the food ceases to be available.

(2) Where an indication is given that food of a particular description is or may be for sale only in an indicated period of a day an indication of the price of that food shall be withdrawn before the next such period if the food ceases to be available.

8–5533U 7. Manner of indication of prices and charges. (1) An indication of price shall be unambiguous, easily identifiable and clearly legible by an intending purchaser and shall comply with such of the following provisions of this article as may be applicable.

(2) In the case of an eating area, the indication shall be given at or near the entrance to the eating area so that an intending purchaser can see it before entering that area or, in the case of an eating area in a railway carriage where an intending purchaser requests the supply of food at the place at which it is to be consumed, at that place.

(3) In the case of a supply area, the indication shall be given at the place where an intending purchaser chooses the food and, if that indication cannot be seen by an intending purchaser

before entering the supply area, a further indication shall be given at or near the entrance to the supply area.

(4) In the case of a take-away area the indication shall be given at the place where an intending purchaser chooses the food.

(5) Any additional charge or minimum charge payable shall be indicated at least as prominently as the price of any food to which it relates.

(6) An indication of price or charge shall be in sterling.

(7) If a person indicates his willingness to accept foreign currency in payment for the sale of food, he shall, in addition to the price indication in sterling, either—

(a)

    (i)   give an indication of the price of that food in the foreign currency in question together with any commission to be charged; or

    (ii) clearly identify the conversion rate on the basis of which the foreign currency price will be calculated together with any commission to be charged; and

(b) indicate that such price or conversion rate does not apply to transactions via a payment card to be applied to accounts denominated in currencies other than sterling, the conversion rate for which will be that applied by the relevant payment scheme which processes the transaction.

8–5533V   **8. Savings for other enactments.**   Nothing in article 7 above shall require anything to be done if it would be a contravention by any person of a regulation made under, or having effect as if made under, sections 220, 221 or 224 of the Town and Country Planning Act 1990 or sections 182, 183 or 186 of the Town and Country Planning (Scotland) Act 1997.

Price Marking Order 2004[1]
(2004/102)

8–5533W   **1. Citation, commencement and interpretation.**   (1) This Order may be cited as the Price Marking Order 2004 and shall come into force on 22nd July 2004.

(2) In this Order—

"advertisement" means any form of advertisement which is made in order to promote the sale of a product but does not include any advertisement by means of which the trader intends to encourage a consumer to enter into a distance contract, a catalogue, a price list, a container or a label;

"consumer" means any individual who buys a product for purposes that do not fall within the sphere of his commercial or professional activity;

"cosmetic products" means any substance or preparation intended to be placed in contact with an external part of the human body, or with the teeth, inside of the mouth or throat with a view exclusively or mainly to one or more of the following purposes: cleaning, perfuming, changing the appearance of, protecting, and keeping in good condition it or them or correcting body odour;

"distance contract" means any contract concerning products concluded between a trader and a consumer, by any means, without the simultaneous physical presence of the trader and the consumer;

"itinerant trader" means any trader who, as a pedestrian, or from a train, aircraft, vessel, vehicle, stall, barrow, or other mobile sales unit, offers products to consumers other than by means of pre-printed material;

"liquid medium" has the meaning given for the purposes of paragraph 4 of Article 8 of Directive 2000/13/EC of the European Parliament and of the Council on the approximation of the laws of the Member States relating to the labelling, presentation and advertising of foodstuffs;

"make-up products" means cosmetic products solely intended temporarily to change the appearance of the face or nails, including (but not limited to) lipsticks, mascaras, eye shadows, blushers and concealers;

"net drained weight" means the weight of a solid food product when it is presented in a liquid medium;

"precious metal" means gold, silver or platinum, or any other metal to which by an order under section 17 of the Hallmarking Act 1973 the provisions of that Act are applied;

"products sold from bulk" means products which are not pre-packaged and are weighed or measured at the request of the consumer;

"relevant floor area" in relation to a shop means the internal floor area of the shop excluding any area not used for the retail sale of products or for the display of such products for retail sale;

"selling price" means the final price for a unit of a product, or a given quantity of a product, including VAT and all other taxes;

"shop" includes a store, kiosk and a franchise or concession within a shop;

"small shop" means any shop which has a "relevant floor area" not exceeding 280 square metres;

"standard of fineness" means any one of the standards of fineness specified in column (2) of paragraph 2 of Schedule 2 to the Hallmarking Act 1973;

"trader" means any person who sells or offers or exposes for sale products which fall within his commercial or professional activity;

"unit price" means the final price, including VAT and all other taxes, for one kilogram, one litre, one metre, one square metre or one cubic metre of a product, except (i) in respect of the products specified in Schedule 1, where unit price means the final price including VAT and all other taxes for the corresponding units of quantity set out in that Schedule; and (ii) in respect of products sold by number, where unit price means the final price including VAT and all other taxes for an individual item of the product.

---

1. Made by the Secretary of State, in exercise of the powers under s 4 of the Prices Act 1974.

8–5533X 2. Revocation. The Price Marking Order 1999 is hereby revoked.

8–5533Y 3. Scope of application of the Order. (1) This Order shall not apply:

   (a) to products which are supplied in the course of the provision of a service; or
   (b) to sales by auction or sales of works of art or antiques.

(2) The Electronic Commerce (EC Directive) Regulations 2002 shall apply to this Order notwithstanding Regulation 3(2) of those Regulations.

8–5533Z 4. Obligation to indicate selling price. (1) Subject to paragraph (2) and articles 9 and 10, where a trader indicates that any product is or may be for sale to a consumer, he shall indicate the selling price of that product in accordance with the provisions of this Order.

(2) The requirement in paragraph (1) above shall not apply in respect of:

   (a) products sold from bulk; or
   (b) an advertisement for a product.

8–5534 5. Obligation to indicate unit price. (1) Subject to paragraph (2), (3) and (4) and article 9, where a trader indicates that any product is or may be for sale to a consumer, he shall indicate the unit price of that product in accordance with the provisions of this Order.

(2) The requirement in paragraph (1) only applies in respect of products sold from bulk or required by or under Parts IV or V of the Weights and Measures Act 1985 to be:

   (a) marked with an indication of quantity; or
   (b) made up in a quantity prescribed by or under that Act.

(3) The requirement in paragraph (1) shall not apply in relation to:

   (a) any product which falls within Schedule 2;
   (b) any product the unit price of which is identical to its selling price;
   (c) bread made up in a prescribed quantity which is or may be for sale in a small shop, by an itinerant trader or from a vending machine; or
   (d) any product which is pre-packaged in a constant quantity which is or may be for sale in a small shop, by an itinerant trader or from a vending machine.

(4) The requirement in paragraph (1) applies in relation to an advertisement for a product only where the selling price of the product is indicated in the advertisement.

8–5534A 6. Manner of indication of selling price and unit price. (1) The indication of selling price and unit price shall be in sterling.

(2) If a trader indicates his willingness to accept foreign currency in payment for a product, he shall, in addition to the required price indications in sterling:

   (a) give an indication of the selling price and any unit price required for the product in the foreign currency in question together with any commission to be charged; or
   (b) clearly identify the conversion rate on the basis of which the foreign currency price will be calculated together with any commission to be charged; and

indicate that such selling price, unit price or conversion rate as the case may be does not apply to transactions via a payment card to be applied to accounts denominated in currencies other than sterling, the conversion rate for which will be that applied by the relevant payment scheme which processes the transaction.

8–5534B 7. (1) An indication of selling price, unit price, commission, conversion rate or a change in the rate or coverage of value added tax given in accordance with article 11 shall be—

   (a) unambiguous, easily identifiable and clearly legible;
   (b) subject to paragraph 2, given in proximity to:

      (i) the product; or
      (ii) in the case of distance contracts and advertisements, a visual or written description of the product; and

(c)   so placed as to be available to consumers without the need for them to seek assistance from the trader or someone on his behalf in order to ascertain it.

(2) Paragraph (1)(b)(i) does not apply to an indication given in relation to any item of jewellery, item of precious metal, or watch displayed in a window of the premises where it is or may be for sale and the selling price of which is in excess of £3,000.

(3) The indication of any charges for postage, package or delivery of a product shall be unambiguous, easily identifiable and clearly legible.

(4) Where, in addition to a unit price, a price per quantity is indicated in relation to a supplementary indication of quantity the unit price shall predominate and the price per supplementary indication of quantity shall be expressed in characters no larger than the unit price.

(5) In paragraph (4) "supplementary indication of quantity" refers to an indication of quantity expressed in a unit of measurement other than a metric unit as authorised by section 8(5A) of the Weights and Measures Act 1985.

8–5534C   8.   In the case of a pre-packaged solid food product presented in a liquid medium, the unit price shall refer to the net drained weight of the product. Where a unit price is also given with reference to the net weight of the product, it shall be clearly indicated which unit price relates to net drained weight and which to net weight.

8–5534D   9. Special provisions relating to general reductions.   Where a trader proposes to sell products to which this Order applies at less than the selling price or the unit price previously applicable and indicated in accordance with article 7(1), he may comply with the obligations specified in articles 4(1) (to indicate the selling price) and 5(1) (to indicate the unit price) by indicating by a general notice or any other visible means that the products are or may be for sale at a reduction, provided that the details of the reduction are prominently displayed, unambiguous, easily identifiable and clearly legible.

8–5534E   10. Special provisions relating to precious metals.   In the case of products the selling price of which varies from day to day according to the price of the precious metals contained in them the obligation to indicate the selling price referred to in article 4(1) may be complied with by indicating in a manner which is unambiguous, easily identifiable and clearly legible:

(a)   the weight, type and standard of fineness of each precious metal contained in the product; and

(b)   any element of the selling price which is not referable to weight,

accompanied by a clearly legible and prominent notice stating the price per unit of weight for the type and standard of fineness of each precious metal contained in the product.

8–5534F   11. Change in Value Added Tax etc.   Where there is a change in the rate or coverage of VAT or any other tax, a trader who adjusts his prices in consequence may comply with the provisions of this Order—

(a)   by means of a general notice or notices for a period of 14 days from the date any such change takes effect, indicating that any products subject to that change are not for sale at the price indicated and that such price will be adjusted to take account of the change; and

(b)   if he continues to distribute any catalogue or sales literature printed or ordered to be printed before a change is announced and there is firmly attached to it a label which prominently states that some or all of the prices printed in it are to be adjusted to reflect the change, and:

     (i)   the label includes sufficient information to enable consumers to establish the adjusted price of any product listed, or

     (ii)   the label refers to and is accompanied by a supplement which enables them to do so.

8–5534G   12. Decimal places and rounding of unit prices.   Where the unit price of a product falls below £1 it shall be expressed to the nearest 0.1p. Where the figure denoting one hundredths of one penny in the unit price is 5 or higher, it shall be rounded up and where it is 4 or lower it shall be rounded down.

8–5534H   13.   Where the unit price of a product falls above £1 it may be expressed to the nearest:

(a)   1p, in which case where the figure denoting tenths of one penny in the unit price is 5 or higher, it shall be rounded up and where it is 4 or lower it shall be rounded down; or

(b)   0.1p, in which case where the figure denoting one hundredths of one penny in the unit price is 5 or higher it shall be rounded up and where it is 4 or lower it shall be rounded down.

8–5534I   14. Units of Quantity.   For the purposes of Schedule 1, the figure denoting the relevant units of quantity in the second column of the table for the corresponding product in the first column of the table refers, as indicated by or under the Weights and Measures Act 1985, and unless specified otherwise to:

(a) grams where the product is sold by weight;
(b) millilitres where the product is sold by volume; and
(c) either grams or millilitres, as indicated by the manufacturer of the product, where the product is permitted to be sold by either weight or volume.

8–5534J 15. Enforcement. For the purpose of ascertaining whether any trader enjoys exemption from unit pricing under article 5(3)(c) or (d) in respect of a small shop, a local weights and measures authority may require that trader to produce such documentary evidence relating to the shop in question as it considers necessary.

8–5534K
Articles 1(2) and 14   SCHEDULE 1
RELEVANT UNITS OF QUANTITY FOR SPECIFIED PRODUCTS FOR THE PURPOSE OF THE DEFINITION OF "UNIT PRICE"

Product	Units of Quantity
Flavouring essences	10
Food colourings	10
Herbs	10
Make-up Products	10 (except where sold by number)
Seeds other than pea, bean, grass and wild bird seeds	10
Spices	10
Biscuits and shortbread	100 (except where sold by number)
Bread	100 (except where sold by number)
Breakfast cereal products	100 (except where required to be quantity marked by number)
Chocolate confectionery and sugar confectionery	100
Coffee	100
Cooked or ready-to-eat fish, seafoods and crustacea	100
Cooked or ready-to-eat meat including game and poultry	100
Cosmetic products other than make-up products	100
Cream and non-dairy alternatives to cream	100
Dips and spreads excluding edible fats	100
Dry sauce mixes	100
Fresh processed salad	100
Fruit juices, soft drinks	100
Handrolling and pipe tobacco	100
Ice cream and frozen desserts	100
Lubricating oils other than oils for internal combustion engines	100
Pickles	100
Pies, pasties, sausage rolls, puddings and flans indicating net quantity	100 (except where sold by number)
Potato crisps and similar products commonly known as snack foods	100
Preserves including honey	100
Ready to eat desserts	100
Sauces, edible oils	100
Soups	100
Tea and other beverages prepared with liquid	100
Waters, including spa waters and aerated waters	100
Wines, sparkling wine, liqueur wine, fortified wine	75 cl
Coal, where sold by the kilogram	50 kg
Ballast, where sold by the kilogram	1,000 kg

8–5534L
Article 5(3)   SCHEDULE 2
PRODUCTS IN RESPECT OF WHICH A TRADER IS EXEMPT FROM THE REQUIREMENT TO UNIT PRICE

1. Any product which is offered by traders to consumers by means of an advertisement which is:

(a) purely aural;
(b) broadcast on television;
(c) shown at a cinema; or
(d) inside a small shop.

2. Any product the price of which has been reduced from the usual price at which it is sold, on account of:

(a) its damaged condition; or
(b) the danger of its deterioration.

3. Any product which comprises an assortment of different items sold in a single package.
4. Any product the unit price of which is 0.0p as a result of article 12 (Decimal places and rounding of unit prices) of this Order.

General Product Safety Regulations 2005
(SI 2005/1803 amended by SI 2005/2759)

PART 1
GENERAL

8–5535 1. Citation, commencement and revocation. (1) These Regulations may be cited as the General Product Safety Regulations 2005 and shall come into force on 1st October 2005 with the exception of the reference to a civil partner in regulation 43(2) which shall come into force on 5th December 2005.

(2) The General Product Safety Regulations 1994 are hereby revoked.

8–5535A   2. Interpretation.   In these Regulations:

"the 1987 Act" means the Consumer Protection Act 1987;

"Community law" includes a law in any part of the United Kingdom which implements a Community obligation;

"contravention" includes a failure to comply and cognate expressions shall be construed accordingly;

"dangerous product" means a product other than a safe product;

"distributor" means a professional in the supply chain whose activity does not affect the safety properties of a product;

"enforcement authority" means the Secretary of State, any other Minister of the Crown in charge of a government department, any such department and any authority or council mentioned in regulation 10;

"general safety requirement" means the requirement that only safe products should be placed on the market;

"the GPS Directive" means Directive 2001/95/EC of the European Parliament and of the Council of 3 December 2001 on general product safety;

"magistrates' court" in relation to Northern Ireland, means a court of summary jurisdiction;

"Member State" means a member State, Norway, Iceland or Liechtenstein;

"notice" means a notice in writing;

"officer", in relation to an enforcement authority, means a person authorised in writing to assist the authority in carrying out its functions under or for the purposes of the enforcement of these Regulations and safety notices, except in relation to an enforcement authority which is a government department where it means an officer of that department;

"producer" means—

    (a) the manufacturer of a product, when he is established in a Member State and any other person presenting himself as the manufacturer by affixing to the product his name, trade mark or other distinctive mark, or the person who reconditions the product;

    (b) when the manufacturer is not established in a Member State—

        (i) if he has a representative established in a Member State, the representative,

        (ii) in any other case, the importer of the product from a state that is not a Member State into a Member State;

    (c) other professionals in the supply chain, insofar as their activities may affect the safety properties of a product;

"product" means a product which is intended for consumers or likely, under reasonably foreseeable conditions, to be used by consumers even if not intended for them and which is supplied or made available, whether for consideration or not, in the course of a commercial activity and whether it is new, used or reconditioned and includes a product that is supplied or made available to consumers for their own use in the context of providing a service. "product" does not include equipment used by service providers themselves to supply a service to consumers, in particular equipment on which consumers ride or travel which is operated by a service provider;

"recall" means any measure aimed at achieving the return of a dangerous product that has already been supplied or made available to consumers;

"recall notice" means a notice under regulation 15;

"record" includes any book or document and any record in any form;

"requirement to mark" means a notice under regulation 12;

"requirement to warn" means a notice under regulation 13;

"safe product" means a product which, under normal or reasonably foreseeable conditions of use including duration and, where applicable, putting into service, installation and maintenance requirements, does not present any risk or only the minimum risks compatible with the product's use, considered to be acceptable and consistent with a high level of protection for the safety and health of persons. In determining the foregoing, the following shall be taken into account in particular—

    (a) the characteristics of the product, including its composition, packaging, instructions for assembly and, where applicable, instructions for installation and maintenance,

    (b) the effect of the product on other products, where it is reasonably foreseeable that it will be used with other products,

    (c) the presentation of the product, the labelling, any warnings and instructions for its use and disposal and any other indication or information regarding the product, and

    (d) the categories of consumers at risk when using the product, in particular children and the elderly.

The feasibility of obtaining higher levels of safety or the availability of other products presenting a lesser degree of risk shall not constitute grounds for considering a product to be a dangerous product;

"safety notice" means a suspension notice, a requirement to mark, a requirement to warn, a withdrawal notice or a recall notice;

"serious risk" means a serious risk, including one the effects of which are not immediate, requiring rapid intervention;

"supply" in relation to a product includes making it available, in the context of providing a service, for use by consumers;

"suspension notice" means a notice under regulation 11;

"withdrawal" means any measure aimed at preventing the distribution, display or offer of a dangerous product to a consumer;

"withdrawal notice" means a notice under regulation 14.

8–5535B   **3. Application.**   (1) Each provision of these Regulations applies to a product in so far as there are no specific provisions with the same objective in rules of Community law governing the safety of the product other than the GPS Directive.

(2) Where a product is subject to specific safety requirements imposed by rules of Community law other than the GPS Directive, these Regulations shall apply only to the aspects and risks or category of risks not covered by those requirements. This means that:

(a) the definition of "safe product" and "dangerous product" in regulation 2 and regulations 5 and 6 shall not apply to such a product in so far as concerns the risks or category of risks covered by the specific rules, and

(b) the remainder of these Regulations shall apply except where there are specific provisions governing the aspects covered by those regulations with the same objective.

8–5535C   **4.**   These Regulations do not apply to a second-hand product supplied as a product to be repaired or reconditioned prior to being used, provided the supplier clearly informs the person to whom he supplies the product to that effect.

PART 2
OBLIGATIONS OF PRODUCERS AND DISTRIBUTORS

8–5535D   **5. General safety requirement.**   (1) No producer shall place a product on the market unless the product is a safe product.

(2) No producer shall offer or agree to place a product on the market or expose or possess a product for placing on the market unless the product is a safe product.

(3) No producer shall offer or agree to supply a product or expose or possess a product for supply unless the product is a safe product.

(4) No producer shall supply a product unless the product is a safe product.

8–5535E   **6. Presumption of conformity.**   (1) Where, in the absence of specific provisions in rules of Community law governing the safety of a product, the product conforms to the specific rules of the law of part of the United Kingdom laying down the health and safety requirements which the product must satisfy in order to be marketed in the United Kingdom, the product shall be deemed safe so far as concerns the aspects covered by such rules.

(2) Where a product conforms to a voluntary national standard of the United Kingdom giving effect to a European standard the reference of which has been published in the Official Journal of the European Union in accordance with Article 4 of the GPS Directive, the product shall be presumed to be a safe product so far as concerns the risks and categories of risk covered by that national standard. The Secretary of State shall publish the reference number of such national standards in such manner as he considers appropriate.

(3) In circumstances other than those referred to in paragraphs (1) and (2), the conformity of a product to the general safety requirement shall be assessed taking into account—

(a) any voluntary national standard of the United Kingdom giving effect to a European standard, other than one referred to in paragraph (2),

(b) other national standards drawn up in the United Kingdom,

(c) recommendations of the European Commission setting guidelines on product safety assessment,

(d) product safety codes of good practice in the sector concerned,

(e) the state of the art and technology, and

(f) reasonable consumer expectations concerning safety.

(4) Conformity of a product with the criteria designed to ensure the general safety requirement is complied with, in particular the provisions mentioned in paragraphs (1) to (3), shall not bar an enforcement authority from exercising its powers under these Regulations in relation to that product where there is evidence that, despite such conformity, it is dangerous.

8–5535F   **7. Other obligations of producers.**   (1) Within the limits of his activities, a producer shall provide consumers with the relevant information to enable them—

(a) to assess the risks inherent in a product throughout the normal or reasonably foreseeable period of its use, where such risks are not immediately obvious without adequate warnings, and

(b) to take precautions against those risks.

(2) The presence of warnings does not exempt any person from compliance with the other requirements of these Regulations.

(3) Within the limits of his activities, a producer shall adopt measures commensurate with the characteristics of the products which he supplies to enable him to—

(a) be informed of the risks which the products might pose, and

(b) take appropriate action including, where necessary to avoid such risks, withdrawal, adequately and effectively warning consumers as to the risks or, as a last resort, recall.

(4) The measures referred to in paragraph (3) include—

(a) except where it is not reasonable to do so, an indication by means of the product or its packaging of—

(i) the name and address of the producer, and

(ii) the product reference or where applicable the batch of products to which it belongs; and

(b) where and to the extent that it is reasonable to do so—

(i) sample testing of marketed products,

(ii) investigating and if necessary keeping a register of complaints concerning the safety of the product, and

(iii) keeping distributors informed of the results of such monitoring where a product presents a risk or may present a risk.

8–5535G **8. Obligations of distributors.** (1) A distributor shall act with due care in order to help ensure compliance with the applicable safety requirements and in particular he—

(a) shall not expose or possess for supply or offer or agree to supply, or supply, a product to any person which he knows or should have presumed, on the basis of the information in his possession and as a professional, is a dangerous product; and

(b) shall, within the limits of his activities, participate in monitoring the safety of a product placed on the market, in particular by—

(i) passing on information on the risks posed by the product,

(ii) keeping the documentation necessary for tracing the origin of the product,

(iii) producing the documentation necessary for tracing the origin of the product, and cooperating in action taken by a producer or an enforcement authority to avoid the risks.

(2) Within the limits of his activities, a distributor shall take measures enabling him to cooperate efficiently in the action referred to in paragraph (1)(b)(iii).

8–5535H **9. Obligations of producers and distributors.** (1) Subject to paragraph (2), where a producer or a distributor knows that a product he has placed on the market or supplied poses risks to the consumer that are incompatible with the general safety requirement, he shall forthwith notify an enforcement authority in writing of that information and—

(a) the action taken to prevent risk to the consumer; and

(b) where the product is being or has been marketed or otherwise supplied to consumers outside the United Kingdom, of the identity of each Member State in which, to the best of his knowledge, it is being or has been so marketed or supplied.

(2) Paragraph (1) shall not apply—

(a) in the case of a second-hand product supplied as an antique or as a product to be repaired or reconditioned prior to being used, provided the supplier clearly informed the person to whom he supplied the product to that effect,

(b) in conditions concerning isolated circumstances or products.

(3) In the event of a serious risk the notification under paragraph (1) shall include the following—

(a) information enabling a precise identification of the product or batch of products in question,

(b) a full description of the risks that the product presents,

(c) all available information relevant for tracing the product, and

(d) a description of the action undertaken to prevent risks to the consumer.

(4) Within the limits of his activities, a person who is a producer or a distributor shall co-operate with an enforcement authority (at the enforcement authority's request) in action taken to avoid the risks posed by a product which he supplies or has supplied. Every enforcement authority shall maintain procedures for such co-operation, including procedures for dialogue with the producers and distributors concerned on issues related to product safety.

PART 3
ENFORCEMENT

8–5535I **10. Enforcement.** (1) It shall be the duty of every authority to which paragraph (4) applies to enforce within its area these Regulations and safety notices.

(2) An authority in England or Wales to which paragraph (4) applies shall have the power to investigate and prosecute for an alleged contravention of any provision imposed by or under these Regulations which was committed outside its area in any part of England and Wales.

(3) A district council in Northern Ireland shall have the power to investigate and prosecute for an alleged contravention of any provision imposed by or under these Regulations which was committed outside its area in any part of Northern Ireland.

(4) The authorities to which this paragraph applies are:

(a) in England, a county council, district council, London Borough Council, the Common Council of the City of London in its capacity as a local authority and the Council of the Isles of Scilly,

(b) in Wales, a county council or a county borough council,

(c) in Scotland, a council constituted under section 2 of the Local Government etc (Scotland) Act 1994,

(d) in Northern Ireland any district council.

(5) An enforcement authority shall in enforcing these Regulations act in a manner proportionate to the seriousness of the risk and shall take due account of the precautionary principle. In this context, it shall encourage and promote voluntary action by producers and distributors. Notwithstanding the foregoing, an enforcement authority may take any action under these Regulations urgently and without first encouraging and promoting voluntary action if a product poses a serious risk.

8–5535J   11. Suspension notices.   (1) Where an enforcement authority has reasonable grounds for suspecting that a requirement of these Regulations has been contravened in relation to a product, the authority may, for the period needed to organise appropriate safety evaluations, checks and controls, serve a notice ("a suspension notice") prohibiting the person on whom it is served from doing any of the following things without the consent of the authority, that is to say—

(a) placing the product on the market, offering to place it on the market, agreeing to place it on the market or exposing it for placing on the market, or

(b) supplying the product, offering to supply it, agreeing to supply it or exposing it for supply.

(2) A suspension notice served by an enforcement authority in relation to a product may require the person on whom it is served to keep the authority informed of the whereabouts of any such product in which he has an interest.

(3) A consent given by the enforcement authority for the purposes of paragraph (1) may impose such conditions on the doing of anything for which the consent is required as the authority considers appropriate.

8–5535K   12. Requirements to mark.   (1) Where an enforcement authority has reasonable grounds for believing that a product is a dangerous product in that it could pose risks in certain conditions, the authority may serve a notice ("a requirement to mark") requiring the person on whom the notice is served at his own expense to undertake either or both of the following, as specified in the notice—

(a) to ensure that the product is marked in accordance with requirements specified in the notice with warnings as to the risks it may present,

(b) to make the marketing of the product subject to prior conditions as specified in the notice so as to ensure the product is a safe product.

(2) The requirements referred to in paragraph (1)(a) shall be such as to ensure that the product is marked with a warning which is suitable, clearly worded and easily comprehensible.

8–5535L   13. Requirements to warn.   Where an enforcement authority has reasonable grounds for believing that a product is a dangerous product in that it could pose risks for certain persons, the authority may serve a notice ("a requirement to warn") requiring the person on whom the notice is served at his own expense to undertake one or more of the following, as specified in the notice—

(a) where and to the extent it is practicable to do so, to ensure that any person who could be subject to such risks and who has been supplied with the product be given warning of the risks in good time and in a form specified in the notice,

(b) to publish a warning of the risks in such form and manner as is likely to bring those risks to the attention of any such person,

(c) to ensure that the product carries a warning of the risks in a form specified in the notice.

8–5535M   14. Withdrawal notices.   (1) Where an enforcement authority has reasonable grounds for believing that a product is a dangerous product, the authority may serve a notice ("a withdrawal notice") prohibiting the person on whom it is served from doing any of the following things without the consent of the authority, that is to say—

(a) placing the product on the market, offering to place it on the market, agreeing to place it on the market or exposing it for placing on the market, or

(b) supplying the product, offering to supply it, agreeing to supply it or exposing it for supply.

(2) A withdrawal notice may require the person on whom it is served to take action to alert consumers to the risks that the product presents.

(3) In relation to a product that is already on the market, a withdrawal notice may only be served by an enforcement authority where the action being undertaken by the producer or the distributor concerned in fulfilment of his obligations under these Regulations is unsatisfactory or insufficient to prevent the risks concerned to the health and safety of persons.

(4) Paragraph (3) shall not apply in the case of a product posing a serious risk requiring, in the view of the enforcement authority, urgent action.

(5) A withdrawal notice served by an enforcement authority in relation to a product may require the person on whom it is served to keep the authority informed of the whereabouts of any such product in which he has an interest.

(6) A consent given by the enforcement authority for the purposes of paragraph (1) may impose such conditions on the doing of anything for which the consent is required as the authority considers appropriate.

8–5535N   15. Recall notices.   (1) Subject to paragraph (4), where an enforcement authority has reasonable grounds for believing that a product is a dangerous product and that it has already been supplied or made available to consumers, the authority may serve a notice ("a recall notice") requiring the person on whom it is served to use his reasonable endeavours to organise the return of the product from consumers to that person or to such other person as is specified in the notice.

(2) A recall notice may require—

(a) the recall to be effected in accordance with a code of practice applicable to the product concerned, or

(b) the recipient of the recall notice to—

    (i) contact consumers who have purchased the product in order to inform them of the recall, where and to the extent it is practicable to do so,

    (ii) publish a notice in such form and such manner as is likely to bring to the attention of purchasers of the product the risk the product poses and the fact of the recall, or

    (iii) make arrangements for the collection or return of the product from consumers who have purchased it or for its disposal,

and may impose such additional requirements on the recipient of the notice as are reasonable and practicable with a view to achieving the return of the product from consumers to the person specified in the notice or its disposal.

(3) In determining what requirements to include in a recall notice, the enforcement authority shall take into consideration the need to encourage distributors, users and consumers to contribute to its implementation.

(4) A recall notice may only be issued by an enforcement authority where—

(a) other action which it may require under these Regulations would not suffice to prevent the risks concerned to the health and safety of persons,

(b) the action being undertaken by the producer or the distributor concerned in fulfilment of his obligations under these Regulations is unsatisfactory or insufficient to prevent the risks concerned to the health and safety of persons, and

(c) the authority has given not less than seven days notice to the person on whom the recall notice is to be served of its intention to serve such a notice and where that person has before the expiry of that period by notice required the authority to seek the advice of such person as the Institute determines on the questions of—

    (i) whether the product is a dangerous product,

    (ii) whether the issue of a recall notice is proportionate to the seriousness of the risk, and

the authority has taken account of such advice.

(5) Paragraphs (4)(b) and (c) shall not apply in the case of a product posing a serious risk requiring, in the view of the enforcement authority, urgent action.

(6) Where a person requires an enforcement authority to seek advice as referred to in paragraph (4)(c), that person shall be responsible for the fees, costs and expenses of the Institute and of the person appointed by the Institute to advise the authority.

(7) In paragraphs 4(c) and (6) "the Institute" means the charitable organisation with registered number 803725 and known as the Chartered Institute of Arbitrators.

(8) A recall notice served by an enforcement authority in relation to a product may require the person on whom it is served to keep the authority informed of the whereabouts of any such product to which the recall notice relates, so far as he is able to do so.

(9) Where the conditions in paragraph (1) for serving a recall notice are satisfied and either the enforcement authority has been unable to identify any person on whom to serve a recall notice, or the person on whom such a notice has been served has failed to comply with it, then the authority may itself take such action as could have been required by a recall notice.

(10) Where—

(a) an authority has complied with the requirements of paragraph (4); and

(b) the authority has exercised its powers under paragraph (9) to take action following the failure of the person on whom the recall notice has been served to comply with that notice, then the authority may recover from the person on whom the notice was served summarily as a civil debt, any costs or expenses reasonably incurred by it in undertaking the action referred to in sub-paragraph (b).

(11) A civil debt recoverable under the preceding paragraph may be recovered—

(a) in England and Wales by way of complaint (as mentioned in section 58 of the Magistrates' Courts Act 1980,

(b) in Northern Ireland in proceedings under Article 62 of the Magistrate's Court (Northern Ireland) Order 1981.

8–5535O   16. Supplementary provisions relating to safety notices. (1) Whenever feasible, prior to serving a safety notice the authority shall give an opportunity to the person on whom the notice is to be served to submit his views to the authority. Where, due to the urgency of the situation, this is not feasible the person shall be given an opportunity to submit his views to the authority after service of the notice.

(2) A safety notice served by an enforcement authority in respect of a product shall—

(a) describe the product in a manner sufficient to identify it;

(b) state the reasons on which the notice is based;

(c) indicate the rights available to the recipient of the notice under these Regulations and (where applicable) the time limits applying to their exercise; and

(d) in the case of a suspension notice, state the period of time for which it applies.

(3) A safety notice shall have effect throughout the United Kingdom.

(4) Where an enforcement authority serves a suspension notice in respect of a product, the authority shall be liable to pay compensation to a person having an interest in the product in respect of any loss or damage suffered by reason of the notice if—

(a) there has been no contravention of any requirement of these Regulations in relation to the product; and

(b) the exercise by the authority of the power to serve the suspension notice was not attributable to any neglect or default by that person.

(5) Where an enforcement authority serves a withdrawal notice in respect of a product, the authority shall be liable to pay compensation to a person having an interest in the product in respect of any loss or damage suffered by reason of the notice if—

(a) the product was not a dangerous product; and

(b) the exercise by the authority of the power to serve the withdrawal notice was not attributable to any neglect or default by that person.

(6) Where an enforcement authority serves a recall notice in respect of a product, the authority shall be liable to pay compensation to the person on whom the notice was served in respect of any loss or damage suffered by reason of the notice if—

(a) the product was not a dangerous product; and

(b) the exercise by the authority of the power to serve the recall notice was not attributable to any neglect or default by that person.

(7) An enforcement authority may vary or revoke a safety notice which it has served provided that the notice is not made more restrictive for the person on whom it is served or more onerous for that person to comply with.

(8) Wherever feasible prior to varying a safety notice the authority shall give an opportunity to the person on whom the original notice was served to submit his views to the authority.

8–5535P   17. Appeals against safety notices. (1) A person on whom a safety notice has been served and a person having an interest in a product in respect of which a safety notice (other than a recall notice) has been served may, before the end of the period of 21 days beginning with the day on which the notice was served, apply for an order to vary or set aside the terms of the notice.

(2) On an application under paragraph (1) the court or the sheriff, as the case may be, shall make an order setting aside the notice only if satisfied that—

(a) in the case of a suspension notice, there has been no contravention in relation to the product of any requirement of these Regulations,

(b) in the case of a requirement to mark or a requirement to warn, the product is not a dangerous product,

(c) in the case of a withdrawal notice—

   (i) the product is not a dangerous product, or

   (ii) where applicable, regulation 14(3) has not been complied with by the enforcement authority concerned,

(d) in the case of a recall notice—

   (i) the product is not a dangerous product, or

   (ii) regulation 15(4) has not been complied with,

(e) in any case, the serving of the safety notice concerned was not proportionate to the seriousness of the risk.

(3) On an application concerning the period of time specified in a suspension notice as the

period for which it applies, the court or the sheriff, as the case may be, may reduce the period to such period as it considers sufficient for organising appropriate safety evaluations, checks and controls.

(4) On an application to vary the terms of a notice, the court or the sheriff, as the case may be, may vary the requirements specified in the notice as it considers appropriate.

(5) A person on whom a recall notice has been served and who proposes to make an application under paragraph (1) in relation to the notice may, before the end of the period of seven days beginning with the day on which the notice was served, apply to the court or the sheriff for an order suspending the effect of the notice and the court or the sheriff may, in any case where it considers it appropriate to do so, make an order suspending the effect of the notice.

(6) If the court or the sheriff makes an order suspending the effect of a recall notice under paragraph (5) in the absence of the enforcement authority, the enforcement authority may apply for the revocation of such order.

(7) An order under paragraph (5) shall take effect from the time it is made until—

(a) it is revoked under paragraph (6),

(b) where no application is made under paragraph (1) in respect of the recall notice within the time specified in that paragraph, the expiration of that time,

(c) where such an application is made but is withdrawn or dismissed for want of prosecution, the date of dismissal or withdrawal of the application, or

(d) where such an application is made and is not withdrawn or dismissed for want of prosecution, the determination of the application.

(8) Subject to paragraph (6), in Scotland the sheriff's decision under paragraph (5) shall be final.

(9) An application under this regulation may be made—

(a) by way of complaint to any magistrates' court in which proceedings have been brought in England and Wales or Northern Ireland—

(i) in respect of a contravention in relation to the product of a requirement imposed by or under these Regulations; or

(ii) for the forfeiture of the product under regulation 18;

(b) where no such proceedings have been brought, by way of complaint to any magistrates' court; or

(c) in Scotland, by summary application to the sheriff.

(10) A person aggrieved by an order made pursuant to an application under paragraph (1) by a magistrates' court in England, Wales or Northern Ireland, or by a decision of such a court not to make such an order, may appeal against that order or decision—

(a) in England and Wales, to the Crown Court;

(b) in Northern Ireland, to the county court.

8–5535Q **18. Forfeiture: England and Wales and Northern Ireland.** (1) An enforcement authority in England and Wales or Northern Ireland may apply for an order for the forfeiture of a product on the grounds that the product is a dangerous product.

(2) An application under paragraph (1) may be made—

(a) where proceedings have been brought in a magistrates' court for an offence in respect of a contravention in relation to the product of a requirement imposed by or under these Regulations, to that court,

(b) where an application with respect to the product has been made to a magistrates' court under regulation 17 (appeals against safety notices) or 25 (appeals against detention of products and records) to that court, and

(c) otherwise, by way of complaint to a magistrates' court.

(3) An enforcement authority making an application under paragraph (1) shall serve a copy of the application on any person appearing to it to be the owner of, or otherwise to have an interest in, the product to which the application relates, together with a notice giving him the opportunity to appear at the hearing of the application to show cause why the product should not be forfeited.

(4) A person on whom notice is served under paragraph (3) and any other person claiming to be the owner of, or otherwise to have an interest in, the product to which the application relates shall be entitled to appear at the hearing of the application and show cause why the product should not be forfeited.

(5) The court shall not make an order for the forfeiture of a product—

(a) if any person on whom notice is served under paragraph (3) does not appear, unless service of the notice on that person is proved, or

(b) if no notice under paragraph (3) has been served, unless the court is satisfied that in the circumstances it was reasonable not to serve notice on any person.

(6) The court may make an order for the forfeiture of a product only if it is satisfied that the product is a dangerous product.

(7) Any person aggrieved by an order made by a magistrates' court for the forfeiture of a product, or by a decision of such a court not to make such an order, may appeal against that order or decision—

(a) in England and Wales, to the Crown Court;

(b) in Northern Ireland, to the county court.

(8) An order for the forfeiture of a product shall not take effect until the later of—

(i) the end of the period within which an appeal under paragraph (7) may be brought or within which an application under section 111 of the Magistrates' Courts Act 1980 or article 146 of the Magistrates' Courts (Northern Ireland) Order 1981 (statement of case) may be made, or

(ii) if an appeal or an application is so made, when the appeal or application is determined or abandoned.

(9) Subject to the following paragraph, where a product is forfeited it shall be destroyed in accordance with such directions as the court may give.

(10) On making an order for forfeiture of a product a magistrates' court may, if it considers it appropriate to do so, direct that the product shall (instead of being destroyed) be delivered up to such person as the court may specify, on condition that the person—

(a) does not supply the product to any person otherwise than as mentioned in paragraph (11), and

(b) on condition, if the court considers it appropriate, that he complies with any order to pay costs or expenses (including any order under regulation 28) which has been made against him in the proceedings for the order for forfeiture.

(11) The supplies which may be permitted under the preceding paragraph are—

(a) a supply to a person who carries on a business of buying products of the same description as the product concerned and repairing or reconditioning them,

(b) a supply to a person as scrap (that is to say, for the value of materials included in the product rather than for the value of the product itself),

(c) a supply to any person, provided that being so supplied the product is repaired by or on behalf of the person to whom the product was delivered up by direction of the court and that following such repair it is not a dangerous product.

8–5535R   19. Forfeiture: Scotland.   (1) In Scotland a sheriff may make an order for forfeiture of a product on the grounds that the product is a dangerous product—

(a) on an application by a procurator-fiscal made in the manner specified in section 134 of the Criminal Procedure (Scotland) Act 1995, or

(b) where a person is convicted of any offence in respect of a contravention in relation to the product of a requirement imposed by or under these Regulations, in addition to any other penalty which the sheriff may impose.

(2) The procurator-fiscal making an application under paragraph (1)(a) shall serve on any person appearing to him to be the owner of, or otherwise to have an interest in, the product to which the application relates a copy of the application, together with a notice giving him the opportunity to appear at the hearing of the application to show cause why the product should not be forfeited.

(3) Service under paragraph (2) shall be carried out, and such service may be proved, in the manner specified for citation of an accused in summary proceedings under the Criminal Procedure (Scotland) Act 1995.

(4) A person upon whom notice is served under paragraph (2) and any other person claiming to be the owner of, or otherwise to have an interest in, the product to which the application relates shall be entitled to appear at the hearing of the application to show cause why the product should not be forfeited.

(5) The sheriff shall not make an order following an application under paragraph (1)(a)—

(a) if any person on whom notice is served under paragraph (2) does not appear, unless service of the notice on that person is proved; or

(b) if no notice under paragraph (2) has been served, unless the sheriff is satisfied that in the circumstances it was reasonable not to serve notice on any person.

(6) The sheriff may make an order under this regulation only if he is satisfied that the product is a dangerous product.

(7) Where an order for the forfeiture of a product is made following an application by the procurator-fiscal under paragraph (1)(a), any person who appeared, or was entitled to appear to show cause why the product should not be forfeited may, within twenty-one days of the making of the order, appeal to the High Court by Bill of Suspension on the ground of an alleged miscarriage of justice; and section 182(5)(a) to (e) of the Criminal Procedure (Scotland) Act 1995 shall apply to an appeal under this paragraph as it applies to a stated case under Part X of that Act.

(8) An order following an application under paragraph (1)(a) shall not take effect—

(a) until the end of the period of twenty-one days beginning with the day after the day on which the order is made; or

(b) if an appeal is made under paragraph (7) within that period, until the appeal is determined or abandoned.

(9) An order under paragraph (1)(b) shall not take effect—

(a) until the end of the period within which an appeal against the order could be brought under the Criminal Procedure (Scotland) Act 1995; or

(b) if an appeal is made within that period, until the appeal is determined or abandoned.

(10) Subject to paragraph (11), a product forfeited under this regulation shall be destroyed in accordance with such directions as the sheriff may give.

(11) If he thinks fit, the sheriff may direct that the product be released to such person as he may specify, on condition that that person does not supply the product to any other person otherwise than as mentioned in paragraph (11) of regulation 18.

8–5535S   20. Offences.   (1) A person who contravenes regulations 5 or 8(1)(a) shall be guilty of an offence and liable on conviction on indictment to imprisonment for a term not exceeding 12 months or to a fine not exceeding £20,000 or to both, or on summary conviction to imprisonment for a term not exceeding three months or to a fine not exceeding the statutory maximum or to both.

(2) A person who contravenes regulation 7(1), 7(3) (by failing to take any of the measures specified in regulation 7(4)), 8(1)(b)(i), (ii) or (iii) or 9(1) shall be guilty of an offence and liable on summary conviction to imprisonment for a term not exceeding three months or to a fine not exceeding level 5 on the standard scale or to both.

(3) A producer or distributor who does not give notice to an enforcement authority under regulation 9(1) in respect of a product he has placed on the market or supplied commits an offence where it is proved that he ought to have known that the product poses risks to consumers that are incompatible with the general safety requirement and he shall be liable on summary conviction to imprisonment for a term not exceeding three months or to a fine not exceeding level 5 on the standard scale or to both.

(4) A person who contravenes a safety notice shall be guilty of an offence and liable on conviction on indictment to imprisonment for a term not exceeding 12 months or to a fine not exceeding £20,000 or to both, or on summary conviction to imprisonment for a term not exceeding three months or to a fine not exceeding the statutory maximum or to both.

8–5535T   21. Test purchases.   (1) An enforcement authority shall have power to organise appropriate checks on the safety properties of a product, on an adequate scale, up to the final stage of use or consumption and for that purpose may make a purchase of a product or authorise an officer of the authority to make a purchase of a product.

(2) Where a product purchased under paragraph (1) is submitted to a test and the test leads to —

(a) the bringing of proceedings for an offence in respect of a contravention in relation to the product of any requirement imposed by or under these Regulations or for the forfeiture of the product under regulation 18 or 19, or

(b) the serving of a safety notice in respect of the product, and

(c) the authority is requested to do so and it is practicable for the authority to comply with the request,

then the authority shall allow the person from whom the product was purchased, a person who is a party to the proceedings, on whom the notice was served or who has an interest in the product to which the notice relates, to have the product tested.

8–5535U   22. Powers of entry and search etc.   (1) An officer of an enforcement authority may at any reasonable hour and on production, if required, of his credentials exercise any of the powers conferred by the following provisions of this regulation.

(2) The officer may, for the purposes of ascertaining whether there has been a contravention of a requirement imposed by or under these Regulations, enter any premises other than premises occupied only as a person's residence and inspect any record or product.

(3) The officer may, for the purpose of ascertaining whether there has been a contravention of a requirement imposed by or under these Regulations, examine any procedure (including any arrangements for carrying out a test) connected with the production of a product.

(4) If the officer has reasonable grounds for suspecting that the product has not been placed on the market or supplied in the United Kingdom since it was manufactured or imported he may for the purpose of ascertaining whether there has been a contravention in relation to the product of a requirement imposed by or under these Regulations—

(a) require a person carrying on a commercial activity, or employed in connection with a commercial activity, to supply all necessary information relating to the activity, including by the production of records,

(b) require any record which is stored in an electronic form and is accessible from the premises to be produced in a form—

(i) in which it can be taken away, and

(ii) in which it is visible and legible.

(c) for the purpose of ascertaining (by testing or otherwise) whether there has been any such contravention, seize and detain samples of the product,

(d) take copies of, or of an entry in, any records produced by virtue of sub-paragraph (a).

(5) If the officer has reasonable grounds for suspecting that there has been a contravention in relation to a product of a requirement imposed by or under these Regulations, he may—

(a) for the purpose of ascertaining whether there has been any such contravention, require a person carrying on a commercial activity, or employed in connection with a commercial activity, to supply all necessary information relating to the activity, including by the production of records,

(b) for the purpose of ascertaining whether there has been any such contravention, require any record which is stored in an electronic form and is accessible from the premises to be produced in a form—

(i) in which it can be taken away, and

(ii) in which it is visible and legible,

(c) for the purpose of ascertaining (by testing or otherwise) whether there has been any such contravention, seize and detain samples of the product,

(d) take copies of, or of an entry in, any records produced by virtue of sub-paragraph (a).

(6) The officer may seize and detain any products or records which he has reasonable grounds for believing may be required as evidence in proceedings for an offence in respect of a contravention of any requirement imposed by or under these Regulations.

(7) If and to the extent that it is reasonably necessary to do so to prevent a contravention of any requirement imposed by or under these Regulations, the officer may, for the purpose of exercising his power under paragraphs (4) to (6) to seize products or records—

(a) require any person having authority to do so to open any container or to open any vending machine; and

(b) himself open or break open any such container or machine where a requirement made under sub-paragraph (a) in relation to the container or machine has not been complied with.

8–5535V   23. Provisions supplemental to regulation 22 and search warrants etc.   (1) An officer seizing any products or records shall, before he leaves the premises, provide to the person from whom they were seized a written notice—

(a) specifying the products (including the quantity thereof) and records seized,

(b) stating the reasons for their seizure, and

(c) explaining the right of appeal under regulation 25.

(2) References in paragraph (1) and regulation 25 to the person from whom something has been seized, in relation to a case in which the power of seizure was exercisable by reason of the product having been found on any premises, are references to the occupier of the premises at the time of the seizure.

(3) If a justice of the peace—

(a) is satisfied by written information on oath that there are reasonable grounds for believing either—

(i) that any products or records which an officer has power to inspect under regulation 22 are on any premises and that their inspection is likely to disclose evidence that there has been a contravention of any requirement imposed by or under these Regulations, or

(ii) that such a contravention has taken place, is taking place or is about to take place on any premises, and

(b) is also satisfied by such information either—

(i) that admission to the premises has been or is likely to be refused and that notice of the intention to apply for a warrant under this paragraph has been given to the occupier, or

(ii) that an application for admission, or the giving of such a notice, would defeat the object of the entry or that the premises are unoccupied or that the occupier is temporarily absent and it might defeat the object of the entry to await his return.

the justice may by warrant under his hand, which shall continue in force for a period of one month, authorise any officer of an enforcement authority to enter the premises, if need be by force.

(4) An officer entering premises by virtue of regulation 22 or a warrant under paragraph (3) may take him such other persons and equipment as may appear to him necessary.

(5) On leaving any premises which a person is authorised to enter by a warrant under paragraph (3), that person shall, if the premises are unoccupied or the occupier is temporarily absent—

(a) leave the premises as effectively secured against trespassers as he found them,

(b) attach a notice such as is mentioned in paragraph (1) in a prominent place at the premises.

(6) Where a product seized by an officer of an enforcement authority under regulation 22 or 23 is submitted to a test, the authority shall inform the person mentioned in paragraph (1) of the result of the test and, if—

(a) proceedings are brought for an offence in respect of a contravention in relation to the product of any requirement imposed by or under these Regulations or for the forfeiture of the product under regulation 18 or 19; or

(b) a safety notice is served in respect of the product; and

(c) the authority is requested to do so and it is practicable for him to comply with the request,

then the authority shall allow a person who is a party to the proceedings or, on whom the notice was served or who has an interest in the product to which the notice relates to have the product tested.

(7) If a person who is not an officer of an enforcement authority purports to act as such under regulation 22 or under this regulation he shall be guilty of an offence and liable on summary conviction to a fine not exceeding level 5 on the standard scale.

(8) In the application of this section to Scotland, the reference in paragraph (3) to a justice of the peace shall include a reference to a sheriff and the reference to written information on oath shall be construed as a reference to evidence on oath.

(9) In the application of this section to Northern Ireland, the reference in paragraph (3) to a justice of the peace shall include a reference to a lay magistrate and the references to an information on oath shall be construed as a reference to a complaint on oath.

8–5535W 24. Obstruction of officers. (1) A person who—

(a) intentionally obstructs an officer of an enforcement authority who is acting in pursuance of any provision of regulations 22 or 23; or

(b) intentionally fails to comply with a requirement made of him by an officer of an enforcement authority under any provision of those regulations; or

(c) without reasonable cause fails to give an officer of an enforcement authority who is so acting any other assistance or information which the officer may reasonably require of him for the purposes of the exercise of the officer's functions under any provision of those regulations,

shall be guilty of an offence and liable on summary conviction to a fine not exceeding level 5 on the standard scale.

(2) A person shall be guilty of an offence if, in giving any information which is required by him by virtue of paragraph (1)(c)—

(a) he makes a statement which he knows is false in a material particular; or

(b) he recklessly makes a statement which is false in a material particular.

(3) A person guilty of an offence under paragraph (2) shall be liable—

(a) on conviction on indictment, to a fine;

(b) on summary conviction, to a fine not exceeding the statutory maximum.

8–5535X 25. Appeals against detention of products and records. (1) A person referred to in regulation 23(1) may apply for an order requiring any product or record which is for the time being detained under regulation 22 or 23 by an enforcement authority or by an officer of such an authority to be released to him or to another person.

(2) An application under the preceding paragraph may be made—

(a) to any magistrates' court in which proceedings have been brought in England and Wales or Northern Ireland—

    (i) for an offence in respect of a contravention in relation to the product of a requirement imposed by or under these Regulation, or

    (ii) for the forfeiture of the product under regulation 18,

(b) where no such proceedings have been brought, by way of complaint to a magistrates' court;

(c) in Scotland, by summary application to the sheriff.

(3) On an application under paragraph (1) to a magistrates' court or to the sheriff, the court or the sheriff may make an order requiring a product or record to be released only if the court or sheriff is satisfied—

(a) that proceedings

    (i) for an offence in respect of any contravention in relation to the product or, in the case of a record, the product to which the record relates, of any requirement imposed by or under these Regulations; or

    (ii) for the forfeiture of the product or, in the case of a record, the product to which the record relate, under regulation 18 or 19,

have not been brought or, having been brought, have been concluded without the product being forfeited; and

(b) where no such proceedings have been brought, that more than six months have elapsed since the product or records was seized.

(4) In determining whether to make an order under this regulation requiring the release of a product or record the court or sheriff shall take all the circumstances into account including the results of any tests on the product which have been carried out by or on behalf of the enforcement authority and any statement made by the enforcement authority to the court or sheriff as to its intention to bring proceedings for an offence in respect of a contravention in relation to the product of any requirement imposed by or under these Regulations.

(5) Where—

(a) more than 12 months have elapsed since a product or records were seized and the enforcement authority has not commenced proceedings for an offence in respect of a contravention in relation to the product (or, in the case of records, the product to which the records relate) of any requirement imposed by or under these Regulations or for the forfeiture of the product under regulation 18 or 19, or

(b) an enforcement authority has brought proceedings for an offence as mentioned in sub-paragraph (a) and the proceedings were dismissed and all rights of appeal have been exercised or the time for appealing has expired,

the authority shall be under a duty to return the product or records detained under regulation 22 or 23 to the person from whom they were seized.

(6) Where the authority is satisfied that some other person has a better right to a product or record than the person from whom they were seized, the authority shall, instead of the duty in paragraph (5), be under a duty to return it to that other person or, as the case may be, to the person appearing to the authority to have the best right to the product or record in question.

(7) Where different persons claim to be entitled to the return of a product or record that is required to be returned under paragraph (5), then it may be retained for as long as it reasonably necessary for the determination in accordance with paragraph (6) of the person to whom it must be returned.

(8) A person aggrieved by an order made under this regulation by a magistrates' court in England and Wales or Northern Ireland, or by a decision of such a court not to make such an order, may appeal against that order or decision—

(a) in England and Wales, to the Crown Court;
(b) in Northern Ireland, to the county court;

and an order so made may contain such provision as appears to the court to be appropriate for delaying the coming into force of the order pending the making and determination of any appeal (including any application under section 111 of the Magistrates' Courts Act 1980 or article 146 of the Magistrates' Courts (Northern Ireland) Order 1981 (statement of case)).

8–5535Y   26. Compensation for seizure and detention.   Where an officer of an enforcement authority exercises any power under regulation 22 or 23 to seize and detain a product, the enforcement authority shall be liable to pay compensation to any person having an interest in the product in respect of any loss or damage caused by reason of the exercise of the power if—

(a) there has been no contravention in relation to the product of any requirement imposed by or under these Regulations, and
(b) the exercise of the power is not attributable to any neglect or default by that person.

8–5535Z   27. Recovery of expenses of enforcement.   (1) This regulation shall apply where a court—

(a) convicts a person of an offence in respect of a contravention in relation to a product of any requirement imposed by or under these Regulations, or
(b) makes an order under regulation 18 or 19 for the forfeiture of a product.

(2) The court may (in addition to any other order it may make as to costs or expenses) order the person convicted or, as the case may be, any person having an interest in the product to reimburse an enforcement authority for any expenditure which has been or may be incurred by that authority—

(a) in connection with any seizure or detention of the product by or on behalf of the authority, or
(b) in connection with any compliance by the authority with directions given by the court for the purposes of any order for the forfeiture of the product.

8–5536   28. Power of Secretary of State to obtain information.   (1) If the Secretary of State considers that, for the purposes of deciding whether to serve a safety notice, or to vary or revoke a safety notice which he has already served, he requires information or a sample of a product he may serve on a person a notice requiring him:

(a) to furnish to the Secretary of State, within a period specified in the notice, such information as is specified;
(b) to produce such records as are specified in the notice at a time and place so specified (and to produce any such records which are stored in any electronic form in a form in which they are visible and legible) and to permit a person appointed by the Secretary of State for that purpose to take copies of the records at that time and place;
(c) to produce such samples of a product as are specified in the notice at a time and place so specified.

(2) A person shall be guilty of an offence if he—

(a) fails, without reasonable cause, to comply with a notice served on him under paragraph (1); or
(b) in purporting to comply with a requirement which by virtue of paragraph (1)(a) or (b) is contained in such a notice—

    (i) furnishes information or records which he knows are false in a material particular, or

    (ii) recklessly furnishes information or records which are false in a material particular.

(3) A person guilty of an offence under paragraph (2) shall—

(a) in the case of an offence under sub-paragraph (a) of that paragraph, be liable on summary conviction to a fine not exceeding level 5 on the standard scale; and

(b) in the case of an offence under sub-paragraph (b) of that paragraph, be liable—

    (i) on conviction on indictment, to a fine;

    (ii) on summary conviction, to a fine not exceeding the statutory maximum.

8–5536A 29. Defence of due diligence. (1) Subject to the following provisions of this regulation, in proceedings against a person for an offence under these Regulations it shall be a defence for that person to show that he took all reasonable steps and exercised all due diligence to avoid committing the offence.

(2) Where in any proceedings against any person for such an offence the defence provided by paragraph (1) involves an allegation that the commission of the offence was due—

(a) to the act or default of another, or

(b) to reliance on information given by another,

that person shall not, without the leave of the court, be entitled to rely on the defence unless, not less than seven clear days before, in England, Wales and Northern Ireland, the hearing of the proceedings or, in Scotland, the trial diet, he has served a notice under paragraph (3) on the person bringing the proceedings.

(3) A notice under this paragraph shall give such information identifying or assisting in the identification of the person who—

(a) committed the act or default, or

(b) gave the information,

as is in the possession of the person serving the notice at the time he serves it.

(4) A person may not rely on the defence provided by paragraph (1) by reason of his reliance on information supplied by another, unless he shows that it was reasonable in all the circumstances to have relied on the information, having regard in particular—

(a) to the steps which he took, and those which might reasonably have been taken, for the purpose of verifying the information; and

(b) to whether he had any reason to disbelieve the information.

8–5536B 30. Defence in relation to antiques. (1) This regulation shall apply in proceedings against any person for an offence under regulation 20(1) in respect of the supply, offer or agreement to supply or exposure or possession for supply of second hand products supplied as antiques.

(2) It shall be a defence for that person to show that the terms on which he supplied the product or agreed or offered to supply the product or, in the case of a product which he exposed or possessed for supply, the terms on which he intended to supply the product, contemplated the acquisition of an interest in the product by the person supplied or to be supplied.

(3) Paragraph (2) applies only if the producer or distributor clearly informed the person to whom he supplied the product, or offered or agreed to supply the product or, in the case of a product which he exposed or possessed for supply, he intended to so inform that person, that the product is an antique.

8–5536C 31. Liability of person other than principal offender. (1) Where the commission by a person of an offence under these Regulations is due to an act or default committed by some other person in the course of a commercial activity of his, the other person shall be guilty of the offence and may be proceeded against and punished by virtue of this paragraph whether or not proceedings are taken against the first-mentioned person.

(2) Where a body corporate is guilty of an offence under these Regulations (including where it is so guilty by virtue of paragraph (1)) in respect of any act or default which is shown to have been committed with the consent or connivance of, or to be attributable to any neglect on the part of, any director, manager, secretary or other similar officer of the body corporate or any person who was purporting to act in any such capacity he, as well as the body corporate, shall be guilty of that offence and shall be liable to be proceeded against and punished accordingly.

(3) Where the affairs of a body corporate are managed by its members, paragraph (2) shall apply in relation to the acts and defaults of a member in connection with his functions of management as if he were a director of the body corporate.

(4) Where a Scottish partnership is guilty of an offence under these Regulations (including where it is so guilty by virtue of paragraph (1)) in respect of any act or default which is shown to have been committed with the consent or connivance of, or to be attributable to any neglect on the part of, a partner in the partnership, he, as well as the partnership, shall be guilty of that offence and shall be liable to be proceeded against and punished accordingly.

PART 4

MISCELLANEOUS

8–5536D 32. Reports. (1) It shall be the duty of the Secretary of State to lay before each House of Parliament a report on the exercise during the period to which the report relates of the functions which are exercisable by enforcement authorities under these Regulations.

(2) The first such report shall relate to the period beginning on the day on which these Regulations come into force and ending on 31 March 2008 and subsequent reports shall relate to a period of not more than five years beginning on the day after the day on which the period to which the previous report relates ends.

(3) The Secretary of State may from time to time prepare and lay before each House of Parliament such other reports on the exercise of those functions as he considers appropriate.

(4) The Secretary of State may direct an enforcement authority to report at such intervals as he may specify in the direction on the discharge by that authority of the functions exercisable by it under these Regulations.

(5) A report under paragraph (4) shall be in such form and shall contain such particulars as are specified in the direction of the Secretary of State.

8–5536E   33. Duty to notify Secretary of State and Commission.   (1) An enforcement authority which has received a notification under regulation 9(1) shall immediately pass the same on to the Secretary of State, who shall immediately pass it on to the competent authorities appointed for the purpose in the Member States where the product in question is or has been marketed or otherwise supplied to consumers.

(2) Where an enforcement authority takes a measure which restricts the placing on the market of a product, or requires its withdrawal or recall, it shall immediately notify the Secretary of State, specifying its reasons for taking the action. It shall also immediately notify the Secretary of State of any modification or lifting of such a measure.

(3) On receiving a notification under paragraph (2), or if he takes a measure which restricts the placing on the market of a product, or requires its withdrawal or recall, the Secretary of State shall (to the extent that such notification is not required under article 12 of the GPS Directive or any other Community legislation) immediately notify the European Commission of the measure taken, specifying the reasons for taking it. The Secretary of State shall also immediately notify the European Commission of any modification or lifting of such a measure. If the Secretary of State considers that the effects of the risk do not or cannot go beyond the territory of the United Kingdom, he shall notify the European Commission of the measure concerned insofar as it involves information likely to be of interest to Member States from the product safety standpoint, and in particular if it is in response to a new risk which has not yet been reported in other notifications.

(4) Where an enforcement authority adopts or decides to adopt, recommend or agree with producers and distributors, whether on a compulsory or voluntary basis, a measure or action to prevent, restrict or impose specific conditions on the possible marketing or use of a product (other than a pharmaceutical product) by reason of a serious risk, it shall immediately notify the Secretary of State. It shall also immediately notify the Secretary of State of any modification or withdrawal of any such measure or action.

(5) On receiving a notification under paragraph (4), or if he adopts or decides to adopt, recommend or agree with producers and distributors, whether on a compulsory or voluntary basis, a measure or action to prevent, restrict or impose specific conditions on the possible marketing or use of a product (other than a pharmaceutical product) by reason of a serious risk, the Secretary of State shall immediately notify the European Commission of it through the Community Rapid Information System, known as RAPEX. The Secretary of State shall also inform the European Commission without delay of any modification or withdrawal of any such measure or action.

(6) If the Secretary of State considers that the effects of the risk do not or cannot go beyond the territory of the United Kingdom, he shall notify the European Commission of the measures or action concerned insofar as they involve information likely to be of interest to Member States of the European Union from the product safety standpoint, and in particular if they are in response to a new risk which has not been reported in other notifications.

(7) Before deciding to adopt such a measure or take such an action as is referred to in paragraph (5), the Secretary of State may pass on to the European Commission any information in his possession regarding the existence of a serious risk. Where he does so, he must inform the European Commission, within 45 days of the day of passing the information to it, whether he confirms or modifies that information.

(8) Upon receipt of a notification from the European Commission under article 12(2) of the GPS Directive, the Secretary of State shall notify the Commission of the following—

(a) whether the product the subject of the notification has been marketed in the United Kingdom;

(b) what measure concerning the product the enforcement authorities in the United Kingdom may be adopting, stating the reasons, including any differing assessment of risk or any other special circumstance justifying the decision as to the measure, in particular lack of action or follow-up; and

(c) any relevant supplementary information he has obtained on the risk involved, including the results of any test or analysis carried out.

(9) The Secretary of State shall notify the European Commission without delay of any modification or withdrawal of any measures notified to it under paragraph (8)(b).

(10) In this regulation—

(a) references to a product excludes a second hand product supplied as an antique or as a product to be repaired or reconditioned prior to being used, provided the supplier clearly informs the person to whom he supplies the product to that effect;

(b) "pharmaceutical product" means a product falling within Council Directive 2001/83/EC of the European Parliament and of the Council on the Community code relating to medicinal products for human use as amended by Directive 2002/98/EC of the European Parliament and of the Council setting standards of quality and safety for the collection, testing, processing, storage and distribution of human blood and blood components, Commission Directive 2003/63/EC amending Directive 2001/83/EC on the Community code relating to medicinal products for human use, Directive 2004/24/EC of the European Parliament and of the Council amending, as regards traditional herbal medicinal products, Directive 2001/83/EC on the Community code relating to medicinal products for human use and Directive 2004/27/EC of the European Parliament and of the Council amending Directive 2001/83/EC on the Community code relating to medicinal products for human use.

8–5536F   34. Provisions supplemental to regulation 33.   (1) A notification under regulation 33(2) to (6), (8) or (9) to the Secretary of State or the Commission shall be in writing and shall provide all available details and at least the following information—

(a) information enabling the product to be identified,
(b) a description of the risk involved, including a summary of the results of any test or analysis and of their conclusions which are relevant to assessing the level of risk,
(c) the nature and the duration of the measures or action taken or decided on, if applicable,
(d) information on supply chains and distribution of the product, in particular on destination countries.

(2) Where a measure notified to the Commission under regulation 33 seeks to limit the marketing or use of a chemical substance or preparation, the Secretary of State shall provide to the Commission as soon as possible either a summary or the references of the relevant data relating to the substance or preparation considered and to known and available substitutes, where such information is available. The Secretary of State shall also notify the Commission of the anticipated effects of the measure on consumer health and safety together with the assessment of the risk carried out in accordance with the general principles for the risk evaluation of chemical substances as referred to in article 10(4) of Council Regulation (EEC) No 793/93 of 23 March 1993 on the evaluation and control of the risks of existing substances, in the case of an existing substance, or in article 3(2) of Council Directive 67/548/EEC on the approximation of laws, regulations and administrative provisions relating to the classification, packaging and labelling of dangerous substances in the case of a new substance.

(3) Where the Commission carries out an investigation under paragraph 5 of Annex II to the GPS Directive, the Secretary of State shall supply the Commission with such information as it requests, to the best of his ability.

8–5536G   35. Implementation of Commission decisions.   (1) This regulation applies where the Commission adopts a decision pursuant to article 13 of the GPS Directive.

(2) The Secretary of State shall—

(a) take such action under these Regulations, or
(b) direct another enforcement authority to take such action under these Regulations

as is necessary to comply with the decision.

(3) Where an enforcement authority serves a safety notice pursuant to paragraph (2), the following provisions of these Regulations shall not apply in relation to that notice, namely regulations 14(3), 15(4) to (6) and 16(1), 16(2)(c) and (d), 16(5) to (7) and 17.

(4) Unless the Commission's decision provides otherwise, export from the Community of a dangerous product which is the subject of such a decision is prohibited with effect from the date the decision comes into force.

(5) The enforcement of the prohibition in paragraph (4) shall be treated as an assigned matter within the meaning of section 1(1) of the Customs and Excise Management Act 1979.

(6) The measures necessary to implement the decision shall be taken within 20 days, unless the decision specifies a different period.

(7) The Secretary of State or, where the Secretary of State has directed another enforcement authority to take action under paragraph (2)(b), that enforcement authority shall, within one month, give the parties concerned an opportunity to submit their views and shall inform the Commission accordingly.

8–5536H   36. Market surveillance.   In order to ensure a high level of consumer health and safety protection, enforcement authorities shall within the limits of their responsibility and to the extent of their ability undertake market surveillance of products employing appropriate means and procedures and co-operating with other enforcement authorities and competent authorities of other Member States which may include:

(a) establishment, periodical updating and implementation of sectoral surveillance programmes by categories of products or risks and the monitoring of surveillance activities, findings and results,
(b) follow-up and updating of scientific and technical knowledge concerning the safety of products,

(c) the periodical review and assessment of the functioning of the control activities and their effectiveness and, if necessary revision of the surveillance approach and organisation put in place.

8–5536I 37. Complaints procedures. An enforcement authority shall maintain and publish a procedure by which complaints may be submitted by any person on product safety and on surveillance and control activities, which complaints shall be followed up as appropriate.

8–5536J 38. Co-operation between enforcement authorities. (1) It shall be the duty of an enforcement authority to co-operate with other enforcement authorities in carrying out the functions conferred on them by these Regulations. In particular—

(a) enforcement authorities shall share their expertise and best practices with each other;
(b) enforcement authorities shall undertake collaborative working where they have a shared interest.

(2) The Secretary of State shall inform the European Commission as to the arrangements for the enforcement of these Regulations, including which bodies are enforcement authorities.

8–5536K 39. Information. (1) An enforcement authority shall in general make available to the public such information as is available to it on the following matters relating to the risks to consumer health and safety posed by a product—

(a) the nature of the risk,
(b) the product identification,

and the measures taken in respect of the risk, without prejudice to the need not to disclose information for effective monitoring and investigation activities.

(2) Paragraph (1) shall not apply to any information obtained by an enforcement authority for the purposes of these Regulations which, by its nature, is covered by professional secrecy, unless the circumstances require such information to be made public in order to protect the health and safety of consumers.

(3) The Enterprise Act 2002 (Part 9 Restrictions on Disclosure of Information) (Amendment and Specification) Order 2003 is amended—

(i) by the omission of the "General Product Safety Regulations 1994" from Schedules 3 and 4; and
(ii) by the insertion of the "General Product Safety Regulations 2005" at the end of Schedules 3 and 4.

8–5536L 40. Service of documents. (1) A document required or authorised by virtue of these Regulations to be served on a person may be so served—

(a) on an individual by delivering it to him or by leaving it at his proper address or by sending it by post to him at that address;
(b) on a body corporate other than a limited liability partnership, by serving it in accordance with sub-paragraph (a) on the secretary of the body;
(c) on a limited liability partnership, by serving it in accordance with sub-paragraph (a) on a member of the partnership; or
(d) on a partnership, by serving it in accordance with sub-paragraph (a) on a partner or a person having the control or management of the partnership business;
(e) on any other person by leaving it at his proper address or by sending it by post to him at that address.

(2) For the purposes of paragraph (1), and for the purposes of section 7 of the Interpretation Act 1978 (which relates to the service of documents by post) in its application to that paragraph, the proper address of a person on whom a document is to be served by virtue of these Regulations shall be his last known address except that—

(a) in the case of a body corporate (other than a limited liability partnership) or its secretary, it shall be the address of the registered or principal office of the body;
(b) in the case of a limited liability partnership or a member of the partnership, it shall be the address of the registered or principal office of the partnership;
(c) in the case of a partnership or a partner or a person having the control or management of a partnership business, it shall be the address of the principal office of the partnership,

and for the purposes of this paragraph the principal officer of a company constituted under the law of a country or territory outside the United Kingdom or of a partnership carrying on business outside the United Kingdom is its principal office within the United Kingdom.

(3) A document required or authorised by virtue of these Regulations to be served on a person may also be served by transmitting the request by any means of electronic communication to an electronic address (which includes a fax number and an e-mail address) being an address which the person has held out as an address at which he or it can be contacted for the purposes of receiving such documents.

(4) A document transmitted by any means of electronic communication in accordance with the preceding paragraph is, unless the contrary is proved, deemed to be received on the business day after the notice was transmitted over a public electronic communications network.

8–5536M 41. Extension of time for bringing summary proceedings. (1) Notwithstanding section 127 of the Magistrates' Courts Act 1980 or article 19 of the Magistrates' Courts (Northern Ireland) Order 1981, in England, Wales and Northern Ireland a magistrates' court may try an information (in the case of England and Wales) or a complaint (in the case of Northern Ireland) in respect of an offence under these Regulations if (in the case of England and Wales) the information is laid or (in the case of Northern Ireland) the complaint is made within three years from the date of the offence or within one year from the discovery of the offence by the prosecutor whichever is the earlier.

(2) Notwithstanding section 136 of the Criminal Procedure (Scotland) Act 1995, in Scotland summary proceedings for an offence under these Regulations may be commenced within three years from the date of the offence or within one year from the discovery of the offence by the prosecutor whichever is the earlier.

(3) For the purposes of paragraph (2), section 136(3) of the Criminal Procedure (Scotland) Act 1995 shall apply as it applies for the purposes of that section.

8–5536N 42. Civil proceedings. These Regulations shall not be construed as conferring any right of action in civil proceedings in respect of any loss or damage suffered in consequence of a contravention of these Regulations.

8–5536O 43. Privileged information. (1) Nothing in these Regulations shall be taken as requiring a person to produce any records if he would be entitled to refuse to produce those records in any proceedings in any court on the grounds that they are the subject of legal professional privilege or, in Scotland, that they contain a confidential communication made by or to an advocate or solicitor in that capacity, or as authorising a person to take possession of any records which are in the possession of a person who would be so entitled.

(2) Nothing in these Regulations shall be construed as requiring a person to answer any question or give any information if to do so would incriminate that person or that person's spouse or civil partner.

8–5536P 44. Evidence in proceedings for offence relating to regulation 9(1). (1) This regulation applies where a person has given a notification to an enforcement authority pursuant to regulation 9(1).

(2) No evidence relating to that statement may be adduced and no question relating to it may be asked by the prosecution in any criminal proceedings (other than proceedings in which that person is charged with an offence under regulation 20 for a contravention of regulation 9(1)), unless evidence relating to it is adduced, or a question relating to it is asked, in the proceedings by or on behalf of that person.

8–5536Q 45. Transitional provisions. Where, in relation to a product, a suspension notice (within the meaning of the 1987 Act) has (by virtue of regulation 11(b) of the General Product Safety Regulations 1994) been served under section 14 of the 1987 Act and is in force immediately prior to the coming into force of these Regulations, it shall continue in force notwithstanding the revocation of the General Product Safety Regulations 1994 by these Regulations, and those Regulations shall continue to apply accordingly.

8–5536R 46. Amendments to the Consumer Protection Act 1987

8–5536S 47. Consequential amendments to other legislation. (1) Omit paragraph 15(1) of Schedule 4 to the Gas Act 1995.

(2) The Criminal Justice and Police Act 2001 is amended as follows.

(3) In section 66(4), insert the following after paragraph (n)—

"(o) regulation 22 of the General Product Safety Regulations 2005 (powers of entry and search etc)".

(4) In Schedule 1, insert the following after paragraph 73F—

"General Product Safety Regulations 2005

73G. Each of the powers of seizure conferred by the provisions of regulation 22(4) to (6) of the General Product Safety Regulations 2005 (seizure for the purposes of ascertaining whether safety provisions have been contravened etc).".

(5) In Schedule 2—

(a) insert the following after paragraph 4—

"4A. Regulation 23(6) of the General Product Safety Regulations 2005 (provision about the testing of seized products) shall apply in relation to items seized under section 50 of this Act in reliance on the power of seizure conferred by regulation 23 of those Regulations as it applies in relation to items seized under regulation 22 of those Regulations.".

(b) insert the following after paragraph 9—

"9A. Regulation 26 of the General Product Safety Regulations 2005 (compensation for seizure and detention) shall apply in relation to the seizure of items under section 50 of this Act in reliance on the power of seizure conferred by regulation 22 of those Regulations, and the retention of products under regulations 22 of those Regulations.".

COPYRIGHT, DESIGNS AND PATENTS

8–5560   This title contains references to the following statutes—

This title contains the following statutory instrument—

Chartered Associations (Protection of Names and Uniforms) Act 1926
(16 & 17 Geo 5 c 26)

8–5580   **1. Protection of name, uniform, etc of chartered associations.**   (1)–(2) *Protection by means of Order in Council.*

(3) Where the use by an association[1] of any name, designation, uniform or badge has been so protected[2] a person shall not, without the authority of the association, use the name, designation, uniform or badge the use of which is so protected, or any name, designation, uniform or badge so closely resembling the name, designation, uniform or badge, the use of which is protected as to lead to the belief that it is that name, designation, uniform or badge.

(4) If any person acts in contravention of this section he shall be liable in respect of each offence, on summary conviction, to a fine not exceeding **level 1** on the standard scale; provided that this section shall not prevent any person from wearing or using any uniform, badge or distinctive marking in the course or for the purpose of a stage play or representation, or a music-hall or circus performance, pageant or production of a cinematograph film, if the uniform, badge or distinctive mark is not worn or used in such a manner or under such circumstances as to bring it into contempt.

(5) Where on an application made by or on behalf of an association to which this Act applies any such uniform or badge as is mentioned in subsection (1) of this section has at any time been registered under Part II of the Patents and Designs Act 1907 an Order in Council under this Act may be made on the application of that association for protecting that uniform or badge, notwithstanding that the right in the registered design has expired.

[Chartered Associations (Protection of Names and Uniforms) Act 1926, s 1, as amended by the Criminal Law Act 1977, s 31, the Criminal Justice Act 1982, s 46 and the Copyright, Designs and Patents Act 1988, Sch 7.]

---

1. As association incorporated by Royal Charter not being an association representative of any profession or business (Chartered Associations (Protection of Names and Uniforms) Act 1926, s 1(1)).

2. The protection will be by Order in Council made on application of the Association, provided that nothing in the Order or the Act shall deprive any *bona fide* national organisation of the right to use any designation, uniform or badge which on 4th August 1926 is in regular use by that organisation (Chartered Associations (Protection of Names and Uniforms) Act 1926, s 1(1)). As to associations of Boy Scouts, Girl Guides, St John of Jerusalem, British Legion, and Royal Life Saving Society, see SR & O 1927 Nos 1057, 1058 and 1959, SR & O 1931 Nos 999 and 1099, SI 1962/407 and SI 1967/1678. Nothing in the Act prevents the continued use of any mark or device which has been *bona fide* used as a trade mark before 25 August 1926 (s 3).

Patents Act 1949
(12, 13 and 14 Geo 6 c 87)

Offences

8–5590   **92. Unauthorised assumption of Royal Arms.**   (1) The grant of a patent[1] under this Act shall not be deemed to authorise the patentee[2] to use the Royal Arms or to place the Royal Arms on any patented article.

(2) *Repealed.*

[Patents Act 1949, s 92, as amended by the Criminal Law Act 1977, s 31, the Criminal Justice Act 1982, s 46 and the Trade Marks Act 1994, Sch 5.]

---

1. "Patent" means Letters Patent for an invention (s 101(1)). "Invention" means any manner of new manufacture the subject of letters patent and grant of privilege within s 6 of the Statute of Monopolies and any new method or process of testing applicable to the improvement or control of manufacture, and includes an alleged invention (s 101(1)).

2. "Patentee" means the person or persons for the time being entered on the register of patents as grantee or proprietor of the patent (s 101(1)).

Registered Designs Act 1949

(12, 13 & 14 Geo 6 c 88)

Registrable designs and proceedings for registration

8–5600   1. Designs registrable under Act[1]. (1) In this Act "design" means features of shape, configuration, pattern or ornament applied to an article by any industrial process, being features which in the finished article appeal to and are judged by the eye, but does not include—

(a)   a method or principle of construction, or

(b)   features of shape or configuration of an article which—

(i)   are dictated solely by the function which the article has to perform, or

(ii)   are dependent upon the appearance of another article of which the article is intended by the author of the design to form an integral part.

(2)   A design which is new may, upon application by the person claiming to be the proprietor, be registered under this Act in respect of any article, or set of articles, specified in the application.

(3)   A design shall not be registered in respect of an article if the appearance of the article is not material, that is, if aesthetic considerations are not normally taken into account to a material extent by persons acquiring or using articles of that description, and would not be so taken into account if the design were to be applied to the article.

(4)   A design shall not be regarded as new for the purposes of this Act if it is the same as a design—

(a)   registered in respect of the same or any other article in pursuance of a prior application, or

(b)   published in the United Kingdom in respect of the same or any other article before the date of the application,

or if it differs from such a design only in immaterial details or in features which are variants commonly used in the trade.

This subsection has effect subject to the provisions of sections 4, 6 and 16[2] of this Act.

(5)   The Secretary of State may by rules[3] provide for excluding from registration under this Act designs for such articles of a primarily literary or artistic character as the Secretary of State thinks fit.

(6)   A design shall not be registered if it consists of or contains a controlled representation within the meaning of the Olympic Symbol etc (Protection) Act 1995 unless it appears to the registrar—

(a)   that the application is made by the person for the time being appointed under section 1(2) of the Olympic Symbol etc (Protection) Act 1995 (power of Secretary of State to appoint a person as the proprietor of the Olympics association right), or

(b)   that consent has been given by or on behalf of the person mentioned in paragraph (a) of this subsection.

[Registered Designs Act 1949, s 1, as substituted by the Copyright, Designs and Patents Act 1988, s 265 and amended by the Olympic Symbol etc (Protection) Act 1995, s 13.]

---

1. For provisions with respect to certain designs registered in pursuance of an application made before the commencement, namely 1 August 1989, of Part IV of the Copyright, Designs and Patents Act 1988, which substituted the new s 1, reference should be made to s 266 of the Copyright, Designs and Patents Act 1988.

2. These sections are not printed in this work.

3. See the Registered Designs Rules 1995, SI 1995/2912 amended by SI 1999/3196 and SI 2001/3950.

8–5600A   1A. Substantive grounds for refusal of registration.   (1) The following shall be refused registration under this Act—

(a)   anything which does not fulfil the requirements of section 1(2) of this Act;

(b)   designs which do not fulfil the requirements of sections 1B to 1D of this Act;

(c)   designs to which a ground of refusal mentioned in Schedule A1 to this Act applies.

(2)   A design ("the later design") shall be refused registration under this Act if it is not new or does not have individual character when compared with a design which—

(a)   has been made available to the public on or after the relevant date; but

(b)   is protected as from a date prior to the relevant date by virtue of registration under this Act or the Community Design Regulation or an application for such registration.

(3)   In subsection (2) above "the relevant date" means the date on which the application for the registration of the later design was made or is treated by virtue of section 3B(2), (3) or (5) or 14(2) of this Act as having been made.

[Registered Designs Act 1949, s 1A, as substituted by SI 2001/3949, reg 2 and amended by SI 2003/550.]

8–5600B   1B. requirement of novelty and individual character.   (1) A design shall be protected by a right in a registered design to the extent that the design is new and has individual character.

(2) For the purposes of subsection (1) above, a design is new if no identical design or no design whose features differ only in immaterial details has been made available to the public before the relevant date.

(3) For the purposes of subsection (1) above, a design has individual character if the overall impression it produces on the informed user differs from the overall impression produced on such a user by any design which has been made available to the public before the relevant date.

(4) In determining the extent to which a design has individual character, the degree of freedom of the author in creating the design shall be taken into consideration.

(5) For the purposes of this section, a design has been made available to the public before the relevant date if—

(*a*) it has been published (whether following registration or otherwise), exhibited, used in trade or otherwise disclosed before that date; and

(*b*) the disclosure does not fall within subsection (6) below.

(6) A disclosure falls within this subsection if—

(*a*) it could not reasonably have become known before the relevant date in the normal course of business to persons carrying on business in the European Economic Area and specialising in the sector concerned;

(*b*) it was made to a person other than the designer, or any successor in title of his, under conditions of confidentiality (whether express or implied);

(*c*) it was made by the designer, or any successor in title of his, during the period of 12 months immediately preceding the relevant date;

(*d*) it was made by a person other than the designer, or any successor in title of his, during the period of 12 months immediately preceding the relevant date in consequence of information provided or other action taken by the designer or any successor in title of his; or

(*e*) it was made during the period of 12 months immediately preceding the relevant date as a consequence of an abuse in relation to the designer or any successor in title of his.

(7) In subsections (2), (3), (5) and (6) above "the relevant date" means the date on which the application for the registration of the design was made or is treated by virtue of section 3B(2), (3) or (5) or 14(2) of this Act as having been made.

(8) For the purposes of this section, a design applied to or incorporated in a product which constitutes a component part of a complex product shall only be considered to be new and to have individual character—

(*a*) if the component part, once it has been incorporated into the complex product, remains visible during normal use of the complex product; and

(*b*) to the extent that those visible features of the component part are in themselves new and have individual character.

(9) In subsection (8) above "normal use" means use by the end user; but does not include any maintenance, servicing or repair work in relation to the product.
[Registered Designs Act 1949, s 1B, as substituted by SI 2001/3949, reg 2.]

8–5600C 1C. Designs dictated by their technical function. (1) A right in a registered design shall not subsist in features of appearance of a product which are solely dictated by the product's technical function.

(2) A right in a registered design shall not subsist in features of appearance of a product which must necessarily be reproduced in their exact form and dimensions so as to permit the product in which the design is incorporated or to which it is applied to be mechanically connected to, or placed in, around or against, another product so that either product may perform its function.

(3) Subsection (2) above does not prevent a right in a registered design subsisting in a design serving the purpose of allowing multiple assembly or connection of mutually interchangeable products within a modular system.
[Registered Designs Act 1949, s 1C, as substituted by SI 2001/3949, reg 2.]

8–5600D 1D. Designs contrary to public policy or morality. A right in a registered design shall not subsist in a design which is contrary to public policy or to accepted principles of morality.
[Registered Designs Act 1949, s 1D, as substituted by SI 2001/3949, reg 2.]

8–5601 2. Proprietorship of designs. (1) The author of a design shall be treated for the purposes of this Act as the original proprietor of the design, subject to the following provisions.

(1A) Where a design is created in pursuance of a commission for money or money's worth, the person commissioning the design shall be treated as the original proprietor of the design.

(1B) Where, in a case not falling within subsection (1A), a design is created by an employee in the course of his employment, his employer shall be treated as the original proprietor of the design.

(2) Where a design, or the right to apply a design to any article, becomes vested, whether by assignment, transmission or operation of law, in any person other than the original proprietor, either alone or jointly with the original proprietor, that other person, or as the case may be the original

proprietor and that other person, shall be treated for the purposes of this Act as the proprietor of the design or as the proprietor of the design in relation to that article.

(3) In this Act the "author" of a design means the person who creates it.

(4) In the case of a design generated by computer in circumstances such that there is no human author, the person by whom the arrangements necessary for the creation of the design are made shall be taken to be the author.

[Registered Designs Act 1949, s 2, as amended by the Copyright, Designs and Patents Act 1988, s 267.]

8–5602   3–4. *Proceedings for registration; registration of same design in respect of other articles, etc.*

8–5603   5. Provisions for secrecy of certain designs[1]**.** (1) Where, either before or after the commencement of this Act, an application for the registration of a design has been made, and it appears to the registrar that the design is one of a class notified to him by the Secretary of State as relevant for defence purposes, he may give directions for prohibiting or restricting the publication of information with respect to the design, or the communication of such information to any person or class of persons specified in the directions.

(2) The Secretary of State shall by rules[2] make provision for securing that where such directions are given—

(a) the representation or specimen of the design, and

(b) any evidence filed in support of the applicant's contention that the appearance of an article is material (for the purposes of section 1(3) of this Act),

shall not be open to public inspection[3] at the Patent Office during the continuance in force of the directions.

(3) Where the registrar gives any such directions as aforesaid, he shall give notice of the application and of the directions to the Secretary of State, and thereupon the following provisions shall have effect, that is to say—

(a) the Secretary of State shall, upon receipt of such notice, consider whether the publication of the design would be prejudicial to the defence of the realm and unless a notice under paragraph (c) of this subsection has previously been given by [him] to the registrar, shall reconsider that question before the expiration of nine months from the date of filing of the application for registration of the design and at least once in every subsequent year;

(b) for the purpose aforesaid, the Secretary of State may, at any time after the design has been registered or, with the consent of the applicant, at any time before the design has been registered, inspect the representation or specimen of the design, or any such evidence as is mentioned in subsection (2)(b) above, filed in pursuance of the application;

(c) if upon consideration of the design at any time it appears to the Secretary of State that the publication of the design would not, or would no longer, be prejudicial to the defence of the realm, he shall give notice to the registrar to that effect;

(d) on the receipt of any such notice the registrar shall revoke the directions and may, subject to such conditions, if any, as he thinks fit, extend the time for doing anything required or authorised to be done by or under this Act in connection with the application or registration, whether or not that time has previously expired.

(4) No person resident in the United Kingdom shall, except under the authority of a written permit granted by or on behalf of the registrar, make or cause to be made any application outside the United Kingdom for the registration of a design of any class prescribed for the purposes of this subsection unless—

(a) an application for registration of the same design has been made in the United Kingdom not less than six weeks before the application outside the United Kingdom; and

(b) either no directions have been given under subsection (1) of this section in relation to the application in the United Kingdom or all such directions have been revoked:

Provided that this subsection shall not apply in relation to a design for which an application for protection has first been filed in a country outside the United Kingdom by a person resident outside the United Kingdom.

(5) (*Repealed*).

[Registered Designs Act 1949, s 5, as amended by the Copyright, Designs and Patents Act 1988, Schs 3 and 8.]

---

1. For penalty for failure to comply with a direction given under this section or making an application for registration in contravention of the section, see s 33, post.

2. See the Registered Designs Rules 1995, SI 1995/2912 amended by SI 1999/3196 and SI 2001/3950.

3. As to when designs are normally open to inspection, see s 22 of the Act.

Offences

8–5604   33. Offences under section 5. (1) If any person fails to comply with any direction given under section five of this Act or makes or causes to be made an application for the registration of a design[1] in contravention of that section, he shall be guilty of an offence and liable[2]—

(*a*) on conviction on indictment to imprisonment for a term not exceeding **two years** or a **fine**, or both;

(*b*) on summary conviction to imprisonment for a term not exceeding **six months** or a fine not exceeding **the statutory maximum**, or both.

(2) (*Repealed*).

[Registered Designs Act 1949, s 33, as amended by the Criminal Law Act 1977, s 32, and the Copyright, Designs and Patents Act 1988, Schs 3 and 8.]

----

1. For the meaning of "design", see s 1, ante.
2. For procedure in respect of this offence which is triable either way, see the Magistrates' Courts Act 1980, ss 17A–21, in PART I: MAGISTRATES' COURTS, PROCEDURE, ante.

8–5605   34. Falsification of register, etc.   If any person makes or causes to be made a false entry in the register of designs[1], or a writing falsely purporting to be a copy of an entry in that register, or produces or tenders or causes to be produced or tendered in evidence any such writing, knowing the entry or writing to be false, he shall be guilty of an offence and liable[2]—

(*a*) on conviction on indictment to imprisonment for a term not exceeding **two years** or a **fine**, or both;

(*b*) on summary conviction to imprisonment for a term not exceeding **six months** or a fine not exceeding **the statutory maximum**, or both.

[Registered Designs Act 1949, s 34, as amended by the Copyright, Designs and Patents Act 1988, Sch 3.]

----

1. For provisions relating to the register of designs, see ss 17–23.
2. For procedure in respect of this offence which is triable either way, see the Magistrates' Courts Act 1980, ss 17A–21, in PART I: MAGISTRATES' COURTS, PROCEDURE, ante.

8–5606   35. Fine for falsely representing a design as registered.   (1) If any person falsely represents that a design[1] applied to any article[2] sold by him is registered in respect of that article, he shall be liable on summary conviction to a fine not exceeding **level 3** on the standard scale; and for the purposes of this provision a person who sells an article having stamped, engraved or impressed thereon or otherwise applied thereto the word "registered", or any other word expressing or implying that the design applied to the article is registered, shall be deemed to represent that the design applied to the article is registered in respect of the article.

(2) If any person, after the right in a registered design has expired, marks any article to which the design has been applied with the word "registered", or any word or words implying that there is a subsisting right in the design under this Act, or causes any such article to be so marked, he shall be liable on summary conviction to a fine not exceeding **level 1** on the standard scale.

(3) For the purposes of this section, the use in the United Kingdom in relation to a design—

(*a*) of the word "registered", or

(*b*) of any other word or symbol importing a reference (express or implied) to registration,

shall be deemed to be a representation as to registration under this Act unless it is shown that the reference is to registration elsewhere than in the United Kingdom and that the design is in fact so registered.

[Registered Designs Act 1949, s 35, as amended by the Criminal Justice Act 1967, Sch 3, the Criminal Law Act 1977, s 31, the Criminal Justice Act 1982, ss 38 and 46, the Copyright, Designs and Patents Act 1988, Sch 3 and SI 2005/2339.]

----

1. For the meaning of "design", see s 1, ante.
2. For the meaning of "article", see s 44, post.

8–5607   35A. Offence by body corporate: liability of officers.   (1) Where an offence under this Act committed by a body corporate is proved to have been committed with the consent or connivance of a director, manager, secretary or other similar officer of the body, or a person purporting to act in any such capacity, he as well as the body corporate is guilty of the offence and liable to be proceeded against and punished accordingly.

(2) In relation to a body corporate whose affairs are managed by its members "director" means a member of the body corporate.

[Registered Designs Act 1949, s 35A, as inserted by the Copyright, Designs and Patents Act 1988, Sch 3.]

8–5608   44. Interpretation.   (1) In this Act, except where the context otherwise requires, the following expressions have the meanings hereby respectively assigned by them, that is to say—

"Appeal Tribunal" means the Appeal Tribunal constituted and acting in accordance with section 28 of this Act as amended by the Administration of Justice Act 1969;

"assignee" includes the personal representative of a deceased assignee, and references to the assignee of any person include references to the assignee of the personal representative or assignee of that person;

"author" in relation to a design, has the meaning given by section 2(3) and (4):

"Community Design Regulation" means Council Regulation (EC) 6/2002 of 12th December 2001 on Community Designs;

"complex product" has the meaning assigned to it by section 1(3) of this Act;"the court" shall be construed in accordance with section 27 of this Act;

"design" has the meaning assigned to it by section 1(1) of this Act;

"employee", "employment" and "employer" refer to employment under a contract of service or of apprenticeship,

"national unregistered design right" means design right within the meaning of Part III of the Copyright, Designs and Patents Act 1988;

"prescribed" means prescribed by rules made by the Secretary of State under this Act;

"product" has the meaning assigned to it by section 1(3) of this Act;

"proprietor" has the meaning assigned to it by section two of this Act;

"registered Community design" means a design that complies with the conditions contained in, and is registered in the manner provided for in, the Community Design Regulation;

"registered proprietor" means the person or persons for the time being entered in the register of designs as proprietor of the design;

"registrar" means the Comptroller-General of Patents, Designs and Trade Marks;

(2) *(Revoked)*.

(3) *(Revoked)*.

(4) For the purposes of subsection (1) of section fourteen and of section sixteen of this Act, the expression "personal representative", in relation to a deceased person, includes the legal representative of the deceased appointed in any country outside the United Kingdom.

[Registered Designs Act 1949, s 44, as amended by the Copyright Act 1956, s 44, the Administration of Justice Act 1969, s 35 and Sch 1, the Patents Act 1977, s 132 and Sch 5, the Copyright, Designs and Patents Act 1988, Schs 3 and 8, SI 2001/3949 and SI 2003/550.]

Hallmarking Act 1973
(1973 c 43)

8–5609 **1. Prohibited descriptions of unhallmarked articles.** (1) Subject to the provisions of this Act, any person who, in the course of a trade or business—

(a) applies to an unhallmarked article a description indicating that it is wholly or partly made of gold, silver or platinum, or

(b) supplies, or offers to supply, an unhallmarked article to which such a description is applied,

shall be guilty of an offence[1].

(2) Subsection (1) above shall not apply to a description which is permitted by Part I of Schedule 1 to this Act.

(3) Subsection (1) above shall not apply to an article within Part II of the said Schedule.

(4) Notwithstanding section 3(1) of the Trade Descriptions Act 1968 (definition of "false trade description" as one which is false to a material degree) a trade description which indicates the fineness (whether in parts per thousand or otherwise) of any precious metal shall be a false trade description if that indication is false to any extent or degree (except by understating the fineness).

The Trade Descriptions Act 1968 is in this Act referred to as "the Act of 1968".

(5) Part III of the said Schedule shall apply for construing descriptions relating to the fineness of precious metals.

(6) The provisions of this section have effect subject to Part IV of the said Schedule.

(7) For the purposes of this section—

(a) "advertisement" includes a catalogue, a circular and a price list,

(b) section 4 of the Act of 1968 (which defines "applies a trade description") shall apply to paragraphs (a) and (b) of subsection (1), for the interpretation of references to a description being applied to any article, as it applies for the interpretation of references in that Act to applying a trade description,

(c) a person exposing articles for supply, or having articles in his possession for supply, "offers to supply" them.

(8) Where in an advertisement a description is used in relation to any class of articles, the description shall be taken as referring to all articles of the class, whether or not in existence at the time the advertisement is published—

(a) for the purpose of determining whether an offence has been committed under subsection (1)(a) above, and

(b) where articles of the class are supplied or offered to be supplied by a person publishing or displaying the advertisement, also for the purpose of determining whether an offence has been committed under subsection (1)(b) above;

and section 5(3) of the Act of 1968 (defining goods of the class in question) shall apply for determining whether any articles are of a class to which a description used in an advertisement relates.

(9) Section 39(2) of the Act of 1968 (descriptions in publication or broadcasts) shall apply for the purposes of this section.
[Hallmarking Act 1973, s 1.]

---

1. For penalty and other provisions as to offences, see Sch 3 and s 10, post. An offence under s 1(1)(*b*) is an offence of strict liability thus the prosecution do not have to establish *mens rea* (*Chilvers v Rayner* [1984] 1 All ER 843, [1984] 1 WLR 328, 148 JP 50).

8–5610   2. Meaning of approved hallmarks, etc.   (1) In this Act, unless the context otherwise requires, "approved hallmarks" means—

   (*a*)   marks struck by an assay office in the United Kingdom, whether before or after the commencement of this Act, under the law for the time being in force, or

   (*b*)   marks struck by the Wardens and Commonalty of Goldsmiths of the City of Dublin before 1st April 1923, or

   (*c*)   marks struck by an assay office under the law of a country outside the United Kingdom, being marks designated for the purposes of this section by order[1] of the Secretary of State as marks recognised pursuant to any international convention or treaty to which Her Majesty's Government in the United Kingdom is a party, or

   (*d*)   marks struck in an EEA State other than the United Kingdom, being marks which—

      (i)   have been struck by an independent body in accordance with the law of that State; and

      (ii)   provide information which is equivalent to the information provided by the marks mentioned in section 4(1)(*a*)(i) and (ii) of this Act and which is intelligible to consumers in the United Kingdom.

(2) Marks within subsection (1)(*c*) above are in this Act called "convention hallmarks", and marks within subsection (1)(*d*) above are in this Act called "EEA hallmarks".

(2A) In this section "EEA State" means a Contracting Party to the Agreement on the European Economic Area signed at Oporto on 2nd May 1992 as adjusted by the Protocol signed at Brussels on 17th March 1993.

(3) The Secretary of State may by order make such provision as appears to him appropriate for enabling articles submitted to an assay office in the United Kingdom to be struck with marks which, pursuant to any convention or treaty falling within subsection (1)(*c*) above, will, or will with other marks, be accorded recognition under the law of any other country, and for making consequential or incidental provisions, including provision for excluding or modifying any of the provisions of this Act.

(4) For the purposes of this Act an article is unhallmarked—

   (*a*)   if it does not bear the approved hallmarks and the sponsor's mark, or

   (*b*)   if the article has been the subject of any improper alteration.

(5) In this Act "improper alteration" means an addition, alteration or repair which has been made to an article bearing approved hallmarks and—

   (*a*)   which contravened section 5 of this Act, or

   (*b*)   which was made before the coming into force of that section, and would have required the consent of an assay office if that section had been in force, or

   (*c*)   in the case of an article which bears a convention hallmark or an EEA hallmark, would have required that consent if the addition, alteration or repair had been made in the United Kingdom:

Provided that paragraphs (*b*) and (*c*) of this subsection shall not apply if, after the marking of the addition, alteration or repair, the article has been re-assayed and struck with any further approved hallmark.
[Hallmarking Act 1973, s 2 as amended by SI 1998/2798.]

---

1. The Hallmarking (International Convention) Order 2002, SI 2002/506

8–5611   3. Sponsors' marks.   (1) Before an article is submitted to an assay office to be struck with the approved hallmarks there shall be struck on the article a mark indicative of the manufacturer or sponsor and known as the sponsor's mark:

Provided that the assay office and the manufacturer or sponsor of an article may make arrangements for the sponsor's mark to be struck by that assay office upon submission of the article to be struck with the approved hallmarks.

(2) After 31st December 1975 all sponsors' marks for the time being in use shall cease to be authorised for striking on any article intended to be struck with the approved hallmarks and thenceforth a sponsor's mark shall be authorised (whether or not of the same design as any sponsor's mark which authorised before 1st January 1976) only if it is for the time being registered under the following provisions of this section with an assay office by which the article is intended to be so struck.

(3)–(7) *Registration of sponsor's mark.*

(8) Any person who without authority strikes an article with a mark purporting to be a sponsor's mark authorised under this section shall be guilty of an offence[1].
[Hallmarking Act 1973, s 3.]

---

1. For penalty and other provisions as to offences, see Sch 3 and s 10, post.

8–5612 4. Approved hallmarks. (1), (3), (5)–(7) *Striking of approved hallmarks by assay office.*

(2) If it is shown to the satisfaction of the assay office that the article was made in the United Kingdom, the assay office mark and the standard mark shall be those specified for that assay office in column (2) of paragraph 1 of Schedule 2 to this Act, and in column (3) of paragraph 2 of that Schedule; and otherwise the marks shall be those specified in column (3) of the said paragraph 1 and column (4) of the said paragraph 2.

(4) A person who knowingly makes a false statement in furnishing any information to an assay office for the purposes of subsection (2) above shall be guilty of an offence[1].
[Hallmarking Act 1973, s 4 as amended by SI 1998/2798.]

---

1. For penalty and other provisions as to offences, see Sch 3 and s 10, post.

8–5613 5. Alterations to hallmarked articles. (1) Subject to subsection (3) to (5) below, it shall be an offence[1] for any person to make an addition, alteration or repair to an article bearing approved hallmarks, except in accordance with the written consent of an assay office.

(2) Subject to subsection (3) below, it shall be an offence for any person to remove, alter or deface any mark struck on an article, except in accordance with the written consent of an assay office.

For the purposes of this subsection "mark" means a sponsor's mark, any approved hallmark, the word "filled", the word "metal" or any other word for the time being prescribed by or under section 4 of, or Schedule 2 to, this Act.

(3) It shall not be an offence under subsection (1) or (2) above to batter an article so as to render it fit only for remanufacture.

(4) It shall not be an offence under subsection (1) above to make an addition to an article which is not a new ware if the character of the article, and the purposes for which it can be used, remain unaltered and—

(a) the addition is of the same precious metal as that of the article;

(b) the metal added to the article is of a fineness not less than the standard of fineness of the article; and

(c) the amount of metal does not exceed the lesser of—

(i) 1 gram of gold, 5 grams of silver or 0·5 grams of platinum, as the case may be; and

(ii) 50 per cent of the weight of the article immediately before the addition was made.

(5) It shall not be an offence under subsection (1) above to add a coating, of a thickness not exceeding 2 micrometres at any point, to the whole or any part of—

(a) an article of gold, if the coating is of gold of a fineness not less than the standard of fineness of the article; or

(b) an article of silver, if the coating is of silver of a fineness not less than the standard of fineness of the article; or

(c) an article of silver, if the coating is of gold of not less than the minimum fineness; or

(d) an article of gold, silver or platinum, if the coating is of rhodium.

(6)–(8) *Power of assay office to give consent subject to conditions.*
[Hallmarking Act 1973, s 5.]

---

1. For penalty and other provisions as to offences, see Sch 3 and s 10, post.

8–5614 6. Counterfeiting, etc of dies and marks. (1) Any person who—

(a) with intent to defraud or deceive, makes a counterfeit of any die or mark; or

(b) removes any mark from an article of precious metal with intent to transpose it to any other article (whether of precious metal or not) or affixes to any article (whether of precious metal or not) any mark which has been removed from an article of precious metal; or

(c) utters any counterfeit of a die or any article bearing a counterfeit of a mark; or

(d) without lawful authority or excuse, has in his custody or under his control anything which is, and which he knows or believes to be, a counterfeit of a die or an article (whether of precious metal or not) which bears a counterfeit of any mark,

shall be guilty of an offence[1] and liable on summary conviction to a fine not exceeding **the statutory maximum**, or on conviction on indictment to a fine or imprisonment for a term not exceeding **ten years**.

(2) In subsection (1) above—

"die" means the whole or part of any plate, tool or instrument by means whereof any mark of the nature of a sponsor's mark or a hallmark is struck on any metal; and "mark" means any mark of the nature of a sponsor's mark or hallmark.

(3) For the purposes of subsection (1) above, a person utters any counterfeit die or article bearing a counterfeit of a mark if, knowing or believing the die or mark, as the case may be, to be a counterfeit, he supplies, offers to supply, or delivers the die or article.
[Hallmarking Act 1973, s 6, as amended by the Criminal Law Act 1977, s 28.]

---

1. For penalty and other provisions as to offences, see Sch 3 and s 10, post.

8–5615 7. Treatment by assay offices of unauthorised marks. (1)–(5), (7) *Power of assay office to cancel or obliterate marks.*

(6) It shall be an offence[1] for any person knowingly or any dealer to supply or offer to supply any article bearing any mark of the character of a hallmark and which under subsection (1) of this section may, if the article is in the possession of an assay office, be cancelled, obliterated or defaced, unless the article has been first submitted to an assay office to enable them at their discretion so to cancel, obliterate or deface that mark.
[Hallmarking Act 1973, s 7.]

---

1. For penalty and other provisions as to offences, see Sch 3 and s 10, post.

8–5616 9. Enforcement of Act. (1) It shall be the duty of every local weights and measures authority to enforce the provisions of this within their area; and section 26 of the Act of 1968 (enforcing authorities) shall apply in relation to the enforcement of this Act, by such an authority, as it applies in relation to the enforcement of that Act.

(2) The Council and the assay offices may also enforce the provisions of this Act.

(3) Subject to subsection (7) below[1], the following provisions of the Act of 1968 shall apply in relation to the enforcement of this Act as they apply in relation to the enforcement of the Act of 1968, that is to say—

section 27 (power to make test purchases);
section 28 (power to enter premises and inspect and seize goods and documents);
section 29 (obstruction of authorised offices);
section 30 (notice of test and intended prosecution);
section 31 (evidence by certificate); and
section 33 (compensation for loss, etc, of goods seized).

(4) Any reference, in the provisions of the Act of 1968 mentioned in subsection (3) above (other than those of subsection (2) to (4) of the said section 30), to a local weights and measures authority and a duly authorised officer of such an authority shall be construed, in relation to the enforcement of this Act, as including respectively a reference to the Council and an assay office and a duly authorised officer of the Council and of an assay office.
[Hallmarking Act 1973, s 9.]

---

1. Sub-s (7) relates to Northern Ireland.

8–5617 10. Treatment of articles following convictions. (1) Upon the conviction of any person of an offence under this Act the court may order any article the subject of the proceedings to be delivered to an assay office who (subject to the order) may exercise the like powers under this Act in relation to the article as if it had been submitted to them for hallmarking.

(2) Any article delivered to an assay office pursuant to such an order as is mentioned in subsection (1) of this section shall be returned to the person entitled thereto.
[Hallmarking Act 1973, s 10.]

8–5618 11. Dealers to exhibit notices as to hallmarks. (1) Any dealer shall keep exhibited at all times, in a conspicuous position in a part of his premises to which those with whom he deals are commonly admitted, a notice in terms approved and in a form supplied by the Council describing such approved hallmarks and including such explanatory matters as the Council think fit; and it shall be an offence[1] for any dealer to fail to exhibit or keep exhibited a notice required to be exhibited under this subsection.

(2) The Council may make a reasonable charge for the supply of any copy of a notice required to be exhibited under this section.
[Hallmarking Act 1973, s 11.]

---

1. For penalty and other provisions as to offences, see Sch 3, post.

8–5619 17. *Power of Secretary of State to apply by order provisions of this Act to metals other than gold, silver and platinum.*

8–5620 18. Local Acts and instruments. (1) Any local statutory provision which is inconsistent with any provision of this Act shall cease to have effect.

(2)–(4) *Power of Secretary of State to repeal or amend any local statutory provision.*
[Hallmarking Act 1973, s 18.]

8–5621 21. *Power to make regulations.*

8–5622 22. Interpretation. (1) In this Act, unless the subject or context otherwise requires—

"the Act of 1968" means the Trade Description Act 1968;

"approved hallmarks" has the meaning given by section 2 of this Act;

"assay office" means (subject to subsection (2) of this section) each of the following bodies—

The Wardens and Commonalty of the Mystery of Goldsmiths of the City of London (in this Act referred to as "the London Assay Office");

The Incorporation of Goldsmiths of the City of Edinburgh (in this Act referred to as "the Edinburgh Assay Office");

The Guardians of the Standard of Wrought Plate in Birmingham (in this Act referred to as " the Birmingham Assay Office");

The Guardians of the Standard of Wrought Plate within the town of Sheffield (in this Act referred to as "the Sheffield Assay Office");

and any other body duly authorised under any enactment, order, charter or franchise for the assaying and hallmarking of precious metals, and includes—

(*a*) a body for the time being established under section 16(1)(*a*) of this Act, and

(*b*) (when the context so admits) a body which, whilst it has been so authorised at any time before or after the passing of this Act, has since being so authorised been dissolved or has ceased business in such assaying and hallmarking;

"convention hallmark" has the meaning given by section 2 of this Act;

"the Council" means the British Hallmarking Council constituted under section 13 of this Act;

"dealer" means a person engaged in the business of making, supplying, selling (including selling by auction) or exchanging articles of precious metal or in other dealings in such articles;

"EEA hallmark" has the meaning given by section 2 of this Act;

"enactment" includes an enactment of the Parliament of Northern Ireland and (without prejudice to subsection (3) of this section) any reference in this Act to an enactment shall include a reference to any enactment re-enacting it with or without modifications;

"fineness" in relation to any precious metal means the number of parts by weight of that fine metal in one thousand parts by weight of alloy; "standard of fineness" means any one of the standards of fineness specified in column (2) of paragraph 2 of Schedule 2 to this Act and reference to an article as being of one of those standards means that the article is of a fineness in all its parts of not less than that standard; and "minimum fineness" in relation to any precious metal means the lowest standard of fineness therefore so specified, namely, for gold the standard of 375, for silver the standard of 800, and for platinum the standard of 850;

"functions" includes powers and duties;

"improper alteration" has the meaning given by section 2 of this Act;

"local statutory provision" means a provision of local Act (including an Act confirming a provisional order), or a provision of public general Act passed with respect only to any particular locality, or provision of an instrument made under any such local or public general Act or of an instrument in the nature of a local enactment made under any other Act or a provision of a charter or franchise;

"new ware" means—

(*a*) any article which is a substantially complete manufacture and which has not as such been supplied on a sale by retail, and

(*b*) any article which has been the subject of any improper alteration;

"precious metal" in relation to any article means gold, silver or platinum, or any other metal to which by an order under section 17 of this Act the provisions of this Act are applied;

"sponsor's mark" means—

(*a*) a sponsor's mark applied under section 3 of this Act, or under the corresponding provisions of the law in force in the United Kingdom before section 3 of this Act came into force; or

(*b*) a mark designated by order of the Secretary of State—

(i) as a mark recognised pursuant to any international convention or treaty to which Her Majesty's Government in the United Kingdom is a party; and

(ii) as a sponsor's mark for the purposes of this Act; or

(*c*) a mark struck on an article in an EEA State which indicates the manufacturer or sponsor of the article;

"unhallmarked" has the meaning given by section 2(4) of this Act.

(2) Reference in this Act to an assay office shall, as respects an assay office who are engaged in the business of an assay office and who carry on any other activity, include reference to so much only of

the undertaking of that assay office as relates wholly to their business as such an assay office and as may be certified in that behalf by that assay office.

(3) References in this enactment shall be construed as references to that enactment as amended or extended by or under any other enactment including this Act.

[Hallmarking Act 1973, s 22 as amended by SI 1998/2978.]

Section 1

SCHEDULE 1
UNHALLMARKED ARTICLES

(As amended by SI 1975/1883 and SI 1998/979.)

PART I
PERMISSIBLE DESCRIPTIONS

8–5623 **1.** (1) Subject to the provisions of this paragraph—

(*a*) "gold" is permissible if qualified by the word "plated" or "rolled";
(*b*) "silver" is permissible if qualified by the word "plated";
(*c*) "platinum" is permissible if qualified by the word "plated".

(2) If the description is in writing the lettering of "plated" or "rolled" is to be at least as large as any other lettering in the description.

(3) This paragraph does not apply if the description is false or is applied to an article for which the description is inappropriate.

2. A description is permissible if it is implicitly or in express terms confined to the colour of the article.

PART II
EXEMPTED ARTICLES

1. An article which is intended for despatch to a destination outside the United Kingdom.

2. An article which is outside the United Kingdom, or which is in course of consignment from outside the United Kingdom to an assay office in the United Kingdom.

3. Any coin which is, or was formerly at any time, current coin of the United Kingdom or any other territory.

4. Any article which has been used, or is intended to be used, for medical, dental, veterinary, scientific or industrial purposes.

5. Any battered article fit only to be remanufactured.

6. Any article of gold or silver thread.

7. Any raw material (including any bar, plate, sheet, foil, rod, wire, strip or tube) or bullion.

8. Any manufactured article which is not substantially complete, and which is intended for further manufacture.

9. Any article which is wholly or mainly of platinum, and which was manufactured before 1st January 1975.

Articles exempt if of minimum fineness

10. Any article which—

(*a*) is wholly or mainly of gold or of silver or of gold and silver assaying in all its gold parts not less than 375 parts per thousand and in all its silver parts not less than 800 parts per thousand; and
(*b*) was manufactured before the year 1920 and has not since the beginning of the year 1920 been the subject of any alteration which would be an improper alteration if the article had previously borne approved hallmarks.

11. Subject to paragraph 14AA below, Any musical instrument, where the description is applied to the mouthpiece, and the mouthpiece is of minimum fineness.

12. (1) Subject to paragraph 14AA and the provisions of this paragraph, any article containing only one precious metal, being a metal of minimum fineness and of a weight less than that specified in the following table—

gold .. .. 1 gram
silver .. .. 7.78 grams
platinum .. .. 0.5 gram.

(2) This paragraph does not apply to any article containing materials other than precious metal, unless the article satisfies the conditions for hallmarking of Part III of Schedule 2 to this Act.

13. Subject to paragraph 14AA below, any article, except an article made of chainwork, which is wholly of one or more precious metals of minimum fineness and which is so small or thin that it cannot be hallmarked.

14. Any article which is of minimum fineness and which is imported temporarily (whether as a trade sample, or as intended for exhibition or otherwise) and for the time being remains under the control of the Commissioners of Customs and Excise.

14A. (1) Subject to the provisions of this paragraph, any article, any precious metal which is of minimum fineness, and which either—

(*a*) contains gold and platinum but not silver, and the weight of the gold parts of which exceeds 50 per cent of the total weight of the precious metals in the article, that total weight being less than 1 gram; or
(*b*) contains silver and either gold or platinum or both gold and platinum, and the weight of the silver parts of which exceeds 50 per cent of the total weight of the precious metals in the article, that total weight being less than 7·78 grams.

(2) This paragraph does not apply to any article containing materials other than precious metal, unless the article satisfies the conditions for hallmarking of Part III of Schedule 2 to this Act.

Existing exemptions

15. The following articles of gold, if manufactured before 1st January 1975, and (except in the case of articles mentioned in sub-paragraph (*d*) below) of minimum fineness—

(a) rings, except wedding rings, pencil cases, lockets, watch chains and thimbles,
(b) articles consisting entirely of filigree work,
(c) articles so heavily engraved or set with stones that it is impossible to mark them without damage,
(d) jewellers' works, that is the actual setting only in which stones or other jewels are set, and jointed sleeper earrings.

16. (1) Subject to the exceptions below, the following articles of silver, if manufactured before 1st January 1975, and (except in the case of articles mentioned in paragraph (e) below) of minimum fineness:

(a) lockets, watch chains and stamped medals,
(b) mounts the weight of which is less than 15·55 grams,
(c) articles consisting entirely of filigree work,
(d) silver articles the weight of which is less than 7·78 grams,
(e) jewellers' works, that is the actual setting only in which stones or other jewels are set.

(2) The following articles are not exempt under sub-paragraph (1) above—

(a) necks and collars for bottles on cruet stands,
(b) buttons and studs, seals, wine labels, shoe clasps, buckles, or patch boxes,
(c) salt spoons, shovels, or ladles, teaspoons, tea strainers, caddy ladles or spoons,
(d) ornaments for cabinets, knife cases, tea caddies, bridles, stands or frames.

17. Articles of gold or silver manufactured before 1st January 1975, other than articles mentioned in paragraphs 15 or 16 above, and being of such descriptions as, under any enactment in force immediately before the passing of this Act, to be specifically exempt from hallmarking.

Articles manufactured before a given date

18. Where under this Part of this Schedule an exemption depends on the date of manufacture, or the date of any alteration, the manufacture or alteration shall be presumed to be after that date until the contrary is proved.

PART III
USE OF THE WORDS "CARATS", "STERLING" AND "BRITANNIA"

1. This Part of this Schedule applies for the purposes of section 1 of this Act, this Schedule and the Act of 1968.
2. (1) A description indicating that an article, or the metal in an article, is of so many carats is to be presumed to be an indication that the article or metal is of gold, and that its fineness is that specified in the following table for that number of carats.

(2) This paragraph shall not apply if (as in a case where the article is a precious stone) the word "carat" is used as a measure of weight for precious stones, and not as a measure of fineness.

TABLE

Number of carats	Indicates gold of a standard of fineness of
9	375 parts per thousand
12	500 parts per thousand
14	585 parts per thousand
15	625 parts per thousand
18	750 parts per thousand
22	916.6 parts per thousand

and so in proportion for any other number of carats.

3. (1) A description of an article, or of the metal in an article, as "sterling" or (except in the phrase "Britannia metal") "Britannia" is to be presumed to be an indication that the article, or the metal, is of silver.

(2) If "sterling" is the word used, the description is to be presumed to be an indication that the silver is of a standard of fineness of 925.

(3) If the word used is "Britannia" the description is to be presumed to be an indication that the silver is of a standard of fineness of 958.4.

PART IV
POWER OF SECRETARY OF STATE TO AMEND

Section 8

SCHEDULE 3
PROVISIONS AS TO OFFENCES

(As amended by the Criminal Law Act 1977, Sch 13.)

Penalties for offences

8–5624 **1.** A person guilty of an offence under this Act for which no other penalty is specified shall be liable[1]—

(a) on summary conviction, to a fine not exceeding **the statutory maximum**; and
(b) on conviction on indictment, to a fine or imprisonment for a term not exceeding two years or both.

Time limit for prosecutions

2. (1) No prosecution for an offence under this Act shall be commenced after the expiration of three years from the commission of the offence or one year from its discovery by the prosecutor whichever is the earlier.
(2) *Repealed.*

(3) *Scotland.*
(4) *Northern Ireland.*
(5) Sub-paragraph (3) above does not apply where—

(a) the offence was one under section 1(1)(a) of this Act and was committed by making of an oral statement; or

(b) the offence was one under section 1(1)(b) of this Act and—

    (i) the description was applied by an oral statement; or

    (ii) the description is deemed to have been applied to the article concerned by virtue of subsection (7)(b) of the said section 1 and the article was supplied in pursuance of an oral request.

Offences by corporations

3. (1) Where an offence under this Act which has been committed by a body corporate is proved to have been committed with the consent and connivance of, or to be attributable to any neglect on the part of, any director, manager, secretary or other similar officer of the body corporate, or any person who was purporting to act in any such capacity, he as well as the body corporate shall be guilty of that offence and shall be liable to be proceeded against and punished accordingly.

(2) In this paragraph "director" in relation to any body corporate established by or under any enactment for the purpose of carrying on under national ownership any industry or part of an industry or undertaking, being a body corporate whose affairs are managed by the members thereof, means a member of that body corporate.

Offences due to fault of other person

4. Where the commission by any person of an offence under this Act is due to the act or default of some other person that other person shall be guilty of the offence, and a person may be charged with and convicted of the offence by virtue of this paragraph whether or not proceedings are taken against the first-mentioned person.

Innocent publication of advertisement

5. In proceedings for an offence under this Act committed by the publication of an advertisement it shall be a defence for the person charged to prove that he is a person whose business it is to publish or arrange for the publication of advertisements and that he received the advertisement for publication in the ordinary course of business and did not know and had no reason to suspect that its publication would amount to an offence under this Act.

Defence in proceedings under section 1

6. In any proceedings for an offence under section 1 of this Act, it shall be a defence for the person charged to prove that—

(a) in reliance on information supplied by another person, he believed that the article concerned was one which was exempt from hallmarking by virtue of Part II of Schedule 1 to this Act; and

(b) that he could not with reasonable diligence have ascertained that it was not such an article.

---

1. For procedure in respect of this offence which is triable either way, see the Magistrates' Courts Act 1980, ss 17A–21, in PART I: MAGISTRATES' COURTS, PROCEDURE, *ante.*

Patents Act 1977
(1977 c 37)

PART I[1]
NEW DOMESTIC LAW
Security and safety

8–5625 22. Information prejudicial to national security or safety of public. (1) Where an application for a patent is filed in the Patent Office (whether under this Act or any treaty or international convention to which the United Kingdom is a party and whether before or after the appointed day) and it appears to the comptroller that the application contains information of a description notified to him by the Secretary of State as being information the publication of which might be prejudicial to national security, the comptroller may give directions prohibiting or restricting the publication of that information or its communication to any specified person or description of persons.

(2) If it appears to the comptroller that any application so filed contains information the publication of which might be prejudicial to the safety of the public, he may give directions prohibiting or restricting the publication of that information or its communication to any specified person or description of persons until the end of a period not exceeding three months from the end of the period prescribed for the purposes of section 16 above.

(3) While directions are in force under this section with respect to an application—

(a) if the application is made under this Act, it may proceed to the stage where it is in order for the grant of a patent, but it shall not be published and that information shall not be so communicated and no patent shall be granted in pursuance of the application;

(b) if it is an application for a European patent, it shall not be sent to the European Patent Office; and

(c) if it is an international application for a patent, a copy of it shall not be sent to the International Bureau or any international searching authority appointed under the Patent Co-operation Treaty.

(4) Subsection (3)(b) above shall not prevent the comptroller from sending the European Patent Office any information which it is his duty to send that office under the European Patent Convention.

(5) Where the comptroller gives directions under this section with respect to any application, he shall give notice of the application and of the directions to the Secretary of State, and the following provisions shall then have effect:—

(a) the Secretary of State shall, on receipt of the notice, consider whether the publication of the application or the publication or communication of the information in question would be prejudicial to national security or the safety of the public;

(b) if the Secretary of State determines under paragraph (a) above that the publication of the application or the publication or communication of that information would be prejudicial to the safety of the public, he shall notify the comptroller who shall continue his directions under subsection (2) above until they are revoked under paragraph (e) below;

(c) if the Secretary of State determines under paragraph (a) above that the publication of the application or the publication or communication of that information would be prejudicial to national security or the safety of the public, he shall (unless a notice under paragraph (d) below has previously been given by the Secretary of State to the comptroller) reconsider that question during the period of nine months from the date of filing the application and at least once in every subsequent period of twelve months;

(d) if on consideration of an application at any time it appears to the Secretary of State that the publication of the application or the publication or communication of the information contained in it would not, or would no longer, be prejudicial to national security or the safety of the public, he shall give notice to the comptroller to that effect; and

(e) on receipt of such a notice the comptroller shall revoke the directions and may, subject to such conditions (if any) as he thinks fit, extend the time for doing anything required or authorised to be done by or under this Act in connection with the application, whether or not that time has previously expired.

(6) The Secretary of State may do the following for the purpose of enabling him to decide the question referred to in subsection (5)(c) above—

(a) where the application contains information relating to the production or use of atomic energy or research into matters connected with such production or use, he may at any time do one or both of the following, that is to say,

(i) inspect the application and any documents sent to the comptroller in connection with it;

(ii) authorise a government body with responsibility for the production of atomic energy or for research into matters connected with its production or use, or a person appointed by such a government body, to inspect the application and any documents sent to the comptroller in connection with it; and

(b) in any other case, he may at any time after (or, with the applicant's consent, before) the end of the period prescribed for the purposes of section 16 above inspect the application and any such documents;

and where a government body or a person appointed by a government body carries out an inspection which the body or person is authorised to carry out under paragraph (a) above, the body or (as the case may be) the person shall report on the inspection to the Secretary of State as soon as practicable.

(7) Where directions have been given under this section in respect of an application for a patent for an invention and, before the directions are revoked, that prescribed period expires and the application is brought in order for the grant of a patent, then—

(a) if while the directions are in force the invention is worked by (or with the written authorisation of or to the order of) a government department, the provisions of sections 55 to 59 below shall apply as if—

(i) the working were use made by virtue of section 55;

(ii) the application had been published at the end of that period; and

(iii) a patent had been granted for the invention at the time the application is brought in order for the grant of a patent (taking the terms of the patent to be those of the application as it stood at the time it was so brought in order); and

(b) if it appears to the Secretary of State that the applicant for the patent has suffered hardship by reason of the continuance in force of the directions, the Secretary of State may, with the consent of the Treasury, make such payment (if any) by way of compensation to the applicant as appears to the Secretary of State and the Treasury to be reasonable having regard to the inventive merit and utility of the invention, the purpose for which it is designed and any other relevant circumstances.

(8) Where a patent is granted in pursuance of an application in respect of which directions have been given under this section, no renewal fees shall be payable in respect of any period during which those directions were in force.

(9) A person who fails to comply with any direction under this section shall be liable—

(a)   on summary conviction, to a fine not exceeding the prescribed sum; or

(b)   on conviction on indictment, to imprisonment for a term not exceeding two years or a fine, or both.

[Patents Act 1977, s 22 as amended by the Magistrates' Courts Act 1980, s 32 and the Patents Act 2004, Sch 2.]

---

1.   Part I contains ss 1–76.
2.   For procedure in respect of this offence which is triable either way, see the Magistrates' Courts Act 1980, ss 17A–21, in PART I: MAGISTRATES' COURTS, PROCEDURE, ante.

8–5626   23. Restrictions on applications abroad by United Kingdom residents.   (1) Subject to the following provisions of this section, no person resident in the United Kingdom shall, without written authority granted by the comptroller, file or cause to be filed outside the United Kingdom an application for a patent for an invention if subsection (1A) below applies to that application, unless—

(a)   an application for a patent for the same invention has been filed in the Patent Office (whether before, on or after the appointed day) not less than six weeks before the application outside the United Kingdom; and

(b)   either no directions have been given under section 22 above in relation to the application in the United Kingdom or all such directions have been revoked.

(1A)   This subsection applies to an application if—

(a)   the application contains information which relates to military technology or for any other reason publication of the information might be prejudicial to national security; or

(b)   the application contains information the publication of which might be prejudicial to the safety of the public.

(2) Subsection (1) above does not apply to an application for a patent for an invention for which an application for a patent has first been filed (whether before or after the appointed day) in a country outside the United Kingdom by a person resident outside the United Kingdom.

(3) A person who files or causes to be filed an application for the grant of a patent in contravention of this section shall be liable—

(a)   on summary conviction, to a fine not exceeding the prescribed sum]; or

(b)   on conviction on indictment, to imprisonment for a term not exceeding two years or a fine, or both.

(3A)   A person is liable under subsection (3) above only if—

(a)   he knows that filing the application, or causing it to be filed, would contravene this section; or

(b)   he is reckless as to whether filing the application, or causing it to be filed, would contravene this section.

(4) In this section—

(a)   any reference to an application for a patent includes a reference to an application for other protection for an invention;

(b)   any reference to either kind of application is a reference to an application under this Act, under the law of any country other than the United Kingdom or under any treaty or international convention to which the United Kingdom is a party.

[Patents Act 1977, s 23 as amended by the Magistrates' Courts Act 1980, s 32 and the Patents Act 2004, s 7.]

PART III[1]
MISCELLANEOUS AND GENERAL

Offences

8–5627   109. Falsification of register etc.   If a person makes or causes to be made a false entry in any register kept under this Act, or a writing falsely purporting to be a copy or reproduction of an entry in any such register, or produces or tenders or causes to be produced or tendered in evidence any such writing, knowing the entry or writing to be false, he shall be liable[2]—

(a)   on summary conviction, to a fine not exceeding **the statutory maximum**;

(b)   on conviction on indictment, to imprisonment for a term not exceeding **two years** or a **fine**, or both.

[Patents Act 1977, s 109.]

8–5628   110. Unauthorised claim of patent rights.   (1) If a person falsely represents that anything disposed of by him for value is a patented product he shall, subject to the following provisions of this section, be liable on summary conviction to a fine not exceeding **level 3** on the standard scale.

(2) For the purposes of subsection (1) above a person who for value disposes of an article having stamped, engraved or impressed on it or otherwise applied to it the word "patent" or "patented" or anything expressing or implying that the article is a patented product, shall be taken to represent that the article is a patented product.

(3) Subsection (1) above does not apply where the representation is made in respect of a product after the patent for that product or, as the case may be, the process in question has expired or been revoked and before the end of a period which is reasonably sufficient to enable the accused to take steps to ensure that the representation is not made (or does not continue to be made).

(4) In proceedings for an offence under this section it shall be a defence for the accused to prove that he used due diligence to prevent the commission of the offence.
[Patents Act 1977, s 110 as amended by the Criminal Justice Act 1982, s 46.]

8–5629   111. Unauthorised claim that patent has been applied for.   (1) If a person represents that a patent has been applied for in respect of any article disposed of for value by him and—

(*a*)   no such application has been made, or
(*b*)   any such application has been refused or withdrawn,

he shall, subject to the following provisions of this section, be liable on summary conviction to a fine not exceeding **level 3** on the standard scale.

(2) Subsection (1)(*b*) above does not apply where the representation is made (or continues to be made) before the expiry of a period which commences with the refusal or withdrawal and which is reasonably sufficient to enable the accused to take steps to ensure that the representation is not made (or does not continue to be made).

(3) For the purposes of subsection (1) above a person who for value disposes of an article having stamped, engraved or impressed on it or otherwise applied to it the words "patent applied for" or "patent pending", or anything expressing or implying that a patent has been applied for in respect of the article, shall be taken to represent that a patent has been applied for in respect of it.

(4) In any proceedings for an offence under this section it shall be a defence for the accused to prove that he used due diligence to prevent the commission of such an offence.
[Patents Act 1977, s 111 as amended by the Criminal Justice Act 1982, s 46.]

8–5630   112. Misuse of title "Patent Office".   If any person uses on his place of business, or on any document issued by him, or otherwise, the words "Patent Office" or any other words suggesting that his place of business is, or is officially connected with, the Patent Office, he shall be liable on summary conviction to a fine not exceeding **level 4** on the standard scale.
[Patents Act 1977, s 112 as amended by the Criminal Justice Act 1982, s 46.]

8–5631   113. Offences by corporations.   (1) Where an offence under this Act which has been committed by a body corporate is proved to have been committed with the consent or connivance of, or to be attributable to any neglect on the part of, a director, manager, secretary or other similar officer of the body corporate, or any person who was purporting to act in any such capacity, he, as well as the body corporate, shall be guilty of that offence and shall be liable to be proceeded against and punished accordingly.

(2) Where the affairs of a body corporate are managed by its members subsection (1) above shall apply in relation to the acts and defaults of a member in connection with his functions of management as if he were a director of the body corporate.
[Patents Act 1977, s 113.]

Supplemental

8–5632   130. Interpretation[1].   (1) In this Act, except so far as the context otherwise requires—

"application fee" means the fee prescribed for the pruposes of section 14(1A) above;
"biological material" means any material containing genetic information and capable of reproducing itself or being reproduced in a biological system;* "biotechnological invention" means an invention which concerns a product consisting of or containing biological material or a process by means of which biological material is produced, processed or used;"
"comptroller" means the Comptroller-General of Patents, Designs and Trade Marks;
"electronic communication" has the same meaning as in the Electronic Communications Act 2000;

"European Patent Convention" means the Convention on the Grant of European Patents, "European patent" means a patent granted under that convention, "European patent (UK)" means a European patent designating the United Kingdom, "European Patent Bulletin" means the bulletin of that name published under that convention, and "European Patent Office" means the office of that name established by that convention;

"international application for a patent" means an application made under the Patent Co-operation Treaty;

"International Bureau" means the secretariat of the World Intellectual Property Organisation established by a convention signed at Stockholm on 14th July 1967;

"1949 Act" means the Patent Act 1949;

"patent" means a patent under this Act;

"Patent Co-operation Treaty" means the treaty of that name signed at Washington on 19th June 1970;

"patented invention" means an invention for which a patent is granted and "patented process" shall be construed accordingly;

"patented product" means a product which is a patented invention or, in relation to a patented process, a product obtained directly by means of the process or to which the process has been applied;

"register" and cognate expressions have the meanings assigned to them by section 32[2] above.

[Patents Act 1977, s 130 amended by the Armed Forces Act 1981, s 22, the Administration of Justice Act 1985, s 60, the Copyright, Designs and Patents Act 1988, Schs 7 and 8, SI 2000/2037 and SI 2004/2357.]

---

1. Only selected definitions are printed in this manual.
2. Section 32 provides for the keeping of a register of patents of the Patents Office, according to rules.

Copyright, Designs and Patents Act 1988[1]
(1988 c 48)

PART I[2]
COPYRIGHT

CHAPTER I
SUBSISTENCE, OWNERSHIP AND DURATION OF COPYRIGHT

Introductory

8–5640   1. Copyright and copyright works.   (1) Copyright is a property right which subsists in accordance with this Part in the following descriptions of work—

(*a*)   original literary, dramatic, musical or artistic works,
(*b*)   sound recordings, films or broadcasts, and
(*c*)   the typographical arrangement of published editions[3].

(2) In this Part "copyright work" means a work of any of those descriptions in which copyright subsists.

(3) Copyright does not subsist in a work unless the requirements of this Part with respect to qualification for copyright protection are met (see section 153[4] and the provisions referred to there).
[Copyright, Designs and Patents Act 1988, s 1, as amended by SI 2003/2498.]

---

1. This Act restates the law of copyright, makes fresh provision as to the rights of performers and others in performances, and amends the law with regard to designs and patents. All those provisions of the Act which are printed in this manual have been brought into force.
2. Part I contains Chapters I–X, ss 1–179. Chapter I contains ss 1–15. For the application of provisions in this Part to publication rights, see the Copyright and Related Rights Regulations 1996, SI 1996/2967, reg 17.
3. In this form of copyright, the copyright is in the typographical arrangement and the work or works of which it is the arrangement is or are of subsidiary importance. What is important is the entire edition which the publisher has published, whether or not it consists of a single literary, dramatic or musical work, or part of such a work or several such works. In respect of a newspaper this refers to the typographical arrangement of the whole newspaper and not the typographical arrangement of each article. Accordingly it was not established that any of the newspaper cuttings distributed by a company to its executives could be regarded as a substantial part of the published edition of the newspaper from which it came for the purposes of s 16(3)(*a*) of this Act. *Newspaper Licensing Agency Ltd v Marks and Spencer plc* [2000] 4 All ER 239, [2000] 3 WLR 1256, CA; affd [2001] UKHL 38, [2001] 3 All ER 977, [2001] 3 WLR 290.
4. See para **8–5752**, post.

8–5641   2. Rights subsisting in copyright works.   (1) The owner of the copyright in a work of any description has the exclusive right to do the acts specified in Chapter II as the acts restricted by the copyright in a work of that description.

(2) In relation to certain descriptions of copyright work the following rights conferred by Chapter IV (moral rights) subsist in favour of the author, director or commissioner of the work, whether or not he is the owner of the copyright—

(a)   section 77 (right to be identified as author or director),[1]
(b)   section 80 (right to object to derogatory treatment of work)[1], and
(c)   section 85 (right to privacy of certain photographs and films)[1].
[Copyright, Designs and Patents Act 1988, s 2.]

---

1. These sections are not printed in this work.

Descriptions of work and related provisions

8–5642   3. Literary, dramatic and musical works.   (1) In this Part—

"literary work" means any work, other than a dramatic or musical work, which is written, spoken or sung, and accordingly includes—

     (a)   a table or compilation other than a database,
     (b)   a computer program;
     (c)   preparatory design material for a computer program; and
     (d)   a database;

"dramatic work" includes a work of dance or mime; and
"musical work" means a work consisting of music, exclusive of any words or action intended to be sung, spoken or performed with the music.

(2) Copyright does not subsist in a literary, dramatic or musical work unless and until it is recorded, in writing or otherwise; and references in this Part to the time at which such a work is made are to the time at which it is so recorded.

(3) It is immaterial for the purposes of subsection (2) whether the work is recorded by or with the permission of the author; and where it is not recorded by the author, nothing in that subsection affects the question whether copyright subsists in the record as distinct from the work recorded.
[Copyright, Designs and Patents Act 1988, s 3 as amended by SI 1992/3233 and SI 1997/3032.]

8–5642A   3A. Databases.   (1) In this Part "database" means a collection of independent works, data or other materials which—

     (a)   are arranged in a systematic or methodical way, and
     (b)   are individually accessible by electronic or other means.

(2) For the purposes of this Part a literary work consisting of a database is original if, and only if, by reason of the selection or arrangement of the contents of the database the database constitutes the author's own intellectual creation.
[Copyright, Designs and Patents Act 1988, s 3A as inserted by SI 1997/3032.]

8–5643   4. Artistic works.   (1) In this Part "artistic work" means—

     (a)   a graphic work, photograph, sculpture or collage, irrespective of artistic quality,
     (b)   a work of architecture being a building or a model for a building, or
     (c)   a work of artistic craftsmanship.

(2) In this Part—

"building" includes any fixed structure, and a part of a building or fixed structure;
"graphic work" includes—

     (a)   any painting, drawing, diagram, map, chart or plan, and
     (b)   any engraving, etching, lithograph, woodcut or similar work;

"photograph" means a recording of light or other radiation on any medium on which an image is produced or from which an image may by any means be produced, and which is not part of a film;
"sculpture" includes a cast or model made for purposes of sculpture.
[Copyright, Designs and Patents Act 1988, s 4.]

8–5644   5A. Sound recordings.   (1) In this Part "sound recording" means—

     (a)   a recording of sounds, from which the sounds may be reproduced, or
     (b)   a recording of the whole or any part of a literary, dramatic or musical work, from which sounds reproducing the work or part may be produced,

regardless of the medium on which the recording is made or the method by which the sounds are reproduced or produced.

(2) Copyright does not subsist in a sound recording which is, or to the extent that it is, a copy taken from a previous sound recording.
[Copyright, Designs and Patents Act 1988, s 5A as substituted by SI 1995/3297.]

8–5644A   5B. Films.   (1) In this Part "film" means a recording on any medium from which a moving image may by any means be produced.

(2) The sound track accompanying a film shall be treated as part of the film for the purposes of this Part.

(3) Without prejudice to the generality of subsection (2), where that subsection applies—

(a) references in this Part to showing a film include playing the film sound track to accompany the film, and

(b) references in this Part to playing a sound recording, or to communicating a sound recording to the public, do not include playing or communicating the film sound track to accompany the film,

(c) references in this Part to copying a work, so far as they apply to a sound recording, do not include copying the film sound track to accompany the film, and

(d) references in this Part to the issuing, rental or lending of copies of a work, so far as they apply to a sound recording, do not include the issuing, rental or lending of copies of the sound track to accompany the film.

(4) Copyright does not subsist in a film which is, or to the extent that it is, a copy taken from a previous film.

(5) Nothing in this section affects any copyright subsisting in a film sound track as a sound recording.

[Copyright, Designs and Patents Act 1988, s 5B as substituted by SI 1995/3297 and amended by SI 2006/18.]

8–5645 6. Broadcasts. (1) In this Part a "broadcast" means an electronic transmission of visual images, sounds or other information which—

(a) is transmitted for simultaneous reception by members of the public and is capable of being lawfully received by them, or

(b) is transmitted at a time determined solely by the person making the transmission for presentation to members of the public,

and which is not excepted by subsection (1A); and references to broadcasting shall be construed accordingly.

(1A) Excepted from the definition of "broadcast" is any internet transmission unless it is—

(a) a transmission taking place simultaneously on the internet and by other means,

(b) a concurrent transmission of a live event, or

(c) a transmission of recorded moving images or sounds forming part of a programme service offered by the person responsible for making the transmission, being a service in which programmes are transmitted at scheduled times determined by that person.

(2) An encrypted transmission shall be regarded as capable of being lawfully received by members of the public only if decoding equipment has been made available to members of the public by or with the authority of the person making the transmission or the person providing the contents of the transmission.

(3) References in this Part to the person making a broadcast or a transmission which is a broadcast are—

(a) to the person transmitting the programme, if he has responsibility to any extent for its contents, and

(b) to any person providing the programme who makes with the person transmitting it the arrangements necessary for its transmission;

and references in this Part to a programme, in the context of broadcasting, are to any item included in a broadcast.

(4) For the purposes of this Part, the place from which a wireless broadcast is made is the place where, under the control and responsibility of the person making the broadcast, the programme-carrying signals are introduced into an uninterrupted chain of communication (including, in the case of a satellite transmission, the chain leading to the satellite and down towards the earth).

(4A) Subsections (3) and (4) have effect subject to section 6A (safeguards in case of certain satellite broadcasts).

(5) References in this Part to the reception of a broadcast include reception of a broadcast relayed by means of a telecommunications system.

(5A) The relaying of a broadcast by reception and immediate re-transmission shall be regarded for the purposes of this Part as a separate act of broadcasting from the making of the broadcast which is so re-transmitted.

(6) Copyright does not subsist in a broadcast which infringes, or to the extent that it infringes, the copyright in another broadcast.

[Copyright, Designs and Patents Act 1988, s 6 as amended by SI 1996/2967 and SI 2003/2498.]

8–5645A 6A. Safeguards in case of certain satellite broadcasts. (1) This section applies where the place from which a broadcast by way of satellite transmission is made is located in a country other than an EEA State and the law of that country fails to provide at least the following level of protection—

(a)   exclusive rights in relation to wireless broadcasting equivalent to those conferred by section 20 (infringement by communication to the public) on the authors of literacy, dramatic, musical and artistic works, films and broadcasts;

(b)   a right in relation to live wireless broadcasting equivalent to that conferred on a performer by section 182(1)(b) (consent required for live broadcast of performance); and

(c)   a right for authors of sound recordings and performers to share in a single equitable remuneration in respect of the wireless broadcasting of sound recordings.

(2) Where the place from which the programme-carrying signals are transmitted to the satellite ("the uplink station") is located in an EEA State—

(a)   that place shall be treated as the place from which the broadcast is made, and

(b)   the person operating the uplink station shall be treated as the person making the broadcast.

(3) Where the uplink station is not located in an EEA State but a person who is established in an EEA State has commissioned the making of the broadcast—

(a)   that person shall be treated as the person making the broadcast, and

(b)   the place in which he has his principal establishment in the European Economic Area shall be treated as the place from which the broadcast is made.

[Copyright, Designs and Patents Act 1988, s 6A as inserted by SI 1996/2967 and amended by SI 2003/2498.]

8–5646   7. Cable programmes.   (*Repealed*).

8–5647   8. Published editions.   (1) In this Part "published edition", in the context of copyright in the typographical arrangement of a published edition, means a published edition of the whole or any part of one or more literary, dramatic or musical works.

(2) Copyright does not subsist in the typographical arrangement of a published edition if, or to the extent that, it reproduces the typographical arrangement of a previous edition.

[Copyright, Designs and Patents Act 1988, s 8.]

Authorship and ownership of copyright

8–5648   9. Authorship of work.   (1) In this Part "author", in relation to a work, means the person who creates it.

(2) That person shall be taken to be—

(aa)   in the case of a sound recording, the producer;

(ab)   in the case of a film, the producer and the principal director;

(b)   in the case of a broadcast, the person making the broadcast (see section 6(3)) or, in the case of a broadcast which relays another broadcast by reception and immediate re-transmission, the person making that other broadcast;

(c)   repealed

(d)   in the case of the typographical arrangement of a published edition, the publisher.

(3) In the case of a literary, dramatic, musical or artistic work which is computer-generated, the author shall be taken to be the person by whom the arrangements necessary for the creation of the work are undertaken.

(4) For the purposes of this Part a work is of "unknown authorship" if the identity of the author is unknown or, in the case of a work of joint authorship, if the identity of none of the authors is known.

(5) For the purposes of this Part the identity of an author shall be regarded as unknown if it is not possible for a person to ascertain his identity by reasonable inquiry; but if his identity is once known it shall not subsequently be regarded as unknown.

[Copyright, Designs and Patents Act 1988, s 9 as amended by SI 1996/2967 and SI 2003/2498.]

8–5649   10. Works of joint authorship.   (1) In this Part a "work of joint authorship" means a work produced by the collaboration of two or more authors in which the contribution of each author is not distinct from that of the other author or authors.

(1A) A film shall be treated as a work of joint authorship unless the producer and the principal director are the same person.

(2) A broadcast shall be treated as a work of joint authorship in any case where more than one person is to be taken as making the broadcast (see section 6(3)).

(3) References in this Part to the author of a work shall, except as otherwise provided, be construed in relation to a work of joint authorship as references to all the authors of the work.

[Copyright, Designs and Patents Act 1988, s 10 as amended by SI 1996/2967.]

8–5650   11. First ownership of copyright.   (1) The author of a work is the first owner of any copyright in it, subject to the following provisions.

(2) Where a literary, dramatic, musical or artistic work, or a film, is made by an employee in the course of his employment, his employer is the first owner of any copyright in the work subject to any agreement to the contrary.

(3) This section does not apply to Crown copyright or Parliamentary copyright (see sections 163 and 165) or to copyright which subsists by virtue of section 168 (copyright of certain international organisations).

[Copyright, Designs and Patents Act 1988, s 11 as amended by SI 1996/2967.]

Duration of copyright

8–5651 **12. Duration of copyright in literary, dramatic, musical or artistic works.** (1) The following provisions have effect with respect to the duration of copyright in a literary, dramatic, musical or artistic work.

(2) Copyright expires at the end of the period of 70 years from the end of the calendar year in which the author dies, subject as follows.

(3) If the work is of unknown authorship, copyright expires—

(a) at the end of the period of 70 years from the end of the calendar year in which the work was made, or

(b) if during that period the work is made available to the public, at the end of the period of 70 years from the end of the calendar year in which it is first so made available;

subject as follows.

(4) Subsection (2) applies if the identity of the author becomes known before the end of the period specified in paragraph (a) or (b) of subsection (3).

(5) For the purposes of subsection (3) making available to the public includes—

(a) in the case of a literary, dramatic or musical work—

   (i) performance in public, or

   (ii) communication to the public;

(b) in the case of an artistic work—

   (i) exhibition in public,

   (ii) a film including the work being shown in public, or

   (iii) communication to the public;

but in determining generally for the purposes of that subsection whether a work has been made available to the public no account shall be taken of any unauthorised act.

(6) Where the country of origin of the work is not an EEA state and the author of the work is not a national of an EEA state, the duration of copyright is that to which the work is entitled in the country of origin, provided that does not exceed the period which would apply under subsections (2) to (5).

(7) If the work is computer-generated the above provisions do not apply and copyright expires at the end of the period of 50 years from the end of the calendar year in which the work was made.

(8) The provisions of this section are adapted as follows in relation to a work of joint authorship—

(a) the reference in subsection (2) to the death of the author shall be construed—

   (i) if the identity of all the authors is known, as a reference to the death of the last of them to die, and

   (ii) if the identity of one or more of the authors is known and the identity of one or more others is not, as a reference to the death of the last whose identity is known;

(b) the reference in subsection (4) to the identity of the author becoming known shall be construed as a reference to the identity of any of the authors becoming known;

(c) the reference in subsection (6) to the author not being a national of an EEA state shall be construed as a reference to none of the authors being a national of an EEA state.

(9) This section does not apply to Crown copyright or Parliamentary copyright (see sections 163 to 166) or to copyright which subsists by virtue of section 168 (copyright of certain international organisations).

[Copyright, Designs and Patents Act 1988, s 12, as substituted by SI 1995/3297 and amended by SI 2003/2498.]

8–5652 **13A. Duration of copyright in sound recording.** (1) The following provisions have effect with respect to the duration of copyright in a sound recording.

(2) Subject to subsections (4) and (5), copyright expires—

(a) at the end of the period of 50 years from the end of the calendar year in which the recording is made, or

(b) if during that period the recording is published, 50 years from the end of the calendar year in which it is first published, or

(c) if during that period the recording is not published but is made available to the public by being played in public or communicated to the public, 50 years from the end of the calendar year in which it is first so made available,

but in determining whether a sound recording has been published, played in public or communicated to the public, no account shall be taken of any unauthorised act.

(3) *Repealed.*

(4) Where the author of a sound recording is not a national of an EEA state, the duration of copyright is that to which the sound recording is entitled in the country of which the author is a national, provided that does not exceed the period which would apply under subsection (2).

(5) If or to the extent that the application of subsection (4) would be at variance with an international obligation to which the United Kingdom became subject prior to 29 October 1993, the duration of copyright shall be as specified in subsection (2).

[Copyright, Designs and Patents Act 1988, s 13A, as substituted by SI 1995/3297 and amended by SI 2003/2498.]

8–5652A   13B. Duration of copyright in films.   (1) The following provisions have effect with respect to the duration of copyright in a film.

(2) Copyright expires at the end of the period of 70 years from the end of the calendar year in which the death occurs of the last to die of the following persons—

    (a)   the principal director,
    (b)   the author of the screenplay,
    (c)   the author of the dialogue, or
    (d)   the composer of music specially created for and used in the film;

subject as follows.

(3) If the identity of one or more of the persons referred to in subsection (2)(a) to (d) is known and the identity of one or more others is not, the reference in that subsection to the death of the last of them to die shall be construed as a reference to the death of the last whose identity is known.

(4) If the identity of the persons referred to in subsection (2)(a) to (d) is unknown, copyright expires at—

    (a)   the end of the period of 70 years from the end of the calendar year in which the film was made, or
    (b)   if during that period the film is made available to the public, at the end of the period of 70 years from the end of the calendar year in which it is first so made available.

(5) Subsections (2) and (3) apply if the identity of any of those persons becomes known before the end of the period specified in paragraph (a) or (b) of subsection (4).

(6) For the purposes of subsection (4) making available to the public includes—

    (a)   showing in public, or
    (b)   communicating to the public;

but in determining generally for the purposes of that subsection whether a film has been made available to the public no account shall be taken of any unauthorised act.

(7) Where the country of origin is not an EEA state and the author of the film is not a national of an EEA state, the duration of copyright is that to which the work is entitled in the country of origin, provided that does not exceed the period which would apply under subsections (2) to (6).

(8) In relation to a film of which there are joint authors, the reference in subsection (7) to the author not being a national of an EEA state shall be construed as a reference to none of the authors being a national of an EEA state.

(9) If in any case there is no person falling within paragraphs (a) to (d) of subsection (2), the above provisions do not apply and copyright expires at the end of the period of 50 years from the end of the calendar year in which the film was made.

(10) For the purposes of this section the identity of any of the persons referred to in subsection 2(a) to (d) shall be regarded as unknown if it is not possible for a person to ascertain his identity by reasonable inquiry; but if the identity of any such person is once known it shall not subsequently be regarded as unknown.

[Copyright, Designs and Patents Act 1988, s 13B, as substituted by SI 1995/3297 and amended by SI 2003/2498.]

8–5653   14. Duration of copyright in broadcasts.   (1) The following provisions have effect with respect to the duration of copyright in a broadcast.

(2) Copyright in a broadcast expires at the end of the period of 50 years from the end of the calendar year in which the broadcast was made, subject as follows.

(3) Where the author of the broadcast is not a national of an EEA state, the duration of copyright in the broadcast is that to which it is entitled in the country of which the author is a national, provided that does not exceed the period which would apply under subsection (2).

(4) If or to the extent that the application of subsection (3) would be at variance with an international obligation to which the United Kingdom became subject prior to 29th October 1993, the duration of copyright shall be as specified in subsection (2).

(5) Copyright in a repeat broadcast expires at the same time as the copyright in the original broadcast; and accordingly no copyright arises in respect of a repeat broadcast which is broadcast after the expiry of the copyright in the original broadcast.

(6) A repeat broadcast means one which is a repeat of a broadcast previously made.

[Copyright, Designs and Patents Act 1988, s 14 as substituted by SI 1995/3297 and amended by SI 2003/2498.]

8–5654   15. Duration of copyright in typographical arrangement of published editions.
Copyright in the typographical arrangement of a published edition expires at the end of the period of 25 years from the end of the calendar year in which the edition was first published.

[Copyright, Designs and Patents Act 1988, s 15.]

8–5654A   15A. Meaning of country of origin.   (1) For the purposes of the provisions of this Part relating to the duration of copyright the country of origin of a work shall be determined as follows.

(2) If the work is first published in a Berne Convention country and is not simultaneously published elsewhere, the country of origin is that country.

(3) If the work is first published simultaneously in two or more countries only one of which is a Berne Convention country, the country of origin is that country.

(4) If the work is first published simultaneously in two or more countries of which two or more are Berne Convention countries, then—

(a) if any of those countries is an EEA state, the country of origin is that country; and
(b) if none of those countries is an EEA state, the country of origin is the Berne Convention country which grants the shorter or shortest period of copyright protection.

(5) If the work is unpublished or is first published in a country which is not a Berne Convention country (and is not simultaneously published in a Berne Convention country), the country of origin is—

(a) if the work is a film and the maker of the film has his headquarters in, or is domiciled or resident in a Berne Convention country, that country;
(b) if the work is—

(i)   a work of architecture constructed in a Berne Convention country, or
(ii) an artistic work incorporated in a building or other structure situated in a Berne Convention country,

that country;

(c) in any other case, the country of which the author of the work is a national.

(6) In this section—

(a) a "Berne Convention country" means a country which is a party to any Act of the International Convention for the Protection of Literary and Artistic Works signed at Berne on 9 September 1886; and
(b) references to simultaneous publication are to publication within 30 days of first publication.
[Copyright, Designs and Patents Act 1988, s 15A as inserted by SI 1995/3297.]

CHAPTER II[1]
RIGHTS OF COPYRIGHT OWNER

The acts restricted by copyright

8–5655   16. The acts restricted by copyright in a work.   (1) The owner of the copyright in a work has, in accordance with the following provisions of this Chapter, the exclusive right to do the following acts in the United Kingdom—

(a) to copy the work (see section 17);
(b) to issue copies of the work to the public (see section 18);
(ba) to rent or lend the work to the public (see section 18A);
(c) to perform, show or play the work in public (see section 19);
(d) to communicate the work to the public;
(e) to make an adaptation of the work or do any of the above in relation to an adaptation (see section 21);

and those acts are referred to in this Part as the "acts restricted by the copyright".

(2) Copyright in a work is infringed by a person who without the licence of the copyright owner does, or authorises another to do, any of the acts restricted by the copyright.

(3) References in this Part to the doing of an act restricted by the copyright in a work are to the doing of it—

(a) in relation to the work as a whole or any substantial part of it, and
(b) either directly or indirectly;

and it is immaterial whether any intervening acts themselves infringe copyright.

(4) This Chapter has effect subject to—

(a) the provisions of Chapter III (acts permitted in relation to copyright works), and
(b) the provisions of Chapter VII (provisions with respect to copyright licensing).
[Copyright, Designs and Patents Act 1988, s 16 as amended by SI 1996/2967 and SI 2003/2498.]

---

1. Chapter II contains ss 16–27.

8–5656   17. Infringement of copyright by copying.   (1) The copying of the work is an act restricted by the copyright in every description of copyright work; and references in this Part to copying and copies shall be construed as follows.

(2) Copying in relation to a literary, dramatic, musical or artistic work means reproducing the work in any material form.

This includes storing the work in any medium by electronic means.

(3) In relation to an artistic work copying includes the making of a copy in three dimensions of a two-dimensional work and the making of a copy in two dimensions of a three-dimensional work.

(4) Copying in relation to a film or broadcast includes making a photograph of the whole or any substantial part of any image forming part of the film or broadcast.

(5) Copying in relation to the typographical arrangement of a published edition means making a facsimile copy of the arrangement.

(6) Copying in relation to any description of work includes the making of copies which are transient or are incidental to some other use of the work.

[Copyright, Designs and Patents Act 1988, s 17, as amended by SI 2003/2498.]

8–5657   18. Infringement by issue of copies to the public.   (1) The issue to the public of copies of the work is an act restricted by the copyright in every description of copyright work.

(2) References in this Part to the issue to the public of copies of a work are to—

(*a*)   the act of putting into circulation in the EEA copies not previously put into circulation in the EEA by or with the consent of the copyright owner, or

(*b*)   the act of putting into circulation outside the EEA copies not previously put into circulation in the EEA or elsewhere.

(3) References in this Part to the issue to the public of copies of a work do not include—

(*a*)   any subsequent distribution, sale, hiring or loan of copies previously put into circulation (but see section 18A: infringement by rental or lending), or

(*b*)   any subsequent importation of such copies into the United Kingdom or another EEA state,

except so far as paragraph (*a*) of subsection (2) applies to putting into circulation in the EEA copies previously put into circulation outside the EEA.

(4) References in this Part to the issue of copies of a work include the issue of the original.

[Copyright, Designs and Patents Act 1988, s 18 as amended by SI 1992/3233 and SI 1996/2967.]

8–5657A   18A. Infringement by rental or lending of work to the public.   (1) The rental or lending of copies of the work to the public is an act restricted by the copyright in—

(*a*)   a literary, dramatic or musical work,

(*b*)   an artistic work, other than—

    (i)   a work of architecture in the form of a building or a model for a building, or

    (ii) a work of applied art, or

(*c*)   a film or a sound recording.

(2) In this Part, subject to the following provisions of this section—

(*a*)   "rental" means making a copy of the work available for use, on terms that it will or may be returned, for direct or indirect economic or commercial advantage, and

(*b*)   "lending" means making a copy of the work available for use, on terms that it will or may be returned, otherwise than for direct or indirect economic or commercial advantage, through an establishment which is accessible to the public.

(3) The expression "rental" and "lending" do not include—

(*a*)   making available for the purpose of public performance, playing or showing in public or communication to the public, broadcasting or inclusion in a cable programme service;

(*b*)   making available for the purpose of exhibition in public; or

(*c*)   making available for on-the-spot reference use.

(4) The expression "lending" does not include making available between establishments which are accessible to the public.

(5) Where lending by an establishment accessible to the public gives rise to a payment the amount of which does not go beyond what is necessary to cover the operating costs of the establishment, there is no direct or indirect economic or commercial advantage for the purposes of this section.

(6) References in this Part to the rental or lending of copies of a work include the rental or lending of the original.

[Copyright, Designs and Patents Act 1988, s 18A as inserted by SI 1996/2967 and amended by SI 2003/2498.]

8–5658   19. Infringement by performance, showing or playing of work in public.   (1) The performance of the work in public is an act restricted by the copyright in a literary, dramatic or musical work.

(2) In this Part "performance", in relation to a work—

(*a*)   includes delivery in the case of lectures, addresses, speeches and sermons, and

(*b*)   in general, includes any mode of visual or acoustic presentation, including presentation by means of a sound recording, film or broadcast.

(3) The playing or showing of the work in public is an act restricted by the copyright in a sound recording, film or broadcast.

(4) Where copyright in a work is infringed by its being performed, played or shown in public by means of apparatus for receiving visual images or sounds conveyed by electronic means, the person by whom the visual images or sounds are sent, and in the case of a performance the performers, shall not be regarded as responsible for the infringement.

[Copyright, Designs and Patents Act 1988, s 19, as amended by SI 2003/2498.]

8–5659   20. Infringement by communication to the public. (1) The communication to the public of the work is an act restricted by the copyright in—

(*a*) a literary, dramatic, musical or artistic work,
(*b*) a sound recording or film, or
(*c*) a broadcast.

(2) References in this Part to communication to the public are to communication to the public by electronic transmission, and in relation to a work include—

(*a*) the broadcasting of the work;
(*b*) the making available to the public of the work by electronic transmission in such a way that members of the public may access it from a place and at a time individually chosen by them.

[Copyright, Designs and Patents Act 1988, s 20, as substituted by SI 2003/2498.]

8–5670   21. Infringement by making adaptation or act done in relation to adaptation. (1) The making of an adaptation of the work is an act restricted by the copyright in a literary, dramatic or musical work.

For this purpose an adaptation is made when it is recorded, in writing or otherwise.

(2) The doing of any of the acts specified in sections 17 to 20, or subsection (1) above, in relation to an adaptation of the work is also an act restricted by the copyright in a literary, dramatic or musical work.

For this purpose it is immaterial whether the adaptation has been recorded, in writing or otherwise, at the time the act is done.

(3) In this Part "adaptation"—

(*a*) in relation to a literary work, other than a computer program or database, or in relation to a dramatic work, means—

(i) a translation of the work;
(ii) a version of a dramatic work in which it is converted into a non-dramatic work or, as the case may be, of a non-dramatic work in which it is converted into a dramatic work;
(iii) a version of the work in which the story or action is conveyed wholly or mainly by means of pictures in a form suitable for reproduction in a book, or in a newspaper, magazine or similar periodical;

(*ab*) in relation to a computer program, means an arrangement or altered version of the program or a translation of it;
(*ac*) in relation to a database, means an arrangement or altered version of the database or a translation of it;
(*b*) in relation to a musical work, means an arrangement or transcription of the work.

(4) In relation to a computer program a "translation" includes a version of the program in which it is converted into or out of a computer language or code or into a different computer language or code.

(5) No inference shall be drawn from this section as to what does or does not amount to copying a work.

[Copyright, Designs and Patents Act 1988, s 21 as amended by SI 1992/3233 and SI 1997/3032.]

Secondary infringement of copyright

8–5671   22. Secondary infringement: importing infringing copy. The copyright in a work is infringed by a person who, without the licence of the copyright owner, imports into the United Kingdom, otherwise than for his private and domestic use, an article which is, and which he knows or has reason to believe is, an infringing copy of the work.

[Copyright, Designs and Patents Act 1988, s 22.]

8–5672   23. Secondary infringement: possessing or dealing with infringing copy. The copyright in a work is infringed by a person who, without the licence of the copyright owner—

(*a*) possesses in the course of a business,
(*b*) sells or lets for hire, or offers or exposes for sale or hire,
(*c*) in the course of a business exhibits in public or distributes, or
(*d*) distributes otherwise than in the course of a business to such an extent as to affect prejudicially the owner of the copyright,

an article which is, and which he knows or has reason to believe[1] is, an infringing copy of the work.

[Copyright, Designs and Patents Act 1988, s 23.]

1. For availability of this defence to a distributor acting on representations of a recording company, see *ZYX Music GmbH v King* [1997] 2 All ER 129, CA.

8–5673   24. Secondary infringement: providing means for making infringing copies.
(1) Copyright in a work is infringed by a person who, without the licence of the copyright owner—

(a) makes,
(b) imports into the United Kingdom,
(c) possesses in the course of a business, or
(d) sells or lets for hire, or offers or exposes for sale or hire,

an article specifically designed or adapted for making copies of that work, knowing or having reason to believe that it is to be used to make infringing copies.

(2) Copyright in a work is infringed by a person who without the licence of the copyright owner transmits the work by means of a telecommunications system (otherwise than by communication to the public), knowing or having reason to believe that infringing copies of the work will be made by means of the reception of the transmission in the United Kingdom or elsewhere.
[Copyright, Designs and Patents Act 1988, s 24, as amended by SI 2003/2498.]

8–5674   25. Secondary infringement: permitting use of premises for infringing performance.
(1) Where the copyright in a literary, dramatic or musical work is infringed by a performance at a place of public entertainment, any person who gave permission for that place to be used for the performance is also liable for the infringement unless when he gave permission he believed on reasonable grounds that the performance would not infringe copyright.

(2) In this section "place of public entertainment" includes premises which are occupied mainly for other purposes but are from time to time made available for hire for the purposes of public entertainment.
[Copyright, Designs and Patents Act 1988, s 25.]

8–5675   26. Secondary infringement: provision of apparatus for infringing performance, etc. (1) Where copyright in a work is infringed by a public performance of the work, or by the playing or showing of the work in public, by means of apparatus for—

(a) playing sound recordings,
(b) showing films, or
(c) receiving visual images or sounds conveyed by electronic means,

the following persons are also liable for the infringement.

(2) A person who supplied the apparatus, or any substantial part of it, is liable for the infringement if when he supplied the apparatus or part—

(a) he knew or had reason to believe that the apparatus was likely to be so used as to infringe copyright, or
(b) in the case of apparatus whose normal use involves a public performance, playing or showing, he did not believe on reasonable grounds that it would not be so used as to infringe copyright.

(3) An occupier of premises who gave permission for the apparatus to be brought onto the premises is liable for the infringement if when he gave permission he knew or had reason to believe that the apparatus was likely to be so used as to infringe copyright.

(4) A person who supplied a copy of a sound recording or film used to infringe copyright is liable for the infringement if when he supplied it he knew or had reason to believe that what he supplied, or a copy made directly or indirectly from it, was likely to be so used as to infringe copyright.
[Copyright, Designs and Patents Act 1988, s 26.]

Infringing copies

8–5676   27. Meaning of "infringing copy". (1) In this Part "infringing copy", in relation to a copyright work, shall be construed in accordance with this section.

(2) An article is an infringing copy if its making constituted an infringement of the copyright in the work in question.

(3) An article is also an infringing copy if—

(a) it has been or is proposed to be imported into the United Kingdom, and
(b) its making in the United Kingdom would have constituted an infringement of the copyright in the work in question, or a breach of an exclusive licence agreement relating to that work.

(3A) *(Repealed).*

(4) Where in any proceedings the question arises whether an article is an infringing copy and it is shown—

(a) that the article is a copy of the work, and
(b) that copyright subsists in the work or has subsisted at any time,

it shall be presumed until the contrary is proved that the article was made at a time when copyright subsisted in the work.

(5) Nothing in subsection (3) shall be construed as applying to an article which may lawfully be imported into the United Kingdom by virtue of any enforceable Community right within the meaning of section 2(1) of the European Communities Act 1972.

(6) In this Part "infringing copy" includes a copy falling to be treated as an infringing copy by virtue of any of the following provisions—

section 31A(6) and (9) (making a single accessible copy for personal use),

section 31B(9) and (10) (multiple copies for visually impaired persons),

section 31C(2) (intermediate copies held by approved bodies),

section 32(5)[1] (copies made for purposes of instruction or examination),

section 35(3)[1] (recordings made by educational establishments for educational purposes),

section 36(5)[1] (reprographic copying by educational establishments for purposes of instruction),

section 37(3)(b)[1] (copies made by librarian or archivist in reliance on false declaration),

section 56(2)[2] (further copies, adaptations, etc of work in electronic form retained on transfer of principal copy),

section 63(2)[2] (copies made for purpose of advertising artistic work for sale),

section 68(4)[2] (copies made for purpose of broadcast),

section 70(2) (recording for the purposes of time-shifting),

section 71(2) (photographs of broadcasts), or

any provision of an order under section 141[1] (statutory licence for certain reprographic copying by educational establishments).

[Copyright, Designs and Patents Act 1988, s 27 as amended by SI 1992/3233, SI 1996/2967, the Copyright (Visually Impaired Persons) Act 2002, s 7(1) and SI 2003/2498.]

---

1. This provision is not printed in this work.
2. See paras **8–5704, 8–5711, 8–5716**, post.

CHAPTER III[1]

ACTS PERMITTED IN RELATION TO COPYRIGHT WORKS

Introductory

8–5677   28. Introductory provisions.   (1) The provisions of this Chapter specify acts which may be done in relation to copyright works notwithstanding the subsistence of copyright; they relate only to the question of infringement of copyright and do not affect any other right or obligation restricting the doing of any of the specified acts.

(2) Where it is provided by this Chapter that an act does not infringe copyright, or may be done without infringing copyright, and no particular description of copyright work is mentioned, the act in question does not infringe the copyright in a work of any description.

(3) No inference shall be drawn from the description of any act which may by virtue of this Chapter be done without infringing copyright as to the scope of the acts restricted by the copyright in any description of work.

(4) The provisions of this Chapter are to be construed independently of each other, so that the fact that an act does not fall within one provision does not mean that it is not covered by another provision.

[Copyright, Designs and Patents Act 1988, s 28.]

---

1. Chapter III contains ss 28–76.

8–5677A   28A. Making of temporary copies.   Copyright in a literary work, other than a computer program or a database, or in a dramatic, musical or artistic work, the typographical arrangement of a published edition, a sound recording or a film, is not infringed by the making of a temporary copy which is transient or incidental, which is an integral and essential part of a technological process and the sole purpose of which is to enable—

(a) a transmission of the work in a network between third parties by an intermediary; or

(b) a lawful use of the work;

and which has no independent economic significance.

[Copyright, Designs and Patents Act 1988, s 28A, as inserted by SI 2003/2498.]

General

8–5678   29. Research and private study.   (1) Fair dealing with a literary, dramatic, musical or artistic work for the purposes of research for a non-commercial purpose does not infringe any copyright in the work provided that it is accompanied by a sufficient acknowledgement.

(1B) No acknowledgement is required in connection with fair dealing for the purposes mentioned in subsection (1) where this would be impossible for reasons of practicality or otherwise.

(1C) Fair dealing with a literary, dramatic, musical or artistic work for the purposes of private study does not infringe any copyright in the work.

(2) Fair dealing with the typographical arrangement of a published edition for the purposes of research or private study does not infringe any copyright in the arrangement.

(3) Copying by a person other than the researcher or student himself is not fair dealing if—

(a) in the case of a librarian, or a person acting on behalf of a librarian, he does anything which regulations under section 40 would not permit to be done under section 38 or 39 (articles or parts of published works: restriction on multiple copies of same material), or

(b) in any other case, the person doing the copying knows or has reason to believe that it will result in copies of substantially the same material being provided to more than one person at substantially the same time and for substantially the same purpose.

(4) It is not fair dealing—

(a) to convert a computer program expressed in a low level language into a version expressed in a higher level language, or

(b) incidentally in the course of so converting the program, to copy it,

(these acts being permitted if done in accordance with section 50B (decompilation)).

(4A) It is not fair dealing to observe, study or test the functioning of a computer program in order to determine the ideas and principles which underlie any element of the program (these acts being permitted if done in accordance with section 50BA (observing, studying and testing)).

(5) *(Repealed).*

[Copyright, Designs and Patents Act 1988, s 29 as amended by SI 1992/3233, SI 1997/3032 and SI 2003/2498.]

8–5679   30.   Criticism, review and news reporting. (1) Fair dealing with a work for the purpose of criticism or review, of that or another work or of a performance of a work, does not infringe any copyright in the work provided that it is accompanied by a sufficient acknowledgement and provided that the work has been made available to the public.

(1A) For the purposes of subsection (1) a work has been made available to the public if it has been made available by any means, including—

(a) the issue of copies to the public;

(b) making the work available by means of an electronic retrieval system;

(c) the rental or lending of copies of the work to the public;

(d) the performance, exhibition, playing or showing of the work in public;

(e) the communication to the public of the work,

but in determining generally for the purposes of that subsection whether a work has been made available to the public no account shall be taken of any unauthorised act.

(2) Fair dealing with a work (other than a photograph) for the purpose of reporting current events does not infringe any copyright in the work provided that (subject to subsection (3)) it is accompanied by a sufficient acknowledgement.

(3) No acknowledgement is required in connection with the reporting of current events by means of a sound recording, film or broadcast where this would be impossible for reasons of practicality or otherwise.

[Copyright, Designs and Patents Act 1988, s 30, as amended by SI 2003/2498.]

8–5680   31.   Incidental inclusion of copyright material. (1) Copyright in a work is not infringed by its incidental inclusion in an artistic work, sound recording, film or broadcast.

(2) Nor is the copyright infringed by the issue to the public of copies, or the playing, showing or communication to the public, of anything whose making was, by virtue of subsection (1), not an infringement of the copyright.

(3) A musical work, words spoken or sung with music, or so much of a sound recording or broadcast as includes a musical work or such words, shall not be regarded as incidentally included in another work if it is deliberately included.*

[Copyright, Designs and Patents Act 1988, s 31, as amended by SI 2003/2498.]

8–5680A   31A.   Making a single accessible copy for personal use. (1) If a visually impaired person has lawful possession or lawful use of a copy ("the master copy") of the whole or part of—

(a) a literary, dramatic, musical or artistic work; or

(b) a published edition,

which is not accessible to him because of the impairment, it is not an infringement of copyright in the work, or in the typographical arrangement of the published edition, for an accessible copy of the master copy to be made for his personal use.

(2) Subsection (1) does not apply—

(a) if the master copy is of a musical work, or part of a musical work, and the making of an accessible copy would involve recording a performance of the work or part of it; or

(b) if the master copy is of a database, or part of a database, and the making of an accessible copy would infringe copyright in the database.

(3) Subsection (1) does not apply in relation to the making of an accessible copy for a particular

visually impaired person if, or to the extent that, copies of the copyright work are commercially available, by or with the authority of the copyright owner, in a form that is accessible to that person.

(4) An accessible copy made under this section must be accompanied by—

(*a*) a statement that it is made under this section; and

(*b*) a sufficient acknowledgement.

(5) If a person makes an accessible copy on behalf of a visually impaired person under this section and charges for it, the sum charged must not exceed the cost of making and supplying the copy.

(6) If a person holds an accessible copy made under subsection (1) when he is not entitled to have it made under that subsection, the copy is to be treated as an infringing copy, unless he is a person falling within subsection (7)(b).

(7) A person who holds an accessible copy made under subsection (1) may transfer it to—

(*a*) a visually impaired person entitled to have the accessible copy made under subsection (1); or

(*b*) a person who has lawful possession of the master copy and intends to transfer the accessible copy to a person falling within paragraph (a).

(8) The transfer by a person ("V") of an accessible copy made under subsection (1) to another person ("T") is an infringement of copyright by V unless V has reasonable grounds for believing that T is a person falling within subsection (7)(a) or (b).

(9) If an accessible copy which would be an infringing copy but for this section is subsequently dealt with—

(*a*) it is to be treated as an infringing copy for the purposes of that dealing; and

(*b*) if that dealing infringes copyright, is to be treated as an infringing copy for all subsequent purposes.

(10) In subsection (9), "dealt with" means sold or let for hire or offered or exposed for sale or hire or communicated to the public.

[Copyright, Designs and Patents Act 1988, s 31A, as inserted by the Copyright (Visually Impaired Persons) Act 2002, s 1, and amended by SI 2003/2498.]

8–5680B   31B. Multiple copies for visually impaired persons.   (1) If an approved body has lawful possession of a copy ("the master copy") of the whole or part of—

(*a*) a commercially published literary, dramatic, musical or artistic work; or

(*b*) a commercially published edition,

it is not an infringement of copyright in the work, or in the typographical arrangement of the published edition, for the body to make, or supply, accessible copies for the personal use of visually impaired persons to whom the master copy is not accessible because of their impairment.

(2) Subsection (1) does not apply—

(*a*) if the master copy is of a musical work, or part of a musical work, and the making of an accessible copy would involve recording a performance of the work or part of it; or

(*b*) if the master copy is of a database, or part of a database, and the making of an accessible copy would infringe copyright in the database.

(3) Subsection (1) does not apply in relation to the making of an accessible copy if, or to the extent that, copies of the copyright work are commercially available, by or with the authority of the copyright owner, in a form that is accessible to the same or substantially the same degree.

(4) Subsection (1) does not apply in relation to the supply of an accessible copy to a particular visually impaired person if, or to the extent that, copies of the copyright work are commercially available, by or with the authority of the copyright owner, in a form that is accessible to that person.

(5) An accessible copy made under this section must be accompanied by—

(*a*) a statement that it is made under this section; and

(*b*) a sufficient acknowledgement.

(6) If an approved body charges for supplying a copy made under this section, the sum charged must not exceed the cost of making and supplying the copy.

(7) An approved body making copies under this section must, if it is an educational establishment, ensure that the copies will be used only for its educational purposes.

(8) If the master copy is in copy-protected electronic form, any accessible copy made of it under this section must, so far as it is reasonably practicable to do so, incorporate the same, or equally effective, copy protection (unless the copyright owner agrees otherwise).

(9) If an approved body continues to hold an accessible copy made under subsection (1) when it would no longer be entitled to make or supply such a copy under that subsection, the copy is to be treated as an infringing copy.

(10) If an accessible copy which would be an infringing copy but for this section is subsequently dealt with—

(*a*) it is to be treated as an infringing copy for the purposes of that dealing; and

(*b*) if that dealing infringes copyright, is to be treated as an infringing copy for all subsequent purposes.

(11) In subsection (10), "dealt with" means sold or let for hire or offered or exposed for sale or hire or communicated to the public.

(12) "Approved body" means an educational establishment or a body that is not conducted for profit.

(13) "Supplying" includes lending.

[Copyright, Designs and Patents Act 1988, s 31B, as inserted by the Copyright (Visually Impaired Persons) Act 2002, s 2, and amended by SI 2003/2498.]

8–5680C   31C. Intermediate copies and records.   (1) An approved body entitled to make accessible copies under section 31B may hold an intermediate copy of the master copy which is necessarily created during the production of the accessible copies, but only—

   (*a*)   if and so long as the approved body continues to be entitled to make accessible copies of that master copy; and

   (*b*)   for the purposes of the production of further accessible copies.

(2) An intermediate copy which is held in breach of subsection (1) is to be treated as an infringing copy.

(3) An approved body may lend or transfer the intermediate copy to another approved body which is entitled to make accessible copies of the work or published edition under section 31B.

(4) The loan or transfer by an approved body ("A") of an intermediate copy to another person ("B") is an infringement of copyright by A unless A has reasonable grounds for believing that B—

   (*a*)   is another approved body which is entitled to make accessible copies of the work or published edition under section 31B; and

   (*b*)   will use the intermediate copy only for the purposes of the production of further accessible copies.

(5) If an approved body charges for lending or transferring the intermediate copy, the sum charged must not exceed the cost of the loan or transfer.

(6) An approved body must—

   (*a*)   keep records of accessible copies made under section 31B and of the persons to whom they are supplied;

   (*b*)   keep records of any intermediate copy lent or transferred under this section and of the persons to whom it is lent or transferred; and

   (*c*)   allow the copyright owner or a person acting for him, on giving reasonable notice, to inspect the records at any reasonable time.

(7) Within a reasonable time of making an accessible copy under section 31B, or lending or transferring an intermediate copy under this section, the approved body must—

   (*a*)   notify each relevant representative body; or

   (*b*)   if there is no such body, notify the copyright owner.

(8) A relevant representative body is a body which—

   (*a*)   represents particular copyright owners, or owners of copyright in the type of copyright work concerned; and

   (*b*)   has given notice to the Secretary of State of the copyright owners, or the classes of copyright owner, represented by it.

(9) The requirement to notify the copyright owner under subsection (7)(b) does not apply if it is not reasonably possible for the approved body to ascertain the name and address of the copyright owner.

[Copyright, Designs and Patents Act 1988, s 31C, as inserted by the Copyright (Visually Impaired Persons) Act 2002, s 3.]

8–5680D   31D. Licensing schemes.   (1) Section 31B does not apply to the making of an accessible copy in a particular form if—

   (*a*)   a licensing scheme operated by a licensing body is in force under which licences may be granted by the licensing body permitting the making and supply of copies of the copyright work in that form;

   (*b*)   the scheme is not unreasonably restrictive; and

   (*c*)   the scheme and any modification made to it have been notified to the Secretary of State by the licensing body.

(2) A scheme is unreasonably restrictive if it includes a term or condition which—

   (*a*)   purports to prevent or limit the steps that may be taken under section 31B or 31C; or

   (*b*)   has that effect.

(3) But subsection (2) does not apply if—

   (*a*)   the copyright work is no longer published by or with the authority of the copyright owner; and (*b*) there are reasonable grounds for preventing or restricting the making of accessible copies of the work.

(4) If section 31B or 31C is displaced by a licensing scheme, sections 119 to 122 apply in relation to the scheme as if it were one to which those sections applied as a result of section 117.
[Copyright, Designs and Patents Act 1988, s 31D, as inserted by the Copyright (Visually Impaired Persons) Act 2002, s 4.]

8–5680E   31E. Limitations, etc following infringement of copyright.   (1) The Secretary of State may make an order under this section if it appears to him that the making of copies—

(*a*) under section 31B; or
(*b*) under a licence granted under a licensing scheme that has been notified under section 31D,

has led to infringement of copyright on a scale which, in the Secretary of State's opinion, would not have occurred if section 31B had not been in force, or the licence had not been granted.

(2) The order may prohibit one or more named approved bodies, or one or more specified categories of approved body, from—

(*a*) acting under section 31B; or
(*b*) acting under a licence of a description specified in the order.

(3) The order may disapply—

(*a*) the provisions of section 31B; or
(*b*) the provisions of a licence, or a licensing scheme, of a description specified in the order,

in respect of the making of copies of a description so specified.

(4) If the Secretary of State proposes to make an order he must, before making it, consult—

(*a*) such bodies representing copyright owners as he thinks fit; and
(*b*) such bodies representing visually impaired persons as he thinks fit.

(5) If the Secretary of State proposes to make an order which includes a prohibition he must, before making it, consult—

(*a*) if the proposed order is to apply to one or more named approved bodies, that body or those bodies;
(*b*) if it is to apply to one or more specified categories of approved body, to such bodies representing approved bodies of that category or those categories as he thinks fit.

(6) An approved body which is prohibited by an order from acting under a licence may not apply to the Copyright Tribunal under section 121(1) in respect of a refusal or failure by a licensing body to grant such a licence.
[Copyright, Designs and Patents Act 1988, s 31E, as inserted by the Copyright (Visually Impaired Persons) Act 2002, s 5.]

8–5680F   31F. Definitions and other supplementary provision for sections 31A to 31E.
(1) This section supplements sections 31A to 31E and includes definitions.

(2) A copy of a copyright work (other than an accessible copy made under section 31A or 31B) is to be taken to be accessible to a visually impaired person only if it is as accessible to him as it would be if he were not visually impaired.

(3) "Accessible copy", in relation to a copyright work, means a version which provides for a visually impaired person improved access to the work.

(4) An accessible copy may include facilities for navigating around the version of the copyright work but may not include—

(*a*) changes that are not necessary to overcome problems caused by visual impairment; or
(*b*) changes which infringe the right (provided by section 80) not to have the work subjected to derogatory treatment.

(5) "Approved body" has the meaning given in section 31B(12).

(6) "Lending", in relation to a copy, means making it available for use, otherwise than for direct or indirect economic or commercial advantage, on terms that it will or may be returned.

(7) For the purposes of subsection (6), a loan is not to be treated as being for direct or indirect economic or commercial advantage if a charge is made for the loan which does not exceed the cost of making and supplying the copy.

(8) The definition of "lending" in section 18A does not apply for the purposes of sections 31B and 31C.

(9) "Visually impaired person" means a person—

(*a*) who is blind;
(*b*) who has an impairment of visual function which cannot be improved, by the use of corrective lenses, to a level that would normally be acceptable for reading without a special level or kind of light;
(*c*) who is unable, through physical disability, to hold or manipulate a book; or

(d) who is unable, through physical disability, to focus or move his eyes to the extent that would normally be acceptable for reading.

(10) The Secretary of State may by regulations prescribe—

(a) the form in which; or

(b) the procedure in accordance with which,

any notice required under section 31C(7) or (8), or 31D(1), must be given.

(11) Any power to make regulations or orders is exercisable by statutory instrument subject to annulment in pursuance of a resolution of either House of Parliament.

[Copyright, Designs and Patents Act 1988, s 31F, as inserted by the Copyright (Visually Impaired Persons) Act 2002, s 6.]

8–5681   32–36A. *Education.*

8–5682   37–44A. *Libraries and archives.*

Public administration

8–5683   45. Parliamentary and judicial proceedings. (1) Copyright is not infringed by anything done for the purposes of parliamentary or judicial proceedings.

(2) Copyright is not infringed by anything done for the purposes of reporting such proceedings; but this shall not be construed as authorising the copying of a work which is itself a published report of the proceedings.

[Copyright, Designs and Patents Act 1988, s 45.]

8–5684   46. Royal Commissions and statutory inquiries. (1) Copyright is not infringed by anything done for the purposes of the proceedings of a Royal Commission or statutory inquiry.

(2) Copyright is not infringed by anything done for the purpose of reporting any such proceedings held in public; but this shall not be construed as authorising the copying of a work which is itself a published report of the proceedings.

(3) Copyright in a work is not infringed by the issue to the public of copies of the report of a Royal Commission or statutory inquiry containing the work or material from it.

(4) In this section—

"Royal Commission" includes a Commission appointed for Northern Ireland by the Secretary of State in pursuance of the prerogative powers of Her Majesty delegated to him under section 7(2) of the Northern Ireland Constitution Act 1973; and

"statutory inquiry" means an inquiry held or investigation conducted in pursuance of a duty imposed or power conferred by or under an enactment.

[Copyright, Designs and Patents Act 1988, s 46.]

8–5685   47. Material open to public inspection or on official register. (1) Where material is open to public inspection pursuant to a statutory requirement, or is on a statutory register, any copyright in the material as a literary work is not infringed by the copying of so much of the material as contains factual information of any description, by or with the authority of the appropriate person, for a purpose which does not involve the issuing of copies to the public.

(2) Where material is open to public inspection pursuant to a statutory requirement, copyright is not infringed by the copying or issuing to the public of copies of the material, by or with the authority of the appropriate person, for the purpose of enabling the material to be inspected at a more convenient time or place or otherwise facilitating the exercise of any right for the purpose of which the requirement is imposed.

(3) Where material which is open to public inspection pursuant to a statutory requirement, or which is on a statutory register, contains information about matters of general scientific, technical, commercial or economic interest, copyright is not infringed by the copying or issuing to the public of copies of the material, by or with the authority of the appropriate person, for the purpose of disseminating that information.

(4) The Secretary of State may by order[1] provide that subsection (1), (2) or (3) shall, in such cases as may be specified in the order, apply only to copies marked in such manner as may be so specified.

(5) The Secretary of State may by order[2] provide that subsections (1) to (3) apply, to such extent and with such modifications as may be specified in the order—

(a) to material made open to public inspection by—

(i) an international organisation specified in the order, or

(ii) a person so specified who has functions in the United Kingdom under an international agreement to which the United Kingdom is party, or

(b) to a register maintained by an international organisation specified in the order,

as they apply in relation to material open to public inspection pursuant to a statutory requirement or to a statutory register.

(6) In this section—

"appropriate person" means the person required to make the material open to public inspection or, as the case may be, the person maintaining the register;

"statutory register" means a register maintained in pursuance of a statutory requirement; and

"statutory requirement" means a requirement imposed by provision made by or under an enactment.

(7) An order under this section shall be made by statutory instrument which shall be subject to annulment in pursuance of a resolution of either House of Parliament.
[Copyright, Designs and Patents Act 1988, s 47.]

---

1. The Copyright (Material Open to Public Inspection) (Marking of Copies of Maps) Order 1989, SI 1989/1099, and the Copyright (Material Open to Public Inspection) (Marking of Copies of Plans and Drawings) Order 1990, SI 1990/1427 have been made.

2. The Copyright (Material Open to Public Inspection) (International Organisations) Order 1989, SI 1989/1098, has been made.

8–5686   48. Material communicated to the Crown in the course of public business.   (1) This section applies where a literary, dramatic, musical or artistic work has in the course of public business been communicated to the Crown for any purpose, by or with the licence of the copyright owner and a document or other material thing recording or embodying the work is owned by or in the custody or control of the Crown.

(2) The Crown may, for the purpose for which the work was communicated to it, or any related purpose which could reasonably have been anticipated by the copyright owner, copy the work and issue copies of the work to the public without infringing any copyright in the work.

(3) The Crown may not copy a work, or issue copies of a work to the public, by virtue of this section if the work has previously been published otherwise than by virtue of this section.

(4) In subsection (1) "public business" includes any activity carried on by the Crown.

(5) This section has effect subject to any agreement to the contrary between the Crown and the copyright owner.

(6) In this section "the Crown" includes a health service body, as defined in section 60(7) of the National Health Service and Community Care Act 1990, a Primary Care Trust established under section 16A of the National Health Service Act 1977, the Commission for Social Care Inspection, the Commission for Healthcare Audit and Inspection and a National Health Service trust established under Part I of that Act or the National Health Service (Scotland) Act 1978 and an NHS foundation trust and also includes a health and social services body, as defined in Article 7(6) of the Health and Personal Social Services (Northern Ireland) Order 1991, and a health and social services trust established under that Order; and the reference in subsection (1) above to public business shall be construed accordingly.
[Copyright, Designs and Patents Act 1988, s 48, as amended by the National Health Service and Community Care Act 1990, Sch 8, SI 1991/194, SI 1999/2795, SI 2000/90, the Health and Social Care (Community Health and Standards) Act 2003, Sch 4 and and SI 2004/2987.]

8–5687   49. Public records.   Material which is comprised in public records within the meaning of the Public Records Act 1958, the Public Records (Scotland) Act 1937 or the Public Records Act (Northern Ireland) 1923, or in Welsh public records (as defined in the Government of Wales Act 1998), which are open to public inspection in pursuance of that Act, may be copied, and a copy may be supplied to any person, by or with the authority of any officer appointed under that Act, without infringement of copyright.
[Copyright, Designs and Patents Act 1988, s 49, as amended by the Government of Wales Act 1998, Sch 12.]

8–5688   50. Acts done under statutory authority.   (1) Where the doing of a particular act is specifically authorised by an Act of Parliament, whenever passed, then, unless the Act provides otherwise, the doing of that act does not infringe copyright.

(2) Subsection (1) applies in relation to an enactment contained in Northern Ireland legislation as it applies in relation to an Act of Parliament.

(3) Nothing in this section shall be construed as excluding any defence of statutory authority otherwise available under or by virtue of any enactment.
[Copyright, Designs and Patents Act 1988, s 50.]

Computer programs: lawful users

8–5689   50A. Back up copies.   (1) It is not an infringement of copyright for a lawful user of a copy of a computer program to make any back up copy of it which it is necessary for him to have for the purposes of his lawful use.

(2) For the purposes of this section and sections 50B, 50BA and 50C a person is a lawful user of a computer program if (whether under a licence to do any acts restricted by the copyright in the program or otherwise), he has a right to use the program.

(3) Where an act is permitted under this section, it is irrelevant whether or not there exists any

term or condition in an agreement which purports to prohibit or restrict the act (such terms being, by virtue of section 296A, void).
[Copyright, Designs and Patents Act 1988, s 50A as inserted by SI 1992/3233 and amended by SI 2003/2498.]

8–5690   50B. Decompilation.   (1) It is not an infringement of copyright for a lawful user of a copy of a computer program expressed in a low level language—

    (*a*)   to convert it into a version expressed in a higher level language, or
    (*b*)   incidentally in the course of so converting the program, to copy it,

(that is, to "decompile" it), provided that the conditions in subsection (2) are met.
    (2) The conditions are that—

    (*a*)   it is necessary to decompile the program to obtain the information necessary to create an independent program which can be operated with the program decompiled or with another program ("the permitted objective"); and
    (*b*)   the information so obtained is not used for any purpose other than the permitted objective.

    (3) In particular, the conditions in subsection (2) are not met if the lawful user—

    (*a*)   has readily available to him the information necessary to achieve the permitted objective;
    (*b*)   does not confine the decompiling to such acts as are necessary to achieve the permitted objective;
    (*c*)   supplies the information obtained by the decompiling to any person to whom it is not necessary to supply it in order to achieve the permitted objective; or
    (*d*)   uses the information to create a program which is substantially similar in its expression to the program decompiled or to do any act restricted by copyright.

    (4) Where an act is permitted under this section, it is irrelevant whether or not there exists any term or condition in an agreement which purports to prohibit or restrict the act (such terms being, by virtue of section 296A, void).
[Copyright, Designs and Patents Act 1988, s 50B as inserted by SI 1992/3233.]

8–5690A   50BA. Observing, studying and testing of computer programs.   (1) It is not an infringement of copyright for a lawful user of a copy of a computer program to observe, study or test the functioning of the program in order to determine the ideas and principles which underlie any element of the program if he does so while performing any of the acts of loading, displaying, running, transmitting or storing the program which he is entitled to do.
    (2) Where an act is permitted under this section, it is irrelevant whether or not there exists any term or condition in an agreement which purports to prohibit or restrict the act (such terms being, by virtue of section 296A, void).
[Copyright, Designs and Patents Act 1988, s 50BA as inserted by SI 2003/2498.]

8–5691   50C. Other acts permitted to lawful users.   (1) It is not an infringement of copyright for a lawful user of a copy of a computer program to copy or adapt it, provided that the copying or adapting—

    (*a*)   is necessary for his lawful use; and
    (*b*)   is not prohibited under any term or condition of an agreement regulating the circumstances in which his use is lawful.

    (2) It may, in particular, be necessary for the lawful use of a computer program to copy it or adapt it for the purpose of correcting errors in it.
    (3) This section does not apply to any copying or adapting permitted under section 50A, 50B or 50BA.
[Copyright, Designs and Patents Act 1988, s 50C as inserted by SI 1992/3233 and amended by SI 2003/2498.]

Databases: permitted acts

8–5691A   50D. Acts permitted in relation to databases.   (1) It is not an infringement of copyright in a database for a person who has a right to use the database or any part of the database, (whether under a licence to do any of the acts restricted by the copyright in the database or otherwise) to do, in the exercise of that right, anything which is necessary for the purposes of access to and use of the contents of the database or of that part of the database.
    (2) Where an act which would otherwise infringe copyright in a database is permitted under this section, it is irrelevant whether or not there exists any term or condition in any agreement which purports to prohibit or restrict the act (such terms being, by virtue of section 296B, void).
[Copyright, Designs and Patents Act 1988, s 50D as inserted by SI 1997/3032.]

Designs

8–5692   51. Design documents and models.   (1) It is not an infringement of any copyright in a design document or model recording or embodying a design for anything other than an artistic work or a typeface to make an article to the design or to copy an article made to the design.

(2) Nor is it an infringement of the copyright to issue to the public, or include in a film or communicate to the public anything the making of which was, by virtue of subsection (1), not an infringement of that copyright.

(3) In this section—

"design" means the design of any aspect of the shape or configuration (whether internal or external) of the whole or part of an article, other than surface decoration; and

"design document" means any record of a design, whether in the form of a drawing, a written description, a photograph, data stored in a computer or otherwise.

[Copyright, Designs and Patents Act 1988, s 51, as amended by SI 2003/2498.]

8–5700   52. Effect of exploitation of design derived from artistic work.   (1) This section applies where an artistic work has been exploited, by or with the licence of the copyright owner, by—

(a) making by an industrial process articles falling to be treated for the purposes of this Part as copies of the work, and

(b) marketing such articles, in the United Kingdom or elsewhere.

(2) After the end of the period of 25 years from the end of the calendar year in which such articles are first marketed, the work may be copied by making articles of any description, or doing anything for the purpose of making articles of any description, and anything may be done in relation to articles so made, without infringing copyright in the work.

(3) Where only part of an artistic work is exploited as mentioned in subsection (1), subsection (2) applies only in relation to that part.

(4) The Secretary of State may by order[1] make provision—

(a) as to the circumstances in which an article, or any description of article, is to be regarded for the purposes of this section as made by an industrial process;

(b) excluding from the operation of this section such articles of a primarily literary or artistic character as he thinks fit.

(5) An order shall be made by statutory instrument which shall be subject to annulment in pursuance of a resolution of either House of Parliament.

(6) In this section—

(a) references to articles do not include films; and

(b) references to the marketing of an article are to its being sold or let for hire or offered or exposed for sale or hire.

[Copyright, Designs and Patents Act 1988, s 52.]

---

1. The Copyright (Industrial Process and Excluded Articles) (No 2) Order 1989, SI 1989/1070, has been made.

8–5701   53. Things done in reliance on registration of design.   (1) The copyright in an artistic work is not infringed by anything done—

(a) in pursuance of an assignment or licence made or granted by a person registered under the Registered Designs Act 1949 as the proprietor of a corresponding design, and

(b) in good faith in reliance on the registration and without notice of any proceedings for the cancellation or invalidation of the registration or for rectifying the relevant entry in the register of designs;

and this is so notwithstanding that the person registered as the proprietor was not the proprietor of the design for the purposes of the 1949 Act.

(2) In subsection (1) a "corresponding design", in relation to an artistic work, means a design within the meaning of the 1949 Act which if applied to an article would produce something which would be treated for the purposes of this Part as a copy of the artistic work.

[Copyright, Designs and Patents Act 1988, s 53, as amended by SI 2001/3949.]

Typefaces

8–5702   54. Use of typeface in ordinary course of printing.   (1) It is not an infringement of copyright in an artistic work consisting of the design of a typeface—

(a) to use the typeface in the ordinary course of typing, composing text, typesetting or printing,

(b) to possess an article for the purpose of such use, or

(c) to do anything in relation to material produced by such use;

and this is so notwithstanding that an article is used which is an infringing copy of the work.

(2) However, the following provisions of this Part apply in relation to persons making, importing or dealing with articles specifically designed or adapted for producing material in a particular typeface, or possessing such articles for the purpose of dealing with them, as if the production of material as mentioned in subsection (1) did infringe copyright in the artistic work consisting of the design of the typeface—

section 24 (secondary infringement: making, importing, possessing or dealing with article for making infringing copy),

sections 99 and 100 (order for delivery up and right of seizure),

section 107(2) (offence of making or possessing such an article), and

section 108 (order for delivery up in criminal proceedings).

(3) The references in subsection (2) to "dealing with" an article are to selling, letting for hire, or offering or exposing for sale or hire, exhibiting in public, or distributing.
[Copyright, Designs and Patents Act 1988, s 54.]

8–5703 55. Articles for producing material in particular typeface. (1) This section applies to the copyright in an artistic work consisting of the design of a typeface where articles specifically designed or adapted for producing material in that typeface have been marketed by or with the licence of the copyright owner.

(2) After the period of 25 years from the end of the calendar year in which the first such articles are marketed, the work may be copied by making further such articles, or doing anything for the purpose of making such articles, and anything may be done in relation to articles so made, without infringing copyright in the work.

(3) In subsection (1) "marketed" means sold, let for hire or offered or exposed for sale or hire, in the United Kingdom or elsewhere.
[Copyright, Designs and Patents Act 1988, s 55.]

Works in electronic form

8–5704 56. Transfers of copies of works in electronic form. (1) This section applies where a copy of a work in electronic form has been purchased on terms which, expressly or impliedly or by virtue of any rule of law, allow the purchaser to copy the work, or to adapt it or make copies of an adaptation, in connection with his use of it.

(2) If there are no express terms—

(*a*) prohibiting the transfer of the copy by the purchaser, imposing obligations which continue after a transfer, prohibiting the assignment of any licence or terminating any licence on a transfer, or

(*b*) providing for the terms on which a transferee may do the things which the purchaser was permitted to do,

anything which the purchaser was allowed to do may also be done without infringement of copyright by a transferee; but any copy, adaptation or copy of an adaptation made by the purchaser which is not also transferred shall be treated as an infringing copy for all purposes after the transfer.

(3) The same applies where the original purchased copy is no longer usable and what is transferred is a further copy used in its place.

(4) The above provisions also apply on a subsequent transfer, with the substitution for references in subsection (2) to the purchaser of references to the subsequent transferor.
[Copyright, Designs and Patents Act 1988, s 56.]

Miscellaneous: literary, dramatic, musical and artistic works

8–5705 57. Anonymous or pseudonymous works: acts permitted on assumptions as to expiry of copyright or death of author. (1) Copyright in a literary, dramatic, musical or artistic work is not infringed by an act done at a time when, or in pursuance of arrangements made at a time when—

(*a*) it is not possible by reasonable inquiry to ascertain the identity of the author, and

(*b*) it is reasonable to assume—

  (i) that copyright has expired, or

  (ii) that the author died 70 years or more before the beginning of the calendar year in which the act is done or the arrangements are made.

(2) Subsection (1)(*b*)(ii) does not apply in relation to—

(*a*) a work in which Crown copyright subsists, or

(*b*) a work in which copyright originally vested in an international organisation by virtue of section 168 and in respect of which an Order under that section specifies a copyright period longer than 70 years.

(3) In relation to a work of joint authorship—

(*a*) the reference in subsection (1) to its being possible to ascertain the identity of the author shall be construed as a reference to its being possible to ascertain the identity of any of the authors, and

(*b*) the reference in subsection (1)(*b*)(ii) to the author having died shall be construed as a reference to all the authors having died.
[Copyright, Designs and Patents Act 1988, s 57 as amended by SI 1995/3297.]

8–5706   **58. Use of notes or recordings of spoken words in certain cases.**   (1) Where a record of spoken words is made, in writing or otherwise, for the purpose—

(*a*)   of reporting current events, or

(*b*)   of communicating to the public the whole or part of the work,

it is not an infringement of any copyright in the words as a literary work to use the record or material taken from it (or to copy the record, or any such material, and use the copy) for that purpose, provided the following conditions are met.

(2)   The conditions are that—

(*a*)   the record is a direct record of the spoken words and is not taken from a previous record or from a broadcast;

(*b*)   the making of the record was not prohibited by the speaker and, where copyright already subsisted in the work, did not infringe copyright;

(*c*)   the use made of the record or material taken from it is not of a kind prohibited by or on behalf of the speaker or copyright owner before the record was made; and

(*d*)   the use is by or with the authority of a person who is lawfully in possession of the record.

[Copyright, Designs and Patents Act 1988, s 58, as amended by SI 2003/2498.]

8–5707   **59. Public reading or recitation.**   (1) The reading or recitation in public by one person of a reasonable extract from a published literary or dramatic work does not infringe any copyright in the work if it is accompanied by a sufficient acknowledgement.

(2)   Copyright in a work is not infringed by the making of a sound recording, or the communication to the public, of a reading or recitation which by virtue of subsection (1) does not infringe copyright in the work, provided that the recording or communication to the public consists mainly of material in relation to which it is not necessary to rely on that subsection.

[Copyright, Designs and Patents Act 1988, s 59, as amended by SI 2003/2498.]

8–5708   **60. Abstracts of scientific or technical articles.**   (1) Where an article on a scientific or technical subject is published in a periodical accompanied by an abstract indicating the contents of the article, it is not an infringement of copyright in the abstract, or in the article, to copy the abstract or issue copies of it to the public.

(2)   This section does not apply if or to the extent that there is a licensing scheme certified for the purposes of this section under section 143 providing for the grant of licences.

[Copyright, Designs and Patents Act 1988, s 60.]

8–5709   **61. Recordings of folksongs.**   (1) A sound recording of a performance of a song may be made for the purpose of including it in an archive maintained by a designated body without infringing any copyright in the words as a literary work or in the accompanying musical work, provided the conditions in subsection (2) below are met.

(2)   The conditions are that—

(*a*)   the words are unpublished and of unknown authorship at the time the recording is made,

(*b*)   the making of the recording does not infringe any other copyright, and

(*c*)   its making is not prohibited by any performer.

(3)   Copies of a sound recording made in reliance on subsection (1) and included in an archive maintained by a designated body may, if the prescribed conditions are met, be made and supplied by the archivist without infringing copyright in the recording or the works included in it.

(4)   The prescribed conditions shall include the following—

(*a*)   that copies are only supplied to persons satisfying the archivist that they require them for the purposes of—

(i)   research for a non-commercial purpose; or

(ii)   private study,

and will not use them for any other purpose, and

(*b*)   that no person is furnished with more than one copy of the same recording.

(5)   In this section—

(*a*)   "designated" means designated for the purposes of this section by order[1] of the Secretary of State, who shall not designate a body unless satisfied that it is not established or conducted for profit,

(*b*)   "prescribed" means prescribed for the purposes of this section by order[1] of the Secretary of State, and

(*c*)   references to the archivist include a person acting on his behalf.

(6)   An order under this section shall be made by statutory instrument which shall be subject to annulment in pursuance of a resolution of either House of Parliament.

[Copyright, Designs and Patents Act 1988, s 61, as amended by SI 2003/2498.]

---

1. See the Copyright (Recordings of Folksongs for Archives) (Designated Bodies) Order 1989, SI 1989/1012.

8–5710   62. Representation of certain artistic works on public display.   (1) This section applies to—

   (*a*)   buildings, and

   (*b*)   sculptures, models for buildings and works of artistic craftsmanship, if permanently situated in a public place or in premises open to the public.

   (2)   The copyright in such a work is not infringed by—

   (*a*)   making a graphic work representing it,

   (*b*)   making a photograph or film of it, or

   (*c*)   making a broadcast of a visual image of it.

   (3)   Nor is the copyright infringed by the issue to the public of copies, or the communication to the public, of anything whose making was, by virtue of this section, not an infringement of the copyright.

[Copyright, Designs and Patents Act 1988, s 62, as amended by SI 2003/2498.]

8–5711   63. Advertisement of sale of artistic work.   (1) It is not an infringement of copyright in an artistic work to copy it, or to issue copies to the public, for the purpose of advertising the sale of the work.

   (2)   Where a copy which would otherwise be an infringing copy is made in accordance with this section but is subsequently dealt with for any other purpose, it shall be treated as an infringing copy for the purposes of that dealing, and if that dealing infringes copyright for all subsequent purposes.

   For this purpose "dealt with" means sold or let for hire, offered or exposed for sale or hire, exhibited in public, distributed or communicated to the public.

[Copyright, Designs and Patents Act 1988, s 63, as amended by SI 2003/2498.]

8–5712   64. Making of subsequent works by same artist.   Where the author of an artistic work is not the copyright owner, he does not infringe the copyright by copying the work in making another artistic work, provided he does not repeat or imitate the main design of the earlier work.

[Copyright, Designs and Patents Act 1988, s 64.]

8–5713   65. Reconstruction of buildings.   Anything done for the purposes of reconstructing a building does not infringe any copyright—

   (*a*)   in the building, or

   (*b*)   in any drawings or plans in accordance with which the building was, by or with the licence of the copyright owner, constructed.

[Copyright, Designs and Patents Act 1988, s 65.]

Miscellaneous: lending of works and playing of sound recordings

8–5714   66. Lending to public of copies of certain works.   (1) The Secretary of State may by order provide that in such cases as may be specified in the order the lending to the public of copies of literary, dramatic, musical or artistic works, sound recordings or films shall be treated as licensed by the copyright owner subject only to the payment of such reasonable royalty or other payment as may be agreed or determined in default of agreement by the Copyright Tribunal.

   (2)   No such order shall apply if, or to the extent that, there is a licensing scheme certified for the purposes of this section under section 143 providing for the grant of licences.

   (3)   An order may make different provision for different cases and may specify cases by reference to any factor relating to the work, the copies lent, the lender or the circumstances of the lending.

   (4)   An order shall be made by statutory instrument; and no order shall be made unless a draft of it has been laid before and approved by a resolution of each House of Parliament.

   (5)   Nothing in this section affects any liability under section 23 (secondary infringement: possessing or dealing with infringing copy) in respect of the lending of infringing copies.

[Copyright, Designs and Patents Act 1988, s 66 as substituted by SI 1996/2967.]

Miscellaneous: films and sound recordings

8–5714A   66A. Films: acts permitted on assumptions as to expiry of copyright, &c.
(1) Copyright in a film is not infringed by an act done at a time when, or in pursuance of arrangements made at a time when—

   (*a*)   it is not possible by reasonable inquiry to ascertain the identity of any of the persons referred to in section 13B(2)(*a*) to (*d*) (persons by reference to whose life the copyright period is ascertained), and

   (*b*)   it is reasonable to assume—

      (i)   that copyright has expired, or

      (ii)   that the last to die of those persons died 70 years or more before the beginning of the calendar year in which the act is done or the arrangements are made.

   (2)   Subsection (1)(*b*)(ii) does not apply in relation to—

(*a*) a film in which Crown copyright subsists, or

(*b*) a film in which copyright originally vested in an international organisation by virtue of section 168 and in respect of which an Order under that section specifies a copyright period longer than 70 years.

[Copyright, Designs and Patents Act 1988, s 66A as inserted by SI 1995/3297 and amended by SI 2003/2498.]

8–5715 67. Playing of sound recordings for purposes of club, society, etc. (1) It is not an infringement of the copyright in a sound recording to play it as part of the activities of, or for the benefit of, a club, society or other organisation if the following conditions are met.

(2) The conditions are—

(*a*) that the organisation is not established or conducted for profit and its main objects are charitable or are otherwise concerned with the advancement of religion, education or social welfare, and

(*b*) that the sound recording is played by a person who is acting primarily and directly for the benefit of the organisation and who is not acting with a view to gain,

(*c*) that the proceeds of any charge for admission to the place where the recording is to be heard are applied solely for the purposes of the organisation, and

(*d*) that the proceeds from any goods or services sold by, or on behalf of, the organisation—

(i) in the place where the sound recording is heard, and

(ii) on the occasion when the sound recording is played,

are applied solely for the purposes of the organisation.

[Copyright, Designs and Patents Act 1988, s 67, as amended by SI 2003/2498.]

Miscellaneous: broadcasts and cable programmes

8–5716 68. Incidental recording for purposes of broadcast. (1) This section applies where by virtue of a licence or assignment of copyright a person is authorised to broadcast—

(*a*) a literary, dramatic or musical work, or an adaptation of such a work,

(*b*) an artistic work, or

(*c*) a sound recording or film.

(2) He shall by virtue of this section be treated as licensed by the owner of the copyright in the work to do or authorise any of the following for the purposes of the broadcast—

(*a*) in the case of a literary, dramatic or musical work, or an adaptation of such a work, to make a sound recording or film of the work or adaptation;

(*b*) in the case of an artistic work, to take a photograph or make a film of the work;

(*c*) in the case of a sound recording or film, to make a copy of it.

(3) That licence is subject to the condition that the recording, film, photograph or copy in question—

(*a*) shall not be used for any other purpose, and

(*b*) shall be destroyed within 28 days of being first used for broadcasting the work.

(4) A recording, film, photograph or copy made in accordance with this section shall be treated as an infringing copy—

(*a*) for the purposes of any use in breach of the condition mentioned in subsection (3)(*a*), and

(*b*) for all purposes after that condition or the condition mentioned in subsection (3)(*b*) is broken.

[Copyright, Designs and Patents Act 1988, s 68, as amended by SI 2003/2498.]

8–5717 69. Recording for purposes of supervision and control of broadcasts and other services. (1) Copyright is not infringed by the making or use by the British Broadcasting Corporation, for the purpose of maintaining supervision and control over programmes broadcast by them, of recordings of those programmes.

(2) Copyright is not infringed by anything done in pursuance of—

(*a*) section 167(1) of the Broadcasting Act 1990, section 115(4) or (6) or 117 of the Broadcasting Act 1996 or paragraph 20 of Schedule 12 to the Communications Act 2003;

(*b*) a condition which, by virtue of section 334(1) of the Communications Act 2003, is included in a licence granted under Part I or III of that Act or Part I or II of the Broadcasting Act 1996;

(*c*) a direction given under section 109(2) of the Broadcasting Act 1990 (power of OFCOM to require production of recordings etc);

(*d*) section 334(3) of the Communications Act 2003.

(3) Copyright is not infringed by the use by OFCOM in connection with the performance of any of their functions under the Broadcasting Act 1990, the Broadcasting Act 1996 or the Communications Act 2003 of—

(*a*) any recording, script or transcript which is provided to them under or by virtue of any provision of those Acts; or (*b*) any existing material which is transferred to them by a scheme made under section 30 of the Communications Act 2003.

(4) In subsection (3), "existing material" means—

(*a*) any recording, script or transcript which was provided to the Independent Television Commission or the Radio Authority under or by virtue of any provision of the Broadcasting Act 1990 or the Broadcasting Act 1996; and

(*b*) any recording or transcript which was provided to the Broadcasting Standards Commission under section 115(4) or (6) or 116(5) of the Broadcasting Act 1996.

[Copyright, Designs and Patents Act 1988, s 69 as amended by the Broadcasting Act 1990, Sch 20, the Broadcasting Act 1996, Sch 10, SI 2003/2498 and the Communications Act 2003, s 411.]

8–5718   70. Recording for purposes of time-shifting.   (1) The making in domestic premises for private and domestic use of a recording of a broadcast solely for the purpose of enabling it to be viewed or listened to at a more convenient time does not infringe any copyright in the broadcast or in any work included in it.

(2) Where a copy which would otherwise be an infringing copy is made in accordance with this section but is subsequently dealt with—

(*a*) it shall be treated as an infringing copy for the purposes of that dealing; and

(*b*) if that dealing infringes copyright, it shall be treated as an infringing copy for all subsequent purposes.

(3) In subsection (2), "dealt with" means sold or let for hire, offered or exposed for sale or hire or communicated to the public.

[Copyright, Designs and Patents Act 1988, s 70, as amended by SI 2003/2498.]

8–5719   71. Photographs of broadcasts.   (1) The making in domestic premises for private and domestic use of a photograph of the whole or any part of an image forming part of a broadcast, or a copy of such a photograph, does not infringe any copyright in the broadcast or in any film included in it.

(2) Where a copy which would otherwise be an infringing copy is made in accordance with this section but is subsequently dealt with—

(*a*) it shall be treated as an infringing copy for the purposes of that dealing; and

(*b*) if that dealing infringes copyright, it shall be treated as an infringing copy for all subsequent purposes.

(3) In subsection (2), "dealt with" means sold or let for hire, offered or exposed for sale or hire or communicated to the public.

[Copyright, Designs and Patents Act 1988, s 71, as substituted by SI 2003/2498.]

8–5720   72. Free public showing or playing of broadcast.   (1) The showing or playing in public of a broadcastto an audience who have not paid for admission to the place where the broadcast is to be seen or heard does not infringe any copyright in—

(*a*) the broadcast;

(*b*) any sound recording (except so far as it is an excepted sound recording) included in it; or

(*c*) any film included in it.

(1A) For the purposes of this Part an "excepted sound recording" is a sound recording—

(*a*) whose author is not the author of the broadcast in which it is included; and

(*b*) which is a recording of music with or without words spoken or sung.

(1B) Where by virtue of subsection (1) the copyright in a broadcast shown or played in public is not infringed, copyright in any excepted sound recording included in it is not infringed if the playing or showing of that broadcast in public—

(*a*) forms part of the activities of an organisation that is not established or conducted for profit; or

(*b*) is necessary for the purposes of—

(i) repairing equipment for the reception of broadcasts;

(ii) demonstrating that a repair to such equipment has been carried out; or

(iii) demonstrating such equipment which is being sold or let for hire or offered or exposed for sale or hire.

(2) The audience shall be treated as having paid for admission to a place—

(*a*) if they have paid for admission to a place of which that place forms part; or

(*b*) if goods or services are supplied at that place (or a place of which it forms part)—

(i) at prices which are substantially attributable to the facilities afforded for seeing or hearing the broadcast, or

(ii) at prices exceeding those usually charged there and which are partly attributable to those facilities.

(3) The following shall not be regarded as having paid for admission to a place—

(*a*) persons admitted as residents or inmates of the place;

(*b*) persons admitted as members of a club or society where the payment is only for membership of the club or society and the provision of facilities for seeing or hearing broadcasts is only incidental to the main purposes of the club or society.

(4) Where the making of the broadcast was an infringement of the copyright in a sound recording or film, the fact that it was heard or seen in public by the reception of the broadcast shall be taken into account in assessing the damages for that infringement.

[Copyright, Designs and Patents Act 1988, s 72, as amended by SI 2003/2498.]

8–5721 73. Reception and re-transmission of wireless broadcast by cable. (1) This section applies where a wireless broadcast made from a place in the United Kingdom is received and immediately re-transmitted by cable.

(2) The copyright in the broadcast is not infringed—

(*a*) if the re-transmission by cable is in pursuance of a relevant requirement, or

(*b*) if and to the extent that the broadcast is made for reception in the area in which it is re-transmitted by cable and forms part of a qualifying service.

(3) The copyright in any work included in the broadcast is not infringed if and to the extent that the broadcast is made for reception in the area in which it is re-transmitted by cable; but where the making of the broadcast was an infringement of the copyright in the work, the fact that the broadcast was re-transmitted by cable shall be taken into account in assessing the damages for that infringement.

(4) Where—

(*a*) the re-transmission by cable is in pursuance of a relevant requirement, but

(*b*) to any extent, the area in which re-transmission by cable takes place ("the cable area") falls outside the area for reception in which the broadcast is made ("the broadcast area"),

the re-transmission by cable(to the extent that it is provided for so much of the cable area as falls outside the broadcast area) of any work included in the broadcast shall, subject to subsection (5), be treated as licensed by the owner of the copyright in the work, subject only to the payment to him by the person making the broadcast of such reasonable royalty or other payment in respect of the re-transmission by cable of the broadcast as may be agreed or determined in default of agreement by the Copyright Tribunal.

(5) Subsection (4) does not apply if, or to the extent that, the re-transmission of the work by cable is (apart from that subsection) licensed by the owner of the copyright in the work.

(6) In this section "qualifying service" means, subject to subsection (8), any of the following services—

(*a*) a regional or national Channel 3 service,

(*b*) Channel 4, Channel 5 and S4C,

(*c*) the public teletext service,

(*d*) S4C Digital, and

(*e*) the television broadcasting services and teletext service of the British Broadcasting Corporation;

and expressions used in this subsection have the same meaning as in Part 3 of the Communications Act 2003.

(7) In this section "relevant requirement" means a requirement imposed by a general condition (within the meaning of Chapter 1 of Part 2 of the Communications Act 2003) the setting of which is authorised under section 64 of that Act (must-carry obligations).

(8) The Secretary of State may by order amend subsection (6) so as to add any service to, or remove any service from, the definition of "qualifying service".

(9) The Secretary of State may also by order—

(*a*) provide that in specified cases subsection (3) is to apply in relation to broadcasts of a specified description which are not made as mentioned in that subsection, or

(*b*) exclude the application of that subsection in relation to broadcasts of a specified description made as mentioned in that subsection.

(10) Where the Secretary of State exercises the power conferred by subsection (9)(*b*) in relation to broadcasts of any description, the order may also provide for subsection (4) to apply, subject to such modifications as may be specified in the order, in relation to broadcasts of that description.

(11) An order under this section may contain such transitional provision as appears to the Secretary of State to be appropriate.

(12) An order under this section shall be made by statutory instrument which shall be subject to annulment in pursuance of a resolution of either House of Parliament.

(13) In this section references to re-transmission by cable include the transmission of microwave energy between terrestrial fixed points.

[Copyright, Designs and Patents Act 1988, s 73 as substituted by the Broadcasting Act 1996, Sch 9, as amended by SI 2003/2498 and the Communications Act 2003, Sch 17.]

8–5721A   73A. *Royalty or other sum payable in pursuance of section 73(4)*

8–5722   74. Provision of sub-titled copies of broadcast.   (1) A designated body may, for the purpose of providing people who are deaf or hard of hearing, or physically or mentally handicapped in other ways, with copies which are sub-titled or otherwise modified for their special needs, make copies of broadcasts and issue or lend copies to the public, without infringing any copyright in the broadcasts or works included in them.

(2) A "designated body" means a body designated for the purposes of this section by order[1] of the Secretary of State, who shall not designate a body unless he is satisfied that it is not established or conducted for profit.

(3) An order under this section shall be made by statutory instrument which shall be subject to annulment in pursuance of a resolution of either House of Parliament.

(4) This section does not apply if, or to the extent that, there is a licensing scheme certified for the purposes of this section under section 143 providing for the grant of licences.
[Copyright, Designs and Patents Act 1988, s 74, as amended by SI 2003/2498.]

1. The Copyright (Sub-titling of Broadcasts and Cable Programmes) (Designated Body) Order 1989, SI 1989/1013, has been made.

8–5723   75. Recording for archival purposes.   (1) A recording of a broadcast of a designated class, or a copy of such a recording, may be made for the purpose of being placed in an archive maintained by a designated body without thereby infringing any copyright in the broadcast or in any work included in it.

(2) In subsection (1) "designated" means designated for the purposes of this section by order[1] of the Secretary of State, who shall not designate a body unless he is satisfied that it is not established or conducted for profit.

(3) An order under this section shall be made by statutory instrument which shall be subject to annulment in pursuance of a resolution of either House of Parliament.
[Copyright, Designs and Patents Act 1988, s 75, as amended by SI 2003/2498.]

1. The Copyright (Recording for Archives of Designated Class of Broadcasts and Cable Programmes) (Designated Bodies) Order 1993, SI 1993/74, has been made.

Adaptations

8–5724   76. Adaptations.   An act which by virtue of this Chapter may be done without infringing copyright in a literary, dramatic or musical work does not, where that work is an adaptation, infringe any copyright in the work from which the adaptation was made.
[Copyright, Designs and Patents Act 1988, s 76.]

8–5725

CHAPTER IV[1]
MORAL RIGHTS

1. Chapter IV, which is not printed in this work, contains ss 77–89.

8–5726

CHAPTER V[1]
DEALINGS WITH RIGHTS IN COPYRIGHT WORKS

1. Chapter V, which is not printed in this work, contains ss 90–95.

CHAPTER VI[1]
REMEDIES FOR INFRINGEMENT

Rights and remedies of copyright owner

8–5734   96–98. *Infringement of copyright actionable by the copyright owner; infringement proceedings.*

1. Chapter VI contains ss 96–115.

8–5735   99. Order for delivery up.   *Owner of copyright may apply to High Court or county court for an order that the infringing copy or article be delivered up to him.*

8–5736   100. Right to seize infringing copies and other articles.   (1) An infringing copy of a work which is found exposed or otherwise immediately available for sale or hire, and in respect of which the copyright owner would be entitled to apply for an order under section 99, may be seized and detained by him or a person authorised by him.

The right to seize and detain is exercisable subject to the following conditions and is subject to any decision of the court under section 114.

(2) Before anything is seized under this section notice of the time and place of the proposed seizure must be given to a local police station.

(3) A person may for the purpose of exercising the right conferred by this section enter premises to which the public have access but may not seize anything in the possession, custody or control of a person at a permanent or regular place of business of his, and may not use any force.

(4) At the time when anything is seized under this section there shall be left at the place where it was seized a notice in the prescribed form[1] containing the prescribed particulars as to the person by whom or on whose authority the seizure is made and the grounds on which it is made.

(5) In this section—

"premises" includes land, buildings, moveable structures, vehicles, vessels, aircraft and hovercraft; and

"prescribed" means prescribed by order of the Secretary of State.

(6) An order of the Secretary of State under this section shall be made by statutory instrument which shall be subject to annulment in pursuance of a resolution of either House of Parliament.
[Copyright, Designs and Patents Act 1988, s 100.]

---

1. See the Copyright and Rights in Performances (Notice of Seizure) Order 1989, SI 1989/1006.

Presumptions

8–5737　104. Presumptions relevant to literary, dramatic, musical and artistic works.
(1) The following presumptions apply in proceedings brought by virtue of this Chapter with respect to a literary, dramatic, musical or artistic work.

(2) Where a name purporting to be that of the author appeared on copies of the work as published or on the work when it was made, the person whose name appeared shall be presumed, until the contrary is proved—

(a) to be the author of the work;

(b) to have made it in circumstances not falling within section 11(2), 163, 165 or 168 (works produced in course of employment, Crown copyright, Parliamentary copyright or copyright of certain international organisations).

(3) In the case of a work alleged to be a work of joint authorship, subsection (2) applies in relation to each person alleged to be one of the authors.

(4) Where no name purporting to be that of the author appeared as mentioned in subsection (2) but—

(a) the work qualifies for copyright protection by virtue of section 155 (qualification by reference to country of first publication), and

(b) a name purporting to be that of the publisher appeared on copies of the work as first published,

the person whose name appeared shall be presumed, until the contrary is proved, to have been the owner of the copyright at the time of publication.

(5) If the author of the work is dead or the identity of the author cannot be ascertained by reasonable inquiry, it shall be presumed, in the absence of evidence to the contrary—

(a) that the work is an original work, and

(b) that the plaintiff's allegations as to what was the first publication of the work and as to the country of first publication are correct.
[Copyright, Designs and Patents Act 1988, s 104.]

8–5738　105. Presumptions relevant to sound recordings and films.　(1) In proceedings brought by virtue of this Chapter with respect to a sound recording, where copies of the recording as issued to the public bear a label or other mark stating—

(a) that a named person was the owner of copyright in the recording at the date of issue of the copies, or

(b) that the recording was first published in a specified year or in a specified country,

the label or mark shall be admissible as evidence of the facts stated and shall be presumed to be correct until the contrary is proved.

(2) In proceedings brought by virtue of this Chapter with respect to a film, where copies of the film as issued to the public bear a statement—

(a) that a named person was the director or producer of the film,

(aa) that a named person was the principal director of the film, the author of the screenplay, the author of the dialogue or the composer of music specifically created for and used in the film,

(b) that a named person was the owner of copyright in the film at the date of issue of the copies, or

(c) that the film was first published in a specified year or in a specified country, the statement shall be admissible as evidence of the facts stated and shall be presumed to be correct until the contrary is proved.

(3) In proceedings brought by virtue of this Chapter with respect to a computer program, where copies of the program are issued to the public in electronic form bearing a statement—

(*a*)   that a named person was the owner of copyright in the program at the date of issue of the copies, or

(*b*)   that the program was first published in a specified country or that copies of it were first issued to the public in electronic form in a specified year,

the statement shall be admissible as evidence of the facts stated and shall be presumed to be correct until the contrary is proved.

(4) The above presumptions apply equally in proceedings relating to an infringement alleged to have occurred before the date on which the copies were issued to the public.

(5) In proceedings brought by virtue of this Chapter with respect to a film, where the film as shown in public or communicated to the public bears a statement—

(*a*)   that a named person was the director or producer of the film, or

(*aa*) that a named person was the principal director, the author of the screenplay, the author of the dialogue or the composer of music specifically created for and used in the film, or

(*b*)   that a named person was the owner of copyright in the film immediately after it was made,

the statement shall be admissible as evidence of the facts stated and shall be presumed to be correct until the contrary is proved.

This presumption applies equally in proceedings relating to an infringement alleged to have occurred before the date on which the film was shown in public or communicated to the public.

(6) For the purposes of this section, a statement that a person was the director of a film shall be taken, unless a contrary indication appears, as meaning that he was the principal director of the film.

[Copyright, Designs and Patents Act 1988, s 105 as amended by SI 1995/3297, SI 1996/2967 and SI 2003/2498.]

8–5739   106. Presumptions relevant to works subject to Crown copyright.   In proceedings brought by virtue of this Chapter with respect to a literary, dramatic or musical work in which Crown copyright subsists, where there appears on printed copies of the work a statement of the year in which the work was first published commercially, that statement shall be admissible as evidence of the fact stated and shall be presumed to be correct in the absence of evidence to the contrary.

[Copyright, Designs and Patents Act 1988, s 106.]

Offences

8–5740   107. Criminal liability for making or dealing with infringing articles, etc.   (1) A person[1] commits an offence[2] who, without the licence of the copyright owner[3]—

(*a*)   makes for sale or hire, or

(*b*)   imports into the United Kingdom otherwise than for his private and domestic use, or

(*c*)   possesses in the course of a business with a view to committing any act infringing[4] the copyright[5], or

(*d*)   in the course of a business—

    (i)   sells or lets for hire, or

    (ii)   offers or exposes for sale or hire, or

    (iii)   exhibits in public, or

    (iv)   distributes, or

(*e*)   distributes otherwise than in the course of a business to such an extent as to affect prejudicially the owner of the copyright,

an article which is, and which he knows or has reason to believe is, an infringing copy[6] of a copyright work[7].

(2) A person commits an offence who—

(*a*)   makes an article specifically designed or adapted for making copies of a particular copyright work, or

(*b*)   has such an article in his possession,

knowing or having reason to believe that it is to be used to make infringing copies for sale or hire or for use in the course of a business.

(2A) A person who infringes copyright in a work by communicating the work to the public—

(*a*)   in the course of a business, or

(*b*)   otherwise than in the course of a business to such an extent as to affect prejudicially the owner of the copyright,

commits an offence if he knows or has reason to believe that, by doing so, he is infringing copyright in that work.

(3) Where copyright is infringed (otherwise than by reception of a communication to the public[8]—

(*a*)   by the public performance of a literary, dramatic or musical work, or (*b*) by the playing or showing in public of a sound recording or film,

any person who caused the work to be so performed, played or shown is guilty of an offence if he knew or had reason to believe that copyright would be infringed.

(4) A person guilty of an offence under subsection (1)(*a*), (*b*), (*d*)(iv) or (*e*) is liable[9]—

(*a*) on summary conviction[10] to imprisonment for a term not exceeding **six months** or a fine not exceeding **the statutory maximum**, or both;

(*b*) on conviction on indictment to a **fine** or imprisonment for a term not exceeding **ten**[11] **years**, or both.★

(4A) A person guilty of an offence under subsection (2A) is liable—

(*a*) on summary conviction to imprisonment for a term not exceeding three months or a fine not exceeding the statutory maximum, or both;

(*b*) on conviction on indictment to a fine or imprisonment for a term not exceeding two years, or both.

(5) A person guilty of any other offence under this section is liable on summary conviction[10] to imprisonment for a term not exceeding **six months** or a fine not exceeding **level 5** on the standard scale, or both.

(6) Sections 104 to 106[12] (presumptions as to various matters connected with copyright) do not apply to proceedings for an offence under this section; but without prejudice to their application in proceedings for an order under section 108 below.

[Copyright, Designs and Patents Act 1988, s 107 as amended by the Copyright, etc and Trade Marks (Offences and Enforcement) Act 2002, s 1 and SI 2003/2498.]

★Sub-section (4)(*b*) printed as amended by the Copyright, etc and Trade Marks (Offences and Enforcement) Act 2002, s 1, in force from 20 November 2002, except in relation to any offence committed before that date.

1. For a body corporate see s 110, post. The class of offenders caught by s 107 is not restricted to "pirates" and may involve parties to a commercial dispute (*Thames and Hudson Ltd v Design and Artists Copyright Society Ltd* [1995] FSR 153).

2. In *R v Carter* (1992) 13 Cr App Rep (S) 576, the Court of Appeal held that counterfeiting of video tapes was a serious offence, and to distribute pirated copies of film was in effect to steal from the copyright's true owner property for which he had had to pay money in order to possess.

3. For the construction of references to "copyright owner", see s 173, post.

4. For acts which may amount to an infringement of copyright, see ss 16–26, ante.

5. For the meaning of "copyright", see generally, s 1, ante.

6. For the meaning of "infringing copy", see s 27, ante.

7. For the meaning of "copyright work", see s 1(2), ante.

8. For the meaning of "communication to the public", see s 20, ante.

9. For procedure in respect of these offences which are triable either way, see the Magistrates' Courts Act 1980, ss 17A–21, in PART I: MAGISTRATES' COURTS, PROCEDURE, ante.

10. In relation to offences concerning publication rights the maximum punishment on summary conviction is imprisonment for a term not exceeding **three months** or a fine not exceeding **level 5** on the standard scale, or both: see the Copyright and Related Rights Regulations 1996, SI 1996/2967.

11. Increased from two years by s 1 of the Copyright, etc, and Trade Marks (Offences and Enforcement) Act 2002 in relation to offences committed on or after 20 November 2002.

12. See, ante.

8–5741   107A. Enforcement by local weights and measures authority.   (1) It is the duty of every local weights and measures authority to enforce within their area the provisions of section 107.

(2) The following provisions of the Trade Descriptions Act 1968 apply in relation to the enforcement of that section by such an authority as in relation to the enforcement of that Act—

section 27 (power to make test purchases),
section 28 (power to enter premises and inspect and seize goods and documents),
section 29 (obstruction of authorised officers), and
section 33 (compensation for loss, etc of goods seized).

(3) *Northern Ireland.*

(4) Any enactment which authorises the disclosure of information for the purpose of facilitating the enforcement of the Trade Descriptions Act 1968 shall apply as if section 107 were contained in that Act and as if the functions of any person in relation to the enforcement of that section were functions under that Act.

(5) *Scotland.*★

[Copyright, Designs and Patents Act 1988, s 107A, as inserted by the Criminal Justice and Public Order Act 1994, s 165.]

★Section 107A is prospectively inserted by the Criminal Justice and Public Order Act 1994, s 165(2), when in force.

8–5742   108. Order for delivery up in criminal proceedings.   (1) The court before which proceedings are brought against a person for an offence under section 107 may, if satisfied that at the time of his arrest or charge—

(a) he had in his possession, custody or control in the course of a business an infringing copy of a copyright work, or

(b) he had in his possession, custody or control an article specifically designed or adapted for making copies of a particular copyright work, knowing or having reason to believe that it had been or was to be used to make infringing copies,

order that the infringing copy or article be delivered up to the copyright owner or to such other person as the court may direct.

(2) For this purpose a person shall be treated as charged with an offence—

(a) in England, Wales and Northern Ireland, when he is orally charged or is served with a summons or indictment;

(b) Scotland.

(3) An order may be made by the court of its own motion or on the application of the prosecutor (or, in Scotland, the Lord Advocate or procurator-fiscal), and may be made whether or not the person is convicted of the offence, but shall not be made—

(a) after the end of the period specified in section 113 (period after which remedy of delivery up not available), or

(b) if it appears to the court unlikely that any order will be made under section 114 (order as to disposal of infringing copy or other article).

(4) An appeal lies from an order made under this section by a magistrates' court—

(a) in England and Wales, to the Crown Court, and

(b) Northern Ireland;

and in Scotland, . . .

(5) A person to whom an infringing copy or other article is delivered up in pursuance of an order under this section shall retain it pending the making of an order, or the decision not to make an order, under section 114.

(6) Nothing in this section affects the powers of the court under section 143 of the Powers of Criminal Courts (Sentencing) Act 2000[1], Part II of the Proceeds of Crime (Scotland) Act 1995 or Article 11 of the Criminal Justice (Northern Ireland) Order 1994 (general provisions as to forfeiture in criminal proceedings).

[Copyright, Designs and Patents Act 1988, s 108 as amended by SI 1994/2795, the Criminal Justice (Scotland) Act 1995, Sch 6, the Criminal Procedure (Consequential Provisions) (Scotland) Act 1995, Sch 4 and the Powers of Criminal Courts (Sentencing) Act 2000, Sch 9.]

---

1. See PART III: SENTENCING, ante.

8–5743 109. Search warrants.   (1) Where a justice of the peace (in Scotland, a sheriff or justice of the peace) is satisfied by information on oath given by a constable (in Scotland, by evidence on oath) that there are reasonable grounds for believing—

(a) that an offence under section 107(1), (2) or (2A) has been or is about to be committed in any premises, and

(b) that evidence that such an offence has been or is about to be committed is in those premises,

he may issue a warrant authorising a constable to enter and search the premises, using such reasonable force as is necessary.

(2) The power conferred by subsection (1) does not, in England and Wales, extend to authorising a search for material of the kinds mentioned in section 9(2) of the Police and Criminal Evidence Act 1984[1] (certain classes of personal or confidential material).

(3) A warrant under this section—

(a) may authorise persons to accompany any constable executing the warrant, and

(b) remains in force for 28 days from the date of its issue.

(4) In executing a warrant issued under this section a constable may seize an article if he reasonably believes that it is evidence that any offence under section 107(1), (2) or (2A) has been or is about to be committed.

(5) In this section "premises" includes land, buildings, fixed or moveable structures, vehicles, vessels, aircraft and hovercraft.

[Copyright, Designs and Patents Act 1988, s 109 as amended by the Copyright, etc and Trade Marks (Offences and Enforcement) Act 2002, s 2 and SI 2003/2498.]

---

1. See PART I: MAGISTRATES' COURTS, PROCEDURE, ante.

8–5744 110. Offence by body corporate: liability of officers.   (1) Where an offence under section 107 committed by a body corporate is proved to have been committed with the consent or connivance of a director, manager, secretary or other similar officer of the body, or a person purporting to act in any such capacity, he as well as the body corporate is guilty of the offence and liable to be proceeded against and punished accordingly.

(2) In relation to a body corporate whose affairs are managed by its members "director" means a member of the body corporate.

[Copyright, Designs and Patents Act 1988, s 110.]

Provision for preventing importation of infringing copies

8–5745　111. Infringing copies may be treated as prohibited goods. (1) The owner of the copyright in a published literary, dramatic or musical work may give notice[1] in writing to the Commissioners of Customs and Excise—

    (a) that he is the owner of the copyright in the work, and

    (b) that he requests the Commissioners, for a period specified in the notice, to treat as prohibited goods printed copies of the work which are infringing copies.

(2) The period specified in a notice under subsection (1) shall not exceed five years and shall not extend beyond the period for which copyright is to subsist.

(3) The owner of the copyright in a sound recording or film may give notice[1] in writing to the Commissioners of Customs and Excise—

    (a) that he is the owner of the copyright in the work,

    (b) that infringing copies of the work are expected to arrive in the United Kingdom at a time and a place specified in the notice, and

    (c) that he requests the Commissioners to treat the copies as prohibited goods.

(3A) The Commissioners may treat as prohibited goods only infringing copies of works which arrive in the United Kingdom—

    (a) from outside the European Economic Area, or

    (b) from within that Area but not having been entered for free circulation.

(3B) This section does not apply to goods placed in, or expected to be placed in, one of the situations referred to in Article 1(1), in respect of which an application may be made under Article 5(1), of Coucil Regulation (EC) No 1383/2003 concerning customs action against goods suspected of infringing certain intellectual property rights and the measures to be taken against goods found to have infringed such rights.

(4) When a notice is in force under this section the importation of goods to which the notice relates, otherwise than by a person for his private and domestic use, is prohibited; but a person is not by reason of the prohibition liable to any penalty other than forfeiture of the goods.

[Copyright, Designs and Patents Act 1988, s 111 as amended by SI 1995/1445 and SI 2004/1473.]

---

    1. Notice shall be in the form prescribed by the Copyright (Customs) Regulations 1989, SI 1989/1178.

8–5746　112. Power of Commissioners of Customs and Excise to make regulations[1]. *The Commissioners of Customs and Excise may make regulations[1] prescribing the form in which notice is to be given under section 111 and requiring a person giving notice to furnish the Commissioners with such evidence as may be specified in the regulations.*

---

    1. The Copyright (Customs) Regulations 1989, SI 1989/1178, have been made.

Supplementary

8–5747　113. Period after which remedy of delivery up not available. (1) An application for an order under section 99 (order for delivery up in civil proceedings) may not be made after the end of the period of six years from the date on which the infringing copy or article in question was made, subject to the following provisions.

(2) If during the whole or any part of that period the copyright owner—

    (a) is under a disability, or

    (b) is prevented by fraud or concealment from discovering the facts entitling him to apply for an order,

an application may be made at any time before the end of the period of six years from the date on which he ceased to be under a disability or, as the case may be, could with reasonable diligence have discovered those facts.

(3) In subsection (2) "disability"—

    (a) in England and Wales, has the same meaning as in the Limitation Act 1980;

    (b) Scotland,

    (c) Northern Ireland,

(4) An order under section 108 (order for delivery up in criminal proceedings) shall not, in any case, be made after the end of the period of six years from the date on which the infringing copy or article in question was made.

[Copyright, Designs and Patents Act 1988, s 113.]

8–5748   **114. Order as to disposal of infringing copy or other article.**   (1) An application may be made to the court for an order that an infringing copy or other article delivered up in pursuance of an order under section 99 or 108, or seized and detained in pursuance of the right conferred by section 100, shall be—

     (*a*)   forfeited to the copyright owner, or
     (*b*)   destroyed or otherwise dealt with as the court may think fit,

or for a decision that no such order should be made.

     (2) In considering what order (if any) should be made, the court shall consider whether other remedies available in an action for infringement of copyright would be adequate to compensate the copyright owner and to protect his interests.

     (3) Provision shall be made by rules of court as to the service of notice on persons having an interest in the copy or other articles, and any such person is entitled—

     (*a*)   to appear in proceedings for an order under this section, whether or not he was served with notice, and
     (*b*)   to appeal against any order made, whether or not he appeared;

and an order shall not take effect until the end of the period within which notice of an appeal may be given or, if before the end of that period notice of appeal is duly given, until the final determination or abandonment of the proceedings on the appeal.

     (4) Where there is more than one person interested in a copy or other article, the court shall make such order as it thinks just and may (in particular) direct that the article be sold, or otherwise dealt with, and the proceeds divided.

     (5) If the court decides that no order should be made under this section, the person in whose possession, custody or control the copy or other article was before being delivered up or seized is entitled to its return.

     (6) References in this section to a person having an interest in a copy or other article include any person in whose favour an order could be made in respect of it under this section or under section 204 or 231 of this Act or section 19 of the Trade Marks Act 1994 (which make similar provision in relation to infringement of rights in performances, design right and trade marks).
[Copyright, Designs and Patents Act 1988, s 114 as amended by the Trade Marks Act 1994, Sch 4.]

8–5748A   **114A. Forfeiture of infringing copies, etc: England and Wales or Northern Ireland.** (1) In England and Wales or Northern Ireland where there have come into the possession of any person in connection with the investigation or prosecution of a relevant offence—

     (*a*)   infringing copies of a copyright work, or
     (*b*)   articles specifically designed or adapted for making copies of a particular copyright work,

that person may apply under this section for an order for the forfeiture of the infringing copies or articles.

     (2) For the purposes of this section "relevant offence" means—

     (*a*)   an offence under section 107(1), (2) or (2A) (criminal liability for making or dealing with infringing articles, etc),
     (*b*)   an offence under the Trade Descriptions Act 1968 (c 29), or
     (*c*)   an offence involving dishonesty or deception.

     (3) An application under this section may be made—

     (*a*)   where proceedings have been brought in any court for a relevant offence relating to some or all of the infringing copies or articles, to that court, or
     (*b*)   where no application for the forfeiture of the infringing copies or articles has been made under paragraph (*a*), by way of complaint to a magistrates' court.

     (4) On an application under this section, the court shall make an order for the forfeiture of any infringing copies or articles only if it is satisfied that a relevant offence has been committed in relation to the infringing copies or articles.

     (5) A court may infer for the purposes of this section that such an offence has been committed in relation to any infringing copies or articles if it is satisfied that such an offence has been committed in relation to infringing copies or articles which are representative of the infringing copies or articles in question (whether by reason of being of the same design or part of the same consignment or batch or otherwise).

     (6) Any person aggrieved by an order made under this section by a magistrates' court, or by a decision of such a court not to make such an order, may appeal against that order or decision—

     (*a*)   in England and Wales, to the Crown Court, or
     (*b*)   in Northern Ireland, to the county court.

     (7) An order under this section may contain such provision as appears to the court to be appropriate for delaying the coming into force of the order pending the making and determination of any appeal (including any application under section 111 of the Magistrates' Courts Act 1980 (c 43)

or Article 146 of the Magistrates' Courts (Northern Ireland) Order 1981 (SI 1981/1675 (NI 26)) (statement of case)).

(8) Subject to subsection (9), where any infringing copies or articles are forfeited under this section they shall be destroyed in accordance with such directions as the court may give.

(9) On making an order under this section the court may direct that the infringing copies or articles to which the order relates shall (instead of being destroyed) be forfeited to the owner of the copyright in question or dealt with in such other way as the court considers appropriate.

[Copyright, Designs and Patents Act 1988, s 114A as inserted by the Copyright, etc and Trade Marks (Offences and Enforcement) Act 2002, s 3 and SI 2003/2498.]

8–5748B   114B.   *Scotland.*

8–5749   115.   *Jurisdiction of county court and sheriff court.*

<h3 style="text-align:center">CHAPTER VII[1]
COPYRIGHT LICENSING</h3>

8–5750

---

1. Chapter VII, which is not printed in this work, contains ss 116–144.

<h3 style="text-align:center">CHAPTER VIII[1]
THE COPYRIGHT TRIBUNAL</h3>

8–5751

---

1. Chapter VIII, which is not printed in this work, contains ss 145–152.

<h3 style="text-align:center">CHAPTER IX[1]
QUALIFICATION FOR AND EXTENT OF COPYRIGHT PROTECTION</h3>

Qualification for copyright protection

8–5752   153.   Qualification for copyright protection.   (1) Copyright does not subsist in a work unless the qualification requirements of this Chapter are satisfied as regards—

(*a*)   the author (see section 154), or
(*b*)   the country in which the work was first published (see section 155), or
(*c*)   in the case of a broadcast, the country from which the broadcast was made (see section 156).

(2) Subsection (1) does not apply in relation to Crown copyright or Parliamentary copyright (see sections 163 to 166) or to copyright subsisting by virtue of section 168 (copyright of certain international organisations).

(3) If the qualification requirements of this Chapter, or section 163, 165 or 168, are once satisfied in respect of a work, copyright does not cease to subsist by reason of any subsequent event.

[Copyright, Designs and Patents Act 1988, s 153 and SI 2003/2498.]

---

1. Chapter IX contains ss 153–162.

8–5760   154.   Qualification by reference to author.   (1) A work qualifies for copyright protection if the author was at the material time a qualifying person, that is—

(*a*)   a British citizen, a British overseas territories citizen, a British National (Overseas), a British Overseas citizen, a British subject or a British protected person within the meaning of the British Nationality Act 1981, or
(*b*)   an individual domiciled or resident in the United Kingdom or another country to which the relevant provisions of this Part extend, or
(*c*)   a body incorporated under the law of a part of the United Kingdom or of another country to which the relevant provisions of this Part extend.

(2) Where, or so far as, provision is made by Order under section 159 (application of this Part to countries to which it does not extend), a work also qualifies for copyright protection if at the material time the author was a citizen or subject of, an individual domiciled or resident in, or a body incorporated under the law of, a country to which the Order relates.

(3) A work of joint authorship qualifies for copyright protection if at the material time any of the authors satisfies the requirements of subsection (1) or (2); but where a work qualifies for copyright protection only under this section, only those authors who satisfy those requirements shall be taken into account for the purposes of—

section 11(1) and (2) (first ownership of copyright; entitlement of author or author's employer),
section 12 (duration of copyright), and section 9(4) (meaning of "unknown authorship") so far as it applies for the purposes of section 12, and

section 57 (anonymous or pseudonymous works: acts permitted on assumptions as to expiry of copyright or death of author).

(4) The material time in relation to a literary, dramatic, musical or artistic work is—

(*a*) in the case of an unpublished work, when the work was made or, if the making of the work extended over a period, a substantial part of that period;

(*b*) in the case of a published work, when the work was first published or, if the author had died before that time, immediately before his death.

(5) The material time in relation to other descriptions of work is as follows—

(*a*) in the case of a sound recording or film, when it was made;

(*b*) in the case of a broadcast, when the broadcast was made;

(*c*) (*revoked*)

(*d*) in the case of the typographical arrangement of a published edition, when the edition was first published.

[Copyright, Designs and Patents Act 1988, s 154 as amended by SI 1995/3297, the British Overseas Territories Act 2002, s 2(3) and SI 2003/2498.]

8–5761   155. Qualification by reference to country of first publication.   (1) A literary, dramatic, musical or artistic work, a sound recording or film, or the typographical arrangement of a published edition, qualifies for copyright protection if it is first published—

(*a*) in the United Kingdom, or

(*b*) in another country to which the relevant provisions of this Part extend.

(2) Where, or so far as, provision is made by Order under section 159 (application of this Part to countries to which it does not extend), such a work also qualifies for copyright protection if it is first published in a country to which the Order relates.

(3) For the purposes of this section, publication in one country shall not be regarded as other than the first publication by reason of simultaneous publication elsewhere; and for this purpose publication elsewhere within the previous 30 days shall be treated as simultaneous.

[Copyright, Designs and Patents Act 1988, s 155.]

8–5762   156. Qualification by reference to place of transmission.   (1) A broadcast qualifies for copyright protection if it is made from a place in—

(*a*) the United Kingdom, or

(*b*) another country to which the relevant provisions of this Part extend.

(2) Where, or so far as, provision is made by Order under section 159 (application of this Part to countries to which it does not extend), a broadcast also qualifies for copyright protection if it is made from a place in a country to which the Order relates.

[Copyright, Designs and Patents Act 1988, s 156, as amended by SI 2003/2498.]

Extent and application of this Part

8–5763   157. Countries to which this Part extends.   (1) This Part extends to England and Wales, Scotland and Northern Ireland.

(2) Her Majesty may by Order in Council direct that this Part shall extend, subject to such exceptions and modifications as may be specified in the Order, to—

(*a*) any of the Channel Islands,

(*b*) the Isle of Man, or

(*c*) any colony.

(3)–(5) *Supplementary provisions.*

[Copyright, Designs and Patents Act 1988, s 157.]

8–5764   158–160.   *Countries ceasing to be colonies; application[1] of this Part to countries to which it does not extend; denial of copyright protection to citizens of countries not giving adequate protection to British works.*

---

1. The Copyright (Application to the Isle of Man) Order 1992, SI 1992/1313, the Copyright (Application to Other Countries) Order 1999, SI 1999/1751 and SI 2003/774 and the Copyright and Performances (Application to Other Countries) Order 2005, SI 2005/852 have been made.

Supplementary

8–5765   161. Territorial waters and the continental shelf.   (1) For the purposes of this Part the territorial waters of the United Kingdom shall be treated as part of the United Kingdom.

(2) This Part applies to things done in the United Kingdom sector of the continental shelf on a structure or vessel which is present there for purposes directly connected with the exploration of the sea bed or subsoil or the exploitation of their natural resources as it applies to things done in the United Kingdom.

(3) The United Kingdom sector of the continental shelf means the areas designated by order under section 1(7) of the Continental Shelf Act 1964.
[Copyright, Designs and Patents Act 1988, s 161.]

8–5766   162. British ships, aircraft and hovercraft.   (1) This Part applies to things done on a British ship, aircraft or hovercraft as it applies to things done in the United Kingdom.

(2) In this section—

"British ship" means a ship which is a British ship for the purposes of the Merchant Shipping Act 1995 otherwise than by virtue of registration in a country outside the United Kingdom; and

"British aircraft" and "British hovercraft" mean an aircraft or hovercraft registered in the United Kingdom.

[Copyright, Designs and Patents Act 1988, s 162 as amended by the Merchant Shipping Act 1995, Sch 13.]

CHAPTER X[1]
MISCELLANEOUS AND GENERAL

8–5767   163–167. *Crown and Parliamentary copyright*

---

1. Chapter X contains ss 163–179.

Interpretation

8–5768   172. General provisions as to construction.   (1) This Part restates and amends the law of copyright, that is, the provisions of the Copyright Act 1956, as amended.

(2) A provision of this Part which corresponds to a provision of the previous law shall not be construed as departing from the previous law merely because of a change of expression.

(3) Decisions under the previous law may be referred to for the purpose of establishing whether a provision of this Part departs from the previous law, or otherwise for establishing the true construction of this Part.

[Copyright, Designs and Patents Act 1988, s 172.]

8–5768A   172A. Meaning of EEA and related expressions.   (1) In this Part—

"the EEA" means the European Economic Area;

"EEA national" means a national of an EEA state; and

"EEA state" means a state which is a contracting party to the EEA Agreement.

(2) References in this Part to a person being an EEA national shall be construed in relation to a body corporate as references to its being incorporated under the law of an EEA state.

(3) The "EEA Agreement" means the Agreement on the European Economic Area signed at Oporto on 2 May 1992, as adjusted by the Protocol signed at Brussels on 17 March 1993.

[Copyright, Designs and Patents Act 1988, s 172A, as inserted by SI 1995/3297 and amended by SI 1996/2967.]

8–5769   173. Construction of references to copyright owner.   (1) Where different persons are (whether in consequence of a partial assignment or otherwise) entitled to different aspects of copyright in a work, the copyright owner for any purpose of this Part is the person who is entitled to the aspect of copyright relevant for that purpose.

(2) Where copyright (or any aspect of copyright) is owned by more than one person jointly, references in this Part to the copyright owner are to all the owners, so that, in particular, any requirement of the licence of the copyright owner requires the licence of all of them.

[Copyright, Designs and Patents Act 1988, s 173.]

8–5770   174. *Meaning of "educational establishment" and related expressions.*

8–5771   175. Meaning of publication and commercial publication.   (1) In this Part "publication", in relation to a work—

(a) means the issue of copies to the public, and

(b) includes, in the case of a literary, dramatic, musical or artistic work, making it available to the public by means of an electronic retrieval system;

and related expressions shall be construed accordingly.

(2) In this Part "commercial publication", in relation to a literary, dramatic, musical or artistic work means—

(a) issuing copies of the work to the public at a time when copies made in advance of the receipt of orders are generally available to the public, or

(b) making the work available to the public by means of an electronic retrieval system;

and related expressions shall be construed accordingly.

(3) In the case of a work of architecture in the form of a building, or an artistic work incorporated in a building, construction of the building shall be treated as equivalent to publication of the work.

(4) The following do not constitute publication for the purposes of this Part and references to commercial publication shall be construed accordingly—

(a) in the case of a literary, dramatic or musical work—

(i) the performance of the work, or
(ii) the communication to the public of the work (otherwise than for the purposes of an electronic retrieval system);

(b) in the case of an artistic work—

(i) the exhibition of the work
(ii) the issue to the public of copies of a graphic work representing, or of photographs of, a work of architecture in the form of a building or a model for a building, a sculpture or a work of artistic craftsmanship,
(iii) the issue to the public of copies of a film including the work, or
(iv) the communication to the public of the work (otherwise than for the purposes of an electronic retrieval system);

(c) in the case of a sound recording or film—

(i) the work being played or shown in public, or
(ii) the communication to the public of the work.

(5) References in this Part to publication or commercial publication do not include publication which is merely colourable and not intended to satisfy the reasonable requirements of the public.

(6) No account shall be taken for the purposes of this section of any unauthorised act.

[Copyright, Designs and Patents Act 1988, s 175, as amended by SI 2003/2498.]

8–5772   178. Minor definitions.   In this Part—

"article", in the context of an article in a periodical, includes an item of any description;

"business" includes a trade or profession;

"collective work" means—

(a) a work of joint authorship, or
(b) a work in which there are distinct contributions by different authors or in which works or parts of works of different authors are incorporated;

"computer-generated", in relation to a work, means that the work is generated by computer in circumstances such that there is no human author of the work;

"country" includes any territory;

"the Crown" includes the Crown in right of Her Majesty's Government in Northern Ireland or in any country outside the United Kingdom to which this Part extends;

"electronic" means actuated by electric, magnetic, electro-magnetic, electro-chemical or electro-mechanical energy, and "in electronic form" means in a form usable only by electronic means;

"employed", "employee", "employer" and "employment" refer to employment under a contract of service or of apprenticeship;

"facsimile copy" includes a copy which is reduced or enlarged in scale;

"international organisation" means an organisation the members of which include one or more states;

"judicial proceedings" includes proceedings before any court, tribunal or person having authority to decide any matter affecting a person's legal rights or liabilities;

"parliamentary proceedings" includes proceedings of the Northern Ireland Assembly of the Scottish Parliament or of the European Parliament;

"private study" does not include which is directly or indirectly for a commercial purpose;

"producer", in relation to a sound recording or a film, means the person by whom the arrangements necessary for the making of the sound recording or film are undertaken;

"public library" means a library administered by or on behalf of—

(a) in England and Wales, a library authority within the meaning of the Public Libraries and Museums Act 1964;
(b) in Scotland, a statutory library authority within the meaning of the Public Libraries (Scotland) Act 1955;
(c) in Northern Ireland, an Education and Library Board within the meaning of the Education and Libraries (Northern Ireland) Order 1986;

"rental right" means the right of a copyright owner to authorise or prohibit the rental of copies of the work (see section 18A);

"reprographic copy" and "reprographic copying" refer to copying by means of a reprographic process;

"reprographic process" means a process—

(a) for making facsimile copies, or
(b) involving the use of an appliance for making multiple copies,

and includes, in relation to a work held in electronic form, any copying by electronic means, but does not include the making of a film or sound recording;

"sufficient acknowledgement" means an acknowledgement identifying the work in question by its title or other description, and identifying the author unless—

    (a) in the case of a published work, it is published anonymously;

    (b) in the case of an unpublished work, it is not possible for a person to ascertain the identity of the author by reasonable inquiry;

"sufficient disclaimer", in relation to an act capable of infringing the right conferred by section 80 (right to object to derogatory treatment of work), means a clear and reasonably prominent indication—

    (a) given at the time of the act, and

    (b) if the author or director is then identified, appearing along with the identification,

that the work has been subjected to treatment to which the author or director has not consented;

"telecommunications system" means a system for conveying visual images, sounds or other information by electronic means;

"typeface" includes an ornamental motif used in printing;

"unauthorised", as regards anything done in relation to a work, means done otherwise than—

    (a) by or with the licence of the copyright owner, or

    (b) if copyright does not subsist in the work, by or with the licence of the author or, in a case where section 11(2) would have applied, the author's employer or, in either case, persons lawfully claiming under him, or

    (c) in pursuance of section 48 (copying, &c of certain material by the Crown);

"wireless broadcast" means a broadcast by means of wireless telegraphy;

"wireless telegraphy" means the sending of electro-magnetic energy over paths not provided by a material substance constructed or arranged for that purpose, but does not include the transmission of microwave energy between terrestrial fixed points;

"writing" includes any form of notation or code, whether by hand or otherwise and regardless of the method by which, or medium in or on which, it is recorded, and "written" shall be construed accordingly.

[Copyright, Designs and Patents Act 1988, s 178 as amended by SI 1996/2967 and SI 2003/2498.]

8–5773   179. Index of defined expressions.   The following Table shows provisions defining or otherwise explaining expressions used in this Part (other than provisions defining or explaining an expression used only in the same section)—

database	section 3A(1)
defendant (in Scotland)	section 177
delivery up (in Scotland)	section 177
dramatic work	section 3(1)
educational establishment	section 174(1) to (4)
EEA, EEA national and EEA state	section 172A
electronic and electronic form	section 178
employed, employee, employer and employment	section 178
excepted sound recording	section 72(1A)
exclusive licence	section 92(1)
existing works (in Schedule 1)	paragraph 1(3) of that Schedule
facsimile copy	section 178
film	section 5B
future copyright	section 91(2)
general licence (in sections 140 and 141)	section 140(7)
graphic work	section 4(2)
infringing copy	section 27
injunction (in Scotland)	section 177
interlocutory relief (in Scotland)	section 177
international organisation	section 178
issue of copies to the public	section 18
joint authorship (work of)	sections 10(1) and (2)
judicial proceedings	section 178
lawful user (in sections 50A to 50C)	section 50A(2)
lending	section 18A(2) to (6)
librarian (in sections 37 to 43)	section 37(6)
licence (in sections 125 to 128)	section 124
licence of copyright owner	sections 90(4), 91(3) and 173
licensing body (in Chapter VII)	section 116(2)
licensing scheme (generally)	section 116(1)
licensing scheme (in sections 118 to 121)	section 117
literary work	section 3(1)
made (in relation to a literary, dramatic or musical work)	section 3(2)
musical work	section 3(1)
needletime	section 135A
the new copyright provisions (in Schedule 1)	paragraph 1(1) of that Schedule
the 1911 Act (in Schedule 1)	paragraph 1(1) of that Schedule
the 1956 Act (in Schedule 1)	paragraph 1(1) of that Schedule
on behalf of (in relation to an educational establishment)	section 174(5)
original (in relation to a database)	section 3A(2)
Parliamentary copyright	sections 165(2) and (7), 166(6) 166A(3) and 166B(3)
parliamentary proceedings	section 178
performance	section 19(2)
photograph	section 4(2)
plaintiff (in Scotland)	section 177
prescribed conditions (in sections 38 to 43)	section 37(1)(*b*)
prescribed library or archive (in sections 38 to 43)	section 37(1)(*a*)
private study	section 178
producer (in relation to a sound recording or film)	section 178
programme (in the context of broadcasting)	section 6(3)
prospective owner (of copyright)	section 91(2)
publication and related expressions	section 175
public library	section 178
published edition (in the context of copyright in the typographical arrangement)	section 8
pupil	section 174(5)
rental	section 18A(2) to (6)
rental right	section 178
reprographic copies and reprographic copying	section 178
reprographic process	section 178
sculpture	section 4(2)
signed	section 176
sound recording	sections 5A and 135A
sufficient acknowledgement	section 178
sufficient disclaimer	section 178
teacher	section 174(5)

telecommunications system	section 178
terms of payment	section 135A
typeface	section 178
unauthorised (as regards things done in relation to a work)	section 178
unknown (in relation to the author of a work)	section 9(5)
unknown authorship (work of)	section 9(4)
visually impaired person	section 31F(9)
wireless broadcast	section 178
wireless telegraphy	section 178
work (in Schedule 1)	paragraph 2(1) of that Schedule
work of more than one author (in Chapter VII)	section 116(4)
writing and written	section 178

[Copyright, Designs and Patents Act 1988, s 179 as amended by the Broadcasting Act 1990, s 175, SI 1992/3233, SI 1995/3297, SI 1996/2967, SI 1997/3032, the Copyright (Visually Impaired Persons) Act 2002, s 7 and SI 2003/2498.]

PART II[1]
RIGHTS IN PERFORMANCES

CHAPTER 1
INTRODUCTORY

8–5774　**180. Rights conferred on performers and persons having recording rights.**
(1) Chapter 2 of this Part (economic rights) confers rights—

(a) on a performer, by requiring his consent to the exploitation of his performances (see sections 181 to 184), and

(b) on a person having recording rights in relation to a performance, in relation to recordings made without his consent or that of the performer (see sections 185 to 188),

and creates offences in relation to dealing with or using illicit recordings and certain other related acts (see sections 198 and 201).

(1A) Rights are also conferred on a performer by the following provisions of Chapter 3 of this Part (moral rights)—

(a) section 205C (right to be identified);
(b) section 205F (right to object to derogatory treatment of performance).

(2) In this Part—

"performance" means—

(a) a dramatic performance (which includes dance and mime),
(b) a musical performance,
(c) a reading or recitation of a literary work, or
(d) a performance of a variety act or any similar presentation,

which is, or so far as it is, a live performance given by one or more individuals; and

"recording", in relation to a performance, means a film or sound recording—

(a) made directly from the live performance,
(b) made from a broadcast of the performance, or
(c) made, directly or indirectly, from another recording of the performance.

(3) The rights conferred by this Part apply in relation to performances taking place before the commencement of this Part; but no act done before commencement, or in pursuance of arrangements made before commencement, shall be regarded as infringing those rights.

(4) The rights conferred by this Part are independent of—

(a) any copyright in, or moral rights relating to, any work performed or any film or sound recording of, or broadcast the performance, and
(b) any other right or obligation arising otherwise than under this Part.

[Copyright, Designs and Patents Act 1988, s 180, as amended by SI 2003/2498 and SI 2006/18.]

---

1. Part II contains ss 180–212.

8–5775　**181. Qualifying performances.**　A performance is a qualifying performance for the purposes of the provisions of this Part relating to performers' rights if it is given by a qualifying individual (as defined in section 206) or takes place in a qualifying country (as so defined).
[Copyright, Designs and Patents Act 1988, s 181.]

Chapter 2

Economic Rights

Performers' rights

8–5776   182. Consent required for recording, etc of live performance.   (1) A performer's rights are infringed by a person who, without his consent—

    (*a*)   makes a recording of the whole or any substantial part of a qualifying performance directly from the live performance,

    (*b*)   broadcasts live the whole or any substantial part of a qualifying performance,

    (*c*)   makes a recording of the whole or any substantial part of a qualifying performance directly from a broadcast the live performance.

(2) (*Repealed*).

(3) In an action for infringement of a performer's rights brought by virtue of this section damages shall not be awarded against a defendant who shows that at the time of the infringement he believed on reasonable grounds that consent had been given.

[Copyright, Designs and Patents Act 1988, s 182 as substituted by SI 1996/2967 and amended by SI 2003/2498.]

8–5777   182A. Consent required for copying or recording.   (1) A performer's rights are infringed by a person who, without his consent, makes a copy of a recording of the whole or any substantial part of a qualifying performance.

(1A) In subsection (1), making a copy of a recording includes making a copy which is transient or is incidental to some other use of the original recording.

(2) It is immaterial whether the copy is made directly or indirectly.

(3) The right of a performer under this section to authorise or prohibit the making of such copies is referred to in this Chapter as "reproduction right".

[Copyright, Designs and Patents Act 1988, s 182A as inserted by SI 1996/2967 and amended by SI 2003/2498 and SI 2005/18.]

8–5778   182B. Consent required for issue of copies to public.   (1) A performer's rights are infringed by a person who, without his consent, issues to the public copies of a recording of the whole or any substantial part of a qualifying performance.

(2) References in this Part to the issue to the public of copies of a recording are to—

    (*a*)   the act of putting into circulation in the EEA copies not previously put into circulation in the EEA by or with the consent of the performer, or

    (*b*)   the act of putting into circulation outside the EEA copies not previously put into circulation in the EEA or elsewhere.

(3) References in this Part to the issue to the public of copies of a recording do not include—

    (*a*)   any subsequent distribution, sale, hiring or loan of copies previously put into circulation (but see section 182C: consent required for rental or lending), or

    (*b*)   any subsequent importation of such copies into the United Kingdom or another EEA state,

except so far as paragraph (*a*) of subsection (2) applies to putting into circulation in the EEA copies previously put into circulation outside the EEA.

(4) References in this Part to the issue of copies of a recording of a performance include the issue of the original recording of the live performance.

(5) The right of a performer under this section to authorise or prohibit the issue of copies to the public is referred to in this Chapter as "distribution right".

[Copyright, Designs and Patents Act 1988, s 182B as inserted by SI 1996/2967 and amended by SI 2005/18.]

8–5779   182C. Consent required for rental or lending of copies to public.   (1) A performer's rights are infringed by a person who, without his consent, rents or lends to the public copies of a recording of the whole or any substantial part of a qualifying performance.

(2) In this Chapter, subject to the following provisions of this section—

    (*a*)   "rental" means making a copy of a recording available for use, on terms that it will or may be returned, for direct or indirect economic or commercial advantage, and

    (*b*)   "lending" means making a copy of a recording available for use, on terms that it will or may be returned, otherwise than for direct or indirect economic or commercial advantage, through an establishment which is accessible to the public.

(3) The expressions "rental" and "lending" do not include—

    (*a*)   making available for the purpose of public performance, playing or showing in public or communication to the public;

    (*b*)   making available for the purpose of exhibition in public; or

    (*c*)   making available for on-the-spot reference use.

(4) The expression "lending" does not include making available between establishments which are accessible to the public.

(5) Where lending by an establishment accessible to the public gives rise to a payment the amount of which does not go beyond what is necessary to cover the operating costs of the establishment, there is no direct or indirect economic or commercial advantage for the purposes of this section.

(6) References in this Chapter to the rental or lending of copies of a recording of a performance include the rental or lending of the original recording of the live performance.

(7) In this Chapter—

"rental right" means the right of a performer under this section to authorise or prohibit the rental of copies to the public, and

"lending right" means the right of a performer under this section to authorise or prohibit the lending of copies to the public.

[Copyright, Designs and Patents Act 1988, s 182C as inserted by SI 1996/2967 and amended by SI 2005/18.]

8–5779A 182CA. Consent required for making available to the public.   (1) A performer's rights are infringed by a person who, without his consent, makes available to the public a recording of the whole or any substantial part of a qualifying performance by electronic transmission in such a way that members of the public may access the recording from a place and at a time individually chosen by them.

(2) The right of a performer under this section to authorise or prohibit the making available to the public of a recording is referred to in this Chapter as "making available right.

[Copyright, Designs and Patents Act 1988, s 182CA as inserted by SI 2003/2498 and amended by SI 2005/18.]

8–5780 182D. Right to equitable remuneration for exploitation of sound recording.
(1) Where a commercially published sound recording of the whole or any substantial part of a qualifying performance—

(*a*) is played in public, or

(*b*) is communicated to the public otherwise than by its being made available to the public in the way mentioned in section 182CA(1),

the performer is entitled to equitable remuneration from the owner of the copyright in the sound recording.

(1A) In subsection (1), the reference to publication of a sound recording includes making it available to the public by electronic transmission in such a way that members of the public may access it from a place and at a time individually chosen by them.

(2) The right to equitable remuneration under this section may not be assigned by the performer except to a collecting society for the purpose of enabling it to enforce the right on his behalf.

The right is, however, transmissible by testamentary disposition or by operation of law as personal or moveable property; and it may be assigned or further transmitted by any person into whose hands it passes.

(3) The amount payable by way of equitable remuneration is as agreed by or on behalf of the persons by and to whom it is payable, subject to the following provisions.

(4) In default of agreement as to the amount payable by way of equitable remuneration, the person by or to whom it is payable may apply to the Copyright Tribunal to determine the amount payable.

(5) A person to or by whom equitable remuneration is payable may also apply to the Copyright Tribunal—

(*a*) to vary any agreement as to the amount payable, or

(*b*) to vary any previous determination of the Tribunal as to that matter;

but except with the special leave of the Tribunal no such application may be made within twelve months from the date of a previous determination.

An order made on an application under this subsection has effect from the date on which it is made or such later date as may be specified by the Tribunal.

(6) On an application under this section the Tribunal shall consider the matter and make such order as to the method of calculating and paying equitable remuneration as it may determine to be reasonable in the circumstances, taking into account the importance of the contribution of the performer to the sound recording.

(7) An agreement is of no effect in so far as it purports—

(*a*) to exclude or restrict the right to equitable remuneration under this section, or

(*b*) to prevent a person questioning the amount of equitable remuneration or to restrict the powers of the Copyright Tribunal under this section.

(8) In this section "collecting society" means a society or other organisation which has as its main object, or one of its main objects, the exercise of the right to equitable remuneration on behalf of more than one performer.

[Copyright, Designs and Patents Act 1988, s 182D as inserted by SI 1996/2967 and amended by SI 2003/2498 and SI 2006/18.]

8–5781   183. Infringement of performer's rights by use of recording made without consent.
A performer's rights are infringed by a person who, without his consent—

(a)   shows or plays in public the whole or any substantial part of a qualifying performance, or

(b)   communicates to the public the whole or any substantial part of a qualifying performance,

by means of a recording which was, and which that person knows or has reason to believe was, made without the performer's consent.

[Copyright, Designs and Patents Act 1988, s 183, as amended by SI 2003/2498.]

8–5782   184. Infringement of performer's rights by importing, possessing or dealing with illicit recording.   (1) A performer's rights are infringed by a person who, without his consent—

(a)   imports into the United Kingdom otherwise than for his private and domestic use, or

(b)   in the course of a business possesses, sells or lets for hire, offers or exposes for sale or hire, or distributes,

a recording of a qualifying performance which is, and which that person knows or has reason to believe is, an illicit recording.

(2) Where in an action for infringement of a performer's rights brought by virtue of this section a defendant shows that the illicit recording was innocently acquired by him or a predecessor in title of his, the only remedy available against him in respect of the infringement is damages not exceeding a reasonable payment in respect of the act complained of.

(3) In subsection (2) "innocently acquired" means that the person acquiring the recording did not know and had no reason to believe that it was an illicit recording.

[Copyright, Designs and Patents Act 1988, s 184.]

Rights of person having recording rights

8–5783   185. Exclusive recording contracts and persons having recording rights.   (1) In this Chapter an "exclusive recording contract" means a contract between a performer and another person under which that person is entitled to the exclusion of all other persons (including the performer) to make recordings of one or more of his performances with a view to their commercial exploitation.

(2) References in this Chapter to a "person having recording rights", in relation to a performance, are (subject to subsection (3)) to a person—

(a)   who is party to and has the benefit of an exclusive recording contract to which the performance is subject, or

(b)   to whom the benefit of such a contract has been assigned,

and who is a qualifying person.

(3) If a performance is subject to an exclusive recording contract but the person mentioned in subsection (2) is not a qualifying person, references in this Chapter to a "person having recording rights" in relation to the performance are to any person—

(a)   who is licensed by such a person to make recordings of the performance with a view to their commercial exploitation, or

(b)   to whom the benefit of such a licence has been assigned,

and who is a qualifying person.

(4) In this section "with a view to commercial exploitation" means with a view to the recordings being sold or let for hire, or shown or played in public.

[Copyright, Designs and Patents Act 1988, s 185 as amended by SI 2005/18.]

8–5790   186. Consent required for recording of performance subject to exclusive contract.

(1) A person infringes the rights of a person having recording rights in relation to a performance who, without his consent or that of the performer, makes a recording of the whole or any substantial part of the performance.

(2) In an action for infringement of those rights brought by virtue of this section damages shall not be awarded against a defendant who shows that at the time of the infringement he believed on reasonable grounds that consent had been given.

[Copyright, Designs and Patents Act 1988, s 186, as amended by SI 2003/2498.]

8–5791   187. Infringement of recording rights by use of recording made without consent.

(1) A person infringes the rights of a person having recording rights in relation to a performance who, without his consent or, in the case of a qualifying performance, that of the performer—

(a)   shows or plays in public the whole or any substantial part of the performance, or

(b)   communicates to the public the whole or any substantial part of the performance,

by means of a recording which was, and which that person knows or has reason to believe was, made without the appropriate consent.

(2) The reference in subsection (1) to "the appropriate consent" is to the consent of—

(a)   the performer, or

(b)   the person who at the time the consent was given had recording rights in relation to the performance (or, if there was more than one such person, of all of them).

[Copyright, Designs and Patents Act 1988, s 187, as amended by SI 2003/2498.]

8–5792   188. Infringement of recording rights by importing, possessing or dealing with illicit recording.   (1) A person infringes the rights of a person having recording rights in relation to a performance who, without his consent or, in the case of a qualifying performance, that of the performer—

(*a*)   imports into the United Kingdom otherwise than for his private and domestic use, or

(*b*)   in the course of a business possesses, sells or lets for hire, offers or exposes for sale or hire, or distributes,

a recording of the performance which is, and which that person knows or has reason to believe is, an illicit recording.

(2) Where in an action for infringement of those rights brought by virtue of this section a defendant shows that the illicit recording was innocently acquired by him or a predecessor in title of his, the only remedy available against him in respect of the infringement is damages not exceeding a reasonable payment in respect of the act complained of.

(3) In subsection (2) "innocently acquired" means that the person acquiring the recording did not know and had no reason to believe that it was an illicit recording.
[Copyright, Designs and Patents Act 1988, s 188.]

Exceptions to rights conferred

8–5793   189. Acts permitted notwithstanding rights conferred by this Chapter.   The provisions of Schedule 2[1] specify acts which may be done notwithstanding the rights conferred by this Chapter, being acts which correspond broadly to certain of those specified in Chapter III of Part I (acts permitted notwithstanding copyright).
[Copyright, Designs and Patents Act 1988, s 189 as amended by SI 2005/18.]

---

1. See, post.

8–5794   190. Power of tribunal to give consent on behalf of performer in certain cases.
(1) The Copyright Tribunal may, on the application of a person wishing to make a copy of a recording of a performance, give consent in a case where the identity or whereabouts of the person entitled to the reproduction right cannot be ascertained by reasonable inquiry.

(2) Consent given by the Tribunal has effect as consent of the person entitled to the reproduction right for the purposes of—

(*a*)   the provisions of this Chapter relating to performers' rights, and

(*b*)   section 198(3)(*a*) (criminal liability: sufficient consent in relation to qualifying performances),

and may be given subject to any conditions specified in the Tribunal's order.

(3)–(6)   *Powers of the Tribunal.*
[Copyright, Designs and Patents Act 1988, s 190 as amended by SI 1996/2967 and SI 2005/18.]

Duration of rights

8–5795   191. Duration of rights.   (1) The following provisions have effect with respect to the duration of the rights conferred by this Chapter.

(2) The rights conferred by this Chapter in relation to a performance expire—

(*a*)   at the end of the period of 50 years from the end of the calendar year in which the performance takes place, or

(*b*)   if during that period a recording of the performance is released, 50 years from the end of the calendar year in which it is released,

subject as follows.

(3) For the purposes of subsection (2) a recording is "released" when it is first published, played or shown in public or communicated to the public; but in determining whether a recording has been released no account shall be taken of any unauthorised act.

(4) Where a performer is not a national of an EEA state, the duration of the rights conferred by this Chapter in relation to his performance is that to which the performance is entitled in the country of which he is a national, provided that does not exceed the period which would apply under subsections (2) and (3).

(5) If or to the extent that the applica tion of subsection (4) would be at variance with an international obligation to which the United Kingdom became subject prior to 29 October 1993, the duration of the rights conferred by this Chapter shall be as specified in subsections (2) and (3).
[Copyright, Designs and Patents Act 1988, s 191 as substituted by SI 1995/3297 and amended by SI 2003/2498 and SI 2005/18.]

8–5796   191A–191M.   *Performers' property rights.*

8–5796A   192A–B.   *Non-property rights.*

8–5797   193. Consent.   (1) Consent for the purposes of this Chapter by a person having a performer's non-property rights, or by a person having recording rights, may be given in relation to a specific performance, a specified description of performances or performances generally, and may relate to past or future performances.

(2) A person having recording rights in a performance is bound by any consent given by a person through whom he derives his rights under the exclusive recording contract or licence in question, in the same way as if the consent had been given by him.

(3) Where a performer's non-property right passes to another person, any consent binding on the person previously entitled binds the person to whom the right passes in the same way as if the consent had been given by him.

[Copyright, Designs and Patents Act 1988, s 193 as amended by SI 1996/2967 and SI 2005/18.]

8–5798   194. Infringement actionable as breach of statutory duty.   An infringement of—

(*a*)   a performer's non-property rights, or
(*b*)   any right conferred by this Chapter on a person having recording rights,

is actionable by the person entitled to the right as a breach of statutory duty.

[Copyright, Designs and Patents Act 1988, s 194 as amended by SI 1996/2967.]

Delivery up or seizure of illicit recordings

8–5799   195. Order for delivery up.   A person having performer's rights or recording rights in relation to a performance under this Chapter may apply to the High Court or county court for an order that the recording be delivered up to him or to such other person as the court may direct.

[Copyright, Designs and Patents Act 1988, s 195 as amended by SI 2005/18—summarised.]

8–5800   196. Right to seize illicit recordings.   (1) An illicit recording of a performance which is found exposed or otherwise immediately available for sale or hire, and in respect of which a person would be entitled to apply for an order under section 195, may be seized and detained by him or a person authorised by him.

The right to seize and detain is exercisable subject to the following conditions and is subject to any decision of the court under section 204 (order as to disposal of illicit recording).

(2) Before anything is seized under this section notice of the time and place of the proposed seizure must be given to a local police station.

(3) A person may for the purpose of exercising the right conferred by this section enter premises to which the public have access but may not seize anything in the possession, custody or control of a person at a permanent or regular place of business of his and may not use any force.

(4) At the time when anything is seized under this section there shall be left at the place where it was seized a notice in the prescribed form[1] containing the prescribed particulars as to the person by whom or on whose authority the seizure is made and the grounds on which it is made.

(5) In this section—

"premises" includes land, buildings, fixed or moveable structures, vehicles, vessels, aircraft and hovercraft; and

"prescribed" means prescribed by order of the Secretary of State.

(6) An order of the Secretary of State under this section shall be made by statutory instrument which shall be subject to annulment in pursuance of a resolution of either House of Parliament.

[Copyright, Designs and Patents Act 1988, s 196.]

---

1. See the Copyright and Rights in Performances (Notice of Seizure) Order 1989, SI 1989/1006.

8–5801   197. Meaning of "illicit recording".   (1) In this Chapter "illicit recording", in relation to a performance, shall be construed in accordance with this section.

(2) For the purposes of a performer's rights, a recording of the whole or any substantial part of a performance of his is an illicit recording if it is made, otherwise than for private purposes, without his consent.

(3) For the purposes of the rights of a person having recording rights, a recording of the whole or any substantial part of a performance subject to the exclusive recording contract is an illicit recording if it is made, otherwise than for private purposes, without his consent or that of the performer.

(4) For the purposes of sections 198 and 199 (offences and orders for delivery up in criminal proceedings), a recording is an illicit recording if it is an illicit recording for the purposes mentioned in subsection (2) or subsection (3).

(5) In this Chapter "illicit recording" includes a recording falling to be treated as an illicit recording by virtue of any of the following provisions of Schedule 2—

paragraph 4(3) (recordings made for purposes of instruction or examination),
paragraph 6(2) (recordings made by educational establishments for educational purposes),
paragraph 12(2) (recordings of performance in electronic form retained on transfer of principal recording),

paragraph 16(3) (recordings made for purposes of broadcast),
paragraph 17A(2) (recording for the purposes of time-shifting), or
paragraph 17B(2) (Photographs of broadcasts),

but otherwise does not include a recording made in accordance with any of the provisions of that Schedule.

(6) It is immaterial for the purposes of this section where the recording was made.

[Copyright, Designs and Patents Act 1988, s 197, as amended by SI 2003/2498 and SI 2005/18.]

Offences

8–5802   198. Criminal liability for making, dealing with or using illicit recordings.   (1) A person commits an offence who without sufficient consent—

(*a*)   makes for sale or hire, or
(*b*)   imports into the United Kingdom otherwise than for his private and domestic use, or
(*c*)   possesses in the course of a business with a view to committing any act infringing the rights conferred by this Chapter, or
(*d*)   in the course of a business—

  (i)   sells or lets for hire, or
  (ii)   offers or exposes for sale or hire, or
  (iii)   distributes,

a recording which is, and which he knows or has reason to believe is, an illicit recording.

(1A)   A person who infringes a performer's making available right—

(*a*)   in the course of a business, or
(*b*)   otherwise than in the course of a business to such an extent as to affect prejudicially the owner of the making available right,

commits an office if he knows or has reason to believe that, by doing so, he is infringing the making available right in the recording.

(2)   A person commits an offence who causes a recording of a performance made without sufficient consent to be—

(*a*)   shown or played in public, or
(*b*)   communicated to the public,

thereby infringing any of the rights conferred by this Chapter, if he knows or has reason to believe that those rights are thereby infringed.

(3)   In subsections (1) and (2) "sufficient consent" means—

(*a*)   in the case of a qualifying performance, the consent of the performer, and
(*b*)   in the case of a non-qualifying performance subject to an exclusive recording contract—

  (i)   for the purposes of subsection (1)(*a*) (making of recording), the consent of the performer or the person having recording rights, and
  (ii)   for the purposes of subsection (1)(*b*), (*c*) and (*d*) and subsection (2) (dealing with or using recording), the consent of the person having recording rights.

The references in this subsection to the person having recording rights are to the person having those rights at the time the consent is given or, if there is more than one such person, to all of them.

(4)   No offence is committed under subsection (1) or (2) by the commission of an act which by virtue of any provision of Schedule 2 may be done without infringing the rights conferred by this Chapter.

(5)   A person guilty of an offence under subsection (1)(*a*), (*b*) or (*d*)(iii) is liable[1]—

(*a*)   on summary conviction to imprisonment for a term not exceeding **six months** or a fine not exceeding **the statutory maximum**, or both;
(*b*)   on conviction on indictment to a **fine** or imprisonment for a term not exceeding **ten**[2] **years**, or **both**.*

(5A)   A person guilty of an offence under subsection (1A) is liable—

(*a*)   on summary conviction to imprisonment for a term not exceeding three months or a fine not exceeding the statutory maximum, or both;
(b)   on conviction on indictment to a fine or imprisonment for a term not exceeding two years, or both.

(6)   A person guilty of any other offence under this section is liable on summary conviction to a fine not exceeding **level 5** on the standard scale or imprisonment for a term not exceeding six months, or both.

[Copyright, Designs and Patents Act 1988, s 198 as amended by the Copyright, etc and Trade Marks (Offences and Enforcement) Act 2002, s 1, SI 2003/2498 and SI 2005/18.]

---

*Sub-section (5)(*b*) reproduced as amended by the Copyright, etc and Trade Marks (Offences and Enforcement) Act 2002, s 1, in force from 20 November 2002, except in relation to any offence committed before that date.

1. For procedure in respect of these offences which are triable either way, see the Magistrates' Courts Act 1980, ss 17A–21, in PART I: MAGISTRATES' COURTS, PROCEDURE, ante.

2. Increased from two years by s 1 of the Copyright, etc, and Trade Marks (Offences and Enforcement) Act 2002 in relation to offences committed on or after 20 November 2002.

8–5802A   198A. Enforcement by local weights and measures authority.   (1) It is the duty of every local weights and measures authority to enforce within their area the provisions of section 198.

(2) The following provisions of the Trade Descriptions Act 1968 apply in relation to the enforcement of that section by such an authority as in relation to the enforcement of that Act—

section 27 (power to make test purchases),

section 28 (power to enter premises and inspect and seize goods and documents),

section 29 (obstruction of authorised officers), and

section 33 (compensation for loss, & c. of goods seized).

(3) *Northern Ireland.*

(4) Any enactment which authorises the disclosure of information for the purpose of facilitating the enforcement of the Trade Descriptions Act 1968 shall apply as if section 198 were contained in that Act and as if the functions of any person in relation to the enforcement of that section were functions under that Act—

(5) *Scotland.* ★

[Copyright, Designs and Patents Act 1988, s 198A as inserted by the Criminal Justice and Public Order Act 1994, s 165.]

★**Section 198A is prospectively inserted by the Criminal Justice and Public Order Act 1994, s 165(3), when in force.**

8–5803   199. Order for delivery up in criminal proceedings.   (1) The court before which proceedings are brought against a person for an offence under section 198 may, if satisfied that at the time of his arrest or charge he had in his possession, custody or control in the course of a business an illicit recording of a performance, order that it be delivered up to a person having performers' rights or recording rights in relation to the performance or to such other person as the court may direct.

(2) For this purpose a person shall be treated as charged with an offence—

(a) in England, Wales and Northern Ireland, when he is orally charged or is served with a summons or indictment;

(b) *Scotland.*

(3) An order may be made by the court of its own motion or on the application of the prosecutor (or, in Scotland, the Lord Advocate or procurator-fiscal), and may be made whether or not the person is convicted of the offence, but shall not be made—

(a) after the end of the period specified in section 203 (period after which remedy of delivery up not available), or

(b) if it appears to the court unlikely that any order will be made under section 204 (order as to disposal of illicit recording).

(4) An appeal lies from an order made under this section by a magistrates' court—

(a) in England and Wales, to the Crown Court, and

(b) *Northern Ireland;*

and in Scotland, . . .

(5) A person to whom an illicit recording is delivered up in pursuance of an order under this section shall retain it pending the making of an order, or the decision not to make an order, under section 204.

(6) Nothing in this section affects the powers of the court under section 143 of the Powers of Criminal Courts (Sentencing) Act 2000[1], Part II of the Proceeds of Crime (Scotland) Act 1995 or Article 11 of the Criminal Justice (Northern Ireland) Order 1994 (general provisions as to forfeiture in criminal proceedings).

[Copyright, Designs and Patents Act 1988, s 199 as amended by SI 1994/2795, the Criminal Justice (Scotland) Act 1995, Sch 6, the Criminal Procedure (Consequential Provisions) (Scotland) Act 1995, Sch 4 and the Powers of Criminal Courts (Sentencing) Act 2000, Sch 9.]

---

1. See PART III: SENTENCING, ante.

8–5804   200. Search warrants.   (1) Where a justice of the peace (in Scotland, a sheriff or justice of the peace) is satisfied by information on oath given by a constable (in Scotland, by evidence on oath) that there are reasonable grounds for believing—

(a) that an offence under section 198(1) or (1A) (offences of making, importing, possessing, selling etc or distributing illicit recordings) has been or is about to be committed in any premises, and

(b) that evidence that such an offence has been or is about to be committed is in those premises, he may issue a warrant authorising a constable to enter and search the premises, using such reasonable force as is necessary.

(2) The power conferred by subsection (1) does not, in England and Wales, extend to authorising a search for material of the kinds mentioned in section 9(2) of the Police and Criminal Evidence Act 1984[1] (certain classes of personal or confidential material).

(3) A warrant under subsection (1)—

(a) may authorise persons to accompany any constable executing the warrant, and
(b) remains in force for 28 days from the date of its issue.

(3A) In executing a warrant issued under section 198(1) or (1A) a constable may seize an article if he reasonably believes that it is evidence that any offence under section 198(1) has been or is about to be committed.

(4) In this section "premises" includes land, buildings, fixed or moveable structures, vehicles, vessels, aircraft and hovercraft.

[Copyright, Designs and Patents Act 1988, s 200 as amended by the Copyright, etc and Trade Marks (Offences and Enforcement) Act 2002, s 2 and SI 2003/2498.]

---

1. See PART I: MAGISTRATES' COURTS, PROCEDURE, ante.

8–5805   201. False representation of authority to give consent.   (1) It is an offence for a person to represent falsely that he is authorised by any person to give consent for the purposes of this Chapter in relation to a performance, unless he believes on reasonable grounds that he is so authorised.

(2) A person guilty of an offence under this section is liable on summary conviction to imprisonment for a term not exceeding **six months** or a fine not exceeding **level 5** on the standard scale or both.

[Copyright, Designs and Patents Act 1988, s 201 as amended by SI 2005/18.]

8–5806   202. Offence by body corporate: liability of officers.   (1) Where an offence under this Chapter committed by a body corporate is proved to have been committed with the consent or connivance of a director, manager, secretary or other similar officer of the body, or a person purporting to act in any such capacity, he as well as the body corporate is guilty of the offence and liable to be proceeded against and punished accordingly.

(2) In relation to a body corporate whose affairs are managed by its members "director" means a member of the body corporate.

[Copyright, Designs and Patents Act 1988, s 202 as amended by SI 2005/18.]

Supplementary provisions with respect to delivery up and seizure

8–5807   203. Period after which remedy of delivery up not available.   (1) An application for an order under section 195 (order for delivery up in civil proceedings) may not be made after the end of the period of six years from the date on which the illicit recording in question was made, subject to the following provisions.

(2) If during the whole or any part of that period a person entitled to apply for an order—

(a) is under a disability, or
(b) is prevented by fraud or concealment from discovering the facts entitling him to apply,

an application may be made by him at any time before the end of the period of six years from the date on which he ceased to be under a disability or, as the case may be, could with reasonable diligence have discovered those facts.

(3) In subsection (2) "disability"—

(a) in England and Wales, has the same meaning as in the Limitation Act 1980;
(b) *Scotland*;
(c) *Northern Ireland*.

(4) An order under section 199 (order for delivery up in criminal proceedings) shall not, in any case, be made after the end of the period of six years from the date on which the illicit recording in question was made.

[Copyright, Designs and Patents Act 1988, s 203.]

8–5808   204. Order as to disposal of illicit recording.   (1) An application may be made to the court[1] for an order that an illicit recording of a performance delivered up in pursuance of an order under section 195 or 199, or seized and detained in pursuance of the right conferred by section 196, shall be—

(a) forfeited to such person having performer's rights or recording rights in relation to the performance as the court may direct, or
(b) destroyed or otherwise dealt with as the court may think fit,

or for a decision that no such order should be made.

(2)–(6) *Supplementary provisions related to orders under this section.*

1. Jurisdiction is conferred on the High Court or a county court; see s 205.

8–5808A   204A. Forfeiture of illicit recordings: England and Wales or Northern Ireland.
(1) In England and Wales or Northern Ireland where illicit recordings of a performance have come into the possession of any person in connection with the investigation or prosecution of a relevant offence, that person may apply under this section for an order for the forfeiture of the illicit recordings.

(2) For the purposes of this section "relevant offence" means—

(*a*) an offence under section 198(1) or (1A) (criminal liability for making or dealing with illicit recordings),

(*b*) an offence under the Trade Descriptions Act 1968 (c 29), or

(*c*) an offence involving dishonesty or deception.

(3) An application under this section may be made—

(*a*) where proceedings have been brought in any court for a relevant offence relating to some or all of the illicit recordings, to that court, or

(*b*) where no application for the forfeiture of the illicit recordings has been made under paragraph (*a*), by way of complaint to a magistrates' court.

(4) On an application under this section, the court shall make an order for the forfeiture of any illicit recordings only if it is satisfied that a relevant offence has been committed in relation to the illicit recordings.

(5) A court may infer for the purposes of this section that such an offence has been committed in relation to any illicit recordings if it is satisfied that such an offence has been committed in relation to illicit recordings which are representative of the illicit recordings in question (whether by reason of being part of the same consignment or batch or otherwise).

(6) Any person aggrieved by an order made under this section by a magistrates' court, or by a decision of such a court not to make such an order, may appeal against that order or decision—

(*a*) in England and Wales, to the Crown Court, or

(*b*) in Northern Ireland, to the county court.

(7) An order under this section may contain such provision as appears to the court to be appropriate for delaying the coming into force of the order pending the making and determination of any appeal (including any application under section 111 of the Magistrates' Courts Act 1980 (c 43) or Article 146 of the Magistrates' Courts (Northern Ireland) Order 1981 (SI 1987/1675 (NI 26)) (statement of case)).

(8) Subject to subsection (9), where any illicit recordings are forfeited under this section they shall be destroyed in accordance with such directions as the court may give.

(9) On making an order under this section the court may direct that the illicit recordings to which the order relates shall (instead of being destroyed) be forfeited to the person having the performers' rights or recording rights in question or dealt with in such other way as the court considers appropriate.

8–5808B   204B.   *Scotland.*

8–5809   205.   *Jurisdiction of county court and sheriff court.*

8–5809A   205A.   *Licensing of performers' property rights.*

8–5809B   205B.   *Jurisdiction of Copyright Tribunal.*

CHAPTER 3
MORAL RIGHTS

Right to be identified as performer

8–5809C   205C.   *Right to be identified as performer*

8–5809D   205D.   *Requirement that right be asserted*

8–5809E   205E.   *Exceptions to right*

Right to object to derogatory treatment

8–5809F   205F.   *Right to object to derogatory treatment of performance*

8–5809G   205G.   *Exceptions to right*

8–5809H   205H.   *Infringement of right by possessing or dealing with infringing article*

Supplementary

8–5809I   205I.   *Duration of rights*

8–5809J   2O5J.   *Consent and waiver of rights*

8–5809K   205K.   *Application of provisions to parts of performances*

8–5809L   205L.   *Moral rights not assignable*

8–5809M   205M.   *Transmission of moral rights on death*

8–5809N   205N.   *Remedies for infringement of moral rights*

CHAPTER 4
QUALIFICATION FOR PROTECTION, EXTENT AND INTERPRETATION

QUALIFICATION FOR PROTECTION AND EXTENT

8–5810   206. Qualifying countries, individuals and persons.   (1) In this Part—
"qualifying country" means—

    (*a*)   the United Kingdom,
    (*b*)   another member State of the European Economic Community, or
    (*c*)   to the extent that an Order under section 208 so provides, a country designated under
    that section as enjoying reciprocal protection;

"qualifying individual" means a citizen or subject of, or an individual resident in, a qualifying
    country; and
"qualifying person" means a qualifying individual or a body corporate or other body having legal
    personality which—

    (*a*)   is formed under the law of a part of the United Kingdom or another qualifying country,
    and
    (*b*)   has in any qualifying country a place of business at which substantial business activity is
    carried on.

(2) The reference in the definition of "qualifying individual" to a person's being a British overseas
territories' citizen or subject of a qualifying country shall be construed—

    (*a*)   in relation to the United Kingdom, as a reference to his being a British citizen, and
    (*b*)   in relation to a colony of the United Kingdom, as a reference to his being a British Dependent
    Territories' citizen by connection with that colony.

(3) In determining for the purpose of the definition of "qualifying person" whether substantial
business activity is carried on at a place of business in any country, no account shall be taken of
dealings in goods which are at all material times outside that country.
[Copyright, Designs and Patents Act 1988, s 206, as amended by the British Overseas Territories Act 2002,
s 2(3).]

8–5811   207. Countries to which this Part extends.   This Part extends to England and Wales,
Scotland and Northern Ireland.
[Copyright, Designs and Patents Act 1988, s 207.]

8–5812   208. Countries enjoying reciprocal protection.   (1) Her Majesty may by Order in
Council designate as enjoying reciprocal protection under this Part—

    (*a*)   a Convention country[1], or
    (*b*)   a country as to which Her Majesty is satisfied that provision has been or will be made under
    its law giving adequate protection for British performances.

(2) A "Convention country" means a country which is a party to a Convention relating to
performers' rights to which the United Kingdom is also a party.
(3) A "British performance" means a performance—

    (*a*)   given by an individual who is a British citizen or resident in the United Kingdom, or
    (*b*)   taking place in the United Kingdom.

(4) If the law of that country provides adequate protection only for certain descriptions of
performance, an Order under subsection (1)(*b*) designating that country shall contain provision

limiting to a corresponding extent the protection afforded by this Part in relation to performances connected with that country.

(5) The power conferred by subsection (1)(*b*) is exercisable in relation to any of the Channel Islands, the Isle of Man or any colony of the United Kingdom, as in relation to a foreign country.

(6) A statutory instrument containing an Order in Council under this section shall be subject to annulment in pursuance of a resolution of either House of Parliament.
[Copyright, Designs and Patents Act 1988, s 208.]

---

1. The Performances (Reciprocal Protection) (Convention Countries and Isle of Man) Order 2003, SI 2003/773, designates the countries enjoying reciprocal protection under the provisions of this Act relating to rights in performances. They are all parties to the International Convention for the Protection of Performers, Producers of Phonograms and Broadcasting Organisations (the Rome Convention) (Cmnd 2425).

8–5813   209. Territorial waters and the continental shelf.   (1) For the purposes of this Part the territorial waters of the United Kingdom shall be treated as part of the United Kingdom.

(2) This Part applies to things done in the United Kingdom sector of the continental shelf on a structure or vessel which is present there for purposes directly connected with the exploration of the sea bed or subsoil or the exploitation of their natural resources as it applies to things done in the United Kingdom.

(3) The United Kingdom sector of the continental shelf means the areas designated by order under section 1(7) of the Continental Shelf Act 1964.
[Copyright, Designs and Patents Act 1988, s 209.]

8–5814   210. British ships, aircraft and hovercraft.   (1) This Part applies to things done on a British ship, aircraft or hovercraft as it applies to things done in the United Kingdom.

(2) In this section—

"British ship" means a ship which is a British ship for the purposes of the Merchant Shipping Act 1995 otherwise than by virtue of registration in a country outside the United Kingdom; and

"British aircraft" and "British hovercraft" mean an aircraft or hovercraft registered in the United Kingdom.
[Copyright, Designs and Patents Act 1988, s 210 as amended by the Merchant Shipping Act 1995, Sch 13.]

Interpretation

210A. Requirement of signature: application in relation to body corporate.   (1) The requirement in the following provisions that an instrument be signed by or on behalf of a person is also satisfied in the case of a body corporate by the affixing of its seal—

section 191B(3) (assignment of performer's property rights);
section 191C(1) (assignment of future performer's property rights);
section 191D(1) (grant of exclusive licence).

(2) The requirement in the following provisions that an instrument be signed by a person is also satisfied in the case of a body corporate by signature on behalf of the body or by the affixing of its seal—

section 205D(2)(*a*) (assertion of performer's moral rights);
section 205J(2) (waiver of performer's moral rights).
[Copyright, Designs and Patents Act 1988, s 210A as inserted by SI 2005/18.]

8–5815   211. Expressions having same meaning as in copyright provisions.   (1) The following expressions have the same meaning in this Part as in Part I (copyright)—

assignment (in Scotland),
broadcast,
business,
communication to the public,
country,
defendant (in Scotland),
delivery up (in Scotland),
EEA national,
film,
injunction (in Scotland),
literary work,
published,
signed,
sound recording, and
wireless broadcast.

(2) The provisions of—

(*a*) section 5B(2) and (3) (supplementary provisions relating to films), and (*b*)   section 6(3) to (5A) and section 19(4) (supplementary provisions relating to broadcasting),

apply for the purposes of this Part, and in relation to an infringement of the rights conferred by this Part, as they apply for the purposes of Part I and in relation to an infringement of copyright.
[Copyright, Designs and Patents Act 1988, s 211 as amended by SI 1995/3297, SI 2003/2498 and SI 2006/18.]

8–5816   212. Index of defined expressions.   The following Table shows provisions defining or otherwise explaining expressions used in this Part (other than provisions defining or explaining an expression used only in the same section)—

assignment (in Scotland)	section 211(1) (and section 177)
broadcast (and related expressions)	section 211 (and section 6)
business	section 211(1) (and section 178)
communication to the public	section 211(1) (section 20)
consent of performer (in relation to performer's property rights)	section 191A(2)
country	section 211(1) (and section 178)
defendant (in Scotland)	section 211(1) (and section 177)
delivery up (in Scotland)	section 211(1) (and section 177)
distribution right	section 182B(5)
EEA national	section 211(1) (and section 172A)
exclusive recording contract	section 185(1)
film	section 211(1) (and section 5B)
group	section 205C(4)
illicit recording	section 197
injunction (in Scotland)	section 211(1) (and section 177)
issue to the public	section 182B
lending right	section 182C(7)
literary work	section 211(1) (and section 3(1))
making available right	section 182CA
performance	section 180(2)
performer's non-property rights	section 192A(1)
performer's property rights	section 191A(1)
published	section 211(1) (and section 175)
qualifying country	section 206(1)
qualifying individual	section 206(1) and (2)
qualifying performance	section 181
qualifying person	section 206(1) and (3)
recording (of a performance)	section 180(2)
recording rights (person having)	section 185(2) and (3)
rental right	section 182C(7)
reproduction right	section 182A(3)
rights owner (in relation to performer's property rights)	section 191A(3) and (4)
signed	section 211(1) (and section 176)
sound recording	section 211(1) (and section 5A)
wireless broadcast	section 211(1) (and section 178)

[Copyright, Designs and Patents Act 1988, s 212 as amended by SI 1995/3297 and SI 1996/2967 and SI 2003/2498.]

PART III[1]
DESIGN RIGHT

8–5817

----

1. Part III, which is not printed in this work, contains Chapters I–V, ss 213–264.

PART IV[1]
REGISTERED DESIGNS

8–5818

----

1. Part IV, which is not printed in this work, contains ss 265–273.

PART V[1]
PATENT AGENTS AND TRADE MARK AGENTS
Patent agents

8–5819   274. Persons permitted to carry on business of a patent agent.   (1) Any individual, partnership or body corporate may, subject to the following provisions of this Part, carry on the business of acting as agent for others for the purpose of—

(a) applying for or obtaining patents, in the United Kingdom or elsewhere, or

(b) conducting proceedings before the comptroller relating to applications for, or otherwise in connection with, patents.

(2) This does not affect any restriction under the European Patent Convention as to who may act on behalf of another for any purpose relating to European patents.

[Copyright, Designs and Patents Act 1988, s 274.]

---

1. Part V contains ss 274–286.

8–5820 275. The register of patent agents. *Power of the Secretary of State to make rules requiring the keeping of a register of persons who act as agent for others for the purposes of applying for or obtaining patents.*

8–5821 276. Persons entitled to describe themselves as patent agents. (1) An individual who is not a registered patent agent shall not—

(a) carry on a business (otherwise than in partnership) under any name or other description which contains the words "patent agent" or "patent attorney"; or

(b) in the course of a business otherwise describe himself, or permit himself to be described, as a "patent agent" or "patent attorney".

(2) A partnership shall not—

(a) carry on a business under any name or other description which contains the words "patent agent" or "patent attorney"; or

(b) in the course of a business otherwise describe itself, or permit itself to be described as, a firm of "patent agents" or "patent attorneys",

unless all the partners are registered patent agents or the partnership satisfies such conditions as may be prescribed for the purposes of this section.

(3) A body corporate shall not—

(a) carry on a business (otherwise than in partnership) under any name or other description which contains the words "patent agent" or "patent attorney"; or

(b) in the course of a business otherwise describe itself, or permit itself to be described as, a "patent agent" or "patent attorney",

unless all the directors of the body corporate are registered patent agents or the body satisfies such conditions as may be prescribed for the purposes of this section.

(4) Subsection (3) does not apply to a company which began to carry on business as a patent agent before 17th November 1917 if the name of a director or the manager of the company who is a registered patent agent is mentioned as being so registered in all professional advertisements, circulars or letters issued by or with the company's consent on which its name appears.

(5) Where this section would be contravened by the use of the words "patent agent" or "patent attorney" in reference to an individual, partnership or body corporate, it is equally contravened by the use of other expressions in reference to that person, or his business or place of business, which are likely to be understood as indicating that he is entitled to be described as a "patent agent" or "patent attorney".

(6) A person who contravenes this section commits an offence and is liable on summary conviction to a fine not exceeding **level 5** on the standard scale; and proceedings for such an offence may be begun at any time within a year from the date of the offence.

(7) This section has effect subject to—

(a) section 277 (persons entitled to describe themselves as European patent attorneys, etc), and

(b) section 278(1) (use of term "patent attorney" in reference to solicitors).

[Copyright, Designs and Patents Act 1988, s 276.]

8–5822 277. Persons entitled to describe themselves as European patent attorneys, etc.

(1) The term "European patent attorney" or "European patent agent" may be used in the following cases without any contravention of section 276.

(2) An individual who is on the European list may—

(a) carry on business under a name or other description which contains the words "European patent attorney" or "European patent agent", or

(b) otherwise describe himself, or permit himself to be described, as a "European patent attorney" or "European patent agent".

(3) A partnership of which not less than the prescribed number or proportion of partners is on the European list may—

(a) carry on a business under a name or other description which contains the words "European patent attorneys" or "European patent agents", or

(b) otherwise describe itself, or permit itself to be described, as a firm which carries on the business of a "European patent attorney" or "European patent agent".

(4) A body corporate of which not less than the prescribed number or proportion of directors is on the European list may—

(a) carry on a business under a name or other description which contains the words "European patent attorney" or "European patent agent", or

(b) otherwise describe itself, or permit itself to be described as, a company which carries on the business of a "European patent attorney" or "European patent agent".

(5) Where the term "European patent attorney" or "European patent agent" may, in accordance with this section, be used in reference to an individual, partnership or body corporate, it is equally permissible to use other expressions in reference to that person, or to his business or place of business, which are likely to be understood as indicating that he is entitled to be described as a "European patent attorney" or "European patent agent."
[Copyright, Designs and Patents Act 1988, s 277.]

8–5823   278. Use of the term "patent attorney": supplementary provisions. (1) The term "patent attorney" may be used in reference to a solicitor, and a firm of solicitors may be described as a firm of "patent attorneys", without any contravention of section 276.

(2) No offence is committed under the enactments restricting the use of certain expressions in reference to persons not qualified to act as solicitors—

(a) by the use of the term "patent attorney" in reference to a registered patent agent, or

(b) by the use of the term "European patent attorney" in reference to a person on the European list.

(3) The enactments referred to in subsection (2) are section 21 of the Solicitors Act 1974, section 31 of the Solicitors (Scotland) Act 1980 and Article 22 of the Solicitors (Northern Ireland) Order 1976.
[Copyright, Designs and Patents Act 1988, s 278.]

8–5824   279. Power to prescribe conditions, etc for mixed partnerships and bodies corporate. (1) The Secretary of State may make rules¹—

(a) prescribing the conditions to be satisfied for the purposes of section 276 (persons entitled to describe themselves as patent agents) in relation to a partnership where not all the partners are qualified persons or a body corporate where not all the directors are qualified persons, and

(b) imposing requirements to be complied with by such partnerships and bodies corporate.

(2) *Supplementary provisions as to rules under subsection (1).*

(3) Contravention of a requirement imposed by the rules is an offence for which a person is liable on summary conviction to a fine not exceeding **level 5** on the standard scale.

(4) The Secretary of State may make rules prescribing for the purposes of section 277 the number or proportion of partners of a partnership or directors of a body corporate who must be qualified persons in order for the partnership or body to take advantage of that section.

(5) In this section "qualified person"—

(a) in subsections (1) and (2), means a person who is a registered patent agent, and

(b) in subsection (4), means a person who is on the European list.

(6) Rules under this section shall be made by statutory instrument which shall be subject to annulment in pursuance of a resolution of either House of Parliament.
[Copyright, Designs and Patents Act 1988, s 279.]

---

1. The Patent Agents (Mixed Partnerships and Bodies Corporate) Rules 1994, SI 1994/362 have been made.

8–5825   280. Privilege for communications with patent agents. (1) This section applies to communications as to any matter relating to the protection of any invention, design, technical information or trade mark, or as to any matter involving passing off.

(2) Any such communication—

(a) between a person and his patent agent, or

(b) for the purpose of obtaining, or in response to a request for, information which a person is seeking for the purpose of instructing his patent agent,

is privileged from disclosure in legal proceedings in England, Wales or Northern Ireland in the same way as a communication between a person and his solicitor or, as the case may be, a communication for the purpose of obtaining, or in response to a request for, information which a person seeks for the purpose of instructing his solicitor.

(3) In subsection (2) "patent agent" means—

(a) a registered patent agent or a person who is on the European list,

(b) a partnership entitled to describe itself as a firm of patent agents or as a firm carrying on the business of a European patent attorney, or

(c) a body corporate entitled to describe itself as a patent agent or as a company carrying on the business of a European patent attorney.

(4) It is hereby declared that in Scotland the rules of law which confer privilege from disclosure in legal proceedings in respect of communications extend to such communications as are mentioned in this section.

[Copyright, Designs and Patents Act 1988, s 280 as amended by the Trade Marks Act 1994, Sch 4.]

8–5826   281. Power of comptroller to refuse to deal with certain agents. *The Secretary of State may make rules authorising the comptroller to refuse to recognise as agent in respect of any business to which the section applies.*

Supplementary

8–5830   285. Offences committed by partnerships and bodies corporate. (1) Proceedings for an offence under this Part alleged to have been committed by a partnership shall be brought in the name of the partnership and not in that of the partners; but without prejudice to any liability of theirs under subsection (4) below.

(2) The following provisions apply for the purposes of such proceedings as in relation to a body corporate—

(a) any rules of court relating to the service of documents;

(b) in England, Wales or Northern Ireland, Schedule 3 to the Magistrates' Courts Act 1980 or Schedule 4 to the Magistrates' Courts (Northern Ireland) Order 1981 (procedure on charge of offence).

(3) A fine imposed on a partnership on its conviction in such proceedings shall be paid out of the partnership assets.

(4) Where a partnership is guilty of an offence under this Part, every partner, other than a partner who is proved to have been ignorant of or to have attempted to prevent the commission of the offence, is also guilty of the offence and liable to be proceeded against and punished accordingly.

(5) Where an offence under this Part committed by a body corporate is proved to have been committed with the consent or connivance of a director, manager, secretary or other similar officer of the body, or a person purporting to act in any such capacity, he as well as the body corporate is guilty of the offence and liable to be proceeded against and punished accordingly.

[Copyright, Designs and Patents Act 1988, s 285.]

8–5831   286. Interpretation. In this Part—

"the comptroller" means the Comptroller-General of Patents, Designs and Trade Marks;

"director", in relation to a body corporate whose affairs are managed by its members, means any member of the body corporate;

"the European list" means the list of professional representatives maintained by the European Patent Office in pursuance of the European Patent Convention;

"registered patent agent" has the meaning given by section 275(1);

[Copyright, Designs and Patents Act 1988, s 286 as amended by the Trade Marks Act 1994, Sch 5.]

8–5832

PART VI[1]

PATENTS

---

1. Part VI, which is not printed in this work, contains ss 287–295.

PART VII[1]

MISCELLANEOUS AND GENERAL

Circumvention of protection measures

8–5832A   296. Circumvention of technical devices applied to computer programs

8–5832B   296ZA. Circumvention of technological measures

8–5832C   296ZB. Devices and services designed to circumvent technological measures.

(1) A person commits an offence if he—

(a) manufactures for sale or hire, or

(b) imports otherwise than for his private and domestic use, or

(c) in the course of a business—

(i) sells or lets for hire, or

(ii) offers or exposes for sale or hire, or

(iii) advertises for sale or hire, or

(iv) possesses, or

(v) distributes, or

(*d*) distributes otherwise than in the course of a business to such an extent as to affect prejudicially the copyright owner,

any device, product or component which is primarily designed, produced, or adapted for the purpose of enabling or facilitating the circumvention of effective technological measures.

(2) A person commits an offence if he provides, promotes, advertises or markets—

(*a*) in the course of a business, or

(*b*) otherwise than in the course of a business to such an extent as to affect prejudicially the copyright owner,

a service the purpose of which is to enable or facilitate the circumvention of effective technological measures.

(3) Subsections (1) and (2) do not make unlawful anything done by, or on behalf of, law enforcement agencies or any of the intelligence services—

(*a*) in the interests of national security; or

(*b*) for the purpose of the prevention or detection of crime, the investigation of an offence, or the conduct of a prosecution,

and in this subsection "intelligence services" has the meaning given in section 81 of the Regulation of Investigatory Powers Act 2000.

(4) A person guilty of an offence under subsection (1) or (2) is liable—

(*a*) on summary conviction, to imprisonment for a term not exceeding three months, or to a fine not exceeding the statutory maximum, or both;

(*b*) on conviction on indictment to a fine or imprisonment for a term not exceeding two years, or both.

(5) It is a defence to any prosecution for an offence under this section for the defendant to prove that he did not know, and had no reasonable ground for believing, that—

(*a*) the device, product or component; or

(*b*) the service,

enabled or facilitated the circumvention of effective technological measures.]
[Copyright, Designs and Patents 1998, s 296B, as substituted by SI 2003/2498.]

8–5832D   296ZC. Devices and services designed to circumvent technological measures: search warrants and forfeiture.   (1) The provisions of sections 297B (search warrants), 297C (forfeiture of unauthorised decoders: England and Wales or Northern Ireland) and 297D (forfeiture of unauthorised decoders: Scotland) apply to offences under section 296ZB with the following modifications.

(2) In section 297B the reference to an offence under section 297A(1) shall be construed as a reference to an offence under section 296ZB(1) or (2).

(3) In sections 297C(2)(a) and 297D(15) the references to an offence under section 297A(1) shall be construed as a reference to an offence under section 296ZB(1).

(4) In sections 297C and 297D references to unauthorised decoders shall be construed as references to devices, products or components for the purpose of circumventing effective technological measures.
[Copyright, Designs and Patents 1998, s 296C, as substituted by SI 2003/2498.]

8–5832E   296ZD. Rights and remedies in respect of devices and services designed to circumvent technological measures

8–5832F   296ZE. Remedy where effective technological measures prevent permitted acts

8–5832G   296ZF. Interpretation of sections 296ZA to 296ZE.   (1) In sections 296ZA to 296ZE, "technological measures" are any technology, device or component which is designed, in the normal course of its operation, to protect a copyright work other than a computer program.

(2) Such measures are "effective" if the use of the work is controlled by the copyright owner through—

(*a*) an access control or protection process such as encryption, scrambling or other transformation of the work, or

(*b*) a copy control mechanism,

which achieves the intended protection.

(3) In this section, the reference to—

(*a*) protection of a work is to the prevention or restriction of acts that are not authorised by the copyright owner of that work and are restricted by copyright; and

(*b*) use of a work does not extend to any use of the work that is outside the scope of the acts restricted by copyright.

6135 Copyright, Designs and Patents Act 1988

(4) Expressions used in sections 296ZA to 296ZE which are defined for the purposes of Part 1 of this Act (copyright) have the same meaning as in that Part.
[Copyright, Designs and Patents 1998, s 296F, as substituted by SI 2003/2498.]

8–5832H   296ZG. Electronic rights management information.   (1) This section applies where a person (D), knowingly and without authority, removes or alters electronic rights management information which—

    (*a*) is associated with a copy of a copyright work, or
    (*b*) appears in connection with the communication to the public of a copyright work, and

where D knows, or has reason to believe, that by so doing he is inducing, enabling, facilitating or concealing an infringement of copyright.

(2) This section also applies where a person (E), knowingly and without authority, distributes, imports for distribution or communicates to the public copies of a copyright work from which electronic rights management information—

    (*a*) associated with the copies, or
    (*b*) appearing in connection with the communication to the public of the work,

has been removed or altered without authority and where E knows, or has reason to believe, that by so doing he is inducing, enabling, facilitating or concealing an infringement of copyright.

(3) A person issuing to the public copies of, or communicating, the work to the public, has the same rights against D and E as a copyright owner has in respect of an infringement of copyright.

(4) The copyright owner or his exclusive licensee, if he is not the person issuing to the public copies of, or communicating, the work to the public, also has the same rights against D and E as he has in respect of an infringement of copyright.

(5) The rights conferred by subsections (3) and (4) are concurrent, and sections 101(3) and 102(1) to (4) apply, in proceedings under this section, in relation to persons with concurrent rights as they apply, in proceedings mentioned in those provisions, in relation to a copyright owner and exclusive licensee with concurrent rights.

(6) The following provisions apply in relation to proceedings under this section as in relation to proceedings under Part 1 (copyright)—

    (*a*) sections 104 to 106 of this Act (presumptions as to certain matters relating to copyright); and
    (*b*) section 72 of the Supreme Court Act 1981, section 15 of the Law Reform (Miscellaneous Provisions) (Scotland) Act 1985 and section 94A of the Judicature (Northern Ireland) Act 1978 (withdrawal of privilege against self-incrimination in certain proceedings relating to intellectual property).

(7) In this section—

    (*a*) expressions which are defined for the purposes of Part 1 of this Act (copyright) have the same meaning as in that Part; and
    (*b*) "rights management information" means any information provided by the copyright owner or the holder of any right under copyright which identifies the work, the author, the copyright owner or the holder of any intellectual property rights, or information about the terms and conditions of use of the work, and any numbers or codes that represent such information.

(8) Subsections (1) to (5) and (6)(b), and any other provision of this Act as it has effect for the purposes of those subsections, apply, with any necessary adaptations, to rights in performances, publication right and database right.

(9) The provisions of regulation 22 (presumptions relevant to database right) of the Copyright and Rights in Databases Regulations 1997 (SI 1997/3032) apply in proceedings brought by virtue of this section in relation to database right.
[Copyright, Designs and Patents 1998, s 296G, as substituted by SI 2003/2498.]

8–5833   297. Offence of fraudulently receiving programmes.   (1) A person who dishonestly receives a programme included in a broadcasting service provided from a place in the United Kingdom with intent to avoid payment of any charge applicable to the reception of the programme commits an offence and is liable on summary conviction to a fine not exceeding **level 5** on the standard scale.

(2) Where an offence under this section committed by a body corporate is proved to have been committed with the consent or connivance of a director, manager, secretary or other similar officer of the body, or a person purporting to act in any such capacity, he as well as the body corporate is guilty of the offence and liable to be proceeded against and punished accordingly.

In relation to a body corporate whose affairs are managed by its members "director" means a member of the body corporate.
[Copyright, Designs and Patents Act 1988, s 297, as amended by SI 2003/2498.]

---

1. Part VII contains ss 296–306.

8–5834   297A.   Unauthorised decoders.   (1)   A person commits an offence if he—

    (*a*)   makes, imports, distributes, sells or lets for hire or offers or exposes for sale or hire any unauthorised decoder;

    (*b*)   has in his possession for commercial purposes any unauthorised decoder;

    (*c*)   instals, maintains or replaces for commercial purposes any unauthorised decoder; or

    (*d*)   advertises any unauthorised decoder for sale or hire or otherwise promotes any unauthorised decoder by means of commercial communications.

(2)   A person guilty of an offence under subsection (1) is liable[1]—

    (*a*)   on summary conviction, to imprisonment for a term not exceeding six months, or to a fine not exceeding the statutory maximum, or to both; and

    (*b*)   on conviction on indictment, to imprisonment for a term not exceeding ten years, or to a fine, or to both.*

(3)   It is a defence to any prosecution for an offence under this section for the defendant to prove that he did not know, and had no reasonable ground for believing, that the decoder was an unauthorised decoder.

(4)   In this section—

"apparatus" includes any device, component or electronic data (including software);

"conditional access technology" means any technical measure or arrangement whereby access to encrypted transmissions in an intelligible form is made conditional on prior individual authorisation;

"decoder" means any apparatus which is designed or adapted to enable (whether on its own or with any other apparatus) an encrypted transmission to be decoded;

"encrypted" includes subjected to scrambling or the operation of cryptographic envelopes, electronic locks, passwords or any other analogous application;

"transmission" means—

    (*a*)   any programme included in a broadcasting service which is provided from a place in the United Kingdom or any other member State; or

    (*b*)   an information society service (within the meaning of Directive 98/34/EC of the European Parliament and of the Council of 22nd June 1998, as amended by Directive 98/48/EC of the European Parliament and of the Council of 20th July 1998) which is provided from a place in the United Kingdom or any other member State; and

"unauthorised", in relation to a decoder, means that the decoder is designed or adapted to enable an encrypted transmission, or any service of which it forms part, to be accessed in an intelligible form without payment of the fee (however imposed) which the person making the transmission, or on whose behalf it is made, charges for accessing the transmission or service (whether by the circumvention of any conditional access technology related to the transmission or service or by any other means).

[Copyright, Designs and Patents Act 1988, s 297A, as substituted by SI 2000/1175 and amended by the Copyright etc, and Trade Marks (Offences and Enforcement) Act 2002, s 1 and SI 2003/2498.]

---

    *Sub-section (2) printed as amended by the Copyright, etc and Trade Marks (Offences and Enforcement) Act 2002, s 1, in force from 20 November 2002, except in relation to any offence committed before that date.

    1.   For procedure in respect of this offence which is triable either way, see the Magistrates' Courts Act 1980, ss 17A–21, in PART I: MAGISTRATES' COURTS, PROCEDURE, ante.

8–5835   297B.   Search warrants.   (1)   Where a justice of the peace (in Scotland, a sheriff or justice of the peace) is satisfied by information on oath given by a constable (in Scotland, by evidence on oath) that there are reasonable grounds for believing—

    (*a*)   that an offence under section 297A(1) has been or is about to be committed in any premises, and

    (*b*)   that evidence that such an offence has been or is about to be committed is in those premises,

he may issue a warrant authorising a constable to enter and search the premises, using such reasonable force as is necessary.

(2)   The power conferred by subsection (1) does not, in England and Wales, extend to authorising a search for material of the kinds mentioned in section 9(2) of the Police and Criminal Evidence Act 1984 (c 60) (certain classes of personal or confidential material).

(3)   A warrant under subsection (1)—

    (*a*)   may authorise persons to accompany any constable executing the warrant, and

    (*b*)   remains in force for 28 days from the date of its issue.

(4)   In executing a warrant issued under subsection (1) a constable may seize an article if he reasonably believes that it is evidence that any offence under section 297A(1) has been or is about to be committed.

(5)   In this section "premises" includes land, buildings, fixed or moveable structures, vehicles, vessels, aircraft and hovercraft.

[Copyright, Designs and Patents Act 1988, s 297B, as inserted by the Copyright etc, and Trade Marks (Offences and Enforcement) Act 2002, s 2.]

8–5836   297C.   Forfeiture of unauthorised decoders: England and Wales or Northern Ireland.
(1) In England and Wales or Northern Ireland where unauthorised decoders have come into the possession of any person in connection with the investigation or prosecution of a relevant offence, that person may apply under this section for an order for the forfeiture of the unauthorised decoders.

(2) For the purposes of this section "relevant offence" means—

(a)   an offence under section 297A(1) (criminal liability for making, importing, etc unauthorised decoders),

(b)   an offence under the Trade Descriptions Act 1968, or

(c)   an offence involving dishonesty or deception.

(3) An application under this section may be made—

(a)   where proceedings have been brought in any court for a relevant offence relating to some or all of the unauthorised decoders, to that court, or

(b)   where no application for the forfeiture of the unauthorised decoders has been made under paragraph (a), by way of complaint to a magistrates' court.

(4) On an application under this section, the court shall make an order for the forfeiture of any unauthorised decoders only if it is satisfied that a relevant offence has been committed in relation to the unauthorised decoders.

(5) A court may infer for the purposes of this section that such an offence has been committed in relation to any unauthorised decoders if it is satisfied that such an offence has been committed in relation to unauthorised decoders which are representative of the unauthorised decoders in question (whether by reason of being of the same design or part of the same consignment or batch or otherwise).

(6) Any person aggrieved by an order made under this section by a magistrates' court, or by a decision of such a court not to make such an order, may appeal against that order or decision—

(a)   in England and Wales, to the Crown Court, or

(b)   in Northern Ireland, to the county court.

(7) An order under this section may contain such provision as appears to the court to be appropriate for delaying the coming into force of the order pending the making and determination of any appeal (including any application under section 111 of the Magistrates' Courts Act 1980 (c 43) or Article 146 of the Magistrates' Courts (Northern Ireland) Order 1981 (SI 1981/1675 (NI 26)) (statement of case)).

(8) Subject to subsection (9), where any unauthorised decoders are forfeited under this section they shall be destroyed in accordance with such directions as the court may give.

(9) On making an order under this section the court may direct that the unauthorised decoders to which the order relates shall (instead of being destroyed) be forfeited to a person who has rights or remedies under section 298 in relation to the unauthorised decoders in question, or dealt with in such other way as the court considers appropriate.
[Copyright, Designs and Patents Act 1988, s 297C, as inserted by the Copyright etc, and Trade Marks (Offences and Enforcement) Act 2002, s 5.]

8–5837   297D.   *Scotland.*

8–5851   304–306.   *Extent; commencement; short title.*

Section 189   SCHEDULE 2
RIGHTS IN PERFORMANCES: PERMITTED ACTS

(As amended by the Broadcasting Act 1990, Schs 20 and 21, the Broadcasting Act 1996, Schs 9 and 10, SI 1996/2967, the Government of Wales Act 1998, Sch 12, SI 2003/2498, SI 2005/18 and the Communications Act 2003, Schs 17 and 19.)

Introductory

8–5852   1. (1) The provisions of this Schedule specify acts which may be done in relation to a performance or recording notwithstanding the rights conferred by this Chapter; they relate only to the question of infringement of those rights and do not affect any other right or obligation restricting the doing of any of the specified acts.

(2) No inference shall be drawn from the description of any act which may by virtue of this Schedule be done without infringing the rights conferred by this Chapter as to the scope of those rights.

(3) The provisions of this Schedule are to be construed independently of each other, so that the fact that an act does not fall within one provision does not mean that it is not covered by another provision.

Making of temporary copies

8–5852A   1A. The rights conferred by this Chapter are not infringed by the making of a temporary copy of a recording of a performance which is transient or incidental, which is an integral and essential part of a technological process and the sole purpose of which is to enable—

  (*a*) a transmission of the recording in a network between third parties by an intermediary; or

  (*b*) a lawful use of the recording;

and which has no independent economic significance.

Criticism, reviews and news reporting

8–5853 **2.** (1) Fair dealing with a performance or recording for the purpose of criticism or review, of that or another performance or recording, or of a work, does not infringe any of the rights conferred by this Chapter provided that the performance or recording has been made available to the public.

  (1A) Fair dealing with a performance or recording for the purpose of reporting current events does not infringe any of the rights conferred by this Chapter.

  (2) Expressions used in this paragraph have the same meaning as in section 30.

Incidental inclusion of performance or recording

8–5854 **3.** (1) The rights conferred by this Chapter are not infringed by the incidental inclusion of a performance or recording in a sound recording, film or broadcast.

  (2) Nor are those rights infringed by anything done in relation to copies of, or the playing, showing or communication to the public of, anything whose making was, by virtue of sub-paragraph (1), not an infringement of those rights.

  (3) A performance or recording so far as it consists of music, or words spoken or sung with music, shall not be regarded as incidentally included in a sound recording or broadcast if it is deliberately included.

  (4) Expressions used in this paragraph have the same meaning as in section 31.

Things done for purposes of instruction or examination

8–5855 **4.** (1) The rights conferred by this Chapter are not infringed by the copying of a recording of a performance in the course of instruction, or of preparation for instruction, in the making of films or film sound-tracks, provided the copying is done by a person giving or receiving instruction and the instruction is for a non-commercial purpose.

  (2) The rights conferred by this Chapter are not infringed—

  (*a*) by the copying of a recording of a performance for the purposes of setting or answering the questions in an examination, or

  (*b*) by anything done for the purposes of an examination by way of communicating the questions to the candidates.

  (3) Where a recording which would otherwise be an illicit recording is made in accordance with this paragraph but is subsequently dealt with, it shall be treated as an illicit recording for the purposes of that dealing, and if that dealing infringes any right conferred by this Chapter for all subsequent purposes.

For this purpose "dealt with" means—

  (*a*) sold or let for hire, offered or exposed for sale or hire; or

  (*b*) communicated to the public, unless that communication, by virtue of sub-paragraph (2)(b), is not an infringement of the rights conferred by Part 2.

  (4) Expressions used in this paragraph have the same meaning as in section 32.

Playing or showing sound recording, film or broadcast at educational establishment

8–5856 **5.** (1) The playing or showing of a sound recording, film or broadcast at an educational establishment for the purposes of instruction before an audience consisting of teachers and pupils at the establishment and other persons directly connected with the activities of the establishment is not a playing or showing of a performance in public for the purposes of infringement of the rights conferred by this Chapter.

  (2) A person is not for this purpose directly connected with the activities of the educational establishment simply because he is the parent of a pupil at the establishment.

  (3) Expressions used in this paragraph have the same meaning as in section 34 and any provision made under section 174(2) with respect to the application of that section also applies for the purposes of this paragraph.

Recording of broadcasts by educational establishments

8–5857 **6.** (1) A recording of a broadcast, or a copy of such a recording, may be made by or on behalf of an educational establishment for the educational purposes of that establishment without thereby infringing any of the rights conferred by this Chapter in relation to any performance or recording included in it, provided that the educational purposes are non-commercial.

  (1A) The rights conferred by this Chapter are not infringed where a recording of a broadcast or a copy of such a recording, whose making was by virtue of sub-paragraph (1) not an infringement of such rights, is communicated to the public by a person situated within the premises of an educational establishment provided that the communication cannot be received by any person situated outside the premises of that establishment.

  (1B) This paragraph does not apply if or to the extent that there is a licensing scheme certified for the purposes of this paragraph under paragraph 16 of Schedule 2A providing for the grant of licences.

  (2) Where a recording which would otherwise be an illicit recording is made in accordance with this paragraph but is subsequently dealt with, it shall be treated as an illicit recording for the purposes of that dealing, and if that dealing infringes any right conferred by this Chapter for all subsequent purposes.

For this purpose "dealt with" means sold or let for hire, or offered or exposed for sale or hire, offered or exposed for sale or hire, or communicated from within the premises of an educational establishment to any person situated outside those premises.

  (3) Expressions used in this paragraph have the same meaning as in section 35 and any provision made under section 174(2) with respect to the application of that section also applies for the purposes of this paragraph.

Lending of copies by educational establishments

8–5857A   6A. (1) The rights conferred by this Chapter are not infringed by the lending of copies of a recording of a performance by an educational establishment.

(2) Expressions used in this paragraph have the same meaning as in section 36A; and any provision with respect to the application of that section made under section 174(2) (instruction given elsewhere than an educational establishment) applies also for the purposes of this paragraph.

Lending of copies by libraries or archives

8–5857B   6B. (1) The rights conferred by this Chapter are not infringed by the lending of copies of a recording of a performance by a prescribed library or archive (other than a public library) which is not conducted for profit.

(2) Expressions used in this paragraph have the same meaning as in section 40A(2); and any provision under section 37 prescribing libraries or archives for the purposes of that section applies also for the purposes of this paragraph.

Copy of work required to be made as condition of export

8–5858   7. (1) If an article of cultural or historical importance or interest cannot lawfully be exported from the United Kingdom unless a copy of it is made and deposited in an appropriate library or archive, it is not an infringement of any right conferred by this Chapter to make that copy.

(2) Expressions used in this paragraph have the same meaning as in section 44.

Parliamentary and judicial proceedings

8–5859   8. (1) The rights conferred by this Chapter are not infringed by anything done for the purposes of parliamentary or judicial proceedings or for the purpose of reporting such proceedings.

(2) Expressions used in this paragraph have the same meaning as in section 45.

Royal Commissions and statutory inquiries

8–5860   9. (1) The rights conferred by this Chapter are not infringed by anything done for the purposes of the proceedings of a Royal Commission or statutory inquiry or for the purpose of reporting any such proceedings held in public.

(2) Expressions used in this paragraph have the same meaning as in section 46.

Public records

8–5861   10. (1) Material which is comprised in public records within the meaning of the Public Records Act 1958, the Public Records (Scotland) Act 1937 or the Public Records Act (Northern Ireland) 1923, or in Welsh public records (as defined in the Government of Wales Act 1998) which are open to public inspection in pursuance of that Act, may be copied, and a copy may be supplied to any person, by or with the authority of any officer appointed under that Act, without infringing any right conferred by this Chapter.

(2) Expressions used in this paragraph have the same meaning as in section 49.

Acts done under statutory authority

8–5862   11. (1) Where the doing of a particular act is specifically authorised by an Act of Parliament, whenever passed, then, unless the Act provides otherwise, the doing of that act does not infringe the rights conferred by this Chapter.

(2) Sub-paragraph (1) applies in relation to an enactment contained in Northern Ireland legislation as it applies to an Act of Parliament.

(3) Nothing in this paragraph shall be construed as excluding any defence of statutory authority otherwise available under or by virtue of any enactment.

(4) Expressions used in this paragraph have the same meaning as in section 50.

Transfer of copies of works in electronic form

8–5863   12. (1) This paragraph applies where a recording of a performance in electronic form has been purchased on terms which, expressly or impliedly or by virtue of any rule of law, allow the purchaser to make further recordings in connection with his use of the recording.

(2) If there are no express terms—

(a) prohibiting the transfer of the recording by the purchaser, imposing obligations which continue after a transfer, prohibiting the assignment of any consent or terminating any consent on a transfer, or

(b) providing for the terms on which a transferee may do the things which the purchaser was permitted to do,

anything which the purchaser was allowed to do may also be done by a transferee without infringement of the rights conferred by this Chapter, but any recording made by the purchaser which is not also transferred shall be treated as an illicit recording for all purposes after the transfer.

(3) The same applies where the original purchased recording is no longer usable and what is transferred is a further copy used in its place.

(4) The above provisions also apply on a subsequent transfer, with the substitution for references in sub-paragraph (2) to the purchaser of references to the subsequent transferor.

(5) This paragraph does not apply in relation to a recording purchased before the commencement of this Chapter.

(6) Expressions used in this paragraph have the same meaning as in section 56.

Use of recordings of spoken works in certain cases

8–5864   13. (1) Where a recording of the reading or recitation of a literary work is made for the purpose—

(*a*) of reporting current events, or

(*b*) of communicating to the public the whole or part of the reading or recitation,

it is not an infringement of the rights conferred by this Chapter to use the recording (or to copy the recording and use the copy) for that purpose, provided the following conditions are met.

(2) The conditions are that—

(*a*) the recording is a direct recording of the reading or recitation and is not taken from a previous recording or from a broadcast;

(*b*) the making of the recording was not prohibited by or on behalf of the person giving the reading or recitation;

(*c*) the use made of the recording is not a kind prohibited by or on behalf of that person before the recording was made; and

(*d*) the use is by or with the authority of a person who is lawfully in possession of the recording.

(3) Expressions used in this paragraph have the same meaning as in section 58.

Recordings of folksongs

8–5865   14. (1) A recording of a performance of a song may be made for the purpose of including it in an archive maintained by a designated body without infringing any of the rights conferred by this Chapter, provided the conditions in sub-paragraph (2) below are met.

(2) The conditions are that—

(*a*) the words are unpublished and of unknown authorship at the time the recording is made,

(*b*) the making of the recording does not infringe any copyright, and

(*c*) its making is not prohibited by any performer.

(3) Copies of a recording made in reliance on sub-paragraph (1) and included in an archive maintained by a designated body may, if the prescribed conditions are met, be made and supplied by the archivist without infringing any of the rights conferred by this Chapter.

(4) In this paragraph—

"designated body" means a body designated for the purposes of section 61, and

"the prescribed conditions" means the conditions prescribed for the purposes of subsection (3) of that section;

and other expressions used in this paragraph have the same meaning as in that section.

Lending of certain recordings

8–5865A   14A. (1) The Secretary of State may by order provide that in such cases as may be specified in the order the lending to the public of copies of films or sound recordings shall be treated as licensed by the performer subject only to the payment of such reasonable royalty or other payment as may be agreed or determined in default of agreement by the Copyright Tribunal.

(2) No such order shall apply if, or to the extent that, there is a licensing scheme certified for the purposes of this paragraph under paragraph 16 of Schedule 2A providing for the grant of licences.

(3) An order may make different provision for different cases and may specify cases by reference to any factor relating to the work, the copies lent, the lender or the circumstances of the lending.

(4) An order shall be made by statutory instrument; and no order shall be made unless a draft of it has been laid before and approved by a resolution of each House of Parliament.

(5) Nothing in this section affects any liability under section 184(1)(*b*) (secondary infringement: possessing or dealing with illicit recording) in respect of the lending of illicit recordings.

(6) Expressions used in this paragraph have the same meaning as in section 66.

Playing of sound recordings for purposes of club, society, etc

8–5866   15. (1) It is not an infringement of any right conferred by this Chapter to play a sound recording as part of the activities of, or for the benefit of, a club, society or other organisation if the following conditions are met.

(2) The conditions are—

(*a*) that the organisation is not established or conducted for profit and its main objects are charitable or are otherwise concerned with the advancement of religion, education or social welfare, and

(*b*) that the sound recording is played by a person who is acting primarily and directly for the benefit of the organisation and who is not acting with a view to gain,

(*c*) that the proceeds of any charge for admission to the place where the recording is to be heard are applied solely for the purposes of the organisation, and

(*d*) that the proceeds from any goods or services sold by, or on behalf of, the organisation—

(i) in the place where the sound recording is heard, and

(ii) on the occasion when the sound recording is played,

are applied solely for the purposes of the organisation.

(3) Expressions used in this paragraph have the same meaning as in section 67.

Incidental recording for purposes of broadcast

8–5867   16. (1) A person who proposes to broadcast a recording of a performance in circumstances not infringing the rights conferred by this Chapter shall be treated as having consent for the purposes of that Part for the making of a further recording for the purposes of the broadcast.

(2) That consent is subject to the condition that the further recording—

(a) shall not be used for any other purpose, and
(b) shall be destroyed within 28 days of being first used for broadcasting the performance.

(3) A recording made in accordance with this paragraph shall be treated as an illicit recording—

(a) for the purposes of any use in breach of the condition mentioned in sub-paragraph (2)(a), and
(b) for all purposes after that condition or the condition mentioned in sub-paragraph (2)(b) is broken.

(4) Expressions used in this paragraph have the same meaning as in section 68.

Recordings for purposes of supervision and control of broadcasts and other services

8–5868 **17.** (1) The rights conferred by this Chapter are not infringed by the making or use by the British Broadcasting Corporation, for the purpose of maintaining supervision and control over programmes broadcast by them, of recordings of those programmes.
(2) The rights conferred by this Chapter are not infringed by anything done in pursuance of—

(a) section 167(1) of the Broadcasting Act 1990, section 115(4) or (6) or 117 of the Broadcasting Act 1996 or paragraph 20 of Schedule 12 to the Communications Act 2003;
(b) a condition which, by virtue of section 334(1) of the Communications Act 2003, is included in a licence granted under Part I or III of that Act or Part I or II of the Broadcasting Act 1996;
(c) a direction given under section 109(2) of the Broadcasting Act 1990 (power of OFCOM to require production of recordings etc);
(d) section 334(3) of theCommunications Act 2003.

(3) The rights conferred by this Chapter are not infringed by the use by OFCOM in connection with the performance of any of their functions under the Broadcasting Act 1990, the Broadcasting Act 1996 or the Communications Act 2003 of—

(a) any recording, script or transcript which is provided to them under or by virtue of any provision of those Acts; or
(b) any existing material which is transferred to them by a scheme made under section 30 of the Communications Act 2003.

(4) In subsection (3), "existing material" means—

(a) any recording, script or transcript which was provided to the Independent Television Commission or the Radio Authority under or by virtue of any provision of the Broadcasting Act 1990 or the Broadcasting Act 1996; and
(b) any recording or transcript which was provided to the Broadcasting Standards Commission under section 115(4) or (6) or 116(5) of the Broadcasting Act 1996.

Recording for the purposes of time-shifting

8–5868A **17A.** (1) The making in domestic premises for private and domestic use of a recording of a broadcast solely for the purpose of enabling it to be viewed or listened to at a more convenient time does not infringe any right conferred by this Chapter in relation to a performance or recording included in the broadcast.
(2) Where a recording which would otherwise be an illicit recording is made in accordance with this paragraph but is subsequently dealt with—

(a) it shall be treated as an illicit recording for the purposes of that dealing; and
(b) if that dealing infringes any right conferred by this Chapter, it shall be treated as an illicit recording for all subsequent purposes.

(3) In sub-paragraph (2), "dealt with" means sold or let for hire, offered or exposed for sale or hire or communicated to the public.
(4) Expressions used in this paragraph have the same meaning as in section 70.

Photographs of broadcasts

8–5868B **17B.** (1) The making in domestic premises for private and domestic use of a photograph of the whole or any part of an image forming part of a broadcast, or a copy of such a photograph, does not infringe any right conferred by this Chapter in relation to a performance or recording included in the broadcast.
(2) Where a recording which would otherwise be an illicit recording is made in accordance with this paragraph but is subsequently dealt with—

(a) it shall be treated as an illicit recording for the purposes of that dealing; and
(b) if that dealing infringes any right conferred by this Chapter, it shall be treated as an illicit recording for all subsequent purposes.

(3) In sub-paragraph (2), "dealt with" means sold or let for hire, offered or exposed for sale or hire or communicated to the public.
(4) Expressions used in this paragraph have the same meaning as in section 71.

Free public showing or playing of broadcast

8–5869 **18.** (1) The showing or playing in public of a broadcast to an audience who have not paid for admission to the place where the broadcast is to be seen or heard does not infringe any right conferred by this Chapter in relation to a performance or recording included in—

(a) the broadcast, or
(b) any sound recording (except so far as it is an excepted sound recording) or film which is played or shown in public by reception of the broadcast.

(1A) The showing or playing in public of a broadcast to an audience who have not paid for admission to the place where the broadcast is to be seen or heard does not infringe any right conferred by this Chapter in relation to a performance or recording included in any excepted sound recording which is played in public by reception of the broadcast, if the playing or showing of that broadcast in public—

    (*a*) forms part of the activities of an organisation that is not established or conducted for profit; or

    (*b*) is necessary for the purposes of—

        (i) repairing equipment for the reception of broadcasts;

        (ii) demonstrating that a repair to such equipment has been carried out; or

        (iii) demonstrating such equipment which is being sold or let for hire or offered or exposed for sale or hire.

(2) The audience shall be treated as having paid for admission to a place—

    (*a*) if they have paid for admission to a place of which that place forms part; or

    (*b*) if goods or services are supplied at that place (or a place of which it forms part)—

        (i) at prices which are substantially attributable to the facilities afforded for seeing or hearing the broadcast, or

        (ii) at prices exceeding those usually charged there and which are partly attributable to those facilities.

(3) The following shall not be regarded as having paid for admission to a place—

    (*a*) persons admitted as residents or inmates of the place;

    (*b*) persons admitted as members of a club or society where the payment is only for membership of the club or society and the provision of facilities for seeing or hearing broadcasts is only incidental to the main purposes of the club or society.

(4) Where the making of the broadcast was an infringement of the rights conferred by this Chapter in relation to a performance or recording, the fact that it was heard or seen in public by the reception of the broadcast shall be taken into account in assessing the damages for that infringement.

(5) Expressions used in this paragraph have the same meaning as in section 72.

Reception and re-transmission of wireless broadcast by cable

8–5880 19. (1) This paragraph applies where a wireless broadcast made from a place in the United Kingdom is received and immediately re-transmitted by cable.

(2) The rights conferred by this Chapter in relation to a performance or recording included in the broadcast are not infringed if and to the extent that the broadcast is made for reception in the area in which it is re-transmitted by cable; but where the making of the broadcast was an infringement of those rights, the fact that the broadcast was re-transmitted by cable shall be taken into account in assessing the damages for that infringement.

(3) Where—

    (*a*) the re-transmission by cable is in pursuance of a relevant requirement, but

    (*b*) to any extent, the area in which the re-transmission by cable takes place ("the cable area") falls outside the area for reception in which the broadcast is made ("the broadcast area"),

the re-transmission by cable (to the extent that it is provided for so much of the cable area as falls outside the broadcast area) of any performance or recording included in the broadcast shall, subject to sub-paragraph (4), be treated as licensed by the owner of the rights conferred by this Chapter in relation to the performance or recording, subject only to the payment to him by the person making the broadcast of such reasonable royalty or other payment in respect of the re-transmission by cable as may be agreed or determined in default of agreement by the Copyright Tribunal.

(4) Sub-paragraph (3) does not apply if, or to the extent that, the re-transmission of the performance or recording by cable is (apart from that sub-paragraph) licensed by the owner of the rights conferred by this Chapter in relation to the performance or recording.

(5) The Secretary of State may by order—

    (*a*) provide that in specified cases sub-paragraph (2) is to apply in relation to broadcasts of a specified description which are not made as mentioned in that sub-paragraph, or

    (*b*) exclude the application of that sub-paragraph in relation to broadcasts of a specified description made as mentioned in that sub-paragraph.

(6) Where the Secretary of State exercises the power conferred by sub-paragraph (5)(*b*) in relation to broadcasts of any description, the order may also provide for sub-paragraph (3) to apply, subject to such modifications as may be specified in the order, in relation to broadcasts of that description.

(7) An order under this paragraph may contain such transitional provision as appears to the Secretary of State to be appropriate.

(8) An order under this paragraph shall be made by statutory instrument which shall be subject to annulment in pursuance of a resolution of either House of Parliament.

(9) Expressions used in this paragraph have the same meaning as in section 73.

8–5880A 19A. *Application to settle the royalty or other sum payable under paragraph 19(3) may be made to the Copyright Tribunal.*

Provision of sub-titled copies of broadcast or cable programme

8–5881 20. (1) A designated body may, for the purpose of providing people who are deaf or hard of hearing, or physically or mentally handicapped in other ways, with copies which are sub-titled or otherwise modified for their special needs, make recordings of broadcasts and copies of such recordings, and issue or lend copies to the public, without infringing any right conferred by this Chapter in relation to a performance or recording included in the broadcast.

(1A) This paragraph does not apply if, or to the extent that, there is a licensing scheme certified for the purposes of this paragraph under paragraph 16 of Schedule 2A providing for the grant of licences.

(2) In this paragraph "designated body" means a body designated for the purposes of section 74 and other expressions used in this paragraph have the same meaning as in that section.

Recording of broadcast for archival purposes

8–5882 21. (1) A recording of a broadcast of a designated class, or a copy of such a recording, may be made for the purpose of being placed in an archive maintained by a designated body without thereby infringing any right conferred by this Chapter in relation to a performance or recording included in the broadcast.

(2) In this paragraph "designated class" and "designated body" means a class or body designated for the purposes of section 75 and other expressions used in this paragraph have the same meaning as in that section.

SCHEDULE 2A
LICENSING OF PERFORMERS' PROPERTY RIGHTS

(Inserted by SI 1996/2967, amended by SI 1999/506, SI 2000/311,SI 2003/2498 and the Enterprise Act 2002, Sch 25 and SI 2005/18.)

Trade Marks Act 1994
(1994 c 26)

PART I[1]
REGISTERED TRADE MARKS

Introductory

8–5890 1. Trade marks. (1) In this Act a "trade mark" means any sign capable of being represented graphically which is capable of distinguishing goods or services of one undertaking from those of other undertakings.

A trade mark may, in particular, consist of words (including personal names), designs, letters, numerals or the shape of goods or their packaging[2].

(2) References in this Act to a trade mark include, unless the context otherwise requires, references to a collective mark (see section 49) or certification mark (see section 50).
[Trade Marks Act 1994, s 1.]

---

1. Part I comprises ss 1–50, Schs 1 and 2.
2. Sections 3–13 make detailed provision as to what signs may be registered as a trade mark. The fact that a trade description is a trade mark, or part of a trade mark, within the meaning of this Act, does not prevent it from being a false trade description when applied to any goods, except when certain conditions are satisfied; see the Trade Descriptions Act 1968, s 34, in this PART, title, CONSUMER PROTECTION, ante.

8–5891 2. Registered trade marks. (1) A registered trade mark is a property right obtained by the registration of the trade mark under this Act and the proprietor of a registered trade mark has the rights and remedies provided by this Act.

(2) No proceedings lie to prevent or recover damages for the infringement of an unregistered trade mark as such; but nothing in this Act affects the law relating to passing off.
[Trade Marks Act 1994, s 2.]

PART II[1]
COMMUNITY TRADE MARKS AND INTERNATIONAL MATTERS
Community trade marks

---

1. Part II comprises ss 51–61.

51. Powers exercisable in consequence of report of Competition Commission

52. Opposition, appeal and arbitration[1]

---

1. The Community Trade Marks Regulations 1996, SI 1966/1908 amended by SI 2004/1908 and SI 2005/440, the Trade Marks (International Registrations Designating the European Community, etc.) Regulations 2004, SI 2004/2332 amended by SI 2005/440 and the Community Trade Mark (Designation of Community Trade Mark Courts) Regulations 2005, SI 2005/440 have been made.

PART III[1]
ADMINISTRATIVE AND OTHER SUPPLEMENTARY PROVISIONS
Legal proceedings and appeals

8–5892 72. Registration to be *prima facie* evidence of validity. In all legal proceedings relating to a registered trade mark[2] (including proceedings for rectification of the register) the registration of a person as proprietor of a trade mark shall be prima facie evidence of the validity of the original registration and of any subsequent assignment or other transmission of it.
[Trade Marks Act 1994, s 72.]

1. Part III comprises ss 62–98.
2. For "trade mark" and "registered trade mark", see ss 1 and 2 above.

Trade mark agents

8–5893   83. *The register of trade mark agents.*

8–5894   84. Unregistered persons not to be described as registered trade mark agents.
(1) An individual who is not a registered trade mark agent shall not—

(*a*) carry on a business (otherwise than in partnership) under any name or other description which contains the words "registered trade mark agent"; or

(*b*) in the course of a business otherwise describe or hold himself out, or permit himself to be described or held out, as a registered trade mark agent.

(2) A partnership[1] shall not—

(*a*) carry on a business under any name or other description which contains the words "registered trade mark agent"; or

(*b*) in the course of a business otherwise describe or hold itself out, or permit itself to be described or held out, as a firm of registered trade mark agents,

unless all the partners are registered trade mark agents or the partnership satisfies such conditions as may be prescribed for the purposes of this section.

(3) A body corporate[1] shall not—

(*a*) carry on a business (otherwise than in partnership) under any name or other description which contains the words "registered trade mark agent"; or

(*b*) in the course of a business otherwise describe or hold itself out, or permit itself to be described or held out, as a registered trade mark agent,

unless all the directors of the body corporate are registered trade mark agents or the body satisfies such conditions as may be prescribed for the purposes of this section.

(4) A person who contravenes this section commits an offence and is liable on summary conviction to a fine not exceeding **level 5** on the standard scale; and proceedings for such an offence may be begun at any time within a year from the date of the offence.
[Trade Marks Act 1994, s 84.]

1. For offences committed by partnerships and bodies corporate, see s 101, post.

8–5895   85. Power to prescribe conditions, etc for mixed partnerships and bodies corporate.
(1) The Secretary of State may make rules[1] prescribing the conditions to be satisfied for the purposes of section 84 (persons entitled to be described as registered trade mark agents)—

(*a*) in relation to a partnership where not all the partners are qualified persons, or

(*b*) in relation to a body corporate where not all the directors are qualified persons,

and imposing requirements to be complied with by such partnerships or bodies corporate.

(2) *Rules.*

(3) Contravention of a requirement imposed by the rules is an offence for which a person is liable on summary conviction to a fine not exceeding **level 5** on the standard scale.

(4) In this section "qualified person" means a registered trade mark agent.
[Trade Marks Act 1994, s 85.]

1. The Registered Trade Mark Agents (Mixed Partnerships and Bodies Corporate) Rules 1994, SI 1994/363 have been made.

8–5896   87. Privilege for communications with registered trade mark agents.   (1) This section applies to communications as to any matter relating to the protection of any design or trade mark, or as to any matter involving passing off.

(2) Any such communication—

(*a*) between a person and his trade mark agent, or

(*b*) for the purpose of obtaining, or in response to a request for, information which a person is seeking for the purpose of instructing his trade mark agent,

is privileged from, or in Scotland protected against, disclosure in legal proceedings in the same way as a communication between a person and his solicitor or, as the case may be, a communication for the purpose of obtaining, or in response to a request for, information which a person is seeking for the purpose of instructing his solicitor.

(3) In subsection (2) "trade mark agent" means—

(*a*) a registered trade mark agent, or

(*b*) a partnership entitled to describe itself as a firm of registered trade mark agents, or

(*c*)   a body corporate entitled to describe itself as a registered trade mark agent.
[Trade Marks Act 1994, s 87.]

8–5897   91. Power of Commissioners of Customs and Excise to disclose information.   Where information relating to infringing goods, material or articles has been obtained by the Commissioners of Customs and Excise for the purposes of, or in connection with, the exercise of their functions in relation to imported goods, the Commissioners may authorise the disclosure of that information for the purpose of facilitating the exercise by any person of any function in connection with the investigation or prosecution of an offence under section 92 below (unauthorised use of trade mark, etc in relation to goods) or under the Trade Descriptions Act 1968.
[Trade Marks Act 1994, s 91.]

Offences

8–5898   92. Unauthorised use of trade mark, etc in relation to goods.   (1) A person[1] commits an offence[2] who with a view to gain for himself or another, or with intent to cause loss to another, and without the consent of the proprietor—

(*a*)   applies to goods or their packaging a sign identical to, or likely to be mistaken for, a registered trade mark[3], or

(*b*)   sells or lets for hire, offers or exposes for sale or hire or distributes goods which bear, or the packaging of which bears, such a sign, or

(*c*)   has in his possession, custody or control in the course of a business any such goods with a view to the doing of anything, by himself or another, which would be an offence under paragraph (*b*).

(2) A person[1] commits an offence[2] who with a view to gain for himself or another, or with intent to cause loss to another, and without the consent of the proprietor—

(*a*)   applies a sign identical to, or likely to be mistaken for, a registered trade mark to material intended to be used—

   (i)   for labelling or packaging goods,

   (ii)   as a business paper in relation to goods, or

   (iii)   for advertising goods, or

(*b*)   uses in the course of a business material bearing such a sign for labelling or packaging goods, as a business paper in relation to goods, or for advertising goods, or

(*c*)   has in his possession, custody or control in the course of a business any such material with a view to the doing of anything, by himself or another, which would be an offence under paragraph (*b*).

(3) A person[1] commits an offence[2] who with a view to gain for himself or another, or with intent to cause loss to another, and without the consent of the proprietor—

(*a*)   makes an article specifically designed or adapted for making copies of a sign identical to, or likely to be mistaken for, a registered trade mark, or

(*b*)   has such an article in his possession, custody or control in the course of a business,

knowing or having reason to believe that it has been, or is to be, used to produce goods, or material for labelling or packaging goods, as a business paper in relation to goods, or for advertising goods.

(4) A person does not commit an offence under this section unless—

(*a*)   the goods are goods in respect of which the trade mark is registered, or

(*b*)   the trade mark has a reputation in the United Kingdom and the use of the sign takes or would take unfair advantage of, or is or would be detrimental to, the distinctive character or the repute of the trade mark.

(5) It is a defence[4] for a person charged with an offence under this section to show that he believed on reasonable grounds that the use of the sign in the manner[5] in which it was used, or was to be used, was not an infringement of the registered trade mark.

(6) A person[1] guilty of an offence under this section is liable[6]—

(*a*)   on summary conviction to imprisonment for a term not exceeding **six months** or a fine not exceeding the **statutory maximum**, or both;

(*b*)   on conviction on indictment to a **fine** or imprisonment for a term not exceeding **ten years**, or both.

[Trade Marks Act 1994, s 92.]

---

1. For offences committed by partnerships and bodies corporate, see s 101, post.

2. There is no legitimate objection, as a matter of law, in a prosecution for an offence under this section to the court hearing expert evidence on whether there has been an infringement of the section (*Akhtar v Grant* (1998) 162 JP 714). A criminal offence under s 92 cannot be committed unless there is a civil infringement of a trade mark; the civil defences will not apply in every case, and it is for the defendant to raise a defence under ss 10, 11 and 12 and then for the prosecution to disprove it (*R v Johnstone* [2003] UKHL 28, [2003] 3 All ER 884, [2003] 1 WLR 1736. See also *R v Isaac* [2004] EWCA Crim 1082, (2004) 168 JP 417).

3. The validity of the registration of a trade mark cannot be tried in criminal proceedings, therefore, if a defendant seeks

to challenge the validity the court must adjourn to allow that challenge to be determined against the trademark owner, though the court may refuse to adjourn is the challenge is made late or is frivolous (*R v Johnstone*, supra).

4. On its true construction, s 92(5) imposes a persuasive or legal burden on the defendant and this is not incompatible with the right to a fair trial under art 6(2) of the Convention (*S v London Borough of Havering* [2002] EWCA Crim 2558, [2002] All ER (D) 300 (Nov), sub nom *R v S* [2003] 1 Cr App R 35).

5. It was held in *Torbay Council v Singh* [1999] 2 Cr App Rep 451, [1999] 163 JP 744 that to establish criminal liability for offences under this section it was not necessary for the prosecution to prove knowledge or intent to infringe a registered trademark; the statutory defence related to a reasonable belief that the manner of use of a sign did not infringe the registered trademark and it presupposed an awareness of the registration. This view was doubted, however, in *R v Johnstone* [2003] UKHL 28, [2003] 3 All ER 884, [2003] 1 WLR 1736, 167 JP 281 (which concerned "bootleg" CDs that bore the names of the performers and those performers had previously registered their names as trademarks). "Section 92(5) is concerned to provide a defence where the person charged has a reasonable belief in the lawfulness of what he did. Those who act honestly and reasonably are not to be visited with criminal sanctions. It makes no sense to confine this defence to cases where the defendant is aware of the existence of the registered trade mark and exclude altogether those cases where the defendant is not. Section 92(5) provides a defence where the defendant believes on reasonable grounds his use of the sign does not infringe a registered trade mark of whose existence he is aware. It would be extraordinary if the subsection does not equally furnish a defence in the stronger case where the reason why the defendant believes his use of the sign does not infringe a registered trade mark is that he reasonably believes no relevant trade mark is registered. Section 92(5) is to be interpreted as including the latter case as well as the former" (per Lord Nicholls at para 43).

The burden upon the defendant of establishing the defence under s 92(5) is a persuasive, and not merely evidential, burden: *R v Johnstone*, supra.

6. For procedure in respect of this offence which is triable either way, see the Magistrates' Courts Act 1980, ss 17A–21 in PART I: MAGISTRATES' COURTS, PROCEDURE, ante.

8–5898A   92A. Search warrants.   (1) Where a justice of the peace (in Scotland, a sheriff or justice of the peace) is satisfied by information on oath given by a constable (in Scotland, by evidence on oath) that there are reasonable grounds for believing—

     (*a*)   that an offence under section 92 (unauthorised use of trade mark, etc in relation to goods) has been or is about to be committed in any premises, and

     (*b*)   that evidence that such an offence has been or is about to be committed is in those premises,

he may issue a warrant authorising a constable to enter and search the premises, using such reasonable force as is necessary.

     (2) The power conferred by subsection (1) does not, in England and Wales, extend to authorising a search for material of the kinds mentioned in section 9(2) of the Police and Criminal Evidence Act 1984 (c 60) (certain classes of personal or confidential material).

     (3) A warrant under subsection (1)—

     (*a*)   may authorise persons to accompany any constable executing the warrant, and

     (*b*)   remains in force for 28 days from the date of its issue.

     (4) In executing a warrant issued under subsection (1) a constable may seize an article if he reasonably believes that it is evidence that any offence under section 92 has been or is about to be committed.

     (5) In this section "premises" includes land, buildings, fixed or moveable structures, vehicles, vessels, aircraft and hovercraft.

[Trade Marks Act 1994, s 92A as inserted by the Copyright, etc and Trade Marks (Offences and Enforcement) Act 2002, s 6.]

8–5899   93. Enforcement function of local weights and measures authority.   (1) It is the duty of every local weights and measures authority to enforce within their area the provisions of section 92 (unauthorised use of trade mark, etc in relation to goods).

     (2) The following provisions of the Trade Descriptions Act 1968[1] apply in relation to the enforcement of that section as in relation to the enforcement of that Act—

section 27 (power to make test purchases),
section 28 (power to enter premises and inspect and seize goods and documents),
section 29 (obstruction of authorised officers), and
section 33 (compensation for loss, etc of goods seized).

     (3) *Northern Ireland*.

     (4) Any enactment which authorises the disclosure of information for the purpose of facilitating the enforcement of the Trade Descriptions Act 1968 shall apply as if section 92 above were contained in that Act and as if the functions of any person in relation to the enforcement of that section were functions under that Act.

     (5) Nothing in this section shall be construed as authorising a local weights and measures authority to bring proceedings in Scotland for an offence.

[Trade Marks Act 1994, s 93.]

---

     1. See this PART, title CONSUMER PROTECTION, ante.

8–5900   94. Falsification of register, etc.   (1) It is an offence for a person[1] to make, or cause to be made, a false entry in the register of trade marks, knowing or having reason to believe that it is false.

     (2) It is an offence for a person—

(a) to make or cause to be made anything falsely purporting to be a copy of an entry in the register, or

(b) to produce or tender or cause to be produced or tendered in evidence any such thing,

knowing or having reason to believe that it is false.

(3) A person guilty of an offence under this section is liable[2]—

(a) on conviction on indictment, to imprisonment for a term not exceeding **two years** or a **fine**, or both;

(b) on summary conviction, to imprisonment for a term not exceeding **six months** or a fine not exceeding the **statutory maximum**, or both.

[Trade Marks Act 1994, s 94.]

---

1. For offences committed by partnerships and bodies corporate, see s 101, post.

2. For procedure in respect of this offence which is triable either way, see the Magistrates' Courts Act 1980, ss 17A–21 in PART I: MAGISTRATES' COURTS, PROCEDURE, ante.

8–5901 95. Falsely representing trade mark as registered.   (1) It is an offence for a person[1]—

(a) falsely to represent that a mark is a registered trade mark, or

(b) to make a false representation as to the goods or services for which a trade mark is registered

knowing or having reason to believe that the representation is false.

(2) For the purposes of this section, the use in the United Kingdom in relation to a trade mark—

(a) of the word "registered", or

(b) of any other word or symbol importing a reference (express or implied) to registration,

shall be deemed to be a representation as to registration under this Act unless it is shown that the reference is to registration elsewhere than in the United Kingdom and that the trade mark is in fact so registered for the goods or services in question.

(3) A person[1] guilty of an offence under this section is liable on summary conviction to a fine not exceeding **level 3** on the standard scale.

[Trade Marks Act 1994, s 95.]

---

1. For offences committed by partnerships and bodies corporate, see s 101, post.

Forfeiture of counterfeit goods, etc

8–5902 97. Forfeiture: England and Wales or Northern Ireland.   (1) In England and Wales or Northern Ireland where there has come into the possession of any person in connection with the investigation or prosecution of a relevant offence—

(a) goods which, or the packaging of which, bears a sign identical to or likely to be mistaken for a registered trade mark,

(b) material bearing such a sign and intended to be used for labelling or packaging goods, as a business paper in relation to goods, or for advertising goods, or

(c) articles specifically designed or adapted for making copies of such a sign,

that person may apply under this section for an order for the forfeiture of the goods, material or articles.

(2) An application under this section may be made—

(a) where proceedings have been brought in any court for a relevant offence relating to some or all of the goods, material or articles, to that court;

(b) where no application for the forfeiture of the goods, material or articles has been made under paragraph (a), by way of complaint to a magistrate's court.

(3) On an application under this section the court shall make an order for the forfeiture of any goods, material or articles only if it is satisfied that a relevant offence has been committed in relation to the goods, material or articles.

(4) A court may infer for the purposes of this section that such an offence has been committed in relation to any goods, material or articles if it is satisfied that such an offence has been committed in relation to goods, material or articles which are representative of them (whether by reason of being of the same design or part of the same consignment or batch or otherwise).

(5) Any person aggrieved by an order made under this section by a magistrates' court, or by a decision of such a court not to make such an order, may appeal against that order or decision—

(a) in England and Wales, to the Crown Court;

(b) *Northern Ireland;*

and an order so made may contain such provision as appears to the court to be appropriate for delaying the coming into force of the order pending the making and determination of any appeal (including any application under section 111 of the Magistrates' Courts Act 1980 (statement of case)).

(6) Subject to subsection (7), where any goods, material or articles are forfeited under this section they shall be destroyed in accordance with such directions as the court may give.

(7) On making an order under this section the court may, if it considers it appropriate to do so, direct that the goods, material or articles to which the order relates shall (instead of being destroyed) be released, to such person as the court may specify, on condition that that person—

(*a*) causes the offending sign to be erased, removed or obliterated, and
(*b*) complies with any order to pay costs which has been made against him in the proceedings for the order for forfeiture.

(8) For the purposes of this section a "relevant offence" means an offence under section 92 above (unauthorised use of trade mark, etc in relation to goods) or under the Trade Descriptions Act 1968 or any offence involving dishonesty or deception.
[Trade Marks Act 1994, s 97.]

PART IV[1]
MISCELLANEOUS AND GENERAL PROVISIONS

Miscellaneous

8–5903   99. Unauthorised use of Royal arms, etc.   (1) A person shall not without the authority of Her Majesty use in connection with any business the Royal arms (or arms so closely resembling the Royal arms as to be calculated to deceive) in such manner as to be calculated to lead to the belief that he is duly authorised to use the Royal arms.

(2) A person shall not without the authority of Her Majesty or of a member of the Royal family use in connection with any business any device, emblem or title in such a manner as to be calculated to lead to the belief that he is employed by, or supplies goods or services to, Her Majesty or that member of the Royal family.

(3) A person who contravenes subsection (1) commits an offence and is liable on summary conviction to a fine not exceeding level 2 on the standard scale.

(4) Contravention of subsection (1) or (2) may be restrained by injunction in proceedings brought by—

(*a*) any person who is authorised to use the arms, device, emblem or title in question, or
(*b*) any person authorised by the Lord Chamberlain to take such proceedings.

(5) Nothing in this section affects any right of the proprietor of a trade mark containing any such arms, device, emblem or title to use that trade mark.
[Trade Marks Act 1994, s 99.]

---

1. Part IV comprises ss 99–110 and Schs 3–5.

8–5904   101. Offences committed by partnerships and bodies corporate.   (1) Proceedings for an offence under this Act alleged to have been committed by a partnership shall be brought against the partnership in the name of the firm and not in that of the partners; but without prejudice to any liability of the partners under subsection (4) below.

(2) The following provisions apply for the purposes of such proceedings as in relation to a body corporate—

(*a*) any rules of court relating to the service of documents;
(*b*) in England and Wales Schedule 3 to the Magistrates' Courts Act 1980 (procedure on charge of offence).

(3) A fine imposed on a partnership on its conviction in such proceedings shall be paid out of the partnership assets.

(4) Where a partnership is guilty[1] of an offence under this Act, every partner, other than a partner who is proved to have been ignorant of or to have attempted to prevent the commission of the offence, is also guilty of the offence and liable to be proceeded against and punished accordingly.

(5) Where an offence under this Act committed by a body corporate is proved to have been committed with the consent or connivance of a director, manager, secretary or other similar officer of the body, or a person purporting to act in any such capacity, he as well as the body corporate is guilty of the offence and liable to be proceeded against and punished accordingly.
[Trade Marks Act 1994, s 101.]

---

1. Where a partnership has ceased to exist at the time of the trial of the individual partners, the prosecution are entitled to proceed on the basis that the partnership could be said to have been guilty of the offence under s 92 at the time the offence was committed. The consequence is that the defendants are liable pursuant to s 101(4) if the prosecution establish that the partnership is guilty but there need be no conviction of the partnership. There is no duplicity arising from the defences in ss 92(5) and 101(4) as the court when determining whether the partnership is guilty, must consider the extent to which the defence in s 92(5) has been made out (*R v Wakefield and Purseglove* [2004] EWCA Crim 2278, 168 JP 505).

Interpretation

8–5905   103. Minor definitions.   (1) In this Act—

"business" includes a trade or profession;

"director", in relation to a body corporate whose affairs are managed by its members, means any member of the body;

"infringement proceedings", in relation to a registered trade mark, includes proceedings under section 16 (order for delivery up of infringing goods, etc);

"publish" means make available to the public, and references to publication—

(a) in relation to an application for registration, are to publication under section 38(1), and

(b) in relation to registration, are to publication under section 40(4);

"statutory provisions" includes provisions of subordinate legislation within the meaning of the Interpretation Act 1978;

"trade" includes any business or profession.

(2) References in this Act to use (or any particular description of use) of a trade mark, or of a sign identical with, similar to, or likely to be mistaken for a trade mark, include use (or that description of use) otherwise than by means of a graphic representation.

(3) References in this Act to a Community instrument include references to any instrument amending or replacing that instrument.

[Trade Marks Act 1994, s 103.]

Olympic Symbol etc (Protection) Act 1995[1]
(1995 c 32)

The Olympics association right

8–5910   1. Creation.   (1) There shall be a right, to be known as the Olympics association right.

(2) The right shall carry with it the rights and remedies provided by this Act, which shall be exercisable by such person as the Secretary of State may by order[2] made by statutory instrument appoint for the purposes of this subsection.

(3)–(4) *Supplementary.*

[Olympic Symbol etc (Protection) Act 1995, s 1.]

---

1. The Act creates a right (the Olympics association right (s 1(1)) to the commercial use of the Olympics symbol and certain words associated with the Olympic games. The Secretary of State may appoint by order a "proprietor" (s 2(1)) who may exploit the right but not otherwise dispose of it. Civil remedies are provided for any infringement of the right (ss 6–7).

Criminal sanctions are also provided (s 8) but it is a defence for the defendant to show that he believed on reasonable grounds that what he did was not an infringement. This is defined extensively in ss 3, 4 and supplemented by any order made under s 5. Powers of forfeiture of counterfeit goods are provided by s 11.

2. The British Olympic Association has been appointed for the purposes of this section: Olympic Association Right (Appointment of Proprietor) Order 1995, SI 1995/2473.

8–5911   2. Rights conferred.   (1) The Olympics association right shall confer exclusive rights in relation to the use of the Olympic symbol[1], the Olympic motto[1] and the protected words[1].

(2) Subject to sections 4 and 5 below, the rights conferred by subsection (1) above shall be infringed by any act done in the United Kingdom which—

(a) constitutes infringement under section 3 below, and

(b) is done without the consent of the person for the time being appointed under section 1(2) above (in this Act referred to as "the proprietor").

(3) The proprietor may exploit the rights conferred by subsection (1) above for gain, but may not make any disposition of, or of any interest in or over, them.

(4) This section shall not have effect to permit the doing of anything which would otherwise be liable to be prevented by virtue of a right—

(a) subsisting immediately before the day on which this Act comes into force, or

(b) created by—

(i) the registration of a design under the Registered Designs Act 1949 on or after the day on which this Act comes into force, or

(ii) the registration of a trade mark under the Trade Marks Act 1994 on or after that day.

(5) Consent given for the purposes of subsection (2)(b) above by a person appointed under section 1(2) above shall, subject to its terms, be binding on any person subsequently appointed under that provision; and references in this Act to doing anything with, or without, the consent of the proprietor shall be construed accordingly.

[Olympic Symbol etc (Protection) Act 1995, s 2.]

---

1. Defined in s 18, post.

8–5912   3. Infringement.   (1) A person infringes the Olympics association right if in the course of trade he uses—

(*a*)   a representation of the Olympic symbol[1], the Olympic motto[1] or a protected word[1], or

(*b*)   a representation of something so similar to the Olympic symbol or the Olympic motto as to be likely to create in the public mind an association with it,

(in this Act referred to as "a controlled representation").

(2) For the purposes of this section, a person uses a controlled representation if, in particular, he—

(*a*)   affixes it to goods or the packaging thereof,

(*b*)   incorporates it in a flag or banner,

(*c*)   offers or exposes for sale, puts on the market or stocks for those purposes goods which bear it or whose packaging bears it,

(*d*)   imports or exports goods which bear it or whose packaging bears it,

(*e*)   offers or supplies services under a sign which consists of or contains it, or

(*f*)   uses it on business papers or in advertising.

[Olympic Symbol etc (Protection) Act 1995, s 3.]

---

1. Defined in s 18, post.

8–5913   4. Limits on effect.   (1) The Olympics association right is not infringed by use of a controlled representation where—

(*a*)   the use consists of use in a work of any of the descriptions mentioned in subsection (3) below, and

(*b*)   the person using the representation does not intend the work to be used in relation to goods or services in circumstances which would involve an infringement of the Olympics association right,

provided the use is in accordance with honest practices in industrial or commercial matters.

(2) The Olympics association right is not infringed by use of a controlled representation where—

(*a*)   the use consists of use of a work of any of the descriptions mentioned in subsection (3) below, and

(*b*)   the use of the work is not in relation to goods or services,

provided the use of the representation is in accordance with honest practices in industrial or commercial matters.

(3) The descriptions of work referred to in subsections (1)(*a*) and (2)(*a*) above are a literary work, a dramatic work, a musical work, an artistic work, a sound recording, a film and a broadcast, in each case within the meaning of Part I of the Copyright, Designs and Patents Act 1988.

(4) For the purposes of subsection (2)(*b*) above, there shall be disregarded any use in relation to a work which—

(*a*)   is of any of the descriptions mentioned in subsection (3) above, and

(*b*)   is to any extent about the Olympic games or the Olympic movement.

(5) For the purposes of subsection (2)(*b*) above, use of a work in relation to goods shall be disregarded where—

(*a*)   the work is to any extent about the Olympic games or the Olympic movement, and

(*b*)   the person using the work does not do so with a view to gain for himself or another or with the intent to cause loss to another.

(6) In the case of a representation of a protected word, the Olympics association right is not infringed by use which is not such as ordinarily to create an association with—

(*a*)   the Olympic games or the Olympic movement, or

(*b*)   a quality ordinarily associated with the Olympic games or the Olympic movement.

(7) In the case of a representation of a protected word, the Olympics association right is not infringed by use which creates an association between the Olympic games or the Olympic movement and any person or thing where the association fairly represents a connection between the two, provided the use is in accordance with honest practices in industrial or commercial matters.

(8) The Olympics association right is not infringed by use of a controlled representation where—

(*a*)   the use is in relation to goods which bear, or whose packaging bears, the representation,

(*b*)   the goods are not infringing goods by virtue of paragraph (*a*) or (*b*) of section 7(2) below, and

(*c*)   the use involves doing any of the things mentioned in section 3(2)(*c*) or (*d*) above.

(9) The Olympics association right is not infringed by use of a controlled representation where—

(*a*)   the use is in relation to goods,

(*b*)   the goods have been put on the market in the European Economic Area by the proprietor or with his consent, and

(*c*)   the representation was used in relation to the goods when they were so put on the market.

(10) Subsection (9) above shall not apply where there exist legitimate reasons for the proprietor to oppose further dealings in the goods (in particular, where the condition of the goods has been changed or impaired after they have been put on the market).

(11) The Olympics association right is not infringed by use of a controlled representation where—

(*a*) the use is for the purposes of an undertaking, and

(*b*) the way in which the representation is used for the purposes of the undertaking is a way in which it has been continuously used for those purposes since a date prior to the commencement of this Act.

(12) In the case of a representation of a protected word, the Olympics association right is not infringed by use as part of—

(*a*) the name of a company, being a name which was the company's corporate name immediately before the day on which this Act comes into force, or

(*b*) the name under which a business is carried on, being a business which was carried on under that name immediately before the day on which this Act comes into force.

(13) The Olympics association right is not infringed by use of a controlled representation where the use—

(*a*) takes place under a right subsisting immediately before the day on which this Act comes into force, or

(*b*) is liable to be prevented by virtue of such a right.

(14) The Olympics association right is not infringed by use of a controlled representation where the use—

(*a*) takes place under a right created by—

(i) the registration of a design under the Registered Designs Act 1949 on or after the day on which this Act comes into force, or

(ii) the registration of a trade mark under the Trade Marks Act 1994 on or after that day, or

(*b*) is liable to be prevented by virtue of such a right.

(15) The Olympics association right is not infringed by use of a controlled representation for the purposes of—

(*a*) judicial or parliamentary proceedings, or

(*b*) a Royal Commission or statutory inquiry.

(16) In subsection (15) above—

"judicial proceedings" includes, proceedings before any court, tribunal or person having authority to decide any matter affecting a person's legal rights or liabilities;

"parliamentary proceedings" includes proceedings of the Northern Ireland Assembly or of the European Parliament;

"Royal Commission" includes a Commission appointed for Northern Ireland by the Secretary of State in pursuance of the prerogative powers of Her Majesty delegated to him under section 7(2) of the Northern Ireland Constitution Act 1973; and

"statutory inquiry" means an inquiry held or investigation conducted in pursuance of a duty imposed or power conferred by or under an enactment.

(17) In this section, references to use of a work in relation to goods include use of a work on goods.

[Olympic Symbol etc (Protection) Act 1995, s 4, as amended by SI 2003/2498.]

8–5914 **5.** *Secretary of State may by order specify additional cases in which the Olympics association right is not infringed.*

Criminal sanctions

8–5915 **8. Offences in relation to goods.** (1) A person shall be guilty of an offence if with a view to gain for himself or another, or with intent to cause loss to another, and without the consent of the proprietor[1], he—

(*a*) applies a controlled representation[2] to goods or their packaging,

(*b*) sells or lets for hire, offers or exposes for sale or hire or distributes goods which bear, or the packaging of which bears, such a representation, or

(*c*) has in his possession, custody or control in the course of a business any such goods with a view to the doing of anything, by himself or another, which would be an offence under paragraph (*b*) above.

(2) A person shall be guilty of an offence if with a view to gain for himself or another, or with intent to cause loss to another, and without the consent of the proprietor[1], he—

(*a*) applies a controlled representation[2] to material intended to be used—

(i) for labelling or packaging goods,

    (ii) as a business paper in relation to goods, or

    (iii) for advertising goods,

  (*b*) uses in the course of a business material bearing such a representation for labelling or packaging goods, as a business paper in relation to goods, or for advertising goods, or

  (*c*) has in his possession, custody or control in the course of a business any such material with a view to the doing of anything, by himself or another, which would be an offence under paragraph (*b*) above.

(3) A person shall be guilty of an offence if with a view to gain for himself or another, or with intent to cause loss to another, and without the consent of the proprietor[1], he—

  (*a*) makes an article specifically designed or adapted for making copies of a controlled representation[2], or

  (*b*) has such an article in his possession, custody or control in the course of a business,

knowing or having reason to believe that it has been, or is to be, used to produce goods, or material for labelling or packaging goods, as a business paper in relation to goods, or for advertising goods.

(4) It shall be a defence for a person charged with an offence under this section to show[3] that he believed on reasonable grounds that the use of the representation in the manner in which it was used, or was to be used, was not an infringement of the Olympics association right.

(5) A person[4] guilty of an offence under this section shall be liable—

  (*a*) on summary conviction, to a fine not exceeding the **statutory maximum**, and

  (*b*) on conviction on indictment, to a **fine**[5].

[Olympic Symbol etc (Protection) Act 1995, s 8.]

---

  1. Defined in s 2(2), ante.
  2. Defined in s 3(1), ante.
  3. The onus of proof is less than that which lies on the prosecution in proving a case beyond reasonable doubt and it may be discharged on the balance of probability (*R v Carr-Briant* [1943] KB 607, [1943] 2 All ER 156, 107 JP 167).
  4. For offences committed by partnerships and bodies corporate, see s 10, post.
  5. For procedure in respect of this offence which is triable either way see the Magistrates' Courts Act 1980, ss 17A–21 in PART I: MAGISTRATES' COURTS, PROCEDURE, ante.

8–5916 10. Partnerships and bodies corporate. Section 101 of the Trade Marks Act 1994 (offences committed by partnerships and bodies corporate)[1] shall apply in relation to an offence under this Act as it applies in relation to an offence under that Act.
[Olympic Symbol etc (Protection) Act 1995, s 10.]

---

  1. In this PART, ante.

Forfeiture of counterfeit goods, etc

8–5917 11. Forfeiture; England and Wales or Northern Ireland. (1) Section 97 of the Trade Marks Act 1994[1] (which makes provision about the forfeiture of certain goods, material or articles which come into the possession of any person in connection with the investigation or prosecution of a relevant offence) shall also have effect with the following modifications.

(2) In subsection (1) (which describes the goods, material or articles concerned)—

  (*a*) in paragraph (*a*), for "sign identical to or likely to be mistaken for a registered trade mark" there shall be substituted "representation within paragraph (*a*) or (*b*) of section 3(1) of the Olympic Symbol etc (Protection) Act 1995", and

  (*b*) in paragraphs (*b*) and (*c*), for "sign" there shall be substituted "representation".

(3) In subsection (7)(*a*) (power of court to direct release instead of destruction on condition that offending sign erased etc) for "sign" there shall be substituted "representation".

(4) In subsection (8) (which defines "relevant offence") for "section 92 above (unauthorised use of trade mark etc in relation to goods)" there shall be substituted "section 8 of the Olympic Symbol etc (Protection) Act 1995".
[Olympic Symbol etc (Protection) Act 1995, s 11.]

---

  1. In this PART, ante.

8–5918 17. Burden of proof. (1) Subject to subsection (2) below, if in any civil proceedings under this Act a question arises as to the use to which a controlled representation has been put, it shall be for the proprietor to show what use was made of it.

(2) If in any civil proceedings under this Act a question arises as to the application of any of subsections (1), (2) and (6) to (15) of section 4 above or any case specified under section 5 above, it shall be for the person who alleges that the subsection or case applies to show that it does.
[Olympic Symbol etc (Protection) Act 1995, s 17.]

General

8–5919 **18. Interpretation.** (1) In this Act—

"business' includes a trade or profession;

"controlled representation" has the meaning given by section 3(1) above;

"infringing articles" has the meaning given by section 7(4) above;

"infringing goods" has the meaning given by section 7(2) above;

"infringing material" has the meaning given by section 7(3) above;

"Olympic motto" means the motto of the International Olympic Committee, "Citius, altius, fortius";

"Olympic symbol" means the symbol of the International Olympic Committee, consisting of five interlocking rings;

"proprietor" has the meaning given by section 2(2) above; and

"trade" includes a business or profession.

(2) For the purposes of this Act each of the following is a protected word, namely, "Olympiad", "Olympiads", "Olympian", "Olympians", "Olympic" and "Olympics".

(3) In this Act, references to the Olympic motto or a protected word include the motto or word in translation into any language.

(4) *Scotland.*

[Olympic Symbol etc (Protection) Act 1995, s 18.]

8–5920 **19.** *Short title, commencement and extent.*

Copyright and Rights in Databases Regulations 1997[1]

(*SI 1997/3032 amended by SI 2003/2501 and the Legal Deposit Libraries Act 2003, s 8*)

PART I
INTRODUCTORY PROVISIONS

8–5925 **1. Citation, commencement and extent.** (1) These Regulations may be cited as the Copyright and Rights in Databases Regulations 1997.

(2) These Regulations come into force on 1st January 1998.

(3) These Regulations extend to the whole of the United Kingdom.

1. Made by the Secretary of State in exercise of the powers conferred on him under s 2 of the European Communities Act 1972.

8–5926 **2. Implementation of Directive.** (1) These Regulations make provision for the purpose of implementing—

(*a*) Council Directive No 96/9/EC[1] of 11 March 1996 on the legal protection of databases,

(*b*) certain obligations of the United Kingdom created by or arising under the EEA Agreement so far as relating to the implementation of that Directive, and

(*c*) an Agreement in the form of an exchange of letters between the United Kingdom of Great Britain and Northern Ireland on behalf of the Isle of Man and the European Community extending to the Isle of Man the legal protection of dtabases as provided for in Chapter III of that Directive.

(2) In this Regulation "the EEA Agreement" means the Agreement on the European Economic Area signed at Oporto on 2nd May 1992, as adjusted by the Protocol signed at Brussels on 17th March 1993.

1. EC Council Directive 96/9 harmonises the laws of member States in relation to the protection of copyright in databases and also introduces a new sui generis right to prevent extraction and re-utilisation of the contents of the database.

8–5927 **3. Interpretation.** In these Regulations "the 1988 Act" means the Copyright, Designs and Patents Act 1988.

8–5928 **4. Scheme of the Regulations.** (1) The 1988 Act is amended in accordance with the provisions of Part II of these Regulations, subject to the savings and transitional provisions in Part IV of these Regulations.

(2) Part III of these Regulations has effect subject to those savings and transitional provisions.

PART II
AMENDMENT OF THE COPYRIGHT, DESIGNS AND PATENTS ACT 1988

PART III
DATABASE RIGHT

8–5929 **12. Interpretation.** (1) In this Part—

"database" has the meaning given by section 3A(1) of the 1988 Act (as inserted by Regulation 6);

"extraction", in relation to any contents of a database, means the permanent or temporary transfer of those contents to another medium by any means or in any form;

"insubstantial", in relation to part of the contents of a database, shall be construed subject to Regulation 16(2);

"investment" includes any investment, whether of financial, human or technical resources;

"jointly", in relation to the making of a database, shall be construed in accordance with Regulation 14(6);

"lawful user", in relation to a database, means any person who (whether under a licence to do any of the acts restricted by any database right in the database or otherwise) has a right to use the database;

"maker", in relation to a database, shall be construed in accordance with Regulation 14;

"re-utilisation", in relation to any contents of a database, means making those contents available to the public by any means;

"substantial", in relation to any investment, extraction or re-utilisation, means substantial in terms of quantity or quality or a combination of both.

(2) The making of a copy of a database available for use, on terms that it will or may be returned, otherwise than for direct or indirect economic or commercial advantage, through an establishment which is accessible to the public shall not be taken for the purposes of this Part to constitute extraction or re-utilisation of the contents of the database.

(3) Where the making of a copy of a database available through an establishment which is accessible to the public gives rise to a payment the amount of which does not go beyond what is necessary to cover the costs of the establishment, there is no direct or indirect economic or commercial advantage for the purposes of paragraph (2).

(4) Paragraph (2) does not apply to the making of a copy of a database available for on-the-spot reference use.

(5) Where a copy of a database has been sold within the EEA or the Isle of Man by, or with the consent of, the owner of the database right in the database, the further sale within the EEA or the Isle of Man of that copy shall not be taken for the purposes of this Part to constitute extraction or re-utilisation of the contents of the database.

8–5930 13. Database right. (1) A property right ("database right") subsists, in accordance with this Part, in a database if there has been a substantial investment in obtaining, verifying or presenting the contents of the database.

(2) For the purposes of paragraph (1) it is immaterial whether or not the database or any of its contents is a copyright work, within the meaning of Part I of the 1988 Act.

(3) This Regulation has effect subject to Regulation 18.

8–5931 14. The maker of a database. (1) Subject to paragraphs (2) to (4), the person who takes the initiative in obtaining, verifying or presenting the contents of a database and assumes the risk of investing in that obtaining, verification or presentation shall be regarded as the maker of, and as having made, the database.

(2) Where a database is made by an employee in the course of his employment, his employer shall be regarded as the maker of the database, subject to any agreement to the contrary.

(3) Subject to paragraph (4), where a database is made by Her Majesty or by an officer or servant of the Crown in the course of his duties, Her Majesty shall be regarded as the maker of the database.

(4) Where a database is made by or under the direction or control of the House of Commons or the House of Lords—

    (*a*) the House by whom, or under whose direction or control, the database is made shall be regarded as the maker of the database, and

    (*b*) if the database is made by or under the direction or control of both Houses, the two Houses shall be regarded as the joint makers of the database.

(4A) Where a database is made by or under the direction or control of the Scottish Parliament, the Scottish Parliamentary Corporate Body shall be regarded as the maker of the database.

(5) For the purposes of this Part a database is made jointly if two or more persons acting together in collaboration take the initiative in obtaining, verifying or presenting the contents of the database and assume the risk of investing in that obtaining, verification or presentation.

(6) References in this Part to the maker of a database shall, except as otherwise provided, be construed, in relation to a database which is made jointly, as references to all the makers of the database.

8–5932 15. First ownership of database right. The maker of a database is the first owner of database right in it.

8–5933 16. Acts infringing database right. (1) Subject to the provisions of this Part, a person infringes database right in a database if, without the consent of the owner of the right, he extracts or re-utilises all or a substantial part of the contents of the database.

(2) For the purposes of this Part, the repeated and systematic extraction or re-utilisation of

insubstantial parts of the contents of a database may amount to the extraction or re-utilisation of a substantial part of those contents.

8–5934   17. Term of protection.   (1) Database right in a database expires at the end of the period of fifteen years from the end of the calendar year in which the making of the database was completed.

(2) Where a database is made available to the public before the end of the period referred to in paragraph (1), database right in the database shall expire fifteen years from the end of the calendar year in which the database was first made available to the public.

(3) Any substantial change to the contents of a database, including a substantial change resulting from the accumulation of successive additions, deletions or alterations, which would result in the database being considered to be a substantial new investment shall qualify the database resulting from that investment for its own term of protection.

(4) This Regulation has effect subject to Regulation 30.

8–5935   18. Qualification for database right.   (1) Database right does not subsist in a database unless, at the material time, its maker, or if it was made jointly, one or more of its makers, was—

(a)   an individual who was a national of an EEA state or habitually resident within the EEA,

(b)   a body which was incorporated under the law of an EEA state and which, at that time, satisfied one of the conditions in paragraph (2),

(c)   a partnership or other unincorporated body which was formed under the law of an EEA state and which, at that time, satisfied the condition in paragraph (2)(a),

(d)   an individual who was habitually resident within the Isle of Man,

(e)   a body which was incorporated under the law of the Isle of Man and which, at that time, satisfied one of the conditions in paragraph (2A), or

(f)   a partnership or other unincorporated body which was formed under the law of the Isle of Man and which, at that time, satisfied the condition in paragraph (2A)(a).

(2) The conditions mentioned in paragraphs (1)(b) and (c) are—

(a)   that the body has its central administration or principal place of business within the EEA, or

(b)   that the body has its registered office within the EEA and the body's operations are linked on an ongoing basis with the economy of an EEA state.

(2A) The conditions mentioned in paragraphs (1)(e) and (f) are—

(a)   that the body has its central administration or principal place of business within the Isle of Man, or

(b)   that the body has its registered office within the Isle of Man and the body's operations are linked on an ongoing basis with the economy of the Isle of Man.

(3) Paragraph (1) does not apply in any case falling within Regulation 14(4).

(4) In this Regulation—

(a)   "EEA" and "EEA state" have the meaning given by section 172A of the 1988 Act;

(b)   "the material time" means the time when the database was made, or if the making extended over a period, a substantial part of that period.

8–5936   19. Avoidance of certain terms affecting lawful users.   (1) A lawful user of a database which has been made available to the public in any manner shall be entitled to extract or re-utilise insubstantial parts of the contents of the database for any purpose.

(2) Where under an agreement a person has a right to use a database, or part of a database, which has been made available to the public in any manner, any term or condition in the agreement shall be void in so far as it purports to prevent that person from extracting or re-utilising insubstantial parts of the contents of the database, or of that part of the database, for any purpose.

8–5937   20. Exceptions to database right.   (1) Database right in a database which has been made available to the public in any manner is not infringed by fair dealing with a substantial part of its contents if—

(a)   that part is extracted from the database by a person who is apart from this paragraph a lawful user of the database,

(b)   it is extracted for the purpose of illustration for teaching or research and not for any commercial purpose, and

(c)   the source is indicated.

(2) The provisions of Schedule 1 specify other acts which may be done in relation to a database notwithstanding the existence of database right.

8–5937A   20A. Exceptions to database right: deposit libraries.   (1) Database right in a database is not infringed by the copying of a work from the internet by a deposit library or person acting on its behalf if—

(a)   the work is of a description prescribed by regulations under section 10(5) of the 2003 Act,

(b) its publication on the internet, or a person publishing it there, is connected with the United Kingdom in a manner so prescribed, and

(c) the copying is done in accordance with any conditions so prescribed.

(2) Database right in a database is not infringed by the doing of anything in relation to relevant material permitted to be done under regulations under section 7 of the 2003 Act.

(3) Regulations under section 44A(3) of the 1988 Act exclude the application of paragraph (2) in relation to prescribed activities in relation to relevant material as (and to the extent that) they exclude the application of section 44A(2) of that Act in relation to those activities.

(4) In this Regulation—

(a) "the 2003 Act" means the Legal Deposit Libraries Act 2003;

(b) "deposit library" and "relevant material" have the same meaning as in section 7 of the 2003 Act.

8–5938   21. Acts permitted on assumption as to expiry of database right.   (1) Database right in a database is not infringed by the extraction or re-utilisation of a substantial part of the contents of the database at a time when, or in pursuance of arrangements made at a time when—

(a) it is not possible by reasonable inquiry to ascertain the identity of the maker, and

(b) it is reasonable to assume that database right has expired.

(2) In the case of a database alleged to have been made jointly, paragraph (1) applies in relation to each person alleged to be one of the makers.

8–5939   22. Presumptions relevant to database right.   (1) The following presumptions apply in proceedings brought by virtue of this Part of these Regulations with respect to a database.

(2) Where a name purporting to be that of the maker appeared on copies of the database as published, or on the database when it was made, the person whose name appeared shall be presumed, until the contrary is proved—

(a) to be the maker of the database, and

(b) to have made it in circumstances not falling within Regulation 14(2) to (4).

(3) Where copies of the database as published bear a label or a mark stating—

(a) that a named person was the maker of the database, or

(b) that the database was first published in a specified year,

the label or mark shall be admissible as evidence of the facts stated and shall be presumed to be correct until the contrary is proved.

(4) In the case of a database alleged to have been made jointly, paragraphs (2) and (3), so far as is applicable, apply in relation to each person alleged to be one of the makers.

8–5940   23. Application of copyright provisions to database right.   The following provisions of the 1988 Act—

sections 90 to 93 (dealing with rights in copyright works);
sections 96 to 98 (rights and remedies of copyright owner);
sections 101 and 102 (rights and remedies of exclusive licensee);

apply in relation to database right and databases in which that right subsists as they apply in relation to copyright and copyright works.

8–5941   24. Licensing of database right.   The provisions of Schedule 2 have effect with respect to the licensing of database right.

8–5942   25. Database right: jurisdiction of Copyright Tribunal.   (1) The Copyright Tribunal has jurisdiction under this Part to hear and determine proceedings under the following provisions of Schedule 2—

(a) paragraph 3, 4 or 5 (reference of licensing scheme);

(b) paragraph 6 or 7 (application with respect to licence under licensing scheme);

(c) paragraph 10, 11 or 12 (reference or application with respect to licence by licensing body).

(2) The provisions of Chapter VIII of Part I of the 1988 Act (general provisions relating to the Copyright Tribunal) apply in relation to the Tribunal when exercising any jurisdiction under this Part.

(3) Provision shall be made by rules under section 150 of the 1988 Act prohibiting the Tribunal from entertaining a reference under paragraph 3, 4 or 5 of Schedule 2 (reference of licensing scheme) by a representative organisation unless the Tribunal is satisfied that the organisation is reasonably representative of the class of persons which it claims to represent.

PART IV
SAVINGS AND TRANSITIONAL PROVISIONS

8–5943   26. Introductory.   Expressions used in this Part which are defined for the purposes of Part I of the 1988 Act have the same meaning as in that Part.

8–5944 **27. General rule.** Subject to Regulations 28 and 29, these Regulations apply to databases made before or after commencement.

8–5945 **28. General savings.** (1) Nothing in these Regulations affects any agreement made before 1st January 1998.

(2) Nothing in these Regulations affects any agreement made after 31st December 1997 and before 1st November 2003 in so far as the effect would only arise as a result of the amendment of these Regulations by the Copyright and Rights in Databases (Amendment) Regulations 2003.

(3) No act done in respect of any database, in which database right subsists by virtue of the maker of the database (or one or more of its makers) falling within one of the provisions contained in Regulations 14(4) and 18(1)(a), (b) and (c),—

(a) before 1st January 1998, or
(b) after 31st December 1997, in pursuance of an agreement made before 1st January 1998,

shall be regarded as an infringement of database right in the database.

(4) No act done in respect of any database, in which database right subsists by virtue of its maker (or one or more of its makers) falling within one of the provisions contained in Regulation 18(1)(d), (e) and (f),—

(a) before 1st November 2003, or
(b) after 31st October 2003, in pursuance of an agreement made before 1st November 2003,

shall be regarded as an infringement of database right in the database.

8–5946 **29. Saving for copyright in certain existing databases.** (1) Where a database—

(a) was created on or before 27th March 1996, and
(b) is a copyright work immediately before 1st January 1998,

copyright shall continue to subsist in the database for the remainder of its copyright term.

(2) In this Regulation "copyright term" means the period of the duration of copyright under section 12 of the 1988 Act (duration of copyright in literary, dramatic, musical or artistic works).

8–5947 **30. Database right: term applicable to certain existing databases.** Where—

(a) the making of any database is completed on or after 1st January 1983, and before 1st January 1998, and
(b) either—

(i) the database is a database in which database right subsists by virtue of the maker of the database (or one or more of its makers) falling within one of the provisions contained in Regulations 14(4) and 18(1)(a), (b) and (c) and database right begins to subsist in the database on 1st January 1998, or

(ii) the database is a database in which database right subsists by virtue of its maker (or one or more of its makers) falling within one of the provisions contained in Regulation 18(1)(d), (e) and (f) and database right begins to subsist in the database on 1st November 2003,

then database right shall subsist in the database for a period of fifteen years beginning with 1st January 1998.

Regulation 20(2)

SCHEDULE 1
EXCEPTIONS TO DATABASE RIGHT FOR PUBLIC ADMINISTRATION

(*As amended by SI 1999/1042, Sch 1.*)

Parliamentary and judicial proceedings

8–5948 **1.** Database right in a database is not infringed by anything done for the purposes of parliamentary or judicial proceedings or for the purposes of reporting such proceedings.

Royal Commissions and statutory inquiries

8–5949 **2.** (1) Database right in a database is not infringed by anything done for—

(a) the purposes of the proceedings of a Royal Commission or statutory inquiry, or
(b) the purpose of reporting any such proceedings held in public.

(2) Database right in a database is not infringed by the issue to the public of copies of the report of a Royal Commission or statutory inquiry containing the contents of the database.

(3) In this paragraph "Royal Commission" and "statutory inquiry" have the same meaning as in section 46 of the 1988 Act.

Material open to public inspection or on official register

8–5950 **3.** (1) Where the contents of a database are open to public inspection pursuant to a statutory requirement, or are on a statutory register, database right in the database is not infringed by the extraction of all or a substantial part of the contents containing factual information of any description, by or with the authority of the appropriate person, for a purpose which does not involve re-utilisation of all or a substantial part of the contents.

(2) Where the contents of a database are open to public inspection pursuant to a statutory requirement, database right in the database is not infringed by the extraction or re-utilisation of all or a substantial part of

the contents, by or with the authority of the appropriate person, for the purpose of enabling the contents to be inspected at a more convenient time or place or otherwise facilitating the exercise of any right for the purpose of which the requirement is imposed.

(3) Where the contents of a database which is open to public inspection pursuant to a statutory requirement, or which is on a statutory register, contain information about matters of general scientific, technical, commercial or economic interest, database right in the database is not infringed by the extraction or re-utilisation of all or a substantial part of the contents, by or with the authority of the appropriate person, for the purpose of disseminating that information.

(4) In this paragraph—

"appropriate person" means the person required to make the contents of the database open to public inspection or, as the case may be, the person maintaining the register;

"statutory register" means a register maintained in pursuance of a statutory requirement; and

"statutory requirement" means a requirement imposed by provision made by or under an enactment.

Material communicated to the Crown in the course of public business

8–5951   **4.** (1) This paragraph applies where the contents of a database have in the course of public business been communicated to the Crown for any purpose, by or with the licence of the owner of the database right and a document or other material thing recording or embodying the contents of the database is owned by or in the custody or control of the Crown.

(2) The Crown may, for the purpose for which the contents of the database were communicated to it, or any related purpose which could reasonably have been anticipated by the owner of the database right in the database, extract or re-utilise all or a substantial part of the contents without infringing database right in the database.

(3) The Crown may not re-utilise the contents of a database by virtue of this paragraph if the contents have previously been published otherwise than by virtue of this paragraph.

(4) In sub-paragraph (1) "public business" includes any activity carried on by the Crown.

(5) This paragraph has effect subject to any agreement to the contrary between the Crown and the owner of the database right in the database.

Public records

8–5952   **5.** The contents of a database which are comprised in public records within the meaning of the Public Records Act 1958, the Public Records (Scotland) Act 1937 or the Public Records Act (Northern Ireland) 1923 which are open to public inspection in pursuance of that Act, may be re-utilised by or with the authority of any officer appointed under that Act, without infringement of database right in the database.

Acts done under statutory authority

8–5953   **6.** (1) Where the doing of a particular act is specifically authorised by an Act of Parliament, whenever passed, then, unless the Act provides otherwise, the doing of that act does not infringe database right in a database.

(2) Sub-paragraph (1) applies in relation to an enactment contained in Northern Ireland legislation as it applies in relation to an Act of Parliament.

(3) Nothing in this paragraph shall be construed as excluding any defence of statutory authority otherwise available under or by virtue of any enactment.

SCHEDULE 2
LICENSING OF DATABASE RIGHT

CORONERS

Coroners Act 1988[1]

(1988 c 13)

Coroners

8–6230   **1–2.** *Appointment of coroners; qualifications for appointment.*

---

1. This Act consolidates the Coroners Acts 1887 to 1980 and certain related enactments with amendments. Only those provisions of the Act which are relevant to magistrates' courts are included in this manual.

8–6231   3. Terms on which coroners hold office. (1) The provisions of Schedule 1[1] to this Act shall have effect with respect to the payment of salaries and the grant of pensions to coroners.

(2) Except as authorised by this or any other Act, a coroner shall not take any fee or remuneration in respect of anything done by him in the execution of his office.

(3) A coroner may resign his office by giving notice in writing to the relevant council, but the resignation shall not take effect unless and until it is accepted by that council.

(4) The Lord Chancellor may, if he thinks fit, remove any coroner from office for inability or misbehaviour in the discharge of his duty.

(5) A coroner who is guilty of corruption, wilful neglect of his duty or misbehaviour in the discharge of his duty shall be guilty of an offence and liable on conviction on indictment to imprisonment for a term not exceeding **two years** or to a fine or to **both**.

(6) Where a coroner is convicted of an offence under subsection (5) above, the court may, unless his office as coroner is annexed to any other office, order that he be removed from office and be disqualified for acting as coroner.
[Coroners Act 1988, s 3.]

---

1. Schedule 1 is not printed in this work.

8–6232 4–5. *Coroners' districts; jurisdiction of coroners.*

Inquests: general

8–6233 8. Duty to hold inquest. (1) Where a coroner is informed that the body of a person ("the deceased") is lying within his district and there is reasonable cause to suspect that the deceased—

(a) has died a violent or an unnatural death;

(b) has died a sudden death of which the cause is unknown; or

(c) has died in prison or in such a place or in such circumstances as to require an inquest under any other Act,

then, whether the cause of death arose within his district or not, the coroner shall as soon as practicable hold an inquest into the death of the deceased either with or, subject to subsection (3) below, without a jury.

(2) In the case of an inquest with a jury—

(a) the coroner shall summon by warrant not less than seven nor more than eleven persons to appear before him at a specified time and place, there to inquire as jurors into the death of the deceased; and

(b) when not less than seven jurors are assembled, they shall be sworn by or before the coroner diligently to inquire into the death of the deceased and to give a true verdict according to the evidence.

(3) If it appears to a coroner, either before he proceeds to hold an inquest or in the course of an inquest begun without a jury, that there is reason to suspect—

(a) that the death occurred in prison or in such a place or in such circumstances as to require an inquest under any other Act;

(b) that the death occurred while the deceased was in police custody, or resulted from an injury caused by a police officer in the purported execution of his duty;

(c) that the death was caused by an accident, poisoning or disease notice of which is required to be given under any Act to a government department, to any inspector or other officer of a government department or to an inspector appointed under section 19 of the Health and Safety at Work etc Act 1974; or

(d) that the death occurred in circumstances the continuance or possible recurrence of which is prejudicial to the health or safety of the public or any section of the public,

he shall proceed to summon a jury in the manner required by subsection (2) above.

(4) If it appears to a coroner, before he proceeds to hold an inquest, on resuming an inquest begun with a jury after the inquest has been adjourned and the jury discharged or in the course of an inquest begun without a jury, that there is any reason for summoning a jury, he may proceed to summon a jury in the manner required by subsection (2) above.

(5) In the case of an inquest or any part of an inquest held without a jury, anything done by or before the coroner alone shall be as validly done as if it had been done by or before the coroner and a jury.

(6) Where an inquest is held into the death of a prisoner who dies within a prison, neither a prisoner in the prison nor any person engaged in any sort of trade or dealing with the prison shall serve as a juror at the inquest.
[Coroners Act 1988, s 8 as amended by the Access to Justice Act 1999, s 71.]

8–6234 9. Qualifications of jurors. (1) A person shall not be qualified to serve as a juror at an inquest held by a coroner unless he is for the time being qualified to serve as a juror in the Crown Court, the High Court and county courts in accordance with section 1 of the Juries Act 1974.

(2) If a person serves on a jury knowing that he is ineligible for such service under Group A, B or C in Part I of Schedule 1 to that Act, he shall be guilty of an offence and liable on summary conviction to a fine not exceeding **level 3** on the standard scale.

(3) If a person serves on a jury knowing that he is disqualified for such service under Part II of that Schedule, he shall be guilty of an offence and liable on summary conviction to a fine not exceeding **level 5** on the standard scale.

(4) The appropriate officer may at any time put or cause to be put to any person who is summoned under section 8 above such questions as he thinks fit in order to establish whether or not the person is qualified to serve as a juror at an inquest.

(5) Where a question is put to any person under subsection (4) above, if that person—

(a) refuses without reasonable excuse to answer;

(b)   gives an answer which he knows to be false in a material particular; or

(c)   recklessly gives an answer which is false in a material particular,

he shall be guilty of an offence and liable on summary conviction to a fine not exceeding **level 3** on the standard scale.

(6)   If any person—

(a)   duly summoned as a juror at an inquest makes, or causes or permits to be made on his behalf, any false representation to the coroner or the appropriate officer with the intention of evading service as such juror; or

(b)   makes or causes to be made on behalf of another person who has been so summoned any false representation to the coroner or the appropriate officer with the intention of enabling that other person to evade such service,

he shall be guilty of an offence and liable on summary conviction to a fine not exceeding **level 3** on the standard scale.

(7)   A coroner may authorise a person to perform the functions conferred on the appropriate officer by subsection (4) above and references in this section to the appropriate officer shall be construed as references to the person so authorised.

[Coroners Act 1988, s 9.]

8–6235   10. Attendance of jurors and witnesses.   (1) Where a person duly summoned as a juror at an inquest—

(a)   does not, after being openly called three times, appear to the summons; or

(b)   appears to the summons but refuses without reasonable excuse to serve as a juror,

the coroner may impose on that person a fine[1] not exceeding £1,000.

(2) Where a person duly summoned to give evidence at an inquest—

(a)   does not, after being openly called three times, appear to the summons; or

(b)   appears to the summons but refuses without lawful excuse to answer a question put to him,

the coroner may impose on that person a fine[1] not exceeding £1,000.

(3) The powers conferred upon a coroner by this section shall be in addition to and not in derogation of any other power which the coroner may possess—

(a)   for compelling any person to appear and give evidence before him in any inquest or other proceeding; or

(b)   for punishing any person for contempt of court in not so appearing and giving evidence;

but a person shall not be fined by the coroner under this section and also be punished under any such other power.

(4) Notwithstanding anything in the foregoing provisions of this section, a juror shall not be liable to any penalty for non-attendance on a coroner's jury unless the summons requiring him to attend was duly served on him no later than six days before the day on which he was required to attend.

[Coroners Act 1988, s 10 amended by the Criminal Justice Act 1991, Sch 4.]

---

1. A fine imposed by a coroner shall be treated for purposes of its collection, enforcement and remission as having been imposed by the magistrates' court for the area in which the coroner's court was held; see the Criminal Justice Act 1988, s 67, in PART I: MAGISTRATES' COURTS, PROCEDURE, ante.

8–6236   11–12.   *Proceedings at inquest.*

Inquests: special cases

8–6237   16. Adjournment of inquest in event of criminal proceedings.   (1) If on an inquest into a death the coroner before the conclusion of the inquest—

(a)   is informed by the designated officer for a magistrates' court under section 17(1) below that some person has been charged before a magistrates' court with—

(i)   the murder, manslaughter or infanticide of the deceased;

(ii)   an offence under section 1 or 3A of the Road Traffic Act 1988 (dangerous driving or careless driving when under the influence of drink or drugs) committed by causing the death of the deceased;

(iii)   an offence under section 2(1) of the Suicide Act 1961 consisting of aiding, abetting, counselling or procuring the suicide of the deceased; or

(iv)   an offence under section 5 of the Domestic Violence, Crime and Victims Act 2004 (causing or allowing the death of a child or vulnerable adult); or

(b)   is informed by the Director of Public Prosecutions that some person has been charged before examining justices[1] with an offence (whether or not involving the death of a person other than the deceased) alleged to have been committed in circumstances connected with the death of the deceased, not being an offence within paragraph (a) above, and is requested by the Director to adjourn the inquest, then, subject to subsection (2) below, the coroner shall, in the absence of reason to the contrary, adjourn the inquest until after the conclusion of the relevant criminal proceedings and, if a jury has been summoned, may, if he thinks fit, discharge them.

(2) The coroner—

(a) need not adjourn the inquest in a case within subsection (1)(a) above if, before he has done so, the Director of Public Prosecutions notifies him that adjournment is unnecessary; and

(b) may in any case resume the adjourned inquest before the conclusion of the relevant criminal proceedings if notified by the Director that it is open to him to do so.

(3) After the conclusion of the relevant criminal proceedings, or on being notified under paragraph (b) of subsection (2) above before their conclusion, the coroner may, subject to the following provisions of this section, resume the adjourned inquest if in his opinion there is sufficient cause to do so.

(4) Where a coroner adjourns an inquest in compliance with subsection (1) above, he shall send to the registrar of deaths a certificate under his hand stating, so far as they have been ascertained at the date of the certificate, the particulars which under the 1953 Act are required to be registered concerning the death.

(5) Where a coroner does not resume an inquest which he has adjourned in compliance with subsection (1) above, he shall (without prejudice to subsection (4) above) send to the registrar of deaths a certificate under his hand stating the result of the relevant criminal proceedings.

(6) Where a coroner resumes an inquest which has been adjourned in compliance with subsection (1) above and for that purpose summons a jury (but not where he resumes without a jury, or with the same jury as before the adjournment)—

(a) he shall proceed in all respects as if the inquest had not previously been begun; and

(b) subject to subsection (7) below, the provisions of this Act shall apply accordingly as if the resumed inquest were a fresh inquest.

(7) Where a coroner resumes an inquest which has been adjourned in compliance with subsection (1) above—

(a) the finding of the inquest as to the cause of death must not be inconsistent with the outcome of the relevant criminal proceedings;

(b) the coroner shall supply to the registrar of deaths after the termination of the inquest a certificate under his hand stating the result of the relevant criminal proceedings; and

(c) the provisions of section 11(7) above shall not apply in relation to that inquest.

(8) In this section "the relevant criminal proceedings" means the proceedings before examining justices and before any court to which the person charged is committed for trial.*

[Coroners Act 1988, s 16 as amended by the Road Traffic (Consequential Provisions) Act 1988, Sch 3, the Road Traffic Act 1991, Sch 4, the Access to Justice Act 1999, s 71 and Sch 13, the Domestic Violence, Crime and Victims Act 2004, Schs 10 and 11 and the Courts Act 2003, Sch 8.]

---

*Substituted by the Criminal Justice Act 2003, Sch 3 from a date to be appointed.

1. This provision applies only to proceedings before examining justices. Where proceedings to be tried summarily are pending, as a matter of good practice, justices ought not to proceed with the hearing, but adjourn it until after the inquest has been held; see *Smith v DPP* [2000] RTR 36, 164 JP 96.

8–6238 17. Provisions supplementary to section 16. (1) Where a person is charged before a magistrates' court with—

(a) murder, manslaughter or infanticide;

(b) an offence under section 1 or 3A of the Road Traffic Act 1988 (dangerous driving or careless driving when under the influence of drink or drugs);

(c) an offence under section 2(1) of the Suicide Act 1961 consisting of aiding, abetting, counselling or procuring the suicide of another; or

(d) an offence under section 5 of the Domestic Violence, Crime and Victims Act 2004 (causing or allowing the death of a child or vulnerable adult),

the designated officer for the court shall inform the coroner who is responsible for holding an inquest into the death of the making of the charge and of the result of the proceedings before that court.

(2) Where a person charged with—

(a) murder, manslaughter or infanticide;

(b) an offence under section 1 or 3A of the Road Traffic Act 1988 (dangerous driving or careless driving when under the influence of drink or drugs);

(c) an offence under section 2(1) of the Suicide Act 1961 consisting of aiding, abetting, counselling or procuring the suicide of another; or

(d) an offence under section 5 of the Domestic Violence, Crime and Victims Act 2004 (causing or allowing the death of a child or vulnerable adult),

is committed* for trial to the Crown Court, the appropriate officer of the Crown Court at the place where the person charged is tried shall inform the coroner of the result of the proceedings before that court.

(3) Where the Director of Public Prosecutions has under section 16(1)(*b*) above requested a coroner to adjourn an inquest, then, whether or not the inquest is adjourned as a result, the Director shall—

(*a*) inform the coroner of the result of the proceedings before the magistrates' court in the case of the person charged as mentioned in that paragraph; and
(*b*) if that person is committed for trial to the Crown Court, inform the coroner of the result of the proceedings before that court.

[Coroners Act 1988, s 17 as amended by the Road Traffic (Consequential Provisions) Act 1988, Sch 3, the Road Traffic Act 1991, the Access to Justice Act 1999, Sch 13 and the Domestic Violence, Crime and Victims Act 2004, Schs 10 and 11 and the Courts Act 2003, Sch 8.]

---

*"Sent" substituted by the Criminal Justice Act 2003, Sch 3 from a date to be appointed.

8–6238A   17A. Adjournment of inquest in event of judicial inquiry.   (1) If on an inquest into a death the coroner is informed by the Lord Chancellor before the conclusion of the inquest that—

(*a*) a public inquiry conducted or chaired by a judge is being, or is to be, held into the events surrounding the death; and
(*b*) the Lord Chancellor considers that the cause of death is likely to be adequately investigated by the inquiry,

the coroner shall, in the absence of any exceptional reason to the contrary, adjourn the inquest and, if a jury has been summoned, may, if he thinks fit, discharge them.

(2) Where a coroner adjourns an inquest in compliance with subsection (1) above, he shall send to the registrar of deaths a certificate under his hand stating, so far as they have been ascertained at the date of the certificate, the particulars which under the 1953 Act are required to be registered concerning the death.

(3) Where a coroner has adjourned an inquest in compliance with subsection (1) above, the Lord Chancellor shall send him the findings of the public inquiry as soon as reasonably practicable after their publication.

(4) A coroner may only resume an inquest which has been adjourned in compliance with subsection (1) above if in his opinion there is exceptional reason for doing so; and he shall not do so—

(*a*) before the end of the period of 28 days beginning with the day on which the findings of the public inquiry are published; or
(*b*) if the Lord Chancellor notifies the coroner that this paragraph applies, before the end of the period of 28 days beginning with the day on which the public inquiry is concluded.

(5) Where a coroner resumes an inquest which has been adjourned in compliance with subsection (1) above—

(*a*) the provisions of section 8(3) above shall not apply in relation to that inquest; and
(*b*) if he summons a jury (but not where he resumes without a jury, or with the same jury as before the adjournment), he shall proceed in all respects as if the inquest had not previously begun and the provisions of this Act shall apply accordingly as if the resumed inquest were a fresh inquest.

(6) Where a coroner does not resume an inquest which he has adjourned in compliance with subsection (1) above, he shall (without prejudice to subsection (2) above) send to the registrar of deaths a certificate under his hand stating any findings of the public inquiry in relation to the death.

[Coroners Act 1988, s 17A as inserted by the Access to Justice Act 1999, s 71.]

Medical witnesses and post-mortem examinations etc

8–6239   21. Summoning of medical witnesses and direction of post-mortem examinations.
(1) In the case of an inquest into a death, the coroner may summon as a witness—

(*a*) any legally qualified medical practitioner appearing to him to have attended at the death of the deceased or during the last illness of the deceased; or
(*b*) where it appears to him that no such practitioner so attended the deceased, any legally qualified medical practitioner in actual practice in or near the place where the death occurred;

and any medical witness summoned under this section may be asked to give evidence as to how, in his opinion, the deceased came by his death.

(2) Subject to subsection (3) below, the coroner may, either in his summons for the attendance of a medical witness or at any time between the issuing of that summons and the end of the inquest, direct the medical witness to make a post-mortem examination of the body of the deceased.

(3) Where a person states upon oath before the coroner that in his belief the death of the deceased was caused partly or entirely by the improper or negligent treatment of a medical practitioner or other person, that medical practitioner or other person shall not be allowed to perform or assist at the post-mortem examination of the deceased.

(4) If, in the case of an inquest with a jury, a majority of the jury are of opinion that the cause of

death has not been satisfactorily explained by the evidence of the medical practitioner or of other witnesses brought before them, they may in writing require the coroner—

  (*a*)   to summon as a witness some other legally qualified medical practitioner named by them; and
  (*b*)   to direct a post-mortem examination of the deceased to be made by a practitioner summoned under this subsection, whether or not such an examination has been previously made;

and if the coroner fails to comply with such a requisition, he shall be liable on conviction on indictment to a term of imprisonment not exceeding **two years** or to a **fine** or to **both**.★

  (5)   Where a medical practitioner fails to obey a summons of a coroner issued in pursuance of this section, he shall, unless he shows a good and sufficient cause for not having obeyed the summons, be liable on summary conviction, on the prosecution of the coroner or of any two of the jury, to a fine not exceeding **£1,000**.
[Coroners Act 1988, s 21 as amended by the Criminal Justice Act 1991, Sch 4.]

★New sub-s (4A) inserted by the Human Tissue Act 2004, Sch 6 from a date to be appointed.

Supplemental

8–6240   32. Power to make rules.   (1) The Lord Chancellor may, with the concurrence of the Secretary of State, make rules[1] for regulating the practice and procedure at or in connection with inquests and post-mortem examinations and, in particular (without prejudice to the generality of the foregoing provision), such rules may provide—

  (*a*)   as to the procedure at inquests held without a jury;
  (*b*)   as to the issue by coroner of orders authorising burials;
  (*c*)   for empowering a coroner or his deputy or assistant deputy to alter the date fixed for the holding of any adjourned inquest within the district of the coroner;
  (*d*)   as to the procedure to be followed where a coroner decides not to resume an adjourned inquest; and
  (*e*)   as to the notices to be given, and as to the variation or discharge of any recognisances[2] entered into by jurors or witnesses, where the date fixed for an adjourned inquest is altered or where a coroner decides not to resume an adjourned inquest.

  (2)   Without prejudice to the generality of subsection (1) above, rules under this section may make provision for persons to be excused service as jurors at inquests in such circumstances as the rules may specify.
  (3)   The power of the Lord Chancellor under this section to make rules with respect to any matter shall include power—

  (*a*)   to prescribe the forms to be used in connection with that matter;
  (*b*)   to revoke or amend, or substitute new forms for, any forms which are directed or authorised by or under any enactment to be used in connection with that matter.

  (4)   The power to make rules under this section shall be exercisable by statutory instrument.★
[Coroners Act 1988, s 32.]

★Amended by the Constitutional Reform Act 2005, Sch 1 from a date to be appointed.
1.   See the Coroners Rules 1984, SI 1984/552, amended by SI 1985/1414, SI 1999/3325, SI 2004/921 and SI 2005/420 and 2114.
2.   Where a recognizance is forfeited at an inquest held before a coroner, the coroner shall proceed as if he had imposed a fine upon the person forfeiting that recognizance. Such sum shall be treated for purposes of its collection, enforcement and remission as having been imposed by the magistrates' court for the area in which the coroner's court was held; see the Criminal Justice Act 1988, s 67, in Part I: MAGISTRATES' COURTS, PROCEDURE, ante.

8–6241   34. Application of Act to Isles of Scilly.   (1) Subject to subsection (2) below, this Act shall apply in relation to the Isles of Scilly as if those Isles were a non-metropolitan county and the Council of those Isles were the council of that county.
  (2)   The power conferred on the Secretary of State by section 265 of the Local Government Act 1972 (application of that Act to the Isles of Scilly) shall include power to make an order providing for regulating the application of this Act to those Isles otherwise than as mentioned in subsection (1) above and such an order may amend or repeal that subsection accordingly.
[Coroners Act 1988, s 34.]

8–6242   35. Interpretation.   (1) In this Act, unless the context otherwise requires—

  "the 1953 Act" means the Births and Deaths Registration Act 1953;
  "administrative area" means a metropolitan or non-metropolitan county in England or Greater London;
  "the Common Council" means the Common Council of the City of London and "common councillor" shall be construed accordingly;
  "the City" means the City of London (including the Inner Temple and the Middle Temple);
  "Greater London" does not include the City;
  "relevant council" has the meaning given by section 1(1) above;

"Welsh principal area" means Welsh county or county borough.

(2)   In this Act references to an inquest held with a jury include, and references to an inquest held without a jury do not include, references to an inquest part of which is held with a jury.
[Coroners Act 1988, s 35 amended by the Local Government (Wales) Act 1994, Sch 16.]

8–6243   36. *Consequential amendments, repeals, transitional provisions and savings.*

8–6244   37. Short title, commencement and extent.   (1) This Act may be cited as the Coroners Act 1988.

(2) This Act shall come into force at the end of the period of two months beginning with the day on which it is passed.

(3) This Act extends to England and Wales only.
[Coroners Act 1988, s 37.]

COUNTY COURTS

County Courts Act 1984

(1984 c 28)

PART I[1]
CONSTITUTION AND ADMINISTRATION

Miscellaneous provisions as to officers

8–6350   13. Officers of court not to act as legal representatives in that court.   (1) Subject to the provisions of this section, no officer[2] of a court[2] shall, either by himself or his partner, be directly or indirectly engaged as legal representative or agent for any party[2] in any proceedings[2] in that court.

(2) Every person who contravenes this section shall for each offence be liable on summary conviction to a fine of an amount not exceeding **level 3** on the standard scale.

(3) Subsection (1) does not apply to a person acting as registrar by virtue of s 6(5).

(4) Subsection (1) does not apply to a deputy registrar; but a deputy registrar shall not act as such in relation to any proceedings in which he is, either by himself or his partner, directly or indirectly engaged as legal representative or agent for any party.
[County Courts Act 1984, s 13 as amended by the Courts and Legal Services Act 1990, Sch 18.]

---

1. Part I contains ss 1–14.
2. For meaning of "officer", "court", "party" and "proceedings", see s 147, post.

8–6351   14. Penalty for assaulting officers.   (1) If any person assaults an officer[1] of a court while in the execution[2] of his duty, he shall be liable—

(a) on summary conviction, to imprisonment for a term not exceeding **3 months*** or to a fine of an amount not exceeding **level 5** on the standard scale, or both; or

(b) on an order made by the judge in that behalf to be committed for a specified period not exceeding **3 months** to prison or to such a fine as aforesaid, or to be so committed and to such a fine,

and a bailiff of the court may take the offender into custody, with or without warrant, and bring him before the judge.

(2) The judge may at any time revoke an order committing a person to prison under this section and, if he is already in custody, order his discharge.

(3) A district judge, assistant district judge or deputy district judge shall have the same powers under this section as a judge.
[County Courts Act 1984, s 14, as amended by the Statute Law (Repeals) Act 1986, Sch 1 and the Courts and Legal Services Act 1990, s 74.]

---

*· **Words substituted by "51 weeks" by the Criminal Justice Act 2003, Sch 26, from a date to be appointed.**
1. For meaning of "Officer", see s 147, post. The section does not require proof by the Crown that the defendant knew either that the complainant was an officer of the court or that he was acting in the execution of his duty, but it does require proof of assault (*Blackburn v Bowering* [1994] 3 All ER 380).
2. A bailiff or constable is not acting in the execution of his duty when he forces an outer door in order to execute civil process, such as distress warrants (*Broughton v Wilkerson* (1880) 44 JP 781; *Rossiter v Conway* (1893) 58 JP 350). But a bailiff is in the execution of his duty when he re-enters, he having previously taken possession of the goods and left the premises for a short time without abandoning the levy (*Coffin v Dyke* (1884) 48 JP 757). The warrant shall be deemed sufficient proof of the court previous to its issue (s 127). No officer is to be deemed a trespasser by reason of irregularity in the warrant or mode of executing it, but the party aggrieved may bring an action for special damage (s 125). As to illegal seizure of a bailiff's warrant, see *R v Bailey* (1872) LR 1 CCR 347, 36 JP 324.

PART II[1]

JURISDICTION AND TRANSFER OF PROCEEDINGS

8–6352

Actions of contract and tort

---

1. Part II contains ss 15–45.

8–6353 16. Money recoverable by statute. A county court shall have jurisdiction[1] to hear and determine an action for the recovery of a sum recoverable by virtue of any enactment for the time being in force, if—

    (*a*) it is not provided by that or any other enactment that such sums shall only be recoverable in the High Court or shall only be recoverable summarily

    (*b*) *Repealed.*

[County Courts Act 1984, s 16 as amended by SI 1991/724.]

---

1. A county court has jurisdiction under this section whatever the amount involved in the proceedings and whatever the value of any fund or asset connected with the proceedings (High Court and County Courts Jurisdiction Order 1991, SI 1991/724, art 2).

PART III[1]

PROCEDURE

Witnesses and evidence

8–6354 58. Persons who may take affidavits for use in county courts. (1) An affidavit to be used in a county court may be sworn before—

    (*a*) the judge or registrar of any court; or

    (*b*) any justice of the peace; or

    (*c*) an officer of any court appointed by the judge of that court for the purpose,

as well as before a commissioner for oaths or any other person authorised to take affidavits under the Commissioners for Oaths Acts 1889 and 1891.

(2) An affidavit sworn before a judge or registrar or before any such officer may be sworn without the payment of any fee.

[County Courts Act 1984, s 58 as amended by the Administration of Justice Act 1985, Schs 7 and 8.]

---

1. Part III contains ss 46–76.

PART V[1]

ENFORCEMENT OF JUDGMENTS AND ORDERS

Seizure and custody of goods etc

8–6355 90. Custody of goods seized. Goods seized in execution under process of a county court[2] shall, until sale,—

    (*a*) be deposited by the bailiff[2] in some fit place; or

    (*b*) remain in the custody of a fit person approved by the registrar[2] to be put in possession by the bailiff; or

    (*c*) be safeguarded in such other manner as the registrar directs.

[County Courts Act 1984, s 90.]

---

1. Part V contains ss 85–111.
2. For meaning of "county court", "bailiff" and "registrar", see s 147, post.

8–6356 92. Penalty for rescuing goods seized. (1) If any person rescues or attempts to rescue any goods seized in execution under process of a county court, he shall be liable—

    (*a*) on summary conviction, to imprisonment for a term not exceeding **one month**★ or to a fine of an amount not exceeding **level 4** on the standard scale, or both; or

    (*b*) on an order made by the judge[1] in that behalf, to be committed for a specified period not exceeding **one month** to prison or to a fine of an amount not exceeding **level 4** on the standard scale or to be so committed and to such a fine,

and a bailiff of the court may take the offender into custody with or without warrant, and bring him before the judge.

(2) The judge[1] may at any time revoke an order committing a person to prison under this section and, if he is already in custody, order his discharge.

[County Courts Act 1984, s 92 as amended by the Statute Law (Repeals) Act 1986, Sch 1.]

★ **Words substituted by "51 weeks" by the Criminal Justice Act 2003, Sch 26, from a date to be appointed.**
1. For meaning of "judge", see s 147, post.

PART IX[1]

MISCELLANEOUS AND GENERAL

Financial Provisions

8–6357   129. Enforcement of fines.   Payment of any fine imposed by any court under this Act may be enforced upon the order of the judge in like manner—

(*a*)   as payment of a debt adjudged by the court to be paid may be enforced under this Act; or

(*b*)   as payment of a sum adjudged to be paid by a conviction of a magistrates' court may be enforced under the Magistrates' Courts Act 1980 (disregarding s 81(1) of that Act).

[County Courts Act 1984, s 129.]

---

1.   Part IX contains ss 128–151.

8–6358   130. Payment and application of fees, fines, etc.   (1) Subject to subsection (2), all fees, forfeitures and fines payable under this Act and any penalty payable to an officer of a county court under any other Act shall be paid to officers designated by the Lord Chancellor and dealt with by them in such manner as the Lord Chancellor, after consultation with the Treasury, may direct.

(2) Subsection (1) does not apply to fines imposed on summary conviction or to so much of a fine as is applicable under section 55(4) to indemnify a party injured.

(3) *Power of the Lord Chancellor to make Rules.*

[County Courts Act 1984, s 130.]

Summonses and other documents

8–6359   133. Proof of service of summonses etc.   (1) Where any summons or other process issued from a county court is served by an officer of a court, the service may be proved by a certificate in a prescribed form under the hand of that officer showing the fact and mode of the service.

(2) Any officer of a court wilfully and corruptly giving a false certificate under subsection (1) in respect of the service of a summons or other process shall be guilty of an offence and, on conviction thereof, shall be removed from office and shall be liable[1]—

(*a*)   on conviction on indictment, to imprisonment for any term not exceeding **2 years**; or

(*b*)   on summary conviction, to imprisonment for any term not exceeding **6 months** or to a fine not exceeding **the statutory maximum** or to both such imprisonment and fine.

[County Courts Act 1984, s 133.]

---

1.   For procedure in respect of this offence which is triable either way, see the Magistrates' Courts Act 1980, ss 17A–21, in PART I: MAGISTRATES' COURTS, PROCEDURE, ante.

8–6360   135. Penalty for falsely pretending to act under authority of court.   Any person who—

(*a*)   delivers or causes to be delivered to any other person any paper falsely purporting[1] to be a copy of any summons or other process of a county court, knowing it to be false; or

(*b*)   acts or professes to act under any false colour or pretence of the process or authority of a county court;

shall be guilty of an offence and shall for each offence be liable on conviction on indictment to imprisonment for a term not exceeding **7 years**.

[County Courts Act 1984, s 135.]

---

1.   See *R v Evans* (1857) Dears & B 236, 21 JP 391, and *R v Richmond* (1859) Bell CC 142, 23 JP 325. A mere notice, though headed "In the County Court of L," is not enough and does not purport to be a process (*R v Castle* (1857) Dears & B 363, 21 JP 775). See now s 136, post.

8–6361   136. Penalty for falsely representing document to have been issued from county court.   (1) It shall not be lawful to deliver or cause to be delivered to any person any document which was not issued under the authority of a county court but which, by reason of its form or contents or both, has the appearance of having been issued under such authority.

(2) If any person contravenes this section, he shall for each offence be liable on summary conviction to a fine of an amount not exceeding **level 3** on the standard scale.

(3) Nothing in this section shall be taken to prejudice s 135.

[County Courts Act 1984, s 136.]

General

8–6362   147. Interpretation.   (1) In this Act, unless the context otherwise requires—

"action" means any proceedings in a county court which may be commenced as prescribed by plaint;

"Admiralty county court" means a county court appointed to have Admiralty jurisdiction by order under this Act;

"Admiralty proceedings" means proceedings in which the claim would not be within the jurisdiction of a county court but for ss 26 and 27;

"bailiff" includes a registrar;

"the Civil Procedure Rule Committee" means the committee constituted under s 2 of the Civil Procedure Act 1987;

"the county court limit" means—

　(a)　in relation to any enactment contained in this Act for which a limit is for the time being specified by an Order under s 145, that limit,

　(b)　*repealed*;

　(c)　in relation to any enactment contained in this Act and not within para (a), the county court limit for the time being being specified by any other Order in Council or order defining the limit of county court jurisdiction for the purposes of that enactment;

"court" and "county court" mean a court held for a district under this Act;

"deposit-taking institution" means any person who may, in the course of his business, lawfully accept deposits in the United Kingdom;

"district" and "county court district" mean a district for which a court is to be held under s 2;

"hearing" includes trial, and "hear" and "heard" shall be construed accordingly;

"hereditament" includes both a corporeal and an incorporeal hereditament;

"judge", in relation to a county court, means a judge assigned to the district of that court under subsection (1) of s 5 and any person sitting as a judge for that district under subsection (3) or (4) of that section;

"judgment summons" means a summons issued on the application of a person entitled to enforce a judgment or order under s 5 of the Debtors Act 1869 requiring a person, or where two or more persons are liable under the judgment or order, requiring any one or more of them, to attend court;

"landlord", in relation to any land, means the person entitled to the immediate reversion or, if the property therein is held in joint tenancy, any of the persons entitled to the immediate reversion;

"legal representative" means an authorised advocate or authorised litigator, as defined by section 119(1) of the Courts and Legal Services Act 1990.

"matter" means every proceeding in a county court which may be commenced as prescribed otherwise than by plaint;

"officer", in relation to a court, means any registrar, deputy registrar or assistant registrar of that court, and any clerk, bailiff, usher or messenger in the service of that court;

"part-time registrar" and "part-time assistant registrar" have the meaning assigned to them by s 10(3);

"party" includes every person served with notice of, or attending, any proceeding, whether named as a party to that proceeding or not;

"prescribed" means prescribed by county court rules;

"probate proceedings" means proceedings brought in a county court by virtue of s 32 or transferred to that court under s 40;

"proceedings" includes both actions and matters;

"registrar" and "registrar of a county court" mean a registrar appointed for a district under this Act, or in a case where two or more registrars are appointed jointly, either or any of those registrars;

"return day" means the day appointed in any summons or proceeding for the appearance of the defendant or any other day fixed for the hearing of any proceedings;

"ship" includes any description of vessel used in navigation;

"solicitor" means solicitor of the Supreme Court.

[County Courts Act 1984, s 147(1) as amended by the Matrimonial and Family Proceedings Act 1984, Sch 3, the Banking Act 1987, Sch 6, the Courts and Legal Services Act 1990, Sch 18, SI 1991/724, the Statute Law (Repeals) Act 1993, Sch 2, the Civil Procedure Act 1997, s 10 and Sch 2, SI 1999/1009, SI 2001/3649, SI 2002/439 and the Courts Act 2003, Sch 8.]

CROWN AND GOVERNMENT, OFFENCES AGAINST[1]

8–6380　Treason　"... when a man[2] doth compass or imagine[3] the death of our Lord the King[4], or of our lady his Queen, or of their eldest son and heir; or if a man do violate the King's companion, or the King's eldest daughter unmarried, or the wife of the King's eldest son and heir; or if a man do levy war[5] against our lord the King in his realm, or be adherent to the King's enemies in his realm, giving them aid and comfort in the realm, or elsewhere[6] and thereof be provably attainted of open deed by the people of their condition ... and if a man slea the chancellor, treasurer or the King's justices ... assigned to hear and determine, being in their places doing their offices".

There are various subsequent Treason Acts; 1695 (three-year limitation period), 1702 (acts to hinder the succession), 1795 (plots to kill, maim, imprison the sovereign, his heirs and successors), 1814 (imprison for life) as amended by the Crime and Disorder Act 1998, s 36. The Treason Act

1842, s 2, makes it an offence to attempt to injure or alarm the sovereign by, for example, presenting or firing a gun or striking with an offensive weapon, or throwing any substance. The terms of the section are wide. Punishable on indictment with a maximum seven years imprisonment.

1. This area of the law has been reviewed in Working Paper No 72 of the Law Commission (HMSO, 10 May 1977).
2. Only a person owing allegiance to the Crown can commit treason: see Smith and Hogan, *Criminal Law*, 6th Ed. 1988, p 829.
3. An overt act is necessary (*R v Thistlewood* (1820) 33 State Tr 681).
4. This has developed into a breach of duty to the constitutional system of the realm; see *R v Sheares* (1798) 27 State Tr 255.
5. Military array is not necessary (*R v Dowling* (1848) 7 State Tr NS 381).
6. See *R v Casement* [1917] 1 KB 98; *Joyce v DPP* [1946] AC 347. As to the mental element in treason, see *R v Ahlers* [1915] 1 KB 616, 79 JP 255 and the Criminal Justice Act 1967, s 8.

8–6390   Treason-felony[1].   "If any person whatsoever shall, within the United Kingdom or without, compass, imagine, invent, devise or intend to deprive or depose our most gracious lady the Queen . . . from the style, honour, or royal name of the imperial crown of the United Kingdom, or of any other of Her Majesty's dominions and countries, or to levy war against Her Majesty . . . within any part of the United Kingdom, or order by force of constraint to compel Her . . . to change Her . . . measures or counsels, or in order to, put any force or constraint upon, or in order to intimidate or overawe both houses or either house of parliament, or to move or stir any foreigner or stranger with force to invade the United Kingdom, or any other of Her Majesty's dominions or countries under the obeisance of Her Majesty . . . and such compassings, imaginations, inventions, devices or intentions or any of them, shall express, utter or declare by publishing any printing or writing . . . or by any overt act or deed, every person so offending . . . shall be liable . . . to be imprisoned for the term of his or her natural life".

1. The part of s 3 of the 1848 Act which appears to criminalise the advocacy of republicanism is part of a bygone age, and the idea that it can survive scrutiny under the 1998 Act is unreal; it is not the function of the courts to bring the statute book up to date: *R (on the application of Rusbridger) v A-G* [2003] UKHL 38, [2003] 3 All ER 784.

8–6391   Sedition.   This common law[1] offence consists in endeavouring by writing or spoken words to vilify or degrade the Queen in the esteem of her subjects, or to create discontent or disaffection, or to incite the people to tumult, violence and disorder or to bring the government, the laws or constitution into hatred and contempt, or to effect any change in the laws by the recommendation of physical force. It must however be observed that the people have an undoubted right to meet and assert their opinions, and discuss their grievances, or supposed wrongs, and it is only when their written or spoken words exceed the bounds of fair and temperate argument or discussion that they constitute the offence. Triable on indictment.

1. See *R v Sullivan* (1868) 11 Cox CC 44; *Boucher v R* [1951] 2 DLR 369 (a Canadian case) and *R v Burns* (1886) 16 Cox CC 355. An intention to cause violence must, it seems, also be proved (*R v Burns, supra*; *R v Collins* (1839) 9 C & P 456; *R v Aldred* (1909) 22 Cox CC 1).

8–6392   Terrorism.   See the Prevention of Terrorism (Temporary Provisions) Act 1989, the Internationally Protected Persons Act 1978 in title PERSONS, OFFENCES AGAINST, post and the Suppression of Terrorism Act 1978, in title EXTRADITION, FUGITIVE OFFENDERS, ETC, post.

8–6393   Piracy[1].   Comprises any illegal acts of violence, detention or any act of depredation committed for private ends by the crew or the passengers of a private ship or private aircraft, and directed (*a*) on the high seas, against another ship or aircraft or against persons or property on board such ship or aircraft; (*b*) against a ship, aircraft, persons or property in a place outside the jurisdiction of any State.

1. The Piracy Act 1837 deals with piracy with violence, punishment for piracy to be life imprisonment. See also the United Nations Convention on the Law of the Sea 1982 incorporated into the law of the United Kingdom by the Merchant Shipping and Maritime Security Act 1997, s 26 and Sch 5 and which may be extended by Order in Council to the Isle of Man, the Channel Islands or any colony.

Unlawful Drilling Act 1819
(60 Geo 3 & 1 Geo 4 c 1)

8–6410   1. Unauthorised meetings of persons for the purpose of being trained, or of practising military exercise prohibited.   All meetings and assemblies of persons for the purpose of training or drilling themselves, or of being trained or drilled to the use of arms, or for the purpose of practising military exercise, movements, or evolutions, without any lawful authority from his Majesty, or [a Secretary of State or by any officer deputed by him for the purpose,] by commission or otherwise, for so doing, shall be and the same are hereby prohibited as dangerous to the peace and security of his Majesty's liege subjects and of his government; and every person who shall be present at or attend any such meeting or assembly for the purpose of training and drilling any other person or persons to the use of arms or the practice of military exercise, movements, or evolutions or who shall train or drill any other person or persons to the use of arms, or the practice of military exercise, movements, or evolutions or who shall aid or assist therein, being legally convicted thereof, shall be liable to imprisonment for any term not exceeding seven years; and every person who shall attend or be present at any such meeting or assembly as aforesaid, for the purpose of being, or who shall at any such meeting or assembly be trained or drilled to the use of arms, or the practice of military exercise, movements, or evolutions being legally convicted thereof, shall be liable to be punished by fine and imprisonment not exceeding two years, at the discretion of the court in which such conviction shall be had.

[Unlawful Drilling Act 1819, s 1—summarised as amended by the Penal Servitude Act 1857, s 2, the Statute Law Revision Act 1890, the Firearms Act 1920, s 16, the Criminal Justice Act 1948, s 1(1) and the Statute Law (Repeals) Act 1995.]

8–6411 Public Stores. See the Public Stores Act 1875 and the Supply Powers Act 1975, in title **PROPERTY, OFFENCES AGAINST**, post. See also titles **PUBLIC MEETING AND PUBLIC ORDER AND OFFICIAL SECRETS**, post.

CURRENCY

8–6429 This title contains the following statute—

    8–6470   COINAGE ACT 1971

The following Act is relevant to this title but it is not reproduced in this Manual—

    8–6449   DECIMAL CURRENCY ACT 1969

8–6430 The Currency Act 1982, s 1(1), provides that the denominations of money in the currency of the United Kingdom shall be the pound sterling and the penny or new penny, being one hundredth part of a pound sterling. The Decimal Currency Act 1969, printed below, made provision for the introduction of decimal currency.

8–6449

Decimal Currency Act 1969
(1969 c 19)

(Not reproduced in this Manual)

Coinage Act 1971
(1971 c 24)

8–6470 2. Legal tender. (1) Gold coins shall be legal tender for payment of any amount, but shall not be legal tender if their weight has become less than that specified in Schedule 1 to this Act, or in the proclamation under which they are made, as the least current weight.

(1A) Subject to any provision made by proclamation under section 3 of this Act, coins of cupro-nickel, silver or bronze shall be legal tender as follows—

(a) coins of cupro-nickel or silver of denominations of more than 10 pence, for payment of any amount not exceeding £10;

(b) coins of cupro-nickel or silver of denominations of not more than 10 pence, for payment of any amount not exceeding £5;

(c) coins of bronze, for payment of any amount not exceeding 20 pence.

(1B) Other coins, if made current by a proclamation under section 3 of this Act, shall be legal tender in accordance with the provision made by that proclamation or by any later proclamation made under that section.

(2) References in subsection (1A) of this section to coins of any denomination include references to coins treated as being of such a denomination by virtue of a proclamation made in pursuance of section 15(5) of the Decimal Currency Act 1969; and silver coins of the Queen's Maundy money issued before 15th February 1971 shall be treated for the purposes of this section as being denominated in the same number of new pence as the number of pence in which they were denominated.

(3) In this section "coins" means coins made by the Mint in accordance with this Act and not called in by proclamation under section 3 of this Act.
[Coinage Act 1971, s 2 as amended by the Currency Act 1983, s 1.]

8–6471   10. Restrictions on melting or breaking of metal coins.   (1) No person shall, except under the authority of a licence granted by the Treasury, melt down or break up any metal coin which is for the time being current in the United Kingdom or which, having been current there, has at any time after 16th May 1969 ceased to be so.

(2) Any person who contravenes subsection (1) of this section shall be liable[1]—

(*a*)   on summary conviction, to a fine not exceeding **the statutory maximum**;

(*b*)   on conviction on indictment, to a fine or to imprisonment for a term not exceeding **two years**, or both.

(3) If any condition attached to a licence granted under subsection (1) of this section is contravened or not complied with, the person to whom the licence was granted shall be liable on summary conviction to a fine not exceeding **level 5** on the standard scale unless he proves that the contravention or non-compliance occurred without his consent or connivance and that he exercised all due diligence to prevent it.

(4) The court by or before which any person is convicted of an offence under this section may, whether or not it imposes any other punishment, order the articles in respect of which the offence was committed to be forfeited to Her Majesty.

(5) Where an offence under this section committed by a body corporate is proved to have been committed with the consent or connivance of, or to be attributable to any neglect on the part of, any director, manager, secretary or other similar officer of the body corporate or any person who was purporting to act in any such capacity, he as well as the body corporate shall be guilty of that offence and shall be liable to be proceeded against and punished accordingly.
[Coinage Act 1971, s 10 as amended by the Criminal Law Act 1977, s 28 and the Criminal Justice Act 1982, ss 38 and 46.]

---

1. For procedure in respect of this offence which is triable either way, see the Magistrates' Courts Act 1980, ss 17A–21, in PART I: MAGISTRATES' COURTS, PROCEDURE, ante.

CUSTOMS AND EXCISE

8–6490   This title contains the following statutes—

and the following statutory instruments—

The customs and excise law, with the exception of the law on betting and gaming, value added tax and car tax, has been consolidated by the following Acts: the Customs and Excise Management Act 1979, the Customs and Excise Duties (General Reliefs) Act 1979, the Alcoholic Liquor Duties Act 1979, the Hydrocarbon Oil Duties Act 1979, the Tobacco Products Duty Act 1979, and the Excise Duties (Surcharge and Rebates) Act 1979. These Acts create many offences and only those offences which are likely to be of more importance to magistrates' courts are included in this work.

The consolidation Acts leave unrepealed those sections of the Customs Consolidation Act 1876 and other statutes which contain prohibitions and restrictions upon the importation into the United Kingdom of various articles and substances, all of which are liable to be forfeited and, subject to the provisions of Sch 3 to the Customs and Excise Management Act 1979[1], may be disposed of in such manner as the Commissioners of Customs and Excise direct (Customs and Excise Management Act 1979, ss 49 and 139).

The Betting and Gaming Duties Act 1981 regulates betting duties and gaming duties, and the Finance Act 1993, Part I, Chapter II, regulates the excise duty known as lottery duty.

1. Post.

8–6500   European Communities Act 1972: regulations.   Within the scope of the title Customs and Excise would logically fall the subject matter of a number of regulations made under the very wide enabling powers provided in section 2(2) of the European Communities Act 1972. Where such regulations create offences they are noted below in chronological order:

Free Zone Regulations 1991, SI 1991/2727 amended by SI 1993/3014;
Customs Controls on Importation of Goods Regulations 1991, SI 1991/2724, amended by SI 1992/3095;
Customs and Excise (Transit) Regulations 1993, this title, post;
Dual-Use Items (Export Control) Regulations 2000, SI 2000/2620 amended by SI 2000/3304, SI 2001/1344, SI 2002/50 and 2033 and SI 2003/504.

Customs Consolidation Act 1876
(39 & 40 Vict c 36)

As to the Importation, Prohibitions, Entry, Examination, Landing, and Warehousing of Goods

8–6510   42. Prohibitions and restrictions[1].   The goods enumerated and described in the following table of prohibitions and restrictions inwards are hereby prohibited to be imported[2] or brought into the United Kingdom.

A Table of Prohibitions and Restrictions Inwards

Goods prohibited to be imported[3]

Indecent or obscene[4] prints, paintings, photographs, books, cards, lithographic or other engravings, or any other indecent or obscene articles[5].
[Customs Consolidation Act 1876, s 42, as amended by the Statute Law Revision Act 1883; the Revenue Act 1883, s 19, Sch; the Finance Act 1896, s 5; the Finance Act 1917, s 6; the Copyright Act 1911, s 36, Sch 2; the Finance Act 1929, ss 5, 6, Sch; the Finance Act 1946, ss 2(1), 67(10), Sch 12, Pt I; the Isle of Man (Customs) Act 1946, s 1(1); the Customs and Excise Act 1952, s 320, Sch 12, Pt I; the Hallmarking Act 1973, s 23, Sch 7, Pt I; the Diseases of Animals Act 1975, ss 4(3), 5(3), Sch 2; the Forgery and Counterfeiting Act 1981, s 30, Sch, Pt II and the Statute Law (Repeals) Act 1993, Sch I.]

1. Other enactments containing prohibitions on the importation of goods include: the Customs and Inland Revenue Act 1879, s 5 (articles marked so as to imply any sanction or guarantee of the Government); the Customs Amendment Act 1886, s 2 (foreign coin); the Foreign Prison-made Goods Act 1897, s 1 (foreign prison-made goods); the Revenue Act 1898, s 1 (certain advertisements of lotteries); the Factories Act 1961, s 77 (matches made with white phosphorus); the Trade Descriptions Act 1968, s 16 (goods bearing a false indication of origin); the Misuse of Drugs Act 1971, s 3 (controlled drugs); the Animal Heath Act 1981, s 10 (certain animals, carcases, etc), and the Forgery and Counterfeiting Act 1981, s 20 (counterfeit notes and coins).
2. Any law of a member state of the European Economic Community which prohibits the importation of pornographic material constitutes a measure having the equivalent effect to a quantitative restriction and accordingly is prima facie in conflict with Art 30 of the EEC Treaty, in this Part, title European Communities, post. Nevertheless, the power to impose prohibitions on the importation from other member states of articles of an indecent or obscene character on the grounds of public morality is within the powers reserved to member states under Art 36 of the Treaty, in this Part, title European Communities, post; accordingly, s 42 of this Act is effective to prevent the importation of pornographic articles from a member state notwithstanding Arts 30 and 36 of the EEC Treaty (*Henn and Darby v DPP* [1981] AC 850, [1980] 2 All ER 166, HL; applied in *Wright v Customs and Excise Comrs* (1998) 162 JP 207). However, a member state may not rely on the ground of public morality within the meaning of Art 36 of the Treaty in order to prohibit the importation of goods on the ground that they are indecent or obscene, where the same goods may be manufactured freely in its territory and marketed in that territory subject only to an absolute prohibition on their transmission by post, a restriction on their display or a system of licensing premises for the sale of such goods (Case 121/85: *Conegate Ltd v Customs and Excise Comrs* [1987] QB 254, [1986] 2 All ER 688).
3. For forfeiture of goods improperly imported and penalty for improper importation of goods prohibited or restricted by or under any enactment, see the Customs and Excise Management Act 1979, ss 49 and 50, this title, post. For general provisions as to forfeiture and proceedings for condemnation of goods liable to forfeiture, see the Customs and Excise Management Act 1979, s 139 and Sch 3, this title, post.
4. In applying s 42 to the importation of obscene books, in respect of which there are condemnation proceedings, in deciding whether the books are obscene, the test to be applied is the definition of the word "obscene" in s 1(1) of the Obscene Publications Act 1959, but there is no requirement for the court to hear evidence as to whether publication of the books could be justified as being for the public good on the grounds specified in s 4 of the 1959 Act (*R v Bow Street Metropolitan Stipendiary Magistrate, ex p Noncyp Ltd* [1990] 1 QB 123, [1989] 3 WLR 467, CA).
5. The ejusdem generis rule does not apply to the concluding words of the prohibition, "or any other indecent or obscene articles", so as to exclude from those words cinematograph films (*Derrick v Customs and Excise Comrs* [1972] 2 QB 28, [1972] 1 All ER 993).

Finance Act 1966
(1966 c 18)

PART I
CUSTOMS AND EXCISE
Duties relating to betting and gaming

8–6511   **12. General betting duty.**   *Repealed.*

8–6512   **15. Additional or supplementary provisions as to duties on betting or gaming.**
(1)–(4) *Repealed).*
(5) The supplemental provisions set out in Schedule 3 to this Act shall have effect with respect to the duties relating to betting and gaming.
(6) *Repealed.*
[Finance Act 1966, s 15 as amended by the Betting and Gaming Duties Act 1972, s 29 and Sch 7.]

PART VII
MISCELLANEOUS

8–6513   **53. Short title, construction, extent and repeals.**   (1) This Act may be cited as the Finance Act 1966.
(2) In this Act Part I shall be construed as one with the Customs and Excise Management Act 1979.
(3) Any reference in this Act to any other enactment shall, except so far as the context otherwise requires, be construed as a reference to that enactment as amended or applied by or under any other enactment, including this Act.
(4) Except as otherwise expressly provided, such of the provisions of this Act as relate to matters in respect of which the Parliament of Northern Ireland has power to make laws shall not extend to Northern Ireland.
(5)–(6) *(Repealed).*
(7) The enactments mentioned in Schedule 13 to this Act are hereby repealed to the extent mentioned in the third column of that Schedule, but subject to any provision in relation thereto made at the end of any part of that Schedule.
[Finance Act 1966, s 53 as amended by the Income and Corporation Taxes Act 1970, s 538 and Sch 16, the Finance Act 1975, ss 52, 59 and Sch 13, the Statute Law (Repeals) Act 1978, the Customs and Excise Management Act 1979, s 177 and Sch 4 and the Statute Law (Repeals) Act 1989.]

Section 15   SCHEDULE 3
SUPPLEMENTARY PROVISIONS AS TO DUTIES RELATING TO BETTING AND GAMING

(As amended by the Betting and Gaming Duties Act 1972, s 29 and Sch 7.)

PART I
DUTIES RELATING TO BETTING

8–6514   **1–5.** *(Repealed).*
6. In Schedule 1 to the Betting, Gaming and Lotteries Act 1963 (which relates to the grant, renewal and cancellation of bookmaker's permits, betting agency permits and betting office licences)—

(*a*) any reference to the appropriate officer of police—

(i) in paragraph 5, 7(*b*), 21(3), 25 or 27(1) shall include a reference to the Collector of Customs and Excise for the area in which the relevant premises within the meaning of that Schedule are, or are to be, situated;

(ii) in paragraph 11 or 27(2) shall include a reference to the Commissioners;

(*b*) in paragraph 34 (which relates to the right to inspect registers of bookmaker's permits and betting agency permits), the reference to any constable shall include a reference to any officer;

and in considering for the purposes of paragraph 16(1), 17(*b*) or 27(4)(*a*) of that Schedule whether a person is or is not a fit and proper person to hold a bookmaker's permit or, as the case may be, whether the applicant for the grant or renewal of a betting agency permit is or is not a fit and proper person to hold a betting office licence, the appropriate authority shall have regard to any failure of that person or applicant to pay any amount due from him by way of the general betting duty or the pool betting duty.

8–6515

Section 53   SCHEDULE 13
REPEALS

Customs and Excise Management Act 1979[1]

(1979 c 2)

PART I[2]

PRELIMINARY

8–6540   1. Interpretation.   (1) In this Act, unless the context otherwise requires—

"aerodrome" means any area of land or water designed, equipped, set apart or commonly used for affording facilities for the landing and departure of aircraft;

"approved wharf" has the meaning given by section 20A below;

"armed forces" means the Royal Navy, the Royal Marines, the regular army and the regular air force, and any reserve or auxiliary force of any of those services which has been called out on permanent service, or embodied;

"assigned matter"[3] means any matter in relation to which the Commissioners are for the time being required in pursuance of any enactment to perform any duties;

"boarding station" means a boarding station for the time being appointed under section 19 below;

"boundary" means the land boundary of Northern Ireland;

"British ship" means a British ship within the meaning of the Merchant Shipping Act 1995;

"claimant", in relation to proceedings for the condemnation of any thing as being forfeited, means a person claiming that the thing is not liable to forfeiture;

"coasting ship" has the meaning given by section 69 below;

"commander", in relation to an aircraft, includes any person having or taking the charge or command of the aircraft;

"the Commissioners" means the Commissioners of Customs and Excise;

"Community transit goods"—

    (*a*)   in relation to imported goods, means—

        (i)   goods which have been imported under the internal or external Community transit procedure for transit through the United Kingdom with a view to exportation where the importation was and the transit and exportation are to be part of one Community transit operation; or

        (ii)   goods which have, at the port or airport at which they were imported, been placed under the internal or external Community transit procedure for transit through the United Kingdom with a view to exportation where the transit and exportation are to be part of one Community transit operation;

    (*b*)   in relation to goods for exportation, means—

        (i)   goods which have been imported as mentioned in paragraph (*a*) (i) of this definition and are to be exported as part of the Community transit operation in the course of which they were imported; or

        (ii)   goods which have, under the internal or external Community transit procedure, transited the United Kingdom from the port or airport at which they were imported and are to be exported as part of the Community transit operation which commenced at that port or airport;

"container" includes any bundle or package and any box, cask or other receptacle whatsoever;

"the customs and excise Acts"[4] means the Customs and Excise Acts 1979 and any other enactment for the time being in force relating to customs or excise;

"the Customs and Excise Acts 1979"[4] means—

    this Act,

    the Customs and Excise Duties (General Reliefs) Act 1979,

    the Alcoholic Liquor Duties Act 1979,

    the Hydrocarbon Oil Duties Act 1979, and

    the Tobacco Products Duty Act 1979;

"customs and excise airport" has the meaning given by section 21(7) below;

"customs and excise station" has the meaning given by section 26 below;

"designation order" has the meaning given by s 100A(5);

"drawback goods" means goods in the case of which a claim for drawback has been or is to be made;

"dutiable goods", except in the expression "dutiable or restricted goods", means goods of a class or description subject to any duty of customs or excise, whether or not those goods are in fact chargeable with that duty, and whether or not that duty has been paid thereon;

"dutiable or restricted goods" has the meaning given by section 52 below;

"examination station" has the meaning given by section 22A below;

"excise duty point" has the meaning given by section 1 of the Finance (No 2) A 1992;

"excise licence trade" means, subject to subsection (5) below, a trade or business for the carrying on of which an excise licence is required;

"excise warehouse" means a place of security approved by the Commissioners under subsection (1) (whether or not it is also approved under subsection (2)) of section 92 below, and, except in that section, also includes a distiller's warehouse;

"exporter", in relation to goods for exportation or for use as stores, includes the shipper of the goods and any person performing in relation to an aircraft functions corresponding with those of a shipper;

"free zone" has the meaning given by section 100A(2);

"free zone goods" are goods which are within a free zone;

"goods" includes stores and baggage;

"holiday", in relation to any part of the United Kingdom, means any day that is a bank holiday in that part of the United Kingdom under the Banking and Financial Dealings Act 1971, Christmas Day, Good Friday and the day appointed for the purposes of customs and excise for the celebration of Her Majesty's birthday;

"hovercraft" means a hovercraft within the meaning of the Hovercraft Act 1968;

"importer", in relation to any goods at any time between their importation and the time when they are delivered out of charge, includes any owner or other person for the time being possessed of or beneficially interested in the goods and, in relation to goods imported by means of a pipe-line, includes the owner of the pipe-line;

"justice" and "justice of the peace" in Scotland includes a sheriff and in Northern Ireland, in relation to any powers and duties which can under any enactment for the time being in force be exercised and performed only by a resident magistrate, means a resident magistrate;

"land" and "landing", in relation to aircraft, include alighting on water;

"law officer of the Crown" means the Attorney General or for the purpose of criminal proceedings in Scotland, the Lord Advocate or, for the purpose of civil proceedings in Scotland, the appropriate Law Officer within the meaning of section 4A of the Crown Suits (Scotland) Act 1857 or in Northern Ireland the Attorney General for Northern Ireland;

"licence year", in relation to an excise licence issuable annually, means the period of 12 months ending on the date on which that licence expires in any year;

"master", in relation to a ship, includes any person having or taking the charge or command of the ship;

"night" means the period between 11 pm. and 5 am;

"occupier", in relation to any bonded premises, includes any person who has given security to the Crown in respect of those premises;

"officer" means, subject to section 8(2) below, a person commissioned by the Commissioners;

"owner", in relation to an aircraft, includes the operator of the aircraft;

"owner", in relation to a pipe-line, means (except in the case of a pipe-line vested in the Crown which in pursuance of arrangements in that behalf is operated by another) the person in whom the line is vested and, in the said excepted case, means the person operating the line;

"perfect entry" means an entry made in accordance with regulation 5 of the Customs Controls on Importation of Goods Regulations 1991;

"pipe-line" has the meaning given by section 65 of the Pipe-lines Act 1962 (that Act being taken, for the purposes of this definition, to extend to Northern Ireland);

"port" means a port appointed by the Commissioners under section 19 below;

"prescribed area" means such an area in Northern Ireland adjoining the boundary as the Commissioners may by regulations prescribe;

"prescribed sum", in relation to the penalty provided for an offence, has the meaning given by section 171(2) below;

"prohibited or restricted goods" means goods of a class or description of which the importation, exportation or carriage coastwise is for the time being prohibited or restricted under or by virtue of any enactment;

"proper", in relation to the person by, with or to whom, or the place at which, anything is to be done, means the person or place appointed or authorised in that behalf by the Commissioners;

"proprietor", in relation to any goods, includes any owner, importer, exporter, shipping or other person for the time being possessed of or beneficially interested in those goods;

"Queen's warehouse" means any place provided by the Crown or appointed by the Commissioners for the deposit of goods for security thereof and of the duties chargeable thereon;

"registered excise dealer and shipper" means a revenue trader approved and registered by the Commissioners under section 100G below;

"registered excise dealers and shippers regulations" means regulations under section 100G below;

"representative", in relation to any person from whom the Commissioners assess an amount as being excise duty due, means his personal representative, trustee in bankruptcy or interim or permanent trustee, any receiver or liquidator appointed in relation to him or any of his property or any other person acting in a representative capacity in relation to him;

"the revenue trade provisions of the customs and excise Acts" means—

    (*a*) the provisions of the customs and excise Acts relating to the protection, security, collection or management of the revenues derived from the duties of excise on goods produced or manufactured in the United Kingdom;

(b) the provisions of the customs and excise Acts relating to any activity or facility for the carrying on or provision of which an excise licence is required;

(c) the provisions of the Betting and Gaming Duties Act 1981 (so far as not included in paragraph (b) above);

(d) the provisions of Chapter II of Part I of the Finance Act (e) the provisions of sections 10 to 15 of, and Schedule 1 to, the Finance Act 1997;

(e) the provisions of sections 10 to 15 of, and Schedule 1 to, the Finance Act 1997;

"revenue trader" means (a) any person carrying on a trade or business subject to any of the revenue trade provisions of the customs and excise Acts, or which consists of or includes—

(i) the buying, selling, importation, exportation, dealing in or handling of any goods of a class or description which is subject to a duty of excise (whether or not duty is chargeable on the goods);

(ia) the buying, selling, importation, exportation, dealing in or handling of tickets or chances on the taking of which lottery duty is or will be chargeable;

(ib) being (within the meaning of sections 10 to 15 of the Finance Act 1997) the provider of any premises for gaming;

(ic) the organisation, management or promotion of any gaming (within the meaning of the Gaming Act 1968 or the Betting, Gaming, Lotteries and Amusements (Northern Ireland) Order 1985); or

(ii) the financing or facilitation of any such transactions or activities as are mentioned in sub-paragraph (i), (ia), (ib) or (ic) above,

whether or not that trade or business is an excise licence trade; and (b) any person who is a wholesaler or an occupier of an excise warehouse (so far as not included in paragraph (a) above), and includes a registered club;

"ship" and "vessel" include any boat or other vessel whatsoever (and, to the extent provided in section 2 below, any hovercraft);

"shipment" includes loading into an aircraft, and "shipped" and cognate expressions shall be construed accordingly;

"stores" means subject to subsection (4) below, goods for use in a ship or aircraft and includes fuel and spare parts and other articles of equipment, whether or not for immediate fitting;

"tons register" means the tons of a ship's net tonnage as ascertained and registered according to the tonnage regulations of the Merchant Shipping Act 1995 or, in the case of a ship which is not registered under that Act, ascertained in like manner as if it were to be so registered;

"transit goods", except in the expression "Community transit goods", means imported goods entered on importation for transit or transhipment;

"transit or transhipment", in relation to the entry of goods, means transit through the United Kingdom or transhipment with a view to the re-exportation of the goods in question or transhipment of those goods for use as stores;

"transit shed" has the meaning given by section 25A below;

"United Kingdom waters" means any waters (including inland waters) within the seaward limits of the territorial sea of the United Kingdom;

"vehicle" includes a railway vehicle;

"warehouse", except in the expressions "Queen's warehouse" and "distiller's warehouse", means a place of security approved by the Commissioners under subsection (1) or (2) or subsections (1) and (2) of section 92 below and, except in that section, also includes a distiller's warehouse; and "warehoused" and cognate expressions shall, subject to subsection (4) of that section and any regulations made by virtue of section 93(2)(da)(i) or (ee) or (4) below, be construed accordingly;

"warehousing regulations" means regulations under section 93 below;

"victualling warehouse" means a place of security approved by the Commissioners under subsection (2) (whether or not it is also a place approved under subsection (1) of section 92 below).

(2) This Act and the other Acts included in the Customs and Excise Acts 1979 shall be construed as one Act but where a provision of this Act refers to this Act that reference is not to be construed as including a reference to any of the others.

(3) Any expression used in this Act or in any instrument made under this Act to which a meaning is given by any other Act included in the Customs and Excise Acts 1979 has, except where the context otherwise requires, the same meaning in this Act or any such instrument as in that Act; and for ease of reference the Table below indicates the expressions used in this Act to which a meaning is given by any other such Act—

Alcoholic Liquor Duties Act 1979

"beer"

"brewer" and "registered brewers"

"cider"

"compounder"
"distiller"
"distiller's warehouse"
"dutiable alcoholic liquor"
"licensed", in relation to producers of wine or made-wine
"made-wine"
"producer of made-wine"
"producer of wine"
"proof"
"rectifier"
"registered club"
"spirits"
"wholesaler"
"wine"

Hydrocarbon Oil Duties Act 1979

"rebate"
"refinery"

Tobacco Products Duty Act 1979

"tobacco products"

Finance Act 1999

(4) Goods for use in a ship or aircraft as merchandise for sale to persons carried in the ship of aircraft shall be treated for the purposes of the customs and excise Acts as stores if, and only if—

> (a) the goods are to be sold by retail either—
>> (i)   in the course of a relevant journey, or
>> (ii) for consumption on board;

and

> (b) the goods are not treated as exported by virtue of regulations under section 12 of the Customs and Excise Duties (General Reliefs) Act 1979 (goods for use in naval ships or establishments).

(4A) For the purposes of subsection (4) above, a relevant journey is any journey beginning in the United Kingdom and having an immediate destination outside the member states.

(4B) In relation to goods treated as stores by virtue of subsection (4) above, any reference in the customs and excise Acts to the consumption of stores shall be construed as referring to the sale of the goods as mentioned in paragraph (a) of that subsection.

(5)–(6) *Supplementary provisions as to interpretation.*

[Customs and Excise Management Act 1979, s 1 as amended by the Finance Act 1981, Sch 8, the Betting and Gaming Duties Act 1981, Sch 5,the Finance Act 1984, Sch 4, the Finance (No 2) Act 1987, s 103, the Territorial Sea Act, Schs 1 and 2, the Finance Act 1991, s 11 and Sch 2, SI 1991/2724. 2725 and 2727, SI 1992/3095, the Finance (No 2) Act 1992, Schs 1, 2 and 18, the Finance Act 1993, s 30 and Sch 23, the Value Added Tax Act 1994, Sch 14, the Merchant Shipping Act 1995, Sch 13, the Finance Act 1997, Schs 2, 6 and 18 and the Finance Act 1999, s 10, SI 1998/3086 and SI 1999/1042.]

---

*Amended by the Finance Act 1993, s 30 and Sch 23, when in force.

1. The Channel Tunnel (Customs and Excise) Order 1990, SI 1990/2167 has been made under ss 11 and 13 of the Channel Tunnel Act 1987 and modifies certain provisions of the 1979 Act. The Order also makes provision for the loading and unloading of goods and associated requirements, contravention of which is a summary offence.

2. Part I contains ss 1–5.

3. For meaning of "document" in connection with any "assigned matter", see the Finance Act 1985, s 10, this title, post.

4. The Police and Criminal Evidence Act 1984, s 114(1) provides that "arrested", "arresting", "arrest" and "to arrest" shall be substituted for "detained", "detaining", "detention" and "to detain" wherever in the customs and excise Acts as here defined, those words are used in relation to persons.

8–6541 2. Application to hovercraft. (1) This Part, Parts III to VII and Parts X to XII of this Act shall apply as if references to ships or vessels included references to hovercraft, and the said Parts III to VII shall apply in relation to an approved wharf or transit shed which is not in a port as if it were in a port.

(2) All other provisions of the customs and excise Acts shall apply as if references (however expressed) to goods or passengers carried in or moved by ships or vessels included references to goods or passengers carried in or moved by hovercraft.

(3) In all the provisions of the customs and excise Acts "landed", "loaded", "master", "shipped", "shipped as stores", "transhipment", "voyage", "waterborne" and cognate expressions shall be construed in accordance with subsections (1) and (2) above.

(4) References in the customs and excise Acts to goods imported or exported by land, or conveyed into or out of Northern Ireland by land, include references to goods imported, exported or conveyed

across any part of the boundary of Northern Ireland; and it is hereby declared that in those Acts references to vehicles include references to hovercraft proceeding over land or water or partly over land and partly over water.

(5) Any power of making regulations or other instruments relating to the importation or exportation of goods conferred by the customs and excise Acts may be exercised so as to make provision for the importation or exportation of goods by hovercraft which is different from the provision made for the importation or exportation of goods by other means.

[Customs and Excise Management Act 1979, s 2.]

8–6542 3. Application to pipe-lines. (1) In the customs and excise Acts "shipping" and "loading" and cognate expressions, where used in relation to importation or exportation, include, in relation to importation or exportation by means of a pipe-line, the conveyance of goods by means of the pipe-line and the charging and discharging of goods into and from the pipe-line, but subject to any necessary modifications.

(2) In the customs and excise Acts "importer", in relation to goods imported by means of a pipe-line, includes the owner of the pipe-line.

(3) Any power of making regulations or other instruments relating to the importation or exportation of goods conferred by the customs and excise Acts may be exercised so as to make a provision for the importation or exportation of goods by means of a pipe-line which is different from the provision made for the importation or exportation of goods by other means.

[Customs and Excise Management Act 1979, s 3.]

8–6543 4. *Application to certain Crown aircraft.*

8–6544 5. Time of importation, exportation, etc. (1) The provisions of this section shall have effect for the purposes of the customs and excise Acts.

(2) Subject to subsections (3) and (6) below, the time of importation of any goods shall be deemed to be—

(a) where the goods are brought by sea, the time when the ship carrying them comes within the limits of a port;

(b) where the goods are brought by air, the time when the aircraft carrying them lands in the United Kingdom or the time when the goods are unloaded in the United Kingdom, whichever is the earlier;

(c) where the goods are brought by land, the time when the goods are brought across the boundary into Northern Ireland.

(3) In the case of goods brought by sea of which entry is not required under regulation 5 of the Customs Controls on Importation of Goods Regulations 1991, the time of importation shall be deemed to be the time when the ship carrying them came within the limits of the port at which the goods are discharged.

(4) Subject to subsections (5) and (7) below, the time of exportation of any goods from the United Kingdom shall be deemed to be—

(a) where the goods are exported by sea or air, the time when the goods are shipped for exportation;

(b) where the goods are exported by land, the time when they are cleared by the proper officer at the last customs and excise station on their way to the boundary.

(5) In the case of goods of a class or description with respect to the exportation of which any prohibition or restriction is for the time being in force under or by virtue of any enactment which are exported by sea or air, the time of exportation shall be deemed to be the time when the exporting ship or aircraft departs from the last port or customs and excise airport at which it is cleared before departing for a destination outside the United Kingdom.

(6) Goods imported by means of a pipe-line shall be treated as imported at the time when they are brought within the limits of a port or brought across the boundary into Northern Ireland.

(7) Goods exported by means of a pipe-line shall be treated as exported at the time when they are charged into that pipe-line for exportation.

(8) A ship shall be deemed to have arrived at or departed from a port at the time when the ship comes within or, as the case may be, leaves the limits of that port.

[Customs and Excise Management Act 1979, s 5 as amended by SI 1992/3095.]

PART II[1].—ADMINISTRATION

Appointment and duties of Commissioners, officers, etc

8–6545 11. Assistance to be rendered by police, etc. It shall be the duty of every constable and every member of Her Majesty's armed forces or coastguard to assist in the enforcement of the law relating to any assigned matter[2].

[Customs and Excise Management Act 1979, s 11.]

1. Part II contains ss 6–16.
2. For meaning of "assigned matter", see s 1, ante.

8–6546 12. Power to hold inquiries. (1) The Commissioners may hold or cause to be held such inquiries as they consider necessary or desirable for the purposes of any assigned matter[1], including inquiries into the conduct of any officer or of any person appointed by them.

(2) The person holding any such inquiry—

(a) may require any person, subject to the tender of the reasonable expenses of his attendance, to attend as a witness and give evidence or to produce any document in his possession or control which relates to any matter in question at the inquiry and is such as would be subject to production in a court of law; and

(b) may require evidence to be given on oath, and for that purpose shall have power to administer oaths.

(3) If any person fails without reasonable excuse to comply with any such requirement as aforesaid, he shall be liable on summary conviction to a penalty of **level 1** on the standard scale.

(4) Subject to the foregoing provisions of this section, the procedure and conduct of any inquiry under this section shall be such as the Commissioners may direct.

[Customs and Excise Management Act 1979, s 12 as amended by the Criminal Justice Act 1982, s 46.]

1. For meaning of "assigned matter", see s 1, ante.

Offences in connection with Commissioners, officers, etc

8–6547 13. Unlawful assumption of character of officer, etc. If, for the purpose of obtaining admission to any house or other place, or of doing or procuring to be done any act which he would not be entitled to do or procure to be done of his own authority, or for any other unlawful purpose, any person falsely assumes the name, designation or character of a Commissioner or officer or of a person appointed by the Commissioners he may be detained and shall, in addition to any other punishment to which he may have rendered himself liable, be liable[1]—

(a) on summary conviction, to a penalty of **the prescribed sum**[2], or to imprisonment for a term not exceeding **3 months**, or to both; or

(b) on conviction on indictment, to a penalty of any amount, or to imprisonment for a term not exceeding **2 years**, or to both.

[Customs and Excise Management Act 1979, s 13.]

1. For procedure in respect of this offence which is triable either way, see s 147, post, and the Magistrates' Courts Act 1980, ss 17A–21, in PART I: MAGISTRATES' COURTS, PROCEDURE, ante.
2. For meaning of the "prescribed sum", see s 171, post.

8–6548 14. Failure to surrender commission, etc. (1) If any person to whom a commission or other written authority has been issued by the Commissioners is required by the Commissioners to deliver up or account to their satisfaction for that commission or authority and fails to comply within such period as may be specified in the requirement, he shall be liable on summary conviction to a penalty of **level 1** on the standard scale.

(2) If the failure continues after he is convicted thereof he shall be guilty of a further offence and be liable on summary conviction to a penalty of £5 for every day on which the failure has so continued.

[Customs and Excise Management Act 1979, s 14 as amended by the Criminal Justice Act 1982, ss 38 and 46.]

8–6549 14A. Exception for Customs and Excise. *This section is printed in the Police and Criminal Evidence Act 1984 (Application to Customs and Excise) Order 1985, in* PART I: MAGISTRATES' COURTS: PROCEDURE, *ante and, subject to the provisions of that Order, relates to the investigation of offences by officers of Customs and Excise.*

8–6550 15. Bribery and collusion. (1) If any Commissioner or officer or any person appointed or authorised by the Commissioners to discharge any duty relating to an assigned matter—

(a) directly or indirectly asks for or takes in connection with any of his duties any payment or other reward whatsoever, whether pecuniary or other, or any promise or security for any such payment or reward, not being a payment or reward which he is lawfully entitled to claim or receive; or

(b) enters into or acquiesces in any agreement to do, abstain from doing, permit, conceal or connive at any act or thing whereby Her Majesty is or may be defrauded or which is otherwise unlawful, being an act or thing relating to an assigned matter,

he shall be guilty of an offence under this section.

(2) If any person—

(a) directly or indirectly offers or gives to any Commissioner or officer or to any person appointed or authorised by the Commissioners as aforesaid any payment or other reward whatsoever, whether pecuniary or other, or any promise or security for any such payment or reward; or

(b) proposes or enters into any agreement with any Commissioner, officer or person appointed or authorised as aforesaid,

in order to induce him to do, abstain from doing, permit, conceal or connive at any act or thing whereby Her Majesty is or may be defrauded or which is otherwise unlawful, being an act or thing relating to an assigned matter, or otherwise to take any course contrary to his duty, he shall be guilty of an offence under this section.

(3) Any person committing an offence under this section shall be liable on summary conviction to a penalty of **level 5** on the standard scale and may be arrested.

[Customs and Excise Management Act 1979, s 15 as amended by the Criminal Justice Act 1982, ss 38 and 46 and the Police and Criminal Evidence Act 1984, s 114.]

8–6551   16. Obstruction of officers, etc.   (1) Any person who—

(a) obstructs[1], hinders, molests or assaults[2] any person duly engaged in the performance of any duty or the exercise of any power imposed or conferred on him by or under any enactment relating to an assigned matter, or any person acting in his aid; or

(b) does anything which impedes or is calculated to impede the carrying out of any search for anything liable to forfeiture under any such enactment or the detention, seizure or removal of any such thing; or

(c) rescues, damages or destroys any thing so liable to forfeiture or does anything calculated to prevent the procuring or giving of evidence as to whether or not any thing is so liable to forfeiture; or

(d) prevents the detention of any person by a person duly engaged or acting as aforesaid or rescues any person so detained,

or who attempts to do any of the aforementioned things, shall be guilty of an offence under this section.

(2) A person guilty of an offence under this section shall be liable[3]—

(a) on summary conviction, to a penalty of **the prescribed sum**[4], or to imprisonment for a term not exceeding **3 months**, or to both; or

(b) on conviction on indictment, to a penalty of any amount, or to imprisonment for a term not exceeding **2 years**, or to both.

(3) Any person committing an offence under this section and any person aiding or abetting the commission of such an offence may be arrested.

[Customs and Excise Management Act 1979, s 16 as amended by the Police and Criminal Evidence Act 1984, s 114.]

---

1. A person who gave a false vehicle owner's name to Customs and Excise officers who wished to give notice of the taking of a sample of fuel from a vehicle's tank, as required by the Hydrocarbon Oil Duties Act 1979, Sch 5, was held to have been properly convicted of obstruction (*R v George and Davies* [1981] Crim LR 185).

2. The court has no jurisdiction to enquire into the reasonableness of a search by a customs officer (*Anderson v Reid* (1902) 66 JP 564). As to assault generally, see title PERSONS, OFFENCES AGAINST, post, and *Logdon v DPP* [1976] Crim LR 121.

3. For procedure in respect of this offence which is triable either way, see s 147, post, and the Magistrates' Courts Act 1980, ss 17A–21, in PART I: MAGISTRATES' COURTS, PROCEDURE, ante.

4. For meaning of the "prescribed sum", see s 171, post.

PART III[1]
CUSTOMS AND EXCISE CONTROL AREAS

8–6552   19. *Appointment of ports, etc.*

---

1. Part III contains ss 19–34.

8–6553   20. Approval of wharves.   (1) The Commissioners may approve, for such periods and subject to such conditions and restrictions as they think fit, places for the loading or unloading of goods or of any class or description of goods.

(2) The Commissioners may at any time for reasonable cause revoke or vary the terms of any approval given under this section.

(3) This section shall not apply in relation to goods imported on or after 1st January 1992 from a place outside the customs territory of the Community or to any goods which are moving under the procedure specified in Article 165 of Council Regulation (EEC) No 2913/92 and Article 311 of Commission Regulation (EEC) No 2454/93 (transit procedures).

[Customs and Excise Management Act 1979, s 20 as substituted by SI 1991/2724 and amended by SI 1992/3095 and SI 1993/3014.]

8–6554   20A. Approved wharves.   (1) In this Act, references to an approved wharf are to—

(*a*)   a place approved under section 20 above; or

(*b*)   a place specified or approved under Article 46 of Council Regulation (EEC) No 2913/92 (equivalent provision for goods imported on or after 1st January 1992 from a place outside the customs territory of the Community), other than an examination station.

(2) Any person contravening or failing to comply with any condition or restriction attaching to an approval by virtue of which a place is an approved wharf shall be liable on summary conviction to a penalty of **level 3** on the standard scale.

(3) An officer may at any time enter an approved wharf and inspect it and any goods for the time being at the wharf.

[Customs and Excise Management Act 1979, s 20A as substituted by SI 1991/2724 and amended by SI 1993/3014.]

8–6555   21. Control of movement of aircraft, etc into and out of the United Kingdom.
(1) Save as permitted by the Commissioners, the commander of an aircraft entering the United Kingdom from a place outside the United Kingdom shall not cause or permit the aircraft to land—

(*a*)   for the first time after its arrival in the United Kingdom; or

(*b*)   at any time while it is carrying passengers or goods brought in that aircraft from a place outside the United Kingdom and not yet cleared,

at any place other than a customs and excise airport.

(1A) Subsection (1) above shall not apply by virtue only of the fact that the aircraft is carrying goods brought in it from a place outside the customs territory of the Community.

(2) Save as permitted by the Commissioners, no person importing from a place within the customs territory of the Community or concerned in so importing any goods in any aircraft shall bring the goods into the United Kingdom at any place other than a customs and excise airport.

(3) Save as permitted by the Commissioners—

(*a*)   no person shall depart on a flight to a place or area outside the United Kingdom from any place in the United Kingdom other than a customs and excise airport; and

(*b*)   the commander of any aircraft engaged in a flight from a customs and excise airport to a place or area outside the United Kingdom shall not cause or permit it to land at any place in the United Kingdom other than a customs and excise airport specified in the application for clearance for that flight.

(4) Subsections (1) to (3) above shall not apply in relation to any aircraft flying from or to any place or area outside the United Kingdom to or from any place in the United Kingdom which is required by or under any enactment relating to air navigation, or is compelled by accident, stress of weather or other unavoidable cause, to land at a place other than a customs and excise airport; but, subject to subsection (5) below,—

(*a*)   the commander of any such aircraft—

(i)   shall immediately report the landing to an officer or constable and shall on demand produce to him the journey log book belonging to the aircraft,

(ii)   shall not without the consent of an officer permit any goods carried in the aircraft to be unloaded from, or any of the crew or passengers to depart from the vicinity of, the aircraft, and

(iii)   shall comply with any directions given by an officer with respect to any such goods; and

(*b*)   no passenger or member of the crew shall without the consent of an officer or constable leave the immediate vicinity of any such aircraft.

(4A) Subsection 4(*a*)(ii) and (iii) above shall not apply in relation to goods brought in the aircraft from a place outside the customs territory of the Community.

(5) Nothing in subsection (4) above shall prohibit—

(*a*)   the departure of passengers or crew from the vicinity of an aircraft; or

(*b*)   the removal of goods from an aircraft,

where that departure or removal is necessary for reasons of health, safety or the preservation of life or property.

(6) Any person contravening or failing to comply with any provision of this section shall be liable on summary conviction to a penalty of **level 4** on the standard scale or to imprisonment for a term not exceeding **3 months★**, or to both.

(7) In this Act "customs and excise airport" means an aerodrome for the time being designated as a place for the landing or departure of aircraft for the purposes of the customs and excise Acts by an order made by the Secretary of State with the concurrence of the Commissioners which is in force under an Order in Council made in pursuance of section 60 of the Civil Aviation Act 1982.

[Customs and Excise Management Act 1979, s 21 as amended by the Civil Aviation Act 1982, Sch 15, the Criminal Justice Act 1982, ss 38 and 46 and SI 1991/2724.]

★Words substituted by "51 weeks" by the Criminal Justice Act 2003, Sch 26, from a date to be appointed.

8–6556 22. Approval of examination stations at customs and excise airports. (1) The Commissioners may approve, for such periods and subject to such conditions and restrictions as they think fit, a part of, or a place at, any customs and excise airport for the loading and unloading of goods and the embarkation and disembarkation of passengers.

(2) The Commissioners may at any time for reasonable cause revoke or vary the terms of any approval given under this section.

(3) This section shall not apply in relation to goods imported on or after 1st January 1992 from a place outside the customs territory of the Community or to any goods which are moving under the procedure specified in Article 165 of Council Regulation (EEC) No 2913/92 and Article 311 of Commission Regulation (EEC) No 2454/93 (transit procedures).
[Customs and Excise Management Act 1979, s 22, as substituted by SI 1991/2724 and amended by SI 1992/3095 and SI 1993/3014.]

8–6558 22A. Examination stations. (1) In this Act, references to an examination station are to—

(a) a part of, or a place at, a customs and excise airport approved under section 22 above; or
(b) a place at such an airport specified or approved under Article 46 of Council Regulation (EEC) No 2913/92 (equivalent provision for goods imported on or after 1st January 1992 from a place outside the customs territory of the Community).

(2) Any person contravening or failing to comply with any condition or restriction attaching to an approval by virtue of which a part of, or place at, a customs and excise airport is an examination station shall be liable on summary conviction to a penalty of **level 3** on the standard scale.
[Customs and Excise Management Act 1979, s 22A, as inserted by SI 1991/2724 and amended by SI 1993/3014.]

8–6559 23. *Control of movement of hovercraft.*

8–6560 24. Control of movement of goods by pipe-line. (1) Goods shall not be imported or exported by means of a pipe-line that is not for the time being approved by the Commissioners for the purposes of this section.

(2) Uncleared goods, that is to say—

(a) imported goods, whether or not chargeable with duty, which have not been cleared out of charge, and in particular goods which are, or are to be, moved under section 30 below; or
(b) dutiable goods moved from warehouse without payment of duty,

shall not be moved by means of a pipe-line that is not for the time being approved by the Commissioners for the purposes of this section.

(3) The Commissioners may give their approval under this section for such period and subject to such conditions as they think fit, and may at any time for reasonable cause—

(a) vary the terms of their approval; and
(b) (if they have given to the owner of the pipe-line not less than 3 months' written notice of their intention so to do) revoke their approval.

(4) Section 49 of the Pipe-lines Act 1962 (procedure for service of documents under that Act) shall apply to a notice required by sub-section (3) (b) above to be served on the owner of a pipe-line as it applies to a document required by that Act to be so served.

(5) A person who—

(a) contravenes subsection (1) or (2) above, or contravenes or fails to comply with a condition imposed by the Commissioners under subsection (3) above; or
(b) except with the authority of the proper officer or for just and sufficient cause, obtains access to goods which are in, or in course of conveyance by, a pipe-line approved under this section,

shall be guilty of an offence under this section and may be detained; and any goods in respect of which the offence was committed shall be liable to forfeiture.

(6) A person guilty of an offence under this section shall be liable[1]—

(a) on summary conviction, to a penalty of **the prescribed sum**[2], or to such imprisonment for a term not exceeding **6 months**, or to both; or
(b) on conviction on indictment, to a penalty of any amount, or to imprisonment for a term not exceeding **2 years**, or to both.

(7) *Northern Ireland.*
[Customs and Excise Management Act 1979, s 24.]

1. For procedure in respect of this offence which is triable either way, see s 147, post, and the Magistrates' Court Act 1980, ss 17A–21, in PART I: MAGISTRATES' COURTS, PROCEDURE, ante.
2. For meaning of the "prescribed sum", see s 171, post.

8–6562 25. Approval of transit sheds. (1) The Commissioners may approve, for such periods and subject to such conditions and restrictions as they think fit, places for the deposit of goods imported and not yet cleared out of charge, including goods not yet reported and entered under regulation 5 of the Customs Controls on Importation of Goods Regulations 1991.

(2) The Commissioners may at any time for reasonable cause revoke or vary the terms of any approval given under this section.

(3) Subsection (1) above shall not apply in relation to goods imported on or after 1st January 1992 from a place outside the customs territory of the Community or to any goods which are moving under the procedure specified in Article 165 of Council Regulation (EEC) No 2913/92 and Article 311 of Commission Regulation (EEC) No 2454/93 (transit procedures).

(4) Where, by any local Act, provision is made for the landing of goods without entry for deposit in transit sheds authorised thereunder, the provisions of this Act relating to goods deposited in transit sheds approved under this section shall have effect in relation to goods deposited in transit sheds authorised under that Act.

[Customs and Excise Management Act 1979, s 25, as substituted by SI 1991/2724 and amended by SI 1992/3095 and SI 1993/3014.]

8–6563   25A. Transit sheds. (1) In this Act, references to a transit shed are to a place approved—

(a) under section 25 above; or

(b) under Article 51 of Council Regulation (EEC) No 2913/92 (equivalent provision for goods imported on or after 1st January 1992 from a place outside the customs territory of the Community).

(2) Any person contravening or failing to comply with any condition or restriction attaching to an approval by virtue of which a place is a transit shed shall be liable on summary conviction to a penalty of **level 3** on the standard scale.

(3) An officer may at any time enter a transit shed and inspect it and any goods for the time being in the transit shed.

[Customs and Excise Management Act 1979, s 25A, as inserted by SI 1991/2724 and amended by SI 1993/3014.]

8–6564   27. *Officers' powers of boarding.*

8–6570   28. *Officers' powers of access, etc.*

8–6571   29. *Officers' powers of detention of ships, etc.*

8–6572   30. Control of movement of uncleared goods within or between port or airport and other places. (1) The Commissioners may from time to time give general or special directions as to the manner in which, and the conditions under which, goods to which this section applies, or any class or description of such goods, may be moved within the limits of any port or customs and excise airport or between any port or customs and excise airport and any other place.

(2) This section applies to goods chargeable with any duty which has not been paid, to drawback goods, and to any other goods which have not been cleared out of charge.

(3) Any directions under subsection (1) above may require that any goods to which this section applies shall be moved only—

(a) by persons licensed by the Commissioners for that purpose;

(b) in such ships, aircraft or vehicles or by such other means as may be approved by the Commissioners for that purpose;

and any such licence or approval may be granted for such period and subject to such conditions and restrictions as the Commissioners think fit and may be revoked at any time by the Commissioners.

(4) Any person contravening or failing to comply with any direction given or condition or restriction imposed, or the terms of any licence granted, by the Commissioners under this section shall be liable on summary conviction to a penalty of **level 2** on the standard scale.

[Customs and Excise Management Act 1979, s 30 as amended by the Criminal Justice Act 1982, s 46.]

8–6573   31. Control of movement of goods to and from inland clearance depot, etc. (1) The Commissioners may by regulations[1] impose conditions and restrictions as respects—

(a) the movement of imported goods between the place of importation and a place approved by the Commissioners for the clearance out of charge of such goods, a free zone or the place of exportation of such goods; and

(aa) the movement of goods between—

(i) a free zone and a place approved by the Commissioners for the clearance out of charge of such goods,

(ii) such a place and a free zone, and

(iii) a free zone and another free zone;

(b) the movement of goods intended for export between a place approved by the Commissioners for the examination of such goods, or a place designated by the proper officer under section 53(4) or 58(3) below, and the place of exportation.

(2) Regulations under subsection (1) above may in particular—

(a) require the goods to be moved within such period and by such route as may be specified by or under the regulations;

(b) require the goods to be carried in a vehicle or container complying with such requirements and secured in such manner as may be so specified;

(c) prohibit, except in such circumstances as may be so specified, any unloading or loading of the vehicle or container or any interference with its security.

(2A) Any documents required to be made or produced as a result of regulations made under subsection (1) above shall be made or produced in such form and manner and contain such particulars as the Commissioners may direct; but the Commissioners may relax any requirement imposed under the regulations that any specific document be made or produced and if they do so may impose substituted requirements.

(3) If any person contravenes or fails to comply with any regulation under subsection (1) above or any requirement imposed by or under any such regulation or a direction made under subsection (2A) above or any requirement imposed under that subsection, that person and the person then in charge of the goods shall each be liable on summary conviction to a penalty of **level 4** on the standard scale and any goods in respect of which the offence was committed shall be liable to forfeiture.

[Customs and Excise Management Act 1979, s 31, as amended by the Finance Act 1981, Sch 7, the Criminal Justice Act 1982, s 46 and the Finance Act 1984, Sch 4.]

---

1. See the Control of Movement of Goods Regulations 1984, SI 1984/1176.

8–6574 32. Penalty for carrying away officers. (1) If any ship or aircraft departs from any place carrying on board without his consent any officer of customs and excise, the master of the ship or commander of the aircraft shall be liable on summary conviction to a penalty of **level 3** on the standard scale.

[Customs and Excise Management Act 1979, s 32 as amended by the Criminal Justice Act 1982, ss 38 and 46—summarised.]

8–6575 33. Power to inspect aircraft, aerodromes, records, etc. (1) The commander of an aircraft shall permit an officer at any time to board the aircraft and inspect—

(a) the aircraft and any goods loaded therein; and

(b) all documents relating to the aircraft or to goods or persons carried therein;

and an officer shall have the right of access at any time to any place to which access is required for the purpose of any such inspection.

(2) The person in control of any aerodrome shall permit an officer at any time to enter upon and inspect the aerodrome and all buildings and goods thereon.

(3) The person in control of an aerodrome licensed under any enactment relating to air navigation and, if so required by the Commissioners, the person in control of any other aerodrome shall—

(a) keep a record in such form and manner as the Commissioners may approve of all aircraft arriving at or departing from the aerodrome;

(b) keep that record available and produce it on demand to any officer, together with all other documents kept on the aerodrome which relate to the movement of aircraft; and

(c) permit any officer to make copies of and take extracts from any such record or document.

(4) If any person contravenes or fails to comply with any of the provisions of this section he shall be liable on summary conviction to a penalty of **level 4** on the standard scale or to imprisonment for a term not exceeding **3 months***, or to both.

[Customs and Excise Management Act 1979, s 33 as amended by the Criminal Justice Act 1982, ss 38 and 46.]

---

*Words substituted by "51 weeks" by the Criminal Justice Act 2003, Sch 26, from a date to be appointed.

8–6576 34. Power to prevent flight of aircraft. (1) If it appears to any officer or constable that an aircraft is intended or likely to depart for a destination outside the United Kingdom from—

(a) any place other than a customs and excise airport; or

(b) a customs and excise airport before clearance outwards is given,

he may give such instructions and take such steps by way of detention of the aircraft or otherwise as appear to him necessary in order to prevent the flight.

(2) Any person who contravenes any instructions given under subsection (1) above shall be liable on summary conviction to a penalty of **level 4** on the standard scale, or to imprisonment for a term not exceeding **3 months***, or to both.

(3) If an aircraft flies in contravention of any instruction given under subsection (1) above or notwithstanding any steps taken to prevent the flight, the owner and the commander thereof shall, without prejudice to the liability of any other person under subsection (2) above, each be liable on summary conviction to a penalty of **level 4** on the standard scale, or to imprisonment for a term not

exceeding **3 months***, or to both, unless he proves that the flight took place without his consent or connivance.

[Customs and Excise Management Act 1979, s 34 as amended by the Criminal Justice Act 1982, ss 38 and 46.]

*Words substituted by "51 weeks" by the Criminal Justice Act 2003, Sch 26, from a date to be appointed.

PART IV[1]
CONTROL OF IMPORTATION

Inward entry and clearance

8–6577   **35. Report inwards.**   (1) Report shall be made in such form and manner and containing such particulars as the Commissioners may direct of every ship and aircraft to which this section applies.

(2) This section applies to every ship arriving at a port—

(a) from any place outside the United Kingdom; or

(b) carrying any goods brought in that ship from some place outside the United Kingdom and not yet cleared on importation.

(3) This section applies to every aircraft arriving at any place in the United Kingdom—

(a) from any place or area outside the United Kingdom; or

(b) carrying passengers or goods taken on board that aircraft at a place outside the United Kingdom, being passengers or goods either—

(i) bound for a destination in the United Kingdom and not already cleared at a customs and excise airport; or

(ii) bound for a destination outside the United Kingdom.

(4) The Commissioners may make regulations[2] prescribing the procedure for making report under this section.

(5) If the person by whom the report should be made fails to make report as required by or under this section—

(a) he shall be liable on summary conviction to a penalty of **level 3** on the standard scale; and

(b) any goods required to be reported which are not duly reported may be detained by any officer until so reported or until the omission is explained to the satisfaction of the Commissioners and may in the meantime be deposited in Queen's warehouse.

(6) The person making the report shall at the time of making it answer all such questions relating to the ship or aircraft, to the goods carried therein, to the crew and to the voyage or flight as may be put to him by the proper officer; and if he refuses to answer he shall be liable on summary conviction to a penalty of **level 3** on the standard scale.

(7) If at any time after a ship or aircraft carrying goods brought therein from any place outside the United Kingdom arrives in or over United Kingdom waters and before report has been made in accordance with this section—

(a) bulk is broken; or

(b) any alteration is made in the stowage of any goods carried so as to facilitate the unloading of any part thereof before due report has been made; or

(c) any part of the goods is staved, destroyed or thrown overboard or any container is opened

and the matter is not explained to the satisfaction of the Commissioners, the master of the ship or commander of the aircraft shall be liable on summary conviction to a penalty of **level 3** on the standard scale.

(8) *(Repealed)*.

[Customs and Excise Management Act 1979, s 35 as amended by the Criminal Justice Act 1982, ss 38 and 46, the Territorial Sea Act 1987, Sch 1 and SI 1992/3095.]

1. Part IV contains ss 35–51.
2. The Pleasure Craft (Arrival and Report) Regulations 1996, SI 1996/1406 and the Ship's Report, Importation and Exportation by Sea Regulations 1981, SI 1981/1260, as amended by SI 1986/1819 and SI 1992/3095, and the Aircraft (Customs and Excise) Regulations 1981, SI 1981/1259 amended by SI 1992/3095, have been made.

8–6579   **37A. Initial and supplementary entries.**   (1) The Commissioners may—

(a) give such directions as they think fit for enabling an entry under regulation 5 of the Customs Controls on Importation of Goods Regulations 1991 to consist of an initial entry and a supplementary entry where the importer is authorised for the purposes of this section in accordance with the directions; and

(b) include in the directions such supplementary provision in connection with entries consisting of initial and supplementary entries as they think fit.

(1A) Without prejudice to section 37 above, a direction under that section may—

(a) provide that where the importer is not authorised for the purposes of this section but a person who is so authorised is appointed as his agent for the purpose of entering the goods, the entry may consist of an initial entry made by the person so appointed and a supplementary entry so made; and

(b) make such supplementary provision in connection with entries consisting of initial and supplementary entries made as mentioned in paragraph (a) above as the Commissioners think fit.

(2) Where—

(a) an initial entry made under subsection (1) above has been accepted and the importer has given security by deposit of money or otherwise to the satisfaction of the Commissioners for payment of the unpaid duty, or

(b) an initial entry made under subsection (1A) above has been accepted and the person making the entry on the importer's behalf has given such security as is mentioned in paragraph (a) above,

the goods may be delivered without payment of any duty chargeable in respect of the goods, but any such duty shall be paid within such time as the Commissioners may direct.

(3) An importer who makes an initial entry under subsection (1) above shall complete the entry by delivering the supplementary entry within such time as the Commissioners may direct.

(3A) A person who makes an initial entry under subsection (1A) above on behalf of an importer shall complete the entry by delivering the supplementary entry within such time as the Commissioners may direct.

(4) For the purposes of the customs and excise Acts an entry of goods shall be taken to have been delivered when an initial entry of the goods has been delivered, and accepted when an initial entry has been accepted.

[Customs and Excise Management Act 1979, s 37A, as inserted by the Finance Act 1984, Sch 5, and amended by the Finance Act 1990, Schs 3 and 19 and SI 1992/3095.]

8–6580 37B. Postponed entry. (1) The Commissioners may, if they think fit, direct that where—

(a) such goods as may be specified in the direction are imported by an importer authorised for the purposes of this subsection;

(b) the importer has delivered a document relating to the goods to the proper officer, in such form and manner, containing such particulars and accompanied by such documents as the Commissioners may direct; and

(c) the document has been accepted by the proper officer,

the goods may be delivered before an entry of them has been delivered or any duty chargeable in respect of them has been paid.

(1A) The Commissioners may, if they think fit, direct that where—

(a) such goods as may be specified in the direction are imported by an importer who is not authorised for the purposes of this subsection;

(b) a person who is authorised for the purposes of this subsection is appointed as his agent for the purpose of entering the goods;

(c) the person so appointed has delivered a document relating to the goods to the proper officer, in such form and manner, containing such particulars and accompanied by such documents as the Commissioners may direct; and

(d) the document has been accepted by the proper officer,

the goods may be delivered before an entry of them has been delivered or any duty chargeable in respect of them has been paid.

(2) The Commissioners may, if they think fit, direct that where—

(a) such goods as may be specified in the direction are imported by an importer authorised for the purposes of this subsection;

(b) the goods have been removed from the place of importation to a place approved by the Commissioners for the clearance out of charge of such goods; and

(c) the conditions mentioned in subsection (3) below have been satisfied,

the goods may be delivered before an entry of them has been delivered or any duty chargeable in respect of them has been paid.

(3) The conditions are that—

(a) on the arrival of the goods at the approved place the importer delivers to the proper officer a notice of the arrival of the goods in such form and containing such particulars as may be required by the directions;

(b) within such time as may be so required the importer enters such particulars of the goods and such other information as may be so required in a record maintained by him at such place as the proper officer may require; and

(c) the goods are kept secure in the approved place for such period as may be required by the directions.

(3A)　The Commissioners may, if they think fit, direct that where—

(a)　such goods as may be specified in the direction are imported by an importer who is not authorised for the purposes of this subsection;

(b)　a person who is authorised for the purposes of this subsection is appointed as his agent for the purpose of entering the goods;

(c)　the goods have been removed from the place of importation to a place approved by the Commissioners for the clearance out of charge of such goods; and

(d)　the conditions mentioned in subsection (3B) below have been satisfied,

the goods may be delivered before an entry of them has been delivered or any duty chargeable in respect of them has been paid.

(3B)　The conditions are that—

(a)　on the arrival of the goods at the approved place the person appointed as the agent of the importer for the purpose of entering the goods delivers to the proper officer a notice of the arrival of the goods in such form and containing such particulars as may be required by the directions;

(b)　within such time as may be so required the person appointed as the agent of the importer for the purpose of entering the goods enters such particulars of the goods and such other information as may be so required in a record maintained by him at such place as the proper officer may require; and

(c)　the goods are kept secure in the approved place for such period as may be required by the directions.

(4)　The Commissioners may direct that the condition mentioned in subsection (3)(a) or (3B)(a) above shall not apply in relation to any goods specified in the direction and such a direction may substitute another condition.

(5)　No goods shall be delivered under subsection (1) or (2) above unless the importer gives security by deposit of money or otherwise to the satisfaction of the Commissioners for the payment of any duty chargeable in respect of the goods which is unpaid.

(5A)　No goods shall be delivered under subsection (1A) or (3A) above unless the person appointed as the agent of the importer for the purpose of entering the goods gives security by deposit of money or otherwise to the satisfaction of the Commissioners for the payment of any duty chargeable in respect of the goods which is unpaid.

(6)　Where goods of which no entry has been made have been delivered under subsection (1) or (2) above, the importer shall deliver an entry of the goods under s 37(1) above within such time as the Commissioners may direct.

(6A)　Where goods of which no entry has been made have been delivered under subsection (1A) or (3A) above, the person appointed as the agent of the importer for the purpose of entering the goods shall deliver an entry of the goods under regulation 5 of the Customs Controls on Importation of Goods Regulations 1991 within such time as the Commissioners may direct.

(7)　For the purposes of s 43(2)(a) below such an entry shall be taken to have been accepted—

(a)　in the case of goods delivered by virtue of a direction under subsection (1) or (1A) above, on the date on which the document mentioned in that subsection was accepted; and

(b)　in the case of goods delivered by virtue of a direction under subsection (2) above, on the date on which particulars of the goods were entered as mentioned in subsection (3)(b) above; and

(c)　in the case of goods delivered by virtue of a direction under subsection (3A) above, on the date on which particulars of the goods were entered as mentioned in subsection (3B)(b) above.

[Customs and Excise Management Act 1979, s 37B, as inserted by the Finance Act 1984, Sch 5, and as amended by the Finance Act 1990, Sch 3 and SI 1992/3095.]

8–6581　37C.　Provisions supplementary to ss 37A and 37B.　　(1)　The Commissioners may, if they think fit—

(a)　authorise any person for the purposes of ss 37A, or 37B(1), (1A), (2) or (3A) above; and

(b)　suspend or cancel the authorisation of any person where it appears to them that he has failed to comply with any requirement imposed on him by or under this Part of this Act or that there is other reasonable cause for suspension or cancellation.

(2)　The Commissioners may give directions—

(a)　imposing such requirements as they think fit on any person authorised under this section; or

(b)　varying any such requirements previously imposed.

(3)　If any person without reasonable excuse contravenes any requirement imposed by or under s 37A, 37B or this section he shall be liable on summary conviction to a penalty of **level 4** on the standard scale.

[Customs and Excise Management Act 1979, s 37C, as inserted by the Finance Act 1984, Sch 5 and as amended by the Finance Act 1990, Sch 3.]

8–6582　38–38A.　(*Repealed*).

8–6584 38B. Correction and cancellation of entry.   (1) Where goods have been entered for home use or for free circulation the importer may correct any of the particulars contained in an entry of the goods after it has been accepted if—

(a) the goods have not been cleared from customs and excise charge;

(b) he has not been notified by an officer that the goods are to be examined; and

(c) the entry has not been found by an officer to be incorrect.

(2) The proper officer may permit or require any correction allowed by subsection (1) above to be made by the delivery of a substituted entry.

(3) An entry of goods may at the request of the importer be cancelled at any time before the goods are cleared from customs and excise charge if the importer proves to the satisfaction of the Commissioners that the entry was delivered by mistake or that the goods cannot be cleared for free circulation.

[Customs and Excise Management Act 1979, s 38B, as inserted by the Finance Act 1981, Sch 6.]

8–6585 39. Entry of surplus stores.   (1) With the permission of the proper officer, surplus stores of any ship or aircraft—

(a) if intended for private use and in quantities which do not appear to him to be excessive, may be entered and otherwise treated as if they were goods imported in the ship or aircraft; or

(b) in any other case may, subject to subsection (2) below, be entered for warehousing notwithstanding that they could not lawfully be imported as merchandise.

(2) Goods entered for warehousing by virtue of subsection (1)(b) above shall not, except with the sanction of the Commissioners, be further entered, or be removed from the warehouse, otherwise than for use as stores.

[Customs and Excise Management Act 1979, s 39.]

8–6586 40. *Removal of uncleared goods to Queen's warehouse.*

8–6587 41. Failure to comply with provisions as to entry.   Without prejudice to any liability under any other provision of the Customs and Excise Acts 1979, any person making entry of goods on their importation who fails to comply with any of the requirements of this Part of this Act in connection with that entry shall be liable on summary conviction to a penalty of **level 2** on the standard scale, and the goods in question shall be liable to forfeiture but—

(a) any failure which has been or may be remedied by virtue of section 38 (B) (1); or

(b) any failure in respect of an entry which by virtue of section 38 (B)(3) has been or may be cancelled at his request.

[Customs and Excise Management Act 1979, s 41 as amended by the Finance Act 1981, Sch 6 and the Criminal Justice Act 1982, s 46.]

Forfeiture, offences etc in connection with importation

8–6588 49. Forfeiture of goods improperly imported.   (1) Where—

(a) except as provided by or under the Customs and Excise Acts 1979, any imported goods, being goods chargeable on their importation with customs or excise duty, are, without payment of that duty—

(i) unshipped in any port,

(ii) unloaded from any aircraft in the United Kingdom,

(iii) unloaded from any vehicle in, or otherwise brought across the boundary into, Northern Ireland, or

(iv) removed from their place of importation or from any approved wharf, examination station or transit shed; or

(b) any goods are imported, landed or unloaded contrary to any prohibition or restriction for the time being in force with respect thereto under or by virtue of any enactment[1]; or

(c) any goods, being goods chargeable with any duty or goods the importation of which is for the time being prohibited or restricted by or under any enactment, are found, whether before or after the unloading thereof, to have been concealed in any manner on board any ship or aircraft or, while in Northern Ireland, in any vehicle; or

(d) any goods are imported concealed in a container holding goods of a different description; or

(e) any imported goods are found, whether before or after delivery, not to correspond with the entry made thereof; or

(f) any imported goods are concealed or packed in any manner appearing to be intended to deceive an officer,

those goods shall, subject to subsection (2) below, be liable to forfeiture.

(2) Where any goods, the importation of which is for the time being prohibited or restricted by or under any enactment, are on their importation either—

(a) reported as intended for exportation in the same ship, aircraft or vehicle; or

(b)   entered for transit or transhipment; or

(c)   entered to be warehoused for exportation or for use as stores,

the Commissioners may, if they see fit, permit the goods to be dealt with accordingly.
[Customs and Excise Management Act 1979, s 49.]

---

1. See in particular, the Customs Consolidation Act 1876, s 42, and notes thereto, this title, ante.

8–6589   50. Penalty for improper importation of goods.   (1) Subsection (2) below applies to goods of the following descriptions, that is to say—

(a)   goods chargeable with a duty which has not been paid; and

(b)   goods the importation, landing or unloading of which is for the time being prohibited or restricted by or under any enactment.

(2) If any person with intent to defraud Her Majesty of any such duty or to evade any such prohibition or restriction as is mentioned in subsection (1) above[1]—

(a)   unships or lands in any port of unloads from any aircraft in the United Kingdom or from any vehicle in Northern Ireland any goods to which this subsection applies, or assists or is otherwise concerned in such unshipping, landing or unloading; or

(b)   removes from their place of importation or from any approved wharf, examination station, transit shed or customs and excise station any goods to which this subsection applies or assists or is otherwise concerned in such removal,

he shall be guilty of an offence under this subsection and may be arrested.

(3) If any person imports or is concerned in importing any goods contrary to any prohibition or restriction for the time being in force under or by virtue of any enactment with respect to those goods, whether or not the goods are unloaded, and does so with intent to evade the prohibition or restriction, he shall be guilty of an offence under this subsection and may be arrested.

(4) Subject to subsection (5), (5A) or (5B) below, a person guilty of an offence under subsection (2) or (3) above shall be liable[2]—

(a)   on summary conviction, to a penalty of **the prescribed sum**[3] or of three times the value of the goods, whichever is the greater, or to imprisonment for a term not exceeding **6 months**, or to both; or

(b)   on conviction on indictment, to a penalty of any amount, or to imprisonment for a term not exceeding **7 years**, or to both.

(5) In the case of an offence under subsection (2) or (3) above in connection with a prohibition or restriction on importation having effect by virtue of section 3 of the Misuse of Drugs Act 1971, subsection (4) above shall have effect subject to the modifications specified in Schedule 1 to this Act[4].

(5A) In the case of—

(a)   an offence under subsection (2) or (3) above committed in Great Britain in connection with a prohibition or restriction on the importation of any weapon or ammunition that is of a kind mentioned in section 5(1)(a), (ab), (aba), (ac), (ad), (ae), (af) or (c) or (1A)(a) of the Firearms Act 1968,

(b)   any such offence committed in Northern Ireland in connection with a prohibition or restriction on the importation of any weapon or ammunition that is of a kind mentioned in Article 45(1)(a), (aa), (b), (c), (d), (e) or (g) or (2)(a) of the Firearms (Northern Ireland) Order 2004, or

(c)   any such offence committed in connection with the prohibition contained in section 20 of the Forgery and Counterfeiting Act 1981,

subsection (4)(b) above shall have effect as if for the words "7 years" there were substituted the words "10 years".

(5B) In the case of an offence under subsection (2) or (3) above in connection with the prohibition contained in regulation 2 of the Import of Seal Skins Regulations 1996, subsection (4) above shall have effect as if—

(a)   for paragraph (a) there were substituted the following—

     "(a) on summary conviction, to a fine not exceeding the statutory maximum or to imprisonment for a term not exceeding three months, or to both"; and

(b)   in paragraph (b) for the words "7 years" there were substituted the words "2 years".

(6) If any person—

(a)   imports or causes to be imported any goods concealed in a container holding goods of a different description; or

(b)   directly or indirectly imports or causes to be imported or entered any goods found, whether before or after delivery, not to correspond with the entry made thereof,

he shall be liable on summary conviction to a penalty of three times the value of the goods or of **level 3** on the standard scale, whichever is the greater.

(7) In any case where a person would, apart from this subsection, be guilty of—

    (*a*) an offence under this section in connection with the importation of goods contrary to a prohibition or restriction; and

    (*b*) a corresponding offence under the enactment or other instrument imposing the prohibition or restriction, being an offence for which a fine or other penalty is expressly provided by that enactment or other instrument,

he shall not be guilty of the offence mentioned in paragraph (*a*) of this subsection.

[Customs and Excise Management Act 1979, s 50, as amended by the Forgery and Counterfeiting Act 1981, s 23, the Criminal Justice Act 1982, ss 38 and 46, the Police and Criminal Evidence Act 1984, s 114, the Finance Act 1988 s 12, SI 1996/2686, the Criminal Justice Act 2003, s 293, SI 2004/702 and SI 2005/1966.]

    1. See *Fox v Kooman* (1919) 83 JP 239. An intention to contravene the prohibition is a necessary ingredient of the offence (*Frailey v Charlton* [1920] 1 KB 147, 83 JP 249), and should be alleged in the charge or summons (*R v Franks* [1950] 2 All ER 1172, 115 JP 21). See also *Garrett v Arthur Churchill (Glass) Ltd* [1970] 1 QB 92, [1969] 2 All ER 1141, 133 JP 509.

    2. For procedure in respect of this offence which is triable either way, see s 147, post, and the Magistrates' Courts Act 1980, ss 17A–21, in PART I: MAGISTRATES' COURTS, PROCEDURE, ante.

    3. For meaning of the "prescribed sum", see s 171, post.

    4. Post.

PART V[1]

CONTROL OF EXPORTATION

Offences in relation to exportation

8–6596 67. Offences in relation to exportation of goods. (1) If any goods which have been loaded or retained on board any ship or aircraft for exportation are not exported to and discharged at a place outside the United Kingdom but are unloaded in the United Kingdom, then, unless—

    (*a*) the unloading was authorised by the proper officer; and

    (*b*) except where that officer otherwise permits, any duty chargeable and unpaid on the goods is paid and any drawback or allowance paid in respect thereof is repaid,

the master of the ship or the commander of the aircraft and any person concerned in the unshipping, relanding, landing, unloading or carrying of the goods from the ship or aircraft without such authority, payment or repayment shall each be guilty of an offence under this section.

    (2) The Commissioners may impose such conditions as they see fit with respect to any goods loaded or retained as mentioned in subsection (1) above which are permitted to be unloaded in the United Kingdom.

    (3) If any person contravenes or fails to comply with, or is concerned in any contravention of or failure to comply with, any condition imposed under subsection (2) above he shall be guilty of an offence under this section.

    (4) Where any goods loaded or retained as mentioned in subsection (1) above or brought to a customs and excise station for exportation by land are—

    (*a*) goods from warehouse, other than goods which have been kept, without being warehoused, in a warehouse by virtue of section 92(4) below;

    (*b*) transit goods;

    (*c*) other goods chargeable with a duty which has not been paid; or

    (*d*) drawback goods,

then if any container in which the goods are held is without the authority of the proper officer opened, or any mark, letter or device on any such container or on any lot of the goods is without that authority cancelled, obliterated or altered, every person concerned in the opening, cancellation, obliteration or alteration shall be guilty of an offence under this section.

    (5) Any goods in respect of which an offence under this section is committed shall be liable to forfeiture and any person guilty of an offence under this section shall be liable on summary conviction to a penalty of three times the value of the goods or of **level 3** on the standard scale, whichever is the greater.

[Customs and Excise Management Act 1979, s 67 as amended by the Criminal Justice Act 1982, ss 38 and 46.]

    1. Part V contains ss 52–68B. Sections 53 to 58 have been substituted by the sections set out in Pt I of Sch 7 to the Finance Act 1981.

8–6597 68. Offences in relation to exportation of prohibited or restricted goods. (1) If any goods are—

    (*a*) exported or shipped as stores; or

    (*b*) brought to any place in the United Kingdom for the purpose of being exported or shipped as stores,

and the exportation or shipment is or would be contrary to any prohibition or restriction for the time being in force with respect to those goods under or by virtue of any enactment, the goods shall be liable to forfeiture and the exporter or intending exporter of the goods and any agent of his concerned in the exportation or shipment or intended exportation or shipment shall be liable on summary conviction to a penalty of three times the value of the goods or of **level 3** on the standard scale, whichever is the greater.

(2) Any person knowingly concerned[1] in the exportation or shipment as stores, or in the attempted exportation or shipment as stores, of any goods[2] with intent to evade any such prohibition or restriction as is mentioned in subsection (1) above shall be guilty of an offence under this subsection and may be arrested.

(3) Subject to subsection (4) or (4A) below, a person guilty of an offence under subsection (2) above shall be liable[3]—

(*a*)   on summary conviction, to a penalty of **the prescribed sum**[4] or of three times the value of the goods, whichever is the greater, or to imprisonment for a term not exceeding **6 months**, or to both; or

(*b*)   on conviction on indictment, to a penalty of any amount, or to imprisonment for a term not exceeding **7 years**, or to both.

(4) In the case of an offence under subsection (2) above in connection with a prohibition or restriction on exportation having effect by virtue of section 3 of the Misuse of Drugs Act 1971, subsection (3) above shall have effect subject to the modifications specified in Schedule 1 to this Act[5].

(4A) In the case of—

(*a*)   an offence under subsection (2) or (3) above committed in Great Britain in connection with a prohibition or restriction on the exportation of any weapon or ammunition that is of a kind mentioned in section 5(1)(*a*), (*ab*), (*aba*), (*ac*), (*ad*), (*ae*), (*af*) or (*c*) or (1A)(*a*) of the Firearms Act 1968,

(*b*)   any such offence committed in Northern Ireland in connection with a prohibition or restriction on the exportation of any weapon or ammunition that is of a kind mentioned in Article 45(1)(*a*), (*aa*), (*b*), (*c*), (*d*), (*e*) or (*g*) or (2)(*a*) of the Firearms (Northern Ireland) Order 2004, or

(*c*)   any such offence committed in connection with the prohibition contained in section 21 of the Forgery and Counterfeiting Act 1981,

subsection (3)(b) above shall have effect as if for the words "7 years" there were substituted the words "10 years".

(5) If by virtue of any such restriction as is mentioned in subsection (1) above any goods may be exported only when consigned to a particular place or person and any goods so consigned are delivered to some other place or person, the ship, aircraft or vehicle in which they were exported shall be liable to forfeiture unless it is proved to the satisfaction of the Commissioners that both the owner of the ship, aircraft or vehicle and the master of the ship, commander of the aircraft or person in charge of the vehicle—

(*a*)   took all reasonable steps to secure that the goods were delivered to the particular place to which or person to whom they were consigned; and

(*b*)   did not connive at or, except under duress, consent to the delivery of the goods to that place or person.

(6) In any case where a person would, apart from this subsection, be guilty of—

(*a*)   an offence under subsection (1) or (2) above; and

(*b*)   a corresponding offence under the enactment or instrument imposing the prohibition or restriction in question, being an offence for which a fine or other penalty is expressly provided by that enactment or other instrument,

he shall not be guilty of the offence mentioned in paragraph (*a*) of this subsection.

[Customs and Excise Management Act 1979, s 68, as amended by the Forgery and Counterfeiting Act 1981, s 23, the Criminal Justice Act 1982, ss 38 and 46, the Police and Criminal Evidence Act 1984, s 114, the Finance Act 1988, s 12, the Criminal Justice Act 2003, s 293, SI 2004/702 and SI 2005/1966.]

---

1. The question whether a defendant was knowingly concerned in the exportation of goods with intent to evade the prohibition should be treated as one question (*Garrett v Arthur Churchill (Glass) Ltd* [1970] 1 QB 92, [1969] 2 All ER 1141, 133 JP 509).

2. Destruction of the goods will not necessarily prejudice the defendant or breach natural justice where secondary evidence can be put before the court (*R v Uxbridge Justices, ex p Sofaer* (1986) 85 Cr App Rep 367).

3. For procedure in respect of this offence which is triable either way, see s 147, post, and the Magistrates' Courts Act 1980, ss 17A–21, in PART I: MAGISTRATES' COURTS, PROCEDURE, ante.

4. For meaning of the "prescribed sum", see s 171, post.

5. Post.

8–6598   68A. Offences in relation to agricultural levies[1]**.** (1) Without prejudice to section 11(1) of the Finance Act 1982, if any person is, in relation to any goods, in any way knowingly concerned in any fraudulent evasion of any agricultural levy chargeable on the export of the goods, he shall be guilty of an offence and may be detained.

(2) A person guilty of an offence under this section shall be liable[2]—

(a) on summary conviction, to a penalty of the **prescribed sum** or of **three times the value** of the goods, whichever is the greater, or to imprisonment for a term not exceeding **6 months**, or to both; or

(b) on conviction on indictment, to a penalty of any amount, or to imprisonment for a term not exceeding **7 years**, or to both.

(3) Any goods in respect of which an offence under this section is committed shall be liable to forfeiture.

(4) In this section "agricultural levy" has the same meaning as in section 6 of the European Communities Act 1972 and the provisions of this section apply notwithstanding that any such levy may be payable to the Secretary of State, the Scottish Ministers, the National Assembly for Wales or (in relation to Northern Ireland) the Department of Agriculture and Rural Development, as the case may be.
[Customs and Excise Management Act 1979, s 68A, as inserted by the Finance Act 1982, s 11, the Criminal Justice Act 1982, s 46, the Finance Act 1988, s 12 and SI 2001/3686.]

---

1. Proceedings for an offence under the Theft Act 1968 or the Theft Act 1978 relating to agricultural levies or payments made by virtue of Community arrangements by the Intervention Board for Agricultural Produce may be instituted by the Commissioners (Finance Act 1982, s 11(1)).
2. For procedure in respect of this offence which is triable either way, see s 147, post, and the Magistrates' Courts Act 1980, ss 17A–21 in PART I: MAGISTRATES' COURTS, PROCEDURE, ante.

8–6598A

PART VI[1]
CONTROL OF COASTWISE TRAFFIC

---

1. Part VI contains ss 69–74. These sections, which are not reproduced in this work, make provision for the control of ships engaged in the trade of carrying goods coastwise between places in the UK and create a number of offences relating to such control.

PART VII[1]
CUSTOMS AND EXCISE CONTROL: SUPPLEMENTARY PROVISIONS
Special requirements as to movement of certain goods

8–6599 75. Explosives. (1) No goods which are explosives within the meaning of the Explosives Act 1875 shall be loaded into any ship or aircraft for exportation, exported by land or shipped for carriage coastwise as cargo, until due entry has been made of the goods in such form and manner and containing such particulars as the Commissioners may direct.

(2) Without prejudice to sections 53 and 60 above, any goods required to be entered under this section which are loaded, exported or shipped as mentioned in subsection (1) above without being entered under this section shall be liable to forfeiture, and the exporter or, as the case may be, shipper shall be liable on summary conviction to a penalty of **level 3** on the standard scale.
[Customs and Excise Management Act 1979, s 75 as amended by the Criminal Justice Act 1982, ss 38 and 46.]

---

1. Part VII contains ss 75–91.

Keeping and preservation of records

8–6600 75A. Records relating to importation and exportation. (1) Every person who is concerned (in whatever capacity) in the importation or exportation of goods of which for that purpose an entry is required by regulation 5 of the Customs Controls on Importation of Goods Regulations 1991 or an entry or specification is required by or under this Act shall keep such records as the Commissioners may require.

(2) The Commissioners may require any records kept in pursuance of this section to be preserved for such period not exceeding four years as they may require.

(3) The duty under this section to preserve records may be discharged by the preservation of the information contained therein by such means as the Commissioners may approve; and where that information is so preserved a copy of any document forming part of the records shall, subject to the following provisions of this section, be admissible in evidence in any proceedings, whether civil or criminal, to the same extent as the records themselves.

(4) The Commissioners may, as a condition of an approval under subsection (3) above of any means of preserving information, impose such reasonable requirements as appear to them necessary for securing that the information will be as readily available to them as if the records themselves had been preserved.

(5) The Commissioners may at any time for reasonable cause revoke or vary the conditions of any approval given under subsection (3) above.

(6) A statement contained in a document produced by a computer shall not by virtue of subsection (3) above be admissible in evidence—

(a) (*Repealed*);

(b) (*Repealed*);

(c)–(d) *Northern Ireland.*

[Customs and Excise Management Act 1979, s 75A, as inserted by the Finance Act 1987, s 9 and amended by SI 1992/3095, the Civil Evidence Act 1995, Sch 2 and the Youth Justice and Criminal Evidence Act 1999, Sch 6.]

8–6601   75B. Records relating to firearms.   (1) Every person who is concerned (in whatever capacity) in the importation or exportation of weapons or firearms within the meaning of Council Directive 91/477/EEC (control of acquisition and possession of such goods) shall keep such records as the Commissioners may require for the purposes of that Directive.

(2) Subsections (2) to (6) of section 75A above shall apply in relation to any requirement under this section and to the records kept in pursuance of this section as they apply in relation to any requirement under that section and to the records kept in pursuance of that section.

[Customs and Excise Management Act 1979, s 75B, as inserted by SI 1992/3095.]

8–6602   75C. Records relating to goods subject to certain transit arrangements.   (1) Every person who is concerned (in whatever capacity) in the importation or exportation of goods which are subject to the transit arrangements set out in Title II of Part II of Commission Regulation (EEC) No 2454/93 shall keep such records as the Commissioners may require for the purposes of Article 324 of that Regulation (verification of procedures and documents).

(2) Subsections (2) to (6) of section 75A above shall apply in relation to any requirement under this section and to the records kept in pursuance of this section as they apply in relation to any requirement under that section and to the records kept in pursuance of that section.

[Customs and Excise Management Act 1979, s 75C, as inserted by SI 1992/3095 and amended by SI 1993/3014.]

Additional provisions as to information

8–6603   77. Information in relation to goods imported or exported.   (1) An officer may require any person—

(a) concerned with the shipment for carriage coastwise of goods of which for that purpose an entry is required by regulation 5 of the Customs Controls on Importation of Goods Regulations 1991 or an entry or specification is required by or under this Act; or

(b) concerned in the carriage, unloading, landing or loading of goods which are being or have been imported or exported,

to furnish in such form as the officer may require any information relating to the goods and to produce and allow the officer to inspect and take extracts from or make copies of any invoice, bill of lading or other book or document whatsoever relating to the goods.

(2) If any person without reasonable cause fails to comply with a requirement imposed on him under subsection (1) above he shall be liable on summary conviction to a penalty of **level 3** on the standard scale.

(3) Where any prohibition or restriction to which this subsection applies, that is to say, any prohibition or restriction under or by virtue of any enactment with respect to—

(a) the exportation of goods to any particular destination; or

(b) the exportation of goods of any particular class or description to any particular destination,

is for the time being in force, then, if any person about to ship for exportation or to export any goods or, as the case may be, any goods of that class or description, in the course of making entry thereof before shipment or exportation makes a declaration as to the ultimate destination thereof, and the Commissioners have reason to suspect that the declaration is untrue in any material particular, the goods may be detained until the Commissioners are satisfied as to the truth of the declaration, and if they are not so satisfied the goods shall be liable to forfeiture.

(4) Any person concerned in the exportation of any goods which are subject to any prohibition or restriction to which subsection (3) above applies shall, if so required by the Commissioners, satisfy the Commissioners that those goods have not reached any destination other than that mentioned in the entry delivered in respect of the goods.

(5) If any person required under subsection (4) above to satisfy the Commissioners as mentioned in that subsection fails to do so, then, unless he proves—

(a) that he did not consent to or connive at the goods reaching any destination other than mentioned in the entry delivered in respect of the goods; and

(b) that he took all reasonable steps to secure that the ultimate destination of the goods was not other than that so mentioned,

he shall be liable on summary conviction to a penalty of three times the value of the goods or of **level 3** on the standard scale, whichever is the greater.

[Customs and Excise Management Act 1979, s 77 as amended by the Criminal Justice Act 1982, ss 38 and 46 and the Finance Act 1987, s 10 and Sch 16 and SI 1992/3095.]

8–6604   77A. Information powers.   (1) Every person who is concerned (in whatever capacity) in the importation or exportation of goods for which for that purpose an entry is required by regulation

5 of the Customs Controls on Importation of Goods Regulations 1991 or an entry or specification is required by or under this Act shall—

    (*a*) furnish to the Commissioners, within such time and in such form as they may reasonably require, such information relating to the goods or to the importation or exportation as the Commissioners may reasonably specify; and

    (*b*) if so required by an officer, produce or cause to be produced for inspection by the officer—

        (i) at the principal place of business of the person upon whom the demand is made or at such other place as the officer may reasonably require, and

        (ii) at such time as the officer may reasonably require,

any documents relating to the goods or to the importation or exportation.

(2) Where, by virtue of subsection (1) above, an officer has power to require the production of any documents from any such person as is referred to in that subsection, he shall have the like power to require production of the documents concerned from any other person who appears to the officer to be in possession of them; but where any such other person claims a lien on any document produced by him, the production shall be without prejudice to the lien.

(3) An officer may take copies of, or make extracts from, any document produced under subsection (1) or subsection (2) above.

(4) If it appears to him to be necessary to do so, an officer may, at a reasonable time and for a reasonable period, remove any document produced under subsection (1) or subsection (2) above and shall, on request, provide a receipt for any document so removed; and where a lien is claimed on a document produced under subsection (2) above, the removal of the document under this subsection shall not be regarded as breaking the lien.

(5) Where a document removed by an officer under subsection (4) above is reasonably required for the proper conduct of a business, the officer shall, as soon as practicable, provide a copy of the document, free of charge, to the person by whom it was produced or caused to be produced.

(6) Where any documents removed under the powers conferred by this section are lost or damaged, the Commissioners shall be liable to compensate their owner for any expenses reasonably incurred by him in replacing or repairing the documents.

(7) If any person fails to comply with a requirement under this section, he shall be liable on summary conviction to a penalty of **level 3** on the standard scale.

[Customs and Excise Management Act 1979, s 77A, as inserted by the Finance Act 1987, s 10 and amended by SI 1992/3095.]

8–6605   **77B. Information powers relating to firearms.**   (1) Every person who is concerned (in whatever capacity) in the importation or exportation of weapons or firearms within the meaning of the Directive mentioned in section 75B(1) above shall—

    (*a*) furnish to the Commissioners, within such time and in such form as they may reasonably require, such information relating to such goods or to the importation or exportation as the Commissioners may specify for the purposes of that Directive; and

    (*b*) if so required by an officer for such purposes, produce or cause to be produced for inspection by the officer—

        (i) at the principal place of business of the person upon whom the demand is made or at such other place as the officer may reasonably require, and

        (ii) at such time as the officer may reasonably require, any documents relating to such goods or to the importation or exportation.

(2) Subsections (2) to (7) of section 77A above shall apply in relation to any requirement under this section as they apply in relation to any requirement under that section.

[Customs and Excise Management Act 1979, s 77B, as inserted by SI 1992/3095.]

8–6606   **77C. Information powers relating to goods subject to certain transit arrangements.**
(1) Every person who is concerned (in whatever capacity) in the importation or exportation of goods which are subject to the transit arrangements set out in the Commission Regulation mentioned in section 75C(1) above shall—

    (*a*) furnish to the Commissioners, within such time and in such form as they may reasonably require, such information relating to the goods or to the importation or exportation as the Commissioners may specify for the purposes of Article 324 of that Regulation (verification of procedures and documents); and

    (*b*) if so required by an officer for such purposes, produce or cause to be produced for inspection by the officer—

        (i) at the principal place of business of the person upon whom the demand is made or at such other place as the officer may reasonably require, and

        (ii) at such time as the officer may reasonably require, any documents relating to such goods or to the importation or exportation.

(2) Subsections (2) to (7) of section 77A above shall apply in relation to any requirement under this section as they apply in relation to any requirement under that section.
[Customs and Excise Management Act 1979, s 77C, as inserted by SI 1992/3095 and amended by SI 1993/3014.]

8–6607 78. Customs and excise control of persons entering or leaving the United Kingdom.
(1) Any person entering the United Kingdom shall, at such place and in such manner as the Commissioners may direct, declare any thing contained in his baggage or carried with him which—

(a) he has obtained outside the United Kingdom; or

(b) being dutiable goods or chargeable goods, he has obtained in the United Kingdom without payment of duty or tax,

and in respect of which he is not entitled to exemption from duty and tax by virtue of any order under section 13 of the Customs and Excise Duties (General Reliefs) Act 1979 (personal reliefs).

In this subsection "chargeable goods" means goods on the importation of which value added tax is chargeable or goods obtained in the United Kingdom before 1st April 1973 which are chargeable goods within the meaning of the Purchase Tax Act 1963; and "tax" means value added tax or purchase tax.

(1A) *Isle of Man.*

(1B) Subsection (1) above does not apply to a person entering the United Kingdom from another member State, except—

(a) where he arrives at a customs and excise airport in an aircraft in which he began his journey in a place outside the member States; or

(b) as respects such of his baggage as—

(i) is carried in the hold of the aircraft in which he arrives at a customs and excise airport, and

(ii) notwithstanding that it was transferred on one or more occasions from aircraft to aircraft at an airport in a member State, began its journey by air from a place outside the member States.

(2) Any person entering or leaving the United Kingdom shall answer such questions as the proper officer may put to him with respect to his baggage and any thing contained therein or carried[1] with him, and shall, if required by the proper officer, produce that baggage and any such thing for examination at such place as the Commissioners may direct.

(2A) Subject to subsection (1A) above, where the journey of a person arriving by air in the United Kingdom is continued or resumed by air to a destination in the United Kingdom which is not the place where he is regarded for the purposes of this section as entering the United Kingdom, subsections (1) and (2) above shall apply in relation to that person on his arrival at that destination as they apply in relation to a person entering the United Kingdom.

(3) Any person failing to declare[2] any thing or to produce any baggage or thing as required by this section shall be liable on summary conviction to a penalty of three times the value of the thing not declared or of the baggage or thing not produced, as the case may be, or of **level 3** on the standard scale, whichever is the greater.

(4) Any thing chargeable with any duty or tax which is found concealed, or is not declared, and any thing which is being taken into or out of the United Kingdom contrary to any prohibition or restriction for the time being in force with respect thereto under or by virtue of any enactment, shall be liable to forfeiture.
[Customs and Excise Management Act 1979, s 78 as amended by the Isle of Man Act 1979, s 13 and Sch 1, the Criminal Justice Act 1982, ss 38 and 46 and the Finance (No 2) Act 1992, s 5 and SI 1992/3095.]

---

1. For this purpose anything carried with a person means carried by sea, air or train, and includes an article of clothing which the person is wearing (*R v Lucien* [1995] Crim LR 807, CA).

2. The offence created by this section is an absolute one; accordingly, an offence is committed if a person fails to declare goods, to which no exemption from duty applies, at such place as the Commissioners direct, namely in the "red channel", *R v Customs and Excise Comrs, ex p Claus* (1987) 86 Cr App Rep 189, [1987] Crim LR 756).

8–6608 83. Penalty for removing seals, etc. (1) Where, in pursuance of any power conferred by the customs and excise Acts or of any requirement imposed by or under those Acts, a seal, lock or mark is used to secure or identify any goods for any of the purposes of those Acts and—

(a) at any time while the goods are in the United Kingdom or within the limits of any port or on passage between ports in the United Kingdom, the seal, lock or mark is wilfully and prematurely removed or tampered with by any person; or

(b) at any time before the seal, lock or mark is lawfully removed, any of the goods are wilfully removed by any person,

that person and the person then in charge of the goods shall each be liable on summary conviction to a penalty of **level 4** on the standard scale.

(2) For the purposes of subsection (1) above, goods in a ship or aircraft shall be deemed to be in the charge of the master of the ship or commander of the aircraft.

(3) Where, in pursuance of any Community requirement or practice which relates to the

movement of goods between countries or of any international agreement to which the United Kingdom is a party and which so relates,—

(*a*) a seal, lock or mark is used (whether in the United Kingdom or elsewhere) to secure or identify any goods for customs or excise purposes; and

(*b*) at any time while the goods are in the United Kingdom, the seal, lock or mark is wilfully and prematurely removed or tampered with by any person.

that person and the person then in charge of the goods shall each be liable on summary conviction to a penalty of **level 4** on the standard scale.
[Customs and Excise Management Act 1979, s 83 as amended by the Criminal Justice Act 1982, s 46.]

8–6609 84. Penalty for signalling to smugglers. (1) In this section references to a "prohibited signal" or a "prohibited message" are references to a signal or message connected with the smuggling or intended smuggling of goods into or out of the United Kingdom.

(2) Any person who by any means makes any prohibited signal or transmits any prohibited message from any part of the United Kingdom or from any ship or aircraft for the information of a person in any ship or aircraft or across the boundary shall be liable on summary conviction to a penalty of **level 3** on the standard scale, or to imprisonment for a term not exceeding **6 months**, or to both, and may be detained, and any equipment or apparatus used for sending the signal or message shall be liable to forfeiture.

(3) Subsection (2) above applies whether or not the person for whom the signal or message is intended is in a position to receive it or is actually engaged at the time in smuggling goods.

(4) If, in any proceedings under subsection (2) above, any question arises as to whether any signal or message was a prohibited signal or message, the burden of proof shall lie upon the defendant or claimant.

(5) If any officer or constable or any member of Her Majesty's armed forces or coastguard has reasonable grounds for suspecting that any prohibited signal or message is being or is about to be made or transmitted from any ship, aircraft, vehicle, house or place, he may board or enter that ship, aircraft, vehicle, house or place and take such steps as are reasonably necessary to stop or prevent the sending of the signal or message.
[Customs and Excise Management Act 1979, s 84 as amended by the Criminal Justice Act 1982, ss 38 and 46.]

8–6610 85. Penalty for interfering with revenue vessels, etc. (1) Any person who save for just and sufficient cause interferes in any way with any ship, aircraft, vehicle, buoy, anchor, chain, rope or mark which is being used for the purposes of any functions of the Commissioners under Parts III to VII of this Act shall be liable on summary conviction to a penalty of **level 1** on the standard scale.

(2) Any person who fires upon any vessel, aircraft or vehicle in the service of Her Majesty while that vessel, aircraft or vehicle is engaged in the prevention of smuggling shall be liable on conviction on indictment to imprisonment for a term not exceeding **5 years**.
[Customs and Excise Management Act 1979, s 85 as amended by the Criminal Justice Act 1982, s 46.]

8–6611 86. Special penalty where offender armed or disguised. Any person concerned in the movement, carriage or concealment of goods—

(*a*) contrary to or for the purpose of contravening any prohibition or restriction for the time being in force under or by virtue of any enactment with respect to the importation or exportation thereof; or

(*b*) without payment having been made of or security given for any duty payable thereon,

who, while so concerned, is armed[1] with any offensive weapon or disguised in any way, and any person so armed or disguised found in the United Kingdom in possession of any goods liable to forfeiture under any provision of the customs and excise Acts relating to imported goods or prohibited or restricted goods, shall be liable on conviction on indictment to imprisonment for a term not exceeding **3 years** and may be arrested.
[Customs and Excise Management Act 1979, s 86 as amended by the Police and Criminal Evidence Act 1984, s 114.]

---

1. "Armed" should be given its ordinary meaning and involves either physically carrying arms or proof that the defendant knows that they are immediately available; but it is not necessary for the prosecution to prove an intent to use the offensive weapon (*R v Jones* [1987] 2 All ER 692, [1987] 1 WLR 692, CA).

8–6612 87. Penalty for offering goods for sale as smuggled goods. If any person offers any goods for sale as having been imported without payment of duty, or as having been otherwise unlawfully imported, then, whether or not the goods were so imported or were in fact chargeable with duty, the goods shall be liable to forfeiture and the person so offering them for sale shall be liable on summary conviction to a penalty of three times the value of the goods or of **level 3** on the standard scale, whichever is the greater, and may be arrested.
[Customs and Excise Management Act 1979, s 87 as amended by the Criminal Justice Act 1982, ss 38 and 46 and the Police and Criminal Evidence Act 1984, s 114.]

PART VIII[1]
WAREHOUSES AND QUEEN'S WAREHOUSES AND RELATED PROVISIONS ABOUT PIPE-LINES

8–6613   100. General offences relating to warehouses and warehoused goods.   (1) Any person who, except with the authority of the proper officer or for just and sufficient cause, opens any of the doors or locks of a warehouse or Queen's warehouse or makes or obtains access to any such warehouse or to any goods warehoused therein shall be liable on summary conviction to a penalty of **level 5** on the standard scale and may be arrested.

(2)   Where—

(a)   any goods which have been entered for warehousing or are otherwise required to be deposited in a warehouse are taken into the warehouse without the authority of, or otherwise than in accordance with any directions given by, the proper officer; or

(b)   save as permitted by the Customs and Excise Acts 1979 or by or under warehousing regulations, any goods which have been entered for warehousing or are otherwise required to be deposited in a warehouse are removed without being duly warehoused or are otherwise not duly warehoused; or

(c)   any goods which have been deposited in a warehouse or Queen's warehouse are unlawfully removed therefrom or are unlawfully loaded into any ship, aircraft or vehicle for removal or for exportation or use as stores; or

(d)   any goods are concealed at a time before they are warehoused when they have been entered for warehousing or are otherwise required to be deposited in a warehouse or when they are required to be in the custody or under the control of the occupier of a warehouse; or

(e)   any goods which have been lawfully permitted to be removed from a warehouse or Queen's warehouse without payment of duty for any purpose are not duly delivered at the destination to which they should have been taken in accordance with that permission,

those goods shall be liable to forfeiture.

(3)   If any person who took, removed, loaded or concealed any goods as mentioned in subsection (2) above did so with intent to defraud Her Majesty of any duty chargeable thereon or to evade any prohibition or restriction for the time being in force with respect thereto under or by virtue of any enactment, he shall be guilty of an offence under this subsection and may be arrested.

(4)   A person guilty of an offence under subsection (3) above shall be liable—

(a)   on summary conviction, to a penalty of **the prescribed sum**[2] or of three times the value of the goods, whichever is the greater, or to imprisonment for a term not exceeding **6 months**, or to both; or

(b)   on conviction on indictment, to a penalty of any amount, or to imprisonment for a term not exceeding **7 years**, or to both.

[Customs and Excise Management Act 1979, s 100 as amended by the Criminal Justice Act 1982, ss 38 and 46, the Police and Criminal Evidence Act 1984, s 114, the Finance Act 1988, s 12 and the Finance (No 2) Act 1992, Sch 2.]

---

1. Part VIII contains ss 92–100.
2. For the meaning of the "prescribed sum", see s 171 post.

PART VIIIA[1]
FREE ZONES

8–6614   100A. Designation of free zones.   (1) The Treasury may by order[2] designate any area in the United Kingdom as a special area for customs purposes.

(2)   An area so designated shall be known as a "free zone".

(3)   An order under subsection (1) above—

(a)   shall have effect for such period as shall be specified in the order;

(b)   may be made so as to take effect, in relation to the area or any part of the area designated by a previous order under this section, on the expiry of the period specified in the previous order;

(c)   shall appoint one or more persons as the responsible authority or authorities for the free zone;

(d)   may impose on any responsible authority such conditions or restrictions as may be specified; and

(e)   may be revoked if the Commissioners are satisfied that there has been a failure to comply with any condition or restriction.

(4)   The Treasury may by order—

(a)   from time to time vary—

(i)   the conditions or restrictions imposed by a designation order; or

(ii)   with the agreement of the responsible authority, the area designated; or

(b)   appoint one or more persons as the responsible authority or authorities for a free zone either in addition to or in substitution for any person appointed as such by a designation order.

(5)   In this Act "designation order" means an order made under subsection (1) above.

(6) Any order under this section shall be made by statutory instrument.

[Customs and Excise Management Act 1979, s 100A, as inserted by the Finance Act 1984, Sch 4.]

---

1. Part VIIIA was inserted by the Finance Act 1984, Sch 4, and contains ss 100A–100F.

2. The following designation orders have been made: SI 1984/1206 amended by SI 1986/1643 (Belfast Airport); SI 1984/1208 (Cardiff); SI 1991/1737 (Birmingham); SI 1991/1738 (Liverpool); SI 1991/1739 amended by SI 1994/143 (Prestwick Airport); SI 1991/1740 amended by SI 1994/1410 and SI 1996/2615 (Southampton); SI 1992/1282 amended by SI 1994/2216 (Port of Tilbury); SI 1994/144 (Humberside); SI 1994/2509 (Birmingham Airport); SI 1994/2898 (Port of Sheerness).

8–6615   100B–100E. *(Repealed).*

8–6619   100F. Powers of search. (1) Any person entering or leaving a free zone shall answer such questions as any officer may put to him with respect to any goods and shall, if required by the officer, produce those goods for examination at such place as the Commissioners may direct.

(2) At any time while a vehicle is entering or leaving a free zone, any officer may board the vehicle and search any part of it.

(3) Any officer may at any time enter upon and inspect a free zone and all buildings and goods within the zone.

[Customs and Excise Management Act 1979, s 100F, as inserted by the Finance Act 1984, Sch 4.]

PART VIIIB[1]
REGISTERED EXCISE DEALERS AND SHIPPERS

8–6620   100G–100H. Registered excise dealers and shippers. *Power of the Commissioners to make regulations[2] for the purpose of administering, collecting or protecting the revenues derived from duties of excise.*

---

1. Part VIIIB, inserted by the Finance Act 1991, s 11 and Sch 4, contains ss 100G–100J.

2. See the Excise Goods (Holding, Movement, Warehousing and REDS) Regulations 1992, SI 1992/3135 amended by SI 2002/501, SI 2004/1003 and SI 2005/3472, the Beer Regulations 1993, SI 1993/1228 amended by SI 2002/501 and 1265 and SI 2004/1003, the Warehousekeepers and Owners of Warehoused Goods Regulations 1999, SI 1999/1278 amended by SI 2002/501 and SI 2005/3472, the Excise Goods (Export Shops) Regulations 2000, SI 2000/645, the Tobacco Products Regulations 2001, SI 2001/1712 amended by SI 2004/1003, the Excise Duty Points (Duty Suspended Movements of Excise Goods) Regulations 2001, SI 2001/3022, the Excise Goods (Accompanying Documents) Regulations 2002, SI 2002/501, the Hydrocarbon Oil (Registered Dealers in Controlled Oil) Regulations 2002, SI 2002/3057, the Excise Warehousing (Energy Products) Regulations 2004, SI 2004/2064, the Biofuels and Other Fuel Substitutes (Payment of Excise Duty etc) Regulations 2004, SI 2004/2065 and the Hydrocarbon Oil (Registered Remote Markers) Regulations 2005, SI 2005/3472.

8–6621   100J. Contravention of regulations etc. If any person contravenes any provision of registered excise dealers and shippers regulations or fails to comply with any condition or restriction which the Commissioners impose upon him under section 100G above or by or under any such regulations, his contravention or failure to comply shall attract a penalty under section 9 of the Finance Act 1994 (civil penalties), and any goods in respect of which any person contravenes any provision of any such regulations, or fails to comply with any such condition or restriction, shall be liable to forfeiture.

[Customs and Excise Management Act 1979, s 100J, as inserted by the Finance Act 1991, Sch 4 and the Finance Act 1994, Sch 4.]

PART IX[1]
CONTROL OF EXCISE LICENCE TRADES AND REVENUE TRADERS

Excise licences—general provisions

8–6622   101. Excise licences. (1) An excise licence shall be in such form and contain such particulars as the Commissioners may direct and, subject to the provisions of any enactment relating to any licence or trade in question, may be granted by the proper officer on payment of the appropriate duty.

(2) An excise licence for the carrying on of a trade shall be granted in respect of one set of premises only, but a licence for the same trade may be granted to the same person in respect of each of two or more sets of premises.

(3) Where an excise licence trade is carried on at any set of premises by two or more persons in partnership, then, subject to the provisions of any enactment relating to the licence or trade in question, not more than one licence shall be required to be held by those persons in respect of those premises at any one time.

(4) Without prejudice to any other requirement as to the production of licences contained in the Customs and Excise Acts 1979, if any person who is the holder of an excise licence to carry on any trade or to manufacture or sell any goods fails to produce his licence for examination within one month after being so requested by an officer his failure shall attract a penalty under section 9 of the Finance Act 1994 (civil penalties).

[Customs and Excise Management Act 1979, s 101 as amended by the Criminal Justice Act 1982, s 46, the Finance Act 1986, Sch 5 and the Finance Act 1994, Sch 4.]

---

1. Part IX contains ss 101–118.

8–6623 102. Payment for excise licences by cheque. (1) Any government department or local authority having power to grant an excise licence may, if they think fit, grant the licence upon receipt of a cheque for the amount of any duty payable thereon.

(2) Where a licence is granted to any person on receipt of a cheque and the cheque is subsequently dishonoured, the licence shall be void as from the time when it was granted, and the department or authority who granted it shall send to that person, by letter sent by registered post or the recorded delivery service and addressed to him at the address given by him when applying for the licence, a notice requiring him to deliver up the licence within the period of 7 days from the date when the notice was posted.

(3) If a person who has been required under subsection (2) above to deliver up a licence fails to comply with the requirement[1] within the period mentioned in that subsection he shall be liable on summary conviction to a penalty of the following amount, that is to say—

(*a*) where the licence is a gaming licence or an amusement machine licence, a penalty of **level 5** on the standard scale;

(*aa*) where the licence is a licence under the Vehicle Excise and Registration Act 1994, a penalty of whichever is the greater of—

(i) **level 3** on the standard scale, or

(ii) an amount equal to five times the annual rate of duty that was payable on the grant of the licence or would have been so payable if it had been taken out for a period of twelve months.

(*b*) in any other case, a penalty of **level 3** on the standard scale.

[Customs and Excise Management Act 1979, s 102 as amended by the Criminal Justice Act 1982, ss 38 and 46, the Finance Act 1986, Sch 5, the Finance Act 1987, Sch 1, the Vehicle Excise and Registration Act 1994, Sch 3 and the Finance Act 1995, Sch 3.]

---

1. It is sufficient to establish the offence for the prosecution to prove that the notice requiring the defendant to deliver up the licence was sent to him by letter sent by registered post or recorded delivery and addressed to him at the address given by him when applying for the licence. It is not necessary also to prove that the notice was actually brought to the attention of the defendant (*Department of Transport v Ladd* (1995) Times, 29 May).

PART IXA[1]
PROTECTION OF THE REVENUES DERIVED FROM EXCISE DUTIES

8–6627 118A. Duty of revenue traders to keep records. (1) The Commissioners may by regulations[2] require every revenue trader—

(*a*) to keep such records as may be prescribed in the regulations; and

(*b*) to preserve those records for such period not exceeding six years as may be prescribed in the regulations or for such lesser period as the Commissioners may require.

(2) Regulations under this section—

(*a*) may make different provision for different cases; and

(*b*) may be framed by reference to such records as may be specified in any notice published by the Commissioners in pursuance of the regulations and not withdrawn by a further notice.

(3) Any duty imposed under this section to preserve records may be discharged by the preservation of the information contained therein by such means as the Commissioners may approve.

(4) Where any information is preserved in accordance with subsection (3) above, a copy of any document forming part of the records in question shall, subject to the following provisions of this section, be admissible in evidence in any proceedings, whether civil or criminal, to the same extent as the records themselves.

(5) The Commissioners may, as a condition of approving under subsection (3) above any means of preserving information contained in any records, impose such reasonable requirements as appear to them necessary for securing that the information will be as readily available to them as if the records themselves had been preserved.

(6) A statement contained in a document produced by a computer shall not by virtue of subsection (4) above be admissible in evidence—

(*a*) (*Repealed*);

(*b*) in criminal proceedings in England and Wales, except in accordance with Part II of the Criminal Justice Act 1988;

(*c*)–(*f*) *Scotland and Northern Ireland.*

(7) (*Repealed*).

[Customs and Excise Management Act 1979, s 118A, as inserted by the Finance Act 1991, Sch 5 and amended by the Finance Act 1994, s 256 and Sch 26, the Civil Evidence Act 1995, Sch 2 and Youth Justice and Criminal Evidence Act 1999, Sch 6.]

---

1. Part IXA inserted by the Finance Act 1991, s 12 and Sch 5, contains ss 118A–118G.
2. The the Beer Regulations 1993, SI 1993/1228 amended by SI 2002/501 and 1265 and SI 2004/1003, the Revenue Traders (Accounts and Records) Regulations 1993, SI 1993/3150, the Aircraft Operators (Accounts and Records) Regulations 1994, SI 1994/1734 amended by SI 2001/837, the Other Fuel Substitutes (Payment of Excise Duty etc) Regulations 1995, SI 1995/2717, the Excise Goods (Sales on Board Ships and Aircraft) Regulations 1999, SI 1999/1565 amended by SI 2005/3472, the Tobacco Products Regulations 2001, SI 2001/1712, the Excise Goods (Accompanying Documents) Regulations 2002, SI 2002/501, the Biofuels and Other Fuel Substitutes (Payment of Excise Duty etc) Regulations 2004, SI 2004/2065 and the Duty Stamps Regulations 2006, SI 2006/202 have been made.

8–6628   118B. Duty of revenue traders and others to furnish information and produce documents.   (1) Every revenue trader shall—

(a) furnish to the Commissioners, within such time and in such form as they may reasonably require, such information relating to—

(i) any goods or services supplied by or to him in the course or furtherance of a business, or

(ii) any goods in the importation or exportation of which he is concerned in the course or furtherance of a business, or

(iii) any transaction or activity effected or taking place in the course or furtherance of a business,

as they may reasonably specify; and

(b) upon demand made by an officer, produce or cause to be produced for inspection by that officer—

(i) at the principal place of business of the revenue trader or at such other place as the officer may reasonably require, and

(ii) at such time as the officer may reasonably require,

any documents relating to the goods or services or to the supply, importation or exportation or to the transaction or activity.

(2) Where, by virtue of subsection (1) above, an officer has power to require the production of any documents from a revenue trader—

(a) he shall have the like power to require production of the documents concerned from any other person who appears to the officer to be in possession of them; but

(b) if that other person claims a lien on any document produced by him, the production shall be without prejudice to the lien.

(3) For the purposes of this section, the documents relating to the supply of goods or services, or the importation or exportation of goods, in the course or furtherance of any business, or to any transaction or activity effected or taking place in the course or furtherance of any business, shall be taken to include—

(a) any profit and loss account and balance sheet, and

(b) any records required to be kept by virtue of section 118A above,

relating to that business.

(4) An officer may take copies of, or make extracts from, any document produced under subsection (1) or (2) above.

(5) If it appears to an officer to be necessary to do so, he may, at a reasonable time and for a reasonable period, remove any document produced under subsection (1) or (2) above and shall, on request, provide a receipt for any document so removed.

(6) Where a lien is claimed on a document produced under subsection (2) above, the removal of the document under subsection (5) above shall not be regarded as breaking the lien.

(7) Where a document removed by an officer under subsection (5) above is reasonably required for the proper conduct of a business he shall, as soon as practicable, provide a copy of the document, free of charge, to the person by whom it was produced or caused to be produced.

(8) Where any documents removed under the powers conferred by this section are lost or damaged, the Commissioners shall be liable to compensate their owner for any expenses reasonably incurred by him in replacing or repairing the documents.

[Customs and Excise Management Act 1979, s 118B, as inserted by the Finance Act 1991, Sch 5 and amended by the Finance Act 1997, Sch 2.]

8–6629   118C. Entry and search of premises and persons.   (1) For the purpose of exercising any powers under the customs and excise Acts an officer may at any reasonable time enter premises used in connection with the carrying on of a business.

(2) Where an officer has reasonable cause to believe that any premises are used in connection with the supply, importation or exportation of goods of a class or description chargeable with a duty of excise and that any such goods are on those premises, he may at any reasonable time enter and inspect those premises and inspect any goods found on them.

(2A) Where an officer has reasonable cause to believe that any premises are premises where gaming to which section 10 of the Finance Act 1997 (gaming duty) applies is taking place, has taken place or is about to take place, he may at any reasonable time enter and inspect those premises and inspect any relevant materials found on them.

(2B) In subsection (2A) above "relevant materials" means—

(*a*) any accounts, records or other documents found on the premises in the custody or control of any person who is engaging, or whom the officer reasonably suspects of engaging—

(i) in any such gaming, or

(ii) in any activity by reason of which he is or may become liable to gaming duty,

and

(*b*) any equipment which is being, or which the officer reasonably suspects of having been or of being intended to be, used on the premises for or in connection with any such gaming.

(3) If a justice of the peace or, in Scotland, a justice (within the meaning of section 307 of the Criminal Procedure (Scotland) Act 1995) is satisfied on information on oath—

(*a*) that there is reasonable ground for suspecting that a fraud offence which appears to be of a serious nature is being, has been or is about to be committed on any premises, or

(*b*) that evidence of the commission of such an offence is to be found there, or

(*c*) that there is reasonable ground for suspecting—

(i) that gaming to which section 10 of the Finance Act 1997 applies is taking place, has taken place or is about to take place on any premises, or

(ii) that evidence of the commission of a gaming duty offence is to be found there,

he may issue a warrant in writing authorising, subject to subsections (6) and (7) below, any officer to enter those premises, if necessary by force, at any time within the period of one month beginning with the date of the issue of the warrant and search them.

(4) Any officer who enters premises under the authority of a warrant under subsection (3) above may—

(*a*) take with him such other persons as appear to him to be necessary;

(*b*) seize and remove any documents or other things whatsoever found on the premises which he has reasonable cause to believe may be required as evidence for the purposes of proceedings in respect of a fraud offence which appears to him to be of a serious nature or in respect of a gaming duty offence; and

(*c*) search or cause to be searched any person found on the premises whom he has reasonable cause to believe to be in possession of any such documents or other things;

but no woman or girl shall be searched by virtue of this subsection except by a woman.

(5) In subsections (3) and (4) above "a fraud offence" means an offence under any provision of section 167(1), 168 or 170 below and "a gaming duty offence" means an offence under paragraph 12(2) of Schedule 1 to the Finance Act 1997 (offences in connection with gaming duty).

(6) The powers conferred by a warrant under this section shall not be exercisable—

(*a*) by more than such number of officers as may be specified in the warrant; nor

(*b*) outside such times of day as may be so specified; nor

(*c*) if the warrant so provides, otherwise than in the presence of a constable in uniform.

(7) An officer seeking to exercise the powers conferred by a warrant under this section or, if there is more than one such officer, that one of them who is in charge of the search shall provide a copy of the warrant endorsed with his name as follows—

(*a*) if the occupier of the premises concerned is present at the time the search is to begin, the copy shall be supplied to the occupier;

(*b*) if at the time the occupier is not present but a person who appears to the officer to be in charge of the premises is present, the copy shall be supplied to that person; and

(*c*) if neither paragraph (*a*) nor paragraph (*b*) above applies, the copy shall be left in a prominent place on the premises.

[Customs and Excise Management Act 1979, s 118C, as inserted by the Finance Act 1991, Sch 5 and amended by the Criminal Procedure (Consequential Provisions) (Scotland) Act 1995, Sch 4 and the Finance Act 1997, Sch 2.]

8–6630 **118D. Order for access to recorded information, etc.** (1) Where, on an application by an officer, a justice of the peace or, in Scotland, a justice (within the meaning of section 307 of the Criminal Procedure (Scotland) Act 1995) is satisfied that there are reasonable grounds for believing[1]—

(*a*) that an offence in connection with a duty of excise is being, has been or is about to be committed, and

(*b*) that any recorded information (including any document of any nature whatsoever) which may be required as evidence for the purpose of any proceedings in respect of such an offence is in the possession of any person, he may make an order under this section.

(2) An order under this section is an order that the person who appears to the justice to be in possession of the recorded information to which the application relates shall—

(a) give an officer access to it, and

(b) permit an officer to remove and take away any of it which he reasonably considers necessary,

not later than the end of the period of seven days beginning with the date of the order or the end of such longer period as the order may specify.

(3) The reference to subsection (2)(a) above to giving an officer access to the recorded information to which the application relates includes a reference to permitting the officer to take copies of it or to make extracts from it.

(4) Where the recorded information consists of information stored in any electronic form, an order under this section shall have effect as an order to produce the information in a form in which it is visible and legible or from which it can readily be produced in a visible and legible form and, if the officer wishes to remove it, in a form in which it can be removed.

(5) This section is without prejudice to sections 118B and 118C above.

[Customs and Excise Management Act 1991, s 118D, as inserted by the Finance Act 1991, Sch 5 and amended by the Criminal Procedure (Consequential Provisions) (Scotland) Act 1995, Sch 4 and the Criminal Justice and Police Act 2001, Sch 2.]

1. The magistrate himself must be satisfied that all the criteria are met; it is not sufficient that the person making the application is so satisfied *R v Thames Magistrates' Court, ex p Hormoz* (1998) 163 JP 19, [1998] Crim LR 732, DC (magistrate erroneously relied on the suspicion of the applicant that money had been received by the company whose premises were to searched).

8–6631 118E. Procedure when documents etc are removed. (1) An officer who removes anything in the exercise of a power conferred by or under section 118C or 118D above shall, if so requested by a person showing himself—

(a) to be the occupier of premises from which it was removed, or

(b) to have had custody or control of it immediately before the removal,

provide that person with a record of what he removed.

(2) The officer shall provide the record within a reasonable time from the making of the request for it.

(3) Subject to subsection (7) below, if a request for permission to be granted access to anything which—

(a) has been removed by an officer, and

(b) is retained by the Commissioners for the purposes of investigating an offence,

is made to the officer in overall charge of the investigation by a person who had custody or control of the thing immediately before it was so removed or by someone acting on behalf of such a person, the officer shall allow the person who made the request access to it under the supervision of an officer.

(4) Subject to subsection (7) below, if a request for a photograph or copy of any such thing is made to the officer in overall charge of the investigation by a person who had custody or control of the thing immediately before it was so removed, or by someone acting on behalf of such a person, the officer shall—

(a) allow the person who made the request access to it under the supervision of an officer for the purpose of photographing it or copying it, or

(b) photograph or copy it, or cause it to be photographed or copied.

(5) Where anything is photographed or copied under subsection (4)(b) above, the photograph or copy shall be supplied to the person who made the request.

(6) The photograph or copy shall be supplied within a reasonable time from the making of the request.

(7) There is no duty under this section to grant access to, or to supply a photograph or copy of, anything if the officer in overall charge of the investigation for the purposes of which it was removed has reasonable grounds for believing that to do so would prejudice—

(a) that investigation;

(b) the investigation of an offence other than the offence for the purposes of the investigation of which the thing was removed; or

(c) any criminal proceedings which may be brought as a result of—

(i) the investigation of which he is in charge; or

(ii) any such investigation as is mentioned in paragraph (b) above.

(8) Any reference in this section to the officer in overall charge of the investigation is a reference to the person whose name and address are endorsed on the warrant or order concerned as being the officer so in charge.

[Customs and Excise Management Act 1979, s 118E, as inserted by the Finance Act 1991, Sch 5.]

8–6632   118F. Failure of officer to comply with requirements under section 118E.
(1) Where, on an application made as mentioned in subsection (2) below, the appropriate judicial authority is satisfied that a person has failed to comply with a requirement imposed by section 118E above, the authority may order that person to comply with the requirement within such time and in such manner as may be specified in the order.

(2) An application under subsection (1) above shall be made—

(*a*) in the case of a failure to comply with any of the requirements imposed by subsections (1) and (2) of section 118E above, by the occupier of the premises from which the thing in question was removed or by the person who had custody or control of it immediately before it was so removed, and

(*b*) in any other case, by the person who has such custody or control.

(3) In this section "the appropriate judicial authority" means—

(*a*) in England and Wales, a magistrates' court;
(*b*) *Scotland*; and
(*c*) *Northern Ireland*.

(4) Any application for an order under this section—

(*a*) in England and Wales, shall be made by way of complaint; or
(*b*) *Northern Ireland*.

(5) *Northern Ireland*.

[Customs and Excise Management Act 1979, s 118F, as inserted by the Finance Act 1991, Sch 5.]

8–6633   118G. Offences under Part IXA.   If any person fails to comply with any requirement imposed under section 118A(1) or section 118B above, his failure to comply shall attract a penalty under section 9 of the Finance Act 1994 (civil penalties) and, in the case of any failure to keep records, shall also attract daily penalties.

[Customs and Excise Management Act 1979, s 118G, as inserted by the Finance Act 1991, Sch 5 and amended by the Finance Act 1994, s 256 and Sch 26.]

PART X[1]
DUTIES AND DRAWBACKS—GENERAL PROVISIONS
General provisions relating to imported goods

8–6635   125. Valuation of goods for purpose of ad valorem duties.   (1) For the purposes of any duty for the time being chargeable on any imported goods by reference to their value (whether a Community customs duty or not), the value of the goods shall, subject to subsection (2) below, be taken according to the rules applicable in the case of Community customs duties, and duty shall be paid on that value.

(2) In relation to an importation in the course of trade within the Communities the value of any imported goods for the purposes mentioned in subsection (1) above shall be determined on the basis of a delivery to the buyer at the port or place of importation into the United Kingdom.

(3) The Commissioners may make regulations for the purpose of giving effect to the foregoing provisions of this section, and in particular for requiring any importer or other person concerned with the importation of goods—

(*a*) to furnish to the Commissioners in such form as they may require, such information as is in their opinion necessary for a proper valuation of the goods; and

(*b*) to produce any books of account or other documents of whatever nature relating to the purchase, importation or sale of the goods by that person.

(4) If any person contravenes or fails to comply with any regulation made under subsection (3) above he shall be liable on summary conviction to a penalty of **level 3** on the standard scale.

[Customs and Excise Management Act 1979, s 125 as amended by the Criminal Justice Act 1982, ss 38 and 46.]

---

1. Part X contains ss 119–137.

Drawbacks, allowances, duties, etc—general

8–6636   136. Offences in connection with claims for drawback, etc.   (1) If any person, with intent to defraud Her Majesty, obtains or attempts to obtain, or does anything whereby there might be obtained by any person, any amount by way of drawback, allowance, remission or repayment of, or any rebate from, any duty in respect of any goods which—

(*a*) is not lawfully payable or allowable in respect thereof; or
(*b*) is greater than the amount so payable or allowable,

he shall be guilty of an offence under this subsection.

(1A) If any person, without such intent as is mentioned in subsection (1) above, does any of the things there mentioned, he shall be guilty of an offence under this subsection.

(2) A person guilty of an offence under subsection (1) above shall be liable[1]—

(a) on summary conviction, to a penalty of **the prescribed sum** or of **three times the value** of the goods, whichever is the greater, or to imprisonment for a term not exceeding **6 months**, or to both; or

(b) on conviction on indictment, to a penalty of any amount, or to imprisonment for a term not exceeding **7 years**, or to both;

and a person guilty of an offence under subsection (1A) above shall be liable on summary conviction to a penalty of **level 3** on the standard scale or three times the amount which was or might have been improperly obtained or allowed, whichever is the greater.

(3) Any goods in respect of which an offence under subsection (1) or (1A) above is committed shall be liable to forfeiture; but in the case of a claim for drawback, the Commissioners may, if they see fit, instead of seizing the goods either refuse to allow any drawback thereon or allow only such drawback as they consider proper.

(4) Without prejudice to the foregoing provisions of this section, if, in the case of any goods upon which a claim for drawback, allowance, remission or repayment of duty has been made, it is found that those goods do not correspond with any entry made thereof in connection with that claim, the goods shall be liable to forfeiture and any person by whom any such entry or claim was made shall be liable on summary conviction to a penalty of three times the amount or of **level 3** on the standard scale, whichever is the greater.

(5) Subsection (4) above applies in the case of any goods upon which a claim for drawback, allowance, remission or repayment of duty has been made where it is found that the goods, if sold for home use, would realise less than the amount claimed as it applies where the finding specified in that subsection is made except that it does not apply by virtue of this subsection to any claim under—

(a) section 123 or 134(2) above; or

(b) section 46, 61 or 64 of the Alcoholic Liquor Duties Act 1979 (remission or repayment of duty on certain spoilt liquors).

(6) Without prejudice to section 6(5) of the European Communities Act 1972 (which provides for the application of certain enactments, including this section, if the Commissioners are charged or entrusted with the performance of certain duties in relation to the payment of refunds or allowances on goods exported or to be exported from the United Kingdom)—

(a) references in this section to amounts by way of drawback include amounts payable by or on behalf of the Secretary of State, the Scottish Ministers, the National Assembly for Wales or (in relation to Northern Ireland) the Department of Agriculture and Rural Development by virtue of Community arrangements to which section 6(3) of the European Communities Act 1972 applies; and

(b) in relation to such amounts, subsection (3) above shall have effect with the omission of the words from "but in the case" onwards.

[Customs and Excise Management Act 1979, s 136 as amended by the Finance Act 1982, s 11, the Criminal Justice Act 1982, ss 38 and 46, the Finance Act 1988, s 12 and SI 2001/3686.]

---

1. For procedure in respect of this offence which is triable either way, see s 147, post, and the Magistrates' Courts Act 1980, ss 17A–21 in PART I: MAGISTRATES' COURTS, PROCEDURE, ANTE.

PART XI[1]

ARREST OF PERSONS, FORFEITURE AND LEGAL PROCEEDINGS

Arrest of persons

8–6637   138. Provisions as to arrest of persons.   (1) Any person who has committed, or whom there are reasonable grounds to suspect of having committed, any offence for which he is liable to be arrested[2] under the customs and excise Acts may be arrested[3] by any officer or any member of Her Majesty's armed forces or coastguard at any time within 20 years from the date of the commission of the offence.

(2) Where it was not practicable to arrest any person so liable at the time of the commission of the offence, or where any such person having been then or subsequently arrested for that offence has escaped, he may be arrested by any officer or any member of Her Majesty's armed forces or coastguard at any time and may be proceeded against in like manner as if the offence had been committed at the date when he was finally arrested.

(3) Where any person who is a member of the crew of any ship in Her Majesty's employment or service is arrested by an officer for an offence under the customs and excise Acts, the commanding officer of the ship shall, if so required by the arresting officer, keep that person secured on board that ship until he can be brought before a court and shall then deliver him up to the proper officer.

(4) Where any person has been arrested by a person who is not an officer—

(a) by virtue of this section; or

(b) by virtue of section 24 of the Police and Criminal Evidence Act 1984 in its application to offences under the customs and excise Acts,

the person arresting him shall give notice of the arrest to an officer at the nearest convenient office of customs and excise.

[Customs and Excise Management Act 1979, s 138 as amended by the Police and Criminal Evidence Act 1984, s 114, and Schs 6 and 7 and the Finance Act 1988, s 11.]

1. Part XI contains ss 138–156.
2. Such offences are arrestable offences by virtue of Sch 1A to the Police and Criminal Evidence Act 1984.
3. Neither customs officers nor police officers have any right to detain somebody for the purpose of getting them to help with their inquiries; see *R v Lemsatef* [1977] 2 All ER 835, 141 JP 462.

Forfeiture

8–6638 **139. Provisions as to detention, seizure and condemnation of goods, etc[1].** (1) Any thing liable to forfeiture under the customs and excise Acts may be seized or detained[2] by any officer or constable or any member of Her Majesty's armed forces or coastguard.

(2) Where any thing is seized or detained as liable to forfeiture under the customs and excise Acts by a person other than an officer, that person shall, subject to subsection (3) below, either—

(a) deliver that thing to the nearest convenient office of customs and excise; or
(b) if such delivery is not practicable, give to the Commissioners at the nearest convenient office of customs and excise notice in writing of the seizure or detention with full particulars of the thing seized or detained.

(3) Where the person seizing or detaining any thing as liable to forfeiture under the customs and excise Acts is a constable and that thing is or may be required for use in connection with any proceedings to be brought otherwise than under those Acts it may, subject to sub-section (4) below, be retained in the custody of the police until either those proceedings are completed or it is decided that no such proceedings shall be brought.

(4) The following provisions apply in relation to things retained in the custody of the police by virtue of subsection (3) above, that is to say—

(a) notice in writing of the seizure or detention and of the intention to retain the thing in question in the custody of the police, together with full particulars as to that thing, shall be given to the Commissioners at the nearest convenient office of customs and excise;
(b) any officer shall be permitted to examine that thing and take account thereof at any time while it remains in the custody of the police;
(c) nothing in the Police (Property) Act 1897[3] shall apply in relation to that thing.

(5) Subject to subsections (3) and (4) above and to Schedule 3 to this Act, any thing seized or detained under the customs and excise Acts shall, pending the determination as to its forfeiture or disposal, be dealt with, and, if condemned or deemed to have been condemned or forfeited, shall be disposed of in such manner as the Commissioners may direct.

(6) Schedule 3[4] to this Act shall have effect for the purpose of forfeitures, and of proceedings for the condemnation of any thing as being forfeited, under the customs and excise Acts.

(7) If any person, not being an officer, by whom any thing is seized or detained or who has custody thereof after its seizure or detention, fails to comply with any requirement of this section or with any direction of the Commissioners given thereunder, he shall be liable on summary conviction to a penalty of **level 2** on the standard scale.

(8) Subsections (2) to (7) above shall apply in relation to any dutiable goods seized or detained by any person other than an officer notwithstanding that they were not so seized as liable to forfeiture under the customs and excise Acts.

[Customs and Excise Management Act 1979, s 139 as amended by the Criminal Justice Act 1982, s 46.]

1. By virtue of the Customs and Excise (Community Transit) (No 2) Regulations 1987, this title, post, reg 5(1), this section and Sch 3, post, apply to any goods liable to forfeiture under reg 4 of those Regulations.
2. For the distinction between 'seized' and 'detained' see the comments of Harrison J in *Customs and Excise Comrs v Venn* [2001] EWHC Admin 1055, 166 JP 53. 'Detained' connotes that a person already has possession of the thing which has already come into the possession of Customs and Excise other than through a seizure under s 139 of the 1979 Act, eg under the Police and Criminal Evidence Act 1984.
3. See title, POLICE, post.
4. See, post.

8–6639 **140. Forfeiture of spirits.** Where, by any provision of, or of any instrument made under, the Customs and Excise Acts 1979, any spirits become liable to forfeiture by reason of some offence committed by a revenue trader, then—

(a) where that provision specifies the quantity of those spirits but does not specify the spirits so liable, the Commissioners may seize the equivalent of that quantity . . . from any spirits in the stock of that trader; and
(b) where that provision specifies the spirits so liable the Commissioners may, if they think fit, seize instead of the spirits so specified an equivalent quantity . . . of any other spirits in the stock of that trader.

[Customs and Excise Management Act 1979, s 140, as amended by SI 1979/241.]

8-6640 141. Forfeiture of ships, etc used in connection with goods liable to forfeiture.
(1) Without prejudice to any other provision of the Customs and Excise Acts 1979, where any thing has become liable to forfeiture under the customs and excise Acts—

    (a) any ship[1], aircraft, vehicle, animal, container (including any article of passengers' baggage) or other thing whatsoever which has been used[2] for the carriage[3], handling, deposit or concealment of the thing so liable to forfeiture, either at a time when it was so liable or for the purposes of the commission of the offence for which it later became so liable; and

    (b) any other thing[4] mixed, packed or found with the thing so liable[5],

shall also be liable to forfeiture[6].

(2) Where any ship, aircraft, vehicle or animal has become liable to forfeiture under the customs and excise Acts, whether by virtue of subsection (1) above or otherwise, all tackle, apparel or furniture thereof shall also be liable to forfeiture.

(3) Where any of the following, that is to say—

    (a) any ship not exceeding 100 tons register;
    (b) any aircraft; or
    (c) any hovercraft,

becomes liable to forfeiture under this section by reason of having been used in the importation, exportation or carriage of goods contrary to or for the purpose of contravening any prohibition or restriction for the time being in force with respect to those goods, or without payment having been made of, or security given for, any duty payable thereon, the owner and the master or commander shall each be liable on summary conviction to a penalty equal to the value of the ship, aircraft or hovercraft or **level 5** on the standard scale, whichever is the less.
[Customs and Excise Management Act 1979, s 141, as amended by the Criminal Justice Act 1982, ss 38 and 46.]

---

    1. For special provision as to forfeiture of larger ships, see s 142, post.
    2. The forfeiture provisions are absolute and it is not necessary for the seizing authority to establish the state of mind or the degree of knowledge of the owner or user of the aircraft. Where the cargo unloaded from an aircraft on a scheduled international flight, unknown to the operator, was found to contain cannabis resin, it was held that the Commissioners were entitled to seize the aircraft under s 141 (*Customs and Excise Comrs v Air Canada* [1991] 2 QB 446, [1991] 1 All ER 570, CA).
    3. Where kerosene oil which was liable to forfeiture was found in the fuel tanks of vehicles, the vehicles were also held liable to forfeiture since they had "been used for the carriage" of such oil; see *Customs and Excise Comrs v Jack Bradley (Accrington) Ltd* [1959] 1 QB 219, [1958] 3 All ER 487. But where cargo unloaded from an aircraft on a scheduled international flight was found to contain cannabis resin, it was held that the aircraft had not "been used for the carriage" of the prohibited goods because, unknown to the operator amd without any recklessness on his part, those goods had been placed on the aircraft (*Customs and Excise Comrs v Air Canada* [1989] QB 234, [1989] 2 All ER 22).
    4. This is to be interpreted in accordance with the ejusdem generis rule, ie only including things of a like kind. Therefore forfeiture of obscene video tapes found in a persons luggage would not justify forfeiture of other items such as his shaver or items of clothing (*R v Uxbridge Justices, ex p Webb* (1998) 162 JP 198, DC).
    5. Paragraphs (a) and (b) of s 141(1) are to be read disjunctively, and therefore anything found with items liable to forfeiture is itself liable to forfeiture, subject to the discretion of the Customs and Excise not to require such forfeiture (*Travell v Customs and Excise Comrs* (1997) 162 JP 181). Where goods liable to forfeiture are jointly owned, and one co-owner declines to make a claim or to attend the hearing, this does not prevent the other co-owner from challenging the contention that the former's goods were liable to forfeiture; s 141(1)(b) only bites where the court finds as a fact in the proceedings relating to the seized goods that other goods are liable to forfeiture and that the seized goods are mixed, etc, with those other goods (*Fox v Customs and Excise Comrs* [2002] EWHC 1244 (Admin), [2003] 1 WLR 1331, (2002) 166 JP 578).
    6. Section 141(1)(a) of, and para 6 of Sch 3 to, the Act mean precisely what they say; once there has been a finding that something has become liable to forfeiture any vehicle, etc, used for its carriage and seized under s 139 must also be condemned as forfeited (*R (on the application of Customs and Excise Comrs) v Helman* [2002] EWHC 2254 (Admin), (2002) 166 JP 725.) However, the liability to forfeiture in sub-s (1)(a) and (b) is subject to European Law on the enforcement of penalties in the case of seized goods which themselves are not liable to duty and article one of the First Protocol to the European Convention on Human Rights in respect of interference with property such as a motor vehicle where any forfeiture must strike a fair balance between the rights of the individual and the public interest; there must be a reasonable relationship of proportionality between the means employed and the aim pursued (*Customs and Excise Comrs v Newbury* [2003] EWHC 702 (Admin), [2003] 2 All ER 964, [2003] 1 WLR 2209).

8-6641 142. Special provision as to forfeiture of larger ships. (1) Notwithstanding any other provision of the Customs and Excise Acts 1979, a ship of 250 or more tons register shall not be liable to forfeiture under or by virtue of any provision of the Customs and Excise Acts 1979, except under section 88 above, unless the offence in respect of or in connection with which the forfeiture is claimed—

    (a) was substantially the object of the voyage during which the offence was committed; or
    (b) was committed while the ship was under chase by a vessel in the service of Her Majesty after failing to bring to when properly summoned to do so by that vessel.

(2) For the purposes of this section, a ship shall be deemed to have been properly summoned to bring to—

    (a) if the vessel making the summons did so by means of an international signal code or other recognised means and while flying her proper ensign; and (*b*) in the case of a ship which is not a British ship, if at the time when the summons was made the ship was in United Kingdom waters.

(3) For the purposes of this section, all hovercraft (of whatever size) shall be treated as ships of less than 250 tons register.

(4) The exemption from forfeiture of any ship under this section shall not affect any liability to forfeiture of goods carried therein.

[Customs and Excise Management Act 1979, s 142, as amended by the Territorial Sea Act 1987, Sch 1.]

8–6642 143. Penalty in lieu of forfeiture of larger ship where responsible officer implicated in offence. *Power of Commissioners to fine a ship.*

8–6643 144. Protection of officers, etc in relation to seizure and detention of goods, etc.
(1) Where, in any proceedings for the condemnation[1] of any thing seized as liable to forfeiture under the customs and excise Acts, judgment is given for the claimant, the court may, if it sees fit, certify that there were reasonable grounds for the seizure.

(2) Where any proceedings, whether civil or criminal, are brought against the Commissioners, a law officer of the Crown or any person authorised by or under the Customs and Excise Acts 1979 to seize or detain any thing liable to forfeiture under the customs and excise Acts on account of the seizure or detention of any thing, and judgment is given for the plaintiff or prosecutor, then if either—

(*a*) a certificate relating to the seizure has been granted under subsection (1) above; or
(*b*) the court is satisfied that there were reasonable grounds for seizing or detaining that thing under the customs and excise Acts,

the plaintiff or prosecutor shall not be entitled to recover any damages or costs and the defendant shall not be liable to any punishment.

(3) Nothing in subsection (2) above shall affect any right of any person to the return of the thing seized or detained or to compensation in respect of any damage to the thing or in respect of the destruction thereof.

(4) Any certificate under subsection (1) above may be proved by the production of either the original certificate or a certified copy thereof purporting to be signed by an officer of the court by which it was granted.

[Customs and Excise Management Act 1979, s 144.]

---

1. For provisions as to detention, seizure and condemnation of goods, etc, see s 139, ante, and Sch 3, post.

General provisions as to legal proceedings

8–6644 145. Institution of proceedings. (1) Subject to the following provisions of this section, no proceedings for an offence under the customs and excise Acts or for condemnation under Schedule 3[1] to this Act shall be instituted except by order of the Commissioners[2].

(2) Subject to the following provisions of this section, any proceedings under the customs and excise Acts instituted in a magistrates' court, and any such proceedings instituted in a court of summary jurisdiction in Northern Ireland, shall be commenced in the name of an officer.

(3) Subsections (1) and (2) above shall not apply to proceedings on indictment in Scotland.

(4) In the case of the death, removal, discharge or absence of the officer in whose name the proceedings were commenced under subsection (2) above, those proceedings may be continued by any officer authorised in that behalf by the Commissioners.

(5) Nothing in the foregoing provisions of this section shall prevent the institution of proceedings for an offence under the customs and excise Acts by order and in the name of a law officer of the Crown in any case in which he thinks it proper that proceedings should be so instituted.

(6) Notwithstanding anything in the foregoing provisions of this section, where any person has been arrested for any offence for which he is liable to be arrested under the customs and excise Acts, any court before which he is brought may proceed to deal with the case[3] although the proceedings have not been instituted by order of the Commissioners or have not been commenced in the name of an officer.

[Customs and Excise Management Act 1979, s 145 as amended by the Police and Criminal Evidence Act 1984, s 114.]

---

1. Schedule 3, post, contains provisions relating to forfeiture of goods that have been seized. For an example of such proceedings, see *Mizel v Warren* [1973] 2 All ER 1140. The provisions of Sch 3 also apply to proceedings under s 143 of the Act when the Commissioners desire to recover from a ship owner a penalty in lieu of forfeiture exceeding £50. The court (which includes a magistrates' court) may make an order for the condemnation of the ship in a sum not exceeding £500 if satisfied that a responsible officer of the ship is implicated in an offence that would give rise to forfeiture. Proceedings for condemnation are civil proceedings (Sch 3, para 8) (and are not classified as "criminal" for the purposes of art 6(2) of the Convention: *Goldsmith v Customs and Excise Comrs* [2001] EWHC Admin 285, [2001] 1 WLR 1673).; the issue is limited to whether the goods should be forfeited. The identity of an importer, for instance, is irrelevant (*Denton v John Lister Ltd* [1971] 3 All ER 669).

2. Notwithstanding this provision, by virtue of s 176, post, a local authority in England or Wales may authorise the bringing by any constable of proceedings for an offence relating to excise duties on licences to kill game or to deal in game.

See also *R v Whitehead* [1982] QB 1272, [1982] 3 All ER 96, [1982] Crim LR 666, CA which applies (what is now) sub-s (6) to proceedings for conspiracy to evade the prohibition on the importation of drugs.

3. This provision is sufficiently wide to enable the Crown Court to deal with defendants who have been committed for the substantive offence of being knowingly concerned in the fraudulent evasion of the prohibition on importation of a controlled drug, for an indictment of conspiracy to commit the offence (*R v Keyes* [2000] 2 Cr App Rep 181, [2000] Crim LR 571, CA).

8–6645   146. Service of process.   (1) Any summons or other process issued anywhere in the United Kingdom for the purpose of any proceedings under the customs and excise Acts may be served on the person to whom it is addressed in any part of the United Kingdom without any further endorsement, and shall be deemed to have been duly served—

   (a)   if delivered to him personally; or
   (b)   if left at his last known place of abode or business or, in the case of a body corporate, at their registered or principal office; or
   (c)   if left on board any vessel or aircraft to which he may belong or have lately belonged.

   (2) Any summons, notice, order or other document issued for the purposes of any proceedings under the customs and excise Acts, or of any appeal from the decision of the court in any such proceedings, may be served by an officer.
   In this subsection "appeal" includes an appeal by way of case stated[1].
   (3) This section shall not apply in relation to proceedings instituted in the High Court or Court of Session.
[Customs and Excise Management Act 1979, s 146.]

---

1. For the right of appeal by the prosecutor to the Crown Court, see s 147(3), post.

8–6646   146A. Time limits for proceedings.   (1) Except as otherwise provided in the customs and excise Acts, and notwithstanding anything in any other enactment, the following provisions shall apply in relation to proceedings for an offence under those Acts.
   (2) Proceedings for an indictable offence shall not be commenced after the end of the period of 20 years beginning with the day on which the offence was committed.
   (3) Proceedings for a summary offence shall not be commenced after the end of the period of 3 years beginning with that day but, subject to that, may be commenced at any time within 6 months from the date on which sufficient evidence to warrant the proceedings came to the knowledge of the prosecuting authority[1].
   (4) For the purposes of subsection (3) above, a certificate of the prosecuting authority as to the date on which such evidence as is there mentioned came to that authority's knowledge shall be conclusive evidence of that fact.
   (5) *Scotland.*
   (6) *Northern Ireland.*
   (7) In this section, "prosecuting authority" means the Commissioners and includes, in Scotland, the procurator fiscal.
[Customs and Excise Management Act 1979, s 146A, as inserted by the Finance Act 1989, s 16.]

---

1. This provision overrides the general limitation of six months contained in the Magistrates' Courts Act 1980, s 127, in PART I: MAGISTRATES' COURTS, PROCEDURE, ante.

8–6647   147. Proceedings for offences.   (1) *Repealed.*
   (2) Where, in England or Wales, a magistrates' court has begun to inquire into an information charging a person with an offence under the customs and excise Acts as examining justices the court shall not proceed under section 25(3) of the Magistrates' Courts Act 1980 to try the information summarily without the consent of—

   (a)   the Attorney General, in a case where the proceedings were instituted by his order and in his name; or
   (b)   the Commissioners, in any other case.*

   (3) In the case of proceedings in England or Wales, without prejudice to any right to require the statement of a case for the opinion of the High Court, the prosecutor may appeal to the Crown Court against any decision[1] of a magistrates' court in proceedings for an offence under the customs and excise Acts.
   (4) *Northern Ireland.*
[Customs and Excise Management Act 1979, s 147, as amended by the Magistrates' Courts Act 1980, Sch 7, the Criminal Justice Act 1982, Schs 14 and 16, the Finance Act 1988 s 11, the Finance Act 1989, s 16 and Sch 17.]

---

*Subsection (2) repealed by the Criminal Justice Act 2003, Sch 3, from a date to be appointed.
1. This allows the prosecutor to appeal to the Crown Court against any decision of the justices including their exercise of discretion on mode of trial (*R v Customs and Excise Comrs, ex p Wagstaff* (1997) 162 JP 186, [1998] Crim LR 287) or sentence (*R v Customs and Excise Comrs, ex p Brunt* (1998) 163 JP 161).

8–6648   148. Place of trial for offences.   (1) Proceedings for an offence under the customs and excise Acts may be commenced—

(a) in any court having jurisdiction in the place where the person charged with the offence resides or is found; or

(b) if any thing was detained or seized in connection with the offence, in any court having jurisdiction in the place where that thing was so detained or seized or was found or condemned as forfeited; or

(c) in any court having jurisdiction anywhere in that part of the United Kingdom, namely—

(i) England and Wales,
(ii) Scotland, or
(iii) Northern Ireland,

in which the place where the offence was committed is situated.

(2) Where any such offence was committed at some place outside the area of any commission of the peace, the place of the commission of the offence shall, for the purposes of the jurisdiction of any court, be deemed to be any place in the United Kingdom where the offender is found or to which he is first brought after the commission of the offence.

(3) The jurisdiction under subsection (2) above shall be in addition to and not in derogation of any jurisdiction or power of any court under any other enactment.
[Customs and Excise Management Act 1979, s 148.]

8–6649   149. Non-payment of penalties, etc: maximum terms of imprisonment.   (1) Where, in any proceedings for an offence under the customs and excise Acts, a magistrates' court in England or Wales or a court of summary jurisdiction in Scotland, in addition to ordering the person convicted to pay a penalty for the offence—

(a) orders him to be imprisoned for a term in respect of the same offence; and

(b) further (whether at the same time or subsequently) orders him to be imprisoned for a term in respect of non-payment of that penalty or default of a sufficient distress to satisfy the amount of that penalty,

the aggregate of the terms for which he is so ordered to be imprisoned shall not exceed 15 months.

(2) *(Repealed)*.

(3) *Northern Ireland*.
[Customs and Excise Management Act 1979, s 149, as amended by the Criminal Justice (Scotland) Act 1980, Sch 8.]

8–6660   150. Incidental provisions as to legal proceedings.   (1) Whereby liability for any offence under the customs and excise Acts is incurred by two or more persons jointly, those persons shall each be liable for the full amount of any pecuniary penalty and may be proceeded against jointly or severally as the Commissioners may see fit.

(2) In any proceedings for an offence under the customs and excise Acts instituted in England, Wales or Northern Ireland, any court by whom the matter is considered may mitigate any pecuniary penalty as they see fit.

(3) In any proceedings for an offence or for the condemnation of any thing as being forfeited under the customs and excise Acts, the fact that security has been given by bond or otherwise for the payment of any duty or for compliance with any condition in respect of the non-payment of which or non-compliance with which the proceedings are instituted shall not be a defence.
[Customs and Excise Management Act 1979, s 150.]

8–6661   151. Application of penalties.   The balance of any sum paid or recovered on account of any penalty imposed under the customs and excise Acts after paying any such compensation or costs as are mentioned in s 139 of the Magistrates' Courts Act 1980 to persons other than the Commissioners shall, notwithstanding any local or other special right of privilege of whatever origin, be accounted for and paid to the Commissioners or as they direct.
[Customs and Excise Management Act 1979, s 151, as amended by the Magistrates' Courts Act 1980, Sch 7.]

8–6662   152. Power of Commissioners to mitigate penalties, etc.   The Commissioners may, as they see fit—

(a) stay, sist or compound[1] any proceedings for an offence or for the condemnation of any thing as being forfeited under the customs and excise Acts; or

(b) restore[2], subject to such conditions (if any) as they think proper, any thing forfeited or seized under those Acts; or

(c) after judgment, mitigate or remit any pecuniary penalty imposed under those Acts; or

(d) order any person who has been imprisoned to be discharged before the expiration of his term of imprisonment, being a person imprisoned for any offence under those Acts or in respect of the non-payment of a penalty or other sum adjudged to be paid or awarded in relation to such an offence or in respect of the default of a sufficient distress to satisfy such a sum;

but paragraph (*a*) above shall not apply to proceedings on indictment in Scotland.
[Customs and Excise Management Act 1979, s 152.]

---

1. See *Patel v Spencer* [1976] 1 WLR 1268, where the Commissioners were allowed to release an offender on his own request from an agreement to compound proceedings but would not have been allowed to resile from the agreement themselves.

It is the Commissioners invariable practice to offer to the courts for sentencing purposes after conviction details of any previously compounded settlements for similar offences where the earlier settlement occurred within the preceding 5 years; see HM Customs and Excise Circular letter to courts, dated 6 June 1989.

2. A policy that any car or light goods vehicle, save rented vehicles, used for smuggling goods would be seized on the first occasion of detection and not restored, save in exceptional circumstances, failed to pay due regard to the principle of proportionality if it did not require, in the case of not-for-profit importation, consideration of the particular facts, including the scale of the importation, whether it was a first offence, whether there was any attempt at concealment or dissimulation, the value of the vehicle and the degree of hardship that forfeiture would cause (*Lindsay v Customs and Excise Comrs* [2002] EWCA Civ 267, [2002] RTR 313), applied in *Gascoyne v Customs and Excise Comrs* [2003] EWHC 257 (Ch), [2003] Ch 292, [2003] 2 WLR 1311.

A single document can represent both an application for restoration under s 152 of the 1979 Act and a notice of claim under para 3 of Sch 3 (*Gascoyne v Customs and Excise Comrs*, supra). On appeal, Buxton LJ stated obiter that in a case where the deeming provisions under para 5 of Sch 3 were applied, the tribunal could reopen those issues in a s 152 application (*Gascoyne v Customs and Excise Comrs* [2004] EWCA Civ 1162, [2005] Ch 215, [2005] 2 WLR 222, at para 55).

See also *Customs and Excise Comrs v Newbury* [2003] EWHC 702 (Admin), [2003] 2 All ER 964, [2003] 1 WLR 2209 and Sch 3 para 8 and notes thereto.

8–6663   153. Proof of certain documents.   (1) Any document purporting to be signed either by one or more of the Commissioners, or by their order, or by any other person with their authority, shall, until the contrary is proved, be deemed to have been so signed and to be made and issued by the Commissioners, and may be proved by the production of a copy thereof purporting to be so signed.

(2) Without prejudice to subsection (1) above, the Documentary Evidence Act 1868 shall apply in relation to—

    (*a*)   any document issued by the Commissioners;

    (*b*)   any document issued before 1st April 1909, by the Commissioners of Customs or the Commissioners of Customs and the Commissioners of Inland Revenue jointly;

    (*c*)   any document issued before that date in relation to the revenue of excise by the Commissioners of Inland Revenue,

as it applies in relation to the documents mentioned in that Act.

(3) That Act shall, as applied by subsection (2) above, have effect as if the persons mentioned in paragraphs (*a*) to (*c*) of that subsection were included in the first column of the Schedule to that Act, and any of the Commissioners or any secretary or assistant secretary to the Commissioners were specified in the second column of that Schedule in connection with those persons.

(4) A photograph of any document delivered to the Commissioners for any customs or excise purpose and certified by them to be such a photograph shall be admissible in any proceedings, whether civil or criminal, to the same extent as the document itself.
[Customs and Excise Management Act 1979, s 153 as amended by the Finance Act 1981, Sch 8.]

8–6664   154. Proof of certain other matters.   (1) An averment in any process in proceedings under the customs and excise Acts—

    (*a*)   that those proceedings were instituted by the order of the Commissioners; or

    (*b*)   that any person is or was a Commissioner, officer or constable, or a member of her Majesty's armed forces or coastguard; or

    (*c*)   that any person is or was appointed or authorised by the Commissioners to discharge, or was engaged by the orders or with the concurrence of the Commissioners in the discharge of, any duty; or

    (*d*)   that the Commissioners have or have not been satisfied as to any matter as to which they are required by any provision of those Acts to be satisfied; or

    (*e*)   that any ship is a British ship; or

    (*f*)   that any goods thrown overboard, staved or destroyed were so dealt with in order to prevent or avoid the seizure of those goods,

shall, until the contrary is proved, be sufficient evidence of the matter in question.

(2) Where in any proceedings relating to customs or excise any question arises as to the place from which any goods have been brought or as to whether or not—

    (*a*)   any duty has been paid or secured in respect of any goods; or

    (*b*)   any goods or other things whatsoever are of the description[1] or nature alleged in the information, writ or other process; or

    (*c*)   any goods have been lawfully imported or lawfully unloaded from any ship or aircraft; or

    (*d*)   any goods have been lawfully loaded into any ship or aircraft or lawfully exported or were lawfully water-borne; or (*e*) any goods were lawfully brought to any place for the purpose of being loaded into any ship or aircraft or exported; or

(*f*) any goods are or were subject to any prohibition of or restriction on their importation or exportation,

then, where those proceedings are brought by or against the Commissioners, a law officer of the Crown or an officer, or against any other person in respect of anything purporting to have done in pursuance of any power or duty conferred or imposed on him by or under the customs and excise Acts, the burden of proof[2] shall lie upon the other party to the proceedings.

[Customs and Excise Management Act 1979, s 154.]

---

1. This is wide enough in its ordinary meaning to include the country of origin (*Mizel v Warren* [1973] 2 All ER 1140).

2. The onus of proof is on the defendant where the crown seeks to recover penalties under the Customs Acts, whether goods have been seized or not (*R v Fitzpatrick* [1948] 2 KB 203, [1948] 1 All ER 769, 112 JP 251). See *R v Cohen* [1951] 1 KB 505, [1951] 1 All ER 203, 115 JP 91; *Sayce v Coupe* [1953] 1 QB 1, [1952] 2 All ER 715, 116 JP 552; *Schneider v Dawson* [1960] 2 QB 106, [1959] 3 All ER 583, 124 JP 7. The reversal of the onus of proof effected by s 154(2) which requires the owner of obscene goods that have been seized as being liable to forfeiture to show that the material is not obscene is not contrary to European law (*Wright v Customs and Excise Comrs* (1998) 162 JP 207). Provisions regarding the proof of official documents are contained in s 153, ante.

8–6665   155. Persons who may conduct proceedings. (1) Any officer or any other person authorised[1] in that behalf by the Commissioners may, although he is not a barrister, advocate or solicitor, conduct any proceedings before any magistrates' court in England or Wales or court of summary jurisdiction in Scotland or Northern Ireland or before any examining justices, being proceedings under any enactment relating to an assigned matter[2] or proceedings arising out of the same circumstances as any proceedings commenced under any such enactment, whether or not the last mentioned proceedings are persisted in.

(2) Any person who has been admitted as a solicitor and is employed by the Commissioners may act as a solicitor in any proceedings in England, Wales or Northern Ireland relating to any assigned matter notwithstanding that he does not hold a current practising certificate.

[Customs and Excise Management Act 1979, s 155.]

---

1. It is unnecessary to prove a special authority (*Dyer v Tulley* (1894) 58 JP 656).

2. For meaning of "assigned matter", see s 1, ante.

Saving for outlying enactments of certain general provisions as to offences

8–6666   156. Saving for outlying enactments of certain general provisions as to offences. (1) In subsections (2), (3) and (4) below (which reproduce certain enactments not required as general provisions for the purposes of the enactments re-enacted in the Customs and Excise Acts 1979) "the outlying provisions of the customs and excise Acts" means—

(*a*) the Betting and Gaming Duties Act 1972, as for the time being amended; and

(*b*) all other provisions of the customs and excise Acts, as for the time being amended, which were passed before the commencement of this Act and are not re-enacted in the Customs and Excise Acts 1979.

(2) It is hereby declared that any act or omission in respect of which a pecuniary penalty (however described) is imposed by any of the outlying provisions of the customs and excise Acts is an offence under that provision; and accordingly in this Part of this Act any reference to an offence under the customs and excise Acts includes a reference to such an act or omission.

(3) Subject to any express provision made by the enactment in question, an offence under any of the outlying provisions of the customs and excise Acts—

(*a*) where it is punishable with imprisonment for a term of 2 years, with or without a pecuniary penalty, shall be punishable either on summary conviction or on conviction on indictment;

(*b*) in any other case, shall be punishable on summary conviction.

(4)–(5) *Scotland.*

[Customs and Excise Management Act 1979, s 156 as amended by the Criminal Justice Act 1982, Schs 14 and 16.]

PART XII[1]
GENERAL AND MISCELLANEOUS

General powers, etc

8–6667   158. Power to require provision of facilities. (1) A person to whom this section applies, that is to say, a revenue trader and any person required by the Commissioners under the Customs and Excise Acts 1979 to give security in respect of any premises or place to be used for the examination of goods by an officer, shall—

(*a*) provide and maintain such appliances and afford such other facilities reasonably necessary to enable an officer to take any account or make any examination or search or to perform any other of his duties on the premises of that trader or at the bonded premises or place as the Commissioners may direct;

(b) keep any appliances so provided in a convenient place approved by the proper officer for that purpose; and

(c) allow the proper officer at any time to use anything so provided and give him any assistance necessary for the performance of his duties.

(2) Any person who contravenes or fails to comply with any provision of subsection (1) above shall be liable on summary conviction to a penalty of **level 3** on the standard scale.

(3) A person to whom this section applies shall provide and maintain any fitting required for the purpose of affixing any lock which the proper officer may require to affix to the premises of that person or any part thereof or to any vessel, utensil or other apparatus whatsoever kept thereon, and in default—

(a) the fitting may be provided or any work necessary for its maintenance may be carried out by the proper officer, and any expenses so incurred shall be paid on demand by that person; and

(b) if that person fails to pay those expenses on demand, he shall in addition be liable on summary conviction to a penalty of **level 3** on the standard scale.

(4) If any person to whom this section applies or any servant of his—

(a) wilfully destroys or damages any such fitting as is mentioned in subsection (3) above or any lock or key provided for use therewith, or any label or seal placed on any such lock; or

(b) improperly obtains access to any place or article secured by any such lock; or

(c) has any such fitting or any article intended to be secured by means thereof so constructed that that intention is defeated,

he shall be liable on summary conviction to a penalty of **level 5** on the standard scale and may be arrested.

[Customs and Excise Management Act 1979, s 158 as amended by the Criminal Justice Act 1982, ss 38 and 46 and the Police and Criminal Evidence Act 1984, s 114.]

---

1. Part XII contains ss 157–178.

8–6668 **159. Power to examine and take account of goods.** (1) Without prejudice to any other power conferred by the Customs and Excise Acts 1979, an officer may examine and take account of any goods—

(a) which are imported; or

(b) which are in a warehouse or Queen's warehouse; or

(bb) which are in a free zone; or

(c) which have been loaded into any ship or aircraft at any place in the United Kingdom; or

(d) which are entered for exportation or for use as stores; or

(e) which are brought to any place in the United Kingdom for exportation or for shipment for exportation or as stores; or

(f) in the case of which any claim for drawback, allowance, rebate, remission or repayment of duty is made;

and may for that purpose require any container to be opened or unpacked.

(2)–(4) *Supplementary provisions as to examination.*

(5) If any imported goods which an officer has power under the Customs and Excise Acts 1979 to examine are without the authority of the proper officer removed from customs and excise charge before they have been examined, those goods shall be liable to forfeiture.

(6) If any goods falling within subsection (5) above are removed by a person with intent to defraud Her Majesty of any duty chargeable thereon or to evade any prohibition or restriction for the time being in force with respect thereto under or by virtue of any enactment, that person shall be guilty of an offence under this subsection and may be arrested.

(7) A person guilty of an offence under subsection (6) above shall be liable[1]—

(a) on summary conviction, to a penalty of **the prescribed sum**[2] or of three times the value of the goods, whichever is the greater, or to imprisonment for a term not exceeding **6 months**, or to both; or

(b) on conviction on indictment, to a penalty of any amount, or to imprisonment for a term not exceeding **7 years**, or to both.

[Customs and Excise Management Act 1979, s 159 as amended by the Finance Act 1984, Sch 4, the Police and Criminal Evidence Act 1984, s 114 and the Finance Act 1988, s 12.]

---

1. For procedure in respect of this offence which is triable either way, see s 147, ante, and the Magistrates' Courts Act 1980, ss 17A–21, in PART I: MAGISTRATES' COURTS, PROCEDURE, ANTE.

2. For the meaning of "prescribed sum", see s 171 post.

8–6669 **160.** *Power to take samples.*

8–6670 161. Power to search premises: writ of assistance. (1) The powers conferred by this section are exercisable by an officer having a writ of assistance if there are reasonable grounds to suspect that anything liable to forfeiture under the customs and excise Acts—

(a) is kept or concealed in any building or place, and

(b) is likely to be removed, destroyed or lost before a search warrant can be obtained and executed.

(2) The powers are—

(a) to enter the building or place at any time, whether by day or night, on any day, and search for, seize, and detain or remove any such thing, and

(b) so far as is necessary for the purpose of such entry, search, seizure, detention or removal, to break open any door, window or container and force and remove any other impediment or obstruction.

(3) An officer shall not exercise the power of entry conferred by this section by night unless accompanied by a constable.

(4) A writ of assistance shall continue in force during the reign in which it is issued and for six months thereafter.

[Customs and Excise Management Act 1979, s 161 as amended by the Finance Act 2000, s 25.]

8–6670A 161A. Power to search premises: search warrant. (1) If a justice of the peace is satisfied by information upon oath given by an officer that there are reasonable grounds to suspect that anything liable to forfeiture under the customs and excise Acts is kept or concealed in any building or place, he may by warrant under his hand authorise any officer, and any person accompanying an officer, to enter and search the building or place named in the warrant.

(2) An officer or other person so authorised has power—

(*a*) to enter the building or place at any time, whether by day or night, on any day, and search for, seize, and detain or remove any such thing, and

(*b*) so far as is necessary for the purpose of such entry, search, seizure, detention or removal, to break open any door, window or container and force and remove any other impediment or obstruction.

(3) Where there are reasonable grounds to suspect that any still, vessel, utensil, spirits or materials for the manufacture of spirits is or are unlawfully kept or deposited in any building or place, subsections (1) and (2) above apply in relation to any constable as they would apply in relation to an officer.

(4) The powers conferred by a warrant under this section are exercisable until the end of the period of one month beginning with the day on which the warrant is issued.

(5) A person other than a constable shall not exercise the power of entry conferred by this section by night unless accompanied by a constable.

[Customs and Excise Management Act 1979, s 161A as inserted by the Finance Act 2000, s 25.]

8–6671 162. *Power to enter land for or in connection with access to pipelines.*

8–6671A 163. Power to search vehicles or vessels. (1) Without prejudice to any other power conferred by the Customs and Excise Acts 1979, where there are reasonable grounds to suspect[1] that any vehicle or vessel is or may be carrying any goods which are—

(*a*) chargeable with any duty which has not been paid or secured; or

(*b*) in the course of being unlawfully removed from or to any place; or

(*c*) otherwise liable to forfeiture under the customs and excise Acts,

any officer or constable or member of Her Majesty's armed forces or coast-guard may stop and search that vehicle or vessel.

(2) If when so required by any such officer, constable or member the person in charge of any such vehicle or vessel refuses to stop or to permit the vehicle or vessel to be searched, he shall be liable on summary conviction to a penalty of **level 3** on the standard scale.

(3) This section shall apply in relation to aircraft as it applies in relation to vehicles or vessels but the power to stop and search in subsection (1) above shall not be available in respect of aircraft which are airborne.

[Customs and Excise Management Act 1979, s 163 as inserted by the Finance Act 2000, s 26.]

---

1. Where customs officers could not provide any positive reason for suspicion, the fact that they had decided to check a particular individual who in fact turned out to be in possession of cigarettes and alcohol in quantities exceeding those mentioned in art 9 of Council Directive (EEC) 92/12 and the Schedule to the Excise Duties (Personal Reliefs) Order 1992, did not give rise to an inference that the customs officers had "reasonable grounds to suspect" (though "reasonable grounds to suspect" within the meaning of ss 163 and 163A of the Act might, in appropriate circumstances, derive from information by way of profiles or trends – the nature and legitimate practicalities of the work carried out by customs officers made profiles and trends an understandable and important part of it); however, any seizure of cigarettes and alcohol from a person was not axiomatically invalid merely because it was in consequence of a check that was invalid though lack of "reasonable grounds to suspect" (*R (on the application of Hoverspeed Ltd) v Customs and Excise Comrs* [2002] EWCA Civ 1804, [2003] QB 1041, [2003] 2 All ER 553, [2003] 2 WLR 950.

8–6671B   163A. Power to search articles. (1) Without prejudice to any other power conferred by the Customs and Excise Acts 1979, where there are reasonable grounds to suspect[1] that a person in the United Kingdom (referred to in this section as "the suspect") has with him, or at the place where he is, any goods to which this section applies, an officer may—

(a)   require the suspect to permit a search of any article that he has with him or at that place, and

(b)   if the suspect is not under arrest, detain him (and any such article) for so long as may be necessary to carry out the search.

(2)   The goods to which this section applies are dutiable alcoholic liquor, or tobacco products, which are—

(a)   chargeable with any duty of excise, and

(b)   liable to forfeiture under the customs and excise Acts.

(3)   Notwithstanding anything in subsection (4) of section 24 of the Criminal Law (Consolidation) (Scotland) Act 1995 (detention and questioning by customs officers), detention of the suspect under subsection (1) above shall not prevent his subsequent detention under subsection (1) of that section. [Customs and Excise Management Act 1979, s 163A as inserted by the Finance Act 2000, s 26.]

---

1. See note to "reasonable grounds to suspect" in para *8–6671A*, ante

8–6672   164. Power to search persons. (1) Where there are reasonable grounds to suspect that any person to whom this section applies (referred to in this section as "the suspect") is carrying any article—

(a)   which is chargeable with any duty which has not been paid or secured; or

(b)   with respect to the importation or exportation of which any prohibition or restriction is for the time being in force under or by virtue of any enactment,

an officer[1] may exercise the powers conferred by subsection (2) below and, if the suspect is not under arrest, may detain him for so long as may be necessary for the exercise of those powers and (where applicable) the exercise of the rights conferred by subsection (3) below.

(2)   The officer[1] may require the suspect—

(a)   to permit such a search of any article which he has with him; and

(b)   subject to subsection (3) below, to submit to such searches of his person, whether rub-down, strip or intimate,

as the officer may consider necessary or expedient; but no such requirement may be imposed under paragraph (b) above without the officer informing the suspect of the effect of subsection (3) below.

(3)   If the suspect is required to submit to a search of his person, he may require to be taken—

(a)   except in the case of a rub-down search, before a justice of the peace or a superior of the officer concerned; and

(b)   in the excepted case, before such a superior;

and the justice or superior shall consider the grounds for suspicion and direct accordingly whether the suspect is to submit to the search.

(3A)   A rub-down or strip search shall not be carried out except by a person of the same sex as the suspect; and an intimate search shall not be carried out except by a suitably qualified person.

(4)   This section applies to the following persons, namely—

(a)   any person who is on board or has landed from any ship or aircraft;

(b)   any person entering or about to leave the United Kingdom;

(c)   any person within the dock area of a port;

(d)   any person at a customs and excise airport;

(e)   any person in, entering or leaving any approved wharf or transit shed which is not in a port;

(ee) any person in, entering or leaving a free zone;

(f)   in Northern Ireland, any person travelling from or to any place which is on or beyond the boundary.

(5)   In this section—

"intimate search" means any search which involves a physical examination (that is, an examination which is more than simply a visual examination) of a person's body orifices;

"rub-down search" means any search which is neither an intimate search nor a strip search;

"strip search" means any search which is not an intimate search but which involves the removal of an article of clothing which—

(a)   is being worn (wholly or partly) on the trunk; and

(b)   is being so worn either next to the skin or next to an article of underwear;

"suitably qualified person" means a registered medical practitioner or a registered nurse.

(6)   Notwithstanding anything in subsection (4) of section 48 of the Criminal Justice (Scotland) Act 1987 (detention and questioning by customs officers), detention of the suspect under subsection (1) above shall not prevent his subsequent detention under subsection (1) of that section.

[Customs and Excise Management Act 1979, s 164 as amended by the Finance Act 1984, Sch 4 and the Finance Act 1988, s 10.]

1. "Officer" is defined by s 1, ante.

General offences

8–6673   167. Untrue declarations, etc[1]. (1) If any person either knowingly or recklessly—

(a) makes or signs, or causes to be made or signed, or delivers or causes to be delivered to the Commissioners or an officer, any declaration, notice, certificate or other document[2] whatsoever; or

(b) makes any statement in answer to any question put to him by an officer which he is required by or under any enactment to answer,

being a document or statement produced or made for any purpose of any assigned matter, which is untrue in any material particular, he shall be guilty of an offence[1] under this subsection and may be detained; and any goods in relation to which the document or statement was made shall be liable to forfeiture.

(2) Without prejudice to subsection (4) below, a person who commits an offence under subsection (1) above shall be liable[1]—

(a) on summary conviction, to a penalty of **the prescribed sum**[3], or to imprisonment for a term not exceeding **6 months**, or to both; or

(b) on conviction on indictment, to a penalty of any amount, or to imprisonment for a term not exceeding **2 years**, or to both.

(3) If any person—

(a) makes or signs, or causes to be made or signed, or delivers or causes to be delivered to the Commissioners or an officer, any declaration, notice, certificate or other document whatsoever; or

(b) makes any statement in answer to any question put to him by an officer which he is required by or under any enactment to answer,

being a document or statement produced or made for any purpose of any assigned matter, which is untrue in any material particular, then, without prejudice to subsection (4) below, he shall be liable[1] on summary conviction to a penalty of **level 4** on the standard scale.

(4) Where by reason of any such document or statement as is mentioned in subsection (1) or (3) above the full amount of any duty payable is not paid or any overpayment is made in respect of any drawback, allowance, rebate or repayment of duty, the amount of the duty unpaid or of the overpayment shall be recoverable as a debt due to the Crown or may be summarily recovered as a civil debt.

(5) An amount of excise duty, or the amount of an overpayment in respect of any drawback, allowance, rebate or repayment of any excise duty, shall not be recoverable as mentioned in subsection (4) above unless the Commissioners have assessed the amount of the duty or of the overpayment as being excise duty due from the person mentioned in subsection (1) or (3) above and notified him or his representative accordingly.

[Customs and Excise Management Act 1979, s 167 as amended by the Criminal Justice Act 1982, ss 38 and 46 and the Finance Act 1997, Sch 6.]

1. This section creates two separate offences. One is triable summarily (pursuant to s 167(3)); the other is triable either way (pursuant to s 167(2)) if the elements of knowledge or recklessness are charged. For procedure in respect of the offence triable either way, see s 147, ante, and the Magistrates' Courts Act 1980, ss 17A–21, in PART I: MAGISTRATES' COURTS, PROCEDURE, ante. The offence under s 167(3) is absolute, and in either case no question of intent to defraud arises (cf s 170, post, and *Parker v Pexton* (1961) reported in 1976 at 63 Cr App Rep 91).

2. "Document" has the same meaning as in Pt I of the Civil Evidence Act 1968; see the Finance Act 1985, s 10, this title, post.

3. For meaning of the "prescribed sum", see s 171, post.

8–6674   168. Counterfeiting documents, etc. (1) If any person—

(a) counterfeits or falsifies any document[1] which is required by or under any enactment relating to an assigned matter or which is used in the transaction of any business relating to an assigned matter; or

(b) knowingly accepts, receives or uses any such document[1] so counterfeited or falsified; or

(c) alters any such document after it is officially issued; or

(d) counterfeits any seal, signature, initials or other mark of, or used by, any officer for the verification of such a document or for the security of goods or for any other purpose relating to an assigned matter,

he shall be guilty of an offence under this section and may be detained.

(2) A person guilty of an offence under this section shall be liable[2]—

    (*a*)   on summary conviction, to a penalty of **the prescribed sum**[3], or to imprisonment for a term not exceeding **6 months**, or to both; or

    (*b*)   on conviction on indictment, to a penalty of any amount, or to imprisonment for a term not exceeding **2 years**, or to both.

[Customs and Excise Management Act 1979, s 168.]

---

    1.   "Document" has the same meaning as in Part I of the Civil Evidence Act 1968; see the Finance Act 1985, s 10, this title, post.

    2.   For procedure in respect of this offence which is triable either way, see s 147, ante and the Magistrates' Courts Act 1980, ss 17A–21, in PART I: MAGISTRATES' COURTS, PROCEDURE, ante.

    3.   For meaning of "the prescribed sum", see s 171, post.

8–6675   169. False scales, etc.   (1)   If any person required by or under the customs and excise Acts to provide scales for any purpose of those Acts provides, uses or permits to be used any scales which are false or unjust he shall be guilty of an offence under this section.

    (2)   Where any article is or is to be weighed, counted, gauged or measured for the purposes of the taking of an account or the making of an examination by an officer, then if—

    (*a*)   any such person as is mentioned in subsection (1) above; or

    (*b*)   any person by whom or on whose behalf the article is weighed, counted, gauged or measured,

does anything whereby the officer is or might he prevented from, or hindered or deceived in, taking a true and just account or making a due examination, he shall be guilty of an offence under this section.

This subsection applies whether the thing is done before, during or after the weighing, counting, gauging or measuring of the article in question.

    (3)   Any person committing an offence under this section shall be liable on summary conviction to a penalty of **level 4** on the standard scale and any false or unjust scales, and any article in connection with which the offence was committed, shall be liable to forfeiture.

    (4)   In this section "scales" includes weights, measures and weighing or measuring machines or instruments.

[Customs and Excise Management Act 1979, s 169 as amended by the Criminal Justice Act 1982, ss 38 and 46.]

8–6676   170. Penalty for fraudulent evasion of duty, etc.   (1)   Without prejudice to any other provision of the Customs and Excise Acts 1979, if any person—

    (*a*)   knowingly acquires possession of any of the following goods, that is to say—

        (i)   goods which have been unlawfully removed from a warehouse or Queen's warehouse;

        (ii)   goods which are chargeable with a duty which has not been paid[1];

        (iii)   goods with respect to the importation[2] or exportation[3] of which any prohibition[4] or restriction is for the time being in force under or by virtue of any enactment[5]; or

    (*b*)   is in any way knowingly[6] concerned in carrying, removing, depositing, harbouring, keeping or concealing or in any manner dealing with any such goods,

and does so with intent to defraud Her Majesty of any duty payable on the goods or to evade any such prohibition or restriction with respect to the goods he shall be guilty of an offence under this section and may be arrested.

    (2)   Without prejudice to any other provision of the Customs and Excise Acts 1979, if any person is, in relation to any goods, in any way knowingly concerned[7] in any fraudulent[8] evasion or attempt[9] at evasion—

    (*a*)   of any duty chargeable on the goods;

    (*b*)   of any prohibition or restriction for the time being in force with respect to the goods under or by virtue of any enactment[10]; or

    (*c*)   of any provision of the Customs and Excise Acts 1979 applicable to the goods,

he shall be guilty of an offence[11] under this section and may be arrested.

    (3)   Subject to subsection (4), (4A) or (4B) below, a person guilty of an offence under this section shall be liable[12]—

    (*a*)   on summary conviction, to a penalty of **the prescribed sum**[13] or of three times the value of the goods, whichever is the greater, or to imprisonment for a term not exceeding **6 months**, or to both; or

    (*b*)   on conviction on indictment, to a penalty of any amount, or to imprisonment for a term not exceeding **7 years**, or to both.

    (4)   In the case of an offence[14] under this section in connection with a prohibition or restriction on importation or exportation having effect by virtue of section 3 of the Misuse of Drugs Act 1971, subsection (3) above shall have effect subject to the modifications specified in Schedule 1 to this Act.

    (4A)   In the case of—

    (*a*)   an offence under subsection (2) or (3) above committed in Great Britain in connection with a prohibition or restriction on the importation or exportation of any weapon or ammunition that is of a kind mentioned in section 5(1)(*a*), (*ab*), (*aba*), (*ac*), (*ad*), (*ae*), (*af*) or (*c*) or (1A)(*a*) of the Firearms Act 1968,

(*b*) any such offence committed in Northern Ireland in connection with a prohibition or restriction on the importation or exportation of any weapon or ammunition that is of a kind mentioned in Article 45(1)(*a*), (*aa*), (*b*), (*c*), (*d*), (*e*) or (*g*) or (2)(*a*) of the Firearms (Northern Ireland) Order 2004, or

(*c*) any such offence committed in connection with the prohibitions contained in sections 20 and 21 of the Forgery and Counterfeiting Act 1981,

subsection (3)(*b*) above shall have effect as if for the words "7 years" there were substituted the words "10 years".

(4B) In the case of an offence under subsection (1) or (2) above in connection with the prohibition contained in regulation 2 of the Import of Seal Skins Regulations 1996, subsection (3) above shall have effect as if—

(*a*) for paragraph (*a*) there were substituted the following—

"(*a*) on summary conviction, to a fine not exceeding the statutory maximum or to imprisonment for a term not exceeding three months, or to both"; and

(*b*) in paragraph (*b*) for the words "7 years" there were substituted the words "2 years".

(5) In any case where a person would, apart from this subsection, be guilty of—

(*a*) an offence under this section in connection with a prohibition or restriction; and

(*b*) a corresponding offence under the enactment or other instrument imposing the prohibition or restriction, being an offence for which a fine or other penalty is expressly provided by that enactment or other instrument,

he shall not be guilty of the offence mentioned in paragraph (*a*) of this subsection.

(6) Where any person is guilty of an offence under this section, the goods in respect of which the offence was committed shall be liable to forfeiture.

[Customs and Excise Management Act 1979, s 170, as amended by the Forgery and Counterfeiting Act 1981, s 23, the Police and Criminal Evidence Act 1984, s 114 and the Finance Act 1988, s 12, the Finance (No 2) Act 1992, Sch 2, SI 1996/2686, the Criminal Justice Act 2003, s 293, SI 2004/702 and SI 2005/1966.]

---

1. The burden of proof that duty has been paid lies upon the defendant (s 154(2)(*a*), ante). The possession by a defendant of dutiable goods raises a presumption that they were knowingly in his possession; the intent to defraud may be inferred from the surrounding circumstances (*R v Cohen* [1951] 1 KB 505, [1951] 1 All ER 203, 115 JP 91; *Sayce v Coupe* [1953] 1 QB 1, [1952] 2 All ER 715, 116 JP 552; *Schneider v Dawson* [1960] 2 QB 106, [1959] 3 All ER 584, 124 JP 7). Where a person has in his possession dutiable goods in excess of the quantities in the Schedule to the Excise (Personal Reliefs) Order 1992, SI 1992/3155, there is a presumption by virtue of para 5 of the order that the goods had been imported for a commercial purpose unless the Commissioners of Customs and Excise are satisfied to the contrary. The exemption in art 3 of the Excise Duties (Personal Reliefs) Order 1992, SI 1992/3155 for goods imported for personal use does not extend to the importation of goods as a favour to a friend etc, on a reimbursement basis (*Customs and Excise Comrs v Newbury* [2003] EWHC 702 (Admin), [2003] 2 All ER 964, [2003] 1 WLR 2209). In the case of a prosecution under s 170 (1) or (2) for fraudulent evasion it is not a requirement for the prosecution to show that more than the quantities set out in para 5 of the Schedule to the Excise (Personal Reliefs) Order 1992, SI 1992/3155 were intended to be imported nor that if more than those quantities were intended to be imported to establish that Customs were not satisfied that the purpose was for personal use. The proper course is to concentrate on establishing beyond reasonable doubt that the goods were being imported for a commercial purpose without any presumption flowing from quantities (*R v Travers* [1998] Crim LR 655, CA).

2. The prosecution must produce evidence to show there has been importation and must establish a link between the offence alleged and the particular prohibited importation before it can seek to shift the burden of proof by using s 154, ante, (*R v Watts and Stack* (1979) 71 Cr App Rep 136, [1980] Crim LR 38. This does not mean that the offence could only be committed by a person involved in the actual smuggling operation; it is simply intended to discourage the Crown from prosecuting under this section where the only evidence is of possession; see *R v Neal* [1984] 3 All ER 156, 77 Cr App Rep 283, CA.

3. See the cases of *R v Smith* [1973] QB 924, [1973] 2 All ER 1161, and *R v Wall* [1974] 2 All ER 245, in note 7, post.

4. Where the material comprises indecent films, the public can be excluded from any showing, but not normally the press (For guidance on the procedure to be adopted, see *R v Waterfield* [1975] 2 All ER 40, 139 JP 400; and see also *R v Uxbridge Justices, ex p Webb* (1993) 162 JP 198, DC (press excluded)). The Import of Goods (Control) Order 1954, SI 1954/23, as amended, made under s 1 of the Import, Export and Customs Powers (Defence) Act 1939, provides a penalty on summary conviction of £500 and/or 6 months imprisonment for making a false statement to obtain an import licence. The Export of Goods (Control) Order 1994, SI 1994/1191 amended by SI 1994/1632, 2518 and 2711, SI 1995/271, 3060 and 3249, SI 1996/1124, 1341 and 2663, SI 1997/323, 1008 and 2758, and SI 1999/63, 335, 1777, 2609, 2627, 3411 and SI 2000/109 similarly provides on summary conviction a penalty not exceeding the statutory maximum, and on conviction on indictment to a fine and/or imprisonment for a term not exceeding 2 years, for offences in connection with applications for export licences etc. These Orders in so far as they control import and export of gold and silver alloy coins, are not incompatible with Community Law (*Case 7/78 R v Thompson, Johnson and Woodiwiss* [1980] QB 229, [1980] 2 All ER 102, [1978] ECR 2247.)

5. See in particular, the Customs Consolidation Act 1876, s 42, and notes thereto, this title, ante.

6. The prosecution do not have to prove that the accused knew precisely what the prohibited goods were as long as he knew they were prohibited (*R v Shivpuri* [1987] AC 1, [1986] 2 All ER 334, 150 JP 353, HL).

7. Section 170(2) is intended as a "sweep up" section to deal with persons who, while not involved with the importation as such, are involved in criminal acts relating to the goods after the importation (*R v Neal* (1983) 77 CR App Rep 283, [1983] Crim LR 677). Trans-shipment of cannabis en route from Kenya to Bermuda, within Heathrow Airport customs area from one aircraft to another, was within the section, and a party to it was "knowingly concerned" (*R v Smith* [1973] QB 924, [1973] 2 All ER 1161). In general, an act committed abroad cannot be the subject of criminal proceedings in England, but steps taken abroad leading to fraudulent evasion in this country can make a defendant "knowingly concerned"

(*R v Wall* [1974] 2 All ER 245; loading cannabis in Kandahar). Where customs officers (unknown to the defendant) removed the offending goods (ie cannabis) and substituted peat, the defendant's *subsequent* actions in arranging for delivery of what he thought was cannabis was held to be "fraudulent evasion", being a continuing offence: see *R v Green* [1976] QB 985, [1975] 3 All ER 1011, 140 JP 112 (*Haughton v Smith* [1975] AC 476, [1973] 3 All ER 1109 distinguished). A customs officer may make a mistake in determining the amount of duty; provided the importer has not induced the mistake or made an untrue declaration, he has not committed an offence, even if he is aware of the mistake (*Customs and Excise Comrs v Tan* [1977] AC 650, [1977] 1 All ER 432, 141 JP 159). Being "knowingly concerned" involves not merely knowledge of a smuggling operation but also knowledge that the substance in question was one the importation of which is prohibited: thus a defendant who smuggles cannabis believing it to be currency cannot be convicted of smuggling cannabis, even though he thought (wrongly) that the smuggling of currency was prohibited (*R v Taaffe* [1984] AC 539, [1984] 1 All ER 747, 148 JP 510, HL), but a person who smuggles controlled drugs believing that they are pornographic goods, which he knows to be subject to a prohibition and which are in fact so subject, may be convicted of fraudulently evading the prohibition on the importation of controlled drugs (*R v Ellis* (1987) 84 Cr App Rep 235, [1987] Crim LR 44). Similarly, a defendant who believes that the obscene videos he is carrying are recordings of sporting events is entitled to be acquitted, but if he is aware of the true nature of the articles he is importing, he will be guilty if the court concludes that the articles have the tendencies to deprave and corrupt the persons specified in s 1(1) of the Obscene Publications Act 1959 (*R v Dunne* (1998) 162 JP 399). It was confirmed in *R v Forbes* [2001] UKHL 40, [2002] 2 AC 512, [2001] 4 All ER 97, [2001] 3 WLR 428, [2002] 1 Cr App Rep 1, that the prosecution does not have to prove that the defendant knew the precise nature of the goods being imported; it is sufficient to prove that he knew that the goods were subject to a prohibition on importation and that the operation in which he was engaged was an evasion of that prohibition. A defendant who is prepared to look after a parcel for a friend which is to be sent from abroad and knows that the parcel might contain controlled drugs, having been told that he could keep a small portion of the drugs for himself, is liable to be convicted of being knowingly concerned in the fraudulent evasion of the prohibition on the importation of a controlled drug (*A-G's Reference (No 1 of 1998)* (1998) 163 JP 390). The mens rea to support an offence under s 170(2) will not necessarily support a charge of conspiracy to commit this offence; see *R v Siracusa* [1989] Crim LR 712. Unsolicited receipt of drugs followed by knowing retention may lead to conviction (*R v Mitchell* [1992] Crim LR 594).

8. The prosecution must prove fraudulent conduct in the sense of dishonest conduct deliberately intended to evade the prohibition or restriction with respect to, or the duty chargeable on, goods as the case may be. There is no necessity for the prosecution to prove acts of deceit practised on a customs officer in his presence (*Re A-G's Reference (No 1 of 1981)* [1982] QB 848, [1982] 2 All ER 417). Where goods normally subject to excise duty are moved within the European Union under duty suspension arrangements under Regulations, excise duty is usually payable in the country of destination. However, where the appropriate accompanying documents have been falsified, the duty suspension arrangements lapse and excise duty immediately becomes chargeable. It has been held that in such circumstances it makes no difference to the issue of guilt on a charge of being knowingly concerned in the fraudulent evasion of excise duty whether the defendant eventually sold the goods free of excise duty in France or England (*R v Hayward* [1999] Crim LR 71).

9. Where an undercover customs officer undertook the importation of drugs from Pakistan to England, the organizer of the undertaking was guilty of the offence of attempting to evade a prohibition in respect of the goods (*R v Latif* [1996] 1 All ER 353, [1996] 1 WLR 104, [1996] 2 Cr App Rep 92, HL).

10. This includes Council Regulations directly applicable within member states (*R v Sissen* [2001] 1 WLR 902, [2001] Crim LR 232, CA).

11. This is an "activity" offence; sometimes it will arise in relation to only one transaction and in other cases there will be many giving rise to continuity of activity which may be charged as one offence. Nevertheless s 170 (2) does not permit two different activities to charged as one offence, see *R v Martin* [1998] 2 Cr App Rep 385 CA.

12. For procedure in respect of this offence which is triable either way, see s 147, ante, and the Magistrates' Courts Act 1980, ss 17A–21, in PART I: MAGISTRATES' COURTS, PROCEDURE, ante.

13. For the meaning of the "prescribed sum", sees 171 post.

14. The sentence will vary according to whether the drugs were intended for personal consumption or distribution to others, but where the quantity was substantial, the offence is grave irrespective of the intention because of the risk they will find their way on to the home market (*R v Ribas* (1976) 63 Cr App Rep 147).

15. "2 years" was the term of imprisonment on conviction on indictment prescribed by s 170(3)(*b*) before its amendment by the Finance Act 1988, s 12.

8–6677   **170B. Offence of taking preparatory steps for evasion of excise duty.** (1) If any person is knowingly concerned in the taking of any steps with a view to the fraudulent evasion, whether by himself or another, of any duty of excise on any goods, he shall be liable[1]—

    (*a*)   on summary conviction, to a penalty of **the prescribed sum**[2] or of three times the amount of the duty, whichever is the greater, or to imprisonment for a term not exceeding **six months** or to both; and

    (*b*)   on conviction on indictment, to a penalty of any amount or to imprisonment for a term not exceeding **seven years** or to both.

(2) Where any person is guilty of an offence under this section, the goods in respect of which the offence was committed shall be liable to forfeiture.

[Customs and Excise Management Act 1979, s 170B, as inserted by the Finance (No 2) Act 1992, Sch 2.]

---

1. For procedure in respect of this offence which is triable either way, see s 147 ante, and the Magistrates' Courts Act 1980, ss 17A–21, in PART I: MAGISTRATES' COURTS, PROCEDURE, ante.

2. For the meaning of "the prescribed sum", see s 171, post.

8–6678   **171. General provisions as to offences and penalties.** (1) Where—

    (*a*)   by any provision of any enactment relating to an assigned matter[1] a punishment is prescribed for any offence thereunder or for any contravention of or failure to comply with any regulation, direction, condition or requirement made, given or imposed thereunder; and

    (*b*)   any person is convicted in the same proceedings of more than one such offence, contravention or failure, that person shall be liable to that punishment for each such offence, contravention or failure of which he is so convicted.

(2) In this Act the "prescribed sum", in relation to the penalty provided for an offence, means—

(*a*) if the offence was committed in England, or Wales, the prescribed sum within the meaning of section 32 of the Magistrates' Courts Act 1980 (£1,000 or other sum substituted by order[2] under section 143(1) of that Act);

(*b*)–(*c*) *Scotland, Northern Ireland*;

and in subsection (1)(*a*) above, the reference to a provision by which a punishment is prescribed includes a reference to a provision which makes a person liable to a penalty of the prescribed sum within the meaning of this subsection.

(2A) (*Repealed*).

(3) Where a penalty for an offence under any enactment relating to an assigned matter[1] is required to be fixed by reference to the value of any goods, that value shall be taken as the price which those goods might reasonably be expected to have fetched, after payment of any duty or tax chargeable thereon, if they had been sold in the open market[3] at or about the date of the commission of the offence for which the penalty is imposed.

(4) Where an offence under any enactment relating to an assigned matter[1] which has been committed by a body corporate is proved to have been committed with the consent or connivance of, or to be attributable to any neglect[4] on the part of, any director, manager, secretary or other similar officer of the body corporate or any person purporting to act in any such capacity, he as well as the body corporate shall be guilty of that offence and shall be liable to be proceeded against and punished accordingly.

In this subsection "director", in relation to any body corporate established by or under any enactment for the purpose of carrying on under national ownership any industry or part of an industry or undertaking, being a body corporate whose affairs are managed by the members thereof, means a member of that body corporate.

(5) Where in any proceedings for an offence under the customs and excise Acts any question arises as to the duty or the rate thereof chargeable on any imported goods, and it is not possible to ascertain the relevant time specified in section 43[5] above or the relevant excise duty point, that duty or rate shall be determined as if the goods had been imported without entry at the time when the proceedings were commenced or, as the case may be, as if the time when the proceedings were commenced was the relevant excise duty point.

[Customs and Excise Management Act 1979, s 171, as amended by the Magistrates' Courts Act 1980, Sch 7, the Finance Act 1984, Sch 4, SI 1984/703 (NI 3), the Finance (No 2) Act 1992, Sch 2 and the Statute Law (Repeals) Act 1993, Sch 1.]

---

1. For meaning of "assigned matter", see s 1, ante.
2. The Criminal Justice Act 1991, s 17(2) now specifies **£5,000** as the prescribed sum.
3. See *Byrne v Low* [1972] 3 All ER 526.
4. It is perfectly proper for a director to leave matters to a co-director or to an official of the company, and to do so would not amount to "neglect" in the absence of factors indicating that the director should distrust the co-director or the official or should feel he was not carrying out his duty (*Huckerby v Elliott* [1970] 1 All ER 189, 134 JP 175).
5. Section 43 provides the times at which rates of duty on imported goods are to be determined.

Miscellaneous

8–6680   176. Game licences.   (1) Subject to the following provisions of this section, and save as expressly provided in section 102 above, the provisions of this Act relating to excise shall not apply in relation to the excise duties on licences to kill game and on licences to deal in game (which, by virtue of the Order in Council made under section 6 of the Finance Act 1908, are leviable by local authorities).

(2) The Treasury may by order provide that, subject to such modifications, if any, as may be specified in the order, any provision of this Act so specified which confers or imposes powers, duties or liabilities with respect to excise duties and to the issue and cancellation of excise licences on which those duties are imposed and to other matters relating to excise duties and licences shall have effect in relation to a local authority and their officers with respect to the duties and licences referred to in subsection (1) above as they have effect in relation to the Commissioners and officers with respect to other excise duties and licences; and those provisions and, subject as aforesaid, any provisions relating to punishments and penalties in connection therewith shall have effect accordingly.

(3) Any order under this section shall be made by statutory instrument and may amend the Order in Council made under section 6 of the Finance Act 1908.

(4) Notwithstanding anything in section 145 above as applied under subsection (2) above, a local authority may authorise the bringing by any constable of proceedings, or any particular proceedings, for an offence under this or any other Act relating to the duties referred to in subsection (1) above.

(5) A document purporting to be a copy of a resolution authorising the bringing of proceedings in accordance with subsection (4) above and to be signed by an officer of the local authority shall be evidence, until the contrary is shown, that the bringing of the proceedings was duly authorised.

(6) This section extends to England and Wales only.

[Customs and Excise Management Act 1979, s 176.]

SCHEDULES

SCHEDULE 1

CONTROLLED DRUGS: VARIATION OF PUNISHMENTS FOR CERTAIN OFFENCES UNDER THIS ACT

(As amended by the Controlled Drugs (Penalties) Act 1985, s 1 and the Criminal Justice Act 2003, Sch 28.)

8–6681   **1.** Section 50(4), 68(3) and 170(3) of this Act shall have effect in a case where the goods in respect of which the offence referred to in that subsection was committed were a Class A drug or a Class B drug as if for the words from "shall be liable" onwards there were substituted the following words, that is to say—
"shall be liable—

    (a)   on summary conviction, to a penalty of **the prescribed sum**[1] or of three times the value of the goods, whichever is the greater, or to imprisonment for a term not exceeding **6 months**, or to both;

    (b)   on conviction on indictment—

        (i)   where the goods were a Class A drug, to a penalty of any amount, or to imprisonment for **life**, or to both; and

        (ii)   where they were a Class B drug, to a penalty of any amount, or to imprisonment for a term not exceeding **14 years**, or to both."

    2. Section 50(4), 68(3) and 170(3) of this Act shall have effect in a case where the goods in respect of which the offence referred to in that subsection was committed were a Class C drug as if for the words from "shall be liable" onwards there were substituted the following words, that is to say—
"shall be liable—

    (a)   on summary conviction, to a penalty of three times the value of the goods or £500, whichever is the greater, or to imprisonment for a term not exceeding **3 months**, or to both;

    (b)   *Northern Ireland;*

    (c)   on conviction on indictment, to a penalty of any amount, or to imprisonment for a term not exceeding <u>14 years</u>, or to both."

    3. In this Schedule "Class A drug", "Class B drug" and "Class C drug" have the same meanings as in the Misuse of Drugs Act 1971.

---

1. For the meaning of the "prescribed sum", see s 171 ante.

SCHEDULE 3

PROVISIONS RELATING TO FORFEITURE[1]

Notice of seizure

8–6690   **1.** (1) The Commissioners shall, except as provided in sub-paragraph (2) below, give notice of the seizure of any thing as liable to forfeiture and of the grounds therefor to any person who to their knowledge was at the time of the seizure the owner or one of the owners thereof.

    (2) Notice need not be given under this paragraph if the seizure was made in the presence of—

    (a)   the person whose offence or suspected offence occasioned the seizure; or

    (b)   the owner or any of the owners of the thing seized, or any servant or agent of his; or

    (c)   in the case of any thing seized in any ship or aircraft, the master or commander.

    2. Notice under paragraph 1, above shall be given in writing and shall be deemed to have been duly served on the person concerned—

    (a)   if delivered to him personally; or

    (b)   if addressed to him and left or forwarded by post to him at his usual or last known place of abode or business or, in the case of a body corporate, at their registered or principal office; or

    (c)   where he has no address within the United Kingdom, or his address is unknown, by publication of notice of the seizure in the London, Edinburgh or Belfast Gazette.

---

1. Where goods are seized in the absence of the persons specified in para 1(2) of Sch 3 notice of seizure has to be given. There is no time limit for giving of such notice but an unreasonable delay could be challenged by an action in detinue. Where the parties are present no written notice need be given but it must be made clear unequivocally to such a person that the goods are being seized as being liable to forfeiture so that he may give a notice of claim within the one month time limit in accordance with para 3. Where no notice of claim is given, any goods are condemned as forfeited. Where a notice of claim is given proceedings for condemnation in a magistrates' court in accordance with para 5 are commenced by way of complaint which must be laid within six months of the date of the notice of claim, see *Customs and Excise v Venn* [2001] EWHC Admin 1055, 166 JP 53.

Notice of claim

8–6691   **3.** Any person claiming that any thing seized as liable to forfeiture is not so liable shall, within one month of the date of the notice of seizure or, where no such notice has been served on him, within one month of the date of the seizure, give notice of his claim in writing to the Commissioners at any office of customs and excise.

    4. (1) Any notice under paragraph 3 above shall specify the name and address of the claimant and, in the case of a claimant who is outside the United Kingdom, shall specify the name and address of a solicitor in the United Kingdom who is authorised to accept service of process and to act on behalf of the claimant.

    (2) Service of process upon a solicitor so specified shall be deemed to be proper service upon the claimant.

Condemnation

8–6692   **5.** If on the expiration of the relevant period under paragraph 3 above for the giving of notice of claim in respect of any thing no such notice has been given to the Commissioners, or if, in the case of any such notice given, any requirement of paragraph 4 above is not complied with, the thing in question shall be deemed to have been duly condemned as forfeited.

6. Where a notice of claim in respect of any thing is duly given in accordance with paragraphs 3 and 4 above, the Commissioners shall take proceedings[1] for the condemnation of that thing by the court, and if the court finds that the thing was at the time of seizure liable to forfeiture the court shall condemn it as forfeited[2].

7. Where any thing is in accordance with either of paragraphs 5 or 6 above condemned or deemed to have been condemned as forfeited, then, without prejudice to any delivery up or sale of the thing by the Commissioners under paragraph 16 below, the forfeiture shall have effect as from the date when the liability to forfeiture arose.

---

1. It was stated *per curiam* in *Gascoyne v Customs and Excise Comrs* [2003] EWHC 257 (Ch), [2003] Ch 292, [2003] 2 WLR 1311 that since condemnation proceedings were excluded from the ambit of the Limitation Act 1980 by s 37(2)(*b*) thereof and since there is, in relation to the High Court, no equivalent to s 127 of the Magistrates' Courts Act 1980 (by virtue of which a six-month time limit applies to bringing condemnation proceedings in a magistrates' court), it would not be an abuse of process if the commissioners were to bring condemnation proceedings in the High Court once the six-month limit for bringing such proceedings in a magistrates' court had expired, although such proceedings might be struck out if there were an unjustifiable or oppressive period of delay or if some assurance or indication had been given that condemnation proceedings would not be issued in the High Court.

2. Where the commissioners failed to bring condemnation proceedings under this para following the issue of a notice of claim they were obliged to exercise their discretion by returning the assets: *Gascoyne v Customs and Excise Comrs*, supra.

Once it is established that the thing in question does come within the class of articles or substances which are liable to forfeiture, justices are not entitled to take into consideration mitigating circumstances so as to remove the thing from that class, but are bound to condemn it (*De Keyser v British Railway Traffic and Electric Co Ltd* [1936] 1 KB 224, 99 JP 403). See also *R (on the application of Customs and Excise Comrs) v Helman* [2002] EWHC 2254 (Admin), (2002) 166 JP 725: s 141(1)(*a*) of, and para 6 of Sch 3 to, the Act mean precisely what they say; once there has been a finding that something has become liable to forfeiture any vehicle, etc, used for its carriage and seized under s 139 must also be condemned as forfeited. However, the liability to forfeiture under s 141(1)(*a*) and (*b*) is subject to European Law on the enforcement of penalties in the case of seized goods which themselves are not liable to duty and article one of the First Protocol to the European Convention on Human Rights in respect of interference with property such as a motor vehicle where any forfeiture must strike a fair balance between the rights of the individual and the public interest; there must be a reasonable relationship of proportionality between the means employed and the aim pursued (*Customs and Excise Comrs v Newbury* [2003] EWHC 702 (Admin), [2003] 2 All ER 964, [2003] 1 WLR 2209. (See also, s 152 post as to the power of Commissioners to restore, etc, items forfeited or seized under the Customs and Excise Acts and *Lindsay v Customs and Excise Comrs* [2002] EWCA Civ 267, [2002] RTR 313. On appeal in *Gascoyne v Customs and Excise Comrs* [2004] EWCA Civ 1162, [2005] Ch 215, [2005] 2 WLR 222, Buxton LJ stated obiter, at para 55, that in a case where the deeming provisions under para 5 of Sch 3 were applied, the tribunal could reopen those issues in a s 152 application.)

Proceedings for condemnation by court

8–6693   **8.** Proceedings for condemnation shall be civil[1] proceedings and may be instituted—

    (*a*) in England or Wales either in the High Court or in a magistrates' court;
    (*b*) in Scotland either in the Court of Session or in the sheriff court;
    (*c*) in Northern Ireland either in the High Court or in a court of summary jurisdiction.

---

1. Though the domestic classification as "civil" carries little weight, condemnation proceedings were concerned only to determine whether the goods were liable to seizure and did not necessarily involve proof of blameworthy conduct, and since the court under para 6 of Sch 3 to the 1979 Act merely declared whether goods were liable to forfeiture and imposed no penalty, they were not in substance in the nature of a criminal charge for the purposes of art 6 of the Convention. As these are civil proceedings there is no power for a magistrates' court to make a representation order under s 12 of the Access to Justice Act 1999: *R (Mudie) v Dover Magistrates' Court* [2003] EWCA Civ 237, [2003] QB 1238, [2003] 2 WLR 1344, [2003] RTR 25.

9. Proceedings for the condemnation of any thing instituted in a magistrates' court in England or Wales, in the sheriff court in Scotland or in a court of summary jurisdiction in Northern Ireland may be so instituted—

    (*a*) in any such court having jurisdiction in the place where any offence in connection with that thing was committed or where any proceedings for such an offence are instituted; or
    (*b*) in any such court having jurisdiction in the place where the claimant resides or, if the claimant has specified a solicitor under paragraph 4 above, in the place where that solicitor has his office; or
    (*c*) in any such court having jurisdiction in the place where that thing was found, detained or seized or to which it is first brought after being found, detained or seized.

10. (1) In any proceedings for condemnation instituted in England, Wales or Northern Ireland, the claimant or his solicitor shall make oath that the thing seized was, or was to the best of his knowledge and belief, the property of the claimant at the time of the seizure.

(2) In any such proceedings instituted in the High Court, the claimant shall give such security for the costs of the proceedings as may be determined by the Court.

(3) If any requirement of this paragraph is not complied with, the court shall give judgment for the Commissioners.

11. (1) In the case of any proceedings for condemnation instituted in a magistrates' court in England or Wales, without prejudice to any right to require the statement of a case for the opinion of the High Court, either party may appeal against the decision of that court to the Crown Court[1].

(2) *Northern Ireland.*

12. Where an appeal, including an appeal by way of case stated, has been made against the decision of the court in any proceedings for the condemnation of any thing, that thing shall, pending the final determination of the matter, be left with the Commissioners or at any convenient office of customs and excise.

---

1. Although the goods must have been physically present within the jurisdiction at the time they were seized, the physical availability of the goods, whether in terms of their being within the jurisdiction or still in existence at all, is not critical at the time of the forfeiture proceedings. Accordingly, where proceedings for condemnation of a pair of ivory reliefs

imported without an import permit or import certificate under Council Regulation EEC 3626/82, were dismissed by the magistrates' court and the reliefs were not retained under para 12, post, but were immediately taken out of the jurisdiction, the Crown Court nevertheless had jurisdiction to entertain an appeal against the refusal to make a condemnation order (*Hashwani v Letherby* (1997) 162 JP 153, DC).

Provisions as to proof

8–6694   **13.** In any proceedings arising out of the seizure of any thing, the fact, form and manner of the seizure shall be taken to have been as set forth in the process without any further evidence thereof, unless the contrary is proved.

     14. In any proceedings, the condemnation by a court of any thing as forfeited may be proved by the production either of the order or certificate of condemnation or of a certified copy thereof purporting to be signed by an officer of the court by which the order or certificate was made or granted.

Special provisions as to certain claimants

8–6695   **15.** For the purposes of any claim to, or proceedings for the condemnation of, anything, where that thing is at the time of seizure the property of a body corporate, of two or more partners or of any number of persons exceeding five, the oath required by paragraph 10 above to be taken and any other thing required by this Schedule or by any rules of the court to be done by, or by any other person authorised by, the claimant or owner may be taken or done by, or by any other person authorised by, the following persons respectively, that is to say—

     (a)   where the owner is a body corporate, the secretary or some duly authorised officer of that body;

     (b)   where the owners are in partnership, any one of those owners;

     (c)   where the owners are any number of persons exceeding five not being in partnership, any two of those persons on behalf of themselves and their co-owners.

8–6696   **16–17.** *Power to deal with seizures before condemnation, etc.*

Customs and Excise Duties (General Reliefs) Act 1979
(1979 c 3)

Personal reliefs

8–6700   **13. Power to provide, in relation to persons entering the United Kingdom, for reliefs from duty and value added tax and for simplified computation of duty and tax.**   (1) The Commissioners may by order[1] make provision for conferring on persons entering the United Kingdom reliefs from duty and value added tax; and any such relief may take the form either of an exemption from payment of duty and tax or of a provision whereby the sum payable by way of duty or tax is less than it would otherwise be.

     (1A) The Commissioners may by order make provision supplementing any Community relief in such manner as they think necessary or expedient.

     (2) Without prejudice to subsection (1) above, the Commissioners may by order make provision whereby, in such cases and to such extent as may be specified in the order, a sum calculated at a rate specified in the order is treated as the aggregate amount payable by way of duty and tax in respect of goods imported by a person entering the United Kingdom; but any order making such provision shall enable the person concerned to elect that duty and tax shall be charged on the goods in question at the rate which would be applicable apart from that provision.

     (3) An order under this section—

     (a)   may make any relief for which it provides, or any Community relief, subject to conditions, including conditions which are to be complied with after the importation of the goods to which the relief applies and conditions with respect to the conduct in relation to the goods of persons other than the person on whom the relief is conferred and of persons whose identity cannot be ascertained at the time of importation;

     (b)   may, in relation to any relief conferred by order made under this section, contain such incidental and supplementary provisions as the Commissioners think necessary or expedient, including provisions requiring any person to whom a condition of the relief at any time relates to notify the Commissioners of any non-compliance with the condition and provisions for the forfeiture of goods in the event of non-compliance with any condition subject to which they have been relieved from duty or tax; and

     (c)   may make different provision for different cases.

     (3A) An order under this section may provide, in relation to any relief which under such an order is made subject to a condition, for there to be a presumption that, in such cases as may be described in the order by reference—

     (a)   to the quantity of goods in question; or

     (b)   to any other factor which the Commissioners consider appropriate,

the condition is to be treated, unless the Commissioners are satisfied to the contrary, as not being complied with.

     (3B) An order under this section may provide, in relation to any requirement of such an order for the Commissioners to be notified of non-compliance of such an order for the Commissioners to be notified of non-compliance with a condition to which any relief from payment of any duty of excise is made subject, for goods to be exempt from forfeiture under section 124 of the Customs and Excise Management Act 1979 (forfeiture for breach of certain conditions) in respect of non-compliance with that condition if—

(a)   the non-compliance is notified to the Commissioners in accordance with that requirement;

(b)   any duty which becomes payable on those goods by virtue of the non-compliance is paid; and

(c)   the circumstances are otherwise such as may be described in the order.

(3C)   If any person fails to comply with any requirement of an order under this section to notify the Commissioners of any non-compliance with a condition to which any relief is made subject—

(a)   he shall be liable, on summary conviction, to a penalty of an amount not exceeding **level 5** on the standard scale; and

(b)   the goods in respect of which the offence was committed shall be liable to forfeiture.

(4)   In this section—

"Community relief" means any relief which is conferred by a Community instrument and is of a kind, or of a kind similar to that, which would otherwise be conferred by order made under this section;

"conduct", in relation to any person who has or may acquire possession or control of any goods, includes that person's intentions at any time in relation to those goods;

"duty" means customs or excise duty chargeable on goods imported into the United Kingdom and, in the case of excise duty, includes any addition thereto by virtue of section 1 of the Excise Duties (Surcharges or Rebates) Act 1979; and

"value added tax" or "tax" means value added tax chargeable on the importation of goods from places outside the member States or on the acquisition of goods from member States other than the United Kingdom.

(5)   Nothing in any order under this section shall be construed as authorising any person to import any thing in contravention of any prohibition or restriction for the time being in force with respect thereto under or by virtue of any enactment.

[Customs and Excise Duties (General Reliefs) Act 1979, s 13, as amended by the Finance Act 1984, s 15, and the Finance (No 2) Act 1992, Schs 1 and 3.]

---

1. The Customs and Excise (Personal Reliefs for Special Visitors) Order 1992, SI 1992/3156 amended by SI 2005/2114 provides certain reliefs for diplomats, members of international organisations and visiting forces and other persons which were formerly allowed by extra-statutory concession.

The relief from excise duties for travellers arriving from places within the EC are set out in the Excise Duties (Personal Reliefs) Order 1992, SI 1992/3155 amended by SI 1999/1617; and SI 1992/3156 (special visitors). For applicability of personal reliefs to new Member States, see the Customs and Excise Duties (Travellers' Allowances and Personal Reliefs) (New Member States) Order 2004, SI 2004/1002 and the Excise Duty Points (Etc) (New Member States) Regulations 2004, SI 2004/1003 give effect to derogations contained in the Act concerning the Accession of the Czech Republic, Cyprus, Estonia, Latvia, Lithuania, Hungary, Malta, Poland, Slovenia and Slovakia to the European Union so that existing member States can maintain limits on the amount of cigarettes or other tobacco products which may be brought into their territory, without further excise duty payment, from new member States who have obtained derogations from the relevant Council Directives. See also the Travellers' Reliefs (Fuel and Lubricants) Order 1995, SI 1995/1777 (relief for fuel and lubricants contained in commercial vehicles).

In addition the Travellers' Allowances Order 1994, SI 1994/955 amended by SI 1995/3044 and SI 2004/1002 applies relief from VAT and excise duties to travellers arriving from places outside the EC.

Where for the purposes of the Excise Duties (Personal Reliefs) Order 1992 the quantity of excise goods being imported is above the prescribed levels, the Customs and Excise are to presume that the goods are imported for a commercial purpose rather than for personal use, but such presumption is rebutted if the importer satisfies the Customs and Excise that the goods are held or used for personal use. Accordingly, the Customs and Excise are obliged to give the person a fair opportunity to satisfy them that the goods are not being held or used for a commercial purpose. The Commissioners are not to treat the condition for relief as not being complied with where a court or tribunal has found it to be complied with. See also *R v Customs and Excise Comrs, ex p Mortimer* [1998] 3 All ER 229, 162 JP 663.

A decision by the Commissioners of Customs and Excise that the condition that excise goods afforded relief under the Excise Duties (Personal Reliefs) Order 1992, SI 1992/3155 are not held or used for a commercial purpose has not been complied with, does not bind a VAT and duties tribunal or Court, see art 5 as amended by SI 1999/1617.

8–6701   13A. reliefs from duties and taxes for persons enjoying certain immunities and privileges.   (1) The Commissioners may by order[1] make provision for conferring in respect of any persons to whom this section applies reliefs, by way of remission or repayment, from payment by them or others of duties of customs or excise, value added tax or car tax.

(2)   An order under this section may make any relief for which it provides subject to such conditions binding the person in respect of whom the relief is conferred and, if different, the person liable apart from the relief for payment of the tax or duty (including conditions which are to be complied with after the time when, apart from the relief, the duty or tax would become payable) as may be imposed by or under the order.

(3)   An order under this section may include any of the provisions mentioned in subsection (4) below for cases where—

(a)   relief from payment of any duty of customs or excise, value added tax or car tax chargeable on any goods, or on the supply of any goods or services or the importation of any goods has been conferred (whether by virtue of an order under this section or otherwise) in respect of any person to whom this section applies, and

   (b)   any condition required to be complied with in connection with the relief is not complied with.

  (4)   The provisions referred to in subsection (3) above are—

   (a)   provision for payment to the Commissioners of the tax or duty by—

     (i)   the person liable, apart from the relief, for its payment, or

     (ii)   any person bound by the condition, or

     (iii)   any person who is or has been in possession of the goods or has received the benefit of the services,

     or for two or more of those persons to be jointly and severally liable for such payment, and

   (b)   in the case of goods, provision for forfeiture of the goods.

  (5)   An order under this section—

   (a)   may contain such incidental and supplementary provisions as the Commissioners think necessary or expedient, and

   (b)   may make different provision for different cases.

  (6)   In this section and section 13C of this Act—

"duty of customs" includes any agricultural levy within the meaning of section 6 of the European Communities Act 1972 chargeable on goods imported into the United Kingdom, and

"duty of excise" means any duty of excise chargeable on goods and includes any addition to excise duty by virtue of section 1 of the Excise Duties (Surcharges or Rebates) Act 1979.

  (7)   For the purposes of this section and section 13C of this Act, where in respect of any person to whom this section applies relief is conferred (whether by virtue of an order under this section or otherwise) in relation to the use of goods by any persons or for any purposes, the relief is to be treated as conferred subject to a condition binding on him that the goods will be used by those persons or for those purposes.

  (8)   Nothing in any order under this section shall be construed as authorising a person to import any thing in contravention of any prohibition of restriction for the time being in force with respect to it under or by virtue of any enactment.

[Customs and Excise Duties (General Reliefs) Act 1979, s 13A, as inserted by the Finance Act 1989, s 28.]

---

1.   The Customs and Excise (Personal Reliefs for Special Visitors) Order 1992, SI 1992/3156 amended by SI 2005/2114, has been made.

8–6702   13B. Persons to whom section 13A applies.   (1) The persons to whom section 13A of this Act applies are—

   (a)   any person who, for the purposes of any provision of the Visiting Forces Act 1952 or the International Headquarters and Defence Organisations Act 1964 is—

     (i)   a member of a visiting force or of a civilian component of such a force or a dependant of such a member, or

     (ii)   a headquarters, a member of a headquarters or a dependant of such a member,

   (b)   any person enjoying any privileges or immunities under or by virtue of—

     (i)   the Diplomatic Privileges Act 1964,

     (ii)   the Commonwealth Secretariat Act 1966,

     (iii)   the Consular Relations Act 1968,

     (iv)   the International Organisations Act 1968, or

     (v)   the International Development Act 2002,

   (c)   any person enjoying, under or by virtue of section 2 of the European Communities Act 1972, any privileges or immunities similar to those enjoyed under or by virtue of the enactments referred to in paragraph (b) above.

  (2)   The Secretary of State may by order amend subsection (1) above to include any persons enjoying any privileges or immunities similar to those enjoyed under or by virtue of the enactments referred to in paragraph (b) of that subsection.

  (3)   No order shall be made under this section unless a draft of the order has been laid before and approved by resolution of each House of Parliament.

[Customs and Excise Duties (General Reliefs) Act 1979, s 13B, as inserted by the Finance Act 1989, s 28 and amended by the International Development Act 2002, s 19(1), Sch 3.]

8–6703   13C. Offence where relieved goods used, etc, in breach of condition.   (1) Subsection (2) below applies where—

   (a)   any relief from payment of any duty of customs or excise, value added tax or car tax chargeable on, or on the supply or importation of, any goods has been conferred (whether by virtue of an order under section 13A of this Act or otherwise) in respect of any person to whom that section applies subject to any condition as to the persons by whom or the purposes for which the goods may be used, and

(b) if the tax or duty has subsequently become payable, it has not been paid.

(2) If any person—

(a) acquires the goods for his own use, where he is not permitted by the condition to use them, or for use for a purpose that is not permitted by the condition or uses them for such a purpose, or

(b) acquires the goods for use, or causes or permits them to be used, by a person not permitted by the condition to use them or by a person for a purpose that is not permitted by the condition or disposes of them to a person not permitted by the condition to use them,

with intent to evade payment of any tax or duty that has become payable or that, by reason of the disposal, acquisition or use, becomes or will become payable, he is guilty of an offence.

(3) For the purposes of this section—

(a) in the case of a condition as to the persons by whom goods may be used, a person is not permitted by the condition to use them unless he is a person referred to in the condition as permitted to use them, and

(b) in relation to a condition as to the purposes for which goods may be used, a purpose is not permitted by the condition unless it is a purpose referred to in the condition as a permitted purpose,

and in this section "dispose" includes "lend" and "let on hire", and "acquire" shall be interpreted accordingly.

(4) A person guilty of an offence under this section may be detained and shall be liable[1]—

(a) on summary conviction, to a penalty of **the statutory maximum** or of three times the value of the goods (whichever is the greater), or to imprisonment for a term not exceeding **six months**, or to both, or

(b) on conviction on indictment, to a **penalty** of any amount, or to imprisonment for a term not exceeding **seven years**, or to both.

(5) Where any person is guilty of an offence under this section, the goods in respect of which the offence was committed shall be liable to forfeiture.

[Customs and Excise Duties (General Reliefs) Act 1979, s 13C, as inserted by the Finance Act 1989, s 28, and amended by the Finance (No 2) Act 1992, Sch 2.]

---

1. For procedure in respect of this offence which is triable either way, see s 147 of the Customs and Excise Management Act 1979, ante, and the Magistrates' Courts Act 1980, ss 17A–21, in PART I, MAGISTRATES' COURTS, PROCEDURE, ante.

False statements etc in connection with reliefs from customs duties

8–6800 15. False statements etc in connection with reliefs from customs duties. (1) If a person—

(a) for the purpose of an application for relief from customs duty under section 1 or 3 above or under a Community instrument; or

(b) for the purpose of an application for an authorisation under regulations made under section 2 above,

makes any statement or furnishes any document[1] which is false in a material particular to any government department or to any authority or person on whom functions are conferred by or under section 1, 3 or 4 above or a Community instrument, then—

(i) any decision allowing the relief or granting the authorisation applied for shall be of no effect; and

(ii) if the statement was made or the document was furnished knowingly or recklessly, that person shall be guilty of an offence under this section.

(2) A person guilty of an offence under this section shall be liable[2]—

(a) on summary conviction, to a fine not exceeding **the prescribed sum**, or to imprisonment for a term not exceeding **3 months**, or to both; or

(b) on conviction on indictment, to a fine of any amount or to imprisonment for a term not exceeding **2 years**, or to both.

(3) In subsection (2)(a) above "the prescribed sum" means—

(a) if the offence was committed in England, Wales or Northern Ireland, the prescribed sum within the meaning of section 32 of the Magistrates' Courts Act 1980 (£1,000 or other sum substituted by order under section 143(1) of that Act);

(b) *Scotland.*

(4) References in Parts XI and XII of the Customs and Excise Management Act 1979 to an offence under the customs and excise Acts shall not apply to an offence under this section.

[Customs and Excise Duties (General Reliefs) Act 1979, s 15, as amended by the Magistrates' Courts Act 1980, Sch 7.]

---

1. "Document" has the same meaning as in Pt I of the Civil Evidence Act 1968; see the Finance Act 1985, s 10, this title, post.

2. For procedure in respect of this offence which is triable either way, see the Magistrates' Courts Act 1980, ss 17A–21, in PART I: MAGISTRATES' COURTS, PROCEDURE, ante.

8–6801 18. Interpretation. (1) This Act and the other Acts included in the Customs and Excise Acts 1979 shall be construed as one Act but where a provision of this Act refers to this Act that reference is not to be construed as including a reference to any of the others.

(2) Any expression used in this Act or in any instrument made under this Act to which a meaning is given by any other Act included in the Customs and Excise Acts 1979 has, except where the context otherwise requires, the same meaning in this Act or in any such instrument as in that Act; and for ease of reference the Table below indicates the expressions used in this Act to which a meaning is given by any other such Act—

Customs and Excise Management Act 1979

"the Commissioners"
"the Customs and Excise Acts 1979"
"the customs and excise Acts"
"customs and excise airport"
"goods"
"hovercraft"
"importer"
"master"
"officer" and "proper" in relation to an officer
"port"
"ship"
"transit and transhipment"
"warehouse"

Alcoholic Liquor Duties Act 1979

"spirits"
"wine"

(3) This Act applies as if references to ships included references to hovercraft.
[Customs and Excise Duties (General Reliefs) Act 1979, s 18.]

Alcoholic Liquor Duties Act 1979
(1979 c 4)

PART I[1]
PRELIMINARY

8–6810 1. The alcoholic liquors dutiable under this Act. (1) Subsections (2) to (8) below define for the purposes of this Act the alcoholic liquors which are subject to excise duty under this Act, that is to say—

(a) spirits,
(b) beer,
(c) wine,
(d) made-wine, and
(e) cider;

and in this Act "dutiable alcoholic liquor" means any of those liquors and "duty" means excise duty.

(2) "Spirits" means, subject to subsections (7) to (9) below—

(a) spirits of any description which are of a strength exceeding 1.2 per cent,
(b) any such mixture, compound or preparation made with spirits as of a strength exceeding 1.2 per cent, or
(c) liquors contained with any spirits, in any mixture which is of a strength exceeding 1.2 per cent.

(3) "Beer" includes ale, porter, stout and any other description of beer, and any liquor which is made or sold as a description of beer or as a substitute for beer and which is of a strength exceeding 0.5 per cent, but does not include—

(a) black beer the worts whereof before fermentation were of a specific gravity of 1200° or more;
(b) (*Repealed*).

(4) "Wine" means any liquor which is of a strength exceeding 1.2 per cent and which is obtained from the alcoholic fermentation of fresh grapes or of the must of fresh grapes, whether or not the liquor is fortified with spirits or flavoured with aromatic extracts.

(5) "Made-wine" means subject to subsection (10) and section 55B (1) below any liquor which is of a strength exceeding 1.2 per cent and which is obtained from the alcoholic fermentation of any substance or by mixing a liquor so obtained or derived from a liquor so obtained with any other liquor or substance but does not include wine, beer, black beer, spirits or cider.

(6) "Cider" means, subject to section 55B (1), below, cider (or perry) of a strength exceeding 1.2 per cent but less than 8.5 per cent obtained from the fermentation of apple or pear juice without the addition at any time of any alcoholic liquor or of any liquor or substance which communicates colour or flavour other than such as the Commissioners may allow as appearing to them to be necessary to make cider (or perry).

(7) Angostura bitters, that is to say, the aromatic flavouring essence commonly known as angostura bitters, shall be deemed not to be spirits, but this subsection does not apply for the purposes of sections 2, 5, 6 and 27 to 30 below.

(8) Methyl alcohol, notwithstanding that it is so purified or prepared as to be drinkable, shall not be deemed to be spirits nor shall naphtha or any mixture or preparation containing naphtha or methyl alcohol and not containing spirits as defined in subsection (2) above.

(9) Any beverage of an alcoholic strength exceeding 1.2 per cent but not exceeding 5.5 per cent which is made with spirits and is not of a description specified in an order made by the Treasury by statutory instrument shall be deemed not to be spirits.

(10) The Treasury may by order[2] made by statutory instrument provide that any beverage of an alcoholic strength exceeding 1.2 per cent but not exceeding 5.5 per cent which is made with beer or cider and is of a description specified in the order shall be deemed to be beer or, as the case may be, cider, and not to be made-wine.

[Alcoholic Liquor Duties Act 1979, s 1, as amended by SI 1979/241, the Finance Act 1988, Schs 1 and 14, the Finance Act 1991, Schs 2 and 19, the Finance Act 1993, s 3, the Excise Duty (Amendment of the Alcoholic Liquor Duties Act 1979) Regulations 1992, SI 1992/3158, the Finance Act 1995, s 1 and Sch 29 and the Finance Act 1997, s 5.]

---

1. Part I contains ss 1–4.
2. See the Alcoholic Liquor Duties (Beer-based Beverages) Order 1988, SI 1988/1684.

8–6811   4. Interpretation.   (1) In this Act, unless the context otherwise requires—

"alcohol" has the meaning given by section 2 above;

"authorised denaturer" means a person authorised under section 75(1) below to denature dutiable alcoholic liquor;

"beer" has the meaning given by section 1 above;

"black beer" means beer or the description called or similar to black beer, mum, spruce beer or Berlin white beer, and any other preparation (whether fermented or not) of a similar character;

"British compounded spirits" means spirits which have, in the United Kingdom, had any flavour communicated thereto or ingredient or material mixed therewith, not being denatured alcohol;

"case", in relation to dutiable alcoholic liquor, means 1 dozen units each consisting of a container holding not less than 65 nor more than 80 centilitres, or the equivalent of that number of such units made up wholly or partly of containers of a larger or smaller size;

"cider" has the meaning given by section 1 above;

"compounder" means a person holding a licence as a compounder under section 18 below;*

"denatured alcohol" means denatured alcohol within the meaning of section 5 of the Finance Act 1995, and references to denaturing a liquor are references to subjecting it to any process by which it becomes denatured alcohol;

"distiller" means a person holding a distiller's licence under section 12 below;

"distiller's licence" has the meaning given by section 12(1) below;

"distiller's warehouse" means a place of security provided by a distiller and approved by the Commissioners under section 15(1) below;

"distillery" means premises where spirits are manufactured, whether by distillation of a fermented liquor or by any other process;

"dutiable alcoholic liquor" has the meaning given by section 1(1) above;

"duty" has the meaning given by section 1(1) above and "duty-paid", "duty-free" and references to drawback shall be construed accordingly;

"gravity" and "original gravity" have the meanings given by section 3 above;

"justices' licence" and "justices on-licence"—

   (a) revoked
   (b) *Northern Ireland*;

"licensed", in relation to a producer of wine or of made-wine, means a producer who holds a licence to produce wine or made-wine respectively under subsection (2) of section 54 or 55 below;

"licensed denaturer" means a person holding a license under section 75(2) below;

"made-wine" has the meaning given by section 1 above;

"the Management Act" means the Customs and Excise Management Act 1979;

"package", in relation to beer, means to put beer into tanks, casks, kegs, cans, bottles or any other receptacles of a kind in which beer is distributed to wholesalers or retailers;

"packager", in relation to beer, means a person carrying on the business of packaging beer;

"the prescribed sum" in relation to the penalty provided for an offence, means—

    (a) if the offence was committed in England or Wales or in Northern Ireland, the prescribed sum within the meaning of section 32 of the Magistrates' Courts Act 1980 (£1,000 or other sum substituted by order under section 143(1) of that Act);

    (b) *Scotland.*

    (c) *Northern Ireland.*

"producer of made-wine" includes a person who renders made-wine sparkling, and "produce", in relation to made-wine, shall be construed accordingly;

"producer of wine" includes a person who renders wine sparkling, and "produce", in relation to wine, shall be construed accordingly;

"rectifier" means a person holding a licence as a rectifier under section 18 below;

"registered brewer" has the meaning given by section 47(1) below;

"registered club" means a club which is for the time being a registered club within the meaning of the Licensing (Scotland) Act 1976 or which is for the time being a registered club within the meaning of the Registration of Clubs Act (Northern Ireland) 1967;

"retailer" means—

    (a) in relation to dutiable alcoholic liquor, a person who sells such liquor by retail;

    (b) *(Repealed)*;

"*Scottish licence*"

"spirits" has the meaning given by section 1 above;

"spirits of wine" means plain spirits of a strength of not less than 80 per cent manufactured in the United Kingdom;

"strength", in relation to any liquor, has the meaning given by section 2 above;

"wholesale", in relation to dealing in dutiable alcoholic liquor, means the sale at any one time to any person of quantities not less than the following, namely—

    (a) in the case of spirits, wine or made-wine, 9 litres or 1 case; or

    (b) in the case of beer or cider, 20 litres or 2 cases;

"wholesaler" means a person who deals wholesale in dutiable alcoholic liquor;

"wine" has the meaning given by section 1 above.

(2) This Act and the other Acts included in the Customs and Excise Acts 1979 shall be construed as one Act but where a provision of this Act refers to this Act that reference is not to be construed as including a reference to any of the others.

(3) Any expression used in this Act or in any instrument made under this Act to which a meaning is given by any other Act included in the Customs and Excise Acts 1979 has, except where the context otherwise requires, the same meaning in this Act or in any such instrument as in that Act; and for ease of reference the Table below indicates the expressions used in this Act to which a meaning is given by any other such Act—

Management Act

"the Commissioners"

"container"

"the Customs and Excise Acts 1979"

"excise warehouse"

"goods"

"hovercraft"

"importer"

"night"

"occupier"

"officer" and "proper" in relation to an officer

"ship" and "British ship"

"shipped"

"shipment"

"stores"

"tons register"

"United Kingdom waters"

"warehouse"

"warehousing regulations".

(4) For the purposes of this Act, selling by retail, in relation to dutiable alcoholic liquor, means the sale at any one time to any one person of quantities not exceeding the following, that is to say—

    (*a*) in the case of spirits, wine or made-wine, 9 litres or 1 case;
    (*b*) in the case of beer or cider, 21 litres or 2 cases.

[Alcoholic Liquor Duties Act 1979, s 4, as amended by SI 1979/241, the Magistrates' Courts Act 1980, Sch 7, the Finance Act 1981, Sch 8, the Finance Act 1986, Sch 23, the Territorial Sea Act 1987, Schs 1 and 2, the Finance Act 1990, s 8, the Finance Act 1991, Sch 2 and 19, SI 1992/3157, the Finance Act 1995, Sch 2 and the Licensing Act 2003, Sch 6.]

PART II[1]
SPIRITS
MANUFACTURE OF SPIRITS

8–6812   17. Offences in connection with removal of spirits from distillery, etc.   (1) If any person—

    (*a*) conceals in or without the consent of the proper officer removes from a distillery any wort, wash, low wines, feints or spirits; or
    (*b*) knowingly buys or receives any wort, wash, low wines, feints or spirits so concealed or removed; or
    (*c*) knowingly buys or receives or has in his possession any spirits which have been removed from the place where they ought to have been charged with duty before the duty payable thereon has been charged and either paid or secured, not being spirits which have been condemned or are deemed to have been condemned as forfeited,

he shall be guilty of an offence under this section and may be arrested, and the goods shall be liable to forfeiture.

   (2) A person guilty of an offence under this section shall be liable[2]—

    (*a*) on summary conviction, to a penalty of **the prescribed sum** or three times the value of the goods, whichever is the greater, or to imprisonment for a term not exceeding **6 months**, or to both; or
    (*b*) on conviction on indictment, to a penalty of any amount, or to imprisonment for a term not exceeding **2 years**, or to both.

[Alcoholic Liquor Duties Act 1979, s 17 as amended by the Police and Criminal Evidence Act 1984, s 114.]

---

   1. Part II contains ss 5–35.
   2. For procedure in respect of this offence which is triable either way, see s 147 of the Customs and Excise Management Act 1979, ante, and the Magistrates' Courts Act 1980, ss 17A–21, in PART I: MAGISTRATES' COURTS, PROCEDURE, ante.

General provisions relating to manufacture of spirits and British compounds

8–6813   25. Penalty for unlawful manufacture of spirits, etc.   (1) Save as provided by or under this Act, any person who, otherwise than under and in accordance with an excise licence under this Act so authorising him—

    (*a*) manufactures spirits, whether by distillation of a fermented liquor or by any other process; or
    (*b*) uses a still for distilling, rectifying or compounding spirits; or
    (*c*) distils or has in his possession any low wines or feints; or
    (*d*) not being a vinegar-maker, brews or makes or has in his possession any wort or wash fit for distillation,

shall be liable on summary conviction to a penalty of **level 5** on the standard scale.

   (2) Where there is insufficient evidence to convict a person of an offence under subsection (1) above, but it is proved that such an offence has been committed on some part of premises belonging to or occupied by that person in such circumstances that it could not have been committed without his knowledge, that person shall be liable on summary conviction to a penalty of **level 3** on the standard scale.

   (3) Any person found on premises on which spirits are being unlawfully manufactured or on which a still is being unlawfully used for rectifying or compounding spirits may be arrested.

   (4) All spirits and stills, vessels, utensils, wort, wash and other materials for manufacturing, distilling or preparing spirits—

    (*a*) found in the possession of any person who commits an offence under subsection (1) above; or
    (*b*) found on any premises on which such an offence has been committed,

shall be liable to forfeiture.

   (5) Notwithstanding any other provision of the Customs and Excise Acts 1979 relating to goods seized as liable to forfeiture, any officer by whom any thing is seized as liable to forfeiture under subsection (4) above may at his discretion forthwith spill, break up or destroy that thing.

   (6) *Northern Ireland.*

[Alcoholic Liquor Duties Act 1979, s 25 as amended by the Criminal Justice Act 1982, ss 38 and 46, the Police and Criminal Evidence Act 1984, s 114 and the Finance Act 1986, Sch 23.]

Brewing of beer

8–6815   74. Liquor to be deemed wine or spirits.   For the purposes of this Act, as against any person selling or offering for sale the liquor in question—

(a)   any liquor sold or offered for sale as wine or under the name by which any wine is usually designated or known shall be deemed to be wine; and

(b)   any fermented liquor which is of a strength exceeding 23 per cent not being imported wine delivered for home use in that state on which the appropriate duty has been duly paid, shall be deemed to be spirits.

Paragraph (a) above is without prejudice to any liability under section 71 above.
[Alcoholic Liquor Duties Act 1979, s 74, as amended by SI 1979/241.]

8–6816   80. Prohibition of use of denatured alcohol, etc as a beverage or medicine.   (1) If any person—

(a)   prepares or attempts to prepare any liquor to which this section applies for use as a beverage or as a mixture with a beverage; or

(b)   sells any such liquor, whether so prepared or not, as a beverage or mixed with a beverage; or

(c)   uses any such liquor or any derivative thereof in the preparation of any article capable of being used wholly or partially as a beverage or internally as a medicine; or

(d)   sells or has in his possession any such article in the preparation of which any such liquor or any derivative thereof has been used; or

(e)   except as permitted by the Commissioners and in accordance with any conditions imposed by them, purifies or attempts to purify any such liquor or, after any such liquor has once been used, recovers or attempts to recover the spirit or alcohol contained therein by distillation or condensation or in any other manner,

he shall be liable on summary conviction to a penalty of **level 3** on the standard scale and the liquor in respect of which the offence was committed shall be liable to forfeiture.

(2)   Nothing in this section shall prohibit the use of any liquor to which this section applies or any derivative thereof—

(a)   in the preparation for use as a medicine of sulphuric ether, chloroform, or any other article which the Commissioners may by order specify; or

(b)   in the making for external use only of any article sold or supplied in accordance with regulations made by the Commissioners under section 77 above; or

(c)   in any art or manufacture,

or the sale or possession of any article permitted to be prepared or made by virtue of paragraph (a) or (b) above where the article is sold or possessed for use as mentioned in that paragraph.

(3)   The liquors to which this section applies are denatured alcohol, methyl alcohol, and any mixture containing denatured alcohol or methyl alcohol.
[Alcoholic Liquor Duties Act 1979, s 80 as amended by the Criminal Justice Act 1982, ss 38 and 46 and the Finance Act 1995, Sch 2.]

Betting and Gaming Duties Act 1981[1]
(1981 c 63)

PART I[2]
BETTING DUTIES

General betting duty

8–7050   1. General betting duty.   A duty of excise to be known as general betting duty shall be charged in accordance with sections 2 to 5D.
[Betting and Gaming Duties Act 1981, s 1 as substituted by the Finance Act 2001, s 6.]

---

1. This Act shall be construed as one with the Customs and Excise Management Act 1979, ante, (s 35(2) post).
2. Part I contains ss 1–12.

8–7051   2–5. *Payment and recovery of general betting duty, etc.*

8–7052   6–8. *Pool Betting duty.*

General

8–7053   9. Prohibitions for protection of revenue.   (1) Any person who—

(*a*) conducts in the United Kingdom any business or agency for the negotiation, receipt or transmission of bets to which this section applies, or

(*b*) knowingly issues, circulates or distributes in the United Kingdom, or has in his possession for that purpose, any advertisement[1] or other document inviting or otherwise relating to the making of such bets, or

(*c*) being a bookmaker in the United Kingdom, makes or offers to make any such bet with a bookmaker outside the United Kingdom,

shall be guilty of an offence.

(2) Except as mentioned in subsection (3) below, this section applies to—

(*a*) all bets made by way of pool betting or coupon betting unless—

    (i) in the case of bets made by means of a totalisator, the totalisator is situated in the United Kingdom,

    (ii) in the case of bets made otherwise than by means of a totalisator, the promoter of the betting is in the United Kingdom; and

(*b*) all bets made with a bookmaker outside the United Kingdom (whether or not made by way of pool betting or coupon betting).

(3) This section does not apply—

(*a*) to any bet which is made by way of pool betting or coupon betting if—

    (i) the bet is not made by means of a totalisator,

    (ii) the promoter is in the Isle of Man,

    (iii) the bet is chargeable with a duty imposed by or under an Act of Tynwald which corresponds to pool betting duty, and

    (iv) the duty mentioned in sub-paragraph (iii) is chargeable on the bet at a rate not less than the appropriate rate of pool betting duty; or

(*aa*) to any bet which is made with a bookmaker if—

    (i) it is not made by way of pool betting or coupon betting,

    (ii) the bookmaker is in the Isle of Man,

    (iii) a duty is imposed by or under an Act of Tynwald in respect of bookmaker's receipts from bets of that kind, and

    (iv) the rates and method of calculation of that duty result in no less duty being charged in respect of bets of that kind than is charged by way of general betting duty in respect of bets of that kind; or

(*b*) to any bet made by means of a totalisator situated in a country outside the United Kingdom on a horse race taking place in that country; or

(*c*) to any bet in respect of an event taking place outside the United Kingdom made by a bookmaker in the United Kingdom—

    (i) by means of a totalisator situated outside the United Kingdom, or

    (ii) with a bookmaker outside the United Kingdom,

    if it is shown that bets in respect of that event have been made in [the United Kingdom with the first-mentioned bookmaker by other persons.

(4) *Repealed.*

(5) A person who makes or tries to make a bet, or who gets or tries to get any advertisement or other document given or sent to him, shall not be guilty of an offence by reason of his thereby procuring or inciting some other person to commit, or aiding or abetting the commission of, an offence under this section.

(6) Section 8C(1) to (3) above shall have effect for the purposes of subsections (2)(*a*) and (5) above as it has effect for the purposes of sections 6 to 8A above.

[Betting and Gaming Duties Act 1981, s 9 as amended by the Finance Act 1986, Schs 4 and 23, the Finance Act 2001, s 6 and the Finance Act 2002, ss 14(3), 141.]

---

1. Section 9(1)(*b*) extends to advertisements arranged by an offshore bookmaker for his services to be made available for viewing on television screens in the United Kingdom by being broadcast on Teletext (*Victor Chandler International Ltd v Customs and Excise Comrs* [2000] 2 All ER 315, [2000] 1 WLR 1296, CA).

2. For procedure in respect of this offence which is triable either way, see s 147 of the Customs and Excise Management Act 1979, ante, and ss 17A–21 of the Magistrates' Courts Act 1980, PART I, MAGISTRATES' COURTS, PROCEDURE, ante.

8–7053A   9A. Further prohibitions for protection of revenue.   (1) A person shall be guilty of an offence if—

(*a*) he knowingly issues, circulates or distributes in the United Kingdom, or has in his possession for that purpose, any advertisement or other document inviting the use of or otherwise relating to bet-broking services, and

(*b*) any person providing any of the bet-broking services concerned—

    (i) is outside the United Kingdom, and

(ii) provides them in the course of a business.

(2) In this section "bet-broking services" means—

(a) facilities provided by a person that may be used by other persons in making bets with third persons, or

(b) a person's services of acting as agent for other persons in making bets on their behalf with third parties (whether the persons on whose behalf the bets are made are disclosed principals or undisclosed principals).

(3) In subsection (2) "bet" means a bet other than one made by way of pool betting.

(4) A person who gets or tries to get any advertisement or other document given or sent to him shall not be guilty of an offence by reason of his thereby procuring or inciting some other person to commit, or aiding or abetting the commission of, an offence under this section.

[Betting and Gaming Duties Act 1981, s 9A as inserted by the Finance Act 2002, s 14(1).]

8–7053B 9B. Offences under sections 9 and 9A: penalties. (1) This section applies where a person is guilty of an offence under section 9 or 9A (a "relevant offence").

(2) In the case of the person's first conviction for a relevant offence, he is liable—

(a) on summary conviction to a penalty of the prescribed sum, or

(b) on conviction on indictment to a penalty of any amount.

(3) In the case of a second or subsequent conviction of the person for a relevant offence, he is liable—

(a) on summary conviction to a penalty of the prescribed sum or to imprisonment for a term not exceeding three months or both, or

(b) on conviction on indictment to a penalty of any amount or to imprisonment for a term not exceeding one year or to both.

[Betting and Gaming Duties Act 1981, s 9B as inserted by the Finance Act 2002, s 14(1).]

8–7054 10. Definition of pool betting. (1) For the purposes of this Part of this Act, a bet shall be deemed to be made by way of pool betting unless it is a bet at fixed odds, and, in particular, bets shall be held to be made by way of pool betting wherever a number of persons make bets—

(a) on terms that the winnings of such of those persons as are winners shall be, or be a share of, or be determined by reference to, the stake money paid or agreed to be paid by those persons, whether the bets are made by means of a totalisator, or by filling up and returning coupons or other printed or written forms, or in any other way, or

(b) on terms that the winnings of such of those persons as are winners shall be, or shall include, an amount (not determined by reference to the stake money paid or agreed to be paid by those persons) which is divisible in any proportions among such of those persons as are winners, or

(c) on the basis that the winners or their winnings shall, to any extent, be at the discretion of the promoter or some other person.

(2) A bet is a bet at fixed odds within the meaning of this section only if each of the persons making it knows or can know, at the time he makes it, the amount he will win, except in so far as that amount is to depend on the result of the event or events betted on, or on any such event taking place or producing a result, or on the numbers taking part in any such event, or on the starting prices or totalisator odds for any such event, or on there being totalisator odds on any such event, or on the time when his bet is received by any person with or through whom it is made.

In this subsection—

"starting prices" means, in relation to any event, the odds ruling at the scene of the event immediately before the start, and

"totalisator odds" means—

(a) in relation to a race which is a recognised horse race within the meaning of section 55(1) of the Betting, Gaming and Lotteries Act 1963, the odds paid on bets on that race made by way of sponsored pool betting, and

(b) in relation to any other event, the odds paid on bets made by means of a totalisator at the scene of the event.

(3) A bet made with or through a person carrying on a business of receiving or negotiating bets, being a bet made in the course of that business, shall be deemed not to be a bet at fixed odds within the meaning of this section if the winnings of the person by whom it is so made consist or may consist wholly or in part of something other than money.

(4) Where a person carries on a business of receiving or negotiating bets and there is or has been issued in connection with that business any advertisement or other publication calculated to encourage in persons making bets of any description with or through him a belief that the bets are made on the basis mentioned in subsection (1)(c) above, then any bets of that description subsequently made with

or through him in the course of that business shall be deemed for the purposes of this section to be made on that basis.
[Betting and Gaming Duties Act 1981, s 10.]

8–7055 11. Definition of coupon betting.   For the purposes of this Part of this Act, bets shall be deemed to be made by way of coupon betting where they are made in pursuance of an invitation which offers stated odds for a choice of bets, being bets of a description not commonly made without such an invitation, unless made by way of pool betting, and not of a description commonly made by means of a totalisator.
[Betting and Gaming Duties Act 1981, s 11.]

8–7056 12. Supplementary provisions.   (1) Where particulars of an intended bet on which general betting duty or pool betting duty would be chargeable and the stake on that bet are collected for transmission to the person by whom that duty would fall to be paid by some other person, whether or not a bookmaker, who holds himself out as available for so collecting and transmitting them, but are in fact not so transmitted, the bet shall be deemed to have been made but the duty in respect of it shall be paid by that other person.

(2) The provisions of Schedule 1 to this Act (supplementary provisions as to betting duties) shall have effect.

(3) In sections 1 to 10 above (except in sections 6, 7, 8, 9(2)(*a*) and 9(5) in their application to coupon betting), in subsection (1) above and in paragraph 10 of Schedule 1 to this Act, "bet" does not include any bet made or stake hazarded in the course of, or incidentally to, any gaming.

(4) In this Part of this Act—

"betting office licence"—

    (*a*) in Great Britain, has the meaning given by section 9(1) of the Betting, Gaming and Lotteries Act 1963, and
    (*b*) in Northern Ireland, means a bookmaking office licence as defined in Article 2(2) of the Betting, Gaming, Lotteries and Amusements (Northern Ireland) Order 1985;

"bookmaker"—

    (*a*) in Great Britain, has the meaning given by section 55(1) of the said Act of 1963, and
    (*b*) in Northern Ireland, has the meaning given by Article 2(2) of the said Order of 1985;

    and (in either case) the expression "bookmaking" shall be construed accordingly;

"bookmaker's permit"—

    (*a*) in Great Britain, has the meaning given by section 2(1) of the said Act of 1963, and
    (*b*) in Northern Ireland, means a bookmaker's licence as defined in Article 2(2) of the said Order of 1985;

"meeting" means any occasion on any one day on which events take place on any track;
"on-course bet" means a bet made in the course of a horse or dog race meeting, either by means of a totalisator situated on premises forming part of the track or with a bookmaker present at the meeting, where—

    (*a*) the person making the bet (that is to say, the person originating the bet and not any agent or intermediary) is present at the meeting, or
    (*b*) the bet is made by a person carrying on a bookmaking business acting as principal (and not acting as agent for, or on behalf of, some other person);

"operator", in relation to bets made by means of a totalisator, means the person who, as principal, operates the totalisator;
"promoter", in relation to any betting, means the person to whom the persons making the bets look for the payment of their winnings, if any;
"sponsored pool betting" has the meaning given by section 55(1) of the said Act of 1963;
"totalisator" has the meaning given by section 55(1) of the said Act of 1963 and Article 2(2) of the said Order of 1985;
"track"—

    (*a*) in Great Britain, has the meaning given by section 55(1) of the said Act of 1963, and
    (*b*) in Northern Ireland, has the meaning given by Article 2(2) of the said Order of 1985;

"winnings" includes winnings of any kind, and references to amount and to payment in relation to winnings shall be construed accordingly;

(5) In this Part of this Act references to this Part of this Act include Schedule 1 to this Act.
[Betting and Gaming Duties Act 1981, s 12 as amended by the Finance Act 1986, Schs 4 and 23 and the Finance Act 2003, s 8.]

8–7061 **17–20.** *Bingo duty*[1].

---

1. The Bingo Duty Regulations 2003, SI 2003/2503.

Gaming machine licence duty

8–7062 **21. Gaming machine licences.** (1) Except in the cases specified in Part I of Schedule 4 to this Act, no amusement machine (other than an excepted machine) shall be provided for play on any premises situated in [the United Kingdom unless there is for the time being in force a licence granted under this Part of this Act with respect to the premises or the machine.

(2) Such a licence shall be known as an amusement machine licence and, if it is granted with respect to a machine, rather than with respect to premises, as a special amusement machine licence.

(3) An amusement machine licence may be granted for a period of a month, or of any number of months not exceeding twelve, beginning on any day of any month.

(3AA) A special amusement machine licence shall not be granted except where—

(a) the machine with respect to which it is granted is of a description of machine for which special amusement machine licences are available;

(b) such conditions as may be prescribed by regulations made by the Commissioners are satisfied in relation to the application for the licence, the machine and the person by whom the application is made; and

(c) the licence is for twelve months.

(3AB) Special amusement machine licences shall be available for amusement machines of each of the following descriptions—

(a) machines that are not gaming machines; and

(b) small prize machines.]

(3A) For the purposes of this section an excepted machine is—

(a) a two-penny machine, or

(b) a ten-penny machine which is a small prize machine; or

(c) a thirty-five-penny machine which is not a prize machine or which, if it is a prize machine, is not a gaming machine; or

(d) an excepted video machine.

(3B) For the purposes of this section an amusement machine is a "fifty-penny machine" if, and only if—

(a) where it is a machine on which a game can be played solo, the cost for each time the game is played on it solo—

(i) does not exceed 50p, or

(ii) where the machine provides differing numbers of games in different circumstances, cannot exceed 50p;

and

(b) where it is a machine on which a game can be played by more than one person at a time, the cost per player for each time the game is played on it simultaneously by more than one player—

(i) does not exceed 50p, or

(ii) where the machine provides differing numbers of games in different circumstances, cannot exceed 50p.

(3C) For the purposes of this section the price for a solo game on a machine does not exceed 35p if the denomination or aggregate denomination of the coin or coins that must be inserted into the machine to play the game solo does not or, where the machine provides differing numbers of games in different circumstances, cannot exceed 35p for each time the game is played.

(3D) For the purposes of this section the price to participate in a game on the machine for two or more players does not exceed 50p if the denomination or aggregate denomination of the coin or coins that must be inserted into the machine to play the game simultaneously with more than one player does not exceed or, where the machine provides differing numbers of games in different circumstances, cannot exceed 50p per player for each time the game is played.

(3E) For the purposes of this section a game is played solo if it is played by one person at a time (whether or not against a previous player).

(4) (*Repealed*)

[Betting and Gaming Duties Act 1981, s 21, as substituted by the Finance Act 1984, Sch 3 and amended by the Finance Act 1985, Sch 5, the Finance Act 1987, s 5 and Sch 16 and the Finance Act 1993, s 16, the Finance Act 1994, Sch 3, the Finance Act 1995, Sch 3, the Finance Act 1996, s 12, the Finance Act 1998, ss 13 and 14, the Finance Act 2000, Sch 2 and the Finance Act 2003, s 10.]

---

1. See the Amusement Machine Licence Duty (Special Licences) Regulations 1996, SI 1996/1423.

8–7063   22–23. *Gaming machine licence duty*[1].

1. Arrangements for the payment of duty are by the Amusement Machine Licence Duty (Special Licences) Regulations 1996, SI 1996/1423, the Amusement Machine Licence Duty (Small-Prize Machines) Order 1998, SI 1998/2207and the Amusement Machine Licence Duty (Medium-prize Machines) Order 2001, SI 2001/4028.

8–7064   24. Restrictions on provision of gaming machines. (1)–(2) *Repealed.*

(3) Amusement machines chargeable at a particular rate shall not be provided on any premises in excess of the number authorised by the licence or licences authorising the provision of amusement machines chargeable at that rate.

(4) Where a licence which authorises the provision of amusement machines chargeable at one rate only is in force in respect of any premises, amusement machines chargeable at any other rate shall not be provided for play on those premises unless another licence authorising the provision of amusement machines chargeable at that other rate is also in force in respect of the premises or the machines.

(5) If any amusement machine is provided for play on any premises in contravention of section 21(1) above or this section, the provision of the machine shall attract a penalty under section 9 of the Finance Act 1994 (civil penalties) and, for the purposes of the application of that section to the conduct attracting the penalty, the provision of the machine shall be treated as the conduct of each of the persons who, at the time when the amusement machine is provided—

(a)   is the owner, lessee or occupier of the premises, or
(b)   is for the time being responsible to the owner, lessee or occupier for the management of the premises, or
(c)   is a person responsible for controlling the use of any amusement machine on the premises, or
(d)   is for the time being responsible for controlling the admission of persons to the premises or for providing persons resorting thereto with any goods or services, or
(e)   is the owner or hirer of the machine, or
(f)   is a party to any contract under which an amusement machine may, or is required to, be on the premises at that time.

(6) If any amusement machine is provided for play on any premises in contravention of section 21(1) above or this section and any such person as is mentioned in subsection (5) above knowingly or recklessly brought about the contravention or took any steps with a view to procuring it he shall be guilty of an offence and liable[1]—

(a)   on summary conviction to a penalty—

(i)   of the prescribed sum,
(ii)   or to imprisonment for a term not exceeding **six months** or to both such penalty and imprisonment; or

(b)   on conviction on indictment[2] to a penalty of any amount or to imprisonment for a term not exceeding two years or to both.

[Betting and Gaming Duties Act 1981, s 24 as amended by the Finance Act 1982, Sch 6, the Criminal Justice Act 1982, ss 38 and 46, the Finance Act 1984, Schs 3 and 23, the Finance Act 1985, Sch 5, the Finance Act 1994, Schs 3, 4 and 26, the Finance Act 1995, Sch 3, the Finance Act 1996, s 12 and the Finance Act 2003, s 12.]

1. For procedure in respect of this offence which is triable either way, see s 147 of the Customs and Excise Management Act 1979, ante and ss 17A–21 of the Magistrates' Courts Act 1980, in Part I, Magistrates' Courts, Procedure, ante.
2. The Crown Court would probably have no jurisdiction to try an offence unless knowledge or recklessness was alleged, (see *A-G's Reference (No 3 of 1975)* [1976] 2 All ER 798, 140 JP 466).

8–7064A   24A. Unlicensed machines: duty chargeable. Schedule 4A to this Act (which provides for the recovery of amusement machine licence duty in relation to unlawfully unlicensed machines) shall have effect.
[Betting and Gaming Duties Act 1981, s 24A as inserted by the Finance Act 2000, Sch 2].

8–7065   25. Meaning of "gaming machine". (1) A machine is an amusement machine for the purposes of this Act if—

(a)   the machine is constructed or adapted for the playing of any game (whether a game of chance, a game of skill or a game of chance and skill combined);
(b)   the game is one played by means of the machine (whether automatically or by the operation of the machine by the player or players);
(c)   a player pays to play the game (except where he has an opportunity to play without payment as a result of having previously played successfully) either by inserting a coin, token or other thing into the machine or in some other way;
(d)   the machine automatically—

(i)   applies some or all of the rules of the game or displays or records scores in the game; and

    (ii)   determines when a player who has paid to play a game by means of the machine can no longer play without paying again; and

  (*e*)   the machine is a gaming machine, a video machine or a pinball machine.

(1A)   A machine constructed or adapted for the playing of a game is a gaming machine for the purposes of this Act if—

  (*a*)   it is a prize machine;

  (*b*)   the game which is played by means of the machine is a game of chance, a game of chance and skill combined or a pretended game of chance or of chance and skill combined; and

  (*c*)   the outcome of the game is determined by the chances inherent in the action of the machine, whether or not provision is made for manipulation of the machine by a player;

and for the purposes of this subsection a game in which the elements of chance can be overcome by skill shall be treated as a game of chance and skill combined if there is an element of chance in the game that cannot be overcome except by superlative skill.

(1B)   A machine constructed or adapted for the playing of a game is a video machine for the purposes of this Act if—

  (*a*)   a micro-processor is used to control some or all of the machine's functions; and

  (*b*)   the playing of the game involves information or images being communicated or displayed to the player or players by means of any description of screen.

(1C)   For the purposes of this Act an amusement machine is a prize machine unless it is constructed or adapted so that a person playing it once and successfully either receives nothing or receives only—

  (*a*)   an opportunity, afforded by the automatic action of the machine, to play again (once or more often) without paying, or

  (*b*)   a prize, determined by the automatic action of the machine and consisting in either—

    (i)   money of an amount not exceeding the sum payable to play the machine once, or

    (ii)   a token which is, or two or more tokens which in the aggregate are, exchangeable for money of an amount not exceeding that sum.

(2)–(3)   *Repealed.*

(4)   Subject to subsection (5) below, for the purposes of determining whether a machine is a machine of any description other than an excepted video machine falling within section 21(3A)(*d*) above it is immaterial whether it is capable of being played by only one person at a time, or is capable of being played by more than one person.

(5)   For the purposes of sections 21 to 24 above a machine (the actual machine) in relation to which the number determined in accordance with subsection (5A) below is more than one shall be treated (instead of as one machine) as if it were a number of machines (accountable machines) equal to the number so determined.

(5A)   That number is—

  (*a*)   except where paragraph (*b*) below applies, the number of individual playing positions provided on the machine for persons to play simultaneously (whether or not while participating in the same game); and

  (*b*)   where—

    (i)   that machine is a video machine but not a gaming machine, and

    (ii)   the number of such playing positions is more than the number of different screens used for the communication or display of information or images to any person or persons playing a game by means of the machine,

the number of such screens.

(6)   Subsection (5) above does not apply for the purpose of determining whether a machine is an excepted video machine falling within section 21(3A)(*d*) above, or in the case of a pinball machine or a machine that is an excepted machine.

(7)   Any question whether the accountable machines are, or are not, machines falling within any of the following descriptions, that is to say—

  (*a*)   gaming machines,

  (*b*)   prize machines,

  (*c*)   small-prize machines,

  (*cc*) medium-prize machines,

  (*cd*) ten-penny machines, or

  (*d*)   five-penny machines,

shall be determined according to whether or not the actual machine is a machine of that description, with the accountable machines being taken to be machines of the same description as the actual machine.

(8)–(9)   (*Repealed*).

[Betting and Gaming Duties Act 1981, s 25 as amended by the Finance Act 1982, Schs 6 and 22, the Finance Act

1993, s 16, the Finance Act 1995, Sch 3, the Finance Act 1998, s 14, the Finance Act 2000, Schs 2 and 40 and the Finance Act 2003, s 10.]

8–7065A   25A. Power to modify definition of "amusement machine".   (1) The Treasury may by order modify the provisions of section 25 above—

     (*a*)   by adding to the machines for the time being specified in subsection (1)(*e*) of that section any description of machines which it appears to them, having regard to the use to which the machines are put, to be appropriate for the protection of the revenue so to add to those machines; or

     (*b*)   by deleting any description of machines for the time being so specified.

(2) An order under this section may make such incidental, consequential or transitional provision as the Treasury think fit, including provision modifying section 21 or section 25(5A) above for the purpose of—

     (*a*)   specifying the circumstances (if any) in which a machine added to section 25(1)(*e*) above is to be an excepted machine for the purposes of section 21 above; or

     (*b*)   determining the number which, in the case of a machine so added, is to be taken into account for the purposes of section 25(5) above.

[Betting and Gaming Duties Act 1981, s 25A, as inserted by the Finance Act 1995, Sch 3.]

8–7066   26. Supplementary provisions as to amusement machine licence duty.   (1) The provisions of Part II of Schedule 4 to this Act (supplementary provisions as to amusement machine licence duty) shall have effect.

(2) In sections 21 to 25 above and in Schedule 4 to this Act—

"United Kingdom" includes the territorial waters of the United Kingdom;
"small-prize machine" has the meaning given by section 22(2) above;
"two-penny machine" means an amusement machine in relation to which the cost for each time a game is played on it—

     (*a*)   does not exceed 2p, or

     (*b*)   where the machine provides differing numbers of games in different circumstances, cannot exceed 2p,

and "five-penny machine" and "ten-penny machine" have a corresponding meaning;

"thirty-five-penny machine" means an amusement machine which can only be played by the insertion into the machine of coins of an aggregate denomination not exceeding 35p;
"premises" includes any place whatsoever and any means of transport;
"video machine" has the meaning given by section 25(1B) above;
"prize machine" has the meaning given by section 25(1C) above.

(2A) References in sections 21 to 25 above and in this section and Schedule 4 to this Act to a game, in relation to any machine, include references to a game in the nature of a quiz or puzzle and to a game which is played solely by way of a pastime or against the machine, as well as one played wholly or partly against one or more contemporaneous or previous players.

(3) A machine is provided for play on any premises if it is made available on those premises in such a way that persons resorting[1] to them can play it; and subject to subsection (3A) below where on any premises one or more amusement machines are so made available, any such machine anywhere on the premises shall be treated as provided for play on those premises, notwithstanding that it is not so made available or is not in a state in which it can be played.

(3A) The Commissioners may by regulations make provision for the purpose of enabling spare amusement machines to be kept on premises for use in the case of the breakdown of other amusement machines on those premises; and such regulations may provide that, in such circumstances and subject to such conditions as may be specified in the regulations, an amusement machine on any premises which is not made available as mentioned in subsection (3) above, or is not in a state in which it can be played, shall not be treated by virtue of that subsection as provided for play on those premises.

(4) (*Repealed*).

[Betting and Gaming Duties Act 1981, s 26 as amended by the Finance Act 1982, Sch 6, the Finance Act 1985, Sch 5, the Finance Act 1987, s 5, the Finance Act 1993, s 16, the Finance Act 1994, Schs 3 and 26, the Finance Act 1995, Sch 3, the Finance Act 2000, Sch 2 and the Finance Act 2003, s 10, 11 and Sch 43.]

---

     1. A person resorts to premises from the moment of entry on to those premises and for the period of time while he remains on them (*R v Customs and Excise Comrs, ex p Ferrymatics Ltd* (1995) Times, 23 February).

8–7066A   26A. Amounts in currencies other than sterling.   (1) Any reference in this Part of this Act to a amount in sterling, in the context of—

     (*a*)   the cost of playing a game, or

     (*b*)   the amount of the prize for a game,

includes a reference to the equivalent amount in another currency.

(2) The equivalent amount in another currency, in relation to any day, shall be determined by reference to the London closing exchange rate for the previous day.

(3) For the purposes of determining what duty is payable on an amusement machine licence in a case where this section applies, the equivalent in another currency of an amount in sterling shall be taken to be its equivalent on the day on which the application for the licence is received by the Commissioners, or the due date in the case of a default licence.

(4) In subsection (3) above—

"default licence" means a licence granted under paragraph 3(1) of Schedule 4A to this Act;
"due date" has the meaning given by paragraph 2(4) of that Schedule.

[Betting and Gaming Duties Act 1981, s 26A, as inserted by the Finance Act 2003, s 11.]

PART III[1]
GENERAL

8–7067 27. Offences by bodies corporate. Where an offence under section 24 above, paragraph 13(1) or (3) or 14(1) of Schedule 1, paragraph 16 of Schedule 3 or paragraph 16 of Schedule 4 to this Act has been committed by a body corporate, every person who at the date of the commission of the offence was a director, general manager, secretary or other similar officer of the body corporate, or was purporting to act in any such capacity, shall be deemed to be guilty of that offence unless he proves—

(a) that the offence was committed without his consent or connivance, and

(b) that he exercised all such diligence to prevent the commission of the offence as he ought to have exercised having regard to the nature of his functions in that capacity and in all the circumstances.

[Betting and Gaming Duties Act 1981, s 27 as amended by the Finance Act 1997, Sch 18.]

---

1. Part III contains ss 27–35.

8–7068 29A. Evidence by certificate, etc. (1) A certificate of the Commissioners—

(a) that any notice required by or under this Act to be given to them had or had not been given at any date, or

(b) that any permit, licence or authority required by or under this Act had or had not been issued at any date, or

(c) that any return required by or under this Act had not been made at any date, or

(d) that any duty shown as due in any return or estimate made in pursuance of this Act had not been paid at any date,

shall be sufficient evidence of that fact until the contrary is proved.

(2) A photograph of any document furnished to the Commissioners for the purposes of this Act and certified by them to be such a photograph shall be admissible in any proceedings, whether civil or criminal, to the same extent as the document itself.

(3) Any document purporting to be a certificate under subsection (1) or (2) above shall be deemed to be such a certificate until the contrary is proved.

[Betting and Gaming Duties Act 1981, s 29A, as inserted by the Finance Act 1986, s 7.]

8–7080 33. Interpretation. (1) In this Act—

"the Commissioners" means the Commissioners of Customs and Excise;
"gaming" has the same meaning as in section 52 of the Gaming Act 1968;
"the prescribed sum" in relation to the penalty provided for an offence, means—

(a) if the offence was committed in England or Wales, the prescribed sum within the meaning of section 32 of the Magistrates' Courts Act 1980 (£1,000 or other sum substituted by order under section 143(1) of that Act); and

(b)–(c) *Scotland, Northern Ireland.*

(2) For the avoidance of doubt it is hereby declared that the imposition by this Act of general betting duty, pool betting duty, bingo duty or the duty on amusement machine licences does not make lawful anything which is unlawful apart from this Act.

[Betting and Gaming Duties Act 1981, s 33 as amended by the Finance Act 1985, Sch 5 and the Finance Act 1995, Schs 3 and 29.]

8–7081 35. Short title, construction, commencement and extent. (1) This Act may be cited as the Betting and Gaming Duties Act 1981.

(2) This Act shall be construed as one with the Customs and Excise Management Act 1979.

(3) *Northern Ireland.*

(4) *Repealed.*

[Betting and Gaming Duties Act 1981, s 35 as amended by the Finance Act 1985, Sch 5 and the Finance Act 1986, Schs 4 and 23.]

SCHEDULES

Section 12(2)   SCHEDULE 1
                                  BETTING DUTIES

(As amended by the Criminal Justice Act 1982, ss 38 and 46, the Police and Criminal Evidence Act 1984, Sch 6, the Finance Act 1986, Sch 4, the Finance Act 1987, s 3, the Finance Act 1988, s 12 and Sch 14, the Finance Act 1994, Schs 4 and 26, the Access To Justice Act 1999, s 120, the Finance Act 2001, ss 6, 110, Sch 1, Sch 33 and the Finance Act 2002, ss 12(1), 141 and Sch 4.)

Definitions

8–7082   1. In this Schedule—

"general betting business" means a business the carrying on of which involves or may involve any sums becoming payable by the person carrying on the business by way of general betting duty or would or might involve such sums becoming so payable if on-course bets were not excluded from that duty;

"general betting operations" means betting operations which do not involve liability to pool betting duty;

"pool betting business" means a business the carrying on of which involves or may involve any sums becoming payable by the person carrying on the business by way of pool betting duty.

General administration

8–7083   2. (1) General betting duty shall be under the care and management of the Commissioners and shall be accounted for by such persons, and accounted for and paid at such times and in such manner, as may be required by or under regulations of the Commissioners.

(2) Without prejudice to any other provision of this Schedule, the Commissioners may make regulations[1] providing for any matter for which provision appears to them to be necessary for the administration or enforcement of general betting duty or for the protection of the revenue from general betting duty.

(3) Regulations[1] under this paragraph may in particular—

(a) provide for payments on account of the duty which may become chargeable to be made in advance by means of stamps or otherwise, and for that purpose apply, with any necessary adaptations, any of the provisions of the Stamp Duties Management Act 1891 (including the penal provisions repealed save as to Scotland by the Forgery Act 1913);

(b) provide for such payments to be made through the persons providing, at the place where any event is or is to be held, facilities for persons engaging or proposing to engage at that place in an activity by reason of which they are or may be or become liable for duty;

(c) require persons providing such facilities as aforesaid at any place to perform other functions in connection with the payment of or accounting for duty by persons engaging or proposing to engage as aforesaid at that place, including the refusal to any of the last-mentioned persons of access to that place unless the requirements of any regulations made by virtue of paragraph (a) or (b) above have been complied with;

(d) otherwise provide for the giving of security by means of a deposit or otherwise for duty due or to become due.

(4) Regulations under this paragraph may also in particular include provision—

(a) for the furnishing to such persons or displaying in such manner in such information or records as the regulations may require by persons engaging or proposing to engage in any activity by reason of which they are or may be or become liable for duty or would be or might be or become liable for duty if on-course bets were not excluded from duty, and by persons providing facilities for another to engage in such an activity or entering into any transaction with another in the course of any such activity of his;

(b) Repealed;

(c) Repealed.

2A. (1) Pool betting duty shall be under the care and management of the Commissioners.

(2) Without prejudice to any other provision of this Schedule, the Commissioners may make regulations providing for any matter for which provision appears to them to be necessary for the administration or enforcement of pool betting duty or for the protection of the revenue from pool betting duty.

(3) Regulations under sub-paragraph (2) above may in particular—

(a) provide for payments on account of pool betting duty which may become chargeable to be made in advance;

(b) provide for the giving of security by means of a deposit or otherwise for duty due or to become due.

3. Pool betting duty shall be paid at such times as the Commissioners may direct.

---

1. See the General Betting Duty Regulations 2001, SI 2001/3088 amended by SI 2003/2631 and SI 2004/768.

Notification to Commissioners as to carrying on of betting business

8–7084   4. (1) Any person who intends to carry on a general betting business which is not also a pool betting business shall, not less than one week before he begins to carry on the business, notify the Commissioners that he intends to carry it on.

(2) Subject to sub-paragraph (3) below, any person who intends to carry on a general betting business or a pool betting business shall, not later than the date when he first uses any premises or totalisator for the purposes of the business, make entry of those premises or that totalisator with the Commissioners.

(3) A person shall not be required by sub-paragraph (2) above to make entry of premises used for the purposes of the business in connection only with general betting operations; but he shall, not later than the date when he first uses any premises for the purposes of the business in connection with general betting operations, notify the Commissioners of those premises being so used (whether or not he is also required by sub-paragraph (2) above to make entry of them).

(4) (*Repealed*).
(5) (*Repealed*).
(6) (*Repealed*).

Requirement of permit for carrying on pool betting business

8–7085 **5.** (1) No person shall carry on a pool betting business unless he holds a permit authorising him to carry on that business granted by the Commissioners in respect of any premises or totalisator in respect of which he has made entry or given notice in accordance with paragraph 4(2) or (4) above.

(2) A permit under this paragraph shall be granted by the Commissioners within fourteen days of the date when application is made for it, and shall continue in force unless and until revoked under sub-paragraph (3) below.

Books, records, accounts, etc

8–7086 **6.** (1) Any person for the time being carrying on a general betting business or a pool betting business shall—

(*a*) keep in relation to the business such books, records and accounts in such form as the Commissioners may direct,

(*b*) for at least six months or such shorter or longer period as the Commissioners may direct, preserve any books, records and accounts directed to be kept by him under paragraph (*a*) above and any other books, records, accounts or documents relating to the business, on premises specified in sub-paragraph (2) below,

(*c*) permit any officer authorised in that behalf by the Commissioners to enter on any premises used for the purposes of the business, and, where the business is a general betting business, to remain on the premises at any time while they are being used, or when the officer has reasonable cause to believe that they are likely to be used, for the conduct of betting operations, and

(*d*) permit any officer so authorised to inspect any totalisator used for the purposes of the business, and to inspect and take copies of any books, records, accounts or other documents in his possession or power or on any premises used for the purposes of the business, being books, records, accounts or documents which relate or appear to relate to the business.

(2) The premises on which a person is to preserve any books, records, accounts or other documents under sub-paragraph (1)(*b*) above are—

(*a*) in the case of books, records, accounts and other documents relating to general betting operations, such of the premises used for the purposes of the business as the Commissioners may direct;

(*b*) (*repealed*)

(*c*) in any other case, premises of which entry has been made in accordance with paragraph 4(2) above.

(3) The power of the Commissioners under sub-paragraph (1)(*b*) above to give directions as to the period for which a person is to preserve any books, records, accounts or documents relating to the business carried on by him shall be exercisable either in any particular case or in relation to any particular class of such books, records, accounts or documents.

7. Any person for the time being carrying on a general betting business or a pool betting business, and any other person employed in, or having functions in connection with, any such business (including in particular the accountant referred to in Schedule 5 to the Betting, Gaming and Lotteries Act 1963 or Schedule 8 to the Betting, Gaming, Lotteries and Amusements (Northern Ireland) Order 1985), shall, if required so to do by the Commissioners or any officer authorised in that behalf by the Commissioners—

(*a*) produce, at a time and place to be specified by the Commissioners or the officer, any such books, records, accounts or documents relating to the business,

(*b*) make, at times and to persons to be so specified, such returns relating to the business, and

(*c*) give such other information relating to the business,

as the Commissioners or the officer may require.

8. *Repealed.*

9. (1) The provisions of this paragraph shall apply to a bookmaker at any time when any person is for the time being, or has at any time during the immediately preceding two months been, authorised by that bookmaker to act as his agent for receiving or negotiating bets or otherwise conducting betting operations, other than such bets or operations as involve liability only to pool betting duty.

(2) The bookmaker shall maintain at any of his premises to which bets received by any such person as aforesaid as the bookmakers's agent are or were transmitted, or, if in the case of any such premises the Commissioners think fit, at such other places as the Commissioners may allow, a record in such form and containing such particulars as the Commissioners may direct in respect of any such person who is for the time being, and any such person who has at any time during the said two months been but is no longer authorised as aforesaid, being in either case a person by or on whose behalf bets received as aforesaid are or were transmitted to those premises.

(3) A bookmaker shall not be guilty of contravening or failing to comply with the provisions of sub-paragraph (2) above by reason of a failure to make an entry or alteration in the record if that entry or alteration is made before six o'clock in the evening of the day after that on which the happening which necessitated the entry or alteration took place.

Powers to enter premises and obtain information

8–7087 **10.** (1) Where in the case of any track or other premises an officer has reason to believe that bookmaking on events taking place thereon is being or is to be carried on, or that facilities for sponsored pool betting on those events are being or are to be provided, or that a totalisator is being or is to be operated in connection with those events, at a place on those premises or on any ground or premises adjacent thereto, he shall be entitled for the purpose of exercising the powers conferred by this paragraph to be admitted without payment to that place, and he may require—

(a) any person who appears to him to be or intend carrying on bookmaking, providing such facilities or operating a totalisator there to give such information as he may demand and to produce to him any accounts, records, or other documents which appear to him to be connected with the business of bookmaking or with the provision of those facilities or the operation of that totalisator or which it appears to him will establish the identity of that person; and

(b) any person who appears to him to have made a bet there with any bookmaker, or through the persons providing any such facilities, or by means of a totalisator, to give such information with respect to the bet as he may demand and to produce to him any document in connection with the bet supplied to that person by the bookmaker, the persons providing those facilities, or the operator of that totalisator, as the case may be,

and any such person as aforesaid shall comply with any such requirement.

(2) Where an officer—

(a) has reason to believe that any person who is not a bookmaker is holding himself out as mentioned in section 12(1) of this Act at any place, and

(b) has reason to suspect that person to have become liable by virtue of that section to pay an amount by way of general betting duty or pool betting duty,

the officer shall have the like powers with respect to that place as if the person so holding himself out were a bookmaker and that place were such a place as is mentioned in sub-paragraph (1) above.

11–12. *Repealed.*

Enforcement

8–7088   **13.** (1) Where any person—

(a) fails to pay any general betting duty or pool betting duty payable by him, or

(b) contravenes or fails to comply with any of the provisions of, or of any regulations made under, any of paragraphs 2, 2A, 4 and 6 to 10 above,

his failure to pay, contravention or failure to comply shall attract a penalty under section 9 of the Finance Act 1994 (civil penalties) which, in the case of a failure to pay, shall be calculated by reference to the amount of duty payable.

(2) Any such failure to pay as is mentioned in sub-paragraph (1)(a) above shall also attract daily penalties.

(2A) Any person who obstructs any officer in the exercise of his functions in relation to general betting duty or pool betting duty shall be guilty of an offence and liable on summary conviction to a penalty of **level 4** on the standard scale.

(3) Any person who—

(a) in connection with general betting duty or pool betting duty, makes any statement which he knows to be false in a material particular or recklessly makes any statement which is false in a material particular, or

(aa) in that connection, with intent to deceive, produces or makes use of any book, account, record, return or other document[1] which is false in a material particular, or

(b) is knowingly concerned in, or in the taking of steps with a view to the fraudulent evasion by him or any other person of general betting duty or pool betting duty,

shall be guilty of an offence and liable[2]—

(i) on summary conviction to a penalty of **the prescribed sum** or, if greater, treble the amount of the duty which is unpaid or payment of which is sought to be avoided, as the case may be, or to imprisonment for a term not exceeding **six months** or to both, or

(ii) on conviction on indictment to a penalty of any amount or to imprisonment for a term not exceeding the maximum term or to both.

(4) In sub-paragraph (3) above, "the maximum term" means two years in the case of an offence under paragraph (a) and seven years in the case of an offence under paragraph (aa) or (b) of that sub-paragraph.

14. (1) If any person carries on any business in contravention of paragraph 5(1) above he shall be guilty of an offence and liable[2]—

(a) on summary conviction to a penalty of **the prescribed sum** or to imprisonment for a term not exceeding **six months** or to both; or

(b) on conviction on indictment to a penalty of any amount or to imprisonment for a term not exceeding **two years** or to both;

(2) Where a person is convicted of an offence under sub-paragraph (1) above and the offence continues after the conviction, he shall be guilty of a further offence under that sub-paragraph and may, on conviction, be punished accordingly.

(3) If at any time the holder of a permit under paragraph 5 above fails to produce his permit for examination within such period, and at such time and place, as may be required by an officer, his failure shall attract a penalty under section 9 of the Finance Act 1994 (civil penalties).

15. (1) Where, on the conviction of any person of an offence under paragraph 13(3) above in connection with general betting duty the Commissioners—

(a) certify to the court by or before whom that person is so convicted that there has been at least one previous occasion on which that or another person has been either—

(i) convicted of an offence under paragraph 13(3) above; or

(ii) assessed to a penalty to which he was liable under section 8 of the Finance Act 1994 (penalty for evasion),

in respect of conduct taking place in the course of the operation of the same premises as a betting office and while the same person has been the holder of a betting office licence in respect thereof, and

(b) make application to that court for effect to be given to this sub-paragraph,

that court shall order that the betting office licence in respect of those premises shall be forfeited and cancelled.

(2) A licence shall not be forfeited or cancelled under such an order made by a court in England and Wales or Northern Ireland—

(a) until the date of expiration of the period within which notice of appeal against the conviction which gave rise to the order may be given, or

(b) if notice of appeal against that conviction is duly given within the period aforesaid, until the date of the determination or abandonment of the appeal, or

(c) if on any such appeal the appeal is allowed.

(3) A licence shall not be forfeited or cancelled under such an order made by a court in Scotland—

(a) until the expiration of the period of fourteen days commencing with the date on which the order was made, or

(b) if an appeal against the conviction which gave rise to the order is begun within the said period, until the date when that appeal is determined or abandoned or deemed to have been abandoned, or

(c) if on any such appeal the appeal is allowed.

(4) Where a betting office licence held by any person in respect of any premises in England, Wales or Scotland is forfeited and cancelled in pursuance of an order under sub-paragraph (1) above, the proper officer of the court by whom the order was made shall, unless he is also proper officer of the appropriate authority who last either granted or renewed the licence, send a copy of the order to the proper officer of that authority; and, without prejudice to the renewal by that authority of any other betting office licence held by that person, that authority shall, notwithstanding anything in paragraph 20(1) of the said Schedule 1, refuse any application by that person for the grant of a new betting office licence in respect of those or any other premises made less than twelve months after that forfeiture and cancellation.

(4A) In sub-paragraph (4) above—

"proper officer of the court" means—

(a) in relation to a magistrates' court in England and Wales, the justices' chief executive for the court; and

(b) in relation to any other court, the clerk of the court, and

"appropriate authority" and "proper officer of the appropriate authority" have the same meaning as in Schedule 1 to the Betting, Gaming and Lotteries Act 1963.

(5)–(6) *Northern Ireland.*

16. (1) If a justice of the peace or, in Scotland, a justice (within the meaning of section 462 of the Criminal Procedure (Scotland) Act 1975) is satisfied on information on oath that there is reasonable ground for suspecting that an offence in connection with general betting duty is being, has been, or is about to be committed on any premises, he may issue a warrant in writing authorising any officer to enter those premises (if necessary by force) at any time within one month from the time of the issue of the warrant and search them.

(2) An officer who enters premises under the authority of such a warrant may—

(a) seize and remove any records, accounts or other documents, money or valuable thing, instrument or other thing whatsoever found on the premises which he has reasonable cause to believe may be required as evidence for the purposes of proceedings in respect of such an offence, and

(b) search any person found on the premises whom he has reasonable cause to believe to be carrying on bookmaking on the premises.

---

1. "Document" has the same meaning as in Part I of the Civil Evidence Act 1968; see the Finance Act 1985, s 10, this title, post.

2. For procedure in respect of this offence which is triable either way, see s 147 of the Customs and Excise Management Act 1979, ante, and ss 17A–21 of the Magistrates' Courts Act 1980, in PART I, MAGISTRATES' COURTS, PROCEDURE, ante.

SCHEDULE 3
BINGO DUTY

(As amended by the Finance Act 1982, Sch 6, the Criminal Justice Act 1982, ss 38 and 46, the Police and Criminal Evidence Act 1984, Sch 6, the Finance Act 1986, Sch 4, the Finance (No 2) Act 1992, s 7, the Finance Act 1994, Schs 4 and 26, the Finance Act 1995, Sch 3. SI 1999/3205 and the Finance Act 2003, s 9.)

PART II
SUPPLEMENTARY PROVISIONS

Definitions

8–7091   **8.** In this Part of this Schedule—

"bingo-promoter" means a person who promotes the playing of bingo chargeable with bingo duty;

"prescribed" means prescribed by regulations;

"regulations" means regulations of the Commissioners made under this Part of this Schedule.

Notification to Commissioners by, and registration of, bingo-promoters

8–7092   **10.** (1) Any person who intends to promote the playing of bingo in connection with which bingo duty may be chargeable shall, not less than fourteen days before the first day on which bingo is to be played, notify the Commissioners of his intention, specifying the premises on which the bingo is to be played, and applying to be registered as a bingo-promoter.

(1A) Any person who is a bingo-promoter but is not registered as such and is not a person to whom sub-paragraph (1) above applies shall within five days of the date on which he became a bingo-promoter (disregarding any day which is a Saturday or a Sunday or a Bank Holiday) notify the Commissioners of that fact and of the place where the bingo was and (if he intends to continue to promote the playing of bingo which will or may be chargeable with duty) is to be played and apply to be registered as a bingo-promoter.

(2) Where a person gives notice to the Commissioners under sub-paragraph (1) or (1A) above, he shall be

entitled to be registered by the Commissioners, except that the Commissioners may, where it appears to them to be requisite for the security of the revenue to do so, impose as a condition of a person's registration, or may subsequently impose as a condition of the continuance in force of his registration, a requirement that he shall give such security (or further security) by way of deposit or otherwise for any bingo duty which he is, or may become, liable to pay as the Commissioners may from time to time require.

Conditions shall not be imposed under this sub-paragraph if the premises at which the bingo in question is or is to be played are not licensed under the Gaming Act 1968 or under Chapter II of Part III of the Betting, Gaming, Lotteries and Amusements (Northern Ireland) Order 1985.

(3) Where, in the case of a person who is for the time being registered as a bingo-promoter, the Commissioners exercise their power under sub-paragraph (2) above to impose, as a condition of the continuance in force of his registration, a requirement that he shall give security or further security, and he does not give it, the Commissioners may cancel his registration but without prejudice to his right to apply again to be registered.

Enforcement

8–7093   **16.** (1) Any person who is knowingly concerned in or in taking steps with a view to the fraudulent evasion by him or any other person of bingo duty shall be guilty of an offence and liable[1]—

   (*a*)   on summary conviction to a penalty of **the prescribed sum** or, if greater, treble the amount of the duty payment of which is sought to be evaded or to imprisonment for a term not exceeding **six months** or to both, or

   (*b*)   on conviction on indictment to a penalty of any amount or to imprisonment for a term not exceeding **two years** or to both.

   (2) Any person who—

   (*a*)   is knowingly concerned with the promotion of bingo (being bingo in connection with which bingo duty may be chargeable) where the promoter is not registered by the Commissioners in accordance with paragraph 10 above

   (*b*)   (*repealed*)

shall be guilty of an offence and liable[1]—

   (i)   on summary conviction to a penalty of **the prescribed sum** or to imprisonment for a term not exceeding **six months** or to both; or

   (ii)   on conviction on indictment, to a penalty of any amount or to imprisonment for a term not exceeding **two years** or to both.

   (3) Where any person—

   (*a*)   contravenes or fails to comply with any provision of this Part of this Schedule or of regulations, or

   (*b*)   fails to comply with any requirement made of him by or under any such provision,

his contravention or failure to comply shall attract a penalty under section 9 of the Finance Act 1994 (civil penalties).

   (4) (*Repealed*).

   17. (1) If a justice of the peace or, in Scotland, a justice (within the meaning of section 462 of the Criminal Procedure (Scotland) Act 1975) is satisfied on information on oath that there is reasonable ground for suspecting that an offence under paragraph 16 above is being, has been, or is about to be committed on any premises, he may issue a warrant in writing authorising any officer to enter those premises (if necessary by force) at any time within one month from the time of the issue of the warrant and search them.

   (2) An officer who enters premises under the authority of such a warrant may—

   (*a*)   seize and remove any books, records, accounts, documents, money or valuable thing, and any instrument, device, apparatus or other thing whatsoever found on the premises, which he has reasonable cause to believe may be required as evidence for the purposes of proceedings in respect of such an offence, and

   (*b*)   search any person found on the premises whom he has reasonable cause to believe to be concerned with the promotion of bingo or, as the case may be, with the management of any premises used for the purpose of playing bingo.

---

1. For procedure in respect of this offence which is triable either way, see s 147 of the Customs and Excise Management Act 1979, *ante*, and ss 17A–21 of the Magistrates' Courts Act 1980, in PART I, MAGISTRATES' COURTS, PROCEDURE, *ante*.

Sections 21 (1), 24 (1) and 26   SCHEDULE 4
AMUSEMENT MACHINE LICENCE DUTY

(As amended by the Finance Act 1982, Sch 6, the Criminal Justice Act 1982, ss 38 and 46, the Finance Act 1983, s 5, the Finance Act 1984, Schs 3 and 23, the Police and Criminal Evidence Act 1984, Sch 6, the Finance Act 1985, Sch 5, SI 1986/2069, the Finance Act 1987, s 5 and Sch 16, SI 1992/2954, the Finance Act 1993, s 16, the Finance Act 1994, Schs 3, 4 and 26, the Finance Act 1995, Schs 3 and 29, SI 1995/2374, the Finance Act 1996, s 12, the Access To Justice Act 1999, s 121 and the Finance Act 2000, Sch 2.)

PART I
EXEMPTIONS FROM REQUIREMENT OF EXCISE LICENCE

Charitable entertainments, etc

8–7094   **1.** (1) An amusement machine licence shall not be required in order to authorise the provision of an amusement machine at an entertainment (whether limited to one day or extending over two or more days), being a bazaar, sale of work, fête, dinner, dance, sporting or athletic event or other entertainment of a similar character, where the conditions of this paragraph are complied with in relation to the entertainment.

   (2) The conditions of this paragraph are that—

(a) the whole proceeds of the entertainment (including the proceeds from any amusement machines) after deducting the expenses of the entertainment, including any expenses incurred in connection with the provision of amusement machines and of prizes to successful players of the machines will be devoted to purposes other than private gain; and

(b) the opportunity to win prizes by playing the machine (or that machine and any other amusement machines provided at the entertainment) does not constitute the only, or the only substantial, inducement for persons to attend the entertainment.

(3) In construing sub-paragraph (2)(a) above, proceeds of an entertainment promoted on behalf of a society falling within this sub-paragraph which are applied for any purpose calculated to benefit the society as a whole shall not be held to be applied for purposes of private gain by reason only that their application for that purpose results in benefit to any person as an individual.

(4) A society falls within sub-paragraph (3) above if it is established and conducted either—

(a) wholly for purposes other than purposes of any commercial undertaking, or
(b) wholly or mainly for the purpose of participation in or support of athletic sports or athletic games;

and in this paragraph "society" includes any club, institution, organisation or association of persons, by whatever name called, and any separate branch or section of such a club, institution, organisation or association.

Pleasure fairs

8–7095 **2.** (1) An amusement machine licence shall not be required in order to authorise the provision of an amusement machine at a pleasure fair, consisting wholly or mainly of amusements provided by travelling showmen, which is held on any day of a year on premises not previously used in that year for more than twenty-seven days for the holding of such a pleasure fair, where the conditions of this paragraph are complied with in relation to the machine.

(2) The conditions of this paragraph are that—

(a) the amount payable to play the machine once does not exceed 25p;
(b) a person playing the machine once and successfully does not receive any thing other than one of the following prizes or combinations of prizes—

(i) a money prize not exceeding £4 or a token which is, or two or more tokens which in the aggregate are, exchangeable only for such a money prize;
(ii) a non-monetary prize or prizes of a value or aggregate value not exceeding £8 or a token exchangeable only for such a non-monetary prize or such non-monetary prizes;
(iii) a money prize not exceeding £4 together with a non-monetary prize of a value which does not exceed £8 less the amount of the money prize;
(iv) one or more tokens which can be exchanged for a non-monetary prize or non-monetary prizes at the appropriate rate; and

(c) the opportunity to play the machine (or that machine and any other amusement machines provided at the fair) does not constitute the only, or the only substantial, inducement for persons to attend the fair.

(3) In sub-paragraph (2)(b) above, "non-monetary prize", in relation to a machine, means a prize which does not consist of or include any money and does not consist of or include any token which can be exchanged for money or money's worth or be used for playing the machine; and, for the purposes of sub-paragraph (2)(b)(iv), a token or tokens shall be taken to be exchanged for a non-monetary prize or prizes at the appropriate rate if either—

(a) the value or aggregate value of the prize or prizes does not exceed £8 and the token or tokens exchanged represent the maximum number of tokens which can be won by playing the machine once, or
(b) in any other case, the value or aggregate value of the prize or prizes does not exceed £8 and bears to £8 a proportion not exceeding that which the number of tokens exchanged bears to the maximum number of tokens which can be won by playing the machine once.

(4) The condition specified in sub-paragraph (2)(b) above shall not, in relation to a machine, be taken to be contravened by reason only that a successful player of the machine receives an opportunity to play again (once or more often) without paying, so long as the most which he can receive if he wins each time he plays again is a money prize or money prizes of an amount, or aggregate amount, of £4 or less.

3. The Commissioners may by order provide that any provision of paragraph 2 above which is specified in the order and which mentions a sum shall have effect, as from a date so specified, as if for that sum there were substituted such larger sum as may be specified in the order.

Seasonal licences

8–7096 **4.** (1) If at any time during March of any year there has previously been granted a seasonal licence for that year authorising the provision of any number of relevant machines on any premises and that licence has not been surrendered, it shall be treated for the purposes of this Act as authorising the provision at that time of that number of relevant machines on the premises.

(2) Where a seasonal licence is granted for any year authorising the provision of any number of relevant machines on any premises, and the licence is not surrendered, it shall be treated for the purposes of this Act as authorising the provision of that number of relevant machines on the premises during the period in that year—

(a) beginning with 1st October; and
(b) ending with the Sunday before the first Monday in November.

(3) Subject to sub-paragraph (4) below, in this Schedule "seasonal licence", in relation to any year, means an amusement machine licence expressed to authorise only the provision of relevant machines on any premises for the period of six months beginning with 1 April in that year.

(4) A licence in respect of any premises is not a seasonal licence in relation to any year if any amusement machine licence has been granted in respect of those premises for any period which includes the whole or any part of the preceding winter period.

(5) If in relation to any year—

(a) a seasonal licence is granted in respect of any premises, and
(b) another amusement machine licence is granted (whether before or after the grant of the seasonal licence or after the surrender of the seasonal licence) in respect of those premises for any period which includes the whole or any part of the following winter period (and does not include the whole or any part of the preceding winter period),

there shall (unless an amount has already become payable under this sub-paragraph in respect of the seasonal licence) be payable on the seasonal licence on the relevant date an additional amount of duty.

(6) The additional amount is the difference between the duty payable (apart from this paragraph) on that licence at the time it was granted and the amount that would have been so payable if the licence had been granted for a period of eight months or, in a case where the seasonal licence has been surrendered before the beginning of September, seven months.

(7) In sub-paragraph (5) above, the "relevant date" means—

(a) the date on which the seasonal licence is granted, or
(b) the date on which the other licence is granted,

whichever is the later.

(7AA) Sub-paragraph (4) and (5) above shall have effect where—

(a) an amusement machine is provided on any premises at any time in a winter period, and
(b) the provision of that machine on those premises at that time is authorised by a special amusement machine licence,

as if an amusement machine licence had been granted in respect of those premises for that winter period.

(7A) An amusement machine is a relevant machine for the purposes of this paragraph unless it is a gaming machine which is not a small-prize machine.

(8) In this paragraph "winter period" means the period beginning with the first Monday in November and ending with the last day of February.

PART II
SUPPLEMENTARY PROVISIONS

General administration

8–7097 **5.** The duty on amusement machine licences shall be under the care and management of the Commissioners, who may (without prejudice to any other provision of this Schedule) make regulations[1] providing for any matter for which provision appears to them to be necessary for the administration or enforcement of the duty, or for the protection of the revenue in respect thereof; and in this Schedule—

(a) "regulations" means regulations of the Commissioners made thereunder; and
(b) "prescribed" means prescribed by regulations.

---

1. See the Amusement Machine Licence Duty Regulations 1995, SI 1995/2631 and the Amusement Machine Licence Duty (Special Licences) Regulations 1996, SI 1996/1423.

Requirements to be observed by licence-holder

8–7098 **12.** The holder of an amusement machine licence in respect of any premises shall secure that the licence is displayed on the premises at such times and in such manner as may be prescribed, and shall on demand by an officer at any time produce the licence for the officer's inspection.

Power to enter premises and obtain information

8–7099 **14.** Any officer may (without payment) enter on any premises on which he knows or has reasonable cause to suspect that amusement machines are or have been provided for play and inspect those premises and require any person who is concerned in the management of the premises, or who is on the premises and appears to the officer to have any responsibility whatsoever in respect of their management or of the control of the admission of persons thereto—

(a) to produce or secure the production of any amusement machine licence for the time being in force in respect of the premises, or
(b) to provide information with respect to any use to which the premises are or have been put, or to any machine which is or has been on the premises and any game which may have been played by means of such a machine or to the way in which the machine works, or to the amount which is or has been payable to play it.

Registers of permits, etc

8–7110 **15.** (1) The proper officer of the appropriate authority shall keep a register in the prescribed form and containing the prescribed particulars of—

(a) all permits issued by the authority for the purposes of section 16 of the Lotteries and Amusements Act 1976 (permitted gaming in the form of amusements with prizes),
(b) all permits so issued for the purposes of section 34 of the Gaming Act 1968 (conditions under which gaming may be carried on by means of machines), and
(c) all directions given by the authority under section 32 of the Gaming Act 1968 (approval for provision of more than two gaming machines);

and any such register shall be open during reasonable hours for inspection by any officer.

(2) In sub-paragraph (1) above, "the appropriate authority"—

(*a*) in relation to permits issued for the purposes of section 16 of the Lotteries and Amusements Act 1976, means the local authority within the meaning of Schedule 3 to that Act,

(*b*) in relation to permits issued for the purposes of section 34 of the Gaming Act 1968, has the same meaning as in Schedule 9 to that Act, and

(*c*) in relation to directions under section 32 of the Gaming Act 1968, means the licensing authority under that Act.

(3) In sub-paragraph (1) above "proper officer of the appropriate authority" means—

(a) where the appropriate authority is a committee of the justices acting for a petty sessions area, the chief executive to the justices; and

(b) in any other case, the clerk to the authority.

Enforcement

8–7111 16. (1) If any person contravenes or fails to comply with any provision of this Part of this Schedule or regulations, or fails or refuses to comply with any requirement lawfully made of him under this Part of this Schedule or regulations, his contravention, failure to comply or refusal shall attract a penalty under section 9 of the Finance Act 1994 (civil penalties).

(1A) This paragraph does not apply to any contravention or failure to comply with arrangements under paragraph 7A above or to any failure or refusal to comply with a requirement made under or for the purposes of any such arrangements.

(2) (*Repealed*).

17. (1) If a justice of the peace or, in Scotland, a justice (within the meaning of section 462 of the Criminal Procedure (Scotland) Act) is satisfied on information on oath that there is reasonable ground for suspecting that amusement machines are or have been, or are to be, provided for play on any premises in contravention of section 21(1) or 24 of this Act, he may issue a warrant in writing authorising an officer to enter the premises (if necessary by force) at any time within one month of the issue of the warrant and search them.

(2) An officer who enters premises under the authority of such a warrant may—

(*a*) seize and remove any records, accounts or other documents, or any amusement machine (including any machine appearing to the officer to be an amusement machine or to be capable of being used as such), or any tokens or other thing whatsoever, found on the premises which he has reasonable cause to believe may be required as evidence for the purposes of proceedings in respect of an offence under section 24 of this Act or paragraph 16 above;

(*b*) search any person found on the premises whom he has reasonable cause to believe to be or have been concerned with the provision of amusement machines on the premises, or with the management of the premises, or to be or have been responsible for controlling the admission of persons to the premises.

18. Where an officer finds amusement machines provided on any premises in such circumstances that an amusement machine licence is required so as to authorise them so to be provided and the officer is satisfied, having regard to the number and description of those machines which are authorised by the amusement machine licence or licences produced to him that there has been a contravention of section 21(1) or 24 of this Act, all amusement machines found on the premises shall be liable to forfeiture.

Finance Act 1985

(1985 c 54)

Part I[1]
Customs and Excise and Value Added Tax

Chapter I
Customs and Excise

Other provisions

8–7200 10. Computer records etc. (1) Any provision made by or under any enactment which requires a person, in connection with any assigned matter,—

(*a*) to produce, furnish or deliver any document, or cause any document to be produced, furnished or delivered, or

(*b*) to permit the Commissioners of Customs and Excise (in this section referred to as "the Commissioners") or a person authorised by them—

(i) to inspect any document, or

(ii) to make or take extracts from or copies of or remove any document,

shall have effect as if any reference in that provision to a document were a reference to anything in which information of any description is recorded and any reference to a copy of a document were a reference to anything onto which information recorded in the document has been copied, by whatever means and whether directly or indirectly.

(2) In connection with any assigned matter, a person authorised by the Commissioners to exercise the powers conferred by this subsection—

(*a*) shall be entitled at any reasonable time to have access to, and inspect and check the operation of, any computer and any associated apparatus or material which is or has been in use in connection with any document to which this subsection applies; and (*b*)   may require—

    (i)   the person by whom or on whose behalf the computer is or has been so used, or

    (ii)   any person having charge of, or otherwise concerned with the operation of, the computer, apparatus or material,

to afford him such reasonable assistance as he may require for the purposes of paragraph (*a*) above.

(3)   Subsection (2) above applies to any document, within the meaning given by subsection (1) above, which, in connection with any assigned matter, a person is or may be required by or under any enactment—

(*a*)   to produce, furnish or deliver, or cause to be produced, furnished or delivered; or

(*b*)   to permit the Commissioners or a person authorised by them to inspect, make or take extracts from or copies of or remove.

(4)   Any person who—

(*a*)   obstructs a person authorised under subsection (2) above in the exercise of his powers under paragraph (*a*) of that subsection, or

(*b*)   without reasonable excuse fails to comply within a reasonable time with a requirement under paragraph (*b*) of that subsection,

shall be liable on summary conviction to a penalty of **level 4** on the standard scale.

(5)   In each of the enactments mentioned in subsection (6) below (which create offences in relation, among other matters, to false documents) "document" shall have the meaning given by subsection (1) above.

(6)   The enactments referred to in subsection (5) above are—

(*a*)–(*b*)   *Northern Ireland*;

(*c*)   section 167 of the Customs and Excise Management Act 1979 (untrue declarations etc);

(*d*)   section 168 of that Act (counterfeit documents etc);

(*e*)   section 15 of the Customs and Excise Duties (General Reliefs) Act 1979 (false statements and documents in connection with reliefs);

(*f*)   paragraph 13(3) of Schedule 1 to the Betting and Gaming Duties Act 1981 (false statements and documents in connection with betting duty);

(*g*)   paragraph 7(3) of Schedule 2 to that Act (false statements and documents in connection with gaming licence duty);

(*h*)   paragraph 8(2) of Schedule 1 to the Car Tax Act 1983 (false documents etc).

(7)   (*Repealed*).

(8)   In this section "assigned matter" means any matter which is an assigned matter for the purposes of the Customs and Excise Management Act 1979.

[Finance Act 1985, s 10 amended by the Statute Law (Repeals) Act 1993, Sch 1 and the Civil Evidence Act 1995, Schs 1 and 2.]

---

1.   Part I contains Chapter 1, ss 1–10, and Chapter 11, ss 11–33.

Finance Act 1993

(1993 c 34)

Part I[1]
Customs and Excise and Value Added Tax

Chapter II
Lottery Duty

The duty

8–7210   **24. Lottery duty.**   (1) Subject to subsections (3) and (4) below, a duty of excise called "lottery duty" is chargeable—

(*a*)   on the taking in the United Kingdom of a ticket or chance in a lottery, and

(*b*)   in such cases as may be determined by regulations[2], on the taking outside the United Kingdom of a ticket or chance in a lottery promoted in the United Kingdom.

(2)   Regulations[2] may make provision for determining when and where the taking of a ticket or chance in a lottery is to be treated as occurring for the purposes of this Chapter.

(3)   Lottery duty is not chargeable in respect of a lottery that constitutes a game of bingo (or any version of bingo, by whatever name called).

(4)   Lottery duty is not chargeable in respect—

(a) of a lottery promoted as an incident of an exempt entertainment within the meaning of the Lotteries and Amusements Act 1976 or the Betting, Gaming, Lotteries and Amusements (Northern Ireland) Order 1985;

(b) of a private lottery within the meaning of that Act or Order;

(c) of a society's lottery within the meaning of that Act or Order in respect of which the conditions set out in section 5(3) of that Act or Article 135(1) of that Order are satisfied;

(d) of a local lottery within the meaning of that Act in respect of which the conditions set out in section 6(2) of that Act are satisfied;

(e) *repealed.*

(5) The Treasury may by order amend subsection (4) above so as to add to the descriptions of lottery for the time being mentioned in that subsection, so as to omit any of them or so as to substitute a different description of lottery for any of them.

[Finance Act 1993, s 24, as amended by the Statute Law (Repeals) Act 2004.]

---

1. Part I contains Chapters I–III; Chapter II contains ss 24–41. Chapter II shall come into force on such day as the Commissioners may by order appoint (s 41 post). The Finance Act 1993, Chapter II, (Appointed Day) Order 1993, SI 1993/2842, appointed the day on which Chapter II came into force (with the exception of sections 24(1)(a), 29(1) and 39) as 1 December 1993, and appointed the day on which all remaining provisions not then already in force are to come into force on 1 February 1994.

2. The Lottery Duty Regulations 1993, SI 1993/3212 amended by SI 2002/2355 and the Lottery Duty (Instant Chances) Regulations 1995, SI 1995/2815 amended by SI 2002/2354 have been made.

8–7211 27. Persons liable for duty. (1) Any lottery duty or payment on account of lottery duty that under section 26 above or regulations under that section is payable in respect of a lottery shall be paid (subject to any regulations under subsection (2) below) by the promoter of the lottery.

(2) Regulations[1] may require any lottery duty or payment on account of lottery duty that is payable in respect of a lottery of a description specified in the regulations to be paid by a person specified in the regulations (being a person who occupies or has occupied a position of responsibility in relation to the lottery) instead of by the promoter.

(3) Any lottery duty that is payable in respect of a lottery may be recovered jointly and severally from—

(a) the promoter of the lottery,

(b) any other person who occupies or has occupied a position of responsibility in relation to the lottery or who has or has had any degree of control over any of its proceeds, and

(c) where the promoter or a person within paragraph (b) above is a body corporate, any director of that body corporate.

(4) Where a person does not make a payment that he is required to make by subsection (1) above or regulations under subsection (2) above at the time the payment becomes payable his failure so to make the payment shall attract a penalty under section 9 of the Finance Act 1994 (civil penalties) which shall be calculated by reference to the amount which has not been paid and shall also attract daily penalties.

[Finance Act 1993, s 27 as amended by the Finance Act 1994, Sch 4.]

---

1. The Lottery Duty Regulations 1993, SI 1993/3212 amended by SI 2002/2355 and 4021 have been made.

Administration and enforcement

8–7212 28. General. (1) Lottery duty shall be under the care and management of the Commissioners.

(2) Regulations[1] may provide for any matter for which provision appears to the Commissioners to be necessary or expedient for the administration or enforcement of lottery duty or for the protection of the revenue derived from lottery duty.

(3) Where a person contravenes or does not comply with any regulations under subsection (2) above his contravention or failure to comply shall attract a penalty under section 9 of the Finance Act 1994 (civil penalties).

[Finance Act 1993, s 28 as amended by the Finance Act 1994, Sch 4.]

---

1. The Lottery Duty Regulations 1993, SI 1993/3212 amended by SI 2002/2355 and 4021 and the Lottery Duty (Instant Chances) Regulations 1995, SI 1995/2815 amended by SI 2002/2354 have been made.

8–7213 29. Registration of promoters etc. (1) A lottery in respect of which lottery duty is chargeable (or, on the taking of a ticket or chance, will be chargeable) shall not be promoted in the United Kingdom unless the chargeable person is registered with the Commissioners under this section.

(2) In this section "the chargeable person", in relation to a lottery, means—

(a) subject to paragraph (b) below, the promoter of the lottery;

(b) in the case of a lottery of a description specified in regulations under section 27(2) above, the other person referred to in that subsection.

(3) Regulations[1] may make provision—

(a) as to the time at which an application for registration is to be made, as to the form and manner of such an application and as to the information to be contained in or provided with it,

(b) as to the requirements that must be satisfied as a condition of a person's registration or continued registration, and

(c) as to other requirements that must be observed by a person while he remains registered.

(4) The requirements imposed by virtue of subsection (3)(b) above may include requirements as to the giving of security or further security (by means of a deposit or otherwise) for any lottery duty that may become due.

(5) Subject to regulations under subsection (3)(a) and (b) above, the Commissioners—

(a) shall register any person applying to them for registration who satisfies them that he will be the chargeable person in relation to a lottery that is to be promoted, and

(b) shall not remove any person from the register unless it appears to them that no lottery is being or is to be promoted in relation to which he is or will be the chargeable person.

(6) Where—

(a) the Commissioners determine that a person should be removed from the register because any requirement imposed by regulations under subsection (3)(b) above is not (or is no longer) satisfied in relation to him, and

(b) a lottery in relation to which he is the chargeable person is being promoted at the time they make that determination,

they shall not remove him from the register until the promotion of that lottery has come to an end.

(7) If subsection (1) above is contravened in relation to a lottery at any time during its promotion, the chargeable person is guilty of an offence and liable[2]—

(a) on summary conviction, to a penalty of **the statutory maximum** or to imprisonment for a term not exceeding **six months**, or to **both**, or

(b) on conviction on indictment, to a **penalty** of any amount or to imprisonment for a term not exceeding **two years**, or to **both**.

(8) Where any person contravenes or fails to comply with any requirements imposed by regulations under subsection (3)(c) above his contravention or failure to comply shall attract a penalty under section 9 of the Finance Act 1994 (civil penalties).
[Finance Act 1993, s 29 as amended by the Finance Act 1994, Sch 4.]

---

1. For procedure in respect of this offence which is triable either way, see s 147 of the Customs and Excise Management Act 1979, ante, and the Magistrates' Courts Act 1980, ss 17A–21, in PART I: MAGISTRATES' COURTS, PROCEDURE, ante.
2. The Lottery Duty Regulations 1993, SI 1993/3212 amended by SI 2001/2355 and 4021 have been made.

8–7214 31. General offences. (1) A person who is knowingly concerned—

(a) in the fraudulent evasion (by him or another person) of lottery duty, or

(b) in taking steps with a view to such fraudulent evasion,

is guilty of an offence.

(2) A person guilty of an offence under subsection (1) above is liable[1]—

(a) on summary conviction, to a penalty of **the statutory maximum** or, if greater, treble the amount of the duty evaded or sought to be evaded or to imprisonment for a term no exceeding **six months**, or to **both**, or

(b) on conviction on indictment, to a **penalty** of any amount or to imprisonment for a term not exceeding **seven years**, or to **both**.

(3) A person who in connection with lottery duty—

(a) makes a statement that he knows to be false in a material particular or recklessly makes a statement that is false in a material particular, or

(b) with intent to deceive, produces or makes use of a book, account, return or other document that is false in a material particular,

is guilty of an offence.

(4) A person guilty of an offence under subsection (3) above is liable—

(a) on summary conviction, to a penalty of **the statutory maximum** or to imprisonment for a term not exceeding **six months**, or to **both**, or

(b) on conviction on indictment, to a penalty of any amount or to imprisonment for a term not exceeding **two years**, or to **both**.
[Finance Act 1993, s 31.]

---

1. For procedure in respect of this offence which is triable either way, see s 147 of the Customs and Excise Management Act 1979, ante, and the Magistrates' Courts Act 1980, ss 17A–21, in PART I: MAGISTRATES' COURTS, PROCEDURE, ante.

8–7215 32. Offences by bodies corporate. Where an offence under this Chapter is committed by a body corporate, every person who at the date of the commission of the offence is a director, manager, secretary or other similar officer of the body corporate (or is purporting to act in such a capacity) is also guilty of the offence unless—

(*a*) the offence is committed without his consent or connivance, and

(*b*) he has exercised all such diligence to prevent its commission as he ought to have exercised, having regard to the nature of his functions in that capacity and to all the circumstances.

[Finance Act 1993, s 32.]

8–7216 33. Forfeiture. (1) Where a person has committed an offence under section 31(1) or (3) above, any goods used in the promotion of, or in any other way related to, a relevant lottery are liable to forfeiture.

(2) In subsection (1) above "relevant lottery"—

(*a*) in relation to an offence under section 31(1) above, means a lottery in respect of which lottery duty was fraudulently evaded or (as the case may be) in respect of which the fraudulent evasion of lottery duty was sought, and

(*b*) in relation to an offence under section 31(3) above, means a lottery to which the false statement or (as the case may be) false document related.

[Finance Act 1993, s 33.]

8–7217 34. Protection of officers etc. Where a person takes an action in pursuance of instructions of the Commissioners given in connection with the enforcement of this Chapter or of regulations under it and, apart from this section, the person would in taking that action be committing an offence under any enactment relating to lotteries, he shall not be guilty of that offence.

[Finance Act 1993, s 34.]

8–7218 35. Evidence by certificate etc. (1) A certificate of the Commissioners—

(*a*) that a person was or was not, at any date, registered under section 29 above,

(*b*) that any return required by regulations under this Chapter had not been made at any date, or

(*c*) that any lottery duty shown as due in a return made in pursuance of such regulations or in an estimate made under section 116A of the Customs and Excise Management Act 1979 had not been paid at any date,

is sufficient evidence of that fact until the contrary is proved.

(2) A photograph of any document furnished to the Commissioners for the purposes of this Chapter and certified by them to be such a photograph is admissible in any proceedings, whether civil or criminal, to the same extent as the document itself.

(3) Any document purporting to be a certificate under subsection (1) or (2) above shall be taken to be such a certificate until the contrary is proved.

[Finance Act 1993, s 35.]

8–7219 37. Disclosure of information. (1) Notwithstanding any obligation not to disclose information that would otherwise apply, the Commissioners may disclose information—

(*a*) to the Secretary of State,

(*b*) to the Gaming Board for Great Britain, or

(*c*) to an authorised officer of the Secretary of State or Gaming Board,

for the purpose of assisting the Secretary of State or Gaming Board (as the case may be) in the performance of duties imposed by or under any enactment in relation to lotteries.

(2) Notwithstanding any such obligation as is mentioned in subsection (1) above—

(*a*) the Secretary of State,

(*b*) the Gaming Board for Great Britain, or

(*c*) an authorised officer of the Secretary of State or Gaming Board,

may disclose information to the Commissioners or to an authorised officer of the Commissioners for the purpose of assisting the Commissioners in the performance of duties in relation to lottery duty.

(3) Information that has been disclosed to a person by virtue of this section shall not be disclosed by him except—

(*a*) to another person to whom (instead of him) disclosure could by virtue of this section have been made, or

(*b*) for the purpose of any proceedings connected with the operation of any enactment in relation to lotteries or lottery duty.

(4) References above in this section to the Secretary of State include any person who has been designated by the Secretary of State as a person to and by whom information may be disclosed under this section.

(5) The Secretary of State shall notify the Commissioners in writing if he designates a person under subsection (4) above.
[Finance Act 1993, s 37.]

Supplementary

8–7220   38. *Regulations and orders.*

8–7221   40. Interpretation etc.   (1) In this Chapter—

"the Commissioners" means the Commissioners of Customs and Excise,

"document" includes a document of any kind whatsoever and, in particular, a record kept by means of a computer,

"promotion", in relation to a lottery, includes the conduct of the lottery (and "promoted" is to be read accordingly), and

"regulations" means regulations made by the Commissioners.

(2) This Chapter applies in relation to lotteries promoted on behalf of the Crown in pursuance of any enactment as it applies in relation to lotteries not so promoted.

(3) The imposition by this Chapter of lottery duty does not make lawful anything that is unlawful apart from this Chapter.
[Finance Act 1993, s 40.]

8–7222   41. Commencement.   This Chapter shall come into force on such day as the Commissioners may by order[1] appoint, and different days may be appointed for different provisions or for different purposes.
[Finance Act 1993, s 41.]

---

1. At the date of going to press no such order had been made.

Finance Act 1994
(1994 c 9)

PART I[1]
CUSTOMS AND EXCISE

CHAPTER II[2]
APPEALS AND PENALTIES

Civil penalties

8–7230   8. Penalty for evasion of excise duty.   (1) Subject to the following provisions of this section, in any case where—

(*a*) any person engages in any conduct for the purpose of evading any duty of excise, and

(*b*) his conduct involves dishonesty (whether or not such as to give rise to any criminal liability),

that person shall be liable to a penalty of an amount equal to the amount of duty evaded or, as the case may be, sought to be evaded.

(2) References in this section to a person's evading a duty of excise shall include references to his obtaining or securing, without his being entitled to it—

(*a*) any repayment, rebate or drawback of duty;

(*b*) any relief or exemption from or any allowance against duty; or

(*c*) any deferral or other postponement of his liability to pay any duty or of the discharge by payment of any such liability,

and shall also include references to his evading the cancellation of any entitlement to, or the withdrawal of, any such repayment, rebate, drawback, relief, exemption or allowance.

(3) In relation to any such evasion of duty as is mentioned in subsection (2) above, the reference in subsection (1) above to the amount of duty evaded or sought to be evaded shall be construed as a reference to the amount of the repayment, rebate, drawback, relief, exemption or allowance or, as the case may be, the amount of the payment which, or the liability to make which, is deferred or otherwise postponed.

(4) Where a person is liable to a penalty under this section—

(*a*) the Commissioners or, on appeal, an appeal tribunal may reduce the penalty to such amount (including nil) as they think proper; and

(*b*) an appeal tribunal, on an appeal relating to a penalty reduced by the Commissioners under this subsection, may cancel the whole or any part of the reduction made by the Commissioners.

(5) Neither of the following matters shall be a matter which the Commissioners or any appeal

tribunal shall be entitled to take into account in exercising their powers under subsection (4) above, that is to say—

    (a) the insufficiency of the funds available to any person for paying any duty of excise or for paying the amount of the penalty;

    (b) the fact that there has, in the case in question or in that case taken with any other cases, been no or no significant loss of duty.

(6) Statements made or documents produced by or on behalf of a person shall not be inadmissible in—

    (a) any criminal proceedings against that person in respect of any offence in connection with or in relation to any duty of excise, or

    (b) any proceedings against that person for the recovery of any sum due from him in connection with or in relation to any duty of excise,

by reason only that any of the matters specified in subsection (7) below has been drawn to his attention and that he was, or may have been, induced by that matter having been brought to his attention to make the statements or produce the documents.

(7) The matters mentioned in subsection (6) above are—

    (a) that the Commissioners have power, in relation to any duty of excise, to assess an amount due by way of a civil penalty, instead of instituting criminal proceedings;

    (b) that it is the Commissioners' practice, without being able to give an undertaking as to whether they will make such an assessment in any case, to be influenced in determining whether to make such an assessment by the fact (where it is the case) that a person has made a full confession of any dishonest conduct to which he has been a party and has given full facilities for an investigation;

    (c) that the Commissioners or, on appeal, an appeal tribunal have power to reduce a penalty under this section, as provided in subsection (4) above; and

    (d) that, in determining the extent of such a reduction in the case of any person, the Commissioners or tribunal will have regard to the extent of the co-operation which he has given to the Commissioners in their investigation.

(8) Where, by reason of conduct falling within subsection (1) above, a person is convicted of an offence, that conduct shall not also give rise to liability to a penalty under this section.
[Finance Act 1994, s 8.]

---

    1. Part I contains ss 1–44.
    2. Chapter II contains ss 7–19.

8–7230A   **9. Penalties for contraventions of statutory requirements.**   (1) This section applies, subject to section 10 below, to any conduct in relation to which any enactment (including an enactment contained in this Act or in any Act passed after this Act) provides for the conduct to attract a penalty under this section.

(2) Any person to whose conduct this section applies shall be liable—

    (a) in the case of conduct in relation to which provision is made by subsection (4) below, or by or under any other enactment, for the penalty attracted to be calculated by reference to an amount of, or an amount payable on account of, any duty of excise, to a penalty of whichever is the greater of 5 per cent of that amount and £250; and

    (b) in any other case, to a penalty of £250.

(3) Subject to section 13(3) and (4) below, in the case of any conduct to which this section applies which is conduct in relation to which provision is made by subsection (4) or (5) below or any other enactment for that conduct to attract daily penalties, the person whose conduct it is—

    (a) shall be liable, in addition to an initial penalty under subsection (2) above, to a penalty of £20 for every day, after the first, on which the conduct continues, but

    (b) shall not, in respect of the continuation of that conduct, be liable to further penalties under subsection (2) above.

(4) Where any conduct to which this section applies consists in a failure, in contravention of any subordinate legislation, to pay any amount of any duty of excise or an amount payable on account of any such duty, then, in so far as that would not otherwise be the case—

    (a) the penalty attracted to that contravention shall be calculated by reference to the amount unpaid; and

    (b) the contravention shall also attract daily penalties.

(5) Where—

    (a) a contravention of any provision made by or under any enactment consists in or involves a failure, before such time as may be specified in or determined in accordance with that provision, to send a return to the Commissioners showing the amount which any person is or may become required to pay by way of, or on account of, any duty of excise, and (*b*) that contravention attracts a penalty under this section,

that contravention shall also attract daily penalties.

(6) Where, by reason of any conduct to which this section applies, a person is convicted of an offence, that conduct shall not also give rise to liability to a penalty under this section.

(7) If it appears to the Treasury that there has been a change in the value of money since the passing of this Act or, as the case may be, the last occasion when the power conferred by this subsection was exercised, they may by order substitute for any sum for the time being specified in subsection (2) or (3) above such other sum as appears to them to be justified by the change.

(8) The power to make an order under subsection (7) above—

(*a*) shall be exercisable by statutory instrument subject to annulment in pursuance of a resolution of the House of Commons; but

(*b*) shall not be exercisable so as to vary the penalty for any conduct occurring before the coming into force of the order.

(9) *Schedule 4—consequential amendments.*

[Finance Act 1994, s 9 as amended by the Finance Act 2000, s 28.]

8–7230B   10. Exceptions to liability under section 9.   (1) Subject to subsection (2) below and to any express provision to the contrary made in relation to any conduct to which section 9 above applies, such conduct shall not give rise to any liability to a penalty under that section if the person whose conduct it is satisfies the Commissioners or, on appeal, an appeal tribunal that there is a reasonable excuse for the conduct.

(2) Where it appears to the Commissioners or, on appeal tribunal that there is no reasonable excuse for a continuation of conduct for which there was at first a reasonable excuse, liability for a penalty under section 9 above shall be determined as if the conduct began at the time when there ceased to be a reasonable excuse for its continuation.

(3) For the purposes of this section—

(*a*) an insufficiency of funds available for paying any duty or penalty due shall not be a reasonable excuse; and

(*b*) where reliance is placed by any person on another to perform any task, then neither the fact of that reliance nor the fact that any conduct to which section 9 above applies was attributable to the conduct of that other person shall be a reasonable excuse.

[Finance Act 1994, s 10.]

CHAPTER III[1]
CUSTOMS: ENFORCEMENT POWERS

8–7230C   20. Interpretation, etc.   (1) This Chapter applies to any person carrying on a trade or business which consists of or includes any of the following activities—

(*a*) importing or exporting any goods of a class or description subject to a duty of customs (whether or not in fact chargeable with that duty);

(*b*) producing, manufacturing or applying a process to them;

(*c*) buying, selling or dealing in them;

(*d*) handling or storing them;

(*e*) financing or facilitating any activity mentioned in paragraphs (*a*) to (*d*) above.

(2) In subsection (1) above "duty of customs" includes any agricultural levy of the European Community.

(3) In this Chapter—

(*a*) "customs goods" means any goods mentioned in paragraph (*a*) of subsection (1) above; and

(*b*) any reference to the business of a person to whom this Chapter applies is a reference to the trade or business carried on by him as mentioned in that subsection.

(4) This Chapter shall have effect and be construed as if it were contained in the Customs and Excise Management Act 1979.

(5) In consequence of the provision made by sections 21 to 27 below, any power under—

(*a*) section 75A, 75B or 75C of the Customs and Excise Management Act 1979 to require a person importing or exporting goods to keep or preserve records, or

(*b*) section 77A, 77B or 77C of that Act to require a person to furnish information or produce documents relating to imported or exported goods,

shall cease to be exercisable in relation to a person to the extent that the goods in question are customs goods.

[Finance Act 1994, s 20.]

---

1. Chapter III contains ss 20–27.

8–7231   21. Requirements about keeping records.   (1) The Commissioners may by regulations require any person to whom this Chapter applies—

(*a*)   to keep such records as may be prescribed in the regulations; and

(*b*)   to preserve those records—

     (i)   for such period not exceeding four years as may be prescribed in the regulations, or

     (ii)   for such lesser period as the Commissioners may require.

(2)   The Commissioners may also require any person mentioned in subsection (3) below—

(*a*)   to keep such records as they may specify; and

(*b*)   to preserve those records for such period not exceeding four years as they may require.

(3)   The person referred to is any person who—

(*a*)   is not carrying on a trade or business which consists of or includes the importation or exportation of customs goods, but

(*b*)   is concerned in some other capacity in such importation or exportation.

(4)   A duty imposed under subsection (1)(*b*) or (2)(*b*) above to preserve records may be discharged by the preservation of the information contained in them by such means as the Commissioners may approve.

(5)   On giving approval under subsection (4) above, the Commissioners may impose such reasonable requirements as appear to them necessary for securing that the information will be as readily available to them as if the records themselves had been preserved.

(6)   Regulations under this section may—

(*a*)   make different provision for different cases; and

(*b*)   be framed by reference to such records as may be specified in any notice published by the Commissioners in pursuance of the regulations and not withdrawn by a further notice.

(7)   Any person who fails to comply with a requirement imposed by virtue of this section shall be liable on summary conviction to a penalty not exceeding **level 3** on the standard scale.

[Finance Act 1994, s 21.]

8–7231A   22. Records and rules of evidence.   (1) Where any information is preserved by approved means as mentioned in section 21(4) above, a copy of any document in which it is contained shall, subject to subsection (2) below, be admissible in evidence in any proceedings, whether civil or criminal, to the same extent as the records themselves.

(2)   A statement contained in a document produced by a computer shall not by virtue of subsection (1) above be admissible in evidence—

(*a*)   *Repealed.*

(*b*)   in criminal proceedings in England and Wales, except in accordance with Part II of the Criminal Justice Act 1988;

(*c*)–(*f*)   *Scotland; Northern Ireland. Para (f) repealed.*

[Finance Act 1994, s 22 as amended by the Civil Evidence Act 1995, Sch 2 and the Youth Justice and Criminal Evidence Act 1999, Sch 6.]

8–7231B   23. Furnishing of information and production of documents.   (1) Every person to whom this Chapter applies shall furnish the Commissioners, within such time and in such form as they may reasonably require, with such information relating to his business as they may reasonably specify.

(2)   Every person to whom this Chapter applies shall, if required to do so by an officer, produce or cause to be produced for inspection by the officer—

(*a*)   at that person's principal place of business or at such other place as the officer may reasonably require, and

(*b*)   at such time as the officer may reasonably require,

any documents which relate to his business.

(3)   Where it appears to an officer that any documents which relate to a business of a person to whom this Chapter applies are in the possession of another person, the officer may require that other person, at such time and place as the officer may reasonably require, to produce those documents or cause them to be produced.

(4)   For the purposes of this section, the documents which relate to a business of a person to whom this Chapter applies shall be taken to include—

(*a*)   any profit and loss account and balance sheet, and

(*b*)   any documents required to be kept by virtue of section 21(1) above.

(5)   Every person mentioned in section 21(3) above shall furnish the Commissioners, within such time and in such form as they may reasonably require, with such information relating to the importation or exportation of customs goods in which he is concerned as they may reasonably specify.

(6)   Every person mentioned in section 21(3) above shall, if required to do so by an officer, produce or cause to be produced for inspection by the officer at such time and place as the officer

may reasonably require, any documents which relate to the importation or exportation of customs goods in which he is concerned.

(7) An officer may take copies of, or make extracts from, any document produced under this section.

(8) If it appears to an officer to be necessary to do so, he may, at a reasonable time and for a reasonable period, remove any document produced under this section.

(9) Where a document is removed under subsection (8) above—

(a) if the person from whom the document is removed so requests, he shall be given a record of what was removed;

(b) if the document is reasonably required for the proper conduct of any business, the person by whom the document was produced or caused to be produced shall be provided as soon as practicable with a copy of the document free of charge;

(c) if the document is lost or damaged, the Commissioners shall be liable to compensate the owner of it for any expenses reasonably incurred by him in replacing or repairing it.

(10) If a person claims a lien on any document produced by him under subsection (3) or (6) above—

(a) the production of the document shall be without prejudice to the lien; and

(b) the removal of the document under subsection (8) above shall not be regarded as breaking the lien.

(11) Any person who fails to comply with a requirement imposed under this section shall be liable on summary conviction to a penalty not exceeding **level 3** on the standard scale.
[Finance Act 1994, s 23.]

8–7231C   24. Power of entry.   Where an officer has reasonable cause to believe that—

(a) any premises are used in connection with a business of a person to whom this Chapter applies, and

(b) any customs goods are on those premises,

he may at any reasonable time enter and inspect those premises and inspect any goods found on them.
[Finance Act 1994, s 24.]

8–7232   25. Order for production of documents.   (1) Where, on an application by an officer, a justice is satisfied that there are reasonable grounds for believing—

(a) that an offence in connection with a duty of customs is being, has been or is about to be committed, and

(b) that any information or documents which may be required as evidence for the purpose of any proceedings in respect of such an offence is in the possession of any person,

he may make an order under this section.

(2) An order under this section is an order that the person who appears to the justice to be in possession of the information or documents to which the application relates shall—

(a) furnish an officer with the information or produce the document,

(b) permit an officer to take copies of or make extracts of any document produced, and

(c) permit an officer to remove any document which he reasonably considers necessary,

not later than the end of the period of seven days beginning with the date of the order or the end of such longer period as the order may specify.

(3) In this section "justice" means a justice of the peace or, in relation to Scotland, a justice within the meaning of section 308 of the Criminal Procedure (Scotland) Act 1995.
[Finance Act 1994, s 25 as amended by the Criminal Procedure (Consequential Provisions) (Scotland) Act 1995, Sch 4.]

8–7232A   26. Procedure when documents are removed.   (1) An officer who removes any document in the exercise of a power conferred under section 25 above shall, if so requested by a person showing himself—

(a) to be the occupier of premises from which it was removed, or

(b) to have had custody or control of it immediately before the removal,

provide that person with a record of what he removed.

(2) The officer shall provide the record within a reasonable time from the making of the request for it.

(3) Subject to subsection (7) below, if a request for permission to be granted access to any document which—

(a) has been removed by an officer, and

(b) is retained by the Commissioners for the purposes of investigating an offence,

is made to the officer in charge of the investigation by a person who had custody or control of the document immediately before it was so removed or by someone acting on behalf of such a person, the officer shall allow the person who made the request access to it under the supervision of an officer.

(4) Subject to subsection (7) below, if a request for a photograph or copy of any such document is made to the officer in charge of the investigation by a person who had custody or control of the document immediately before it was so removed, or by someone acting on behalf of such a person, the officer shall—

    (a)   allow the person who made the request access to it under the supervision of an officer for the purpose of photographing it or copying it, or

    (b)   photograph or copy it, or cause it to be photographed or copied.

(5) Where any document is photographed or copied under subsection (4)(b) above, the photograph or copy shall be supplied to the person who made the request.

(6) The photograph or copy shall be supplied within a reasonable time from the making of the request.

(7) There is no duty under this section to grant access to, or to supply a photograph or copy of, any document if the officer in charge of the investigation for the purposes of which it was removed has reasonable grounds for believing that to do so would prejudice—

    (a)   that investigation;

    (b)   the investigation of an offence other than the offence for the purposes of the investigation of which the document was removed; or

    (c)   any criminal proceedings which may be brought as a result of—

        (i)   the investigation of which he is in charge; or

        (ii)   any such investigation as is mentioned in paragraph (b) above.

(8) Any reference in this section to the officer in charge of the investigation is a reference to the person whose name and address are endorsed on the order concerned as being the officer in charge of it.

[Finance Act 1994, s 26.]

8–7232B **27. Failure of officer to comply with requirements under section 26.** (1) Where, on an application made as mentioned in subsection (2) below, the appropriate judicial authority is satisfied that a person has failed to comply with a requirement imposed by section 26 above, the authority may order that person to comply with the requirement within such time and in such manner as may be specified in the order.

(2) An application under subsection (1) above shall be made—

    (a)   in the case of a failure to comply with any of the requirements imposed by subsections (1) and (2) of section 26 above, by the occupier of the premises from which the document in question was removed or by the person who had custody or control of it immediately before it was so removed, and

    (b)   in any other case, by the person who has such custody or control.

(3) In this section "the appropriate judicial authority" means—

    (a)   in England and Wales, a magistrates' court;

    (b)   in Scotland, the sheriff; and

    (c)   in Northern Ireland, a court of summary jurisdiction, as defined in Article 2(2)(a) of the Magistrates' Courts (Northern Ireland) Order 1981.

(4) Any application for an order under this section—

    (a)   in England and Wales, shall be made by way of complaint; or

    (b)   in Northern Ireland, shall be made by way of civil proceedings upon complaint.

(5) *Northern Ireland.*

[Finance Act 1994, s 27.]

CHAPTER IV[1]

AIR PASSENGER DUTY

The duty

8–7232C **28. Air passenger duty.** (1) A duty to be known as air passenger duty shall be charged in accordance with this Chapter on the carriage on a chargeable aircraft of any chargeable passenger.

(2) Subject to the provisions of this Chapter about accounting and payment, the duty in respect of any carriage on an aircraft of a chargeable passenger—

    (a)   becomes due when the aircraft first takes off on the passenger's flight, and

    (b)   shall be paid by the operator of the aircraft.

(3) Subject to section 29 below, every aircraft designed or adapted to carry persons in addition to the flight crew is a chargeable aircraft for the purposes of this Chapter.

(4) Subject to sections 31 and 32 below, every passenger on an aircraft is a chargeable passenger for the purposes of this Chapter if his flight begins at an airport in the United Kingdom.

(5) In this Chapter, "flight", in relation to any person, means his carriage on an aircraft; and for the purposes of this Chapter, a person's flight is to be treated as beginning when he first boards the aircraft and ending when he finally disembarks from the aircraft.
[Finance Act 1994, s 28.]

---

1. Chapter IV contains ss 28–44.

8–7233   29. Chargeable aircraft.   (1) Where—

(a)   the authorised take-off weight in respect of an aircraft is less than ten tonnes, or
(b)   an aircraft is not authorised to seat twenty or more persons (excluding members of the flight crew and cabin attendants),

the aircraft is not a chargeable aircraft for the purposes of this Chapter.

(2) In this section "take-off weight", in relation to an aircraft, means the total weight of the aircraft and its contents when taking off; and for the purposes of this section the authorised take-off weight of an aircraft is less than ten tonnes if—

(a)   there is a certificate of airworthiness in force in respect of the aircraft showing that the maximum authorised take-off weight (assuming the most favourable circumstances for take-off) is less than ten tonnes, or
(b)   the Commissioners are satisfied that the aircraft is not designed or adapted to take off when its take-off weight is ten tonnes or more (assuming the most favourable circumstances for take-off) or the aircraft belongs to a class or description of aircraft in respect of which the Commissioners are so satisfied.

(3) For the purposes of this section an aircraft is not authorised as mentioned in subsection (1)(b) above if—

(a)   there is a certificate of airworthiness in force in respect of the aircraft showing that the maximum number of persons who may be seated on the aircraft (excluding members of the flight crew and cabin attendants) is less than twenty, or
(b)   the Commissioners are satisfied that the aircraft is not designed or adapted to seat twenty or more persons (excluding members of the flight crew and cabin attendants) or the aircraft belongs to a class or description of aircraft in respect of which the Commissioners are so satisfied.

(4) In this section "certificate of airworthiness" has the same meaning as in the Air Navigation Order.
[Finance Act 1994, s 29.]

8–7233A   30. The rate of duty.   (1) Air passenger duty shall be charged on the carriage of each chargeable passenger at the rate determined in accordance with subsections (2) to (4) below.

(2) If the place where the passenger's journey ends] is in the area specified in subsection (3) below and in—

(a)   the United Kingdom or another EEA State,
(b)   any territory for whose external relations the United Kingdom or another member State is responsible, or
(c)   any qualifying territory (so long as not falling within paragraph (a) above),

the rate shall be determined in accordance with subsection (3A) below.

(3) The area referred to in subsection (2) above is the area bounded by the meridians of longitude 32 degrees W and [45 degrees E] and the parallels of latitude 26 degrees N and 81 degrees N

(3A) In a case falling within subsection (2) above—

(a)   if the passenger's agreement for carriage provides for standard class travel in relation to every flight on his journey, the rate is £5;
(b)   in any other case, the rate is £10.

(4) In a case not falling within subsection (2) above—

(a)   if the passenger's agreement for carriage provides for standard class travel in relation to every flight on his journey, the rate is £20;
(b)   in any other case, the rate is £40.

(5) Subject to subsection (6) below, the journey of a passenger whose agreement for carriage is evidenced by a ticket ends for the purposes of this section at his final place of destination.

(6) Where in the case of such a passenger—

(a)   his journey includes two or more flights, and
(b)   any of those flights is not followed by a connected flight,

his journey ends for those purposes where the first flight not followed by a connected flight ends.

(7) The journey of any passenger whose agreement for carriage is not evidenced by a ticket ends for those purposes where his flight ends.

(8) For the purposes of this Chapter, successive flights are connected if (and only if) they are treated under an order[1] as connected.

(9) In this section "EEA State" means a State which is a Contracting Party to the EEA Agreement but until the EEA Agreement comes into force in relation to Liechtenstein does not include the State of Liechtenstein; and "EEA Agreement" here means the Agreement on the European Economic Area signed at Oporto on 2nd May 1992 as adjusted by the Protocol signed at Brussels on 17th March 1993.

(9A) In this section "qualifying territory" means each of the following territories—

Bulgaria	Latvia	Slovak Republic
Cyprus	Lithuania	Slovenia
Czech Republic	Malta	Switzerland
Estonia	Poland	Turkey.
Hungary	Romania	

(9B) The Treasury may by order amend the definition of "qualifying territory" in subsection (9A) above by adding, removing, or varying the description of, any territory.

(10) In this section "standard class travel", in relation to carriage on an aircraft, means—

(*a*) in the case of an aircraft on which only one class of travel is available, that class of travel;

(*b*) in any other case, the lowest class of travel available on the aircraft.

[Finance Act 1994, s 30 as amended by the Finance Act 1995, s 15, the Finance Act 1997, s 9, the Finance Act 2000, s 18 and the Finance Act 2002, s 121.]

---

1. See the Air Passenger Duty (Connected Flights) Order 1994, SI 1994/1821 amended by SI 2001/809.

8–7233B   **31. Passengers: exceptions**(1) (*Repealed*).

.   (2) (*Repealed*).

(3) A passenger whose agreement for carriage is evidenced by a ticket is not a chargeable passenger in relation to a flight which is the second or a subsequent flight on his journey if—

(*a*) the prescribed[1] particulars of the flight are shown on the ticket, and

(*b*) that flight and the previous flight are connected.

(4) A child who—

(*a*) has not attained the age of two years, and

(*b*) is not allocated a separate seat before he first boards the aircraft,

is not a chargeable passenger.

(4A) A passenger is not a chargeable passenger in relation to a flight if under his agreement for carriage (whether or not it is evidenced by a ticket)—

(*a*) the flight is to depart from and return to the same airport, and

(*b*) the duration of the flight (excluding any period during which the aircraft's doors are open for boarding or disembarkation) is not to exceed 60 minutes.

(4B) A passenger is not a chargeable passenger in relation to a flight if under his agreement for carriage (whether or not it is evidenced by a ticket) the flight is to depart from an airport which is in a region of the United Kingdom designated by order[3].

(4C) An order may be made for the purposes of subsection (4B) above in respect of any region which has a population density of not more than 12.5 persons per square kilometre.

(4D) In subsections (4B) and (4C) above, references to a region are references to an area which is determined by the Treasury to constitute a region for the purposes of those subsections.

(5) A passenger not carried for reward is not a chargeable passenger if he is carried—

(*a*) in pursuance of any requirement imposed under any enactment, or

(*b*) for the purpose only of inspecting matters relating to the aircraft or the flight crew.

(6) (*Repealed*)

[Finance Act 1994, s 31 as amended by the Finance Act 1996, s 13 and the Finance Act 2000, s 19 and Sch 40.]

---

1. See the Air Passenger Duty Regulations 1994, SI 1994/1738 amended by SI 2001/836.

2. See note 1, ante.

3. The Air Passenger Duty (Designated Region of the United Kingdom) Order 2001, SI 2001/808 designates certain areas of Scotland.

8–7233C   **32. Change of circumstances after ticket issued etc.** (1) Subsections (2) and (3) below apply in the case of a person whose agreement for carriage is evidenced by a ticket.

(2) Where—

(*a*) at the time the ticket is issued or, if it is altered, at the time it is last altered, he would not (assuming there is no change of circumstances) be a chargeable passenger in relation to any flight in the course of his journey, and

(*b*) by reason only of a change of circumstances not attributable to any act or default of his, he arrives at or departs from an airport in the course of that journey on a flight the prescribed[1] particulars of which were not shown on his ticket at that time, he shall not by reason of the change of circumstances be treated as a chargeable passenger in relation to that flight.

(3) Where—

(*a*) at the time the ticket is issued or, if it is altered, at the time it is last altered, he would (assuming there is no change of circumstances) be a chargeable passenger in relation to one or more flights ("the proposed chargeable flights") in the course of his journey,

(*b*) by reason only of a change of circumstances not attributable to any act or default of his, he arrives at or departs from an airport in the course of that journey on a flight the prescribed[2] particulars of which were not shown on his ticket at that time, and

(*c*) but for this subsection he would by reason of the change be a chargeable passenger in relation to a number of flights exceeding the number of the proposed chargeable flights,

he shall not by reason of the change of circumstances be treated as a chargeable passenger in relation to that flight.

(4) Where—

(*a*) at the time a passenger's flight begins, by virtue of section 31 (4A) above he would not (assuming there is no change of circumstances) be a chargeable passenger in relation to the flight, and

(*b*) by reason only of a change of circumstances not attributable to any act or default of his, the flight does not return to the airport from which it departed or exceeds 60 minutes in duration (excluding any period during which the aircraft's doors are open for boarding or disembarkation),

he shall not by reason of the change of circumstances be treated as a chargeable passenger in relation to that flight.

[Finance Act 1994, s 32 as amended by the Finance Act 1996, s 13.]

---

1. See the Air Passenger Duty Regulations 1994, SI 1994/1738 amended by SI 2001/826.
2. See note 1, ante.

Persons liable for the duty

8–7234 33. Registration of aircraft operators.   (1) The Commissioners shall under this section keep a register of aircraft operators.

(2) The operator of a chargeable aircraft becomes liable to be registered under this section if the aircraft is used for the carriage of any chargeable passengers.

(3) A person who has become liable to be registered under this section ceases to be so liable if the Commissioners are satisfied at any time—

(*a*) that he no longer operates any chargeable aircraft, or

(*b*) that no chargeable aircraft which he operates will be used for the carriage of chargeable passengers.

(4) A person who is not registered and has not given notice under this subsection shall, if he becomes liable to be registered at any time, give written notice of that fact to the Commissioners not later than the end of the prescribed[1] period beginning with that time.

(5) Notice under subsection (4) above shall be in such form, be given in such manner and contain such information as the Commissioners may direct.

(6) If a person who is required to give notice under subsection (4) above fails to do so, his failure shall attract a penalty under section 9 above which, if any amount of duty is then due from him and unpaid, shall be calculated by reference to that amount.

(7) Regulations[2] may make provision as to the information to be included in, and the correction of, the register kept under this section.

(8) In particular, the regulations[3] may provide—

(*a*) for the inclusion in the register of persons who have not given notice under this section but appear to the Commissioners to be liable to be registered,

(*b*) for persons who are liable to be registered—

(i) not to be included in, or
(ii) to be removed from,

the register in prescribed circumstances,

(*c*) for the removal from the register of persons who have ceased to be so liable, and

(*d*) for the time from which an entry in the register is to be effective (which may be earlier than the time when the entry is first made in the register).

[Finance Act 1994, s 33.]

---

1. See the Air Passenger Duty Regulations 1994, SI 1994/1738 amended by SI 2001/836.
2. See note 1, ante.
3. See note 1, ante.

Administration and enforcement

8–7234A 40. Administration and enforcement. (1) Air passenger duty shall be a duty of excise and, accordingly, shall be under the care and management of the Commissioners.

(2) Schedule 6 to this Act (administration and enforcement) shall have effect.
[Finance Act 1994, s 40.]

8–7234B 41. Offences. (1) A person who is knowingly concerned—

(a) in the fraudulent evasion (by him or another person) of duty, or

(b) in taking steps with a view to such fraudulent evasion,

is guilty of an offence.

(2) A person guilty of an offence under subsection (1) above is liable[1]—

(a) on summary conviction, to a penalty of—

(i) the **statutory maximum**, or

(ii) if greater, treble the amount of the duty evaded or sought to be evaded,

or to imprisonment for a term not exceeding **six months**, or to both, or

(b) on conviction on indictment, to a penalty of any amount or to imprisonment for a term not exceeding **seven years**, or to both.

(3) A person who in connection with duty—

(a) makes a statement that he knows to be false in a material particular or recklessly makes a statement that is false in a material particular, or

(b) with intent to deceive, produces or makes use of a book account, return or other document that is false in a material particular,

is guilty of an offence.

(4) A person guilty of an offence under subsection (3) above is liable—

(a) on summary conviction, to a penalty of the **statutory maximum** or to imprisonment for a term not exceeding **six months**, or to both, or

(b) on conviction on indictment, to a penalty of any amount or to imprisonment for a term not exceeding **two years**, or to both.

[Finance Act 1994, s 4.]

---

1. For procedure in respect of this offence which is triable either way, see s 147 of the Customs and Excise Management Act 1979, this PART ante, and the Magistrates' Courts Act 1980, ss 17A–21, in PART I: MAGISTRATES' COURTS, PROCEDURE, ante.

Supplementary

8–7234C 42. Regulations and orders. (1) In this Chapter "regulations" means regulations made by the Commissioners and "order" means an order made by the Treasury.

(2) Regulations and orders may make different provision for different cases or circumstances and make incidental, supplemental, saving or transitional provision.

(3) Any power to make regulations or an order is exercisable by statutory instrument.

(4) No order which appears to the Treasury to extend the circumstances in which passengers are to be treated as chargeable passengers shall be made unless a draft of the order has been laid before and approved by the House of Commons.

(5) Any other order, and any regulations, shall be subject to annulment in pursuance of a resolution of the House of Commons.
[Finance Act 1994, s 42.]

8–7235 43. Interpretation. (1) In this Chapter—

"accounting period" means any period prescribed or allowed for the purposes of section 38 above.

"agreement for carriage", in relation to the carriage of any person, means the agreement or arrangement under which he is carried, whether the carriage is by a single carrier or successive carriers,

"Air Navigation Order" has the same meaning as in the Civil Aviation Act 1982,

"airport" means any aerodrome (within the meaning of that Act),

"carriage" means carriage wholly or partly by air, and "carried" is to be read accordingly,

"connected', in relation to any flights, has the meaning given by section 30(8) above,

"document" includes information recorded in any form,

"duty" means air passenger duty,

"fiscal representative" has the meaning given by section 34(2) above,

"flight" has the meaning given by section 28(5) above,

"operator", in relation to any aircraft, means the person having the management of the aircraft for the time being,

"passenger", in relation to any aircraft, means—

(*a*) where the operator is an air transport undertaking (within the meaning of the Air Navigation Order), any person carried on the aircraft other than—

    (i) a member of the flight crew,

    (ii) a cabin attendant, or

    (iii) a person who is not carried for reward, who is an employee of any aircraft operator and who satisfies such other requirements as may be prescribed, and

(*b*) in any other case, any person carried on the aircraft for reward,

"prescribed" means prescribed by regulations,

"reward", in relation to the carriage of any person, includes any form of consideration received or to be received wholly or partly in connection with the carriage, irrespective of the person by whom or to whom the consideration has been or is to be given, and

"ticket" means a document or documents evidencing an agreement (wherever made) for the carriage of any person.

(2) In this Chapter, in relation to a passenger whose agreement for carriage is evidenced by a ticket—

"journey" means the journey from his original place of departure to his final place of destination, and

"original place of departure" and "final place of destination" mean the original place of departure and the final place of destination indicated on his ticket.

(3) (*Repealed*)

(4) Subject to the preceding provisions of this section, expressions used in this Chapter and in the Customs and Excise Management Act 1979 have the same meaning as in that Act.

[Finance Act 1994, s 43 as amended by the Finance Act 2000, Sch 40.]

8–7235A   44. *Commencement.*

Part III[1]
Insurance Premium Tax

The basic provisions

8–7235B   48. Insurance premium tax.   (1) A tax, to be known as insurance premium tax, shall be charged in accordance with this Part.

(2) The tax shall be under the care and management of the Commissioners of Customs and Excise.

[Finance Act 1994, s 48.]

---

1. Part III contains ss 48–74.

8–7235C   49. Charge to tax.   Tax shall be charged on the receipt of a premium by an insurer if the premium is received—

(*a*) under a taxable insurance contract, and

(*b*) on or after 1 October 1994.

[Finance Act 1994, s 49.]

8–7236   50. Chargeable amount.   (1) Tax shall be charged by reference to the chargeable amount.

(2) For the purposes of this Part, the chargeable amount is such amount as, with the addition of the tax chargeable, is equal to the amount of the premium.

(3) Subsections (1) and (2) above shall have effect subject to section 69 below.

[Finance Act 1994, s 50 as amended by the Finance Act 1997, s 23.]

8–7236A   51. *Rate of tax*

8–7236B   52. Liability to pay tax.   (1) Tax shall be payable by the person who is the insurer in relation to the contract under which the premium is received.

(2) Subsection (1) above shall have effect subject to any regulations made under section 65 below.

[Finance Act 1994, s 52.]

Administration

8–7236C   53. Registration of insurers.   (1) A person who—

(*a*) receives, as insurer, premiums in the course of a taxable business, and

(*b*) is not registered,

is liable to be registered.

(1A) The register kept under this section may contain such information as the Commissioners think is required for the purposes of the care and management of the tax.

(2) A person who—

(*a*) at any time forms the intention of receiving, as insurer, premiums in the course of a taxable business, and

(*b*) is not already receiving, as insurer, premiums in the course of another taxable business,

shall notify the Commissioners of those facts.

(3) A person who at any time—

(*a*) ceases to have the intention of receiving, as insurer, premiums in the course of a taxable business, and

(*b*) has no intention of receiving, as insurer, premiums in the course of another taxable business,

shall notify the Commissioners of those facts.

(4) Where a person is liable to be registered by virtue of subsection (1) above the Commissioners shall register him with effect from the time when he begins to receive premiums in the course of the business concerned; and it is immaterial whether or not he notifies the Commissioners under subsection (2) above.

(5) Where a person—

(*a*) notifies the Commissioners under subsection (3) above, and

(*b*) satisfies them of the facts there mentioned,

the Commissioners shall cancel his registration with effect from the earliest practicable time after he ceases to receive, as insurer, premiums in the course of any taxable business.

(5A) In a case where—

(*a*) the Commissioners are satisfied that a person has ceased to receive, as insurer, premiums in the course of any taxable business, but

(*b*) he has not notified them under subsection (3) above,

they may cancel his registration with effect from the earliest practicable time after he so ceased.

(6) For the purposes of this section regulations[1] may make provision—

(*a*) as to the time within which a notification is to be made;

(*b*) as to the circumstances in which premiums are to be taken to be received in the course of a taxable business;

(*c*) as to the form and manner in which any notification is to be made and as to the information to be contained in or provided with it;

(*d*) requiring a person who has made a notification to notify the Commissioners if any information contained in or provided in connection with it is or becomes inaccurate;

(*e*) as to the correction of entries in the register.

(7) References in this section to receiving premiums are to receiving premiums on or after 1 October 1994.

[Finance Act 1994, s 53 as amended by the Finance Act 1995, Schs 5 and 29.]

---

1. The Insurance Premium Tax Regulations 1994, SI 1994/1774, amended by SI 1995/1587, SI 1996/2099 and SI 1997/1157, have been made.

8–7236D 53AA. *Registration of taxable intermediaries*

8–7236E 53A. Information required to keep register up to date. *Regulations may make provision as to notification of information to Commissioners.*

Supplementary

8–7237 70. Interpretation: taxable insurance contracts. (1) Subject to subsection (1A) below, any contract of insurance is a taxable insurance contract.

(1A) A contract is not a taxable insurance contract if it falls within one or more of the paragraphs of Part I of Schedule 7A to this Act.

(1B) Part II of Schedule 7A to this Act (interpretation of certain provisions of Part I) shall have effect.

(2) (*Repealed*).

(3) The conditions referred to in subsection (2)(*c*) above are that—

(*a*) the vehicle is used, or intended for use, by a handicapped person in receipt of a disability living allowance by virtue of entitlement to the mobility component or of a mobility supplement,

(*b*) the insured lets such vehicles on hire to such persons in the course of a business consisting predominantly of the provision of motor vehicles to such persons, and

(*c*) the insured does not in the course of the business let such vehicles on hire to such persons on terms other than qualifying terms.

(4) For the purposes of subsection (3)(*c*) above a vehicle is let on qualifying terms to a person

(the lessee) if the consideration for the letting consists wholly or partly of sums paid to the insured by—

(a)   the Department of Social Security,
(b)   the Department of Health and Social Services for Northern Ireland, or
(c)   the Ministry of Defence,

on behalf of the lessee in respect of the disability living allowance or mobility supplement to which the lessee is entitled.

(5)   For the purposes of subsection (2)(d) and (e) above the relevant classes are classes 1, 6 and 12 of the classes specified in Part I of Schedule 2 to the Insurance Companies Act 1982 (ships, accident, third-party etc).

(6)   For the purposes of subsection (2)(g) above the relevant classes are classes 1, 5 and 11 of the classes specified in Part I of Schedule 2 to the Insurance Companies Act 1982 (aircraft, accident, third-party etc).

(7)   In deciding whether a contract relates to lifeboat equipment the nature of the risks concerned is immaterial, and they may (for example) be risks of dying or sustaining injury or of loss or damage.

(8)   For the purposes of subsection (2)(l) above relevant supplies are—

(a)   any supply of goods where the supply is to be made outside the United Kingdom or where the goods are to be exported from the United Kingdom;

(b)   any supply of services where the services are to be performed outside the United Kingdom.

(9)   Regulations may make provision for determining for the purposes of subsection (8) above—

(a)   the place where a supply of goods is to be regarded as made;
(b)   the place where services are to be regarded as performed.

(10)   (*Repealed*).

(11)   This section has effect subject to section 71 below.

(12)   This section and section 71 below have effect for the purposes of this Part.

[Finance Act 1994, s 70 amended by SI 1994/1698.]

8–7237A   71. Taxable insurance contracts: power to change definition.   (1)   Provision may be made by order that—

(a)   a contract of insurance that would otherwise not be a taxable insurance contract shall be a taxable insurance contract if it falls within a particular description;

(b)   a contract of insurance that would otherwise be a taxable insurance contract shall not be a taxable insurance contract if it falls within a particular description.

(2)   A description referred to in subsection (1) above may be by reference to the nature of the insured or by reference to such other factors as the Treasury think fit.

(3)   Provision under this section may be made in such way as the Treasury think fit, and in particular may be made by amending this Part.

(4)   An order under this section may amend or modify the effect of section 69 above in such way as the Treasury think fit.

[Finance Act 1994, s 71.]

8–7237B   72. Interpretation: premium.   (1)   In relation to a taxable insurance contract, a premium is any payment received under the contract by the insurer, and in particular includes any payment wholly or partly referable to—

(a)   any risk,
(b)   costs of administration,
(c)   commission,
(d)   any facility for paying in instalments or making deferred payment (whether or not payment for the facility is called interest), or
(e)   tax.

(1A)   Where an amount is charged to the insured by any person in connection with a taxable insurance contract, any payment in respect of that amount is to be regarded as a payment received under that contract by the insurer unless—

(a)   the payment is chargeable to tax at the higher rate by virtue of section 52A above; or
(b)   the amount is charged under a separate contract and is identified in writing to the insured as a separate amount so charged.

(2)   A premium may consist wholly or partly of anything other than money, and references to payment in subsection (1) above shall be construed accordingly.

(3)   Where a premium is to any extent received in a form other than money, its amount shall be taken to be—

(a)   an amount equal to the value of whatever is received in a form other than money, or
(b)   if money is also received, the aggregate of the amount found under paragraph (a) above and the amount received in the form of money.

(4) The value to be taken for the purposes of subsection (3) above is open market value at the time of the receipt by the insurer.

(5) The open market value of anything at any time shall be taken to be an amount equal to such consideration in money as would be payable on a sale of it at that time to a person standing in no such relationship with any person as would affect that consideration.

(6) Where (apart from this subsection) anything received under a contract by the insurer would be taken to be an instalment of a premium, it shall be taken to be a separate premium.

(7) Where anything is received by any person on behalf of the insurer—

(a) it shall be treated as received by the insurer when it is received by the other person, and

(b) the later receipt of the whole or any part of it by the insurer shall be disregarded.

(7A) Where any person is authorised by or on behalf of an employee to deduct from anything due to the employee under his contract of employment an amount in respect of a payment due under a taxable insurance contract, subsection (7) above shall not apply to the receipt on behalf of the insurer by the person so authorised of the amount deducted.

(8) In a case where—

(a) a payment under a taxable insurance contract is made to a person (the intermediary) by or on behalf of the insured, and

(b) the whole or part of the payment is referable to commission to which the intermediary is entitled,

in determining for the purposes of subsection (7) above whether, or how much of, the payment is received by the intermediary on behalf of the insurer any of the payment that is referable to that commission shall be regarded as received by the intermediary on behalf of the insurer notwithstanding the intermediary's entitlement.

(8A) Where, by virtue of subsection (7A) above, subsection (7) above does not apply to the receipt of an amount by a person and the whole or part of the amount is referable to commission to which he is entitled—

(a) if the whole of the amount is so referable, the amount shall be treated as received by the insurer when it is deducted by that person; and

(b) otherwise, the part of the amount that is so referable shall be treated as received by the insurer when the remainder of the payment concerned is or is treated as received by him.

(9) References in subsection (8) above to a payment include references to a payment in a form other than money.

(10) This section has effect for the purposes of this Part.

[Finance Act 1994, s 72 as amended by the Finance Act 1997, ss 28 and 30.]

8–7237C   73. Interpretation: other provisions.   (1) Unless the context otherwise requires—

"accounting period" shall be construed in accordance with section 54 above;

"appeal tribunal" means a VAT and duties tribunal;

"authorised person" means any person acting under the authority of the Commissioners;

"the Commissioners" means the Commissioners of Customs and Excise;

"conduct" includes any act, omission or statement;

"the higher rate" shall be construed in accordance with section 51 above;

"insurance business" means a business which consists of or includes the provision of insurance;

"insurer" means a person or body of persons (whether incorporated or not) carrying on insurance business;

"legislation relating to insurance premium tax" means this Part (as defined by subsection (9) below), any other enactment (whenever passed) relating to insurance premium tax, and any subordinate legislation made under any such enactment;

"prescribed" means prescribed by an order or regulations under this Part;

"the standard rate" shall be construed in accordance with section 51 above;

"tax" means insurance premium tax;

"tax representative" shall be construed in accordance with section 57 above;

"taxable business" means a business which consists of or includes the provision of insurance under taxable insurance contracts;

"taxable insurance contract" shall be construed in accordance with section 70 above.

"taxable intermediary" shall be construed in accordance with section 52A above;

"taxable intermediary's fees" has the meaning given by section 53AA(9) above.

(2) *Repealed.*

(3) Subject to subsection (3A) below, a registrable person is a person who—

(a) is registered under section 53 above, or

(b) is liable to be registered under that section.

(3A) *Meaning of registrable person.*

(4)–(8) *Repealed.*

(9) A reference to this Part includes a reference to any order or regulations made under it and a

reference to a provision of this Part includes a reference to any order or regulations made under the provision, unless otherwise required by the context or any order or regulations.

(10) This section has effect for the purposes of this Part.

[Finance Act 1994, s 73 as amended by the Finance Act 1995, Sch 5, SI 1994/1698 and the Finance Act 1997, ss 21 and 27.]

8–7238   74. *Orders and regulations.*

Section 40   SCHEDULE 6

AIR PASSENGER DUTY: ADMINISTRATION AND ENFORCEMENT

(Amended by the Finance Act 1995, s 16, the Finance Act 2001, Sch 3 and the Enterprise Act 2002, Sch 26.)

Application of excise enactments

8–7239   1. (1) The Customs and Excise Management Act 1979[1] shall have effect for the purposes of Chapter IV of Part I of this Act in relation to—

(a) any person who is or is liable to be registered,

(b) any fiscal representative, and

(c) any handling agent where a notice given to him under section 37 of this Act is effective,

as it has effect in relation to revenue traders, but with the modifications mentioned in sub-paragraph (2), and paragraphs 3 and 4, below.

(2) That Act shall have effect, in relation to any person to whom sub-paragraph (1) above applies, as if—

(a) the reference in section 112(1) (power of entry) to vehicles included aircraft,

(b) section 116 (payment of duty) were omitted,

(c) in section 117 (execution and distress)—

(i) the references to goods liable to any excise duty included tickets, and

(ii) the references to the trade in respect of which duty is imposed were to the trade or business by virtue of which sub-paragraph (1) above applies to him, and

(d) any power under section 118B(1)(b) to require any person who is or is liable to be registered to produce or cause to be produced any such documents as are referred to in that subsection included power to require his fiscal representative to produce them.

---

1. See also the Aircraft Operators (Accounts and Records) Regulations 1994, SI 1994/1737 amended by SI 2001/837, which are made under the Customs and Excise Management Act 1979, and which require aircraft operators who are registered or liable to be registered for air passenger duty to keep and preserve records containing information relevant to calculations of duty due.

2. Section 118B of that Act shall have effect for the purposes of Chapter IV of Part I of this Act in relation to any person who, in the course of a trade or business carried on by him, issues or arranges for the issue of tickets as if—

(a) he were a revenue trader, and

(b) the references to services supplied by or to him in the course or furtherance of a business were to services supplied by or to him in the course of issuing or arranging for the issue of tickets.

3. (1) A notice may require any person to whom paragraph 1 above applies to furnish, at specified times and in the specified form, any such information to the Commissioners as he could be required by the Commissioners to furnish under subsection (1) of section 118B; and any such requirement shall have effect as a requirement under that subsection.

(2) A notice may require any person to whom paragraph 1 or 2 above applies to produce or cause to be produced for inspection by an officer, at specified places and times, any such documents as he could be required by the officer to produce under that subsection; and any such requirement shall have effect as a requirement under that subsection.

(3) In this paragraph—

"notice" means a notice published, and not withdrawn, by the Commissioners, and

"specified" means specified in such a notice.

4. In relation to any person to whom paragraph 1 or 2 above applies—

(a) that Act shall have effect as if "document" had the same meaning as in Chapter IV of Part I of this Act, and

(b) that Act and this Schedule shall have effect as if any reference to the production of any document, in the case of information recorded otherwise than in legible form, were to producing a copy of the information in legible form.

5–11A. *Information; Appeals; Interest payable etc (paras 9–11 repealed)*

Evidence by certificate

8–7239A   12. (1) A certificate of the Commissioners—

(a) that a person was or was not, on any date specified in the certificate, registered or liable to be registered under section 33 of this Act,

(b) that the name of any person was or was not, on any date so specified, shown as the fiscal representative of any person in the register kept under that section,

(c) that any aircraft was or was not, on any date so specified, a chargeable aircraft,

(d) that any return required to be made under regulations made by virtue of section 38 of this Act had not, on any date so specified, been made, or

(e)   that any duty shown as due in such a return, or in an assessment under section 12 of this Act, had not, on any date so specified, been paid,

shall be sufficient evidence of that fact until the contrary is proved.

(2) A photograph of any document furnished to the Commissioners for the purposes of Chapter IV of Part I of this Act and certified by them to be such a photograph shall be admissible in any proceedings, whether civil or criminal, to the same extent as the document itself.

(3) Any document purporting to be a certificate under sub-paragraph (1) or (2) above shall be taken to be such a certificate until the contrary is proved.

13. *Repealed.*

SCHEDULE 6A
PREMIUMS LIABLE TO TAX AT THE HIGHER RATE

(Inserted by the Finance Act 1997, Sch 4.)

Section 64   SCHEDULE 7
INSURANCE PREMIUM TAX

(As amended by the Finance Act 1995, Sch 5, the Criminal Procedure (Consequential Provisions) (Scotland) Act 1995, Sch 4, the Civil Evidence Act 1995, Sch 2, the Finance Act 1997, ss 27 and 113, the Youth Justice and Criminal Evidence Act 1999, Sch 6, the Criminal Justice and Police Act 2001, Sch 2 and SI 2004/1501.)

PART I
INFORMATION

Records

8–7239B   **1.** (1) Regulations may require registrable persons to keep records.

(2) Regulations under sub-paragraph (1) above may be framed by reference to such records as may be specified in any notice published by the Commissioners in pursuance of the regulations and not withdrawn by a further notice.

(3) Regulations may require any records kept in pursuance of the regulations to be preserved for such period not exceeding six years as may be specified in the regulations.

(4) Any duty under regulations to preserve records may be discharged by the preservation of the information contained in them by such means as the Commissioners may approve; and where that information is so preserved a copy of any document forming part of the records shall (subject to the following provisions of this paragraph) be admissible in evidence in any proceedings, whether civil or criminal, to the same extent as the records themselves.

(5) The Commissioners may, as a condition of approving under sub-paragraph (4) above any means of preserving information contained in any records, impose such reasonable requirements as appear to them necessary for securing that the information will be as readily available to them as if the records themselves had been preserved.

(6) A statement contained in a document produced by a computer shall not by virtue of sub-paragraph (4) above be admissible in evidence—

(a)   *Repealed;*

(b)   in criminal proceedings in England and Wales, except in accordance with Part II of the Criminal Justice Act 1988;

(c)–(f)   *Scotland; Northern Ireland.*

Other provisions

8–7239C   **2.** (1) Every person who is concerned (in whatever capacity) in an insurance business shall furnish to the Commissioners such information relating to contracts of insurance entered into in the course of the business as the Commissioners may reasonably require.

(2) Every person who makes arrangements for other persons to enter into any contract of insurance shall furnish to the Commissioners such information relating to that contract as the Commissioners may reasonably require.

(3) Every person who—

(a)   is concerned in a business that is not an insurance business, and

(b)   has been involved in the entry into any contract of insurance providing cover for any matter associated with the business,

shall furnish to the Commissioners such information relating to that contract as the Commissioners may reasonably require.

(4) The information mentioned in sub-paragraph (1), (2) or (3) above shall be furnished within such time and in such form as the Commissioners may reasonably require.

3. (1) Every person who is concerned (in whatever capacity) in an insurance business shall upon demand made by an authorised person produce or cause to be produced for inspection by that person any documents relating to contracts of insurance entered into in the course of the business.

(2) Every person who makes arrangements for other persons to enter into any contract of insurance shall upon demand made by an authorised person produce or cause to be produced for inspection by that person any documents relating to that contract.

(3) Every person who—

(a)   is concerned in a business that is not an insurance business, and

(b)   has been involved in the entry into any contract of insurance providing cover for any matter associated with the business,

shall upon demand made by an authorised person produce or cause to be produced for inspection by that person any documents relating to that contract.

(4) Where, by virtue of any of sub-paragraphs (1) to (3) above, an authorised person has power to require the

production of any documents from any person, he shall have the like power to require production of the documents concerned from any other person who appears to the authorised person to be in possession of them; but where any such other person claims a lien on any document produced by him, the production shall be without prejudice to the lien.

(5) The documents mentioned in sub-paragraphs (1) to (4) above shall be produced—

(a) at the principal place of business of the person on whom the demand is made or at such other place as the authorised person may reasonably require, and

(b) at such time as the authorised person may reasonably require.

(6) An authorised person may take copies of, or make extracts from, any document produced under any of sub-paragraphs (1) to (4) above.

(7) If it appears to him to be necessary to do so, an authorised person may, at a reasonable time and for a reasonable period, remove any document produced under any of sub-paragraphs (1) to (4) above and shall, on request, provide a receipt for any document so removed; and where a lien is claimed on a document produced under sub-paragraph (4) above the removal of the document under this sub-paragraph shall not be regarded as breaking the lien.

(8) Where a document removed by an authorised person under sub-paragraph (7) above is reasonably required for the proper conduct of a business he shall, as soon as practicable, provide a copy of the document, free of charge, to the person by whom it was produced or caused to be produced.

(9) Where any documents removed under the powers conferred by this paragraph are lost or damaged the Commissioners shall be liable to compensate their owner for any expenses reasonably incurred by him in replacing or repairing the documents.

PART II
POWERS

Entry, arrest, etc

8–7240 **4.** (1) For the purpose of exercising any powers under this Part of this Act an authorised person may at any reasonable time enter premises used in connection with the carrying on of a business.

(2) In a case where—

(a) a justice of the peace is satisfied on information on oath that there is reasonable ground for suspecting that a fraud offence which appears to be of a serious nature is being, has been or is about to be committed on any premises or that evidence of the commission of such an offence is to be found there, or

(b) in Scotland a justice, within the meaning of section 308 of the Criminal Procedure (Scotland) Act 1995, is satisfied by evidence on oath as mentioned in paragraph (a) above,

he may issue a warrant in writing authorising any authorised person to enter those premises, if necessary by force, at any time within one month from the time of the issue of the warrant and search them.

(3) A person who enters the premises under the authority of the warrant may—

(a) take with him such other persons as appear to him to be necessary;

(b) seize and remove any documents or other things whatsoever found on the premises which he has reasonable cause to believe may be required as evidence for the purposes of proceedings in respect of a fraud offence which appears to him to be of a serious nature;

(c) search or cause to be searched any person found on the premises whom he has reasonable cause to believe to be in possession of any such documents or other things;

but no woman or girl shall be searched except by a woman.

(4) The powers conferred by a warrant under this paragraph shall not be exercisable—

(a) by more than such number of authorised persons as may be specified in the warrant,

(b) outside such times of day as may be so specified, or

(c) if the warrant so provides, otherwise than in the presence of a constable in uniform.

(5) An authorised person seeking to exercise the powers conferred by a warrant under this paragraph or, if there is more than one such authorised person, that one of them who is in charge of the search shall provide a copy of the warrant endorsed with his name as follows—

(a) if the occupier of the premises concerned is present at the time the search is to begin, the copy shall be supplied to the occupier;

(b) if at that time the occupier is not present but a person who appears to the authorised person to be in charge of the premises is present, the copy shall be supplied to that person;

(c) if neither paragraph (a) nor paragraph (b) above applies, the copy shall be left in a prominent place on the premises.

(6) Where an authorised person has reasonable grounds for suspecting that a fraud offence has been committed he may arrest anyone whom he has reasonable grounds for suspecting to be guilty of the offence.

(7) In this paragraph "a fraud offence" means an offence under any provision of paragraph 9(1) to (5) below.

Order for access to recorded information etc

8–7240A **4A.** (1) Where, on an application by an authorised person, a justice of the peace or, in Scotland, a justice (within the meaning of section 462 of the Criminal Procedure (Scotland) Act 1975) is satisfied that there are reasonable grounds for believing—

(a) that an offence in connection with tax is being, has been or is about to be committed, and

(b) that any recorded information (including any document of any nature whatsoever) which may be required as evidence for the purpose of any proceedings in respect of such an offence is in the possession of any person,

he may make an order under this paragraph.

(2) An order under this paragraph is an order that the person who appears to the justice to be in possession of the recorded information to which the application relates shall—

(*a*) give an authorised person access to it, and
(*b*) permit an authorised person to remove and take away any of it which he reasonably considers necessary,

not later than the end of the period of 7 days beginning on the date of the order or the end of such longer period as the order may specify.

(3) The reference in sub-paragraph (2)(*a*) above to giving an authorised person access to the recorded information to which the application relates includes a reference to permitting the authorised person to take copies of it or to make extracts from it.

(4) Where the recorded information consists of information stored in any electronic form, an order under this paragraph shall have effect as an order to produce the information in a form in which it is visible and legible or from which it can readily be produced in a visible and legible form and, if the authorised person wishes to remove it, in a form in which it can be removed.

(5) This paragraph is without prejudice to paragraphs 3 and 4 above.

Removal of documents etc

8–7240B 5. (1) An authorised person who removes anything in the exercise of a power conferred by or under paragraph 4 or 4A above shall, if so requested by a person showing himself—

(*a*) to be the occupier of premises from which it was removed, or
(*b*) to have had custody or control of it immediately before the removal,

provide that person with a record of what he removed.

(2) The authorised person shall provide the record within a reasonable time from the making of the request for it.

(3) Subject to sub-paragraph (7) below, if a request for permission to be allowed access to anything which—

(*a*) has been removed by an authorised person, and
(*b*) is retained by the Commissioners for the purposes of investigating an offence,

is made to the officer in overall charge of the investigation by a person who had custody or control of the thing immediately before it was so removed or by someone acting on behalf of such a person, the officer shall allow the person who made the request access to it under the supervision of an authorised person.

(4) Subject to sub-paragraph (7) below, if a request for a photograph or copy of any such thing is made to the officer in overall charge of the investigation by a person who had custody or control of the thing immediately before it was so removed, or by someone acting on behalf of such a person, the officer shall—

(*a*) allow the person who made the request access to it under the supervision of an authorised person for the purpose of photographing it or copying it, or
(*b*) photograph or copy it, or cause it to be photographed or copied.

(5) Subject to sub-paragraph (7) below, where anything is photographed or copied under sub-paragraph (4)(*b*) above the officer shall supply the photograph or copy, or cause it to be supplied, to the person who made the request.

(6) The photograph or copy shall be supplied within a reasonable time from the making of the request.

(7) There is no duty under this paragraph to allow access to, or to supply a photograph or copy of, anything if the officer in overall charge of the investigation for the purposes of which it was removed has reasonable grounds for believing that to do so would prejudice—

(*a*) that investigation,
(*b*) the investigation of an offence other than the offence for the purposes of the investigation of which the thing was removed, or
(*c*) any criminal proceedings which may be brought as a result of the investigation of which he is in charge or any such investigation as is mentioned in paragraph (*b*) above.

(8) Any reference in this paragraph to the officer in overall charge of the investigation is a reference to the person whose name and address are endorsed on the warrant concerned as being the officer so in charge.

8–7240C 6. (1) Where, on an application made as mentioned in sub-paragraph (2) below, the appropriate judicial authority is satisfied that a person has failed to comply with a requirement imposed by paragraph 5 above, the authority may order that person to comply with the requirement within such time and in such manner as may be specified in the order.

(2) An application under sub-paragraph (1) above shall be made—

(*a*) in the case of a failure to comply with any of the requirements imposed by sub-paragraphs (1) and (2) of paragraph 5 above, by the occupier of the premises from which the thing in question was removed or by the person who had custody or control of it immediately before it was so removed, and
(*b*) in any other case, by the person who had such custody or control.

(3) In this paragraph "the appropriate judicial authority" means—

(*a*) in England and Wales, a magistrates' court;
(*b*) in Scotland, the sheriff;
(*c*) in Northern Ireland, a court of summary jurisdiction, as defined in Article 2(2)(*a*) of the Magistrates' Court (Northern Ireland) Order 1981.

(4) In England and Wales and Northern Ireland, an application for an order under this paragraph shall be made by way of complaint; and sections 21 and 42(2) of the Interpretation Act (Northern Ireland) 1954 shall apply as if any reference in those provisions to any enactment included a reference to this paragraph.

Part III

Recovery

8–7240D   **7.** *Repealed.*

     8. *Recovery of overpaid tax*

Part IV

Penalties

Criminal offences

8–7240E   **9.**—(1) A person is guilty of an offence if—

   (*a*) being a registrable person, he is knowingly concerned in, or in the taking of steps with a view to, the fraudulent evasion of tax by him or another registrable person, or

   (*b*) not being a registrable person, he is knowingly concerned in, or in the taking of steps with a view to, the fraudulent evasion of tax by a registrable person.

   (2) Any reference in sub-paragraph (1) above to the evasion of tax includes a reference to the obtaining of a payment under regulations under section 55(3)(*c*) or (*d*) or (*f*) of this Act.

   (3) A person is guilty of an offence if with the requisite intent—

   (*a*) he produces, furnishes or sends, or causes to be produced, furnished or sent, for the purposes of this Part of this Act any document which is false in a material particular, or

   (*b*) he otherwise makes use for those purposes of such a document;

and the requisite intent is intent to deceive or to secure that a machine will respond to the document as if it were a true document.

   (4) A person is guilty of an offence if in furnishing any information for the purposes of this Part of this Act he makes a statement which he knows to be false in a material particular or recklessly makes a statement which is false in a material particular.

   (5) A person is guilty of an offence by virtue of this sub-paragraph if his conduct during any specified period must have involved the commission by him of one or more offences under the preceding provisions of this paragraph; and the preceding provisions of this sub-paragraph apply whether or not the particulars of that offence or those offences are known.

   (6) A person is guilty of an offence if—

   (*a*) he enters into a taxable insurance contract, or

   (*b*) he makes arrangements for other persons to enter into a taxable insurance contract,

with reason to believe that tax in respect of the contract will be evaded.

   (7) A person is guilty of an offence if he enters into taxable insurance contracts without giving security (or further security) he has been required to give under paragraph 24 below.

Criminal penalties

8–7241   **10.**—(1) A person guilty of an offence under paragraph 9(1) above shall be liable[1]—

   (*a*) on summary conviction, to a penalty of the **statutory maximum** or of three times the amount of the tax, whichever is the greater, or to imprisonment for a term not exceeding **six months** or to **both**;

   (*b*) on conviction on indictment, to a **penalty of any amount** or to imprisonment for a term not exceeding **seven years** or to **both**.

   (2) The reference in sub-paragraph (1) above to the amount of the tax shall be construed, in relation to tax itself or a payment falling within paragraph 9(2) above, as a reference to the aggregate of—

   (*a*) the amount (if any) falsely claimed by way of credit, and

   (*b*) the amount (if any) by which the gross amount of tax was falsely understated.

   (3) A person guilty of an offence under paragraph 9(3) or (4) above shall be liable[1]—

   (*a*) on summary conviction, to a penalty of the **statutory maximum** or, where sub-paragraph (4) below applies, to the alternative penalty there specified if it is greater, or to imprisonment for a term not exceeding **six months** or to **both**;

   (*b*) on conviction on indictment, to a **penalty of any amount** or to imprisonment for a term not exceeding **seven years** or to **both**.

   (4) In a case where—

   (*a*) the document referred to in paragraph 9(3) above is a return required under this Part of this Act, or

   (*b*) the information referred to in paragraph 9(4) above is contained in or otherwise relevant to such a return,

the alternative penalty is a penalty equal to three times the aggregate of the amount (if any) falsely claimed by way of credit and the amount (if any) by which the gross amount of tax was understated.

   (5) A person guilty of an offence under paragraph 9(5) above shall be liable[1]—

   (*a*) on summary conviction, to a penalty of the **statutory maximum** or (if greater) three times the amount of any tax that was or was intended to be evaded by his conduct, or to imprisonment for a term not exceeding **six months** or to **both**;

   (*b*) on conviction on indictment, to a **penalty of any amount** or to imprisonment for a term not exceeding **seven years** or to **both**;

and paragraph 9(2) and sub-paragraph (2) above shall apply for the purposes of this sub-paragraph as they apply respectively for the purposes of paragraph 9(1) and sub-paragraph (1) above.

   (6) A person guilty of an offence under paragraph 9(6) above shall be liable on summary conviction to a penalty of **level 5** on the standard scale or three times the amount of the tax, whichever is the greater.

(7) A person guilty of an offence under paragraph 9(7) above shall be liable on summary conviction to a penalty of **level 5** on the standard scale.

(8) In this paragraph—

(*a*) "credit" means credit for which provision is made by regulations under section 55 of this Act;

(*b*) "the gross amount of tax" means the total amount of tax due before taking into account any deduction for which provision is made by regulations under section 55(3) of this Act.

---

1. For procedure in respect of this offence which is triable either way, see s 147 of the Customs and Excise Management Act 1979, this PART, ante; and the Magistrates' Courts Act 1980, ss 17A–21, in PART I: MAGISTRATES' COURTS, PROCEDURE, ante.

Criminal proceedings etc

8–7241A **11.** Sections 145 to 155 of the Customs and Excise Management Act 1979 (proceedings for offences, mitigation of penalties and certain other matters) shall apply in relation to offences under paragraph 9 above and penalties imposed under paragraph 10 above as they apply in relation to offences and penalties under the customs and excise Acts as defined in that Act.

12–20. *Civil penalties.*

PART V
INTEREST

8–7241B **21–23.** *Interest on tax etc.*

PART VI
MISCELLANEOUS

8–7241C **24–28B.** *Security for tax; assessments; disclosure of information.*

Evidence by certificate

8–7242 **29.** (1) A certificate of the Commissioners—

(*a*) that a person was or was not at any time registered under section 53 of this Act,

(*b*) that any return required by regulations under section 54 of this Act has not been made or had not been made at any time, or

(*c*) that any tax shown as due in a return made in pursuance of regulations made under section 54 of this Act, or in an assessment made under section 56 of this Act, has not been paid,

shall be sufficient evidence of that fact until the contrary is proved.

(2) Any document purporting to be a certificate under sub-paragraph (1) above shall be taken to be such a certificate until the contrary is proved.

Service of notices etc

8–7242A **30.** Any notice, notification or requirement to be served on, given to or made of any person for the purposes of this Part of this Act may be served, given or made by sending it by post in a letter addressed to that person or his tax representative at the last or usual residence or place of business of that person or representative.

31–35. *Miscellaneous provisions.*

SCHEDULE 7A
INSURANCE PREMIUM TAX: CONTRACTS THAT ARE NOT TAXABLE

(Inserted by SI 1994/1698 and as amended by SI 1996/2955, SI 2001/3649 and SI 2002/1397.)

PART I
DESCRIPTIONS OF CONTRACT

Contracts of reinsurance

8–7243 **1.** A contract falls within this paragraph if it is a contract of reinsurance.

Contracts constituting long term business

2. (1) A contract falls within this paragraph if it is one whose effecting and carrying out constitutes business of one or more of the classes specified in Schedule 1 to the Insurance Companies Act 1982 (long term business) and constitutes only such business.

(2) In deciding whether the effecting and carrying out of a contract constitutes only such business as is mentioned in sub-paragraph (1) above where—

(*a*) the contract includes cover for risks not falling within the descriptions in any of the classes specified in Schedule 1 to the Insurance Companies Act 1982;

(*b*) the effecting and carrying out of the contract is treated for the purposes of that Act as constituting business of one or more of those classes and only such business by virtue of the application to it of section 1(3) of that Act; and

(*c*) the contract was not entered into after 30th November 1993,

the inclusion of such cover shall be ignored.

Contracts relating to motor vehicles for use by handicapped persons

3. (1) A contract falls within this paragraph if it relates only to a motor vehicle and the conditions mentioned in sub-paragraph (2) below are satisfied.

(2) The conditions referred to in sub-paragraph (1) above are that—

(*a*) the vehicle is used, or intended for use, by a handicapped person in receipt of a disability living allowance by virtue of entitlement to the mobility component or of a mobility supplement;

(*b*) the insured lets such vehicles on hire to such persons in the course of a business consisting predominantly of the provision of motor vehicles to such persons; and

(*c*) the insured does not in the course of the business let such vehicles on hire to such persons on terms other than qualifying terms.

(3) For the purposes of sub-paragraph (2)(*c*) above a vehicle is let on qualifying terms to a person (the lessee) if the consideration for the letting consists wholly or partly of sums paid to the insured by—

(*a*) the Department for Work and Pensions;

(*b*) the Department of Health and Social Services for Northern Ireland; or

(*c*) the Ministry of Defence,

on behalf of the lessee in respect of the disability living allowance or mobility supplement to which the lessee is entitled.

(4) For the purposes of this paragraph—

(*a*) "handicapped" means chronically sick or disabled;

(*b*) "disability living allowance" means a disability living allowance within the meaning of section 71 of the Social Security Contributions and Benefits Act 1992 or section 71 of the Social Security Contributions and Benefits (Northern Ireland) Act 1992;

(*c*) "mobility supplement" means a mobility supplement within the meaning of article 26A of the Naval, Military and Air Forces etc (Disablement and Death) Service Pensions Order 1983, article 25A of the Personal Injuries (Civilians) Scheme 1983, article 3 of the Motor Vehicles (Exemption from Vehicles Excise Duty) Order 1985 or article 3 of the Motor Vehicles (Exemption from Vehicles Excise Duty) (Northern Ireland) Order 1985.

Contracts relating to commercial ships

4. (1) A contract falls within this paragraph if it relates only to a commercial ship and is a contract whose effecting and carrying out constitutes business of one or more of the relevant classes and constitutes only such business.

(2) For the purposes of this paragraph the relevant classes are classes 1, 6 and 12 of the classes specified in Part I of Schedule 2 to the Insurance Companies Act 1982 (ships, accident, third-party etc).

(3) For the purposes of this paragraph a commercial ship is a ship which is—

(*a*) of a gross tonnage of 15 tons or more; and

(*b*) not designed or adapted for use for recreation or pleasure.

Contracts relating to lifeboats and lifeboat equipment

5. (1) A contract falls within this paragraph if it relates only to a lifeboat and is a contract whose effecting and carrying out constitutes business of one or more of the relevant classes and constitutes only such business.

(2) For the purposes of this paragraph the relevant classes are classes 1, 6 and 12 of the classes specified in Part I of Schedule 2 to the Insurance Companies Act 1982 (ships, accident, third-party etc).

(3) For the purposes of this paragraph a lifeboat is a vessel used or to be used solely for rescue or assistance at sea.

6. (1) A contract falls within this paragraph if it relates only to a lifeboat and lifeboat equipment and is such that, if it related only to a lifeboat, it would fall within paragraph 5 above.

(2) In deciding whether a contract relates to lifeboat equipment the nature of the risks concerned is immaterial, and they may (for example) be risks of dying or sustaining injury or of loss or damage.

(3) For the purposes of this paragraph—

(*a*) "lifeboat" has the meaning given by paragraph 5(3) above; and

(*b*) "lifeboat equipment" means anything used or to be used solely in connection with a lifeboat.

Contracts relating to commercial aircraft

7. (1) A contract falls within this paragraph if it relates only to a commercial aircraft and is a contract whose effecting and carrying out constitutes business of one or more of the relevant classes and constitutes only such business.

(2) For the purposes of this paragraph the relevant classes are classes 1, 5 and 11 of the classes specified in Part I of Schedule 2 to the Insurance Companies Act 1982 (aircraft, accident, third-party etc).

(3) For the purposes of this paragraph a commercial aircraft is an aircraft which is—

(*a*) of a weight of 8,000 kilogrammes or more; and

(*b*) not designed or adapted for use for recreation or pleasure.

Contracts relating to risks outside the United Kingdom

8. (1) A contract falls within this paragraph if it relates only to a risk which is situated outside the United Kingdom.

(2) Section 96A(3) of the Insurance Companies Act 1982 shall apply to determine whether a risk is situated in the United Kingdom for the purposes of this paragraph as it applies to determine that question for the purposes of that Act, but as if for paragraph (*a*) of that section there were substituted the following—

"(*a*) where the insurance relates to a building, its contents or both (whether or not the contents are covered by the same policy), to the member State in which the building is situated;".

Contracts relating to foreign or international railway rolling stock

9. (1) A contract falls within this paragraph if it relates only to foreign or international railway rolling stock and is a contract whose effecting and carrying out constitutes business of one or more of the relevant classes and constitutes only such business.

(2) For the purposes of this paragraph the relevant classes are classes 4 and 13 of the classes specified in Part I of Schedule 2 to the Insurance Companies Act 1982 (railway rolling stock, third party etc).

(3) For the purposes of this paragraph foreign or international railway rolling stock is railway rolling stock used principally for journeys taking place wholly or partly outside the United Kingdom.

Contracts relating to the Channel tunnel

10. (1) A contract falls within this paragraph if it relates only to the Channel tunnel system and is a contract whose effecting and carrying out constitutes business of one or more of the relevant classes and constitutes only such business.

(2) For the purposes of this paragraph the relevant classes are classes 8, 9 and 13 of the classes specified in Part I of Schedule 2 to the Insurance Companies Act 1982 (fire, damage to property, third party etc).

(3) For the purposes of this paragraph "the Channel tunnel system" means—

(*a*) the tunnels described in section 1(7)(*a*) of the Channel Tunnel Act 1987;
(*b*) the control towers situated in the terminal areas described in section 1(7)(*b*) of that Act; and
(*c*) the shuttle crossovers, wherever situated.

11. (1) A contract falls within this paragraph if it relates only to relevant Channel tunnel equipment and is a contract whose effecting and carrying out constitutes business of one or more of the relevant classes and constitutes only such business.

(2) For the purposes of this paragraph the relevant classes are classes 8, 9 and 13 of the classes specified in Part I of Schedule 2 to the Insurance Companies Act 1982 (fire, damage to property, third party etc).

(3) For the purposes of this paragraph "the Channel tunnel system" has the meaning given by paragraph 10(3) above.

(4) For the purposes of this paragraph "relevant Channel tunnel equipment" means, subject to sub-paragraph (5) below, the fixed or movable equipment needed for the operation of the Channel tunnel system or for the operation of trains through any tunnel forming part of it and in particular includes—

(*a*) any ventilation, cooling or electrical plant used or to be used in connection with any such operation; and
(*b*) any safety, signalling and control equipment which is or is to be so used.

(5) Equipment which consists of or forms part of—

(*a*) roads, bridges, platforms, ticket offices and other facilities for the use of passengers or motor vehicles;
(*b*) administrative buildings and maintenance facilities; and
(*c*) railway track or signalling equipment which is not situated in any part of the Channel tunnel system,

is not relevant Channel tunnel equipment for the purposes of this paragraph.

Contracts relating to goods in foreign or international transit

12. (1) A contract falls within this paragraph if it relates only to loss of or damage to goods in foreign or international transit and the insured enters into the contract in the course of a business carried on by him.

(2) For the purposes of this paragraph goods in foreign or international transit are goods in transit, and any container in which they are carried, where their carriage—

(*a*) begins and ends outside the United Kingdom;
(*b*) begins outside but ends in the United Kingdom; or
(*c*) ends outside but begins in the United Kingdom.

(3) For the purposes of sub-paragraph (2) above "container" has the same meaning as in regulation 38(3) of the Value Added Tax (General) Regulations 1985.

Contracts relating to credit

13. (1) A contract falls within this paragraph if it relates only to credit granted in relation to goods or services supplied under a relevant contract by a person carrying on business in the United Kingdom.

(2) For the purposes of this paragraph a relevant contract is—

(*a*) a contract to make a relevant supply of goods, or a supply of services, or both, to an overseas customer;
(*b*) a contract to supply goods to a person who is to—

(i) export those goods; or
(ii) incorporate those goods in other goods which he is to export,

where the condition mentioned in sub-paragraph (3) below is satisfied;

(*c*) a contract to supply to a person who is to export goods services consisting of the valuation or testing of, or other work carried out on, those goods where the condition mentioned in sub-paragraph (3) below is satisfied;
(*d*) a contract to supply services to a person in order that he may comply with a legally binding obligation to make a supply of services to an overseas customer.

(3) The condition referred to in sub-paragraph (2)(*b*) and (*c*) above is that the goods to be exported are to be exported in order that the person exporting them may comply with a legally binding obligation to make a relevant supply of goods to an overseas customer.

(4) For the purposes of this paragraph—

(*a*) "export" means export from the United Kingdom and cognate expressions shall be construed accordingly; and

(*b*) any reference to a person who is to export goods shall be taken as including a reference to a person at whose direction the insured is to export them and the reference in sub-paragraph (3) above to the person exporting goods shall be construed accordingly.

(5) Where a contract relates to—

(*a*) credit of the description in sub-paragraph (1) above; and

(*b*) loss resulting from the insured or any third party being required to pay the amount of any bond or guarantee against non-performance by the insured of the contract which involves him making the supply,

the contract shall be treated for the purposes of sub-paragraph (1) above as if it did not relate to loss of the description in paragraph (*b*) above.

Contracts relating to exchange losses

14. (1) A contract falls within this paragraph if—

(*a*) it relates only to loss resulting from a change in the rate at which the price for a supply which is or may be made by the insured may be exchanged for another currency; and

(*b*) the conditions mentioned in sub-paragraph (2) below are satisfied.

(2) The conditions referred to in sub-paragraph (1) above are that—

(*a*) the insured is a person carrying on business in the United Kingdom;

(*b*) the contract of insurance concerns a contract to make a relevant supply of goods, or a supply of services, or both, to an overseas customer (whether or not the contract to make the supply is one into which the insured has entered, or one for which he has tendered or intends to tender); and

(*c*) the period of cover for the risk expires no later than the date by which the whole of the price for the supply is to be paid or, where the contract has not been entered into, would be required to be paid.

(3) Where the contract relates to—

(*a*) loss of the description in sub-paragraph (1)(*a*) above; and

(*b*) loss relating from a change in the rate at which the price of goods which the insured imports into the United Kingdom for the purpose of enabling him to make the supply concerned may be exchanged for another currency,

the contract shall be treated for the purposes of sub-paragraphs (1) and (2) above as if it did not relate to loss of the description in paragraph (*b*) above.

Contracts relating to the provision of financial facilities

15. (1) A contract falls within this paragraph if it relates only to the provision of a relevant financial facility and the conditions mentioned in sub-paragraph (2) below are satisfied.

(2) The conditions referred to in sub-paragraph (1) above are that—

(*a*) the person to whom the relevant financial facility is provided is an overseas customer;

(*b*) it is provided in order that he may comply with a legally binding obligation to receive a relevant supply of goods, or a supply of services, or both, from a person carrying on business; and

(*c*) the contract of insurance is a contract whose effecting and carrying out constitutes business of one or both of classes 14 and 15 of the classes specified in Part I of Schedule 2 to the Insurance Companies Act 1982 (credit, suretyship etc).

(3) For the purposes of this paragraph a relevant financial facility is—

(*a*) the making of an advance;

(*b*) the issue of a letter of credit or acceptance of a bill of exchange;

(*c*) the giving of a guarantee or bond; or

(*d*) any other similar transaction entered into in order to provide a customer with the means to pay, or a supplier with the right to call upon a third party for, the consideration for goods or services.

Part II
Interpretation

8–7244 **16.** (1) This Part of this Schedule applies for the purposes of Part I of this Schedule.

(2) A relevant supply of goods is any supply of goods where the supply is to be made outside the United Kingdom or where the goods are to be exported from the United Kingdom.

(3) An overseas customer, in relation to a supply of goods or services, is a person who—

(*a*) does not have any business establishment in the United Kingdom but has such an establishment elsewhere;

(*b*) has such establishments both in the United Kingdom and elsewhere, provided that the establishment at which, or for the purposes of which, the goods or services which are to be supplied to him are most directly to be used is not in the United Kingdom; or

(*c*) has not such establishment in any place and does not have his usual place of residence in the United Kingdom.

Finance Act 1996
(1996 c 8)

PART III[1]
LANDFILL TAX

The basic provisions

8–7245 39. Landfill tax.   (1) A tax, to be known as landfill tax, shall be charged in accordance with this Part.

(2) The tax shall be under the care and management of the Commissioners of Customs and Excise.

[Finance Act 1996, s 39.]

---

1. Part III contains ss 39–71. Only those provisions of this Part which are relevant to the work of magistrates' courts are included in this Manual.

8–7245A 40. Charge to tax.   (1) Tax shall be charged on a taxable disposal.

(2) A disposal is a taxable disposal if—

(a) it is a disposal of material as waste,
(b) it is made by way of landfill,
(c) it is made at a landfill site, and
(d) it is made on or after 1st October 1996.

(3) For this purpose a disposal is made at a landfill site if the land on or under which it is made constitutes or falls within land which is a landfill site at the time of the disposal.

[Finance Act 1996, s 40.]

8–7245B 41. Liability to pay tax.   (1) The person liable to pay tax charged on a taxable disposal is the landfill site operator.

(2) The reference here to the landfill site operator is to the person who is at the time of the disposal the operator of the landfill site which constitutes or contains the land on or under which the disposal is made.

[Finance Act 1996, s 41.]

8–7245C 42. *Amount of tax*

8–7245D 43–46. *Exemptions*

Administration

8–7245E 47. Registration.   (1) The register kept under this section may contain such information as the Commissioners think is required for the purposes of the care and management of the tax.

(2) A person who—

(a) carries out taxable activities, and
(b) is not registered,

is liable to be registered.

(3) Where—

(a) a person at any time forms the intention of carrying out taxable activities, and
(b) he is not registered,

he shall notify the Commissioners of his intention.

(4) A person who at any time ceases to have the intention of carrying out taxable activities shall notify the Commissioners of that fact.

(5) Where a person is liable to be registered by virtue of subsection (2) above the Commissioners shall register him with effect from the time when he begins to carry out taxable activities; and this subsection applies whether or not he notifies the Commissioners under subsection (3) above.

(6) Where the Commissioners are satisfied that a person has ceased to carry out taxable activities they may cancel his registration with effect from the earliest practicable time after he so ceased; and this subsection applies whether or not he notifies the Commissioners under subsection (4) above.

(7) Where—

(a) a person notifies the Commissioners under subsection (4) above,
(b) they are satisfied that he will not carry out taxable activities,
(c) they are satisfied that no tax which he is liable to pay is unpaid,
(d) they are satisfied that no credit to which he is entitled under regulations made under section 51 below is outstanding, and
(e) subsection (8) below does not apply,

the Commissioners shall cancel his registration with effect from the earliest practicable time after he ceases to carry out taxable activities.

(8) Where—

(*a*) a person notifies the Commissioners under subsection (4) above, and

(*b*) they are satisfied that he has not carried out, and will not carry out, taxable activities,

the Commissioners shall cancel his registration with effect from the time when he ceased to have the intention to carry out taxable activities.

(9) For the purposes of this section regulations may make provision—

(*a*) as to the time within which a notification is to be made;

(*b*) as to the form and manner in which any notification is to be made and as to the information to be contained in or provided with it;

(*c*) requiring a person who has made a notification to notify the Commissioners if any information contained in or provided in connection with it is or becomes inaccurate;

(*d*) as to the correction of entries in the register.

(10) References in this Part to a registrable person are to a person who—

(*a*) is registered under this section, or

(*b*) is liable to be registered under this section.

[Finance Act 1996, s 47.]

8–7245F   48. Information required to keep register up to date.   (1) Regulations may make provision requiring a registrable person to notify the Commissioners of particulars which—

(*a*) are of changes in circumstances relating to the registrable person or any business carried on by him,

(*b*) appear to the Commissioners to be required for the purpose of keeping the register kept under section 47 above up to date, and

(*c*) are of a prescribed description.

(2) Regulations may make provision—

(*a*) as to the time within which a notification is to be made;

(*b*) as to the form and manner in which a notification is to be made;

(*c*) requiring a person who has made a notification to notify the Commissioners if any information contained in it is inaccurate.

[Finance Act 1996, s 48.]

8–7245G   49. Accounting for tax and time for payment.   Regulations may provide that a registrable person shall—

(*a*) account for tax by reference to such periods (accounting periods) as may be determined by or under the regulations;

(*b*) make, in relation to accounting periods, returns in such form as may be prescribed and at such times as may be so determined;

(*c*) pay tax at such times and in such manner as may be so determined.

[Finance Act 1996, s 49.]

8–7245GA   50. Power to assess.   *Where a person has failed to make any returns required to be made under this Part, the Commissioners may assess the amount of tax due.*

Interpretation

8–7245H   64. Disposal of material as waste.   (1) A disposal of material is a disposal of it as waste if the person making the disposal does so with the intention of discarding the material.

(2) The fact that the person making the disposal or any other person could benefit from or make use of the material is irrelevant.

(3) Where a person makes a disposal on behalf of another person, for the purposes of subsections (1) and (2) above the person on whose behalf the disposal is made shall be treated as making the disposal.

(4) The reference in subsection (3) above to a disposal on behalf of another person includes references to a disposal—

(*a*) at the request of another person;

(*b*) in pursuance of a contract with another person.

[Finance Act 1996, s 64.]

8–7245I   65. Disposal by way of landfill.   (1) There is a disposal of material by way of landfill if—

(*a*) it is deposited on the surface of land or on a structure set into the surface, or

(*b*) it is deposited under the surface of land.

(2) Subsection (1) above applies whether or not the material is placed in a container before it is deposited.

(3) Subsection (1)(*b*) above applies whether the material—

(*a*) is covered with earth after it is deposited, or

(*b*) is deposited in a cavity (such as a cavern or mine).

(4) If material is deposited on the surface of land (or on a structure set into the surface) with a view to it being covered with earth the disposal must be treated as made when the material is deposited and not when it is covered.

(5) An order may provide that the meaning of the disposal of material by way of landfill (as it applies for the time being) shall be varied.

(6) An order under subsection (5) above may make provision in such way as the Treasury think fit, whether by amending any of subsections (1) to (4) above or otherwise.

(7) In this section "land" includes land covered by water where the land is above the low water mark of ordinary spring tides.

(8) In this section "earth" includes similar matter (such as sand or rocks).
[Finance Act 1996, s 65.]

8–7245J 66. Landfill sites. Land is a landfill site at a given time if at that time—

(*a*) a licence which is a site licence for the purposes of Part II of the Environmental Protection Act 1990 (waste on land) is in force in relation to the land and authorises disposals in or on the land,

(*b*) *Scotland;*

(*ba*) a permit under regulations under section 2 of the Pollution Prevention and Control Act 1999 is in force in relation to the land and authorises deposits or disposals in or on the land,

(*c*)–(*e*) *Northern Ireland.*
[Finance Act 1996, s 66 as amended by the Pollution Prevention and Control Act 1999, Sch 2.]

8–7245K 67. Operators of landfill sites. The operator of a landfill site at a given time is—

(*a*) the person who is at the time concerned the holder of the licence, where section 66(*a*) above applies;

(*b*) the waste disposal authority which at the time concerned occupies the landfill site, where section 66(*b*) above applies;

(*ba*) the person who is at the time concerned the holder of the permit, where the section 66(*ba*) above applies;

(*c*) the person who is at the time concerned the holder of the licence, where section 66(*c*) above applies;

(*d*) the district council which passed the resolution, where section 66(*d*) above applies;

(*e*) the person who is at the time concerned the holder of the licence, where section 66(*e*) above applies.
[Finance Act 1996, s 67 as amended by SI 2000/1973 and SSI 2000/323.]

8–7245L 68. Weight of material disposed of. (1) The weight of the material disposed of on a taxable disposal shall be determined in accordance with regulations.

(2) The regulations may—

(*a*) prescribe rules for determining the weight;

(*b*) authorise rules for determining the weight to be specified by the Commissioners in a prescribed manner;

(*c*) authorise rules for determining the weight to be agreed by the person liable to pay the tax and an authorised person.

(3) The regulations may in particular prescribe, or authorise the specification or agreement of, rules about—

(*a*) the method by which the weight is to be determined;

(*b*) the time by reference to which the weight is to be determined;

(*c*) the discounting of constituents (such as water).

(4) The regulations may include provision that a specification authorised under subsection (2)(*b*) above may provide—

(*a*) that it is to have effect only in relation to disposals of such descriptions as may be set out in the specification;

(*b*) that it is not to have effect in relation to particular disposals unless the Commissioners are satisfied that such conditions as may be set out in the specification are met in relation to the disposals;

and the conditions may be framed by reference to such factors as the Commissioners think fit (such as the consent of an authorised person to the specification having effect in relation to disposals).

(5) The regulations may include provision that—

(*a*) where rules are agreed as mentioned in subsection (2)(*c*) above, and

(*b*) the Commissioners believe that they should no longer be applied because they do not given an accurate indication of the weight or they are not being fully observed or for some other reason,

the Commissioners may direct that the agreed rules shall no longer have effect.

(6) The regulations shall be so framed that where in relation to a given disposal—

(*a*) no specification of the Commissioners has effect, and

(*b*) no agreed rules have effect,

the weight shall be determined in accordance with rules prescribed in the regulations.
[Finance Act 1996, s 68.]

8–7245M 69. Taxable activities. (1) A person carries out a taxable activity if—

(*a*) he makes a taxable disposal in respect of which he is liable to pay tax, or

(*b*) he permits another person to make a taxable disposal in respect of which he (the first-mentioned person) is liable to pay tax.

(2) Where—

(*a*) a taxable disposal is made, and

(*b*) it is made without the knowledge of the person who is liable to pay tax in respect of it,

that person shall for the purposes of this section be taken to permit the disposal.
[Finance Act 1996, s 69.]

8–7245N 70. Interpretation: other provisions. (1) Unless the context otherwise requires—

"accounting period" shall be construed in accordance with section 49 above;

"appeal tribunal" means a VAT and duties tribunal;

"authorised person" means any person acting under the authority of the Commissioners;

"the Commissioners" means the Commissioners of Customs and Excise;

"conduct" includes any act, omission or statement;

"material" means material of all kinds, including objects, substances and products of all kinds;

"prescribed" means prescribed by an order or regulations under this Part;

"registrable person" has the meaning given by section 47(10) above;

"tax" means landfill tax;

"taxable disposal" has the meaning given by section 40 above.

(2) A landfill disposal is a disposal—

(*a*) of material as waste, and

(*b*) made by way of landfill.

(3) A reference to this Part includes a reference to any order or regulations made under it and a reference to a provision of this Part includes a reference to any order or regulations made under the provision, unless otherwise required by the context or any order or regulations.

(4) This section and sections 64 to 69 above apply for the purposes of this Part.
[Finance Act 1996, s 70.]

Supplementary

8–7245O 71. *Orders and regulations*

8–7246

Section 60

SCHEDULE 5
LANDFILL TAX

(*As amended by SI 1997/2983, the Youth Justice and Criminal Evidence Act 1999, Sch 6, the Finance Act 2000, Sch 37, the Criminal Justice and Police Act 2001, Sch 2 and the Criminal Justice Act 2003, Sch 37.*)

PART I
INFORMATION

General

1. (1) Every person who is concerned (in whatever capacity) with any landfill disposal shall furnish to the Commissioners such information relating to the disposal as the Commissioners may reasonably require.

(2) The information mentioned in sub-paragraph (1) above shall be furnished within such time and in such form as the Commissioners may reasonably require.

Records

2. (1) Regulations may require registrable persons to make records.

(2) Regulations under sub-paragraph (1) above may be framed by reference to such records as may be stipulated in any notice published by the Commissioners in pursuance of the regulations and not withdrawn by a further notice.

(3) Regulations may—

(a) require registrable persons to preserve records of a prescribed description (whether or not the records are required to be made in pursuance of regulations) for such period not exceeding six years as may be specified in the regulations;

(b) authorise the Commissioners to direct that any such records need only be preserved for a shorter period than that specified in the regulations;

(c) authorise a direction to be made so as to apply generally or in such cases as the Commissioners may stipulate.

(4) Any duty under regulations to preserve records may be discharged by the preservation of the information contained in them by such means as the Commissioners may approve; and where that information is so preserved a copy of any document forming part of the records shall (subject to the following provisions of this paragraph) be admissible in evidence in any proceedings, whether civil or criminal, to the same extent as the records themselves.

(5) The Commissioners may, as a condition of approving under sub-paragraph (4) above any means of preserving information contained in any records, impose such reasonable requirements as appear to them necessary for securing that the information will be as readily available to them as if the records themselves had been preserved.

(6) A statement contained in a document produced by a computer shall not by virtue of sub-paragraph (4) above be admissible in evidence—

(a) repealed;

(b) in civil proceedings in Scotland, except in accordance with sections 5 and 6 of the Civil Evidence (Scotland) Act 1988;

(c) in criminal proceedings in Scotland, except in accordance with Schedule 8 to the Criminal Procedure (Scotland) Act 1995;

(d) repealed;

(e) in criminal proceedings in Northern Ireland, except in accordance with Article 68 of the Police and Criminal Evidence (Northern Ireland) Order 1989 and Part II of the Criminal Justice (Evidence, Etc.) (Northern Ireland) Order 1988.*

(7) In the case of civil proceedings in England and Wales to which sections 5 and 6 of the Civil Evidence Act 1968 apply, a statement contained in a document produced by a computer shall not be admissible in evidence by virtue of sub-paragraph (4) above except in accordance with those sections.

Documents

3. (1) Every person who is concerned (in whatever capacity) with any landfill disposal shall upon demand made by an authorised person produce or cause to be produced for inspection by that person any documents relating to the disposal.

(2) Where, by virtue of sub-paragraph (1) above, an authorised person has power to require the production of any documents from any person, he shall have the like power to require production of the documents concerned from any other person who appears to the authorised person to be in possession of them; but where any such other person claims a lien on any document produced by him, the production shall be without prejudice to the lien.

(3) The documents mentioned in sub-paragraphs (1) and (2) above shall be produced—

(a) at such place as the authorised person may reasonably require, and

(b) at such time as the authorised person may reasonably require.

(4) An authorised person may take copies of, or make extracts from, any document produced under sub-paragraph (1) or (2) above.

(5) If it appears to him to be necessary to do so, an authorised person may, at a reasonable time and for a reasonable period, remove any document produced under sub-paragraph (1) or (2) above and shall, on request, provide a receipt for any document so removed; and where a lien is claimed on a document produced under sub-paragraph (2) above the removal of the document under this sub-paragraph shall not be regarded as breaking the lien.

(6) Where a document removed by an authorised person under sub-paragraph (5) above is reasonably required for any purpose he shall, as soon as practicable, provide a copy of the document, free of charge, to the person by whom it was produced or caused to be produced.

(7) Where any documents removed under the powers conferred by this paragraph are lost or damaged the Commissioners shall be liable to compensate their owner for any expenses reasonably incurred by him in replacing or repairing the documents.

---

*Repealed by SI 2004/1501 from a date to be appointed.

Part II
Powers

Entry and inspection

4. For the purpose of exercising any powers under this Part of this Act an authorised person may at any reasonable time enter and inspect premises used in connection with the carrying on of a business.

Entry and search

5. (1) Where—

(a) a justice of the peace is satisfied on information on oath that there is reasonable ground for suspecting that a fraud offence which appears to be of a serious nature is being, has been or is about to be committed on any premises or that evidence of the commission of such an offence is to be found there, or

(b) in Scotland a justice, within the meaning of section 307 of the Criminal Procedure (Scotland) Act 1995, is satisfied by evidence on oath as mentioned in paragraph (a) above, he may issue a warrant in writing authorising any authorised person to enter those premises, if necessary by force, at any time within one month from the time of the issue of the warrant and search them.

(2) A person who enters the premises under the authority of the warrant may—

(*a*) take with him such other persons as appear to him to be necessary;

(*b*) seize and remove any documents or other things whatsoever found on the premises which he has reasonable cause to believe may be required as evidence for the purposes of proceedings in respect of a fraud offence which appears to him to be of a serious nature;

(*c*) search or cause to be searched any person found on the premises whom he has reasonable cause to believe to be in possession of any such documents or other things;

but no woman or girl shall be searched except by a woman.

(3) The powers conferred by a warrant under this paragraph shall not be exercisable—

(*a*) by more than such a number of authorised persons as may be specified in the warrant,

(*b*) outside such times of day as may be so specified, or

(*c*) if the warrant so provides, otherwise than in the presence of a constable in uniform.

(4) An authorised person seeking to exercise the powers conferred by a warrant under this paragraph or, if there is more than one such authorised person, that one of them who is in charge of the search shall provide a copy of the warrant endorsed with his name as follows—

(*a*) if the occupier of the premises concerned is present at the time the search is to begin, the copy shall be supplied to the occupier;

(*b*) if at that time the occupier is not present but a person who appears to the authorised person to be in charge of the premises is present, the copy shall be supplied to that person;

(*c*) if neither paragraph (*a*) nor paragraph (*b*) above applies, the copy shall be left in a prominent place on the premises.

(5) In this paragraph "a fraud offence" means an offence under any provision of paragraph 15(1) to (5) below.

Arrest

6. (1) Where an authorised person has reasonable grounds for suspecting that a fraud offence has been committed he may arrest anyone whom he has reasonable grounds for suspecting to be guilty of the offence.

(2) In this paragraph "a fraud offence" means an offence under any provision of paragraph 15(1) to (5) below.

Order for access for recorded information etc.

7. (1) Where, on an application by an authorised person, a justice of the peace or, in Scotland, a justice (within the meaning of section 307 of the Criminal Procedure (Scotland) Act 1995) is satisfied that there are reasonable grounds for believing—

(*a*) that an offence in connection with tax is being, has been or is about to be committed, and

(*b*) that any recorded information (including any document of any nature whatsoever) which may be required as evidence for the purpose of any proceedings in respect of such an offence is in the possession of any person,

he may make an order under this paragraph.

(2) An order under this paragraph is an order that the person who appears to the justice to be in possession of the recorded information to which the application relates shall—

(*a*) give an authorised person access to it, and

(*b*) permit an authorised person to remove and take away any of it which he reasonably considers necessary,

not later than the end of the period of 7 days beginning with the date of the order or the end of such longer period as the order may specify.

(3) The reference in sub-paragraph (2)(*a*) above to giving an authorised person access to the recorded information to which the application relates includes a reference to permitting the authorised person to take copies of it or to make extracts from it.

(4) Where the recorded information consists of information stored in any electronic form, an order under this paragraph shall have effect as an order to produce the information in a form in which it is visible and legible or from which it can readily be produced in a visible and legible form and, if the authorised person wishes to remove it, in a form in which it can be removed.

(5) This paragraph is without prejudice to paragraphs 3 to 5 above.

Removal of documents etc.

8. (1) An authorised person who removes anything in the exercise of a power conferred by or under paragraph 5 or 7 above shall, if so requested by a person showing himself—

(*a*) to be the occupier of premises from which it was removed, or

(*b*) to have had custody or control of it immediately before the removal,

provide that person with a record of what he removed.

(2) The authorised person shall provide the record within a reasonable time from the making of the request for it.

(3) Subject to sub-paragraph (7) below, if a request for permission to be allowed access to anything which—

(*a*) has been removed by an authorised person, and

(*b*) is retained by the Commissioners for the purposes of investigating an offence,

is made to the officer in overall charge of the investigation by a person who had custody or control of the thing immediately before it was so removed or by someone acting on behalf of such a person, the officer shall allow the person who made the request access to it under the supervision of an authorised person.

(4) Subject to sub-paragraph (7) below, if a request for a photograph or copy of any such thing is made to the

officer in overall charge of the investigation by a person who had custody or control of the thing immediately before it was so removed, or by someone acting on behalf of such a person, the officer shall—

(a) allow the person who made the request access to it under the supervision of an authorised person for the purpose of photographing it or copying it, or

(b) photograph or copy it, or cause it to be photographed or copied.

(5) Subject to sub-paragraph (7) below, where anything is photographed or copied under sub-paragraph (4)(b) above the officer shall supply the photograph or copy, or cause it to be supplied, to the person who made the request.

(6) The photograph or copy shall be supplied within a reasonable time from the making of the request.

(7) There is no duty under this paragraph to allow access to, or to supply a photograph or copy of, anything if the officer in overall charge of the investigation for the purposes of which it was removed has reasonable grounds for believing that to do so would prejudice—

(a) that investigation,

(b) the investigation of an offence other than the offence for the purposes of the investigation of which the thing was removed, or

(c) any criminal proceedings which may be brought as a result of the investigation of which he is in charge or any such investigation as is mentioned in paragraph (b) above.

(8) Any reference in this paragraph to the officer in overall charge of the investigation is a reference to the person whose name and address are endorsed on the warrant concerned as being the officer so in charge.

9. (1) Where, on an application made as mentioned in sub-paragraph (2) below, the appropriate judicial authority is satisfied that a person has failed to comply with a requirement imposed by paragraph 8 above, the authority may order that person to comply with the requirement within such time and in such manner as may be specified in the order.

(2) An application under sub-paragraph (1) above shall be made—

(a) in the case of a failure to comply with any of the requirements imposed by sub-paragraphs (1) and (2) or paragraph 8 above, by the occupier of the premises from which the thing in question was removed or by the person who had custody or control of it immediately before it was so removed, and

(b) in any other case, by the person who had such custody or control.

(3) In this paragraph "the appropriate judicial authority" means—

(a) in England and Wales, a magistrates' court;

(b) in Scotland, the sheriff;

(c) in Northern Ireland, a court of summary jurisdiction, as defined in Article 2(2)(a) of the Magistrates' Court (Northern Ireland) Order 1981.

(4) In England and Wales and Northern Ireland, an application for an order under this paragraph shall be made by way of complaint; and sections 21 and 42(2) of the Interpretation Act (Northern Ireland) 1954 shall apply as if any reference in those provisions to any enactment included a reference to this paragraph.

Power to take samples

10. (1) An authorised person, if it appears to him necessary for the protection of the revenue against mistake or fraud, may at any time take, from material which he has reasonable cause to believe is intended to be, is being, or has been disposed of as waste by way of landfill, such samples as he may require with a view to determining how the material ought to be or to have been treated for the purposes of tax.

(2) Any sample taken under this paragraph shall be disposed of in such manner as the Commissioners may direct.

PART III

RECOVERY

General

11. Tax due from any person shall be recoverable as a debt due to the Crown.

12. *Preferential and preferred debts.*

13. *Distress and diligence.*

14. *Recovery of overpaid tax.*

PART IV

CRIMINAL PENALTIES

Criminal offences

15. (1) A person is guilty of an offence if—

(a) being a registrable person, he is knowingly concerned in, or in the taking of steps with a view to, the fraudulent evasion of tax by him or another registrable person, or

(b) not being a registrable person, he is knowingly concerned in, or in the taking of steps with a view to, the fraudulent evasion of tax by a registrable person.

(2) Any reference in sub-paragraph (1) above to the evasion of tax includes a reference to the obtaining of a payment under regulations under section 51(2)(c) or (d) or (f) of this Act.

(3) A person is guilty of an offence if with the requisite intent—

(a) he produces, furnishes or sends, or causes to be produced, furnished or sent, for the purposes of this Part of this Act any document which is false in a material particular, or

(b) he otherwise makes use for those purposes of such a document;

and the requisite intent is intent to deceive or to secure that a machine will respond to the document as if it were a true document.

(4) A person is guilty of an offence if in furnishing any information for the purposes of this Part of this Act he makes a statement which he knows to be false in a material particular or recklessly makes a statement which is false in a material particular.

(5) A person is guilty of an offence by virtue of this sub-paragraph if his conduct during any specified period must have involved the commission by him of one or more offences under the preceding provisions of this paragraph; and the preceding provisions of this sub-paragraph apply whether or not the particulars of that offence or those offences are known.

(6) A person is guilty of an offence if—

(a) he enters into a taxable landfill contract, or
(b) he makes arrangements for other persons to enter into such a contract, with reason to believe that tax in respect of the disposal concerned will be evaded.

(7) A person is guilty of an offence if he carries out taxable activities without giving security (or further security) he has been required to give under paragraph 31 below.

(8) For the purposes of this paragraph a taxable landfill contract is a contract under which there is to be a taxable disposal.

Criminal penalties

16. (1) A person guilty of an offence under paragraph 15(1) above is liable[1]—

(a) on summary conviction, to a penalty of **the statutory maximum** or of **three times the amount of the tax**, whichever is the greater, or to imprisonment for a term not exceeding **six months** or to both;
(b) on conviction on indictment, to a penalty of any amount or to imprisonment for a term not exceeding **seven years** or to both.

(2) The reference in sub-paragraph (1) above to the amount of the tax shall be construed, in relation to tax itself or a payment falling within paragraph 15(2) above, as a reference to the aggregate of—

(a) the amount (if any) falsely claimed by way of credit, and
(b) the amount (if any) by which the gross amount of tax was falsely understated.

(3) A person guilty of an offence under paragraph 15(3) or (4) above is liable[1]—

(a) on summary conviction, to a penalty of **the statutory maximum** (or, where sub-paragraph (4) below applies, to the alternative penalty there specified if it is greater) or to imprisonment for a term not exceeding **six months** or to both;
(b) on conviction on indictment, to a penalty of any amount or to imprisonment for a term not exceeding **seven years** or to both.

(4) Where—

(a) the document referred to in paragraph 15(3) above is a return required under this Part of this Act, or
(b) the information referred to in paragraph 15(4) above is contained in or otherwise relevant to such a return,

the alternative penalty is a penalty equal to three times the aggregate of the amount (if any) falsely claimed by way of credit and the amount (if any) by which the gross amount of tax was understated.

(5) A person guilty of an offence under paragraph 15(5) above is liable[1]—

(a) on summary conviction, to a penalty of **the statutory maximum** (or, if greater, **three times the amount of any tax** that was or was intended to be evaded by his conduct) or to imprisonment for a term not exceeding **six months** or to both;
(b) on conviction on indictment, to a penalty of any amount or to imprisonment for a term not exceeding **seven years** or to both;

and paragraph 15(2) and sub-paragraph (2) above shall apply for the purposes of this sub-paragraph as they apply respectively for the purposes of paragraph 15(1) and sub-paragraph (1) above.

(6) A person guilty of an offence under paragraph 15(6) above is liable on summary conviction to a penalty of **level 5** on the standard scale or **three times the amount of the tax**, whichever is the greater.

(7) A person guilty of an offence under paragraph 15(7) above is liable on summary conviction to a penalty of **level 5** on the standard scale.

(8) In this paragraph—

(a) "credit" means credit for which provision is made by regulations under section 51 of this Act;
(b) "the gross amount of tax" means the total amount of tax due before taking into account any deduction for which provision is made by regulations under section 51(2) of this Act.

Criminal proceedings etc.

17. Sections 145 to 155 of the Customs and Excise Management Act 1979[1] (proceedings for offences, mitigation of penalties and certain other matters) shall apply in relation to offences under paragraph 15 above and penalties imposed under paragraph 16 above as they apply in relation to offences and penalties under the customs and excise Acts as defined in that Act.

---

1. See this title, ante.

PART VII

MISCELLANEOUS[1]

Evidence by certificate etc.

37. (1) A certificate of the Commissioners—

    (*a*)   that a person was or was not at any time registered under section 47 of this Act,

    (*b*)   that any return required by regulations made under section 49 of this Act has not been made or had not been made at any time, or

    (*c*)   that any tax shown as due in a return made in pursuance of regulations made under section 49 of this Act, or in an assessment made under section 50 of this Act, has not been paid,

shall be sufficient evidence of that fact until the contrary is proved.

(2) A photograph of any document furnished to the Commissioners for the purposes of this Part of this Act and certified by them to be such a photograph shall be admissible in any proceedings, whether civil or criminal, to the same extent as the document itself.

(3) Any document purporting to be a certificate under sub-paragraph (1) or (2) above shall be taken to be such a certificate until the contrary is proved.

---

1. For procedure in respect of this offence which is triable either way, see s 147 of the Customs and Excise Management Act 1979, ante, and the Magistrates' Courts Act 1980, ss 17A–21, in PART I: MAGISTRATES' COURTS, PROCEDURE, ante.

8-7246A

PART VIII

SECONDARY LIABILITY: CONTROLLERS OF LANDFILL SITES

Finance Act 1997[1]

(1997 c 16)

PART I[1]

EXCISE DUTIES

Gaming duty

8-7247   **10. Gaming duty to replace gaming licence duty.**   (1) A gaming licence shall not be required under section 13 of the Betting and Gaming Duties Act 1981 (gaming licence duty) for any gaming on or after 1 October 1997; but a duty of excise (to be known as "gaming duty") shall be charged in accordance with section 11 below on any premises in the United Kingdom where gaming to which this section applies ("dutiable gaming") takes place on or after that date.

(2) Subject to subsections (3) and (4) below, this section applies to gaming by way of any of the following games, that is to say, baccarat, punto banco, big six, blackjack, boule, casino stud poker, chemin de fer, chuck-a-luck, craps, crown and anchor, faro, faro bank, hazard, poker dice, pontoon, French roulette, American roulette, super pan 9, trente et quarante, vingt-et-un, and wheel of fortune.

(3) This section does not apply to any lawful gaming which is gaming to which any of the following provisions applies and takes place in accordance with the requirements of that provision, that is to say—

    (*a*)   section 2(2) of the Gaming Act 1968 or Article 55(2) of the Betting, Gaming, Lotteries and Amusements (Northern Ireland) Order 1985 (private parties);

    (*b*)   section 6 of that Act (premises licensed for the sale of liquor);

    (*c*)   section 34 of that Act or Article 108 of that Order (certain gaming machines);

    (*d*)   section 41 of that Act or Article 126 of that Order (gaming at entertainments not held for private gain);

    (*e*)   section 15 or 16 of the Lotteries and Amusements Act 1976 or Article 153 or 154 of that Order (amusements with prizes).

(4) This section does not apply to any gaming which takes place on premises in respect of which a club or miners' welfare institute is for the time being registered under Part II of the Gaming Act 1968[2].

(5) The Treasury may by order made by statutory instrument add to the games mentioned in subsection (2) above if it appears to them, having regard to the character of the game and the circumstances in which it is played, that it is appropriate to do so.

(6) Any reference in this section, or in an order under subsection (5) above, to a particular game shall be taken to include a reference to any game (by whatever name called) which is essentially similar to that game.

[Finance Act 1997, s 10.]

---

1. Part I contains ss 1 to 20.

8-7248   **11. Rate of gaming duty.**   (1) Gaming duty shall be charged on premises for every accounting period which contains a time when dutiable gaming takes place on those premises.

(2)–(11) *Calculation of gaming duty; power of Commissioners to make Regulations[1] and directions.*

1. The Gaming Duty Regulations 1997, SI 1997/2196 amended by SI 1999/2489, SI 2000/2408, SI 2001/3021, SI 2002/2310, SI 2003/2247 and SI 2004/2243 have been made.
[Finance Act 1997, s 11.]

8–7249   12. *Liability to pay gaming duty*

8–7250   13. Supplemental provisions relating to gaming duty.   (1) Schedule 1 to this Act[1] (which makes supplemental provision with respect to gaming duty) shall have effect.
   (2) Amendments to the *Customs and Excise Management Act 1979.*
[Finance Act 1997, s 13.]

---

   1. See post.

8–7251   14. *Subordinate legislation relating to gaming duty*

8–7252   15. Interpretation of gaming duty provisions.   (1) This section shall have effect for the purposes of construing the gaming duty provisions of this Act, that is to say, sections 10 to 14 above, this section and Schedule 1 to this Act.
   (2) The gaming duty provisions of this Act shall be construed as one with the Customs and Excise Management Act 1979.
   (3) In the gaming duty provisions of this Act—

"accounting period" means, subject to the provisions of Schedule 1 to this Act, a period of six months beginning with 1 April or 1 October;
"dutiable gaming" means gaming to which section 10 above applies;
"gaming" means gaming within the meaning of the Gaming Act 1968 or the Betting, Gaming, Lotteries and Amusements (Northern Ireland) Order 1985;
"the gaming duty register" means the register maintained under paragraph 1 of Schedule 1 to this Act;
"premises" includes any place and any means of transport and shall be construed subject to section 11(6) above;
"provider", in relation to any premises where gaming takes place, means any person having a right to control the admission of persons to those premises, whether or not he has a right to control the admission of persons to the gaming.

   (4) For the avoidance of doubt it is hereby declared that the imposition or payment of gaming duty does not make lawful any gaming which is otherwise unlawful.
[Finance Act 1997, s 15.]

8–7253

Section 13

SCHEDULE 1
GAMING DUTY: ADMINISTRATION, ENFORCEMENT ETC
PART I
THE GAMING DUTY REGISTER
The Register

1. The Commissioners shall establish and maintain a register of persons involved in the provision of dutiable gaming.

Interpretation

2. (1) In this Part of this Schedule—

"the register" means the gaming duty register;
"registered person" means a person registered on the register; and
"registrable person" has the meaning given by paragraph 3 below.

   (2) For the purposes of this Part of this Schedule premises in the United Kingdom are "unlicensed premises" unless they are premises in Great Britain—

   (*a*) in respect of which a licence under the Gaming Act 1968 is for the time being in force, or
   (*b*) in respect of which a club or miners' welfare institute is for the time being registered under Part II of that Act.

   (3) References in this Part of this Schedule to being a member of a group and to being the representative member of a group shall be construed in accordance with paragraph 8 below.
   3–8. *Registration; notification of premises and civil penalties.*

PART II
OTHER PROVISIONS
   9. *Accounting periods.*

Directions as to the making of returns

10. (1) The commissioners may give directions as to the making of returns in connection with gaming duty by—

(*a*) persons registered on the gaming duty register;

(*b*) persons liable to pay any gaming duty.

(2) Directions under this paragraph may, in particular, make provision as to—

(*a*) when any returns are to be made;

(*b*) the persons by whom any returns are to be made;

(*c*) the form in which any returns are to be made;

(*d*) the information to be given in any returns;

(*e*) the declarations to be contained in returns and the manner in which returns are to be authenticated;

(*f*) returns being treated as not made until received by the Commissioners;

(*g*) the places to which returns are to be made.

(3) Where a person fails to comply with any provision of a direction given under this paragraph, that failure shall attract a penalty under section 9 of the Finance Act 1994 (civil penalties) and shall also attract daily penalties.

11. *Regulations.*

Offences

12. (1) Any person who obstructs any officer in the exercise of his functions in relation to gaming duty shall be guilty of an offence and liable, on summary conviction, to a penalty of **level 5** on the standard scale.

(2) Any person who—

(*a*) in connection with gaming duty, makes any statement which he knows to be false in a material particular or recklessly makes any statement which is false in a material particular,

(*b*) in that connection, with intent to deceive, produces or makes use of any book, account, record, return or other document which is false in a material particular, or

(*c*) is knowingly concerned in, or in the taking of steps with a view to, the fraudulent evasion (by him or any other person) of any gaming duty or of any obligation to make a payment on account of gaming duty,

shall be guilty of an offence.

(3) A person guilty of an offence under sub-paragraph (2) above shall be liable[1]—

(*a*) on summary conviction, to a penalty of—

(i) **the statutory maximum**, or

(ii) if greater, **three times the duty** or other amount which is unpaid or the payment of which is sought to be avoided,

or to imprisonment for a term not exceeding **six months**, or to both;

(*b*) on conviction on indictment, to a penalty of any amount, or to imprisonment for a term not exceeding—

(i) **two years** in the case of an offence by virtue of sub-paragraph (2)(*a*) above, and

(ii) **seven years** in any other case,

or to both.

(4) Section 27 of the Betting and Gaming Duties Act 1981 (offences by bodies corporate) shall have effect for the purposes of any offence under this paragraph as it has effect for the purposes of the offences mentioned in that section.

(5) Where a person has committed an offence under sub-paragraph (2) above, all designated items related to the relevant gaming shall be liable to forfeiture if—

(*a*) at the time the offence was committed that person was not registered on the gaming duty register; and

(*b*) the relevant gaming did not take place on premises which, at the time the offence was committed, were specified in any person's entry on that register.

(6) In sub-paragraph (5) above, "the relevant gaming" means—

(*a*) in relation to an offence under sub-paragraph (2)(*a*) or (*b*) above, any gaming to which the false statement or (as the case may be) the false document related; and

(*b*) in relation to an offence under sub-paragraph (2)(*c*) above, any gaming on the premises the gaming duty on which was, or was sought to be, fraudulently evaded.

(7) For the purposes of sub-paragraph (5) above, the designated items related to any gaming are—

(*a*) any furniture, machines and other articles and equipment which—

(i) are on the premises where the gaming takes place; and

(ii) have been or are being, or are capable of being, used for or in connection with gaming;

and

(*b*) any cash and gaming chips in the custody or under the control of any person who—

(i) is a provider of the premises on which the gaming takes place, or

(ii) is in any way concerned with the organisation or management of the gaming.

(8) For the purposes of sub-paragraph (7)(*b*) above the cash and gaming chips taken to be under the control of a person who is the provider of any premises or is concerned with the organisation or management of gaming on any premises shall include all cash and gaming chips in play or left on a gaming table on those premises.

Disclosure of information

14. (1) No obligation as to secrecy or other restriction on the disclosure of information imposed by statute or otherwise shall prevent—

(a) the Commissioners or an authorised officer of the Commissioners from disclosing to the Gaming Board for Great Britain or to an authorised officer of that Board, or

(b) that Board or an authorised officer of that Board from disclosing to the Commissioners or an authorised officer of the Commissioners,

information for the purpose of assisting the Commissioners in the carrying out of their functions with respect to gaming duty or, as the case may be, that Board in the carrying out of that Board's functions under the Gaming Act 1968.

(2) Information obtained by virtue of a disclosure authorised by this paragraph shall not be disclosed except—

(a) to the Commissioners or the Gaming Board for Great Britain or to an authorised officer of the Commissioners or that Board; or

(b) for the purposes of any proceedings connected with a matter in relation to which the Commissioners or that Board carry out the functions mentioned in sub-paragraph (1) above.

Evidence by certificate

15. Section 29A of the Betting and Gaming Duties Act 1981 (evidence by certificate) shall apply for the purposes of sections 10 to 15 of this Act and this Schedule as it applies for the purposes of that Act.

Protection of officers

16. Section 31 of the Betting and Gaming Duties Act 1981 (protection of officers) shall apply for the purposes of gaming duty as it applies for the purposes of general betting duty.

---

1. For procedure in respect of this offence which is triable either way, see s 147 of the Customs and Excise Management Act 1979, ante, and ss 17A–21 of the Magistrates' Courts Act 1980, in PART I, MAGISTRATES' COURTS, PROCEDURE, ante.

Finance Act 2000
(2000 c 17)

PART I[1]
EXCISE DUTIES
Vehicle excise duty

8–7254   20. Threshold for reduced general rate.   (1) In paragraph 1 of Schedule 1 to the Vehicle Excise and Registration Act 1994[2] (rate of duty applicable where no other rate specified), in sub-paragraphs (2) and (2A) for "1,100 cubic centimetres" (the reduced rate threshold) substitute "1,200 cubic centimetres".

This amendment applies to licences issued on or after 1st March 2001.

(2) Refunds shall be made by the Secretary of State, in accordance with the following provisions of this section, in respect of licences—

(a) issued in the period beginning with 1st March 2000 and ending with 28th February 2001, and

(b) not surrendered before the end of that period,

where the amount of vehicle excise duty chargeable on the licence would have been less if the amendment in subsection (1) had applied.

(3) The amount of the refund is—

(a) £55 for a 12 month licence, and

(b) £27.50 for a 6 month licence.

(4) The person entitled to the refund is—

(a) in the case of a licence in force on 28th February 2001, the keeper of the vehicle on that date;

(b) in the case of a licence that has ceased to be in force before that date, the keeper of the vehicle when the licence expired.

(5) For the purposes of subsection (4) the keeper of the vehicle shall be taken to be—

(a) the person registered as keeper of the vehicle on the date in question, or

(b) if the Secretary of State has received notification of a change of ownership of the vehicle as a result of which another person is on that date entitled to be registered as the new keeper of the vehicle, that person.

(6) A refund shall only be made if an application is made for it in such form, and containing such particulars and supported by such documents, as the Secretary of State may require.

(7) The Secretary of State shall give notice in writing to any person appearing to him to be entitled to a refund—

(a) informing him that he appears to be entitled to a refund,

(b) enclosing an application form, and

(c) specifying the particulars and supporting documents to be provided.

(8) An application for, or the making of, a refund under this section in respect of a licence does not affect the validity of the licence.

(9) For the purposes of section 19 of the Vehicle Excise and Registration Act 1994[2] (surrender of licences) as it applies to the surrender on or after 1st March 2001 of a licence in respect of which a refund under this section has been made, or applied for, the annual rate of duty chargeable on the licence shall be taken to be that which would have been chargeable if the amendment in subsection (1) above had applied.

(10) Section 45 of that Act[2] (offence of false or misleading declaration) applies to a declaration in connection with an application for a refund under this section as it applies to a declaration in connection with an application for a vehicle licence.

(11) *Northern Ireland*

[Finance Act 2000, s 20.]

---

1. Part I comprises ss 1 to 29.
2. See Part VII, Transport, ante.

8–7255   23. Enforcement provisions for graduated rates.   Schedule 4[1] to this Act has effect with respect to vehicle licences for vehicles in respect of which vehicle excise duty is chargeable at different rates.

[Finance Act 2000, s 23.]

---

1. See, post.

8–7256   30. Climate change levy.   (1) Schedule 6[2] to this Act (which makes provision for a new tax that is to be known as climate change levy) shall have effect.

(2) Schedule 7[3] to this Act (climate change levy: consequential amendments) shall have effect.

(3) Part V of Schedule 6 to this Act (registration for the purposes of climate change levy) shall not come into force until such date as the Treasury may appoint by order[4] made by statutory instrument; and different days may be appointed under this subsection for different purposes.

[Finance Act 2000, s 30.]

---

1. Part II comprises s 30.
2. See, post.
3. Schedule 7 is not reproduced in this work.
4. See the Finance Act 2000, Schedule 6 Part V (Appointed Day) Order 2000, SI 2000/3350, which brought the provisions contained in Part V into force on either 2 or 29 January 2001.

Compliance

8–7257   144. Offence of fraudulent evasion of income tax.   (1) A person commits an offence if he is knowingly concerned in the fraudulent evasion of income tax by him or any other person.

(2) A person guilty of an offence under this section is liable[2]—

(*a*) on summary conviction, to imprisonment for a term not exceeding **six months** or a fine not exceeding the **statutory maximum**, or both;

(*b*) on conviction on indictment, to imprisonment for a term not exceeding **seven years** or a fine, or both.

(3) This section applies to things done or omitted on or after 1st January 2001.

[Finance Act 2000, s 144.]

---

1. Part VI comprises ss 143 to 157.
2. For procedure in respect of this offence which is triable either way, see the Magistrates' Courts Act 1980, ss 17A–21, in PART I: MAGISTRATES' COURTS, PROCEDURE, ante..

Section 23   SCHEDULE 4
VEHICLE EXCISE DUTY: ENFORCEMENT PROVISIONS FOR GRADUATED RATES

Introduction

8–7257A   1. (1) This Schedule applies to vehicles in respect of which different rates of vehicle excise duty are, under the provisions listed below, chargeable in respect of vehicles by reference to characteristics of the vehicle.

(2) The provisions referred to in sub-paragraph (1) are—

Part I of Schedule 1 to the Vehicle Excise and Registration Act 1994[1] (the general rate),

Part IA of that Schedule (graduated rates for light passenger vehicles first registered on or after 1st March 2001), or

Part II of that Schedule (motorcycles).

Particulars to be furnished on application for licence

2. (1) The Secretary of State may make provision by regulations as to the particulars to be furnished on an application for a vehicle licence in respect of a vehicle to which this Schedule applies.

(2) The regulations may make different provision for different descriptions of vehicle and different descriptions of licence.

(3) The prescribed particulars may include—

(a) particulars other than those required for the purposes of vehicle excise duty, and
(b) particulars other than with respect to the vehicle in respect of which the licence is to be taken out.

(4) Every person making an application with respect to which regulations under this paragraph are in force shall—

(a) furnish such particulars as may be prescribed by the regulations, and
(b) make such a declaration as may be specified by the Secretary of State.

(5) A person applying for a licence need not make the declaration specified for the purposes of sub-paragraph (4)(b) if he agrees to comply with such conditions as may be specified in relation to him by the Secretary of State. The conditions which may be specified include—

(a) a condition that the prescribed particulars are furnished by being transmitted to the Secretary of State by such electronic means as he may specify; and
(b) a condition requiring such payments as may be specified by the Secretary of State to be made to him in respect of—

 (i) steps taken by him for facilitating compliance by any person with any condition falling within paragraph (a); and
 (ii) in such circumstances as may be so specified, the processing of applications for vehicle licences where particulars are transmitted in accordance with that paragraph.

(6) In relation to applications with respect to which regulations under this paragraph are in force, the preceding provisions of this paragraph have effect in place of the provisions of subsections (1) to (3B) of section 7 of the Vehicle Excise and Registration Act 1994.

Power to require evidence in support of application

3. The Secretary of State may make provision by regulations—

(a) requiring an application for a vehicle licence in respect of a vehicle to which this Schedule applies to be supported by such documentary or other evidence as may be specified in the regulations, and
(b) authorising him to refuse to issue the licence applied for if such evidence is not provided.

Powers exercisable where licence issued on basis of incorrect application

4. The powers conferred by paragraphs 5 to 11 below are exercisable in a case where—

(a) a vehicle licence is issued to a person on the basis of an application stating that the vehicle—

 (i) is a vehicle to which this Schedule applies, or
 (ii) is a vehicle to which this Schedule applies in respect of which a particular amount of vehicle excise duty falls to be paid, and

(b) the vehicle is not such a vehicle or, as the case may be, is one in respect of which duty falls to be paid at a higher rate.

Power to declare licence void

5. The Secretary of State may by notice sent by post to the person inform him that the licence is void as from the time when it was granted.

If he does so, the licence shall be void as from the time when it was granted.

Power to require payment of balance of duty

6. (1) The Secretary of State may by notice sent by post to the person require him to secure that the additional duty payable is paid within such reasonable period as is specified in the notice.

(2) If that requirement is not complied with, the Secretary of State may by notice sent by post to the person inform him that the licence is void as from the time when it was granted.

If he does so, the licence shall be void as from the time when it was granted.

Power to require delivery up of licence

7. The Secretary of State may in a notice under paragraph 5 or 6(2) require the person to whom it is sent to deliver up the licence within such reasonable period as is specified in the notice.

Power to require delivery up of licence and payment in respect of duty

8. (1) The Secretary of State may in a notice under paragraph 5 or 6(2) require the person to whom it is sent—

(a) to deliver up the licence within such reasonable period as is specified in the notice, and
(b) on doing so to pay an amount equal to the monthly duty shortfall for each month, or part of a month, in the relevant period.

(2) The "monthly duty shortfall" means one-twelfth of the difference between—

(a) the duty that would have been payable for a licence for a period of twelve months if the vehicle had been correctly described in the application, and
(b) that duty payable in respect of such a licence on the basis of the description in the application as made.

For this purpose the amount of the duty payable shall be ascertained by reference to the rates in force at the beginning of the relevant period.

Failure to deliver up licence

9. (1) A person who—

(*a*) is required by notice under paragraph 7 or 8(1)(a) above to deliver up a licence, and

(*b*) fails to comply with the requirement contained in the notice,

commits an offence.

(2) A person committing such an offence is liable on summary conviction to a penalty not exceeding whichever is the greater of—

(*a*) **level 3** on the standard scale, and

(*b*) **five times** the annual duty shortfall.

(3) The "annual duty shortfall" means the difference between—

(*a*) the duty that would have been payable for a licence for a period of twelve months if the vehicle had been correctly described in the application, and

(*b*) that duty payable in respect of a licence for a period of twelve months in respect of the vehicle as described in the application.

For this purpose the amount of the duty payable shall be ascertained by reference to the rates in force at the beginning of the relevant period.

Failure to deliver up licence: additional liability

10. (1) Where a person has been convicted of an offence under paragraph 9, the court shall (in addition to any penalty which it may impose under that paragraph) order him to pay an amount equal to the monthly duty shortfall for each month, or part of a month, in the relevant period (or so much of the relevant period as falls before the making of the order).

(2) In sub-paragraph (1) the "monthly duty shortfall" has the meaning given by paragraph 8(2).

(3) Where—

(*a*) a person has been convicted of an offence under paragraph 9, and

(*b*) a requirement to pay an amount with respect to that licence has been imposed on that person by virtue of paragraph 8(1)(*b*),

the order to pay an amount under this paragraph has effect instead of that requirement and the amount to be paid under the order shall be reduced by any amount actually paid in pursuance of the requirement.

Meaning of the "relevant period"

11. References in this Schedule to the "relevant period" are to the period—

(*a*) beginning with the first day of the period for which the licence was applied for or, if later, the day on which the licence first was to have effect, and

(*b*) ending with whichever is the earliest of the following times—

(i) the end of the month during which the licence was required to be delivered up;

(ii) the end of the month during which the licence was actually delivered up;

(iii) the date on which the licence was due to expire;

(iv) the end of the month preceding that in which there first had effect a new vehicle licence for the vehicle in question.

Construction and effect

12. (1) This Schedule and the Vehicle and Excise Registration Act 1994 shall be construed and have effect as if this Schedule were contained in that Act.

(2) References in any other enactment to that Act shall be construed and have effect accordingly as including references to this Schedule.

---

1. See PART VII, TRANSPORT, ante.

Section 30

SCHEDULE 6[1]

CLIMATE CHANGE LEVY

(As amended by the Criminal Justice and Police Act 2001, Sch 2 and the Finance Act 2003, ss 188, 192 and SI 2004/1501.)

PART I

THE LEVY

Climate change levy

8–7257B 1. (1) A tax to be known as climate change levy ("the levy") shall be charged in accordance with this Schedule.

(2) The levy is under the care and management of the Commissioners of Customs and Excise.

Levy charged on taxable supplies

2. (1) The levy is charged on taxable supplies.

(2) Any supply of a taxable commodity is a taxable supply, subject to the provisions of Part II of this Schedule.

Meaning of "taxable commodity"

3. (1) The following are taxable commodities for the purposes of this Schedule, subject to sub-paragraph (2) and to any regulations under sub-paragraph (3)—

    (*a*)   electricity;
    (*b*)   any gas in a gaseous state that is of a kind supplied by a gas utility;
    (*c*)   any petroleum gas, or other gaseous hydrocarbon, in a liquid state;
    (*d*)   coal and lignite;
    (*e*)   coke, and semi-coke, of coal or lignite;
    (*f*)   petroleum coke.

(2) The following are not taxable commodities—

    (*a*)   hydrocarbon oil or road fuel gas within the meaning of the Hydrocarbon Oil Duties Act 1979;
    (*b*)   waste within the meaning of Part II of the Environmental Protection Act 1990 or the meaning given by Article 2(2) of the Waste and Contaminated Land (Northern Ireland) Order 1997.

(3) The Treasury may by regulations provide that a commodity of a description specified in the regulations is, or is not, a taxable commodity for the purposes of this Schedule.

---

1. Only those provisions of Schedule 6 which are relevant to the work of magistrates' courts are included in this work.

PART VIII
EVASION, MISDECLARATION AND NEGLECT

Criminal offences: Evasion

8–7257C   **92.** (1) A person is guilty of an offence if he is knowingly concerned in, or in the taking of steps with a view to—

    (*a*)   the fraudulent evasion by that person of any levy with which he is charged; or
    (*b*)   the fraudulent evasion by any other person of any levy with which that other person is charged.

(2) The references in sub-paragraph (1) to the evasion of levy include references to obtaining, in circumstances where there is no entitlement to it, either a tax credit or a repayment of levy.

(3) A person guilty of an offence under this paragraph shall be liable[1] (subject to sub-paragraph (4))—

    (*a*)   on summary conviction, to a penalty of **the statutory maximum** or to imprisonment for a term not exceeding **six months**, or to both;
    (*b*)   on conviction on indictment, to a penalty of any amount or to imprisonment for a term not exceeding **seven years**, or to both.

(4) In the case of any offence under this paragraph, where the statutory maximum is less than three times the sum of the amounts of levy which are shown to be amounts that were or were intended to be evaded, the penalty on summary conviction shall be the amount equal to three times that sum (instead of the statutory maximum).

(5) For the purposes of sub-paragraph (4) the amounts of levy that were or were intended to be evaded shall be taken to include—

    (*a*)   the amount of any tax credit, and
    (*b*)   the amount of any repayment of levy,

which was, or was intended to be, obtained in circumstances where there was no entitlement to it.

(6) In determining for the purposes of sub-paragraph (4) how much levy (in addition to any amount falling within sub-paragraph (5)) was or was intended to be evaded, no account shall be taken of the extent (if any) to which any liability to levy of any person fell, or would have fallen, to be reduced by the amount of any tax credit or repayment of levy to which he was, or would have been, entitled.

Criminal offences: Misstatements

93. (1) A person is guilty of an offence if, with the requisite intent and for purposes connected with the levy—

    (*a*)   he produces or provides, or causes to be produced or provided, any document which is false in a material particular, or
    (*b*)   he otherwise makes use of such a document;

and in this sub-paragraph "the requisite intent" means the intent to deceive any person or to secure that a machine will respond to the document as if it were a true document.

(2) A person is guilty of an offence if, in providing any information under any provision made by or under this Schedule—

    (*a*)   he makes a statement which he knows to be false in a material particular; or
    (*b*)   he recklessly makes a statement which is false in a material particular.

(3) A person guilty of an offence under this paragraph shall be liable[1] (subject to sub-paragraph (4))—

    (*a*)   on summary conviction, to a penalty of **the statutory maximum** or to imprisonment for a term not exceeding **six months**, or to both;
    (*b*)   on conviction on indictment, to a penalty of any amount or to imprisonment for a term not exceeding **seven years**, or to both.

(4) In the case of any offence under this paragraph, where—

    (*a*)   the document referred to in sub-paragraph (1) is a return or other notification required under any provision made by or under this Schedule, or
    (*b*)   the information referred to in sub-paragraph (2) is contained in or otherwise relevant to such a return or notification,

the amount of the penalty on summary conviction shall be whichever is the greater of the statutory maximum and the amount equal to three times the sum of the amounts (if any) by which the return or notification understates any person's liability to levy.

(5) In sub-paragraph (4) the reference to the amount by which any person's liability to levy is understated shall be taken to be equal to the sum of—

(a) the amount (if any) by which his gross liability was understated; and

(b) the amount (if any) by which any entitlements of his to tax credits and repayments of levy were overstated.

(6) In sub-paragraph (5) "gross liability" means liability to levy before any deduction is made in respect of any entitlement to any tax credit or repayments of levy.

Criminal offences: Conduct involving evasions or misstatements

94. (1) A person is guilty of an offence under this paragraph if his conduct during any particular period must have involved the commission by him of one or more offences under the preceding provisions of this Part of this Schedule.

(2) For the purposes of any proceedings for an offence under this paragraph it shall be immaterial whether the particulars of the offence or offences that must have been committed are known.

(3) A person guilty of an offence under this paragraph shall be liable[1] (subject to sub-paragraph (4))—

(a) on summary conviction, to a penalty of the **statutory maximum** or to imprisonment for a term not exceeding **six months**, or to both;

(b) on conviction on indictment, to a penalty of any amount or to imprisonment for a term not exceeding **seven years**, or to both.

(4) In the case of any offence under this paragraph, where the statutory maximum is less than three times the sum of the amounts of levy which are shown to be amounts that were or were intended to be evaded by the conduct in question, the penalty on summary conviction shall be the amount equal to three times that sum (instead of the statutory maximum).

(5) For the purposes of sub-paragraph (4) the amounts of levy that were or were intended to be evaded by any conduct shall be taken to include—

(a) the amount of any tax credit, and

(b) the amount of any repayment of levy,

which was, or was intended to be, obtained in circumstances where there was no entitlement to it.

(6) In determining for the purposes of sub-paragraph (4) how much levy (in addition to any amount falling within sub-paragraph (5)) was or was intended to be evaded, no account shall be taken of the extent (if any) to which any liability to levy of any person fell, or would have fallen, to be reduced by the amount of any tax credit or repayments of levy to which he was, or would have been, entitled.

Criminal offences: Preparations for evasion

95. (1) Where a person—

(a) becomes a party to any agreement under or by means of which a supply of a taxable commodity is or is to be made, or

(b) makes arrangements for any other person to become a party to such an agreement,

he is guilty of an offence if he does so in the belief that levy chargeable on the supply will be evaded.

(2) Subject to sub-paragraph (3), a person guilty of an offence under this paragraph shall be liable, on summary conviction, to a penalty of **level 5** on the standard scale.

(3) In the case of any offence under this paragraph, where level 5 on the standard scale is less than three times the sum of the amounts of levy which are shown to be amounts that were or were intended to be evaded in respect of the supply in question, the penalty shall be the amount equal to three times that sum (instead of level 5 on the standard scale).

(4) For the purposes of sub-paragraph (3) the amounts of levy that were or were intended to be evaded shall be taken to include—

(a) the amount of any tax credit, and

(b) the amount of any repayment of levy,

which was, or was intended to be, obtained in circumstances where there was no entitlement to it.

(5) In determining for the purposes of sub-paragraph (3) how much levy (in addition to any amount falling within sub-paragraph (4)) was or was intended to be evaded, no account shall be taken of the extent (if any) to which any liability to levy of any person fell, or would have fallen, to be reduced by the amount of any tax credit or repayments of levy to which he was, or would have been, entitled.

Offences under paragraphs 92 to 95: procedural matters

96. Sections 145 to 155 of the Customs and Excise Management Act 1979 (proceedings for offences, mitigation of penalties and certain other matters) shall apply in relation to offences and penalties under paragraphs 92 to 95 as they apply in relation to offences and penalties under the customs and excise Acts.

Arrest for offences under paragraphs 92 to 94

97. (1) Where an authorised person has reasonable grounds for suspecting that a fraud offence has been committed he may arrest anyone whom he has reasonable grounds for suspecting to be guilty of the offence.

(2) In this paragraph—

"authorised person" means any person acting under the authority of the Commissioners; and

"a fraud offence" means an offence under any of paragraphs 92 to 94.

98. *Civil penalties: Evasion*

Liability of directors etc for penalties under paragraph 98

Interpretation of Part VIII

102. (1) References in this Part of this Schedule to obtaining a tax credit are references to bringing an amount into account as a tax credit for the purposes of levy on the basis that that amount is an amount which may be so brought into account in accordance with tax credit regulations.

(2) References in this Part of this Schedule to obtaining a repayment of levy are references to obtaining either—

    (*a*)   the payment or repayment of any amount, or
    (*b*)   the acknowledgement of a right to receive any amount,

on the basis that that amount is the amount of a repayment of levy to which there is an entitlement.

PART XII
INFORMATION AND EVIDENCE

8–7257D

124 Provision of information
Records

126. Evidence of records that are required to be preserved.   (1) Subject to the following provisions of this paragraph, where any obligation to preserve records is discharged in accordance with paragraph 125(4), a copy of any document forming part of the records shall be admissible in evidence in any proceedings, whether civil or criminal, to the same extent as the records themselves.

(2) A statement contained in a document produced by a computer shall not by virtue of this paragraph be admissible in evidence—

    (*a*)   repealed
    (*b*)–(*d*)   Scotland; Northern Ireland

Production of documents

127. (1) Every person involved (in whatever capacity) in making or receiving supplies of taxable commodities, or in any connected activities, shall upon demand made by an authorised person produce or cause to be produced for inspection by that person any documents relating to the matters in which he is or has been involved.

(2) Where, by virtue of sub-paragraph (1), an authorised person has power to require the production of any documents from any person—

    (*a*)   he shall have the like power to require production of the documents concerned from any other person who appears to the authorised person to be in possession of them; and
    (*b*)   the production of any document by that other person in pursuance of a requirement under this sub-paragraph shall be without prejudice to any lien claimed by that other person on that document.

(3) The documents mentioned in sub-paragraphs (1) and (2) shall be produced at such time and place as the authorised person may reasonably require.

(4) Subject to sub-paragraphs (5) and (6) and to paragraph 107(5) (which relates to supplementary assessments of daily penalties), if a person fails to produce any document which he is required to produce under this paragraph, he shall be liable—

    (*a*)   to a penalty of £250; and
    (*b*)   to a further penalty of £20 for every day after the last relevant date and before the day after that on which the document is produced.

(5) Liability to a penalty specified in sub-paragraph (4) shall not arise if the person required to produce the document in question satisfies the Commissioners or, on appeal, an appeal tribunal—

    (*a*)   in the case of the penalty under paragraph (*a*) of that sub-paragraph, that there is a reasonable excuse—

        (i)   for the initial failure to produce the document at the required time; and
        (ii)   for every subsequent failure to produce it;

    and

    (*b*)   in the case of any penalty under paragraph (b) of that sub-paragraph for any day, that there is a reasonable excuse for the failure to produce the document on or before that day.

(6) Where, by reason of any failure by any person to provide information required under this paragraph—

    (*a*)   that person is convicted of an offence (whether under this Act or otherwise), or
    (*b*)   that person is assessed to a penalty under paragraph 98 (penalty for evasion),

that person shall not by reason of that failure be liable also to a penalty under this paragraph.

(7) In this paragraph "the last relevant date" means the last day of the period within which the person in question was required to produce the document.

Powers in relation to documents produced

128. (1) An authorised person may take copies of, or make extracts from, any document produced under paragraph 127.

(2) If it appears to him to be necessary to do so, an authorised person may, at a reasonable time and for a reasonable period, remove any document produced under paragraph 127.

(3) An authorised person who removes any document under sub-paragraph (2) shall, if requested to do so, provide a receipt for the document so removed.

(4) Where a lien is claimed on a document produced under paragraph 127(2), the removal of the document under sub-paragraph (2) shall not be regarded as breaking the lien.

(5) Where a document removed by an authorised person under sub-paragraph (2) is reasonably required for any purpose he shall, as soon as practicable, provide a copy of the document, free of charge, to the person by whom it was produced or caused to be produced.

(6) Where any documents removed under the powers conferred by this paragraph are lost or damaged, the Commissioners shall be liable to compensate their owner for any expenses reasonably incurred by him in replacing or repairing the documents.

Entry and inspection

129. For the purpose of exercising any powers under this Schedule, an authorised person may at any reasonable time enter and inspect premises used in connection with the carrying on of a business.

Entry and search

130. (1) Where—

(a) a justice of the peace is satisfied on information on oath that there is reasonable ground for suspecting that a fraud offence which appears to be of a serious nature is being, has been or is about to be committed on any premises or that evidence of the commission of such an offence is to be found there, or

(b) in Scotland a justice (within the meaning of section 307 of the Criminal Procedure (Scotland) Act 1995) is satisfied by evidence on oath as mentioned in paragraph (a),

he may issue a warrant in writing authorising any authorised person to enter those premises, if necessary by force, at any time within one month from the time of the issue of the warrant and to search them.

(2) A person who enters the premises under the authority of the warrant may—

(a) take with him such other persons as appear to him to be necessary;

(b) seize and remove any such documents or other things at all found on the premises as he has reasonable cause to believe may be required as evidence for the purposes of proceedings in respect of a fraud offence which appears to him to be of a serious nature;

(c) search, or cause to be searched, any person found on the premises whom he has reasonable cause to believe to be in possession of any documents or other things which may be so required.

(3) Sub-paragraph (2) shall not authorise any person to be searched by a member of the opposite sex.

(4) The powers conferred by a warrant under this paragraph shall not be exercisable—

(a) by more than such number of authorised persons as may be specified in the warrant;

(b) outside such periods of the day as may be so specified; or

(c) if the warrant so provides, otherwise than in the presence of a constable in uniform.

(5) An authorised person seeking to exercise the powers conferred by a warrant under this paragraph or, if there is more than one such authorised person, such one of them as is in charge of the search shall provide a copy of the warrant endorsed with his name as follows—

(a) if the occupier of the premises concerned is present at the time the search is to begin, the copy shall be supplied to the occupier;

(b) if at that time the occupier is not present but a person who appears to the authorised person to be in charge of the premises is present, the copy shall be supplied to that person;

(c) if neither paragraph (a) nor paragraph (b) applies, the copy shall be left in a prominent place on the premises.

(6) In this paragraph "a fraud offence" means an offence under any of paragraphs 92 to 94.

Order for access to recorded information etc

131. (1) Where, on an application by an authorised person, a justice of the peace or, in Scotland, a justice (within the meaning of section 307 of the Criminal Procedure (Scotland) Act 1995) is satisfied that there are reasonable grounds for believing—

(a) that an offence in connection with levy is being, has been or is about to be committed, and

(b) that any recorded information (including any document of any nature at all) which may be required as evidence for the purpose of any proceedings in respect of such an offence is in the possession of any person,

he may make an order under this paragraph.

(2) An order under this paragraph is an order that the person who appears to the justice to be in possession of the recorded information to which the application relates shall—

(a) give an authorised person access to it, and

(b) permit an authorised person to remove and take away any of it which he reasonably considers necessary,

not later than the end of the period of seven days beginning with the date of the order or the end of such longer period as the order may specify.

(3) The reference in sub-paragraph (2)(a) to giving an authorised person access to the recorded information to which the application relates includes a reference to permitting the authorised person to take copies of it or to make extracts from it.

(4) Where the recorded information consists of information stored in any electronic form,, an order under this paragraph shall have effect as an order to produce the information—

(a) in a form in which it is visible and legible or from which it can readily be produced in a visible and legible form; and

(b) if the authorised person wishes to remove it, in a form in which it can be removed.

(5) This paragraph is without prejudice to the preceding paragraphs of this Part of this Schedule.

Removal of documents etc

132. (1) An authorised person who removes anything in the exercise of a power conferred by or under paragraph 130 or 131 shall, if so requested by a person showing himself—

(*a*) to be the occupier of premises from which it was removed, or
(*b*) to have had custody or control of it immediately before the removal,

provide that person with a record of what he removed.

(2) The authorised person shall provide the record within a reasonable time from the making of the request for it.

(3) Subject to sub-paragraph (7), if a request for permission to be allowed access to anything which—

(*a*) has been removed by an authorised person, and
(*b*) is retained by the Commissioners for the purposes of investigating an offence,

is made to the officer in overall charge of the investigation by a person who had custody or control of the thing immediately before it was so removed, or by someone acting on behalf of such a person, the officer shall allow the person who made the request access to it under the supervision of an authorised person.

(4) Subject to sub-paragraph (7), if a request for a photograph or copy of any such thing is made to the officer in overall charge of the investigation by a person who had custody or control of the thing immediately before it was so removed, or by someone acting on behalf of such a person, the officer shall—

(*a*) allow the person who made the request access to it under the supervision of an authorised person for the purpose of photographing it or copying it; or
(*b*) photograph or copy it, or cause it to be photographed or copied.

(5) Subject to sub-paragraph (7), where anything is photographed or copied under sub-paragraph (4)(*b*), the officer shall supply the photograph or copy, or cause it to be supplied, to the person who made the request.

(6) The photograph or copy shall be supplied within a reasonable time from the making of the request.

(7) There is no duty under this paragraph to allow access to anything, or to supply a photograph or copy of anything, if the officer in overall charge of the investigation for the purposes of which it was removed has reasonable grounds for believing that to do so would prejudice—

(*a*) that investigation;
(*b*) the investigation of an offence other than the offence for the purposes of the investigation of which the thing was removed; or
(*c*) any criminal proceedings which may be brought as a result of the investigation of which he is in charge or any such investigation as is mentioned in paragraph (b).

(8) Any reference in this paragraph to the officer in overall charge of the investigation is a reference to the person whose name and address are endorsed on the warrant concerned as being the officer so in charge.

Enforcement of paragraph 132

133. (1) Where, on an application made as mentioned in sub-paragraph (2), the appropriate judicial authority is satisfied that a person has failed to comply with a requirement imposed by paragraph 132, the authority may order that person to comply with the requirement within such time and in such manner as may be specified in the order.

(2) An application under sub-paragraph (1) shall not be made except—

(*a*) in the case of a failure to comply with any of the requirements imposed by paragraph 132(1) and (2)—

(i) by the occupier of the premises from which the thing in question was removed, or
(ii) by the person who had custody or control of it immediately before it was so removed;

(*b*) in any other case, by the person who had such custody or control.

(3) In this paragraph "the appropriate judicial authority" means—

(*a*) in England and Wales, a magistrates' court;
(*b*) in Scotland, the sheriff;
(*c*) in Northern Ireland, a court of summary jurisdiction, as defined in Article 2(2)(a) of the Magistrates' Courts (Northern Ireland) Order 1981.

(4) In England and Wales and Northern Ireland, an application for an order under this paragraph shall be made by way of complaint; and sections 21 and 42(2) of the Interpretation Act (Northern Ireland) 1954 shall apply as if any reference in those provisions to any enactment included a reference to this paragraph.

Power to take samples and examine meters

134. (1) An authorised person, if it appears to him necessary for the protection of the revenue against mistake or fraud, may at any time take, from material which he has reasonable cause to believe is—

(*a*) a taxable commodity which is intended to be, is being or has been the subject of a taxable supply, or
(*b*) a product of the burning of a taxable commodity (other than electricity) which is being or has been the subject of a taxable supply,

such samples as he may require with a view to determining how the material ought to be treated, or to have been treated, for the purposes of the levy.

(2) An authorised person, if it appears to him necessary for the protection of the revenue against mistake or fraud, may at any time examine any meter which he has reasonable cause to believe is intended to be, is being or has been used for ascertaining the quantity of any taxable commodity supplied by a taxable supply.

(3) Any sample taken under sub-paragraph (1) shall be disposed of in such manner as the Commissioners may direct.

Evidence by certificate

135. (1) In any proceedings a certificate of the Commissioners—

(a) that a person was or was not at any time registered for the purposes of the levy,

(b) that any return required by regulations made under paragraph 41 has not been made or had not been made at any time,

(c) that any levy shown as due in a return or other notification made in pursuance of regulations made under paragraph 41 has not been paid, or

(d) that any amount shown as due in any assessment made under this Schedule has not been paid,

shall be evidence or, in Scotland, sufficient evidence of that fact.

(2) A photograph of any document provided to the Commissioners for the purposes of this Schedule and certified by them to be such a photograph shall be admissible in any proceedings, whether civil or criminal, to the same extent as the document itself.

(3) In any proceedings any document purporting to be a certificate under sub-paragraph (1) or (2) shall be taken to be such a certificate unless the contrary is shown.

Inducements to provide information

136. (1) This paragraph applies—

(a) to any criminal proceedings against a person in respect of an offence in connection with or in relation to levy; and

(b) to any proceedings against a person for the recovery of any sum due from him in connection with or in relation to levy.

(2) Statements made or documents produced or provided by or on behalf of a person shall not be inadmissible in any proceedings to which this paragraph applies by reason only that—

(a) a matter falling within sub-paragraph (3) or (4) has been drawn to that person's attention; and

(b) he was or may have been induced, as a result, to make the statements or to produce or provide the documents.

(3) The matters falling within this sub-paragraph are—

(a) that, in relation to levy, the Commissioners may assess an amount due by way of a civil penalty instead of instituting criminal proceedings;

(b) that it is the practice of the Commissioners (without giving any undertaking as to whether they will make such an assessment in any case) to be influenced by whether a person—

(i) has made a full confession of any dishonest conduct to which he has been a party; and

(ii) has otherwise co-operated to the full with any investigation.

(4) The matter falling within this sub-paragraph is the fact that the Commissioners or, on appeal, an appeal tribunal have power under any provision of this Schedule to reduce a penalty.

Disclosure of information

137. (1) Notwithstanding any obligation not to disclose information that would otherwise apply, but subject to sub-paragraph (2), the Commissioners may disclose any information obtained or held by them in or in connection with the carrying out of their functions in relation to the levy to any of the following—

(a) any Minister of the Crown;

(b) the Scottish Ministers;

(c) any Minister, within the meaning of the Northern Ireland Act 1998, or any Northern Ireland department;

(d) the National Assembly for Wales;

(e) the Environment Agency;

(f) the Scottish Environment Protection Agency;

(g) the Gas and Electricity Markets Authority;

(h) the Director General of Electricity Supply for Northern Ireland;

(i) the Director General of Gas for Northern Ireland;

(j) an authorised officer of any person mentioned in paragraphs (a) to (i).

(2) Information shall not be disclosed under sub-paragraph (1) except for the purpose of assisting a person falling within paragraphs (a) to (j) of that sub-paragraph in the performance of his duties.

(3) Notwithstanding any such obligation as is mentioned in sub-paragraph (1), any person mentioned in sub-paragraph (1)(a) to (j) may disclose information—

(a) to the Commissioners, or

(b) to an authorised officer of the Commissioners,

for the purpose of assisting the Commissioners in the performance of duties in relation to the levy.

(4) Information that has been disclosed to a person by virtue of this paragraph shall not be disclosed by him except—

(a) to another person to whom (instead of him) disclosure could by virtue of this paragraph have been made; or

(b) for the purpose of any proceedings connected with the operation of any provision made by or under any enactment relating to the environment or to levy.

(5) References in the preceding provisions of this paragraph to an authorised officer of any person ("the principal") are to any person who has been designated by the principal as a person to and by whom information may be disclosed by virtue of this paragraph.

(6) Where the principal is a person falling within any of paragraphs (a) to (c) of sub-paragraph (1), the principal

shall notify the Commissioners in writing of the name of any person designated by the principal for the purposes of this paragraph.

(7) No charge may be made for any disclosure made by virtue of this paragraph.

(8) In this paragraph "enactment" includes an enactment contained in an Act of the Scottish Parliament or in any Northern Ireland legislation.

Meaning of "authorised person"

138. In this Part of this Schedule "authorised person" means any person acting under the authority of the Commissioners.

PART XIII
MISCELLANEOUS AND SUPPLEMENTARY

Security for levy

8–7257E   **139.** (1) Where it appears to the Commissioners necessary to do so for the protection of the revenue they may require any person who is or is required to be registered for the purposes of the levy to give security, or further security, for the payment of any levy which is or may become due from him.

(2) The power of the Commissioners to require any security, or further security, under this paragraph shall be a power to require security, or further security, of such amount and in such manner as they may determine.

(3) A person who is liable to account for the levy on a taxable supply that he makes is guilty of an offence if, at the time the supply is made—

(*a*) he has been required to give security under this paragraph, and

(*b*) he has not complied with that requirement.

(4) A person who is liable to account for the levy on a taxable supply that another person makes to him is guilty of an offence if he makes any arrangements for the making of the supply at a time when—

(*a*) he has been required to give security under this paragraph, and

(*b*) he has not complied with that requirement.

(5) A person guilty of an offence under this paragraph shall be liable, on summary conviction, to a penalty of level 5 on the standard scale.

(6) Sections 145 to 155 of the Customs and Excise Management Act 1979 (proceedings for offences, mitigation of penalties and certain other matters) shall apply in relation to an offence under this paragraph as they apply in relation to offences and penalties under the customs and excise Acts.

Service of notices etc

144. (1) Any notice, notification or requirement that is to be or may be served on, given to or imposed on any person for the purposes of any provision made by or under this Schedule may be served, given or imposed by sending it to that person or his tax representative by post in a letter addressed to that person or his representative at the latest or usual residence or place of business of that person or representative.

(2) Any direction required or authorised by or under this Schedule to be given by the Commissioners may be given by sending it by post in a letter addressed to each person affected by it at his latest or usual residence or place of business.

Variation and withdrawal of directions etc

145. Any direction, notice or notification required or authorised by or under this Schedule to be given by the Commissioners may be withdrawn or varied by them by a direction, notice or notification given in the same manner as the one withdrawn or varied.

Regulations and orders

146. (1) Any power under this Schedule to make regulations shall be exercisable by statutory instrument.

(2) A statutory instrument that—

(*a*) contains regulations made under this Schedule, and

(*b*) is not subject to a requirement that a draft of the instrument be laid before Parliament and approved by a resolution of the House of Commons,

shall be subject to annulment in pursuance of a resolution of the House of Commons.

(3) A statutory instrument that contains (whether alone or with other provisions) regulations under paragraph 3(3), 14(3), 15(4)(*a*), 16, 18(2), 18A, 52, 113(1), 148(4), 149 or 151(2) (regulations made by the Treasury) shall not be made unless a draft of the statutory instrument containing the regulations has been laid before Parliament and approved by a resolution of the House of Commons.

(4) Where regulations under this Schedule made by the Commissioners impose a relevant requirement on any person, they may provide that if the person fails to comply with the requirement he shall be liable, subject to sub-paragraph (5), to a penalty of £250.

(5) Where by reason of any conduct—

(*a*) a person is convicted of an offence (whether under this Act or otherwise), or

(*b*) a person is assessed to a penalty under paragraph 98,

that person shall not by reason of that conduct be liable also to a penalty under any regulations under this Schedule.

(6) In sub-paragraph (4) "relevant requirement" means any requirement other than one the penalty for a contravention of which is specified in paragraph 41(3), 114(3) or 125(6).

(7) A power under this Schedule to make any provision by regulations—

(a) may be exercised so as to apply the provision only in such cases as may be described in the regulations;
(b) may be exercised so as to make different provision for different cases or descriptions of case; and
(c) shall include power by the regulations to make such supplementary, incidental, consequential or transitional provision as the authority making the regulations may think fit.

PART XIV
INTERPRETATION[1]

General

8–7257F   147. In this Schedule—

"accounting period" means a period which, in pursuance of any regulations under paragraph 41, is an accounting period for the purposes of the levy;

"agreement" includes any arrangement or understanding (whether or not legally enforceable), and cognate expressions shall be construed accordingly;

"appeal tribunal" means a VAT and duties tribunal;

"auto-generator" has the meaning given by paragraph 152;

"climate change agreement" has the meaning given by paragraph 46;

"climate change levy accounting document" has the meaning given by paragraph 143(2);

"combined heat and power station" has the meaning given by paragraph 148(1);

"the Commissioners" means the Commissioners of Customs and Excise;

"conduct" includes acts and omissions;

"electricity utility" has the meaning given by paragraph 150(2) (but see paragraph 150(4));

"fully exempt combined heat and power station" has the meaning given by paragraph 148(2);

"gas utility" has the meaning given by paragraph 150(3) (but see paragraph 150(4));

"half-rate supply" has the meaning given by paragraph 43(1);

"member", in relation to a group, shall be construed in accordance with regulations under paragraph 116;

"non-resident taxpayer" means a person who—

(a) is or is required to be registered for the purposes of the levy, and
(b) is not resident in the United Kingdom;

"partly exempt combined heat and power station" has the meaning given by paragraph 148(3);

"prescribed" (except in paragraphs 14(3), 16(3), 18A and 148(4)) means prescribed by regulations made by the Commissioners under this Schedule;

"produced"—

(a) in relation to electricity, means generated, and
(b) in relation to any other commodity, includes extracted;

"reduced-rate supply" has the meaning given by paragraph 44(3) (which, by virtue of paragraph 44(4), has effect subject to paragraph 45);

"registered" means registered in the register maintained under paragraph 53(2);

"representative member", in relation to a group, shall be construed in accordance with regulations under paragraph 116;

"resident in the United Kingdom" has the meaning given by paragraph 156;

"ship" includes hovercraft;

"special utility scheme" has the meaning given by paragraph 29(1);

"subordinate legislation" has the same meaning as in the Interpretation Act 1978;

"supply for charity use" shall be construed in accordance with paragraph 8;

"supply for domestic use" shall be construed in accordance with paragraphs 8 and 9;

"tax credit" means a tax credit for which provision is made by tax credit regulations;

"tax credit regulations" means regulations under paragraph 62;

"tax representative", in relation to any person, means the person who, in accordance with any regulations under paragraph 114, is for the time being that person's tax representative for the purposes of the levy;

"taxable commodity" shall be construed in accordance with paragraph 3;

"taxable supply" shall be construed in accordance with paragraphs 2(2) and 4;

"the United Kingdom" includes the territorial waters adjacent to any part of the United Kingdom;

"utility" has the meaning given by paragraph 150(1).

148. *Meaning of other words and expressions used in this Schedule*

---

1. For procedure in respect of this offence which is triable either way, see s 147 of the Customs and Excise Management Act 1979, *ante*, and the Magistrates' Courts Act 1980, ss 17A–21, in PART I: MAGISTRATES' COURTS, PROCEDURE, *ante*.

Finance Act 2003

(2003 c 14)

PART 3[1]

TAXES AND DUTIES ON IMPORTATION AND EXPORTATION: PENALTIES

Preliminary

8–7257G   24. Introductory.   (1) This Part makes provision for and in connection with the imposition of liability to a penalty where a person—

(a) engages in any conduct for the purpose of evading any relevant tax or duty, or
(b) engages in any conduct by which he contravenes a duty, obligation, requirement or condition imposed by or under legislation relating to any relevant tax or duty.

(2) For the purposes of this Part "relevant tax or duty" means any of the following—

(*a*)   customs duty;
(*b*)   Community export duty;
(*c*)   Community import duty;
(*d*)   import VAT;
(*e*)   customs duty of a preferential tariff country.

(3) In this Part—

"appeal tribunal" means a VAT and duties tribunal;

"the Commissioners" means the Commissioners of Customs and Excise;

"the Community Customs Code" means Council Regulation 2913/92/EEC establishing the Community Customs Code;

"Community export duty" means any of the duties, charges or levies which are export duties within the meaning of the Community Customs Code (as at 9th April 2003, see the definition of "export duties" in Article 4(11) of that Code);

"Community import duty" means any of the duties, charges or levies which are import duties within the meaning of the Community Customs Code (as at 9th April 2003, see the definition of "import duties" in Article 4(10) of that Code);

"contravene" includes fail to comply with;

"customs duty of a preferential tariff country" includes a reference to any charge imposed by a preferential tariff country and having an equivalent effect to customs duty payable on the importation of goods into the territory of that country;

"demand notice" means a demand notice within the meaning of section 30;

"import VAT" means value added tax chargeable by virtue of section 1(1)(c) of the Value Added Tax Act 1994 (c 23) (importation of goods from places outside the member States);

"notice" means notice in writing;

"preferential tariff country" means a country outside the European Community which is, or is a member of a group of countries which is, party to an agreement falling within Article 20(3)(d) of the Community Customs Code (preferential tariff agreements with the Community);

"prescribed" means specified in, or determined in accordance with, regulations made by the Treasury;

"relevant rule", in relation to any relevant tax or duty, has the meaning given by subsection (8) of section 26 (as read with subsection (9) of that section);

"representative", in relation to any person, means—

(*a*)   his personal representative,
(*b*)   his trustee in bankruptcy or interim or permanent trustee,
(*c*)   any receiver or liquidator appointed in relation to that person or any of his property,

or any other person acting in a representative capacity in relation to that person.

(4) References in this Part to the Community Customs Code are references to that Code as from time to time amended, whether before or after the coming into force of this Part.

(5) The Treasury may by order amend this Part for the purpose of replacing any reference to, or to a provision of,—

(*a*)   the Community Customs Code, or
(*b*)   any instrument referred to in this Part by virtue of an order under this subsection,

with a reference to, or (as the case may be) to a provision of, a different instrument.

(6) A statutory instrument containing an order under subsection (5) may not be made unless a draft of the instrument has been laid before, and approved by a resolution of, the House of Commons.

(7) Except for this subsection and section 41 (which accordingly come into force on the passing of this Act), this Part comes into force on such day as the Treasury may by order appoint.
[Finance Act 2003, s 24.]

---

1. Part I comprises ss 24 to 41.

The penalties

8–7257H   25. Penalty for evasion. (1) In any case where—

(*a*)   a person engages in any conduct for the purpose of evading any relevant tax or duty, and
(*b*)   his conduct involves dishonesty (whether or not such as to give rise to any criminal liability),

that person is liable to a penalty of an amount equal to the amount of the tax or duty evaded or, as the case may be, sought to be evaded.

(2) Subsection (1) is subject to the following provisions of this Part.

(3) Nothing in this section applies in relation to any customs duty of a preferential tariff country.

(4) Any reference in this section to a person's "evading" any relevant tax or duty includes a reference to his obtaining or securing, without his being entitled to it,—

(*a*)   any repayment, rebate or drawback of any relevant tax or duty, (*b*) any relief or exemption from, or any allowance against, any relevant tax or duty, or

(*c*) any deferral or other postponement of his liability to pay any relevant tax or duty or of the discharge by payment of any such liability,

and also includes a reference to his evading the cancellation of any entitlement to, or the withdrawal of, any such repayment, rebate, drawback, relief, exemption or allowance.

(5) In relation to any such evasion of any relevant tax or duty as is mentioned in subsection (4), the reference in subsection (1) to the amount of the tax or duty evaded or sought to be evaded is a reference to the amount of—

(*a*) the repayment, rebate or drawback,

(*b*) the relief, exemption or allowance, or

(*c*) the payment which, or the liability to make which, is deferred or otherwise postponed,

as the case may be.

(6) Where, by reason of conduct falling within subsection (1) in the case of any relevant tax or duty, a person—

(*a*) is convicted of an offence,

(*b*) is given, and has not had withdrawn, a demand notice in respect of a penalty to which he is liable under section 26, or

(*c*) is liable to a penalty imposed upon him under any other provision of the law relating to that relevant tax or duty,

that conduct does not also give rise to liability to a penalty under this section in respect of that relevant tax or duty.

[Finance Act 2003, s 25.]

8–7257I   26. Penalty for contravention of relevant rule.   (1) If, in the case of any relevant tax or duty, a person of a prescribed description engages in any conduct by which he contravenes—

(*a*) a prescribed relevant rule, or

(*b*) a relevant rule of a prescribed description,

he is liable to a penalty under this section of a prescribed amount.

(2) Subsection (1) is subject to the following provisions of this Part.

(3) The power conferred by subsection (1) to prescribe a description of person includes power to prescribe any person (without further qualification) as such a description.

(4) Different penalties may be prescribed under subsection (1) for different cases or different circumstances.

(5) Any amount prescribed under subsection (1) as the amount of a penalty must not be more than £2,500.

(6) The Treasury may by order amend subsection (5) by substituting a different amount for the amount for the time being specified in that subsection.

(7) A statutory instrument containing an order under subsection (6) may not be made unless a draft of the instrument has been laid before, and approved by a resolution of, the House of Commons.

(8) In this Part "relevant rule", in relation to any relevant tax or duty, means any duty, obligation, requirement or condition imposed by or under any of the following—

(*a*) the Customs and Excise Management Act 1979 (c 2), as it applies in relation to the relevant tax or duty;

(*b*) any other Act, or any statutory instrument, as it applies in relation to the relevant tax or duty;

(*c*) in the case of customs duty, Community export duty or Community import duty, Community customs rules;

(*d*) in the case of import VAT, Community customs rules as they apply in relation to import VAT;

(*e*) any directly applicable Community legislation relating to the relevant tax or duty;

(*f*) any relevant international rules applying in relation to the relevant tax or duty.

(9) In subsection (8)—

"Community customs rules" means customs rules, as defined in Article 1 of the Community Customs Code;

"relevant international rules" means international agreements so far as applying in relation to a relevant tax or duty and having effect as part of the law of any part of the United Kingdom by virtue of—

(*a*) any Act or statutory instrument, or

(*b*) any directly applicable Community legislation.

[Finance Act 2003, s 26.]

8–7257J   27. Exceptions from section 26.   (1) A person is not liable to a penalty under section 26 if he satisfies—

(*a*) the Commissioners, or

(b) on appeal, an appeal tribunal,

that there is a reasonable excuse for his conduct.

(2) For the purposes of subsection (1) none of the following is a reasonable excuse—

(a) an insufficiency of funds available to any person for paying any relevant tax or duty or any penalty due;

(b) that reliance was placed by any person on another to perform any task;

(c) that the contravention is attributable, in whole or in part, to the conduct of a person on whom reliance to perform any task was so placed.

(3) Where, by reason of conduct falling within subsection (1) of section 26 in the case of any relevant tax or duty, a person—

(a) is prosecuted for an offence,

(b) is given, and has not had withdrawn, a demand notice in respect of a penalty to which he is liable under section 25, or

(c) is liable to a penalty imposed upon him under any other provision of the law relating to that relevant tax or duty,

that conduct does not also give rise to liability to a penalty under section 26 in respect of that relevant tax or duty.

(4) A person is not liable to a penalty under section 26 in respect of any conduct, so far as relating to import VAT, if in respect of that conduct—

(a) he is liable to a penalty under any of sections 62 to 69A of the Value Added Tax Act 1994 (c 23) (penalty for contravention of statutory requirements as to VAT), or

(b) he would be so liable but for section 62(4), 63(11), 64(6), 67(9), 69(9) or 69A(7) of that Act (conduct resulting in conviction, different penalty etc).

[Finance Act 2003, s 27.]

8–7257K 28. Liability of directors etc where body corporate liable to penalty for evasion.

(1) Where it appears to the Commissioners—

(a) that a body corporate is liable to a penalty under section 25, and

(b) that the conduct giving rise to the penalty is, in whole or in part, attributable to the dishonesty of a person who is, or at the material time was, a director or managing officer of the body corporate (a "relevant officer"),

the Commissioners may give a notice under this section to the body corporate (or its representative) and to the relevant officer (or his representative).

(2) A notice under this section must state—

(a) the amount of the penalty referred to in subsection (1)(a) (the "basic penalty"), and

(b) that the Commissioners propose, in accordance with this section, to recover from the relevant officer such portion (which may be the whole) of the basic penalty as is specified in the notice.

(3) If a notice is given under this section, this Part shall apply in relation to the relevant officer as if he were personally liable under section 25 to a penalty which corresponds to that portion of the basic penalty specified in the notice.

(4) If a notice is given under this section—

(a) the amount which may be recovered from the body corporate under this Part is limited to so much (if any) of the basic penalty as is not recoverable from the relevant officer by virtue of subsection (3), and

(b) the body corporate is to be treated as discharged from liability for so much of the basic penalty as is so recoverable from the relevant officer.

(5) In this section "managing officer", in relation to a body corporate, means—

(a) a manager, secretary or other similar officer of the body corporate, or

(b) a person purporting to act in any such capacity or as a director.

(6) Where the affairs of a body corporate are managed by its members, this section applies in relation to the conduct of a member in connection with his functions of management as if he were a director of the body corporate.

[Finance Act 2003, s 28.]

Reduction of amount of penalty

8–7257L 29. Reduction of penalty under section 25 or 26. (1) Where a person is liable to a penalty under section 25 or 26—

(a) the Commissioners (whether originally or on review) or, on appeal, an appeal tribunal may reduce the penalty to such amount (including nil) as they think proper; and

(b) the Commissioners on a review, or an appeal tribunal on an appeal, relating to a penalty reduced by the Commissioners under this subsection may cancel the whole or any part of the reduction previously made by the Commissioners.

(2) In exercising their powers under subsection (1), neither the Commissioners nor an appeal tribunal are entitled to take into account any of the matters specified in subsection (3).

(3) Those matters are—

(a) the insufficiency of the funds available to any person for paying any relevant tax or duty or the amount of the penalty,

(b) the fact that there has, in the case in question or in that case taken with any other cases, been no or no significant loss of any relevant tax or duty,

(c) the fact that the person liable to the penalty, or a person acting on his behalf, has acted in good faith.

[Finance Act 2003, s 29.]

Demand notices

8–7257M   30. Demands for penalties.   (1) Where a person is liable to a penalty under this Part, the Commissioners may give to that person or his representative a notice in writing (a "demand notice") demanding payment of the amount due by way of penalty.

(2) An amount demanded as due from a person or his representative in accordance with subsection (1) is recoverable as if it were an amount due from the person or, as the case may be, the representative as an amount of customs duty.

This subsection is subject to—

(a) any appeal under section 36 (appeals to tribunal); and

(b) subsection (3).

(3) An amount so demanded is not recoverable if or to the extent that—

(a) the demand has subsequently been withdrawn; or

(b) the amount has been reduced under section 29.

[Finance Act 2003, s 30.]

8–7257N   31. Time limits for demands for penalties.   (1) A demand notice may not be given—

(a) in the case of a penalty under section 25, more than 20 years after the conduct giving rise to the liability to the penalty ceased, or

(b) in the case of a penalty under section 26, more than 3 years after the conduct giving rise to the liability to the penalty ceased.

(2) A demand notice may not be given more than 2 years after there has come to the knowledge of the Commissioners evidence of facts sufficient in the opinion of the Commissioners to justify the giving of the demand notice.

(3) A demand notice—

(a) may be given in respect of a penalty to which a person was liable under section 25 or 26 immediately before his death, but

(b) in the case of a penalty to which the deceased was so liable under section 25, may not be given more than 3 years after his death.

[Finance Act 2003, s 31.]

8–7257O   32. No prosecution after demand notice for penalty under section 26.   Where a demand notice is given demanding payment of an amount due by way of penalty under section 26 in respect of any conduct of a person, no proceedings may be brought against that person for any offence constituted by that conduct (whether or not the demand notice is subsequently withdrawn).

[Finance Act 2003, s 32.]

Reviews

8–7257P   33. Right to review of certain decisions.   (1) If, in the case of any relevant tax or duty, the Commissioners give a person or his representative a notice informing him—

(a) that they have decided that the person has engaged in conduct by which he contravenes a relevant rule, and

(b) that the person is, in consequence, liable to a penalty under section 26, but

(c) that they do not propose to give a demand notice in respect of the penalty,

the person or his representative may give a notice to the Commissioners requiring them to review the decision mentioned in paragraph (a).

(2) Where the Commissioners give a demand notice to a person or his representative, the person or his representative may by notice require the Commissioners to review—

(a) their decision that the person is liable to a penalty under section 25 or 26, or

(b) their decision as to the amount of the liability.

(3) Where the Commissioners give a notice under section 28 to a body corporate and to a relevant officer—

(a) subsection (2) does not apply to any demand notice given in respect of the liability of either of them to a penalty under this Part in respect of the conduct in question, but

(b) subsections (4) and (5) have effect instead in relation to any such demand notice.

(4) Where the Commissioners give a demand notice to the relevant officer or his representative for a penalty which corresponds to the portion of the basic penalty specified in the notice under section 28, the relevant officer or his representative may by notice require the Commissioners to review—

(a) their decision that the conduct of the body corporate referred to in section 28(1)(b) is, in whole or in part, attributable to the relevant officer's dishonesty, or

(b) their decision as to the portion of the basic penalty which the Commissioners are seeking to recover from the relevant officer or his representative.

(5) Where the Commissioners give a demand notice to the body corporate or its representative for so much of the basic penalty as is not recoverable from the relevant officer by virtue of section 28(3), the body corporate or its representative may by notice require the Commissioners to review—

(a) their decision that the body corporate is liable to a penalty under section 25, or

(b) their decision as to amount of the basic penalty as if it were the amount specified in the demand notice.

(6) A person may not under this section require a review of a decision under section 35 (decision on review).

[Finance Act 2003, s 33.]

8–7257Q   34. Time limit and right to further review.   (1) The Commissioners are not required under section 33 to review any decision unless the notice requiring the review is given before the end of the permitted period.

(2) For the purposes of this section the "permitted period" is the period of 45 days beginning with the day on which the relevant notice is given.

(3) For the purposes of subsection (2) the "relevant notice" is—

(a) in the case of a review by virtue of subsection (1) of section 33, the notice mentioned in that subsection; or

(b) in any other case, the demand notice in question.

(4) Nothing in subsection (1) prevents the Commissioners from agreeing on request to review a decision in a case where the notice required by that subsection is not given within the permitted period.

(5) A person may give notice under section 33 requiring a decision to be reviewed a second or subsequent time only if—

(a) the grounds on which he requires the further review are that the Commissioners did not, on any previous review, have the opportunity to consider any particular facts or matters; and

(b) he does not, on the further review, require the Commissioners to consider any facts or matters which were considered on a previous review of the decision, except in so far as they are relevant to any issue to which the facts or matters not previously considered relate.

[Finance Act 2003, s 34.]

8–7257R   35. Powers of Commissioners on a review.   (1) Where the Commissioners—

(a) are required in accordance with section 33 to review a decision, or

(b) agree to do so on such a request as is mentioned in section 34(4),

the following provisions of this section apply.

(2) On any such review, the Commissioners may—

(a) confirm the decision,

(b) withdraw the decision, or

(c) vary the decision.

(3) Where the Commissioners withdraw or vary the decision, they may also take such further steps (if any) in consequence of the withdrawal or variation as they may consider appropriate.

(4) If the Commissioners do not within the permitted period give notice of their determination on the review to the person who required the review or his representative, they shall be taken for the purposes of this Part to have confirmed the decision.

(5) For the purposes of subsection (4), the "permitted period" is the period of 45 days beginning with the day on which the review—

(a) is required by the person or his representative in accordance with section 33, or

(b) is agreed to by the Commissioners as mentioned in section 34(4).

[Finance Act 2003, s 35.]

Appeals

8–7257S   36. Appeals to a tribunal.   (1) Where the Commissioners—

(a) are required in accordance with section 33 to review a decision, or

(b) agree to do so on such a request as is mentioned in section 34(4),

an appeal lies to an appeal tribunal against any decision by the Commissioners on the review (including any confirmation under section 35(4)).

(2) An appeal lies under this section only if the appellant is one of the following persons—

(a) the person who required the review in question,

(b) where the person who required the review in question did so as representative of another person, that other person, or

(c) a representative of a person falling within paragraph (a) or (b).

(3) The powers of an appeal tribunal on an appeal under this section include—

(a) power to quash or vary a decision; and

(b) power to substitute the tribunal's own decision for any decision so quashed.

(4) On an appeal under this section—

(a) the burden of proof as to the matters mentioned in section 25(1) or 26(1) lies on the Commissioners; but

(b) it is otherwise for the appellant to show that the grounds on which any such appeal is brought have been established.

[Finance Act 2003, s 36.]

8–7257T   37. Appeal tribunals.   (1) Sections 85 and 87 of the Value Added Tax Act 1994 (c 23) (settling of appeals by agreement and enforcement of decisions of tribunal) have effect as if—

(a) any reference to section 83 of that Act included a reference to section 36 above, and

(b) any reference to VAT included a reference to any relevant tax or duty.

(2) The provision that may be made by rules under paragraph 9 of Schedule 12 to the Value Added Tax Act 1994 (rules of procedure for tribunals) includes provision for costs awarded against an appellant on an appeal by virtue of this Part to be recoverable as if the amount awarded were an amount of customs duty which the appellant is required to pay.

[Finance Act 2003, s 37.]

Evidence

8–7257U   38. Admissibility of certain statements and documents.   (1) Statements made or documents produced by or on behalf of a person are not inadmissible in—

(a) any criminal proceedings against that person in respect of any offence in connection with or in relation to any relevant tax or duty, or

(b) any proceedings against that person for the recovery of any sum due from him in connection with or in relation to any relevant tax or duty,

by reason only that any of the matters specified in subsection (2) has been drawn to his attention and that he was, or may have been, induced by that matter having been brought to his attention to make the statements or produce the documents.

(2) The matters mentioned in subsection (1) are—

(a) that the Commissioners have power, in relation to any relevant tax or duty, to demand by means of a written notice an amount by way of a civil penalty, instead of instituting criminal proceedings;

(b) that it is the Commissioners' practice, without being able to give an undertaking as to whether they will make such a demand in any case, to be influenced in determining whether to make such a demand by the fact (where it is the case) that a person has made a full confession of any dishonest conduct to which he has been a party and has given full facilities for an investigation;

(c) that the Commissioners or, on appeal, an appeal tribunal have power to reduce a penalty under section 25, as provided in subsection (1) of section 29; and

(d) that, in determining the extent of such a reduction in the case of any person, the Commissioners or tribunal will have regard to the extent of the co-operation which he has given to the Commissioners in their investigation.

(3) References in this section to a relevant tax or duty do not include a reference to customs duty of a preferential tariff country.

[Finance Act 2003, s 38.]

Miscellaneous and supplementary

8–7257V   39. Service of notices.   Any notice to be given to any person for the purposes of this Part may be given by sending it by post in a letter addressed to that person or his representative at the last or usual residence or place of business of that person or representative.

[Finance Act 2003, s 39.]

8–7257W   40. Penalties not to be deducted for income tax or corporation tax purposes.   In section 827 of the Taxes Act 1988 (no deduction for penalties etc) after subsection (1D) insert—

"(1E)   Where a person is liable to make a payment by way of a penalty under section 25 or 26 of the Finance Act 2003 (evasion of, or contravention of relevant rule relating to, certain taxes and duties under the management of the Commissioners of Customs and Excise etc) the payment shall not be allowed as a deduction in computing any income, profits or losses for any tax purposes.".

[Finance Act 2003, s 40.]

8–7257X   41. Regulations and orders.   (1) Any power conferred on the Treasury by this Part to make regulations or an order includes power—

(*a*)   to make different provision for different cases, and

(*b*)   to make incidental, consequential, supplemental or transitional provision or savings.

(2)   Any power conferred on the Treasury by this Part to make regulations or an order shall be exercisable by statutory instrument.

(3)   Any statutory instrument containing regulations under this Part shall be subject to annulment in pursuance of a resolution of the House of Commons.

[Finance Act 2003, s 41.]

Transferred Excise Duties (Application of Enactments) Order 1952[1]
(SI 1952/2205)

8–7258   1. In the case of any local authority to whom the power to levy any excise duty has been transferred under s 6 of the Finance Act, 1908, or s 15 of the Finance Act, 1949, the provisions of the Customs and Excise Act, 1952, set out in the Schedule to this Order shall have effect in relation to that authority and their officers with respect to the transferred duties and the licences on which those duties are imposed as they have effect in relation to the Commissioners and officers of Customs and Excise with respect to other excise duties and licences, subject, however, to the modifications, if any, specified in that Schedule.

---

1. Made by the Lords Commissioners of Her Majesty's Treasury pursuant to s 313 of the Customs and Excise Act 1952 (now s 176 of the Customs and Excise Management Act 1979).
The Transferred Excise Duties (Application of Enactments) Order 1963, SI 1963/2014, applies to local authorities so much of s 4(1) of the Customs and Excise Act 1952 (now s 8 of the Customs and Excise Management Act 1979) as is necessary to enable a local authority to delegate to a duly authorised officer the functions of ordering the institution of proceedings in connection with transferred duties and of authorising the continuance of such proceedings by another officer in specified circumstances. The Order no longer applies to money lenders' and pawnbrokers' licences (Consumer Credit Act 1974).

SCHEDULE
SECTIONS OF CUSTOMS AND EXCISE ACT, 1952, TO APPLY IN RELATION TO TRANSFERRED EXCISE DUTIES

8–7259   Section 5[1], so far as it relates to a constable.
Section 10[2].
Section 233[3], except for the words in subsection (1) from "shall be" to "direct and".
Sections 235[4], 236[5], 239[6], 281[7] and 282[8].
Section 283[9], except for subsections (1) and (3).
Sections 284[10] and 286[11].
Section 287[12], so, however, as not to prejudice the operation of section 27[13] of the Justices of the Peace Act, 1949.
In relation to duties levied in England or Wales, section 288[14], except for paragraph (*d*).
In section 290[15], subsection (1) except for paragraphs (*b*), (*e*), and (*f*).
In section 305[16], subsections (1) and (3).

---

1. This relates to assistance to be rendered by police.
2. This relates to obstruction of officers. See now s 11 of the Customs and Excise Management Act 1979.
3. This relates to the form and production of excise licences. See now s 16 of the Customs and Excise Management Act 1979.
4. This relates to the renewal of excise licences. See now s 101 of the Customs and Excise Management Act 1979.
5. This relates to the transfer and removal of excise licences. See now s 103 of the Customs and Excise Management Act 1979.
6. This relates to offences in connection with excise licences. See now s 104 of the Customs and Excise Management Act 1979.
7. This relates to the institution of proceedings. See now s 106 of the Customs and Excise Management Act 1979.
8. This relates to the service of process. See now s 145 of the Customs and Excise Management Act 1979.
9. This relates to proceedings for offences. See now s 146 of the Customs and Excise Management Act 1979.
10. This relates to venue. See now s 147 of the Customs and Excise Management Act 1979.
11. Incidental provisions as to legal proceedings including the mitigation of penalties by the court. See now s 148 of the Customs and Excise Management Act 1979.
12. This relates to the application of penalties. See now s 150 of the Customs and Excise Management Act 1979.

13. The reference to s 287 seems to be a transitional provision which ceased to be effective when s 27 of the Justices of the Peace Act 1949 (now s 61 of the Justices of the Peace Act 1979) came into operation on 1 April, 1953. See now s 151 of the Customs and Excise Management Act 1979.

14. This relates to the prosecutor's power to mitigate penalties after conviction. See now s 152 of the Customs and Excise Management Act 1979.

15. This relates to matters of proof. See now s 154 of the Customs and Excise Management Act 1979.

16. General provisions as to offences and penalties. See now s 171 of the Customs and Excise Management Act 1979.

Customs and Excise (Transit) Regulations 1993[1]

(SI 1993/1353 amended by SI 1993/3014)

8–7260   **1.** *Citation, commencement and interpretation*

1. Made by the Commissioners of Customs and Excise, in exercise of the powers conferred upon them by s 2(2) of the European Communities Act 1972.

8–7261   **2.** In these Regulations—

"Consignment Note CIM" and "TR transfer note"—

    (*a*) in relation to Community transit, have the same meanings as in Articles 413 and 427 respectively of Commission Regulation (EEC) No 2454/93[1];

    (*b*) in relation to common transit, have the same meanings as in Articles 72 and 86 respectively of Appendix II to the Convention[2];

"the Convention" means the Convention of 20th May 1987 on a common transit procedure entered into by the Economic Community, Austria, Finland, Iceland, Norway, Sweden and the Swiss Confederation[3];

"the customs and excise Acts" has the same meaning as in section 1 of the Customs and Excise Management Act 1979;

"relevant Community provision" means—

    (*a*) in relation to Community transit, any provision of a Community Regulation specified in the first or second columns of the Schedule to these Regulations and shall include any such provisions as applied by—

        (i) Article 163(3) of Council Regulation (EEC) No 2913/92 and Article 381(2) of Commission Regulation (EEC) No 2454/93[4];

        (ii) Articles 422(1) and 437(1) of Commission Regulation (EEC) No 2454/93;

    (*b*) in relation to common transit, any provision of the Convention specified in the third or fourth columns of the Schedule to these Regulations and shall include any such provisions as applied by—

        (i) Article 37(3) of Appendix I[5] to the Convention;

        (ii) Articles 81(1) and 96(1) of Appendix II to the Convention.

1. OJ No L132, 16.5.92, p 1. This Regulation has been amended by Commission Regulation (EEC) No 3712/92 (OJ No L378, 23.12.92, p 15).

2. OJ No L226, 13.8.87, p 2. Appendix II was substituted by Article 1 of, and Annex I to, Decision No 2/92 of the EEC-EFTA Joint Committee on Common Transit (OJ No L402, 31.12.92, p 9).

3. OJ No L226, 13.8.87, p 2.

4. OJ No L262, 26.9.90, p 1.

5. OJ No L402, 31.12.92. Appendix I was substituted by Article 1 of, and Annex I to, Decision No 1/91 of the EEC-EFTA Joint Committee on Common Transit (OJ No L402, 31.12.92, p 1).

Offences, penalty and forfeiture

8–7262   **3.** In the event of any contravention or failure to comply with—

    (*a*) any relevant Community provision, or

    (*b*) any requirement or condition imposed by or under any such provision,

the person responsible for the contravention or failure and the person then in charge of the goods shall each be liable on summary conviction to a penalty of **level 5** on the standard scale and any goods in respect of which the offence was committed shall be liable to forfeiture.

Supplementary

8–7263   **4.** (1) Section 139 of and Schedule 3 to the Customs and Excise Management Act 1979 (detention, seizure and condemnation of goods) shall apply to any goods liable to forfeiture under regulation 3 above as if the goods were liable to forfeiture under the customs and excise Acts.

(2) Sections 144 to 148 and 150 to 155 of the Customs and Excise Management Act 1979 (proceedings for offences, mitigation of penalties, proof and other matters) shall apply in relation to offences and penalties under regulation 3 above and proceedings for such offences or for

condemnation of anything as being forfeited under that regulation as they apply in relation to offences and penalties and proceedings for offences or for condemnation under the customs and excise Acts.

8–7264   5. *Revocation*

8–7265

Regulation 2

SCHEDULE
RELEVANT COMMUNITY PROVISIONS

EC REGULATIONS (COMMUNITY TRANSIT)			THE CONVENTION (1) (COMMON TRANSIT)	
(1) COUNCIL REGULATION (EEC) No 2913/92	(2) COMMISSION REGULATION (EEC) No 2454/93	(3) APPENDIX I	(4) APPENDIX II	(5) SUBJECT MATTER OF PROVISIONS
Article 96(1)	Article 356(1)	Article 11(1) (a) and (b)		Principal's responsibility for production of goods and T1 document at office of destination and for observance of time limits, identification measures and provisions relating, as the case may be, to Community transit or common transit.
Article 96(2)		Article 11(2)		Responsibility of carrier and recipient for production of goods at office of destination and for observance of time limits and identification measures.
	Article 350	Article 15(1)		Copies of T1 document to accompany the goods.
	Article 352(1)	Article 18(1)		Consignment and copies of T1 document to be produced at each office of transit.
	Article 352(2)	Article 18(2)		Carrier to give each office of transit a transit advice note.
	Article 354(1) 1st sentence	Article 20(1) 1st sentence		Transfer of goods under supervision of customs authorities.
Article 94(1)	Article 359	Article 24(1) 1st sub-paragraph		Principal to furnish guarantee.
	Article 219(2)		Article 20(1)	Document for dispatch or export of goods to be presented to office of departure together with declaration to which it relates.
	Article 464			Restriction etc on exportation from Community to be stated on Community transit document.
	Article 465(1)			When restricted etc goods placed under a transit procedure other than the Community transit procedure Control Copy T5 to be endorsed with statement of restriction on export.
	Article 419(1)		Article 78(1)	Consignment Note CIM to be produced at office of departure.
	Article 421(1)		Article 80(1)	Railway authority to forward to office of destination sheets of Consignment Note CIM.
	Article 434(1)		Article 93(1)	TR transfer note to be produced at office of departure.
	Article 434(7)		Article 93(10)	TR transfer note to be produced at office of destination.
	Article 436(1)		Article 95(1)	Transport undertaking to deliver to office of destination sheets of TR transfer note.
	Article 405(1)(a)		Article 110(1)(a)	Authorised consignor to comply with simplified formalities applicable at the office of departure and conditions of authorisation.

	EC REGULATIONS (COMMUNITY TRANSIT)		THE CONVENTION (1) (COMMON TRANSIT)	
(1) COUNCIL REGULATION (EEC) No 2913/92	(2) COMMISSION REGULATION (EEC) No 2454/93	(3) APPENDIX I	(4) APPENDIX II	(5) SUBJECT MATTER OF PROVISIONS
	Article 409(1)		Article 114(1)	Authorised consignee to notify excess quantities, shortages etc, and to send documents to office of destination.
	Article 395(1)(*a*)		Article 125(1)(*a*)	Formalities to be complied with by authorised consignor under T2L simplified procedure.
	Article 472(2)			Goods to be put to declared use and dispatched to a declared destination.
	Article 493(1)			Authorised consignor to comply with simplified formalities applicable at office of departure and conditions of authorisation.

1. OJ No L226, 13.8.87, p 2. The Appendices to the Convention were substituted by Decision Nos 1/91 and 2/92 of the EEC-EFTA Joint Committee on Common Transit (OJ No L402, 31.12.92, pp 1 and 9 respectively).

DATA PROTECTION

8–7266   This title contains the following statutes—

     8–7337   COMPUTER MISUSE ACT 1990
     8–7355   DATA PROTECTION ACT 1998

Computer Misuse Act 1990

(1990 c 18)

Computer misuse offences

8–7337   **1. Unauthorised access to computer material.**   (1) A person is guilty of an offence[1] if—

(*a*)   he causes a computer to perform any function with intent to secure access to any program or data held in any computer;

(*b*)   the access he intends to secure is unauthorised; and

(*c*)   he knows at the time when he causes the computer to perform the function that that is the case.

(2) The intent a person has to have to commit an offence under this section need not be directed at—

(*a*)   any particular program or data;

(*b*)   a program or data of any particular kind; or

(*c*)   a program or data held in any particular computer.

(3) A person guilty of an offence under this section shall be liable on summary conviction to imprisonment for a term not exceeding **six months** or to a fine not exceeding **level 5** on the standard scale or to both.

[Computer Misuse Act 1990, s 1.]

---

1. Section 1 of this Act is not concerned with authority to assess kinds of data, but rather with authority to assess the actual data involved (*R v Bow Street Metropolitan Stipendiary Magistrates, ex p United States Government* [2000] 2 AC 216, [1999] 4 All ER 1, [1999] 3 WLR 620, HL). The computer which the person causes to perform any function with the required intent does not have to be a different computer from the one into which he intends to secure unauthorised access to any program or data held therein (*A-G's Reference (No 1 of 1991)* [1993] QB 94, [1992] 3 All ER 897, CA).

A person who does not have control access but who accesses a computer at the point of entry does not commit an offence under s 1 if he obtains access of any of the kinds set out in s 17(2)(*a*) to (*d*), post, and he has the consent to do so of a person having control access (*DPP v Bignell* [1998] 1 Cr App Rep 1, 161 JP 541, [1998] Crim LR 53).

8–7338   **2. Unauthorised access with intent to commit or facilitate commission of further offences.**   (1) A person is guilty of an offence under this section if he commits an offence under section 1 above ("the unauthorised access offence") with intent—

(*a*)   to commit an offence to which this section applies; or

(*b*)   to facilitate the commission of such an offence (whether by himself or by any other person);

and the offence he intends to commit or facilitate is referred to below in this section as the further offence.

(2) This section applies to offences—

(a) for which the sentence is fixed by law; or

(b) for which a person of twenty-one years of age or over (not previously convicted)* may be sentenced to imprisonment for a term of five years (or, in England and Wales, might be so sentenced but for the restrictions imposed by section 33 of the Magistrates' Courts Act 1980).

(3) It is immaterial for the purposes of this section whether the further offence is to be committed on the same occasion as the unauthorised access offence or on any future occasion.

(4) A person may be guilty of an offence under this section even though the facts are such that the commission of the further offence is impossible.

(5) A person guilty of an offence under this section shall be liable[1]—

(a) on summary conviction, to imprisonment for a term not exceeding **six months** or to a fine not exceeding the **statutory maximum** or to both; and

(b) on conviction on indictment, to imprisonment for a term not exceeding **five years** or to a **fine** or to both.

[Computer Misuse Act 1990, s 2.]

---

*Amended by the Criminal Justice and Court Services Act 2000, Sch 7 from a date to be appointed.
1. For procedure in respect of this offence which is triable either way, see the Magistrates' Courts Act 1980, ss 17A–21, in PART I: MAGISTRATES' COURTS, PROCEDURE, ante.

8–7339   3. Unauthorised modification of computer material.   (1) A person is guilty of an offence if—

(a) he does any act which causes an unauthorised modification of the contents of any computer; and

(b) at the time when he does the act he has the requisite intent and the requisite knowledge.

(2) For the purposes of subsection (1)(b) above the requisite intent is an intent to cause a modification of the contents of any computer and by so doing—

(a) to impair the operation of any computer;

(b) to prevent or hinder access to any program or data held in any computer; or

(c) to impair the operation of any such program or the reliability of any such data[1].

(3) The intent need not be directed at—

(a) any particular computer;

(b) any particular program or data or a program or data of any particular kind; or

(c) any particular modification or a modification of any particular kind.

(4) For the purposes of subsection (1)(b) above the requisite knowledge is knowledge that any modification he intends to cause is unauthorised.

(5) It is immaterial for the purposes of this section whether an unauthorised modification or any intended effect of it of a kind mentioned in subsection (2) above is, or is intended to be, permanent or merely temporary.

(6) For the purposes of the Criminal Damage Act 1971 a modification of the contents of a computer shall not be regarded as damaging any computer or computer storage medium unless its effect on that computer or computer storage medium impairs its physical condition.

(7) A person guilty of an offence under this section shall be liable[2]—

(a) on summary conviction, to imprisonment for a term not exceeding **six months** or to a fine not exceeding the **statutory maximum** or to both; and

(b) on conviction on indictment, to imprisonment for a term not exceeding **five years** or to a **fine** or to both.

[Computer Misuse Act 1990, s 3.]

---

1. This offence is not confined to damage to the computer so that it does not record information fed into it but includes the feeding in of information which affects the reliability of the information stored in the computer such as where a bogus e-mail which by misusing the password purported to be from the password holder when it was not (*Re Zezev* [2002] EWHC Admin 589, [2002] Crim LR 648).
2. For procedure in respect of this offence which is triable either way, see the Magistrates' Courts Act 1980, ss 17A–21, in PART I: MAGISTRATES' COURTS, PROCEDURE, ante.

Jurisdiction

8–7340   4. Territorial scope of offences under this Act.   (1) Except as provided below in this section, it is immaterial for the purposes of any offence under section 1 or 3 above—

(a) whether any act or other event proof of which is required for conviction of the offence occurred in the home country concerned; or

(b) whether the accused was in the home country concerned at the time of any such act or event.

(2) Subject to subsection (3) below, in the case of such an offence at least one significant link with domestic jurisdiction must exist in the circumstances of the case for the offence to be committed.

(3) There is no need for any such link to exist for the commission of an offence under section 1 above to be established in proof of an allegation to that effect in proceedings for an offence under section 2 above.

(4) Subject to section 8 below, where—

(*a*) any such link does in fact exist in the case of an offence under section 1 above; and

(*b*) commission of that offence is alleged in proceedings for an offence under section 2 above;

section 2 above shall apply as if anything the accused intended to do or facilitate in any place outside the home country concerned which would be an offence to which section 2 applies if it took place in the home country concerned were the offence in question.

(5) This section is without prejudice to any jurisdiction exercisable by a court in Scotland apart from this section.

(6) References in this Act to the home country concerned are references—

(*a*) in the application of this Act to England and Wales, to England and Wales;

(*b*) in the application of this Act to Scotland, to Scotland; and

(*c*) in the application of this Act to Northern Ireland, to Northern Ireland.

[Computer Misuse Act 1990, s 4.]

8–7341   5. Significant links with domestic jurisdiction.   (1) The following provisions of this section apply for the interpretation of section 4 above.

(2) In relation to an offence under section 1, either of the following is a significant link with domestic jurisdiction—

(*a*) that the accused was in the home country concerned at the time when he did the act which caused the computer to perform the function; or

(*b*) that any computer containing any program or data to which the accused secured or intended to secure unauthorised access by doing that act was in the home country concerned at that time.

(3) In relation to an offence under section 3, either of the following is a significant link with domestic jurisdiction—

(*a*) that the accused was in the home country concerned at the time when he did the act which caused the unauthorised modification; or

(*b*) that the unauthorised modification took place in the home country concerned.

[Computer Misuse Act 1990, s 5.]

8–7342   6. Territorial scope of inchoate offences related to offences under this Act.   (1) On a charge of conspiracy to commit an offence under this Act the following questions are immaterial to the accused's guilt—

(*a*) the question where any person became a party to the conspiracy; and

(*b*) the question whether any act, omission or other event occurred in the home country concerned.

(2) On a charge of attempting to commit an offence under section 3 above the following questions are immaterial to the accused's guilt—

(*a*) the question where the attempt was made; and

(*b*) the question whether it had an effect in the home country concerned.

(3) On a charge of incitement to commit an offence under this Act the question where the incitement took place is immaterial to the accused's guilt.

(4) This section does not extend to Scotland.

[Computer Misuse Act 1990, s 6.]

8–7343   7. Territorial scope of inchoate offences related to offences under external law corresponding to offences under this Act.   (1) and (2) (*Repealed*).

(3) *Consequential amendments.*

(4) Subject to section 8 below, if any act done by a person in England and Wales would amount to the offence of incitement to commit an offence under this Act but for the fact that what he had in view would not be an offence triable in England and Wales—

(*a*) what he had in view shall be treated as an offence under this Act for the purposes of any charge of incitement brought in respect of that act; and

(*b*) any such charge shall accordingly be triable in England and Wales.

[Computer Misuse Act 1990, s 7 as amended by the Criminal Justice (Terrorism and Conspiracy) Act 1998, Sch 2.]

8–7344   8. Relevance of external law.   (1) A person is guilty of an offence triable by virtue of section 4(4) above only if what he intended to do or facilitate would involve the commission of an offence under the law in force where the whole or any part of it was intended to take place.

(2) *(Repealed)*.

(3) A person is guilty of an offence triable by virtue of section 1(1A) of the Criminal Attempts Act 1981 or by virtue of section 7(4) above only if what he had in view would involve the commission of an offence under the law in force where the whole or any part of it was intended to take place.

(4) Conduct punishable under the law in force in any place is an offence under that law for the purposes of this section, however it is described in that law.

(5) Subject to subsection (7) below, a condition specified in subsection (1) or (3) above shall be taken to be satisfied unless not later than rules of court may provide the defence serve on the prosecution a notice—

(a) stating that, on the facts as alleged with respect to the relevant conduct, the condition is not in their opinion satisfied;
(b) showing their grounds for that opinion; and
(c) requiring the prosecution to show that it is satisfied.

(6) In subsection (5) above "the relevant conduct" means—

(a) where the condition in subsection (1) above is in question, what the accused intended to do or facilitate;
(b) *(Repealed)*.
(c) where the condition in subsection (3) above is in question, what the accused had in view.

(7) The court, if it thinks fit, may permit the defence to require the prosecution to show that the condition is satisfied without the prior service of a notice under subsection (5) above.

(8) *Scotland*.

(9) In the Crown Court the question whether the condition is satisfied shall be decided by the judge alone.

(10) *Scotland*.

[Computer Misuse Act 1990, s 8 as amended by the Criminal Justice (Terrorism and Conspiracy) Act 1998, Schs 1 and 2.]

8-7345   9. British citizenship immaterial.   (1) In any proceedings brought in England and Wales in respect of any offence to which this section applies it is immaterial to guilt whether or not the accused was a British citizen at the time of any act, omission or other event proof of which is required for conviction of the offence.

(2) This section applies to the following offences—

(a) any offence under this Act;
(b) *(Repealed)*;
(c) any attempt to commit an offence under section 3 above; and
(d) incitement to commit an offence under this Act.

[Computer Misuse Act 1990, s 9 as amended by the Criminal Justice (Terrorism and Conspiracy) Act 1998, Schs 1 and 2.]

Miscellaneous and general

8-7346   10. Saving for certain law enforcement powers.   Section 1(1) above has effect without prejudice to the operation—

(a) in England and Wales of any enactment relating to powers of inspection, search or seizure; and
(b) in Scotland of any enactment or rule of law relating to powers of examination, search or seizure

and nothing designed to indicate a withholding of consent to access to any program or data from persons as enforcement officers shall have effect to make access unauthorised for the purposes of the said section 1(1).

In this section "enforcement officer" means a constable or other person charged with the duty of investigating offences; and withholding consent from a person "as" an enforcement officer of any description includes the operation, by the person entitled to control access, of rules whereby enforcement officers of that description are, as such, disqualified from membership of a class of persons who are authorised to have access.

[Computer Misuse Act 1990, s 10 as amended by the Criminal Justice and Public Order Act 1994, s 162.]

8-7347   11. Proceedings for offences under section 1.   (1) A magistrates' court shall have jurisdiction to try an offence under section 1 above if—

(a) the accused was within its commission area at the time when he did the act which caused the computer to perform the function; or (*b*) any computer containing any program or data to which the accused secured or intended to secure unauthorised access by doing that act was in its commission area at that time.

(2) Subject to subsection (3) below, proceedings for an offence under section 1 above may be brought within a period of six months from the date on which evidence sufficient in the opinion of the prosecutor to warrant the proceedings came to his knowledge[1].

(3) No such proceedings shall be brought by virtue of this section more than three years after the commission of the offence.

(4) For the purposes of this section, a certificate signed by or on behalf of the prosecutor and stating the date on which evidence sufficient in his opinion to warrant the proceedings came to his knowledge shall be conclusive evidence of that fact.

(5) A certificate stating that matter and purporting to be so signed shall be deemed to be so signed unless the contrary is proved.

(6) (*Repealed*).

(7) This section does not extend to Scotland.

[Computer Misuse Act 1990, s 11 as amended by the Justices of the Peace Act 1997, Sch 5 and the Access To Justice Act 1990, Sch 15].

---

1. Time begins to run once evidence comes to the knowledge of the prosecutor and not when the prosecutor comes to the opinion that the evidence is sufficient to warrant proceedings (*Morgans v DPP* [1999] 1 WLR 968, [1999] 2 Cr App Rep 99, sub nom *Morgans v Southwark Crown Court* (1998) 163 JP 543, DC).

8–7348   12. Conviction of an offence under section 1 in proceedings for an offence under section 2 or 3.   (1) If on the trial on indictment of a person charged with—

(*a*) an offence under section 2 above; or
(*b*) an offence under section 3 above or any attempt to commit such an offence;

the jury find him not guilty of the offence charged, they may find him guilty of an offence under section 1 above if on the facts shown he could have been found guilty of that offence in proceedings for that offence brought before the expiry of any time limit under section 11 above applicable to such proceedings.

(2) The Crown Court shall have the same powers and duties in relation to a person who is by virtue of this section convicted before it of an offence under section 1 above as a magistrates' court would have on convicting him of the offence.

(3) This section is without prejudice to section 6(3) of the Criminal Law Act 1967 (conviction of alternative indictable offence on trial on indictment).

(4) This section does not extend to Scotland.

[Computer Misuse Act 1990, s 12.]

8–7349   13. *Scotland.*

8–7350   14. Search warrants for offences under section 1.   (1) Where a circuit judge★ is satisfied by information on oath given by a constable that there are reasonable grounds for believing—

(*a*) that an offence under section 1 above has been or is about to be committed in any premises; and
(*b*) that evidence that such an offence has been or is about to be committed is in those premises;

he may issue a warrant authorising a constable to enter and search the premises, using such reasonable force as is necessary.

(2) The power conferred by subsection (1) above does not extend to authorising a search for material of the kinds mentioned in section 9(2) of the Police and Criminal Evidence Act 1984 (privileged, excluded and special procedure material).

(3) A warrant under this section—

(*a*) may authorise persons to accompany any constable executing the warrant; and
(*b*) remains in force for twenty-eight days from the date of its issue.

(4) In executing a warrant issued under this section a constable may seize an article if he reasonably believes that it is evidence that an offence under section 1 above has been or is about to be committed.

(5) In this section "premises" includes land, buildings, movable structures, vehicles, vessels, aircraft and hovercraft.

(6) This section does not extend to Scotland.

[Computer Misuse Act 1990, s 14.]

★**Words "or a District Judge (Magistrates' Courts)" inserted by the Courts Act 2003, Sch 4, from a date to be appointed.**

8–7351 15. Extradition where Schedule 1 to the Extradition Act 1989 applies. *Repealed.*

8–7352 16. *Northern Ireland.*

8–7353 17. Interpretation.   (1) The following provisions of this section apply for the interpretation of this Act.

(2) A person secures access to any program or data held in a computer if by causing a computer to perform any function he—

(*a*) alters or erases the program or data;

(*b*) copies or moves it to any storage medium other than that in which it is held or to a different location in the storage medium in which it is held;

(*c*) uses it; or

(*d*) has it output from the computer in which it is held (whether by having it displayed or in any other manner);

and references to access to a program or data (and to an intent to secure such access) shall be read accordingly.

(3) For the purposes of subsection (2)(*c*) above a person uses a program if the function he causes the computer to perform—

(*a*) causes the program to be executed; or

(*b*) is itself a function of the program.

(4) For the purposes of subsection (2)(*d*) above—

(*a*) a program is output if the instructions of which it consists are output; and

(*b*) the form in which any such instructions or any other data is output (and in particular whether or not it represents a form in which, in the case of instructions, they are capable of being executed or, in the case of data, it is capable of being processed by a computer) is immaterial.

(5) Access of any kind by any person to any program or data held in a computer is unauthorised if—

(*a*) he is not himself entitled to control[1] access of the kind in question to the program or data; and

(*b*) he does not have consent to access by him of the kind in question to the program or data from any person who is so entitled but this subjection is subject to section 10.

(6) References to any program or data held in a computer include references to any program or data held in any removable storage medium which is for the time being in the computer; and a computer is to be regarded as containing any program or data held in any such medium.

(7) A modification of the contents of any computer takes place if, by the operation of any function of the computer concerned or any other computer—

(*a*) any program or data held in the computer concerned is altered or erased; or

(*b*) any program or data is added to its contents;

and any act which contributes towards causing such a modification shall be regarded as causing it.

(8) Such a modification is unauthorised if—

(*a*) the person whose act causes it is not himself entitled to determine whether the modification should be made; and

(*b*) he does not have consent to the modification from any person who is so entitled.

(9) References to the home country concerned shall be read in accordance with section 4(6) above.

(10) References to a program include references to part of a program.

[Computer Misuse Act 1990, s 17 as amended by the Criminal Justice and Public Order Act 1994, s 162.]

---

1. The word "control" is not used in the physical sense of the ability to operate or manipulate the computer, but rather to authorise and forbid (*R v Bow Street Metropolitan Stipendiary Magistrate, ex p United States Government* [2000] 2 AC 216, [1999] 4 All ER 1, [1999] 3 WLR 620, HL).

8–7354 18. Citation, commencement etc.   (1) This Act may be cited as the Computer Misuse Act 1990.

(2) This Act shall come into force at the end of the period of two months beginning with the day on which it is passed.

(3) An offence is not committed under this Act unless every act or other event proof of which is required for conviction of the offence takes place after this Act comes into force.

[Computer Misuse Act 1990, s 18.]

---

1. This Act was passed on 29 June 1990.

Data Protection Act 1998[1]

(1998 c 29)

PART I[2]
PRELIMINARY

8–7355 1. Basic interpretative provisions.   (1) In this Act, unless the context otherwise requires—

"data" means information which—

(*a*) is being processed by means of equipment operating automatically in response to instructions given for that purpose,

(*b*) is recorded with the intention that it should be processed by means of such equipment,

(*c*) is recorded as part of a relevant filing system or with the intention that it should form part of a relevant filing system,

(*d*) does not fall within paragraph (*a*), (*b*) or (*c*) but forms part of an accessible record as defined by section 68; or

(*e*) is recorded information held by a public authority and does not fall within any of paragraphs (*a*) to (*d*);

"data controller" means, subject to subsection (4), a person who (either alone or jointly or in common with other persons) determines the purposes for which and the manner in which any personal data are, or are to be, processed;

"data processor", in relation to personal data, means any person (other than an employee of the data controller) who processes the data on behalf of the data controller;

"data subject" means an individual who is the subject of personal data;

"personal data" means data which relate to a living individual who can be identified—

(*a*) from those data, or

(*b*) from those data and other information which is in the possession of, or is likely to come into the possession of, the data controller,

and includes any expression of opinion about the individual and any indication of the intentions of the data controller or any other person in respect of the individual;

"processing"[3], in relation to information or data, means obtaining, recording or holding the information or data or carrying out any operation or set of operations on the information or data, including—

(*a*) organisation, adaptation or alteration of the information or data,

(*b*) retrieval, consultation or use of the information or data,

(*c*) disclosure of the information or data by transmission, dissemination or otherwise making available, or

(*d*) alignment, combination, blocking, erasure or destruction of the information or data;

"public authority" means a public authority as defined by the Freedom of Information Act 2000 or a Scottish public authority as defined by the Freedom of Information (Scotland) Act 2002;

"relevant filing system" means any set of information relating to individuals to the extent that, although the information is not processed by means of equipment operating automatically in response to instructions given for that purpose, the set is structured, either by reference to individuals or by reference to criteria relating to individuals, in such a way that specific information relating to a particular individual is readily accessible.

(2) In this Act, unless the context otherwise requires—

(*a*) "obtaining" or "recording", in relation to personal data, includes obtaining or recording the information to be contained in the data, and

(*b*) "using" or "disclosing", in relation to personal data, includes using or disclosing the information contained in the data.

(3) In determining for the purposes of this Act whether any information is recorded with the intention—

(*a*) that it should be processed by means of equipment operating automatically in response to instructions given for that purpose, or

(*b*) that it should form part of a relevant filing system,

it is immaterial that it is intended to be so processed or to form part of such a system only after being transferred to a country or territory outside the European Economic Area.

(4) Where personal data are processed only for purposes for which they are required by or under any enactment to be processed, the person on whom the obligation to process the data is imposed by or under that enactment is for the purposes of this Act the data controller.

(5) In paragraph (*e*) of the definition of "data" in subsection (1), the reference to information "held" by a public authority shall be construed in accordance with section 3(2) of the Freedom of Information Act 2000 or (*Scotland*).

(6) Where

(a) section 7 of the Freedom of Information Act 2000 prevents Parts I to V of that Act or
(b) *Scotland*

from applying to certain information held by a public authority, that information is not to be treated for the purposes of paragraph (e) of the definition of "data" in subsection (1) as held by a public authority.
[Data Protection Act 1998, s 1 as amended by the Freedom of Information Act 2000, s 68.]

1. This Act makes new provision for the regulation of the processing of information relating to individuals, including the obtaining, holding, use or disclosure of such information.
   The Act is to be brought into force in accordance with s 75, post. At the date of going to press, with the exception of s 56, the whole of the Act had been brought into force.
2. Part I contains ss 1 to 6.
3. The Act is largely concerned with the automated processing of personal information, but while neither the activity of obtaining information and using it at the other end of the process might amount to "processing", the entire set of operations might fall within the scope of the legislation if the activity is carried on by, or at the instigation of a data controller for example, the publication of "hard copies" (such as newspapers) which reproduced data that has previously been processed by means of equipment operating automatically, see *Campbell v Mirror Group Newspapers* [2002] EWCA Civ 1373, [2003] QB 633, [2003] 1 All ER 224.

8–7356   2. Sensitive personal data.   In this Act "sensitive personal data" means personal data consisting of information as to—

(a) the racial or ethnic origin of the data subject,
(b) his political opinions,
(c) his religious beliefs or other beliefs of a similar nature,
(d) whether he is a member of a trade union (within the meaning of the Trade Union and Labour Relations (Consolidation) Act 1992,
(e) his physical or mental health or condition,
(f) his sexual life,
(g) the commission or alleged commission by him of any offence, or
(i) any proceedings for any offence committed or alleged to have been committed by him, the disposal of such proceedings or the sentence of any court in such proceedings.
[Data Protection Act 1998, s 2.]

8–7357   3. The special purposes.   In this Act "the special purposes" means any one or more of the following—

(a) the purposes of journalism,
(b) artistic purposes, and
(c) literary purposes.
[Data Protection Act 1998, s 3.]

8–7358   4. The data protection principles.   (1) References in this Act to the data protection principles are to the principles set out in Part I of Schedule 1.
   (2) Those principles are to be interpreted in accordance with Part II of Schedule 1.
   (3) Schedule 2 (which applies to all personal data) and Schedule 3 (which applies only to sensitive personal data) set out conditions applying for the purposes of the first principle; and Schedule 4 sets out cases in which the eighth principle does not apply.
   (4) Subject to section 27(1), it shall be the duty of a data controller to comply with the data protection principles in relation to all personal data with respect to which he is the data controller.
[Data Protection Act 1998, s 4.]

8–7359   5. Application of Act.   (1) Except as otherwise provided by or under section 54, this Act applies to a data controller in respect of any data only if—

(a) the data controller is established in the United Kingdom and the data are processed in the context of that establishment, or
(b) the data controller is established neither in the United Kingdom nor in any other EEA State but uses equipment in the United Kingdom for processing the data otherwise than for the purposes of transit through the United Kingdom.

   (2) A data controller falling within subsection (1)(b) must nominate for the purposes of this Act a representative established in the United Kingdom.
   (3) For the purposes of subsections (1) and (2), each of the following is to be treated as established in the United Kingdom—

(a) an individual who is ordinarily resident in the United Kingdom,
(b) a body incorporated under the law of, or of any part of, the United Kingdom,
(c) a partnership or other unincorporated association formed under the law of any part of the United Kingdom, and

(*d*) any person who does not fall within paragraph (*a*), (*b*) or (*c*) but maintains in the United Kingdom—

    (i) an office, branch or agency through which he carries on any activity, or
    (ii) a regular practice;

and the reference to establishment in any other EEA State has a corresponding meaning.
[Data Protection Act 1998, s 5.]

8–7360 6. The Commissioner and the Tribunal. (1) For the purposes of this Act and of the Freedom of Information Act 2000 there shall be an officer known as the Information Commissioner (in this Act referred to as "the Commissioner").

(2) The Commissioner shall be appointed by Her Majesty by Letters Patent.

(3) For the purposes of this Act and of the Freedom of Information Act 2000 there shall be a tribunal known as the Information Tribunal (in this Act referred to as "the Tribunal").

(4)–(7) *Further provisions with respect to the Commissioner and the Tribunal.*
[Data Protection Act 1998, s 6 as amended by the Freedom of Information Act 2000, Sch 2.]

PART II[1]
RIGHTS OF DATA SUBJECTS AND OTHERS

8–7361 7. Right of access to personal data. (1) Subject to the following provisions of this section and to sections 8, 9 and 9A, an individual is entitled—

(*a*) to be informed by any data controller whether personal data of which that individual is the data subject are being processed by or on behalf of that data controller,

(*b*) if that is the case, to be given by the data controller a description of—

    (i) the personal data of which that individual is the data subject,
    (ii) the purposes for which they are being or are to be processed, and
    (iii) the recipients or classes of recipients to whom they are or may be disclosed,

(*c*) to have communicated to him in an intelligible form—

    (i) the information constituting any personal data of which that individual is the data subject, and
    (ii) any information available to the data controller as to the source of those data, and

(*d*) where the processing by automatic means of personal data of which that individual is the data subject for the purpose of evaluating matters relating to him such as, for example, his performance at work, his creditworthiness, his reliability or his conduct, has constituted or is likely to constitute the sole basis for any decision significantly affecting him, to be informed by the data controller of the logic involved in that decision-taking.

(2) A data controller is not obliged to supply any information under subsection (1) unless he has received—

(*a*) a request in writing, and

(*b*) except in prescribed cases, such fee (not exceeding the prescribed maximum[2]) as he may require.

(3) Where a data controller—

(*a*) reasonably requires further information in order to satisfy himself as to the identity of the person making a request under this section and to locate the information which that person seeks, and

(*b*) has informed him of that requirement,

the data controller is not obliged to comply with the request unless he is supplied with that further information.

(4) Where a data controller cannot comply with the request without disclosing information relating to another individual who can be identified from that information, he is not obliged to comply with the request unless—

(*a*) the other individual has consented to the disclosure of the information to the person making the request, or

(*b*) it is reasonable in all the circumstances to comply with the request without the consent of the other individual.

(5) In subsection (4) the reference to information relating to another individual includes a reference to information identifying that individual as the source of the information sought by the request; and that subsection is not to be construed as excusing a data controller from communicating so much of the information sought by the request as can be communicated without disclosing the identity of the other individual concerned, whether by the omission of names or other identifying particulars or otherwise.

(6) In determining for the purposes of subsection (4)(*b*) whether it is reasonable in all the

circumstances to comply with the request without the consent of the other individual concerned, regard shall be had, in particular, to—

(a) any duty of confidentiality owed to the other individual,
(b) any steps taken by the data controller with a view to seeking the consent of the other individual,
(c) whether the other individual is capable of giving consent, and
(d) any express refusal of consent by the other individual.

(7) An individual making a request under this section may, in such cases as may be prescribed, specify that his request is limited to personal data of any prescribed description.

(8) Subject to subsection (4), a data controller shall comply with a request under this section promptly and in any event before the end of the prescribed period[2] beginning with the relevant day.

(9) If a court is satisfied on the application of any person who has made a request under the foregoing provisions of this section that the data controller in question has failed to comply with the request in contravention of those provisions, the court may order him to comply with the request.

(10) In this section—

"prescribed" means prescribed by the Secretary of State[3] by regulations;
"the prescribed maximum" means such amount as may be prescribed;
"the prescribed period" means forty days or such other period as may be prescribed;
"the relevant day", in relation to a request under this section, means the day on which the data controller receives the request or, if later, the first day on which the data controller has both the required fee and the information referred to in subsection (3).

(11) Different amounts or periods may be prescribed under this section in relation to different cases.

[Data Protection Act 1998, s 7, as amended by the Freedom of Information Act 2000, Sch 6, SI 2001/3500 and SI 2003/1887.]

---

1. Part II contains ss 7–15.
2. The Data Protection (Subject Access) (Fees and Miscellaneous Provisions) Order 2000, SI 2000/191 amended by SI 2001/3223 prescribe inter alia the extent of access to personal information to which an individual is entitled when he makes a request for data and the maximum fees which may be payable – £10 subject to specified exceptions.
3. The functions of the Minister, so far as exercisable in relation to Wales, have been transferred to the National Assembly for Wales, by the National Assembly for Wales (Transfer of Functions) Order 1999, SI 1999/672, art 2, Sch 1.

8–7362   8. Provisions supplementary to section 7.   (1) The Secretary of State may by regulations provide that, in such cases as may be prescribed, a request for information under any provision of subsection (1) of section 7 is to be treated as extending also to information under other provisions of that subsection.

(2) The obligation imposed by section 7(1)(c)(i) must be complied with by supplying the data subject with a copy of the information in permanent form unless—

(a) the supply of such a copy is not possible or would involve disproportionate effort, or
(b) the data subject agrees otherwise;

and where any of the information referred to in section 7(1)(c)(i) is expressed in terms which are not intelligible without explanation the copy must be accompanied by an explanation of those terms.

(3) Where a data controller has previously complied with a request made under section 7 by an individual, the data controller is not obliged to comply with a subsequent identical or similar request under that section by that individual unless a reasonable interval has elapsed between compliance with the previous request and the making of the current request.

(4) In determining for the purposes of subsection (3) whether requests under section 7 are made at reasonable intervals, regard shall be had to the nature of the data, the purpose for which the data are processed and the frequency with which the data are altered.

(5) Section 7(1)(d) is not to be regarded as requiring the provision of information as to the logic involved in any decision-taking if, and to the extent that, the information constitutes a trade secret.

(6) The information to be supplied pursuant to a request under section 7 must be supplied by reference to the data in question at the time when the request is received, except that it may take account of any amendment or deletion made between that time and the time when the information is supplied, being an amendment or deletion that would have been made regardless of the receipt of the request.

(7) For the purposes of section 7(4) and (5) another individual can be identified from the information being disclosed if he can be identified from that information, or from that and any other information which, in the reasonable belief of the data controller, is likely to be in, or to come into, the possession of the data subject making the request.

[Data Protection Act 1998, s 8, as amended by SI 2001/3500 and SI 2003/1887.]

8–7363   9. Application of section 7 where data controller is credit reference agency.
(1) Where the data controller is a credit reference agency, section 7 has effect subject to the provisions of this section.

(2) An individual making a request under section 7 may limit his request to personal data relevant

to his financial standing, and shall be taken to have so limited his request unless the request shows a contrary intention.

(3) Where the data controller receives a request under section 7 in a case where personal data of which the individual making the request is the data subject are being processed by or on behalf of the data controller, the obligation to supply information under that section includes an obligation to give the individual making the request a statement, in such form as may be prescribed by the Secretary of State by regulations, of the individual's rights—

(a) under section 159 of the Consumer Credit Act 1974 , and

(b) to the extent required by the prescribed form, under this Act.

[Data Protection Act 1998, s 9, as amended by SI 2001/3500 and SI 2003/1887.]

8–7363A 9A. Unstructured personal data held by public authorities. (1) In this section "unstructured personal data" means any personal data falling within paragraph (e) of the definition of "data" in section 1(1), other than information which is recorded as part of, or with the intention that it should form part of, any set of information relating to individuals to the extent that the set is structured by reference to individuals or by reference to criteria relating to individuals.

(2) A public authority is not obliged to comply with subsection (1) of section 7 in relation to any unstructured personal data unless the request under that section contains a description of the data.

(3) Even if the data are described by the data subject in his request, a public authority is not obliged to comply with subsection (1) of section 7 in relation to unstructured personal data if the authority estimates that the cost of complying with the request so far as relating to those data would exceed the appropriate limit.

(4) Subsection (3) does not exempt the public authority from its obligation to comply with paragraph (a) of section 7(1) in relation to the unstructured personal data unless the estimated cost of complying with that paragraph alone in relation to those data would exceed the appropriate limit.

(5) In subsections (3) and (4) "the appropriate limit" means such amount as may be prescribed by the Secretary of State by regulations[1], and different amounts may be prescribed in relation to different cases.

(6) Any estimate for the purposes of this section must be made in accordance with regulations under section 12(5) of the Freedom of Information Act 2000.

[Data Protection Act 1998, s 9A, as inserted by the Freedom of Information Act 2000, s 69 and amended by SI 2003/1887.]

---

1. See the Freedom of Information and Data Protection (Appropriate Limit and Fees) Regulations 2004, in the title CIVIL RIGHTS, ante.

8–7364 10. Right to prevent processing likely to cause damage or distress. (1) Subject to subsection (2), an individual is entitled at any time by notice in writing to a data controller to require the data controller at the end of such period as is reasonable in the circumstances to cease, or not to begin, processing, or processing for a specified purpose or in a specified manner, any personal data in respect of which he is the data subject, on the ground that, for specified reasons—

(a) the processing of those data or their processing for that purpose or in that manner is causing or is likely to cause substantial damage or substantial distress to him or to another, and

(b) that damage or distress is or would be unwarranted.

(2) Subsection (1) does not apply—

(a) in a case where any of the conditions in paragraphs 1 to 4 of Schedule 2 is met, or

(b) in such other cases as may be prescribed by the Secretary of State by order.

(3) The data controller must within twenty-one days of receiving a notice under subsection (1) ("the data subject notice") give the individual who gave it a written notice—

(a) stating that he has complied or intends to comply with the data subject notice, or

(b) stating his reasons for regarding the data subject notice as to any extent unjustified and the extent (if any) to which he has complied or intends to comply with it.

(4) If a court is satisfied, on the application of any person who has given a notice under subsection (1) which appears to the court to be justified (or to be justified to any extent), that the data controller in question has failed to comply with the notice, the court may order him to take such steps for complying with the notice (or for complying with it to that extent) as the court thinks fit.

(5) The failure by a data subject to exercise the right conferred by subsection (1) or section 11(1) does not affect any other right conferred on him by this Part.

[Data Protection Act 1998, s 10, as amended by SI 2001/3500 and SI 2003/1887.]

8–7365 11. Right to prevent processing for purposes of direct marketing. (1) An individual is entitled at any time by notice in writing to a data controller to require the data controller at the end of such period as is reasonable in the circumstances to cease, or not to begin, processing for the purposes of direct marketing personal data in respect of which he is the data subject.

(2) If the court is satisfied, on the application of any person who has given a notice under

subsection (1), that the data controller has failed to comply with the notice, the court may order him to take such steps for complying with the notice as the court thinks fit.

(2A) This section shall not apply in relation to the processing of such data as are mentioned in paragraph (1) of regulation 8 of the Telecommunications (Data Protection and Privacy) Regulations 1999 (processing of telecommunications billing data for certain marketing purposes) for the purposes mentioned in paragraph (2) of that regulation.

(3) In this section "direct marketing" means the communication (by whatever means) of any advertising or marketing material which is directed to particular individuals.

[Data Protection Act 1998, s 11, as amended by SI 1999/2093.]

8–7366 12. Rights in relation to automated decision-taking. (1) An individual is entitled at any time, by notice in writing to any data controller, to require the data controller to ensure that no decision taken by or on behalf of the data controller which significantly affects that individual is based solely on the processing by automatic means of personal data in respect of which that individual is the data subject for the purpose of evaluating matters relating to him such as, for example, his performance at work, his creditworthiness, his reliability or his conduct.

(2) Where, in a case where no notice under subsection (1) has effect, a decision which significantly affects an individual is based solely on such processing as is mentioned in subsection (1)—

  (*a*) the data controller must as soon as reasonably practicable notify the individual that the decision was taken on that basis, and
  (*b*) the individual is entitled, within twenty-one days of receiving that notification from the data controller, by notice in writing to require the data controller to reconsider the decision or to take a new decision otherwise than on that basis.

(3) The data controller must, within twenty-one days of receiving a notice under subsection (2)(*b*) ("the data subject notice") give the individual a written notice specifying the steps that he intends to take to comply with the data subject notice.

(4) A notice under subsection (1) does not have effect in relation to an exempt decision; and nothing in subsection (2) applies to an exempt decision.

(5) In subsection (4) "exempt decision" means any decision—

  (*a*) in respect of which the condition in subsection (6) and the condition in subsection (7) are met, or
  (*b*) which is made in such other circumstances as may be prescribed by the Secretary of State by order.

(6) The condition in this subsection is that the decision—

  (*a*) is taken in the course of steps taken—

    (i) for the purpose of considering whether to enter into a contract with the data subject,
    (ii) with a view to entering into such a contract, or
    (iii) in the course of performing such a contract, or

  (*b*) is authorised or required by or under any enactment.

(7) The condition in this subsection is that either—

  (*a*) the effect of the decision is to grant a request of the data subject, or
  (*b*) steps have been taken to safeguard the legitimate interests of the data subject (for example, by allowing him to make representations).

(8) If a court is satisfied on the application of a data subject that a person taking a decision in respect of him ("the responsible person") has failed to comply with subsection (1) or (2)(*b*), the court may order the responsible person to reconsider the decision, or to take a new decision which is not based solely on such processing as is mentioned in subsection (1).

(9) An order under subsection (8) shall not affect the rights of any person other than the data subject and the responsible person.

[Data Protection Act 1998, s 12, as amended by SI 2001/3500 and SI 2003/1887.]

8–7366A 12A. Rights of data subjects in relation to exempt manual data. (1) A data subject is entitled at any time by notice in writing—

  (*a*) to require the data controller to rectify, block, erase or destroy exempt manual data which are inaccurate or incomplete, or
  (*b*) to require the data controller to cease holding exempt manual data in a way incompatible with the legitimate purposes pursued by the data controller.

(2) A notice under subsection (1)(*a*) or (*b*) must state the data subject's reasons for believing that the data are inaccurate or incomplete or, as the case may be, his reasons for believing that they are held in a way incompatible with the legitimate purposes pursued by the data controller.

(3) If the court is satisfied, on the application of any person who has given a notice under subsection (1) which appears to the court to be justified (or to be justified to any extent) that the data

controller in question has failed to comply with the notice, the court may order him to take such steps for complying with the notice (or for complying with it to that extent) as the court thinks fit.

(4) In this section "exempt manual data" means—

(a) in relation to the first transitional period, as defined by paragraph 1(2) of Schedule 8, data to which paragraph 3 or 4 of that Schedule applies, and

(b) in relation to the second transitional period, as so defined, data to which paragraph 14 or 14A of that Schedule applies.

(5) For the purposes of this section personal data are incomplete if, and only if, the data, although not inaccurate, are such that their incompleteness would constitute a contravention of the third or fourth data protection principles, if those principles applied to the data.★

[Data Protection Act 1998, s 12A, as amended by the Freedom of Information Act 2000, Sch 13.]

★**Temporarily inserted by the Data Protection Act 1998, s 72, Sch 13, para 1, until 23 October 2007.**

8–7367 13. Compensation for failure to comply with certain requirements. (1) An individual who suffers damage by reason of any contravention by a data controller of any of the requirements of this Act is entitled to compensation from the data controller for that damage.

(2) An individual who suffers distress by reason of any contravention by a data controller of any of the requirements of this Act is entitled to compensation from the data controller for that distress if—

(a) the individual also suffers damage by reason of the contravention, or

(b) the contravention relates to the processing of personal data for the special purposes.

(3) In proceedings brought against a person by virtue of this section it is a defence to prove that he had taken such care as in all the circumstances was reasonably required to comply with the requirement concerned.

[Data Protection Act 1998, s 13.]

8–7368 14. Rectification, blocking, erasure and destruction. (1) If a court is satisfied on the application of a data subject that personal data of which the applicant is the subject are inaccurate, the court may order the data controller to rectify, block, erase or destroy those data and any other personal data in respect of which he is the data controller and which contain an expression of opinion which appears to the court to be based on the inaccurate data.

(2) Subsection (1) applies whether or not the data accurately record information received or obtained by the data controller from the data subject or a third party but where the data accurately record such information, then—

(a) if the requirements mentioned in paragraph 7 of Part II of Schedule 1 have been complied with, the court may, instead of making an order under subsection (1), make an order requiring the data to be supplemented by such statement of the true facts relating to the matters dealt with by the data as the court may approve, and

(b) if all or any of those requirements have not been complied with, the court may, instead of making an order under that subsection, make such order as it thinks fit for securing compliance with those requirements with or without a further order requiring the data to be supplemented by such a statement as is mentioned in paragraph (a).

(3) Where the court

(a) makes an order under subsection (1), or

(b) is satisfied on the application of a data subject that personal data of which he was the data subject and which have been rectified, blocked, erased or destroyed were inaccurate,

it may, where it considers it reasonably practicable, order the data controller to notify third parties to whom the data have been disclosed of the rectification, blocking, erasure or destruction.

(4) If a court is satisfied on the application of a data subject—

(a) that he has suffered damage by reason of any contravention by a data controller of any of the requirements of this Act in respect of any personal data, in circumstances entitling him to compensation under section 13, and

(b) that there is a substantial risk of further contravention in respect of those data in such circumstances,

the court may order the rectification, blocking, erasure or destruction of any of those data.

(5) Where the court makes an order under subsection (4) it may, where it considers it reasonably practicable, order the data controller to notify third parties to whom the data have been disclosed of the rectification, blocking, erasure or destruction.

(6) In determining whether it is reasonably practicable to require such notification as is mentioned in subsection (3) or (5) the court shall have regard, in particular, to the number of persons who would have to be notified.

[Data Protection Act 1998, s 14.]

8–7369 15. Jurisdiction and procedure. (1) The jurisdiction conferred by sections 7 to 14 is exercisable by the High Court or a county court or, in Scotland, by the Court of Session or the sheriff.

(2) For the purpose of determining any question whether an applicant under subsection (9) of section 7 is entitled to the information which he seeks (including any question whether any relevant data are exempt from that section by virtue of Part IV) a court may require the information constituting any data processed by or on behalf of the data controller and any information as to the logic involved in any decision-taking as mentioned in section 7(1)(*d*) to be made available for its own inspection but shall not, pending the determination of that question in the applicant's favour, require the information sought by the applicant to be disclosed to him or his representatives whether by discovery (or, in Scotland, recovery) or otherwise.
[Data Protection Act 1998, s 15.]

PART III¹
NOTIFICATION BY DATA CONTROLLERS

8–7370 16. Preliminary. (1) In this Part "the registrable particulars", in relation to a data controller, means—

    (*a*) his name and address,
    (*b*) if he has nominated a representative for the purposes of this Act, the name and address of the representative,
    (*c*) a description of the personal data being or to be processed by or on behalf of the data controller and of the category or categories of data subject to which they relate,
    (*d*) a description of the purpose or purposes for which the data are being or are to be processed,
    (*e*) a description of any recipient or recipients to whom the data controller intends or may wish to disclose the data,
    (*f*) the names, or a description of, any countries or territories outside the European Economic Area to which the data controller directly or indirectly transfers, or intends or may wish directly or indirectly to transfer, the data,
    (*ff*) where the data controller is a public authority, a statement of that fact, and
    (*g*) in any case where—

        (i) personal data are being, or are intended to be, processed in circumstances in which the prohibition in subsection (1) of section 17 is excluded by subsection (2) or (3) of that section, and
        (ii) the notification does not extend to those data,

    a statement of that fact.

(2) In this Part—

"fees regulations" means regulations made by the Secretary of State under section 18(5) or 19(4) or (7);
"notification regulations" means regulations made by the Secretary of State under the other provisions of this Part;
"prescribed", except where used in relation to fees regulations, means prescribed by notification regulations.

(3) For the purposes of this Part, so far as it relates to the addresses of data controllers—

    (*a*) the address of a registered company is that of its registered office, and
    (*b*) the address of a person (other than a registered company) carrying on a business is that of his principal place of business in the United Kingdom.
[Data Protection Act 1998, s 16, as amended by SI 2001/3500, SI 2003/1887 and the Freedom of Information Act 2000, s 71.]

---

  1. Part III contains ss 16 to 26.

8–7371 17. Prohibition on processing without registration. (1) Subject to the following provisions of this section, personal data must not be processed unless an entry in respect of the data controller is included in the register maintained by the Commissioner under section 19 (or is treated by notification regulations made by virtue of section 19(3) as being so included).

(2) Except where the processing is assessable processing for the purposes of section 22, subsection (1) does not apply in relation to personal data consisting of information which falls neither within paragraph (*a*) of the definition of "data" in section 1(1) nor within paragraph (*b*) of that definition.

(3) If it appears to the Secretary of State that processing of a particular description is unlikely to prejudice the rights and freedoms of data subjects, notification regulations¹ may provide that, in such cases as may be prescribed, subsection (1) is not to apply in relation to processing of that description.

(4) Subsection (1) does not apply in relation to any processing whose sole purpose is the maintenance of a public register.
[Data Protection Act 1998, s 17, as amended by SI 2001/3500 and SI 2003/1887.]

1. See the Data Protection (Notification and Notification Fees) Regulations 2000, SI 2000/ 188 amended by SI 2001/3214.

8–7372   18. Notification by data controllers.   (1) Any data controller who wishes to be included in the register maintained under section 19 shall give a notification to the Commissioner under this section.

(2) A notification under this section must specify in accordance with notification regulations[1]—

(*a*)   the registrable particulars, and

(*b*)   a general description of measures to be taken for the purpose of complying with the seventh data protection principle.

(3) Notification regulations made by virtue of subsection (2) may provide for the determination by the Commissioner, in accordance with any requirements of the regulations, of the form in which the registrable particulars and the description mentioned in subsection (2)(*b*) are to be specified, including in particular the detail required for the purposes of section 16(1)(*c*), (*d*), (*e*) and (*f*) and subsection (2)(*b*).

(4) Notification regulations[1] may make provision as to the giving of notification—

(*a*)   by partnerships, or

(*b*)   in other cases where two or more persons are the data controllers in respect of any personal data.

(5) The notification must be accompanied by such fee as may be prescribed by fees regulations.

(6) Notification regulations[1] may provide for any fee paid under subsection (5) or section 19(4) to be refunded in prescribed circumstances.

[Data Protection Act 1998, s 18.]

1. See the Data Protection (Notification and Notification Fees) Regulations 2000, SI 2000/188 amended by SI 2001/3214.

8–7373   19. Register of notifications.   (1) The Commissioner shall—

(*a*)   maintain a register of persons who have given notification under section 18, and

(*b*)   make an entry in the register in pursuance of each notification received by him under that section from a person in respect of whom no entry as data controller was for the time being included in the register.

(2) Each entry in the register shall consist of—

(*a*)   the registrable particulars notified under section 18 or, as the case requires, those particulars as amended in pursuance of section 20(4), and

(*b*)   such other information as the Commissioner may be authorised or required by notification regulations[1] to include in the register.

(3) Notification regulations[1] may make provision as to the time as from which any entry in respect of a data controller is to be treated for the purposes of section 17 as having been made in the register.

(4) No entry shall be retained in the register for more than the relevant time except on payment of such fee as may be prescribed by fees regulations[1].

(5) In subsection (4) "the relevant time" means twelve months or such other period as may be prescribed by notification regulations[1]; and different periods may be prescribed in relation to different cases.

(6) The Commissioner—

(*a*)   shall provide facilities for making the information contained in the entries in the register available for inspection (in visible and legible form) by members of the public at all reasonable hours and free of charge, and

(*b*)   may provide such other facilities for making the information contained in those entries available to the public free of charge as he considers appropriate.

(7) The Commissioner shall, on payment of such fee, if any, as may be prescribed[2] by fees regulations, supply any member of the public with a duly certified copy in writing of the particulars contained in any entry made in the register.

[Data Protection Act 1998, s 19.]

1. See the Data Protection (Notification and Notification Fees) Regulations 2000, SI 2000/188 amended by SI 2001/3214.
2. The sum of £2 has been prescribed by the Data Protection (Fees under Section 19(7)) Regulations 2000, SI 2000/187.

8–7374   20. Duty to notify changes.   (1) For the purpose specified in subsection (2), notification regulations[1] shall include provision imposing on every person in respect of whom an entry as a data controller is for the time being included in the register maintained under section 19 a duty to notify to the Commissioner, in such circumstances and at such time or times and in such form as may be prescribed, such matters relating to the registrable particulars and measures taken as mentioned in section 18(2)(*b*) as may be prescribed.

(2) The purpose referred to in subsection (1) is that of ensuring, so far as practicable, that at any time—

(*a*) the entries in the register maintained under section 19 contain current names and addresses and describe the current practice or intentions of the data controller with respect to the processing of personal data, and

(*b*) the Commissioner is provided with a general description of measures currently being taken as mentioned in section 18(2)(*b*).

(3) Subsection (3) of section 18 has effect in relation to notification regulations made by virtue of subsection (1) as it has effect in relation to notification regulations made by virtue of subsection (2) of that section.

(4) On receiving any notification under notification regulations made by virtue of subsection (1), the Commissioner shall make such amendments of the relevant entry in the register maintained under section 19 as are necessary to take account of the notification.
[Data Protection Act 1998, s 20.]

---

1. See the Data Protection (Notification and Notification Fees) Regulations 2000, SI 2000/188 amended by SI 2001/3214.

8–7375　21. Offences.　(1) If section 17(1) is contravened, the data controller is guilty of an offence[1].

(2) Any person who fails to comply with the duty imposed by notification regulations made by virtue of section 20(1) is guilty of an offence[1].

(3) It shall be a defence for a person charged with an offence under subsection (2) to show that he exercised all due diligence to comply with the duty.
[Data Protection Act 1998, s 21.]

---

1. For procedure and penalties, see s 60 post.

8–7376　22. Preliminary assessment by Commissioner.　(1) In this section "assessable processing" means processing which is of a description specified in an order made by the Secretary of State as appearing to him to be particularly likely—

(*a*) to cause substantial damage or substantial distress to data subjects, or

(*b*) otherwise significantly to prejudice the rights and freedoms of data subjects.

(2) On receiving notification from any data controller under section 18 or under notification regulations made by virtue of section 20 the Commissioner shall consider—

(*a*) whether any of the processing to which the notification relates is assessable processing, and

(*b*) if so, whether the assessable processing is likely to comply with the provisions of this Act.

(3) Subject to subsection (4), the Commissioner shall, within the period of twenty-eight days beginning with the day on which he receives a notification which relates to assessable processing, give a notice to the data controller stating the extent to which the Commissioner is of the opinion that the processing is likely or unlikely to comply with the provisions of this Act.

(4) Before the end of the period referred to in subsection (3) the Commissioner may, by reason of special circumstances, extend that period on one occasion only by notice to the data controller by such further period not exceeding fourteen days as the Commissioner may specify in the notice.

(5) No assessable processing in respect of which a notification has been given the Commissioner as mentioned in subsection (2) shall be carried on unless either—

(*a*) the period of twenty-eight days beginning with the day on which the notification is received by the Commissioner (or, in a case falling within subsection (4), that period as extended under that subsection) has elapsed, or

(*b*) before the end of that period (or that period as so extended) the data controller has received a notice from the Commissioner under subsection (3) in respect of the processing.

(6) Where subsection (5) is contravened, the data controller is guilty of an offence[1].

(7) The Secretary of State may by order amend subsections (3), (4) and (5) by substituting for the number of days for the time being specified there a different number specified in the order.
[Data Protection Act 1998, s 22, as amended by SI 2001/3500 and SI 2003/1887.]

---

1. For procedure and penalties, see s 60, post.

8–7377　23. Power to make provision for appointment of data protection supervisors.
(1) The Secretary of State may by order—

(*a*) make provision under which a data controller may appoint a person to act as a data protection supervisor responsible in particular for monitoring in an independent manner the data controller's compliance with the provisions of this Act, and

(b) provide that, in relation to any data controller who has appointed a data protection supervisor in accordance with the provisions of the order and who complies with such conditions as may be specified in the order, the provisions of this Part are to have effect subject to such exemptions or other modifications as may be specified in the order.

(2) An order under this section may—

(a) impose duties on data protection supervisors in relation to the Commissioner, and
(b) confer functions on the Commissioner in relation to data protection supervisors.

[Data Protection Act 1998, s 23, as amended by SI 2001/3500 and SI 2003/1887.]

8–7378 24. Duty of certain data controllers to make certain information available.
(1) Subject to subsection (3), where personal data are processed in a case where—

(a) by virtue of subsection (2) or (3) of section 17, subsection (1) of that section does not apply to the processing, and
(b) the data controller has not notified the relevant particulars in respect of that processing under section 18,

the data controller must, within twenty-one days of receiving a written request from any person, make the relevant particulars available to that person in writing free of charge.

(2) In this section "the relevant particulars" means the particulars referred to in paragraphs (a) to (f) of section 16(1).

(3) This section has effect subject to any exemption conferred for the purposes of this section by notification regulations.

(4) Any data controller who fails to comply with the duty imposed by subsection (1) is guilty of an offence[1].

(5) It shall be a defence for a person charged with an offence under subsection (4) to show that he exercised all due diligence to comply with the duty.

[Data Protection Act 1998, s 24.]

---

1. For procedure and penalties, see s 60, post.

8–7379 25. Functions of Commissioner in relation to making of notification regulations.
(1) As soon as practicable after the passing of this Act, the Commissioner shall submit to the Secretary of State proposals as to the provisions to be included in the first notification regulations.

(2) The Commissioner shall keep under review the working of notification regulations and may from time to time submit to the Secretary of State proposals as to amendments to be made to the regulations.

(3) The Secretary of State may from time to time require the Commissioner to consider any matter relating to notification regulations and to submit to him proposals as to amendments to be made to the regulations in connection with that matter.

(4) Before making any notification regulations, the Secretary of State shall—

(a) consider any proposals made to him by the Commissioner under subsection (2) or (3), and
(b) consult the Commissioner.

[Data Protection Act 1998, s 25, as amended by SI 2001/3500 and SI 2003/1887.]

8–7380 26. *Fees regulations*

PART IV[1]
EXEMPTIONS

8–7381 27. Preliminary.   (1) References in any of the data protection principles or any provision of Parts II and III to personal data or to the processing of personal data do not include references to data or processing which by virtue of this Part are exempt from that principle or other provision.

(2) In this Part "the subject information provisions" means—

(a) the first data protection principle to the extent to which it requires compliance with paragraph 2 of Part II of Schedule 1, and
(b) section 7.

(3) In this Part "the non-disclosure provisions" means the provisions specified in subsection (4) to the extent to which they are inconsistent with the disclosure in question.

(4) The provisions referred to in subsection (3) are—

(a) the first data protection principle, except to the extent to which it requires compliance with the conditions in Schedules 2 and 3,
(b) the second, third, fourth and fifth data protection principles, and
(c) sections 10 and 14(1) to (3).

(5) Except as provided by this Part, the subject information provisions shall have effect

notwithstanding any enactment or rule of law prohibiting or restricting the disclosure, or authorising the withholding, of information.
[Data Protection Act 1998, s 27.]

----

1. Part IV contains ss 27 to 39.

8–7382   28. National security.   (1) Personal data are exempt from any of the provisions of—

    (a)   the data protection principles,
    (b)   Parts II, III and V, and
    (c)   section* 55,

if the exemption from that provision is required for the purpose of safeguarding national security.

    (2) Subject to subsection (4), a certificate signed by a Minister of the Crown certifying that exemption from all or any of the provisions mentioned in subsection (1) is or at any time was required for the purpose there mentioned in respect of any personal data shall be conclusive evidence of that fact.

    (3) A certificate under subsection (2) may identify the personal data to which it applies by means of a general description and may be expressed to have prospective effect.

    (4) Any person directly affected by the issuing of a certificate under subsection (2) may appeal to the Tribunal against the certificate.

    (5) If on an appeal under subsection (4), the Tribunal finds that, applying the principles applied by the court on an application for judicial review, the Minister did not have reasonable grounds for issuing the certificate, the Tribunal may allow the appeal and quash the certificate.

    (6) Where in any proceedings under or by virtue of this Act it is claimed by a data controller that a certificate under subsection (2) which identifies the personal data to which it applies by means of a general description applies to any personal data, any other party to the proceedings may appeal to the Tribunal on the ground that the certificate does not apply to the personal data in question and, subject to any determination under subsection (7), the certificate shall be conclusively presumed so to apply.

    (7) On any appeal under subsection (6), the Tribunal may determine that the certificate does not so apply.

    (8) A document purporting to be a certificate under subsection (2) shall be received in evidence and deemed to be such a certificate unless the contrary is proved.

    (9) A document which purports to be certified by or on behalf of a Minister of the Crown as a true copy of a certificate issued by that Minister under subsection (2) shall in any legal proceedings be evidence (or, in Scotland, sufficient evidence) of that certificate.

    (10) The power conferred by subsection (2) on a Minister of the Crown shall not be exercisable except by a Minister who is a member of the Cabinet or by the Attorney General or the Advocate General for Scotland.

    (11) No power conferred by any provision of Part V may be exercised in relation to personal data which by virtue of this section are exempt from that provision.

    (12) Schedule 6 shall have effect in relation to appeals under subsection (4) or (6) and the proceedings of the Tribunal in respect of any such appeal.
[Data Protection Act 1998, s 28 as amended by SI 1999/679.]

----

*"sections 54A and" prospectively substituted by the Crime (International Co-operation) Act 2003, Sch 5, from a date to be appointed.

8–7383   29. Crime and taxation.   (1) Personal data processed for any of the following purposes—

    (a)   the prevention or detection of crime,
    (b)   the apprehension or prosecution of offenders, or
    (c)   the assessment or collection of any tax or duty or of any imposition of a similar nature,

are exempt from the first data protection principle (except to the extent to which it requires compliance with the conditions in Schedules 2 and 3) and section 7 in any case to the extent to which the application of those provisions to the data would be likely to prejudice any of the matters mentioned in this subsection.

    (2) Personal data which—

    (a)   are processed for the purpose of discharging statutory functions, and
    (b)   consist of information obtained for such a purpose from a person who had it in his possession
        for any of the purposes mentioned in subsection (1),

are exempt from the subject information provisions to the same extent as personal data processed for any of the purposes mentioned in that subsection.

    (3) Personal data are exempt from the non-disclosure provisions in any case in which—

    (a)   the disclosure is for any of the purposes mentioned in subsection (1), and
    (b)   the application of those provisions in relation to the disclosure would be likely to prejudice
        any of the matters mentioned in that subsection.

(4) Personal data in respect of which the data controller is a relevant authority and which—

(a) consist of a classification applied to the data subject as part of a system of risk assessment which is operated by that authority for either of the following purposes—

(i) the assessment or collection of any tax or duty or any imposition of a similar nature, or

(ii) the prevention or detection of crime, or apprehension or prosecution of offenders, where the offence concerned involves any unlawful claim for any payment out of, or any unlawful application of, public funds, and

(b) are processed for either of those purposes,

are exempt from section 7 to the extent to which the exemption is required in the interests of the operation of the system.

(5) In subsection (4)—

"public funds" includes funds provided by any Community institution;
"relevant authority" means—

(a) a government department,

(b) a local authority, or

(c) any other authority administering housing benefit or council tax benefit.

[Data Protection Act 1998, s 29.]

8–7384   30. Health, education and social work.   (1) The Secretary of State may by order[1] exempt from the subject information provisions, or modify those provisions in relation to, personal data consisting of information as to the physical or mental health or condition of the data subject.

(2) Secretary of State may by order exempt from the subject information provisions, or modify those provisions in relation to—

(a) personal data in respect of which the data controller is the proprietor of, or a teacher at, a school, and which consist of information relating to persons who are or have been pupils at the school, or

(b) personal data in respect of which the data controller is an education authority in Scotland, and which consist of information relating to persons who are receiving, or have received, further education provided by the authority.

(3) The Secretary of State may by order exempt from the subject information provisions, or modify those provisions in relation to, personal data of such other descriptions as may be specified in the order, being information—

(a) processed by government departments or local authorities or by voluntary organisations or other bodies designated by or under the order, and

(b) appearing to him to be processed in the course of, or for the purposes of, carrying out social work in relation to the data subject or other individuals;

but the Secretary of State shall not under this subsection confer any exemption or make any modification except so far as he considers that the application to the data of those provisions (or of those provisions without modification) would be likely to prejudice the carrying out of social work.

(4) An order[1] under this section may make different provision in relation to data consisting of information of different descriptions.

(5) In this section—

"education authority" and "further education" have the same meaning as in the Education (Scotland) Act 1980 ("the 1980 Act"), and
"proprietor"—

(a) in relation to a school in England or Wales, has the same meaning as in the Education Act 1996,

(b) in relation to a school in Scotland, means—

(i) in the case of a self-governing school, the board of management within the meaning of the Self-Governing Schools etc (Scotland) Act 1989,*

(ii) in the case of an independent school, the proprietor within the meaning of the 1980 Act,

(iii) in the case of a grant-aided school, the managers within the meaning of the 1980 Act, and

(iv) in the case of a public school, the education authority within the meaning of the 1980 Act, and

(c) in relation to a school in Northern Ireland, has the same meaning as in the Education and Libraries (Northern Ireland) Order 1986 and includes, in the case of a controlled school, the Board of Governors of the school.

[Data Protection Act 1998, s 30, as amended by SI 2001/3500 and SI 2003/1887.]

---

*Repealed by the Standards in Scotland's Schools etc Act 2000, Sch 3 from a date to be appointed.
1. The following Data Protection (Subject Access Modification) Orders have been made which provide for partial

exemption from the provisions of the Act for subject access to personal data: Health, SI 2000/413; Education, SI 2000/414; Social Work, SI 2000/415 amended by SI 2002/2469 and 3220 and SI 2005/467.

8–7385   31. Regulatory activity.   (1) Personal data processed for the purposes of discharging functions to which this subsection applies are exempt from the subject information provisions in any case to the extent to which the application of those provisions to the data would be likely to prejudice the proper discharge of those functions.

(2) Subsection (1) applies to any relevant function which is designed—

(*a*)   for protecting members of the public against—

(i)   financial loss due to dishonesty, malpractice or other seriously improper conduct by, or the unfitness or incompetence of, persons concerned in the provision of banking, insurance, investment or other financial services or in the management of bodies corporate,

(ii)   financial loss due to the conduct of discharged or undischarged bankrupts, or

(iii)   dishonesty, malpractice or other seriously improper conduct by, or the unfitness or incompetence of, persons authorised to carry on any profession or other activity,

(*b*)   for protecting charities or community interest companies against misconduct or mismanagement (whether by trustees, directors or other persons) in their administration,

(*c*)   for protecting the property of charities or community interest companies from loss or misapplication,

(*d*)   for the recovery of the property of charities or community interest companies,

(*e*)   for securing the health, safety and welfare of persons at work, or

(*f*)   for protecting persons other than persons at work against risk to health or safety arising out of or in connection with the actions of persons at work.

(3) In subsection (2) "relevant function" means—

(*a*)   any function conferred on any person by or under any enactment,

(*b*)   any function of the Crown, a Minister of the Crown or a government department, or

(*c*)   any other function which is of a public nature and is exercised in the public interest.

(4) Personal data processed for the purpose of discharging any function which—

(*a*)   is conferred by or under any enactment on—

(i)   the Parliamentary Commissioner for Administration,

(ii)   the Commission for Local Administration in England or,,

(iii) the Health Service Commissioner for England,

(iv)   the Public Services Ombudsman for Wales,

(v)   the Assembly Ombudsman for Northern Ireland,

(vi)   the Northern Ireland Commissioner for Complaints, or

(vii) the Scottish Public Services Ombudsman, and

(*b*)   is designed for protecting members of the public against—

(i)   maladministration by public bodies,

(ii)   failures in services provided by public bodies, or

(iii) a failure of a public body to provide a service which it was a function of the body to provide,

are exempt from the subject information provisions in any case to the extent to which the application of those provisions to the data would be likely to prejudice the proper discharge of that function.

(4A) Personal data processed for the purpose of discharging any function which is conferred by or under Part XVI of the Financial Services and Markets Act 2000 on the body established by the Financial Services Authority for the purposes of that Part are exempt from the subject information provisions in any case to the extent to which the application of those provisions to the data would be likely to prejudice the proper discharge of the function.

(5) Personal data processed for the purpose of discharging any function which—

(*a*)   is conferred by or under any enactment on the Office of Fair Trading, and

(*b*)   is designed—

(i)   for protecting members of the public against conduct which may adversely affect their interests by persons carrying on a business,

(ii)   for regulating agreements or conduct which have as their object or effect the prevention, restriction or distortion of competition in connection with any commercial activity, or

(iii) for regulating conduct on the part of one or more undertakings which amounts to the abuse of a dominant position in a market,

are exempt from the subject information provisions in any case to the extent to which the application of those provisions to the data would be likely to prejudice the proper discharge of that function.

(6) Personal data processed for the purpose of the function of considering a complaint under section 113(1) or (2) or 114(1) or (3) of the Health and Social Care (Community Health and Standards) Act 2003, or section 24D, 26, 26ZA or 26ZB of the Children Act 1989, are exempt from

the subject information provisions in any case to the extent to which the application of those provisions to the data would be likely to prejudice the proper discharge of that function.
[Data Protection Act 1998, s 31 as amended by the Financial Services and Markets Act 2000, s 233, the Companies (Audit, Invesitgations and Community Enterprise) at 2004, s 59, SI 2004/1823, the Health and Social Care (Community Health and Standards) Act 2003, s 119 and the Public Services Ombudsman (Wales) Act 2005, Sch 6.]

8–7386 32. Journalism, literature and art.   (1) Personal data which are processed only for the special purposes are exempt from any provision to which this subsection relates if—

(*a*)   the processing is undertaken with a view to the publication by any person of any journalistic[1], literary or artistic material,

(*b*)   the data controller reasonably believes that, having regard in particular to the special importance of the public interest in freedom of expression, publication would be in the public interest, and

(*c*)   the data controller reasonably believes that, in all the circumstances, compliance with that provision is incompatible with the special purposes.

(2) Subsection (1) relates to the provisions of—

(*a*)   the data protection principles except the seventh data protection principle,

(*b*)   section 7,

(*c*)   section 10,

(*d*)   section 12,

(*dd*) section 12A, and★

(*e*)   section 14(1) to (3).

(3) In considering for the purposes of subsection (1)(*b*) whether the belief of a data controller that publication would be in the public interest was or is a reasonable one, regard may be had to his compliance with any code of practice[2] which—

(*a*)   is relevant to the publication in question, and

(*b*)   is designated by the Secretary of State by order[3] for the purposes of this subsection.

(4) Where at any time ("the relevant time") in any proceedings against a data controller under section 7(9), 10(4), 12(8), 12A or 14 or by virtue of section 13 the data controller claims, or it appears to the court, that any personal data to which the proceedings relate are being processed—

(*a*)   only for the special purposes, and

(*b*)   with a view to the publication by any person of any journalistic, literary or artistic material which, at the time twenty-four hours immediately before the relevant time, had not previously been published by the data controller,

the court shall stay the proceedings until either of the conditions in subsection (5) is met.

(5) Those conditions are—

(*a*)   that a determination of the Commissioner under section 45 with respect to the data in question takes effect, or

(*b*)   in a case where the proceedings were stayed on the making of a claim, that the claim is withdrawn.

(6) For the purposes of this Act "publish", in relation to journalistic, literary or artistic material, means make available to the public or any section of the public.
[Data Protection Act 1998, s 32 as amended by the Data Protection Act 1998, s 72, Sch 13, SI 2001/3500 and SI 2003/1887.]

★**Section 32(2)(*dd*) temporarily inserted until 23 October 2007.**
1. For an exposition of the application of this Act to newspapers, see *Campbell v Mirror Group Newspapers* [2002] EWCA Civ 1373, [2003] QB 633, [2003] 1 All ER 224.
2. See the Data Protection (Designated Codes of Practice) Order 2000, SI 2000/418.
3. The Data Protection (Designated Codes of Practice) (No 2) Order 2000, SI 2000/1864 designates codes of practice issued by various media organisations.

8–7387 33. Research, history and statistics.   (1) In this section—

"research purposes" includes statistical or historical purposes;
"the relevant conditions", in relation to any processing of personal data, means the conditions—

(*a*)   that the data are not processed to support measures or decisions with respect to particular individuals, and

(*b*)   that the data are not processed in such a way that substantial damage or substantial distress is, or is likely to be, caused to any data subject.

(2) For the purposes of the second data protection principle, the further processing of personal data only for research purposes in compliance with the relevant conditions is not to be regarded as incompatible with the purposes for which they were obtained.

(3) Personal data which are processed only for research purposes in compliance with the relevant conditions may, notwithstanding the fifth data protection principle, be kept indefinitely.

(4) Personal data which are processed only for research purposes are exempt from section 7 if—

(*a*) they are processed in compliance with the relevant conditions, and

(*b*) the results of the research or any resulting statistics are not made available in a form which identifies data subjects or any of them.

(5) For the purposes of subsections (2) to (4) personal data are not to be treated as processed otherwise than for research purposes merely because the data are disclosed—

(*a*) to any person, for research purposes only,

(*b*) to the data subject or a person acting on his behalf,

(*c*) at the request, or with the consent, of the data subject or a person acting on his behalf, or

(*d*) in circumstances in which the person making the disclosure has reasonable grounds for believing that the disclosure falls within paragraph (*a*), (*b*) or (*c*).

[Data Protection Act 1998, s 33.]

8–7387A   33A. Manual data held by public authorities.   (1) Personal data falling within paragraph (*e*) of the definition of "data" in section 1(1) are exempt from—

(*a*) the first, second, third, fifth, seventh and eighth data protection principles,

(*b*) the sixth data protection principle except so far as it relates to the rights conferred on data subjects by sections 7 and 14,

(*c*) sections 10 to 12,

(*d*) section 13, except so far as it relates to damage caused by a contravention of section 7 or of the fourth data protection principle and to any distress which is also suffered by reason of that contravention,

(*e*) Part III, and

(*f*) section 55.

(2) Personal data which fall within paragraph (e) of the definition of "data" in section 1(1) and relate to appointments or removals, pay, discipline, superannuation or other personnel matters, in relation to—

(*a*) service in any of the armed forces of the Crown,

(*b*) service in any office or employment under the Crown or under any public authority, or

(*c*) service in any office or employment, or under any contract for services, in respect of which power to take action, or to determine or approve the action taken, in such matters is vested in Her Majesty, any Minister of the Crown, the National Assembly for Wales, any Northern Ireland Minister (within the meaning of the Freedom of Information Act 2000) or any public authority,

are also exempt from the remaining data protection principles and the remaining provisions of Part II.

[Data Protection Act 1998, s 33A, as inserted by the Freedom of Information Act 2000, s 70.]

8–7388   34. Information available to the public by or under enactment.   Personal data are exempt from—

(*a*) the subject information provisions,

(*b*) the fourth data protection principle and sections 12A and 14(1) to (3)★, and

(*c*) the non-disclosure provisions,

if the data consist of information which the data controller is obliged by or under any enactment other than an enactment contained in the Freedom of Information Act 2000 to make available to the public, whether by publishing it, by making it available for inspection, or otherwise and whether gratuitously or on payment of a fee.

[Data Protection Act 1998, s 34 as amended by the Data Protection Act 1998, Sch 13 and the Freedom of Information Act 2000, s 72.]

★**Reproduced as in force until 23 October 2007.**

8–7389   35. Disclosures required by law or made in connection with legal proceedings etc.

(1) Personal data are exempt from the non-disclosure provisions where the disclosure is required by or under any enactment, by any rule of law or by the order of a court.

(2) Personal data are exempt from the non-disclosure provisions where the disclosure is necessary—

(*a*) for the purpose of, or in connection with, any legal proceedings (including prospective legal proceedings), or

(*b*) for the purpose of obtaining legal advice,

or is otherwise necessary for the purposes of establishing, exercising or defending legal rights.

[Data Protection Act 1998, s 35.]

8–7389A 35A. Parliamentary privilege. Personal data are exempt from—

  (a) the first data protection principle, except to the extent to which it requires compliance with the conditions in Schedules 2 and 3,

  (b) the second, third, fourth and fifth data protection principles,

  (c) section 7, and

  (d) sections 10 and 14(1) to (3),

if the exemption is required for the purpose of avoiding an infringement of the privileges of either House of Parliament.

[Data Protection Act 1998, s 35A, as inserted by the Freedom of Information Act 2000, Sch 6.]

8–7390 36. Domestic purposes. Personal data processed by an individual only for the purposes of that individual's personal, family or household affairs (including recreational purposes) are exempt from the data protection principles and the provisions of Parts II and III.

[Data Protection Act 1998, s 36.]

8–7391 37. Miscellaneous exemptions. Schedule 7 (which confers further miscellaneous exemptions) has effect.

[Data Protection Act 1998, s 37.]

8–7392 38. Powers to make further exemptions by order[1]. (1) The Secretary of State may by order[1] exempt from the subject information provisions personal data consisting of information the disclosure of which is prohibited or restricted by or under any enactment if and to the extent that he considers it necessary for the safeguarding of the interests of the data subject or the rights and freedoms of any other individual that the prohibition or restriction ought to prevail over those provisions.

  (2) The Secretary of State may by order exempt from the non-disclosure provisions any disclosures of personal data made in circumstances specified in the order, if he considers the exemption is necessary for the safeguarding of the interests of the data subject or the rights and freedoms of any other individual.

[Data Protection Act 1998, s 38, as amended by SI 2001/3500 and SI 2003/1887.]

---

1. The Data Protection (Miscellaneous subject Access Exemptions) Order 2000, SI 2000/419 amended by SI 2000/1865 and SI 2005/3504 exempts the following information from disclosure under s 7 of this Act: human fertilisation and embryology information in the UK; information contained in adoption and parental order records and reports; statements and records of the special educational needs of children.

8–7393 39. Transitional relief. Schedule 8 (which confers transitional exemptions) has effect.]

[Data Protection Act 1998, s 39.]

PART V[1]

ENFORCEMENT

8–7394 40. Enforcement notices. (1) If the Commissioner is satisfied that a data controller has contravened or is contravening any of the data protection principles, the Commissioner may serve him with a notice (in this Act referred to as "an enforcement notice") requiring him, for complying with the principle or principles in question, to do either or both of the following—

  (a) to take within such time as may be specified in the notice, or to refrain from taking after such time as may be so specified, such steps as are so specified, or

  (b) to refrain from processing any personal data, or any personal data of a description specified in the notice, or to refrain from processing them for a purpose so specified or in a manner so specified, after such time as may be so specified.

  (2) In deciding whether to serve an enforcement notice, the Commissioner shall consider whether the contravention has caused or is likely to cause any person damage or distress.

  (3) An enforcement notice in respect of a contravention of the fourth data protection principle which requires the data controller to rectify, block, erase or destroy any inaccurate data may also require the data controller to rectify, block, erase or destroy any other data held by him and containing an expression of opinion which appears to the Commissioner to be based on the inaccurate data.

  (4) An enforcement notice in respect of a contravention of the fourth data protection principle, in the case of data which accurately record information received or obtained by the data controller from the data subject or a third party, may require the data controller either—

  (a) to rectify, block, erase or destroy any inaccurate data and any other data held by him and containing an expression of opinion as mentioned in subsection (3), or

  (b) to take such steps as are specified in the notice for securing compliance with the requirements specified in paragraph 7 of Part II of Schedule 1 and, if the Commissioner thinks fit, for supplementing the data with such statement of the true facts relating to the matters dealt with by the data as the Commissioner may approve.

  (5) Where—

(*a*) an enforcement notice requires the data controller to rectify, block, erase or destroy any personal data, or

(*b*) the Commissioner is satisfied that personal data which have been rectified, blocked, erased or destroyed had been processed in contravention of any of the data protection principles,

an enforcement notice may, if reasonably practicable, require the data controller to notify third parties to whom the data have been disclosed of the rectification, blocking, erasure or destruction; and in determining whether it is reasonably practicable to require such notification regard shall be had, in particular, to the number of persons who would have to be notified.

(6) An enforcement notice must contain—

(*a*) a statement of the data protection principle or principles which the Commissioner is satisfied have been or are being contravened and his reasons for reaching that conclusion, and

(*b*) particulars of the rights of appeal conferred by section 48.

(7) Subject to subsection (8), an enforcement notice must not require any of the provisions of the notice to be complied with before the end of the period within which an appeal can be brought against the notice and, if such an appeal is brought, the notice need not be complied with pending the determination or withdrawal of the appeal.

(8) If by reason of special circumstances the Commissioner considers that an enforcement notice should be complied with as a matter of urgency he may include in the notice a statement to that effect and a statement of his reasons for reaching that conclusion; and in that event subsection (7) shall not apply but the notice must not require the provisions of the notice to be complied with before the end of the period of seven days beginning with the day on which the notice is served.

(9) Notification regulations (as defined by section 16(2)) may make provision as to the effect of the service of an enforcement notice on any entry in the register maintained under section 19 which relates to the person on whom the notice is served.

(10) This section has effect subject to section 46(1).

[Data Protection Act 1998, s 40.]

---

1. Part V contains ss 40 to 50. Part V is modified in respect of Telecommunications by the Telecommunications (Data Protection and Privacy) Regulations 1999, in this title, post.

8–7395 41. Cancellation of an enforcement notice. (1) If the Commissioner considers that all or any of the provisions of an enforcement notice need not be complied with in order to ensure compliance with the data protection principle or principles to which it relates, he may cancel or vary the notice by written notice to the person on whom it was served.

(2) A person on whom an enforcement notice has been served may, at any time after the expiry of the period during which an appeal can be brought against that notice, apply in writing to the Commissioner for the cancellation or variation of that notice on the ground that, by reason of a change of circumstances, all or any of the provisions of that notice need not be complied with in order to ensure compliance with the data protection principle or principles to which that notice relates.

[Data Protection Act 1998, s 41.]

8–7396 42. Request for assessment. (1) A request may be made to the Commissioner by or on behalf of any person who is, or believes himself to be, directly affected by any processing of personal data for an assessment as to whether it is likely or unlikely that the processing has been or is being carried out in compliance with the provisions of this Act.

(2) On receiving a request under this section, the Commissioner shall make an assessment in such manner as appears to him to be appropriate, unless he has not been supplied with such information as he may reasonably require in order to—

(*a*) satisfy himself as to the identity of the person making the request, and

(*b*) enable him to identify the processing in question.

(3) The matters to which the Commissioner may have regard in determining in what manner it is appropriate to make an assessment include—

(*a*) the extent to which the request appears to him to raise a matter of substance,

(*b*) any undue delay in making the request, and

(*c*) whether or not the person making the request is entitled to make an application under section 7 in respect of the personal data in question.

(4) Where the Commissioner has received a request under this section he shall notify the person who made the request—

(*a*) whether he has made an assessment as a result of the request, and

(*b*) to the extent that he considers appropriate, having regard in particular to any exemption from section 7 applying in relation to the personal data concerned, of any view formed or action taken as a result of the request.

[Data Protection Act 1998, s 42.]

8–7397 **43. Information notices.** (1) If the Commissioner—

    (a) has received a request under section 42 in respect of any processing of personal data, or

    (b) reasonably requires any information for the purpose of determining whether the data controller has complied or is complying with the data protection principles,

he may serve the data controller with a notice (in this Act referred to as "an information notice") requiring the data controller, within such time as is specified in the notice, to furnish the Commissioner, in such form as may be so specified, with such information relating to the request or to compliance with the principles as is so specified.

    (2) An information notice must contain—

    (a) in a case falling within subsection (1)(a), a statement that the Commissioner has received a request under section 42 in relation to the specified processing, or

    (b) in a case falling within subsection (1)(b), a statement that the Commissioner regards the specified information as relevant for the purpose of determining whether the data controller has complied, or is complying, with the data protection principles and his reasons for regarding it as relevant for that purpose.

    (3) An information notice must also contain particulars of the rights of appeal conferred by section 48.

    (4) Subject to subsection (5), the time specified in an information notice shall not expire before the end of the period within which an appeal can be brought against the notice and, if such an appeal is brought, the information need not be furnished pending the determination or withdrawal of the appeal.

    (5) If by reason of special circumstances the Commissioner considers that the information is required as a matter of urgency, he may include in the notice a statement to that effect and a statement of his reasons for reaching that conclusion; and in that event subsection (4) shall not apply, but the notice shall not require the information to be furnished before the end of the period of seven days beginning with the day on which the notice is served.

    (6) A person shall not be required by virtue of this section to furnish the Commissioner with any information in respect of—

    (a) any communication between a professional legal adviser and his client in connection with the giving of legal advice to the client with respect to his obligations, liabilities or rights under this Act, or

    (b) any communication between a professional legal adviser and his client, or between such an adviser or his client and any other person, made in connection with or in contemplation of proceedings under or arising out of this Act (including proceedings before the Tribunal) and for the purposes of such proceedings.

    (7) In subsection (6) references to the client of a professional legal adviser include references to any person representing such a client.

    (8) A person shall not be required by virtue of this section to furnish the Commissioner with any information if the furnishing of that information would, by revealing evidence of the commission of any offence other than an offence under this Act, expose him to proceedings for that offence.

    (9) The Commissioner may cancel an information notice by written notice to the person on whom it was served.

    (10) This section has effect subject to section 46(3).

[Data Protection Act 1998, s 43.]

8–7398 **44. Special information notices.** If the Commissioner—

    (a) has received a request under section 42 in respect of any processing of personal data, or

    (b) has reasonable grounds for suspecting that, in a case in which proceedings have been stayed under section 32, the personal data to which the proceedings relate—

        (i) are not being processed only for the special purposes, or

        (ii) are not being processed with a view to the publication by any person of any journalistic, literary or artistic material which has not previously been published by the data controller,

he may serve the data controller with a notice (in this Act referred to as a "special information notice") requiring the data controller, within such time as is specified in the notice, to furnish the Commissioner, in such form as may be so specified, with such information as is so specified for the purpose specified in subsection (2).

    (2) That purpose is the purpose of ascertaining—

    (a) whether the personal data are being processed only for the special purposes, or

    (b) whether they are being processed with a view to the publication by any person of any journalistic, literary or artistic material which has not previously been published by the data controller.

    (3) A special information notice must contain—

(a)   in a case falling within paragraph (a) of subsection (1), a statement that the Commissioner has received a request under section 42 in relation to the specified processing, or

(b)   in a case falling within paragraph (b) of that subsection, a statement of the Commissioner's grounds for suspecting that the personal data are not being processed as mentioned in that paragraph.

(4) A special information notice must also contain particulars of the rights of appeal conferred by section 48.

(5) Subject to subsection (6), the time specified in a special information notice shall not expire before the end of the period within which an appeal can be brought against the notice and, if such an appeal is brought, the information need not be furnished pending the determination or withdrawal of the appeal.

(6) If by reason of special circumstances the Commissioner considers that the information is required as a matter of urgency, he may include in the notice a statement to that effect and a statement of his reasons for reaching that conclusion; and in that event subsection (5) shall not apply, but the notice shall not require the information to be furnished before the end of the period of seven days beginning with the day on which the notice is served.

(7) A person shall not be required by virtue of this section to furnish the Commissioner with any information in respect of—

(a)   any communication between a professional legal adviser and his client in connection with the giving of legal advice to the client with respect to his obligations, liabilities or rights under this Act, or

(b)   any communication between a professional legal adviser and his client, or between such an adviser or his client and any other person, made in connection with or in contemplation of proceedings under or arising out of this Act (including proceedings before the Tribunal) and for the purposes of such proceedings.

(8) In subsection (7) references to the client of a professional legal adviser include references to any person representing such a client.

(9) A person shall not be required by virtue of this section to furnish the Commissioner with any information if the furnishing of that information would, by revealing evidence of the commission of any offence other than an offence under this Act, expose him to proceedings for that offence.

(10) The Commissioner may cancel a special information notice by written notice to the person on whom it was served.
[Data Protection Act 1998, s 44.]

8–7399   45. Determination by Commissioner as to the special purposes.   (1) Where at any time it appears to the Commissioner (whether as a result of the service of a special information notice or otherwise) that any personal data—

(a)   are not being processed only for the special purposes, or

(b)   are not being processed with a view to the publication by any person of any journalistic, literary or artistic material which has not previously been published by the data controller,

he may make a determination in writing to that effect.

(2) Notice of the determination shall be given to the data controller; and the notice must contain particulars of the right of appeal conferred by section 48.

(3) A determination under subsection (1) shall not take effect until the end of the period within which an appeal can be brought and, where an appeal is brought, shall not take effect pending the determination or withdrawal of the appeal.
[Data Protection Act 1998, s 45.]

8–7400   46. Restriction on enforcement in case of processing for the special purposes. (1) The Commissioner may not at any time serve an enforcement notice on a data controller with respect to the processing of personal data for the special purposes unless—

(a)   a determination under section 45(1) with respect to those data has taken effect, and

(b)   the court has granted leave for the notice to be served.

(2) The court shall not grant leave for the purposes of subsection (1)(b) unless it is satisfied—

(a)   that the Commissioner has reason to suspect a contravention of the data protection principles which is of substantial public importance, and

(b)   except where the case is one of urgency, that the data controller has been given notice, in accordance with rules of court, of the application for leave.

(3) The Commissioner may not serve an information notice on a data controller with respect to the processing of personal data for the special purposes unless a determination under section 45(1) with respect to those data has taken effect.
[Data Protection Act 1998, s 46.]

8–7401   47. Failure to comply with notice.   (1) A person who fails to comply with an enforcement notice, an information notice or a special information notice is guilty of an offence.

(2) A person who, in purported compliance with an information notice or a special information notice—

(a) makes a statement which he knows to be false in a material respect, or

(b) recklessly makes a statement which is false in a material respect,

is guilty of an offence[1].

(3) It is a defence for a person charged with an offence under subsection (1) to prove that he exercised all due diligence to comply with the notice in question.

[Data Protection Act 1998, s 47.]

---

1. For procedure and penalties, see s 60, post.

8–7402 48. Rights of appeal. (1) A person on whom an enforcement notice, an information notice or a special information notice has been served may appeal to the Tribunal against the notice.

(2) A person on whom an enforcement notice has been served may appeal to the Tribunal against the refusal of an application under section 41(2) for cancellation or variation of the notice.

(3) Where an enforcement notice, an information notice or a special information notice contains a statement by the Commissioner in accordance with section 40(8), 43(5) or 44(6) then, whether or not the person appeals against the notice, he may appeal against—

(a) the Commissioner's decision to include the statement in the notice, or

(b) the effect of the inclusion of the statement as respects any part of the notice.

(4) A data controller in respect of whom a determination has been made under section 45 may appeal to the Tribunal against the determination.

(5) Schedule 6 has effect in relation to appeals under this section and the proceedings of the Tribunal in respect of any such appeal.

[Data Protection Act 1998, s 48.]

8–7403 49. Determination of appeals. (1) If on an appeal under section 48(1) the Tribunal considers—

(a) that the notice against which the appeal is brought is not in accordance with the law, or

(b) to the extent that the notice involved an exercise of discretion by the Commissioner, that he ought to have exercised his discretion differently,

the Tribunal shall allow the appeal or substitute such other notice or decision as could have been served or made by the Commissioner; and in any other case the Tribunal shall dismiss the appeal.

(2) On such an appeal, the Tribunal may review any determination of fact on which the notice in question was based.

(3) If on an appeal under section 48(2) the Tribunal considers that the enforcement notice ought to be cancelled or varied by reason of a change in circumstances, the Tribunal shall cancel or vary the notice.

(4) On an appeal under subsection (3) of section 48 the Tribunal may direct—

(a) that the notice in question shall have effect as if it did not contain any such statement as is mentioned in that subsection, or

(b) that the inclusion of the statement shall not have effect in relation to any part of the notice,

and may make such modifications in the notice as may be required for giving effect to the direction.

(5) On an appeal under section 48(4), the Tribunal may cancel the determination of the Commissioner.

(6) Any party to an appeal to the Tribunal under section 48 may appeal from the decision of the Tribunal on a point of law to the appropriate court; and that court shall be—

(a) the High Court of Justice in England if the address of the person who was the appellant before the Tribunal is in England or Wales,

(b) the Court of Session if that address is in Scotland, and

(c) the High Court of Justice in Northern Ireland if that address is in Northern Ireland.

(7) For the purposes of subsection (6)—

(a) the address of a registered company is that of its registered office, and

(b) the address of a person (other than a registered company) carrying on a business is that of his principal place of business in the United Kingdom.

[Data Protection Act 1998, s 49.]

8–7404 50. Powers of entry and inspection. Schedule 9 (powers of entry and inspection) has effect.

[Data Protection Act 1998, s 50.]

PART VI[1]

MISCELLANEOUS AND GENERAL

Functions of Commissioner

8–7405 51. General duties of Commissioner. (1) It shall be the duty of the Commissioner to promote the following of good practice by data controllers and, in particular, so to perform his functions under this Act as to promote the observance of the requirements of this Act by data controllers.

(2) The Commissioner shall arrange for the dissemination in such form and manner as he considers appropriate of such information as it may appear to him expedient to give to the public about the operation of this Act, about good practice, and about other matters within the scope of his functions under this Act, and may give advice to any person as to any of those matters.

(3) Where—

(a) the Secretary of State so directs by order, or
(b) the Commissioner considers it appropriate to do so,

the Commissioner shall, after such consultation with trade associations, data subjects or persons representing data subjects as appears to him to be appropriate, prepare and disseminate to such persons as he considers appropriate codes of practice for guidance as to good practice.

(4) The Commissioner shall also—

(a) where he considers it appropriate to do so, encourage trade associations to prepare, and to disseminate to their members, such codes of practice, and
(b) where any trade association submits a code of practice to him for his consideration, consider the code and, after such consultation with data subjects or persons representing data subjects as appears to him to be appropriate, notify the trade association whether in his opinion the code promotes the following of good practice.

(5) An order under subsection (3) shall describe the personal data or processing to which the code of practice is to relate, and may also describe the persons or classes of persons to whom it is to relate.

(6) The Commissioner shall arrange for the dissemination in such form and manner as he considers appropriate of—

(a) any Community finding as defined by paragraph 15(2) of Part II of Schedule 1,
(b) any decision of the European Commission, under the procedure provided for in Article 31(2) of the Data Protection Directive, which is made for the purposes of Article 26(3) or (4) of the Directive, and
(c) such other information as it may appear to him to be expedient to give to data controllers in relation to any personal data about the protection of the rights and freedoms of data subjects in relation to the processing of personal data in countries and territories outside the European Economic Area.

(7) The Commissioner may, with the consent of the data controller, assess any processing of personal data for the following of good practice and shall inform the data controller of the results of the assessment.

(8) The Commissioner may charge such sums as he may with the consent of the Secretary of State determine for any services provided by the Commissioner by virtue of this Part.

(9) In this section—

"good practice" means such practice in the processing of personal data as appears to the Commissioner to be desirable having regard to the interests of data subjects and others, and includes (but is not limited to) compliance with the requirements of this Act;
"trade association" includes any body representing data controllers.
[Data Protection Act 1998, s 51, as amended by SI 2001/3500 and SI 2003/1887.]

---

1. Part VI contains ss 51 to 75.

8–7406 52. Reports and codes of practice to be laid before Parliament. (1) The Commissioner shall lay annually before each House of Parliament a general report on the exercise of his functions under this Act.

(2) The Commissioner may from time to time lay before each House of Parliament such other reports with respect to those functions as he thinks fit.

(3) The Commissioner shall lay before each House of Parliament any code of practice prepared under section 51(3) for complying with a direction of the Secretary of State, unless the code is included in any report laid under subsection (1) or (2).
[Data Protection Act 1998, s 52, as amended by SI 2001/3500 and SI 2003/1887.]

8–7407 53. Assistance by Commissioner in cases involving processing for the special purposes. (1) An individual who is an actual or prospective party to any proceedings under section 7(9), 10(4), 12(8) or 14 or by virtue of section 13 which relate to personal data processed for the special purposes may apply to the Commissioner for assistance in relation to those proceedings.

(2) The Commissioner shall, as soon as reasonably practicable after receiving an application under subsection (1), consider it and decide whether and to what extent to grant it, but he shall not grant the application unless, in his opinion, the case involves a matter of substantial public importance.

(3) If the Commissioner decides to provide assistance, he shall, as soon as reasonably practicable after making the decision, notify the applicant, stating the extent of the assistance to be provided.

(4) If the Commissioner decides not to provide assistance, he shall, as soon as reasonably

practicable after making the decision, notify the applicant of his decision and, if he thinks fit, the reasons for it.

(5) In this section—

(a) references to "proceedings" include references to prospective proceedings, and

(b) "applicant", in relation to assistance under this section, means an individual who applies for assistance.

(6) Schedule 10 has effect for supplementing this section.

[Data Protection Act 1998, s 53.]

8–7408   **54. International co-operation.**   (1) The Commissioner—

(a) shall continue to be the designated authority in the United Kingdom for the purposes of Article 13 of the Convention, and

(b) shall be the supervisory authority in the United Kingdom for the purposes of the Data Protection Directive.

(2) The Secretary of State may by order[1] make provision as to the functions to be discharged by the Commissioner as the designated authority in the United Kingdom for the purposes of Article 13 of the Convention.

(3) The Secretary of State may by order[2] make provision as to co-operation by the Commissioner with the European Commission and with supervisory authorities in other EEA States in connection with the performance of their respective duties and, in particular, as to—

(a) the exchange of information with supervisory authorities in other EEA States or with the European Commission, and

(b) the exercise within the United Kingdom at the request of a supervisory authority in another EEA State, in cases excluded by section 5 from the application of the other provisions of this Act, of functions of the Commissioner specified in the order.

(4) The Commissioner shall also carry out any data protection functions which the Secretary of State by order direct him to carry out for the purpose of enabling Her Majesty's Government in the United Kingdom to give effect to any international obligations of the United Kingdom.

(5) The Commissioner shall, if so directed by the Secretary of State, provide any authority exercising data protection functions under the law of a colony specified in the direction with such assistance in connection with the discharge of those functions as the Secretary of State may direct or approve, on such terms (including terms as to payment) as the Secretary of State may direct or approve.

(6) Where the European Commission makes a decision for the purposes of Article 26(3) or (4) of the Data Protection Directive under the procedure provided for in Article 31(2) of the Directive, the Commissioner shall comply with that decision in exercising his functions under paragraph 9 of Schedule 4 or, as the case may be, paragraph 8 of that Schedule.

(7) The Commissioner shall inform the European Commission and the supervisory authorities in other EEA States—

(a) of any approvals granted for the purposes of paragraph 8 of Schedule 4, and

(b) of any authorisations granted for the purposes of paragraph 9 of that Schedule.

(8) In this section—

"the Convention" means the Convention for the Protection of Individuals with regard to Automatic Processing of Personal Data which was opened for signature on 28th January 1981;

"data protection functions" means functions relating to the protection of individuals with respect to the processing of personal information.

[Data Protection Act 1998, s 54, as amended by SI 2001/3500 and SI 2003/1887.]

---

1. The Date Protection (Functions of Designated Authority) Order 2000, SI 2000/186 has been made.
2. The Data Protection (International Cooperation) Order 2000, SI 2000/190 has been made.

8–7408A   **54A. Inspection of overseas information systems.**   (1) The Commissioner may inspect any personal data recorded in—

(a) the Schengen information system,

(b) the Europol information system,

(c) the Customs information system.

(2) The power conferred by subsection (1) is exercisable only for the purpose of assessing whether or not any processing of the data has been or is being carried out in compliance with this Act.

(3) The power includes power to inspect, operate and test equipment which is used for the processing of personal data.

(4) Before exercising the power, the Commissioner must give notice in writing of his intention to do so to the data controller.

(5) But subsection (4) does not apply if the Commissioner considers that the case is one of urgency.

(6) Any person who—

(*a*) intentionally obstructs a person exercising the power conferred by subsection (1), or

(*b*) fails without reasonable excuse to give any person exercising the power any assistance he may reasonably require,

is guilty of an offence.

(7) In this section—

"the Customs information system" means the information system established under Chapter II of the Convention on the Use of Information Technology for Customs Purposes,

"the Europol information system" means the information system established under Title II of the Convention on the Establishment of a European Police Office,

"the Schengen information system" means the information system established under Title IV of the Convention implementing the Schengen Agreement of 14th June 1985, or any system established in its place in pursuance of any Community obligation.

[Data Protection Act 1998, s 54A, as inserted by the Crime (International Co-operation) Act 2003, s 81.]

Unlawful obtaining etc of personal data

8–7409   55. Unlawful obtaining etc of personal data.   (1) A person must not knowingly or recklessly, without the consent of the data controller—

(*a*) obtain or disclose personal data or the information contained in personal data, or

(*b*) procure the disclosure to another person of the information contained in personal data.

(2) Subsection (1) does not apply to a person who shows—

(*a*) that the obtaining, disclosing or procuring—

  (i) was necessary for the purpose of preventing or detecting crime, or

  (ii) was required or authorised by or under any enactment, by any rule of law or by the order of a court,

(*b*) that he acted in the reasonable belief that he had in law the right to obtain or disclose the data or information or, as the case may be, to procure the disclosure of the information to the other person,

(*c*) that he acted in the reasonable belief that he would have had the consent of the data controller if the data controller had known of the obtaining, disclosing or procuring and the circumstances of it, or

(*d*) that in the particular circumstances the obtaining, disclosing or procuring was justified as being in the public interest.

(3) A person who contravenes subsection (1) is guilty of an offence[1].

(4) A person who sells personal data is guilty of an offence[1] if he has obtained the data in contravention of subsection (1).

(5) A person who offers to sell personal data is guilty of an offence[1] if—

(*a*) he has obtained the data in contravention of subsection (1), or

(*b*) he subsequently obtains the data in contravention of that subsection.

(6) For the purposes of subsection (5), an advertisement indicating that personal data are or may be for sale is an offer to sell the data.

(7) Section 1(2) does not apply for the purposes of this section; and for the purposes of subsections (4) to (6), "personal data" includes information extracted from personal data.

(8) References in this section to personal data do not include references to personal data which by virtue of section 28 or 33A are exempt from this section.

[Data Protection Act 1998, s 55, as amended by the Freedom of Information Act 2000, s 70.]

---

1. For procedure and penalties, see s 60, post.

Records obtained under data subject's right of access

8–7409A   56. Prohibition of requirement as to production of certain records[1].   (1) A person must not, in connection with—

(*a*) the recruitment of another person as an employee,

(*b*) the continued employment of another person, or

(*c*) any contract for the provision of services to him by another person,

require that other person or a third party to supply him with a relevant record or to produce a relevant record to him.

(2) A person concerned with the provision (for payment or not) of goods, facilities or services to the public or a section of the public must not, as a condition of providing or offering to provide any goods, facilities or services to another person, require that other person or a third party to supply him with a relevant record or to produce a relevant record to him.

(3) Subsections (1) and (2) do not apply to a person who shows—

    (*a*)   that the imposition of the requirement was required or authorised by or under any enactment, by any rule of law or by the order of a court, or

    (*b*)   that in the particular circumstances the imposition of the requirement was justified as being in the public interest.

(4) Having regard to the provisions of Part V of the Police Act 1997 (certificates of criminal records etc), the imposition of the requirement referred to in subsection (1) or (2) is not to be regarded as being justified as being in the public interest on the ground that it would assist in the prevention or detection of crime.

    (5) A person who contravenes subsection (1) or (2) is guilty of an offence[2].

    (6) In this section "a relevant record" means any record which—

    (*a*)   has been or is to be obtained by a data subject from any data controller specified in the first column of the Table below in the exercise of the right conferred by section 7, and

    (*b*)   contains information relating to any matter specified in relation to that data controller in the second column,

and includes a copy of such a record or a part of such a record.

Data controller	*Subject-matter*

1 Any of the following persons—
  (*a*) a chief officer of police of a police force in England and Wales.
  (*b*) a chief constable of a police force in Scotland.
  (*c*) the Chief Constable of the Police Service of Northern Ireland.
  (*d*) the Director General of the National Criminal Intelligence Service.
  (*e*) the Director General of the National Crime Squad.
	(*a*) Convictions.
	(*b*) Cautions.

2 The Secretary of State.	(*a*) Convictions. (*b*) Cautions. (*c*) His functions under section 92 of the Powers of Criminal Courts (Sentencing) Act 2000, section 205(2) or 208 of the Criminal Procedure (Scotland) Act 1995 or section 73 of the Children and Young Persons Act (Northern Ireland) 1968 in relation to any person sentenced to detention. (*d*) His functions under the Prison Act 1952, the Prisons (Scotland) Act 1989 or the Prison Act (Northern Ireland) 1953 in relation to any person imprisoned or detained. (*e*) His functions under the Social Security Contributions and Benefits Act 1992, the Social Security Administration Act 1992 or the Jobseekers Act 1995. (*f*) His functions under Part V of the Police Act 1997.
3 The Department of Health and Social Services for Northern Ireland.	Its functions under the Social Security Contributions and Benefits (Northern Ireland) Act 1992, the Social Security Administration (Northern Ireland) Act 1992 or the Jobseekers (Northern Ireland) Order 1995.

(6A) A record is not a relevant record to the extent that it relates, or is to relate, only to personal data falling within paragraph (*e*) of the definition of "data" in section 1(1).

    (7) In the Table in subsection (6)—

"caution" means a caution given to any person in England and Wales or Northern Ireland in respect of an offence which, at the time when the caution is given, is admitted;

"conviction" has the same meaning as in the Rehabilitation of Offenders Act 1974 or the Rehabilitation of Offenders (Northern Ireland) Order 1978.

    (8) The Secretary of State may by order amend—

    (*a*)   the Table in subsection (6), and

    (*b*)   subsection (7).

(9) For the purposes of this section a record which states that a data controller is not processing any personal data relating to a particular matter shall be taken to be a record containing information relating to that matter.

(10) In this section "employee" means an individual who—

(a) works under a contract of employment, as defined by section 230(2) of the Employment Rights Act 1996, or

(b) holds any office,

whether or not he is entitled to remuneration; and "employment" shall be construed accordingly.
[Data Protection Act 1998, s 56 as amended by the Powers of Criminal Courts (Sentencing) Act 2000, Sch 9, the Police (Northern Ireland) Act 2000, s 78(2)(a), SI 2001/3500, SI 2003/1887 and the Freedom of Information Act 2000, s 68.]

1. At the date of going to press, s 56 had not been brought into force.
2. For procedure and penalties, see s 60, post.

8–7409B   57. Avoidance of certain contractual terms relating to health records. (1) Any term or condition of a contract is void in so far as it purports to require an individual—

(a) to supply any other person with a record to which this section applies, or with a copy of such a record or a part of such a record, or

(b) to produce to any other person such a record, copy or part.

(2) This section applies to any record which—

(a) has been or is to be obtained by a data subject in the exercise of the right conferred by section 7, and

(b) consists of the information contained in any health record as defined by section 68(2).
[Data Protection Act 1998, s 57.]

Information provided to Commissioner or Tribunal

8–7409C   58. Disclosure of information. No enactment or rule of law prohibiting or restricting the disclosure of information shall preclude a person from furnishing the Commissioner or the Tribunal with any information necessary for the discharge of their functions under this Act.
[Data Protection Act 1998, s 58.]

8–7409D   59. Confidentiality of information. (1) No person who is or has been the Commissioner, a member of the Commissioner's staff or an agent of the Commissioner shall disclose any information which—

(a) has been obtained by, or furnished to, the Commissioner under or for the purposes of this Act,

(b) relates to an identified or identifiable individual or business, and

(c) is not at the time of the disclosure, and has not previously been, available to the public from other sources,

unless the disclosure is made with lawful authority.

(2) For the purposes of subsection (1) a disclosure of information is made with lawful authority only if, and to the extent that—

(a) the disclosure is made with the consent of the individual or of the person for the time being carrying on the business,

(b) the information was provided for the purpose of its being made available to the public (in whatever manner) under any provision of this Act,

(c) the disclosure is made for the purposes of, and is necessary for, the discharge of—

(i) any functions under this Act, or
(ii) any Community obligation,

(d) the disclosure is made for the purposes of any proceedings, whether criminal or civil and whether arising under, or by virtue of, this Act or otherwise, or

(e) having regard to the rights and freedoms or legitimate interests of any person, the disclosure is necessary in the public interest.

(3) Any person who knowingly or recklessly discloses information in contravention of subsection (1) is guilty of an offence[1].
[Data Protection Act 1998, s 59.]

1. For procedure and penalties, see s 60, post.

General provisions relating to offences

8–7409E 60. Prosecutions and penalties. (1) No proceedings for an offence under this Act shall be instituted—

(a) in England or Wales, except by the Commissioner or by or with the consent of the Director of Public Prosecutions;

(b) in Northern Ireland, except by the Commissioner or by or with the consent of the Director of Public Prosecutions for Northern Ireland.

(2) A person guilty of an offence under any provision of this Act other than* paragraph 12 of Schedule 9 is liable[1]—

(a) on summary conviction, to a fine not exceeding **the statutory maximum**, or

(b) on conviction on indictment, to a **fine**.

(3) A person guilty of an offence under* paragraph 12 of Schedule 9 is liable on summary conviction to a fine not exceeding **level 5** on the standard scale.

(4) Subject to subsection (5), the court by or before which a person is convicted of—

(a) an offence under section 21(1), 22(6), 55 or 56,

(b) an offence under section 21(2) relating to processing which is assessable processing for the purposes of section 22, or

(c) an offence under section 47(1) relating to an enforcement notice,

may order any document or other material used in connection with the processing of personal data and appearing to the court to be connected with the commission of the offence to be forfeited, destroyed or erased.

(5) The court shall not make an order under subsection (4) in relation to any material where a person (other than the offender) claiming to be the owner of or otherwise interested in the material applies to be heard by the court, unless an opportunity is given to him to show cause why the order should not be made.

[Data Protection Act 1998, s 60.]

***Words "section 54A and" inserted by the Crime (International Co-operation) Act 2003, Sch 5 from a date to be appointed.**

1. For procedure in respect of this offence which is triable either way, see the Magistrates' Courts Act 1980, ss 17A–21, in PART I: MAGISTRATES' COURTS, PROCEDURE, ante.

8–7409F 61. Liability of directors etc. (1) Where an offence under this Act has been committed by a body corporate and is proved to have been committed with the consent or connivance of or to be attributable to any neglect on the part of any director, manager, secretary or similar officer of the body corporate or any person who was purporting to act in any such capacity, he as well as the body corporate shall be guilty of that offence and be liable to be proceeded against and punished accordingly.

(2) Where the affairs of a body corporate are managed by its members subsection (1) shall apply in relation to the acts and defaults of a member in connection with his functions of management as if he were a director of the body corporate.

(3) Where an offence under this Act has been committed by a Scottish partnership and the contravention in question is proved to have occurred with the consent or connivance of, or to be attributable to any neglect on the part of, a partner, he as well as the partnership shall be guilty of that offence and shall be liable to be proceeded against and punished accordingly.

[Data Protection Act 1998, s 61.]

Amendments of Consumer Credit Act 1974

8–7409G 62. *Amendments of Consumer Credit Act 1974*

General

8–7409H 63. Application to Crown. (1) This Act binds the Crown.

(2) For the purposes of this Act each government department shall be treated as a person separate from any other government department.

(3) Where the purposes for which and the manner in which any personal data are, or are to be, processed are determined by any person acting on behalf of the Royal Household, the Duchy of Lancaster or the Duchy of Cornwall, the data controller in respect of those data for the purposes of this Act shall be—

(a) in relation to the Royal Household, the Keeper of the Privy Purse,

(b) in relation to the Duchy of Lancaster, such person as the Chancellor of the Duchy appoints, and

(c) in relation to the Duchy of Cornwall, such person as the Duke of Cornwall, or the possessor for the time being of the Duchy of Cornwall, appoints.

(4) Different persons may be appointed under subsection (3)(b) or (c) for different purposes.

(5) Neither a government department nor a person who is a data controller by virtue of subsection (3) shall be liable to prosecution under this Act, but sections 54A and 55 and paragraph 12 of Schedule 9 shall apply to a person in the service of the Crown as they apply to any other person.
[Data Protection Act 1998, s 63 as amended by the Crime (International Co-operation) Act 2003, Sch 5.]

8–7409HA   63A. Application to Parliament.   (1) Subject to the following provisions of this section and to section 35A, this Act applies to the processing of personal data by or on behalf of either House of Parliament as it applies to the processing of personal data by other persons

(2) Where the purposes for which and the manner in which any personal data are, or are to be, processed are determined by or on behalf of the House of Commons, the data controller in respect of those data for the purposes of this Act shall be the Corporate Officer of that House.

(3) Where the purposes for which and the manner in which any personal data are, or are to be, processed are determined by or on behalf of the House of Lords, the data controller in respect of those data for the purposes of this Act shall be the Corporate Officer of that House.

(4) Nothing in subsection (2) or (3) is to be taken to render the Corporate Officer of the House of Commons or the Corporate Officer of the House of Lords liable to prosecution under this Act, but section 55 and paragraph 12 of Schedule 9 shall apply to a person acting on behalf of either House as they apply to any other person.
[Data Protection Act 1998, s 63A, as inserted by the Freedom of Information Act 2000, Sch 6.]

8–7409I   64. Transmission of notices etc by electronic or other means.   (1) This section applies to

(a) a notice or request under any provision of Part II,
(b) a notice under subsection (1) of section 24 or particulars made available under that subsection, or
(c) an application under section 41(2),

but does not apply to anything which is required to be served in accordance with rules of court.

(2) The requirement that any notice, request, particulars or application to which this section applies should be in writing is satisfied where the text of the notice, request, particulars or application—

(a) is transmitted by electronic means,
(b) is received in legible form, and
(c) is capable of being used for subsequent reference.

(3) The Secretary of State may by regulations provide that any requirement that any notice, request, particulars or application to which this section applies should be in writing is not to apply in such circumstances as may be prescribed by the regulations.
[Data Protection Act 1998, s 64, as amended by SI 2001/3500 and SI 2003/1887.]

8–7409J   65. Service of notices by Commissioner.   (1) Any notice authorised or required by this Act to be served on or given to any person by the Commissioner may—

(a) if that person is an individual, be served on him—

   (i) by delivering it to him, or
   (ii) by sending it to him by post addressed to him at his usual or last-known place of residence or business, or
   (iii) by leaving it for him at that place;

(b) if that person is a body corporate or unincorporate, be served on that body—

   (i) by sending it by post to the proper officer of the body at its principal office, or
   (ii) by addressing it to the proper officer of the body and leaving it at that office;

(c) if that person is a partnership in Scotland, be served on that partnership—

   (i) by sending it by post to the principal office of the partnership, or
   (ii) by addressing it to that partnership and leaving it at that office.

(2) In subsection (1)(b) "principal office", in relation to a registered company, means its registered office and "proper officer", in relation to any body, means the secretary or other executive officer charged with the conduct of its general affairs.

(3) This section is without prejudice to any other lawful method of serving or giving a notice.
[Data Protection Act 1998, s 65.]

8–7409K   66. Exercise of rights in Scotland by children.   (1) Where a question falls to be determined in Scotland as to the legal capacity of a person under the age of sixteen years to exercise any right conferred by any provision of this Act, that person shall be taken to have that capacity where he has a general understanding of what it means to exercise that right.

(2) Without prejudice to the generality of subsection (1), a person of twelve years of age or more

shall be presumed to be of sufficient age and maturity to have such understanding as is mentioned in that subsection.

[Data Protection Act 1998, s 66.]

8–7409L 67. Orders, regulations and rules.   (1) Any power conferred by this Act on the Secretary of State to make an order, regulations or rules shall be exercisable by statutory instrument.

(2) Any order, regulations or rules made by the Secretary of State under this Act may—

(a) make different provision for different cases, and
(b) make such supplemental, incidental, consequential or transitional provision or savings as the Secretary of State considers appropriate;

and nothing in section 7(11), 19(5), 26(1) or 30(4) limits the generality of paragraph (a).

(3) Before making—

(a) an order under any provision of this Act other than section 75(3),
(b) any regulations under this Act other than notification regulations (as defined by section 16(2)),

the Secretary of State shall consult the Commissioner.

(4) A statutory instrument containing (whether alone or with other provisions) an order under—

section 10(2)(b),
section 12(5)(b),
section 22(1),
section 30,
section 32(3),
section 38,
section 56(8),
paragraph 10 of Schedule 3, or
paragraph 4 of Schedule 7,

shall not be made unless a draft of the instrument has been laid before and approved by a resolution of each House of Parliament.

(5) A statutory instrument which contains (whether alone or with other provisions)—

(a) an order under—

section 22(7),
section 23,
section 51(3),
section 54(2), (3) or (4),
paragraph 3, 4 or 14 of Part II of Schedule 1,
paragraph 6 of Schedule 2,
paragraph 2, 7 or 9 of Schedule 3,
paragraph 4 of Schedule 4,
paragraph 6 of Schedule 7,

(b) regulations under section 7 which—

(i) prescribe cases for the purposes of subsection (2)(b),
(ii) are made by virtue of subsection (7), or
(iii) relate to the definition of "the prescribed period",

(c) regulations under section 8(1), 9(3) or 9A(5),
(d) regulations under section 64,
(e) notification regulations (as defined by section 16(2)), or
(f) rules under paragraph 7 of Schedule 6,

and which is not subject to the requirement in subsection (4) that a draft of the instrument be laid before and approved by a resolution of each House of Parliament, shall be subject to annulment in pursuance of a resolution of either House of Parliament.

(6) A statutory instrument which contains only—

(a) regulations prescribing fees for the purposes of any provision of this Act, or
(b) regulations under section 7 prescribing fees for !he purposes of any other enactment,

shall be laid before Parliament after being made.

[Data Protection Act 1998, s 67, as amended by SI 2001/3500, SI 2003/1887 and the Freedom of Information Act 2000, s 69.]

8–7409M 68. Meaning of "accessible record".   (1) In this Act "accessible record" means—

(a) a health record as defined by subsection (2),
(b) an educational record as defined by Schedule 11, or
(c) an accessible public record as defined by Schedule 12.

(2) In subsection (1)(a) "health record" means any record which—

(a) consists of information relating to the physical or mental health or condition of an individual, and

(b) has been made by or on behalf of a health professional in connection with the care of that individual.

[Data Protection Act 1998, s 68.]

8–7409N 69. Meaning of "health professional". (1) In this Act "health professional" means any of the following—

(a) a registered medical practitioner,

(b) a registered dentist as defined by section 53(1) of the Dentists Act 1984,

(bb) a Primary Care Trust established under section 16A of that Act,

(c) a registered dispensing optician or a registered optometrist within the meaning of the Opticians Act 1989,

(d) a registered pharmaceutical chemist as defined by section 24(1) of the Pharmacy Act 1954 or a registered person as defined by Article 2(2) of the Pharmacy (Northern Ireland) Order 1976,

(e) a registered nurse or midwife,

(f) a registered osteopath as defined by section 41 of the Osteopaths Act 1993,

(g) a registered chiropractor as defined by section 43 of the Chiropractors Act 1994,

(h) any person who is registered as a member of a profession to which the Health Professions Order 2001 for the time being extends,

(i) a clinical psychologist or child psychotherapist,

(j) (*revoked*) and

(k) a scientist employed by such a body as head of a department.

(2) In subsection (1)(a) "registered medical practitioner" includes any person who is provisionally registered under section 15 or 21 of the Medical Act 1983 and is engaged in such employment as is mentioned in subsection (3) of that section.

(3) In subsection (1) "health service body" means—

(a) a Strategic Health Authority or a Health Authority established under section 8 of the National Health Service Act 1977,

(b) a Special Health Authority established under section 11 of that Act,

(bb) a Primary Care Trust established under section 16A of that Act,

(bbb) a Local Health Board established under section 16B of that Act,

(c) a Health Board within the meaning of the National Health Service (Scotland) Act 1978,

(d) a Special Health Board within the meaning of that Act,

(e) the managers of a State Hospital provided under section 102 of that Act,

(f) a National Health Service trust first established under section 5 of the National Health Service and Community Care Act 1990 or section 12A of the National Health Service (Scotland) Act 1978,

(fa) an NHS foundation trust,

(g) a Health and Social Services Board established under Article 16 of the Health and Personal Social Services (Northern Ireland) Order 1972,

(h) a special health and social services agency established under the Health and Personal Social Services (Special Agencies) (Northern Ireland) Order 1990, or

(i) a Health and Social Services trust established under Article 10 of the Health and Personal Social Services (Northern Ireland) Order 1991.

[Data Protection Act 1998, s 69 as amended by SI 2000/90, SI 2002/254 and 2469, the National Health Service Reform and Health Care Professions Act 2002, s 6(2), SI 2003/1590, SI 2002/253, the Health and Social Care (Community Health and Standards) Act 2003, Sch 4 and SI 2005/848.]

8–7409O 70. Supplementary definitions. (1) In this Act, unless the context otherwise requires—

"business" includes any trade or profession;

"the Commissioner" means the Information Commissioner;

"credit reference agency" has the same meaning as in the Consumer Credit Act 1974;

"the Data Protection Directive" means Directive 95/46/EC on the protection of individuals with regard to the processing of personal data and on the free movement of such data;

"EEA State" means a State which is a contracting party to the Agreement on the European Economic Area signed at Oporto on 2nd May 1992 as adjusted by the Protocol signed at Brussels on 17th March 1993;

"enactment" includes an enactment passed after this Act and any enactment comprised in, or in any instrument made under, an Act of the Scottish Parliament;

"government department" includes a Northern Ireland department and any body or authority exercising statutory functions on behalf of the Crown;

"Minister of the Crown" has the same meaning as in the Ministers of the Crown Act 1975;

"public register" means any register which pursuant to a requirement imposed—

(a) by or under any enactment, or

    (*b*)   in pursuance of any international agreement,

is open to public inspection or open to inspection by any person having a legitimate interest;

"pupil"—

    (*a*)   in relation to a school in England and Wales, means a registered pupil within the meaning of the Education Act 1996,

    (*b*)   in relation to a school in Scotland, means a pupil within the meaning of the Education (Scotland) Act 1980, and

    (*c*)   in relation to a school in Northern Ireland, means a registered pupil within the meaning of the Education and Libraries (Northern Ireland) Order 1986;

"recipient", in relation to any personal data, means any person to whom the data are disclosed, including any person (such as an employee or agent of the data controller, a data processor or an employee or agent of a data processor) to whom they are disclosed in the course of processing the data for the data controller, but does not include any person to whom disclosure is or may be made as a result of, or with a view to, a particular inquiry by or on behalf of that person made in the exercise of any power conferred by law;

"registered company" means a company registered under the enactments relating to companies for the time being in force in the United Kingdom;

"school"—

    (*a*)   in relation to England and Wales, has the same meaning as in the Education Act 1996,

    (*b*)   in relation to Scotland, has the same meaning as in the Education (Scotland) Act 1980, and

    (*c*)   in relation to Northern Ireland, has the same meaning as in the Education and Libraries (Northern Ireland) Order 1986;

"teacher" includes—

    (*a*)   in Great Britain, head teacher, and

    (*b*)   in Northern Ireland, the principal of a school;

"third party", in relation to personal data, means any person other than—

    (*a*)   the data subject,

    (*b*)   the data controller, or

    (*c*)   any data processor or other person authorised to process data for the data controller or processor;

"the Tribunal" means the Information Tribunal.

(2) For the purposes of this Act data are inaccurate if they are incorrect or misleading as to any matter of fact.

[Data Protection Act 1998, s 70 as amended by SI 1999/1820, Schedule 2 and the Freedom of Information Act 2000, Sch 2.]

8–7409P   **71. Index of defined expressions.**   The following Table shows provisions defining or otherwise explaining expressions used in this Act (other than provisions defining or explaining an expression only used in the same section or Schedule)—

accessible record	section 68
address (in Part III)	section 16(3)
Business	section 70(1)
the Commissioner	section 70(1)
credit reference agency	section 70(1)
Data	section 1(1)
data controller	sections 1(1) and (4) and 63(3)
data processor	section 1(1)
the Data Protection Directive	section 70(1)
data protection principles	section 4 and Schedule 1
data subject	section 1(1)
disclosing (of personal data)	section 1(2)(*b*)
EEA State	section 70(1)
Enactment	section 70(1)
enforcement notice	section 40(1)
fees regulations (in Part III)	section 16(2)
government department	section 70(1)
health professional	section 69
inaccurate (in relation to data)	section 70(2)
information notice	section 43(1)
Minister of the Crown	section 70(1)
the non-disclosure provisions (in Part IV)	section 27(3)
notification regulations (in Part III)	section 16(2)

obtaining (of personal data)	section 1(2)(*a*)
personal data	section 1(1)
prescribed (in Part III)	section 16(2)
processing (of information or data)	section 1(1) and paragraph 5 of Schedule 8
public authority	section 1(1)
public register	section 70(1)
publish (in relation to journalistic, literary or artistic material)	section 32(6)
pupil (in relation to a school)	section 70(1)
recipient (in relation to personal data)	section 70(1)
recording (of personal data)	section 1(2)(*a*)
registered company	section 70(1)
registrable particulars (in Part III)	section 16(1)
relevant filing system	section 1(1)
School	section 70(1)
sensitive personal data	section 2
special information notice	section 44(1)
the special purposes	section 3
the subject information provisions (in Part IV)	section 27(2)
Teacher	section 70(1)
third party (in relation to processing of personal data)	section 70(1)
the Tribunal	section 70(1)
using (of personal data)	section 1(2)(*b*).

[Data Protection Act 1998, s 71, as amended by the Freedom of Information Act 2000, s 68.]

8–7409Q   72. Modifications of Act.   During the period beginning with the commencement of this section and ending with 23rd October 2007, the provisions of this Act shall have effect subject to the modifications set out in Schedule 13.
[Data Protection Act 1998, s 72.]

8–7409R   73. Transitional provisions and savings.   Schedule 14 (which contains transitional provisions and savings) has effect.
[Data Protection Act 1998, s 73.]

8–7409S   74. Minor and consequential amendments and repeals and revocations.
(1)   Schedule 15 (which contains minor and consequential amendments) has effect.
(2)   The enactments and instruments specified in Schedule 16 are repealed or revoked to the extent specified.
[Data Protection Act 1998, s 74.]

8–7409T   75. Short title, commencement and extent.   (1) This Act may be cited as the Data Protection Act 1998.
(2)   The following provisions of this Act—

(*a*)   sections 1 to 3,
(*b*)   section 25(1) and (4),
(*c*)   section 26,
(*d*)   sections 67 to 71,
(*e*)   this section,
(*f*)   paragraph 17 of Schedule 5,
(*g*)   Schedule 11,
(*h*)   Schedule 12, and
(*i*)   so much of any other provision of this Act as confers any power to make subordinate legislation,

shall come into force on the day on which this Act is passed.
(3)   The remaining provisions of this Act shall come into force on such day as the Secretary of State may by order[1] appoint; and different days may be appointed for different purposes.
(4)   The day appointed under subsection (3) for the coming into force of section 56 must not be earlier than the first day on which sections 112, 113 and 115 of the Police Act 1997 (which provide for the issue by the Secretary of State of criminal conviction certificates, criminal record certificates and enhanced criminal record certificates) are all in force.
(5)   Subject to subsection (6), this Act extends to Northern Ireland.
(6)   Any amendment, repeal or revocation made by Schedule 15 or 16 has the same extent as that of the enactment or instrument to which it relates.
[Data Protection Act 1998, s 75, as amended by SI 2001/3500 and SI 2003/1887.]

---

1. The Data Protection Act 1998 (Commencement) Order 2000, SI 2000/183, brought all provisions of the Act, except for s 56, into force on 1 March 2000.

Section 4(1) and (2)   SCHEDULE 1
THE DATA PROTECTION PRINCIPLES

(Amended by SI 2001/3500 and SI 2003/1887.)

8–7409U

PART I
THE PRINCIPLES

1. Personal data shall be processed fairly and lawfully and, in particular, shall not be processed unless—

(*a*) at least one of the conditions in Schedule 2 is met, and
(*b*) in the case of sensitive personal data, at least one of the conditions in Schedule 3 is also met.

2. Personal data shall be obtained only for one or more specified and lawful purposes, and shall not be further processed in any manner incompatible with that purpose or those purposes.

3. Personal data shall be adequate, relevant and not excessive in relation to the purpose or purposes for which they are processed.

4. Personal data shall be accurate and, where necessary, kept up to date.

5. Personal data processed for any purpose or purposes shall not be kept for longer than is necessary for that purpose or those purposes.

6. Personal data shall be processed in accordance with the rights of data subjects under this Act.

7. Appropriate technical and organisational measures shall be taken against unauthorised or unlawful processing of personal data and against accidental loss or destruction of, or damage to, personal data.

8. Personal data shall not be transferred to a country or territory outside the European Economic Area unless that country or territory ensures an adequate level of protection for the rights and freedoms of data subjects in relation to the processing of personal data.

8–7409V

PART II
INTERPRETATION OF THE PRINCIPLES IN PART I

The first principle

1. (1) In determining for the purposes of the first principle whether personal data are processed fairly, regard is to be had to the method by which they are obtained, including in particular whether any person from whom they are obtained is deceived or misled as to the purpose or purposes for which they are to be processed.

(2) Subject to paragraph 2, for the purposes of the first principle data are to be treated as obtained fairly if they consist of information obtained from a person who—

(*a*) is authorised by or under any enactment to supply it, or
(*b*) is required to supply it by or under any enactment or by any convention or other instrument imposing an international obligation on the United Kingdom.

2. (1) Subject to paragraph 3, for the purposes of the first principle personal data are not to be treated as processed fairly unless—

(*a*) in the case of data obtained from the data subject, the data controller ensures so far as practicable that the data subject has, is provided with, or has made readily available to him, the information specified in sub-paragraph (3), and
(*b*) in any other case, the data controller ensures so far as practicable that, before the relevant time or as soon as practicable after that time, the data subject has, is provided with, or has made readily available to him, the information specified in sub-paragraph (3).

(2) In sub-paragraph (1)(*b*) "the relevant time" means—

(*a*) the time when the data controller first processes the data, or
(*b*) in a case where at that time disclosure to a third party within a reasonable period is envisaged—

    (i) if the data are in fact disclosed to such a person within that period, the time when the data are first disclosed,
    (ii) if within that period the data controller becomes, or ought to become, aware that the data are unlikely to be disclosed to such a person within that period, the time when the data controller does become, or ought to become, so aware, or
    (iii) in any other case, the end of that period.

(3) The information referred to in sub-paragraph (1) is as follows, namely—

(*a*) the identity of the data controller,
(*b*) if he has nominated a representative for the purposes of this Act, the identity of that representative,
(*c*) the purpose or purposes for which the data are intended to be processed, and
(*d*) any further information which is necessary, having regard to the specific circumstances in which the data are or are to be processed, to enable processing in respect of the data subject to be fair.

3. (1) Paragraph 2(1)(*b*) does not apply where either of the primary conditions in sub-paragraph (2), together with such further conditions as may be prescribed by the Secretary of State by order[1], are met.

(2) The primary conditions referred to in sub-paragraph (1) are—

(*a*) that the provision of that information would involve a disproportionate effort, or
(*b*) that the recording of the information to be contained in the data by, or the disclosure of the data by, the data controller is necessary for compliance with any legal obligation to which the data controller is subject, other than an obligation imposed by contract.

4. (1) Personal data which contain a general identifier falling within a description prescribed by the Secretary of State by order are not to be treated as processed fairly and lawfully unless they are processed in compliance with any conditions so prescribed in relation to general identifiers of that description.

(2) In sub-paragraph (1) "a general identifier" means any identifier (such as, for example, a number or code used for identification purposes) which—

(a) relates to an individual, and

(b) forms part of a set of similar identifiers which is of general application.

The second principle

5. The purpose or purposes for which personal data are obtained may in particular be specified—

(a) in a notice given for the purposes of paragraph 2 by the data controller to the data subject, or

(b) in a notification given to the Commissioner under Part III of this Act.

6. In determining whether any disclosure of personal data is compatible with the purpose or purposes for which the data were obtained, regard is to be had to the purpose or purposes for which the personal data are intended to be processed by any person to whom they are disclosed.

The fourth principle

7. The fourth principle is not to be regarded as being contravened by reason of any inaccuracy in personal data which accurately record information obtained by the data controller from the data subject or a third party in a case where—

(a) having regard to the purpose or purposes for which the data were obtained and further processed, the data controller has taken reasonable steps to ensure the accuracy of the data, and

(b) if the data subject has notified the data controller of the data subject's view that the data are inaccurate, the data indicate that fact.

The sixth principle

8. A person is to be regarded as contravening the sixth principle if, but only if—

(a) he contravenes section 7 by failing to supply information in accordance with that section,

(b) he contravenes section 10 by failing to comply with a notice given under subsection (1) of that section to the extent that the notice is justified or by failing to give a notice under subsection (3) of that section,

(c) he contravenes section 11 by failing to comply with a notice given under subsection (1) of that section,

(d) he contravenes section 12 by failing to comply with a notice given under subsection (1) or (2)(b) of that section or by failing to give a notification under subsection (2)(a) of that section or a notice under subsection (3) of that section, or

(e) he contravenes section 12A by failing to comply with a notice given under subsection (1) of that section to the extent that the notice is justified.

The seventh principle

9. Having regard to the state of technological development and the cost of implementing any measures, the measures must ensure a level of security appropriate to—

(a) the harm that might result from such unauthorised or unlawful processing or accidental loss, destruction or damage as are mentioned in the seventh principle, and

(b) the nature of the data to be protected.

10. The data controller must take reasonable steps to ensure the reliability of any employees of his who have access to the personal data.

11. Where processing of personal data is carried out by a data processor on behalf of a data controller, the data controller must in order to comply with the seventh principle—

(a) choose a data processor providing sufficient guarantees in respect of the technical and organisational security measures governing the processing to be carried out, and

(b) take reasonable steps to ensure compliance with those measures.

12. Where processing of personal data is carried out by a data processor on behalf of a data controller, the data controller is not to be regarded as complying with the seventh principle unless—

(a) the processing is carried out under a contract—

    (i) which is made or evidenced in writing, and

    (ii) under which the data processor is to act only on instructions from the data controller, and

(b) the contract requires the data processor to comply with obligations equivalent to those imposed on a data controller by the seventh principle.

The eighth principle

13. An adequate level of protection is one which is adequate in all the circumstances of the case, having regard in particular to—

(a) the nature of the personal data,

(b) the country or territory of origin of the information contained in the data,

(c) the country or territory of final destination of that information,

(d) the purposes for which and period during which the data are intended to be processed,

(e) the law in force in the country or territory in question,

(f) the international obligations of that country or territory,

(g) any relevant codes of conduct or other rules which are enforceable in that country or territory (whether generally or by arrangement in particular cases), and (*h*) any security measures taken in respect of the data in that country or territory.

14. The eighth principle does not apply to a transfer falling within any paragraph of Schedule 4, except in such circumstances and to such extent as the Secretary of State may by order provide.

15. (1) Where—

(*a*) in any proceedings under this Act any question arises as to whether the requirement of the eighth principle as to an adequate level of protection is met in relation to the transfer of any personal data to a country or territory outside the European Economic Area, and

(*b*) a Community finding has been made in relation to transfers of the kind in question,

that question is to be determined in accordance with that finding.

(2) In sub-paragraph (1) "Community finding" means a finding of the European Commission, under the procedure provided for in Article 31(2) of the Data Protection Directive, that a country or territory outside the European Economic Area does, or does not, ensure an adequate level of protection within the meaning of Article 25(2) of the Directive.

---

1. The Data Protection (Conditions under Paragraph 3 of Part II of Schedule 1) Order 2000, SI 2000/185 has been made which requires that any data controller claiming the benefit of the disapplication of the information requirements must still provide the relevant information to any individual who requests it in writing, and where, owing to lack of identifying information, the data controller cannot readily determine whether he is processing data relating to that individual, he must write explaining the position. A record must be kept of the reasons why a data controller believes it would involve disproportionate effort to provide information in those cases where the exemption from the information requirements is claimed.

8–7409W

Section 4(3)   SCHEDULE 2
CONDITIONS RELEVANT FOR PURPOSES OF THE FIRST PRINCIPLE: PROCESSING OF ANY PERSONAL DATA

(Amended by SI 2003/1887 and the Freedom of Information Act 2000, Sch 6.)

1. The data subject has given his consent to the processing.

2. The processing is necessary—

(*a*) for the performance of a contract to which the data subject is a party, or

(*b*) for the taking of steps at the request of the data subject with a view to entering into a contract.

3. The processing is necessary for compliance with any legal obligation to which the data controller is subject, other than an obligation imposed by contract.

4. The processing is necessary in order to protect the vital interests of the data subject.

5. The processing is necessary—

(*a*) for the administration of justice,

(*aa*) for the exercise of any functions of either House of Parliament,

(*b*) for the exercise of any functions conferred on any person by or under any enactment,

(*c*) for the exercise of any functions of the Crown, a Minister of the Crown or a government department, or

(*d*) for the exercise of any other functions of a public nature exercised in the public interest by any person.

6. (1) The processing is necessary for the purposes of legitimate interests pursued by the data controller or by the third party or parties to whom the data are disclosed, except where the processing is unwarranted in any particular case by reason of prejudice to the rights and freedoms or legitimate interests of the data subject.

(2) The Secretary of State may by order specify particular circumstances in which this condition is, or is not, to be taken to be satisfied.

8–7409X

Section 4(3)   SCHEDULE 3
CONDITIONS RELEVANT FOR PURPOSES OF THE FIRST PRINCIPLE: PROCESSING OF SENSITIVE PERSONAL DATA

(Amended by SI 2003/1887 and the Freedom of Information Act 2000, Sch 6.)

1. The data subject has given his explicit consent to the processing of the personal data.

2. (1) The processing is necessary for the purposes of exercising or performing any right or obligation which is conferred or imposed by law on the data controller in connection with employment.

(2) The Secretary of State may by order—

(*a*) exclude the application of sub-paragraph (1) in such cases as may be specified, or

(*b*) provide that, in such cases as may be specified, the condition in subparagraph (1) is not to be regarded as satisfied unless such further conditions as may be specified in the order are also satisfied.

3. The processing is necessary—

(*a*) in order to protect the vital interests of the data subject or another person, in a case where—

(i) consent cannot be given by or on behalf of the data subject, or

(ii) the data controller cannot reasonably be expected to obtain the consent of the data subject, or

(*b*) in order to protect the vital interests of another person, in a case where consent by or on behalf of the data subject has been unreasonably withheld.

4. The processing—

(*a*) is carried out in the course of its legitimate activities by any body or association which—

(i) is not established or conducted for profit, and

(ii) exists for political, philosophical religious or trade-union purposes,

(*b*) is carried out with appropriate safeguards for the rights and freedoms of data subjects,

(*c*) relates only to individuals who either are members of the body or association or have regular contact with it in connection with its purposes, and (*d*) does not involve disclosure of the personal data to a third party without the consent of the data subject.

5. The information contained in the personal data has been made public as a result of steps deliberately taken by the data subject.

6. The processing—

(*a*) is necessary for the purpose of, or in connection with, any legal proceedings (including prospective legal proceedings),

(*b*) is necessary for the purpose of obtaining legal advice, or

(*c*) is otherwise necessary for the purposes of establishing, exercising or defending legal rights.

7. (1) The processing is necessary—

(*a*) for the administration of justice,

(*aa*) for the exercise of any functions of either House of Parliament,

(*b*) for the exercise of any functions conferred on any person by or under an enactment, or

(*c*) for the exercise of any functions of the Crown, a Minister of the Crown or a government department.

(2) The Secretary of State may by order—

(*a*) exclude the application of sub-paragraph (1) in such cases as may be specified, or

(*b*) provide that, in such cases as may be specified, the condition in subparagraph (1) is not to be regarded as satisfied unless such further conditions as may be specified in the order are also satisfied.

8. (1) The processing is necessary for medical purposes and is undertaken by—

(*a*) a health professional, or

(*b*) a person who in the circumstances owes a duty of confidentiality which is equivalent to that which would arise if that person were a health professional.

(2) In this paragraph "medical purposes" includes the purposes of preventative medicine, medical diagnosis, medical research, the provision of care and treatment and the management of healthcare services.

9. (1) The processing—

(*a*) is of sensitive personal data consisting of information as to racial or ethnic origin,

(*b*) is necessary for the purpose of identifying or keeping under review the existence or absence of equality of opportunity or treatment between persons of different racial or ethnic origins, with a view to enabling such equality to be promoted or maintained, and

(*c*) is carried out with appropriate safeguards for the rights and freedoms of data subjects.

(2) The Secretary of State may by order specify circumstances in which processing falling within sub-paragraph (1)(*a*) and (*b*) is, or is not, to be taken for the purposes of sub-paragraph (1)(*c*) to be carried out with appropriate safeguards for the rights and freedoms of data subjects.

10. The personal data are processed in circumstances specified in an order[1] made by the Secretary of State for the purposes of this paragraph.

---

1. See the Data Protection (Processing of Sensitive Personal Data) Order 2000, SI 2000/417 amended by SI 2001/3649; see also the Data Protection (Processing of Sensitive Personal data) (Elected Representatives) Order 2002, SI 2002/2905.

8–7409Y

Section 4(3)   SCHEDULE 4

CASES WHERE THE EIGHTH PRINCIPLE DOES NOT APPLY

(*Amended by SI 2003/1887.*)

1. The data subject has given his consent to the transfer.

2. The transfer is necessary—

(*a*) for the performance of a contract between the data subject and the data controller, or

(*b*) for the taking of steps at the request of the data subject with a view to his entering into a contract with the data controller.

3. The transfer is necessary—

(*a*) for the conclusion of a contract between the data controller and a person other than the data subject which—

(i) is entered into at the request of the data subject, or

(ii) is in the interests of the data subject, or

(*b*) for the performance of such a contract.

4. (1) The transfer is necessary for reasons of substantial public interest.

(2) The Secretary of State may by order specify—

(*a*) circumstances in which a transfer is to be taken for the purposes of subparagraph (1) to be necessary for reasons of substantial public interest, and

(*b*) circumstances in which a transfer which is not required by or under an enactment is not to be taken for the purpose of sub-paragraph (1) to be necessary for reasons of substantial public interest.

5. The transfer—

(*a*) is necessary for the purpose of, or in connection with, any legal proceedings (including prospective legal proceedings),

(*b*) is necessary for the purpose of obtaining legal advice, or

(*c*) is otherwise necessary for the purposes of establishing, exercising or defending legal rights.

6. The transfer is necessary in order to protect the vital interests of the data subject.

7. The transfer is of part of the personal data on a public register and any conditions subject to which the register is open to inspection are complied with by any person to whom the data are or may be disclosed after the transfer.

8. The transfer is made on terms which are of a kind approved by the Commissioner as ensuring adequate safeguards for the rights and freedoms of data subjects.

9. The transfer has been authorised by the Commissioner as being made in such a manner as to ensure adequate safeguards for the rights and freedoms of data subjects.

8–7409Z

Section 6(7)

SCHEDULE 5
THE DATA PROTECTION COMMISSIONER AND THE DATA PROTECTION TRIBUNAL

8–7409AA

Sections 28(12), 48(5)

SCHEDULE 6
APPEAL PROCEEDINGS

(Amended by the Freedom of Information Act 2000, Sch 4 and SI 2003/1887.)

Hearing of appeals

1. For the purpose of hearing and determining appeals or any matter preliminary or incidental to an appeal the Tribunal shall sit at such times and in such places as the chairman or a deputy chairman may direct and may sit in two or more divisions.

Constitution of Tribunal in national security cases

2. (1) The Lord Chancellor shall from time to time designate, from among the chairman and deputy chairmen appointed by him under section 6(4)(*a*) and (*b*), those persons who are to be capable of hearing appeals under section 28(4) or (6) or under section 60(1) or (4) of the Freedom of Information Act 2000.

(2) A designation under sub-paragraph (1) may at any time be revoked by the Lord Chancellor.

3. The Tribunal shall be duly constituted—

(*a*) for an appeal under section 28(4) or (6) in any case where the application of paragraph 6(1) is excluded by rules under paragraph 7, or

(*b*) for an appeal under section 60(1) or (4) of the Freedom of Information Act 2000,

if it consists of three of the persons designated under paragraph 2(1), of whom one shall be designated by the Lord Chancellor to preside.

Constitution of Tribunal in other cases

4. (1) Subject to any rules made under paragraph 7, the Tribunal shall be duly constituted for an appeal under section 48(1), (2) or (4) if it consists of—

(*a*) the chairman or a deputy chairman (who shall preside), and

(*b*) an equal number of the members appointed respectively in accordance with paragraphs (*a*) and (*b*) of section 6(6).

(1A) Subject to any rules made under paragraph 7, the Tribunal shall be duly constituted for an appeal under section 57(1) or (2) of the Freedom of Information Act 2000 if it consists of—

(*a*) the chairman or a deputy chairman (who shall preside), and

(*b*) an equal number of the members appointed respectively in accordance with paragraphs (*aa*) and (*bb*) of section 6(6).

(2) The members who are to constitute the Tribunal in accordance with subparagraph (1) shall be nominated by the chairman or, if he is for any reason unable to act, by a deputy chairman.

Determination of questions by full Tribunal

5. The determination of any question before the Tribunal when constituted in accordance with paragraph 3 or 4 shall be according to the opinion of the majority of the members hearing the appeal.

Ex parte proceedings

6. (1) Subject to any rules made under paragraph 7, the jurisdiction of the Tribunal in respect of an appeal under section 28(4) or (6) shall be exercised ex parte by one or more persons designated under paragraph 2(1).

(2) Subject to any rules made under paragraph 7, the jurisdiction of the Tribunal in respect of an appeal under section 48(3) shall be exercised ex parte by the chairman or a deputy chairman sitting alone.

Rules of procedure

7. (1) The Secretary of State may make rules[1] for regulating—

(a) the exercise of the rights of appeal conferred—

    (i) by sections 28(4) and (6) and 48, and

    (ii) by sections 57(1) and (2) and section 60(1) and (4) of the Freedom of Information Act 2000, and

(b) the practice and procedure of the Tribunal.

(2) Rules under this paragraph may in particular make provision—

(a) with respect to the period within which an appeal can be brought and the burden of proof on an appeal,

(aa) for the joinder of any other person as a party to any proceedings on an appeal under the Freedom of Information Act 2000, (*ab*) for the hearing of an appeal under this Act with an appeal under the Freedom of Information Act 2000,

(*c*) for securing the production of documents and material used for the processing of personal data,

(*d*) for the inspection, examination, operation and testing of any equipment or material used in connection with the processing of personal data,

(*e*) for the hearing of an appeal wholly or partly in camera,

(*f*) for hearing an appeal in the absence of the appellant or for determining an appeal without a hearing,

(*g*) for enabling an appeal under section 48(1) against an information notice to be determined by the chairman or a deputy chairman,

(*h*) for enabling any matter preliminary or incidental to an appeal to be dealt with by the chairman or a deputy chairman,

(*i*) for the awarding of costs or, in Scotland, expenses,

(*j*) for the publication of reports of the Tribunal's decisions, and

(*k*) for conferring on the Tribunal such ancillary powers as the Secretary of State thinks necessary for the proper discharge of its functions.

(3) In making rules under this paragraph which relate to appeals under section 28(4) or (6) the Secretary of State shall have regard, in particular, to the need to secure that information is not disclosed contrary to the public interest.

Obstruction etc

8. (1) If any person is guilty of any act or omission in relation to proceedings before the Tribunal which, if those proceedings were proceedings before a court having power to commit for contempt, would constitute contempt of court, the Tribunal may certify the offence to the High Court or, in Scotland, the Court of Session.

(2) Where an offence is so certified, the court may inquire into the matter and, after hearing any witness who may be produced against or on behalf of the person charged with the offence, and after hearing any statement that may be offered in defence, deal with him in any manner in which it could deal with him if he had committed the like offence in relation to the court.

---

1. The Data Protection Tribunal (Enforcement Appeals) Rules 2000, SI 2000/189 amended by SI 2002/2722 and SI 2005/540, the Data Protection Tribunal (National Security Appeals) Rules 2000, SI 2000/206, the Data Protection Tribunal (National Security Appeals) (Telecommunications) Rules 2000, SI 2000/731, the Information Tribunal (National Security Appeals) Rules 2005, SI 2005/13 and the Information Tribunal (Enforcement Appeals) Rules 2005, SI 2005/14 have been made.

8–7409AB

Section 37

SCHEDULE 7

MISCELLANEOUS EXEMPTIONS

(*Amended by the Northern Ireland Act 1998, Sch 1, the Freedom of Information Act 2000, Sch 4, SI 2002/1555 and SI 2003/1887.*)

Confidential references given by the data controller

1. Personal data are exempt from section 7 if they consist of a reference given or to be given in confidence by the data controller for the purposes of—

(*a*) the education, training or employment, or prospective education, training or employment, of the data subject,

(*b*) the appointment, or prospective appointment, of the data subject to any office, or

(*c*) the provision, or prospective provision, by the data subject of any service.

Armed forces

2. Personal data are exempt from the subject information provisions in any case to the extent to which the application of those provisions would be likely to prejudice the combat effectiveness of any of the armed forces of the Crown.

Judicial appointments and honours

3. Personal data processed for the purposes of—

(*a*) assessing any person's suitability for judicial office or the office of Queen's Counsel, or

(*b*) the conferring by the Crown of any honour or dignity,

are exempt from the subject information provisions.

Crown employment and Crown or Ministerial appointments

4. (1) The Secretary of State may by order[1] exempt from the subject information provisions personal data processed for the purposes of assessing any person's suitability for—

(*a*) employment by or under the Crown, or

(*b*) any office to which appointments are made by Her Majesty, by a Minister of the Crown or by a Northern Ireland authority.

(2) In this paragraph "Northern Ireland authority" means the First Minister, the deputy First Minister, a Northern Ireland Minister or a Northern Ireland department.

Management forecasts etc

5. Personal data processed for the purposes of management forecasting or management planning to assist the data controller in the conduct of any business or other activity are exempt from the subject information provisions in any case to the extent to which the application of those provisions would be likely to prejudice the conduct of that business or other activity.

Corporate finance

6. (1) Where personal data are processed for the purposes of, or in connection with, a corporate finance service provided by a relevant person—

    (a) the data are exempt from the subject information provisions in any case to the extent to which either—

        (i) the application of those provisions to the data could affect the price of any instrument which is already in existence or is to be or may be created, or

        (ii) the data controller reasonably believes that the application of those provisions to the data could affect the price of any such instrument, and

    (b) to the extent that the data are not exempt from the subject information provisions by virtue of paragraph (a), they are exempt from those provisions if the exemption is required for the purpose of safeguarding an important economic or financial interest of the United Kingdom.

(2) For the purposes of sub-paragraph (1)(b) the Secretary of State may by order[2] specify—

    (a) matters to be taken into account in determining whether exemption from the subject information provisions is required for the purpose of safeguarding an important economic or financial interest of the United Kingdom, or

    (b) circumstances in which exemption from those provisions is, or is not, to be taken to be required for that purpose.

(3) In this paragraph—

"corporate finance service" means a service consisting in—

    (a) underwriting in respect of issues of, or the placing of issues of, any instrument,

    (b) advice to undertakings on capital structure, industrial strategy and related matters and advice and service relating to mergers and the purchase of undertakings, or

    (c) services relating to such underwriting as is mentioned in paragraph (a);

"instrument" means any instrument listed in section B of the Annex to the Council Directive on investment services in the securities field (93/22/EEC);

"price" includes value;

"relevant person" means—

    (a) any person who, by reason of any permission he has under Part IV of the Financial Services and Markets Act 2000, is able to carry on a corporate finance service without contravening the general prohibition, within the meaning of section 19 of that Act,

    (b) an EEA firm of the kind mentioned in paragraph 5(a) or (b) of Schedule 3 to that Act which has qualified for authorisation under paragraph 12 of that Schedule, and may lawfully carry on a corporate finance service,

    (c) any person who is exempt from the general prohibition in respect of any corporate finance service—

        (i) as a result of an exemption order made under section 38(1) of that Act, or

        (ii) by reason of section 39(1) of that Act (appointed representatives),

    (cc) any person, not falling within paragraph (a), (b) or (c) who may lawfully carry on a corporate finance service without contravening the general prohibition,

    (d) any person who, in the course of his employment, provides to his employer a service falling within paragraph (b) or (c) of the definition of "corporate finance service", or

    (e) any partner who provides to other partners in the partnership a service falling within either of those paragraphs.

Negotiations

7. Personal data which consist of records of the intentions of the data controller in relation to any negotiations with the data subject are exempt from the subject information provisions in any case to the extent to which the application of those provisions would be likely to prejudice those negotiations.

Examination marks

8. (1) Section 7 shall have effect subject to the provisions of sub-paragraphs (2) to (4) in the case of personal data consisting of marks or other information processed by a data controller—

    (a) for the purpose of determining the results of an academic, professional or other examination or of enabling the results of any such examination to be determined, or

    (b) in consequence of the determination of any such results.

(2) Where the relevant day falls before the day on which the results of the examination are announced, the period mentioned in section 7(8) shall be extended until—

    (a) the end of five months beginning with the relevant day, or

    (b) the end of forty days beginning with the date of the announcement,

whichever is the earlier.

(3) Where by virtue of sub-paragraph (2) a period longer than the prescribed period elapses after the relevant day before the request is complied with, the information to be supplied pursuant to the request shall be supplied both by reference to the data in question at the time when the request is received and (if different) by reference to the data as from time to time held in the period beginning when the request is received and ending when it is complied with.

(4) For the purposes of this paragraph the results of an examination shall be treated as announced when they are first published or (if not published) when they are first made available or communicated to the candidate in question.

(5) In this paragraph—

"examination" includes any process for determining the knowledge, intelligence, skill or ability of a candidate by reference to his performance in any test, work or other activity;

"the prescribed period" means forty days or such other period as is for the time being prescribed under section 7 in relation to the personal data in question;

"relevant day" has the same meaning as in section 7.

Examination scripts etc

9. (1) Personal data consisting of information recorded by candidates during an academic, professional or other examination are exempt from section 7.

(2) In this paragraph "examination" has the same meaning as in paragraph 8.

Legal professional privilege

10. Personal data are exempt from the subject information provisions if the data consist of information in respect of which a claim to legal professional privilege or, in Scotland, to confidentiality of communications could be maintained in legal proceedings.

Self-incrimination

11. (1) A person need not comply with any request or order under section 7 to the extent that compliance would, by revealing evidence of the commission of any offence other than an offence under this Act, expose him to proceedings for that offence.

(2) Information disclosed by any person in compliance with any request or order under section 7 shall not be admissible against him in proceedings for an offence under this Act.

---

1. See the Data Protection (Crown Appointments) Order 2000, SI 2000/416.
2. The Data Protection Tribunal (Corporate Finance Exemption) Order 2000, SI 2000/184 has been made.

Section 39   SCHEDULE 8
TRANSITIONAL RELIEF

(Amended by the Freedom of Information Act 2000, s 70.)

8–7409AC

PART I
INTERPRETATION OF SCHEDULE

1. (1) For the purposes of this Schedule, personal data are "eligible data" at any time if, and to the extent that, they are at that time subject to processing which was already under way immediately before 24th October 1998.

(2) In this Schedule—

"eligible automated data" means eligible data which fall within paragraph (*a*) or (*b*) of the definition of "data" in section 1(1);

"eligible manual data" means eligible data which are not eligible automated data;

"the first transitional period" means the period beginning with the commencement of this Schedule and ending with 23rd October 2001;

"the second transitional period" means the period beginning with 24th October 2001 and ending with 23rd October 2007.

8–7409AD

PART II
EXEMPTIONS AVAILABLE BEFORE 24TH OCTOBER 2001

Manual data

2. (1) Eligible manual data, other than data forming part of an accessible record, are exempt from the data protection principles and Parts II and III of this Act during the first transitional period.

(2) This paragraph does not apply to eligible manual data to which paragraph 4 applies.

3. (1) This paragraph applies to—

(*a*) eligible manual data forming part of an accessible record, and

(*b*) personal data which fall within paragraph (*d*) of the definition of "data" in section 1(1) but which, because they are not subject to processing which was already under way immediately before 24th October 1998, are not eligible data for the purposes of this Schedule.

(2) During the first transitional period, data to which this paragraph applies are exempt from—

(*a*) the data protection principles, except the sixth principle so far as relating to sections 7 and 12A,

(*b*) Part II of this Act, except—

(i) section 7 (as it has effect subject to section 8) and section 12A, and

(ii) section 15 so far as relating to those sections, and

(*c*) Part III of this Act.

4. (1) This paragraph applies to eligible manual data which consist of information relevant to the financial standing of the data subject and in respect of which the data controller is a credit reference agency.

(2) During the first transitional period, data to which this paragraph applies are exempt from—

(a) the data protection principles, except the sixth principle so far as relating to sections 7 and 12A,

(b) Part II of this Act, except—

    (i) section 7 (as it has effect subject to sections 8 and 9) and section 12A, and

    (ii) section 15 so far as relating to those sections, and

(c) Part III of this Act.

Processing otherwise than by reference to the data subject

5. During the first transitional period, for the purposes of this Act (apart from paragraph 1), eligible automated data are not to be regarded as being "processed" unless the processing is by reference to the data subject.

Payrolls and accounts

6. (1) Subject to sub-paragraph (2), eligible automated data processed by a data controller for one or more of the following purposes—

(a) calculating amounts payable by way of remuneration or pensions in respect of service in any employment or office or making payments of, or of sums deducted from, such remuneration or pensions, or

(b) keeping accounts relating to any business or other activity carried on by the data controller or keeping records of purchases, sales or other transactions for the purpose of ensuring that the requisite payments are made by or to him in respect of those transactions or for the purpose of making financial or management forecasts to assist him in the conduct of any such business or activity,

are exempt from the data protection principles and Parts II and III of this Act during the first transitional period.

(2) It shall be a condition of the exemption of any eligible automated data under this paragraph that the data are not processed for any other purpose, but the exemption is not lost by any processing of the eligible data for any other purpose if the data controller shows that he had taken such care to prevent it as in all the circumstances was reasonably required.

(3) Data processed only for one or more of the purposes mentioned in subparagraph (1)(a) may be disclosed—

(a) to any person, other than the data controller, by whom the remuneration or pensions in question are payable,

(b) for the purpose of obtaining actuarial advice,

(c) for the purpose of giving information as to the persons in any employment or office for use in medical research into the health of, or injuries suffered by, persons engaged in particular occupations or working in particular places or areas,

(d) if the data subject (or a person acting on his behalf) has requested or consented to the disclosure of the data either generally or in the circumstances in which the disclosure in question is made, or

(e) if the person making the disclosure has reasonable grounds for believing that the disclosure falls within paragraph (d).

(4) Data processed for any of the purposes mentioned in sub-paragraph (1) may be disclosed—

(a) for the purpose of audit or where the disclosure is for the purpose only of giving information about the data controller's financial affairs, or

(b) in any case in which disclosure would be permitted by any other provision of this Part of this Act if sub-paragraph (2) were included among the non-disclosure provisions.

(5) In this paragraph "remuneration" includes remuneration in kind and "pensions" includes gratuities or similar benefits.

Unincorporated members' clubs and mailing lists

7. Eligible automated data processed by an unincorporated members' club and relating only to the members of the club are exempt from the data protection principles and Parts II and III of this Act during the first transitional period.

8. Eligible automated data processed by a data controller only for the purposes of distributing, or recording the distribution of, articles or information to the data subjects and consisting only of their names, addresses or other particulars necessary for effecting the distribution, are exempt from the data protection principles and Parts II and III of this Act during the first transitional period.

9. Neither paragraph 7 nor paragraph 8 applies to personal data relating to any data subject unless he has been asked by the club or data controller whether he objects to the data relating to him being processed as mentioned in that paragraph and has not objected.

10. It shall be a condition of the exemption of any data under paragraph 7 that the data are not disclosed except as permitted by paragraph 11 and of the exemption under paragraph 8 that the data are not processed for any purpose other than that mentioned in that paragraph or as permitted by paragraph 11, but—

(a) the exemption under paragraph 7 shall not be lost by any disclosure in breach of that condition, and

(b) the exemption under paragraph 8 shall not be lost by any processing in breach of that condition,

if the data controller shows that he had taken such care to prevent it as in all the circumstances was reasonably required.

11. Data to which paragraph 10 applies may be disclosed—

(a) if the data subject (or a person acting on his behalf) has requested or consented to the disclosure of the data either generally or in the circumstances in which the disclosure in question is made,

(b) if the person making the disclosure has reasonable grounds for believing that the disclosure falls within paragraph (a), or

(c) in any case in which disclosure would be permitted by any other provision of this Part of this Act if paragraph 10 were included among the non-disclosure provisions.

Back-up data

12. Eligible automated data which are processed only for the purpose of replacing other data in the event of the latter being lost, destroyed or impaired are exempt from section 7 during the first transitional period.

Exemption of all eligible automated data from certain requirements

13.—(1) During the first transitional period, eligible automated data are exempt from the following provisions—

(*a*) the first data protection principle to the extent to which it requires compliance with—

　(i) paragraph 2 of Part II of Schedule 1,
　(ii) the conditions in Schedule 2, and
　(iii) the conditions in Schedule 3,

(*b*) the seventh data protection principle to the extent to which it requires compliance with paragraph 12 of Part II of Schedule 1;
(*c*) the eighth data protection principle,
(*d*) in section 7(1), paragraphs (*b*), (*c*)(ii) and (*d*),
(*e*) sections 10 and 11,
(*f*) section 12, and
(*g*) section 13, except so far as relating to—

　(i) any contravention of the fourth data protection principle,
　(ii) any disclosure without the consent of the data controller,
　(iii) loss or destruction of data without the consent of the data controller, or
　(iv) processing for the special purposes.

(2) The specific exemptions conferred by sub-paragraph (1)(*a*), (*c*) and (*e*) do not limit the data controller's general duty under the first data protection principle to ensure that processing is fair.

8–7409AE

PART III

EXEMPTIONS AVAILABLE AFTER 23RD OCTOBER 2001 BUT BEFORE 24TH OCTOBER 2007

14.—(1) This paragraph applies to—

(*a*) eligible manual data which were held immediately before 24th October 1998, and
(*b*) personal data which fall within paragraph (d) of the definition of "data" in section 1(1) but do not fall within paragraph (a) of this subparagraph,

but does not apply to eligible manual data to which the exemption in paragraph 16 applies.

(2) During the second transitional period, data to which this paragraph applies are exempt from the following provisions—

(*a*) the first data protection principle except to the extent to which it requires compliance with paragraph 2 of Part II of Schedule 1,
(*b*) the second, third, fourth and fifth data protection principles, and
(*c*) section 14(1) to (3).

14A.—(1) This paragraph applies to personal data which fall within paragraph (*e*) of the definition of "data" in section 1(1) and do not fall within paragraph 14(1)(*a*), but does not apply to eligible manual data to which the exemption in paragraph 16 applies.

(2) During the second transitional period, dat to which this paragrpah applies are exempt from—

(*a*) the fourth data protection principle, and
(*b*) section 14(1) to (3).

8–7409AF

PART IV

EXEMPTIONS AFTER 23RD OCTOBER 2001 FOR HISTORICAL RESEARCH

15. In this Part of this Schedule "the relevant conditions" has the same meaning as in section 33.

16.—(1) Eligible manual data which are processed only for the purpose of historical research in compliance with the relevant conditions are exempt from the provisions specified in sub-paragraph (2) after 23rd October 2001.

(2) The provisions referred to in sub-paragraph (1) are—

(*a*) the first data protection principle except in so far as it requires compliance with paragraph 2 of Part II of Schedule 1,
(*b*) the second, third, fourth and fifth data protection principles, and
(*c*) section 14(1) to (3).

17.—(1) After 23rd October 2001 eligible automated data which are processed only for the purpose of historical research in compliance with the relevant conditions are exempt from the first data protection principle to the extent to which it requires compliance with the conditions in Schedules 2 and 3.

(2) Eligible automated data which are processed—

(*a*) only for the purpose of historical research,
(*b*) in compliance with the relevant conditions, and
(*c*) otherwise than by reference to the data subject,

are also exempt from the provisions referred to in sub-paragraph (3) after 23rd October 2001.

(3) The provisions referred to in sub-paragraph (2) are—

(*a*) the first data protection principle except in so far as it requires compliance with paragraph 2 of Part II of Schedule 1,

(b) the second, third, fourth and fifth data protection principles, and

(c) section 14(1) to (3).

18. For the purposes of this Part of this Schedule personal data are not to be treated as processed otherwise than for the purpose of historical research merely because the data are disclosed—

(a) to any person, for the purpose of historical research only,

(b) to the data subject or a person acting on his behalf,

(c) at the request, or with the consent, of the data subject or a person acting on his behalf, or

(d) in circumstances in which the person making the disclosure has reasonable grounds for believing that the disclosure falls within paragraph (a), (b) or (c).

8–7409AG

PART V

EXEMPTION FROM SECTION 22

19. Processing which was already under way immediately before 24th October 1998 is not assessable processing for the purposes of section 22.

8–7409AH

Section 50

SCHEDULE 9

POWERS OF ENTRY AND INSPECTION

Issue of warrants

1. (1) If a circuit judge★ is satisfied by information on oath supplied by the Commissioner that there are reasonable grounds for suspecting—

(a) that a data controller has contravened or is contravening any of the data protection principles, or

(b) that an offence under this Act has been or is being committed,

and that evidence of the contravention or of the commission of the offence is to be found on any premises specified in the information, he may, subject to subparagraph (2) and paragraph 2, grant a warrant to the Commissioner.

(2) A judge shall not issue a warrant under this Schedule in respect of any personal data processed for the special purposes unless a determination by the Commissioner under section 45 with respect to those data has taken effect.

(3) A warrant issued under sub-paragraph (1) shall authorise the Commissioner or any of his officers or staff at any time within seven days of the date of the warrant to enter the premises, to search them, to inspect, examine, operate and test any equipment found there which is used or intended to be used for the processing of personal data and to inspect and seize any documents or other material found there which may be such evidence as is mentioned in that sub-paragraph.

★**Words "or a District Judge (Magistrates' Courts)" inserted by the Courts Act 2003, Sch 4, from a date to be appointed.**

2. (1) A judge shall not issue a warrant under this Schedule unless he is satisfied—

(a) that the Commissioner has given seven days' notice in writing to the occupier of the premises in question demanding access to the premises, and

(b) that either—

(i) access was demanded at a reasonable hour and was unreasonably refused, or

(ii) although entry to the premises was granted, the occupier unreasonably refused to comply with a request by the Commissioner or any of the Commissioner's officers or staff to permit the Commissioner or the officer or member of staff to do any of the things referred to in paragraph 1(3), and

(c) that the occupier, has, after the refusal, been notified by the Commissioner of the application for the warrant and has had an opportunity of being heard by the judge on the question whether or not it should be issued.

(2) Sub-paragraph (1) shall not apply if the judge is satisfied that the case is one of urgency or that compliance with those provisions would defeat the object of the entry.

3. A judge who issues a warrant under this Schedule shall also issue two copies of it and certify them clearly as copies.

Execution of warrants

4. A person executing a warrant issued under this Schedule may use such reasonable force as may be necessary.

5. A warrant issued under this Schedule shall be executed at a reasonable hour unless it appears to the person executing it that there are grounds for suspecting that the evidence in question would not be found if it were so executed.

6. If the person who occupies the premises in respect of which a warrant is issued under this Schedule is present when the warrant is executed, he shall be shown the warrant and supplied with a copy of it; and if that person is not present a copy of the warrant shall be left in a prominent place on the premises.

7. (1) A person seizing anything in pursuance of a warrant under this Schedule shall give a receipt for it if asked to do so.

(2) Anything so seized may be retained for so long as is necessary in all the circumstances but the person in occupation of the premises in question shall be given a copy of anything that is seized if he so requests and the person executing the warrant considers that it can be done without undue delay[1].

---

1. See the Criminal Justice and Police Act 2001, Part 2 (PART I, *ante*). These provisions confer, by ss 50 and 51, additional powers of seizure of property in relation to searches carried out under existing powers. However, s 57 (retention of seized items) does not authorise the retention of any property which could not be retained under the provisions listed in s 57(1), which include para 7(2) of Sch 9 to the Data Protection Act 1998, if the property was seized under the new

powers (i.e. those conferred by ss 50 and 51) in reliance on one of those powers (i.e. those conferred by the provisions listed in s 57(1)). Section 57(4) further provides that nothing in any of the provisions listed in s 57(1) authorises the retention of anything after an obligation to return it has arisen under Part 2.

Matters exempt from inspection and seizure

8. The powers of inspection and seizure conferred by a warrant issued under this Schedule shall not be exercisable in respect of personal data which by virtue of section 28 are exempt from any of the provisions of this Act.

9. (1) Subject to the provisions of this paragraph, the powers of inspection and seizure conferred by a warrant issued under this Schedule shall not be exercisable in respect of—

(a) any communication between a professional legal adviser and his client in connection with the giving of legal advice to the client with respect to his obligations, liabilities or rights under this Act, or

(b) any communication between a professional legal adviser and his client, or between such an adviser or his client and any other person, made in connection with or in contemplation of proceedings under or arising out of this Act (including proceedings before the Tribunal) and for the purposes of such proceedings.

(2) Sub-paragraph (1) applies also to—

(a) any copy or other record of any such communication as is there mentioned, and

(b) any document or article enclosed with or referred to in any such communication if made in connection with the giving of any advice or, as the case may be, in connection with or in contemplation of and for the purposes of such proceedings as are there mentioned.

(3) This paragraph does not apply to anything in the possession of any person other than the professional legal adviser or his client or to anything held with the intention of furthering a criminal purpose.

(4) In this paragraph references to the client of a professional legal adviser include references to any person representing such a client.

10. If the person in occupation of any premises in respect of which a warrant is issued under this Schedule objects to the inspection or seizure under the warrant of any material on the grounds that it consists partly of matters in respect of which those powers are not exercisable, he shall, if the person executing the warrant so requests, furnish that person with a copy of so much of the material as is not exempt from those powers.

Return of warrants

11. A warrant issued under this Schedule shall be returned to the court from which it was issued—

(a) after being executed, or

(b) if not executed within the time authorised for its execution;

and the person by whom any such warrant is executed shall make an endorsement on it stating what powers have been exercised by him under the warrant.

Offences

12. Any person who—

(a) intentionally obstructs a person in the execution of a warrant issued under this Schedule, or

(b) fails without reasonable excuse to give any person executing such a warrant such assistance as he may reasonably require for the execution of the warrant,

is guilty of an offence[1].

Vessels, vehicles etc

13. In this Schedule "premises" includes any vessel, vehicle, aircraft or hovercraft, and references to the occupier of any premises include references to the person in charge of any vessel, vehicle, aircraft or hovercraft.

14–15. *Scotland and Northern Ireland.*

---

1. For procedure and penalties, see s 60, ante.

8–7409AI

Section 53(6)

SCHEDULE 10
FURTHER PROVISIONS RELATING TO ASSISTANCE UNDER SECTION 53

1. In this Schedule "applicant" and "proceedings" have the same meaning as in section 53.

2. The assistance provided under section 53 may include the making of arrangements for, or for the Commissioner to bear the costs of—

(a) the giving of advice or assistance by a solicitor or counsel, and

(b) the representation of the applicant, or the provision to him of such assistance as is usually given by a solicitor or counsel—

(i) in steps preliminary or incidental to the proceedings, or

(ii) in arriving at or giving effect to a compromise to avoid or bring an end to the proceedings.

3. Where assistance is provided with respect to the conduct of proceedings—

(a) it shall include an agreement by the Commissioner to indemnify the applicant (subject only to any exceptions specified in the notification) in respect of any liability to pay costs or expenses arising by virtue of any judgment or order of the court in the proceedings,

(b) it may include an agreement by the Commissioner to indemnify the applicant in respect of any liability to pay costs or expenses arising by virtue of any compromise or settlement arrived at in order to avoid the proceedings or bring the proceedings to an end, and

(c) it may include an agreement by the Commissioner to indemnify the applicant in respect of any liability to pay damages pursuant to an undertaking given on the grant of interlocutory relief (in Scotland, an interim order) to the applicant.

4. Where the Commissioner provides assistance in relation to any proceedings, he shall do so on such terms, or make such other arrangements, as will secure that a person against whom the proceedings have been or are commenced is informed that assistance has been or is being provided by the Commissioner in relation to them.

5. In England and Wales or Northern Ireland, the recovery of expenses incurred by the Commissioner in providing an applicant with assistance (as taxed or assessed in such manner as may be prescribed by rules of court) shall constitute a first charge for the benefit of the Commissioner—

(a) on any costs which, by virtue of any judgment or order of the court, are payable to the applicant by any other person in respect of the matter in connection with which the assistance is provided, and

(b) on any sum payable to the applicant under a compromise or settlement arrived at in connection with that matter to avoid or bring to an end any proceedings.

6. In Scotland, the recovery of such expenses (as taxed or assessed in such manner as may be prescribed by rules of court) shall be paid to the Commissioner, in priority to other debts—

(a) out of any expenses which, by virtue of any judgment or order of the court, are payable to the applicant by any other person in respect of the matter in connection with which the assistance is provided, and

(b) out of any sum payable to the applicant under a compromise or settlement arrived at in connection with that matter to avoid or bring to an end any proceedings.

8–7409AJ

Section 68(1)(b)

SCHEDULE 11
EDUCATIONAL RECORDS

Meaning of "educational record"

1. For the purposes of section 68 "educational record" means any record to which paragraph 2, 5 or 7 applies.

England and Wales

2. This paragraph applies to any record of information which—

(a) is processed by or on behalf of the governing body of, or a teacher at, any school in England and Wales specified in paragraph 3,

(b) relates to any person who is or has been a pupil at the school, and

(c) originated from or was supplied by or on behalf of any of the persons specified in paragraph 4,

other than information which is processed by a teacher solely for the teacher's own use.

3. The schools referred to in paragraph 2(a) are—

(a) a school maintained by a local education authority, and

(b) a special school, as defined by section 6(2) of the Education Act 1996, which is not so maintained.

4. The persons referred to in paragraph 2(c) are—

(a) an employee of the local education authority which maintains the school,

(b) in the case of—

(i) a voluntary aided, foundation or foundation special school (within the meaning of the School Standards and Framework Act 1998), or

(ii) a special school which is not maintained by a local education authority,

a teacher or other employee at the school (including an educational psychologist engaged by the governing body under a contract for services),

(c) the pupil to whom the record relates, and

(d) a parent, as defined by section 576(1) of the Education Act 1996, of that pupil.

5–6. *Scotland.*

7–8. *Northern Ireland.*

England and Wales: transitory provisions

9. (1) Until the appointed day within the meaning of section 20 of the School Standards and Framework Act 1998, this Schedule shall have effect subject to the following modifications.

(2) Paragraph 3 shall have effect as if for paragraph (b) and the "and" immediately preceding it there were substituted—

"(aa) a grant-maintained school, as defined by section 183(1) of the Education Act 1996,

(ab) a grant-maintained special school, as defined by section 337(4) of that Act, and

(b) a special school, as defined by section 6(2) of that Act, which is neither a maintained special school, as defined by section 337(3) of that Act, nor a grant-maintained special school.".

(3) Paragraph 4(b)(i) shall have effect as if for the words from "foundation", in the first place where it occurs, to "1998)" there were substituted "or grant-maintained school".

8–7409AK

Section 68(1)(c)

SCHEDULE 12
ACCESSIBLE PUBLIC RECORDS

Meaning of "accessible public record"

1. For the purposes of section 68 "accessible public record" means any record which is kept by an authority specified—

(a) as respects England and Wales, in the Table in paragraph 2,
(b) as respects Scotland, in the Table in paragraph 4, or
(c) as respects Northern Ireland, in the Table in paragraph 6,

and is a record of information of a description specified in that Table in relation to that authority.

Housing and social services records: England and Wales

2. The following is the Table referred to in paragraph 1(a).

The authorities	*The accessible information*
Housing Act local authority.	Information held for the purpose of any of the authority's tenancies.
Local social services authority.	Information held for any purpose of the authority's social services functions.

3. (1) The following provisions apply for the interpretation of the Table in paragraph 2.

(2) Any authority which, by virtue of section 4(e) of the Housing Act 1985, is a local authority for the purpose of any provision of that Act is a "Housing Act local authority" for the purposes of this Schedule, and so is any housing action trust established under Part III of the Housing Act 1988.

(3) Information contained in records kept by a Housing Act local authority is "held for the purpose of any of the authority's tenancies" if it is held for any purpose of the relationship of landlord and tenant of a dwelling which subsists, has subsisted or may subsist between the authority and any individual who is, has been or, as the case may be, has applied to be, a tenant of the authority.

(4) Any authority which, by virtue of section 1 or 12 of the Local Authority Social Services Act 1970, is or is treated as a local authority for the purposes of that Act is a "local social services authority" for the purposes of this Schedule; and information contained in records kept by such an authority is "held for any purpose of the authority's social services functions" if it is held for the purpose of any past, current or proposed exercise of such a function in any case.

(5) Any expression used in paragraph 2 or this paragraph and in Part II of the Housing Act 1985 or the Local Authority Social Services Act 1970 has the same meaning as in that Act.

4–7. *Housing and social services records: Scotland and Northern Ireland.*

Section 72

SCHEDULE 13
MODIFICATIONS OF ACT HAVING EFFECT BEFORE 24TH OCTOBER 2007

(*Amended by the Freedom of Information Act 2000, s 70.*)

1. After section 12 there is inserted—

"12A. Rights of data subjects in relation to exempt manual data. (1) A data subject is entitled at any time by notice in writing—

(a) to require the data controller to rectify, block, erase or destroy exempt manual data which are inaccurate or incomplete, or
(b) to require the data controller to cease holding exempt manual data in a way incompatible with the legitimate purposes pursued by the data controller.

(2) A notice under subsection (1)(a) or (b) must state the data subject's reasons for believing that the data are inaccurate or incomplete or, as the case may be, his reasons for believing that they are held in a way incompatible with the legitimate purposes pursued by the data controller.

(3) If the court is satisfied, on the application of any person who has given a notice under subsection (1) which appears to the court to be justified (or to be justified to any extent) that the data controller in question has failed to comply with the notice, the court may order him to take such steps for complying with the notice (or for complying with it to that extent) as the court thinks fit.

(4) In this section "exempt manual data" means—

(a) in relation to the first transitional period, as defined by paragraph 1(2) of Schedule 8, data to which paragraph 3 or 4 of that Schedule applies, and
(b) in relation to the second transitional period, as so defined, data to which paragraph 14 or 14A of that Schedule applies.

(5) For the purposes of this section personal data are incomplete if, and only if, the data, although not inaccurate, are such that their incompleteness would constitute a contravention of the third or fourth data protection principles, if those principles applied to the data.".

2. In section 32—

(a) in subsection (2) after "section 12" there is inserted—

"(dd)section 12A,", and

(b) in subsection (4) after "12(8)" there is inserted ", 12A(3)".

3. In section 34 for "section 14(1) to (3)" there is substituted "sections 12A and 14(1) to (3)."

4. In section 53(1) after "12(8)" there is inserted ", 12A(3)".

5. In paragraph 8 of Part II of Schedule 1, the word "or" at the end of paragraph (c) is omitted and after paragraph (d) there is inserted

"or

(e) he contravenes section 12A by failing to comply with a notice given under subsection (1) of that section to the extent that the notice is justified.".

Section 73

SCHEDULE 14

TRANSITIONAL PROVISIONS AND SAVINGS

Interpretation

1. In this Schedule—

"the 1984 Act" means the Data Protection Act 1984;

"the old principles" means the data protection principles within the meaning of the 1984 Act;

"the new principles" means the data protection principles within the meaning of this Act.

Effect of registration under Part II of 1984 Act

2. (1) Subject to sub-paragraphs (4) and (5) any person who, immediately before the commencement of Part III of this Act—

(a) is registered as a data user under Part II of the 1984 Act, or

(b) is treated by virtue of section 7(6) of the 1984 Act as so registered,

is exempt from section 17(1) of this Act until the end of the registration period or, if earlier, 24th October 2001.

(2) In sub-paragraph (1) "the registration period", in relation to a person, means—

(a) where there is a single entry in respect of that person as a data user, the period at the end of which, if section 8 of the 1984 Act had remained in force, that entry would have fallen to be removed unless renewed, and

(b) where there are two or more entries in respect of that person as a data user, the period at the end of which, if that section had remained in force, the last of those entries to expire would have fallen to be removed unless renewed.

(3) Any application for registration as a data user under Part II of the 1984 Act which is received by the Commissioner before the commencement of Part III of this Act (including any appeal against a refusal of registration) shall be determined in accordance with the old principles and the provisions of the 1984 Act.

(4) If a person falling within paragraph (b) of sub-paragraph (1) receives a notification under section 7(1) of the 1984 Act of the refusal of his application, sub-paragraph (1) shall cease to apply to him—

(a) if no appeal is brought, at the end of the period within which an appeal can be brought against the refusal, or

(b) on the withdrawal or dismissal of the appeal.

(5) If a data controller gives a notification under section 18(1) at a time when he is exempt from section 17(1) by virtue of sub-paragraph (1), he shall cease to be so exempt.

(6) The Commissioner shall include in the register maintained under section 19 an entry in respect of each person who is exempt from section 17(1) by virtue of sub-paragraph (1); and each entry shall consist of the particulars which, immediately before the commencement of Part III of this Act, were included (or treated as included) in respect of that person in the register maintained under section 4 of the 1984 Act.

(7) Notification regulations under Part III of this Act may make provision modifying the duty referred to in section 20(1) in its application to any person in respect of whom an entry in the register maintained under section 19 has been made under sub-paragraph (6).

(8) Notification regulations under Part III of this Act may make further transitional provision in connection with the substitution of Part III of this Act for Part II of the 1984 Act (registration), including provision modifying the application of provisions of Part III in transitional cases.

Rights of data subjects

3. (1) The repeal of section 21 of the 1984 Act (right of access to personal data) does not affect the application of that section in any case in which the request (together with the information referred to in paragraph (a) of subsection (4) of that section and, in a case where it is required, the consent referred to in paragraph (b) of that subsection) was received before the day on which the repeal comes into force.

(2) Sub-paragraph (1) does not apply where the request is made by reference to this Act.

(3) Any fee paid for the purposes of section 21 of the 1984 Act before the commencement of section 7 in a case not falling within sub-paragraph (1) shall be taken to have been paid for the purposes of section 7.

4. The repeal of section 22 of the 1984 Act (compensation for inaccuracy) and the repeal of section 23 of that Act (compensation for loss or unauthorised disclosure) do not affect the application of those sections in relation to damage or distress suffered at any time by reason of anything done or omitted to be done before the commencement of the repeals.

5. The repeal of section 24 of the 1984 Act (rectification and erasure) does not affect any case in which the application to the court was made before the day on which the repeal comes into force.

6. Subsection (3)(b) of section 14 does not apply where the rectification, blocking, erasure or destruction occurred before the commencement of that section.

Enforcement and transfer prohibition notices served under Part V of 1984 Act

7. (1) If, immediately before the commencement of section 40—

(a) an enforcement notice under section 10 of the 1984 Act has effect, and

(b) either the time for appealing against the notice has expired or any appeal has been determined,

then, after that commencement, to the extent mentioned in sub-paragraph (3), the notice shall have effect for the purposes of sections 41 and 47 as if it were an enforcement notice under section 40.

(2) Where an enforcement notice has been served under section 10 of the 1984 Act before the commencement of section 40 and immediately before that commencement either—

(*a*) the time for appealing against the notice has not expired, or
(*b*) an appeal has not been determined,

the appeal shall be determined in accordance with the provisions of the 1984 Act and the old principles and, unless the notice is quashed on appeal, to the extent mentioned in sub-paragraph (3) the notice shall have effect for the purposes of sections 41 and 47 as if it were an enforcement notice under section 40.

(3) An enforcement notice under section 10 of the 1984 Act has the effect described in sub-paragraph (1) or (2) only to the extent that the steps specified in the notice for complying with the old principle or principles in question are steps which the data controller could be required by an enforcement notice under section 40 to take for complying with the new principles or any of them.

8. (1) If, immediately before the commencement of section 40—

(*a*) a transfer prohibition notice under section 12 of the 1984 Act has effect, and
(*b*) either the time for appealing against the notice has expired or any appeal has been determined,

then, on and after that commencement, to the extent specified in sub-paragraph (3), the notice shall have effect for the purposes of sections 41 and 47 as if it were an enforcement notice under section 40.

(2) Where a transfer prohibition notice has been served under section 12 of the 1984 Act and immediately before the commencement of section 40 either—

(*a*) the time for appealing against the notice has not expired, or
(*b*) an appeal has not been determined,

the appeal shall be determined in accordance with the provisions of the 1984 Act and the old principles and, unless the notice is quashed on appeal, to the extent mentioned in sub-paragraph (3) the notice shall have effect for the purposes of sections 41 and 47 as if it were an enforcement notice under section 40.

(3) A transfer prohibition notice under section 12 of the 1984 Act has the effect described in sub-paragraph (1) or (2) only to the extent that the prohibition imposed by the notice is one which could be imposed by an enforcement notice under section 40 for complying with the new principles or any of them.

Notices under new law relating to matters in relation to which 1984 Act had effect

9. The Commissioner may serve an enforcement notice under section 40 on or after the day on which that section comes into force if he is satisfied that, before that day, the data controller contravened the old principles by reason of any act or omission which would also have constituted a contravention of the new principles if they had applied before that day.

10. Subsection (5)(*b*) of section 40 does not apply where the rectification, blocking, erasure or destruction occurred before the commencement of that section.

11. The Commissioner may serve an information notice under section 43 on or after the day on which that section comes into force if he has reasonable grounds for suspecting that, before that day, the data controller contravened the old principles by reason of any act or omission which would also have constituted a contravention of the new principles if they had applied before that day.

12. Where by virtue of paragraph 11 an information notice is served on the basis of anything done or omitted to be done before the day on which section 43 comes into force, subsection (2)(*b*) of that section shall have effect as if the reference to the data controller having complied, or complying, with the new principles were a reference to the data controller having contravened the old principles by reason of any such act or omission as is mentioned in paragraph 11.

Self-incrimination, etc

13. (1) In section 43(8), section 44(9) and paragraph 11 of Schedule 7, any reference to an offence under this Act includes a reference to an offence under the 1984 Act.

(2) In section 34(9) of the 1984 Act, any reference to an offence under that Act includes a reference to an offence under this Act.

Warrants issued under 1984 Act

14. The repeal of Schedule 4 to the 1984 Act does not affect the application of that Schedule in any case where a warrant was issued under that Schedule before the commencement of the repeal.

Complaints under section 36(2) of 1984 Act and requests for assessment under section 42

15. The repeal of section 36(2) of the 1984 Act does not affect the application of that provision in any case where the complaint was received by the Commissioner before the commencement of the repeal.

16. In dealing with a complaint under section 36(2) of the 1984 Act or a request for an assessment under section 42 of this Act, the Commissioner shall have regard to the provisions from time to time applicable to the processing, and accordingly—

(*a*) in section 36(2) of the 1984 Act, the reference to the old principles and the provisions of that Act includes, in relation to any time when the new principles and the provisions of this Act have effect, those principles and provisions, and
(*b*) in section 42 of this Act, the reference to the provisions of this Act includes, in relation to any time when the old principles and the provisions of the 1984 Act had effect, those principles and provisions.

Applications under Access to Health Records Act 1990 or corresponding Northern Ireland legislation

17. (1) The repeal of any provision of the Access to Health Records Act 1990 does not affect—

(*a*) the application of section 3 or 6 of that Act in any case in which the application under that section was received before the day on which the repeal comes into force, or
(*b*) the application of section 8 of that Act in any case in which the application to the court was made before the day on which the repeal comes into force.

(2) Sub-paragraph (1)(a) does not apply in relation to an application for access to information which was made by reference to this Act.

18. (1) The revocation of any provision of the Access to Health Records (Northern Ireland) Order 1993 does not affect—

(a) the application of Article 5 or 8 of that Order in any case in which the application under that Article was received before the day on which the repeal comes into force, or

(b) the application of Article 10 of that Order in any case in which the application to the court was made before the day on which the repeal comes into force.

(2) Sub-paragraph (1)(a) does not apply in relation to an application for access to information which was made by reference to this Act.

Applications under regulations under Access to Personal Files Act 1987 or corresponding Northern Ireland legislation

19. (1) The repeal of the personal files enactments does not affect the application of regulations under those enactments in relation to—

(a) any request for information,

(b) any application for rectification or erasure, or

(c) any application for review of a decision,

which was made before the day on which the repeal comes into force.

(2) Sub-paragraph (1)(a) does not apply in relation to a request for information which was made by reference to this Act.

(3) In sub-paragraph (1) "the personal files enactments" means—

(a) in relation to Great Britain, the Access to Personal Files Act 1987, and

(b) in relation to Northern Ireland, Part II of the Access to Personal Files and Medical Reports (Northern Ireland) Order 1991.

Applications under section 158 of Consumer Credit Act 1974

20. Section 62 does not affect the application of section 158 of the Consumer Credit Act 1974 in any case where the request was received before the commencement of section 62, unless the request is made by reference to this Act.

DEVELOPMENT OF TOURISM

8–7439 This title contains the following statutory provisions—

Development of Tourism Act 1969

(1969 c 51)

8–7440 This Act set up the British Tourist Authority and Tourist Boards responsible for promoting and developing tourism to and within Great Britain; financial assistance may be given for tourist projects, the provision of new hotels and the extension, alteration and improvement of existing hotels; and Orders[1] maybe made requiring the registration of tourist accommodation and the display of prices and providing, on default, for a penalty not exceeding **level 4** on the standard scale.

1. See the Tourism (Sleeping Accommodation Price Display) Order 1977, SI 1977/1877, this title, post.

SCHEDULE 2
ENFORCEMENT OF CONDITIONS OF GRANT

(*Amended by the Criminal Law Act 1977, Sch 13, the Criminal Justice Act 1982, ss 35, 38 and 46 and SI 2005/3225.*)

Power to call for information

8–7441 **1.** (1) A Tourist Board may by notice require any person who has received a grant from the Board under this Act, and any person acting on his behalf, to furnish to the Board such information, or to produce for examination on behalf of the Board such books, records or other documents, as may be specified in the notice for the purpose of enabling the Board to determine whether any condition subject to which the grant was made is satisfied or is being complied with or whether the grant has become repayable in whole or in part in accordance with any such condition.

(1A) Sub-paragraph (1) applies in relation to the National Assembly for Wales and any person who has received a grant from the Assembly (and any person acting on that person's behalf) as it applies in relation to a Tourist Borad and the corresponding persons.

(2) A notice under this paragraph may require the information to which it relates to be furnished within such time as may be specified in the notice, and may require the documents to which it relates to be produced at such time and place as may be so specified:

Provided that the time specified in such a notice for furnishing any information or producing any document shall not be earlier than the end of the period of twenty-eight days beginning with the service of the notice.

(3) A notice under this paragraph may be served—

(a) by delivering it to the person on whom it is to be served;

(b) by leaving it at the usual or last known place of abode of that person;

(c) by sending it in a prepaid registered letter, or by the recorded delivery service, addressed to that person at his usual or last known place of abode; or

(d) in the case of an incorporated company or body, by delivering it to the secretary or clerk of the company or body at their registered or principal office, or sending it in a prepaid registered letter, or by the recorded delivery service, addressed to the secretary or clerk of the company or body at that office.

(4) Any person who without reasonable excuse fails to comply with a notice under this paragraph shall be guilty of an offence and liable on summary conviction to a fine not exceeding **level 5** on the standard scale.

Power to enter and inspect premises

8–7442   **2.** (1) Any person duly authorised in that behalf by a Tourist Board or the national Assembly for Wales may, on production (if so required) of written evidence of his authority, at all reasonable times enter and inspect any premises in relation to which a grant has been made by the Board or (as the case may be) the Assembly under this Act for the purpose of determining whether any condition subject to which the grant was made is satisfied or is being complied with or whether the grant has become repayable in whole or in part in accordance with any such condition.

(2) Any person who wilfully obstructs any person in the exercise of a right of entry conferred by this paragraph shall be guilty of an offence and liable on summary conviction to a fine not exceeding **level 3** on the standard scale.

Failure to comply with condition requiring notification of event on which grant becomes repayable

8–7443   **3.** (1) Any person who without reasonable excuse fails to comply with any conditions subject to which a grant was made to him under this Act requiring him to inform a Tourist Board or the National Assembly for Wales of any event whereby the grant becomes repayable in whole or in part shall be guilty of an offence and liable to a fine which, if imposed on summary conviction, shall not exceed **level 5** on the standard scale.

(2) *Repealed.*

(3) Summary proceedings in Scotland for an offence under this paragraph shall not be commenced after the expiration of three years from the commission of the offence, but subject to the foregoing limitation and notwithstanding anything in section 23 of the Summary Jurisdiction (Scotland) Act 1954, such proceedings may be commenced at any time within twelve months after the date on which evidence sufficient in the opinion of the Lord Advocate to justify the proceedings comes to his knowledge; and subsection (2) of the said section 23 shall apply for the purposes of this sub-paragraph as it applies for the purposes of that section.

(4) For the purposes of sub-paragraph (3) of this paragraph, a certificate of the Lord Advocate, as to the date on which such evidence as aforesaid came to his knowledge, shall be conclusive evidence of that fact.

Offences by bodies corporate

8–7444   **4.** (1) Where an offence under this Schedule committed by a body corporate is proved to have been committed with the consent or connivance of, or to be attributable to any neglect on the part of, any director, manager, secretary or other similar officer of the body corporate, or any person who was purporting to act in any such capacity, he as well as the body corporate shall be guilty of that offence and shall be liable to be proceeded against and punished accordingly.

(2) In this paragraph "director", in relation to a body corporate established by or under any enactment for the purpose of carrying on under national ownership any industry or undertaking or part of an industry or undertaking, being a body corporate of that body.

Tourism (Sleeping Accommodation Price Display) Order 1977
(SI 1977/1877 as amended by SI 1985/1778)

8–7460   **1.** *Commencement and application of Interpretation Act [1978].*

8–7461   **2.** In this Order, "hotel" means any establishment in Great Britain at which sleeping accommodation is provided by way of trade or business—

(a) which for the purposes of letting has not fewer than four bedrooms or eight beds (including beds situate in dormitories), excluding any which are normally in the same occupation for more than 21 consecutive nights, and

(b) at which such accommodation is offered, whether for one night or for a longer period, to any person who wishes to avail himself thereof and appears able and willing to pay therefor and is in a fit state to be received—

but excluding any establishment which a bona fide members' club and provides such accommodation as a benefit of membership and any establishment where accommodation is normally provided for a price which includes the provision of other services and those other services are not merely ancillary to the accommodation.

8–7463   **3.** (1) At each hotel there shall be displayed in a prominent position in the reception area or, if none, at the entrance, where it can easily be read by a person seeking to engage sleeping accommodation at the hotel, a legible notice stating the current prices (which, wherever appropriate, shall include, and be stated to include, any service charge) payable per night by any such person for sleeping accommodation at the hotel consisting of:—

 (a) a bedroom for occupation by one adult person,
 (b) a bedroom for occupation by two adult persons, and
 (c) a bed, other than as in (a) or (b) above, for occupation by an adult person and stating also whether it is situate in a dormitory or room to be shared with other guests.

 (2) Where Value Added Tax is payable, then either—

 (a) the price shall include and be stated to include the amount of tax, or
 (b) the price shall be stated to exclude the amount of tax and that amount shall be stated with equal prominence in money terms as the amount of tax payable in addition to the price.

 (3) If the accommodation is only provided inclusive of meals, the price of the accommodation shall be stated to be inclusive thereof and the meals so provided shall be suitably identified.

 (4) If the prices in respect of each of the above categories of sleeping accommodation are not standard throughout the hotel it shall be sufficient to state the lowest and highest current price for accommodation of each category (disregarding any bedroom or bed which is normally in the same occupation for more than 21 consecutive nights).

 (5) Additional information may be included in the notice provided it does not detract from the prominence to be given to the above information.

8–7464 **4.** If any person who provides sleeping accommodation in a hotel fails to display a notice which complies with Article 3 he shall, unless he proves that he had reasonable excuse for the failure, be liable on summary conviction to a penalty not exceeding a fine of £200.

8–7465 **5.** (1) A duly authorised officer of a local weights and measures authority may, at all reasonable hours and on production, if required, of his credentials, enter and inspect any establishment within the area of that authority at which sleeping accommodation is provided by way of trade or business for the purpose of determining whether the provisions of this Order are being complied with; and where a local weights and measures authority has made arrangements for the discharge of any of its functions as such by another local authority the power conferred by this Article shall also be exercisable by a duly authorised officer of that other local authority.

 (2) Any person who wilfully obstructs any person in the exercise of a right of entry and inspection conferred by paragraph (1) of this Article shall be guilty of an offence and be liable on summary conviction to a penalty not exceeding a fine of £100.

8–7466 **6.** (1) Where an offence under this Order committed by a body corporate is committed with the consent or connivance of, or is attributable to any neglect on the part of, any director, manager, secretary or other similar officer of the body corporate, or any other person who was purporting to act in any such capacity, he as well as the body corporate shall also be guilty of an offence.

 (2) Where the affairs of a body corporate are managed by its members, paragraph (1) of this Article shall apply in relation to the acts and defaults of a member in connection with his functions of management as if he were a director of the body corporate.

8–7467 **7.** The Secretary of State as respects England, the Secretary of State for Scotland as respects Scotland and the Secretary of State for Wales as respects Wales may make regulations to exclude from the definition of "hotel" in Article 2 of this Order any class of establishment and to make consequential amendments to this Order.

DISORDERLY HOUSES

8–7480 **Bawdy house, or other disorderly house[1].** Any person acting or appearing as the master or mistress, or as having the care or management of any such house, is to be deemed the owner[2] and liable to prosecution as such, although not in fact the real keeper thereof (Disorderly Houses Act 1751, 25 Geo 2, c 36, s 8). *Misdemeanour*, punishable by fine or imprisonment, or both[3].

8–7490 **Brothels.** Keeping a bawdy-house is a nuisance at common law (*Halsbury's Laws of England*, 4th edn, Vol 11, para 1057). See *R v Morris* [1951] 1 KB 394, [1950] 2 All ER 965, 115 JP 5, for punishment; alternatively proceedings may be taken under provisions for the suppression of brothels contained in the Sexual Offences Act 1956, ss 33–36, post.

---

 1. A disorderly house is a house kept open, not necessarily to the public at large, and so conducted as to violate law and good order (*R v Berg, Britt, Carré and Lummies* (1927) 20 Cr App Rep 38). In *R v Quinn, R v Bloom* [1961] 3 All ER 88 at 91, the Court of Criminal Appeal recorded the principles to be applied where the essence of the charge is the presentation of an indecent performance. A conviction for keeping a disorderly house will be supported, although there is no evidence of indecency or disorderly conduct perceptible from the exterior of the house (*R v Rice* (1866) LR 1 CCR 21).

 In order to establish the offence of keeping a disorderly house at common law, the prosecutor must show that the defendant habitually or persistently kept such a house and did so with knowledge of the use to which the premises were put; accordingly, a single performance of an indecent exhibition was held to be insufficient to establish the necessary element of habit or persistency to constitute the offence (*Moores v DPP* [1992] QB 125, [1991] 4 All ER 521).

2. The owner of a house, letting it out in different apartments to several young women, who use the apartments for the purposes of prostitution, cannot be indicted for keeping a disorderly house (*R v Stannard* (1863) Le & Ca 349, 28 JP 20; see also *R v Barrett* (1863) Le & Ca 263, 26 JP 805).

3. An offence under section 8 of the Disorderly Houses Act 1751 is triable either way (Magistrates' Courts Act 1980, Sch 1). For procedure in respect of this offence which is triable either way, see the Magistrates' Courts Act 1980, §s 17A–21, in PART I: MAGISTRATES' COURTS, PROCEDURE, ante.

DOGS

8–7500　This title contains the following statutes—

8–7510	DOGS ACT 1871
8–7530	DOGS ACT 1906
8–7550	DOGS (PROTECTION OF LIVESTOCK) ACT 1953
8–7570	BREEDING OF DOGS ACT 1973
8–7590	GUARD DOGS ACT 1975
8–7610	DANGEROUS DOGS ACT 1989
8–7612	BREEDING OF DOGS ACT 1991
8–7615	DANGEROUS DOGS ACT 1991
8–7625	BREEDING AND SALE OF DOGS (WELFARE) ACT 1999

and the following statutory instruments—

8–7630	Dangerous Dogs Compensation and Exemption Schemes Order 1991
8–7641	Control of Dogs Order 1992

Dogs Act 1871

(34 & 35 Vict c 56)

8–7510　**2. Dangerous dogs may be destroyed.**　Any court of summary jurisdiction may take cognisance of a complaint[1], that a dog is dangerous[2], and not kept under proper control[3], and if it appears to the court having cognisance of such complaint that such dog is dangerous, the court may[4] make an order[5] in a summary way directing the dog to be kept by the owner[6] under proper control[7] or destroyed[8].

[Dogs Act 1871, s 2, as amended by the Dangerous Dogs Act 1989, s 2.]

1. Proceedings instituted by "information" are invalid (*R v Nottingham Justices, ex p Brown* [1960] 3 All ER 625, 125 JP 49). A valid complaint may be preferred by a police officer (*Smith v Baker* [1960] 3 All ER 653, 125 JP 53). By way of an assignment made by the Attorney General under s 3(2)(*g*) of the Prosecution of Offences Act 1985, in PART I: MAGISTRATES' COURTS, PROCEDURE, ante, the Director of Public Prosecutions may conduct proceedings under s 2 of the Dogs Act 1871 instituted on behalf of a police force. The court has jurisdiction to hear a complaint under s 2 even though the conduct relied upon to show dangerousness occurred outside the court's Commission area; s 2 is aimed at the mischief of dog owners that owned dogs, wherever the dogs may be located, the conduct of which, in any location, showed that the dogs were dangerous and out of control: *Shufflebottom v Chief Constable of Greater Manchester* (2003) 167 JP 153. It is a better practice to hear a complaint under this section separately from any related criminal proceedings and after the criminal proceedings have been determined (*R v Dunmow Justices, ex p Anderson* [1964] 2 All ER 943, 128 JP 468).

2. It was held in a case stated prior to the coming into operation of the Dogs Act 1906, that the word "dangerous" in this section is not confined to meaning dangerous to mankind (*Williams v Richards* [1907] 2 KB 88, 71 JP 222). The term "dangerous" is to be given its ordinary everyday meaning. For a dog to be dangerous it is not necessary for it to present a danger to human beings or livestock such as sheep, cattle, horses or poultry and it may be considered dangerous even if the only danger it presents is to another dog (*Briscoe v Shattock* [1999] 1 WLR 432, (1998) 163 JP 201, [1999] Crim LR 396, DC. See Dogs Act 1906, s 1(4), post, for power to deal with a dog who has injured cattle or poultry or chased sheep as a dangerous dog under this section. A dog may yet be "dangerous" even though it has been held not to be "ferocious" within the terms of that Act (*Keddle v Payn* [1964] 1 All ER 189, 128 JP 144). A dog which on only one occasion killed two pet rabbits was held not to be dangerous because it was in the nature of dogs to chase, wound and kill other small animals (*Sansom v Chief Constable of Kent* [1981] Crim LR 617).

3. "Under control" is a question of fact to be decided by the justices. If a dog is under control the order cannot apply to it. An order may be made although the dog is found to be dangerous on owner's private property to which other persons have a right of access (*Philp v Wright* 1940 JC 9).

4. An order may be made whether or not the dog is shown to have injured any person (Dangerous Dogs Act 1991, s 3(5)(*a*), post).

5. Costs may be ordered under the Magistrates' Courts Act 1980, s 64. The fact that the dog is out of the jurisdiction of the particular court where the complaint is preferred and heard does not prevent the justices making an order (*Lockett v Withey* (1908) 72 JP 492). Where the court makes an order directing a dog to be destroyed it may appoint a person to undertake its destruction and require any person having custody of the dog to deliver it up for that purpose (Dangerous Dogs Act 1989, s 1(1), post). The court may also make an order disqualifying the owner for having custody of a dog for a specified period (Dangerous Dogs Act 1989, s 1(1), post).

For right of appeal to the Crown Court against any order made under s 2, see the Dangerous Dogs Act 1989, s 1(2), post.

For penalty on failure to comply with an order under s 2, see the Dangerous Dogs Act 1989, s 1(3), post.

6. No order can be made upon a person who was the owner of the dog when it was dangerous and not kept under

proper control if before the hearing the dog has been transferred *bona fide* to another person's ownership (*R v Jones, ex p Daunton* [1963] 1 All ER 368, 127 JP 349): but an order may be made against the new owner (*R v Leicester Justices, ex p Workman* [1964] 2 All ER 346). Knowledge of the owner that the dog is dangerous is not necessary (*Parker v Walsh* (1885) 1 TLR 583).

7. The court may specify the measures to be taken for keeping the dog under proper control, whether by muzzling, keeping on a lead, excluding it from specified places or otherwise (Dangerous Dogs Act 1991, s 3(5)(b), post).

8. The justices may, at their option, direct the dog to be kept or destroyed without giving the owner the option of keeping it under proper control (*Pickering v Marsh*(1874) 38 JP 678). This decision was followed in*R v Dymock*, and *R v Moger* (1901) 49 WR 618.

8–7520   6. Saving of local Acts.   This Act shall not affect the powers contained in any local or other Act of Parliament for the same or like purposes; and in places where any such local or other Act is in force, proceedings may be taken under such local or other Act, or under this Act, as may be deemed expedient.

[Dogs Act 1871, s 6, as amended by the Dangerous Dogs Act 1989, s 2.]

Dogs Act 1906
(6 Edw 7 c 32)

8–7530   1. Liability of owner of dog for injury to cattle.   (4) Where a dog is proved to have injured cattle or poultry[1] or chased sheep, it may be dealt with under section 2 of the Dogs Act 1871, as a dangerous dog.

[Dogs Act 1906, s 1, as amended by the Dogs (Amendment) Act 1928, s 1.]

---

1. Originally the definition of "poultry" in the Poultry Act 1911 was applied to this section by the Dogs (Amendment) Act 1928, s 1, but was replaced by the definition contained in s 84(2) of the Diseases of Animals Act 1950, by s 89(3) thereof; see now the Animal Health Act 1981, s 87, title ANIMALS ante.

8–7531   3. Seizure of stray dogs.   (1) Where a police officer has reason to believe that any dog found in a highway or place of public resort is a stray dog, he may seize the dog and may detain it until the owner has claimed it and paid all expenses incurred by reason of its detention.

(2) Where any dog so seized wears a collar having inscribed thereon or attached thereto the address of any person, or the owner of the dog is known, the chief officer of police, or any person authorised by him in that behalf, shall serve on the person whose address is given on the collar, or on the owner, a notice in writing stating that the dog has been so seized, and will be liable to be sold or destroyed if not claimed within seven clear days after the service of notice.

(3) A notice under this section may be served either—

(a)   by delivering it to the person on whom it is to be served; or

(b)   by leaving it at that person's usual or last known place of abode, or at the address given on the collar; or

(c)   by forwarding it by post in a prepaid letter addressed to that person at his usual or last known place of abode, or the address given on the collar.

(4) Where any dog so seized has been detained for seven clear days after the seizure, or, in the case of such a notice as aforesaid having been served with respect to the dog, then for seven clear days after the service of the notice, and the owner has not claimed the dog and paid all expenses incurred by reason of its detention, the chief officer of police, or any person authorised by him in that behalf, may cause the dog to be sold or destroyed in a manner to cause as little pain as possible.

(5) No dog so seized shall be given or sold for the purposes of vivisection.

(6) The chief officer of police of a police area shall keep, or cause to be kept, one or more registers of all dogs seized under this section in that area which are not transferred to an establishment for the reception of stray dogs. The register shall contain a brief description of the dog, the date of seizure, and particulars as to the manner in which the dog is disposed of, and every such register shall be open to inspection at all reasonable times by any member of the public on payment of a fee of 5p.

(7) The police shall not dispose of any dog seized under this section by transferring it to an establishment for the reception of stray dogs unless a register is kept for that establishment containing such particulars as to dogs received in the establishment as are above mentioned, and such register is open to inspection by the public on payment of a fee not exceeding 5p.

(8) The police officer or other person having charge of any dog detained under this section shall cause the dog to be properly fed and maintained.

(9) All expenses incurred by the police under this section shall be defrayed out of the police fund, and any money received by the police under this section shall be paid to the account of the police fund.

(10) (*Repealed*).*

[Dogs Act 1906, s 3, as amended by the Police Act 1964, ss 64 and 65, and Sch 10, the Decimal Currency Act 1969, s 10, the Local Government Act 1988, s 39 and the Environmental Protection Act 1990, Sch 15.]

*Repealed, in relation to England and Wales, by the Clean Neighbourhoods and Environment Act 2005, Sch 5 from a date to be appointed.

8–7532   4. Delivery of stray dogs to police.   (1) *Repealed.*

(2) Where a dog has been taken to a police station in pursuance of section 150(1) of the Environmental Protection Act 1990 then—(*a*) if the finder desires to keep the dog, he shall inform the said police officer of this fact and shall furnish his name and address, and the police officer shall, having complied with the procedure (if any) prescribed under subsection (5) below, allow the finder to remove the dog and thereupon the finder may remove the dog, but shall be under obligation to keep it for not less than one month; (*b*) if the finder does not desire to keep the dog, the said police officer shall treat it as if it had been seized by him in pursuance of s 3 of this Act.

(3) If the finder removes the dog but fails to keep it for at least one month, he shall be liable on summary conviction to a fine not exceeding **level 1** on the standard scale.

(4) The Secretary of State may, by regulations made by statutory instrument, prescribe the procedure to be followed under subsection (2)(*a*) above and any instrument containing regulations under this subsection shall be subject to annulment in pursuance of a resolution of either House of Parliament.*

[Dogs Act 1906, s 4, substituted by Dogs (Amendment) Act 1928, s 2 and amended by the Criminal Law Act 1977, s 31, the Criminal Justice Act 1982, s 46, the Local Government Act 1988, s 39 and the Environmental Protection Act 1990, Sch 15.]

---

*Repealed, in relation to England and Wales, by the Clean Neighbourhoods and Environment Act 2005, Sch 5 from a date to be appointed.

1. This form is prescribed by Order dated 4 August 1928, SR & O 1928/612.

8–7533   6. Burying of carcases.   Any person who shall knowingly and without reasonable excuse permit the carcase of any head of cattle belonging to him, or under his control, to remain unburied in a field or other place to which dogs can gain access shall be liable on conviction under the Magistrates' Courts Act 1952[1] to a fine not exceeding **level 1** on the standard scale.*

[Dogs Act 1906, s 6, as amended by Dogs (Amendment) Act 1928, s 3, Criminal Justice Act 1967, 3rd Sch and the Criminal Justice Act 1982, ss 38 and 46.]

---

*Repealed in relation to England by SI 2005/2347.

1. Now the Magistrates' Courts Act 1980.

8–7534   7. Definition of cattle.   In this Act, the expression "cattle"[1] includes horses, mules, asses, sheep, goats and swine.

[Dogs Act 1906, s 7.]

---

1. Note also the definition in s 89(1) of the Animal Health Act 1981, in title ANIMALS, ante. Rabbits kept for commercial purposes are not "cattle" (*Tallents v Bell and Goddard* [1944] 2 All ER 474).

Dogs (Protection of Livestock) Act 1953
(1 & 2 Eliz 2 c 28)

8–7550   1. Penalty where dog worries livestock on agricultural land.   (1) Subject to the provisions of this section, if a dog worries livestock[1] on any agricultural land[2], the owner of the dog, and, if it is in the charge of a person other than its owner, that person also, shall be guilty of an offence under this Act.

(2) For the purposes of this Act worrying livestock[1] means—

(*a*) attacking livestock, or

(*b*) chasing livestock in such a way as may reasonably be expected to cause injury or suffering to the livestock or, in the case of females, abortion, or loss of or diminution in their produce, or

(*c*) being at large (that is to say not on a lead or otherwise under close control) in a field or enclosure in which there are sheep.

(2A) Subsection (2)(*c*) of this section shall not apply in relation to—

(*a*) a dog owned by, or in the charge of, the occupier of the field or enclosure or the owner of the sheep or a person authorised by either of those persons; or

(*b*) a police dog, a guide dog, a trained sheep dog, a working gun dog or a dog lawfully used to hunt.

(3) A person shall not be guilty of an offence under this Act by reason of anything done by a dog, if at the material time the livestock are trespassing on the land in question and the dog is owned by, or in the charge of, the occupier of that land or a person authorised by him, except in a case where the said person causes the dog to attack the livestock.

(4) The owner of a dog shall not be convicted of an offence under this Act in respect of the

worrying of livestock by the dog if he proves that at the time when the dog worried the livestock it was in the charge of some other person, whom he reasonably believed to be a fit and proper person to be in charge of the dog.

(5) Where the Minister[3] is satisfied that it is inexpedient that subsection (1) of this section should apply to land in any particular area, being an area appearing to him to consist wholly or mainly of mountain, hill, moor, heath or down land, he may by order direct that that subsection shall not apply to land in that area.

(6) A person guilty of an offence under this Act shall be liable on summary conviction to a fine not exceeding **level 3** on the standard scale.

[Dogs (Protection of Livestock) Act 1953, s 1, as amended by Criminal Justice Act 1967, 3rd Sch, the Criminal Law Act 1977, Sch 6, the Wildlife and Countryside Act 1981, Sch 7, the Criminal Justice Act 1982, s 46 and the Protection of Wild Mammals (Scotland) Act 2002, s 11.]

1. "Livestock" means cattle, sheep, goats, swine, horses, or poultry, and for the purposes of this definition "cattle" means bulls, cows, oxen, heifers or calves, "horses" includes asses and mules and "poultry" means domestic fowls, turkeys, geese or ducks (s 3(1)).

2. "Agricultural land" means land used as arable, meadow or grazing land or for the purposes of poultry farming, pig farming, market gardens, allotments, nursery grounds or orchards (s 3(1)).

3. In England, the Minister for Agriculture, Fisheries and Food (s 8(2)). The functions of the Minister, so far as exercisable in relation to Wales have been transferred to the National Assemblt for Wales, by the National Assembly for Wales (Transfer of Functions) Order 1999, SI 1999/672, art 2, Sch 1.

8–7551 2. Enforcement. (1) As respects an offence under this Act alleged to have been committed in respect of a dog on any agricultural land in England or Wales, no proceedings shall be brought except—

(a) by or with the consent of the chief officer of police for the police area in which the land is situated, or

(b) by the occupier of the land, or

(c) by the owner of any of the livestock in question.

(2) Where in the case of a dog found on any land—

(a) a police officer has reasonable cause to believe that the dog has been worrying livestock on that land, and the land appears to him to be agricultural land, and

(b) no person is present who admits to being the owner of the dog or in charge of it,

then for the purpose of ascertaining who is the owner of the dog the police officer may seize it and may detain it until the owner has claimed it and paid all expenses incurred by reason of its detention.

(3) Subsections (4) to (10) of section 3 of the Dogs Act 1906[1] (which provide for the disposal of dogs seized under subsection (1) of that section if unclaimed after seven days) shall apply in relation to dogs seized under the last preceding subsection as they apply in relation to dogs seized under subsection (1) of that section (which provides for the seizure and detention of dogs found in highways and places of public resort and believed to be stray dogs).

[Dogs (Protection of Livestock) Act 1953, s 2.]

1. See this title, ante.

8–7552 2A. Power of justice of the peace to authorise entry and search. If on an application made by a constable a justice of the peace is satisfied that there are reasonable grounds for believing—

(a) that an offence under this Act has been committed; and

(b) that the dog in respect of which the offence has been committed is on premises specified in the application,

he may issue a warrant authorising a constable to enter and search the premises in order to identify the dog.

[Dogs (Protection of Livestock) Act 1953, s 2A added by the Police and Criminal Evidence Act 1984, Sch 6.]

Breeding of Dogs Act 1973[1]
(1973 c 60)

8–7570 1. Licensing of breeding establishments for dogs. (1) No person shall keep a breeding establishment for dogs except under the authority of a licence granted in accordance with the provisions of this Act.

(2) Every local authority may, on application being made to them for that purpose by a person who is not for the time being disqualified—

(a) from keeping a breeding establishment for dogs; or

(b) under the Pet Animals Act 1951, from keeping a pet shop; or

(c), (d) (*Repealed*);

    (*e*)   under the Protection of Animals (Amendment) Act 1954, from having the custody of animals; or

    (*f*)   under the Animal Boarding Establishments Act 1963, from the boarding of animals,

grant a licence to that person to keep a breeding establishment for dogs at such premises in their area as may be specified in the application and subject to compliance with such conditions as may be specified in the licence.

    (2A)   On receipt of an application by a person to a local authority for the grant of a licence under this Act in respect of any premises—

    (*a*)   if a licence under this Act has not previously been granted to the person in respect of the premises, the authority shall arrange for the inspection of the premises by a veterinary surgeon or veterinary practitioner and by an officer of the authority; and

    (*b*)   in any other case, the authority shall arrange for the inspection of the premises by a veterinary surgeon or veterinary practitioner or by an officer of the authority (or by both).

    (2B)   Where an inspection is arranged under subsection (2A) of this section, the local authority shall arrange for the making of a report about the premises, the applicant and any other relevant matter; and the authority shall consider the report before determining whether to grant a licence.

    (3)   (*Repealed*).

    (4)   In determining whether to grant a licence for the keeping of a breeding establishment for dogs by any person at any premises, a local authority shall in particular (but without prejudice to their discretion to withhold a licence on other grounds) have regard to the need for securing—

    (*a*)   that the dogs will at all times be kept in accommodation suitable as respects construction, size of quarters, number of occupants, exercising facilities, temperature, lighting, ventilation and cleanliness;

    (*b*)   that the dogs will be adequately supplied with suitable food, drink and bedding material, adequately exercised, and visited at suitable intervals;

    (*c*)   that all reasonable precautions will be taken to prevent and control the spread among dogs of infectious or contagious diseases;

    (*d*)   that appropriate steps will be taken for the protection of the dogs in case of fire or other emergency;

    (*e*)   that all appropriate steps will be taken to secure that the dogs will be provided with suitable food, drink and bedding material and adequately exercised when being transported to or from the breeding establishment;

    (*f*)   that bitches are not mated if they are less than one year old;

    (*g*)   that bitches do not give birth to more than six litters of puppies each;

    (*h*)   that bitches do not give birth to puppies before the end of the period of twelve months beginning with the day on which they last gave birth to puppies; and

    (*i*)   that accurate records in a form prescribed by regulations[2] are kept at the premises and made available for inspection there by any officer of the local authority, or any veterinary surgeon or veterinary practitioner, authorised by the local authority to inspect the premises;

and shall specify such conditions in the licence, if granted by them, as appear to the local authority necessary or expedient in the particular case for securing all the objects specified in paragraphs (*a*) to (*i*) of this subsection.

    (4A)   Regulations[2] under paragraph (*i*) of subsection (4) of this section shall be made by the Secretary of State by statutory instrument; and a statutory instrument containing regulations made under that paragraph shall be subject to annulment in pursuance of a resolution of either House of Parliament.

    (5)   Any person aggrieved by the refusal of a local authority to grant such a licence, or by any condition subject to which such a licence is proposed to be granted, may appeal to a magistrates' court; and the court may on such an appeal give such directions with respect to the issue of a licence or, as the case may be, with respect to the conditions subject to which a licence is to be granted as it thinks proper.

    (5A)   A local authority shall determine whether to grant such a licence before the end of the period of three months beginning with the day on which the application for the licence is received.

    (6)–(8)   *Duration of licence.*

    (9)   Any person who contravenes the provisions of subsection (1) of this section shall be guilty of an offence; and if any condition subject to which a licence is granted in accordance with the provisions of this Act is contravened or not complied with, the person to whom the licence was granted shall be guilty of an offence.

[Breeding of Dogs Act 1973, s 1, as amended by the Local Government, Planning and Land Act 1980, Schs 6 and 34, the Protection of Animals (Amendment) Act 1988, Sch, and the Breeding and Sale of Dogs (Welfare) Act 1999, s 11(2).]

---

    1. This Act shall not apply to the breeding of dogs for use in regulated procedures within the meaning of the Animals (Scientific Procedures) Act 1986 if they are bred at a designated breeding establishment (Animals (Scientific Procedures) Act 1986, s 27(3), title ANIMALS, ante. The Breeding of Dogs Act 1991, post, extends the powers of inspection for the purposes of this Act to premises not covered by a licence.

    2. The Breeding of Dogs (Licensing Records) Regulations 1999, SI 1999/3192, set out the form of record to be kept by a licensed dog breeder for each breeding bitch.

8–7571   **2. Inspection of breeding establishments for dogs.**   (1) A local authority may authorise in writing any of its officers or any veterinary surgeon or veterinary practitioner to inspect (subject to compliance with such precautions as the authority may specify to prevent the spread among animals of infectious or contagious diseases) any premises in their area as respects which a licence granted in accordance with the provisions of this Act is for the time being in force, and any person authorised under this section may, on producing his authority if so required, enter any such premises at all reasonable times and inspect them and any animals found thereon or any thing therein, for the purpose of ascertaining whether an offence has been or is being committed against this Act.

(2) Any person who wilfully obstructs or delays any person in the exercise of his powers of entry or inspection under this section shall be guilty of an offence.

[Breeding of Dogs Act 1973, s 2.]

8–7572   **3. Offences and disqualifications.**   (1) Any person guilty of an offence under any provision of this Act other than the last foregoing section shall be liable on summary conviction to—

     (a)   imprisonment for a term not exceeding three months; or

     (b)   a fine not exceeding level 4 on the standard scale,

or to both.

(2) Any person guilty of an offence under the last foregoing section shall be liable on summary conviction to a fine not exceeding **level 3** on the standard scale.

(3) Where a person is convicted of any offence under this Act ", the court by which he is convicted may (in addition to or in substitution for any penalty under subsection (1) or (2) of this section) make an order providing for any one or more of the following—

     (a)   the cancellation of any licence held by him under this Act;

     (b)   his disqualification, for such period as the court thinks fit, from keeping an establishment the keeping of which is required to be licensed under this Act; and

     (c)   his disqualification, for such period as the court thinks fit, from having custody of any dog of a description specified in the order.

(4) A court which has made an order under this section, or his disqualification, in pursuance of the last foregoing subsection may, if it thinks fit, suspend the operation of the order pending an appeal.

(5) Where a court makes an order under subsection (3)(c) of this section in relation to a description of dogs it may also make such order as it thinks fit in respect of any dog of that description which—

     (a)   was in the offender's custody at the time when the offence was committed; or

     (b)   has been in his custody at any time since that time.

(6) An order under subsection (5) of this section may (in particular)—

     (a)   require any person who has custody of the dog to deliver it up to a specified person; and

     (b)   (if it does) also require the offender to pay specified amounts to specified persons for the care of the dog from the time when it is delivered up in pursuance of the order until permanent arrangements are made for its care or disposal.

(7) A person who—

     (a)   has custody of a dog in contravention of an order under subsection (3)(c) of this section; or

     (b)   fails to comply with a requirement imposed on him under subsection (6) of this section,

shall be guilty of an offence.

(8) Where a court proposes to make an order under subsection (5) of this section in respect of a dog owned by a person other than the offender, the court shall notify the owner who may make representations to the court; and if an order is made the owner may, within the period of seven days beginning with the date of the order, appeal to—

     (a)   in England and Wales, the Crown Court; or

     (b)   in Scotland, the High Court of Justiciary,

against the order.

(9) A person who is subject to a disqualification by virtue of an order under subsection (3)(c) of this section may, at any time after the end of the period of one year beginning with the date of the order, apply to the court which made the order (or, in England and Wales, any magistrates' court acting for the same petty sessions area) for a direction terminating the disqualification from such date as the court considers appropriate.

(10) On an application under subsection (9) of this section the court—

     (a)   shall notify the relevant local authority which may make representations to the court;

     (b)   shall, having regard to the applicant's character and his conduct since the disqualification was imposed, any representations made by the relevant local authority and any other circumstances of the case, grant or refuse the application; and

     (c)   may order the applicant to pay all or any part of the costs, or (in Scotland) expenses, of the application (including any costs, or expenses, of the relevant local authority in making representations);

and in this subsection "the relevant local authority" means the local authority in whose area are situated the premises in relation to which the offence which led to the disqualification was committed.

(11) Where an application under subsection (9) of this section in respect of a disqualification is refused, no further application under that subsection in respect of that disqualification shall be entertained if made before the end of the period of one year beginning with the date of the refusal.
[Breeding of Dogs Act 1973, s 3 as amended by the Criminal Justice Act 1982, ss 38 and 46 and the Breeding and Sale of dogs (welfare) Act 1999.]

---

1. He may also be disqualified from keeping any dangerous wild animal (Dangerous Wild Animals Act 1976, s 6(2), title ANIMALS, ante). A magistrates' court shall not in a person's absence impose any disqualification on him except after an adjournment after convicting and before sentencing him, see Magistrates' Courts Act 1980, s 11(4), ante.

8–7572A 3A. Fees.

(1) The costs of inspecting premises under this Act and the Breeding of Dogs Act 1991 shall be met by the local authority concerned.

(2) A local authority may charge fees—

(*a*) in respect of applications for the grant of licences under this Act; and
(*b*) in respect of inspections of premises under section 1(2A) of this Act.

(3) A local authority may set the level of fees to be charged by virtue of subsection (2) of this section—

(*a*) with a view to recovering the reasonable costs incurred by them in connection with the administration and enforcement of this Act and the Breeding of Dogs Act 1991; and
(*b*) so that different fees are payable in different circumstances.

[Breeding of Dogs Act 1973, s 3A as inserted by the Breeding and Sale of dogs (Welfare) Act 1999.]

8–7572B 4A. Breeding establishments for dogs.

(1) References in this Act to the keeping of a breeding establishment for dogs shall be construed in accordance with this section.

(2) A person keeps a breeding establishment for dogs at any premises if he carries on at those premises a business of breeding dogs for sale (whether by him or any other person).

(3) Subject to subsection (5) of this section, where—

(*a*) a person keeps a bitch at any premises at any time during any period of twelve months; and
(*b*) the bitch gives birth to a litter of puppies at any time during that period,

he shall be treated as carrying on a business of breeding dogs for sale at the premises throughout the period if a total of four or more other litters is born during the period to bitches falling within subsection (4) of this section.

(4) The bitches falling within this subsection are—

(*a*) the bitch mentioned in subsection (3)(*a*) and (*b*) of this section and any other bitches kept by the person at the premises at any time during the period;
(*b*) any bitches kept by any relative of his at the premises at any such time;
(*c*) any bitches kept by him elsewhere at any such time; and
(*d*) any bitches kept (anywhere) by any person at any such time under a breeding arrangement made with him.

(5) Subsection (3) of this section does not apply if the person shows that none of the puppies born to bitches falling within paragraph (*a*), (*b*) or (*d*) of subsection (4) of this section was in fact sold during the period (whether by him or any other person).

(6) In subsection (4) of this section "breeding arrangement" means a contract or other arrangement under which the person agrees that another person may keep a bitch of his on terms that, should the bitch give birth, the other person is to provide him with either—

(*a*) one or more of the puppies; or
(*b*) the whole or part of the proceeds of selling any of them;

and "relative" means the person's parent or grandparent, child or grandchild, sibling, aunt or uncle or niece or nephew or someone with whom he lives as a couple.

(7) In this section "premises" includes a private dwelling.
[Breeding of Dogs Act 1973, s 4A as inserted by the Breeding and Sale of dogs (Welfare) Act 1999.]

8–7572C 4B. Rearing establishments for dogs.

(1) For the purposes of the application of this Act in relation to Scotland, a person keeps a rearing establishment for dogs at any premises if he carries on at those premises a business of rearing dogs for sale (whether by him or any other person).

(2) In subsection (1) of this section "premises" includes a private dwelling.
[Breeding of Dogs Act 1973, s 4B as inserted by the Breeding and Sale of dogs (Welfare) Act 1999.]

8–7573 5. Interpretation.

(1) nothing in this Act shall apply to the keeping of a dog at any premises in pursuance of a requirement imposed under, or having effect by virtue of, the Diseases of Animals Act 1950.

(2) In this Act, unless the context otherwise requires, the following expressions have the meanings hereby respectively assigned to them, that is to say:—

"local authority" means in England the council of a London borough the council of a district or the Common Council of the City of London and in Wales the council of a county or county borough; and in Scotland a council constituted under section 2 of the Local Government etc. (Scotland) Act 1994;

"veterinary practitioner" means a person who is for the time being registered in the Supplementary Veterinary Register;

"veterinary surgeon" means a person who is for the time being registered in the Register of Veterinary Surgeons.

[Breeding of Dogs Act 1973, s 5, as amended by the Local Government Act 1974, Sch 7, the Local Government (Wales) Act 1994, Sch 16 and the Breeding and Sale of Dogs (Welfare) Act 1999, Sch.]

Guard Dogs Act 1975

(1975 c 50)

8–7590 *By SI 1975/1767 this Act, except ss 2 to 4, 5 (so far as its provisions relate to ss 2 to 4 and 6, were brought into force on 1st February 1976.*

8–7591 1. Control of guard dogs. (1) A person shall not use or permit the use of a guard dog at any premises unless a person ("the handler") who is capable of controlling the dog is present on the premises and the dog is under the control of the handler at all times while it is being so used except while it is secured so that it is not at liberty to go freely about the premises[1].

(2) The handler of a guard dog shall keep the dog under his control at all times while it is being used as a guard dog at any premises except—

(a) while another handler has control over the dog; or

(b) while the dog is secured so that it is not at liberty to go freely about the premises.

(3) A person shall not use or permit the use of a guard dog at any premises unless a notice containing a warning that a guard dog is present is clearly exhibited at each entrance to the premises.
[Guard Dogs Act 1975, s 1.]

---

1. It is not necessary for the handler to be on the premises at all times provided that the dog is properly secured (*Hobson v Gledhill* [1978] 1 All ER 945, [1978] 1 WLR 215, 142 JP 250).

8–7592 2. Restriction on keeping guard dogs without a licence. (1) A person shall not keep a dog at guard dog kennels unless he holds a licence under section 3 of this Act in respect of the kennels.

(2) A person shall not use or permit the use at any premises of a guard dog if he knows or has reasonable cause to suspect that the dog (when not being used as a guard dog) is normally kept at guard dog kennels in breach of subsection (1) of this section.
[Guard Dogs Act 1975, s 2.]

8–7593 3. Guard dog licences. (1)–(3) Power of local authority to grant licences and impose conditions therein.

(4) Where a person is convicted of an offence under this Act, the Protection of Animals Act 1911, the Protection of Animals (Scotland) Act 1912, the Pet Animals Act 1951, the Animal Boarding Establishments Act 1963 or the Breeding of Dogs Act 1973, the court by which he is convicted may cancel any licence held by him under this Act.

(5) The court may suspend the operation of the cancellation pending an appeal.

(6) For the purposes of this Act the Inner and Middle Temples shall be deemed to be in the City of London.
[Guard Dogs Act 1975, s 3.]

8–7594 4. Appeals. (1) The applicant or, as the case may be, the licence holder may appeal to a magistrates' court or (*Scotland*), against—

(a) the refusal of a local authority to grant a licence; or

(b) the conditions (other than the prescribed conditions) to which the licence is subject; or

(c) the authority's refusal to vary the conditions; or

(d) the revocation of a licence.

(2) On an appeal the court may, if it thinks fit, give directions to the local authority with respect to the licence or the conditions, and it shall be the duty of the local authority to comply with such directions.
[Guard Dogs Act 1975, s 4.]

8–7595 5. Offences, penalties and civil liability. (1) A person who contravenes section 1 or 2 of this Act shall be guilty of an offence and liable on summary conviction to a fine not exceeding **level 5** on the standard scale.

(2) The provisions of this Act shall not be construed as—

(*a*) conferring a right of action in any civil proceedings (other than proceedings or the recovery of a fine or any prescribed fee) in respect of any contravention of this Act or of any regulations made under this Act or of any of the terms or conditions of a licence granted under section 3 of this Act; or

(*b*) derogating from any right of action or other remedy (whether civil or criminal) in proceedings instituted otherwise than by virtue of this Act.

[Guard Dogs Act 1975, s 5 as amended by the Criminal Justice Act 1982, ss 38 and 46.]

8–7596   6. *Power to make regulations.*

8–7597   7. Interpretation.   In this Act, unless the context otherwise requires—

"agricultural land" has the same meaning as in the Dogs (Protection of Livestock) Act 1953;
"guard dog" means a dog which is being used to protect—

(*a*) premises; or
(*b*) property kept on the premises; or
(*c*) a person guarding the premises or such property;

"guard dog kennels" means a place where a person in the course of business keeps a dog which (notwithstanding that it is used for other purposes) is used as a guard dog elsewhere, other than a dog which is used as a guard dog only at premises belonging to its owner;
"local authority" means, in relation to England, a district council, a London borough council and the Common Council of the City of London, in relation to Wales means a county or a county borough council, and, in relation to Scotland, an islands council or a district council;
"premises" means land other than agricultural land and land within the curtilage of a dwelling-house, and buildings, including parts of buildings, other than dwelling-houses;
"prescribed" means prescribed by regulations;
"regulations" means regulations made by the Secretary of State.

[Guard Dogs Act 1975, s 7 amended by the Local Government (Wales) Act 1994, Sch 16.]

Dangerous Dogs Act 1989[1]
(1989 c 30)

8–7610   1. Additional powers of court on complaint about dangerous dog.   (1) Where a magistrates' court makes an order under section 2 of the Dogs Act 1871[2] directing a dog to be destroyed it may also—

(*a*) appoint a person to undertake its destruction and require any person having custody of the dog to deliver it up for that purpose; and

(*b*) if it thinks fit, make an order disqualifying the owner for having custody of a dog for such period as is specified in the order.

(2) An appeal shall lie to the Crown Court against any order under section 2 of that Act or under subsection (1) above; and, unless the owner of a dog which is ordered to be delivered up and destroyed gives notice to the court that made the order that he does not intend to appeal against it, the dog shall not be destroyed pursuant to the order—

(*a*) until the end of the period within which notice of appeal to the Crown Court against the order can be given; and

(*b*) if notice of appeal is given within that period, until the appeal is determined or withdrawn.

(3) Any person who fails to comply with an order under section 2 of the said Act of 1871 to keep a dog under proper control or to deliver a dog up for destruction as required by an order under subsection (1)(*a*) above is guilty of an offence and liable on summary conviction to a fine not exceeding **level 3** on the standard scale and the court may, in addition, make an order disqualifying[3] him for having custody of a dog for such period as is specified in the order.

(4) A person who is disqualified for having custody of a dog by virtue of an order made under subsection (1)(*b*) or (3) above may, at any time after the end of the period of one year beginning with the date of the order, apply[4] to the court that made it (or any magistrates' court acting for the same petty sessions area as that court) for a direction terminating the disqualification.

(5) On an application under subsection (4) above the court may—

(*a*) having regard to the applicant's character, his conduct since the disqualification was imposed and any other circumstances of the case, grant or refuse the application; and

(*b*) order the applicant to pay all or any part of the costs of the application;

and where an application in respect of an order is refused no further application in respect of that order shall be entertained if made before the end of the period of one year beginning with the date of the refusal.

(6) Any person who has custody of a dog in contravention of an order made under subsection

(1)(*b*) or (3) above is guilty of an offence and liable on summary conviction to a fine not exceeding **level 5** on the standard scale.

(7) *Scotland.*
[Dangerous Dogs Act 1989, s 1.]

1. This Act extends the powers available to a court on a complaint under s 2 of the Dogs Act 1871 and provides additional rights of appeal and enhanced penalties. The Act came into force on 27 August 1989 (s 2(4)).

2. See this title, ante.

3. A magistrates' court shall not in a person's absence impose any disqualification on him, except after an adjournment after convicting and before sentencing him (Magistrates' Courts Act 1980, s 11(4), in PART I: MAGISTRATES' COURTS, PROCEDURE, ante).

4. No procedure is laid down for making an application, but it would seem desirable that the informant or complainant in the proceedings in which the disqualification order was made should be given notice of the hearing of the application and an opportunity of being heard; see, for example, r 55.2 of the Criminal Procedure Rules 2005 relating to application for removal of disqualification for holding or obtaining a licence to drive a motor vehicle.

8–7611 **2.** *Short title, consequential amendment and repeals, commencement and extent.*

Breeding of Dogs Act 1991[1]
(1991 c 64)

8–7612 **1. Power to inspect premises not covered by licence under Breeding of Dogs Act 1973.** (1) If a justice of the peace is satisfied by information on oath laid by an officer of a local authority authorised in writing for the purposes of this section by the authority, or any veterinary surgeon or veterinary practitioner so authorised, that there are reasonable grounds for suspecting that an offence against section 1(1) of the Breeding of Dogs Act 1973[2] (breeding establishments for dogs to be covered by a licence) has been or is being committed at any premises in the area of the authority, the justice may issue a warrant authorising any such officer, surgeon or practitioner to enter those premises, by reasonable force if need be, and inspect them and any animals or any thing found there.

(2) No warrant shall be issued under subsection (1) above authorising entry to any premises for the time being used as a private dwelling.

(3) The reference in subsection (2) above to premises for the time being used as a private dwelling does not include a reference to any garage, outhouse or other structure (whether or not forming part of the same building as the premises) which belongs to or is usually enjoyed with the premises.

(4) A warrant issued under subsection (1) above—

(*a*) may authorise persons to accompany the person who is executing the warrant; and
(*b*) shall continue in force for the period of one month commencing with the date of issue.

(5) The power of entry conferred by the warrant may be exercised at all reasonable times and any person entering the premises in exercise of that power shall—

(*a*) produce the warrant if so required; and
(*b*) comply with such precautions (if any) as the justice of the peace may specify to prevent the spread among animals of infectious or contagious diseases.

(6) In the application of this section to Scotland, any reference to a justice of the peace shall include a reference to a sheriff and the reference in subsection (1) to written information on oath shall be construed as a reference to evidence on oath.

(7) In this section "local authority", "veterinary practitioner" and "veterinary surgeon" have the same meanings as in the Breeding of Dogs Act 1973[2].
[Breeding of Dogs Act 1991, s 1.]

1. This Act extends the powers of inspection for the purposes of the Breeding of Dogs Act 1973, ante, to premises not covered by a licence under that Act. This Act came into force on 25 September 1991.

2. See this title, ante.

8–7613 **2. Offence and disqualification.** (1) Any person who intentionally obstructs or delays any person in the exercise of his powers of entry or inspection under section 1 above is guilty of an offence and liable on summary conviction to a fine not exceeding **level 3** on the standard scale.

(2) Where a person is convicted of an offence under subsection (1) above, the court by which he is convicted may make an order providing for either or both of the following—

(*a*) his disqualification, for such period as the court thinks fit, from keeping an establishment the keeping of which is required to be licensed under the Breeding of Dogs Act 1973; and
(*b*) his disqualification, for such period as the court thinks fit, from having custody of any dog of a description specified in the order.

(2A) A court which has made an order under or by virtue of this section may, if it thinks fit, suspend the operation of the order pending an appeal.

(2B) Subsections (5) to (11) of section 3 of the Breeding of Dogs Act 1973 (provisions about disqualification) apply in relation to an order made under subsection (2)(*b*) above as they apply in relation to an order made under subsection (3)(*c*) of that section.

(3) (*Repealed*).

[Breeding of Dogs Act 1991, s 2 as amended by the Breeding and Sale of Dogs (Welfare) Act 1999.]

8–7614 3. Short title, commencement and extent. (1) This Act may be cited as the Breeding of Dogs Act 1991.

(2) This Act shall come into force at the end of the period of two months beginning with the date on which it is passed.

(3) This Act does not extend to Northern Ireland.

[Breeding of Dogs Act 1991, s 3.]

Dangerous Dogs Act 1991[1]
(1991 c 65)

8–7615 1. Dogs bred for fighting. (1) This section applies to—

(*a*) any dog of the type[2] known as the pit bull terrier;
(*b*) any dog of the type[2] known as the Japanese tosa; and
(*c*) any dog of any type[2] designated for the purposes of this section by an order[3] of the Secretary of State, being a type appearing to him to be bred for fighting or to have the characteristics of a type bred for that purpose.

(2) No person shall—

(*a*) breed, or breed from, a dog to which this section applies;
(*b*) sell or exchange such a dog or offer, advertise or expose such a dog for sale or exchange;
(*c*) make or offer to make a gift of such a dog or advertise or expose such a dog as a gift;
(*d*) allow[4] such a dog of which he is the owner or of which he is for the time being in charge to be in a public place[5] without being muzzled and kept on a lead; or
(*e*) abandon such a dog of which he is the owner or, being the owner or for the time being in charge of such a dog, allow it to stray.

(3) After such day[6] as the Secretary of State may by order appoint for the purposes of this subsection no person shall have any dog to which this section applies in his possession or custody except—

(*a*) in pursuance of the power of seizure conferred by the subsequent provisions of this Act; or
(*b*) in accordance with an order for its destruction made under those provisions;

but the Secretary of State shall by order[7] make a scheme for the payment to the owners of such dogs who arrange for them to be destroyed before that day of sums specified in or determined under the scheme in respect of those dogs and the cost of their destruction.

(4) Subsection (2)(*b*) and (*c*) above shall not make unlawful anything done with a view to the dog in question being removed from the United Kingdom before the day appointed under subsection (3) above.

(5) The Secretary of State may by order[8] provide that the prohibition in subsection (3) above shall not apply in such cases and subject to compliance with such conditions as are specified in the order and any such provision may take the form of a scheme of exemption containing such arrangements (including provision for the payment of charges or fees) as he thinks appropriate.

(6) A scheme under subsection (3) or (5) above may provide for specified functions under the scheme to be discharged by such persons or bodies as the Secretary of State thinks appropriate.

(7) Any person who contravenes this section is guilty of an offence and liable on summary conviction to imprisonment for a term not exceeding **six months** or a fine not exceeding **level 5** on the standard scale or both except that a person who publishes an advertisement in contravention of subsection (2)(*b*) or (*c*)—

(*a*) shall not on being convicted be liable to imprisonment if he shows that he published the advertisement to the order of someone else and did not himself devise it; and
(*b*) shall not be convicted if, in addition, he shows that he did not know and had no reasonable cause to suspect that it related to a dog which this section applies.

(8) An order under subsection (1)(*c*) above adding dogs of any type to those to which this section applies may provide that subsections (3) and (4) above shall apply in relation to those dogs with the substitution for the day appointed under subsection (3) of a later day specified in the order.

(9) The power to make orders under this section shall be exercisable by statutory instrument which, in the case of an order under subsection (1) or (5) or an order containing a scheme under subsection (3), shall be subject to annulment in pursuance of a resolution of either House of Parliament.

[Dangerous Dogs Act 1991, s 1.]

1. This Act was brought fully into force on 12 August 1991 by the Dangerous Dogs Act 1991 (Commencement and Appointed Day) Order 1991, SI 1991/1742, made in accordance with ss 1(3) and 10(4) of the Act. This Act is printed as amended by the Dangerous Dogs (Amendment) Act 1997 which came into force on 8 June 1997 (SI 1997/1151). The Dangerous Dogs (Amendment) Act 1997 shall apply in relation to cases where proceedings have been instituted before, as well as after, the commencement of that Act. In a case where, before the commencement of the 1997 Act—

    (a) the court has ordered the destruction of a dog in respect of which an offence under section 1, or an aggravated offence under section 3(1) or (3), of the 1991 Act has been committed, but

    (b) the dog has not been destroyed,

       that destruction order shall cease to have effect and the case shall be remitted to the court for reconsideration.

Where a case is so remitted, the court may make any order in respect of the dog which it would have power to make if the person in question had been convicted of the offence after the commencement of the 1997 Act (Dangerous Dogs (Amendment) Act 1997, s 5).

2. "Type" is not synonymous with the word "breed', but has a meaning different from and wider than the word "breed". Accordingly, s 1(1)(a) applies to any dog having a substantial number or most of the physical characteristics of a pit bull terrier (*R v Crown Court at Knightsbridge, ex p Dunne* [1993] 4 All ER 491, [1994] 1 WLR 296).

3. The Dangerous Dogs (Designated Types) Order 1991, SI 1991/1743 designates two types of dog, Dogo Argentino and Fila Braziliero.

4. Voluntary intoxication of the owner or person in charge of the dog is no defence to a charge of allowing a dog to be in a public place without being muzzled or kept on a lead (*DPP v Kellett* (1994) 158 JP 1138, [1994] Crim LR 916). A defence of necessity is not available to a defendant charged with an offence contrary to s 1(2)(d) notwithstanding that he can show he did what he did to avoid serious harm to the dog (*Cichon v DPP* [1994] Crim LR 918).

5. If such a dog is in a car which itself is in a public place, then the dog is likewise in a public place (*Bates v DPP* (1993) 157 JP 1004).

6. The day appointed for the purposes of s 1(3) of the Act was 30 November 1991 (SI 1991/1742).

7. See Pt II of the Dangerous Dogs Compensation and Exemption Schemes Order 1991, post.

8. See Pt III of the Dangerous Dogs Compensation and Exemption Schemes Order 1991, post.

8–7616 2. Other specially dangerous dogs. (1) If it appears to the Secretary of State that dogs of any type to which section 1 above does not apply present a serious danger to the public he may by order impose in relation to dogs of that type restrictions corresponding, with such modifications, if any, as he thinks appropriate, to all or any of those in subsection (2)(d) and (e) of that section.

(2) An order under this section may provide for exceptions from any restriction imposed by the order in such cases and subject to compliance with such conditions as are specified in the order.

(3) An order under this section may contain such supplementary or transitional provisions as the Secretary of State thinks necessary or expedient and may create offences punishable on summary conviction with imprisonment for a term not exceeding **six months** or a fine not exceeding **level 5** on the standard scale or both.

(4) In determining whether to make an order under this section in relation to dogs of any type and, if so, what the provisions of the order should be, the Secretary of State shall consult with such persons or bodies as appear to him to have relevant knowledge or experience, including a body concerned with animal welfare, a body concerned with veterinary science and practice and a body concerned with breeds of dogs.

(5) The power to make an order under this section shall be exercisable by statutory instrument and no such order shall be made unless a draft of it has been laid before and approved by a resolution of each House of Parliament.

[Dangerous Dogs Act 1991, s 2.]

8–7617 3. Keeping dogs under proper control. (1) If a dog is dangerously out of control[1] in a public place[2]—

    (a) the owner; and

    (b) if different, the person for the time being in charge of the dog,

is guilty of an offence, or, if the dog while so out of control injures any person, an aggravated offence, under this subsection[3].

(2) In proceedings for an offence under subsection (1) above against a person who is the owner of a dog but was not at the material time in charge of it, it shall be a defence[4] for the accused to prove that the dog was at the material time in the charge of a person whom he reasonably believed to be a fit and proper person to be in charge of it.

(3) If the owner or, if different, the person for the time being in charge of a dog allows[5] it to enter a place which is not a public place but where it is not permitted to be and while it is there—

    (a) it injures any person; or

    (b) there are grounds for reasonable apprehension that it will do so,

he is guilty of an offence, or, if the dog injures any person, an aggravated offence, under this subsection.

(4) A person guilty of an offence under subsection (1) or (3) above other than an aggravated offence is liable on summary conviction to imprisonment for a term not exceeding **six months** or a fine not exceeding **level 5** on the standard scale or both; and a person guilty of an aggravated offence under either of those subsections is liable[6]—

    (a) on summary conviction, to imprisonment for a term not exceeding **six months** or a fine not exceeding the **statutory maximum** or both;

(*b*) on conviction on indictment, to imprisonment for a term not exceeding **two years** or a **fine** or both.

(5) It is hereby declared for the avoidance of doubt that an order under section 2 of the Dogs Act 1871 (order on complaint that dog is dangerous and not kept under proper control)—

(*a*) may be made whether or not the dog is shown to have injured any person; and

(*b*) may specify the measures to be taken for keeping the dog under proper control, whether by muzzling, keeping on a lead, excluding it from specified places or otherwise.

(6) If it appears to a court on a complaint under section 2 of the said Act of 1871 that the dog to which the complaint relates is a male and would be less dangerous if neutered the court may under that section make an order requiring it to be neutered.

(7) The reference in section 1(3) of the Dangerous Dogs Act 1989 (penalties)[7] to failing to comply with an order under section 2 of the said Act of 1871 to keep a dog under proper control shall include a reference to failing to comply with any other order made under that section; but no order shall be made under that section by virtue of subsection (6) above where the matters complained of arose before the coming into force of that subsection.
[Dangerous Dogs Act 1991, s 3.]

  1. For the meaning of the words "dangerously out of control", see s 10(3), and note thereto, post.

  2. For the meaning of "public place", see s 10(2) post.

  3. Section 3(1) imposes an absolute liability upon the owner or the person for the time being in charge of the dog; it is no defence that the owner had no realisation that his dog might behave in such a way (*R v Bezzina* [1994] 1 WLR 1057, 158 JP 671). Natural justice requires that the known owner of the dog be notified of any prosecution where a conviction will result in the destruction of the dog (*R v Trafford Magistrates' Court, ex p Riley* (1995) 160 JP 418, DC).

  4. This subsection operates only if there is plain evidence that the dog has been placed in the charge of someone other than the owner. In order for there to be a transfer of the charge of the dog, it is necessary for there to be evidence which establishes, or permits the inference to be drawn, that the owner had, for the time being, divested himself of responsibility in favour of an identifiable person: see *R v Huddart* [1999] Crim LR 568.

  5. The word "allows" includes both taking and omitting to take a positive step. *Mens rea* is not a necessary ingredient of the offence under s 3(3) of the Act. However, the prosecution must establish on the facts that as a matter of ordinary language and causation, the owner has allowed the dog to enter the place in question (*R v Greener* (1996) 160 JP 265).

  6. For procedure in respect of this offence which is triable either way, see the Magistrates' Courts Act 1980, ss 17A–21, in PART I: MAGISTRATES' COURTS, PROCEDURE, ante. The offence of *aggravated keeping dogs dangerously out of control* requires courts to look at the consequences of the offence when determining the appropriate penalty, and it is entirely appropriate to pass a custodial sentence for such an offence: *R v Jacqueline Cox* [2004] EWCA Crim 282, [2004] 2 Cr App R (S) 54 (9 months' imprisonment reduced to 3; 10 years' disqualification upheld).

  7. See this title, ante.

8–7618   4. Destruction and disqualification orders.   (1) Where a person[1] is convicted of an offence under section 1 or 3(1) or (3) above or of an offence under an order made under section 2 above the court—

(*a*) may order the destruction of any dog in respect of which the offence was committed and, subject to subsection (1A) below, shall do so in the case of an offence under section 1 or an aggravated offence under section 3(1) or (3) above[2]; and

(*b*) may order the offender to be disqualified[3], for such period as the court thinks fit, for having custody of a dog.

(1A) Nothing in subsection (1)(*a*) above shall require the court to order the destruction of a dog if the court is satisfied—

(*a*) that the dog would not constitute a danger to public safety; and

(*b*) where the dog was born before 30 November 1991 and is subject to the prohibition in section 1(3) above, that there is a good reason why the dog has not been exempted from that prohibition.

(2) Where a court makes an order under subsection (1)(*a*) above for the destruction of a dog owned by a person other than the offender, the owner may appeal to the Crown Court against the order.

(3) A dog shall not be destroyed pursuant to an order under subsection (1)(*a*) above—

(*a*) until the end of the period for giving notice of appeal against the conviction or, against the order; and

(*b*) if notice of appeal is given within that period, until the appeal is determined or withdrawn,

unless the offender and, in a case to which subsection (2) above applies, the owner of the dog give notice to the court that made the order that there is to be no appeal.

(4) Where a court makes an order under subsection (1)(*a*) above it may—

(*a*) appoint a person to undertake the destruction of the dog and require any person having custody of it to deliver it up for that purpose; and

(*b*) order the offender to pay such sum as the court may determine to be the reasonable expenses of destroying the dog and of keeping it pending its destruction.

(5) Any sum ordered to be paid under subsection (4)(*b*) above shall be treated for the purposes of enforcement as if it were a fine imposed on conviction.

(6) Any person who is disqualified for having custody of a dog by virtue of an order under subsection (1)(*b*) above may, at any time after the end of the period of one year beginning with the date of the order, apply to the court that made it (or a magistrates' court acting for the same petty sessions area as that court) for a direction terminating the disqualification.

(7) On an application under subsection (6) above the court may—

    (*a*) having regard to the applicant's character, his conduct since the disqualification was imposed and any other circumstances of the case, grant or refuse the application; and

    (*b*) order the applicant to pay all or any part of the costs of the application;

and where an application in respect of an order is refused no further application in respect of that order shall be entertained if made before the end of the period of one year beginning with the date of the refusal.

(8) Any person who—

    (*a*) has custody of a dog in contravention of an order under subsection (1)(*b*) above; or

    (*b*) fails to comply with a requirement imposed on him under subsection (4)(*a*) above,

is guilty of an offence and liable on summary conviction to a fine not exceeding **level 5** on the standard scale.

(9) *Scotland.*

[Dangerous Dogs Act 1991, s 4 as amended by the Dangerous Dogs (Amendment) Act 1997, s 1.]

---

1. The rules of natural justice require a known owner of the dog at least to be given an opportunity to be heard accordingly, where the person convicted is not the owner of the dog, notice of hearing must be given to any known owner before an order for destruction is made (*R v Trafford Magistrates' Court, ex p Riley* (1995) 160 JP 418; *R v Ealing Magistrates' Court, ex p Fanneran* (1995) 160 JP 409).

2. See, by way of example, *R v Holland* [2002] EWCA Crim 1585, [2003] 1 Cr App R (S), in which the court upheld a 10-year disqualification and indicated the kind of matters that might be relevant in the determination of any application under s 4(6) or (7) below.

3. There is no power to order a defendant to be disqualified from keeping more than one dog, nor to make a qualified disqualification order, nor to specify conditions that must be met if the defendant is to be permitted to retain one or more dogs; however, in deciding whether or not to make a disqualification order or whether or not to order the forfeiture of any dogs the court is entitled to have regard to any voluntary undertaking offered by the defendant as to his future conduct: *R v Rodney Haynes* [2003] EWCA Crim 3247, [2004] 2 Cr App R (S) 9.

8–7618A   **4A. Contingent destruction orders.** (1) Where—

    (*a*) a person is convicted of an offence under section 1 above or an aggravated offence under section 3(1) or (3) above;

    (*b*) the court does not order the destruction of the dog under section 4(1)(*a*) above; and

    (*c*) in the case of an offence under section 1 above, the dog is subject to the prohibition in section 1(3) above,

the court shall order that, unless the dog is exempted from that prohibition within the requisite period, the dog shall be destroyed.

(2) Where an order is made under subsection (1) above in respect of a dog, and the dog is not exempted from the prohibition in section 1(3) above within the requisite period, the court may extend that period.

(3) Subject to subsection (2) above, the requisite period for the purposes of such an order is the period of two months beginning with the date of the order.

(4) Where a person is convicted of an offence under section 3(1) or (3) above, the court may order that, unless the owner of the dog keeps it under proper control, the dog shall be destroyed.

(5) An order under subsection (4) above—

    (*a*) may specify the measures to be taken for keeping the dog under proper control, whether by muzzling, keeping on a lead, excluding it from specified places or otherwise; and

    (*b*) if it appears to the court that the dog is a male and would be less dangerous if neutered, may require it to be neutered.

(6) Subsections (2) to (4) of section 4 above shall apply in relation to an order under subsection (1) or (4) above as they apply in relation to an order under subsection (1)(*a*) of that section.

[Dangerous Dogs Act 1991, s 4A, as inserted by the Dangerous Dogs (Amendment) Act 1997, s 2.]

8–7618B   **4B. Destruction orders otherwise than on a conviction.** (1) Where a dog is seized under section 5(1) or (2) below and it appears to a justice of the peace, or in Scotland a justice of the peace or sheriff—

    (*a*) that no person has been or is to be prosecuted[1] for an offence under this Act or an order under section 2 above in respect of that dog (whether because the owner cannot be found or for any other reason); or

    (*b*) that the dog cannot be released into the custody or possession of its owner without the owner contravening the prohibition in section 1(3) above,

he may order the destruction of the dog and, subject to subsection (2) below, shall do so if it is one to which section 1 above applies.

(2) Nothing in subsection (1)(*b*) above shall require the justice or sheriff to order the destruction of a dog if he is satisfied—

    (*a*) that the dog would not constitute a danger to public safety; and

    (*b*) where the dog was born before 30 November 1991 and is subject to the prohibition in section 1(3) above, that there is a good reason why the dog has not been exempted from that prohibition.

(3) Where in a case falling within subsection (1)(*b*) above the justice or sheriff does not order the destruction of the dog, he shall order that, unless the dog is exempted from the prohibition in section 1(3) above within the requisite period, the dog shall be destroyed.

(4) Subsections (2) to (4) of section 4 above shall apply in relation to an order under subsection (1)(*b*) or (3) above as they apply in relation to an order under subsection (1)(*a*) of that section.

(5) Subsections (2) and (3) of section 4A above shall apply in relation to an order under subsection (3) above as they apply in relation to an order under subsection (1) of that section, except that the reference to the court in subsection (2) of that section shall be construed as a reference to the justice or sheriff.

[Dangerous Dogs Act 1991, s 4B, as inserted by the Dangerous Dogs (Amendment) Act 1997, s 3.]

---

1. The power may not be exercised where a prosecution has been initiated but discontinued (*R v Walton Street Justices, ex p Crothers* (1992) 157 JP 171) but the fact that a prosecution was once initiated against somebody does not mean that the dog is protected thereafter and a fresh and a new case arises when there is a re-seizure (*R v Walton Street Magistrates' Court, ex p Crothers* (1994) 160 JP 427, DC). Where the owner of a dog is known natural justice requires that notice be given of an application for destruction (*R v Walton Street Justices, ex p Crothers*, ibid.) Where there has been an acquittal on a charge under s 1, ante, it is an abuse of the process of the court for fresh proceedings to be taken under s 5(4) in relation to the same dog which has remained in the same ownership throughout (*R v Haringey Magistrates' Court, ex p Cragg* (1996) 161 JP 61).

7–7619 5. Seizure, entry of premises and evidence. (1) A constable or an officer of a local authority authorised by it to exercise the powers conferred by this subsection may seize—

    (*a*) any dog which appears to him to be a dog to which section 1 above applies and which is in a public place—

        (i) after the time when possession or custody of it has become unlawful by virtue of that section; or

        (ii) before that time, without being muzzled and kept on a lead;

    (*b*) any dog in a public place which appears to him to be a dog to which an order under section 2 above applies and in respect of which an offence against the order has been or is being committed; and

    (*c*) any dog in a public place (whether or not one to which that section or such an order applies) which appears to him to be dangerously out of control.

(2) If a justice of the peace is satisfied by information on oath, or in Scotland a justice of the peace or sheriff is satisfied by evidence on oath, that there are reasonable grounds for believing—

    (*a*) that an offence under any provision of this Act or of an order under section 2 above is being or has been committed; or

    (*b*) that evidence of the commission of any such offence is to be found,

on any premises he may issue a warrant authorising a constable to enter those premises (using such force as is reasonably necessary) and to search them and seize any dog or other thing found there which is evidence of the commission of such an offence.

(3) A warrant issued under this section in Scotland shall be authority for opening lockfast places and may authorise persons named in the warrant to accompany a constable who is executing it.

(4) (*Repealed*).

(5) If in any proceedings[1] it is alleged by the prosecution that a dog is one to which section 1 or an order under section 2 above applies it shall be presumed that it is such a dog unless the contrary is shown by the accused by such evidence as the court considers sufficient; and the accused shall not be permitted to adduce such evidence unless he has given the prosecution notice of his intention to do so not later than the fourteenth day before that on which the evidence is to be adduced.

[Dangerous Dogs Act 1991, s 5 as amended by the Dangerous Dogs (Amendment) Act 1997, s 3.]

---

1. This provision envisages criminal proceedings and the requirement to give notice does not apply where a person is contesting proceedings for a destruction order under s 4B(1) (*R v Walton Street Magistrates' Court, ex p Crothers* (1994) 160 JP 427, DC).

8–7620 6. Dogs owned by young persons. Where a dog is owned by a person who is less than sixteen years old any reference to its owner in section 1(2)(*d*) or (*e*) or 3 above shall include a reference to the head of the household, if any, of which that person is a member or, in Scotland, to the person who has his actual care and control.

[Dangerous Dogs Act 1991, s 6.]

8–7621   **7. Muzzling and leads.**   (1) In this Act—

(a) references to a dog being muzzled are to its being securely fitted with a muzzle sufficient to prevent it biting any person; and

(b) references to its being kept on a lead are to its being securely held on a lead by a person who is not less than sixteen years old.

(2) If the Secretary of State thinks it desirable to do so he may by order prescribe the kind of muzzle or lead to be used for the purpose of complying, in the case of a dog of any type, with section 1 or an order under section 2 above; and if a muzzle or lead of a particular kind is for the time being prescribed in relation to any type of dog the references in subsection (1) above to a muzzle or lead shall, in relation to any dog of that type, be construed as references to a muzzle or lead of that kind.

(3) The power to make an order under subsection (2) above shall be exercisable by statutory instrument subject to annulment in pursuance of a resolution of either House of Parliament.
[Dangerous Dogs Act 1991, s 7.]

8–7622   **8.** *Power to make corresponding provision for Northern Ireland.*

8–7623   **9.** *Expenses.*

8–7624   **10. Short title, interpretation, commencement and extent.**   (1) This Act may be cited as the Dangerous Dogs Act 1991.

(2) In this Act—

"advertisement" includes any means of bringing a matter to the attention of the public and "advertise" shall be construed accordingly;

"public place"[1] means any street, road or other place (whether or not enclosed) to which the public have or are permitted to have access whether for payment or otherwise and includes the common parts of a building containing two or more separate dwellings[2].

(3) For the purposes of this Act a dog shall be regarded as dangerously out of control on any occasion on which there are grounds for reasonable apprehension that it will injure any person, whether or not it actually does so, but references to a dog injuring a person or there being grounds for reasonable apprehension that it will do so do not include references to any case in which the dog is being used for a lawful purpose by a constable or a person in the service of the Crown[3].

(4) Except for section 8, this Act shall not come into force until such day as the Secretary of State may appoint by an order[4] made by statutory instrument and different days may be appointed for different provisions or different purposes.

(5) Except for section 8, this Act does not extend to Northern Ireland.
[Dangerous Dogs Act 1991, s 10.]

---

1. It may be inferred that an area is a public place from the fact that it is publicly owned, in which case there is no need for the prosecution to adduce evidence of public use of it (*Cummings v DPP* (1999) Times, 26 March).

2. A garden path has been held not be a "public place" for the purposes of this section (*DPP v Fellowes* [1993] Crim LR 523). Evidence from photographs that a cul-de-sac contained a number of warehouses and from a police officer who recollected from her time on the beat two years before that she had seen children playing there and that sometimes cars parked there was prima facie evidence that it was a public place (*R (DPP) v Zhao* [2003] EWHC Admin 1724, 167 JP 521).

3. Section 10(3) sets an objective standard of reasonable apprehension, not related to the state of mind of the dog owner; see *R v Bezzina* [1994] 1 WLR 1057, 158 JP 671. Where a dog inflicts a bite without reasonable apprehension immediately before that, the use of the word "any occasion" is sufficient to impose a liability because there are grounds thereafter for reasonable apprehension that it will injure some other person (*Rafiq v DPP* (1997) 161 JP 412).

4. See note 1 to the title of this Act, ante

Breeding and Sale of Dogs (Welfare) Act 1999

(1999 c 11)

Sale of dogs

8–7625   **8.** (1) The keeper of a licensed breeding establishment is guilty of an offence if—

(a) he sells a dog otherwise than at a licensed breeding establishment, a licensed pet shop or a licensed Scottish rearing establishment,

(b) he sells a dog otherwise than to the keeper of a licensed pet shop or a licensed Scottish rearing establishment knowing or believing that the person who buys it intends that it should be sold (by him or any other person),

(c) he sells a dog which is less than eight weeks old otherwise than to the keeper of a licensed pet shop or a licensed Scottish rearing establishment,

(d) he sells to the keeper of a licensed pet shop or a licensed Scottish rearing establishment a dog which was not born at a licensed breeding establishment, or

(e) he sells to the keeper of a licensed pet shop or a licensed Scottish rearing establishment a dog which, when delivered, is not wearing a collar with an identifying tag or badge.

(2) *Scotland.*

(3) The keeper of a licensed pet shop is guilty of an offence if he sells a dog which, when delivered to him, was wearing a collar with an identifying tag or badge but is not wearing such a collar when delivered to the person to whom he sells it.

(4) In proceedings against any person for an offence under this section it shall be a defence for that person to show that he took all reasonable steps and exercised all due diligence to avoid committing the offence.

(5) In this section—

"identifying tag or badge", in relation to a dog, means a tag or badge which clearly displays information indicating the licensed breeding establishment at which it was born and any other information required by regulations[1],

"licensed breeding establishment" means a breeding establishment for dogs the keeping of which by its keeper (or, where more than one, each of its keepers) is licensed under the 1973 Act,

"licensed pet shop" means a pet shop the keeping of which by its keeper (or, where more than one, each of its keepers) is licensed under the Pet Animals Act 1951,

"licensed Scottish rearing establishment" means a rearing establishment for dogs the keeping of which by its keeper (or, where more than one, each of its keepers) is licensed under the 1973 Act (as it applies in relation to Scotland), and

"regulations" means regulations made by the Secretary of State by statutory instrument;

and a statutory instrument containing regulations made under this section shall be subject to annulment in pursuance of a resolution of either House of Parliament.

[Breeding and Sale of Dogs (Welfare) Act 1999, s 8.]

---

1. The Sale of Dogs (Identification Tag) Regulations 1999, SI 1999/3191 require the following additional information: (a) the date of birth of the dog; and (b) an identifying number, if any, allocated to the dog by the licensed breeding establishment at which it was born.

8–7625A   9. Penalties.   (1) A person guilty of an offence under section 8 is liable on summary conviction to—

(*a*)   imprisonment for a term not exceeding **three months**, or
(*b*)   a fine not exceeding **level 4** on the standard scale,

or to both.

(2) Where a person is convicted of an offence under section 8(1) or (2), the court before which he is convicted may (in addition to or in substitution for any penalty under subsection (1)) make an order providing for any one or more of the following—

(*a*)   the cancellation of any licence held by him under the 1973 Act,
(*b*)   his disqualification, for such period as the court thinks fit, from keeping an establishment the keeping of which is required to be licensed under the 1973 Act, and
(*b*)   his disqualification, for such period as the court thinks fit, from having custody of any dog of a description specified in the order.

(3) A court which has made an order under this section may, if it thinks fit, suspend the operation of the order pending an appeal.

(4) Where a court makes an order under subsection (2)(*c*) in relation to a description of dogs it may also make such order as it thinks fit in respect of any dog of that description which—

(*a*)   was in the offender's custody at the time when the offence was committed, or
(*b*)   has been in custody at any time since then.

(5) An order under subsection (4) may (in particular)—
(*a*)   require any person who has custody of the dog to deliver it up to a specified person,
(*b*)   (if it does) also require the offender to pay specified amounts to specified persons for the care of the dog from the time when it is delivered up in pursuance of the order until permanent arrangements are made for its care or disposal.

(6) A person who—

(*a*)   has custody of a dog in contravention of an order under subsection (2)(*c*), or
(*b*)   fails to comply with a requirement imposed on him under subsection (5),

is guilty of an offence.

(7) A person guilty of an offence under subsection (6) is liable on summary conviction to—

(*a*)   imprisonment for a term not exceeding **three months**, or
(*b*)   a fine not exceeding **level 4** on the standard scale,

or to both.

(8) Where a court proposes to make an order under subsection (4) in respect of a dog owned by a person other than the offender, the court shall notify the owner who may make representations to the court; and if an order is made the owner may, within the period of seven days beginning with the date of the order, appeal to—

(a) in England and Wales, the Crown Court, or

(b) in Scotland, the High Court of Justiciary,

against the order.

(9) A person who is subject to a disqualification by virtue of an order under subsection (2)(c) may, at any time after the end of the period of one year beginning with the date of the order, apply to the court which made the order (or, in England and Wales, any magistrates' court acting for the same petty sessions area) for a direction terminating the disqualification from such date as the court considers appropriate.

(10) On an application under subsection (9) the court shall, having regard to—

(a) the applicant's character

(b) his conduct since the disqualification was imposed, and

(c) any other circumstances of the case,

grant or refuse the application; and where an application under subsection (9) in respect of a disqualification is refused, no further application under that subsection in respect of that disqualification shall be entertained if made before the end of the period of one year beginning with the date of the refusal.

[Breeding and Sale of Dogs (Welfare) Act 1999, s 9.]

Supplementary

8–7625B   10. *(Repealed).*

8–7625C   11. Short title, commencement and extent. (1) This Act may be cited as the Breeding and sale of Dogs (Welfare) Act 1999.

(2) This Act shall come into force at the end of the period of six months beginning with the day on which it was passed.

(3) This Act does not extend to Northern Ireland.

[Breeding and Sale of Dogs (Welfare) Act 1999, s 11.]

Dangerous Dogs Compensation and Exemption Schemes Order 1991[1]

(SI 1991/1744 amended by SI 1991/2297, SI 1991/2636 and SI 1997/1152)

Part I
Preliminary

8–7630   1. (1) *Citation and commencement.*

(2) In this Order—

(a) "the Act" means the Dangerous Dogs Act 1991;

(b) "the Agency" means the person or body for the time being designated by the Secretary of State to discharge those functions under this Order, which, in pursuance thereof, are functions falling to be discharged by the Agency;

(c) "the appointed day" means the day appointed for the purposes of section 1(3) of the Act; and

(d) unless the context otherwise requires, any reference to an article is to an article of this Order and any reference in an article to a paragraph is to a paragraph of that article.

---

1. Made by the Secretary of State in exercise of the powers conferred upon me by subsections (3), (5) and (6) of section 1 of the Dangerous Dogs Act 1991.

8–7631

Part II
Compensation Scheme

Part III[1]
Exemption Scheme

8–7632   3. The prohibition contained in subsection (3) of section 1 of the Act (no person to have in his possession or custody after the appointed day a dog to which that section applies) shall not apply to a dog born before the appointed day in respect of which the conditions specified in article 4, or as the case may be, article 5 are complied with.

---

1. Where an order is made under ss 4A(1) or 4B(3) of the Dangerous Dogs Act 1991, Part III of this Order shall have effect as if—

(a) any reference to the appointed day were a reference to the end of the requisite period within the meaning of s 4A or, as the case may be, section 4B of the 1991 Act;

(b) paragraph (a) of Article 4 and Article 6 were omitted; and
(c) the fee payable to the Agency under Article 9 were a fee of such amount as the Secretary of State may by order prescribe.

[Dangerous Dogs (Amendment) Act 1997, s 4.]

Conditions for adult dogs

8–7633 **4.** In the case of a dog which is over the age of six months on the appointed day, the conditions referred to in article 3 are—

(a) that article 6 has been complied with;
(b) that the requirements of article 7 have been complied with;
(c) that there is in force in respect of the dog third party insurance which complies with article 8;
(d) that the fee specified in article 9 has been paid;
(e) that a certificate of exemption issued in accordance with article 10 is in force; and
(f) that the requirements specified in the certificate, in accordance with article 10, are complied with.

Conditions for puppies

8–7634 **5.** In the case of a dog which is under the age of six months on the appointed day, the conditions referred to in article 3 are those specified in article 4 except that the conditions contained in paragraphs (b) to (f) of article 4 need not be complied with until after the appointed day as long as they are complied with within one month of the dog's attaining the age of six months.

Reporting to the Police

8–7635 **6.** The owner of a dog to which section 1 of the Act applies who wishes to claim compensation in accordance with Part II of this Order and a person who wishes such a dog to be exempt from the provisions of section 1(3) of the Act shall, in the case of a dog to which article 4 applies, before 12 October 1991, and in the case of a dog to which article 5 applies, before the appointed day, report to a police station and provide the police with such information concerning the dog as may reasonably be required by the Secretary of State for the purpose of establishing—

(a) that the dog is one to which section 1 of the Act applies; and
(b) the address at which the dog is kept; and
(c) the name, age and gender of the dog.

Neutering and Identification

8–7636 **7.** (1) A male dog which is to be exempted from the provisions of section 1(3) of the Act shall be castrated, and a female dog which is to be so exempted shall be spayed, in either case by a veterinary surgeon or veterinary practitioner, and the dog shall be provided with permanent identification in such form as may be prescribed by the Agency in order that it may be readily ascertained that the relevant operation has been performed on it.

(2) A person wishing to claim exemption shall provide the Agency with such evidence as they may require of the fact that the requirements of paragraph (1) have been met.

Third Party Insurance

8–7637 **8.** (1) There shall be in force in respect of a dog which is to be exempted from the provisions of section 1(3) of the Act a policy of insurance which, subject to such terms, conditions, limitations and exclusions as may be contained in the policy insures the person specified in the policy (the policyholder) in respect of the death of, or bodily injury to, any person caused by the dog other than the death of, or bodily injury to, a member of the policyholder's family who resides permanently with him or a person in respect of whom the policyholder is required to maintain a policy of insurance by virtue of the Employer's Liability (Compulsory Insurance) Act 1969.

(2) A person wishing to claim exemption shall provide the Agency with such evidence as they may require of the fact that the dog is insured in accordance with paragraph (1).

8–7638 **9.** *Fees.*

Certificate of Exemption

8–7639 **10.** (1) If satisfied that the conditions referred to in paragraphs (a) to (d) of article 4 have been met, the Agency shall issue a certificate of exemption in respect of the dog.

(2) Such a certificate shall contain the following requirements—

(a) a requirement to notify the Agency of any change of address at which the dog to which it relates is kept for a period in excess of 30 days;

(*b*) a requirement to notify the Agency of the death or export of the dog;

(*c*) a requirement, on request by a person specified in section 5(1) of the Act, to produce the certificate to such a person within five days of being requested to do so;

(*d*) a requirement, on request by a person specified in section 5(1) of the Act, to display the dog's permanent identification pursuant to article 7 to such a person;

(*e*) a requirement to satisfy the Agency that a policy of insurance which complies with article 8 continues in force;

(*f*) a requirement to keep the dog to which it relates in sufficiently secure conditions to prevent its escape;

(*g*) a requirement to keep the dog to which it relates muzzled and on a lead when in a public place;

(*h*) a requirement to provide the Agency before 1st March 1992 with such evidence as they may require that (in addition to the permanent identification required by article 7(1) the dog has been tattooed in such manner as may be prescribed by them;

(*i*) a requirement, on request on or after 1st March 1992 by a person specified in section 5(1) of the Act to display the dog's tattoo pursuant to paragraph (*h*) to such a person.

(3) Such a certificate may also contain such additional requirements, including the imposition of time limits, as the Agency may reasonably require for the purpose of ensuring that the requirements of this article are complied with.

8–7640 **11.** *Payments to agency.*

Control of Dogs Order 1992[1]
(SI 1992/901)

8–7641 **1.** *Title and commencement.*

---

1. Made by the Minister of Agriculture, Fisheries and Food, in relation to England, the Secretary of State for Scotland in relation to Scotland, and the Secretary of State for Wales in relation to Wales, in exercise of the powers conferred on them by sections 13(2) and (3) and 72 of the Animal Health Act 1981.

[Wearing of collars by dogs]

8–7642 **2.** (1) Subject to paragraph (2) below, every dog while in a highway or in a place of public resort shall wear a collar with the name and address of the owner inscribed on the collar or on a plate or badge attached to it.

(2) Paragraph (1) above shall not apply to—

(*a*) any pack of hounds,

(*b*) any dog while being used for sporting purposes,

(*c*) any dog while being used for the capture or destruction of vermin,

(*d*) any dog while being used for the driving or tending of cattle or sheep,

(*e*) any dog while being used on official duties by a member of Her Majesty's Armed Forces or Her Majesty's Customs and Excise or the police force for any area,

(*f*) any dog while being used in emergency rescue work, or

(*g*) any dog registered with the Guide Dogs for the Blind Association.

[Offences]

8–7643 **3.** The owner of a dog or the person in charge of a dog who, without lawful authority or excuse, proof of which shall lie on him, causes or permits the dog to be in a highway or in a place of public resort not wearing a collar as prescribed in article 2(1) above shall be guilty of an offence against the Animal Health Act 1981.

[Seizure of dogs]

8–7644 **4.** Any dog in respect of which an offence is being committed against this Order may be seized and treated as a stray dog under section 3 of the Dogs Act 1906 or under section 149 of the Environmental Protection Act 1990.

[Enforcement]

8–7645 **5.** (1) This Order shall be executed and enforced by the officers of a local authority (and not by the police force for any area).

(2) In this article "local authority" and "officer" have the same meaning as in section 149 of the Environmental Protection Act 1990.

8–7646 **6.** *Revocations.*

EDUCATION[1]

8–7651   This title contains the following statutes—

With the passing of the Education Act 1996, the Education Acts 1962 to 1996 and that Act may be cited together as "the Education Acts" (Education Act 1996, s 578).

---

1. Article 2 of Protocol 1 of the European Convention on Human Rights provides that:
No person shall be denied the right to education. In the exercise of any functions which it assumes in relation to education and to teaching, the State shall respect the right of parents to ensure such education and teaching in conformity with their own religious and philosophical aims.'
The UK has entered a reservation in respect of this right in the following terms:

'... in view of certain provisions of the Education Acts in the United Kingdom, the principle affirmed in the second sentence of Article 2 is accepted by the United Kingdom only in so far as it is compatible with the provision of efficient instruction and training, and the avoidance of unreasonable public expenditure.'

Under the Human Rights Act 1998 this reservation has effect in domestic law. But see *SP v United Kingdom* (1997) 23 EHRR CD 139 where the European Commission of Human Rights raised doubts about the continued validity of this reservation.

Education Reform Act 1988

(1988 c 40)

PART IV[1]
MISCELLANEOUS AND GENERAL

Unrecognised degrees

8–7700   214. Unrecognised degrees.   (1) Any person who, in the course of business, grants, offers to grant or issues any invitation relating to any award—

(a)   which may reasonably be taken to be an award granted or to be granted by a United Kingdom institution; and

(b)   which either—

(i)   is described as a degree; or

(ii)   purports to confer on its holder the right to the title of bachelor, master or doctor and may reasonably be taken to be a degree;

shall be guilty of an offence and liable on summary conviction to a fine not exceeding **level 5** on the standard scale.

(2)   Subsection (1) above does not apply as respects anything done in relation to any recognised award; and for the purposes of this section a "recognised award" means—

(a)   any award granted or to be granted by a university, college or other body which is authorised by Royal Charter or by or under Act of Parliament to grant degrees;

(b)   any award granted or to be granted by any body for the time being permitted by any body falling within paragraph (a) above to act on its behalf in the granting of degrees; or

(c)   such other award as the Secretary of State[2] may by order[3] designate as a recognised award for the purposes of this section.

(3)   An order under subsection (2)(c) above may designate as a recognised award either—

(a)   a specified award granted or to be granted by a person named in the order; or

(b)   any award granted or to be granted by such a person.

(4)   Where in any proceedings for an offence under this section it is shown—

(a)   that the defendant granted, offered to grant or issued an invitation relating to an award; and

(b)   that an address in the United Kingdom was given in any document issued by the defendant certifying the granting of the award or containing the offer or invitation in question;

the award shall be presumed to fall within subsection (1)(a) above unless it is shown that the defendant took reasonable steps to inform the person to whom the award was granted or any member of the public or particular individual to whom the offer or invitation was addressed that the award was not granted or to be granted by a United Kingdom institution.

(5)   In any proceedings for an offence under this section it shall be a defence for the defendant to show—

(a) that the award in question was granted or to be granted by virtue of authority conferred on or before 5th July 1988 by a foreign institution on the body granting the award; and

(b) that the defendant took reasonable steps to inform the person to whom the award was granted or any member of the public or particular individual to whom the offer was addressed that the award was granted or was to be granted by virtue of authority conferred by a foreign institution.

(6) For the purposes of subsection (5) above, where—

(a) on or before 5th July 1988 authority was conferred by a foreign institution on a body to grant awards of any description for a period expiring after that date; and

(b) new authority is conferred by the institution (whether before or after the expiry of that period) on the body to grant awards of that description;

the new authority shall be taken to have been granted on or before that date.

(7) Where an offence under this section which has been committed by a body corporate is proved to have been committed with the consent and connivance of, or to be attributable to any neglect on the part of, any director, manager, secretary or other similar officer of the body corporate, or any person who was purporting to act in any such capacity, he as well as the body corporate shall be guilty of that offence and shall be liable to be proceeded against and punished accordingly.

(8) Proceedings for an offence under this section shall not, in England and Wales, be instituted except by or on behalf of a local weights and measures authority or the chief officer of police for a police area.

(9) Nothing in this section shall apply in relation to the granting of an award to a candidate who—

(a) before 12th May 1988 began to undertake a course of education approved by the person granting the award in preparation for an examination to qualify for the award; and

(b) whether before or after that date, passes the examination;

and in this subsection "examination" includes any form of assessment and the reference to passing an examination shall be construed accordingly.

(9A) For the purposes of this section and section 215, as they extend to Scotland, the reference to the Secretary of State is to be read as a reference to the Scottish Ministers.

(10) For the purposes of this section—

(a) a "United Kingdom institution" means any institution established in the United Kingdom, other than one which is, or is affiliated to or forms part of, an institution whose principal establishment is situated outside the United Kingdom;

(b) a "foreign institution" means any institution other than a United Kingdom institution; and

(c) the reference to issuing an invitation relating to any award includes in particular the issuing of any circular, prospectus or advertisement relating to an award, whether addressed to the public generally, to any section of the public, or to any particular individual or individuals.

[Education Reform Act 1988, s 214 as amended by the Further and Higher Education Act 1992, Sch 8 and SI 1999/1820.]

---

1. Part IV contains ss 197–238.
2. The functions of the Secretary of State, so far as exercisable in relation to Wales have been transferred to the National Assembly for Wales, by the National Assembly for Wales (Transfer of Functions) Order 1999, SI 1999/672, art 2, Sch 1.
3. See the Education (Recognised Awards) Order 1988, SI 1988/2035, amended by SI 1989/598 and SI 1990/1085.

8–7701 215. Unrecognised degrees: enforcement. (1) It shall be the duty of every local weights and measures authority to enforce the provisions of section 214 of this Act within their area; and such an authority shall, whenever the Secretary of State so directs, make to him a report on the exercise of their functions under this section and section 214 of this Act in such form and containing such particulars as he may direct.

(2) A duly authorised officer of a local weights and measures authority may, at all reasonable hours and on production, if required, of his credentials, exercise the following powers, that is to say—

(a) he may, for the purpose of ascertaining whether any offence under section 214 of this Act has been committed, enter and search any premises which he reasonably believes may be used for or in connection with the carrying on of a business which is concerned with the granting of awards which are not recognised awards;

(b) he may, for that purpose, require any person carrying on or employed in connection with any such business to produce any documents or other items relating to the business and may take copies of any such document;

(c) he may require any information which is contained in a computer and is accessible from the premises to be produced in a form in which it can be taken away and in which it is visible and legible if he has reason to believe that it may be evidence of the commission of an offence under that section; and

(d) he may seize and detain anything which he has reason to believe may be evidence of the commission of an offence under that section.

(3) In subsection (2) above "recognised award" has the same meaning as in section 214 of this Act.

(4) If a justice of the peace, on sworn information in writing—

(a) is satisfied that there is reasonable ground to believe that any documents or other items which a duly authorised officer has power under this section to inspect are on any premises and that their inspection is likely to disclose evidence of the commission of an offence under section 214 of this Act; and

(b) is also satisfied either—

(i) that admission to the premises has been or is likely to be refused and that notice of intention to apply for a warrant under this subsection has been given to the occupier; or

(ii) that an application for admission, or the giving of such a notice, would defeat the object of the entry or that the premises are unoccupied or that the occupier is temporarily absent and it might defeat the object of the entry to await his return;

the justice may by warrant under his hand, which shall continue in force for a period of one month, authorise an officer of a local weights and measures authority to enter the premises, if need be by force.

In the application of this subsection to Scotland, "justice of the peace" shall be construed as including a sheriff.

(5) An officer seizing any documents or other items in the exercise of his powers under this section shall inform the person from whom they are seized.

(6) An officer entering any premises by virtue of this section may take with him such other persons and such equipment as may appear to him necessary; and on leaving any premises which he has entered by virtue of a warrant under subsection (4) above he shall, if the premises are unoccupied or the occupier is temporarily absent, leave them as effectively secured against trespassers as he found them.

(7) Section 29 of the Trade Descriptions Act 1968[1] (penalty for obstruction of authorised officers) shall apply as respect the obstruction of an officer acting in pursuance of this section as it applies as respects the obstruction of an officer acting in pursuance of that Act but with the substitution in subsection (1)—

(a) of a reference to this section for the reference to section 28 of that Act; and

(b) of a reference to his functions under this section for the reference to his functions under that Act.

(8) Nothing in this section shall be taken to compel the production by a solicitor of a document or other item containing a privileged communication made by or to him in that capacity or to authorise the taking of possession of any such item which is in his possession.

(9) Nothing in this section shall be taken as authorising a local weights and measures authority in Scotland to institute proceedings for an offence.
[Education Reform Act 1988, s 215.]

------

1. See title Consumer Protection, ante.

8–7702   216. Identification of bodies granting or providing courses for recognised awards.
(1) For the purposes of sections 214 and 215 of this Act, any body for the time being designated by order[1] made by the Secretary of State as appearing to him to be a recognised body shall be conclusively presumed to be such a body.

(2) The Secretary of State shall compile, maintain and publish by order[1] a list including the name of every body which appears to him to fall for the time being within subsection (3) below.

(2A) For the purposes of this section, as it extends to Scotland, the references in subsections (1) and (2) above to the Secretary of State are to be read as references to the Scottish Ministers."

(3) A body falls within this subsection if it is not a recognised body and either—

(a) provides any course which is in preparation for a degree to be granted by a recognised body and is approved by or on behalf of the recognised body; or

(b) is a constituent college, school or hall or other institution of a university which is a recognised body.

(4) In this section "recognised body" means a body falling within section 214(2)(a) or (b) of this Act.
[Education Reform Act 1988, s 216 as amended by SI 1999/1820, Sch 2.]

------

1. The Education (Recognised Bodies) Order 1999, SI 1999/833 revoked in so far as it applies to England by SI 2000/3327; and the Education (Recognised Bodies) (England) Order 2000, SI 2000/3332 and the Education (Listed Bodies) Order 1999, SI 1999/834 revoked in so far as it applies to England by SI 2000/3332 and the Education (Listed Bodies) (England) Order 2000, SI 2000/3332 have been made.

Further and Higher Education Act 1992
(1992 c 13)

PART I[1]

CHAPTER III
GENERAL

8–7800   55. Inspection etc of local education authority institutions, other than schools, and advice to Secretary of State[2].   (1) *Repealed.*

(2) *Repealed.*

(3) *Repealed.*

(4) In relation to any local education authority institution maintained or assisted by them, a local education authority—

(a)   shall keep under review the quality of education provided, the educational standards achieved and whether the financial resources made available are managed efficiently, and

(b)   may cause an inspection to be made by persons authorised by them.

(5) A local education authority shall not authorise any person to inspect any institution under this section unless they are satisfied that he is suitably qualified to do so.

(6) A person who wilfully obstructs any person authorised to inspect an institution under or by virtue of this section in the exercise of his functions shall be guilty of an offence and liable on summary conviction to a fine not exceeding **level 4** on the standard scale.

(7) In this section—

(a)   *repealed*

(b)   Her Majesty's Chief Inspector of Education and Training in Wales or Prif Arolygydd Ei Mawrhydi dros Addysg a Hyfforddiant yng Nghymru and "his inspectors" means Her Majesty's Inspectors of Education and Training in Wales or Arolgwyr Ei Mawrhydi dros Addysg a Hyfforddiant yng Nghymru, and★

(c)   "local education authority institution" means an educational institution, other than a school, maintained or assisted by a local education authority.

[Further and Higher Education Act 1992, s 55, as amended by the Learning and Skills Act 2000, Sch 9.]

★Repealed by the Learning and Skills Act 2000, Sch 9, when in force.

1. Part I contains Chapters I–III; Chapter III contains ss 54 to 61.

2. The functions of the Secretary of State, so far as exercisable in relation to Wales, have been transferred to the National Assembly for Wales, by the National Assembly for Wales (Transfer of Functions) Order 1999, SI 1999/672, art 2, Sch 1.

Education Act 1996[1]
(1996 c 56)[2]

PART I
GENERAL

8–7801   The statutory system of public education consists of three progressive stages: primary education, secondary education and further education (s 1). In England, the local education authority for a county having a county council is the County Council; for a district not in a county having a county council, it is the district council; for a London Borough it is the borough council and for the City of London the Common Council. In Wales, the local education authority for a county is the County Council and for a county borough the county borough council (s 12).

It is the duty of every local education authority (so far as their powers enable them to do so) to secure that efficient primary education, secondary education and further education★ are available to meet the needs of the population of their area (s 13) and to promote high standards in primary and secondary education (s 13A).

★Section 13 is amended by the Learning and Skills Act 2000, Sch 9, when in force.

1. The functions of the Minister, so far as exercisable in relation to Wales, have been transferred to the National Assembly for Wales, by the National Assembly for Wales (Transfer of Functions) Order 1999, SI 1999/672, art 2, Sch 1.

2. Part I comprises ss 1–30.

CHAPTER I
THE STATUTORY SYSTEM OF EDUCATION

General

8–7802   3. Definition of pupil etc.   (1) In this Act "pupil" means a person for whom education is being provided at a school, other than—

(a)   a person who has attained the age of 19 for whom further education is being provided, or (*b*) a person for whom part-time education suitable to the requirements of persons of any age over compulsory school age is being provided,

and references to pupils in the context of the admission of pupils to, or the exclusion of pupils from, a school are references to persons who following their admission will be, or (as the case may be) before their exclusion were, pupils as defined by this subsection.

(1A) A person is not for the purposes of this Act to be treated as a pupil at a school merely because any education is provided for him at the school in the exercise of the powers conferred by section 27 of the Education Act 2002 (power of governing body of maintained school to provide community facilities etc).

(2) In this Act—

"junior pupil", means a child who has not attained the age of 12; and

"senior pupil", means a person who has attained the age of 12 but not the age of 19.

(3) Subsection (1) and (1A) also apply (unless the context otherwise requires) for the purposes of any instrument made or having effect as if made under the Education Acts.

[Education Act 1996, s 3 as amended by the Education Act 1997, Sch 7 and the Education Act 2002, s 215.]

---

1. Chapter I comprises ss 1–9.

Educational institutions

8–7804 4. Schools: general. (1) In this Act "school" means an educational institution which is outside the further education sector and the higher education sector and is an institution for providing—

(*a*) primary education,

(*b*) secondary education, or

(*c*) both primary and secondary education,

whether or not the institution also provides part-time education suitable to the requirements of junior pupils or* further education.

(2) Nothing in subsection (1) shall be taken to preclude the making of arrangements under section 19(1) (exceptional educational provision) under which part-time education is to be provided at a school; and for the purposes of this Act an educational institution that would fall within subsection (1) but for the fact that it provides part-time rather than full-time education shall nevertheless be treated as a school if that part-time education is provided under arrangements made under section 19(1).

(3) For the purposes of this Act an institution is outside the further education sector if it is not—

(*a*) an institution conducted by a further education corporation established under section 15 or 16 of the Further and Higher Education Act 1992, or

(*b*) a designated institution for the purposes of Part I of that Act (defined in section 28(4) of that Act);

and references to institutions within that sector shall be construed accordingly.

(4) For the purposes of this Act an institution is outside the higher education sector if it is not—

(*a*) a university receiving financial support under section 65 of that Act,

(*b*) an institution conducted by a higher education corporation within the meaning of that Act, or

(*c*) a designated institution for the purposes of Part II of that Act (defined in section 73(3) of that Act);

and references to institutions within that sector shall be construed accordingly.

[Education Act 1996, s 4 as amended by the Education Act 1997, s 51, Schs 7 and 8 and the Education Act 2002, s 215.]

---

*Sub-section (1) words repealed by the Education Act 2002, s 215. In force in relation to England from 2 September 2002, as regards Wales, in force from a date to be appointed.

1. Chapter I comprises ss 1–9.

Compulsory education

8–7805 7. Duty of parents to secure education of children of compulsory school age. The parent of every child of compulsory school age shall cause him to receive efficient full-time education suitable—

(*a*) to his age, ability and aptitude, and

(*b*) to any special educational needs he may have, either by regular attendance at school or otherwise[1].

[Education Act 1996, s 7.]

---

1. The duty imposed by this section does not attach where it is not practicable for the parent to arrange for the child to become a registered pupil at the beginning, but during the currency of, a school term (Education Act 1996, s 433, post).

8–7806　8. Compulsory school age. (1) Subsections (2) and (3) apply to determine for the purposes of any enactment whether a person is of compulsory school age.

(2)　A person begins to be of compulsory school age—

(a)　when he attains[1] the age of five[2], if he attains that age on a prescribed day, and

(b)　otherwise at the beginning of the prescribed day next following his attaining that age.

(3)　A person ceases to be of compulsory school age at the end of the day which is the school leaving date for any calendar year—

(*a*)　if he attains[1] the age of 16[2] after that day but before the beginning of the school year next following,

(*b*)　if he attains that age on that day, or

(*c*)　(unless paragraph (*a*) applies) if that day is the school leaving date next following his attaining that age.

(4)　The Secretary of State may by order[3]—

(a)　provide that such days in the year as are specified in the order shall be, for each calendar year, prescribed days for the purposes of subsection (2);

(b)　determine the day in any calendar year which is to be the school leaving date for that year[4].

[Education Act 1996, s 8 as amended by the Education Act 1997, s 52.]

1.　A person attains an age at the commencement of the relevant anniversary of the date of his birth; see the Family Law Reform Act 1969, s 9 in PART IV: FAMILY LAW, ante.

2.　As to evidence of age, see s 565(1), post.

3.　The Education (Start of Compulsory School Age) Order 1998, SI 1998/1607 provides that for the purposes of s 8(2) above the 31 March, 31 August and 31 December are prescribed days in each year. The Education (School Leaving Date) Order 1997, SI 1997/1970 has been made which provides for the school leaving date for 1998 and successive years to be the last Friday in June.

4.　Section 52(4) and (5) (when in force) of the Education Act 1997 further provide:

> (4)　The Secretary of State may also make an order providing that such days in the year as are specified in the order shall be, for each calendar year during the whole or part of which section 8 of the Education Act 1996 is not wholly in force, prescribed days for the purposes of paragraph 1(2) of Schedule 40 to that Act (transitory provisions pending coming into force of section 8 of that Act) as it has effect in accordance with subsection (5) below.

> (5)　Where a person does not attain the age of five on any of those prescribed days, he shall be regarded for the purposes of paragraph 1(2) of that Schedule—

> (*a*)　as not attaining that age, and

> (*b*)　accordingly as not being of compulsory school age,

> until the beginning of the prescribed day next following his fifth birthday.

PART IV[1]
SPECIAL EDUCATIONAL NEEDS

8–7807　Part IV makes provision for children with special educational needs. A child has "special educational needs" if he has a learning difficulty which calls for "special educational provision" to be made for him. Special educational provision in relation to children of compulsory school age means educational provision which is additional to, or otherwise different from, the educational provision made generally for children of his age in schools maintained by the local education authority in their area (s 312 amended by the Education Act 1997, Sch 7). So far as is reasonably practicable and is compatible with the provision of the special educational provision that the child's learning difficulty calls for, the provision of efficient education for the children with whom the child will be educated and the efficient use of resources, children with special educational needs are to be educated in mainstream schools (s 317).

A local education authority is under a duty to identify children with special educational needs and where necessary determine the special educational provision that they need (s 321). Although assessment of special educational needs may take place within the school and appropriate special educational provision be arranged, the local education authority may determine that a formal assessment is required with a view to preparing a statement of special educational needs in order to ensure protection for the child (s 323). Thereafter it is the duty of the local education authority to ensure the special educational provision specified in the statement is made for the child (s 324). The child's parent may appeal to a Special Educational Needs Tribunal against the refusal to make a statement, or the contents of a statement (ss 325–326).

1.　Part IV comprises ss 312–349.

CHAPTER I[1]
CHILDREN WITH SPECIAL EDUCATIONAL NEEDS

Introductory

8–7808　312. Meaning of "special educational needs" and "special educational provision" etc. (1) A child has "special educational needs" for the purposes of this Act if he has a learning difficulty which calls for special educational provision to be made for him.

(2) Subject to subsection (3) (and except for the purposes of section 15A or 15B) a child has a "learning difficulty" for the purposes of this Act if—

(a) he has a significantly greater difficulty in learning than the majority of children of his age,

(b) he has a disability which either prevents or hinders him from making use of educational facilities of a kind generally provided for children of his age in schools within the area of the local education authority, or

(c) he is under compulsory school age and is, or would be if special educational provision were not made for him, likely to fall within paragraph[1] or[2] when of that age.

(3) A child is not to be taken as having a learning difficulty solely because the language (or form of the language) in which he is, or will be, taught is different from a language (or form of a language) which has at any time been spoken in his home.

(4) In this Act "special educational provision" means—

(a) in relation to a child who has attained the age of two, educational provision which is additional to, or otherwise different from, the educational provision made generally for children of his age in schools maintained by the local education authority (other than special schools), and

(b) in relation to a child under that age, educational provision of any kind.

(5) In this Part—

"child" includes any person who has not attained the age of 19 and is a registered pupil at a school; "maintained school" means any community, foundation or voluntary school or any community or foundation special school not established in a hospital.

[Education Act 1996, s 312 as amended by the School Standards and Framework Act 1998, Sch 30, the Education Act 1997, Schs 7 and 8 and the Learning Skills Act 2000, Sch 9.]

---

1. Chapter I comprises ss 312–336.

Identification of children with special educational needs

8-7809   321. General duty of local education authority towards children for whom they are responsible.   (1) A local education authority shall exercise their powers with a view to securing that, of the children for whom they are responsible, they identify those to whom subsection (2) below applies.

(2) This subsection applies to a child if—

(a) he has special educational needs, and

(b) it is necessary for the authority to determine the special educational provision which any learning difficulty he may have calls for.

(3) For the purposes of this Part a local education authority are responsible for a child if he is in their area and—

(a) he is a registered pupil at a maintained school or maintained nursery school,

(b) education is provided for him at a school which is not a maintained school or maintained nursery school but is so provided at the expense of the authority,

(c) he does not come within paragraph (a) or (b) above but is a registered pupil at a school and has been brought to the authority's attention as having (or probably having) special educational needs, or

(d) he is not a registered pupil at a school but is not under the age of two or over compulsory school age and has been brought to their attention as having (or probably having) special educational needs.

[Education Act 1996, s 321 as amended by the School Standards and Framework Act 1998, Sch 30 and the Education Act 2002, s 215.]

---

1. Chapter I comprises ss 1–9.

8-7810   322. *Duty of Health Authority or local authority to help local education authority.*

8-7811   323. Assessment of educational needs.   (1) Where a local education authority are of the opinion that a child for whom they are responsible falls, or probably falls, within subsection (2), they shall serve a notice on the child's parent informing him—

(a) that they are considering whether to make an assessment of the child's educational needs,

(b) of the procedure to be followed in making the assessment,

(c) of the name of the officer of the authority from whom further information may be obtained, and

(d) of the parent's rights to make representations, and submit written evidence, to the authority within such period (which must not be less than 29 days beginning with the date on which the notice is served) as may be specified in the notice.

(2) A child falls within this subsection if—

(*a*) he has special educational needs, and

(*b*) it is necessary for the authority to determine the special educational provision which any learning difficulty he may have calls for.

(3) Where—

(*a*) a local education authority have served a notice under subsection (1) and the period specified in the notice in accordance with subsection (1)(*d*) has expired, and

(*b*) the authority remain of the opinion, after taking into account any representations made and any evidence submitted to them in response to the notice, that the child falls, or probably falls, within subsection (2),

they shall make an assessment of his educational needs.

(4) Where a local education authority decide to make an assessment under this section, they shall give notice in writing to the child's parent of that decision and of their reasons for making it.

(5) Schedule 26[1] has effect in relation to the making of assessments under this section.

(6) Where, at any time after serving a notice under subsection (1), a local education authority decide not to assess the educational needs of the child concerned they shall give notice in writing to the child's parent of their decision.

[Education Act 1996, s 323, as amended by the Special Educational Needs and Disability Act 2001, s 42.]

---

1. See post.

8–7812   324. Statement of special educational needs[1]. (1) If, in the light of an assessment under section 323 of any child's educational needs and of any representations made by the child's parent in pursuance of Schedule 27[2], it is necessary for the local education authority to determine the special education provision which any learning difficulty he may have calls for, the authority shall make and maintain a statement of his special educational needs.

(2) The statement shall be in such form and contain such information as may be prescribed[3]

(3) In particular, the statement shall—

(*a*) give details of the authority's assessment of the child's special educational needs, and

(*b*) specify the special educational provision to be made for the purpose of meeting those needs, including the particulars required by subsection (4).

(4) The statement shall—

(*a*) specify the type of school or other institution which the local education authority consider would be appropriate for the child,

(*b*) if they are not required under Schedule 27[2] to specify the name of any school in the statement, specify the name of any school or institution (whether in the United Kingdom or elsewhere) which they consider would be appropriate for the child and should be specified in the statement, and

(*c*) specify any provision for the child for which they make arrangements under section 319 and which they consider should be specified in the statement.

(4A) Subsection (4)(*b*) does not require the name of a school or institution to be specified if the child's parent has made suitable arrangements for the special educational provision specified in the statement to be made for the child.

(5) Where a local education authority maintain a statement under this section, then—

(*a*) unless the child's parent has made suitable arrangements, the authority—

(i) shall arrange that the special educational provision specified in the statement is made for the child, and

(ii) may arrange that any non-educational provision specified in the statement is made for him in such manner as they consider appropriate, and

(*b*) if the name of a maintained school or maintained nursery school is specified in the statement, the governing body of the school shall admit the child to the school.

(5A) Subsection (5)(*b*) has effect regardless of any duty imposed on the governing body of a school by section 1(6) of the School Standards and Framework Act 1998.

(6) Subsection (5)(*b*) does not affect any power to exclude from a school a pupil who is already a registered pupil there.

(7) Schedule 27[2] has effect in relation to the making and maintenance of statements under this section.

[Education Act 1996, s 324 as amended by the School Standards and Framework Act 1998, Sch 30 and the Special Educational Needs and Disability Act 2001, s 9 and the Education Act 2002, s 215.]

---

1. The special educational provision for any pupil specified in a statement made under this section may include any provision excluding the National Curriculum for England or applying it with modifications: s 92 of the Education Act 2002.

2. Schedule 27 is not reproduced in this work.

3. The Education (Special Educational Needs) Regulations 1994, SI 1994/1047 amended by SI 1994/1251 revoked

and replaced in so far as they apply to England by the Education (Special Educational Needs) (England) (Consolidation) Regulations 2001, SI 2001/3455 have been made.

Special Educational Needs Tribunal

8–7813   333. *Constitution of Tribunal.*

8–7814   336. Tribunal procedure.   (1) Regulations may make provision about the proceedings of the Tribunal on an appeal under this Part and the initiation of such an appeal.

(2) The regulations may, in particular, include provision—

(*a*)–(*f*)

(*g*) for granting any person such disclosure or inspection of documents or right to further particulars as might be granted by a county court,

(*h*) requiring persons to attend to give evidence and produce documents,

(*i*)–(*o*)

(2A) Proceeding before the Tribunal shall be held in private, except in prescribed circumstances.

(3) The Secretary of State may pay such allowances for the purpose of or in connection with the attendance of persons at the Tribunal as he may, with the consent of the Treasury, determine.

(4) Part I of the Arbitration Act 1996 shall not apply to any proceedings before the Tribunal but regulations may make provision corresponding to any provision of that Part.

(4A) The regulations may make provision for an appeal under this Part to be heard, in prescribed circumstances, with a claim under Chapter 1 of Part 4 of the Disability Discrimination Act 1995.

(5) Any person who without reasonable excuse fails to comply with—

(*a*) any requirement in respect of the discovery or inspection of documents imposed by the regulations by virtue of subsection (2)(*g*), or

(*b*) any requirement imposed by the regulations by virtue of subsection (2)(*h*),

is guilty of an offence.

(6) A person guilty of an offence under subsection (5) is liable on summary conviction to a fine not exceeding **level 3** on the standard scale.

[Education Act 1996, s 336, as amended by the Special Educational Needs and Disability Act 2001, s 42.]

PART VI[1]
SCHOOL ADMISSIONS, ATTENDANCE AND CHARGES

CHAPTER I[2]
ADMISSION, REGISTRATION AND WITHDRAWAL OF PUPILS

Time for admission of pupils

8–7815   433. Time for admission of pupils.   (1) Section 14 (which requires a local education authority to secure that sufficient schools for providing primary and secondary education are available for their area) shall not be construed as imposing any obligation on the proprietor of a school to admit children as pupils otherwise than at the beginning of a school term.

(2) Where, however, a child was prevented from entering a school at the beginning of a term—

(*a*) by his being ill or by other circumstances beyond his parent's control, or

(*b*) by his parent's having been then resident at a place from which the school was not accessible with reasonable facility,

the school's proprietor is not entitled by virtue of subsection (1) to refuse to admit him as a pupil during the currency of the term.

(3) In cases where subsection (2) does not apply, the governing body of a school maintained by a local education authority shall comply with any general directions given by the authority as to the time of admission of children as pupils.

(4) (*Repealed*).

(5) Despite section 7 (duty of parent of child of compulsory school age to cause him to receive full-time education), a parent is not under a duty to cause a child to receive full-time education during any period during which, having regard to subsections (1) and (2), it is not practicable for the parent to arrange for him to be admitted as a pupil at a school.

[Education Act 1996, s 433 as amended by the School Standards and Framework Act 1998, Sch 30.]

---

1. Part VI comprises ss 411–462.
2. Chapter I comprises ss 411–436.

Registration of pupils

8–7816   434. Registration of pupils.   (1) The proprietor of a school shall cause to be kept, in accordance with regulations[1], a register containing the prescribed particulars in respect of all persons who are pupils at the school.

(2) Without prejudice to the generality of subsection (1), the prescribed particulars shall include

particulars of the name and address of every person known to the proprietor to be a parent of a pupil at the school.

(3) The regulations shall prescribe the grounds on which names are to be deleted from a register kept under this section; and the name of a person entered in such a register as a pupil at a school—

(a) shall, when any of the prescribed grounds is applicable, be deleted from the register on that ground; and

(b) shall not be deleted from the register otherwise than on any such ground.

(4) The regulations may make provision—

(a) for enabling registers kept under this section to be inspected;

(b) for enabling extracts from such registers to be taken for the purposes of this Act by persons authorised to do so under the regulations; and

(c) for requiring the person by whom any such register is required to be kept to make to—

(i) the Secretary of State; and

(ii) local education authorities,

such periodical or other returns as to the contents of the register as may be prescribed.

(5) In this Act—

"registered pupil", in relation to a school, means a person registered as a pupil at the school in the register kept under this section; and

"registered", in relation to the parents of pupils at a school or in relation to the names or addresses of such parents or pupils, means shown in that register.

(6) A person who contravenes of fails to comply with any requirement imposed on him by regulations under this section is guilty of an offence and liable on summary conviction to a fine not exceeding **level 1** on the standard scale.

[Education Act 1996, s 434 as amended by the School Standards and Framework Act 1998, Sch 30.]

1. The Education (Pupil Registration) Regulations 1995, SI 1995/2089 amended by SI 1997/2624 and SI 2001/1109 (Wales), have been made.

CHAPTER II[1]
SCHOOL ATTENDANCE

8–7817 **437. School attendance orders.** (1) If it appears to a local education authority[2] that a child of compulsory school age[3] in their area is not receiving suitable education, either by regular attendance at school or otherwise, they shall serve a notice in writing[4] on the parent[5] requiring him to satisfy them within the period specified in the notice that the child is receiving such education.

(2) That period shall not be less than 15 days beginning with the day on which the notice is served.

(3) If—

(a) a parent[5] on whom a notice has been served under subsection (1) fails to satisfy the local education authority, within the period specified in the notice, that the child is receiving suitable education, and

(b) in the opinion of the authority it is expedient that the child should attend school,

the authority shall serve on the parent[5] an order (referred to in this Act as a "school attendance order"), in such form as may be prescribed, requiring him to cause the child to become a registered pupil at a school named in the order.

(4) A school attendance order shall (subject to any amendment made by the local education authority) continue in force for so long as the child is of compulsory school age[3], unless—

(a) it is revoked by the authority, or

(b) a direction is made in respect of it under section 443(2) or 447(5).

(5) Where a maintained school is named in a school attendance order, the local education authority shall inform the governing body and the head teacher.

(6) Where a maintained or grant-maintained school is named in a school attendance order, the governing body (and, in the case of a maintained school, the local education authority) shall admit the child to the school.

(7) Subsection (6) does not affect any power to exclude from a school a pupil who is already a registered pupil there.

(8) In this Chapter—

"maintained school" means any community, foundation or voluntary school or any community or foundation special school not established in a hospital; and

"suitable education", in relation to a child, means efficient full-time education suitable to his age, ability and aptitude and to any special educational needs he may have.

[Education Act 1996, s 437 as amended by the School Standards and Framework Act 1998, Sch 30.]

1. Chapter II comprises ss 437–448.
2. For the meaning of "local education authority" see para **8–7951**, post.

3. For the meaning of "compulsory school age" see s 8, ante.
4. As to the service of notices, see s 572, post.
5. For the meaning of "parent" see s 576, post.

8–7818   438. Choice of school: child without statement of special educational needs.
(1) This section applies where a local education authority are required by virtue of section 437(3) to serve a school attendance order in respect of a child, other than a child for whom they maintain a statement under section 324.

(2) Before serving the order, the authority shall serve on the parent a notice in writing—

(a) informing him of their intention to serve the order,
(b) specifying the school which the authority intend to name in the order and, if they think fit, one or more other schools which they regard as suitable alternatives, and
(c) stating the effect of subsections (3) to (6).

(3) If the notice specifies one or more alternative schools and the parent selects one of them within the period of 15 days beginning with the day on which the notice is served, the school selected by him shall be named in the order.

(4) If—

(a) within the period mentioned in subsection (3), the parent applies for the child to be admitted to a school maintained by a local education authority and, where that authority are not the authority by whom the notice was served, notifies the latter authority of the application, and
(b) the child is offered a place at the school as a result of the application,

that school shall be named in the order.

(5) If—

(a) within the period mentioned in subsection (3), the parent applies to the local education authority by whom the notice was served for education to be provided at a school which is not a school maintained by the local education authority, and
(b) the child is offered a place at the school and the authority are required by virtue of regulations under section 18(3) to pay the fees payable in respect of the education provided for him at the school,

that school shall be named in the order.

(6) If, within the period mentioned in subsection (3)—

(a) the parent—

(i) applies for the child to be admitted to a school which is not maintained by a local education authority, and in respect of which no application is made under subsection (5), and
(ii) notifies the local education authority by whom the notice was served of the application,

(b) the child is offered a place at the school as a result of the application, and
(c) the school is suitable to his age, ability and aptitude and to any special educational need he may have,

that school shall be named in the order.
[Education Act 1996, s 438 as amended by the School Standards and Framework Act 1998, Sch 30.]

8–7819   439. Specification of schools in notices under s 438(2).   (1) Subject to subsection (3), a local education authority shall not, if it appears to them that subsection (2) applies in relation to any school, specify the school in a notice under section 438(2) unless they are responsible for determining the arrangements for the admission of pupils to the school.

(2) This subsection applies where, if the child concerned were admitted to the school in accordance with a school attendance order resulting from the notice, the number of pupils at the school in the child's age group would exceed the number determined in accordance with section 89 of the School Standards and Framework Act 1998 (determination of admission numbers) as the number of pupils in that age group which it is intended to admit to the school in the school year in which he would be admitted.*

(3) Subsection (1) does not prevent a local education authority specifying in a notice under section 438(2) any maintained school if—

(a) there is no maintained school in their area which—

(i) the authority are not (apart from this subsection) prevented by subsection (1) from specifying, and
(ii) is, in the opinion of the authority, a reasonable distance from the home of the child concerned, and

(b) in the opinion of the authority, the school in question is a reasonable distance from the home of the child concerned.

(4) A local education authority shall not specify in a notice under section 438(2) a school from which the child concerned is permanently excluded.

(4A) A local education authority shall not specify a school in a notice under section 438(2) if the admission of the child concerned would result in prejudice of the kind referred to in section 86(3)(*a*) of the School Standards and Framework Act 1998 (parental preferences) by reason of measures required to be taken as mentioned I subsection (4) of that section.

(5) Before deciding to specify a particular maintained school in a notice under section 438(2) a local education authority shall consult—

(*a*) the governing body, and

(*b*) if another local education authority are responsible for determining the arrangements for the admission of pupils to the school, that authority.

(6) Where a local education authority decide to specify a particular maintained school in a notice under section 438(2) they shall, before serving the notice, serve notice in writing of their decision on—

(*a*) the governing body and head teacher of the school, and

(*b*) if another local education authority are responsible for determining the arrangements for the admission of pupils to the school, that authority.

(7) A governing body or local education authority on whom notice is served under subsection (6) may, within the period of 15 days beginning with the day on which the notice was received, apply to the Secretary of State for a direction under this section, and if they do so, shall inform the local education authority which served the notice.

(8) Where the Secretary of State gives a direction under this section, the school or schools to be specified in the notice under section 438(2) shall be determined in accordance with the direction.

[Education Act 1996, s 439 as amended by the School Standards and Framework Act 1998, Sch 30.]

8–7820　440. Amendment of order at request of parent: child without statement of special educational needs.　(1) This section applies where a school attendance order is in force in respect of a child, other than a child for whom the local education authority maintain a statement under section 324.

(2) If at any time—

(*a*) the parent applies for the child to be admitted to a school maintained by a local education authority which is different from the school named in the order,

(*b*) the child is offered a place at the school as a result of the application, and

(*c*) the parent requests the local education authority by whom the order was served to amend it by substituting that school for the one currently named,

the authority shall comply with the request.

(3) If at any time—

(*a*) the parent applies to the authority for education to be provided for the child at a school which is not a school maintained by a local education authority or grant-maintained school and which is different from the school named in the order,

(*b*) the child is offered a place and the authority are required by virtue of regulations under section 18(3) to pay the fees payable in respect of the education provided for him at the school, and

(*c*) the parent requests the authority to amend the order by substituting that school for the one currently named,

the authority shall comply with the request.

(4) If at any time—

(*a*) the parent applies for the child to be admitted to a school which is not maintained by a local education authority, which is different from the school named in the order and in respect of which no application is made under subsection (3),

(*b*) as a result of the application, the child is offered a place at the school, being a school which is suitable to his age, ability and aptitude and to any special educational needs he may have, and

(*c*) the parent requests the authority to amend the order by substituting that school for the one currently named,

the authority shall comply with the request.

[Education Act 1996, s 440 as amended by the School Standards and Framework Act 1998, Sch 30.]

8–7821　441. Choice of school: child with statement of special educational needs.　(1) Subsections (2) and (3) apply where a local education authority are required by virtue of section 437(3) to serve a school attendance order in respect of a child for whom they maintain a statement under section 324.

(2) Where the statement specifies the name of a school, that school shall be named in the order.

(3) Where the statement does not specify the name of a school—

(*a*) the authority shall amend the statement so that it specifies the name of a school, and

(*b*) that school shall then be named in the order.

(3A) An amendment to a statement required to be made under subsection (3)(a) shall be treated for the purposes of Schedule 27 as if it were an amendment proposed following a periodic review (within the meaning of that Schedule).

　(4) Where—

　　(*a*)　a school attendance order is in force in respect of a child for whom the local education authority maintain a statement under section 324, and

　　(*b*)　the name of the school specified in the statement is changed, the local education authority shall amend the order accordingly.

[Education Act 1996, s 441, as amended by the Special Educational Needs and Disability Act 2001, s 42.]

8–7822　442. Revocation of order at request of parent.　(1) This section applies where a school attendance order is in force in respect of a child.

　(2) If at any time the parent applies to the local education authority requesting that the order be revoked on the ground that arrangements have been made for the child to receive suitable education otherwise than at school, the authority shall comply with the request, unless they are of the opinion that no satisfactory arrangements have been made for the education of the child otherwise than at school.

　(3) If a parent is aggrieved by a refusal of the local education authority to comply with a request under subsection (2), he may refer the question to the Secretary of State.

　(4) Where a question is referred to the Secretary of State under subsection (3), he shall give such direction determining the question as he thinks fit.

　(5) Where the child in question is one for whom the authority maintain a statement under section 324—

　　(*a*)　subsections (2) to (4) do not apply if the name of a school or other institution is specified in the statement, and

　　(*b*)　in any other case a direction under subsection (4) may require the authority to make such amendments in the statement as the Secretary of State considers necessary or expedient in consequence of his determination.

[Education Act 1996, s 442.]

School attendance: offences and education supervision orders

8–7823　443. Offence: failure to comply with school attendance order.　(1) If a parent[1] on whom a school attendance order is served fails to comply with the requirements of the order, he is guilty of an offence[2], unless he proves that he is causing the child to receive suitable education otherwise than at school[3].

　(2) If, in proceedings for an offence under this section, the parent[3] is acquitted, the court may direct that the school attendance order shall cease to be in force.

　(3) A direction under subsection (2) does not affect the duty of the local education authority to take further action under section 437 if at any time the authority are of the opinion that, having regard to any change of circumstances, it is expedient to do so.

　(4) A person guilty of an offence under this section is liable on summary conviction to a fine not exceeding **level 3** on the standard scale.

[Education Act 1996, s 443.]

---

　1. For "parent" see s 576, post.

　2. This is a continuing offence in the sense that failure is a continuing condition; however s 443(1) creates only one offence of failure in regard to any particular school attendance order and after conviction of failing to comply with the requirements of an order there can be no second prosecution with reference to the same order (*Enfield London Borough Council v Forsyth and Forsyth* (1986) 151 JP 113, [1987] 2 FLR 126, [1987] Fam Law 163). As to presumption of age, see s 445 and the institution of proceedings, see s 446.

　3. For "school", see s 4, ante.

8–7824　444. Offence: failure to secure regular attendance at school of registered pupil.

　(1) If a child of compulsory school age[1] who is a registered pupil[2] at a school[3] fails to attend[4] regularly at the school, his parent[5] is guilty of an offence[6].

　(1A) If in the circumstances mentioned in subsection (1) the parent knows that his child is failing to attend regularly at the school and fails without reasonable justification to cause him to do so, he is guilty of an offence.

　(2) Subsections (3) to (6) below apply in proceedings for an offence under this section in respect of a child who is not a boarder at the school at which he is a registered pupil.

　(3) The child shall not be taken to have failed to attend regularly at the school by reason of his absence from the school—

　　(*a*)　with leave[7],

　　(*b*)　at any time when he was prevented from attending by reason of sickness or any unavoidable cause[8], or

　　(*c*)　on any day exclusively set apart for religious observance[9] by the religious body to which his parent belongs.

　(4) The child shall not be taken to have failed to attend regularly at the school if the parent proves—

(a) that the school at which the child is a registered pupil is not within walking distance[10] of the child's home, and

(b) that no suitable[11] arrangements have been made by the local education authority for any of the following—

  (i) his transport to and from the school,
  (ii) boarding accommodation for him at or near the school, or
  (iii) enabling him to become a registered pupil at a school nearer to his home.

(5) In subsection (4) "walking distance"—

(a) in relation to a child who is under the age of eight, means 3.218688 kilometres (two miles), and

(b) in relation to a child who has attained the age of eight, means 4.828032 kilometres (three miles),

in each case measured by the nearest available route[12].

(6) If it is proved that the child has no fixed abode, subsection (4) shall not apply, but the parent[4] shall be acquitted if he proves—

(a) that he is engaged in a trade or business of such a nature as to require him to travel from place to place,

(b) that the child has attended at a school as a registered pupil[2] as regularly as the nature of that trade or business permits, and

(c) if the child has attained the age of six, that he has made at least 200 attendances during the period of 12 months ending with the date on which the proceedings were instituted.

(7) In proceedings for an offence under this section in respect of a child who is a boarder at the school at which he is a pupil[2], the child shall be taken to have failed to attend regularly at the school if he is absent from it without leave during any part of the school term at a time when he was not prevented from being present by reason of sickness or any unavoidable cause[8].

(8) A person guilty of an offence under this subsection (1) is liable on summary conviction to a fine not exceeding **level 3** on the standard scale.

(8A) A person guilty of an offence under subsection (1A) is liable on summary conviction—

(a) to a fine not exceeding level 4 on the standard scale, or

(b) to imprisonment for a term not exceeding <u>three months</u>*,

or both.

(8B) If, on the trial of an offence under subsection (1A), the court finds the defendant not guilty of that offence but is satisfied that he is guilty of an offence under subsection (1), the court may find him guilty of that offence.

(9) In this section "leave", in relation to a school, means leave granted by any person authorised to do so by the governing body or proprietor of the school[7].
[Education Act 1996, s 444 as amended by the School Standards and Framework Act 1998 and the Court Services and Criminal Justice Act 2000, s 72.]

---

*"51 weeks" substituted by the Criminal Justice Act 2003, Sch 26, from a date to be appointed.
1. For "compulsory school age", see s 8 and for presumption of age, see s 445, post.
2. "Registered pupil" in relation to a school, means a person registered as a pupil at the school in the register kept under s 434, ante.
3. For the meaning of "school", see s 4, ante.
4. For the meaning of "parent", see s 576, post.
5. Absence when the attendance register is closed may be treated as non-attendance so as to affect "regular attendance" (*Hinchley v Rankin* [1961] 1 All ER 692, [1961] 1 WLR 421, 125 JP 293). As to evidence of attendance, see s 566, post. As to defence where a child has been excluded by any reason of being infested with vermin, or in a foul condition, see s 524(2), post.
6. Subject to the defences set out in the subsequent provisions of s 444, this is an offence of strict liability and the lack of a defence does not contravene art 6 of the Convention; art 6(2) provides a criterion against which the court could scrutinise procedural and evidential matters but not the substantive elements of an offence: *Barnfather v Islington Education Authority* [2003] EWHC 418 (Admin), [2003] 1 WLR 2318. Where parents have been acquitted by justices, the local authority must give careful consideration before making a decision to appeal and any decision to appeal is the personal responsibility of the chief education officer. He should take into account the distress an appeal would cause to the parent in question: *Sutton London Borough Council v S* (2004) Times 1 November, DC).
7. Exclusion of a child from school, being a disciplinary measure, does not constitute leave (*Happe v Lay* (1978) 8 Fam Law 54, 76 LGR 313). As to absence through taking part in an entertainment, see the Children and Young Persons Act 1963, s 37(7), in PART V: YOUTH COURTS, ante.
8. Chronic illness of a parent, or other family responsibilities or duties, are not an "unavoidable cause" within the meaning of this section. (*Jenkins v Howell* [1949] 2 KB 218, [1949] 1 All ER 942, 113 JP 292). "Unavoidable cause" is not to be equated with reasonable cause (*Jarman v Mid Glamorgan Education Authority* [1985] LS Gaz R 1249).
9. Ascension Day is a "day exclusively set apart for religious observance" by the Church of England; and a member of that church who withdrew his child from school for the purpose of sending him to church on that day was exempt from prosecution (*Marshall v Graham, Bell v Graham* [1907] 2 KB 112, 71 JP 270).
10. See sub-s (5).
11. See *Surrey County Council v Ministry of Education* [1953] 1 All ER 705, 117 JP 194. "Suitable" refers to the arrangements not to the suitability of any proposed school nearer to the pupil's home (*Re S (minors)* [1995] ELR 98, sub nom *R v Dyfed County Council, ex p S* (minors) [1995] 1 FCR 113, CA).
12. This means a route along which a child accompanied as necessary can walk with reasonable safety; it does not fail

to qualify as "available" because of dangers which would arise if the child is unaccompanied (*Essex County Council v Rogers* [1987] AC 66, [1986] 3 All ER 321, [1986] 3 WLR 689, HL); considered in *Devon County Council v George* [1989] AC 573, [1988] 3 All ER 1002, [1988] 3 WLR 1386, HL (provision of free transport for pupils living outside the statutory walking distance).

8–7824ZA   444ZA. Application of section 444 to alternative educational provision.
(1) Where, in the case of a child of compulsory school age who is not a registered pupil at any school—

(*a*) a local education authority has made arrangements under section 19 for the provision of education for him otherwise than at a school or at his home, and

(*b*) notice in writing of the arrangements has been given to the child's parent,

subsections (1) to (7) of section 444 have effect as if the place at which the education is provided were a school and the child were a registered pupil at that school.

(2) Where—

(*a*) a child of compulsory school age has been excluded from a relevant school,

(*b*) he remains for the time being a registered pupil at the school,

(*c*) he is required by the appropriate authority for the school to attend at a place outside the school premises for the purpose of receiving any instruction or training, and

(*d*) notice in writing of the requirement has been given to the child's parent,

subsections (1) to (7) of section 444 have effect as if the place at which the child is required to attend were a school and the child were a registered pupil at that school (and not at the school mentioned in paragraph (*b*)).

(3) In relation to a maintained school or a pupil referral unit—

(*a*) the reference in subsection (2)(*a*) to exclusion is a reference to exclusion under section 52 of the Education Act 2002, and

(*b*) the requirement referred to in subsection (2)(*c*) is a requirement imposed under section 29(3) of that Act.

(4) A child shall not be taken to have failed to attend regularly—

(*a*) in a case falling within subsection (1), at the place at which education is provided for him, or

(*b*) in a case falling within subsection (2), at the place at which he is required to attend,

unless he has failed to attend regularly since the giving of the notice mentioned in subsection (1)(*b*) or (2)(*d*).

(5) Section 572, which provides for the methods by which notices may be served under this Act, does not preclude the notice mentioned in subsection (1)(*b*) or (2)(*d*) from being given to a child's parent by any other effective method.

(6) In proceedings for an offence under section 444 in a case falling within subsection (1) of this section, the parent shall be acquitted if he proves that the child is receiving suitable education otherwise than by regular attendance at a school or at the place mentioned in subsection (1).

(7) In section 444 "leave"—

(*a*) in relation to a place at which education is provided as mentioned in subsection (1) of this section, means leave granted by any person authorised to do so by the local education authority;

(*b*) in relation to a place at which a child is required to attend as mentioned in subsection (2)(*c*) of this section, means leave granted by any person authorised to do so by the appropriate authority for the school.

(8) In this section—

(*a*) "relevant school" means—

   (i) a maintained school,
   (ii) a pupil referral unit,
   (iii) an Academy,
   (iv) a city technology college, or
   (v) a city college for the technology of the arts;

(*b*) "appropriate authority" means—

   (i) in relation to a maintained school, the governing body,
   (ii) in relation to a pupil referral unit, the local education authority, and
   (iii) in relation to a school falling within paragraph (*a*)(iii), (iv) or (v), the proprietor of the school.*

[Education Act 1996, s 444ZA, as inserted by the Education Act 2005, s 116.]

---

*Reproduced as in force in England; in force in Wales from a date to be appointed.

8–7824A   444A. Penalty notice in respect of failure to secure regular attendance at school of registered pupil.   (1) Where an authorised officer has reason to believe—

(a) that a person has committed an offence under section 444(1), and
(b) that the offence relates—

   (i) to a relevant school in England,
   (ii) in a case falling within subsection (1) of section 444ZA, to a place at which education is provided by a local education authority in England, or
   (iii) in a case falling within subsection (2) of that section, to a place at which a child is required to attend by the appropriate authority (within the meaning of that section) for a relevant school in England,

he may give the person a penalty notice in respect of the offence.

(2) A penalty notice is a notice offering a person the opportunity of discharging any liability to conviction for the offence under section 444(1) to which the notice relates by payment of a penalty in accordance with the notice.

(3) Where a person is given a penalty notice, proceedings for the offence to which the notice relates (or an offence under section 444(1A) arising out of the same circumstances) may not be instituted before the end of such period as may be prescribed.

(4) Where a person is given a penalty notice, he cannot be convicted of the offence to which the notice relates (or an offence under section 444(1A) arising out of the same circumstances) if he pays a penalty in accordance with the notice.

(5) Penalties under this section shall be payable to local education authorities in England.

(6) Sums received by a local education authority under this section may be used by the authority for the purposes of any of its functions which may be specified in regulations.
[Education Act 1996, s 444A, as inserted by Anti-social Behaviour Act 2003, s 23.]

8–7824B   444B. Penalty notices: supplemental.   (1) Regulations[1] may make—

(a) provision as to the form and content of penalty notices,
(b) provision as to the monetary amount of any penalty and the time by which it is to be paid,
(c) provision for determining the local education authority to which a penalty is payable,
(d) provision as to the methods by which penalties may be paid,
(e) provision as to the records which are to be kept in relation to penalty notices,
(f) provision as to the persons who may be authorised by a local education authority or a head teacher to give penalty notices,
(g) provision limiting the circumstances in which authorised officers of a prescribed description may give penalty notices,
(h) provision for or in connection with the withdrawal, in prescribed circumstances, of a penalty notice, including—

   (i) repayment of any amount paid by way of penalty under a penalty notice which is withdrawn, and
   (ii) prohibition of the institution or continuation of proceedings for the offence to which the withdrawn notice relates (and any offence under section 444(1A) arising out of the same circumstances),

(i) provision for a certificate—

   (i) purporting to be signed by or on behalf of a prescribed person, and
   (ii) stating that payment of any amount paid by way of penalty was or, as the case may be, was not received on or before a date specified in the certificate,

to be received in evidence of the matters so stated,

(j) provision as to the action to be taken if a penalty is not paid in accordance with a penalty notice,
(k) provision for or in connection with the preparation of codes of conduct in relation to the giving of penalty notices,
(l) such other provision in relation to penalties or penalty notices as the Secretary of State thinks necessary or expedient.

(2) Without prejudice to the generality of subsection (1) or section 569(4), regulations under subsection (1)(b) may make provision for penalties of different amounts to be payable in different cases or circumstances (including provision for the penalty payable under a penalty notice to differ according to the time by which it is paid).

(3) Local education authorities, head teachers and authorised officers shall, in carrying out their functions in relation to penalty notices, have regard to any guidance which is published by the Secretary of State from time to time in relation to penalty notices.

(4) In this section and section 444A—

"authorised officer" means—

   (a) a constable,
   (b) an officer of a local education authority in England who is authorised by the authority to give penalty notices, or
   (c) an authorised staff member,

"authorised staff member" means—

(*a*) a head teacher of a relevant school in England, or

(*b*) a member of the staff of a relevant school in England who is authorised by the head teacher of the school to give penalty notices,

"penalty" means a penalty under a penalty notice,

"penalty notice" has the meaning given by section 444A(2),

"relevant school" means—

(*a*) a maintained school,

(*b*) a pupil referral unit,

(*c*) an Academy,

(*d*) a city technology college, or

(*e*) a city college for the technology of the arts.

[Education Act 1996, s 444B, as inserted by Anti-social Behaviour Act 2003, s 23.]

---

1. The Education (Penalty Notices) (England) Regulations 2004, SI 2004/181 amended by SI 2004/920 and SI 2005/2029 (E) have been made which provide inter alia that the amount of the penalty to be paid shall be (*a*) £50 where the amount is paid within 28 days of receipt of the notice; (*b*) £100 where the amount is paid within 42 days of receipt of the notice.

8–7825 445. Presumption of age. (1) This section applies for the purposes of any proceedings for an offence under section 443 or 444.

(2) In so far as it is material, the child in question shall be presumed to have been of compulsory school age[1] at any time unless the parent proves the contrary.

(3) Where a court is obliged by virtue of subsection (2) to presume a child to have been of compulsory school age[1], section 565 (1) (provisions as to evidence) does not apply.

[Education Act 1996, s 445.]

---

1. For "compulsory school age", see s 8, ante.

8–7826 446. Institution of proceedings. Proceedings for an offence under section 443 or 444 shall not be instituted except by a local education authority[1].

[Education Act 1996, s 446.]

---

1. For "local education authority", see para **8–7951**, post.

8–7827 447. Education supervision orders. (1) Before instituting proceedings for an offence under section 443 or 444, a local education authority shall consider whether it would be appropriate (instead of or as well as instituting the proceedings) to apply for an education supervision order[1] with respect to the child.

(2) The court—

(*a*) by which a person is convicted of an offence under section 443, or

(*b*) before which a person is charged with an offence under section 444,

may direct the local education authority instituting the proceedings to apply for an education supervision order[1] with respect to the child unless the authority, having consulted the appropriate local authority, decide that the child's welfare will be satisfactorily safeguarded even though no education supervision order is made.

(3) Where, following such a direction, a local education authority decide not to apply for an education supervision order, they shall inform the court of the reasons for their decision.

(4) Unless the court has directed otherwise, the information required under subsection (3) shall be given to the court before the end of the period of eight weeks beginning with the date on which the direction was given.

(5) Where—

(*a*) a local education authority apply for an education supervision order with respect to a child who is the subject of a school attendance order, and

(*b*) the court decides that section 36(3) of the Children Act 1989[2] (education supervision orders) prevents it from making the order,

the court may direct that the school attendance order shall cease to be in force.

(6) In this section—

"the appropriate local authority" has the same meaning as in section 36(9) of the Children Act 1989[2], and

"education supervision order" means an education supervision order under that Act.

[Education Act 1944, s 447.]

1. As to education supervision orders, see the Children Act 1989, s 36 and Part III of Sch 3, in PART IV: FAMILY LAW, ante. As to procedure for making an application for an education supervision order, see the Family Proceedings Courts (Children Act 1989) Rules 1991, in PART IV: FAMILY LAW, ante.
2. See the Children Act 1989, in PART IV: FAMILY LAW, ante.

8–7828   448. *Repealed*

PART VII[1]
INDEPENDENT SCHOOLS

CHAPTER I[2]
PRELIMINARY

8–7829   463. Meaning of "independent school". (1) In this Act "independent school" means any school at which full-time education is provided for—

(*a*)   five or more pupils of compulsory school age, or
(*b*)   at least one pupil of that age for whom a statement is maintained under section 324, or who is looked after by a local authority (within the meaning of section 22 of the Children Act 1989),

and which is not a school maintained by a local education authority or a special school not so maintained.

(2) For the purposes of subsection (1)(a) and (b) it is immaterial if full-time education is also provided at the school for pupils under or over compulsory school age.

[Education Act 1996, s 463 as amended by the School Standards and Framework Act 1998, Sch 30 and the Education Act 2002, s 216(4).]

1. Part VII comprises ss 463–483.
2. Chapter I comprises s 463.

CHAPTER II[1]
REGISTRATION OF INDEPENDENT SCHOOLS

Registration

8–7830   464. *Separate registration for England and Wales.*
Repealed.

1. Chapter II comprises ss 464–478.

8–7831   465. *Provisional and final registration of a school.*
Repealed.

8–7832   466. Enforcement of registration: offences. *Repealed.*

Complaints about registered and provisionally registered schools

8–7833   470. *Determination of complaint by an Independent Schools Tribunal.*
Repealed.

8–7834   471. *Determination of complaint by Secretary of State.*
Repealed.

8–7835   473. Enforcement of disqualification. *Repealed.*

8–7835A   473A. Removal of disqualification: persons no longer unsuitable to work with children. *Repealed.*

8–7835B   473B. Conditions for application under section 473A. *Repealed.*

8–7836   477. Disqualification in Scotland. *Repealed.*

8–7837   478. Offences: institution of proceedings and punishment. *Repealed.*

PART IX[1]
ANCILLARY FUNCTIONS

CHAPTER I[2]
ANCILLARY FUNCTIONS OF SECRETARY OF STATE

Medical examinations

8–7838   506. Power to require medical examination of pupils. (1) Where—

(*a*)   a question is referred to the Secretary of State under section 442(3) or 495, and (*b*) in his opinion the examination of any pupil by a registered medical practitioner appointed by him for the purpose would assist in determining the question,

he may serve a notice on the parent of that pupil requiring the parent to present the pupil for examination by such a practitioner.

(2) Any parent who without reasonable excuse fails to comply with any requirements of a notice served on him under subsection (1) is guilty of an offence.

(3) A person guilty of an offence under this section is liable on summary conviction to a fine not exceeding **level 1** on the standard scale.

[Education Act 1996, s 506.]

---

1. Part IX comprises ss 495–541.
2. Chapter I comprises ss 495–507.

CHAPTER II[1]

ANCILLARY FUNCTIONS OF LOCAL EDUCATION AUTHORITIES

Cleanliness of pupils

8–7839 521. Examination of pupils for cleanliness. (1) A local education authority may by directions in writing authorise a medical officer[2] of theirs to have the persons and clothing of pupils in attendance at relevant schools examined whenever in his opinion such examinations are necessary in the interests of cleanliness[3].

(2) Directions under subsection (1) may be given with respect to—

(*a*) all relevant schools, or

(*b*) any relevant schools named in the directions.

(3) An examination under this section shall be made by a person authorised by the authority to make such examinations; and, if the examination is of a girl, it shall not be made by a man unless he is a registered medical practitioner.

(4) For the purposes of this section "relevant schools" are schools maintained by the authority

[Education Act 1996, s 521 as amended by the School Standards and Framework Act 1998, Sch 30.]

---

1. Chapter II comprises ss 508–532.
2. For the definition of "medical officer", see s 579(1), post.
3. This section imposes an obligation on the parent and child to allow the medical examination (*Fox v Burgess* [1922] 1 KB 623, 86 JP 66). The powers conferred by s 85 of the Public Health Act 1936, shall be in addition to the powers conferred by this section (Public Health Act 1936, ss 85 and 328, post).

8–7840 522. Compulsory cleansing of a pupil. (1) If, on an examination under section 521, the person or clothing of a pupil is found to be infested with vermin or in a foul condition, any officer of the local education authority may serve a notice[1] on the pupil's parent[2] requiring him to cause the pupil's person and clothing to be cleansed.

(2) The notice shall inform the parent[2] that, unless within the period specified in the notice the pupil's person and clothing are cleansed to the satisfaction of such person as is specified in the notice, the cleansing will be carried out under arrangements made by the authority.

(3) The period so specified shall not be less than 24 hours from the service of the notice.

(4) If, on a report being made to him by the specified person at the end of the specified period, a medical officer of the authority is not satisfied that the pupil's person and clothing have been properly cleansed, he may by order direct that they shall be cleansed under arrangements made by the authority under section 523.

(5) An order made under section (4) shall be sufficient to authorise any officer of the authority—

(*a*) to cause the pupil's person and clothing to be cleansed in accordance with arrangements made by the authority under section 523, and

(*b*) for that purpose to convey the pupil to, and detain him at, any premises provided in accordance with such arrangements.

[Education Act 1996, s 522.]

---

1. As to service, see s 572, post.
2. For the definition of parent, see s 576, post.

8–7841 523. Arrangements for cleansing of pupils. (1) A local education authority shall make arrangements for securing that the person or clothing of any pupil required to be cleansed under section 522 may be cleansed (whether at the request of a parent or in pursuance of an order under section 522(4)) at suitable premises, by suitable persons and with suitable appliances.

(2) Where the council of a district in the area of the authority are entitled to the use of any premises or appliances for cleansing the person or clothing of persons infested with vermin, the authority may require the council to permit the authority to use those premises or appliances for such purposes upon such terms as may be determined—

(*a*) by agreement between the authority and the council, or (b)　in default of such agreement, by the Secretary of State.

(3)　Subsection (2) does not apply in relation to Wales.

(4)　A girl may be cleansed under arrangements under this section only by a registered medical practitioner or by a woman authorised for the purpose by the authority.
[Education Act 1996, s 523.]

8–7842　524.　Suspension of pupil pending examination or cleansing.　(1) Where—

(a)　a medical officer of a local education authority suspects that the person or clothing of a pupil in attendance at a relevant school is infested with vermin or in a foul condition, but

(b)　action for the examination or cleansing of the pupil's person and clothing cannot be taken immediately,

the medical officer may direct that the pupil is to be suspended from the school until such action has been taken, if he considers it necessary to do so in the interests either of the pupil or of other pupils in attendance at the school.

(2)　A direction under subsection (1) is a defence to any proceedings under Chapter II or Part VI in respect of the failure of the pupil to attend school on any day on which he is excluded in pursuance of the direction, unless it is proved that the giving of the direction was necessitated by the wilful default of the pupil or his parent.

(3)　For the purposes of this section a "relevant school" is a school maintained by the local education authority.
[Education Act 1996, s 524 as amended by the School Standards and Framework Act 1998, Sch 30.]

8–7843　525.　Offence of neglecting the cleanliness of a pupil.　(1) If, after the person or clothing of a pupil has been cleansed under section 522—

(a)　his person or clothing is again infested with vermin, or in a foul condition, at any time while he is in attendance at a relevant school, and

(b)　the condition of his person or clothing is due to neglect on the part of his parent,

the parent is guilty of an offence.

(2)　A person guilty of an offence under this section is liable on summary conviction to a fine not exceeding **level 1** on the standard scale.

(3)　For the purposes of this section a "relevant school" is a school maintained by a local education authority.
[Education Act 1996, s 525 as amended by the School Standards Framework Act 1998, Sch 30.]

1.　For the definition of "parent", see s 576, post. It may be either the father or the mother, and proceedings under sub-s (1) will lie against either (or both) whose neglect is proved (*Plunkett v Alker* [1954] 1 QB 420, [1954] 1 All ER 396, [1954] 2 WLR 280).

PART X[1]
MISCELLANEOUS AND GENERAL

CHAPTER I[2]
EDUCATIONAL PREMISES

Nuisance or disturbance on school premises

8–7844　547.　Nuisance or disturbance on school premises.　(1) Any person who without lawful authority is present on premises to which this section applies and causes or permits nuisance or disturbance to the annoyance of persons who lawfully use those premises (whether or not any such persons are present at the time) is guilty of an offence and liable on summary conviction to a fine not exceeding **level 2** on the standard scale.

(2)　This section applies to premises, including playgrounds, playing fields and other premises for outdoor recreation, of—

(a)　any school maintained by a local education authority,

(aa)　any special school not so maintained, and

(ab)　any independent school,

(b)　(repealed).★

(2A)　This section also applies to any premises which are—

(a)　provided by a local education authority under section 508, and

(b)　used wholly or mainly in connection with the provision of instruction or leadership in sporting, recreational or outdoor activities.★

(3)　If—

(a)　a police constable, or

(b)　(subject to subsection (5)) a person whom the appropriate authority has authorised to exercise the power conferred by this subsection,★

has reasonable cause to suspect that any person is committing or has committed an offence under this section, he may remove him from the premises in question.

(4) In subsection (3) "the appropriate authority" means—

(*a*) in relation to premises of a foundation, voluntary aided or foundation special school, a local education authority or the governing body,

(*b*) in relation to—

    (i) premises of any other school maintained by a local education authority, and

    (ii) premises provided by a local education authority as mentioned in subsection (2A),

a local education authority, and

(*c*) in relation to premises of a special school which is not so maintained or of an independent school, the proprietor of the school.

(5) A local education authority may not authorise a person to exercise the power conferred by subsection (3) in relation to premises of a foundation, voluntary or foundation special school without first obtaining the consent of the governing body.

(6) No proceedings for an offence under this section shall be brought by any person other than—

(*a*) a police constable, or

(*b*) an authorised person.

(7) In subsection (6) "authorised person" means—

(*a*) in relation to an offence committed on premises of a foundation, voluntary aided or foundation special school, a local education authority or a person whom the governing body have authorised to bring such proceedings,

(*b*) in relation to an offence committed—

    (i) on premises of any other school maintained by a local education authority, or

    (ii) on premises provided by a local education authority as mentioned in subsection (2A),

a local education authority, and

(*c*) in relation to an offence committed on premises of a special school which is not so maintained or of an independent school, a person whom the proprietor of the school has authorised to bring such proceedings.*

(8) A local education authority may not bring proceedings for an offence under this section committed on premises of a voluntary or grant-maintained school without first obtaining the consent of the governing body.

[Education Act 1996, s 547 as amended by the School Standards Framework Act 1998, Sch 30 and the Education Act 2002, s 206.]

---

1. Part X comprises ss 542–583.
2. Chapter I comprises s 542–547.

CHAPTER II
PUNISHMENT AND RESTRAINT OF PUPILS

Corporal Punishment

8–7844A   548. No right to give corporal punishment. (1) Corporal punishment given by, or on the authority of, a member of staff to a child—

(*a*) for whom education is provided at any school, or

(*b*) for whom education is provided, otherwise than at school, under any arrangements made by a local education authority, or

(*c*) for whom specified nursery education is provided otherwise than at school,

cannot be justified in any proceedings on the ground that it was given in pursuance of a right exercisable by the member of staff by virtue of his position as such[1].

(2) Subsection (1) applies to corporal punishment so given to a child at any time, whether at the school or other place at which education is provided for the child, or elsewhere.

(3) The following provisions have effect for the purposes of this section.

(4) Any reference to giving corporal punishment to a child is to doing anything for the purpose of punishing that child (whether or not there are other reasons for doing it) which, apart from any justification, would constitute battery.

(5) However, corporal punishment shall not be taken to be given to a child by virtue of anything done for reasons that include averting—

(*a*) an immediate danger of personal injury to, or

(*b*) an immediate danger to the property of,

any person (including the child himself).

(6) "Member of staff", in relation to the child concerned, means—

(a) any person who works as a teacher at the school or other place at which education is provided for the child, or

(b) any other person who (whether in connection with the provision of education for the child or otherwise)—

    (i) works at that school or place, or

    (ii) otherwise provides his services there (whether or not for payment),

and has lawful control or charge of the child.

(7) "Child" (except in subsection (8)) means a person under the age of 18.

(8) "Specified nursery education" means full-time or part-time education suitable for children who have not attained compulsory school age which is provided—

(a) by a local education authority; or

(b) by any other person—

    (i) who is (or is to be) in receipt of financial assistance given by such an authority and whose provision of nursery education is taken into account by the authority in formulating proposals for the purposes of section 120(2)(a) of the School Standards and Framework Act 1998, or

    (ii) who is (or is to be) in receipt of grants under section 1 of the Nursery Education and Grant-Maintained Schools Act 1996; or★

(c) *repealed.*

[Education Act 1996, s 548 as substituted by the School Standards and Framework Act 1998, s 131(1) and the Education Act 2002, Sch 22.]

★Paragraph (b) and preceding "or" repealed in relation to England by the Education Act 2002, Sch 22, in force in relation to Wales from a date to be appointed: see the Education Act 2002, s 216(4).

1. This phrase limits the application of s 548(1) to corporal punishment administered by a teacher while discharging his functions as such and not, for example, as a parent punishing his own child. Parents may not therefore expressly authorise a teacher to administer corporal punishment on their behalf (*R (Williamson) v Secretary of State for Education and Employment* [2005] UKHL 15, [2005] 2 AC 246, [2005] 2 All ER 1, [2005] 1 FCR 497, [2005] 2 FLR 374.

8–7844B   550A. Power of members of staff to restrain pupils.   (1) A member of the staff of a school may use, in relation to any pupil at the school, such force as is reasonable in the circumstances for the purpose of preventing the pupil from doing (or continuing to do) any of the following, namely—

(a) committing any offence,

(b) causing personal injury to, or damage to the property of, any person (including the pupil himself), or

(c) engaging in any behaviour prejudicial to the maintenance of good order and discipline at the school or among any of its pupils, whether that behaviour occurs during a teaching session or otherwise.

(2) Subsection (1) applies where a member of the staff of a school is—

(a) on the premises of the school, or

(b) elsewhere at a time when, as a member of its staff, he has lawful control or charge of the pupil concerned;

but it does not authorise anything to be done in relation to a pupil which constitutes the giving of corporal punishment within the meaning of section 548.

(3) Subsection (1) shall not be taken to prevent any person from relying on any defence available to him otherwise than by virtue of this section.

(4) In this section—

"member of the staff", in relation to a school, means any teacher who works at the school and any other person who, with the authority of the head teacher, has lawful control or charge of pupils at the school;

"offence" includes anything that would be an offence but for the operation of any presumption that a person under a particular age is incapable of committing an offence.

[Education Act 1996, s 550A as inserted by the Education Act 1997, s 4.]

8–7844C   550B. Detention outside school hours lawful despite absence of parental consent.

(1) Where a pupil to whom this section applies is required on disciplinary grounds to spend a period of time in detention at his school after the end of any school session, his detention shall not be rendered unlawful by virtue of the absence of his parent's consent to it if the conditions set out in subsection (3) are satisfied.

(2) This section applies to any pupil who has not attained the age of 18 and is attending—

(a) a school maintained by a local education authority;

(b) *repealed* or

(c) a city technology college, city college for the technology of the arts or Academy.

(3) The conditions referred to in subsection (1) are as follows—

(*a*) the head teacher of the school must have previously determined, and have—

(i) made generally known within the school, and

(ii) taken steps to bring to the attention of the parent of every person who is for the time being a registered pupil there,

that the detention of pupils after the end of a school session is one of the measures that may be taken with a view to regulating the conduct of pupils;

(*b*) the detention must be imposed by the head teacher or by another teacher at the school specifically or generally authorised by him for the purpose;

(*c*) the detention must be reasonable in all the circumstances; and

(*d*) the pupil's parent must have been given at least 24 hours' notice in writing that the detention was due to take place.

(4) In determining for the purposes of subsection (3)(*c*) whether a pupil's detention is reasonable, the following matters in particular shall be taken into account—

(*a*) whether the detention constitutes a proportionate punishment in the circumstances of the case; and

(*b*) any special circumstances relevant to its imposition on the pupil which are known to the person imposing it (or of which he ought reasonably to be aware) including in particular—

(i) the pupil's age,

(ii) any special educational needs he may have,

(iii) any religious requirements affecting him, and

(iv) where arrangements have to be made for him to travel from the school to his home, whether suitable alternative arrangements can reasonably be made by his parent.

(5) Section 572, which provides for the methods by which notices may be served under this Act, does not preclude a notice from being given to a pupil's parent under this section by any other effective method.

[Education Act 1996, s 550B as inserted by the Education Act 1997, s 5 and amended by the School Standards and Framework Act 1998, Sch 30, the Learning and Skills Act 2000, Sch 9 and the Education Act 2002, Sch 7.]

Chapter IV[1]

Employment of Children and Young Persons

8–7845 558. Meaning of "child" for purposes of enactments relating to employment of children or young persons. For the purposes of any enactment relating to the prohibition or regulation of the employment of children or young persons[2], any person who is not over compulsory school age shall be deemed to be a child within the meaning of that enactment.

[Education Act 1996, s 558.]

1. See the Employment of Women, Young Persons and Children Act 1920, title Health and Safety, post; the Children and Young Persons Act 1933, s 18, in Part V: Youth Courts, ante, and the Factories Act 1961, ss 20 and 21, title Health and Safety, post.

2. "Young person" means a person over compulsory school age but under the age of 18, see s 579(1), post.

8–7846 559. Power of local education authorities to prohibit or restrict employment of children. (1) If it appears to a local education authority that a child[1] who is a registered pupil at a community, foundation, voluntary or special school is being employed in such a manner as to be prejudicial to his health, or otherwise to render him unfit to obtain the full benefit of the education provided for him, the authority may serve a notice[2] in writing on the employer—

(*a*) prohibiting him from employing the child, or

(*b*) imposing such restrictions upon his employment of the child as appear to them to be expedient in the interests of the child.

(2) A local education authority may serve a notice in writing on the parent[3] or employer of a child who is a registered pupil at a community, foundation, voluntary or special school requiring the parent or employer to provide the authority, within such period as may be specified in the notice, with such information as appears to the authority to be necessary for the purpose of enabling them to ascertain whether the child is being employed in such a manner as to render him unfit to obtain the full benefit of the education provided for him.

(3) A person who—

(*a*) employs[4] a child in contravention of any prohibition or restriction imposed under subsection (1), or

(*b*) fails to comply with the requirements of a notice served under subsection (2),

shall be guilty of an offence.

(4) A person guilty of an offence under this section shall be liable on summary conviction—

(*a*) to a fine not exceeding **level 1** on the standard scale, or (*b*)   to imprisonment for a term not exceeding **one month***,

or both.

(5) Section 28(1) and (3) of the Children and Young Persons Act 1933[5] (powers of entry for the enforcement of the provisions of Part II of that Act as to the employment of children) shall apply with respect to the provisions of any notice served under this section as they apply with respect to the provisions of Part II of that Act.

[Education Act 1996, s 559 as amended by the School Standards Framework Act 1998, Sch 30.]

---

*"51 weeks" substituted by the Criminal Justice Act 2003, Sch 25, from a date to be appointed.

1.   "Child" means a person who is not over compulsory school age, s 579(1), post.
2.   As to service, see s 572, post
3.   As to "parent", see s 576, post.
4.   See *Morgan v Parr* [1921] 2 KB 379, 85 JP 165, and *Sweet v Williams* (1922) 87 JP 51, where it was held that "employ" applies not merely to the relationship of master and servant, but also to that of principal and agent.
5.   see PART V: YOUTH COURTS, ante.

8–7847   560. Work experience in last year of compulsory schooling. (1) The enactments relating to the prohibition or regulation of the employment of children[1] shall not apply to the employment of a child in his last year of compulsory schooling if the employment is in pursuance of arrangements made or approved—

(*a*)   by the local education authority, or
(*b*)   in the case of a child at a grant-maintained school, by the governing body of the school

with a view to providing him with work experience as a part of his education.

(2)[2] For the purposes of subsection (1) a child shall be taken to be in his last year of compulsory schooling from the beginning of the term at his school which precedes the beginning of the school year in which he would cease to be of compulsory school age.

(3) Subsection (1) shall not be taken to permit the employment of a person in any way contrary to—

(*a*)   an enactment which in terms applies to persons of less than, or not over, a specified age expressed as a number of years, or
(*b*)   section 1(2) of the Employment of Women, Young Persons and Children Act 1920 or section 55(1) of the Merchant Shipping Act 1995 (which prohibit the employment of children in ships).

(4) No arrangements shall be made under subsection (1) for a child to be employed in any way which would be contrary to an enactment prohibiting or regulating the employment of young persons if he were a young person (within the meaning of the enactment) and not a child.

(5) Where a child is employed in pursuance of arrangements made under subsection (1), so much of any enactment as—

(*a*)   regulates the employment of young persons (whether by excluding them from any description of work, prescribing the conditions under which they may be permitted to do it or in any other way), and
(*b*)   would apply in relation to him if he were of an age to be treated as a young person for the purposes of that enactment,

shall apply in relation to him, in and in respect of the employment arranged for him, in all respects as if he were of an age to be so treated.

(6) Nothing in section 495 or 496 applies in relation to any power conferred on a local education authority or the governing body of a grant-maintained school by subsection (1).

(7) In this section "enactment" includes any byelaw, regulation or other provision having effect under an enactment.

[Education Act 1996, s 560.]

---

1.   See the Employment of Women, Young Persons and Children Act 1920, title HEALTH AND SAFETY, post; the Children and Young Persons Act 1933, s 18, in PART V: YOUTH COURTS, ante, and the Factories Act 1961, ss 20 and 21, title HEALTH AND SAFETY, post.
2.   Until the date appointed under s 583(3) for the coming into force of s 8, sub-s (2) shall have effect as if "by virtue of para 1 of Sch 40 he would be entitled to leave school" were substituted for "he would cease to be of compulsory school age". (See also s 8, ante.)

CHAPTER V[1]

8–7848   561. *Act not to apply to persons in service of the Crown.*

---

1.   Chapter V comprises ss 561 and 562.

8–7849   562. *Act not to apply to persons detained under order of a court.*

CHAPTER VI[1]
GENERAL

Documents and evidence

8–7850   564. Certificates of birth and registrars' returns.   (1) Where the age of any person is required to be proved for the purposes of this Act or of any enactment relating to the employment of children or young persons, the registrar having the custody of the register of births and deaths containing the entry relating to the birth of that person shall—

(a)   on being presented by any person ("the applicant") with a written requisition in such form and containing such particulars as may be determined by regulations, and

(b)   on payment of a fee of £3.50[2],

supply the applicant with a copy of the entry certified under his hand.

(2) A registrar shall, on being requested so to do, supply free of charge a form of requisition for the purposes of subsection (1).

(3) A registrar shall supply to a local education authority such particulars of the entries contained in any register of births and deaths in his custody, and in such form, as (subject to regulations) the authority may from time to time require.

(4) In this section—

"register of births and deaths" means a register of births and deaths kept under the Births and Deaths Registration Act 1953, and

"registrar" includes a registrar of births and deaths and a superintendent registrar.

[Education Act 1996, s 564.]

---

1. Chapter VI comprises ss 563–583.
2. A fee of £3.50 is now payable for the copy of an entry issued by a registrar, and £7.00 for the copy of an entry issued by a superintendent registrar (Registration of Births, Deaths and Marriages (Fees) Order 2002, SI 2002/3076 amended by SI 2005/1997).

8–7851   565. Evidence; presumption as to age.   (1) Where in any proceedings under this Act the person by whom the proceedings are brought—

(a)   alleges that any person whose age is material to the proceedings is under, of, or over, any age, and

(b)   satisfies the court that, having used all reasonable diligence to obtain evidence as to the age of that person, he has been unable to do so,

the court may, unless the contrary is proved[1], presume that person to be under, of, or (as the case may be) over, the age alleged.

(2) This section has effect subject to section 445(3).

[Education Act 1996, s 565.]

---

1. See *R v Carr-Briant* [1943] KB 607, [1943] 2 All ER 156, 107 JP 167.

8–7852   566. Evidence documents.   (1) In any legal proceedings, any of the following documents, namely—

(a)   a document purporting to be a document issued by a local education authority, and to be signed by the clerk of that authority or by the chief education officer of that authority* or by any other officer of the authority authorised to sign it,

(b)   a document purporting to be an extract from the minutes of the proceedings of the governing body of a maintained school, and to be signed by the chairman of the governing body or by their clerk,

(c)   a document purporting to be a certificate giving particulars of the attendance of a child or young person at a school, and to be signed by the head teacher of the school, and

(d)   a document purporting to be a certificate issued by a medical officer of a local education authority, and to be signed by such an officer,

shall be received in evidence and shall be treated, without further proof, as the document which it purports to be and as having been signed by the person by whom it purports to have been signed, unless the contrary is proved.

(2) In any legal proceedings, any such extract or certificate as is mentioned in subsection (1)(b), (c) or (d) shall be evidence of the matters stated in it.

(3) Where a child of compulsory school age is required to attend at—

(a)   any place at which education is provided for him in the circumstances mentioned in subsection (1) of section 444ZA, or

(b)   any place in the circumstances mentioned in subsection (2) of that section,

subsection (1)(c) has effect as if the place in question were a school and the person in charge of the provision of education or training at that place were its head teacher (and subsection (2) has effect accordingly).

[Education Act 1996, s 566 as amended by the School Standards and Framework Act 1998, Sch 30 and the Education Act 2005, Sch 18.]

---

*Words substituted by the Children Act 2004, Sch 2 from a date to be appointed.

8–7853 572. Service of notices and other documents. Any order, notice or other document required or authorised by this Act to be served on, or given to, any person may be served or given—

   (*a*) by delivering it to that person, or
   (*b*) by leaving it at his usual or last known place of residence, or
   (*c*) by sending it in a prepaid letter addressed to him at that place[1].

[Education Act 1996, s 572, as amended by the Anti-social Behaviour Act 2003, s 23.]

---

   1. See Magistrates' Courts Rules 1981, r 99, also the Criminal Procedure Rules 2005, Part 4, in PART I: MAGISTRATES' COURTS, PROCEDURE, ante.

8–7854 576. Meaning of "parent". (1) In this Act, unless the context otherwise requires, "parent," in relation to a child or young person, includes any person—

   (*a*) who is not a parent of his but who has parental responsibility for him, or
   (*b*) who has care of him,

except that in section 499(8) it only includes such a person if he is an individual.
   (2) (*Repealed*).
   (3) In subsection (1) "parental responsibility" has the same meaning as in the Children Act 1989.
   (4) In determining for the purposes of subsection (1) whether an individual has care of a child or young person, any absence of the child or young person at a hospital or boarding school and any other temporary absence shall be disregarded.

[Education Act 1996, s 576 as amended by the School Standards and Framework Act 1998, Sch 30.]

8–7855 579. General interpretation. (1) In this Act, unless the context otherwise requires—

   "assist", in relation to any school, institution or university, shall be construed in accordance with subsections (5) to (7) below;
   "boarder" includes a pupil who boards during the week but not at weekends;
   "child" means a person who is not over compulsory school age;
   "clothing" includes footwear;
   "financial year" means a period of twelve months ending with 31st March;
   "functions" includes powers and duties;
   "head teacher" includes acting head teacher;
   "land" includes buildings and other structures, land covered with water, and any interest in land;
   "local authority" means a county council, a county borough council, a district council, a London borough council or the Common Council of the City of London;
   "maintained nursery school" has the meaning given by section 22(9) of the School Standards and Framework Act 1998;
   "medical officer", in relation to a local education authority, means a registered medical practitioner who is employed or engaged (whether regularly or for the purposes of any particular case) by the authority or whose services are made available to the authority by the Secretary of State;
   "the National Curriculum" (without more) means—

   (*a*) in relation to England, the National Curriculum for England, and
   (*b*) in relation to Wales, the National Curriculum for Wales;

   "premises", in relation to a school, includes any detached playing fields but, except where otherwise expressly provided, does not include a teacher's dwelling-house;
   "prescribed" means prescribed by regulations;
   "proprietor", in relation to a school, means the person or body of persons responsible for the management of the school (so that, in relation to a community, foundation or voluntary or community or foundation special school, or a maintained nursery school, it means the governing body);
   "regulations" means regulations made by the Secretary of State;
   "sex education" includes education about—

   (*a*) Acquired Immune Deficiency Syndrome and Human Immunodeficiency Virus, and
   (*b*) any other sexually transmitted disease;

   "school buildings", in relation to a school, means any building or part of a building forming part of the school premises, other than a building or part required only—

   (*a*) as a caretaker's dwelling,
   (*b*) for use in connection with playing fields,
   (*c*) to afford facilities for enabling the Secretary of State facilities to carry out his functions under section 5(1) or (1A) of, and Schedule 1 to, the National Health Service Act 1977 (which relate to the provision of medical and dental services for pupils), or

(*d*)　to afford facilities for providing milk, meals or other refreshments for pupils in attendance at the school;

"school day", in relation to a school, means any day on which at that school there is a school session;

"school year", in relation to a school, means the period beginning with the first school term to begin after July and ending with the beginning of the first such term to begin after the following July;

"trust deed" includes any instrument (other than an instrument of government) regulating the constitution of the school's governing body or the maintenance, management or conduct of the school;

"young person" means a person over compulsory school age but under the age of 18.

(2)　References in this Act to an interest in land include any easement, right or charge in, to or over land.

(3)　*Repealed.*

(4)–(7)　*Not reproduced.*

[Education Act 1996, s 579 as amended by the Education Act 1997, Sch 7, the School Standards and Framework Act 1998, Sch 30, the Education Act 2002, s 215, SI 2003/2045 (E) and SI 2005/2913 (W).]

1.　Only those definitions relevant to this work are reproduced.

8–7856　**580.**　*Index*

8–7857　**581.**　*Application to Isles of Scilly.*

8–7858　**582.**　*Consequential amendments, repeals, transitional provisions etc.*

8–7859　**583.**　*Short title, commencement and extent.*

Section 323.

SCHEDULE 26

Making of assessments under section 323

(*Amended by the Special educational Needs and Disability Act 2001, s 42.*)

Introductory

8–7860　**1.**　In this Schedule, "assessment" means an assessment of a child's educational needs under section 323.

Medical and other advice

2.　(1)　Regulations shall make provision as to the advice which a local education authority are to seek in making assessments.

(2)　Without prejudice to the generality of sub-paragraph (1), the regulations shall require the authority, except in such circumstances as may be prescribed, to seek medical, psychological and educational advice and such other advice as may be prescribed.

Manner, and timing, of assessments, etc.

3.　(1)　Regulations may make provision—

(*a*)　as to the manner in which assessments are to be conducted,

(*b*)　requiring the local education authority, where, after conducting an assessment under section 323 of the educational needs of a child for whom a statement is maintained under section 324, they determine not to amend the statement, to serve on the parent of the child a notice giving the prescribed information, and

(*c*)　in connection with such other matters relating to the making of assessments as the Secretary of State considers appropriate.

(2)　Sub-paragraph (1)(*b*) does not apply to a determination made following the service of notice under paragraph 2A of Schedule 27 (amendment of statement by LEA) of a proposal to amend the statement.

(3)　Regulations may provide—

(*a*)　that where a local education authority are under a duty under section 323, 329 or 329A to serve any notice, the duty must be performed within the prescribed period,

(*b*)　that where a local education authority have served a notice under section 323(1) or 329A(3) on a child's parent, they must decide within the prescribed period whether or not to make an assessment of the child's educational needs,

(*c*)　that where a request has been made to a local education authority under section 329(1), they must decide within the prescribed period whether or not to comply with the request, and

(*d*)　that where a local education authority are under a duty to make an assessment, the duty must be performed within the prescribed period.

(4)　Provision made under sub-paragraph (3)—

(*a*)　may be subject to prescribed exceptions, and

(*b*)　does not relieve the authority of the duty to serve a notice, or make a decision or assessment, which has not been served or made within the prescribed period.

Attendance at examinations

4. (1) Where a local education authority are considering whether to make an assessment, they may serve a notice on the parent of the child concerned requiring the child's attendance for examination in accordance with the provisions of the notice.

(2) The parent of a child examined under this paragraph may be present at the examination if he so desires.

(3) A notice under this paragraph shall—

(*a*) state the purpose of the examination,
(*b*) state the time and place at which the examination will be held,
(*c*) name an officer of the authority from whom further information may be obtained,
(*d*) inform the parent that he may submit such information to the authority as he may wish, and
(*e*) inform the parent of his right to be present at the examination.

Offence

5. (1) Any parent who fails without reasonable excuse to comply with any requirements of a notice served on him under paragraph 4 above commits an offence if the notice relates to a child who is not over compulsory school age at the time stated in it as the time for holding the examination.

(2) A person guilty of an offence under this paragraph is liable on summary conviction to a fine not exceeding **level 2** on the standard scale.

School Inspections Act 1996

(1996 c 57)

PART I
SCHOOL INSPECTIONS

CHAPTER I
SCHOOL INSPECTORS AND INSPECTIONS CARRIED OUT BY THEM

Her Majesty's Inspectorate for England

8–7861 **1. Her Majesty's Inspectorate of Schools in England.** *Repealed.*

8–7862 **2.** *Repealed.*

8–7863 **3. Power of Chief Inspector for England to arrange for inspections.** *Repealed.*

Registered inspectors

8–7864 **7. Registration of inspectors.** (1) No person shall conduct an inspection of any school in England under section 10(1) unless he is registered as an inspector in a register kept by the Chief Inspector for England for the purposes of this Part.

(2) No person shall conduct an inspection of any school in Wales under section 10(2) unless he is registered as an inspector in a register kept by the Chief Inspector for Wales for the purposes of this Part.

(3)–(9) Supplementary provision with respect to registration.

(10) Subsections (1) and (2) have effect subject to section 12.★

[School Inspections Act 1996, s 7.]

★Repealed by the Education Act 2005, Sch 19, in England from 1 September 2005, in Wales from a date to be appointed.

Inspections by registered inspectors

8–7865 **10. Inspection of certain schools by registered inspectors.** (1) It shall be the duty of the Chief Inspector for England to secure that every school in England to which this section applies is inspected, at such intervals as may be prescribed[1], by an inspector registered under section 7(1).

(2) It shall be the duty of the Chief Inspector for Wales to secure that every school in Wales to which this section applies is inspected, at such intervals as may be prescribed, by an inspector registered under section 7(2).

(3) Subject to subsection (4A), the schools to which this section applies are—

(*a*) community, foundation and voluntary schools;
(*b*) *(repealed)*.
(*c*) community and foundation special schools;
(*d*) special schools which are not community or foundation special schools but are for the time being approved by the Secretary of State under section 342 of the Education Act 1996 (approval of special schools);
(*e*) *(repealed)*.
(*f*) city technology colleges;

(g)   city colleges for the technology of the arts;
(gg) Acadamies; and
(h)   maintained nursery schools.

(4)   *(Repealed)*.
(4A)   This section does not apply to any school—

(a)   which is a closing school (as defined by subsection (4B)), and
(b)   in respect of which the Chief Inspector has decided, having regard to the date on which the closure is to take effect, that no useful purpose would be served by the school being inspected under this section.

(4B)   In subsection (4A) a "closing school" means—

(a)   a community, foundation or voluntary or community or foundation special school or maintained nursery school in respect of which proposals to discontinue the school have been approved, adopted or determined under any enactment;*
(b)   a foundation or voluntary school in respect of which the governing body have given notice of discontinuance under section 30 of that Act;
(c)   a community, foundation or voluntary or community or foundation special school in respect of which the Secretary of State has given a direction to discontinue the school under section 19 or 32 of that Act;
(d)   a city technology college or city college for the technology of the arts or city academy in respect of which notice of termination of an agreement made under section 482 of the Education Act 1996 has been given;
(e)   a special school which is not a community or foundation special school but which is for the time being approved by the Secretary of State under section 342 of the Education Act 1996 and which the proprietor has decided to close;
(f)   *(repealed)*.

(5)   It shall be the general duty of any registered inspector conducting an inspection under this section to report on—

(a)   the quality of the education provided by the school;
(b)   the educational standards achieved in the school;
(c)   the quality of the leadership in and management of the school, including whether the financial resources made available to the school are managed efficiently; and
(d)   the spiritual, moral, social and cultural development of pupils at the school.

(6)   In prescribing[1] the intervals mentioned in subsections (1) and (2) the Secretary of State may make provision as to the period within which the first inspection of a school under this section is to begin.
(7)   Subsections (1) and (2) have effect subject to section 12.
(8)   An inspection which is required under this section shall not extend to—

(a)   denominational education, or
(aa) education which is brought within the remit of Her Majesty's Chief Inspector of Education and Training in Wales by Part IV of the Learning and Skills Act 2000, or
(b)   the content of collective worship which falls to be inspected under section 23.

(9)   Schedule 3 makes further provision with respect to inspections under this section.**
[School Inspections Act 1996, s 10 as amended by the School Standards and Framework Act 1998, Sch 30, the Learning and Skills Act 2000, Sch 9 and the Education Act 2002, s 65(3) and Schs 16, 21 and 22.]

---

*Reproduced as in force in England (date in force for Wales to be appointed).
**Repealed by the Education Act 2005, Sch 19, in England from 1 September 2005, in Wales from a date to be appointed.
1.   The Education (Schools Inspection) (No 2) Regulations 1993, SI 1993/1986, have been made.

Construction

8–7866   46. Interpretation[1]. (1)   In this Act—

"Chief Inspector" (without more) shall be read—

     (a)   in relation to any school in England or registration under section 7(1), as a reference to the Chief Inspector for England; and
     (b)   in relation to any school in Wales or registration under section 7(2), as a reference to the Chief Inspector for Wales;

"Chief Inspector for England" means the person referred to in section 1(1);
"Chief Inspector for Wales" means the person referred to in section 4(1);
"Church in Wales school", "Church of England school" and "Roman Catholic Church school", and "appropriate diocesan authority" in each case, have the meaning given by section 142 of the School Standards and Framework Act 1998;

"delegated budget" has the same meaning as in section 49 of the School Standards and Framework Act 1998; "denominational education" has the meaning given in section 23(4);

"member of the Inspectorate" means the Chief Inspector, any of Her Majesty's Inspectors of Schools in England or, as the case may be, Wales and any additional inspector authorised under paragraph 2 of Schedule 1;

"prescribed" means prescribed by regulations;

"registered inspector" means a person registered under section 7(1) or (2);

"regulations" means regulations made by the Secretary of State under this Act;

(2) References in this Act to special measures being, or not being, required to be taken in relation to a school shall be construed in accordance with section 13(9).

(3) For the purposes of this Act any reference to a condition imposed under section 7(5)(c) includes a reference to a condition imposed under section 8(3).

(4) This Act and the Education Act 1996 shall be construed as one.*

[School Inspections Act 1996, s 46 as amended by the School Standards and Framework Act 1998, Sch 30.]

---

*Repealed by the Education Act 2005, Sch 19, in England from 1 September 2005, in Wales from a date to be appointed.**

1. Only those definitions which are relevant to the provisions of the Act contained in this work are printed here.

8–7867 47. *Consequential amendments, repeals and transitional provisions.**

---

*Repealed by the Education Act 2005, Sch 19, in England from 1 September 2005, in Wales from a date to be appointed.**

8–7868 48. *Short title, commencement, extent etc.**

---

*Repealed by the Education Act 2005, Sch 19, in England from 1 September 2005, in Wales from a date to be appointed.**

Section 10. SCHEDULE 3

(As amended by the School Standards and Framework Act 1998, Schs 28 and 30 and the Education Act 2002, Schs 16 and 21, 22.)

Inspections Under Section 10

8–7869 1. In this Schedule—

"appropriate authority" means—

  (a) in relation to a community, foundation or voluntary or community or foundation special school or a maintained nursery school, the school's governing body or, if the school does not have a delegated budget within the meaning of section 49 of the School Standards and Framework Act 1998, the local education authority;

  (b) in relation to a maintained nursery school, the local education authority;

  (c) in the case of a school falling within paragraph (d), (f) or (g) of section 10(3), the proprietor of the school;]

"inspection" means an inspection under section 10.

Selection of registered inspectors

2. (1) Before entering into any arrangement for an inspection, the Chief Inspector shall invite tenders from at least two persons who can reasonably be expected to tender for the proposed inspection and to do so at arm's length from each other, and each of whom is either—

  (a) a registered inspector, or

  (b) a person who the Chief Inspector is satisfied would, if his tender were successful, arrange with a registered inspector for the inspection to be carried out.

(2) Before an inspection takes place the Chief Inspector shall consult the appropriate authority about the inspection.

Inspection teams

3. (1) Every inspection shall be conducted by a registered inspector with the assistance of a team (an "inspection team"); and no person shall act as a member of an inspection team unless—

  (a) he is enrolled in the list kept by the Chief Inspector under paragraph 3A; or

  (b) he is a member of the Inspectorate and (if he is not the Chief Inspector) is authorised so to act by the Chief Inspector.

((2) It shall be the duty of the registered inspector to ensure that—

(a)   at least one member of the inspection team is a person—

    (i)   without personal experience in the management of any school or the provision of education in any school (otherwise than as a governor or in any other voluntary capacity); and

    (ii)   whose primary function on the team is not that of providing financial or business expertise; and

(b)   no member of the inspection team falls within a category of person prescribed for the purposes of this sub-paragraph.

(3)   Otherwise, the composition of the inspection team shall be determined by the registered inspector, subject to his complying with any condition imposed under section 7(5)(c).

(4)   Any experience of a kind mentioned in sub-paragraph (2)(a) which it is reasonable to regard as insignificant, having regard to the purposes of sub-paragraph (2), may be ignored by the registered inspector.

(5)   It shall be the duty of the registered inspector to ensure that no person takes any part in an inspection if he has, or has at any time had, any connection with—

(a)   the school in question,

(b)   any person who is employed at the school,

(c)   any person who is a member of the school's governing body, or

(d)   the proprietor of the school,

of a kind which might reasonably be taken to raise doubts about his ability to act impartially in relation to that school.

Enrolment of persons to act as team members

3A. (1)   The Chief Inspector shall keep a list of persons who may act as members of an inspection team by virtue of paragraph 3(1)(a) ("the list").

(2)   The Chief Inspector shall not enrol any person in the list unless, having regard to any conditions that he proposes to impose under section 7(5)(c) (as it applies in accordance with sub-paragraph (4) below), it appears to him that that person—

(a)   is a fit and proper person for carrying out an inspection, and

(b)   will be capable of assisting in an inspection competently and effectively.

(3)   An application for enrolment in the list shall (except in such circumstances as may be prescribed) be accompanied by the prescribed fee.

(4)   Subsections (5) to (9) of section 7 shall apply in relation to the enrolment of a person in the list and to acting as a member of an inspection team as they apply in relation to the registration of a person under subsection (1) or (2) of that section and to acting as a registered inspector.

(5)   Sections 8 and 9 and Schedule 2 shall (with any necessary modifications) apply in relation to enrolment in the list and to a person so enrolled as they apply in relation to registration under section 7(1) or (2) and to a person so registered.

(6)   In its application to an enrolled person in accordance with subparagraph (5) above, section 8 shall have effect as if the conditions mentioned in subsection (2) of that section were that—

(a)   that person is no longer a fit and proper person to act as a member of an inspection team;

(b)   he is no longer capable of assisting in an inspection competently and effectively;

(c)   there has been a significant failure on his part to comply with any condition imposed under section 7(5)(c) (as it applies in accordance with sub-paragraph (4) above).

(7)   Without prejudice to the generality of paragraph 2(1) of Schedule 2, regulations under that provision may provide that, where a person s appealing simultaneously—

(a)   against a decision of the Chief Inspector relating to that person's registration, and

(b)   against a decision of the Chief Inspector relating to that person's enrolment in the list,

both appeals are to be heard at the same time.

4–5. *Training for inspections.*

6. *Meeting with parents.*

Rights of entry etc

7.   A registered inspector conducting an inspection, and the members of his inspection team, shall have at all reasonable times—

(a)   a right of entry to the premises of the school concerned; and

(b)   a right to inspect, and take copies of, any records kept by the school, and any other documents containing information relating to the school, which he requires for the purposes of the inspection.

Offence of obstructing inspector or inspection team

8. (1)   It shall be an offence wilfully to obstruct—

(a)   a registered inspector, or

(b)   a member of an inspection team,

in the exercise of his functions in relation to the inspection of a school.

(2) Any person guilty of an offence under sub-paragraph (1) shall be liable on summary conviction to a fine not exceeding **level four** on the standard scale.*

---

*Repealed by the Education Act 2005, Sch 19, in England from 1 September 2005, in Wales from a date to be appointed.**

Learning and Skills Act 2000[1]

(2000 c 21)

PART III
INSPECTIONS IN ENGLAND

CHAPTER I
THE ADULT LEARNING INSPECTORATE

The Inspectorate

8–7870   52. The Inspectorate.   (1) There shall be a body corporate called the Adult Learning Inspectorate.

(2) The Inspectorate is to consist of 9 members appointed by the Secretary of State.

(3) The Secretary of State must appoint one of the members as chairman and another of the members as the Inspectorate's chief officer.

(4) The chief officer is to be known as the Chief Inspector of Adult Learning.

(5) In appointing any member, the Secretary of State must have regard to the desirability of appointing a person who has experience relevant to the Inspectorate's functions.

(6) The Secretary of State may make grants to the Inspectorate of such amounts and subject to such conditions as he thinks fit.

(7) The conditions may—

(a)   set the Inspectorate's budget for any of its financial years;

(b)   require it to use the grants for specified purposes;

(c)   enable the Secretary of State to require the repayment, in whole or in part, of sums paid by him if any condition imposed is not complied with;

(d)   require the payment of interest in respect of any period during which a sum due to the Secretary of State in accordance with any of the conditions remains unpaid.

(8) Schedule 6 contains provisions about the Inspectorate.
[Learning and Skills Act 2000, s 52.]

---

1. Commencement of this Act was completed by the Learning and Skills Act 2000 (Commencement Number 4) Order 2002, SI 2002/279.

8–7871   53. The Inspectorate's remit.   (1) The Inspectorate's remit is—

(a)   further education for persons aged 19 or over which is wholly or partly funded by the Learning and Skills Council for England;

(b)   training for persons aged 16 or over so far as it takes place wholly or partly at the premises of an employer and is wholly or partly funded by the Council;

(c)   further education funded by a local education authority in England for persons aged 19 or over;

(d)   training for persons aged 16 or over which is funded by the Secretary of State under section 2 of the Employment and Training Act 1973;

(e)   such other education or training as may be prescribed by regulations made by the Secretary of State.

(2) Regulations made under subsection (1)(e) may include within the Inspectorate's remit training of or for teachers, lecturers, trainers or other persons engaged in the provision of education or training which otherwise falls within the Inspectorate's remit.

(3) "Further education" has the same meaning as it has in the Education Act 1996.
[Learning and Skills Act 2000, s 53.]

Functions of the Inspectorate and the Chief Inspector

8–7872   54. Functions of the Inspectorate and Chief Inspector.   (1) The Inspectorate must keep the Secretary of State informed about—

(a)   the quality of the education and training within its remit;

(b)   the standards achieved by those receiving that education and training; and

(c)   whether the financial resources made available to those providing that education and training are managed efficiently and used in a way which provides value for money.

(2) When asked to do so by the Secretary of State, the Inspectorate must give the Secretary of State advice on such matters relating to education or training within its remit as he may specify.

(3) When asked to do so by the Secretary of State, the Chief Inspector of Adult Learning must conduct inspections of such education or training, or such class of education or training, within the Inspectorate's remit, at such intervals, as the Secretary of State may specify.

(4) The Inspectorate is to have such other functions in connection with education and training within its remit as the Secretary of State may specify.

(5) The Chief Inspector is to have such other functions in connection with education and training within the Inspectorate's remit as the Secretary of State may specify.

(6) The functions specified under subsection (4) or (5) may include functions with respect to training of or for teachers, lecturers, trainers or other persons engaged in the provision of education or training which falls within the Inspectorate's remit.

(7) In exercising their functions, the Inspectorate and the Chief Inspector must have regard to such aspects of government policy as the Secretary of State may specify.
[Learning and Skills Act 2000, s 54.]

8–7873   55. Inspections under section 54.   (1) When an inspection asked for under section 54(3) has been completed, the Chief Inspector of Adult Learning must make a written report on it if asked to do so by the Secretary of State.

(2) The report—

(a) must state whether the Chief Inspector considers the education or training inspected to be of a quality adequate to meet the reasonable needs of those receiving it; and

(b) may deal with such other matters as he considers relevant.

(3) The Chief Inspector must send copies of the report to—

(a) the Secretary of State;

(b) the Learning and Skills Council for England;

(c) any local education authority providing funds for the education or training inspected; and

(d) the provider of the inspected education or training.

(4) Copies may also be sent to such other persons as the Chief Inspector considers appropriate.

(5) The Chief Inspector must arrange for the report to be published in such manner as he considers appropriate.
[Learning and Skills Act 2000, s 55.]

8–7874   56. General powers.   (1) The Inspectorate may give advice to the Secretary of State on any matter relating to education or training within its remit.

(2) The Inspectorate may inspect, and report on, any education or training within its remit.

(3) The Inspectorate may inspect any education or training—

(a) which is not within its remit, but

(b) which would be if it were funded in one of the ways mentioned in section 53,

if asked to do so by the provider of the education or training.

(4) The Inspectorate may charge for the cost of an inspection conducted under subsection (3).

(5) The Inspectorate must send copies of a report of an inspection conducted under this section otherwise than as a result of a request under subsection (3) to—

(a) the Secretary of State;

(b) the Learning and Skills Council for England;

(c) any local education authority providing funds for the education or training inspected; and

(d) the provider of the inspected education or training.

(6) Copies may also be sent to such other persons as the Inspectorate considers appropriate.

(7) The Inspectorate must arrange for the report to be published in such manner as it considers appropriate.

(8) The Inspectorate may arrange for a report of an inspection carried out as a result of a request under subsection (3) to be published.
[Learning and Skills Act 2000, s 56.]

8–7875   57. Right of entry and offences.   (1) This section applies to an inspection conducted under this Chapter other than one conducted as a result of a request under section 56(3).

(2) An inspector taking part in the inspection has, at all reasonable times—

(a) a right of entry to premises on which the education or training being inspected is provided;

(b) a right of entry to premises of the person providing that education or training used in connection with that provision;

(c) a right to inspect, and take copies of, any records kept by that person, and any other documents containing information relating to the education or training, which the inspector requires for the purposes of the inspection.

(3) In respect of education or training provided by an employer in the workplace, the right of

entry conferred by subsection (2) may be exercised only if the employer has been given reasonable notice in writing.

(4) The right to inspect records conferred by subsection (2)(*c*) includes the right to have access to, and to inspect and check the operation of, any computer and any associated apparatus or material which is or has been in use in connection with the records in question.

(5) That right also includes the right to require—

(*a*) the person by whom or on whose behalf the computer is or has been so used, or

(*b*) any person having charge of, or otherwise concerned with the operation of, the computer, apparatus or material,

to afford the Inspectorate or any inspector such assistance as he may reasonably require.

(6) It is an offence wilfully to obstruct any person exercising functions in relation to an inspection.

(7) A person guilty of such an offence is liable on summary conviction to a fine not exceeding level 4 on the standard scale.

(8) "Inspector", in relation to an inspection, means an employee of the Inspectorate taking part in the inspection or any person appointed by the Inspectorate to assist with the inspection and includes the Chief Inspector of Adult Learning where the inspection is being conducted by him.
[Learning and Skills Act 2000, s 57.]

8–7876 **58.** *Action plans*

8–7877 **59.** *Annual report*

CHAPTER II
HER MAJESTY'S CHIEF INSPECTOR OF SCHOOLS IN ENGLAND

The Chief Inspector's extended remit

8–7878 **60. The extended remit.** (1) The following kinds of education and training are brought within the remit of Her Majesty's Chief Inspector of Schools in England by this Chapter—

(*a*) secondary education provided in institutions which are in England and within the further education sector;

(*b*) further education provided in the further education sector which is suitable to the requirements of those aged 16 or over but under 19 and funded wholly or partly by the Learning and Skills Council for England;

(*c*) further education provided by local education authorities in England for persons aged under 19;

(*d*) such other education or training (which may, in particular, include training of or for teachers or lecturers) as may be prescribed by regulations made by the Secretary of State.

(2) "Secondary education" and "further education" have the same meaning as they have in the Education Act 1996.
[Learning and Skills Act 2000, s 60.]

Additional functions

8–7879 **61. Additional functions of the Chief Inspector.** (1) Her Majesty's Chief Inspector of Schools in England must keep the Secretary of State informed about—

(*a*) the quality of the education and training brought within the Chief Inspector's remit by this Chapter;

(*b*) the standards achieved by those receiving that education and training; and

(*c*) whether the financial resources made available to those providing it are managed efficiently and used so as to provide value for money.

(2) When asked to do so by the Secretary of State, the Chief Inspector must—

(*a*) give him advice on such matters, relating to education or training brought within the Chief Inspector's remit by this Chapter, as the Secretary of State may specify;

(*b*) inspect such education or training, or such class of education or training, within that remit as the Secretary of State may specify;

(*c*) report on the result of an inspection conducted under this section.

(3) The Chief Inspector is to have such other functions in connection with education and training brought within the Chief Inspector's remit by this Chapter, including functions with respect to the training of or for teachers or lecturers, as the Secretary of State may specify.
[Learning and Skills Act 2000, s 61.]

8–7880 **62. Inspection of further education institutions.** (1) Her Majesty's Chief Inspector of Schools in England must inspect all institutions within the further education sector other than those providing education or training falling wholly within the remit of the Adult Learning Inspectorate.

(2) Inspections are to be conducted at such intervals as may be specified by the Secretary of State.

(3) When the Chief Inspector has completed an inspection under this section he must make a written report.

(4) The report—

(a) must state whether the Chief Inspector considers the education or training inspected to be adequate to meet the reasonable needs of those receiving it; and

(b) may deal with such other matters as the Chief Inspector considers relevant.

(5) Copies of the report must be sent to—

(a) the Secretary of State;

(b) the Learning and Skills Council for England;

(c) the provider of the education or training inspected.

(6) Copies may also be sent to such other persons as the Chief Inspector considers appropriate.

(7) The Chief Inspector must arrange for the report to be published in such manner as he considers appropriate.

[Learning and Skills Act 2000, s 62.]

8–7881   63. Right of entry and offences.   (1) This section applies to an inspection conducted under section 61(2)(*b*), 62, 65 or 68(2).

(2) When conducting an inspection, Her Majesty's Chief Inspector of Schools in England has, at all reasonable times—

(a) a right of entry to premises on which the education or training being inspected is provided;

(b) a right of entry to premises of the provider of that education or training used in connection with that provision;

(c) a right to inspect, and take copies of, any records kept by that person, and any other documents containing information relating to the education or training, which the Chief Inspector requires for the purposes of the inspection.

(3) The right to inspect conferred by subsection (2)(*c*) includes the right to have access to, and to inspect and check the operation of, any computer and any associated apparatus or material which is or has been in use in connection with the records in question.

(4) That right also includes the right to require—

(a) the person by whom or on whose behalf the computer is or has been so used, or

(b) any person having charge of, or otherwise concerned with the operation of, the computer, apparatus or material,

to afford the Chief Inspector such assistance as he may reasonably require.

(5) It is an offence wilfully to obstruct the Chief Inspector in the exercise of functions in relation to an inspection.

(6) A person guilty of such an offence is liable on summary conviction to a fine not exceeding level 4 on the standard scale.

[Learning and Skills Act 2000, s 63.]

8–7882   64. *Action plans*

8–7883   65. *Area inspections*

8–7884   66. *Reports of area inspections*

8–7885   67. *Action plans following section 65 inspections*

8–7886   68. *Further powers of the chief inspector*

PART IV

INSPECTIONS IN WALES

New titles

8–7887   73. Inspectors of Education and Training in Wales.   (1) Her Majesty's Chief Inspector of Schools in Wales is renamed Her Majesty's Chief Inspector of Education and Training in Wales or Prif Arolygydd Ei Mawrhydi dros Addysg a Hyfforddiant yng Nghymru.

(2) Her Majesty's Inspectors of Schools in Wales are renamed Her Majesty's Inspectors of Education and Training in Wales or Arolgwyr Ei Mawrhydi dros Addysg a Hyfforddiant yng Nghymru.

(3) In any provision of, or made under, any enactment—

(a) for "Her Majesty's Chief Inspector of Schools in Wales" substitute "Her Majesty's Chief Inspector of Education and Training in Wales or Prif Arolygydd Ei Mawrhydi dros Addysg a Hyfforddiant yng Nghymru"; and (*b*) for "Her Majesty's Inspectors of Schools in Wales" substitute "Her Majesty's Inspectors of Education and Training in Wales or Arolgwyr Ei Mawrhydi dros Addysg a Hyfforddiant yng Nghymru".

[Learning and Skills Act 2000, s 73.]

8–7888   74. Some defined terms.   (1) In this Part—

"the National Assembly" means the National Assembly for Wales.

    (2) In this Part, any reference to the Chief Inspector for Wales is to be read as a reference to the person mentioned in section 73(1).

[Learning and Skills Act 2000, s 74 as amended by SI 2005/3238.]

Extended remit

8–7889   75. The extended remit of the Chief Inspector for Wales.   (1) The following kinds of education and training are brought within the remit of the Chief Inspector for Wales by this Part—

    (*a*) education or training for persons aged 16 or over where the provider of the education or training is given financial support by the National Assembly in the discharge of its functions under Part 2 or by a local education authority in Wales (either generally or for a specific purpose);

    (*b*) education or training for persons aged 16 or over where the National Assembly in the discharge of its functions under Part 2 is, or a local education authority in Wales are, contemplating giving the provider of the education financial support (either generally or for a specific purpose);

    (*c*) education or training provided for persons of compulsory school age in an institution in Wales which is within the further education sector;

    (*d*) further education provided by a school under section 80 of the School Standards and Framework Act 1998;

    (*e*) such other education or training in Wales as may be prescribed by regulations made by the National Assembly.

    (2) Neither paragraph (*a*) nor paragraph (*b*) of subsection (1) applies—

    (*a*) to education of a kind that may be inspected under the Schools Inspections Act 1996; or★

    (*b*) if the financial support mentioned in that paragraph is given for a specific purpose, to education or training at which that support is not directed.

[Learning and Skills Act 2000, s 75 as amended by SI 2005/3238.]

★Amended by the Education Act 2005, Sch 9 from a date to be appointed.

8–7890   76. *Additional functions of the Chief Inspector for Wales*

8–7891   77. *Inspections*

8–7892   78. *General powers*

8–7893   79. Right of entry and offences.   (1) When conducting an inspection under this Part, the Chief Inspector for Wales has, at all reasonable times—

    (*a*) a right of entry to premises on which the education or training being inspected is provided;

    (*b*) a right of entry to premises of the provider of that education or training which are used in connection with that provision;

    (*c*) a right to inspect, and take copies of, any records kept by that person, and any other documents containing information relating to the education or training, which the inspector requires for the purposes of the inspection.

    (2) In respect of education or training provided by an employer in the workplace, the right of entry conferred by subsection (1) may be exercised only if the employer has been given reasonable notice in writing.

    (3) The right to inspect records conferred by subsection (1)(*c*) includes the right to have access to, and to inspect and check the operation of, any computer and any associated apparatus or material which is or has been in use in connection with the records in question.

    (4) That right also includes the right to such assistance from—

    (*a*) the person by whom or on whose behalf the computer is or has been so used, or

    (*b*) any person having charge of, or otherwise concerned with the operation of, the computer, apparatus or material,

as the Chief Inspector for Wales may reasonably require.

    (5) It is an offence wilfully to obstruct the Chief Inspector for Wales in the exercise of functions in relation to an inspection under this Part.

(6) A person guilty of such an offence is liable on summary conviction to a fine not exceeding level 4 on the standard scale.
[Learning and Skills Act 2000, s 79.]

8–7894 80. Action plans. (1) This section applies if the Chief Inspector for Wales publishes a report of an inspection.

(2) But it does not apply to a report of an inspection conducted—

(*a*) as a result of a request under section 78(3); or
(*b*) under section 83.

(3) The provider of the education or training which is the subject of the report must prepare a written statement of the action which he proposes to take in the light of the report and the period within which he proposes to take it.

(4) The person making the statement must—

(*a*) publish it within such period, and in such manner, as may be prescribed by regulations[1] made by the National Assembly; and
(*b*) send copies of it to such persons as may be so prescribed.

[Learning and Skills Act 2000, s 80.]

_____

1. The Inspection of Education and Training (Wales) Regulations 2001, SI 2001/2501 have been made.

8–7895 82. Inspections of education and training provided under 1973 Act arrangements.
(1) The Chief Inspector for Wales may, at the request of the Secretary of State or the Adult Learning Inspectorate, inspect any education or training provided in Wales by the Secretary of State in accordance with arrangements made under section 2 of the Employment and Training Act 1973.

(2) A report of an inspection conducted under this section at the request of the Secretary of State must be given to the Secretary of State.

(3) The Secretary of State may arrange for the report to be published in such manner as he considers appropriate.

(4) A report of an inspection conducted under this section at the request of the Adult Learning Inspectorate must be given to that Inspectorate.

(5) The Adult Learning Inspectorate may arrange for the report to be published in such manner as it considers appropriate.

(6) The Chief Inspector for Wales must send a copy of any report under subsection (2) or (4) to the National Assembly.
[Learning and Skills Act 2000, s 82.]

8–7896 83. Area inspections. (1) If asked to do so by the National Assembly, the Chief Inspector for Wales must inspect—

(*a*) the quality and availability of a specified description of education or training, in a specified area in Wales, for persons who are aged 15 or over;
(*b*) the standards achieved by those receiving that education or training; and
(*c*) whether the financial resources made available to those providing that education and training are managed efficiently and used in a way which provides value for money.

(2) The Chief Inspector for Wales may, without being asked to, conduct such an inspection.

(3) If financial resources have been applied by the National Assembly or a local education authority in respect of education or training which is being inspected under this section, the inspection may extend to considering the manner in which those resources have been applied and whether they have been applied in a way which provides value for money.

(4) The education or training that may be made the subject of an area inspection is any education or training within the remit of the Chief Inspector for Wales (whether as a result of this Part or of any other enactment).

(5) A provider of education or training which is the subject of an area inspection must provide such information as the Chief Inspector for Wales may reasonably require in connection with the inspection.

(6) The National Assembly and any local education authority within the area which is the subject of an area inspection must provide such information as the Chief Inspector for Wales may reasonably require in connection with the inspection.

(7) The National Assembly may by regulations[1] make further provision with respect to the obligation to provide information imposed by this section.

(8) On completing an area inspection, the Chief Inspector for Wales must make a written report.

(9) Subsections (4), (5)(*a*) to (*c*) and (6) to (9) of section 77 apply to a report under this section as they apply to a report under that section.

(10) "Area inspection" means an inspection under this section.

(11) In subsection (1)(*a*) "persons who are aged 15" includes persons for whom education is

being provided at a school who will attain that age in the current school year: and for this purpose "school" and "school year" have the same meaning as in the Education Act 1996.

[Learning and Skills Act 2000, s 83, as amended by the Education Act 2002, s 178 and SI 2005/3238.]

---

1. The Inspection of Education and Training (Wales) Regulations 2001, SI 2001/2501 have been made.

8–7897 84. *Action plans following section 83 inspections*

8–7898 85. *Studies across Wales or of provision made outside Wales*

8–7899 86. *Annual reports*

8–7900 87. *Annual plan of the Chief Inspector for Wales*

8–7901 88. *Defamation*

Education Act 2002[1]

(2002 c 32)

---

1. This Act, which received the Royal Assent on 24 July 2002, is in 11 parts with 217 sections and 22 schedules. PART 1 introduces new legal frameworks, including powers to promote innovation. PART 2 deals with financial assistance and replaces a significant number of powers to fund education with a general one. PART 3 makes provision for the governance of maintained schools. PART 4 makes provision for intervention in schools with serious weaknesses or requiring special measures; it also extends the power of the Secretary of State (or the National Assembly of Wales) to intervene in weak local education authorities. PART 5 provides for the setting up of new schools and the alteration and discontinuance of existing schools. PARTS 6 and 7 deal with the curricula in England and Wales, respectively. PART 8 makes provision for teachers' pay and conditions. PART 9 deals with childcare and nursery education. PART 10 deals with independent schools. PART 11 deals with miscellaneous and general matters.

Most of the provisions of the Act are to be brought into force in accordance with commencement orders made under s 216. At the time of going to press the following commencement orders had been made: Education Act 2002 (Commencement No 1) Order 2002, SI 2002/2002, as amended by SI 2002/2018; Education Act 2002 (Commencement No 2 and Savings and Transitional Provisions) Order 2002, SI 2002/24391, as amended by SI 2003/606 (revoked), SI 2003/2992; Education Act 2002 (Commencement No 3 and Savings and Transitional Provisions) Order 2002, SI 2002/29522; Education Act 2002 (Commencement No 1) (Wales) Order 2002, SI 2002/31853; Education Act 2002 (Commencement No 4 and Transitional and Saving Provisions) Order 2003, SI 2003/1244; Education Act 2002 (Commencement No 5 and Transitional and Saving Provisions) Order 2003, SI 2003/11155; Education Act 2002 (Commencement No 6 and Transitional and Saving Provisions) Order 2003, SI 2003/16676; Education Act 2002 (Commencement No 2) (Wales) Order 2003, SI 2003/1718; Education Act 2002 (Commencement No 7 and Transitional Provision) Order 2003, SI 2003/2071; Education Act 2002 (Commencement No 3) (Wales) Order 2003, SI 2003/2961; Education Act 2002 (Commencement No 4 and Transitional Provisions) (Wales) Order 2004, SI 2004/912; Education Act 2002 (Commencement No 8) Order 2004, SI 2004/1318; and Education Act 2002 (Commencement No 5) (Wales) Order 2004, SI 2004/1728; Education Act 2002 (Commencement No 6 and Transitional Provisions) (Wales) Order 2005, SI 2005/1395; and Education Act 2002 (Commencement No 7) (Wales) Order 2005, SI 2005/2910.

PART 8[1]
TEACHERS

---

[1] Part 8 contains ss 119–148.

Misconduct etc

8–7910 142. Prohibition from teaching, etc. (1) The Secretary of State, in relation to England, or the Secretary of State and the National Assembly for Wales concurrently, in relation to Wales, may direct that a person—

(a) may not carry out work to which this section applies;

(b) may carry out work to which this section applies only in circumstances specified in the direction;

(c) may carry out work to which this section applies only if conditions specified in the direction are satisfied.

(2) This section applies to—

(a) providing education at a school,

(b) providing education at a further education institution,

(c) providing education under a contract of employment or for services where the other party to the contract is a local education authority or a person exercising a function relating to the provision of education on behalf of a local education authority, and

(d) taking part in the management of an independent school.

(3) This section also applies to work of a kind which—

(a) brings a person regularly into contact with children, and

(b) is carried out at the request of or with the consent of a relevant employer (whether or not under a contract).

(4) A direction under this section may be given in respect of a person only—

(a) on the grounds that the person is included (otherwise than provisionally) in the list kept under section 1 of the Protection of Children Act 1999 (c 14) (list of individuals considered unsuitable to work with children),

(b) on the grounds that the person is unsuitable to work with children,

(c) on grounds relating to the person's misconduct,

(d) on grounds relating to the person's health, or

(e) in the case of a direction given by virtue of subsection (2)(d), on grounds relating to the person's professional incompetence (or on a ground mentioned in any of paragraphs (a) to (d)).

(5) The Secretary of State, in relation to England, or the Secretary of State and the National Assembly for Wales concurrently, in relation to Wales, may by regulations[1] prescribe the procedure for giving a direction under this section (including provision about notification of persons who are subject to directions).

(6) The Secretary of State, in relation to England, or the Secretary of State and the National Assembly for Wales concurrently, in relation to Wales, may vary or revoke a direction under this section except in a case where—

(a) the direction was given on the grounds that a person is unsuitable to work with children, and

(b) the person claims that he is no longer unsuitable to work with children.

(7) The Secretary of State, in relation to England, or the Secretary of State and the National Assembly for Wales concurrently, in relation to Wales, may by regulations prescribe the grounds on which a person subject to a direction under this section may seek to have it varied or revoked under subsection (6).

(8) Where a person is subject to a direction under this section, a relevant employer shall not use the person to carry out work in contravention of the direction.

(9) In this section—

"child" means a person who has not attained the age of 18 years,

"education" includes vocational, social, physical and recreational training,

"further education institution" has the meaning given by section 140,

"relevant employer" means—

(a) a local education authority,

(b) a person exercising a function relating to the provision of education on behalf of a local education authority,

(c) the proprietor of a school, or

(d) the governing body of a further education institution, and

"school" includes an independent school.

This section shall come into force in accordance with provision made, in relation to England, by the Secretary of State and in relation to Wales, by the National Assembly for Wales, by order: see s 216(4).

[Education Act 2002, s 142.]

---

1. See the Education (Prohibition from Teaching or Working with Children) Regulations 2003, SI 2003/1184 amended by SI 2004/1493.

8–7911   143. Directions under section 142: contractor, agency, etc.   (1) A person shall not arrange for an individual who is subject to a direction under section 142 to carry out work in contravention of the direction.

(2) If the Secretary of State thinks that a person is likely to fail to comply with the duty under this section in relation to work in England, the Secretary of State may direct the person to take or refrain from taking specified steps with a view to securing compliance with that duty.

(3) If the National Assembly for Wales thinks that a person is likely to fail to comply with the duty under this section in relation to work in Wales, the National Assembly may direct the person to take or refrain from taking specified steps with a view to securing compliance with that duty.

(4) A direction under subsection (2) shall be enforceable, on the application of the Secretary of State, by a mandatory order.

(5) A direction under subsection (3) shall be enforceable, on the application of the National Assembly, by a mandatory order.

This section shall come into force in accordance with provision made, in relation to England, by the Secretary of State and in relation to Wales, by the National Assembly for Wales, by order: see s 216(4).

[Education Act 2002, s 143.]

8–7912   144. *Directions under section 142: appeal*[1]

---

1. In summary, s 144 provides that a person in respect of whom a direction has been made under s 142 may appeal to the Tribunal established under s 9 of the Protection of Children Act 1999. In a case where the direction was given on the ground of unsuitability to work with children, the Tribunal has granted leave to apply for a review of the direction, such an application is made and the Tribunal is satisfied that the applicant is no longer unsuitable to work with children, the Tribunal may revoke the direction.

PART 10[1]
INDEPENDENT SCHOOLS

Chapter 1[2]

Requirement of registration

8–7913   158. The registers.   (1) There shall continue to be—

     (a) a register of independent schools in England, and
     (b) a register of independent schools in Wales.

     (2) The register of independent schools in England shall be kept by the Secretary of State.

     (3) The register of independent schools in Wales shall be kept by the National Assembly for Wales.

This section shall come into force in accordance with provision made, in relation to England, by the Secretary of State and in relation to Wales, by the National Assembly for Wales, by order: see s 216(4).

[Education Act 2002, s 158.]

---

1. Part 10 contains ss 157–174.
2. Chapter 1 contains ss 157–171.

8–7914   159. Unregistered schools.   (1) A person who conducts an independent school which is not a registered school is guilty of an offence.

     (2) A person guilty of an offence under subsection (1) is liable on summary conviction to—

     (a) a fine not exceeding level 5 on the standard scale, or
     (b) imprisonment for a term not exceeding six months, or to both.

     (3) No proceedings shall be instituted for an offence under subsection (1) except with the consent of the registration authority.

     (4) Where the Chief Inspector has reasonable cause to believe that an offence under subsection (1) is being committed on any premises, he may at any reasonable time—

     (a) enter and inspect the premises, and
     (b) inspect and take copies of any records or other documents which he has reasonable cause to believe may be required for the purposes of proceedings in relation to such an offence.

     (5) Section 58 of the Education Act 2005 (computer records) applies in relation to the inspection of records or other documents under subsection (4)(b).*

     (6) It is an offence wilfully to obstruct the Chief Inspector in the exercise of his functions under subsection (4).

     (7) A person guilty of an offence under subsection (6) is liable on summary conviction to a fine not exceeding level 4 on the standard scale.

This section shall come into force in accordance with provision made, in relation to England, by the Secretary of State and in relation to Wales, by the National Assembly for Wales, by order: see s 216(4).

[Education Act 2002, s 159 as amended by SI 2005/2034.]

---

*Reproduced as in force in England.

8–7914A   162A. Power to inspect registered schools in England.   (1) The registration authority may at any time—

     (*a*) require the Chief Inspector for England to inspect any registered school in England, or
     (*b*) arrange for the inspection of any registered school in England by a body approved by the registration authority for the purposes of this subsection.

     (2) The inspection of a school under this section shall relate to—

     (*a*) such of the independent school standards as are, at the time of the inspection, specified by the registration authority for the purposes of this section in relation to any category of school into which that school falls, or
     (*b*) if the registration authority so determines, such of the independent school standards as the registration authority may specify in relation to that school.

(3) When conducting an inspection under this section, the Chief Inspector for England shall—

(a) make a report to the registration authority on the extent to which the school meets the standard or standards to which the inspection relates, and

(b) if the registration authority so requires, arrange for the publication of the report in the prescribed manner.

(4) A report published under subsection (3) is privileged for the purposes of the law of defamation unless the publication is shown to be made with malice (but without prejudice to any privilege subsisting apart from this subsection).

(5) In this section and section 162B "the Chief Inspector for England" means Her Majesty's Chief Inspector of Schools in England.

[Education Act 2002, s 162A as inserted by the Education Act 2005, Sch 8.]

8–7914B 162B Inspections under section 162A: supplementary. (1) This section applies to the inspection of a school which is conducted by the Chief Inspector for England under section 162A(1)(a).

(2) The Chief Inspector for England shall have at all reasonable times—

(a) a right of entry to the premises of the school, and

(b) a right to inspect and take copies of any records kept by the school and any other documents containing information relating to the school which are required for the purposes of the inspection.

(3) Section 58 of the Education Act 2005 (computer records) applies in relation to the inspection of records or other documents under subsection (2)(b).

(4) It is an offence intentionally to obstruct a person in the exercise of his functions in relation to the inspection.

(5) A person guilty of an offence under subsection (4) is liable on summary conviction to a fine not exceeding level 4 on the standard scale.

(6) The proprietor of the school shall pay the Chief Inspector for England, in respect of the inspection, a fee of such amount, and by such time, as may be specified in or determined under regulations.

(7) Where the proprietor fails to comply with subsection (6), the registration authority may remove the school from the register.

(8) The Chief Inspector for England shall pay the amount of any fee received under subsection (7) into the Consolidated Fund."

[Education Act 2002, s 162B as inserted by the Education Act 2005, Sch 8.]

Enforcement of standards after registration

8–7915 163. Power to inspect registered schools in Wales. (1) The registration authority may at any time—

(a) require the Chief Inspector for Wales to inspect any registered school in Wales, or to secure its inspection by one or more registered inspectors, or

(b) arrange for the inspection of any registered school by a body approved by the registration authority for the purposes of this subsection.

(2) The inspection of a school under this section shall relate to—

(a) such of the independent school standards as are, at the time of the inspection, specified by the registration authority for the purposes of this section in relation to any category of school into which that school falls, or

(b) if the registration authority so determines, such of the independent school standards as the registration authority may specify in relation to that school.

(3) A person who conducts an inspection under this section shall—

(a) make a report to the registration authority on the extent to which the school meets the standard or standards to which the inspection relates, and

(b) if the registration authority so requires, arrange for the publication of the report in the prescribed manner[1].

(4) A report published under subsection (3) is privileged for the purposes of the law of defamation unless the publication is shown to be made with malice (but without prejudice to any privilege subsisting apart from this subsection).

(5) In this section and section 164—

"the Chief Inspector for Wales" means Her Majesty's Chief Inspector of Education and Training in Wales;

"registered inspector" means a person registered under section 25 of the Education Act 2005.*

[Education Act 2002, s 163 as substituted by the Education Act 2005, Sch 8.]

*Reproduced as in force in England; in force in Wales from a date to be appointed.
1. The following regulations have been made under s 163(3)(*b*): Education (Independent School Inspection Fees and Publication) (England) Regulations 2003, SI 2003/1926; and Independent Schools (Publication of Inspection Reports) (Wales) Regulations 2003, SI 2003/3232.

8–7916   164. Inspections under section 163: supplementary.   (1) This section applies to the inspection of a school which is conducted by the Chief Inspector for Wales or a registered inspector under section 163(1)(*a*).

(2) If the inspection is conducted by a registered inspector—

(*a*) he may, by agreement with the Chief Inspector for Wales, be assisted by the Chief Inspector for Wales, and

(*b*) he may be assisted by such one or more persons enrolled in the list kept under paragraph 4 of Schedule 4 to the Education Act 2005 as he may determine, subject to paragraph 3(5) of that Schedule and subsection (3) below.

(3) If the Chief Inspector for Wales so requires, a registered inspector shall be assisted by at least one person enrolled in the list referred to in subsection (2)(*b*)—

(*a*) who is without personal experience in the management of any school or the provision of education in any school (otherwise than as a governor or in any other voluntary capacity, and disregarding any experience which it is reasonable to regard as insignificant), and

(*b*) whose primary function in the inspection is not that of providing financial or business expertise.

(4) If the inspection is conducted by a registered inspector, it may be monitored by the Chief Inspector for Wales.

(5) The person conducting the inspection, any person assisting him pursuant to subsection (2) or (3) and any person monitoring the inspection shall have at all reasonable times—

(*a*) a right of entry to the premises of the school, and

(*b*) a right to inspect and take copies of any records kept by the school and any other documents containing information relating to the school which are required for the purposes of the inspection.

(6) Section 58 of the Education Act 2005 (computer records) applies in relation to the inspection of records or other documents under subsection (5)(*b*).

(7) It is an offence intentionally to obstruct a person in the exercise of his functions in relation to the inspection.

(8) A person guilty of an offence under subsection (7) is liable on summary conviction to a fine not exceeding level 4 on the standard scale.

(9) The proprietor of the school shall pay the Chief Inspector for Wales, in respect of the inspection, a fee of such amount, and by such time, as may be specified in or determined under regulations[1].

(10) Where the proprietor fails to comply with subsection (9), the registration authority may remove the school from the register.

(11) The Chief Inspector for Wales shall pay the amount of any fee received under subsection (9) into the Consolidated Fund.

(12) Subsection (11) has effect subject to paragraph 4 of Schedule 6 to the Government of Wales Act 1998 (Treasury power to direct that requirement for payment into Consolidated Fund not to apply in relation to specified sums received by the Chief Inspector for Wales).*
[Education Act 2002, s 164 as substituted by the Education Act 2005, Sch 8.]

*Reproduced as in force in England; in force in Wales from a date to be appointed.
1. The following regulations have been made under s 164(9): Education (Independent School Inspection Fees and Publication) (England) Regulations 2003, SI 2003/1926.

8–7917   166. *Appeals*[1]

1. The proprietor of a registered school may appeal against certain decisions to the Tribunal established under s 9 of the Protection of Children Act 1999.

Supplementary

8–7918   169. Unsuitable persons.   The registration authority may remove a registered school from the register where it is satisfied that any person who, in relation to the school, carries out any work to which section 142 applies—

(a) is carrying out that work in contravention of a direction under that section, or

(b) is subject to an order under section 28 or 29 of the Criminal Justice and Court Services Act 2000 (c 43) (disqualification from working with children).

This section shall come into force in accordance with provision made, in relation to England, by the Secretary of State and in relation to Wales, by the National Assembly for Wales, by order: see s 216(4).
[Education Act 2002, s 169.]

8–7919　171. Interpretation of Chapter 1.　In this Chapter—
"appeal period" has the meaning given by section 165;
"Chief Inspector" means—

(a)　in relation to a school in England, Her Majesty's Chief Inspector of Schools in England, and
(b)　in relation to a school in Wales, Her Majesty's Chief Inspector of Education and Training in Wales;

"independent school standards" has the meaning given by section 157;
"the register" means—

(a)　in relation to a school in England, the register of independent schools in England, and
(b)　in relation to a school in Wales, the register of independent schools in Wales;

"registered" means entered in the register;
"registration authority" means—

(a)　in relation to a school in England, the Secretary of State, and
(b)　in relation to a school in Wales, the National Assembly for Wales.

This section shall come into force in accordance with provision made, in relation to England, by the Secretary of State and in relation to Wales, by the National Assembly for Wales, by order: see s 216(4). *
[Education Act 2002, s 171 as amended by SI 2005/2034.]

---

*Reproduced as in force in England.

PART 11[1]
MISCELLANEOUS AND GENERAL

---

1. Part 11 contains ss 175–217 and Schs 1–22.

Education Act 2005[1]
(2005 c 18)

PART 1[2]
SCHOOL INSPECTIONS AND OTHER INSPECTIONS BY SCHOOL INSPECTORS

CHAPTER 1[3]
School Inspectors and School Inspections: England

Her Majesty's Inspectorate for England

8–7920　1. Her Majesty's Inspectorate of Schools in England.　(1) Her Majesty may by Order in Council appoint a person to the office of Her Majesty's Chief Inspector of Schools in England ("the Chief Inspector").

(2)　Her Majesty may by Order in Council appoint persons as Her Majesty's Inspectors of Schools in England.

(3)　Any person appointed as one of Her Majesty's Inspectors of Schools in England is to serve, in accordance with the terms and conditions on which he is appointed, as a member of the staff of the Chief Inspector.

(4)　The Chief Inspector holds and vacates office in accordance with the terms of his appointment, but—

(a)　must not be appointed for a term of more than five years,
(b)　may at any time resign by giving written notice to the Secretary of State, and
(c)　may be removed from office by Her Majesty on the ground of incapacity or misconduct.

(5)　The previous appointment of a person as Chief Inspector does not affect his eligibility for appointment.

(6)　Schedule 1 makes further provision about the Chief Inspector and his staff.
[Education Act 2005, s 1.]

1.　This Act received the Royal Assent on 7 April 2005. It is principally concerned with reform of school inspection, establishing a new accountability framework and extending the remit of the Teacher Training Agency. It also contains, inter alia, provisions for enforcing the attendance of excluded children at alternative educational provision, and the funding of limited higher education in maintained schools.

　　The Act is divided into five parts:

Part 1 reforms school inspection and deals with schools causing concern.
Part 2 extends the circumstances in which a local education authority must invite proposals for a new or replacement secondary school.
Part 3 broadens the objectives of the Teacher Training Agency and rationalises its functions.
Part 4 contains miscellaneous provisions relating to maintained schools, information sharing and the attendance of excluded children at alternative educational provision.

Part 5 contains general incidental and supplemental provisions.

Some of the Act's provisions came into force on the day it was passed. The remaining provisions will be brought into force in accordance with commencement orders made under s 125. At the time of going to press the Education Act 2005 (Commencement No 1 and Savings and Transitional Provisions) Order 2005, SI 2005/2034, had been made.

Only the provisions relevant to powers of entry and offences are reproduced below.

2. Part 1 contains ss 1-63. At the time of going to press, ss 1-18, 48 and 49 were in force in relation to both England and Wales; ss 44 and 45, 46 (to the extent that it relations to certain specified paras of Sch 5), ss 47, 51, 54, 58, 60, and 61 (to the extent that it relates to certain specified paras of Sch 9 were in force in relation to England only: see Education Act 2005 (Commencement No 1 and Savings and Transitional Provisions) Order 2005, SI 2005/2034. Sections 62 and 63 came into force when the Act was passed.

3. Chapter 1 contains ss 1–12.

8–7921 2. Functions of Her Majesty's Chief Inspector of Schools in England. (1) The Chief Inspector has the general duty of keeping the Secretary of State informed about—

(a) the quality of the education provided by schools in England,
(b) how far that education meets the needs of the range of pupils at those schools,
(c) the educational standards achieved in those schools,
(d) the quality of the leadership in and management of those schools, including whether the financial resources made available to those schools are managed efficiently,
(e) the spiritual, moral, social and cultural development of pupils at those schools,
(f) the contribution made by those schools to the well-being of those pupils,
(g) the extent to which those schools are developing rigorous internal procedures of self-evaluation, and
(h) the behaviour and attendance of pupils at those schools.

(2) When asked to do so by the Secretary of State, the Chief Inspector must—

(a) give advice to the Secretary of State on such matters as may be specified in the Secretary of State's request, and
(b) inspect and report on such school, or class of school, in England as may be so specified.

(3) In addition, the Chief Inspector must keep under review the extent to which any requirement imposed by or under this Part, or any other enactment, on any local education authority, proprietor of a school or governing body in relation to inspections of schools in England is complied with.

(4) The Chief Inspector may at any time give advice to the Secretary of State on any matter connected with schools, or a particular school, in England.

(5) The Chief Inspector is to have such other functions in connection with schools in England, including functions with respect to the training of teachers for such schools, as may be assigned to him by the Secretary of State.

(6) In exercising his functions, the Chief Inspector must have regard to such aspects of government policy as the Secretary of State may direct.

[Education Act 2005, s 2.]

8–7922 4. Powers of entry etc for purposes of section 2. (1) For the purposes of the exercise of any function conferred by or under section 2, the Chief Inspector has at all reasonable times, in relation to any school in England—

(a) a right of entry to the premises of the school, and
(b) a right to inspect, and take copies of, any records kept by the school, and any other documents containing information relating to the school, which he requires for those purposes.

(2) For the purposes of the exercise of any function conferred by or under section 2, the Chief Inspector has at all reasonable times—

(a) a right of entry to any premises (other than school premises) on which, by virtue of arrangements made by a school in England, any pupils who—
    (i) are registered at the school, and
    (ii) have attained the age of 15, or will attain that age in the current school year, but have not ceased to be of compulsory school age,
    are provided with part of their education by any person ("the provider"),
(b) a right of entry to any premises of the provider used in connection with the provision by him of that education, and
(c) a right to inspect and take copies of—
    (i) any records kept by the provider relating to the provision of that education, and
    (ii) any other documents containing information so relating,
    which the Chief Inspector requires for those purposes.

(3) It is an offence intentionally to obstruct the Chief Inspector—

(a) in the exercise of his functions in relation to the inspection of a school for the purposes of section 2(2)(b), or

(b) in the exercise of any right under subsection (1) or (2) for the purposes of the exercise of any other function.

(4) A person guilty of an offence under subsection (3) is liable on summary conviction to a fine not exceeding level 4 on the standard scale.
[Education Act 2005, s 4.]

Inspections

8–7923 5. Duty to inspect certain schools at prescribed intervals. (1) It is the duty of the Chief Inspector—

(a) to inspect under this section every school in England to which this section applies, at such intervals as may be prescribed, and
(b) when the inspection has been completed, to make a report of the inspection in writing.

(2) Subject to subsection (3), the schools to which this section applies are—

(a) community, foundation and voluntary schools,
(b) community and foundation special schools,
(c) maintained nursery schools,
(d) Academies,
(e) city technology colleges,
(f) city colleges for the technology of the arts, and
(g) special schools which are not community or foundation special schools but are for the time being approved by the Secretary of State under section 342 of the Education Act 1996 (c 56) (approval of special schools).

(3) This section does not apply to any school—

(a) which is a closing school (as defined by subsection (4)), and
(b) in respect of which the Chief Inspector has decided, having regard to the date on which the closure is to take effect, that no useful purpose would be served by the school being inspected under this section.

(4) In subsection (3)(a) a "closing school" means—

(a) any community, foundation or voluntary school, community or foundation special school or maintained nursery school in respect of which proposals to discontinue the school have been approved, adopted or determined under any enactment,
(b) a foundation or voluntary school in respect of which the governing body have given notice of discontinuance under section 30 of the School Standards and Framework Act 1998 (c 31),
(c) a community, foundation or voluntary or community or foundation special school in respect of which the Secretary of State has given a direction to discontinue the school under section 19 or 32 of that Act,
(d) a city technology college, city college for the technology of the arts or Academy in respect of which notice of termination of an agreement made under section 482 of the Education Act 1996 has been given, or
(e) a special school which is not a community or foundation special school but is for the time being approved by the Secretary of State under section 342 of the Education Act 1996 and which the proprietor has decided to close.

(5) It is the general duty of the Chief Inspector, when conducting an inspection under this section, to report on—

(a) the quality of the education provided in the school,
(b) how far the education provided in the school meets the needs of the range of pupils at the school,
(c) the educational standards achieved in the school,
(d) the quality of the leadership in and management of the school, including whether the financial resources made available to the school are managed effectively,
(e) the spiritual, moral, social and cultural development of the pupils at the school, and
(f) the contribution made by the school to the well-being of those pupils.

(6) Subsection (1) has effect subject to section 9.
(7) An inspection which is required under this section must not extend to—

(a) denominational education, or
(b) the content of collective worship which falls to be inspected under section 48.
[Education Act 2005, s 5.]

6. Duty to notify parents of section 5 inspection

7. Duty to have regard to views of certain persons

8–7924   8. Inspection at discretion of Chief Inspector.   The Chief Inspector may inspect any school in England, in circumstances where he is not required by section 2(2)(b) or 5 to do so.
[Education Act 2005, s 8.]

9. Power of Chief Inspector to treat other inspection as section 5 inspection

8–7925   10. Power of entry etc for purposes of inspection under section 5 or 8.   (1) When inspecting a school under section 5 or 8, the Chief Inspector has at all reasonable times—

  (a) a right of entry to the premises of the school,
  (b) a right of entry to any other premises on which, by virtue of arrangements made by the school, any pupils who—

   (i) are registered at the school, and
   (ii) have attained the age of 15, or will attain that age in the current school year, but have not ceased to be of compulsory school age,

   are receiving part of their education from any person ("the provider"),

  (c) a right of entry to any premises of the provider used in connection with the provision by him of that education,
  (d) a right to inspect, and take copies of, any records kept by the school, and any other documents containing information relating to the school, which he considers relevant to the discharge of his functions, and
  (e) a right to inspect and take copies of—

   (i) any records kept by the provider relating to the provision of education for pupils registered at the school, and
   (ii) any other documents containing information relating to the provision of such education by the provider,

   which the Chief Inspector considers relevant to the discharge of his functions.
   (2) It is an offence intentionally to obstruct the Chief Inspector in relation to the inspection of a school for the purposes of section 5 or 8.
   (3) A person guilty of an offence under subsection (2) is liable on summary conviction to a fine not exceeding level 4 on the standard scale.
[Education Act 2005, s 10.]

CHAPTER 3[1]
School Inspectors and School Inspections: Wales

Her Majesty's Inspectorate for Wales

8–7926   19. Her Majesty's Inspectorate of Education and Training in Wales.   (1) Her Majesty may by Order in Council appoint a person to the office of Her Majesty's Chief Inspector of Education and Training in Wales or Prif Arolygydd Ei Mawrhydi dros Addysg a Hyfforddiant yng Nghymru ("the Chief Inspector").
   (2) Her Majesty may by Order in Council appoint persons as Her Majesty's Inspectors of Education and Training in Wales or Arolgwyr Ei Mawrhydi dros Addysg a Hyfforddiant yng Nghymru.
   (3) Any person appointed as one of Her Majesty's Inspectors of Education and Training in Wales is to serve, in accordance with the terms and conditions on which he is appointed, as a member of the staff of the Chief Inspector.
   (4) The Chief Inspector holds and vacates office in accordance with the terms of his appointment, but—

  (a) must not be appointed for a term of more than five years,
  (b) may at any time resign by giving written notice to the Assembly, and
  (c) may be removed from office by Her Majesty on the ground of incapacity or misconduct.

   (5) The previous appointment of a person as Chief Inspector does not affect his eligibility for appointment.
   (6) If the Assembly considers that any of the powers conferred by subsection (1), (2) and (4)(c) ought to be exercised, the Assembly must advise the Secretary of State on any recommendation to be made to Her Majesty as to the exercise of the power.
   (7) The terms of a person's appointment under subsection (2) are to be determined by the Chief Inspector with the approval of the Assembly.
   (8) Schedule 2 makes further provision about the Chief Inspector and his staff.
[Education Act 2005, s 19.]

---

1. Chapter 3 contains ss 19–31.

8–7927 20. Functions of Chief Inspector. (1) The Chief Inspector has the general duty of keeping the Assembly informed about—

(a) the quality of the education provided by schools in Wales,

(b) how far that education meets the needs of the range of pupils at those schools,

(c) the educational standards achieved in those schools,

(d) the quality of the leadership in and management of those schools, including whether the financial resources made available to those schools are managed efficiently,

(e) the spiritual, moral, social and cultural development of pupils at those schools, and

(f) the contribution made by those schools to the well-being of those pupils.

(2) When asked to do so by the Assembly, the Chief Inspector must—

(a) give advice to the Assembly on such matters as may be specified in the Assembly's request, and

(b) inspect and report on such school, or class of school, in Wales as may be so specified.

(3) In addition, the Chief Inspector has the following specific duties—

(a) establishing and maintaining the register mentioned in section 25(1);

(b) giving guidance to inspectors registered in that register, and such other persons as he considers appropriate, in connection with inspections of schools in Wales under section 28 and the making of reports of such inspections;

(c) keeping under review the system of inspecting schools under that section and, in particular, the standard of such inspections and of the reports made by registered inspectors;

(d) keeping under review the extent to which any requirement imposed by or under this Part, or any other enactment, on any registered inspector, local education authority, proprietor of a school or governing body in relation to inspections of schools in Wales is complied with;

(e) promoting efficiency in the conduct and reporting of inspections of schools in Wales by encouraging competition in the provision of services by registered inspectors.

(4) The Chief Inspector may at any time give advice to the Assembly on any matter connected with schools, or a particular school, in Wales.

(5) The Chief Inspector is to have such other functions in connection with schools in Wales, including functions with respect to the training of teachers for such schools, as may be assigned to him by the Assembly.

(6) In exercising his functions, the Chief Inspector must have regard to such aspects of policy adopted or formulated by the Assembly as the Assembly may direct.

(7) This section does not apply in relation to education which is brought within the remit of the Chief Inspector by Part 4 of the Learning and Skills Act 2000 (c 21).

[Education Act 2005, s 20.]

8–7928 23. Powers of entry etc of Chief Inspector. (1) For the purposes of the exercise of any function conferred by or under section 20, the Chief Inspector has at all reasonable times, in relation to any school in Wales—

(a) a right of entry to the premises of the school, and

(b) a right to inspect, and take copies of, any records kept by the school, and any other documents containing information relating to the school, which he requires for those purposes.

(2) For the purposes of the exercise of any function conferred by or under section 20, the Chief Inspector has at all reasonable times—

(a) a right of entry to any premises (other than school premises) on which, by virtue of arrangements made by a school in Wales, any pupils who—

(i) are registered at the school, and

(ii) have attained the age of 15, or will attain that age in the current school year, but have not ceased to be of compulsory school age,

are provided with part of their education by any person ("the provider"),

(b) a right of entry to any premises of the provider used in connection with the provision by him of that education, and

(c) a right to inspect and take copies of—

(i) any records kept by the provider relating to the provision of that education, and

(ii) any other documents containing information so relating,

which the Chief Inspector requires for those purposes.

(3) It is an offence intentionally to obstruct the Chief Inspector—

(a) in the exercise of his functions in relation to the inspection of a school for the purposes of section 20(2)(b), or

(b) in the exercise of any right under subsection (1) or (2) for the purposes of the exercise of any other function.

(4) A person guilty of an offence under subsection (3) is liable on summary conviction to a fine not exceeding level 4 on the standard scale.

[Education Act 2005, s 23.]

8–7929   24. Power of Chief Inspector to arrange for inspections.   (1) The Chief Inspector may cause any school in Wales to be inspected by one or more of Her Majesty's Inspectors of Education and Training in Wales (in this section referred to as "Inspectors").

(2) Where an inspection of a school in Wales is being conducted by a registered inspector under section 28, the Chief Inspector may arrange for that inspection to be monitored by one or more Inspectors.

(3) An Inspector inspecting a school, or monitoring an inspection, under this section has at all reasonable times—

(a) a right of entry to the premises of the school,

(b) a right of entry to any other premises on which, by virtue of arrangements made by the school, any pupils who—

    (i) are registered at the school, and

    (ii) have attained the age of 15, or will attain that age in the current school year, but have not ceased to be of compulsory school age,

are receiving part of their education from any person ("the provider"),

(c) a right of entry to any premises of the provider used in connection with the provision by him of that education,

(d) a right to inspect, and take copies of, any records kept by the school, and any other documents containing information relating to the school, which he considers relevant to the discharge of his functions, and

(e) a right to inspect and take copies of—

    (i) any records kept by the provider relating to the provision of education for pupils registered at the school, and

    (ii) any other documents containing information relating to the provision of such education by the provider,

which the Inspector considers relevant to the discharge of his functions.

(4) It is an offence intentionally to obstruct any Inspector in the exercise of any of his functions under this section.

(5) A person guilty of an offence under subsection (4) is liable on summary conviction to a fine not exceeding level 4 on the standard scale.

(6) An inspection of a school conducted under subsection (1) may not extend to any education of a kind brought within the remit of the Chief Inspector by Part 4 of the Learning and Skills Act 2000 (c 21) that is provided by the school.

[Education Act 2005, s 24.]

CHAPTER 6[1]
Other Inspections: England and Wales

8–7930   55. Inspection of careers services in Wales.   (1) This section applies to relevant services provided in Wales in pursuance of arrangements made or directions given by the Assembly under section 10 of the Employment and Training Act 1973 (c 50).

(2) The Chief Inspector has the general duty of keeping the Assembly informed about the quality of the relevant services provided in Wales in accordance with such arrangements or directions.

(3) In subsections (4) to (7) "a service provider" means a person who provides, or arranges for the provision of, relevant services in accordance with such arrangements or directions.

(4) The Chief Inspector must inspect any service provider under this section at prescribed intervals.

(5) When asked to do so by the Assembly, the Chief Inspector must—

(a) give advice to the Assembly on such matters relating to the provision of relevant services in Wales in pursuance of such arrangements or directions as may be specified in the Assembly's request, or

(b) inspect any service provider under this section.

(6) The Chief Inspector may at any time—

(a) give advice to the Assembly relating to the provision of relevant services in Wales in pursuance of such arrangements or directions, or

(b) inspect any service provider under this section.

(7) An inspection of any service provider under this section is to consist of a review of the way in which he is discharging his responsibilities under or by virtue of the arrangements or directions in question, having regard to any guidance given by the Assembly with respect to the provision of relevant services.

(8) In this section and sections 56 and 57—

"the Chief Inspector" means Her Majesty's Chief Inspector for Education and Training in Wales;
"prescribed" means prescribed by regulations;
"regulations" means regulations made by the Assembly;
"relevant services" has the same meaning as in sections 8 and 9 of the Employment and Training Act 1973 (provision of careers services).
[Education Act 2005, s 55.]

---

1. Chapter 6 contains ss 47–57.

8–7931 56. Inspection of services related to careers services in Wales. (1) This section applies if a person ("a relevant provider") who provides a relevant service to which section 55 applies also provides in Wales education, training or an advisory service—

(a) in pursuance of arrangements made by the Assembly under section 2 of the Employment and Training Act 1973 (c 50), or

(b) with the assistance of a grant or loan made under section 12(1) of the Industrial Development Act 1982 (c 52).

(2) The Chief Inspector has the general duty of keeping the Assembly informed about the quality of any education, training or advisory services falling within subsection (1) provided by relevant providers in Wales.

(3) The Chief Inspector must inspect any relevant provider under this section at prescribed intervals.

(4) When asked to do so by the Assembly, the Chief Inspector must—

(a) give advice to the Assembly on such matters relating to the provision of education, training or advisory services falling within subsection (1) by relevant providers, or

(b) inspect any relevant provider under this section.

(5) The Chief Inspector may at any time—

(a) give advice to the Assembly relating to the provision of education, training or advisory services falling within subsection (1) by relevant providers, or

(b) inspect any relevant provider under this section.

(6) An inspection of any relevant provider under this section is to consist of a review of the way in which he is providing the education, training or advisory service falling within subsection (1)(a) or (b).
[Education Act 2005, s 56.]

PART 4[1]
MISCELLANEOUS

Information

8–7932 108. Supply of information: education maintenance allowances. (1) This subsection applies to information which—

(a) is held for the purposes of functions relating to tax or tax credits—

(i) by the Commissioners of Inland Revenue, or

(ii) by a person providing services to the Commissioners of Inland Revenue, in connection with the provision of those services, or

(b) is held for the purposes of functions relating to social security—

(i) by the Secretary of State or a Northern Ireland department, or

(ii) by a person providing services to the Secretary of State or such a department, in connection with the provision of those services.

(2) Information to which subsection (1) applies may be supplied to a person falling within subsection (3) for use for purposes relating to eligibility for education maintenance allowances.

(3) The following persons fall within this subsection—

(a) the Secretary of State,

(b) the Learning and Skills Council for England,

(c) the Assembly,

(d) a Northern Ireland department,

(e) the Scottish Ministers, and

(f) any person providing services to the Secretary of State, the Learning and Skills Council for England, the Assembly, a Northern Ireland department or the Scottish Ministers.

(4) Information received by virtue of subsection or this subsection (2) by a person other than the Scottish Ministers may be supplied to a person falling within subsection (5) for use for purposes relating to eligibility for education maintenance allowances.

(5) The following persons fall within this subsection—

(a) the Assembly,

(b) a Northern Ireland department,

(c) the Scottish Ministers,

(d) any person by whom functions in relation to education maintenance allowances falling within subsection (8)(a) are exercisable by virtue of section 14 or 17 of the 2002 Act,

(e) any person by whom functions under regulations under section 181 of the 2002 Act are exercisable by virtue of section 183 or 184 of that Act, and

(f) any person providing services to the Assembly or a Northern Ireland department.

(6) A person other than the Scottish Ministers may, in making any request for the supply to him of information by virtue of subsection (2) or (4), supply to any person who holds, or is to be supplied with, the information—

(a) the name, address and date of birth of any person to whom the request relates ("the student"),

(b) the name, address and date of birth of—

(i) any parent of the student, or

(ii) any other person whose financial circumstances are relevant to the student's eligibility for an education maintenance allowance, and

(c) any other information (whether relating to the student, any parent of his or any person falling within paragraph (b)(ii)) which is required for the purpose of determining the student's eligibility for an education maintenance allowance.

(7) This section does not limit the circumstances in which information may be supplied apart from this section.

(8) In this section and section 109 "education maintenance allowance" means—

(a) financial assistance under section 14 of the 2002 Act paid to or in respect of a person who is over compulsory school age in connection with his undertaking any course of education or training,

(b) an allowance under section 181 of the 2002 Act,

(c) an award under Article 51(1)(b) of the Education and Libraries (Northern Ireland) Order 1986 (No 594/NI 3) paid to or in respect of a person who is over compulsory school age (within the meaning of that Order) in connection with his undertaking any course of education or training,

(d) an allowance under section 73(f) of the Education (Scotland) Act 1980 (c 44) paid to or in respect of a relevant person attending a course of education, other than higher education, or

(e) financial assistance provided under section 12(2)(c) of the Further and Higher Education (Scotland) Act 1992 (c 37).

(9) In subsection (8)(d)—

"higher education" has the same meaning as in Part 2 of the Further and Higher Education (Scotland) Act 1992;

"relevant person" means a person who—

(a) is deemed to have attained the age of 16 years under section 33 of the Education (Scotland) Act 1980, and

(b) has not, on the first day of the term of the course of education, attained the age of 20 years.

[Education Act 2005, s 108.]

---

1. Part 4 contains ss 101–118. At the time of going to press, ss 105, 116 and 116, 117 (to the extent that it relates to certain specified paras of s 19 and 118 were in force: see Education Act 2005 (Commencement No 1 and Savings and Transitional Provisions) Order 2005, SI 2005/2034.

8–7933 109. Unauthorised disclosure of information received under section 108. (1) A person ("X") who discloses information which he has received by virtue of subsection (2) or (4) of section 108 and which relates to a particular person commits an offence unless the information is disclosed—

(a) in accordance with subsection (4) of that section,

(b) in the course of any duty X has in connection with the exercise of functions relating to eligibility for education maintenance allowances,

(c) in accordance with an enactment or an order of a court,

(d) for the purpose of instituting, or otherwise for the purposes of, civil or criminal proceedings, or

(e) with consent given by or on behalf of the person to whom the information relates.

(2) It is a defence for a person charged with an offence under subsection (1) to prove that he reasonably believed that his disclosure was lawful.

(3) A person guilty of an offence[1] under subsection (1) is liable—

(a) on conviction on indictment, to imprisonment for a term not exceeding two years, to a fine or to both;

(b)　on summary conviction in England and Wales, to imprisonment for a term not exceeding 12 months, to a fine not exceeding the statutory maximum or to both;

(c)　on summary conviction in Scotland or Northern Ireland, to imprisonment for a term not exceeding 6 months, to a fine not exceeding the statutory maximum or to both.

(4)　In relation to an offence committed before the commencement of section 154(1) of the Criminal Justice Act 2003 (c 44), the reference in subsection (3)(b) to 12 months is to be read as a reference to 6 months.

(5)　The reference in subsection (1)(c) to an enactment includes a reference to an enactment comprised in, or in an instrument made under—

(a)　an Act of the Scottish Parliament, or

(b)　any Northern Ireland legislation as defined in section 24(5) of the Interpretation Act 1978 (c 30).

[Education Act 2005, s 109.]

1.　For procedure in respect of an offence triable either way, see the Magistrates' Courts Act 1980 ss 17A–21, in Part 1: Magistrates' Courts, Procedure, ante.

8–7934　110. Supply of information: free school lunches etc.　(1) This subsection applies to information held for the purposes of functions relating to tax credits—

(a)　by the Commissioners of Inland Revenue, or

(b)　by a person providing services to them, in connection with the provision of those services.

(2)　This subsection applies to information held for the purposes of functions relating to social security—

(a)　by the Secretary of State, or

(b)　by a person providing services to him, in connection with the provision of those services.

(3)　Information to which subsection (1) or (2) applies may be supplied—

(a)　to the Secretary of State, or any person providing services to him, or

(b)　to the Assembly, or any person providing services to the Assembly,

for use for the purpose of determining eligibility for free school lunches and milk.

(4)　Information to which subsection (2) applies may be supplied to a local education authority for use for that purpose.

(5)　Information received by virtue of subsection (3) may be supplied—

(a)　to another person to whom it could have been supplied under that subsection, or

(b)　to a local education authority,

for use for that purpose.

(6)　The references in subsections (4) and (5)(b) to a local education authority include references to any person exercising on behalf of such an authority functions relating to eligibility for free school lunches and milk.

(7)　For the purposes of this section, a person is eligible for free school lunches and milk if school lunches and milk are required to be provided for him, on request, free of charge—

(a)　in accordance with section 512ZB(2) and (3) of the Education Act 1996 (c 56),

(b)　in accordance with regulations under section 342 of that Act (non-maintained special schools), or

(c)　in accordance with an agreement under section 482 of that Act (Academies, etc).

(8)　In this section, "school lunch" has the same meaning as in section 512 of the Education Act 1996.

(9)　This section does not limit the circumstances in which information may be supplied apart from this section.

[Education Act 2005, s 110.]

8–7935　111. Unauthorised disclosure of information received under section 110.　(1) A person ("X") who discloses information which he has received by virtue of any of subsections (3) to (5) of section 110 and which relates to a particular person commits an offence unless the information is disclosed—

(a)　in the case of information received by virtue of subsection (3) of that section, in accordance with subsection (5) of that section,

(b)　in the course of any duty X has in connection with the exercise of functions relating to eligibility for free school lunches and milk,

(c)　in accordance with an enactment or an order of a court, or

(d)　with consent given by or on behalf of the person to whom the information relates.

(2)　In subsection (1)(b), "eligibility for free school lunches and milk" is to be read in accordance with section 110(7).

(3) It is a defence for a person charged with an offence under subsection (1) to prove that he reasonably believed that his disclosure was lawful.

(4) A person guilty of an offence[1] under subsection (1) is liable—

(a) on conviction on indictment, to imprisonment for a term not exceeding two years, to a fine or to both, or

(b) on summary conviction, to imprisonment for a term not exceeding 12 months, to a fine not exceeding the statutory maximum or to both.

(5) In relation to an offence committed before the commencement of section 154(1) of the Criminal Justice Act 2003 (c 44), the reference in subsection (4)(b) to 12 months is to be read as a reference to 6 months.

[Education Act 2005, s 111.]

---

1. For procedure in respect of an offence triable either way, see the Magistrates' Courts Act 1980 ss 17A–21, in PART 1: MAGISTRATES' COURTS, PROCEDURE, ante.

PART 5[1]
GENERAL

8–7936   **125. Commencement.**   (1) The following provisions of this Act come into force on the day on which this Act is passed—

(a) in Part 1, sections 62 and 63;

(b) in Part 3—

section 75(5),
section 78(3),
sections 96 and 97,
section 100, and
paragraph 3 of Schedule 15 (and section 99 so far as relating to that paragraph); and

(c) in this Part—

sections 119 to 122,
section 124,
this section, and
sections 126 to 128.

(2) The following provisions of Part 4 come into force at the end of the period of two months beginning with the day on which this Act is passed—

section 102,
sections 107 to 114, and
Schedule 17.

(3) The following provisions come into force on 1st September 2005 or, if this Act is passed after 1st July 2005, at the end of the period of two months beginning with the day on which it is passed—

(a) Part 3 (including Schedules 13 to 15), except the provisions specified in subsection (1)(b), and

(b) Part 3 of Schedule 19 (and section 123 so far as relating to that Part of that Schedule).

(4) The remaining provisions of this Act come into force in accordance with provision made by the appropriate authority (as defined in section 126) by order.

[Education Act 2005, s 125.]

---

1. Part 5 contains ss 119–128. At the time of going to press, s 123 (to the extent that it relation to certain specified provisions of Sch 9) was in force see Education Act 2005 (Commencement No 1 and Savings and Transitional Provisions) Order 2005, SI 2005/2034. Sections 119–122, and 124–128 came into force when the Act was passed.

8–7937   **126. The appropriate authority by whom commencement order is made.**   (1) This section has effect for determining who is the appropriate authority for the purposes of section 125(4).

(2) In relation to Part 1, the appropriate authority is—

(a) the Secretary of State, for the following provisions—

Chapters 1 and 2 (including Schedule 1);
sections 48 and 49;
paragraphs 1 to 4 of Schedule 7 (and section 53 so far as relating to those paragraphs);
paragraphs 1 to 5, 23 and 26 of Schedule 9 (and section 61 so far as relating to those paragraphs),

(b) the Assembly, for the following provisions—

Chapters 3 and 4 (including Schedules 2 to 4);
section 50 (including Schedule 6);
section 52;

sections 55 to 57;

paragraph 5 of Schedule 7 (and section 53 so far as relating to that paragraph);

paragraphs 6, 7, 22, 24, 25 and 27 of Schedule 9 (and section 61 so far as relating to those paragraphs), and

(c) for the other provisions of the Part—

   (i) in relation to England, the Secretary of State, and

   (ii) in relation to Wales, the Assembly.

(3) In relation to Part 2, the appropriate authority is—

(a) for sections 70 and 71 and paragraph 9 of Schedule 12 (and section 72 so far as relating to that paragraph)—

   (i) in relation to England, the Secretary of State, and

   (ii) in relation to Wales, the Assembly, and

(b) for the other provisions of the Part, the Secretary of State.

(4) In relation to Part 4, the appropriate authority is—

(a) the Secretary of State, for the following provisions—

sections 103 and 104;

paragraph 8 of Schedule 16 (and section 101 so far as relating to that paragraph);

paragraphs 2 to 4 of Schedule 18 (and section 117 so far as relating to those paragraphs), and

(b) for the other provisions of the Part—

   (i) in relation to England, the Secretary of State, and

   (ii) in relation to Wales, the Assembly.

(5) In relation to section 123 and Schedule 19, the appropriate authority is—

(a) the Secretary of State, for a repeal contained in Part 2 of the Schedule, and

(b) for a repeal contained in Part 1 or 4 of the Schedule, the appropriate authority for the purposes of section 125(4) in relation to the provision on which the repeal is consequential.

[Education Act 2005, s 126.]

8–7938 127. Extent. (1) Subject to subsections (2) and (3), this Act extends to England and Wales only.

(2) The following provisions extend also to Scotland and Northern Ireland—

sections 108 and 109 (supply of information: education maintenance allowances),

section 124, so far as relating to those sections, and

the other provisions of this Part except sections 119, 122 and 123.

(3) Any amendment or repeal made by this Act has the same extent as the enactment amended or repealed.

[Education Act 2005, s 127.]

8–7939 128. Short title, etc. (1) This Act may be cited as the Education Act 2005.

(2) This Act shall be included in the list of Education Acts set out in section 578 of the Education Act 1996 (c 56).

[Education Act 2005, s 128.]

8–7940

Section 28

SCHEDULE 4[1]

SCHOOL INSPECTIONS IN WALES UNDER SECTION 28

Rights of entry etc

7. (1) An inspector conducting an inspection, and the members of his inspection team, have at all reasonable times—

(a) a right of entry to the premises of the school concerned, and

(b) a right to inspect, and take copies of, any records kept by the school, and any other documents containing information relating to the school, which he requires for the purposes of the inspection.

(2) Where—

(a) pupils registered at the school concerned are, by arrangement with another school, receiving part of their education at the other school, and

(b) the inspector is satisfied that he cannot properly discharge his duty under section 28(5) in relation to the school concerned without inspecting the provision made for those pupils at that other school,

sub-paragraph (1) applies in relation to that other school as it applies in relation to the school concerned.

(3) An inspector conducting an inspection of a school, and the members of his inspection team, also have at all reasonable times—

(a) a right of entry to any premises (other than school premises) on which, by virtue of arrangements made by the school, any pupils who—

(i) are registered at the school, and
(ii) have attained the age of 15, or will attain that age in the current school year, but have not ceased to be of compulsory school age,

are receiving part of their education from any person ("the provider");

(b) a right of entry to any premises of the provider used in connection with the provision by him of that education, and
(c) a right to inspect and take copies of—

(i) any records kept by the provider relating to the provision of that education, and
(ii) any other documents containing information so relating,

which the inspector or (as the case may be) member of the team requires for the purposes of the inspection.

8. Offence of obstructing inspector or inspection team. (1) It is an offence intentionally to obstruct—

(a) the inspector conducting the inspection, or
(b) a member of an inspection team,

in the exercise of his functions in relation to an inspection of a school.

(2) A person guilty of an offence under sub-paragraph (1) is liable on summary conviction to a fine not exceeding level 4 on the standard scale.

---

1. At the time of going to press, none of the provisions of Sch 4 were in force.

ELECTIONS

8–7961 This title contains the following statutory provisions—

Representation of the People Act 1983
(1983 c 2)

PART I[1]
PARLIAMENTARY AND LOCAL GOVERNMENT FRANCHISE AND ITS EXERCISE

8–7970 **53.** *Power to make regulations as to registration etc[2].*

---

1. Part I comprises ss 1–66.
2. The Representation of the People (England and Wales) Regulations 2001, SI 2001/341 amended by SI 2001/1700, SI 2002/881, SI 2003/3075, SI 2004/294, 1771 and 1848 and SI 2005/2114 and the Representation of the People (Combination of Polls) (England and Wales) Regulations 2004, SI 2004/294 have been made. Failure to comply with, or the giving of false information in pursuance of a registration officer's requisition is punishable on summary conviction by a fine not exceeding **level 3**. If any person without lawful authority destroys, mutilates, defaces or removes any notice published by the registration officer in connection with his registration duties or any copies of a document which have been made available for inspection in pursuance of those duties he shall be liable on summary conviction to a fine not exceeding **level 3**.

Offences

8–7971 **60. Personation.** (1) A person shall be guilty of a corrupt practice[1] if he commits, or aids, abets, counsels or procures the commission of, the offence of personation.

(2) A person shall be deemed to be guilty of a personation[2] at a parliamentary or local government election if he—

(a) votes in person or by post as some other person, whether as an elector or as proxy, and whether that other person is living or dead or is a fictitious person; or
(b) votes in person or by post as proxy—

(i) for a person whom he knows or has reasonable grounds for supposing to be dead or to be a fictitious person; or
(ii) when he knows or has reasonable grounds for supposing that his appointment as proxy is no longer in force.

(3) For the purposes of this section, a person who has applied for a ballot paper for the purpose of voting in person or who has marked, whether validly or not, and returned a ballot paper issued for the purpose of voting by post, shall be deemed to have voted.

[Representation of the People Act 1983, s 60.]

1. For procedure for prosecutions for corrupt or illegal practices see ss 168–171, and generally, see ss 176–181.
2. The evidence of not less than two credible witnesses is necessary (s 168(5), post).

8–7972   61. Other voting offences.   (1) A person shall be guilty of an offence if—

(a)   he votes in person or by post, whether as an elector or as proxy, or applies to vote by proxy or by post as elector, at a parliamentary or local government election, or at parliamentary or local government elections, knowing that he is subject to a legal incapacity to vote at the election or, as the case may be, at elections of that kind; or

(b)   he applies for the appointment of a proxy to vote for him at any parliamentary or local government election or at parliamentary or local government elections knowing that he is or the person to be appointed is subject to a legal incapacity to vote at the election or, as the case may be, at elections of that kind; or

(c)   he votes, whether in person or by post, as proxy for some other person at a parliamentary or local government election, knowing that that person is subject to a legal incapacity to vote.

For the purposes of this subsection references to a person being subject to a legal incapacity to vote do not, in relation to things done before polling day at the election or first election at or for which they are done, include his being below voting age if he will be of voting age on that day.

(2) A person shall be guilty of an offence if—

(a)   he votes as elector otherwise than by proxy either—

(i)   more than once in the same constituency at any parliamentary election, or more than once in the same electoral area at any local government election; or

(ii)   in more than one constituency at a general election, or in more than one electoral area at an ordinary election of councillors for a local government area which is not a single electoral area; or

(iii)   in any constituency at a general election, or in any electoral area at such an ordinary election as mentioned above, when there is in force an appointment of a person to vote as his proxy at the election in some other constituency or electoral area; or

(b)   he votes as elector in person at a parliamentary or local government election at which he is entitled to vote by post; or

(c)   he votes as elector in person at a parliamentary or local government election, knowing that a person appointed to vote as his proxy at the election either has already voted in person at the election or is entitled to vote by post at the election; or

(d)   he applies for a person to be appointed as his proxy to vote for him at parliamentary elections in any constituency without applying for the cancellation of a previous appointment of a third person then in force in respect of that or another constituency or without withdrawing a pending application for such an appointment in respect of that or another constituency.

(2A) In the case of Authority elections, paragraph (a) of subsection (2) above shall not have effect; but a person shall be guilty of an offence under this subsection if he votes as an elector otherwise than by proxy—

(a)   more than once at the same election of the Mayor of London;

(b)   more than once at the same election of the London members of the London Assembly at an ordinary election;

(c)   more than once in the same Assembly constituency at the same election of a constituency member of the London Assembly;

(d)   in more than one Assembly constituency at the same ordinary election; or

(e)   in any Assembly constituency at an ordinary election, or an election of the Mayor of London held under section 16 of the 1999 Act, when there is in force an appointment of a person to vote as his proxy at the election in some other Assembly constituency.

(3) A person shall be guilty of an offence if—

(a)   he votes as proxy for the same elector either—

(i)   more than once in the same constituency at any parliamentary election, or more than once in the same electoral area at any local government election; or

(ii)   in more than one constituency at a general election, or in more than one electoral area at an ordinary election of councillors for a local government area which is not a single electoral area; or

(b)   he votes in person as proxy for an elector at a parliamentary or local government election at which he is entitled to vote by post as proxy for that elector; or

(c)   *repealed*

(d)   he votes in person as proxy for an elector at a parliamentary or local government election knowing that the elector has already voted in person at the election.

(3A) In the case of Authority elections, paragraph (a) of subsection (3) above shall not have effect; but a person shall be guilty of an offence under this subsection if he votes as proxy for the same elector—

(*a*)   more than once at the same election of the Mayor of London;

(*b*)   more than once at the same election of the London members of the London Assembly at an ordinary election;

(*c*)   more than once in the same Assembly constituency at the same election of a constituency member of the London Assembly; or

(*d*)   in more than one Assembly constituency at the same ordinary election.

(4) A person shall also be guilty of an offence if he votes at a parliamentary election in any constituency or at a local government election in any electoral area as proxy for more than two persons of whom he is not the spouse, civil partner, parent, grandparent, brother, sister, child or grandchild.

(5) A person shall also be guilty of an offence if he knowingly induces or procures some other person to do an act which is, or but for that other person's want of knowledge would be, an offence by that other person under the foregoing subsections of this section.

(6) For the purposes of this section a person who has applied for a ballot paper for the purpose of voting in person, or who has marked, whether validly or not, and returned a ballot paper issued for the purpose of voting by post, shall be deemed to have voted, but for the purpose of determining whether an application for a ballot paper constitutes an offence under subsection (4) above, a previous application made in circumstances which entitle the applicant only to mark a tendered ballot paper shall, if he does not exercise that right, be disregarded.

(7) An offence under this section shall be an illegal practice[1] but—

(*a*)   the court before whom a person is convicted of any such offence may, if they think it just in the special circumstances of the case, mitigate or entirely remit any incapacity imposed by virtue of section 173 below; and

(*b*)   a candidate shall not be liable, nor shall his election be avoided, for an illegal practice under this section of any agent of his other than an offence under subsection (5) above.

[Representation of the People Act 1983, s 61, as amended by the Repesentation of the People Act 1985, Sch 2, the Greater London Authority Act 1999, Sch 3 and the Civil Partnership Act 2004, Sch 27.]

---

1. For procedure for prosecutions for corrupt or illegal practices see ss 168–171, and generally see ss 176–181, post.

8–7973   **62. Offences as to declarations.**   (1) A person who—

(*a*)   makes a declaration of local connection or a service declaration—

    (i)   when he is not authorised to do so by section 7B(1) or section 15(1) above, or

    (ii)   except as permitted by this Act, when he knows that he is subject to a legal incapacity to vote, or

    (iii)   when he knows that it contains a statement which is false, or

(*b*)   attests a service declaration when he knows—

    (i)   that he is not authorised to do so, or

    (ii)   that it contains a false statement as to any particulars required by regulations under section 16 above,

shall be guilty of an offence and liable on summary conviction to a fine not exceeding **level 5** on the standard scale.

(2) Where the declaration is available only for local government elections the reference in subsection (1) above to a legal incapacity to vote refers to a legal incapacity to vote at local government elections.

[Representation of the People Act 1983, s 62 as amended by the Representation of the People Act 1985, Schs 1, 3 and 4.]

8–7974   **63. Breach of official duty.**   (1) If a person to whom this section applies is, without reasonable cause, guilty of any act or omission in breach of his official duty, he shall be liable on summary conviction to a fine not exceeding **level 5** on the standard scale.

(2) No person to whom this section applies shall be liable for breach of his official duty to any penalty at common law and no action for damages shall lie in respect of the breach by such a person of his official duty.

(3) The persons to whom this section applies are—

(*a*)   the Clerk of the Crown (or, in Northern Ireland, the Clerk of the Crown for Northern Ireland),

(*b*)   any sheriff clerk, registration officer, returning officer or presiding officer,

(*c*)   any other person whose duty it is to be responsible after a local government election for the used ballot papers and other documents (including returns and declarations as to expenses),

(*d*)   any postmaster, and

(*e*)   any deputy of a person mentioned in any of paragraphs (*a*) to (*d*) above or any person appointed to assist or in the course of his employment assisting a person so mentioned in connection with his official duties;

and "official duty" shall for the purposes of this section be construed accordingly, but shall not

include duties imposed otherwise than by the law relating to parliamentary or local government elections or the registration of parliamentary or local government electors.
[Representation of the People Act 1983, s 63 as substituted by the Representation of the People Act 1985, Sch 4.]

8–7975 65. Tampering with nomination papers, ballot papers, etc. (1) A person shall be guilty of an offence, if, at a parliamentary or local government election, he—

(a) fraudulently defaces or fraudulently destroys any nomination paper; or
(b) fraudulently defaces or fraudulently destroys any ballot paper, or the official mark on any ballot paper, or any declaration of identity or official envelope used in connection with voting by post; or
(c) without due authority supplies any ballot paper to any person; or
(d) fraudulently puts into any ballot box any paper other than the ballot paper which he is authorised by law to put in; or
(e) fraudulently takes out of the polling station any ballot paper; or
(f) without due authority destroys, takes, opens or otherwise interferes with any ballot box or packet of ballot papers then in use for the purposes of the election; or
(g) fraudulently or without due authority, as the case may be, attempts to do any of the foregoing acts.

(2) *Scotland.*

(3) If a returning officer, a presiding officer or a clerk appointed to assist in taking the poll, counting the votes or assisting at the proceedings in connection with the issue or receipt of postal ballot papers is guilty of an offence under this section, he shall be liable[1]—

(a) on conviction on indictment to a fine, or to imprisonment for a term not exceeding **2 years**, or to both;
(b) on summary conviction, to a fine not exceeding the **statutory maximum**, or to imprisonment for a term not exceeding **6 months, or to both**.

(4) If any other person is guilty of an offence under this section, he shall be liable on summary conviction to a fine not exceeding **level 5** on the standard scale, or to imprisonment for a term not exceeding **6 months, or to both**.
[Representation of the People Act 1983, s 65 as amended by the Representation of the People Act 1985, Sch 3.]

---

1. For procedure in respect of this offence which is triable either way, see Magistrates' Courts Act 1980, ss 17A–21 in PART I: MAGISTRATES' COURTS, PROCEDURE, *ante.*

8–7975A 65A. False statements in nomination papers etc. (1) A person is guilty of a corrupt practice if, in the case of any relevant election, he causes or permits to be included in a document delivered or otherwise furnished to a returning officer for use in connection with the election—

(a) a statement of the name or home address of a candidate at the election which he knows to be false in any particular; or
(b) anything which purports to be the signature of an elector who proposes, seconds or assents to, the nomination of such a candidate but which he knows—

(i) was not written by the elector by whom it purports to have been written, or
(ii) if written by that elector, was not written by him for the purpose of signifying that he was proposing, seconding, or (as the case may be) assenting to, that candidate's nomination.

(2) In this section "relevant election" means—

(a) any parliamentary election, or
(b) any local government election in England or Wales.
[Representation of the People Act 1983, s 65A inserted by the Representation of the People Act 2000, s 15(1), Sch 6, paras 3, 5.]

8–7976 66. Requirement of secrecy. (1) The following persons—

(a) every returning officer and every presiding officer or clerk attending at a polling station,
(b) every candidate or election agent or polling agent so attending,

shall maintain and aid in maintaining the secrecy of voting and shall not, except for some purpose authorised by law, communicate to any person before the poll is closed any information as to—

(i) the name of any elector or proxy for an elector who has or has not applied for a ballot paper or voted at a polling station;
(ii) the number on the register of electors of any elector who, or whose proxy, has or has not applied for a ballot paper or voted at a polling station; or
(iii) the official mark.

(2) Every person attending at the counting of the votes shall maintain and aid in maintaining the secrecy of voting and shall not—

(a) ascertain or attempt to ascertain at the counting of the votes the number on the back of any ballot paper;

(b) communicate any information obtained at the counting of the votes as to the candidate for whom any vote is given on any particular ballot paper.

(3) No person shall—

(a) interfere with or attempt to interfere with a voter when recording his vote;

(b) otherwise obtain or attempt to obtain in a polling station information as to the candidate for whom a voter in that station is about to vote or has voted;

(c) communicate at any time to any person any information obtained in a polling station as to the candidate for whom a voter in that station is about to vote or has voted, or as to the number on the back of the ballot paper given to a voter at that station;

(d) directly or indirectly induce a voter to display his ballot paper after he has marked it so as to make known to any person the name of the candidate for whom he has or has not voted.

(4) Every person attending the proceedings in connection with the issue or the receipt of ballot papers for persons voting by post shall maintain and aid in maintaining the secrecy of the voting and shall not—

(a) except for some purpose authorised by law, communicate, before the poll is closed, to any person any information obtained at those proceedings as to the official mark; or

(b) except for some purpose authorised by law, communicate to any person at any time any information obtained at those proceedings as to the number on the back of the ballot paper sent to any person; or

(c) except for some purpose authorised by law, attempt to ascertain at the proceedings in connection with the receipt of ballot papers the number on the back of any ballot paper; or

(d) attempt to ascertain at the proceedings in connection with the receipt of the ballot papers the candidate for whom any vote is given in any particular ballot paper or communicate any information with respect thereto obtained at those proceedings.

(5) No person having undertaken to assist a blind voter to vote shall communicate at any time to any person any information as to the candidate for whom that voter intends to vote or has voted, or as to the number on the back of the ballot paper given for the use of that voter.

(6) If a person acts in contravention of this section he shall be liable on summary conviction to a fine not exceeding **level 5** on the standard scale or to imprisonment for a term not exceeding **six months**.

[Representation of the People Act 1983, s 66 as amended by the Representation of the People Act 1985, Sch 3.]

8–7976A   **66A. Prohibition on publication of exit polls.**   (1) No person shall, in the case of an election to which this section applies, publish before the poll is closed—

(a) any statement relating to the way in which voters have voted at the election where that statement is (or might reasonably be taken to be) based on information given by voters after they have voted, or

(b) any forecast as to the result of the election which is (or might reasonably be taken to be) based on information so given.

(2) This section applies to—

(a) any parliamentary election; and

(b) any local government election in England or Wales.

(3) If a person acts in contravention of subsection (1) above, he shall be liable on summary conviction to a fine not exceeding level 5 on the standard scale or to imprisonment for a term not exceeding six months.

(4) In this section—

"forecast" includes estimate;

"publish" means make available to the public at large, or any section of the public, in whatever form and by whatever means;

and any reference to the result of an election is a reference to the result of the election either as a whole or so far as any particular candidate or candidates at the election is or are concerned.

[Representation of the People Act 1983, s 66A as inserted by the Representation of the People Act 2000, s 15(1), Sch 6, paras 3, 6.]

PART II[1]

THE ELECTION CAMPAIGN

Election expenses

8–7977   **Provision for expenses.**   Payment of expenses to be made through election agent, and money provided to be paid to the candidate or his election agent; any payment advance or deposit paid otherwise is an illegal practice[2] (Representation of the People Act 1983 s 73 amended by the Representation of the People Act 1985, s 14, and the Political Parties, Elections and Referendums

Act 2000, Sch 18, *summarised*). Prohibition of expenses not authorised by election agent, to incur or aid, abet, counsel or procure any person to incur such expenses[3] or make false declaration thereon is a corrupt practice; failure to send declaration as required is an illegal practice[2] (Representation of the People Act 1983, s 75 amended by the Cable and Broadcasting Act 1984, Sch 5, the Representation of the People Act 1985, s 14 and Sch 4, the Broadcasting Act 1990, Sch 20, the Broadcasting Act 1996, Sch 10 and the Political Parties, Elections and Referendums Act 2000, s 131, *summarised*). Exceeding election expense limits knowingly is an illegal practice[2] (Representation of the People Act 1983, s 76 amended by the Representation of the People Act 1985, Schs 4 and 5, the Local Government Act 1985, Schs 9 and 17, the Representation of the People Act 1989, s 6, the Representation of the People Act 2000, Schs 1 and 7 and the Political Parties, Elections and Referendums Act 2000, s 132, *summarised*). Limitations on election expenses may raise issues under Article 3 of Protocol 1 of the European Convention (the duty to hold free elections). Since a statutory limitation on election expenses can operate as a barrier to the publication of information intended to influence voters, it will breach the Convention unless it is proportionate[4]. See also the Representation of the People (Variation of Limits of Candidates' Election Expenses Order 2005, SI 2005/269.

1. Part II comprises ss 67–119.
2. For procedure for prosecutions for corrupt or illegal practices see ss 168–171, and generally see ss 176–181, post.
3. As to advertisements in national newspapers, see *R v Tronoh Mines Ltd* [1952] 1 All ER 697, 116 JP 180, and as to sufficiency of an intention to *prevent* the election of a candidate see *DPP v Luft* [1977] AC 962, [1976] 2 All ER 569.
4. See *Bowman v United Kingdom* (1998) 26 EHRR 1.

8–7978 Returns and declarations as to election expenses. Election agent to deliver to appropriate officer a true return of election expenses within 35 days of election result (Representation of the People Act 1983, s 81 amended by the Representation of the People Act 1985, Sch 4 and the Political Parties, Elections and Referendums Act 2000, Sch 18—*summarised*). Return to be accompanied by declaration; if false, a corrupt practice[1] (Representation of the People Act 1983, s 82 amended by the Local Government Act 1985, Schs 9 and 17, the Representation of the People Act 1985, Sch 4 and the Local Government (Wales) Act 1994, Sch 16—*summarised*). Failure to comply with ss 81 or 82 an illegal practice[1] (Representation of the People Act 1983, s 84—*summarised*). Candidate sitting or voting in the council for the local government area for which election held without return and declarations being delivered is liable on summary conviction to a fine not exceeding £50[2]; (Representation of the People Act 1983, s 85 amended by the Representation of the People Act 1985, Sch 4—*summarised*).

1. For procedure for prosecutions for corrupt or illegal practices see ss 168–171, and generally see ss 176–181, post.
2. The section visualises civil proceedings for a penalty, but as an alternative summary proceedings in a magistrates' court may be taken with the penalty not to exceed the penalty recoverable in civil proceedings.

Election meetings

8–7979 97. Disturbances at election meetings. (1) A person who at a lawful public meeting to which this section applies acts, or incites others to act, in a disorderly manner for the purpose of preventing the transaction of the business for which the meeting was called together shall be guilty of an illegal practice.

(2) This section applies to—

(a) a political meeting held in any constituency between the date of the issue of a writ for the return of a member of Parliament for the constituency and the date at which a return to the writ is made;

(b) a meeting held with reference to a local government election in the electoral area for that election on, in the period beginning with the last date on which notice of the election may be published in accordance with rules made under section 36, or, in Scotland, section 42 above and ending with the day of election.

(3) If a constable reasonably suspects any person of committing an offence under subsection (1) above, he may if requested so to do by the chairman of the meeting require that person to declare to him immediately his name and address and, if that person refuses or fails so to declare his name and address or gives a false name and address, he shall be liable on summary conviction to a fine not exceeding **level 1** on the standard scale.

This subsection shall not apply to Northern Ireland.

[Representation of the People Act 1983, s 97 as amended by the Police and Criminal Evidence Act 1984, Sch 7, and the Representation of the People Act 1985, Sch 4.]

8–7980 Summary of other offences in relation to elections. Official acting for candidate, liable on summary conviction to a fine not exceeding **level 4** on the standard scale (s 99). Illegal canvassing by police officers, liable on summary conviction to a fine not exceeding **level 3** on the standard scale unless act done in discharge of his duty (s 100 amended by the Representation of the People Act 1985, Sch 3). Let, lend or employ public vehicle for conveyance of electors or their proxies to or from the poll, or hire, borrow or use a public vehicle the owner of which is known to be prohibited for that purpose is an illegal hiring[1] (s 101). Payment or contract for payment for conveyance of voters an illegal practice[2] (s 102). Saving from ss 101 and 102 for electors themselves hiring etc (s 103 amended by the Representation of the People Act 1985, Sch 4), and for access to polling places by sea (s 105). False statements as to candidates an illegal practice[2] (s 106). Corruptly inducing or procuring withdrawal from candidature or withdrawing is an illegal payment[1] (s 107). Premises licensed for the sale of, or where supply takes place, of intoxicating liquor, and school premises not to be used as committee rooms, otherwise an illegal hiring[2] (s 108 amended by the Representation of the People Act 1985, Sch 4). Payment or contract for payment for exhibition of election notices unless to person whose ordinary business it is to exhibit bills and advertisements is an illegal practice[2] (s 109). Printer's name and address to appear on election publications, otherwise candidate or election agent guilty of illegal practice[2] and any other person liable on summary conviction to a fine not exceeding **level 5** on the standard scale (s 110 amended by the Representation of the People Act 1985, Sch 3). Person engaging or employing paid canvasser and person so engaged or employed guilty of illegal employment[1] (s 111). Knowingly provide money for illegal purposes is an illegal payment[1] (s 112). Bribery a corrupt practice[1] (s 113); treating a corrupt practice[2] (s 114); undue influence a corrupt practice[2] (s 115).

---

1. For procedure, penalties etc in relation to illegal payments, employment or hiring, see s 175, post; and see ss 176–181 for general provisions as to prosecutions.
2. For procedure for prosecutions for corrupt or illegal practices see ss 168–171, and generally see ss 176–181, post.

8–7981   118. Interpretation of Part II[1].   In this Part of this Act, unless the context otherwise requires—

"candidate" shall be construed in accordance with section 118A below;

"committee room" does not include any house or room occupied by a candidate as a dwelling, by reason only of the candidate transacting business there with his agents in relation to the election, and no room or building shall be deemed to be a committee room by reason only of the candidate or any agent of the candidate addressing in it electors, committee members or others;

"declaration as to election expenses" means a declaration made under section 82 above, or, as the case may be, paragraph 3 of Schedule 4 to this Act;

"election expenses", in relation to an election, shall be construed in accordance with sections 90A to 90D above;

"money" and "pecuniary reward" shall (except in sections 71A, 113 and 114 above and Schedule 2A to this Act) be deemed to include—

    (*a*)   any office, place or employment, and
    (*b*)   any valuable security or other equivalent of money, and
    (*c*)   any valuable consideration,

and expressions referring to money shall be construed accordingly;

"payment" includes any pecuniary or other reward;

"personal expenses" as used with respect to the expenditure of any candidate in relation to any election includes the reasonable travelling expenses of the candidate, and the reasonable expenses of his living at hotels or elsewhere for the purposes of and in relation to the election;

"return as to election expenses" means a return (including the bills and receipts to be delivered with it) to be made under section 81(1) above, or, as the case may be paragraph 3 of Schedule 4 to this Act.

[Representation of the People Act 1983, s 118 as amended by the Representation of the People Act 1985, Sch 4 and the Political Parties, Elections and Referendums Act 2000, s 135(1)—abridged.]

---

1. Only definitions of immediate relevance to the provisions included in this Manual are printed here.

PART III[1]
LEGAL PROCEEDINGS

Director of Public Prosecutions' Duty to report corrupt practice

8–7982   161. Justice of the Peace.   Where a justice of the peace is reported by an election court to have been guilty of any corrupt practice in reference to an election, the court shall report the case to the Lord Chancellor or (*Scotland*) with such evidence as may have been given of the corrupt practice.*

[Representation of the People Act 1983, s 161 as amended by the Representation of the People Act 1985, Schs 4 and 5.]

---

*Amended by the Constitutional Reform Act 2005, Sch 4 from a date to be appointed.
1. Part III comprises ss 120–186.

8–7983   162. Member of legal and certain other professions.   Where a barrister, advocate, solicitor or any person who belongs to any profession the admission to which is regulated by law is reported by an election court to have been guilty of any corrupt practice in reference to an election—

(*a*) the court shall bring the matter before the Inn of Court, Faculty of Advocates, High Court or tribunal having power to take cognizance of any misconduct of the person in his profession; and

(*b*) the Inn of Court, Faculty of Advocates, High Court or tribunal may deal with him as if the corrupt practice were misconduct by him in his profession.

[Representation of the People Act 1983, s 162 as amended by the Representation of the People Act 1985, Schs 4 and 5.]

8–7984   163. Holder of licence or certificate under Licensing Acts.   (1) Licence or certificate holder who knowingly permits bribery or treating on his licensed premises to be reported to licensing authority by the court and the licensing authority to enter report in register of licences.

(2) Report to be taken into consideration when considering renewal and may be ground for refusal.

[Representation of the People Act 1983, s 163 as amended by the Representation of the People Act 1985, Schs 4 and 5—summarised.]

Prosecutions for corrupt or illegal practices

8–7985   168. Prosecutions for corrupt practices.   (1) A person who is guilty of a corrupt practice shall be liable[1]—

(*a*) on conviction on indictment—

(i) in the case of a corrupt practice under section 60 above, to imprisonment for a term not exceeding two years, or to a fine, or to both,

(ii) in any other case, to imprisonment for a term not exceeding one year, or to a fine, or to both;

(*b*) on summary conviction, to imprisonment for a term not exceeding **6 months**, or to a fine not exceeding the **statutory maximum, or to both**.

(5), (6) (*Repealed*).

(7) If it appears to the court by which any person holding a licence or certificate under the Licensing Acts is convicted of the offence of bribery or treating that the offence was committed on his licensed premises—

(*a*) the court shall direct the conviction to be entered in the proper register of licences, and

(*b*) the entry shall be taken into consideration by the licensing authority in determining whether they will or will not grant a renewal of the licence or certificate, and may be a ground, if the authority think fit, for refusing its renewal.

[Representation of the People Act 1983, s 168 as amended by the Representation of the People Act 1985, Schs 3, 4 and 5.]

---

1. For procedure in respect of this offence which is triable either way, see the Magistrates' Courts Act 1980, ss 17A–21 in PART I: MAGISTRATES' COURTS, PROCEDURE, ante.

8–7986   169. Prosecutions for illegal practices.   A person guilty of an illegal practice shall on summary conviction be liable to a fine not exceeding **level 5** on the standard scale, . . .; and on a prosecution for an illegal practice it shall be sufficient to allege that the person charged was guilty of an illegal practice.

[Representation of the People Act 1983, s 169 as amended by the Representation of the People Act 1985, Schs 3 and 5.]

8–7987   170. Conviction of illegal practice on charge of corrupt practice, etc.   A person charged with a corrupt practice may, if the circumstances warrant such a finding, be found guilty of an illegal practice (which offence shall for that purpose be an indictable offence), and a person charged with an illegal practice may be found guilty of that offence notwithstanding that the act constituting the offence amounted to a corrupt practice.

[Representation of the People Act 1983, s 170.]

Illegal payments, employments or hirings

8–7988   175. Illegal payments, etc.   (1) A person guilty of an offence of illegal payment or employment or hiring shall, on summary conviction, be liable to a fine not exceeding **level 5** on the standard scale, and on a prosecution for such an offence it shall be sufficient to allege that the person charged was guilty of an illegal payment or employment or hiring as the case may be.

(2) A candidate or election agent who is personally guilty of an offence of illegal payment or employment or hiring shall be guilty of an illegal practice, and if an offence of illegal payment or employment or hiring is committed with the candidate's knowledge and consent at an election where candidates are not required to have election agents, the candidate shall be guilty of an illegal practice.

(3) Any person charged with an offence of illegal payment or employment or hiring may be found guilty of that offence, notwithstanding that the act constituting the offence amounted to a corrupt or illegal practice.

[Representation of the People Act 1983, s 175 as amended by the Representation of the People Act 1985, Sch 3 and the Political Parties, Elections and Referendums Act 2000, Sch 21.]

General provisions as to prosecutions

8–7989   176. Time limit for prosecutions.   (1) A proceeding against a person in respect of any offence under any provision contained in or made under this Act shall be commenced within one year after the offence was committed, and the time so limited by this section shall, in the case of any proceedings under the Magistrates' Courts Act 1980 . . . for any such offence be substituted for any limitation of time contained in that Act . . .

(2) For the purposes of this section—

(*a*)   in England and Wales, the laying of an information;

(*b*), (*c*)   *Scotland, Northern Ireland,*

shall be deemed to be the commencement of a proceeding.

(3) *(Repealed).*

[Representation of the People Act 1983, s 176 as amended by the Representation of the People Act 1985, Schs 4 and 5.]

8–8000   177. Local election offence punishable summarily.   (1) A prosecution for any offence punishable summarily committed in reference to an election under the local government Act—

(*a*)   may be instituted before any magistrates' court in the county[1] in which the local government area for which the election was held is situated or which it adjoins; and

(*b*)   the offence shall be deemed for all purposes to have been committed within the jurisdiction of that court.

This section does not apply in Scotland.

(2) *Repealed.*

[Representation of the People Act 1983, s 177 amended by the Local Government (Wales) Act 1994, Sch 2 and SI 1996/675.]

---

1. This reference to a county shall be construed in relation to any area in England (outside Greater London) or Wales as meaning a commission area (as defined in the Justices of the Peace Act 1979, s 1 in PART I: MAGISTRATES' COURTS, PROCEDURE, ante) (Local Government Changes for England Regulations 1996, SI 1996/674 and the Magistrates' Courts (Wales) (Consequences of Local Changes) Order 1996, SI 1996/675).

8–8001   178. Prosecution of offences committed outside the United Kingdom.   Proceedings in respect of an offence under this Act alleged to have been committed outside the United Kingdom by a Commonwealth citizen or citizen of the Republic of Ireland may be taken, and the offence may for all incidental purposes be treated as having been committed, in any place in the United Kingdom.

[Representation of the People Act 1983, s 178 as substituted by the Representation of the People Act 1985, Sch 4.]

8–8002   179. Offences by associations.   Where—

(*a*)   any corrupt or illegal practice or any illegal payment, employment or hiring, or

(*b*)   any offence under section 110 above,

is committed by any association or body of persons, corporate or unincorporate, the members of the association or body who have taken part in the commission of the offence shall be liable to any fine or punishment imposed for that offence by this Act.

[Representation of the People Act 1983, s 179.]

8–8003   180. Evidence by certificate of holding of elections.   On—

(*a*)   any prosecution for a corrupt or illegal practice or for any illegal payment, employment or hiring, and

(*b*)   any proceedings for a penalty under section 85 above or paragraph 4 of Schedule 4 to this Act,

the certificate of the returning officer at an election—

(i)   that the election mentioned in the certificate was duly held, and

(ii)   that the person named in the certificate was a candidate at the election,

shall be sufficient evidence of the facts stated in it.

[Representation of the People Act 1983, s 180.]

8–8003A   180A. Evidence by certificate of electoral registration.   The certificate of a registration officer that any person is or is not, or was or was not at any particular time, duly registered in one of the officer's registers in respect of any address shall be sufficient evidence of the facts stated in it; and a document purporting to be such a certificate shall be received in evidence and presumed to be such a certificate unless the contrary is proved.

[Representation of the People Act 1983, s 180A, as inserted by the Representation of the People Act 2000, Sch 1.]

8–8004 185. Interpretation of Part III. In this Part of this Act, unless the context otherwise requires[1]—

"judicial office" includes the office of justice of the peace;
"Licensing Acts" means the Licensing (Scotland) Act 1976 and the Licensing (Northern Ireland) Order 1996 (as that Act or Order may from time to time have effect);
"money" and "pecuniary reward" shall be deemed to include—

> (*a*) any office, place or employment, and
> (*b*) any valuable security or other equivalent of money, and
> (*c*) any valuable consideration,

and expressions referring to money shall be construed accordingly;

"payment" includes any pecuniary or other reward:
[Representation of the People Act 1983, s 185 as amended by the Licensing Act 2003, Sch 6—abridged.]

------

1. Only definitions of immediate relevance to the provisions included in this Manual are printed here.

PART V
GENERAL AND SUPPLEMENTAL

Interpretation

8–8005 202. General provisions as to interpretation. (1) In this Act, unless the context otherwise requires—

"dwelling" includes any part of a house where that part is occupied separately as a dwelling;
"election" means a parliamentary election or an election under the local government Act.
"election court" means—

> (*a*) in relation to a parliamentary election petition, the judges presiding at the trial;
> (*b*) in relation to a petition questioning an election under the local government Act, the court constituted under this Act for the trial of that petition;

"election petition" means a petition presented in pursuance of Part III of this Act;
"elector" in relation to an election, means any person whose name is for the time being on the register to be used at that election, but does not include those shown in the register as below voting age on the day fixed for the poll;
"legal incapacity" includes (in addition to any incapacity by virtue of any subsisting provision of the common law) any disqualification imposed by this Act or any other Act;
"legal process" means a claim form, application notice, writ, summons or other process;
"parliamentary election petition" means an election petition questioning a parliamentary election or return;
"person" includes (without prejudice to the provisions of the Interpretation Act 1978) an association corporate or unincorporate;
"prescribed" except in Part III of this Act means prescribed by regulations;
"proper officer" means in England and Wales one within the meaning of section 270(3) and (4) of the Local Government Act 1972, and (*Scotland*).
"qualifying address" shall be construed in accordance with section 9(8) above;
"service voter" means a person who has made a service declaration and is registered or entitled to be registered in pursuance of it;
"universal postal service provider" means a universal service provider (within the meaning of the Postal Services Act 2000);
"voter" means a person voting at an election and includes a person voting as proxy and, except in the parliamentary elections rules, and the rules under section 36 and 42 above, a person voting by proxy, and "vote" (whether noun or verb) shall be construed accordingly, except that in those rules any reference to an elector voting or an elector's vote shall include a reference to an elector voting by proxy or an elector's vote given by proxy.

(2) For the purposes of the Representation of the People Acts a person shall be deemed not to have attained a given age until the commencement of the relevant anniversary of the day of his birth.
[Representation of the People Act 1983, s 202 as amended by the Representation of the People Act 1985, Schs 4 and 5, the Statute Law (Repeals) Act 1993, Sch 1, the Law Officers Act 1997, Schedule and the Representation of the People Act 2000, Sch 1—abridged.]

8–8006 203. Local government provisions as to England and Wales. (1) In this Act, unless the context otherwise requires, in relation to England and Wales—

"electoral area" means any electoral division, London borough, ward, district, parish, community or other area for which the election of councillors is held under the local government Act;

"local authority" means a county council, a county borough council, a district council, a London borough council, or a parish or community council;

"local government Act" means the Local Government Act 1972;

"local government area" means a county, county borough, London borough, district, parish or community;

"local government election" means the election of councillors for any electoral area.

(2)–(5) *London, Isles of Scilly.*

[Representation of the People Act 1983, s 203 as amended by the Local Government Act 1985, Schs 9 and 17, the Education Reform Act 1988, Sch 13 and the Local Government (Wales) Act 1994, Sch 16.]

Representation of the People Act 1985[1]

(1985 c 50)

8-8110 This Act extends the entitlement to vote as an elector in a parliamentary election to British citizens overseas, and makes comparable arrangements for European Parliamentary elections (ss 1–4)[2]. It provides for the manner of voting including proxy votes (ss 5–11)[3].

A person making an overseas elector's declaration knowing that he is subject to a legal incapacity or that it contains a false statement, or a person who attests a declaration when he knows he is not authorised or it contains a false statement, is guilty of an offence and liable on summary conviction to a fine not exceeding **level 5** on the standard scale (s 12).

---

1. Although many consequential amendments in the Act were brought into force by SI 1985/1185, these sections are not among them.

2. Amendments were made by the Representation of the People Act 1989 (c 28), the European Parliamentary Elections Act 1999, Schs 3 and 4 and the Representation of the People Act 2000, Schs 2 and 7.

3. Amendments were made by SI 1997/138 and the Representation of the People Act 2000, Sch 6.

Political Parties, Elections and Referendums Act 2000

(2000 c 41)

This Act establishes the Electoral Commission and bodies with related functions as defined in Part I (**ss 1–21 and Schs 1–3**). Part II (**ss 22–40 and Sch 4**) makes provision for registration of political parties. Nominations may only be received from registered parties or persons who represent no party ('independent candidates') in relevant elections i.e. parliamentary and local elections, elections to the European Parliament and to the National Assembly for Wales (**s 22**). The Electoral Commission maintains a register for Great Britain and one for Northern Ireland (**s 23**). A registered party is required to register its office holders including campaign officers (**ss 24–25**) and to adopt a scheme setting out the arrangements for regulating its financial affairs (**ss 26–27**). Registration may include up to three emblems to be used by the party on ballot papers (**s 29**). Alterations to the register may be made on application and any changes in a party's entry must be notified to the Commission (**ss 30–32**). Special provision is made for minor parties (**s 34**). Part III (**ss 41–49 and Sch 5**) makes requirements for the keeping of accounting records.

PART IV[1]

CONTROL OF DONATIONS TO REGISTERED PARTIES AND THEIR MEMBERS ETC

CHAPTER I

DONATIONS TO REGISTERED PARTIES

8-8112 50. Donations for purposes of Part IV. (1) The following provisions have effect for the purposes of this Part.

(2) "Donation", in relation to a registered party, means (subject to section 52)—

(*a*) any gift to the party of money or other property;

(*b*) any sponsorship provided in relation to the party (as defined by section 51);

(*c*) any subscription or other fee paid for affiliation to, or membership of, the party;

(*d*) any money spent (otherwise than by or on behalf of the party) in paying any expenses incurred directly or indirectly by the party;

(*e*) any money lent to the party otherwise than on commercial terms;

(*f*) the provision otherwise than on commercial terms of any property, services or facilities for the use or benefit of the party (including the services of any person).

(3) Where—

(a)　any money or other property is transferred to a registered party pursuant to any transaction or arrangement involving the provision by or on behalf of the party of any property, services or facilities or other consideration of monetary value, and

(b)　the total value in monetary terms of the consideration so provided by or on behalf of the party is less than the value of the money or (as the case may be) the market value of the property transferred,

the transfer of the money or property shall (subject to subsection (5)) constitute a gift to the party for the purposes of subsection (2)(*a*).

(4) In determining—

(a)　for the purposes of subsection (2)(*e*), whether any money lent to a registered party is so lent otherwise than on commercial terms, or

(b)　for the purposes of subsection (2)(*f*), whether any property, services or facilities provided for the use or benefit of a registered party is or are so provided otherwise than on such terms,

regard shall be had to the total value in monetary terms of the consideration provided by or on behalf of the party in respect of the loan or the provision of the property, services or facilities.

(5) Where (apart from this subsection) anything would be a donation both by virtue of subsection (2)(*b*) and by virtue of any other provision of this section, subsection (2)(*b*) (together with section 51) shall apply in relation to it to the exclusion of the other provision of this section.

(6) Anything given or transferred to any officer, member, trustee or agent of a registered party in his capacity as such (and not for his own use or benefit) is to be regarded as given or transferred to the party (and references to donations received by a party accordingly include donations so given or transferred).

(7) Except so far as a contrary intention appears, references to a registered party in the context of—

(a)　the making of donations to, or the receipt or acceptance of donations by, a registered party, or

(b)　any provision having effect for or in connection with determining what constitutes a donation to such a party,

shall, in the case of a party with accounting units, be construed as references to the central organisation of the party or any of its accounting units.

(8) In this section—

(a)　any reference to anything being given or transferred to a party or any person is a reference to its being so given or transferred either directly or indirectly through any third person;

(b)　"gift" includes bequest.

(9) Nothing in this Part applies in relation to donations received by a minor party.

[Political Parties, Elections and Referendums Act 2000, s 50.]

---

1. Part IV contains ss 50–71 and Schs 6–7.

8–8113 51. Sponsorship.　(1) For the purposes of this Part sponsorship is provided in relation to a registered party if—

(a)　any money or other property is transferred to the party or to any person for the benefit of the party, and

(b)　the purpose (or one of the purposes) of the transfer is (or must, having regard to all the circumstances, reasonably be assumed to be)—

(i)　to help the party with meeting, or to meet, to any extent any defined expenses incurred or to be incurred by or on behalf of the party, or

(ii)　to secure that to any extent any such expenses are not so incurred.

(2) In subsection (1) "defined expenses" means expenses in connection with—

(a)　any conference, meeting or other event organised by or on behalf of the party;

(b)　the preparation, production or dissemination of any publication by or on behalf of the party; or

(c)　any study or research organised by or on behalf of the party.

(3) The following do not, however, constitute sponsorship by virtue of subsection (1)—

(a)　the making of any payment in respect of—

(i)　any charge for admission to any conference, meeting or other event, or

(ii)　the purchase price of, or any other charge for access to, any publication;

(b)　the making of any payment in respect of the inclusion of an advertisement in any publication where the payment is made at the commercial rate payable for the inclusion of such an advertisement in any such publication;

and subsection (1) also has effect subject to section 52(3).

(4) The Secretary of State may by order made on the recommendation of the Commission amend subsection (2) or (3).

(5) In this section "publication" means a publication made available in whatever form and by whatever means (whether or not to the public at large or any section of the public).

[Political Parties, Elections and Referendums Act 2000, s 51.]

8–8114   52. Payments, services etc not to be regarded as donations.   (1) For the purposes of this Part none of the following shall be regarded as a donation—

(a)   any policy development grant (within the meaning of section 12);

(b)   any grant under section 170 of the Criminal Justice and Public Order Act 1994 (security costs at party conferences);

(c)   any payment made by or on behalf of the European Parliament for the purpose of assisting members of the Parliament to perform their functions as such members;

(d)   the transmission by a broadcaster, free of charge, of a party political broadcast or a referendum campaign broadcast (within the meaning of section 127);

(e)   any other facilities provided in pursuance of any right conferred on candidates or a party at an election or a referendum by any enactment;

(f)   the provision of assistance by a person appointed under section 9 of the Local Government and Housing Act 1989;

(g)   the provision by any individual of his own services which he provides voluntarily in his own time and free of charge;

(h)   any interest accruing to a registered party in respect of any donation which is dealt with by the party in accordance with section 56(2)(a) or (b).

(2) For the purposes of this Part there shall be disregarded—

(a)   any donation which (in accordance with any enactment) falls to be included in a return as to election expenses in respect of a candidate or candidates at a particular election; and

(b)   except for the purposes of section 68, any donation whose value (as determined in accordance with section 53) is not more than £200.

(3) Nothing in section 50 or 51 shall have the result that a payment made in respect of the hire of a stand at a party conference organised by or on behalf of a registered party is to constitute a donation to the party for the purposes of this Part if or to the extent that the payment does not exceed such of the maximum rates which the Commission determine to be reasonable for the hire of stands at party conferences as is applicable to the hire of the stand in question.

[Political Parties, Elections and Referendums Act 2000, s 52.]

8–8115   53. Value of donations.   (1) The value of any donation falling within section 50(2)(a) (other than money) shall be taken to be the market value of the property in question.

(2) Where, however, section 50(2)(a) applies by virtue of section 50(3), the value of the donation shall be taken to be the difference between—

(a)   the value of the money, or the market value of the property, in question, and

(b)   the total value in monetary terms of the consideration provided by or on behalf of the party.

(3) The value of any donation falling within section 50(2)(b) shall be taken to be the value of the money, or (as the case may be) the market value of the property, transferred as mentioned in section 51(1); and accordingly any value in monetary terms of any benefit conferred on the person providing the sponsorship in question shall be disregarded.

(4) The value of any donation falling within section 50(2)(e) or (f) shall be taken to be the amount representing the difference between—

(a)   the total value in monetary terms of the consideration that would have had to be provided by or on behalf of the party in respect of the loan or the provision of the property, services or facilities if—

    (i)   the loan had been made, or

    (ii)   the property, services or facilities had been provided,

    on commercial terms, and

(b)   the total value in monetary terms of the consideration (if any) actually so provided by or on behalf of the party.

(5) Subsection (6) applies where a donation such as is mentioned in subsection (3) confers an enduring benefit on the party during the whole or part of—

(a)   any period for which a report is to be prepared under this Part, or

(b)   two or more such periods.

(6) In such a case, the amount to be recorded in any such report shall be so much of the total value of the donation (as determined in accordance with subsection (3)) as accrues during the whole or part of the period to which the report relates.

[Political Parties, Elections and Referendums Act 2000, s 53.]

CHAPTER II

RESTRICTIONS ON DONATIONS TO REGISTERED PARTIES

Permissible donations

8–8116   54. Permissible donors.   (1) A donation received by a registered party must not be accepted by the party if—

(*a*)   the person by whom the donation would be made is not, at the time of its receipt by the party, a permissible donor; or

(*b*)   the party is (whether because the donation is given anonymously or by reason of any deception or concealment or otherwise) unable to ascertain the identity of that person.

(2)   For the purposes of this Part the following are permissible donors—

(*a*)   an individual registered in an electoral register;

(*b*)   a company—

   (i)   registered under the Companies Act 1985 or the Companies (Northern Ireland) Order 1986, and

   (ii)   incorporated within the United Kingdom or another member State,

   which carries on business in the United Kingdom;

(*c*)   a registered party;

(*d*)   a trade union entered in the list kept under the Trade Union and Labour Relations (Consolidation) Act 1992 or the Industrial Relations (Northern Ireland) Order 1992;

(*e*)   a building society (within the meaning of the Building Societies Act 1986);

(*f*)   a limited liability partnership registered under the Limited Liability Partnerships Act 2000, or any corresponding enactment in force in Northern Ireland, which carries on business in the United Kingdom;

(*g*)   a friendly society registered under the Friendly Societies Act 1974 or a society registered (or deemed to be registered) under the Industrial and Provident Societies Act 1965 or the Industrial and Provident Societies Act (Northern Ireland) 1969; and

(*h*)   any unincorporated association of two or more persons which does not fall within any of the preceding paragraphs but which carries on business or other activities wholly or mainly in the United Kingdom and whose main office is there.

(3)   In relation to a donation in the form of a bequest subsection (2)(*a*) shall be read as referring to an individual who was, at any time within the period of five years ending with the date of his death, registered in an electoral register.

(4)   Where any person ("the principal donor") causes an amount ("the principal donation") to be received by a registered party by way of a donation—

(*a*)   on behalf of himself and one or more other persons, or

(*b*)   on behalf of two or more other persons,

then for the purposes of this Part each individual contribution by a person falling within paragraph (*a*) or (*b*) of more than £200 shall be treated as if it were a separate donation received from that person.

(5)   In relation to each such separate donation, the principal donor must ensure that, at the time when the principal donation is received by the party, the party is given—

(*a*)   (except in the case of a donation which the principal donor is treated as making) all such details in respect of the person treated as making the donation as are required by virtue of paragraph 2 of Schedule 6 to be given in respect of the donor of a recordable donation; and

(*b*)   (in any case) all such details in respect of the donation as are required by virtue of paragraph 4 of Schedule 6 to be given in respect of a recordable donation.

(6)   Where—

(*a*)   any person ("the agent") causes an amount to be received by a registered party by way of a donation on behalf of another person ("the donor"), and

(*b*)   the amount of that donation is more than £200,

the agent must ensure that, at the time when the donation is received by the party, the party is given all such details in respect of the donor as are required by virtue of paragraph 2 of Schedule 6 to be given in respect of the donor of a recordable donation.

(7)   A person commits an offence if, without reasonable excuse, he fails to comply with subsection (5) or (6).

(8)   In this section "electoral register" means any of the following—

(*a*)   a register of parliamentary or local government electors maintained under section 9 of the Representation of the People Act 1983;

(*b*)   a register of relevant citizens of the European Union prepared under the European Parliamentary Elections (Franchise of Relevant Citizens of the Union) Regulations 2001; or (*c*)   a register of peers prepared under regulations under section 3 of the Representation of the People Act 1985.

[Political Parties, Elections and Referendums Act 2000, s 54, as amended by SI 2001/1184.]

8–8117   **55. Payments etc which are (or are not) to be treated as donations by permissible donors.**   (1) The following provisions have effect for the purposes of this Part.

(2) Any payment out of public funds received by a registered party shall (subject to section 52(1)(*a*) and (*b*)) be regarded as a donation received by the party from a permissible donor.

(3) Any donation received by a registered party shall (if it would not otherwise fall to be so regarded) be regarded as a donation received by the party from a permissible donor if and to the extent that—

(*a*)   the purpose of the donation is to meet qualifying costs incurred or to be incurred in connection with a visit by any member or officer of the party to a country or territory outside the United Kingdom, and

(*b*)   the amount of the donation does not exceed a reasonable amount in respect of such costs.

(4) In subsection (3) "qualifying costs", in relation to any member or officer of the party, means costs relating to that person in respect of—

(*a*)   travelling between the United Kingdom and the country or territory in question, or

(*b*)   travelling, accommodation or subsistence while within that country or territory.

(5) Any exempt trust donation received by a registered party shall be regarded as a donation received by the party from a permissible donor.

(6) But any donation received by a registered party from a trustee of any property (in his capacity as such) which is not—

(*a*)   an exempt trust donation, or

(*b*)   a donation transmitted by the trustee to the party on behalf of beneficiaries under the trust who are—

(i)   persons who at the time of its receipt by the party are permissible donors, or

(ii)   the members of an unincorporated association which at that time is a permissible donor,

shall be regarded as a donation received by the party from a person who is not a permissible donor.

[Political Parties, Elections and Referendums Act 2000, s 55.]

8–8118   **56. Acceptance or return of donations: general.**   (1) Where—

(*a*)   a donation is received by a registered party, and

(*b*)   it is not immediately decided that the party should (for whatever reason) refuse the donation,

all reasonable steps must be taken forthwith by or on behalf of the party to verify (or, so far as any of the following is not apparent, ascertain) the identity of the donor, whether he is a permissible donor, and (if that appears to be the case) all such details in respect of him as are required by virtue of paragraph 2 of Schedule 6 to be given in respect of the donor of a recordable donation.

(2) If a registered party receives a donation which it is prohibited from accepting by virtue of section 54(1), or which it is decided that the party should for any other reason refuse, then—

(*a*)   unless the donation falls within section 54(1)(*b*), the donation, or a payment of an equivalent amount, must be sent back to the person who made the donation or any person appearing to be acting on his behalf,

(*b*)   if the donation falls within that provision, the required steps (as defined by section 57(1)) must be taken in relation to the donation,

within the period of 30 days beginning with the date when the donation is received by the party.

(3) Where—

(*a*)   subsection (2)(*a*) applies in relation to a donation, and

(*b*)   the donation is not dealt with in accordance with that provision,

the party and the treasurer of the party are each guilty of an offence.

(4) Where—

(*a*)   subsection (2)(*b*) applies in relation to a donation, and

(*b*)   the donation is not dealt with in accordance with that provision,

the treasurer of the party is guilty of an offence.

(5) For the purposes of this Part a donation received by a registered party shall be taken to have been accepted by the party unless—

(*a*)   the steps mentioned in paragraph (*a*) or (*b*) of subsection (2) are taken in relation to the donation within the period of 30 days mentioned in that subsection; and

(*b*)   a record can be produced of the receipt of the donation and—

(i)   of the return of the donation, or the equivalent amount, as mentioned in subsection (2)(*a*), or

(ii) of the required steps being taken in relation to the donation as mentioned in subsection (2)(*b*),

as the case may be.

(6) Where a donation is received by a registered party in the form of an amount paid into any account held by the party with a financial institution, it shall be taken for the purposes of this Part to have been received by the party at the time when the party is notified in the usual way of the payment into the account.

[Political Parties, Elections and Referendums Act 2000, s 56.]

8–8119   57. Return of donations where donor unidentifiable.   (1) For the purposes of section 56(2)(*b*) the required steps are as follows—

(*a*) if the donation mentioned in that provision was transmitted by a person other than the donor, and the identity of that person is apparent, to return the donation to that person;

(*b*) if paragraph (*a*) does not apply but it is apparent that the donor has, in connection with the donation, used any facility provided by an identifiable financial institution, to return the donation to that institution; and

(*c*) in any other case, to send the donation to the Commission.

(2) In subsection (1) any reference to returning or sending a donation to any person or body includes a reference to sending a payment of an equivalent amount to that person or body.

(3) Any amount sent to the Commission in pursuance of subsection (1)(*c*) shall be paid by them into the Consolidated Fund.

[Political Parties, Elections and Referendums Act 2000, s 57.]

Forfeiture of certain donations

8–8119A   60. Supplementary provisions about orders under section 58.   (1) Provision may be made by rules of court[1]—

(*a*) with respect to applications or appeals to any court under section 58 or 59,

(*b*) for the giving of notice of such applications or appeals to persons affected,

(*c*) for the joinder, or in Scotland sisting, of such persons as parties,

and generally with respect to the procedure under those sections before any court.

(2) Subsection (1) is without prejudice to the generality of any existing power to make rules.

(3) Any amount forfeited by an order under section 58 or 59 shall be paid into the Consolidated Fund.

(4) Subsection (3) does not apply—

(*a*) where an appeal is made under section 59(2) or (5), before the appeal is determined or otherwise disposed of; and

(*b*) in any other case—

(i) where the forfeiture was ordered by a magistrates' court or a court of summary jurisdiction in Northern Ireland, before the end of the period of 30 days mentioned in section 59(2); or

(ii) where the forfeiture was ordered by the sheriff, before the end of any period within which, in accordance with rules of court, an appeal under section 59(5) must be made.

(5) In the case of a registered party which is not a body corporate—

(*a*) proceedings under section 58 or 59 shall be brought against or by the party in its own name (and not in that of any of its members);

(*b*) for the purposes of any such proceedings any rules of court relating to the service of documents apply as if the party were a body corporate; and

(*c*) any amount forfeited by an order under section 58 or 59 shall be paid out of the funds of the party.

[Political Parties, Elections and Referendums Act 2000, s 60.]

---

1. See the Magistrates' Courts (Forfeiture of Political Donations) Rules 2003, SI 2003/1645 in Part I: Magistrates' Courts, Procedure, *ante*. The Crown Court (Forfeiture of Political donations) Rules 2003, SI 2003/1646 have also been made.

Evasion of restrictions on donations

8–8119B   61. Offences concerned with evasion of restrictions on donations.   (1) A person commits an offence if he—

(*a*) knowingly enters into, or

(*b*) knowingly does any act in furtherance of,

any arrangement which facilitates or is likely to facilitate, whether by means of any concealment or disguise or otherwise, the making of donations to a registered party by any person or body other than a permissible donor.

(2) A person commits an offence if—

(a) he knowingly gives the treasurer of a registered party any information relating to—

(i) the amount of any donation made to the party, or
(ii) the person or body making such a donation,

which is false in a material particular; or

(b) with intent to deceive, he withholds from the treasurer of a registered party any material information relating to a matter within paragraph (a)(i) or (ii).

[Political Parties, Elections and Referendums Act 2000, s 61.]

CHAPTER III
REPORTING OF DONATIONS TO REGISTERED PARTIES

Reports to be made by registered parties

8-8119C   62. Quarterly donation reports.   (1) The treasurer of a registered party shall, in the case of each year, prepare a report under this subsection in respect of each of the following periods—

(a) January to March;
(b) April to June;
(c) July to September;
(d) October to December.

(2) In this section—

"donation report" means a report prepared under subsection (1);
"reporting period", in relation to such a report, means the period mentioned in any of paragraphs (a) to (d) of that subsection to which the report relates.

(3) The donation reports for any year shall, in the case of each permissible donor from whom any donation is accepted by the party during that year, comply with the following provisions of this section so far as they require any such donation to be recorded in a donation report; and in those provisions any such donation is referred to, in relation to the donor and that year, as a "relevant donation".

(4) Where no previous relevant donation or donations has or have been required to be recorded under this subsection, a relevant donation must be recorded—

(a) if it is a donation of more than £5,000, or
(b) if, when it is added to any other relevant donation or donations, the aggregate amount of the donations is more than £5,000.

(5) A donation to which subsection (4) applies must—

(a) (if within paragraph (a) of that subsection) be recorded in the donation report for the reporting period in which it is accepted, or
(b) (if within paragraph (b) of that subsection) be recorded (as part of the aggregate amount mentioned in that paragraph) in the donation report for the reporting period in which the donation which causes that aggregate amount to be more than £5,000 is accepted.

(6) Where any previous relevant donation or donations has or have been required to be recorded under subsection (4), a relevant donation must be recorded at the point when there has or have been accepted—

(a) since the donation or donations required to be recorded under subsection (4), or
(b) if any relevant donation or donations has or have previously been required to be recorded under this subsection, since the donation or donations last required to be so recorded,

any relevant donation or donations of an amount or aggregate amount which is more than £1,000.

(7) A donation to which subsection (6) applies on any occasion must—

(a) if it is the only donation required to be recorded on that occasion, be recorded in the donation report for the reporting period in which it is accepted, or
(b) in any other case be recorded (as part of the aggregate amount mentioned in that subsection) in the donation report for the reporting period in which the donation which causes that aggregate amount to be more than £1,000 is accepted.

(8) For the purposes of subsections (4) to (7) as they apply in relation to any year—

(a) each payment to which section 55(2) applies and which is accepted by the party during that year shall be treated as a relevant donation in relation to that year, and
(b) each payment to which section 55(3) applies and which is received from a particular donor and accepted by the party during that year shall be treated as a relevant donation in relation to the donor and that year;

and the donation reports for the year shall accordingly comply with subsections (4) to (7) so far as they operate, by virtue of paragraph (a) or (b) above, to require any relevant donation falling within that paragraph to be recorded in a donation report.

(9) A donation report must also record every donation falling within section 54(1)(*a*) or (*b*) and dealt with during the reporting period in accordance with section 56(2).

(10) If during any reporting period—

(*a*) no donations have been accepted by the party which, by virtue of the preceding provisions of this section, are required to be recorded in the donation report for that period, and

(*b*) no donations have been dealt with as mentioned in subsection (9),

the report shall contain a statement to that effect.

(11) Where a registered party is a party with accounting units, subsections (3) to (10) shall apply separately in relation to the central organisation of the party and each of its accounting units—

(*a*) as if any reference to the party were a reference to the central organisation or (as the case may be) to such an accounting unit; but

(*b*) with the substitution, in relation to such an accounting unit, of "£1,000" for "£5,000" in each place where it occurs in subsections (4) and (5).

(12) However, for the purposes of subsections (3) to (7) in their application in relation to the central organisation and any year by virtue of subsection (11), any donation—

(*a*) which is accepted from a permissible donor by any of the accounting units during that year, but

(*b*) which is not required to be recorded under subsection (4) or (6) (as they apply by virtue of subsection (11)) as a donation accepted by the accounting unit,

shall be treated as a donation accepted from the donor during that year by the central organisation.

(13) Schedule 6 has effect with respect to the information to be given in donation reports.

[Political Parties, Elections and Referendums Act 2000, s 62.]

8–8119D **63. Weekly donation reports during general election periods.** (1) Subject to section 64, the treasurer of a registered party shall, in the case of any general election period, prepare a report under this section in respect of each of the following periods—

(*a*) the period of seven days beginning with the first day of the general election period;

(*b*) each succeeding period of seven days falling within the general election period; and

(*c*) any final period of less than seven days falling within that period.

(2) In this section—

"weekly report" means a report prepared under subsection (1);

"reporting period", in relation to such a report, means the period mentioned in any of paragraphs (*a*) to (*c*) of that subsection to which the report relates.

(3) The weekly report for any reporting period shall record each donation of more than £5,000 received during that period—

(*a*) by the party (if it is not a party with accounting units); or

(*b*) by the central organisation of the party (if it is a party with accounting units).

(4) If during any reporting period no donations falling within subsection (3) have been received as mentioned in that subsection, the weekly report for that period shall contain a statement to that effect.

(5) Schedule 6 has effect with respect to the information to be given in weekly reports.

(6) In this section and section 64 "general election period" means the period—

(*a*) beginning with the date on which Her Majesty's intention to dissolve Parliament is announced in connection with a forthcoming parliamentary general election, and

(*b*) ending with the date of the poll.

[Political Parties, Elections and Referendums Act 2000, s 63.]

8–8119E **64. Exemptions from section 63.** (1) Section 63(1) shall not apply in relation to a registered party in respect of a general election period if the party has made an exemption declaration which covers the general election in question.

(2) A registered party shall be taken to have made an exemption declaration which covers a particular general election if a declaration that the party does not intend to have any candidates at that election—

(*a*) is signed by the responsible officers of the party; and

(*b*) is sent to the Commission within the period of seven days beginning with the date mentioned in section 63(6)(*a*).

(3) A registered party shall also be taken to have made an exemption declaration which covers a particular general election if the party's application for registration was accompanied by a declaration that the party was not intending to have candidates at parliamentary elections and either—

(*a*) the poll for the general election in question takes place within the period of twelve months beginning with the date of its registration; or

(b)   the declaration has been confirmed in the party's most recent notification given to the Commission under section 32 and the poll for the general election in question takes place within the period of twelve months beginning with the date when that notification was so given.

(4)   An exemption declaration shall, however, not cover a particular general election if the party in question withdraws its declaration by a notice—

(a)   signed by the responsible officers of the party, and
(b)   sent to the Commission,

before the beginning of the general election period.

(5)   Where—

(a)   a registered party has made an exemption declaration which (apart from this subsection) would cover a particular general election, but
(b)   the party has one or more candidates at that election,

the exemption declaration shall be treated as if it had been withdrawn at the beginning of the general election period (and the requirements of section 63 shall accordingly apply retrospectively as from the beginning of that period).

(6)   Subsection (3) shall apply to a party registered immediately before the date on which this section comes into force as if it referred to a declaration in the terms mentioned in that subsection having been—

(a)   signed by the responsible officers of the party, and
(b)   sent to the Commission within the period of six weeks beginning with that date.

(7)   For the purposes of this section "the responsible officers" are—

(a)   the registered leader;
(b)   the registered nominating officer; and
(c)   where the leader and the nominating officer are the same person, any other registered officer.

(8)   If any responsible officer is unable to sign a declaration or notice for the purposes of any provision of this section—

(a)   the holder of some other office in the party may sign in his place, and
(b)   the declaration or notice must include a statement of the reason why the responsible officer is unable to sign and a declaration that the holder of the other office is authorised to sign in his place.

(9)   For the purposes of this section and section 65 a registered party shall be taken to have a candidate at a general election if any statement published, in connection with the election, under rule 14 of the rules set out in Schedule 1 to the Representation of the People Act 1983 (parliamentary election rules) contains the name of a candidate standing in the name of the party.

[Political Parties, Elections and Referendums Act 2000, s 64.]

8–8119F   65. Submission of donation reports to Commission.   (1) A donation report under section 62 shall be delivered to the Commission by the treasurer of the party in question within the period of 30 days beginning with the end of the reporting period to which it relates.

(2)   A donation report under section 63 shall be delivered to the Commission by the treasurer of the party in question—

(a)   within the period of 7 days beginning with the end of the reporting period to which it relates; or
(b)   (if that is not possible in the case of any party to which section 63(1) applies by virtue of section 64(5)) within the period of 7 days beginning with the first day on which the party has a candidate at the election in question.

(3)   The treasurer of a registered party commits an offence if he fails to comply with the requirements of subsection (1) or (2) in relation to a donation report.

(4)   The treasurer of a registered party also commits an offence if he delivers a donation report to the Commission which does not comply with any requirements of this Part as regards the recording of donations in such a report.

(5)   Where a person is charged with an offence under this section, it shall be a defence to prove that he took all reasonable steps, and exercised all due diligence, to ensure that any such requirements were complied with in relation to donations received by the party during the relevant reporting period.

(6)   Where the court is satisfied, on an application made by the Commission, that any failure to comply with any such requirements in relation to any donation to a registered party was attributable to an intention on the part of any person to conceal the existence or true amount of the donation, the court may order the forfeiture by the party of an amount equal to the value of the donation.

(7)   The following provisions, namely—

(a)   subsections (3) to (5) of section 58, and
(b)   sections 59 and 60,

shall apply for the purposes, or in connection with the operation, of subsection (6) above as they apply for the purposes, or in connection with the operation, of section 58.

(8) Section 64(9) applies for the purposes of this section.

[Political Parties, Elections and Referendums Act 2000, s 65.]

8-8119G 66. Declaration by treasurer in donation report. (1) Each donation report under section 62 or 63 must, when delivered to the Commission, be accompanied by a declaration made by the treasurer which complies with subsection (2), (3) or (4).

(2) In the case of a report under section 62 (other than one making a nil return), the declaration must state that, to the best of the treasurer's knowledge and belief—

(a) all the donations recorded in the report as having been accepted by the party are from permissible donors, and

(b) during the reporting period—

(i) no other donations required to be recorded in the report have been accepted by the party, and

(ii) no donation from any person or body other than a permissible donor has been accepted by the party.

(3) For the purposes of subsection (2) a return under section 62 makes a nil return if it contains such a statement as is mentioned in subsection (10) of that section; and in the case of such a report the declaration must state that, to the best of the treasurer's knowledge and belief—

(a) that statement is accurate; and

(b) during the reporting period no donation from any person or body other than a permissible donor has been accepted by the party.

(4) In the case of a report under section 63, the declaration must state that, to the best of the treasurer's knowledge and belief, no donations have been received by the party, or (if section 63(3)(b) applies) by its central organisation, during the reporting period which—

(a) are required to be recorded in the report, but

(b) are not so recorded.

(5) A person commits an offence if he knowingly or recklessly makes a false declaration under this section.

[Political Parties, Elections and Referendums Act 2000, s 66.]

Extension of reporting requirements

8-8119H 67. Weekly donation reports in connection with elections other than general elections. (1) The Secretary of State may, after consulting the Commission and all registered parties, by order make provision for—

(a) sections 63 and 64, together with Schedule 6,

(b) sections 65 and 66, and

(c) section 147 so far as applying in relation to section 65(1) or (2),

to apply in relation to the specified election period in the case of one or more relevant elections with such modifications as are specified in the order.

(2) In this section—

(a) "specified election period", in relation to a relevant election, means such period ending with the date of the poll for the election as may be specified in an order under subsection (1);

(b) "relevant election" means—

(i) an election to the European Parliament;

(ii) an election to the Scottish Parliament;

(iii) an election to the National Assembly for Wales; or

(iv) an election to the Northern Ireland Assembly.

[Political Parties, Elections and Referendums Act 2000, s 67.]

Reports to be made by donors

8-8119I 68. Reporting of multiple small donations. (1) This section applies where a person ("the donor") has during the course of a calendar year made small donations to a registered party whose aggregate value is more than £5,000.

(2) The donor must make a report to the Commission in respect of the donations which gives the following details—

(a) the aggregate value of the donations and the year in which they were made;

(b) the name of the registered party to whom they were made; and

(c) the full name and address of the donor (if an individual) and (in any other case) such details in respect of the donor as are required by virtue of paragraph 2 of Schedule 6 to be given in respect of the donor of a recordable donation.

(3) The report must be delivered to the Commission by 31st January in the year following that in which the donations were made.

(4) The report must, when delivered to the Commission, be accompanied by a declaration by the donor stating—

(a) that small donations whose aggregate value was that specified in the report were made by him to the specified registered party during the specified year, and

(b) that no other small donations were made by him to that party during that year.

(5) A person commits an offence if—

(a) he delivers a report under this section which does not comply with subsection (2); or

(b) he fails to deliver such a report in accordance with subsection (3) or such a report, when delivered by him, is not accompanied by a declaration under subsection (4); or

(c) he knowingly or recklessly makes a false declaration under that subsection.

(6) In this section—

(a) "small donation" means a donation whose value is not more than £200; and

(b) "specified" means specified in the report in question.

[Political Parties, Elections and Referendums Act 2000, s 68.]

Register of donations

8–8119J 69. Register of recordable donations. (1) The Commission shall maintain a register of all donations reported to them under this Chapter.

(2) The register shall be maintained by the Commission in such form as they may determine and shall contain the following details in the case of each such donation—

(a) the amount or value of the donation;

(b) (subject to subsection (4)) such other details as have been given in relation to the donation in pursuance of paragraph 2, 3, 6 or 7(a) or (c) of Schedule 6; and

(c) the relevant date for the donation within the meaning of paragraph 5 of that Schedule, and (in the case of a donation falling within sub-paragraph (2) of that paragraph) the details given in pursuance of that sub-paragraph.

(3) In the case of any donations reported to them under section 68, the register shall (subject to subsection (4)) contain the details given in pursuance of subsection (2) of that section.

(4) The details required by virtue of subsection (2) or (3) do not include, in the case of any donation by an individual, the donor's address.

(5) Where any donation or donations is or are reported to the Commission under this Chapter, they shall cause the details mentioned in subsection (2) or (3) to be entered in the register in respect of the donation or donations as soon as is reasonably practicable.

[Political Parties, Elections and Referendums Act 2000, s 69.]

8–8119K

CHAPTER IV
POWER TO MAKE SPECIAL PROVISION

8–8119L

CHAPTER V
CONTROL OF DONATIONS TO INDIVIDUALS AND MEMBERS ASSOCIATIONS

71. *Provides for Schedule 7 (not reproduced in this work) which makes provision for controlling donations to individual members of registered parties, assocoaitions of such members and certain elected office holders (summarised).*

8–8119M

PART V[1]
CONTROL OF CAMPAIGN EXPENDITURE

---

1. Part V contains ss 72–84 and Schs 8–9.

8–8119N

PART VI[1]
CONTROLS RELATING TO THIRD PARTY NATIONAL ELECTION CAMPAIGNS

---

1. Part VI contains ss 85–100 and Schs 10–11 and relates to expenditure incurred by or on behalf of a third party in connection with the production or publication of election material which is made available to the public to promote the electoral success at a relevant election for one or more registered parties or their candidates.

8–8119O

PART VII[1]
REFERENDUMS

---

1. Part VII contains ss 101–129 and Schs 1215.

8–8119P

PART VIII[1]

ELECTION CAMPAIGNS AND PROCEEDINGS

1. Part VIII contains ss 130–138 and Schs 16–18 which amend the Representation of the People Act 1983.

8–8119Q

PART IX[1]

POLITICAL DONATIONS AND EXPENDITURE BY COMPANIES

1. Part IX contains ss 139–140 and Sch 19.

PART X[1]

MISCELLANEOUS AND GENERAL

Overseas electors

8–8119R   141. *Reduction of qualifying period for overseas electors.*

1. Part X contains ss 141–163 and Sch 20–23.

Pre-consolidation amendments

8–8119S   142. *Pre-consolidation amendments*

Election material

8–8119T   143. Details to appear on election material.   (1) No election material shall be published unless—

(a) in the case of material which is, or is contained in, such a printed document as is mentioned in subsection (3), (4) or (5), the requirements of that subsection are complied with; or

(b) in the case of any other material, any requirements falling to be complied with in relation to the material by virtue of regulations under subsection (6) are complied with.

(2) For the purposes of subsections (3) to (5) the following details are "the relevant details" in the case of any material falling within subsection (1)(a), namely—

(a) the name and address of the printer of the document;

(b) the name and address of the promoter of the material; and

(c) the name and address of any person on behalf of whom the material is being published (and who is not the promoter).

(3) Where the material is a document consisting (or consisting principally) of a single side of printed matter, the relevant details must appear on the face of the document.

(4) Where the material is a printed document other than one to which subsection (3) applies, the relevant details must appear either on the first or the last page of the document.

(5) Where the material is an advertisement contained in a newspaper or periodical—

(a) the name and address of the printer of the newspaper or periodical must appear either on its first or last page; and

(b) the relevant details specified in subsection (2)(b) and (c) must be included in the advertisement.

(6) The Secretary of State may, after consulting the Commission, by regulations make provision for and in connection with the imposition of requirements as to the inclusion in material falling within subsection (1)(b) of the following details, namely—

(a) the name and address of the promoter of the material; and

(b) the name and address of any person on behalf of whom the material is being published (and who is not the promoter).

(7) Regulations under subsection (6) may in particular specify—

(a) the manner and form in which such details must be included in any such material for the purpose of complying with any such requirement;

(b) circumstances in which—

    (i) any such requirement does not have to be complied with by a person of any description specified in the regulations, or

    (ii) a breach of any such requirement by a person of any description so specified is not to result in the commission of an offence under this section by that person or by a person of any other such description;

(c) circumstances in which material is, or is not, to be taken for the purposes of the regulations to be published or (as the case may be) published by a person of any description so specified.

(8) Where any material falling within subsection (1)(*a*) is published in contravention of subsection (1), then (subject to subsection (10))—

    (*a*) the promoter of the material,

    (*b*) any other person by whom the material is so published, and

    (*c*) the printer of the document,

shall be guilty of an offence.

(9) Where any material falling within subsection (1)(*b*) is published in contravention of subsection (1), then (subject to regulations made by virtue of subsection (7)(*b*) and to subsection (10))—

    (*a*) the promoter of the material, and

    (*b*) any other person by whom the material is so published,

shall be guilty of an offence.

(10) It shall be a defence for a person charged with an offence under this section to prove—

    (*a*) that the contravention of subsection (1) arose from circumstances beyond his control; and

    (*b*) that he took all reasonable steps, and exercised all due diligence, to ensure that that contravention would not arise.

(11) In this section—

"election material" has the meaning given by section 85(3);

"print" means print by whatever means, and "printer" shall be construed accordingly;

"the promoter", in relation to any election material, means the person causing the material to be published;

"publish" means make available to the public at large, or any section of the public, in whatever form and by whatever means1[1].

[Political Parties, Elections and Referendums Act 2000, s 143.]

---

1. Despite the commencement by the Political Parties, Elections and Referendums Act 2000 (Commencement No 1 and Transitional Provisions) Order 2001 (SI 2001/222) of s 143 and the repeals consequential upon it, the Election Publications Act 2001 (not reproduced in this work) restored the previous law relating to election publications (ie the Representation of the People Act 1983, s 110 in the form it was in before it was replaced as provided by para 14 of Sch 8 to the 2000 Act) and empowered the Secretary of State by statutory instrument to re-introduce the new provisions (ie s 143 of the 2000 Act and the new s 110 of the 1983 Act) at a later date. Any act done in compliance with, or any omission made in reliance on, the new provisions during the brief period they were in force shall not be deemed unlawful despite the restoration of the former provisions: the Elections Publications Act 2001, s 3.

Broadcasting during election period

8–8119U   **144.** *Broadcasting of local items during election period*

Enforcement of Act

8–8119V   **145.** *General function of Commission with respect to monitoring compliance with controls imposed by the Act etc*

8–8119W   **146.** *Supervisory powers of Commission*

8–8119X   **147.** *Civil penalty for failure to deliver documents etc*

8–8119Y   **148. General offences.** (1) A person commits an offence if he—

    (*a*) alters, suppresses, conceals or destroys, or

    (*b*) causes or permits the alteration, suppression, concealment or destruction of,

any document or other record relating to the financial affairs or transactions of a supervised organisation or individual which is or is liable to be required to be produced for inspection under section 146(1), and does so with the intention of falsifying the document or record or enabling that organisation or individual to evade any of the provisions of this Act.

(2) Where the relevant person in the case of a supervised organisation, or a person acting on his behalf, requests a person holding an office in any such organisation ("the office-holder") to supply the relevant person with any information which he reasonably requires for the purposes of any of the provisions of this Act, the office-holder commits an offence if—

    (*a*) without reasonable excuse, he fails to supply the relevant person with that information as soon as is reasonably practicable, or

    (*b*) in purporting to comply with the request, he knowingly supplies the relevant person with any information which is false in a material particular.

(3) A person commits an offence if, with intent to deceive, he withholds—

    (*a*) from the relevant person in the case of a supervised organisation, or

    (*b*) from a supervised individual,

any information required by the relevant person or that individual for the purposes of any of the provisions of this Act.

(4) In subsections (1) to (3) any reference to a supervised organisation or individual includes a reference to a former supervised organisation or individual.

(5) Subsections (1) and (3) shall apply in relation to a person who is (or has been)—

(*a*) a candidate at an election (other than a local government election in Scotland), or

(*b*) the election agent for such a candidate,

as they apply in relation to a supervised individual (or a former supervised individual), except that in their application in relation to any such person any reference to any of the provisions of this Act includes a reference to any other enactment imposing any restriction or other requirement falling within section 145(1)(*b*).

(6) In this section—

(*a*) "supervised individual" means an individual who is a regulated donee, a recognised third party or a permitted participant;

(*b*) "supervised organisation" means—

(i) a registered party or (in the case of such a party with accounting units) the central organisation of the party or any of its accounting units,

(ii) a regulated donee which is a members association,

(iii) a recognised third party other than an individual, or

(iv) a permitted participant other than an individual;

(*c*) "relevant person" means a person who is (or has been)—

(i) in relation to a registered party (other than a minor party) or the central organisation of such a party, the treasurer of the party,

(ii) in relation to any accounting unit of such a party, the registered treasurer of the unit,

(iii) in relation to a regulated donee which is a members association, the responsible person for the purposes of Schedule 7,

(iv) in relation to a recognised third party, the responsible person for the purposes of Part VI,

(v) in relation to a permitted participant, the responsible person for the purposes of Part VII;

(*d*) "regulated donee" and "members association" have the same meaning as in Schedule 7;

(*e*) "recognised third party" and "permitted participant" have the same meaning as in Parts VI and VII respectively.

[Political Parties, Elections and Referendums Act 2000, s 148.]

Inspection of registers

8–8119Z   149. *Inspection of Commission registers etc*

Provisions relating to offences

8–8119ZA   150. Punishment of offences.   (1) Schedule 20 makes provision for the punishment of offences under this Act.

(2) In relation to an offence under any provision specified in the first column of that Schedule, the second column shows—

(*a*) whether the offence is punishable on summary conviction only or is punishable either on summary conviction or on conviction on indictment; and

(*b*) the maximum punishment (or, in the case of a fine on a conviction on indictment, the punishment) which may be imposed by way of fine or imprisonment on a person convicted of the offence in the way specified;

and, where that column shows two alternative penalties that may be imposed on a person convicted in the way specified, as a further alternative both of those penalties may be imposed on him.

(3) In the second column of that Schedule—

(*a*) "Level 5" means a fine not exceeding level 5 on the standard scale;

(*b*) "statutory maximum" means a fine not exceeding the statutory maximum; and

(*c*) any reference to 1 year or 6 months is a reference to a term of imprisonment not exceeding 1 year or 6 months (as the case may be).

[Political Parties, Elections and Referendums Act 2000, s 150.]

8–8119ZB   151. Summary proceedings.   (1) Summary proceedings for any offence under this Act may, without prejudice to any jurisdiction exercisable apart from this subsection, be taken against any body, including an unincorporated association, at any place at which it has a place of business, and against an individual at any place at which he is for the time being.

(2) Despite anything in section 127(1) of the Magistrates' Courts Act 1980, any information relating to an offence under this Act which is triable by a magistrates' court in England and Wales may be so tried if it is laid at any time within three years after the commission of the offence and within six months after the relevant date.

(3) Despite anything in section 136 of the Criminal Procedure (Scotland) Act 1995, summary proceedings for such an offence may be commenced in Scotland at any time within three years after the commission of the offence and within six months after the relevant date; and subsection (3) of that section shall apply for the purposes of this subsection as it applies for the purposes of that section.

(4) Despite anything in Article 19(1) of the Magistrates' Courts (Northern Ireland) Order 1981, a complaint relating to such an offence which is triable by a court of summary jurisdiction in Northern Ireland may be so tried if it is made at any time within three years after the commission of the offence and within six months after the relevant date.

(5) In this section "the relevant date" means the date on which evidence sufficient in the opinion of the prosecutor to justify proceedings comes to his knowledge.

(6) For the purposes of subsection (5) a certificate of any prosecutor as to the date on which such evidence as is there mentioned came to his knowledge shall be conclusive evidence of that fact.

[Political Parties, Elections and Referendums Act 2000, s 151.]

8–8119ZC   152. Offences committed by bodies corporate.   (1) Where an offence under this Act committed by a body corporate is proved to have been committed with the consent or connivance of, or to be attributable to any neglect on the part of—

(a) any director, manager, secretary or other similar officer of the body corporate, or

(b) any person who was purporting to act in any such capacity,

he, as well as the body corporate, shall be guilty of that offence and be liable to be proceeded against and punished accordingly.

(2) Where the affairs of a body corporate are managed by its members, subsection (1) shall apply in relation to the acts and defaults of a member in connection with his functions of management as if he were a director of the body corporate.

[Political Parties, Elections and Referendums Act 2000, s 152.]

8–8119ZD   153. Offences committed by unincorporated associations.   (1) Proceedings for an offence alleged to have been committed under this Act by an unincorporated association shall be brought against the association in its own name (and not in that of any of its members) and, for the purposes of any such proceedings, any rules of court relating to the service of documents shall have effect as if the association were a corporation.

(2) A fine imposed on an unincorporated association on its conviction of an offence under this Act shall be paid out of the funds of the association.

(3) Section 33 of the Criminal Justice Act 1925 and Schedule 3 to the Magistrates' Courts Act 1980 (procedure on charge of offence against a corporation) shall have effect in a case in which an unincorporated association is charged in England or Wales with an offence under this Act in like manner as they have effect in the case of a corporation so charged.

(4) In relation to any proceedings on indictment in Scotland for an offence alleged to have been committed under this Act by an unincorporated association, section 70 of the Criminal Procedure (Scotland) Act 1995 (proceedings on indictment against bodies corporate) shall have effect as if the association were a body corporate.

(5) Section 18 of the Criminal Justice Act (Northern Ireland) 1945 and Schedule 4 to the Magistrates' Courts (Northern Ireland) Order 1981 (procedure on charge of offence against a corporation) shall have effect in a case in which an unincorporated association is charged in Northern Ireland with an offence under this Act in like manner as they have effect in the case of a corporation so charged.

(6) Where a partnership is guilty of an offence under this Act and the offence is proved to have been committed with the consent or connivance of, or to be attributable to any neglect on the part of, any partner, he as well as the partnership shall be guilty of that offence and be liable to be proceeded against and punished accordingly.

(7) Where any other unincorporated association is guilty of an offence under this Act and the offence is proved to have been committed with the consent or connivance of, or to be attributable to any neglect on the part of—

(a) any officer of the association, or

(b) any member of the committee or other similar governing body of the association,

he, as well as the association, shall be guilty of that offence and be liable to be proceeded against and punished accordingly.

[Political Parties, Elections and Referendums Act 2000, s 153.]

8–8119ZE   154. Duty of court to report convictions to Commission.   The court by or before which a person is convicted of—

(a) an offence under this Act, or

(b) an offence committed in connection with a relevant election (within the meaning of Part II),

shall notify the Commission of his conviction as soon as is practicable.

[Political Parties, Elections and Referendums Act 2000, s 154.]

Variation of specified sums

8–8119ZF   **155.**   *Power to vary specified sums*

Supplementary

8–8119ZG   **156.**   *Orders and regulations*

8–8119ZH   **157. Documents for purposes of the Act.**   (1) Any application, notice or notification required or authorised to be made or given under this Act must be in writing.

(2) Any document required or authorised to be given or sent under this Act may be sent by post.
[Political Parties, Elections and Referendums Act 2000, s 157.]

8–8119ZI   **158.**   *Minor and consequential amendments and repeals*

8–8119ZJ   **159.**   *Financial provisions*

8–8119ZK   **160.**   *General interpretation*

8–8119ZL   **161. Interpretation: donations.**   (1) This section has effect for the purposes of the provisions of this Act relating to donations.

(2) Where any provision of this Act refers to a donation for the purpose of meeting a particular kind of expenses incurred by or on behalf of a person of a particular description—

(a) the reference includes a reference to a donation for the purpose of securing that any such expenses are not so incurred; and

(b) a donation shall be taken to be a donation for either of those purposes if, having regard to all the circumstances, it must be reasonably assumed to be such a donation.

(3) Subsections (4) and (5) apply to any provision of this Act which provides, in relation to a person of a particular description ("the donee"), that money spent (otherwise than by or on behalf of the donee) in paying any expenses incurred directly or indirectly by the donee is to constitute a donation to the donee.

(4) The reference in any such provision to money so spent is a reference to money so spent by a person, other than the donee, out of his own resources (with no right to reimbursement out of the resources of the donee).

(5) Where by virtue of any such provision any amount of money so spent constitutes a donation to the donee, the donee shall be treated as receiving an equivalent amount on the date on which the money is paid to the creditor in respect of the expenses in question.

(6) For the purposes of this Act it is immaterial whether a donation received by a registered party or a person of any other description is so received in the United Kingdom or elsewhere.
[Political Parties, Elections and Referendums Act 2000, s 161.]

8–8119ZM   **162.**   *Interpretation: exempt trust donations*

8–8119ZN   **163. Short title, commencement, transitional provisions and extent[1].**   (1) This Act may be cited as the Political Parties, Elections and Referendums Act 2000.

(2) Subject to subsections (3) and (4), this Act does not come into force until such day as the Secretary of State may by order appoint; and different days may be so appointed for different purposes.

(3) The following provisions come into force on the day on which this Act is passed—

(a) sections 1 to 3 and Schedules 1 and 2,

(b) sections 156, 159 and 160, and paragraph 12(1) and (4) of Schedule 21,

(c) this section, and Part II of Schedule 23, and

(d) any other provision so far as it confers power to make an order or regulations.

(4) The following provisions come into force at the end of the period of two weeks beginning with the day on which this Act is passed—

(a) section 36,

(b) Part I of Schedule 23, and

(c) any provision of Part II of this Act so far as necessary for the purposes of the operation of any provision of Part I of that Schedule.

(5) An order under subsection (2) may contain such transitional provisions and savings (including provisions modifying enactments) as the Secretary of State considers appropriate.

(6) Such an order may, in particular, make provision as respects the operation of any financial limit imposed by any provision of this Act in cases where a period in relation to which any such limit is imposed would otherwise begin at a time before the commencement of that provision of this Act.

(7) The transitional provisions contained in Schedule 23 shall have effect.

(8) Subject to subsections (9) and (10), this Act extends to the whole of the United Kingdom.

(9) Part IX and paragraphs 2 and 3 of Schedule 12 and paragraphs 12 and 13 of Schedule 23 extend to England, Wales and Scotland.

(10) Subject to any express limitation contained in this Act, the extent of any amendment or repeal made by this Act is the same as that of the enactment amended or repealed.

[Political Parties, Elections and Referendums Act 2000, s 163.]

---

1. The following orders have been made: Commencement (No 1 and Transitional Provisions) Order 2001, SI 2001/222; Commencement (No 2) Order 2001, SI 2001/3526. All of the provisions reproduced here had been brought into force.

8–8119ZO

Section 150   SCHEDULE 20
                                PENALTIES

Provision creating offence	*Penalty*
Section 24(8) (registration as treasurer where convicted of certain offences)	On summary conviction: Level 5
Section 39 (false statements)	On summary conviction: Level 5
Section 43(7) (failure to deliver statement relating to auditor's resignation etc)	On summary conviction: statutory maximum or 6 months On indictment: fine or 1 year
Section 44(4) (making false statement to auditor)	On summary conviction: statutory maximum or 6 months On indictment: fine or 1 year
Section 47(1)(*a*) (failure to deliver proper statement of accounts)	On summary conviction: Level 5
Section 47(1)(*b*) (failure to deliver accounts within time limits)	On summary conviction: Level 5
Section 54(7) (failure to provide information about donors)	On summary conviction: statutory maximum or 6 months On indictment: fine or 1 year
Section 56(3) or (4) (failure to return donations)	On summary conviction: statutory maximum or 6 months On indictment: fine or 1 year
Section 61(1) (facilitating the making of donations by impermissible donors)	On summary conviction: statutory maximum or 6 months On indictment: fine or 1 year
Section 61(2)(*a*) (knowingly giving treasurer false information about donations)	On summary conviction: statutory maximum or 6 months On indictment: fine or 1 year
Section 61(2)(*b*) (withholding information about donations from treasurer with intent to deceive)	On summary conviction: statutory maximum or 6 months On indictment: fine or 1 year
Section 65(3) (failure to deliver donation reports to Commission within time limits)	On summary conviction: Level 5
Section 65(4) (failure to comply with requirements for recording donations in donation report)	On summary conviction: statutory maximum or 6 months On indictment: fine or 1 year
Section 66(5) (making a false declaration about donation report)	On summary conviction: statutory maximum or 6 months On indictment: fine or 1 year
Section 68(5) (failure to report multiple small donations; false declaration about such donations)	On summary conviction: statutory maximum or 6 months On indictment: fine or 1 year
Section 73(8) (making a false declaration about value of property etc)	On summary conviction: statutory maximum or 6 months On indictment: fine or 1 year
Section 74(4) (acceptance by ineligible person of office of deputy treasurer)	On summary conviction: Level 5
Section 75(2) (incurring campaign expenditure without authority)	On summary conviction: Level 5
Section 76(4)(*a*) (making payments in respect of campaign expenditure without authority)	On summary conviction: Level 5
Section 76(4)(*b*) (failure to notify treasurer of payments in respect of campaign expenditure)	On summary conviction: Level 5
Section 77(3)(*a*) (paying claim in respect of campaign expenditure where failure to comply with procedure)	On summary conviction: Level 5
Section 77(3)(*b*) (paying claim in respect of campaign expenditure outside specified time period)	On summary conviction: Level 5
Section 79(2) (exceeding limits on campaign expenditure)	On summary conviction: statutory maximum On indictment: fine
Section 82(4)(*a*) (failure of treasurer to deliver return and auditor's report to Commission)	On summary conviction: Level 5

Provision creating offence	Penalty
Section 82(4)(b) (failure to comply with requirements for returns)	On summary conviction: statutory maximum or 6 months
	On indictment: fine or 1 year
Section 82(4)(c) (failure of treasurer to deliver return and court order to Commission)	On summary conviction: Level 5
Section 83(3)(a) (making a false declaration to Commission when delivering return)	On summary conviction: statutory maximum or 6 months
	On indictment: fine or 1 year
Section 83(3)(b) (failure to deliver signed declaration with return to Commission)	On summary conviction: statutory maximum or 6 months
	On indictment: fine or 1 year
Section 86(8) (making false declaration about value of property etc)	On summary conviction: statutory maximum or 6 months
	On indictment: fine or 1 year
Section 90(2) (incurring controlled expenditure without authority)	On summary conviction: Level 5
Section 91(4)(a) (making payments in respect of controlled expenditure without authority)	On summary conviction: Level 5
Section 91(4)(b) (failure to notify responsible person of payments in respect of controlled expenditure)	On summary conviction: Level 5
Section 92(3)(a) (paying claim in respect of controlled expenditure where failure to comply with procedure)	On summary conviction: Level 5
Section 92(3)(b) (paying claim in respect of controlled expenditure outside specified time period)	On summary conviction: Level 5
Section 94(2) or (4) (exceeding limits on controlled expenditure)	On summary conviction: statutory maximum
	On indictment: fine
Section 98(4)(a) (failure of responsible person to deliver return and auditor's report to Commission)	On summary conviction: Level 5
Section 98(4)(b) (failure to comply with requirements for returns)	On summary conviction: statutory maximum or 6 months
	On indictment: fine or 1 year
Section 98(4)(c) (failure to deliver return and court order to Commission)	On summary conviction: Level 5
Section 99(4)(a) (making a false declaration to Commission when delivering return)	On summary conviction: statutory maximum or 6 months
	On indictment: fine or 1 year
Section 99(4)(b) (failure to deliver signed declaration with return to Commission)	On summary conviction: statutory maximum or 6 months
	On indictment: fine or 1 year
Section 112(8) (making a false declaration about value of property etc)	On summary conviction: statutory maximum or 6 months
	On indictment: fine or 1 year
Section 113(2) (incurring referendum expenses without authority)	On summary conviction: Level 5
Section 114(4)(a) (making payments in respect of referendum expenses without authority)	On summary conviction: Level 5
Section 114(4)(b) (failure to notify responsible person of payments in respect of referendum expenses)	On summary conviction: Level 5
Section 115(3)(a) (paying claim in respect of referendum expenses where failure to comply with procedure)	On summary conviction: Level 5
Section 115(3)(b) (paying claim in respect of referendum expenses outside specified time period)	On summary conviction: Level 5
Section 117(2) (individual (other than permitted participant) exceeding limits on referendum expenses)	On summary conviction: statutory maximum or 6 months
	On indictment: fine or 1 year
Section 117(3) or (4) (body (other than permitted participant) exceeding limits on referendum expenses)	On summary conviction: statutory maximum or 6 months
	On indictment: fine or 1 year
Section 118(2) (permitted participant exceeding limits on referendum expenses)	On summary conviction: statutory maximum
	On indictment: fine
Section 122(4)(a) (failure to deliver return and auditor's report to Commission)	On summary conviction: Level 5
Section 122(4)(b) (failure to comply with requirements for returns)	On summary conviction: statutory maximum or 6 months
	On indictment: fine or 1 year
Section 122(4)(c) (failure to deliver return and court order to Commission)	On summary conviction: Level 5
Section 123(4)(a) (making a false declaration to Commission when delivering return)	On summary conviction: statutory maximum or 6 months
	On indictment: fine or 1 year
Section 123(4)(b) (failure to deliver signed declaration with return to Commission)	On summary conviction: statutory maximum or 6 months

Provision creating offence	Penalty
	On indictment : fine or 1 year
Section 126(8) or (9) (printing or publishing referendum material without details of printer or publisher)	On summary conviction: Level 5
Section 143(8) or (9) (printing or publishing election material without details of printer or publisher)	On summary conviction: Level 5
Section 146(5) (failure to comply with supervision requirement)	On summary conviction: Level 5
Section 146(6) (intentional obstruction of person exercising right of entry etc)	On summary conviction: Level 5
Section 148(1) (alteration of documents etc)	On summary conviction: statutory maximum or 6 months On indictment: fine or 1 year
Section 148(2)(a) (failure to supply relevant person with information)	On summary conviction: Level 5
Section 148(2)(b) (supplying relevant person with false information)	On summary conviction: statutory maximum or 6 months On indictment: fine or 1 year
Section 148(3) (withholding information from relevant person with intent to deceive)	On summary conviction: statutory maximum or 6 months On indictment: fine or 1 year
Paragraph 6(5) of Schedule 7 (failure to provide information about donors)	On summary conviction: statutory maximum or 6 months On indictment: fine or 1 year
Paragraph 12(1) of Schedule 7 (failure to deliver donation report to Commission within time limit)	On summary conviction: Level 5
Paragraph 12(2) of Schedule 7 (failure to comply with requirements for recording donations in donation reports)	On summary conviction: statutory maximum or 6 months On indictment: fine or 1 year
Paragraph 13(4) of Schedule 7 (making a false declaration about donation report)	On summary conviction: statutory maximum or 6 months On indictment: fine or 1 year
Paragraph 14(5) of Schedule 7 (failure to report multiple small donations; false declaration about such donations)	On summary conviction: statutory maximum or 6 months On indictment: fine or 1 year
Paragraph 6(7) of Schedule 11 (failure to provide information about donors)	On summary conviction: statutory maximum or 6 months On indictment: fine or 1 year
Paragraph 6(8) of Schedule 15 (failure to provide information about donors)	On summary conviction: statutory maximum or 6 months On indictment: fine or 1 year

European Parliamentary Elections Act 2002[1]

(2002 c 24)

8–8119ZP   **8. Persons entitled to vote.**   (1) A person is entitled to vote as an elector at an election to the European Parliament in an electoral region if he is within any of subsections (2) to (5).

(2) A person is within this subsection if on the day of the poll he would be entitled to vote as an elector at a parliamentary election in a parliamentary constituency wholly or partly comprised in the electoral region, and—

- (a) the address in respect of which he is registered in the relevant register of parliamentary electors is within the electoral region, or
- (b) his registration in the relevant register of parliamentary electors results from an overseas elector's declaration which specifies an address within the electoral region.

(3) A person is within this subsection if—

- (a) he is a peer who on the day of the poll would be entitled to vote at a local government election in an electoral area wholly or partly comprised in the electoral region, and
- (b) the address in respect of which he is registered in the relevant register of local government electors is within the electoral region.

(4) A person is within this subsection if he is entitled to vote in the electoral region by virtue of section 3 of the Representation of the People Act 1985 (c 50) (peers resident outside the United Kingdom).

(5) A person is within this subsection if he is entitled to vote in the electoral region by virtue of the European Parliamentary Elections (Franchise of Relevant Citizens of the Union[2]) Regulations 2001 (SI 2001/1184) (citizens of the European Union other than Commonwealth and Republic of Ireland citizens).

(6) Subsection (1) has effect subject to any provision of regulations made under this Act which provides for alterations made after a specified date in a register of electors to be disregarded.

(7) In subsection (3) "local government election" includes a municipal election in the City of London (that is, an election to the office of mayor, alderman, common councilman or sheriff and also the election of any officer elected by the mayor, aldermen and liverymen in common hall).

(8) The entitlement to vote under this section does not apply to voting in Gibraltar.

[European Parliamentary Elections Act 2002, s 8, as amended by the European Parliament (Representation) Act 2003, 15.]

---

1. This Act, which came into force on 24 October 2002, consolidates the European Parliamentary Elections Acts 1978, 1993 and 1999. The UK elects 87 Members of the European Parliament according to the voting systems that the Act prescribes. The Treaty of Nice, however, provides for the number of United Kingdom seat to be reduced to 72 in consequence of the potential enlargement of the EU to 27 Member States. The European Parliament (Representation) Act 2003 has been passed to provide the mechanism for this reduction (and to enfranchise the Gibraltar electorate for the purpose of European Parliamentary elections, as of 2004).

2. Section 17 provides that "Citizen of the European Union" is to be determined in accordance with art 17.1 of the Treaty establishing the European Community.

8–8119ZQ 9. Double voting.   (1) A person is guilty of an offence if, on any occasion when elections to the European Parliament are held in all the member states under Article 9 of the Act annexed to Council Decision 76/787, he votes as an elector more than once in those elections, whether in the United Kingdom or elsewhere.

(2) Subsection (1) is without prejudice to any enactment relating to voting offences, as applied by regulations under this Act to elections of MEPs held in the United Kingdom.

(3) The provisions of the Representation of the People Act 1983 (c 2), as applied by regulations under this Act, have effect in relation to an offence under this section as they have effect in relation to an offence under section 61(2) of that Act (double voting).

(4) In particular, the following provisions of that Act apply—

(a) section 61(7) (which makes an offence under section 61(2) an illegal practice but allows any incapacity resulting from conviction to be mitigated by the convicting court), and

(b) section 178 (prosecutions for offences committed outside the United Kingdom).

[European Parliamentary Elections Act 2002, s 8.]

European Parliament (Representation) Act 2003[1]
(2003 c 7)

8–8119ZR

---

1. This Act enables alterations to be made to the total number of Members of the European Parliament to be elected for the United Kingdom and to their distribution between the electoral regions. It further makes provision for and in connection with the establishment of an electoral region including Gibraltar for the purposes of European Parliamentary elections. The Act is not reproduced in this work.

European Parliamentary and Local Elections (Pilots) Act 2004[1]
(2004 c 2)

8–8119ZS 6. Personation: arrestable offence.   (1) For the purposes of any election held in accordance with provision made by a pilot order, the offence of personation under section 60 of the Representation of the People Act 1983 (c 2) must be treated as if it is an offence to which section 24(2) of the Police and Criminal Evidence Act 1984 (c 60) (offences which are arrestable offences) applies.

(2) Subsection (1) does not affect anything which may be done in pursuance of Rule 36 of Schedule 1 to the Representation of the People Act 1983 (arrest of challenged voter).

[European Parliamentary and Local Elections (Pilots) Act 2004, s 6.]

---

1. This Act provided for postal voting only in certain regions in respect of the European Parliamentary election of 2004 and any local government elections due to be held in those regions at the same time. The postal voting had to be in accordance with the provisions contained in a pilot order made by the Secretary of State.

8–8119ZT 7. Time limit for prosecution of offences.   (1) This section applies for the purposes of any election held in accordance with provision made by a pilot order.

(2) A magistrates' court may act under subsection (3) if it is satisfied on an application by a constable or Crown Prosecutor—

(a) that there are exceptional circumstances which justify the granting of the application, and

(b) that there has been no undue delay in the investigation of the offence to which the application relates.

(3) The magistrates' court may extend the time within which proceedings for an offence must be commenced in pursuance of section 176(1) of the Representation of the People Act 1983 (time limit for prosecution of offences under that Act) to not more than 24 months after the offence is committed. [European Parliamentary and Local Elections (Pilots) Act 2004, s 7.]

EMBRACERY

8–8120   Embracery is an attempt by bribes, or any corrupt means, other than evidence and argument in open court, to influence or corrupt a jury. It is a misdemeanour indictable at common law, punishable by fine and imprisonment.

EMERGENCY POWERS

Emergency Powers Act 1920
(10 & 11 Geo 5 c 55)

8–8139   This Act empowers Her Majesty to issue proclamations of emergency if, at any time, it appears that there have occurred, or are about to occur, events of such a nature as to be calculated, by interfering with the supply and distribution of food, water, fuel, or light, or with the means of locomotion, to deprive the community, or any substantial portion of the community, of the essentials of life. No single proclamation is to be in force for more than one month, and Parliament, if not sitting, is to be at once summoned to meet (s 1, amended by Emergency Power Act 1964, s 1). Power is given to Her Majesty, by Order in Council, to make regulations for securing the essentials of life, and to confer on a Secretary of State or other Government department certain powers and duties as are therein mentioned. Any regulations are to be laid before Parliament as soon as may be after they are made, and are not to continue in force after the expiration of seven days from the time when they are so laid unless a resolution is passed by both Houses providing for the continuance thereof. The regulations may provide for the trial, by courts of summary jurisdiction, of persons found guilty of offences against the regulations, the maximum penalty to be imprisonment for a term of **three months** or a fine not exceeding **level 5** on the standard scale, or not exceeding a lesser amount, or both such imprisonment and fine, together with the forfeiture of any goods or money in respect of which the offence has been committed; but no such regulations are to alter any existing procedure in criminal cases, or confer any right to punish by fine or imprisonment without trial. The regulations are to have effect as if enacted in the Act, but may be added to, altered, or revoked by resolution of both Houses of Parliament or by regulations made in like manner and subject to the like provisions as the original regulations (s 2 amended by the Criminal Justice Act 1982, s 41 and the Statute Law (Repeals) Act 1993, Sch 1).

EMPLOYMENT

8–8140   This title includes the following statutes—

and the following statutory instruments—

8–8141   European Communities Act 1972: regulations.   The Secretary of State has, in exercise of the powers conferred on him by s 2(2) of the European Communities Act 1972, made the Maternity (Compulsory Leave) Regulations 1994, SI 1994/2479. These regulations make it an offence, punishable with a fine not exceeding **level 2** on the standard scale, to work or be permitted to work during the period of two weeks starting with the date on which the child is born if the employee is entitled to leave in accordance with the Employment Protection (Consolidation) Act 1978.

The Working Time Regulations 1998, SI 1998/1833, amended by SI 1999/3372 and SI 2003/1684, implement Council Directive 93/104/EC concerning certain aspects of the organization of working time. Regulations 4 to 9 impose obligations on employers, enforceable by the Health and Safety Executive and local authorities. Failing to comply is an offence triable either way, punishable on summary conviction by a fine not exceeding the statutory maximum.

Servants' Characters Act 1792
(32 Geo 3 c 56)

8–8160 False character, etc. Falsely personating a master, or his executor, administrator, wife, relation, housekeeper, steward, agent or servant, and personally giving any false character[1] to any person offering himself to be hired as a servant (Servants' Characters Act 1792, 32 Geo 3, c 56, s 1 amended by the Forgery and Counterfeiting Act 1981, Sch): or knowingly or wilfully pretending[2] or falsely asserting in writing, that any servant has been hired for any period other than the time for which he shall have been hired or retained (Servants' Characters Act 1792, s 2); or that any servant was discharged or left his service at any other time than that at which he actually left, or that any servant had not been hired or employed in any previous service (Servants' Characters Act 1792, s. 3)—*Penalty* (in each section), on summary conviction a fine not exceeding **level 2** on the standard scale.

---

1. A master is not bound to give a servant a character (*Carrol v Bird* (1800) 3 Esp 201). If a testimonial from a former employer be maliciously damaged by a new employer, the servant may recover substantial and not merely nominal damages; but there is a distinction between a letter written to a would-be employer, in answer to an inquiry about a servant's character, and a general testimonial of good character (*Wennhak v Morgan* (1888) 20 QBD 635, 52 JP 470).

2. A false character may be verbally given. There are two distinct offences, "knowingly and wilfully pretending" and "falsely asserting in writing" (*R v Connolly and Costello* [1910] 1 KB 28, 74 JP 15).

8–8161 False statements by servants. Any person offering himself as a servant, asserting or pretending that he has served in any service in which he had not actually served; or with a false, certificate of character; or altering, effacing, or erasing any word, date, or thing contained in any certificate given by, or by the authority of, any former master (Servants' Characters Act 1792, s 4 amended by the Forgery and Counterfeiting Act 1981, Sch); or if any person having before been in service shall, when offering to hire himself, falsely or wilfully pretend not to have been hired or retained in any previous service (Servants' Characters Act 1792, s 5)—*Penalty*, on summary conviction a fine not exceeding **level 2** on the standard scale.

Conspiracy, and Protection of Property Act 1875
(38 & 39 Vict c 86)

8–8182 6. Neglect to provide food, etc, for servant or apprentice. If a master, being legally bound to provide for his servant or apprentice[1] necessary food, clothing, medical aid, or lodging, wilfully and without lawful excuse refuses or neglects to provide the same, whereby the health of the servant or apprentice is or is likely to be seriously or permanently injured—*Penalty*, on summary conviction, not exceeding **level 2** on the standard scale or to be imprisoned for not exceeding **six months**.
[Conspiracy, and Protection of Property Act 1875, s 6, as amended by the Criminal Law Act 1977, s 31 and the Criminal Justice Act 1982, s 46.]

---

1. See also the Offences Against the Persons Act 1861, s 26, as to not providing food, etc, or doing bodily harm whereby life is endangered, title PERSONS (OFFENCES AGAINST), post.

8–8183 Exceptions. Nothing in this Act is to apply to seamen or to apprentices to the sea service.
[Conspiracy, and Protection of Property Act 1875, s 16.]

Employers' Liability (Compulsory Insurance) Act 1969
(1969 c 57)

8–8340 1. Insurance against liability for employees. (1) Except as otherwise provided by this Act, every employer carrying on any business in Great Britain shall insure, and maintain insurance, under one or more approved policies with an authorised insurer or insurers against liability for bodily injury or disease sustained by his employees, and arising out of and in the course of their employment in Great Britain in that business, but except in so far as regulations otherwise provide not including injury or disease suffered or contracted outside Great Britain.

(2) Regulations[1] may provide that the amount for which an employer is required by this Act to insure and maintain insurance shall, either generally or in such cases or classes of case as may be prescribed by the regulations, be limited in such manner as may be so prescribed.

(3) For the purposes of this Act—

(a) "approved policy" means a policy of insurance not subject to any conditions or exceptions prohibited for those purposes by regulations[1];

(b) "authorised insurer" means a person or body of persons lawfully carrying on in the United Kingdom insurance business of a class specified in Schedule 1 or 2 to the Insurance Companies Act 1982 and issuing the policy or policies in the course thereof;

(c) "business; includes a trade or profession, and includes any activity carried on by a body of persons, whether corporate or unincorporate;

(d) except as otherwise provided by regulations, an employer not having a place of business in Great Britain shall be deemed not to carry on business there.

[Employers' Liability (Compulsory Insurance) Act 1969, s 1 as amended by the Insurance Companies Act 1981, Sch 4 and the Insurance Companies Act 1982, Sch 5.]

---

1. The Employers' Liability (Compulsory Insurance) Regulations 1998, SI 1998/2573 amended by SI 1999/1820, SI 2000/253, SI 2003/1615 and SI 2004/2882 have been made.

8–8341   2. Employees to be covered.   (1) For the purposes of this Act the term "employee" means an individual who has entered into or works under a contract of service or apprenticeship with an employer whether by way of manual labour, clerical work or otherwise, whether such contract is expressed or implied, oral or in writing.

(2) This Act shall not require an employer to insure—

(a) in respect of an employee of whom the employer is the husband, wife,★ father, mother, grandfather, grandmother, step-father, step-mother, son, daughter, grandson, granddaughter, stepson, stepdaughter, brother, sister, half-brother or half-sister; or

(b) except as otherwise provided by regulations[1], in respect of employees not ordinarily resident in Great Britain.

[Employers' Liability (Compulsory Insurance) Act 1969, s 2.]

★**"Civil partner" inserted by the Civil Partnership Act 2004, Sch 27 from a date to be appointed.**
1. The Employers' Liability (Compulsory Insurance) Regulations 1998, SI 1998/2573 amended by SI 1999/1820, SI 2000/253, SI 2003/1615 and SI 2004/2882 have been made.

8–8342   3. Employers exempted from insurance.   (1) This Act shall not require any insurance to be effected by—

(a) any such authority as is mentioned in subsection (2) below; or

(b) any body corporate established by or under any enactment for the carrying on of any industry or part of an industry, or of any undertaking, under national ownership or control; or

(c) in relation to any such cases as may be specified in the regulations, any employer exempted by regulations[1].

(2) The authorities referred to in subsection (1)(a) above are—

(a) a health service body, as defined in section 60(7) of the National Health Service and Community Care Act 1990, a National Health Service trust established under Part I of that Act or the National Health Service (Scotland) Act 1978, an NHS foundation trust, a Primary Care Trust established under s 16A of the National Health Service Act 1977 and a Local Health Board established under section 16BA of that Act; and★

(b) the Common Council of the City of London, the council of a London borough, the council of a county, or county district in England, the council of a county or county borough in Wales, the Broads Authority, a National Park authority, a county, town or district council in Scotland, any joint board or joint committee in England and Wales or joint committee in Scotland which is so constituted as to include among its members representatives of any such council, a joint authority established by Part IV of the Local Government Act 1985, the London Fire and Emergency Planning Authority and any police authority.★★

[Employers' Liability (Compulsory Insurance) Act 1969, s 3, as amended by the Local Government Act 1972, Sch 30, the Local Government Act 1985, Schs 14 and 17, the Norfolk and Suffolk Broads Act 1988, Sch 6, the National Health Service and Community Care Act 1990, Sch 8, the Local Government (Wales) Act 1994, Sch 16, the Environment Act 1995, Sch 10 the Police Act 1997, Sch 9, the Greater London Authority Act 1999, Sch 29, SI 2000/90, the Criminal Justice and Police Act 2001, Sch 6, the National Health Service Reform and Health Care Professions Act 2002, Sch 5 and the Health and Social Care (Community Health and Standards) Act 2003, Sch 4.]

★**Reproduced as in force in England and Wales.**
★★**Para (2)(c) to be inserted by the Equality Act 2006, Sch 1 from a date to be appointed.**

1. The Employers' Liability (Compulsory Insurance) Regulations 1998, SI 1998/2573 amended by SI 1999/1820, SI 2000/253, SI 2003/1615 and SI 2004/2882 have been made.

8–8343 4. Certificates of insurance. (1) Provision may be made by regulations[1] for securing that certificates of insurance in such form and containing such particulars as may be prescribed by the regulations, are issued by insurers to employers entering into contracts of insurance in accordance with the requirements of this Act, and for the surrender in such circumstances as may be so prescribed of certificates so issued.

(2) Where a certificate of insurance is required to be issued to an employer in accordance with regulations[1] under subsection (1) above, the employer (subject to any provision made by the regulations as to the surrender of the certificate) shall during the currency of the insurance and such further period (if any) as may be provided by regulations—

(a) comply with any regulations requiring him to display copies of the certificate of insurance for the information of his employees;

(b) produce the certificate of insurance or a copy thereof on demand to any inspector duly authorised by the Secretary of State for the purposes of this Act and produce or send the certificate or a copy thereof to such other persons, at such place and in such circumstances as may be prescribed by regulations;

(c) permit the policy of insurance or a copy thereof to be inspected by such persons and in such circumstances as may be so prescribed.

(3) A person who fails to comply with a requirement imposed by or under this section shall be liable on summary conviction to a fine not exceeding **level 3** on the standard scale.
[Employers' Liability (Compulsory Insurance) Act 1969, s 4, as amended by the Criminal Law Act 1977, Sch 6 and the Criminal Justice Act 1982, s 46.]

---

1. The Employers' Liability (Compulsory Insurance) Regulations 1998, SI 1998/2573 amended by SI 1999/1820, SI 2000/253, SI 2003/1615 and SI 2004/2882 have been made.

8–8344 5. Penalty for failure to insure. An employer who on any day is not insured in accordance with this Act when required to be so shall be guilty of an offence and shall be liable on summary conviction to a fine not exceeding **level 4** on the standard scale; and where an offence under this section committed by a corporation has been committed with the consent or connivance of, or facilitated by any neglect on the part of, any director, manager, secretary or other officer of the corporation, he, as well as the corporation shall be deemed to be guilty of that offence and shall be liable to be proceeded against and punished accordingly.
[Employers' Liability (Compulsory Insurance) Act 1969, s 5, as amended by the Criminal Law Act 1977, Sch 6 and the Criminal Justice Act 1982, s 46.]

8–8345 6. *Power to make regulations*

Employment Agencies Act 1973
(1973 c 35)

Prohibition orders

8–8360 3A. Power to make orders. (1) On application by the Secretary of State, an industrial tribunal may by order prohibit a person from carrying on, or being concerned with the carrying on of—

(a) any employment agency or employment business; or

(b) any specified description of employment agency or employment business.

(2) An order under subsection (1) of this section (in this Act referred to as "a prohibition order") may either prohibit a person from engaging in an activity altogether or prohibit him from doing so otherwise than in accordance with specified conditions.

(3) A prohibition order shall be made for a period beginning with the date of the order and ending—

(a) on a specified date, or

(b) on the happening of a specified event,

in either case, not more than ten years later.

(4) Subject to subsections (5) and (6) of this section, an industrial tribunal shall not make a prohibition order in relation to any person unless it is satisfied that he is, on account of his misconduct or for any other sufficient reason, unsuitable to do what the order prohibits.

(5) An industrial tribunal may make a prohibition order in relation to a body corporate if it is satisfied that—

(a) any director, secretary, manager or similar officer of the body corporate,

(b) any person who performs on behalf of the body corporate the functions of a director, secretary, manager or similar officer, or

(c) any person in accordance with whose directions or instructions the directors of the body corporate are accustomed to act,

is unsuitable, on account of his misconduct or for any other sufficient reason, to do what the order prohibits.

(6) An industrial tribunal may make a prohibition order in relation to a partnership if it is satisfied that any member of the partnership, or any manager employed by the partnership, is unsuitable, on account of his misconduct or for any other sufficient reason, to do what the order prohibits.

(7) For the purposes of subsection (4) of this section, where an employment agency or employment business has been improperly conducted, each person who was carrying on, or concerned with the carrying on of, the agency or business at the time, shall be deemed to have been responsible for what happened unless he can show that it happened without his connivance or consent and was not attributable to any neglect on his part.

(8) A person shall not be deemed to fall within subsection (5)(c) of this section by reason only that the directors act on advice given by him in a professional capacity.

(9) In this section—

"director", in relation to a body corporate whose affairs are controlled by its members, means a member of the body corporate; and

"specified", in relation to a prohibition order, means specified in the order.

[Employment Agencies Act 1973, s 3A inserted by the Deregulation and Contracting Out Act 1994, s 35 and Sch 10.]

8–8361   3B. Enforcement.   Any person who, without reasonable excuse, fails to comply with a prohibition order shall be guilty of an offence and liable on summary conviction to a fine not exceeding **level 5** on the standard scale.

[Employment Agencies Act 1973, s 3B inserted by the Deregulation and Contracting Out Act 1994, s 35 and Sch 10.]

8–8361A   3C. Variation and revocation of orders.   (1) On application by the person to whom a prohibition order applies, an industrial tribunal may vary or revoke the order if the tribunal is satisfied that there has been a material change of circumstances since the order was last considered.

(2) An industrial tribunal may not, on an application under this section, so vary a prohibition order as to make it more restrictive.

(3) The Secretary of State shall be a party to any proceedings before an industrial tribunal with respect to an application under this section, and be entitled to appear and be heard accordingly.

(4) When making a prohibition order or disposing of an application under this section, an industrial tribunal may, with a view to preventing the making of vexatious or frivolous applications, by order prohibit the making of an application, or further application, under this section in relation to the prohibition order before such date as the tribunal may specify in the order under this subsection.

[Employment Agencies Act 1973, s 3C inserted by the Deregulation and Contracting Out Act 1994, s 35 and Sch 10.]

8–8361B   3D. Appeals.   (1) An appeal shall lie to the Employment Appeal Tribunal on a question of law arising from any decision of, or arising in proceedings before, an industrial tribunal under section 3A or 3C of this Act.

(2) No other appeal shall lie from a decision of an industrial tribunal under section 3A or 3C of this Act; and section 11 of the Tribunals and Inquiries Act 1992 (appeals from certain tribunals to High Court or Court of Session) shall not apply to proceedings before an industrial tribunal under section 3A or 3C of this Act.

[Employment Agencies Act 1973, s 3D inserted by the Deregulation and Contracting Out Act 1994, s 35 and Sch 10.]

8–8362   5. General Regulations.   (1)–(1A) Power of Secretary of State to make regulations[1].★

(2) Any person who contravenes or fails to comply with any regulation made under this section shall be guilty of an offence and liable on summary conviction to a fine not exceeding **level 5** on the standard scale.

[Employment Agencies Act 1973, s 5 as amended by the Criminal Justice Act 1982, ss 38 and 46 and the Employment Relations Act 1999, Sch 7.]

★**Amended by the Employment Relations Act 1999, Sch 7, when in force.**

1. The Conduct of Employment Agencies and Employment Businesses Regulations 2003, SI 2003/3319 amended by SI 2005/2114, have been made.

8–8363   6. Restriction on charging persons seeking employment, etc.   (1) Except in such cases or classes of case as the Secretary of State may prescribe[1] (*a*) a person carrying on an employment agency shall not request or directly or indirectly receive any fee from any person for providing services (whether by the provision of information or otherwise) for the purpose of finding him employment or seeking to find him employment[2];

(*b*) a person carrying on an employment business shall not request or directly or indirectly receive any fee from an employee for providing services (whether by the provision of information or otherwise) for the purpose of finding or seeking to find another person, with a view to the employee acting for and under the control of that other person;

(*c*) a person carrying on an employment business shall not request or directly or indirectly receive any fee from a second person for providing services (whether by the provision of information or otherwise) for the purpose of finding or seeking to find a third person, with a view to the second person becoming employed by the first person and acting for and under the control of the third person).

(2) Any person who contravenes this section shall be guilty of an offence and liable on summary conviction to a fine not exceeding **level 5** on the standard scale.
[Employment Agencies Act 1973, s 6 as amended by the Criminal Justice Act 1982, ss 38 and 46, the Employment Relations Act 1999, Sch 7 and the Employment Relations Act 1973, Sch 7.]

---

1. In *First Point International Ltd v Department of Trade and Industry* (1999) 164 JP 89, which was decided on the wording of this section before its amendment by the Employment Relations Act 1999, Sch 7, it was held that the collection of information which was required for the purposes of a personal appraisal was capable, as a matter of law, of being part of the seeking of employment provided that that information collection was sufficiently proximate to what went on thereafter.

2. See the Conduct of Employment Agencies and Employment Business Regulations 2003, SI 2003/3319 amended by SI 2005/2114.

8–8364   7. *(Repealed).*

8–8365   9. Inspection.   (1) Any officer duly authorised in that behalf by the Secretary of State may at all reasonable times on producing, if so required, written evidence of his authority—

(*a*) enter any relevant business premises; and
(*b*) inspect those premises and any records or other documents kept in pursuance of this Act or of any regulations made thereunder; and
(*c*) subject to subsection (2) of this section, require any person on those premises to furnish him with such information as he may reasonably require for the purpose of ascertaining whether the provisions of this Act and of any regulations made thereunder are being complied with or of enabling the Secretary of State to exercise his functions under this Act; and
(*d*) take copies of records and other documents inspected under paragraph (*b*).★

(1A) If an officer seeks to inspect or acquire, in accordance with subsection (1)(*b*) or (*c*), a record or other document or information which is not kept at the premises being inspected, he may require any person on the premises—

(*a*) to inform him where and by whom the record, other document or information is kept, and
(*b*) to make arrangements, if it is reasonably practicable for the person to do so, for the record, other document or information to be inspected by or furnished to the officer at the premises at a time specified by the officer.

(1B) In subsection (1) "relevant business premises" means premises—

(*a*) which are used, have been used or are to be used for or in connection with the carrying on of an employment agency or employment business,
(*b*) which the officer has reasonable cause to believe are used or have been used for or in connection with the carrying on of an employment agency or employment business, or
(*c*) which the officer has reasonable cause to believe are used for the carrying on of a business by a person who also carries on or has carried on an employment agency or employment business, if the officer also has reasonable cause to believe that records or other documents which relate to the employment agency or employment business are kept there.

(1C) For the purposes of subsection (1)—

(*a*) "document" includes information recorded in any form, and
(*b*) information is kept at premises if it is accessible from them.

(2) Nothing in this section shall require a person to produce, provide access to or make arrangements for the production of anything which he could not be compelled to produce in civil proceedings before the High Court or (in Scotland) the Court of Session.★
(2A) Subject to subsection (2B), a statement made by a person in compliance with a requirement under this section may be used in evidence against him in criminal proceedings.★

(2B) Except in proceedings for an offence under section 5 of the Perjury Act 1911 (false statements made otherwise than on oath), no evidence relating to the statement may be adduced, and no question relating to it may be asked, by or on behalf of the prosecution unless—

(a) evidence relating to it is adduced, or

(b) a question relating to it is asked,

by or on behalf of the person who made the statement.*

(3) Any person who obstructs an officer in the exercise of his powers under paragraph (a),(b) or (d) of subsection (1) of this section shall be guilty of an offence and liable on summary conviction to a fine not exceeding **level 3** on the standard scale and any person who, without reasonable excuse, fails to comply with a requirement under paragraph (c) of that subsection or under subsection (1A) shall be guilty of an offence and liable on summary conviction to a fine not exceeding **level 3** on the standard scale.*

(4)

(a) No information obtained in the course of exercising the powers conferred by subsection (1) of this section shall be disclosed except—

(i) with the consent of the person by whom the information was furnished or, where the information was furnished on behalf of another person, with the consent of that other person or with the consent of the person carrying on or proposing to carry on the employment agency or employment business concerned; or

(ii) to the Secretary of State, or an officer or servant appointed by, or person exercising functions on behalf of, the Secretary of State for the purposes of the exercise of their respective functions under this Act; or

(iii) by the Secretary of State, or an officer or servant appointed by, or persons exercising functions on behalf of, the Secretary of State to the person carrying on or proposing to carry on the employment agency or employment business concerned, to any person in his employment or, in the case of information relating to a person availing himself of the services of such an agency or business, to that person; or

(iv) with a view to the institution of, or otherwise for the purposes of, any criminal proceedings or for the purposes of any proceedings under section 3A, 3C or 3D of this Act.*

(b) Any person who contravenes paragraph (a) of this subsection shall be guilty of an offence and liable on summary conviction to a fine not exceeding **level 5** on the standard scale.
[Employment Agencies Act 1973, s 9, as amended by the Employment Protection Act 1975, Sch 13, the Criminal Justice Act 1982, ss 38 and 46, the Deregulation and Contracting Out Act 1994, s 35 and Sch 10, the Employment Relations Act 1999, Schs 7 and 9 and the Employment Relations Act 1999, Sch 7.]

---

*Sub-s 9(4)(a)(iv) is prospectively repealed by the Employment Relations Act 1999, Sch 9, when in force.

8–8366 10. Fraudulent applications and entries. (1) (*Repealed*).

(2) Any person who makes or causes to be made or knowingly allows to be made any entry in a record or other document required to be kept in pursuance of this Act or of any regulations made thereunder which he knows to be false in a material particular shall be guilty of an offence.

(3) Any person guilty of an offence under this section shall be liable on summary conviction to a fine not exceeding **level 5** on the standard scale.
[Employment Agencies Act 1973, s 10 as amended by the Criminal Justice Act 1982, ss 38 and 46.]

8–8367 11. Offences by bodies corporate. Where an offence under this Act committed by a body corporate is proved to have been committed with the consent or connivance of, or to have been attributable to any neglect on the part of, any director, manager, secretary or other similar officer of the body corporate or a person who was purporting to act in any such capacity, he, as well as the body corporate, shall be guilty of the offence and shall be liable to be proceeded against and punished accordingly.
[Employment Agencies Act 1973, s 11.]

8–8367A 11A. Offences: extension of time limit. (1) For the purposes of subsection (2) of this section a relevant offence is an offence under section 3B, 5(2), 6(2), 9(4)(b) or 10(2) of this Act for which proceedings are instituted by the Secretary of State.

(2) Notwithstanding section 127(1) of the Magistrates' Court Ac t1980 (information to be laid within 6 months of offence) as information relating to a relevant offence which is triable by a magistrates' court in England and Wales may be so tried if it is laid at any time—

(a) within 3 years after the date of the commission of the offence, and

(b) within 6 months after the date on which evidence sufficient in the opinion of the Secretary of State to justify proceedings came to his knowledge.

(3) Notwithstanding section 136 of the Criminal Procedure (Scotland) Act 1995 (time limit for prosecuting certain statutory offences) in Scotland proceedings in respect of an offence under section 3B, 5(2), 6(2). 9(4)(*b*) or 10(2) of this Act may be commenced at any time—

(*a*) within 3 years after the date of the commission of the offence, and

(*b*) within 6 months after the date on which evidence sufficient in the opinion of the Lord Advocate to justify the proceedings came to his knowledge.

For the purposes of this section a certificate of the Secretary of State of Lord Advocate (as the case may be) as to the date on which evidence came to his knowledge is conclusive evidence.
[Employment Agencies Act 1973, s 11A.]

8–8367B   11B. Offences: cost of investigation.   The court in which a person is convicted of an offence under this Act may order him to pay to the Secretary of State a sum which appears to the court not to exceed the costs of the investigation which resulted in the conviction.
[Employment Agencies Act 1973, s 11B, as inserted by the Employment Relations Act 1999, Sch 7.]

8–8368   13. Interpretation.   (1) In this Act—

"employment" includes—

(*a*) employment by way of a professional engagement or otherwise under a contract for services;

(*b*) the reception in a private household of a person under an arrangement whereby that person is to assist in the domestic work of the household in consideration of receiving hospitality and pocket money or hospitality only;

and "worker" and "employer" shall be construed accordingly;

"employment agency" has the meaning assigned by subsection (2) of this section but does not include any arrangements, services, functions or business to which this Act does not apply by virtue of subsection (7) of this section;

"employment business" has the meaning assigned by subsection (3) of this section but does not include any arrangements, services, functions or business to which this Act does not apply by virtue of subsection (7) of this section;

"fee" includes any charge however described;

"local authority", in relation to England, means a county council, the Common Council of the City of London, a district council or a London borough council and in relation to Wales, means a county council or a county borough council and, in relation to Scotland means a council constituted under section 2 of the Local Government etc (Scotland) Act 1994;

"organisation" includes an association of organisations;

"organisation of employers" means an organisation which consists wholly or mainly of employers and whose principal objects include the regulation of relations between employers and workers or organisations or workers;

"organisation of workers" means an organisation which consists wholly or mainly of workers and whose principal objects include the regulation of relations between workers and employers or organisations of employers;

"prescribed" means prescribed by regulations made under this Act by the Secretary of State;

"prohibition order" has the meaning given by section 3A(2) of this Act.

(2) For the purposes of this Act "employment agency" means the business (whether or not carried on with a view to profit and whether or not carried on in conjunction with any other business) of providing services (whether by the provision of information or otherwise) for the purpose of finding persons employment with employers or of supplying employers with persons for employment by them.

(3) For the purposes of this Act "employment business" means the business (whether or not carried on with a view to profit and whether or not carried on in conjunction with any other business) of supplying persons in the employment of the person carrying on the business, to act for, and under the control of, other persons in any capacity.

(4) The reference in subsection (2) of this section to providing services does not include a reference—

(*a*) to publishing a newspaper or other publication unless it is published wholly or mainly for the purpose mentioned in that subsection;

(*b*) to the display by any person of advertisements on premises occupied by him otherwise than for the said purpose;

(*c*) to providing a programme service (within the meaning of the Broadcasting Act 1990).

(5) For the purposes of section 269 of the Local Government Act 1972, this Act shall be deemed to have been passed after 1st April 1974.

(6) In this Act, except where the content otherwise requires, references to any enactment shall be construed as references to that enactment as amended, extended or applied by or under any other enactment.

(7) This Act does not apply to—

(a) any business which is carried on exclusively for the purpose of obtaining employment for—

(i) persons formerly members of Her Majesty's naval, military or air forces; or
(ii) persons released from a custodial sentence passed by a criminal court in the United Kingdom, the Channel Islands or the Isle of Man;

and which is certified annually by or on behalf of the Admiralty Board of the Defence Council, the Army Board of the Defence Council or the Air Force Board of the Defence Council or by the Secretary of State (as the case may be) to be properly conducted;

(b) *repealed*;
(c) *repealed*;
(d) services which are ancillary to the letting upon hire of any aircraft, vessel, vehicle, plant or equipment;
(e) *repealed*;
(f) the exercise by a local authority, a police authority established under section 3 of the Police Act 1996, the Service Authority for the National Criminal Intelligence Service, the Service Authority for the National Crime Squad or a joint authority established by Part IV of the Local Government Act 1985 of any of their functions;
(ff) the exercise by the Broads Authority of any of its functions;
(fa) the exercise by the Metropolitan Police Authority of any of its functions;
(fg) the exercise by the National Park authority of any of its functions;
(fh) the exercise by the London Fire and Emergency Planning Authority of any of its functions;
(g) services provided by any organisation of employers or organisation of workers for its members;
(ga) services provided in pursuance of arrangements made, or a direction given, under section 10 of the Employment and Training Act 1973;
(h) services provided by an appointments board or service controlled by—

(i) one or more universities;
(ii) *repealed*;

(i) any prescribed business or service, or prescribed class of business or service or business or service carried on or provided by prescribed persons or classes of person[1].

(8) *Scotland*.

[Employment Agencies Act 1973, s 13, as amended by the Employment Protection Act 1975, Sch 13, the Cable and Broadcasting Act 1984, Schs 5 and 6, the Local Government Act 1985, Schs 14 and 17, the Criminal Justice Act 1988, Sch 8, the Norfolk and Suffolk Broads Act 1988, Sch 6, the Education Reform Act 1988, Sch 13, the Broadcasting Act 1990, Sch 20, the Police and Magistrates' Courts Act 1994, Sch 4, the Trade Union Reform and Employment Rights Act 1993, Sch 8, the Deregulation and Contracting Out Act 1994, s 35 and Sch 10, Local Government (Wales) Act 1994, Sch 16, the Environment Act 1995, Sch 10, the Police Act 1996, Sch 7, the Police Act 1997, Sch 9, the Employment Relations Act 1999, Sch 7, the Greater London Authority Act 1999, Schs 27 and 29 and the Care Standards Act 2000, Sch 6.]

---

1. See the Employment Agencies Act 1973 (Exemption) Regulations 1976, SI 1976/710, the Employment Agencies Act 1973 (Exemption) (No 2) Regulations 1979, SI 1979/1741 and the Employment Agencies Act 1973 (Exemption) (No 2) Regulations 1984, SI 1984/978.

Industrial Training Act 1982[1]
(1982 c 10)

Functions of boards

8–8400   6. Power to obtain information from employers.   (1) An industrial training board[2] may require employers[3] in the industry to furnish such returns and other information of a kind approved by the Secretary of State and to keep such records of a kind approved by him and produce them for examination on behalf of the board as appear to the board to be necessary for carrying out its functions.

(2) Subject to subsection (3) below, returns and other information furnished in pursuance of subsection (1) above and any information obtained on an examination made in pursuance of that subsection shall not, without the consent of the employer[3] to whose business the returns or information relate, be disclosed otherwise than to the Secretary of State or one of his officers, or to an industrial training board or a committee appointed by such a board, or an officer if such a board or committee or any person entitled to take part in the proceedings of such a board.

(3) Subsection (2) above shall not apply—

(a) to the disclosure of returns or information in the form of a summary of similar returns or information furnished by or obtained from a number of employers, if the summary is so framed as not to enable particulars relating to any individual business to be ascertained from it;

(b) to any disclosure of information made for the purposes of any legal proceedings pursuant to this Act or any criminal proceedings, whether pursuant to this Act or not, or for the purposes of any report of any such proceedings.

(4) A certificate purporting to be issued by or on behalf of the Secretary of State and stating that he has approved any kind of information, return or record for the purposes of subsection (1) above shall in any legal proceedings be evidence, and in Scotland sufficient evidence, of the facts stated in the certificate.

(5) If any person fails to comply with any requirement made under subsection (1) above he shall be liable on summary conviction to a fine not exceeding **level 4** on the standard scale.

(6) If any person—

(a) knowingly or recklessly furnishes, in pursuance of any requirement made under subsection (1) above, any return or other information which is false in a material particular, or

(b) wilfully makes a false entry in any record required to be produced under that subsection or, with intent to deceive, makes use of any such entry which he knows to be false, or

(c) discloses any information in contravention of subsection (2) above,

he shall be liable[4] on summary conviction to imprisonment for a term not exceeding **three months** or to a fine not exceeding **the prescribed sum** or to both, or on conviction on indictment to imprisonment for a term not exceeding **two years** or to a fine or to both.

(7) In subsection (6) above "the prescribed sum" means—

(a) if the offence was committed in England or Wales, the prescribed sum within the meaning of section 32 of the Magistrates' Courts Act 1980 (£1,000 or other sum substituted by order under section 143(1) of that Act); and

(b) Scotland.

(8) Where an offence under this section committed by a body corporate is proved to have been committed with the consent or connivance of, or to be attributable to any neglect on the part of, any director, manager, secretary or other similar officer of the body corporate, or any person who was purporting to act in any such capacity, he, as well as the body corporate, shall be guilty of that offence and be liable to be proceeded against and punished accordingly.

[Industrial Training Act 1982, s 6 as amended by the Criminal Justice Act 1982, ss 35, 38 and 46 and the Employment Act 1989, Schs 4 and 7.]

---

1. This Act consolidates the law relating to industrial training boards.
2. "Industrial training board" means (subject to s 20(2) of the Act) a board established under s 1 of the Act or s 1 of the Industrial Training Act 1964, (s 1(2)).
3. "Employee" includes a person engaged under a contract for services, and "employer" shall be construed accordingly, (s 1(2)).
4. For procedure in respect of this offence which is triable either way, see the Magistrates' Courts Act 1980, ss 17A–21, in PART I, ante.

8–8401   **7. Provisions supplementary to s 6.** (1) The Secretary of State may direct an industrial training board to exercise the power to require the furnishing of information which is conferred on the board by section 6(1) above (in this section referred to as "the information power") so as to require employers in the industry to furnish to the board, in such form and on such occasions as are specified in the direction, such information as the Secretary of State considers that he needs for the purposes of his functions and as is so specified; and it shall be the duty of the board to comply with the direction.

(2) An industrial training board shall not exercise the information power except—

(a) in pursuance of a direction given by virtue of subsection (1) above; or

(b) with the approval of the Secretary of State and in accordance with the conditions, if any, of the approval;

and any application by a board for approval in pursuance of paragraph (b) above must be made to the Secretary of State and contains such information as he may require with respect to the proposed exercise of the information power.

(3) *(Repealed)*.

(4) An approval of an application given by the Secretary of State in pursuance of subsection (2) (b) above may be given subject to conditions that the board in question may exercise the information power only for the purpose of requiring the furnishing of information in such forms and on such occasions as are specified in the instrument of approval.

[Industrial Training Act 1982, s 7 as amended by the Employment Act 1989, Schs 4 and 7.]

Trade Union and Labour Relations (Consolidation) Act 1992

(1992 c 52)

PART I[1]
TRADE UNIONS

CHAPTER I
INTRODUCTORY

Meaning of "trade union"

8–8500   1. Meaning of "trade union".   In this Act a "trade union" means an organisation (whether temporary or permanent)—

(a)   which consists wholly or mainly of workers of one or more descriptions and whose principal purposes include the regulation of relations between workers of that description or those descriptions and employers or employers' associations; or

(b)   which consist wholly or mainly of—

(i)   constituent or affiliated organisations which fulfil the conditions in paragraph (a) (or themselves consist wholly or mainly of constituent or affiliated organisations which fulfil those conditions), or

(ii)   representatives of such constituent or affiliated organisations,

and whose principal purposes include the regulation of relations between workers and employers or between workers and employers' associations, or the regulation or relations between its constituent or affiliated organisations.

[Trade Union and Labour Relations (Consolidation) Act 1992, s 1.]

---

1.   Part I contains ss 1–121. The Certification Officer is responsible for keeping a list of trade unions.

CHAPTER II
STATUS AND PROPERTY OF TRADE UNIONS

General

8–8501   10. Quasi-corporate status of trade unions.   (1) A trade union is not a body corporate but—

(a)   it is capable of making contracts;

(b)   it is capable of suing and being sued in its own name, whether in proceedings relating to property or founded on contract or tort or any other cause of action; and

(c)   proceedings for an offence alleged to have been committed by it or on its behalf may be brought against it in its own name.

(2)   A trade union shall not be treated as if it were a body corporate except to the extent authorised by the provisions of this Part.

(3)   A trade union shall not be registered—

(a)   as a company under the Companies Act 1985, or

(b)   under the Friendly Societies Act 1974 or the Industrial and Provident Societies Act 1965;

and any such registration of a trade union (whenever effected) is void.

[Trade Union and Labour Relations (Consolidation) Act 1992, s 10.]

8–8502   11. Exclusion of common law rules as to restraint of trade.   (1) The purposes of a trade union are not, by reason only that they are in restraint of trade, unlawful so as—

(a)   to make any member of the trade union liable to criminal proceedings for conspiracy or otherwise, or

(b)   to make any agreement or trust void or voidable.

(2)   No rule of a trade union is unlawful or unenforceable by reason only that it is in restraint of trade.

[Trade Union and Labour Relations (Consolidation) Act 1992, s 11.]

Property of trade union

8–8503   12. Property to be vested in trustees.   (1) All property belonging to a trade union shall be vested in trustees in trust for it[1].

(2)   A judgment, order or award made in proceedings of any description brought against a trade union is enforceable, by way of execution, diligence, punishment for contempt or otherwise, against any property held in trust for it to the same extent and in the same manner as if it were a body corporate[1].

(3) Subsection (2) has effect subject to section 23 (restriction on enforcement of awards against certain property).
[Trade Union and Labour Relations (Consolidation) Act 1992, s 12.]

---

1. Section 12(1) and (2) applies as well to an unincorporated employers' association (Trade Union and Labour Relations (Consolidation) Act 1992, s 129(1)).

8–8504 45. Offences[1]. (1) If a trade union refuses or wilfully neglects to perform a duty imposed on it by or under any of the provisions of—

section 27 (duty to supply copy of rules),
sections 28 to 30 (accounting records),
sections 32 to 37 (annual return, statement for members, accounts and audit), or
sections 38 to 42 (members' superannuation schemes),

it commits an offence.

(2) The offence shall be deemed to have been also committed by—

(a) every officer of the trade union who is bound by the rules of the union to discharge on its behalf the duty breach of which constitutes the offence, or
(b) if there is no such officer, every member of the general committee of management of the union.

(3) In any proceedings brought against an officer or member by virtue of subsection (2) in respect of a breach of duty, it is a defence for him to prove that he had reasonable cause to believe, and did believe, that some other person who was competent to discharge that duty was authorised to discharge it instead of him and had discharged it or would do so.

(4) A person who wilfully alters or causes to be altered a document which is required for the purposes of any of the provisions mentioned in subsection (1), with intent to falsify the document or to enable a trade union to evade any of those provisions, commits an offence.

(5) If a person contravenes any duty, or requirement imposed, under section 37A (power of Certification officer to require production of documents etc) or 37B (investigations by inspectors) he commits an offence.

(6) In any proceedings brought against a person in respect of a contravention of a requirement imposed under section 37A(3) or 37B(4) to produce documents it is a defence for him to prove—

(a) that the documents were not in his possession, and
(b) that it was not reasonably practicable for him to comply with the requirement.

(7) If an official or agent of a trade union—

(a) destroys, mutilates or falsifies, or is privy to the destruction, mutilation or falsification of, a document relating to the financial affairs of the trade union, or
(b) makes, or is privy to the making of, a false entry in any such document,

he commits an offence unless he proves that he had no intention to conceal the financial affairs of the trade union or to defeat the law.

(8) If such a person fraudulently—

(a) parts with, alters or deletes anything in any such document, or
(b) is privy to the fraudulent parting with, fraudulent alteration of or fraudulent deletion in, any such document,

he commits an offence.

(9) If a person in purported compliance with a duty, or requirement imposed, under section 37A or 37B to provide an explanation or make a statement—

(a) provides or makes an explanation or statement which he knows to be false in a material particular, or
(b) recklessly provides or makes an explanation or statement which is false in a material particular,

he commits an offence.
[Trade Union and Labour Relations (Consolidation) Act 1992, s 45 amended by the Trade Union Reform and Employments Rights Act 1993, s 11 and Sch 8.]

---

1. This section applies as well to an employers' association (Trade Union and Labour Relations (Consolidation) Act 1992, s 131) as do ss 27, 28, 32–37, 38–42, 43(1), 44(1), (2) and (4). The Certification Officer keeps a list of employers' associations. For penalties see s 45A ante.

8–8505 45A. Penalties and prosecution time limits. (1) A person guilty of an offence under section 45 is liable on summary conviction—

(a) in the case of an offence under subsection (1) or (5), to a fine not exceeding **level 5** on the standard scale;
(b) in the case of an offence under subsection (4), (7), (8) or (9), to imprisonment for a term not exceeding **six months** or to a fine not exceeding **level 5** on the standard scale or to **both**.

(2) Proceedings for an offence under section 45(1) relating to the duty imposed by section 32 (duty to send annual return to Certification Officer) may be commenced at any time before the end of the period of three years beginning with the date when the offence was committed.

(3) Proceedings for any other offence under section 45(1) may be commenced—

(a) at any time before the end of the period of six months beginning with the date when the offence was committed, or

(b) at any time after the end of that period but before the end of the period of twelve months beginning with the date when evidence sufficient in the opinion of the Certification Officer or, in Scotland, the procurator fiscal, to justify the proceedings came to his knowledge;

but no proceedings may be commenced by virtue of paragraph (b) after the end of the period of three years beginning with the date when the offence was committed.

(4) For the purposes of subsection (3)(b), a certificate signed by or on behalf of the Certification Officer or the procurator fiscal which states the date on which evidence sufficient in his opinion to justify the proceedings came to his knowledge shall be conclusive evidence of that fact.

(5) A certificate stating that matter and purporting to be so signed shall be deemed to be so signed unless the contrary is proved.

(6) For the purposes of this section—

(a) in England and Wales, proceedings are commenced when an information is laid, and

(b) in Scotland, subsection (3) of section 136 of the Criminal Procedure (Scotland) Act 1995 (date of commencement of proceedings) applies as it applies for the purposes of that section.

[Trade Union and Labour Relations (Consolidation) Act 1992, s 45A inserted by the Trade Union Reform and Employment Rights Act 1993, s 11 and amended by the Criminal Procedure (Consequential Provisions) (Scotland) Act 1995, Sch 4.]

8–8506   **193.** *Duty of employer to notify Secretary of State of certain redundancies.*

PART IV[1]
INDUSTRIAL RELATIONS

CHAPTER II
PROCEDURE FOR HANDLING REDUNDANCIES

8–8507   **194. Offence of failure to notify.**   (1) An employer who fails to give notice to the Secretary of State in accordance with section 193 commits an offence and is liable on summary conviction to a fine not exceeding **level 5** on the standard scale.

(2) Proceedings in England or Wales for such an offence shall be instituted only by or with the consent of the Secretary of State or by an officer authorised for that purpose by special or general directions of the Secretary of State.

An officer so authorised may, although not of counsel or a solicitor, prosecute or conduct proceedings for such an offence before a magistrates' court.

(3) Where an offence under this section committed by a body corporate is proved to have been committed with the consent or connivance of, or to be attributable to neglect on the part of, any director, manager, secretary or other similar officer of the body corporate, or any person purporting to act in any such capacity, he as well as the body corporate is guilty of the offence and liable to be proceeded against and punished accordingly.

(4) Where the affairs of a body corporate are managed by its members, subsection (3) applies in relation to the acts and defaults of a member in connection with his functions of management as if he were a director of the body corporate.

[Trade Union and Labour Relations (Consolidation) Act 1992, s 194.]

---

1. Part IV contains sections 178–218.

PART V[1]
INDUSTRIAL ACTION

8–8508   **220. Peaceful picketing.**   (1) It is lawful for a person in contemplation or furtherance of a trade dispute to attend—

(a) at or near his own place of work, or

(b) if he is an official of a trade union, at or near the place of work of a member of the union whom he is accompanying and whom he represents,

for the purpose only of peacefully obtaining or communicating information, or peacefully persuading any person to work or abstain from working.

(2) If a person works or normally works—

(a) otherwise than at any one place, or

(b) at a place the location of which is such that attendance there for a purpose mentioned in subsection (1) is impracticable, his place of work for the purposes of that subsection shall be any premises of his employer from which he works or from which his work is administered.

(3) In the case of a worker not in employment where—

(*a*) his last employment was terminated in connection with a trade dispute, or

(*b*) the termination of his employment was one of the circumstances giving rise to a trade dispute,

in relation to that dispute in his former place of work shall be treated for the purposes of subsection (1) as being his place of work.

(4) A person who is an official of a trade union by virtue only of having been elected or appointed to be a representative of some of the members of the union shall be regarded for the purposes of subsection (1) as representing only those members; but otherwise an official of a union shall be regarded for those purposes as representing all its members.

[Trade Union and Labour Relations (Consolidation) Act 1992, s 220.]

---

1. Part V contains ss 219–246.

Criminal offences

8–8509　240. Breach of contract involving injury to persons or property.　(1) A person commits an offence who wilfully and maliciously breaks a contract of service or hiring, knowing or having reasonable cause to believe that the probable consequences of his so doing, either alone or in combination with others, will be—

(*a*) to endanger human life or cause serious bodily injury, or

(*b*) to expose valuable property, whether real or personal, to destruction or serious injury.

(2) Subsection (1) applies equally whether the offence is committed from malice conceived against the person endangered or injured or, as the case may be, the owner of the property destroyed or injured, or otherwise.

(3) A person guilty of an offence under this section is liable on summary conviction to imprisonment for a term not exceeding **three months** or to a fine not exceeding **level 2** on the standard scale **or both**.

(4) This section does not apply to seamen.

[Trade Union and Labour Relations (Consolidation) Act 1992, s 240.]

8–8510　241. Intimidation or annoyance by violence or otherwise.　(1) A person commits an offence[1] who, with a view to compelling another person to abstain from doing or to do any act which that person has a legal right to do or abstain from doing, wrongfully and without legal authority—

(*a*) uses violence to or intimidates that person or his spouse or civil partner or children, or injures his property,

(*b*) persistently follows that person about from place to place,

(*c*) hides any tools, clothes or other property owned or used by that person, or deprives him of or hinders him in the use thereof,

(*d*) watches or besets the house or other place where that person resides, works, carries on business or happens to be, or the approach to any such house or place, or

(*e*) follows that person with two or more other persons in a disorderly manner in or through any street or road.

(2) A person guilty of an offence under this section is liable on summary conviction to imprisonment for a term not exceeding **six months** or a fine not exceeding **level 5** on the standard scale, **or both**.

(3) A constable may arrest without warrant anyone he reasonably suspects is committing an offence under this section.

[Trade Union and Labour Relations (Consolidation) Act 1992, s 241 as amended by the Civil Partnership Act 2004, Sch 27.]

---

1. Section 241 is not restricted to circumstances of trade disputes or industrial action, and may therefore be applied to the actions of an anti-roads protester (*Todd v DPP* [1996] Crim LR 344).

8–8511　242. Restriction of offence of conspiracy: England and Wales.　(1) Where in pursuance of any such agreement as is mentioned in section 1(1) of the Criminal Law Act 1977 (which provides for the offence of conspiracy) the acts in question in relation to an offence are to be done in contemplation or furtherance of a trade dispute, the offence shall be disregarded for the purposes of that subsection if it is a summary offence which is not punishable with imprisonment.

(2) This section extends to England and Wales only.

[Trade Union and Labour Relations (Consolidation) Act 1992, s 242.]

Supplementary

8–8512   244. Meaning of "trade dispute" in Part V.   (1) In this Part a "trade dispute" means a dispute between workers and their employer which relates wholly or mainly to one or more of the following—

(a)   terms and conditions of employment, or the physical conditions in which any workers are required to work;

(b)   engagement or non-engagement, or termination or suspension of employment or the duties of employment, of one or more workers;

(c)   allocation of work or the duties of employment between workers or groups of workers;

(d)   matters of discipline;

(e)   a worker's membership or non-membership of a trade union;

(f)   facilities for officials of trade unions; and

(g)   machinery for negotiation or consultation, and other procedures, relating to any of the above matters, including the recognition by employers or employers' associations of the right of a trade union to represent workers in such negotiation or consultation or in the carrying out of such procedures.

(2) A dispute between a Minister of the Crown and any workers shall, notwithstanding that he is not the employer of those workers, be treated as a dispute between those workers and their employer if the dispute relates to matters which—

(a)   have been referred for consideration by a joint body on which, by virtue of provision made by or under any enactment, he is represented, or

(b)   cannot be settled without him exercising a power conferred on him by or under an enactment.

(3) There is a trade dispute even though it relates to matters occurring outside the United Kingdom, so long as the person or persons whose actions in the United Kingdom are said to be in contemplation or furtherance of a trade dispute relating to matters occurring outside the United Kingdom are likely to be affected in respect of one or more of the matters specified in subsection (1) by the outcome of the dispute.

(4) An act, threat or demand done or made by one person or organisation against another which, if resisted, would have led to a trade dispute with that other, shall be treated as being done or made in contemplation of a trade dispute with that other, notwithstanding that because that other submits to the act or threat or accedes to the demand no dispute arises.

(5) In this section—

"employment" includes any relationship whereby one person personally does work or performs services for another; and

"worker", in relation to a dispute with an employer, means—

(a)   a worker employed by that employer; or

(b)   a person who has ceased to be so employed if his employment was terminated in connection with the dispute or if the termination of his employment was one of the circumstances giving rise to the dispute.

[Trade Union and Labour Relations (Consolidation) Act 1992, s 244.]

PART VII[1]

MISCELLANEOUS AND GENERAL

Interpretation

8–8513   295. Meaning of "employee" and related expressions.   (1) In this Act—

"contract of employment" means a contract of service or of apprenticeship,

"employee" means an individual who has entered into or works under (or, where the employment has ceased, worked under) a contract of employment, and

"employer", in relation to an employee, means the person by whom the employee is (or, where the employment has ceased, was) employed.

(2) Subsection (1) has effect subject to section 235 and other provisions conferring a wider meaning on "contract of employment" or related expressions.

[Trade Union and Labour Relations (Consolidation) Act 1992, s 295.]

---

1. Part VII contains ss 273–303.

8–8514   296. Meaning of "worker" and related expressions.   (1) In this Act "worker" means an individual who works, or normally works or seeks to work—

(a)   under a contact of employment, or

(b)   under any other contract whereby he undertakes to do or perform personally any work or services for another party to the contract who is not a professional client of his, or (*c*)   in employment under or for the purposes of a government department (otherwise than as a member of the naval, military or air forces of the Crown) in so far as such employment does not fall within paragraph (*a*) or (*b*) above.

(2)   In this Act "employer", in relation to a worker, means a person for whom one or more workers work, or have worked or normally work or seek to work.

(3)   This section has effect subject to sections 68(4), 145F(3) and 151(1B).

[Trade Union and Labour Relations (Consolidation) Act 1992, s 296 as amended by the Trade Union Reform and Employment Rights Act 1993, Sch 8 and the Employment Relations Act 2004, Sch 1.]

Employment Tribunals Act 1996[1]

(1996 c 17)

Part I[2]

EMPLOYMENT TRIBUNALS

Introductory

8–8520   1. Employment tribunals.   (1) The Secretary of State may by regulations make provision for the establishment of tribunals to be known as employment tribunals.

(2)   Regulations made wholly or partly under section 128(1) of the Employment Protection (Consolidation) Act 1978 and in force immediately before this Act comes into force shall, so far as made under that provision, continue to have effect (until revoked) as if made under subsection (1).

[Employment Tribunals Act 1996, s 1 as amended by the Employment Rights (Dispute Resolution) Act 1998, s 1 and Sch 2.]

---

1.   This Act consolidates enactments relating to industrial tribunals and the Employment Appeal Tribunal. Industrial tribunals have since been renamed as employment tribunals and the citation of the Act has been changed to the "Employment Tribunals Act 1996" by the Employment Rights (Dispute Resolution) Act 1998, s 1.

2.   The Act came into force on 22 August 1996 (s 46). Part I contains ss 1–19.

Procedure

8–8521   6. Conduct of hearings.   (1) A person may appear before an employment tribunal in person or be represented by—

(*a*)   counsel or a solicitor,

(*b*)   a representative of a trade union or an employers' association, or

(*c*)   any other person whom he desires to represent him.

(2)   Part I of the Arbitration Act 1996 does not apply to any proceedings before an employment tribunal.

[Employment Tribunals Act 1996, s 6 as amended by the Arbitration Act 1996, Sch 3 and the Employment Rights (Dispute Resolution) Act 1998, s 1.]

8–8522   7. Employment tribunal procedure regulations.   (1) The Secretary of State may by regulations[1] ("employment tribunal procedure regulations") make such provision as appears to him to be necessary or expedient with respect to proceedings before employment tribunals.

(2)   Proceedings before employment tribunals shall be instituted in accordance with employment tribunal procedure regulations.

(3)   Employment tribunal procedure regulations[1] may, in particular, include provision—

(*a*)   for determining by which tribunal any proceedings are to be determined,

(*b*)   for enabling an employment tribunal to hear and determine proceedings brought by virtue of section 3 concurrently with proceedings brought before the tribunal otherwise than by virtue of that section,

(*c*)   for treating the Secretary of State (either generally or in such circumstances as may be prescribed by the regulations) as a party to any proceedings before an employment tribunal (where he would not otherwise be a party to them) and entitling him to appear and to be heard accordingly,

(*d*)   for requiring persons to attend to give evidence and produce documents and for authorising the administration of oaths to witnesses,

(*e*)   for enabling an employment tribunal, on the application of any party to the proceedings before it or of its own motion, to order—

(i)   in England and Wales, such discovery or inspection of documents, or the furnishing of such further particulars, as might be ordered by a county court on application by a party to proceedings before it, or

(ii)   in Scotland, such recovery or inspection of documents as might be ordered by a sheriff,

(*f*)   for prescribing the procedure to be followed in any proceedings before an employment tribunal, including provision—

    (i)   (*repealed*),*

  (ia) for postponing fixing a time and place for a hearing, or postponing a time fixed for a hearing, for such period as may be determined in accordance with the regulations for the purpose of giving an opportunity for the proceedings to be settled by way of conciliation and withdrawn, and

   (ii) for enabling an employment tribunal to review its decisions, and revoke or vary its orders and awards, in such circumstances as may be determined in accordance with the regulations,

  (g) for the appointment of one or more assessors for the purposes of any proceedings before an employment tribunal, where the proceedings are brought under an enactment which provides for one or more assessors to be appointed,

  (h) for authorising an employment tribunal to require persons to furnish information and produce documents to a person required for the purposes of section 2A(1)(*b*) of the Equal Pay Act 1970 to prepare a report, and

  (j) for the registration and proof of decisions, orders and awards of employment tribunals.

(3ZA) Employment tribunal procedure regulations may—

  (a) authorise the Secretary of State to prescribe, or prescribe requirements in relation to, any form which is required by such regulations to be used for the purpose of instituting, or entering an appearance to, proceedings before employment tribunals,

  (b) authorise the Secretary of State to prescribe requirements in relation to documents to be supplied with any such form, and

  (c) make provision about the publication of anything prescribed under authority conferred by virtue of this subsection.

(3A) Employment tribunal procedure regulations may authorise the determination of proceedings without any hearing in such circumstances as the regulations may prescribe.

(3B) Employment tribunal procedure regulations may authorise the determination of proceedings without hearing anyone other than the person or persons by whom the proceedings are brought (or his or their representatives) where—

  (a) the person (or, where more than one, each of the persons) against whom the proceedings are brought has done nothing to contest the case, or

  (b) it appears from the application made by the person (or, where more than one, each of the persons) bringing the proceedings that he is not (or they are not) seeking any relief which an employment tribunal has power to give or that he is not (or they are not) entitled to any such relief.

(3C) Employment tribunal procedure regulations may authorise the determination of proceedings without hearing anyone other than the person or persons by whom, and the person or persons against whom, the proceedings are brought (or his or their representatives) where—

  (a) an employment tribunal is on undisputed facts bound by the decision of a court in another case to dismiss the case of the person or persons by whom, or of the person or persons against whom, the proceedings are brought, or

  (b) the proceedings relate only to a preliminary issue which may be heard and determined in accordance with regulations under section 9(4).

(4) A person who without reasonable excuse fails to comply with—

  (a) any requirement imposed by virtue of subsection (3)(*d*) or (*h*), or

  (b) any requirement with respect to the discovery, recovery or inspection of documents imposed by virtue of subsection (3)(*e*), or

  (c) any requirement imposed by virtue of employment tribunal procedure regulations to give written answers for the purpose of facilitating the determination of proceedings as mentioned in subsection (3A), (3B) or (3C),

is guilty of an offence and liable on summary conviction to a fine not exceeding **level 3** on the standard scale.

(5) Subject to any regulations[1] under section 11(1)(*a*), employment tribunal procedure regulations may include provision authorising or requiring an employment tribunal, in circumstances specified in the regulations, to send notice or a copy of—

  (a) any document specified in the regulations which relates to any proceedings before the tribunal, or

  (b) any decision, order or award of the tribunal,

to any government department or other person or body so specified.

(6) Where in accordance with employment tribunal procedure regulations an employment tribunal determines in the same proceedings—

  (a) a complaint presented under section 111 of the Employment Rights Act 1996, and

  (b) a question referred under section 163 of that Act,

subsection (2) of that section has no effect for the purposes of the proceedings in so far as they relate to the complaint under section 111.

[Employment Tribunals Act 1996, s 7 as amended by the Employment Rights (Dispute Resolution) Act, ss 1, 2 and Schs 1 and 2 and the Employment Act 2002, ss 24–26.]

---

1. See the Employment Tribunals (Constitution and Rules of Procedure) Regulations 2004, SI 2004/1861 amended by SI 2004/2351 and SI 2005/435 and 1865.

8–8522A 7A. Practice directions. (1) Employment tribunal procedure regulations may include provision—

   (*a*) enabling the President to make directions about the procedure of employment tribunals, including directions about the exercise by tribunals of powers under such regulations,

   (*b*) for securing compliance with such directions, and

   (*c*) about the publication of such directions.

(2) Employment tribunal procedure regulations may, instead of providing for any matter, refer to provision made or to be made about that matter by directions made by the President.

(3) In this section, references to the President are to a person appointed in accordance with regulations under section 1(1) as—

   (*a*) President of the Employment Tribunals (England and Wales), or

   (*b*) President of the Employment Tribunals (Scotland)★

[Employment Tribunals Act 1996, s 7A, as inserted by the Employment Act 2002, s 27.]

★Section printed as prospectively inserted by the Employment Act 2000, s 27, from a date to be appointed.

8–8522AB 10. National security. (1) If on a complaint under—

   (*a*) section 145A, 145B or 146 of the Trade Union and Labour Relations (Consolidation) Act 1992 (inducements and detriments in respect of trade union membership), or

   (*b*) section 111 of the Employment Rights Act 1996 (unfair dismissal),

it is shown that the action complained of was taken for the purpose of safeguarding national security, the employment tribunal shall dismiss the complaint.

(2) Employment tribunal procedure regulations may make provision about the composition of the tribunal (including provision disapplying or modifying section 4) for the purposes of proceedings in relation to which—

   (*a*) a direction is given under subsection (3), or

   (*b*) an order is made under subsection (4),

(3) A direction may be given under this subsection by a Minister of the Crown if—

   (*a*) it relates to particular Crown employment proceedings, and

   (*b*) the Minister considers it expedient in the interests of national security.

(4) An order may be made under this subsection by the President or a Regional Chairman in relation to particular proceedings if he considers it expedient in the interests of national security.

(5) Employment tribunal procedure regulations may make provision enabling a Minister of the Crown, if he considers it expedient in the interests of national security—

   (*a*) to direct a tribunal to sit in private for all or part of particular Crown employment proceedings;

   (*b*) to direct a tribunal to exclude the applicant from all or part of particular Crown employment proceedings;

   (*c*) to direct a tribunal to exclude the applicant's representatives from al or part of particular Crown employment proceedings;

   (*d*) to direct a tribunal to take steps to conceal the identity of a particular witness in particular Crown employment proceedings;

   (*e*) to direct a tribunal to take steps to keep secret all or part of the reasons for its decision in particular crown employment proceedings.

(6) Employment tribunal procedure regulations may enable a tribunal, if it considers it expedient in the interests of national security, to do anything of a kind which a tribunal can be required to do by direction under subsection (5) (*a*) to (*e*).★

(7) In relation to cases where a person has been excluded by virtue of subsection (5) (*b*) or (*c*) or (6), employment tribunal procedure regulations[1] may make provision—

   (*a*) for the appointment by the Attorney General, or by the Advocate General for Scotland, of a person to represent the interests of the applicant;

   (*b*) about the publication and registration of reasons for the tribunal's decision;

   (*c*) permitting an excluded person to make a statement to the tribunal before the commencement of the proceedings, or the part of the proceedings, from which he is excluded.

(8) Proceedings are Crown employment proceedings for the purposes of this section if the employment to which the complaint relates—

    (*a*) is Crown employment, or

    (*b*) is connected with the performance of functions on behalf of the Crown.

(9) The reference in subsection (4) to the President or a Regional Chairman is to a person appointed in accordance with regulations under section 1(1) as—

    (*a*) a regional Chairman,

    (*b*) President of the Employment Tribunals (England and Wales), or

    (*c*) President of the Employment tribunals (Scotland).

[Employment Tribunals Act 1996, s 10, substituted together with ss 10A, 10B for s 10 as originally enacted, by the Employment Relations Act 1999, Sch 8 and amended by the Employment Relations Act 2004, Sch 1.]

---

*Substituted by the Employment Relations Act 2004, s 36 from a date to be appointed.

1. See the Employment Tribunals (Constitution and Rules of Procedure) Regulations 2004, SI 2004/1861 amended by SI 2004/2351 and SI 2005/435 and 1865.

8–8522B　10A. Confidential information.   (1) Employment tribunal procedure regulations may enable an employment tribunal to sit in private for the purpose of hearing evidence from any person which in the opinion of the tribunal is likely to consist of—

    (*a*) information which he could not disclose without contravening a prohibition imposed by or by virtue of any enactment,

    (*b*) information which has been communicated to him in confidence or which he has otherwise obtained in consequence of the confidence reposed in him by another person, or

    (*c*) information the disclosure of which would, for reasons other than its effect on negotiations with respect to any of the matters mentioned in section 178(2) of the Trade Union and Labour Relations (Consolidation) Act 1992, cause substantial injury to any undertaking of his or in which he works.

(2) The reference in subsection (1)(*c*) to any undertaking of a person or in which he works shall be construed—

    (*a*) in relation to a person in Crown employment, as a reference to the national interest,

    (*b*) in relation to a person who is a relevant member of the House of Lords staff, as a reference to the national interest or (if the case so requires) the interests of the House of Lords, and

    (*c*) in relation to a person who is a relevant member of the House of Commons staff, as a reference to the national interest or (if the case so requires) the interests of the House of Commons.

[Employment Tribunals Act 1996, s 10A, substituted together with ss 10, 10B for s 10 as originally enacted, by the Employment Relations Act 1999, Sch 8.]

8–8522C　10B. Restriction of publicity in cases involving national security.   (1) This section applies where a tribunal has been directed under section 10(5) or has determined under section 10(6)—

    (*a*) to take steps to conceal the identity of a particular witness, or

    (*b*) to take steps to keep secret all or part of the reasons for its decision.

(2) It is an offence to publish—

    (*a*) anything likely to lead to the identification of the witness, or

    (*b*) the reasons for the tribunal's decision or the part of its reasons which it is directed or has determined to keep secret.

(3) A person guilty of an offence under this section is liable on summary conviction to a fine not exceeding level 5 on the standard scale.

(4) Where a person is charged with an offence under this section it is a defence to prove that at the time of the alleged offence he was not aware, and neither suspected nor had reason to suspect, that the publication in question was of, or included, the matter in question.

(5) Where an offence under this section committed by a body corporate is proved to have been committed with the consent or connivance of, or to be attributable to any neglect on the part of—

    (*a*) a director, manager, secretary or other similar officer of the body corporate, or

    (*b*) a person purporting to act in any such capacity, he as well as the body corporate is guilty of the offence and liable to be proceeded against and punished accordingly.

(6) A reference in this section to publication includes a reference to inclusion in a programme which is included in a programme service, within the meaning of the Broadcasting Act 1990.

[Employment Tribunals Act 1996, s10B substituted together with ss 10, 10A for s 10 as originally enacted, by the Employment Relations Act 1999, Sch 8.]

8–8523　11. Restriction of publicity in cases involving sexual misconduct.   (1) Employment tribunal procedure regulations may include provision—

    (*a*) for cases involving allegations of the commission of sexual offences, for securing that the registration or other making available of documents or decisions shall be so effected as to prevent the identification of any person affected by or making the allegation, and (*b*)　for cases involving allegations of sexual misconduct, enabling an employment tribunal, on the application of any party to proceedings before it or of its own motion, to make a restricted reporting order having effect (if not revoked earlier) until the promulgation of the decision of the tribunal.

(2)　If any identifying matter is published or included in a relevant programme in contravention of a restricted reporting order—

(*a*)　in the case of publication in a newspaper or periodical, any proprietor, any editor and any publisher of the newspaper or periodical,

(*b*)　in the case of publication in any other form, the person publishing the matter, and

(*c*)　in the case of matter included in a relevant programme—

　　(i)　any body corporate engaged in providing the service in which the programme is included, and

　　(ii)　any person having functions in relation to the programme corresponding to those of an editor of a newspaper,

shall be guilty of an offence and liable on summary conviction to a fine not exceeding **level 5** on the standard scale.

(3)　Where a person is charged with an offence under subsection (2) it is a defence to prove that at the time of the alleged offence he was not aware, and neither suspected nor had reason to suspect, that the publication or programme in question was of, or included, the matter in question.

(4)　Where an offence under subsection (2) committed by a body corporate is proved to have been committed with the consent or connivance of, or to be attributable to any neglect on the part of—

(*a*)　a director, manager, secretary or other similar officer of the body corporate, or

(*b*)　a person purporting to act in any such capacity.

he as well as the body corporate is guilty of the offence and liable to be proceeded against and punished accordingly.

(5)　In relation to a body corporate whose affairs are managed by its members "director", in subsection (4), means a member of the body corporate.

(6)　In this section—

"identifying matter", in relation to a person, means any matter likely to lead members of the public to identify him as a person affected by, or as the person making, the allegation,

"relevant programme" has the same meaning as in the Sexual Offences (Amendment) Act 1992,

"restricted reporting order" means an order—

(*a*)　made in exercise of a power conferred by regulations made by virtue of this section, and

(*b*)　prohibiting the publication in Great Britain of identifying matter in a written publication available to the public or its inclusion in a relevant programme for reception in Great Britain.

"sexual misconduct" means the commission of a sexual offence, sexual harassment or other adverse conduct (of whatever nature) related to sex, and conduct is related to sex whether the relationship with sex lies in the character of the conduct or in its having reference to the sex or sexual orientation of the person at whom the conduct is directed,

"sexual offence" means any offence to which section 4 of the Sexual Offences (Amendment) Act 1976, the Sexual Offences (Amendment) Act 1992 or section 274(2) of the Criminal Procedure (Scotland) Act 1995 applies (offences under the Sexual Offences Act 1956, Part I of the Criminal Law (Consolidation) (Scotland) Act 1995 and certain other enactments), and

"written publication" has the same meaning as in the Sexual Offences (Amendment) Act 1992.

[Employment Tribunals Act 1996, s 11 as amended by the Employment Rights (Dispute Resolution) Act 1998, s 1.]

8–8524　12. Restriction of publicity in disability cases. (1)　This section applies to proceedings on a complaint under section 17A or 25(8) of the Disability Discrimination Act 1995 in which evidence of a personal nature is likely to be heard by the employment tribunal hearing the complaint.

(2)　Employment tribunal procedure regulations may include provision in relation to proceedings to which this section applies for—

(*a*)　enabling an employment tribunal, on the application of the complainant or of its own motion, to make a restricted reporting order having effect (if not revoked earlier) until the promulgation of the decision of the tribunal, and

(*b*)　where a restricted reporting order is made in relation to a complaint which is being dealt with by the tribunal together with any other proceedings, enabling the tribunal to direct that the order is to apply also in relation to those other proceedings or such part of them as the tribunal may direct.

(3)　If any identifying matter is published or included in a relevant programme in contravention of a restricted reporting order—

(a) in the case of publication in a newspaper or periodical, any proprietor, any editor and any publisher of the newspaper or periodical,

(b) in the case of publication in any other form, the person publishing the matter, and

(c) in the case of matter included in a relevant programme—

    (i) any body corporate engaged in providing the service in which the programme is included, and

    (ii) any person having functions in relation to the programme corresponding to those of an editor of a newspaper,

shall be guilty of an offence and liable on summary conviction to a fine not exceeding **level 5** on the standard scale.

(4) Where a person is charged with an offence under subsection (3), it is a defence to prove that at the time of the alleged offence he was not aware, and neither suspected nor had reason to suspect, that the publication or programme in question was of, or included, the matter in question.

(5) Where an offence under subsection (3) committed by a body corporate is proved to have been committed with the consent or connivance of, or to be attributable to any neglect on the part of—

(a) a director, manager, secretary or other similar officer of the body corporate, or

(b) a person purporting to act in any such capacity,

he as well as the body corporate is guilty of the offence and liable to be proceeded against and punished accordingly.

(6) In relation to a body corporate whose affairs are managed by its members "director", in subsection (5), means a member of the body corporate.

(7) In this section—

"evidence of a personal nature" means any evidence of a medical, or other intimate, nature which might reasonably be assumed to be likely to cause significant embarrassment to the complainant if reported,

"identifying matter" means any matter likely to lead members of the public to identify the complainant or such other persons (if any) as may be named in the order,

"promulgation" has such meaning as may be prescribed by regulations made by virtue of this section,

"relevant programme" means a programme included in a programme service, within the meaning of the Broadcasting Act 1990,

"restricted reporting order" means an order—

(a) made in exercise of a power conferred by regulations made by virtue of this section, and

(b) prohibiting the publication in Great Britain of identifying matter in a written publication available to the public or its inclusion in a relevant programme for reception in Great Britain, and

"written publication" includes a film, a sound track and any other record in permanent form but does not include an indictment or other document prepared for use in particular legal proceedings.

[Employment Tribunals Act 1996, s 12 as amended by the Employment Rights (Dispute Resolution) Act 1998, s 1 and SI 2003/1673.]

PART II[1]

THE EMPLOYMENT APPEAL TRIBUNAL

Introductory

8–8525 20. The Appeal Tribunal. (1) The Employment Appeal Tribunal ("the Appeal Tribunal") shall continue in existence.

(2) The Appeal Tribunal shall have a central office in London but may sit at any time and in any place in Great Britain.

(3) The Appeal Tribunal shall be a superior court of record and shall have an official seal which shall be judicially noticed.

(4) Subsection (2) is subject to regulation 34 of the Transnational Information and Consultation of Employees Regulations 1999 and regulation 46(1) of the European Public Limited-Liability Company Regulations 2004.

[Employment Tribunals Act 1996, s 20 as amended by the Employment Rights (Dispute Resolution) Act 1998, s 1, SI 1999/3323 and SI 2004/2326.]

---

1. Part II contains ss 20–37.

Procedure

8–8526 29. Conduct of hearings. (1) A person may appear before the Appeal Tribunal in person or be represented by—

(a) counsel or a solicitor,

(b)   a representative of a trade union or an employers' association, or

(c)   any other person whom he desires to represent him.

(2)   The Appeal Tribunal has in relation to—

(a)   the attendance and examination of witnesses,

(b)   the production and inspection of documents, and

(c)   all other matters incidental to its jurisdiction,

the same powers, rights, privileges and authority (in England and Wales) as the High Court and (in Scotland) as the Court of Session.

[Employment Tribunals Act 1996, s 29 as amended by the Employment Rights (Dispute Resolution) Act 1998, s 1.]

8–8527   30. Appeal Tribunals procedure rules.   *Power of the Lord Chancellor to make rules with respect to proceedings before the Appeal Tribunal.*

8–8528   31. Restriction of publicity in cases involving sexual misconduct.   (1) Appeal Tribunal procedure rules may, as respects proceedings to which this section applies, include provision—

(a)   for cases involving allegations of the commission of sexual offences, for securing that the registration or other making available of documents or decisions shall be so effected as to prevent the identification of any person affected by or making the allegation, and

(b)   for cases involving allegations of sexual misconduct, enabling the Appeal Tribunal, on the application of any party to the proceedings before it or of its own motion, to make a restricted reporting order having effect (if not revoked earlier) until the promulgation of the decision of the Appeal Tribunal.

(2)   This section applies to—

(a)   proceedings on an appeal against a decision of an employment tribunal to make, or not to make, a restricted reporting order, and

(b)   proceedings on an appeal against any interlocutory decision of an employment tribunal in proceedings in which the employment tribunal has made a restricted reporting order which it has not revoked.

(3)   If any identifying matter is published or included in a relevant programme in contravention of a restricted reporting order—

(a)   in the case of publication in a newspaper or periodical, any proprietor, any editor and any publisher of the newspaper or periodical,

(b)   in the case of publication in any other form, the person publishing the matter, and

(c)   in the case of matter included in a relevant programme—

(i)   any body corporate engaged in providing the service in which the programme is included, and

(ii)   any person having functions in relation to the programme corresponding to those of an editor of a newspaper,

shall be guilty of an offence and liable on summary conviction to a fine not exceeding **level 5** on the standard scale.

(4)   Where a person is charged with an offence under subsection (3) it is a defence to prove that at the time of the alleged offence he was not aware, and neither suspected nor had reason to suspect, that the publication or programme in question was of, or included, the matter in question.

(5)   Where an offence under subsection (3) committed by a body corporate is proved to have been committed with the consent or connivance of, or to be attributable to any neglect on the part of—

(a)   a director, manager, secretary or other similar officer of the body corporate, or

(b)   a person purporting to act in any such capacity,

he as well as the body corporate is guilty of the offence and liable to be proceeded against and punished accordingly.

(6)   In relation to a body corporate whose affairs are managed by its members "director", in subsection (5), means a member of the body corporate.

(7)   "Restricted reporting order" means—

(a)   in subsections (1) and (3), an order—

(i)   made in exercise of a power conferred by rules made by virtue of this section, and

(ii)   prohibiting the publication in Great Britain of identifying matter in a written publication available to the public or its inclusion in a relevant programme for reception in Great Britain, and

(b)   in subsection (2), an order which is a restricted reporting order for the purposes of section 11.

(8)   In this section—

"identifying matter", in relation to a person, means any matter likely to lead members of the public to identify him as a person affected by, or as the person making, the allegation,

"relevant programme" has the same meaning as in the Sexual Offences (Amendment) Act 1992,

"sexual misconduct" means the commission of a sexual offence, sexual harassment or other adverse conduct (of whatever nature) related to sex, and conduct is related to sex whether the relationship with sex lies in the character of the conduct or in its having reference to the sex or sexual orientation of the person at whom the conduct is directed,

"sexual offence" means any offence to which section 4 of the Sexual Offences (Amendment) Act 1976, the Sexual Offences (Amendment) Act 1992 or section 274(2) of the Criminal Procedure (Scotland) Act 1995 applies (offences under the Sexual Offences Act 1956, Part I of the Criminal Law (Consolidation) (Scotland) Act 1995 and certain other enactments), and

"written publication" has the same meaning as in the Sexual Offences (Amendment) Act 1992.

[Employment Tribunals Act 1996, s 31 as amended by the Employment Rights (Dispute Resolution) Act 1998, s 1.]

8–8529 32. Restriction of publicity in disability cases. (1) This section applies to proceedings—

   (a)   on an appeal against a decision of an employment tribunal to make, or not to make, a restricted reporting order, or

   (b)   on an appeal against any interlocutory decision of an employment tribunal in proceedings in which the employment tribunal has made a restricted reporting order which it has not revoked.

(2) Appeal Tribunal procedure rules may, as respects proceedings to which this section applies, include provision for—

   (a)   enabling the Appeal Tribunal, on the application of the complainant or of its own motion, to make a restricted reporting order having effect (if not revoked earlier) until the promulgation of the decision of the Appeal Tribunal, and

   (b)   where a restricted reporting order is made in relation to an appeal which is being dealt with by the Appeal Tribunal together with any other proceedings, enabling the Appeal Tribunal to direct that the order is to apply also in relation to those other proceedings or such part of them as the Appeal Tribunal may direct.

(3) If any identifying matter is published or included in a relevant programme in contravention of a restricted reporting order—

   (a)   in the case of publication in a newspaper or periodical, any proprietor, any editor and any publisher of the newspaper or periodical,

   (b)   in the case of publication in any other form, the person publishing the matter, and

   (c)   in the case of matter included in a relevant programme—

      (i)   any body corporate engaged in providing the service in which the programme is included, and

      (ii)   any person having functions in relation to the programme corresponding to those of an editor of a newspaper,

shall be guilty of an offence and liable on summary conviction to a fine not exceeding **level 5** on the standard scale.

(4) Where a person is charged with an offence under subsection (3), it is a defence to prove that at the time of the alleged offence he was not aware, and neither suspected nor had reason to suspect, that the publication or programme in question was of, or included, the matter in question.

(5) Where an offence under subsection (3) committed by a body corporate is proved to have been committed with the consent or connivance of, or to be attributable to any neglect on the part of—

   (a)   a director, manager, secretary or other similar officer of the body corporate, or

   (b)   a person purporting to act in any such capacity,

he as well as the body corporate is guilty of the offence and liable to be proceeded against and punished accordingly.

(6) In relation to a body corporate whose affairs are managed by its members "director", in subsection (5), means a member of the body corporate.

(7) "Restricted reporting order" means—

   (a)   in subsection (1), an order which is a restricted reporting order for the purposes of section 12, and

   (b)   in subsections (2) and (3), an order—

      (i)   made in exercise of a power conferred by rules made by virtue of this section, and

      (ii)   prohibiting the publication in Great Britain of identifying matter in a written publication available to the public or its inclusion in a relevant programme for reception in Great Britain.

(8) In this section—

"complainant" means the person who made the complaint to which the proceedings before the Appeal Tribunal relate, "identifying matter" means any matter likely to lead members of the public to identify the complainant or such other persons (if any) as may be named in the order,

"promulgation" has such meaning as may be prescribed by rules made by virtue of this section,

"relevant programme" means a programme included in a programme service, within the meaning of the Broadcasting Act 1990, and

"written publication" includes a film, a sound track and any other record in permanent form but does not include an indictment or other document prepared for use in particular legal proceedings.

[Employment Tribunals Act 1996, s 32 as amended by the Employment Rights (Dispute Resolution) Act 1998, s 1.]

Decisions and further appeals

8–8530　36. Enforcement of decisions etc.　(1) Any sum payable in England and Wales in pursuance of an award of the Appeal Tribunal—

(*a*)　made under section 67 or 176 of the Trade Union and Labour Relations (Consolidation) Act 1992, and

(*b*)　registered in accordance with Appeal Tribunal procedure rules,

is, if a county court so orders, recoverable by execution issued from the county court or otherwise as if it were payable under an order of that court.

(2) Any order by the Appeal Tribunal for the payment in Scotland of any sum in pursuance of such an award (or any copy of such an order certified by the Secretary of the Tribunals) may be enforced as if it were an extract registered decree arbitral bearing a warrant for execution issued by the sheriff court of any sheriffdom in Scotland.

(3) Any sum payable in pursuance of an award of the Appeal Tribunal under section 67 or 176 of the Trade Union and Labour Relations (Consolidation) Act 1992 shall be treated as if it were a sum payable in pursuance of a decision of an employment tribunal for the purposes of section 14 of this Act.*

(4) No person shall be punished for contempt[1] of the Appeal Tribunal except by, or with the consent of, a judge.

(5) A magistrates' court shall not remit the whole or part of a fine[1] imposed by the Appeal Tribunal unless it has the consent of a judge who is a member of the Appeal Tribunal.

[Employment Tribunals Act 1996, s 36 as amended by the Employment Rights (Dispute Resolution) Act 1998, s 1.]

---

*Repealed by the Employment Relations Act 2004, Sch 1 from a date to be appointed.

1. A fine for contempt of the Appeal Tribunal may be enforced upon the order of the Appeal Tribunal as if it were a fine imposed by the Crown Court, and the provisions of ss 31 and 32 of the Powers of Criminal Courts Act 1973 shall apply to such fine (Contempt of Court Act 1981, s 16, in PART I: MAGISTRATES' COURTS, PROCEDURE, *ante*). Therefore, in accordance with s 32 of the Powers of Criminal Courts Act 1973, in PART III: SENTENCING, *ante*, the fine shall be treated for the purposes of collection and enforcement as having been imposed by a magistrates' court.

PART III[1]
SUPPLEMENTARY

General

8–8531　41. Orders, regulations and rules

---

1. Part III contains ss 38–48.

8–8532　42. *Interpretation*

8–8533　46–48. *Commencement; Extent; Short title (summarised)*

Employment Rights Act 1996[1]

(1996 c 18)

PART VI[2]
TIME OFF WORK

Public duties

8–8540　50. Right to time off for public duties.　(1) An employer shall permit an employee of his who is a justice of the peace to take time off during the employee's working hours for the purpose of performing any of the duties of his office.

(2) An employer shall permit an employee of his who is a member of—

(*a*)　a local authority,

- (b) a statutory tribunal,
- (c) a police authority,
- (ca) the Service Authority for the National Criminal Intelligence Service or the Service Authority for the National Crime Squad,
- (d) a board of prison visitors or a prison visiting committee,
- (e) a relevant health body,
- (f) a relevant education body,
- (g) the Environment Agency or the Scottish Environment Protection Agency, or
- (h) Scottish Water or a Water Customer Consultation Panel,

to take time off during the employee's working hours for the purposes specified in subsection (3).

(3) The purposes referred to in subsection (2) are—

- (a) attendance at a meeting of the body or any of its committees or sub-committees, and
- (b) the doing of any other thing approved by the body, or anything of a class so approved, for the purpose of the discharge of the functions of the body or of any of its committees or sub-committees, and
- (c) in the case of a local authority which are operating executive arrangements—
  - (i) attendance at a meeting of the executive of that local authority or committee of that executive; and
  - (ii) the doing of any other thing, by an individual member of that executive, for the purposes of the discharge of any function which is to any extent the responsibility of that executive.

(4) The amount of time off which an employee is to be permitted to take under this section, and the occasions on which and any conditions subject to which time off may be so taken, are those that are reasonable in all the circumstances having regard, in particular, to—

- (a) how much time off is required for the performance of the duties of the office or as a member of the body in question, and how much time off is required for the performance of the particular duty,
- (b) how much time off the employee has already been permitted under this section or sections 168 and 170 of the Trade Union and Labour Relations (Consolidation) Act 1992 (time off for trade union duties and activities), and
- (c) the circumstances of the employer's business and the effect of the employee's absence on the running of that business.

(5) In subsection (2)(a) "a local authority" means—

- (a) a local authority within the meaning of the Local Government Act 1972,
- (b) a council constituted under section 2 of the Local Government etc (Scotland) Act 1994,
- (c) the Common Council of the City of London,
- (d) a National Park authority, or
- (e) the Broads Authority.

(6) The reference in subsection (2) to a member of a police authority is to a person appointed as such a member under Schedule 2 to the Police Act 1996.

(7) In subsection (2)(d)—

- (a) "a board of prison visitors" means a board of visitors appointed under section 6(2) of the Prison Act 1952, and
- (b) "a prison visiting committee" means a visiting committee appointed under section 19(3) of the Prisons (Scotland) Act 1989 or constituted by virtue of rules made under section 39 (as read with section 8(1)) of that Act.

(8) *Meaning of "a relevant health body".*

(9) *Meaning of "a relevant education body".*

(9A) In subsection (3)(c) of this section "executive" and "executive arrangements" have the same meaning as in Part II of the Local Government Act 2000.

(10) The Secretary of State may by order—

- (a) modify the provisions of subsections (1) and (2) and (5) to (9) by adding any office or body, removing any office or body or altering the description of any office or body, or
- (b) modify the provisions of subsection (3).

(11) For the purposes of this section the working hours of an employee shall be taken to be any time when, in accordance with his contract of employment, the employee is required to be at work.

[Employment Rights Act 1996, s 50 as amended by the Police Act 1997, Sch 9, the School Standards and Framework Act 1998, Sch 31, the Standards in Scotland's Schools etc Act 2000, Sch 3, SI 2000/90, 1737 and 2463, SI 2001/2237, SI 2002/808, 2469 and SI 2000/1737.]

---

1. This Act consolidates enactments relating to employment rights. The Act came into force on 22 August 1996 (s 243).

2. Part VI contains ss 50–63.

8–8541   51. Complaints to employment tribunals.   (1) An employee may present a complaint to an employment tribunal that his employer has failed to permit him to take time off as required by section 50.

(2) An employment tribunal shall not consider a complaint under this section that an employer has failed to permit an employee to take time off unless it is presented—

(*a*)   before the end of the period of three months beginning with the date on which the failure occurred, or

(*b*)   within such further period as the tribunal considers reasonable in a case where it is satisfied that it was not reasonably practicable for the complaint to be presented before the end of that period of three months.

(3) Where an employment tribunal finds a complaint under this section well-founded, the tribunal—

(*a*)   shall make a declaration to that effect, and

(*b*)   may make an award of compensation to be paid by the employer to the employee.

(4) The amount of the compensation shall be such as the tribunal considers just and equitable in all the circumstances having regard to—

(*a*)   the employer's default in failing to permit time off to be taken by the employee, and

(*b*)   any loss sustained by the employee which is attributable to the matters to which the complaint relates.

[Employment Rights Act 1996, s 51 as amended by the Employment Rights (Dispute Resolution) Act 1998, s 1.]

PART XI[1]
REDUNDANCY PAYMENTS ETC.

CHAPTER V
OTHER PROVISIONS ABOUT REDUNDANCY PAYMENTS

8–8542   165. Written particulars of redundancy payment.   (1) On making any redundancy payment, otherwise than in pursuance of a decision of a tribunal which specifies the amount of the payment to be made, the employer shall give to the employee a written statement indicating how the amount of the payment has been calculated.

(2) An employer who without reasonable excuse fails to comply with subsection (1) is guilty of an offence and liable on summary conviction to a fine not exceeding **level 1** on the standard scale.

(3) If an employer fails to comply with the requirements of subsection (1), the employee may by notice in writing to the employer require him to give to the employee a written statement complying with those requirements within such period (not being less than one week beginning with the day on which the notice is given) as may be specified in the notice.

(4) An employer who without reasonable excuse fails to comply with a notice under subsection (3) is guilty of an offence and liable on summary conviction to a fine not exceeding **level 3** on the standard scale.

[Employment Rights Act 1996, s 165.]

---

1. Part XI contains ss 135–181.

CHAPTER VI
PAYMENTS BY SECRETARY OF STATE

8–8543   166. Applications for payments.   (1) Where an employee claims that his employer is liable to pay to him an employer's payment and either—

(*a*)   that the employee has taken all reasonable steps, other than legal proceedings, to recover the payment from the employer and the employer has refused or failed to pay it, or has paid part of it and has refused or failed to pay the balance, or

(*b*)   that the employer is insolvent and the whole or part of the payment remains unpaid,

the employee may apply to the Secretary of State for a payment under this section.

[Employment Rights Act 1996, s 166(1).]

8–8544   169. Information relating to applications for payments.   (1) Where an employee makes an application to the Secretary of State under section 166, the Secretary of State may, by notice in writing given to the employer, require the employer—

(*a*)   to provide the Secretary of State with such information, and

(*b*)   to produce for examination on behalf of the Secretary of State documents in his custody or under his control of such description,

as the Secretary of State may reasonably require for the purpose of determining whether the application is well-founded.

(2) Where a person on whom a notice is served under subsection (1) fails without reasonable

excuse to comply with a requirement imposed by the notice, he is guilty of an offence and liable on summary conviction to a fine not exceeding **level 3** on the standard scale.

(3) A person is guilty of an offence if—

(a) in providing any information required by a notice under subsection (1), he makes a statement which he knows to be false in a material particular or recklessly makes a statement which is false in a material particular, or

(b) he produces for examination in accordance with a notice under subsection (1) a document which to his knowledge has been wilfully falsified.

(4) A person guilty of an offence under subsection (3) is liable[1]—

(a) on summary conviction, to a fine not exceeding **the statutory maximum** or to imprisonment for a term not exceeding **three months**, or to both, or

(b) on conviction on indictment, to a **fine** or to imprisonment for a term not exceeding **two years**, or to both.

[Employment Rights Act 1996, s 169.]

---

1. For procedure in respect of this offence which is triable either way, see the Magistrates' Courts Act 1980, ss 17A–21, in PART I: MAGISTRATES' COURTS, PROCEDURE, ante.

CHAPTER VII
SUPPLEMENTARY

Other supplementary provisions

8–8545 180. Offences.   (1) Where an offence under this Part committed by a body corporate is proved—

(a) to have been committed with the consent or connivance of, or

(b) to be attributable to any neglect on the part of,

any director, manager, secretary or other similar officer of the body corporate, or any person who was purporting to act in any such capacity, he (as well as the body corporate) is guilty of the offence and liable to be proceeded against and punished accordingly.

(2) In this section "director", in relation to a body corporate established by or under any enactment for the purpose of carrying on under national ownership any industry or part of an industry or undertaking, being a body corporate whose affairs are managed by its members, means a member of that body corporate.

[Employment Rights Act 1996, s 180.]

8–8546 181. Interpretation.   (1) In this Part—

"counter-notice" shall be construed in accordance with section 149(a),

"dismissal" and "dismissed" shall be construed in accordance with sections 136 to 138,

"employer's payment" has the meaning given by section 166,

"notice of intention to claim" shall be construed in accordance with section 148(1),

"obligatory period of notice" has the meaning given by section 136(4), and

"trial period" shall be construed in accordance with section 138(3).

(2) In this Part—

(a) references to an employee being laid off or being eligible for a redundancy payment by reason of being laid off, and

(b) references to an employee being kept on short-time or being eligible for a redundancy payment by reason of being kept on short-time,

shall be construed in accordance with sections 147 and 148.

[Employment Rights Act 1996, s 181.]

PART XII[1]
INSOLVENCY OF EMPLOYERS

8–8547 182. Employee's rights on insolvency of employer.   If, on an application made to him in writing by an employee, the Secretary of State is satisfied that—

(a) the employee's employer has become insolvent,

(b) the employee's employment has been terminated, and

(c) on the appropriate date the employee was entitled to be paid the whole or part of any debt to which this Part applies,

the Secretary of State shall, subject to section 186, pay the employee out of the National Insurance Fund the amount to which, in the opinion of the Secretary of State, the employee is entitled in respect of the debt.

[Employment Rights Act 1996, s 182.]

1. Part XII contains ss 182–190.

8–8548   190. Power to obtain information.   (1) Where an application is made to the Secretary of State under section 182 in respect of a debt owed by an employer, the Secretary of State may require—

(*a*)   the employer to provide him with such information as he may reasonably require for the purpose of determining whether the application is well-founded, and

(*b*)   any person having the custody or control of any relevant records or other documents to produce for examination on behalf of the Secretary of State any such document in that person's custody or under his control which is of such a description as the Secretary of State may require.

(2) Any such requirement—

(*a*)   shall be made by notice in writing given to the person on whom the requirement is imposed, and

(*b*)   may be varied or revoked by a subsequent notice so given.

(3) If a person refuses or wilfully neglects to furnish any information or produce any document which he has been required to furnish or produce by a notice under this section he is guilty of an offence and liable on summary conviction to a fine not exceeding **level 3** on the standard scale.

(4) If a person, in purporting to comply with a requirement of a notice under this section, knowingly or recklessly makes any false statement he is guilty of an offence and liable on summary conviction to a fine not exceeding **level 5** on the standard scale.

(5) Where an offence under this section committed by a body corporate is proved—

(*a*)   to have been committed with the consent or connivance of, or

(*b*)   to be attributable to any neglect on the part of,

any director, manager, secretary or other similar officer of the body corporate, or any person who was purporting to act in any such capacity, he (as well as the body corporate) is guilty of the offence and liable to be proceeded against and punished accordingly.

(6) Where the affairs of a body corporate are managed by its members, subsection (5) applies in relation to the acts and defaults of a member in connection with his functions of management as if he were a director of the body corporate.

[Employment Rights Act 1996, s 190.]

PART XV[1]

GENERAL AND SUPPLEMENTARY

General

8–8549   236. *Orders and regulations.*

1. Part XV contains ss 236–245.

Final provisions

8–8550   243. *Commencement.*

8–8551   244. *Extent.*

8–8552   245. *Short title.*

National Minimum Wage Act 1998[1]

(1998 c 39)

Entitlement to the national minimum wage

8–8560   1. Workers to be paid at least the national minimum wage.   (1) A person who qualifies for the national minimum wage shall be remunerated by his employer in respect of his work in any pay reference period at a rate which is not less than the national minimum wage.

(2) A person qualifies for the national minimum wage if he is an individual who—

(*a*)   is a worker;

(*b*)   is working, or ordinarily works, in the United Kingdom under his contract; and

(*c*)   has ceased to be of compulsory school age.

(3) The national minimum wage shall be such single hourly rate as the Secretary of State may from time to time prescribe[2].

(4) For the purposes of this Act a "pay reference period" is such period as the Secretary of State may prescribe for the purpose.

(5) Subsections (1) to (4) above are subject to the following provisions of this Act.
[National Minimum Wage Act 1998, s 1.]

---

1. For provisions as to commencement, see s 56 and note thereto, post.
2. The National Minimum Wage Regulations 1999, SI 1999/584 amended by SI 2000/1411 and 1989, SI 2001/1108 and 2763, SI 2002/1999, SI 2003/1923, SI 2004/1161 and 1930 and SI 2005/2019 have been made which prescribe inter alia the minimum wage as £5.05, £4.25 (workers who qualify for the national minimum wage at a different rate, including those aged 18–21) and £3.00 (workers who qualify for the national minimum wage at a different rate, below the age of 18 who have ceased to be of compulsory school age) as from 1 October 2005.

Records

8–8561 9. Duty of employers to keep records. For the purposes of this Act, the Secretary of State may by regulations make provision requiring employers—

(a) to keep, in such form and manner as may be prescribed, such records as may be prescribed; and

(b) to preserve those records for such period as may be prescribed.
[National Minimum Wage Act 1998, s 9.]

Enforcement

8–8562 17. Non-compliance: worker entitled to additional remuneration. (1) If a worker who qualifies for the national minimum wage is remunerated for any pay reference period by his employer at a rate which is less than the national minimum wage, the worker shall be taken to be entitled under his contract to be paid, as additional remuneration in respect of that period, the amount described in subsection (2) below.

(2) That amount is the difference between—

(a) the relevant remuneration received by the worker for the pay reference period; and

(b) the relevant remuneration which the worker would have received for that period had he been remunerated by the employer at a rate equal to the national minimum wage.

(3) In subsection (2) above, "relevant remuneration" means remuneration which falls to be brought into account for the purposes of regulations under section 2 above.
[National Minimum Wage Act 1998, s 17.]

Offences

8–8563 31. Offences. (1) If the employer of a worker who qualifies for the national minimum wage refuses or wilfully neglects to remunerate the worker for any pay reference period at a rate which is at least equal to the national minimum wage, that employer is guilty of an offence.

(2) If a person who is required to keep or preserve any record in accordance with regulations under section 9 above fails to do so, that person is guilty of an offence.

(3) If a person makes, or knowingly causes or allows to be made, in a record required to be kept in accordance with regulations under section 9 above any entry which he knows to be false in a material particular, that person is guilty of an offence.

(4) If a person, for purposes connected with the provisions of this Act, produces or furnishes, or knowingly causes or allows to be produced or furnished, any record or information which he knows to be false in a material particular, that person is guilty of an offence.

(5) If a person—

(a) intentionally delays or obstructs an officer acting for the purposes of this Act in the exercise of any power conferred by this Act, or

(b) refuses or neglects to answer any question, furnish any information or produce any document when required to do so under section 14(1) above,

that person is guilty of an offence.

(6) Where the commission by any person of an offence under subsection (1) or (2) above is due to the act or default of some other person, that other person is also guilty of the offence.

(7) A person may be charged with and convicted of an offence by virtue of subsection (6) above whether or not proceedings are taken against any other person.

(8) In any proceedings for an offence under subsection (1) or (2) above it shall be a defence for the person charged to prove[1] that he exercised all due diligence and took all reasonable precautions to secure that the provisions of this Act, and of any relevant regulations made under it, were complied with by himself and by any person under his control.

(9) A person guilty of an offence under this section shall be liable on summary conviction to a fine not exceeding **level 5** on the standard scale.
[National Minimum Wage Act 1998, s 17.]

---

1. An accused who raises this defence is not required to establish it beyond reasonable doubt, but on the balance of probabilities: see *R v Carr-Briant* [1943] KB 607, [1943] 2 All ER 156, 107 JP 167.

8–8564 32. Offences by bodies corporate etc. (1) This section applies to any offence under this Act.

(2) If an offence committed by a body corporate is proved—

(*a*) to have been committed with the consent or connivance of an officer of the body, or

(*b*) to be attributable to any neglect on the part of such an officer,

the officer as well as the body corporate is guilty of the offence and liable to be proceeded against and punished accordingly.

(3) In subsection (2) above "officer", in relation to a body corporate, means a director, manager, secretary or other similar officer of the body, or a person purporting to act in any such capacity.

(4) If the affairs of a body corporate are managed by its members, subsection (2) above applies in relation to the acts and defaults of a member in connection with his functions of management as if he were a director of the body corporate.

(5) If an offence committed by a partnership in Scotland is proved—

(*a*) to have been committed with the consent or connivance of a partner, or

(*b*) to be attributable to any neglect on the part of a partner,

the partner as well as the partnership is guilty of the offence and liable to be proceeded against and punished accordingly.

(6) In subsection (5) above, "partner" includes a person purporting to act as a partner.
[National Minimum Wage Act 1998, s 32.]

8–8565 33. Proceedings for offences. (1) The persons who may conduct proceedings for an offence under this Act—

(*a*) in England and Wales, before a magistrates' court, or

(*b*) in Northern Ireland, before a court of summary jurisdiction,

shall include any person authorised for the purpose by the Secretary of State even if that person is not a barrister or solicitor.

(2) In England and Wales or Northern Ireland, proceedings for an offence under this Act may be begun at any time within whichever of the following periods expires the later, that is to say—

(*a*) the period of 6 months from the date on which evidence, sufficient in the opinion of the Secretary of State to justify a prosecution for the offence, comes to the knowledge of the Secretary of State, or

(*b*) the period of 12 months from the commission of the offence,

notwithstanding anything in any other enactment (including an enactment comprised in Northern Ireland legislation) or in any instrument made under an enactment.

(3) For the purposes of subsection (2) above, a certificate purporting to be signed by or on behalf of the Secretary of State as to the date on which such evidence as is mentioned in paragraph (a) of that subsection came to the knowledge of the Secretary of State shall be conclusive evidence of that date.

(4)–(5) *Scotland*
[National Minimum Wage Act 1998, s 33.]

Exclusions

8–8566 43. *Share fisherman*

8–8567 44. *Voluntary workers*

8–8567A 44A. *Religious and other communities: resident workers*

8–8568 45. *Prisoners*

Agricultural Workers

8–8569 46. Relationship of this Act and agricultural wages legislation. (1) A person who has been prosecuted for an offence which falls within paragraph (*a*) or (*b*) below, that is to say—

(*a*) an offence under any provision of this Act in its application for the purposes of the agricultural wages legislation, or

(*b*) an offence under any provision of this Act in its application otherwise than for the purposes of the agricultural wages legislation,

shall not also be liable to be prosecuted for an offence which falls within the other of those paragraphs but which is constituted by the same conduct or alleged conduct for which he was prosecuted.

(2) No amount shall be recoverable both—

(*a*) under or by virtue of this Act in its application for the purposes of the agricultural wages legislation, and

(b)   under or by virtue of this Act in its application otherwise than for those purposes,

in respect of the same work.

(3)   Nothing in the agricultural wages legislation, or in any order under that legislation, affects the operation of this Act in its application otherwise than for the purposes of that legislation.

(4)   In this section "the agricultural wages legislation" means—

(a)   the Agricultural Wages Act 1948;

(b)   the Agricultural Wages (Scotland) Act 1949; and

(b)   the Agricultural Wages (Regulation) (Northern Ireland) Order 1977.

[National Minimum Wage Act 1998, s 46.]

Miscellaneous

8–8570. Application of Act to superior employers
Where—

(a)   the immediate employer of a worker is himself in the employment of some other person, and

(b)   the worker is employed on the premises of that other person,

that other person shall be deemed for the purposes of this Act to be the employer of the worker jointly with the immediate employer.

[National Minimum Wage Act 1998, s 48.]

8–8571   54. Meaning of "worker", "employer" etc.   (1) In this Act "employee" means an individual who has entered into or works under (or, where the employment has ceased, worked under) a contract of employment.

(2)   In this Act "contract of employment" means a contract of service or apprenticeship, whether express or implied, and (if it is express) whether oral or in writing.

(3)   In this Act "worker" (except in the phrases "agency worker" and "home worker") means an individual who has entered into or works under (or, where the employment has ceased, worked under)—

(a)   a contract of employment; or

(b)   any other contract, whether express or implied and (if it is express) whether oral or in writing, whereby the individual undertakes to do or perform personally any work or services for another party to the contract whose status is not by virtue of the contract that of a client or customer of any profession or business undertaking carried on by the individual;

and any reference to a worker's contract shall be construed accordingly.

(4)   In this Act "employer", in relation to an employee or a worker, means the person by whom the employee or worker is (or, where the employment has ceased, was) employed.

(5)   In this Act "employment"—

(a)   in relation to an employee, means employment under a contract of employment; and

(b)   in relation to a worker, means employment under his contract;

and "employed" shall be construed accordingly.

[National Minimum Wage Act 1998, s 54.]

8–8572   55. Interpretation.   (1) In this Act, unless the context otherwise requires,—

"civil proceedings" means proceedings before an employment tribunal or civil proceedings before any other court;

"enforcement notice" shall be construed in accordance with section 19 above;

"government department" includes a Northern Ireland department, except in section 52(a) above;

"industrial tribunal" means a tribunal established under Article 3 of the Industrial Tribunals (Northern Ireland) Order 1996;

"notice" means notice in writing;

"pay reference period" shall be construed in accordance with section 1(4) above;

"penalty notice" shall be construed in accordance with section 21 above;

"person who qualifies for the national minimum wage" shall be construed in accordance with section 1(2) above; and related expressions shall be construed accordingly;

"prescribe" means prescribe by regulations;

"regulations" means regulations made by the Secretary of State, except in the ca0se of regulations under section 47(2) or (4) above made by the Secretary of State and the Minister of Agriculture, Fisheries and Food acting jointly or by the Department of Agriculture for Northern Ireland.

(2)   Any reference in this Act to a person being remunerated for a pay reference period is a reference to the person being remunerated by his employer in respect of his work in that pay reference period.

(3)   Any reference in this Act to doing work includes a reference to performing services; and "work" and other related expressions shall be construed accordingly.

(4)   *Scotland.*

(5)–(6)   *Northern Ireland.*

[National Minimum Wage Act 1998, s 55.]

8–8573　56. Short title, commencement and extent.　(1) This Act may be cited as the National Minimum Wage Act 1998.

(2) Apart from this section and any powers to make an Order in Council or regulations or an order (which accordingly come into force on the day on which this Act is passed) the provisions of this Act shall come into force on such day or days as the Secretary of State may by order appoint[1]; and different days may be appointed for different purposes.

(3) Northern Ireland.

[National Minimum Wage Act 1998, s 56.]

---

　1. Section 56 and powers to make an Order in Council or regulations were brought into force on the commencement of this Act, 31 July 1998. The remaining provisions reproduced in this Manual with the exception of s 46 were brought in force on 1 November 1998 and 1 April 1999 by the National Minimum Wage Act 1998 (Commencement No 1 and Transitional Provisions) Order 1998, SI 1998/2574.

Employment Relations Act 1999[1]
(1999 c 26)

8–8574　3. Blacklists.　(1) The Secretary of State may make regulations prohibiting the compilation of lists which—

(*a*)　contain details of members of trade unions or persons who have taken part in the activities of trade unions, and

(*b*)　are compiled with a view to being used by employers or employment agencies for the purposes of discrimination in relation to recruitment or in relation to the treatment of workers.

(2) The Secretary of State may make regulations prohibiting—

(*a*)　the use of lists to which subsection (1) applies;

(*b*)　the sale or supply of lists to which subsection (1) applies.

(3) Regulations under this section may, in particular—

(*a*)　confer jurisdiction (including exclusive jurisdiction) on employment tribunals and on the Employment Appeal Tribunal;

(*b*)　include provision for or about the grant and enforcement of specified remedies by courts and tribunals;

(*c*)　include provision for the making of awards of compensation calculated in accordance with the regulations;

(*d*)　include provision permitting proceedings to be brought by trade unions on behalf of members in specified circumstances;

(*e*)　include provision about cases where an employee is dismissed by his employer and the reason or principal reason for the dismissal, or why the employee was selected for dismissal, relates to a list to which subsection (1) applies;

(*f*)　create criminal offences;

(*g*)　in specified cases or circumstances, extend liability for a criminal offence created under paragraph (*f*) to a person who aids the commission of the offence or to a person who is an agent, principal, employee, employer or officer of a person who commits the offence;

(*h*)　provide for specified obligations or offences not to apply in specified circumstances;

(*i*)　include supplemental, incidental, consequential and transitional provision, including provision amending an enactment;

(*j*)　make different provision for different cases or circumstances.

(4) Regulations under this section creating an offence may not provide for it to be punishable—

(*a*)　by imprisonment,

(*b*)　by a fine in excess of level 5 on the standard scale in the case of an offence triable only summarily, or

(*c*)　by a fine in excess of the statutory maximum in the case of summary conviction for an offence triable either way.

(5) In this section—

"list" includes any index or other set of items whether recorded electronically or by any other means, and

"worker" has the meaning given by section 13.

(6) Subject to subsection (5), expressions used in this section and in the Trade Union and Labour Relations (Consolidation) Act 1992 have the same meaning in this section as in that Act.

[Employment Relations Act 1999, s 3.]

---

　1. The Employment Relations Act 1999 amends the law relating to employment, to trade unions and to employment agencies and businesses. Only those provisions of the Act which are relevant to the work of magistrates' courts are set out below. While these provisions had all been brought into force, other provisions of the Act, including consequential

amendments and repeals, had not been brought into force when we went to press.. For commencement provisions, see s 45, post.

Other rights of individuals

8–8575   19. Part-time work: discrimination.   (1) The Secretary of State shall make regulations[1] for the purpose of securing that persons in part-time employment are treated, for such purposes and to such extent as the regulations may specify, no less favourably than persons in full-time employment.

(2) The regulations may—

(a) specify classes of person who are to be taken to be, or not to be, in part-time employment;
(b) specify classes of person who are to be taken to be, or not to be, in full-time employment;
(c) specify circumstances in which persons in part-time employment are to be taken to be, or not to be, treated less favourably than persons in full-time employment;
(d) make provision which has effect in relation to persons in part-time employment generally or provision which has effect only in relation to specified classes of persons in part-time employment.

(3) The regulations may—

(a) confer jurisdiction (including exclusive jurisdiction) on employment tribunals and on the Employment Appeal Tribunal;
(b) create criminal offences in relation to specified acts or omissions by an employer, by an organisation of employers, by an organisation of workers or by an organisation existing for the purposes of a profession or trade carried on by the organisation's members;
(c) in specified cases or circumstances, extend liability for a criminal offence created under paragraph (b) to a person who aids the commission of the offence or to a person who is an agent, principal, employee, employer or officer of a person who commits the offence;
(d) provide for specified obligations or offences not to apply in specified circumstances;
(e) make provision about notices or information to be given, evidence to be produced and other procedures to be followed;
(f) amend, apply with or without modifications, or make provision similar to any provision of the Employment Rights Act 1996 (including, in particular, Parts V, X and XIII) or the Trade Union and Labour Relations (Consolidation) Act 1992;
(g) provide for the provisions of specified agreements to have effect in place of provisions of the regulations to such extent and in such circumstances as may be specified;
(h) include supplemental, incidental, consequential and transitional provision, including provision amending an enactment;
(i) make different provision for different cases or circumstances.

(4) Without prejudice to the generality of this section the regulations may make any provision which appears to the Secretary of State to be necessary or expedient—

(a) for the purpose of implementing Council Directive 97/81/EC on the framework agreement on part-time work in its application to terms and conditions of employment;
(b) for the purpose of dealing with any matter arising out of or related to the United Kingdom's obligations under that Directive;
(c) for the purpose of any matter dealt with by the framework agreement or for the purpose of applying the provisions of the framework agreement to any matter relating to part-time workers.

(5) Regulations under this section which create an offence—

(a) shall provide for it to be triable summarily only, and
(b) may not provide for it to be punishable by imprisonment or by a fine in excess of level 5 on the standard scale.

[Employment Relations Act 1999, s 19.]

---

1. The Part-time Workers (Prevention of Less Favourable Treatment) Regulations 2000, SI 2000/1551 amended by SI 2002/2035 and SI 2005/2240 have been made.

8–8576   20. Part-time work: code of practice.   (1) The Secretary of State may issue codes of practice containing guidance for the purpose of—

(a) eliminating discrimination in the field of employment against part-time workers;
(b) facilitating the development of opportunities for part-time work;
(c) facilitating the flexible organisation of working time taking into account the needs of workers and employers;
(d) any matter dealt with in the framework agreement on part-time work annexed to Council Directive 97/81/EC.

(2) The Secretary of State may revise a code and issue the whole or part of the revised code.
(3) A person's failure to observe a provision of a code does not make him liable to any proceedings.
(4) A code—

(a)   is admissible in evidence in proceedings before an employment tribunal, and

(b)   shall be taken into account by an employment tribunal in any case in which it appears to the tribunal to be relevant.

[Employment Relations Act 1999, s 20.]

8–8577   21. Code of practice: supplemental.   (1) Before issuing or revising a code of practice under section 20 the Secretary of State shall consult such persons as he considers appropriate.

(2) Before issuing a code the Secretary of State shall—

(a)   publish a draft code,

(b)   consider any representations made to him about the draft,

(c)   if he thinks it appropriate, modify the draft in the light of any representations made to him.

(3) If, having followed the procedure under subsection (2), the Secretary of State decides to issue a code, he shall lay a draft code before each House of Parliament.

(4) If the draft code is approved by resolution of each House of Parliament, the Secretary of State shall issue the code in the form of the draft.

(5) In this section and section 20(3) and (4)—

(a)   a reference to a code includes a reference to a revised code,

(b)   a reference to a draft code includes a reference to a draft revision, and

(c)   a reference to issuing a code includes a reference to issuing part of a revised code.

[Employment Relations Act 1999, s 21.]

8–8578   42. Orders and regulations.   (1) Any power to make an order or regulations under this Act shall be exercised by statutory instrument.

(2) No order or regulations shall be made under section 3, 17, 19 or 23 unless a draft has been laid before, and approved by resolution of, each House of Parliament.

8–8579   43. Finance.   There shall be paid out of money provided by Parliament—

(a)   any increase attributable to this Act in the sums so payable under any other enactment;

(b)   any other expenditure of the Secretary of State under this Act.

8–8580   44. Repeals.   The provisions mentioned in Schedule 9[1] are repealed (or revoked) to the extent specified in column 3.

[Employment Relations Act 1999, s 44.]

---

1.   Schedule 9 is not set out below.

8–8581   45. Commencement.   (1) The preceding provisions of this Act shall come into force in accordance with provision made by the Secretary of State by order[1] made by statutory instrument.

(2) An order under this section—

(a)   may make different provision for different purposes;

(b)   may include supplementary, incidental, saving or transitional provisions.

[Employment Relations Act 1999, s 45.]

---

1.   At the date of going to press, the Employment Relations act 1999 (Commencement No 1 and Transitional Provisions) Order 1999, SI 1999/2509, the Employment Relations Act 1999 (Commencement No 2 and Transitional and Saving Provisions) Order 1999, SI 1999/2830, the Employment Relations Act 1999 (Commencement No 3 and Transitional Provision) Order 1999, SI 1999/3374, the Employment Relations Act 1999 (Commencement No 4 and Transitional Provision) Order 2000, SI 2000/420; the Employment Relations Act 1999 (Commencement No 5 and Transitional Provision) Order 2000, SI 2000/875, the Employment Relations Act 1999 (Commencement No 6 and Transitional Provisions) Order 2000, SI 2000/1338, and the Employment Relations Act 1999, (Commencement No 7 and Transitional Provisions) Order 2000, SI 2000/2242, had been made.

8–8582   46. Extent.   (1) Any amendment or repeal in this Act has the same extent as the provision amended or repealed.

(2) An Order in Council under paragraph 1(1)(b) of Schedule 1 to the Northern Ireland Act 1974 (legislation for Northern Ireland in the interim period) which contains a statement that it is made only for purposes corresponding to any of the purposes of this Act—

(a)   shall not be subject to paragraph 1(4) and (5) of that Schedule (affirmative resolution of both Houses of Parliament), but

(b)   shall be subject to annulment in pursuance of a resolution of either House of Parliament.

(3) Apart from sections 39 and 45 and subject to subsection (1), the preceding sections of this Act shall not extend to Northern Ireland.

[Employment Relations Act 1999, s 46.]

8–8583   47. Citation.   This Act may be cited as the Employment Relations Act 1999.

[Employment Relations Act 1999, s 47.]

Employment Act 2002[1]

(2002 c 22)

8–8583A

1. The Employment Act 2002 received the Royal Assent on July 8, 2002. The Act is in 4 Parts. Part 1 is concerned with paternity and adoption leave and pay, and maternity leave and pay. Its object is to help parents devote more time to their children while the latter are in the early stages of life. Part 2 is concerned with tribunal reform in relation to costs and expenses, conciliation, forms, determinations without hearings, practice directions and pre-hearing reviews. Part 3 is concerned with dispute resolution and employment particulars. Part 4 is concerned with miscellaneous and general matters.

At the time of going to press the following commencement orders had been made: Employment Act 2002 (Commencement No 1) Order 2002, SI 2002/1989; Employment Act 2002 (Commencement No 2) Order 2002, SI 2002/2256; Employment Act 2002 (Commencement No 3 and Transitional and Saving Provisions) Order 2002, SI 2002/2866; Employment Act 2002 (Commencement No 4 and Transitional Provisions) Order 2003, SI 2003/1190; Employment Act 2002 (Commencement No 5) Order 2003, SI 2003/1666; Employment Act 2002 (Commencement No 6 and Transitional Provision) Order 2004, SI 2004/1717; Employment Act 2002 (Commencement No 7) Order 2004, SI 2004/2185; and Employment Act 2002 (Commencement No 8) Order 2004, SI 2004/2822.

The Act is not reproduced in this work.

Gangmasters (Licensing) Act 2004[1]

(2004 c 11)

The Gangmasters Licensing Authority

8–8583B **1. The Gangmasters Licensing Authority.** (1) There shall be a body known as the Gangmasters Licensing Authority (in this Act referred to as "the Authority").

(2) The functions of the Authority shall be—

(a) to carry out the functions relating to licensing that are conferred on it by this Act,

(b) to ensure the carrying out of such inspections as it considers necessary of persons holding licences under this Act,

(c) to keep under review generally the activities of persons acting as gangmasters,

(d) to supply information held by it to specified persons in accordance with the provisions of this Act,

(e) to keep under review the operation of this Act, and

(f) such other functions as may be prescribed in regulations made by the Secretary of State.

(3) The Authority may do anything that it considers is calculated to facilitate, or is incidental or conducive to, the carrying out of any of its functions.

(4) The Authority shall not be regarded—

(a) as the servant or agent of the Crown, or

(b) as enjoying any status, immunity or privilege of the Crown,

and the property of the Authority shall not be regarded as property of, or property held on behalf of, the Crown.

(5) The Secretary of State may by regulations[2] make provision as to—

(a) the status and constitution of the Authority,

(b) the appointment of its members,

(c) the payment of remuneration and allowances to its members, and

(d) such other matters in connection with its establishment and operation as he thinks fit.

(6) Schedule 1 amends certain enactments in consequence of the establishment of the Authority.
[Gangmasters (Licensing) Act 2004, s 1.]

1. This Act makes provision for the licensing of activities involving the supply or use of workers in connection with agricultural work, the gathering of wild creatures and wild plants, the harvesting of fish from fish farms, and certain processing and packaging. The Act is to be brought into force in accordance with Commencement Orders made under s 29. At the time of going to press the following commencement orders had been made: Gangmasters (Licensing) Act 2004 (Commencement No 1) Order 2004, SI 2004/2857; and Gangmasters (Licensing) Act 2004 (Commencement No 2) Order 2005, SI 2005/447. The only provisions of the Act that remain prospective are: ss 11–14 and 27, and paras 12–14 of Sch 1.

2. The Gangmasters (Licensing Authority) Regulations 2005, SI 2005/448 have been made.

8–8583C **2. Directions etc by the Secretary of State**

Scope of Act

8–8583D **3. Work to which this Act applies.** (1) The work to which this Act applies is—

(a) agricultural work,

(b) gathering shellfish, and

(*c*) processing or packaging—

    (i) any produce derived from agricultural work, or

    (ii) shellfish, fish or products derived from shellfish or fish.

This is subject to any provision made by regulations under subsection (5) below and to section 5 (territorial scope of application).

(2) In subsection (1)(a) "agricultural work" means work in agriculture.

(3) In this Act "agriculture" includes—

(*a*) dairy-farming,

(*b*) the production for the purposes of any trade, business or other undertaking (whether carried on for profit or not) of consumable produce,

(*c*) the use of land as grazing, meadow or pasture land,

(*d*) the use of land as an orchard or as osier land or woodland, and

(*e*) the use of land for market gardens or nursery grounds.

In paragraph (*b*) "consumable produce" means produce grown for sale, consumption or other use after severance from the land on which it is grown.

(4) In this Act "shellfish" means crustaceans and molluscs of any kind, and includes any part of a shellfish and any (or any part of any) brood, ware, halfware or spat of shellfish, and any spawn of shellfish, and the shell, or any part of the shell, of a shellfish.

(5) The Secretary of State may by regulations make provision—

(*a*) excluding work of a prescribed description from being work to which this Act applies;

(*b*) including work of the following nature as being work to which this Act applies—

    (i) the gathering (by any manner) of wild creatures, or wild plants, of a prescribed description and the processing and packaging of anything so gathered, and

    (ii) the harvesting of fish from a fish farm (within the meaning of the Diseases of Fish Act 1937 (c 33)).

[Gangmasters (Licensing) Act 2004, s 3.]

8–8583E 4. Acting as a gangmaster. (1) This section defines what is meant in this Act by a person acting as a gangmaster.

(2) A person ("A") acts as a gangmaster if he supplies a worker to do work to which this Act applies for another person ("B").

(3) For the purposes of subsection (2) it does not matter—

(*a*) whether the worker works under a contract with A or is supplied to him by another person,

(*b*) whether the worker is supplied directly under arrangements between A and B or indirectly under arrangements involving one or more intermediaries,

(*c*) whether A supplies the worker himself or procures that the worker is supplied,

(*d*) whether the work is done under the control of A, B or an intermediary,

(*e*) whether the work done for B is for the purposes of a business carried on by him or in connection with services provided by him to another person.

(4) A person ("A") acts as a gangmaster if he uses a worker to do work to which this Act applies in connection with services provided by him to another person.

(5) A person ("A") acts as a gangmaster if he uses a worker to do any of the following work to which this Act applies for the purposes of a business carried on by him—

(*a*) harvesting or otherwise gathering agricultural produce following—

    (i) a sale, assignment or lease of produce to A, or

    (ii) the making of any other agreement with A,

where the sale, assignment, lease or other agreement was entered into for the purpose of enabling the harvesting or gathering to take place;

(*b*) gathering shellfish;

(*c*) processing or packaging agricultural produce harvested or gathered as mentioned in paragraph (a).

In this subsection "agricultural produce" means any produce derived from agriculture.

(6) For the purposes of subsection (4) or (5) A shall be treated as using a worker to do work to which this Act applies if he makes arrangements under which the worker does the work—

(*a*) whether the worker works for A (or for another) or on his own account, and

(*b*) whether or not he works under a contract (with A or another).

(7) Regulations under section 3(5)(b) may provide for the application of subsections (5) and (6) above in relation to work that is work to which this Act applies by virtue of the regulations.

[Gangmasters (Licensing) Act 2004, s 4.]

8–8583F 5. Territorial scope of application. (1) The work to which this Act applies is work—

(*a*) in the United Kingdom,

(*b*)   on any portion of the shore or bed of the sea, or of an estuary or tidal river, adjacent to the United Kingdom, whether above or below (or partly above and partly below) the low water mark, or

(*c*)   in UK coastal waters.

(2) In subsection (1)(*c*) "UK coastal waters" means waters adjacent to the United Kingdom to a distance of six miles measured from the baselines from which the breadth of the territorial sea is measured.

In this subsection "miles" means international nautical miles of 1,852 metres.

(3) The provisions of this Act apply where a person acts as a gangmaster, whether in the United Kingdom or elsewhere, in relation to work to which this Act applies.

[Gangmasters (Licensing) Act 2004, s 5.]

Licensing

8–8583G   6. Prohibition of unlicensed activities.   (1) A person shall not act as a gangmaster except under the authority of a licence.

(2) Regulations made by the Secretary of State may specify circumstances in which a licence is not required.

[Gangmasters (Licensing) Act 2004, s 6.]

8–8583H   7. Grant of licence.   (1) The Authority may grant a licence if it thinks fit.

(2) A licence shall describe the activities authorised by it and shall be granted for such period as the Authority thinks fit.

(3) A licence authorises activities—

(*a*)   by the holder of the licence, and

(*b*)   by persons employed or engaged by the holder of the licence who are named or otherwise specified in the licence.

(4) In the case of a licence held otherwise than by an individual, the reference in subsection (3)(*a*) to activities by the holder of the licence shall be read as a reference only to such activities as are mentioned in whichever of the following provisions applies—

section 20(2) (body corporate);

section 21(2) (unincorporated association);

section 22(4) (partnership that is regarded as a legal person under the law of the country or territory under which it is formed).

(5) A licence shall be granted subject to such conditions as the Authority considers appropriate.

[Gangmasters (Licensing) Act 2004, s 7.]

8–8583I   8. General power of Authority to make rules

8–8583J   9. Modification, revocation or transfer of licence

8–8583K   10. Appeals

8–8583L   11. Register of licences

Offences

8–8583M   12. Offences: acting as a gangmaster, being in possession of false documents etc.

(1) A person commits an offence if he acts as a gangmaster in contravention of section 6 (prohibition of unlicensed activities).

For this purpose a person acting as a gangmaster does not contravene section 6 by reason only of the fact that he breaches a condition of the licence which authorises him to so act.

(2) A person commits an offence if he has in his possession or under his control—

(*a*)   a relevant document that is false and that he knows or believes to be false,

(*b*)   a relevant document that was improperly obtained and that he knows or believes to have been improperly obtained, or

(*c*)   a relevant document that relates to someone else,

with the intention of inducing another person to believe that he or another person acting as a gangmaster in contravention of section 6 is acting under the authority of a licence.

(3) A person guilty of an offence under subsection (1) or (2) is liable on summary conviction—

(*a*)   in England and Wales, to imprisonment for a term not exceeding twelve months, or to a fine not exceeding the statutory maximum, or to both;

(*b*)   in Scotland or Northern Ireland, to imprisonment for a term not exceeding six months, or to a fine not exceeding the statutory maximum, or to both.

In relation to an offence committed before the commencement of section 154(1) of the Criminal Justice Act 2003 (c 44), for "twelve months" in paragraph (a) substitute "six months".

(4) A person guilty of an offence under subsection (1) or (2) is liable on conviction on indictment to imprisonment for a term not exceeding ten years, or to a fine, or to both[1].

(5) For the purposes of this section—

(*a*) except in Scotland, a document is false only if it is false within the meaning of Part 1 of the Forgery and Counterfeiting Act 1981 (c 45) (see section 9(1) of that Act), and

(*b*) a document is improperly obtained if false information was provided, in or in connection with the application for its issue or an application for its modification, to the person who issued it or (as the case may be) to a person entitled to modify it,

and references to the making of a false document include references to the modification of a document so that it becomes false.

(6) In this section "relevant document" means—

(*a*) a licence, or

(*b*) any document issued by the Authority in connection with a licence.

[Gangmasters (Licensing) Act 2004, s 12.]

---

1. For procedure in respect of offences triable either way see the Magistrates' Courts Act 1980, ss 17A–21 in PART I: MAGISTRATES' COURTS' PROCEDURE, ante.

8–8583N   13. Offences: entering into arrangements with gangmasters.   (1) A person commits an offence if—

(*a*) he enters into arrangements under which a person ("the gangmaster") supplies him with workers or services, and

(*b*) the gangmaster in supplying the workers or services contravenes section 6 (prohibition of unlicensed activities).

(2) In proceedings against a person for an offence under subsection (1) it is a defence for him to prove that he—

(*a*) took all reasonable steps to satisfy himself that the gangmaster was acting under the authority of a valid licence, and

(*b*) did not know, and had no reasonable grounds for suspecting that the gangmaster was not the holder of a valid licence.

(3) The Secretary of State may by regulations make provision as to what constitutes "reasonable steps" for the purposes of subsection (2)(*a*).

(4) A person guilty of an offence under subsection (1) is liable—

(*a*) on summary conviction in England and Wales, to imprisonment for a term not exceeding 51 weeks, or to a fine not exceeding the statutory maximum, or to both,

(*b*) *Scotland and Northern Ireland.*

In relation to an offence committed before the commencement of section 281(5) of the Criminal Justice Act 2003 (c 44), for "51 weeks" in paragraph (a) substitute "six months".

[Gangmasters (Licensing) Act 2004, s 13.]

8–8583O   14. Offences: supplementary provisions.   (1) An enforcement officer (see section 15) has the powers of arrest mentioned in subsection (2) (in addition to powers under section 24(4) and (5) of the Police and Criminal Evidence Act 1984 (c 60)) in relation to any of the following offences—

(*a*) an offence under section 12(1) or (2),

(*b*) conspiring to commit any such offence,

(*c*) attempting to commit any such offence,

(*d*) inciting, aiding, abetting, counselling or procuring the commission of any such offence.

(2) Those powers are as follows—

(*a*) if he has reasonable grounds for suspecting that such an offence has been committed, he may arrest without warrant anyone whom he has reasonable grounds for suspecting to be guilty of the offence;

(*b*) he may arrest without warrant—

(i) anyone who is about to commit such an offence;

(ii) anyone whom he has reasonable grounds for suspecting to be about to commit such an offence.

(3) Subsections (1) and (2) do not apply in Scotland.

(4) In Schedules 2, 4 and 5 to the Proceeds of Crime Act 2002 (c 29), after paragraph 9 insert—

"**9A.** An offence under section 12(1) or (2) of the Gangmasters (Licensing) Act 2004 (acting as a gangmaster other than under the authority of a licence, possession of false documents etc).".

[Gangmasters (Licensing) Act 2004, s 14.]

Enforcement

8–8583P   15. Enforcement and compliance officers.   (1) The Secretary of State may appoint officers ("enforcement officers") to act for the purposes of this Act—

(*a*)   in enforcing the provisions of section 6 (prohibition of unlicensed activities), and

(*b*)   in taking action in circumstances in which it appears that an offence under section 13 (persons entering into arrangements with gangmasters) has been, is being, or may be committed.

(2)   The Secretary of State may, instead of or in addition to appointing enforcement officers under subsection (1), make arrangements with a relevant authority for officers of that authority to be enforcement officers.

(3)   The following are relevant authorities for this purpose—

(*a*)   the Authority,

(*b*)   any Minister of the Crown or government department,

(*c*)   the National Assembly for Wales,

(*d*)   the Scottish Ministers,

(*e*)   any body performing functions on behalf of the Crown.

(4)   The Authority may appoint officers ("compliance officers") to act for the purposes of this Act in verifying, from time to time or in such circumstances as the Authority may determine, compliance by a licence holder with the conditions of the licence.

(5)   When acting for the purposes of this Act, an enforcement officer or a compliance officer shall, if so required, produce some duly authenticated document showing his authority to act.

(6)   If it appears to an enforcement officer or a compliance officer that any person with whom he is dealing while acting for the purposes of this Act does not know that he is an officer so acting, the officer shall identify himself as such to that person.

[Gangmasters (Licensing) Act 2004, s 15.]

8–8583Q   16. Powers of officers.   (1) An enforcement officer or a compliance officer acting for the purposes of this Act shall have power for the performance of his duties—

(*a*)   to require the production by a relevant person of any records required to be kept by virtue of this Act, to inspect and examine those records, to remove those records from the premises where they are kept and to copy any material part of them,

(*b*)   to require a relevant person to furnish to him (either alone or in the presence of any other person, as the officer thinks fit) an explanation of any such records,

(*c*)   to require a relevant person to furnish to him (either alone or in the presence of any other person, as the officer thinks fit) any additional information known to the relevant person which might reasonably be needed in order to establish whether—

(i)   any provision of this Act, or

(ii)   any condition of any licence granted under it,

is being complied with,

(*d*)   at all reasonable times to enter any relevant premises in order to exercise any power conferred on the officer by virtue of paragraphs (*a*) to (*c*).

(2)   The powers conferred by subsection (1) include power, on reasonable written notice, to require a relevant person—

(*a*)   to produce any such records as are mentioned in paragraph (*a*) of that subsection to an officer at such time and place as may be specified in the notice, or

(*b*)   to attend before an officer at such time and place as may be specified in the notice to furnish any such explanation or additional information as is mentioned in paragraph (*b*) or (*c*) of that subsection.

(3)   The power conferred by subsection (1)(*a*) includes, in relation to records which are kept by means of a computer, power to require the records to be produced in a form in which they are legible and can be taken away.

(4)   A person authorised by virtue of subsection (1)(*a*) to inspect any records is entitled to have access to, and to check the operation of, any computer and any associated apparatus or material which is or has been in use in connection with the records in question.

(5)   In this section "relevant person" means any person whom an officer acting for the purposes of this Act has reasonable cause to believe to be—

(*a*)   a person acting as a gangmaster,

(*b*)   a person supplied with workers or services by a person acting as a gangmaster,

(*c*)   any employee or agent of a person falling within paragraph (*a*) or (*b*).

(6)   In this section and section 17—

"relevant premises" means any premises which an officer acting for the purposes of this Act has reasonable cause to believe to be—

(*a*) premises at which a person mentioned in subsection (5)(a) or (b) carries on business, and

(*b*) premises which such a person uses in connection with his business,

"premises" includes any place and, in particular, includes—

(*a*) any vehicle, vessel, aircraft or hovercraft, and

(*b*) any tent or movable structure.

[Gangmasters (Licensing) Act 2004, s 16.]

8–8583R   17. Entry by warrant.   (1) If a justice of the peace is satisfied by written information on oath that there are reasonable grounds for an enforcement officer to enter relevant premises for the purpose of ascertaining whether there has been any contravention of section 6 (prohibition of unlicensed activities), and is also satisfied—

(*a*) that admission to the premises has been refused, or that a refusal is expected, and (in either case) that notice of the intention to apply for a warrant has been given to the occupier,

(*b*) that an application for admission, or the giving of such a notice, would defeat the object of the entry,

(*c*) that the case is one of extreme urgency, or

(*d*) that the premises are unoccupied or the occupier is temporarily absent,

the justice may issue a warrant authorising the enforcement officer to enter the premises, if necessary using reasonable force.

(2) An enforcement officer entering any premises by virtue of a warrant under this section may—

(*a*) take with him when he enters those premises such other persons and such other equipment as he considers necessary,

(*b*) carry out on those premises such inspections and examinations as he considers necessary for the purpose of ascertaining whether there has been any contravention of section 6, and

(*c*) take possession of any book, document, data, record (in whatever form it is held) or product which is on the premises and retain it for as long as he considers necessary for that purpose.

(3) On leaving any premises which an enforcement officer is authorised to enter by a warrant under this section, that officer shall, if the premises are unoccupied or the occupier is temporarily absent, leave the premises as effectively secured against trespassers as he found them.

(4) Where by virtue of subsection (2)(c) an enforcement officer takes possession of any item, he shall leave on the premises from which the item was removed a statement giving particulars of what he has taken and stating that he has taken possession of it.

(5) *Scotland.*

[Gangmasters (Licensing) Act 2004, s 17.]

8–8583S   18. Obstruction of officers.   (1) A person commits an offence who—

(*a*) intentionally obstructs an enforcement officer or compliance officer who is acting in the exercise of his functions under this Act, or

(*b*) without reasonable cause, fails to comply with any requirement made of him by such an officer who is so acting.

(2) A person who, in giving any information which is required of him by an enforcement officer or compliance officer, makes a statement which is false in a material particular commits an offence.

(3) A person guilty of an offence under this section is liable—

(*a*) on summary conviction in England and Wales, to imprisonment for a term not exceeding 51 weeks, or to a fine not exceeding the statutory maximum, or to both,

(*b*) *Scotland and Northern Ireland.*

In relation to an offence committed before the commencement of section 281(5) of the Criminal Justice Act 2003 (c 44), for "51 weeks" in paragraph (*a*) substitute "six months".

[Gangmasters (Licensing) Act 2004, s 18.]

8–8583T   19. Information relating to gangmasters

Supplementary

8–8583U   20. Application of Act to bodies corporate.   (1) A licence under this Act may be granted to a body corporate.

(2) A licence granted to a body corporate authorises activities carried on by the body through such persons representing, or acting on behalf of, the body as are named or otherwise specified in the licence.

(3) If an offence under this Act committed by a body corporate is shown—

(*a*) to have been committed with the consent or connivance of an officer of the body corporate, or

(*b*) to be attributable to any neglect on his part,

the officer, as well as the body corporate, is guilty of the offence and liable to be proceeded against and punished accordingly.

(4) In subsection (3) "officer" means—

(a) any director, manager, secretary or other similar officer of the body corporate, or

(b) any person purporting to act in any such capacity.

(5) If the affairs of a body corporate are managed by its members, subsection (3) applies in relation to the acts and defaults of a member in connection with his functions of management as if he were a director of the body corporate.

[Gangmasters (Licensing) Act 2004, s 20.]

8–8583V 21. Application of Act to unincorporated associations. (1) A licence under this Act may be granted to an unincorporated association (other than a partnership).

(2) A licence granted to an unincorporated association authorises activities carried on by the association through such persons representing, or acting on behalf of, the association as are named or otherwise specified in the licence.

(3) Proceedings for an offence under this Act alleged to have been committed by an unincorporated association may be brought against the association in the name of the association.

(4) For the purposes of such proceedings—

(a) rules of court relating to the service of documents have effect as if the association were a body corporate, and

(b) the following provisions apply as they apply in relation to a body corporate—

section 33 of the Criminal Justice Act 1925 (c 86) and Schedule 3 to the Magistrates' Courts Act 1980 (c 43),

sections 70 and 143 of the Criminal Procedure (Scotland) Act 1995,

section 18 of the Criminal Justice Act (Northern Ireland) 1945 (c 15 (NI)) and Schedule 4 to the Magistrates' Courts (Northern Ireland) Order 1981 (SI 1981/ 1675 (NI 26)).

(5) A fine imposed on the association on its conviction of an offence shall be paid out of the funds of the association.

(6) If an offence under this Act committed by an unincorporated association is shown—

(a) to have been committed with the consent or connivance of an officer of the association, or

(b) to be attributable to any neglect on his part,

the officer, as well as the association, is guilty of the offence and liable to be proceeded against and punished accordingly.

(7) In subsection (6) "officer", in relation to any association, means—

(a) any officer of the association or any member of its governing body, or

(b) any person purporting to act in such a capacity.

[Gangmasters (Licensing) Act 2004, s 21.]

8–8583W 22. Application of Act to partnerships. (1) A licence under this Act may be granted to a partnership in the firm name.

(2) Where the partnership is not regarded as a legal person under the law of the country or territory under which it is formed, the grant of a licence to the partnership in the firm name—

(a) continues to have effect notwithstanding a change of partners, so long as at least one of the persons who was a partner before the change remains a partner after it; and

(b) has effect as the grant of a licence to those partners named in the licence.

(3) If in the case of such a partnership an offence under this Act committed by a partner is shown—

(a) to have been committed with the consent or connivance of another partner, or

(b) to be attributable to any neglect on the part of another partner,

that other partner, as well as the first-mentioned partner, is guilty of the offence and liable to be proceeded against and punished accordingly.

(4) A licence granted to a partnership that is regarded as a legal person under the law of the country or territory under which it is formed authorises activities carried on by the partnership through those partners named in the licence.

(5) Proceedings for an offence under this Act alleged to have been committed by such a partnership may be brought against the partnership in the firm name.

(6) For the purposes of such proceedings—

(a) rules of court relating to the service of documents have effect as if the partnership were a body corporate, and

(b) the following provisions apply as they apply in relation to a body corporate—

section 33 of the Criminal Justice Act 1925 (c 86) and Schedule 3 to the Magistrates' Courts Act 1980 (c 43),

sections 70 and 143 of the Criminal Procedure (Scotland) Act 1995, section 18 of the Criminal Justice Act (Northern Ireland) 1945 (c 15 (NI)) and Schedule 4 to the Magistrates' Courts (Northern Ireland) Order 1981 (SI 1981/ 1675 (NI 26)).

(7) A fine imposed on a partnership on its conviction of an offence shall be paid out of the funds of the partnership.

(8) If an offence under this Act committed by a partnership is shown—

(*a*) to have been committed with the consent or connivance of a partner, or

(*b*) to be attributable to any neglect on the part of a partner,

the partner, as well as the partnership, is guilty of the offence and liable to be proceeded against and punished accordingly.

(9) In subsections (3) and (8) "partner" includes a person purporting to act as a partner.
[Gangmasters (Licensing) Act 2004, s 22.]

Miscellaneous and general

8–8583X   23. Annual report

8–8583Y   24. Financial provision

8–8583Z   25. Regulations, rules and orders

8–8583ZA   26. Meaning of "worker".   (1) In this Act "worker" means an individual who does work to which this Act applies.

(2) A person is not prevented from being a worker for the purposes of this Act by reason of the fact that he has no right to be, or to work, in the United Kingdom.
[Gangmasters (Licensing) Act 2004, s 26.]

8–8583ZB   27. Exclusion of provisions relating to employment agencies and businesses

8–8583ZC   28. Application of Act to Northern Ireland

8–8583ZD   29. Commencement and transitional provision.   (1) The provisions of this Act come into force on such day as the Secretary of State may by order appoint[1].

(2) Different days may be appointed for different purposes and for different areas.

(3) The Secretary of State may by order make such transitional provision as he considers appropriate in connection with the coming into force of any provision of this Act.
[Gangmasters (Licensing) Act 2004, s 29.]

---

1. At the time of going to press the following Commencement Orders had been made: Gangmasters (Licensing) Act 2004 (Commencement No 1) Order 2004, SI 2004/2857; and Gangmasters (Licensing) Act 2004 (Commencement No 2) Order 2005, SI 2005/447. The only provisions of the Act that remain prospective are: ss 11-14 and 27, and paras 12-14 of Sch 1.

8–8583ZE   SCHEDULE 1
                      THE AUTHORITY: CONSEQUENTIAL AMENDMENTS OF ENACTMENTS
8–8583ZF   SCHEDULE 2
                        APPLICATION OF ACT TO NORTHERN IRELAND

Working Time Regulations 1998
(SI 1998/1833 as amended by SI 1999/3242 and 3372, SI 2001/3256, SI 2002/3128, SI 2003/1684 and 3049, 2004/1713 and 2516, SI 2005/2241 and SI 2006/99)

PART I
GENERAL

8–8584   1. Citation, commencement and extent.   (1) These Regulations may be cited as the Working Time Regulations 1998 and shall come into force on 1st October 1998.

(2) These Regulations extend to Great Britain only.

8–8585   2. Interpretation.   (1) In these Regulations—

"the 1996 Act" means the Employment Rights Act 1996;

"adult worker" means a worker who has attained the age of 18;

"the armed forces" means any of the naval, military and air forces of the Crown;

"calendar year" means the period of twelve months beginning with 1st January in any year;

"the civil protection services" includes the police, fire brigades and ambulance services, the security and intelligence services, customs and immigration officers, the prison service, the coastguard, and lifeboat crew and other voluntary rescue services;

"collective agreement" means a collective agreement within the meaning of section 178 of the Trade Union and Labour Relations (Consolidation) Act 1992, the trade union parties to which are independent trade unions within the meaning of section 5 of that Act;

"day" means a period of 24 hours beginning at midnight;

"employer", in relation to a worker, means the person by whom the worker is (or, where the employment has ceased, was) employed;

"employment", in relation to a worker, means employment under his contract, and "employed" shall be construed accordingly;

"night time", in relation to a worker, means a period—

    (*a*) the duration of which is not less than seven hours, and

    (*b*) which includes the period between midnight and 5 am,

which is determined for the purposes of these Regulations by a relevant agreement, or, in default of such a determination, the period between 11 pm and 6 am;

"night work" means work during night time;

"night worker" means a worker—

    (*a*) who, as a normal course, works at least three hours of his daily working time during night time, or

    (*b*) who is likely, during night time, to work at least such proportion of his annual working time as may be specified for the purposes of these Regulations in a collective agreement or a workforce agreement;

and, for the purpose of paragraph (*a*) of this definition, a person works hours as a normal course (without prejudice to the generality of that expression) if he works such hours on the majority of days on which he works;

"relevant agreement", in relation to a worker, means a workforce agreement which applies to him, any provision of a collective agreement which forms part of a contract between him and his employer, or any other agreement in writing which is legally enforceable as between the worker and his employer;

"relevant training" means work experience provided pursuant to a training course or programme, training for employment, or both, other than work experience or training—

    (*a*) the immediate provider of which is an educational institution or a person whose main business is the provision of training, and

    (*b*) which is provided on a course run by that institution or person;

"rest period", in relation to a worker, means a period which is not working time, other than a rest break or leave to which the worker is entitled under these Regulations;

"the restricted period", in relation to a worker, means the period between 10 pm and 6 am or, where the worker's contract provides for him to work after 10 pm., the period between 11 pm and 7 am

"worker" means an individual who has entered into or works under (or, where the employment has ceased, worked under)—

    (*a*) a contract of employment; or

    (*b*) any other contract, whether express or implied and (if it is express) whether oral or in writing, whereby the individual undertakes to do or perform personally any work or services for another party to the contract whose status is not by virtue of the contract that of a client or customer of any profession or business undertaking carried on by the individual;

and any reference to a worker's contract shall be construed accordingly;

"worker employed in agriculture" has the same meaning as in the Agricultural Wages Act 1948 or the Agricultural Wages (Scotland) Act 1949, and a reference to a worker partly employed in agriculture is to a worker employed in agriculture whose employer also employs him for non-agricultural purposes;

"workforce agreement" means an agreement between an employer and workers employed by him or their representatives in respect of which the conditions set out in Schedule 1 to these Regulations are satisfied;

"working time", in relation to a worker, means—

    (*a*) any period during which he is working, at his employer's disposal and carrying out his activity or duties,

    (*b*) any period during which he is receiving relevant training, and

    (*c*) any additional period which is to be treated as working time for the purpose of these Regulations under a relevant agreement;

and "work" shall be construed accordingly;

"Working Time Directive" means Council Directive 93/104/EC of 23rd November 1993 concerning certain aspects of the organization of working time;

"young worker" means a worker who has attained the age of 15 but not the age of 18 and who, as respects England and Wales, is over compulsory school age (construed in accordance with section 8 of the Education Act 1996) and, as respects Scotland, is over school age (construed in accordance with section 31 of the Education (Scotland) Act 1980), and

"Young Workers Directive" means Council Directive 94/33/EC of 22nd June 1994 on the protection of young people at work.

(2) In the absence of a definition in these Regulations, words and expressions used in particular provisions which are also used in corresponding provisions of the Working Time Directive or the Young Workers Directive have the same meaning as they have in those corresponding provisions.

(3) In these Regulations—

(a) a reference to a numbered regulation is to the regulation in these Regulations bearing that number;

(b) a reference in a regulation to a numbered paragraph is to the paragraph in that regulation bearing that number; and

(c) a reference in a paragraph to a lettered sub-paragraph is to the sub-paragraph in that paragraph bearing that letter.

PART II
RIGHTS AND OBLIGATIONS CONCERNING WORKING TIME

8–8586 **3. General.** (1) The provisions of this Part have effect subject to the exceptions provided for in Part III of these Regulations.

(2) Where, in this Part, separate provision is made as respects the same matter in relation to workers generally and to young workers, the provision relating to workers generally applies only to adult workers and those young workers to whom, by virtue of any exception in Part 3, the provision relating to young workers does not apply.

8–8587 **4. Maximum weekly working time.** (1) Unless his employer has first obtained the worker's agreement in writing to perform such work, a worker's working time, including overtime, in any reference period which is applicable in his case shall not exceed an average of 48 hours for each seven days.

(2) An employer shall take all reasonable steps, in keeping with the need to protect the health and safety of workers, to ensure that the limit specified in paragraph (1) is complied with in the case of each worker employed by him in relation to whom it applies and shall keep up-to-date records of all workers who carry out work to which it does not apply by reason of the fact that the employer has obtained the worker's agreement as mentioned in paragraph (1).

(3) Subject to paragraphs (4) and (5) and any agreement under regulation 23(b), the reference periods which apply in the case of a worker are—

(a) where a relevant agreement provides for the application of this regulation in relation to successive periods of 17 weeks, each such period, or

(b) in any other case, any period of 17 weeks in the course of his employment.

(4) Where a worker has worked for his employer for less than 17 weeks, the reference period applicable in his case is the period that has elapsed since he started work for his employer.

(5) Paragraphs (3) and (4) shall apply to a worker who is excluded from the scope of certain provisions of these Regulations by regulation 21 as if for each reference to 17 weeks there were substituted a reference to 26 weeks.

(6) For the purposes of this regulation, a worker's average working time for each seven days during a reference period shall be determined according to the formula—

$$\frac{(A + B)}{C}$$

where—

A is the aggregate number of hours comprised in the worker's working time during the course of the reference period;

B is the aggregate number of hours comprised in his working time during the course of the period beginning immediately after the end of the reference period and ending when the number of days in that subsequent period on which he has worked equals the number of excluded days during the reference period; and

C is the number of weeks in the reference period.

(7) In paragraph (6), "excluded days" means days comprised in—

(a) any period of annual leave taken by the worker in exercise of his entitlement under regulation 13;

(b) any period of sick leave taken by the worker;

(c) any period of maternity, paternity, adoption or parental leave taken by the worker; and

(d) any period in respect of which the limit specified in paragraph (1) did not apply in relation to the worker by reason of the fact that the employer has obtained the worker's agreement as mentioned in paragraph (1).

8–8588 **5. Agreement to exclude the maximum.** (1) (*Revoked*)

(2) An agreement for the purposes of regulation 4—

(a) may either relate to a specified period or apply indefinitely; and

(b) subject to any provision in the agreement for a different period of notice, shall be terminable by the worker by giving not less than seven days' notice to his employer in writing.

(3) Where an agreement for the purposes of regulation 4 makes provision for the termination of the agreement after a period of notice, the notice period provided for shall not exceed three months.

(4) *Revoked.*

8–8588A 5A. Maximum working time for young workers. (1) A young worker's working time shall not exceed—

(a) eight hours a day, or
(b) 40 hours a week.

(2) If, on any day, or, as the case may be, during any week, a young worker is employed by more than one employer, his working time shall be determined for the purpose of paragraph (1) by aggregating the number of hours worked by him for each employer.

(3) For the purposes of paragraphs (1) and (2), a week starts at midnight between Sunday and Monday.

(4) An employer shall take all reasonable steps, in keeping with the need to protect the health and safety of workers, to ensure that the limits specified in paragraph (1) are complied with in the case of each worker employed by him and in relation to whom they apply.

8–8589 6. Length of night work. (1) A night worker's normal hours of work in any reference period which is applicable in his case shall not exceed an average of eight hours for each 24 hours.

(2) An employer shall take all reasonable steps, in keeping with the need to protect the health and safety of workers, to ensure that the limit specified in paragraph (1) is complied with in the case of each night worker employed by him.

(3) The reference periods which apply in the case of a night worker are—

(a) where a relevant agreement provides for the application of this regulation in relation to successive periods of 17 weeks, each such period, or
(b) in any other case, any period of 17 weeks in the course of his employment.

(4) Where a worker has worked for his employer for less than 17 weeks, the reference period applicable in his case is the period that has elapsed since he started work for his employer.

(5) For the purposes of this regulation, a night worker's average normal hours of work for each 24 hours during a reference period shall be determined according to the formula—

$$\frac{A}{(B - C)}$$

where—

A is the number of hours during the reference period which are normal working hours for that worker;
B is the number of days during the reference period, and
C is the total number of hours during the reference period comprised in rest periods spent by the worker in pursuance of his entitlement under regulation 11, divided by 24.

(6) (*Revoked*).

(7) An employer shall ensure that no night worker employed by him whose work involves special hazards or heavy physical or mental strain works for more than eight hours in any 24-hour period during which the night worker performs night work.

(8) For the purposes of paragraph (7), the work of a night worker shall be regarded as involving special hazards or heavy physical or mental strain if—

(a) it is identified as such in—

(i) a collective agreement, or
(ii) a workforce agreement,

which takes account of the specific effects and hazards of night work, or

(b) it is recognised in a risk assessment made by the employer under regulation 3 of the Management of Health and Safety at Work Regulations 1999 as involving a significant risk to the health or safety of workers employed by him.

8–8589A 6A. Night work by young workers. An employer shall ensure that no young worker employed by him works during the restricted period.

8–8590 7. Health assessment and transfer of night workers to day work. (1) An employer—

(a) shall not assign an adult worker to work which is to be undertaken during periods such that the worker will become a night worker unless—

(i) the employer has ensured that the worker will have the opportunity of a free health assessment before he takes up the assignment; or

(ii) the worker had a health assessment before being assigned to work to be undertaken during such periods on an earlier occasion, and the employer has no reason to believe that that assessment is no longer valid, and

(b) shall ensure that each night worker employed by him has the opportunity of a free health assessment at regular intervals of whatever duration may be appropriate in his case.

(2) Subject to paragraph (4), an employer—

(a) shall not assign a young worker to work during the restricted period unless—

(i) the employer has ensured that the young worker will have the opportunity of a free assessment of his health and capacities before he takes up the assignment; or

(ii) the young worker had an assessment of his health and capacities before being assigned to work during the restricted period on an earlier occasion, and the employer has no reason to believe that that assessment is no longer valid; and

(b) shall ensure that each young worker employed by him and assigned to work during the restricted period has the opportunity of a free assessment of his health and capacities at regular intervals of whatever duration may be appropriate in his case.

(3) For the purposes of paragraphs (1) and (2), an assessment is free if it is at no cost to the worker to whom it relates.

(4) The requirements in paragraph (2) do not apply in a case where the work a young worker is assigned to do is of an exceptional nature.

(5) No person shall disclose an assessment made for the purposes of this regulation to any person other than the worker to whom it relates, unless—

(a) the worker has given his consent in writing to the disclosure, or

(b) the disclosure is confined to a statement that the assessment shows the worker to be fit—

(i) in a case where paragraph (1)(a)(i) or (2)(a)(i) applies, to take up an assignment, or

(ii) in a case where paragraph (1)(b) or (2)(b) applies, to continue to undertake an assignment.

(6) Where—

(a) a registered medical practitioner has advised an employer that a worker employed by the employer is suffering from health problems which the practitioner considers to be connected with the fact that the worker performs night work, and

(b) it is possible for the employer to transfer the worker to work—

(i) to which the worker is suited, and

(ii) which is to be undertaken during periods such that the worker will cease to be a night worker,

the employer shall transfer the worker accordingly.

8–8591 **8. Pattern of work.** Where the pattern according to which an employer organizes work is such as to put the health and safety of a worker employed by him at risk, in particular because the work is monotonous or the work-rate is predetermined, the employer shall ensure that the worker is given adequate rest breaks.

8–8592 **9. Records.** An employer shall—

(a) keep records which are adequate to show whether the limits specified in regulations 4(1), 5A(1) and 6(1) and (7) and the requirements in regulations 6A and 7(1) and (2) are being complied with in the case of each worker employed by him in relation to whom they apply; and

(b) retain such records for two years from the date on which they were made.

8–8593 **10. Daily rest.** (1) A worker is entitled to a rest period of not less than eleven consecutive hours in each 24-hour period during which he works for his employer.

(2) Subject to paragraph (3), a young worker is entitled to a rest period of not less than twelve consecutive hours in each 24-hour period during which he works for his employer.

(3) The minimum rest period provided for in paragraph (2) may be interrupted in the case of activities involving periods of work that are split up over the day or of short duration.

8–8594 **11. Weekly rest period.** (1) Subject to paragraph (2), a worker is entitled to an uninterrupted rest period of not less than 24 hours in each seven-day period during which he works for his employer.

(2) If his employer so determines, a worker shall be entitled to either—

(a) two uninterrupted rest periods each of not less than 24 hours in each 14-day period during which he works for his employer; or

(b) one uninterrupted rest period of not less than 48 hours in each such 14-day period, in place of the entitlement provided for in paragraph (1).

(3) Subject to paragraph (8), a young worker is entitled to a rest period of not less than 48 hours in each seven-day period during which he works for his employer.

(4) For the purpose of paragraphs (1) to (3), a seven-day period or (as the case may be) 14-day period shall be taken to begin—

(a) at such times on such days as may be provided for the purposes of this regulation in a relevant agreement; or

(b) where there are no provisions of a relevant agreement which apply, at the start of each week or (as the case may be) every other week.

(5) In a case where, in accordance with paragraph (4), 14-day periods are to be taken to begin at the start of every other week, the first such period applicable in the case of a particular worker shall be taken to begin—

(a) if the worker's employment began on or before the date on which these Regulations come into force, on 5th October 1998; or

(b) if the worker's employment begins after the date on which these Regulations come into force, at the start of the week in which that employment begins.

(6) For the purposes of paragraphs (4) and (5), a week starts at midnight between Sunday and Monday.

(7) The minimum rest period to which a worker is entitled under paragraph (1) or (2) shall not include any part of a rest period to which the worker is entitled under regulation 10(1), except where this is justified by objective or technical reasons or reasons concerning the organization of work.

(8) The minimum rest period to which a young worker is entitled under paragraph (3)—

(a) may be interrupted in the case of activities involving periods of work that are split up over the day or are of short duration; and

(b) may be reduced where this is justified by technical or organization reasons, but not to less than 36 consecutive hours.

8–8595 **12. Rest breaks.** (1) Where a worker's daily working time is more than six hours, he is entitled to a rest break.

(2) The details of the rest break to which a worker is entitled under paragraph (1), including its duration and the terms on which it is granted, shall be in accordance with any provisions for the purposes of this regulation which are contained in a collective agreement or a workforce agreement.

(3) Subject to the provisions of any applicable collective agreement or workforce agreement, the rest break provided for in paragraph (1) is an uninterrupted period of not less than 20 minutes, and the worker is entitled to spend it away from his workstation if he has one.

(4) Where a young worker's daily working time is more than four and a half hours, he is entitled to a rest break of at least 30 minutes, which shall be consecutive if possible, and he is entitled to spend it away from his workstation if he has one.

(5) If, on any day, a young worker is employed by more than one employer, his daily working time shall be determined for the purpose of paragraph (4) by aggregating the number of hours worked by him for each employer.

8–8596 **13. Entitlement to annual leave.** (1) Subject to paragraph (5), a worker is entitled to four weeks' annual leave in each leave year.

(2) *Revoked.*

(3) A worker's leave year, for the purposes of this regulation, begins—

(a) on such date during the calendar year as may be provided for in a relevant agreement; or

(b) where there are no provisions of a relevant agreement which apply—

(i) if the worker's employment began on or before 1st October 1998, on that date and each subsequent anniversary of that date; or

(ii) if the worker's employment begins after 1st October 1998, on the date on which that employment begins and each subsequent anniversary of that date.

(4) Paragraph (3) does not apply to a worker to whom Schedule 2 applies (workers employed in agriculture) except where, in the case of a worker partly employed in agriculture, a relevant agreement so provides.

(5) Where the date on which a worker's employment begins is later than the date on which (by virtue of a relevant agreement) his first leave year begins, the leave to which he is entitled in that leave year is a proportion of the period applicable under paragraph (1) equal to the proportion of that leave year remaining on the date on which his employment begins.

(6) Where by virtue of paragraph (5) the period of leave to which a worker is entitled is or includes a proportion of a week, the proportion shall be determined in days and any fraction of a day shall be treated as a whole day.

(7) *Revoked.*

(8) *Revoked.*

(9) Leave to which a worker is entitled under this regulation may be taken in instalments, but—

(a) it may only be taken in the leave year in respect of which it is due, and

(b) it may not be replaced by a payment in lieu except where the worker's employment is terminated.

8-8597　14. Compensation related to entitlement to leave.　(1) This regulation applies where—

(a) a worker's employment is terminated during the course of his leave year, and

(b) on the date on which the termination takes effect ("the termination date"), the proportion he has taken of the leave to which he is entitled in the leave year under regulation 13 differs from the proportion of the leave year which has expired.

(2) Where the proportion of leave taken by the worker is less than the proportion of the leave year which has expired, his employer shall make him a payment in lieu of leave in accordance with paragraph (3).

(3) The payment due under paragraph (2) shall be—

(a) such sum as may be provided for the purposes of this regulation in a relevant agreement, or

(b) where there are no provisions of a relevant agreement which apply, a sum equal to the amount that would be due to the worker under regulation 16 in respect of a period of leave determined according to the formula—

$$(A \times B) - C$$

where—

A is the period of leave to which the worker is entitled under regulation 13;

B is the proportion of the worker's leave year which expired before the termination date, and

C is the period of leave taken by the worker between the start of the leave year and the termination date.

(4) A relevant agreement may provide that, where the proportion of leave taken by the worker exceeds the proportion of the leave year which has expired, he shall compensate his employer, whether by a payment, by undertaking additional work or otherwise.

8-8598　15. Dates on which leave is taken.　(1) A worker may take leave to which he is entitled under regulation 13 on such days as he may elect by giving notice to his employer in accordance with paragraph (3), subject to any requirement imposed on him by his employer under paragraph (2).

(2) A worker's employer may require the worker—

(a) to take leave to which he is entitled under regulation 13; or

(b) not to take such leave,

on particular days, by giving notice to the worker in accordance with paragraph (3).

(3) A notice under paragraph (1) or (2)—

(a) may relate to all or part of the leave to which a worker is entitled in a leave year;

(b) shall specify the days on which leave is or (as the case may be) is not to be taken and, where the leave on a particular day is to be in respect of only part of the day, its duration; and

(c) shall be given to the employer or, as the case may be, the worker before the relevant date.

(4) The relevant date, for the purposes of paragraph (3), is the date—

(a) in the case of a notice under paragraph (1) or (2)(a), twice as many days in advance of the earliest day specified in the notice as the number of days or part-days to which the notice relates, and

(b) in the case of a notice under paragraph (2)(b), as many days in advance of the earliest day so specified as the number of days or part-days to which the notice relates.

(5) Any right or obligation under paragraphs (1) to (4) may be varied or excluded by a relevant agreement.

(6) This regulation does not apply to a worker to whom Schedule 2 applies (workers employed in agriculture) except where, in the case of a worker partly employed in agriculture, a relevant agreement so provides.

8-8598A　15A. Leave during the first year of employment.　(1) During the first year of his employment, the amount of leave a worker may take at any time in exercise of his entitlement under regulation 13 is limited to the amount which is deemed to have accrued in his case at that time under paragraph (2), as modified under paragraph (3) in a case where that paragraph applies, less the amount of leave (if any) that he has already taken during that year.

(2) For the purposes of paragraph (1), leave is deemed to accrue over the course of the worker's first year of employment, at the rate of one-twelfth of the amount specified in regulation 13(1) on the first day of each month of that year.

(3) Where the amount of leave that has accrued in a particular case includes a fraction of a day other than a half-day, the fraction shall be treated as a half-day if it is less than a half-day and as a whole day if it is more than a half-day.

(4) This regulation does not apply to a worker whose employment began on or before 25th October 2001.

8-8599　16. Payment in respect of periods of leave.　(1) A worker is entitled to be paid in respect of any period of annual leave to which he is entitled under regulation 13, at the rate of a week's pay in respect of each week of leave.

(2) Sections 221 to 224 of the 1996 Act shall apply for the purpose of determining the amount of a week's pay for the purposes of this regulation, subject to the modifications set out in paragraph (3).

(3) The provisions referred to in paragraph (2) shall apply—

(a) as if references to the employee were references to the worker;

(b) as if references to the employee's contract of employment were references to the worker's contract;

(c) as if the calculation date were the first day of the period of leave in question; and

(d) as if the references to sections 227 and 228 did not apply.

(4) A right to payment under paragraph (1) does not affect any right of a worker to remuneration under his contract ("contractual remuneration").

(5) Any contractual remuneration paid to a worker in respect of a period of leave goes towards discharging any liability of the employer to make payments under this regulation in respect of that period; and, conversely, any payment of remuneration under this regulation in respect of a period goes towards discharging any liability of the employer to pay contractual remuneration in respect of that period.

8–8600   17. Entitlements under other provisions.   Where during any period a worker is entitled to a rest period, rest break or annual leave both under a provision of these Regulations and under a separate provision (including a provision of his contract), he may not exercise the two rights separately, but may, in taking a rest period, break or leave during that period, take advantage of whichever right is, in any particular respect, the more favourable.

PART III

EXCEPTIONS

8–8601   18. Excluded sectors.   (1) These Regulations do not apply—

(a) to workers to whom the European Agreement on the organisation of working time of seafarers dated 30th September 1998 and put into effect by Council Directive 1999/63/EC of 21st June 1999 applies;

(b) to workers to whom the Fishing Vessels (Working Time: Sea-fishermen) Regulations 2004 apply; or

(c) to workers to whom the Merchant Shipping (Working Time: Inland Waterways) Regulations 2003 apply.

(2) Regulations 4(1) and (2), 6(1), (2) and (7), 7(1) and (6), 8, 10(1), 11(1) and (2), 12(1), 13 and 16 do not apply—

(a) where characteristics peculiar to certain specific services such as the armed forces or the police, or to certain specific activities in the civil protection services, inevitably conflict with the provisions of these Regulations;

(b) to workers to whom the European Agreement on the organisation of working time of mobile staff in civil aviation concluded on 22nd March 2000 and implemented by Council Directive 2000/79/EC of 27th November 2000 applies; or

(c) to the activities of workers who are doctors in training.

(3) Paragraph (2)(c) has effect only until 31st July 2004.

(4) Regulations 4(1) and (2), 6(1), (2) and (7), 8, 10(1), 11(1) and (2) and 12(1) do not apply to workers to whom Directive 2002/15/EC of the European Parliament and of the Council on the organisation of the working time of persons performing mobile road transport activities, dated 11th March 2002 applies.

8–8602   19. Domestic service.   Regulations 4(1) and (2), 6(1), (2) and (7), 7(1), (2) and (6) and 8 do not apply in relation to a worker employed as a domestic servant in a private household.

8–8603   20. Unmeasured working time.   (1) Regulations 4(1) and (2), 5A(1) and (4), 6(1), (2) and (7), 6A, 10(1), 11(1) and (2) and 12(1) do not apply in relation to a worker where, on account of the specific characteristics of the activity in which he is engaged, the duration of his working time is not measured or predetermined or can be determined by the worker himself, as may be the case for—

(a) managing executives or other persons with autonomous decision-taking powers;

(b) family workers; or

(c) workers officiating at religious ceremonies in churches and religious communities.

(2) *Revoked.*

8–8604   21. Other special cases.   Subject to regulation 24, regulations 6(1), (2) and (7), 10(1), 11(1) and (2) and 12(1) do not apply in relation to a worker—

(a) where the worker's activities are such that his place of work and place of residence are distant from one another or his different places of work are distant from one another;

(b)　where the worker is engaged in security and surveillance activities requiring a permanent presence in order to protect property and persons, as may be the case for security guards and caretakers or security firms;

(c)　where the worker's activities involve the need for continuity of service or production, as may be the case in relation to—

(i)　services relating to the reception, treatment or care provided by hospitals or similar establishments, residential institutions and prisons;

(ii)　work at docks or airports;

(iii)　press, radio, television, cinematographic production, postal and telecommunications services and civil protection services;

(iv)　gas, water and electricity production, transmission and distribution, household refuse collection and incineration;

(v)　industries in which work cannot be interrupted on technical grounds;

(vi)　research and development activities;

(vii)　agriculture;

(d)　where there is a foreseeable surge of activity, as may be the case in relation to—

(i)　agriculture;

(ii)　tourism; and

(iii)　postal services;

(e)　where the worker's activities are affected by—

(i)　an occurrence due to unusual and unforeseeable circumstances, beyond the control of the worker's employer;

(ii)　exceptional events, the consequences of which could not have been avoided despite the exercise of all due care by the employer; or

(iii)　an accident or the imminent risk of an accident.

8–8605　22. Shift workers.　(1)　Subject to regulation 24—

(a)　regulation 10(1) does not apply in relation to a shift worker when he changes shift and cannot take a daily rest period between the end of one shift and the start of the next one;

(b)　paragraphs (1) and (2) of regulation 11 do not apply in relation to a shift worker when he changes shift and cannot take a weekly rest period between the end of one shift and the start of the next one; and

(c)　neither regulation 10(1) nor paragraphs (1) and (2) of regulation 11 apply to workers engaged in activities involving periods of work split up over the day, as may be the case for cleaning staff.

(2)　For the purposes of this regulation—

"shift worker" means any worker whose work schedule is part of shift work; and

"shift work" means any method of organizing work in shifts whereby workers succeed each other at the same workstations according to a certain pattern, including a rotating pattern, and which may be continuous or discontinuous, entailing the need for workers to work at different times over a given period of days or weeks.

8–8606　23. Collective and workforce agreements.　A collective agreement or a workforce agreement may—

(a)　modify or exclude the application of regulations 6(1) to (3) and (7), 10(1), 11(1) and (2) and 12(1), and

(b)　for objective or technical reasons or reasons concerning the organization of work, modify the application of regulation 4(3) and (4) by the substitution, for each reference to 17 weeks, of a different period, being a period not exceeding 52 weeks,

in relation to particular workers or groups of workers.

8–8607　24. Compensatory rest.　Where the application of any provision of these Regulations is excluded by regulation 21 or 22, or is modified or excluded by means of a collective agreement or a workforce agreement under regulation 23(a), and a worker is accordingly required by his employer to work during a period which would otherwise be a rest period or rest break—

(a)　his employer shall wherever possible allow him to take an equivalent period of compensatory rest, and

(b)　in exceptional cases in which it is not possible, for objective reasons, to grant such a period of rest, his employer shall afford him such protection as may be appropriate in order to safeguard the worker's health and safety.

8–8608　25. Workers in the armed forces.　(1)　Regulation 9 does not apply in relation to a worker serving as a member of the armed forces.

(2)　Regulations 5A, 6A, 10(2) and 11(3) do not apply in relation to a young worker serving as a member of the armed forces.

(3)　In a case where a young worker is accordingly required to work during the restricted period, or is not permitted the minimum rest period provided for in regulation 10(2) or 11(3), he shall be allowed an appropriate period of compensatory rest.

8–8608A 25A. Doctors in training. (1) Paragraph (1) of regulation 4 is modified in its application to workers who are doctors in training as follows—

- (a) for the reference to 48 hours there is substituted a reference to 58 hours with effect from 1st August 2004 until 31st July 2007;
- (b) for the reference to 48 hours there is substituted a reference to 56 hours with effect from 1st August 2007 until 31st July 2009.

(2) In the case of workers who are doctors in training, paragraphs (3)–(5) of regulation 4 shall not apply and paragraphs (3) and (4) of this regulation shall apply in their place.

(3) Subject to paragraph (4), the reference period which applies in the case of a worker who is a doctor in training is, with effect from 1st August 2004—

- (a) where a relevant agreement provides for the application of this regulation in relation to successive periods of 26 weeks, each such period; and
- (b) in any other case, any period of 26 weeks in the course of his employment.

(4) Where a doctor in training has worked for his employer for less than 26 weeks, the reference period applicable in his case is the period that has elapsed since he started work for his employer.

8–8609 26. Young workers employed on ships. Regulations 5A, 6A, 7(2), 10(2), 11(3) and 12(4) do not apply in relation to a young worker whose employment is subject to regulation under section 55(2)(*b*) of the Merchant Shipping Act 1995.

8–8610 27. Young workers: force majeure. (1) Regulations 5A, 6A, 10(2) and 12(4) do not apply in relation to a young worker where his employer requires him to undertake work which no adult worker is available to perform and which—

- (a) is occasioned by either—
  - (i) an occurrence due to unusual and unforseeable circumstances, beyond the employer's control, or
  - (ii) exceptional events, the consequences of which could not have been avoided despite the exercise of all due care by the employer;
- (b) is of a temporary nature; and
- (c) must be performed immediately.

(2) Where the application of regulation 5A, 6A, 10(2) or 12(4) is excluded by paragraph (1), and a young worker is accordingly required to work during a period which would otherwise be a rest period or rest break, his employer shall allow him to take an equivalent period of compensatory rest within the following three weeks.

8–8610A 27A. Other exceptions relating to young workers. (1) Regulation 5A does not apply in relation to a young worker where—

- (a) the young worker's employer requires him to undertake work which is necessary either to maintain continuity of service or production or to respond to a surge in demand for a service or product;
- (b) no adult worker is available to perform the work, and
- (c) performing the work would not adversely affect the young worker's education or training.

(2) Regulation 6A does not apply in relation to a young worker employed—

- (a) in a hospital or similar establishment, or
- (b) in connection with cultural, artistic, sporting or advertising activities,

in the circumstances referred to in paragraph (1).

(3) Regulation 6A does not apply, except in so far as it prohibits work between midnight and 4 a.m., in relation to a young worker employed in—

- (a) agriculture;
- (b) retail trading;
- (c) postal or newspaper deliveries;
- (d) a catering business;
- (e) a hotel, public house, restaurant, bar or similar establishment, or
- (f) a bakery,

in the circumstances referred to in paragraph (1).

(4) Where the application of regulation 6A is excluded by paragraph (2) or (3), and a young worker is accordingly required to work during a period which would otherwise be a rest period or rest break—

- (a) he shall be supervised by an adult worker where such supervision is necessary for the young worker's protection, and
- (b) he shall be allowed an equivalent period of compensatory rest.

PART IV
MISCELLANEOUS

8–8611   28. Enforcement.   (1) In this regulation and regulation 29—

"the 1974 Act" means the Health and Safety at Work etc Act 1974;
"the relevant requirements" means the following provisions—

    (*a*) regulations 4(2), 5A(4), 6(2) and (7), 6A, 7(1), (2) and (6), 8, 9 and 27A(4)(*a*); and
    (*b*) regulation 24, in so far as it applies where regulation 6(1), (2) or (7) is modified or excluded, and

"the relevant statutory provisions" has the same meaning as in the 1974 Act.

(2) It shall be the duty of the Health and Safety Executive to make adequate arrangements for the enforcement of the relevant requirements except to the extent that a local authority is made responsible for their enforcement by paragraph (3).

(3) Where the relevant requirements apply in relation to workers employed in premises in respect of which a local authority is responsible, under the Health and Safety (Enforcing Authority) Regulations 1998, for enforcing any of the relevant statutory provisions, it shall be the duty of that authority to enforce those requirements.

(4) The duty imposed on local authorities by paragraph (3) shall be performed in accordance with such guidance as may be given to them by the Health and Safety Commission.

(5) The following provisions of the 1974 Act shall apply in relation to the enforcement of the relevant requirements as they apply in relation to the enforcement of the relevant statutory provisions, and as if any reference in those provisions to an enforcing authority were a reference to the Health and Safety Executive and any local authority made responsible for the enforcement of the relevant requirements—

    (*a*) section 19;
    (*b*) section 20(1), (2)(*a*) to (*d*) and (*j*) to (*m*), (7) and (8); and
    (*c*) sections 21, 22, 23(1), (2) and (5), 24 and 26; and
    (*d*) section 28, in so far as it relates to information obtained by an inspector in pursuance of a requirement imposed under section 22(2)(j) or (k).

(6) Any function of the Health and Safety Commission under the 1974 Act which is exercisable in relation to the enforcement by the Health and Safety Executive of the relevant statutory provisions shall be exercisable in relation to the enforcement by the Executive of the relevant requirements.

8–8612   29. Offences.   (1) An employer who fails to comply with any of the relevant requirements shall be guilty of an offence.

(2) The following provisions of section 33(1) of the 1974 Act shall apply where an inspector is exercising or has exercised any power conferred by a provision specified in regulation 28(5)—

    (*a*) paragraph (*e*), in so far as it refers to section 20;
    (*b*) paragraphs (*f*) and (*g*);
    (*c*) paragraph (*h*), in so far as it refers to an inspector;
    (*d*) paragraph (*j*) in so far as it refers to section 28; and
    (*e*) paragraph (*k*).

(3) An employer guilty of an offence under paragraph (1) shall be liable—

    (*a*) on summary conviction, to a fine not exceeding the statutory maximum;
    (*b*) on conviction on indictment, to a fine.

(4) A person guilty of an offence under a provision of section 33(1) of the 1974 Act as applied by paragraph (2) shall be liable to the penalty prescribed in relation to that provision by subsection (2), (2A) or (3) of section 33, as the case may be.

(5) Sections 36(1), 37 to 39 and 42(1) to (3) of the 1974 Act shall apply in relation to the offences provided for in paragraphs (1) and (2) as they apply in relation to offences under the relevant statutory provisions.

8–8613   30. *Remedies*

8–8614   31. *Right not to suffer detriment*

8–8615   32. *Unfair dismissal*

8–8616   33. *Conciliation*

8-8617   34. *Appeals*

8–8618   35. *Restrictions on contracting out*

8–8619   35A.   (1) The Secretary of State shall, after consulting persons appearing to him to represent the two sides of industry, arrange for the publication, in such form and manner as he considers appropriate, of information and advice concerning the operation of these Regulations.

(2) The information and advice shall be such as appear to him best calculated to enable employers and workers affected by these Regulations to understand their respective rights and obligations under them.

PART V

SPECIAL CLASSES OF PERSON

8–8620 **36. Agency workers not otherwise "workers".** (1) This regulation applies in any case where an individual ("the agency worker")—

- (a) is supplied by a person ("the agent") to do work for another ("the principal") under a contract or other arrangements made between the agent and the principal; but
- (b) is not, as respects that work, a worker, because of the absence of a worker's contract between the individual and the agent or the principal; and
- (c) is not a party to a contract under which he undertakes to do the work for another party to the contract whose status is, by virtue of the contract, that of a client or customer of any profession or business undertaking carried on by the individual.

(2) In a case where this regulation applies, the other provisions of these Regulations shall have effect as if there were a worker's contract for the doing of the work by the agency worker made between the agency worker and—

- (a) whichever of the agent and the principal is responsible for paying the agency worker in respect of the work; or
- (b) if neither the agent nor the principal is so responsible, whichever of them pays the agency worker in respect of the work,

and as if that person were the agency worker's employer.

8–8621 **37. Crown employment.** (1) Subject to paragraph (4) and regulation 38, these Regulations have effect in relation to Crown employment and persons in Crown employment as they have effect in relation to other employment and other workers.

(2) In paragraph (1) "Crown employment" means employment under or for the purposes of a government department or any officer or body exercising on behalf of the Crown functions conferred by a statutory provision.

(3) For the purposes of the application of the provisions of these Regulations in relation to Crown employment in accordance with paragraph (1)—

- (a) references to a worker shall be construed as references to a person in Crown employment; and
- (b) references to a worker's contract shall be construed as references to the terms of employment of a person in Crown employment.

(4) No act or omission by the Crown which is an offence under regulation 29 shall make the Crown criminally liable, but the High Court or, in Scotland, the Court of Session may, on the application of a person appearing to the Court to have an interest, declare any such act or omission unlawful.

8–8622 **38. Armed forces.** (1) Regulation 37 applies—

- (a) subject to paragraph (2), to service as a member of the armed forces, and
- (b) to employment by an association established for the purposes of Part XI of the Reserve Forces Act 1996.

(2) No complaint concerning the service of any person as a member of the armed forces may be presented to an employment tribunal under regulation 30 unless—

- (a) that person has made a complaint in respect of the same matter to an officer under the service redress procedures, and
- (b) that complaint has not been withdrawn.

(3) For the purpose of paragraph (2)(b), a person shall be treated as having withdrawn his complaint if, having made a complaint to an officer under the service redress procedures, he fails to submit the complaint to the Defence Council under those procedures.

(4) Where a complaint of the kind referred to in paragraph (2) is presented to an employment tribunal, the service redress procedures may continue after the complaint is presented.

(5) In this regulation, "the service redress procedures" means the procedures, excluding those which relate to the making of a report on a complaint to Her Majesty, referred to in section 180 of the Army Act 1955, section 180 of the Air Force Act 1955 and section 130 of the Naval Discipline Act 1957.

8–8623 **39.** *House of Lords staff*

8–8624 **40.** *House of Commons staff*

8–8625 **41.** *Police service*

8–8626   42. Non-employed trainees.   For the purposes of these Regulations, a person receiving relevant training, otherwise than under a contract of employment, shall be regarded as a worker, and the person whose undertaking is providing the training shall be regarded as his employer.

8–8627   43. Agricultural workers.   The provisions of Schedule 2 have effect in relation to workers employed in agriculture.

8–8628

Regulation 2   SCHEDULE 1
                                                       WORKFORCE AGREEMENTS

Regulations 13(4), 15(6) and 43   SCHEDULE 2
                                                   WORKERS EMPLOYED IN AGRICULTURE

8–8629   1. Except where, in the case of a worker partly employed in agriculture, different provision is made by a relevant agreement—

   (a) for the purposes of regulation 13, the leave year of a worker employed in agriculture begins on 6th April each year or such other date as may be specified in an agricultural wages order which applies to him; and

   (b) the dates on which leave is taken by a worker employed in agriculture shall be determined in accordance with an agricultural wages order which applies to him.

   2. Where, in the case referred to in paragraph 1 above, a relevant agreement makes provision different from sub-paragraph (a) or (b) of that paragraph—

   (a) neither section 11 of the Agricultural Wages Act 1948 nor section 11 of the Agricultural Wages (Scotland) Act 1949 shall apply to that provision; and

   (b) an employer giving effect to that provision shall not thereby be taken to have failed to comply with the requirements of an agricultural wages order.

   3. In this Schedule, "an agricultural wages order" means an order under section 3 of the Agricultural Wages Act 1948 or section 3 of the Agricultural Wages (Scotland) Act 1949.

ENERGY

8–8669   This includes the following statutes—

       8–8670   ATOMIC ENERGY ACT 1946
       8–8980   RIGHTS OF ENTRY (GAS AND ELECTRICITY BOARDS) ACT 1954
       8–9120   GAS ACT 1965
       8–9140   NUCLEAR INSTALLATIONS ACT 1965
       8–9151   ENERGY ACT 1976
       8–9182   NUCLEAR SAFEGUARDS AND ELECTRICITY (FINANCE) ACT 1978
       8–9410   NUCLEAR MATERIAL (OFFENCES) ACT 1983
       8–9447   GAS ACT 1986
       8–9570   ELECTRICITY ACT 1989
       8–9664   RADIOACTIVE MATERIAL (ROAD TRANSPORT) ACT 1991
       8–9666   RADIOACTIVE SUBSTANCES ACT 1993
       8–9693   NUCLEAR SAFEGUARDS ACT 2000
       8–9693G   ENERGY ACT 2004

8–8669A   European Communities Act 1972: Regulations.   Within the scope of the title ENERGY there falls the subject matter of regulations made under the enabling powers provided in s 2(2) of the European Communities Act 1972. The following regulations which create offences have been made—

   Measuring Instruments (EC Requirements) (Electrical Energy Meters) Regulations 1995, SI 1995/2607,

   Energy Efficiency (Ballasts for Fluorescent Lighting) Regulations 2001, SI 2001/3316;

   Uranium Enrichment Technology (Prohibition on Disclosure) Regulations 2004, SI 2004/1818.

Atomic Energy Act 1946
(9 & 10 Geo 6 c 80)

8–8670   This Act, the Radioactive Substances Act 1948, and the Atomic Energy Authority Act 1954, which may be cited together as the Atomic Energy and Radioactive Substances Acts 1946 to 1954, provide for the development of atomic energy and the control of such development by the Minister of Science[1] and the Atomic Energy Authority.

   The Minister of Science[1] may by notice require information; failure to comply with such a notice or knowingly or recklessly making an untrue statement is an offence. (Atomic Energy Act 1946, s 4—*SUMMARISED*.) On production of his authority, an authorised person has power to enter and inspect premises and to make copies of drawings, etc and for the purpose he may remove them and

retain them in his possession for not exceeding seven days: the wilful obstruction of such a person is an offence. (Atomic Energy Act 1946, s 5—*SUMMARISED*.) Similarly, it is an offence wilfully to obstruct or interfere with persons authorised by the Minister of Science[1] engaged in work for the purpose of discovering minerals. (Atomic Energy Act 1946, s 6—*SUMMARISED*.) For purposes connected with the control of production and use of atomic energy, the Minister of Science[1] may make provisions by order and may grant certain licences; contravention of, or non-compliance with, such an order or any condition of such a licence is an offence.
[Atomic Energy Act 1946, s 10, summarised.]

It is an offence to disclose information relating to plant. (Atomic Energy Act 1946, s 11—*SUMMARISED*), but proceedings for such an offence shall not be instituted except by, or with the consent of, the Director of Public Prosecutions. (Atomic Energy Act 1946, s 14(4)—*SUMMARISED*.) The Comptroller General of Patents, etc may give directions for prohibiting or restricting the publication of information respecting applications made to him, and contravention of such a direction is an offence. (Atomic Energy Act 1946, s 12(1)—*SUMMARISED*.) It is an offence, with prescribed exceptions, for a person resident in the United Kingdom, without the consent of a patent for an invention relating to atomic energy. (Atomic Energy Act 1946, s 12(1)—*SUMMARISED*.) An offence is committed by a person who discloses information obtained by him under the Act.
[Atomic Energy Act 1946, s 13—summarised.]

Penalties for offences under this Act: on summary conviction, imprisonment for a term not exceeding **three months** or a fine not exceeding **the statutory maximum**, or both; or, on indictment, imprisonment for not exceeding **five years** or a fine or both. There are special provisions where the person convicted is a body corporate.
[Atomic Energy Act 1946, s 14, as amended by the Criminal Law Act 1977, ss 28 and 32—summarised.]

---

1. Ministerial functions have now been transferred to the Minister of Technology; SI 1964/2048.

Rights of Entry (Gas and Electricity Boards) Act 1954
(2 & 3 Eliz 2 c 21)

8–8980 1. Restriction on exercise of rights of entry. (1) No right of entry to which this Act applies shall be exercisable in respect of any premises except—

   (*a*) with consent given by or on behalf of the occupier of the premises, or
   (*b*) under the authority of a warrant granted under the next following section:

Provided that this subsection shall not apply where entry is required in a case of emergency.
(2) This Act applies to all rights[1] of entry conferred by—

   (*a*) the Gas Act 1986, regulations made under it or any other enactment relating to gas,
   (*b*) Schedule 6 to the Electricity Act 1989[2], and
   (*c*) any local[3] enactment relating to gas or electricity,

in so far as those rights are exercisable for the purposes of a gas operator or an electricity supplier.
(3) No person shall be liable to a penalty, under the enactment relating to obstruction[4] of the exercise of a right of entry to which this Act applies, by reason only of his refusing admission to a person who seeks to exercise the right of entry without a warrant granted under the next following section.
[Rights of Entry (Gas and Electricity Boards) Act 1954, s 1, as amended by the Gas Act 1972, Sch 6, the Gas Act 1986, Sch 7, the Electricity Act 1989, Sch 16, the Gas Act 1995, Sch 4 and the Utilities Act 2000, Sch 6.]

---

1. "Right of entry" includes a power of entry (s 3).
2. See this title, post.
3. "Local enactment" means a local or private Act, or an order made under or confirmed by, an Act (whether a public general Act or a local or private Act) (s 3).
4. See eg, Gas Act 1986, Sch 5, para 18(3), post.

8–8981 2. Warrant to authorise entry. (1) Where it is shown to the satisfaction of a justice of the peace, on sworn information in writing—

   (*a*) that admission to premises specified in the information is reasonably required by a gas operator[1] that admission to premises specified in the information is reasonably required by a gas operator or an electricity operator or by an employee of a gas operator or an electricity operator;
   (*b*) that the operator or any employee of the operator as the case may be, would, apart from the preceding section, be entitled for that purpose to exercise in respect of the premises a right of entry[2] to which this Act applies; and
   (*c*) that the requirements (if any) of the relevant enactment have been complied with,

then subject to the provisions of this section the justice may by warrant under his hand authorise the operator or any employee of the operator as the case may be, to enter the premises, if need be by force.

(2) If, in a case to which the preceding subsection applies, the relevant enactment does not require notice of an intended entry to be given to the occupier of the premises, the justice shall not grant a warrant under this section in respect of the right of entry in question unless he is satisfied—

(a) that admission to the premises for the purpose specified in the information was sought by a person lawfully requiring entry in the exercise of that right, and was so sought after not less than twenty-four hours' notice of the intended entry had been given to the occupier; or

(b) that admission to the premises for that purpose was sought in a case of emergency and was refused by or on behalf of the occupier; or

(c) that the premises are unoccupied; or

(d) that an application for admission to the premises would defeat the object of the entry.

(3) Where paragraph (a) of subsection (2) above applies—

(a) section 46 of the Gas Act 1986 (if entry is required for the purposes of a gas operator); or

(b) section 109 of the Electricity Act 1989 (if entry is required for the purposes of an electricity supplier),

shall apply to the service of the notice required by that paragraph.

(4) Every warrant granted under this section shall continue in force until—

(a) the time when the purpose for which the entry is required is satisfied; or

(b) the end of the period of 28 days beginning with the day on which the warrant was granted,

whichever is the earlier.

(5) Any person who, in the exercise of a right of entry under the authority of a warrant granted under this section, enters any premises which are unoccupied, or premises of which the occupier is temporarily absent, shall leave the premises as effectually secured against trespassers as he found them.

(6) Where a warrant is granted under this section in respect of a right of entry, then for the purposes of any enactment whereby—

(a) an obligation is imposed to make good damage, or to pay compensation, or to take any other step, in consequence of the exercise of the right of entry, or

(b) a penalty is imposed for obstructing the exercise of that right,

any entry effected, or sought to be effected, under the authority of the warrant shall be treated as an entry effected, or sought to be effected, in the exercise of that right of entry.

(7) *Application to Scotland.*

[Rights of Entry (Gas and Electricity Boards) Act 1954, s 2, as amended by the Gas Act 1972, Sch 6, the Gas Act 1986, Sch 7, the Electricity Act 1989, s 101 and Sch 16, the Gas Act 1995, Sch 4 and the Utilities Act 2000, Sch 6.]

---

1. "Gas operator" is defined in s 3, post.
2. See eg Gas Act 1986, Sch 5, para 18.

8–8982 3. Interpretation.   (1) In this Act the following expressions have the meanings hereby assigned to them respectively, that is to say,—

"employee" means—

(a) in relation to a gas operator, an officer, servant or agent of the operator and any servant or officer of such an agent; and

(b) in relation to an electricity supplier, an officer, servant or agent of the operator and any person authorised by such an agent;

"enactment" includes a local enactment;

"local enactment" means a local or private Act, or an order made under, or confirmed by, an Act (whether a public general Act or a local or private Act);

"premises" means a building or a part of a building;

"electricity operator" means an electricity distributor or an electricity supplier (within the meaning of Part I of the Electricity Act 1989);

"gas operator" means a gas transporter, gas supplier or gas shipper within the meaning of Part I of the Gas Act 1986;

"right of entry" includes a power of entry.

(2) In this Act—

(a) references to a person lawfully requiring entry to premises in the exercise of a right of entry to which this Act applies are references to a person seeking admission to those premises by virtue of that right and in accordance with the requirements (if any) of the relevant enactment; and

(b) references to the relevant enactment, in relation to a right of entry, are references to the enactment conferring that right, and references to the requirements of the relevant enactment are references to any requirements of that enactment as to the giving of notices or the taking of any other step before, or at the time of, the exercise of the right.

(3) References in this Act to a case of emergency are references to a case in which a person lawfully requiring entry to the premises in question, in the exercise of a right of entry to which this Act applies, has reasonable cause to believe that circumstances exist which are likely to endanger life or property, and that immediate entry to the premises is necessary to verify the existence of those circumstances or to ascertain their cause or to effect a remedy.

[Rights of Entry (Gas and Electricity Boards) Act 1954, s 3, as amended by the Gas Act 1972, s 49, Schs 6 and 8, the Gas Act 1986, Schs 7 and 9, the Electricity Act 1989, Schs 16 and 18, the Gas Act 1995, Sch 4 and the Utilities Act 2000, Sch 6.]

Gas Act 1965
(1965 c 36)

8–9120 5. Control of mining and other operations in storage area and protective area.
(1) This section shall apply to controlled operations in a storage area and, if a storage authorisation order so provides as respects any area outside the storage area[1], in that other area (in this Part of this Act referred to as "the protective area"), and for the purposes of this section controlled operations are any description of excavation, mining, quarrying or boring operations in the storage area or the protective area which are carried out wholly or partly below the depth prescribed by the storage authorisation order (which may be a different depth for different parts of either area) and which are begun or continued after the coming into force of the storage authorisation order.

(2) No person, other than the gas transporter authorised to operate the underground gas storage, shall carry out any controlled operations without the consent of the Minister[2].

(3)–(12) *Application for the consent of the Minister under this section; powers of the Minister include power to give consent with or without conditions.*

(13) If any person contravenes subsection (2) of this section or fails to comply with any conditions imposed under this section he shall be guilty of an offence under this Part of this Act and shall be liable[3]—

(a) on summary conviction to imprisonment for a term not exceeding **three months** or to a fine not exceeding **the statutory maximum**, or to both, and

(b) on conviction on indictment to imprisonment for a term not exceeding **two years** or to a fine, or to both.

[Gas Act 1965, s 5, as amended by the Gas Act 1972, Sch 6, the Criminal Law Act 1977, s 28, the Gas Act 1986, Sch 7, the Gas Act 1995, Sch 4 and the Utilities Act 2000, s 76.]

---

1. A "storage area" is the area within the surface perimeter specified in a storage authorisation order made by the Minister of Power (Sch 2, para 1 (2)).
2. Ie, the Minister of Power (s 32).
3. For procedure in respect of this offence which is triable either way, see the Magistrates' Courts Act 1980, ss 17A–21, in PART I, ante.

8–9121 6. Controlled operations: carrying out of works to remedy a default. (1) If a gas transporter applies in England or Wales to a magistrates' court or in Scotland to the sheriff, and satisfies the court that any controlled operations have been carried out without the consent of the Minister, or that there has been a failure to comply with any conditions subject to which the Minister's consent to the carrying out of any controlled operations has been granted, and that the works specified in the application which consist of the filling in of an excavation, well, borehole or shaft made or sunk in contravention of the last foregoing section, or the taking of any other steps to make good the default, ought to be carried out in the interests of safety, or in order to safeguard property, to preserve water resources or to prevent the suspension, or continued suspension, of the operations of an underground gas storage, the court may make an order authorising the gas transporter to execute those works in such manner as he thinks fit.

(2) Any person having an interest in the land in which the controlled operations have been carried out shall be entitled to appear and be heard on the application by the gas transporter to the court, and the court shall not entertain the application unless satisfied that the gas transporter has taken reasonable steps to give notice of the application to all such persons who are known to him.

(3) The gas transporter shall, as against all persons interested in the land in which the works are to be carried out, and any other land to which entry is required for the purpose of obtaining access to that land, have all such rights as are necessary in order to enable him to execute the order.

(4) Except in a case of emergency, a gas transporter shall not in pursuance of subsection (3) of this section demand admission as of right to any land which is occupied unless twenty-four hours' notice of the intended entry has been given to the occupier, and where a gas transporter in exercising his powers under subsection (3) of this section causes any damage to land or chattels, any person interested in the land or chattels shall be entitled to compensation in respect of that damage from the gas transporter.

(5) *Expenses.*

(6) Any person who wilfully obstructs a person acting under the authority of the order of a court under this section shall be guilty of an offence and shall be liable on summary conviction to a fine not exceeding **level 1** on the standard scale.

(7) Any application under this section to a magistrates' court shall be made by complaint.

(8) *Scotland.*

[Gas Act 1965, s 6, as amended by the Gas Act 1972, Sch 6, the Criminal Justice Act 1982, ss 38 and 46, the Gas Act 1986, Sch 7, the Gas Act 1995, Sch 4 and the Utilities Act 2000, s 76.]

8–9122 **16–18.** A gas transporter is liable to penalties for failing to comply with safety conditions imposed by the Minister of Power (s 16 amended by the Gas Act 1995, Sch 4); or failing to comply with a notice of the Minister relating to a leakage of gas from an underground gas storage or other event (s 17); or failing to comply with an order of the Minister requiring discontinuance of an underground gas storage (s 18).

8–9123 **19. Appointment of Inspectors.** (1) The Minister[1] may appoint as inspectors to assist him in the execution of this Part of this Act such number of persons as appear to him to be qualified—*summarised.*

(5) An inspector shall, for the purpose of the execution of this Part of this Act, have power (subject to production, if so requested, of written evidence of this authority), to do all or any of the following things that is—

(a) at all reasonable times to carry out inspections and tests of any underground gas storage, and of the equipment and apparatus used for the storage, and to take samples of any gas, fluid or other matter,

(b) to require the production of, and to inspect, any documents which are in the possession or under the control of the gas transporter and which relate to the storage,

(c) to require any officer or servant of the gas transporter having responsibilities as respects the storage to give to the inspector such facilities and assistance with respect to any matters or things to which the responsibilities of that officer or servant extend as are necessary for the purpose of enabling the inspector to exercise the powers conferred on him by paragraph (a) of this subsection.

(6) A person who—

(a) fails to comply with a requirement imposed under this section by an inspector, or

(b) obstructs an inspector in the exercise of the powers conferred by this section,

shall be guilty of an offence under this Part of this Act, and shall be liable on summary conviction to a fine not exceeding **level 3** on the standard scale.

[Gas Act 1965, s 19 as amended by the Gas Act 1972, Sch 6, the Criminal Justice Act 1982, ss 38 and 46, the Gas Act 1986, Sch 7, the Gas Act 1995, Sch 4 and the Utilities Act 2000, s 76.]

---

1. Ie, the Minister of Power (s 32).

8–9124 **20. Powers of entry.** Schedule 6[1] to this Act (which confers powers of entry on land and powers of prospecting and surveying land) shall have effect for the purposes of this Part of this Act.

[Gas Act 1965, s 20.]

---

1. This lengthy Schedule is not printed in this work. It provides (in para 8) for a fine not exceeding **level 1** on the standard scale for wilful obstruction of a person acting in the exercise of powers under the Schedule: and (in para 9) for a fine not exceeding **level 3** on the standard scale or imprisonment not exceeding **three months** for wrongful disclosure of information obtained in premises entered under the Schedule.

8–9125 **21. General provisions as to offences under Part II.** (1) Section 43(1) of the principal Act[1] (punishment for false information given for purposes of Act) shall apply as if references in that subsection to any provision of that Act included references to any provision of this Part of this Act.

(2) Section 43(2) of the principal Act[2] (restriction on institution of prosecutions) shall apply as if the reference in that section to an offence under the said section 43(1) included a reference to an offence under any provision of this Part of this Act.

(3) Where a body corporate is guilty of an offence under any provision of this Part of this Act and that offence is proved to have been committed with the consent or connivance of, or to be attributable to any neglect on the part of, any director, manager, secretary or other similar officer of the body corporate or of any person who was purporting to act in any such capacity, he, as well as the body corporate, shall be guilty of that offence and shall be liable to be proceeded against and punished accordingly.

In this subsection, the expression "director", in relation to any other body corporate established by or under any enactment for the purpose of carrying on under national ownership any industry or part of an industry or undertaking, being a body corporate whose affairs are managed by its members, means a member of that body corporate.

(4) Without prejudice to the operation, as respects England and Wales, of section 8 of the

Accessories and Abettors Act 1961 and section 44 of the Magistrates' Courts Act 1980, any person who aids, abets, counsels or procures[3] the commission of an offence under this Part of this Act shall be guilty of that offence and shall be liable to be proceeded against and punished accordingly.

(5) If by virtue of either of the two last foregoing subsections an individual is guilty of an offence under section 16(5)[4] or section 18(9)[5] of this Act the individual shall be liable[6]—

(a) on summary conviction to imprisonment for a term not exceeding **three months** or to a fine not exceeding **the statutory maximum** or to both, and

(b) on conviction on indictment to imprisonment for a term not exceeding **two years** or to a fine of any amount or to both.

[Gas Act 1965, s 21, as amended by the Gas Act 1972, Sch 6, the Criminal Law Act 1977, s 28, the Magistrates' Courts Act 1980, Sch 7 and the Gas Act 1986, Sch 7.]

---

1. The Gas Act 1986, post.
2. See Gas Act 1986, post, which requires that proceedings for an offence may not be instituted except by or with the consent of the Secretary of State or by the Director of Public Prosecutions.
3. See PART I: MAGISTRATES' COURTS, PROCEDURE, para **1–301 Aid, abet, counsel or procure**, ante.
4. This subsection provides for a penalty to be imposed on a public gas transporter for failure to comply with the Minister's directions as to safety conditions.
5. This subsection provides for a penalty to be imposed on a public gas transporter for failure to comply with an order relating to the discontinuance of an underground gas storage.
6. For procedure in respect of this offence which is triable either way, see the Magistrates' Courts Act 1980, ss 17A–21, in PART I, ante.

8–9126   22. Notices.   (1) Section 46 of the principal Act[1] (service of notices) shall apply as if any reference in that section to the principal Act included a reference to this Part of this Act.

(2) *Inquiries held by Minister.*

[Gas Act 1965, s 22 as amended by the Gas Act 1972, Sch 6, and the Gas Act 1986, Sch 7.]

---

1. The Gas Act 1986, post.

Nuclear Installations Act 1965
(1965 c 57)

8–9140   This Act provides for the licensing of sites for nuclear installations. The Act has been amended by SI 1974/2056 consequent upon the enactment of the Health and Safety at Work etc Act 1974. It provides that dangerous occurrences in connection with such sites shall be reported by the licensee to the Secretary of State. The Secretary of State may appoint inspectors to assist in the execution of the Act. Non-compliance with or contravention of the Act's several provisions is an offence punishable in varying degrees on summary conviction or on indictment. As a result of amendments by SI 1974/2056 the punishment for some offences is that prescribed by s 33 of the Health and Safety at Work etc Act 1974. Certain proceedings may be instituted only by the Minister of Power or by or with the consent of the Director of Public Prosecutions.

Energy Act 1976
(1976 c 76)

Permanent and reserve powers for energy conservation and control

8–9151   1. General control by order.   (1) The Secretary of State may by order[1] provide for regulating or prohibiting the production, supply, acquisition or use of—

(a) any of the following substances, namely—

(i) crude liquid petroleum, natural gas[2] and petroleum products[2];

(ii) any substance, whether solid, liquid or gaseous, not falling within sub-paragraph (i) above but used as fuel, whether for the propulsion of vehicles or for any other purposes;

(b) electricity.

(2)–(3) *Procedure for making orders under subsection* (1).

(4) The Secretary of State may by order provide for regulating the price at which crude liquid petroleum, natural gas or petroleum products may be supplied.

This power is exercisable at any time in the case of petroleum products, but otherwise only when an Order in Council under section 3 is in force.

[Energy Act 1976, s 1.]

---

1. Contravention of or failure to comply with an order made under s 1 is an offence (see s 18, post; for penalties, see s 19, post). For restrictions on instituting proceedings under sub-s (4), see Sch 2, para 6(2), post. By virtue of s 22 and

Sch 4, Pt III, the Fuel and Electricity (Heating) (Control) Order 1974, SI 1974/2160, amended by SI 1980/1013, continues in force as if made under sub-s (1).

   2. For meaning of "natural gas" and "petroleum products", see s 21, post.

8–9152   2. Reserve power to control by government directions.   (1) When an Order in Council under section 3 of this Act is in force the Secretary of State may give directions[1]—

   (*a*) to any person carrying on an undertaking in the course of which he produces any substance mentioned in section 1(1) above, as to the production and use of that subject;

   (*b*) to any person carrying on an undertaking in the course of which he supplies any such substance, as to the supply by him of that substance; and

   (*c*) to any person carrying on an undertaking which involves the use of any such substance, as to the use by him of that substance for the purposes of the undertaking.

   (2) Without prejudice to the generality of subsection (1) above—

   (*a*) a direction under subsection (1)(*a*) may prohibit or restrict the use of any material for the production of a substance mentioned in section 1(1) and may extend to the disposal of stocks of such a substance or of any such material;

   (*b*) a direction under subsection (1)(*b*) may—

      (i) prohibit or restrict the supply (anywhere in the world) of any such substance to specified persons, and

      (ii) require the supply (anywhere in the world) of any such substance to specified persons in accordance with specified requirements, including, in the case of crude liquid petroleum, natural gas[2] or petroleum products[2], requirements as to price; and

   (*c*) a direction under subsection (1)(*c*) may prohibit or restrict the use of any substance mentioned in section 1(1) for specified purposes or during specified periods.

   (3) In this section "specified" means specified by the Secretary of State's directions.

   (4) This section (except subsection (2)(*b*)(ii) so far as it relates to requirements as to price) applies in relation to electricity as it applies in relation to the substances mentioned in section 1(1). [Energy Act 1976, s 2.]

----

   1. Contravention of or failure to comply with a direction under s 2 is an offence (see s 18, post; for penalties, see s 19, post).

   2. For meaning of "natural gas" and "petroleum products", see s 21, post.

8–9153   3. Implementation of reserve powers.   (1) Her Majesty may by Order in Council declare the powers of sections 1 and 2 above exercisable to their fullest extent.

   (2) Any such Order in Council shall cease to be in force on the expiration of 28 days beginning on the date on which it was made, unless before the end of that period it is approved by resolution of each House of Parliament. [Energy Act 1976, s 3—summarised.]

8–9154   4. Other powers.   (1) A person supplying or using a substance mentioned in section 1(1) above may, if authorised to do so by the Secretary of State by any general or special authority granted for the purpose, and while acting in accordance with that authority, disregard or fall short in discharging any obligation imposed by or under an enactment, or any contractual obligation, relating to or involving the supply or use of that substance.

   This subsection has effect only at a time when there is in force an Order in Council under section 3(1).

   (2) At any time when an Order in Council is in force, the Secretary of State may grant, or enable any person to grant on his behalf, a general or special authority for the doing, during the whole or any part of the period for which the Order remains in force, of all or any of the things mentioned in Schedule 1 to this Act (relaxations of road traffic and transport law).

   (3) Her Majesty may by Order in Council make provision for modifying or excluding any obligation or restriction imposed, or extending any power conferred, by or under an enactment which directly or indirectly affects the use of a substance mentioned in section 1(1).

   (4) While an Order in Council is in force under section 3(1)—

   (*a*) subsection (3) above has effect as if for "affects the use" there were substituted "affects the supply or use"; and

   (*b*) without prejudice to the generality of the subsection, the powers under it extend to making such provision for modifying an order under section 2 of the Counter-Inflation Act 1973 as appears to Her Majesty to be necessary or expedient for the purpose of price controls under this Act.

   (5) This section applies in relation to electricity as it applies in relation to substances mentioned in section 1(1). [Energy Act 1976, s 4.]

8–9155   **5. Sections 1 to 4: territorial application.**   (1) A power under sections 1 to 4 may be exercised in relation to anything which is wholly or partly situated in, or to activity wholly of partly in—

    (*a*)   the United Kingdom,

    (*b*)   the territorial sea of the United Kingdom, or

    (*c*)   an area designated under the Continental Shelf Act 1964 (c 29),

    (2)   Subsection (1) is without prejudice to section 2(2)(*b*).

[Energy Act 1976, s 5 as inserted by the Civil Contigencies Act 2004, Sch 2.]

Maintenance of fuel reserves

8–9156   **6. Bulk stocks of petroleum, etc.**   (1) Directions[1] under this section may be given to any person who in the course of an undertaking[2] carried on by him produces, supplies or uses crude liquid petroleum, or petroleum products[2].

    (2)   The Secretary of State may—

    (*a*)   direct any such person to make such arrangements with respect to his United Kingdom stocks of crude liquid petroleum, or of petroleum products, as will—

       (i)   enable those stocks to be brought within a specified time to, and thereafter maintained at, a specified level, and

       (ii)   ensure that they do not fall below that level, except as may be permitted by the terms of the direction or by authority of the Secretary of State;

    (*b*)   in the case of any person who is a substantial supplier to the United Kingdom market, direct him to create such stocks and make such arrangements with respect to them.

    (3)   In giving such directions, the Secretary of State shall have regard in particular to—

    (*a*)   the quantities of crude liquid petroleum, or of petroleum products, which have been supplied by the undertaking to the United Kingdom market in past periods; and

    (*b*)   the extent to which crude liquid petroleum and petroleum products produced or supplied by the undertaking are, or will be, indigenous.

"Indigenous", in relation to crude liquid petroleum, means won under the authority of licences granted under United Kingdom legislation[3], and in relation to petroleum products means produced in the United Kingdom from indigenous crude.

    (4)   A direction given to a person under this section may require a specified portion of his stocks to be held in Northern Ireland.

    (5)   Before giving a direction under this section the Secretary of State shall notify the substance of the proposed direction to the person to whom he proposes to give it and shall afford him a reasonable opportunity to make representations.

    (6)   In this section "specified" means specified by the Secretary of State's direction; and the Secretary of State may by order[4] prescribe, as respects the effect of, and compliance with, directions under this section—

    (*a*)   the cases and circumstances in which stocks (in the United Kingdom or elsewhere) are to be treated, in relation to any person, as his United Kingdom stocks, and those in which a person is to be treated as a substantial supplier to the United Kingdom market;

    (*b*)   the extent to which stocks of a particular kind are to count towards compliance with a direction specifying stocks of another kind; and

    (*c*)   the method by which quantities are to be measured for different purposes.

[Energy Act 1976, s 6.]

---

   1.   Contravention of or failure to comply with a direction under s 6 is an offence (see s 18, post; for penalties, see s 19, post). For restrictions on instituting proceedings under this section, see Sch 2, para 6(1), post.

   2.   For meaning of "undertaking" and "petroleum products", see s 21, post.

   3.   "United Kingdom legislation" includes any enactment for the time being in force in any part of the United Kingdom (s 21).

   4.   The Petroleum Stocks Order 1976, SI 1976/2162, amended by SI 1980/1609 and SI 1983/909, has been made.

Other measures for controlling energy sources and promoting economy

8–9157   **14. Fuelling of new and converted power stations[1].**   (1) A person who proposes to carry out works—

    (*a*)   for the establishment of an electricity generating station to be fuelled by crude liquid petroleum, any petroleum product[2] or natural gas[2]; or

    (*b*)   for the conversion of an electricity generating station with a view to its being so fuelled,

shall, unless his case is one excepted by order of the Secretary of State under subsection (4), give written notice of the proposal to him.

    (2)   A person who proposes—

(*a*) to enter into contractual or other arrangements for obtaining a supply of natural gas as fuel for an electricity generating station; or

(*b*) to extend the duration of any such arrangements (whether made before or after the passing of this Act),

shall unless the arrangements fall within the scope of a general authority granted by the Secretary of State by order under subsection (5), give written notice of the proposal to him.

(3) The Secretary of State may, if he thinks it expedient having regard to current energy policies, direct that a proposal notified to him under this section be not carried out, or be carried out in accordance with conditions specified in the direction.

(4) The Secretary of State may by order[3] prescribe cases in which notice under subsection (1) above need not be given; and the cases prescribed may be those where—

(*a*) the plant is of less than specified capacity or is used only for specified purposes; or

(*b*) such other circumstances obtain as make it unnecessary in the Secretary of State's opinion for him to be given notice under the subsection.

(5) The Secretary of State may by order grant authority for the purposes of subsection (2) above for fuel supply arrangements of any description specified in the order[3].

(6) This section does not affect section 36 of the Electricity Act 1989 (which operates so as, in certain circumstances, to require the Secretary of State's consent for power station construction etc).
[Energy Act 1976, s 14 as amended by the Energy Act 1983, Sch 4 and the Electricity Act 1989, Sch 16.]

---

1. Contravention of or failure to comply with the provisions of subsections (1), (2) and (3) is an offence (see s 18, post; for penalties, see s 19, post).
2. For meaning of "petroleum product" and "natural gas", see s 21, post.
3. See the Electricity Generating Stations (Fuel Control) Order 1987, SI 1987/2175 and the Electricity Generating Stations (Gas Contracts) Order 1995, SI 1995/2450.

8–9158 15. Passenger car fuel consumption[1]. (1) Subject to the provisions of this section, the Secretary of State may in relation to passenger cars make orders[2]—

(*a*) requiring fuel consumption to be determined by means of officially approved tests; and

(*b*) providing for test results, showing the consumption of different classes or descriptions of cars in standard conditions, to be recorded in official fuel economy certificates and published in the special manner.

(2) The orders may provide—

(*a*) for requiring manufacturers or importers of cars to carry out officially approved tests, or to arrange for such tests to be carried out (by making available a car to officers of the Secretary of State's department for that purpose, or otherwise);

(*b*) for tests to be repeated from time to time with a view to the issue, where appropriate, of amended or amplified certificates;

(*c*) for payment of fees in connection with testing; and

(*d*) for official approval to be extended to tests carried out in other countries, and for the results of such tests to be adopted, certified and published in the United Kingdom.

(3) As from a date appointed by such an order[2] in relation to any class or description of cars—

(*a*) no person shall, in the course of a business, deal in or offer for sale new cars of that class or description unless the relevant official tests have been carried out;

(*b*) every person who issues material to the general public with a view to promoting sales of cars of that class or description (especially advertisements, technical specifications, sales brochures and the like) shall, if the material contains any statement about fuel consumption, include specified information as to the results of the relevant official tests;

(*c*) every manufacturer or, in the case of imported cars, importer of cars of that class or description shall secure that any manual or handbook compiled with a view to a copy of it being issued to any first purchaser of such a car includes specified information as to the results of the relevant official tests;

(*d*) every person who, in the course of a business, deals in or offers for sale new cars of that class or description shall make available for inspection by his customers at any place where he causes such cars to be offered for sale, or regularly transacts business with customers relating to the sale of such cars, specified information as to the results of officially approved tests on all cars which have been subjected to the tests, including not only cars which he deals in or offers for sale, but also those which he does not; and

(*e*) no person shall, with a view to promoting the sale of new cars of that class or description, display such a car on premises where he carries on a business unless the car has affixed to it, so as to be clearly visible to those to whom the car is displayed, a label in specified form containing specified information including—

(i) the results of the relevant official tests; and

(ii) the fact that the results of officially approved tests on other cars are available for inspection by customers.

(4) The cars about whose fuel consumption provision may be made by orders under this section are road vehicles constructed solely for carrying passengers and their effects and adapted to carry not more than eight passengers excluding the driver.

(5) *Secretary of State to consult with the motor industry with respect to orders under this section.*

(6) Orders under this section may classify and describe cars by reference to—

(a) manufacturer, mark, serial number, trade appellation or country of origin;

(b) design and application (including passenger and baggage carrying capacity);

(c) technical characteristics (including engine size, mode of transmission and carburation system); or

(d) date of manufacture, date of issue from factory or date of importation into the United Kingdom,

or to any such combination of those matters, or of those and other similar matters, as the Secretary of State thinks best adapted to keeping the public informed about the fuel consumption of cars on the market.

(7) In this section—

(a) "relevant official tests", in relation to any car, means the officially approved tests carried out or, as the case may be, required to be carried out (pursuant to orders under this section) on cars of that class or description; and

(b) "specified" means specified by such orders;

and the orders may specify the cases in which a car is to be regarded as a new car and those in which a person is, or is not, to be regarded as one who deals in new cars.

[Energy Act 1976, s 15.]

---

1. Contravention of or failure to comply with the provisions of s 15 or an order made thereunder is an offence (see s 18, post; for penalties, see s 19, post).

2. The Passenger Car Fuel Consumption Order 1983, SI 1983/1486 amended by SI 1996/1132, has been made. The functions of the Secretary of State under s 15 and the Passenger Car Fuel Consumption Order 1977 were transferred to him by SI 1980/1719 and SI 1981/238.

Miscellaneous and general

8–9159 **17.** *Orders and directions.*

8–9160 **18. Administration, enforcement and offences.** (1) Schedule 2 to this Act has effect with respect to the administration and enforcement of this Act and provision made under it, including powers of obtaining information, powers of entry, consent for taking proceedings and other matters.

(2) A person commits an offence if—

(a) without reasonable excuse he contravenes or fails to comply with any provision made by this Act, or made under it by order, direction or otherwise (but subject to subsection (3) below in the case of sections 8, 9 and 12); or

(b) he wilfully obstructs any person exercising a power conferred, or performing a duty imposed, by or under this Act; or

(c) he contravenes or fails to comply with any directly applicable Community obligation specified in Schedule 3[1] to this Act; or

(d) in furnishing any information—

(i) in purported compliance with such a Community obligation; or

(ii) for the purposes of this Act, or of an order made or direction given under it,

or in a notice given for any of those purposes, he makes or causes to be made on his behalf a statement which he knows to be false or does not believe to be true; or

(e) he has in his possession without lawful excuse a document purporting to be one issued for the purposes of this Act, or of an order made or direction given under it, which is not such a document but so closely resembles it as to be calculated to deceive.

(3) In respect of contraventions of, or failure to comply with—

(a) any provision made by section 9 or 12 of this Act; or

(b) any condition of a consent given by the Secretary of State thereunder,

criminal proceedings do not lie; but this is without prejudice to other methods of obtaining compliance with statutory obligations.

(4) Where an offence under this Act committed by a body corporate is proved to have been committed with the consent or connivance of, or to be attributable to any neglect on the part of, any director, manager, secretary or other similar officer of a body corporate, or any person who was purporting to act in any such capacity, he as well as the body corporate is guilty of that offence and liable to be proceeded against and punished accordingly.

(5) Where the affairs of a body corporate are managed by its members subsection (4) applies in relation to the acts and defaults of a member in connection with his functions of management as if he were a director of the body corporate.

[Energy Act 1976, s 18 as amended by the Oil and Gas (Enterprise) Act 1982, Sch 4 and the Gas Act 1986, Sch 9.]

---

1. The following EEC Council Regulations are specified in Schedule 3:

    (*a*)   Council Regulation (EEC) No 1055/72 on notification of imports of crude oil and natural gas;
    (*b*)   Council Regulation (EEC) No 1056/72 on notification of certain investment projects;
    (*c*)   Council Regulation (EEC) No 293/74 on information for the purposes of Community energy policy;
    (*d*)   Council Regulation (EEC) No 3254/74 on notification of imports of certain petroleum products;
    (*e*)   Council Regulation (EEC) No 388/75 on notification of exports of crude oil and natural gas.

8–9161   **19. Penalties.**   (1) Subject to subsections (2) and (3) below, a person guilty of an offence under this Act is liable on summary conviction to a fine of not more than **level 5** on the standard scale.

(2) In the case of a contravention of, or failure to comply with—

    (*a*)   price controls; or
    (*b*)   section 14(1) or (2); or
    (*c*)   a direction of the Secretary of State given under section 6, 7 or 14(3),

the person guilty is liable[1] either as provided in subsection (1) or on conviction on indictment to a fine.

(3) In the case of a contravention of, or failure to comply with—

    (*a*)   a direction under section 2; or
    (*b*)   a provision or an order under this Act to which this subsection has been applied in accordance with subsection (4) below,

and in the case of an offence under section 18(2)(*d*) or (*e*), the person guilty is liable[1] on summary conviction to imprisonment for a term of not more than **three months**, or to a fine of not more than **the statutory maximum** or both, or on conviction on indictment to imprisonment for a term of not more than **two years** or to a fine, or both.

(4) An order under section 1 of this Act made at a time when there is in force an Order in Council under section 3 may apply the higher penalties of subsection (3) above to a contravention of, or failure to comply with, particular provisions of the order committed at a time when such an Order in Council is in force; and those penalties then apply in place of those provided by subsections (1) and (2).

[Energy Act 1976, s 19, as amended by the Criminal Law Act 1977, s 28 and the Criminal Justice Act 1982, ss 38 and 46.]

---

1. For procedure in respect of this offence which is triable either way, see the Magistrates' Courts Act 1980, ss 17A–21, in PART I, ante. On summary conviction the maximum fine for an offence triable either way is £5,000 (Magistrates' Court Act 1980, s 32 as amended); the penalty in sub-s (1), therefore, no longer applies to offences triable either way.

8–9162   **21. Interpretation.**   In this Act—

    "enactment" includes an enactment of the Parliament of Northern Ireland and a Measure of the Northern Ireland Assembly;
    "International Energy Agency" and "International Energy Agreement" mean, respectively, the body established by the Decision of the Council of the Organisation for Economic Co-operation and Development on 15th November 1974, and the Agreement on an International Energy Program signed at Paris on 18th November 1974;
    "natural gas" means any gas derived from natural strata;
    "petroleum products" means the following substances produced directly or indirectly from crude, that is to say, fuels, lubricants, bitumen, wax, industrial spirits and any wide-range substance (meaning a substance whose final boiling point at normal atmospheric pressure is more than 50˚C higher than its initial boiling point);
    "price controls" means orders under section 1(4) of this Act and directions under section 2 imposing requirements as to price;
    "Standard Industrial Classification" means the revised edition published by Her Majesty's Stationery Office in 1968 of the publication of that name prepared by the Central Statistical Office;
    "undertaking" includes a business, and also any activity carried on by a body of persons, whether corporate or unincorporate; and
    "United Kingdom legislation" includes any enactment for the time being in force in any part of the United Kingdom.

[Energy Act 1976, s 21 as amended by the Industrial Development Act 1982, Sch 2 and the Co-operative Development Agency and Industrial Development Act 1984, Sch 1.]

SCHEDULES

Section 4(2)   SCHEDULE 1
RELAXATIONS OF ROAD TRAFFIC AND TRANSPORT LAW PERMISSIBLE UNDER SECTION 4(2)

(As amended by the Transport Act 1980, Schs 5 and 9, the Public Passenger Vehicles Act 1981 Sch 7, the Transport Act 1985, Sch 8, the Road Traffic (Consequential Provisions) Act 1988, Sch 3, the Electricity Act 1989, Sch 18, the Road Traffic (Driver Licensing and Information Systems) Act 1989, Sch 3 and SI 1996/1974.)

8–9163   **1.** (1) A person acting under and in accordance with a general or special authority granted by the Secretary of State under section 4(2) of this Act may provide any stage carriage service or use, any vehicle on a road as a stage carriage, an express carriage or a contract carriage—

    (*a*)   without a licence, certificate, agreement or consent otherwise required; and
    (*b*)   notwithstanding that the vehicle does not comply with regulations; and
    (*c*)   notwithstanding that any conditions attached to any licence under Part II of the Public Passenger Vehicles Act 1981 are not complied with;
    (*d*)   *Repealed.*

(2) The regulations here referred to are those made under the Public Passenger Vehicles Act 1981, or such of the regulations made or having effect as if made under section 41 of the Road Traffic Act 1988 (construction and use of motor vehicles and their equipment) as apply to a vehicle used as mentioned in this paragraph and do not apply to a vehicle not so used.

  2. (1) A person acting under and in accordance with such an authority may—

    (*a*)   drive a passenger-carrying vehicle notwithstanding that his licence does not authorise him to do so; or
    (*b*)   cause or permit to drive any such vehicle a person whose licence does not so authorise him.

(2) In this paragraph—

"Community licence" has the same meaning as in Part III of the Road Traffic Act 1988;
"licence" means a licence under that Part or a Community licence; and
"passenger-carrying vehicle" has the same meaning as in Part IV of that Act.

  3. A person acting under and in accordance with such an authority may, to such extent and in accordance with such conditions as may be specified in the authority, act, or cause or permit another person to act, as the driver of a vehicle without complying with the requirements of section 96(1) to (6) of the Transport Act 1968 (as for the time being in force).

  4. (1) A person charged under section 143 of the Road Traffic Act 1988 with the offence of using, or causing or permitting the use, of a motor vehicle so as to contravene that section (driving uninsured) may prove as a defence that the vehicle was being used by authority of the Secretary of State under section 4(2) of this Act and that—

    (*a*)   it was at the material time the subject of insurance or security complying with Part VI of the 1988 Act; and
    (*b*)   pursuant to arrangements made by or with the Secretary of State for the purposes of section 4(2), the insurance or security is treated as extending to its use on that occasion.

(2) A person charged under section 165 or 170 of the Road Traffic Act 1988 with an offence of failing to produce the relevant certificate of insurance or certificate of security within the meaning of Part VI of that Act may prove as a defence that the vehicle was being used by authority of the Secretary of State under section 4(2) of this Act and that—

    (*a*)   he produced a certificate of insurance or certificate of security complying with Part VI of that Act; and
    (*b*)   pursuant to arrangements made by or with the Secretary of State for the purposes of section 4(2), the insurance or security to which the certificate relates is treated as extending to the use in question.

Section 18(1)   SCHEDULE 2
ADMINISTRATION AND OTHER MATTERS[1]

Power to obtain information

8–9164   **1.** (1) Subject to the provisions of this paragraph, the Secretary of State may direct any person carrying on an undertaking[2]—

    (*a*)   to keep such books, accounts and records relating to a substance mentioned in section 1(1) of this Act, or to electricity, as may be specified;
    (*b*)   to furnish, as and when specified, estimates, forecasts, returns and information relating to such a substance, or to electricity;
    (*c*)   to furnish, as and when specified, information and forecasts relating to the undertaking itself or its activities, including the way in which the undertaking is organised and administered and the character and extent of its operations.

(2) All the powers of this paragraph are exercisable by the Secretary of State where it appears to him expedient for the purpose of implementing obligations incumbent on the United Kingdom as a member of the European Communities or the International Energy Agency[2] or as a party to the International Energy Agreement[2], and the powers conferred by paragraphs (*a*) and (*b*) of sub-paragraph (1) are also exercisable where it appears to the Secretary of State expedient for any purpose connected with the operation of this Act or the effective performance by him of his functions under it.

(3) In this paragraph "specified" means specified by the Secretary of State's directions.

---

1. Contravention of or failure to comply with any provision of this Schedule or a direction made thereunder is an offence (see s 18, *ante*; for penalties, see s 19, *ante*).

2. For meaning of "undertaking", "International Energy Agency" and "International Energy Agreement", see s 21, ante.

Power to call for documents

8–9165　2. (1) The powers of this paragraph are exercisable—

(a) by a person authorised by or on behalf of the Secretary of State, on production (if so required) of his authorisation;

(b) for the purpose of securing compliance with any provision made by or under this Act, and of checking estimates and forecasts or verifying returns and information provided in response to directions under paragraph 1 above.

(2) The powers are—

(a) to require any person to produce for inspection, or to deliver up, any document in his possession or control which has been issued by or on the authority of the Secretary of State in connection with the administration and enforcement of this Act, or any provision made under it;

(b) to require any person with executive functions in an undertaking, or the persons carrying it on, to produce documents relating to the undertaking or its operations, and allow copies or extracts to be made from them;

(c) to require any such person, or one who has in the preceding 5 years exercised such functions, to provide further particulars as to the whereabouts, contents or subject matter of such documents.

Access to premises etc for enforcement purposes

8–9166　3. (1) Subject to sub-paragraph (2) below, a person authorised by or on behalf of the Secretary of State may for the purpose—

(a) of securing compliance with orders made and directions given by the Secretary of State under this Act;

(b) of checking estimates and forecasts or verifying returns and information provided in response to directions under paragraph 1 of this Schedule;

at all reasonable hours and on production (if so required) of his authorisation, go on any premises and there make such enquiries and inspections, and purchase or take such samples of any substance, as are allowed by the terms of his authorisation or he thinks necessary for those purposes.

(2) The powers of this paragraph are not exercisable—

(a) for the purposes only of securing compliance with orders under section 15 of this Act;

(b) except when an Order in Council under section 3 of this Act is in force, for the purpose only of securing compliance with orders under section 1(1).

(3) The reference in this paragraph to premises includes vehicles and vessels, but not any premises used as a dwelling.

Entry with warrant

8–9167　4. (1) Subject to sub-paragraph (4) below, if a justice of the peace (in Scotland a justice of the peace or a sheriff) is satisfied, on sworn information in writing submitted on behalf of the Secretary of State, that—

(a) admission to premises is reasonably required for any of the purposes mentioned in paragraph 3(1) above; and

(b) the circumstances specified in sub-paragraph (2) or, as the case may be, sub-paragraph (3) below are present,

the justice or sheriff may issue a warrant naming a person authorised by the Secretary of State and authorising that person to enter the premises, by force if necessary.

(2) If no Order in Council under section 3 of this Act is for the time being in force the circumstances in which a warrant may be issued are that either—

(a) admission to the premises has been refused after, if the case is not one of urgency, not less than seven days' notice of the intention to enter had been given to the occupier; or

(b) application for admission would defeat the object for the entry or the premises are unoccupied.

(3) If such an Order in Council is for the time being in force the circumstances in which a warrant may be issued are that either—

(a) admission to the premises has been refused, or a refusal is apprehended, and notice of intention to apply for a warrant has been given to the occupier; or

(b) application for admission would defeat the object of the entry, or the case is one of urgency, or the premises are unoccupied or the occupier is temporarily absent.

(4) A warrant under this paragraph—

(a) is not to be issued authorising entry for the purpose only of securing compliance with orders under section 15 of this Act;

(b) except when an Order in Council under section 3 of this Act is in force, is not to be issued authorising entry for the purpose only of securing compliance with orders under section 1(1).

(5) A person entering premises under the authority of the warrant may search the premises and take possession of any documents which he finds there and which appear to him to be relevant to the purposes for which the warrant was obtained.

(6) Any documents of which possession is taken under this paragraph may be retained for a period of 3 months or, if within that period there are commenced any proceedings for an offence under this Act to which they are relevant, until the conclusion of those proceedings.

(7) If the premises are unoccupied or the occupier is temporarily absent, the person entering them under the authority of the warrant shall leave them as effectively secured against trespassers as he found them.

(8) The warrant continues in force until the end of one month beginning with the date on which it was issued.

(9) References in this paragraph to premises include vehicles and vessels, but not any premises used only as a dwelling.

Price control enforcement

8–9168   5. (1) The Secretary of State may designate a local weights and measures authority for the purposes of the enforcement within its area of price controls[1] in relation to supplies to the general public.

(2) The powers of paragraphs 2 and 3 above are also exercisable by a duly authorised officer of a designated local weights and measures authority, for the purpose of securing compliance with price controls in relation to such supplies.

(3) If a justice of the peace (in Scotland, a justice of the peace or a sheriff) is satisfied, on sworn information in writing submitted on behalf of a designated local weights and measures authority, that—

    (a)   admission to premises is reasonably required for that purpose; and

    (b)   the circumstances specified in paragraph 4(2) or, as the case may be (3) above are present,

the justice or sheriff may issue a warrant authorising a duly authorised officer of the authority (naming him) to enter the premises, by force if necessary; and paragraph 4(5) to (9) above also applies in relation to this warrant.

---

1. For meaning of "price controls", see s 21, ante.

Proceedings

8–9169   6. (1) Proceedings for an offence of contravening or failing to comply with a direction of the Secretary of State given under section 6 of this Act shall be instituted only by, or with the consent of, the Secretary of State or the Director of Public Prosecutions.

(2) Proceedings for an offence of contravening or failing to comply with price controls[1] shall be instituted only—

    (a)   by or on behalf of a local weights and measures authority designated under paragraph 5 above; or

    (b)   by, or with the consent of, the Secretary of State or the Director of Public Prosecutions.

(3)–(4) *Scotland and Northern Ireland.*

---

1. For meaning of "price controls", see s 21, ante.

Non-disclosure of information

8–9180   7. No information obtained by virtue of this Act shall be disclosed except—

    (a)   with the consent of the person by whom or on whose behalf the information was given or supplied and, where applicable, of the owner of any goods, or the occupier of any premises, to which the information relates;

    (b)   for the purpose of the exercise of any of its functions, to a government department (including a department of the government of Northern Ireland);

    (c)   to any institution of the European Communities, or to the International Energy Agency, in pursuance of obligations incumbent on the United Kingdom to transmit the information or see to its transmission;

    (d)   in the form of statistics or otherwise, so that it cannot readily be recognised as relating to any particular person or undertaking;

    (e)   with a view to the institution, or otherwise for the purposes, of any criminal proceedings.

Proof of documents

8–9181   8. (1) Every document purporting to be an instrument made by any person in pursuance of this Act and to be signed by or on behalf of that person shall be received in evidence and shall until the contrary is proved be deemed to be such an instrument.

(2) Prima facie evidence of any such instrument may in any legal proceedings (including arbitrations) be given by the production of a document purporting to be certified to be a true copy of the instrument by or on behalf of the person having power to make or issue the instrument.

(3) Prima facie evidence of—

    (a)   any general authority granted under section 4(1) or (2) of this Act;

    (b)   any exemption under section 17(4)(b) relating to a class of persons, premises or undertakings; or

    (c)   the variation or revocation of such an authority or exemption,

may be given in any legal proceedings (including arbitrations) by the production of a copy of the London, Edinburgh or Belfast Gazette purporting to contain such an authority or exemption or (as the case may be) the variation or revocation.

Nuclear Safeguards and Electricity (Finance) Act 1978[1]

(1978 c 25)

Safeguards on nuclear material

8–9182   2. Rights of Agency inspectors.   (1) Subject to subsection (2) below, for the purpose of—

    (a)   making any inspection permitted by articles 71 to 84; or

    (b)   verifying design information, as mentioned in article 50,

any person designated as an inspector of the International Atomic Energy Agency under article 85 of the Safeguards Agreement or Article 11 of the Additional Protocol (within the meaning of the Nuclear Safeguards Act 2000) may enter any facility or part thereof and there make any inspection or do any other thing which may reasonably be required for that purpose.

(2) The powers conferred by subsection (1) above shall be exercisable only in the cases specified in, and subject to the provisions of, the Safeguards Agreement and, in particular—

(*a*) shall be exercisable only in accordance with articles 5, 9(*c*) and 87 and the provisions of the Protocol which forms part of the Safeguards Agreement; and

(*b*) where article 83 applies, shall not be exercisable unless any advance notice required by that article has been given.

(3) *Repealed.*

(4) Any person who—

(*a*) intentionally obstructs any person exercising a power conferred by subsection (1) above; or

(*b*) without reasonable excuse refuses or fails to provide any information or to permit any inspection reasonably required by any such person; or

(*c*) without reasonable excuse refuses or fails to carry out in a facility any operation which he is requested to carry out by a person designated as mentioned in subsection (1) above,

shall be guilty of an offence[2].

(4A) A person guilty of an offence under subsection (4) above shall be liable[2]—

(*a*) on summary conviction, to a fine not exceeding the statutory maximum; and

(*b*) on conviction on indictment, to a fine.

(5) If any person in giving any information reasonably required by any person exercising a power conferred by subsection (1) above makes any statement which he knows to be false in a material particular or recklessly makes any statement which is false in a material particular he shall be liable[2]—

(*a*) on summary conviction to a fine not exceeding **the statutory maximum**; and

(*b*) on conviction on indictment, to imprisonment for a term not exceeding **two years**, or a fine, or both.

(6) *Repealed.*

(7) In this section "facility" has the meaning assigned to it by article 92(2).

(8) If in any proceedings any question arises whether a person at any time when purporting to exercise powers under this section was or was not a person designated as mentioned in subsection (1) above, a certificate issued by or under the authority of the Secretary of State stating any fact relevant to that question shall be conclusive evidence of that fact.

[Nuclear Safeguards and Electricity (Finance) Act 1978, s 2, amended by the Magistrates' Courts Act 1980, Sch 7, the Criminal Justice Act 1982, s 46, the Statute Law (Repeals) Act 1993, Sch 1 and the Nuclear Safeguards Act 2000, s 11.]

---

1. This Act makes provision for giving effect to an International Agreement for the application of safeguards in the United Kingdom in connection with the Treaty on the Non-Proliferation of Nuclear Weapons. This Act came into force on Royal Assent, 30 June 1978.

2. For procedure in respect of this offence which is triable either way, see the Magistrates' Courts Act 1980, ss 17A–21 in PART I: MAGISTRATES' COURTS, PROCEDURE, ante.

8–9183 3. Regulations. (1) The Secretary of State may make regulations for giving effect to certain provisions of the Safeguards Agreement. (2) Such regulations may provide that any person contravening or failing to comply with any provision of the regulations shall be liable on summary conviction to a fine not exceeding **level 4** on the standard scale.

[Nuclear Safeguards and Electricity (Finance) Act 1978, s 3 as amended by the Criminal Justice Act 1983, s 46—summarised.]

8–9184 4. Offences by bodies corporate. (1) Where an offence under section 2 above or under regulations made under section 3 above which has been committed by a body corporate is proved to have been committed with the consent or connivance of, or to be attributable to any neglect on the part of, any director, manager, secretary or other similar officer of the body corporate, or any person who was purporting to act in any such capacity, he, as well as the body corporate, shall be guilty of that offence and be liable to be proceeded against and punished accordingly.

(2) Where the affairs of a body corporate are managed by its members, subsection (1) above shall apply in relation to the acts and defaults of a member in connection with his functions of management as if he were a director of the body corporate.

[Nuclear Safeguards and Electricity (Finance) Act 1978, s 4.]

Nuclear Material (Offences) Act 1983[1]

(1983 c 18)

8–9410 1. Extended scope of certain offences. (1) If a person, whatever his nationality, does outside the United Kingdom, in relation to or by means of nuclear material, any act which, had he done it in any part of the United Kingdom, would have made him guilty of—

(a)   the offence of murder, manslaughter, culpable homicide, assault to injury, malicious mischief or causing injury, or endangering the life of the lieges, by reckless conduct, or

(b)   an offence under section 18 or 20 of the Offences against the Person Act 1861 or section 1 of the Criminal Damage Act 1971 or Article 3 of the Criminal Damage (Northern Ireland) Order 1977 or section 78 of the Criminal Justice (Scotland) Act 1980, or

(c)   the offence of theft, embezzlement, robbery, assault with intent to rob, burglary or aggravated burglary, or

(d)   the offence of fraud or extortion or an offence under section 15 or 21 of the Theft Act 1968 or section 15 or 20 of the Theft Act (Northern Ireland) 1969,

he shall in any part of the United Kingdom be guilty of such of the offences mentioned in paragraphs (a) to (d) above as are offences of which the act would have made him guilty had he done it in that part of the United Kingdom.

(2) In this section and in section 2 below, "act" includes omission.
[Nuclear Material (Offences) Act 1983, s 1.]

---

1. This Act implements the Convention on the Physical Protection of Nuclear Material. This Act was brought into force on 2 October 1991 (SI 1991/1716).

8–9411   2. Offences involving preparatory acts and threats.   (1) If a person, whatever his nationality, in the United Kingdom or elsewhere contravenes subsection (2), (3) or (4) below he shall be guilty of an offence.

(2) A person contravenes this subsection if he receives, holds or deals with nuclear material—

(a)   intending, or for the purpose of enabling another, to do by means of that material an act which is an offence mentioned in paragraph (a) or (b) of subsection (1) of section 1 above; or

(b)   being reckless as to whether another would so do such an act.

(3) A person contravenes this subsection if he—

(a)   makes to another person a threat that he or any other person will do by means of nuclear material such an act as is mentioned in paragraph (a) of subsection (2) above; and

(b)   intends that the person to whom the threat is made shall fear that it will be carried out.

(4) A person contravenes this subsection if, in order to compel a State, international governmental organisation or person to do, or abstain from doing, any act, he threatens that he or any other person will obtain nuclear material by an act which is an offence mentioned in paragraph (c) of subsection (1) of section 1 above.

(5) A person guilty of an offence under this section shall be liable on conviction on indictment to imprisonment for a term not exceeding fourteen years and not exceeding the term of imprisonment to which a person would be liable for the offence constituted by doing the contemplated act at the place where the conviction occurs and at the time of the offence to which the conviction relates.

(6) In subsection (5) above "contemplated act" means,—

(a)   where the conviction relates to an offence under subsection (2) above, the act intended or as to the doing of which the person convicted was reckless, as the case may be; and

(b)   where the conviction relates to an offence under subsection (3) or (4) above, the act threatened.

(7) In this section references to an act which is an offence mentioned in paragraph (a), (b) or (c) of subsection (1) of section 1 above are references to an act which, by virtue of that subsection or otherwise, is an offence so mentioned.
[Nuclear Material (Offences) Act 1983, s 2.]

8–9412   3. Supplemental.   (1) Proceedings for an offence which (disregarding the provisions of the Internationally Protected Persons Act 1978, the Suppression of Terrorism Act 1978, the United Nations Personnel Act 1997 and the Terrorism Act 2000) would not be an offence apart from the preceding provisions of this Act shall not be begun—

(a)   in England and Wales, except by or with the consent of the Attorney General; or

(b)   in Northern Ireland, except by or with the consent of the Attorney General for Northern Ireland.★

(2) *Scotland.*
[Nuclear Material (Offences) Act 1983, s 3 as amended by the United Nations Personnel Act 1997, Schedule and the Crime (International Co-operation) Act 2003, Sch 5.]

★**Sub-section (1)(b) words substituted by the Justice (Northern Ireland) Act 2002, s 28(2) from a date to be appointed.**

8–9413   4. Amendments of other Acts.   (1) In consequence of the provisions of this Act—

(a)   in subsections (1) and (2) of section 2 of the Internationally Protected Persons Act 1978 (which relates to certain offences committed outside the United Kingdom) after the words

"Suppression of Terrorism Act 1978" there shall be inserted in each place the words "and the Nuclear Material (Offences) Act 1983"; and

(b) in subsections (4) and (5) of section 4 of the Suppression of Terrorism Act 1978 (which also relates to certain offences committed outside the United Kingdom) after the words "Internationally Protected Persons Act 1978" there shall be inserted in each place the words "and the Nuclear Material (Offences) Act 1983".

(2) In the Schedule to the Visiting Forces Act 1952 (which specifies the offences which are offences against the person and against property for the purposes of section 3 of that Act)—

(a) at the end of each of paragraphs 1, 2 and 4 there shall be inserted the following sub-paragraph—

"(d) an offence under section 2 of the Nuclear Material (Offences) Act 1983, where the circumstances are that—

  (i) in the case of a contravention of subsection (2), the act falling within paragraph (a) or (b) of that subsection would, had it been done, have constituted an offence falling within sub-paragraph (a) or (b) of this paragraph, or

  (ii) in the case of a contravention of subsection (3) or (4), the act threatened would, had it been done, have constituted such an offence"; and

(b) at the end of paragraph 3 there shall be inserted the following sub-paragraph—

"(k) an offence under section 2 of the Nuclear Material (Offences) Act 1983, where the circumstances are that

  (i) in the case of a contravention of subsection (2), the act falling within paragraph (a) or (b) of that subsection would, had it been done, have constituted an offence falling within the foregoing sub-paragraphs, or

  (ii) in the case of a contravention of subsection (3) or (4), the act threatened would, had it been done, have constituted such an offence."

(3) In Part I of Schedule 4 to the Northern Ireland (Emergency Provisions) Act 1978 (scheduled offences for the purposes of that Act),—

(a) in paragraph 12, for the words "note 4" there shall be substituted the words "notes 4 and 5" and at the end there shall be added the following sub-paragraphs—

"(c) section 1 (theft);
(d) section 9 (burglary);
(e) section 15 (obtaining property by deception);
(f) section 20 (blackmail);"

(b) the paragraph inserted by section 2(3) of the Taking of Hostages Act 1982 as paragraph 19A shall be renumbered 19B and after that paragraph there shall be inserted the following—

"Nuclear Material (Offences) Act 1983

19C. Offences under section 2 of the Nuclear Material (Offences) Act 1983 (offences involving nuclear material: preparatory acts and threats)"; and

(c) in the Notes, for note 4 there shall be substituted the following notes—

"4. Robbery and aggravated burglary are scheduled offences only where it is charged—

(a) that an explosive, firearm, imitation firearm or weapon of offence was used to commit the offence; or

(b) that the offence was committed in relation to or by means of nuclear material within the meaning of the Nuclear Material (Offences) Act 1983;

and expressions defined in section 10 of the Theft Act (Northern Ireland) 1969 have the same meaning when used in this note.

5. An offence under section 1, 9, 15 or 20 of the Theft Act (Northern Ireland) 1969 is a scheduled offence only where it is charged that the offence was committed in relation to or by means of nuclear material within the meaning of the Nuclear Material (Offences) Act 1983."
[Nuclear Material (Offences) Act 1983, s 4.]

8–9414 6. Material to which the Act applies. (1) References in this Act to nuclear material are references to material which, within the meaning of the Convention, is nuclear material used for peaceful purposes.

(2) If in any proceedings a question arises whether any material was used for peaceful purposes, a certificate issued by or under the authority of the Secretary of State and stating that it was, or was not, so used at a time specified in the certificate shall be conclusive of that question.

(3) In any proceedings a document purporting to be such a certificate as is mentioned in subsection (2) above shall be taken to be such a certificate unless the contrary is proved.

(4) Paragraphs (a) and (b) of Article 1 of the Convention (which give the definition of "nuclear material" for the purposes of the Convention) are set out in the Schedule to this Act.

(5) In this section "the Convention" means the Convention on the Physical Protection of Nuclear Material opened for signature at Vienna and New York on 3rd March 1980.
[Nuclear Material (Offences) Act 1983, s 6 as amended by the Extradition Act 1989, s 36.]

8–9415   7. Application to Channel Islands, Isle of Man, etc.   (1) *Repealed.*

(2) Her Majesty may by Order in Council[1] make provision for extending the other provisions of this Act, with such exceptions, adaptations or modifications as may be specified in the Order, to any of the Channel Islands, the Isle of Man or any colony.
[Nuclear Material (Offences) Act 1983, s 7 as amended by the Extradition Act 1989, Sch 2.]

---

1. Orders have been made in respect of Guernsey (SI 1991/1717), Jersey (SI 1991/1718) and the Isle of Man (SI 1991/1719).

8–9416
Section 6   SCHEDULE
             ARTICLE 1(*A*) AND (*B*) OF THE CONVENTION
                     ARTICLE 1

For the purposes of this Convention:

  (*a*)   "nuclear material" means plutonium except that with isotopic concentration exceeding 80% in plutonium-238; uranium-233; uranium enriched in the isotopes 235 or 233; uranium containing the mixture of isotopes as occurring in nature other than in the form of ore or ore-residue; any material containing one or more of the foregoing;

  (*b*)   "uranium enriched in the isotope 235 or 233" means uranium containing the isotopes 235 or 233 or both in an amount such that the abundance ratio of the sum of these isotopes to the isotope 238 is greater than the ratio of the isotope 235 to the isotope 238 occurring in nature.

Gas Act 1986[1]

(1986 c 44)

PART I[2]
GAS SUPPLY
Introductory

8–9447   3. Abolition of Corporation's special privilege.   *Repealed.*

---

1. This Act provides for the appointment and functions of a Director General of Gas Supply and the establishment and functions of a Gas Consumers' Council; abolishes the privilege conferred on the British Gas Corporation and makes provision for the dissolution of that Corporation, and makes new provision with respect to the supply of gas through pipes and related matters.

    At the date of going to press all the provisions of the Act referred to below had been brought into force in accordance with s 68.
2. Part I contains ss 1–48.
3. The date appointed for the purposes of s 3 was 23 August 1986 (SI 1986/1316).

Licensing of activities relating to gas

8–9448   5. Prohibition on unlicensed activities.   (1) Subject to section 6A below and Schedule 2A[1] to this Act*, a person who—

  (*a*)   conveys gas through pipes to any premises, or to a pipe-line system operated by a gas transporter;**

  (*b*)   supplies to any premises gas which has been conveyed to those premises through pipes; or

  (*c*)   arranges with a gas transporter for gas to be introduced into, conveyed by means of or taken out of a pipe-line system operated by that transporter,

shall be guilty of an offence unless he is authorised to do so by a licence.

(2) The exceptions to subsection (1) above which are contained in Schedule 2A to this Act shall have effect.*

(3) A person guilty of an offence under this section shall be liable[2]—

  (*a*)   on summary conviction to a fine not exceeding **the statutory maximum**;

  (*b*)   on conviction on indictment, to a **fine**.

(4) No proceedings shall be instituted in England and Wales in respect of an offence under this section except by or on behalf of the Secretary of State or the Authority.

(5) Any reference in this Part to the conveyance by any person of gas through pipes to any premises is a reference to the conveyance by him of gas through pipes to those premises with a view to the gas being supplied to those premises by any person, or being used in those premises by the holder of a licence under section 7A(2) below.

(6) A reference in this Part to participating in the operation of a gas interconnector is a reference to—

(*a*)   co-ordinating and directing the conveyance of gas into or through a gas interconnector; or

(*b*)   making such an interconnector available for use for the conveyance of gas.

(7)   For the purposes of subsection (6)(*b*) a person shall not be regarded as making something available just because he consents to its being made available by another.

(8)   In this Part "gas interconnector" means so much of any pipeline system as—

(*a*)   is situated at a place within the jurisdiction of Great Britain; and

(*b*)   subsists wholly or primarily for the purposes of the conveyance of gas (whether in both directions or in only one) between Great Britain and another country or territory.

(9)   For the purposes of this section a place is within the jurisdiction of Great Britain if it is in Great Britain, in the territorial sea adjacent to Great Britain or in an area designated under section 1(7) of the Continental Shelf Act 1964.

(10)   In this section "pipe-line system" includes the pipes and any associated apparatus comprised in that system.

[Gas Act 1986, s 5, as substituted by the Gas Act 1995, s 3, as amended by the Utilities Act 2000, s 76 and Sch 6 and the Energy Act 2004, s 149.]

---

*Repealed by the Utilities Act 2000, Sch 8, when in force.

**Amended and new para (*aa*) inserted by the Energy Act Act 2004, s 149 from a date to be appointed.

1.   See, post.

2.   For procedure in respect of this offence which is triable either way, see the Magistrates' Courts Act 1980, ss 17A–21, in PART I: MAGISTRATES' COURTS, PROCEDURE, ante.

8–9449   6A. Exemptions from prohibition.   (1) The Secretary of State may by order[1] grant exemption from paragraph (*a*),* (*b*) or (*c*) of section 5(1) above—

(*a*)   either to a person or to persons of a class;

(*b*)   either generally or to such extent as may be specified in the order; and

(*c*)   either unconditionally or subject to such conditions as may be so specified.

(1A)   Before making an order under subsection (1) the Secretary of State shall give notice—

(*a*)   stating that he proposes to make such an order and setting out the terms of the proposed order;

(*b*)   stating the reasons why he proposes to make the order in the terms proposed; and

(*c*)   specifying the time (not being less than 28 days from the date of publication of the notice) within which representations with respect to the proposals may be made,

and shall consider any representations which are duly made in respect of the proposals and not withdrawn.

(1B)   The notice required by subsection (1A) shall be given—

(*a*)   by serving a copy of it on the Authority and the Council; and

(*b*)   by publishing it in such manner as the Secretary of State considers appropriate for bringing it to the attention of those likely to be affected by the proposed order.

(2)   Notice of an exemption granted to a person shall be given—

(*a*)   by serving a copy of the exemption on him; and

(*b*)   by publishing the exemption in such manner as the Secretary of State considers appropriate for bringing it to the attention of other persons who may be affected by it.

(2A)   Notice of an exemption granted to persons of a class shall be given by publishing the exemption in such manner as the Secretary of State considers appropriate for bringing it to the attention of—

(*a*)   persons of that class; and

(*b*)   other persons who may be affected by it.

(3)   An exemption may be granted—

(*a*)   indefinitely; or

(*b*)   for a period specified in, or determined by or under, the exemption.

(4)   Without prejudice to the generality of paragraph (*c*) of subsection (1) above, conditions included by virtue of that paragraph in an exemption may require any person carrying on any activity in pursuance of the exemption—

(*a*)   to comply with any direction given by the Secretary of State or the Authority as to such matters as are specified in the exemption or are of a description so specified;

(*b*)   except in so far as the Secretary of State or the Authority consents to his doing or not doing them, not to do or to do such things as are specified in the exemption or are of a description so specified; and

(*c*)   to refer for determination by the Secretary of State or the Authority such questions arising under the exemption as are specified in the exemption or are of a description so specified.

(5)   If any condition of an exemption granted to persons of a class is not complied with by any

person of that class, the Secretary of State may give to that person a direction declaring that the exemption is revoked, so far as relating to that person, to such extent and as from such date as may be specified in the direction.

[Gas Act 1986, s 6A, as substituted by the Gas Act 1995, s 4 and amended by the Utilities Act 2000, ss 3 and 86.]

---

*Reference "(aa)" inserted by the Energy Act Act 2004, s 149 from a date to be appointed.

1. See the following Gas Act 1986 (Exemptions) Orders: 1996, SI 1996/449, 471, 1354 and 2795; 1997, SI 1997/2427; 1998, SI 1998/1779; 1999, SI 1999/2639, 3026; 2005, SI 2005/16 and 3089; 2000, SI 2000/3206; 2005, SI 2005/280.

8–9450   7. Licensing of gas transporters.   (1) In this Part "gas transporter" means the holder of a licence under this section except where the holder is acting otherwise than for purposes connected with—

   (a) the carrying on of activities authorised by the licence;

   (b) the conveyance of gas through pipes which—

      (i) are situated in an authorised area of his; or

      (ii) are situated in an area which was an authorised area of his, or an authorised area of a previous holder of the licence, and were so situated at a time when it was such an area; or

   (c) the conveyance through pipes of gas which is in the course of being conveyed to or from a country or territory outside Great Britain.*

(2) Subject to subsection (3) below, the Authority may grant a licence authorising any person to do either or both of the following, namely—

   (a) to convey gas through pipes to any premises in an authorised area of the Authority, that is to say, any area specified in the licence as it has effect for the time being;

   (b) to convey gas through pipes either to any pipe-line system operated by another gas transporter, or to any pipe-line system so operated which is specified in the licence or an extension of the licence.

(3) A licence shall not be granted under this section to a person who is the holder of a licence under section 7ZA or 7A below.

(4) The Authority may, with the consent of the licence holder, direct that any licence under this section shall have effect—

   (a) as if any area or pipe-line system specified in the direction were specified in the licence;

   (b) in the case of a licence under subsection (2)(a) above, as if it were also a licence under subsection (2)(b) above and any pipe-line system specified in the direction were specified in the licence; or

   (c) in the case of a licence under subsection (2)(b) above, as if it were also a licence under subsection (2)(a) above and any area specified in the direction were specified in the licence;

and references in this Part to, or to the grant of, an extension under this section, or an extension of such a licence, shall be construed as references to, or to the giving of, such a direction.

(4A) The Authority may, with the consent of the licence holder, direct that any licence under this section shall have effect as if any area or pipe-line system specified in the direction were not specified in the licence; and references in this Part to, or to the grant of, a restriction under this section, or a restriction of such a licence, shall be construed as references to, or to the giving of, such a direction.

(5) Before granting a licence under this section, the Authority shall give notice—

   (a) stating that it proposes to grant the licence;

   (b) stating the reasons why it proposes to grant the licence; and

   (c) specifying the time from the date of publication of the notice (not being less than two months) within which representations or objections with respect to the proposed licence may be made,

and shall consider any representations or objections which are duly made and not withdrawn.

(6) A notice under subsection (5) above shall be given—

   (a) by publishing the notice in such manner as the Authority considers appropriate for bringing it to the attention of persons likely to be affected by the grant of the licence or extension; and

   (b) by sending a copy of the notice to the Secretary of State, to the Health and Safety Executive and to any gas transporter whose area includes the whole or any part of the area proposed to be specified in the licence.

(7) *Repealed.*

(8) *Repealed.*

(9) As soon as practicable after the granting of a licence under this section, the gas transporter shall publish, in such manner as the Authority considers appropriate for bringing it to the attention of persons who are likely to do business with the transporter, a notice—

   (a) stating that the licence has been granted; and

   (b) explaining that, as a result, it might be necessary for those persons to be licensed under section 7A below.

(10) In this section—

(*a*) "relevant main" has the same meaning as in section 10 below;

(*b*) references to an area specified in a licence or direction include references to an area included in an area so specified; and

(*c*) references to a pipe-line system specified in a licence or direction include references to a pipe-line system of a description, or situated in an area, so specified.

(11) *Repealed.*

[Gas Act 1986, s 7, as substituted by the Gas Act 1995, s 5 and amended by the Utilities Act 2000, ss 7, 76 and Sch 6.]

---

*Repealed by the Energy Act 2004, Sch 23 from a date to be appointed.

8–9450ZA 7ZA. Licences for operation of gas interconnectors. (1) Subject to subsection (2), the Authority may grant a licence authorising any person to participate in the operation of a gas interconnector.

(2) A licence shall not be granted under this section to a person who is the holder of a licence under section 7 or 7A.

(3) A licence under this section—

(*a*) must specify the interconnector or interconnectors in relation to which participation is authorised; and

(*b*) may limit the forms of participation in the operation of an interconnector which are authorised by the licence.]

[Gas Act 1986, s 7ZA, as inserted by the Energy Act 2004, s 149.]

8–9450A 7A. Licensing of gas suppliers and gas shippers. (1) Subject to subsection (3) below, the Authority may grant a licence authorising any person to do either or both of the following, namely—

(*a*) to supply, to any premises specified in the licence, gas which has been conveyed through pipes to those premises; and

(*b*) to supply, to any premises at a rate which, at the time when he undertakes to give the supply, he reasonably expects to exceed 2,500 therms a year, gas which has been conveyed through pipes to those premises.

(2) Subject to subsection (3) below, the Authority may grant a licence authorising any person to arrange with any gas transporter for gas to be introduced into, conveyed by means of or taken out of a pipe-line system operated by that transporter, either generally or for purposes connected with the supply of gas to any premises specified in the licence.

(3) A licence shall not be granted under this section to a person who is the holder of a licence under section 7 or 7ZA above.

(4) The Authority may, with the consent of the licence holder, direct that any licence under this section shall have effect—

(*a*) as if any premises specified in the direction were specified in the licence; or

(*b*) in the case of a licence under subsection (1)(*b*) above, as if it were also a licence under subsection (1)(*a*) above and any premises specified in the direction were specified in the licence,

and references in this Part to, or to the grant of, an extension under this section, or an extension of such a licence, shall be construed as references to, or to the giving of, such a direction.

(5) Subsection (4) above shall not apply in relation to a licence under subsection (1) above which authorises only the supply to premises of gas which has been conveyed to the premises otherwise than by a gas transporter.

(6) The Authority may, with the consent of the licence holder, direct that any licence under this section shall have effect as if any premises specified in the direction were not specified in the licence; and references in this Part to, or to the grant of, a restriction under this section, or a restriction of such a licence, shall be construed as references to, or to the giving of, such a direction.

(7) In this section references to premises specified in a licence or direction include references to premises of a description, or situated in an area, so specified.

(8) The Authority shall not, in any licence under subsection (1) above, or in any extension or restriction of such a licence, specify any premises by description or area if he is of the opinion that the description or area has been so framed as—

(*a*) in the case of a licence or extension, artificially to exclude from the licence or extension; or

(*b*) in the case of a restriction, artificially to include in the restriction,

premises likely to be owned or occupied by persons who are chronically sick, disabled or of pensionable age, or who are likely to default in the payment of charges.

(9) If the holder of a licence under subsection (1) above applies to the Authority for a restriction of the licence, or for the revocation of the licence in accordance with any term contained in it, the Authority shall, subject to subsection (8) above, accede to the application if the Authority is satisfied that such arrangements have been made as—

(a) will secure continuity of supply for all relevant consumers; and

(b) in the case of each such consumer who is supplied with gas in pursuance of a contract, will secure such continuity on the same terms as nearly as may be as the terms of the contract.

(10) A person is a relevant consumer for the purposes of subsection (9) above if—

(a) immediately before the restriction or revocation takes effect, he is being supplied with gas by the holder of the licence; and

(b) in the case of a restriction, his premises are excluded from the licence by the restriction;

and in that subsection "contract" does not include any contract which, by virtue of paragraph 8 of Schedule 2B to this Act, is deemed to have been made.

(11) In this Part "gas supplier" and "gas shipper" mean respectively the holder of a licence under subsection (1) above, and the holder of a licence under subsection (2) above, except (in either case) where the holder is acting otherwise than for purposes connected with the carrying on of activities authorised by the licence.

(12) Any reference in this Part (however expressed) to activities authorised by a licence under subsection (1) above shall be construed without regard to any exception contained in Schedule 2A to this Act.*

[Gas Act 1986, s 7A, as inserted by the Gas Act 1995, s 6 and amended by the Utilities Act 2000, s 3 and Sch 8 and the Energy Act 2004, s 149.]

---

*Repealed by the Utilities Act 2000, Sch 8, when in force.

8–9450B   7B. *Licences: general*

8–9451   8. Standard conditions of licences.   (1) Subject to subsections (2) and (3) , each condition which by virtue of section 8(2) of the Utilities Act 2000 is a standard condition for the purposes of—

(a) licences under section 7 above;

(b) licences under subsection (1) of section 7A above; or

(c) licences under subsection (2) of that section,

shall be incorporated (that is to say, incorporated by reference) in each licence under that section or, as the case may be, that subsection.*

(2) Subsection (1) above shall not apply in relation to a licence under section 7A(1) above which authorises only the supply to premises of gas which has been conveyed to the premises otherwise than by a gas transporter.

(3) Subject to the following provisions of this section, the Authority may, in granting a licence, modify any of the standard conditions to such extent as it considers requisite to meet the circumstances of the particular case.

(4) Before making any modifications under subsection (3) above, the Authority shall give notice—

(a) stating that it proposes to make the modifications and setting out their effect;

(b) stating the reasons why it proposes to make the modifications; and

(c) specifying the time (not being less than 28 days from the date of publication of the notice) within which representations or objections with respect to the proposed modifications may be made,

and shall consider any representations or objections which are duly made and not withdrawn.

(5) A notice under subsection (4) above shall be given—

(a) by publishing the notice in such manner as the Authority considers appropriate for the purpose of bringing the notice to the attention of persons likely to be affected by the making of the modifications; and

(b) by sending a copy of the notice to the Secretary of State, to the Health and Safely Executive and to the Council.

(6) If, within the time specified in the notice under subsection (4) above, the Secretary of State directs the Authority not to make any modification, the Authority shall comply with the direction.

(6A) The Authority shall not make any modifications under subsection (3) above of a condition of a licence under section 7ZA unless it is of the opinion that the modifications are such that—

(a) the licence holder would not be unduly disadvantaged in competing with one or more other holders of licences under that section; and

(b) no other holder of a licence under that section would be unduly disadvantaged in competing with the holder of the licence to be modified or with any one or more other holders of licences under that section.

(7) The Authority shall not make any modifications under subsection (3) above of a condition of a licence under subsection (1) or (2) of section 7A above unless it is of the opinion that the modifications are such that no other holder of such a licence would be unduly disadvantaged in competing with other holders of such licences (including the holder of the licence).

(8) The modification under subsection (3) above of a condition of a licence shall not prevent so

much of the condition as is not so modified being regarded as a standard condition for the purposes of this Part.

(9) In this section "modify" includes fail to incorporate and "modification" shall be construed accordingly.

[Gas Act 1986, s 8, as substituted by the Gas Act 1995, s 8 and amended by the Utilities Act 2000, s 3 and Sch 5 and the Energy Act 2004, s 150.]

---

*Amended by the Energy Act 2004, s 150 from a date to be appointed.

8–9452   8AA. *Transfer of licences*

8–9453   8A. Modification or removal of the 25,000 therm limits. *Power of the Secretary of State by order to amend s 4(2)(d), s 8(5)(b), s 10(5) or s 14(3) or (4)(b) by modifying or removing the references to therms.*

The gas code

8–9453A   8B. The gas code. The provisions of Schedule 2B[1] to this Act (which relate to rights and obligations of licence holders and consumers and related matters) shall have effect.

[Gas Act 1986, s 8B, as inserted by the Gas Act 1995, s 9.]

---

1. See this title, post.

8–9454   16. Standards of gas quality. (1) The Authority may, with the consent of the Secretary of State, prescribe—

(a) standards of pressure and purity to be complied with by gas transporters in conveying gas to premises or to pipe-line systems operated by other gas transporters; and

(b) other standards with respect to the properties, condition and composition of gas so conveyed.

(2) Before making any regulations under this section the Authority shall consult such persons and organisations as it considers appropriate and such gas transporters as appear to it to be affected by the regulations.

(3) The Authority shall appoint competent and impartial persons for the purpose of—

(a) carrying out tests of gas, apparatus or equipment in accordance with regulations under this section; and

(b) assisting the Authority in exercising functions under this section and regulations made under it.

(4) Regulations under this section may make provision—

(a) for requiring tests of gas conveyed by gas transporters to be carried out by persons appointed under subsection (3) or by gas transporters for the purpose of ascertaining whether the gas conforms with the standards prescribed by the regulations;

(b) for requiring such tests to be carried out on the basis of samples taken by persons appointed under subsection (3) or by gas transporters; and

(c) for requiring samples of gas taken under paragraph (b) to be provided by gas transporters for the purpose of carrying out such tests.

(5) Regulations under this section may make provision—

(a) for requiring such premises, apparatus and equipment as the Authority may direct to be provided and maintained by gas transporters for the purpose of carrying out tests required under subsection (4)(a);

(b) for requiring tests of apparatus and equipment so provided to be carried out by persons appointed under subsection (3); and

(c) for requiring gas transporters to carry out tests of apparatus and equipment so provided and maintained by them.

(6) Regulations under this section may make provision—

(a) as to the places or premises and the times at which, and the manner in which—

(i)   tests under this section are to be carried out;

(ii) samples of gas are to be taken and provided under this section; and

(iii) results of tests under this section are to be notified or made available;

(b) for the Authority to require by direction any matter which may be required by regulations by virtue of paragraph (a);

(c) for persons representing the gas transporter concerned to be present during the carrying out of any tests carried out by persons appointed under subsection (3);

(d) for the results of tests under this section to be made available to other licence holders and to the public;

(e) for requiring gas transporters to notify the results of such tests carried out by them to the Authority or to any person appointed under subsection (3);

(f) for conferring powers of entry on property owned or occupied by gas transporters for the purpose of carrying out tests under this section and otherwise for the purposes of the regulations.

(7) Subject to subsection (8), the Authority may by notice in writing require a gas transporter to give to the Authority, or to any person appointed by it for the purpose, within such time and at such place as may be specified in the notice, such information as the Authority may reasonably require for the purpose of making regulations under this section or of giving directions under such regulations.

(8) A gas transporter shall not be required under subsection (7) to give any information which he could not be compelled to give in evidence in civil proceedings before the High Court or, in Scotland, the Court of Session.

(9) Every person who is a gas transporter during any period shall pay to the Authority such proportion as the Authority may determine of such part of its expenses for that period as the Authority may determine to be attributable to its functions in connection with the testing of gas for the purposes of this section.

(10) It shall be the duty of every gas transporter to conduct his business in such a way as can reasonably be expected to secure compliance with the standards set under subsection (1).

[Gas Act 1986, s 16, as substituted by the Utilitites Act 2000, s 101.]

---

1. At the date of going to press, no regulations had been made under this section. However, by virtue of s 17(3) of the Gas Act 1995 and the Gas Act 1995 (Transitional Provisions and Savings) (No 1) Order 1996, SI 1996/219, the Gas Quality Regulations 1983, SI 1983/363 as amended by SI 1996/219, which prescribe standards of pressure, purity and smell to be complied with by any person supplying gas through pipes, shall have effect as though they were made under s 16.

2. No regulations have been made; however, by s 17(3) of the Gas Act 1995 and the Gas Act 1995 (Transitional Provisions and Savings) (No 1) Order 1996, SI 1996/219, the Gas (Testing) Regulations 1949, SI 1949/789 amended by SI 1983/363 and SI 1996/219, are saved and have effect under this section.

8–9455 17. Meter testing and stamping. (1) No meter shall be used for the purpose of ascertaining the quantity of gas supplied through pipes to any person unless it is stamped[1] either by, or on the authority of, a meter examiner appointed under this section or in such other manner as may be authorised by regulations[2] under this section.

(2) Subject to subsections (3) to (5) below, it shall be the duty of a meter examiner who is a member of the Authority's staff, on being required to do so by any person and on payment of the requisite fee—

(a) to examine any meter used or intended to be used for ascertaining the quantity of gas supplied to any person; and

(b) to stamp, or authorise the stamping of, that meter.

(3) A meter examiner shall not stamp, or authorise the stamping of, any meter unless he is satisfied that it is of such pattern and construction and is marked in such manner as is approved by the Authority and that the meter conforms with such standards as may be prescribed for the purposes of this subsection.

(4) A meter examiner may stamp or authorise another person to stamp a meter, notwithstanding that he has not himself examined it, if—

(a) the meter was manufactured or repaired by the person submitting it to the examiner;

(b) that person has obtained the consent of the Director* to his submission; and

(c) any conditions subject to which the consent was given have been satisfied.

(5) A meter examiner may authorise another person to stamp a meter, notwithstanding that he has not himself examined it, if—

(a) the meter was manufactured or repaired by that person;

(b) that person has obtained the consent of the Authority to his stamping of the meter; and

(c) any conditions subject to which the consent was given have been satisfied.

(6) The Director* shall appoint competent and impartial persons as meter examiners for the purposes of this section.

(7)–(8) *Expenses.*

(9) Regulations[2] under this section, which shall be made by the Authority with the consent of the Secretary of State, may make provision—

(a) for re-examining meters already stamped, and for the cancellation of stamps in the case of meters which no longer conform with the prescribed standards and in such other circumstances as may be prescribed;

(b) for requiring meters to be periodically overhauled; and

(c) for the revocation of any approval given by the Authority to any particular pattern or construction of meter, and for requiring existing meters of that pattern or construction to be replaced within such period as may be prescribed for the purposes of this subsection.

(10) *Fees.*

(11) If any person supplies gas through a meter which has not been stamped under this section, he shall be guilty of an offence and liable on summary conviction to a fine not exceeding **level 3** on the standard scale.

(12) Where the commission by any person of an offence under subsection (11) above is due to the act or default of some other person, that other person shall be guilty of the offence; and a person may be charged with and convicted of the offence by virtue of this subsection whether or not proceedings are taken against the first-mentioned person.

(13) In any proceedings for an offence under subsection (11) above it shall be a defence for the person charged to prove that he took all reasonable steps and exercised all due diligence to avoid committing the offence.

(14) The preceding provisions of this section shall not have effect in relation to the supply of gas to a person under any agreement providing for the quantity of gas supplied to him to be ascertained by a meter designed for rates of flow which, if measured at a temperature of 15°C and a pressure of 1013.25 millibars, would exceed 1600 cubic metres an hour.

(15) Regulations under this section may provide that subsection (14) above shall have effect as if for the number of cubic metres an hour which is for the time being applicable for the purposes of that subsection there were substituted such lower number of cubic metres an hour as the Director considers appropriate.

[Gas Act 1986, s 17, as substituted by the Gas Act 1995, Sch 3 and amended by the Utilities Act 2000, s 3.]

---

1. Any meter which immediately before the appointed day was, or was treated as, stamped under s 30 of the Gas Act 1972 shall be treated as stamped under this section (Sch 8, para 5).
2. See the Gas (Meters) Regulations 1983, SI 1983/684, amended by SI 1991/1471, SI 1993/1521 and SI 1995/1251, and the Measuring Instruments (EEC Requirements) (Gas Volume Meters) Regulations 1988, SI 1988/296.

8–9456   18. Safety regulations.   (1) *Repealed.*

(2) *The Secretary of State may by regulations[1] make provision for empowering any officer authorised by the relevant authority to enter premises.*

(3)–(4) *Further provisions as to Regulations under this section.*

(5) Where in pursuance of any powers conferred by regulations made under subsection (2) above, entry is made on any premises by an officer authorised by the relevant authority—

(a) the officer shall ensure that the premises are left no less secure by reason of the entry; and

(b) the relevant authority shall make good, or pay compensation for, any damage caused by the officer, or by any person accompanying him in entering the premises, in taking any action therein authorised by the regulations, or in making the premises secure.

(6) Any officer exercising powers of entry conferred by regulations made under subsection (2) above may be accompanied by such persons as may be necessary or expedient for the purpose for which entry is made, or for the purposes of subsection (5) above.

(7) If any person intentionally obstructs any officer exercising powers of entry conferred by regulations made under subsection (2) above, he shall be guilty of an offence and liable on summary conviction to a fine not exceeding **level 3** on the standard scale.

(8) The Rights of Entry (Gas and Electricity Boards) Act 1954 (entry under a justice's warrant) shall apply in relation to any powers of entry conferred by regulations made under subsection (2) above as if any reference to a gas operator were a reference to the relevant authority.

(9) In this section "the relevant authority"—

(a) in relation to dangers arising from the conveyance of gas by a gas transporter, or from the use of gas conveyed by such a transporter, means that transporter; and

(b) in relation to dangers arising from the conveyance of gas by a person other than a gas transporter, or from the use of gas conveyed by such a person, means the Secretary of State.

(10) Where the relevant authority is a gas transporter, any reference in this section to any officer authorised by the authority includes a reference to any officer authorised by another such transporter with whom the authority has made arrangements for officers authorised by the other transporter to discharge any functions of the authority under this section.

(11) Except in cases of emergency, no officer shall be authorised by a gas transporter to exercise any powers of entry conferred by regulations under this section unless the transporter has taken all reasonable steps to ensure that he is a fit and proper person to exercise those powers.

[Gas Act 1986, s 18 as amended by the Offshore Safety Act 1992, s 3, the Gas Act 1995, Sch 3 and the Utilities Act 2000, Sch 6.]

---

1. By virtue of Sch 8, para 6, regulations made under s 31 of the Gas Act 1972 (now repealed) shall continue to have effect, subject to modifications, as if made under s 15 of the Health and Safety at Work etc Act 1974 for the general purpose mentioned in s 18(1) of this Act. See the Gas Safety Regulations 1972, SI 1972/1178 amended by SI 1980/1851, SI 1984/1358 and SI 1996/470, the Gas Safety (Rights of Entry) Regulations 1996, SI 1996/2535 and the Gas Safety (Installation and Use) Regulations 1994, SI 1994/1886 amended by SI 1996/252 and 550. The provisions of these regulations conferring powers of entry have effect subject to the provisions of the Rights of Entry (Gas and Electricity Boards) Act 1954, ss 1 and 2, ante.

8–9457   18A. Gas escape regulations.   (1) The Secretary of State may by regulations[1] make provision—

    (*a*) for empowering any officer authorised by a gas transporter, if the transporter has reasonable cause to suspect—

       (i)   that gas conveyed by the transporter is escaping, or may escape, in any premises; or

       (ii) that gas so conveyed which has escaped has entered, or may enter, any premises,

to enter the premises, to carry out any work necessary to prevent the escape of gas and to take any other steps necessary to avert danger to life or property; and

    (*b*) for empowering any officer so authorised, if the transporter has reasonable cause to suspect—

       (i)   that gas conveyed through pipes by some other person is escaping, or may escape, in any premises; or

       (ii) that gas so conveyed which has escaped has entered, or may enter, any premises,

to enter the premises and take any steps necessary to avert danger to life or property.

  (2) Subsections (5) to (7) and (11) of section 18 above shall apply for the purposes of this section as if—

    (*a*) any reference to subsection (2) of that section were a reference to subsection (1) above;

    (*b*) any reference to the relevant authority were a reference to a gas transporter;

    (*c*) any reference to subsection (5) of that section were a reference to that subsection as applied by this subsection; and

    (*d*) the reference in subsection (11) of that section to regulations under that section were a reference to regulations under this section.

  (3) The Rights of Entry (Gas and Electricity Boards) Act 1954[2] (entry under a justice's warrant) shall apply in relation to any powers of entry conferred by regulations made under subsection (1) above.

  (4) Any reference in this section to any officer authorised by a gas transporter includes a reference to any officer authorised by another such transporter with whom the transporter has made arrangements for officers authorised by the other transporter to discharge any functions under this section of officers authorised by the transporter.

[Gas Act 1986, s 18A, as inserted by the Gas Act 1995, Sch 3 and amended by the Utilities Act 2000, Sch 6.]

---

  1. See the Gas Safety (Rights of Entry) Regulations 1996, SI 1996/2535.

  2. See this title, ante.

Other functions of Director

8–9458   38. Power to require information etc.   (1) Where it appears to the Authority that a licence holder may be contravening, or may have contravened, any relevant condition or requirement, or may be failing, or may have failed, to achieve any standard of performance prescribed under section 33A or 33AA, the Authority may, for any purpose connected with the exercise of its functions under section 28 or 30A to 30F above in relation to that matter, by notice in writing—

    (*a*) require any person to produce, at a time and place specified in the notice, to the Authority or to any person appointed by it for the purpose, any documents which are specified or described in the notice and are in that person's custody or under his control; or

    (*b*) require any person carrying on any business to furnish to the Authority such information as may be specified or described in the notice, and specify the time, the manner and the form in which any such information is to be furnished.

  (1A) Where a licence has been or is to be revoked or suspended, or has expired or is about to expire by effluxion of time, and it appears to the Authority, having regard to the duties imposed by section 4AA, 4AB or 4A, to be requisite or expedient to do so for any purpose connected with the revocation, suspension or expiry, the Authority may, with the consent of the Secretary of State, by notice signed by it—

    (*a*) require the licence holder to produce, at a time and place specified in the notice, to the Authority, or to any person so specified, any records which are specified or described in the notice and are in the licence holder's custody or under his control; or

    (*b*) require the licence holder to furnish to the Authority, or to any person specified in the notice, such information as may be specified or described in the notice, and specify the time, the manner and the form in which any such information is to be furnished.

  (1B) No person shall be compelled for any such purpose as is mentioned in subsection (1) or (1A) above to produce any documents or records which he could not be compelled to produce in civil proceedings before the court or, in complying with any requirement for the furnishing of information, to give any information which he could not be compelled to give in evidence in such proceedings.

  (2) A person who without reasonable excuse fails to do anything duly required of him by a notice

under subsection (1) or (1A) above shall be guilty of an offence and liable on summary conviction to a fine not exceeding **level 5** on the standard scale.

(3) A person who intentionally alters, suppresses or destroys any document or record which he has been required by any such notice to produce shall be guilty of an offence and liable[1]—

(*a*)   on summary conviction, to a fine not exceeding **the statutory maximum**;

(*b*)   on conviction on indictment, to a **fine**.

(4) If a person makes default in complying with a notice under subsection (1) or (1A) above, the court may, on the application of the Authority, make such order as the court thinks fit for requiring the default to be made good; and any such order may provide that all the costs or expenses of and incidental to the application shall be borne by the person in default or by any officers of a company or other association who are responsible for its default.

(5) In this section—

"relevant condition" and "relevant requirement" have the same meanings as in section 28 above; "the court" has the same meaning as in section 30 above.

[Gas Act 1986, s 38 as amended by the Competition and Service (Utilities) Act 1992, Sch 1, the Gas Act 1995, Schs 3 and 6 and the Utilities Act 2000, ss 3, 95 and Sch 6.]

---

1. For procedure in respect of this offence which is triable either way, see the Magistrates' Courts Act 1980, ss 17A–21, in PART I: MAGISTRATES' COURTS, PROCEDURE, ante.

Miscellaneous

8–9459   42. General restrictions on disclosure of information.   *Repealed.*

8–9460   43. Making of false statements etc.   (1) If any person, in giving any information or making any application for the purposes of any provision of this Part, or of any regulation made under any provision of this Part, makes any statement which he knows to be false in a material particular, or recklessly makes any statement which is false in a material particular, he shall be guilty of an offence and liable[1]—

(*a*)   on summary conviction, to a fine not exceeding **the statutory maximum**;

(*b*)   on conviction on indictment, to a **fine**.

(1A) Any person who with intent to deceive—

(*a*)   impersonates an officer of a gas transporter, gas supplier or gas shipper for the purpose of obtaining entry to any premises; or

(*b*)   for that purpose makes any statement or does any act calculated falsely to suggest that he is an officer, or an authorised officer, of such a transporter, supplier or shipper,

shall be guilty of an offence and liable on summary conviction to a fine not exceeding **level 4** on the standard scale.

(2) Proceedings for an offence under subsection (1) above shall not in England and Wales be instituted except by or with the consent of the Secretary of State or the Director of Public Prosecutions.

[Gas Act 1986, s 43 amended by the Gas Act 1995, Sch 3 and the Utilities Act 2000, Sch 6.]

---

1. For procedure in respect of this offence which is triable either way, see the Magistrates' Courts Act 1980, ss 17A–21, in PART I: MAGISTRATES' COURTS, PROCEDURE, ante.

Supplemental

8–9461   45. Offences by bodies corporate.   (1) Where a body corporate is guilty of an offence under this Part and that offence is proved to have been committed with the consent or connivance of, or to be attributable to any neglect on the part of, any director, manager, secretary or other similar officer of the body corporate or any person who was purporting to act in any such capacity he, as well as the body corporate, shall be guilty of that offence and shall be liable to be proceeded against and punished accordingly.

(2) Where the affairs of a body corporate are managed by its members, subsection (1) above shall apply in relation to the acts and defaults of a member in connection with his functions of management as if he were a director of the body corporate.

[Gas Act 1986, s 45.]

8–9462   46. Service of notices etc.   (1) Any notice or other document required or authorised to be given, delivered or served under this Part or regulations made under this Part may be given, delivered or served either—

(*a*)   by delivering it to the person to whom it is to be given or delivered or on whom it is to be served;

(*b*)   by leaving it at the usual or last known place of abode of that person;

    (*c*) by sending it in a prepaid letter addressed to that person at his usual or last known place of abode;

    (*d*) in the case of a body corporate, by delivering it to the secretary or clerk of the body at their registered or principal office, or sending it in a prepaid letter addressed to the secretary or clerk of the body at that office; or

    (*e*) if it is not practicable after reasonable inquiry to ascertain the name or address of a person to whom it should be given or delivered, or on whom it should be served, as being a person having any interest in premises, by addressing it to him by the description of the person having that interest in the premises (naming them) to which it relates and delivering it to some responsible person on the premises, or affixing it or a copy of it to some conspicuous part of the premises.

(2) Without prejudice to subsection (1) above, where this subsection applies in relation to a gas transporter or gas supplier, any notice to be given to or served on the transporter or supplier under—

    (*a*) any condition of his licence;

    (*b*) any provision of Schedule 2B to this Act; or

    (*c*) in the case of a transporter, section 10 above,

may be given or served by delivering it at, or sending it in a prepaid letter to, an appropriate office of the transporter or supplier.

(3) Subsection (2) above applies in relation to a gas transporter if he divides any authorised area of his into such areas as he thinks fit and—

    (*a*) in the case of each area, fixes offices of his which are to be appropriate offices in relation to notices relating to matters arising in that area; and

    (*b*) publishes in each area, in such manner as he considers adequate, the addresses of the offices fixed by him for that area.

(4) Subsection (2) above applies in relation to a gas supplier if he divides the premises specified in his licence into such areas as he thinks fit and—

    (*a*) in the case of each area, fixes offices of his which are to be appropriate offices in relation to notices relating to matters arising in that area;

    (*b*) publishes in each area, in such manner as he considers adequate, the addresses of the offices fixed by him for that area; and

    (*c*) endorses on every demand note for gas charges payable to him the addresses of the offices fixed for the area in question.

(5) In this section references to premises specified in a licence include references to premises of a description, or situated in an area, so specified.

[Gas Act 1986, s 46, as amended by the Gas Act 1995, Schs 3 and 6 and the Utilities Act 2000, Sch 6.]

8–9463   **47. Provisions as to regulations.**   (1) Regulations made under any provision of this Part may provide for the determination of questions of fact or of law which may arise in giving effect to the regulations and for regulating (otherwise than in relation to any court proceedings) any matters relating to the practice and procedure to be followed in connection with the determination of such questions, including provision—

    (*a*) as to the mode of proof of any matter;

    (*b*) as to parties and their representation;

    (*c*) for the right to appear before and be heard by the Secretary of State, the Authority and other authorities; and

    (*d*) as to awarding costs or expenses of proceedings for the determination of such questions, determining the amount thereof and the enforcement of awards thereof.

(2) Regulations made under any provision of this Part which prescribe a period within which things are to be done may provide for extending the period so prescribed.

(3) Regulations made under any provision of this Part may—

    (*aa*) provide for anything falling to be determined under the regulations to be determined—

       (i) by the Authority or by such other person as may be prescribed by the regulations; and

       (ii) in accordance with such procedure and by reference to such matters and to the opinion of such persons as may be so prescribed;

    (*a*) make different provision for different areas or in relation to different cases or different circumstances; and

    (*b*) provide for such exceptions, limitations and conditions, and make such supplementary, incidental or transitional provision, as the Secretary of State or, as the case may be, the Authority considers necessary or expedient.

(4) Regulations[1] made under any provision of this Part may provide that any person contravening the regulations shall be guilty of an offence and liable on summary conviction to a fine not exceeding **level 5** on the standard scale.

(5) Proceedings for an offence under any regulations[2] made under any provision of this Part shall

not in England and Wales be instituted except by or with the consent of the Secretary of State, the Authority or the Director of Public Prosecutions.

(6) In any proceedings against any person for an offence under any regulations made under any provision of this Part, it shall be a defence for that person to show—

(a) that he was prevented from complying with the regulations by circumstances not within his control; or

(b) that circumstances existed by reason of which compliance with the regulations would or might have involved danger to the public and that he took all such steps as it was reasonable for him to take both to prevent the circumstances from occurring and to prevent them from having that effect.

(7) Any power to make regulations conferred by this Part on the Secretary of State or the Authority shall be exercisable by statutory instrument.

(8) Any statutory instrument containing regulations under this Part made by the Secretary of State shall, except as otherwise provided by this Act, be subject to annulment in pursuance of a resolution of either House of Parliament.

[Gas Act 1986, s 47 as amended by the Competition and Service (Utilities) Act 1992, Sch, the Gas Act 1995, Sch 3 and the Utilities Act 2000, ss 3 and 100.]

---

1. The Gas (Alternative Methods of Charge) Regulations 1990, SI 1990/1634, the Gas (Testing of Apparatus and Equipment) Regulations 1990, SI 1990/1635, and the Gas (Calculation of Thermal Energy) Regulations 1996, SI 1996/439 amended by SI 1997/937 and SI 2003/3130, made under s 13, create offences.

2. Sub-s (5) is repealed in so far as it relates to proceedings for offences created by regulations made or having effect under s 16 so far as relating to standards affecting safety (Offshore Safety Act 1992, s 3).

8–9464   48. Interpretation of Part I and savings.   (1) In this Part, unless the context otherwise requires—

"authorised area", in relation to a gas transporter, has the meaning given by section 7(2) above;

"authorised supplier" means a person authorised by a licence or exemption to supply to any premises gas which has been conveyed to those premises through pipes;

"authorised transporter" means a person authorised by a licence or exemption to convey gas through pipes to any premises or to a pipe-line system operated by a gas transporter;

"calorific value" has the meaning given by section 12(2) above;

"declared calorific value" has the meaning given by section 12(2) above;

"distribution main", in relation to a gas transporter, means any main of the transporter through which the transporter is for the time being distributing gas and which is not being used only for the purpose of conveying gas in bulk;

"exemption" means an exemption under section 6A;

"gas" means—

(a) any substance in a gaseous state which consists wholly or mainly of—

(i) methane, ethane, propane, butane, hydrogen or carbon monoxide;

(ii) a mixture of two or more of those gases; or

(iii) a combustible mixture of one or more of those gases and air; and

(b) any other substance in a gaseous state which is gaseous at a temperature of 15°C and a pressure of 1013·25 millibars and is specified in an order made by the Secretary of State;

"gas fittings" means gas pipes and meters, and fittings, apparatus and appliances designed for use by consumers of gas for heating, lighting, motive power and other purposes for which gas can be used;

"gas interconnector" has the meaning given by section 5(8);

"gas supplier" and "gas shipper" have the meanings given by section 7A(11) above;

"holding company" has the meaning given by section 736 of the Companies Act 1985;

"information" includes accounts, estimates and returns;

"kilowatt hour" means 3.6 megajoules;

"licence" means a licence under section 7, 7ZA or 7A and "licence holder" shall be construed accordingly;

"notice" means notice in writing;

"officer", in relation to any person, includes any servant or agent of that person, and any officer or servant of such an agent;

"owner", in relation to any premises or other property, includes a lessee, and cognate expressions shall be construed accordingly;

"prescribed" means prescribed by regulations made, unless the context otherwise requires, by the Secretary of State;

"gas transporter" has the meaning given by section 7(1) above;

"service pipe" means a pipe, other than a distribution main of a gas transporter, which is used for the purpose of conveying gas from such a main to any premises, and includes part of any such pipe;

"storage", in relation to gas, means storage in, or in a facility which is connected (directly or indirectly) to, a pipe-line system operated by a gas transporter;

"subsidiary" has the meaning given by section 736 of the Companies Act 1985.

(1A) In this Part any reference to an officer authorised by any person includes, in relation to an officer who is an officer or servant of an agent of that person, an officer who, in accordance with the terms of any written authority given by that person to the agent, is authorised by the agent on behalf of that person.

(2) In this Part, except in section 18, references to the supply of gas do not include references to the supply of gas (directly or indirectly) to a gas transporter, gas supplier or gas shipper.

(2A) In relation to any time after 31st December 1999—

(a) references in this Part to 2,500, 75,000 and 2 million therms shall be construed as references to 73,200, 2,196,000 and 58 million kilowatt hours respectively; and

(b) other references in this Part to therms, and references in this Part to therms or kilowatt hours, shall be construed as references to kilowatt hours.

(2B) *Person of pensionable age.*

(3) *Repealed.*

(4) *Repealed.*

[Gas Act 1986, s 48 as amended by the Companies Act 1989, Sch 18, the Competition and Service (Utilities) Act 1992, Sch 1 and the Gas Act 1995, Schs 3 and 6, SI 1999/506, the Utilities Act 2000, s 108 and the Energy Act 2004, s 149.]

8–9465

PART II[1]

Transfer of Undertaking of Corporation

1. Part II contains ss 49–61.

PART III[1]

MISCELLANEOUS AND GENERAL

8–9466 66. General interpretation.   In this Act, unless the context otherwise requires—

"the 1972 Act" means the Gas Act 1972;

"the appointed day" has the meaning given by section 3 above;

"the Authority" means the Gas and Electricity Markets Authority;

"contravention", in relation to any direction, condition, requirement, regulation or order, includes any failure to comply with it and cognate expressions shall be construed accordingly;

"the Corporation" means the British Gas Corporation;

"the Council" means the Gas and Electricity Consumer Council;

"modifications" includes additions, alterations and omissions and cognate expressions shall be construed accordingly;

"subordinate legislation" has the same meaning as in the Interpretation Act 1978;

"the successor company" has the meaning given by section 49(1) above;

"the transfer date" has the meaning given by section 49(1) above;

"the transitional period" has the meaning given by section 57(1) above.

[Gas Act 1986, s 66, as amended by the Utilities Act 2000, s 108.]

1. Part III contains ss 62–68.

Section 3(2)   SCHEDULE 2A
                   EXCEPTIONS TO PROHIBITION ON UNLICENSED ACTIVITIES

(As inserted by the Gas Act 1995, Sch 1.)

Conveyance or supply by landlords etc. *

8–9467   **1.** Section 5(1) of this Act is not contravened by a person—

(a) conveying within a building or part of a building in which he has an interest; or

(b) supplying for use in such a building or part of a building,

gas supplied to the building by a person authorised to supply it by or under section 6A or 7A of this Act or this Schedule.

Conveyance or supply to associated companies

2. Section 5(1) of this Act is not contravened by a company conveying or supplying gas to any premises occupied by a subsidiary or holding company of the company, or by a subsidiary of a holding company of the company.

Conveyance or supply of propane or butane

3. (1) Section 5(1) of this Act is not contravened by a person conveying or supplying to any premises gas which consists wholly or mainly of propane or butane.

(2) In the case of a supply, this paragraph does not apply unless—

(a) the contract for the supply contains provisions empowering a person authorised by the supplier to enter the premises where in his opinion it is necessary to do so for the purpose of averting danger to life or property;

(b) those provisions are in terms approved for the purposes of this paragraph by the Secretary of State; and

(c) the gas is conveyed to the premises otherwise than by a public gas transporter.

Conveyance for supply to large consumers

4. Section 5(1) of this Act is not contravened by a person conveying gas to any premises at any time if they are supplied with gas at a rate which, at any time within the period of 12 months immediately preceding that time, he reasonably expected to exceed 75,000 therms a year.

Supply to very large consumers

5. (1) Sub-paragraph (2) below applies where a person (in this paragraph referred to as a "supplier") notifies the Director—

(a) that he proposes to undertake a supply of gas to any premises at a rate in excess of 2,000,000 therms a year (in this paragraph referred to as "the required rate"); or

(b) that, in such circumstances as may be described in the notification, he would undertake a supply of gas to any premises, at a rate in excess of the required rate, for such period as may be so described.

(2) Section 5(1) of this Act is not contravened by a supply of gas to the premises (or, as the case may require, a supply of gas to the premises in the circumstances and for the period described in the notification) unless, within six weeks of receiving the notification, the Director notifies the supplier either—

(a) that he is of the opinion that the rate of supply to those premises would be unlikely to exceed the required rate; or

(b) that he is unable to form an opinion as to whether the rate of supply to those premises would or would not be likely to exceed the required rate.

(3) Where a supplier has given the Director a notification under sub-paragraph (1)(a) above and—

(a) the rate of supply to the premises to which the notification relates fails to exceed the required rate for three successive periods of twelve months;

(b) the supplier fails to furnish the Director with such information as he may require for the purpose of determining whether the condition in paragraph (a) above is fulfilled; or

(c) the supplier fails to afford to the Director such facilities as he may require for the purpose of verifying any information furnished in pursuance of such a requirement as is mentioned in paragraph (b) above,

the Director may direct that the supplier's notification shall be treated as invalid for the purposes of that sub-paragraph except as regards gas previously supplied.

(4) As soon as practicable after receiving a notification under sub-paragraph (1) above, giving a notification under sub-paragraph (2) above or giving a direction under sub-paragraph (3) above, the Director shall send a copy of the notification or direction to the Health and Safety Executive.*

---

*Repealed by the Utilities Act 2000, Sch 8, when in force.

Section 9(2)   SCHEDULE 2B
                              THE GAS CODE

(As inserted by the Gas Act 1995, Sch 2 and amended by SI 1996/551, SI 1996/3293, SI 1998/2451, the Utilities Act 2000, s 108, the Debt Arrangement and Attachment (Scotland) Act 2002, s 61 and the Energy Act, s 181.)

Preliminary

8–9468   **1.** (1) In this Schedule, unless the context otherwise requires—

"the appointed day" means the day appointed¹ under section 18(2) of the Gas Act 1995;

"connect", in relation to any premises, means connect to a main of a gas transporter, whether directly or by means of a service pipe, and "disconnect" and "re-connect" have corresponding meanings except that they also include discontinuing or, as the case may be, resuming the conveyance of gas to the premises;

"consumer" means a person who is supplied with gas conveyed to particular premises (in this Schedule referred to as his premises) by a gas transporter;

"relevant gas supplier" and "relevant gas shipper", in relation to a consumer, mean respectively any gas supplier who is supplying him with gas conveyed to his premises and any gas shipper who has made arrangements in pursuance of which gas is conveyed to those premises.

(2) In so far as the provisions of this Schedule, other than paragraphs 20 to 22 below, apply in relation to a gas transporter, gas supplier or gas shipper, they shall have effect subject to any conditions of his licence.

---

1. The date appointed for the purposes of s 18(2) of the Gas Act 1995 was the 1 March 1996 (Gas Act 1995 (Appointed Day and Commencement) Order 1996, SI 1996/218).

Consumption of gas to be ascertained by meter

2. (1) Every consumer shall take his supply through a meter—

   (a) the use of which does not contravene section 17 of this Act; and

   (b) which is of a type appropriate for registering the quantity of gas supplied.

   (2) In default of the consumer's doing so or agreeing to do so—

   (a) the gas transporter may disconnect or, as the case may be, refuse to connect his premises; and

   (b) any relevant gas supplier may cut off the supply of gas to his premises.

Meters to be kept in proper order

3. (1) Every consumer shall at all times, at his own expense, keep all meters—

   (a) which belong to him, or which are lent or hired to him and are owned otherwise than by the gas transporter or a relevant gas supplier; and

   (b) by which the quantity of gas supplied is registered,

in proper order for correctly registering the quantity of gas.

   (2) In default of the consumer's doing so—

   (a) the gas transporter may disconnect his premises; and

   (b) any relevant gas supplier may cut off the supply of gas to his premises.

   (3) In the case of any consumer, the gas transporter or any relevant gas supplier shall at all times, without charge to the consumer, keep any meter which is owned by him and is lent or hired to the consumer in proper order for correctly registering the quantity of gas supplied.

   (4) Sub-paragraph (3) above is without prejudice to any remedy the transporter or supplier may have against the consumer for failure to take proper care of the meter.

   (5) In the case of any consumer, the gas transporter, any relevant gas supplier and any relevant gas shipper—

   (a) shall have power to remove, inspect and re-install any meter by which the quantity of gas supplied is registered; and

   (b) shall, while any such meter is removed, fix a substitute meter on the premises;

and, subject to sub-paragraph (6) below, the cost of removing, inspecting and re-installing a meter and of fixing a substitute meter shall be defrayed by the transporter, supplier or shipper.

   (6) Where such a meter is removed for the purpose of being examined by a meter examiner in accordance with section 17 of this Act, the expenses incurred in removing, examining and re-installing the meter and fixing a substitute meter shall be defrayed as follows—

   (a) if the examination is carried out at the request of any person and the meter is found in proper order, by that person;

   (b) if the meter is not so found, by the person required by sub-paragraph (1) or (3) above to keep the meter in proper order.

   (7) A meter is found in proper order for the purposes of sub-paragraph (6) above if it is found to register correctly or to register erroneously to a degree not exceeding the degree permitted by regulations under section 17 of this Act.

   (8) Nothing in this paragraph shall apply in relation to any meter which, in pursuance of an agreement falling within section 17(14) of this Act, is used for ascertaining the quantity of gas supplied to a consumer if either—

   (a) the agreement was entered into before the appointed day; or

   (b) the gas transporter and each relevant gas shipper have agreed that the meter should be kept in proper order by a person other than the consumer.

Meter as evidence of quantity of gas supplied

4. (1) This paragraph applies where a consumer is supplied with gas through a meter at a rate not exceeding 75,000 therms a year.

   (2) Subject to sub-paragraph (3) below, the register of the meter shall be prima facie evidence of the quantity of gas supplied.

   (3) Where the meter is found, when examined by a meter examiner appointed under section 17 of this Act, to register erroneously to a degree exceeding the degree permitted by regulations under that section, the meter shall be deemed to have registered erroneously to the degree so found since the relevant date, except in a case where it is proved to have begun to do so on some later date.

   (4) In sub-paragraph (3) above "the relevant date" means—

   (a) the penultimate date on which, otherwise than in connection with the examination, the register of the meter was ascertained; or

   (b) if regulations so provide, such other date as may be determined by or under the regulations.

   (5) *Installation of meters in new premises etc.*

Meters for disabled persons

6. Where, in the case of any consumer, the gas transporter or a relevant gas supplier, for the purpose of meeting the needs of a disabled person—

   (a) alters the position of any gas meter which is owned by the transporter or supplier and is lent or hired to the consumer; or

   (b) replaces such a meter with one which has been specially adapted,

the transporter or supplier shall not charge the consumer for the alteration or replacement.

Use of pre-payment meters

6A. (1) A pre-payment meter installed by an authorised supplier through which a consumer takes his supply of gas shall not be used to recover a sum unless—

(*a*) the sum is owed to an authorised supplier in respect of the supply of gas to the premises on which the meter is installed or in respect of the provision of the meter; or

(*b*) the recovery of the sum in that manner is permitted by both—

(i) regulations made by the Authority; and

(ii) an agreement falling within sub-paragraph (2) below between the consumer and the person to whom the sum is owed.

(2) An agreement falls within this sub-paragraph if—

(*a*) the person to whom the sum is owed is a person who is authorised by regulations made by the Authority to enter into agreements falling within this sub-paragraph;

(*b*) the agreement permits that person to use the meter in question to recover such sums as may be specified in or determined under the agreement; and

(*c*) the agreement complies with the requirements specified for the purposes of this sub-paragraph by regulations made by the Authority.

(3) The sums that regulations under this paragraph may permit the recovery of through a pre-payment meter include—

(*a*) sums owed to a person other than an authorised supplier;

(*b*) sums owed in respect of premises other than the premises on which the meter is installed;

(*c*) sums owed in respect of matters other than the supply of gas.

(4) Before making regulations under this paragraph the Authority must consult—

(*a*) the Council;

(*b*) all authorised suppliers;

(*c*) such other persons as the Authority considers appropriate.

(5) The approval of the Secretary of State is required for the making of regulations under this paragraph.

Recovery of gas charges etc.

7. (1) Sub-paragraphs (3) and (4) below apply where—

(*a*) a demand in writing is made by a gas supplier for the payment of any of the charges due to him from a consumer in respect of the supply of gas to any premises of his (in this paragraph referred to as "the premises"); and

(*b*) the consumer does not pay those charges within 28 days after the making of the demand.

(2) *Repealed.*

(3) If the supplier is a relevant supplier, he may, after giving not less than 7 days' notice of his intention—

(*a*) cut off the supply to the consumer's premises by disconnecting the service pipe at the meter or by such other means as he thinks fit; and

(*b*) recover any expenses incurred in so doing from the consumer.

(4) If—

(*a*) the supplier is not a relevant supplier but another supplier ("the new supplier") is such a supplier; and

(*b*) the supplier has assigned to the new supplier his right to recover any of the charges due to him from the consumer,

sub-paragraph (3) above shall apply as if any reference to the supplier were a reference to the new supplier.

(5) The powers conferred by sub-paragraphs (3) and (4) above shall not be exercisable as respects any charges or deposit the amount of which is genuinely in dispute.

Deemed contracts in certain cases

8. (1) Where a gas supplier supplies gas to a consumer otherwise than in pursuance of a contract, the supplier shall be deemed to have contracted with the consumer for the supply of gas as from the time ("the relevant time") when he began so to supply gas to the consumer.

(2) Where—

(*a*) the owner or occupier of any premises takes a supply of gas which has been conveyed to those premises by a gas transporter in pursuance of arrangements made with the transporter by a gas shipper, or by a person authorised to make the arrangements by an exemption granted under section 6A of this Act;

(*b*) that supply is not made by a gas supplier, or by a person authorised to make it by an exemption granted under section 6A of this Act or an exception contained in Schedule 2A to this Act; and

(*c*) a supply of gas so conveyed has been previously made by a gas supplier,

the owner or occupier shall be deemed to have contracted with the appropriate supplier for the supply of gas as from the time ("the relevant time") when he began to take such a supply; but nothing in this sub-paragraph shall be taken to afford a defence in any criminal proceedings.

(3) In sub-paragraph (2) above "the appropriate supplier" means—

(*a*) the gas supplier who previously supplied gas to the premises or, if more than one, the gas supplier who last supplied gas to the premises; or

(*b*) where that supplier's licence has been assigned generally, or has been assigned so far as relating to the premises, the person to whom the licence was so assigned; or

(c) where that supplier's licence has been revoked on his application, or has been so restricted on his application as to exclude the premises, the gas supplier with whom that supplier made arrangements for securing continuity of supply to the premises.

(4)–(6) *Repealed.*

(7) The express terms and conditions of a contract which, by virtue of sub-paragraph (1) or (2) above, is deemed to have been made shall be provided for by a scheme made under this paragraph.

(8) Each gas supplier shall make, and from time to time revise, a scheme for determining the terms and conditions which are to be incorporated in the contracts which, by virtue of sub-paragraph (1) or (2) above, are to be deemed to have been made.

(9) The terms and conditions so determined may include terms and conditions for enabling the gas supplier to determine, in any case where the meter is not read immediately before the relevant time, the number of therms or kilowatt hours which are to be treated as supplied to the consumer, or taken by the owner or occupier of the premises, during the period beginning with the relevant time and ending with—

(a) the time when the meter is first read after the relevant time; or

(b) the time when the supplier ceases to supply gas to the consumer, or the owner or occupier ceases to take a supply of gas,

whichever is the earlier.

(10) A scheme under this paragraph may make different provisions for different cases or classes of cases, or for different areas, determined by, or in accordance with, the provisions of the scheme.

(11) As soon as practicable after a gas supplier makes a scheme under this paragraph, or a revision of such a scheme, he shall—

(a) publish, in such manner as he considers appropriate for bringing it to the attention of persons likely to be affected by it, a notice stating the effect of the scheme or revision;

(b) send a copy of the scheme or revision to the Authority and to the Council; and

(c) if so requested by any other person, send such a copy to that person without charge to him.

Supplies of gas illegally taken

9. (1) Where any person takes a supply of gas which is in the course of being conveyed by a gas transporter, the transporter shall be entitled to recover from that person the value of the gas so taken.

(2) Where—

(a) any person at premises which have been reconnected in contravention of paragraph 11(1) below takes a supply of gas which has been conveyed to those premises by the gas transporter; and

(b) the supply is taken otherwise than in pursuance of a contract made with a gas supplier, or deemed to have been made with such a supplier by virtue of paragraph 8 above or paragraph 19 of Schedule 5 to the Gas Act 1995,

the transporter shall be entitled to recover from that person the value of the gas so taken.

(3) Each gas transporter shall make, and from time to time revise, a scheme providing for the manner in which, and the persons by whom, the number of therms or kilowatt hours represented by a supply of gas taken in such circumstances as are mentioned in sub-paragraph (1) or (2) above is to be determined for the purposes of that sub-paragraph.

(4) Sub-paragraphs (10) and (11) of paragraph 8 above shall apply in relation to a scheme under this paragraph as they apply in relation to a scheme under that paragraph.

(5) In this paragraph—

"gas supplier" includes a person authorised to supply gas by an exemption granted under section 6A of this Act or an exception contained in Schedule 2A to this Act*;

"value", in relation to any gas taken in such circumstances as are mentioned in sub-paragraph (1) or (2) above, means the amount which, if the gas had been taken in such circumstances as are mentioned in sub-paragraph (2) of paragraph 8 above, could reasonably be expected to have been payable in respect of the gas under a contract deemed to have been made by virtue of that sub-paragraph.

***Repealed by the Utilities Act 2000, Sch 8 when in force.**

Injury to gas fittings and interference with meters

10. (1) If any person intentionally or by culpable negligence—

(a) injures or allows to be injured any gas fitting provided by a gas transporter or gas supplier, or any service pipe by which any premises are connected to such a transporter's main;

(b) alters the index to any meter used for measuring the quantity of gas conveyed or supplied by such a transporter or supplier; or

(c) prevents any such meter from duly registering the quantity of gas conveyed or supplied,

he shall be guilty of an offence and liable on summary conviction to a fine not exceeding **level 3** on the standard scale[1].

(2) In the case of any offence under sub-paragraph (1) above, the transporter or supplier may disconnect the premises of, or cut off the supply of gas to, the person so offending.

(3) Where any person is prosecuted for an offence under sub-paragraph (1)(b) or (c) above, the possession by him of artificial means for causing an alteration of the index of the meter or, as the case may be, for preventing the meter from duly registering shall, if the meter was in his custody or under his control, be prima facie evidence that the alteration or prevention was intentionally caused by him.

---

1. Gas may be stolen if it is appropriated at a point before that at which the consumer is contractually entitled to use it (*R v Firth* (1869) LR 1 CCR 172, 33 JP 212; *R v White* (1853) Dears CC 203, 17 JP 391).

Restoration of supply without consent

11. (1) Where a consumer's premises have been disconnected by a gas transporter, or a supply of gas to a consumer's premises has been cut off by a gas supplier, otherwise than in the exercise of a power conferred by—

(*a*) paragraph 20, 21 or 22 below;

(*b*) regulations under section 18(2) or 18A(1) of this Act; or

(*c*) regulations under section 15 of the Health and Safety at Work etc. Act 1974 (health and safety regulations),

no person shall, without the relevant consent, reconnect the premises or restore the supply.

(2) If any person acts in contravention of sub-paragraph (1) above—

(*a*) he shall be guilty of an offence and liable on summary conviction to a fine not exceeding **level 3** on the standard scale; and

(*b*) the transporter or supplier may again disconnect the premises or, as the case may be, cut off the supply.

(3) In this paragraph "the relevant consent" means—

(*a*) where the premises are reconnected, the consent of the gas transporter to whose main the reconnection is made;

(*b*) where the supply is restored, the consent of the supplier who cut off the supply, or the consent of a person who is or is about to become a relevant gas supplier.

Failure to notify connection or disconnection of service pipe

12. (1) No person shall connect any meter with a service pipe through which gas is conveyed to any premises by a gas transporter, or disconnect any meter from any such pipe, unless he has given—

(*a*) in a case where gas is supplied to the premises by a relevant gas supplier whose name and address are known to him, to the supplier; and

(*b*) in any other case, to the transporter,

so that it is received by the supplier or transporter at least 48 hours before he does so, notice in the prescribed form of his intention to do so.

(2) Subject to sub-paragraph (3) below, a notice under sub-paragraph (1) above shall contain—

(*a*) details of the time and place of the proposed connection or disconnection; and

(*b*) such other information as may be prescribed.

(3) In so far as it is not reasonably practicable for a notice under sub-paragraph (1) above to contain any information required by sub-paragraph (2)(*b*) above, it shall be a sufficient compliance with that requirement if the information is given to the relevant gas supplier or, as the case may be, the gas transporter within 48 hours after the connection or disconnection is effected.

(4) If any person acts in contravention of this paragraph, he shall be guilty of an offence and liable on summary conviction to a fine not exceeding **level 3** on the standard scale.

Failure to notify disconnection of meter

13. (1) Subject to sub-paragraph (2) below, this paragraph applies where any meter through which gas has been supplied to any premises is completely disconnected, that is to say, is disconnected both from the service pipe and from all other pipes within the premises.

(2) This paragraph does not apply where the meter—

(*a*) is disconnected for the purposes of an examination under section 17 of this Act or an inspection under paragraph 3(5) above; or

(*b*) is disconnected for a particular purpose (whether repair or repositioning of the meter, detection of a gas leak or otherwise) and is intended to be reconnected.

(3) Except in so far as it is not reasonably practicable for him to do so, the person making the disconnection shall—

(*a*) ascertain the name and address of the owner of the meter; and

(*b*) inform that owner of the disconnection and of the address at which the meter will be available for collection.

(4) If any person fails to comply with sub-paragraph (3) above, he shall be guilty of an offence and liable on summary conviction to a fine not exceeding **level 2** on the standard scale.

Failure to maintain shipping arrangements

14. (1) Where—

(*a*) any arrangements for the conveyance of gas by a gas transporter to a consumer's premises at a rate reasonably expected to exceed 2,500 therms a year have been made by a gas shipper, or by a person authorised to make the arrangements by an exemption granted under section 6A of this Act; and

(*b*) those arrangements have ceased to operate and have not been replaced by arrangements made for the like purpose,

the transporter may, after giving 21 days' notice to the relevant persons, disconnect the premises.

(2) The relevant persons for the purposes of sub-paragraph (1) above are—

(*a*) the occupier, or the owner of the premises if they are unoccupied; and

(*b*) any gas supplier who, to the knowledge of the transporter, has contracted to supply gas to the premises.

(3) The notice required to be given by sub-paragraphs (1) and (2)(*a*) above may, in the case of unoccupied premises the owner of which is unknown to the gas transporter and cannot be ascertained after diligent inquiry, be given by affixing it upon a conspicuous part of the premises.

Maintenance etc. of service pipes

15. (1) A gas transporter shall carry out any necessary work of maintenance, repair or renewal of any service pipe by which gas is conveyed by him to a consumer's premises, whether or not the service pipe was supplied and laid at the transporter's expense.

(2) The cost of any work carried out in accordance with sub-paragraph (1) above shall be defrayed as follows—

(a) if the work was made necessary by any intentional act or culpable negligence of the consumer and the transporter so requires, by the consumer;

(b) in any other case, by the transporter.

Alterations etc. of burners on change of calorific value

16. (1) This paragraph applies where there is a change in the properties of any gas which is conveyed by a gas transporter to a consumer's premises at a rate not exceeding 75,000 therms a year.

(2) It shall be the duty of the gas transporter to take without charge to the consumer such steps as may be necessary to alter, adjust or replace the burners in appliances at the premises which burn that gas in such manner as to secure that the gas can be burned with safety and efficiency.

Use of antifluctuators and valves

17. (1) Where a consumer uses gas for working or supplying a compressor, that is to say—

(a) an engine, gas compressor or other similar apparatus; or

(b) any apparatus liable to produce in any main of the gas transporter a pressure less than atmospheric pressure,

he shall, if so required by the transporter by notice, fix in a suitable position and keep in use an appliance provided by him which will effectually prevent inconvenience being caused to persons by reason that he and they are supplied with gas conveyed through the same system.

(2) Where a consumer uses for or in connection with the consumption of gas—

(a) any air at high pressure ("compressed air"); or

(b) any gaseous substance not conveyed by the gas transporter ("extraneous gas"),

he shall, if so required other than for the purpose of preventing danger by the transporter by notice, fix in a suitable position and keep in use an appliance provided by him which will effectually prevent the admission of the compressed air or extraneous gas into the service pipe or into any main through which gas is conveyed by the transporter.

(3) Where a person is required by this paragraph to keep in use any appliance, he shall at his own expense keep it in proper order and repair, and repair, renew or replace it if it is not in proper order or repair.

(4) A consumer shall not be entitled to use a compressor, or any apparatus for using compressed air or extraneous gas, unless he has given to the gas transporter not less than 14 days' notice of his intention to do so; but this sub-paragraph shall not apply to the use of any compressor or apparatus which was lawfully in use immediately before the appointed day.

(5) If a consumer makes default in complying with any provision of this paragraph or regulation 38 of the Gas Safety (Installation and Use) Regulations [1998] or directions made thereunder, the gas transporter may disconnect the consumer's premises.

(6) The gas transporter shall have power to disconnect, remove, test and replace any appliance which a consumer is required by this paragraph or regulation 38 of the Gas Safety (Installation and Use) Regulations [1998] or directions made thereunder to keep in use; and any expenses incurred by the transporter under this sub-paragraph shall, if the appliance is found in proper order and repair, be paid by the transporter, but otherwise shall be paid by the consumer.

Improper use of gas

18. If a consumer improperly uses or deals with gas so as to interfere with the efficient conveyance of gas by the gas transporter (whether to the consumer or to any other person), the transporter may, if he thinks fit, disconnect the consumer's premises.

No obligation to restore supply where consumer in default

19. (1) This paragraph applies where—

(a) a consumer's premises have been disconnected by a gas transporter in pursuance of paragraph 2(2)(a), 3(2)(a), 5(4), 10(2), 11(2)(b), 14(1), 17(5) or 18 above; or

(b) a supply of gas to a consumer's premises has been cut off by a gas supplier in pursuance of paragraph 2(2)(b), 3(2)(b), 7(3) or (4), 10(2) or 11(2)(b) above.

(2) The transporter or supplier shall not be under any obligation to reconnect the consumer's premises or, as the case may be, resume the supply of gas to the consumer's premises until the consumer either is no longer an owner or occupier of the premises or—

(a) has made good the default, or remedied the matter, in consequence of which the premises were disconnected or the supply was cut off; and

(b) has paid the reasonable expenses of disconnecting and reconnecting the premises or, as the case may be, of cutting off the supply and restoring the supply.

(3) In this paragraph "consumer", in relation to a disconnection or cutting off under paragraph 11(2)(b) above, means—

(a) the owner of the premises at the time when the reconnection was made, or the supply was restored, without the relevant consent—

    (i) if the premises were unoccupied at that time, or

    (ii) if that reconnection or restoration of supply was made by him or on his behalf; and

  (b) the occupier of the premises at that time in any other case;

and in this sub-paragraph "relevant consent" has the same meaning as in paragraph 11 above.

20–23. *Repealed.*

23. (1) Any officer authorised by a gas transporter may at all reasonable times, on the production of some duly authenticated document showing his authority, enter a consumer's premises for the purpose of—

  (a) inspecting gas fittings;

  (b) ascertaining the quantity of gas conveyed to the premises;

  (c) exercising the power conferred on the transporter by paragraph 3(5) above;

  (d) performing the duty imposed on the transporter by paragraph 15 or 16 above;

  (e) exercising the power conferred on the transporter by paragraph 17(6) above; or

  (f) in the case of premises where the transporter has reason to believe that a compressor or compressed air or extraneous gas is being used, inspecting the premises and ascertaining whether the provisions of paragraph 17 above are being complied with.

(2) Any officer authorised by a relevant gas supplier or relevant gas shipper may at all reasonable times, on the production of some duly authenticated document showing his authority, enter a consumer's premises for the purpose of—

  (a) inspecting gas fittings;

  (b) ascertaining the quantity of gas supplied or conveyed to the premises; or

  (c) exercising a power conferred by paragraph 3(5) or 7(3)(a) (and testing gas fittings, and making any adjustments required for their safe operation, after the exercise of the power).

(3) In this paragraph "compressor", "compressed air" and "extraneous gas" have the same meanings as in paragraph 17 above, and any reference to a relevant gas supplier or relevant gas shipper includes a reference to a person who has been or is about to become such a supplier or shipper.

Entry on discontinuance of supply

24. (1) This paragraph applies where—

  (a) a gas transporter or gas supplier is authorised by any provision of this Act to disconnect any premises, or, as the case may be, to cut off or discontinue the supply of gas to any premises;

  (b) a person occupying premises supplied with gas by a gas supplier ceases to require a supply of gas; or

  (c) a person entering into occupation of any premises previously supplied with gas by a gas supplier does not take a supply of gas.

(2) Any officer authorised by the gas transporter or gas supplier, after 24 hours' notice to the occupier, or to the owner of the premises if they are unoccupied, may at all reasonable times, on production of some duly authenticated document showing his authority, enter the premises for the purpose of—

  (a) disconnecting the premises, or cutting off or discontinuing the supply of gas to the premises; or

  (b) removing any meter or other gas fitting owned by the transporter or supplier.

(3) The notice required to be given by sub-paragraph (2) above may, in the case of unoccupied premises the owner of which is unknown to the gas transporter or gas supplier and cannot be ascertained after diligent inquiry, be given by affixing it upon a conspicuous part of the premises not less than 48 hours before the premises are entered.

Entry following discontinuance of supply

25. (1) This paragraph applies where a consumer's premises have been disconnected by a gas transporter, or a supply of gas to a consumer's premises has been cut off by a gas supplier, otherwise than in the exercise of a power conferred by—

  (a) paragraph 20, 21 or 22 above;

  (b) regulations under section 18(2) or 18A(1) of this Act; or

  (c) regulations under section 15 of the Health and Safety at Work etc. Act 1974 (health and safety regulations).

(2) Any officer authorised by the gas transporter or gas supplier may at all reasonable times, on production of some duly authenticated document showing his authority, enter the premises for the purpose of ascertaining whether the premises have been reconnected, or the supply has been restored, without the relevant consent.

(3) In this paragraph "the relevant consent" has the same meaning as in paragraph 11 above.

Entry for removing fittings and meters

26. (1) This paragraph applies where—

  (a) a person occupying premises supplied with gas through a meter or other gas fitting owned by a gas transporter or gas supplier ceases to take a supply through that meter or fitting; or

  (b) a person entering into occupation of any premises previously supplied with gas through a meter or other gas fitting so owned does not take a supply of gas through that meter or fitting.

(2) Any officer authorised by the gas transporter or gas supplier, after 24 hours' notice to the occupier, or to the owner of the premises if they are unoccupied, may at all reasonable times, on production of some duly authenticated document showing his authority, enter the premises for the purpose of removing the meter or other gas fitting.

(3) Sub-paragraph (3) of paragraph 24 above applies for the purposes of this paragraph as it applies for the purposes of that paragraph.

Entry for replacing, repairing or altering pipes

27. (1) Any officer authorised by a gas transporter, after 7 clear days' notice to the occupier of any premises, or to the owner of any premises which are unoccupied, may at all reasonable times, on production of some duly authenticated document showing his authority, enter the premises for the purpose of—

(a) placing a new pipe in the place of any existing pipe which has already been lawfully placed; or

(b) repairing or altering any such existing pipe.

(2) The notice required to be given by sub-paragraph (1) above may, in the case of unoccupied premises the owner of which is unknown to the gas transporter and cannot be ascertained after diligent inquiry, be given by affixing it upon a conspicuous part of the premises.

(3) In cases of emergency arising from defects in any pipes entry may be made under sub-paragraph (1) above without the notice required to be given by that sub-paragraph, but notice of the entry and the justification for it shall then be given as soon as possible after the occurrence of the emergency.

Provisions as to powers of entry

28. (1) No officer shall be authorised by a gas transporter, gas supplier or gas shipper to exercise any powers of entry conferred by this Schedule unless—

(a) the transporter, supplier or shipper has taken all reasonable steps to ensure that he is a fit and proper person to exercise those powers; or

(b) in cases of emergency, those powers are powers conferred by paragraph 22 above.

(2) Where in pursuance of any powers of entry conferred by this Schedule, entry is made on any premises by an officer authorised by a gas transporter, gas supplier or gas shipper—

(a) the officer shall ensure that the premises are left no less secure by reason of the entry; and

(b) the transporter, supplier or shipper shall make good, or pay compensation for, any damage caused by the officer, or by any person accompanying him in entering the premises, in taking any action therein authorised by this Schedule, or in making the premises secure.

(3) Any officer exercising powers of entry conferred by this Schedule may be accompanied by such persons as may be necessary or expedient for the purpose for which the entry is made, or for the purposes of sub-paragraph (2) above.

(4) If any person intentionally obstructs any officer exercising powers of entry conferred by this Schedule, he shall be guilty of an offence and liable on summary conviction to a fine not exceeding **level 3** on the standard scale.

(5) The Rights of Entry (Gas and Electricity Boards) Act 1954[1] (entry under a justice's warrant) shall apply in relation to any powers of entry conferred by this Schedule.

---

1. See this title, ante.

Gas meters and fittings not to be subject to distress

29. (1) Any gas meter which is connected to a service pipe, and any gas fitting in a consumer's premises which is owned by a gas transporter or gas supplier and is marked or impressed with a sufficient mark or brand indicating its owner—

(a) shall not be subject to distress or be liable to be taken in execution under process of any court or any proceedings in bankruptcy against the person in whose possession it may be; and

(b) shall be deemed not to be a landlord's fixture, notwithstanding that it may be fixed or fastened to any part of the premises in which it may be situated.

(2) In the application of sub-paragraph (1)(a) above to Scotland, for the word "distress" and the words "in bankruptcy against" there shall be substituted respectively the word "attachment" and the words "for the sequestration of the estate of".

Electricity Act 1989[1]
(1989 c 29)

PART I[2]
ELECTRICITY SUPPLY

Introductory

8–9570 **1. The Director General of Electricity Supply.** *Repealed.*

---

1. This Act makes new provision with respect to the supply of electricity through electric lines and the generation and transmission of electricity for such supply.
2. Part I contains ss 1–64.

Licensing of supply etc

8–9571 **4. Prohibition on unlicensed supply etc.** (1) A person who—

(a) generates electricity for the purpose of giving a supply to any premises or enabling a supply to be so given;

(b) participates in the transmission of electricity for that purpose; or*

(bb) distributes electricity for that purpose;

   (*c*) supplies electricity to any premises,*

shall be guilty of an offence unless he is authorised to do so by a licence.

   (2) A person guilty of an offence under this section shall be liable[1]—

   (*a*) on summary conviction, to a fine not exceeding **the statutory maximum**;
   (*b*) on conviction on indictment, to a **fine**.

   (3) No proceedings shall be instituted in England and Wales in respect of an offence under this section except by or on behalf of the Secretary of State or the Authority.

   (3A) In subsection (1)(*b*) above, the reference to a person who participates in the transmission of electricity is to a person who—

   (*a*) co-ordinates, and directs, the flow of electricity onto and over a transmission system by means of which the transmission of electricity takes place, or
   (*b*) makes available for use for the purposes of such a transmission system anything which forms part of it.

   (3B) For the purposes of subsection (3A)(*b*), a person shall not be regarded as making something available just because he consents to its being made available by another.

   (3C) A reference in this Part to participating in the operation of an electricity interconnector is a reference to—

   (*a*) co-ordinating and directing the flow of electricity into or through an electricity interconnector; or
   (*b*) making such an interconnector available for use for the conveyance of electricity;

and a person is not to be regarded as participating in the transmission of electricity by reason only of activities constituting participation in the operation of an electricity interconnector.

   (3D) For the purposes of subsection (3C)(*b*), a person shall not be regarded as making something available just because he consents to its being made available by another.

   (3E) In this Part "electricity interconnector" means so much of an electric line or other electrical plant as—

   (*a*) is situated at a place within the jurisdiction of Great Britain; and
   (*b*) subsists wholly or primarily for the purposes of the conveyance of electricity (whether in both directions or in only one) between Great Britain and a place within the jurisdiction of another country or territory.

   (3F) For the purposes of this section—

   (*a*) a place is within the jurisdiction of Great Britain if it is in Great Britain, in the territorial sea adjacent to Great Britain or in an area designated under section 1(7) of the Continental Shelf Act 1964; and
   (*b*) a place is within the jurisdiction of another country or territory if it is in that country or territory or in waters in relation to which authorities of that country or territory exercise jurisdiction.

   (4) In this Part, unless the context otherwise requires—

"distribute", in relation to electricity, means distribute by means of a distribution system, that is to say, a system which consists (wholly or mainly) of low voltage lines and electrical plant and is used for conveying electricity to any premises or to any other distribution system;

"supply", in relation to electricity, means supply of electricity conveyed by a distribution system to premises other than premises occupied by a licence holder for the purpose of carrying on the activities which he is authorised by his licence to carry on;*

"transmission", in relation to electricity, means transmission by means of a transmission system;
"transmission system" means a system which—

   (*a*) consists (wholly or mainly) of high voltage lines and electrical plant, and
   (*b*) is used for conveying electricity from a generating station to a substation, from one generating station to another or from one substation to another.

   (5) In this section—

"relevant place" means a place in Great Britain, in the territorial sea adjacent to Great Britain or in a Renewable Energy Zone; and
"system" means a system the whole or a part of which is at a relevant place;

and references in this section to premises are references to premises situated at a relevant place, or at a place that is not in a Renewable Energy Zone but is in an area designated under section 1(7) of the Continental Shelf Act 1964.**

[Electricity Act 1989, s 4, as amended by the Utilities Act 2000, s 28 and Sch 8 and the Energy Act 2004, ss 89, 135, 145, 179 and 197.]

---

*Definition "supply" substituted and new definition "generate" inserted by the Energy Act 2004, ss 89 and 179 from a date to be appointed.
**Sub-section (5) in force for the purpose of defining "relevant place" as used in s 36(1): SI 2005/442.

8–9572 5. Exemptions from prohibition. (1) The Secretary of State may by order[1] grant exemption from paragraph (a), (b), (bb) or (c)* of section 4(1)—

   (*a*) either to a person or to persons of a class;
   (*b*) either generally or to such extent as may be specified in the order; and
   (*c*) either unconditionally or subject to such conditions as may be so specified.

(2) Before making an order under subsection (1) the Secretary of State shall give notice—

   (*a*) stating that he proposes to make such an order and setting out the terms of the proposed order;
   (*b*) stating the reasons why he proposes to make the order in the terms proposed; and
   (*c*) specifying the time (not being less than 28 days from the date of publication of the notice) within which representations with respect to the proposals may be made,

and shall consider any representations which are duly made in respect of the proposals and not withdrawn.

(3) The notice required by subsection (2) shall be given—

   (*a*) by serving a copy of it on the Authority and the Council; and
   (*b*) by publishing it in such manner as the Secretary of State considers appropriate for bringing it to the attention of those likely to be affected by the proposed order.

(4) Notice of an exemption granted to a person shall be given—

   (*a*) by serving a copy of the exemption on him; and
   (*b*) by publishing the exemption in such manner as the Secretary of State considers appropriate for bringing it to the attention of other persons who may be affected by it.

(5) Notice of an exemption granted to persons of a class shall be given by publishing the exemption in such manner as the Secretary of State considers appropriate for bringing it to the attention of—

   (*a*) persons of that class; and
   (*b*) other persons who may be affected by it.

(6) An exemption may be granted—

   (*a*) indefinitely; or
   (*b*) for a period specified in, or determined by or under, the exemption.

(7) Conditions subject to which an exemption is granted may (in particular) require any person carrying on any activity in pursuance of the exemption—

   (*a*) to comply with any direction given by the Secretary of State or the Authority as to such matters as are specified in the exemption or are of a description so specified;
   (*b*) except in so far as the Secretary of State or the Authority consents to his doing or not doing them, not to do or to do such things as are specified in the exemption or are of a description so specified; and
   (*c*) to refer for determination by the Secretary of State or the Authority such questions arising under the exemption as are specified in the exemption or are of a description so specified.

(8) The Secretary of State may by order revoke an order by which an exemption was granted to a person or vary an order by which more than one exemption was so granted so as to terminate any of the exemptions—

   (*a*) at the person's request;
   (*b*) in accordance with any provision of the order by which the exemption was granted; or
   (*c*) if it appears to the Secretary of State inappropriate that the exemption should continue to have effect.

(9) The Secretary of State may by order revoke an order by which an exemption was granted to persons of a class or vary an order by which more than one exemption was so granted so as to terminate any of the exemptions—

   (*a*) in accordance with any provision of the order by which the exemption was granted; or
   (*b*) if it appears to the Secretary of State inappropriate that the exemption should continue to have effect.

(10) The Secretary of State may by direction withdraw an exemption granted to persons of a class from any person of that class—

   (*a*) at the person's request;
   (*b*) in accordance with any provision of the order by which the exemption was granted; or
   (*c*) if it appears to the Secretary of State inappropriate that the exemption should continue to have effect in the case of the person.

(11) Before—

   (*a*) making an order under subsection (8)(*b*) or (*c*) or (9); or (*b*)　giving a direction under subsection (10)(*b*) or (*c*),

the Secretary of State shall consult the Authority and give notice of his proposal to do so (with reasons) and of a period within which representations may be made to him.

(12)　The notice under subsection (11) shall be given—

(*a*)　where the Secretary of State is proposing to make an order under subsection (8)(*b*) or (*c*), by serving a copy of it on the person to whom the exemption was granted;

(*b*)　where he is proposing to make an order under subsection (9), by publishing it in such manner as the Secretary of State considers appropriate for bringing it to the attention of persons of the class of persons to whom the exemption was granted; and

(*c*)　where he is proposing to give a direction under subsection (10)(*b*) or (*c*), by serving a copy of it on the person from whom he proposes to withdraw the exemption.

[Electricity Act 1989, s 5, as substituted by the Utilities Act 2000, s 29.]

---

*Words substituted by the Energy Act 2004, s 145 from a date to be appointed.
1. See the Electricity (Class Exemptions from Requirement for a Licence) Order 1997, SI 1997/989 amended by SI 2000/2424 and SI 2001/3270, the Electricity (Class Exemptions from the Requirement for a Licence) Order 2001, SI 2001/3270 amended by SI 2005/488, the Electricity (Exemption from the Requirement for a Generation Licence) (England and Wales) Order 2002, SI 2002/823 and the Electricity (Exemption from the Requirement for a Generation Licence) Order 2004, SI 2004/1179, the Electricity (Exemption form the Requirement for a Generation Licence) (No 2) Order 2004, SI 2004/1776 and the Electricity (Exemption form the Requirement for a Generation Licence) (England and Wales) Order 2005, SI 2005/2242.

8–9573　**6. Licences authorising supply, etc.**　　(1)　The Authority may grant any of the following licences—

(*a*)　a licence authorising a person to generate electricity for the purpose of giving a supply to any premises or enabling a supply to be so given ("a generation licence");

(*b*)　a licence authorising a person to participate in the transmission of electricity for that purpose ("a transmission licence");

(*c*)　a licence authorising a person to distribute electricity for that purpose ("a distribution licence");

(*d*)　a licence authorising a person to supply electricity to premises ("a supply licence"); or

(*e*)　a licence authorising a person to participate in the operation of an electricity interconnector ("an interconnector licence").

(2)　The same person may not be the holder of both a distribution licence and a supply licence.

(2A)　The same person may not be the holder of an interconnector licence and the holder of a licence falling within any of paragraphs (*a*) to (*d*) of subsection (1).

(3)–(8)　*Further provisions relating to application for and grant of a licence*[1].

(9)　In this Part—

"electricity distributor" means any person who is authorised by a distribution licence to distribute electricity except where he is acting otherwise than for purposes connected with the carrying on of activities authorised by the licence;

"electricity supplier" means any person who is authorised by a supply licence to supply electricity except where he is acting otherwise than for purposes connected with the carrying on of activities authorised by the licence.*

[Electricity Act 1989, s 6, as amended by the Utilities Act 2000, s 30 and the Energy Act 2004, ss 136, 143, 145 and 197.]

---

*New sub-s (10) inserted by the Energy Act 2004, s 89 from a date to be appointed.
1. The Electricity (Applications for Licences and Extensions of Licences) Regulations 1990, SI 1990/192 have been made.

8–9573A　**6A.**　*Procedure for licence applications*

8–9573B　**6B.**　*Applications for transmission licences*

8–9573C　**6C.**　*Competitive tenders for offshore transmission licences*

8–9574　**7.**　*Conditions of licences: general*

Supply by public electricity suppliers

8–9575　**16. Duty to connect on request.**　　(1)　An electricity distributor is under a duty—

(*a*)　to make a connection between a distribution system of his and any premises, when required to do so by—

(i)　the owner or occupier of the premises; or

(ii)　an authorised supplier acting with the consent of the owner or occupier of the premises,

for the purpose of enabling electricity to be conveyed to or from the premises;

(b) to make a connection between a distribution system of his and any distribution system of another authorised distributor, when required to do so by that authorised distributor for the purpose of enabling electricity to be conveyed to or from that other system.

(2) Any duty under subsection (1) includes a duty to provide such electric lines or electrical plant as may be necessary to enable the connection to be used for the purpose for which it is required.

(3) The duties under this section shall be performed subject to such terms as may be agreed under section 16A for so long as the connection is required.

(4) In this section and sections 16A to 23—

(a) any reference to making a connection includes a reference to maintaining the connection (and continuing to provide the necessary electric lines or electrical plant);

(b) any reference to requiring a connection includes a reference to requiring the connection to be maintained (and the continued provision of the necessary electric lines and electrical plant); and

(c) any reference to the provision of any electric line or electrical plant is a reference to the provision of such a line or an item of electrical plant either by the installation of a new one or by the modification of an existing one.

(5) The duties under this section are subject to the following provisions of this Part and any regulations made under those provisions.

[Electricity Act 1989, s 16, as amended by the Utilities Act 2000, s 44.]

8–9575A 16A. Procedure for requiring a connection. (1) Where a person requires a connection to be made by an electricity distributor in pursuance of section 16(1), he shall give the distributor a notice requiring him to offer terms for making the connection.

(2) That notice must specify—

(a) the premises or distribution system to which a connection to the distributor's system is required;

(b) the date on or by which the connection is to be made; and

(c) the maximum power at which electricity may be required to be conveyed through the connection.

(3) The person requiring a connection shall also give the distributor such other information in relation to the required connection as the distributor may reasonably request.

(4) A request under subsection (3) shall be made as soon as practicable after the notice under subsection (1) is given (if not made before that time).

(5) As soon as practicable after receiving the notice under subsection (1) and any information requested under subsection (3) the distributor shall give to the person requiring the connection a notice—

(a) stating the extent (if any) to which his proposals are acceptable to the distributor and specifying any counter proposals made by him;

(b) specifying any payment which that person will be required to make under section 19(1) or regulations under section 19(2);

(c) specifying any security which that person will be required to give under section 20; and

(d) stating any other terms which that person will be required to accept under section 21.

(6) A notice under subsection (5) shall also contain a statement of the effect of section 23.

[Electricity Act 1989, s 16A as inserted by the Utilities Act 2000 , s 44.]

8–9576 17. Exceptions from duty to connect. (1) Nothing in section 16(1) requires an electricity distributor to make a connection if and to the extent that—

(a) he is prevented from doing so by circumstances not within his control;

(b) circumstances exist by reason of which his doing so would or might involve his being in breach of regulations under section 29, and he has taken all such steps as it was reasonable to take both to prevent the circumstances from occurring and to prevent them from having that effect; or

(c) it is not reasonable in all the circumstances for him to be required to do so.

(2) Without prejudice to the generality of subsection (1) an electricity distributor is not required to make a connection if—

(a) making the connection involves the distributor doing something which, without the consent of another person, would require the exercise of a power conferred by any provision of Schedule 3 or 4;

(b) the distributor's licence does not provide for that provision to have effect in relation to him; and

(c) any necessary consent has not, at the time the request is made, been given.

(3) Subsection (1)(c) does not permit an electricity distributor to disconnect any premises or distribution system to which a connection is being maintained by him unless the distributor gives—

   (*a*) where the connection is to premises, to the occupier or to the owner if the premises are not
       occupied;

   (*b*) where the connection is to another distribution system, to the person who is authorised by a
       licence or exemption to run that system,

not less than seven working days' notice of his intention to disconnect the premises or distribution
system.
[Electricity Act 1989, s 17, as amended by the Utilities Act 2000, s 44.]

8-9577 18. Power to recover charges[1]. *Repealed.*

---

   1. The rights and liabilities as between tariff customers and public electricity suppliers are regulated by statute and not
by contract. The recovery of electricity charges is provided for by Sch 6 and is not subject to s 40 of the Administration of
Justice Act 1970 (unlawful harrassment of debtors) in PART I: MAGISTRATES' COURTS, PROCEDURE, ante (*Norweb plc v
Dixon* [1995] 3 All ER 952, [1995] 1 WLR 636).

8-9578 19. Power to recover expenditure. (1) Where any electric line or electrical plant is
provided by an electricity distributor in pursuance of section 16(1) above, the distributor may require
any expenses reasonably incurred in providing it to be defrayed by the person requiring the
connection to such extent as is reasonable in all the circumstances.

   (2) The Secretary of State may, after consultation with the Authority, make provision by
regulations[1] for entitling an electricity distributor to require a person requiring a connection in
pursuance of section 16(1) to pay to the distributor, in respect of any expenses reasonably incurred
in providing any electric line or electrical plant used for the purpose of making the connection, such
amount as may be reasonable in all the circumstances if—

   (*a*) the connection is required within the prescribed period after the provision of the line or plant;
       and

   (*b*) a person ("the initial contributor") has made a payment to the distributor in respect of those
       expenses, the line or plant having been provided for the purpose of making a connection to
       any premises or distribution system as required by that person.

   (3) Regulations under subsection (2) above may require an electricity distributor who, in
pursuance of this section or the regulations, has recovered any amount in respect of expenses
reasonably incurred in providing any electric line or electrical plant—

   (*a*) to exercise his rights under the regulations in respect of those expenses; and

   (*b*) to apply any payments received by him in the exercise of those rights in making such payments
       as may be appropriate towards reimbursing the initial contributor and any persons previously
       required to make payments under the regulations.

   (4) Any reference in this section to any expenses reasonably incurred in providing an electric line
or electrical plant includes a reference to the capitalised value of any expenses likely to be so incurred
in continuing to provide it.
[Electricity Act 1989, s 19, as amended by the Utilities Act 2000, s 46.]

---

   1. The Electricity (Connection Charges) Regulations 2002, SI 2002/93 and 3232 have been made.

8-9579 20. Power to require security. (1) Subject to the following provisions of this section, an
electricity distributor may require any person who requires a connection in pursuance of section
16(1) to give him reasonable security for the payment to him under section 19 in respect of the
provision of any electric line or electrical plant.

   (1A) If a person fails to give any security required under subsection (1), or the security given has
become invalid or insufficient, and he fails to provide alternative or additional security, the electricity
distributor may if he thinks fit—

   (*a*) if the connection has not been made, refuse to provide the line or plant for so long as the
       failure continues; or

   (*b*) if the connection is being maintained, disconnect the premises or distribution system in
       question.

   (2) *Repealed.*

   (3) Where any money is deposited with an electricity distributor by way of security in pursuance
of this section, the distributor shall pay interest, at such rate as may from time to time be fixed by the
distributor with the approval of the Authority, on every sum of 50p so deposited for every three
months during which it remains in the hands of the distributor.

   (4) *Repealed.*
[Electricity Act 1989, s 20, as amended by the Utilities Act 2000, s 47.]

8-9580 21. Additional terms of connection. An electricity distributor may require any person
who requires a connection in pursuance of section 16(1) above to accept in respect of the making of
the connection—

(a) any restrictions which must be imposed for the purpose of enabling the distributor to comply with regulations under section 29;

(b) any terms which it is reasonable in all the circumstances for that person to be required to accept; and

(c) without prejudice to the generality of paragraph (b), any terms restricting any liability of the distributor for economic loss resulting from negligence which it is reasonable in all the circumstances for that person to be required to accept.]

[Electricity Act 1989, s 21, as amended by the Utilities Act 2000, s 48.]

8–9581 22. Special agreements with respect to connection. (1) Notwithstanding anything in sections 16 to 21, a person who requires a connection in pursuance of section 16(1) may enter into an agreement with the electricity distributor (referred to in this Part as a "special connection agreement") for the making of the connection on such terms as may be agreed by the parties.

(2) So long as a special connection agreement is effective, the rights and liabilities of the parties shall be those arising under the agreement and not those provided for by sections 16 to 21.

(3) Nothing in subsection (2) prevents the giving of a notice under section 16A(1) requiring a connection to be made as from the time when a special connection agreement ceases to be effective.

[Electricity Act 1989, s 22, as amended by the Utilities Act 2000, s 49.]

8–9582 23. Determination of disputes. (1) This section applies (in addition to any disputes to which it applies by virtue of any other provision of this Act) to any dispute[1] arising under sections 16 to 21 between an electricity distributor and a person requiring a connection.

(1A) A dispute to which this section applies—

(a) may be referred to the Authority by either party, or with the agreement of either party, by the Council; and

(b) on such a reference, shall be determined by order made either by the Authority or, if the Authority thinks fit, by an arbitrator (or in Scotland an arbiter) appointed by the Authority.

(1B) The practice and procedure to be followed in connection with any such determination shall be such as the Authority may consider appropriate.

(1C) No dispute arising under sections 16 to 21 which relates to the making of a connection between any premises and a distribution system may be referred to the Authority after the end of the period of 12 months beginning with the time when the connection is made.

(2) Where a dispute arising under sections 16 to 21 between an electricity distributor and a person requiring a connection falls to be determined under this section, the Authority may give directions as to the circumstances in which, and the terms on which, the distributor is to make or (as the case may be) to maintain a connection pending the determination of the dispute[2].

(3) Where any dispute arising under section 20(1) above falls to be determined under this section, the Authority may give directions as to the security (if any) to be given pending the determination of the dispute.

(4) Directions under subsection (2) or (3) above may apply either in cases of particular descriptions or in particular cases.

(4A) A person making an order under this section shall include in the order his reasons for reaching his decision with respect to the dispute.

(5) An order under this section—

(a) may include such incidental, supplemental and consequential provision (including provision requiring either party to pay a sum in respect of the costs or expenses incurred by the person making the order) as that person considers appropriate; and

(b) shall be final and—

(i) in England and Wales, shall be enforceable, in so far as it includes such provision as to costs or expenses, as if it were a judgment of the county court;

(ii) *Scotland.*

(6) In including in an order under this section any such provision as to costs or expenses as is mentioned in subsection (5) above, the person making the order shall have regard to the conduct and means of the parties and any other relevant circumstances.

(7) Section 16(4)(a) does not apply to the references in this section to making a connection.

[Electricity Act 1989, s 23 as amended by the Competition and Service (Utilities) Act 1992, s 25 and Schs 1 and 2 and the Utilities Act 2000, s 3 and Sch 6.]

---

1. Includes not only an unresolved dispute but any dispute even where the charges have been paid, and there is no time limit within which a person requiring a supply of electricity might refer a dispute (*R v Director General of Electricity Supply, ex p Redrow Homes (Northern) Ltd* (1995) Times, 21 February).

2. Note: the Queen's Printers's copy of the Utilities Act 2000 provides, Sch 6, Pt II, paras 24, 26(1), (2), that the new sub-ss (1), (1A), (1B), (1C), (2) should be substituted for the existing sub-ss (1), (2). This amendment makes no reference to the prior existence of sub-s (1A) as inserted by the Competition and Service (Utilities) Act 1992, s 56(6), Sch 1, para 11. It is believed that this is an error and that the new subsections should replace all of the existing sub-ss (1), (1A), (2). It should also be noted that the existing sub-s (1A), as inserted by the 1992 Act, is almost identical to the new sub-s (4A) above, as inserted by s 108 of, and Sch 6, Pt II, paras 24, 26(1), (3) to, the 2000 Act.

8–9583   24. The public electricity supply code.   The provisions of Schedule 6[1] to this Act (which relate to the distribution and supply of electricity) shall have effect.
[Electricity Act 1989, s 24, as amended by the Utilities Act 2000.]

---

1. See, post.

Enforcement of preceding provisions

8–9584   28. Power to require information etc.   (1) Where it appears to the Authority that a licence holder—

(*a*)   may be contravening, or may have contravened, any relevant condition or requirement; or

(*b*)   may be failing, or may have failed, to achieve any standard of performance prescribed under section 39 or 39A,

the Authority may, for any purpose connected with such of its functions under section 25 or 27A to 27F as are exercisable in relation to that matter, serve a notice under subsection (2) below on any person.

(2)   A notice under this subsection is a notice signed by the Authority and—

(*a*)   requiring the person on whom it is served to produce, at a time and place specified in the notice, to the Authority or to any person appointed by the Authority for the purpose, any documents which are specified or described in the notice and are in that person's custody or under his control; or

(*b*)   requiring that person, if he is carrying on a business, to furnish, at a time and place and in the form and manner specified in the notice, to the Authority such information as may be specified or described in the notice.

(2A)   Where a licence has been or is to be revoked or suspended, or has expired or is about to expire by effluxion of time, and it appears to the Authority, having regard to the duties imposed by section 3A, 3B or 3C, to be requisite or expedient to do so for any purpose connected with the revocation, suspension or expiry, the Authority may, with the consent of the Secretary of State, by notice in writing—

(*a*)   require the licence holder to produce, at a time and place specified in the notice, to the Authority, or to any person so specified, any records which are specified or described in the notice and are in the licence holder's custody or under his control; or

(*b*)   require the licence holder to furnish to the Authority, or to any person specified in the notice, such information as may be specified or described in the notice, and specify the time, the manner and the form in which any such information is to be furnished.

(3)   No person shall be required under this section to produce any documents or records which he could not be compelled to produce in civil proceedings in the court or, in complying with any requirement for the furnishing of information, to give any information which he could not be compelled to give in evidence in any such proceedings.

(4)   A person who without reasonable excuse fails to do anything required of him by notice under subsection (2) or (2A) above shall be liable on summary conviction to a fine not exceeding **level 5** on the standard scale.

(5)   A person who intentionally alters, suppresses or destroys any document or record which he has been required by any notice under subsection (2) or (2A) above to produce shall be liable[1]—

(*a*)   on summary conviction, to a fine not exceeding **the statutory maximum**;

(*b*)   on conviction on indictment, to a **fine**.

(6)   If a person makes default in complying with a notice under subsection (2) or (2A) above, the court may, on the application of the Authority, make such order as the court thinks fit for requiring the default to be made good; and any such order may provide that all the costs or expenses of and incidental to the application shall be borne by the person in default or by any officers of a company or other association who are responsible for its default.
[Electricity Act 1989, s 28 as amended by the Competition and Service (Utilities) Act 1992, Sch 1 and the Utilities Act 2000, Sch 6.]

---

1. For procedure in respect of this offence which is triable either way, see the Magistrates' Courts Act 1980, ss 17A–21, in PART I: MAGISTRATES' COURTS, PROCEDURE, ante.

Provisions with respect to supply generally

8–9585   29. Regulations relating to supply and safety.   (1) The Secretary of State may make such regulations[1] as he thinks fit for the purpose of—

(*a*)   securing that supplies of electricity are regular and efficient;

(*b*)   protecting the public from dangers arising from the generation, transmission, distribution or supply of electricity, from the use of electricity interconnectors, from the use of electricity supplied or from the installation, maintenance or use of any electric line or electrical plant; and

(c) without prejudice to the generality of paragraph (b) above, eliminating or reducing the risks of personal injury, or damage to property or interference with its use, arising as mentioned in that paragraph.

(1A) Regulations under this section may include provision for securing the purposes mentioned in subsection (1) in relation to the territorial sea adjacent to Great Britain or any Renewable Energy Zone.

(2) Without prejudice to the generality of subsection (1) above, regulations under this section may—

(a) prohibit the distribution or transmission of electricity except by means of a system approved by the Secretary of State;

(b) make provision requiring notice in the prescribed form to be given to the Secretary of State, in such cases as may be specified in the regulations, of accidents and of failures in the distribution or transmission of electricity or in the use of electricity interconnectors;

(c) make provision as to the keeping, by persons authorised by a licence or exemption to distribute or participate in the transmission of electricity or to participate in the transmission of an electricity interconnector, of maps, plans and sections and as to their production (on payment, if so required, of a reasonable fee) for inspection or copying;

(d) make provision for relieving electricity distributors from any duty under section 16 or authorising them to disconnect any premises or distribution system in such cases as may be prescribed;

(e) make provision requiring compliance with notices given by the Secretary of State specifying action to be taken in relation to any electric line or electrical plant, or any electrical appliance under the control of a consumer, for the purpose of—

(i) preventing or ending a breach of regulations under this section; or

(ii) eliminating or reducing a risk of personal injury or damage to property or interference with its use;

(f) provide for particular requirements of the regulations to be deemed to be complied with in the case of any electric line or electrical plant complying with specified standards or requirements;

(g) provide for the granting of exemptions from any requirement of the regulations for such periods as may be determined by or under the regulations.

(3) Regulations under this section may provide that any person—

(a) who contravenes any specified provision of the regulations; or

(b) who does so in specified circumstances,

shall be liable on summary conviction to a fine not exceeding **level 5** on the standard scale; but nothing in this subsection shall affect any liability of any such person to pay compensation in respect of any damage or injury which may have been caused by the contravention.

(4) No proceedings shall be instituted in England and Wales in respect of an offence under this section except by or on behalf of the Secretary of State or the Director of Public Prosecutions.

[Electricity Act 1989, s 29, as amended by the Utilities Act 2000, Sch 6 and the Energy Act 2004, ss 94, 143 and 147.]

---

1. The Electricity Safety, Quality and Continuity Regulations 2002, SI 2002/2665 amended by SI 2003/2155 have been made.

8–9586 30. Electrical inspectors.   (1) The Secretary of State may appoint competent and impartial persons to be electrical inspectors under this Part.

(2) The duties of an electrical inspector under this Part shall be as follows—

(a) to inspect and test, periodically and in special cases, electric lines and electrical plant belonging to persons authorised by a licence or exemption to generate, distribute or participate in the transmission of electricity or to participate in the operation of electricity interconnectors;

(b) to examine, periodically and in special cases, the generation, transmission, distribution or supply of electricity by such persons;

(c) to inspect and test, if and when required by any consumer, any such lines and plant on the consumer's premises, for the purpose of determining whether any requirement imposed by or under this Part in respect of the lines or plant or the conveyance of electricity through them has been complied with; and

(d) such other duties as may be imposed by regulations under this section or as the Secretary of State may determine.

(3) The Secretary of State may by regulations—

(a) prescribe the manner in which and the times at which any duties are to be performed by electrical inspectors;

(b) require persons authorised by a licence or exemption to carry on licensable activities—

(i) to furnish electrical inspectors with records or other information; and

    (ii)   to allow such inspectors access to premises and the use of electrical plant and other facilities;

  (c)   make provision for relieving electricity distributors from any duty under section 16 or authorising them to disconnect any premises or distribution system in such cases as may be prescribed; and

  (d)   prescribe the amount of the fees which are to be payable to such inspectors.

(3A)   The regulations that may be made under this section include regulations—

  (a)   imposing duties on electrical inspectors in relation to anything in the territorial sea adjacent to Great Britain or a Renewable Energy Zone; or

  (b)   making any other provision authorised by this section in relation to activities carried on there.

(4)   *Fees.*

[Electricity Act 1989, s 30, as amended by the Utilities Act 2000, Sch 6 and the Energy Act 2004, ss 94, 147 and Sch 19.]

8–9587   31. Use etc of meters.   The provisions of Schedule 7[1] to this Act (which relate to the use, certification, testing and maintenance of electricity meters) shall have effect.
[Electricity Act 1989, s 31.]

---

  1. See, post.

Protection of public interest

8–9589   34. Fuel stocks etc at generating stations.   (1) This section applies to any generating station which—

  (a)   is of a capacity not less than 10 megawatts; and

  (b)   is fuelled otherwise than by waste or manufactured gases;

and in this subsection "waste" has the same meaning as in the Control of Pollution Act 1974.

(2)   The Secretary of State may by order provide that subsection (1) above shall have effect as if for the capacity mentioned in paragraph (a) there were substituted such other capacity (not exceeding 100 megawatts) as may be specified in the order.

(3)   In respect of any generating station to which this section applies, the Secretary of State may give a direction requiring the person who operates it—

  (a)   to make such arrangements with respect to stocks of fuel and other materials held at or near that generating station for the purposes of its operation as will—

    (i)   enable those stocks to be brought within a specified time to, and thereafter maintained at, a specified level; and

    (ii)   ensure that they do not fall below that level, except as may be permitted by the terms of the direction or by a direction under subsection (4) below;

  (b)   to create such stocks and make such arrangements with respect to them;

and the amount of any stocks may be specified by reference to the period for which it would enable the generating station to be maintained in operation.

(4)   In respect of any generating station to which this section applies, the Secretary of State may give a direction—

  (a)   authorising or requiring the person who operates it to make such use as may be specified of any stocks held at or near that generating station; and

  (b)   requiring that person to operate, or not to operate, that generating station for specified periods, at specified levels of capacity or using specified fuels.

(5)   In subsections (3) and (4) above "specified" means specified by or under the Secretary of State's direction; and a direction may—

  (a)   specify the cases and circumstances in which any stocks are to be treated as held at or near any generating station;

  (b)   specify the extent to which the direction may be treated as complied with where, under arrangements made or approved by the Secretary of State, access can be had to stocks held for the use of a number of consumers;

  (c)   specify the manner in which any period mentioned in subsection (3) or (4) above is to be determined;

  (d)   require anything falling to be specified under the direction to be specified by such persons and by reference to such matters as may be specified.

(6)   A direction under subsection (3) or (4) above which confers on any person the function of specifying anything falling to be specified under the direction may require that person to exercise that function in such manner as may be specified by the direction.

[Electricity Act 1989, s 34, amended by SI 1990/1066.]

8–9590   **35. Provisions supplementary to section 34.**   (1) The Secretary of State may give a direction requiring the holder of a transmission licenceto give to the Secretary of State, after consultation with specified persons, any information or advice which the Secretary of State may reasonably require for purposes connected with the exercise of his functions under section 34 above.

(2) The Secretary of State may give a direction requiring any person who is authorised by a licence to participate in the transmission of electricity to carry on the activities which the licence authorises (or any of them), at any time when a direction under section 34(4) above is in force, either in a specified manner or with a view to achieving specified objectives.

(3) In subsections (1) and (2) above "specified" means specified by or under the Secretary of State's direction; and a person subject to a direction under subsection (2) above shall give effect to it notwithstanding any other duty imposed on him by or under this Part.

(4) The Secretary of State shall lay before each House of Parliament a copy of every direction given under section 34 above or this section unless he is of the opinion that disclosure of the direction is against the interests of national security or the commercial interests of any person.

(5) A person who, without reasonable excuse, contravenes or fails to comply with a direction of the Secretary of State under section 34 above or this section shall be liable[1]—

    (a)   on summary conviction, to a fine not exceeding **the statutory maximum**;

    (b)   on conviction on indictment, to a **fine**.

(6) No proceedings shall be instituted in England and Wales in respect of an offence under this section except by or on behalf of the Secretary of State.

(7) Paragraphs 1 to 4, 7 and 8 of Schedule 2 to the Energy Act 1976 (administration of Act and other matters) shall have effect as if—

    (a)   section 34 above were contained in that Act;

    (b)   the powers of paragraph 1 were exercisable for any purpose connected with securing compliance with a direction under that section;

    (c)   information obtained by virtue of that paragraph could lawfully be disclosed to any person by whom anything falls to be specified under such a direction; and

    (d)   the powers conferred by sub-paragraph (1)(c) of that paragraph included power to direct that information and forecasts be furnished to any such person.

[Electricity Act 1989, s 35 as amended by the Energy Acy 2004, Sch 19.]

---

1. For procedure in respect of this offence which is triable either way, see the Magistrates' Courts Act 1980, ss 17A–21, in PART I: MAGISTRATES' COURTS, PROCEDURE, ante.

8–9591   **36. Consent required for construction etc of generating stations.**   (1) Subject to subsections (2) and (4) below, a generating station shall not be constructed, at a relevant place (within the meaning of section 4), and a generating station at such a place shall not be extended or operated except in accordance with a consent granted by the Secretary of State.★

(2) Subsection (1) above shall not apply to a generating station whose capacity—

    (a)   does not exceed the permitted capacity, that is to say, 50 megawatts; and

    (b)   in the case of a generating station which is to be constructed or extended, will not exceed the permitted capacity when it is constructed or extended;

and an order under this subsection may make different provision for generating stations of different classes or descriptions.

(3) The Secretary of State may by order provide that subsection (2) above shall have effect as if for the permitted capacity mentioned in paragraph (a) there were substituted such other capacity as may be specified in the order.

(4) The Secretary of State may by order[1] direct that subsection (1) above shall not apply to generating stations of a particular class or description, either generally or for such purposes as may be specified in the order.

(5) A consent under this section—

    (a)   may include such conditions (including conditions as to the ownership or operation of the station) as appear to the Secretary of State to be appropriate; and

    (b)   shall continue in force for such period as may be specified in or determined by or under the consent.

(6) Any person who without reasonable excuse contravenes the provisions of this section shall be liable on summary conviction to a fine not exceeding **level 5** on the standard scale.

(7) No proceedings shall be instituted in England and Wales in respect of an offence under this section except by or on behalf of the Secretary of State.

(8) The provisions of Schedule 8[2] to this Act (which relate to consents under this section and section 37 below) shall have effect.

(9) In this Part "extension", in relation to a generating station, includes the use by the person operating the station of any land or area of waters (wherever situated) for a purpose directly related to the generation of electricity by that station and "extend" shall be construed accordingly.★

[Electricity Act 1989, s 36 as amended by the Energy Act 2004, s 93.]

*Sub-sections (1) and (9) amended, and new ss 36A and 36B inserted by the Energy Act 2004, ss 93 and 99 from a date to be appointed.**

1. The Offshore Generating Stations (Exemption) Order 1990, SI 1990/443 and the Electricity Act 1989 (Requirement of Consent for Offshore Wind and Water Driven Generating Stations) (England and Wales) Order 2001, SI 2001/3642 have been made.

2. Schedule 8 is not printed in this work.

8–9591A 36A. Declarations extinguishing etc public rights of navigation. (1) Where a consent is granted by the Secretary of State or the Scottish Ministers in relation to—

(a) the construction or operation of a generating station that comprises or is to comprise (in whole or in part) renewable energy installations situated at places in relevant waters, or

(b) an extension of a generating station that is to comprise (in whole or in part) renewable energy installations situated at places in relevant waters or an extension of such an installation,

he or (as the case may be) they may, at the same time, make a declaration under this section as respects rights of navigation so far as they pass through some or all of those places.

(2) The Secretary of State or the Scottish Ministers may make such a declaration only if the applicant for the consent made an application for such a declaration when making his application for the consent.

(3) A declaration under this section is one declaring that the rights of navigation specified or described in it—

(a) are extinguished;

(b) are suspended for the period that is specified in the declaration;

(c) are suspended until such time as may be determined in accordance with provision contained in the declaration; or

(d) are to be exercisable subject to such restrictions or conditions, or both, as are set out in the declaration.

(4) A declaration under this section—

(a) has effect, in relation to the rights specified or described in it, from the time at which it comes into force; and

(b) continues in force for such period as may be specified in the declaration or as may be determined in accordance with provision contained in it.

(5) A declaration under this section—

(a) must identify the renewable energy installations, or proposed renewable energy installations, by reference to which it is made;

(b) must specify the date on which it is to come into force, or the means by which that date is to be determined;

(c) may modify or revoke a previous such declaration, or a declaration under section 100 of the Energy Act 2004; and

(d) may make different provision in relation to different means of exercising a right of navigation.

(6) Where a declaration is made under this section by the Secretary of State or the Scottish Ministers, or a determination is made by him or them for the purposes of a provision contained in such a declaration, he or (as the case may be) they must either—

(a) publish the declaration or determination in such manner as appears to him or them to be appropriate for bringing it, as soon as is reasonably practicable, to the attention of persons likely to be affected by it; or

(b) secure that it is published in that manner by the applicant for the declaration.

(7) In this section—

"consent" means a consent under section 36 above;

"extension", in relation to a renewable energy installation, has the same meaning as in Chapter 2 of Part 2 of the Energy Act 2004;

"relevant waters" means waters in or adjacent to Great Britain which are between the mean low water mark and the seaward limits of the territorial sea.

[Electricity Act 1989, s 36A as inserted by the Energy Act 2004, s 99.]

8–9591B 36B. Duties in relation to navigation. (1) Neither the Secretary of State nor the Scottish Ministers may grant a consent in relation to any particular offshore generating activities if he considers, or (as the case may be) they consider, that interference with the use of recognised sea lanes essential to international navigation—

(a) is likely to be caused by the carrying on of those activities; or

(b) is likely to result from their having been carried on.

(2) It shall be the duty both of the Secretary of State and of the Scottish Ministers, in determining—

(a) whether to give a consent for any particular offshore generating activities, and

(b) what conditions to include in such a consent,

to have regard to the extent and nature of any obstruction of or danger to navigation which (without amounting to interference with the use of such sea lanes) is likely to be caused by the carrying on of the activities, or is likely to result from their having been carried on.

(3) In determining for the purposes of this section what interference, obstruction or danger is likely and its extent and nature, the Secretary of State or (as the case may be) the Scottish Ministers must have regard to the likely overall effect (both while being carried on and subsequently) of—

(a) the activities in question; and

(b) such other offshore generating activities as are either already the subject of consents or are activities in respect of which it appears likely that consents will be granted.

(4) For the purposes of this section the effects of offshore generating activities include—

(a) how, in relation to those activities, the Secretary of State and the Scottish Ministers have exercised or will exercise their powers under section 36A above and section 100 of the Energy Act 2004 (extinguishment of public rights of navigation); and

(b) how, in relation to those activities, the Secretary of State has exercised or will exercise his powers under sections 95 and 96 and Chapter 3 of Part 2 of that Act (safety zones and decommissioning).

(5) If the person who has granted a consent in relation to any offshore generating activities thinks it appropriate to do so in the interests of the safety of navigation, he may at any time vary conditions of the consent so as to modify in relation to any of the following matters the obligations imposed by those conditions—

(a) the provision of aids to navigation (including, in particular, lights and signals);

(b) the stationing of guard ships in the vicinity of the place where the activities are being or are to be carried on; or

(c) the taking of other measures for the purposes of, or in connection with, the control of the movement of vessels in that vicinity.

(6) A modification in exercise of the power under subsection (5) must be set out in a notice given by the person who granted the consent to the person whose obligations are modified.

(7) In this section—

"consent" means a consent under section 36 above;
"offshore generating activities" means—

(a) the construction or operation of a generating station that is to comprise or comprises (in whole or in part) renewable energy installations; or

(b) an extension of a generating station that is to comprise (in whole or in part) renewable energy installations or an extension of such an installation;

"the use of recognised sea lanes essential to international navigation" means—

(a) anything that constitutes the use of such a sea lane for the purposes of Article 60(7) of the United Nations Convention on the Law of the Sea 1982 (Cmnd 8941); or

(b) any use of waters in the territorial sea adjacent to Great Britain that would fall within paragraph (a) if the waters were in a Renewable Energy Zone.

(8) In subsection (7) "extension", in relation to a renewable energy installation, has the same meaning as in Chapter 2 of Part 2 of the Energy Act 2004.
[Electricity Act 1989, s 36B as inserted by the Energy Act 2004, s 99.]

8–9592 37. Consent required for overhead lines. (1) Subject to subsection (2) below, an electric line shall not be installed or kept installed above ground except in accordance with a consent granted by the Secretary of State.

(2) Subsection (1) above shall not apply—

(a) in relation to an electric line which has a nominal voltage not exceeding 20 kilovolts and is used or intended to be used for supplying a single consumer;

(b) in relation to so much of an electric line as is or will be within premises in the occupation or control of the person responsible for its installation; or

(c) in such other cases as may be prescribed[1].

(3) A consent under this section—

(a) may include such conditions (including conditions as to the ownership and operation of the line) as appear to the Secretary of State to be appropriate;

(b) may be varied or revoked by the Secretary of State at any time after the end of such period as may be specified in the consent; and

(c) subject to paragraph (b) above, shall continue in force for such period as may be specified in or determined by or under the consent.

(4) Any person who without reasonable excuse contravenes the provisions of this section shall be liable on summary conviction to a fine not exceeding **level 3** on the standard scale.

(5) No proceedings shall be instituted in England and Wales in respect of an offence under this section except by or on behalf of the Secretary of State.
[Electricity Act 1989, s 37.]

---

1. See the Overhead Lines (Exemption) Regulations 1990, SI 1990/2035 and the Overhead Lines (Exemption) Regulations 1992, SI 1992/3074.

Consumer protection: standards of performance

8–9593   39. Electricity supply: performance in individual cases.   (1) The Authority may, with the consent of the Secretary of State, make regulations[1] prescribing such standards of performance in connection with the activities of electricity suppliers, so far as affecting customers or potential customers of theirs, as in the Authority's opinion ought to be achieved in individual cases.

(2) Regulations under this section may—

(a) prescribe circumstances in which electricity suppliers are to inform persons of their rights under this section or their rights under section 39A;

(b) prescribe such standards of performance in relation to any duty arising under paragraph (a) above as, in the Authority's opinion, ought to be achieved in all cases; and

(c) prescribe circumstances in which electricity suppliers are to be exempted from any requirements of the regulations or this section,

and, if the Authority is of the opinion that the differences are such that no electricity supplier would be unduly disadvantaged in competing with other electricity suppliers, may make different provision for different electricity suppliers.

(3) If an electricity supplier fails to meet a prescribed standard, he shall make to any person who is affected by the failure and is of a prescribed description such compensation as may be determined by or under the regulations.

(4) The making of compensation under this section in respect of any failure by an electricity supplier to meet a prescribed standard shall not prejudice any other remedy which may be available in respect of the act or omission which constituted that failure.

(5) *Repealed.*

(5A) *Repealed.*

(6) *Repealed.*

(7) In this section "prescribed" means prescribed by regulations under this section.
[Electricity Act 1989, s 39 amended by the Competition and Service (Utilities) Act 1992, s 20 and Schs 1 and 2 and the Utilities Act 2000, Sch 6.]

---

1. See the Electricity (Standards of Performance) Regulations 2001, SI 2001/3265 amended by SI 2002/476 and 742.

8–9593A   39A. Standards of performance in individual cases: electricity distributors.
(1) The Authority may with the consent of the Secretary of State make regulations[1] prescribing such standards of performance in connection with the activities of electricity distributors, so far as affecting customers or potential customers of electricity suppliers, as in the Authority's opinion ought to be achieved in individual cases.

(2) If an electricity distributor fails to meet a prescribed standard, he shall make to any person who is affected by the failure and is of a prescribed description such compensation as may be determined by or under the regulations.

(3) The regulations may—

(a) prescribe circumstances in which electricity distributors are to inform customers or potential customers of electricity suppliers of their rights under this section;

(b) prescribe such standards of performance in relation to any duty arising under paragraph (a) as, in the Authority's opinion, ought to be achieved in all cases;

(c) make provision as to the manner in which compensation under this section is to be made;

(d) prescribe circumstances in which electricity distributors are to be exempted from any requirements of the regulations or this section; and

(e) if the Authority is of the opinion that the differences are such that no electricity distributor would be unduly disadvantaged in competing with other electricity distributors, make different provision with respect to different electricity distributors.

(4) Provision made under subsection (3)(c) may—

(a) require or permit compensation to be made on behalf of electricity distributors by electricity suppliers to customers or potential customers; and

(b) require electricity suppliers to provide services to electricity distributors in connection with the making of compensation under this section.

(5) The making of compensation under this section in respect of any failure to meet a prescribed standard shall not prejudice any other remedy which may be available in respect of the act or omission which constituted that failure.

(6) In this section "prescribed" means prescribed by regulations under this section.
[Electricity Act 1989, s 39A, as inserted by the Utilities Act 2000, s 54(2).]

---

1. The Electricity (Standards of Performance) Regulations 2001, SI 2002/3265 amended by SI 2002/476 and 742 have been made.

8–9593B   39B. Standards of performance in individual cases: disputes. (1) Any dispute arising under section 39 or 39A or regulations made under either of those sections—

(a)   may be referred to the Authority by either party or, with the agreement of either party, by the Council; and

(b)   on such a reference, shall be determined by order made by the Authority or, if it thinks fit, by such person (other than the Council) as may be prescribed.

(2) A person making an order under subsection (1) shall include in the order his reasons for reaching his decision with respect to the dispute.

(3) The practice and procedure to be followed in connection with any such determination shall be such as may be prescribed.

(4) An order under subsection (1) shall be final and shall be enforceable—

(a)   in England and Wales, as if it were a judgment of a county court; and

(b)   in Scotland, as if it were an extract registered decree arbitral bearing a warrant for execution issued by the sheriff.

(5) In this section "prescribed" means prescribed by regulations[1] made by the Authority with the consent of the Secretary of State.
[Electricity Act 1989, s 39B, as inserted by the Utilities Act 2000, s 54(2).]

---

1. The Electricity (Standards of Performance) Regulations 2001, SI 2002/3265 amended by SI 2002/476 and 742 have been made.

8–9594   40. Electricity supply: overall performance. (1) The Authority may from time to time—

(a)   determine such standards of overall performance in connection with the provision of electricity supply services as, in its opinion, ought to be achieved by electricity suppliers; and

(b)   arrange for the publication, in such form and in such manner as it considers appropriate, of the standards so determined.

(1A) *Repealed.*

(2) Different standards may be determined under this section for different electricity suppliers if the Authority is of the opinion that the differences are such that no electricity supplier would be unduly disadvantaged in competing with other electricity suppliers.

(3) It shall be the duty of every electricity supplier to conduct his business in such a way as can reasonably be expected to lead to his achieving the standards set under this section.
[Electricity Act 1989, s 40 as amended by the Competition and Service (Utilities) Act 1992, ss 20 and 24 and Sch 2 and the Utilities Act 2000, Sch 6.]

8–9594A   40A. Overall standards of performance: electricity distributors. (1) The Authority may from time to time—

(a)   determine such standards of overall performance in connection with the activities of electricity distributors as, in its opinion, ought to be achieved by them; and

(b)   arrange for the publication, in such form and in such manner as it considers appropriate, of the standards so determined.

(2) Different standards may be determined for different electricity distributors if the Authority is of the opinion that the differences are such that no electricity distributor would be unduly disadvantaged in competing with other electricity distributors.

(3) It shall be the duty of every electricity distributor to conduct his business in such a way as can reasonably be expected to lead to his achieving the standards set under this section.]
[Electricity Act 1989, s 40A, as inserted by the Utilities Act 2000, s 55.]

8–9594B   40B. Procedures for prescribing or determining standards of performance.
(1) Before prescribing standards of performance in regulations under section 39 or 39A, or determining standards of performance under section 40 or 40A, the Authority shall—

(a)   arrange for such research as the Authority considers appropriate with a view to discovering the views of a representative sample of persons likely to be affected and consider the results;

(b)   publish a notice of its proposals in accordance with subsections (2) and (3) and consider any representations which are duly made in respect of those proposals; and

(c)   consult the Council and other persons or bodies mentioned in subsection (4).

(2) The notice required by subsection (1)(b) is a notice—

(a) stating that the Authority proposes to prescribe or determine standards of performance and setting out the standards of performance proposed;

(b) stating the reasons why it proposes to prescribe or determine those standards of performance; and

(c) specifying the time (not being less than 28 days from the date of publication of the notice) within which representations with respect to the proposals may be made.

(3) A notice required by subsection (1)(b) shall be published in such manner as the Authority considers appropriate for the purpose of bringing it to the attention of those likely to be affected by the proposals.

(4) The persons or bodies to be consulted by the Authority under subsection (1)(c) are—

(a) electricity suppliers (in the case of standards of performance under section 39 or 40) or electricity distributors and electricity suppliers (in the case of standards of performance under section 39A or 40A); and

(b) persons or bodies appearing to the Authority to be representative of persons likely to be affected by the regulations or determination.

(5) The Authority shall make arrangements for securing that notices under subsection (1)(b), regulations under section 39 or 39A and determinations under section 40 or 40A are made available to the public by whatever means it considers appropriate.]

[Electricity Act 1989, s 40B, as inserted by the Utilities Act 2000, s 56.]

8–9595 41A. Promotion of efficient use by consumers of electricity. (1) The Secretary of State may by order[1] impose—

(*a*) on each electricity distributor (or each electricity distributor of a specified description); and

(*b*) on each electricity supplier (or each electricity supplier of a specified description),

an obligation to achieve, within a specified period and in accordance with the order, the energy efficiency target to be determined by the Authority under the order for that distributor or supplier (and that obligation is referred to in this section as an "energy efficiency obligation").

(2) In this section "energy efficiency target" means a target for the promotion of improvements in energy efficiency, that is to say, efficiency in the use by consumers of electricity, gas conveyed through pipes or any other source of energy which is specified in the order.

(3) An order under this section may specify criteria by reference to which the Authority is to determine energy efficiency targets for the electricity distributors or electricity suppliers on whom obligations are imposed by the order.

(4) The Secretary of State and the Authority shall carry out their respective functions under this section in the manner he or it considers is best calculated to ensure that no electricity distributor is unduly disadvantaged in competing with other electricity distributors and no electricity supplier is unduly disadvantaged in competing with other electricity suppliers.

(5) The order may make provision generally in relation to the energy efficiency obligations which it imposes, including in particular provision—

(*a*) as to the treatment of persons who become electricity distributors or electricity suppliers after the beginning of the period to which the order relates;

(*b*) as to the action which qualifies for the purpose of meeting the whole or any part of an energy efficiency target;

(*c*) as to the method by which improvements in energy efficiency attributable to any qualifying action are to be assessed;

(*d*) requiring distributors and suppliers to give to the Authority specified information, or information of a specified nature, about their proposals for complying with their energy efficiency obligations;

(*e*) requiring the Authority to determine—

(i) whether any proposed action qualifies for the purpose of achieving the whole or any part of a person's energy efficiency target; and

(ii) if so, what improvement in energy efficiency is to be attributed for that purpose to the proposed action or to any result of that action specified in the determination; and

(*f*) requiring distributors or suppliers to produce to the Authority evidence of a specified kind demonstrating that they have complied with their energy efficiency obligations.

(6) The order may make provision authorising the Authority to require a distributor or supplier to provide it with specified information, or information of a specified nature, relating to—

(*a*) his proposals for complying with his energy efficiency obligation; or

(*b*) the question whether he has complied with that obligation.

(7) The order may make provision as to circumstances in which—

(*a*) a person's energy efficiency target may be altered during the period to which the order relates;

(*b*) the whole or any part of a person's energy efficiency target may be treated as having been achieved by action taken otherwise than by or on behalf of that person;

(c) any action taken before the period to which the order relates may be treated as qualifying action taken during that period;

(d) the whole or any part of a person's energy efficiency target may be transferred to another electricity distributor or electricity supplier or to a gas transporter or gas supplier (within the meaning of Part I of the Gas Act 1986); or

(e) a person may carry forward the whole or any part of his energy efficiency target for the period to which the order relates to a subsequent period.

(8) The order may—

(a) provide for exceptions from any requirement of the order;

(b) provide that any specified requirement contained in it is to be treated as a relevant requirement for the purposes of this Part;

(c) make supplementary, incidental and transitional provision; and

(d) subject to subsection (4), make different provision for different cases (including different provision in relation to different distributors or suppliers).

(9) The order may include provision for treating the promotion of the supply to premises of—

(a) electricity generated by a generating station which is operated for the purposes of producing heat, or a cooling effect, in association with electricity;

(b) heat produced in association with electricity or steam produced from (or air or water heated by) such heat;

(c) any gas or liquid subjected to a cooling effect produced in association with electricity,

as promotion of energy efficiency.

(10) No person shall be required by virtue of this section to provide any information which he could not be compelled to give in evidence in civil proceedings in the High Court or, in Scotland, the Court of Session.

(11) Before making an order under this section the Secretary of State shall consult the Authority, the Council, electricity distributors and electricity suppliers and such other persons as he considers appropriate.

(12) An order under this section shall not be made unless a draft of the instrument containing it has been laid before, and approved by a resolution of, each House of Parliament.

[Electricity Act 1989, s 41A as substituted for s 41 as originally enacted by the Utilities Act 2000, s 70]

---

1. The Electicity and Gas (Energy Efficiency Obligations) Order 2004, SI 2004/3392 has been made.

8–9596 42. Information with respect to levels of performance. (1) The Authority shall from time to time collect information with respect to—

(a) the compensation made by electricity suppliers under section 39 above;

(b) the levels of overall performance achieved by such suppliers in connection with the provision of electricity supply services

(c) *Repealed.*

(1A) The Authority shall from time to time collect information with respect to—

(a) the compensation made by electricity distributors under section 39A above;

(b) the levels of overall performance achieved by electricity distributors.

(2) At such times as may be specified in a direction given by the Authority, each electricity supplier shall furnish to the Authority the following information, namely—

(a) as respects each standard prescribed by regulations under section 39 above, the number of cases in which compensation was made and the aggregate amount or value of that compensation; and

(b) as respects each standard determined under section 40 or 41 above, such information with respect to the level of performance achieved by the supplier as may be so specified.

(2A) At such times as may be specified in a direction given by the Authority, each electricity distributor shall furnish to the Authority the following information, namely—

(a) as respects each standard prescribed by regulations under section 39A, the number of cases in which compensation was made and the aggregate amount or value of that compensation; and

(b) as respects each standard determined under section 40A, such information with respect to the level of performance achieved by the distributor as may be so specified.

(3)–(5) *Repealed.*

[Electricity Act 1989, s 42, as amended by the Utilities Act 2000, ss 3, 57 and 108.]

8–9597 42A. *Information to be given to customers about overall performance.*

Miscellaneous

8–9607 57. General restrictions on disclosure of information. *Repealed.*

8–9608   58. *Directions restricting the use of certain information.*

8–9609   59. Making of false statements etc.   (1) If any person, in giving any information or making any application under or for the purposes of any provision of this Part, or of any regulations made under this Part, makes any statement which he knows to be false in a material particular, or recklessly makes any statement which is false in a material particular, he shall be liable[1]—

(*a*) on summary conviction, to a fine not exceeding **the statutory maximum**;
(*b*) on conviction on indictment, to a **fine**.

(2) Any person who seeks to obtain entry to any premises by falsely pretending to be—

(*a*) an employee of, or other person acting on behalf of an electricity distributor or electricity supplier;
(*b*) an electrical inspector; or
(*c*) a meter examiner,

shall be liable on summary conviction to a fine not exceeding **level 4** on the standard scale.

(3) No proceedings shall be instituted in England and Wales in respect of an offence under subsection (1) above except by or with the consent of the Secretary of State or the Director of Public Prosecutions.
[Electricity Act 1989, s 59, as amended by the Utilities Act 2000, Sch 6.]

1. For procedure in respect of an offence which is triable either way, see the Magistrates' Courts Act 1980, ss 17A–21, in PART I: MAGISTRATES' COURTS, PROCEDURE, ante.

Supplemental

8–9610   60. *Powers to make regulations.*

8–9611   64. Interpretation etc of Part I.   (1) In this Part, unless the context otherwise requires—

"the 1973 Act" means the Fair Trading Act 1973;
"the 1980 Act" means the Competition Act 1980;
"authorised distributor" means a person who is authorised by a licence or exemption to distribute electricity;
"authorised supplier" means a person who is authorised by a licence or exemption to supply electricity;
"construct" and "construction", in relation to so much of a generating station as comprises or is to comprise renewable energy installations, has the same meaning as in Chapter 2 of Part 2 of the Energy Act 2004;
"distribute", in relation to electricity, has the meaning given by section 4(4), and cognate expressions shall be construed accordingly;
"electrical plant" means any plant, equipment, apparatus or appliance used for, or for purposes connected with, the generation, transmission, distribution or supply of electricity, other than—

(*a*) an electric line;
(*b*) a meter used for ascertaining the quantity of electricity supplied to any premises; or
(*c*) an electrical appliance under the control of a consumer;

"electricity distributor" and "electricity supplier" have the meanings given by section 6(9);
"electricity interconnector" has the meaning given by section 4(3E);
"electric line" means any line which is used for carrying electricity for any purpose and includes, unless the context otherwise requires—

(*a*) any support for any such line, that is to say, any structure, pole or other thing in, on, by or from which any such line is or may be supported, carried or suspended;
(*b*) any apparatus connected to any such line for the purpose of carrying electricity; and
(*c*) any wire, cable, tube, pipe or other similar thing (including its casing or coating) which surrounds or supports, or is surrounded or supported by, or is installed in close proximity to, or is supported, carried or suspended in association with, any such line;

"exemption" means an exemption under section 5 above;
"extension", in relation to a generating station, has the meaning given by section 36(8) above and "extend" shall be construed accordingly;
"final order" and "provisional order" have the meanings given by section 25(8) above;*
"generating station", in relation to a generating station wholly or mainly driven by water, includes all structures and works for holding or channelling water for a purpose directly related to the generation of electricity by that station;
"high voltage line" means—

(*a*) in relation to England and Wales, an electric line of a nominal voltage exceeding 132 kilovolts;
(*b*) in relation to Scotland, an electric line of a nominal voltage not less than 132 kilovolts,*

and "low voltage line" shall be construed accordingly;

"information" includes accounts, estimates and returns;

"licence" means a licence under section 6 above and "licence holder" shall be construed accordingly;

"licensable activity" means an activity which, if carried on without the authority of a licence or exemption, constitutes an offence under section 4(1);

"line" means any wire, cable, tube, pipe or other similar thing (including its casing or coating) which is designed or adapted for use in carrying electricity;

"notice" means notice in writing;

"premises" includes any land, building or structure;

"prescribed" means prescribed by regulations made unless the context otherwise requires, by the Secretary of State;

"relevant condition" and "relevant requirement" have the meanings given by section 25(8) above;

"renewable energy installation" and "Renewable Energy Zone" have the same meanings as in Chapter 2 of Part 2 of the Energy Act 2004;

"special connection agreement" means a special agreement under section 22;

"supply", in relation to electricity, has the meaning given by section 4(4) above, and cognate expressions shall be construed accordingly;

"transmission", in relation to electricity, has the meaning given by section 4(4) above;

"transmission system" has the same meaning given by section 4(4) above;

"working day" means any day other than a Saturday, a Sunday, Christmas Day, Good Friday or a day which is a bank holiday within the meaning of the Banking and Financial Dealings Act 1971.*

(1B) In this Part, references to participation, in relation to the transmission of electricity, are to be construed in accordance with section 4(3A) and (3B) above.

(2) *Scotland.*

[Electricity Act 1989, s 64 as amended by SI 1999/506, the Utilities Act 2000, Sch 6 and the Energy Acy 2004, ss 102, 143, 147 and Sch 23.]

---

*Definition "high voltage line", new definition "generate" and new sub-s (1A) inserted by the Energy Act 2004, s 89 and 180 from a date to be appointed.

8–9612

PART II[1]
REORGANISATION OF THE INDUSTRY

---

1. Part II, which is not printed in this work, contains ss 65–95.

PART III[1]
MISCELLANEOUS AND SUPPLEMENTAL
Miscellaneous

8–9613   98. Provision of statistical information. (1) The Secretary of State may, if he considers it expedient for the purpose of obtaining statistical information relating to the generation, transmission or supply of electricity or the use of electricity interconnectors, serve a notice under this section on any licence holder or any person who is authorised by an exemption to generate or supply electricity or to participate in the operation of electricity interconnectors.

(2) A notice under this section may require the person on whom it is served to furnish, at a time and place specified in the notice, to the Secretary of State such statistical information about that person's business as may be so specified.

(3) Subject to subsections (4) and (5) below, no information with respect to any particular business which—

(*a*) has been obtained under this section; and

(*b*) relates to the affairs of any individual or to any particular business,

shall, during the lifetime of that individual or so long as that business continues to be carried on, be published or otherwise disclosed without the consent of that individual or the person for the time being carrying on that business.

(4) Subsection (3) above does not apply in relation to any disclosure which is made after consultation with the individual concerned, or the person for the time being carrying on the business concerned, and is of information relating to—

(*a*) the quantities of electricity generated by particular methods or by the use of particular fuels;

(*b*) the quantities of particular fuels used for the generation of electricity;

(*c*) the quantities of electricity transferred between Great Britain and countries or territories outside Great Britain, or between England and Wales on the one hand and Scotland on the other; or (*d*)　the quantities of electricity supplied in England, Scotland or Wales either generally or to persons of any particular class or description.

(5)　Subsection (3) above does not apply in relation to any disclosure which is made to the Minister in charge of any Government department or to the Scottish Ministers or for the purposes of any proceedings under this section.

(6)　The Secretary of State may, after consultation with persons or bodies appearing to him to be representative of persons likely to be affected, by order amend subsection (4) above so as to add other descriptions of information which may be disclosed notwithstanding that it may relate to a particular person or business.

(7)　Any person who without reasonable excuse fails to furnish information in compliance with a requirement under this section shall be liable on summary conviction to a fine not exceeding **level 1** on the standard scale.

(8)　Any person who publishes or discloses any information in contravention of subsection (3) above or, in purported compliance with a requirement under this section, knowingly or recklessly furnishes any information which is false in any material particular shall be liable[2]—

(*a*)　on summary conviction, to imprisonment for a term not exceeding **three months** or a fine not exceeding **the statutory maximum** or both;

(*b*)　on conviction on indictment, to imprisonment for a term not exceeding **two years** or a **fine** or both.

(9)　In this section "information" does not include estimates as to future matters but, subject to that, expressions which are used in Part I have the same meanings as in that Part.
[Electricity Act 1989, s 98 as amended by SI 1999/1820, Sch 4 and the Energy Act 2004, s 147.]

---

1. Part III contains ss 96–113.
2. For procedure in respect of this offence which is triable either way, see the Magistrates' Courts Act 1980, ss 17A–21, in Part I: Magistrates' Courts, Procedure, ante.

Amendment of enactments

8–9614　101. Rights of entry.　In section 2 of the Rights of Entry (Gas and Electricity Boards) Act 1954 (warrant to authorise entry), for subsection (4) there shall be substituted the following subsection—

"(4)　Every warrant granted under this section shall continue in force until—

(*a*)　the time when the purpose for which the entry is required is satisfied; or
(*b*)　the end of the period of 28 days beginning with the day on which the warrant was granted,

whichever is the earlier."
[Electricity Act 1989, s 101.]

Supplemental

8–9615　106. Regulations and orders.　(1)　Any power under this Act to make regulations, and any power of the Secretary of State under this Act to make orders (other than the powers conferred by paragraph 9(6) of Schedule 4 and paragraph 2 of Schedule 5), shall be exercisable by statutory instrument.

(2)　Any statutory instrument containing—

(*a*)　regulations under this Act made by the Secretary of State; or
(*b*)　an order under this Act (other than an order appointing a day or nominating a company, an order under section 11A, 27A, 32, 41A, 43A or 56A, or an order under paragraph 4 of Schedule 12 to this Act),

shall be subject to annulment in pursuance of a resolution of either House of Parliament.
[Electricity Act 1989, s 106, as amended by the Utilities Act 2000, Sch 6.]

8–9616　107. Directions.　(1)　It shall be the duty of any person to whom a direction is given under this Act to give effect to that direction.

(2)　Any power conferred by this Act to give a direction shall, unless the context otherwise requires, include power to vary or revoke the direction.

(3)　Any direction given under this Act shall be in writing.
[Electricity Act 1989, s 107.]

8–9617　108. Offences by bodies corporate.　(1)　Where a body corporate is guilty of an offence under this Act and that offence is proved to have been committed with the consent or connivance of, or to be attributable to any neglect on the part of, any director, manager, secretary or other similar officer of the body corporate or any person who was purporting to act in any such capacity he, as well as the body corporate, shall be guilty of that offence and shall be liable to be proceeded against and punished accordingly.

(2)　Where the affairs of a body corporate are managed by its members, subsection (1) above shall apply in relation to the acts and defaults of a member in connection with his functions of management as if he were a director of the body corporate.

[Electricity Act 1989, s 108.]

8–9617A 108. Extraterritorial operation of Act. (1) Where by virtue of this Act an act or omission taking place outside Great Britain constitutes an offence, proceedings for the offcence may be taken, and the offence may for all incidental purposes be treated as having been committed, in any place in Great Britain.

(2) Provision made by or under this Act in relation to places outside Great Britain—

(*a*) so far as it applies to individuals, applies to them whether or not they are British citizens; and

(*b*) so far as it applies to bodies corporate, applies to them whether or not they are incorporated under the law of a part of the United Kingdom.

[Electricity Act 1989, s 108A as inserted by the Energy Act 2004, s 102.]

8–9618 109. Service of documents. (1) Any document required or authorised by virtue of this Act to be served on any person may be served—

(*a*) by delivering it to him or by leaving it at his proper address or by sending it by post to him at that address; or

(*b*) if the person is a body corporate, by serving it in accordance with paragraph (*a*) above on the secretary of that body; or

(*c*) if the person is a partnership, by serving it in accordance with paragraph (*a*) above on a partner or a person having the control or management of the partnership business.

(2) For the purposes of this section and section 7 of the Interpretation Act 1978 (which relates to the service of documents by post) in its application to this section, the proper address of any person on whom a document is to be served shall be his last known address, except that—

(*a*) in the case of service on a body corporate or its secretary, it shall be the address of the registered or principal office of the body;

(*b*) in the case of service on a partnership or a partner or a person having the control or management of a partnership business, it shall be the address of the principal office of the partnership;

and for the purposes of this subsection the principal office of a company registered outside the United Kingdom or of a partnership carrying on business outside the United Kingdom is its principal office within the United Kingdom.

(3) If a person to be served by virtue of this Act with any document by another has specified to that other an address within the United Kingdom other than his proper address (as determined in pursuance of subsection (2) above) as the one at which he or someone on his behalf will accept documents of the same description as that document, that address shall also be treated as his proper address for the purposes of this section and for the purposes of the said section 7 in its application to this section.

(4) If the name or address of any owner or occupier of land on whom by virtue of this Act any document is to be served cannot after reasonable inquiry be ascertained, the document may be served by—

(*a*) addressing it to him by the description of "owner" or "occupier" of the land (describing it); and

(*b*) either leaving it in the hands of a person who is or appears to be resident or employed on the land or leaving it conspicuously affixed to some building or object on or near the land.

(5) This section shall not apply to any document in relation to the service of which provision is made by rules of court.

(6) In this section "secretary", in relation to a local authority within the meaning of the Local Government Act 1972 or the Local Government (Scotland) Act 1973, means the proper officer within the meaning of that Act.

[Electricity Act 1989, s 109.]

8–9619 110. *Financial provisions.*

8–9620 111. General interpretation. (1) In this Act, unless the context otherwise requires—

"Area Board" has the same meaning as in the Electricity Act 1947;

"the Authority" means the Gas and Electricity Markets Authority;

"contravention", in relation to any direction, condition, requirement, regulation or order, includes any failure to comply with it and cognate expressions shall be construed accordingly;

"the Council" means the Gas and Electricity Consumer Council;

"Electricity Board" means an Area Board, the Generating Board or a Scottish Board;

"the Generating Board" means the Central Electricity Generating Board;

"modifications" includes additions, alterations and omissions and cognate expressions shall be construed accordingly;

"Scottish Board" means either the North of Scotland Hydro-Electric Board or the South of Scotland Electricity Board.

(2) For the purposes of this Act any class or description may be framed by reference to any matters or circumstances whatever.

[Electricity Act 1989, s 111, as amended by the Utilities Act 2000, Sch 6.]

8–9630　112. *Amendments, transitional provisions, savings and repeals.*

8–9631　113. *Short title, commencement and extent.*

Section 24

SCHEDULE 6
THE ELECTRICITY CODE

(As substituted by the Utilities Act 2000, Sch 4.)

Suppliers' charges relating to meters for disabled persons

8–9632　1. (1) Where an electricity supplier, for the purpose of meeting the needs of a disabled person—

(a) alters the position of any electricity meter provided by him for a customer of his; or
(b) replaces such a meter with one which has been specially adapted,

the supplier shall not charge the customer for the alteration or replacement.

(2) Section 23 applies to any dispute arising under this paragraph.

Non-payment of suppliers' charges

8–9633　2. (1) Where a customer has not, within the requisite period, paid all charges due from him to an electricity supplier in respect of the supply of electricity to any premises or the provision of an electricity meter, the supplier may—

(a) install a pre-payment meter on the premises; or
(b) disconnect the premises,

and the supplier may recover any expenses incurred in so doing from the customer.

(2) The power of a supplier under sub-paragraph (1)(a) or (b) may not be exercised—

(a) as respects any amount which is genuinely in dispute (disregarding for this purpose a dispute under section 39 or regulations made under it); and
(b) unless not less than seven working days' notice has been given to the occupier of the premises (or the owner of the premises if they are unoccupied) of his intention to exercise it.

(3) In this paragraph the "requisite period" means the period of 28 days after the making by the supplier of a demand in writing for payment of the charges due.

Deemed contracts in certain cases

8–9634　3. (1) Where an electricity supplier supplies electricity to any premises otherwise than in pursuance of a contract, the supplier shall be deemed to have contracted with the occupier (or the owner if the premises are unoccupied) for the supply of electricity as from the time ("the relevant time") when he began so to supply electricity.

(2) Where—

(a) the owner or occupier of any premises takes a supply of electricity which has been conveyed to those premises by an electricity distributor;
(b) that supply is not made by an authorised supplier; and
(c) a supply of electricity so conveyed has been previously made by an electricity supplier,

the owner or occupier shall be deemed to have contracted with the appropriate supplier for the supply of electricity as from the time ("the relevant time") when he began to take such a supply.

(3) Nothing in sub-paragraph (2) shall be taken to afford a defence in any criminal proceedings.

(4) The Authority shall publish a document containing provision for determining the "appropriate supplier" for the purposes of sub-paragraph (2).

(5) The Authority may revise the current document published under sub-paragraph (4); and where it does so it shall publish the revised document.

(6) The express terms and conditions of a contract which, by virtue of sub-paragraph (1) or (2), is deemed to have been made shall be provided for by a scheme made under this paragraph.

(7) Each electricity supplier shall make (and may from time to time revise), a scheme for determining the terms and conditions which are to be incorporated in the contracts which, by virtue of sub-paragraph (1) or (2), are to be deemed to have been made.

(8) The terms and conditions so determined may include terms and conditions for enabling the electricity supplier to determine, in any case where the meter is not read immediately before the relevant time, the quantity of electricity which is to be treated as supplied by the supplier to the premises, or taken by the owner or occupier of the premises, during the period beginning with the relevant time and ending with—

(a) the time when the meter is first read after the relevant time; or
(b) the time when the supplier ceases to supply electricity to the premises, or the owner or occupier ceases to take a supply of electricity,

whichever is the earlier.

(9) A scheme under this paragraph may (subject to section 7B) make different provision for different cases or classes of cases, or for different areas, determined by, or in accordance with, the provisions of the scheme.

(10) As soon as practicable after an electricity supplier makes a scheme under this paragraph, or a revision of such a scheme, he shall—

    (a) publish, in such manner as he considers appropriate for bringing it to the attention of persons likely to be affected by it, a notice stating the effect of the scheme or revision;

    (b) send a copy of the scheme or revision to the Authority and to the Council; and

    (c) if so requested by any other person, send such a copy to that person without charge to him.

Supplies of electricity illegally taken

8–9635   **4.** (1) Where any person takes a supply of electricity which is in the course of being conveyed by an electricity distributor, the distributor shall be entitled to recover from that person the value of the electricity so taken.

(2) Where—

    (a) any person at premises at which a connection has been restored in contravention of paragraph 5(1) takes a supply of electricity which has been conveyed to those premises by an electricity distributor; and

    (b) the supply is taken otherwise than in pursuance of a contract made with an authorised supplier, or of a contract deemed to have been made with an electricity supplier by virtue of paragraph 3 above or paragraph 23 (former tariff customers) of Schedule 7 to the Utilities Act 2000,

the distributor shall be entitled to recover from that person the value of the electricity so taken.

(3) Each electricity distributor shall make, and from time to time revise, a scheme providing for the manner in which, and the persons by whom, the quantity of electricity taken in such circumstances as are mentioned in sub-paragraph (1) or (2) is to be determined for the purposes of this sub-paragraph.

(4) Sub-paragraphs (9) and (10) of paragraph 3 shall apply in relation to a scheme under this paragraph as they apply in relation to a scheme under that paragraph.

(5) In this paragraph "value", in relation to any electricity taken in such circumstances as are mentioned in sub-paragraph (1) or (2), means the amount which, if the electricity had been taken in such circumstances as are mentioned in sub-paragraph (2) of paragraph 3, could reasonably be expected to have been payable in respect of the electricity under a contract deemed to have been made by virtue of that sub-paragraph.

Restoration of connection without consent

8–9636   **5.** (1) Where, otherwise than in the exercise of a power conferred by regulations under section 29, premises have been disconnected by an electricity supplier or an electricity distributor, no person shall, without the consent of the supplier or, as the case may be, the distributor, restore the connection.

(2) A person who acts in contravention of this paragraph shall be liable on summary conviction to a fine not exceeding level 3 on the standard scale.

(3) A connection restored in contravention of this paragraph may be disconnected by the distributor to whose distribution system the connection is made or, if the original disconnection was carried out by an electricity supplier, by that supplier.

Damage to electrical plant etc

8–9637   **6.** (1) A person who intentionally or by culpable negligence damages or allows to be damaged—

    (a) any electric line or electrical plant provided by an electricity distributor; or

    (b) any electricity meter provided by an electricity supplier,

shall be liable on summary conviction to a fine not exceeding level 3 on the standard scale.

(2) Where an offence has been committed under sub-paragraph (1) by the occupier of any premises (or by the owner of the premises if they are unoccupied when the offence is committed) in relation to any electric line or electrical plant provided by an electricity distributor for making or maintaining a connection to the premises, the distributor may disconnect the premises.

(3) Where an offence has been committed under sub-paragraph (1) in relation to an electricity meter provided by an electricity supplier which is situated on any premises, by the occupier (or by the owner of the premises if they are unoccupied when the offence is committed), the supplier may disconnect the premises and may remove the meter.

(4) A meter removed under sub-paragraph (3) shall be kept safely by the supplier until the Authority authorises its destruction or disposal.

(5) The distributor or supplier shall not be under any obligation to reconnect (and in the case of a supplier to restore the supply to) any premises disconnected under sub-paragraph (2) or (3) until—

    (a) the offender is no longer the occupier or, as the case may be, the owner of the premises; or

    (b) the matter in consequence of which the premises were disconnected has been remedied.

Entry during continuance of connection or supply

8–9638   **7.** (1) Any officer or other person authorised by an electricity distributor may at all reasonable times enter any premises to which the distributor is maintaining a connection, for the purpose of inspecting any electric line or electrical plant provided by him.

(2) Any officer or other person authorised by an electricity supplier may at all reasonable times enter any premises to which electricity is being supplied by him for the purpose of—

    (a) ascertaining the register of any electricity meter and, in the case of a pre-payment meter, removing any money or tokens belonging to the supplier;

    (b) removing, inspecting or re-installing any electricity meter or installing any substitute meter.

(3) The supplier shall provide a substitute meter while a meter is removed under sub-paragraph (2)(b).

(4) Where an electricity supplier is authorised by paragraph 2(1) to install a pre-payment meter on any

premises, any officer or other person authorised by the supplier may at all reasonable times enter the premises for the purpose of installing such a meter.

(5) A power of entry for the purpose of removing or installing an electricity meter may not be exercised unless at least two working days' notice has been given to the occupier (or the owner of the premises if they are unoccupied).

Entry on discontinuance of supply or connection

8–9639   8. (1) Where an electricity supplier or an electricity distributor is authorised by paragraph 6(2) or (3) above or paragraph 11(3) of Schedule 7 to this Act—

(*a*) to disconnect any premises; or
(*b*) to remove an electricity meter,

any officer or other person authorised by the supplier or distributor may at all reasonable times enter the premises for the purpose of disconnecting the premises or removing the meter.

(2) Where—

(*a*) an electricity distributor is authorised by any provision of this Act (other than one mentioned in sub-paragraph (1)) or of regulations made under it to disconnect any premises;
(*b*) a person occupying premises which are connected to a distribution system of an electricity distributor ceases to require a connection; or
(*c*) a person entering into occupation of any premises connected to a distribution system of an electricity distributor does not require such a connection,

any officer or other person authorised by the distributor may at all reasonable times enter the premises for the purpose of disconnecting the premises or removing any electrical plant or electric line provided by the distributor.

(3) Where—

(*a*) an electricity supplier is authorised by any provision of this Act (other than one mentioned in sub-paragraph (1)), or of regulations made under it, to disconnect any premises or to discontinue the supply to any premises;
(*b*) a person occupying premises which are supplied with electricity by an electricity supplier ceases to require such a supply; or
(*c*) a person entering into occupation of any premises previously supplied with electricity by an electricity supplier does not require such a supply;

any officer or other person authorised by the supplier may at all reasonable times enter the premises for the purpose of disconnecting the premises or removing any electricity meter provided by the supplier.

(4) A power of entry under sub-paragraph (2) or (3) may not be exercised unless at least two working day's notice has been given to the occupier (or to the owner of the premises if they are unoccupied).

Entry for replacing, repairing or altering lines or plant

8–9640   9. (1) Any officer or other person authorised by an electricity distributor may at all reasonable times enter any premises for the purpose of—

(*a*) placing a new electric line or any new electrical plant in the place of or in addition to any existing line or plant which has already been lawfully placed; or
(*b*) repairing or altering any such existing line or plant.

(2) A power of entry under sub-paragraph (1) may not be exercised unless at least five working days' notice has been given to the occupier of any premises (or to the owner of the premises if they are unoccupied).

(3) In the case of emergency arising from faults in an electric line or any electrical plant entry may be made under sub-paragraph (1) above without the notice required by sub-paragraph (2), but notice shall then be given as soon as possible after the occurrence of the emergency.

Provisions as to powers of entry

8–9640A   10. (1) The Rights of Entry (Gas and Electricity Boards) Act 1954 (entry under a justice's warrant) shall apply in relation to the powers of entry conferred by this Schedule.

(2) Any reference in this Schedule to an officer or other person authorised by an electricity supplier or an electricity distributor includes a reference to a person who, in accordance with a written authority given by the supplier or distributor to an agent of the supplier or distributor, is authorised by the agent on behalf of the supplier or distributor.

(3) Where in pursuance of any power of entry conferred by this Schedule, entry is made on any premises by a person authorised to do so—

(*a*) that person shall ensure that the premises are left no less secure by reason of the entry; and
(*b*) the supplier or distributor shall make good, or pay compensation for, any damage caused by that person (or by any other person accompanying him under sub-paragraph (5)) in entering the premises, in taking any action on the premises or in making them secure.

(4) A person may only exercise a power of entry conferred by this Schedule on production of some duly authenticated document showing his authority.

(5) Any person exercising a power of entry conferred by this Schedule may be accompanied by such other persons as may be necessary or expedient for the purpose for which the entry is made or for the purposes of sub-paragraph (3)(*a*) or (*b*) above.

(6) A person who intentionally obstructs a person exercising powers of entry conferred by this Schedule shall be liable on summary conviction to a fine not exceeding level 3 on the standard scale.

Electrical plant etc not to be subject to distress

8–9640B **11.** (1) This paragraph applies to any electric line, electrical plant or electricity meter belonging to or provided by an electricity distributor or electricity supplier which is marked or impressed with a sufficient mark or brand indicating an electricity supplier or electricity distributor as the owner or provider thereof.

(2) Anything to which this paragraph applies—

(a) shall be deemed not to be landlord's fixtures, notwithstanding that they may be fixed or fastened to any part of any premises; and

(b) shall not in England and Wales be subject to distress or be liable to be taken in execution under process of any court or any proceedings in bankruptcy against the person in whose possession they may be.

Section 31
SCHEDULE 7
USE ETC OF ELECTRICITY METERS

(As amended by the Utilities Act 2000, Sch 5 and the Energy Act 2004, s 181.)

Consumption to be ascertained by appropriate meter

8–9641 **1.** (1) Where a customer of an authorised supplier is to be charged for his supply wholly or partly by reference to the quantity of electricity supplied, the supply shall be given through, and the quantity of electricity shall be ascertained by, an appropriate meter.

(1A) An authorised supplier may give a supply otherwise than through an appropriate meter in such circumstances as may be prescribed[1].

(2) If the authorised supplier agrees, the meter may be provided by the customer (who may provide a meter which belongs to him or is made available otherwise than in pursuance of arrangements made by the supplier); but otherwise it shall be provided by the authorised supplier (who may provide a meter which belongs to him or to any person other than the customer).

(2A) An authorised supplier may refuse to allow one of his customers to provide a meter only if there are reasonable grounds for his refusal.

(3) The meter shall be installed on the customer's premises in a position determined by the authorised supplier, unless in all the circumstances it is more reasonable to place it outside those premises or in some other position.

(4) The authorised supplier may require the replacement of any meter provided and installed in accordance with sub-paragraphs (2) and (3) above where its replacement—

(a) is necessary to secure compliance with this Schedule or any regulations made under it; or

(b) is otherwise reasonable in all the circumstances;

and any replacement meter shall be provided and installed in accordance with those sub-paragraphs.

(5) If the customer refuses or fails to take his supply through an appropriate meter provided and installed in accordance with sub-paragraphs (2) and (3) above, the supplier may refuse to give or may discontinue the supply.

(6) For the purposes of this paragraph a meter is an appropriate meter for use in connection with any particular supply if it is of a pattern or construction which, having regard to the terms on which the supply is to be charged for, is particularly suitable for such use.

(7) Section 23 of this Act shall apply in relation to any dispute arising under this paragraph between an electricity supplier and a customer.

(8) Pending the determination under section 23 of this Act of any dispute arising under this paragraph, the meter and its provision and installation shall be such as the Authority may direct; and directions under this sub-paragraph may apply either in cases of particular descriptions or in particular cases.

(9) Part I of this Act shall apply as if any duty or other requirement imposed on an electricity supplier by directions under sub-paragraph (8) above were imposed by directions under section 23 of this Act.

(10) In this Schedule "exempt supply" means a supply of electricity to any premises where—

(a) the premises are not premises used wholly or mainly for domestic purposes; or

(b) the authorised supplier or the customer is a person authorised by an exemption to supply electricity to those premises.

1. See the Electricity (Unmetered Supply) Regulations 2001, SI 2001/3263.

Restrictions on use of meters

8–9642 **2.** (1) No meter shall be used for ascertaining the quantity of electricity supplied by an authorised supplier to a customer unless the meter—

(a) is of an approved pattern or construction and is installed in an approved manner; and

(b) subject to sub-paragraph (2) below, is certified under paragraph 5 below;

and in this Schedule "approved" means approved by or under regulations made under this paragraph.

(2) Paragraph (b) of sub-paragraph (1) above shall not apply to a meter used in connection with an exempt supply if the authorised supplier and the customer have agreed in writing to dispense with the requirements of that paragraph.

(3) Regulations under this paragraph may provide—

(a) for determining the fees to be paid for approvals given by or under the regulations;

(b) for revoking an approval so given to any particular pattern or construction of meter and requiring meters of that pattern or construction which have been installed to be replaced with meters of an approved pattern or construction within a prescribed period;

(c) for revoking an approval so given to any particular manner of installation and requiring meters which have been installed in that manner to be installed in an approved manner within such a period;

and may make different provision for meters of different descriptions or for meters used or intended to be used for different purposes.

8–9643　**3.**—(1) If an authorised supplier supplies electricity through a meter which is used for ascertaining the quantity of electricity supplied and—

    (*a*) is not of an approved pattern or construction or is not installed in an approved manner; or

    (*b*) in the case of a meter to which paragraph 2(1)(*b*) above applies, is not certified under paragraph 5 below,

he shall be liable on summary conviction to a fine not exceeding level 3 on the standard scale.

(1A) Regulations under paragraph 1(1A) may provide for this paragraph not to apply in such circumstances as may be prescribed (being circumstances in which an authorised supplier is not required to supply electricity through an appropriate meter).

(2) Where the commission by any person of an offence under this paragraph is due to the act or default of some other person, that other person shall be guilty of the offence; and a person may be charged with and convicted of the offence by virtue of this sub-paragraph whether or not proceedings are taken against the first-mentioned person.

(3) In any proceedings in respect of an offence under this paragraph it shall be a defence for the person charged to prove that he took all reasonable steps and exercised all due diligence to avoid committing the offence.

(4) No proceedings shall be instituted in England and Wales in respect of an offence under this paragraph except by or on behalf of the Authority.

Meter examiners

8–9644　**4.**—(1) The Authority shall appoint competent and impartial persons as meter examiners for the purposes of this Schedule.

(2) There shall be paid out of money provided by Parliament to meter examiners such remuneration and such allowances as may be determined by the Authority with the approval of the Treasury; and such pensions as may be so determined may be paid out of money provided by Parliament to or in respect of such examiners.

(3) All fees payable in respect of the examination of meters by meter examiners shall be paid to the Authority; and any sums received by it under this sub-paragraph shall be paid into the Consolidated Fund.

Certification of meters

8–9645　**5.**—(1) Subject to sub-paragraph (2) below, a meter may be certified—

    (*a*) by a meter examiner appointed under paragraph 4 above; or

    (*b*) by a person who is authorised to certify meters of that description by or under regulations made under this paragraph;

and in this paragraph "examiner" means a meter examiner or a person so authorised.

(2) No meter shall be certified unless the examiner is satisfied—

    (*a*) that the meter is of an approved pattern or construction; and

    (*b*) that the meter conforms to such standards (including standards framed by reference to margins of error) as may be prescribed;

and references in this Schedule to prescribed margins of error shall be construed accordingly.

(3) An examiner may certify any meter submitted to him, notwithstanding that he has not himself examined or tested it, if—

    (*a*) the meter is submitted to him by a person authorised by the Authority for the purposes of this sub-paragraph;

    (*b*) the meter is accompanied by a report stating that the meter has been examined and tested by the person submitting it and containing such other information as may be prescribed;

    (*c*) the examiner considers that the report indicates that the meter is entitled to be certified;

    (*d*) the meter is one of a number submitted at the same time by the same person,

and the examiner has himself examined and tested as many of those meters as he may consider sufficient to provide a reasonable test of all of them.

(4) Regulations[1] under this paragraph may make different provision for meters of different descriptions or for meters used or intended to be used for different purposes and may include provision—

    (*a*) for the termination of certification in the case of meters which no longer conform to the prescribed standards and in such other cases as may be prescribed;

    (*b*) for determining the fees to be paid for examining, testing and certifying meters, and the persons by whom they are to be paid; and

    (*c*) as to the procedure to be followed in examining, testing and certifying meters.

(5) Regulations under this paragraph above may also include provision—

    (*a*) for determining the fee to be paid in respect of any authorisation under sub-paragraph (1) or (3) above;

    (*b*) for imposing conditions on any such authorisation; and

    (*c*) for withdrawing any such authorisation before the end of any period for which it is given if any of those conditions is not satisfied.

---

    1. See the Meters (Approval of Pattern or Construction and Manner of Installation) Regulations 1998, SI 1998/1565 amended by SI 2002/3129.

Apparatus for testing etc of meters

8–9646　**6.**—(1) It shall be the duty of a person to whom this paragraph applies, that is to say, a person authorised by the Authority for the purposes of paragraph 5(3) above—

    (*a*) to provide and maintain such apparatus for the examination, testing and regulation of meters, and such apparatus for the sealing and unsealing of meters, as may be specified by a direction of the Authority;

(b) to use apparatus so provided and maintained to carry out such examination, testing and regulation of meters, or to seal or unseal meters in such circumstances, as may be so specified; and

(c) to keep such records and make such reports of things done in pursuance of paragraph (b) above as may be so specified.

(2) It shall also be the duty of a person to whom this paragraph applies to afford to meter examiners, acting in the exercise of their functions under this Schedule, all necessary facilities for the use of apparatus provided and maintained in pursuance of sub-paragraph (1) above.

(3) If the Authority considers that any person to whom this paragraph applies has made satisfactory arrangements whereby apparatus provided by some other person is available for the examination, testing or regulation of the first mentioned person's meters, the Authority may direct that this paragraph shall not apply to that person to such extent as may be specified in the direction.

(4) Any two or more persons to whom this paragraph applies may with the approval of the Authority enter and carry into effect arrangements whereby apparatus provided by one or more of the parties is to be available to all or any of them for the purposes of fulfilling their obligations under this paragraph.

(5) *Repealed.*

Testing etc of meters

8–9647 7. (1) It shall be the duty of a meter examiner, on being required to do so by any person and after giving notice to such persons as may be prescribed—

(a) to examine and test any meter used or intended to be used for ascertaining the quantity of electricity supplied to any premises;

(b) to determine whether it is of an approved pattern or construction and, if it is installed for use, whether it is installed in an approved manner;

(c) to determine whether it is in proper order for ascertaining the quantity of electricity supplied within the prescribed margins of error and, if it has been in use and there is a dispute as to whether it registered correctly at any time, to determine if possible whether it registered within those margins at that time; and

(d) to make a written report of his conclusions as to the matters mentioned in paragraphs (b) and (c) above.

(2) If a meter examiner determines that a meter is, or was at any time, operating outside the prescribed margins of error, he shall if possible give an opinion as to—

(a) any period for which the meter has or may have been so operating; and

(b) the accuracy (if any) with which it was or may have been operating for any such period.

(3) Regulations under this paragraph may make provision for determining the fees to be paid for examining and testing meters, and the persons by whom and the circumstances in which they are to be paid.

(4) In relation to a meter used or intended to be used in connection with an exempt supply, this paragraph shall have effect as if any reference to the prescribed margins of error included a reference to any margins of error agreed between the authorised supplier and the customer (in this Schedule referred to as "agreed margins of error").

8–9648 8. (1) This paragraph applies where there is a genuine dispute as to the accuracy of a meter used for ascertaining the quantity of electricity supplied to any premises and notice of the dispute—

(a) is given to the authorised supplier by the customer, or to the customer by the authorised supplier; or

(b) is given to the authorised supplier and to the customer by any other person interested.

(2) Except with the approval of a meter examiner and, if he so requires, under his supervision, the meter shall not be removed or altered by the supplier or the customer until after the dispute is resolved by agreement or the meter is examined and tested under paragraph 7 above, whichever first occurs.

(3) If the supplier or the customer removes or alters the meter in contravention of sub-paragraph (2) above, he shall be liable on summary conviction to a fine not exceeding level 2 on the standard scale.

Presumptions and evidence

8–9649 9. (1) This paragraph applies to meters used for ascertaining the quantity of electricity supplied to any premises.

(2) The register of a meter to which this paragraph applies shall be admissible in any proceedings as evidence of the quantity of electricity supplied through it.

(3) Where electricity has been supplied for any period through such a meter which is of an approved pattern or construction and is installed in an approved manner, the register of the meter shall be presumed to have been registering for that period—

(a) within the prescribed margins of error; and

(b) in the case of a meter used in connection with an exempt supply, within any agreed margins of error,

unless the contrary is proved.

(4) Where a meter to which this paragraph applies has been operating for any period—

(a) within the prescribed margins of error; and

(b) in the case of a meter used in connection with an exempt supply, within any agreed margins of error,

the meter shall be conclusively presumed to have been correctly registering for that period the quantity of electricity supplied through it.

(5) The report of a meter examiner on any question relating to such a meter shall be admissible in evidence in any proceedings in which that question is raised; and any conclusions in the report as to the accuracy of the meter when it was tested shall be presumed to be correct unless the contrary is proved.

Meters to be kept in proper order

8–9660   10. (1) A customer of an authorised supplier shall at all times, at his own expense, keep any meter provided by him in proper order for correctly registering the quantity of electricity supplied to him; and in default of his doing so the supplier may discontinue the supply of electricity through that meter.

(2) An authorised supplier shall at all times, at his own expense, keep any meter provided by him to any customer in proper order for correctly registering the quantity of electricity supplied and, in the case of pre-payment meters, for operating properly on receipt of the necessary payment.

(2A) Section 23 of this Act shall apply in relation to any dispute arising under this paragraph between an electricity supplier and a customer.

(3) *Repealed.*

(4) Sub-paragraphs (2) and (3) above are without prejudice to any remedy the supplier may have against the customer for failure to take proper care of the meter.

Interference with meters

8–9661   11. (1) If any person intentionally or by culpable negligence—

(*a*) alters the register of any meter used for measuring the quantity of electricity supplied to any premises by an authorised supplier; or

(*b*) prevents any such meter from duly registering the quantity of electricity supplied,

he shall be liable on summary conviction to a fine not exceeding level 3 on the standard scale.

(2) Where any person is prosecuted for an offence under sub-paragraph (1) above, the possession by him of artificial means for causing an alteration of the register of the meter or, as the case may be, the prevention of the meter from duly registering shall, if the meter was in his custody or under his control, be prima facie evidence (or in Scotland sufficient evidence) that the alteration or prevention was intentionally caused by him.

(3) Where an offence under sub-paragraph (1) above has been committed, the supplier may discontinue the supply of electricity to the premises until the matter has been remedied and remove the meter in respect of which the offence was committed.

(4) Where an authorised supplier removes a meter under sub-paragraph (3) above, he shall keep it safely until the Authority authorises him to destroy or otherwise dispose of it.

Special provision for pre-payment meters

8–9662   12. (1) A customer of an authorised supplier who takes his supply through a pre-payment meter shall be under a duty to take all reasonable precautions for the safekeeping of any money or tokens which are inserted into that meter.

(2) A pre-payment meter installed by an authorised supplier[1] through which a customer of such a supplier takes his supply of electricity shall not be used to recover a sum unless—

(*a*) the sum is owed to an authorised supplier in respect of the supply of electricity to the premises on which the meter is installed or in respect of the provision of the meter; or

(*b*) the recovery of the sum in that manner is permitted by both—

(i)   regulations; and

(ii) an agreement falling within sub-paragraph (3) below between the customer and the person to whom the sum is owed.

(3) An agreement falls within this sub-paragraph if—

(*a*) the person to whom the sum is owed is a person who is authorised by regulations to enter into agreements falling within this sub-paragraph;

(*b*) the agreement permits that person to use the meter in question to recover such sums as may be specified in or determined under the agreement; and

(*c*) the agreement complies with the requirements specified for the purposes of this sub-paragraph by regulations.

(4) The sums that regulations under this paragraph may permit the recovery of through a pre-payment meter include—

(*a*) sums owed to a person other than an authorised supplier;

(*b*) sums owed in respect of premises other than the premises on which the meter is installed;

(*c*) sums owed in respect of matters other than the supply of electricity.

(5) Before making regulations under this paragraph the Authority must consult—

(*a*) the Council;

(*b*) all authorised suppliers;

(*c*) such other persons as the Authority considers appropriate.

---

1. It is not reasonably incidental to the carrying out of an authorised supplier's functions to recover charges unrelated to the supply of electricity such as water charges by means of a two-in-one prepayment meter (*South Wales Electricity plc v Director General of Electricity Supply* [1999] 44 LS Gaz R 40.

Interpretation

8–9663   13. In this Schedule—

"agreed margins of error" has the meaning given by paragraph 7(4) above;

"approved" means approved by or under regulations made under paragraph 2 above;

"exempt supply" has the meaning given in paragraph 1(10) above;

"prescribed" means prescribed by regulations;

"prescribed margins of error" has the meaning given by paragraph 5(2) above;

"regulations" means regulations made by the Authority with the consent of the Secretary of State.

Radioactive Material (Road Transport) Act 1991
(1991 c 27)

8–9664   5. Powers of entry. (1) An inspector or examiner shall, on producing, if so required, some duly authenticated document showing his authority, have a right at all reasonable hours—

   (a)   to enter any vehicle used to transport radioactive packages for the purpose of ascertaining—

       (i)   whether the vehicle, or any radioactive package which is being transported by it, fails to comply with any regulations under section 2 above;

       (ii)   whether the vehicle, or any radioactive package which is or was being transported by it, has been involved in an accident; and

       (iii)   whether any radioactive package which was being transported by the vehicle, or any radioactive material which was contained in such a package, has been lost or stolen; and

   (b)   in the case of an inspector, to enter any premises for the purpose of ascertaining whether there is on the premises any vehicle used for transporting radioactive packages, or any radioactive package or packaging component which fails to comply with regulations under section 2 above.

(2) If a justice of the peace, on sworn information in writing or, in Scotland, on evidence on oath, is satisfied that there are reasonable grounds for entering any vehicle or premises for any such purpose as is mentioned in subsection (1) above and either—

   (a)   that admission to the vehicle or premises has been refused, or a refusal is apprehended, and (in the case of premises) that notice of the intention to apply for the warrant has been given to the occupier; or

   (b)   that an application for admission, or the giving of such a notice, would defeat the object of the entry, or that the case is one of urgency, or (in the case of premises) that they are unoccupied or the occupier temporarily absent,

he may by warrant signed by him authorise the inspector or examiner to enter and search the vehicle or premises, using reasonable force if need be.

(3) A warrant granted under this section shall continue in force until executed.

(4) An inspector or examiner who enters any vehicle or premises by virtue of this section, or of a warrant issued under it, may seize anything which he has reasonable grounds for believing is evidence in relation to an offence under section 2(4) above.

(5) Any person who intentionally obstructs any person exercising any power conferred by this section, or by a warrant issued under it, shall be guilty of an offence.

(6) If any person who enters any vehicle or premises by virtue of this section, or of a warrant issued under it, discloses any information thereby obtained with respect to any manufacturing process or trade secret, he shall, unless the disclosure was made in the performance of his duty, be guilty of an offence.

(7) *Scotland.*

[Radioactive Material (Road Transport) Act 1991, s 5.]

8–9665   6. Offences and penalties. (1) Where an offence under this Act which has been committed by a body corporate is proved to have been committed with the consent or connivance of, or to be attributable to any neglect on the part of—

   (a)   any director, manager, secretary or other similar officer of the body corporate; or

   (b)   any person who was purporting to act in any such capacity,

he as well as the body corporate shall be deemed to be guilty of that offence and shall be liable to be proceeded against and punished accordingly.

(2) Any person guilty of an offence under section 5(5) above shall be liable on summary conviction to a fine not exceeding **level 3** on the standard scale.

(3) Any person guilty of any other offence[1] under this Act shall be liable[2]—

   (a)   on conviction on indictment, to a fine or to imprisonment for a term not exceeding two years or to both;

   (b)   on summary conviction, to a fine not exceeding the **statutory maximum** or to imprisonment for a term not exceeding **two months or to both**.

(4) The court by or before which any person is convicted of an offence under section 2(4) or 3(8) above in respect of any radioactive material[3] may order the material to be destroyed or disposed of and any expenses reasonably incurred in connection with the destruction or disposal to be defrayed by that person.

[Radioactive Material (Road Transport) Act 1991, s 6.]

---

1. Offences under this Act are: s 2(4) contravene or fail to comply with regulations unde s 2; s 3(1) contravene a prohibition to drive a vehicle used to transport radioactive packages; s 3(2) contravene a prohibition concerning transport of a radioactive package or the use of a packaging component; s 3(4) fail to comply with direction to move a vehicle or trailer as specified in writing; s 4 fail to comply with an enforcement notice. See also the Radioactive Material (Road

Transport) Regulations 2002, SI 2002/1093 amended by SI 2005/2929 (W), made under s 2 of the Act, and which make further provision concerning the transport by road of radioactive material.

2. For procedure in respect of this offence which is triable either way, see the Magistrates' Courts Act 1980 ss 17A–22 ante in PART I, MAGISTRATES' COURTS, PROCEDURE.

3. Radioactive material is defined by s 1 as meaning any material having a specific activity in excess of 70 kilobecquerels per kilogram or such less specific activity as may be specified by an Order. 0.1 kilobecquerels per kilogram has been specified as the specific activity for the purposes of section 1(1) of the Radioactive Material (Road Transport) Act 1991 by the Radioactive Material (Road Transport) (Definition of Radioactive Material) Order 2002, SI 2002/1092.

Radioactive Substances Act 1993
(1993 c 12)

Preliminary

8–9666   1. Meaning of "radioactive material".   (1) In this Act "radioactive material" means anything which, not being waste, is either a substance to which this subsection applies or an article made wholly or partly from, or incorporating, such a substance.

(2) Subsection (1) applies to any substance falling within either or both of the following descriptions, that is to say,—

(a) a substance containing an element specified in the first column of Schedule 1, in such a proportion that the number of becquerels of that element contained in the substance, divided by the number of grams which the substance weighs, is a number greater than that specified in relation to that element in the appropriate column of that Schedule;

(b) a substance possessing radioactivity which is wholly or partly attributable to a process of nuclear fission or other process of subjecting a substance to bombardment by neutrons or to ionising radiations, not being a process occurring in the course of nature, or in consequence of the disposal of radioactive waste, or by way of contamination in the course of the application of a process to some other substance.

(3) In subsection (2)(a) "the appropriate column"—

(a) in relation to a solid substance, means the second column,

(b) in relation to a liquid substance, means the third column, and

(c) in relation to a substance which is a gas or vapour, means the fourth column.

(4) For the purposes of subsection (2)(b), a substance shall not be treated as radioactive material if the level of radioactivity is less than such level as may be prescribed for substances of that description.

(5) The Secretary of State may by order vary the provisions of Schedule 1, either by adding further entries to any column of that Schedule or by altering or deleting any entry for the time being contained in any column.

(6) *Northern Ireland.*

[Radioactive Substances Act 1993, s 1.]

8–9667   2. Meaning of "radioactive waste".   In this Act "radioactive waste" means waste which consists wholly or partly of—

(a) a substance or article which, if it were not waste, would be radioactive material, or

(b) a substance or article which has been contaminated in the course of the production, keeping or use of radioactive material, or by contact with or proximity to other waste falling within paragraph (a) or this paragraph.

[Radioactive Substances Act 1993, s 2.]

8–9668   3. Meaning of "mobile radioactive apparatus".   In this Act "mobile radioactive apparatus" means any apparatus, equipment, appliance or other thing which is radioactive material and—

(a) is constructed or adapted for being transported from place to place, or

(b) is portable and designed or intended to be used for releasing radioactive material into the environment or introducing it into organisms.

[Radioactive Substances Act 1993, s 3.]

Registration relating to use of radioactive material and mobile radioactive apparatus

8–9669   6. Prohibition of use of radioactive material without registration[1].   No person shall, on any premises which are used for the purposes of an undertaking carried on by him, keep or use, or cause or permit to be kept or used, radioactive material of any description, knowing or having reasonable grounds for believing it to be radioactive material, unless either—

(a) he is registered under section 7 in respect of those premises and in respect of the keeping and use on those premises of radioactive material of that description, or

(b) he is exempted from registration under that section in respect of those premises and in respect of the keeping and use on those premises of radioactive material of that description, or

(c) the radioactive material in question consists of mobile radioactive apparatus in respect of which a person is registered under section 10 or is exempted from registration under that section.

[Radioactive Substances Act 1993, s 6.]

---

1. For the creation of offences and their punishment see s 32, post.

8–9670 7. Registration of users of radioactive material. (1) Any application for registration under this section shall be made to the appropriate Agency and shall—

(a) specify the particulars mentioned in subsection (2),

(b) contain such other information as may be prescribed, and

(c) be accompanied by the charge prescribed for the purpose by a charging scheme under section 41 of the Environment Act 1995.

(2) The particulars referred to in subsection (1)(a) are—

(a) the premises to which the application relates,

(b) the undertaking for the purposes of which those premises are used,

(c) the description or descriptions of radioactive material proposed to be kept or used on the premises, and the maximum quantity of radioactive material of each such description likely to be kept or used on the premises at any one time, and

(d) the manner (if any) in which radioactive material is proposed to be used on the premises.

(3) On any application being made under this section, the appropriate Agency shall, subject to directions under section 25, send a copy of the application to each local authority in whose area the premises are situated.

(4) Subject to the following provisions of this section, where an application is made to the appropriate Agency for registration under this section in respect of any premises, the appropriate Agency may either—

(a) register the applicant in respect of those premises and in respect of the keeping and use on those premises of radioactive material of the description to which the application relates, or

(b) if the application relates to two or more descriptions of radioactive material, register the applicant in respect of those premises and in respect of the keeping and use on those premises of such one or more of those descriptions of radioactive material as may be specified in the registration, or

(c) refuse the application.

(5) An application for registration under this section which is duly made to the appropriate Agency may be treated by the applicant as having been refused if it is not determined within the prescribed period for determinations or within such longer period as may be agreed with the applicant.

(6) Any registration under this section in respect of any premises may (subject to subsection (7)) be effected subject to such limitations or conditions as the appropriate Agency thinks fit, and in particular (but without prejudice to the generality of this subsection) may be effected subject to conditions of any of the following descriptions—

(a) conditions imposing requirements (including, if the appropriate Agency thinks fit, requirements involving structural or other alterations) in respect of any part of the premises, or in respect of any apparatus, equipment or appliance used or to be used on any part of the premises for the purposes of any use of radioactive material from which radioactive waste is likely to arise,

(b) conditions requiring the person to whom the registration relates, at such times and in such manner as may be specified in the registration, to furnish the appropriate Agency with information as to the removal of radioactive material from those premises to any other premises, and

(c) conditions prohibiting radioactive material from being sold or otherwise supplied from those premises unless it (or the container in which it is supplied) bears a label or other mark—

(i) indicating that it is radioactive material, or

(ii) if the conditions so require, indicating the description of radioactive material to which it belongs,

and (in either case) complying with any relevant requirements specified in the conditions.

(7) In the exercise of any power conferred on it by subsection (4) or (6), the appropriate Agency shall have regard exclusively to the amount and character of the radioactive waste likely to arise from the keeping or use of radioactive material on the premises in question.

(7A) Subsection (7) does not apply—

(a) in relation to high-activity sources and to other sealed sources which, in the opinion of the appropriate Agency or the chief inspector, are of a similar level of potential hazard to high-activity sources, or

(*b*) in determining whether to impose any conditions falling within paragraph (*b*) or (*c*) of subsection (6).

(8) On registering a person under this section in respect of any premises, the appropriate Agency—

(*a*) shall furnish him with a certificate which contains all material particulars of the registration or gives sufficient information as to the particulars to enable them to be ascertained, and

(*b*) subject to directions under section 25, shall send a copy of the certificate to each local authority in whose area the premises are situated.

[Radioactive Substances Act 1993, s 7 as amended by the Environment Act 1995, Sch 22 and SI 2005/2686.]

8–9671   8. Exemptions from registration under section 7.   (1) At any time while a nuclear site licence is in force in respect of a site, and at any time after the revocation or surrender of such a licence but before the period of responsibility of the licensee has come to an end, the licensee (subject to subsection (2)) is exempted from registration under section 7 in respect of any premises situated on that site and in respect of the keeping and use on those premises of radioactive material of every description.

(2) Where, in the case of any such premises as are mentioned in subsection (1), it appears to the appropriate Agency that, if the licensee had been required to apply for registration under section 7 in respect of those premises, the appropriate Agency would have imposed conditions such as are mentioned in paragraph (*b*) or (*c*) of subsection (6) of that section, the appropriate Agency may direct that the exemption conferred by subsection (1) of this section shall have effect subject to such conditions (being conditions which in the opinion of the appropriate Agency correspond to those which it would so have imposed) as may be specified in the direction.

(3) On giving a direction under subsection (2) in respect of any premises, the appropriate Agency shall furnish the licensee with a copy of the direction.

(4) Except as provided by subsection (5), in respect of all premises all persons are exempted from registration under section 7 in respect of the keeping and use on the premises of clocks and watches which are radioactive material.

(5) Subsection (4) does not exempt from registration under section 7 any premises on which clocks or watches are manufactured or repaired by processes involving the use of luminous material.

(6) The Secretary of State may by order[1] grant further exemptions from registration under section 7, by reference to such classes of premises and undertakings, and such descriptions of radioactive material, as may be specified in the order.

(7) Any exemption granted by an order under subsection (6) may be granted subject to such limitations or conditions as may be specified in the order.

(8) *Northern Ireland.*

[Radioactive Substances Act 1993, s 8 as amended by the Environment Act 1995, Sch 22.]

---

1. The Radioactive Substances (Natural Gas) Exemption Order 2002, SI 2002/1177 has been made.

8–9672   9. Prohibition of use of mobile radioactive apparatus without registration[1].   (1) No person shall, for the purpose of any activities to which this section applies—

(*a*) keep, use, lend or let on hire mobile radioactive apparatus of any description, or

(*b*) cause or permit mobile radioactive apparatus of any description to be kept, used, lent or let on hire,

unless he is registered under section 10 in respect of that apparatus or is exempted from registration under that section in respect of mobile radioactive apparatus of that description.

(2) This section applies to activities involving the use of the apparatus concerned for—

(*a*) testing, measuring or otherwise investigating any of the characteristics of substances or articles, or

(*b*) releasing quantities of radioactive material into the environment or introducing such material into organisms.

[Radioactive Substances Act 1993, s 9.]

---

1. For the creation of offences and their punishment see s 32, post.

8–9673   10. Registration of mobile radioactive apparatus.   (1) Any application for registration under this section shall be made to the appropriate Agency and—

(*a*) shall specify—

(i) the apparatus to which the application relates, and

(ii) the manner in which it is proposed to use the apparatus,

(*b*) shall contain such other information as may be prescribed, and

(*c*) shall be accompanied by the charge prescribed for the purpose by a charging scheme under section 41 of the Environment Act 1995.

(2) Where an application is made to the appropriate Agency for registration under this section in

respect of any apparatus, the appropriate Agency may register the applicant in respect of that apparatus, either unconditionally or subject to such limitations or conditions as the appropriate Agency thinks fit, or may refuse the application.

(3) On any application being made the appropriate Agency shall, subject to directions under section 25, send a copy of the application to each local authority in whose area it appears to the appropriate Agency the apparatus will be kept or will be used for releasing radioactive material into the environment.

(4) An application for registration under this section which is duly made to the appropriate Agency may be treated by the applicant as having been refused if it is not determined within the prescribed period for determinations or within such longer period as may be agreed with the applicant.

(5) On registering a person under this section in respect of any mobile radioactive apparatus, the appropriate Agency—

(a) shall furnish him with a certificate which contains all material particulars of the registration or gives sufficient information as to the particulars to enable them to be ascertained, and

(b) shall, subject to directions under section 25, send a copy of the certificate to each local authority in whose area it appears to the appropriate Agency the apparatus will be kept or will be used for releasing radioactive material into the environment.

[Radioactive Substances Act 1993, s 10 as amended by the Environment Act 1995, Sch 22 and SI 2005/2686.]

8–9674 11. Exemptions from registration under section 10.   (1) The Secretary of State may by order grant exemptions from registration under section 10, by reference to such classes of persons, and such descriptions of mobile radioactive apparatus, as may be specified in the order.

(2) Any exemption granted by an order under subsection (1) may be granted subject to such limitations or conditions as may be specified in the order.

(3) *Northern Ireland.*

[Radioactive Substances Act 1993, s 11.]

8–9675 12. Cancellation and variation of registration.   (1) Where any person is for the time being registered under section 7 or 10, the appropriate Agency may at any time cancel the registration, or may vary it—

(a) where the registration has effect without limitations or conditions, by attaching limitations or conditions to it, or

(b) where the registration has effect subject to limitations or conditions, by revoking or varying any of those limitations or conditions or by attaching further limitations or conditions to the registration.

(1A) The powers of the appropriate Agency and of the chief inspector under this section are exercisable with or without the making of an application by the person holding the registration.

(2) On cancelling or varying a registration by virtue of this section, the appropriate Agency shall—

(a) give notice of the cancellation or variation to the person to whom the registration relates, and

(b) if a copy of the certificate was sent to a local authority in accordance with section 7(8) or 10(5), send a copy of the notice to that local authority.

[Radioactive Substances Act 1993, s 12 as amended by the Environment Act 1995, Sch 22 and SI 2005/2686.]

Authorisation of disposal and accumulation of radioactive waste

8–9676 13. Disposal of radioactive waste[1].   (1) Subject to section 15, no person shall, except in accordance with an authorisation granted in that behalf under this subsection, dispose of any radioactive waste on or from any premises which are used for the purposes of any undertaking carried on by him, or cause or permit any radioactive waste to be so disposed of, if (in any such case) he knows or has reasonable grounds for believing it to be radioactive waste.

(2) Where any person keeps any mobile radioactive apparatus for the purpose of its being used in activities to which section 9 applies, he shall not dispose of any radioactive waste arising from any such apparatus so kept by him, or cause or permit any such radioactive waste to be disposed of, except in accordance with an authorisation granted in that behalf under this subsection.

(3) Subject to subsection (4) and to section 15, where any person, in the course of the carrying on by him of an undertaking, receives any radioactive waste for the purpose of its being disposed of by him, he shall not, except in accordance with an authorisation granted in that behalf under this subsection, dispose of that waste, or cause or permit it to be disposed of, knowing or having reasonable grounds for believing it to be radioactive waste.

(4) The disposal of any radioactive waste does not require an authorisation under subsection (3) if it is waste which falls within the provisions of an authorisation granted under subsection (1) or (2), and it is disposed of in accordance with the authorisation so granted.

(5) In relation to any premises which—

(a) are situated on a nuclear site, but

(b) have ceased to be used for the purposes of an undertaking carried on by the licensee,

subsection (1) shall apply (subject to section 15) as if the premises were used for the purposes of an undertaking carried on by the licensee.
[Radioactive Substances Act 1993, s 13.]

---

1. For the creation of offences and their punishment see s 32, post.

8–9677   14. Accumulation of radioactive waste[1].   (1) Subject to the provisions of this section and section 15, no person shall, except in accordance with an authorisation granted in that behalf under this section, accumulate any radioactive waste (with a view to its subsequent disposal) on any premises which are used for the purposes of an undertaking carried on by him, or cause or permit any radioactive waste to be so accumulated, if (in any such case) he knows or has reasonable grounds for believing it to be radioactive waste.

(2) Where the disposal of any radioactive waste has been authorised under section 13, and in accordance with that authorisation the waste is required or permitted to be accumulated with a view to its subsequent disposal, no further authorisation under this section shall be required to enable the waste to be accumulated in accordance with the authorisation granted under section 13.

(3) Subsection (1) shall not apply to the accumulation of radioactive waste on any premises situated on a nuclear site.

(4) For the purposes of this section, where radioactive material is produced, kept or used on any premises, and any substance arising from the production, keeping or use of that material is accumulated in a part of the premises appropriated for the purpose, and is retained there for a period of not less than three months, that substance shall, unless the contrary is proved, be presumed—

    (*a*)   to be radioactive waste, and

    (*b*)   to be accumulated on the premises with a view to the subsequent disposal of the substance.
[Radioactive Substances Act 1993, s 14.]

---

1. For the creation of offences and their punishment see s 32, post.

8–9678   15. Further exemptions from sections 13 and 14.   (1) Sections 13(1) and (3) and 14(1) shall not apply to the disposal or accumulation of any radioactive waste arising from clocks or watches on or from any premises in the circumstances described in subsection (1A)—

    (*a*)   where the total quantity taken together of each of the radionuclides listed in column 1 of Table A below present in the clocks and watches on any premises does not exceed the amount set out in column 2—

TABLE A

Radioactive material	Relevant value
Tritium	10^9 becquerels
Promethium 147	10^7 becquerels
Radium 226	10^4 becquerels

    or

    (*b*)   where

        (i)   the total quantity of the radionuclides listed in column 2 of Table B below present in each such clock or watch of the type listed in column 1 of that table does not exceed the amount set out in column 3—

TABLE B

Type of clock or watch	Radioactive material	Relevant value (becquerels)
(i) Luminised time measurement instruments—		
(*a*) worn or carried on the person	Tritium	2.8×10^8
	Promethium 147	5.5×10^6
(*b*) not worn or carried on the person	Tritium	3.7×10^8
	Promethium 147	7.4×10^6
(ii) Special luminised time measurement instruments	Tritium	9.3×10^8
	Promethium 147	1.9×10^7
(iii) Watches containing gaseous tritium light sources	Tritium	7.4×10^9

Type of clock or watch	Radioactive material	Relevant value (becquerels)
(iv) Radium luminised time-pieces—		
(a) wristwatches	Radium 226	3.7×10^3
(b) alarm clocks	Radium 226	5.5×10^3
(c) special time measurement instruments	Radium 226	5.6×10^4

and

(ii) no more than five items falling within Table B which constitute radioactive waste are present on any premises,

but this subsection does not affect the operation of section 13(1) or section 14(1) in relation to the disposal or accumulation of radioactive waste arising from clocks or watches on or from premises which, by virtue of subsection (5) of section 8, are excluded from the operation of subsection (4) of that section.

(1A) The circumstances referred to in subsection (1) are that—

(a) no radionuclide other than tritium, promethium 147 or radium 226 is present in any clock or watch on the premises (whether or not any radioactive waste arises from it),

(b) no such clock or watch contains more than one of those radionuclides, and

(c) either subsection (1B) or subsection (1C) is satisfied.

(1B) This subsection is satisfied if the total quantity of tritium divided by 109, plus the total quantity of promethium 147 divided by 107, plus the total quantity of radium 226 divided by 104, in all such clocks and watches does not exceed 1 (quantity in each case being measured in becquerels).

(1C) This subsection is satisfied if—

(a) all such clocks and watches fall within a description specified in the first column of the Table below;

(b) radioactive waste arises from no more than five of them; and

(c) none of them gives rise to a quantity of radioactive waste exceeding the figure in the third column of the Table corresponding to the relevant radionuclide listed in the second column.

TABLE

Description of clock or watch	Radionuclide	Relevant quantity (in becquerels)
(i) Clocks or watches having their dials marked at the time of manufacture with "T 25" (Tritium), "Pm 0.5" (Promethium 147) or "Ra 1.5" (Radium 226)	Tritium Promethium 147 Radium 226	9.3×10^8 1.9×10^7 5.6×10^4
(ii) Clocks bearing radioluminescent deposits and not falling within category (i)	Tritium Promethium 147 Radium 226	3.7×10^8 7.4×10^6 7.4×10^3
(iii) Watches bearing radioluminescent deposits and not falling within category (i)	Tritium Promethium 147 Radium 226	2.8×10^8 5.5×10^6 5.6×10^3
(iv) Watches containing small sealed glass tubes internally coated with a phosphor and filled with tritium gas	Tritium	7.4×10^9]

(2) Without prejudice to subsection (1), the Secretary of State may by order[1] exclude particular descriptions of radioactive waste from any of the provisions of section 13 or 14, either absolutely or subject to limitations or conditions; and accordingly such of those provisions as may be specified in an order under this subsection shall not apply to a disposal or accumulation of radioactive waste if it

is radioactive waste of a description so specified, and (where the exclusion is subject to limitations or conditions) the limitations or conditions specified in the order are complied with.

(3) *Northern Ireland.*

[Radioactive Substances Act 1993, s 15, as amended by SI 2001/4005.]

1. The Radioactive Substances (Natural Gas) Exemption Order 2002, SI 2002/1177 has been made.

8–9679   16–18. *Authorisations.*

Further obligations relating to registration or authorisation

8–9680   19. Duty to display documents[1]. At all times while—

(*a*)   a person is registered in respect of any premises under section 7, or

(*b*)   an authorisation granted in respect of any premises under section 13(1) or 14 is for the time being in force,

the person to whom the registration relates, or to whom the authorisation was granted, as the case may be, shall cause copies of the certificate of registration or authorisation issued to him under this Act to be kept posted on the premises, in such characters and in such positions as to be conveniently read by persons having duties on those premises which are or may be affected by the matters set out in the certificate.

[Radioactive Substances Act 1993, s 19.]

1. For the creation of offences and their punishment see s 32, post.

8–9681   20. Retention and production of site or disposal records[1]. (1) The appropriate Agency may, by notice served on any person to whom a registration under section 7 or 10 relates or who holds an authorisation under section 13 or 14 has been granted, impose on him such requirements authorised by this section in relation to site, source transfer or disposal records kept by that person as the appropriate Agency may specify in the notice.

(2) The requirements that may be imposed on a person under this section in relation to site or disposal records are—

(*a*)   to retain copies of the records for a specified period after he ceases to carry on the activities regulated by his registration or authorisation, or

(*b*)   to furnish the appropriate Agency with copies of the records in the event of his registration being cancelled or his authorisation being revoked or in the event of his ceasing to carry on the activities regulated by his registration or authorisation.

(3) *Repealed.*

(4) In this section, in relation to a registration and the person registered or an authorisation and the person authorised—

"the activities regulated" by his registration or authorisation means—

(*a*)   in the case of registration under section 7, the keeping or use of radioactive material,

(*b*)   in the case of registration under section 10, the keeping, using, lending or hiring of the mobile radioactive apparatus,

(*c*)   in the case of an authorisation under section 13, the disposal of radioactive waste, and

(*d*)   in the case of an authorisation under section 14, the accumulation of radioactive waste,

"records" means records required to be kept by virtue of the conditions attached to the registration or authorisation relating to the activities regulated by the registration or authorisation, and "site records" means records relating to the condition of the premises on which those activities are carried on or, in the case of registration in respect of mobile radioactive apparatus, of any place where the apparatus is kept, "source transfer records" means records relating to the transfer of control of high-activity sources and "disposal records" means records relating to the disposal of radioactive waste on or from the premises on which the activities are carried on, and "specified" means specified in a notice under this section.

[Radioactive Substances Act 1993, s 20 as amended by the Environment Act 1995, Schs 22 and 24, the Energy Act 2004, Sch 15 and SI 2005/2686.]

1. For the creation of offences and their punishment see s 32, post.

Enforcement notices and prohibition notices

8–9682   21. Enforcement notices. (1) Subject to the provisions of this section, if the appropriate Agency is of the opinion that a person to whom a registration under section 7 or 10 relates or who holds an authorisation under section 13 or 14—

(*a*)   is failing to comply with any limitation or condition subject to which the registration or authorisation has effect, or

(*b*)   is likely to fail to comply with any such limitation or condition, it may serve a notice under this section on that person.

(2) A notice under this section shall—

(a) state that the appropriate Agency is of that opinion,

(b) specify the matters constituting the failure to comply with the limitations or conditions in question or the matters making it likely that such a failure will occur, as the case may be, and

(c) specify the steps that must be taken to remedy those matters and the period within which those steps must be taken.

(3) *Repealed.*

(4) Where a notice is served under this section the appropriate Agency shall—

(a) in the case of a registration, if a certificate relating to the registration was sent to a local authority under section 7(8) or 10(5), or

(b) in the case of an authorisation, if a copy of the authorisation was sent to a public or local authority under section 16(9)(b) or 16A(8)(d),

send a copy of the notice to that authority.

[Radioactive Substances Act 1993, s 21 as amended by the Environment Act 1995, Schs 22 and 24 and the Energy Act 2004, Sch 15.]

8–9683 22. Prohibition notices. (1) Subject to the provisions of this section, if the appropriate Agency is of the opinion, as respects the keeping or use of radioactive material or of mobile radioactive apparatus, or the disposal or accumulation of radioactive waste, by a person in pursuance of a registration or authorisation under this Act, that the continuing to carry on that activity (or the continuing to do so in a particular manner) involves an imminent risk of pollution of the environment or of harm to human health, it may serve a notice under this section on that person.

(2) A notice under this section may be served whether or not the manner of carrying on the activity in question complies with any limitations or conditions to which the registration or authorisation in question is subject.

(3) A notice under this section shall—

(a) state the appropriate Agency's opinion,

(b) specify the matters giving rise to the risk involved in the activity, the steps that must be taken to remove the risk and the period within which those steps must be taken, and

(c) direct that the registration or authorisation shall, until the notice is withdrawn, wholly or to the extent specified in the notice cease to have effect.

(4) Where the registration or authorisation is not wholly suspended by the direction given under subsection (3), the direction may specify limitations or conditions to which the registration or authorisation is to be subject until the notice is withdrawn.

(5) *Repealed.*

(6) Where a notice is served under this section the appropriate Agency shall—

(a) in the case of a registration, if a certificate relating to the registration was sent to a local authority under section 7(8) or 10(5), or

(b) in the case of an authorisation, if a copy of the authorisation was sent to a public or local authority under section 16(9)(b) or 16A(8)(d),

send a copy of the notice to that authority.

(7) The appropriate Agency shall, by notice to the recipient, withdraw a notice under this section when that Agency is satisfied that the risk specified in it has been removed; and on so doing that Agency shall send a copy of the withdrawal notice to any public or local authority to whom a copy of the notice under this section was sent.

[Radioactive Substances Act 1993, s 22 as amended by the Environment Act 1995, Schs 22 and 24 and the Energy Act 2004, Sch 15.]

8–9684 23–25. *Powers of Secretary of State in relation to applications etc.*

8–9685 26–28. *Appeals in respect of authorisations.*

8–9686 29–30A. *Further powers of Secretary of State in relation to radioactive waste.*

Offences

8–9687 32. Offences relating to registration or authorisation. (1) Any person who—

(a) contravenes section 6, 9, 13(1), (2) or (3) or 14(1), or

(b) being a person registered under section 7 or 10, or being (wholly or partly) exempted from registration under either of those sections, does not comply with a limitation or condition subject to which he is so registered or exempted, or

(c) being a person who holds an authorisation under section 13 or 14, does not comply with a limitation or condition subject to which that authorisation has effect, or (*d*) being a person who is registered under section 7 or 10 or who holds an authorisation under section 13 or 14, fails to comply with any requirement of a notice served on him under section 21 or 22,

shall be guilty of an offence.

(2) A person guilty of an offence under this section shall be liable[1]—

(*a*) on summary conviction, to a fine not exceeding £20,000 or to imprisonment for a term not exceeding six months, or both;

(*b*) on conviction on indictment, to a fine or to imprisonment for a term not exceeding five years, or both.

(3) If the appropriate Agency is of the opinion that proceedings for an offence under subsection (1)(*d*) would afford an ineffectual remedy against a person who has failed to comply with the requirements of a notice served on him under section 21 or 22, that Agency may take proceedings in the High Court or, in Scotland, in any court of competent jurisdiction, for the purpose of securing compliance with the notice.

[Radioactive Substances Act 1993, s 32 as amended by the Environment Act 1995, Sch 22 and the Energy Act 2004, Sch 15.]

---

1. For procedure in respect of this offence which is triable either way, see the Magistrates' Courts Act 1980, ss 17A–21, in PART I: MAGISTRATES' COURTS, PROCEDURE, ANTE.

8–9688   33. Offences relating to sections 19 and 20.   (1) Any person who contravenes section 19 shall be guilty of an offence and liable[1]—

(*a*) on summary conviction, to a fine not exceeding the **statutory maximum**;

(*b*) on conviction on indictment, to a fine.

(2) Any person who without reasonable cause pulls down, injures or defaces any document posted in pursuance of section 19 shall be guilty of an offence and liable on summary conviction to a fine not exceeding **level 2** on the standard scale.

(3) Any person who fails to comply with a requirement imposed on him under section 20 shall be guilty of an offence and liable[1]—

(*a*) on summary conviction, to a fine not exceeding the **statutory maximum** or to imprisonment for a term not exceeding **three months**, or **both**;

(*b*) on conviction on indictment, to a fine or to imprisonment for a term not exceeding two years, or both.

[Radioactive Substances Act 1993, s 33.]

---

1. For procedure in respect of this offence which is triable either way, see the Magistrates' Courts Act 1980, ss 17A–21, in PART I: MAGISTRATES' COURTS, PROCEDURE, ANTE.

8–9689   34. Disclosure of trade secrets.   (1) If any person discloses any information relating to any relevant process or trade secret used in carrying on any particular undertaking which has been given to or obtained by him under this Act or in connection with the execution of this Act, he shall be guilty of an offence, unless the disclosure is made—

(*a*) with the consent of the person carrying on that undertaking, or

(*b*) in accordance with any general or special directions given by the Secretary of State, or

(*bb*) under or by virtue of section 113 of the Environment Act 1995, or

(*c*) in connection with the execution of this Act, or

(*d*) for the purposes of any legal proceedings arising out of this Act or of any report of any such proceedings.

(2) A person guilty of an offence under this section shall be liable[1]—

(*a*) on summary conviction, to a fine not exceeding the **statutory maximum** or to imprisonment for a term not exceeding **three months**, or **both**;

(*b*) on conviction on indictment, to a fine or to imprisonment for a term not exceeding two years, or both.

(3) In this section "relevant process" means any process applied for the purposes of, or in connection with, the production or use of radioactive material.

(4) *Northern Ireland.*

[Radioactive Substances Act 1993, s 34 as amended by the Environment Act 1995, Sch 22.]

---

1. For procedure in respect of this offence which is triable either way, see the Magistrates' Courts Act 1980, ss 17A–21, in PART I: MAGISTRATES' COURTS, PROCEDURE, ANTE.

8–9690   34A. Offences of making false or misleading statements or false entries.   (1) Any person who—

(a) for the purpose of obtaining for himself or another any registration under section 7 or 10, any authorisation under section 13 or 14, any transfer of such authorisation under section 16A or any variation of such an authorisation under section 17, or

(b) in purported compliance with a requirement to furnish information imposed under section 31(1)(d),

makes a statement which he knows to be false or misleading in a material particular, or recklessly makes a statement which is false or misleading in a material particular, shall be guilty of an offence.

(2) Any person who intentionally makes a false entry in any record—

(a) which is required to be kept by virtue of a registration under section 7 or 10, an authorisation under section 13 or 14 or a transfer under 16A or an authorisation under section 13 or 14, or

(b) which is kept in purported compliance with a condition which must be complied with if a person is to have the benefit of an exemption under section 8, 11 or 15,

shall be guilty of an offence.

(3) A person guilty of an offence under this section shall be liable[1]—

(a) on summary conviction, to a fine not exceeding **the statutory maximum**;

(b) on conviction on indictment, to a **fine** or to imprisonment for a term not exceeding **two years**, or to both.

[Radioactive Substances Act 1993, s 34A, as inserted by the Environment Act 1995, Sch 19 and the Energy Act 2004, Sch 15.]

---

1. For procedure in respect of an offence which is triable either way, see the Magistrates' Courts Act 1980, ss 17A–21, in PART I: MAGISTRATES' COURTS, PROCEDURE, ante.

8–9691   36. Offences by bodies corporate.   (1) Where a body corporate is guilty of an offence under this Act, and that offence is proved to have been committed with the consent or connivance of, or to be attributable to any neglect on the part of, any director, manager, secretary or other similar officer of the body corporate, or any person who was purporting to act in any such capacity, he, as well as the body corporate, shall be guilty of that offence, and shall be liable to be proceeded against and punished accordingly.

(2) In this section "director", in relation to a body corporate established by or under any enactment for the purpose of carrying on under national ownership any industry or part of an industry or undertaking, being a body corporate whose affairs are managed by its members, means a member of that body corporate.

[Radioactive Substances Act 1993, s 36.]

8–9691A   37. Offence due to another's fault.   Where the commission by any person of an offence under this Act is due to the act or default of some other person, that other person may by virtue of this section be charged with and convicted of the offence whether or not proceedings for the offence are taken against the first-mentioned person.

[Radioactive Substances Act 1993, s 37.]

8–9691B   38. Restriction on prosecutions.   (1) Proceedings in respect of any offence under this Act shall not be instituted in England or Wales except—

(a) by the Secretary of State,

(b) by the Environment Agency, or

(c) by or with the consent of the Director of Public Prosecutions.

(2), (3) *Northern Ireland.*

[Radioactive Substances Act 1993, s 38 as amended by the Environment Act 1995, Sch 22.]

8–9691C   39. *Public access to documents and records.*

Operation of other statutory provisions

8–9691D   40. Radioactivity to be disregarded for purposes of certain statutory provisions.   (1) For the purposes of the operation of any statutory provision to which this section applies, and for the purposes of the exercise or performance of any power or duty conferred or imposed by, or for the enforcement of, any such statutory provision, no account shall be taken of any radioactivity possessed by any substance or article or by any part of any premises.

(2) This section applies—

(a) to any statutory provision contained in, or for the time being having effect by virtue of, any of the enactments specified in Schedule 3, or any enactment for the time being in force whereby an enactment so specified is amended, extended or superseded, and (*b*) to any statutory provision contained in, or for the time being having effect by virtue of, a local enactment whether passed or made before or after the passing of this Act (in whatever terms the provision is expressed) in so far as—

    (i) the disposal or accumulation of waste or any description of waste, or of any substance which is a nuisance, or so as to be a nuisance, or of any substance which is, or so as to be, prejudicial to health, noxious, polluting or of any similar description, is prohibited or restricted by the statutory provision, or

    (ii) a power or duty is conferred or imposed by the statutory provision on the Environment Agency or SEPA or on any local authority, relevant water body or other public or local authority, or on any officer of a public or local authority, to take any action (whether by way of legal proceedings or otherwise) for preventing, restricting or abating such disposals or accumulations as are mentioned in sub-paragraph (i).

(3) In this section—

"statutory provision"—

    (*a*) in relation to Great Britain, means a provision, whether of a general or a special nature, contained in, or in any document made or issued under, any Act, whether of a general or a special nature, and

    (*b*) *Northern Ireland*

"local enactment" means—

    (*a*) a local or private Act (including a local or private Act of the Parliament of Northern Ireland or a local or private Measure of the Northern Ireland Assembly), or

    (*b*) an order confirmed by Parliament (or by the Parliament of Northern Ireland or the Northern Ireland Assembly) or brought into operation in accordance with special parliamentary procedure,

and any reference to disposal, in relation to a statutory provision, is a reference to discharging or depositing a substance or allowing a substance to escape or to enter a stream or other place, as may be mentioned in that provision.

(4) The references to provisions of the Water Resources Act 1991 in Part I of Schedule 3 shall have effect subject to the power conferred by section 98 of that Act.

[Radioactive Substances Act 1993, s 40 as amended by the Environment Act 1995, Sch 22.]

General

8–9691E   41. Service of documents.   (1) Any notice required or authorised by or under this Act to be served on or given to any person may be served or given by delivering it to him, or by leaving it at his proper address, or by sending it by post to him at that address.

(2) Any such notice may—

    (*a*) in the case of a body corporate, be served on or given to the secretary or clerk of that body;

    (*b*) in the case of a partnership, be served on or given to a partner or a person having the control or management of the partnership business.

(3) For the purposes of this section and of section 7 of the Interpretation Act 1978 (service of documents by post) in its application to this section, the proper address of any person on or to whom any such notice is to be served or given shall be his last known address, except that—

    (*a*) in the case of a body corporate or their secretary or clerk, it shall be the address of the registered or principal office of that body;

    (*b*) in the case of a partnership or person having the control or the management of the partnership business, it shall be the principal office of the partnership;

and for the purposes of this subsection the principal office of a company registered outside the United Kingdom or of a partnership carrying on business outside the United Kingdom shall be their principal office within the United Kingdom.

(4) If the person to be served with or given any such notice has specified an address in the United Kingdom other than his proper address within the meaning of subsection (3) as the one at which he or someone on his behalf will accept notices of the same description as that notice, that address shall also be treated for the purposes of this section and section 7 of the Interpretation Act 1978 as his proper address.

(5) The preceding provisions of this section shall apply to the sending or giving of a document as they apply to the giving of a notice.

[Radioactive Substances Act 1993, s 41.]

8–9691F   42. Application of Act to Crown.   (1) Subject to the following provisions of this section, the provisions of this Act shall bind the Crown.

(2) Subsection (1) does not apply in relation to premises—

    a) occupied on behalf of the Crown for naval, military or air force purposes or for the purposes of the department of the Secretary of State having responsibility for defence, or

(b)   occupied by or for the purposes of a visiting force.

(3) No contravention by the Crown of any provision of this Act shall make the Crown criminally liable; but the High Court or, in Scotland, the Court of Session may, on the application of any authority charged with enforcing that provision, declare unlawful any act or omission of the Crown which constitutes such a contravention.

(4) Notwithstanding anything in subsection (3), the provisions of this Act shall apply to persons in the public service of the Crown as they apply to other persons.

(5) *Repealed.*

(6) Where, in the case of any such premises as are mentioned in subsection (2)—

   (a)   arrangements are made whereby radioactive waste is not to be disposed of from those premises except with the approval of the appropriate Agency, and

   (b)   in pursuance of those arrangements the appropriate Agency proposes to approve, or approves, the removal of radioactive waste from those premises to a place provided by a local authority as a place for the deposit of refuse,

the provisions of section 18 shall apply as if the proposal to approve the removal of the waste were an application for an authorisation under section 13 to remove it, or (as the case may be) the approval were such an authorisation.

(7) Nothing in this section shall be taken as in any way affecting Her Majesty in her private capacity; and this subsection shall be construed as if section 38(3) of the Crown Proceedings Act 1947 (interpretation of references in that Act to Her Majesty in her private capacity) were contained in this Act.

(8) In this section "visiting force" means any such body, contingent or detachment of the forces of any country as is a visiting force for the purposes of any of the provisions of the Visiting Forces Act 1952.

(9) *Northern Ireland.*

[Radioactive Substances Act 1993, s 42 as amended by the Environment Act 1995, Schs 22 and 24.]

8–9691G   44. Regulations and orders: Great Britain.   (1) The Secretary of State may make regulations under this Act for any purpose for which regulations are authorised or required to be made under this Act.

(2) For the purpose of facilitating the exercise of any power under this Act to effect registrations, or grant authorisations, subject to limitations or conditions, the Secretary of State may make regulations setting out general limitations or conditions applicable to such classes of cases as may be specified in the regulations; and any limitations or conditions so specified shall, for the purposes of this Act, be deemed to be attached to any registration or authorisation falling within the class of cases to which those limitations or conditions are expressed to be applicable, subject to such exceptions or modifications (if any) as may be specified in any such registration or authorisation.

(3) Any power conferred by this Act to make regulations or orders shall be exercisable by statutory instrument.

(4) Any statutory instrument containing regulations or an order made under this Act, other than an order under Schedule 5, shall be subject to annulment in pursuance of a resolution of either House of Parliament.

(5) This section does not extend to Northern Ireland.

[Radioactive Substances Act 1993, s 44.]

8–9691H   45. *Northern Ireland, Regulations.*

8–9691I   46. Effect of Act on other rights and duties.   Subject to the provisions of section 40 of this Act, and of section 18 of the Interpretation Act 1978 (which relates to offences under two or more laws), nothing in this Act shall be construed as—

   (a)   conferring a right of action in any civil proceedings (other than proceedings for the recovery of a fine) in respect of any contravention of this Act, or

   (b)   affecting any restriction imposed by or under any other enactment, whether contained in a public general Act or in a local or private Act, or

   (c)   derogating from any right of action or other remedy (whether civil or criminal) in proceedings instituted otherwise than under this Act.

[Radioactive Substances Act 1993, s 46.]

8–9691J   47. General interpretation provisions.   (1) In this Act, except in so far as the context otherwise requires—

"the appropriate Agency" means—

   (a)   in relation to England and Wales, the Environment Agency; and

   (b)   in relation to Scotland, SEPA;

"the appropriate Minister" means—

   (a), (b)   *Repealed,*

   (c)   *Northern Ireland,*

"article" includes a part of an article,

"the chief inspector" means—

    (*a*), (*b*) *Repealed*,
    (*c*) *Northern Ireland*,

"disposal", in relation to waste, includes its removal, deposit, destruction, discharge (whether into water or into the air or into a sewer or drain or otherwise) or burial (whether underground or otherwise) and "dispose of" shall be construed accordingly,

"the HASS Directive" means Council Directive 2003/122/EURATOM on the control of high-activity sealed radioactive sources and orphan sources;

"high-activity source" has the same meaning as it has in the HASS Directive but excluding any such source once its activity level has fallen below the exemption levels specified in column 2 of Table A to Annex I to Council Directive 96/29/EURATOM laying down basic safety standards for the protection of the health of workers and the general public against the dangers arising from ionising radiation,

"local authority" (except where the reference is to a public or local authority) means—

    (*a*) in England, the council of a county, district or London borough or the Common Council of the City of London or an authority established by the Waste Regulation and Disposal (Authorities) Order 1985,
    (*aa*) in Wales, the council of a county or county borough;
    (*b*) *Scotland*,
    (*c*) *Northern Ireland*,

"nuclear site" means—

    (*a*) any site in respect of which a nuclear site licence is for the time being in force, or
    (*b*) any site in respect of which, after the revocation or surrender of a nuclear site licence, the period of responsibility of the licensee has not yet come to an end,

"nuclear site licence", "licensee" and "period of responsibility" have the same meaning as in the Nuclear Installations Act 1965,

"orphan source" has the same meaning as it has in the HASS Directive,

"premises" includes any land, whether covered by buildings or not, including any place underground and any land covered by water,

"prescribed"—

    (*a*) in relation to a charging scheme under section 41 of the Environment Act 1995, has the same meaning as in that section;
    (*b*) in relation to fees or charges payable in Northern Ireland in accordance with a scheme under section 43 of this Act, nmeans prescirbed under that scheme; and
    (*c*) in other contexts, means prescribed by regualtions under this Act,

"the prescribed period for determinations", in relation to any application under this Act, means, subject to subsection (2), the period of four months beginning with the day on which the application was received,

"public or local authority", in relation to England and Wales, includes a water undertaker or a sewerage undertaker,

"relevant water body" means—

    (*a*) in England and Wales, a water undertaker, a sewerage undertaker or a local fisheries committee,
    (*b*) *Scotland*,
    (*c*) *Northern Ireland*,

"SEPA" means the Scottish Environment Protection Agency;

"substance" means any natural or artificial substance, whether in solid or liquid form or in the form of a gas or vapour,

"undertaking" includes any trade, business or profession and—

    (*a*) in relation to a public or local authority, includes any of the powers or duties of that authority, and
    (*b*) in relation to any other body of persons, whether corporate or unincorporate, includes any of the activities of that body, and

"waste" includes any substance which constitutes scrap material or an effluent or other unwanted surplus substance arising from the application of any process, and also includes any substance or article which requires to be disposed of as being broken, worn out, contaminated or otherwise spoilt.

(2) The Secretary of State may by order substitute for the period for the time being specified in subsection (1) as the prescribed period for determinations such other period as he considers appropriate.

(3) In determining, for the purposes of this Act, whether any radioactive material is kept or used on any premises, no account shall be taken of any radioactive material kept or used in or on any railway vehicle, road vehicle, vessel or aircraft if either—

    (*a*) the vehicle, vessel or aircraft is on those premises in the course of a journey, or

(b) in the case of a vessel which is on those premises otherwise than in the course of a journey, the material is used in propelling the vessel or is kept in or on the vessel for use in propelling it.

(4) Any substance or article which, in the course of the carrying on of any undertaking, is discharged, discarded or otherwise dealt with as if it were waste shall, for the purposes of this Act, be presumed to be waste unless the contrary is proved.

(5) Any reference in this Act to the contamination of a substance or article is a reference to its being so affected by either or both of the following, that is to say,—

(a) absorption, admixture or adhesion of radioactive material or radioactive waste, and
(b) the emission of neutrons or ionising radiations,

as to become radioactive or to possess increased radioactivity.

(5A) A reference in this Act to the keeping or use of radioactive material means, in relation to a high-activity source, any practice in relation to that source except the disposal or accumulation of the source: and "practice" must be construed in accordance with Council Directive 96/29/EURATOM laying down basic safety standards for the protection of the health of workers and the general public against the dangers arising from ionising radiation.

(6) *Northern Ireland.*

[Radioactive Substances Act 1993, s 47 amended by the Local Government (Wales) Act 1994, Sch 16, the Environment Act 1995, Schs 22 and 24, the Energy Act 2004, Sch 15 and 2005/2686.]

8–9691K   48. Index of defined expressions. The following Table shows provisions defining or otherwise explaining expressions for the purposes of this Act—

the appropriate Agency	section 47(1)
the appropriate Minister	section 47(1)
article	section 47(1)
contamination	section 47(5)
disposal	section 47(1)
the HASS Directive	section 47(1)
high-activity source	section 47(1)
licensee (in relation to a nuclear site licence)	section 47(1)
local authority	section 47(1)
mobile radioactive apparatus	section 3
nuclear site	section 47(1)
nuclear site licence	section 47(1)
orphan source	section 47(1)
period of responsibility (in relation to a nuclear site licence)	section 47(1)
premises	section 47(1)
prescribed	section 47(1)
the prescribed period for determinations	section 47(1) and (2)
public or local authority	section 47(1)
radioactive material	section 1
radioactive waste	section 2
relevant water body	section 47(1)
SEPA	section 47(1)
substance	section 47(1)
undertaking	section 47(1)
waste	section 47(1) and (4)

[Radioactive Substances Act 1993, s 48 as amended by the Environment Act 1995, Schs 22 and 24 and SI 2005/2686.]

8–9691L

SCHEDULES

Section 1

SCHEDULE 1
SPECIFIED ELEMENTS

Element	Becquerels per gram (Bq g (to the power of -1))		
	Solid	Liquid	Gas or Vapour
1. Actinium	0.37	$7.40 \times (10$ to the power of $-2)$	$2.59 \times (10$ to the power of $-6)$
2. Lead	0.74	$3.70 \times (10$ to the power of $-3)$	$1.11 \times (10$ to the power of $-4)$
3. Polonium	0.37	$2.59 \times (10$ to the power of $-2)$	$2.22 \times (10$ to the power of $-4)$
4. Protoactinium	0.37	$3.33 \times (10$ to the power of $-2)$	$1.11 \times (10$ to the power of $-6)$
5. Radium	0.37	$3.70 \times (10$ to the power of $-4)$	$3.70 \times (10$ to the power of $-5)$
6. Radon	—	—	$3.70 \times (10$ to the power of $-2)$
7. Thorium	2.59	$3.70 \times (10$ to the power of $-2)$	$2.22 \times (10$ to the power of $-5)$
8. Uranium	11.1	0.74	$7.40 \times (10$ to the power of $-5)$

Section 40
SCHEDULE 3
ENACTMENTS, OTHER THAN LOCAL ENACTMENTS, TO WHICH S 40 APPLIES

(Amended by Clean Air Act 1993 and the Environment Act 1995, Schs 22 and 24.)

PART I
ENGLAND AND WALES

8–9692   Sections 48, 81, 82, 141, 259 and 261 of the Public Health Act 1936.

8–9692A   **2.** Section 16 of the Clean Air 1993.

8–9692B   **3.** Section 5 of the Sea Fisheries Regulation Act 1966.

8–9692C   **4.** Section 4 of the Salmon and Freshwater Fisheries Act 1975.

8–9692D   **5.** Section 59 of the Building Act 1984.

8–9692E   **6.** The Planning (Hazardous Substances) Act 1990.

8–9692F   **7.** Part III of the Environmental Protection Act 1990.

8–9692G   **8.** Sections 72, 111 and 113(6) and Chapter III of Part IV of the Water Industry Act 1991 and paragraphs 2 to 4 of Schedule 8 to that Act so far as they re-enact provisions of sections 43 and 44 of the Control of Pollution Act 1974.

8–9692H   **9.** Sections 82, 84, 85, 86, 87(1), 88(2), 92, 93, 99, 161, 190, 202 and 203 of and paragraph 6 of Schedule 25 to the Water Resources Act 1991.

8–9692I   **10.** Section 18 of the Water Act 1945 so far as it continues to have effect by virtue of Schedule 2 to the Water Consolidation (Consequential Provisions) Act 1991 or by virtue of provisions of the Control of Pollution Act 1974 not having been brought into force.

Nuclear Safeguards Act 2000[1]
(2000 c 5)

8–9693   This Act enables effect to be given to the protocol signed at Vienna on 22 September 1998 (Cm. 4282) additional to the agreement made on 6 September 1976 between the United Kingdom, the European Atomic Energy Community and the International Atomic Energy Agency for the application of safeguards in the United Kingdom in connection with the Treaty on the Non-Proliferation of Nuclear Weapons (**s 1**).

---

1. This Act is to be brought into force by order made under s 12, post.

8–9694   **2. Information and records for purposes of the Additional Protocol.**   (1) No obligation as to secrecy or other restriction on disclosure (whether imposed by statute or otherwise) prevents a person voluntarily giving information to the Secretary of State if that person has reasonable cause to believe that it is Additional Protocol information.

(2) The Secretary of State may serve a notice on any person requiring him to give the Secretary of State information, or information of a description, specified in the notice—

(*a*) within a period or at times specified in the notice; and

(*b*) if the notice so provides, in such form as the notice may require.

(3) The information required by a notice—

(*a*) must be information which the Secretary of State has reasonable cause to believe is Additional Protocol information; and

(*b*) may relate to a state of affairs subsisting before the coming into force of this Act or of the Additional Protocol.

(4) A notice shall not require a person to give information which is required only for the purposes of sub-paragraph (ii) of Article 2.a unless the notice sets out the terms, agreed by the United Kingdom, in which the Agency has identified information for the purposes of that sub-paragraph.

(5) A person who refuses or fails without reasonable excuse to comply with a notice is guilty of an offence.

(6) The duty to comply with a notice is not affected by any obligation or restriction mentioned in subsection (1).

(7) A person on whom a notice is served shall keep and retain such records of information in his possession (and retain any existing records) as may be necessary to enable him to comply with the notice; and a failure to do so shall be taken into account in proceedings for an offence under

subsection (5) in determining whether a reasonable excuse exists for a refusal or failure to comply with the notice.

(8) In this section "notice" means a notice served under subsection (2).
[Nuclear Safeguards Act 2000, s 2.]

8–9695 **3. Identifying persons who have information.** (1) The Secretary of State may make regulations[1] requiring persons of any description specified in the regulations to inform him that they are of such a description and to give such supplementary particulars as may be so specified.

(2) Any such description must be so framed that persons within it are—

(a) persons about whose activities the United Kingdom is or will be obliged under the Additional Protocol to provide information to the Agency; or

(b) other persons likely to be in possession of information which the Secretary of State has reasonable cause to believe is Additional Protocol information.

(3) The regulations may—

(a) require persons to notify the Secretary of State of changes in their circumstances; and

(b) include incidental and supplementary provisions.

(4) Regulations under this section shall be made by statutory instrument subject to annulment in pursuance of a resolution of either House of Parliament.

(5) If regulations are made under this section the Secretary of State shall arrange for a statement of the fact that they have been made to be published in such manner as is likely to bring them to the attention of persons affected by them.

(6) A person who fails without reasonable excuse to comply with a requirement imposed by regulations under this section is guilty of an offence.
[Nuclear Safeguards Act 2000, s 3.]

---

1. The Nuclear Safeguards (Notification) Regulations 2004, SI 2004/1255 have been made.

8–9696 **4. Powers of entry in relation to Additional Protocol information.** (1) If a justice of the peace is satisfied, on information on oath, that a person served with a notice under section 2(2) has refused to give all or any of the information required by the notice, or has failed to give all or any of that information within the period or at the time required by the notice, and that there are reasonable grounds for believing—

(a) that the Secretary of State is not in possession of all or any of the information which that person has refused or failed to give; and

(b) that a document or other thing, containing any of the information which that person has refused or failed to give and which is not in the possession of the Secretary of State, is to be found on any premises,

he may issue a warrant authorising an authorised officer to enter the premises, if necessary by force, at any reasonable hour within one month from the time of the issue of the warrant and to search them.

(2) If a justice of the peace is satisfied, on information on oath, that the Secretary of State has specified information, or information of a description, in a notice served under section 2(2) or in a certificate for the purposes of this subsection, and that there are reasonable grounds for believing—

(a) that the Secretary of State is not in possession of all or any of the information so specified or all or any information of the description so specified;

(b) that a document or other thing containing any of the information so specified or any information of the description so specified is to be found on any premises; and

(c) that the document or other thing is likely to be altered, destroyed or otherwise disposed of without all the information so specified or all the information of the description so specified which is contained in it and is not in the possession of the Secretary of State having been given to him,

he may issue a warrant authorising an authorised officer to enter the premises, if necessary by force, at any reasonable hour within one month from the time of the issue of the warrant and to search them.

(3) For the purposes of subsection (2) there may be specified in a certificate only information, or information of a description, which could be specified in a notice under section 2(2).

(4) *Scotland*

(5) The powers of an authorised officer who enters premises under the authority of a warrant under this section include power—

(a) to take with him such other persons and such equipment as appear to him to be necessary;

(b) to inspect anything found on the premises;

(c) to require any information which is held in electronic form and is accessible from the premises to be produced in a form in which he can read and copy it; and (*d*) to copy, or to seize and remove, any document or other thing which he has reasonable cause to believe is something which contains Additional Protocol information.

(6) A constable who enters premises under the authority of a warrant or by virtue of subsection (5)(*a*) may—

(*a*) give such assistance as an authorised officer may request for the purpose of facilitating the exercise of any power under this section; and

(*b*) search or cause to be searched any person on the premises who the constable has reasonable cause to believe may have in his possession any document or other thing falling within subsection (5)(*d*).

(7) No constable shall, by virtue of subsection (6)(*b*), search a person of the opposite sex.

(8) The powers conferred by a warrant under this section shall only be exercisable, if the warrant so provides, in the presence of a constable.

(9) A person who—

(*a*) wilfully obstructs an authorised officer in the exercise of a power conferred by a warrant under this section; or

(*b*) fails without reasonable excuse to comply with a reasonable request made by an authorised officer or a constable for the purpose of facilitating the exercise of such a power,

is guilty of an offence.

(10) In this section any reference to information contained in a document or other thing includes a reference to information which may be obtained from that document or other thing.
[Nuclear Safeguards Act 2000, s 4.]

8–9697 5. Rights of access etc for Agency inspectors.   (1) This section has effect for securing that the Agency's rights under the Additional Protocol—

(*a*) of access to locations of a description mentioned in Article 5, for purposes permitted by Article 4 or any other provision of the Additional Protocol in relation to locations of that description;

(*b*) of access to locations specified by the Agency for the purposes of Article 9, for the purpose of carrying out wide-area environmental sampling; and

(*c*) to carry out activities at those locations,

are exercisable in the United Kingdom by Agency inspectors.

(2) An Agency inspector may, at any location falling within subsection (1)—

(*a*) exercise such rights of access and entry as are required for the purposes of the Additional Protocol; and

(*b*) do anything which the Agency is entitled to do by virtue of Article 6 (if the location falls within subsection (1)(*a*)) or Article 9 (if it falls within subsection (1)(*b*));

but only in accordance with and subject to the provisions of the Additional Protocol and the Safeguards Agreement (including any arrangements for managed access made under Article 7, procedural arrangements for wide-area environmental sampling approved under Article 9, or subsidiary arrangements agreed under Article 13).

(3) For the purposes of subsection (2)—

(*a*) the reference to "other objective measures" in any paragraph of Article 6 shall be taken to refer only to measures specified by the Secretary of State in relation to that paragraph in an order made by statutory instrument; and

(*b*) the reference to procedural arrangements for wide-area environmental sampling in Article 9 shall be taken to refer only to arrangements specified by the Secretary of State in an order made by statutory instrument.

(4) An authorised officer may accompany an Agency inspector while he is exercising powers under this section.

(5) A constable may—

(*a*) give such assistance as an Agency inspector, or an authorised officer accompanying that inspector, may request for the purpose of facilitating the exercise of powers under this section; and

(*b*) use such reasonable force as he considers necessary for that purpose.

(6) If in any proceedings any question arises whether a person at any time when purporting to exercise powers under this section was or was not an Agency inspector, a certificate issued by or under the authority of the Secretary of State stating any fact relevant to that question shall be conclusive evidence of that fact.

(7) A person who—

(*a*) wilfully obstructs an Agency inspector or authorised officer in the exercise of a power under this section;

(b) fails without reasonable excuse to comply with a reasonable request made by an Agency inspector, an authorised officer or a constable for the purpose of facilitating the exercise of such a power; or

(c) interferes without reasonable excuse with anything placed on any land in exercise of such a power,

is guilty of an offence.

(8) In this section "wide-area environmental sampling" has the meaning given by Article 18.g.
[Nuclear Safeguards Act 2000, s 5.]

8–9698   6. Restriction on disclosure.   (1) This section applies to information if—

(a) it is obtained by any person under, or in connection with anything done under, this Act or the Additional Protocol; and

(b) it relates to a particular business or other activity carried on by any person.

(2) So long as the business or activity continues to be carried on the information shall not be disclosed except—

(a) with the consent of the person for the time being carrying on the business or activity;

(b) in connection with anything done for the purposes of this Act, the Additional Protocol or the Safeguards Agreement;

(c) in connection with the investigation of a criminal offence or for the purposes of criminal proceedings;

(d) in connection with the enforcement of a restriction on imports or exports;

(e) in dealing with an emergency involving danger to the public; or

(f) with a view to ensuring the security of the United Kingdom.

(3) A person who discloses information in contravention of this section is guilty of an offence.

(4) It is not an offence under this section to disclose information which has previously been disclosed to the public otherwise than in contravention of this section.

(5) A disclosure of any information to which this section applies may be made in circumstances in which any of paragraphs (b) to (f) of subsection (2) prevents there being a contravention of this section, notwithstanding any obligation as to secrecy or other restriction on disclosure that would otherwise apply.
[Nuclear Safeguards Act 2000, s 6.]

8–9698A   7. Giving false or misleading information.   A person who knowingly or recklessly makes a statement which is false or misleading in a material particular in giving—

(a) any information to the Secretary of State or an authorised officer for the purposes of this Act or the Additional Protocol;

(b) any information to the Secretary of State in response to a requirement of regulations under section 3; or

(c) any information to an Agency inspector exercising powers under section 5,

is guilty of an offence.
[Nuclear Safeguards Act 2000, s 7.]

8–9698B   8. Power to search and obtain evidence.   (1) If—

(a) a justice of the peace is satisfied on information on oath that there are reasonable grounds for suspecting that evidence of the commission of an offence under this Act is to be found on any premises; or

(b) in Scotland a justice (within the meaning of section 307 of the Criminal Procedure (Scotland) Act 1995) is satisfied by evidence on oath as mentioned in paragraph (a) above,

he may issue a warrant authorising an authorised officer to enter the premises, if necessary by force, at any time within one month from the time of the issue of the warrant and to search them.

(2) The powers of an authorised officer who enters the premises under the authority of the warrant include power—

(a) to take with him such other persons and such equipment as appear to him to be necessary;

(b) to inspect anything found on the premises;

(c) to require any information which is held in electronic form and is accessible from the premises to be produced in a form in which he can read and copy it;

(d) to copy, or to seize and remove, any document or other thing which he has reasonable cause to believe may be required as evidence for the purposes of proceedings in respect of an offence under this Act; and

(e) to sample any substance found on the premises which he has reasonable cause to believe may be required as such evidence.

(3) A constable who enters premises under the authority of a warrant or by virtue of subsection (2)(a) may—

(a) give such assistance as an authorised officer may request for the purpose of facilitating the exercise of any power under this section; and

(b) search or cause to be searched any person on the premises who the constable has reasonable cause to believe may have in his possession any document or other thing which may be required as evidence for the purposes of proceedings in respect of an offence under this Act.

(4) No constable shall, by virtue of subsection (3)(b), search a person of the opposite sex.

(5) The powers conferred by a warrant under this section shall only be exercisable, if the warrant so provides, in the presence of a constable.

(6) A person who—

(a) wilfully obstructs an authorised officer in the exercise of a power conferred by a warrant under this section; or

(b) fails without reasonable excuse to comply with a reasonable request made by an authorised officer or a constable for the purpose of facilitating the exercise of such a power,

is guilty of an offence.

[Nuclear Safeguards Act 2000, s 8, as amended by the Criminal Justice and Police Act 2001, Sch 2.]

8–9698C   **9. Penalty for offences and offences by bodies corporate.**   (1) A person guilty of an offence under any provision of this Act except section 6 or 7 is liable[1]—

(a) on summary conviction, to a fine not exceeding the statutory maximum; and

(b) on conviction on indictment, to a fine.

(2) A person guilty of an offence under section 6 or 7 is liable[1]—

(a) on summary conviction, to a fine not exceeding the statutory maximum; and

(b) on conviction on indictment, to imprisonment for a term not exceeding two years or to a fine (or both).

(3) Where an offence under this Act committed by a body corporate is proved to have been committed with the consent or connivance of, or to be attributable to any neglect on the part of—

(a) a director, manager, secretary or other similar officer of the body corporate; or

(b) a person who was purporting to act in any such capacity,

he as well as the body corporate is guilty of that offence and liable to be proceeded against and punished accordingly.

(4) In subsection (3) "director", in the case of a body corporate whose affairs are managed by its members, means a member of the body corporate.

(5) Where an offence under this Act committed by a Scottish partnership is proved to have been committed with the consent or connivance of, or to be attributable to any neglect on the part of, a partner, he as well as the partnership is guilty of the offence and may be proceeded against and punished accordingly.

[Nuclear Safeguards Act 2000, s 9.]

---

1. For procedure in respect of an offence triable either way, see the Magistrates' Courts Act 1980, ss 17A–21, in PART I: MAGISTRATES' COURTS, PROCEDURE, *ante.*

8–9698D   **10. Service of notices.**   (1) Any notice under this Act may be served on a person by delivering it to him, by leaving it at his proper address or by sending it by post to him at that address.

(2) Any such notice may be served—

(a) in the case of a body corporate, on the secretary or clerk of that body;

(b) in the case of a partnership, on any partner or a person having control or management of the partnership business; and

(c) in the case of an unincorporated association (other than a partnership), on any member of its governing body.

(3) For the purposes of this section and section 7 of the Interpretation Act 1978 (service of documents) in its application to this section, the proper address of any person is—

(a) in the case of a body corporate, its secretary or clerk, the address of its registered or principal office in the United Kingdom;

(b) in the case of an unincorporated association (other than a partnership) or a member of its governing body, the address of its principal office in the United Kingdom; and

(c) in any other case, his usual or last-known address (whether of his residence or of a place where he carries on business or is employed).

[Nuclear Safeguards Act 2000, s 10.]

11. *Minor and consequential amendments*

12. *Short title etc*[1]

1. The following commencement order has been made under this section: (No 1) SI 2004/1242 (1 May 2004 except s 5(1)(*b*) and in s 5(2), the words "or Article 9 (if it falls within subsection (1)(*b*))" and "procedural arrangements for wide-area environmental sampling approved under Article 9").

The provisions of this Act are extended to Jersey (Nuclear Safeguards (Jersey) Order 2004, SI 2004/1288); the Isle of Man (Nuclear Safeguards (Isle of Man) Order 2004, SI 2004/1289); Guernsey (Nuclear Safeguards (Guernsey) Order 2004, SI 2004/1290).

Energy Act 2004[1]

(2004 c 20)

PART 1[2]

CHAPTER 3[3]

1. The Act deals with three main areas: the civil nuclear industry; sustainability and renewable energy sources; and energy markets and regulation.

The Act is in four parts with 23 Schedules.

Part 1 is concerned with the Civil Nuclear Industry. It establishes the Nuclear Decommissioning Authority as a new public body with the primary role of ensuring the decommissioning and clean up of Britain's civil public sector nuclear sites. It creates a new Civil Nuclear Police Authority to oversee a reconstituted nuclear constabulary (the present United Kingdom Atomic Energy Authority ("UKAEA" Constabulary), directly accountable to the Secretary of State. It amends the Anti-terrorism, Crime and Security Act 2001 to extend the regulation of the security of uranium enrichment technologies and sensitive nuclear information. Finally, it provides statutory authority for the Secretary of State to spend money under his options to acquire British Energy's power stations and/or its stake in Nirex, which is a company owned by the major nuclear industry waste producers and tasked with investigating feasibility of a deep intermediate and low level waste disposal facility.

Part 2 is concerned with sustainable and renewable energy sources. It amends the Sustainable Energy Act 2003 to require the Government to publish information about the development and bringing into use of new energy sources, actions taken to ensure that the requisite scientific and engineering expertise is available to develop new energy sources, and actions taken to achieve the statutory energy efficiency aim or aims designated under ss 2 and 3 of the Sustainable Energy Act. This information will be published as part of the annual report required under section 1 of the Sustainable Energy Act 2003. It provides for publication and implementation of a microgeneration strategy. It places a new duty on the Secretary of State and the Gas and Electricity Markets Authority to carry out their respective functions under Part 1 of both the Gas Act 1986 (c 44) and the Electricity Act 1989 (c 29), in a manner best calculated to contribute to the achievement of sustainable development. It establishes a comprehensive legal framework to support renewable energy developments beyond territorial waters and augment the regime for inshore waters. It provides the Secretary of State with a power to specify shorter obligation periods under the Renewables Obligation, impose surcharges to be made on late payments to the Renewables buy-out fund and to require mutualisation payments from electricity suppliers to cover a shortfall in the buy-out fund. It makes provision regarding the mutual recognition of Northern Ireland and UK Renewables Obligation Certificates. It makes provision regarding the issue of Renewables Obligation Certificates in respect of electricity generated from renewable sources outside Northern Ireland and supplied to customers in Northern Ireland. Finally, it enables the Secretary of State to introduce a renewable transport fuel obligation.

Part 3 is concerned with energy regulation. It create a single wholesale electricity market for Great Britain. It introduces a new licensing regime for gas and electricity interconnectors to enable the Gas and Electricity Markets Authority ('GEMA') to regulate their operation. It creates a special administration regime for gas transportation and electricity transmission and distribution companies facing actual or threatened insolvency. It places a duty on the Secretary of State to publish an annual report on the security of energy supplies and lay that report before Parliament. It establishes a mechanism allowing energy market participants to appeal GEMA's decisions on modifications to the Codes that govern activities in the gas and electricity markets. It places a duty on the Secretary of State and GEMA to have regard to the principles of best regulatory practice in carrying out their functions under the Gas Act 1986 and the Electricity Act 1989. It amends the definition of electricity supply in the Electricity Act 1989 to include supply over a transmission line. It defines 'high voltage line' in respect of offshore electric lines. It creates a power for GEMA (with the consent of the Secretary of State) to make regulations to extend the range of sums that can be collected from a prepayment meter. It reforms the planning system for large energy projects handled by the Department for Trade and Industry ('DTI') to enable the appointment of additional inspectors to speed up public inquiries. It amends the Electricity Act 1989 and the Gas Act 1986 to allow GEMA, when entering information on registers it is required to maintain under s 49 of the Electricity Act 1989 and s 36 of the Gas Act 1986, to exclude details in certain circumstances. It creates a power for the Secretary of State to adjust transmission charges for renewable generators within a single area that can be shown to be of high renewable energy potential and where evidence would suggest that unadjusted transmission charges might have a material impact on the development of generation of electricity from renewable sources. Finally, it provides for the use of surpluses arising under the Fossil Fuel Levy in Scotland.

Part 4 is concerned with miscellaneous and supplementary matters.

The Act will be brought into force in accordance with Commencement Orders made under s 148. At the time of going to press the Energy Act 2004 (Commencement No 1) Order 2004, SI 2004/1973; Energy Act 2004 (Commencement No 2) Order 2004, SI 2004/2184; Energy Act 2004 (Commencement No 3) Order 2004, SI 2004/2575; Energy Act 2004 (Commencement No 4) Order 2005, SI 2005/442; Energy Act 2004 (Commencement No 5) Order 2005, SI 2005/877 and Energy Act 2004 (Commencement No 6) Order 2005, SI 2005/2965 had been made. The majority of the Act's provisions remain, however, prospective. Only those provisions which are relevant to the work of magistrates' court are reproduced in this work.

2. Part 1 contains ss 1–80.

3. Chapter 3 contains ss 51–71.

8–9698G   51. The Civil Nuclear Police Authority.   (1) There shall be a body corporate to be known as the Civil Nuclear Police Authority ("the Police Authority").

(2) Schedule 10 (which makes further provision about the Police Authority) has effect.

[Energy Act 2004, s 51.]

Civil Nuclear Constabulary

8–9698H   52. The Civil Nuclear Constabulary.   (1) It shall be the function of the Police Authority to secure the maintenance of an efficient and effective constabulary, to be known as the Civil Nuclear Constabulary ("the Constabulary").

(2) The primary function of the Constabulary is—

(a) the protection of licensed nuclear sites which are not used wholly or mainly for defence purposes; and

(b) safeguarding nuclear material in Great Britain and elsewhere.

(3) The Police Authority may allocate to the Constabulary the function of carrying on such other activities relating to, or connected with, the security of—

(a) nuclear material, or

(b) sites where such material is being, has been or is to be used, processed or stored,

as the Police Authority thinks fit.

(4) The Constabulary shall have the function of carrying on such other activities as may be allocated to it by the Police Authority in accordance with directions given to that Authority for the purposes of this section by the Secretary of State.

(5) The Secretary of State may give the Police Authority directions restricting the exercise of its powers under subsection (3).

(6) Subject to the provisions of this Chapter, the Police Authority may do anything which appears to it to be likely to facilitate the carrying out of its functions, or to be incidental to carrying them out.

(7) Nothing in this section limits what a member of the Constabulary may do in the exercise of the powers and privileges conferred on him by section 56.

[Energy Act 2004, s 52.]

8–9698I   53. Chief constable and other senior officers

8–9698J   54. Functions of senior officers

8–9698K   55. Members of the Constabulary.   (1) The Police Authority may appoint persons to be members of the Constabulary.

(2) Members of the Constabulary are to be employees of the Police Authority and (apart from the chief constable himself) under the direction and control of the chief constable.

(3) A person appointed as a member of the Constabulary must, on appointment—

(a) be attested as a constable by making the required declaration before a justice of the peace in England and Wales; or

(b) make the required declaration before a sheriff or a justice of the peace in Scotland.

(4) The required declaration is—

(a) in the case of a declaration before a justice of the peace in England and Wales, the declaration required by section 29 of the Police Act 1996 (c 16) in the case of a member of a police force maintained under that Act; and

(b) in the case of a declaration before a sheriff or a justice of the peace in Scotland, a declaration faithfully to execute the duties of the office of a member of the Civil Nuclear Constabulary.

[Energy Act 2004, s 55.]

Jurisdiction and powers of Constabulary

8–9698L   56. Jurisdiction of Constabulary.   (1) A member of the Constabulary shall have the powers and privileges of a constable—

(a) at every place comprised in a relevant nuclear site; and

(b) everywhere within 5 kilometres of such a place.

(2) A member of the Constabulary shall have the powers and privileges of a constable at every trans-shipment site where it appears to him expedient to be in order to safeguard nuclear material while it is at the site.

(3) A member of the Constabulary shall have the powers and privileges of a constable at every other place where it appears to him expedient to be in order to safeguard nuclear material which is in transit.

(4) A member of the Constabulary shall have the powers and privileges of a constable at every place where it appears to him expedient to be in order to pursue or to detain a person whom he reasonably believes—

(a) to have unlawfully removed or interfered with nuclear material being safeguarded by members of the Constabulary; or

(b) to have attempted to do so.

(5) A member of the Constabulary shall have the powers and privileges of a constable throughout Great Britain for purposes connected with—

(a) a place mentioned in subsections (1) to (4);

(b) anything that he or another member of the Constabulary is proposing to do, or has done, at such a place; or

(c) anything which he reasonably believes to have been done, or to be likely to be done, by another person at or in relation to such a place.

(6) This section has effect in United Kingdom waters adjacent to Great Britain as it has effect in Great Britain, but as if references to the powers and privileges of a constable were references to the powers and privileges of a constable in the nearest part of Great Britain.

(7) In this section—

"detain", in relation to a person, includes transferring him to the custody of another or to a place where he may be held in custody;

"relevant nuclear site" means a licensed nuclear site other than a designated defence site;

"trans-shipment site" means a place which a member of the Constabulary reasonably believes to be—

(a) a place where a consignment of nuclear material in transit is trans-shipped or stored; or

(b) a place to which a consignment of nuclear material may be brought to be trans-shipped or stored while it is in transit;

"United Kingdom waters" means waters within the seaward limits of the territorial sea;

and nuclear material is "in transit" for the purposes of this section if it is being carried (or is being trans-shipped or stored incidentally to carriage) before its delivery at its final destination.

(8) In subsection (7) "designated defence site" means a site designated by order made by the Secretary of State as a site which appears to him to be used wholly or mainly for defence purposes.

(9) An order under subsection (8) must be laid before Parliament after being made.

(10) Where an order designating a site for the purposes of section 76(2) of the Anti-terrorism, Crime and Security Act 2001 (c 24) (jurisdiction of Atomic Energy Authority special constables) is in force immediately before the commencement of this section, that order shall have effect after the commencement of this section as an order made under and for the purposes of subsection (8).
[Energy Act 2004, s 56.]

8–9698M 57. Stop and search under Terrorism Act 2000. *Amends ss 44 and 46 of the Terrorism Act 2000.*

8–9698N 68. Application of offences etc applying to constables. *Amends the Police Act 1996.*

8–9698O 71. Interpretation of Chapter 3 of Part 1. (1) In this Chapter—

"chief constable" means the chief constable of the Constabulary;

"the Civil Nuclear Police Federation" is to be construed in accordance with section 64(2);

"the Constabulary" means the Civil Nuclear Constabulary;

"licensed nuclear site" means a site in respect of which a nuclear site licence is or is required to be in force;

"nuclear material" means—

(a) any fissile material in the form of—

(i) uranium metal, alloy or chemical compound; or

(ii) plutonium metal, alloy or chemical compound;

(b) any other fissile material prescribed by regulations made by the Secretary of State;

"the Police Authority" means the Civil Nuclear Police Authority;

"rank-related association" is to be construed in accordance with section 65(2);

"senior officer" means the chief constable or the deputy chief constable or an assistant chief constable of the Constabulary.

(2) References in this Chapter to the functions of the Police Authority include references to securing that the functions of the Constabulary are carried out.

(3) Any power of the Secretary of State under this Chapter to give directions—

(a) restricting the exercise by the Police Authority of its powers,

(b) requiring functions to be carried out or objectives to be met by the Constabulary or the Police Authority, or

(c) imposing obligations on the Police Authority or any of its members or employees, includes power to impose restrictions, confer functions, require objectives to be met or impose obligations at or in relation to places outside Great Britain.

(4) Regulations under subsection (1) are subject to the negative resolution procedure.

(5) Where regulations under subsection (7) of section 76 of the Anti-terrorism, Crime and Security Act 2001 (c 24) (jurisdiction of Atomic Energy Authority special constables) prescribing material to be treated as nuclear material for the purposes of that section are in force immediately before the commencement of this section, those regulations shall have effect after the commencement of this section as regulations made under and for the purposes of subsection (1).

[Energy Act 2004, s 71.]

PART 2[1]

CHAPTER 2[2]

8–9698P   84. Exploitation of areas outside the territorial sea for energy production

---

1. Part 2 contains ss 81–132.
2. Chapter 2 contains ss 84–104.

8–9698Q   85. Application of criminal law to renewable energy installations etc.   (1) Her Majesty may by Order in Council provide that acts and omissions which—

   (a)   fall within subsection (2), and
   (b)   would, if they took place in a part of the United Kingdom, constitute an offence under the law in force in that part,

are to be treated for the purposes of that law as taking place in that part.

(2) An act or omission falls within this subsection if it takes place on, under or above—

   (a)   a renewable energy installation situated in waters to which this section applies; or
   (b)   waters to which this section applies that are within a safety zone.

(3) Her Majesty may by Order in Council provide that a constable is to have—

   (a)   on, under and above a renewable energy installation situated in waters to which this section applies, and
   (b)   on, under and above any waters to which this section applies that are within a safety zone,

all the powers and privileges that he has in the area of the force of which he is a member.

(4) Subsection (3) is in addition to any other enactment or any rule of law or subordinate legislation conferring a power or privilege on constables; and this section is to be disregarded in determining the extent of those other powers and privileges.

(5) The waters to which this section applies are—

   (a)   tidal waters and parts of the sea in or adjacent to Great Britain up to the seaward limits of the territorial sea; and
   (b)   waters in a Renewable Energy Zone.

(6) Proceedings for anything that is an offence by virtue only of an Order in Council under this section may be taken, and the offence may for all incidental purposes be treated as having been committed, in any place in the United Kingdom.

(7) In this section "subordinate legislation" includes an instrument made under an Act of the Scottish Parliament.

[Energy Act 2004, s 85.]

8–9698R   86. Prosecutions.   (1) Subject to subsection (2), this section applies to an offence alleged to have been committed on, under or above—

   (a)   a renewable energy installation situated in waters to which section 85 applies; or
   (b)   waters to which section 85 applies that, at the time of the alleged offence, were within a safety zone.

(2) This section does not apply to an offence created by or under—

   (a)   the Health and Safety at Work etc Act 1974 (c 37);
   (b)   the Customs and Excise Acts 1979, or any enactment that has to be construed as one with those Acts or any of them;
   (c)   the Civil Aviation Act 1982 (c 16) or any enactment that has to be construed as one with that Act;
   (d)   section 23 of the Petroleum Act 1987 (c 12);
   (e)   the Pilotage Act 1987 (c 21);
   (f)   section 4, 29, 35, 36, 37 or 59 of the 1989 Act, or paragraph 3 of Schedule 7 to that Act;
   (g)   the Value Added Tax Act 1994 (c 23) or any enactment that has to be construed as one with that Act;
   (h)   the Merchant Shipping Act 1995 (c 21);

(*i*) section 97 of this Act or Chapter 3 of this Part.

(3) No proceedings for an offence to which this section applies shall be instituted—

(*a*) in England and Wales, except by or with the consent of the Director of Public Prosecutions; or

(*b*) in Northern Ireland, except by or with the consent of the Director of Public Prosecutions for Northern Ireland.

(4) Subsection (3) does not require the consent of the Director of Public Prosecutions, or of the Director of Public Prosecutions for Northern Ireland, where the proceedings in question are proceedings for which the consent of the Attorney General, or of the Advocate General for Northern Ireland, is required apart from this section.

(5) In relation to times before the coming into force of section 27(1) of the Justice (Northern Ireland) Act 2002 (c 26), the reference in subsection (4) to the Advocate General for Northern Ireland is to be read as a reference to the Attorney General for Northern Ireland.

(6) Section 3 of the Territorial Waters Jurisdiction Act 1878 (c 73) (consents to prosecution of offences committed on the open sea by persons who are not British citizens) does not apply to proceedings for an offence to which this section applies.
[Energy Act 2004, s 86.]

8–9698S **87. Application of civil law to renewable energy installations etc**

8–9698T **88. Orders in Council under ss 85 and 87**

8–9698U **89. Activities offshore requiring 1989 Act licences**

8–9698V **90. Modification of licence conditions for offshore transmission and distribution**

8–9698W **91. Extension of transmission licences offshore**

8–9698X **92. Competitive tenders for offshore transmission licences.** *Inserts new s 6B in the Electricity Act 1989.*

8–9698Y **93. Consents for generating stations offshore.** *Amends, and inserts new s 7A, in the Electricity Act 1989.*

8–9698Z **94. Application of regulations under 1989 Act offshore.** *Amends ss 29 and 30 of the Electricity Act 1989.*

8–9699 **95. Safety zones around renewable energy installations.** (1) This section applies where—

(*a*) there is a proposal to construct a renewable energy installation in waters subject to regulation under this section, or to extend or to decommission a renewable energy installation situated in such waters;

(*b*) there is a proposal to operate a renewable energy installation on completion of its construction in such waters, or of any extension of it in such waters; or

(*c*) a renewable energy installation is being constructed, extended, operated or decommissioned in such waters.

(2) If the Secretary of State considers it appropriate to do so for the purpose of securing the safety of—

(*a*) the renewable energy installation or its construction, extension or decommissioning,

(*b*) other installations in the vicinity of the installation or the place where it is to be constructed or extended,

(*c*) individuals in or on the installation or other installations in that vicinity, or

(*d*) vessels in that vicinity or individuals on such vessels,

he may issue a notice declaring that such areas as are specified or described in the notice are to be safety zones for the purposes of this Chapter.

(3) The power of the Secretary of State to issue a notice under this section shall be exercisable by him either—

(*a*) on an application made to him for the purpose by any person; or

(*b*) where no such application is made, on his own initiative.

(4) Before issuing a notice under this section which relates, wholly or partly, to—

(*a*) an area of Scottish waters, or

(*b*) an area of waters in a Scottish part of a Renewable Energy Zone,

the Secretary of State must consult the Scottish Ministers.

(5) An area may be declared to be a safety zone only if it is an area of waters around or adjacent

to a place where a renewable energy installation is to be, or is being, constructed, extended, operated or decommissioned; but a safety zone may extend to waters outside the waters subject to regulation under this section.

(6) A notice under this section—

(a) must identify the renewable energy installation, or proposed renewable energy installation, by reference to which it is issued;

(b) must specify the date on which it is to come into force, or the means by which that date is to be determined;

(c) may contain provision by virtue of which the area of a safety zone varies from time to time by reference to factors specified in, or determinations made in accordance with, the provisions of the notice;

(d) may contain provision imposing prohibitions on the carrying on in a safety zone of activities specified in, or determined in accordance with, the provisions of the notice, or for the imposition of such prohibitions;

(e) may contain provision granting permission for vessels to enter or remain in a safety zone or for persons to carry on prohibited activities, or for the grant of such permissions;

(f) may confer discretions, with respect to the making of determinations for the purposes of such a notice, on such persons as may be specified or described in the notice;

(g) may modify or revoke a previous notice; and

(h) may make different provision in relation to different cases.

(7) Where a notice is issued under this section or a determination is made for the purposes of such a notice, the Secretary of State must either—

(a) himself publish the notice or determination in such manner as he considers appropriate for bringing it, as soon as is reasonably practicable, to the attention of persons likely to be affected by it; or

(b) secure that it is published in that manner—

(i) by the applicant for the notice; or

(ii) in the case of a determination made by a person other than the Secretary of State, by the applicant for the notice or by the person who made the determination.

(8) References in this section to a determination for the purposes of a notice include references to a determination made for those purposes in accordance with the notice, or with regulations under section 96—

(a) to impose a prohibition;

(b) to grant a permission; or

(c) to impose conditions in relation to a permission.

(9) Schedule 16 (which makes provision about the procedure for the declaration of safety zones) has effect.

(10) The waters subject to regulation under this section are—

(a) waters in or adjacent to Great Britain which are between the mean low water mark and the seaward limits of the territorial sea; and

(b) waters within a Renewable Energy Zone.

[Energy Act 2004, s 95.]

8–9699A 96. Prohibited activities in safety zones. (1) A vessel is not to enter or remain in a safety zone except where permission for it to do so is granted—

(a) by or in accordance with provision contained in a notice under section 95; or

(b) by or in accordance with provision contained in regulations made by the Secretary of State.

(2) A person must not carry on an activity wholly or partly in a safety zone if his doing so is prohibited by or in accordance with provision contained in a notice under section 95.

(3) Subsection (2) does not apply to the extent that carrying on the activity is permitted—

(a) by or in accordance with provision contained in such a notice; or

(b) by or in accordance with provision contained in regulations made by the Secretary of State.

(4) The provision that may be made with respect to permissions for the purposes of this section includes—

(a) provision for the permissions to apply in relation only to such times and such periods as may be specified or described in that provision; and

(b) provision for the permissions to apply only to such vessels, such persons and such purposes as may be specified or described in that provision.

(5) The provision that may be made with respect to a permission for the purposes of this section includes provision imposing conditions in relation to a permission.

(6) The conditions may include—

(a) conditions imposing obligations in relation to a vessel, or individuals on it, that must be satisfied while the vessel is in the safety zone; and

(b) conditions imposing obligations as to the manner in which any activity to which the permission relates is to be carried on.

(7) Regulations under this section may confer discretions, with respect to the granting or imposition in accordance with the regulations of permissions or conditions, on such persons as may be specified or described in the regulations.

(8) Regulations under this section are subject to the negative resolution procedure.
[Energy Act 2004, s 96.]

8–9699B   97. Offences relating to safety zones.   (1) Where a vessel enters or remains in a safety zone in contravention of section 96(1), the vessel's owner and her master are each guilty of an offence.

(2) Where—

(a) a vessel enters or remains in a safety zone with a permission granted for the purposes of section 96, and

(b) there is a contravention of a condition of that permission in relation to the vessel or individuals on the vessel,

the vessel's owner and her master are each guilty of an offence.

(3) A person who carries on an activity wholly or partly in a safety zone in contravention of section 96(2) is guilty of an offence.

(4) Where—

(a) a person carries on an activity wholly or partly in a safety zone with a permission granted for the purposes of section 96, and

(b) there is a contravention of a condition of that permission in relation to the carrying on of that activity,

that person is guilty of an offence.

(5) A person guilty of an offence under this section shall be liable—

(a) on summary conviction, to a fine not exceeding the statutory maximum;

(b) on conviction on indictment, to imprisonment for a term not exceeding two years or to a fine, or to both.

(6) In proceedings against a person as the owner of a vessel for an offence under subsection (1) or (2), it is a defence for him to show that the existence of the safety zone—

(a) was not known to the master of the vessel in question at the time of the offence; and

(b) would not have become known to the master had he made reasonable inquiries before that time.

(7) In any other proceedings against a person for an offence under this section, it is a defence for that person to show that the existence of the safety zone—

(a) was not known to him at the time of the offence; and

(b) would not have become known to him had he made reasonable inquiries before that time.

(8) It is also a defence in proceedings against a person for an offence under this section for that person to show that he took all reasonable steps to prevent the contravention in question.
[Energy Act 2004, s 97.]

8–9699C   98. Supplementary provisions relating to offences under s 97.   (1) Where the commission of an offence under section 97 is due—

(a) in the case of an offence under subsection (1) or (2) of that section, to an act or omission of a person other than the owner or master of the vessel in question, or

(b) in the case of an offence under subsection (3) or (4) of that section, to an act or omission of a person other than the person carrying on the activity in question,

that person is also guilty of that offence and shall be liable to be proceeded against and dealt with accordingly.

(2) Where an offence under section 97 is committed by a body corporate and is proved to have been committed with the consent or connivance of, or to be attributable to any neglect on the part of—

(a) a director, manager, secretary or other similar officer of the body corporate, or

(b) a person who was purporting to act in any such capacity,

he (as well as the body corporate) is guilty of that offence and shall be liable to be proceeded against and dealt with accordingly.

(3) Where an offence under section 97—

(a) is committed by a Scottish firm, and

(b) is proved to have been committed with the consent or connivance of, or to be attributable to any neglect on the part of, a partner of the firm, he (as well as the firm) is guilty of that offence and shall be liable to be proceeded against and dealt with accordingly.

(4) Where an offence under section 97 is committed outside of the United Kingdom, proceedings for the offence may be taken, and the offence may for all incidental purposes be treated as having been committed, in any place in the United Kingdom.

(5) Section 3 of the Territorial Waters Jurisdiction Act 1878 (c 73) (consents to prosecution of offences committed on the open sea by persons who are not British citizens) does not apply to proceedings for an offence under section 97.

(6) In this section "director", in relation to a body corporate whose affairs are managed by its members, means a member of the body corporate.

[Energy Act 2004, s 98.]

8–9699D   99. Navigation.   *Inserts new ss 36A and 36B in the Electricity Act 1989.*

8–9699E   100. Further provision relating to public rights of navigation.   (1) This section applies where a consent falling within subsection (2) has been granted by the Secretary of State or the Scottish Ministers ("the consenting authority") under section 36 of the 1989 Act (consent required for construction etc of generating stations) before the commencement of section 99.

(2) A consent falls within this subsection if it relates to—

(*a*)   the construction or operation of a generating station that comprises or is to comprise (in whole or in part) renewable energy installations situated in relevant waters; or

(*b*)   an extension of a generating station that comprises or is to comprise (in whole or in part) renewable energy installations so situated or an extension of such an installation.

(3) On an application made by the generator, the consenting authority may make a declaration under this section as respects rights of navigation—

(*a*)   so far as they pass through the places where the renewable energy installations are situated or are to be situated; or

(*b*)   so far as they pass through some of those places.

(4) A declaration under this section is one declaring that the rights of navigation specified or described in it—

(*a*)   are extinguished;

(*b*)   are suspended for the period that is specified in the declaration;

(*c*)   are suspended until such time as may be determined in accordance with provision contained in the declaration; or

(*d*)   are to be exercisable subject to such restrictions or conditions, or both, as are set out in the declaration.

(5) Subsections (4) to (6) of section 36A of the 1989 Act (declarations extinguishing etc rights of navigation upon grant of consent under section 36 of that Act) shall apply in relation to declarations under this section as they apply in relation to declarations under that section, but with the omission of subsection (5)(c).

(6) Before making a declaration under this section, the consenting authority must—

(*a*)   publish details of the generator's application in such manner as that authority considers appropriate;

(*b*)   give notice of that application to such persons as that authority considers appropriate;

(*c*)   consult the persons to whom notice has been given;

(*d*)   make such arrangements as that authority considers appropriate for a copy of the application to be made available for inspection by members of the public; and

(*e*)   give such opportunities to such persons as that authority considers appropriate to make representations to the authority about the application.

(7) The consenting authority may satisfy the requirements of paragraphs (*a*) to (*d*) of subsection (6) by securing that the things that it is required to do under those paragraphs are done on its behalf by the generator.

(8) In this section—

"generator", in relation to a consent under section 36 of the 1989 Act, means the person who is constructing or operating the station in question, or making the extension in question, or who is proposing to do so;

"relevant waters" has the same meaning as in section 36A of the 1989 Act.

[Energy Act 2004, s 100.]

8–9699F   101. Application of civil aviation regulations to renewable energy installations

8–9699G   102. Amendments of 1989 Act consequential on Chapter 2 of Part 2

8–9699H   103. Other amendments consequential on Chapter 2 of Part 2

8–9699I   **104. Interpretation of Chapter 2 of Part 2.**   (1) In this Chapter—

"construct", in relation to an installation or an electric line or in relation to a generating station so far as it is to comprise renewable energy installations, includes—

(a)   placing it in or upon the bed of any waters;
(b)   attaching it to the bed of any waters;
(c)   assembling it;
(d)   commissioning it; and
(e)   installing it;

and "construction" is to be construed accordingly;

"decommission", in relation to an installation or an electric line, includes—

(a)   removing it from the bed of any waters;
(b)   demolishing it; and
(c)   dismantling it;

"distribution" and "electric line" have the same meanings as in Part 1 of the 1989 Act;

"extend" and "extension"—

(a)   in relation to a generating station, have the same meanings as in Part 1 of the 1989 Act; and
(b)   in relation to an installation, have the same meanings as in relation to a generating station;

"installation" includes artificial island, structure and device;

"master" includes—

(a)   in relation to a hovercraft, the captain;
(b)   in relation to any submersible apparatus, the person in charge of the apparatus; and
(c)   in relation to an installation in transit, the person in charge of the transit operation;

"renewable energy installation" is to be construed in accordance with subsections (3) to (5);

"Renewable Energy Zone" has the meaning given by section 84(4);

"safety zone" means an area which is a safety zone for the purposes of this Chapter by virtue of section 95;

"Scottish part", in relation to a Renewable Energy Zone, means so much of that Zone as is designated under section 84(5);

"Scottish waters" means—

(a)   the internal waters of the United Kingdom that are in or are adjacent to Scotland; or
(b)   so much of the territorial sea of the United Kingdom as is adjacent to Scotland;

"submersible apparatus" has the meaning given by section 88(4) of the Merchant Shipping Act 1995 (c 21);

"supply", in relation to electricity, has the same meaning as in Part 1 of the 1989 Act;

"transmission", in relation to electricity, has the same meaning as in Part 1 of the 1989 Act;

"vessel" includes—

(a)   a hovercraft;
(b)   any submersible apparatus; and
(c)   an installation in transit.

(2) References in this Chapter to the production of energy from water include, in particular, references to its production from currents and tides.

(3) In this Chapter "renewable energy installation" means—

(a)   an offshore installation used for purposes connected with the production of energy from water or winds;
(b)   an installation in the course of construction at a place where it is to be used as an offshore installation within paragraph (a);
(c)   an installation that has ceased to be an installation within paragraph (a) while remaining an offshore installation (whether or not at the same place);
(d)   an installation that is being decommissioned at a place where it has been an installation within paragraph (a) or (c);
(e)   an installation in transit to or from a place where it is to be, or has been, used for purposes that would make it, or made it, an installation within paragraph (a);
(f)   an installation in transit to or from a place where it is to be, or was, an installation within paragraph (c).

(4) In subsection (3) "offshore installation" means an installation which is situated in waters where—

(a)   it permanently rests on, or is permanently attached to, the bed of the waters; and
(b)   it is not connected with dry land by a permanent structure providing access at all times for all purposes.

(5) The purposes referred to in subsection (3)(a) include, in particular—

(*a*)   the transmission, distribution and supply of electricity generated using water or winds; and

(*b*)   the doing of anything (whether by way of investigations, trials or feasibility studies or otherwise) with a view to ascertaining whether the generation of electricity in that manner is, in a particular case, practicable or commercially viable, or both.

(6)   Provision made by or under this Chapter in relation to places outside the United Kingdom—

(*a*)   so far as it applies to individuals, applies to them whether or not they are British citizens; and

(*b*)   so far as it applies to bodies corporate, applies to them whether or not they are incorporated under the law of a part of the United Kingdom.

[Energy Act 2004, s 104.]

<h2 style="text-align:center">CHAPTER 3[1]</h2>

8–9699J   105. Requirement to prepare decommissioning programmes.   (1) This section applies where—

(*a*)   there is a proposal by a person to construct a relevant object in waters regulated under this Chapter, or to extend a relevant object in such waters;

(*b*)   there is a proposal by a person to operate or to use a relevant object in such waters on the completion of its construction, or of any extension of it in such waters; or

(*c*)   a person is constructing, extending, operating or using a relevant object in such waters or has begun in such waters to decommission such an object.

(2)   The Secretary of State may by notice require that person to submit to him a programme for decommissioning the relevant object (a "decommissioning programme").

(3)   The Secretary of State may require a person to submit a decommissioning programme in respect of proposals made by that person only if the Secretary of State is satisfied that at least one of the statutory consents required for enabling that person to give effect to those proposals—

(*a*)   has been given; or

(*b*)   has been applied for and is likely to be given;

but for this purpose it is immaterial that a statutory consent that has been or may be given will have no effect before a particular time or unless particular conditions are satisfied.

(4)   Where there is more than one person to whom a notice under this section may be given—

(*a*)   it may be given to any one or more of them; and

(*b*)   where it is given to more than one of them, the requirement to submit a programme must be satisfied by all those persons acting jointly.

(5)   Before giving a notice under this section in relation to a relevant object which is to be or is, wholly or partly—

(*a*)   in an area of Scottish waters; or

(*b*)   in an area of waters in a Scottish part of a Renewable Energy Zone,

the Secretary of State must consult the Scottish Ministers.

(6)   A notice under this section must either—

(*a*)   specify the date by which the decommissioning programme is to be submitted; or

(*b*)   require it to be submitted on or before such date as the Secretary of State may direct.

(7)   A notice under this section may require the recipient of the notice to carry out the consultations specified in the notice before submitting the programme required of him.

(8)   A decommissioning programme—

(*a*)   must set out measures to be taken for decommissioning the relevant object;

(*b*)   must contain an estimate of the expenditure likely to be incurred in carrying out those measures;

(*c*)   must make provision for the determination of the times at which, or the periods within which, those measures will have to be taken;

(*d*)   if it proposes that the relevant object will be wholly or partly removed from a place in waters regulated under this Chapter, must include provision about restoring that place to the condition that it was in prior to the construction of the object; and

(*e*)   if it proposes that the relevant object will be left in position at a place in waters regulated under this Chapter or will not be wholly removed from a place in such waters, must include provision about whatever continuing monitoring and maintenance of the object will be necessary.

(9)   A notice under this section may require the recipient of the notice to submit any of the following with the decommissioning programme—

(*a*)   such information and documents relating to the place where the relevant object is or is to be situated as may be specified in the notice;

(*b*)   such specifications relating to the relevant object as may be specified in the notice;

(*c*)   such information and documents relating to the financial affairs of the recipient as may be specified in the notice; and (*d*)   details of the security (if any) that the recipient proposes to provide in relation to the carrying out of the decommissioning programme and for his compliance with any conditions of its approval.

(10) In this Chapter—

"relevant object" means the whole or any part of—

(*a*)   a renewable energy installation; or

(*b*)   an electric line that is or has been a related line;

"waters regulated under this Chapter" means—

(*a*)   waters in or adjacent to Great Britain which are between the mean low water mark and the seaward limits of the territorial sea; and

(*b*)   waters in a Renewable Energy Zone.

(11) In this section—

"related line" means an electric line which is a line for the conveyance of electricity to or from a renewable energy installation but is not an electricity interconnector (within the meaning of Part 1 of the 1989 Act); and

"statutory consent" means a consent, licence or approval required by or under any enactment.
[Energy Act 2004, s 105.]

---

1.   Chapter 3 contains ss 105–114.

8–9699K   106. Approval of decommissioning programmes.   (1) The Secretary of State may either approve or reject a programme submitted to him under section 105.

(2) Before approving or rejecting a decommissioning programme relating to a relevant object which is to be or is, wholly or partly—

(*a*)   in an area of Scottish waters, or

(*b*)   in an area of waters in a Scottish part of a Renewable Energy Zone,

the Secretary of State must consult the Scottish Ministers.

(3) If the Secretary of State approves a programme, he may do so—

(*a*)   with or without modifications; and

(*b*)   either subject to conditions or unconditionally.

(4) His power to approve it subject to conditions includes, in particular, power to approve it subject to a condition that the person who submitted the programme—

(*a*)   provides such security in relation to the carrying out of the programme, and for his compliance with the conditions (if any) of its approval, as may be specified by the Secretary of State; and

(*b*)   provides that security at such time, and in accordance with such requirements, as may be specified by the Secretary of State.

(5) Before approving a programme with modifications or subject to conditions, the Secretary of State must give the person who submitted it an opportunity of making representations about the proposed modifications or conditions.

(6) The power of the Secretary of State to approve a programme subject to conditions includes power, where more than one person submitted it, to impose different conditions in relation to different persons.

(7) If he rejects a programme, the Secretary of State—

(*a*)   must inform the person who submitted it of his reasons for doing so; and

(*b*)   may exercise his power under section 105 to require the submission of a new one.

(8) The Secretary of State must act without unreasonable delay in reaching a decision as to whether to approve or reject a programme.
[Energy Act 2004, s 106.]

8–9699L   107. Failure to submit or rejection of decommissioning programmes.   (1) Where—

(*a*)   a notice given under section 105 is not complied with, or

(*b*)   the Secretary of State rejects a programme submitted to him,

the Secretary of State may himself prepare a decommissioning programme in relation to the relevant object in question.

(2) Before himself preparing a decommissioning programme relating to a relevant object which is to be or is, wholly or partly—

(*a*)   in an area of Scottish waters, or

(*b*)   in an area of waters in a Scottish part of a Renewable Energy Zone,

the Secretary of State must consult the Scottish Ministers.

(3) Where the Secretary of State prepares a decommissioning programme under this section—

(a)   he must give notice informing the recipient of the notice given under section 105 that he has done so; and

(b)   this Chapter shall have effect subsequently as if the Secretary of State's programme were a programme submitted to him by the person informed and had been approved by the Secretary of State subject to the conditions specified by the Secretary of State.

(4) Where the Secretary of State informs a person under subsection (3) that he has prepared his own decommissioning programme, he may by notice to that person require him—

(a)   to provide such security in relation to the carrying out of the programme, and for his compliance with its conditions (if any), as may be specified by the Secretary of State; and

(b)   to provide it at such time, and in accordance with such requirements, as may be specified by the Secretary of State;

and a requirement under this subsection has effect as if it were a condition of the deemed approval of the programme.

(5) The Secretary of State may by notice require the recipient of a notice under section 105 to provide him with such information and documents as he may require for the purpose of exercising his powers under subsections (1) and (4).

(6) Information and documents required to be provided under subsection (5) must be provided within such period as may be specified in the notice under that subsection.

(7) A person who fails, without reasonable excuse, to comply with a notice under subsection (5) is guilty of an offence.

(8) The power of the Secretary of State to impose requirements under this section includes power, where there is more than one person on whom he may impose them, to impose different requirements in relation to different persons.

(9) Where, having given a notice under section 105, the Secretary of State prepares his own decommissioning programme, he may recover expenditure incurred by him in, or in connection with, the exercise of his powers under this section from the recipient of the notice.

(10) A person liable to pay a sum to the Secretary of State by virtue of subsection (9) must also pay interest on that sum for the period which—

(a)   begins with the day on which the Secretary of State notified him of the sum payable; and

(b)   ends with the date of payment.

(11) The rate of interest shall be a rate determined by the Secretary of State to be comparable with commercial rates.

[Energy Act 2004, s 107.]

8–9699M   **108. Reviews and revisions of decommissioning programmes.**   (1) The Secretary of State must, from time to time, conduct such reviews of a decommissioning programme approved by him as he considers appropriate.

(2) A proposal—

(a)   to modify a decommissioning programme approved by the Secretary of State, or

(b)   to modify a condition to which such a programme is subject,

may be made by the Secretary of State, or by the person who submitted the programme or (if there is more than one of them) by all of them acting jointly.

(3) A proposal—

(a)   to relieve a person of his duty under section 109(1) in relation to a decommissioning programme approved by the Secretary of State, or

(b)   as respects such a programme, to impose that duty upon a person not previously subject to it (whether in addition to or in substitution for another person),

may be made by the Secretary of State or by the person for the time being subject to that duty or (if there is more than one person subject to that duty) by any one or more of them.

(4) A proposal under subsection (2) or (3) may be made only by way of notice given—

(a)   if the proposal is the Secretary of State's, to every person whose duty under section 109(1) in relation to the programme would be affected or relieved under the proposal or who would become subject to such a duty; and

(b)   in any other case, to the Secretary of State.

(5) An opportunity of making representations to the Secretary of State about a proposal of his under this section must be given by him to every person to whom notice of the proposal is required to have been given.

(6) It is to be for the Secretary of State, after considering any representations made to him, to determine whether or not effect should be given to a proposal of his, or of any other person, under this section.

(7) Before making a determination under subsection (6) with respect to a proposal in relation to a decommissioning programme relating to a relevant object which is to be or is, wholly or partly—

(a)   in an area of Scottish waters, or

(*b*) in an area of waters in a Scottish part of a Renewable Energy Zone,

the Secretary of State must consult the Scottish Ministers.

(8) Where the Secretary of State makes a determination under subsection (6), he must give notice of his determination, and of his reasons for it, to—

(*a*) every person who, before the determination, had a duty under section 109(1) in relation to the programme; and

(*b*) every person who will become subject to such a duty as a result of the determination.

(9) Where the Secretary of State gives notice under subsection (8) in respect of a proposal, this Chapter shall have effect after the giving of that notice—

(*a*) in the case of a proposal under subsection (2), as if the programme in question had been approved subject to the modifications specified in the determination; and

(*b*) in the case of a proposal under subsection (3), as if that programme had been submitted to the Secretary of State by the person or persons so specified.

(10) Where the Secretary of State gives notice under subsection (8) to a person that he is to become subject to a duty under section 109(1) in relation to a programme, the Secretary of State may by notice to that person require him—

(*a*) to provide such security in relation to the carrying out of the programme, and for his compliance with any conditions of its approval, as may be specified by the Secretary of State; and

(*b*) to provide it at such time, and in accordance with such requirements, as may be specified by the Secretary of State;

and a requirement under this subsection has effect as if it were a condition of the approval of the programme.
[Energy Act 2004, s 108.]

8–9699N   109. Carrying out of decommissioning programmes. (1) Where a decommissioning programme is approved by the Secretary of State, it shall be the duty of the person who submitted the programme to secure—

(*a*) that it is carried out in every respect; and

(*b*) that all the conditions to which the approval is subject are complied with.

(2) Where a relevant object is subject to a decommissioning programme approved by the Secretary of State, it is an offence for a person to take any measures for decommissioning that object unless he does so—

(*a*) in accordance with the programme; or

(*b*) with the agreement of the Secretary of State.
[Energy Act 2004, s 109.]

8–9699O   110. Default in carrying out decommissioning programmes. (1) Where—

(*a*) a decommissioning programme approved by the Secretary of State is not carried out in a particular respect, or

(*b*) a condition to which the approval is subject is contravened,

the Secretary of State may, by notice, require a person subject to the duty under section 109(1) in relation to the programme to take such remedial action as may be specified in the notice.

(2) Remedial action required by a notice under this section must be taken within such period as may be specified in the notice.

(3) A person who fails to comply with a notice given to him under this section is guilty of an offence.

(4) In proceedings against a person for an offence under this section it is a defence for him to show that he exercised due diligence to avoid the contravention in question.

(5) If a notice under this section is not complied with, the Secretary of State may—

(*a*) himself secure the carrying out of the remedial action required by the notice; and

(*b*) recover any expenditure incurred by him in doing so from the person to whom the notice was given.

(6) A person liable to pay a sum to the Secretary of State by virtue of subsection (5) must also pay interest on that sum for the period which—

(*a*) begins with the day on which the Secretary of State notified him of the sum payable; and

(*b*) ends with the date of payment.

(7) The rate of interest shall be a rate determined by the Secretary of State to be comparable with commercial rates.
[Energy Act 2004, s 110.]

8–9699P   111. Regulations about decommissioning

8–9699Q 112. Duty to inform Secretary of State. (1) A person who becomes responsible for a relevant object must notify the Secretary of State that he has become so responsible.

(2) For the purposes of this section a person becomes responsible for a relevant object if—

(*a*) he makes a proposal to construct the object in waters regulated under this Chapter;

(*b*) he makes a proposal for the extension or decommissioning in such waters of the object;

(*c*) he makes a proposal to operate or use the object on completion of its construction in such waters;

(*d*) he makes a proposal to operate or use the object on completion in such waters of any extension of it;

(*e*) he becomes a party to a proposal mentioned in paragraphs (a) to (d);

(*f*) he begins in such waters to construct, to extend, to operate or use or to decommission the object;

(*g*) he begins to participate in any of the following activities carried on in such waters, the construction, extension, operation or use or decommissioning of the object.

(3) A person is not required to notify the Secretary of State that he has made a proposal, or become a party to a proposal, at any time before at least one of the statutory consents required for enabling effect to be given to the proposal has been given or applied for.

(4) A person who notifies the Secretary of State under this section that he has made a proposal, or has become a party to a proposal—

(*a*) must specify in the notification what statutory consents required for giving effect to the proposal have been given, and what applications for such consents have been made; and

(*b*) must notify him subsequently whenever such a consent or application is given or made.

(5) A notification under this section must be given within such period after the obligation to give the notification arises as may be prescribed by regulations made by the Secretary of State.

(6) A person who contravenes the requirements of this section is guilty of an offence.

(7) Regulations under this section are subject to the negative resolution procedure.

(8) A reference in this section to participation in activities does not include a reference—

(*a*) to participation on behalf of another person; or

(*b*) to participation by acting in pursuance of an agreement to provide a service or services to a person carrying on those activities.

(9) In this section "statutory consent" has the same meaning as in section 105.

[Energy Act 2004, s 112.]

8–9699R 113. Offences relating to decommissioning programmes. (1) A person guilty of an offence under a provision of this Chapter is liable—

(*a*) on summary conviction, to a fine not exceeding the statutory maximum;

(*b*) on conviction on indictment, to imprisonment for a term not exceeding two years or to a fine, or to both.

(2) No proceedings for a decommissioning offence shall be instituted in England and Wales or Northern Ireland except—

(*a*) by the Secretary of State;

(*b*) by a person authorised in that behalf by the Secretary of State; or

(*c*) by or with the consent of the Director of Public Prosecutions or (as the case may be) the Director of Public Prosecutions for Northern Ireland.

(3) Where a decommissioning offence is committed by a body corporate and is proved to have been committed with the consent or connivance of, or to be attributable to any neglect on the part of—

(*a*) a director, manager, secretary or other similar officer of the body corporate, or

(*b*) a person who was purporting to act in any such capacity,

he (as well as the body corporate) is guilty of that offence and shall be liable to be proceeded against and dealt with accordingly.

(4) Where such an offence—

(*a*) is committed by a Scottish firm, and

(*b*) is proved to have been committed with the consent or connivance of, or to be attributable to any neglect on the part of, a partner of the firm,

he (as well as the firm) is guilty of that offence and shall be liable to be proceeded against and dealt with accordingly.

(5) Where a decommissioning offence is committed outside the United Kingdom, proceedings for the offence may be taken, and the offence may for all incidental purposes be treated as having been committed, in any place in the United Kingdom.

(6) Section 3 of the Territorial Waters Jurisdiction Act 1878 (c 73) (consents to prosecution of offences committed on the open sea by persons who are not British citizens) does not apply to proceedings for a decommissioning offence.

(7) In this section—

"decommissioning offence" means an offence under—

    (*a*) a provision of this Chapter; or
    (*b*) regulations made under section 111;

"director", in relation to a body corporate whose affairs are managed by its members, means a member of the body corporate.
[Energy Act 2004, s 113.]

8–9699S   114. Interpretation of Chapter 3 of Part 2.   (1) Expressions used in this Chapter and in Chapter 2 of this Part have the same meanings in this Chapter as in that Chapter.

(2) In this Chapter—

"decommissioning programme" has the meaning given by section 105(2);
"extend" and "extension", in relation to an electric line, have the same meanings as they have in Chapter 2 of this Part and this Chapter in relation to a renewable energy installation;
"recipient", in relation to a notice under section 105, means the person or any one or more of the persons to whom that notice was given;
"relevant object" has the meaning given by section 105(10);
"security" includes—

    (*a*) a charge over a bank account or any other asset;
    (*b*) a deposit of money;
    (*c*) a performance bond or guarantee;
    (*d*) a letter of credit; and
    (*e*) a letter of comfort;

"waters regulated under this Chapter" has the meaning given by section 105(10).

(3) References in this Chapter to providing a security include references—

    (*a*) to securing its maintenance or renewal; and
    (*b*) to ensuring that its value is adjusted from time to time to take account of changes to the likely costs of the matters in respect of which it is given.

(4) References in this Chapter to the person by whom a decommissioning programme was submitted are references, in the case of a programme submitted jointly by more than one person, to each of them.

(5) Provision made by or under this Chapter in relation to places outside the United Kingdom—

    (*a*) so far as it applies to individuals, applies to them whether or not they are British citizens; and
    (*b*) so far as it applies to bodies corporate, applies to them whether or not they are incorporated under the law of any part of the United Kingdom.
[Energy Act 2004, s 114.]

PART 3[1]

CHAPTER 1[2]

8–9699T   134. Power to modify licence conditions.   (1) If the Secretary of State considers it necessary or expedient to do so for the purpose of implementing the new trading and transmission arrangements (whether wholly or partly), he may modify—

    (*a*) the conditions of a particular licence under section 6 of the 1989 Act (licences authorising supply etc), or
    (*b*) the standard conditions of licences of any of the types of licence mentioned in subsection (1) of that section (generation, transmission, distribution or supply licences).

(2) The power under subsection (1) includes—

    (*a*) power to make modifications relating to the operation of distribution systems, and
    (*b*) power to make incidental, consequential or transitional modifications.

(3) Before making modifications under this section, the Secretary of State shall consult the holder of any licence being modified and such other persons as he considers appropriate.

(4) Subsection (3) may be satisfied by consultation before, as well as by consultation after, the commencement of this section.

(5) The Secretary of State shall publish any modifications under subsection (1) in such manner as he considers appropriate.

(6) Any modification under subsection (1)(a) of part of a standard condition of a licence shall not prevent any other part of the condition from continuing to be regarded as a standard condition for the purposes of Part 1 of the 1989 Act.

(7) Where the Secretary of State modifies the standard conditions of licences of any type under subsection (1)(*b*), GEMA shall—

    (*a*) make (as nearly as may be) the same modifications of those standard conditions for the purposes of their incorporation in licences of that type granted after that time, and
    (*b*) publish the modifications in such manner as it considers appropriate.

(8) The power under subsection (1) may not be exercised after the end of the period of eighteen months beginning with the day on which that subsection comes into force.

(9) In subsection (2)(*a*), the reference to distribution systems is to be construed in accordance with section 4(4) of the 1989 Act.
[Energy Act 2004, s 134.]

---

 1. Part 3 contains ss 133–171.
 2. Chapter 1 contains ss 133–144.

8–9699U   135. Alteration of transmission activities requiring licence. *Amends s 4 of the Electricity Act 1989.*

8–9699V   136. Transmission licences. *Amends ss 6 and 7 of the Electricity Act 1989.*

8–9699W   137. New standard conditions for transmission licences

8–9699X   138. Conversion of existing transmission licences

8–9699Y   139. Grant of transmission licences

8–9699Z   140. Duties to provide information etc to Secretary of State

8–9699ZA   141. Property arrangements schemes

8–9699ZB   142. Interpretation of Chapter 1 of Part 3. In this Chapter—

"transmission licence" means a licence under section 6(1)(b) of the 1989 Act;

and references to the new trading and transmission arrangements are to be construed in accordance with section 133.
[Energy Act 2004, s 142.]

8–9699ZC   143. Amendments consequential on Chapter 1 of Part 3

CHAPTER 2[1]

8–9699ZD   145. Operators of electricity interconnectors to be licensed. *Amends ss 4, 5 and 6 of the Electricitiy Act 1989.*

---

 1. Chapter 2 contains ss 145–153.

8–9699ZE   146. Standard conditions for electricity interconnectors

8–9699ZF   147. Consequential amendments of the 1989 Act

8–9699ZG   148. Grant of electricity interconnector licences to existing operators

8–9699ZH   149. Operators of gas interconnectors to be licensed. *Amends, and inserts new provisions, in the Gas Act 1986.*

8–9699ZI   150. Standard conditions for gas interconnectors

8–9699ZJ   151. Disapplication of existing regimes

8–9699ZK   152. Grant of gas interconnector licences to existing operators

8–9699ZL   153. Extraterritorial application of Gas Act 1986. *Inserts new s 64A in the Gas Act 1986.*

CHAPTER 3[1]
Special Administration Regime for Energy Licensees

8–9699ZM   154. Energy administration orders. (1) In this Chapter "energy administration order" means an order which—

(*a*) is made by the court in relation *to* a protected energy company; and

(*b*) directs that, while the order is in force, the affairs, business and property of the company are to be managed by a person appointed by the court.

(2) The person appointed in relation to a company for the purposes of an energy administration order is referred to in this Chapter as the energy administrator of the company.

(3) The energy administrator of a company must manage its affairs, business and property, and exercise and perform all his powers and duties as such, so as to achieve the objective set out in section 155.

(4) In relation to an energy administration order applying to a non-GB company, references in this section to the affairs, business and property of the company are references only to its affairs and business so far as carried on in Great Britain and to its property in Great Britain.

(5) In this Chapter—

"protected energy company" means a company which is the holder of a relevant licence; and "relevant licence" means—

(a) a licence granted under section 6(1)(b) or (c) of the 1989 Act (transmission and distribution licences for electricity); or

(b) a licence granted under section 7 of the Gas Act 1986 (licensing of gas transporters).

[Energy Act 2004, s 154.]

---

1. Chapter 3 contains ss 154–171.

8–9699ZN 155. Objective of an energy administration. (1) The objective of an energy administration is to secure—

(a) that the company's system is and continues to be maintained and developed as an efficient and economical system; and

(b) that it becomes unnecessary, by one or both of the following means, for the energy administration order to remain in force for that purpose.

(2) Those means are—

(a) the rescue as a going concern of the company subject to the energy administration order; and

(b) transfers falling within subsection (3).

(3) A transfer falls within this subsection if it is a transfer as a going concern—

(a) to another company, or

(b) as respects different parts of the undertaking of the company subject to the energy administration order, to two or more different companies,

of so much of that undertaking as it is appropriate to transfer for the purpose of achieving the objective of the energy administration.

(4) The means by which transfers falling within subsection (3) may be effected include, in particular—

(a) a transfer of the undertaking of the company subject to the energy administration order, or of a part of its undertaking, to a wholly-owned subsidiary of that company; and

(b) a transfer to a company of securities of a wholly-owned subsidiary to which there has been a transfer falling within paragraph (a).

(5) The objective of an energy administration may be achieved by transfers falling within subsection (3) to the extent only that—

(a) the rescue as a going concern of the company subject to the energy administration order is not reasonably practicable or is not reasonably practicable without such transfers;

(b) the rescue of that company as a going concern will not achieve that objective or will not do so without such transfers;

(c) such transfers would produce a result for the company's creditors as a whole that is better than the result that would be produced without them; or

(d) such transfers would, without prejudicing the interests of those creditors as a whole, produce a result for the company's members as a whole that is better than the result that would be produced without them.

(6) In this section "the company's system", in relation to an energy administration, means—

(a) the system of electricity distribution or of electricity transmission, or

(b) the pipe-line system for the conveyance of gas,

which the company subject to the energy administration order has been maintaining as the holder of a relevant licence.

(7) In this section "efficient and economical", in relation to a system for electricity distribution or electricity transmission, includes co-ordinated.

[Energy Act 2004, s 155.]

8–9699ZR   171. Interpretation of Chapter 3 of Part 3

PART 4[1]

8–9699ZS   196. General interpretation.   (1) In this Act—

"the 1965 Act" means the Nuclear Installations Act 1965 (c 57);

"the 1989 Act" means the Electricity Act 1989 (c 29);

"the 1993 Act" means the Radioactive Substances Act 1993 (c 12);

"affirmative resolution procedure" is to be construed in accordance with section 192(3);

"BNFL" means the Nuclear Fuels Company (within the meaning of the Atomic Energy Authority Act 1971 (c 11));

"contravention" includes a failure to comply, and cognate expressions are to be construed accordingly;

"documents" includes accounts, drawings, written representations and records of any description;

"electronic communications network" has the same meaning as in the Communications Act 2003 (c 21);

"enactment" includes Acts of the Scottish Parliament and Northern Ireland legislation;

"financial year" means a period of twelve months ending with 31st March;

"GEMA" means the Gas and Electricity Markets Authority;

"modification" includes omission, addition or alteration, and cognate expressions are to be construed accordingly;

"the NDA" means the Nuclear Decommissioning Authority established by section 1;

"negative resolution procedure" is to be construed in accordance with section 192(2);

"nuclear site licence" has the same meaning as in the 1965 Act;

"nuclear transfer scheme" means a scheme under section 38;

"pensions, allowances or gratuities" is to be construed in accordance with subsection (2);

"securities", in relation to a body corporate, includes shares, debentures, debenture stock, bonds and other securities of the body corporate, whether or not constituting a charge on the assets of the body corporate;

"shares" includes stock;

"subordinate legislation" has the same meaning as in the Interpretation Act 1978 (c 30);

"subsidiary" and "wholly-owned subsidiary" have the meanings given by section 736 of the Companies Act 1985 (c 6);

"the UKAEA" means the United Kingdom Atomic Energy Authority.

(2) In this Act—

(*a*)   references to pensions, allowances or gratuities include references to any similar benefits provided on death or retirement; and

(*b*)   references to the payment of pensions, allowances or gratuities to or in respect of a person include references to the making of payments towards the provision of the payment of pensions, allowances or gratuities to or in respect of that person.

[Energy Act 2004, s 196.]

1. Part 4 contains ss 188–198.

8–9699ZT   198. Short title, commencement and extent.   (1) This Act may be cited as the Energy Act 2004.

(2) This Act (apart from this section) shall come into force on such day as the Secretary of State may by order appoint; and different days may be appointed for different purposes[1].

(3) Subject to subsection (4) of this section, this Act extends to Northern Ireland.

(4) The following provisions of this Act do not extend to Northern Ireland—

(*a*)   Chapter 3 of Part 1 (with the exception of section 59 and paragraphs 1, 5, 6, 8, 10(1) and (2) and 11 of Schedule 14);

(*b*)   so much of Part 2 as amends the 1989 Act;

(*c*)   sections 82, 90, 91 and 100; and

(*d*)   Part 3 (with the exception of section 151(5)).

[Energy Act 2004, s 198.]

1. At the time of going to press, the following Commencement Order had been made: Commencement provisions: s 198; Energy Act 2004 (Commencement No 1) Order 2004, SI 2004/1973; Energy Act 2004 (Commencement No 2) Order 2004, SI 2004/2184.

8–9699ZU

SCHEDULE 1
THE NUCLEAR DECOMMISSIONING AUTHORITY
SCHEDULE 10
THE CIVIL NUCLEAR POLICE AUTHORITY

SCHEDULE 14
Minor Amendments Relating to Constabulary[1]

1. Where these amendments relate to provisions reproduced in this work their effect will be noted when they come into force.

SCHEDULE 15
Amendments of 1993 Act[1]

1. Where these amendments relate to provisions of the Radioactive Substances Act 1993 that are reproduced, ante, in this work their effect will be noted when they come into force.

SCHEDULE 19
Consequential Amendments Relating to Chapter 1 of Part 3[1]

1. Where these amendments relate to provisions reproduced in this work their effect will be noted when they come into force.

SCHEDULE 23
Repeals[1]

1. Where these repeals relate to provisions reproduced in this work their effect will be noted when they come into force.

ESCAPE

8–9700 An escape is where one who is arrested gains his liberty before he is delivered by the due course of the law. And it may be by the party himself: either without force before he is put in hold or with force after he is restrained of his liberty: or it may be by others; and this also either without force by their permission or negligence, or with force by rescuing the party from custody. For a concise statement of the law on this subject, and of prison escape by the party confined, either serving a sentence or awaiting trial, see *Halsbury's Laws of England*, 4th edn, Vol 11(1), pp 256 *et seq*; *R v Waters* (1873) 12 Cox CC 390; *R v Hinds* (1957) 41 Cr App Rep 143; *R v Timmis* [1976] Crim LR 129. For assisting a prisoner to escape, see Prison Act 1952, s 39, in title Prisons, post.

In *E v DPP* [2002] All ER (D) 348 (Feb) a youth was remanded into the care of the local authority, in secure accommodation, and had been brought to court by the persons who were responsible for him. Owing to lack of space he was not detained there in secure accommodation. He absconded before his case was called on. An argument that he was not under the direct control of the youth offending team and thus not in lawful custody was rejected and he was liable for escaping from lawful custody. "Lawful custody" in such cases is a question of fact. For escape where the defendant has absconded after surrendering to bail, see the Bail Act 1976, s 2 and note thereto. For sentence in cases of escape, see para **3–240** in Part III: Sentencing, ante.

EUROPEAN COMMUNITIES

8–9800 This title contains the following statutory provisions—

8–9801 The United Kingdom has many substantial obligations by reason of its membership of the European Community. Their implementation is provided for by the European Communities Act 1972 in Part I: Magistrates' Courts, Procedure—Statutes on Procedure, ante) which refers to binding provisions of law and to consequential statutory instruments not listed elsewhere in this work.

Certain provisions of the Treaty establishing the European Community which may be referred to in proceedings in magistrates' courts are set out below.

Treaty Establishing the European Community

(The Community Treaties listed in the European Communities Act 1972 included the three main treaties that establish the European Economic Community (now the Economic Community). Further treaties have been added to the list by later Acts of Parliament, the last of which was the Treaty of Amsterdam 1998. The European Communities (Amendment) Act 2002 will enable the United Kingdom to ratify the Treaty of Nice 2001, which contains provisions to reform the institutions of the European Union.)

PART ONE
PRINCIPLES

Article 1

8–9802   By this Treaty, the High Contracting Parties establish among themselves a EUROPEAN COMMUNITY.

Article 2

8–9803   The Community shall have as its task, by establishing a common market and an economic and monetary union and by implementing the common policies or activities referred to in Articles 3 and 3A, to promote throughout the Community a harmonious and balanced development of economic activities, sustainable and non-inflationary growth respecting the environment, a high degree of convergence of economic performance, a high level of employment and of social protection, the raising of the standard of living and quality of life, and economic and social cohesion and solidarity among Member States.

Article 3

8–9804   For the purposes set out in Article 2, the activities of the Community shall include, as provided in this Treaty and in accordance with the timetable set out therein:

   (a)   the elimination, as between Member States, of customs duties and quantitative restrictions on the import and export of goods, and of all other measures having equivalent effect;
   (b)   a common commercial policy;
   (c)   an internal market characterized by the abolition, as between Member States, of obstacles to the free movement of goods, persons, services and capital;
   (d)   measures concerning the entry and movement of persons in the internal market as provided for in Article 100C;
   (e)   a common policy in the sphere of agriculture and fisheries;
   (f)   a common policy in the sphere of transport;
   (g)   a system ensuring that competition in the internal market is not distorted;
   (h)   the approximation of the laws of Member States to the extent required for the functioning of the common market;
   (i)   a policy in the social sphere comprising a European Social Fund;
   (j)   the strengthening of economic and social cohesion;
   (k)   a policy in the sphere of the environment;
   (l)   the strengthening of the competitiveness of Community industry;
   (m) the promotion of research and technological development;
   (n)   encouragement for the establishment and development of trans-European networks;
   (o)   a contribution to the attainment of a high level of health protection;
   (p)   a contribution to education and training of quality and to the flowering of the cultures of the Member States;
   (q)   a policy in the sphere of development co-operation;
   (r)   the association of the overseas countries and territories in order to increase trade and promote jointly economic and social development;
   (s)   a contribution to the strengthening of consumer protection;
   (t)   measures in the spheres of energy, civil protection and tourism.

Article 3A[1]

8–9804A   **1.** For the purposes set out in Article 2, the activities of the Member States and the Community shall include, as provided in this Treaty and in accordance with the timetable set out therein, the adoption of an economic policy which is based on the close co-ordination of Member States' economic policies, on the internal market and on the definition of common objectives, and conducted in accordance with the principle of an open market economy with free competition.

   2. [1] Concurrently with the foregoing, and as provided in this Treaty and in accordance with the timetable and the procedures set out therein, these activities shall include the irrevocable fixing of exchange rates leading to the introduction of a single currency, the Ecu, and the definition and conduct of a single monetary policy and exchange rate policy the primary objective of both of which shall be to maintain price stability and, without prejudice to this objective, to support the general economic policies in the Community, in accordance with the principle of an open market economy with free competition.

   3. These activities of the Member States and the Community shall entail compliance with the following guiding principles: stable prices, sound public finances and monetary conditions and a sustainable balance of payments.

---

1. If the United Kingdom notifies the Council that it does not intend to move to the third stage of Economic and Monetary Union, Article 3A(2) of this Treaty shall not apply to the United Kingdom (Protocol on Certain Provisions Relating to the United Kingdom annexed to the Treaty on European Union).

Article 3B

8–9804B The Community shall act within the limits of the powers conferred upon it by this Treaty and of the objectives assigned to it therein.

In areas which do not fall within its exclusive competence, the Community shall take action, in accordance with the principle of subsidiarity, only if and in so far as the objectives of the proposed action cannot be sufficiently achieved by the Member States and can therefore, by reason of the scale or effects of the proposed action, be better achieved by the Community.

Any action by the Community shall not go beyond what is necessary to achieve the objectives of this Treaty.

8–9805 Article 4 1. The tasks entrusted to the Community shall be carried out by the following institutions:

—a European Parliament,
—a Council,
—a Commission,
—a Court of Justice,
—a Court of Auditors.

Each institution shall act within the limits of the powers conferred upon it by this Treaty.

2. The Council and the Commission shall be assisted by an Economic and Social Committee and a Committee of the Regions acting in an advisory capacity.

8–9805A Article 4A. A European System of Central Banks (hereinafter referred to as "ESCB") and a European Central Bank (hereinafter referred to as "ECB") shall be established in accordance with the procedures laid down in this Treaty; they shall act within the limits of the powers conferred upon them by this Treaty and by the Statute of the ESCB and of the ECB (hereinafter referred to as "Statute of the ESCB") annexed thereto.

8–9805B Article 4B. A European Investment Bank is hereby established, which shall act within the limits of the powers conferred upon it by this Treaty and the Statute annexed thereto.

8–9806 Article 5. Member States shall take all appropriate measures, whether general or particular, to ensure fulfilment of the obligations arising out of this Treaty or resulting from action taken by the institutions of the Community. They shall facilitate the achievement of the Community's tasks.

They shall abstain from any measure which could jeopardise the attainment of the objectives of this Treaty.

8–9807 Article 6. Within the scope of application of this Treaty, and without prejudice to any special provisions contained therein, any discrimination on grounds of nationality shall be prohibited.

The Council, acting in accordance with the procedure referred to in Article 189C, may adopt rules designed to prohibit such discrimination.

PART TWO
CITIZENSHIP OF THE UNION

8–9808 Article 8 1. Citizenship of the Union is hereby established.

Every person holding the nationality of a Member State shall be a citizen of the Union.

2. Citizens of the Union shall enjoy the rights conferred by this Treaty and shall be subject to the duties imposed thereby.

8–9809 Article 8A 1. Every citizen of the Union shall have the right to move and reside freely within the territory of the Member States, subject to the limitations and conditions laid down in this Treaty and by the measures adopted to give it effect.

2. The Council may adopt provisions with a view to facilitating the exercise of the rights referred to in paragraph 1; save as otherwise provided in this Treaty, the Council shall act unanimously on a proposal from the Commission and after obtaining the assent of the European Parliament.

8–9810 Article 8B 1. Every citizen of the Union residing in a Member State of which he is not a national shall have the right to vote and to stand as a candidate at municipal elections in the Member State in which he resides, under the same conditions as nationals of that State. This right shall be exercised subject to detailed arrangements to be adopted before 31 December 1994 by the Council, acting unanimously on a proposal from the Commission and after consulting the European Parliament; these arrangements may provide for derogations where warranted by problems specific to a Member State.

2. Without prejudice to Article 138(3) and to the provisions adopted for its implementation, every citizen of the Union residing in a Member State of which he is not a national shall have the right to vote and to stand as a candidate in elections to the European Parliament in the Member State in which he resides, under the same conditions as nationals of that State. This right shall be exercised subject to detailed arrangements to be adopted before 31 December 1993 by the Council, acting unanimously on a proposal from the Commission and after consulting the European Parliament; these arrangements may provide for derogations where warranted by problems specific to a Member State.

8–9811   Article 8C. Every citizen of the Union shall, in the territory of a third country in which the Member State of which he is a national is not represented, be entitled to protection by the diplomatic or consular authorities of any Member State, on the same conditions as the nationals of that State. Before 31 December 1993, Member States shall establish the necessary rules among themselves and start the international negotiations required to secure this protection.

8–9812   Article 8D. Every citizen of the Union shall have the right to petition the European Parliament in accordance with Article 138D.

Every citizen of the Union may apply to the Ombudsman established in accordance with Article 138E.

8–9813   Article 8E. The Commission shall report to the European Parliament, to the Council and to the Economic and Social Committee before 31 December 1993 and then every three years on the application of the provisions of this Part. This report shall take account of the development of the Union.

On this basis, and without prejudice to the other provisions of this Treaty, the Council, acting unanimously on a proposal from the Commission and after consulting the European Parliament, may adopt provisions to strengthen or to add to the rights laid down in this Part, which it shall recommend to the Member States for adoption in accordance with their respective constitutional requirements.

PART THREE
COMMUNITY POLICIES

TITLE I
FREE MOVEMENT OF GOODS

8–9814   Article 9   1. The Community shall be based upon a customs union which shall cover all trade in goods and which shall involve the prohibition between Member States of customs duties on imports and exports and of all charges having equivalent effect, and the adoption of a common customs tariff in their relations with third countries.

2. The provisions of Chapter 1, Section 1, and of Chapter 2 of this Title shall apply to products originating in Member States and to products coming from third countries which are in free circulation in Member States.

CHAPTER 1—THE CUSTOMS UNION

Section 1—*Elimination of customs duties between Member States*

8–9815   Article 12. Member States shall refrain from introducing between themselves any new customs duties on imports or exports or any charges having equivalent effect, and from increasing those which they already apply in their trade with each other.

CHAPTER 2—ELIMINATION OF QUANTITATIVE RESTRICTIONS BETWEEN MEMBER STATES

8–9816   Article 30. Quantitative restrictions on imports and all measures having equivalent effect shall, without prejudice to the following provisions, be prohibited between Member States.

8–9817   Article 31. Member States shall refrain from introducing between themselves any new quantitative restrictions or measures having equivalent effect.

This obligation shall, however, relate only to the degree of liberalisation attained in pursuance of the decisions of the Council of the Organisation for European Co-operation of 14 January 1955. Member States shall supply the Commission, not later than six months after the entry into force of this Treaty, with lists of the products liberalised by them in pursuance of these decisions. These lists shall be consolidated between Member States.

8–9818   Article 36. The provisions of Articles 30 to 34 shall not preclude prohibitions or restrictions on imports, exports or goods in transit justified on grounds of public morality, public policy or public security; the protection of health and life of humans, animals or plants; the protection of national treasures possessing artistic, historic or archaeological value; or the protection of industrial and commercial property. Such prohibitions or restrictions shall not, however, constitute a means of arbitrary discrimination or a disguised restriction on trade between Member States.

8–9819 Article 37 1. Member States shall progressively adjust any State monopolies of a commercial character so as to ensure that when the transitional period has ended no discrimination regarding the conditions under which goods are procured and marketed exists between nationals of Member States.

The provisions of this Article shall apply to any body through which a Member State, in law or in fact, either directly or indirectly supervises, determines or appreciably influences imports or exports between Member States. These provisions shall likewise apply to monopolise delegated by the State to others.

2. Member States shall refrain from introducing any new measure which is contrary to the principles laid down in paragraph 1 or which restricts the scope of the Articles dealing with the abolition of customs duties and quantitative restrictions between Member States.

3. The timetable for the measures referred to in paragraph 1 shall be harmonised with the abolition of quantitative restrictions on the same products provided for in Articles 30 to 34.

If a product is subject to a State monopoly of a commercial character in only one or some Member States, the Commission may authorise the other Member States to apply protective measures until the adjustment provided for in paragraph 1 has been effected; the Commission shall determine the conditions and details of such measures.

4. If a State monopoly of a commercial character has rules which are designed to make it easier to dispose of agricultural products or obtain for them the best return, steps should be taken in applying the rules contained in this Article to ensure equivalent safeguards for the employment and standard of living of the producers concerned, account being taken of the adjustments that will be possible and the specialisation that will be needed with the passage of time.

5. The obligations on Member States shall be binding only in so far as they are compatible with existing international agreements.

6. With effect from the first stage the Commission shall make recommendations as to the manner in which and the timetable according to which the adjustment provided for in this Article shall be carried out.

TITLE III

FREE MOVEMENT OF PERSONS, SERVICES AND CAPITAL

CHAPTER I—WORKERS

8–9820 Article 48 1. Freedom of movement for workers shall be secured within the Community by the end of the transitional period at the latest.

2. Such freedom of movement shall entail the abolition of any discrimination based on nationality between workers of the Member States as regards employment, remuneration and other conditions of work and employment.

3. It shall entail the right, subject to limitations justified on grounds of public policy, public security or public health:

    (*a*) to accept offers of employment actually made;

    (*b*) to move freely within the territory of Member States for this purpose;

    (*c*) to stay in a Member state for the purpose of employment in accordance with the provisions governing the employment of nationals of that State laid down by law, regulation or administrative action;

    (*d*) to remain in the territory of a Member State after having been employed in that State, subject to conditions which shall be embodied in implementing regulations to be drawn up by the Commission.

4. The provisions of this Article shall not apply to employment in the public service.

Article 49

8–9821 As soon as this Treaty enters into force, the Council shall, acting in accordance with the procedure referred to in Article 189B and after consulting the Economic and Social Committee, issue directives or make regulations setting out the measures required to bring about, by progressive stages, freedom of movement for workers, as defined in Article 48, in particular:

    (*a*) by ensuring close co-operation between national employment services;

    (*b*) by systematically and progressively abolishing those administrative procedures and practices and those qualifying periods in respect of eligibility for available employment, whether resulting from national legislation or from agreements previously concluded between Member States, the maintenance of which would form an obstacle to liberalisation of the movement of workers;

    (*c*) by systematically and progressively abolishing all such qualifying periods and other restrictions provided for either under national legislation or under agreements previously concluded between Member States as imposed on workers of other Member States conditions regarding the free choice of employment other than those imposed on workers of the State concerned;

    (*d*) by setting up appropriate machinery to bring offers of employment into touch with applications for employment and to facilitate the achievement of a balance between supply and demand in the employment market in such a way as to avoid serious threats to the standard of living and level of employment in the various regions and industries[1].

---

1. This Article is printed as amended by the Single European Act, art 6(3).

8–9822 Article 50. Member states shall, within the framework of a joint programme, encourage the exchange of young workers.

8–9823 Article 51. The council shall, acting unanimously on a proposal from the Commission, adopt such measures in the field of social security as are necessary to provide freedom of movement for workers; to this end, it shall make arrangements to secure for migrant workers and their dependants:

(a) aggregation, for the purpose of acquiring and retaining the right to benefit and of calculating the amount of benefit, of all periods taken into account under the laws of the several countries;

(b) payment of benefits to persons resident in the territories of Member States.

European Communities (Services of Lawyers) Order 1978[1]

(SI 1978/1910 amended by SI 1980/1964 amended by SI 2004/1117)

8–9830 1. *Citation and commencement.*

---

1. Made in exercise of powers conferred by s 2(2) of the European Communities Act 1972.

Interpretation

8–9831 2. In this Order, unless the context otherwise requires—

"advocate", "barrister" and "solicitor" mean, in relation to any part of the United Kingdom, a person practising in that part as an advocate, barrister or solicitor as the case may be;

"country of origin", in relation to a European lawyer, means the country or countries in which he is established;

"the Directive" means the European Communities Council Directive No 77/249EEC to facilitate the effective exercise by lawyers of freedom to provide services[1];

""European lawyer" means a person entitled to pursue his professional activities in a state in column 1 under the designation referred to in column 2—

State	Designation(s)
Austria	Rechtsanwalt
Belgium	Avocat/Advocaat
Cyprus	Δικηγορος
Czech Republic	Advokát
Denmark	Advokat
Estonia	Vandeadvokaat
Finland	Asianajaja/Advokat
France	Avocat
Germany	Rechtsanwalt
Hellenic Republic	Dikegoros
Hungary	Ügyvéd
Iceland	Lögmaður
Republic of Ireland	Barrister/solicitor
Italy	Avvocato
Latvia	Zverinats advokats
Liechtenstein	Rechtsanwalt
Lithuania	Advokatas
Luxembourg	Avocat-avoué
Malta	Avukat/Prokuratur Legali
Netherlands	Advocaat
Norway	Advokat
Poland	Adwokat/Radca prawny
Portugal	Advogado
Slovakia	Advokát/Komercný právnik
Slovenia	Odvetnik/Odvetnica
Spain	Abogado/Advocat/Avogado/Abokatu
Sweden	Advokat
Switzerland	Avocat/Advokat/Rechtsanwalt/Anwalt/Für-sprecher/Fürsprech/Avvocato

"own professional authority", in relation to a European lawyer, means an authority entitled to exercise disciplinary authority over him in his member State of origin.

1. OJ No L78, 26 March 1977, p 17.

8–9832   **3.** (1) The Interpretation Act 1978 shall apply to this Order as it applies to subordinate legislation made after the commencement of that Act.

(2) Unless the context otherwise requires, any reference in this Order to a numbered article or to the Schedule is a reference to an article of, or the Schedule to, this Order.

Purpose of Order

8–9833   **4.** The provisions of this Order shall have effect for the purpose of enabling a European lawyer to pursue his professional activities in any part of the United Kingdom by providing, under the conditions specified in or permitted by the Directive, services otherwise reserved to advocates, barristers and solicitors; and services which may be so provided are hereafter in this Order referred to as services.

Representation in legal proceedings

8–9834   **5.** No enactment or rule of law or practice shall prevent a European lawyer from providing any service in relation to any proceedings, whether civil or criminal, before any court, tribunal or public authority (including appearing before and addressing the court, tribunal or public authority) by reason only that he is not an advocate, barrister or solicitor; provided that throughout he is instructed with, and acts in conjunction with, an advocate, barrister or solicitor who is entitled to practise before the court, tribunal or public authority concerned and who could properly provide the service in question.

8–9835   **6.** Nothing in this Order shall enable a European lawyer:—

(a) if he is established in practice as a barrister in the Republic of Ireland, to provide in the course of any proceedings any service which could not properly be provided by an advocate or barrister;

(b) if he is instructed with and acts in conjunction with an advocate or barrister in any proceedings, to provide in the course of those proceedings, or of any related proceedings, any service which an advocate or barrister could not properly provide;

(c) if he is instructed with and acts in conjunction with a solicitor in any proceedings, to provide in the course of those proceedings, or of any related proceedings, any service which a solicitor could not properly provide.

8–9836   **7.** A European lawyer in salaried employment who is instructed with and acts in conjunction with an advocate or barrister in any proceedings may provide a service on behalf of his employer in those proceedings only in so far as an advocate or barrister in such employment could properly do so.

Drawing of documents, etc not related to legal proceedings

8–9837   **8.** No enactment or rule of law or practice shall prevent a European lawyer from drawing or preparing for remuneration:—

(i) in England, Wales or Northern Ireland, an instrument relating to personal estate, or

(ii) in Scotland, a writ relating to moveable property,

by reason only that he is not an advocate, barrister or solicitor.

8–9838   **9.** Nothing in this Order shall entitle a European lawyer to draw or prepare for remuneration any instrument, or in Scotland any writ:—

(i) creating or transferring an interest in land; or

(ii) for obtaining title to administer the estate of a deceased person.

Legal aid

8–9839   **10.** Services may be provided by a European lawyer by way of legal advice and assistance or legal aid under the enactments specified in Part 1 of the Schedule; and references to counsel and solicitors in those and any other enactments relating to legal advice and assistance or legal aid shall be construed accordingly.

Title and description to be used by European lawyers

8–9840   **11.** In providing any services, a European lawyer shall use the professional title and description applicable to him in his country of origin, expressed in the language or one of the languages of that country, together with the name of the professional organisation by which he is authorised to practise or the court of law before which he is entitled to practise in that country.

Power to require a European lawyer to verify his status

8–9841   **12.** A competent authority may at any time request a person seeking to provide any services to verify his status as a European lawyer.

8–9842   13. Where a request has been made under article 12, the person to whom it is made shall not, except to the extent (if any) allowed by the competent authority making the request, be entitled to provide services in the United Kingdom until he has verified his status as a European lawyer to the satisfaction of that authority.

8–9843   14. For the purposes of articles 12 and 13, a competent authority is:—

  (*a*) where the services which the person concerned seeks to provide are reserved to advocates or barristers, or in any case where the person concerned claims to be a barrister established in practice in the Republic of Ireland, the Senate of the Inns of Court and the Bar, the Faculty of Advocates, or the Benchers of the Inn of Court of Northern Ireland, according to the part of the United Kingdom concerned; or

  (*b*) where subparagraph (*a*) does not apply, the Law Society, the Law Society of Scotland, or the Incorporated Law Society of Northern Ireland, according to the part of the United Kingdom concerned; or

  (*c*) in any case, any court, tribunal or public authority before which the person concerned seeks to provide services.

Professional misconduct

8–9844   15. (1) A complaint may be made to a disciplinary authority that a European lawyer providing any services has failed to observe a condition or rule of professional conduct referred to in article 4 of the Directive and applicable to him.

(2) Where a complaint is made under paragraph (1), the disciplinary authority concerned shall consider and adjudicate upon it in accordance with the same procedure, and subject to the same rights of appeal, as apply in relation to an advocate, barrister or solicitor (as the case may be) over whom that authority has jurisdiction.

(3) For the purposes of this article and article 16, a disciplinary authority is:—

  (*a*) where the services in question are reserved to advocates or barristers, or in any case where the person whose conduct is in question is established in practice as a barrister in the Republic of Ireland, an authority having disciplinary jurisdiction over advocates or barristers (as the case may be) in the part of the United Kingdom concerned;

  (*b*) where subparagraph (*a*) does not apply, an authority having disciplinary jurisdiction over solicitors in the part of the United Kingdom concerned.

8–9845   16. (1) Where a disciplinary authority finds that a European lawyer against whom a complaint has been made under article 15(1) has committed a breach of a condition or a rule of professional conduct mentioned in that article, that authority—

  (*a*) shall report that finding to the European lawyer's own professional authority; and

  (*b*) may, if it thinks fit, direct him not to provide services in the United Kingdom, except to such extent and under such conditions (if any) as the disciplinary authority may specify in the direction.

(2) A disciplinary authority may at any time, if it thinks fit, vary, cancel or suspend the operation of a direction given by it under paragraph (1)(*b*).

8–9846   17. A European lawyer in respect of whom a direction is made under article 16(1)(*b*) shall not be entitled to provide services in the United Kingdom except as allowed by the direction.

Modification of enactments

8–9847   18. (1) Without prejudice to the generality of articles 5 and 8, the enactments specified in Part 2 of the Schedule (being enactments which reserve the provision of certain services to advocates, barristers, solicitors and other qualified persons) shall be construed subject to those articles.

(2) Notwithstanding anything in the Solicitors (Scotland) Act 1933, the Solicitors Act 1974 or the Solicitors (Northern Ireland) Order 1976, references to unqualified persons, however expressed, in the enactments specified in Part 3 of the Schedule (being enactments relating to unqualified persons acting as solicitors) shall not include a European lawyer providing services within the meaning of this Order.

(3) *Scotland.*

8–9848   SCHEDULE

PART 1
ENACTMENTS RELATING TO THE PROVISION OF LEGAL ADVICE AND ASSISTANCE AND LEGAL AID

Article 10

Legal Aid and Advice Act (Northern Ireland) 1965 (c 8).
Legal Aid (Scotland) Act 1967 (c 43)[1].
Legal Advice and Assistance Act 1972 (c 50).
Legal Aid, Advice and Assistance (Northern Ireland) Order 1977 (SI No 1252 (NI 19)).
Access to Justice Act 1999 (c 22).

Financial Services and Markets Act 2000 (c 8).
Access to Justice (Northern Ireland) Order 2003.

PART 2
ENACTMENTS RESERVING THE PROVISION OF SERVICES TO ADVOCATES, BARRISTERS, SOLICITORS, ETC

Article 18(1)

Solicitors (Scotland) Act 1933 (c 21), section 39.
Magistrates' Courts (Northern Ireland) Order 1981, article 164(1).County Courts (Northern Ireland) Order 1980, article 50.Solicitors Act 1974 (c 47), sections 20, 22 and 23.
Solicitors (Northern Ireland) Order 1976 (SI No 582 (NI12)), articles 19, 23.

PART 3
ENACTMENTS RELATING TO UNQUALIFIED PERSONS ACTING AS SOLICITORS

Article 18(2)

Solicitors (Scotland) Act 1933 (c 21), sections 37, 38[2].
Solicitors Act 1974 (c 47), section 25(1).
Solicitors (Northern Ireland) Order 1976 (SI No 582 (NI 12)), articles 25(1), 27.

---

1. See now the Legal Aid (Scotland) Act 1986.
2. See now the Solicitors (Scotland) Act 1980, ss 26 and 27.

EXTRADITION, FUGITIVE OFFENDERS AND BACKING OF WARRANTS

8–9859 This title contains the following statutes—

8–9880	INDICTABLE OFFENCES ACT 1848
8–10040	SUPPRESSION OF TERRORISM ACT 1978
8–10220	INTERNATIONAL CRIMINAL COURT ACT 2001
8–10243	EXTRADITION ACT 2003

and the following statutory instruments—

8–10340	Backing of Warrants (Republic of Ireland) (Rule of Speciality) Order 1994
8–10347	International Criminal Court Act 2001 (Enforcement of Fines, Forfeiture and Reparation Orders) Regulations 2001
8–10348	Extradition Act 2003 (Designation of Part 2 Territories) Order 2003
8–10349	International Criminal Court Act 2001 (Elements of Crimes) (No 2) Regulations 2004

8–9860 NOTE 1.—This title deals with arrangements between countries as regards fugitive criminals, and these arise under a mixture of Acts which are complex in their provisions. The following scheme summarises the provisions; the descriptions refer to the place of the alleged offence and not to the nationality of the alleged offender:

Offender from Isle of Man or Channel Islands in England; English offender in Isle of Man or Channel Islands	Indictable Offences Act 1848, s 13
Irish offender in England	Backing of Warrants (Republic of Ireland) Act 1965, s 1
English offender in Ireland	See Note 2.
Commonwealth or Dependencies offender in England	Extradition Act 1989
English offender in Commonwealth or Dependencies country	See below, Note 2.
Foreign offenders in England	Extradition Act 1989
English offender in foreign country	See below, Note 2.
English offender in Scotland or Northern Ireland; or Scottish or Northern Irish offender in England	Criminal Justice and Public Order Act 1994, s 136 (execution of warrants), s 137 (cross-borders powers of arrest)[1]

---

1. In PART I: MAGISTRATES' COURT PROCEDURE, ante.

8–9870 NOTE 2.—The action to be taken by an English court depends on where the fugitive criminal is believed to be:

(*a*) *Ireland*[1]—The Irish Parliament has enacted[2] provisions which correspond with those of the Backing of Warrants (Republic of Ireland) Act 1965, of which Act note especially s 2(2) (restriction of proceedings to indictable offences and summary offences specially defined for the purpose) and s 1(2) (restriction of proceedings involving summary offences) post[3]. A warrant may be sent to the Commissioner of the Garda Siochana for execution, accompanied by the required papers[4].

(*b*) *Commonwealth or Dependencies country*[5]—Application is made to the Home Secretary together with a warrant of arrest, statement of the facts of the case, description of the fugitive and any other information facilitating his arrest, and a statement that the offence is a relevant offence. The Home Office will advise on details. See also paragraph (*c*) below.

(*c*) *Foreign countries*[6]—Application is made to the Home Secretary together with a warrant of arrest or certificate of conviction, statement of the facts of the case, description of the fugitive and any other information facilitating his arrest, any other forms required by the particular treaty with the country in question, and an indemnity in respect of expenses. It should be made clear that the offence is an extradition crime. Two systems of extradition to foreign states are in force. The new system which is contained in the Extradition Act 1989[7], applies not only as between the United Kingdom and foreign states, but also as between the United Kingdom and the Commonwealth. The old system which is derived from the Extradition Act 1870 and re-enacted in the Extradition Act 1989[8], will continue to operate until all the treaties by virtue of which it operates have been replaced or denounced. The Home Office will advise on details. Once a person is in lawful custody within the jurisdiction, the court has no power to refuse to try that person for the offence in question, and no power to inquire into the circumstances in which he had been brought into the jurisdiction[9].

---

1. See Home Office Circular 178/1965 which gives all the requisite detail.

2. The Irish Acts which govern extradition from the Republic of Ireland to the United Kingdom are the Extradition Act 1965 and the Extradition (Amendment) Act 1987.

3. The Irish Act, the Extradition Act 1965, is not quoted in this work, but one can gain an accurate impression if the actual terms of these sections of the English Act are read as it were in "mirror image" so they are made to relate to offences in England and not in Ireland. The Extradition Act 1965 must now be read subject to the provisions of a further enactment by the Irish Parliament, namely the Extradition (Amendment) Act 1987.

4. Detailed in Home Office Circular 178/1965.

5. These may be designated by Order in Council for the purposes of s 5(1) of the Extradition Act 1989 (previously s 1 of the Fugitive Offenders Act 1967); many Orders in Council have been made, see note to s 5 of the Extradition Act 1989, post.

6. These are countries which have entered into an extradition treaty with the United Kingdom; various statutory instruments contain the relevant Orders in Council. Those Orders in Council which were made under s 2 of the Extradition Act 1870 and which continue to have effect are listed in note 1 to the Extradition Act 1989, Sch 1, para 2, post. Note that someone extradited from the United States of America may only be dealt with here for the offence for which he has been extradited; see *R v Uxbridge Justices, ex p Davies* [1981] 1 WLR 1080.

7. For the new procedure, see Pt III of the Extradition Act 1989, post.

8. See Sch 1 to the Extradition Act 1989, post.

9. *R v Plymouth Justices, ex p Driver* [1986] QB 95, [1985] 2 All ER 681, 149 JP 465 ("disguised extradition" from Turkey).

8–9871 Simplified extradition procedure. The European Union Extradition Regulations 2002, SI 2002/419 amended by SI 2002/1662 have been made under s 111 of the Anti-terrorism, Crime and Security Act 2001 which give effect to the 1995 and 1996 Conventions drawn up on the basis of Article K.3 of the Treaty on Simplified Extradition Procedure between the Member States of the European Union under which Member States undertake to surrender to each other under simplified procedures as provided for by the Convention persons sought for the purpose of extradition, subject to consent of such persons and the agreement of the requested State given in accordance with this Convention.

8–9872 European Communities Act 1972: regulations. The International Criminal Tribunal for the Former Yugoslavia (Financial Sanctions Against Indictees) Regulations 2005, SI 2005/1527 have been made which inter alia provide that breaches of certain provisions of Council Regulation (EC) No 1763/2004 of 11 October 2004 relating to financial sanctions are criminal offences.

Indictable Offences Act 1848

(11 & 12 Vict c 42)

8–9880 13. Backing English warrants in the Isles of Man, Guernsey, Jersey, Alderney, or Sark, and vice versa. If any person against whom a warrant shall be issued in England or Wales, by any justice of the peace, or by any judge of her Majesty's Court of Queen's Bench, or the Crown Court for any indictable offence, shall escape, go into, reside, or be, or be supposed or suspected to be, in any of the Isles of Man, Guernsey, Jersey, Alderney, or Sark, it shall be lawful for any officer within the district into which such accused person shall escape or go, or where he shall reside or be, or be supposed or suspected to be, who shall have jurisdiction to issue any warrant or process in the

nature of a warrant for the apprehension of offenders within such district, to indorse such warrant in the manner herein-before mentioned, or to the like effect; or if any person against whom any warrant, or process in the nature of a warrant, shall be issued in any of the isles aforesaid shall escape, go into, reside, or be, or be supposed or suspected to be, in England or Wales, it shall be lawful for any justice of the peace in England and Wales to indorse such warrant or process in manner herein-before mentioned; and every such warrant or process so indorsed shall be a sufficient authority to the person or persons bringing the same, and to all persons to whom the same respectively was originally directed, and also to all constables and peace officers in the county, district, or jurisdiction within which such warrant or process shall be so indorsed, to execute the same within the county, district, or place where the justice or officer indorsing the same is acting or has jurisdiction, and to convey such offender, when apprehended, into the county or district wherein the justice or person who issued such warrant or process is acting or has jurisdiction, and carry him before such justice or person, or before some other justice or person within the same county or district who shall have jurisdiction to commit such offender to prison for trial, and such justice or person may thereupon proceed in such and the same manner as if the said offender had been apprehended in England or Wales or (as the case may be) within his jurisdiction.
[Indictable Offences Act 1848, s 13, as amended by the Courts Act 1971, Sch 8 and the Courts Act 2003, Sch 8.]

---

1. For application of this section to warrants issued under the Magistrates' Courts Act 1980, for offences other than indictable offences, and to warrants of commitment, see Magistrates' Courts Act 1980, s 126, in PART I: MAGISTRATES' COURTS, PROCEDURE, ante.
2. As to the proper authority to indorse warrants in the Channel Islands, see the Criminal Justice Administration Act 1851, s 18.

8–9881 32. Berwick-upon-Tweed, Scotland, Ireland, and Isles of Man, Jersey, and Guernsey. That the town of Berwick-upon-Tweed shall be deemed to be within England for all the purposes of this Act, but nothing in this Act shall be deemed or taken to extend to Scotland or Ireland, or to the Isles of Man, Jersey, or Guernsey, save and except the several provisions[1] respectively hereinbefore contained respecting the backing of warrants.
[Indictable Offences Act 1848, s 32, as amended by the Courts Act 1971, Sch 11.]

---

1. See s 13, ante.

Suppression of Terrorism Act 1978
(1978 c 26)

8–10040 1. Cases in which certain offences are not to be regarded as of a political character.
(1) This section applies to any offence of which a person is accused or has been convicted outside the United Kingdom if the act constituting the offence, or the equivalent act, would, if it took place in any part of the United Kingdom or, in the case of an extra-territorial offence, in corresponding circumstances outside the United Kingdom, constitute one of the offences listed in Schedule 1 to this Act.
(2) For the purposes mentioned in subsection (3) below—
(a) no offence to which this section applies shall be regarded as an offence of a political character; and
(b) no proceedings in respect of an offence to which this section applies shall be regarded as a criminal matter of a political character or as criminal proceedings of a political character.
(3) Those purposes are—
(a)–(b) (Repealed).
(c) the purposes of the Backing of Warrants (Republic of Ireland) Act 1965[1] in relation to any warrant issued in the Republic of Ireland to which this paragraph applies by virtue of an order under subsection (4) below;
(d) (Repealed).
(4) The Secretary of State may by order[2] direct that subsection (3)(c) above shall apply to warrants of the kind mentioned in section 11(a) of the said Act of 1965 issued while the order is in force.
(5) On the revocation of an order made under subsection (4) above—
(a) subsection (3)(c) above shall cease to apply to any warrant issued while the order was in force;
(b) (Repealed).
but without prejudice to the validity of anything done while the order was in force.*
[Suppression of Terrorism Act 1978, s 1, as amended by the Extradition Act 1989, Sch 2 and the Criminal Justice (International Co-operation) Act 1990, Sch 5.]

---

*Repealed by the Extradition Act 2003, Sch 4 (except in relation to any extradition made or request for extradition received by the relevant authority in the United Kingdom on or before 31 December 2003).
1. See, ante.

2. The Suppression of Terrorism Act 1978 (Application of Provisions) (Republic of Ireland) Order 1989, SI 1989/2313 has been made.

8–10041   2. Restrictions on return of criminal to Republic of Ireland, in certain cases.
(1) (*Repealed*).

(2) In relation to any warrant issued in the Republic of Ireland which specifies an offence to which section 1 above applies, being a warrant to which paragraph (*c*) of subsection (3) of that section applies as mentioned in that paragraph, the Backing of Warrants (Republic of Ireland) Act 1965[1] shall have effect as if at the end of section 2(2), as amended by the Criminal Jurisdiction Act 1975, (cases where warrant from Republic of Ireland is not to be executed) there were added the following words—

"or

(*e*)   that there are substantial grounds for believing—

(i)   that the warrant was in fact issued in order to secure the return of the person named or described in it to the Republic for the purpose of prosecuting or punishing him on account of his race, religion, nationality or political opinions; or

(ii)   that he would, if returned there, be prejudiced at his trial or punished, detained or restricted in his personal liberty by reason of his race, religion, nationality or political opinions.".*

[Suppression of Terrorism Act 1978, s 2, as amended by the Extradition Act 1989, Sch 2.]

---

*Repealed by the Extradition Act 2003, Sch 4 (except in relation to any extradition made or request for extradition received by the relevant authority in the United Kingdom on or before 31 December 2003).
1. See, ante.

8–10042   4. Jurisdiction in respect of offences committed outside United Kingdom.   (1) If a person, whether a citizen of the United Kingdom and Colonies or not, does in a convention country[1] any act which, if he had done it in a part of the United Kingdom, would have made him guilty in that part of the United Kingdom of—

(*a*)   an offence mentioned in paragraph 1, 2, 4, 5, 10, 11B, 12, 13, 14 or 15 of Schedule 1 to this Act; or

(*b*)   an offence of attempting to commit any offence so mentioned,

he shall, in that part of the United Kingdom, be guilty of the offence or offences aforesaid of which the act would have made him guilty if he had done it there.

(2) *Repealed.*

(3) If a person who is a national of a convention country but not a citizen of the United Kingdom and Colonies does outside the United Kingdom and that convention country any act which makes him in that convention country guilty of an offence and which, if he had been a citizen of the United Kingdom and Colonies, would have made him in any part of the United Kingdom guilty of an offence mentioned in paragraph 1, 2 or 13 of Schedule 1 to this Act, he shall, in any part of the United Kingdom, be guilty of the offence or offences aforesaid of which the act would have made him guilty if he had been such a citizen.

(4) Proceedings for an offence which (disregarding the provisions of the Internationally Protected Persons Act 1978, the Nuclear Material (Offences) Act 1983, the United Nations Personnel Act 1997 and the Terrorism Act 2000) would not be an offence apart from this section shall not be instituted—'

(*a*)   in Northern Ireland, except by or with the consent of the Attorney General for Northern Ireland; or

(*b*)   in England and Wales, except by or with the consent of the Attorney General;

and references to a consent provision in Article 7(3) to (5) of the Prosecution of Offences (Northern Ireland) Order 1972 (which relates to consents to prosecutions) shall include so much of this subsection as precedes paragraph (*b*).*

(5) *Applies to Scotland only.*

(6) *Repealed.*

(7) For the purposes of this section any act done—

(*a*)   on board a ship registered in a convention country, being an act which, if the ship had been registered in the United Kingdom, would have constituted an offence within the jurisdiction of the Admiralty; or

(*b*)   on board an aircraft registered in a convention country while the aircraft is in flight elsewhere than in or over that country; or

(*c*)   on board a hovercraft registered in a convention country while the hovercraft is in journey elsewhere than in or over that country,

shall be treated as done in that convention country; and subsection (4) of section 92 of the Civil Aviation Act 1982 (definition of "in flight" or, as applied to hovercraft, "in journey") shall apply for the purposes of this subsection as it applies for the purposes of that section.

[Suppression of Terrorism Act 1978, s 4, as amended by the Internationally Protected Persons Act 1978, s 5, the Civil Aviation Act 1982, s 109 and Sch 15, the Nuclear Material (Offences) Act 1983; s 4, the Child Abduction Act 1984, s 11, the United Nations Personnel Act 1997, Schedule, the Sexual Offences Act 2003, Sch 7 and the Crime (International Co-operation) Act 2003, Sch 5.]

---

*Sub-section (4) words repealed by the Justice (Northern Ireland) Act 2002, s 86, from a date to be appointed.
1. The following countries are designated as convention countries; Austria, Denmark, Federal Republic of Germany and West Berlin, Sweden (SI 1978/1245); Cyprus (SI 1979/497); Norway (SI 1980/357); Iceland (SI 1980/1392); Spain, Republic of Turkey (SI 1981/1389); Luxembourg (SI 1981/1507); Belgium, The Netherlands, Portugal, Switzerland (SI 1986/271); Italy and Liechtenstein (SI 1986/1137, France (SI 1987/2137), the Republic of Ireland (SI 1989/2210), Finland and Greece (SI 1990/1272), the Czech Republic and Slovakia (SI 1994/2978), Albania; Bulgaria; Estonia; Georgia; Hungary; Latvia; Lithuania; Malta; Moldova; Poland; Romania; Russian Federation; San Marino; Slovenia; Ukraine (SI 2003/6), Croatia, Serbia and Montenegro (SI 2003/1863).

In addition the Act has been applied to the United States of America by the Suppression of Terrorism Act 1978 (Application of Provisions) (United States of America) Order 1986, SI 1986/2146, and to India by the Suppression of Terrorism Act 1978 (Application of Provisions) (India) Order 1993, SI 1993/2533.

8–10043 5. *Power to apply[1] section 4 to non-convention countries.*
[Suppression of Terrorism Act 1978, s 5 amended by the Extradition Act 1989, s 36 and substituted by the Extradition Act 2003, Sch 3—summarised.]

---

1. The Suppression of Terrorism Act 1978 (Application of Provisions) (United States of America) Order 1986, SI 1986/2146, applies provisions of this Act to the extradition of offenders to the United States of America in pursuance of a Supplementary Treaty between the UK and the USA. The provisions apply also to India (SI 1993/2533) from a date to be notified.

8–10044 7. *Extension to Channel Islands, Isle of Man and other countries[1].*

---

1. The Act has been extended to Guernsey (SI 1978/1529), the Isle of Man (SI 1978/1530) and Jersey (SI 1978/1531) under s 7(1); and under s 7(3) the Act has been extended to Anguilla, Bermuda, British Indian Ocean Territory, British Virgin Islands, Cayman Islands, Falkland Islands, Falkland Islands Dependencies, Gibraltar, Montserrat, Pitcairn, Henderson, Ducie and Oeno Islands, St Helena Dependencies, Akrotiri and Dhekalia and the Turks and Caicos Islands (SI 1986/2019) and to Hong Kong (SI 1987/2045).

8–10045 8. Provisions as to interpretation and orders. (1) In this Act—

"act" includes omission;
"convention country", means a country for the time being designated in an order made by the Secretary of State as a party to the European Convention on the Suppression of Terrorism signed at Strasbourg on the 27th January 1977;
"country" includes any territory;
"enactment" includes an enactment of the Parliament of Northern Ireland, a Measure of the Northern Ireland Assembly, and an Order in Council under the Northern Ireland (Temporary Provisions) Act 1972 or the Northern Ireland Act 1974.

(2) Except so far as the context otherwise requires, any reference in this Act to an enactment is a reference to it as amended by or under any other enactment, including this Act.

(3) For the purpose of construing references in this Act to other Acts, section 38(1) of the Interpretation Act 1889 shall apply in cases of repeal and re-enactment by a Measure of the Northern Ireland Assembly or by an Order in Council under the Northern Ireland Act 1974 as it applies in cases of repeal and re-enactment by an Act.

(4) Any power to make an order conferred on the Secretary of State by any provision of this Act—

(a) shall be exercisable by statutory instrument; and
(b) shall include power to revoke or vary a previous order made under that provision.

(5) No order shall be made—

(a) repealed
(b) under section 5 above at any time,

unless a draft of the order has been laid before Parliament and approved by a resolution of each House of Parliament.

(6) Any statutory instrument containing an order made under subsection (1) above shall be laid before Parliament after being made.
[Suppression of Terrorism Act 1978, s 8, as amended by the Extradition Act 2003, Sch 4.]

8–10046 9. *Short title, repeals and commencement.*

8–10047

SCHEDULES

Sections 1, 4   ## SCHEDULE 1
LIST OF OFFENCES

(As amended by the Firearms (Northern Ireland) Order 1981, SI 1981/155, the Taking of Hostages Act 1982, s 3, the Aviation Security Act 1982, s 40 and Sch 2, the Child Abduction Act 1984, s 11, the Criminal Justice Act 1988, s 22, the Prevention of Terrorism (Temporary Provisions) Act 1989, Sch 8, the Aviation and Maritime Act 1990, Sch 3, the Terroriam Act 2000, Sch 15, the Sexual Offences Act 2003, Sch 7 and SI 2004/702.)

Common law offences

1. Murder.
2. Manslaughter or culpable homicide.
3. Rape.
4. Kidnapping, abduction or plagium.
5. False imprisonment.
6. Assault occasioning actual bodily harm or causing injury.
7. Wilful fire-raising.

Offences against the person

8. An offence under any of the following provisions of the Offences against the Person Act 1861—

(*za*)   section 4 (soliciting etc to commit murder);
(*a*)   section 18 (wounding with intent to cause grievous bodily harm);
(*b*)   section 20 (causing grievous bodily harm);
(*c*)   section 21 (attempting to choke etc in order to commit or assist in the committing of any indictable offence);
(*d*)   section 22 (using chloroform etc to commit or assist in the committing of any indictable offence);
(*e*)   section 23 (maliciously administering poison etc so as to endanger life or inflict grievous bodily harm);
(*f*)   section 24 (maliciously administering poison etc with intent to injure etc);
(*g*)   section 48 (rape).

9. An offence under any of the following provisions of the Sexual Offences Act 2003—

(*a*)   sections 1 or 2 (rape, assault by penetration);
(*b*)   section 4 (causing a person to engage in sexual activity without consent), where the activity caused involved penetration within subsection (4)(*a*) to (*d*) of that section;
(*c*)   section 5 or 6 (rape of a child under 13, assault of a child under 13 by penetration);
(*d*)   section 8 (causing or inciting a child under 13 to engage in sexual activity), where an activity involving penetration within subsection (3)(*a*) to (*d*) of that section was caused;
(*e*)   section 30 (sexual activity with a person with a mental disorder impeding choice), where the touching involved penetration within subsection (3)(*a*) to (*d*) of that section;
(*f*)   section 31 (causing or inciting a person, with a mental disorder impeding choice, to engage in sexual activity), where an activity involving penetration within subsection (3)(*a*) to (*d*) of that section was caused.

9A. The offence of torture under section 134 of the Criminal Justice Act 1988.

Abduction

10. An offence under any of the following provisions of the Offences against the Person Act 1861—

(*a*)   section 55 (abduction of unmarried girl under 16);
(*b*)   section 56 (child-stealing or receiving stolen child).

11. *Repealed.*

Taking of hostages

11A. An offence under the Taking of Hostages Act 1982.
11B. An offence under section 2 of the Child Abduction Act 1984 (abduction of child by person other than parent etc) or any corresponding provision in force in Northern Ireland.

Explosives

12. An offence under any of the following provisions of the Offences against the Person Act 1861—

(*a*)   section 28 (causing bodily injury by gunpowder);
(*b*)   section 29 (causing gunpowder to explode etc with intent to do grievous bodily harm);
(*c*)   section 30 (placing gunpowder near a building etc with intent to cause bodily injury).

13. An offence under any of the following provisions of the Explosive Substances Act 1883—

(*a*)   section 2 (causing explosion likely to endanger life or property);
(*b*)   section 3 (doing any act with intent to cause such an explosion, conspiring to cause such an explosion, or making or possessing explosive with intent to endanger life or property).

Nuclear material

13A. An offence under any provision of the Nuclear Material (Offences) Act 1983

Firearms

14. The following offences under the Firearms Act 1968—

(*a*) an offence under section 16 (possession of firearm with intent to injure);

(*b*) an offence under subsection (1) of section 17 (use of firearm or imitation firearm to resist arrest) involving the use or attempted use of a firearm within the meaning of that section.

15. The following offences under the Firearms (Northern Ireland) Order 2004—

(*a*) an offence under Article 58(1) consisting of a person's having in his possession any firearm or ammunition within the meaning of that Article with intent by that means to endanger life, or to enable another person by that means to endanger life;

(*b*) an offence under Article 59(1) (use of firearm or imitation firearm to resist arrest) involving the use or attempted use of a firearm within the meaning of that Article.

Offences against property

16. An offence under section 1(2) of the Criminal Damage Act 1971 (destroying or damaging property intending to endanger life or being reckless as to danger to life).

17. An offence under Article 3(2) of the Criminal Damage (Northern Ireland) Order 1977 (destroying or damaging property intending to endanger life or being reckless as to danger to life).

Offences in relation to aircraft

18. An offence under Part I of the Aviation Security Act 1982 (other than an offence under section 4 or 7 of that Act.

18A. An offence under section 1 of the Aviation and Maritime Security Act 1990.

Offences relating to ships and fixed platforms

18B. An offence under Part II of the Aviation and Maritime Security Act 1990 (other than an offence under section 15 of that Act).

Financing terrorism

19A. An offence under Part III of the Prevention of Terrorism (Temporary Provisions) Act 1989.

Attempts

20. An offence of attempting to commit any offence mentioned in a preceding paragraph of this Schedule.

Conspiracy

21. An offence of conspiring to commit any offence mentioned in a preceding paragraph of this Schedule.

International Criminal Court Act 2001
(2001 c 17)

8–10220 The inter-governmental treaty that forms the Rome Statute of the International Criminal Court ('the Statute') was adopted on 17 July 1998. The purpose of the International Court Act 2001 ('the Act'), together with corresponding legislation in the Scottish Parliament, is to enable the UK to comply with its obligations under the Statute and accordingly to ratify.

The International Criminal Court ('ICC') will be created when 60 states ('States Parties') have ratified the Statute. The ICC will be a permanent court, situated in the Hague[1]. It will try individuals accused of genocide, crimes against humanity and war crimes. It will also be able to investigate crimes committed by nationals of, or within the territory of, States Parties, and to exercise jurisdiction over crimes, wherever committed, which are referred to the ICC by the UN Security Council. States Parties will be obliged to co-operate with the ICC, including by gathering evidence and arresting suspects.

The ICC will be complementary to national courts. States Parties will retain jurisdiction unless they are unable or unwilling genuinely to investigate and prosecute a crime.

Part 1 of the Act defines certain terms. Part 2 enables the arrest and surrender of suspects at the request of the ICC. Part 3 provides for various forms of co-operation with ICC investigations. Part 4 makes provision for persons convicted by the ICC to serve their sentences in UK prisons and for the enforcement in the UK of fines, forfeitures and reparations ordered by the ICC. Part 5 incorporates into domestic law the offences of genocide, crimes against humanity and war crimes[2] and criminalises conduct ancillary to an act that would constitute such an offence if it were committed in England and Wales. This Part also provides that offences in relation to the ICC may be dealt with as for the corresponding domestic offence. The new offences have extra-territorial effect in relation to UK nationals and residents, and persons subject to UK Service legislation[3]. Part 6 contains general provisions. There are 10 schedules to the Act.

The provisions of the Act came into force on royal assent or on 1 September 2001 (see the International Criminal Court (Commencement Order) 2001, SI 2001/2161). However, with the exception of Part 5, and provisions ancillary to that Part, the Act is not reproduced in this work due to uncertainty as to when there will be sufficient signatory states for the ICC to come into being.

1. Schedule 1 to the Act provides power for the ICC to sit in the UK.
2. As defined in the relevant Articles of the Statute, which are set out in Sch 8 to the Act.
3. Defined in s 67.

PART 4
ENFORCEMENT OF SENTENCES AND ORDERS
Other Orders

8–10220A   **49.** *Power to make provision for enforcement of other orders*[1]

1. See the International Criminal Court Act 2001 (Enforcement of Fines, Forfeiture and Reparation Orders) Regulations 2001, in this Title, post.

PART 5[1]
OFFENCES UNDER DOMESTIC LAW
Introduction

8–10221   **50. Meaning of "genocide", "crime against humanity" and "war crime".**   (1) In this Part—

"genocide" means an act of genocide as defined in article 6,
"crime against humanity" means a crime against humanity as defined in article 7, and
"war crime" means a war crime as defined in article 8.2.

(2) In interpreting and applying the provisions of those articles the court shall take into account—

(*a*) any relevant Elements of Crimes adopted in accordance with article 9, and
(*b*) until such time as Elements of Crimes are adopted under that article, any relevant Elements of Crimes contained in the report of the Preparatory Commission for the International Criminal Court adopted on 30th June 2000.

(3) The Secretary of State shall set out in regulations the text of the Elements of Crimes referred to in subsection (2), as amended from time to time.
The regulations shall be made by statutory instrument which shall be laid before Parliament after being made[2].

(4) The articles referred to in subsection (1) shall for the purposes of this Part be construed subject to and in accordance with any relevant reservation or declaration made by the United Kingdom when ratifying any treaty or agreement relevant to the interpretation of those articles.
Her Majesty may by Order in Council—

(*a*) certify that such a reservation or declaration has been made and the terms in which it was made;
(*b*) if any such reservation or declaration is withdrawn (in whole or part), certify that fact and revoke or amend any Order in Council containing the terms of that reservation or declaration[3].

(5) In interpreting and applying the provisions of the articles referred to in subsection (1) the court shall take into account any relevant judgment or decision of the ICC.
Account may also be taken of any other relevant international jurisprudence.

(6) The relevant provisions of the articles of the ICC Statute referred to in this section are set out in Schedule 8 to this Act.
No account shall be taken for the purposes of this Part of any provision of those articles omitted from the text set out in that Schedule.
[International Criminal Court Act 2001, s 50.]

1. Part 5 contains ss 50–74.
2. See the International Criminal Court Act 2001 (Elements of Crimes) Regulations 2001, SI 2001/2505, this PART, post.
3. The International Criminal Court Act 2001 (Reservations and Declarations) Order 2001, SI 2001/2559 (not reproduced in this work) has been made.

England and Wales

8–10222   **51. Genocide, crimes against humanity and war crimes.**   (1) It is an offence against the law of England and Wales for a person to commit genocide, a crime against humanity or a war crime.

(2) This section applies to acts committed—

(*a*) in England or Wales, or

(b)   outside the United Kingdom by a United Kingdom national, a United Kingdom resident or a person subject to UK service jurisdiction.

[International Criminal Court Act 2001, s 51.]

8–10223   52.   Conduct ancillary to genocide, etc committed outside jurisdiction.   (1) It is an offence against the law of England and Wales for a person to engage in conduct ancillary to an act to which this section applies.

(2) This section applies to an act that if committed in England or Wales would constitute—

(a)   an offence under section 51 (genocide, crime against humanity or war crime), or

(b)   an offence under this section,

but which, being committed (or intended to be committed) outside England and Wales, does not constitute such an offence.

(3) The reference in subsection (1) to conduct ancillary to such an act is to conduct that would constitute an ancillary offence in relation to that act if the act were committed in England or Wales.

(4) This section applies where the conduct in question consists of or includes an act committed—

(a)   in England or Wales, or

(b)   outside the United Kingdom by a United Kingdom national, a United Kingdom resident or a person subject to UK service jurisdiction.

[International Criminal Court Act 2001, s 52.]

8–10224   53.   Trial and punishment of main offences.   (1) The following provisions apply in relation to—

(a)   offences under section 51 (genocide, crimes against humanity and war crimes),

(b)   offences under section 52 (conduct ancillary to genocide, etc committed outside jurisdiction), and

(c)   offences ancillary to an offence within paragraph (a) or (b) above.

(2) The offence is triable only on indictment.

(3) Proceedings for an offence shall not be instituted except by or with the consent of the Attorney General.

(4) If the offence is not committed in England or Wales—

(a)   proceedings may be taken, and

(b)   the offence may for incidental purposes be treated as having been committed,

in any place in England or Wales.

(5) A person convicted of—

(a)   an offence involving murder, or

(b)   an offence ancillary to an offence involving murder,

shall be dealt with as for an offence of murder or, as the case may be, the corresponding ancillary offence in relation to murder.

In this subsection "murder" means the killing of a person in such circumstances as would, if committed in England or Wales, constitute murder.

(6) In any other case a person convicted of an offence is liable to imprisonment for a term not exceeding 30 years.

[International Criminal Court Act 2001, s 53.]

8–10225   54.   *Offences in relation to the ICC*

8–10226   55.   Meaning of "ancillary offence".   (1) References in this Part to an ancillary offence under the law of England and Wales are to—

(a)   aiding, abetting, counselling or procuring the commission of an offence,

(b)   inciting a person to commit an offence,

(c)   attempting or conspiring to commit an offence, or

(d)   assisting an offender or concealing the commission of an offence.

(2) In subsection (1)(a) the reference to aiding, abetting, counselling or procuring is to conduct that in relation to an indictable offence would be punishable under section 8 of the Accessories and Abettors Act 1861 (c 94).

(3) In subsection (1)(b) the reference to incitement is to conduct amounting to an offence of incitement at common law.

(4) In subsection (1)(c)—

(a)   the reference to an attempt is to conduct amounting to an offence under section 1 of the Criminal Attempts Act 1981 (c 47); and

(b)   the reference to conspiracy is to conduct amounting to an offence of conspiracy under section 1 of the Criminal Law Act 1977 (c 45).

(5) In subsection (1)(d)—

(a) the reference to assisting an offender is to conduct that in relation to an arrestable offence would amount to an offence under section 4(1) of the Criminal Law Act 1967 (c 58); and

(b) the reference to concealing an offence is to conduct that in relation to an arrestable offence would amount to an offence under section 5(1) of that Act.

[International Criminal Court Act 2001, s 55.]

8–10227 56. Saving for general principles of liability, etc. (1) In determining whether an offence under this Part has been committed the court shall apply the principles of the law of England and Wales.

(2) Nothing in this Part shall be read as restricting the operation of any enactment or rule of law relating to—

(a) the extra-territorial application of offences (including offences under this Part), or

(b) offences ancillary to offences under this Part (wherever committed).

[International Criminal Court Act 2001, s 56.]

8–10228 57. Protection of victims and witnesses. (1) The enactments specified below (which make provision for the protection of victims and witnesses of certain offences) have effect—

(a) as if any reference in those provisions to a specific substantive offence included an offence under section 51 involving conduct constituting that offence; and

(b) as if any reference in those provisions to a specific ancillary offence included—

(i) that ancillary offence in relation to an offence under section 51 involving conduct constituting the substantive offence in question, and

(ii) an offence under section 52 involving conduct constituting that ancillary offence in relation to an act to which that section applies involving conduct constituting the substantive offence in question.

(2) The enactments are—

the Sexual Offences (Amendment) Act 1976 (c 82) and the Sexual Offences (Amendment) Act 1992 (c 34) (protection of victims of sexual offences);

Chapters 1 to 3 of Part 2 of the Youth Justice and Criminal Evidence Act 1999 (c 23) (protection of witnesses and complainants); and

the Sexual Offences (Protected Material) Act 1997 (c 39) (restrictions on access by defendants and others to material disclosed in connection with proceedings for offences).

(3) In subsection (1) above—

(a) "substantive offence" means an offence other than an ancillary offence; and

(b) the reference to conduct constituting an offence is to conduct that would constitute that offence if committed in England and Wales.

[International Criminal Court Act 2001, s 57.]

8–10229 58–64. *Provisions relating to Northern Ireland*

Supplementary provisions

8–10230 65. Responsibility of commanders and other superiors. (1) This section applies in relation to—

(a) offences under this Part, and

(b) offences ancillary to such offences.

(2) A military commander, or a person effectively acting as a military commander, is responsible for offences committed by forces under his effective command and control, or (as the case may be) his effective authority and control, as a result of his failure to exercise control properly over such forces where—

(a) he either knew, or owing to the circumstances at the time, should have known that the forces were committing or about to commit such offences, and

(b) he failed to take all necessary and reasonable measures within his power to prevent or repress their commission or to submit the matter to the competent authorities for investigation and prosecution.

(3) With respect to superior and subordinate relationships not described in subsection (2), a superior is responsible for offences committed by subordinates under his effective authority and control, as a result of his failure to exercise control properly over such subordinates where—

(a) he either knew, or consciously disregarded information which clearly indicated, that the subordinates were committing or about to commit such offences,

(b) the offences concerned activities that were within his effective responsibility and control, and

(c) he failed to take all necessary and reasonable measures within his power to prevent or repress their commission or to submit the matter to the competent authorities for investigation and prosecution.

(4) A person responsible under this section for an offence is regarded as aiding, abetting, counselling or procuring the commission of the offence.

(5) In interpreting and applying the provisions of this section (which corresponds to article 28) the court shall take into account any relevant judgment or decision of the ICC.

Account may also be taken of any other relevant international jurisprudence.

(6) Nothing in this section shall be read as restricting or excluding—

(a) any liability of the commander or superior apart from this section, or

(b) the liability of persons other than the commander or superior.

[International Criminal Court Act 2001, s 65.]

8–10231 66. Mental element. (1) References in this Part to a person committing—

(a) genocide,

(b) a crime against humanity,

(c) a war crime, or

(d) any of the acts mentioned in article 70.1 (offences against the administration of justice in relation to the ICC),

shall be construed in accordance with this section.

(2) Unless otherwise provided by—

(a) the articles mentioned in the definition in section 50(1) of the crimes specified in subsection (1)(a) to (c) above, or any relevant Elements of Crimes (see section 50(2)),

(b) section 54(1) or 61(1) or article 70.1 (offences in relation to the ICC), or

(c) section 65 (responsibility of commanders and other superiors),

a person is regarded as committing such an act or crime only if the material elements are committed with intent and knowledge.

(3) For this purpose—

(a) a person has intent—

(i) in relation to conduct, where he means to engage in the conduct, and

(ii) in relation to a consequence, where he means to cause the consequence or is aware that it will occur in the ordinary course of events; and

(b) "knowledge" means awareness that a circumstance exists or a consequence will occur in the ordinary course of events.

(4) In interpreting and applying the provisions of this section (which corresponds to article 30) the court shall take into account any relevant judgment or decision of the ICC.

Account may also be taken of any other relevant international jurisprudence.

[International Criminal Court Act 2001, s 66.]

8–10232 67. Meaning of "UK national", "UK resident" and "person subject to UK service jurisdiction". (1) In this Part a "United Kingdom national" means an individual who is—

(a) a British citizen, a British Dependent Territories citizen, a British National (Overseas) or a British Overseas Citizen,

(b) a person who under the British Nationality Act 1981 (c 61) is a British subject, or

(c) a British protected person within the meaning of that Act.

(2) In this Part a "United Kingdom resident" means a person who is resident in the United Kingdom.

(3) In this Part a "person subject to UK service jurisdiction" means—

(a) a person subject to military law, air force law or the Naval Discipline Act 1957 (c 53);

(b) any such person as is mentioned in section 208A or 209(1) or (2) of the Army Act 1955 (c 18) or the Air Force Act 1955 (c 19) (application of Act to passengers in HM ships and aircraft and to certain civilians); or

(c) any such person as is mentioned in section 117 or 118 of the Naval Discipline Act 1957 (application of Act to passengers in HM ships and to certain civilians).

[International Criminal Court Act 2001, s 67.]

8–10233 68. Proceedings against persons becoming resident within the jurisdiction.

(1) This section applies in relation to a person who commits acts outside the United Kingdom at a time when he is not a United Kingdom national, a United Kingdom resident or a person subject to UK service jurisdiction and who subsequently becomes resident in the United Kingdom.

(2) Proceedings may be brought against such a person in England and Wales or Northern Ireland for a substantive offence under this Part if—

(a) he is resident in the United Kingdom at the time the proceedings are brought, and

(b) the acts in respect of which the proceedings are brought would have constituted that offence if they had been committed in that part of the United Kingdom.

(3) Proceedings may be brought against such a person in England and Wales or Northern Ireland

for an offence ancillary to a substantive offence under this Part (or what would be such a substantive offence if committed in that part of the United Kingdom) if—

(*a*)   he is resident in the United Kingdom at the time the proceedings are brought, and
(*b*)   the acts in respect of which the proceedings are brought would have constituted that offence if they had been committed in that part of the United Kingdom.

(4)   In this section a "substantive offence" means an offence other than an ancillary offence.
(5)   Nothing in this section shall be read as restricting the operation of any other provision of this Part.
[International Criminal Court Act 2001, s 68.]

8–10234   69. References to acts to include omissions, etc.   In this Part "act", except where the context otherwise requires, includes an omission, and references to conduct have a corresponding meaning.
[International Criminal Court Act 2001, s 69.]

Consequential provisions

8–10235   70. *Offences under section 1 of the Geneva Conventions Act 1957*[1]

1.   Amends s 1 of the Geneva Conventions Act 1957 (punishment of grave breaches of the Conventions).

8–10236   71. Extradition: Orders in Council under the 1870 Act.   (1)   This section applies in relation to extradition under Schedule 1 to the Extradition Act 1989 (c 33) (extradition where an Order in Council under section 2 of the Extradition Act 1870 (c 52) is in force in relation to the foreign state).
(2)   The offences to which such an Order in Council can apply include any Part 5 offence.
(3)   "Part 5 offence" means—

(*a*)   an offence under section 51 or 58 (genocide, crimes against humanity and war crimes),
(*b*)   an offence under section 52 or 59 (conduct ancillary to genocide etc committed outside the jurisdiction), or
(*c*)   an ancillary offence in relation to any such offence.

(4)   For the purposes of Schedule 1 to the 1989 Act, conduct, wherever committed, which constitutes—

(*a*)   a Part 5 offence, and
(*b*)   an offence against the law of any state in relation to which that Schedule has effect,

shall be deemed to be an offence committed within the jurisdiction of that state.
(5)   If any conduct would constitute a Part 5 offence if committed in the United Kingdom then, notwithstanding that it does not constitute such an offence—

(*a*)   a person whose surrender is sought in respect of that conduct may be surrendered by the United Kingdom in pursuance of an Order in Council to which subsection (2) applies, and
(*b*)   subsection (4) applies to the conduct as if it constituted a Part 5 offence.

(6)   References in this section to an offence under any provision of this Part, or to an offence ancillary to such an offence, include any corresponding offence under the law of Scotland.*
[International Criminal Court Act 2001, s 71.]

*Repealed by the Extradition Act 2003, Sch 4 (except in relation to any extradition made or request for extradition received by the relevant authority in the United Kingdom on or before 31 December 2003).

8–10237   72. *Extradition: exception to dual criminality rule under the 1989 Act*[1]*

*Repealed by the Extradition Act 2003, Sch 4 (except in relation to any extradition made or request for extradition received by the relevant authority in the United Kingdom on or before 31 December 2003).
1.   Section 73(1) substitutes a new s 23 of the Extradition Act 1989. Section 73(2) inserts a new s 6D in the Backing of Warrants (Republic of Ireland) Act 1965.

8–10238   74. *Consequential amendments of armed forces legislation*

Section 50(6)   SCHEDULE 8
GENOCIDE, CRIMES AGAINST HUMANITY AND WAR CRIMES: ARTICLES 6 TO 9
ARTICLE 6

Genocide

8–10239   For the purpose of this Statute, "genocide" means any of the following acts committed with intent to destroy, in whole or in part, a national, ethnical, racial or religious group, as such:

(a) Killing members of the group;
(b) Causing serious bodily or mental harm to members of the group;
(c) Deliberately inflicting on the group conditions of life calculated to bring about its physical destruction in whole or in part;
(d) Imposing measures intended to prevent births within the group;
(e) Forcibly transferring children of the group to another group.

ARTICLE 7

Crimes against humanity

8–10240 **1.** For the purpose of this Statute, "crime against humanity" means any of the following acts when committed as part of a widespread or systematic attack directed against any civilian population, with knowledge of the attack:

(a) Murder;
(b) Extermination;
(c) Enslavement;
(d) Deportation or forcible transfer of population;
(e) Imprisonment or other severe deprivation of physical liberty in violation of fundamental rules of international law;
(f) Torture;
(g) Rape, sexual slavery, enforced prostitution, forced pregnancy, enforced sterilization, or any other form of sexual violence of comparable gravity;
(h) Persecution against any identifiable group or collectivity on political, racial, national, ethnic, cultural, religious, gender as defined in paragraph 3, or other grounds that are universally recognized as impermissible under international law, in connection with any act referred to in this paragraph or any crime within the jurisdiction of the Court;
(i) Enforced disappearance of persons;
(j) The crime of apartheid;
(k) Other inhumane acts of a similar character intentionally causing great suffering, or serious injury to body or to mental or physical health.

2. For the purpose of paragraph 1:

(a) "Attack directed against any civilian population" means a course of conduct involving the multiple commission of acts referred to in paragraph 1 against any civilian population, pursuant to or in furtherance of a State or organizational policy to commit such attack;
(b) "Extermination" includes the intentional infliction of conditions of life, inter alia the deprivation of access to food and medicine, calculated to bring about the destruction of part of a population;
(c) "Enslavement" means the exercise of any or all of the powers attaching to the right of ownership over a person and includes the exercise of such power in the course of trafficking in persons, in particular women and children;
(d) "Deportation or forcible transfer of population" means forced displacement of the persons concerned by expulsion or other coercive acts from the area in which they are lawfully present, without grounds permitted under international law;
(e) "Torture" means the intentional infliction of severe pain or suffering, whether physical or mental, upon a person in the custody or under the control of the accused; except that torture shall not include pain or suffering arising only from, inherent in or incidental to, lawful sanctions;
(f) "Forced pregnancy" means the unlawful confinement of a woman forcibly made pregnant, with the intent of affecting the ethnic composition of any population or carrying out other grave violations of international law;
(g) "Persecution" means the intentional and severe deprivation of fundamental rights contrary to international law by reason of the identity of the group or collectivity;
(h) "The crime of apartheid" means inhumane acts of a character similar to those referred to in paragraph 1, committed in the context of an institutionalized regime of systematic oppression and domination by one racial group over any other racial group or groups and committed with the intention of maintaining that regime;
(i) "Enforced disappearance of persons" means the arrest, detention or abduction of persons by, or with the authorization, support or acquiescence of, a State or a political organization, followed by a refusal to acknowledge that deprivation of freedom or to give information on the fate or whereabouts of those persons, with the intention of removing them from the protection of the law for a prolonged period of time.

3. For the purpose of this Statute, it is understood that the term "gender" refers to the two sexes, male and female, within the context of society. The term "gender" does not indicate any meaning different from the above.

ARTICLE 8

War crimes

8–10241 **2.** For the purpose of this Statute, "war crimes" means:

(a) Grave breaches of the Geneva Conventions of 12 August 1949, namely, any of the following acts against persons or property protected under the provisions of the relevant Geneva Convention:

(i) Wilful killing;
(ii) Torture or inhuman treatment, including biological experiments;
(iii) Wilfully causing great suffering, or serious injury to body or health;
(iv) Extensive destruction and appropriation of property, not justified by military necessity and carried out unlawfully and wantonly;

(v)   Compelling a prisoner of war or other protected person to serve in the forces of a hostile Power;

(vi) Wilfully depriving a prisoner of war or other protected person of the rights of fair and regular trial;

(vii) Unlawful deportation or transfer or unlawful confinement;

(viii) Taking of hostages.

(b) Other serious violations of the laws and customs applicable in international armed conflict, within the established framework of international law, namely, any of the following acts:

(i)   Intentionally directing attacks against the civilian population as such or against individual civilians not taking direct part in hostilities;

(ii) Intentionally directing attacks against civilian objects, that is, objects which are not military objectives;

(iii) Intentionally directing attacks against personnel, installations, material, units or vehicles involved in a humanitarian assistance or peacekeeping mission in accordance with the Charter of the United Nations, as long as they are entitled to the protection given to civilians or civilian objects under the international law of armed conflict;

(iv) Intentionally launching an attack in the knowledge that such attack will cause incidental loss of life or injury to civilians or damage to civilian objects or widespread, long-term and severe damage to the natural environment which would be clearly excessive in relation to the concrete and direct overall military advantage anticipated;

(v)   Attacking or bombarding, by whatever means, towns, villages, dwellings or buildings which are undefended and which are not military objectives;

(vi) Killing or wounding a combatant who, having laid down his arms or having no longer means of defence, has surrendered at discretion;

(vii) Making improper use of a flag of truce, or of the flag or of the military insignia and uniform of the enemy or of the United Nations, as well as of the distinctive emblems of the Geneva Conventions, resulting in death or serious personal injury;

(viii) The transfer, directly or indirectly, by the Occupying Power of parts of its own civilian population into the territory it occupies, or the deportation or transfer of all or parts of the population of the occupied territory within or outside this territory;

(ix) Intentionally directing attacks against buildings dedicated to religion, education, art, science or charitable purposes, historic monuments, hospitals and places where the sick and wounded are collected, provided they are not military objectives;

(x)   Subjecting persons who are in the power of an adverse party to physical mutilation or to medical or scientific experiments of any kind which are neither justified by the medical, dental or hospital treatment of the person concerned nor carried out in his or her interest, and which cause death to or seriously endanger the health of such person or persons;

(xi) Killing or wounding treacherously individuals belonging to the hostile nation or army;

(xii) Declaring that no quarter will be given;

(xiii) Destroying or seizing the enemy's property unless such destruction or seizure be imperatively demanded by the necessities of war;

(xiv) Declaring abolished, suspended or inadmissible in a court of law the rights and actions of the nationals of the hostile party;

(xv) Compelling the nationals of the hostile party to take part in the operations of war directed against their own country, even if they were in the belligerent's service before the commencement of the war;

(xvi) Pillaging a town or place, even when taken by assault;

(xvii) Employing poison or poisoned weapons;

(xviii) Employing asphyxiating, poisonous or other gases, and all analogous liquids, materials or devices;

(xix) Employing bullets which expand or flatten easily in the human body, such as bullets with a hard envelope which does not entirely cover the core or is pierced with incisions;

(xxi) Committing outrages upon personal dignity, in particular humiliating and degrading treatment;

(xxii) Committing rape, sexual slavery, enforced prostitution, forced pregnancy as defined in article 7, paragraph 2(f), enforced sterilisation, or any other form of sexual violence also constituting a grave breach of the Geneva Conventions;

(xxiii) Utilizing the presence of a civilian or other protected person to render certain points, areas or military forces immune from military operations;

(xxiv) Intentionally directing attacks against buildings, material, medical units and transport, and personnel using the distinctive emblems of the Geneva Conventions in conformity with international law;

(xxv) Intentionally using starvation of civilians as a method of warfare by depriving them of objects indispensable to their survival, including wilfully impeding relief supplies as provided for under the Geneva Conventions;

(xxvi) Conscripting or enlisting children under the age of fifteen years into the national armed forces or using them to participate actively in hostilities.

(c) In the case of an armed conflict not of an international character, serious violations of article 3 common to the four Geneva Conventions of 12 August 1949, namely, any of the following acts committed against persons taking no active part in the hostilities, including members of armed forces who have laid down their arms and those placed *hors de combat* by sickness, wounds, detention or any other cause:

(i)   Violence to life and person, in particular murder of all kinds, mutilation, cruel treatment and torture;

(ii) Committing outrages upon personal dignity, in particular humiliating and degrading treatment;

(iii) Taking of hostages;

(iv) The passing of sentences and the carrying out of executions without previous judgement pronounced by a regularly constituted court, affording all judicial guarantees which are generally recognised as indispensable.

(d) Paragraph 2(c) applies to armed conflicts not of an international character and thus does not apply to situations of internal disturbances and tensions, such as riots, isolated and sporadic acts of violence or other acts of a similar nature.

(e) Other serious violations of the laws and customs applicable in armed conflicts not of an international character, within the established framework of international law, namely, any of the following acts:

(i) Intentionally directing attacks against the civilian population as such or against individual civilians not taking direct part in hostilities;

(ii) Intentionally directing attacks against buildings, material, medical units and transport, and personnel using the distinctive emblems of the Geneva Conventions in conformity with international law;

(iii) Intentionally directing attacks against personnel, installations, material, units or vehicles involved in a humanitarian assistance or peacekeeping mission in accordance with the Charter of the United Nations, as long as they are entitled to the protection given to civilians or civilian objects under the international law of armed conflict;

(iv) Intentionally directing attacks against buildings dedicated to religion, education, art, science or charitable purposes, historic monuments, hospitals and places where the sick and wounded are collected, provided they are not military objectives;

(v) Pillaging a town or place, even when taken by assault;

(vi) Committing rape, sexual slavery, enforced prostitution, forced pregnancy, as defined in article 7, paragraph 2(*f*), enforced sterilization, and any other form of sexual violence also constituting a serious violation of article 3 common to the four Geneva Conventions;

(vii) Conscripting or enlisting children under the age of fifteen years into armed forces or groups or using them to participate actively in hostilities;

(viii) Ordering the displacement of the civilian population for reasons related to the conflict, unless the security of the civilians involved or imperative military reasons so demand;

(ix) Killing or wounding treacherously a combatant adversary;

(x) Declaring that no quarter will be given;

(xi) Subjecting persons who are in the power of another party to the conflict to physical mutilation or to medical or scientific experiments of any kind which are neither justified by the medical, dental or hospital treatment of the person concerned nor carried out in his or her interest, and which cause death to or seriously endanger the health of such person or persons;

(xii) Destroying or seizing the property of an adversary unless such destruction or seizure be imperatively demanded by the necessities of the conflict.

(*f*) Paragraph 2(*e*) applies to armed conflicts not of an international character and thus does not apply to situations of internal disturbances and tensions, such as riots, isolated and sporadic acts of violence or other acts of a similar nature. It applies to armed conflicts that take place in the territory of a State when there is protracted armed conflict between governmental authorities and organized armed groups or between such groups.

ARTICLE 9

Elements of crimes

8–10242   **1.** Elements of Crimes shall assist the Court in the interpretation and application of articles 6, 7 and 8. They shall be adopted by a two-thirds majority of the members of the Assembly of States Parties.

2. Amendments to the Elements of Crimes may be proposed by:

(*a*)   Any State Party;

(*b*)   The judges acting by an absolute majority;

(*c*)   The Prosecutor.

Such amendments shall be adopted by a two-thirds majority of the members of the Assembly of States Parties.

3. The Elements of Crimes and amendments thereto shall be consistent with this Statute.

Extradition Act 2003[1]

(2003 c 41)

PART 1[2]
EXTRADITION TO CATEGORY 1 TERRITORIES

Introduction

8–10243   **1. Extradition to category 1 territories.**   (1) This Part deals with extradition from the United Kingdom to the territories designated for the purposes of this Part by order[3] made by the Secretary of State.

(2) In this Act references to category 1 territories are to the territories designated for the purposes of this Part.

(3) A territory may not be designated for the purposes of this Part if a person found guilty in the territory of a criminal offence may be sentenced to death for the offence under the general criminal law of the territory.

[Extradition Act 2003, s 1.]

---

1. This Act establishes new, comprehensive extradition procedures. The Extradition Act 1989 and the Backing of Warrants (Republic of Ireland) Act 1965 have been repealed in their entirety (though see below as to transitional arrangements).

The main features of the Act are:

1.   the establishment of a system where each of the UK's extradition partners is in one of two categories. Each country is designated by order of the Secretary of State for a particular category and it will, therefore, be possible for a country to move from one category to the other when appropriate, depending on the extradition procedures that the UK negotiates with each extradition partner;

2. the adoption of the Framework Decision on the European Arrest Warrant creating a fast-track extradition arrangement with Member States of the EU and Gibraltar;
3. the retention of the current arrangements for extradition with non-EU countries with important modifications to reduce duplication and complexity;
4. the simplification of the rules governing the authentication of foreign documents;
5. the abolition of the requirement to provide prima facie evidence in certain cases; and
6. a simplified single avenue of appeal for all cases.

Part I contains ss 1–68.

2. The provisions of the Act were brought into force, subject to specified savings, on 1 January 2004, by the Extradition Act 2003 (Commencement and Savings) Order 2003, SI 2003/3103, as amended by SI 2003/3258 and 3312. Extradition requests received before the above date will continue, however, to be dealt with under the provisions of the Extradition Act 1989, as will any post extradition requests made in respect of a person extradited from the UK before that date. All requests received by the British Overseas Territories (with the exception of Gibraltar which will be designated as a category 1 territory), the Bailiwick of Jersey, the Bailiwick of Guernsey and the Isle of Man will also continue to be dealt with under the provisions of the Extradition Act 1989 until Orders in Council are made under ss 177, 178 or 222 or until any of those territories passes their own legislation to deal with extradition.

3. The Extradition Act 2003 (Designation of Part 1 Territories) Order 2003, SI 2003/3333 amended by SI 2004/1898 and SI 2005/365 and 2036 has been made which designates the following countries: Austria; Belgium; Czech Republic; Cyprus; Denmark; Estonia; France; Finland; Germany; Greece; Hungary; Ireland; Italy; Latvia; Lithuania; Luxembourg; Malta; The Netherlands; Poland; Portugal; Slovakia; Slovenia; Spain and Sweden.

8–10244   2. Part 1 warrant and certificate.   (1) This section applies if the designated authority receives a Part 1 warrant in respect of a person.

(2) A Part 1 warrant is an arrest warrant which is issued by a judicial authority of a category 1 territory and which contains—

(a) the statement referred to in subsection (3) and the information referred to in subsection (4), or
(b) the statement referred to in subsection (5) and the information referred to in subsection (6).

(3) The statement is one that—

(a) the person in respect of whom the Part 1 warrant is issued is accused in the category 1 territory of the commission of an offence specified in the warrant, and
(b) the Part 1 warrant is issued with a view to his arrest and extradition to the category 1 territory for the purpose of being prosecuted for the offence.

(4) The information is—

(a) particulars of the person's identity;
(b) particulars of any other warrant issued in the category 1 territory for the person's arrest in respect of the offence;
(c) particulars of the circumstances in which the person is alleged to have committed the offence, including the conduct alleged to constitute the offence, the time and place at which he is alleged to have committed the offence and any provision of the law of the category 1 territory under which the conduct is alleged to constitute an offence;
(d) particulars of the sentence which may be imposed under the law of the category 1 territory in respect of the offence if the person is convicted of it.

(5) The statement is one that—

(a) the person in respect of whom the Part 1 warrant is issued is alleged to be unlawfully at large after conviction of an offence specified in the warrant by a court in the category 1 territory, and
(b) the Part 1 warrant is issued with a view to his arrest and extradition to the category 1 territory for the purpose of being sentenced for the offence or of serving a sentence of imprisonment or another form of detention imposed in respect of the offence.

(6) The information is—

(a) particulars of the person's identity;
(b) particulars of the conviction;
(c) particulars of any other warrant issued in the category 1 territory for the person's arrest in respect of the offence;
(d) particulars of the sentence which may be imposed under the law of the category 1 territory in respect of the offence, if the person has not been sentenced for the offence;
(e) particulars of the sentence which has been imposed under the law of the category 1 territory in respect of the offence, if the person has been sentenced for the offence.

(7) The designated authority may issue a certificate under this section if it believes that the authority which issued the Part 1 warrant has the function of issuing arrest warrants in the category 1 territory.

(8) A certificate under this section must certify that the authority which issued the Part 1 warrant has the function of issuing arrest warrants in the category 1 territory.

(9) The designated authority is the authority designated for the purposes of this Part by order[1] made by the Secretary of State.

(10) An order[1] made under subsection (9) may—

(a) designate more than one authority;
(b) designate different authorities for different parts of the United Kingdom.

[Extradition Act 2003, s 2.]

---

1. The National Criminal Intelligence Service and the Crown Agent of the Crown Office are designated for these purposes by the Extradition Act 2003 (Part 1 Designated Authorities) Order 2003, SI 2003/3109.

Arrest

8-10245 3. Arrest under certified Part 1 warrant. (1) This section applies if a certificate is issued under section 2 in respect of a Part 1 warrant issued in respect of a person.

(2) The warrant may be executed by a constable or a customs officer in any part of the United Kingdom.

(3) The warrant may be executed by a service policeman, but only if the service policeman would have power to arrest the person under the appropriate service law if the person had committed an offence under that law.

(4) If a service policeman has power to execute the warrant under subsection (3), he may execute the warrant in any place where he would have power to arrest the person under the appropriate service law if the person had committed an offence under that law.

(5) The warrant may be executed even if neither the warrant nor a copy of it is in the possession of the person executing it at the time of the arrest.

(6) The appropriate service law is—

(a) the Army Act 1955 (3 & 4 Eliz 2 c 18), if the person in respect of whom the warrant is issued is subject to military law;
(b) the Air Force Act 1955 (3 & 4 Eliz 2 c 19), if that person is subject to air-force law;
(c) the Naval Discipline Act 1957 (c 53), if that person is subject to that Act.

[Extradition Act 2003, s 3.]

8-10246 4. Person arrested under Part 1 warrant. (1) This section applies if a person is arrested under a Part 1 warrant.

(2) A copy of the warrant must be given to the person as soon as practicable after his arrest.

(3) The person must be brought as soon as practicable before the appropriate judge.

(4) If subsection (2) is not complied with and the person applies to the judge to be discharged, the judge may order his discharge.

(5) If subsection (3) is not complied with and the person applies to the judge to be discharged, the judge must order his discharge.

(6) A person arrested under the warrant must be treated as continuing in legal custody until he is brought before the appropriate judge under subsection (3) or he is discharged under subsection (4) or (5).

[Extradition Act 2003, s 4.]

8-10247 5. Provisional arrest. (1) A constable, a customs officer or a service policeman may arrest a person without a warrant if he has reasonable grounds for believing—

(a) that a Part 1 warrant has been or will be issued in respect of the person by an authority of a category 1 territory, and
(b) that the authority has the function of issuing arrest warrants in the category 1 territory.

(2) A constable or a customs officer may arrest a person under subsection (1) in any part of the United Kingdom.

(3) A service policeman may arrest a person under subsection (1) only if the service policeman would have power to arrest the person under the appropriate service law if the person had committed an offence under that law.

(4) If a service policeman has power to arrest a person under subsection (1), the service policeman may exercise the power in any place where he would have power to arrest the person for an offence under the appropriate service law if the person had committed an offence under that law.

(5) The appropriate service law is—

(a) the Army Act 1955 (3 & 4 Eliz 2 c 18), if the person to be arrested is subject to military law;
(b) the Air Force Act 1955 (3 & 4 Eliz 2 c 19), if that person is subject to air-force law;
(c) the Naval Discipline Act 1957 (c 53), if that person is subject to that Act.

[Extradition Act 2003, s 5.]

8-10248 6. Person arrested under section 5. (1) This section applies if a person is arrested under section 5.

(2) The following must occur within the required period—

(a) the person must be brought before the appropriate judge;
(b) the documents specified in subsection (4) must be produced to the judge.

(3) The required period is 48 hours starting with the time when the person is arrested.

(4) The documents are—

(a) a Part 1 warrant in respect of the person;

(b) a certificate under section 2 in respect of the warrant.

(5) A copy of the warrant must be given to the person as soon as practicable after his arrest.

(6) If subsection (2) is not complied with and the person applies to the judge to be discharged, the judge must order his discharge.

(7) If subsection (5) is not complied with and the person applies to the judge to be discharged, the judge may order his discharge.

(8) The person must be treated as continuing in legal custody until he is brought before the appropriate judge under subsection (2) or he is discharged under subsection (6) or (7).

(9) Subsection (10) applies if—

(a) a person is arrested under section 5 on the basis of a belief that a Part 1 warrant has been or will be issued in respect of him;

(b) the person is discharged under subsection (6) or (7).

(10) The person must not be arrested again under section 5 on the basis of a belief relating to the same Part 1 warrant.

The initial hearing

[Extradition Act 2003, s 6.]

8–10249 7. Identity of person arrested. (1) This section applies if—

(a) a person arrested under a Part 1 warrant is brought before the appropriate judge under section 4(3), or

(b) a person is arrested under section 5 and section 6(2) is complied with in relation to him.

(2) The judge must decide whether the person brought before him is the person in respect of whom—

(a) the warrant referred to in subsection (1)(a) was issued, or

(b) the warrant referred to in section 6(4) was issued.

(3) The judge must decide the question in subsection (2) on a balance of probabilities.

(4) If the judge decides the question in subsection (2) in the negative he must order the person's discharge.

(5) If the judge decides that question in the affirmative he must proceed under section 8.

(6) In England and Wales, the judge has the same powers (as nearly as may be) as a magistrates' court would have if the proceedings were the summary trial of an information against the person.

(7) (*Scotland*).

(8) (*Northern Ireland*).

(9) If the judge exercises his power to adjourn the proceedings he must remand the person in custody or on bail.

(10) If the judge remands the person in custody he may later grant bail.

[Extradition Act 2003, s 7.]

8–10250 8. Remand etc. (1) If the judge is required to proceed under this section he must—

(a) fix a date on which the extradition hearing is to begin;

(b) inform the person of the contents of the Part 1 warrant;

(c) give the person the required information about consent;

(d) remand the person in custody or on bail.

(2) If the judge remands the person in custody he may later grant bail.

(3) The required information about consent is—

(a) that the person may consent to his extradition to the category 1 territory in which the Part 1 warrant was issued;

(b) an explanation of the effect of consent and the procedure that will apply if he gives consent;

(c) that consent must be given before the judge and is irrevocable.

(4) The date fixed under subsection (1) must not be later than the end of the permitted period, which is 21 days starting with the date of the arrest referred to in section 7(1)(a) or (b).

(5) If before the date fixed under subsection (1) (or this subsection) a party to the proceedings applies to the judge for a later date to be fixed and the judge believes it to be in the interests of justice to do so, he may fix a later date; and this subsection may apply more than once.

(6) Subsections (7) and (8) apply if the extradition hearing does not begin on or before the date fixed under this section.

(7) If the person applies to the judge to be discharged the judge must order his discharge, unless reasonable cause is shown for the delay.

(8) If no application is made under subsection (7) the judge must order the person's discharge on

the first occasion after the date fixed under this section when the person appears or is brought before the judge, unless reasonable cause is shown for the delay.

The extradition hearing

[Extradition Act 2003, s 8.]

8–10251   9. Judge's powers at extradition hearing.   (1) In England and Wales, at the extradition hearing the appropriate judge has the same powers (as nearly as may be) as a magistrates' court would have if the proceedings were the summary trial of an information against the person in respect of whom the Part 1 warrant was issued.

(2) *(Scotland).*

(3) *(Northern Ireland).*

(4) If the judge adjourns the extradition hearing he must remand the person in custody or on bail.

(5) If the judge remands the person in custody he may later grant bail.

[Extradition Act 2003, s 9.]

8–10252   10. Initial stage of extradition hearing.   (1) This section applies if a person in respect of whom a Part 1 warrant is issued appears or is brought before the appropriate judge for the extradition hearing.

(2) The judge must decide whether the offence specified in the Part 1 warrant is an extradition offence.

(3) If the judge decides the question in subsection (2) in the negative he must order the person's discharge.

(4) If the judge decides that question in the affirmative he must proceed under section 11.

[Extradition Act 2003, s 10.]

8–10253   11. Bars to extradition.   (1) If the judge is required to proceed under this section he must decide whether the person's extradition to the category 1 territory is barred by reason of—

(a)   the rule against double jeopardy;

(b)   extraneous considerations;

(c)   the passage of time;

(d)   the person's age;

(e)   hostage-taking considerations;

(f)   speciality;

(g)   the person's earlier extradition to the United Kingdom from another category 1 territory;

(h)   the person's earlier extradition to the United Kingdom from a non-category 1 territory.

(2) Sections 12 to 19 apply for the interpretation of subsection (1).

(3) If the judge decides any of the questions in subsection (1) in the affirmative he must order the person's discharge.

(4) If the judge decides those questions in the negative and the person is alleged to be unlawfully at large after conviction of the extradition offence, the judge must proceed under section 20.

(5) If the judge decides those questions in the negative and the person is accused of the commission of the extradition offence but is not alleged to be unlawfully at large after conviction of it, the judge must proceed under section 21.

[Extradition Act 2003, s 11.]

8–10254   12. Rule against double jeopardy.   A person's extradition to a category 1 territory is barred by reason of the rule against double jeopardy if (and only if) it appears that he would be entitled to be discharged under any rule of law relating to previous acquittal or conviction on the assumption—

(a)   that the conduct constituting the extradition offence constituted an offence in the part of the United Kingdom where the judge exercises jurisdiction;

(b)   that the person were charged with the extradition offence in that part of the United Kingdom.

[Extradition Act 2003, s 12.]

8–10255   13. Extraneous considerations.   A person's extradition to a category 1 territory is barred by reason of extraneous considerations if (and only if) it appears that—

(a)   the Part 1 warrant issued in respect of him (though purporting to be issued on account of the extradition offence) is in fact issued for the purpose of prosecuting or punishing him on account of his race, religion, nationality, gender, sexual orientation or political opinions, or

(b)   if extradited he might be prejudiced at his trial or punished, detained or restricted in his personal liberty by reason of his race, religion, nationality, gender, sexual orientation or political opinions.

[Extradition Act 2003, s 13.]

8–10256   14. Passage of time.   A person's extradition to a category 1 territory is barred by reason of the passage of time if (and only if) it appears that it would be unjust or oppressive to extradite him by reason of the passage of time since he is alleged to have committed the extradition offence or since he is alleged to have become unlawfully at large (as the case may be).

[Extradition Act 2003, s 14.]

8–10257   15. Age.   A person's extradition to a category 1 territory is barred by reason of his age if (and only if) it would be conclusively presumed because of his age that he could not be guilty of the extradition offence on the assumption—

(a)   that the conduct constituting the extradition offence constituted an offence in the part of the United Kingdom where the judge exercises jurisdiction;

(b)   that the person carried out the conduct when the extradition offence was committed (or alleged to be committed);

(c)   that the person carried out the conduct in the part of the United Kingdom where the judge exercises jurisdiction.

[Extradition Act 2003, s 15.]

8–10258   16. Hostage-taking considerations.   (1) A person's extradition to a category 1 territory is barred by reason of hostage-taking considerations if (and only if) the territory is a party to the Hostage-taking Convention and it appears that—

(a)   if extradited he might be prejudiced at his trial because communication between him and the appropriate authorities would not be possible, and

(b)   the act or omission constituting the extradition offence also constitutes an offence under section 1 of the Taking of Hostages Act 1982 (c 28) or an attempt to commit such an offence.

(2)   The appropriate authorities are the authorities of the territory which are entitled to exercise rights of protection in relation to him.

(3)   A certificate issued by the Secretary of State that a territory is a party to the Hostage-taking Convention is conclusive evidence of that fact for the purposes of subsection (1).

(4)   The Hostage-taking Convention is the International Convention against the Taking of Hostages opened for signature at New York on 18 December 1979.

[Extradition Act 2003, s 16.]

8–10259   17. Speciality.   (1) A person's extradition to a category 1 territory is barred by reason of speciality if (and only if) there are no speciality arrangements with the category 1 territory.

(2)   There are speciality arrangements with a category 1 territory if, under the law of that territory or arrangements made between it and the United Kingdom, a person who is extradited to the territory from the United Kingdom may be dealt with in the territory for an offence committed before his extradition only if—

(a)   the offence is one falling within subsection (3), or

(b)   the condition in subsection (4) is satisfied.

(3)   The offences are—

(a)   the offence in respect of which the person is extradited;

(b)   an extradition offence disclosed by the same facts as that offence;

(c)   an extradition offence in respect of which the appropriate judge gives his consent under section 55 to the person being dealt with;

(d)   an offence which is not punishable with imprisonment or another form of detention;

(e)   an offence in respect of which the person will not be detained in connection with his trial, sentence or appeal;

(f)   an offence in respect of which the person waives the right that he would have (but for this paragraph) not to be dealt with for the offence.

(4)   The condition is that the person is given an opportunity to leave the category 1 territory and—

(a)   he does not do so before the end of the permitted period, or

(b)   if he does so before the end of the permitted period, he returns there.

(5)   The permitted period is 45 days starting with the day on which the person arrives in the category 1 territory.

(6)   Arrangements made with a category 1 territory which is a Commonwealth country or a British overseas territory may be made for a particular case or more generally.

(7)   A certificate issued by or under the authority of the Secretary of State confirming the existence of arrangements with a category 1 territory which is a Commonwealth country or a British overseas territory and stating the terms of the arrangements is conclusive evidence of those matters.

[Extradition Act 2003, s 17.]

8–10260 **18. Earlier extradition to United Kingdom from category 1 territory.** A person's extradition to a category 1 territory is barred by reason of his earlier extradition to the United Kingdom from another category 1 territory if (and only if)—

    (a) the person was extradited to the United Kingdom from another category 1 territory (the extraditing territory);

    (b) under arrangements between the United Kingdom and the extraditing territory, that territory's consent is required to the person's extradition from the United Kingdom to the category 1 territory in respect of the extradition offence under consideration;

    (c) that consent has not been given on behalf of the extraditing territory.

[Extradition Act 2003, s 18.]

8–10261 **19. Earlier extradition to United Kingdom from non-category 1 territory.** A person's extradition to a category 1 territory is barred by reason of his earlier extradition to the United Kingdom from a non-category 1 territory if (and only if)—

    (a) the person was extradited to the United Kingdom from a territory that is not a category 1 territory (the extraditing territory);

    (b) under arrangements between the United Kingdom and the extraditing territory, that territory's consent is required to the person's being dealt with in the United Kingdom in respect of the extradition offence under consideration;

    (c) consent has not been given on behalf of the extraditing territory to the person's extradition from the United Kingdom to the category 1 territory in respect of the extradition offence under consideration.

[Extradition Act 2003, s 19.]

8–10262 **20. Case where person has been convicted.** (1) If the judge is required to proceed under this section (by virtue of section 11) he must decide whether the person was convicted in his presence.

(2) If the judge decides the question in subsection (1) in the affirmative he must proceed under section 21.

(3) If the judge decides that question in the negative he must decide whether the person deliberately absented himself from his trial.

(4) If the judge decides the question in subsection (3) in the affirmative he must proceed under section 21.

(5) If the judge decides that question in the negative he must decide whether the person would be entitled to a retrial or (on appeal) to a review amounting to a retrial.

(6) If the judge decides the question in subsection (5) in the affirmative he must proceed under section 21.

(7) If the judge decides that question in the negative he must order the person's discharge.

(8) The judge must not decide the question in subsection (5) in the affirmative unless, in any proceedings that it is alleged would constitute a retrial or a review amounting to a retrial, the person would have these rights—

    (a) the right to defend himself in person or through legal assistance of his own choosing or, if he had not sufficient means to pay for legal assistance, to be given it free when the interests of justice so required;

    (b) the right to examine or have examined witnesses against him and to obtain the attendance and examination of witnesses on his behalf under the same conditions as witnesses against him.

[Extradition Act 2003, s 20.]

8–10263 **21. Human rights.** (1) If the judge is required to proceed under this section (by virtue of section 11 or 20) he must decide whether the person's extradition would be compatible with the Convention rights within the meaning of the Human Rights Act 1998 (c 42).

(2) If the judge decides the question in subsection (1) in the negative he must order the person's discharge.

(3) If the judge decides that question in the affirmative he must order the person to be extradited to the category 1 territory in which the warrant was issued.

(4) If the judge makes an order under subsection (3) he must remand the person in custody or on bail to wait for his extradition to the category 1 territory.

(5) If the judge remands the person in custody he may later grant bail.

[Extradition Act 2003, s 21.]

Matters arising before end of extradition hearing

8–10264 **22. Person charged with offence in United Kingdom.** (1) This section applies if at any time in the extradition hearing the judge is informed that the person in respect of whom the Part 1 warrant is issued is charged with an offence in the United Kingdom.

(2) The judge must adjourn the extradition hearing until one of these occurs—

(a) the charge is disposed of;

(b) the charge is withdrawn;

(c) proceedings in respect of the charge are discontinued;

(d) an order is made for the charge to lie on the file, or in relation to Scotland, the diet is deserted *pro loco et tempore.*

(3) If a sentence of imprisonment or another form of detention is imposed in respect of the offence charged, the judge may adjourn the extradition hearing until the sentence has been served.

(4) If before he adjourns the extradition hearing under subsection (2) the judge has decided under section 11 whether the person's extradition is barred by reason of the rule against double jeopardy, the judge must decide that question again after the resumption of the hearing.

[Extradition Act 2003, s 22.]

8–10265   23. Person serving sentence in United Kingdom.   (1) This section applies if at any time in the extradition hearing the judge is informed that the person in respect of whom the Part 1 warrant is issued is serving a sentence of imprisonment or another form of detention in the United Kingdom.

(2) The judge may adjourn the extradition hearing until the sentence has been served.

[Extradition Act 2003, s 23.]

8–10266   24. Extradition request.   (1) This section applies if at any time in the extradition hearing the judge is informed that—

(a) a certificate has been issued under section 70 in respect of a request for the person's extradition;

(b) the request has not been disposed of;

(c) an order has been made under section 179(2) for further proceedings on the warrant to be deferred until the request has been disposed of.

(2) The judge must remand the person in custody or on bail.

(3) If the judge remands the person in custody he may later grant bail.

[Extradition Act 2003, s 24.]

8–10267   25. Physical or mental condition.   (1) This section applies if at any time in the extradition hearing it appears to the judge that the condition in subsection (2) is satisfied.

(2) The condition is that the physical or mental condition of the person in respect of whom the Part 1 warrant is issued is such that it would be unjust or oppressive to extradite him.

(3) The judge must—

(a) order the person's discharge, or

(b) adjourn the extradition hearing until it appears to him that the condition in subsection (2) is no longer satisfied.

[Extradition Act 2003, s 25.]

Appeals

8–10268   26. Appeal against extradition order.   (1) If the appropriate judge orders a person's extradition under this Part, the person may appeal to the High Court against the order.

(2) But subsection (1) does not apply if the order is made under section 46 or 48.

(3) An appeal under this section may be brought on a question of law or fact.

(4) Notice of an appeal under this section must be given in accordance with rules of court before the end of the permitted period, which is 7 days starting with the day on which the order is made.

[Extradition Act 2003, s 26.]

8–10269   27. Court's powers on appeal under section 26.   (1) On an appeal under section 26 the High Court may—

(a) allow the appeal;

(b) dismiss the appeal.

(2) The court may allow the appeal only if the conditions in subsection (3) or the conditions in subsection (4) are satisfied.

(3) The conditions are that—

(a) the appropriate judge ought to have decided a question before him at the extradition hearing differently;

(b) if he had decided the question in the way he ought to have done, he would have been required to order the person's discharge.

(4) The conditions are that—

(a) an issue is raised that was not raised at the extradition hearing or evidence is available that was not available at the extradition hearing;
(b) the issue or evidence would have resulted in the appropriate judge deciding a question before him at the extradition hearing differently;
(c) if he had decided the question in that way, he would have been required to order the person's discharge.

(5) If the court allows the appeal it must—

(a) order the person's discharge;
(b) quash the order for his extradition.

[Extradition Act 2003, s 27.]

8–10270 **28. Appeal against discharge at extradition hearing.** (1) If the judge orders a person's discharge at the extradition hearing the authority which issued the Part 1 warrant may appeal to the High Court against the relevant decision.
(2) But subsection (1) does not apply if the order for the person's discharge was under section 41.
(3) The relevant decision is the decision which resulted in the order for the person's discharge.
(4) An appeal under this section may be brought on a question of law or fact.
(5) Notice of an appeal under this section must be given in accordance with rules of court before the end of the permitted period, which is 7 days starting with the day on which the order for the person's discharge is made.

[Extradition Act 2003, s 28.]

8–10271 **29. Court's powers on appeal under section 28.** (1) On an appeal under section 28 the High Court may—

(a) allow the appeal;
(b) dismiss the appeal.

(2) The court may allow the appeal only if the conditions in subsection (3) or the conditions in subsection (4) are satisfied.
(3) The conditions are that—

(a) the judge ought to have decided the relevant question differently;
(b) if he had decided the question in the way he ought to have done, he would not have been required to order the person's discharge.

(4) The conditions are that—

(a) an issue is raised that was not raised at the extradition hearing or evidence is available that was not available at the extradition hearing;
(b) the issue or evidence would have resulted in the judge deciding the relevant question differently;
(c) if he had decided the question in that way, he would not have been required to order the person's discharge.

(5) If the court allows the appeal it must—

(a) quash the order discharging the person;
(b) remit the case to the judge;
(c) direct him to proceed as he would have been required to do if he had decided the relevant question differently at the extradition hearing.

(6) A question is the relevant question if the judge's decision on it resulted in the order for the person's discharge.

[Extradition Act 2003, s 29.]

8–10272 **30. Detention pending conclusion of appeal under section 28.** (1) This section applies if immediately after the judge orders the person's discharge the judge is informed by the authority which issued the Part 1 warrant that it intends to appeal under section 28.
(2) The judge must remand the person in custody or on bail while the appeal is pending.
(3) If the judge remands the person in custody he may later grant bail.
(4) An appeal under section 28 ceases to be pending at the earliest of these times—

(a) when the proceedings on the appeal are discontinued;
(b) when the High Court dismisses the appeal, if the authority does not immediately inform the court that it intends to apply for leave to appeal to the House of Lords;
(c) at the end of the permitted period, which is 28 days starting with the day on which leave to appeal to the House of Lords against the decision of the High Court on the appeal is granted;
(d) when there is no further step that can be taken by the authority which issued the Part 1 warrant in relation to the appeal (ignoring any power of a court to grant leave to take a step out of time).

(5) The preceding provisions of this section apply to Scotland with these modifications—

(a) in subsection (4)(b) omit the words from "if" to the end;
(b) omit subsection (4)(c).

[Extradition Act 2003, s 30.]

8–10273 31. Appeal to High Court: time limit for start of hearing.   (1) Rules of court must prescribe the period (the relevant period) within which the High Court must begin to hear an appeal under section 26 or 28.

(2) Rules of court must provide for the relevant period to start with the date on which the person in respect of whom a Part 1 warrant is issued—

(a) was arrested under section 5, if he was arrested under that section;
(b) was arrested under the Part 1 warrant, if he was not arrested under section 5.

(3) The High Court must begin to hear the appeal before the end of the relevant period.

(4) The High Court may extend the relevant period if it believes it to be in the interests of justice to do so; and this subsection may apply more than once.

(5) The power in subsection (4) may be exercised even after the end of the relevant period.

(6) If subsection (3) is not complied with and the appeal is under section 26—

(a) the appeal must be taken to have been allowed by a decision of the High Court;
(b) the person whose extradition has been ordered must be taken to have been discharged by the High Court;
(c) the order for the person's extradition must be taken to have been quashed by the High Court.

(7) If subsection (3) is not complied with and the appeal is under section 28 the appeal must be taken to have been dismissed by a decision of the High Court.

[Extradition Act 2003, s 31.]

8–10274 32. Appeal to House of Lords

8–10275 33. Powers of House of Lords on appeal under section 32

8–10276 34. Appeals: general.   A decision of the judge under this Part may be questioned in legal proceedings only by means of an appeal under this Part.

Time for extradition

[Extradition Act 2003, s 34.]

8–10277 35. Extradition where no appeal.   (1) This section applies if—

(a) the appropriate judge orders a person's extradition to a category 1 territory under this Part, and
(b) no notice of an appeal under section 26 is given before the end of the period permitted under that section.

(2) But this section does not apply if the order is made under section 46 or 48.

(3) The person must be extradited to the category 1 territory before the end of the required period.

(4) The required period is—

(a) 10 days starting with the day on which the judge makes the order, or
(b) if the judge and the authority which issued the Part 1 warrant agree a later date, 10 days starting with the later date.

(5) If subsection (3) is not complied with and the person applies to the appropriate judge to be discharged the judge must order his discharge, unless reasonable cause is shown for the delay.

(6) These must be ignored for the purposes of subsection (1)(b)—

(a) any power of a court to extend the period permitted for giving notice of appeal;
(b) any power of a court to grant leave to take a step out of time.

[Extradition Act 2003, s 35.]

8–10278 36. Extradition following appeal.   (1) This section applies if—

(a) there is an appeal to the High Court under section 26 against an order for a person's extradition to a category 1 territory, and
(b) the effect of the decision of the relevant court on the appeal is that the person is to be extradited there.

(2) The person must be extradited to the category 1 territory before the end of the required period.

(3) The required period is—

(a) 10 days starting with the day on which the decision of the relevant court on the appeal becomes final or proceedings on the appeal are discontinued, or

(b) if the relevant court and the authority which issued the Part 1 warrant agree a later date, 10 days starting with the later date.

(4) The relevant court is—

(a) the High Court, if there is no appeal to the House of Lords against the decision of the High Court on the appeal;

(b) the House of Lords, if there is such an appeal.

(5) The decision of the High Court on the appeal becomes final—

(a) when the period permitted for applying to the High Court for leave to appeal to the House of Lords ends, if there is no such application;

(b) when the period permitted for applying to the House of Lords for leave to appeal to it ends, if the High Court refuses leave to appeal and there is no application to the House of Lords for leave to appeal;

(c) when the House of Lords refuses leave to appeal to it;

(d) at the end of the permitted period, which is 28 days starting with the day on which leave to appeal to the House of Lords is granted, if no such appeal is brought before the end of that period.

(6) These must be ignored for the purposes of subsection (5)—

(a) any power of a court to extend the period permitted for applying for leave to appeal;

(b) any power of a court to grant leave to take a step out of time.

(7) The decision of the House of Lords on the appeal becomes final when it is made.

(8) If subsection (2) is not complied with and the person applies to the appropriate judge to be discharged the judge must order his discharge, unless reasonable cause is shown for the delay.

(9) The preceding provisions of this section apply to Scotland with these modifications—

(a) in subsections (1) and (3) for "relevant court" substitute "High Court";

(b) omit subsections (4) to (7).

[Extradition Act 2003, s 36.]

8–10279   37. Undertaking in relation to person serving sentence in United Kingdom.
(1) This section applies if—

(a) the appropriate judge orders a person's extradition to a category 1 territory under this Part;

(b) the person is serving a sentence of imprisonment or another form of detention in the United Kingdom.

(2) But this section does not apply if the order is made under section 46 or 48.

(3) The judge may make the order for extradition subject to the condition that extradition is not to take place before he receives an undertaking given on behalf of the category 1 territory in terms specified by him.

(4) The terms which may be specified by the judge in relation to a person accused in a category 1 territory of the commission of an offence include terms—

(a) that the person be kept in custody until the conclusion of the proceedings against him for the offence and any other offence in respect of which he is permitted to be dealt with in the category 1 territory;

(b) that the person be returned to the United Kingdom to serve the remainder of his sentence on the conclusion of those proceedings.

(5) The terms which may be specified by the judge in relation to a person alleged to be unlawfully at large after conviction of an offence by a court in a category 1 territory include terms that the person be returned to the United Kingdom to serve the remainder of his sentence after serving any sentence imposed on him in the category 1 territory for—

(a) the offence, and

(b) any other offence in respect of which he is permitted to be dealt with in the category 1 territory.

(6) Subsections (7) and (8) apply if the judge makes an order for extradition subject to a condition under subsection (3).

(7) If the judge does not receive the undertaking before the end of the period of 21 days starting with the day on which he makes the order and the person applies to the appropriate judge to be discharged, the judge must order his discharge.

(8) If the judge receives the undertaking before the end of that period—

(a) in a case where section 35 applies, the required period for the purposes of section 35(3) is 10 days starting with the day on which the judge receives the undertaking;

(b) in a case where section 36 applies, the required period for the purposes of section 36(2) is 10 days starting with the day on which the decision of the relevant court on the appeal becomes final (within the meaning of that section) or (if later) the day on which the judge receives the undertaking.

[Extradition Act 2003, s 37.]

8–10280 **38. Extradition following deferral for competing claim.** (1) This section applies if—

(a) an order is made under this Part for a person to be extradited to a category 1 territory in pursuance of a Part 1 warrant;

(b) before the person is extradited to the territory an order is made under section 44(4)(b) or 179(2)(b) for the person's extradition in pursuance of the warrant to be deferred;

(c) the appropriate judge makes an order under section 181(2) for the person's extradition in pursuance of the warrant to cease to be deferred.

(2) But this section does not apply if the order for the person's extradition is made under section 46 or 48.

(3) In a case where section 35 applies, the required period for the purposes of section 35(3) is 10 days starting with the day on which the order under section 181(2) is made.

(4) In a case where section 36 applies, the required period for the purposes of section 36(2) is 10 days starting with the day on which the decision of the relevant court on the appeal becomes final (within the meaning of that section) or (if later) the day on which the order under section 181(2) is made.

[Extradition Act 2003, s 38.]

8–10281 **39. Asylum claim.** (1) This section applies if—

(a) a person in respect of whom a Part 1 warrant is issued makes an asylum claim at any time in the relevant period;

(b) an order is made under this Part for the person to be extradited in pursuance of the warrant.

(2) The relevant period is the period—

(a) starting when a certificate is issued under section 2 in respect of the warrant;

(b) ending when the person is extradited in pursuance of the warrant.

(3) The person must not be extradited in pursuance of the warrant before the asylum claim is finally determined; and sections 35, 36, 47 and 49 have effect subject to this.

(4) Subsection (3) is subject to section 40.

(5) If the Secretary of State allows the asylum claim, the claim is finally determined when he makes his decision on the claim.

(6) If the Secretary of State rejects the asylum claim, the claim is finally determined—

(a) when the Secretary of State makes his decision on the claim, if there is no right to appeal against the Secretary of State's decision on the claim;

(b) when the period permitted for appealing against the Secretary of State's decision on the claim ends, if there is such a right but there is no such appeal;

(c) when the appeal against that decision is finally determined or is withdrawn or abandoned, if there is such an appeal.

(7) An appeal against the Secretary of State's decision on an asylum claim is not finally determined for the purposes of subsection (6) at any time when a further appeal or an application for leave to bring a further appeal—

(a) has been instituted and has not been finally determined or withdrawn or abandoned, or

(b) may be brought.

(8) The remittal of an appeal is not a final determination for the purposes of subsection (7).

(9) The possibility of an appeal out of time with leave must be ignored for the purposes of subsections (6) and (7).

[Extradition Act 2003, s 39.]

8–10282 **40. Certificate in respect of asylum claimant.** (1) Section 39(3) does not apply in relation to a person if the Secretary of State has certified that the conditions in subsection (2) or the conditions in subsection (3) are satisfied in relation to him.

(2) The conditions are that—

(a) the category 1 territory to which the person's extradition has been ordered has accepted that, under standing arrangements, it is the responsible State in relation to the person's asylum claim;

(b) in the opinion of the Secretary of State, the person is not a national or citizen of the territory.

(3) The conditions are that, in the opinion of the Secretary of State—

(a) the person is not a national or citizen of the category 1 territory to which his extradition has been ordered;

(b) the person's life and liberty would not be threatened in that territory by reason of his race, religion, nationality, political opinion or membership of a particular social group;

(c) the government of the territory would not send the person to another country otherwise than in accordance with the Refugee Convention.

(4) In this section—

"the Refugee Convention" has the meaning given by section 167(1) of the Immigration and Asylum Act 1999 (c 33);

"standing arrangements" means arrangements in force between the United Kingdom and the category 1 territory for determining which State is responsible for considering applications for asylum.

[Extradition Act 2003, s 40.]

Withdrawal of Part 1 warrant

8–10283   41. Withdrawal of warrant before extradition.   (1) This section applies if at any time in the relevant period the appropriate judge is informed by the designated authority that a Part 1 warrant issued in respect of a person has been withdrawn.

(2) The relevant period is the period—

(a) starting when the person is first brought before the appropriate judge following his arrest under this Part;

(b) ending when the person is extradited in pursuance of the warrant or discharged.

(3) The judge must order the person's discharge.

(4) If the person is not before the judge at the time the judge orders his discharge, the judge must inform him of the order as soon as practicable.

[Extradition Act 2003, s 41.]

8–10284   42. Withdrawal of warrant while appeal to High Court pending

8–10285   43. Withdrawal of warrant while appeal to House of Lords pending

Competing Part 1 warrants

[Extradition Act 2003, s 43.]

8–10286   44. Competing Part 1 warrants.   (1) This section applies if at any time in the relevant period the conditions in subsection (3) are satisfied in relation to a person in respect of whom a Part 1 warrant has been issued.

(2) The relevant period is the period—

(a) starting when the person is first brought before the appropriate judge following his arrest under this Part;

(b) ending when the person is extradited in pursuance of the warrant or discharged.

(3) The conditions are that—

(a) the judge is informed that another Part 1 warrant has been issued in respect of the person;

(b) the other warrant falls to be dealt with by the judge or by a judge who is the appropriate judge in another part of the United Kingdom;

(c) the other warrant has not been disposed of.

(4) The judge may—

(a) order further proceedings on the warrant under consideration to be deferred until the other warrant has been disposed of, if the warrant under consideration has not been disposed of;

(b) order the person's extradition in pursuance of the warrant under consideration to be deferred until the other warrant has been disposed of, if an order for his extradition in pursuance of the warrant under consideration has been made.

(5) If the judge makes an order under subsection (4) and the person is not already remanded in custody or on bail, the judge must remand the person in custody or on bail.

(6) If the judge remands the person in custody he may later grant bail.

(7) In applying subsection (4) the judge must take account in particular of these matters—

(a) the relative seriousness of the offences concerned;

(b) the place where each offence was committed (or was alleged to have been committed);

(c) the date on which each warrant was issued;

(d) whether, in the case of each offence, the person is accused of its commission (but not alleged to have been convicted) or is alleged to be unlawfully at large after conviction.

Consent to extradition

[Extradition Act 2003, s 44.]

8–10287   45. Consent to extradition.   (1) A person arrested under a Part 1 warrant may consent to his extradition to the category 1 territory in which the warrant was issued.

(2) A person arrested under section 5 may consent to his extradition to the category 1 territory referred to in subsection (1) of that section.

(3) If a person consents to his extradition under this section he must be taken to have waived any right he would have (apart from the consent) not to be dealt with in the category 1 territory for an offence committed before his extradition.

(4) Consent under this section—

(a) must be given before the appropriate judge;

(b) must be recorded in writing;

(c) is irrevocable.

(5) A person may not give his consent under this section unless—

(a) he is legally represented before the appropriate judge at the time he gives consent, or

(b) he is a person to whom subsection (6) applies.

(6) This subsection applies to a person if—

(a) he has been informed of his right to apply for legal aid and has had the opportunity to apply for legal aid, but he has refused or failed to apply;

(b) he has applied for legal aid but his application has been refused;

(c) he was granted legal aid but the legal aid was withdrawn.

(7) In subsection (6) "legal aid" means—

(a) in England and Wales, a right to representation funded by the Legal Services Commission as part of the Criminal Defence Service;

(b) in Scotland, such legal aid as is available by virtue of section 183(a) of this Act;

(c) in Northern Ireland, such free legal aid as is available by virtue of sections 184 and 185 of this Act.

(8) For the purposes of subsection (5) a person is to be treated as legally represented before the appropriate judge if (and only if) he has the assistance of counsel or a solicitor to represent him in the proceedings before the appropriate judge.

[Extradition Act 2003, s 45.]

8–10288   46. Extradition order following consent.   (1) This section applies if a person consents to his extradition under section 45.

(2) The judge must remand the person in custody or on bail.

(3) If the judge remands the person in custody he may later grant bail.

(4) If the judge has not fixed a date under section 8 on which the extradition hearing is to begin he is not required to do so.

(5) If the extradition hearing has begun the judge is no longer required to proceed or continue proceeding under sections 10 to 25.

(6) The judge must within the period of 10 days starting with the day on which consent is given order the person's extradition to the category 1 territory.

(7) Subsection (6) has effect subject to sections 48 and 51.

(8) If subsection (6) is not complied with and the person applies to the judge to be discharged the judge must order his discharge.

[Extradition Act 2003, s 46.]

8–10289   47. Extradition to category 1 territory following consent.   (1) This section applies if the appropriate judge makes an order under section 46(6) for a person's extradition to a category 1 territory.

(2) The person must be extradited to the category 1 territory before the end of the required period.

(3) The required period is—

(a) 10 days starting with the day on which the order is made, or

(b) if the judge and the authority which issued the Part 1 warrant agree a later date, 10 days starting with the later date.

(4) If subsection (2) is not complied with and the person applies to the judge to be discharged the judge must order his discharge, unless reasonable cause is shown for the delay.

(5) If before the person is extradited to the category 1 territory the judge is informed by the designated authority that the Part 1 warrant has been withdrawn—

(a) subsection (2) does not apply, and

(b) the judge must order the person's discharge.

[Extradition Act 2003, s 47.]

8–10290   48. Other warrant issued following consent.   (1) This section applies if—

(a) a person consents under section 45 to his extradition to a category 1 territory, and

(b) the conditions in subsection (2) are satisfied before the judge orders his extradition under section 46(6).

(2) The conditions are that—

(a) the judge is informed that another Part 1 warrant has been issued in respect of the person;

(b) the warrant falls to be dealt with by the judge or by a judge who is the appropriate judge in another part of the United Kingdom;

(c) the warrant has not been disposed of.

(3) Section 46(6) does not apply but the judge may—

(a) order the person's extradition in pursuance of his consent, or

(b) order further proceedings on the warrant under consideration to be deferred until the other warrant has been disposed of.

(4) Subsection (3) is subject to section 51.

(5) In applying subsection (3) the judge must take account in particular of these matters—

(a) the relative seriousness of the offences concerned;

(b) the place where each offence was committed (or was alleged to have been committed);

(c) the date on which each warrant was issued;

(d) whether, in the case of each offence, the person is accused of its commission (but not alleged to have been convicted) or is alleged to be unlawfully at large after conviction.

[Extradition Act 2003, s 48.]

8–10291   49. Other warrant issued: extradition to category 1 territory.   (1) This section applies if the appropriate judge makes an order under section 48(3)(a) for a person's extradition to a category 1 territory.

(2) The person must be extradited to the category 1 territory before the end of the required period.

(3) The required period is—

(a) 10 days starting with the day on which the order is made, or

(b) if the judge and the authority which issued the Part 1 warrant agree a later date, 10 days starting with the later date.

(4) If subsection (2) is not complied with and the person applies to the judge to be discharged the judge must order his discharge, unless reasonable cause is shown for the delay.

(5) If before the person is extradited to the category 1 territory the judge is informed by the designated authority that the Part 1 warrant has been withdrawn—

(a) subsection (2) does not apply, and

(b) the judge must order the person's discharge.

[Extradition Act 2003, s 49.]

8–10292   50. Other warrant issued: proceedings deferred.   (1) This section applies if the appropriate judge makes an order under section 48(3)(b) for further proceedings on a Part 1 warrant to be deferred.

(2) The judge must remand the person in respect of whom the warrant was issued in custody or on bail.

(3) If the judge remands the person in custody he may later grant bail.

(4) If an order is made under section 180 for proceedings on the warrant to be resumed, the period specified in section 46(6) must be taken to be 10 days starting with the day on which the order under section 180 is made.

[Extradition Act 2003, s 50.]

8–10293   51. Extradition request following consent.   (1) This section applies if—

(a) a person in respect of whom a Part 1 warrant is issued consents under section 45 to his extradition to the category 1 territory in which the warrant was issued, and

(b) the condition in subsection (2) is satisfied before the judge orders his extradition under section 46(6) or 48(3)(a).

(2) The condition is that the judge is informed that—

(a) a certificate has been issued under section 70 in respect of a request for the person's extradition;

(b) the request has not been disposed of.

(3) The judge must not make an order under section 46(6) or 48(3) until he is informed what order has been made under section 179(2).

(4) If the order under section 179(2) is for further proceedings on the warrant to be deferred until the request has been disposed of, the judge must remand the person in custody or on bail.

(5) If the judge remands the person in custody he may later grant bail.

(6) If—

(a) the order under section 179(2) is for further proceedings on the warrant to be deferred until the request has been disposed of, and

(b) an order is made under section 180 for proceedings on the warrant to be resumed,

the period specified in section 46(6) must be taken to be 10 days starting with the day on which the order under section 180 is made.

(7) If the order under section 179(2) is for further proceedings on the request to be deferred until the warrant has been disposed of, the period specified in section 46(6) must be taken to be 10 days starting with the day on which the judge is informed of the order.

[Extradition Act 2003, s 51.]

8–10294 52. Undertaking in relation to person serving sentence. (1) This section applies if—

(a) the appropriate judge makes an order under section 46(6) or 48(3)(a) for a person's extradition to a category 1 territory;

(b) the person is serving a sentence of imprisonment or another form of detention in the United Kingdom.

(2) The judge may make the order for extradition subject to the condition that extradition is not to take place before he receives an undertaking given on behalf of the category 1 territory in terms specified by him.

(3) The terms which may be specified by the judge in relation to a person accused in a category 1 territory of the commission of an offence include terms—

(a) that the person be kept in custody until the conclusion of the proceedings against him for the offence and any other offence in respect of which he is permitted to be dealt with in the category 1 territory;

(b) that the person be returned to the United Kingdom to serve the remainder of his sentence on the conclusion of those proceedings.

(4) The terms which may be specified by the judge in relation to a person alleged to be unlawfully at large after conviction of an offence by a court in a category 1 territory include terms that the person be returned to the United Kingdom to serve the remainder of his sentence after serving any sentence imposed on him in the category 1 territory for—

(a) the offence, and

(b) any other offence in respect of which he is permitted to be dealt with in the category 1 territory.

(5) If the judge makes an order for extradition subject to a condition under subsection (2) the required period for the purposes of sections 47(2) and 49(2) is 10 days starting with the day on which the judge receives the undertaking.

[Extradition Act 2003, s 52.]

8–10295 53. Extradition following deferral for competing claim. (1) This section applies if—

(a) an order is made under section 46(6) or 48(3)(a) for a person to be extradited to a category 1 territory in pursuance of a Part 1 warrant;

(b) before the person is extradited to the territory an order is made under section 44(4)(b) or 179(2)(b) for the person's extradition in pursuance of the warrant to be deferred;

(c) the appropriate judge makes an order under section 181(2) for the person's extradition in pursuance of the warrant to cease to be deferred.

(2) The required period for the purposes of sections 47(2) and 49(2) is 10 days starting with the day on which the order under section 181(2) is made.

[Extradition Act 2003, s 53.]

Post-extradition matters

8–10296 54. Request for consent to other offence being dealt with. (1) This section applies if—

(a) a person is extradited to a category 1 territory in respect of an offence in accordance with this Part;

(b) the appropriate judge receives a request for consent to the person being dealt with in the territory for another offence;

(c) the request is certified under this section by the designated authority.

(2) The designated authority may certify a request for consent under this section if it believes that the authority making the request—

(a) is a judicial authority of the territory, and

(b) has the function of making requests for the consent referred to in subsection (1)(b) in that territory.

(3) A certificate under subsection (2) must certify that the authority making the request falls within paragraphs (a) and (b) of that subsection.

(4) The judge must serve notice on the person that he has received the request for consent, unless he is satisfied that it would not be practicable to do so.

(5) The consent hearing must begin before the end of the required period, which is 21 days starting with the day on which the request for consent is received by the designated authority.

(6) The judge may extend the required period if he believes it to be in the interests of justice to do so; and this subsection may apply more than once.

(7) The power in subsection (6) may be exercised even after the end of the required period.

(8) If the consent hearing does not begin before the end of the required period and the judge does not exercise the power in subsection (6) to extend the period, he must refuse consent.

(9) The judge may at any time adjourn the consent hearing.

(10) The consent hearing is the hearing at which the judge is to consider the request for consent.

[Extradition Act 2003, s 54.]

8–10297   55. Questions for decision at consent hearing.   (1) At the consent hearing under section 54 the judge must decide whether consent is required to the person being dealt with in the territory for the offence for which consent is requested.

(2) If the judge decides the question in subsection (1) in the negative he must inform the authority making the request of his decision.

(3) If the judge decides that question in the affirmative he must decide whether the offence for which consent is requested is an extradition offence.

(4) If the judge decides the question in subsection (3) in the negative he must refuse consent.

(5) If the judge decides that question in the affirmative he must decide whether he would order the person's extradition under sections 11 to 25 if—

(a) the person were in the United Kingdom, and

(b) the judge were required to proceed under section 11 in respect of the offence for which consent is requested.

(6) If the judge decides the question in subsection (5) in the affirmative he must give consent.

(7) If the judge decides that question in the negative he must refuse consent.

(8) Consent is not required to the person being dealt with in the territory for the offence if the person has been given an opportunity to leave the territory and—

(a) he has not done so before the end of the permitted period, or

(b) if he did so before the end of the permitted period, he has returned there.

(9) The permitted period is 45 days starting with the day on which the person arrived in the territory following his extradition there in accordance with this Part.

(10) Subject to subsection (8), the judge must decide whether consent is required to the person being dealt with in the territory for the offence by reference to what appears to him to be the law of the territory or arrangements made between the territory and the United Kingdom.

[Extradition Act 2003, s 55.]

8–10298   56. Request for consent to further extradition to category 1 territory.   (1) This section applies if—

(a) a person is extradited to a category 1 territory (the requesting territory) in accordance with this Part;

(b) the appropriate judge receives a request for consent to the person's extradition to another category 1 territory for an offence;

(c) the request is certified under this section by the designated authority.

(2) The designated authority may certify a request for consent under this section if it believes that the authority making the request—

(a) is a judicial authority of the requesting territory, and

(b) has the function of making requests for the consent referred to in subsection (1)(b) in that territory.

(3) A certificate under subsection (2) must certify that the authority making the request falls within paragraphs (a) and (b) of that subsection.

(4) The judge must serve notice on the person that he has received the request for consent, unless he is satisfied that it would not be practicable to do so.

(5) The consent hearing must begin before the end of the required period, which is 21 days starting with the day on which the request for consent is received by the designated authority.

(6) The judge may extend the required period if he believes it to be in the interests of justice to do so; and this subsection may apply more than once.

(7) The power in subsection (6) may be exercised even after the end of the required period.

(8) If the consent hearing does not begin before the end of the required period and the judge does not exercise the power in subsection (6) to extend the period, he must refuse consent.

(9) The judge may at any time adjourn the consent hearing.

(10) The consent hearing is the hearing at which the judge is to consider the request for consent.

[Extradition Act 2003, s 56.]

8-10299   57. Questions for decision at consent hearing.   (1) At the consent hearing under section 56 the judge must decide whether consent is required to the person's extradition to the other category 1 territory for the offence.

(2) If the judge decides the question in subsection (1) in the negative he must inform the authority making the request of his decision.

(3) If the judge decides that question in the affirmative he must decide whether the offence is an extradition offence in relation to the category 1 territory referred to in section 56(1)(b).

(4) If the judge decides the question in subsection (3) in the negative he must refuse consent.

(5) If the judge decides that question in the affirmative he must decide whether he would order the person's extradition under sections 11 to 25 if—

(a) the person were in the United Kingdom, and

(b) the judge were required to proceed under section 11 in respect of the offence for which consent is requested.

(6) If the judge decides the question in subsection (5) in the affirmative he must give consent.

(7) If the judge decides that question in the negative he must refuse consent.

(8) Consent is not required to the person's extradition to the other territory for the offence if the person has been given an opportunity to leave the requesting territory and—

(a) he has not done so before the end of the permitted period, or

(b) if he did so before the end of the permitted period, he has returned there.

(9) The permitted period is 45 days starting with the day on which the person arrived in the requesting territory following his extradition in accordance with this Part.

(10) Subject to subsection (8), the judge must decide whether consent is required to the person's extradition to the other territory for the offence by reference to what appears to him to be the arrangements made between the requesting territory and the United Kingdom.

[Extradition Act 2003, s 57.]

8-10299A   58. Consent to further extradition to category 2 territory.   (1) This section applies if—

(a) a person is extradited to a category 1 territory (the requesting territory) in accordance with this Part;

(b) the Secretary of State receives a request for consent to the person's extradition to a category 2 territory for an offence;

(c) the request is certified under this section by the designated authority.

(2) The designated authority may certify a request for consent under this section if it believes that the authority making the request—

(a) is a judicial authority of the requesting territory, and

(b) has the function of making requests for the consent referred to in subsection (1)(b) in that territory.

(3) A certificate under subsection (2) must certify that the authority making the request falls within paragraphs (a) and (b) of that subsection.

(4) The Secretary of State must serve notice on the person that he has received the request for consent, unless he is satisfied that it would not be practicable to do so.

(5) The Secretary of State must decide whether the offence is an extradition offence within the meaning given by section 137 in relation to the category 2 territory.

(6) If the Secretary of State decides the question in subsection (5) in the negative he must refuse consent.

(7) If the Secretary of State decides that question in the affirmative he must decide whether the appropriate judge would send the case to him (for his decision whether the person was to be extradited) under sections 79 to 91 if—

(a) the person were in the United Kingdom, and

(b) the judge were required to proceed under section 79 in respect of the offence for which the Secretary of State's consent is requested.

(8) If the Secretary of State decides the question in subsection (7) in the negative he must refuse his consent.

(9) If the Secretary of State decides that question in the affirmative he must decide whether, if the person were in the United Kingdom, his extradition to the category 2 territory in respect of the offence would be prohibited under section 94, 95 or 96.

(10) If the Secretary of State decides the question in subsection (9) in the negative he may give consent.

(11) If the Secretary of State decides that question in the affirmative he must refuse consent.

(12) This section applies in relation to any function which falls under this section to be exercised in relation to Scotland only as if the references in this section to the Secretary of State were to the Scottish Ministers.

[Extradition Act 2003, s 58.]

8–10299B   59. Return of person to serve remainder of sentence.   (1) This section applies if—

     (a)   a person who is serving a sentence of imprisonment or another form of detention in the United Kingdom is extradited to a category 1 territory in accordance with this Part;

     (b)   the person is returned to the United Kingdom to serve the remainder of his sentence.

(2) The person is liable to be detained in pursuance of his sentence.

(3) If he is at large he must be treated as being unlawfully at large.

(4) Time during which the person was not in the United Kingdom as a result of his extradition does not count as time served by him as part of his sentence.

(5) But subsection (4) does not apply if—

     (a)   the person was extradited for the purpose of being prosecuted for an offence, and

     (b)   the person has not been convicted of the offence or of any other offence in respect of which he was permitted to be dealt with in the category 1 territory.

(6) In a case falling within subsection (5), time during which the person was not in the United Kingdom as a result of his extradition counts as time served by him as part of his sentence if (and only if) it was spent in custody in connection with the offence or any other offence in respect of which he was permitted to be dealt with in the territory.

[Extradition Act 2003, s 59.]

Costs

8–10299C   60. Costs where extradition ordered.   (1) This section applies if any of the following occurs in relation to a person in respect of whom a Part 1 warrant is issued—

     (a)   an order for the person's extradition is made under this Part;

     (b)   the High Court dismisses an appeal under section 26;

     (c)   the High Court or the House of Lords dismisses an application for leave to appeal to the House of Lords under section 32, if the application is made by the person;

     (d)   the House of Lords dismisses an appeal under section 32, if the appeal is brought by the person.

(2) In a case falling within subsection (1)(a), the appropriate judge may make such order as he considers just and reasonable with regard to the costs to be paid by the person.

(3) In a case falling within subsection (1)(b), (c) or (d), the court by which the application or appeal is dismissed may make such order as it considers just and reasonable with regard to the costs to be paid by the person.

(4) An order for costs under this section—

     (a)   must specify their amount;

     (b)   may name the person to whom they are to be paid.

[Extradition Act 2003, s 60.]

8–10299D   61. Costs where discharge ordered.   (1) This section applies if any of the following occurs in relation to a person in respect of whom a Part 1 warrant is issued—

     (a)   an order for the person's discharge is made under this Part;

     (b)   the person is taken to be discharged under this Part;

     (c)   the High Court dismisses an appeal under section 28;

     (d)   the High Court or the House of Lords dismisses an application for leave to appeal to the House of Lords under section 32, if the application is made by the authority which issued the warrant;

     (e)   the House of Lords dismisses an appeal under section 32, if the appeal is brought by the authority which issued the warrant.

(2) In a case falling within subsection (1)(a), an order under subsection (5) in favour of the person may be made by—

     (a)   the appropriate judge, if the order for the person's discharge is made by him;

     (b)   the High Court, if the order for the person's discharge is made by it;

     (c)   the House of Lords, if the order for the person's discharge is made by it.

(3) In a case falling within subsection (1)(b), the appropriate judge may make an order under subsection (5) in favour of the person.

(4) In a case falling within subsection (1)(c), (d) or (e), the court by which the application or appeal is dismissed may make an order under subsection (5) in favour of the person.

(5) An order under this subsection in favour of a person is an order for a payment of the appropriate amount to be made to the person out of money provided by Parliament.

(6) The appropriate amount is such amount as the judge or court making the order under subsection (5) considers reasonably sufficient to compensate the person in whose favour the order is made for any expenses properly incurred by him in the proceedings under this Part.

(7) But if the judge or court making an order under subsection (5) is of the opinion that there are circumstances which make it inappropriate that the person in whose favour the order is made should recover the full amount mentioned in subsection (6), the judge or court must—

(a) assess what amount would in his or its opinion be just and reasonable;

(b) specify that amount in the order as the appropriate amount.

(8) Unless subsection (7) applies, the appropriate amount—

(a) must be specified in the order, if the court considers it appropriate for it to be so specified and the person in whose favour the order is made agrees the amount;

(b) must be determined in accordance with regulations made by the Lord Chancellor for the purposes of this section, in any other case.

[Extradition Act 2003, s 61.]

8–10299E   **62. Costs where discharge ordered: supplementary.**   (1) In England and Wales, subsections (1) and (3) of section 20 of the Prosecution of Offences Act 1985 (c 23) (regulations for carrying Part 2 of that Act into effect) apply in relation to section 61 as those subsections apply in relation to Part 2 of that Act.

(2) As so applied those subsections have effect as if an order under section 61(5) were an order under Part 2 of that Act for a payment to be made out of central funds.

(3) In Northern Ireland, section 7 of the Costs in Criminal Cases Act (Northern Ireland) 1968 (c 10) (rules relating to costs) applies in relation to section 61 as that section applies in relation to sections 2 to 5 of that Act.

[Extradition Act 2003, s 62.]

8–10299F

Repatriation cases

63. Persons serving sentences outside territory where convicted.   (1) This section applies if an arrest warrant is issued in respect of a person by an authority of a category 1 territory and the warrant contains the statement referred to in subsection (2).

(2) The statement is one that—

(a) the person is alleged to be unlawfully at large from a prison in one territory (the imprisoning territory) in which he was serving a sentence after conviction of an offence specified in the warrant by a court in another territory (the convicting territory), and

(b) the person was serving the sentence in pursuance of international arrangements for prisoners sentenced in one territory to be repatriated to another territory in order to serve their sentence, and

(c) the warrant is issued with a view to his arrest and extradition to the category 1 territory for the purpose of serving a sentence or another form of detention imposed in respect of the offence.

(3) If the category 1 territory is either the imprisoning territory or the convicting territory, section 2(2)(b) has effect as if the reference to the statement referred to in subsection (5) of that section were a reference to the statement referred to in subsection (2) of this section.

(4) If the category 1 territory is the imprisoning territory—

(a) section 2(6)(e) has effect as if "the category 1 territory" read "the convicting territory";

(b) section 10(2) has effect as if "an extradition offence" read "an extradition offence in relation to the convicting territory";

(c) section 20(5) has effect as if after "entitled" there were inserted "in the convicting territory";

(d) section 37(5) has effect as if "a category 1 territory" read "the convicting territory" and as if "the category 1 territory" in both places read "the convicting territory";

(e) section 52(4) has effect as if "a category 1 territory" read "the convicting territory" and as if "the category 1 territory" in both places read "the convicting territory";

(f) section 65(1) has effect as if "a category 1 territory" read "the convicting territory";

(g) section 65(2) has effect as if "the category 1 territory" in the opening words and paragraphs (a) and (c) read "the convicting territory" and as if "the category 1 territory" in paragraph (b) read "the imprisoning territory";

(h) in section 65, subsections (3), (4), (5), (6) and (8) have effect as if "the category 1 territory" in each place read "the convicting territory".

[Extradition Act 2003, s 63.]

Interpretation

64. Extradition offences: person not sentenced for offence. (1) This section applies in relation to conduct of a person if—

(a) he is accused in a category 1 territory of the commission of an offence constituted by the conduct, or

(b) he is alleged to be unlawfully at large after conviction by a court in a category 1 territory of an offence constituted by the conduct and he has not been sentenced for the offence.

(2) The conduct constitutes an extradition offence in relation to the category 1 territory if these conditions are satisfied—

(a) the conduct occurs in the category 1 territory and no part of it occurs in the United Kingdom;

(b) a certificate issued by an appropriate authority of the category 1 territory shows that the conduct falls within the European framework list;

(c) the certificate shows that the conduct is punishable under the law of the category 1 territory with imprisonment or another form of detention for a term of 3 years or a greater punishment.

(3) The conduct also constitutes an extradition offence in relation to the category 1 territory if these conditions are satisfied—

(a) the conduct occurs in the category 1 territory;

(b) the conduct would constitute an offence under the law of the relevant part of the United Kingdom if it occurred in that part of the United Kingdom;

(c) the conduct is punishable under the law of the category 1 territory with imprisonment or another form of detention for a term of 12 months or a greater punishment (however it is described in that law).

(4) The conduct also constitutes an extradition offence in relation to the category 1 territory if these conditions are satisfied—

(a) the conduct occurs outside the category 1 territory;

(b) the conduct is punishable under the law of the category 1 territory with imprisonment or another form of detention for a term of 12 months or a greater punishment (however it is described in that law);

(c) in corresponding circumstances equivalent conduct would constitute an extra-territorial offence under the law of the relevant part of the United Kingdom punishable with imprisonment or another form of detention for a term of 12 months or a greater punishment.

(5) The conduct also constitutes an extradition offence in relation to the category 1 territory if these conditions are satisfied—

(a) the conduct occurs outside the category 1 territory and no part of it occurs in the United Kingdom;

(b) the conduct would constitute an offence under the law of the relevant part of the United Kingdom punishable with imprisonment or another form of detention for a term of 12 months or a greater punishment if it occurred in that part of the United Kingdom;

(c) the conduct is so punishable under the law of the category 1 territory (however it is described in that law).

(6) The conduct also constitutes an extradition offence in relation to the category 1 territory if these conditions are satisfied—

(a) the conduct occurs outside the category 1 territory and no part of it occurs in the United Kingdom;

(b) the conduct is punishable under the law of the category 1 territory with imprisonment or another form of detention for a term of 12 months or a greater punishment (however it is described in that law);

(c) the conduct constitutes or if committed in the United Kingdom would constitute an offence mentioned in subsection (7).

(7) The offences are—

(a) an offence under section 51 or 58 of the International Criminal Court Act 2001 (c 17) (genocide, crimes against humanity and war crimes);

(b) an offence under section 52 or 59 of that Act (conduct ancillary to genocide etc committed outside the jurisdiction);

(c) an ancillary offence, as defined in section 55 or 62 of that Act, in relation to an offence falling within paragraph (a) or (b);

(d) an offence under section 1 of the International Criminal Court (Scotland) Act 2001 (asp 13) (genocide, crimes against humanity and war crimes);

(e) an offence under section 2 of that Act (conduct ancillary to genocide etc committed outside the jurisdiction);

(f)   an ancillary offence, as defined in section 7 of that Act, in relation to an offence falling within paragraph (d) or (e).

(8) For the purposes of subsections (3)(b), (4)(c) and (5)(b)—

(a)   if the conduct relates to a tax or duty, it is immaterial that the law of the relevant part of the United Kingdom does not impose the same kind of tax or duty or does not contain rules of the same kind as those of the law of the category 1 territory;

(b)   if the conduct relates to customs or exchange, it is immaterial that the law of the relevant part of the United Kingdom does not contain rules of the same kind as those of the law of the category 1 territory.

(9) This section applies for the purposes of this Part.

[Extradition Act 2003, s 64.]

8–10299H 65. Extradition offences: person sentenced for offence.   (1) This section applies in relation to conduct of a person if—

(a)   he is alleged to be unlawfully at large after conviction by a court in a category 1 territory of an offence constituted by the conduct, and

(b)   he has been sentenced for the offence.

(2) The conduct constitutes an extradition offence in relation to the category 1 territory if these conditions are satisfied—

(a)   the conduct occurs in the category 1 territory and no part of it occurs in the United Kingdom;

(b)   a certificate issued by an appropriate authority of the category 1 territory shows that the conduct falls within the European framework list;

(c)   the certificate shows that a sentence of imprisonment or another form of detention for a term of 12 months or a greater punishment has been imposed in the category 1 territory in respect of the conduct.

(3) The conduct also constitutes an extradition offence in relation to the category 1 territory if these conditions are satisfied—

(a)   the conduct occurs in the category 1 territory;

(b)   the conduct would constitute an offence under the law of the relevant part of the United Kingdom if it occurred in that part of the United Kingdom;

(c)   a sentence of imprisonment or another form of detention for a term of 4 months or a greater punishment has been imposed in the category 1 territory in respect of the conduct.

(4) The conduct also constitutes an extradition offence in relation to the category 1 territory if these conditions are satisfied—

(a)   the conduct occurs outside the category 1 territory;

(b)   a sentence of imprisonment or another form of detention for a term of 4 months or a greater punishment has been imposed in the category 1 territory in respect of the conduct;

(c)   in corresponding circumstances equivalent conduct would constitute an extra-territorial offence under the law of the relevant part of the United Kingdom punishable with imprisonment or another form of detention for a term of 12 months or a greater punishment.

(5) The conduct also constitutes an extradition offence in relation to the category 1 territory if these conditions are satisfied—

(a)   the conduct occurs outside the category 1 territory and no part of it occurs in the United Kingdom;

(b)   the conduct would constitute an offence under the law of the relevant part of the United Kingdom punishable with imprisonment or another form of detention for a term of 12 months or a greater punishment if it occurred in that part of the United Kingdom;

(c)   a sentence of imprisonment or another form of detention for a term of 4 months or a greater punishment has been imposed in the category 1 territory in respect of the conduct.

(6) The conduct also constitutes an extradition offence in relation to the category 1 territory if these conditions are satisfied—

(a)   the conduct occurs outside the category 1 territory and no part of it occurs in the United Kingdom;

(b)   a sentence of imprisonment or another form of detention for a term of 4 months or a greater punishment has been imposed in the category 1 territory in respect of the conduct;

(c)   the conduct constitutes or if committed in the United Kingdom would constitute an offence mentioned in subsection (7).

(7) The offences are—

(a)   an offence under section 51 or 58 of the International Criminal Court Act 2001 (c 17) (genocide, crimes against humanity and war crimes);

(b)   an offence under section 52 or 59 of that Act (conduct ancillary to genocide etc committed outside the jurisdiction);

(c) an ancillary offence, as defined in section 55 or 62 of that Act, in relation to an offence falling within paragraph (a) or (b);

(d) an offence under section 1 of the International Criminal Court (Scotland) Act 2001 (asp 13) (genocide, crimes against humanity and war crimes);

(e) an offence under section 2 of that Act (conduct ancillary to genocide etc committed outside the jurisdiction);

(f) an ancillary offence, as defined in section 7 of that Act, in relation to an offence falling within paragraph (d) or (e).

(8) For the purposes of subsections (3)(b), (4)(c) and (5)(b)—

(a) if the conduct relates to a tax or duty, it is immaterial that the law of the relevant part of the United Kingdom does not impose the same kind of tax or duty or does not contain rules of the same kind as those of the law of the category 1 territory;

(b) if the conduct relates to customs or exchange, it is immaterial that the law of the relevant part of the United Kingdom does not contain rules of the same kind as those of the law of the category 1 territory.

(9) This section applies for the purposes of this Part.

[Extradition Act 2003, s 65.]

8–10299I 66. Extradition offences: supplementary. (1) Subsections (2) to (4) apply for the purposes of sections 64 and 65.

(2) An appropriate authority of a category 1 territory is a judicial authority of the territory which the appropriate judge believes has the function of issuing arrest warrants in that territory.

(3) The law of a territory is the general criminal law of the territory.

(4) The relevant part of the United Kingdom is the part of the United Kingdom in which the relevant proceedings are taking place.

(5) The relevant proceedings are the proceedings in which it is necessary to decide whether conduct constitutes an extradition offence.

[Extradition Act 2003, s 66.]

8–10299J 67. The appropriate judge. (1) The appropriate judge is—

(a) in England and Wales, a District Judge (Magistrates' Courts) designated for the purposes of this Part by the Lord Chancellor;

(b) in Scotland, the sheriff of Lothian and Borders;

(c) in Northern Ireland, such county court judge or resident magistrate as is designated for the purposes of this Part by the Lord Chancellor.

(2) A designation under subsection (1) may be made for all cases or for such cases (or cases of such description) as the designation stipulates.

(3) More than one designation may be made under subsection (1).

(4) This section applies for the purposes of this Part.

[Extradition Act 2003, s 67.]

8–10299K 68. The extradition hearing. (1) The extradition hearing is the hearing at which the appropriate judge is to decide whether a person in respect of whom a Part 1 warrant was issued is to be extradited to the category 1 territory in which it was issued.

(2) This section applies for the purposes of this Part.

[Extradition Act 2003, s 68.]

PART 2[1]
EXTRADITION TO CATEGORY 2 TERRITORIES

Introduction

8–10299L 69. Extradition to category 2 territories. (1) This Part deals with extradition from the United Kingdom to the territories designated for the purposes of this Part by order[2] made by the Secretary of State.

(2) In this Act references to category 2 territories are to the territories designated for the purposes of this Part.

[Extradition Act 2003, s 69.]

---

1. Part 2 contains ss 69–141.
2. The Extradition Act 2003 (Designation of Territories) Order, SI 2003/3334, amended by SI 2004/1898, SI 2005/365 (made under sub-s (1)) and SI 2005/2036 has been made: see this title, post.

8–10299M   70. Extradition request and certificate.   (1) The Secretary of State must issue a certificate under this section if he receives a valid request for the extradition to a category 2 territory of a person who is in the United Kingdom.

(2) But subsection (1) does not apply if the Secretary of State decides under section 126 that the request is not to be proceeded with.

(3) A request for a person's extradition is valid if—

(a)   it contains the statement referred to in subsection (4), and

(b)   it is made in the approved way.

(4) The statement is one that the person—

(a)   is accused in the category 2 territory of the commission of an offence specified in the request, or

(b)   is alleged to be unlawfully at large[1] after conviction by a court in the category 2 territory of an offence specified in the request.

(5) A request for extradition to a category 2 territory which is a British overseas territory is made in the approved way if it is made by or on behalf of the person administering the territory.

(6) A request for extradition to a category 2 territory which is the Hong Kong Special Administrative Region of the People's Republic of China is made in the approved way if it is made by or on behalf of the government of the Region.

(7) A request for extradition to any other category 2 territory is made in the approved way if it is made—

(a)   by an authority of the territory which the Secretary of State believes has the function of making requests for extradition in that territory, or

(b)   by a person recognised by the Secretary of State as a diplomatic or consular representative of the territory.

(8) A certificate under this section must certify that the request is made in the approved way.

(9) If a certificate is issued under this section the Secretary of State must send these documents to the appropriate judge—

(a)   the request;

(b)   the certificate;

(c)   a copy of any relevant Order in Council.

[Extradition Act 2003, s 70.]

---

1. Where an extradition request does not contain a statement in the actual words of this subsection, the Secretary of State may examine the request and the documents incorporated into it by reference but it is only in a clear case that he should conclude that the person was not only at large but unlawfully at large (*R (Bleta) v Secretary of State for the Home Department*) [2004] EWHC 2034 (Admin), [2005] 1 All ER 810).

Arrest

8–10299N   71. Arrest warrant following extradition request.   (1) This section applies if the Secretary of State sends documents to the appropriate judge under section 70.

(2) The judge may issue a warrant for the arrest of the person whose extradition is requested if the judge has reasonable grounds for believing that—

(a)   the offence in respect of which extradition is requested is an extradition offence, and

(b)   there is evidence falling within subsection (3).

(3) The evidence is—

(a)   evidence that would justify the issue of a warrant for the arrest of a person accused of the offence within the judge's jurisdiction, if the person whose extradition is requested is accused of the commission of the offence;

(b)   evidence that would justify the issue of a warrant for the arrest of a person unlawfully at large after conviction of the offence within the judge's jurisdiction, if the person whose extradition is requested is alleged to be unlawfully at large after conviction of the offence.

(4) But if the category 2 territory to which extradition is requested is designated for the purposes of this section by order[1] made by the Secretary of State, subsections (2) and (3) have effect as if "evidence" read "information".

(5) A warrant issued under this section may—

(a)   be executed by any person to whom it is directed or by any constable or customs officer;

(b)   be executed even if neither the warrant nor a copy of it is in the possession of the person executing it at the time of the arrest.

(6) If a warrant issued under this section in respect of a person is directed to a service policeman, it may be executed in any place where the service policeman would have power to arrest the person under the appropriate service law if the person had committed an offence under that law.

(7) In any other case, a warrant issued under this section may be executed in any part of the United Kingdom.

(8) The appropriate service law is—

(a) the Army Act 1955 (3 & 4 Eliz 2 c 18), if the person in respect of whom the warrant is issued is subject to military law;
(b) the Air Force Act 1955 (3 & 4 Eliz 2 c 19), if that person is subject to air-force law;
(c) the Naval Discipline Act 1957 (c 53), if that person is subject to that Act.

[Extradition Act 2003, s 71.]

---

1. For the list of countries so designated see The Extradition Act 2003 (Designation of Territories) Order, SI 2003/3334, amended by SI 2004/1898, SI 2005/365 and SI 2005/2036 (see this TITLE, post).

8–10299O 72. Person arrested under section 71. (1) (*Scotland*).
(2) A copy of the warrant must be given to the person as soon as practicable after his arrest.
(3) The person must be brought as soon as practicable before the appropriate judge.
(4) But subsection (3) does not apply if—

(a) the person is granted bail by a constable following his arrest, or
(b) the Secretary of State decides under section 126 that the request for the person's extradition is not to be proceeded with.

(5) If subsection (2) is not complied with and the person applies to the judge to be discharged, the judge may order his discharge.
(6) If subsection (3) is not complied with and the person applies to the judge to be discharged, the judge must order his discharge.
(7) When the person first appears or is brought before the appropriate judge, the judge must—

(a) inform him of the contents of the request for his extradition;
(b) give him the required information about consent;
(c) remand him in custody or on bail.

(8) The required information about consent is—

(a) that the person may consent to his extradition to the category 2 territory to which his extradition is requested;
(b) an explanation of the effect of consent and the procedure that will apply if he gives consent;
(c) that consent must be given in writing and is irrevocable.

(9) If the judge remands the person in custody he may later grant bail.
(10) Subsection (4)(a) applies to Scotland with the omission of the words "by a constable".

[Extradition Act 2003, s 72.]

8–10299P 73. Provisional warrant. (1) This section applies if a justice of the peace is satisfied on information in writing and on oath that a person within subsection (2)—

(a) is or is believed to be in the United Kingdom, or
(b) is or is believed to be on his way to the United Kingdom.

(2) A person is within this subsection if—

(a) he is accused in a category 2 territory of the commission of an offence, or
(b) he is alleged to be unlawfully at large after conviction of an offence by a court in a category 2 territory.

(3) The justice may issue a warrant for the arrest of the person (a provisional warrant) if he has reasonable grounds for believing that—

(a) the offence of which the person is accused or has been convicted is an extradition offence, and
(b) there is written evidence falling within subsection (4).

(4) The evidence is—

(a) evidence that would justify the issue of a warrant for the arrest of a person accused of the offence within the justice's jurisdiction, if the person in respect of whom the warrant is sought is accused of the commission of the offence;
(b) evidence that would justify the issue of a warrant for the arrest of a person unlawfully at large after conviction of the offence within the justice's jurisdiction, if the person in respect of whom the warrant is sought is alleged to be unlawfully at large after conviction of the offence.

(5) But if the category 2 territory is designated[1] for the purposes of this section by order made by the Secretary of State, subsections (3) and (4) have effect as if "evidence" read "information".
(6) A provisional warrant may—

(a) be executed by any person to whom it is directed or by any constable or customs officer;
(b) be executed even if neither the warrant nor a copy of it is in the possession of the person executing it at the time of the arrest.

(7) If a warrant issued under this section in respect of a person is directed to a service policeman,

it may be executed in any place where the service policeman would have power to arrest the person under the appropriate service law if the person had committed an offence under that law.

(8) In any other case, a warrant issued under this section may be executed in any part of the United Kingdom.

(9) The appropriate service law is—

(a) the Army Act 1955 (3 & 4 Eliz 2 c 18), if the person in respect of whom the warrant is issued is subject to military law;
(b) the Air Force Act 1955 (3 & 4 Eliz 2 c 19), if that person is subject to air-force law;
(c) the Naval Discipline Act 1957 (c 53), if that person is subject to that Act.

(10) (*Scotland*).
(11) (*Northern Ireland*).

[Extradition Act 2003, s 73.]

---

1. For the list of the countries so designated see The Extradition Act 2003 (Designation of Part 2 Territories) Order, SI 2003/3334 (see this PART, post).

8–10299Q   74. Person arrested under provisional warrant.   (1) This section applies if a person is arrested under a provisional warrant.

(2) A copy of the warrant must be given to the person as soon as practicable after his arrest.
(3) The person must be brought as soon as practicable before the appropriate judge.
(4) But subsection (3) does not apply if—

(a) the person is granted bail by a constable following his arrest, or
(b) in a case where the Secretary of State has received a valid request for the person's extradition, the Secretary of State decides under section 126 that the request is not to be proceeded with.

(5) If subsection (2) is not complied with and the person applies to the judge to be discharged, the judge may order his discharge.
(6) If subsection (3) is not complied with and the person applies to the judge to be discharged, the judge must order his discharge.
(7) When the person first appears or is brought before the appropriate judge, the judge must—

(a) inform him that he is accused of the commission of an offence in a category 2 territory or that he is alleged to be unlawfully at large after conviction of an offence by a court in a category 2 territory;
(b) give him the required information about consent;
(c) remand him in custody or on bail.

(8) The required information about consent is—

(a) that the person may consent to his extradition to the category 2 territory in which he is accused of the commission of an offence or is alleged to have been convicted of an offence;
(b) an explanation of the effect of consent and the procedure that will apply if he gives consent;
(c) that consent must be given in writing and is irrevocable.

(9) If the judge remands the person in custody he may later grant bail.
(10) The judge must order the person's discharge if the documents referred to in section 70(9) are not received by the judge within the required period.
(11) The required period is—

(a) 45 days starting with the day on which the person was arrested, or
(b) if the category 2 territory is designated[1] by order made by the Secretary of State for the purposes of this section, any longer period permitted by the order.

(12) Subsection (4)(a) applies to Scotland with the omission of the words "by a constable".

[Extradition Act 2003, s 74.]

---

1. For the list of countries so designated, and the length of the periods permitted, see The Extradition Act 2003 (Designation of Territories) Order, SI 2003/3334, amended by SI 2004/1898, SI 2005/365 (made under sub-s (1)) and SI 2005/2036 has been made (see this TITLE, post).

8–10299R

The extradition hearing

75. Date of extradition hearing: arrest under section 71.   (1) When a person arrested under a warrant issued under section 71 first appears or is brought before the appropriate judge, the judge must fix a date on which the extradition hearing is to begin.

(2) The date fixed under subsection (1) must not be later than the end of the permitted period, which is 2 months starting with the date on which the person first appears or is brought before the judge.

(3) If before the date fixed under subsection (1) (or this subsection) a party to the proceedings

applies to the judge for a later date to be fixed and the judge believes it to be in the interests of justice to do so, he may fix a later date; and this subsection may apply more than once.

(4) If the extradition hearing does not begin on or before the date fixed under this section and the person applies to the judge to be discharged, the judge must order his discharge.

[Extradition Act 2003, s 75.]

8–10299S   76. Date of extradition hearing: arrest under provisional warrant.   (1) Subsection (2) applies if—

(a)   a person is arrested under a provisional warrant, and

(b)   the documents referred to in section 70(9) are received by the appropriate judge within the period required under section 74(10).

(2) The judge must fix a date on which the extradition hearing is to begin.

(3) The date fixed under subsection (2) must not be later than the end of the permitted period, which is 2 months starting with the date on which the judge receives the documents.

(4) If before the date fixed under subsection (2) (or this subsection) a party to the proceedings applies to the judge for a later date to be fixed and the judge believes it to be in the interests of justice to do so, he may fix a later date; and this subsection may apply more than once.

(5) If the extradition hearing does not begin on or before the date fixed under this section and the person applies to the judge to be discharged, the judge must order his discharge.

[Extradition Act 2003, s 76.]

8–10299T   77. Judge's powers at extradition hearing.   (1) In England and Wales, at the extradition hearing the appropriate judge has the same powers (as nearly as may be) as a magistrates' court would have if the proceedings were the summary trial of an information against the person whose extradition is requested.

(2) *(Scotland)*.

(3) *(Northern Ireland)*.

(4) If the judge adjourns the extradition hearing he must remand the person in custody or on bail.

(5) If the judge remands the person in custody he may later grant bail.

[Extradition Act 2003, s 77.]

8–10299U   78. Initial stages of extradition hearing.   (1) This section applies if a person alleged to be the person whose extradition is requested appears or is brought before the appropriate judge for the extradition hearing.

(2) The judge must decide whether the documents sent to him by the Secretary of State consist of (or include)—

(a)   the documents referred to in section 70(9);

(b)   particulars of the person whose extradition is requested;

(c)   particulars of the offence specified in the request;

(d)   in the case of a person accused of an offence, a warrant for his arrest issued in the category 2 territory;

(e)   in the case of a person alleged to be unlawfully at large after conviction of an offence, a certificate issued in the category 2 territory of the conviction and (if he has been sentenced) of the sentence.

(3) If the judge decides the question in subsection (2) in the negative he must order the person's discharge.

(4) If the judge decides that question in the affirmative he must decide whether—

(a)   the person appearing or brought before him is the person whose extradition is requested;

(b)   the offence specified in the request is an extradition offence;

(c)   copies of the documents sent to the judge by the Secretary of State have been served[1] on the person.

(5) The judge must decide the question in subsection (4)(a) on a balance of probabilities.

(6) If the judge decides any of the questions in subsection (4) in the negative he must order the person's discharge.

(7) If the judge decides those questions in the affirmative he must proceed under section 79.

(8) The reference in subsection (2)(d) to a warrant for a person's arrest includes a reference to a judicial document authorising his arrest.

[Extradition Act 2003, s 78.]

---

1. The statute does not specify who is to effect service, although normally the CPS will do so. Service is not required to be made prior to the commencement of the hearing. Service may be effected at the hearing and the court may grant an adjournment if the interests of justice require it. If late service would cause prejudice, this may be met by the granting of an adjournment to the defendant or the refusal of an adjournment to effect service (*Government of Germany v Kleinschmidt* [2005] EWHC 1373 (Admin), [2005] 3 All ER 759, [2006] 1 WLR 1).

8–10299V   79. Bars to extradition.   (1) If the judge is required to proceed under this section he must decide whether the person's extradition to the category 2 territory is barred by reason of—

  (a) the rule against double jeopardy;
  (b) extraneous considerations;
  (c) the passage of time;
  (d) hostage-taking considerations.

  (2) Sections 80 to 83 apply for the interpretation of subsection (1).

  (3) If the judge decides any of the questions in subsection (1) in the affirmative he must order the person's discharge.

  (4) If the judge decides those questions in the negative and the person is accused of the commission of the extradition offence but is not alleged to be unlawfully at large after conviction of it, the judge must proceed under section 84.

  (5) If the judge decides those questions in the negative and the person is alleged to be unlawfully at large after conviction of the extradition offence, the judge must proceed under section 85.

   [Extradition Act 2003, s 79.]

8–10299W   80. Rule against double jeopardy.   A person's extradition to a category 2 territory is barred by reason of the rule against double jeopardy if (and only if) it appears that he would be entitled to be discharged under any rule of law relating to previous acquittal or conviction if he were charged with the extradition offence in the part of the United Kingdom where the judge exercises his jurisdiction.

   [Extradition Act 2003, s 80.]

8–10299X   81. Extraneous considerations.   A person's extradition to a category 2 territory is barred by reason of extraneous considerations if (and only if) it appears that—

  (a) the request for his extradition (though purporting to be made on account of the extradition offence) is in fact made for the purpose of prosecuting or punishing him on account of his race, religion, nationality, gender, sexual orientation or political opinions, or
  (b) if extradited he might be prejudiced at his trial or punished, detained or restricted in his personal liberty by reason of his race, religion, nationality, gender, sexual orientation or political opinions.

   [Extradition Act 2003, s 81.]

8–10299Y   82. Passage of time.   A person's extradition to a category 2 territory is barred by reason of the passage of time if (and only if) it appears that it would be unjust or oppressive to extradite him by reason of the passage of time since he is alleged to have committed the extradition offence or since he is alleged to have become unlawfully at large (as the case may be).

   [Extradition Act 2003, s 82.]

8–10299Z   83. Hostage-taking considerations.   (1) A person's extradition to a category 2 territory is barred by reason of hostage-taking considerations if (and only if) the territory is a party to the Hostage-taking Convention and it appears that—

  (a) if extradited he might be prejudiced at his trial because communication between him and the appropriate authorities would not be possible, and
  (b) the act or omission constituting the extradition offence also constitutes an offence under section 1 of the Taking of Hostages Act 1982 (c 28) or an attempt to commit such an offence.

  (2) The appropriate authorities are the authorities of the territory which are entitled to exercise rights of protection in relation to him.

  (3) A certificate issued by the Secretary of State that a territory is a party to the Hostage-taking Convention is conclusive evidence of that fact for the purposes of subsection (1).

  (4) The Hostage-taking Convention is the International Convention against the Taking of Hostages opened for signature at New York on 18 December 1979.

   [Extradition Act 2003, s 83.]

8–10299ZA   84. Case where person has not been convicted.   (1) If the judge is required to proceed under this section he must decide whether there is evidence which would be sufficient to make a case requiring an answer by the person if the proceedings were the summary trial of an information against him.

  (2) In deciding the question in subsection (1) the judge may treat a statement made by a person in a document as admissible evidence of a fact if—

  (a) the statement is made by the person to a police officer or another person charged with the duty of investigating offences or charging offenders, and
  (b) direct oral evidence by the person of the fact would be admissible.

(3) In deciding whether to treat a statement made by a person in a document as admissible evidence of a fact, the judge must in particular have regard—

    (a) to the nature and source of the document;

    (b) to whether or not, having regard to the nature and source of the document and to any other circumstances that appear to the judge to be relevant, it is likely that the document is authentic;

    (c) to the extent to which the statement appears to supply evidence which would not be readily available if the statement were not treated as being admissible evidence of the fact;

    (d) to the relevance of the evidence that the statement appears to supply to any issue likely to have to be determined by the judge in deciding the question in subsection (1);

    (e) to any risk that the admission or exclusion of the statement will result in unfairness to the person whose extradition is sought, having regard in particular to whether it is likely to be possible to controvert the statement if the person making it does not attend to give oral evidence in the proceedings.

(4) A summary in a document of a statement made by a person must be treated as a statement made by the person in the document for the purposes of subsection (2).

(5) If the judge decides the question in subsection (1) in the negative he must order the person's discharge.

(6) If the judge decides that question in the affirmative he must proceed under section 87.

(7) If the judge is required to proceed under this section and the category 2 territory to which extradition is requested is designated[1] for the purposes of this section by order made by the Secretary of State—

    (a) the judge must not decide under subsection (1), and

    (b) he must proceed under section 87.

    (8) (*Scotland*).

    (9) (*Northern Ireland*).

[Extradition Act 2003, s 84.]

---

1. For the list of countries so designated see The Extradition Act 2003 (Designation of Territories) Order, SI 2003/3334, amended by SI 2004/1898, SI 2005/365 and SI 2005/2036 (see this TITLE, post).

8–10299ZB   85. Case where person has been convicted.   (1) If the judge is required to proceed under this section he must decide whether the person was convicted in his presence.

(2) If the judge decides the question in subsection (1) in the affirmative he must proceed under section 87.

(3) If the judge decides that question in the negative he must decide whether the person deliberately absented himself from his trial.

(4) If the judge decides the question in subsection (3) in the affirmative he must proceed under section 87.

(5) If the judge decides that question in the negative he must decide whether the person would be entitled to a retrial or (on appeal) to a review amounting to a retrial.

(6) If the judge decides the question in subsection (5) in the affirmative he must proceed under section 86.

(7) If the judge decides that question in the negative he must order the person's discharge.

(8) The judge must not decide the question in subsection (5) in the affirmative unless, in any proceedings that it is alleged would constitute a retrial or a review amounting to a retrial, the person would have these rights—

    (a) the right to defend himself in person or through legal assistance of his own choosing or, if he had not sufficient means to pay for legal assistance, to be given it free when the interests of justice so required;

    (b) the right to examine or have examined witnesses against him and to obtain the attendance and examination of witnesses on his behalf under the same conditions as witnesses against him.

[Extradition Act 2003, s 85.]

8–10299ZC   86. Conviction in person's absence.   (1) If the judge is required to proceed under this section he must decide whether there is evidence which would be sufficient to make a case requiring an answer by the person if the proceedings were the summary trial of an information against him.

(2) In deciding the question in subsection (1) the judge may treat a statement made by a person in a document as admissible evidence of a fact if—

    (a) the statement is made by the person to a police officer or another person charged with the duty of investigating offences or charging offenders, and

    (b) direct oral evidence by the person of the fact would be admissible.

(3) In deciding whether to treat a statement made by a person in a document as admissible evidence of a fact, the judge must in particular have regard—

(a) to the nature and source of the document;
(b) to whether or not, having regard to the nature and source of the document and to any other circumstances that appear to the judge to be relevant, it is likely that the document is authentic;
(c) to the extent to which the statement appears to supply evidence which would not be readily available if the statement were not treated as being admissible evidence of the fact;
(d) to the relevance of the evidence that the statement appears to supply to any issue likely to have to be determined by the judge in deciding the question in subsection (1);
(e) to any risk that the admission or exclusion of the statement will result in unfairness to the person whose extradition is sought, having regard in particular to whether it is likely to be possible to controvert the statement if the person making it does not attend to give oral evidence in the proceedings.

(4) A summary in a document of a statement made by a person must be treated as a statement made by the person in the document for the purposes of subsection (2).

(5) If the judge decides the question in subsection (1) in the negative he must order the person's discharge.

(6) If the judge decides that question in the affirmative he must proceed under section 87.

(7) If the judge is required to proceed under this section and the category 2 territory to which extradition is requested is designated[1] for the purposes of this section by order made by the Secretary of State—

(a) the judge must not decide under subsection (1), and
(b) he must proceed under section 87.

(8) (*Scotland*).
(9) (*Northern Ireland*).

[Extradition Act 2003, s 86.]

---

1. For the list of countries so designated see The Extradition Act 2003 (Designation of Territories) Order, SI 2003/3334, amended by SI 2004/1898, SI 2005/365 and SI 2005/2036 (see this TITLE, post).

8–10299ZD   87. Human rights.   (1) If the judge is required to proceed under this section (by virtue of section 84, 85 or 86) he must decide whether the person's extradition would be compatible with the Convention rights within the meaning of the Human Rights Act 1998 (c 42).

(2) If the judge decides the question in subsection (1) in the negative he must order the person's discharge.

(3) If the judge decides that question in the affirmative he must send the case to the Secretary of State for his decision whether the person is to be extradited.

[Extradition Act 2003, s 87.]

8–10299ZE   88. Person charged with offence in United Kingdom.   (1) This section applies if at any time in the extradition hearing the judge is informed that the person is charged with an offence in the United Kingdom.

(2) The judge must adjourn the extradition hearing until one of these occurs—

(a) the charge is disposed of;
(b) the charge is withdrawn;
(c) proceedings in respect of the charge are discontinued;
(d) an order is made for the charge to lie on the file, or in relation to Scotland, the diet is deserted *pro loco et tempore.*

(3) If a sentence of imprisonment or another form of detention is imposed in respect of the offence charged, the judge may adjourn the extradition hearing until the sentence has been served.

(4) If before he adjourns the extradition hearing under subsection (2) the judge has decided under section 79 whether the person's extradition is barred by reason of the rule against double jeopardy, the judge must decide that question again after the resumption of the hearing.

[Extradition Act 2003, s 88.]

8–10299ZF   89. Person serving sentence in United Kingdom.   (1) This section applies if at any time in the extradition hearing the judge is informed that the person is serving a sentence of imprisonment or another form of detention in the United Kingdom.

(2) The judge may adjourn the extradition hearing until the sentence has been served.

[Extradition Act 2003, s 89.]

8–10299ZG   90. Competing extradition claim.   (1) This section applies if at any time in the extradition hearing the judge is informed that the conditions in subsection (2) or (3) are met.

(2) The conditions are that—

(a) the Secretary of State has received another valid request for the person's extradition to a category 2 territory;

(b) the other request has not been disposed of;

(c) the Secretary of State has made an order under section 126(2) for further proceedings on the request under consideration to be deferred until the other request has been disposed of.

(3) The conditions are that—

(a) a certificate has been issued under section 2 in respect of a Part 1 warrant issued in respect of the person;

(b) the warrant has not been disposed of;

(c) the Secretary of State has made an order under section 179(2) for further proceedings on the request to be deferred until the warrant has been disposed of.

(4) The judge must remand the person in custody or on bail.

(5) If the judge remands the person in custody he may later grant bail.

[Extradition Act 2003, s 90.]

8–10299ZH 91. Physical or mental condition. (1) This section applies if at any time in the extradition hearing it appears to the judge that the condition in subsection (2) is satisfied.

(2) The condition is that the physical or mental condition of the person is such that it would be unjust or oppressive to extradite him.

(3) The judge must—

(a) order the person's discharge, or

(b) adjourn the extradition hearing until it appears to him that the condition in subsection (2) is no longer satisfied.

[Extradition Act 2003, s 91.]

8–10299ZI 92. Case sent to Secretary of State. (1) This section applies if the appropriate judge sends a case to the Secretary of State under this Part for his decision whether a person is to be extradited.

(2) The judge must inform the person in ordinary language that—

(a) he has a right to appeal to the High Court;

(b) if he exercises the right the appeal will not be heard until the Secretary of State has made his decision.

(3) But subsection (2) does not apply if the person has consented to his extradition under section 127.

(4) The judge must remand the person in custody or on bail—

(a) to wait for the Secretary of State's decision, and

(b) to wait for his extradition to the territory to which extradition is requested (if the Secretary of State orders him to be extradited).

(5) If the judge remands the person in custody he may later grant bail.

[Extradition Act 2003, s 92.]

Secretary of State's functions

8–10299ZJ 93. Secretary of State's consideration of case. (1) This section applies if the appropriate judge sends a case to the Secretary of State under this Part for his decision whether a person is to be extradited.

(2) The Secretary of State must decide whether he is prohibited from ordering the person's extradition under any of these sections—

(a) section 94 (death penalty);

(b) section 95 (speciality);

(c) section 96 (earlier extradition to United Kingdom from other territory).

(3) If the Secretary of State decides any of the questions in subsection (2) in the affirmative he must order the person's discharge.

(4) If the Secretary of State decides those questions in the negative he must order the person to be extradited to the territory to which his extradition is requested unless—

(a) he is informed that the request has been withdrawn,

(b) he makes an order under section 126(2) or 179(2) for further proceedings on the request to be deferred and the person is discharged under section 180, or

(c) he orders the person's discharge under section 208.

(5) In deciding the questions in subsection (2), the Secretary of State is not required to consider any representations received by him after the end of the permitted period.

(6) The permitted period is the period of 6 weeks starting with the appropriate day.

[Extradition Act 2003, s 93.]

8–10299ZK   94. Death penalty.   (1) The Secretary of State must not order a person's extradition to a category 2 territory if he could be, will be or has been sentenced to death for the offence concerned in the category 2 territory.

(2) Subsection (1) does not apply if the Secretary of State receives a written assurance which he considers adequate that a sentence of death—

(a) will not be imposed, or
(b) will not be carried out (if imposed).

[Extradition Act 2003, s 94.]

8–10299ZL   95. Speciality.   (1) The Secretary of State must not order a person's extradition to a category 2 territory if there are no speciality arrangements with the category 2 territory.

(2) But subsection (1) does not apply if the person consented to his extradition under section 127 before his case was sent to the Secretary of State.

(3) There are speciality arrangements with a category 2 territory if (and only if) under the law of that territory or arrangements made between it and the United Kingdom a person who is extradited to the territory from the United Kingdom may be dealt with in the territory for an offence committed before his extradition only if—

(a) the offence is one falling within subsection (4), or
(b) he is first given an opportunity to leave the territory.

(4) The offences are—

(a) the offence in respect of which the person is extradited;
(b) an extradition offence disclosed by the same facts as that offence, other than one in respect of which a sentence of death could be imposed;
(c) an extradition offence in respect of which the Secretary of State consents to the person being dealt with;
(d) an offence in respect of which the person waives the right that he would have (but for this paragraph) not to be dealt with for the offence.

(5) Arrangements made with a category 2 territory which is a Commonwealth country or a British overseas territory may be made for a particular case or more generally.

(6) A certificate issued by or under the authority of the Secretary of State confirming the existence of arrangements with a category 2 territory which is a Commonwealth country or a British overseas territory and stating the terms of the arrangements is conclusive evidence of those matters.

[Extradition Act 2003, s 95.]

8–10299ZM   96. Earlier extradition to United Kingdom from other territory.   The Secretary of State must not order a person's extradition to a category 2 territory if—

(a) the person was extradited to the United Kingdom from another territory (the extraditing territory);
(b) under arrangements between the United Kingdom and the extraditing territory, that territory's consent is required to the person's extradition from the United Kingdom to the category 2 territory in respect of the extradition offence under consideration;
(c) that consent has not been given on behalf of the extraditing territory.

[Extradition Act 2003, s 96.]

8–10299ZN   97. Deferral: person charged with offence in United Kingdom.   (1) This section applies if—

(a) the appropriate judge sends a case to the Secretary of State under this Part for his decision whether a person is to be extradited;
(b) the person is charged with an offence in the United Kingdom.

(2) The Secretary of State must not make a decision with regard to the person's extradition until one of these occurs—

(a) the charge is disposed of;
(b) the charge is withdrawn;
(c) proceedings in respect of the charge are discontinued;
(d) an order is made for the charge to lie on the file or, in relation to Scotland, the diet is deserted *pro loco et tempore*.

(3) If a sentence of imprisonment or another form of detention is imposed in respect of the offence charged, the Secretary of State may defer making a decision with regard to the person's extradition until the sentence has been served.

[Extradition Act 2003, s 97.]

8–10299ZO   98. Deferral: person serving sentence in United Kingdom.   (1) This section applies if—

(a) the appropriate judge sends a case to the Secretary of State under this Part for his decision whether a person is to be extradited;

(b) the person is serving a sentence of imprisonment or another form of detention in the United Kingdom.

(2) The Secretary of State may defer making a decision with regard to the person's extradition until the sentence has been served.

[Extradition Act 2003, s 98.]

8–10299ZP   99. Time limit for order for extradition or discharge.   (1) This section applies if—

(a) the appropriate judge sends a case to the Secretary of State under this Part for his decision whether a person is to be extradited;

(b) within the required period the Secretary of State does not make an order for the person's extradition or discharge.

(2) If the person applies to the High Court to be discharged, the court must order his discharge.

(3) The required period is the period of 2 months starting with the appropriate day.

(4) If before the required period ends the Secretary of State applies to the High Court for it to be extended the High Court may make an order accordingly; and this subsection may apply more than once.

[Extradition Act 2003, s 99.]

8–10299ZQ   100. Information.   (1) If the Secretary of State orders a person's extradition under this Part he must—

(a) inform the person of the order;

(b) inform him in ordinary language that he has a right of appeal to the High Court;

(c) inform a person acting on behalf of the category 2 territory of the order.

(2) But subsection (1)(b) does not apply if the person has consented to his extradition under section 127.

(3) If the Secretary of State orders a person's extradition under this Part and he has received an assurance such as is mentioned in section 94(2), he must give the person a copy of the assurance when he informs him under subsection (1) of the order.

(4) If the Secretary of State orders a person's discharge under this Part he must—

(a) inform him of the order;

(b) inform a person acting on behalf of the category 2 territory of the order.

[Extradition Act 2003, s 100.]

8–10299ZR   101. Making of order for extradition or discharge

8–10299ZS   102. The appropriate day.   (1) This section applies for the purposes of sections 93 and 99 if the appropriate judge sends a case to the Secretary of State under this Part for his decision whether a person is to be extradited.

(2) If the person is charged with an offence in the United Kingdom, the appropriate day is the day on which one of these occurs—

(a) the charge is disposed of;

(b) the charge is withdrawn;

(c) proceedings in respect of the charge are discontinued;

(d) an order is made for the charge to lie on the file, or in relation to Scotland, the diet is deserted *pro loco et tempore*.

(3) If under section 97(3) or 98(2) the Secretary of State defers making a decision until the person has served a sentence, the appropriate day is the day on which the person finishes serving the sentence.

(4) If section 126 applies in relation to the request for the person's extradition (the request concerned) the appropriate day is—

(a) the day on which the Secretary of State makes an order under that section, if the order is for proceedings on the other request to be deferred;

(b) the day on which an order under section 180 is made, if the order under section 126 is for proceedings on the request concerned to be deferred and the order under section 180 is for the proceedings to be resumed.

(5) If section 179 applies in relation to the request for the person's extradition, the appropriate day is—

(a) the day on which the Secretary of State makes an order under that section, if the order is for proceedings on the warrant to be deferred;

(b) the day on which an order under section 180 is made, if the order under section 179 is for proceedings on the request to be deferred and the order under section 180 is for the proceedings to be resumed.

(6) If more than one of subsections (2) to (5) applies, the appropriate day is the latest of the days found under the subsections which apply.

(7) In any other case, the appropriate day is the day on which the judge sends the case to the Secretary of State for his decision whether the person is to be extradited.

[Extradition Act 2003, s 102.]

Appeals

8–10299ZT 103. Appeal where case sent to Secretary of State. (1) If the judge sends a case to the Secretary of State under this Part for his decision whether a person is to be extradited, the person may appeal to the High Court against the relevant decision.

(2) But subsection (1) does not apply if the person consented to his extradition under section 127 before his case was sent to the Secretary of State.

(3) The relevant decision is the decision that resulted in the case being sent to the Secretary of State.

(4) An appeal under this section may be brought on a question of law or fact.

(5) If an appeal is brought under this section before the Secretary of State has decided whether the person is to be extradited the appeal must not be heard until after the Secretary of State has made his decision.

(6) If the Secretary of State orders the person's discharge the appeal must not be proceeded with.

(7) No appeal may be brought under this section if the Secretary of State has ordered the person's discharge.

(8) If notice of an appeal under section 110 against the decision which resulted in the order for the person's discharge is given in accordance with subsection (5) of that section—

(a) subsections (6) and (7) do not apply;
(b) no appeal may be brought under this section if the High Court has made its decision on the appeal.

(9) Notice of an appeal under this section must be given in accordance with rules of court before the end of the permitted period, which is 14 days starting with the day on which the Secretary of State informs the person under section 100(1) or (4) of the order he has made in respect of the person.

[Extradition Act 2003, s 103.]

8–10299ZU 104. Court's powers on appeal under section 103. (1) On an appeal under section 103 the High Court may—

(a) allow the appeal;
(b) direct the judge to decide again a question (or questions) which he decided at the extradition hearing;
(c) dismiss the appeal.

(2) The court may allow the appeal only if the conditions in subsection (3) or the conditions in subsection (4) are satisfied.

(3) The conditions are that—

(a) the judge ought to have decided a question before him at the extradition hearing differently;
(b) if he had decided the question in the way he ought to have done, he would have been required to order the person's discharge.

(4) The conditions are that—

(a) an issue is raised that was not raised at the extradition hearing or evidence is available that was not available at the extradition hearing;
(b) the issue or evidence would have resulted in the judge deciding a question before him at the extradition hearing differently;
(c) if he had decided the question in that way, he would have been required to order the person's discharge.

(5) If the court allows the appeal it must—

(a) order the person's discharge;
(b) quash the order for his extradition.

(6) If the judge comes to a different decision on any question that is the subject of a direction under subsection (1)(b) he must order the person's discharge.

(7) If the judge comes to the same decision as he did at the extradition hearing on the question that is (or all the questions that are) the subject of a direction under subsection (1)(b) the appeal must be taken to have been dismissed by a decision of the High Court.

[Extradition Act 2003, s 104.]

8–10299ZV   **105. Appeal against discharge at extradition hearing.**   (1) If at the extradition hearing the judge orders a person's discharge, an appeal to the High Court may be brought on behalf of the category 2 territory against the relevant decision.

(2) But subsection (1) does not apply if the order for the person's discharge was under section 122.

(3) The relevant decision is the decision which resulted in the order for the person's discharge.

(4) An appeal under this section may be brought on a question of law or fact.

(5) Notice of an appeal under this section must be given in accordance with rules of court before the end of the permitted period, which is 14 days starting with the day on which the order for the person's discharge is made.

[Extradition Act 2003, s 105.]

8–10299ZW   **106. Court's powers on appeal under section 105.**   (1) On an appeal under section 105 the High Court may—

(a) allow the appeal;

(b) direct the judge to decide the relevant question again;

(c) dismiss the appeal.

(2) A question is the relevant question if the judge's decision on it resulted in the order for the person's discharge.

(3) The court may allow the appeal only if the conditions in subsection (4) or the conditions in subsection (5) are satisfied.

(4) The conditions are that—

(a) the judge ought to have decided the relevant question differently;

(b) if he had decided the question in the way he ought to have done, he would not have been required to order the person's discharge.

(5) The conditions are that—

(a) an issue is raised that was not raised at the extradition hearing or evidence is available that was not available at the extradition hearing;

(b) the issue or evidence would have resulted in the judge deciding the relevant question differently;

(c) if he had decided the question in that way, he would not have been required to order the person's discharge.

(6) If the court allows the appeal it must—

(a) quash the order discharging the person;

(b) remit the case to the judge;

(c) direct him to proceed as he would have been required to do if he had decided the relevant question differently at the extradition hearing.

(7) If the court makes a direction under subsection (1)(b) and the judge decides the relevant question differently he must proceed as he would have been required to do if he had decided that question differently at the extradition hearing.

(8) If the court makes a direction under subsection (1)(b) and the judge does not decide the relevant question differently the appeal must be taken to have been dismissed by a decision of the High Court.

[Extradition Act 2003, s 106.]

8–10299ZX   **107. Detention pending conclusion of appeal under section 105.**   (1) This section applies if immediately after the judge orders the person's discharge the judge is informed on behalf of the category 2 territory of an intention to appeal under section 105.

(2) The judge must remand the person in custody or on bail while the appeal is pending.

(3) If the judge remands the person in custody he may later grant bail.

(4) An appeal under section 105 ceases to be pending at the earliest of these times—

(a) when the proceedings on the appeal are discontinued;

(b) when the High Court dismisses the appeal, if the court is not immediately informed on behalf of the category 2 territory of an intention to apply for leave to appeal to the House of Lords;

(c) at the end of the permitted period, which is 28 days starting with the day on which leave to appeal to the House of Lords against the decision of the High Court on the appeal is granted;

(d) when there is no further step that can be taken on behalf of the category 2 territory in relation to the appeal (ignoring any power of a court to grant leave to take a step out of time).

(5) The preceding provisions of this section apply to Scotland with these modifications—

(a) in subsection (4)(b) omit the words from "if" to the end;

(b) omit subsection (4)(c).

[Extradition Act 2003, s 107.]

8–10299ZY   108. Appeal against extradition order.   (1) If the Secretary of State orders a person's extradition under this Part, the person may appeal to the High Court against the order.

(2) But subsection (1) does not apply if the person has consented to his extradition under section 127.

(3) An appeal under this section may be brought on a question of law or fact.

(4) Notice of an appeal under this section must be given in accordance with rules of court before the end of the permitted period, which is 14 days starting with the day on which the Secretary of State informs the person of the order under section 100(1).

[Extradition Act 2003, s 108.]

8–10299ZZ   109. Court's powers on appeal under section 108.   (1) On an appeal under section 108 the High Court may—

(a)   allow the appeal;

(b)   dismiss the appeal.

(2) The court may allow the appeal only if the conditions in subsection (3) or the conditions in subsection (4) are satisfied.

(3) The conditions are that—

(a)   the Secretary of State ought to have decided a question before him differently;

(b)   if he had decided the question in the way he ought to have done, he would not have ordered the person's extradition.

(4) The conditions are that—

(a)   an issue is raised that was not raised when the case was being considered by the Secretary of State or information is available that was not available at that time;

(b)   the issue or information would have resulted in the Secretary of State deciding a question before him differently;

(c)   if he had decided the question in that way, he would not have ordered the person's extradition.

(5) If the court allows the appeal it must—

(a)   order the person's discharge;

(b)   quash the order for his extradition.

[Extradition Act 2003, s 109.]

8–10299ZZA   110. Appeal against discharge by Secretary of State.   (1) If the Secretary of State makes an order for a person's discharge under this Part, an appeal to the High Court may be brought on behalf of the category 2 territory against the relevant decision.

(2) But subsection (1) does not apply if the order for the person's discharge was under section 123.

(3) The relevant decision is the decision which resulted in the order for the person's discharge.

(4) An appeal under this section may be brought on a question of law or fact.

(5) Notice of an appeal under this section must be given in accordance with rules of court before the end of the permitted period, which is 14 days starting with the day on which (under section 100(4)) the Secretary of State informs a person acting on behalf of the category 2 territory of the order.

[Extradition Act 2003, s 110.]

8–10299ZZB   111. Court's powers on appeal under section 110.   (1) On an appeal under section 110 the High Court may—

(a)   allow the appeal;

(b)   dismiss the appeal.

(2) The court may allow the appeal only if the conditions in subsection (3) or the conditions in subsection (4) are satisfied.

(3) The conditions are that—

(a)   the Secretary of State ought to have decided a question before him differently;

(b)   if he had decided the question in the way he ought to have done, he would have ordered the person's extradition.

(4) The conditions are that—

(a)   an issue is raised that was not raised when the case was being considered by the Secretary of State or information is available that was not available at that time;

(b)   the issue or information would have resulted in the Secretary of State deciding a question before him differently;

(c)   if he had decided the question in that way, he would have ordered the person's extradition.

(5) If the court allows the appeal it must—

(a) quash the order discharging the person;

(b) order the person's extradition.

[Extradition Act 2003, s 111.]

8–10299ZZC 112. Detention pending conclusion of appeal under section 110. (1) This section applies if immediately after the Secretary of State orders the person's discharge under this Part the Secretary of State is informed on behalf of the category 2 territory of an intention to appeal under section 110.

(2) The judge must remand the person in custody or on bail while the appeal is pending.

(3) If the judge remands the person in custody he may later grant bail.

(4) An appeal under section 110 ceases to be pending at the earliest of these times—

(a) when the proceedings on the appeal are discontinued;

(b) when the High Court dismisses the appeal, if the court is not immediately informed on behalf of the category 2 territory of an intention to apply for leave to appeal to the House of Lords;

(c) at the end of the permitted period, which is 28 days starting with the day on which leave to appeal to the House of Lords against the decision of the High Court on the appeal is granted;

(d) when there is no further step that can be taken on behalf of the category 2 territory in relation to the appeal (ignoring any power of a court to grant leave to take a step out of time).

(5) The preceding provisions of this section apply to Scotland with these modifications—

(a) in subsection (4)(b) omit the words from "if" to the end;

(b) omit subsection (4)(c).

[Extradition Act 2003, s 112.]

8–10299ZZD 113. Appeal to High Court: time limit for start of hearing. (1) Rules of court must prescribe the period (the relevant period) within which the High Court must begin to hear an appeal under section 103, 105, 108 or 110.

(2) The High Court must begin to hear the appeal before the end of the relevant period.

(3) The High Court may extend the relevant period if it believes it to be in the interests of justice to do so; and this subsection may apply more than once.

(4) The power in subsection (3) may be exercised even after the end of the relevant period.

(5) If subsection (2) is not complied with and the appeal is under section 103 or 108—

(a) the appeal must be taken to have been allowed by a decision of the High Court;

(b) the person whose extradition has been ordered must be taken to have been discharged by the High Court;

(c) the order for the person's extradition must be taken to have been quashed by the High Court.

(6) If subsection (2) is not complied with and the appeal is under section 105 or 110 the appeal must be taken to have been dismissed by a decision of the High Court.

[Extradition Act 2003, s 113.]

8–10299ZZE 114. Appeal to House of Lords

8–10299ZZF 115. Powers of House of Lords on appeal under section 114

8–10299ZZG 116. Appeals: general. A decision under this Part of the judge or the Secretary of State may be questioned in legal proceedings only by means of an appeal under this Part.

[Extradition Act 2003, s 116.]

Time for extradition

8–10299ZZH 117. Extradition where no appeal. (1) This section applies if—

(a) the Secretary of State orders a person's extradition to a category 2 territory under this Part, and

(b) no notice of an appeal under section 103 or 108 is given before the end of the permitted period, which is 14 days starting with the day on which the Secretary of State informs the person under section 100(1) that he has ordered his extradition.

(2) The person must be extradited to the category 2 territory before the end of the required period, which is 28 days starting with the day on which the Secretary of State makes the order.

(3) If subsection (2) is not complied with and the person applies to the appropriate judge to be discharged the judge must order his discharge, unless reasonable cause is shown for the delay.

(4) These must be ignored for the purposes of subsection (1)(b)—

(a) any power of a court to extend the period permitted for giving notice of appeal;

(b) any power of a court to grant leave to take a step out of time.

[Extradition Act 2003, s 117.]

8–10299ZZI 118. Extradition following appeal. (1) This section applies if—

(a) there is an appeal to the High Court under section 103, 108 or 110 against a decision or order relating to a person's extradition to a category 2 territory, and

(b) the effect of the decision of the relevant court on the appeal is that the person is to be extradited there.

(2) The person must be extradited to the category 2 territory before the end of the required period, which is 28 days starting with—

(a) the day on which the decision of the relevant court on the appeal becomes final, or

(b) the day on which proceedings on the appeal are discontinued.

(3) The relevant court is—

(a) the High Court, if there is no appeal to the House of Lords against the decision of the High Court on the appeal;

(b) the House of Lords, if there is such an appeal.

(4) The decision of the High Court on the appeal becomes final—

(a) when the period permitted for applying to the High Court for leave to appeal to the House of Lords ends, if there is no such application;

(b) when the period permitted for applying to the House of Lords for leave to appeal to it ends, if the High Court refuses leave to appeal and there is no application to the House of Lords for leave to appeal;

(c) when the House of Lords refuses leave to appeal to it;

(d) at the end of the permitted period, which is 28 days starting with the day on which leave to appeal to the House of Lords is granted, if no such appeal is brought before the end of that period.

(5) These must be ignored for the purposes of subsection (4)—

(a) any power of a court to extend the period permitted for applying for leave to appeal;

(b) any power of a court to grant leave to take a step out of time.

(6) The decision of the House of Lords on the appeal becomes final when it is made.

(7) If subsection (2) is not complied with and the person applies to the appropriate judge to be discharged the judge must order his discharge, unless reasonable cause is shown for the delay.

(8) The preceding provisions of this section apply to Scotland with these modifications—

(a) in subsections (1) and (2) for "relevant court" substitute "High Court";

(b) omit subsections (3) to (6).

[Extradition Act 2003, s 118.]

8–10299ZZJ 119. Undertaking in relation to person serving sentence in United Kingdom. (1) This section applies if—

(a) the Secretary of State orders a person's extradition to a category 2 territory under this Part;

(b) the person is serving a sentence of imprisonment or another form of detention in the United Kingdom.

(2) The Secretary of State may make the order for extradition subject to the condition that extradition is not to take place before he receives an undertaking given on behalf of the category 2 territory in terms specified by him.

(3) The terms which may be specified by the Secretary of State in relation to a person accused in a category 2 territory of the commission of an offence include terms—

(a) that the person be kept in custody until the conclusion of the proceedings against him for the offence and any other offence in respect of which he is permitted to be dealt with in the category 2 territory;

(b) that the person be returned to the United Kingdom to serve the remainder of his sentence on the conclusion of those proceedings.

(4) The terms which may be specified by the Secretary of State in relation to a person alleged to be unlawfully at large after conviction of an offence by a court in a category 2 territory include terms that the person be returned to the United Kingdom to serve the remainder of his sentence after serving any sentence imposed on him in the category 2 territory for—

(a) the offence, and

(b) any other offence in respect of which he is permitted to be dealt with in the category 2 territory.

(5) Subsections (6) and (7) apply if the Secretary of State makes an order for extradition subject to a condition under subsection (2).

(6) If the Secretary of State does not receive the undertaking before the end of the period of 21

days starting with the day on which he makes the order and the person applies to the High Court to be discharged, the court must order his discharge.

(7) If the Secretary of State receives the undertaking before the end of that period—

(a) in a case where section 117 applies, the required period for the purposes of section 117(2) is 28 days starting with the day on which the Secretary of State receives the undertaking;

(b) in a case where section 118 applies, the required period for the purposes of section 118(2) is 28 days starting with the day on which the decision of the relevant court on the appeal becomes final (within the meaning of that section) or (if later) the day on which the Secretary of State receives the undertaking.

[Extradition Act 2003, s 119.]

8–10299ZZK   120. Extradition following deferral for competing claim.   (1) This section applies if—

(a) an order is made under this Part for a person to be extradited to a category 2 territory in pursuance of a request for his extradition;

(b) before the person is extradited to the territory an order is made under section 126(2) or 179(2) for the person's extradition in pursuance of the request to be deferred;

(c) the appropriate judge makes an order under section 181(2) for the person's extradition in pursuance of the request to cease to be deferred.

(2) In a case where section 117 applies, the required period for the purposes of section 117(2) is 28 days starting with the day on which the order under section 181(2) is made.

(3) In a case where section 118 applies, the required period for the purposes of section 118(2) is 28 days starting with the day on which the decision of the relevant court on the appeal becomes final (within the meaning of that section) or (if later) the day on which the order under section 181(2) is made.

[Extradition Act 2003, s 120.]

8–10299ZZL   121. Asylum claim.   (1) This section applies if—

(a) a person whose extradition is requested makes an asylum claim at any time in the relevant period;

(b) an order is made under this Part for the person to be extradited in pursuance of the request.

(2) The relevant period is the period—

(a) starting when a certificate is issued under section 70 in respect of the request;

(b) ending when the person is extradited in pursuance of the request.

(3) The person must not be extradited in pursuance of the request before the asylum claim is finally determined; and sections 117 and 118 have effect subject to this.

(4) If the Secretary of State allows the asylum claim, the claim is finally determined when he makes his decision on the claim.

(5) If the Secretary of State rejects the asylum claim, the claim is finally determined—

(a) when the Secretary of State makes his decision on the claim, if there is no right to appeal against the Secretary of State's decision on the claim;

(b) when the period permitted for appealing against the Secretary of State's decision on the claim ends, if there is such a right but there is no such appeal;

(c) when the appeal against that decision is finally determined or is withdrawn or abandoned, if there is such an appeal.

(6) An appeal against the Secretary of State's decision on an asylum claim is not finally determined for the purposes of subsection (5) at any time when a further appeal or an application for leave to bring a further appeal—

(a) has been instituted and has not been finally determined or withdrawn or abandoned, or

(b) may be brought.

(7) The remittal of an appeal is not a final determination for the purposes of subsection (6).

(8) The possibility of an appeal out of time with leave must be ignored for the purposes of subsections (5) and (6).

[Extradition Act 2003, s 121.]

Withdrawal of extradition request

8–10299ZZM   122. Withdrawal of request before end of extradition hearing.   (1) This section applies if at any time in the relevant period the appropriate judge is informed by the Secretary of State that a request for a person's extradition has been withdrawn.

(2) The relevant period is the period—

(a) starting when the person first appears or is brought before the appropriate judge following his arrest under this Part;

(b) ending when the judge orders the person's discharge or sends the case to the Secretary of State for his decision whether the person is to be extradited.

(3) The judge must order the person's discharge.

(4) If the person is not before the judge at the time the judge orders his discharge, the judge must inform him of the order as soon as practicable.

[Extradition Act 2003, s 122.]

8–10299ZZN 123. *Withdrawal of request after case sent to Secretary of State*

8–10299ZZO 124. *Withdrawal of request while appeal to High Court pending*

8–10299ZZP 125. *Withdrawal of request while appeal to House of Lords pending*

Competing extradition requests

8–10299ZZQ 126. Competing extradition requests. (1) This section applies if—

(a) the Secretary of State receives a valid request for a person's extradition to a category 2 territory;
(b) the person is in the United Kingdom;
(c) before the person is extradited in pursuance of the request or discharged, the Secretary of State receives another valid request for the person's extradition.

(2) The Secretary of State may—

(a) order proceedings (or further proceedings) on one of the requests to be deferred until the other one has been disposed of, if neither of the requests has been disposed of;
(b) order the person's extradition in pursuance of the request under consideration to be deferred until the other request has been disposed of, if an order for his extradition in pursuance of the request under consideration has been made.

(3) In applying subsection (2) the Secretary of State must take account in particular of these matters—

(a) the relative seriousness of the offences concerned;
(b) the place where each offence was committed (or was alleged to have been committed);
(c) the date when each request was received;
(d) whether, in the case of each offence, the person is accused of its commission (but not alleged to have been convicted) or is alleged to be unlawfully at large after conviction.

[Extradition Act 2003, s 126.]

Consent to extradition

8–10299ZZR 127. Consent to extradition: general. (1) A person arrested under a warrant issued under section 71 may consent to his extradition to the category 2 territory to which his extradition is requested.

(2) A person arrested under a provisional warrant may consent to his extradition to the category 2 territory in which he is accused of the commission of an offence or is alleged to have been convicted of an offence.

(3) Consent under this section—

(a) must be given in writing;
(b) is irrevocable.

(4) Consent under this section which is given by a person before his case is sent to the Secretary of State for the Secretary of State's decision whether he is to be extradited must be given before the appropriate judge.

(5) Consent under this section which is given in any other case must be given to the Secretary of State.

(6) A person may not give his consent under this section before the appropriate judge unless—

(a) he is legally represented before the appropriate judge at the time he gives consent, or
(b) he is a person to whom subsection (7) applies.

(7) This subsection applies to a person if—

(a) he has been informed of his right to apply for legal aid and has had the opportunity to apply for legal aid, but he has refused or failed to apply;
(b) he has applied for legal aid but his application has been refused;
(c) he was granted legal aid but the legal aid was withdrawn.

(8) In subsection (7) "legal aid" means—

(a) in England and Wales, a right to representation funded by the Legal Services Commission as part of the Criminal Defence Service;

(b) in Scotland, such legal aid as is available by virtue of section 183(a) of this Act;

(c) in Northern Ireland, such free legal aid as is available by virtue of sections 184 and 185 of this Act.

(9) For the purposes of subsection (6) a person is to be treated as legally represented before the appropriate judge if (and only if) he has the assistance of counsel or a solicitor to represent him in the proceedings before the appropriate judge.

[Extradition Act 2003, s 127.]

8–10299ZZS 128. Consent to extradition before case sent to Secretary of State. (1) This section applies if a person gives his consent under section 127 to the appropriate judge.

(2) If the judge has not fixed a date under section 75 or 76 on which the extradition hearing is to begin he is not required to do so.

(3) If the extradition hearing has begun the judge is no longer required to proceed or continue proceeding under sections 78 to 91.

(4) The judge must send the case to the Secretary of State for his decision whether the person is to be extradited.

(5) The person must be taken to have waived any right he would have (apart from the consent) not to be dealt with in the category 2 territory for an offence committed before his extradition.

[Extradition Act 2003, s 128.]

Post-extradition matters

8–10299ZZT 129. *Consent to other offence being dealt with*

8–10299ZZU 130. *Consent to further extradition to category 2 territory*

8–10299ZZV 131. *Consent to further extradition to category 1 territory*

8–10299ZZW 132. Return of person to serve remainder of sentence. (1) This section applies if—

(a) a person who is serving a sentence of imprisonment or another form of detention in the United Kingdom is extradited to a category 2 territory in accordance with this Part;

(b) the person is returned to the United Kingdom to serve the remainder of his sentence.

(2) The person is liable to be detained in pursuance of his sentence.

(3) If he is at large he must be treated as being unlawfully at large.

(4) Time during which the person was not in the United Kingdom as a result of his extradition does not count as time served by him as part of his sentence.

(5) But subsection (4) does not apply if—

(a) the person was extradited for the purpose of being prosecuted for an offence, and

(b) the person has not been convicted of the offence or of any other offence in respect of which he was permitted to be dealt with in the category 2 territory.

(6) In a case falling within subsection (5), time during which the person was not in the United Kingdom as a result of his extradition counts as time served by him as part of his sentence if (and only if) it was spent in custody in connection with the offence or any other offence in respect of which he was permitted to be dealt with in the territory.

[Extradition Act 2003, s 132.]

Costs

8–10299ZZX 133. Costs where extradition ordered. (1) This section applies if any of the following occurs in relation to a person whose extradition is requested under this Part—

(a) an order for the person's extradition is made under this Part;

(b) the High Court dismisses an appeal under section 103 or 108;

(c) the High Court or the House of Lords dismisses an application for leave to appeal to the House of Lords under section 114, if the application is made by the person;

(d) the House of Lords dismisses an appeal under section 114, if the appeal is brought by the person.

(2) In a case falling within subsection (1)(a), the appropriate judge may make such order as he considers just and reasonable with regard to the costs to be paid by the person.

(3) In a case falling within subsection (1)(b) by virtue of section 104(7), the judge who decides the question that is (or all the questions that are) the subject of a direction under section 104(1)(b) may make such order as he considers just and reasonable with regard to the costs to be paid by the person.

(4) In any other case falling within subsection (1)(b), the High Court may make such order as it considers just and reasonable with regard to the costs to be paid by the person.

(5) In a case falling within subsection (1)(c) or (d), the court by which the application or appeal is dismissed may make such order as it considers just and reasonable with regard to the costs to be paid by the person.

(6) An order for costs under this section—

(a) must specify their amount;

(b) may name the person to whom they are to be paid.

[Extradition Act 2003, s 133.]

8–10299ZZY   134. Costs where discharge ordered.   (1) This section applies if any of the following occurs in relation to a person whose extradition to a category 2 territory is requested under this Part—

(a) an order for the person's discharge is made under this Part;

(b) the person is taken to be discharged under this Part;

(c) the High Court dismisses an appeal under section 105 or 110;

(d) the High Court or the House of Lords dismisses an application for leave to appeal to the House of Lords under section 114, if the application is made on behalf of the category 2 territory;

(e) the House of Lords dismisses an appeal under section 114, if the appeal is brought on behalf of the category 2 territory.

(2) In a case falling within subsection (1)(a), an order under subsection (5) in favour of the person may be made by—

(a) the appropriate judge, if the order for the person's discharge is made by him or by the Secretary of State;

(b) the High Court, if the order for the person's discharge is made by it;

(c) the House of Lords, if the order for the person's discharge is made by it.

(3) In a case falling within subsection (1)(b), the appropriate judge may make an order under subsection (5) in favour of the person.

(4) In a case falling within subsection (1)(c), (d) or (e), the court by which the application or appeal is dismissed may make an order under subsection (5) in favour of the person.

(5) An order under this subsection in favour of a person is an order for a payment of the appropriate amount to be made to the person out of money provided by Parliament.

(6) The appropriate amount is such amount as the judge or court making the order under subsection (5) considers reasonably sufficient to compensate the person in whose favour the order is made for any expenses properly incurred by him in the proceedings under this Part.

(7) But if the judge or court making an order under subsection (5) is of the opinion that there are circumstances which make it inappropriate that the person in whose favour the order is made should recover the full amount mentioned in subsection (6), the judge or court must—

(a) assess what amount would in his or its opinion be just and reasonable;

(b) specify that amount in the order as the appropriate amount.

(8) Unless subsection (7) applies, the appropriate amount—

(a) must be specified in the order, if the court considers it appropriate for it to be so specified and the person in whose favour the order is made agrees the amount;

(b) must be determined in accordance with regulations made by the Lord Chancellor for the purposes of this section, in any other case.

[Extradition Act 2003, s 134.]

8–10299ZZZ   135. Costs where discharge ordered: supplementary.   (1) In England and Wales, subsections (1) and (3) of section 20 of the Prosecution of Offences Act 1985 (c 23) (regulations for carrying Part 2 of that Act into effect) apply in relation to section 134 as those subsections apply in relation to Part 2 of that Act.

(2) As so applied those subsections have effect as if an order under section 134(5) were an order under Part 2 of that Act for a payment to be made out of central funds.

(3) (*Northern Ireland*).

[Extradition Act 2003, s 135.]

Repatriation cases

8–10299ZZZA   136. Persons serving sentences outside territory where convicted.   (1) This section applies if—

(a) a request is made for a person's extradition to a category 2 territory and the request contains the statement referred to in subsection (2), or

(b) a provisional warrant for a person's arrest is sought on behalf of a category 2 territory and the information laid before the justice contains the statement referred to in subsection (2).

(2) The statement is one that the person—

(a) is alleged to be unlawfully at large from a prison in one territory (the imprisoning territory) in which he was serving a sentence after conviction of an offence specified in the request by a court in another territory (the convicting territory), and

(b) was serving the sentence in pursuance of international arrangements for prisoners sentenced in one territory to be repatriated to another territory in order to serve their sentence.

(3) If the category 2 territory is either the imprisoning territory or the convicting territory—

(a) section 70(3) has effect as if the reference to the statement referred to in subsection (4) of that section were a reference to the statement referred to in subsection (2) of this section;

(b) section 73(1) has effect as if the reference to a person within subsection (2) of that section were a reference to the person referred to in subsection (1)(b) of this section.

(4) If the category 2 territory is the imprisoning territory—

(a) sections 71(2)(a), 73(3)(a) and 78(4)(b) have effect as if "an extradition offence" read "an extradition offence in relation to the convicting territory";

(b) sections 74(8)(a) and 127(2) have effect as if "the category 2 territory in which he is accused of the commission of an offence or is alleged to have been convicted of an offence" read "the imprisoning territory";

(c) section 74(11)(b) has effect as if "the category 2 territory" read "the imprisoning territory";

(d) section 78(2)(e) has effect as if "the category 2 territory" read "the convicting territory";

(e) section 85(5) has effect as if after "entitled" there were inserted "in the convicting territory";

(f) section 119(4) has effect as if "a category 2 territory" read "the convicting territory" and as if "the category 2 territory" in both places read "the convicting territory";

(g) section 138(1) has effect as if "a category 2 territory" read "the convicting territory";

(h) in section 138, subsections (2), (3), (4), (5) and (7) have effect as if "the category 2 territory" read "the convicting territory".

(5) (*Scotland*).

(6) (*Northern Ireland*).

[Extradition Act 2003, s 136.]

Interpretation

8–10299ZZZB   **137. Extradition offences: person not sentenced for offence.** (1) This section applies in relation to conduct of a person if—

(a) he is accused in a category 2 territory of the commission of an offence constituted by the conduct, or

(b) he is alleged to be unlawfully at large after conviction by a court in a category 2 territory of an offence constituted by the conduct and he has not been sentenced for the offence.

(2) The conduct constitutes an extradition offence in relation to the category 2 territory if these conditions are satisfied—

(a) the conduct occurs in the category 2 territory;

(b) the conduct would constitute an offence under the law of the relevant part of the United Kingdom punishable with imprisonment or another form of detention for a term of 12 months or a greater punishment if it occurred in that part of the United Kingdom;

(c) the conduct is so punishable under the law of the category 2 territory (however it is described in that law).

(3) The conduct also constitutes an extradition offence in relation to the category 2 territory if these conditions are satisfied—

(a) the conduct occurs outside the category 2 territory;

(b) the conduct is punishable under the law of the category 2 territory with imprisonment or another form of detention for a term of 12 months or a greater punishment (however it is described in that law);

(c) in corresponding circumstances equivalent conduct would constitute an extra-territorial offence under the law of the relevant part of the United Kingdom punishable with imprisonment or another form of detention for a term of 12 months or a greater punishment.

(4) The conduct also constitutes an extradition offence in relation to the category 2 territory if these conditions are satisfied—

(a) the conduct occurs outside the category 2 territory and no part of it occurs in the United Kingdom;

(b) the conduct would constitute an offence under the law of the relevant part of the United Kingdom punishable with imprisonment or another form of detention for a term of 12 months or a greater punishment if it occurred in that part of the United Kingdom;

(c) the conduct is so punishable under the law of the category 2 territory (however it is described in that law).

(5) The conduct also constitutes an extradition offence in relation to the category 2 territory if these conditions are satisfied—

   (a)   the conduct occurs outside the category 2 territory and no part of it occurs in the United Kingdom;

   (b)   the conduct is punishable under the law of the category 2 territory with imprisonment for a term of 12 months or another form of detention or a greater punishment (however it is described in that law);

   (c)   the conduct constitutes or if committed in the United Kingdom would constitute an offence mentioned in subsection (6).

(6) The offences are—

   (a)   an offence under section 51 or 58 of the International Criminal Court Act 2001 (c 17) (genocide, crimes against humanity and war crimes);

   (b)   an offence under section 52 or 59 of that Act (conduct ancillary to genocide etc committed outside the jurisdiction);

   (c)   an ancillary offence, as defined in section 55 or 62 of that Act, in relation to an offence falling within paragraph (a) or (b);

   (d)   an offence under section 1 of the International Criminal Court (Scotland) Act 2001 (asp 13) (genocide, crimes against humanity and war crimes);

   (e)   an offence under section 2 of that Act (conduct ancillary to genocide etc committed outside the jurisdiction);

   (f)   an ancillary offence, as defined in section 7 of that Act, in relation to an offence falling within paragraph (d) or (e).

(7) If the conduct constitutes an offence under the military law of the category 2 territory but does not constitute an offence under the general criminal law of the relevant part of the United Kingdom it does not constitute an extradition offence; and subsections (1) to (6) have effect subject to this.

(8) The relevant part of the United Kingdom is the part of the United Kingdom in which—

   (a)   the extradition hearing took place, if the question of whether conduct constitutes an extradition offence is to be decided by the Secretary of State;

   (b)   proceedings in which it is necessary to decide that question are taking place, in any other case.

(9) Subsections (1) to (7) apply for the purposes of this Part.

[Extradition Act 2003, s 137.]

8–10299ZZZC   138. Extradition offences: person sentenced for offence.   (1) This section applies in relation to conduct of a person if—

   (a)   he is alleged to be unlawfully at large after conviction by a court in a category 2 territory of an offence constituted by the conduct, and

   (b)   he has been sentenced for the offence.

(2) The conduct constitutes an extradition offence in relation to the category 2 territory if these conditions are satisfied—

   (a)   the conduct occurs in the category 2 territory;

   (b)   the conduct would constitute an offence under the law of the relevant part of the United Kingdom punishable with imprisonment or another form of detention for a term of 12 months or a greater punishment if it occurred in that part of the United Kingdom;

   (c)   a sentence of imprisonment or another form of detention for a term of 4 months or a greater punishment has been imposed in the category 2 territory in respect of the conduct.

(3) The conduct also constitutes an extradition offence in relation to the category 2 territory if these conditions are satisfied—

   (a)   the conduct occurs outside the category 2 territory;

   (b)   a sentence of imprisonment or another form of detention for a term of 4 months or a greater punishment has been imposed in the category 2 territory in respect of the conduct;

   (c)   in corresponding circumstances equivalent conduct would constitute an extra-territorial offence under the law of the relevant part of the United Kingdom punishable with imprisonment or another form of detention for a term of 12 months or a greater punishment.

(4) The conduct also constitutes an extradition offence in relation to the category 2 territory if these conditions are satisfied—

   (a)   the conduct occurs outside the category 2 territory and no part of it occurs in the United Kingdom;

   (b)   the conduct would constitute an offence under the law of the relevant part of the United Kingdom punishable with imprisonment or another form of detention for a term of 12 months or a greater punishment if it occurred in that part of the United Kingdom;

   (c)   a sentence of imprisonment or another form of detention for a term of 4 months or a greater punishment has been imposed in the category 2 territory in respect of the conduct.

(5) The conduct also constitutes an extradition offence in relation to the category 2 territory if these conditions are satisfied—

(a) the conduct occurs outside the category 2 territory and no part of it occurs in the United Kingdom;

(b) a sentence of imprisonment or another form of detention for a term of 4 months or a greater punishment has been imposed in the category 2 territory in respect of the conduct;

(c) the conduct constitutes or if committed in the United Kingdom would constitute an offence mentioned in subsection (6).

(6) The offences are—

(a) an offence under section 51 or 58 of the International Criminal Court Act 2001 (c 17) (genocide, crimes against humanity and war crimes);

(b) an offence under section 52 or 59 of that Act (conduct ancillary to genocide etc committed outside the jurisdiction);

(c) an ancillary offence, as defined in section 55 or 62 of that Act, in relation to an offence falling within paragraph (a) or (b);

(d) an offence under section 1 of the International Criminal Court (Scotland) Act 2001 (asp 13) (genocide, crimes against humanity and war crimes);

(e) an offence under section 2 of that Act (conduct ancillary to genocide etc committed outside the jurisdiction);

(f) an ancillary offence, as defined in section 7 of that Act, in relation to an offence falling within paragraph (d) or (e).

(7) If the conduct constitutes an offence under the military law of the category 2 territory but does not constitute an offence under the general criminal law of the relevant part of the United Kingdom it does not constitute an extradition offence; and subsections (1) to (6) have effect subject to this.

(8) The relevant part of the United Kingdom is the part of the United Kingdom in which—

(a) the extradition hearing took place, if the question of whether conduct constitutes an extradition offence is to be decided by the Secretary of State;

(b) proceedings in which it is necessary to decide that question are taking place, in any other case.

(9) Subsections (1) to (7) apply for the purposes of this Part.

[Extradition Act 2003, s 138.]

8–10299ZZZD   139. The appropriate judge.   (1) The appropriate judge is—

(a) in England and Wales, a District Judge (Magistrates' Courts) designated for the purposes of this Part by the Lord Chancellor;

(b) in Scotland, the sheriff of Lothian and Borders;

(c) in Northern Ireland, such county court judge or resident magistrate as is designated for the purposes of this Part by the Lord Chancellor.

(2) A designation under subsection (1) may be made for all cases or for such cases (or cases of such description) as the designation stipulates.

(3) More than one designation may be made under subsection (1).

(4) This section applies for the purposes of this Part.

[Extradition Act 2003, s 139.]

8–10299ZZZE   140. The extradition hearing.   (1) The extradition hearing is the hearing at which the appropriate judge is to deal with a request for extradition to a category 2 territory.

(2) This section applies for the purposes of this Part.

[Extradition Act 2003, s 140.]

8–10299ZZZF   141. Scotland: references to Secretary of State

PART 3[1]
EXTRADITION TO THE UNITED KINGDOM

Extradition from category 1 territories

8–10299ZZZG   142. Issue of Part 3 warrant.   (1) The appropriate judge may issue a Part 3 warrant in respect of a person if—

(a) a constable or an appropriate person applies to the judge for a Part 3 warrant, and

(b) the condition in subsection (2) is satisfied.

(2) The condition is that a domestic warrant has been issued in respect of the person and there are reasonable grounds for believing—

(a) that the person has committed an extradition offence, or

(b) that the person is unlawfully at large after conviction of an extradition offence by a court in the United Kingdom.

(3) A Part 3 warrant is an arrest warrant which contains—

(a) the statement referred to in subsection (4) or the statement referred to in subsection (5), and
(b) the certificate referred to in subsection (6).

(4) The statement is one that—

(a) the person in respect of whom the warrant is issued is accused in the United Kingdom of the commission of an extradition offence specified in the warrant, and
(b) the warrant is issued with a view to his arrest and extradition to the United Kingdom for the purpose of being prosecuted for the offence.

(5) The statement is one that—

(a) the person in respect of whom the warrant is issued is alleged to be unlawfully at large after conviction of an extradition offence specified in the warrant by a court in the United Kingdom, and
(b) the warrant is issued with a view to his arrest and extradition to the United Kingdom for the purpose of being sentenced for the offence or of serving a sentence of imprisonment or another form of detention imposed in respect of the offence.

(6) The certificate is one certifying—

(a) whether the conduct constituting the extradition offence specified in the warrant falls within the European framework list;
(b) whether the offence is an extra-territorial offence;
(c) what is the maximum punishment that may be imposed on conviction of the offence or (if the person has been sentenced for the offence) what sentence has been imposed.

(7) The conduct which falls within the European framework list must be taken for the purposes of subsection (6)(a) to include conduct which constitutes—

(a) an attempt, conspiracy or incitement to carry out conduct falling within the list, or
(b) aiding, abetting, counselling or procuring the carrying out of conduct falling within the list.

(8) A domestic warrant is a warrant for the arrest or apprehension of a person which is issued under any of these—

(a) section 72 of the Criminal Justice Act 1967 (c 80);
(b) section 7 of the Bail Act 1976 (c 63);
(c) section 51 of the Judicature (Northern Ireland) Act 1978 (c 23);
(d) section 1 of the Magistrates' Courts Act 1980 (c 43);
(e) Article 20 or 25 of the Magistrates' Courts (Northern Ireland) Order 1981 (SI 1981/ 1675 (NI 26));
(f) the Criminal Procedure (Scotland) Act 1995 (c 46).

(9) An appropriate person is a person of a description specified in an order[2] made by the Secretary of State for the purposes of this section.
(10) (*Scotland*).

[Extradition Act 2003, s 142.]

---

1. Part 3 contains ss 142–155.
2. The Extradition Act 2003 (Part 3 Designation) Order, SI 2003/3335 amended by SI 2005/1127, provides that "appropriate persons" for the purposes of s 142 are– (*a*) the Director of the Revenue and Customs Prosecutions Office; (*b*) any member of the Serious Fraud Office designated by the Director of the Serious Fraud Office under s 1(7) of the Criminal Justice Act 1987; (*c*) the Director of Public Prosecutions, any Crown Prosecutor and any counsel or solicitor instructed by the Crown Prosecution Service for the purposes of the case concerned.

8–10299ZZZH 143. *Undertaking in relation to person serving sentence*

8–10299ZZZI 144. *Return to extraditing territory to serve sentence*

8–10299ZZZJ 145. *Service of sentence in territory executing Part 3 warrant*

8–10299ZZZK **146. Dealing with person for other offences.** (1) This section applies if a person is extradited to the United Kingdom from a category 1 territory in pursuance of a Part 3 warrant.
(2) The person may be dealt with in the United Kingdom for an offence committed before his extradition only if—

(a) the offence is one falling within subsection (3), or
(b) the condition in subsection (4) is satisfied.

(3) The offences are—

(a) the offence in respect of which the person is extradited;
(b) an offence disclosed by the information provided to the category 1 territory in respect of that offence;

(c) an extradition offence in respect of which consent to the person being dealt with is given on behalf of the territory;

(d) an offence which is not punishable with imprisonment or another form of detention;

(e) an offence in respect of which the person will not be detained in connection with his trial, sentence or appeal;

(f) an offence in respect of which the person waives the right that he would have (but for this paragraph) not to be dealt with for the offence.

(4) The condition is that the person has been given an opportunity to leave the United Kingdom and—

(a) he has not done so before the end of the permitted period, or

(b) he has done so before the end of the permitted period and has returned to the United Kingdom.

(5) The permitted period is 45 days starting with the day on which the person arrives in the United Kingdom.

[Extradition Act 2003, s 146.]

8–10299ZZZL   147. Effect of consent to extradition to the United Kingdom. (1) This section applies if—

(a) a person is extradited to the United Kingdom from a category 1 territory in pursuance of a Part 3 warrant;

(b) the person consented to his extradition to the United Kingdom in accordance with the law of the category 1 territory.

(2) Section 146(2) does not apply if the conditions in subsection (3) or the conditions in subsection (4) are satisfied.

(3) The conditions are that—

(a) under the law of the category 1 territory, the effect of the person's consent is to waive his right under section 146(2);

(b) the person has not revoked his consent in accordance with that law, if he is permitted to do so under that law.

(4) The conditions are that—

(a) under the law of the category 1 territory, the effect of the person's consent is not to waive his right under section 146(2);

(b) the person has expressly waived his right under section 146(2) in accordance with that law;

(c) the person has not revoked his consent in accordance with that law, if he is permitted to do so under that law;

(d) the person has not revoked the waiver of his right under section 146(2) in accordance with that law, if he is permitted to do so under that law.

[Extradition Act 2003, s 147.]

8–10299ZZZM   148. Extradition offences. (1) Conduct constitutes an extradition offence in relation to the United Kingdom if these conditions are satisfied—

(a) the conduct occurs in the United Kingdom;

(b) the conduct is punishable under the law of the relevant part of the United Kingdom with imprisonment or another form of detention for a term of 12 months or a greater punishment.

(2) Conduct also constitutes an extradition offence in relation to the United Kingdom if these conditions are satisfied—

(a) the conduct occurs outside the United Kingdom;

(b) the conduct constitutes an extra-territorial offence punishable under the law of the relevant part of the United Kingdom with imprisonment or another form of detention for a term of 12 months or a greater punishment.

(3) But subsections (1) and (2) do not apply in relation to conduct of a person if—

(a) he is alleged to be unlawfully at large after conviction by a court in the United Kingdom of the offence constituted by the conduct, and

(b) he has been sentenced for the offence.

(4) Conduct also constitutes an extradition offence in relation to the United Kingdom if these conditions are satisfied—

(a) the conduct occurs in the United Kingdom;

(b) a sentence of imprisonment or another form of detention for a term of 4 months or a greater punishment has been imposed in the United Kingdom in respect of the conduct.

(5) Conduct also constitutes an extradition offence in relation to the United Kingdom if these conditions are satisfied—

(a)   the conduct occurs outside the United Kingdom;
(b)   the conduct constitutes an extra-territorial offence;
(c)   a sentence of imprisonment or another form of detention for a term of 4 months or a greater punishment has been imposed in the United Kingdom in respect of the conduct.

(6)   The relevant part of the United Kingdom is the part of the United Kingdom in which the relevant proceedings are taking place.

(7)   The relevant proceedings are the proceedings in which it is necessary to decide whether conduct constitutes an extradition offence.

(8)   Subsections (1) to (5) apply for the purposes of sections 142 to 147.

[Extradition Act 2003, s 148.]

8–10299ZZZN   149. The appropriate judge.   (1) The appropriate judge is—

(a)   in England and Wales, a District Judge (Magistrates' Courts), a justice of the peace or a judge entitled to exercise the jurisdiction of the Crown Court;
(b)   in Scotland, a sheriff;
(c)   in Northern Ireland, a justice of the peace, a resident magistrate or a Crown Court judge.

(2)   This section applies for the purposes of sections 142 to 147.

[Extradition Act 2003, s 149.]

Extradition from category 2 territories

8–10299ZZZO   150. Dealing with person for other offences: Commonwealth countries etc.
(1)   This section applies if—

(a)   a person is extradited to the United Kingdom from a category 2 territory under law of the territory corresponding to Part 2 of this Act, and
(b)   the territory is a Commonwealth country, a British overseas territory or the Hong Kong Special Administrative Region of the People's Republic of China.

(2)   The person may be dealt with in the United Kingdom for an offence committed before his extradition only if—

(a)   the offence is one falling within subsection (3), or
(b)   the condition in subsection (6) is satisfied.

(3)   The offences are—

(a)   the offence in respect of which the person is extradited;
(b)   a lesser offence disclosed by the information provided to the category 2 territory in respect of that offence;
(c)   an offence in respect of which consent to the person being dealt with is given by or on behalf of the relevant authority.

(4)   An offence is a lesser offence in relation to another offence if the maximum punishment for it is less severe than the maximum punishment for the other offence.

(5)   The relevant authority is—

(a)   if the person has been extradited from a Commonwealth country, the government of the country;
(b)   if the person has been extradited from a British overseas territory, the person administering the territory;
(c)   if the person has been extradited from the Hong Kong Special Administrative Region of the People's Republic of China, the government of the Region.

(6)   The condition is that the protected period has ended.

(7)   The protected period is 45 days starting with the first day after his extradition to the United Kingdom on which the person is given an opportunity to leave the United Kingdom.

(8)   A person is dealt with in the United Kingdom for an offence if—

(a)   he is tried there for it;
(b)   he is detained with a view to trial there for it.

[Extradition Act 2003, s 150.]

8–10299ZZZP   151. Dealing with person for other offences: other category 2 territories.
(1)   This section applies if—

(a)   a person is extradited to the United Kingdom from a category 2 territory under law of the territory corresponding to Part 2 of this Act, and
(b)   the territory is not one falling within section 150(1)(b).

(2)   The person may be dealt with in the United Kingdom for an offence committed before his extradition only if—

(a)   the offence is one falling within subsection (3), or

(b) the condition in subsection (4) is satisfied.

(3) The offences are—

(a) the offence in respect of which the person is extradited;

(b) an offence disclosed by the information provided to the category 2 territory in respect of that offence;

(c) an offence in respect of which consent to the person being dealt with is given on behalf of the territory.

(4) The condition is that—

(a) the person has returned to the territory from which he was extradited, or

(b) the person has been given an opportunity to leave the United Kingdom.

(5) A person is dealt with in the United Kingdom for an offence if—

(a) he is tried there for it;

(b) he is detained with a view to trial there for it.

[Extradition Act 2003, s 151.]

General

8–10299ZZZQ   152. Remission of punishment for other offences.   (1) This section applies if—

(a) a person is extradited to the United Kingdom from—

  (i) a category 1 territory under law of the territory corresponding to Part 1 of this Act, or

  (ii) a category 2 territory under law of the territory corresponding to Part 2 of this Act;

(b) before his extradition he has been convicted of an offence in the United Kingdom;

(c) he has not been extradited in respect of that offence.

(2) The punishment for the offence must be treated as remitted but the person's conviction for the offence must be treated as a conviction for all other purposes.

[Extradition Act 2003, s 152.]

8–10299ZZZR   153. Return of person acquitted or not tried.   (1) This section applies if—

(a) a person is accused in the United Kingdom of the commission of an offence;

(b) the person is extradited to the United Kingdom in respect of the offence from—

  (i) a category 1 territory under law of the territory corresponding to Part 1 of this Act, or

  (ii) a category 2 territory under law of the territory corresponding to Part 2 of this Act;

(c) the condition in subsection (2) or the condition in subsection (3) is satisfied.

(2) The condition is that—

(a) proceedings against the person for the offence are not begun before the end of the required period, which is 6 months starting with the day on which the person arrives in the United Kingdom on his extradition, and

(b) before the end of the period of 3 months starting immediately after the end of the required period the person asks the Secretary of State to return him to the territory from which he was extradited.

(3) The condition is that—

(a) at his trial for the offence the person is acquitted or is discharged under any of the provisions specified in subsection (4), and

(b) before the end of the period of 3 months starting immediately after the date of his acquittal or discharge the person asks the Secretary of State to return him to the territory from which he was extradited.

(4) The provisions are—

(a) section 12(1) of the Powers of Criminal Courts (Sentencing) Act 2000 (c 6);

(b) section 246(1), (2) or (3) of the Criminal Procedure (Scotland) Act 1995 (c 46);

(c) Article 4(1) of the Criminal Justice (Northern Ireland) Order 1996 (SI 1996/3160 (NI 24)).

(5) The Secretary of State must arrange for him to be sent back, free of charge and with as little delay as possible, to the territory from which he was extradited to the United Kingdom in respect of the offence.

(6) If the accusation in subsection (1)(a) relates to the commission of an offence in Scotland, subsections (2)(b), (3)(b) and (5) apply as if the references to the Secretary of State were references to the Scottish Ministers.

[Extradition Act 2003, s 153.]

8–10299ZZZS   154. Restriction on bail where undertaking given by Secretary of State.

(1) This section applies in relation to a person if—

(a) the Secretary of State has given an undertaking in connection with the person's extradition to the United Kingdom, and

(b) the undertaking includes terms that the person be kept in custody until the conclusion of any proceedings against him in the United Kingdom for an offence.

(2) A court, judge or justice of the peace may grant bail to the person in the proceedings only if the court, judge or justice of the peace considers that there are exceptional circumstances which justify it.

[Extradition Act 2003, s 154.]

8–10299ZZZT 155. Service personnel.   The Secretary of State may by order provide for the preceding provisions of this Part to have effect with specified modifications in relation to a case where the person whose extradition is sought or ordered is subject to military law, air-force law or the Naval Discipline Act 1957 (c 53).

[Extradition Act 2003, s 155.]

PART 4[1]
POLICE POWERS

Warrants and orders

8–10299ZZZU 156. Search and seizure warrants.   (1) A justice of the peace may, on an application made to him by a constable, issue a search and seizure warrant if he is satisfied that the requirements for the issue of a search and seizure warrant are fulfilled.

(2) The application for a search and seizure warrant must state that—

(a) the extradition of a person specified in the application is sought under Part 1 or Part 2;

(b) the warrant is sought in relation to premises specified in the application;

(c) the warrant is sought in relation to material, or material of a description, specified in the application;

(d) that material, or material of that description, is believed to be on the premises.

(3) If the application states that the extradition of the person is sought under Part 1, the application must also state that the person is accused in a category 1 territory specified in the application of the commission of an offence—

(a) which is specified in the application, and

(b) which is an extradition offence within the meaning given by section 64.

(4) If the application states that the extradition of the person is sought under Part 2, the application must also state that the person is accused in a category 2 territory specified in the application of the commission of an offence—

(a) which is specified in the application, and

(b) which is an extradition offence within the meaning given by section 137.

(5) A search and seizure warrant is a warrant authorising a constable—

(a) to enter and search the premises specified in the application for the warrant, and

(b) to seize and retain any material found there which falls within subsection (6).

(6) Material falls within this subsection if—

(a) it would be likely to be admissible evidence at a trial in the relevant part of the United Kingdom for the offence specified in the application for the warrant (on the assumption that conduct constituting that offence would constitute an offence in that part of the United Kingdom), and

(b) it does not consist of or include items subject to legal privilege, excluded material or special procedure material.

(7) The relevant part of the United Kingdom is the part of the United Kingdom where the justice of the peace exercises jurisdiction.

(8) The requirements for the issue of a search and seizure warrant are that there are reasonable grounds for believing that—

(a) the offence specified in the application has been committed by the person so specified;

(b) the person is in the United Kingdom or is on his way to the United Kingdom;

(c) the offence is an extradition offence within the meaning given by section 64 (if subsection (3) applies) or section 137 (if subsection (4) applies);

(d) there is material on premises specified in the application which falls within subsection (6);

(e) any of the conditions referred to in subsection (9) is satisfied.

(9) The conditions are—

(a) that it is not practicable to communicate with a person entitled to grant entry to the premises;

(b) that it is practicable to communicate with a person entitled to grant entry to the premises but it is not practicable to communicate with a person entitled to grant access to the material referred to in subsection (8)(d);

(c) that entry to the premises will not be granted unless a warrant is produced;

(d) that the purpose of a search may be frustrated or seriously prejudiced unless a constable arriving at the premises can secure immediate entry to them.

(10) (*Scotland*).

[Extradition Act 2003, s 156.]

---

1. Part 4 contains ss 156–176.

8–10299ZZZV   157. Production orders.   (1) A judge may, on an application made to him by a constable, make a production order if he is satisfied that the requirements for the making of a production order are fulfilled.

(2) The application for a production order must state that—

(a) the extradition of a person specified in the application is sought under Part 1 or Part 2;

(b) the order is sought in relation to premises specified in the application;

(c) the order is sought in relation to material, or material of a description, specified in the application;

(d) the material is special procedure material or excluded material;

(e) a person specified in the application appears to be in possession or control of the material.

(3) If the application states that the extradition of the person is sought under Part 1, the application must also state that the person is accused in a category 1 territory specified in the application of the commission of an offence—

(a) which is specified in the application, and

(b) which is an extradition offence within the meaning given by section 64.

(4) If the application states that the extradition of the person is sought under Part 2, the application must also state that the person is accused in a category 2 territory specified in the application of the commission of an offence—

(a) which is specified in the application, and

(b) which is an extradition offence within the meaning given by section 137.

(5) A production order is an order either—

(a) requiring the person the application for the order specifies as appearing to be in possession or control of special procedure material or excluded material to produce it to a constable (within the period stated in the order) for him to take away, or

(b) requiring that person to give a constable access to the special procedure material or excluded material within the period stated in the order.

(6) The period stated in a production order must be a period of 7 days starting with the day on which the order is made, unless it appears to the judge by whom the order is made that a longer period would be appropriate.

(7) Production orders have effect as if they were orders of the court.

(8) In this section "judge"—

(a) in England and Wales, means a circuit judge;

(b) in Northern Ireland, means a Crown Court judge.

[Extradition Act 2003, s 157.]

8–10299ZZZW   158. Requirements for making of production order.   (1) These are the requirements for the making of a production order.

(2) There must be reasonable grounds for believing that—

(a) the offence specified in the application has been committed by the person so specified;

(b) the person is in the United Kingdom or is on his way to the United Kingdom;

(c) the offence is an extradition offence within the meaning given by section 64 (if section 157(3) applies) or section 137 (if section 157(4) applies);

(d) there is material which consists of or includes special procedure material or excluded material on premises specified in the application;

(e) the material would be likely to be admissible evidence at a trial in the relevant part of the United Kingdom for the offence specified in the application (on the assumption that conduct constituting that offence would constitute an offence in that part of the United Kingdom).

(3) The relevant part of the United Kingdom is the part of the United Kingdom where the judge exercises jurisdiction.

(4) It must appear that other methods of obtaining the material—

(a) have been tried without success, or

(b) have not been tried because they were bound to fail.

(5) It must be in the public interest that the material should be produced or that access to it should be given.

[Extradition Act 2003, s 158.]

8–10299ZZZX   159. Computer information.   (1) This section applies if any of the special procedure material or excluded material specified in an application for a production order consists of information stored in any electronic form.

(2) If the order is an order requiring a person to produce the material to a constable for him to take away, it has effect as an order to produce the material in a form—

(a) in which it can be taken away by him;
(b) in which it is visible and legible or from which it can readily be produced in a visible and legible form.

(3) If the order is an order requiring a person to give a constable access to the material, it has effect as an order to give him access to the material in a form—

(a) in which it is visible and legible, or
(b) from which it can readily be produced in a visible and legible form.

[Extradition Act 2003, s 159.]

8–10299ZZZY   160. Warrants: special procedure material and excluded material.   (1) A judge may, on an application made to him by a constable, issue a warrant under this section if he is satisfied that—

(a) the requirements for the making of a production order are fulfilled, and
(b) the further requirement for the issue of a warrant under this section is fulfilled.

(2) The application for a warrant under this section must state that—

(a) the extradition of a person specified in the application is sought under Part 1 or Part 2;
(b) the warrant is sought in relation to premises specified in the application;
(c) the warrant is sought in relation to material, or material of a description, specified in the application;
(d) the material is special procedure material or excluded material.

(3) If the application states that the extradition of the person is sought under Part 1, the application must also state that the person is accused in a category 1 territory specified in the application of the commission of an offence—

(a) which is specified in the application, and
(b) which is an extradition offence within the meaning given by section 64.

(4) If the application states that the extradition of the person is sought under Part 2, the application must also state that the person is accused in a category 2 territory specified in the application of the commission of an offence—

(a) which is specified in the application, and
(b) which is an extradition offence within the meaning given by section 137.

(5) A warrant under this section authorises a constable to enter and search the premises specified in the application for the warrant and—

(a) to seize and retain any material found there which falls within subsection (6) and which is special procedure material, if the application for the warrant states that the warrant is sought in relation to special procedure material;
(b) to seize and retain any material found there which falls within subsection (6) and which is excluded material, if the application for the warrant states that the warrant is sought in relation to excluded material.

(6) Material falls within this subsection if it would be likely to be admissible evidence at a trial in the relevant part of the United Kingdom for the offence specified in the application for the warrant (on the assumption that conduct constituting that offence would constitute an offence in that part of the United Kingdom).

(7) The relevant part of the United Kingdom is the part of the United Kingdom where the judge exercises jurisdiction.

(8) The further requirement for the issue of a warrant under this section is that any of these conditions is satisfied—

(a) it is not practicable to communicate with a person entitled to grant entry to the premises;
(b) it is practicable to communicate with a person entitled to grant entry to the premises but it is not practicable to communicate with a person entitled to grant access to the material referred to in section 158(2)(d);

(c) the material contains information which is subject to a restriction on disclosure or an obligation of secrecy contained in an enactment (including one passed after this Act) and is likely to be disclosed in breach of the restriction or obligation if a warrant is not issued.

(9) In this section "judge"—

(a) in England and Wales, means a circuit judge;
(b) in Northern Ireland, means a Crown Court judge.

[Extradition Act 2003, s 160.]

Search and seizure without warrant

8–10299ZZZZ **161. Entry and search of premises for purposes of arrest.** (1) This section applies if a constable has power to arrest a person under an extradition arrest power.

(2) A constable may enter and search any premises for the purpose of exercising the power of arrest if he has reasonable grounds for believing that the person is on the premises.

(3) The power to search conferred by subsection (2) is exercisable only to the extent that is reasonably required for the purpose of exercising the power of arrest.

(4) A constable who has entered premises in exercise of the power conferred by subsection (2) may seize and retain anything which is on the premises if he has reasonable grounds for believing—

(a) that it has been obtained in consequence of the commission of an offence or it is evidence in relation to an offence, and
(b) that it is necessary to seize it in order to prevent it being concealed, lost, damaged, altered or destroyed.

(5) An offence includes an offence committed outside the United Kingdom.

(6) If the premises contain 2 or more separate dwellings, the power conferred by subsection (2) is a power to enter and search only—

(a) any parts of the premises which the occupiers of any dwelling comprised in the premises use in common with the occupiers of any other dwelling comprised in the premises, and
(b) any dwelling comprised in the premises in which the constable has reasonable grounds for believing that the person may be.

[Extradition Act 2003, s 161.]

8–10299ZZZZA **162. Entry and search of premises on arrest.** (1) This section applies if a person has been arrested under an extradition arrest power at a place other than a police station.

(2) A constable may enter and search any premises in which the person was at the time of his arrest or immediately before his arrest if he has reasonable grounds for believing—

(a) if the person has not been convicted of the relevant offence, that there is on the premises evidence (other than items subject to legal privilege) relating to the relevant offence;
(b) in any case, that there is on the premises evidence (other than items subject to legal privilege) relating to the identity of the person.

(3) The relevant offence is the offence—

(a) referred to in the Part 1 warrant, if the arrest was under a Part 1 warrant;
(b) in respect of which the constable has reasonable grounds for believing that a Part 1 warrant has been or will be issued, if the arrest was under section 5;
(c) in respect of which extradition is requested, if the arrest was under a warrant issued under section 71;
(d) of which the person is accused, if the arrest was under a provisional warrant.

(4) The power to search conferred by subsection (2)—

(a) if the person has not been convicted of the relevant offence, is a power to search for evidence (other than items subject to legal privilege) relating to the relevant offence;
(b) in any case, is a power to search for evidence (other than items subject to legal privilege) relating to the identity of the person.

(5) The power to search conferred by subsection (2) is exercisable only to the extent that it is reasonably required for the purpose of discovering evidence in respect of which the power is available by virtue of subsection (4).

(6) A constable may seize and retain anything for which he may search by virtue of subsections (4) and (5).

(7) A constable who has entered premises in exercise of the power conferred by subsection (2) may seize and retain anything which is on the premises if he has reasonable grounds for believing—

(a) that it has been obtained in consequence of the commission of an offence or it is evidence in relation to an offence, and
(b) that it is necessary to seize it in order to prevent it being concealed, lost, damaged, altered or destroyed.

(8) An offence includes an offence committed outside the United Kingdom.

(9) If the premises contain 2 or more separate dwellings, the power conferred by subsection (2) is a power to enter and search only—

   (a) any dwelling in which the arrest took place or in which the person was immediately before his arrest, and

   (b) any parts of the premises which the occupier of any such dwelling uses in common with the occupiers of any other dwelling comprised in the premises.

[Extradition Act 2003, s 162.]

8–10299ZZZZB 163. Search of person on arrest.   (1) This section applies if a person has been arrested under an extradition arrest power at a place other than a police station.

(2) A constable may search the person if he has reasonable grounds for believing that the person may present a danger to himself or others.

(3) A constable may search the person if he has reasonable grounds for believing that the person may have concealed on him anything—

   (a) which he might use to assist him to escape from lawful custody;

   (b) which might be evidence relating to an offence or to the identity of the person.

(4) The power to search conferred by subsection (3)—

   (a) is a power to search for anything falling within paragraph (a) or (b) of that subsection;

   (b) is exercisable only to the extent that is reasonably required for the purpose of discovering such a thing.

(5) The powers conferred by subsections (2) and (3)—

   (a) do not authorise a constable to require a person to remove any of his clothing in public, other than an outer coat, jacket or gloves;

   (b) authorise a search of a person's mouth.

(6) A constable searching a person in exercise of the power conferred by subsection (2) may seize and retain anything he finds, if he has reasonable grounds for believing that the person searched might use it to cause physical injury to himself or to any other person.

(7) A constable searching a person in exercise of the power conferred by subsection (3) may seize and retain anything he finds if he has reasonable grounds for believing—

   (a) that the person might use it to assist him to escape from lawful custody;

   (b) that it is evidence of an offence or of the identity of the person or has been obtained in consequence of the commission of an offence.

(8) An offence includes an offence committed outside the United Kingdom.

(9) Nothing in this section affects the power conferred by section 43 of the Terrorism Act 2000 (c 11).

[Extradition Act 2003, s 163.]

8–10299ZZZZC 164. Entry and search of premises after arrest.   (1) This section applies if a person has been arrested under an extradition arrest power.

(2) A constable may enter and search any premises occupied or controlled by the person if the constable has reasonable grounds for suspecting—

   (a) if the person has not been convicted of the relevant offence, that there is on the premises evidence (other than items subject to legal privilege) relating to the relevant offence;

   (b) in any case, that there is on the premises evidence (other than items subject to legal privilege) relating to the identity of the person.

(3) The relevant offence is the offence—

   (a) referred to in the Part 1 warrant, if the arrest was under a Part 1 warrant;

   (b) in respect of which the constable has reasonable grounds for believing that a Part 1 warrant has been or will be issued, if the arrest was under section 5;

   (c) in respect of which extradition is requested, if the arrest was under a warrant issued under section 71;

   (d) of which the person is accused, if the arrest was under a provisional warrant.

(4) The power to search conferred by subsection (2)—

   (a) if the person has not been convicted of the relevant offence, is a power to search for evidence (other than items subject to legal privilege) relating to the relevant offence;

   (b) in any case, is a power to search for evidence (other than items subject to legal privilege) relating to the identity of the person.

(5) The power to search conferred by subsection (2) is exercisable only to the extent that it is reasonably required for the purpose of discovering evidence in respect of which the power is available by virtue of subsection (4).

(6) A constable may seize and retain anything for which he may search by virtue of subsections (4) and (5).

(7) A constable who has entered premises in exercise of the power conferred by subsection (2) may seize and retain anything which is on the premises if he has reasonable grounds for believing—

(a) that it has been obtained in consequence of the commission of an offence or it is evidence in relation to an offence, and

(b) that it is necessary to seize it in order to prevent it being concealed, lost, damaged, altered or destroyed.

(8) An offence includes an offence committed outside the United Kingdom.

(9) The powers conferred by subsections (2) and (6) may be exercised only if a police officer of the rank of inspector or above has given written authorisation for their exercise.

(10) But the power conferred by subsection (2) may be exercised without authorisation under subsection (9) if—

(a) it is exercised before the person arrested is taken to a police station, and

(b) the presence of the person at a place other than a police station is necessary for the effective exercise of the power to search.

(11) Subsections (9) and (10) do not apply to Scotland.

[Extradition Act 2003, s 164.]

8–10299ZZZZD   165. Additional seizure powers.   (*Amends the Criminal Justice and Police Act 2001.*)

Treatment following arrest

8–10299ZZZZE   166. Fingerprints and samples.   (1) This section applies if a person has been arrested under an extradition arrest power and is detained at a police station.

(2) Fingerprints may be taken from the person only if they are taken by a constable—

(a) with the appropriate consent given in writing, or

(b) without that consent, under subsection (4).

(3) A non-intimate sample may be taken from the person only if it is taken by a constable—

(a) with the appropriate consent given in writing, or

(b) without that consent, under subsection (4).

(4) Fingerprints or a non-intimate sample may be taken from the person without the appropriate consent only if a police officer of at least the rank of inspector authorises the fingerprints or sample to be taken.

[Extradition Act 2003, s 166.]

8–10299ZZZZF   167. Searches and examination.   (1) This section applies if a person has been arrested under an extradition arrest power and is detained at a police station.

(2) If a police officer of at least the rank of inspector authorises it, the person may be searched or examined, or both, for the purpose of facilitating the ascertainment of his identity.

(3) An identifying mark found on a search or examination under this section may be photographed—

(a) with the appropriate consent, or

(b) without the appropriate consent, if that consent is withheld or it is not practicable to obtain it.

(4) The only persons entitled to carry out a search or examination, or take a photograph, under this section are—

(a) constables;

(b) persons designated for the purposes of this section by the appropriate police officer.

(5) A person may not under this section—

(a) carry out a search or examination of a person of the opposite sex;

(b) take a photograph of any part of the body (other than the face) of a person of the opposite sex.

(6) An intimate search may not be carried out under this section.

(7) Ascertaining a person's identity includes showing that he is not a particular person.

(8) Taking a photograph includes using a process by means of which a visual image may be produced; and photographing a person must be construed accordingly.

(9) Mark includes features and injuries and a mark is an identifying mark if its existence in a person's case facilitates the ascertainment of his identity.

(10) The appropriate police officer is—

(a) in England and Wales, the chief officer of police for the police area in which the police station in question is situated;

(b) in Northern Ireland, the Chief Constable of the Police Service of Northern Ireland.

[Extradition Act 2003, s 167.]

8–10299ZZZZG   168. Photographs.   (1) This section applies if a person has been arrested under an extradition arrest power and is detained at a police station.

(2) The person may be photographed—

(a)   with the appropriate consent, or

(b)   without the appropriate consent, if that consent is withheld or it is not practicable to obtain it.

(3) A person proposing to take a photograph of a person under this section—

(a)   may for the purpose of doing so require the removal of any item or substance worn on or over the whole or any part of the head or face of the person to be photographed, and

(b)   if the requirement is not complied with may remove the item or substance himself.

(4) The only persons entitled to take a photograph under this section are—

(a)   constables;

(b)   persons designated for the purposes of this section by the appropriate police officer.

(5) Taking a photograph includes using a process by means of which a visual image may be produced; and photographing a person must be construed accordingly.

(6) The appropriate police officer is—

(a)   in England and Wales, the chief officer of police for the police area in which the police station in question is situated;

(b)   in Northern Ireland, the Chief Constable of the Police Service of Northern Ireland.

[Extradition Act 2003, s 168.]

8–10299ZZZZH   169. Evidence of identity: England and Wales.   (*Amends the Police and Criminal Evidence Act 1984 by disapplying certain provisions to persons arrested under an extradition arrest power.*)

8–10299ZZZZI   170.   *Evidence of identity: Northern Ireland*

8–10299ZZZZJ   171. Other treatment and rights.   (1) This section applies in relation to cases where a person—

(a)   is arrested under an extradition arrest power at a police station;

(b)   is taken to a police station after being arrested elsewhere under an extradition arrest power;

(c)   is detained at a police station after being arrested under an extradition arrest power.

(2) In relation to those cases the Secretary of State may by order[1] apply the provisions mentioned in subsections (3) and (4) with specified modifications.

(3) The provisions are these provisions of the Police and Criminal Evidence Act 1984 (c 60)—

(a)   section 54 (searches of detained persons);

(b)   section 55 (intimate searches);

(c)   section 56 (right to have someone informed when arrested);

(d)   section 58 (access to legal advice).

(4) (Northern Ireland).

[Extradition Act 2003, s 171.]

---

1. The Extradition Act 2003 (Police Powers) Order 2003, SI 2003/3106 provides:

"**2.**—(1) Sections 54, 55, 56 and 58 of the Police and Criminal Evidence Act 1984 apply in the circumstances described in section 171(1) of the Extradition Act 2003 with the following modifications.

(2) In sections 54(4)(b) and 55(12)(b) for 'an offence' there is substituted 'a relevant offence (within the meaning of section 164(3) of the Extradition Act 2003)'.

(3) In sections 56(2)(a), 56(5)(a), 58(6)(a) and 58(8)(a) for 'a serious arrestable offence' there is substituted 'a relevant offence (within the meaning of section 164(3) of the Extradition Act 2003) that would be a serious arrestable offence if it had been committed in England and Wales'.

(4) Sections 56(5A), 56(5B), 58(8A) and 58(8B) are omitted."

Delivery of seized property

8–10299ZZZZK   172. Delivery of seized property.   (1) This section applies to—

(a)   anything which has been seized or produced under this Part, or

(b)   anything which has been seized under section 50 or 51 of the Criminal Justice and Police Act 2001 (c 16) in reliance on a power of seizure conferred by this Part.

(2) A constable may deliver any such thing to a person who is or is acting on behalf of an authority if the constable has reasonable grounds for believing that the authority—

(a)   is an authority of the relevant territory, and

(b)   has functions such that it is appropriate for the thing to be delivered to it.

(3) If the relevant seizure power was a warrant issued under this Part, or the thing was produced

under an order made under this Part, the relevant territory is the category 1 or category 2 territory specified in the application for the warrant or order.

(4) If the relevant seizure power was section 161(4), 162(6) or (7), 163(6) or (7) or 164(6) or (7), the relevant territory is—

(a) the territory in which the Part 1 warrant was issued, in a case where the applicable extradition arrest power is a Part 1 warrant in respect of which a certificate under section 2 has been issued;

(b) the territory in which a constable has reasonable grounds for believing that a Part 1 warrant has been or will be issued, in a case where the applicable extradition arrest power is section 5;

(c) the territory to which a person's extradition is requested, in a case where the applicable extradition arrest power is a warrant issued under section 71;

(d) the territory in which a person is accused of the commission of an offence or has been convicted of an offence, in a case where the applicable extradition arrest power is a provisional warrant.

(5) The applicable extradition arrest power is—

(a) the extradition arrest power under which a constable had a power of arrest, if the relevant seizure power was section 161(4);

(b) the extradition arrest power under which a person was arrested, if the relevant seizure power was section 162(6) or (7), 163(6) or (7) or 164(6) or (7).

(6) The relevant seizure power is—

(a) the power under which the thing was seized, or

(b) the power in reliance on which the thing was seized under section 50 or 51 of the Criminal Justice and Police Act 2001 (c 16).

(7)–(9) (*Scotland*).

[Extradition Act 2003, s 172.]

Codes of practice

8–10299ZZZZL **173. Codes of practice.** (1) The Secretary of State must issue codes of practice in connection with—

(a) the exercise of the powers conferred by this Part;

(b) the retention, use and return of anything seized or produced under this Part;

(c) access to and the taking of photographs and copies of anything so seized or produced;

(d) the retention, use, disclosure and destruction of fingerprints, a sample or a photograph taken under this Part.

(2) If the Secretary of State proposes to issue a code of practice under this section he must—

(a) publish a draft of the code;

(b) consider any representations made to him about the draft;

(c) if he thinks it appropriate, modify the draft in the light of any such representations.

(3) The Secretary of State must lay the code before Parliament.

(4) When he has done so he may bring the code into operation by order[1].

(5) The Secretary of State may revise the whole or any part of a code issued under this section and issue the code as revised; and subsections (2) to (4) apply to such a revised code as they apply to the original code.

(6) A failure by a constable to comply with a provision of a code issued under this section does not of itself make him liable to criminal or civil proceedings.

(7) A code issued under this section is admissible in evidence in proceedings under this Act and must be taken into account by a judge or court in determining any question to which it appears to the judge or the court to be relevant.

(8) If the Secretary of State publishes a draft code of practice in connection with a matter specified in subsection (1) before the date on which this section comes into force—

(a) the draft is as effective as one published under subsection (2) on or after that date;

(b) representations made to the Secretary of State about the draft before that date are as effective as representations made to him about it after that date;

(c) modifications made by the Secretary of State to the draft in the light of any such representations before that date are as effective as any such modifications made by him on or after that date.

[Extradition Act 2003, s 173.]

---

1. The Extradition Act 2003 (Police Powers: Codes of Practice) Order, SI 2003/3336 has been made which provides that the codes of practice entitled "Extradition Act 2003: Codes of Practice" laid before Parliament on 2nd December 2003 came into operation on 1st January 2004.

General

8–10299ZZZZM **174. Interpretation.** (1) Subsections (2) to (8) apply for the purposes of this Part.

(2) Each of these is an extradition arrest power—

(a) a Part 1 warrant in respect of which a certificate under section 2 has been issued;
(b) section 5;
(c) a warrant issued under section 71;
(d) a provisional warrant.

(3) "Excluded material"—

(a) in England and Wales, has the meaning given by section 11 of the 1984 Act;
(b) in Northern Ireland, has the meaning given by Article 13 of the 1989 Order.

(4) "Items subject to legal privilege"—

(a) in England and Wales, has the meaning given by section 10 of the 1984 Act;
(b) in Scotland, has the meaning given by section 412 of the 2002 Act;
(c) in Northern Ireland, has the meaning given by Article 12 of the 1989 Order.

(5) "Premises"—

(a) in England and Wales, has the meaning given by section 23 of the 1984 Act;
(b) in Scotland, has the meaning given by section 412 of the 2002 Act;
(c) in Northern Ireland, has the meaning given by Article 25 of the 1989 Order.

(6) "Special procedure material"—

(a) in England and Wales, has the meaning given by section 14 of the 1984 Act;
(b) in Northern Ireland, has the meaning given by Article 16 of the 1989 Order.

(7) The expressions in subsection (8) have the meanings given—

(a) in England and Wales, by section 65 of the 1984 Act;
(b) in Northern Ireland, by Article 53 of the 1989 Order.

(8) The expressions are—

(a) appropriate consent;
(b) fingerprints;
(c) intimate search;
(d) non-intimate sample.

(9) The 1984 Act is the Police and Criminal Evidence Act 1984 (c 60).
(10) The 1989 Order is the Police and Criminal Evidence (Northern Ireland) Order 1989 (SI 1989/1341 (NI 12)).
(11) The 2002 Act is the Proceeds of Crime Act 2002 (c 29).

[Extradition Act 2003, s 174.]

8–10299ZZZZN 175. Customs officers. The Treasury may by order provide for any provision of this Part which applies in relation to police officers or persons arrested by police officers to apply with specified modifications in relation to customs officers or persons arrested by customs officers.

[Extradition Act 2003, s 175.]

8–10299ZZZZO 176. Service policemen. The Secretary of State may by order[1] provide for any provision of this Part which applies in relation to police officers or persons arrested by police officers to apply with specified modifications in relation to service policemen or persons arrested by service policemen.

[Extradition Act 2003, s 176.]

Part 5[1]

MISCELLANEOUS AND GENERAL

British overseas territories

8–10299ZZZZP 177. Extradition from British overseas territories. (1) This section applies in relation to extradition—

(a) from a British overseas territory to a category 1 territory;
(b) from a British overseas territory to the United Kingdom;
(c) from a British overseas territory to a category 2 territory;
(d) from a British overseas territory to any of the Channel Islands or the Isle of Man.

(2) An Order in Council may provide for any provision of this Act applicable to extradition from the United Kingdom to apply to extradition in a case falling within subsection (1)(a) or (b).

(3) An Order in Council may provide for any provision of this Act applicable to extradition from the United Kingdom to a category 2 territory to apply to extradition in a case falling within subsection (1)(c) or (d).

(4) An Order in Council under this section may provide that the provision applied has effect with specified modifications.

[Extradition Act 2003, s 177.]

---

1. Part 5 contains ss 177–227 and Schs 1–4.

8–10299ZZZZQ 178. Extradition to British overseas territories. (1) This section applies in relation to extradition—

    (a) to a British overseas territory from a category 1 territory;
    (b) to a British overseas territory from the United Kingdom;
    (c) to a British overseas territory from a category 2 territory;
    (d) to a British overseas territory from any of the Channel Islands or the Isle of Man.

(2) An Order in Council may provide for any provision of this Act applicable to extradition to the United Kingdom to apply to extradition in a case falling within subsection (1)(a) or (b).

(3) An Order in Council may provide for any provision of this Act applicable to extradition to the United Kingdom from a category 2 territory to apply to extradition in a case falling within subsection (1)(c) or (d).

(4) An Order in Council under this section may provide that the provision applied has effect with specified modifications.

[Extradition Act 2003, s 178.]

Competing extradition claims

8–10299ZZZZR 179. Competing claims to extradition. (1) This section applies if at the same time—

    (a) there is a Part 1 warrant in respect of a person, a certificate has been issued under section 2 in respect of the warrant, and the person has not been extradited in pursuance of the warrant or discharged, and
    (b) there is a request for the same person's extradition, a certificate has been issued under section 70 in respect of the request, and the person has not been extradited in pursuance of the request or discharged.

(2) The Secretary of State may—

    (a) order proceedings (or further proceedings) on one of them (the warrant or the request) to be deferred until the other one has been disposed of, if neither the warrant nor the request has been disposed of;
    (b) order the person's extradition in pursuance of the warrant to be deferred until the request has been disposed of, if an order for his extradition in pursuance of the warrant has been made;
    (c) order the person's extradition in pursuance of the request to be deferred until the warrant has been disposed of, if an order for his extradition in pursuance of the request has been made.

(3) In applying subsection (2) the Secretary of State must take account in particular of these matters—

    (a) the relative seriousness of the offences concerned;
    (b) the place where each offence was committed (or was alleged to have been committed);
    (c) the date when the warrant was issued and the date when the request was received;
    (d) whether, in the case of each offence, the person is accused of its commission (but not alleged to have been convicted) or is alleged to be unlawfully at large after conviction.

(4) If both the certificates referred to in subsection (1) are issued in Scotland, the preceding provisions of this section apply as if the references to the Secretary of State were to the Scottish Ministers.

[Extradition Act 2003, s 179.]

8–10299ZZZZS 180. Proceedings on deferred warrant or request. (1) This section applies if—

    (a) an order is made under this Act deferring proceedings on an extradition claim in respect of a person (the deferred claim) until another extradition claim in respect of the person has been disposed of, and
    (b) the other extradition claim is disposed of.

(2) The judge may make an order for proceedings on the deferred claim to be resumed.

(3) No order under subsection (2) may be made after the end of the required period.

(4) If the person applies to the appropriate judge to be discharged, the judge may order his discharge.

(5) If the person applies to the appropriate judge to be discharged, the judge must order his discharge if—

    (a) the required period has ended, and

(b) the judge has not made an order under subsection (2) or ordered the person's discharge.

(6) The required period is 21 days starting with the day on which the other extradition claim is disposed of.

(7) If the proceedings on the deferred claim were under Part 1, section 67 applies for determining the appropriate judge.

(8) If the proceedings on the deferred claim were under Part 2, section 139 applies for determining the appropriate judge.

(9) An extradition claim is made in respect of a person if—

(a) a Part 1 warrant is issued in respect of him;

(b) a request for his extradition is made.

[Extradition Act 2003, s 180.]

8–10299ZZZZT   **181. Proceedings where extradition deferred.** (1) This section applies if—

(a) an order is made under this Act deferring a person's extradition in pursuance of an extradition claim (the deferred claim) until another extradition claim in respect of him has been disposed of;

(b) the other extradition claim is disposed of.

(2) The judge may make an order for the person's extradition in pursuance of the deferred claim to cease to be deferred.

(3) No order under subsection (2) may be made after the end of the required period.

(4) If the person applies to the appropriate judge to be discharged, the judge may order his discharge.

(5) If the person applies to the appropriate judge to be discharged, the judge must order his discharge if—

(a) the required period has ended, and

(b) the judge has not made an order under subsection (2) or ordered the person's discharge.

(6) The required period is 21 days starting with the day on which the other extradition claim is disposed of.

(7) If the person's extradition in pursuance of the deferred claim was ordered under Part 1, section 67 applies for determining the appropriate judge.

(8) If the person's extradition in pursuance of the deferred claim was ordered under Part 2, section 139 applies for determining the appropriate judge.

(9) An extradition claim is made in respect of a person if—

(a) a Part 1 warrant is issued in respect of him;

(b) a request for his extradition is made.

[Extradition Act 2003, s 181.]

Legal aid

8–10299ZZZZU   **182.** *Legal advice, assistance and representation: England and Wales*

8–10299ZZZZV   **183.** *Legal aid: Scotland*

8–10299ZZZZW   **184.** *Grant of free legal aid: Northern Ireland**

---

*Repealed by SI 2005/1965 from a date to be appointed.

8–10299ZZZZX   **185.** *Free legal aid: supplementary**

---

*Repealed by SI 2005/1965 from a date to be appointed.

Re-extradition

8–10299ZZZZY   **186. Re-extradition: preliminary.** (1) Section 187 applies in relation to a person if the conditions in subsections (2) to (6) are satisfied.

(2) The first condition is that the person was extradited to a territory in accordance with Part 1 or Part 2.

(3) The second condition is that the person was serving a sentence of imprisonment or another form of detention in the United Kingdom (the UK sentence) before he was extradited.

(4) The third condition is that—

(a) if the person was extradited in accordance with Part 1, the Part 1 warrant in pursuance of which he was extradited contained a statement that it was issued with a view to his extradition for the purpose of being prosecuted for an offence;

(b) if the person was extradited in accordance with Part 2, the request in pursuance of which the person was extradited contained a statement that the person was accused of the commission of an offence.

(5) The fourth condition is that a certificate issued by a judicial authority of the territory shows that—

(a) a sentence of imprisonment or another form of detention for a term of 4 months or a greater punishment (the overseas sentence) was imposed on the person in the territory;
(b) the overseas sentence was imposed on him in respect of—

    (i) the offence specified in the warrant or request, or
    (ii) any other offence committed before his extradition in respect of which he was permitted to be dealt with in the territory.

(6) The fifth condition is that before serving the overseas sentence the person was returned to the United Kingdom to serve the remainder of the UK sentence.

[Extradition Act 2003, s 186.]

8–10299ZZZZZ   **187. Re-extradition hearing.**   (1) If this section applies in relation to a person, as soon as practicable after the relevant time the person must be brought before the appropriate judge for the judge to decide whether the person is to be extradited again to the territory in which the overseas sentence was imposed.

(2) The relevant time is the time at which the person would otherwise be released from detention pursuant to the UK sentence (whether or not on licence).

(3) If subsection (1) is not complied with and the person applies to the judge to be discharged, the judge must order his discharge.

(4) The person must be treated as continuing in legal custody until he is brought before the appropriate judge under subsection (1) or he is discharged under subsection (3).

(5) If the person is brought before the appropriate judge under subsection (1) the judge must decide whether the territory in which the overseas sentence was imposed is—

(a) a category 1 territory;
(b) a category 2 territory;
(c) neither a category 1 territory nor a category 2 territory.

(6) If the judge decides that the territory is a category 1 territory, section 188 applies.

(7) If the judge decides that the territory is a category 2 territory, section 189 applies.

(8) If the judge decides that the territory is neither a category 1 territory nor a category 2 territory, he must order the person's discharge.

(9) A person's discharge as a result of this section or section 188 or 189 does not affect any conditions on which he is released from detention pursuant to the UK sentence.

(10) Section 139 applies for determining the appropriate judge for the purposes of this section.

[Extradition Act 2003, s 187.]

8–10299ZZZZZA   **188. Re-extradition to category 1 territories.**   (1) If this section applies, this Act applies as it would if—

(a) a Part 1 warrant had been issued in respect of the person;
(b) the warrant contained a statement that—

    (i) the person was alleged to be unlawfully at large after conviction of the relevant offence, and
    (ii) the warrant was issued with a view to the person's arrest and extradition to the territory for the purpose of serving a sentence imposed in respect of the relevant offence;

(c) the warrant were issued by the authority of the territory which issued the certificate referred to in section 186(5);
(d) the relevant offence were specified in the warrant;
(e) the judge were the appropriate judge for the purposes of Part 1;
(f) the hearing at which the judge is to make the decision referred to in section 187(1) were the extradition hearing;
(g) the proceedings before the judge were under Part 1.

(2) As applied by subsection (1) this Act has effect with the modifications set out in Part 1 of Schedule 1.

(3) The relevant offence is the offence in respect of which the overseas sentence is imposed.

[Extradition Act 2003, s 188.]

8–10299ZZZZZB   **189. Re-extradition to category 2 territories.**   (1) If this section applies, this Act applies as it would if—

(a) a valid request for the person's extradition to the territory had been made;

(b) the request contained a statement that the person was alleged to be unlawfully at large after conviction of the relevant offence;
(c) the relevant offence were specified in the request;
(d) the hearing at which the appropriate judge is to make the decision referred to in section 187(1) were the extradition hearing;
(e) the proceedings before the judge were under Part 2.

(2) As applied by subsection (1) this Act has effect with the modifications set out in Part 2 of Schedule 1.
(3) The relevant offence is the offence in respect of which the overseas sentence is imposed.

[Extradition Act 2003, s 189.]

Conduct of extradition proceedings

8–10299ZZZZZC 190. Crown Prosecution Service: role in extradition proceedings. (*Amends the Prosecution of Offences Act 1985.*)

8–10299ZZZZZD 191. *Lord Advocate: role in extradition proceedings*

8–10299ZZZZZE 192. *Northern Ireland DPP and Crown Solicitor: role in extradition proceedings*

Parties to international Conventions

8–10299ZZZZZF 193. Parties to international Conventions. (1) A territory may be designated by order[1] made by the Secretary of State if—

(a) it is not a category 1 territory or a category 2 territory, and
(b) it is a party to an international Convention to which the United Kingdom is a party.

(2) This Act applies in relation to a territory designated by order under subsection (1) as if the territory were a category 2 territory.
(3) As applied to a territory by subsection (2), this Act has effect as if—

(a) sections 71(4), 73(5), 74(11)(b), 84(7), 86(7), 137 and 138 were omitted;
(b) the conduct that constituted an extradition offence for the purposes of Part 2 were the conduct specified in relation to the territory in the order under subsection (1) designating the territory.

(4) Conduct may be specified in relation to a territory in an order under subsection (1) designating the territory only if it is conduct to which the relevant Convention applies.
(5) The relevant Convention is the Convention referred to in subsection (1)(*b*) which is specified in relation to the territory in the order under subsection (1) designating it.

[Extradition Act 2003, s 193.]

---

1. The Extradition Act 2003 (Parties to International Conventions) Order 2005, SI 2005/46 has been made, which establishes extradition relations with territories that are parties to certain international Conventions which give rise to extradition relations in relation to specific conduct. The text of the Order may be found at the HMSO website – http://www.hmso.gov.uk/stat.htm.

Special extradition arrangements

8–10299ZZZZZG 194. Special extradition arrangements. (1) This section applies if the Secretary of State believes that—

(a) arrangements have been made between the United Kingdom and another territory for the extradition of a person to the territory, and
(b) the territory is not a category 1 territory or a category 2 territory.

(2) The Secretary of State may certify that the conditions in paragraphs (a) and (b) of subsection (1) are satisfied in relation to the extradition of the person.
(3) If the Secretary of State issues a certificate under subsection (2) this Act applies in respect of the person's extradition to the territory as if the territory were a category 2 territory.
(4) As applied by subsection (3), this Act has effect—

(a) as if sections 71(4), 73(5), 74(11)(b), 84(7) and 86(7) were omitted;
(b) with any other modifications specified in the certificate.

(5) A certificate under subsection (2) in relation to a person is conclusive evidence that the conditions in paragraphs (a) and (b) of subsection (1) are satisfied in relation to the person's extradition.

[Extradition Act 2003, s 194.]

Human rights

8–10299ZZZZZH 195. Human rights: appropriate tribunal. (1) The appropriate judge is the only appropriate tribunal in relation to proceedings under section 7(1)(a) of the Human Rights Act

1998 (c 42) (proceedings for acts incompatible with Convention rights) if the proceedings relate to extradition under Part 1 or Part 2 of this Act.

(2) If the proceedings relate to extradition under Part 1, section 67 applies for determining the appropriate judge.

(3) If the proceedings relate to extradition under Part 2, section 139 applies for determining the appropriate judge.

[Extradition Act 2003, s 195.]

Genocide etc

8–10299ZZZZZI   196. Genocide, crimes against humanity and war crimes.   (1) This section applies if—

(a) a Part 1 warrant in respect of a person is issued in respect of an offence mentioned in subsection (2), or

(b) a valid request for a person's extradition is made in respect of an offence mentioned in subsection (2).

(2) The offences are—

(a) an offence that if committed in the United Kingdom would be punishable as an offence under section 51 or 58 of the International Criminal Court Act 2001 (c 17) (genocide, crimes against humanity and war crimes);

(b) an offence that if committed in the United Kingdom would be punishable as an offence under section 52 or 59 of that Act (conduct ancillary to genocide, etc committed outside the jurisdiction);

(c) an offence that if committed in the United Kingdom would be punishable as an ancillary offence, as defined in section 55 or 62 of that Act, in relation to an offence falling within paragraph (a) or (b);

(d) an offence that if committed in the United Kingdom would be punishable as an offence under section 1 of the International Criminal Court (Scotland) Act 2001 (asp 13) (genocide, crimes against humanity and war crimes);

(e) an offence that if committed in the United Kingdom would be punishable as an offence under section 2 of that Act (conduct ancillary to genocide etc committed outside the jurisdiction);

(f) an offence that if committed in the United Kingdom would be punishable as an ancillary offence, as defined in section 7 of that Act, in relation to an offence falling within paragraph (d) or (e);

(g) any offence punishable in the United Kingdom under section 1 of the Geneva Conventions Act 1957 (c 52) (grave breach of scheduled conventions).

(3) It is not an objection to extradition under this Act that the person could not have been punished for the offence under the law in force at the time when and in the place where he is alleged to have committed the act of which he is accused or of which he has been convicted.

[Extradition Act 2003, s 196.]

Custody and bail

8–10299ZZZZZJ   197. Custody.   (1) If a judge remands a person in custody under this Act, the person must be committed to the institution to which he would have been committed if charged with an offence before the judge.

(2) If a person in custody following his arrest under Part 1 or Part 2 escapes from custody, he may be retaken in any part of the United Kingdom in the same way as he could have been if he had been in custody following his arrest or apprehension under a relevant domestic warrant.

(3) A relevant domestic warrant is a warrant for his arrest or apprehension issued in the part of the United Kingdom in question in respect of an offence committed there.

(4) Subsection (5) applies if—

(a) a person is in custody in one part of the United Kingdom (whether under this Act or otherwise);

(b) he is required to be removed to another part of the United Kingdom after being remanded in custody under this Act;

(c) he is so removed by sea or air.

(5) The person must be treated as continuing in legal custody until he reaches the place to which he is required to be removed.

(6) An order for a person's extradition under this Act is sufficient authority for an appropriate person—

(a) to receive him;

(b) to keep him in custody until he is extradited under this Act;

(c) to convey him to the territory to which he is to be extradited under this Act.

(7) An appropriate person is—

(a) a person to whom the order is directed;
(b) a constable.

[Extradition Act 2003, s 197.]

8–10299ZZZZZK   198. Bail: England and Wales.   (*Amends the Bail Act 1976.*)

8–10299ZZZZZL   199. Bail: Scotland

8–10299ZZZZZM   200. Appeal against grant of bail.   (*Amends the Bail (Amendment) Act 1993.*)

8–10299ZZZZZN   201. Remand to local authority accommodation.   (*Amends s 23 of the Children and Young Persons Act 1969.*)

Evidence

8–10299ZZZZZO   202. Receivable documents.   (1) A Part 1 warrant may be received in evidence in proceedings under this Act.

(2) Any other document issued in a category 1 territory may be received in evidence in proceedings under this Act if it is duly authenticated.

(3) A document issued in a category 2 territory may be received in evidence in proceedings under this Act if it is duly authenticated.

(4) A document issued in a category 1 or category 2 territory is duly authenticated if (and only if) one of these applies—

(a) it purports to be signed by a judge, magistrate or other judicial authority of the territory;
(b) it purports to be authenticated by the oath or affirmation of a witness.

(5) Subsections (2) and (3) do not prevent a document that is not duly authenticated from being received in evidence in proceedings under this Act.

[Extradition Act 2003, s 202.]

8–10299ZZZZZP   203. Documents sent by facsimile.   (1) This section applies if a document to be sent in connection with proceedings under this Act is sent by facsimile transmission.

(2) This Act has effect as if the document received by facsimile transmission were the document used to make the transmission.

[Extradition Act 2003, s 203.]

8–10299ZZZZZQ   204. Part 1 warrant: transmission by other electronic means.   (1) This section applies if a Part 1 warrant is issued and the information contained in the warrant—

(a) is transmitted to the designated authority by electronic means (other than by facsimile transmission), and
(b) is received by the designated authority in a form in which it is intelligible and which is capable of being used for subsequent reference.

(2) This Act has effect as if the information received by the designated authority were the Part 1 warrant.

(3) A copy of the information received by the designated authority may be received in evidence as if it were the Part 1 warrant.

[Extradition Act 2003, s 204.]

8–10299ZZZZZR   205. Written statements and admissions.   (1) The provisions mentioned in subsection (2) apply in relation to proceedings under this Act as they apply in relation to proceedings for an offence.

(2) The provisions are—

(a) section 9 of the Criminal Justice Act 1967 (c 80) (proof by written statement in criminal proceedings);
(b) section 10 of the Criminal Justice Act 1967 (proof by formal admission in criminal proceedings);
(c) section 1 of the Criminal Justice (Miscellaneous Provisions) Act (Northern Ireland) 1968 (c 28) (proof by written statement in criminal proceedings);
(d) section 2 of the Criminal Justice (Miscellaneous Provisions) Act (Northern Ireland) 1968 (proof by formal admission in criminal proceedings).

(3) As applied by subsection (1) in relation to proceedings under this Act, section 10 of the Criminal Justice Act 1967 and section 2 of the Criminal Justice (Miscellaneous Provisions) Act (Northern Ireland) 1968 have effect as if—

(a) references to the defendant were to the person whose extradition is sought (or who has been extradited);

(b) references to the prosecutor were to the category 1 or category 2 territory concerned;
(c) references to the trial were to the proceedings under this Act for the purposes of which the admission is made;
(d) references to subsequent criminal proceedings were to subsequent proceedings under this Act.

[Extradition Act 2003, s 205.]

8–10299ZZZZZS   206. Burden and standard of proof.   (1) This section applies if, in proceedings under this Act, a question arises as to burden or standard of proof.

(2) The question must be decided by applying any enactment or rule of law that would apply if the proceedings were proceedings for an offence.

(3) Any enactment or rule of law applied under subsection (2) to proceedings under this Act must be applied as if—

(a) the person whose extradition is sought (or who has been extradited) were accused of an offence;
(b) the category 1 or category 2 territory concerned were the prosecution.

(4) Subsections (2) and (3) are subject to any express provision of this Act.

(5) In this section "enactment" includes an enactment comprised in, or in an instrument made under, an Act of the Scottish Parliament.

[Extradition Act 2003, s 206.]

8–10299ZZZZZT

Other miscellaneous provisions

207. Extradition for more than one offence.   The Secretary of State may by order[1] provide for this Act to have effect with specified modifications in relation to a case where—

(a) a Part 1 warrant is issued in respect of more than one offence;
(b) a request for extradition is made in respect of more than one offence.

[Extradition Act 2003, s 207.]

---

1. See the Extradition Act 2003 (Multiple Offences) Order 2003, SI 2003/3150 in Part X: Stop Press, Miscellaneous Legislation, *post*.

8–10299ZZZZZU   208. National security.   (1) This section applies if the Secretary of State believes that the conditions in subsections (2) to (4) are satisfied in relation to a person.

(2) The first condition is that the person's extradition is sought or will be sought under Part 1 or Part 2 in respect of an offence.

(3) The second condition is that—

(a) in engaging in the conduct constituting (or alleged to constitute) the offence the person was acting for the purpose of assisting in the exercise of a function conferred or imposed by or under an enactment, or
(b) as a result of an authorisation given by the Secretary of State the person is not liable under the criminal law of any part of the United Kingdom for the conduct constituting (or alleged to constitute) the offence.

(4) The third condition is that the person's extradition in respect of the offence would be against the interests of national security.

(5) The Secretary of State may certify that the conditions in subsections (2) to (4) are satisfied in relation to the person.

(6) If the Secretary of State issues a certificate under subsection (5) he may—

(a) direct that a Part 1 warrant issued in respect of the person and in respect of the offence is not to be proceeded with, or
(b) direct that a request for the person's extradition in respect of the offence is not to be proceeded with.

(7) If the Secretary of State issues a certificate under subsection (5) he may order the person's discharge (instead of or in addition to giving a direction under subsection (6)).

(8) These rules apply if the Secretary of State gives a direction under subsection (6)(a) in respect of a warrant—

(a) if the designated authority has not issued a certificate under section 2 in respect of the warrant it must not do so;
(b) if the person is arrested under the warrant or under section 5 there is no requirement for him to be brought before the appropriate judge and he must be discharged;
(c) if the person is brought before the appropriate judge under section 4 or 6 the judge is no longer required to proceed or continue proceeding under sections 7 and 8;

(d) if the extradition hearing has begun the judge is no longer required to proceed or continue proceeding under sections 10 to 25;

(e) if the person has consented to his extradition, the judge is no longer required to order his extradition;

(f) if an appeal to the High Court or House of Lords has been brought, the court is no longer required to hear or continue hearing the appeal;

(g) if the person's extradition has been ordered there is no requirement for him to be extradited.

(9) These rules apply if the Secretary of State gives a direction under subsection (6)(b) in respect of a request—

(a) if he has not issued a certificate under section 70 in respect of the request he is no longer required to do so;

(b) if the person is arrested under a warrant issued under section 71 or under a provisional warrant there is no requirement for him to appear or be brought before the appropriate judge and he must be discharged;

(c) if the person appears or is brought before the appropriate judge the judge is no longer required to proceed or continue proceeding under sections 72, 74, 75 and 76;

(d) if the extradition hearing has begun the judge is no longer required to proceed or continue proceeding under sections 78 to 91;

(e) if the person has given his consent to his extradition to the appropriate judge, the judge is no longer required to send the case to the Secretary of State for his decision whether the person is to be extradited;

(f) if an appeal to the High Court or House of Lords has been brought, the court is no longer required to hear or continue hearing the appeal;

(g) if the person's extradition has been ordered there is no requirement for him to be extradited.

(10) These must be made under the hand of the Secretary of State—

(a) a certificate under subsection (5);

(b) a direction under subsection (6);

(c) an order under subsection (7).

(11) The preceding provisions of this section apply to Scotland with these modifications—

(a) in subsection (9)(a) for "he has" substitute "the Scottish Ministers have" and for "he is" substitute "they are";

(b) in subsection (9)(e) for "Secretary of State for his" substitute "Scottish Ministers for their".

(12) In subsection (3) the reference to an enactment includes an enactment comprised in, or in an instrument made under, an Act of the Scottish Parliament.

[Extradition Act 2003, s 208.]

8–10299ZZZZZV   209. Reasonable force.   A person may use reasonable force, if necessary, in the exercise of a power conferred by this Act.

[Extradition Act 2003, s 209.]

8–10299ZZZZZW   210. Rules of court.   (1) Rules of court may make provision as to the practice and procedure to be followed in connection with proceedings under this Act.

(2) In Scotland any rules of court under this Act are to be made by Act of Adjournal.

[Extradition Act 2003, s 210.]

8–10299ZZZZZX   211. Service of notices.   Service of a notice on a person under section 54, 56, 58, 129, 130 or 131 may be effected in any of these ways—

(a) by delivering the notice to the person;

(b) by leaving it for him with another person at his last known or usual place of abode;

(c) by sending it by post in a letter addressed to him at his last known or usual place of abode.

[Extradition Act 2003, s 211.]

8–10299ZZZZZY   212. Article 95 alerts: transitional provision.   (1) This section applies in a case where an article 95 alert is issued before 1 January 2004 by an authority of a category 1 territory.

(2) In such a case, this Act applies as if—

(a) the alert were a Part 1 warrant issued by the authority;

(b) any information sent with the alert relating to the case were included in the warrant.

(3) As applied by subsection (2), this Act has effect with these modifications—

(a) in sections 2(7) and (8), 28(1), 30(1) and (4)(d), 32(2)(b), 33(6)(b), 35(4)(b), 36(3)(b), 47(3)(b), 49(3)(b), 190(3) and 191(2)(a) for "authority which issued the Part 1 warrant" substitute "authority at the request of which the alert was issued";

(b) omit section 5;

(c) in sections 33(4)(b), 42(2)(a), 43(2)(a) and (4) and 61(1)(d) and (e), for "authority which issued the warrant" substitute "authority at the request of which the alert was issued";

(d) in section 66(2), for the words from "believes" to the end substitute "believes is the authority at the request of which the alert was issued".

(4) An article 95 alert is an alert issued pursuant to article 95 of the Convention implementing the Schengen agreement of 14th June 1985.

[Extradition Act 2003, s 212.]

Interpretation

8–10299ZZZZZZ   **213. Disposal of Part 1 warrant and extradition request.**   (1) A Part 1 warrant issued in respect of a person is disposed of—

(a) when an order is made for the person's discharge in respect of the warrant and there is no further possibility of an appeal;

(b) when the person is taken to be discharged in respect of the warrant;

(c) when an order is made for the person's extradition in pursuance of the warrant and there is no further possibility of an appeal.

(2) A request for a person's extradition is disposed of—

(a) when an order is made for the person's discharge in respect of the request and there is no further possibility of an appeal;

(b) when the person is taken to be discharged in respect of the request;

(c) when an order is made for the person's extradition in pursuance of the request and there is no further possibility of an appeal.

(3) There is no further possibility of an appeal against an order for a person's discharge or extradition—

(a) when the period permitted for giving notice of an appeal to the High Court ends, if notice is not given before the end of that period;

(b) when the decision of the High Court on an appeal becomes final, if there is no appeal to the House of Lords against that decision;

(c) when the decision of the House of Lords on an appeal is made, if there is such an appeal.

(4) The decision of the High Court on an appeal becomes final—

(a) when the period permitted for applying to the High Court for leave to appeal to the House of Lords ends, if there is no such application;

(b) when the period permitted for applying to the House of Lords for leave to appeal to it ends, if the High Court refuses leave to appeal and there is no application to the House of Lords for leave to appeal;

(c) when the House of Lords refuses leave to appeal to it;

(d) at the end of the permitted period, which is 28 days starting with the day on which leave to appeal to the House of Lords is granted, if no such appeal is brought before the end of that period.

(5) These must be ignored for the purposes of subsections (3) and (4)—

(a) any power of a court to extend the period permitted for giving notice of appeal or for applying for leave to appeal;

(b) any power of a court to grant leave to take a step out of time.

(6) Subsections (3) to (5) do not apply to Scotland.

[Extradition Act 2003, s 213.]

8–10299ZZZZZZA   **214. Disposal of charge.**   (1) A charge against a person is disposed of—

(a) if the person is acquitted in respect of it, when he is acquitted;

(b) if the person is convicted in respect of it, when there is no further possibility of an appeal against the conviction.

(2) There is no further possibility of an appeal against a conviction—

(a) when the period permitted for giving notice of application for leave to appeal to the Court of Appeal against the conviction ends, if the leave of the Court of Appeal is required and no such notice is given before the end of that period;

(b) when the Court of Appeal refuses leave to appeal against the conviction, if the leave of the Court of Appeal is required and notice of application for leave is given before the end of that period;

(c) when the period permitted for giving notice of appeal to the Court of Appeal against the conviction ends, if notice is not given before the end of that period;

(d) when the decision of the Court of Appeal on an appeal becomes final, if there is no appeal to the House of Lords against that decision;

(e) when the decision of the House of Lords on an appeal is made, if there is such an appeal.

(3) The decision of the Court of Appeal on an appeal becomes final—

(a) when the period permitted for applying to the Court of Appeal for leave to appeal to the House of Lords ends, if there is no such application;

(b) when the period permitted for applying to the House of Lords for leave to appeal to it ends, if the Court of Appeal refuses leave to appeal and there is no application to the House of Lords for leave to appeal;

(c) when the House of Lords refuses leave to appeal to it;

(d) at the end of the permitted period, which is 28 days starting with the day on which leave to appeal to the House of Lords is granted, if no such appeal is brought before the end of that period.

(4) These must be ignored for the purposes of subsections (2) and (3)—

(a) any power of a court to extend the period permitted for giving notice of appeal or of application for leave to appeal or for applying for leave to appeal;

(b) any power of a court to grant leave to take a step out of time.

(5) Subsections (2) to (4) do not apply to Scotland.

[Extradition Act 2003, s 214.]

8–10299ZZZZZZB 215. European framework list. (1) The European framework list is the list of conduct set out in Schedule 2.

(2) The Secretary of State may by order amend Schedule 2 for the purpose of ensuring that the list of conduct set out in the Schedule corresponds to the list of conduct set out in article 2.2 of the European framework decision.

(3) The European framework decision is the framework decision of the Council of the European Union made on 13 June 2002 on the European arrest warrant and the surrender procedures between member states (2002/584/JHA).

[Extradition Act 2003, s 215.]

8–10299ZZZZZZC 216. Other interpretative provisions. (1) References to a category 1 territory must be read in accordance with section 1.

(2) References to a category 2 territory must be read in accordance with section 69.

(3) References to the designated authority must be read in accordance with section 2(9).

(4) References to a Part 1 warrant must be read in accordance with section 2.

(5) References to a Part 3 warrant must be read in accordance with section 142.

(6) References to a valid request for a person's extradition must be read in accordance with section 70.

(7) "Asylum claim" has the meaning given by section 113(1) of the Nationality, Immigration and Asylum Act 2002 (c 41).

(8) A customs officer is a person commissioned by the Commissioners of Customs and Excise under section 6(3) of the Customs and Excise Management Act 1979 (c 2).

(9) "High Court" in relation to Scotland means the High Court of Justiciary.

(10) In relation to Scotland, references to an appeal being discontinued are to be construed as references to its being abandoned.

(11) "Police officer" in relation to Northern Ireland has the same meaning as in the Police (Northern Ireland) Act 2000 (c 32).

(12) A provisional warrant is a warrant issued under section 73(3).

(13) A service policeman is a member of the Royal Navy Regulating Branch, the Royal Marines Police, the Royal Military Police or the Royal Air Force Police.

(14) The Provost Marshal of the Royal Air Force and any officer appointed to exercise the functions conferred on provost officers by the Air Force Act 1955 (3 & 4 Eliz. 2 c. 19) are to be taken to be members of the Royal Air Force Police for the purposes of subsection (13).

(15) This section and sections 213 to 215 apply for the purposes of this Act.

[Extradition Act 2003, s 216.]

General

8–10299ZZZZZZD 217. Form of documents. The Secretary of State may by regulations prescribe the form of any document required for the purposes of this Act.

[Extradition Act 2003, s 217.]

8–10299ZZZZZZE 218. Existing legislation on extradition. These Acts shall cease to have effect—

(a) the Backing of Warrants (Republic of Ireland) Act 1965 (c 45);

(b) the Extradition Act 1989 (c 33).

[Extradition Act 2003, s 218.]

8–10299ZZZZZZF   **219. Amendments.**   (1) Schedule 3 contains miscellaneous and consequential amendments.

(2) The Secretary of State may by order[1] make—

(a) any supplementary, incidental or consequential provision, and

(b) any transitory, transitional or saving provision,

which he considers necessary or expedient for the purposes of, in consequence of, or for giving full effect to any provision of this Act.

(3) An order under subsection (2) may, in particular—

(a) provide for any provision of this Act which comes into force before another such provision has come into force to have effect, until that other provision has come into force, with such modifications as are specified in the order, and

(b) amend, repeal or revoke any enactment other than one contained in an Act passed in a Session after that in which this Act is passed.

(4) The amendments that may be made under subsection (3)(b) are in addition to those made by or under any other provision of this Act.

[Extradition Act 2003, s 219.]

---

1. The Extradition Act 2003 (Repeals) Order 2004, SI 2004/1897, has been made.

8–10299ZZZZZZG   **220. Repeals.**   Schedule 4 contains repeals.

[Extradition Act 2003, s 220.]

8–10299ZZZZZZH   **221. Commencement.**   The preceding provisions of this Act come into force in accordance with provision made by the Secretary of State by order.

[Extradition Act 2003, s 221.]

---

1. The provisions of the Act were brought into force, subject to specified savings, on 1 January, 2004, by the Extradition Act 2003 (Commencement and Savings) Order 2003, SI 2003/3103, as amended by SI 2003/3258 and 3312. Extradition requests received before the above date will continue, however, to be dealt with under the provisions of the Extradition Act 1989, as will any post extradition requests made in respect of a person extradited from the UK before that date. All requests received by the British Overseas Territories (with the exception of Gibraltar which will be designated as a category 1 territory), the Bailiwick of Jersey, the Bailiwick of Guernsey and the Isle of Man will also continue to be dealt with under the provisions of the Extradition Act 1989 until Orders in Council are made under ss 177, 178 or 222 or until any of those territories passes their own legislation to deal with extradition.

8–10299ZZZZZZI   **222. Channel Islands and Isle of Man.**   An Order in Council may provide for this Act to extend to any of the Channel Islands or the Isle of Man with the modifications (if any) specified in the Order.

[Extradition Act 2003, s 222.]

8–10299ZZZZZZJ   **223. Orders and regulations**

8–10299ZZZZZZK   **224. Orders in Council.**   (1) An Order in Council under section 177 or 178 is subject to annulment in pursuance of a resolution of either House of Parliament.

(2) An Order in Council under this Act—

(a) may make different provision for different purposes;

(b) may include supplementary, incidental, saving or transitional provisions.

[Extradition Act 2003, s 224.]

8–10299ZZZZZZL   **225. Finance**

8–10299ZZZZZZM   **226. Extent.**   (1) Sections 157 to 160, 166 to 168, 171, 173 and 205 do not extend to Scotland.

(2) Sections 154, 198, 200 and 201 extend to England and Wales only.

(3) Sections 183 and 199 extend to Scotland only.

(4) Sections 184 and 185 extend to Northern Ireland only.*

[Extradition Act 2003, s 226.]

---

*Repealed by SI 2005/1965 from a date to be appointed.

8–10299ZZZZZZN   **227. Short title.**   This Act may be cited as the Extradition Act 2003.

[Extradition Act 2003, s 227.]

8–10299ZZZZZZO

Sections 188 and 189
SCHEDULE 1
RE-EXTRADITION: MODIFICATIONS

PART 1
CATEGORY 1 TERRITORIES

1. In section 11(1), omit paragraphs (c), (g) and (h).

2. Omit sections 14, 18 and 19.

3. In section 21(3), for "must" substitute "may".

4. In section 31(2), for paragraphs (a) and (b) substitute "would (apart from section 187(1)) be released from detention pursuant to the UK sentence (whether or not on licence)".

5. In section 39(2)(a), for "a certificate is issued under section 2 in respect of the warrant" substitute "the person would (apart from section 187(1)) be released from detention pursuant to the UK sentence (whether or not on licence)".

6. In section 44(2)(a), for "following his arrest under this Part" substitute "under section 187(1)".

7. In section 45(1), for the words from "arrested" to "issued" substitute "brought before the appropriate judge under section 187(1) may consent to his extradition to the territory in which the overseas sentence was imposed".

8–10299ZZZZZZP

PART 2
CATEGORY 2 TERRITORIES

8. In section 78, omit subsections (2), (3), (5) and (8).

9. In section 78, for subsection (4) substitute—

"(4)   The judge must decide whether the offence specified in the request is an extradition offence."

10. In section 78(6), for "any of the questions" substitute "the question".

11. In section 78(7), for "those questions" substitute "that question".

12. In section 79(1), omit paragraph (c).

13. Omit section 82.

14. In section 87(3), for the words from "must send the case" to "extradited" substitute "may order the person to be extradited to the category 2 territory".

15. In section 87, after subsection (3) insert—

"(4)   If the judge makes an order under subsection (3) he must remand the person in custody or on bail to wait for his extradition to the territory.

(5)   If the judge remands the person in custody he may later grant bail."

16. In section 103(1)—

(a)   for the words from "sends a case" to "extradited" substitute "orders a person's extradition under this Part"; and

(b)   for "the relevant decision" substitute "the order".

17. In section 103(2), for the words from "the person" to "the Secretary of State" substitute "the order is made under section 128".

18. In section 103, omit subsections (3), (5), (6), (7) and (8).

19. In section 103(9), for the words from "the Secretary of State" to "person" substitute "the order is made".

20. In section 104, omit subsections (1)(b), (6) and (7).

21. In section 106, omit subsections (1)(b), (7) and (8).

22. In section 117(1)(a), for "the Secretary of State" substitute "the appropriate judge".

23. In section 117(1)(b), for the words from "permitted period" to "extradition" substitute "period permitted under that section".

24. In section 117, after subsection (1) insert—

"(1A)   But this section does not apply if the order is made under section 128."

25. In section 117(2), for "the Secretary of State" substitute "the judge".

26. In section 119(1)(a), for "the Secretary of State" substitute "the appropriate judge".

27. In section 119, in subsections (2) to (6) and in each place in subsection (7), for "the Secretary of State" substitute "the judge".

28. In section 120, after subsection (1) insert—

"(1A)   But this section does not apply if the order for the person's extradition is made under section 128."

29. In section 121(2)(a), for "a certificate is issued under section 70 in respect of the request" substitute "the person would (apart from section 187(1)) be released from detention pursuant to the UK sentence (whether or not on licence)".

30. In section 127(1), for the words from "arrested" to "requested" substitute "brought before the appropriate judge under section 187(1) may consent to his extradition to the territory in which the overseas sentence was imposed".

31. In section 127(3), before paragraph (a) insert—

"(aa) must be given before the appropriate judge;".

32. In section 127, omit subsections (4) and (5).

33. In section 128, after subsection (1) insert—

"(1A)   The judge must remand the person in custody or on bail.

(1B)   If the judge remands the person in custody he may later grant bail."

34. In section 128(4), for the words from "send the case" to "extradited" substitute "within the period of 10 days starting with the day on which consent is given order the person's extradition to the category 2 territory".

35. In section 128, after subsection (5) insert—

"(6)   Subsection (4) has effect subject to section 128B.

(7) If subsection (4) is not complied with and the person applies to the judge to be discharged the judge must order his discharge."

36. After section 128 insert—

"**128A. Extradition to category 2 territory following consent.** (1) This section applies if the appropriate judge makes an order under section 128(4) for a person's extradition to a category 2 territory.

(2) The person must be extradited to the category 2 territory before the end of the required period, which is 28 days starting with the day on which the order is made.

(3) If subsection (2) is not complied with and the person applies to the judge to be discharged the judge must order his discharge, unless reasonable cause is shown for the delay.

128B. Extradition claim following consent. (1) This section applies if—

  (a) a person consents under section 127 to his extradition to a category 2 territory, and
  (b) before the judge orders his extradition under section 128(4), the judge is informed that the conditions in subsection (2) or (3) are met.

(2) The conditions are that—

  (a) the Secretary of State has received another valid request for the person's extradition to a category 2 territory;
  (b) the other request has not been disposed of.

(3) The conditions are that—

  (a) a certificate has been issued under section 2 in respect of a Part 1 warrant issued in respect of the person;
  (b) the warrant has not been disposed of.

(4) The judge must not make an order under section 128(4) until he is informed what order has been made under section 126(2) or 179(2).

(5) If the order under section 126(2) or 179(2) is for further proceedings on the request under consideration to be deferred until the other request, or the warrant, has been disposed of, the judge must remand the person in custody or on bail.

(6) If the judge remands the person in custody he may later grant bail.

(7) If—

  (a) the order under section 126(2) or 179(2) is for further proceedings on the request under consideration to be deferred until the other request, or the warrant, has been disposed of, and
  (b) an order is made under section 180 for proceedings on the request under consideration to be resumed,

the period specified in section 128(4) must be taken to be 10 days starting with the day on which the order under section 180 is made.

(8) If the order under section 126(2) or 179(2) is for further proceedings on the other request, or the warrant, to be deferred until the request under consideration has been disposed of, the period specified in section 128(4) must be taken to be 10 days starting with the day on which the judge is informed of the order.

128C. Extradition following deferral for competing claim. (1) This section applies if—

  (a) an order is made under section 128(4) for a person to be extradited to a category 2 territory in pursuance of a request for his extradition;
  (b) before the person is extradited to the territory an order is made under section 126(2) or 179(2) for the person's extradition in pursuance of the request to be deferred;
  (c) the appropriate judge makes an order under section 181(2) for the person's extradition in pursuance of the request to cease to be deferred.

(2) The required period for the purposes of section 128A(2) is 28 days starting with the day on which the order under section 181(2) is made."

8–10299ZZZZZZQ

Section 215   SCHEDULE 2
EUROPEAN FRAMEWORK LIST

1. Participation in a criminal organisation.
2. Terrorism.
3. Trafficking in human beings.
4. Sexual exploitation of children and child pornography.
5. Illicit trafficking in narcotic drugs and psychotropic substances.
6. Illicit trafficking in weapons, munitions and explosives.
7. Corruption.
8. Fraud, including that affecting the financial interests of the European Communities within the meaning of the Convention of 26 July 1995 on the protection of the European Communities' financial interests.
9. Laundering of the proceeds of crime.
10. Counterfeiting currency, including of the euro.
11. Computer-related crime.
12. Environmental crime, including illicit trafficking in endangered animal species and in endangered plant species and varieties.
13. Facilitation of unauthorised entry and residence.
14. Murder, grievous bodily injury.
15. Illicit trade in human organs and tissue.
16. Kidnapping, illegal restraint and hostage-taking.
17. Racism and xenophobia.
18. Organised or armed robbery.

19. Illicit trafficking in cultural goods, including antiques and works of art.
20. Swindling.
21. Racketeering and extortion.
22. Counterfeiting and piracy of products.
23. Forgery of administrative documents and trafficking therein.
24. Forgery of means of payment.
25. Illicit trafficking in hormonal substances and other growth promoters.
26. Illicit trafficking in nuclear or radioactive materials.
27. Trafficking in stolen vehicles.
28. Rape.
29. Arson.
30. Crimes within the jurisdiction of the International Criminal Court.
31. Unlawful seizure of aircraft/ships.
32. Sabotage.

8–10299ZZZZZZR

SCHEDULE 3
AMENDMENTS

(*The amendments made by Schedule 3, so far as they affect statutory provisions reproduced in this work, are shown in those statutes.*)

8–10299ZZZZZZS

SCHEDULE 4
REPEALS

(*Schedule 4 provides for the repeal in their entirety of the Backing of Warrants (Republic of Ireland) Act 1965 and the Extradition Act 1989. Other, relatively minor repeals are also provided for.*)

Backing of Warrants (Republic of Ireland) (Rule of Speciality) Order 1994
(SI 1994/1952)

8–10340 **1.** (1) and (2) *Citation, commencement and jurisdiction.*

8–10341 **2.** (1) In this Order—

"corresponding arrangements" means arrangements in force in the Republic for the delivery up of a person to the United Kingdom by the Republic corresponding to provisions contained in the 1965 Act for the delivery up of a person to the Republic by the United Kingdom;
"defendant" means a person delivered up to the United Kingdom under corresponding arrangements;
"the 1965 Act" means the Backing of Warrants (Republic of Ireland) Act 1965, including that Act as it has effect in the Channel Islands and the Isle of Man, hereinafter referred to as "the Islands";
"the Republic" means the Republic of Ireland;
except in article 1(3), "the United Kingdom" includes the Islands; and
"a part of the United Kingdom" includes each of the Islands.

(2) For the purposes of this Order, references to a defendant being dealt with for, or in respect of, an offence include a reference to his being dealt with by being proceeded against, sentenced, detained with a view to carrying out a sentence or detention order or otherwise restricted in his personal freedom for or in respect of an offence, and "detention order" means any order involving deprivation of liberty which has been made by a criminal court in addition to or instead of a prison sentence.

(3) For the purposes of this Order, a defendant is not to be regarded as having had an opportunity to leave the United Kingdom, or of having returned to any part of the United Kingdom, at any time whilst he was on bail granted to him in any part of the United Kingdom.

8–10342 **3.** An order shall not be made under section 2(1) of the 1965 Act if it is shown to the satisfaction of the court that no provision is made in the law of the Republic, in respect of a person delivered up to the Republic by the United Kingdom, corresponding to the provision made by articles 4 and 5 of this Order in respect of a person delivered up to the United Kingdom by the Republic.

8–10343 **4.** (1) Unless his case is a specified case for the purposes of this article, no defendant may be dealt with in the United Kingdom for, or in respect of, any offence, other than that for which he was delivered up, committed before his surrender, and accordingly, a provision of law for the time being in force in any part of the United Kingdom which would, but for this article, require or allow that person to be so dealt with, shall not have effect in respect of him unless his case is a specified case for the purposes of this article.

(2) A defendant's case is a specified case for the purposes of this article if—

(a) the Minister for Justice of the Republic has consented by notice in writing given to the Secretary of State to the defendant being dealt with for, or in respect of, the offence in question;

(b) the defendant, having had an opportunity to leave the United Kingdom, has not done so within 45 days of his final discharge in respect of the offence for which he was delivered up;

(c) the defendant has, after being returned to the United Kingdom, left the United Kingdom and subsequently returned to it; or

(d) the description of the offence with which the defendant is charged in the United Kingdom is altered in the course of the proceedings but the offence under its new description is shown by its constituent elements to be an offence for which he could have been delivered up under corresponding arrangements.

(3) A defendant's case is also a specified case for the purposes of this article where the offence in question is, under the law for the time being in force in the part of the United Kingdom in which the warrant was issued, an offence of which, on his trial on a charge for the offence for which he was delivered up, he could (disregarding paragraph (1) of this article) be convicted.

8–10344 **5.** (1) Unless his case is a specified case for the purposes of this article, no defendant may be delivered up to a territory other than the Republic to be dealt with for, in respect of, any offence committed before his surrender to the United Kingdom.

(2) A defendant's case is a specified case for the purposes of this article if—

(a) the Minister for Justice of the Republic has consented by notice in writing given to the Secretary of State to the defendant being so delivered up;

(b) the defendant, having had the opportunity to leave the United Kingdom has not done so within 45 days of his final discharge in respect of the offence for which he was delivered up; or

(c) the defendant has, after being returned to the United Kingdom, left the United Kingdom and subsequently returned to it.

International Criminal Court Act 2001 (Enforcement of Fines, Forfeiture and Reparation Orders) Regulations 2001[1]
(SI 2001/2379)

8–10347 **1. Citation, commencement and extent.** (1) These Regulations may be cited as the International Criminal Court Act 2001 (Enforcement of Fines, Forfeiture and Reparation Orders) Regulations 2001 and shall come into force on 1st August 2001.

(2) These Regulations extend to England and Wales and Northern Ireland.

---

1. Made by the Lord Chancellor, in exercise of the powers conferred upon him by s 144 of the Magistrates' Courts Act 1980, after consultation with the Rule Committee appointed under that section.

2. Interpretation. In these Regulations references to "the Order" have the same meaning as in section 49 of the International Criminal Court Act 2001, that is to say,

(a) a fine or forfeiture ordered by the International Criminal Court ("the ICC"), or

(b) an order by the ICC against a person convicted by the ICC specifying a reparation to, or in respect of, a victim.

3. Person appointed to act for ICC. On receipt of the Order the Secretary of State may,

(a) appoint a person to act on behalf of the ICC for the purposes of enforcing the Order, and

(b) give such directions to the appointed person as appear to him necessary.

4. Registration of Order. (1) If the Secretary of State so directs, the person appointed under regulation 3(a) shall apply to a court in England and Wales or Northern Ireland for registration of the Order for enforcement.

(2) On the application of the person so appointed the court shall register the Order as a pre-condition of enforcement.

(3) The registration of the Order under this regulation shall be cancelled if the Order is satisfied by other means.

5. Effect of registration. For the purposes of enforcement of the Order when registered,

(a) the Order has the same force and effect;

(b) the same powers are exercisable in relation to its enforcement, and

(c) proceedings for its enforcement may be taken in the same way,

as if the Order were an order of a court in England and Wales or Northern Ireland.

6. Disposal of Property. (1) A court may, on the application of the person appointed under regulation 3(a), vest in him any property to which the Order relates, to be disposed of in accordance with the directions of the Secretary of State.

(2) That person shall account to the Secretary of State for the proceeds of disposal.

(3) The Secretary of State shall transmit the proceeds to the ICC.

7. Recovery of Costs.   The reasonable costs of, and incidental to, the registration and enforcement of the Order shall be recoverable as if they were sums recoverable under the Order.

Extradition Act 2003 (Designation of Part 2 Territories) Order 2003[1]

(SI 2003/3334 as amended by SI 2004/1898 and SI 2005/365 and 2036)

8–10348 1.   (1) This Order may be cited as the Extradition Act 2003 (Designation of Part 2 Territories) Order 2003 and shall come into force on 1st January 2004.

(2) In this Order "the Act" means the Extradition Act 2003.

---

1. Made by the Secretary of State, in exercise of the powers conferred upon him by sections 1, 69(1), 71(4), 73(5), 74(11)(*b*), 84(7) and 86(7) of the Extradition Act 2003.

2.   (1) The territories set out in paragraph (2) are hereby designated for the purposes of Part 2 of the Act.

(2) Those territories are—

Albania,
Andorra,
Antigua and Barbuda,
Argentina,
Armenia,
Australia,
Azerbaijan,
The Bahamas,
Bangladesh,
Barbados,
Belize,
Bolivia,
Bosnia and Herzegovina,
Botswana,
Brazil,
Brunei,
Bulgaria,
Canada,
Chile,
Colombia,
Cook Islands,
Croatia,
Cuba,
Dominica,
Ecuador,
El Salvador,
Fiji,
The Gambia,
Georgia,
Ghana,
Grenada,
Guatemala,
Guyana,
Hong Kong Special Administrative Region,
Haiti,
Iceland,
India,
Iraq,
Israel,
Jamaica,
Kenya,
Kiribati,
Lesotho,
Liberia,
Liechtenstein,
Macedonia, FYR,
Malawi,
Malaysia,

Maldives,
Mauritius,
Mexico,
Moldova,
Monaco,
Nauru,
New Zealand,
Nicaragua,
Nigeria,
Norway,
Panama,
Papua New Guinea,
Paraguay,
Peru,
Romania,
Russian Federation,
Saint Christopher and Nevis,
Saint Lucia,
Saint Vincent and the Grenadines,
San Marino,
Serbia and Montenegro,
Seychelles,
Sierra Leone,
Singapore,
Solomon Islands,
South Africa,
Sri Lanka,
Swaziland,
Switzerland,
Tanzania,
Thailand,
Tonga,
Trinidad and Tobago,
Turkey,
Tuvalu,
Uganda,
Ukraine,
Uruguay,
The United States of America,
Vanuatu,
Western Samoa,
Zambia,
Zimbabwe.

3. (1) The territories set out in paragraph (2) are hereby designated for the purposes of section 71(4), 73(5), 84(7) and 86(7) of the Act.
(2) Those territories are—

Albania,
Andorra,
Armenia,
Australia,
Azerbaijan,
Bulgaria,
Canada,
Croatia,
Georgia,
Iceland,
Israel,
Liechtenstein,
Macedonia, FYR,
Moldova,
New Zealand,
Norway,
Romania,
Russian Federation,
Serbia and Montenegro,
South Africa,
Switzerland,
Turkey,
Ukraine,
The United States of America.

(3) The Hong Kong Special Administrative Region is hereby designated for the purposes of section 71(4) and 73(5) of the Act.

4. (1) The territories set out in paragraph (2) are hereby designated for the purposes of section 74(11)(b) with the relevant longer period for each territory following in brackets.
(2) Those territories and relevant periods are—

Argentina (65 days)
Bolivia (65 days)
Bosnia and Herzegovina (65 days)
Brazil (65 days)
Chile (65 days)
Colombia (65 days)
Cuba (65 days)
El Salvador (65 days)
Guatemala (95 days)
Haiti (65 days)
Hong Kong Special Administrative Region (65 days)
Iraq (65 days)
Liberia (95 days)
Mexico (65 days)
Monaco (65 days)
Nicaragua (65 days)
Panama (95 days)
Paraguay (95 days)
Peru (95 days)
San Marino (65 days)
Thailand (65 days)
The United States of America (65 days).

---

1. Made by the Secretary of State, in exercise of the powers conferred on him by section 193 of the Extradition Act 2003.

International Criminal Court Act 2001 (Elements of Crimes) (No 2) Regulations 2004
(SI 2004/3239)

8–10349 1. Citation, commencement and extent. (1) These Regulations may be cited as the International Criminal Court Act 2001 (Elements of Crimes) (No 2) Regulations 2004 and shall come into force on 30th December 2004.
(2) In so far as these Regulations may relate to proceedings in a service court these Regulations extend to any place at which those proceedings are held.

2. The Elements of Crimes. The text of the Elements of Crimes adopted by the Assembly of States Parties on 9th September 2002 in accordance with Article 9(1) of the Rome Statute of the International Criminal Court and referred to in section 50(2)(a) of the International Criminal Court Act 2001 is set out in the Schedule to these Regulations.

3. The International Criminal Court Act 2001 (Elements of Crimes) Regulations 2004 are hereby revoked.

SCHEDULE
ELEMENTS OF CRIMES*

Contents

*Explanatory note: The structure of the elements of the crimes of genocide, crimes against humanity and war crimes follows the structure of the corresponding provisions of articles 6, 7 and 8 of the Rome Statute. Some paragraphs of those articles of the Rome Statute list multiple crimes. In those instances, the elements of crimes appear in separate paragraphs which correspond to each of those crimes to facilitate the identification of the respective elements.

Elements of Crimes. General Introduction

1. Pursuant to article 9, the following Elements of Crimes shall assist the Court in the interpretation and application of articles 6, 7 and 8, consistent with the Statute. The provisions of the Statute, including article 21 and the general principles set out in Part 3, are applicable to the Elements of Crimes.

2. As stated in article 30, unless otherwise provided, a person shall be criminally responsible and liable for punishment for a crime within the jurisdiction of the Court only if the material elements are committed with intent and knowledge. Where no reference is made in the Elements of Crimes to a mental element for any particular conduct, consequence or circumstance listed, it is understood that the relevant mental element, ie, intent, knowledge or both, set out in article 30 applies. Exceptions to the article 30 standard, based on the Statute, including applicable law under its relevant provisions, are indicated below.

3. Existence of intent and knowledge can be inferred from relevant facts and circumstances.

4. With respect to mental elements associated with elements involving value judgement, such as those using the terms "inhumane" or "severe", it is not necessary that the perpetrator personally completed a particular value judgement, unless otherwise indicated.

5. Grounds for excluding criminal responsibility or the absence thereof are generally not specified in the elements of crimes listed under each crime.

6. The requirement of "unlawfulness" found in the Statute or in other parts of international law, in particular international humanitarian law, is generally not specified in the elements of crimes.

7. The elements of crimes are generally structured in accordance with the following principles:

—As the elements of crimes focus on the conduct, consequences and circumstances associated with each crime, they are generally listed in that order;
—When required, a particular mental element is listed after the affected conduct, consequence or circumstance;
—Contextual circumstances are listed last.

8. As used in the Elements of Crimes, the term "perpetrator" is neutral as to guilt or innocence. The elements, including the appropriate mental elements, apply, *mutatis mutandis,* to all those whose criminal responsibility may fall under articles 25 and 28 of the Statute.

9. A particular conduct may constitute one or more crimes.

10. The use of short titles for the crimes has no legal effect.

Article 6
Genocide. Introduction

With respect to the last element listed for each crime:

—The term "in the context of" would include the initial acts in an emerging pattern;
—The term "manifest" is an objective qualification;
—Notwithstanding the normal requirement for a mental element provided for in article 30, and recognising that knowledge of the circumstances will usually be addressed in proving genocidal intent, the appropriate requirement, if any, for a mental element regarding this circumstance will need to be decided by the Court on a case-by-case basis.

Article 6(a)
Genocide by killing. Elements

1. The perpetrator killed one or more persons.
2. Such person or persons belonged to a particular national, ethnical, racial or religious group.
3. The perpetrator intended to destroy, in whole or in part, that national, ethnical, racial or religious group, as such.
4. The conduct took place in the context of a manifest pattern of similar conduct directed against that group or was conduct that could itself effect such destruction.

Article 6(*b*)
Genocide by causing serious bodily or mental harm. Elements
1. The perpetrator caused serious bodily or mental harm to one or more persons.
2. Such person or persons belonged to a particular national, ethnical, racial or religious group.
3. The perpetrator intended to destroy, in whole or in part, that national, ethnical, racial or religious group, as such.
4. The conduct took place in the context of a manifest pattern of similar conduct directed against that group or was conduct that could itself effect such destruction.

Article 6(*c*)
Genocide by deliberately inflicting conditions of life calculated to bring about physical destruction. Elements
1. The perpetrator inflicted certain conditions of life upon one or more persons.
2. Such person or persons belonged to a particular national, ethnical, racial or religious group.
3. The perpetrator intended to destroy, in whole or in part, that national, ethnical, racial or religious group, as such.
4. The conditions of life were calculated to bring about the physical destruction of that group, in whole or in part.
5. The conduct took place in the context of a manifest pattern of similar conduct directed against that group or was conduct that could itself effect such destruction.

Article 6(*d*)
Genocide by imposing measures intended to prevent births. Elements
1. The perpetrator imposed certain measures upon one or more persons.
2. Such person or persons belonged to a particular national, ethnical, racial or religious group.
3. The perpetrator intended to destroy, in whole or in part, that national, ethnical, racial or religious group, as such.
4. The measures imposed were intended to prevent births within that group.
5. The conduct took place in the context of a manifest pattern of similar conduct directed against that group or was conduct that could itself effect such destruction.

Article 6(*e*)
Genocide by forcibly transferring children. Elements
1. The perpetrator forcibly transferred one or more persons.
2. Such person or persons belonged to a particular national, ethnical, racial or religious group.
3. The perpetrator intended to destroy, in whole or in part, that national, ethnical, racial or religious group, as such.
4. The transfer was from that group to another group.
5. The person or persons were under the age of 18 years.
6. The perpetrator knew, or should have known, that the person or persons were under the age of 18 years.
7. The conduct took place in the context of a manifest pattern of similar conduct directed against that group or was conduct that could itself effect such destruction.

Article 7
Crimes against humanity. Introduction
1. Since article 7 pertains to international criminal law, its provisions, consistent with article 22, must be strictly construed, taking into account that crimes against humanity as defined in article 7 are among the most serious crimes of concern to the international community as a whole, warrant and entail individual criminal responsibility, and require conduct which is impermissible under generally applicable international law, as recognised by the principal legal systems of the world.
2. The last two elements for each crime against humanity describe the context in which the conduct must take place. These elements clarify the requisite participation in and knowledge of a widespread or systematic attack against a civilian population. However, the last element should not be interpreted as requiring proof that the perpetrator has knowledge of all characteristics of the attack or the precise details of the plan or policy of the State or organisation. In the case of an emerging widespread or systematic attack against a civilian population, the intent clause of the last element indicates that this mental element is satisfied if the perpetrator intended to further such an attack.
3. "Attack directed against a civilian population" in these context elements is understood to mean a course of conduct involving the multiple commission of acts referred to in article 7, paragraph 1, of the Statute against any civilian population, pursuant to or in furtherance of a State or organisational policy to commit such attack. The acts need not constitute a military attack. It is understood that "policy to commit such attack" requires that the State or organisation actively promote or encourage such an attack against a civilian population.

Article 7(1)(*a*)
Crime against humanity of murder. Elements
1. The perpetrator killed one or more persons.
2. The conduct was committed as part of a widespread or systematic attack directed against a civilian population.
3. The perpetrator knew that the conduct was part of or intended the conduct to be part of a widespread or systematic attack against a civilian population.

Article 7(1)(*b*)
Crime against humanity of extermination. Elements
1. The perpetrator killed one ore more persons, including by inflicting conditions of life calculated to bring about the destruction of part of a population.
2. The conduct constituted, or took place as part of, a mass killing of members of a civilian population.
3. The conduct was committed as part of a widespread or systematic attack directed against a civilian population.
4. The perpetrator knew that the conduct was part of or intended the conduct to be part of a widespread or systematic attack directed against a civilian population.

Article 7(1)(c)
Crime against humanity of enslavement.　Elements

1. The perpetrator exercised any or all of the powers attaching to the right of ownership over one or more persons, such as by purchasing, selling, lending or bartering such a person or persons, or by imposing on them a similar deprivation of liberty.
2. The conduct was committed as part of a widespread or systematic attack directed against a civilian population.
3. The perpetrator knew that the conduct was part of or intended the conduct to be part of a widespread or systematic attack directed against a civilian population.

Article 7(1)(d)
Crime against humanity of deportation or forcible transfer of population.　Elements

1. The perpetrator deported or forcibly transferred, without grounds permitted under international law, one or more persons to another State or location, by expulsion or other coercive acts.
2. Such person or persons were lawfully present in the area from which they were so deported or transferred.
3. The perpetrator was aware of the factual circumstances that established the lawfulness of such presence.
4. The conduct was committed as part of a widespread or systematic attack directed against a civilian population.
5. The perpetrator knew that the conduct was part of or intended the conduct to be part of a widespread or systematic attack directed against a civilian population.

Article 7(1)(e)
Crime against humanity of imprisonment or other severe deprivation of physical liberty.　Elements

1. The perpetrator imprisoned one or more persons or otherwise severely deprived one or more persons of physical liberty.
2. he gravity of the conduct was such that it was in violation of fundamental rules of international law.
3. The perpetrator was aware of the factual circumstances that established the gravity of the conduct.
4. The conduct was committed as part of a widespread or systematic attack directed against a civilian population.
5. The perpetrator knew that the conduct was part of or intended the conduct to be part of a widespread or systematic attack directed against a civilian population.

Article 7(1)(f)
Crime against humanity of torture.　Elements

1. The perpetrator inflicted severe physical or mental pain or suffering upon one or more persons.
2. Such person or persons were in the custody or under the control of the perpetrator.
3. Such pain or suffering did not arise only from, and was not inherent in or incidental to, lawful sanctions.
4. The conduct was committed as part of a widespread or systematic attack directed against a civilian population.
5. The perpetrator knew that the conduct was part of or intended the conduct to be part of a widespread or systematic attack directed against a civilian population.

Article 7(1)(g)–1
Crime against humanity of rape.　Elements

1. The perpetrator invaded the body of a person by conduct resulting in penetration, however slight, of any part of the body of the victim or of the perpetrator with a sexual organ, or of the anal or genital opening of the victim with any object or any other part of the body.
2. The invasion was committed by force, or by threat of force or coercion, such as that caused by fear of violence, duress, detection, psychological oppression or abuse of power, against such person or another person, or by taking advantage of a coercive environment, or the invasion was committed against a person incapable of giving genuine consent.
3. The conduct was committed as part of a widespread or systematic attack directed against a civilian population.
4. The perpetrator knew that the conduct was part of or intended the conduct to be part of a widespread or systematic attack directed against a civilian population.

Article 7(1)(g)–2
Crime against humanity of sexual slavery.　Elements

1. The perpetrator exercised any or all of the powers attaching to the right of ownership over one or more persons, such as by purchasing, selling, lending or bartering such a person or persons, or by imposing on them a similar deprivation of liberty.
2. The perpetrator caused such person or persons to engage in one or more acts of a sexual nature.
3. The conduct was committed as part of a widespread or systematic attack directed against a civilian population.
4. The perpetrator knew that the conduct was part of or intended the conduct to be part of a widespread or systematic attack directed against a civilian population.

Article 7(1)(g)–3
Crime against humanity of enforced prostitution.　Elements

1. The perpetrator caused one or more persons to engage in one or more acts of a sexual nature by force, or by threat of force or coercion, such as that caused by fear of violence, duress, detention, psychological oppression or abuse of power, against such person or persons or another person, or by taking advantage of a coercive environment or such person's or persons' incapacity to give genuine consent.
2. The perpetrator or another person obtained or expected to obtain pecuniary or other advantage in exchange for or in connection with the acts of a sexual nature.
3. The conduct was committed as part of a widespread or systematic attack directed against a civilian population.
4. The perpetrator knew that the conduct was part of or intended the conduct to be part of a widespread or systematic attack directed against a civilian population.

Article 7(1)(g)–4
Crime against humanity of forced pregnancy. Elements

1. The perpetrator confined one or more women forcibly made pregnant, with the intent of affecting the ethnic composition of any population or carrying out other grave violations of international law.
2. The conduct was committed as part of a widespread or systematic attack directed against a civilian population.
3. The perpetrator knew that the conduct was part of or intended the conduct to be part of a widespread or systematic attack directed a civilian population.

Article 7(1)(g)–5
Crime against humanity of enforced sterilization. Elements

1. The perpetrator deprived one or more persons of biological reproductive capacity.
2. The conduct was neither justified by the medical or hospital treatment of the person or persons concerned nor carried out with their genuine consent.
3. The conduct was committed as part of a widespread or systematic attack directed against a civilian population.
4. The perpetrator knew that the conduct was part of or intended the conduct to be part of a widespread or systematic attack directed against a civilian population.

Article 7(1)(g)–6
Crime against humanity of sexual violence. Elements

1. The perpetrator committed an act of a sexual nature against one or more persons or caused such person or persons to engage in an act of a sexual nature by force, or by threat of force or coercion, such as that caused by fear of violence, duress, detention, psychological oppression or abuse or power, against such person or persons or another person, or by taking advantage of a coercive environment or such person's or persons' incapacity to give genuine consent.
2. Such conduct was of a gravity comparable to the other offences in article 7, paragraph 1(g), of the Statute.
3. The perpetrator was aware of the factual circumstances that established the gravity of the conduct.
4. The conduct was committed as part of a widespread or systematic attack directed against a civilian population.
5. The perpetrator knew that the conduct was part of or intended the conduct to be part of widespread or systematic attack directed against a civilian population.

Article 7(1)(h)
Crime against humanity of persecution. Elements

1. The perpetrator severely deprived, contrary to international law, one or more persons of fundamental rights.
2. The perpetrator targeted such person or persons by reason of the identity of a group or collectivity or targeted the group or collectivity as such.
3. Such targeting was based on political, racial, national, ethnic, cultural, religious, gender as defined in article 7, paragraph 3, of the Statute, or other grounds that are universally recognised as impermissible under international law.
4. The conduct was committed in connection with any act referred to in article 7, paragraph 1, of the Statute or any crime within the jurisdiction of the Court.
5. The conduct was committed as part of a widespread or systematic attack directed against a civilian population.
6. The perpetrator knew that the conduct was part of or intended the conduct to be part of a widespread or systematic attack directed against a civilian population.

Article 7(1)(i)
Crime against humanity of enforced disappearance of persons. Elements

1. The perpetrator:

(a) Arrested, detained or abducted one or more persons; or
(b) Refused to acknowledge the arrest, detention or abduction, or to give information on the fate or whereabouts of such person or persons.

2

(a) Such arrest, detention or abduction was followed or accompanied by a refusal to acknowledge that deprivation of freedom or to give information on the fate or whereabouts of such person or persons; or
(b) Such refusal was preceded or accompanied by that deprivation of freedom.

3. The perpetrator was aware that;

(a) Such arrest, detention or abduction would be followed in the ordinary course of events by a refusal to acknowledge that deprivation of freedom or to give information on the fate or whereabouts of such person or persons; or
(b) Such refusal was preceded or accompanied by that deprivation of freedom.

4. Such arrest, detention or abduction was carried out by, or with the authorisation, support or acquiescence of, a State or a political organisation.
5. Such refusal to acknowledge that deprivation of freedom or to give information on the fate or whereabouts of such person or persons was carried out by, or with the authorisation or support of, such State or political organisation.
6. The perpetrator intended to remove such person or persons from the protection of the law for a prolonged period of time.
7. The conduct was committed as part of a widespread or systematic attack directed against a civilian population.
8. The perpetrator knew that the conduct was part of or intended the conduct to be part of a widespread or systematic attack directed against a civilian population.

Article 7(1)(*j*)
Crime against humanity of apartheid. Elements
1. The perpetrator committed an inhumane act against one or more persons.
2. Such act was an act referred to in article 7, paragraph 1, of the Statute, or was an act of a character similar to any of those acts.
3. The perpetrator was aware of the factual circumstances that established the character of the act.
4. The conduct was committed in the context of an institutionalized regime of systematic oppression and domination by one racial group over any other racial group or groups.
5. The perpetrator intended to maintain such regime by that conduct.
6. The conduct was committed as part of a widespread or systematic attack directed against a civilian population.
7. The perpetrator knew that the conduct was part of or intended the conduct to be part of a widespread or systematic attack directed against a civilian population.

Article 7(1)(*k*)
Crime against humanity of other inhumane acts. Elements
1. The perpetrator inflicted great suffering, or serious injury to body or to mental or physical health, by means of an inhumane act.
2. Such act was of a character similar to any other act referred to in article 7, paragraph 1, of the Statute.
3. The perpetrator was aware of the factual circumstances that established the character of the act.
4. The conduct was committed as part of a widespread or systematic attack directed against a civilian population.
5. The perpetrator knew that the conduct was part of or intended the conduct to be part of a widespread or systematic attack directed against a civilian population.

Article 8
War crimes. Introduction
The elements for war crimes under article 8, paragraph 2 (c) and (e), are subject to the limitations addressed in article 8, paragraph 2(d) and (f), which are not elements of crimes.
The elements for war crimes under article 8, paragraph 2, of the Statute shall be interpreted within the established framework of the international law of armed conflict including, as appropriate, the international law of armed conflict applicable to armed conflict at sea.

With respect to the last two elements listed for each crime:
—There is no requirement for a legal evaluation by the perpetrator as to the existence of an armed conflict of its character as international or non-international;
—In that context there is no requirement for awareness by the perpetrator of the facts that established the character of the conflict as international or non-international;
—There is only a requirement for the awareness of the factual circumstances that established the existence of an armed conflict that is implicit in the terms "took place in the context of and was associated with".

Article 8(2)(*a*)

Article 8(2)(*a*)(i)
War crime of wilful killing. Elements
1. The perpetrator killed one or more persons.
2. Such person or persons were protected under one or more of the Geneva Conventions of 1949.
3. The perpetrator was aware of the factual circumstances that established that protected status.
4. The conduct took place in the context of and was associated with an international armed conflict.
5. The perpetrator was aware of factual circumstances that established the existence of an armed conflict.

Article 8(2)(*a*)(ii)–1
War crime of torture. Elements
1. The perpetrator inflicted severe physical or mental pain or suffering upon one or more persons.
2. The perpetrator inflicted the pain or suffering for such purposes as: obtaining information or a confession, punishment, intimidation or coercion or for any reason based on discrimination of any kind.
3. Such person or persons were protected under one or more of the Geneva Conventions of 1949.
4. The perpetrator was aware of the factual circumstances that established that protected status.
5. The conduct took place in the context of and was associated with an international armed conflict.
6. The perpetrator was aware of factual circumstances that established the existence of an armed conflict.

Article 8(2)(*a*)(ii)–2
War crime of inhuman treatment. Elements
1. The perpetrator inflicted severe physical or mental pain or suffering upon one or more persons.
2. Such person or persons were protected under one or more of the Geneva Conventions of 1949.
3. The perpetrator was aware of the factual circumstances that established that protected status.
4. The conduct took place in the context of and was associated with an international armed conflict.
5. The perpetrator was aware of factual circumstances that established the existence of an armed conflict

Article 8(2)(*a*)(ii)–3
War crime of biological experiments. Elements
1. The perpetrator subjected one or more persons to a particular biological experiment.
2. The experiment seriously endangered the physical or mental health or integrity of such person or persons.
3. The intent of the experiment was non-therapeutic and it was neither justified by medical reasons nor carried out in such person's or persons' interest.
4. Such person or persons were protected under one or more of the Geneva Conventions of 1949.
5. The perpetrator was aware of the factual circumstances that established that protected status.
6. The conduct took place in the context of and was associated with an international armed conflict.
7. The perpetrator was aware of factual circumstances that established the existence of an armed conflict.

Article 8(2)(*a*)(iii)
War crime of wilfully causing great suffering.   Elements
1. The perpetrator caused great physical or mental pain or suffering to, or serious injury to body or health of, one or more persons.
2. Such person or persons were protected under one or more of the Geneva Conventions of 1949.
3. The perpetrator was aware of the factual circumstances that established that protected status.
4. The conduct took place in the context of and was associated with an international armed conflict.
5. The perpetrator was aware of factual circumstances that established the existence of an armed conflict.

Article 8(2)(*a*)(iv)
War crime of destruction and appropriation of property.   Elements
1. The perpetrator destroyed or appropriated certain property.
2. The destruction or appropriation was not justified by military necessity.
3. The destruction or appropriation was extensive and carried out wantonly.
4. Such property was protected under one or more of the Geneva Conventions of 1949.
5. The perpetrator was aware of the factual circumstances that established that protected status.
6. The conduct took place in the context of and was associated with an international armed conflict.
7. The perpetrator was aware of factual circumstances that established the existence of an armed conflict.

Article 8(2)(*a*)(v)
War crime of compelling service in hostile forces.   Elements
1. The perpetrator coerced one or more persons, by act or threat, to take part in military operations against that person's own country or forces or otherwise serve in the forces of a hostile power.
2. Such person or persons were protected under one or more of the Geneva Conventions of 1949.
3. The perpetrator was aware of the factual circumstances that established that protected status.
4. The conduct took place in the context of and was associated with an international armed conflict.
5. The perpetrator was aware of factual circumstances that established the existence of an armed conflict.

Article 8(2)(*a*)(vi)
War crime of denying a fair trial.   Elements
1. The perpetrator deprived one or more persons of a fair and regular trial by denying judicial guarantees as defined, in particular, in the third and the fourth Geneva Conventions of 1949.
2. Such person or persons were protected under one or more of the Geneva Conventions of 1949.
3. The perpetrator was aware of the factual circumstances that established that protected status.
4. The conduct took place in the context of and was associated with an international armed conflict.
5. The perpetrator was aware of factual circumstances that established the existence of an armed conflict.

Article 8(2)(*a*)(vii)–1
War crime of unlawful deportation and transfer.   Elements
1. The perpetrator deported or transferred one or more persons to another State or to another location.
2. Such person or persons were protected under one or more of the Geneva Conventions of 1949.
3. The perpetrator was aware of the factual circumstances that established that protected status.
4. The conduct took placed in the context of and was associated with an international armed conflict.
5. The perpetrator was aware of factual circumstances that established the existence of an armed conflict.

Article 8(2)(*a*)(vii)–2
War crime of unlawful confinement.   Elements
1. The perpetrator confined or continued to confine one or more persons to a certain location.
2. Such person or persons were protected under one or more of the Geneva Conventions of 1949.
3. The perpetrator was aware of the factual circumstances that established that protected status.
4. The conduct took place in the context of and was associated with an international armed conflict.
5. The perpetrator was aware of factual circumstances that established the existence of an armed conflict.

Article 8(2)(*a*)(viii)
War crime of taking hostages.   Elements
1. The perpetrator seized, detained or otherwise held hostage one or more persons.
2. The perpetrator threatened to kill, injure or continue to detain such person or persons.
3. The perpetrator intended to compel a State, an international organisation, a natural or legal person or a group of persons to act or refrain from acting as an explicit or implicit condition for the safety or the release of such person or persons.
4. Such person or persons were protected under one or more of the Geneva Conventions of 1949.
5. The perpetrator was aware of the factual circumstances that established that protected status.
6. The conduct took place in the context of and was associated with an international armed conflict.
7. The perpetrator was aware of factual circumstances that established the existence of an armed conflict.

Article 8(2)(*b*)

Article 8(2)(*b*)(i)
War crime of attacking civilians.   Elements
1. The perpetrator directed an attack.
2. The object of the attack was a civilian population as such or individual civilians not taking direct part in hostilities.
3. The perpetrator intended the civilian population as such or individual civilians not taking direct part in hostilities to be the object of the attack.
4. The conduct took place in the context of and was associated with an international armed conflict.
5. The perpetrator was aware of factual circumstances that established the existence of an armed conflict.

Article 8(2)(*b*)(ii)
War crime of attacking civilian objects.   Elements
1. The perpetrator directed an attack.
2. The object of the attack was civilian objects, that is, objects which are not military objectives.

3. The perpetrator intended such civilian objects to be the object of the attack.
4. The conduct took place in the context of and was associated with an international armed conflict.
5. The perpetrator was aware of factual circumstances that established the existence of an armed conflict.

Article 8(2)(*b*)(iii)
War crime of attacking personnel or objects involved in a humanitarian assistance or peacekeeping mission. Elements
1. The perpetrator directed an attack.
2. The object of the attack was personnel, installations, material, units or vehicles involved in a humanitarian assistance or peacekeeping mission in accordance with the Charter of the United Nations.
3. The perpetrator intended such personnel, installations, material, units or vehicles so involved to be the object of the attack.
4. Such personnel, installations, material, units or vehicles were entitled to that protection given to civilians or civilian objects under the international law of armed conflict.
5. The perpetrator was aware of the factual circumstances that established that protection.
6. The conduct took place in the context of and was associated with an international armed conflict.
7. The perpetrator was aware of factual circumstances that established the existence of an armed conflict.

Article 8(2)(*b*)(iv)
War crime of excessive incidental death, injury, or damage. Elements
1. The perpetrator launched an attack.
2. The attack was such that it would cause incidental death or injury to civilians or damage to civilian objects or widespread, long-term and severe damage to the natural environment and that such death, injury or damage would be of such an extent as to be clearly excessive in relation to the concrete and direct overall military advantage anticipated.
3. The perpetrator knew that the attack would cause incidental death or injury to civilians or damage to civilian objects or widespread, long-term and severe damage to the natural environment and that such death, injury or damage would be of such an extent as to be clearly excessive in relation to the concrete and direct overall military advantage anticipated.
4. The conduct took place in the context of and was associated with an international armed conflict.
5. The perpetrator was aware of factual circumstances that established the existence of an armed conflict.

Article 8(2)(*b*)(v)
War crime of attacking undefended places. Elements
1. The perpetrator attacked one or more towns, villages, dwellings or buildings.
2. Such towns, villages, dwellings or buildings were open for unresisted occupation.
3. Such towns, villages, dwellings or buildings did not constitute military objectives.
4. The conduct took place in the context of and was associated with an international armed conflict.
5. The perpetrator was aware of factual circumstances that established the existence of an armed conflict.

Article 8(2)(*b*)(vi)
War crime of killing or wounding a person *hors de combat* . Elements
1. The perpetrator killed or injured one or more persons.
2. Such person or persons were *hors de combat*.
3. The perpetrator was aware of the factual circumstances that established this status.
4. The conduct took place in the context of and was associated with an international armed conflict.
5. The perpetrator was aware of factual circumstances that established the existence of an armed conflict.

Article 8(2)(*b*)(vii)–1
War crime of improper use of a flag of truce. Elements
1. The perpetrator used a flag of truce.
2. The perpetrator made such use in order to feign an intention to negotiate when there was no such intention on the part of the perpetrator.
3. The perpetrator knew or should have known of the prohibited nature of such use.
4. The conduct resulted in death or serious personal injury.
5. The perpetrator knew that the conduct could result in death or serious personal injury.
6. The conduct took place in the context of and was associated with an international armed conflict.
7. The perpetrator was aware of factual circumstances that established the existence of an armed conflict.

Article 8(2)(*b*)(vii)–2
War crime of improper use of a flag, insignia or uniform of the hostile party. Elements
1. The perpetrator used a flag, insignia or uniform of the hostile party.
2. The perpetrator made such use in a manner prohibited under the international law of armed conflict while engaged in an attack.
3. The perpetrator knew or should have known of the prohibited nature of such use.
4. The conduct resulted in death or serious personal injury.
5. The perpetrator knew that the conduct could result in death or serious personal injury.
6. The conduct took place in the context of and was associated with an international armed conflict.
7. The perpetrator was aware of factual circumstances that established the existence of an armed conflict.

Article 8(2)(*b*)(vii)–3
War crime of improper use of a flag, insignia or uniform of the United Nations. Elements
1. The perpetrator used a flag, insignia or uniform of the United Nations.
2. The perpetrator made such use in a manner prohibited under the international law of armed conflict.
3. The perpetrator knew of the prohibited nature of such use.
4. The conduct resulted in death or serious personal injury.
5. The perpetrator knew that the conduct could result in death or serious personal injury.
6. The conduct took place in the context of and was associated with an international armed conflict.
7. The perpetrator was aware of factual circumstances that established the existence of an armed conflict.

6727 International Criminal Court Act 2001 etc Regulations 2004 **8–10349**

Article 8(2)(*b*)(vii)–4
War crime of improper use of the distinctive emblems of the Geneva Conventions. Elements
1. The perpetrator used the distinctive emblems of the Geneva Conventions.
2. The perpetrator made such use for combatant purposes in a manner prohibited under the international law of armed conflict.
3. The perpetrator knew or should have known of the prohibited nature of such use.
4. The conduct resulted in death or serious personal injury.
5. The perpetrator knew that the conduct could result in death or serious personal injury.
6. The conduct took place in the context of and was associated with an international armed conflict.
7. The perpetrator was aware of factual circumstances that established the existence of an armed conflict.

Article 8(2)(*b*)(viii)
The transfer, directly or indirectly, by the Occupying Power of parts of its own civilian population into the territory it occupies, or the deportation or transfer of all or parts of the population of the occupied territory within or outside this territory. Elements
1. The perpetrator:

   (*a*) Transferred, directly or indirectly, parts of its own population into the territory it occupies; or
   (*b*) Deported or transferred all or parts of the population of the occupied territory within or outside this territory.

2. The conduct took place in the context of and was associated with an international armed conflict.
3. The perpetrator was aware of factual circumstances that established the existence of an armed conflict.

Article 8(2)(*b*)(ix)
War crime of attacking protected objects. Elements
1. The perpetrator directed an attack.
2. The object of the attack was one or more buildings dedicated to religion, education, art, science or charitable purposes, historic monuments, hospitals or places where the sick and wounded are collected, which were not military objectives.
3. The perpetrator intended such building or buildings dedicated to religion, education, art, science or charitable purposes, historic monuments, hospitals or places where the sick and wounded are collected, which were not military objectives, to be the object of the attack.
4. The conduct took place in the context of and was associated with an international armed conflict.
5. The perpetrator was aware of factual circumstances that established the existence of an armed conflict.

Article 8(2)(*b*)(x)–1
War crime of mutilation. Elements
1. The perpetrator subjected one or more persons to mutilation, in particular by permanently disfiguring the person or persons, or by permanently disabling or removing an organ or appendage.
2. The conduct caused death or seriously endangered the physical or mental health of such person or persons.
3. The conduct was neither justified by the medical, dental or hospital treatment of the person or persons concerned nor carried out in such person's or persons' interest.
4. Such person or persons were in the power of an adverse party.
5. The conduct took place in the context of and was associated with an international armed conflict.
6. The perpetrator was aware of factual circumstances that established the existence of an armed conflict.

Article 8(2)(*b*)(x)–2
War crime of medical or scientific experiments. Elements
1. The perpetrator subjected one or more persons to a medical or scientific experiment.
2. The experiment caused death or seriously endangered the physical or mental health or integrity of such person or persons.
3. The conduct was neither justified by the medical, dental or hospital treatment of such person or persons concerned nor carried out in such person's or persons' interest.
4. Such person or persons were in the power of an adverse party.
5. The conduct took place in the context of and was associated with an international armed conflict.
6. The perpetrator was aware of factual circumstances that established the existence of an armed conflict.

Article 8(2)(*b*)(xi)
War crime of treacherously killing or wounding. Elements
1. The perpetrator invited the confidence or belief of one or more persons that they were entitled to, or were obliged to accord, protection under rules of international law applicable in armed conflict.
2. The perpetrator intended to betray that confidence or belief.
3. The perpetrator killed or injured such person or persons.
4. The perpetrator made use of that confidence or belief in killing or injuring such person or persons.
5. Such person or persons belonged to an adverse party.
6. The conduct took place in the context of and was associated with an international armed conflict.
7. The perpetrator was aware of factual circumstances that established the existence of an armed conflict.

Article 8(2)(*b*)(xii)
War crime of denying quarter. Elements
1. The perpetrator declared or ordered that there shall be no survivors.
2. Such declaration or order was given in order to threaten an adversary or to conduct hostilities on the basis that there shall be no survivors.
3. The perpetrator was in a position of effective command or control over the subordinate forces to which the declaration or order was directed.
4. The conduct took place in the context of and was associated with an international armed conflict.
5. The perpetrator was aware of factual circumstances that established the existence of an armed conflict.

Article 8(2)(*b*)(xiii)
War crime of destroying or seizing the enemy's property. Elements
1. The perpetrator destroyed or seized certain property.
2. Such property was property of a hostile party.
3. Such property was protected from that destruction or seizure under the international law of armed conflict.
4. The perpetrator was aware of the factual circumstances that established the status of the property.
5. The destruction or seizure was not justified by military necessity.
6. The conduct took place in the context of and was associated with an international armed conflict.
7. The perpetrator was aware of factual circumstances that established the existence of an armed conflict.

Article 8(2)(*b*)(xiv)
War crime of depriving the nationals of the hostile power of rights or actions. Elements
1. The perpetrator effected the abolition, suspension or termination of admissibility in a court of law of certain rights or actions.
2. The abolition, suspension or termination was directed at the nationals of a hostile party.
3. The perpetrator intended the abolition, suspension or termination to be directed at the nationals of a hostile party.
4. The conduct took place in the context of and was associated with an international armed conflict.
5. The perpetrator was aware of factual circumstances that established the existence of an armed conflict.

Article 8(2)(*b*)(xv)
War crime of compelling participation in military operations. Elements
1. The perpetrator coerced one or more persons by act or threat to take part in military operations against that person's own country or forces.
2. Such person or persons were nationals of a hostile party.
3. The conduct took place in the context of and was associated with an international armed conflict.
4. The perpetrator was aware of factual circumstances that established the existence of an armed conflict.

Article 8(2)(*b*)(xvi)
War crime of pillaging. Elements
1. The perpetrator appropriated certain property.
2. The perpetrator intended to deprive the owner of the property and to appropriate it for private or personal use.
3. The appropriation was without the consent of the owner.
4. The conduct took place in the context of and was associated with an international armed conflict.
5. The perpetrator was aware of factual circumstances that established the existence of an armed conflict.

Article 8(2)(*b*)(xvii)
War crime of employing poison or poisoned weapons. Elements
1. The perpetrator employed a substance or a weapon that releases a substance as a result of its employment.
2. The substance was such that it causes death or serious damage to health in the ordinary course of events, through its toxic properties.
3. The conduct took place in the context of and was associated with an international armed conflict.
4. The perpetrator was aware of factual circumstances that established the existence of an armed conflict.

Article 8(2)(*b*)(xviii)
War crime of employing prohibited gases, liquids, materials or devices. Elements
1. The perpetrator employed a gas or other analogous substance or device.
2. The gas, substance or device was such that it causes death or serious damage to health in the ordinary course of events, through its asphyxiating or toxic properties.
3. The conduct took place in the context of and was associated with an international armed conflict.
4. The perpetrator was aware of factual circumstances that established the existence of an armed conflict.

Article 8(2)(*b*)(xix)
War crime of employing prohibited bullets. Elements
1. The perpetrator employed certain bullets.
2. The bullets were such that their use violates the international law of armed conflict because they expand or flatten easily in the human body.
3. The perpetrator was aware that the nature of the bullets was such that their employment would uselessly aggravate suffering or the wounding effect.
4. The conduct took place in the context of and was associated with an international armed conflict.
5. The perpetrator was aware of actual circumstances that established the existence of an armed conflict.

Article 8(2)(*b*)(xx)
War crime of employing weapons, projectiles or materials or methods of warfare listed in the Annex to the Statute. Elements
[Elements will have to be drafted once weapons, projectiles or material of methods of warfare have been included in an annex to the Statute.]

Article 8(2)(*b*)(xxi)
War crime of outrages upon personal dignity. Elements
1. The perpetrator humiliated, degraded or otherwise violated the dignity of one or more persons.
2. The severity of the humiliation, degradation or other violation was of such degree as to be generally recognised as an outrage upon personal dignity.
3. The conduct took place in the context of and was associated with an international armed conflict.
4. The perpetrator was aware of factual circumstances that established the existence of an armed conflict.

Article 8(2)(*b*)(xxii)–1
War crime of rape. Elements
1. The perpetrator invaded the body of a person by conduct resulting in penetration, however slight, of any

part of the body of the victim or of the perpetrator with a sexual organ, or of the anal or genital opening of the victim with any object or any other part of the body.

   2. The invasion was committed by force, or by threat of force or coercion, such as that caused by fear of violence, duress, detention, psychological oppression or abuse of power, against such person or another person, or by taking advantage of a coercive environment, or the invasion was committed against a person incapable of giving genuine consent.

   3. The conduct took place in the context of and was associated with an international armed conflict.

   4. The perpetrator was aware of factual circumstances that established the existence of an armed conflict.

Article 8(2)(*b*)(xxii)–2
War crime of sexual slavery. Elements

   1. The perpetrator exercised any or all of the powers attaching to the right of ownership over one or more persons, such as by purchasing, selling, lending or bartering such a person or persons, or by imposing on them a similar deprivation of liberty.

   2. The perpetrator caused such person or persons to engage in one or more acts of a sexual nature.

   3. The conduct took place in the context of and was associated with an international armed conflict.

   4. The perpetrator was aware of factual circumstances that established the existence of an armed conflict.

Article 8(2)(*b*)(xxii)–3
War crime of enforced prostitution. Elements

   1. The perpetrator caused one or more persons to engage in one or more acts of a sexual nature by force, or by threat of force or coercion, such as that caused by fear of violence, duress, detention, psychological oppression or abuse of power, against such person or persons or another person, or by taking advantage of a coercive environment or such person's or persons' incapacity to give genuine consent.

   2. The perpetrator or another person obtained or expected to obtain pecuniary or other advantage in exchange for or in connection with the acts of a sexual nature.

   3. The conduct took place in the context of and was associated with an international armed conflict.

   4. The perpetrator was aware of factual circumstances that established the existence of an armed conflict.

Article 8(2)(*b*)(xxii)–4
War crime of forced pregnancy. Elements

   1. The perpetrator confined one ore more women forcibly made pregnant, with the intent of affecting the ethnic composition of any population or carrying out other grave violations of international law.

   2. The conduct took place in the context of and was associated with an international armed conflict.

   3. The perpetrator was aware of factual circumstances that established the existence of an armed conflict.

Article 8(2)(*b*)(xxii)–5
War crime of enforced sterilisation. Elements

   1. The perpetrator deprived one or more persons of biological reproductive capacity.

   2. The conduct was neither justified by the medical or hospital treatment of the person or persons concerned nor carried out with their genuine consent.

   3. The conduct took place in the context of and was associated with an international armed conflict.

   4. The perpetrator was aware of factual circumstances that established the existence of an armed conflict.

Article 8(2)(*b*)(xxii)–6
War crime of sexual violence. Elements

   1. The perpetrator committed an act of a sexual nature against one or more persons or caused such person or persons to engage in an act of sexual nature by force, or by threat of force or coercion, such as that caused by fear of violence, duress, detention, psychological oppression or abuse of power, against such person or persons or another person, or by taking advantage of a coercive environment or such person's or persons' incapacity to give genuine consent.

   2. The conduct was of a gravity comparable to that of a grave breach of the Geneva Conventions.

   3. The perpetrator was aware of the factual circumstances that established the gravity of the conduct.

   4. The conduct took place in the context of and was associated with an international armed conflict.

   5. The perpetrator was aware of factual circumstances that established the existence of an armed conflict.

Article 8(2)(*b*)(xxiii)
War crime of using protected persons as shields. Elements

   1. The perpetrator moved or otherwise took advantage of the location of one or more civilians or other persons protected under the international law of armed conflict.

   2. The perpetrator intended to shield a military objective from attack or shield, favour or impede military operations.

   3. The conduct took place in the context of and was associated with an international armed conflict.

   4. The perpetrator was aware of factual circumstances that established the existence of an armed conflict.

Article 8(2)(*b*)(xxiv)
War crime of attacking objects or persons using the distinctive emblems of the Geneva Conventions. Elements

   1. The perpetrator attacked one or more persons, buildings, medical units or transports or other objects using, in conformity with international law, a distinctive emblem or other method of identification indicating protection under the Geneva Conventions.

   2. The perpetrator intended such persons, buildings, units or transports or other objects so using such identification to be the object of the attack.

   3. The conduct took place in the context of and was associated with an international armed conflict.

   4. The perpetrator was aware of factual circumstances that established the existence of an armed conflict.

Article 8(2)(*b*)(xxv)
War crime of starvation as a method of warfare. Elements

   1. The perpetrator deprived civilians of objects indispensable to their survival.

   2. The perpetrator intended to starve civilians as a method of warfare.

   3. The conduct took place in the context of and was associated with an international armed conflict.

   4. The perpetrator was aware of factual circumstances that established the existence of an armed conflict.

Article 8(2)(b)(xxvi)
War crime of using, conscripting or enlisting children. Elements
   1. The perpetrator conscripted or enlisted one or more persons into the national armed forces or used one or more persons to participate actively in hostilities.
   2. Such persons or persons were under the age of 15 years.
   3. The perpetrator knew or should have known that such person or persons were under the age of 15 years.
   4. The conduct took place in the context of and was associated with an international armed conflict.
   5. The perpetrator was aware of factual circumstances that established the existence of an armed conflict.

Article 8(2)(c)

Article 8(2)(c)(i)–1
War crime of murder. Elements
   1. The perpetrator killed one or more persons.
   2. Such person or persons were either *hors de combat*, or were civilians, medical personnel, or religious personnel taking no active part in the hostilities.
   3. The perpetrator was aware of the factual circumstances that established this status.
   4. The conduct took place in the context of and was associated with an armed conflict not of an international character.
   5. The perpetrator was aware of factual circumstances that established the existence of an armed conflict.

Article 8(2)(c)(i)–2
War crime of mutilation. Elements
   1. The perpetrator subjected one or more persons to mutilation, in particular by permanently disfiguring the person or persons, or by permanently disabling or removing an organ or appendage.
   2. The conduct was neither justified by the medical, dental or hospital treatment of the person or persons concerned nor carried out in such person's or persons' interests.
   3. Such person or persons were either *hors de combat*, or were civilians, medical personnel or religious personnel taking no active part in the hostilities.
   4. The perpetrator was aware of the factual circumstances that established this status.
   5. The conduct took place in the context of and was associated with an armed conflict not of an international character.
   6. The perpetrator was aware of factual circumstances that established the existence of an armed conflict.

Article 8(2)(c)(i)–3
War crime of cruel treatment. Elements
   1. The perpetrator inflicted severe physical or mental pain or suffering upon one or more persons.
   2. Such person or persons were either *hors de combat*, or were civilians, medical personnel, or religious personnel taking no active part in the hostilities.
   3. The perpetrator was aware of the factual circumstances that established this status.
   4. The conduct took place in the context of and was associated with an armed conflict not of an international character.
   5. The perpetrator was aware of factual circumstances that established the existence of an armed conflict.

Article 8(2)(c)(i)–4
War crime of torture. Elements
   1. The perpetrator inflicted severe physical or mental pain or suffering upon one or more persons.
   2. The perpetrator inflicted the pain or suffering for such purposes as: obtaining information or a confession, punishment, intimidation or coercion or for any reason based on discrimination of any kind.
   3. Such person or persons were either *hors de combat*, or were civilians, medical personnel or religious personnel taking no active part in the hostilities.
   4. The perpetrator was aware of the factual circumstances that established this status.
   5. The conduct took place in the context of and was associated with an armed conflict not of an international character.
   6. The perpetrator was aware of factual circumstances that established the existence of an armed conflict.

Article 8(2)(c)(ii)
War crime of outrages upon personal dignity. Elements
   1. The perpetrator humiliated, degraded or otherwise violated the dignity of one or more persons.
   2. The severity of the humiliation, degradation or other violation was of such degree as to be generally recognised as an outrage upon personal dignity.
   3. Such person or persons were either *hors de combat*, or were civilians, medical personnel or religious personnel taking no active part in the hostilities.
   4. The perpetrator was aware of the factual circumstances that established this status.
   5. The conduct took place in the context of and was associated with an armed conflict not of an international character.
   6. The perpetrator was aware of factual circumstances that established the existence of an armed conflict.

Article 8(2)(c)(iii)
War crime of taking hostages. Elements
   1. The perpetrator seized, detained or otherwise held hostage one or more persons.
   2. The perpetrator threatened to kill, injure or continue to detain such person or persons.
   3. The perpetrator intended to compel a State, an international organisation, a natural or legal person or a group of persons to act or refrain from acting as an explicit or implicit condition for the safety or the release of such person or persons.
   4. Such person or persons were either *hors de combat*, or were civilians, medical personnel or religious personnel taking no active part in the hostilities.
   5. The perpetrator was aware of the factual circumstances that established this status.

6. The conduct took place in the context of and was associated with an armed conflict not of an international character.

7. The perpetrator was aware of factual circumstances that established the existence of an armed conflict.

Article 8(2)(c)(iv)
War crime of sentencing or execution without due process. Elements

1. The perpetrator passed sentence or executed one or more persons.

2. Such person or persons were either *hors de combat*, or were civilians, medical personnel or religious personnel taking no active part in the hostilities.

3. The perpetrator was aware of the factual circumstances that established this status.

4. There was no previous judgement pronounced by a court, or the court that rendered judgement was not "regularly constituted", that is, it did not afford the essential guarantees or independence and impartiality, or the court that rendered judgement did not afford all other judicial guarantees generally recognised as indispensable under international law.

5. The perpetrator was aware of the absence of a previous judgement or of the denial of relevant guarantees and the fact that they are essential or indispensable to a fair trial.

6. The conduct took place in the context of and was associated with an armed conflict not of an international character.

7. The perpetrator was aware of factual circumstances that established the existence of an armed conflict.

Article 8(2)(e)

Article 8(2)(e)(i)
War crime of attacking civilians. Elements

1. The perpetrator directed an attack.

2. The object of the attack was a civilian population as such or individual civilians not taking direct part in hostilities.

3. The perpetrator intended the civilian population as such or individual civilians not taking direct part in hostilities to be the object of the attack.

4. The conduct took place in the context of and was associated with an armed conflict not of an international character.

5. The perpetrator was aware of factual circumstances that established the existence of an armed conflict.

Article 8(2)(e)(ii)
War crime of attacking objects or persons using the distinctive emblems of the Geneva Conventions. Elements

1. The perpetrator attacked one or more persons, buildings, medical units or transports or other objects using, in conformity with international law, a distinctive emblem or other method of identification indicating protection under the Geneva Conventions.

2. The perpetrator intended such persons, buildings, units or transports or other object so using such identification to be the object of the attack.

3. The conduct took place in the context of and was associated with an armed conflict not of an international character.

4. The perpetrator was aware of factual circumstances that established the existence of an armed conflict.

Article 8(2)(e)(iii)
War crime of attacking personnel or objects involved in a humanitarian assistance or peacekeeping mission. Elements

1. The perpetrator directed an attack.

2. The object of the attack was personnel, installations, material, units or vehicles involved in a humanitarian assistance or peacekeeping mission in accordance with the Charter of the United Nations.

3. The perpetrator intended such personnel, installations, material, units or vehicles so involved to be the object of the attack.

4. Such personnel, installations, material, units or vehicles were entitled to that protection given to civilians or civilian objects under the international law of armed conflict.

5. The perpetrator was aware of the factual circumstances that established that protection.

6. The conduct took place in the context of and was associated with an armed conflict not of an international character.

7. The perpetrator was aware of factual circumstances that established the existence of an armed conflict.

Article 8(2)(e)(iv)
War crime of attacking protected objects. Elements

1. The perpetrator directed an attack.

2. The object of the attack was one or more buildings dedicated to religion, education, art, science or charitable purposes, historic monuments, hospitals or places where the sick and wounded are collected, which were not military objectives.

3. The perpetrator intended such building or buildings dedicated to religion, education, art, science or charitable purposes, historic monuments, hospitals or places where the sick and wounded are collected, which were not military objectives, to be the object of the attack.

4. The conduct took place in the context of and was associated with an armed conflict not of an international character.

5. The perpetrator was aware of factual circumstances that established the existence of an armed conflict.

Article 8(2)(e)(v)
War crime of pillaging. Elements

1. The perpetrator appropriated certain property.

2. The perpetrator intended to deprive the owner of the property and to appropriate it for private or personal use.

3. The appropriation was without the consent of the owner.

4. The conduct took place in the context of and was associated with an armed conflict not of an international character.

5. The perpetrator was aware of factual circumstances that established the existence of an armed conflict.

Article 8(2)(*e*)(vi)–1
War crime of rape. Elements
1. The perpetrator invaded the body of a person by conduct resulting in penetration, however slight, of any part of the body of the victim or of the perpetrator with a sexual organ, or of the anal or genital opening of the victim with any object or any other part of the body.
2. The invasion was committed by force, or by threat of force or coercion, such as that caused by fear of violence, duress, detention, psychological oppression or abuse of power, against such person or another person, or by taking advantage of a coercive environment, or the invasion was committed against a person incapable of giving genuine consent.
3. The conduct took place in the context of and was associated with an armed conflict not of an international character.
4. The perpetrator was aware of factual circumstances that established the existence of an armed conflict.

Article 8(2)(*e*)(vi)–2
War crime of sexual slavery. Elements
1. The perpetrator exercised any or all of the powers attaching to the right of ownership over one or more persons, such as by purchasing, selling, lending or bartering such a person or persons, or by imposing on them a similar deprivation of liberty.
2. The perpetrator caused such person or persons to engage in one or more acts of a sexual nature.
3. The conduct took place in the context of and was associated with an armed conflict not of an international character.
4. The perpetrator was aware of factual circumstances that established the existence of an armed conflict.

Article 8(2)(*e*)(vi)–3
War crime of enforced prostitution. Elements
1. The perpetrator caused one or more persons to engage in one or more acts of a sexual nature by force, or by threat of force or coercion, such as that caused by fear of violence, duress, detention, psychological oppression or abuse of power, against such person or persons or another person, or by taking advantage of a coercive environment or such person's or persons' incapacity to give genuine consent.
2. The perpetrator or another person obtained or expected to obtain pecuniary or other advantage in exchange for or in connection with the acts of a sexual nature.
3. The conduct took place in the context of and was associated with an armed conflict not of an international character.
4. The perpetrator was aware of factual circumstances that established the existence of an armed conflict.

Article 8(2)(*e*)(vi)–4
War crime of forced pregnancy. Elements
1. The perpetrator confined one or more women forcibly made pregnant, with the intent of affecting the ethnic composition of any population or carrying out other grave violations of international law.
2. The conduct took place in the context of and was associated with an armed conflict not of an international character.
3. The perpetrator was aware of factual circumstances that established the existence of an armed conflict.

Article 8(2)(*e*)(vi)–5
War crime of enforced sterilization. Elements
1. The perpetrator deprived one or more persons of biological reproductive capacity.
2. The conduct was neither justified by the medical or hospital treatment of the person or persons concerned nor carried out with their genuine consent.
3. The conduct took place in the context of and was associated with an armed conflict not of an international character.
4. The perpetrator was aware of factual circumstances that established the existence of an armed conflict.

Article 8(2)(*e*)(vi)–6
War crime of sexual violence. Elements
1. The perpetrator committed an act of a sexual nature against one or more persons or caused such person or persons to engage in an act of a sexual nature by force, or by threat of force or coercion, such as that caused by fear of violence, duress, detention, psychological oppression or abuse of power, against such person or persons or another person, or by taking advantage of a coercive environment or such person's or persons' incapacity to give genuine consent.
2. The conduct was of a gravity comparable to that of a serious violation of article 3 common to the four Geneva Conventions.
3. The perpetrator was aware of the factual circumstances that established the gravity of the conduct.
4. The conduct took place in the context of and was associated with an armed conflict not of an international character.
5. The perpetrator was aware of factual circumstances that established the existence of an armed conflict.

Article 8(2)(*e*)(vii)
War crime of using, conscripting and enlisting children. Elements
1. The perpetrator conscripted or enlisted one or more persons into an armed force or group or used one or more persons to participate actively in hostilities.
2. Such person or persons were under the age of 15 years.
3. The perpetrator knew or should have known that such person or persons were under the age of 15 years.
4. The conduct took place in the context of and was associated with an armed conflict not of an international character.
5. The perpetrator was aware of factual circumstances that established the existence of an armed conflict.

Article 8(2)(*e*)(viii)
War crime of displacing civilians. Elements
1. The perpetrator ordered a displacement of a civilian population.
2. Such order was not justified by the security of the civilians involved or by military necessity.
3. The perpetrator was in a position to effect such displacement by giving such order.

4. The conduct took place in the context of and was associated with an armed conflict not of an international character.

5. The perpetrator was aware of factual circumstances that established the existence of an armed conflict.

Article 8(2)(*e*)(ix) War crime of treacherously killing or wounding. Elements

1. The perpetrator invited the confidence or belief of one or more combatant adversaries that they were entitled to, or were obliged to accord, protection under rules of international law applicable in armed conflict.

2. The perpetrator intended to betray that confidence or belief.

3. The perpetrator killed or injured such person or persons.

4. The perpetrator made use of that confidence or belief in killing or injuring such person or persons.

5. Such person or persons belonged to an adverse party.

6. The conduct took place in the context of and was associated with an armed conflict not of an international character.

7. The perpetrator was aware of factual circumstances that established the existence of an armed conflict.

Article 8(2)(*e*)(x) War crime of denying quarter. Elements

1. The perpetrator declared or ordered that there shall be no survivors.

2. Such declaration or order was given in order to threaten an adversary or to conduct hostilities on the basis that there shall be no survivors.

3. The perpetrator was in a position of effective command or control over the subordinate forces to which the declaration or order was directed.

4. The conduct took place in the context of and was associated with an armed conflict not of an international character.

5. The perpetrator was aware of factual circumstances that established the existence of an armed conflict.

Article 8(2)(*e*)(xi)–1 War crime of mutilation. Elements

1. The perpetrator subjected one or more persons to mutilation, in particular by permanently disfiguring the person or persons, or by permanently disabling or removing an organ or appendage.

2. The conduct caused death or seriously endangered the physical or mental health of such person or persons.

3. The conduct was neither justified by the medical, dental or hospital treatment of the person or persons concerned nor carried out in such person's or persons' interest.

4. Such person or persons were in the power of another party to the conflict.

5. The conduct took place in the context of and was associated with an armed conflict not of an international character.

6. The perpetrator was aware of factual circumstances that established the existence of an armed conflict.

Article 8(2)(*e*)(xi)–2 War crime of medical or scientific experiments. Elements

1. The perpetrator subjected one or more persons to a medical or scientific experiment.

2. The experiment caused the death or seriously endangered the physical or mental health or integrity of such person or persons.

3. The conduct was neither justified by the medical, dental or hospital treatment of such person or persons concerned nor carried out in such person's or persons' interest.

4. Such person or persons were in the power of another party to the conflict.

5. The conduct took place in the context of and was associated with an armed conflict not of an international character.

6. The perpetrator was aware of factual circumstances that established the existence of an armed conflict.

Article 8(2)(*e*)(xii) War crime of destroying or seizing the enemy's property. Elements

1. The perpetrator destroyed or seized certain property.

2. Such property was property of an adversary.

3. Such property was protected from that destruction or seizure under the international law of armed conflict.

4. The perpetrator was aware of the factual circumstances that established the status of the property.

5. The destruction or seizure was not required by military necessity.

6. The conduct took place in the context of and was associated with an armed conflict not of an international character.

7. The perpetrator was aware of factual circumstances that established the existence of an armed conflict.

FIREARMS

8–10350   This title contains the following statutes—

and the following statutory instrument—

8–10360   **The Gun Barrel Proof Acts 1868 to 1978** impose powers and duties on The Gunmakers' Company of London and the Guardians of the Birmingham Proof House (two companies to which the Act gives statutory recognition) in relation to the proving and marking of the barrels of small arms (as defined). The Acts provide for penalties on summary conviction for offences in relation to stamping and marking of barrels, and dealing, by way of sale or exchange or export, with small arms the barrels of which have not been proved as the Acts require.

Firearms Act 1968[1,2]

(1968 c 27)

PART I

PROVISIONS AS TO POSSESSION, HANDLING AND DISTRIBUTION OF WEAPONS AND
AMMUNITION; PREVENTION OF CRIME AND MEASURES TO PROTECT PUBLIC SAFETY

General restrictions on possession and handling of firearms and ammunition

8–10370   1. Requirement of firearm certificate[3]. (1) Subject to any exemption[4] under this Act,
it is an offence[5] for a person—

(a) to have in his possession[6], or to purchase or acquire[7] a firearm[8] to which this section applies
without holding a firearm certificate[7] in force at the time, or otherwise than as authorised[9] by
such a certificate;

(b) to have in his possession[6], or to purchase or acquire[8], any ammunition[10] to which this section
applies without holding a firearm certificate in force at the time, or otherwise than as authorised
by such a certificate, or in quantities in excess of those so authorised.

(2) It is an offence[11] for a person to fail to comply with a condition subject to which a firearm
certificate is held by him.

(3) This section applies to every firearm except—

(a) a shot gun within the meaning of this Act, that is to say a smooth-bore[12] gun (not being an air
gun) which—

   (i)   has a barrel not less than 24 inches in length and does not have any barrel with a bore
exceeding 2 inches in diameter;

   (ii) either has no magazine or has a non-detachable magazine incapable of holding more than
two cartridges; and

   (iii) is not a revolver gun; and

(b) an air weapon (that is to say, an air rifle, air gun or air pistol which does not fall within section
5(1) and which is not of a type declared by rules made by the Secretary of State under section
53 of this Act to be specially dangerous)[13].

(3A) A gun which has been adapted to have such a magazine as is mentioned in subsection
(3)(a)(ii) above shall not be regarded as falling within that provision unless the magazine bears a
mark approved by the Secretary of State for denoting that fact and that mark has been made, and the
adaptation has been certified in writing as having been carried out in a manner approved by him,
either by one of the two companies mentioned in section 58(1) of this Act or by such other person as
may be approved by him for that purpose.

(4) This section applies to any ammunition for a firearm, except the following articles, namely:

(a) cartridges containing five or more shot, none of which exceeds ·36 inch in diameter;

(b) ammunition for an air gun, air rifle or air pistol; and

(c) blank cartridges not more than one inch in diameter measured immediately in front of the rim
or cannelure of the base of the cartridge.

[Firearms Act 1968, s 1 as amended by the Firearms (Amendment) Act 1988, s 2 and the Anti-social Behaviour
Act 2003, s 39.]

---

1. This Act, the Firearms Act 1982 and the Firearms (Amendment) Acts 1988, 1992 and 1997 may be cited together
as the Firearms Acts 1968 to 1997. The provisions of this Act should be read in conjunction with those of the Firearms
(Amendment) Act 1988, this title, post. Sections 46, 51(4) and 52 of the Firearms Act 1968 (powers of search, time-limit
for prosecutions and forfeiture and cancellation orders on conviction) shall, subject to certain exceptions, apply also to
offences under the Firearms (Amendment) Act 1988; as to interpretation and construction of these Acts, see generally s 25
of the Firearms (Amendment) Act 1988, post.

2. The Firearms Act 1968 and the Firearms Amendment Act 1988 are amended by the Firearms Acts (Amendment)
Regulations 1992, SI 1992/2823 for the purpose of implementing the requirements of EEC Council Directive 91/477. In
addition provision is made for the exchange of information by removing any obligation as to confidentiality or secrecy with
regard to the disclosure of information which is required to be disclosed in pursuance of the Directive:

   10. —(1) No obligation as to secrecy or other restriction upon the disclosure of information imposed by statute or
otherwise shall preclude—

(a) the disclosure by the Secretary of State or an officer of his to the competent authorities of a member State other
than the United Kingdom of any information which is required to be disclosed in pursuance of the directive of
the Council of the European Communities No 91/477/EEC (directive on the control of the acquisition and
possession of weapons); or

(b) the disclosure to the Secretary of State or any officer of his by a chief officer of police, or by any government
department or officer of a government department, of any information required by the Secretary of State for
the purpose of facilitating the communication or exchange of information in pursuance of that directive.

   (2) The reference in paragraph (1) above to the competent authorities of a member State is a reference to the
persons appointed by that member State to deal with the communication or exchange of information in pursuance of
the directive mentioned in that paragraph.

   (SI 1992/2823, reg 10.)

3. For further provisions as to firearm certificates, see ss 26, 27 and 29–32, post.

4. See ss 8–15, 54 and 58(1) and (2), post.
5. This section is to be construed strictly and proof of *mens rea* is unnecessary (*R v Howells* [1977] QB 614, [1977] 3 All ER 417, 141 JP 641). It is immaterial that the accused did not know the nature of the article in his possession (*R v Hussain* [1981] 2 All ER 287, [1981] 1 WLR 416; *R v Waller* [1991] Crim LR 381, CA approved in *R v Vann and Davis* [1996] Crim LR 52, CA) or that possession of a container was for a matter of minutes without opportunity to discover that it contained a firearm (*R v Steele* [1993] Crim LR 298, CA). For prosecution and punishment, see Sch 6, post.
6. The word "possession" is to be construed strictly; see *Woodage v Moss* [1974] 1 All ER 584, 138 JP 233. So a person who keeps the firearms in a place other than where he lives may nevertheless have possession of them: see *Sullivan v Earl of Caithness* [1976] QB 966, [1976] 1 All ER 844, 140 JP 277.
7. For definition see s 57(4), post.
8. For definition see s 57(1), post. See also sub-s (3) for exceptions.
9. The interpretation of what is authorised by a particular certificate is a matter of law. The commission of an absolute offence of transferring a firearm requiring a certificate to someone who does not produce a certificate authorising its acquisition does not depend on the transferee's intended use of it (*R v Paul* [1999] Crim LR 79, CA (transferee possessing a certificate for a "humane killer" not entitled to acquire a Ruger–357 revolver where the revolver was wanted to shoot pigs)).
10. For definition see s 57(2), post. See also sub-s (4) for exceptions.
11. For prosecution and punishment, see Sch 6, post.
12. For effect of removal of rifling from a rifle, see *R v Hucklebridge, A-G's Reference (No 3 of 1980)* [1980] 3 All ER 273, [1980] 1 WLR 1284, 145 JP 13 (decided on the original wording of s 1(3)(*a*) before its amendment by the Firearms (Amendment) Act 1988, s 2).
13. See the Firearms (Dangerous Air Weapons) Rules 1969, SI 1969/47 amended by SI 1993/1490, declaring certain air weapons to be specially dangerous. The meaning of "air weapon" was not expanded to include a revolver powered by compressed carbon dioxide in *R v Thorpe* [1987] 2 All ER 108, [1987] 1 WLR 383.

8–10371 2. Requirement of certificate for possession of shot guns. (1) Subject to any exemption[1] under this Act, it is an offence[2] for a person to have in his possession, or to purchase or acquire, a shot gun[3] without holding a certificate[4] under this Act authorising him to possess shot guns.

(2) It is an offence[2] for a person to fail to comply with a condition subject to which a shot gun certificate is held by him.
[Firearms Act 1968, s 2.]

1. See ss 8–15, 54 and 58(1) and (2), post.
2. For prosecution and punishment, see Sch 6, post. The offence is not technical as the purpose of a licence is to enable the keeping of shotguns to be inspected and monitored. In fining an accused, the value of the shotgun has no relevance in assessing the amount of the fine (*R v Cowley* (1995) Times, 2 February).
3. For definition of shot gun see s 1(3)(*a*), ante.
4. For definition see s 57(4), post.

8–10372 3. Business and other transactions with firearms and ammunition. (1) A person commits an offence[1] if, by way of trade or business, he—

(*a*) manufactures, sells, transfers[2], repairs, tests or proves any firearm or ammunition to which section 1 of this Act applies, or a shot gun; or

(*b*) exposes for sale or transfer[2], or has in his possession for sale, transfer, repair, test or proof any such firearm or ammunition, or a shot gun,

without being registered under this Act as a firearms dealer.

(2) It is an offence[3] for a person to sell[4] or transfer[2] to any other person in the United Kingdom, other than a registered firearms dealer, any firearm or ammunition to which section 1 of this Act applies, or a shot gun, unless that other produces a firearm certificate[5] authorising him to purchase or acquire it or, as the case may be, his shot gun certificate, or shows that he is by virtue of this Act entitled to purchase or acquire it without holding a certificate.

(3) It is an offence[3] for a person to undertake the repair, test or proof of a firearm or ammunition to which section 1 of this Act applies, or of a shot gun, for any other person in the United Kingdom other than a registered firearm dealer as such, unless that other produces or causes to be produced a firearm certificate authorising him to have possession of the firearm or ammunition or, as the case may be, his shot gun certificate, or shows that he is by virtue of this Act entitled to have possession of it without holding a certificate.

(4) Subsections (1) to (3) above have effect subject to any exemption under subsequent provisions of this Part of this Act[1].

(5) A person commits an offence[3] if, with a view to purchasing or acquiring, or procuring the repair, test or proof of, any firearm or ammunition to which section 1 of this Act applies, or a shot gun, he produces a false certificate or a certificate in which any false entry has been made, or personates a person to whom a certificate has been granted, or knowingly or recklessly makes a statement false in any material particular.

(6) It is an offence[1] for a pawnbroker to take in pawn any firearm or ammunition to which section 1 of this Act applies, or a shot gun.
[Firearms Act 1968, s 3 as amended by the Firearms (Amendment) Act 1997, Sch 2.]

1. For prosecution and punishment, see Sch 6, post.
2. For definition of "transfer" see s 57(4), post, and note thereto.
3. The prohibition on the sale of firearms imposed by this subsection is not avoided by a collateral arrangement that

possession of the firearm shall be retained by the seller, and its use by the buyer permitted only on a lawful occasion, eg, as a member of a rifle club (*Watts v Seymour* [1967] 2 QB 647, [1967] 1 All ER 1044, 131 JP 309).

4. See ss 7 to 15 and 54, post.

5. A firearm certificate gives specific authority for a particular firearm by reference to name, type calibre and serial number; accordingly, variation of a firearm certificate is required prior to a certificate holder changing the firearm in his possession, and shown in the certificate, for one of the same type and calibre (*Wilson v Coombe* [1989] 1 WLR 78, 88 Cr App Rep 322).

8–10373 **4. Conversion of weapons.** (1) Subject to this section, it is an offence[1] to shorten the barrel of a shot gun to a length less than 24 inches[2].

(2) It is not an offence under subsection (1) above for a registered firearms dealer to shorten the barrel of a shot gun for the sole purpose of replacing a defective part of the barrel so as to produce a barrel not less than 24 inches in length[2].

(3) It is an offence[1] for a person other than a registered firearms dealer to convert into a firearm anything which, though having the appearance of being a firearm, is so constructed as to be incapable of discharging any missile through its barrel.

(4) A person who commits an offence under section 1 of this Act by having in his possession, or purchasing or acquiring, a shot gun which has been shortened contrary to subsection (1) above or a firearm which has been converted as mentioned in subsection (3) above (whether by a registered firearms dealer or not), without holding a firearm certificate authorising him to have it in his possession, or to purchase or acquire it, shall be treated for the purposes of provisions of this Act relating to the punishment of offences as committing that offence in an aggravated form.

[Firearms Act 1968, s 4 as amended by the Firearms (Amendment) Act 1988, s 23.]

1. For prosecution and punishment, see Sch 6, post.
2. For interpretation of "length", see s 57(6)(*a*), post.

Prohibition of certain weapons and control of arms traffic

8–10374 **5. Weapons subject to general prohibition[1].** (1) A person commits an offence[2] if, without the authority of the Defence Council[3], he has in his possession, or purchases or acquires[4], or manufactures, sells or transfers[4]—

(*a*) any firearm[5] which is so designed or adapted[6] that two or more missiles can be successively discharged without repeated pressure on the trigger;

(*ab*) any self-loading or pump-action rifled gun other than one which is chambered for .22 rim-fire cartridges;

(*aba*)any firearm which either has a barrel less than 30 centimetres in length or is less than 60 centimetres in length overall, other than an air weapon, a muzzle-loading gun or a firearm as signalling apparatus;

(*ac*) any self-loading or pump-action smooth-bore gun which is not an air weapon or chambered for .22 rim-fire cartridges and either has a barrel less than 24 inches in length or an air weapon or is less than 40 inches in length overall;

(*ad*) any smooth-bore revolver gun other than one which is chambered for 9 mm rim-fire cartridges or a muzzle-loading gun;

(*ae*) any rocket launcher, or any mortar, for projecting a stabilised missile, other than a launcher or mortar designed for line-throwing or pyrotechnic purposes or as signalling apparatus;

(*af*) any air rifle, sir gun or air pistol which uses, or is designed or adapted for use with, a self-contained gas cartridge system;

(*b*) any weapon of whatever description designed or adapted[7] for the discharge[8] of any noxious liquid, gas or other thing; and

(*c*) any cartridge with a bullet designed to explode on or immediately before impact, any ammunition containing or designed or adapted to contain any such noxious thing as is mentioned in paragraph (*b*) above and, if capable of being used with a firearm of any description, any grenade, bomb (or other like missile), or rocket or shell designed to explode as aforesaid.

(1A) Subject to section 5A of this Act, a person commits an offence if, without the authority of the Secretary of State, he has in his possession, or purchases or acquires, or sells or transfers—

(*a*) any firearm which is disguised as another object;

(*b*) any rocket or ammunition not falling within paragraph (*c*) of subsection (1) of this section which consists in or incorporates a missile designed to explode on or immediately before impact and is for military use;

(*c*) any launcher or other projecting apparatus not falling within paragraph (*ae*) of that subsection which is designed to be used with any rocket or ammunition falling within paragraph (*b*) above or with ammunition which would fall within that paragraph but for its being ammunition falling within paragraph (*c*) of that subsection;

(*d*) any ammunition for military use which consists in or incorporates a missile designed so that a substance contained in the missile will ignite on or immediately before impact;

(e) any ammunition for military use which consists in or incorporates a missile designed, on account of its having a jacket and hard-core, to penetrate armour plating, armour screening or body armour;

(f) any ammunition which incorporates a missile designed or adapted to expand on impact;

(g) anything which is designed to be projected as a missile from any weapon and is designed to be, or has been, incorporated in—

(i) any ammunition falling within any of the preceding paragraphs; or

(ii) any ammunition which would fall within any of those paragraphs but for its being specified in subsection (1) of this section.

(2) The weapons and ammunition specified in subsections (1) and (1A) of this section (including, in the case of ammunition, any missiles falling within subsection (1A)(g) of this section) are referred to in this Act as "prohibited weapons" and "prohibited ammunition" respectively.

(3) An authority given to a person by the Defence Council[3] under this section shall be in writing and be subject to conditions specified therein.

(4) The conditions of the authority shall include such as the Defence Council[3], having regard to the circumstances of each particular case, think fit to impose for the purpose of securing that the prohibited weapon or ammunition to which the authority relates will not endanger the public safety or the peace.

(5) It is an offence[2] for a person to whom an authority is given under this section to fail to comply with any condition of the authority.

(6) The Defence Council[3] may at any time, if they think fit, revoke an authority given to a person under this section by notice in writing requiring him to deliver up the authority to such person as may be specified in the notice within twenty-one days from the date of the notice; and it is an offence[2] for him to fail to comply with that requirement.

(7) For the purposes of this section and section 5A of this Act—

(a) any rocket or ammunition which is designed to be capable of being used with a military weapon shall be taken to be for military use;

(b) references to a missile designed so that a substance contained in the missile will ignite on or immediately before impact include references to any missile containing a substance that ignites on exposure to air; and

(c) references to a missile's expanding on impact include references to its deforming in any predictable manner on or immediately after impact.

(8) For the purposes of subsection (1) (aba) and (ac) above, any detachable, folding, retractable or other movable butt-stock shall be disregarded in measuring the length of any firearm.

(9) Any reference in this section to a muzzle-loading gun is a reference to a gun which is designed to be loaded at the muzzle end of the barrel or chamber with a loose charge and a separate ball (or other missile).

[Firearms Act 1968, s 5 as amended by the Firearms (Amendment) Act 1988, s 1, SI 1992/2823 and the Firearms (Amendment) Act 1997, ss 1, 9 and Sch 3, the Firearms (Amendment) (No 2) Act 1997, s 1 and Sch and the Anti-social Behaviour Act 2003, s 39.]

---

1. The provisions of s 5, in relation to certain small firearms etc, must be read in conjunction with ss 1 to 8 of the Firearms (Amendment) Act 1997, post. If it appears to the Secretary of State that the provisions of section 5 relating to prohibited weapons or ammunition should apply to—

(a) any firearm (not being an air weapon) which is not for the time being specified in section 5(1), was not lawfully on sale in Great Britain in substantial numbers at any time before 1988 and appears to him to be—

(i) specially dangerous; or

(ii) wholly or partly composed of material making it not readily detectable by apparatus used for detecting metal objects; or

(b) any ammunition which is not for the time being specified in that subsection but appears to him to be specially dangerous,

he may by order add it to the weapons or ammunition specified in that subsection whether by altering the description of any weapon or ammunition for the time being there specified or otherwise.
(Firearms (Amendment) Act 1988, s 1(4).)

2. This section creates an absolute offence, and it is not open to the defence to prove that the accused did not know and could not reasonably have been expected to know that he was in possession of a prohibited weapon (*R v Bradish* [1990] 1 QB 981, [1990] 1 All ER 460, 154 JP 21, CA). For prosecution and punishment, see Sch 6, post.

3. By the Transfer of Functions (Prohibited Weapons) Order 1968, SI 1968/1200, the functions of the Defence Council were transferred to the Secretary of State.

4. For definition of "acquire" and "transfer", see s 57(4), post.

5. A firearm which is designed or adapted for automatic fire still remains so designed, and is therefore a prohibited weapon, despite the fact that an essential component such as the trigger may be missing (*R v Clarke* [1986] 1 All ER 846, [1986] 1 WLR 209, CA).

6. The weapon does not have to be designed or adapted for the purpose of burst or repeated fire; it is sufficient if it is capable of such fire even if only in the hands of an expert (*R v Law* [1999] Crim LR 837, CA).

7. An empty bottle of Fairy Liquid filled with hydrochloric acid was held not to be a weapon designed or adapted for the discharge of the acid within the meaning of this paragraph because there had been no alteration to the bottle so as to make it fit for such use (*R v Formosa* [1991] 2 QB 1, [1991] 1 All ER 131, 155 JP 97, CA).

8. The emission of electricity from a stun device amounts to a "discharge"; accordingly, a Lightning Strike hand-held

electric stun device was held to be a weapon designed for the discharge of a noxious thing (*Flack v Baldry* [1988] 1 All ER 673, [1988] 1 WLR 393, 152 JP 418, HL).

8–10374A   5A. Exemptions from requirement of authority under s 5.   (1) Subject to subsection (2) below, the authority of the Secretary of State shall not be required by virtue of subsection (1A) of section 5 of this Act for any person to have in his possession, or to purchase, acquire, sell or transfer, any prohibited weapon or ammunition if he is authorised by a certificate under this Act to possess, purchase or acquire that weapon or ammunition subject to a condition that he does so only for the purpose of its being kept or exhibited as part of a collection.

(2) No sale or transfer may be made under subsection (1) above except to a person who—

(a) produces the authority of the Secretary of State under section 5 of this Act for his purchase or acquisition; or

(b) shows that he is, under this section or a licence under the Schedule to the Firearms (Amendment) Act 1988 (museums etc), entitled to make the purchase or acquisition without the authority of the Secretary of State.

(3) The authority of the Secretary of State shall not be required by virtue of subsection (1A) of section 5 of this Act for any person to have in his possession, or to purchase or acquire, any prohibited weapon or ammunition if his possession, purchase or acquisition is exclusively in connection with the carrying on of activities in respect of which—

(a) that person; or

(b) the person on whose behalf he has possession, or makes the purchase or acquisition,

is recognised, for the purposes of the law of another member State relating to firearms, as a collector of firearms or a body concerned in the cultural or historical aspects of weapons.

(4) The authority of the Secretary of State shall not be required by virtue of subsection (1A) of section 5 of this Act for any person to have in his possession, or to purchase or acquire, or to sell or transfer, any expanding ammunition or the missile for any such ammunition if—

(a) he is authorised by a firearm certificate or visitor's firearm permit to possess, or purchase or acquire, any expanding ammunition; and

(b) the certificate or permit is subject to a condition restricting the use of any expanding ammunition to use in connection with any one or more of the following, namely—

(i)   the lawful shooting of deer;

(ii) the shooting of vermin or, in the course of carrying on activities in connection with the management of any estate[1], other wildlife;

(iii) the humane killing of animals;

(iv) the shooting of animals for the protection of other animals or humans.

(5) The authority of the Secretary of State shall not be required by virtue of subsection (1A) of section 5 of this Act for any person to have in his possession any expanding ammunition or the missile for any such ammunition if—

(a) he is entitled, under section 10 of this Act, to have a slaughtering instrument and the ammunition for it in his possession; and

(b) the ammunition or missile in question is designed to be capable of being used with a slaughtering instrument.

(6) The authority of the Secretary of State shall not be required by virtue of subsection (1A) of section 5 of this Act for the sale or transfer of any expanding ammunition or the missile for any such ammunition to any person who produces a certificate by virtue of which he is authorised under subsection (4) above to purchase or acquire it without the authority of the Secretary of State.

(7) The authority of the Secretary of State shall not be required by virtue of subsection (1A) of section 5 of this Act for a person carrying on the business of a firearms dealer, or any servant of his, to have in his possession, or to purchase, acquire, sell or transfer, any expanding ammunition or the missile for any such ammunition in the ordinary course of that business.

(8) In this section—

(a) references to expanding ammunition are references to any ammunition which incorporates a missile which is designed to expand on impact; and

(b) references to the missile for any such ammunition are references to anything which, in relation to any such ammunition, falls within section 5(1)(g) of this Act.

[Firearms Act 1968, s 5A inserted by SI 1992/2823 and amended by the Firearms (Amendment) Act 1997, s 10 and Sch 3.]

---

1. The reference to activities in connection with the management of any estate is limited to the management of an estate in Great Britain (*Lacey v Metropolitan Police Comr* [2000] Crim LR 853).

8–10375   6. Power to prohibit movement of arms and ammunition.   (1) The Secretary of State may by order prohibit the removal of firearms or ammunition—

(a) from one place to another in Great Britain; or

(b) *(Repealed)*;

(c) for export from Great Britain,

unless the removal is authorised by the chief officer of police for the area from which they are to be removed, and unless such other conditions as may be specified in the order are complied with.

(1A) The Secretary of State may by order[1] prohibit the removal of firearms or ammunition from Great Britain to Northern Ireland unless—

(a) the removal is authorised by the chief officer of police for the area from which they are to be removed and by the Chief Constable of the Royal Ulster Constabulary; and

(b) such conditions as may be specified in the order or imposed by the chief officer of police or the Chief Constable are complied with.

(2) An order under this section may apply—

(a) either generally to all such removals, or to removals from and to particular localities specified in the order; and

(b) either to all firearms and ammunition or to firearms and ammunition of such classes and descriptions as may be so specified; and

(c) either to all modes of conveyance or to such modes of conveyance as may be so specified;

but no such order shall prohibit the holder of a firearm certificate from carrying with him any firearm or ammunition authorised by the certificate to be so carried.

(3) It is an offence[2] to contravene any provision of—

(a) an order made under this section; or

(b) an order made under section 9 of the Firearms Act 1920 (the former enactment corresponding to section 18 of the Firearms Act 1937, and this section); or

(c) any corresponding Northern Irish order, that is to say an order made under the said section 9 as extending to Northern Ireland or under any enactment of the Parliament of Northern Ireland repealing and re-enacting that section, prohibiting the removal of firearms or ammunition from Northern Ireland to Great Britain.

(4) An order under this section shall be made by statutory instrument and may be varied or revoked by a subsequent order made thereunder by the Secretary of State.

[Firearms Act 1968, s 6 as amended by the Firearms (Amendment) Act 1988, s 20.]

---

1. The Firearms (Removal to Northern Ireland) Order 1990, SI 1990/2621 has been made.
2. For prosecution and punishment, see Sch 6, post. Note also forfeiture power in Part II thereof.

Special exemptions from sections 1 to 5

8-10376 7. Police permit. (1) A person who has obtained from the chief officer of police[1] for the area in which he resides a permit for the purpose in the prescribed[2] form may, without holding a certificate under this Act, have in his possession a firearm and ammunition in accordance with the terms of the permit.

(2) It is an offence[3] for a person knowingly or recklessly to make a statement false in any material particular for the purpose of procuring, whether for himself or for another person, the grant of a permit under this section.

[Firearms Act 1968, s 7 as amended by the Firearms (Amendment) Act 1997, Sch 2.]

---

1. See s 62 and Sch 8 of the Police Act 1964, title POLICE, post; and s 55, post. As to the adoption of a policy when considering applications, see *R v Crown Court at Wakefield, ex p Oldfield* [1978] Crim LR 164.
2. The form is contained in the Schedule to the Firearms Rules 1998, see r 9(1), this title, post.
3. For prosecution and punishment, see Sch 6, post.

8-10377 8. Authorised dealing with firearms. (1) A person carrying on the business of a firearms dealer[1] and registered[1] as such under this Act, or a servant of such a person may, without holding a certificate, have in his possession, or purchase or acquire, a firearm or ammunition in the ordinary course of that business.

(1A) Subsection (1) above applies to the possession, purchase or acquisition of a firearm or ammunition in the ordinary course of the business of a firearms dealer notwithstanding that the firearm or ammunition is in the possession of, or purchased or acquired by, the dealer or his servant at a place which is not a place of business of the dealer or which he has not registered as a place of business under section 33 or 37 of this Act.

(2) It is not an offence under section 3(2) of this Act for a person—

(a) to part with the possession of any firearm or ammunition, otherwise than in pursuance of a contract of sale or hire or by way of gift or loan, to a person who shows that he is by virtue of this Act entitled to have possession of the firearm or ammunition without holding a certificate; or

(b) to return to another person a shot gun which he has lawfully undertaken to repair, test or prove for the other.

[Firearms Act 1968, s 8 as amended by the Firearms (Amendment) Act 1997, s 42.]

1. Defined in s 57(4), post.

8–10378   9. Carriers, auctioneers, etc.   (1) A person carrying on the business of an auctioneer, carrier or warehouseman, or a servant of such a person, may, without holding a certificate, have in his possession a firearm or ammunition in the ordinary course of that business.

(2) It is not an offence under section 3(1) of this Act for an auctioneer to sell by auction, expose for sale by auction or to have in his possession for sale by auction a firearm or ammunition without being registered as a firearms dealer, if he has obtained from the chief officer of police for the area in which the auction is held a permit for that purpose in the prescribed[1] form and complies with the terms of the permit.

(3) It is an offence[2] for a person knowingly or recklessly to make a statement false in any material particular for the purpose of procuring, either for himself or for another person, the grant of a permit under subsection (2) of this section.

(4) It is not an offence under section 3(2) of this Act for a carrier or warehouseman, or a servant of a carrier or warehouseman, to deliver any firearm or ammunition in the ordinary course of his business or employment as such.
[Firearms Act 1968, s 9 as amended by the Firearms (Amendment) Act 1997, Sch 2.]

1. The form is contained in the Schedule to the Firearms Rules 1998, see r 9(2), this title, post.
2. For prosecution and punishment, see Sch 6, post.

8–10379   10. Slaughter of animals.   (1) A person licensed under the Welfare of Animals (Slaughter or Killing) Regulations 1995[1] to slaughter horses, cattle, sheep, swine or goats, may, without holding a certificate, have in his possession a slaughtering instrument[2] and ammunition therefor in any slaughterhouse or knacker's yard in which he is employed.

(2) The proprietor of a slaughterhouse or knacker's yard or a person appointed by him to take charge of slaughtering instruments and ammunition therefor for the purpose of storing them in safe custody at that slaughterhouse or knacker's yard[3] may, without holding a certificate, have in his possession a slaughtering instrument or ammunition therefor for that purpose.
[Firearms Act 1968, s 10, as amended by the Slaughterhouses Act 1974, Sch 3 and SI 1995/731.]

1. SI 1995/731.
2. Defined in s 57(4), post.
3. Cf definition of "knacker's yard" in s 45 of the Slaughterhouses Act 1974, for the purposes of that Act, title ANIMALS , ante.

8–10380   11. Sports, athletics and other approved activities.   (1) A person carrying a firearm or ammunition belonging to another person holding a certificate under this Act may, without himself holding such a certificate, have in his possession that firearm or ammunition under instructions from, and for the use of, that other person for sporting purposes[1] only.

(2) A person may, without holding a certificate, have a firearm in his possession at an athletic meeting for the purpose of starting races at that meeting.

(3) *Repealed.*

(4) A person conducting or carrying on a miniature rifle range (whether for a rifle club or otherwise) or shooting gallery at which no firearms are used other than air weapons or miniature rifles not exceeding ·23 inch calibre may, without holding a certificate, have in his possession, or purchase or acquire, such miniature rifles and ammunition suitable therefor; and any person may, without holding a certificate, use any such rifle and ammunition at such a range or gallery.

(5) A person may, without holding a shot gun certificate, borrow a shot gun from the occupier of private premises[2] and use it on those premises[2] in the occupier's presence.

(6) A person may, without holding a shot gun certificate, use a shot gun at a time and place approved for shooting at artificial targets by the chief officer of police for the area in which that place is situated.
[Firearms Act 1968, s 11 as amended by the Firearms (Amendment) Act 1988, s 15, the Armed Forces Act 1996, Sch 7 and the Firearms (Amendment) Act 1997, Sch 2.]

1. Shooting rats is not a "sporting purpose" (*Morton v Chaney* [1960] 3 All ER 632, 125 JP 37).
2. "Premises" includes any land: s 57(4), post.

8–10381   12. Theatre and cinema.   (1) A person taking part in a theatrical performance or a rehearsal thereof, or in the production of a cinematograph film, may, without holding a certificate, have a firearm in his possession during and for the purpose of the performance, rehearsal or production.

(2) Where the Defence Council[1] are satisfied, on the application of a person in charge of a theatrical performance, a rehearsal of such a performance or the production of a cinematograph film, that a prohibited weapon is required for the purpose of the performance, rehearsal or production, they may under section 5 of this Act, if they think fit, not only authorise that person to have possession

of the weapon but also authorise such other persons as he may select to have possession of it while taking part in the performance, rehearsal or production.
[Firearms Act 1968, s 12 as amended by the Firearms (Amendment) Act 1988, s 23.]

1. By the Transfer of Functions (Prohibited Weapons) Order 1968 (SI 1968/1200) the functions of the Defence Council were transferred to the Secretary of State.

8–10382   13. Equipment for ships and aircraft.   (1) A person may, without holding a certificate,—

(a) have in his possession a firearm or ammunition on board a ship or a signalling apparatus or ammunition therefor on board an aircraft or at an aerodrome, as part of the equipment of the ship, aircraft or aerodrome;

(b) remove a signalling apparatus or ammunition therefor, being part of the equipment of an aircraft, from one aircraft to another at an aerodrome, or from or to an aircraft at an aerodrome to or from a place appointed for the storage thereof in safe custody at that aerodrome, and keep any such apparatus or ammunition at such a place; and

(c) if he has obtained from a constable a permit for the purpose in the prescribed[1] form, remove a firearm from or to a ship, or a signalling apparatus from or to an aircraft or aerodrome, to or from such place and for such purpose as may be specified in the permit.

(2) It is an offence[2] for a person knowingly or recklessly to make a statement false in any material particular for the purpose of procuring, either for himself or for another person, the grant of a permit under subsection (1)(c) of this section.
[Firearms Act 1968, s 13 as amended by the Firearms (Amendment) Act 1988, s 23 and the Firearms (Amendment) Act 1997, Sch 2.]

1. The form is contained in the Schedule to the Firearms Rules 1998, see r 9(3), this title, post.
2. For prosecution and punishment, see Sch 6, post.

8–10384   15. Holder of Northern Irish certificate.   Section 2(1) of this Act does not apply to a person holding a firearm certificate issued in Northern Ireland authorising him to possess a shot gun.
[Firearms Act 1968, s 15.]

Prevention of crime and preservation of public safety

8–10385   16. Possession of firearm with intent[1] to injure.   It is an offence[2] for a person to have in his possession any firearm[3] or ammunition[4] with intent by means thereof to endanger life[5], or to enable another person by means thereof to endanger life, whether any injury has been caused or not.
[Firearms Act 1968, s 16, as amended by the Criminal Damage Act 1971, Sch]

1. Since both limbs of s 16 are concerned with possession not supply, it is the state of mind of the possessor of the firearm or ammunition that must be considered; the intent required is a specific intent (*R v Jones* [1997] 2 WLR 792).
2. For prosecution and punishment, see Sch 6, post. See *R v Bentham* [1973] QB 357, [1972] 3 All ER 271; and *R v El-Hakkaoui* [1975] 2 All ER 146, 139 JP 467.
3. Defined in s 57(1), post.
4. Defined in s 57(2), post.
5. It will not be an offence if he intended suicide, and not to endanger the life of another; see *R v Norton* and commentary thereon at [1977] Crim LR 478. Lawful self-defence constitutes a defence to a charge under this section (*R v Georgiades* [1989] 1 WLR 759, 89 Cr App Rep 206, CA).

8–10386   16A. Possession of firearm with intent to cause fear of violence.   It is an offence for a person to have in his possession any firearm or imitation firearm with intent—

(a) by means thereof to cause, or
(b) to enable another person by means thereof to cause,

any person to believe that unlawful violence will be used against him or another person.
[Firearms Act 1968, s 16A, as inserted by the Firearms (Amendment) Act 1994, s 1.]

8–10387   17. Use of firearm to resist arrest[1].   (1) It is an offence[2] for a person to make or attempt to make any use whatsoever of a firearm[3] or imitation firearm[4] with intent to resist or prevent the lawful arrest or detention of himself or another person.

(2) If a person, at the time of his committing or being arrested[5] for an offence specified in Schedule 1 to this Act, has in his possession[6] a firearm or imitation firearm, he shall be guilty of an offence[2] under this subsection unless he shows that he had it in his possession for a lawful object.

(3) *Repealed.*

(4) For purposes of this section, the definition of "firearm" in section 57(1) of this Act shall apply without paragraphs (b) and (c) of that subsection, and "imitation firearm" shall be construed accordingly.

(5) In the application of this section to Scotland, a reference to Schedule 2 to this Act shall be substituted for the reference in subsection (2) to Schedule 1.
[Firearms Act 1968, s 17, as amended by the Theft Act 1968.]

1. If the defendant is also charged with an offence listed in Schedule 1 to the Magistrates' Courts Act 1980, see the special procedure set out in Sch 6 para 3, post.

2. For prosecution and punishment, see Sch 6, post.

3. Defined in s 57(1), post.

4. Defined in s 57(4), post.

5. It is not necessary for the prosecution to prove that the defendant actually committed the specified offence; it is sufficient to prove that the defendant was in possession of the firearm or imitation firearm when he was lawfully arrested for a specified offence (*R v Jones* (2000) 164 JP 293, CA and see *R v Nelson* [2000] 3 WLR 300, [2000] Crim LR 591, CA).

6. "Possession" as distinct from the term "has with him" used elsewhere in the Act includes possession other than physical possession. Thus a defendant arrested in a street was rightly convicted of an offence under this provision where a firearm was found during a search of his flat (*R v North* [2001] Crim LR 746, CA). One cannot possess something that is part of oneself, such as an unsevered hand or finger; therefore, using one's fingers through clothing to give the impression of carrying a gun does not amount to possession of an imitation firearm: *R v Bentham* [2005] UKHL 18, [2005] 2 ALL ER 65, [2005] 1 WLR 1057, (2005) 169 JP 181.

8–10388   18. Carrying firearms with criminal intent.   (1) It is an offence[1] for a person to have with him[2] a firearm[3] or imitation firearm[4] with intent[5] to commit an indictable offence, or to resist arrest or prevent the arrest of another, in either case while he has the firearm or imitation firearm with him.

(2) In proceedings for an offence under this section proof that the accused had a firearm or imitation firearm with him and intended to commit an offence, or to resist or prevent arrest, is evidence that he intended to have with him while doing so.

(3) *Applies to Scotland.*

[Firearms Act 1968, s 18.]

1. For prosecution and punishment, see Sch 6, post.

2. To prove that the accused had with him a firearm the prosecution must establish more than mere possession, namely that the accused had a close physical link and immediate control over the firearm; but it is not necessary to establish that he had been carrying it (*R v Kelt* [1977] 3 All ER 1099, 142 JP 60 and see *R v Pawlicki and R v Swindell* [1992] 1 WLR 827, [1992] Crim LR 584, CA).

3. Defined in s 57(1), post. It is not necessary to prove that the accused intended to use the weapon in the crime as the section is wide enough to embrace those who set out to commit an indictable offence whilst intentionally carrying a firearm (*R v Stoddart* [1998] 2 Cr App Rep 25, 162 JP 78, CA).

4. Defined in s 57(4), post.

5. Where a defendant pulled an imitation firearm from a shoulder holster, it was held that it was not essential for the intent to have been formed before the imitation firearm was pulled out of the holster (*R v Houghton* [1982] Crim LR 112).

8–10389   19. Carrying firearm in a public place.   A person commits an offence[1] if, without lawful authority[2] or reasonable excuse (the proof[3] whereof lies on him) he has with him[4] in a public place[5]—

(*a*) a loaded shot gun[6],

(*b*) an air weapon[7] (whether loaded or not),

(*c*) any other firearm[6] (whether loaded or not) together with ammunition suitable for use in that firearm, or

(*d*) an imitation firearm.

[Firearms Act 1968, s 19, as amended by the Anti-social Behaviour Act 2003, s 37.]

1. For prosecution and punishment, see Sch 6, post.

2. A valid shotgun certificate does not give a person lawful authority to have with him a loaded shotgun in a public place (*Ross v Collins* [1982] Crim LR 368). The same reasoning applies *a fortiori* to a firearms certificate and a firearm. Mistaken belief that a certificate is valid and constitutes lawful authority is not a defence (*R v Clarke* (1994) Times, 19 August); followed in *R v Jones (TM)* [1995] QB 235, 159 JP 94, CA where it was held that a certificate for a firearm and ammunition was not in itself lawful authority for the holder of the certificate to have the firearm and ammunition for it in a public place.

3. The onus of proof is less than that which lies on the prosecution in proving a case beyond reasonable doubt and it may be discharged by evidence of probability (*R v Carr-Briant* [1943] KB 607, [1943] 2 All ER 156, 107 JP 167). The mistaken belief by the holder of an invalid firearm certificate that it was valid and that it was lawful authority is not capable of being a reasonable excuse (*R v Jones (TM)* [1995] QB 235, 159 JP 94, CA).

4. See note 2 at para **8–10388**.

5. Defined in s 57(4), post. See *Anderson v Miller* [1976] Crim LR 743.

6. Defined in s 57(1), post.

7. Defined in s 57(6), (*b*), post. The term "air weapon" is not intended to be limited to "firearms" and it is not necessary for an air weapon to have lethal effect to fall within the prohibition in this section (*DPP v Street* (2004) Times, 23 January).

8–10390   20. Trespassing with firearm.   (1) A person commits an offence[1] if, while he has a firearm or imitation firearm[2] with him[3], he enters or is in any building or part of a building as a trespasser and without reasonable excuse (the proof[4] whereof lies on him).

(2) A person commits an offence[1] if, while he has a firearm or imitation firearm[2] with him[3], he enters or is on any land as a trespasser and without reasonable excuse (the proof[4] whereof lies on him).

(3) In subsection (2) of this section the expression "land" includes land covered with water.

[Firearms Act 1968, s 20 as amended by the Firearms (Amendment) Act 1994, s 2.]

1. For prosecution and punishment, see Sch 6, post.

2. Defined in s 57(1), post.

3. To prove that the accused had with him a firearm the prosecution must establish more than mere possession, namely that the accused had a close physical link and immediate control over the firearm; but it is not necessary to establish that he had been carrying it (*R v Kelt* [1977] 3 All ER 1099, 142 JP 60).

4. The onus of proof is less than that which lies on the prosecution in proving a case beyond reasonable doubt and it may be discharged by evidence of probability (*R v Carr-Briant* [1943] KB 607, [1943] 2 All ER 156, 107 JP 167).

8–10400 21. Possession of firearms by persons previously convicted of crime. (1) A person who has been sentenced to custody for life or to preventative detention, or to imprisonment or to corrective training for a term of three years or more[1] or to youth custody or detention in a young offender institution for such a term, or who has been sentenced to be detained for such a term in a young offenders institution in Scotland, shall not at any time have a firearm or ammunition in his possession.

(2) A person who has been sentenced to imprisonment[2] for a term of three months or more but less than three years or to youth custody or detention in a young offender institution for such a term, or who has been sentenced to be detained for such a term in a detention centre or in a young offenders institution in Scotland or who has been subject to a secure training order or a detention and training order, shall not at any time before the expiration of the period of five years from the date of his release have a firearm or ammunition in his possession.

(2A) For the purposes of subsection (2) above, "the date of his release" means—

(*a*) in the case of a person sentenced to imprisonment with an order under section 47(1) of the Criminal Law Act 1977 (prison sentence partly served and partly suspended), the date on which he completes service of so much of the sentence as was by that order required to be served in prison;

(*b*) in the case of a person who has been subject to a secure training order—

(i) the date on which he is released from detention under the order;

(ii) the date on which he is released from detention ordered under section 4 of the Criminal Justice and Public Order Act 1994; or

(iii) the date halfway through the total period specified by the court in making the order,

whichever is the later;

(*c*) in the case of a person who has been subject to a detention and training order—

(i) the date on which he is released from detention under the order;

(ii) the date on which he is released from detention ordered under section 104 of the Powers of Criminal Courts (Sentencing) Act 2000; or

(iii) the date of the halfway point of the term of the order,

whichever is the later.

(*d*) in the case of a person who has been subject to a sentence of imprisonment to which an intermittent custody order under section 183(1)(*b*) of the Criminal Justice Act 2003 relates, the date of his final release.

(2B) A person who is serving a sentence of imprisonment to which an intermittent custody order under section 183 of the Criminal Justice Act 2003 relates shall not during any licence period specified for the purposes of subsection (1)(*b*)(i) of that section have a firearm or ammunition in his possession.

(3) A person who—

(*a*) is the holder of a licence issued under section 53 of the Children and Young Persons Act 1933, or section 57 of the Children and Young Persons (Scotland) Act 1937 (which sections provide for the detention of children and young persons convicted of serious crime, but enable them to be discharged on licence by the Secretary of State); or

(*b*) is subject to a recognisance to keep the peace or to be of good behaviour, a condition of which is that he shall not possess, use or carry a firearm, or is subject to a probation order containing a requirement that he shall not possess, use or carry a firearm; or

(*c*) has, in Scotland, been ordained to find caution a condition of which is that he shall not possess, use or carry a firearm;

shall not, at any time during which he holds the licence or is so subject or has been so ordained, have a firearm or ammunition in his possession.

(3ZA) In subsection (3)(*b*) above, "community order" means—

(a) a community order with the meaning of Part 12 of the Criminal Justice Act 2003 made in England and Wales, or

(b) a probation order made in Scotland.

(3A) Where by section 19 of the Firearms Act (Northern Ireland) 1969, or by any other enactment for the time being in force in Northern Ireland and corresponding to this section, a person is prohibited in Northern Ireland from having a firearm or ammunition in his possession, he shall also be so prohibited in Great Britain at any time when to have it in his possession in Northern Ireland would be a contravention of the said section 19 or corresponding enactment.

(4) It is an offence[3] for a person to contravene any of the foregoing provisions of this section.

(5) It is an offence[3] for a person to sell or transfer[4] a firearm or ammunition to, or to repair, test or

prove a firearm or ammunition for, a person whom he knows or has reasonable ground for believing to be prohibited by this section from having a firearm or ammunition in his possession.

(6) A person prohibited under subsection (1), (2), (2B), (3) or (3A) of this section from having in his possession a firearm or ammunition may apply to the Crown Court[5] or, in Scotland, in accordance with Act of Sederunt to the sheriff for a removal of the prohibition; and if the application is granted that prohibition shall not then apply to him.

(7) Schedule 3 to this Act shall have effect with respect to the courts with jurisdiction to entertain an application under this section and to the procedure appertaining thereto.

[Firearms Act 1968, s 21, as amended by the Courts Act 1971, Sch 9, the Criminal Law Act 1977, Sch 9, the Criminal Justice Act 1982, Sch 14, the Criminal Justice Act 1988, Schs 8 and 16, the Criminal Justice and Public Order Act 1994, Sch 10, the Crime and Disorder Act 1998, Sch 8, the Powers of Criminal Courts (Sentencing) Act 2000, Sch 9 and the Criminal Justice Act 2003, Sch 32.]

---

*Reproduced as amended by the Criminal Justice Act 2003, s 304: para (2A)(*d*), sub-ss (2B) and (3ZA) and "(2B)" in sub-s (6) inserted from a date to be appointed.

1. Where there are several separate shorter sentences it is the total which counts for this purpose (*Davies v Tomlinson* (1980) 71 Cr App Rep 279—two concurrent and one consecutive sentence totalling 2³/₄ years imprisonment plus an activated suspended sentence of six months).

2. The prohibition in subsection (2) was held not to apply to a person whose sentence was suspended: *R v Fordham* [1970] 1 QB 77, [1969] 3 All ER 532, 133 JP 626.

3. For prosecution and punishment, see Sch 6, post.

4. Defined in s 57(4), post.

5. The chief officer of police shall not be ordered to pay the costs of the applicant (Sch 3, para 7).

8–10401　22. Acquisition and possession of firearms by minors.　　(1) It is an offence[1] for a person under the age of seventeen[2] to purchase or hire any firearm[3] or ammunition[4].

(1A) Where a person under the age of eighteen is entitled, as the holder of a certificate under this Act, to have a firearm in his possession, it is an offence for that person to use that firearm for a purpose not authorised by the European weapons directive.

(2) It is an offence[1] for a person under the age of fourteen[2] to have in his possession any firearm[3] or ammunition[4] to which section 1 of this Act applies, except in circumstances where under section 11(1), (3) or (4) of this Act or section 15 of the Firearms (Amendment) Act 1988[5] he is entitled to have possession of it without holding a firearm certificate.

(3) It is an offence[1] for a person under the age of fifteen[2] to have with him[6] an assembled shot gun[7] except while under the supervision of a person of or over the age of twenty-one, or while the shot gun is so covered with a securely fastened gun cover that it cannot be fired.

(4) Subject to section 23 below, it is an offence[1] for a person under the age of seventeen[2] to have with him[6] an air weapon[8] or ammunition for an air weapon.

(5) (*Repealed*).

[Firearms Act 1968, s 22 as amended by the Firearms (Amendment) Act 1988, s 23, SI 1992/2823 and the Anti-social Behaviour Act 2003, s 38.]

---

1. For prosecution and punishment, see Sch 6, post and note forfeiture powers under Part II thereof.

2. The onus of proving that the person is under the relevant age will be on the prosecution.

3. Defined in s 57(1), post.

4. Defined in s 57(2), post.

5. See, post.

6. See note 2 to s 18(1), ante.

7. Defined in s 1(3)(*a*), ante.

8. Defined in s 1(3)(*b*), ante.

8–10402　23. Exceptions from section 22(4).　　(1) It is not an offence under section 22(4) of this Act for a person to have with him an air weapon or ammunition while he is under the supervision of a person of or over the age of twenty-one; but where a person has with him an air weapon on any premises[1] in circumstances where he would be prohibited from having it with him but for this subsection, it is an offence[2]—

(*a*) for him to use it for firing any missile beyond those premises; or

(*b*) for the person under whose supervision he is to allow him so to use it.

(2) It is not an offence under section 22(4) of this Act for a person to have with him an air weapon or ammunition at a time when—

(*a*) being a member of a rifle club or miniature rifle club for the time being approved by the Secretary of State for the purposes of this section or section 15 of the Firearms (Amendment) Act 1988[3], he is engaged as such a member in connection with target shooting; or

(*b*) he is using the weapon or ammunition at a shooting gallery where the only firearms used are either air weapons or miniature rifles not exceeding ·23 inch calibre.

(3) It is not an offence under section 22(4) of this Act for a person of or over the age of fourteen to have with him an air weapon or ammunition on private premises with the consent of the occupier.

(4) But where a person has with him an air weapon on premises in circumstances where he would

be prohibited from having it with him but for subsection (3), it is an offence for him to use it for firing any missile beyond those premises.
[Firearms Act 1968, s 23 as amended by the Firearms (Amendment) Act 1988, s 23 and the Firearms (Amendment) Act 1997, Schs 2 and 3 and the Anti-social Behaviour Act 2003, s 38.]

1. Defined in s 57(4), post.
2. For prosecution and punishment, see Sch 6, post and note forfeiture powers under Part II thereof.
3. See, post.

8–10403 24. Supplying firearms to minors. (1) It is an offence[1] to sell[2] or let on hire any firearm[3] or ammunition[4] to a person under the age of seventeen[5].

(2) It is an offence[1]—

(*a*) to make a gift or lend any firearm[3] or ammunition[4] to which section 1 of this Act applies to a person under the age of fourteen[5]; or

(*b*) to part with the possession of any such firearm or ammunition to a person under that age[5], except in circumstances where that person is entitled under section 11(1), (3) or (4) of this Act or section 15 of the Firearms (Amendment) Act 1988[6] to have possession thereof without holding a firearm certificate.

(3) It is an offence[1] to make a gift of a shot gun[7] or ammunition for a shot gun to a person under the age of fifteen[5].

(4) It is an offence[1]—

(*a*) to make a gift of an air weapon[8] or ammunition for an air weapon to a person under the age of seventeen[5]; or

(*b*) to part with the possession of an air weapon or ammunition for an air weapon to a person under the age of seventeen[5] except where by virtue of section 23 of this Act the person is not prohibited from having it with him.

(5) In proceedings for an offence under any provision of this section it is a defence to prove that the person charged with the offence believed the other person to be of or over the age mentioned in that provision and had reasonable ground for the belief.
[Firearms Act 1968, s 24 as amended by the Firearms (Amendment) Act 1988, s 23 and the Anti-social Behaviour Act 2003, s 39.]

1. For prosecution and punishment, see Sch 6, post and note forfeiture powers under Part II thereof.
2. The prohibition on the sale of firearms is not avoided by a collateral arrangement that possession of the firearm shall be retained by the seller (*Watts v Seymour* [1967] 2 QB 647, [1967] 1 All ER 1044, 131 JP 309).
3. Defined in s 57(1), post.
4. Defined in s 57(2), post.
5. The onus of proving that the person is under the relevant age will be on the prosecution.
6. See, post.
7. Defined in s 1(3)(*a*), ante.
8. Defined in s 1(3)(*b*), ante.

8–10404 25. Supplying firearm to person drunk or insane. It is an offence[1] for a person to sell or transfer any firearm or ammunition to, or to repair, prove or test any firearm or ammunition for, another person whom he knows or has reasonable cause for believing to be drunk or of unsound mind.
[Firearms Act 1968, s 25.]

1. For prosecution and punishment, see Sch 6, post.

PART II
FIREARM AND SHOT GUN CERTIFICATES; REGISTRATION OF FIREARMS DEALERS
Grant, renewal, variation and revocation of firearm and shot gun certificates

8–10405 26A. Application for firearm certificates. (1) An application for the grant of a firearm certificate shall be made in the prescribed form[1] to the chief officer of police[2] for the area[3] in which the applicant resides[4] and shall state such particulars as may be required by the form.

(2) Rules[1] made by the Secretary of State under section 53 of this Act may require any application for a certificate to be accompanied by up to four photographs of the applicant and by the names and addresses of two persons who have agreed to act as referees.

(3) The rules may require that, before considering an application for a firearm certificate, the chief officer of police has the following from each referee nominated by the applicant—

(*a*) verification in the prescribed manner of—

(i) any prescribed particulars; and
(ii) the likeness to the applicant of the photographs submitted with the application;

(*b*) a statement in the prescribed form to the effect that he knows of no reason why the applicant should not be permitted to possess a firearm; and (*c*) such other statements or information in connection with the application or the applicant as may be prescribed.

[Firearms Act 1968, s 26A, as inserted by the Firearms (Amendment) Act 1997, ss 37.]

1. "Prescribed" means prescribed by rules made by the Secretary of State under s 53 (s 57(4)). See the Firearms Rules 1998, this title, post.
2. "Chief officer of police" is defined in the Police Act 1996, s 101(1), title POLICE, post, and that definition is applied to this Act by the Interpretation Act 1978, Sch 1, in PART II: EVIDENCE, ante.
3. "Area" means a police area, see s 57(4).
4. Ownership of property which does not carry with it the right of occupation is not sufficient to show that the applicant resides within the area in which he applies for the certificate (*Burditt v Joslin* [1981] 3 All ER 203).

8–10405A 26B. Applications for shot gun certificates. (1) An application for the grant of a shot gun certificate shall be made in the prescribed[1] form to the chief officer of police[2] for the area[3] in which the applicant resides[4] and shall state such particulars as may be required by the form.

(2) Rules made by the Secretary of State under section 53 of this Act may—

(*a*) require any application for a certificate to be accompanied by up to four photographs of the applicant;

(*b*) require the verification in the prescribed manner of any prescribed particulars and of the likeness of those photographs to the applicant;

(*c*) require any application for a certificate to be accompanied by a statement by the person verifying the matters mentioned in paragraph (*b*) above to the effect that he knows of no reason why the applicant should not be permitted to possess a shot gun.

[Firearms Act 1968, s 26B, as inserted by the Firearms (Amendment) Act 1997, s 37.]

1. "Prescribed" means prescribed by rules made by the Secretary of State under s 53 (s 57(4)). See the Firearms Rules 1998, this title, post.
2. "Chief officer of police" is defined in the Police Act 1996, s 101(1), title POLICE, post, and that definition is applied to this Act by the Interpretation Act 1978, Sch 1, in PART II: EVIDENCE, ante.
3. "Area" means a police area; see s 57(4), post.
4. Ownership of property which does not carry with it the right of occupation is not sufficient to show that the applicant resides within the area in which he applies for the certificate (*Burditt v Joslin* [1981] 3 All ER 203).

8–10406 27. Special provisions about firearm certificates. (1) A firearm certificate shall be granted where the chief officer of police is satisfied—

(*a*) that the applicant is fit to be entrusted with a firearm to which section 1 of this Act applies and is not a person prohibited by this Act from possessing such a firearm;

(*b*) that he has a good reason for having in his possession, or for purchasing or acquiring, the firearm or ammunition in respect of which the application is made[1]; and

(*c*) that in all the circumstances the applicant can be permitted to have the firearm or ammunition in his possession without danger to the public safety or to the peace.

(1A) For the purposes of subsection (1) above a person under the age of eighteen shall be capable of having a good reason for having a firearm or ammunition in his possession, or for purchasing or acquiring it, only if he has no intention of using the firearm or ammunition, at any time before he attains the age of eighteen, for a purpose not authorised by the European weapons directive.

(2) A firearm certificate shall be in the prescribed form[2] and shall specify the conditions (if any) subject to which it is held, the nature and number of the firearms to which it relates, including if known their identification numbers, and, as respects ammunition, the quantities authorised to be purchased or acquired and to be held at any one time thereunder.

(3) This section applies to the renewal of a firearm certificate as it applies to a grant.

[Firearms Act 1968, s 27 as amended by the Firearms (Amendment) Act 1988, s 23, SI 1992/2823 and the Firearms (Amendment) Act 1997, s 38.]

1. Firearms certificates will normally be specific rather than general, necessitating a fresh certificate whenever the original firearm is exchanged (*R v Wilson* [1989] Crim LR 146).
2. The power to prescribe the form of a firearm certificate includes power to require the certificate to bear a photograph of the holder (Firearms (Amendment) Act 1988, s 9).
The form of certificate is given in the Firearms Rules 1998 and certain standard conditions are prescribed by r 3(4); see this title, post.

8–10407 28. Special provisions about shot gun certificates. (1) Subject to subsection (1A) below, a shot gun certificate shall be granted or, as the case may be, renewed by the chief officer of police if he is satisfied that the applicant can be permitted to possess a shot gun without danger to the public safety or to the peace.

(1A) No such certificate shall be granted or renewed if the chief officer of police—

(*a*) has reason to believe that the applicant is prohibited by this Act from possessing a shot gun; or

(*b*) is satisfied that the applicant does not have a good reason for possessing, purchasing or acquiring one.

(1B) For the purposes of paragraph (*b*) of subsection (1A) above an applicant shall, in particular, be regarded as having a good reason if the gun is intended to be used for sporting or competition purposes or for shooting vermin; and an application shall not be refused by virtue of that paragraph merely because the applicant intends neither to use the gun himself nor to lend it for anyone else to use.

(1C) A person under the age of eighteen shall be regarded for the purposes of paragraph (*b*) of subsection (1A) above as not having a good reason for possessing, purchasing or acquiring a shot gun if it is his intention to use the shot gun, at any time before he attains the age of eighteen, for a purpose not authorised by the European weapons directive.

(2) A shot gun certificate shall be in the prescribed form[1] and shall—

(*a*) be granted or renewed subject to any prescribed conditions and no others; and

(*b*) specify the conditions, if any, subject to which it is granted or renewed.

(2A) A shot gun certificate shall specify the description of the shot guns to which it relates including, if known, the identification numbers of the guns.

(3) *Repealed.*

[Firearms Act 1969, s 28 as amended by the Firearms (Amendment) Act 1988, s 3, SI 1992/2823 and the Firearms (Amendment) Act 1997, Sch 3.]

---

1. The power to prescribe the form of a shot gun certificate includes power to require the certificate to bear a photograph of the holder (Firearms (Amendment) Act 1988, s 9).

The form of certificate is given in the Firearms Rules 1998 and certain standard conditions are prescribed by r 5(4); see this title, post.

8–10407A 28A. Certificates: supplementary.

(1) A certificate shall, unless previously revoked or cancelled, continue in force for five years from the date when it was granted or last renewed, but shall be renewable for a further period of five years by the chief officer of police for the area in which the holder resides.

(2) The provisions of this Act apply to the renewal of a certificate as they apply to a grant; but, subject to the power of renewal conferred by this subsection, a certificate granted or last renewed in Northern Ireland shall not continue in force for a period longer than that for which it was so granted or last renewed.

(3) The Secretary of State may by order amend subsection (1) above so as to substitute for any reference to a period for the time being specified in that subsection a reference to such other period as may be specified in the order.

(4) An order made under subsection (3) above shall apply only to certificates granted or renewed after the date on which the order comes into force.

(5) The power to make orders under subsection (3) above shall be exercisable by statutory instrument which shall be subject to annulment in pursuance of a resolution of either House of Parliament.

(6) A person aggrieved by the refusal of a chief officer of police to grant or to renew a certificate under this Act may in accordance with section 44 of this Act appeal against the refusal.

(7) It is an offence[1] for a person knowingly or recklessly to make any statement which is false in any material particular for the purpose of procuring (whether for himself or another) the grant or renewal of a certificate under this Act.

[Firearms Act 1968, s 28A as inserted by the Firearms (Amendment) Act 1997, Sch 2.]

---

1. For prosecution and punishment, see Sch 6, post.

8–10408 29. Variation of firearm certificates.

(1) The chief officer of police for the area in which the holder of a firearm certificate resides may at any time by notice in writing vary the conditions subject to which the certificate is held, except such of them as may be prescribed, and may by the notice require the holder to deliver up the certificate to him within twenty-one days from the date of the notice for the purpose of amending the conditions specified therein.

(2) A firearm certificate may also, on the application of the holder, be varied from time to time by the chief officer of police for the area in which the holder for the time being resides; and a person aggrieved by the refusal of a chief officer of police to vary a firearm certificate may in accordance with section 44 of this Act appeal[1] against the refusal.

(3) It is an offence[2] for a person knowingly or recklessly to make a statement false in any material particular for the purpose of procuring, whether for himself or another person, the variation of a firearm certificate.

[Firearms Act 1968, s 29 as amended by the Firearms (Amendment) Act 1997, Sch 2.]

---

1. There is not right of appear to the Crown Court against a decision not to vary the conditions on a firearm certificate *R v Cambridge Crown Court, ex p Buckland* [1998] 32 LS Gaz R 29.

2. For prosecution and punishment, see Sch 6, post.

8–10409 30A. Revocation of firearm certificates.

(1) A firearm certificate may be revoked by the chief officer of police for the area in which the holder resides on any of the grounds mentioned in subsection (2) to (5) below.

(2) The certificate may be revoked if the chief officer of police has reason to believe—

(*a*) that the holder is of intemperate habits or unsound mind or is otherwise unfitted to be trusted with a firearm; or

(*b*) that the holder can no longer be permitted to have the firearm or ammunition to which the certificate relates in his possession without danger[1] to the public safety or to the peace.

(3) The certificate may be revoked if the chief officer of police is satisfied that the holder is prohibited by this Act from possessing a firearm to which section 1 of this Act applies.

(4) The certificate may be revoked if the chief officer of police is satisfied that the holder no longer has a good reason for having in his possession, or for purchasing or acquiring, the firearm or ammunition which he is authorised by virtue of the certificate to have in his possession or to purchase or acquire.

(5) A firearm certificate may be revoked if the holder fails to comply with a notice under section 29(1) of this Act requiring him to deliver up the certificate.

(6) A person aggrieved by the revocation of a certificate under subsection (2), (3) or (4) of this section may in accordance with section 44 of this Act appeal against the revocation.

[Firearms Act 1968, s 30A, as inserted by the Firearms (Amendment) Act 1997, s 40.]

---

1. See note 1 to s 30C(1), post.

8–10409A 30B. Partial revocation of firearm certificates. (1) The chief officer of police for the area in which the holder of a firearm certificate resides may partially revoke the certificate, that is to say, he may revoke the certificate in relation to any firearm or ammunition which the holder is authorised by virtue of the certificate to have in his possession or to purchase or acquire.

(2) A firearm certificate may be partially revoked only if the chief officer of police is satisfied that the holder no longer has a good reason for having in his possession, or for purchasing or acquiring, the firearm or ammunition to which the partial revocation relates.

(3) A person aggrieved by the partial revocation of a certificate may in accordance with section 44 of this Act appeal against the partial revocation.

[Firearms Act 1968, s 30B, as inserted by the Firearms (Amendment) Act 1997, s 40.]

8–10409B 30C. Revocation of shot gun certificates. (1) A shot gun certificate may be revoked by the chief officer of police for the area in which the holder resides if he is satisfied that the holder is prohibited by this Act from possessing a shot gun or cannot be permitted to possess a shot gun without danger[1] to the public safety or to the peace.

(2) A person aggrieved by the revocation of a shot gun certificate may in accordance with section 44 of this Act appeal against the revocation.

[Firearms Act 1968, s 30C, as inserted by the Firearms (Amendment) Act 1997, s 40.]

---

1. This need not just be a danger of violence; use of the gun for poaching can justify revocation (*Ackers v Taylor* [1974] 1 All ER 771, 138 JP 269). The danger to the peace which must be considered must be a danger to the peace involving the use of a shot gun (*Spencer-Stewart v Chief Constable of Kent* (1988) 89 Cr App Rep 307). Where the holder of a shotgun certificate was married to a man with previous convictions for drug offences, and both she and her husband still associated with drug users, it was held that there was some danger to the public and that the requirements for revocation of the shotgun certificate had been satisfied (*Dabek v Chief Constable of Devon and Cornwall* (1990) 155 JP 55, DC). Similarly, a chief constable is entitled in the exercise of his discretion to take account of irresponsible and uncontroled conduct not involving a shotgun but analogous to it (*Chief Constable of Essex v Germain* (1991) 156 JP 109).

8–10409C 30D. Revocation of certificates: supplementary. (1) Where a certificate is revoked under section 30A or 30C of this Act the chief officer of police shall by notice in writing require the holder to surrender the certificate.

(2) Where a certificate is partially revoked under section 30B of this Act the chief officer of police shall by notice in writing require the holder to deliver up the certificate for the purpose of amending it.

(3) It is an offence[1] for the holder of a certificate to fail to comply with a notice under subsection (1) or (2) above within twenty-one days from the date of the notice.

(4) If an appeal is brought against a revocation or partial revocation—

(*a*) this section shall not apply to that revocation or partial revocation unless the appeal is abandoned or dismissed; and

(*b*) it shall then apply with the substitution, for the reference to the date of the notice, of a reference to the date on which the appeal was abandoned or dismissed.

(5) This section shall not apply in relation to—

(*a*) the revocation of a firearm certificate on any ground mentioned in section 30A(2), (3) or (4) of this Act;

(*b*) the revocation of a shot gun certificate,

if the chief officer of police serves a notice on the holder under section 12 of the Firearms Act 1988 requiring him to surrender forthwith his certificate and any firearms and ammunition in his possession by virtue of the certificate.

[Firearms Act 1968, s 30D, as inserted by the Firearms (Amendment) Act 1997, s 40.]

---

1. For prosecution and punishment, see Sch 6, post.

8–10410 31. Certificate for prohibited weapon. (1) A chief officer of police shall not refuse to grant or renew, and shall not revoke, a firearm certificate in respect of a prohibited weapon or prohibited ammunition if the applicant for the certificate is for the time being authorised by the Defence Council under section 5 of this Act to have possession of that weapon or ammunition.

(2) Where an authority of the Defence Council under that section to have possession of, or to purchase or acquire, a prohibited weapon or prohibited ammunition is revoked, the firearm certificate relating to that weapon or ammunition shall be revoked or varied accordingly by the chief officer of police by whom it was granted.

[Firearms Act 1968, s 31.]

8–10411 32. Fee for certificate and exemption from paying it in certain cases. (1) Subject to this Act, there shall be payable—

(a) on the grant of a firearm certificate, a fee of £50;

(b) on the renewal of a firearm certificate, a fee of £40;

(c) on any variation of a firearm certificate (otherwise than when it is renewed at the same time) so as to increase the number of firearms to which the certificate relates, a fee of £26;

(cc) on the replacement of a firearm certificate which has been lost or destroyed, a fee of £9;

(d) on the grant of a shot gun certificate, a fee of £50;

(e) on the renewal of a shot gun certificate, a fee of £40, and

(f) on the replacement of a shotgun certificate which has been lost or destroyed, a fee of £8.

(2) No fee shall be payable on the grant to a responsible officer of a rifle club, miniature rifle club or muzzle-loading pistol club which is approved under section 15 of the Firearms (Amendment) Act 1988 of a firearm certificate in respect of rifles, miniature rifles or muzzle-loading pistols, or ammunition, to be used solely for target shooting by the members of the club, or on the variation or renewal of a certificate so granted.

(2A) Subsection (2) above—

(a) does not apply if the operation of subsection (1) of section 15 of the Firearms (Amendment) Act 1988 is excluded in relation to the club by a limitation in the approval; or

(b) if the operation of subsection (1) of that section in relation to the club is limited by the approval to target shooting with specified types of rifles, miniature rifles or muzzle-loading pistols, only applies to a certificate in respect of rifles, miniature rifles or pistols of those types.

(2B) *(Repealed).*

(3) No fee shall be payable on the grant, variation or renewal of a firearm certificate if the chief officer of police is satisfied that the certificate relates solely to and, in the case of a variation, will continue when varied to relate solely to—

(a) a firearm or ammunition which the applicant requires as part of the equipment of a ship; or

(b) a signalling apparatus, or ammunition therefor, which the applicant requires as part of the equipment of an aircraft or aerodrome; or

(c) a slaughtering instrument, or ammunition therefor, which the applicant requires for the purpose of the slaughter of animals.

(3A) No fee shall be payable on the grant, variation or renewal of a firearm certificate which relates solely to and, in the case of a variation, will continue when varied to relate solely to a signalling device, which, when assembled and ready to fire, is not more than eight inches long and which is designed to discharge a flare, or to ammunition for such a device.

(4) No fee shall be payable—

(a) on the grant or renewal of a firearm certificate relating solely to a firearm which is shown to the satisfaction of the chief officer of police to be kept by the applicant as a trophy of war; or

(b) on any variation of a certificate the sole effect of which is to add such a firearm as aforesaid to the firearms to which the certificate relates,

if the certificate is granted, renewed or varied subject to the condition that the applicant shall not use the firearm.

[Firearms Act 1968, s 32, as amended by the Firearms (Variation of Fees) Orders 1980, SI 1980/574 and 1986, the Firearms (Amendment) Act 1988, s 15, SI 1994/2615, the Firearms (Amendment) Act 1997, Sch 2, the Firearms (Amendment) (No 2) Act 1997, Sch and SI 2000/3148.]

Issue etc in Great Britain of documents for European purposes

8–10412 32A. Documents for European purposes. (1) Where a person is granted, or is the holder of, a certificate under this Act, he shall be entitled to be issued by the chief officer of police for the area in which he resides with—

(a) a document ('a European firearms pass') containing the required particulars; and

(b) a document stating that, for the purposes of Article 7 of the European weapons directive, the holder of the certificate has the agreement of the United Kingdom authorities, for so long as the certificate remains in force, to any purchase or acquisition by him in another member State of any firearm or ammunition to which the certificate relates;

and an application for the issue of a document falling within paragraph (a) or (b) above may be made at the same time as any application for a certificate the grant of which will entitle him to the issue of the document or subsequently while the certificate is in force.

(2) Where—

(a) a person who resides in Great Britain is proposing to purchase or acquire any firearm or ammunition in another member State;

(b) that person is not for the time being the holder of a certificate under this Act relating to that firearm or ammunition;

(c) the firearm falls within category B for the purposes of Annex I to the European weapons directive or the ammunition is capable of being used with such a firearm; and

(d) that person satisfies the chief officer of police for the area where he resides that he is not proposing to bring that firearm or ammunition into the United Kingdom,

the chief officer of police may, if he thinks fit, issue that person with a document stating that, for the purposes of Article 7 of the European weapons directive, that person has the agreement of the United Kingdom authorities to any purchase or acquisition by him in another member State of that firearm or ammunition.

(3) For the purposes of subsection (1) above the required particulars, in relation to a person issued with a European firearms pass, are—

(a) particulars identifying that person;

(b) particulars identifying every firearm which—

(i) that person has applied to have included in a European firearms pass; and

(ii) is a firearm in relation to which a certificate granted to that person is for the time being in force;

(c) a statement in relation to every firearm identified in the pass as to the category into which it falls for the purposes of Annex I to the European weapons directive;

(d) the date of the issue of the pass and the period from its issue for which the pass is to be valid;

(e) the statements required by paragraph (f) of Annex II to that directive (statements as to travel in the member States with the firearms identified in the pass).

(4) For the purposes of this section the particulars of the firearms to which a shot gun certificate relates which are to be contained in a European firearms pass by virtue of subsection (3)(b) above are—

(a) a description of the shot guns to which that certificate relates; and

(b) any identification numbers specified in or entered on that certificate in pursuance of section 28(2A) of this Act or in consequence of any person's compliance, in accordance with section 32(2)(b) of the Firearms (Amendment) Act 1997 (requirements relating to transfers of firearms), with any instructions contained in the certificate;

and, accordingly, references in this Act to a firearm identified in such a pass shall include references to any shot gun of a description specified in that pass.

(5) A European firearms pass shall contain space for the making of entries by persons authorised to do so under the law of any member State.

(6) The period specified in a European firearms pass as the period for which it is to be valid shall be whichever is the shorter of the following—

(a) the period until the earliest time when a certificate relating to a firearm identified in the pass expires; and

(b) the maximum period for the duration of that pass.

(7) For the purposes of subsection (6) above the maximum period for the duration of a European firearms pass is—

(a) in the case of a pass identifying only a firearm or firearms stated in the pass to fall within category D for the purposes of Annex I to the European weapons directive, ten years; and

(b) in any other case, five years.

[Firearms Act 1968, s 32A inserted by SI 1992/2823 and amended by the Firearms (Amendment) Act 1997, Sch 2.]

8–10413 32B. (1) On an application for the renewal by a chief officer of police of a certificate under this Act relating to a firearm identified in a European firearms pass, the holder of the certificate may apply to the chief officer of police for the renewal of the pass.

(2) Where—

(*a*) a certificate relating to a firearm identified in a European firearms pass is to expire without being renewed; but

(*b*) a certificate relating to another firearm identified in that pass will continue in force after the other certificate expires,

the holder of the pass may apply to the chief officer of police for the area in which he resides for the renewal of the pass subject to the deletion of the reference to any firearm to which the expiring certificate relates.

(3) Where, on an application to a chief officer of police under subsection (1) or (2) above—

(*a*) the pass in question is produced to him; and

(*b*) a certificate relating to a firearm identified in the pass is renewed or will continue in force after the time when the pass would (apart from its renewal) have ceased to be valid,

he shall renew that pass, subject to any appropriate deletion, from that time for whichever is the shorter of the periods specified in section 32A(6)(*a*) and (*b*) of this Act.

(4) Where a European firearms pass ceases to be valid without being renewed under this section, the chief officer of police for the area in which the person to whom it was issued resides may, by notice in writing, require that person, within twenty-one days of the date of the notice, to surrender the pass to him.

(5) It is an offence for any person to fail to comply with a notice given to him under subsection (4) above.

[Firearms Act 1968, s 32B inserted by SI 1992/2823.]

8–10414 32C. (1) Where—

(*a*) a certificate relating to a firearm identified in a European firearms pass or a certificate in respect of which an Article 7 authority has been issued is varied, revoked or cancelled under this Act;

(*b*) the Secretary of State gives notice that any European firearms pass needs to be modified by the addition or variation of any such statement as is mentioned in section 32A(3)(*e*) of this Act; or

(*c*) the holder of a European firearms pass applies to have particulars of another firearm added to the pass,

it shall be the duty of the chief officer of police for the area in which the holder of the pass or authority resides to make such variations of the pass or authority as are appropriate in consequence of the variation, revocation, cancellation, notice or application or, where appropriate, to cancel it.

(2) For the purpose of performing his duty under subsection (1) above the chief officer of police for the area in which any person who is or has been the holder of any certificate resides may, by notice in writing, require that person, within twenty-one days of the date of the notice, to produce or surrender to him any European firearms pass or Article 7 authority issued to that person.

(3) Where a person is for the time being the holder of an Article 7 authority issued under section 32A(2) of this Act by the chief officer of police for any area, the chief officer of police for that area may, if he thinks fit, at any time—

(*a*) revoke that authority; and

(*b*) by notice in writing require that person, within twenty-one days of the date of the notice, to surrender that authority to him.

(4) Where a firearm identified in a European firearms pass which is for the time being valid, is lost or stolen, the holder of the pass shall immediately—

(*a*) inform the chief officer of police for the area in which he resides about the loss or theft; and

(*b*) produce the pass to that chief officer for him to endorse particulars of that loss or theft on the pass.

(5) Where a firearm to which an endorsement under subsection (4) above relates is returned to the possession of the holder of the pass in question, the chief officer of police for the area in which that person resides may, on the production to him of that pass, make such further endorsement on that pass as may be appropriate.

(6) It is an offence for any person to fail to comply with a notice given to him under subsection (2) or (3) above or with any obligation imposed on him by virtue of subsection (4)(*a*) or (*b*) above.

(7) Any reference in this section to the variation of a certificate includes a reference to the making of any entry on a shot gun certificate in pursuance of the requirement under section 32(2)(*b*) of the Firearms (Amendment) Act 1997 (requirements relating to transfers of firearms) to comply with instructions contained in the certificate.

[Firearms Act 1968, s 32C inserted by SI 1992/2823 and amended by the Firearms (Amendment) Act 1997, Sch 2.]

Registration of firearms dealers

8–10415 33. Police register. (1) For purposes of this Act, the chief officer of police for every area shall keep in the prescribed[1] form a register of firearms dealers.

(2) Except as provided by section 34 of this Act, the chief officer of police shall enter in the register the name of any person[2] who, having or proposing to have a place of business in the area, applies to be registered as a firearms dealer.

(3) An applicant for registration as a firearms dealer must furnish the chief officer of police with the prescribed particulars, which shall include particulars of every place of business[3] at which he proposes to carry on business in the area as a firearms dealer and, except as provided by this Act, the chief officer of police shall (if he registers the applicant as a firearms dealer) enter every such place of business in the register.

(4) When a person is registered, the chief officer of police shall grant or cause to be granted to him a certificate of registration[4].

(5) A person for the time being registered shall, on or before the expiration of the period of three years from the grant of the certificate of registration for the time being held by him—

(*a*) surrender his certificate to the chief officer of police; and

(*b*) apply in the prescribed form for a new certificate;

and thereupon the chief officer of police shall, subject to sections 35(3) and 38(1) below, grant him a new certificate of registration.

[Firearms Act 1968, s 33 as amended by the Firearms (Amendment) Act 1988, s 13 and the Firearms (Amendment) Act 1997, s 42.]

1. See the Firearms Rules 1998, this title, post.
2. Where a company carries on business, it should be registered, and not the managing director. See *Staravia Ltd v Gordon* [1973] Crim LR 298.
3. The words "every place of business at which he proposes to carry on business in the area as a firearms dealer" should be given a wide construction. Accordingly, a barn at which a registered firearms dealer stored ammunition was held to be a place of business of which particulars were required to be furnished under s 33(3) of the Act (*R v Bull* (1993) 99 Cr App Rep 193, [1994] Crim LR 224).
4. As to power to impose conditions, see s 36, post.

8–10416 34. Grounds for refusal of registration. (1) The chief officer of police shall not register an applicant as a firearms dealer if he is prohibited to be so registered by order of a court in Great Britain made under section 45 of this Act, or by order of a court in Northern Ireland under section 8(5) of the Firearms Act 1920, or any enactment of the Parliament of Northern Ireland amending or substituted for that section.

(1A) The chief officer of police may refuse to register an applicant unless he is satisfied that the applicant will engage in business as a firearms dealer to a substantial extent or as an essential part of another trade, business or profession.

(2) Subject to subsection (3) below, the chief officer of police may refuse to register an applicant, if he is satisfied that the applicant cannot be permitted to carry on business as a firearms dealer without danger to the public safety or to the peace.

(3) In the case of a person for the time being authorised by the Defence Council under section 5 of this Act to manufacture, sell or transfer prohibited weapons or ammunition, the chief officer of police shall not refuse to enter his name in the register on the ground that he cannot be permitted to carry on business as a firearms dealer without danger to the public safety or to the peace.

(4) The chief of police, if he is satisfied that a place of business notified to him under section 33(3) of this Act by an applicant for registration is a place at which the person cannot be permitted to carry on business as a firearms dealer without danger to the public safety or to the peace, may refuse to enter that place of business in the register.

(5) A person aggrieved by the refusal of a chief officer of police to register him as a firearms dealer, or to enter in the register a place of business of his, may in accordance with section 44 of this Act appeal against the refusal.

[Firearms Act 1968, s 34 as amended by the Firearms (Amendment) Act 1988, s 13.]

8–10417 35. Fee for registration and renewal thereof. (1) Subject to this Act, on the registration of a person as a firearms dealer there shall be payable by him a fee of £150.

(1A) If the chief officer of police for the area in which the applicant has applied to be registered is satisfied—

(*a*) that the only place of business in respect of which the application is made is at a game fair, trade fair or exhibition, agricultural show or an event of a similar character, and

(*b*) that the applicant's principal place of business is entered in the register for another area,

the fee payable shall be £12.

(2) No fee shall be payable if the chief officer of police for the area in which the applicant has applied to be registered is satisfied that the only place of business in respect of which the application is made—

(*a*) has become situated in that area because of an alteration in the boundary of the area and was previously entered in the register for another area; or

(*b*) is one to which the applicant proposes to transfer the business previously carried on by him at a place entered in the register for another area.

(3) Before a person for the time being registered as a firearms dealer can be granted a new certificate of registration under section 33(5) of this Act, he shall pay a fee of £150.
[Firearms Act 1968, s 35, as amended by SI 1980/574, SI 1994/2615 and SI 2000/3148.]

8–10418   36. Conditions of registration.   (1) The chief officer of police may at any time impose conditions subject to which the registration of a person as a firearms dealer is to have effect and may at any time, of his own motion or on the application of the dealer, vary or revoke any such condition.

(2) The chief officer of police shall specify the conditions for the time being in force under this section in the certificate of registration granted to the firearms dealer and, where any such condition is imposed, varied or revoked during the currency of the certificate of registration, the chief officer of police—

(*a*)   shall give to the dealer notice in writing of the condition or variation (giving particulars) or of the revocation, as the case may be; and

(*b*)   may by that notice require the dealer to deliver up to him his certificate of registration within twenty-one days from the date of the notice, for the purpose of amending the certificate.

(3) A person aggrieved by the imposition or variation of, or refusal to vary or revoke, any condition of a firearms dealer's registration may in accordance with section 44 of this Act appeal against the imposition, variation or refusal.
[Firearms Act 1968, s 36.]

8–10419   37. Registration of new place of business.   (1) A person registered in any area as a firearms dealer and proposing to carry on business as such at a place of business in that area which is not entered in the register, shall notify the chief officer of police for that area and furnish him with such particulars as may be prescribed[1]; and the officer shall, subject to the provisions of this section, enter that place of business in the register.

(2) The chief officer of police, if he is satisfied that a place of business notified to him by a person under subsection (1) of this section is a place at which that person cannot be permitted to carry on business as a firearms dealer without danger to the public safety or to the peace, may refuse to enter it in the register.

(3) A person aggrieved by the refusal by a chief officer of police to enter in the register a place of business of his may in accordance with section 44 of this Act appeal against the refusal.
[Firearms Act 1968, s 37.]

---

1. See the Firearms Rules 1998, this title, post.

8–10420   38. Removal from register of dealer's name or place of business.   (1) If the chief officer of police, after giving reasonable notice to a person whose name is on the register, is satisfied that the person—

(*a*)   is no longer carrying on business as a firearms dealer; or

(*b*)   has ceased to have a place of business in the area; or

(*c*)   cannot be permitted to continue to carry on business as a firearms dealer without danger to the public safety or to the peace,

he shall (subject to this section) cause the name of that person to be removed from the register.

(2) In the case of a person for the time being authorised by the Defence Council under section 5 of this Act to manufacture, sell or transfer prohibited weapons or ammunition, the chief officer of police shall not remove his name from the register on the ground that he cannot be permitted to continue to carry on business as a firearms dealer without danger to the public safety or to the peace.

(3) If the chief officer of police is satisfied that a person registered as a firearms dealer has failed to comply with any of the conditions of registration in force under section 36 of this Act, he may remove from the register either that person's name or any place of business of his to which the condition relates.

(4) If the chief officer of police is satisfied that a place entered in the register as a person's place of business is one at which that person cannot be permitted to carry on business as a firearms dealer without danger to the public safety or to the peace, he may remove that place from the register.

(5) The chief officer of police shall cause the name of a person to be removed from the register if the person so desires.

(6) If a person for the time being registered fails to comply with any requirement of section 33(5) of this Act, the chief officer of police shall by notice in writing require him to comply with that requirement and, if the person fails to do so within twenty-one days from the date of the notice or within such further time as the chief officer may in special circumstances allow, shall cause his name to be removed from the register.

(7) A person aggrieved by the removal of his name from the register, or by the removal from the register of a place of business of his, may in accordance with section 44 of this Act appeal against the removal.

(8) Where the chief officer of police causes the name of a firearms dealer to be removed from the register, he shall by notice in writing require the dealer to surrender his certificate of registration and

the register of transactions kept by him under section 40 of this Act (or, if the register is kept by means of a computer, a copy of the information comprised in that register in a visible and legible form); and it is an offence[1] for the dealer to fail to do so within twenty-one days from the date of the notice:

Provided that, if an appeal is brought against the removal, this subsection shall not apply to that removal unless the appeal is abandoned or dismissed and shall than apply with the substitution, for the reference to the date of the notice, of a reference to the date on which the appeal was abandoned or dismissed.

[Firearms Act 1968, s 38 as amended by the Firearms (Amendment) Act 1988, s 13 and the Firearms (Amendment) Act 1997, Sch 2.]

---

1. For prosecution and punishment, see Sch 6, post.

8–10421   39. Offences in connection with registration.   (1) A person commits an offence[1] if, for the purpose—

   (a) of procuring the registration of himself or another person as a firearms dealer; or

   (b) of procuring, whether for himself or another person, the entry of any place of business in a register of firearms dealers,

he knowingly or recklessly makes a statement false in any material particular.

(2) A person commits an offence[1] if, being a registered firearms dealer, he has a place of business which is not entered in the register for the area in which the place of business is situated and carries on business as a firearms dealer at that place.

(3) Without prejudice to section 38(3) above, a person commits an offence[1] if he fails to comply with any of the conditions of registration imposed on him by the chief officer of police under section 36 of this Act.

[Firearms Act 1968, s 39 as amended by the Firearms (Amendment) Act 1997, Sch 2.]

---

1. For prosecution and punishment, see Sch 6, post.

Supplementary

8–10422   40. Compulsory register of transaction in firearms.   (1) Subject to section 41 of this Act, every person who by way of trade or business manufactures, sells or transfers firearms or ammunition shall provide and keep a register of transactions and shall enter or cause to be entered therein the particulars specified in Schedule 4 to this Act.

(2) In subsection (1) above and in the said Schedule 4, any reference to firearms is to be construed as not including a reference to air weapons or component parts of, or accessories to, air weapons; and any reference therein to ammunition is to be construed as not including—

   (a) cartridges containing five or more shot, none of which exceeds ·36 inch in diameter;

   (b) ammunition for an air gun, air rifle or air pistol; or

   (c) blank cartridges not more than one inch in diameter measured immediately in front of the rim or cannelure of the base of the cartridge[1].

(3) Every entry required by subsection (1) of this section to be made in the register shall be made within twenty-four hours after the transaction to which it relates took place and, in the case of a sale or transfer, every person to whom that subsection applies shall at the time of the transaction require the purchaser or transferee, if not known to him, to furnish particulars sufficient for identification and shall immediately enter the said particulars in the register.

(3A) Every person keeping a register in accordance with this section shall (unless required to surrender the register under section 38(8) of this Act) keep it for such a period that each entry made after the coming into force of this subsection will be available for inspection for at least five years from the date on which it was made.

(4) Every person keeping a register in accordance with this section shall on demand allow a constable or a civilian officer, duly authorised in writing in that behalf by the chief officer of police, to enter and inspect all stock in hand and shall on request by a constable or a civilian officer so authorised or by an officer of customs and excise produce the register (or if the register is kept by means of a computer, a copy of the information comprised in that register in a visible and legible form); for inspection[2]:

Provided that, where a written authority is required by this subsection, the authority shall be produced on demand.

(4A) Every person keeping a register in accordance with this section by means of a computer shall secure that the information comprised in the register can readily be produced in a form in which it is visible and legible and can be taken away.

(5) It is an offence[3] for a person to fail to comply with any provision of this section or knowingly to make any false entry in the register required to be kept thereunder.

(6) Nothing in this section applies to the sale of firearms or ammunition by auction in accordance with the terms of a permit issued under section 9(2) of this Act.

(7) Rules[4] made by the Secretary of State under section 53 of this Act may vary or add to Schedule

4 to this Act, and references in this section to that Schedule shall be construed as references to the Schedule as for the time being so varied or added to.
[Firearms Act 1968, s 40 as amended by the Firearms (Amendment) Act 1988, ss 13 and 23 and the Firearms (Amendment) Act 1997, Sch 2.]

1. Therefore these cartridges are included (*Burfitt v A and E Kille* [1939] 2 KB 743, [1939] 2 All ER 372).
2. This includes the right to take notes of the entries therein. Cf *Hart v Cohen and Van der Laan* (1902) 4 F 445.
3. For prosecution and punishment, see Sch 6, post.
4. See the Firearms Rules 1998, this title, post.

8–10423   41. Exemption from s 40 in case of trade in shot gun components. If it appears to the chief officer of police that—

(a) a person required to be registered as a firearms dealer carries on a trade or business in the course of which he manufactures, tests or repairs component parts or accessories for shot guns, but does not manufacture, test or repair complete shot guns; and

(b) it is impossible to assemble a shot gun from the parts likely to come into that person's possession in the course of that trade or business,

the chief officer of police may, if he thinks fit, by notice in writing given to that person exempt his transactions in those parts and accessories, so long as the notice is in force, from all or any of the requirements of section 40 of this Act and Schedule 4 thereto.
[Firearms Act 1968, s 41.]

8–10425   42A. Information as to transactions under visitors' permits. (1) A person who sells, lets on hire, gives or lends a shot gun with a magazine to another person who—

(a) shows that he is entitled to purchase or acquire the weapon as the holder of a visitor's shot gun permit under section 17 of the Firearms (Amendment) Act 1988; but

(b) fails to show that the purchase or acquisition falls within subsection (1A)(c) or (d) of that section (temporary acquisitions or purchases or acquisitions by collectors etc) or that he resides outside the member States.

shall, within forty-eight hours of the transaction, send by registered post or the recorded delivery service notice of the transaction to the chief officer of police who granted that permit.

(2) A notice under subsection (1) above shall—

(a) contain a description of the shot gun (giving the identification number if any);

(b) state the nature of the transaction (giving the name of the person to whom the gun has been sold, let on hire, given or lent, his address in the member State where he resides and the number and place of issue of his passport, if any); and

(c) set out the particulars of any licence granted for the purposes of an order made under section 1 of the Import, Export and Customs Powers (Defence) Act 1939 by virtue of which the transaction is authorised under section 17 of that Act of 1988.

(3) It is an offence for a person to fail to comply with this section.
[Firearms Act 1968, s 42A inserted by SI 1992/2823.]

8–10432   43. *Power of Secretary of State to alter fees.*

8–10433   44. Appeals against police decisions. *Appeals under ss 28A, 29, 30A, 30B, 30C, 34, 36, 37 or 38 lie to the Crown Court*[1].
[Firearms Act 1968, s 44, substituted by the Firearms (Amendment) Act 1997, s 41.]

1. The procedure on appeal is set out in Sch 5. The decision on appeal is within the discretion of the Crown Court and will not be set aside unless there is some error in law (*Greenly v Lawrence* [1949] 1 All ER 241, 113 JP 120).

8–10434   45. Consequences where registered dealer convicted of offence. (1) Where a registered firearms dealer is convicted of an offence relevant for the purposes of this section the court may order—

(a) that the name of the dealer be removed from the register; and

(b) that neither the dealer nor any person who acquires his business, nor any person who took part in the management of the business and was knowingly a party to the offence, shall be registered as a firearms dealer; and

(c) that any person who, after the date of the order, knowingly employs in the management of his business the dealer convicted of the offence or any person who was knowingly a party to the offence, shall not be registered as a firearms dealer or, if so registered, shall be liable to be removed from the register; and

(d) that any stock-in-hand of the business shall be disposed of by sale or otherwise in accordance with such directions as may be contained in the order.

(2) The offences relevant for the purposes of this section are:

(a) all offences under this Act, except an offence under section 2, 22(3) or 24(3) or an offence relating specifically to air weapons[1]; and

(b) offences against the enactments for the time being in force relating to customs or excise in respect of the import or export of firearms or ammunition to which section 1 of this Act applies, or of shot guns.

(3) A person aggrieved by an order made under this section may appeal against the order in the same manner as against the conviction, and the court may, if it thinks fit, suspend the operation of the order pending the appeal.
[Firearms Act 1968, s 45, as amended by the Customs and Excise Management Act 1979, Sch 4.]

---

1. See s 57(3), post.

PART III
LAW ENFORCEMENT AND PUNISHMENT OF OFFENCES

8–10435 46. Power of search with warrant.   (1) If a justice of the peace or, in Scotland, the sheriff, is satisfied by information on oath that there is reasonable ground for suspecting—

(a) that an offence relevant for the purposes of this section has been, is being, or is about to be committed; or

(b) that, in connection with a firearm or ammunition, there is a danger to the public safety or to the peace,

he may grant a warrant[1] for any of the purposes mentioned in subsection (2) below.

(2) A warrant under this section may authorise a constable or civilian officer—

(a) to enter at any time any premises[2] or place named in the warrant, if necessary by force, and to search the premises or place and every person found there;

(b) to seize and detain anything which he may find on the premises or place, or on any such person, in respect of which or in connection with which he has reasonable ground for suspecting—

(i) that an offence relevant for the purposes of this section has been, is being, or is about to be committed; or

(ii) that in connection with a firearm, imitation firearm or ammunition there is a danger to the public safety or to the peace.

(3) The power of a constable or civilian officer under subsection (2)(b) above to seize and detain anything found on any premises or place shall include power to require any information which is stored in any electronic form and is accessible from the premises or place to be produced in a form in which it is visible and legible or from which it can readily be produced in a visible and legible form and can be taken away.

(4) The offences relevant for the purposes of this section are all offences under this Act except an offence under section 22(3) or an offence relating specifically to air weapons[3].

(5) It is an offence[4] for any person intentionally to obstruct a constable or civilian officer in the exercise of his powers under this section.
[Firearms Act 1968, s 46, as substituted by the Firearms (Amendment) Act 1997, s 43, and amended by the Criminal Justice and Police Act 2001, Sch 2.]

---

1. The issue and execution of the warrant must be in conformity with the Police and Criminal Evidence Act 1984, ss 15 and 16, ante in PART II: EVIDENCE.
2. "Premises" includes any land (s 57(4)).
3. See s 57(3), post.
4. For prosecution and punishment, see Sch 6, post.

8–10436 47. Powers of constables to stop and search.   (1) A constable may require any person whom he has reasonable cause to suspect—

(a) of having a firearm[1], with or without ammunition[2], with him in a public place; or

(b) to be committing or about to commit, elsewhere than in a public place[3], an offence relevant[4] for the purposes of this section,

to hand over the firearm or any ammunition for examination by the constable.

(2) It is an offence[5] for a person having a firearm or ammunition with him to fail to hand it over when required to do so by a constable under subsection (1) of this section.

(3) If a constable has reasonable cause to suspect a person of having a firearm with him in a public place, or to be committing or about to commit, elsewhere than in a public place, an offence relevant for the purposes of this section, the constable may search that person and may detain him for the purpose of doing so.

(4) If a constable has reasonable cause to suspect that there is a firearm in a vehicle in a public place, or that a vehicle is being or is about to be used in connection with the commission of an offence relevant for the purposes of this section elsewhere than in a public place, he may search the vehicle and for that purpose require the person driving or in control of it to stop it.

(5) For the purpose of exercising the powers conferred by this section a constable may enter any place.

(6) The offences relevant for the purpose of this section are those, under sections 18(1) and (2) and 20 of this Act.

[Firearms Act 1968, s 47.]

---

1. Defined in s 57(1), post.
2. Defined in s 57(2), post.
3. Defined in s 57(4), post.
4. See sub-s (6).
5. For prosecution and punishment, see Sch 6, post.

8–10437   48. Production of certificates.   (1) A constable may demand, from any person whom he believes to be in possession of a firearm or ammunition to which section 1 of this act applies, or of a shot gun, the production of his firearm certificate or, as the case may be, his shot gun certificate.

(1A) Where a person upon whom a demand has been made by a constable under subsection (1) above and whom the constable believes to be in possession of a firearm fails—

(a) to produce a firearm certificate or, as the case may be, a shot gun certificate;
(b) to show that he is a person who, by reason of his place of residence or any other circumstances, is not entitled to be issued with a document identifying that firearm under any of the provisions which in the other member States correspond to the provisions of this Act for the issue of European firearms passes; or
(c) to show that he is in possession of the firearm exclusively in connection with the carrying on of activities in respect of which, he or the person on whose behalf he has possession of the firearm, is recognised, for the purposes of the law of another member State relating to firearms, as a collector of firearms or a body concerned in the cultural or historical aspects of weapons,

the constable may demand from that person the production of a document which has been issued to that person in another member State under any such corresponding provisions, identifies that firearm as a firearm to which it relates and is for the time being valid.

(2) If a person upon whom a demand is made under this section fails to produce the certificate or document or to permit the constable to read it, or to show that he is entitled by virtue of this Act to have the firearm, ammunition or shot gun in his possession without holding a certificate, the constable may seize and detain the firearm, ammunition or shot gun and may require the person to declare to him immediately his name and address.

(3) If under this section a person is required to declare to a constable his name and address, it is an offence[1] for him to refuse to declare it or to fail to give his true name and address.

(4) It is an offence for a person who is in possession of a firearm to fail to comply with a demand under subsection (1A) above.

[Firearms Act 1968, s 48 amended by SI 1992/2823.]

---

1. For prosecution and punishment, see Sch 6, post.

8–10438   49. Police powers in relation to arms traffic.   (1) A constable may search for and seize any firearms or ammunition which he has reason to believe are being removed, or to have been removed, in contravention of an order made under section 6 of this Act or of a corresponding Northern Irish order within the meaning of subsection (3)(c) of that section.

(2) A person having the control or custody of any firearms or ammunition in course of transit shall, on demand by a constable, allow him all reasonable facilities for the examination and inspection thereof and shall produce any documents in his possession relating thereto.

(3) It is an offence[1] for a person to fail to comply with subsection (2) of this section.

[Firearms Act 1968, s 49 as amended by the Firearms (Amendment) Act 1988, s 23.]

---

1. For prosecution and punishment, see Sch 6, post.

8–10438A   50. *(Repealed).*

8–10439   51. Prosecution and punishment of offences.   (1)–(3) *Modes of prosecution, maximum punishment and powers of the court on conviction to be as set out in Schedule 6.*

(4) Notwithstanding section 127(1) of the Magistrates' Courts Act 1980, or section 23 of the Summary Jurisdiction (Scotland) Act 1954 (limitation of time for taking proceedings) summary proceedings for an offence under this Act, other than an offence under section 22(3) or an offence relating specifically to air weapons, may be instituted at any time within four years after the commission of the offence:

Provided that no such proceedings shall be instituted in England after the expiration of six months after the commission of the offence unless they are instituted by, or by the direction of, the Director of Public Prosecutions.

[Firearms Act 1968, s 51, as amended by the Magistrates' Courts Act 1980, Sch 7.]

8–10440 **52. Forfeiture and disposal of firearms; cancellation of certificate by convicting court.** (1) Where a person—

(a) is convicted of an offence under this Act (other than an offence under section 22(3) or an offence relating specifically to air weapons)[1] or is convicted of a crime for which he is sentenced to imprisonment, or detention in a detention centre or in a young offenders' institution in Scotland or is subject to a detention and training order; or

(b) has been ordered to enter into a recognisance to keep the peace or to be of good behaviour, a condition of which is that he shall not possess, use or carry a firearm; or

(c) is subject to a probation order* containing a requirement that he shall not possess, use or carry a firearm; or

(d) has, in Scotland, been ordained to find caution a condition of which is that he shall not possess, use or carry a firearm,

the court by or before which he is convicted, or by which the order is made, may make such orders as to the forfeiture[2] or disposal of any firearm or ammunition found in his possession as the court thinks fit and may cancel any firearm certificate or shot gun certificate held by him.*

(2) Where the court cancels a certificate under this section—

(a) the court shall cause notice to be sent to the chief officer of police by whom the certificate was granted; and

(b) the chief officer of police shall by notice in writing require the holder of the certificate to surrender it; and

(c) it is an offence[3] for the holder to fail to surrender the certificate within twenty-one days from the date of the notice given him by the chief officer of police.

(3) A constable may seize and detain any firearm or ammunition which may be the subject of an order for forfeiture under this section.

(4) A court of summary jurisdiction or, in Scotland, the sheriff may, on the application of the chief officer of police, order any firearm or ammunition seized and detained by a constable under this Act to be destroyed or otherwise disposed of.

[Firearms Act 1968, s 52 as amended by the Criminal Justice Act 1988, Sch 16, the Criminal Justice and Public Order Act 1994, Sch 10 and the Crime and Disorder Act 1998, Sch 8.]

---

*Para (1)(c) amended and sub-s (1A) inserted by the Criminal Justice Act 2003, s 304.

1. The effect of this provision, when read with s 57(3), post, is that there is no power to order forfeiture *under this section* in respect of offences against ss 22(3), (4) and (5), 23(1) and 24(1). The power to order forfeiture on conviction of those offences is contained in Schedule 6 to the Act and, in this work, is noted to each of the subsections referred to.

2. For manner of disposal of such a forfeiture, see s 140 of the Magistrates' Courts Act 1980, ante.

3. For prosecution and punishment, see Sch 6, post.

PART IV
MISCELLANEOUS AND GENERAL

8–10441 **53.** *Power to make rules*[1].

---

1. See the Firearms Rules 1998, this title, post.

8–10442 **54. Application on Parts I and II to Crown servants.** (1) Sections 1, 2, 7 to 13 and 26A to 32 of this Act apply, subject to the modifications specified in subsection (2) of this section, to persons in the service of Her Majesty in their capacity as such[1] so far as those provisions relate to the purchase and acquisition, but not so far as they relate to the possession, of firearms.

(2) The modifications referred to above are the following—

(a) a person in the service of Her Majesty[2] duly authorised in writing in that behalf may purchase or acquire firearms and ammunition for the public service without holding a certificate under this Act;

(b) a person in the naval, military or air service of Her Majesty shall, if he satisfies the chief officer of police on an application under section 26A of this Act that he is required to purchase a firearm or ammunition for his own use in his capacity as such, be entitled without payment of any fee to the grant of a firearm certificate authorising the purchase or acquisition or, as the case may be, to the grant of a shot gun certificate.

(3) For the purposes of this section and of any rule of law whereby any provision of this Act does not bind the Crown, a person shall be deemed to be in the service of Her Majesty if he is—

(a) a member of a police force, or

(b) a person employed by a police authority who is under the direction and control of a chief officer of police, or

(c) a member of the National Criminal Intelligence Service or the National Crime Squad.*

(3AA) For the puroposes of this section and of any rule of law whereby any provision of this Act does not bind the Crown—

(a) a member of the Civil Nuclear Constabulary shall be deemed to be a person in the service of Her Majesty; and

(b) references to the public service shall be deemed to included references to use by a person in the exercise and performance of his powers and duties as a member of the Civil Nuclear Constabulary.

(3A) An appropriately authorised person who is either a member of the British Transport Police Force or an associated civilian employee does not commit any offence under this Act by reason of having in his possession, or purchasing or acquiring, for use by that Force anything which is—

(a) a prohibited weapon by virtue of paragraph (b) of section 5(1) of this Act; or

(b) ammunition containing or designed or adapted to contain any such noxious thing as is mentioned in that paragraph.

(3B) In subsection (3A) of this section—

(a) "appropriately authorised" means authorised in writing by the Chief Constable of the British Transport Police Force or, if he is not available, by a member of that Force who is of at least the rank of assistant chief constable; and

(b) "associated civilian employee" means a person employed by the British Transport Police Authority who is under the direction and control of the Chief Constable of the British Transport Police Force.

(4) For the purposes of this section and any rule of law whereby any provision of this Act does not bind the Crown, the persons specified in subsection (5) of this section shall be deemed to be in the naval, military or air service of Her Majesty, insofar as they are not otherwise in, or treated as being in, any such service.

(5) The persons referred to in subsection (4) of this section are the following—

(a) members of any foreign force when they are serving with any of the naval, military or air forces of Her Majesty;

(b) members of any cadet corps approved by the Secretary of State when—

(i) they are engaged as members of the corps in connection with, drill or target practice; and

(ii) in the case of possession of prohibited weapons or prohibited ammunition when engaged in target practice, they are on service premises; and

(c) persons providing instruction to any members of a cadet corps who fall within paragraph (b).

(6) In subsection (5) of this section—

"foreign force" means any of the naval, military or air forces of a country other than the United Kingdom; and

"service premises" means premises, including any ship or aircraft, used for any purpose of any of the naval, military or air forces of Her Majesty.

[Firearms Act 1968, s 54 amended by the Police and Magistrates' Courts Act 1994, s 423, the Armed Forces Act 1996, s 28, the Firearms (Amendment) Act 1997, Schs 2 and 3, the Police Act 1997, Sch 9, the Anti-terrorism, Crime and Security Act 2001, Sch 7, SI 2004/1573 and the Energy Act 2004, Sch 14.]

---

*Amended by the Serious Organised Crime and Police Act 2005, Sch 4 from a date to be appointed.

1. Therefore possession by a person in the service of Her Majesty otherwise than in his capacity as such, is an offence (*Heritage v Claxton* (1941) 85 Sol Jo 323; *Tarttelin v Bowen* [1947] 2 All ER 837, 112 JP 99).

2. A constable of the United Kingdom Atomic Energy Authority is deemed to be a person in the service of Her Majesty: Atomic Energy Authority (Special Constables) Act 1976, s 1.

3. For comprehensive application of this section to the service authorities and members of a visiting force, or of an international headquarters, see Visiting Forces and International Headquarters (Application of Law) Order 1965, SI 1965/1536 amended by Post Office Act 1969, Sch 4, British Telecommunications Act 1981, s 87, SI 1987/928, SI 1989/1330 and 2169, SI 1994/1643 and SI 1998/253; and see Art 12 and Schs 2 and 3.

8–10443 55. Exercise of police functions. (1) Rules[1] made under section 53 of this Act may—

(a) regulate the manner in which chief officers of police are to carry out their duties under this Act;

(b) enable all or any of the functions of a chief officer of police to be discharged by a deputy in the event of his illness or absence, or of a vacancy in the office of chief officer of police.

(2) Without prejudice to subsection (1)(b) of this section, the functions of a chief officer of police under this Act shall be exercisable on any occasion by a person, or a person of a particular class, authorised by the chief officer of police to exercise that function on that occasion, or on occasions of that class or on all occasions.

[Firearms Act 1968, s 55.]

---

1. See the Firearms Rules 1998, this title, post.

8–10444 56. Service of notices. Any notice required or authorised by this Act to be given to a person may be sent by registered post or by the recorded delivery service in a letter addressed to him at his last or usual place of abode or, in the case of a registered firearms dealer, at any place of business in respect of which he is registered.

[Firearms Act 1968, s 56.]

8–10445   57. Interpretation.   (1) In this Act, the expression "firearm" means a lethal barrelled weapon[1] of any description from which any shot, bullet or other missile can be discharged and includes—

(a)   any prohibited weapon[2], whether it is such a lethal weapon as aforesaid or not; and

(b)   any component part[3] of such a lethal or prohibited weapon; and

(c)   any accessory[4] to any such weapon designed or adapted to diminish the noise or flash caused by firing the weapon;

and so much of section 1 of this Act as excludes any description of firearm from the category of firearms to which that section applies shall be construed as also excluding component parts of, and accessories to, firearms of that description.

(1A)   *(Repealed)*.

(2)   In this Act, the expression "ammunition" means ammunition for any firearm and includes grenades, bombs and other like missiles, whether capable of use with a firearm or not, and also includes prohibited ammunition[5].

(2A)   In this Act "self-loading" and "pump action" in relation to any weapon mean respectively that it is designed or adapted (otherwise than as mentioned in section 5(1)(a)) so that it is automatically re-loaded or that it is so designed or adapted that it is re-loaded by the manual operation of the fore-end or forestock of the weapon.

(2B)   In this Act "revolver", in relation to a smooth-bore gun, means a gun containing a series of chambers which revolve when the gun is fired.

(3)   For purposes of sections 45, 46, 50, 51(4) and 52 of this Act, the offences under this Act relating specifically to air weapons are those under section 22(4), 22(5), 23(1) and 24(4).

(4)   In this Act—

"acquire" means hire, accept as a gift or borrow and "acquisition" shall be construed accordingly;

"air weapon" has the meaning assigned to it by section 1(3)(b) of this Act;

"another member State" means a member State other than the United Kingdom, and "other member States" shall be construed accordingly;

"area" means a police area[6],

"Article 7 authority" means a document issued by virtue of section 32A(1)(b) or (2) of this Act;

"British Transport Police Force" means the constables appointed under section 53 of the British Transport Commission Act 1949;

"certificate" (except in a context relating to the registration of firearms dealers) and "certificate under this Act" mean a firearm certificate or a shot gun certificate and—

(a)   "firearm certificate" means a certificate granted by a chief officer of police under this Act in respect of any firearm or ammunition to which section 1 of this Act applies and includes a certificate granted in Northern Ireland under section 1 of the Firearms Act 1920, or under an enactment of the Parliament of Northern Ireland amending or substituted for that section; and

(b)   "shot gun certificate" means a certificate granted by a chief officer of police under this act and authorising a person to possess shot guns;

"civilian officer" means—

(a)   a person employed by a police authority or the Corporation of the City of London who is under the direction and control of a chief officer of police;

(b)   *(repealed)*.

"European firearms pass" means a document to which the holder of a certificate under this Act is entitled by virtue of section 32A(1)(a) of this Act;

"European weapons directive" means the directive of the Council of the European Communities No 91/477/EEC (directive on the control of the acquisition and possession of weapons);

"firearms dealer" means a person who, by way of trade or business, manufactures, sells, transfers, repairs, tests or proves firearms or ammunition to which section 1 of this Act applies, or shot guns;

"imitation firearm" means any thing which has the appearance[7] of being a firearm (other than such a weapon as is mentioned in section 5(1)(b) of this Act) whether or not it is capable of discharging any shot, bullet or other missile;

"premises" includes any land;

"prescribed" means prescribed by rules made by the Secretary of State under section 53 of this Act;

"prohibited weapon" and "prohibited ammunition" have the meanings assigned to them by section 5(2) of this Act;

"public place" includes any highway and any other premises or place to which at the material time the public have or are permitted to have access, whether on payment or otherwise[8];

"registered", in relation to a firearms dealer, means registered either—

(*a*) in Great Britain, under section 33 of this Act, or

(*b*) in Northern Ireland, under section 8 of the Firearms Act 1920, or any enactment of the Parliament of Northern Ireland amending or substituted for that section,

and references to "the register", "registration" and a "certificate of registration" shall be construed accordingly, except in section 40;

"rifle" includes carbine;

"shot gun" has the meaning assigned to it by section 1(3)(*a*) of this Act and, in sections 3(1) and 45(2) of this Act and in the definition of "firearms dealer", includes any component part of a shot gun and any accessory to a shot gun designed or adapted to diminish the noise or flash caused by firing the gun;

"slaughtering instruments" means a firearm which is specially designed or adapted for the instantaneous slaughter of animals or for the instantaneous stunning of animals with a view to slaughtering them; and

"transfer" includes let on hire, give, lend and part with possession[9], and "transferee" and "transferor" shall be construed accordingly.

(4A) For the purposes of any reference in this Act to the use of any firearm or ammunition for a purpose not authorised by the European weapons directive, the directive shall be taken to authorise the use of a firearm or ammunition as or with a slaughtering instrument and the use of a firearm and ammunition—

(*a*) for sporting purposes;

(*b*) for the shooting of vermin, or, in the course of carrying on activities in connection with the management of any estate, of other wildlife; and

(*c*) for competition purposes and target shooting outside competitions.

(5) The definitions in subsections (1) to (3) above apply to the provisions of this Act except where the context otherwise requires.

(6) For purposes of this Act—

(*a*) the length of the barrel of a firearm shall be measured from the muzzle to the point at which the charge is exploded on firing; and

(*b*) a shot gun or an air weapon shall be deemed to be loaded if there is ammunition in the chamber or barrel or in any magazine or other device which is in such a position that the ammunition can be fed into the chamber or barrel by the manual or automatic operation of some part of the gun or weapon.

[Firearms Act 1968, s 57 as amended by the Firearms (Amendment) Act 1988, s 25, SI 1992/2823, the Firearms (Amendment) Act 1997, ss 1 and 43, the Firearms (Amendment) (No 2) Act 1997, Sch, the Greater London Authority Act 1999, Sch 27 and Sch 34 and the Anti-terrorism, Crime and Security Act 2001, Sch 7.]

---

1. "Lethal weapon" includes a weapon not designed to kill or inflict injury but capable of doing so if misused (*Read v Donovan* [1947] KB 326, [1947] 1 All ER 37, 111 JP 46 (signal pistol); *Moore v Gooderham* [1960] 3 All ER 575, 124 JP 513 (air gun)); *R v Thorpe* [1987] 2 All ER 108, [1987] 1 WLR 383 (revolver powered by compressed carbon dioxide); *R v Singh* [1989] Crim LR 724 (flare launcher). Nevertheless, an air gun as a species of weapon is not, as a matter of law, a lethal weapon; the prosecution must prove that fact, either by expert evidence or by evidence of someone who has seen the gun fired and can indicate not only that it did work but what its observed effect was when it was fired (*Grace v DPP* (1988) 153 JP 491, DC). However, air rifles which had been tested and classified as in normal working order and capable of killing small vermin or of being used in target practice were held to have been properly found to be lethal barrelled weapons. (*Castle v DPP* (1998) Times 3 April.)

2. See s 5, ante. This includes stripped-down weapons (*R v Pannell* [1982] Crim LR 752, [1982] LS Gaz R 1257, CA).

3. A weapon incapable of discharging a missile because the barrel is solid but capable of being adapted to fire missiles by boring the barrel may fall within the definition of "firearm" as being a part of a firearm: see *Cafferata v Wilson* [1936] 3 All ER 149, 100 JP 489; *R v Freeman* [1970] 2 All ER 413, 134 JP 462. A telescopic sight is not a component part which requires to be included in a firearm certificate (*Watson v Herman* [1952] 2 All ER 70, 116 JP 395).

4. Whether a silencer is an accessory to a firearm for the purposes of s 57(1) is a question of fact which must be answered by considering whether the silencer could be used with that firearm and whether the defendant had it for that purpose; see *R v Buckfield* [1998] Crim LR 673.

5. Cartridges containing only primer are ammunition (*R v Stubbings* [1990] Crim LR 811, CA).

6. For meaning of "police area", see s 62 and Sch 8 of the Police Act 1964, title POLICE, post.

7. The test is whether the thing looked like a firearm at the time when the accused actually had it with him. (*R v Morris and King* (1984) 149 JP 60, 79 Cr App Rep 104, CA).

8. The space behind a counter in a shop was held to be a public place (*Anderson v Miller* [1976] Crim LR 743).

9. The phrase "part with possession" is to be read disjunctively from the word "lend". Where an owner of shotguns left them for safekeeping at the home of a friend who did not have a shotgun certificate, it was held that, although the owner had retained proprietary possession, there had been a parting of possession, and thereby a transfer of the shotguns, because the friend had acquired custodial possession of them (*Hall v Cotton* [1987] QB 504, [1986] 3 All ER 332).

8–10446   58. Particular savings. (1) Nothing in this Act shall apply to the proof houses of the Master, Wardens and Society of the Mystery of Gunmakers of the City of London and the Guardians of the Birmingham Proof House or the rifle range at Small Heath in Birmingham where firearms are sighted and tested, so as to interfere in any way with the operations of those two companies in proving firearms under the provisions of the Gun Barrel Proof Act 1868, or any other Acts for the time being in force, or to any person carrying firearms to or from any such proof house when being taken to such proof house for the purposes of proof or being removed therefrom after proof.

(2) Nothing in this Act relating to firearms shall apply to an antique firearm which is sold, transferred, purchased, acquired or possessed as a curiosity or ornament[1].

(3) The provisions of this Act relating to ammunition shall be in addition to and not in derogation of any enactment relating to the keeping and sale of explosives.

(4) The powers of arrest and entry conferred by Part III of this Act shall be without prejudice to any power of arrest or entry which may exist apart from this Act; and section 52(3) of this Act is not to be taken as prejudicing the power of a constable, when arresting a person for an offence, to seize property found in his possession or any other power of a constable to seize firearms, ammunition or other property, being a power exercisable apart from that subsection.

(5) Nothing in this Act relieves any person using or carrying a firearm from his obligation to take out a licence to kill game under the enactments requiring such a licence.

[Firearms Act 1968, s 58.]

---

1. This subsection does not apply to a firearm which is honestly and reasonably believed to be an antique if in fact it is not an antique (*R v Howells* [1977] QB 614, [1977] 3 All ER 417). Whether a firearm is an antique is a matter of fact and degree in each case (*Richards v Curwen* [1977] 3 All ER 426, 141 JP 651), but a firearm manufactured this century cannot be regarded an antique (*Bennett v Brown* (1980) 71 Cr App Rep 109).

8–10447   59. Repeals and general savings. (1) *Repeals.*

(2) In so far as any certificate, authority or permit granted, order or rule made, registration effected, or other thing done under an enactment repealed by this Act could have been granted, made, effected or done under a corresponding provision of this Act, it shall not be invalidated by the repeal of that enactment but shall have effect as if granted, made, effected or done under that corresponding provision; and for the purposes of this provision anything which under section 33(1) or (2) of the Firearms Act 1937, had effect as if done under any enactment in that Act shall, so far as may be necessary for the continuity of the law, be treated as done under the corresponding enactment in this Act.

(3) Any document referring to an enactment repealed by this Act or by the Firearms Act 1937, shall, so far as may be necessary for preserving its effect, be construed as referring, or as including a reference, to the corresponding enactment in this Act.

(4) The mention of particular matters in this section shall not be taken to affect the general application of section 38 of the Interpretation Act 1889, with regard to the effect of repeals.

[Firearms Act 1968, s 59.]

SCHEDULE 1
OFFENCES TO WHICH 17(2) APPLIES

(*As amended by the Criminal Damage Act 1971, the Criminal Attempts Act 1981, Sch, the Child Abduction Act 1984, s 11 and the Criminal Justice, Public Order Act 1994, Sch 9, the Police Act 1996, Sch 7 and the Sexual Offences Act 2003, Sch 6.*)

8–10448   1. Offences under s 1 of the Criminal Damage Act 1971.
2. Offences under any of the following provisions of the Offences against the Person Act 1861:

sections 20 to 22 (inflicting bodily injury; garrotting; criminal use of stupefying drugs);
section 30 (laying explosive to building, etc);
section 32 (endangering railway passengers by tampering with track);
section 38 (assault with intent to commit felony[1] or resist arrest);
section 47 (criminal assaults);

2A. Offences under Part I of the Child Abduction Act 1984 (abduction of children).
3. *Repealed.*
4. Theft[2], robbery, burglary, blackmail and any offence under section 12(1) (taking of motor vehicle or other conveyance without owner's consent) of the Theft Act 1968.
5. Offences under section 89(1) of the Police Act 1996, or section 41 of the Police (Scotland) Act 1967 (assaulting constable in execution of his duty).
5A. An offence under section 90(1) of the Criminal Justice Act 1991 (assaulting prisoner custody officer).
5B. An offence under section 13(1) of the Criminal Justice and Public Order Act 1994 (assaulting secure training centre custody officer).*
6. Offences under any of the following provisions of the Sexual Offences Act 1956:

section 1 (rape);
sections 17, 18 and 20 (abduction of women).**

7. *Repealed*: Theft Act 1968.
8. Aiding or abetting the commission of any offence specified in paragraphs 1 to 6 of this Schedule.
9. Attempting to commit any offence so specified.

---

*Para 5C inserted by the Immigration and Asylum Act 1999, Sch 14, from a date to be appointed.
1. The words "commit felony or" are no longer appropriate having regard to the repeal by Sch 3 to the Criminal Law Act 1967 of certain words in s 38 of the 1861 Act.

2. Since "robbery" is "theft" with an additional ingredient, namely the use of force or putting a person in fear of being subjected to force, the reference here to theft also includes the offence of robbery (*R v Guy* (1991) 155 JP 778, 93 Cr App Rep 108, CA).

8–10449   SCHEDULE 3

Jurisdiction and Procedure on Application under s 21(6).

8–10460   SCHEDULE 4

Particulars to be entered by firearms dealer in register.

8–10461   SCHEDULE 5

Jurisdiction and Procedure on Appeals under s 44.

8–10462   Section 51

SCHEDULE 6

(As amended by the Criminal Justice Act 1972, s 28 and Sch 6; the Criminal Law Act 1977, Sch 12; the Magistrates' Court Act 1980, Sch 7; the Criminal Justice Act 1982, s 38, 46; the Criminal Justice Act 1988, s 44; the Firearms (Amendment) Act 1988, ss 13 and 23, SI 1992/2823, the Firearms (Amendment) Act 1994, ss 1 and 2; the Criminal Justice and Public Order Act 1994, Sch 8, the Firearms (Amendment) Act 1997, ss 11 and Schs 2 and 3 and the Anti-social Behaviour Act 2003, ss 37, 38.)

PROSECUTION AND PUNISHMENT OF OFFENCES

PART 1

TABLE OF PUNISHMENTS

Section of Act creating offence	General nature of offence	Mode of prosecution	Punishment	Additional provisions
Section 1 (1)	Possessing etc, firearm or ammunition without firearm certificate.	(a) Summary¹	6 months or the **statutory maximum** or both.	
		(b) On indictment	(i) where the offence is committed in the aggravated form within the meaning of section 4(4) of the Act, 7 years, or a fine; or both; (ii) in any other case, 5 years or a fine, or both.	(*Scotland*)
Section 1 (2)	Non-compliance with condition of firearm certificate	Summary	6 months or **level 5** on the standard scale or both.	(*Scotland*)
Section 2 (1)	Possessing, etc, shot gun without shot gun certificate.	(a) Summary¹	6 months or the statutory maximum or both.	(*Scotland*)
		(b) On indictment	5 years or a fine; or both	
Section 2 (2)	Non-compliance with condition of shot gun certificate.	Summary	6 months or **level 5** on the standard scale or both.	(*Scotland*)
Section 3 (1)	Trading in firearms without being registered as firearms dealer.	(a) Summary¹	6 months or the **statutory maximum** or both.	
		(b) On indictment	5 years or a fine; or both.	
Section 3 (2)	Selling firearm to person without a certificate.	(a) Summary¹	6 months or the **statutory maximum** or both.	
		(b) On indictment	5 years or a fine; or both.	
Section 3 (3)	Repairing, testing etc firearm without a certificate.	(a) Summary¹	6 months or the **statutory maximum** or both.	
		(b) On indictment	5 years or a fine; or both.	
Section 3 (5)	Falsifying certificate, etc, with view to acquisition of firearm.	(a) Summary¹	6 months or the **statutory maximum** or both.	
		(b) On indictment	5 years or a fine; or both.	
Section 3 (6)	Pawnbroker taking firearm in pawn.	Summary	3 months or **level 3** on the standard scale or both.	
Section 4 (1) (3)	Shortening a shot gun; conversion of firearms.	(a) Summary¹	6 months or the **statutory maximum** or both.	
		(b) On indictment	7 years or a fine; or both.	

Section of Act creating offence	General nature of offence	Mode of prosecution	Punishment	Additional provisions
Section 5(1)	Possessing or distributing prohibited weapons or ammunition.	(a) Summary[1]	6 months or the **statutory maximum** or both.	
		(b) On indictment	10 years or a fine; or both	
Section 5(1A)	Possessing or distributing other prohibited weapons or ammunition.	(a) Summary	6 months or the **statutory maximum** or both.	
		(b) On indictment	10 years or a fine; or both	
Section 5(5)	Non-compliance with condition of Defence Council authority	Summary	6 months or **level 5** on the standard scale or both.	
Section 5(6)	Non-compliance with requirement to surrender authority to possess, etc, prohibited weapon or ammunition.	Summary	**Level 3** on the standard scale.	
Section 6(3)	Contravention of order under s 6 (or corresponding Northern Irish order) restricting removal of arms.	Summary	3 months or, for each firearm or parcel of ammunition in respect of which the offence is committed, **level 3** on the standard scale; or both.	Paragraph 2 of Part II of this Schedule applies.
Section 7(2)	Making false statement in order to obtain police permit.	Summary	6 months or **level 5** on the standard scale or both.	
Section 9(3)	Making false statement in order to obtain permit for auction of firearms etc.	Summary	6 months or a fine not exceeding **level 5** on the standard scale; or both.	
Section 13(2)	Making false statement in order to obtain permit for removal of signalling apparatus.	Summary	6 months or **level 5** on the standard scale or both.	
Section 16	Possession of firearm with intent to endanger life or injure property.	On indictment	Life imprisonment or a fine; or both.	
Section 16A	Possession of firearm with intent to cause fear of violence.	On indictment	10 years or a fine; or both.	
Section 17(1)	Use of firearms to resist arrest.	On indictment	Life imprisonment or a fine; or both.	
Section 17(2)	Possessing firearm while committing an offence specified in Schedule 1 or, in Scotland, an offence specified in Schedule 2.	On indictment	Life imprisonment or a fine; or both.	
Section 18(1)	Carrying firearms or imitation firearm with intent to commit indictable offence (or, in Scotland, an offence specified in Schedule 2) or to resist arrest.	On indictment	Life imprisonment or a fine; or both.	
Section 19	Carrying firearm or imitation firearm in public place.	(a) Summary[1]	6 months or the **statutory maximum** or both.	Paragraphs 3 to 5 of Part II of this Schedule apply.
		(b) On indictment (but not in the case of an imitation firearm or if the firearm is an air weapon)	7 years or a fine; or both.	
Section 19A	Having small-calibre pistol outside premises of licensed pistol club.	(a) Summary	6 months or a fine of the **statutory maximum**; or both.	
		(b) On indictment	10 years or a fine; or both.	

Section of Act creating offence	General nature of offence	Mode of prosecution	Punishment	Additional provisions
Section 20(1)	Trespassing with firearm or imitation firearm in a building.	(*a*) Summary[1]	6 months or the **statutory maximum** or both.	
		(*b*) On indictment (but not in the case of an imitation firearm or if the firearm is an air weapon)	7 years or a fine; or both.	
Section 20(2)	Trespassing with firearm or imitation firearm on land.	Summary	3 months or **level 4** on the standard scale or both.	
Section 21(4)	Contravention of provisions denying firearms to ex-prisoners and the like.	(*a*) Summary[1]	6 months or the **statutory maximum** or both.	
		(*b*) On indictment	5 years or a fine; or both.	
Section 21(5)	Supplying firearms to person denied them under section 21.	(*a*) Summary[1]	6 months or the **statutory maximum** or both.	
		(*b*) On indictment	5 years or a fine; or both.	
Section 22(1)	Person under 17 acquiring firearm.	Summary	6 months or **level 5** on the standard scale[2] or both.	
Section 22(1A)	Person under 18 using certificated firearm for unauthorised purpose.	Summary	3 months or **level 5** on the standard scale; or both.	
Section 22(2)	Person under 14 having firearm in his possession without lawful authority.	Summary	6 months or **level 5** on the standard scale[2] or both.	
Section 22(3)	Person under 15 having with him a shot gun without adult supervision.	Summary	**Level 3** on the standard scale[2].	Paragraph 8 of Part II of this Schedule applies.
Section 22(4)	Person under 17 having with him an air weapon or ammunition therefor.	Summary	**Level 3** on the standard scale[2].	Paragraphs 7 and 8 of Part II of this Schedule apply.
Section 23(1)	Person under 17 making improper use of air weapon when under supervision; person supervising him permitting such use.	Summary	**Level 3** on the standard scale[2].	Paragraphs 7 and 8 of Part II of this Schedule apply.
Section 23(4)	Person under 17 making improper use of air weapon on private premises.	Summary	A fine of **level 3** on the standard scale.	Paragraphs 7 and 8 of Part II of this Schedule apply.
Section 24(1)	Selling or letting on hire a firearm to person under 17.	Summary	6 months or **level 5** on the standard scale; or both.	
Section 24(2)	Supplying firearm or ammunition (being of a kind to which section 1 of this Act applies) to person under 14.	Summary	6 months or **level 5** on the standard scale; or both.	
Section 24(3)	Making gift of shot gun to person under 15.	Summary	**Level 3** on the standard scale.	
Section 24(4)	Supplying air weapon to person under 17.	Summary	**Level 3** on the standard scale.	Paragraph 9 of Part II of this Schedule applies.
Section 25	Supplying firearm to person drunk or insane.	Summary	3 months or **level 3** on the standard scale; or both.	Paragraphs 7 and 8 of Part II of this Schedule apply.

Section of Act creating offence	General nature of offence	Mode of prosecution	Punishment	Additional provisions
Section 28A(7)	Making false statement in order to procure grant or renewal of a firearm or shot gun certificate.	Summary	6 months or **level 5** on the standard scale; or both.	
Section 29(3)	Making false statement in order to procure variation of a firearm certificate.	Summary	6 months or **level 5** on the standard scale; or both.	
Section 30D(3)	Failing to surrender certificate on revocation	Summary	**Level 3** on the standard scale.	
Section 32B(5)	Failure to surrender expired European firearms pass.	Summary	**Level 3** on the standard scale.	
Section 32C(6)	Failure to produce European firearms pass or Article 7 authority for variation or cancellation etc; failure to notify loss or theft of firearm identified in pass or to produce pass for endorsement.	Summary	3 months or **level 5** on the standard scale; or both.	
Section 38(8)	Failure to surrender certificate of registration or register of transaction on removal of firearms dealer's name from register.	Summary	**Level 3** on the standard scale.	
Section 39(1)	Making false statement in order to secure registration or entry in register of a place of business.	Summary	6 months or **level 5** on the standard scale; or both.	
Section 39(2)	Registered firearms dealer having place of business not entered in the register.	Summary	6 months or **level 5** on the standard scale; or both.	
Section 39(3)	Non-compliance with condition of registration.	Summary	6 months or **level 5** on the standard scale; or both.	
Section 40(5)	Non-compliance by firearms dealer with provisions as to register of transactions; making false entry in register.	Summary	6 months or **level 5** on the standard scale; or both.	
Section 42A	Failure to report transaction authorised by visitor's shot gun permit.	Summary	3 months or **level 5** on the standard scale; or both.	
Section 46	Obstructing constable or civilian officer in exercise of search powers.	Summary	6 months or a fine of **level 5** on the standard scale; or both.	
Section 47(2)	Failure to hand over firearm or ammunition on demand by constable.	Summary	3 months or **level 4** on the standard scale; or both.	
Section 48(3)	Failure to comply with requirement of a constable that a person shall declare his name and address.	Summary	**Level 3** on the standard scale.	
Section 48(4)	Failure to produce firearms pass issued in another member State.	Summary	**Level 3** on the standard scale.	
Section 49(3)	Failure to give constable facilities for examination of firearms in transit, or to produce papers.	Summary	3 months or, for each firearm or parcel of ammunition in respect of which the offence is committed, **level 3** on the standard scale or both.	Paragraph 2 of Part II of this Schedule applies.
Section 52(2)(*c*)	Failure to surrender firearm or shot gun certificate cancelled by court on conviction.	Summary	**Level 3** on the standard scale.	

PART II
SUPPLEMENTARY PROVISIONS AS TO TRIAL AND PUNISHMENT OF OFFENCES

1. *Scotland.*

2. In the case of an offence against section 6(3) or 49(3) of this Act, the court before which the offender is convicted may, if the offender is the owner of the firearms or ammunition, make such order as to the forfeiture of the firearms or ammunition as the court thinks fit.

3. (1) Where in England or Wales a person who has attained the age of seventeen is charged before a magistrates' court with an offence triable either way listed in Schedule 1 to the Magistrates' Courts Act 1980[3] ("the listed offence") and is also charged before that court with an offence under section 17(1) or (2) of this Act, the following provisions of this paragraph shall apply.

(2) Subject to the following sub-paragraph the court shall proceed as if the listed offence were triable only on indictment and sections 18 to 23 of the said Act of 1980 (procedure for determining mode of trial of offences triable either way) shall not apply in relation to that offence.

(3) If the court determines not to commit the accused for trial in respect of the offence under section 17(1) or (2), or if proceedings before the court for that offence are otherwise discontinued, the preceding sub-paragraph shall cease to apply as from the time when this occurs and—

(*a*) if at that time the court has not yet begun to inquire into the listed offence as examining justices, the court shall, in the case of the listed offence, proceed in the ordinary way in accordance with the said sections 18 to 23; but

(*b*) if at that time the court has begun so to inquire into the listed offence, those sections shall continue not to apply and the court shall proceed with its inquiry into that offence as examining justices, but shall have power in accordance with section 25(3) and (4) of the said Act of 1980 to change to summary trial with the accused's consent.*

4. Where a person commits an offence under section 17(1) of this Act in respect of the lawful arrest or detention of himself for any other offence committed by him, he shall be liable to the penalty provided by Part I of this Schedule in addition to any penalty to which he may be sentenced for the other offence.

5. If on the trial of a person for an offence under section 17(1) of this Act the jury are not satisfied that he is guilty of that offence but are satisfied that he is guilty of an offence under section 17(2), the jury may find him guilty of the offence under section 17(2) and he shall then be punishable accordingly.

6. The punishment to which a person is liable for an offence under section 17(2) of this Act shall be in addition to any punishment to which he may be liable for the offence first referred to in section 17(2).

7. The court by which a person is convicted of an offence under section 22(4), 23(1) or (4) or 24(4) of this Act may make such order as it thinks fit as to the forfeiture or disposal of the air weapon or ammunition in respect of which the offence was committed.

8. The court by which a person is convicted of an offence under section 22(3) or (4), 23(1) or (4) or 24(4) may make such order as it thinks fit as to the forfeiture or disposal of any firearm or ammunition found in his possession.

9. The court by which a person is convicted of an offence under section 24(3) of this Act may make such order as it thinks fit as to the forfeiture or disposal of the shot gun or ammunition in respect of which the offence was committed.

---

*Para 3 repealed by the Criminal Justice Act 2003, Sch 3, from a date to be appointed.

1. For procedure in respect of this offence which is triable either way, see the Magistrates' Courts Act 1980, ss 17A–21 in PART I: MAGISTRATES' COURTS, PROCEDURE, ante.

2. The restrictions as to punishment of juvenile offenders will apply; see eg Magistrates' Courts Act 1980, s 36.

3. This reference to an offence triable either way listed in Sch 1 to the 1980 Act includes a reference to an offence under s 1 of the Criminal Attempts Act 1981; Criminal Attempts Act 1981, s 7(2), in PART I: MAGISTRATES' COURTS, PROCEDURE, ante.

Firearms Act 1982
(1982 c 31)

8–10570   1. Control of imitation firearms readily convertible into firearms to which section 1 of the 1958 Act applies. (1) This Act applies to an imitation firearm if—

(*a*) it has the appearance of being a firearm to which section 1 of the 1968 Act (firearms requiring a firearm certificate) applies; and

(*b*) it is so constructed or adapted as to be readily convertible into a firearm to which that section applies.

(2) Subject to section 2(2) of this Act and the following provisions of this section, the 1968 Act shall apply in relation to an imitation firearm to which this Act applies as it applies in relation to a firearm to which section 1 of that Act applies.

(3) Subject to the modifications in subsection (4) below, any expression given a meaning for the purposes of the 1968 Act has the same meaning in this Act.

(4) For the purposes of this section and the 1968 Act, as it applies by virtue of this section—

(*a*) the definition of air weapon in section 1(3)(*b*) of that Act (air weapons excepted from requirement of firearm certificate) shall have effect without the exclusion of any type declared by rules made by the Secretary of State under section 53 of that Act to be specially dangerous; and (*b*)   the definition of firearm in section 57(1) of that Act shall have effect without paragraphs (*b*) and (*c*) of that subsection (component parts and accessories).

(5) In any proceedings brought by virtue of this section for an offence under the 1968 Act involving an imitation firearm to which this Act applies, it shall be a defence for the accused to show that he did not know and had no reason to suspect that the imitation firearm was so constructed or adapted as to be readily convertible into a firearm to which section 1 of that Act applies.

(6) For the purposes of this section an imitation firearm shall be regarded as readily convertible into a firearm to which section 1 of the 1968 Act applies if—

(*a*)   it can be so converted without any special skill on the part of the person converting it in the construction or adaptation of firearms of any description; and

(*b*)   the work involved in converting it does not require equipment or tools other than such as are in common use by persons carrying out works of construction and maintenance in their own homes.

[Firearms Act 1982, s 1.]

8–10571   2. Provisions supplementary to section 1.   (1) Subject to subsection (2) below, references in the 1968 Act, and in any order made under section 6 of that Act (orders prohibiting movement of firearms or ammunition) before this Act comes into force—

(*a*)   to firearms (without qualification); or

(*b*)   to firearms to which section 1 of that Act applies;

shall be read as including imitation firearms to which this Act applies.

(2) The following provisions of the 1968 Act do not apply by virtue of this Act to an imitation firearm to which this Act applies, that is to say—

(*a*)   section 4(3) and (4) (offence to convert anything having appearance of firearm into a firearm and aggravated offence under section 1 involving a converted firearm); and

(*b*)   the provisions of that Act which relate to, or to the enforcement of control over, the manner in which a firearm is used or the circumstances in which it is carried;

but without prejudice, in the case of the provisions mentioned in paragraph (*b*) above, to the application to such an imitation firearm of such of those provisions as apply to imitation firearms apart from this Act.

(3) The provisions referred to in subsection (2)(*b*) above are sections 16 to 20 and section 47.

[Firearms Act 1982, s 2.]

8–10572   3. *Northern Ireland.*

8–10573   4. Citation, interpretation, commencement and extent.   (1) This Act may be cited as the Firearms Act 1982, and this Act and the 1968 Act may be cited together as the Firearms Acts 1968 and 1982.

(2) In this Act "the 1968 Act" means the Firearms Act 1968.

(3) This Act shall come into force on such day as the Secretary of State may by order made by statutory instrument appoint.

(4) This Act, except section 3, does not extend to Northern Ireland.

[Firearms Act 1982, s 4.]

Firearms (Amendment) Act 1988[1, 2]

(1988 c 45)

Specially dangerous weapons

8–10590   1. Prohibited weapons and ammunition.   (1) Section 5 of the Firearms Act 1968 (in this Act referred to as "the principal Act") shall have effect with the following amendments the purpose of which is to extend the class of prohibited weapons and ammunition, that is to say weapons and ammunition the possession, purchase, acquisition, manufacture, sale or transfer of which requires the authority of the Secretary of State.

(2)–(5) *Amendment of the Firearms Act 1968, s 5; power of Secretary of State by order to add to the weapons or ammunition specified in s 5(1) of the principal Act.*

[Firearms (Amendment) Act 1988, s 1.]

---

1. This Act amends the Firearms Act 1968, ante, and makes further provision for regulating the possession of, and transactions relating to, firearms and ammunition.

This Act, the Firearms Acts 1968 and 1982 and the Firearms (Amendment) Act 1992 may be cited together as the Firearms Acts 1968 to 1992. The provisions of this Act should be read in conjunction with those of the Firearms Act 1968. Sections 46, 51(4) and 52 of the Firearms Act 1968 (powers of search, time limit for prosecutions and forfeiture and cancellation orders on conviction) shall, subject to certain exceptions, apply also to offences under this Act; as to interpretation and construction of these Acts, see generally s 25, post.

2. Exchange of information, see note to the Firearms Act 1968, above.

Shot guns requiring firearm certificate

8–10592 5. Restriction on sale of ammunition for smooth-bore guns. (1) This section applies to ammunition to which section 1 of the principal Act does not apply and which is capable of being used in a shot gun or in a smooth-bore gun to which that section applies.

(2) It is an offence for a person to sell any such ammunition to another person in the United Kingdom who is neither a registered firearms dealer nor a person who sells such ammunition by way of trade or business unless that other person—

(*a*) produces a certificate authorising him to possess a gun of a kind mentioned in subsection (1) above; or

(*b*) shows that he is by virtue of that Act or this Act entitled to have possession of such a gun without holding a certificate; or

(*c*) produces a certificate authorising another person to possess such a gun, together with that person's written authority to purchase the ammunition on his behalf.

(3) An offence under this section shall be punishable on summary conviction with imprisonment for a term not exceeding **six months** or a fine not exceeding **level 5** on the standard scale or both.
[Firearms (Amendment) Act 1988, s 5.]

Converted and de-activated weapons

8–10593 6. Shortening of barrels. (1) Subject to subsection (2) below, it is an offence to shorten to a length less than 24 inches the barrel of any smooth-bore gun to which section 1 of the principal Act applies other than one which has a barrel with a bore exceeding 2 inches in diameter; and that offence shall be punishable[1]—

(*a*) on summary conviction, with imprisonment for a term not exceeding **six months** or a fine not exceeding **the statutory maximum** or both;

(*b*) on indictment, with imprisonment for a term not exceeding **five years** or a **fine** or both.

(2) It is not an offence under this section for a registered firearms dealer to shorten the barrel of a gun for the sole purpose of replacing a defective part of the barrel so as to produce a barrel not less than 24 inches in length.
[Firearms (Amendment) Act 1988, s 6.]

---

1. For procedure in respect of this offence which is triable either way, see the Magistrates' Courts Act 1980, ss 17A–21, in PART I: MAGISTRATES' COURTS, PROCEDURE, ante.

8–10594 7. Conversion not to affect classification. (1) Any weapon which—

(*a*) has at any time (whether before or after the passing of the Firearms (Amendment) Act 1997) been a weapon of a kind described in section 5(1) or (1A) of the principal Act (including any amendments to section 5(1) made under section 1(4) of this Act);

(*b*) is not a self-loading or pump-action smooth-bore gun which has at any such time been such a weapon by reason only of having had a barrel less than 24 inches in length,

shall be treated as a prohibited weapon notwithstanding anything done for the purpose of converting it into a weapon of a different kind.

(2) Any weapon which—

(*a*) has at any time since the coming into force of section 2 above been a weapon to which section 1 of the principal Act applies; or

(*b*) would at any previous time have been such a weapon if those sections had then been in force,

shall, if it has, or at any time has had, a rifled barrel less than 24 inches in length, be treated as a weapon to which section 1 of the principal Act applies notwithstanding anything done for the purpose of converting it into a shot gun or an air weapon.

(3) For the purposes of subsection (2) above there shall be disregarded the shortening of a barrel by a registered firearms dealer for the sole purpose of replacing part of it so as to produce a barrel not less than 24 inches in length.
[Firearms (Amendment) Act 1988, s 7 as amended by the Firearms (Amendment) Act 1997, Sch 2.]

8–10595 8. De-activated weapons. For the purposes of the principal Act and this Act it shall be presumed, unless the contrary is shown, that a firearm has been rendered incapable of discharging any shot, bullet or other missile, and has consequently ceased to be a firearm within the meaning of those Acts, if—

(*a*) it bears a mark which has been approved by the Secretary of State for denoting that fact and which has been made either by one of the two companies mentioned in section 58(1) of the principal Act or by such other person as may be approved by the Secretary of State for the purposes of this section; and

(*b*) that company or person has certified in writing that work has been carried out on the firearm in a manner approved by the Secretary of State for rendering it incapable of discharging any shot, bullet or other missile.
[Firearms (Amendment) Act 1988, s 8.]

Firearm and shot gun certificates

8–10596 11. Grant of coterminous certificates. (1) Where a person who holds a firearm certificate applies for the grant or renewal of a shot gun certificate that certificate may, if he so requests, be granted or renewed for such period less than that specified in subsection (1), or in an order made under subsection (3) of section 28A of the principal Act as will secure that it ceases to be in force at the same time as the firearm certificate.

(2) Where a person who holds a shot gun certificate, or both such a certificate and a firearm certificate, applies for the grant of a firearm certificate, or for the renewal of the firearm certificate held by him, he may, on surrendering his shot gun certificate, apply for a new shot gun certificate to take effect on the same day as that on which the firearm certificate is granted or renewed.

(3) Where a shot gun certificate is granted to a person or such a certificate held by him is renewed and on the same occasion he is granted a firearm certificate or such a certificate held by him is renewed the fee payable on the grant or renewal of the shot gun certificate shall be £10 instead of that specified in section 32 of the principal Act.

(4) Subsection (3) above shall be included in the provisions that may be amended by an order under section 43 of the principal Act.
[Firearms (Amendment) Act 1988, s 11 as amended by the Firearms (Amendment) Act 1992, s 1, the Firearms (Amendment) Act 1997, Sch 2 and SI 2000/3148.]

8–10597 12. Revocation of certificates. (1) Where a certificate is revoked by the chief officer of police under section 30A(2), (3) or (4) or 30C of the principal Act he may by notice in writing require the holder of the certificate to surrender forthwith the certificate and any firearms and ammunition which are in the holder's possession by virtue of the certificate.

(2) It is an offence to fail to comply with a notice under subsection (1) above; and that offence shall be punishable on summary conviction with imprisonment for a term not exceeding **three months** or a fine not exceeding **level 4** on the standard scale or both.

(3) Where a firearm or ammunition is surrendered in pursuance of a notice under subsection (1) above, then—

(*a*) if an appeal against the revocation of the certificate succeeds, the firearm or ammunition shall be returned;

(*b*) if such an appeal is dismissed, the court may make such order for the disposal of the firearm or ammunition as it thinks fit;

(*c*) if no such appeal is brought or such an appeal is abandoned, the firearm or ammunition shall be disposed of—

(i) in such manner as the chief officer of police and the owner may agree; or

(ii) in default of agreement, in such manner as the chief officer may decide;

but subject, in a case within sub-paragraph (ii), to the provisions of subsection (4) below.

(4) The chief officer of police shall give the owner notice in writing of any decision under subsection (3)(*c*)(ii) above, the owner may appeal against that decision in accordance with section 44 of the principal Act and on such an appeal the court may either dismiss the appeal or make such order as to the disposal of the firearm or ammunition as it thinks fit.

(5) Paragraph 1 of Part I and paragraphs 1 to 5 of Part II of Schedule 5 to that Act (appeal jurisdiction and procedure) shall apply to an appeal under subsection (4) above as they apply to an appeal against the revocation of a certificate.
[Firearms (Amendment) Act 1988, s 12 as amended by the Firearms (Amendment) Act 1997, Schs 2 and 3.]

Firearms dealers and other businesses

8–10598 14. Auctioneers, carriers and warehousemen. (1) It is an offence for an auctioneer, carrier or warehouseman—

(*a*) to fail to take reasonable precautions for the safe custody of any firearm or ammunition which, by virtue of section 9(1) of the principal Act, he or any servant of his has in his possession without holding a certificate; or

(*b*) to fail to report forthwith to the police the loss or theft of any such firearm or ammunition.

(2) An offence under this section shall be punishable on summary conviction with imprisonment for a term not exceeding **six months** or a fine not exceeding **level 5** on the standard scale or both.
[Firearms (Amendment) Act 1988, s 14.]

Exemptions

8–10599 15. Approved rifle clubs and muzzle-loading pistol clubs. (1) Subject to subsection (4) below, a member of a rifle club approved by the Secretary of State may, without holding a firearm certificate, have in his possession a rifle and ammunition when engaged as a member of the club in connection with target shooting.

(2) Any rifle club may apply for approval, whether or not it is intended that any club members will, by virtue of subsection (1) above, have rifles or ammunition in their possession without holding firearm certificates.

(3) The Secretary of State may publish such guidance as he considers appropriate for the purpose of informing those seeking approval for a club of criteria that must be met before any application for such approval will be considered.

(4) The application of subsection (1) above to members of an approved rifle club may—

(a) be excluded in relation to the club, or
(b) be restricted to target shooting with specified types of rifle,
    by limitations contained in the approval.

(5) An approval—

(a) may be granted subject to such conditions specified in it as the Secretary of State thinks fit;
(b) may at any time be varied or withdrawn by the Secretary of State; and
(c) shall (unless withdrawn) continue in force for six years from the date on which it is granted or last renewed.

(6) There shall be payable on the grant or renewal of an approval a fee of £84 but this subsection shall be included in the provisions which may be amended by an order under section 43 of the principal Act.

(7) A constable or civilian officer authorised in writing in that behalf may, on producing if required his authority, enter any premises occupied or used by an approved rifle club and inspect those premises, and anything on them, for the purpose of ascertaining whether the provisions of this section, and any limitations or conditions in the approval, are being complied with.

(8) The power of a constable or civilian officer under subsection (7) above to inspect anything on club premises shall include power to require any information which is kept by means of a computer and is accessible from the premises to be made available for inspection in a visible and legible form.

(9) It is an offence for a person intentionally to obstruct a constable or civilian officer in the exercise of his powers under subsection (7) above; and that offence shall be punishable on summary conviction with a fine not exceeding **level 3** on the standard scale.

(10) In this section and section 15A below—

"approval", means an approval under this section; and "approved" shall be construed accordingly;
"civilian officer" has the same meaning as in the principal Act; and
"rifle club" includes a miniature rifle club.

(11) This section applies in relation to a muzzle-loading pistol club and its members as it applies to a rifle club and its members with the substitution for any reference to a rifle of a reference to a muzzle-loading pistol.

(12) In subsection (11) above—

"muzzle-loading pistol club" means a club where muzzle-loading pistols are used for target shooting; and
"muzzle-loading pistol" means a pistol designed to be loaded at the muzzle end of the barrel or chamber with a loose charge and a separate ball (or other missile).
[Firearms (Amendment) Act 1988, s 15, as substituted by the Firearms (Amendment) Act 1997, s 45.]

8–10600   16. Borrowed rifles on private premises.   (1) A person of or over the age of seventeen may, without holding a firearm certificate, borrow a rifle from the occupier of private premises and use it on those premises in the presence either of the occupier or of a servant of the occupier if—

(a) the occupier or servant in whose presence it is used holds a firearm certificate in respect of that rifle; and
(b) the borrower's possession and use of it complies with any conditions as to those matters specified in the certificate.

(2) A person who by virtue of subsection (1) above is entitled without holding a firearm certificate to borrow and use a rifle in another person's presence may also, without holding such a certificate, purchase or acquire ammunition for use in the rifle and have it in his possession during the period for which the rifle is borrowed if—

(a) the firearm certificate held by that other person authorises the holder to have in his possession at that time ammunition for the rifle of a quantity not less than that purchased or acquired by, and in the possession of, the borrower; and
(b) the borrower's possession and use of the ammunition complies with any conditions as to those matters specified in the certificate.
[Firearms (Amendment) Act 1988, s 16.]

8–10600A   16A. Possession of firearms on service premises.   (1) A person under the supervision of a member of the armed forces may, without holding a certificate or obtaining the authority of the Secretary of State under section 5 of the principal Act, have in his possession a firearm and ammunition on service premises.

(2) Subsection (1) above does not apply to a person while engaged in providing security protection on service premises.

(3) In this section—

"armed forces" means any of the naval, military or air forces of Her Majesty; and

"service premises" means premises, including any ship or aircraft, used for any purpose of the armed forces.

[Firearms (Amendment) Act 1988, s 16A, as inserted by the Armed Forces Act 1996, s 28.]

8–10600B 16B. Possession of firearms on Ministry of Defence Police premises. (1) A person who is being trained or assessed in the use of firearms under the supervision of a member of the Ministry of Defence Police may, without holding a certificate or obtaining the authority of the Secretary of State under section 5 of the principal Act, have in his possession a firearm and ammunition on relevant premises for the purposes of the training or assessment.

(2) In this section "relevant premises" means premises used for any purpose of the Ministry of Defence Police.

[Firearms (Amendment) Act 1988, s 16A, as inserted by the Police Reform Act 2002, s 81.]

8–10601 17. Visitors' permits. (1) The holder of a visitor's firearm permit may, without holding a firearm certificate, have in his possession any firearm, and have in his possession, purchase or acquire any ammunition, to which section 1 of the principal Act applies; and (subject to subsection (1A) below) the holder of a visitor's shot gun permit may, without holding a shot gun certificate, have shot guns in his possession and purchase or acquire shot guns.

(1A) A visitor's shot gun permit shall not authorise the purchase or acquisition by any person of any shot gun with a magazine except where—

(a) that person is for the time being the holder of a licence granted, for the purposes of any order made under section 1 of the Import, Export and Customs Powers (Defence) Act 1939[1], in respect of the exportation of that shot gun;

(b) the shot gun is to be exported from Great Britain to a place outside the member States without first being taken to another member State;

(c) the shot gun is acquired on terms which restrict that person's possession of the gun to the whole or a part of the period of his visit to Great Britain and preclude the removal of the gun from Great Britain; or

(d) the shot gun is purchased or acquired by that person exclusively in connection with the carrying on of activities in respect of which—

(i) that person; or

(ii) the person on whose behalf he makes the purchase or acquisition,

is recognised, for the purposes of the law of another member State relating to firearms, as a collector of firearms or a body concerned in the cultural or historical aspects of weapons.

(2) The chief officer of police for an area may, on an application in the prescribed[1] form made by a person resident in that area on behalf of a person specified in the application, grant a permit under this section to the specified person if satisfied that he is visiting or intending to visit Great Britain and—

(a) in the case of a visitor's firearm permit, that he has a good reason for having each firearm and the ammunition to which the permit relates in his possession, or, as respects ammunition, for purchasing or acquiring it, while he is a visitor to Great Britain;

(b) in the case of a visitor's shot gun permit, that he has a good reason for having each shot gun to which the permit relates in his possession, or for purchasing or acquiring it, while he is such a visitor.

(3) No permit shall be granted under this section to a person if the chief officer of police has reason to believe—

(a) that his possession of the weapons or ammunition in question would represent a danger to the public safety or to the peace; or

(b) that he is prohibited by the principal Act from possessing them.

(3A) No permit shall be granted under this section as respects any firearm unless—

(a) there is produced to the chief officer of police a document which—

(i) has been issued in another member State under provisions corresponding to the provisions of the principal Act for the issue of European firearms passes;

(ii) identifies that firearm as a firearm to which it relates; and

(iii) is for the time being valid;

(b) the applicant shows that the person specified in the application is a person who, by reason of his place of residence or any other circumstances, is not entitled to be issued with such a document in any of the other member States; or

(c) the applicant shows that the person specified in the application requires the permit exclusively in connection with the carrying on of activities in respect of which—

    (i) that person; or

    (ii) the person on whose behalf he is proposing to make use of the authorisation conferred by the permit,

is recognised, for the purposes of the law of another member State relating to firearms, as a collector of firearms or a body concerned in the cultural or historical aspects of weapons;

and a chief officer of police who grants a permit under this section in a case where a document has been produced to him in pursuance of paragraph (a) above shall endorse on the document a statement which identifies the permit and the firearm to which it relates and briefly describes the effect of the permit.

(4) A permit under this section shall be in the prescribed[1] form, shall specify the conditions subject to which it is held and—

(a) in the case of a visitor's firearm permit, shall specify the number and description of the firearms to which it relates, including their identification numbers, and, as respects ammunition, the quantities authorised to be purchased or acquired and to be held at any one time;

(b) in the case of a visitor's shot gun permit, shall specify the number and description of the shot guns to which it relates, including, if known, their identification numbers.

(5) The chief officer of police by whom a permit under this section is granted may by notice in writing to the holder vary the conditions subject to which the permit is held but, in the case of a visitor's shot gun permit, no condition shall be imposed or varied so as to restrict the premises where the shot gun or guns to which the permit relates may be used.

(6) A permit under this section shall come into force on such date as is specified in it and continue in force for such period, not exceeding twelve months, as is so specified.

(7) A single application (a "group application") may be made under this section for the grant of not more than twenty permits to persons specified in the application if it is shown to the satisfaction of the chief officer of police that their purpose in having the weapons in question in their possession while visiting Great Britain is—

(a) using them for sporting purposes on the same private premises during the same period; or

(b) participating in the same competition or other event or the same series of competitions or other events.

(8) There shall be payable on the grant of a permit under this section a fee of £12 except that where six or more permits are granted on a group application the fee shall be £60 in respect of those permits taken together.

(9) Subsection (8) above shall be included in the provisions that may be amended by an order under section 43 of the principal Act.

(10) It is an offence for a person—

(a) knowingly or recklessly to make a statement false in any material particular for the purpose of procuring the grant of a permit under this section; or

(b) to fail to comply with a condition subject to which such a permit is held by him;

and each of those offences shall be punishable on summary conviction with imprisonment for a term not exceeding **six months** or a fine not exceeding **level 5** on the standard scale or both.
[Firearms (Amendment) Act 1988, s 17 as amended by SI 1992/2823 and the Firearms (Amendment) Act 1997, Sch 2.]

---

1. See the Firearms Rules 1998 this title, post.

8–10602   18. Firearms acquired for export.   (1) A person may, without holding a firearm or shot gun certificate, purchase a firearm from a registered firearms dealer if—

(a) that person has not been in Great Britain for more than thirty days in the preceding twelve months; and

(b) the firearm is purchased for the purpose only of being exported from Great Britain without first coming into that person's possession.

(1A) A person shall not be entitled under subsection (1) above to purchase any firearm which falls within category B for the purposes of Annex I to the European weapons directive unless he—

(a) produces to the dealer from whom he purchases it a document which—

    (i) has been issued under provisions which, in the member State where he resides, correspond to the provisions of the principal Act for the issue of Article 7 authorities; and

    (ii) contains the prior agreement to the purchase of that firearm which is required by Article 7 of the European weapons directive;

(b) shows that he is purchasing the firearm exclusively in connection with the carrying on of activities in respect of which he, or the person on whose behalf he is purchasing the firearm, is recognised, for the purposes of the law of another member State relating to firearms, as a collector of firearms or a body concerned in the cultural or historical aspects of weapons; or

(c) shows that he resides in the United Kingdom or outside the member States.

(2) A registered firearms dealer who sells a firearm to a person who shows that he is entitled by virtue of subsection (1) above to purchase it without holding a certificate shall within forty-eight hours from the transaction send a notice of the transaction to the chief officer of police in whose register the premises where the transaction took place are entered.

(3) The notice of a transaction under subsection (2) above shall contain the particulars of the transaction which the dealer is required to enter in the register kept by him under section 40 of the principal Act and every such notice shall be sent by registered post or the recorded delivery service.

(4) In the case of a transaction to which subsection (2) above applies the particulars to be entered in the register kept under section 40 of the principal Act (and accordingly contained in a notice under subsection (3) above) shall include the number and place of issue of the purchaser's passport, if any and, in a case where the transaction is one for the purposes of which a document such as is mentioned in subsection (1A)(a) above is required to be produced, particulars of the agreement contained in that document.

(5) It is an offence for a registered firearms dealer to fail to comply with subsection (2) above; and that offence shall be punishable on summary conviction with imprisonment for a term not exceeding **six months** or a fine not exceeding **level 5** on the standard scale or both.

(6) In the case of any failure to comply with subsection (2) above which is confined to the omission from a notice of the particulars of an agreement contained in a document such as is mentioned in subsection (1A)(a) above, subsection (5) above shall have effect as if for "six months" there were substituted "three months".

[Firearms (Amendment) Act 1988, s 18 amended by SI 1992/2823.]

8–10603 18A. Purchase or acquisition of firearms in other member States. (1) Subject to subsections (2) and (3) below, where—

(a) a person who resides in Great Britain purchases or acquires a firearm in another member State; and

(b) that firearm is a firearm which falls within category C for the purposes of Annex I to the European weapons directive,

he shall, within fourteen days of the transaction, send notice of the transaction to the chief officer of police for the area where he resides.

(2) A person shall not be required to give notice under subsection (1) above of a transaction under which he acquires a firearm on terms which—

(a) restrict his possession of the firearm to the whole or a part of the period of a visit to the member State where the transaction takes place; and

(b) preclude the removal of the firearm from that member State.

(3) A person shall not be required to give notice under subsection (1) above of a transaction under which he purchases or acquires a firearm if—

(a) he is for the time being the holder of a certificate under the principal Act relating to that firearm and containing, in relation to that firearm, a condition that he may have the firearm in his possession only for the purpose of its being kept or exhibited as part of a collection; or

(b) he would, if in Great Britain, be authorised by virtue of a licence under the Schedule to this Act to have that firearm in his possession.

(4) A notice under subsection (1) above shall contain a description of the firearm (giving the identification number if any) and state the nature of the transaction and the name and address in Great Britain of the person giving the notice.

(5) A notice under subsection (1) above which is sent from a place in Great Britain shall be sent by registered post or by the recorded delivery service and, in any other case, shall be sent in such manner as most closely corresponds to the use of registered post or the recorded delivery service.

(6) It is an offence for a person to fail to comply with this section; and that offence shall be punishable on summary conviction with imprisonment for a term not exceeding **three months** or a fine not exceeding **level 5** on the standard scale or **both**.

[Firearms Act 1968, s 18A inserted by SI 1992/2823.]

8–10604 19. Firearms and ammunition in museums. The Schedule to this Act shall have effect for exempting firearms and ammunition in museums from certain provisions of the principal Act.

[Firearms (Amendment) Act 1988, s 19.]

Miscellaneous and supplementary

8–10605 20. *Removal of arms and ammunition to Northern Ireland. Amendment of s 6 of principal Act.*

8–10606 21. Payments in respect of prohibited weapons. The Secretary of State shall, in accordance with a scheme made by him, make payments to persons who surrender or otherwise dispose of firearms—

(a) which they had, and were entitled to have, in their possession immediately before 23rd September 1987 by virtue of firearm or shot gun certificates held by them; or

(b) which before that date they had contracted to acquire and were entitled to have in their possession on or after that date by virtue of such certificates held by them,

and the possession of which will become, or has become, unlawful by virtue of section 1(2) or 7(1) above.

[Firearms (Amendment) Act 1988, s 21.]

8–10607 22. *Firearms consultative committee.*

8–10608 24. *Expenses and receipts.*

8–10609 25. Interpretation and supplementary provisions. (1) In this Act "the principal Act" means the Firearms Act 1968 and any expression which is also used in that Act has the same meaning as in that Act.

(2)–(3) *Amendment of s 57 of the principal Act.*

(4) Any reference in the principal Act to a person who is by virtue of that Act entitled to possess, purchase or acquire any weapon or ammunition without holding a certificate shall include a reference to a person who is so entitled by virtue of any provision of this Act.

(5) Sections 46, 51(4) and 52 of the principal Act (powers of search, time-limit for prosecutions and forfeiture and cancellation orders on conviction) shall apply also to offences under this Act except that on the conviction of a person for an offence under the Schedule to this Act no order shall be made for the forfeiture of anything in his possession for the purposes of the museum in question.

(6) Sections 53 to 56 and section 58 of the principal Act (rules, Crown application, service of notices and savings) shall have effect as if this Act were contained in that Act.

(7) The provisions of this Act other than sections 15 and 17 shall be treated as contained in the principal Act for the purposes of the Firearms Act 1982 (imitation firearms readily convertible into firearms to which section 1 of the principal Act applies).

[Firearms (Amendment) Act 1988, s 25.]

8–10610 26. *Corresponding provisions for Northern Ireland.*

8–10620 27. Short title, citation, commencement and extent. (1) This Act may be cited as the Firearms (Amendment) Act 1988.

(2) This Act and the Firearms Acts 1968 and 1982 may be cited together as the Firearms Acts 1968 to 1988.

(3) *Commencement.*

(4) Except for* section 26 and this section this Act does not extend to Northern Ireland.

[Firearms (Amendment) Act 1988, s 27.]

---

*Words to be inserted by the Criminal Justice Act 2003, Sch 32, from a date to be appointed.

Section 19   SCHEDULE

(*As amended by the Firearms (Amendment) Act 1997, s 47 and Sch 2.*)

Firearms and Ammunition in Museums
MUSEUM FIREARMS LICENCES

8–10621 1. (1) The Secretary of State may, on an application in writing made on behalf of a museum to which this Schedule applies, grant a museum firearms licence in respect of that museum.

(2) While a museum firearms licence (in this Schedule referred to as a "licence") is in force in respect of a museum the persons responsible for its management and their servants—

(a) may, without holding a firearm certificate or shot gun certificate, have in their possession, and purchase or acquire, for the purposes of the museum firearms and ammunition which are or are to be normally exhibited or kept on its premises or on such of them as are specified in the licence; and

(b) if the licence so provides, may, without the authority of the Secretary of State under section 5 of the principal Act, have in their possession, purchase or acquire for those purposes any prohibited weapons and ammunition which are or are to be normally exhibited or kept as aforesaid.

(3) The Secretary of State shall not grant a licence in respect of a museum unless, after consulting the chief officer of police for the area in which the premises to which the licence is to apply are situated, he is satisfied that the arrangements for exhibiting and keeping the firearms and ammunition in question are or will be such as not to endanger the public safety or the peace.

(4) A licence shall be in writing and be subject to such conditions specified in it as the Secretary of State thinks necessary for securing the safe custody of the firearms and ammunition in question.

(5) A licence shall, unless previously revoked or cancelled, continue in force for five years from the date on which it is granted but shall be renewable for further periods of five years at a time and sub-paragraph (3) above shall apply to the renewal of a licence as it applies to a grant.

(6) The Secretary of State may by order substitute for the periods mentioned in sub-paragraph (5) above such longer or shorter periods as are specified in the order.

(7) The power to make an order under sub-paragraph (6) above shall be exercisable by statutory instrument subject to annulment in pursuance of a resolution of either House of Parliament.

Variation and revocation

8–10622 **2.** (1) The Secretary of State may by notice in writing to the persons responsible for the management of a museum—

(*a*) vary the conditions specified in a licence held in respect of the museum; or
(*b*) vary the licence so as to extend or restrict the premises to which it applies.

(2) A notice under sub-paragraph (1) above may require the persons in question to deliver up the licence to the Secretary of State within twenty-one days of the date of the notice for the purpose of having it amended in accordance with the variation.

(3) The Secretary of State may by notice in writing to the persons responsible for the management of a museum revoke a licence held in respect of the museum if—

(*a*) at any time, after consulting the chief officer of police for the area in which the premises to which it applies are situated, he is satisfied that the continuation of the exemption conferred by the licence would result in danger to the public safety or to the peace; or
(*b*) those persons or any of them or any servant of theirs has been convicted of an offence under this Schedule; or
(*c*) those persons have failed to comply with a notice under this paragraph requiring them to deliver up the licence.

(4) Where a licence is revoked the Secretary of State shall by notice in writing require the persons responsible for the management of the museum in question to surrender the licence to him.

Fees

8–10623 **3.** (1) There shall be payable—

(*a*) on the grant or renewal of a licence a fee of £200 or of such lesser amount as the Secretary of State may in any particular case determine;
(*b*) on the extension of a licence to additional premises, a fee of £75.

(2) This paragraph shall be included in the provisions that may be amended by an order under section 43 of the principal Act.

Offences and enforcement

8–10624 **4.** (1) It is an offence—
(2) This Schedule also applies to any museum or similar institution in Great Britain which is of a description specified in an order[1] made for the purposes of this sub-paragraph by the Secretary of State and whose collection includes or is to include firearms.
(3) An order[1] under sub-paragraph (2) above may specify any description of museum or similar institution which appears to the Secretary of State to have as its purpose, or one of its purposes, the preservation for the public benefit of a collection of historical, artistic or scientific interest.
(4) The power to make an order under sub-paragraph (2) above shall be exercisable by statutory instrument.

(*a*) for a person knowingly or recklessly to make a statement false in any material particular for the purpose of procuring the grant, renewal or variation of a licence;
(*b*) for the persons or any of the persons responsible for the management of a museum to fail to comply or to cause or permit another person to fail to comply with any condition specified in the licence held in respect of that museum.

(2) An offence under sub-paragraph (1) above shall be punishable on summary conviction with imprisonment for a term not exceeding **six months** or a fine not exceeding **level 5** on the standard scale or both.
(3) It is an offence for a person to fail to comply with a notice under paragraph 2(4) above; and that offence shall be punishable on summary conviction with a fine not exceeding **level 3** on the standard scale.
(4) In proceedings against any person for an offence under sub-paragraph (1)(*b*) above it is a defence for him to prove that he took all reasonable precautions and exercised all due diligence to avoid the commission of the offence.
(5) Where an offence under this paragraph committed by a body corporate is proved to have been committed with the consent or connivance of, or to be attributable to any neglect on the part of, any director, manager, secretary or other similar officer of the body corporate, or any person who was purporting to act in any such capacity, he, as well as the body corporate, shall be guilty of that offence and be liable to be proceeded against and punished accordingly.
(6) Where the affairs of a body corporate are managed by its members sub-paragraph (5) above shall apply in relation to the acts and defaults of a member in connection with his functions of management as if he were a director of the body corporate.

Museums to which this Schedule applies

8–10625 **5.** (1) This Schedule applies to the following museums—

The Armouries, HM Tower of London
The National Army Museum
The National Museum of Wales
The Royal Air Force Museum
The Science Museum
The Victoria and Albert Museum
The Royal Marines Museum

The Fleet Air Arm Museum
The Royal Navy Museum
The Royal Navy Submarine Museum
The British Museum
The Imperial War Museum
The National Maritime Museum
The National Museums of Scotland
The National Museums and Galleries on Merseyside
The Wallace Collection

Any other museum or similar institution in Great Britain which has as its purpose, or one of its purposes, the preservation for the public benefit of a collection of historical, artistic or scientific interest which includes or is to include firearms and which is maintained wholly or mainly out of money provided by Parliament or by a local authority.

(2) This Schedule also applies to any museum or similar institution in Great Britain which is of a description specified in an order[1] made for the purposes of this sub-paragraph by the Secretary of State and whose collection includes or is to include firearms.

(3) An order[1] under sub-paragraph (2) above may specify any description of museum or similar institution which appears to the Secretary of State to have as its purpose, or one of its purposes, the preservation for the public benefit of a collection of historical, artistic or scientific interest.

(4) The power to make an order under sub-paragraph (2) above shall be exercisable by statutory instrument.

---

1. See the Firearms (Museums) Order 1997, SI 1997/1692.

Interpretation

8–10626 6. In this Schedule references to the persons responsible for the management of a museum are to the board of trustees, governing body or other person or persons (whether or not incorporated) exercising corresponding functions.

Firearms (Amendment) Act 1997[1]
(1997 c 5)

PART I[2]
PROHIBITION OF WEAPONS AND AMMUNITION AND CONTROL OF SMALL-CALIBRE PISTOLS

General prohibition of small firearms etc

8–10627 1. Extension of section 5 of the 1968 Act to prohibit certain small firearms etc.
(1)–(6) *Amendment of section 5 of the Firearms Act 1968.*

(7) The general prohibition by section 5 of the 1968 Act of firearms falling within subsection (1)(*aba*) of that section is subject to the special exemptions in sections 2 to 8 below.

(8) In sections 2 to 8 below any reference to a firearm certificate shall include a reference to a visitor's firearm permit.

(9) (*Repealed*).

[Firearms (Amendment) Act 1997, s 1 as amended by the Firearms (Amendment) (No 2) Act 1997, Sch.]

---

1. The Firearms (Amendment) Act 1997 amends the Firearms Acts 1968 to 1992; makes provision in relation to the licensing and regulation of pistol clubs and makes further provision for regulating the possession of, and transactions relating to, firearms and ammunition. For commencement of the Act, see s 53(3), post.
2. Part I contains ss 1 to 18.

Special exemptions from prohibition of small firearms

8–10628 2. Slaughtering instruments. The authority of the Secretary of State is not required by virtue of subsection (1)(*aba*) of section 5 of the 1968 Act—

   (*a*) for a person to have in his possession, or to purchase or acquire, or to sell or transfer, a slaughtering instrument if he is authorised by a firearm certificate to have the instrument in his possession, or to purchase or acquire it;

   (*b*) for a person to have a slaughtering instrument in his possession if he is entitled, under section 10 of the 1968 Act, to have it in his possession without a firearm certificate.

[Firearms (Amendment) Act 1997, s 2.]

8–10629 3. Firearms used for humane killing of animals. The authority of the Secretary of State is not required by virtue of subsection (1)(*aba*) of section 5 of the 1968 Act for a person to have in his possession, or to purchase or acquire, or to sell or transfer, a firearm if he is authorised by a firearm certificate to have the firearm in his possession, or to purchase or acquire it, subject to a condition that it is only for use in connection with the humane killing of animals.

[Firearms (Amendment) Act 1997, s 3.]

8–10630 4. Shot pistols used for shooting vermin. (1) The authority of the Secretary of State is not required by virtue of subsection (1)(*aba*) of section 5 of the 1968 Act for a person to have in his possession, or to purchase or acquire, or to sell or transfer, a shot pistol if he is authorised by a firearm certificate to have the shot pistol in his possession, or to purchase or acquire it, subject to a condition that it is only for use in connection with the shooting of vermin.

(2) For the purposes of this section, "shot pistol" means a smooth-bored gun which is chambered for .410 cartridges or 9mm rim-fire cartridges.

[Firearms (Amendment) Act 1997, s 4.]

8–10631   5. Races at athletic meetings. The authority of the Secretary of State is not required by virtue of subsection (1)(*aba*) of section 5 of the 1968 Act—

    (*a*)   for a person to have a firearm in his possession at an athletic meeting for the purpose of starting races at that meeting; or

    (*b*)   for a person to have in his possession, or to purchase or acquire, or to sell or transfer, a firearm if he is authorised by a firearm certificate to have the firearm in his possession, or to purchase or acquire it, subject to a condition that it is only for use in connection with starting races at athletic meetings.

[Firearms (Amendment) Act 1997, s 5.]

8–10632   6. Trophies of war. The authority of the Secretary of State is not required by virtue of subsection (1)(*aba*) of section 5 of the 1968 Act for a person to have in his possession a firearm which was acquired as a trophy of war before 1 January 1946 if he is authorised by a firearm certificate to have it in his possession.

[Firearms (Amendment) Act 1997, s 6.]

8–10633   7. Firearms of historic interest. (1) The authority of the Secretary of State is not required by virtue of subsection (1)(*aba*) of section 5 of the 1968 Act for a person to have in his possession, or to purchase or acquire, or to sell or transfer, a firearm which—

    (*a*)   was manufactured before 1 January 1919; and

    (*b*)   is of a description specified under subsection (2) below,

if he is authorised by a firearm certificate to have the firearm in his possession, or to purchase or acquire it, subject to a condition that he does so only for the purpose of its being kept or exhibited as part of a collection.

(2) The Secretary of State may by order[1] made by statutory instrument specify a description of firearm for the purposes of subsection (1) above if it appears to him that—

    (*a*)   firearms of that description were manufactured before 1 January 1919; and

    (*b*)   ammunition for firearms of that type is not readily available.

(3) [2] The authority of the Secretary of State is not required by virtue of subsection (1)(*aba*) of section 5 of the 1968 Act for a person to have in his possession, or to purchase or acquire, or to sell or transfer, a firearm which—

    (*a*)   is of particular rarity, aesthetic quality or technical interest, or

    (*b*)   is of historical importance,

if he is authorised by a firearm certificate to have the firearm in his possession subject to a condition requiring it to be kept and used only at a place designated for the purposes of this subsection by the Secretary of State.

(4) This section has effect without prejudice to section 58(2) of the 1968 Act (antique firearms).

[Firearms (Amendment) Act 1997, s 7.]

---

1. The Firearms (Amendment) Act 1997 (Firearms of Historic Interest) Order 1997, SI 1997/1537, has been made.
2. See the Firearms (Amendment) Act 1997 (Transitional Provisions and Savings) Regulations 1997, SI 1997/1538, which limit for a certain period the effect of one of the exemptions from the prohibition of large-calibre hand guns.

Weapons and ammunition used for treating animals

8–10634   8. Weapons and ammunition used for treating animals. The authority of the Secretary of State is not required by virtue of subsection (1)(*aba*), (*b*) or (*c*) of section 5 of the 1968 Act for a person to have in his possession, or to purchase or acquire, or to sell or transfer, any firearm, weapon or ammunition designed or adapted for the purpose of tranquillising or otherwise treating any animal, if he is authorised by a firearm certificate to possess, or to purchase or acquire, the firearm, weapon or ammunition subject to a condition restricting its use to use in connection with the treatment of animals.

[Firearms (Amendment) Act 1997, s 8.]

Surrender of firearms, etc and compensation

8–10639   15. Surrender of prohibited small firearms and ammunition. (1) The Secretary of State may make such arrangements as he thinks fit to secure the orderly surrender at designated police stations of firearms or ammunition the possession of which will become or has become unlawful by virtue of section 1 or 9 above.

(2) The chief officer of police for any area may designate any police station in his area as being suitable for the receipt of surrendered firearms or ammunition or surrendered firearms or ammunition of any description.

(3) This section applies in relation to small-calibre pistols with the substitution for the reference in subsection (1) above to section 1 above of a reference to section 1 of the Firearms (Amendment) (No. 2) Act 1997 (prohibition of small-calibre pistols).

[Firearms (Amendment) Act 1997, s 15 as amended by the Firearms (Amendment) (No 2) Act 1997, s 2.]

8–10640 16. Payments in respect of prohibited small firearms and ammunition. (1) The Secretary of State shall, in accordance with a scheme made by him, make payments in respect of firearms and ammunition surrendered at designated police stations in accordance with the arrangements made by him under section 15 above.

(2) A scheme under subsection (1) above shall provide only for the making of payments to persons making claims for such payments in respect of firearms or ammunition—

(a) which they had, and were entitled to have in their possession on or immediately before 16 October 1996 by virtue of firearm certificates held by them or by virtue of their being registered firearms dealers; or

(b) which on or before that date they had contracted to acquire and were entitled to have in their possession after that date by virtue of such certificates held by them or by virtue of their being registered firearms dealers,

and their possession of which will become, or has become, unlawful by virtue of section 1(2) or 9 above.

(3) A scheme under subsection (1) above may—

(a) restrict eligibility for receipt of payments to claims made in respect of firearms or ammunition surrendered within a period specified in the scheme;

(b) provide for the procedure to be followed (including any time within which claims must be made and the provision of information) in respect of claims under the scheme and for the determination of such claims;

(c) make different provision for different descriptions of firearm or ammunition or for different descriptions of claimant.

(4) This section applies in relation to small-calibre pistols surrendered at designated police stations in accordance with the arrangements made under section 15 above with the substitution—

(a) for the reference in paragraph (a) of subsection (2) above to 16th October 1996 of a reference to 14th May 1997; and

(b) for the reference in that subsection to section 1(2) above of a reference to section 1 of the Firearms (Amendment) (No 2) Act 1997 (prohibition of small-calibre pistols).

[Firearms (Amendment) Act 1997, s 16 as amended by the Firearms (Amendment) (No 2) Act 1997, s 2.]

8–10641 17. Payments in respect of ancillary equipment. (1) The Secretary of State shall, in accordance with any scheme which may be made by him, make payments in respect of ancillary equipment of any description specified in the scheme.

(2) For the purposes of subsection (1) above "ancillary equipment" means equipment, other than prohibited ammunition, which—

(a) is designed or adapted for use in connection with firearms prohibited by virtue of section 1(2) above; and

(b) has no practicable use in connection with any firearm which is not a prohibited weapon.

(3) A scheme under subsection (1) above shall provide only for the making of payments to persons making claims for such payments in respect of ancillary equipment—

(a) which they had in their possession on 16 October 1996; or

(b) which they had in their possession after that date, having purchased it by virtue of a contract entered into before that date.

(4) No payments shall be made under a scheme under subsection (1) above in relation to any ammunition unless its possession or, as the case may be, purchase by any person claiming a payment in respect of it was, at all material times, lawful by virtue of a firearm certificate held by him or by virtue of his being a registered firearms dealer.

(5) A scheme under subsection (1) above may require, as a condition of eligibility for receipt of payments under the scheme in respect of any equipment—

(a) the surrender (whether to the police or any other person) of that equipment in accordance with the scheme within a period specified by the scheme; or

(b) the disposal of that equipment by way of sale within a period so specified; or

(c) either such surrender or such disposal of the equipment within a period so specified.

(6) A scheme under subsection (1) above may—

(a) provide for the procedure to be followed (including any time within which claims must be made and the provision of information) in respect of claims under the scheme and for the determination of such claims;

(b) make different provision for different descriptions of equipment or for different descriptions of claimant.

(7) This section applies in relation to equipment designed or adapted for use in connection with small-calibre pistols with the substitution—

(a) for the reference in subsection (2)(a) above to firearms prohibited by virtue of section 1(2) above of a reference to small-calibre pistols; and

(b) for the reference in subsection (3)(a) above to 16th October 1996 of a reference to 14th May 1997.

[Firearms (Amendment) Act 1997, s 17 as amended by the Firearms (Amendment) (No 2) Act 1997, s 2.]

8–10642 18. Parliamentary control of compensation schemes. (1) Before making a compensation scheme the Secretary of State shall lay a draft of it before Parliament.

(2) The Secretary of State shall not make the scheme unless the draft has been approved by resolution of each House.

(3) Subsections (1) and (2) above apply to an alteration to a compensation scheme as they apply to a compensation scheme.

(4) In this section "compensation scheme" means a scheme under section 16 or 17 above.

[Firearms (Amendment) Act 1997, s 18 as amended by the Firearms (Amendment) (No 2) Act 1997, s 2.]

PART III[1]
REGULATION OF FIREARMS AND AMMUNITION

Transfers and other events relating to firearms and ammunition

8–10656 32. Transfers of firearms etc. to be in person. (1) This section applies where, in Great Britain—

(a) a firearm or ammunition to which section 1 of the 1968 Act applies is sold, let on hire, lent or given by any person, or

(b) a shot gun is sold, let on hire or given, or lent for a period of more than 72 hours by any person,

to another person who is neither a registered firearms dealer nor a person who is entitled to purchase or acquire the firearm or ammunition without holding a firearm or shot gun certificate or a visitor's firearm or shot gun permit.

(2) Where a transfer to which this section applies takes place—

(a) the transferee must produce to the transferor the certificate or permit entitling him to purchase or acquire the firearm or ammunition being transferred;

(b) the transferor must comply with any instructions contained in the certificate or permit produced by the transferee;

(c) the transferor must hand the firearm or ammunition to the transferee, and the transferee must receive it, in person.

(3) A failure by the transferor or transferee to comply with subsection (2) above shall be an offence.

[Firearms (Amendment) Act 1997, s 32.]

---

1. Pt III contains ss 32 to 48.

8–10657 33. Notification of transfers involving firearms. (1) This section applies where in Great Britain—

(a) any firearm to which section 1 of the 1968 Act applies is sold, let on hire, lent or given;

(b) any shot gun is sold, let on hire or given, or lent for a period of more than 72 hours.

(2) Any party to a transfer to which this section applies who is the holder of a firearm or shot gun certificate or, as the case may be, a visitor's firearm or shot gun permit which relates to the firearm in question shall within seven days of the transfer give notice to the chief officer of police who granted his certificate or permit.

(3) A notice required by subsection (2) above shall—

(a) contain a description of the firearm in question (giving its identification number if any); and

(b) state the nature of the transaction and the name and address of the other party;

and any such notice shall be sent by registered post or the recorded delivery service.

(4) A failure by a party to a transaction to which this section applies to give the notice required by this section shall be an offence.

[Firearms (Amendment) Act 1997, s 33.]

8–10658   34. Notification of de-activation, destruction or loss of firearms etc.   (1) Where, in Great Britain—

(*a*) a firearm to which a firearm or shot gun certificate relates; or

(*b*) a firearm to which a visitor's firearm or shot gun permit relates,

is de-activated, destroyed or lost (whether by theft or otherwise), the certificate holder who was last in possession of the firearm before that event shall within seven days of that event give notice of it to the chief officer of police who granted the certificate or permit.

(2) Where, in Great Britain, any ammunition to which section 1 of the 1968 Act applies, and a firearm certificate or a visitor's firearm permit relates, is lost (whether by theft or otherwise), the certificate or permit holder who was last in possession of the ammunition before that event shall within seven days of the loss give notice of it to the chief officer of police who granted the certificate or permit.

(3) A notice required by this section shall—

(*a*) describe the firearm or ammunition in question (giving the identification number of the firearm if any);

(*b*) state the nature of the event;

and any such notice shall be sent by registered post or the recorded delivery service.

(4) A failure, without reasonable excuse, to give a notice required by this section shall be an offence.

(5) For the purposes of this section and section 35 below a firearm is de-activated if it would by virtue of section 8 of the 1988 Act be presumed to be rendered incapable of discharging any shot, bullet or other missile.

[Firearms (Amendment) Act 1997, s 34.]

8–10659   35. Notification of events taking place outside Great Britain involving firearms etc.
(1) Where, outside Great Britain, any firearm or shot gun is sold or otherwise disposed of by a transferor whose acquisition or purchase of the firearm or shot gun was authorised by a firearm certificate or shot gun certificate, the transferor shall within 14 days of the disposal give notice of it to the chief officer of police who granted his certificate.

(2) A failure to give a notice required by subsection (1) above shall be an offence.

(3) Where, outside Great Britain—

(*a*) a firearm to which a firearm or shot gun certificate relates is de-activated, destroyed or lost (whether by theft or otherwise); or

(*b*) any ammunition to which section 1 of the 1968 Act applies, and a firearm certificate relates, is lost (whether by theft or otherwise),

the certificate holder who was last in possession of the firearm or ammunition before that event shall within 14 days of the event give notice of it to the chief officer of police who granted the certificate.

(4) A failure, without reasonable excuse, to give a notice required by subsection (3) above shall be an offence.

(5) A notice required by this section shall—

(*a*) contain a description of the firearm or ammunition in question (including any identification number); and

(*b*) state the nature of the event and, in the case of a disposal, the name and address of the other party.

(6) A notice required by this section shall be sent within 14 days of the disposal or other event—

(*a*) if it is sent from a place in the United Kingdom, by registered post or by the recorded delivery service; and

(*b*) in any other case, in such manner as most closely corresponds to the use of registered post or the recorded delivery service.

[Firearms (Amendment) Act 1997, s 35.]

8–10660   36. Penalty for offences under ss 32 to 35.   An offence under section 32, 33, 34 or 35 above shall—

(*a*) if committed in relation to a transfer or other event involving a firearm or ammunition to which section 1 of the 1968 Act applies be punishable[1]—

(i) on summary conviction with imprisonment for a term not exceeding **six months** or a fine not exceeding the **statutory maximum** or **both**;

(ii) on conviction on indictment with imprisonment for a term not exceeding **five years** or a **fine** or **both**;

(*b*) if committed in relation to a transfer or other event involving a shot gun be punishable on summary conviction with imprisonment for a term not exceeding **six months** or a fine not exceeding **level 5** on the standard scale or **both**.

[Firearms (Amendment) Act 1997, s 36.]

1. For procedure in respect of this offence which is triable either way, see the Magistrates' Courts Act 1980, ss 17A–21, in PART I: MAGISTRATES' COURTS, PROCEDURE, ante.

Firearm and shot gun certificates

8–10661   39. Register of holders of shot gun and firearm certificates.   (1) There shall be established a central register of all persons who have applied for a firearm or shot gun certificate or to whom a firearm or shot gun certificate has been granted or whose certificate has been renewed.

(2) The register shall—

(*a*)   record a suitable identifying number for each person to whom a certificate is issued; and
(*b*)   be kept by means of a computer which provides access on-line to all police forces.
[Firearms (Amendment) Act 1997, s 39.]

Miscellaneous

8–10662   44. Firearm certificates for certain firearms used for target shooting: special conditions.   (1) If a chief officer of police is satisfied, on an application for the grant or renewal of a firearm certificate in relation to any rifle or muzzle-loading pistol which is not a prohibited weapon, that the applicant's only reason for having it in his possession is to use it for target shooting, any certificate which may be granted to the applicant or, as the case may be, renewed shall be held subject to the following conditions (in addition to any other conditions), namely—

(*a*)   the rifle or pistol is only to be used for target shooting; and
(*b*)   the holder must be a member of an approved rifle club or, as the case may be, muzzle-loading pistol club specified in the certificate.

(2) In this section, "muzzle loading pistol" means a pistol designed to be loaded at the muzzle end of the barrel or chamber with a loose charge and a separate ball (or other missile).
[Firearms (Amendment) Act 1997, s 44.]

8–10663   45. Approved rifle clubs and muzzle-loading pistol clubs.   (1) *Substitution of a new s 15 in the Firearms (Amendment) Act 1988.*

(2) *(Repealed).*

(3) Any approval of a rifle or miniature rifle club or muzzle-loading pistol club under section 15 of the 1988 Act which is in force immediately before the commencement of this section shall have effect as if it were an approval under section 15 of the 1988 Act as substituted by subsection (1) above.
[Firearms (Amendment) Act 1997, s 45 as amended by the Firearms (Amendment) (No 2) Act 1997, Sch.]

8–10665   47. Museums eligible for a museums firearm licence.   (1) In the Schedule to the 1988 Act (firearms and ammunition in museums to which the Schedule applies)—

(*a*)   the existing provisions of paragraph 5 shall be numbered as sub-paragraph (1) of that paragraph;
(*b*)   after that sub-paragraph there shall be inserted the following sub-paragraphs—

"(2) This Schedule also applies to any museum or similar institution in Great Britain which is of a description specified in an order made for the purposes of this sub-paragraph by the Secretary of State and whose collection includes or is to include firearms.

(3) An order under sub-paragraph (2) above may specify any description of museum or similar institution which appears to the Secretary of State to have as its purpose, or one of its purposes, the preservation for the public benefit of a collection of historical, artistic or scientific interest.

(4) The power to make an order under sub-paragraph (2) above shall be exercisable by statutory instrument.".
[Firearms (Amendment) Act 1997, s 47.]

8–10666   48. Firearms powered by compressed carbon dioxide.   Any reference to an air rifle, air pistol or air gun—

(*a*)   in the Firearms Acts 1968 to 1997; or
(*b*)   in the Firearms (Dangerous Air Weapons) Rules 1969 or the Firearms (Dangerous Air Weapons) (Scotland) Rules 1969,

shall include a reference to a rifle, pistol or gun powered by compressed carbon dioxide.
[Firearms (Amendment) Act 1997, s 48.]

Part IV
FINAL PROVISIONS

8–10667　**49.** *Financial provisions*

8–10668　**50. Interpretation and supplementary provisions.**　(1) In this Act—

"small-calibre pistol" means—

(*a*)　a pistol chambered for .22 or smaller rim-fire cartridges; or

(*b*)　an air pistol to which section 1 of the 1968 Act applies and which is designed to fire .22 or smaller diameter ammunition;

"the 1968 Act" means the Firearms Act 1968;

"the 1988 Act" means the Firearms (Amendment) Act 1988.

(2)　Any expression used in this Act which is also used in the 1968 Act or the 1988 Act has the same meaning as in that Act.

(3)　Any reference in the 1968 Act to a person who is by virtue of that Act entitled to possess, purchase or acquire any weapon or ammunition without holding a certificate shall include a reference to a person who is so entitled by virtue of any provision of this Act.

(4)　Sections 46, 51(4) and 52 of the 1968 Act (powers of search, time-limit for prosecutions and forfeiture and cancellation orders on conviction) shall apply also to offences under this Act.

(5)　Sections 53 to 56 and section 58 of the 1968 Act (rules, Crown application, service of notices and savings) shall have effect as if this Act were contained in that Act.

(6)　The provisions of this Act shall be treated as contained in the 1968 Act for the purposes of the Firearms Act 1982 (imitation firearms readily convertible into firearms to which section 1 of the 1968 Act applies).

[Firearms (Amendment) Act 1997, s 50 as amended by the Firearms (Amendment) (No 2) Act 1997, Sch.]

8–10669　**51. Power to make transitional, consequential etc. provisions.**　(1) The Secretary of State may by regulations make such transitional and consequential provisions and such savings as he considers necessary or expedient in preparation for, in connection with, or in consequence of—

(*a*)　the coming into force of any provision of this Act; or

(*b*)　the operation of any enactment repealed or amended by a provision of this Act during any period when the repeal or amendment is not wholly in force.

(2)　Regulations under this section may make modifications of any enactment contained in this or in any other Act.

(3)　The power to make regulations under subsection (2) above shall be exercisable by statutory instrument which shall be subject to annulment in pursuance of a resolution of either House of Parliament.

[Firearms (Amendment) Act 1997, s 51.]

8–10670　**52. Minor and consequential amendments and repeals.**　(1) Schedule 2 (minor and consequential amendments) shall have effect.

(2)　The enactments mentioned in Schedule 3 (which include spent enactments) are repealed to the extent specified in the third column of that Schedule.

[Firearms (Amendment) Act 1997, s 52.]

8–10671　**53. Short title, commencement and extent.**　(1) This Act may be cited as the Firearms (Amendment) Act 1997.

(2)　This Act and the Firearms Acts 1968 and 1992 may be cited together as the Firearms Acts 1968 to 1997.

(3)　This Act shall come into force on such day as the Secretary of State may by order[1] made by statutory instrument appoint; and different days may be appointed for different purposes and different areas.

(4)　An order under subsection (3) above may contain such transitional provision and savings (whether or not involving the modification of any statutory provision) as appear to the Secretary of State to be necessary or expedient in connection with any provisions brought into force.

(5)　This Act does not extend to Northern Ireland.

[Firearms (Amendment) Act 1997, s 53.]

---

1. At the date of going to press the Firearms (Amendment) Act 1997, (Commencement) (No 1) Order 1997, SI 1997/1076, and the Firearms (Amendment) Act 1997 (Commencement) (No 2) Order 1997, SI 1997/1535, amended by SI 1997/1536, had been made. The effect of these Commencement Orders has been to bring into force all provisions of the Act which are reproduced in this work except for the following:

Part I: ss 11, 12, 13 and 14;
Part II: ss 19 to 31;
Part III: s 46;
Schedule 1.

Firearms Rules 1998[1]
(SI 1998/1941 amended by SI 2005/3344)

8–10730

Citation, commencement and extent.

1. These Rules may be cited as the Firearms Rules 1998 and shall come into force on 1st September 1998.

---

1. Made by the Secretary of State in exercise of the powers conferred on him by the Firearms Act 1968, ss 7(1), 9(2), 13(1), 26A, 26B, 27(2), (3), 28(2), 33(1), (3), (5), 37(1), 40(7), 53, 55(1) and 57(4) and the Firearms (Amendment) Act 1988, s 17(2), (4).

Interpretation

8–10731 **2.** In these Rules—

- (a) "the principal Act" means the Firearms Act 1968;
- (b) "the 1997 Act" means the Firearms (Amendment) Act 1997;
- (c) references to firearms include references to imitation firearms to which the Firearms Act 1982 applies;
- (d) "muzzle-loading pistol", "approved rifle club" and "approved muzzle-loading pistol club" have the same meaning as in section 15 of the Firearms (Amendment) Act 1988;
- (e) "target shooting club" means any club at which shooting at targets is conducted with firearms to which section 1 of the principal Act applies, whether or not an approved rifle or muzzle-loading pistol club;
- (f) any reference to a form includes a reference to any form to the like effect; and
- (g) any reference to a Schedule, except in rule 10(5) below, is a reference to a Schedule to these Rules.

Firearm certificates

8–10732 **3.** (1) An application for the grant, renewal or variation of a firearm certificate shall be in the form set out in Part I of Schedule 1.

(2) The information given by an applicant for the grant or renewal of a firearm certificate in answer to the questions numbered 1 to 16 in the form of application referred to in paragraph (1) above shall be verified in the manner specified in rule 4(1) below.

(3) An application for the grant or renewal of a firearm certificate shall be accompanied by—

- (a) the names and addresses of two persons who have agreed to act as referees and who satisfy the requirements of rule 4(3) below, and
- (b) four photographs of the applicant as specified in rule 7 below.

(4) Subject to paragraph (5) below, a firearm certificate shall be granted or renewed subject to the following conditions (whether or not in addition to any other conditions), namely—

- (i) the holder must, on receipt of the certificate, sign it in ink with his usual signature;
- (ii) the holder of the certificate must inform the chief officer of police by whom the certificate was granted within seven days of the theft, loss or destruction in Great Britain of the certificate;
- (iii) the holder of the certificate must, without undue delay, inform the chief officer of police by whom the certificate was granted of any change in his permanent address;
- (iv)
  - (a) the firearms and ammunition to which the certificate relates must at all times (except in the circumstances set out in paragraph (b) below) be stored securely so as to prevent, so far as is reasonably practicable, access to the firearms or ammunition by an unauthorised person;
  - (b) where a firearm or ammunition to which the certificate relates is in use or the holder of the certificate has the firearm with him for the purpose of cleaning, repairing or testing it or for some other purpose connected with its use, transfer or sale, or the firearm or ammunition is in transit to or from a place in connection with its use or any such purpose, reasonable precautions must be taken for the safe custody of the firearm or the ammunition.

(5) Where a chief officer of police is satisfied on an application for the grant or renewal of a firearm certificate in relation to any firearm, weapon or ammunition to which section 5A(1) or (4) of the principal Act or section 3, 4, 5, 7 or 8 of the 1997 Act apply and that it is to be used only for the purpose or purposes specified in those sections, the certificate shall be subject to an additional condition restricting the use of that firearm, weapon or ammunition to use for that purpose or purposes.

(6) A firearm certificate shall bear a photograph of the holder and, subject to paragraph (5) above, shall be in the form set out in Part II of Schedule 1.

Referees: firearm certificates

8–10732A **4.** (1) The information referred to in rule 3(2) above shall be verified by the signed statement of each of the persons nominated as a referee by the applicant pursuant to rule 3(3)(a) above that the information is, to the best of his knowledge and belief, correct.

(2) An application for a firearm certificate shall not be considered by a chief officer of police until he receives from each referee nominated by the applicant pursuant to rule 3(3)(a) above and who satisfy the requirements of paragraph (3) below a completed reference in the form set out in Part III of Schedule 1 containing a statement to the effect that he knows of no reason why the applicant should not be permitted to possess a firearm.

(3) Subject to paragraph (4) below, to satisfy the requirements of this paragraph a person must not be a member of the applicant's family, a serving police officer or police employee or a registered firearms dealer, and must—

(a) be resident in Great Britain;

(b) have known the applicant personally for at least two years; and

(c) be of good character.

(4) Where the chief officer of police is satisfied pursuant to section 44 of the 1997 Act that the application is for renewal of a firearm certificate in relation to a rifle or muzzle-loading pistol for use only for target shooting, the requirements of paragraph (3) above shall be varied so that one of the referees must be an official of the approved rifle or muzzle-loading pistol club specified in the application who may be a registered firearms dealer and need not have known the applicant personally for at least two years. The other referee must satisfy the requirements of paragraph (3) above and must not be a member of any target shooting club.

Shot gun certificates

8–10733 **5.** (1) An application for the grant or renewal of a shotgun certificate shall be in the form set out in Part I of Schedule 2 and, in the case of an application for renewal, shall be accompanied by the certificate to be renewed if it is available.

(2) The information given by an applicant in answer to the questions numbered 1 to 16 in the form of application for the grant or renewal of a shotgun certificate shall be verified in the manner specified in rule 6(1) below.

(3) An application for the grant or renewal of a shotgun certificate shall be accompanied by—

(a) a signed statement by the person referred to in rule 6(1) below to the effect that he knows of no reason why the applicant should not be permitted to possess a firearm; and

(b) four photographs of the applicant as specified in rule 7 below.

(4) Subject to section 34 of the 1997 Act and paragraph (5) below, a shotgun certificate shall be granted or renewed subject to the following conditions, and no others, namely—

(i) the holder must, on receipt of the certificate, sign it in ink with his usual signature;

(ii) the holder of the certificate must inform the chief officer of police by whom the certificate was granted within seven days of the theft, loss or destruction in Great Britain of the certificate;

(iii) the holder of the certificate must, without undue delay, inform the chief officer of police by whom the certificate was granted of any change in his permanent address;

(iv)

    (a) the shotguns to which the certificate relates must at all times (except in the circumstances set out in paragraph (b) below) be stored securely so as to prevent, so far as is reasonably practicable, access to the guns by an unauthorised person;

    (b) where a shotgun to which the certificate relates is in use or the holder of the certificate has the shotgun with him for the purpose of cleaning, repairing or testing it or for some other purpose connected with its use, transfer or sale, or the gun is in transit to or from a place in connection with its use or any such purpose, reasonable precautions must be taken for the safe custody of the gun.

(5) Where a shotgun which is disguised as another object, is possessed, purchased or acquired by the holder of the certificate for the purpose only of its being kept or exhibited as part of a collection, the certificate shall be subject to an additional condition restricting the use of that shotgun to use for that purpose.

(6) A shotgun certificate shall bear a photograph of the holder and, subject to paragraph (5) above, shall be in the form set out in Part II of Schedule 2.

Verification of application: shotgun certificates

8–10735 **6.** (1) The information referred to in rule 5(2) above shall be verified by the signed statement of a person who satisfies the requirements of paragraph (2) below that the information is, to the best of his knowledge and belief, correct.

(2) To satisfy the requirements of this paragraph a person must not be a member of the applicant's family, and must—

(a) be resident in Great Britain,

(b) have known the applicant personally for at least two years, and

(c) be a member of Parliament, member of the Scottish Parliament, justice of the peace, minister of religion, doctor, lawyer, established civil servant, bank officer or person of similar standing.

Photographs to accompany application

8–10736 **7.** The photographs referred to in rules 3(3)(b) and 5(3)(b) above shall, in the case of each application, be four identical unmounted photographs showing the current true likeness of the applicant and measuring 45mm by 35mm, of which—

(a) one shall be signed in ink, on the back of the photograph, with the applicant's usual signature; and

(b) one for each of the persons referred to in rule 4(1) or 6(1) above as appropriate shall have set out, on the back of the photograph—

(i) a signed statement in ink by that person to the effect that the photograph is a current true likeness of the applicant, and

(ii) the date when the likeness was compared.

Visitors' firearm and shot gun permits

8–10737 8. (1) An application for the grant of a visitor's firearm permit, a visitor's shotgun permit or a group application for the grant of not more than twenty visitors' firearm permits or not more than twenty visitors' shotgun permits shall be in the form set out in Part I of Schedule 3.

(2) A visitor's firearm permit shall be in the form set out in Part II of Schedule 3.

(3) A visitor's shotgun permit shall be in the form set out in Part III of Schedule 3.

Other permits

8–10738 9. (1) A permit issued under section 7(1) of the principal Act (police permit) shall—

(a) in the case of a permit relating to firearms and ammunition to which section 1 of the principal Act applies, be in the form set out in Part I of Schedule 4, or

(b) in the case of a permit relating to shotguns only, be in the form set out in Part II of Schedule 4.

(2) A permit issued under section 9(2) of the principal Act (permit for auctioneers) shall—

(a) in the case of a permit relating to firearms and ammunition to which section 1 of the principal Act applies, be in the form set out in Part III of Schedule 4, or

(b) in the case of a permit relating to shotguns only, be in the form set out in Part IV of Schedule 4.

(3) A permit issued under section 13(1) of the principal Act (permit to remove firearm from or to a ship or to remove signalling apparatus from or to an aircraft or aerodrome) shall be in the form set out in Part V of Schedule 4.

Firearms dealers

8–10739 10. (1) An application under section 33 of the principal Act for registration as a firearms dealer, or for a new certificate of registration as a firearms dealer, shall be in the form set out in Part I of Schedule 5.

(2) A notification under section 37 of the principal Act (notification that a person registered as a firearms dealer proposes to carry on business as such at a place of business not yet entered in the register) shall be in the form set out in Part II of Schedule 5.

(3) The register to be kept by a chief officer of police under section 33 of the principal Act shall be in the form set out in Part III of Schedule 5.

(4) The provisions of Part IV to Schedule 5 shall have effect in relation to the manner in which a register kept under section 40(1) of the principal Act by a person who by way of trade or business manufactures, sells or transfers firearms or ammunition (being firearms or ammunition within the meaning of that subsection) should be kept.

(5) Schedule 4 to the principal Act (particulars to be entered by firearms dealer in register of transactions) shall continue to have effect with the substitution for paragraph 4 of the Schedule of the following paragraph:

"**4.** The quantities and description of firearms and ammunition sold or transferred with the names and addresses of the purchasers or transferees and (except in cases where the purchaser or transferee is a registered dealer) the areas in which the firearm certificates were issued, and the dates of the several transactions.".

Discharge of chief officer's functions

8–10740 11. Any of the functions of a chief officer of police under the principal Act may in the event of his illness or absence, or of a vacancy in the office of the chief officer of police, be discharged—

(a) in the City of London, by an Assistant Commissioner of City of London Police; and

(b) in the metropolitan police district, by an Assistant Commissioner of Police of the Metropolis.

Revocations

8–10741 12. The Rules set out in Schedule 6 are hereby revoked.

8–10742 SCHEDULES 1–5. *Forms*

8–10743 SCHEDULE 6. *Revocations*

FISHERIES

8–10749   This title contains the following statutes—

8–10749A   European Communities Act 1972: regulations.   Within the scope of the title Fisheries would logically fall the subject matter of a number of regulations made under the very wide enabling power provided in section 2(2) of the European Communities Act 1972. In respect of those regulations listed in Sch 1 to the National Assembly for Wales (Transfer of Functions) Order 2000, SI 2000/253, the functions of the Secretary of State, so far as exercisable in relation to Wales, have been transferred to the National Assembly for Wales. Where such regulations create offences they are noted below in chronological order.

Sea Fish (Marketing Standards) Regulations 1986, SI 1986/1272 amended by SI 1989/687 and SI 1994/452;

Agricultural, Fishery and Aquaculture Products (Improvement Grant) Regulations 1991, SI 1991/777;

Sea Fishing (Days in Port) Regulations 1992, SI 1992/130 amended by 1992/670;

Diseases of Fish (Control) Regulations 1994, SI 1994/1447 amended by SI 2002/284;

Fisheries and Aquaculture Structures (Grants) Regulations 1995, SI 1995/1576 amended by SI 1998/1365;

Fish Health Regulations 1997, SI 1997/1881;

Fisheries and Aquaculture Structures (Grants) (England) Regulations 2001, SI 2001/1117;

Fisheries and Aquaculture Structures (Grants) (Wales) Regulations 2002, SI 2002/675;

Registration of Fish Buyers and Sellers and Designation of Fish Auction Sites Regulations 2005, SI 2005/1605.

Whaling Industry (Regulation) Act 1934
(22 & 25 Geo 5 c 49)

8–10750   1. Description of whales to which the Act applies.   (1) Subject to the provisions of this section, references in this Act to whales shall be construed as references to any cetacean, and the reference in section 6(4)(*a*) to whale products shall be construed accordingly.

(2) In their application to a ship registered in or licensed under the law of a colony sections 3 to 6 of this Act shall have effect as if references to whales were references only to the following cetaceans, that is to say—

(*a*)   whales known as whalebone whales or baleen whales; and

(*b*)   whales known as sperm whales, spermacet whales, cachalots or pot whales;

but Her Majesty may by Order in Council direct that those references shall also include references to all other cetaceans or to any description of other cetaceans specified in the Order.

(3) An Order under subsection (2) above may provide that in its application by virtue of the Order this Act shall have effect with such exceptions, adaptations or modifications as may be specified in the Order; and any Order under that subsection may be limited so as to apply only in relation to one or more colonies specified in the Order.

(4) Neither subsection (1) nor subsection (2) above shall be construed as extending, or enabling an Order to extend, to other cetaceans so much of section 3 of this Act as is expressed to apply only to right whales, grey whales, blue whales or fin whales.

[Whaling Industry (Regulation) Act 1934, s 1, as substituted by the Fisheries Act 1981, s 35, and amended by the Statute Law (Repeals) Act 1989, Sch 1.]

8–10751   2. Prohibition of catching or treating whales within the United Kingdom.   It shall be unlawful for any ship[1] to be used within the coastal waters[2] of the United Kingdom for taking or

treating whales[3], and if any ship is so used, the master[3] shall be liable[4] on summary conviction to a fine not exceeding **£50,000** or on conviction on indictment to a fine.
[Whaling Industry (Regulation) Act 1934, s 2 as amended by the Fisheries Act 1981, s 35.]

---

1. "Ship" has the same meaning as in the Merchant Shipping Act 1995 (Whaling Industry (Regulation) Act 1934, s 17(1)). Ship includes every description of vessel used in navigation (Merchant Shipping Act 1995, s 313(1)).

2. "Coastal waters" means (*a*) in relation to the United Kingdom, the Channel Islands and the Isle of Man, so much of the waters adjoining those countries respectively as is within the British fishery limits; and (*b*) in relation to any other country, so much of the waters adjoining that country as is within the distance to which provisions of the law of that country corresponding to the provisions of this Act extend. (Whaling Industry (Regulation) Act 1934, s 17(1), as amended by the Fishery Limits Acts 1964 and 1976, s 1, ante.

3. "Master" in relation to any ship, includes the person for the time being in command or charge of the ship and, in relation to a ship used for treating whales, includes the person for the time being in charge of the operations on board the ship in connection with such treatment (Whaling Industry (Regulation) Act 1934, s 17(1)).

4. For procedure in respect of this offence which is triable either way, see the Magistrates' Courts Act 1980, ss 17A–21, in PART I, ante.

8–10752 3. Protection of certain classes of whales. (1) If any person belonging to a British ship to which this Act applies[1], while outside the coastal waters of the United Kingdom, kills or takes, or attempts to kill or to take—(*a*) a right whale [or a grey whale][2], or (*b*) an immature whale, or (*c*) a female whale which is accompanied by a calf, that person and the master and (subject to the following provisions of this Act) the owner and the charterer (if any) shall each be liable[3] on summary conviction to a fine not exceeding **£50,000** or on conviction on indictment to a fine.

(2) For the purposes of this section a whale of any description shall be seemed to be immature if it is of less than such length[4] as may be prescribed[5] in relation to whales of that description: Provided that the length prescribed for the purposes of this section in relation to blue whales shall not be less than 60 feet, and the length so prescribed in relation to fin whales shall not be less than 50 feet.

(3) In this section—(*a*) the expression "calf" includes a suckling whale; (*b*) the expression "right whale" means a whale known by any of the names set out in Part I of the Schedule[6] to this Act; (*c*) the expression "blue whales" means whales known by any of the names set out in Part II of the Schedule to this Act; (*d*) the expression "fin whales" means whales known by any of the names set out in Part III of the Schedule[6] to this Act, the expression grey whales means a whale known by any of the names set out in Part IV of the Schedule to this Act.
[Whaling Industry (Regulation) Act 1934, s 3, as amended by the Sea Fish Industry Act 1938, s 43 and the Fisheries Act 1981, s 35.]

---

1. "British ship to which this Act applies" means a British ship which is not registered in—(*a*) any of the Dominions of Canada, Australia, New Zealand, and the Irish Free State; or (*b*) a territory administered by Her Majesty's Government in any of the Dominions aforesaid; or (*c*) India (Whaling Industry (Regulation) Act 1934, s 17(1)). The provisions of the Act were extended to ships registered under the laws of territories specified in the Whaling Industry (Regulation) Act (Newfoundland, etc) Order 1936, SR & O 1936/716, but this extension was subsequently restricted by various Independence Acts relating to former colonies; see eg the Namibia Act 1991, Schedule.

2. The words "or a grey whale" were inserted by the Sea Fish Industry Act 1938, s 43. "Grey whale" means a whale known by any of the names set out in Part IV of the Schedule to this Act, as inserted by the Sea Fish Industry Act 1938, s 43.

3. For procedure in respect of this offence which is triable either way, see the Magistrates' Courts Act 1980, ss 17A–21, in PART I: MAGISTRATES' COURTS, PROCEDURE, ante.

4. Regulations prescribing lengths of whales for the purposes of any of the provisions of this Act may also prescribe the manner in which the lengths are to be measured (Whaling Industry (Regulation) Act 1934, s 18(1)).

5. "Prescribed" means by regulations of the licensing authority (Whaling Industry (Regulation) Act 1934, s 17(1)).

6. The Schedule contains in Part I thirteen names of Right Whales, in Part II three names of Blue Whales, in Part III eight names of Fin Whales, and in Part IV, as inserted by s 43 of the Sea Fish Industry Act 1938, seven names of Grey Whales.

8–10753 4. Whaling ships and whale-oil factories to be licensed. (1) Without prejudice to the provisions of the last foregoing section, it shall be unlawful for any British ship to which this Act applies to be used outside the coastal waters of the United Kingdom for taking or treating[1] whales, or for any factory[2] situate in Great Britain to be used for treating whales, unless the owner or charterer of the ship, or the occupier of the factory, is the holder of a licence[3] in force under this Act authorising the ship or the factory, as the case may be, to be so used.

(2) If any ship or factory is used for taking or treating whales in contravention of this section, the master and (subject to the following provisions[4] of this Act) the owner and the charterer (if any) of the ship or the manager and (subject as aforesaid) the occupier of the factory, as the case may be, shall each be liable[5], in respect of each whale taken or treated in contravention of this section, on summary conviction to a fine not exceeding **£50,000** or on conviction on indictment to a fine.
[Whaling Industry (Regulation) Act 1934, s 4 as amended by the Fisheries Act 1981, s 35.]

---

1. The Board of Trade may grant permits for killing, taking and treating whales for purposes of scientific research or other exceptional purposes, subject to such restrictions and conditions as the Board thinks fit (Whaling Industry (Regulation) Act 1934, s 7). As to evidence of permits, see s 10(3), post.

2. "Factory" does not include a ship (Whaling Industry (Regulation) Act 1934, s 17(1)).

3. The licensing authority may grant yearly licences authorising a ship or factory to be used for taking or treating whales, as the case may require (s 5 and the Sea Fish Industry Act 1938, s 44). The licensing authority for a factory situate in

England is the Minister of Agriculture, Fisheries, and Food, and for a ship the Board of Trade (Whaling Industry (Regulation) Act 1934, s 17(1)). As to evidence of licences, see s 10(3), post.

4. See s 10(1), post.

5. For procedure in respect of this offence which is triable either way, see the Magistrates' Courts Act 1980, ss 17A–21, in PART I: MAGISTRATES' COURTS, PROCEDURE, ante.

8–10754 6. Contravening, or failing to keep records required by, condition of licence.
(7) If any condition[1] attached to a licence under this Act is contravened or not complied with, then, in the case of a licence granted in respect of a ship, the master and (subject to the following provisions[2] of this Act) the owner and the charterer, if any, of the ship, or in the case of a licence granted in respect of a factory, the manager and (subject as aforesaid) the occupier of the factory, shall each be liable[3] on summary conviction to a fine not exceeding **£5,000** or on conviction on indictment to a fine; and the court by whom the offender is convicted may, if the court think fit, cancel any licence granted under this Act to the offender, being a licence which is for the time being in force in respect of the ship or factory, as the case may be, and that licence shall thereupon cease to be in force.

(8) Without prejudice to the provisions of the last foregoing subsection, if any person fails to keep any record in accordance with the conditions attached to a licence under this Act or knowingly makes in any record which he is required by such conditions to keep, a statement false in any material particular, he shall be liable[4] on summary conviction to a fine not exceeding **the statutory maximum** or on conviction on indictment to a fine.

[Whaling Industry (Regulation) Act 1934, s 6 as amended by the Fisheries Act 1981, s 35 and the Criminal Justice Act 1991, Sch 4.]

1. These conditions must include provisions as to the remuneration of the gunners and crew of the ship (sub-s (1)); for recording prescribed particulars as to each whale treated; as to the plant with which the ship or factory must be equipped; as to the method of extraction of the oil, and for the utilisation of residual products (sub-s (3)); and may include provisions for preventing any wastage of whales or whale products or the taking of whales during certain seasons (sub-s (4)). A condition as to the substitution of one type of plant for another shall not be made without twelve months' notice (sub-s (5)). The authority may refuse to grant a licence until satisfied that a condition as to the structure or equipment of a ship or factory, which it is proposed to attach to the licence, has been complied with (sub-s (6)). The authority may refuse to grant a licence to any person who has been convicted of an offence under this Act (s 5(4)). Sub-s (3) is amended by the Sea Fish Industry Act 1938, s 44.

2. See s 10(1), post.

3. For procedure in respect of this offence which is triable either way, see the Magistrates' Courts Act 1980, ss 17A–21, in PART I: MAGISTRATES' COURTS, PROCEDURE, ante.

4. For procedure in respect of this offence which is triable either way, see the Magistrates' Courts Act 1980, ss 17A–21, in PART I: MAGISTRATES' COURTS, PROCEDURE, ante.

8–10755 8. Powers of whale fishery inspectors.   (3) Every person who without reasonable excuse refuses to produce to a whale fishery inspector[1] any document which he is required under this section to produce, or without reasonable excuse refuses to answer, or answers falsely, any inquiry duly made of him by such an inspector, or otherwise wilfully obstructs, or without reasonable excuse refuses facilities to, such an inspector in the discharge of his functions under this section, shall be liable[2] on summary conviction to a fine not exceeding **£5,000** or on conviction on indictment to a fine.

[Whaling Industry (Regulation) Act 1934, s 8 as amended by the Fisheries Act 1981, s 35.]

1. A "whale fishery inspector" means—(*a*) any person appointed by, or under the authority of, the Board of Trade to be such an inspector; (*b*) any commissioned officer of any of her Majesty's ships on full pay (sub-s (4)). On producing on demand evidence that he is such an inspector, he may enter and inspect a ship or factory which he believes is used for taking or for treating whales, and its plant and equipment; may require the master and crew, the occupier or manager of a factory and the employees therein, or any of them, to produce licences, records and other documents, and to answer his inquiries; and may take copies of or extracts from any document produced (sub-s (1)). With the written authority of the Board of Trade, he may remain on board the ship and shall then be provided with subsistence and accommodation therein, he paying the prescribed sum (sub-s (2)).

2. For procedure in respect of this offence which is triable either way, see the Magistrates' Courts Act 1980, ss 17A–21, in PART I: MAGISTRATES' COURTS, PROCEDURE, ante.

8–10756 9. Forgery of documents.   (1) If any person with intent to deceive—(*a*) uses, or lends to or allows to be used by any other person, a licence or permit under this Act; or (*b*) makes or has in his possession[1] any document so closely resembling a licence or permit under this Act as to be calculated[2] to deceive; he shall be liable[3] on summary conviction to a fine not exceeding **the statutory maximum** or on conviction on indictment to a fine.

[Whaling Industry (Regulation) Act 1934, s 9 as amended by the Fisheries Act 1981, s 35, the Forgery and Counterfeiting Act 1981, Sch and the Criminal Justice Act 1991, Sch 4.]

1. See *R v Greenberg* [1942] 2 All ER 344, 28 Cr App Rep 160.

2. Cf *Re London and Globe Finance Corpn Ltd* [1903] 1 Ch 728, 82 JP 447.

3. For procedure in respect of this offence which is triable either way, see the Magistrates' Courts Act 1980, ss 17A–21, in PART I: MAGISTRATES' COURTS, PROCEDURE, ante.

8–10757 10. Legal proceedings.   (1) In any proceedings taken by virtue of this Act against the owner or charterer of a ship or against the occupier of a factory in respect of any act or omission on the part of another person, it shall be a good defence for the owner, charterer or occupier, as the case may be, to prove that the act or omission took place without his knowledge or connivance and was not facilitated by any negligence on his part.

(2) Summary proceedings taken by virtue of this Act against any person for an offence committed at sea, may be commenced at any time within six months from the date on which that person first lands in the United Kingdom after the commission of the offence.

(3) In any proceedings a document purporting to be a licence or permit granted under this Act shall, until the contrary is proved, be presumed to be such a licence or permit, as the case may be.

(4) Proceedings against any person for the purposes of this Act may be taken before the court having jurisdiction in the place where that person is for the time being.

[Whaling Industry (Regulation) Act 1934, s 10 as amended by the Fisheries Act 1981, s 35.]

Diseases of Fish Act 1937[1]
(1 Edw 8 & 1 Geo 6 c 33)

8–10770   1. Restriction on importation of live fish and eggs of fish. (1) Subject to subsection (6) of this section, it shall not be lawful to import or bring into Great Britain any fish of the salmon family.[2]

(2) It shall not be lawful to import or bring into Great Britain any live freshwater fish or live eggs of fish of the salmon family, or of freshwater fish, unless the fish or eggs are consigned to a person licensed under this section and the licence is produced at the time of the delivery under the enactments for the time being in force relating to customs or excise of the entry of the consignment.

(3) The Minister[3] may grant a licence[4] to any person to have consigned to him such fish or eggs as are mentioned in the last foregoing subsection, and the following provisions shall have effect in relation to such licences, that is to say—

(a) a licence may be granted subject to such conditions as the Minister thinks fit as to the quantities or kinds of fish or eggs which may be imported or brought in under the licence, as to the disposal, transport, inspection, cleaning and disinfection of the fish or eggs and of the containers or other vessels in which they are to be transported or kept and otherwise as to the precautions which are to be taken for avoiding the spreading of disease among salmon and freshwater fish;

(b) a licence may be granted for any period not exceeding twelve months but may be suspended or revoked by the Minister at any time during the currency thereof;

(c) there shall on the grant of a licence be paid by the person applying therefor to the Minister such sum not exceeding 25p as the Minister may, with the consent of the Treasury, determine.

(4) If any person in contravention of the provisions of this section imports or brings or promises to be imported or brought into Great Britain any live fish or eggs of fish, or being the holder of a licence under this Act, contravenes any condition subject to which the licence was granted, he shall be guilty of any offence[5]; and any officer of police, officer of Customs and Excise, or inspector may seize[6] any fish or eggs with respect to which he has reason to believe that such an offence has been committed and may detain them pending the determination of any proceedings instituted under this Act in respect of that offence or until the Minister is satisfied that no such proceedings are likely to be instituted.

(5) Notwithstanding the foregoing provisions of this section, where it is shown to the satisfaction of the Comrs of Customs and Excise that any live fish or eggs of fish, of which the importation is prohibited or restricted by this section, are being imported or brought into Great Britain is prohibited or restricted by this section, are being imported or brought solely with a view to the re-exportation thereof after transit through Great Britain or by way of transhipment, the Comrs may, subject to such conditions as they think fit to impose for securing the re-exportation of the goods, allow the fish or eggs of fish to be imported or brought as if prohibition did not apply thereto.

(6) Subsection (1) of this section shall not apply to any fish of a description specified in an order[7] made by the Minister under this subsection.

(7) The description may be made by reference to species, place of origin or any other factor.

(8) Where an order under subsection (6) of this section has effect in relation to any fish, subsections (2) to (5) of this section shall have effect as if it were a freshwater fish.

(9) The power to make an order under subsection (6) of this section shall be exercisable by statutory instrument, and no such order shall be made unless a draft of the order has been laid before and approved by resolution of each House of Parliament.

(10) An order under subsection (6) of this section may be varied or revoked by a subsequent order made under that subsection.

[Diseases of Fish Act 1937, s 1, as amended by the Customs and Excise Management Act 1979, Sch 4 and the Diseases of Fish Act 1983, s 1 and Sch.]

---

1. This Act does not extend to Northern Ireland (s 14).
   In the Diseases of Fish Act 1937—

(a) any reference which to any extent is, or falls to be construed as, a reference to the National Rivers Authority shall have effect, in relation to the area which by virtue of s 6(7) of the Environment Act 1995, title PUBLIC HEALTH, post, is the area in relation to which the Environment Agency carries out functions under the Act of 1937, as a reference to the Agency; and

(b) references to an area (including references which fall to be construed as references to the area which by virtue of s 2(6) of the Water Resources Act 1991 is the area in relation to which the National Rivers Authority carries out functions under the Act of 1937), in relation to the Agency, shall have effect as references to the area described in paragraph (a) above (Environment Act 1995, Sch 15, para 4).

2. See further, in relation to the disapplication of this section in relation to imports from another member State of the European Community or other specified countries, in certain circumstances: SI 2000/1673 and SSI 2000/216.

3. The functions of the Minister, so far as exercisable in relation to Wales, have been transferred to the National Assembly for Wales, by the National Assembly for Wales (Transfer of Functions) Order 1999, SI 1999/672, art 2, Sch 1.

4. The form of licence has been prescribed by the Diseases of Fish Regulations 1984, SI 1984/455, amended by SI 1986/538.

5. For penalty, see s 8, post.

6. Any live fish or live eggs of fish which have been seized under the Act and in respect of which there has been a contravention of s 1 of the Act shall be destroyed or otherwise disposed of as the Minister shall direct (Diseases of Fish Regulations 1984, SI 1984/455 as amended, reg 5).

7. By the Importation of Live Fish of the Salmon Family Order 1986, SI 1986/283. Live fish of the Salmon family which have been taken from Northern Ireland and have not at any time been in any country or territory outside Northern Ireland are specified for the purposes of subsection (6).

8–10771   2. Power to designate areas.   (1) If, at any time, the Minister has reasonable grounds for suspecting that any inland or marine waters are or may become infected waters, he may by order designate the waters and such land adjacent to them as he considers appropriate in the circumstances; and in the following provisions of this section "designated area" means anything designated by an order under this section.

(2) The Minister may, to such extent as he considers practicable and desirable for the purpose of preventing the spread of infection among fish, by the same or a subsequent order—

(a) prohibit or regulate the taking into or out of the designated area of such of the following (or of such description of them) as may be specified in the order, namely, live fish, live eggs of fish and foodstuffs for fish;

(b) regulate the movement within the area of such of those things (or of such description of them) as may be specified in the order.

(3) Any person who is the occupier of any inland waters in a designated area, or carries on the business of fish farming in any marine waters in such an area, shall be entitled, on application, to be supplied by the Minister free of charge with a report of the evidence on which the order was made. This subsection does not apply to Scotland.

(4) *Scotland.*

(5) Any order under this section shall be published in the prescribed[1] manner and may be varied or revoked by a subsequent order made under this section.

(6) If any person intentionally contravenes any provision of an order under this section he shall be guilty of an offence[2].

[Diseases of Fish Act 1937, s 2, as substituted by the Diseases of Fish Act 1983, s 2.]

_____

1. See the Diseases of Fish Regulations 1984, SI 1984/455 amended by SI 1986/538.

2. For penalty, see s 8, post.

8–10772   2A. Designated areas; direction to remove fish.   (1) Where an order is in force under section 2 of this Act, the Minister may serve a notice in writing on—

(a) any occupier of inland waters situated in the designated area (that is, the area designated by the order);

(b) any person carrying on the business of fish farming in marine waters situated in the designated area.

(2) A notice served on a person under subsection (1)(a) of this section may direct him to take such practicable steps as are specified in the notice to secure the removal of dead or dying fish from the waters concerned, and may regulate the manner in which any fish removed from the waters, and any parts of such fish, are to be disposed of.

(3) A notice served on a person under subsection (1)(b) of this section may direct him to take such practicable steps as are specified in the notice to secure the removal of dead or dying fish from any cage which is owned or possessed by him, is used for the purposes of the business and is situated in the waters concerned, and may regulate the manner in which any fish removed from such a cage, and any parts of such fish, are to be disposed of.

(4) No notice may be served under subsection (1)(a) of this section in respect of waters in the area of a water authority[1] not being a fish farm.

(5) If the Minister is satisfied that a direction contained in a notice served under this section has not been complied with within the time specified in the notice, he may authorise an inspector to carry out the direction, and any expenses reasonably incurred by the Inspector in so doing shall be recoverable by the Minister from the person upon whom the notice was served; and if any person

intentionally does any act which is prohibited by such a notice, he shall be guilty of an offence[2] unless he shows that he did not know that the act was so prohibited.

[Diseases of Fish Act 1937, s 2A, as inserted by the Diseases of Fish Act 1983, s 2.]

1. This may refer to the National Rivers Authority or a district salmon fishery board, see the Water Act 1989, Sch 17, para 3. For references to the National Rivers Authority, there should now be substituted a reference to the Environment Agency; see note 1 at para **8–10770**.

2. For penalty, see s 8, post.

8–10773   2B. Designated areas; authority to remove fish.   (1) Where an order is in force under section 2 of this Act, the Minister, if he is satisfied that for the protection against disease of the stock of fish in any waters it is necessary to do so, may by a notice served under section 2A of this Act or otherwise in writing give authority falling within subsection (2) or (3) of this section; and in those subsections "the designated area" means the area designated by the order.

(2) Authority falling within this subsection is authority to any occupier of inland waters situated in the designated area to remove, notwithstanding anything in any agreement to the contrary, any fish (or any fish of a description specified in the authorisation) from the waters, and to do so by such agents and by such methods (including methods otherwise illegal) as the Minister considers to be most expedient for the purpose.

(3) Authority falling within this subsection is authority to any person carrying on the business of fish farming in marine waters situated in the designated area to remove, notwithstanding anything in any agreement to the contrary, any fish (or any fish of a description specified in the authorisation) from any cage which is owned possessed by him, is used for the purposes of the business and is situated in the waters, and to do so by such agents and by such methods (including methods otherwise illegal) as the Minister considers to be most expedient for the purpose.

(4) No authority may be given as mentioned in subsection (2) of this section in respect of waters in the area of a water authority[1], not being a fish farm.

(5) Where a person has in pursuance of an authority under this section removed any fish, he shall comply with any directions given to him by the Minister as to the manner in which the fish, and any parts of such fish, are to be disposed of; and if he intentionally fails to comply with any such directions, he shall be guilty of an offence[2].

[Diseases of Fish Act 1937, s 2B, as inserted by the Diseases of Fish Act 1983, s 2.]

1. This may refer to the National Rivers Authority or a district salmon fishery board, see the Water Act 1989, Sch 17, para 3. For references to the National Rivers Authority, there should now be substituted a reference to the Environment Agency; see note 1 at para **8–10770**.

2. For penalty, see s 8, post.

8–10774   3. Powers and duties of fishery boards.   (1) Any fishery board who have reasonable ground for suspecting that any inland waters, not being a fish farm, are infected waters, shall forthwith report the facts to the Minister, and may take any practicable steps for securing the removal of dead or dying fish from the waters. The Minister on receiving any such report as aforesaid with respect to any inland waters, shall forthwith cause an investigation[1] to be made as to whether they are infected waters.

(2) Where an order is in force in relation to an area under section 2 of this Act, the Minister may authorise any water authority[2] to remove any fish (or any fish of a description specified in the authorisation) from any inland waters in that area (not being a fish farm) and to do so by such agents and by such methods (including methods otherwise illegal) as he considers to be most expedient for the purpose.

(3) Every fishery board—

(a) shall destroy or otherwise properly dispose of all fish removed under any powers conferred on them by or under this section; and

(b) shall at such times as the Minister may direct send to him a return stating the number of fish so removed.

[Diseases of Fish Act 1937, s 3 as amended by the Diseases of Fish Act 1983, Schedule.]

1. On the demand of a fishery board, or the occupier of any waters, the Minister will cause an inspector to make an examination of any waters within their district, or in his occupation, as the case may be, and to furnish a report to the board or occupier free of charge (s 5). The functions of fishery boards are now exercised by river authorities.

2. This may refer to the National Rivers Authority or a district salmon fishery board, see the Water Act 1989, Sch 17, para 3. For references to the National Rivers Authority, there should now be substituted a reference to the Environment Agency; see note 1 in para **8–10770**.

8–10775   4. Preliminary precautions: inland waters.   (1) If an inspector has reasonable grounds for suspecting that any inland waters which are the waters of any fish farm are infected waters, he may serve the prescribed[1] notice upon the occupier of the fish farm and (if the inspector serves such a notice) he shall report the facts to the Minister.

(2) Where a notice has been served under sub-section (1) of this section—

(*a*) no live fish and no live eggs of fish shall, without the permission of the Minister, be taken into or out of the fish farm, and

(*b*) no foodstuffs for fish shall, without the permission of the Minister, be taken out of the fish farm,

until after the expiration of thirty days from the service of the notice, unless before the expiration of that period the occupier receives from the Minister a written intimation that such permission is no longer required.

(3) Where a notice has been served upon an occupier under subsection (1) of this section, the Minister may if he thinks it desirable authorise an inspector to serve a further prescribed notice upon the occupier so long as no written intimation under subsection (2) above has been given to the occupier; and if the inspector does so before the expiration of thirty days from the service of the first notice, that subsection shall have effect in relation to the fish farm concerned as if for "thirty" there were substituted "sixty".

(4) A person who intentionally takes any fish, eggs or foodstuff into or out of a fish farm while the taking is prohibited by this section shall be guilty of an offence, unless he shows that he did not know that the taking was prohibited.

(5) If any person entitled to take fish from any inland waters, or employed for the purpose of having the care of any inland waters, has reasonable grounds for suspecting that the waters are infected waters, it shall be his duty forthwith to report the facts in writing to the Minister or, if the waters are not a fish farm, to the water authority in whose area the waters are situated, and if without reasonable excuse he fails to do so, he shall be guilty of an offence[2].

(6) (*Repealed*).

[Diseases of Fish Act 1937, s 4, as substituted by the Diseases of Fish Act 1983, s 3 and amended by the Water Act 1989, Sch 27.]

---

1. See the Diseases of Fish Regulations 1984, SI 1984/455, amended by SI 1986/538.
2. For penalty, see s 8, post.

8–10776 4A. Preliminary precautions: marine waters. (1) If an inspector has reasonable grounds for suspecting that any marine waters are infected waters—

(*a*) he may serve, upon any person who owns or possesses a cage which is situated in the waters and is used by him for the purposes of a business of fish farming carried on by him, the prescribed[1] notice specifying the waters suspected to be infected waters, and

(*b*) if the inspector serves such a notice, he shall report the facts to the Minister,

and in the following provisions of this section "the farmer" means the person so served.

(2) Where a notice has been served under subsection (1) of this section—

(*a*) no live fish and no live eggs of fish shall, without the permission of the Minister, be taken into or out of any cage which is situated in the waters specified in the notice and is used by the farmer for the purposes of a business of fish farming carried on by him, and

(*b*) no foodstuff for fish shall, without the permission of the Minister, be taken out of any such cage,

until after the expiration of thirty days from the service of the notice, unless before the expiration of that period the farmer receives from the Minister a written intimation that such permission is no longer required.

(3) Where a notice has been served upon a farmer under subsection (1) of this section, the Minister may if he thinks it desirable authorise an inspector to serve a further prescribed notice upon the farmer so long as no written intimation under subsection (2) above has been given to the farmer; and if the inspector does so before the expiration of thirty days from the service of the first notice, that subsection shall have effect in relation to any cage concerned as if for "thirty" there were substituted "sixty".

(4) A person who intentionally takes any fish, eggs or foodstuff into or out of a cage while the taking is prohibited by this section shall be guilty of an offence, unless he shows that he did not know that the taking was prohibited.

(5) If any person who—

(*a*) owns or possesses a cage which is situated in marine waters and is used by him for the purposes of a business of fish farming carried on by him, or

(*b*) is employed for the purpose of having the care of a cage so situated and used for the purposes of a business of fish farming,

has reasonable grounds for suspecting that the waters in which the cage is situated are infected waters, it shall be his duty forthwith to report the facts in writing to the Minister; and if without reasonable excuse he fails to do so, he shall be guilty of an offence[2].

(6) *Scotland.*

[Diseases of Fish Act 1937, s 4A, as inserted by the Diseases of Fish Act 1983, s 3.]

---

1. See the Diseases of Fish Regulations 1984, SI 1984/455, amended by SI 1986/538.
2. For penalty, see s 8, post.

8–10777   **6. Powers of entry on land and inspection.**   (1) Any justice of the peace, upon an information on oath that there is reasonable cause to suspect an offence under this Act to have been committed, may, by warrant under his hand, authorise any person named in the warrant to enter on any land mentioned in the warrant at such times as are so mentioned and to seize any fish, eggs of fish, or foodstuff or article which that person suspects to have been imported or brought into Great Britain, removed or otherwise dealt with, or to be about to be removed or otherwise dealt with, in contravention of this Act or any licence granted, order made, or notice served thereunder: Provided that a warrant under this subsection shall not continue in force for more than one week from the date of the granting thereof.

The preceding provisions of this subsection shall have effect for the purpose of authorising the boarding of and entry into a cage situated in marine waters and used for the purposes of a business of fish farming as they have effect for the purpose of authorising entry on land.

(2) Any inspector shall have power (to the extent that he does not have it apart from this subsection)—

     (*a*)   to inspect any inland waters in which fish or the eggs of fish of foodstuffs for fish are likely to be found, and to take therefrom samples of any fish or of any such eggs or foodstuff or of water, mud, vegetation or other matter;

     (*aa*)   to inspect any cage situated in marine waters and used for the purposes of a business of fish farming, and to take therefrom samples of any fish or of any eggs of fish or of foodstuffs for fish or of water or other matter;

     (*ab*)   to inspect any marine waters in which fish of the salmon family or freshwater fish or the eggs of such fish or foodstuff for fish are likely to be found, and to take therefrom samples of any such fish, eggs or foodstuffs or of water, mud, vegetation or other matter;

     (*b*)   for the purpose of exercising any powers or performing any duties under this Act, to enter, upon production on demand of his authority on any land;

     (*c*)   for the purposes of exercising any powers or performing any duties under this Act, to board and enter, upon production on demand of his authority, any cage situated in marine waters and used for the purposes of a business of fish farming.

and any person who refuses to admit or intentionally obstructs an inspector in the exercise or performance of any of the said powers and duties shall be guilty of an offence[1].

(3) If in any sample of fish taken from any inland waters by an inspector under the powers conferred by the last foregoing subsection none is found to be infected, the Minister shall pay to the occupier of the waters, or where there is more than one occupier of the waters, to such of the occupiers as he considers equitable, a sum equal to the market value of the fish taken in that sample.

(3A) If in any sample of fish taken from a cage by an inspector under the powers conferred by subsection (2)(*aa*) of this section none is found to be infected, the Minister shall pay to the person who owns or possesses the cage and uses it for the purposes of a business of fish farming carried on by him a sum equal to the market value of the fish taken in that sample.

(4) Any person authorised in writing in that behalf by a fishery board may, for the purpose of performing any duties imposed on him by the board in the exercise of their functions under this Act enter, upon production on demand of his authority, on any situate within the district of the board not being part of a fish farm, and any person who refuses to admit him or intentionally obstructs him in the carrying out of any of those duties shall be guilty of an offence[1].

(5) Any person exercising powers conferred on him by or under this section on land owned or used for the purposes of any railway or canal undertaking shall conform to such reasonable requirements of the undertakers as are necessary to prevent obstruction to, or interference with, the working of the traffic on their railway or canal, as the case may be, and the undertakers shall not be liable for any accident or injury happening to any person while exercising such powers—

     (*a*)   in the case of a railway undertaking upon any railway or land carrying a railway belonging to them; and

     (*b*)   in the case of a canal undertaking upon any canal or reservoir or the banks of any canal or reservoir belonging to them.

[Diseases of Fish Act 1937, s 6 as amended by the Diseases of Fish Act 1983, Sch.]

---

   1. For penalties, see s 8, post.

8–10778   **7. Service of notices, and authority of agents.**   (1) Any notice required or authorised to be served for the purpose of this Act, upon an occupier of any inland waters may be served by delivering it to him, or to any servant or agent employed by him for the purpose of having the care of any waters, or by sending it by registered post to the usual or last known address of the occupier, or, if his address is not known and cannot reasonably be ascertained, by exhibiting the notice addressed to him in some conspicuous place at or near the waters, and where the identity of the occupier of the waters cannot reasonably be ascertained, the notice, if so exhibited as aforesaid, shall be deemed to be addressed to every person who is an occupier of the waters if it is addressed "The Occupier" without further name or description.

(1A) Any notice required or authorised to be served for the purposes of this Act upon a person carrying on the business of fish farming in marine water may be served by delivering it to him or by sending it by registered post to his usual or last-known address.

(2) Where a notice requiring anything to be done by an occupier of any inland waters has been served under this section by delivering it to a servant or agent having the care of any waters, that servant or agent shall be deemed to have authority from the occupier to do on his behalf and at his expense whatever is required by the notice to be done in relation to any of the waters.

[Diseases of Fish Act 1937, s 7 as amended by the Diseases of Fish Act 1983, Sch.]

8–10779 8. Penalties and legal proceedings. (1) Any person guilty of an offence under this Act shall be liable on summary conviction to a fine not exceeding **level 4** on the standard scale; and the court by whom any person is convicted of an offence under this Act may order to be forfeited[1] any fish, eggs of fish, foodstuff or article in respect of which the offence was committed.

(2) In England and Wales the National Rivers Authority shall have power to take legal proceedings to enforce provisions of this Act as respect inland waters.

(3) Offences against this Act committed in inland waters in Scotland (including offences committed in inland waters with respect to which functions under this Act are exercisable by the Environment Agency) shall be proceeded against and punished in Scotland.

(4) For the purposes of and incidental to the jurisdiction of any magistrates' court or, in Scotland, of the sheriff, any offence under this Act committed in the territorial sea adjacent to Great Britain shall be taken to have been committed in any place in which the offender may for the time being be found.

[Diseases of Fish Act 1937, s 8, as amended by the Water Act 1973, Sch 8, the Criminal Law Act 1977, s 31, the Criminal Justice Act 1982, ss 35, 38 and 46, the Diseases of Fish Act 1983, Sch, the Salmon Act 1986 Sch 4, the Water Act 1989, Schs 17 and 27, the Statute Law (Repeals) Act 1993, Sch 1 and the Environment Act 1995, Sch 15.]

---

1. Any fish, eggs of fish, foodstuffs or articles forfeited under this Act shall be dealt with as the Minister shall direct (Diseases of Fish Regulations 1984, SI 1984/455 as amended, reg 5).

8–10780 10. Interpretation. (1) In this Act, unless the context otherwise requires, the following expressions have the meanings hereby respectively assigned to them, that is to say—

"business of fish farming" means business of keeping live fish (whether or not for profit) with a view to their sale or to their transfer to other waters;

"cage" means any structure for containing live fish;

"fish" does not include shellfish but otherwise means fish of any kind;

"fish farm" means any pond, stew, fish hatchery or other place used for keeping, with a view to their sale or to their transfer to other waters (including any other fish farm), live fish, live eggs of fish, or foodstuff for fish, and includes any buildings used in connection therewith, and the banks and margins of any water therein;

"fish of the salmon family" includes all fish of whatever genus of species belonging to the family Salmonidae;

"fishery board" has the same meaning as in the Salmon and Freshwater Fisheries Act 1923, and, in relation to any waters, means the fishery board within whose district those waters are situated;

"foodstuff for fish" means any substance used, or intended or likely to be used, as food for fish, including natural food;

"freshwater fish" does not include fish of the salmon family, or any kinds of fish which migrate to and from tidal waters, but save as aforesaid includes any fish living in fresh water;

"infected" means, in relation to fish, infected with any of the diseases respectively known as bacterial kidney disease (BKD), furunculosis of salmon gyrodactyliasis caused by *Gyrodactylus salaris*, infectious haematopoietic necrosis (IHN), infectious pancreatic necrosis (IPN), spring viraemia of carp (SVC), viral haemorrhagic septicaemia (VHS), whirling disease (*Myxosoma cerebralis*) and salmon anaemia;

"infected waters" means water in which any of the diseases mentioned in the definition of the expression "infected" exists among fish, or in which the causative organisms of any of those diseases are present;

"inland waters" means waters within Great Britain which do not form part of the sea or of any creek, bay or estuary or of any river as far as the tide flows;

"inspector" means a person authorised by the Minister to act as an inspector under this Act, either generally or for the particular purpose in question;

"land" includes land covered with inland waters;

"marine waters" means waters (other than inland waters) within the seaward limits of the territorial sea adjacent to Great Britain;

"the Minister" means—

(a) in relation to England, and any marine waters adjacent to England, the Minister of Agriculture, Fisheries and Food;

(b) in relation to Wales, and any marine waters adjacent to Wales, the Secretary of State;

(c) in relation to Scotland (including the marine waters thereof), the Secretary of State;

"occupier" means in relation to any inland waters a person entitled, without the permission of any other person, to take fish from the waters;

"prescribed" means prescribed by regulations made under this Act;

"shellfish" includes crustaceans and molluscs of any kind;

"waters" means any waters (including any fish farm) which are frequented by, or used for keeping, live fish, live eggs of fish, or foodstuff for fish, and includes the banks and margins of any such waters and any buildings used in connection therewith.

(2) Notwithstanding anything in the foregoing definition of the expression "occupier", where the persons entitled without the permission of any other person to take fish from any inland waters are so entitled only by reason of their membership of a club or association, the person having the management of the waters on behalf of the club or association shall, to the exclusion of any members of the club or association (other than himself if a member), be deemed to be the occupier of the waters; and where a person is entitled, without the permission of any other person, to take fish from any inland waters only by virtue of a right acquired for a period not exceeding one year, not he, but the person from whom the right was acquired, shall be deemed to be the occupier of the waters.

(3) *(Repealed)*.

[Diseases of Fish Act 1937, s 10, amended by the SI 1973/2093, Diseases of Fish Act 1983, s 4 and Sch, SI 1984/301, SI 1988/195, the Water Act 1989, Sch 27 and SI 1990/616.]

8–10781   13. Power to amend definition of "infected".   (1) The Minister may by order add to or remove any disease for the time being set out in the definition of "infected" in section 10(1) of this Act.

(2) The power to make an order[1] under this section shall be exercisable by statutory instrument subject to annulment in pursuance of a resolution of either House of Parliament.

[Diseases of Fish Act 1937, s 13, as inserted by the Diseases of Fish Act 1983, s 4.]

---

1. A number of orders have been made, s 10 has been amended and the orders noted to that section.

Sea Fisheries Regulation Act 1966
(1966 c 38)

8–10880   The Sea Fisheries Regulation Act 1966 provides for the setting up of local fishery committees. A committee may appoint fishery officers for the purpose of enforcing its bye-laws[1]. Obstruction of such officers is an offence[2]. As to validity of bye-laws made under (what is now) Sea Fisheries Regulation Act 1966, section 5(1)(*b*), see *Friend v Brehout* (1914) 79 JP 25 and the Sea Fisheries (Byelaws) Regulations 1985, 1985/1785.

---

1. Contravention of a byelaw is punishable on summary conviction by a fine not exceeding **level 5** on the standard scale. Where the contravention is of a byelaw restricting fishing etc, the Court may order the forfeiture of any net or other fishing gear used in committing the offence, and any fish in respect of which the offence was committed (Sea Fisheries Regulation Act 1966, s 11, as amended by the Fishery Limits Act 1976, Sch 1 and the Criminal Justice Act 1982, s 46). As to the meaning of "fishing", see *Alexander v Tonkin* [1979] 2 All ER 1009. "Breaking nets" to remove debris is not a method of fishing within the byelaws (*South Wales Sea Fisheries Ccommittee v Saunders* (2003) Times, 5 December). The extent to which byelaws may be made under s 5 of the 1966 Act is enlarged by the Salmon Act 1986 s 37 so that protection for sea fish extends to salmon, and by a new s 5A inserted by the Environment Act 1995, s 102, for marine environmental purposes.
2. Punishable on summary conviction by fine not exceeding **level 5** on the standard scale (Sea Fisheries Regulation Act 1966, s 11, as amended by the Fishery Limits Act 1976, Sch 1 and the Criminal Justice Act 1982, s 46).

Sea Fisheries (Shellfish) Act 1967
(1967 c 83)

8–10890   Fisheries of shellfish.   The Minister of Agriculture, Fisheries and Food[1] may by Order[2] provide for the establishment and maintenance of a fishery for shellfish, that is to say, oysters, mussels, cockles, clams, lobsters, scallops, queens and any other molluscs or crustaceans of a kind specified in regulations[3] made by the appropriate Minister, on "the sea shore" as defined in section 1(1) of the Act.

Such an Order confers the right of fishery within the limits of the prescribed area. It imposes restrictions on and makes regulations respecting the dredging, fishing for and taking of shellfish within such area.

Persons to whom the right of fishery is granted may levy or with the consent of the Minister may vary tolls or royalties on persons fishing for shellfish within the area.

[Sea Fisheries (Shellfish) Act 1967, ss 1–3, as amended by the Sea Fisheries Act 1968, the Fishery Limits Act 1976, Sch 2 and the Sea Fisheries (Shellfish) (Amendment) Act 1997, s 1—summarised.]

1. The functions of the Minister and the appropriate Minister, so far as exercisable in relation to Wales, have been transferred to the National Assembly for Wales, by the National Assembly for Wales (Transfer of Functions) Order 1999, SI 1999/672, art 2, Sch 1. Residual functions of the Secretary of State and the Secretary of State for Wales were transferred to the Minister of Agriculture, Fisheries and Food by the Transfer of Functions (Agriculture and Fisheries) Order 2000, SI 2000/1812, now the Secretary of State for Environment, Food and Rural Affairs (Ministry of Agriculture, Fisheries and Food (Dissolution) Order 2002, SI 2002/794).

2. See the Stanswood Bay Oyster Fishery Order 1973, SI 1973/861 amended by SI 1979/1137, SI 1988/1024 and SI 1995/1257, the Menai Strait (West) Oyster, Mussel and Clam Fishery Order 1978, SI 1978/243, the Solent Oyster Fishery Order 1980, SI 1980/1373 amended by SI 1996/828, the Calshot Oyster Fishery Order 1982, SI 1982/135 amended by SI 1995/1258, the Southampton Water (Chilling) Oyster Fishery Order 1984, SI 1984/907, the Poole Fishery Order 1985, SI 1985/847 the River Nene Fisheries Order 1986, SI 1986/1896, the Portchester Channel Oyster Fisheries Order 1986, SI 1986/1901, the Brancaster Staithe Fishery Order 1979, SI 1979/1066 as amended by SI 1994/2230, the Stanswood Bay Oyster Fishery Order 1988, SI 1988/1024 amended by SI 1995/1257, the Swansea Bay Mussel Fishery Order 1995, SI 1995/2145, the Penrhos Point Mussel Fishery Order 1998, SI 1998/1146 and the Waddeton Fishery Order 2001, SI 2001/1380.

3. The Shellfish (Specification of Molluscs) Regulations 1987, SI 1987/218, the Shellfish (Specification of Crustaceans) Regulations 2001, SI 2001/1381 and the Shellfish (Specification of Crustaceans) (Wales) Regulations 2002, SI 2002/1885 have been made.

8–10891   3. Offences.   (3) Any person who dredges, fishes for or takes shellfish (1) of any description to which any such order applies in contravention of any such restriction or regulation, or without paying such toll or royalty, as aforesaid shall be guilty of an offence and liable on summary conviction to a fine not exceeding **level 5** on the standard scale and to forfeit all such shellfish so taken or, if they have been sold, a sum equal to their value; and any shellfish or sum so forfeited shall be recoverable in like manner as a fine.

(4) The court by which any such forfeiture is imposed may direct the shellfish or sum forfeited to be delivered or paid to the grantees to be applied by them for the improvement and cultivation of the regulated fishery or part.

[Sea Fisheries (Shellfish) Act 1967, s 3(3), (4), as amended by the Criminal Law Act 1977, s 31, the Criminal Justice Act 1982, s 46 and the Criminal Justice and Public Order Act 1994, Sch 8.]

8–10892   7. Protection of fisheries.   (1) The provisions of this section shall have effect where—

(*a*)   an order under section 1 of this Act grants a right of several fishery or

(*b*)   a private oyster bed is owned by any person independently of this Act and is sufficiently marked out or sufficiently known as such.

(2) All shellfish[1] of a description to which the order applies in or on a bed for such shellfish within the area of the fishery with respect to which the right of several fishery is conferred, or, as the case may be, all oysters in or on the private oyster bed, shall be the absolute property of the grantees or, as the case may be, of the owner of the bed and in all courts and for all purposes shall be deemed to be in the actual possession of the grantees or, as the case may be, owner.

(3) All such shellfish[1] removed by any person from a bed for such shellfish within the area of the fishery with respect to which the right of several fishery is conferred, or, as the case may be, all oysters removed by any person from the private oyster bed, shall, unless disposed of by or under the authority of the grantees or, as the case may be, of the owner of the bed, be the absolute property of the grantees or, as the case may be, of the owner, and in all courts and for all purposes the absolute right to the possession thereof shall be deemed to be in the grantees or, as the case may be, owner.

(4) Subject to subsection (5) of this section, if within the limits of the area of the fishery with respect to which the right of several fishery is conferred or in any part of that area described for the purposes of this subsection in the order, or within the limits of any such private oyster bed, any person other than the grantees or an agent or employee of theirs or, as the case may be, the owner or an agent or employee of his knowingly does any of the following things, namely—

(*a*)   uses any implement for fishing except—

(i)   a line and hook; or

(ii)   a net adapted solely for catching floating fish and so used as not to disturb or injure in any manner shellfish of the description in question or any bed therefor or the fishery therefor; or

(iii)   in the case of several fishery, an implement of a type specified in the order and so used as not to disturb or injure in any manner shellfish of the description in question;

(*b*)   dredges for any ballast or other substance except under a lawful authority for improving the navigation;

(*c*)   deposits any ballast, rubbish or other substance;

(*d*)   places any implement, apparatus or thing prejudicial or likely to be prejudicial to any such shellfish, bed or fishery except for a lawful purpose of navigation or anchorage;

(*e*)   disturbs or injures in any manner, except for a lawful purpose of navigation or anchorage, any such shellfish, bed or fishery;

he shall be guilty of an offence and liable on summary conviction to a fine not exceeding **level 5** on the standard scale and shall also be liable to make full compensation to the grantees or, as the case may be, owner for all damage sustained by them or him by reason of the unlawful act; and such compensation in default of payment may be recovered from him by the grantees or owner as the case may be in proceedings in any court of competent jurisdiction whether he has been prosecuted for or convicted of the offence in question or not.

(5) Nothing in subsection (4) of this section shall make it unlawful for any person to do any of the things therein mentioned—

(*a*) in the case of a right of several fishery granted by an order under section 1 of this Act, if at the time of his doing that thing the limits of the area of the fishery within which that right is exercisable or of the part of that area described for the purposes of the said subsection (4) in the order are not sufficiently marked out in manner prescribed by or under the order or if notice of those limits has not been given to that person in manner so prescribed.

(*b*) in the case of a private oyster bed, owned by any person independently of this Act, if the bed is not sufficiently marked out and known as such.

(6) In this section "the grantees" means the persons for the time being entitled to the right of several fishery conferred by the order under section 1 of this Act.

[Sea Fisheries (Shellfish) Act 1967, s 7, as amended by the Criminal Law Act 1977, Sch 6, the Criminal Justice Act 1982, s 46, the Criminal Justice and Public Order Act 1994, Sch 8, the Sale of Goods (Amendment) Act 1994, s 2 and the Sea Fisheries (Shellfish) Amendment (Scotland) Act 2000, s 1.]

---

1. See s 22, post, for definition of "shellfish".

8–10893 8. Proof of certain matters. Whenever it is necessary in any legal proceedings to prove that the requirement of an order under section 1 of this Act or of any other Act as to—

(*a*) the buoying or other marking of the limits of any fishery for shellfish of any description to which the order applies or, as the case may be, of any fishery for oysters or mussels to which that other Act applies, or

(*b*) the publication, posting or distribution of notices of those limits,

have been complied with, or that notice of the provisions of the order or Act relating to the fishery has been duly published, a certificate, purporting to be under the hand of one of the secretaries, under secretaries or assistant secretaries of the appropriate Minister's department, certifying that that Minister is satisfied that those requirements have been complied with or that the said notice was duly published shall be received as evidence of compliance with those requirements or publication of that notice.

[Sea Fisheries (Shellfish) Act 1967, s 8.]

8–10894 10. Fishery to be within county etc for purposes of jurisdiction. (1) The portion of the sea shore to which an order under section 1 of this Act relates shall for all purposes of jurisdiction be deemed to be within the body of the adjoining county, borough or burgh (so far as it is not by law within it) or to be within the body of each of them, of more than one.

(2) In the application of this section in relation to Wales, the reference to a county in subsection (1) of this section includes a reference to a preserved county (as defined by section 64 of the Local Government (Wales) Act 1994).

[Sea Fisheries (Shellfish) Act 1967, s 10, as amended by the Local Government (Wales) Act 1994, Sch 2.]

8–10895 11. Service of certain documents. Without prejudice to any provision made by or under any other Act prescribing the manner in which service of any document may be affected, service of any summons or other document in any proceedings under sections 3(3) or 7(4) of, or paragraph 4(5) of Schedule 1 to, this Act[1] may be effected by leaving the document for the person to be served on board any sea fishing boat to which he belongs with the person being or appearing to be in charge of the boat.

[Sea Fisheries (Shellfish) Act 1967, s 11.]

---

1. See ss 3(3) and 7(4), ante. Paragraph 4(5) of Sch 1 relates to the obstruction of a person appointed to hold an inquiry concerning a proposed Order under s 1.

8–10896 Further provisions with respect to shellfish. The Minister of Agriculture, Fisheries and Food may by Order[1] prohibit the deposit of shellfish in designated waters (s 12, amended by the Diseases of Fish Act 1983, s 6—*SUMMARISED*) and may prohibit the importation of shellfish into an area prescribed by Order[2] (s 13—*SUMMARISED*).

---

1. The Molluscan Shellfish (Control of Deposit) Order 1974, SI 1974/1555, amended by SI 1983/4159, and the Lobsters (Control of Deposit) Order 1981, SI 1981/994, has been made.
2. The Lobsters (Control of Importation) Order 1981, SI 1981/995, has been made.

8–10897 14. Supplementary provisions as to orders under ss 12 and 18. (1) Where the appropriate Minister makes an order under sections 12 or 13 of this Act, he shall take such steps (whether by the publication or display of notices or otherwise) as he may consider most suitable for informing all persons concerned of the effect of the order.

(2) Any person who contravenes the provisions of any order made under the said sections 12 or 13 (including any person who contravenes those provisions by not complying with any conditions specified in a licence granted thereunder) shall be guilty of an offence under this subsection, and shall be liable on summary conviction to imprisonment for a term not exceeding **three months**, or a fine not exceeding **level 5** on the standard scale, or **both**.

(3) A person authorised in that behalf by the appropriate Minister (in this section referred to as an "inspector") shall, subject to subsection (4) of this section, have the right, at any reasonable time, to enter any land designated by an order in pursuance of subsection (1) of that section under the said section 12, or any waters, or land covered by waters, designated by such an order, where either—

(a) the inspector has reasonable grounds for believing that the prohibition imposed by the order is being or has been contravened, or

(b) entry is required for the purpose of removing any shellfish which the appropriate Minister is empowered to remove under subsection (5) of that section;

and an inspector having a right to enter any land or waters under this subsection shall also have the right to obtain and take away samples (which shall be marked, labelled or otherwise made capable of identification) of any shellfish found there, and to dispose of any such sample as the inspector may determine;

Provided that where an inspector enters any land or waters by virtue of paragraph (a) above, he shall retain any shellfish so taken for as long as may be necessary to secure that they are available for production in any proceedings for an offence under this section in respect of the contravention in question.

(4) A right of entry under subsection (3) of this section shall not be exercisable in respect of any occupied land unless not less than twenty-four hours' notice of the intended entry has been given to the occupier; and the inspector shall, if so required, produce written evidence of his authority before entering.

(5) Any person who obstructs an inspector in the exercise of any right conferred by subsection (3) of this section shall be guilty of an offence and liable on summary conviction to a fine not exceeding **level 5** on the standard scale.

[Sea Fisheries (Shellfish) Act 1967, s 14 as amended by the Criminal Justice Act 1982, ss 35, 38 and 46, the Diseases of Fish Act 1983, s 6 and the Criminal Justice and Public Order Act 1994, Sch 8.]

8–10898 16. Oysters not to be sold between certain dates. (1) Subject to subsection (2) of this section, any person who between the 14th May in any year and the following 4th August sells, exposes for sale, buys for sale, or consigns to any person for the purpose of sale, any description of oysters shall be guilty of an offence and liable on summary conviction to a fine not exceeding **level 4** on the standard scale and, in any case, to forfeit the oysters exposed for sale, bought for sale or consigned to any person for the purpose of sale, in contravention of this subsection.

(2) A person shall not be guilty of an offence under this section if he satisfies the court that the oysters alleged to have been sold, exposed for sale, bought for sale or consigned to any person for the purpose of sale—

(a) were originally taken within the waters of a foreign state, or

(b) were preserved in tins or otherwise cured, or

(c) were intended for the purpose of oyster cultivation within the same district in which the oysters were taken, or

(d) were taken from any place for cultivation with the consent of the appropriate Minister, or

(e) were Pacific or Japanese oysters (crassostrea gigas), Portuguese oysters (crassostrea angulata) or other members of the genus Crassostrea.

(3) For the purposes of subsection (2)(c) of this section a district is—

(a) the Thames Estuary, bounded by a line drawn from Orford Ness to the North Foreland, and

(b) any other area for the time being constituted a district for the purposes of this section by an order of the appropriate Minister;

and where the place at which oysters are taken is not within any such district, so much of the area within ten miles of that place as is not included in any such district shall be deemed to be a district for those purposes.

(4) The appropriate Minister may by a subsequent order revoke or vary any order made by him under subsection (3)(b) of this section.

[Sea Fisheries (Shellfish) Act 1967, s 16, as amended by the Sea Fisheries (Shellfish) Act 1973, s 1, the Criminal Law Act 1977, s 31, the Criminal Justice Act 1982, ss 35 and 46 and the Criminal Justice and Public Order Act 1994, Sch 8.]

8–10899 17. Taking and sale of certain crabs and lobsters prohibited. (1) Subject to subsection (2) of this section, any person who takes, has in his possession, sells, exposes for sale, buys for sale, or consigns to any person for the purpose of sale—

(a) any edible crab carrying any spawn attached to the tail or other exterior part of the crab, or

(b) any edible crab which has recently cast its shell,

shall be guilty of an offence.

(2) A person shall not be guilty of an offence under subsection (1) of this section if he satisfies the court that the edible crabs found in his possession or alleged to have been sold, exposed for sale, bought for sale, or consigned to any person for the purpose of sale, were intended for bait for fishing.

(3) If the Minister and the Secretary of State for Scotland and the Secretary of State for Wales by order so direct, no person shall, in Great Britain, land, sell, expose or offer for sale, or have in his possession for the purpose of sale, any lobster which is carrying any spawn attached to the tail or some other exterior part of the lobster, or which is in such a condition as to show that, at the time when it was taken, it was carrying spawn so attached; and any person who contravenes an order under this subsection shall be guilty of an offence.

(4) A person guilty of an offence under this section shall be liable on summary conviction to a fine not exceeding **level 5** on the standard scale, and the court by which the offender is convicted may order the forfeiture of all crabs or lobsters found in his possession or alleged to have been sold, exposed or offered for sale, bought for sale, or consigned to any person for the purpose of sale, in contravention of subsection (1) of this section or of an order under subsection (3) thereof, as the case may be.

(5) An order under subsection (3) of this section may be varied or revoked by a subsequent order thereunder.

[Sea Fisheries (Shellfish) Act 1967, s 17 amended by SI 1978/272, the Criminal Justice Act 1982, ss 35, 38 and 46 and the Criminal Justice and Public Order Act 1994, Sch 8.]

8–10900   18. Power to search for, seize, etc oysters, crabs and lobsters illegally in possession of any person, etc.   Any person who has power under any Act, charter or byelaw to search for, seize, remove or condemn any food unfit for human consumption or to order any such food to be destroyed or otherwise disposed of, may exercise the like power with respect to any oysters, crabs or lobsters which, in contravention of sections 16 or 17 of this Act, are in the possession of any person or exposed or offered by any person for sale or have been bought by, or consigned to, any person for the purpose of sale.

[Sea Fisheries (Shellfish) Act 1967, s 18.]

Supplemental

8–10901   19. Jurisdiction to try certain offences and applications of certain fines.   (1) For the purposes of and incidental to the jurisdiction of any magistrates' court, or (*applies to Scotland*), any offence under sections 16 or 17 of this Act shall be deemed to have been committed either in the place in which its was actually committed or in any place in which the offender may for the time being be found.

(2) (*Applies to Scotland*).

(4) The provisions of this Act referred to in subsections (2) and (3) of this section are sections 3(3) and 7(4) and paragraph 4(5) of Schedule 1.

[Sea Fisheries (Shellfish) Act 1967, s 19, as amended by the Criminal Justice Act 1972, Sch 6.]

8–10902   22. Interpretation.   (1) In this Act "the Minister" means the Minister of Agriculture, Fisheries and Food and "the appropriate Minister", in relation to England and Wales, means the Minister and, in relation to Scotland, means the Secretary of State[1].

(2) In this Act, except in so far as the context otherwise requires, the following expressions have the meaning hereby assigned to them respectively, that is to say—

"land" includes land covered by water;

"sea fish" means fish of any description found in the sea, other than fish of the salmon species, and includes shellfish;

"sea fishing boat" means a vessel of whatever size, and in whatever way propelled, which is used by any person in fishing for sea fish;

"shellfish" includes crustaceans and molluscs of any kind, and includes any part of shellfish and any (or any part of any) brood, ware, half-ware or spat of shellfish, and any spawn of shellfish, and the shell, or any part of the shell, of a shellfish, and references in this Act to shellfish of any particular description shall be construed accordingly;

"shellfish bed" means any bed or ground in which shellfish are usually found or which is used for the propagation or cultivation of shellfish.

[Sea Fisheries (Shellfish) Act 1967, s 22.]

---

1. The functions of the Minister and the appropriate Minister, so far as exercisable in relation to Wales, have been transferred to the National Assembly for Wales, by the National Assembly for Wales (Transfer of Functions) Order 1999, SI 1999/672, art 2, Sch 1.

8–10903   24. *Transitional provisions.*

Sea Fish (Conservation) Act 1967

(1967 c 84)

Restrictions on commercial use of under-sized, etc, sea fish

8–11010   1. Size, Limits, etc for fish.   (1) Subject to the provisions of this section and of section 9(1) of this Act, no person shall land in Great Britain any sea fish[1] of any description, being a fish of a smaller size than such size as may be prescribed in relation to sea fish of that description by an order of the Ministers.

(2) Subject to the provisions of this section, no person shall, in Great Britain, sell, expose or offer for sale or have in his possession for the purpose of sale, any sea fish of any description, being a fish of a smaller size than such size as may be prescribed in relation to sea fish of that description by an order of the Ministers.

(3) Sea fish of any description which are of less than the minimum size prescribed in relation to sea fish of that description by an order[2] of the Ministers[3] shall not be carried, whether within or outside British fishery limits[4], on a British fishing boat; and an order under this subsection may prohibit the carrying by any foreign fishing boat in waters adjacent to the United Kingdom and within British fishery limits of sea fish of any description prescribed by the order which are of less than the minimum size so prescribed in relation to sea fish of that description.

(4) Different sizes may be prescribed for the purposes of each of the foregoing provisions of this section; and an order under subsection (1) above may prescribe different sizes in relation to different areas and in relation to fish of different sexes.

(5) Where an order under subsection (1) above prescribes a size for fish of any description (or of any description and sex), whether generally or in relation to any particular area, then, except so far as provision to the contrary is made by such an order, a person who in Great Britain or, as the case may be, in that area lands a part of a fish of that description (or of that description and sex) shall, subject to section 9(1) of this Act, be deemed to contravene subsection (1) above if the part is of a smaller size than the one so prescribed.

(6) An order under this section may confer exemptions from any prohibition imposed by or by virtue of this section; and any such exemption may be general or subject to conditions and may relate to all fish to which the order applies or to fish of any specified description.

(7) Any person who contravenes subsection (1) or (2) above shall be guilty of an offence[5] under that subsection.

(8) If subsection (3) above is contravened in the case of a British fishing boat the master[1], the owner and the charterer (if any) shall each be guilty of an offence[5] under that subsection; and if a prohibition imposed by virtue of that subsection is contravened in the case of a foreign fishing boat, the master shall be guilty of an offence[5] under that subsection.

(9) In this section

"British fishing boat" means a fishing boat[1] which either is registered in the United Kingdom under Part II of the Merchant Shipping Act 1995 or is owned wholly by persons qualified to own British ships for the purposes of that Part of that Act; and "foreign fishing boat" means any fishing boat other than a British fishing boat.

[Sea Fish (Conservation) Act 1967, s 1, as substituted by the Fisheries Act 1981, s 19 and amended by the Merchant Shipping Act 1995, Sch 13.]

---

1. For definitions of "sea fish", "fishing-boat" and "master", see s 22, post.

2. See the Undersized Crabs Order 1986, SI 1986/497, amended by SI 1989/2443 and SI 2000/2029, the Undersized Velvet Crabs Order 1989, SI 1989/919, the Undersized Bass Order 1989, SI 1989/1285, the Undersized Lobsters Order 1993, SI 1993/1178 (England), the Undersized Spider Crabs Order 2000, SI 2000/1502, the Undersized Lobsters Order 2000, SI 2000/1503, the Undersized Spider Crab (Wales) Order 2002, SI 2002/1897 and the Scallop Fishing Order 2004, SI 2004/12.

3. In England and Wales, the appropriate Minister is the Minister of Agriculture, Fisheries and Food (s 22(1)).

4. See the Fishery Limits Act 1976, post.

5. For penalty, see s 11, post.

8–11011   2. Size limits for fish for use in course of any business.   (1) Subject to any exemption granted under this section no person shall in Great Britain have in his possession any fish to which this section applies for the purpose of processing or otherwise using it in the course of any business.

(2) This section applies to any fish which under section 1(2) of this Act is prohibited from being sold in Great Britain.

(3) Where it appears to an officer authorised in that behalf by the appropriate Minister that any fish which have been caught are fish to which this section applies, the officer may grant to any person such exemption from subsection (1) above as the officer considers requisite to enable the fish to be disposed of.

(4) Any person who contravenes this section shall be guilty of an offence[1] under this section.

[Sea Fish (Conservation) Act 1967, s 2 as amended by the Fisheries Act 1981, s 19.]

---

1. For penalty, see s 11, post.

Regulation of fishing for sea fish

8–11012 3. Regulation of nets and other fishing gear. (1) The Ministers may make an order[1] for securing that the nets and other fishing gear carried in any British fishing boat[2] registered in the United Kingdom comply with such requirements as to construction, design, material, or size, including, in the case of nets, size of mesh, as may be prescribed by the order, and an order under this section, or any provisions of such an order, may be framed so as to apply only in relation to fishing for specified descriptions of sea fish, to specified methods of fishing or to fishing in specified areas or during specified periods[3].

(2) An order under this section may be made so as to extend to nets or other fishing gear carried in any waters adjacent to the United Kingdom and within British fishery limits by fishing boats[4] registered in any country outside the United Kingdom or not registered in any country.

(3) An order under this section prescribing minimum sizes of mesh may also—

(a) prescribe the manner in which the sizes of mesh are to be measured and, in the case of any class of nets, prescribe different sizes for the nets when in different conditions;

(b) make provision for securing that the restrictions imposed by the order are not evaded by the use of any nets in such manner as practically to diminish their mesh, or by the covering of nets with canvas or any other material, or by the use of any other artifice;

(c) provide for exempting any nets from any such restrictions as aforesaid, either generally or in relation to particular fishing boats or[4] classes of fishing boats, if and so long as such conditions as may be imposed by or under the order are complied with.

(4) Without prejudice to subsection (3) above, an order under this section may, in relation to any fishing gear—

(a) restrict the manner in which it may be used;

(b) prescribe the manner in which its size is to be measured;

(c) make provision for securing that the restrictions imposed by the order are not evaded;

(d) make the like provision for exemption as is mentioned in relation to nets in subsection (3)(c) above.

(5) If any order under this section is contravened in the case of any fishing boat[4], the master[4], the owner and the charterer (if any) shall each be guilty of an offence under this section[5].

(6) Any restrictions imposed by an order under this section shall be in addition to, and not in substitution for, any restriction imposed by or under any other Act, and nothing in this section shall affect any power conferred by any Act to regulate sea fishing.

(7) *Application to Scotland and Northern Ireland.*

[Sea Fish (Conservation) Act 1967, s 3, as amended by the Fishery Limits Act 1976, Sch 2.]

---

1. An order shall not affect the carrying of nets for fishing within the fishery limits for authorised fishing for scientific investigation or for transplanting fish from one fishing ground to another (s 9, post). A number of orders have been made. See the Sea Fish (Specified Sea Areas) (Regulation of Nets and Other Fishing Gear) Order 2001, SI 2001/649 amended by SI 2003/1560; the Shrimp Fishing Nets Order 2002, SI 2002/2870; the Prohibition of Fishing with Multiple Trawls Order 2003, SI 2003/1559; the Prohibition of Fishing with Multiple Trawls (Wales) Order 2003, SI 2003/1855; the South-west Territorial Waters (Prohibition of Pair Trawling) Order 2004, SI 2004/3397 amended by SI 2005/49.
2. See note 4, below.
3. Any order made under an enactment repealed by this Act has effect as if made under a corresponding provision of this Act (s 25(1), post).
4. For meaning of "fishing boat", "sea fish", "master" and "vessel", see s 22, post.
5. For penalty, see s 11, post.

8–11013 4. Licensing of fishing boats[1]. (1) The Ministers may by order[2] provide—

(a) that in any specified area within British fishery limits fishing by fishing boats[3] (whether British or foreign) is prohibited unless authorised by a licence granted by one of the Ministers;

(b) that in any specified area outside those limits fishing by British boats is prohibited unless so authorised.

(2) Such an order may apply to fishing generally in the specified area or to fishing—

(a) for a specified description of sea fish[3];

(b) by a specified method;

(c) during a specified season of the year or other period; or

(d) in the case of an order under subsection (1)(a), by fishing boats registered in a specified country,

and whether the order is general or limited in scope it may provide for exceptions from the prohibition contained in it.

(3) Where any fishing boat is used in contravention of any prohibition imposed by an order under this section, the master[3], the owner and the charterer (if any) are each guilty of an offence[4] under this subsection.

(4) An order under this section, if made with the consent of the Treasury given for the purposes of this subsection, may authorise the making of a charge for a licence under this section.

Such an order shall specify a maximum charge and may specify different maxima in relation to different classes of licence.

(5) A licence under this section shall be granted to the owner or charterer in respect of a named vessel[3] and may authorise fishing generally or may confer limited authority by reference to, in particular—

(a) the area within which fishing is authorised;

(b) the periods, times or particular voyages during which fishing is authorised;

(c) the descriptions and quantities of fish which may be taken; or

(d) the method of sea fishing.

(6) [5] A licence under this section may authorise fishing either unconditionally or subject to such conditions as appear to the Minister granting the licence to be necessary or expedient for the regulation of sea fishing (including conditions which do not relate directly to fishing), and in particular a licence may contain conditions—

(a) as to the landing of fish or parts of fish taken under the authority of the licence (including specifying the ports at which the catch is to be landed); or

(b) as to the use to which the fish may be put; or

(c) restricting the time which a vessel named in the licence may spend at sea (whether for the purpose of fishing or otherwise);

and if a licence condition is broken the master, the owner and the charterer (if any) of the vessel named in the licence are each guilty of an offence[4] under this subsection.

(6A) The conditions subject to which a licence may be granted under this section may differ as between different vessels or between vessels of different descriptions.

(6B) A licence containing a condition restricting the time which a vessel may spend at sea may make provision as to the circumstances in which time is, or is not, to count as time spent at sea.

(6C) The Ministers shall by order[6] make provision as to the principles on which the time which vessels may spend at sea is to be arrived at for the purposes of any condition included in a licence by virtue of subsection (6)(c) above.

(6D) Before considering what action to take under subsection (6C) above, the Ministers shall first give due consideration to a scheme of decommissioning in order to achieve a significant reduction in the capacity of the fishing fleet.

(7) The Minister granting a licence under this section may require the master, the owner and the charterer (if any) of the vessel named in the licence to provide him with such information, in such form as he may direct and a person who fails without reasonable excuse to comply with such a requirement is guilty of an offence[4] under this subsection.

(7A) Any person who—

(a) for the purpose of obtaining a licence under this section; or

(b) in purported compliance with subsection (7) above,

furnishes information which he knows to be false in a material particular or recklessly furnishes information which is false in a material particular shall be guilty of an offence under this subsection.

(8) The licensing powers conferred by this section may be exercised so as to limit the number of fishing boats or of any class of fishing boats engaged in fishing in any area, or in fishing in any area for any description of fish, to such extent as appears to the Ministers necessary or expedient for the regulation of sea fishing.

(9) A licence under this section—

(a) may be varied from time to time; and

(b) may be revoked or suspended, if this appears to the Minister who granted the licence to be necessary or expedient for the regulation of sea fishing.

(9A) Where an order under this section prohibits fishing in a specified area for a specified description of sea fish there shall be returned to the sea forthwith—

(a) any sea fish of that description taken on board a fishing boat in contravention of the order; and

(b) except so far as the order otherwise provides, any sea fish of that description taken on board a fishing boat in that area in the course of fishing for sea fish of a different description;

but, where the order applies only to fishing by a specified period or by boats of a specified description, paragraph (b) above applies only if the fish are caught by that method, during that period or by a boat of that description.

(9B) Where subsection (9A) above is not complied with in the case of any fishing boat, the master, the owner and the charterer (if any) shall each be guilty of an offence under that subsection or to be appropriate in a case where there is a contravention of a prohibition imposed by an order under this section or a contravention of a condition of the licence.

(10) If a licence is varied, revoked or suspended the Minister who granted it may, if he considers it appropriate in all the circumstances of the case, refund the whole or part of any charge made for the licence.

(11) The Ministers may make arrangements for any of their licensing powers under this section

(but not the power to make orders under subsection (1)) to be exercised by other persons on their behalf.

(12) In this section "British fishing boat" means a fishing boat which is registered in the United Kingdom or is British-owned, and "foreign fishing boat" means a fishing boat which is not so registered or owned.

[Sea Fish (Conservation) Act 1967, s 4, as substituted by the Fishery Limits Act 1976, s. 3 and as amended by the Fisheries Act 1981, s 20 and the Sea Fish (Conservation) Act 1992, s 1.]

---

1. For application to the Isle of Man, and British fishing boats registered there, see SI 1977/1244. See also the Herring and White Fish (Specified Manx Waters) Licensing Order 1983, SI 1983/1204 amended by SI 1983/1879, SI 1986/1439 and SI 1987/1564.

2. The Sea Fish Licensing Order 1992, SI 1992/2633 amended by SI 1993/188 and 2291 has been made.

3. For meaning of "fishing boat", "sea fish", "master" and "vessel", see s 22, post.

4. For penalty, see s 11, post.

5. Subsection (6) is printed as amended by the Sea Fish (Conservation) Act 1992, s 1(2), which added the words "(including conditions which do not relate directly to fishing)" and para (c); s 11(2) of the 1992 Act provides that these amendments shall not apply in relation to vessels of an overall length of 10 metres or less until such day as may be appointed by Order.

6. The Sea Fish Licensing (Time at Sea) Order 1993, SI 1993/1196 has been made.

8–11013A   4AA. *Restrictions on time spent at sea—appeals.*

8–11014   4A. Licensing of vessels receiving trans-shipped fish.   (1) The Ministers may by order[1] provide that within British fishery limits or in any specified area within those limits the receiving by any vessel (whether British or foreign) of fish trans-shipped from any other vessel is prohibited unless authorised by a licence granted by one of the Ministers.

(2) Such an order may apply to the receiving of fish generally or to the receiving of—

(a)   a specified description of fish; or

(b)   fish caught by a specified method; or

(c)   fish caught in a specified area; or

(d)   fish caught or trans-shipped during a specified season of the year or other period; or

(e)   fish caught or received by vessels of a specified description, including vessels registered in a specified country;

and may provide for exceptions from the prohibitions contained in it.

(3) Where any vessel is used in contravention of a prohibition imposed by an order under this section, the master, the owner and the charterer (if any) are each guilty of an offence under this subsection.

(4) An order under this section, if made with the consent of the Treasury given for the purposes of this subsection, may authorise the making of a charge for a licence under this section, and if it does so it shall specify a maximum charge and may specify different maxima in relation to different classes of licence.

(5) A licence under this section shall be granted to the owner or charterer in respect of a named vessel and may authorise the receiving of fish generally or may confer limited authority by reference to, in particular—

(a)   the area within which the fish was caught or is trans-shipped; or

(b)   the periods, times or particular voyages during which the fish was caught or is trans-shipped; or

(c)   the descriptions and quantities of fish that may be received; or

(d)   the description of vessel or method by which the trans-shipped fish was caught.

(6) A licence under this section may authorise the receiving of fish either unconditionally or subject to such conditions as appear to the Minister granting the licence to be necessary or expedient for the regulation of trans-shipment, including conditions as to the treatment on board the vessel of the fish received by it; and different conditions may be so imposed with respect to different vessels or vessels of different descriptions.

If such a condition is broken the master, the owner and the charterer (if any) are each guilty of an offence under this subsection.

(7) The Minister granting a licence under this section may require the master, the owner and the charterer (if any) of the vessel named in the licence and any agent named in the licence to provide him with such information, in such form as he may direct, and a person who fails without reasonable excuse to comply with such a requirement is guilty of an offence under this subsection.

(8) Any person who—

(a)   for the purpose of obtaining a licence under this section; or

(b)   in purported compliance with subsection (7) above,

furnishes information which he knows to be false in a material particular or recklessly furnishes information which is false in a material particular is guilty of an offence under this subsection.

(9) The licensing power conferred by this section may be exercised so as to limit the number of vessels, or of any description of vessel (including vessels or any description of vessel registered in a

specified country) engaged in receiving fish to such an extent as appears to the Ministers necessary or expedient for the regulation of trans-shipment.

(10) A licence under this section—

(a) may be varied from time to time; and

(b) may be revoked or suspended, if it appears to the Minister who granted it to be necessary or expedient for the regulation of trans-shipment or to be appropriate in a case where there is a contravention of a prohibition imposed by an order under this section or a contravention of a condition of the licence.

(11) If a licence is varied, revoked or suspended, the Minister who granted it may, if he considers it appropriate in all the circumstances of the case, refund the whole or part of any charge made for the licence.

(12) The Ministers may make arrangements for any of their licensing powers under this section (but not the power to make orders under subsection (1)) to be exercised by other persons on their behalf.

[Sea Fish (Conservation) Act 1981, s 4A, as inserted by the Fisheries Act 1981, s 21 and amended by the Sea Fish (Conservation) Act 1992, s 3.]

---

1. The Receiving of Trans-shipped Sea Fish (Licensing) Order 1982, SI 1982/80 amended by SI 1983/1139 has been made.

8–11014A   4B. *Regulations supplementary to sections 4 and 4A.*

8–11014B   4C. Provisions supplementary to sections 4 and 4A—evidence. (1) Where automatic recording equipment—

(a) is used in accordance with a condition included in a licence by virtue of section 4(6) or 4A(6) of this Act, or

(b) is used to record information transmitted or derived from equipment used in accordance with such a condition,

any record produced by means of the automatic recording equipment, or partly by those and partly by other means, shall, in any proceedings for an offence under section 4 or 4A, except proceedings in Scotland, be evidence of the matters appearing from the record.

(2), (3) *Scotland.*

[Sea Fish (Conservation) Act 1967, s 4C added by the Sea Fish (Conservation) Act 1992, s 4.]

---

1. This section has effect in relation to offences committed on and after 17 January 1993.

8–11015   5. Power to restrict fishing for sea fish. (1) Subject to the provisions of this section, the Ministers may by order[1] prohibit in any area specified in the order and either for a period so specified or without limitation of time—

(a) all fishing for sea fish; or

(b) fishing for any description of sea fish specified in the order; or

(c) fishing for sea fish, or for any description of sea fish specified in the order, by any method so specified,

by any fishing boat to which the prohibition applies; and where any fishing boat is used in contravention of any prohibition imposed by an order under this section, the master, the owner and the charterer (if any) shall each be guilty of an offence[2] under this subsection.

(2) Orders under this section may make different provisions in relation to fishing boats of different descriptions.

(3)–(4) *(Repealed).*

(5) Any prohibition imposed by an order under this section may be made so as to have effect either at all times while the order is in force or at such times as (whether by reference to particular months, weeks, days or hours, or to any combination thereof) are specified in the order.

(6) Where an order under this section is made in respect of a description of sea fish specified in the order, and, in the course of any fishing operations conducted in an area so specified and at a time when a prohibition imposed by the order in relation to sea fish of that description has effect in that area, any sea fish of that description (or, if the prohibition applies only to fishing for sea fish of that description by a method specified in the order, any sea fish of that description caught by that method) are taken on board a fishing boat to which the order applies those sea fish shall, subject to s 9 of this Act and except where the order otherwise provides, be returned to the sea forthwith.

(7) Where subsection (6) above is not complied with in the case of any fishing boat, the master, the owner and the charterer (if any) shall each be guilty of an offence[3] under that subsection.

(8) An order under this section relating to an area outside British fishery limits shall not apply to any fishing boat other than—

(a) a British fishing boat registered in the United Kingdom; or (*b*) in so far as the order relates to fishing for salmon or migratory trout, a fishing boat which is British-owned but not registered under the Merchant Shipping Act 1995;

but an order under this section relating to an area within those limits may apply to any fishing boat.
[Sea Fish (Conservation) Act 1967, s 5, as amended by the Fishery Limits Act 1967, Sch 2, the Fisheries Act 1981, s 22, the Merchant Shipping (Registration, etc) Act 1993, Sch 2 and the Merchant Shipping Act 1995, Sch 13.]

---

1. See note 3 to s 3, supra. Several Orders have been made making specific prohibition of fishing for particular fish or in particular waters or by particular fishing methods.
2. For penalty, see s 11, post.
3. For penalty, see s 11, post.

Regulation of the landing of sea fish

8–11016   6. Prohibition on landing of sea fish[1] caught in certain areas.   (1) The Ministers, after consultation with the Board of Trade, may by order, prohibit, in accordance with the provisions of this section, the landing in the United Kingdom of sea fish, or any particular description of sea fish, being fish caught in any such waters as may be specified in the order[2].

(1A) The Ministers, after consultation with the Secretary of State for Trade, may by order prohibit, in accordance with the provisions of this section, the trans-shipment within British fishery limits of sea fish, or any particular description of sea fish, being fish caught in any such waters as may be specified in the order.

(2) Any prohibition imposed by an order under this section in relation to sea fish, or any particular description of sea fish, caught in any waters specified in the order may be so imposed either for a period specified in the order or without limitation of time, and either free from, or subject to, all or any, or any combination, of the following limitations that is to say, limitations whereby the prohibition has effect in relation to sea fish, or sea fish of that description, as the case may be—

(*a*) caught while in a condition specified in the order and not while in any other condition, or caught while in any condition except a condition so specified;

(*b*) caught by a method specified in the order and not by any other method, or caught by any method except a method so specified;

(*c*) caught at any such time as (whether by reference to particular months, weeks, days or hours, or to any combination thereof) are specified in the order.

(3) Without prejudice to subsection (2) above, any prohibition imposed by an order under this section may be imposed subject to such exceptions as may be specified in the order.

(4) Where an order is made under this section the enactments relating to customs shall apply accordingly, but no steps shall be taken under those enactments for the purposes of this section by any officer of customs and excise, except at the request of an officer of the Ministry of Agriculture, Fisheries and Food, the Secretary of State for Scotland or the Ministry of Agriculture for Northern Ireland, as the case may be.

(5) If any sea fish are landed from a vessel in contravention of an order under this section, the master, the owner, and the charterer (if any) of the vessel shall each be guilty of an offence under this subsection[3].

(5A) If any sea fish are—

(*a*) trans-shipped into a vessel in contravention of an order under this section; or

(*b*) trans-shipped from a vessel in contravention of such an order,

the master, the owner and the charterer (if any) of the vessel shall each be guilty of an offence under this subsection.

(6) In this and the next following section "sea fish" includes a salmon and migratory trout.
[Sea Fish (Conservation) Act 1967, s 6 as amended by the Fisheries Act 1981, s 23.]

---

1. Defined by s 22, post.
2. See note 3 to s 3, ante. Annual Orders control the landing of North Sea herring, and salmon and migratory trout; see also the Sea Fishing (Specified Western Waters) (Restrictions on Landing) Order 1987, SI 1987/1566.
3. For penalty, see s 11, post.

8–11017   7. Declarations required for purposes of orders under section 6.   (1) Any British sea-fishery officer[1] may serve on the master[2] of any vessel a notice in writing under the hand of the officer requiring the master to make, on each occasion when any sea fish[2] are about to be landed in the United Kingdom from that vessel while any order under section 6(1) of this Act is in force, a written declaration that those sea fish are not sea fish the landing of which is prohibited by the order, and to deliver the declaration, before any of the sea fish are landed, to such person, or at such place, in the port of landing as may be specified in the notice:

Provided that a notice under this subsection shall not be taken to require the making or delivery of any declaration in respect of the landing of any sea fish after the end of the period of six months from the date on which the notice is served.

(2) Where any sea fish are brought to land in the United Kingdom in any vessel, any British sea

fishery officer may, at any time before the vessel next puts out to sea, request the master to make, in respect of any of those sea fish which have been, or are being, or are about to be, landed from the vessel while any order under section 6(1) of this Act is in force a written declaration that the sea fish in question are not sea fish the landing of which is prohibited by the order, and to deliver the declaration to the officer or to such person, or at such place, in the port of landing as he may designate.

Nothing in this subsection shall be taken to affect the operation of subsection (1) above.

(2A) Any British sea-fishery officer may serve on the master of any vessel a notice in writing under the hand of the officer requiring the master to make, on each occasion when any sea fish are about to be trans-shipped within British fishery limits from that vessel while an order under section 6(1A) of this Act is in force, a written declaration that those sea fish are not sea fish the trans-shipment of which is prohibited by the order, and to deliver the declaration, before any of the sea fish are trans-shipped, to the officer or to such other person or at such place as may be specified in the notice and as appears to the officer to be reasonable in the circumstances:

Provided that a notice under this subsection shall not be taken to require the making or delivery of any declaration in respect of the trans-shipment of any sea fish after the end of the period of six months from the date on which the notice is served.

(2B) Where any sea fish have been or are being trans-shipped, or where a British sea-fishery officer has reasonable grounds for believing that any sea fish are about to be trans-shipped, within British fishery limits from any vessel while an order under section 6(1A) of this Act is in force, any such officer may request the master of the vessel to make and deliver to the officer a written declaration that the sea fish in question are not sea fish the trans-shipment of which is prohibited by the order.

Nothing in this subsection shall be taken to affect the operation of subsection (2A) above.

(3) If the master of any vessel makes for the purposes of this section a declaration which is to his knowledge false in any material particular, he shall be guilty of an offence[3] under this section; and if the master of any vessel fails to make, in respect of any sea fish, a declaration in accordance with the requirements of a notice duly served on him under this section or in accordance with a request duly made under this section by a British sea-fishery officer the said sea fish shall—

(a) where the notice or request was served or made under subsection (1) or (2) above, be presumed until the contrary is proved to be sea fish the landing of which is prohibited under section 6 of this Act; and

(b) where the notice or request was served or made under subsection (2A) or (2B) above, be presumed until the contrary is proved to be sea fish the trans-shipment of which is prohibited under that section.

(4) A notice under subsection (1) or (2A) above relating to any vessel may be addressed to "The Master" of the vessel (identifying it by name or otherwise) and shall be deemed to be duly served if it is delivered or sent by post to, or to the agent of, the owner or the charterer (if any) of the vessel, together with a written request that it be transmitted to the master, and, if the notice is served by being so delivered or sent as aforesaid, it shall be deemed to be served on the master of the vessel for the time being and on every other person who at any material time thereafter is the master of the vessel.

[Sea Fish (Conservation) Act 1967, s 7 as amended by the Fisheries Act 1981, s 23.]

---

1. The definition of "British Sea Fishery Officer" in s 22, post, now refers to s 7 of the Sea Fisheries Act 1968.
2. Defined by s 22, post.
3. For penalty, see s 11, post.

8–11018 8. Regulation of landing of foreign-caught sea fish. The Board of Trade may make orders regulating the landing in the United Kingdom of foreign-caught sea fish.
[Sea Fish (Conservation) Act 1967, s 8—summarised).]

Exemption for certain operations

8–11019 9. Exemption for operations for scientific and other purposes. (1) Nothing in section 1(1) of this Act shall restrict the landing of fish taken in the course of fishing operations which, under the authority of one of the Ministers, are conducted for the purpose of scientific investigation.

(2) Nothing in section 1(3) of this Act or in any order made under section 3 thereof shall apply in relation to fishing operations which, under the authority of one of the Ministers, are conducted for the purpose of scientific investigation or for the purpose of transplanting fish from one fishing ground to another.

(3) Neither a prohibition imposed by an order under section 5 of this Act, nor the obligation imposed by subsection (6) of that section, shall apply in relation to fishing operations conducted under the authority of one of the Ministers for either of the purposes mentioned in subsection (2) above.

(4) No enactment to which this subsection applies, and no order or byelaw made (whether before or after the passing of this Act) under any such enactment, shall restrict the carrying of on any

operations which, under the authority of one of the Ministers, are conducted for the purpose of scientific investigation, or for the purpose of transplanting sea fish from one fishing ground to another, or shall restrict the landing of sea fish caught in the course of any such operations.

(5) Subsection (4) above applies to sections 4, 4A, 5, 6 and 8 of this Act and to any other enactment which provides for regulating the catching or landing of sea fish.

(6) Subsection (4) above shall have effect in addition to, and not in derogation of, subsections (1), (2) and (3) above and any express saving or exemption contained in such other enactment as is referred to in subsection (5) above or in any order or byelaw made under an enactment to which the said subsection (4) applies.

(7) In this section "sea fish" includes salmon and migratory trout.

[Sea Fish (Conservation) Act 1967, s 9 as amended by the Fisheries Act 1981, ss 19 and 21.]

Penalties for, and other provisions as to, offences

8–11020   11. Penalties for offences.   (1) Any person guilty of an offence under this Act shall be liable—

    (*a*)   in the case of an offence under section 4(3) or (6), 4A(3) or (6), 5(1) or 6(5A)(*a*), on summary conviction to a fine[1] not exceeding **£50,000** or on conviction on indictment to a fine;

    (*b*)   in the case of an offence under sections 3, 4(9A), or 5(6), on summary conviction to a fine[1] not exceeding **£5,000** or on conviction on indictment to a fine;

    (*c*)   in the case of an offence under section 1, 2, 4(7) or (7A), 4A(7) or (8), 6(5) or (5A) (*b*) or 7(3), on summary conviction to a fine[1] not exceeding **the statutory maximum** or on conviction on indictment to a fine.

(2) Subject to the following provisions of this section, the court by or before which a person is convicted of an offence under any of the following provisions of this Act, that is to say, ss 1(3), 4(3), (6) and (9A), 4A(3) and (6), 5(1) and (6) and 6(5) and (5A)(*b*) may—

    (*a*)   in the case of an offence under section 1, order the forfeiture[2] of any fish in respect of which the offence was committed;

    (*b*)   in the case of an offence under section 3, order the forfeiture[2] of the net or other fishing gear in respect of which the contravention constituting the offence occurred;

    (*c*)   in the case of an offence under section 4(3), (6) or (9A) or 4A(3) or (6), order that the owner or the charterer (if any) of the vessel used to commit the offence, or, as the case may be, of the vessel named in the licence of which a condition is broken, be disqualified for a specified period from holding a licence under that section in respect of that vessel;

    (*d*)   in the case of an offence under section 4(3), (6) or (9A) or section 5(1) or (6), order the forfeiture[2] of any fish in respect of which the offence was committed and of any net or other fishing gear used in committing the offence;

    (*e*)   in the case of an offence under s 6(5) or (5A)(*b*), order the forfeiture[2] of any fish in respect of which the offence was committed and of any net or other fishing gear used on the vessel in catching any fish landed in contravention of an order under that section.

(3) Any person guilty of an offence under section 1, 3, 4(3), (6) or (9A), 4A(3) or (6), 5(1) or (6) or 6 of this Act shall, subject to subsection (5) below, be liable on summary conviction to a fine[3] not exceeding the value of the fish in respect of which the offence was committed or, in the case of an offence under section 3, the fish caught with the net or other gear in respect of which the contravention constituting the offence occurred.

(4) A person shall not be liable to a fine under subsection (3) above in respect of an offence if, under subsection (2) above, the court orders the forfeiture of the fish in respect of which the offence was committed; and where a fine is imposed under subsection (3) above in respect of any offence, the court shall not have power under subsection (2) above to order the forfeiture of the fish in respect of which the offence was committed.

(5) Subject to subsection (4) above, any fine to which a person is liable under subsection (3) above in respect of an offence shall be in addition to any other penalty (whether pecuniary or otherwise) to which he is liable in respect of that offence under this section or under any other enactment.

[Sea Fish (Conservation) Act 1967, s 11, as amended by the Fishery Limits Act 1976, Schs 1 and 2, the Fisheries Act 1981, s 24, the Criminal Justice Act 1991, Sch 4 and the Sea Fish (Conservation) Act 1992, s 5.]

---

   1. Note also liability to a further "fine" related to the value of fish caught (sub-ss (3)–(5) post).

   2. The method of disposal of forfeitures ordered by this subsection is prescribed by the Magistrates' Courts Act 1980, s 140, Part I: Magistrates' Courts, Procedure, ante.

   3. This "fine" will be in addition to the main penalty under sub-s (1) ante (see sub-s (4) and (5) below).

8–11021   12. Offences committed by bodies corporate.   Where any offence under any of the following provisions of this Act, that is to say, section 1(1), (2) and (3) and sections 3, 4, 4A, 5 and 6, committed by a body corporate is proved to have been committed with the consent or approval of any director, manager, secretary or other officer of the body corporate, he, as well as the body corporate, shall be deemed to be guilty of the offence and shall be liable to be proceeded against and punished accordingly.

[Sea Fish (Conservation) Act 1967, s 12 as amended by the Fisheries Act 1981, ss 19 and 28.]

8–11022   13. Institution of proceedings by local fisheries committee.   (1) A local fisheries committee may take proceedings in respect of any contravention of sections 1, 2 or 3 of this Act occurring within the district of the committee.

(2) For the purposes of subsection (1) above, in so far as it applies to a contravention of the said sections 1 or 2, the district of a local fisheries committee shall be deemed to extend throughout the area of any council liable to pay, or contribute to the payment of, the expenses of the committee, except that the powers conferred by that subsection on the committee shall not be exercisable in respect of any matter arising within the limits of any market under the control of the council of any county borough or county district.

[Sea Fish (Conservation) Act 1967, s 13.]

8–11023   14. Jurisdiction of court to try offences.   Proceedings for an offence under sections 1(3), 3, 4, 4A, 5, 6, 7, 15 or 16 of this Act may be taken, and the offence may for all incidental purposes be treated as having been committed, in any place in the United Kingdom.

[Sea Fish (Conservation) Act 1967, s 14, as substituted by the Fisheries Act 1981, s 29.]

Enforcement of orders, etc

8–11024   15. Powers of British sea-fishery officers for enforcement of Act.   (1) Every British sea-fishery officer shall have the powers conferred by the following provisions of this section.

(2) Any such officer may seize—

(*a*) any fish in respect of which an offence has been or is being committed under section 1(3) of this Act;

(*aa*) any net or other fishing gear in respect of which a contravention of an order under section 3 of this Act has been or is being committed;

(*b*) any fish in respect of which an offence has been or is being committed under sections 4(3), (6) or (9A) or 5(1) or (6) of this Act where the fish are on the fishing boat with or on which the offence has been or is being committed or are in the ownership or custody of, or under the control of, the owner, the master or the charterer (if any) of the fishing boat;

(*c*) any net or other fishing gear used in contravention of a prohibition imposed by an order under the said sections 4 or 5;

(*d*) any fish landed in contravention of an order under section 6 of this Act, and any net or other fishing gear used in catching any fish so landed.

(2A) Any such officer may—

(*a*) enter at any reasonable time any premises (other than a dwelling-house) used for carrying on any business in connection with the operation of fishing boats or activities connected therewith or ancillary thereto or with the treatment, storage or sale of sea fish;

(*b*) require any person on the premises to produce any documents which are in his custody or possession relating to the catching, landing, trans-shipment, sale or disposal of any sea fish;

(*c*) take copies of any such document;

and, if he has reason to suspect that an offence under this Act has been committed, he may also—

(*d*) search the premises for any such document and require any person on the premises to do anything which appears to him to be necessary for facilitating the search;

(*e*) seize and detain any such document produced to him or found on the premises for the purpose of enabling the document to be used as evidence in proceedings for the offence—

(2B) Any such officer may—

(*a*) go on board any vessel into which sea fish are being trans-shipped or into which he has reason to believe that sea fish have been or are about to be trans-shipped;

(*b*) require any person on the vessel to produce any documents which are in his custody or possession relating to sea fish which have been or are to be trans-shipped into that vessel;

(*c*) for the purpose of ascertaining whether an offence has been committed under this Act search the vessel for any such document;

(*d*) take copies of any such document;

(*e*) inspect any sea fish on, and the equipment of, the vessel, and observe any trans-shipment of sea fish into, the vessel;

(*f*) require any person on the vessel to do anything which appears to the officer to be necessary for facilitating the exercise of his powers under paragraph (*a*), (*c*) or (*e*) above.

(2C) Any person who—

(*a*) without reasonable excuse fails to comply with any requirement imposed under subsection (2A) or (2B) above; or (*b*) assaults an officer who is exercising any of the powers conferred on him by either of those subsections or wilfully obstructs an officer in the exercise of any of those powers,

shall be guilty of an offence and liable[1] on summary conviction to a fine not exceeding **£5,000** or on conviction on indictment to a fine.

(3) Any such officer may exercise in relation to any fishing boat in any waters adjacent to the United Kingdom and within British fishery limits, and in relation to any British fishing boat registered in the United Kingdom and any British owned fishing boat (not so registered) anywhere outside those limits, such of the powers of a British sea-fishery officer under section 8(2) to (4) of the Sea Fisheries Act 1968, as may be conferred on him by order of the Ministers, being powers which the Ministers, consider necessary for the enforcement of any of the provisions of sections 1 to 7 of this Act or any order made under any of those sections.

(3A) The powers which may be conferred on any such officer by an order under this section shall include power to—

(*a*) require any person on board the boat to produce—

    (i) any automatic recording equipment or transmitting equipment used in accordance with a condition included in a licence by virtue of section 4(6) or 4A(6) of this Act, or

    (ii) any record produced by means of such equipment, or partly by those and partly by other means;

(*b*) search the boat for any such equipment or record, and require any person on board the boat to do anything which appears to the officer to be necessary to facilitate the search;

(*c*) examine and take copies of any such record;

(*d*) seize and detain any such equipment or record for the purpose of enabling that equipment or record, or any record which may be produced by means of that equipment, to be used as evidence in proceedings for any offence.

(3B) An order under this section shall not permit anything which is required to be carried on board the boat by a condition included in a licence by virtue of section 4(6) or 4A(6) of this Act to be seized and detained except while the boat is detained in a port.

(4) An order under this section may make different provisions for different cases.

(5) Section 10 of the Sea Fisheries Act, 1968, shall apply in relation to the provisions of an order under this section and the powers thereby conferred as they apply in relation to section 8 of that Act and the powers thereby conferred; and, in relation to an offence under the said section 10 as it applies by virtue of this subsection, sections 12 to 14 of that Act shall apply accordingly.

[Sea Fish (Conservation) Act 1967, s 15, as amended by the Sea Fisheries Act 1968, the Fishery Limits Act 1976, Sch 2, the Fisheries Act 1981, s 25 and the Sea Fish (Conservation) Act 1992, s 6.]

---

1. For procedure in respect of this offence which is triable either way, see the Magistrates' Courts Act 1980, ss 17A–21, in PART I: MAGISTRATES' COURTS, PROCEDURE, ante.

8–11025   16. Enforcement of orders under ss 1 and 2. (1) With a view to enforcing any order under section 1 of this Act, and with a view to enforcing section 2 thereof, any of the following officers, that is to say—

(*a*) any officer authorised by the appropriate Minister,

(*aa*) any British sea-fishery officer[1],

(*b*) any police officer,

(*c*) any officer of a market authority, acting within the limits of any market which that authority has power to regulate,

(*d*) any fishery officer of a local fisheries committee acting within the district of the committee, and

(*e*) any officer authorised by the Fishmongers' Company and acting within the City of London,

may, at all reasonable times, go on board any fishing boat or enter any premises used for carrying on any business in connection with the treatment, storage or sale of sea fish, may search for and examine any sea fish in any place, whether on board a fishing boat or elsewhere, and whether in a receptacle or not, and may seize any sea fish which have been landed, sold or exposed or offered for sale by any person in contravention of the said section 1, or which any person has in his possession in contravention of the said section 1 or 2, as the case may be.

(1A) Any person who assaults a officer who is exercising any of the powers conferred on him by subsection (1) above or wilfully obstructs an officer in the exercise of any of those powers shall be guilty of an offence and liable[2] on summary conviction to a fine not exceeding **the statutory maximum** or on conviction on indictment to a fine.

(2) For the purposes of this section the district of a local fisheries committee shall be deemed to extend throughout the area of any council liable to pay, or contribute to the payment of, the expenses of the committee, except that the powers conferred by this section on the committee or any officer thereof shall not be exercisable in respect of any matter arising within the limits of any market under the control of the council of any county borough or county district.

(3) An officer shall not be liable in any civil or criminal proceedings for anything done in the

purported exercise of the powers conferred on him by this section if the court is satisfied that the act was done in good faith and there were reasonable grounds for doing it.
[Sea Fish (Conservation) Act 1967, s 16, as amended by the Fisheries Act 1981, s 25 and the Criminal Justice Act 1991, Sch 4.]

---

1. For the meaning of British sea-fishery officer, see s 22, post.
2. For procedure in respect of this offence which is triable either way, see the Magistrates' Courts Act 1980, ss 17A–21, in PART I: MAGISTRATES' COURTS, PROCEDURE, ante.

8–11026 22. Interpretation. (1) In this Act, except in so far as the context otherwise requires, the following expressions have the meanings hereby assigned to them respectively, that is to say—

"British-owned", in relation to a fishing boat, means owned by a person who is for the purposes of Part II of the Merchant Shipping Act 1995 a person qualified to own a British ship, or owned by two or more persons any one of whom is for those purposes a person so qualified;

"British sea-fishery officer" means any person who by virtue of section 7 of the Sea Fisheries Act 1968[1] is a British sea-fishery officer;

"fishing boat" means a vessel of whatever size, and in whatever way propelled, which is for the time being employed in sea fishing or (except in section 5 and except in section 15 in so far as that section applies to ss 5 and 6 of this Act and orders made under those sections) the sea fishing service;

"the Fishmongers' Company" means the wardens and commonalty of the Mystery of Fishmongers in the City of London;

"local fisheries committee" means a local fisheries committee constituted by an order made, or having effect as if made, under section 1 of the Sea Fisheries Regulations Act 1966;

"market authority" means any person having power to regulate a market;

"master" includes, in relation to any vessel, the person for the time being in command or charge of the vessel;

"migratory trout" means trout which migrate to and from the sea;

"processing" (in relation to fish) includes preserving or preparing fish, or producing any substance or article from fish, by any method for human or animal consumption;

"salmon" includes any fish of the salmon species;

"sea fish" means fish, whether fresh or cured, of any kind found in the sea, including shellfish, and any parts of any such fish but (except in sections 4, 4A, 5, 6, 7 and 9) does not include salmon or migratory trout;

"shellfish" includes crustaceans and molluscs of any kind and any spat or spawn of shellfish;

"vessel" includes any ship or boat or any other description of vessel used in navigation.

(2) In this Act "the appropriate Minister"[2], in relation to England means the Minister of Agriculture, Fisheries and Food, in relation to Wales, means the Secretary of State concerned with the sea fishing industry in Wales, and, in relation to Scotland, means the Secretary of State concerned with the sea fishing industry in Scotland, and "the Ministers"—

(a) except in sections 1(1) and (2) and 9(1) and (4) of this Act means the Minister of Agriculture, Fisheries and Food and the Secretaries of State respectively concerned with the sea fishing industry in Scotland, Wales and Northern Ireland;

(b) in the said sections 1(1) and (2) and 9(1) means the Minister of Agriculture, Fisheries and Food and the Secretaries of State respectively concerned with the sea fishing industry in Scotland and Wales;

(c) in the said section 9(4) means the Minister of Agriculture, Fisheries and Food, the Secretaries of State respectively concerned with the sea fishing industry in Scotland and Wales and the Ministry of Agriculture for Northern Ireland.

(3) Anything which is required or authorised under this Act to be done by the Ministers shall be done by the Ministers acting in conjunction.

(4) Except in so far as the context otherwise requires, references in this Act to any enactment are references to that enactment as amended by or under any other enactment.
[Sea Fish (Conservation) Act 1967, s 22 as amended by the Fisheries Act 1981, ss 19, 21 and 45, and Sch 5, the Merchant Shipping (Registration, etc) Act 1993, Sch 2 and the Merchant Shipping Act 1995, Sch 13.]

---

1. See post.
2. Functions of the Secretary of State, the Secretary of State for Scotland or the Secretary of State for Wales under this Act (except for sections 6, 8 and 19 so far as they relate to any function originally exercisable by the Board of Trade) have been transferred to the Minister of Agriculture, Fisheries and Food by the Transfer of Functions (Agriculture and Fisheries) Order 2000, SI 2000/1812.

8–11027 25. *Repeals, savings and consequential amendment.*

Sea Fisheries Act 1968
(1968 c 77)

Regulation of sea fishing operations

8–11130   5. Regulation of conduct of fishing operations.   (1) The Ministers[1] may, whenever it appears to them necessary or expedient, by order make provision for regulating the conduct of, and safeguarding, fishing operations and operations ancillary thereto, including provision with respect to the identification and marking of fishing boats[2] and fishing gear.

(2) The provisions of any order under subsection (1) above shall, except as provided by the order, apply—

    (*a*)   to all British fishing boats[2], and things done by such boats and their crews, wherever they may be, and

    (*b*)   to all foreign fishing boats[2], and things done by such boats and their crews, in waters within British fishery limits.

(3) The Ministers[1] may by order make such provisions as is mentioned in subsection (1) above with respect to foreign fishing boats[2] which, in pursuance of an arrangement for the time being in force between Her Majesty's Government in the United Kingdom and the government of any other country, enter British fishery limits[3] for the purpose of carrying on fishing operations or operations ancillary thereto, including provisions regulating the movement of those boats within those limits.

(4) Where a provision of an order under this section is not complied with in the case of a fishing boat[2] or its crew, any person prescribed by the order in relation to that provision, being one or more of the following, that is to say the master[2], the owner and the charterer, if any, shall be liable[4] on summary conviction to a fine not exceeding **the statutory maximum** or on conviction on indictment to a fine.

(5) The provisions of any order under this section shall be taken to be in addition to and not to derogate from the provisions of any other enactment or any instrument made under any other enactment.

[Sea Fisheries Act 1968, s 5, as amended by the Fishery Limits Act 1976, s 4 and Schs 1 and 2, the Fisheries Act 1981, s 24 and the Criminal Justice Act 1991, Sch 4.]

---

1. In England and Wales this will be the Minister of Agriculture, Fisheries and Food (s 19, post). (See also the Transfer of Functions (Agriculture and Fisheries) Order 2000, SI 2000/1812.) The functions of the Minister, so far as exercisable in relation to Wales, have been transferred to the National Assembly for Wales, by the National Assembly for Wales (Transfer of Functions) Order 1999, SI 1999/672, art 2, Sch 1.

2. For definition of "fishing boat", "British fishing boat", "foreign fishing boat", and "master" see s 19, post. (See also the Transfer of Functions (Agriculture and Fisheries) Order 2000, SI 2000/1812). The definition of "master" and "fishing boat" should be compared with those in the Sea Fish (Conservation) Act 1967, s 22, ante. The Third Country Fishing (Enforcement) Regulations made under s 2(2) of the European Communities Act 1972 on an annual basis, make breaches of certain Community regulations in British fishery limits, triable either way. Obstruction of a British sea-fishery officer is punishable on summary conviction by a fine not exceeding **level 5** on the standard scale. For other similar regulations see note to s 2 of the European Communities Act 1972, in PART I: MAGISTRATES' COURTS, PROCEDURE, ante.

3. See the Fishery Limits Act 1976, s 1, post.

4. For procedure in respect of this offence which is triable either way, see the Magistrates' Courts Act 1980, ss 17A–21, in PART I: MAGISTRATES' COURTS, PROCEDURE, ante.

8–11131   7. Sea-fishery officers.   (1) The following persons shall be British sea-fishery officers for the purposes of the Sea Fisheries Acts, that is to say—

    (*a*)   officers of the sea-fishery inspectorates of each of the appropriate Ministers other than assistant fishery officers;

    (*b*)   commissioned officers of any of Her Majesty's ships;

    (*c*)   persons in command or charge of any aircraft or hovercraft of the Royal Navy, the Army or the Royal Air Force;

    (*d*)   officers of the fishery protection service of the Secretary of State holding the rank of commander, first officer or second officer;

    (*e*) and (*f*)   (*Repealed*);

    (*g*)   other persons appointed as British sea-fishery officers by one of the appropriate Ministers.

(2) The appropriate Minister may appoint any person to exercise and perform the powers and duties of a British sea-fishery officer subject to such limitations as may be specified in the instrument appointing him; and for the purposes of the Sea Fisheries Acts a person so appointed shall be a British sea-fishery officer within those limitations, but not otherwise.

(3) An appointment made under subsection (2) above may be limited in any one or more of the following ways, that is to say—

    (*a*)   to particular matters;

    (*b*)   to a particular area;

    (*c*)   to a particular order or class of orders.

(4) In this Act, "foreign sea-fishery officer", in relation to any convention with respect to the conduct or safeguarding of fishing operations or operations ancillary thereto to which Her Majesty's

Government in the United Kingdom is a party, means a person of any class specified in an order[1] made by the Ministers, being a person appointed by the government of any other country which is a party to the convention to enforce its provisions or any other person having power under the laws of that other country to enforce those provisions.

(5)　in this section "the appropriate Minister" means—

(a)　in relation to England and Wales[2], the Minister of Agriculture, Fisheries and Food;
(b)　in relation to Scotland, the Secretary of State; and
(c)　in relation to Northern Ireland, the Ministry of Agriculture for Northern Ireland.

[Sea Fisheries Act 1968. s 7, as amended by the Fisheries Act 1981, s 26.]

1.　See for example the Foreign Sea-Fishery Officers Order 1976, SI 1976/1103 (officers appointed by the Icelandic Government).

2.　Functions of the Secretary of State and the Secretary of State for Wales under this section have been transferred to the Minister of Agriculture, Fisheries and Food by the Transfer of Functions (Agriculture and Fisheries) Order 2000, SI 2000/1812.

8–11132　8.　General powers of British officers.　(1)　For the purpose of enforcing the provisions of any order under section 5 above or of section 2 of the Fishery Limits Act 1976 or any order thereunder a British sea-fishery officer may exercise in relation to any fishing boat within British fishery limits and in relation to any British fishing boat anywhere outside those limits the powers conferred by subsections (2) to 4) below.

(2)　He may go on board the boat, with or without persons assigned to assist him in his duties, and for that purpose may require the boat to stop and do anything else which will facilitate the boarding of the boat.

(3)　He may require the attendance of the master and other persons on board the boat and may make any examination and inquiry which appears to him to be necessary for the purpose mentioned in subsection (1) above and, in particular,—

(a)　may examine any fish on the boat and equipment of the boat, including the fishing gear, and require persons on board the boat to do anything which appears to him to be necessary for facilitating the examination; and
(b)　may require any person on board the boat to produce any document relating to the boat, to its fishing operations or other operations ancillary thereto or to the persons on board which is in his custody or possession and may take copies of any such document;
(c)　for the purpose of ascertaining whether the master, owner or charterer of the boat has committed an offence under any of the provisions mentioned in subsection (1) above, may search the boat for any such document and may require any person on board the boat to do anything which appears to him to be necessary for facilitating the search;
(d)　where the boat is one in relation to which he has reason to suspect that such an offence has been committed, may seize and detain any such document produced to him or found on board for the purpose of enabling the document to be used as evidence in proceedings for the offence;

but nothing in paragraph (d) above shall permit any document required by law to be carried on board the boat to be seized and detained except while the boat is detained in a port.

(4)　Where it appears to a British sea-fishery officer that a contravention of any provision of an order under section 5 above or of section 2 of the Fishery Limits Act 1976 or any order thereunder has at any time taken place within British fishery limits, he may—

(a)　require the master of the boat in relation to which the contravention took place to take, or may himself take, the boat and its crew to the port which appears to him to be the nearest convenient port; and
(b)　detain or require the master to detain the boat in the port;

and where such an officer detains or requires the detention of a boat he shall serve on the master a notice in writing stating that the boat will be or is required to be detained until the notice is withdrawn by the service on the master of a further notice in writing signed by a British sea-fishery officer.

(5)　If it appears to a British sea-fishery officer that a British fishing boat or a fishing boat belonging to a country which is party to a convention to which Her Majesty's Government in the United Kingdom is a party is being so navigated or stationed as to interfere or be likely to interfere with fishing operations which are being carried on, or about to be carried on, within British fishery limits, he may require the boat to move away or to move in a direction or to a position specified by him.

(6)　For the purpose of enforcing the collision regulations made under section 85 of the Merchant Shipping Act 1995, so far as they apply to fishing boats, a British sea-fishery officer may exercise, in relation to any fishing boat within British fishery limits and in relation to a British fishing boat anywhere outside those limits, the powers conferred by section 257 of the Merchant Shipping Act 1995 (powers to require production of ships documents), whether or not he is mentioned in section 257, and also the powers conferred by the foregoing provisions of this section, and section 723(2) of that Act so far as it relates to the former powers shall apply accordingly.

[Sea Fisheries Act 1968, s 8, as amended by the Fishery Limits Act 1976, s 2 and Sch 2, the Fisheries Act 1981, s 26 and the Merchant Shipping Act 1995, Sch 13.]

8–11133   9. Powers of sea-fishery officers to enforce conventions.   (1) For the purpose of enforcing the provisions of any convention with respect to the conduct or safeguarding of fishing operations to which Her Majesty's Government in the United Kingdom is a party a foreign sea-fishery officer may, in relation to a British fishing boat, and a British sea-fishery officer may, in relation to any foreign fishing boat, exercise anywhere within the convention area outside British fishery limits the powers conferred by section 8(2) and (3) above.

(2) Nothing in this section shall authorise a British or foreign sea-fishery officer to do anything not authorised by the convention he is purporting to enforce or authorize him to exercise in relation to a boat belonging to a country which is a party to the convention any power which the government of that country has informed the other parties to the convention is not to be exercised in relation to its fishing boats.

[Sea Fisheries Act 1968, s 9, as amended by the Fishery Limits Act 1976, Sch 2.]

8–11134   10. Miscellaneous provisions as to sea-fishery officers.   (1) A British sea-fishery officer shall not be liable in any civil or criminal proceedings for anything done in the purported exercise of the powers conferred on him by section 8 or 9 of this Act, section 15 of the Sea Fish (Convention) Act 1967 or section 27 of the Fisheries Act 1981, and a foreign sea-fishery officer[1] shall not be liable in any such proceedings for anything done in purported exercise of the powers conferred on him by section 9 of this Act, if the court is satisfied that the act was done in good faith and that there were reasonable grounds for doing it.

(2) Any person who on any fishing boat[2] within British fishery limits[3], or on a British fishing boat anywhere outside those limits,—

(a)   fails without reasonable cause to comply with any requirement imposed, or to answer any question asked, by a British sea-fishery officer under section 8 or 9 of this Act;

(b)   prevents, or attempts to prevent, any other person from complying with any such requirement or answering any such question; or

(c)   assaults any such officer while exercising any of the powers conferred on him by or by virtue of section 8 or 9 of this Act or wilfully obstructs any such officer in the exercise of any of those powers;

shall be guilty of an offence.

(2A) Any person who on any vessel within British fishery limits—

(a)   fails without reasonable excuse to comply with any requirement imposed, or to answer any question asked, by a British sea-fishery officer under section 27 of the Fisheries Act 1981;

(b)   prevents, or attempts to prevent, any other person complying with any such requirement or answering any such question; or

(c)   assaults any such officer while exercising any of the powers conferred on him by that section or wilfully obstructs any such officer in the exercise of any of those powers;

shall be guilty of an offence.

(3) Subsection (2) above shall apply in relation to things done on a British fishing boat[2] anywhere within the convention area outside British fishery limits[3] by or in relation to a foreign sea-fishery officer[1] who is exercising powers to enforce the provisions of the convention relating to that area as it applies in relation to things done on any fishing boat within those limits by or in relation to a British sea-fishery officer[1].

(4) A person guilty of an offence under this section shall be liable[4] on summary conviction to a fine not exceeding £5,000 or on conviction on indictment to a fine.

[Sea Fisheries Act 1968, s 10, as amended by the Fishery Limits Act 1976, Schs 1 and 2 and the Fisheries Act 1981, ss 24 and 26.]

---

1. For meaning of British or foreign sea-fishery officer, see s 7, ante.
2. Defined by s 19, post.
3. See the Fishery Limits Act 1976, s 1, post.
4. For procedure in respect of this offence which is triable either way, see the Magistrates' Courts Act 1980, ss 17A–21, in PART I: MAGISTRATES' COURTS, PROCEDURE, ante.

8–11135   11. Evidence.   (1) In any civil or criminal proceedings a written statement purporting to be a report made by a British or foreign sea-fishery officer[1] on matters ascertained in the course of exercising his powers under section 9 above for the purpose of enforcing the provisions of any convention mentioned in that section shall be admissible as evidence to the like extent as oral evidence to the like effect by that officer.

(2) Subsection (1) above shall be taken to be in addition to, and not to derogate from, the provisions of any other enactment relating to the reception or admissibility of documentary evidence.

[Sea Fisheries Act 1968, s 11.]

---

1. For meaning of British or foreign sea-fishery officer, see s 7, ante.

8–11136   12. Recovery of fines imposed on master, etc, or crew.   (1) Where a fine is imposed by a magistrates' court in England and Wales or Northern Ireland on the master[1], owner or charterer or a member of the crew of a fishing boat[1] who is convicted by the court of an offence under section 5 or 10 of this Act, or under section 2 of the Fishery Limits Act 1976, the court may—

(a)   issue a warrant of distress against the boat and its gear and catch and any property of the person convicted for the purpose of levying the amount of the fine; and

(b)   if the boat is a foreign fishing boat[1], order it to be detained for a period not exceeding three months from the date of the conviction or until the fine is paid or the amount of the fine is levied in pursuance of any such warrant, whichever occurs first.

(2) *Applies to Scotland.*

(3) Sections 77(1) and 78 of the Magistrates' Courts Act 1980 (postponement of issue of, and defects in, warrants of distress), shall apply to a warrant of distress issued under this section in England and Wales as they apply to a warrant of distress issued under Part III of that Act.

(4) *Applies to Northern Ireland.*

[Sea Fisheries Act 1968, s 12, as amended by the Fishery Limits Act 1976, s 2 and the Magistrates' Courts Act 1980, Sch 7.]

----

1. "Master", "fishing boat" and "foreign fishing boat" are defined in s 19, post.

8–11137   13. Compensation for damage caused by offence.   (1) (*Repealed*).

(2)–(3) *Applies to Scotland.*

(4) The provisions of this section shall not be taken to derogate from any right of a person who has suffered personal injury or damage to property in consequence of an offence under section 5 or 10 of this Act or under Section 2 of the Fishery Limits Act 1976 to recover damages in respect of the injury or damage in civil proceedings.

[Sea Fisheries Act 1968, s 13, as amended by the Fishery Limits Act 1976, s 2.]

8–11138   14. Jurisdiction to try offences.   Proceedings for an offence under section 5 or 10 of this Act or under Section 2 of the Fishery Limits Act 1976 may be taken, and the offence may for all incidental purposes be treated as having been committed, in any place in the United Kingdom.

[Sea Fisheries Act 1968, s 14, as amended by the Fishery Limits Act 1976, s 2.]

8–11139   19. Interpretation.   (1) In this Act, except so far as the context otherwise requires—

"British fishing boat" means a fishing boat which either is registered in the United Kingdom under Part II of the Merchant Shipping Act 1995 or is wholly British owned";

"convention" includes an agreement or other arrangement;

"convention area" means, in relation to any international convention, the area to which the convention relates;

"enactment" includes an enactment of the Parliament of Northern Ireland;

"fish" includes shellfish, and cognate expressions shall be construed accordingly;

"fishing boat" means any vessel for the time being employed in fishing operations or any operations ancillary thereto;

"foreign fishing boat" means any fishing boat other than a British fishing boat;

"foreign sea-fishery officer" has the meaning assigned to it by section 7 of this Act;

"master" includes, in relation to any fishing boat, the person for the time being in command or charge of the boat;

"the Ministers" means the Minister of Agriculture, Fisheries and Food and the Secretaries of State respectively concerned with the sea fishing industry in Scotland and Northern Ireland;

"Sea Fisheries Acts" means any enactments for the time being in force relating to sea-fishing, including any enactment relating to fishing for shellfish, salmon or migratory trout;

"wholly British-owned" means wholly owned by persons qualified to own British ships for the purposes of Part II of the Merchant Shipping Act 1995.

(2) *Repealed.*

(3) Any reference in this Act to any other enactment is a reference thereto as amended and includes a reference thereto as extended or applied by or under any other enactment, including this Act.

[Sea Fisheries Act 1968, s 19, as amended by Sea Fish Industry Act 1970, Sch, the Fishery Limits Act 1976, Sch 2, the Merchant Shipping Act 1988, Sch 6 and the Merchant Shipping Act 1995, Sch 13.]

Sea Fish Industry Acts 1970

(1970 c 11)

8–11250   By the 1970 Act (as amended by the Sea Fish Industry Act 1973 and the Fishery Limits Act 1976) the White Fish Authority established by the Sea Fish Industry Act 1951, is continued with the Scottish Committee and the White Fish Industry Advisory Council to advise the authority in the exercise and performance of their functions. The general functions of the authority are to reorganise, develop and regulate the white fish industry.

The Authority may make regulations relating to the handling of white fish and for other purposes. Persons engaged in the industry are registered and their fishing vessels licensed.

Prescribed records shall be kept and produced to the Authority as required.

The Authority's officers are given powers of entry and, if necessary, a justice may grant a warrant for this purpose.

Various offences against the Act are punishable on summary conviction but prosecutions have rarely arisen under the previous statute.

Salmon and Freshwater Fisheries Act 1975[1]

(1975 c 51)

PART I[2]
PROHIBITION OF CERTAIN MODES OF TAKING OR DESTROYING FISH, ETC

8–11260 **1. Prohibited implements.** (1) Subject to subsection (4) below, no person shall—

(*a*) use any of the following instruments, that is to say—

    (i) a firearm within the meaning of the Firearms Act 1968;
    (ii) an otter lath or jack, wire or snare;
    (iii) a crossline or setline;
    (iv) a spear, gaff, stroke-haul, snatch or other like instrument[3];
    (v) a light;
    for the purpose of taking or killing salmon, trout or freshwater fish[4];

(*b*) have in his possession any instrument mentioned in paragraph (*a*) above intending to use it to take or kill salmon, trout or freshwater fish; or

(*c*) throw or discharge any stone or other missile for the purpose of taking or killing, or facilitating the taking or killing of any salmon, trout or freshwater fish.

(2) If any person contravenes this section, he shall be guilty of an offence[5] unless he proves to the satisfaction of the court that the act was done for the purpose of the preservation or development of a private fishery and with the previous permission in writing of the National Rivers Authority.

(3) In this section—

"crossline" means a fishing line reaching from bank to bank across water and having attached to it one or more lures or baited hooks;

"otter lath or jack" includes any small boat or vessel, board, stick or other instrument, whether used with a hand line, or as auxiliary to a rod and line, or otherwise for the purpose of running out lures, artificial or otherwise;

"setline" means a fishing line left unattended in water and having attached to it one or more lures or baited hooks;

"stroke-haul or snatch" includes any instrument or device, whether used with a rod and line or otherwise, for the purpose of foul hooking any fish.

(4) This section shall not apply to any person using a gaff (consisting of a plain metal hook without a barb) or tailer as auxiliary to angling with a rod and line or having such a gaff or a tailer in his possession intending to use it as aforesaid.

[Salmon and Freshwater Fisheries Act 1975, s 1 as amended by the Water Act 1989, Schs 17 and 27.]

---

1. For general modification of references to the National Rivers Authority, however framed, in this Act and subordinate legislation, see the Environment Act 1995, Sch 15, title PUBLIC HEALTH, post.
2. Part I contains ss 1–5.
3. A net with a mesh smaller than that allowed by s 3 is not an "instrument" *eiusdem generis* with the other things specified in this section (*Jones v Davies* [1898] 1 QB 405, 62 JP 182).
4. See s 41 for definitions, post.
5. For prosecution and punishment of offences, see Sch 4, post.

8–11261 **2. Roe, spawning and unclean fish, etc.** (1) Subject to subsection (5) below, any person who, for the purposes of fishing for salmon, trout or freshwater fish[1]—

(*a*) uses any fish roe; or
(*b*) buys, sells, or exposes for sale[2], or has in his possession any roe of salmon or trout;

shall be guilty of an offence[3].

(2) Subject to subsections (3) and (5) below, any person who—

(*a*) knowingly takes, kills or injures, or attempts to take, kill or injure, any salmon, trout or freshwater fish which is unclean or immature[4]; or

(*b*) buys, sells, or exposes for sale[5], or has in his possession any salmon, trout or freshwater fish which is unclean or immature[4] or any part of any such fish, shall be guilty of an offence[3].

(3) Subsection (2) above does not apply to any person who takes a fish accidentally and returns it to the water with the least possible injury.

(4) Subject to subsection (5) below, any person who, except in the exercise of a legal right to take materials from any waters, wilfully disturbs any spawn or spawning fish, or any bed, bank or shallow on which any spawn or spawning fish may be, shall be guilty of an offence[5].

(5) A person shall not be guilty of an offence under this section in respect of any act, if he does the act for the purpose of the artificial propagation of salmon, trout or freshwater fish or for some scientific purpose or for the purpose of the preservation or development of a private fishery and has obtained the previous permission in writing of the National Rivers Authority.
[Salmon and Freshwater Fisheries Act 1975, s 2 as amended by the Water Act 1989, Schs 17 and 27.]

---

1. See s 41 for definitions, post.
2. See discussion of the phrases "offers for sale", "exposes for sale" in *Keating v Horwood* (1926) 90 JP 141; also in *British Car Auctions Ltd v Wright* [1972] 3 All ER 462 and in cases therein referred to.
3. For prosecution and punishment of offences, see Sch 4, post.
4. "Unclean" and "immature" are defined by s 41, post. The defendant cannot be convicted if he did not know that the fish were the young of salmon etc (*Hopton v Thirlwall* (1863) 27 JP 743); but a person may be convicted although the constable who found the young of salmon in the defendant's pocket had no right to search him (*Jones v Owens* (1870) 34 JP 759).
5. For prosecution and punishment of offences, see Sch 4, post.
Section 2(4) creates two offences: wilful disturbance of any spawn or spawning fish and wilful disturbance of any bank, bed or shallow on which spawn or spawning fish might be. Only the defences in section 2 may be raised; a person charged is not entitled to raise a defence that he was a riparian owner with the right to cross the river either on foot or by any other means (*National Rivers Authority v Jones* (1992) Times, 10 March).

8–11262   3. Nets.   (1) Any person who shoots or works any seine or draft net for salmon or migratory trout in any waters across more than three-fourths of the width of those waters shall be guilty of an offence[1].

(2) Subject to subsection (3) below, any person who, except in a place where smaller dimensions are authorised by byelaw, takes or attempts to take salmon or migratory trout with any net that has a mesh of less dimensions than 2 inches in extension from knot to knot (the measurement to be made on each side of the square), or 8 inches measured round each mesh when wet, shall be guilty of an offence[1].

(3) In subsection (2) above "net" does not include a landing net in use as auxiliary to angling with rod and line.

(4) The placing of two or more nets the one behind the other or near to each other in such manner as practically to diminish the mesh of the nets used, or the covering of the nets used with canvas, or the using any other device so as to evade subsection (2) above, shall be deemed to be a contravention of that subsection[2].
[Salmon and Freshwater Fisheries Act 1975, s 3.]

---

1. For prosecution and punishment of offences, see Sch 4, post.
2. A trammel net is illegal (*Dodd v Armor* (1867) 31 JP 773).

8–11263   4. Poisonous matter and polluting effluent.   (1) Subject to subsection (2) below, any person who causes[1] or knowingly permits to flow, or puts or knowingly permits to be put, into any waters containing fish or into any tributaries of waters containing fish, any liquid or solid matter to such an extent as to cause the waters to be poisonous or injurious to fish or the spawning grounds, spawn or food of fish, shall be guilty of an offence[2].

(2) A person shall not be guilty of an offence under subsection (1) above for any act done in the exercise of any right to which he is by law entitled[3] or in continuance of a method in use in connection with the same premises before 18 July 1923, if he proves to the satisfaction of the court that he has used the best practicable means, within a reasonable cost, to prevent such matter from doing injury to fish or to the spawning grounds, spawn or food of fish.

(3) Proceedings under this section shall not be instituted except by the National Rivers Authority or by a person who has first obtained a certificate from the Minister that he has a material interest in the waters alleged to be affected.
[Salmon and Freshwater Fisheries Act 1975, s 4 as amended by the Water Act 1989, Schs 17 and 27.]

---

1. See *Alphacell Ltd v Woodward* [1972] AC 824, [1972] 2 All ER 475, 136 JP 505; and cases referred to therein. The offence of "causing" requires proof of some positive act leading to that result (*Price v Cromack* [1975] 2 All ER 113, 139 JP 423).
2. For prosecution and punishment of offences, see Sch 4, post.
3. A person shall not be guilty of an offence under this section in respect of any entry of matter into any controlled waters (within the meaning of Part III of the Water Resources Act 1991) which occurs—(*a*) under and in accordance with a consent under Chapter II of Part III of the Water Resources Act 1991 or under Part II of the Control of Pollution Act 1974 (which makes corresponding provision for Scotland); or (*b*) as a result of any act or omission under and in accordance with such a consent. (Water Consolidation (Consequential Provisions) Act 1991, Sch 1).

8–11264   5. Prohibition of use of explosives, poisons or electrical devices and of destruction of dams, etc.   (1) Subject to subsection (2) below, no person shall use in or near any waters (including waters adjoining the coast of England and Wales to a distance of six nautical miles measured from the baselines from which the breadth of the territorial sea is measured[1] any explosive substance, any poison or other noxious substance, or any electrical device, with intent thereby to take or destroy fish.

(2) Subsection (1) above shall not apply to the use by a person of any substance or device—

(a) for a scientific purpose, or for the purpose of protecting, improving or replacing stocks of fish; and

(b) with the permission in writing of the National Rivers Authority.

(3) No person shall, without lawful excuse, destroy or damage any dam, flood-gate or sluice with intent thereby to take or destroy fish.

(4) A person who contravenes subsection (1) or (3) above or who, for the purpose of contravening subsection (1) above, has in his possession any explosive or noxious substance or any electrical device, shall be guilty of an offence[2].

(5) The use of any substance in any waters for a purpose falling within paragraph (a) of subsection (2) above, and with the permission mentioned in paragraph (b) of that subsection, shall not constitute an offence under—

(a) section 4 above;

(b) any byelaws made under paragraph 31 of Schedule 3 below;

(c) section 85(1) of the Water Resources Act 1991; or

(d) section 22(1)(a) of the Rivers (Prevention of Pollution) (Scotland) Act 1951.

[Salmon and Freshwater Fisheries Act 1975, s 5, as amended by the Fishery Limits Act 1976, Sch 2, the Water Act 1989, Schs 17 and 27, the Water Consolidation (Consequential Provisions) Act 1991, Sch 1 and the Environment Act 1995, Schs 15 and 24.]

---

1. Baselines are drawn in accordance with the Territorial Waters Order in Council, 1964, made on 25 September 1964.
2. For prosecution and punishment of offences, see Sch 4, post.

PART II[1]
OBSTRUCTIONS TO PASSAGE OF FISH

8–11265 6. Fixed engines. (1) Any person who places[2] or uses an unauthorised fixed engine[3] in any inland or tidal waters[4] which are within the area of any water authority shall be guilty of an offence[5].

(2) A person acting under directions to that effect given by the National Rivers Authority may take possession of or destroy an engine placed or used in contravention of this section.

(3) In subsection (1) above "unauthorised fixed engine" means any fixed engine other than—

(a) a fixed engine certified in pursuance of the Salmon Fishery Act 1865 to be a privileged fixed engine; or

(b) a fixed engine which was in use for taking salmon or migratory trout during the open season of 1861, in pursuance of an ancient right[6] or mode of fishing as lawfully exercised during that open season, by virtue of any grant or charter or immemorial usage; or

(c) a fixed engine the placing and use of which is authorised by byelaws made by a water authority or by byelaws made by a local fisheries committee by virtue of section 37(2) of the Salmon Act 1986.

(d) a fixed engine which is placed and used by the Agency with the consent of, or in accordance with a general authorisation given by, the Minister or the Secretary of State.

[Salmon and Freshwater Fisheries Act 1975, s 6 as amended by the Salmon Act 1986 s 33, the Territorial Sea Act 1987, Sch 1, the Water Act 1989, Schs 17 and 27, the Water Consolidation (Consequential Provisions) Act 1991, Sch 3 and the Environment Act 1995, Sch 15.]

---

1. Part II contains ss 6–18.
2. Section 6(1)(a) creates an absolute offence (*Champion v Maughan* [1984] 1 All ER 680, [1984] 1 WLR 469). See also *Gray v Blamey* [1991] 1 All ER 1, [1991] 1 WLR 47, [1990] Crim LR 746, DC.
3. "Fixed engine" is defined by s 41, post.
4. Justices are entitled to use their own local knowledge in finding whether waters are tidal or not. It cannot be concluded that tidal waters do not include the sea itself. It is necessary that there shall be some movement by way of ebb and flow (*Ingram v Percival* [1969] 1 QB 548, [1968] 3 All ER 657, 133 JP 1).
5. For prosecution and punishment of offences, see Sch 4, post.
6. Where an ancient right is set up *bona fide*, the justices must decline to adjudicate (*Raby v Seed* (1854) 29 JP 37).

8–11266 7. Fishing weirs. (1) No unauthorised fishing weir shall be used for taking or facilitating the taking of salmon or migratory trout.

(2) Where a fishing weir extends more than halfway across any river at its lowest state of water, it shall not be used for the purpose of taking salmon or migratory trout unless it has in it a free gap or opening situated in the deepest part of the river between the points where it is intercepted by the weir, and—

(a) the sides of the gap are in a line with and parallel to the direction of the stream at the weir; and

(b) the bottom of the gap is level with the natural bed of the river above and below the gap; and

(c) the width of the gap in its narrowest part is not less than one-tenth part of the width of the river.

(3) A free gap need not be more than 40 feet wide and must not be less than 3 feet wide.

(4) If any person uses a weir in contravention of this section or makes any alteration in the bed of a river in such manner as to reduce the flow of water through a free gap, he shall be guilty of an offence[1].

(5) In subsection (1) above "unauthorised fishing weir" means any fishing weir which was not lawfully in use on 6th August 1861, by virtue of a grant or charter or immemorial usage.
[Salmon and Freshwater Fisheries Act 1975, s 7.]

---

1. For prosecution and punishment of offences, see Sch 4, post.

8-11267   8. Fishing mill dams.   (1) No unauthorised fishing mill dam shall be used for taking or facilitating the taking of salmon or migratory trout.

(2) A fishing mill dam shall not be used for the purpose of taking salmon or migratory trout unless it has attached to it a fish pass of such form and dimensions as may be approved by the Agency, and unless the fish pass is maintained in such a condition and has constantly running through it such a flow of water as will enable salmon and migratory trout to pass up and down the pass.

(3) If any person—

(a) uses an unauthorised fishing mill dam as mentioned in subsection (1) above; or

(b) uses or attempts to use a dam in contravention of subsection (2) above,

he shall be guilty of an offence[1].

(4) If a fishing mill dam has not a fish pass attached to it as required by law, the right of using the fishing mill dam for the purpose of taking fish shall be deemed to have ceased and be for ever forfeited, and the water Agency may remove from it any cage, crib, trap, box, cruive or other obstruction to the free passage of the fish.

(5) In subsection (1) above "unauthorised fishing mill dam" means any fishing mill dam which was not lawfully in use on 6th August 1861, by virtue of a grant or charter or immemorial usage.
[Salmon and Freshwater Fisheries Act 1975, s 8, as amended by the Water Act 1989, s 190 and Sch 27 and the Environment Act 1995, Sch 15.]

---

1. For prosecution and punishment of offences, see Sch 4, post.

8-11268   9. Duty to make and maintain fish passes.   (1) Where in any waters frequented by salmon or migratory trout—

(a) a new dam is constructed or an existing dam is raised or otherwise altered so as to create increased obstruction to the passage of salmon or migratory trout, or any other obstruction to the passage of salmon or migratory trout is created, increased or caused; or

(b) a dam which from any cause has been destroyed or taken down to the extent of one-half of its length is rebuilt or reinstated,

the owner or occupier for the time being of the dam or obstruction shall, if so required by notice given by the water Agency and within such reasonable time as may be specified in the notice, make a fish pass for salmon or migratory trout of such form and dimensions as the Agency may approve as part of the structure of, or in connection with, the dam or obstruction, and shall thereafter maintain it in an efficient state.

(2) If any such owner or occupier fails to make such a fish pass, or to maintain such a fish pass in an efficient state, he shall be guilty of an offence[1].

(3) The water authority may cause to be done any work required by this section to be done, and for that purpose may enter on the dam or obstruction or any land adjoining it, and may recover the expenses of doing the work in a summary manner from any person in default.

(4) Nothing in this section—

(a) shall authorise the doing of anything that may injuriously affect any public waterworks or navigable river, canal, or inland navigation, or any dock, the supply of water to which is obtained from any navigable river, canal or inland navigation, under any Act of Parliament; or

(b) shall prevent any person from removing a fish pass for the purpose of repairing or altering a dam or other obstruction, provided that the fish pass is restored to its former state of efficiency within a reasonable time; or

(c) shall apply to any alteration of a dam or other obstruction, unless—

(i)   the alteration consists of a rebuilding or reinstatement of a dam or other obstruction destroyed or taken down to the extent of one-half of its length, or

(ii) the dam or obstruction as altered causes more obstruction to the passage of salmon or migratory trout than was caused by it as lawfully constructed or maintained at any previous date.

[Salmon and Freshwater Fisheries Act 1975, s 9, as amended by the Water Act 1989, s 190 and Sch 27 and the Environment Act 1995, Sch 15.]

---

1. For prosecution and punishment of offences, see Sch 4, post.

8–11269 **10–11.** *Power of water authority to construct and alter fish passes; Minister's consents and approvals for fish passes.*

8–11270 **12. Penalty for injuring or obstructing fish pass or free gap.** (1) If any person—

(a) wilfully alters or injures a fish pass; or

(b) does any act whereby salmon or trout are obstructed or liable to be obstructed in using a fish pass or whereby a fish pass is rendered less efficient; or

(c) alters a dam or the bed or banks of the river so as to render a fish pass less efficient; or

(d) uses any contrivance or does any act whereby salmon or trout are in any way liable to be scared, hindered or prevented from passing through a fish pass,

he shall be guilty of an offence[1], and shall also in every case pay any expenses which may be incurred in restoring the fish pass to its former state of efficiency; and any such expenses may be recovered in a summary manner.

(2) The owner or occupier of a dam shall be deemed to have altered it if it is damaged, destroyed or allowed to fall into a state of disrepair, and if after notice is served on him by the National Rivers Authority he fails to repair or reconstruct it within a reasonable time so as to render the fish pass as efficient as before the damage or destruction.

(3) If any person—

(a) does any act for the purpose of preventing salmon or trout from passing through a fish pass, or takes, or attempts to take, any salmon or trout in its passage through a fish pass; or

(b) places any obstruction, uses any contrivance or does any act whereby salmon or trout may be scared, deterred or in any way prevented from freely entering and passing up and down a free gap at all periods of the year,

he shall be guilty of an offence[1].

(4) This section shall not apply to a temporary bridge or board used for crossing a free gap, and taken away immediately after the person using it has crossed.

[Salmon and Freshwater Fisheries Act 1975, s 12, as amended by the Water Act 1989, s 190 and Sch 27.]

---

1. For prosecution and punishment of offences, see Sch 4, post.

8–11271 **13. Sluices.** (1) Subject to subsection (3) below, unless permission in writing is granted by the National Rivers Authority, any sluices for drawing off the water which would otherwise flow over any dam in waters frequented by salmon or migratory trout shall be kept shut on Sundays and at all times when the water is not required for milling purposes, in such manner as to cause the water to flow through any fish pass in or connected with the dam or, if there is no such fish pass, over the dam.

(2) If any person fails to comply with this section, he shall be guilty of an offence[1].

(3) This section shall not prevent any person opening a sluice for the purpose of letting off water in cases of flood or for milling purposes or when necessary for the purpose of navigation or, subject to previous notice in writing being given to the water authority, for cleaning or repairing the dam or mill or its appurtenances.

[Salmon and Freshwater Fisheries Act 1975, s 13, as amended by the Water Act 1989, s 190 and Sch 27.]

---

1. For prosecution and punishment of offences, see Sch 4, post.

8–11272 **14. Screens.** (1) This section applies in any case where—

(a) by means of any conduit or artificial channel, water is diverted from waters frequented by salmon or migratory trout; and

(b) any of the water so diverted is used for the purposes of a water or canal undertaking or for the purposes of any mill or fish farm;

and in this section "the responsible person" means the owner of the water or canal undertaking or (as the case may be) the occupier of the mill or the owner or occupier of the fish farm.

(2) Where this section applies, the responsible person shall, unless an exemption from the obligation is granted by the Agency, ensure (at his own cost) that there is placed and maintained at the entrance of, or within, the conduit or channel a screen which-

(a) subject to subsection (4) below, prevents the descent of the salmon or migratory trout; and

(b) in a case where any of the water diverted is used for the purposes of a fish farm, prevents the egress of farmed fish from the fish farm by way of the conduit or channel.

(3) Where this section applies, the responsible person shall also, unless an exemption from the

obligation is granted by the Agency, ensure (at his own cost) that there is placed and maintained across any outfall of the conduit or channel a screen which-

(a) prevents salmon or migratory trout from entering the outfall; and

(b) in a case where any of the water diverted is used for the purposes of a fish farm, prevents the egress of farmed fish from the fish farm by way of the outfall.

(4) Where a screen is placed within any conduit or channel pursuant to subsection (2) above, the responsible person shall ensure that a continuous by-wash is provided immediately upstream of the screen, by means of which salmon or migratory trout may return by as direct a route as practicable to the waters from which they entered the conduit or channel (and accordingly nothing in subsection (2) or (3) above applies in relation to a by-wash provided for the purposes of this subsection).

(5) Any screen placed, or by-wash provided, in pursuance of this section shall be so constructed and located as to ensure, so far as reasonably practicable, that salmon or migratory trout are not injured or damaged by it.

(6) No such screen shall be so placed as to interfere with the passage of boats on any navigable canal.

(7) Any exemption under subsection (2) or (3) above may be granted subject to conditions.

(8) If any person who is required to do so by this section fails to ensure that a screen is placed or maintained, or that a by-wash is provided, in accordance with the provisions of this section, he shall be guilty of an offence[1].

(9) In any proceedings for an offence under subsection (8) above, it shall, subject to subsection (10) below, be a defence for the person charged to prove that he took all reasonable precautions and exercised all due diligence to avoid the commission of the offence by himself or a person under his control.

(10) If in any case the defence provided by subsection (9) above involves the allegation that the commission of the offence was due to an act or default of another person, or to reliance on information supplied by another person, the person charged shall not, without leave of the court, be entitled to rely on that defence unless-

(a) at least seven clear days before the hearing, and

(b) where he has previously appeared before a court in connection with the alleged offence, within one month of his first such appearance,

he has served on the prosecutor a notice in writing giving such information identifying or assisting in the identification of that other person as was then in his possession.

(11) Any reference in subsection (10) above to appearing before a court includes a reference to being brought before a court.

(12) The obligations imposed by subsections (2) to (6) above, except so far as relating to farmed fish, shall not be in force during such period (if any) in each year as may be prescribed by byelaw.

(13) The obligations imposed by subsections (2) to (6) above on the occupier of a mill shall apply only where the conduit or channel was constructed on or after 18th July 1923.

(14) Any reference in this section to ensuring that a screen is placed and maintained includes, in a case where the screen takes the form of apparatus the operation of which prevents the passage of fish of the descriptions in question, a reference to ensuring that the apparatus is kept in continuous operation.

(15) In this section "by-wash" means a passage through which water flows.

[Salmon and Freshwater Fisheries Act 1975, s 14, as substituted by the Environment Act 1995, Sch 15.]

---

1. For prosecution and punishment of offences, see Sch 4, post.

8–11273   15. Power of Agency to use screens etc to limit movements of salmon and trout.

(1) The Agency—

(a) may cause a screen or screens of such form and dimensions as they may determine to be placed and maintained, at the expense of the authority, at a suitable place in any watercourse, mill race, cut, leat, conduit or other channel for conveying water for any purpose from any waters frequented by salmon or migratory trout; and

(b) may cause any watercourse, mill race, cut, leat, conduit or other channel in which a screen is placed under this section to be widened or deepened at the expense of the authority so far as may be necessary to compensate for the diminution of any flow of water caused by the placing of the screen, or shall take some other means to prevent the flow of water being prejudicially diminished or otherwise injured.

(2) If any person—

(a) injures any such screen; or

(b) removes any such screen or part of any such screen, except during any period of the year during which under a byelaw screens need not be maintained; or

(c) opens any such screen improperly; or

(d) permits any such screen to be injured, or removed, except as aforesaid, or improperly opened;

he shall be guilty of an offence[1].

(3) The Agency may adopt such means as in its opinion are necessary for preventing the ingress of salmon or trout into waters in which they or their spawning beds or ova are, from the nature of the channel or other causes, liable to be destroyed.

(4) Nothing in this section shall—

(a) affect the liability under this Act of any person to place and maintain a screen; or

(b) authorise a screen to be so placed or maintained during any period of the year during which under a byelaw screens need not be maintained; or

(c) authorise any screen to be placed or maintained so as to obstruct any conduit or channel used for navigation or in any way interfere with the effective working of any mill;

and nothing in subsection (3) above shall authorise the Agency prejudicially to interfere with water rights used or enjoyed for the purposes of manufacturing or for milling or for milling purposes or for drainage or navigation.

(5) In this section "open", in relation to a screen which consists of apparatus, includes the doing of anything which interrupts, or otherwise interferes with, the operation of the apparatus.
[Salmon and Freshwater Fisheries Act 1975, s 15, as amended by the Environment Act 1995, Schs 15 and 24.]

---

1. For prosecution and punishment of offences, see Sch 4, post.

8–11274   16. Boxes and cribs in weirs and dams.   (1) Any person who uses a fishing weir or fishing mill dam for the taking of salmon or migratory trout by means of boxes or cribs shall be guilty of an offence[1] unless the boxes or cribs satisfy the requirements specified in subsection (2) below.

(2) The requirements mentioned in subsection (1) above are—

(a) the upper surface of the sill of the box or crib must be level with the bed of the river;

(b) the bars or inscales of the heck or upstream side of the box or crib—

(i) must not be nearer to each other than 2 inches;

(ii) must be capable of being removed; and

(iii) must be placed perpendicularly;

(c) there must not be attached to any such box or crib any spur or tail wall, leader or outrigger of a greater length than 20 feet from the upper or lower side of the box or crib.
[Salmon and Freshwater Fisheries Act 1975, s 16.]

---

1. For prosecution and punishment of offences, see Sch 4, post.

8–11275   17. Restrictions on taking salmon or trout above or below an obstruction or in mill races.   (1) Any person who takes or kills, or attempts to take or kill, except with rod and line, or scares or disturbs any salmon or trout—

(a) at any place above or below any dam or any obstruction, whether artificial or natural, which hinders or retards the passage of salmon or trout, being within 50 yards above or 100 yards below the dam or obstruction, or within such other distance from the dam or obstruction as may be prescribed by byelaw; or

(b) in any waters under or adjacent to any mill, or in the head race or tail race of any mill, or in any waste race or pool communicating with a mill; or

(c) in any artificial channel connected with any such dam or obstruction,

shall be guilty of an offence[1].

(2) Nothing in this section shall apply to any legal fishing mill dam not having a crib, box or cruive, or to any fishing box, coop, apparatus, net or mode of fishing in connection with and forming part of such a dam or obstruction for purposes of fishing.

(3) Where a fish pass—

(a) approved by the Agency or

(b) constructed and maintained by the Agency in accordance with section 10(1) above,

is for the time being attached to a dam or obstruction, this section shall not be enforced in respect of the dam or obstruction until compensation has been made by the water authority to the persons entitled to fish in the waters for that right of fishery.
[Salmon and Freshwater Fisheries Act 1975, s 17 as amended by the Environment Act 1995, Sch 15.]

---

1. For prosecution and punishment of offences, see Sch 4, post.

8–11276   18. Provisions supplementary to Part II.   (1) If any person obstructs a person legally authorised whilst he is doing any act authorised by section 9, 10 or 15 above, he shall be guilty of an offence[1].

(2) The Agency shall not—

(a) construct, abolish or alter any fish pass, or abolish or alter any free gap, in pursuance of section 10 above, or

(b) do any work under section 15 above,

unless reasonable notice of its intention to do so (specifying the section in question) has been served on the owner and occupier of the dam, fish pass or free gap, watercourse, mill race, cut, leat, conduit or other channel, with a plan and specification of the proposed work; and the Agency shall take into consideration any objections by the owner or occupier, before doing the proposed work.

(3) If any injury is caused—

    (a) to any dam by reason of the construction, abolition or alteration of a fish pass or the abolition or alteration of a free gap in pursuance of section 10 above; or

    (b) by anything done by the water authority under section 15 above,

any person sustaining any loss as a result may recover from the water authority compensation for the injury sustained.

(4) The amount of any compensation under section 10, 15 or 17 above shall be settled in case of dispute by a single arbitrator appointed by the Minister.

(5) In any case in which a water authority are liable to pay compensation under this Part of this Act in respect of injury or damage caused by the making or maintaining of any work, compensation shall not be recoverable unless proceedings for its recovery are instituted within two years from the completion of the work.

[Salmon and Freshwater Fisheries Act 1975, s 18 as amended by the Environment Act 1995, Sch 15.]

---

1. For prosecution and punishment of offences, see Sch 4, post.

PART III[1]

TIMES OF FISHING AND SELLING AND EXPORTING FISH

8–11277   19. Close seasons and close times.   (1) Schedule 1 to this Act shall have effect in relation to the close seasons and close times for the descriptions of fish there specified.

(2) Subject to subsection (3) below, any person who fishes for, takes, kills or attempts to take or kill salmon[2]—

    (a) except with a rod and line[3] or putts and putchers, during the annual close season or weekly close time; or

    (b) with a rod and line[3] during the annual close season for rod and line; or

    (c) with putts and putchers, during the annual close season for putts and putchers,

shall be guilty of an offence[4].

(3) A person shall not be guilty of an offence under subsection (2) above in respect of any act done for the purpose of the artificial propagation of fish, or for some scientific purpose, if he has obtained the previous permission in writing of the National Rivers Authority.

(4) Subject to subsection (5) below, any person who fishes for, takes, kills or attempts to take or kill trout other than rainbow trout[5]—

    (a) except with a rod and line[3], during the annual close season or weekly close time for trout; or

    (b) with a rod and line[3] during the annual trout close season for rod and line,

shall be guilty of an offence[4].

(5) A person shall not be guilty of an offence under subsection (4) above in respect of any act done for the purpose of the artificial propagation of fish or the stocking or restocking of waters, or for some scientific purpose, if he has obtained the previous permission in writing of the National Rivers Authority.

(6) Subject to subsection (8) below, any person who, during the annual close season for freshwater fish, fishes for, takes, kills, or attempts to take or kill, any freshwater fish[3] in any inland water, or fishes for eels[3] by means of a rod and line[3] in any such water, shall be guilty of an offence[6].

(7) Subject to subsection (8) below, any person who, during the annual close season for rainbow trout, fishes for, takes, kills or attempts to take or kill, any rainbow trout in any inland water, or fishes for eels[3] by means of a rod and line[3] in any such water, shall be guilty of an offence[6].

(8) Subsections (6) and (7) above do not apply—

    (a) to the removal by the owner or occupier[3], from any several fishery[7] where salmon or trout are specially preserved, of any eels, freshwater fish or rainbow trout not so preserved;

    (b) to any person fishing with rod and line[3] in any such fishery with the previous permission in writing of its owner or occupier[3];

    (c) to any person fishing with rod and line[3] for eels[3] in any waters in which such fishing is authorised by a byelaw;

    (d) to the taking of freshwater fish or rainbow trout for scientific purposes;

    (e) to the taking of freshwater fish for bait—

        (i) in a several fishery[7] with the permission in writing of its owner or occupier[3], or

        (ii) in any other fishery, unless the taking would contravene a byelaw.

[Salmon and Freshwater Fisheries Act 1975, s 19 as amended by the Water Act 1989, Schs 17 and 27.]

---

1. Part III contains ss 19–24.
2. To establish an offence under this section there must be an intention to catch salmon (*Cain v Campbell* [1978] Crim LR 292).

3. Defined by s 41, post.
4. For prosecution and punishment of offences, see Sch 4, post.
5. For rainbow trout see sub-s (7), infra.
6. For prosecution and punishment of offences see Sch 4, post.
7. A several fishery is an exclusive right of fishing in a given place either with or without the property in the soil (*Hanbury v Jenkins* [1901] 2 Ch 401, 65 JP 631). "Exclusive" means that no other person has a co-extensive right with the owner.

8–11278   20. Close seasons and close times—fixed engines and obstructions. (1) Subject to subsections (4) and (5) below, immediately after the commencement of the annual close season and the weekly close time, the occupier of any fixed engine[1] for taking salmon or migratory trout shall cause it to be removed or rendered incapable of taking them or obstructing their passage.

(2) Subject to subsections (4) and (5) below, where in pursuance of subsection (1) above a fixed engine has been rendered incapable (whether by removal or otherwise) of taking salmon or migratory trout or obstructing their passage, its occupier shall not replace it or otherwise render it capable of taking them or obstructing their passage until the end of the close season or close time.

(3) If any person—

(a) fails to comply with subsection (1) or (2) above; or
(b) during the annual close season or weekly close time places any obstruction, uses any contrivance or does any act, for the purpose of deterring salmon or migratory trout from passing up a river[2],

he shall be guilty of an offence[3].

(4) Subsections (1) to (3) above only apply to putts and putchers in relation to the close season for putts and putchers.

(5) It shall be a defence for a person charged with an offence under subsection (3) (b) above to show that he placed the obstruction, used the contrivance or did the acts in question in the course of legally fishing for fish other than salmon or migratory trout.

(6) In this section "migratory trout" does not include rainbow trout.
[Salmon and Freshwater Fisheries Act 1975, s 20.]

1. Defined by s 41, post.
2. "River" includes a stream (s 41, post).
3. For prosecution and punishment of offences see Sch 4, post.

8–11279   21. Eel baskets etc. (1) Subject to subsection (2) below, any person who—

(a) before 25th June in any year, hangs, fixes or uses in any waters frequented by salmon or migratory trout any baskets, nets, traps or devices[1] for catching eels[2], or places in any inland water any device whatsoever to catch or obstruct any fish descending the river[3]; or
(b) at any time places upon the apron of any weir any basket, trap or device for taking fish[4], except wheels or leaps for taking lamperns between 1st August and the following 1st March.

shall be guilty of an offence[5].

(2) Subsection (1) above does not prohibit—

(a) the use of eel baskets not exceeding in any part 10 inches in diameter constructed so as to be fished with bait, and not used at any dam[2] or other obstruction or in any conduit or artificial channel by which water is deviated from a river; or
(b) any device for taking eels in such places, during such time and subject to such conditions as may be authorised by the National Rivers Authority.
[Salmon and Freshwater Fisheries Act 1975, s 21 as amended by the Water Act 1989, Schs 17 and 27.]

1. An eel trap forming part of a weir built before the passing of the Salmon Fishery Act 1873, and used for catching eels ever since by opening a sluice, is within these words (*Briggs v Swanwick* (1883) 10 QBD 510, 47 JP 564).
2. Defined in s 41, post.
3. "River" includes a stream (s 41, post).
4. These words include fish ascending and fish descending the weir (*Maw v Holloway* [1914] 3 KB 594, 78 JP 347; also explaining "apron" and "weir").
5. For prosecution and punishment of offences see Sch 4, post.

8–11280   22. Sale of salmon and trout. (1) Subject to subsections (2) and (3) below, any person who buys, sells, or exposes for sale[1] or has in his possession[1] for sale—

(a) any salmon[2] between 31st August and the following 1st February; or
(b) any trout[2] other than rainbow trout between 31st August and the following 1st March,

shall be guilty of an offence[3].

(2) Subsection (1) above shall not apply to any person buying, selling or exposing for sale, or having in his possession for sale—

(a) any salmon or trout which has been canned, frozen, cured, salted, pickled, dried or otherwise preserved outside the United Kingdom; or (b)　any salmon which has been canned, frozen, cured, salted, pickled, dried or otherwise preserved in the United Kingdom between 1st February and 31st August; or

(c)　any trout which has been canned, frozen, cured, salted, pickled, dried or otherwise preserved within the United Kingdom between 1st March and 31st August; or

(d)　any salmon or trout (other than an unclean[4] salmon or trout) caught outside the United Kingdom; or

(e)　any salmon or trout (other than an unclean or immature salmon or trout) caught within the United Kingdom, if its capture by any net, instrument or device was lawful at the time and in the place where it was caught.

(3)　A person shall not be guilty of an offence in respect of trout under this section for any act done for the purpose of the artificial propagation of fish, or the stocking or restocking of waters, or for some scientific purpose.

(4)　The burden of proving that any salmon or trout bought, sold, exposed for sale or in the possession of any person for sale between the dates mentioned in paragraph (a) or (b) of subsection (1) above is not bought, sold, exposed for sale or in the possession of that person for sale in contravention of this section shall lie on the person buying, selling or exposing it for sale, or having it in his possession for sale.

[Salmon and Freshwater Fisheries Act 1975, s 22.]

---

1. For "exposes for sale" see note 2 to s 2(1), ante. "Possession" does not, necessarily mean actual physical possession (*McAttee v Hogg* (1903) 5 F 67 (J)); the expression "possession for sale" relates to a contemplated sale between the prohibited dates (*Birkett v McGlassons Ltd* [1957] 1 All ER 369, 121 JP 126).
2. Defined in s 41, post.
3. For prosecution and punishment of offences see Sch 4, post.
4. Defined in s 41, post.

8–11281　23. Export of salmon and trout.　No person shall export or enter for export any unclean salmon[1] or trout[1] or any salmon or trout caught during the time at which the sale of salmon or trout is prohibited where the salmon or trout was caught.

(2)　All salmon or trout intended for export between 31st August and the following 1st May shall before shipment be entered for that purpose with the proper officer of Customs and Excise, at the port or place of intended export.

(3)　If any salmon or trout is entered for export, or exported or brought to any wharf, quay or other place for export, contrary to this section, or is not entered as required by this section, the salmon or trout and any package containing it shall be deemed to be goods liable to be forfeited under the enactments relating to customs, and the person entering or exporting the salmon or trout, or bringing it for export, or failing to enter the salmon or trout as required by this section, shall be guilty of an offence[2].

(4)　Any officer of Customs and Excise may, between 31st August and the following 1st May, open or cause to be opened any parcel entered or intended for export, or brought to any quay, wharf or other place for that purpose, and suspected by him to contain salmon or trout, and may detain or cause to be detained any salmon or trout found in the parcel until proof is given of the salmon or trout being such as may be legally exported; and if the salmon or trout becomes unfit for human food before such proof is given, the officer may destroy it or cause it to be destroyed.

(5)　The burden of proving that any salmon or trout entered for export between 31st August and the following 1st May is not so entered in contravention of this section shall lie on the person entering it.

[Salmon and Freshwater Fisheries Act 1975, s 23.]

---

1. Defined in s 41, post.
2. For prosecution and punishment of offences see Sch 4, post.

8–11282　24. Consignment of salmon and trout.　(1)　A person who consigns or sends a package containing salmon or trout by any common or other carrier shall be guilty of an offence unless the outside of the package containing it is conspicuously marked "salmon" or "trout", as the case may be.

(2)　An authorised officer[1] may open any package consigned or sent by a carrier, or brought to any place to be so consigned or sent, and suspected to contain salmon or trout.

(3)　If any such package is found to contain salmon or trout and is not marked in accordance with this section, or if there is reasonable cause to suspect that the salmon or trout contained in any marked package is being dealt with contrary to law, an authorised officer[1] may detain the package and its contents until proof is given that the salmon or trout is not being so dealt with.

(4)　The power to detain salmon or trout conferred by subsection (3) above shall be exercisable in relation to salmon or trout not packed in a package.

(5)　If any salmon or trout detained under this section becomes unfit for human food before the proof required by subsection (3) above is given, an authorised officer[1] may destroy it or cause it to be destroyed.

(6) If any person refuses to allow an authorised officer[1] to exercise the powers conferred by this section, or obstructs such an officer in their exercise, he shall be guilty of an offence[2].
[Salmon and Freshwater Fisheries Act 1975, s 24.]

---

1. Defined by s 41, post.
2. For prosecution and punishment of offences see Sch 4, post.

PART IV[1]
FISHING LICENCES

8–11283   25. Licences to fish.   (1) A water authority shall by means of a system of licensing regulate fishing for salmon and trout . . . and, except so far as excused by the Minister, shall by such means regulate fishing for freshwater fish of any description or eels . . .

(2) Subject to the following provisions of this section, a licence granted for the purposes of this section (hereafter in this Act referred to as a "fishing licence") shall entitle the person to whom it was granted and no others to use an instrument specified in the licence to fish for any fish of such a description, in such area or areas and for such period as is so specified.

(3) A fishing licence for the use of an instrument other than a rod and line to fish for salmon or trout shall also authorise the use of the instrument for that purpose by the duly authorised servants or agents of the person to whom it was granted, but subject to the provisions of paragraphs 9 to 13 of Schedule 2 to this Act.

(4) A fishing licence for the use of a rod and line shall entitle the licensee to use as ancillary to that use a gaff, consisting of a plain metal hook without a barb, or a tailer or landing net.

(5) A fishing licence for the use of any instrument for fishing for salmon shall authorise the use of that instrument for fishing for trout.

(6) A fishing licence in respect of any instrument for fishing for salmon or trout shall authorise the use of that instrument for fishing for freshwater fish and eels.

(7) Any person or association entitled to an exclusive right of fishing in any inland waters may be granted a general licence to fish in those waters subject to any conditions agreed between the water authority and the licensee, and the licence shall entitle the licensee and, subject to paragraph 9 of Schedule 4 below, any person authorised by him in writing, or in the case of an association, by its secretary so to fish.

(8) Schedule 2 to this Act shall have effect with respect to fishing licences.

(9) Any licence in force under any provision of section 61 of the Salmon and Freshwater Fisheries Act 1923 immediately before 29th June 1972 shall be treated as having been granted under the corresponding provision of this section.
[Salmon and Freshwater Fisheries Act 1975, s 25, as amended by the Salmon Act 1986, s 36 and the Water Act 1989, ss 141 and 190, and Schs 17 and 27.]

---

1. Part IV contains ss 25–27.

8–11284   26. Limitation of fishing licences.   (1) A water authority may in relation to any such area or areas as are specified in the order by order confirmed by the Minister—

(a) limit for a period not exceeding ten years from the coming into operation of the order the number of fishing licences to be issued in any year for fishing in that area or those areas, for salmon or trout other than rainbow trout with any instrument so specified other than rod and line; and

(b) provide for the selection of the applicants to whom such licences are to be issued where the number of applications exceeds the number of licences which may be granted.

(2) Where the Minister proposes to confirm an order under this section, he shall require the water authority to publish the order and notice of his intention to confirm it in such manner as he may require, together with a notification that within a period specified in the requirement written objections to the order may be made to him.

(3) The Minister shall consider any such objections received by him within the said period, and—

(a) if the number of licences as proposed to be limited by the order is less than the number of licences issued in any of the three years preceding the year in which the order is to come into operation; and

(b) any such objection is made by any person who has during each of the two years preceding that year held a licence of the same description as the licences which it is proposed so to limit in number;

he shall cause a local inquiry to be held before confirming the order.

(4) Subject to subsection (5) below, the Minister shall not confirm an order under this section unless he is satisfied that the terms of the order relating to the selection of applicants for licences are such as to secure that any person who during the year preceding that year held a fishing licence to use an instrument of any description and who is dependent on fishing for his livelihood will be able to obtain a fishing licence to use an instrument of that description.

(5) If it appears to the Minister that the operation of subsection (4) above would be detrimental

to the conservation of any fishery, he may direct that the subsection shall in its application to that fishery have effect with the substitution for the words "the year" of the words "the two years" or, if in his opinion special circumstances justify it, "the three years".

(6) The Minister may with the consent of the water authority vary an order submitted to him under this section before confirming it and may require the water authority to publish the terms of the proposed variation in such manner, if any, as he may specify in the requirement.

(7) An order under this section may be revoked by the Minister, or by an order made by the water authority and confirmed by the Minister.

[Salmon and Freshwater Fisheries Act 1975, s 26, as amended by the Water Act 1989, ss 141 and 190, and Schs 17 and 27.]

8–11285 27. Unlicensed fishing. A person is guilty of an offence if, in any place in which fishing for fish of any description is regulated by a system of licensing[1], he—

(a) fishes for or takes fish of that description otherwise than by means of an instrument which he is entitled to use for that purpose by virtue of a fishing licence or otherwise than in accordance with the conditions of the licence; or

(b) has in his possession with intent to use it for that purpose an instrument other than one which he is authorised to use for that purpose by virtue of such a licence.

[Salmon and Freshwater Fisheries Act 1975, s 27.]

---

1. Section 25 requires the National Rivers Authority to regulate fishing for salmon, trout, freshwater fish and eels, and stipulates what a licence may allow. Section 26 provides for limitation on the number of licences and the selection of licence holders. Schedule 2 makes further provision for licensing, including the offence of entering more than the permitted names on a licence with intent to deceive.

PART V[1]
ADMINISTRATION AND ENFORCEMENT
Regulation of fisheries etc

8–11286 28. General powers and duties of water authorities and Minister[2]. *(Repealed).*

---

1. Part V contains ss 28–37.
2. Contravention of byelaws made under the repealed provisions of this Act was an offence by virtue of s 28(7); such a contravention is now an offence by virtue of s 211(3) of the Water Resources Act 1991, title WATER, post; for penalty, see s 211(3), ibid.

8–11287 30. Introduction of fish into inland waters. A person shall be guilty of an offence if he introduces any fish or spawn of fish into an inland water, or has in his possession any fish or spawn of fish intending to introduce it into an inland water, unless he first obtains the written consent of the Agency or the inland water is one which consists exclusively of, or of part of, a fish farm and which, if it discharges into another inland water, does so only through a conduit constructed or adapted for the purpose.

[Salmon and Freshwater Fisheries Act 1975, s 30 as amended by the Salmon Act 1986 s 34, the Water Act 1989, Schs 17 and 27 and the Environment Act 1995, Schs 15 and 24.]

Powers of water bailiffs etc

8–11288 31. Powers of search etc. (1) Any water bailiff appointed by the National Rivers Authority and any person appointed by the Minister—

(a) may examine any dam, fishing weir, fishing mill dam, fixed engine or obstruction, or any artificial watercourse, and for that purpose enter on any land;

(b) may examine any instrument or bait which he has reasonable cause to suspect of having been or being used or likely to be used in taking fish in contravention of this Act[1] or any container which he has reasonable cause to suspect of having been or being used or likely to be used for holding any such instrument bait or fish;

(c) may stop and search[2] any boat or other vessel used in fishing in a water authority area or any vessel or vehicle which he has reasonable cause to suspect of containing—

(i) fish which had been caught in contravention of this Act[1];
(ii) any such instrument, bait or container as aforesaid;

(d) may seize any fish and any instrument, vessel, vehicle or other thing liable to be forfeited in pursuance of this Act.

(2) If any person refuses to allow a water bailiff or a person appointed by the Minister to make an entry, search or examination which he is by this section authorised to make, or to seize anything which he is so authorised to seize, or resists or obstructs a water bailiff or person so appointed in any such entry, search, examination or seizure, he shall be guilty of an offence[3].

[Salmon and Freshwater Fisheries Act 1975, s 31 as amended by the Water Act 1989, Sch 17.]

1. This includes references to a salmon in respect of which a relevant offence has been committed (Salmon Act 1986 s 32 post).

2. The bailiff must produce his appointment before searching (*Barnacott v Passmore* (1887) 19 QBD 75, 51 JP 821). A bailiff produced his warrant of appointment, but when asked to read it he was unable to do so because it was too dark. The respondent resisted the bailiff; it was held that he should be convicted (*Cowler v Jones* (1890) 54 JP 660).

3. For prosecution and punishment of offences see Sch 4, post.

8–11289   32. *Power to enter lands.*

8–11290   33. Orders and warrants to enter suspected premises.   (1) Where from a statement on oath of a water bailiff or any other officer of the National Rivers Authority, or any person appointed by the Minister, it appears to any justice of the peace that the person making the statement has good reason to suspect that any offence against this Act is being or is likely to be committed on any land situate on or near to any waters, the justice may by order under his hand authorise him, during a period not exceeding 24 hours to be specified in the order, to enter upon and remain on the land during any hours of the day or night for the purpose of detecting the persons committing the offence.

(2) Any justice of the peace upon an information on oath that there is probable cause to suspect any offence against this Act[1] to have been committed on any premises, or any salmon, trout, freshwater fish or eels to have been illegally taken, or any illegal nets or other instruments to be on any premises, by warrant under this hand and seal may authorise any water bailiff or other officer of a water authority, or any person appointed by the Minister, or any constable, to enter the premises for the purpose of detecting the offence of the fish, nets or other instruments, at such times of the day or night as are mentioned in the warrant, and to seize all illegal nets and other instruments and all salmon, trout, freshwater fish or eels suspected to have been illegally taken that may be found on the premises.

(3) A warrant under subsection (2) above shall not continue in force for more than one week.
[Salmon and Freshwater Fisheries Act 1975, s 33 as amended by the Water Act 1989, Sch 17.]

1. This includes offences under s 32 of the Salmon Act 1986 post.

8–11291   34. Power to apprehend persons fishing illegally at night.   If any person, between the end of the first hour after sunset on any day and the beginning of the last hour before sunrise on the following morning, illegally takes or kills salmon, trout, freshwater fish or eels, or is found on or near any waters with intent illegally to take or kill salmon, trout, freshwater fish or eels, or having in his possession for the capture of salmon, trout, freshwater fish or eels any instrument prohibited by this Act, a water bailiff or a person appointed by the Minister, with any assistants, may seize him without warrant and put him as soon as may be into the custody of a police officer.
[Salmon and Freshwater Fisheries Act 1975, s 34.]

8–11292   35. Power to require production of fishing licences.   (1) A water bailiff or other officer of the Agency, or any constable, may require any person who is fishing, or whom he reasonably suspects of being about to fish or to have within the preceding half hour fished in any area, to produce his licence or other authority to fish and to state his name and address.

(1A) Without prejudice to subsection (1) above, a water bailiff or other officer of the Agency who on any occasion finds a person who he has reason to believe is committing, or has on that occasion committed, a fixed penalty offence, within the meaning of section 37A below, may require that person to state his name and address.

(2) A person holding a fishing licence for any area may, on production of his licence, require any person who is fishing in that area to produce his licence or other authority to fish and to state his name and address.

(3) If any person required to produce his fishing licence or other authority or to state his name and address fails to do so, he shall be guilty of an offence[1]; but if within seven days after the production of his licence was so required he produces the licence or other authority at the appropriate office of the Agency he shall not be convicted of an offence under this section for failing to produce it.

(4) In subsection (3) above, "the appropriate office of the Agency" means—

(*a*) in a case where the person requiring the production of the licence or other authority specifies a particular office of the Agency for its production, that office; and

(*b*) in any other case, any office of the Agency;

and for the purposes of that subsection where a licence or other authority which any person has been required to produce is sent by post to an office of the Agency that licence or other authority shall be treated as produced by that person at that office.
[Salmon and Freshwater Fisheries Act 1975, s 35 as amended by the Water Act 1989, Schs 17 and 27 and the Environment Act 1995, s 104 and Sch 15.]

8–11293   36. Provisions supplementary to sections 31 to 35.   (1) A water bailiff and a person appointed by the Minister shall be deemed to be a constable[1] for the purpose of the enforcement of this Act[2], or any order or byelaw under it, and to have all the same powers and privileges, and be subject to the same liabilities as a constable duly appointed has or is subject to by virtue of the common law or of any statute.

(2) The production by a water bailiff or a person appointed by the Minister of evidence of his appointment shall be a sufficient warrant for him exercising the powers conferred on him by this Act.

(3) A police constable whose services are provided under paragraph 39(1)(c) of Schedule 3 below[3] shall have all the powers and privileges of a water bailiff.

[Salmon and Freshwater Fisheries Act 1975, s 36.]

---

1. An occupier of lands ordering him to leave would contravene s 51(3) of the Police Act 1964; cf *Heseltine v Myers* (1894) 58 JP 689.
2. Or the Salmon Act 1986, s 32, post.
3. Schedule 3, para 39(1)(c) enables the Environment Agency to obtain the services of additional constables under s 25 of the Police Act 1996.

Offences

8–11294   37. Prosecution etc of offences.   Parts I and II of Schedule 4 to this Act shall have effect with regard to the prosecution and punishment of offences against this Act and the procedure on such prosecutions.

[Salmon and Freshwater Fisheries Act 1975, s 37.]

8–11294A   37A. Fixed penalty notices for certain offences.   (1) Where on any occasion a water bailiff or other officer of the Agency finds a person who he has reason to believe is committing, or has on that occasion committed, a fixed penalty offence, he may give to that person a notice (in this section referred to as a "fixed penalty notice") offering him the opportunity of discharging any liability to conviction for that offence by payment of a fixed penalty.

(2) Where a person is given a fixed penalty notice in respect of a fixed penalty offence

(a) no proceedings shall be instituted for that offence before the expiration of the period for paying the fixed penalty; and

(b) he shall not be convicted of that offence if the fixed penalty is paid before the expiration of that period.

(3) The Agency may extend the period for paying the fixed penalty in any particular case if it considers it appropriate to do so in all the circumstances of the case.

(4) If, in any particular case, the Agency considers that a fixed penalty notice which has been given ought not to have been given, it may give to the person to whom the fixed penalty notice was given a notice withdrawing the fixed penalty notice; and where notice under this subsection is given—

(a) the Agency shall repay any amount which has been paid by way of fixed penalty in pursuance of the fixed penalty notice; and

(b) no proceedings shall be instituted or continued against that person for the offence in question.

(5) The amount by which the sums received by the Agency by way of fixed penalties exceed the sums repaid by it under subsection (4)(a) above shall be paid into the Consolidated Fund.

(6) In any proceedings, a certificate purporting to be signed by or on behalf of the Chief Executive of the Agency and stating either—

(a) that payment of a fixed penalty was, or (as the case may be) was not, received by the agency on or before a date specified in the certificate, or

(b) that an envelope containing an amount sent by post in payment of a fixed penalty was marked as posted on a date specified in the certificate,

shall be received as evidence of the matters so stated and shall be treated, without further proof, as being so signed unless the contrary is shown.

(7) A fixed penalty notice shall give such reasonable particulars of the circumstances alleged to constitute the fixed penalty offence to which the notice relates as are necessary for giving reasonable information of the offence and shall state—

(a) the monetary amount of the fixed penalty which may be paid;

(b) the person to whom and the address at which—

(i) the fixed penalty may be paid, and

(ii) any correspondence relating to the fixed penalty notice may be sent;

(c) the method or methods by which payment of the fixed penalty may be made;

(d) the period for paying the fixed penalty;

(e) the consequences of the fixed penalty not being paid before the expiration of that period.

(8) A fixed penalty notice may also contain such other information relating to, or for the purpose of facilitating, the administration of the fixed penalty system as the Agency considers necessary or desirable.

(9) Regulations may—

(a) make provision with respect to the giving of fixed penalty notices, including, in particular, provision with respect to—

(i) the methods by which,

(ii) the officers, servants or agents by, to or on whom, and

(iii) the places at which,

fixed penalty notices may be given by, or served on behalf of, a water bailiff or other officer of the Agency;

(b) prescribe the method or methods by which fixed penalties may be paid;

(c) make provision for or with respect to the issue of prescribed documents to persons to whom fixed penalty notices are or have been given.

(10) In this section—

"fixed penalty" means a penalty of such amount as may be prescribed (whether by being specified in, or made calculable under, regulations);

"fixed penalty offence" means, subject to subsection (11) below, any offence—

(a) under this Act,

(b) under the Salmon Act 1986

(c) under or by virtue of regulations or orders made under section 115, 116 or 142 of the Water Resources Act 1991, or

(d) under section 211(3) of that Act, so far as relating to byelaws made by virtue of paragraph 6 of Schedule 25 to that Act, which is for the time being prescribed for the purpose;

"the fixed penalty system" means the system implementing this section and regulations made under it;

"the Ministers" means the Secretary of State and the Minister;

"notice" means notice in writing;

"the period for paying", in relation to any fixed penalty, means such period as may be prescribed for the purpose;

"prescribed" means prescribed by regulations;

"regulations" means regulations made under this section by the Ministers.

(11) The provision that may be made by regulations prescribing fixed penalty offences includes provision for an offence to be a fixed penalty offence—

(a) only if it is committed in such circumstances or manner as may be prescribed; or

(b) except if it is committed in such circumstances or manner as may be prescribed.

(12) Regulations may provide for any offence which is a fixed penalty offence to cease to be such an offence.

(13) An offence which, in consequence of regulations made by virtue of subsection (12) above, has ceased to be a fixed penalty offence shall be eligible to be prescribed as such an offence again.

(14) Regulations may—

(a) make different provision in relation to different cases or classes of case; or

(b) provide for such exceptions, limitations and conditions, or make such incidental, supplemental, consequential or transitional provision, as the Ministers consider necessary or expedient.

(15) Any power to make regulations under this section shall be exercisable by statutory instrument made by the Ministers; and a statutory instrument containing any such regulations shall be subject to annulment pursuant to a resolution of either House of Parliament.

[Salmon and Freshwater Fisheries Act 1975, s 37A, as inserted by the Environment Act 1995, s 104.]

PART VI[1]
MISCELLANEOUS AND SUPPLEMENTARY

8–11295 Works below high-water mark are subject to approval; unauthorised works may be removed and Secretary of State's costs recoverable summarily (s 38). Act[2] does not apply to River Tweed, applies to River Esk in Scotland and to dams and fish passes on the River Severn. Special provisions apply to Solway Firth (ss 39, 40).

[Salmon and Freshwater Fisheries Act 1975, ss 38–40 amended by the Water Act 1989, Schs 17 and 27, the Water Consolidation (Consequential Provisions) Act 1991, Sch 1 and the Environment Act 1995, Sch 15, summarised.]

---

1. Part VI contains ss 38–43.

2. References to this Act include references to the Salmon Act 1986, s 32 post (ibid).

8–11296 41. Interpretation. (1) In this Act, unless the context otherwise requires—

"the Agency" means the Environment Agency;

"authorised officer" means—

(a) any officer of the National Rivers Authority;

(b) any officer of a market authority acting within the area of the jurisdiction of that authority;

(c) any officer appointed by the Minister;

(d) any officer appointed in writing by the Fishmongers Company, or

(e) any police officer;

"byelaw" means a byelaw under this Act;

"dam" includes any weir or other fixed obstruction used for the purposes of damming up water;

"eels" includes elvers and the fry of eels;

"fish farm" has the same meaning as in the Diseases of Fish Act 1937;

"fishing licence" has the meaning assigned to it by section 25(2) above;

"fishing mill dam" means a dam used or intended to be used partly for the purpose of taking or facilitating the taking of fish, and partly for the purpose of supplying water for milling or other purposes;

"fishing weir" means any erection, structure or obstruction to the soil either temporarily or permanently, across or partly across a river or branch of a river, and used for the exclusive purpose of taking or facilitating the taking of fish;

"Fishmongers Company" means the wardens and commonalty of the Mystery of Fishmongers in the City of London;

"fixed engine" includes—

(a) a stake net, bag net, putt or putcher;

(b) any fixed implement or engine for taking or facilitating the taking of fish;

(c) any net secured by anchors[1] and any net or other implement for taking fish fixed to the soil, or made stationary in any other way; and

(d) any net placed or suspended in any inland or tidal waters unattended by the owner or a person duly authorised by the owner to use it for taking salmon or trout[2], and any engine, device, machine or contrivance, whether floating or otherwise, for placing or suspending such a net or maintaining it in working order or making it stationary;

"foreshore" includes the shore and bed of the sea and of every channel, creek, bay, estuary and navigable river as far up as the tide flows;

"freshwater fish" means any fish living in fresh water exclusive of salmon and trout and of any kinds of fish which migrate to and from tidal waters and of eels;

"general licence" means a licence granted under section 25(7) above;

"immature" in relation to salmon means that the salmon is of a length of less than 12 inches, measured from the tip of the snout to the fork or cleft of the tail, and in relation to any other fish means that the fish is of a length less than such length (if any) as may be prescribed by the byelaws applicable to the water in which the fish is taken;

"inland water" means any area of inland waters within the meaning of the Water Resources Act 1991;

"market authority" includes any corporation, local authority, body of trustee or other persons having power to maintain or regulate any market;

"migratory trout" means trout which migrate to and from the sea;

"mill" includes any erection for the purpose of developing water power, and "milling" has a corresponding meaning;

"the Minister" means the Minister of Agriculture, Fisheries and Food[3];

"occupier" in relation to a fishery or premises includes any person for the time being in actual possession of the fishery or premises;

"owner" includes any person who is entitled to receive rents from a fishery or premises;

"river" includes a stream;

"rod and line" means single rod and line;

"salmon" means all fish of the salmon species and includes part of a salmon;

"screen" means a grating or other device which, or any apparatus the operation of which, prevents—

(a) the passage of salmon or migratory trout, and

(b) if the screen is required in connection with a fish farm, the passage of any fish farmed at that fish farm,

or any combination of devices or apparatus which, taken together, achieve that result;

"trout" means any fish of the salmon family commonly known as trout, including migratory trout and char, and also includes part of a trout;

"unclean" in relation to any fish means that the fish is about to spawn, or has recently spawned and has not recovered from spawning.

(2), (2A) *(Repealed).*

(3) *Crown property.*

(4) In any byelaw made under an enactment repealed by the Salmon and Freshwater Fisheries Act 1923 "salmon" and "trout" have the meanings assigned to them by subsection (1) above.

[Salmon and Freshwater Fisheries Act 1975, s 41 as amended by the Water Act 1983, Sch 4, the Water Act 1989, Schs 17 and 27, the Water Consolidation (Consequential Provisions) Act 1991, Sch 1 and the Environment Act 1995, s 104 and Schs 15 and 24.]

1. Where light anchors are attached merely as a brake and the net drifts with the tide, it is not a "fixed engine" (*Percival v Stanton* [1954] 1 All ER 392, 118 JP 171).

2. The words "to use it for taking salmon or trout" do not relate to the placing and subsequent use of the net (*Gray v Blamey* [1991] 1 All ER 1, [1991] 1 WLR 47, DC.

3. Residual functions of the Secretary of State and the Secretary of State for Wales have been transferred to the Minister of Agriculture, Fisheries and Food by the Transfer of Functions (Agriculture and Fisheries) Order 2000, SI 2000/1812.

8–11297 42. *Repeals etc*[1].

1. These have been noted where appropriate. The section also contains savings for instruments made and things done under repealed enactments with which provisions of this Act correspond. The power of the Secretary of State to amend etc enactments by order, contained in s 254(2)(*c*) of the Local Government Act 1972, applies to this Act.

SCHEDULES

Section 19

SCHEDULE 1
CLOSE SEASONS AND CLOSE TIMES

(As amended by the Water Act 1989 Schs 17 and 27 and the Environment Act 1995, Sch 15.)

8–11298 1. It shall be the duty of the Agency to make byelaws fixing for the respective parts of the area in relation to which the National Rivers Authority carries out its functions under this Act, subject to paragraph 3 below, the annual close season and weekly close time for fishing by any method for salmon and trout other than rainbow trout.*

2. *(Repealed)*.

3. The minimum close seasons and close times are specified in the following Table (subject to the power to dispense altogether with a close season for freshwater fish or rainbow trout conferred by paragraph 20 of Schedule 3 below).

TABLE

	Minimum duration
1 Salmon close season	153 days
2 Close season for fishing for salmon with rod and line	92 days
3 Close season for fishing for salmon or trout with putts and putchers	242 days
4 Weekly close time for salmon	42 hours
5 Trout close season	181 days
6 Close season for fishing for trout with rod and line	153 days
7 Weekly close time for trout	42 hours
8 Close season for freshwater fish or rainbow trout	93 days

4. If byelaws neither specify nor dispense with an annual close season for freshwater fish, the annual close season for such fish shall be the period between 14th March and 16th June.

5. The annual close season for rainbow trout for any waters is that fixed for those waters by byelaws.

6. Subject to any byelaws under this Act or the Salmon and Freshwater Fisheries Act 1923—

(*a*) for salmon—

   (i) the annual close season shall be the period between 31st August and the following 1st February;

   (ii) the close season for rods shall be the period between 31st October and the following 1st February;

   (iii) the close season for putts and putchers shall be the period between 31st August and the following 1st May; and

   (iv) the weekly close time shall be the period between 6 am on Saturday and 6 am on the following Monday; and

(*b*) for trout—

   (i) the annual close season shall be the period between 31st August and the following 1st March;

   (ii) the annual close season for rod and line shall be the period between 30th September and the following 1st March; and

   (iii) the weekly close time shall be the period between 6 am on Saturday and 6 am on the following Monday.

8–11299

SCHEDULE 2
LICENCES

8–11300

SCHEDULE 3
ADMINISTRATION: ORDERS AND BYELAWS

8–11301

Section 37

SCHEDULE 4
OFFENCES

(As amended by the Criminal Law Act 1977, s 28 and Sch 6, the Customs and Excise Management Act 1979, Sch 4, the Criminal Justice Act 1982, s 46, the Salmon Act 1986 s 35, the Water Act 1989 Schs 17 and 27 and the Access to Justice Act 1999, Sch 13.)

PART I
PROSECUTION AND PUNISHMENT

1. (1) Column 2 of the Table below gives a description of the offences against the provisions of this Act specified in column 1 of the Table, and in relation to any such offence—

(a)   column 3 shows whether the offence is punishable summarily (that is to say, on summary conviction) or on indictment or either in one way or the other; and

(b)   column 4 shows the maximum punishment by way of fine or imprisonment which may be imposed on a person convicted of the offence in the way specified in column 3 (that is to say, summarily or on indictment), any reference in column 4 to a period of years or months being construed as a reference to a term of imprisonment for that period.

(2)   A person guilty of an offence against any provision of this Act not specified in the Table shall be liable on summary conviction to a fine not exceeding **level 4** on the standard scale.

TABLE

Provision of Act creating the offence (1)	Description of offence (2)	Mode of prosecution (3)	Punishment (4)
Section 1	Fishing with certain instruments for salmon, trout or freshwater fish and possessing certain instruments for fishing for such fish.	(a) Summarily	**Three months** or the statutory maximum or both
		(b) On indictment	Two years or a fine or both.
Section 4	Discharging poisonous or injurious matter into waters containing fish or spawn.	(a) Summarily	The prescribed sum and £40 for each day on which the offence continues after a conviction thereof.
		(b) On indictment	Two years or a fine or both.
Section 5(1)	Using explosives, poisons, noxious substances or electrical devices to take or destroy fish.	(a) Summarily	The prescribed sum.
		(b) On indictment	Two years or a fine or both.
Section 5(3)	Destroying or damaging dams etc, to take or destroy fish.	(a) Summarily	The prescribed sum.
		(b) On indictment	Two years or a fine or both.
Section 19(2)	Fishing for salmon during the annual close season or weekly close time.	Summarily	**Level 4** on the standard scale.
Section 19(4)	Fishing for trout during the annual close season or weekly close time.	Summarily	**Level 4** on the standard scale.
Section 19(6)	Fishing for freshwater fish during the annual close season for freshwater fish and fishing for eels by means of a rod and line during that season.	Summarily	**Level 4** on the standard scale.
Section 19(7)	Fishing for rainbow trout during the annual close season for rainbow trout and fishing for eels by means of a rod and line during that season.	Summarily	**Level 4** on the standard scale.
Section 21	Prohibition on use of certain devices at certain times.	Summarily	**Level 4** on the standard scale.
Section 27	Fishing for fish otherwise than under the authority of a licence and possessing an unlicensed instrument with intent to use it for fishing.	(a) If the instrument in question, or each of the instruments in question, is a rod and line, summarily.	**Level 4** on the standard scale.
		(b) In any other case— (i) summarily	**Three months** or the **statutory maximum** or both;
		(ii) on indictment	Two years or a fine or both.

(3)   A person shall be treated as acting together with another for the purposes of the above Table if both are engaged in committing an offence against section 1 or 27 above, other than one committed by means of a rod and line or without any instrument, or one is aiding, abetting, counselling or procuring the commission of such an offence by the other.

PART II
PROCEDURE[1]

2. Any offence against this Act committed on the sea-coast or at sea beyond the ordinary jurisdiction of a court of summary jurisdiction shall be deemed to have been committed in any place abutting on that sea-coast or adjoining that sea, and may be tried and punished accordingly.

3. Offences against this Act committed in Scotland shall be proceeded against and punished in Scotland.

4. A justice of the peace shall not be disqualified from hearing any case under this Act by reason only of being a subscriber to any society for the protection of fish, but a justice shall not be entitled to hear any case in respect of an offence committed on his own land or in relation to any fishery of which he is owner or occupier[2].

5. The court by which a person is convicted of an offence against this Act may order the forfeiture of—

(a) any fish illegally taken by him or in his possession at the time of the offence;

(b) any instrument, bait or other thing used in the commission of the offence;

(c) in the case of an offence of unlawful possession of any substance or device in contravention of section 5 above, that substance or device; and

(d) on conviction on indictment, any vessel[3] or vehicle used in or in connection with the commission of the offence or in which any substance or device unlawfully in his possession was contained at the time of the offence;

and may order any object so forfeited to be disposed of as the court thinks fit.

6. Schedule 3 to the Customs and Excise Management Act 1979 (provisions relating to the forfeiture of things seized under that Act)[4] shall apply in relation to any vessel or vehicle liable to forfeiture under paragraph 5 above as it applies in relation to anything liable to forfeiture under that Act, but in its application in relation to any such vessel or vehicle shall have effect subject to the following modifications:

(a) paragraphs 1(2) and 5 shall be omitted;

(b) for references to the Comrs of Customs and Excise there shall be substituted references to the National Rivers Authority; and

(c) the court shall not condemn a vehicle or vessel as forfeited under paragraph 6 of that Schedule if satisfied by its owner that that offence was committed without his knowledge and that he could not have reasonably foreseen that it would be used as mentioned in paragraph 5(d) above;

and where notice of claim in respect of anything is duly given in accordance with paragraphs 3 and 4 of that Schedule, as applied by this paragraph, the court shall not exercise its power of ordering forfeiture of the vessel or vehicle under paragraph 5 above.

In this paragraph "owner", in relation to a vessel or vehicle which is the subject of a hire-purchase agreement, means the person in possession of the vehicle under that agreement.

7. An authorised officer[5] may seize any salmon, trout or freshwater fish[5] bought, sold or exposed for sale[6] by, or in the possession[6] for sale of, any person in contravention of this Act.

8. Where any fish or any other thing of a perishable nature is seized as liable to forfeiture under paragraph 5 above, the person by whom it is seized may sell it, and the net proceeds of sale shall be liable to forfeiture in the same manner as the fish or other thing sold, and if and so far as not forfeited shall be paid on demand to the owner; but no person shall be subject to any liability on account of his neglect or failure to exercise the powers conferred on him by this paragraph.

9. If a person is convicted of an offence against this Act, the court may order that any fishing or general licence held by him shall be forfeited, and that he shall be disqualified from holding and obtaining a fishing or general licence for having his name entered on a licence in pursuance of paragraphs 9 to 14 of Schedule 2 to this Act or for fishing (either in a particular area or generally) by virtue of a fishing or general licence for such period not exceeding five years as the court thinks fit.

10. A person who is prosecuted for an offence against this Act and who is the holder of a fishing or general licence shall either—

(a) cause it to be delivered to the proper officer of the court not later than the day before the date appointed for the hearing, or

(b) post it, at such a time that in the ordinary course of post it would be delivered not later than that day, in a letter duly addressed to the clerk and either registered or sent by the recorded delivery service, or

(c) have it with him at the hearing;

and if he is convicted of the offence and the court makes an order under paragraph 9 above the court shall order the licence to be surrendered to it; and if the offender has not posted the licence or caused it to be delivered as aforesaid and does not surrender it as required then he shall be guilty of an offence and the licence shall be revoked from the time when its surrender was ordered.

11. Where a court orders a fishing or general licence to be surrendered to it under paragraph 10 above, or where by an order of a court under paragraph 9 above a person is disqualified from holding or obtaining a licence, the court shall—

(a) send notice of the order to the water authority within whose area the offence was committed, unless the authority prosecuted in the case;

(b) if the licence has been so surrendered, retain it and forward it to that authority, who may dispose of it as they think fit.

12. Where any person is convicted of an offence against this Act, the proper officer of the court before whom he is convicted shall, within one month of the date of conviction, forward a certificate of the conviction to the water authority for the area in which the offence was committed.

13. A certificate under paragraph 12 above shall be receivable in evidence in all legal proceedings.

14. In paragraphs 10 and 12 above "proper oficer" means—

(a) in relation to a magistrates' court, the justices' chief executive for the court; and

(b) in relation to the Crown Court, the appropriate officer.

_____

1. References in Part II to "this Act" include references to s 32 of the Salmon Act 1986 post.

2. Note also Justices of the Peace Act 1979, s 64 (disqualification of justices who are members of local authorities).

3. See title CUSTOMS AND EXCISE, ante.
4. Even if owned by someone else: but see *R v Williams* [1991] Crim LR 793.
5. Defined by s 41, ante.
6. For "exposes for sale" see note to s 2(1), ante, and for "possession", see note to s 22(1), ante.

Fishery Limits Act 1976
(1976 c 86)

8–11400 1. British fishery limits. (1) Subject to the following provisions of this section, British fishery limits extend to 200 miles[1] from the baselines[2] from which the breadth of the territorial sea adjacent to the United Kingdom, the Channel Islands and the Isle of Man is measured.

(2) Her Majesty may by Order in Council, for the purpose of implementing any international agreement or the arbitral award of an international body, or otherwise, declare that British fishery limits extend to such other line as may be specified in the Order.

(3) Where the median line defined below is less than 200 miles[1] from the baselines referred to in subsection (1), and no other line is for the time being specified by Order in Council under subsection (2), British fishery limits extend to the median line.

(4) The median line is a line every point of which is equidistant from the nearest points of, on the one hand, the baselines referred to in subsection (1) and, on the other hand, the corresponding baselines of other countries.

(5) Subject to section 10(2)(*b*) below, references to British fishery limits in any enactment for the time being in force relating to sea fishing[1] or whaling are to the limits set by or under this section.
[Fishery Limits Act 1976, s 1.]

_____

1. For meaning of "miles", "sea fishing", "sea fish", "fishing boat" and "foreign fishing boat", see s 8, post. A requirement for a Spanish fishing vessel to obtain an authorisation for fishing between 12 and 200 miles is not in conflict with Community law even though antecedent rights under the London Fisheries Convention of 1964 required authorisation only up to 12 miles; see Case 812/79: *A-G v Juan C Burgoa* [1980] ECR 2787).
2. Baselines are drawn in accordance with the Territorial Waters Order in Council, 1964, made on 25 September 1964. See *Halsbury's Statutory Instruments*, Vol 23, title WATERS AND WATERCOURSES.

8–11401 2. Access to British fisheries. (1) The Ministers may by order[1] designate any country outside the United Kingdom, the Channel Islands and the Isle of Man and, in relation to it, areas within relevant British fishery limits in which, and descriptions of sea fish[2] for which, fishing boats[2] registered in that country may fish.

(2) A foreign fishing boat[2] not registered in a country for the time being designated under subsection (1) shall not enter British fishery limits except for a purpose recognised by international law or by any convention for the time being in force between Her Majesty's Government in the United Kingdom and the government of the country to which his boat belongs; and any such boat which enters those limits for such a purpose—

(*a*) shall return outside the limits as soon as the purpose has been fulfilled; and
(*b*) shall not fish or attempt to fish while within the limits.

(3) A foreign fishing boat registered in a country designated under subsection (1) shall not fish or attempt to fish within British fishery limits except in an area and for descriptions of fish for the time being designated under this section in relation to that country.

(4) At any time when a foreign fishing boat is in an area within British fishery limits and either—

(*a*) it is prohibited by this section from fishing in that area at all; or
(*b*) it is permitted under this section to fish only for certain descriptions of fish,

then, its fishing gear, or so much of the gear as is not required for permitted fishing, shall be stowed in accordance with an order made by the Ministers.

(5) If this section is contravened in the case of any fishing boat—

(*a*) the master of the boat is liable[3] on summary conviction to a fine not exceeding **£50,000** or on conviction on indictment to a fine;
(*b*) the court may on convicting him of an offence under this section order the forfeiture[4] of any fish or fishing gear found in the boat or taken or used by any person from the boat; and
(*c*) *Applies to Scotland.*

(6) The foregoing provisions of this section do not prohibit or restrict fishing by fishing boats registered in a country outside the United Kingdom in any area with respect to which special provision is made by any arrangement between Her Majesty's Government in the United Kingdom and the government of that country for fishing by such boats for the purpose of scientific research.

(7)–(8) *Annulment of orders; consequential amendments.*
(9) *Applies to Scotland.*
[Fishery Limits Act 1976, s 2, as amended by the Fisheries Act 1981, Sch 5, the Merchant Shipping Act 1988, Sch 7 and SI 1999/1820, Sch 2. A new Sub-s 9 is inserted by SI 1999/1820, Sch 2.]

1. Designation orders have been made in respect of fishing boats registered in countries belonging to the European Economic Community (SI 1983/253 amended by SI 1986/382, SI 1992/3108 and SI 1996/248) and in Norway and the Faroe Islands (SI 1996/1035) amended by SI 1997/1630.

2. For meaning of "miles", "sea fishing", "sea fish", "fishing boat" and "foreign fishing boat", see s 8, post. A requirement for a Spanish fishing vessel to obtain an authorisation for fishing between 12 and 200 miles is not in conflict with Community law even though antecedent rights under the London Fisheries Convention of 1964 required authorisation only up to 12 miles; see Case 812/79: *A-G v Juan C Burgoa* [1980] ECR 2787).

3. For procedure in respect of this offence which is triable either way, see the Magistrates' Courts Act 1980, ss 17A–21, PART I: MAGISTRATES' COURTS, PROCEDURE, ante.

4. For disposal of non-pecuniary forfeitures, see Magistrates' Courts Act 1980, s 140, PART I: MAGISTRATES' COURTS, PROCEDURE, ante.

8–11402   8. Interpretation.   In this Act—

"enactment" includes an enactment of the Parliament of Northern Ireland and a Measure of the Northern Ireland Assembly;

"fishing boat" means any vessel for the time being employed in fishing operations or any operations ancillary thereto;

"foreign fishing boat" means a fishing boat which is not

(a)   registered in the United Kingdom, the Channel Islands or the Isle of Man; or
(b)   wholly British-owned;

"miles" means international nautical miles of 1,852 metres;

"the Ministers" means the Minister of Agriculture, Fisheries and Food and the Secretaries of State concerned with sea fishing in Scotland and Northern Ireland respectively[1];

"sea fish" includes shellfish, salmon and migratory trout, and "sea fishing" has a corresponding meaning.

"wholly British-owned" means wholly owned by persons qualified to own British fishing boats for the purposes of Part II of the Merchant Shipping Act 1995;

[Fishery Limits Act 1976, s 8, as amended by the Merchant Shipping Act 1988, Sch 6 and the Merchant Shipping Act 1995, Sch 13.]

1. The functions of the Minister, so far as exercisable in relation to Wales, have been transferred to the National Assembly for Wales, by the National Assembly for Wales (Transfer of Functions) Order 1999, SI 1999/672, art 2, Sch 1. Residual functions of the Secretary of State and the Secretary of State for Wales have been transferred to the Minister of Agriculture, Fisheries and Food by the Transfer of Functions (Agriculture and Fisheries) Order 2000, SI 2000/1812.

Import of Live Fish (England and Wales) Act 1980
(1980 c 27)

8–11420   1. Power to limit the import etc of fish and fish eggs.   (1) Without prejudice to section 1(1) of the Diseases of Fish Act 1937 and subject to subsection (2) below, the Minister may by order[1] forbid either absolutely or except under a licence granted under this section, the import into, or the keeping or the release, in any part of England and Wales of live fish, or the live eggs of fish, of a species which is not native to England and Wales and which in the opinion of the Minister might compete with, displace, prey on or harm the habitat of any freshwater fish, shellfish or salmon in England and Wales.

(2) Before determining whether or not to make an order under this section, the Minister shall consult English Nature, the Countryside Council for Wales and any other person with whom the Minister considers that consultation is appropriate.

(3) The Minister may, subject to such conditions as he thinks fit, grant a licence to any person to import keep or release live fish, or the live eggs of fish, of a species specified in an order under this section and the Minister may revoke or vary any such licence.

(4) An order under this section may, with the consent of the Treasury, authorise the making of a charge for a licence under this section and shall specify a maximum charge.

(5) The power conferred by this section to make orders shall be exercisable by statutory instrument, which shall be subject to annulment in pursuance of a resolution of either House of Parliament.

[Import of Live Fish (England and Wales) Act 1980, s 1, as amended by the Fisheries Act 1980, s 37, the Environmental Protection Act 1990, Sch 9 and the Countryside and Rights of Way Act 2000, Sch 8.]

1. The Prohibition of Keeping Live Fish (Crayfish) Order 1996, SI 1996/1104 amended by SI 1996/1374 and the Prohibition of Keeping or Release of Live Fish (Specified Species) Order 1998, SI 1998/2409 amended by SI 2003/25 (E) and 416 (W) have been made.

8–11421   2. Powers of entry and inspection.   (1) While an order under section 1 of this Act is in force any officer commissioned by the Comrs of Customs and Excise, or a person duly authorised by the Minister may at all reasonable times, on production of his authority if so required, enter and inspect any land occupied by a person holding a licence granted under that section and any other land upon which he has reason to believe that live fish, or the live eggs of fish, of the species specified in the order are being kept or may be found.

(2) In this section "land" includes land covered with water but does not include a dwelling-house.
[Import of Live Fish (England and Wales) Act 1980, s 2, as amended by the Fisheries Act 1981, s 37 and Sch 5.]

8–11422 3. Offences etc. (1) Subject to subsection (2) below, any person who—

(*a*) imports or attempts to import into, or keeps or releases, in any part of England and Wales any live fish, or the live eggs of fish, of a species specified in an order under section 1 of this Act—

(i) in a case where the order forbids absolutely such import, keeping or release;

(ii) without having a valid licence granted under the said section 1 authorising such import keeping or release, in a case where the order forbids the import keeping or release except under such a licence;

(*b*) being the holder of a licence granted to him under the said section 1, acts in contravention of or fails to comply with any term of the licence;

(*c*) obstructs any person from entering or inspecting any land in pursuance of section 2 of this Act;

shall be guilty of an offence under this Act and shall be liable on summary conviction to a fine not exceeding **level 4** on the standard scale.

(2) A person shall not be guilty of an offence under this Act in respect of any act if he does the act for some scientific or research purpose authorised by the Minister.

(3) The Court by whom any person is convicted of an offence under paragraph (*a*) or (*b*) of subsection (1) above may order any fish or eggs in respect of which the offence was committed to be forfeited and destroyed.

(4) Any person who is empowered to enter land under section 2 of this Act may seize any fish or eggs with respect to which he has reason to believe that an offence under paragraph (*a*) or (*b*) of subsection (1) above has been committed, and may detain them pending the determination of any proceedings to be instituted under the said paragraph (*a*) or (*b*), or until the Minister is satisfied that no such proceedings are likely to be instituted.
[Import of Live Fish (England and Wales) Act 1980, s 3, as amended by the Fisheries Act 1981, s 37 and the Criminal Justice Act 1982, s 45.]

8–11423 4. Interpretation. In this Act—

"eggs" include milt;

"fish" includes shellfish;

"freshwater fish" means any fish living in fresh water including eels and the fry of eels, but excluding salmon;

"Minister" means—

(*a*) in relation to England, the Minister of Agriculture, Fisheries and Food; and

(*b*) in relation to Wales, the Secretary of State for Wales;

"salmon" includes all migratory fish of the species Salmo salar and Salmo trutta commonly known as salmon and sea trout respectively;

"shellfish" includes crustaceans and molluscs of any kind and any spat or spawn of shellfish.
[Import of Live Fish (England and Wales) Act 1980, s 4.]

Fisheries Act 1981
(1981 c 29)

PART I[1]
THE SEA FISH INDUSTRY AUTHORITY

8–11440 1–4. *Constitution, duties and powers of the Sea Fish Industry Authority.*

---

1. Part I contains ss 1–14.

8–11441 5. Records and information for levy purposes. (1) Regulations imposing a levy under section 4 above may require persons engaged in the sea fish industry to keep and preserve such records and to furnish to the Authority such information as may be specified in the regulations.

(2) Any officer authorised by the Authority may, on producing on demand evidence of his authority, require the production of, and take copies of, any records which a person is required to keep by virtue of the regulations and for that purpose may at any reasonable time enter any premises occupied for the purposes of his business by any person who is or may be liable to pay the levy and board any vessel owned by or in the possession of any such person.

(3) Any person who—

(a) fails without reasonable excuse to comply with a requirement imposed by virtue of subsection (1) or (2) above; or

(b) wilfully obstructs an officer in the exercise of his powers under subsection (2) above,

shall be guilty of a offence and liable on summary conviction to a fine not exceeding **level 4** on the standard scale.

(4) Any person who—

(a) in purported compliance with a requirement imposed by virtue of subsection (1) above knowingly makes a record or furnishes any information which is false in a material particular; or

(b) knowingly alters a record made in compliance with any such requirement so that it becomes false as aforesaid; and

(c) for "adjourned" there is substituted "in recess".

shall be guilty of an offence and liable on summary conviction to a fine not exceeding **level 5** on the standard scale or to imprisonment for a term not exceeding **three months** or to both.
[Fisheries Act 1981, s 5 as amended by the Criminal Justice Act 1982, s 46 and SI 2000/2040.]

8–11442   12. Restriction on disclosure of information.   (1) Subject to subsection (2) below, no information with respect to any particular undertaking which has been obtained by or on behalf of the Authority under this Act shall, without the consent of the person carrying on the undertaking, be disclosed otherwise than for the purpose of the discharge of the Authority's functions.

(2) Subsection (1) above shall not preclude the disclosure of information by or on behalf of the Authority—

(a) to the Ministers of any of them for the purposes of any of their functions relating to the sea fish industry or to the regulation of sea fishing; or

(b) for the purposes of any legal proceedings or of any report of any such proceedings; or

(c) to the Department of Agriculture and Rural Development for the purpose of any of its functions relating to the sea fish industry in Northern Ireland or to the regulation of sea fishing.

(3) If any person discloses information in contravention of this section he shall be guilty of an offence and liable[1]—

(a) on conviction on indictment, to a fine or to imprisonment for a term not exceeding **two years** or to both;

(b) on summary conviction, to a fine not exceeding **the prescribed sum** or to imprisonment for a term not exceeding **six months** or to both.

(4) In subsection (3)(b) above "the prescribed sum" means—

(a) in the case of an offence committed in England, Wales or Northern Ireland, the prescribed sum within the meaning of section 32 of the Magistrates' Courts Act 1980 (£1,000 at the passing of this Act);

(b) in the case of an offence committed in Scotland the prescribed sum within the meaning of section 289B of the Criminal Procedure (Scotland) Act 1975 (£1,000 at the passing of this Act);

and for the purposes of the application of this definition in Northern Ireland the provisions of the said Act of 1980 which relate to the sum mentioned in paragraph (a) above shall extend to Northern Ireland.
[Fisheries Act 1981, s 12, as amended by SI 2002/790.]

---

1. For procedure in respect of this offence which is triable either way, see the Magistrates' Courts Act 1980, ss 17A–21, in PART I: MAGISTRATES' COURTS, PROCEDURE, ante.

8–11443   14. Interpretation of Part I.   (1) In this Part of this Act—

"the Authority" means the Sea Fish Industry Authority;

"financial year" means the twelve months ending with 31st March;

"the Ministers" means the Minister of Agriculture, Fisheries and Food and the Secretaries of State respectively concerned with the sea fish industry in Scotland, Wales and Northern Ireland;

"sea fish" means fish of any kind found in the sea, including shellfish and, subject to section 4(8)(a) above, any part of any fish but does not include salmon or migratory trout.

(2) For the purposes of this Part of this Act other than sections 2(2A) and 3(5) "the sea fish industry" means the sea fish industry in the United Kingdom and a person shall be regarded as engaged in the sea fish industry if—

(a) he carries on the business of operating vessels for catching or processing sea fish or for transporting sea fish or sea fish products, being vessels registered in the United Kingdom; or

(b) he carries on in the United Kingdom the business of breeding, rearing or cultivating sea fish for human consumption, of selling sea fish or sea fish products by wholesale or retail, of

buying sea fish or sea fish products by wholesale, of importing sea fish or sea fish products or of processing sea fish (including the business of fish fryer).
[Fisheries Act 1981, s 14, as amended by SI 1989/1190.]

PART II[1]
FINANCIAL ASSISTANCE FOR SEA FISH INDUSTRY

8–11444   15–16. *Schemes of financial assistance*[2]

1. Part II contains ss 15–18.
2. The following Instruments have been made: Fish Producers' Organizations (Formation Grants) Scheme 1982, SI 1982/498 amended by SI 1985/987, Fishing Vessels (Acquisition and Improvement) (Grants) Scheme 1987, SI 1987/1135 amended by 1990/685, Fishing Vessels (Financial Assistance) Scheme 1987, SI 1987/1136, Fishing Vessels (Decommissioning) Schemes: 1993, SI 1993/1345; 1994, SI 1994/1568; 1996, SI 1996/1242, the Fishing Vessels (Safety Improvements) (Grants) Scheme 1995, SI 1995/1609, Fishing Vessels (Decommissioning) Scheme 2001, SI 2001/3390, Fishing Vessels (Decommissioning) Scheme 2003, SI 2003/2669; Fishing Boats (Satellite-Tracking Devices) (England) Scheme 2004, SI 2004/2467.

8–11445   17. Offences in connection with schemes.   Any person who—

(a) in furnishing any information in purported compliance with a requirement imposed by a scheme made under this Part of this Act makes a statement which he knows to be false in a material particular or recklessly makes a statement which is false in a material particular; or

(b) in purported compliance with a requirement imposed by such a scheme produces a document which he knows to be false in a material particular or recklessly produces a document which is false in a material particular; or

(c) wilfully refuses to supply any information, make any return or produce any document when required to do so by or under any such scheme,

shall be guilty of an offence and liable on summary conviction to a fine not exceeding **level 5** on the standard scale.
[Fisheries Act 1981, s 17 as amended by the Criminal Justice Act 1982, s 46.]

PART III[1]
REGULATION OF SEA FISHING

8–11446   27. Enforcement of provisions as to trans-shipment.   (1) For the purpose of enforcing the provisions of an order under section 4A or 6(1A) of the Sea Fish Conservation Act 1967 or the conditions of any licence granted under section 4A of that Act, a British sea-fishery officer may exercise in relation to any vessel (whether British or foreign) within British fishery limits the powers conferred by the following provisions of this section.

(2) He may go on board the vessel, with or without persons assigned to assist him in his duties, and for that purpose may require the vessel to stop and do anything else which will facilitate the boarding of the vessel.

(3) He may require the attendance of the master and other persons on board the vessel and may make any examination and inquiry which appears to him to be necessary for the purpose mentioned in subsection (1) above.

(4) Where it appears to him that a contravention of the order or a breach of a condition of the licence has at any time taken place he may—

(a) require the master of the vessel in relation to which the contravention took place to take, or may himself take, the vessel and its crew to the port which appears to him to be the nearest convenient port, and

(b) detain or require the master to detain the vessel in the port;

and if he detains or requires the detention of the vessel he shall serve on the master a notice in writing stating that the vessel will be or is required to be detained until the notice is withdrawn by the service on the master of a further notice in writing signed by a British sea-fishery officer.
[Fisheries Act 1981, s 27.]

1. Part III contains ss 19–30.

8–11447   30. Enforcement of Community rules.   (1) The following provisions apply in relation to enforceable Community restrictions relating to sea fishing except where, or to the extent that, other provision is made by an order under subsection (2) below—

(a) if any fishing boat fishes within British fishery limits in contravention of any such restriction, the master, the owner and the charterer (if any) are each guilty of an offence;

(b) sections 11, 12, 14 and 15(2) of the Sea Fish (Conservation) Act 1967 (penalties, jurisdiction and powers of seizure) apply to such offences as they apply to offences under section 5(1) of that Act; and (*c*) section 8 of the Sea Fisheries Act 1968 (general powers of British sea fishery officers) has effect in relation to such restrictions as it has effect in relation to the provisions mentioned in subsection (1) of that section.

(2) The Ministers may by order[1] make such provision as appears to them to be requisite for the enforcement of any enforceable Community restriction or other obligation relating to sea fishing; and any such order may in particular contain provisions which (with any necessary modifications) apply or correspond to any relevant provisions of the said Act of 1967 or the said Act of 1968.

(3) In this section—

"enforceable Community restriction" and "enforceable Community obligation" mean a restriction or obligation to which section 2(1) of the European Communities Act 1972 applies;

"fishing boat" means any vessel for the time being employed in fishing operations or any operations ancillary thereto;

"master" includes, in relation to any fishing boat, the person for the time being in command or charge of the boat;

"the Ministers"[2] means the Minister of Agriculture, Fisheries and Food and the Secretaries of State respectively concerned with sea fishing in Scotland, Wales and Northern Ireland.

(4) Any order under subsection (2) above shall be subject to annulment in pursuance of a resolution of either House of Parliament.
[Fisheries Act 1981, s 30.]

---

1. The following regulations have been made:

Sea Fisheries (Enforcement of Community Measures for Spanish and Portuguese Vessels) Order 1986, SI 1986/110;
Sea Fishing (Enforcement of Community Conservation Measures) Order 1986, SI 1986/2090 amended by SI 1988/17, SI 1992/1084 and 2936 and SI 1994/1680;
Sea Fish (Marketing Standards) Regulations 1986, SI 1986/1272 amended by SI 1989/687 and SI 1994/452;
Fishing Boats (Marking and Documentation) (Enforcement) Order 1993, SI 1993/2015;
Sea Fishing (Enforcement of Community Control Measures) Order 1994, SI 1994/451 and amended by SI 1996/2 and revoked in so far as they apply to Wales by SI 2000/1075 and partially revoked (as to England and N Ireland) by SI 2000/51;
Sea Fishing (Enforcement of Community Conservation Measures) Order 1997, SI 1997/1949 amended by SI 1997/2841, SI 1999/424 revoked in relation to Wales and the sea around Wales by SI 2000/1096, SI 2000/1081 (which revokes the regulations except in so far as they have effect in Wales) and SI 2000/2230;
Sea Fishing (Enforcement of Community Quota Measures) Order 1999, SI 1999/424 amended by SI 2000/827 (England);
Sea Fishing (Enforcement of Community Control Measures) Order 2000, SI 2000/51 amended by SI 2003/229, SI 2004/38 and 393 (E) and SI 2005/393 (E) and 2624;
Sea Fishing (Enforcement of Community Quota and Third Country Measures) Order 2000, SI 2000/827 as amended by SI 2000/2008;
Sea Fishing (Enforcement of Community Control Measures) (Wales) Order 2000, SI 2000/1075 amended by SI 2003/559;
Sea Fishing (Enforcement of Community Satellite Monitoring Measures) (Wales) Order 2000, SI 2000/1078 amended by SI 2002/677;
Sea Fishing (Enforcement of Community Conservation Measures) Order 2000, SI 2000/1081 amended by SI 2002/426 and 794;
Sea Fishing (North East Atlantic Control Measures) Order 2000, SI 2000/1843;
Sea Fishing (Enforcement of Community Conservation Measures) (Wales) Order 2000, SI 2000/2230;
Sea Fishing (Enforcement of Community Quota and Third Country Fishing Measures) Order 2002, SI 2002/272 revoked in respect to England by SI 2003/272;
Sea Fishing (Enforcement of Community Quota and Third Country Fishing Measures) (England) Order 2003, SI 2003/772 (revoked in relation to England by SI 2004/1237);
Sea Fishing (Restrictions on Days at Sea) (No 2) Order 2003, SI 2003/1535 amended by SI 2004/38 (revoked in relation to England by SI 2004/398);
Sea Fishing (Restrictions on Days at Sea) Order 2004, SI 2004/398 (revoked in relation to England by SI 2005/393);
Sea Fishing (Enforcement of Community Quota and Third Country Fishing Measures) (England) Order 2004, SI 2004/1237;
Sea Fishing (Enforcement of Community Satellite Monitoring Measures) Order 2004, SI 2004/3226;
Incidental Catches of Cetaceans in Fisheries (England) Order 2005, SI 2005/17;
Sea Fishing (Restrictions on Days at Sea) Order 2005, SI 2005/393.

All these regulations specify certain Council Regulations contravention of which by British boats, or foreign boats in British fishery limits, is made a criminal offence. Offences in relation to false statements and obstrucion are also provided. Various penalties are provided including some for offences triable either way; fines relating to the size of an illegal catch, forfeiture and distress for recovery of fines are also provided.

In addition each year sees the making of a Third Country Fishing (Enforcement) Order: SI 2000/1096 (Wales), SI 2000/827 (England) which make breaches of specified articles of the Community regulations offences.

2. Residual functions of the Secretaries of State under Part I (except s 2(5)) (applicable to Wales) and SI 2001/1631 (applicable to England) s 30(2) of this Act have been transferred to the Minister of Agriculture, Fisheries of Food by the Transfer of Functions (Agriculture and Fisheries) Order 2000, SI 2000/1812.

PART IV[1]
FISH FARMING

8–11448   **31. Financial assistance**[2]**.** (1) The Ministers may, in accordance with a scheme[3] made by them with the approval of the Treasury, make such grants as appear to them to be desirable for the purpose of reorganising, developing or promoting fish farming in Great Britain.

(2) In this section "fish farming" means the breeding, rearing or cultivating of fish (including shellfish) for the purpose of producing food for human consumption.

(3) A scheme under this section may be confined to the making of such grants as appear to the Ministers to be requisite for enabling persons to benefit from any Community instrument which provides for the making of grants by a Community institution where such grants are also provided by a member State.

(4) A scheme under this section may extend to the whole of Great Britain, to England, Wales or Scotland only or to any two of those countries.

(5) In this section "the Ministers" means—

(a) (*Repealed*);

(b) in relation to a scheme extending to England only or to England together with Wales, that Minister or, as the case may be, that Minister and the Secretary of State concerned with fisheries in Wales;

(c) in relation to a scheme extending to Wales, the Secretary of State concerned with fisheries in Wales;

but a scheme made by two or more Ministers may provide for payments under the scheme to be made by any of them.

(6) A scheme under this section shall be laid before Parliament after being made and shall cease to have effect (without prejudice to anything previously done thereunder or to the making of a new scheme) after the expiration of the period of forty days beginning with the day on which it is made unless within that period it has been approved by a resolution of each House of Parliament.

(7) In reckoning any period under subsection (6) above no account shall be taken of any time during which Parliament is dissolved or prorogued or during which both Houses are adjourned for more than four days.

(8) Section 17[4] above shall have effect in relation to a scheme under this section as it has effect in relation to a scheme under Part II of this Act.

(9) *Scotland.*

[Fisheries Act 1981, s 31 as amended by SI 2000/2040.]

---

1. Part IV contains ss 31–34.

2. This section creates certain offences in respect of fraudulent applications for grant, for which there is a maximum penalty not exceeding **level 5** on the standard; see s 31(8) below, and s 17, ante.

3. The Fish Farming (Financial Assistance) Scheme 1984, SI 1984/341, amended by SI 1987/1134, and the Fish Farming (Financial Assistance) Scheme 1987, SI 1987/1134, have been made.

4. Ante.

8–11449 33. Exclusion of offences under conservation legislation. (1) A person shall not be guilty of an offence mentioned in Part I of Schedule 4 to this Act by reason of anything done or omitted by him in the course of fish farming if it is done or omitted under the authority of an exemption conferred by the Minister and in accordance with any conditions attached to the exemption.

(2) The Minister may by regulations confer general exemptions for the purposes of subsection (1) above, and such regulations may—

(a) make different provision for different methods of fish farming and for other different circumstances; and

(b) specify conditions to which the exemptions are subject.

(3) Regulations under subsection (2) above shall be made by statutory instrument which shall be subject to annulment in pursuance of a resolution of either House of Parliament.

(4) In the application of subsections (1) and (2) above to offences under the Salmon and Freshwater Fisheries Act 1975, "the Minister" means, in relation to the area of the Welsh Water Authority, the Secretary of State and, in relation to other areas to which the Act applies, the Minister of Agriculture, Fisheries and Food; and in the application of those subsections to offences under enactments relating to sea fishing, "the Minister" means, in relation to England, the Minister of Agriculture, Fisheries and Food, and, in relation to Wales or Scotland, the Secretary of State concerned with fisheries in that country.

(5) It shall be a defence for a person charged with an offence mentioned in Part II of Schedule 4 to this Act to show that he believed on reasonable grounds that the fish with respect to which the offence is alleged to have been committed were produced by fish farming.

(6) In this section "fish farming" means the breeding, rearing or cultivating of fish (including shellfish) whether or not for the purpose of producing food for human consumption; but the reference in subsection (5) above to fish produced by fish farming does not include fish bred, reared or cultivated in captivity which have later been released to the wild.

[Fisheries Act 1981, s 33.]

8–11450 34. Structures for propagating or cultivating shellfish. In sections 2, 7, 9 and 12 of the Sea Fisheries (Shellfish) Act 1967 references to a bed for shellfish, a shellfish bed or an oyster bed shall include references to any structure floating on or standing or suspended in, water for the propagation or cultivation of shellfish or, as the case may be, oysters; and—

(a) the area of a fishery to which an order under section 1 of that Act relates may, within the limits specified in subsection (1) of that section, include any waters which contain or are to contain any such structure;

(b) the reference in section 5 of that Act to cultivating the ground for shellfish shall include a reference to cultivating shellfish by means of any such structure.

[Fisheries Act 1981, s 34.]

PART V¹
MISCELLANEOUS AND SUPPLEMENTARY

8–11451   42. Offences by bodies corporate.   Where an offence under Part I, II or IV of this Act which has been committed by a body corporate is proved to have been committed with the consent or connivance of or to be attributable to any neglect on the part of any director, manager, secretary or other similar officer of the body corporate, or any person who was purporting to act in any such capacity, he as well as the body corporate shall be deemed to be guilty of that offence and shall be liable to be proceeded against and punished accordingly.

[Fisheries Act 1981, s 42.]

---

1. Part V contains ss 35–46.

8–11452   44. General interpretation.   In this Act—

"salmon" includes any fish of the salmon species;
"shellfish" includes crustaceans and molluscs of any kind;
"migratory trout" means any species of trout which migrates to and from the sea.

[Fisheries Act 1981, s 44.]

Section 33(1)   SCHEDULE 4
                              EXEMPTIONS FOR FISH FARMING

(As amended by the Inshore Fishing (Scotland) Act 1984 and the Water Consolidation (Consequential Provisions) Act 1991, Sch 1.)

PART I
OFFENCES TO WHICH SECTION 33(1) OF THIS ACT APPLIES

Offences under the Salmon and Freshwater Fisheries Act 1975

8–11453   1. Any offence under section 2(2)(a) of the Salmon and Freshwater Fisheries Act 1975 (taking, killing or injuring, or attempting to take, kill or injure, unclean or immature fish).

2. Any offence under section 3 of that Act (restriction on shooting or working seine or draft net in certain waters and prohibition on use of certain nets).

3. Any offence under section 5(1) of that Act (prohibition on use of explosives, poison or electrical devices to take or destroy fish) relating to the use a noxious substance or electrical device, and any offence under section 5(4) of that Act relating to the possession of such substance or device.

4. Any offence under section 19 of that Act (fishing for, taking or killing or attempting to take or kill fish during close seasons or close times).

5. Any offence under section 27 of that Act (fishing for or taking fish without a licence or possession of equipment with intent to use it for an unlicensed purpose).

Offences against byelaws relating to salmon and other freshwater fishing

6. Any offence under section 211 of the Water Resources Act 1991 consisting in a contravention of a byelaw made for any of the following purposes mentioned in paragraph 6(2) of Schedule 25 to that Act—

(a) prohibiting the taking or removal from any water without lawful authority of any fish, whether alive or dead;

(b) prohibiting or regulating the taking of trout or any freshwater fish of a size less than that prescribed by the byelaw;

(c) prohibiting the use for taking salmon, trout, or freshwater fish of any instrument (not being a fixed engine) in such waters and at such times as are prescribed by the byelaw;

(d) specifying the nets and other instruments (not being fixed engines) which may be used for taking salmon, trout, freshwater fish and eels and imposing requirements as to the use of such nets and other instruments;

(e) imposing requirements as to the construction, design, material and dimensions of any such nets or instruments, including in the case of nets the size of mesh;

(f) prohibiting the carrying in any boat or vessel whilst being used in fishing for salmon or trout of any net which is not licensed, or which is without the mark, label or number prescribed by the byelaw;

(g) prohibiting or regulating the carrying in a boat or vessel during the annual close season for salmon of a net capable of taking salmon, other than a net commonly used in the area to which the byelaw applies for sea fishing and carried in a boat or vessel commonly used for that purpose.

Offences relating to sea fishing

8–9. *(Repealed).*

10. Any offence consisting of a contravention of a byelaw made under section 5 of the Sea Fisheries Regulation Act 1966 (byelaws for the regulation of sea fishing).

11. Any offence under section 17 of the Sea Fisheries (Shellfish) Act 1967 of taking an edible crab or landing a lobster in a condition prohibited by subsection (1) or (3) of that section.

12. Any offence under section 1(1) or (3) of the Sea Fish (Conservation) Act 1967 (landing or carrying fish smaller than prescribed size).

13. Any offence under section 3(5) of that Act (contravention of order regulating nets and gear).

14. Any offence under section 4(3) or (3A) of that Act (contravention of order prohibiting fishing without licence and failure to return to sea fish caught in contravention of such a prohibition).

15. Any offence under section 4A(3) of that Act (contravention of order prohibiting trans-shipment of fish without licence).

16. Any offence under section 5(1) or (6) of that Act (contravention of order prohibiting fishing and failure to return to sea fish caught in contravention of such a prohibition).

17. Any offence under section 6 of that Act (landing or trans-shipping fish in contravention of order).

17A. *Scotland.*

PART II

OFFENCES TO WHICH SECTION 33(5) OF THIS ACT APPLIES

Offences relating to freshwater fish and salmon

18–25. *Scotland.**

26. An offence under section 2(2)(b) of the Salmon and Freshwater Fisheries Act 1975 (buying, selling, exposure for sale or possession of unclean or immature fish or parts of such fish).

27. Any offence under section 22(1) of that Act (buying, selling, exposure for sale or possession for sale of fish at prohibited times of year).

28. Any offence under subsection (3) of section 23 of that Act of entering for export or exporting fish contrary to subsection (1) of that section (unclean fish and fish caught at a time when their sale is prohibited).

---

*Repealed, except in relation to the River Tweed and the Uper Esk, by the Salmon and Freshwater Fisheries (Consolidation) (Scotland) Act 2003, Sch 4.

Offences relating to sea fishing

29. *Repealed.*

30. Any offence under section 16 of the Sea Fisheries (Shellfish) Act 1967 (sale, exposure for sale, buying for sale or consignment for the purpose of sale of oysters at prohibited times of year).

31. Any offence under section 17(1) of that Act of possessing, selling or offering for sale, buying for sale or consigning for the purpose of sale an edible crab in a condition prohibited by that subsection.

32. Any offence under section 17(3) of that Act of selling, exposing or offering for sale, or possessing for the purpose of sale a lobster in a condition prohibited by that subsection.

33. Any offence under section 1(2) of the Sea Fisheries (Conservation) Act 1967 (selling, exposing or offering for sale, or possessing for the purpose of sale fish smaller than the prescribed size).

34. Any offence under section 2 of that Act (possession for use in the course of a business of fish prohibited from being sold under section 1(2) of that Act).

34A. *Scotland.*

British Fishing Boats Act 1983

(1983 c 8)

8–11560   1. Restrictions on fishing etc, by British fishing boats. (1) The operations mentioned in subsection (2) below may not be carried out by or from a relevant British fishing boat unless the boat is qualified in accordance with an order[1] made by the Ministers[2] under this subsection for use in carrying out operations of that description.

(2) Those operations are—

(a) fishing for sea fish in any area for the time being specified in an order[1] made by the Ministers;

(b) the trans-shipment of sea fish in any such area; and

(c) the landing of sea fish in the United Kingdom.

References below in this Act to a restricted fishing area are references to any area for the time being specified in an order made by the Ministers under this subsection.

(3) An order[1] under subsection (1) above prescribing qualifications for relevant British fishing boats for use in carrying out any such operations may prescribe conditions for qualification with respect to the nationality of members of the crew of a fishing boat, or of any proportion of those members specified in the order.

(4) The conditions so prescribed shall be such as appear to the Ministers to be necessary or expedient for the protection of the sea fishing industry in England and Wales and Northern Ireland; but any such conditions shall not discriminate between British citizens and persons who are nationals of any other member State.

(5) Where a relevant British fishing boat is not for the time being qualified under this section for use in carrying out operations of any description mentioned in subsection (2)(a) or (b) above in a restricted fishing area, its fishing gear shall be stowed in accordance with an order[1] made by the Ministers at any time when it is within such an area.

(6) If this section is contravened in the case of any fishing boat the master, the owner and the

charterer (if any) of the boat shall be liable[3] on summary conviction to a fine not exceeding £50,000 or on conviction on indictment to a fine.

(7) The court by or before which a person is convicted of an offence under subsection (6) above may order the forfeiture of any fish or fishing gear found in the boat in relation to which the offence was committed or taken or used by any person from the boat; and in Scotland, any fish or fishing gear forfeited under this subsection may be destroyed or disposed of as the court may direct.

(8) Any power to make an order under this section shall be exercisable by statutory instrument, which shall be subject to annulment in pursuance of a resolution of either House of Parliament.
[British Fishing Boats Act 1983, s 1 as amended by SI 1999/1820, art 4, Sch 2, Pt I, paras 70(1), (2)(a), (2)(b).]

---

1. See the British Fishing Boats Order 1983, SI 1983/482.
2. Functions of the Minister, so far as exercisable in relation to Wales, have been transferred to the National Assembly for Wales (Transfer of Functions) Order 1999, SI 1999;/672, art 2, Sch 1. Residual functions of the Secretary of State and the Secretary of State for Wales have been transferred to the Minister of Agriculture, Fisheries and Food by the Transfer of Functions (Agriculture and Fisheries) Order 2000, SI 2000/1812.
3. For procedure in respect of this offence which is triable either way, see the Magistrates' Courts Act 1980, ss 17A–21 in PART I: MAGISTRATES' COURTS, PROCEDURE, ante.

8–11561 2. Powers of British sea-fishery officers in relation to British fishing boats in restricted fishing areas. (1) The powers conferred by the following provisions of this section are exercisable by British sea-fishery officers, in relation to any British fishing boat within a restricted fishing area, for the purpose of enforcing the provisions of section 1 of this Act.

(2) Any such officer may go on board any such boat, with or without persons assigned to assist him in his duties, and for that purpose may require the boat to stop and do anything else which will facilitate the boarding of the boat.

(3) Any such officer may require the attendance of the master and other persons on board any boat he has boarded under subsection (2) above and may make any examination and inquiry which appears to him to be necessary for the purpose of enforcing the provisions of section 1 of this Act.

(4) Without prejudice to the generality of subsection (3) above, any such officer—

(a) may require any person on board any such boat to produce any document he has with him on board that is or may be relevant for determining his nationality and any document relating to the boat, to its fishing operations or other operations ancillary to its fishing operations or to persons on board which is in his custody or possession, and may take copies of any such document;

(b) for the purpose of ascertaining whether an offence under section 1 of this Act has been committed in relation to any such boat, may search the boat for any such document and may require any person on board the boat to do anything which appears to him to be necessary for facilitating the search; and

(c) if he has reason to suspect that any such offence has been committed in relation to any such boat, may seize and detain any such document produced to him or found on board for the purpose of enabling the document to be used as evidence in proceedings for the offence;

but nothing in paragraph (c) above shall permit any document required by law to be carried on board the boat to be seized except while the boat is detained in a port.

(5) Where it appears to any such officer that an offence under section 1 of this Act has been committed in relation to any fishing boat, he may—

(a) require the master of the boat to take, or may himself take, the boat and its crew to the port which appears to him to be the nearest convenient port; and

(b) detain or require the master to detain the boat in the port;

and where such an officer detains or requires the detention of a boat he shall serve on the master a notice in writing stating that the boat will be or is required to be detained until the notice is withdrawn by the service on the master of a further notice in writing signed by a British sea-fishery officer.
[British Fishing Boats Act 1983, s 2.]

8–11562 3. Powers of entry of British sea-fishery officers in relation to premises on land.
(1) Subject to the following provisions of this section, if—

(a) in England, Wales or Northern Ireland, a justice of the peace; or

(b) in Scotland, the sheriff or a justice of the peace;

is satisfied by information on oath that there is reasonable ground for suspecting that an offence under section 1 of this Act has been committed in relation to any fishing boat, and that any document relevant for determining whether such an offence has been committed in relation to that boat may be found on any premises specified in the information, he may grant a search warrant for the purposes of this section.

(2) The premises specified in any information laid for the purposes of subsection (1) above must be premises (other than a dwelling-house) used for carrying on a business in connection with the operation of fishing boats or activities connected with or ancillary to the operation of fishing boats.

(3) For the purposes of this section, a document shall be regarded as relevant for determining

whether an offence under section 1 of this Act has been committed in relation to a fishing boat if it relates—

    (*a*) to that boat, to its fishing operations or to other operations ancillary to its fishing operations; or

    (*b*) to the nationality of members of the crew of that boat.

A warrant granted under subsection (1) above shall authorise any British sea-fishery officer named in the warrant, with or without any constables, to enter the premises specified in the information and to search the premises for any document relevant for determining whether the suspected offence has been committed.

(5) Any such officer may require any person on any premises he has entered in pursuance of any such warrant to produce any document relevant for determining whether the suspected offence has been committed which is in his custody or possession, and may take copies of any such document.

(6) Any such officer may require any such person to do anything which appears to him to be necessary for facilitating any search carried out by him in pursuance of the warrant.

(7) Any such officer may seize and detain any document relevant for determining whether the suspected offence has been committed which is produced to him or found in the course of any such search, for the purpose of enabling the document to be used as evidence in proceedings for the offence.

(8) A warrant granted under subsection (1) above shall remain in force for a period of one month.
[British Fishing Boats Act 1983, s 3.]

8–11563   4. Supplementary provisions with respect to powers of British sea-fishery officers.
  (1) Any person who—

    (*a*) without reasonable excuse fails to comply with any requirement imposed by a British sea-fishery officer under section 2 or 3 of this Act;

    (*b*) prevents, or attempts to prevent, any other person from complying with any such requirement; or

    (*c*) assaults any such officer while exercising any of the powers conferred on him under section 2 or 3 of this Act or wilfully obstructs any such officer in the exercise of any of those powers;

shall be liable[1] on summary conviction to a fine not exceeding **£5,000** or on conviction on indictment to a fine.

(2) A British sea-fishery officer shall not be liable in any civil or criminal proceedings for anything done in purported exercise of the powers conferred on him by section 2 or 3 of this Act if the court is satisfied that the act was done in good faith and with reasonable skill and care and that there were reasonable grounds for doing it.
[British Fishing Boats Act 1983, s 4.]

---

    1. For procedure in respect of this offence which is triable either way, see the Magistrates' Courts Act 1980, ss 17A–21 in PART I: MAGISTRATES' COURTS, PROCEDURE, ante.

8–11564   5. Recovery of fines.   (1) Where a fine is imposed by a magistrates' court in England and Wales or Northern Ireland on the master, owner or charterer or a member of the crew of a fishing boat who is convicted by the court of an offence under section 1 or 4 of this Act, the court may—

    (*a*) issue a warrant of distress against the boat and its gear and catch and any property of the person convicted for the purpose of levying the amount of the fine; and

    (*b*) order the boat to be detained for a period not exceeding three months from the date of the conviction or until the fine is paid or the amount of the fine is levied in pursuance of any such warrant, whichever occurs first.

  (2) *Scotland.*

  (3) Sections 77(1) and 78 of the Magistrates' Courts Act 1980 (postponement of issue of, and defects in, warrants of distress) shall apply to a warrant of distress issued under this section in England and Wales as they apply to a warrant of distress issued under Part III of that Act.

  (4) *Northern Ireland.*
[British Fishing Boats Act 1983, s 5.]

8–11565   6. Offences committed by bodies corporate.   Where any offence under section 1 or 4 of this Act committed by a body corporate is proved to have been committed with the consent or approval of any director, manager, secretary or other officer of the body corporate, he, as well as the body corporate, shall be deemed to be guilty of the offence and shall be liable to be proceeded against and punished accordingly.
[British Fishing Boats Act 1983, s 6.]

8–11566   7. Jurisdiction to try offences.   Proceedings for an offence under section 1 or 4 of this Act may be taken, and the offence may for all incidental purposes be treated as having been committed, in any place in the United Kingdom.
[British Fishing Boats Act 1983, s 7.]

8–11567   9. Interpretation.   In this Act—

"British fishing boat" means a fishing vessel which either is registered in the United Kingdom under Part II of the Merchant Shipping Act 1995 or is wholly British-owned;

"British sea-fishery officer" means any person who by virtue of section 7 of the Sea Fisheries Act 1968 is a British sea-fishery officer;

"fishing boat" means any vessel for the time being employed in fishing operations or any operations ancillary to fishing operations;

"master" includes in relation to any fishing boat, the person for the time being in command or charge of the boat;

"the Ministers" means the Minister of Agriculture, Fisheries and Food and the Secretaries of State respectively concerned with the sea fishing industry in Scotland, Wales and Northern Ireland; and

"relevant British fishing boat" means a British fishing boat which is not a Scottish fishing boat;

"relevant British fishery limits" means British fishery limits so far as they do not relate to the Scottish zone;

""the Scottish zone" has the same meaning as it has for the purposes of the Scotland Act 1998;"; and

"Scottish fishing boat" means a fishing vessel which is registered in the register maintained under section 8 of the Merchant Shipping Act 1995 and whose entry in the register specifies a port in Scotland as the port to which the vessel is to be treated as belonging;

"sea fish" includes shellfish, salmon and migratory trout, and "sea fishing industry" has a corresponding meaning;

"wholly British-owned" means wholly owned by persons qualified to own British ships for the purposes of Part II of the Merchant Shipping Act 1995;

and references to a restricted fishing area shall be read in accordance with section 1(2) of this Act.
[British Fishing Boats Act 1983, s 9.]

8–11567A   9A. (*Scotland*)
[British Fishing Boats Act 1983, s 9A, as amended by the Merchant Shipping Act 1988, Sch 6, the Merchant Shipping (Registration, etc) Act 1993, Sch 2, the Merchant Shipping Act 1995, Sch 13 and the Scotland Act 1998 (Consequential Modifications) (No 2) Order 1999.]

Diseases of Fish Act 1983
(1983 c 30)

Information about fish farming

8–11580   7. Power to require information.   (1) If it appears to the Minister[1] necessary to do so for the purpose of obtaining information with a view to preventing the spread of disease among fish, he may make an order[2] under this section.

(2) An order under this section may require any person who occupies an inland fish farm for the purposes of a business of fish farming carried on by him (whether or not for profit)—

(*a*)   to register the business in a register kept for the purpose by the Minister,

(*b*)   to furnish in writing to the Minister such information as may be specified in the order in relation to the farm and to fish, eggs of fish and foodstuff for fish,

(*c*)   to compile such records as may be so specified in relation to the matters mentioned in paragraph (*b*) above, and

(*d*)   to retain for such period (not exceeding 3 years) as may be so specified any records compiled in accordance with paragraph (*c*) above.

In this subsection "fish" does not include shellfish.

(3) An order under this section may require any person who owns or possesses any cage, pontoon or other structure which is anchored or moored in marine waters and is used by him for the purposes of a business of fish farming carried on by him (whether or not for profit)—

(*a*)   to register the business in a register kept for the purpose by the Minister,

(*b*)   to furnish in writing to the Minister such information as may be specified in the order in relation to any such cage, pontoon or other structure and to fish, eggs of fish and foodstuff for fish,

(*c*)   to compile such records as may be so specified in relation to the matters mentioned in paragraph (*b*) above, and

(*d*)   to retain for such period (not exceeding 3 years) as may be so specified any records compiled in accordance with paragraph (*c*) above.

In this subsection "fish" does not include shellfish.

(4) An order under this section may require any person who carries on a business of shellfish farming (whether or not for profit)—

(a)   to register the business in a register kept for the purpose by the Minister,

(b)   to furnish in writing to the Minister such information as may be specified in the order in relation to any activity carried on (whether in marine or inland waters or on land) for the purpose of cultivating or propagating shellfish in the course of the business, and in relation to shellfish deposited in or on or taken from such waters or land in the course of the business,

(c)   to compile such records as may be so specified in relation to the matters mentioned in paragraph (b) above, and

(d)   to retain for such period (not exceeding 3 years) as may be so specified any records compiled in accordance with paragraph (c) above.

(5) An order under this section may require any person registering a business as mentioned in subsection (2)(a), (3)(a) or 4(a) above to pay to the Minister in respect of each registration such fee (complying with subsection (6) below) as may be specified in the order.

(6) The fee shall be such as the Minister may determine with the Treasury's approval but shall not exceed the cost to the Minister of effecting the registration.

(7) Any person authorised by the Minister may, on producing on demand evidence of his authority, require the production of, and inspect and take copies of, any records which a person is required to retain by virtue of an order under this section.

(8) In this section—

"fish farming" means the keeping of live fish with a view to their sale or to their transfer to other waters;

"inland fish farm" means any place where inland waters are used for the keeping of live fish with a view to their sale or to their transfer to other waters (whether inland or not);

"inland waters" means waters within Great Britain which do not form part of the sea or of any creek, bay or estuary or of any river as far as the tide flows;

"marine waters" means waters (other than inland waters) within the seaward limits of the territorial sea adjacent to Great Britain;

"the Minister" means—

    (a)   in relation to England, and any marine waters adjacent to England, the Secretary of State;

    (b)   in relation to Wales, and any marine waters adjacent to Wales, the Secretary of State;

    (c)   in relation to Scotland (including the marine waters thereof), the Secretary of State;

"shellfish" includes crustaceans and molluscs of any kind, and includes any brood, ware, half-ware, spat or spawn of shellfish;

"shellfish farming" means the cultivation or propagation of shellfish (whether in marine or inland waters or on land) with a view to their sale or to their transfer to other waters or land.

(9) The power to make an order under this section shall be exercisable by statutory instrument subject to annulment in pursuance of a resolution of either House of Parliament.

[Diseases of Fish Act 1983, s 7, as amended by SI 2002/794.]

---

1. Functions of the Minister, so far as exercisable in relation to Wales, transferred to the National Assembly for Wales, by the National Assembly for Wales (Transfer of Functions) Order 1999, SI 1999/672, art 2, Sch 1.

2. The Registration of Fish Farming and Shellfish Farming Businesses Order 1985, SI 1985/1391 has been made.

8–11581   8. Information: enforcement.   (1) Any person who—

(a)   fails without reasonable excuse to comply with a requirement of an order under section 7 above (other than a requirement mentioned in subsection (5) of that section), or

(b)   in purported compliance with a requirement of an order under section 7 above knowingly furnishes any information or compiles a record which is false in a material particular, or

(c)   knowingly alters a record compiled in compliance with a requirement of an order under section 7 above so that the record becomes false in a material particular, or

(d)   fails without reasonable excuse to comply with a requirement imposed by virtue of section 7(7) above, or

(e)   intentionally obstructs a person in the exercise of his powers under section 7(7) above,

shall be guilty of an offence and liable on summary conviction to a fine not exceeding **level 4** on the standard scale.

(2) Where an offence under this section which has been committed by a body corporate is proved to have been committed with the consent or connivance of, or to be attributable to any neglect on the part of, a director, manager, secretary or other similar officer of the body corporate, or any person who was purporting to act in any such capacity, he, as well as the body corporate, shall be guilty of that offence and shall be liable to be proceeded against and punished accordingly.

(3) For the purposes of and incidental to the jurisdiction of any magistrates' court or, in Scotland, of the sheriff, any offence under this section committed in, or in relation to anything in, the territorial sea adjacent to Great Britain shall be taken to have been committed in any place in which the offender may for the time being be found.

[Diseases of Fish Act 1983, s 8 amended by the Statute Law (Repeals) Act 1993, Sch 1.]

8–11582 9. Disclosure of information. (1) Information (including information in records) obtained by any person in pursuance of section 7 above or an order under that section shall not be disclosed except—

(a) with the written consent of the person by whom the information was provided, or

(b) in the form of a summary of similar information obtained from a number of persons, where the summary is so framed as not to enable particulars relating to any one person or business to be ascertained from it, or

(c) for the purpose of any criminal proceedings or for the purpose of a report of any such proceedings or

(d) for the purpose of enabling the Environment Agency to carry out any of its functions, under the 1937 Act.

(2) Any person who discloses any information in contravention of subsection (1) above shall be guilty of an offence and liable on summary conviction to a fine not exceeding **level 4** on the standard scale (as defined in section 75 of the Criminal Justice Act 1982).

(3) In this section "the Minister" has the same meaning as in section 7 above.
[Diseases of Fish Act 1983, s 9 as amended by the Salmon Act 1986 s 38, the Water Act 1989, Sch 17 and the Environment Act 1995, Sch 15.]

Salmon Act 1986[1]

(1986 c 62)

PART III[2]
PROVISIONS APPLYING TO ENGLAND AND WALES

8–11600 31. Dealer licensing in England and Wales. Minister may make Orders prohibiting unlicensed dealing in salmon or purchase from an unlicensed dealer and creating criminal offences therefor. "Deal" in relation to salmon, includes selling any quantity of salmon, whether by way of business or otherwise, and acting on behalf of a buyer or seller of salmon.
[Salmon Act 1986, s 31—summarised.]

---

1. This Act came into force on 7 January 1987.
2. Part III contains ss 31–38.

8–11601 32. Handling salmon in suspicious circumstances. (1) Subject to subsections (3) and (4) below, a person shall be guilty of an offence if, at a time when he believes or it would be reasonable for him to suspect that a relevant offence has at any time been committed in relation to any salmon[1], he receives the salmon, or undertakes or assists in its retention, removal or disposal by or for the benefit of another person, or if he arranges to do so.

(2) For the purposes of this section an offence is a relevant offence in relation to a salmon if—

(a) it is committed by taking, killing or landing that salmon, either in England and Wales or in Scotland; or

(b) that salmon is taken, killed or landed, either in England and Wales or in Scotland, in the course of the commission of the offence.

(3) It shall be immaterial for the purposes of subsection (1) above that a person's belief or the grounds for suspicion relate neither specifically to a particular offence that has been committed nor exclusively to a relevant offence or to relevant offences; but it shall be a defence in proceedings for an offence under this section to show that no relevant offence had in fact been committed in relation to the salmon in question.

(4) A person shall not be guilty of an offence under this section in respect of conduct which constitutes a relevant offence in relation to any salmon or in respect of anything done in good faith for purposes connected with the prevention or detection of crime or the investigation or treatment of disease.

(5) A person guilty of an offence under this section[2] shall be liable[3]—

(a) on summary conviction, to imprisonment for a term not exceeding **three months** or to a fine not exceeding **the statutory maximum** or to both;

(b) on conviction on indictment, to imprisonment for a term not exceeding two years or to a fine or to both.

(6) *Reference to Salmon and Freshwater Fisheries Act 1975.*

(7) In this section "offence", in relation to the taking, killing or landing of a salmon either in England and Wales or in Scotland, means an offence under the law applicable to the place where the salmon is taken, killed or landed.
[Salmon Act 1986, s 32.]

---

1. "Salmon" means all migratory fish of the species *Salmo salar* and *Salmo trutta* and commonly known as salmon and sea trout respectively or any part of any such fish (s 40, ibid).

2. Sub-section (6) below provides that Sch 4, Pt II of the Salmon and Freshwater Fisheries Act 1975 ante (procedure) applies to prosecutions under this section.

3. For procedure in respect of this offence which is triable either way, see the Magistrates' Courts Act 1980, ss 17A–21, in Part I: Magistrates' Courts, Procedure, ante.

FOOD

8–11620 This title contains the following statutes—

    8–11939 Food Act 1984
    8–12180 Milk (Cessation of Production) Act 1985
    8–12200 Food and Environment Protection Act 1985
    8–12235 Food Safety Act 1990
    8–12299 Food Standards Act 1999

The following statute which is relevant to this title is not reproduced in this Manual—

    8–11640   International Carriage of Perishable Foodstuffs Act 1976

This title contains the following statutory instruments—

    8–12820   Control of Pesticides Regulations 1986
    8–13000   Food Labelling Regulations 1996
    8–13057A Regulation (EC) No 178/2002 General principles and requirements of food
                  law, the European Food Safety Authority and matters of food safety
    8–13058   General Food Regulations 2004
    8–13065A Materials and Articles in Contact with Food Regulations 2005
    8–13066   Food Hygiene (England) Regulations 2006

8–11630 European Communities Act 1972: regulations. Within the scope of the title Food there also falls the subject matter of a number of regulations made under the very wide enabling power provided in section 2(2) of the European Communities Act 1972. In respect of those regulations listed in Sch 1 to the National Assembly for Wales (Transfer of Functions) Order 2000, SI 2000/253, the functions of the Secretary of State, so far as exercisable in relation to Wales, have been transferred to the National Assembly for Wales. Where such regulations create offences they are noted below in chronological order:

    Natural Mineral Waters, SI 1985/71 amended by SI 1990/2487 and SI 1991/1476;
    Animals and Fresh Meat (Hormonal Substances), SI 1988/849 amended by SI 1991/2843;
    Milk and Milk Products (Protection of Designations) Regulations 1990, SI 1990/607;
    Preserved Sardines (Marketing Standards), SI 1990/1084;
    Organic Products Regulations 1992/2111 as amended by SI 1993/405 and SI 1994/2286.
    Organic Farming (Aid) Regulations SI 1994/1721;
    Fresh Meat (Hygiene and Inspection) Regulations 1995, SI 1995/539 amended by SI 1995/731,
        1763, 2148, 2200, 3189 (amended by SI 2001/1739) and 3214, SI 1996/1148 and 2235,
        SI 1997/1729 and 2074, SI 2000/2215, SI 2001/1739 and SI 2002/129;
    Animals and Animal Products (Examination for Residues and Maximum Residue Limits)
        Regulations 1997, SI 1997/1729 amended by SI 2001/3590 and SI 2004/147;
    Olive Oil (Designation of Origin) Regulations 1999, SI 1999/1513;
    Meat (Disease Control) (England) Regulations 2000, SI 2000/2215;
    Beef Labelling (Enforcement) (England) Regulations 2000, SI 2000/3047 amended by
        SI 2002/2315;
    Meat (Hazard Analysis and Critical Control Point) (England) Regulations 2002, SI 2002/889;
    Food (Jelly Confectionery) (Emergency Control) (England) Regulations 2002, SI 2002/931
        amended by SI 2004/1151;
    Food (Jelly Confectionery) (Emergency Control) (Wales) Regulations 2002, SI 2002/1090
        amended by SI 2004/1262;
    Meat (Hazard Analysis and Critical Control Point) (Wales) Regulations 2002, SI 2002/1476;
    Food and Animal Feedingstuffs (Products of Animal Origin from China) (Control) (Wales)
        Regulations 2002, SI 2002/1798;
    Food (Peanuts from China) (Emergency Control) (No 2) (Wales) Regulations 2002, SI 2002/2295
        amended by SI 2003/2299;
    Food (Figs, Hazelnuts and Pistachios from Turkey) (Emergency Control) (No 2) (Wales)
        Regulations 2002, SI 2002/2296 amended by SI 2003/2292;
    Food (Peanuts from China) (Emergency Control) (England) (No 2) Regulations 2002,
        SI 2002/2350 amended by SI 2003/1958 and SI 2004/1265;
    Food (Figs, Hazelnuts and Pistachios from Turkey) (Emergency Control) (England) (No 2)
        Regulations 2002, SI 2002/2351 amended by SI 2003/1957 and SI 2004/1265;
    Food (Brazil Nuts) (Emergency Control) (England) Regulations 2003, SI 2003/1722 amended
        by SI 2003/2988 and SI 2004/1265;

Food (Pistachios from Iran) (Emergency Control) (England) Regulations 2003, SI 2003/1956 amended by SI 2004/1265 and SI 2005/208;

Food (Brazil Nuts) (Emergency Control) (Wales) Regulations 2003, SI 2003/2254 amended by SI 2004/245;

Food (Pistachios from Iran) (Emergency Control) (Wales) (No 2) Regulations 2003, SI 2003/2288 amended by SI 2004/245 and SI 2005/257;

Food (Hot Chilli and Hot Chilli Products) (Emergency Control) (Wales) Regulations 2003, SI 2003/2455 amended by SI 2004/245 and 392;

Food (Peanuts from Egypt) (Emergency Control) (England) Regulations 2003, SI 2003/2074 amended by SI 2004/1265;

Collagen and Gelatine (Intra-Community Trade) (England) (No 2) Regulations 2003, SI 2003/3003;

Collagen and Gelatine (Intra-Community Trade) (Wales) Regulations 2003, SI 2003/3229 amended by SI 2005/3292;

Production of Bovine Collagen Intended for Human Consumption in the United Kingdom (England) Regulations 2005, SI 2005/404;

Production of Bovine Collagen Intended for Human Consumption in the United Kingdom (Wales) Regulations 2005, SI 2005/1397;

Food (Chilli, Chilli Products, Curcuma and Palm Oil) (Emergency Control) (England) Regulations 2005, SI 2005/1442;

Food (Chilli, Chilli Products, Curcuma and Palm Oil) (Emergency Control) (Wales) Regulations 2005, SI 2005/1540;

Food Hygiene (England) Regulations 2005, in this title, post;

Meat (Official Controls Charges) (England) Regulations 2005, SI 2005/2983;

Meat (Official Controls) (Charges) (Wales) Regulations 2005, SI 2005/3370;

Food Hygiene (England) Regulations 2006, this title, post;

Food Hygiene (Wales) Regulations 2006, SI 2006/31.

8–11630A   European Communities Act 1972: regulations – appeals to a magistrates' court.
The regulations listed below do not create offences but confer a right of appeal on specified matters to a magistrates' court. Any appeal will be by way of complaint:

Fishery Products (Official Controls Charges) (England) Regulations 2005, SI 2005/2991;
Fishery Products (Official Controls Charges) (Wales) Regulations 2005, SI 2005/3297.

8–11631   Wales.   Where any provision in an instrument made prior to 5 March 1996 made under an Act passed before or in the same Session as the Local Government (Wales) Act 1994, provides for the exclusion from references to a "food authority" of either a district council or a county council, that exclusion shall, notwithstanding the provisions of s 17(5) of the Local Government (Wales) Act 1994, have no effect in relation to a food authority in Wales (Local Government Reorganization (Wales) (Consequential Amendments) Order 1996, SI 1996/525, reg 2).

International Carriage of Perishable Foodstuffs Act 1976
(1976 c 58)

Note

8–11640   The International Carriage of Perishable Foodstuffs Act 1976 is not printed in this work. The Act enables the United Kingdom to accede to the Agreement on the International Carriage of Perishable Foodstuffs and on the Special Equipment to be used for such Carriage which was concluded in Geneva in September 1970. The aim of the agreement is to establish common European standards of thermal efficiency for refrigerated and heat-insulated transport equipment used in the international carriage of perishable foodstuffs.

The Act gives power to make regulations prescribing standards (s 1) and contains regulatory powers for the examination, testing and approval of transport equipment (ss 2–4). Provision is also made for powers of entry and inspection (s 6). The Act imposes penalties for carrying prescribed foodstuffs in international transport contrary to regulations, for offences concerning certificates and designated marks, and for making false statements (ss 7–10). There is power to prohibit the driving of foreign goods vehicles (s 11). There are also general provisions which deal with legal proceedings under the Act (ss 12–15).

For the full text of the Act, see *Halsbury's Statutes*, Fourth Edition, Vol 18 FOOD.

Food Act 1984

(1984 c 30)

PART III[1]
MARKETS

8–11939   50. Establishment or acquisition.   *A local authority may establish a market within their area, or acquire by agreement, either by purchase or on lease, the whole or any part of an existing market undertaking within their area.*

---

1. Part III contains ss 50–61. It is the responsibility of the local authority to enforce the provisions of this Part of the Act (s 74(2), post).

8–11940   51. Power to sell to local authority.   *The owner of a market undertaking, or of any rights in respect of a market and of tolls, may sell or lease to a local authority the whole or any part of his market undertaking or rights.*

8–11941   52. Market days and hours.   A market authority may appoint the days on which, and the hours during which, markets are to be held.
[Food Act 1984, s 52.]

8–11942   53. Charges.   (1) A market authority[1] may demand in respect of the market, such charges[1] as they may from time to time determine.
  (2) A market authority who provide—

  (*a*) a weighing machine for weighing cattle, sheep or swine; or
  (*b*) a cold air store or refrigerator for the storage and preservation of meat and other articles of food,

may demand in respect of the weighing of such animals or, as the case may be. the use of the store or refrigerator such charges as they may from time to time determine.
  (3) The authority—

  (*a*) shall keep exhibited in conspicuous places in the market place, and in any market house, tables stating in large and legibly printed characters the several charges payable under this Part; and
  (*b*) shall keep so much of the tables as relates to charges payable, in respect of the weighing of animals, conspicuously exhibited at every weighing machine provided by them in connection with the market for the purpose.

  (4) A person who demands or accepts a charge greater than that for the time being authorised shall be liable[2] to a fine not exceeding **level 2** on the standard scale.
  (5) Nothing in this section applies in relation to rents charged by a market authority in respect of the letting of accommodation within their market for any period longer than one week.
[Food Act 1984, s 53 as amended by the Food Safety Act 1990, Schs 2 and 5.]

---

1. For meaning of "market authority" and "charges", see s 61, post.
2. This offence is triable summarily; see s 93, post.

8–11943   54. Time for payment of charges.   (1) Charges[1] payable in respect of the market shall be paid from time to time on demand to an authorised market officer[1].
  (2) Charges payable in respect of the weighing of cattle, sheep or swine shall be paid in advance to an authorised market officer by the person bringing the animals to be weighed.
  (3) Charges payable in respect of animals[2] brought to the market for sale shall be payable, and may be demanded by an authorised market officer—

  (*a*) as soon as the animals in respect of which they are payable are brought into the market place, and
  (*b*) before they are put into any pen, or tied up in the market place,

but further charges shall be payable and may be demanded in respect of any of the animals which are not removed within one hour after the close of the market.
[Food Act 1984, s 54 as amended by the Food Safety Act 1990, Sch 2.]

---

1. For meaning of "charges" and "authorised market officer", see s 61, post.
2. For meaning of "animal", see s 132, post.

8–11944   55. Recovery of charges.   If a person liable to pay any charge[1] authorised under this Part does not pay it when lawfully demanded, the market authority[1] may, by any authorised market officer[1], levy it by distress—

  (*a*) of all or any of the animals[2], poultry or other articles[2] in respect of which the charge is payable, or (*b*) of any other animals, poultry or articles in the market belonging to, or in the charge of, the person liable,

and any such charge may also be recovered either summarily[3] as a civil debt or in any court of competent jurisdiction.
[Food Act 1984, s 55.]

1. For meaning of "charge", "market authority" and "authorised market officer", see s 61, post.
2. For meaning of "animal" and "article", see s 132, post.
3. See the Magistrates' Courts Act 1980, ss 58 and 96, in PART I: MAGISTRATES' COURTS, PROCEDURE, ante.

8–11945   56. Prohibited sales in market hours.   (1) A person (other than a pedlar holding a certificate under the Pedlars Act 1871[1]) who on a market day and during market hours sells or exposes for sale any articles[2]—

(*a*)   which are specified in a byelaw made by the market authority[3], and
(*b*)   which are commonly sold in the market,

and such sale or exposure for sale—

(i)   is in any place within the authority's area, and
(ii)   is within such distance from the market as the authority may by byelaw declare,

is liable[4] to a fine not exceeding **level 2** on the standard scale.
    This subsection does not apply to a sale or exposure for sale in a person's own dwelling place or shop, or in, or at the door of, any premises to a person resident in those premises.
    (2) The market authority shall keep exhibited in conspicuous positions in the vicinity of the market notices stating the effect of any byelaw made under this section.
[Food Act 1984, s 56 as amended by the Food Safety Act 1990, Sch 2.]

1. See title PEDLARS, post.
2. For meaning of "article", see s 132, post.
3. For meaning of "market authority", see s 61, post.
4. This offence is triable summarily; see s 93, post.

8–11946   57. Weighing machines and scales.   (1) *Repealed.*
    (2) A market authority[1] in whose market cattle, sheep or swine are sold shall, unless there is in force an order of the Minister declaring that the circumstances are such as to render compliance with this subsection unnecessary—

(*a*)   provide to that Minister's satisfaction one or more weighing machines adapted for weighing such animals; and
(*b*)   appoint officers to attend to the weighing of such animals.

A weighing machine provided under this subsection shall for the purposes of section 1 of the Markets and Fairs (Weighing of Cattle) Act 1926, be deemed to have been provided for the purpose of complying with the provisions of the principal Act referred to in that Act of 1926.
[Food Act 1984, s 57 as amended by the Food Safety Act 1990, Schs 2 and 5.]

1. For meaning of "market authority", see s 61, post.

8–11947   57A. *Provision of cold stores.*

8–11947A   58. *Repealed.*

8–11948   59. Information for market officer.   The person in charge of any vehicle in which, and any other person by whom, animals, poultry or other articles are brought for sale in the market shall give to any authorised market officer[1] such information—

(*a*)   as to their number and kind, or
(*b*)   in the case of articles on which charges are made by reference to weight, as to their weight,

as that officer may require.
[Food Act 1984, s 59.]

1. For meaning of "authorised market officer", see s 61, post.

8–11949   60. Market byelaws.   A local authority who maintain a market, whether or not they are a market authority within the meaning of this Act, may make byelaws—

(*a*)   for regulating the use of the market place, and the buildings, stalls, pens and standings in that market place;
(*b*)   for preventing nuisances or obstructions in the market place, or in the immediate approaches to it;

(*c*)　for regulating porters and carriers resorting to the market, and fixing the charges to be made for carrying articles from the market within the district.

(*d*)　after consulting the fire and rescue authority, for preventing the spread of fires in the market.
[Food Act 1984, s 60 as amended by the Food Safety Act 1990, Sch 2, the Fire and Rescue Services Act 2004, Sch 1 and SI 2005/1541.]

8–11960　61. Interpretation of Part III, and exclusion of City of London.　In this Part, unless the context otherwise requires—

"authorised market officer" means an officer of a market authority specially authorised by them to collect charges in their market,

"charges" includes stallage or tolls,

"fire and rescue authority" in relation to a market, means—

(*a*)　where the Regulatory Reform (Fire Safety) Order 2005 applies to the market, the enforcing authority within the meaning given by article 25 of that Order; or

(*b*)　in any other case, the fire and rescue authority under the Fire and Rescue Services Act 2004 for the area in which the market is situated;

"food" has the same meaning as in the Food Safety Act 1990;

"local authority" means a district council, a London borough council or a parish council, but, in relation to Wales, means a county council, county borough council or community council;

"market authority" means a local authority who maintain a market which has been established or acquired under section 50(1) or under the corresponding provisions of any earlier enactment.
[Food Act 1984, s 61 as amended by the Food Safety Act 1990, Schs 2 and 5, the Local Government (Wales) Act 1994, Sch 9, the Fire and Rescue Services Act 2004, Sch 1 and SI 2005/1541.]

Part V[1]
Sugar Beet and Cold Storage

8–11967　69A. Information.　(1)　For the purpose of facilitating—

(*a*)　the making of a determination under section 69(1); or

(*b*)　the preparation or conduct of discussions concerning Community arrangements for or relating to the regulation of the market for sugar,

the appropriate Minister may serve on any processor of homegrown beet a notice requiring him to furnish in writing, within such period as is specified in the notice, such information as is so specified.

(2)　Subject to subsection (3), information obtained under subsection (1) shall not be disclosed without the previous consent in writing of the person by whom the information was furnished; and a person who discloses any information so obtained in contravention of this subsection shall be liable[2]—

(*a*)　on conviction on indictment, to a **fine** or to imprisonment for a term not exceeding **two years** or to both;

(*b*)　on summary conviction, to a fine not exceeding **the statutory maximum** or to imprisonment for a term not exceeding **three months** or to both.

(3)　Nothing in subsection (2) shall restrict the disclosure of information to any of the Ministers or the disclosure—

(*a*)　of information obtained under subsection (1)(*a*)—

(i)　to a person designated to make a determination under section 69(1); or

(ii)　to a body which substantially represents the growers of home-grown beet; or

(*b*)　of information obtained under subsection (1)(*b*), to the Community institution concerned.

(4)　In this section "the appropriate Minister" means—

(*a*)　in relation to England, the Minister of Agriculture, Fisheries and Food; and

(*b*)　in relation to Scotland or Wales, the Secretary of State[3].
[Food Act 1984, s 69A, as inserted by the Food Safety Act 1990, Sch 2.]

1.　Part V contains ss 68–70. This Part re-enacts the provisions of the Sugar Act 1956 relating to Ministerial functions as to sugar beet, and confers power on a local authority to make provision for the cold storage and preservation of meat and other articles of food.

2.　For procedure in respect of this offence which is triable either way, see the Magistrates Courts Act 1980, ss 17A–21, in Part I: Magistrates' Courts, Procedure, ante.

3.　The functions of the Secretary of State, so far as exercisable in relation to Wales, have been transferred to the National Assembly for Wales, by the National Assembly for Wales (Transfer of Functions) Order 1999, SI 1999/672, art 2, Sch 1.

Part VI[1]
Administration, Enforcement and Legal Proceedings

8–11999　93. Summary offences.　(1)　Any offence to which this section applies is triable summarily.

(2)　The offences to which this section applies are—

(a) an offence under any provision of this Act specified in subsection (3);

(b)–(d) *Repealed*.

(3) The provisions of this Act mentioned in paragraph (a) of subsection (2) are—

(a)–(e) *Repealed*;

(f) section 53(4);

(g) section 56(1);

(h)–(l) *Repealed*;

(4) *Northern Ireland*.

[Food Act 1984, s 93 as amended by the Food Safety Act 1990, Sch 5.]

---

1. Part VI contains ss 71–109.

8–12000 94. Offences by corporations[1]. (1) Where an offence under this Act, or any regulations or order made under this Act, which has been committed by a body corporate is proved to have been committed with the consent or connivance of, or to be attributable to any neglect on the part of—

(a) any director, manager, secretary or other similar officer of the body corporate, or

(b) any person who was purporting to act in any such capacity,

he as well as the body corporate shall be deemed to be guilty of that offence and shall be liable to be proceeded against and punished accordingly.

(2) *Repealed*.

[Food Act 1984, s 94 as amended by the Food Safety Act 1990, Sch 5.]

---

1. Section 94(1) has been repealed, except as regards offences under Part III of the Act, by the Food Safety Act 1990, Sch 5.

8–12001 95. Prosecutions. (1) No prosecution for an offence under this Act or regulations made under this Act which is triable either summarily or on indictment shall be begun after the expiry of—

(a) three years from the commission of the offence, or

(b) one year from its discovery by the prosecutor,

whichever is the earlier.

(2)–(8) *Repealed*.

[Food Act 1984, s 95 as amended by the Food Safety Act 1990, Sch 5.]

PART VII[1]

GENERAL AND SUPPLEMENTAL

Acquisition of land, and order to permit works

8–12026 110. *Compulsory purchase of land.*

---

1. Part VII contains ss 110–136.

8–12037 121. Byelaws. (1) The confirming authority in respect of byelaws made under this Act is the Secretary of State.

(2)–(3) (*Repealed*).

[Food Act 1984, s 121 as amended by the Food Safety Act 1990, Sch 5.]

Interpretation and operation

8–12056 132. Interpretation: further provision. (1) In this Act, unless the context otherwise requires—

"animal" does not include bird or fish;

"the Minister"[1] means the Minister of Agriculture, Fisheries and Food and the Secretary of State, acting jointly, except in paragraph (a) of section 5(1), section 37 so far as it relates to the Minister's power to appoint veterinary inspectors, sections 68(5), 83, 101(4), 114 and paragraph (b) of section 115(1), where it means the Minister of Agriculture, Fisheries and Food;

(2) All powers and duties conferred or imposed by this Act shall be deemed to be in addition to, and not in derogation of, any other powers and duties conferred or imposed by Act of Parliament, law or custom, and, subject to any repeal effected by, or other express provision of, this Act, all such other powers and duties may be exercised and shall be performed in the same manner as if this Act had not been passed.

[Food Act 1984, s 132 as amended by the Food Safety Act 1990, Sch 5.]

---

1. The functions of the Secretary of State under ss 68, 69 and 69A have been transferred to the Minister of Agriculture, Fisheries and Food see the Transfer of Functions (Agriculture and Food) Order 1999, SI 1999/3141.

8–12059　135. *Northern Ireland.*

8–12060　136. *Citation, extent and commencement*[1].

---

1. This Act came into force on 26 September 1984.

Milk (Cessation of Production) Act 1985
(1985 c 4)

This Act provides for payments to be made for the purpose of compensating persons, who are or have been registered in the direct sales register or a wholesale register maintained under the Dairy Produce Quotas Regulations 1984, for discontinuing or reducing milk production and to make provision in connection with payments to such persons whenever made.

8–12180　1. Payments to persons ceasing or reducing milk production.　(1) For the purpose of compensating persons who are registered milk producers for discontinuing milk production or reducing milk production the Minister may prepare a scheme[1] for the making of payments to such persons (s 1—*SUMMARISED*).

---

1. See the Milk (Cessation of Production) (England and Wales) Scheme 1987, SI 1987/908.

8–12181　2. Powers of entry, etc.　(1) Where it is reasonably necessary for him to do so for the purpose of determining whether any person to whom a payment under section 1 has been made is involved or has a substantial interest in the production of milk, a duly authorised officer of the Minister[1] may at all reasonable times—

    (*a*)　enter on any land which is occupied by that person; and
    (*b*)　require any person engaged in milk production to furnish any accounts or records under his control for inspection (s 2—*SUMMARISED*).

---

1. "Minister" means the Minister of Agriculture, Fisheries and Food or the Secretary of State (s 5).

8–12182　3. Offences.　(1) Any person who—

    (*a*)　for the purpose of obtaining a payment under section 1 above for himself or any other person or retaining such a payment or any cessation payment (within the meaning of section 2 above), knowingly or recklessly makes a statement which is false in a material particular, or
    (*b*)　intentionally obstructs any authorised officer acting under section 2 above,

shall be guilty of an offence and liable on summary conviction to a fine not exceeding **level 5** on the standard scale.

(2) Where an offence under this section which has been committed by a body corporate is proved to have been committed with the consent or connivance of, or to be attributable to any neglect on the part of, a director, manager, secretary or other similar officer of the body corporate or any person who was purporting to act in any such capacity, he as well as the body corporate shall be guilty of that offence and shall be liable to be proceeded against and punished accordingly.
[Milk (Cessation of Production) Act 1985, s 3 amended by the Statute Law (Repeals) Act 1993, Sch 1.]

Food and Environment Protection Act 1985[1]
(1985 c 48)

PART I[2]
CONTAMINATION OF FOOD

Emergency orders etc

8–12200　1. Power to make emergency orders.　(1) If in the opinion of a designating authority—

    (*a*)　there exist or may exist circumstances which are likely to create a hazard to human health through human consumption of food;
    (*b*)　in consequence food which is or may be in the future in an area—

        (i)　of land in the United Kingdom;
        (ii)　of sea within British fishery limits; or
        (iii)　both of such land and of such sea,

    or which is or may be in the future derived from anything in such an area, is, or may be, or may become, unsuitable for human consumption,

the designating authority may by statutory instrument make an order[3] designating that area and containing emergency prohibitions.

(2) In this Act—

"designating authority" in relation to England and Wales means the Secretary of State and, in relation to Scotland and the Scottish zone means the Scottish Ministers; and the functions of that authority in relation to Scotland and the Scottish zone shall be treated as exercisable in or as regards Scotland and may be exercised separately;

"emergency order" means an order under this section—

    (*a*) which designates an area; or
    (*b*) which amends or re-enacts an order which designated an area;

"emergency prohibitions" means the prohibitions specified in Schedule 1 to this Act;

"designated area" means an area designated by an emergency order; and

"Scottish zone" has the meaning assigned to it by section 126(1) of the Scotland Act 1998.

(3) Food derived from any creature is to be treated for the purposes of this Act as also derived—

    (*a*) from any feeding stuff which that creature has eaten; and
    (*b*) from anything from which any such feeding stuff was derived,

and references in this Act to anything from which food could be derived shall be construed accordingly.

(4) A designating authority may jointly by order made by statutory instrument amend Schedule 1 to this Act.

(5) An emergency order shall refer to the circumstances or suspected circumstances in consequence of which in the opinion of the designating authority making it food such as is mentioned in subsection (1)(*b*) above is, or may be, or may become, unsuitable for human consumption; and in this Act

"designated circumstances" means the circumstances or suspected circumstances to which an emergency order refers in pursuance of this subsection.

(6) Subject to subsection (7) below, and to section 2(2) below, any person who—

    (*a*) contravenes an emergency prohibition; or
    (*b*) causes or permits any other person to do so,

shall be guilty of an offence.

(7) It shall be a defence for a person charged—

    (*a*) with contravening an emergency prohibition contained in an emergency order by virtue of paragraph 2 or 3 of Schedule 1 to this Act; or
    (*b*) with causing or permitting any other person to contravene such a prohibition,

to show—

    (i)   that the contravention took place on a foreign vessel, foreign aircraft, foreign hovercraft or foreign marine structure; and
    (ii) that nothing to which the prohibition related was landed from it in the United Kingdom.

(8) An emergency order—

    (*a*) shall be laid before Parliament; and
    (*b*) shall cease to have effect at the expiry of a period of 28 days beginning with the date on which it was made unless, before the expiry of that period, the order has been approved by resolution of each House of Parliament, but without prejudice to anything previously done or to the making of a new order.

(9) In reckoning for the purposes of subsection (8) above any period of 28 days, no account shall be taken of any period during which Parliament is dissolved or prorogued or during which both Houses are adjourned for more than 4 days.

(10) An order under this section which—

    (*a*) wholly or partly revokes an emergency order; and
    (*b*) does nothing else, or nothing else except make provision incidental or supplementary to the revocation,

shall be laid before Parliament after being made.

(11) No order under subsection (4) above shall be made unless a draft of the order has been laid before and approved by resolution of each House of Parliament.

(12) Where an order under this section is made by the Scottish Ministers, or is made on their behalf by the Food Standards Agency in accordance with an arrangement made under section 17 of the Food Standards Act 1999, this section shall have effect subject to the following modifications—

    (*a*) any reference to Parliament or to a House of Parliament shall be construed as a reference to the Scottish Parliament; and
    (*b*) in subsection (9), for "Parliament is dissolved or prorogued or during which both Houses are adjourned" there shall be substituted "the Scottish Parliament is dissolved or is in recess".

[Food and Environment Protection Act 1985, s 1 as amended by the Food Safety Act 1990, s 51. SI 1999/1756, the Food Standards Act 1999, Sch 5 and SI 2000/2040.]

1. For commencement of this Act, see s 27, post.
2. Part I contains ss 1–4.
3. The following orders are in force:

Food Protection (Emergency Prohibitions) Radioactivity in Sheep (Wales), SI 1991/5 amended by SI 1991/2780, SI 1993/32, SI 1994/63, SI 1995/46, SI 1996/29 and SI 1998/72;

Food Protection Radioactivity in Sheep (England), SI 1991/6 amended by SI 1991/2776, SI 1993/33, SI 1994/65, SI 1995/39 and SI 1996/62;

Food Protection (Emergency Prohibitions) (Radioactivity in Sheep) Order 1991, SI 1991/20 amended by SI 1991/2766, SI 1993/13, SI 1994/50, SI 1995/48, SI 1997/62, SI 1998/82 and SI 1999/80;

Food Protection (Emergency Prohibitions) (Lead in Ducks and Geese) (England) Order 1992, SI 1992/2726;

Food Protection (Emergency Prohibitions) (Dioxins) (England) (No 2) (Revocation) Order 1992, SI 1992/3188;

Food Protection (Emergency Prohibitions) (Dounreay Nuclear Establishment) Order 1997, SI 1997/2622;

Food Protection (Emergency Provisions) (Amnesiac Shellfish Poisoning) Order 1999, SI 1999/1005.

Food Protection (Emergency Prohibitions) (Paralytic Shellfish Poisoning) (No 2) Order 1998 Partial Revocation Order 1999, SI 1999/649.

Food Protection (Emergency Prohibitions) (Paralytic Shellfish Poisoning) (No 2) Order 1998 Partial Revocation (No 2) Order 1999, SI 1999/1067.

Food Protection (Emergency Prohibitions) (Amnesiac Shellfish Poisoning) Order 1999 Revocation Order 1999, SI 1999/1192.

8–12201　2. Powers of designating authorities when emergency order has been made.　(1) A designating authority or the Food Standards Agency may consent, either unconditionally or subject to any condition that the authority giving consent considers appropriate, to the doing in a particular case of anything prohibited by an emergency order.

(2) It shall be a defence for a person charged with an offence under section 1(6) above to show—

(*a*) that consent had been given under subsection (1) above to the contravention of the emergency prohibition; and

(*b*) that any condition subject to which that consent was given was complied with.

(3) A designating authority or the Food Standards Agency—

(*a*) may give any person such directions as appear to the authority giving the directions to be necessary or expedient for the purpose of preventing human consumption of food which the authority giving the directions believes, on reasonable grounds, is, or may be, or may become, unsuitable for human consumption in consequence of designated circumstances; and

(*b*) may do anything which appears to the designating authority or the Agency (as the case may be) to be necessary or expedient for that purpose;

and such directions may be given and such action may be taken after the emergency order has ceased to be in force.

(4) Any person who—

(*a*) fails to comply with a direction under this section; or

(*b*) causes or permits any other person to do so,

shall be guilty of an offence.

(5) If the designating authority or the Food Standards Agency does anything by virtue of this section in consequence of a failure on the part of any person to comply with such a direction, the authority taking that action may recover from that person any expenses reasonably incurred by that authority under this section.

(6) If the designating authority or the Food Standards Agency does anything by virtue of this section in consequence of any person causing or permitting another person to fail to comply with such a direction, the authority taking that action may recover from the person who caused or permitted the failure to comply any expenses reasonably incurred by that authority under this section. [Food and Environment Protection Act 1985, s 2 as amended by the Food Safety Act 1990, s 51, SI 1999/1756 and the Food Standards Act 1999, Sch 5.]

Investigation and enforcement

8–12202　3. Authorisation of investigating officers and enforcement officers.　(1) A designating authority may authorise—

(*a*) persons (in this Act referred to as "investigating officers") to conduct investigations for the purpose of determining—

(i) whether any of the powers conferred by this Part of this Act should be exercised; and

(ii) the manner in which any such power should be exercised;

(*b*) persons (in this Act referred to as "enforcement officers") to enforce—

(i) emergency orders; and

(ii) directions under section 2 above.

(2) A designating authority may authorise an investigating officer or an enforcement officer who is not an officer of his department to perform any of the designating authority's functions under this Part of this Act which he could perform if he were an officer of the department; and an officer

performing such functions in pursuance of such an authorisation is to be treated in relation to their performance as if he were an officer of the department.

(3) An authorisation under subsection (1) or (2) above may be given subject to such limitations as may be specified in the instrument containing it; and this Act shall be construed, in reference to a person whose authorisation has been given subject to limitations, as subject to those limitations.

(4) The functions of an investigating officer and of an enforcement officer may also be performed by a British sea-fishery officer, and accordingly any reference to an investigating officer or an enforcement officer in the following provisions of this Act includes a reference to a British sea-fishery officer.

[Food and Environment Protection Act 1985, s 3 as amended by SI 1999/1756.]

8–12203 4. Powers of officers. (1) An investigating officer may enter any land, vehicle, vessel, aircraft, hovercraft or marine structure—

(a) if he has reasonable grounds to suspect that food—

    (i) which is on or in it; or

    (ii) which is derived from anything on or in it,

is, or may be, or may become, unsuitable for human consumption in consequence of such circumstances as are mentioned in section 1(1) above; or

(b) if he has reasonable grounds to suspect that there is present on or in it any food—

    (i) which has been in a designated area at any time before or after the making of the emergency order that designated the area; and

    (ii) which is, or may be, or may become, so affected by the designated circumstances as to be unsuitable for human consumption; or

(c) if he has reasonable grounds to suspect that there is present on or in it anything from which food could be derived—

    (i) which has been in a designated area at any such time; and

    (ii) which is, or may be, or may become, so affected by the designated circumstances as to cause any food derived from it to be unsuitable for human consumption.

(2) An enforcement officer may enter any land, vehicle, vessel, aircraft, hovercraft or marine structure—

(a) if a direction under section 2 above has been given in relation to it or in relation to anything that he has reasonable grounds to suspect to be present on or in it; or

(b) if he has reasonable grounds to suspect that there is present on or in it any document, book or other record that may assist him in ascertaining the whereabouts of anything in relation to which such a direction has been given; or

(c) if he has reasonable grounds to suspect that it is for any other reason necessary for him to enter it for the purpose of performing his functions under this Part of this Act.

(3) An investigating officer or an enforcement officer may seize things for the purpose of performing his functions under this Part of this Act.

(4) While an emergency order is in force, an investigating officer or an enforcement officer may enter—

(a) any land, vehicle, vessel, aircraft, hovercraft or marine structure in the designated area; and

(b) any land, vehicle, vessel, aircraft, hovercraft or marine structure not in that area but on or in which he has reasonable grounds to suspect that there is present—

    (i) any food, or anything from which food could be derived, which has been in that area at any time either before or after the making of the emergency order; or

    (ii) any document, book or other record that may assist him in ascertaining the whereabouts of any such food or thing.

(5) An investigating officer or an enforcement officer may exercise any powers conferred on him for the purposes of this Part of this Act—

(a) in relation to a British vessel, British aircraft, British hovercraft or British marine structure, wherever it may be;

(b) in relation to a foreign fishing boat, only if it is within British fishery limits; and

(c) in relation to a foreign vessel other than a fishing boat, or to a foreign aircraft, foreign hovercraft or foreign marine structure, only if—

    (i) it is in the United Kingdom or United Kingdom waters; and

    (ii) the officer has reasonable grounds to suspect that something to which an emergency prohibition contained in an emergency order by virtue of paragraph 2 or 3 of Schedule 1 to this Act relates has been or is being landed from it in the United Kingdom.

(6) Schedule 2 to this Act shall have effect with respect to investigating officers and enforcement officers.

[Food and Environment Protection Act 1985, s 4, as amended by the Food Safety Act 1990, s 51.]

PART II[1]
DEPOSITS IN THE SEA

Licensing

8–12204 5. Requirement of licences for deposit of substances and articles in the sea etc. Subject to the following provisions of this Part of this Act, a licence under this Part of this Act is needed—

(a) for the deposit of substances or articles within United Kingdom waters or United Kingdom controlled waters, either in the sea or under the sea-bed—

   (i) from a vehicle, vessel, aircraft, hovercraft or marine structure;
   (ii) from a container floating in the sea; or
   (iii) from a structure on land constructed or adapted wholly or mainly for the purpose of depositing solids in the sea;

(b) for the deposit of substances or articles anywhere in the sea or under the sea-bed—

   (i) from a British vessel, British aircraft, British hovercraft or British marine structure; or
   (ii) from a container floating in the sea, if the deposit is controlled from a British vessel, British aircraft, British hovercraft or British marine structure;

(c)–(d) *Repealed*;
(e) for the scuttling of vessels—

   (i) in United Kingdom waters or United Kingdom controlled waters; or
   (ii) anywhere at sea, if the scuttling is controlled from a British vessel, British aircraft, British hovercraft or British marine structure; or
   (iii) *Repealed*;

(f) for the loading of a vessel, aircraft, hovercraft, marine structure or floating container in the United Kingdom or United Kingdom waters with substances or articles for deposit anywhere in the sea or under the sea-bed;

(g) for the loading of a vehicle in the United Kingdom with substances or articles for deposit from that vehicle as mentioned in paragraph (a) above; and

(h) for the towing or propelling from the United Kingdom or United Kingdom waters of a vessel for scuttling anywhere at sea.

[Food and Environment Protection Act 1985, s 5 as amended by the Environmental Protection Act 1990, s 146 and Sch 16 and the Statute Law (Repeals) Act 1993, Sch 1.]

_____

1. Part II contains ss 5–15.

8–12205 6. Requirement of licences for incineration at sea etc. (1) Subject to the following provisions of this Part of this Act, a licence is needed—

(a) for the incineration of substances or articles on a vessel or marine structure—

   (i) in United Kingdom waters or United Kingdom controlled waters; or
   (ii) anywhere at sea, if the incineration takes place on a British vessel or British marine structure; or
   (iii) *repealed*; and

(b) for the loading of a vessel or marine structure in the United Kingdom or United Kingdom waters with substances or articles for incineration anywhere at sea.

(2) In this Act "incineration" means any combustion of substances and materials for the purpose of their thermal destruction.

[Food and Environment Protection Act 1985, s 6 as amended by the Environmental Protection Act 1990, s 146 and Sch 16.]

8–12206 7. Exemptions. (1) A licensing authority may by order[1] made by statutory instrument specify operations—

(a) which are not to need a licence; or
(b) which are not to need a licence if they satisfy conditions specified in the order.

(2) The conditions that an order under this section may specify include conditions enabling a licensing authority to require a person to obtain the authority's approval before he does anything for which a licence would be needed but for the order.

(3) Approval under subsection (2) above may be without conditions or subject to such conditions as the authority considers appropriate.

(3A) A licensing authority—

(a) shall consult the Food Standards Agency as to any order the authority contemplates making under this section; and
(b) shall from time to time consult that Agency as to the general approach to be taken by the authority in relation to the granting of approvals and the imposition of conditions under

subsection (2) and (3) (including the identification of circumstances in which it may be desirable for the Agency to be consulted in relation to particular cases).

(4) A statutory instrument containing an order under this section shall be subject to annulment in pursuance of a resolution of either House of Parliament.

[Food and Environment Protection Act 1985, s 7, as amended by SI 1999/1756 and the Food Standards Act 1999, Sch 3.]

---

1. The Deposits in the Sea (Exemptions) Order 1985, SI 1985/1699 amended by SI 1994/1056, has been made.

8–12206A 7A. *Exemption for certain offshore installations*

8–12207 8. *Licences.*

Offences relating to licensing system etc

8–12208 9. Offences relating to licensing system. (1) Subject to subsections (3) to (7) below, a person who—

(a) except in pursuance of a licence and in accordance with its provisions, does anything for which a licence is needed; or

(b) causes or permits any other person to do any such thing except in pursuance of a licence and in accordance with its provisions,

shall be guilty of an offence.

(2) A person who for the purpose of procuring the issue of a licence, or in purporting to carry out any duty imposed on him by the provisions of a licence—

(a) makes a statement which he knows to be false in a material particular;

(b) recklessly makes a statement which is false in a material particular; or

(c) intentionally fails to disclose any material particular,

shall be guilty of an offence.

(3) Subject to subsection (4) below, it shall be a defence for a person charged with an offence under subsection (1) above in relation to any operation to prove—

(a) that the operation was carried out for the purpose of securing the safety of a vessel, aircraft, hovercraft or marine structure or of saving life; and

(b) that he took steps within a reasonable time to inform one or other of the Ministers—

(i) of the operation;

(ii) of the locality and circumstances in which it took place; and

(iii) of any substances or articles concerned.

(4) A person does not have the defence provided by subsection (3) above if the court is satisfied—

(a) that the operation—

(i) was not necessary for any purpose mentioned in paragraph (a) of that subsection; and

(ii) was not a reasonable step to take in the circumstances; or

(b) that it was necessary for one of those purposes but the necessity was due to the fault of the defendant.

(5) It shall be a defence for a person charged with an offence under subsection (1) above in relation to any operation—

(a) which falls within section 5(b) or (e)(ii) or 6(1)(a)(ii) above; and

(b) which was carried out outside United Kingdom controlled waters (and not within United Kingdom waters),

to prove that subsections (6) and (7) below are satisfied in respect of that operation.

(6) This subsection is satisfied—

(a) in respect of an operation falling within section 5(b) above, if the vessel, aircraft, hovercraft, marine structure or container (as the case may be) was loaded in a Convention State or the national or territorial waters of a Convention State with the substances or articles deposited;

(b) in respect of an operation falling within section 5(e)(ii) above, if the vessel scuttled was towed or propelled from a Convention State or the national or territorial waters of a Convention State to the place where the scuttling was carried out; or

(c) in respect of an operation falling within section 6(1)(a)(ii) above, if the vessel or marine structure on which the incineration took place was loaded in a Convention State or the national or territorial waters of a Convention State with the substances or articles incinerated.

(7) This subsection is satisfied in respect of an operation if the operation took place in pursuance of a licence issued by the responsible authority in the Convention State concerned and in accordance with the provisions of that licence.

[Food and Environment Protection Act 1985, s 9 as amended by the Environmental Protection Act 1990, s 146.]

8–12209   **10.** *Power to take remedial action.—Power of a Licensing Authority.*

Enforcement

8–12210   **11. Powers of officers.**   (1) A licensing authority may authorise any person, subject to such limitations as may be specified in the instrument authorising him, to enforce this Part of this Act; and the following provisions of this Act shall be construed, in reference to a person so authorised, as subject to any such limitations.

(2) Subject to the following provisions of this Act, a person so authorised may enter—

(*a*) land and vehicles in the United Kingdom;

(*b*) foreign vessels, foreign aircraft, foreign hovercraft and foreign marine structures in the United Kingdom or within United Kingdom waters or United Kingdom controlled waters;

(*c*) British vessels, British aircraft, British hovercraft and British marine structures, wherever they may be,

if he has reasonable grounds for believing that any substances or articles intended to be deposited in the sea or under the sea-bed or incinerated on a vessel or marine structure at sea are or have been present there.

(3) A person so authorised may board—

(*a*) any vessel within United Kingdom waters or United Kingdom controlled waters; and

(*b*) any British vessel wherever it may be,

if it appears to him that it is intended to be scuttled.

(4) A person so authorised shall not enter premises used only as a dwelling for the purpose of enforcing this Part of this Act.

(5) Schedule 2 to this Act shall have effect with respect to persons authorised to enforce this Part of this Act.

[Food and Environment Protection Act 1985, s 11 as amended by the Environmental Protection Act 1990, s 146 and SI 1999/1756, Schedule.]

8–12211   **12. Enforcement of Conventions.**   (1) A licensing authority may jointly by order made by statutory instrument—

(*a*) declare that any procedure which has been developed for the effective application of the London Convention or the Oslo Convention and is specified in the order is an agreed procedure as between Her Majesty's Government in the United Kingdom and the Government of any Convention State so specified; and

(*b*) specify any of the powers conferred by this Act for the purpose of enforcing this Part of this Act as a power that may be exercised, by such persons in such circumstances and subject to such conditions or modifications as may be specified, for the purpose of enforcing that procedure.

(2) A person who exercises any powers by virtue of an order under this section shall have the same rights and liabilities in relation to their exercise that a person authorised under section 11 above would have in relation to the exercise of any powers for the purpose of enforcing this Part of this Act.

(3) A statutory instrument containing an order under this section shall be subject to annulment in pursuance of a resolution of either House of Parliament.

[Food and Environment Protection Act 1985, s 12 as amended by SI 1999/1756, Schedule.]

Miscellaneous

8–12212   **15.** *Repeal of Dumping at Sea Act 1974, consequential amendments and transitional provisions.*

PART III[1]
PESTICIDES ETC

8–12213   **16. Control of pesticides etc.**   (1) The provisions of this Part of this Act shall have effect—

(*a*) with a view to the continuous development of means—

(i) to protect the health of human beings, creatures and plants;

(ii) to safeguard the environment; and

(iii) to secure safe, efficient and humane methods of controlling pests; and

(*b*) with a view to making information about pesticides available to the public;

and references in this Part of this Act to the general purposes of this Part of this Act are references to the purposes mentioned in this subsection.

(2) The Ministers may jointly by regulations[2]—

(*a*) impose the specified prohibitions in relation to pesticides but exclude from them pesticides of a description specified in the regulations;

(b) provide that the Ministers may jointly give their approval, in relation to pesticides of a description specified in the regulations, to the doing of anything that would otherwise be prohibited by virtue of paragraph (a) above;

(c) provide for the imposition of conditions on an approval, when or after it is given;

(d) provide for the giving of consent by the Ministers or either of them to the doing of anything contrary to a specified prohibition;

(e) provide that a consent given by virtue of paragraph (d) above may be given either without conditions or subject to such conditions as may be specified;

(f) provide—

    (i) for the review, revocation or suspension of an approval;

    (ii) for the amendment of conditions imposed on an approval;

(g) direct that, if there has been a breach, in relation to any pesticide,—

    (i) of any of the specified prohibitions; or

    (ii) of a condition imposed by virtue of this subsection,

either of the Ministers and any local authority shall have power—

    (iii) to seize or dispose of it or to require that some other person shall dispose of it;

    (iv) to seize or dispose of anything treated with it or to require that some other person shall dispose of any such thing;

    (v) to direct some other person to take such remedial action as appears to the Minister or local authority to be necessary as a result of the contravention;

(h) provide that, if any pesticide has been imported into the United Kingdom in contravention of any of the specified prohibitions or of any such condition, either of the Ministers may require that it shall be removed out of the United Kingdom;

(j) provide for the availability to the public, subject to any condition that the Ministers consider appropriate, and to payment of such reasonable fees for furnishing copies as the Ministers may with the consent of the Treasury determine, of information supplied for the purposes of this section;

(k) specify how much pesticide or pesticide residue may be left in any crop, food or feeding stuff; and

(l) provide for information to be made available for the public, subject to—

    (i) any condition that the Ministers consider appropriate; and

    (ii) payment of such amount as the Ministers may, with the consent of the Treasury, determine as representing the cost reasonably attributable to the supply of the information;

and in this Part of this Act "regulations" means regulations under this section and "approval" means approval under regulations.

(2A) In subsection (2)—

(a) in paragraph (g), "local authority" has the same meaning as in section 19; and

(b) in paragraph (j), "information" means any information which has been supplied to a government department or other authority at any time for the purposes of, or otherwise in connection with—

    (i) any provision made by or under this section;

    (ii) the United Kingdom Pesticides Safety Precautions Scheme; or

    (iii) the Agricultural Chemicals Approval Scheme.

(3) In this Part of this Act "the specified prohibitions", in relation to pesticides, means prohibitions of any of the following—

(a) importation;

(b) sale, offer or exposure for sale or possession for the purpose of sale;

(c) supply or offer to supply;

(d) storage;

(e) use;

(f) advertisement.

(4) Pesticides may be identified in any way for the purposes of this Part of this Act.

(5) In determining any provision to be made by virtue of subsection (2)(j) above the Ministers shall have regard to the interests of persons supplying information to which that provision would relate.

(6) Regulations shall be made by statutory instrument and no regulations shall be made unless a draft of them has been laid before and approved by resolution of each House of Parliament.

(7) The Ministers may by order[3] made by statutory instrument jointly establish a committee to give them advice either when requested to do so or otherwise, on any matters relating to the control of pests in furthering the general purposes of this Part of this Act, and Schedule 5 shall have effect with respect to it.

(8) A statutory instrument containing an order under this section shall be subject to annulment in pursuance of a resolution of either House of Parliament.

(9) The Ministers shall consult the committee—

(a) as to regulations which they contemplate making;

(b) as to approvals which they contemplate giving, revoking or suspending; and

(c) as to conditions to which they contemplate making approvals subject.

(9A) The Ministers—

(a) shall consult the Food Standards Agency as to regulations which they contemplate making; and

(b) shall from time to time consult that Agency as to the general approach to be taken by them in relation to the giving, revocation or suspension of approvals and the imposition of conditions on approvals (including the identification of circumstances in which it may be desirable for the Agency to be consulted in relation to particular cases).

(10) If it appears to the Ministers that regulations which they contemplate making are likely to affect the health or safety of persons at work, it shall be their duty to consult the Health and Safety Commission concerning them.

(11) Either of the Ministers may require the provision of such information by importers, exporters, manufacturers, distributors or users of a pesticide as he considers to be necessary—

(a) for the purpose of controlling pesticides in the United Kingdom; or

(b) for the fulfilment by the government of the United Kingdom of any of its international obligations to supply information; or

(c) to enable the government of the United Kingdom to determine what action it should take in order to fulfil an international obligation of any other description.

(12) A person who—

(a) without reasonable excuse, contravenes, or causes or permits any other person to contravene—

(i) any provision of regulations;

(ii) any condition of approval of a pesticide; or

(iii) any requirement imposed by virtue of regulations or of subsection (11) above; or

(b) in purporting to give information required by virtue of subsection (11) above—

(i) makes a statement which he knows to be false in a material particular;

(ii) recklessly makes a statement which is false in a material particular; or

(iii) intentionally fails to disclose any material particular,

shall be guilty of an offence.

(13) In subsection (12) above "contravenes" includes "fails to comply with" and "contravene" has a corresponding meaning.

(14) It shall be a defence in proceedings for an offence—

(a) under section 8(b) of the Protection of Animals Act 1911;

(b) under section 7(b) of the Protection of Animals (Scotland) Act 1912; or

(c) under section 22(2)(b) of the Welfare of Animals Act (Northern Ireland) 1972,

(each of which restricts the placing on land of poison and poisonous substances) for the person charged to show that he acted in accordance with an approval.

(15) In this Act—

"pest" means—

(a) any organism harmful to plants or to wood or other plant products;

(b) any undesired plant; and

(c) any harmful creature;

"pesticide" means any substance, preparation or organism prepared or used for destroying any pest; and

"pesticide residue" means any substance resulting from the use of a pesticide including, without prejudice to the generality of this definition, any such derivative as regulations may specify in relation to a particular pesticide.

(16) This Part of this Act applies to any substance, preparation or organism prepared or used for any of the following purposes—

(a) protecting plants or wood or other plant products from harmful organisms;

(b) regulating the growth of plants;

(c) giving protection against harmful creatures;

(d) rendering such creatures harmless;

(e) controlling organisms with harmful or unwanted effects on water systems, buildings or other structures, or on manufactured products;

(f) protecting animals against ectoparasites,

as if it were a pesticide.

[Food and Environment Protection Act 1985, s 16 as amended by the Pesticides Act1998, s 1 and the Food Standards Act 1999, Sch 3.]

1. Part III contains ss 16–19.
2. See the Control of Pesticides Regulations 1986, in this title, post. See also the Pesticides (Maximum Residue Levels in Crops, Food and Feeding Stuffs) (Amendment) Regulations 1994, SI 1994/1985, amended by SI 1996/1487 and the Plant Protection Products (Basic Conditions) Regulations 1997, SI 1997/189.
3. The Control of Pesticides (Advisory Committee on Pesticides) Order 1985, SI 1985/1516, has been made.

8–12214   17. Codes of practice.   (1) The Ministers may from time to time after consultation with such persons or bodies as seem to them representative of the interests concerned—

   (a)   prepare and issue codes of practice for the purpose of providing practical guidance in respect of any provision of this Part of this Act or of regulations; and
   (b)   revise any such code by revoking, varying, amending or adding to the provisions of the code.

(2) A code prepared in pursuance of this section and any alterations proposed to be made on a revision of such a code shall be laid before both Houses of Parliament, and the Ministers shall not issue the code or revised code, as the case may be, until after the end of the period of 40 days beginning with the day on which the code or the proposed alterations were so laid.

(3) If, within the period mentioned in subsection (2) above, either House resolves that the code be not issued, or the proposed alterations be not made, as the case may be, the Ministers shall not issue the code or revised code (without prejudice to their powers under that subsection to lay further codes or proposed alterations before Parliament).

(4) For the purposes of subsection (2) above—

   (a)   where a code or proposed alterations are laid before each House of Parliament on different days, the later day shall be taken to be the day on which the code or the proposed alterations, as the case may be, were laid before both Houses; and
   (b)   in reckoning any period of 40 days, no account shall be taken of any time during which Parliament is dissolved or prorogued or during which both Houses are adjourned for more than four days.

(5) The Ministers shall cause any code issued or revised under this section to be printed and distributed, and may make such arrangements as they think fit for its distribution, including causing copies of it to be put on sale to the public at such reasonable price as the Ministers may determine.

(6) A failure on the part of any person to follow any guidance contained in a code issued under this section shall not of itself render that person liable to proceedings of any kind.

(7) In all criminal proceedings any such code shall be admissible in evidence; and if any provision of such a code appears to the court conducting the proceedings to be relevant to any question arising in the proceedings, it shall be taken into account in determining that question.

(8) In relation to the exercise by the Scottish Ministers of functions under this section—

   (a)   references in this section to Parliament or to either or both Houses of Parliament shall be read as if they were references to the Scottish Parliament;
   (b)   subsection (4)(a) shall cease to have effect; and
   (c)   in subsection (4)(b) the reference to any time during which Parliament is dissolved or prorogued or during which both Houses are adjourned for more than four days shall be read as if it were a reference to any time during which the Scottish Parliament is dissolved or is in recess for more than four days.

[Food and Environment Protection Act 1985, s 17, as amended by SI 1999/1820, Sch 2.]

8–12215   18. *Fees.*

8–12216   19. Enforcement powers.   (1) Subject to the following provisions of this section, the powers conferred by this section (including Schedule 2 to this Act) ("the enforcement powers") may be exercised—

   (a)   by a person whom either of the Ministers has by instrument in writing authorised to exercise them; or
   (b)   by an officer of a local authority who is authorised to exercise them under subsection (1C) below.

(1A) An instrument issued under subsection (1)(a) above may provide that the person to whom it is issued may only exercise the enforcement powers for specified purposes.

(1B) Either of the Ministers may specify descriptions of local authority officers who may be authorised to exercise the enforcement powers but may direct that an officer of a particular description may only be authorised to exercise them for specified purposes.

(1C) If either of the Ministers specifies a description of local authority officers under subsection (1B) above, a local authority may by instrument in writing authorise any of its officers falling within that description to exercise the enforcement powers.

(1D) The following provisions of this Act are to be construed in reference to a person authorised to exercise the enforcement powers as subject to the terms of the instrument which authorises him to exercise them.

(2) Subject to the following provisions of this Act, a person so authorised may enter any land if he has reasonable grounds to believe—

(a) that any pesticide is being or has been applied to or stored on it; and

(b) that it is necessary for him to enter for any of the general purposes of this Part of this Act.

(3) A person so authorised may enter any vehicle, vessel, aircraft, hovercraft or marine structure if he has reasonable grounds to believe—

(a) that any pesticide is being or has been stored in, transported on or applied by means of it; and

(b) that it is necessary for him to do so for any of the general purposes of this Part of this Act.

(4) For any of those purposes, a person so authorised may require any person to give him information as to the formulation, effects or use of any substance.

(5) If a person so authorised is of the opinion that a person—

(a) is committing an offence under section 16(12)(a) above; or

(b) has committed such an offence in circumstances that make it likely that the offence will be repeated,

he may serve on that person a notice stating that he is of that opinion, specifying the offence as to which he is of that opinion, giving particulars of the reasons why he is of that opinion and directing—

(i) that any land, vehicle, vessel, aircraft, hovercraft or marine structure on or in which it appears to him that the offence was or is being committed or anything which is on or in it, shall be left undisturbed (whether generally or in particular respects) for so long as it appears to him to be reasonably necessary; or

(ii) that any reasonable remedial or preventive measures shall be taken.

(6) If a person so authorised is of the opinion that any activities, as carried on or about to be carried on by or under the control of any person, involve or, as the case may be, will involve a risk of the commission of an offence under section 16(12)(a) above, he may serve on that person a notice—

(a) stating that he is of that opinion;

(b) specifying the matters which in his opinion give or, as the case may be, will give rise to the said risk; and

(c) directing that the activities to which the notice relates shall not be carried on by or under the control of the person on whom the notice is served unless the matters specified in the notice in pursuance of paragraph (b) above have been remedied.

(6A) A notice under subsection (5) or (6) above may at any time be withdrawn by a person so authorised.

(6B) Withdrawal of a notice does not affect the power to serve a fresh notice under subsection (5) or (6).

(7) Schedule 2 to this Act shall have effect with respect to persons authorised to enforce this Part of this Act.

(8) In this section "local authority" means—

(a) any local authority, as defined in the Local Government Act 1972, except a parish or community council;

(b) any local authority, as defined in the Local Government (Scotland) Act 1973;

(c) a district council in Northern Ireland; and

(d) a port health authority.

[Food and Environment Protection Act 1985, s 19 as amended by the Pesticides (Fees and Enforcement) Act 1989, s 2 and the Pesticides Act 1998, s 2.]

PART IV[1]
GENERAL AND SUPPLEMENTARY

8–12217   20. Application to Crown etc. (1) An emergency order operates in relation to land in the designated area in which there is a Crown interest or a Duchy interest.

(2) Subject to subsection (3) below, a person to whom this subsection applies may perform any functions under this Act in relation to land in which there is such an interest.

(3) Such a person shall not perform any functions—

(a) in relation to land in which there is no interest other than a Crown interest or a Duchy interest; or

(b) in relation to land which is exclusively in Crown occupation.

(4) Subsection (2) above applies—

(a) to an investigating officer;

(b) to an enforcement officer; and

(c) to a person authorised to enforce Part II or III of this Act.

(5) In this section—

"Crown interest" means any interest belonging to Her Majesty in right of the Crown or belonging to a government department or held in trust for Her Majesty for the purposes of a government department;

"Crown occupation" means occupation by Her Majesty in right of the Crown or occupation by a government department; and

"Duchy interest" means an interest belonging to Her Majesty in right of the Duchy of Lancaster, or belonging to the Duchy of Cornwall.

[Food and Environment Protection Act 1985, s 20.]

---

1. Part IV contains ss 20–28.

8–12218   21. Offences—penalties etc.   (1) A person guilty of an offence to which this subsection applies shall be liable[1]—

(a)   on summary conviction, to a fine of an amount not exceeding **the statutory maximum**; and

(b)   on conviction on indictment, to a fine or to imprisonment for a term of not more than **two years** or to both.

(2)   The offences to which subsection (1) above applies are offences under sections 1(6) and 2(4) above.

(2A)   A person guilty of an offence under section 9(1) shall be liable[1]—

(a)   on summary conviction, to a fine of an amount not exceeding **£50,000**; and

(b)   on conviction on indictment, to a **fine** or to imprisonment for a term not exceeding **two years** or to both.

(3)   A person guilty of an offence to which this subsection applies shall be liable[1]—

(a)   on summary conviction, to a fine of an amount not exceeding **the statutory maximum**; and

(b)   on conviction on indictment, to a fine.

(4)   The offences to which subsection (3) above applies are offences under sections 9(2) and 16(12) above.

(5)   A person guilty of an offence under Schedule 2 to this Act shall be liable on summary conviction to a fine of an amount not exceeding **level 5** on the standard scale.

(6)   Where an offence under this Act which has been committed by a body corporate is proved to have been committed with the consent or connivance of, or to be attributable to any neglect on the part of, a director, manager, secretary or other similar officer of the body corporate, or any person who was purporting to act in any such capacity, he as well as the body corporate shall be guilty of that offence and be liable to be proceeded against and punished accordingly.

(7)   Where the affairs of a body corporate are managed by its members, subsection (6) above shall apply in relation to the acts and defaults of a member in connection with his functions of management as if he were a director of the body corporate.

(8)   Proceedings for any offence under this Act may be taken, and the offence may for all incidental purposes be treated as having been committed, in any place in the United Kingdom.

[Food and Environment Protection Act 1985, s 21 as amended by the Environmental Protection Act 1990, s 146.]

---

1.   For procedure in respect of this offence which is triable either way, see the Magistrates' Courts Act 1980, ss 17A–21, in PART I: MAGISTRATES' COURTS, PROCEDURE, ante.

8–12219   22. General defence of due diligence.   (1) In any proceedings for an offence under this Act it is a defence for the person charged to prove that he took all reasonable precautions and exercised all due diligence to avoid the commission of the offence.

(2)   Without prejudice to the generality of subsection (1) above, a person is to be taken to have established the defence provided by that subsection if he proves—

(a)   that he acted under instructions given to him by his employer; or

(b)   that he acted in reliance on information supplied by another person without any reason to suppose that the information was false or misleading,

and in either case that he took all such steps as were reasonably open to him to ensure that no offence would be committed.

(3)   If in any case the defence provided by subsection (1) above involves an allegation that the commission of the offence was due to an act or omission by another person, other than the giving of instructions to the person charged with the offence by his employer, or to reliance on information supplied by another person, the person charged shall not, without leave of the court, be entitled to rely on that defence unless within a period ending seven clear days before the hearing, he has served on the prosecutor a notice giving such information identifying or assisting in the identification of that other person as was then in his possession.

[Food and Environment Protection Act 1985, s 22.]

8–12230　24. Interpretation.　(1) In this Act, unless the context otherwise requires—

"adjacent to Scotland", in relation to United Kingdom waters or United Kingdom controlled waters, means—

(a)　those waters so far as lying within the Scottish zone; and

(b)　United Kingdom controlled waters outside that zone, which are nearer to any point on the baselines from which the breadth of the territorial sea adjacent to Scotland is measured than to any point on the baselines in any other part of the United Kingdom;

"agricultural" is to be construed in accordance with section 109(3) of the Agriculture Act 1947, section 86(3) of the Agriculture (Scotland) Act 1948 or section 43(1) of the Agriculture Act (Northern Ireland) 1949;

"British aircraft" means an aircraft registered in the United Kingdom;

"British fishery limits" has the meaning assigned to it by the Fishery Limits Act 1976;

"British hovercraft" means a hovercraft registered in the United Kingdom;

"British marine structure" means a marine structure owned by or leased to an individual residing in or a body corporate incorporated under the law of any part of the United Kingdom;

"British sea-fishery officer" means any person who by virtue of section 7 of the Sea Fisheries Act 1968 is a British sea-fishery officer for the purposes of the Sea Fisheries Acts;

"British vessel" means a vessel registered in the United Kingdom, or a vessel exempted from such registration under the Merchant Shipping Act 1995;

"captain", in relation to a hovercraft, means the person who is designated by the operator to be in charge of it during any journey, or, failing such designation, the person who is for the time being lawfully in charge of it;

"commander", in relation to an aircraft, means the member of the flight crew designated as commander of that aircraft by the operator, or, failing such designation, the person who is for the time being the pilot in command of the aircraft;

"Convention State" means a state which is a party to the London Convention or the Oslo Convention;

"creature" means any living organism other than a human being or a plant;

"crops" includes any form of vegetable produce;

"designated area" and "designating authority" have the meanings assigned to them by section 1(2) above;

"designated circumstances" has the meaning assigned to it by section 1(5) above;

"emergency order" and "emergency prohibitions" have the meanings assigned to them by section 1(2) above;

"enforcement officer" has the meaning assigned to it by section 3 above;

"fish" includes—

(a)　shellfish; and
(b)　part of a fish;

and "fishing" includes fishing for shellfish;

"fishing boat" means any vessel for the time being employed in fishing operations or any operations ancillary thereto;

"food" has the same meaning as in the Food Safety Act 1990;

"human consumption" includes use in the preparation of food for human consumption;

"importation" has the same meaning as in the Customs and Excise Acts 1979;

"incineration" has the meaning assigned to it by section 6 above;

"international organisation" means any organisation established in pursuance of Article XIV of the London Convention or Article 16 of the Oslo Convention;

"investigating officer" has the meaning assigned to it by section 3 above;

"licence" means a licence under Part II of this Act;

licensing authority" means,

(a)　in relation to England and Wales whichever of the Ministers is responsible for fisheries in the place where an operation to which a licence would relate would, or have been, be carried out or commenced and,

(b)　in relation to Scotland—

(i)　as regards operations, so far as relating to oil and gas exploration and exploitation, to which a licence would relate and which would be, or have been, carried out in United Kingdom waters, or United Kingdom controlled waters, adjacent to Scotland but lying outside controlled waters within the meaning of section 30A(1) of the Control of Pollution Act 1974 or which commence in Scotland, the Secretary of State;

(ii)　as regards operations falling within the subject matter of Part VI of the Merchant Shipping Act 1995, to which a licence would relate and which would be, or have been, carried out in United Kingdom waters, or United Kingdom controlled waters, adjacent to Scotland, the Secretary of State;

(iii)　as regards any other operations to which a licence would relate and which would be, or have been, carried out in United Kingdom waters, or United Kingdom controlled waters, adjacent to Scotland or which commence in Scotland, the Secretary of State and the functions of that authority under this sub-paragraph shall be treated as exercisable in or as regards Scotland and may be exercised separately;

"the London Convention" means the Convention on the Prevention of Maritime Pollution by Dumping of Wastes and Other Matter concluded at London in December 1972;

"marine structure" means a platform or other man-made structure at sea, other than a pipe-line;

"master", in relation to any vessel, includes the person for the time being in charge of the vessel;

"the Ministers" means the Minister of Agriculture, Fisheries and Food and the Secretary of State;

"the Oslo Convention" means the Convention for the Prevention of Marine Pollution by Dumping from Ships and Aircraft concluded at Oslo in February 1972;

"pest", "pesticide" and "pesticide residue" are to be construed in accordance with section 16 above;

"plants" means any form of vegetable matter, while it is growing and after it has been harvested, gathered, felled or picked, and in particular, but without prejudice to the generality of this definition, includes—

(a) agricultural crops;
(b) trees and bushes grown for purposes other than those of agriculture;
(c) wild plants; and
(d) fungi;

"Scottish zone" has the meaning assigned to it by section 126(1) of the Scotland Act 1998;

"sea" includes any area submerged at mean high water springs and also includes, so far as the tide flows at mean high water springs, an estuary or arm of the sea and the waters of any channel, creek, bay or river;

"shellfish" includes crustaceans and molluscs of any kind;

"United Kingdom waters" means any part of the sea within the seaward limits of United Kingdom territorial waters and "United Kingdom controlled waters" means any part of the sea within the limits of an area designated under section 1(7) of the Continental Shelf Act 1964; and

"vessel" has the meaning assigned to "ship" by the Merchant Shipping Act 1995.

(2) Any reference in this Act to the London Convention or the Oslo Convention is a reference to it as it has effect from time to time.

(3) Any power conferred by this Act to make orders or regulations may be exercised—

(a) either in relation to all cases to which the power extends, or in relation to all those cases subjected to specified exceptions, or in relation to any specified cases or classes of case; and
(b) so as to make, as respects the cases in relation to which it is exercised—

(i) the full provision to which the power extends or any less provision (whether by way of exception or otherwise);
(ii) the same provision for all cases in relation to which the power is exercised, or different provision for different cases or different classes of case, or different provision as respects the same case or class of case for different purposes of this Act;
(iii) any such provision either unconditionally, or subject to any specified condition,

and includes power to make such incidental or supplemental provision in the orders or regulations as the Minister making them considers appropriate.

[Food and Environment Protection Act 1985, s 24 as amended by the Food Safety Act 1990, Schs 3 and 5, the Environmental Protection Act 1990, s 146, the Statute Law (Repeals) Act 1993, Sch 1, the Merchant Shipping Act 1995, Sch 13 and SI 1999/1756.]

8–12231 27. Commencement. *Repealed by the Statute Law (Repeals) Act 2004.*

SCHEDULES

Section 1

SCHEDULE 1
EMERGENCY PROHIBITIONS

(As amended by SI 1999/1756, Schedule.)

PART I
ACTIVITIES THAT MAY BE PROHIBITED IN A DESIGNATED AREA

8–12233 1. An emergency order may prohibit any of the following in the designated area—

(a) agricultural activities;
(b) the gathering or picking of wild plants;
(c) the slaughter of creatures;
(d) fishing for and taking fish; and
(e) the preparation and processing for supply to purchasers or others of food and anything from which food could be derived.

Part II
Movements of Food Etc that may be Prohibited

2. An emergency order may prohibit the movement of food or anything from which food could be derived—

(a) into or out of the designated area; or
(b) from one place to another within that area.

Part III
Activities that may be Prohibited Throughout the United Kingdom

3. An emergency order may prohibit any of the following—

(a) the use of anything taken from the designated area after a time specified in the order in the preparation or processing for supply to purchasers or others of food or anything from which food could be derived;
(b) the landing of fish or other forms of aquatic produce which were taken from waters in the designated area after a time so specified;
(c) the slaughter of creatures that were in the designated area after a time so specified;
(d) the supply, or the possessing for supply, to purchasers or others of any food or anything from which food could be derived, which was in the designated area after a time so specified;
(e) the feeding to creatures of any feeding stuff—

    (i) that was prepared or processed in contravention of a prohibition under paragraph 1(e) above;
    (ii) that was taken from the designated area after a time specified in the order; or
    (iii) in the preparation or processing of which anything was used in contravention of a prohibition under sub-paragraph (a) above;

(f) the supply, or the possessing for supply, to purchasers or others of any food or anything from which food could be derived,—

    (i) that was prepared or processed in contravention of a prohibition under paragraph 1(e) above; or
    (ii) in the preparation or processing of which anything was used in contravention of a prohibition under sub-paragraph (a) above.

4. A prohibition of a kind specified in paragraph 3 above shall apply in every part of the United Kingdom and United Kingdom waters.

Sections 4, 11 and 19   SCHEDULE 2
Officers and their Powers

(As amended by the Environmental Protection Act 1990, s 146, the Pesticides Act 1998, s 2 and the Civil Partnership Act 2004, Sch 27.)

Introductory

8–12234   **1.** In this Schedule "officer" means—

(a) an investigating officer;
(b) an enforcement officer; and
(c) a person authorised to enforce Part II or III of this Act.

Assistants for officers etc

2. (1) An officer may take with him, to assist him in performing his functions—

(a) any other person; and
(b) any equipment or materials.

(2) A person whom an officer takes with him to assist him may perform any of the officer's functions, but only under the officer's supervision.

2A. (1) If an officer is carrying out functions conferred by Part III of this Act, he may require a person whom he has reasonable cause to believe is able to give information which will assist him in carrying out those functions—

(a) to answer such questions as the officer thinks it appropriate to ask; and
(b) to sign a declaration of truth of his answers.

(2) Any person to whom questions are put under this paragraph may nominate a person to be with him when he gives his answers.

(3) When a person answers any such questions the only other person who may be present (apart from the questioner) are—

(a) the person (if any) nominate under sub-paragraph (2); and
(b) any person authorised by the officer to be present.

(4) A person is not to be excused from complying with a requirement under sub-paragraph (1) on the ground that to do so may incriminate him or his spouse or civil partner of an offence; but a statement or admission made in complying is not admissible in evidence against either of them in proceedings for any offence.

Powers in relation to vessels, aircraft etc

3. (1) In order to perform functions under Part I or II of this Act an officer may require any person—

(a) to give details of any substances or articles on board a vessel, aircraft, hovercraft or marine structure; and
(b) to give information concerning any substances or articles lost from a vessel, aircraft, hovercraft or marine structure.

(2) In order to perform any such functions an officer—

(*a*) may require any vessel, aircraft, hovercraft or marine structure to stop; and
(*b*) may require the attendance—

    (i) of the master, captain or commander of a vessel, aircraft or hovercraft;
    (ii) of the person in charge of a marine structure; and
    (iii) of any other person who is on board a vessel, aircraft, hovercraft or marine structure,

and may require any person on board to assist him in the performance of his functions.
(3) In order to perform functions under Part I or II of this Act an officer—

(*a*) may require—

    (i) the master, captain or commander of a vessel, aircraft or hovercraft; and
    (ii) the person in charge of a marine structure,

to take it and its crew to the port which appears to the officer to be the nearest convenient port; or

(*b*) may take it there himself.

(4) In order to perform any such functions an officer may detain a vessel, aircraft, hovercraft or marine structure.
(5) If an officer detains a vessel, aircraft, hovercraft or marine structure, he shall serve on the master, captain, commander or person in charge a notice in writing stating that it is to be detained until the notice is withdrawn by the service on him of a further notice in writing signed by an officer.

Containers etc

4. (1) Without prejudice to his powers under any other provision of this Act, in order to perform his functions an officer—

(*a*) may open any container;
(*b*) may carry out searches, inspections, measurements and tests;
(*c*) may take samples;
(*d*) may require the production of documents, books and records; and
(*e*) may photograph or copy anything whose production he has power to require under paragraph (*d*) above.

(2) An officer exercising any power of entry conferred by Part III of this Act may photograph anything which he has reasonable cause to believe may be relevant in connection with the exercise of his functions under that Part.
(3) Nothing in sub-paragraph (2) affects the powers conferred by sub-paragraph (1).

Evidence of officers' authority

5. (1) An officer shall be furnished with a certificate of his authorisation, and when he proposes to perform any function under this Act, it shall be his duty, if so requested, to produce that certificate.
(2) It shall also be his duty, if so requested, to state—

(*a*) his name;
(*b*) the function that he proposes to perform; and
(*c*) his grounds for proposing to perform it.

(3) The references to certificates of authorisation in sub-paragraph (1) above are to be construed, in relation to a British sea-fishery officer, as references to his warrant of appointment as a British sea-fishery officer.

Time of performance of functions

6. An officer must perform his functions under this Act at a reasonable hour unless it appears to the officer that there are grounds for suspecting that the purpose of their performance may be frustrated if he seeks to perform them at a reasonable hour.

Entry into dwellings

7. (1) An officer may only enter a dwelling for the purpose of performing his functions under this Act if a justice has issued a warrant authorising him to enter and search that dwelling.
(2) A justice may only issue such a warrant if on an application made by the officer he is satisfied—

(*a*) that the officer has reasonable grounds for believing that there is present in the dwelling anything to which those functions relate, and
(*b*) that—

    (i) It is not practicable to communicate with any person entitled to grant entry to the dwelling; or
    (ii) a person entitled to grant entry to the dwelling has unreasonably refused an officer entry; or
    (iii) entry to the dwelling is unlikely to be granted unless a warrant is produced; or
    (iv) the purpose of entry may be frustrated or seriously prejudiced unless an officer arriving at the dwelling can secure immediate entry to it.

(3) In this paragraph "justice" means—

(*a*) in relation to England and Wales and Northern Ireland, a justice of the peace; and
(*b*) in relation to Scotland, a sheriff, stipendiary magistrate or justice of the peace.

(4) In relation to England and Wales, sections 15 and 16 of the Police and Criminal Evidence Act 1984 (which relate to safeguards in respect of warrants and the execution of warrants) shall have effect in relation to warrants for officers under this paragraph as they have effect in relation to warrants for constables.

Power of officer to use reasonable force

8. An officer may use reasonable force, if necessary, in the performance of his functions.

Protection of officers

9. An officer shall not be liable in any civil or criminal proceedings for anything done in the purported performance of his functions under this Act if the court is satisfied that the act was done in good faith and that there were reasonable grounds for doing it.

Offences

10. Any person who—

(*a*)　intentionally obstructs an officer in the performance of any of his functions under this Act;

(*b*)　fails without reasonable excuse to comply with a requirement made or direction given by an officer in the performance of his functions under this Act; or

(*c*)　in purporting to give information required by an officer for the performance of any of his functions under this Act—

　　(i)　makes a statement which he knows to be false in a material particular;
　　(ii)　recklessly makes a statement which is false in a material particular; or
　　(iii)　intentionally fails to disclose any material particular,

shall be guilty of an offence.

Food Safety Act 1990

(1990 c 16)

PART I[1]

PRELIMINARY

8–12235　**1. Meaning of "food" and other basic expressions.**　(1) In this Act "food" has the same meaning as it has in Regulation (EC) No 178/2002.

(2) In this Act "Regulation (EC) No 178/2002" means Regulation (EC) No 178/2002 of the European Parliament and of the Council laying down the general principles and requirements of food law, establishing the European Food Safety Authority and laying down procedures in matters of food safety.

(*c*)　chewing gum and other products of a like nature and use; and

(*d*)　articles and substances used as ingredients in the preparation of food or anything falling within this subsection.

(2) In this Act "food" does not include—

(*a*)　live animals or birds, or live fish which are not used for human consumption while they are alive;

(*b*)　fodder or feeding stuffs for animals, birds or fish;

(*c*)　controlled drugs within the meaning of the Misuse of Drugs Act 1971; or

(*d*)　subject to such exceptions as may be specified in an order made by the Secretary of State—

　　(i)　medicinal products within the meaning of the Medicines Act 1968[2] in respect of which product licences within the meaning of that Act are for the time being in force; or
　　(ii)　other articles or substances in respect of which such licences are for the time being in force in pursuance of orders under section 104 or 105 of that Act (application of Act to other articles and substances).★

(3) In this Act, unless the context otherwise requires—

"business" includes the undertaking of a canteen, club, school, hospital or institution, whether carried on for profit or not, and any undertaking or activity carried on by a public or local authority;

"commercial operation", in relation to any food or contact material, means any of the following, namely—

　　(*a*)　selling, possessing for sale and offering, exposing or advertising for sale;
　　(*b*)　consigning, delivering or serving by way of sale;
　　(*c*)　preparing for sale or presenting, labelling or wrapping for the purpose of sale;
　　(*d*)　storing or transporting for the purpose of sale;
　　(*e*)　importing and exporting;

　　and, in relation to any food source, means deriving food from it for the purpose of sale or for purposes connected with sale;

"contact material" means any article or substance which is intended to come into contact with food;

"food business" means any business in the course of which commercial operations with respect to food or food sources are carried out;

"food premises" means any premises used for the purposes of a food business;

"food source" means any growing crop or live animal, bird or fish from which food is intended to be derived (whether by harvesting, slaughtering, milking, collecting eggs or otherwise);

"premises" includes any place, any vehicle, stall or moveable structure and, for such purposes as may be specified in an order³ made by the Secretary of State, any ship or aircraft of a description so specified.

(4) The reference in subsection (3) above to preparing for sale shall be construed, in relation to any contact material, as a reference to manufacturing or producing for the purpose of sale.
[Food Safety Act 1990, s 1 amended by SI 1994/3144, the Food Standards Act 1999, Sch 5 and SI 2004/2990.]

1. Part I contains ss 1–6.
2. This section shall have effect as if the reference to medicinal products within the meaning of the Medicines Act 1968, in respect of which product licences within the meaning of the Act are for the time being in force, included a reference to relevant medicinal products in respect of which United Kingdom marketing authorisations under the Medicines for Human Use (Marketing Authorisations etc) Regulations 1994, SI 1994/3144 as amended, or Community marketing authorisations are for the time being in force.
3. The Food Safety (Ships and Aircraft) (Wales) Order 2003, SI 2003/1774 amended by SI 2005/3292 and the Food Safety (Ships and Aircraft) (England and Scotland) Order 2003, SI 2003/1895 amended by SI 2005/2059 (E) have been made which specify ships and aircraft and purposes for which they are "premises" in and under the Food Safety Act 1990.

8–12236   2. Extended meaning of "sale" etc.   (1) For the purposes of this Act—

(a) the supply of food, otherwise than on sale, in the course of a business; and
(b) any other thing which is done with respect to food and is specified in an order made by the Secretary of State,

shall be deemed to be a sale of the food, and references to purchasers and purchasing shall be construed accordingly.
(2) This Act shall apply—

(a) in relation to any food which is offered as a prize or reward or given away in connection with any entertainment to which the public are admitted, whether on payment of money or not, as if the food were, or had been, exposed for sale by each person concerned in the organisation of the entertainment;
(b) in relation to any food which, for the purpose of advertisement or in furtherance of any trade or business, is offered as a prize or reward or given away, as if the food were, or had been, exposed for sale by the person offering or giving away the food; and
(c) in relation to any food which is exposed or deposited in any premises for the purpose of being so offered or given away as mentioned in paragraph (a) or (b) above, as if the food were, or had been, exposed for sale by the occupier of the premises;

and in this subsection "entertainment" includes any social gathering, amusement, exhibition, performance, game, sport or trial of skill.
[Food Safety Act 1990, s 2 as amended by the Food Standards Act 1999, Sch 6.]

8–12237   3. Presumptions that food intended for human consumption.   (1) The following provisions shall apply for the purposes of this Act.
(2) Any food commonly used for human consumption shall, if sold or offered, exposed or kept for sale, be presumed, until the contrary is proved, to have been sold or, as the case may be, to have been or to be intended for sale for human consumption.
(3) The following, namely—

(a) any food commonly used for human consumption which is found on premises used for the preparation, storage, or sale of that food; and
(b) any article or substance commonly used in the manufacture of food for human consumption which is found on premises used for the preparation, storage or sale of that food,

shall be presumed, until the contrary is proved, to be intended for sale, or for manufacturing food for sale, for human consumption.
(4) Any article or substance capable of being used in the composition or preparation of any food commonly used for human consumption which is found on premises on which that food is prepared shall, until the contrary is proved, be presumed to be intended for such use.
[Food Safety Act 1990, s 3.]

8–12238   4. Ministers having functions under Act.   *Repealed.*

8–12239   5. Food authorities and authorised officers.   (1) Subject to subsections (3) and (4) below, the food authorities in England are—

(a) as respects each London borough, district or non-metropolitan county, the council of that borough, district or county;
(b) as respects the City of London (including the Temples), the Common Council;
(c) as respects the Inner Temple or the Middle Temple, the appropriate Treasurer;
(d) as respects the Isles of Scilly, the council of the Isles of Scilly.

(1A) Subject to subsection (3)(a) and (b) below, the food authorities in Wales are, as respects each county or county borough, the council of that county or county borough.

(2) in relation to Scotland, the Secretary of State subject to subsection (3)(*a*) below, the food authorities in Scotland are the islands or district councils.

(3) Where any functions under this Act are assigned—

(*a*) by an order under section 2 or 7 of the Public Health (Control of Disease) Act 1984, to a port health authority or, by an order under section 172 of the Public Health (Scotland) Act 1897, to a port local authority;

(*b*) by an order under section 6 of the Public Health Act 1936, to a joint board for a united district; or

(*c*) by an order under paragraph 15(6) of Schedule 8 to the Local Government Act 1985, to a single authority for a metropolitan county,

any reference in this Act to a food authority shall be construed, so far as relating to those functions, as a reference to the authority to whom they are so assigned.

(4) The Secretary of State may by order[1] provide, either generally or in relation to cases of a particular description, that any functions under this Act which are exercisable concurrently—

(*a*) as respects a non-metropolitan district, by the council of that district and the council of the non-metropolitan county;

(*b*) as respects the Inner Temple or the Middle Temple, by the appropriate Treasurer and the Common Council,

shall be exercisable solely by such one of those authorities as may be specified in the order.*

(5) In this section—

"the appropriate Treasurer" means the Sub-Treasurer in relation to the Inner Temple and the Under Treasurer in relation to the Middle Temple;

"the Common Council" means the Common Council of the City of London;

"port local authority" includes a joint port local authority.

(6) In this Act "authorised officer", in relation to a food authority, means any person (whether or not an officer of the authority) who is authorised by them in writing, either generally or specially, to act in matters arising under this Act; but if regulations[2] made by the Secretary of State so provide, no person shall be so authorised unless he has such qualifications as may be prescribed by the regulations. [Food Safety Act 1990, s 5 amended by the Local Government (Wales) Act 1994, Sch 9 and the Food Standards Act 1999, Sch 5.]

---

1. The Food Safety (Enforcement Authority) (England and Wales) Order 1990, SI 1990/2462 has been made; in non-metropolitan districts enforcement functions under s 12 are to be exercised solely by district councils whilst enforcement functions under s 15 are to be exercised solely by county councils.

2. The Authorised Officers (Meat Inspection) Regulations 1987, SI 1987/133, made under s 73(2) of the Food Act 1984, now repealed, shall have effect as if made under s 5(6) of this Act; see Sch 4, post.

8–12240   6. Enforcement of Act.   (1) In this Act "the enforcement authority", in relation to any provisions of this Act or any regulations or orders made under it, means the authority by whom they are to be enforced and executed.

(2) Every food authority shall enforce and execute within their area the provisions of this Act with respect to which the duty is not imposed expressly or by necessary implication on some other authority.

(3) The Secretary of State may direct, in relation to cases of a particular description or a particular case, that any duty imposed on food authorities by subsection (2) above shall be discharged by the Secretary of State or the Food Standards Agency, and not by those authorities.

(4) Regulations or orders under this Act shall specify which of the following authorities are to enforce and execute them, either generally or in relation to cases of a particular description or a particular area, namely—

(*a*) the Secretary of State, the Food Standards Agency, food authorities and such other authorities as are mentioned in section 5(3) above; and

(*b*) in the case of regulations, the Commissioners of Customs and Excise;

and any such regulations or orders may provide for the giving of assistance and information, by any authority concerned in the administration of the regulations or orders, or of any provisions of this Act, to any other authority so concerned, for the purposes of their respective duties under them.

(5) An enforcement authority in England and Wales may institute proceedings under any provisions of this Act or any regulations or orders made under it.

(5A) The Secretary of State may take over the conduct of any such proceedings which have been instituted by some other person.

(5B) The Secretary of State may direct the Food Standards Agency to take over the conduct of any such proceedings which have been instituted by some person other than the Agency.

(5C) The Food Standards Agency may take over the conduct of any such proceedings which have been instituted by some other person, but (unless the Agency has been directed to do so under subsection (5B) above) only with the consent of the person who instituted them.

(6) In this Act "authorised officer", in relation to an enforcement authority, means any person

(whether or not an officer of the authority) who is authorised by the authority in writing, either generally or specially, to act in matters arising under this Act and regulations and orders made under it; but if regulations made by the Secretary of State so provide, no person shall be so authorised unless he has such qualifications as may be prescribed by the regulations.
[Food Safety Act 1990, s 6 amended by the Deregulation and Contracting Out Act 1994, s 31 and Schs 16 and 9, the Food Standards Act 1999, Schs 5 and 6 and SI 2002/794.]

PART II[1]
MAIN PROVISIONS
FOOD SAFETY

8-12241   7. Rendering food injurious to health.   (1) Any person who renders any food injurious to health by means of any of the following operations, namely—

(a)   adding any article or substance to the food;
(b)   using any article or substance as an ingredient[2] in the preparation of the food;
(c)   abstracting any constituent from the food; and
(d)   subjecting the food to any other process or treatment,

with intent that it shall be sold for human consumption, shall be guilty of an offence.

(2) In determining for the purposes of this section whether any food is injurious to health, regard shall be had to the matters specified in sub–paragraphs (a) to (c) of Article 14(4) of Regulation (EC) No 178/2002.

(3) *Repealed.*
[Food Safety Act 1990, s 7 as amended by SI 2004/3279.]

---

1. Part II contains ss 8–26.
2. The ingredient added must be such as to render the article of food as sold injurious to health; but it is not necessary that the analyst's certificate shall state this (*Hull v Horsnell* (1904) 68 JP 591; cf *Friend v Mapp* (1904) 68 JP 589). An offence may be committed where the article is harmless to adults, but injurious to children or invalids (*Cullen v McNair* (1908) 72 JP 280; and see *Haigh v Aerated Bread Co Ltd* [1916] 1 KB 878, 80 JP 284). Where the sale was to the prejudice of a purchaser, a person may be charged under this section or under s 14 (*Goulder v Rook, Bent v Ormerod*) [1901] 2 KB 290, 65 JP 646).

8-12242   8. Selling food not complying with food safety requirements(1) *Repealed.*
.   (2) For the purposes of this Part food fails to comply with food safety requirements if it is unsafe within the meaning of Article 14 of Regulation (EC) No 178/2002 and references to food safety requirements or to food complying with such requirements shall be construed accordingly.

(3) *Repealed.*

(4) For the purposes of this Part, any part of, or product derived wholly or partly from, an animal—

(a)   which has been slaughtered in a knacker's yard, or of which the carcase has been brought into a knacker's yard; or
(b)   in Scotland, which has been slaughtered otherwise than in a slaugherhouse,

shall be deemed to be unfit for human consumption.

(5) In subsection (4) above, in its application to Scotland, "animal" means any description of cattle, sheep, goat, swine, horse, ass or mule; and paragraph (b) of that subsection shall not apply where accident, illness or emergency affecting the animal in question required it to be slaughtered as mentioned in that paragraph.
[Food Safety Act 1990, s 8 as amended by SI 2004/3279.]

8-12243   9. Inspection and seizure of suspected food.   (1) An authorised officer of a food authority may at all reasonable times inspect any food intended for human consumption which—

(a)   has been sold or is offered or exposed for sale;
(b)   is in the possession of, or has been deposited with or consigned to, any person for the purpose of sale or of preparation for sale; or
(c)   is otherwise placed on the market within the meaning of Regulation (EC) No 178/2002;

and subsections (3) to (9) below shall apply where, on such an inspection, it appears to the authorised officer that any food fails to comply with food safety requirements.

(2) The following provisions shall also apply where, otherwise than on such an inspection, it appears to an authorised officer of a food authority that any food is likely to cause food poisoning or any disease communicable to human beings.

(3) The authorised officer may either—

(a)   give notice to the person in charge of the food that, until the notice is withdrawn, the food or any specified portion of it—

(i)   is not to be used for human consumption; and
(ii)   either is not to be removed or is not to be removed except to some place specified in the notice; or

(b)   seize the food and remove it in order to have it dealt with by a justice of the peace;

and any person who knowingly contravenes the requirements of a notice under paragraph (*a*) above shall be guilty of an offence.

(4) Where the authorised officer exercises the powers conferred by subsection (3)(*a*) above, he shall, as soon as is reasonably practicable and in any event within 21 days, determine whether or not he is satisfied that the food complies with food safety requirements and—

(*a*) if he is so satisfied, shall forthwith withdraw the notice;

(*b*) if he is not so satisfied, shall seize the food and remove it in order to have it dealt with by a justice of the peace.

(5) Where an authorised officer exercises the powers conferred by subsection (3)(*b*) or (4)(*b*) above, he shall inform the person in charge of the food of his intention to have it dealt with by a justice of the peace and—

(*a*) any person who under section 7 or regulation 4(*a*) of the General Food Regulations 2004 might be liable to a prosecution in respect of the food shall, if he attends before the justice of the peace by whom the food falls to be dealt with, be entitled to be heard and to call witnesses; and

(*b*) that justice of the peace may, but need not, be a member of the court before which any person is charged with an offence under that section in relation to that food.

(6) If it appears to a justice of the peace, on the basis of such evidence as he considers appropriate in the circumstances, that any food falling to be dealt with by him under this section fails to comply with food safety requirements, he shall[1] condemn the food and order—

(*a*) the food to be destroyed or to be disposed of as to prevent it from being used for human consumption; and

(*b*) any expenses reasonably incurred in connection with the destruction or disposal to be defrayed by the owner of the food.

(7) If a notice under subsection (3)(*a*) above is withdrawn, or the justice of the peace by whom any food falls to be dealt with under this section refuses to condemn it, the food authority shall compensate the owner of the food for any depreciation in its value resulting from the action taken by the authorised officer.

(8) Any disputed question as to the right to or the amount of any compensation payable under subsection (7) above shall be determined by arbitration.

(9) In the application of this section to Scotland—

(*a*) any reference to a justice of the peace includes a reference to the sheriff and to a magistrate;

(*b*) paragraph (*b*) of subsection (5) above shall not apply;

(*c*) any order made under subsection (6) above shall be sufficient evidence in any proceedings under this Act of the failure of the food in question to comply with food safety requirements; and

(*d*) the reference in subsection (8) above to determination by arbitration shall be construed as a reference to determination by a single arbiter appointed, failing agreement between the parties, by the sheriff.

[Food Safety Act 1990, s 9 as amended by SI 2004/3279.]

----

1. The hearing is a proceeding within the meaning of s 11 of the Magistrates' Courts Act 1980 and it is, accordingly amenable to appeal by way of case stated: *R (on the application of the Food Standards Agency) v Brent Justices and Kelman's Kosher Products* [2004] Admin 459, (2004) 168 JP 241. The word 'shall' in subs(6) indicates that condemnation is mandatory: *R (on the application of the Food Standards Agency) v Brent Justices and Kelman's Kosher Products*, supra.

8–12244   10. Improvement notices.   (1) If an authorised officer of an enforcement authority has reasonable grounds for believing that the proprietor of a food business is failing to comply with any regulations to which this section applies, he may, by a notice served on that proprietor (in this Act referred to as an "improvement notice")—

(*a*) state the officer's grounds for believing that the proprietor is failing to comply with the regulations;

(*b*) specify the matters which constitute the proprietor's failure so to comply;

(*c*) specify the measures which, in the officer's opinion, the proprietor must take in order to secure compliance; and

(*d*) require the proprietor to take those measures, or measures which are at least equivalent to them, within such period (not being less than 14 days) as may be specified in the notice.

(2) Any person who fails to comply with an improvement notice shall be guilty of an offence.

(3) This section and section 11 below apply to any regulations under this Part which make provision—

(*a*) for requiring, prohibiting or regulating the use of any process or treatment in the preparation of food; or

(*b*) for securing the observance of hygienic conditions and practices in connection with the carrying out of commercial operations with respect to food or food sources.

[Food Safety Act 1990, s 10.]

8–12245 **11. Prohibition orders.** (1) If—

(*a*) the proprietor of a food business is convicted of an offence under any regulations to which this section applies; and

(*b*) the court by or before which he is so convicted is satisfied that the health risk condition is fulfilled with respect to that business,

the court shall by an order impose the appropriate prohibition.

(2) The health risk condition is fulfilled with respect to any food business if any of the following involves risk of injury to health, namely—

(*a*) the use for the purposes of the business of any process or treatment;

(*b*) the construction of any premises used for the purposes of the business, or the use for those purposes of any equipment; and

(*c*) the state or condition of any premises or equipment used for the purposes of the business.

(2A) In subsection (2) above and in sections 12(4) and 13(1) "injury" includes any impairment, whether permanent or temporary.

(3) The appropriate prohibition is—

(*a*) in a case falling within paragraph (*a*) of subsection (2) above, a prohibition on the use of the process or treatment for the purposes of the business;

(*b*) in a case falling within paragraph (*b*) of that subsection, a prohibition on the use of the premises or equipment for the purposes of the business or any other food business of the same class or description;

(*c*) in a case falling within paragraph (*c*) of that subsection, a prohibition on the use of the premises or equipment for the purposes of any food business.

(4) If—

(*a*) the proprietor of a food business is convicted of an offence under any regulations to which this section applies by virtue of section 10(3)(*b*) above; and

(*b*) the court by or before which he is so convicted thinks it proper to do so in all the circumstances of the case,

the court may, by an order, impose a prohibition on the proprietor participating in the management of any food business, or any food business of a class or description specified in the order.

(5) As soon as practicable after the making of an order under subsection (1) or (4) above (in this Act referred to as a "prohibition order"), the enforcement authority shall—

(*a*) serve a copy of the order on the proprietor of the business; and

(*b*) in the case of an order under subsection (1) above, affix a copy of the order in a conspicuous position on such premises used for the purposes of the business as they consider appropriate;

and any person who knowingly contravenes such an order shall be guilty of an offence.

(6) A prohibition order shall cease to have effect—

(*a*) in the case of an order under subsection (1) above, on the issue by the enforcement authority of a certificate to the effect that they are satisfied that the proprietor has taken sufficient measures to secure that the health risk condition is no longer fulfilled with respect to the business;

(*b*) in the case of an order under subsection (4) above, on the giving by the court of a direction to that effect.

(7) The enforcement authority shall issue a certificate under paragraph (*a*) of subsection (6) above within three days of their being satisfied as mentioned in that paragraph; and on an application by the proprietor for such a certificate, the authority shall—

(*a*) determine, as soon as is reasonably practicable and in any event within 14 days, whether or not they are so satisfied; and

(*b*) if they determine that they are not so satisfied, give notice to the proprietor of the reasons for that determination.

(8) The court shall give a direction under subsection (6)(*b*) above if, on an application by the proprietor, the court thinks it proper to do so having regard to all the circumstances of the case, including in particular the conduct of the proprietor since the making of the order; but no such application shall be entertained if it is made—

(*a*) within six months after the making of the prohibition order; or

(*b*) within three months after the making by the proprietor of a previous application for such a direction.

(9) Where a magistrates' court or, in Scotland, the sheriff makes an order under section 12(2) below with respect to any food business, subsection (1) above shall apply as if the proprietor of the business had been convicted by the court or sheriff of an offence under regulations to which this section applies.

(10) Subsection (4) above shall apply in relation to a manager of a food business as it applies in

relation to the proprietor of such a business; and any reference in subsection (5) or (8) above to the proprietor of the business, or to the proprietor, shall be construed accordingly.

(11) In subsection (10) above "manager", in relation to a food business, means any person who is entrusted by the proprietor with the day to day running of the business, or any part of the business. [Food Safety Act 1990, s 11 as amended by SI 2004/3279.]

8–12246 12. Emergency prohibition notices and orders. (1) If an authorised officer of an enforcement authority is satisfied that the health risk condition is fulfilled with respect to any food business, he may, by a notice served on the proprietor of the business (in this Act referred to as an "emergency prohibition notice"), impose the appropriate prohibition.

(2) If a magistrates' court or, in Scotland, the sheriff is satisfied, on the application of such an officer, that the health risk condition is fulfilled with respect to any food business, the court or sheriff shall, by an order (in this Act referred to as an "emergency prohibition order"), impose the appropriate prohibition.

(3) Such an officer shall not apply for an emergency prohibition order unless, at least one day before the date of the application, he has served notice on the proprietor of the business of his intention to apply for the order.

(4) Subsections (2) and (3) of section 11 above shall apply for the purposes of this section as they apply for the purposes of that section, but as if the reference in subsection (2) to risk of injury to health were a reference to imminent risk of such injury.

(5) As soon as practicable after the service of an emergency prohibition notice, the enforcement authority shall affix a copy of the notice in a conspicuous position on such premises used for the purposes of the business as they consider appropriate; and any person who knowingly contravenes such a notice shall be guilty of an offence.

(6) As soon as practicable after the making of an emergency prohibition order, the enforcement authority shall—

(*a*) serve a copy of the order on the proprietor of the business; and

(*b*) affix a copy of the order in a conspicuous position on such premises used for the purposes of that business as they consider appropriate;

and any person who knowingly contravenes such an order shall be guilty of an offence.

(7) An emergency prohibition notice shall cease to have effect—

(*a*) if no application for an emergency prohibition order is made within the period of three days beginning with the service of the notice, at the end of that period;

(*b*) if such an application is so made, on the determination or abandonment of the application.

(8) An emergency prohibition notice or emergency prohibition order shall cease to have effect on the issue by the enforcement authority of a certificate to the effect that they are satisfied that the proprietor has taken sufficient measures to secure that the health risk condition is no longer fulfilled with respect to the business.

(9) The enforcement authority shall issue a certificate under subsection (8) above within three days of their being satisfied as mentioned in that subsection; and on an application by the proprietor for such a certificate, the authority shall—

(*a*) determine, as soon as is reasonably practicable and in any event within 14 days, whether or not they are so satisfied; and

(*b*) if they determine that they are not so satisfied, give notice to the proprietor of the reasons for that determination.

(10) Where an emergency prohibition notice is served on the proprietor of a business, the enforcement authority shall compensate him in respect of any loss suffered by reason of his complying with the notice unless—

(*a*) an application for an emergency prohibition order is made within the period of three days beginning with the service of the notice; and

(*b*) the court declares itself satisfied, on the hearing of the application, that the health risk condition was fulfilled with respect to the business at the time when the notice was served;

and any disputed question as to the right to or the amount of any compensation payable under this subsection shall be determined by arbitration or, in Scotland, by a single arbiter appointed, failing agreement between the parties, by the sheriff. [Food Safety Act 1990, s 12.]

8–12247 13. Emergency control orders. (1) If it appears to the Secretary of State that the carrying out of commercial operations with respect to food, food sources or contact materials of any class or description involves or may involve imminent risk of injury to health, he may, by an order[1] (in this Act referred to as an "emergency control order"), prohibit the carrying out of such operations with respect to food, food sources or contact materials of that class or description.

(2) Any person who knowingly contravenes an emergency control order shall be guilty of an offence.

(3) The Secretary of State or the Food Standards Agency may consent, either unconditionally or

subject to any condition that the authority giving the consent considers appropriate, to the doing in a particular case of anything prohibited by an emergency control order.

(4) It shall be a defence for a person charged with an offence under subsection (2) above to show—

(*a*) that consent had been given under subsection (3) above to the contravention of the emergency control order; and

(*b*) that any condition subject to which that consent was given was complied with.

(5) The Secretary of State or the Food Standards Agency—

(*a*) may give such directions as appear to the authority giving the directions to be necessary or expedient for the purpose of preventing the carrying out of commercial operations with respect to any food, food sources or contact materials which the authority giving the directions believes, on reasonable grounds, to be food, food sources or contact materials to which an emergency control order applies; and

(*b*) may do anything which appears to the authority giving the directions to be necessary or expedient for that purpose.

(6) Any person who fails to comply with a direction under this section shall be guilty of an offence.

(7) If the Secretary of State or the Food Standards Agency does anything by virtue of this section in consequence of any person failing to comply with an emergency control order or a direction under this section, that authority may recover from that person any expenses reasonably incurred by that authority under this section.

[Food Safety Act 1990, s13 as amended by the Food Standards Act 1999, Sch 5.]

---

1. The following orders have been made: Food (Pistachios from Iran) (Emergency Control) SI 1997/2238 amended by SI 1997/3046 and SI 2000/656; Food (Peanuts from Egypt) (Emergency Control) Order 2000, SI 2000/375 amended by SI 2000/656; Food (Star Anise from Third Countries) (Emergency Control) (England) Order 2002, SI 2002/334 amended by SI 2002/602; Food (Star Anise from Third Countries) (Emergency Control) (Wales) Order 2002, SI 2002/402. See now, orders made under s 2 of the European Communities Act 1972, listed ante.

Consumer protection

8–12248   14. Selling food not of the nature or substance or quality demanded.   (1) Any person[1] who sells[2] to the purchaser's prejudice[3] any food[4] which is not[5] of the nature or substance[6] or quality[7] demanded[8] by the purchaser[9] shall be guilty of an offence[10].

(2) In subsection (1) above the reference to sale shall be construed as a reference to sale for human consumption; and in proceedings under that subsection it shall not be a defence that the purchaser was not prejudiced because he bought for analysis[11] or examination[12].

[Food Safety Act 1990, s 14.]

---

1. A servant who sells on behalf of his master is liable to be convicted (*Hotchin v Hindmarsh* [1891] 2 QB 181, 55 JP 775; *Goodfellow v Johnson* [1966] 1 QB 83, [1965] 1 All ER 941, 129 JP 283). A master may be liable for a sale by his servant who is acting within the scope of his authority, even though the servant is guilty of misconduct in his methods of selling (*Brown v Foot* (1892) 56 JP 581; see also *Morris v Corbett* (1892) 56 JP 649; *Parker v Alder* [1899] 1 QB 20, 62 JP 772; *Houghton v Mundy* (1910) 74 JP 377). Where the servant has authority to sell, though limited, the master is liable where the servant misuses his authority (*Elder v Bishop Auckland Co-operative Society Ltd* (1917) 81 JP 202; *Buckingham v Duck* (1918) 83 JP 20; see also *Quality Dairies (York) Ltd v Pedley* [1952] 1 KB 275, [1952] 1 All ER 380, 116 JP 123; *United Dairies (London) Ltd v Beckenham Corpn, United Dairies (London) Ltd v Fisher & Sons Ltd* [1963] 1 QB 434, [1961] 1 All ER 579, 125 JP 218). Where milk deficient in milk-fat was supplied by defendant's servant, having been drawn from the bottom of a can after the cream had risen, a Scottish court held that the defendant was liable, notwithstanding that his orders that the milk should be stirred had been disobeyed (*Penrice v Brander* 1921 JC 63).
"Person" includes a limited company (*Pearks, Gunston and Tee Ltd v Ward; Hennen v Southern Counties Dairies Co* [1902] 2 KB 1, 66 JP 774; *R v Ascanio Puck & Co and Paice* (1912) 76 JP 487; *R v ICR Haulage Ltd* [1944] KB 551, [1944] 1 All ER 691, 108 JP 181). Although only a licensee or his servant can lawfully sell alcohol, s 14 applies to all foods and the words of the section should be given their ordinary meaning so that a brewery, as owner of the goods prior to sale may be liable for selling under strength drink (*Nottingham City Council v Wolverhampton and Dudley Breweries plc* [2003] EWHC 2852 (Admin), [2004], [2004] QB 1274, [2004] 1 All ER 1352, 168 JP 37). For liability of a director, etc of a body corporate, see s 36 post.
The admissibility in evidence of statements made by a defendant's servant is considered in PART II: EVIDENCE, para **2–470 Statements and admissions by agents and employees**, ante.
2. No action lies by a person who is not the purchaser for damages caused by a breach of this section in respect of milk containing typhoid bacilli (*Square v Model Farm Dairies (Bournemouth) Ltd* [1939] 2 KB 365, [1939] 1 All ER 259, CA). A purported sale of food takes place even though something different is actually supplied, for example savin instead of saffron (*Knight v Bowers* (1885) 14 QBD 845), caustic soda instead of lemonade (*Meah v Roberts* [1978] 1 All ER 97). For circumstances in which the supply of food is deemed to be a sale, see s 2, ante.
3. A sale is not to the prejudice of the purchaser where it is brought clearly to his notice that the article offered to him is not of the nature or substance or quality of the article he has asked for (*Sandys v Jackson* (1905) 69 JP 171); the offence is in handing to a purchaser something to his prejudice, not necessarily pecuniary prejudice (*Hoyle v Hitchman* (1879) 4 QBD 233, 43 JP 430). The cases on this point were reviewed in *Rodbourn v Hudson* [1925] 1 KB 225, 89 JP 25. The article demanded must be held to be the article which an ordinary purchaser desires to obtain, not something which falls below the standard of an exact scientific definition (*Morton v Green* 1881 8 R (Ct of Sess) 36; *Collins Arden Products Ltd v Barking Corpn* [1943] KB 419, [1943] 2 All ER 249, 107 JP 117; *Robinson (Thomas) Sons & Co v Allardice* (1944) 108 JP 101). The fact that an article is offered below the market price is not *prima facie* an indication to a purchaser that it is below quality (*Heywood v Whitehead* (1897) 76 LT 781).
As "prejudice" must be alleged, it must be proved that the seller acted in a manner prejudicial to the purchaser; and this is not avoided where the ostensible purchaser is a mere agent in connection with the particular purchase, as, *eg*, where an

inspector sends into a shop a person who makes a purchase, the inspector not appearing until the transaction is completed (*Garforth v Esam* (1892) 56 JP 521).

Milk.—Milk is genuine if it is sold as it comes from the cow (*Hunt v Richardson* [1916] 2 KB 446, 80 JP 305). This decision was followed in *Grigg v Smith* (1917) 82 JP 2, where the deficiency in fact was caused by reason of the cow not being fully milked, and in *Williams v Rees* (1918) 82 JP 97, in spite of a finding that the milk was not of merchantable quality, and in *Few v Robinson* [1921] 3 KB 504, 85 JP 257, where the milk was not up to the standard contracted for. The magistrates may find, as a fact, that the milk is of the substance demanded if, as it came from the cow, it contained foreign matter unavoidably present in minute quantities (*Kenny v Cox* (1920) 85 JP 70), but in *Hall v Owen-Jones and Jones* [1967] 3 All ER 209, 131 JP 405, it was held that it is no defence if a substance (in that case penicillin) which ought never to be there at all is in the milk as it leaves the cow. Where a purchaser asks for "hot milk" and is supplied with adulterated milk that has been heated, the fact that "hot milk" and not merely "milk" was asked for is no bar to a conviction (*Herrington v Slater* (1920) 85 JP 83).

As to evidence by analysis of samples from recent corresponding milkings, see *Wilkinson v Clark* [1916] 2 KB 636, 80 JP 334; *Smith v Philpott* [1920] 1 KB 222, 84 JP 5; for cases on evidence necessary to rebut the presumption raised by the analyst's certificate, see *Bowen v Jones* (1917) 81 JP 178; *Kings v Merris* [1920] 3 KB 566, 85 JP 68; *Jenkins v Williams* (1939) 103 JP 183; *Churcher v Reeves* [1942] 1 KB 172, [1942] 1 All ER 69, 106 JP 66.

"Camphorated oil" was held to be a drug and proceedings were rightly taken under this section (*Beardsley v Walton & Co* [1900] 2 QB 1, 64 JP 436). A chemist sold mercury ointment which contained only 12·5 per cent of mercury whereas, according to the British Pharmacopoeia, mercury ointment should contain 48·5 per cent of mercury. The purchaser did not ask specifically for mercury ointment of any particular strength. It was held that an offence had been committed (*Dickins v Randerson* [1901] 1 KB 437, 65 JP 262); but evidence is admissible to show that there is a commercial standard differing from that prescribed by the British Pharmacopoeia (*Boots Cash Chemists (Southern) Ltd v Cowling* (1903) 67 JP 195). And where the British Pharmacopoeia does not prescribe any standard, but only describes the proper process of manufacture (eg, for vinegar of squills, an article liable to certain chemical changes) there was held not be sale to the prejudice of a purchaser (*Hudson v Bridge* (1903) 67 JP 186). Where deficiency in pills was due to wastage in manufacture, an offence was committed: notice should have been given to the purchaser that the pills were, or might be, deficient (*Breed v British Drug Houses Ltd* [1947] 2 All ER 613, 112 JP 36).

Where the appellation of an article, eg, "Demerara sugar" had become a generic term referring to a process of manufacture and not to a place of production, it was held that it was no offence to sell as "Demerara sugar" a similar sugar grown elsewhere (*Anderson v Britcher* (1913) 78 JP 65). If there is no standard of the article purchased, it is the duty of the court to fix one based on the evidence before it, not necessarily a quantitative standard, but to have regard to a minimum and to say that whatever the minimum, this article clearly falls below it (*Bowker v Woodroffe, Bowker v Premier Drug Co* [1928] 1 KB 217, 91 JP 118 (extract of meat and malt wine), following Scots case of *Wilson and McPhee v Wilson* (1903) 68 JP 175 (brandy); *Roberts v Leeming* (1905) 69 JP 417 (margarine); *Rudd v Skelton Co-operative Society Ltd* (1911) 75 JP 326 (lardine); *Riley Bros (Halifax) Ltd v Hallimond* (1927) 44 TLR 238 (rum and butter toffee); *Preston v Jackson* (1928) 73 Sol Jo 712 (table vinegar); *Webb v Jackson Wyness Ltd* [1948] 2 All ER 1054, 113 JP 38 (non-brewed vinegar); *Broughton v Whittaker* [1944] KB 269, [1944] 2 All ER 544, 108 JP 75; *Sopers of Harrow Ltd v Johnston & Son (London) Ltd and Henderson and Liddell Ltd and Collins Arden Products Ltd* [1944] 2 All ER 586 (cordial); *Stott v Green* [1936] 2 All ER 354 (Lysol soap). The standard set by an Order made under an enabling statute is not applicable to a sale before the Order was made (*Thomas Robinson Sons & Co Ltd v Allardice* (1944) 108 JP 101). A standard set by a price control Order has no application to a prosecution under this section (*Highnam v Turier* [1951] 2 All ER 850, 115 JP 606).

4. For meaning of "food", see s 1, ante.

5. An information charging the selling of food "not of the nature or not of the substance or not of the quality" does not conform with (what is now) r 7.3 of the Criminal Procedure Rules 2005 and is bad (*Bastin v Davies* [1950] 2 KB 579, [1950] 1 All ER 1095, 114 JP 302). See also *Moore v Ray* [1951] 1 KB 98, [1950] 2 All ER 561, 114 JP 486, in which Lord GODDARD, CJ, disapproved *obiter* of an information charging the selling of food "not of the nature, substance and quality" demanded. In *Preston v Greenclose Ltd* (1975) 139 JP Jo 245. followed in *Shearer v Rowe* (1985) 149 JP 698. Lord WIDGERY, CJ, said that there was a large area of common ground between the three words "nature", "substance" and "quality" which were not mutually exclusive and on the facts of a particular case the prosecutor might word the charge in whatever way he though appropriate.

6. This offence may be committed where, in the absence of any prescribed minimum standard, the standard falls below what the justices find to be reasonable (*Tonkin v Victor Value Ltd* [1962] 1 All ER 821, 126 JP 169—"mock salmon cutlettes").

7. The bare opinion of an expert witness as to the standard of the "quality" of food cannot be evidence of the quality demanded by a purchaser (*Goldup v John Manson Ltd* [1982] QB 161, [1981] 3 All ER 257). Where there is no fixed standard and none is specified by the purchaser, the implication in terms of contract is that the purchaser is offering to purchase food of a reasonable quality having regard to the general practice of the trade; it is for the justices to determine whether the food sold was of such quality (*T W Lawrence & Sons Ltd v Burleigh* (1982) 146 JP 134). The prosecution does not need to prove that the presence of the extraneous material would be deleterious to the purchaser (*Barber v Co-operative Wholesale Society Ltd* (1983) 147 JP 296, [1983] Crim LR 476). It is not a defence to prove that the article was not defective in all three respects: "quality" is not equivalent to description, but means "commercial quality" (*Anness v Grivell* [1915] 3 KB 685, 79 JP 558). Milk containing a dead house-fly has been held to be not of the "quality" demanded (*Newton v West Vale Creamery Co Ltd* (1956) 120 JP 318). The presence of a harmless article, eg, a metal milk bottle cap, does not necessarily give rise to an offence under this section (*Edwards v Llaethdy Meirion Ltd* (1957) 107 L Jo 133), but the presence of a source of danger, eg, a sliver of glass, is adequate to create an offence (*Southworth v Whitewell Dairies Ltd* (1958) 122 JP 322). The word "description" may on the facts of the case be equivalent to "quality" (*McDonald's Hamburgers Ltd v Windle* (1986) 151 JP 333, conviction for supplying ordinary Cola when Diet Cola demanded).

8. The determining factor in deciding what ought to have been supplied is the demand of the purchaser (*Collins Arden Products Ltd v Barking Corpn* [1943] KB 419, [1943] 2 All ER 249, 107 JP 117). The section imposes an absolute duty quite apart from *mens rea* (*Lindley v George W Horner & Co Ltd* [1950] 1 All ER 234, 114 JP 124).

9. "Purchaser" means an ordinary, not a skilled, purchaser, and the knowledge of the purchaser cannot be taken into account except in so far as it has been derived from information given by the seller, either by notice, by the article itself, or by what passed at the time of sale (*Pearks, Gunston and Tee Ltd v Ward* [1902] 2 KB 1, 66 JP 774).

10. For penalty, see s 35, post.

11. For meaning of "analysis", see s 53, post.

12. By the Licensing Act 1964, s 31(1), a conviction of the holder of a justices' licence under any Act for an offence relating to the adulteration of intoxicating liquor must be entered in the register of licences.

8–12249   15. Falsely describing or presenting food. (1) Any person who gives with any food sold by him, or displays with any food offered or exposed by him for sale or in his possession for the purpose of sale, a label, whether or not attached to or printed on the wrapper or container, which—

(*a*) falsely describes the food; or

(*b*) is likely to mislead as to the nature or substance or quality of the food,

shall be guilty of an offence[1].

(2) Any person who publishes, or is a party to the publication of, an advertisement (not being such a label given or displayed by him as mentioned in subsection (1) above) which—

(*a*) falsely describes any food; or

(*b*) is likely to mislead as to the nature or substance or quality of any food,

shall be guilty of an offence.

(3) Any person who sells, or offers or exposes for sale, or has in his possession for the purpose of sale, any food the presentation of which is likely to mislead as to the nature or substance or quality of the food shall be guilty of an offence.

(4) In proceedings for an offence under subsection (1) or (2) above, the fact that a label or advertisement in respect of which the offence is alleged to have been committed contained an accurate statement of the composition of the food shall not preclude the court from finding that the offence was committed.

(5) In this section references to sale shall be construed as references to sale for human consumption. [Food Safety Act 1990, s 15.]

---

1. Sub-s (1) creates different offences and any summons must make clear which offence is being alleged. Any summons which does not do this may not be amended (*Ward v London Borough of Barking and Dagenham* [1999] Crim LR 920, DC).

Regulations

8–12250 **16. Food safety and consumer protection.** (1) The Secretary of State[1] may by regulations[2] make—

(*a*) provision for requiring, prohibiting or regulating the presence in food or food sources of any specified substance, or any substance of any specified class, and generally for regulating the composition of food;

(*b*) provision for securing that food is fit for human consumption and meets such microbiological standards (whether going to the fitness of the food or otherwise) as may be specified by or under the regulations;

(*c*) provision for requiring, prohibiting or regulating the use of any process or treatment in the preparation of food;

(*d*) provision for securing the observance of hygienic conditions and practices in connection with the carrying out of commercial operations with respect to food or food sources;

(*e*) provision for imposing requirements or prohibitions as to, or otherwise regulating, the labelling, marking, presenting or advertising of food, and the descriptions which may be applied to food; and

(*f*) such other provision with respect to food or food sources, including in particular provision for prohibiting or regulating the carrying out of commercial operations with respect to food or food sources, as appears to them to be necessary or expedient—

(i) for the purpose of securing that food complies with food safety requirements or in the interests of the public health; or

(ii) for the purpose of protecting or promoting the interests of consumers.

(2) The Secretary of State may also by regulations[2] make provision—

(*a*) for securing the observance of hygienic conditions and practices in connection with the carrying out of commercial operations with respect to contact materials which are intended to come into contact with food intended for human consumption;

(*b*) for imposing requirements or prohibitions as to, or otherwise regulating, the labelling, marking or advertising of such materials, and the descriptions which may be applied to them; and

(*c*) otherwise for prohibiting or regulating the carrying out of commercial operations with respect to such materials.

(3) Without prejudice to the generality of subsection (1) above, regulations[2] under that subsection may make any such provision as is mentioned in Schedule 1 to this Act.

(4) In making regulations under subsection (1) above, the Secretary of State shall have regard to the desirability of restricting, so far as practicable, the use of substances of no nutritional value as foods or as ingredients of foods.

(5) In subsection (1) above and Schedule 1 to this Act, unless the context otherwise requires—

(*a*) references to food shall be construed as references to food intended for sale for human consumption; and (*b*) references to food sources shall be construed as references to food sources from which such food is intended to be derived.

[Food Safety Act 1990, s 16 as amended by the Food Standards Act 1999, Sch 5.]

1. The functions of the Secretary of State under Part VI of this Act, so far as exercisable in relation to Wales, have been transferred to the National Assembly for Wales (Transfer of Functions) Order 2000, SI 2000/253 art 2, Sch 1.

2. The following regulations which were made under ss 4, 7, 13 and 33 of the Food Act 1984, now repealed, shall have effect as if made under provisions of this section (Sch 4, post):

Regulations made under s 4 of the Food Act 1984:

Regulations relating to specific foods or additives are set out below; offences under these regulations carry a fine not exceeding the **statutory maximum** where the offences are triable either way and not exceeding **level 5** on the standard scale where the offences are triable summarily only—see the Food (Revision of Penalties) Regulations 1982, SI 1982/1727 (as amended), the Milk and Dairies (Revision of Penalties) Regulations 1982, SI 1982/1703 (as amended), the Food (Revision of Penalties) Regulations 1985, SI 1985/67 (as amended) and the Criminal Justice Act 1988, ss 51 and 52.

Arsenic in Food, SI 1959/831 amended by SI 1973/1052, SI 1973/1340, SI 1982/1727, SI 1984/1304, SI 1985/67, SI 1990/2486, SI 1991/1476, SI 1992/1971, SI 1995/3202 and SI 2005/2626 (E) and 3254 (W);

Mineral Hydrocarbons in Food, SI 1966/1073 amended by SI 1982/1727, SI 1985/67, SI 1990/2486, SI 1991/1476, SI 1992/2597, SI 1995/3187, SI 1999/1136 and SI 2001/60 (England), 1787 (Wales) and 3775 (England);

Butter, SI 1966/1074 amended by SI 1973/1340, SI 1982/1727, SI 1985/67, SI 1990/2486, SI 1991/1476, SI 1992/2596 and SI 2005/2626 (E) and 3254 (W);

Control of Irradiation, SI 1967/385 amended by SI 1972/205, SI 1982/1727 and SI 1985/67;

Ice Cream, SI 1970/752 amended by SI 1982/1727, SI 1985/67 and SI 1990/2486;

Erucic Acid in Food, SI 1977/691 amended by SI 1982/264 and 1727, SI 1985/67, SI 1990/2486, SI 1991/1476 and SI 2005/2626 (E) and 3254 (W);

Antioxidants in Food, SI 1978/105 amended by SI 1980/1831, SI 1982/1727, SI 1983/1211, SI 1984/1304, SI 1985/67, SI 1990/2486, SI 1991/1476 and 2540, SI 1992/1978 and SI 1995/3187;

Chloroform in Food, SI 1980/36 amended by SI 1982/1727, SI 1985/67, SI 1990/2486, SI 1991/1476 and SI 2005/2626 (E) and 3254 (W);

Caseins and Caseinates, SI 1985/2026 amended by SI 1989/2321, SI 1990/2486, SI 1991/1476, SI 1992/2596, SI 1996/1499 and SI 2005/2626 (E) and 3254 (W);

Regulations made under or having effect as if made under s 13 of the Food Act 1984:

The Ungraded Eggs (Hygiene) Regulations 1990, SI 1990/1323 amended by SI 1990/2486 prohibit the sale by a producer of ungraded eggs which have cracks visible to the naked eye an offence is created punishable with a fine not exceeding **level 5** on the standard scale: the offence is triable either way, for procedure see ss 17A–21 Magistrates' Courts Act 1980 in PART I: MAGISTRATES' COURTS: PROCEDURE, ante.

The following regulations have been made under s 16 of this Act:

Food (Control of Irradiation) Regulations 1990, SI 1990/2490 amended by SI 2000/656, SI/2000/2254, SI 2002/1922 and SI 2005/2626 (E) and 3254 (W);

Quick-frozen Foodstuffs Regulations 1990, SI 1990/2615 amended by SI 1992/2596, SI 1994/298, SI 1996/1499 and SI 2004/2145 and 2731 (W);

Imported Food and Feedingstuffs (Safeguard against Cholera) Regulations 1991, SI 1991/2486 amended by SI 1991/2934 and SI 1992/2364;

Imported Food (Bivalve Molluscs and Marine Gastropods from Japan) Regulations 1992, SI 1992/1601;

Flavourings in Food Regulations 1992, SI 1992/1971 amended by SI 1994/1486, SI 1996/1499, SI 2002/890 (England) and 1886 (Wales) and SI 2005/2626 (E) and 3254 (W);

Food Additives Labelling Regulations 1992, SI 1992/1978 amended by SI 1995/3123, 3124 and 3187, SI 1996/1499, SI 1999/1136, SI 2001/60 (England), 1787 (Wales) and 3775 (England), SI 2002/379 (England), SI 2003/1182 (E) and 3047 (W) and SI 2005/2626 (E) and 3254 (W);

Extraction Solvents in Food Regulations 1993, SI 1993/1658, amended by SI 1995/1440, SI 1998/2257 (Wales) and SI 2005/2626 (E) and 3254 (W);

Infant Formula and Follow On Formula Regulations 1995, SI 1995/77 amended by SI 1995/3267, SI 1996/1499, SI 1997/451, SI 2000/1509 (England), SI 2000/1885 (Wales) and 2215, SI 2001/1690 (Wales), SI 2003/3208 (E), SI 2004/313 (W) and SI 2005/2626 (E) and 3254 (W);

Poultry Meat, Farmed Game Bird Meat and Rabbit Meat (Hygiene and Inspection) Regulations 1995, SI 1995/540, amended by SI 1995/1763, 2148, 2200 and 3205, SI 1997/1729, SI 2000/225, 656, 2215 and 2257 (Wales) , SI 2001/2198 (Wales) and 3399 (England), SI 2002/47 (Wales)), 889 (England) and 1476 (Wales) and SI 2005/209 (E), 1310 (W), SI 2005/2059 (E) (revoked in relation to Wales by SI 2005/3292);

Animal By-Products (Identification) Regulations 1995, SI 1995/614, amended by SI 1995/1955, SI 1997/2073, SI 2000/656, SI 2002/1619 and 1472 (Wales) and 3231 (E), SI 2003/1484 (E), 1849 (W) and 2754 (W), SI 2005/3051 (W) and 3068 (E) and SI 2006/14 (E) and 31 (W);

Eggs (Marketing Standards) Regulations 1995, SI 1995/1544, amended by SI 1996/1725, SI 1997/1414, SI 1998/1665, SI 2000/656 and SI 2005/2059 (E) and 3292 (W);

Sweeteners in Food Regulations 1995, SI 1995/3123 amended by SI 1996/1477, SI 1997/814, SI 1999/982 amended by SI 2001/2294 and 2679 (Wales) and SI 2002/330 (Wales) and 379 (England), SI 2003/1182 (E) and 1713 (W), SI 2004/3348 (E) and SI 2005/1156 (W), 2626 and 3254 (W);

Colours in Food Regulations 1995, SI 1995/3124 amended by SI 2000/481 (England) and 1799 (Wales), SI 2001/3442 (England) and 3909 (Wales), SI 2002/890 (England) and 1886 (Wales), SI 2003/1564 (E), 1596 (E), 3037 (W), 3041 (W), 3044 (W) and 3047 (W), SI 2005/519 (E), 1628 (W), 2626 and 3254 (W) and SI 2006/14 (E) and 31 (W);

Miscellaneous Food Additives Regulations 1995, SI 1995/3187 amended by SI 1997/1413, SI 1999/1136, SI 2000/3323 (England) and SI 2001/60 (England), SI 2001/1787 (Wales), 1440 (Wales) and 3775 (England), SI 2002/329 (Wales) and 379 (England), SI 2003/945 (W), 1182 (E), 1563 (E), 1564 (E), 1596 (E), 2243 (E), 3037 (W), 3041 (W), 3044 (W), 3047 (W), 3053 (W), 3122 (E) and 3295 (E), SI 2004/554 (W), 553 (W) and 2601 (E) and SI 2005/259 (W), 1099 (E), 1311 (W), 2626 and 3254 (W);

Cheese and Cream Regulations 1995, SI 1995/3240;

Food Labelling Regulations 1996, in this title, post;

Food (Lot Marking) Regulations 1996, SI 1996/1502;

Novel Foods and Novel Food Ingredients Regulations 1997, SI 1997/1335 amended by SI 1999/3182, SI 2000/253, 656 and 768 (England) and SI 2004/2335 and 3220 (W);

Contaminants in Food Regulations 1997, SI 1997/1499 amended by SI 1999/1603 and 3221;

Animals and Animal Products (Examination for Residues and Maximum Residue Limits) Regulations 1997, SI 1997/1729 amended by SI 2005/2626 (E) and 3254 (W);

Foods Intended for Use in Energy Restricted Diets for Weight Reduction Regulations 1997, SI 1997/2182 amended by SI 2005/2626 (E) and 3254 (W);

Beef Bones Regulations 1997, SI 1997/2959 amended by SI 1999/3371 (England) and 3464 (Wales), SI 2000/6556 and SI 2006/14 (E) and 31 (W);

Specified Risk Material Regulations 1997, SI 1997/2965 amended by SI 1997/3062, SI 1998/539, 2405 and 2431, SI 2000/656, 1973, 2659 (Wales) and 2672 (England), 3381 (England), 3387 (Wales), SI 2001/817 (England), 2672 (England), 2732 (Wales) and 3546 (Wales) and SI 2002/843 (England) and 1416 (Wales) (revoked in relation to England by SI 2006/68);

Bread and Flour Regulations 1998, SI 1998/141 amended by SI 1999/1136 and SI 2005/2626 (E) and 3254 (W);

Plastic Materials and Articles in Contact with Food Regulations 1998, SI 1998/1376 amended by SI 2000/3162 (England), SI 2001/1263 (Wales), SI 2002/2364 (England), 2834 (Wales) and 3008 (England), SI 2003/302 (W), SI 2004/3113(E) and SI 2005/182 (W), 325 (E), 898 (E), 1647 (W), 1649 (W), 2626 and 3254 (W);

Drinking Milk Regulations 1998, SI 1998/2424 amended by SI 2005/2626 (E) and 3254 (W);

Natural Mineral Water, Spring Water and Bottled Drinking Water Regulations 1999, SI 1999/1540 amended by SI 2000/656, SI 2003/666 (E) and 3042 (W), SI 2004/656 (E) and 1509 (W) and SI 2005/2626 (E) and 3254 (W);

Spreadable Fats (Marketing Standards) (England) Regulations 1999, SI 1999/2457 amended by SI 2005/2626;

Food Irradiation Provisions (England) Regulations 2000, SI 2000/2254;

Meat (Disease Control) (Wales) Regulations 2000, SI 2000/2257;

Coffee Extracts and Chicory Extracts (England) Regulations 2000, SI 2000/3323 amended by SI 2005/2626;

Food Irradiation Provisions (Wales) Regulations 2001, SI 2001/1232;

Spreadable Fats (Marketing Standards) (Wales) Regulations 2001, SI 2001/1361 amended by SI 2005/3254;

Coffee Extracts and Chicory Extracts (Wales) Regulations 2001, SI 2001/1440 amended by SI 2003/3047 and SI 2005/3254;

Food for Particular Nutritional Uses (Addition of Substances for Specific Nutritional Purposes) (England) Regulations 2002, SI 2002/1817 amended by SI 2004/649 and SI 2005/2626 and 2630;

Food for Particular Nutritional Uses (Addition of Substances for Specific Nutritional Purposes) (Wales) Regulations 2002, SI 2002/2939 amended by SI 2004/1012 and SI 2005/3254;

Kava-kava in Food (England) Regulations 2002, SI 2002/3169 amended by SI 2004/445;

Fish Labelling Regulations 2003, SI 2003/461;

Food Supplements (England) Regulations 2003, SI 2003/1387 amended by SI 2005/2626 and 2759;

Specified Sugar Products (England) Regulations 2003, SI 2003/1563 amended by SI 2005/2626;

Fruit Juices and Nectars (England) Regulations 2003, SI 2003/1564 amended by SI 2005/2626;

Condensed Milk and Dried Milk (England) Regulations 2003, SI 2003/1596 amended by SI 2004/2145, SI 2005/2626 and SI 2006/14 (E);

Cocoa and Cocoa Products (England) Regulations 2003, SI 2003/1659 amended by SI 2005/2626;

Food Supplements (Wales) Regulations 2003, SI 2003/1719 amended by SI 2005/2759 and 3254;

Meat Products (England) Regulations 2003, SI 2003/2075 amended by SI 2005/2626;

Honey (England) Regulations 2003, SI 2003/2243 amended by SI 2005/1920 and SI 2005/2626;

Cocoa and Cocoa Products (Wales) Regulations 2003, SI 2003/3037 amended by SI 2005/3254;

Fruit Juices and Fruit Nectars (Wales) Regulations 2003, SI 2003/3041 amended by SI 2005/3254;

Honey (Wales) Regulations 2003, SI 2003/3044 amended by SI 2005/3052 and 3254;

Specified Sugar Products (Wales) Regulations 2003, SI 2003/3047 amended by SI 2005/3254;

Condensed Milk and Dried Milk (Wales) Regulations 2003, SI 2003/3053 amended by SI 2004/2731 amended by SI 2005/3254;

Jam and Similar Products (England) Regulations 2003, SI 2003/3120 amended by SI 2005/2626;

Processed Cereal-based Foods and Baby Foods for Infants and Young Children (England) Regulations 2003, SI 2003/3207 amended by SI 2005/2626 and 2630;

Processed Cereal-based Foods and Baby Foods for Infants and Young Children (Wales) Regulations 2004, SI 2004/314 amended by SI 2005/3254;

Jam and Similar Products (Wales) Regulations 2004, SI 2004/553 amended by SI 2005/3254;

Meat Products (Wales) Regulations 2004, SI 2004/1396 amended by SI 2005/3254;

Genetically Modified Food (England) Regulations 2004, SI 2004/2335;

Genetically Modified Food (Wales) Regulations 2004, SI 2004/3220 amended by SI 2005/3254;

General Food Regulations 2004, in this title, post;

Food with Added Phytosterols or Phytostanols (Labelling) (England) Regulations 2004, SI 2004/3344 amended by SI 2005/2626;

Contaminants in Food (Wales) Regulations 2005, SI 2005/364 amended by SI 2005/1629;

Smoke Flavourings (England) Regulations 2005, SI 2005/464;

Materials and Articles in Contact with Food (England) Regulations 2005, SI 2005/898 amended by SI 2005/2626;

Food with Added Phytosterols or Phytostanols (Labelling) (Wales) Regulations 2005, SI 2005/1224 amended by SI 2005/3254;

Smoke Flavourings (Wales) Regulations 2005, SI 2005/1350;

Materials and Articles in Contact with Food (Wales) Regulations 2005, SI 2005/1647 amended by SI 2005/3254

Bovine Products (Restrictions on Placing on the Market) (England) (No 2) Regulations 2005, SI 2005/3068;

Trytophan in Food (Wales) Regulations 2005, SI 2005/3111;

Contaminants in Food (England) Regulations 2005, SI 2005/3251;

Bovine Products (Restrictions on Placing on the Market) (Wales) (No 2) Regulations 2005, SI 2005/3296.

The Food (Control of Irradiation) Regulations 1990, SI 1990/2490 amended by SI 2000/656 control the irradiation of food by a licensing system with further controls on importation, storage and transportation of irradiated food: offences are triable either way and contraventions are punishable by a fine not exceeding the statutory maximum.

8–12251   17. Enforcement of Community provisions.   (1) The Secretary of State[1] may by regulations[2] make such provision with respect to food, food sources or contact materials, including in particular provision for prohibiting or regulating the carrying out of commercial operations with respect to food, food sources or contact materials, as appears to him to be called for by any Community obligation.

(2) As respects any directly applicable Community provision which relates to food, food sources or contact materials and for which, in his opinion, it is appropriate to provide under this Act, the Secretary of State may by regulations³—

(a) make such provision as he considers necessary or expedient for the purpose of securing that the Community provision is administered, executed and enforced under this Act; and

(b) apply such of the provisions of this Act as may be specified in the regulations in relation to the Community provision with such modifications, if any, as may be so specified.

(3) In subsections (1) and (2) above references to food or food sources shall be construed in accordance with section 16(5) above.

[Food Safety Act 1990, s 17 as amended by the Food Standards Act 1999, Sch 5.]

1. In respect of those regulations listed in Sch 1 to the National Assembly of Wales Transfer of Functions Order 2000, SI 2000/253, the functions of the Secretary of State, so far as exercisable in relation to Wales, have been transferred to the National Assembly for Wales.

2. Certain regulations made under s 4 of the Food Act 1984, now repealed, shall have effect as if made under s 17(1) of this Act (Sch 4, post). For regulations made under s 4 of the Food Act 1984, see note 1 to s 16, ante.

The following regulations have been made under s 17(1) of this Act:

Food (Lot Marking) Regulations, SI 1992/1357;

Food Labelling Regulations 1996, this title, post;

Food Safety (Fishery Products and Live Shellfish) (Hygiene) Regulations 1998, SI 1998/994 amended by SIs 1999/399 and 1585;

Notification of Marketing of Food for Particular Nutritional Uses (England and Wales) Regulations 2002, SI 2002/333.

3. Regulations governing the following made under s 119 of the Food Act 1984, now repealed, shall have effect as if made under s 17(2) of this Act (Sch 4, post):

Poultry Meat (Water Content) Regulations 1984, SI 1984/1145, as amended;

Caseins and Caseinates, SI 1985/2026, as amended;

Spirit Drinks, SI 1990/1179, as amended.

The following regulations have been made under s 17 (2) of this Act:

Beef Labelling (Enforcement) Regulations 1998, SI 1998/616 (revoked in so far as they apply to England by SI 2000/3047);

Medical Food (England) Regulations 2000, SI 2000/845 amended by SI 2004/2145 and SI 2005/2626;

Medical Food (Wales) Regulations 2000, SI 2000/1866 amended by SI 2004/2731 and SI 2005/3254;

Genetically Modified and Novel Foods (Labelling) (Wales) Regulations 2000, SI 2000/1925;

Beef Labelling (Enforcement) (Wales) Regulations 2001, SI 2001/1360.

8–12252   18. Special provisions for particular foods etc.   (1) The Secretary of State may by regulations¹ make provision—

(a) for prohibiting the carrying out of commercial operations with respect to novel foods, or food sources from which such foods are intended to be derived, of any class specified in the regulations;

(b) for prohibiting the carrying out of such operations with respect to genetically modified food sources, or foods derived from such food sources, of any class so specified; or

(c) for prohibiting¹ the importation of any food of a class so specified,

and (in each case) for excluding from the prohibition any food or food source which is of a description specified by or under the regulations and, in the case of a prohibition on importation, is imported at an authorised place of entry.

(2) The Secretary of State may also by regulations²—

(a) prescribe, in relation to milk of any description, such a designation (in this subsection referred to as a "special designation") as the Secretary of State considers appropriate;

(b) provide for the issue by enforcement authorities of licences to producers and sellers of milk authorising the use of a special designation; and

(c) prohibit, without the use of a special designation, all sales of milk for human consumption, other than sales made with the Secretary of State's consent.

(3) In this section—

"authorised place of entry" means any port, aerodrome or other place of entry authorised by or under the regulations and, in relation to food in a particular consignment, includes any place of entry so authorised for the importation of that consignment;

"description", in relation to food, includes any description of its origin or of the manner in which is packed;

"novel food" means any food which has not previously been used for human consumption in Great Britain, or has been so used only to a very limited extent.

(4) For the purposes of this section a food source is genetically modified if any of the genes or other genetic material in the food source—

(a) has been modified by means of an artificial technique; or

(b) is inherited or otherwise derived, through any number of replications, from genetic material which was so modified;

and in this subsection "artificial technique" does not include any technique which involves no more

than, or no more than the assistance of, naturally occurring processes of reproduction (including selective breeding techniques or *in vitro* fertilisation).
[Food Safety Act 1990, s 18 as amended by the Food Standards Act 1999, Sch 5.]

1. The Imported Food (Peruvian Foodstuffs) Regulations 1991, SI 1991/370 have been made.
2. The Milk (Special Designation) Regulations 1989, SI 1989/2383, amended by SI 1990/2486, 2492 and SI 1992/1208 and made under s 38 of the Food Act 1984, now repealed, shall have effect as if made under s 18(2); see Sch 4, post.

8–12253 19. Registration and licensing of food premises. (1) The Secretary of State may by regulations[1] make provision—

(*a*) for the registration by enforcement authorities of premises used or proposed to be used for the purposes of a food business, and for prohibiting the use for those purposes of any premises which are not registered in accordance with the regulations; or

(*b*) subject to subsection (2) below, for the issue by such authorities of licences in respect of the use of premises for the purposes of a food business, and for prohibiting the use for those purposes of any premises except in accordance with a licence issued under the regulations.

(2) The Secretary of State shall exercise the power conferred by subsection (1)(*b*) above only where it appears to him to be necessary or expedient to do so—

(*a*) for the purpose of securing that food complies with food safety requirements or in the interests of the public health; or

(*b*) for the purpose of protecting or promoting the interests of consumers.
[Food Safety Act 1990, s 19 as amended by the Food Standards Act 1999, Sch 5.]

1. The Food Premises (Registration) (Welsh Form of Application) Regulations 1993, SI 1993/1270 have been made.

Defences etc

8–12254 20. Offences due to fault of another person. Where the commission by any person of an offence under any of the preceding provisions of this Part is due to an act or default of some other person, that other person shall be guilty of the offence; and a person may be charged with and convicted of the offence by virtue of this section whether or not proceedings are taken against the first-mentioned person.
[Food Safety Act 1990, s 20.]

8–12255 21. Defence of due diligence[1]. (1) In any proceedings for an offence under any of the preceding provisions of this Part (in this section referred to as "the relevant provision"), it shall, subject to subsection (5) below, be a defence for the person charged to prove that he took all reasonable precautions and exercised all due diligence to avoid the commission of the offence by himself or by a person under his control.

(2) Without prejudice to the generality of subsection (1) above, a person charged with an offence under section 14 or 15 above who neither—

(*a*) prepared the food in respect of which the offence is alleged to have been committed; nor

(*b*) imported it into Great Britain,

shall be taken to have established the defence provided by that subsection if he satisfies the requirements of subsection (3) or (4) below.

(3) A person satisfies the requirements of this subsection if he proves—

(*a*) that the commission of the offence was due to an act or default of another person who was not under his control, or to reliance on information supplied by such a person;

(*b*) that he carried out all such checks of the food in question as were reasonable in all the circumstances, or that it was reasonable in all the circumstances for him to rely on checks carried out by the person who supplied the food to him; and

(*c*) that he did not know and had no reason to suspect at the time of the commission of the alleged offence that his act or omission would amount to an offence under the relevant provision.

(4) A person satisfies the requirements of this subsection if he proves—

(*a*) that the commission of the offence was due to an act or default of another person who was not under his control, or to reliance on information supplied by such a person;

(*b*) that the sale or intended sale of which the alleged offence consisted was not a sale or intended sale under his name or mark; and

(*c*) that he did not know, and could not reasonably have been expected to know, at the time of the commission of the alleged offence that his act or omission would amount to an offence under the relevant provision.

(5) If in any case the defence provided by subsection (1) above involves the allegation that the commission of the offence was due to an act or default of another person, or to reliance on information supplied by another person, the person charged shall not, without leave of the court, be entitled to rely on that defence unless—

(*a*) at least seven clear days before the hearing; and
(*b*) where he has previously appeared before a court in connection with the alleged offence, within one month of his first such appearance,

he has served on the prosecutor a notice in writing giving such information identifying or assisting in the identification of that other person as was then in his possession.

(6) In subsection (5) above any reference to appearing before a court shall be construed as including a reference to being brought before a court.
[Food Safety Act 1990, s 21 as amended by SI 2004/3279.]

1. If a court finds in a particular case that it was reasonable for the defendant to rely on a certificate of examination by another, such as a certificate of inspection of a meat inspector, the court may, if it thinks fit, find the defence of due diligence has been made out; see *Carrick District Council v Taunton Vale Meat Traders Ltd* (1994) 158 JP 347.
2. Leave may be applied for where, in the defence closing submissions, the District Judge raises the issue of what the defence position would be if he were to find that the fault arose from the default of an employee not named in the defendant company's notice. Where the defence had misunderstood the import of the judge's comment, the matter may still be raised on the hearing of the case stated and the Divisional Court may grant leave to name the particular employee and quash the conviction under s 28A of the Supreme Court Act 1981 (*Kilhey Court Hotels Ltd v Wigan Metropolitan Borough Council* [2004] EWHC 2890 (Admin), 169 JP 1).

8–12256 22. Defence of publication in the course of business. In proceedings for an offence under any of the preceding provisions of this Part consisting of the advertisement for sale of any food, it shall be a defence for the person charged to prove—

(*a*) that he is a person whose business it is to publish or arrange for the publication of advertisements; and
(*b*) that he received the advertisement in the ordinary course of business and did not know and had no reason to suspect that its publication would amount to an offence under that provision.
[Food Safety Act 1990, s 22.]

Miscellaneous and supplemental

8–12257 23. Provision of food hygiene training. (1) A food authority may provide, whether within or outside their area, training courses in food hygiene for persons who are or intend to become involved in food businesses, whether as proprietors or employees or otherwise.

(2) A food authority may contribute towards the expenses incurred under this section by any other such authority, or towards expenses incurred by any other person in providing, such courses as are mentioned in subsection (1) above.
[Food Safety Act 1990, s 23.]

8–12258 24. Provision of facilities for cleansing shellfish. (1) A food authority may provide, whether within or outside their area, tanks or other apparatus for cleansing shellfish.

(2) A food authority may contribute towards the expenses incurred under this section by any other such authority, or towards expenses incurred by any other person in providing, and making available to the public, tanks or other apparatus for cleansing shellfish.

(3) Nothing in this section authorises the establishment of any tank or other apparatus, or the execution of any other work, on, over or under tidal lands below high-water mark of ordinary spring tides, except in accordance with such plans and sections, and subject to such restrictions and conditions as may before the work is commenced be approved by the Secretary of State.

(4) In this section "cleansing", in relation to shellfish, includes subjecting them to any germicidal treatment.
[Food Safety Act 1990, s 24.]

8–12259 25. Orders for facilitating the exercise of functions. *Repealed.*

8–12260 26. Regulations and orders: supplementary provisions. (1) Regulations under this Part may—

(*a*) make provision for prohibiting or regulating the carrying out of commercial operations with respect to any food, food source or contact material—
  (i) which fails to comply with the regulations; or
  (ii) in relation to which an offence against the regulations has been committed, or would have been committed if any relevant act or omission had taken place in Great Britain; and
(*b*) without prejudice to the generality of section 9 above, provide that any food which, in accordance with the regulations, is certified as being such food as is mentioned in paragraph (*a*) above may be treated for the purposes of that section as failing to comply with food safety requirements.

(2) Regulations under this Part may also—

(*a*) require persons carrying on any activity to which the regulations apply to keep and produce records and provide returns;

(b) prescribe the particulars to be entered on any register required to be kept in accordance with the regulations;

(c) require any such register to be open to inspection by the public at all reasonable times and, subject to that, authorise it to be kept by means of a computer;

(d) prescribe the periods for which and the conditions subject to which licences may be issued, and provide for the subsequent alteration of conditions and for the cancellation, suspension or revocation of licences;

(e) provide for an appeal to a magistrates' court or, in Scotland, to the sheriff, or to a tribunal constituted in accordance with the regulations, against any decision of an enforcement authority, or of an authorised officer of such an authority; and

(f) provide, as respects any appeal to such a tribunal, for the procedure on the appeal (including costs) and for any appeal against the tribunal's decision.

(3) Regulations under this Part may—

(a) provide that an offence under the regulations shall be triable in such way as may be there specified; and

(b) include provisions under which a person guilty of such an offence shall be liable to such penalties (not exceeding those which may be imposed in respect of offences under this Act) as may be specified in the regulations.

[Food Safety Act 1990, s 26 as amended by the Food Standards Act 1999, Sch 6.]

PART III[1]
ADMINISTRATION AND ENFORCEMENT
ADMINISTRATION

8–12261   27. Appointment of public analysts.   (1) Every authority to whom this section applies, that is to say, every food authority in England and Wales and every regional or islands council in Scotland, shall appoint in accordance with this section one or more persons (in this Act referred to as "public analysts") to act as analysts for the purposes of this Act within the authority's area.

(2) No person shall be appointed as a public analyst unless he possesses—

(a) such qualifications as may be prescribed by regulations[2] made by the Secretary of State; or

(b) such other qualifications as the Secretary of State may approve,

and no person shall act as a public analyst for any area who is engaged directly or indirectly in any food business which is carried on in that area.

(3) An authority to whom this section applies shall pay to a public analyst such remuneration as may be agreed, which may be expressed to be payable either—

(a) in addition to any fees received by him under this Part; or

(b) on condition that any fees so received by him are paid over by him to the authority.

(4) An authority to whom this section applies who appoint only one public analyst may appoint also a deputy to act during any vacancy in the office of public analyst, or during the absence or incapacity of the holder of the office, and—

(a) the provisions of this section with respect to the qualifications, appointment, removal and remuneration of a public analyst shall apply also in relation to a deputy public analyst; and

(b) any reference in the following provisions of this Act to a public analyst shall be construed as including a reference to a deputy public analyst appointed under this subsection.

(5) In subsection (1) above "food authority" does not include the council of a non-metropolitan district in England, the Sub-Treasurer of the Inner Temple or the Under Treasurer of the Middle Temple; and in subsection (2) above the reference to being engaged directly or indirectly in a food business includes a reference to having made such arrangements with a food business as may be prescribed[3] by regulations made by the Secretary of State.

[Food Safety Act 1990, s 27 amended by the Local Government (Wales) Act 1994, Sch 9 and the Food Standards Act 1999, Sch 5.]

---

1. Part III contains ss 28–39.
2. The Food Safety (Sampling and Qualifications) Regulations 1990, SI 1990/2463 amended by SI 1991/2843, SI 19995/360 and 1086, SI 1997/1729. SI 1998/1376, SI 1999/1540 and 1603, SI 2002/890 (England), 2364 (England), 2834 (Wales) and 3008 (England), SI 2003/302 (W), 666 (E), 1478 (E), 1721 (W) and 3042 (W) and SI 2004/1509 (W) and 3062 (E), have been made.
3. See reg 5 of the Food Safety (Sampling and Qualifications) Regulations 1990, SI 1990/2463 as amended, as to disqualifications.

8–12262   28. Provision of facilities for examinations.   (1) A food authority, or a regional council in Scotland, may provide facilities for examinations for the purposes of this Act.

(2) In this Act "examination" means a microbiological examination and "examine" shall be construed accordingly.

[Food Safety Act 1990, s 28.]

Sampling and analysis etc

8–12263   29. Procurement of samples[1]. An authorised officer of an enforcement authority may—

(a) purchase a sample of any food, or any substance capable of being used in the preparation of food;

(b) take a sample of any food, or any such substance, which—

(i) appears to him to be intended for sale, or to have been sold, for human consumption; or

(ii) is found by him on or in any premises which he is authorised to enter by or under section 32 below;

(c) take a sample from any food source, or a sample of any contact material, which is found by him on or in any such premises;

(d) take a sample of any article or substance which is found by him on or in any such premises and which he has reason to believe may be required as evidence in proceedings under any of the provisions of this Act or of regulations or orders made under it.

[Food Safety Act 1990, s 29.]

---

1. This section is modified by the Contaminants in Food (England) Regulations 2003, SI 2003/1478 in proceedings to which those regulations apply and in its application to the taking of a sample of any food specified in Sections 1 to 6 of Annex I to the Commission Regulation is modified by the Contaminants in Food (England) Regulations 2004, SI 2004/3062. For modifications in respect of Wales, see the Contaminants in food (Wales) Regulations 2005, SI 2005/364.

8–12264   30. Analysis etc of samples.   (1) An authorised officer of an enforcement authority who has procured a sample under section 29 above shall—

(a) if he considers that the sample should be analysed, submit it to be analysed either—

(i) by the public analyst for the area in which the sample was procured; or

(ii) by the public analyst for the area which consists of or includes the area of the authority;

(b) if he considers that the sample should be examined, submit it to be examined by a food examiner.

(2) A person, other than such an officer, who has purchased any food, or any substance capable of being used in the preparation of food, may submit a sample of it—

(a) to be analysed by the public analyst for the area in which the purchase was made; or

(b) to be examined by a food examiner.

(3) If, in any case where a sample is proposed to be submitted for analysis under this section, the office of public analyst for the area in question is vacant, the sample shall be submitted to the public analyst for some other area.

(4) If, in any case where a sample is proposed to be or is submitted for analysis or examination under this section, the food analyst or examiner determines that he is for any reason unable to perform the analysis or examination, the sample shall be submitted or, as the case may be, sent by him to such other food analyst or examiner as he may determine.

(5) A food analyst or examiner shall analyse or examine as soon as practicable any sample submitted or sent to him under this section, but may, except where—

(a) he is the public analyst for the area in question; and

(b) the sample is submitted to him for analysis by an authorised officer of an enforcement authority,

demand in advance the payment of such reasonable fee as he may require.

(6) A food analyst or examiner who has analysed or examined a sample shall give to the person by whom it was submitted a certificate specifying the result of the analysis or examination.

(7) Any certificate given by a food analyst or examiner under subsection (6) above shall be signed by him, but the analysis or examination may be made by any person acting under his direction.

(8) In any proceedings under this Act, the production by one of the parties—

(a) of a document purporting to be a certificate given by a food analyst or examiner under subsection (6) above; or

(b) of a document supplied to him by the other party as being a copy of such a certificate,

shall be sufficient evidence of the facts stated in it unless, in a case falling within paragraph (a) above, the other party requires that the food analyst or examiner shall be called as a witness.

(9) In this section—

"food analyst" means a public analyst or any other person who possesses the requisite qualifications to carry out analyses for the purposes of this Act;

"food examiner" means any person who possesses the requisite qualifications to carry out examinations for the purposes of this Act;

"the requisite qualifications" means such qualifications as may be prescribed[1] by regulations made by the Secretary of State, or such other qualifications as the Secretary of State may approve;

"sample", in relation to an authorised officer of an enforcement authority, includes any part of a sample retained by him in pursuance of regulations under section 31 below;

and where two or more public analysts are appointed for any area, any reference in this section to the public analyst for that area shall be construed as a reference to either or any of them.
[Food Safety Act 1990, s 30 as amended by the Food Standards Act 1999, Sch 5.]

---

1. See reg 3 (qualification of analysts) and r 4 (qualification of examiners) of the Food Safety (Sampling and Qualifications) Regulations 1990, SI 1990/2463 as amended.

8–12265 31. Regulation of sampling and analysis etc. (1) The Secretary of State may by regulations[1] make provision for supplementing or modifying the provisions of sections 29 and 30 above.

(2) Without prejudice to the generality of subsection (1) above, regulations under that subsection may make provision with respect to—

(a) the matters to be taken into account in determining whether, and at what times, samples should be procured;

(b) the manner of procuring samples, including the steps to be taken in order to ensure that any samples procured are fair samples;

(c) the method of dealing with samples, including (where appropriate) their division into parts;

(d) the persons to whom parts of samples are to be given and the persons by whom such parts are to be retained;

(e) the notices which are to be given to, and the information which is to be furnished by, the persons in charge of any food, substance, contact material or food source of or from which samples are procured;

(f) the methods which are to be used in analysing or examining samples, or parts of samples, or in classifying the results of analyses or examinations;

(g) the circumstances in which a food analyst or examiner is to be precluded, by reason of a conflict of interest, from analysing or examining a particular sample or part of a sample; and

(h) the circumstances in which samples, or parts of samples, are to be or may be submitted for analysis or examination—

(i) to the Government Chemist, or to such other food analyst or examiner as he may direct; or

(ii) to a person determined by or under the regulations.

(3) In this section "food analyst" and "food examiner" have the same meanings as in section 30 above.
[Food Safety Act 1990, s 31 as amended by the Food Standards Act 1999, Sch 5.]

---

1. The Food Safety (Sampling and Qualifications) Regulations 1990, SI 1990/2463 amended by SI 1991/2843, SI 1995/360 and 1086, SI 1997/1729, SI 1998/1376, SI 1999/1540 and 1603, SI 2002/890 (England), 2364 (England), 2834 (Wales) and 3008 (England), SI 2003/302 (W), 666 (E), 1478 (E), 1721 (W) and 3042 (W), SI 2004/1509 (W) and 3062 (E) and SI 2005/364 (W) have been made.

Powers of entry and obstruction etc

8–12266 32. Powers of entry. (1) An authorised officer of an enforcement authority shall, on producing, if so required, some duly authenticated document showing his authority, have a right at all reasonable hours—

(a) to enter any premises within the authority's area for the purpose of ascertaining whether there is or has been on the premises any contravention of the provisions of this Act, or of regulations or orders made under it; and

(b) to enter any business premises, whether within or outside the authority's area, for the purpose of ascertaining[1] whether there is on the premises any evidence of any contravention within that area of any of such provisions; and

(c) in the case of an authorised officer of a food authority, to enter any premises for the purpose of the performance by the authority of their functions under this Act;

but admission to any premises used only as a private dwelling-house shall not be demanded as of right unless 24 hours' notice of the intended entry has been given to the occupier.

(2) If a justice of the peace, on sworn information in writing, is satisfied that there is reasonable ground for entry into any premises for any such purpose as is mentioned in subsection (1) above and either—

(a) that admission to the premises has been refused, or a refusal is apprehended, and that notice of the intention to apply for a warrant has been given to the occupier; or

(b) that an application for admission, or the giving of such a notice, would defeat the object of the entry, or that the case is one of urgency, or that the premises are unoccupied or the occupier temporarily absent,

the justice may by warrant signed by him authorise the authorised officer to enter the premises, if need be by reasonable force.

(3) Every warrant granted under this section shall continue in force for a period of one month.

(4) An authorised officer entering any premises by virtue of this section, or of a warrant issued under it, may take with him such other persons as he considers necessary, and on leaving any unoccupied premises which he has entered by virtue of such a warrant shall leave them as effectively secured against unauthorised entry as he found them.

(5) An authorised officer entering premises by virtue of this section, or of a warrant issued under it, may inspect any records (in whatever form they are held) relating to a food business and, where any such records are stored in any electronic form—

(a) may have access to, and inspect and check the operation of, any computer and any associated apparatus or material which is or has been in use in connection with the records; and

(b) may require any person having charge of, or otherwise concerned with the operation of, the computer, apparatus or material to afford him such assistance as he may reasonably require.

(6) Any officer exercising any power conferred by subsection (5) above may—

(a) seize and detain any records which he has reason to believe may be required as evidence in proceedings under any of the provisions of this Act or of regulations or orders made under it; and

(b) where the records are stored in any electronic form, may require the records to be produced in a form in which they may be taken away.

(7) If any person who enters any premises by virtue of this section, or of a warrant issued under it, discloses to any person any information obtained by him in the premises with regard to any trade secret, he shall, unless the disclosure was made in the performance of his duty, be guilty of an offence.

(8) Nothing in this section authorises any person, except with the permission of the local authority under the Animal Health Act 1981, to enter any premises—

(a) in which an animal or bird affected with any disease to which that Act applies is kept; and

(b) which is situated in a place declared under that Act to be infected with such a disease.

(9) In the application of this section to Scotland, any reference to a justice of the peace includes a reference to the sheriff and to a magistrate.
[Food Safety Act 1990, s 32, as amended by the Criminal Justice and Police Act 2001, Sch 2.]

---

1. While the powers of an "away" team of environmental health officers investigating a possible contravention of the provisions of the Act outside their own authority's area under s 32(1)(b) are more limited than those of a "home" team carrying out an investigation within their own authority's area under s 32(1)(a), the "away" team is entitled by ss 32(1)(b) and 32(5) to inspect the relevant production process and relevant records for the purpose of rebutting a possible "due diligence" defence which might be advanced by the defendant in the event of prosecution (*Walkers Snack Foods Ltd v Coventry City Council* [1998] 3 All ER 163).

8–12267   33. Obstruction etc of officers.   (1) Any person who—

(a) intentionally obstructs any person acting in the execution of this Act; or

(b) without reasonable cause, fails to give to any person acting in the execution of this Act any assistance or information which that person may reasonably require of him for the performance of his functions under this Act,[1]

shall be guilty of an offence.

(2) Any person who, in purported compliance with any such requirement as is mentioned in subsection (1)(b) above—

(a) furnishes information which he knows to be false or misleading in a material particular; or

(b) recklessly furnishes information which is false or misleading in a material particular,

shall be guilty of an offence.

(3) Nothing in subsection (1)(b) above shall be construed as requiring any person to answer any question or give information if to do so might incriminate him.
[Food Safety Act 1990, s 33.]

---

1. Section 33(3) upholds an individual's privilege against self-incrimination by protecting him against answering questions or giving information which might incriminate him, but this, when read in conjunction with s 33(1)(b) does not confer an entitlement not to answer questions or give information in relation to others, including a company by whom he or she is employed (*Walkers Snack Foods Ltd v Coventry City Council* [1998] 3 All ER 163).

Offences

8–12268   34. Time limit for prosecutions.   No prosecution for an offence under this Act which is punishable under section 35(2) below shall be begun after the expiry of—

(a) three years from the commission of the offence; or

(b) one year from its discovery[1] by the prosecutor,

whichever is the earlier.
[Food Safety Act 1990, s 34.]

1. In the case of a continuing offence, "discovery" may take place on any later day during which commission of the offence continues (*R v Thames Metropolitan Stipendiary Magistrate, ex p London Borough of Hackney* (1993) 158 JP 305, 92 LGR 392). See also *R v Gale* [2005] EWCA Crim 286, (2005) 169 JP 166: the court must consider the date of offence that is charged, rather than whether the defendant could have been charged with committing the offence on an earlier date.

8–12269 35. Punishment of offences.   (1) A person guilty of an offence under section 33(1) above shall be liable on summary conviction to a fine not exceeding **level 5** on the standard scale or to imprisonment for a term not exceeding **three months* or to both**.

(2) A person guilty of any other offence under this Act shall be liable—

   (*a*) on conviction on indictment, to a fine or to imprisonment for a term not exceeding two years or to both;

   (*b*) on summary conviction, to a fine not exceeding the **relevant amount** or to imprisonment for a term not exceeding **six months or to both**.

(3) In subsection (2) above "**the relevant amount**" means—

   (*a*) in the case of an offence under section 7 or 14 above, £20,000;

   (*b*) in any other case, the statutory maximum.

(4) If a person who is—

   (*a*) licensed under section 1 of the Slaughterhouses Act 1974 to keep a knacker's yard;

   (*b*) *Repealed*;

   (*c*) licensed under section 6 of the Slaughter of Animals (Scotland) Act 1980 to use any premises as a knacker's yard,

is convicted of an offence under Part II of this Act, the court may, in addition to any other punishment, cancel his licence or registration.

[Food Safety Act 1990, s 35 as amended by SI 1996/2235 and SI 2004/3279.]

---

*Words substituted with "51 weeks" by the Criminal Justice Act 2003, Sch 26 from a date to be appointed.

   1. For procedure in respect of an offence which is triable either way, see the Magistrates' Courts Act 1980, ss 17A–21, in PART I: MAGISTRATES' COURTS, PROCEDURE, ante.

8–12270 36. Offences by bodies corporate.   (1) Where an offence under this Act which has been committed by a body corporate is proved to have been committed with the consent or connivance of, or to be attributable to any neglect on the part of—

   (*a*) any director, manager, secretary or other similar officer of the body corporate; or

   (*b*) any person who was purporting to act in any such capacity,

he as well as the body corporate shall be deemed to be guilty of that offence and shall be liable to be proceeded against and punished accordingly.

(2) In subsection (1) above "director", in relation to any body corporate established by or under any enactment for the purpose of carrying on under national ownership any industry or part of an industry or undertaking, being a body corporate whose affairs are managed by its members, means a member of that body corporate.

[Food Safety Act 1990, s 36.]

8–12270A 36A. Offences by Scottish Partnerships.   Where an offence under this Act which has been committed by a Scottish partnership is proved to have been committed with the consent or connivance of, or to be attributable to any neglect on the part of, a partner, he, as well as the partnership shall be deemed to be guilty of that offence and liable to be proceeded against and punished accordingly.

[Food Safety Act 1990, s 36A, as inserted by the Food Standards Act 1999, Sch 5.]

Appeals

8–12271 37. Appeals to magistrates' court or sheriff.   (1) Any person who is aggrieved by—

   (*a*) a decision of an authorised officer of an enforcement authority to serve an improvement notice;

   (*b*) a decision of an enforcement authority to refuse to issue such a certificate as is mentioned in section 11(6) or 12(8) above; or

   (*c*) subject to subsection (2) below, a decision of such an authority to refuse, cancel, suspend or revoke a licence required by regulations under Part II of this Act,

may appeal to a magistrates' court or, in Scotland, to the sheriff.

(2) Subsection (1)(*c*) above shall not apply in relation to any decision as respects which regulations under Part II of this Act provide for an appeal to a tribunal constituted in accordance with the regulations.

(3) The procedure on an appeal to a magistrates' court under subsection (1) above, or an appeal to such a court for which provision is made by regulations under Part II of this Act, shall be by way of complaint for an order, and the Magistrates' Courts Act 1980 shall apply to the proceedings.

(4) *Scotland.*

(5) The period within which such an appeal as is mentioned in subsection (3) or (4) above may be brought shall be—

(a) one month from the date on which notice of the decision was served on the person desiring to appeal; or

(b) in the case of an appeal under subsection (1)(*a*) above, that period or the period specified in the improvement notice, whichever ends the earlier;

and, in the case of such an appeal as is mentioned in subsection (3) above, the making of the complaint shall be deemed for the purposes of this subsection to be the bringing of the appeal.

(6) In any case where such an appeal as is mentioned in subsection (3) or (4) above lies, the document notifying the decision to the person concerned shall state—

(a) the right of appeal to a magistrates' court or to the sheriff; and

(b) the period within which such an appeal may be brought.

[Food Safety Act 1990, s 37.]

8–12272   38. Appeals to Crown Court.   A person who is aggrieved by—

(a) any dismissal by a magistrates' court of such an appeal as is mentioned in section 37(3) above; or

(b) any decision of such a court to make a prohibition order or an emergency prohibition order, or to exercise the power conferred by section 35(4) above,

may appeal to the Crown Court.

[Food Safety Act 1990, s 38.]

8–12273   39. Appeals against improvement notices.   (1) On an appeal against an improvement notice, the court may either cancel or affirm the notice and, if it affirms it, may do so either in its original form or with such modifications as the court may in the circumstances think fit.

(2) Where, apart from this subsection, any period specified in an improvement notice would include any day on which an appeal against that notice is pending, that day shall be excluded from that period.

(3) An appeal shall be regarded as pending for the purposes of subsection (2) above until it is finally disposed of, is withdrawn or is struck out for want of prosecution.

[Food Safety Act 1990, s 39.]

PART IV[1]

MISCELLANEOUS AND SUPPLEMENTAL

Powers of Ministers

8–12274   40. Power to issue codes of practice.   (1) For the guidance of food authorities, the Secretary of State may issue codes of recommended practice as regards the execution and enforcement of this Act and of regulations and orders made under it; and any such code shall be laid before Parliament, or in the case of a code which applies only to Scotland, before the Scottish Parliament, after being issued.

(1A) The Food Standards Agency may, after consulting the Secretary of State, give a food authority a direction requiring them to take any specified steps in order to comply with a code under this section.

(2) In the exercise of the functions conferred on them by or under this Act, every food authority—

(a) shall have regard to any relevant provision of any such code; and

(b) shall comply with any direction which is given by the Secretary of State under this section and requires them to take any specified steps in order to comply with such a code.

(3) Any direction under subsection (1A) above shall, on the application of the Food Standards Agency, be enforceable by mandamus or, in Scotland, by an order of the Court of Session under section 45 of the Court of Session Act 1988.

(3A) The Food Standards Agency shall consult the Secretary of State before making an application under subsection (3) above.

(4) Before issuing any code under this section, the Secretary of State shall

(a) subject to subsection (4B) below, consult with such organisations as appear to him to be representative of interests likely to be substantially affected by the code; and

(b) have regard to any relevant advice given by the Food Standards Agency.

(4A) If it appears to the Secretary of State that the Food Standards Agency has undertaken any consultation with an organisation that he is required to consult under subsection (4) above, the Secretary of State may treat that consultation as being as effective for the purposes of that subsection as if undertaken by him.

(4B) Subsection (4)(*a*) above shall not apply in any case in which consultation is required by Article 9 of Regulation (EC) No 178/2002.

(5) Any consultation undertaken before the commencement of subsection (4) above shall be as effective, for the purposes of that subsection, as if undertaken after that commencement.
[Food Safety Act 1990, s 40 as amended by SI 1999/1820, the Food Standards Act 1999, Sch 5 and SI 2004/2990.]

8–12275 41. Power to require returns. Every food authority shall send to the Secretary of State or to the Food Standards Agency such reports and returns, and give him or it such information, with respect to the exercise of the functions conferred on them by or under this Act as he or it may require.
[Food Safety Act 1990, s 41 as amended by the Food Standards Act 1999, Sch 5.]

8–12276 42. Default powers. (1) Where the Secretary of State is satisfied that—

    (*a*) a food authority (in this section referred to as "the authority in default") have failed to discharge any duty imposed by or under this Act; and

    (*b*) the authority's failure affects the general interests of consumers of food,

he may by order empower another food authority or the Food Standards Agency (in this section referred to as "the substitute authority"), or one of his officers, to discharge that duty in place of the authority in default.

(2) For the purpose of determining whether the power conferred by subsection (1) above is exercisable, the Secretary of State may cause a local inquiry to be held; and where he does so, the relevant provisions of the Local Government Act shall apply as if the inquiry were a local inquiry held under that Act.

(3) Nothing in subsection (1) above affects any other power exercisable by the Secretary of State with respect to defaults of local authorities.

(4) The substitute authority or the Secretary of State may recover from the authority in default any expenses reasonably incurred by them or him under subsection (1) above; and for the purpose of paying any such amount the authority in default may—

    (*a*) raise money as if the expenses had been incurred directly by them as a local authority; and

    (*b*) if and to the extent that they are authorised to do so by the Secretary of State, borrow money in accordance with the statutory provisions relating to borrowing by a local authority.

(5) In this section "the relevant provisions of the Local Government Act" means subsections (2) to (5) of section 250 of the Local Government Act 1972 in relation to England and Wales and subsections (3) to (8) of section 210 of the Local Government (Scotland) Act 1973 in relation to Scotland.
[Food Safety Act 1990, s 42 as amended by the Food Standards Act 1999, Sch 5.]

Protective provisions

8–12277 43. Continuance of registration or licence on death. (1) This section shall have effect on the death of any person who—

    (*a*) is registered in respect of any premises in accordance with regulations made under Part II of this Act; or

    (*b*) holds a licence issued in accordance with regulations so made.

(2) The registration or licence shall subsist for the benefit of the deceased's personal representative, or widow or widower or surviving civil partner or any other member of the deceased's family, until the end of—

    (*a*) the period of three months beginning with the deceased's death; or

    (*b*) such longer period as the enforcement authority may allow.
[Food Safety Act 1990, s 43 as amended by the Civil Partnership Act 2004, Sch 27.]

8–12278 44. Protection of officers acting in good faith. (1) An officer of a food authority is not personally liable in respect of any act done by him—

    (*a*) in the execution or purported execution of this Act; and

    (*b*) within the scope of his employment,

if he did that act in the honest belief that his duty under this Act required or entitled him to do it.

(2) Nothing in subsection (1) above shall be construed as relieving any food authority from any liability in respect of the acts of their officers.

(3) Where an action has been brought against an officer of a food authority in respect of an act done by him—

    (*a*) in the execution or purported execution of this Act; but

    (*b*) outside the scope of his employment,

the authority may indemnify him against the whole or a part of any damages which he has been ordered to pay or any costs which he may have incurred if they are satisfied that he honestly believed that the act complained of was within the scope of his employment.

(4) A public analyst appointed by a food authority shall be treated for the purposes of this section as being an officer of the authority, whether or not his appointment is a whole-time appointment.
[Food Safety Act 1990, s 44.]

Financial provisions

8–12279   45. *Regulations as to charges.*

8–12280   46. *Expenses of authorised officers and county councils.*

8–12281   47. *Remuneration of tribunal chairmen.*

Instruments and documents

8–12282   48. Regulations and orders.   (1) Any power of the Secretary of State to make regulations or an order under this Act includes power—

- (*a*)   to apply, with modifications and adaptations, any other enactment (including one contained in this Act) which deals with matters similar to those being dealt with by the regulations or order;
- (*b*)   to make different provision in relation to different cases or classes of case (including different provision for different areas or different classes of business); and
- (*c*)   to provide for such exceptions, limitations and conditions, and to make such supplementary, incidental, consequential or transitional provisions, as the Secretary of State considers necessary or expedient.

(2) Any power of the Secretary of State to make regulations or orders under this Act shall be exercisable by statutory instrument.

(3) Any statutory instrument containing—

- (*a*)   regulations under this Act; or
- (*b*)   an order under this Act other than an order under section 60(3) below,

shall be subject to annulment in pursuance of a resolution of either House of Parliament.

(4) Subject to subsection (4C) below, before making—

- (*a*)   any regulations under this Act, other than regulations under section 17(2) or 18(1)(*c*) above; or
- (*b*)   any order under Part I of this Act,

the Secretary of State shall consult with such organisations as appear to them to be representative of interests likely to be substantially affected by the regulations or order.

(4A)   Before making any regulations or order under this Act, the Secretary of State shall have regard to any relevant advice given by the Food Standards Agency.

(4B)   If it appears to the Secretary of State that the Food Standards Agency has undertaken any consultation with an organisation that he is required to consult under subsection (4) above, the Secretary of State may treat that consultation as being as effective for the purposes of that subsection as if undertaken by him.

(4C)   Subsection (4) above shall not apply in any case in which consultation is required by Article 9 of Regulation (EC) No 178/2002.

(5) Any consultation undertaken before the commencement of subsection (4) above shall be as effective, for the purposes of that subsection, as if undertaken after that commencement.

[Food Safety Act 1990, s 48 as amended by the Food Standards Act 1999, Sch 6 and SI 2004/2990.]

8–12283   49. Form and authentication of documents.   (1) The following shall be in writing, namely—

- (*a*)   all documents authorised or required by or under this Act to be given, made or issued by a food authority; and
- (*b*)   all notices and applications authorised or required by or under this Act to be given or made to, or to any officer of, such an authority.

(2) The Secretary of State may by regulations[1] prescribe the form of any document to be used for any of the purposes of this Act and, if forms are so prescribed, those forms or forms to the like effect may be used in all cases to which those forms are applicable.

(3) Any document which a food authority are authorised or required by or under this Act to give, make or issue may be signed on behalf of the authority—

- (*a*)   by the proper officer of the authority as respects documents relating to matters within his province; or
- (*b*)   by any officer of the authority authorised by them in writing to sign documents of the particular kind or, as the case may be, the particular document.

(4) Any document purporting to bear the signature of an officer who is expressed—

- (*a*)   to hold an office by virtue of which he is under this section empowered to sign such a document; or
- (*b*)   to be duly authorised by the food authority to sign such a document or the particular document,

shall for the purposes of this Act, and of any regulations and orders made under it, be deemed, until the contrary is proved, to have been duly given, made or issued by authority of the food authority.

(5) In this section—

"proper officer", in relation to any purpose and to any food authority or any area, means the officer appointed for that purpose by that authority or, as the case may be, for that area;

"signature" includes a facsimile of a signature by whatever process reproduced.

[Food Safety Act 1990, s 48 as amended by the Food Standards Act 1999, Sch 5.]

---

1. Regulations made under s 79(5) of the Food Act 1984, now repealed, shall have effect as if made under s 49(2) of this Act; see Sch 4, post. For regulations made under this Act, see the Food Safety (Sampling and Qualifications) Regulations 1990, SI 1990/2463 amended by SI 1991/2483 , SI 1995/360 and 1086, SI 1997/1729, SI 1998/1376, SI 1999/1540 and 1603 and SI 2002/890 (England), 2364 (England), 2834 (Wales) and 3008 (England), the Detention of Food (Prescribed Forms) Regulations 1990, SI 1990/2614 and the Food Safety (Improvement and Prohibition—Prescribed Forms) Regulations 1991, SI 1991/100.

8–12284 50. Service of documents. (1) Any document which is required or authorised by or under this Act to be given to or served on any person may, in any case for which no other provision is made by this Act, be given or served either—

(*a*) by delivering it to that person;

(*b*) in the case of any officer of an enforcement authority, by leaving it, or sending it in a prepaid letter addressed to him, at his office;

(*c*) in the case of an incorporated company or body, by delivering it to their secretary or clerk at their registered or principal office, or by sending it in a prepaid letter addressed to him at that office; or

(*d*) in the case of any other person, by leaving it, or sending it in a prepaid letter addressed to him, at his usual or last known residence.

(2) Where a document is to be given to or served on the owner or the occupier of any premises and it is not practicable after reasonable inquiry to ascertain the name and address of the person to or on whom it should be given or served, or the premises are unoccupied, the document may be given or served by addressing it to the person concerned by the description of "owner" or "occupier" of the premises (naming them) and—

(*a*) by delivering it to some person on the premises; or

(*b*) if there is no person on the premises to whom it can be delivered, by affixing it, or a copy of it, to some conspicuous part of the premises.

[Food Safety Act 1990, s 50.]

Amendments of other Acts

8–12285 51. Contamination of food: emergency orders. (1) Part I of the Food and Environment Protection Act 1985 (contamination of food) shall have effect, and shall be deemed always to have had effect, subject to the amendments specified in subsection (2) below.

(2) The amendments referred to in subsection (1) above are—

(*a*) in subsection (1) of section 1 (power to make emergency orders), the substitution for paragraph (*a*) of the following paragraph—

"(*a*) there exist or may exist circumstances which are likely to create a hazard to human health through human consumption of food;";

(*b*) in subsection (2) of that section, the omission of the definition of "escape";

(*c*) the substitution for subsection (5) of that section of the following subsection—

"(5) An emergency order shall refer to the circumstances or suspected circumstances in consequence of which in the opinion of the designating authority making it food such as is mentioned in subsection (1)(*b*) above is, or may be, or may become, unsuitable for human consumption; and in this Act "designated circumstances" means the circumstances or suspected circumstances to which an emergency order refers in pursuance of this subsection.";

(*d*) in section 2(3) (powers when emergency order has been made), the substitution for the words "a designated incident" of the words "designated circumstances";

(*e*) in paragraph (*a*) of subsection (1) of section 4 (powers of officers), the substitution for the words "an escape of substances" of the words "such circumstances as are mentioned in section 1(1) above"; and

(*f*) in paragraphs (*b*) and (*c*) of that subsection, the substitution for the words "the designated incident" of the words "the designated circumstances".

[Food Safety Act 1990, s 51.]

8–12286 52. Markets, sugar beet and cold storage. In the Food Act 1984 (in this Act referred to as "the 1984 Act")—

(*a*) Part III (markets); and

(*b*) Part V (sugar beet and cold storage),

shall have effect subject to the amendments specified in Schedule 2 to this Act.
[Food Safety Act 1990, s 52.]

Supplemental

8–12287 53. General interpretation. (1) In this Act, unless the context otherwise requires—

"the 1984 Act" means the Food Act 1984;

"the 1956 Act" means the Food and Drugs (Scotland) Act 1956;

"advertisement" includes any notice, circular, label, wrapper, invoice or other document, and any public announcement made orally or by any means of producing or transmitting light or sound, and "advertise" shall be construed accordingly;

"analysis" includes microbiological assay and any technique for establishing the composition of food, and "analyse" shall be construed accordingly;

"animal" means any creature other than a bird or fish;

"article" does not include a live animal or bird, or a live fish which is not used for human consumption while it is alive;

"container" includes any basket, pail, tray, package or receptacle of any kind, whether open or closed;

"contravention", in relation to any provision, includes any failure to comply with that provision;

"cream" means that part of milk rich in fat which has been separated by skimming or otherwise;

"equipment" includes any apparatus;

"exportation" and "importation" have the same meanings as they have for the purposes of the Customs and Excise Management Act 1979, and "export" and "import" shall be construed accordingly;

"fish" includes crustaceans and molluscs;

"functions" includes powers and duties;

"human consumption" includes use in the preparation of food for human consumption;

"knacker's yard" means any premises used in connection with the business of slaughtering, flaying or cutting up animals the flesh of which is not intended for human consumption;

"milk" includes cream and skimmed or separated milk;

"occupier", in relation to any ship or aircraft of a description specified in an order made under section 1(3) above or any vehicle, stall or place, means the master, commander or other person in charge of the ship, aircraft, vehicle, stall or place;

"officer" includes servant;

"preparation", in relation to food, includes manufacture and any form of processing or treatment, and "preparation for sale" includes packaging, and "prepare for sale" shall be construed accordingly;

"presentation", in relation to food, includes the shape, appearance and packaging of the food, the way in which the food is arranged when it is exposed for sale and the setting in which the food is displayed with a view to sale, but does not include any form of labelling or advertising, and "present" shall be construed accordingly;

"proprietor", in relation to a food business, means the person by whom that business is carried on[1];

"ship" includes any vessel, boat or craft, and a hovercraft within the meaning of the Hovercraft Act 1968, and "master" shall be construed accordingly;

"slaughterhouse" means a place for slaughtering animals, the flesh of which is intended for sale for human consumption, and includes any place available in connection with such a place for the confinement of animals while awaiting slaughter there or for keeping, or subjecting to any treatment or process, products of the slaughtering of animals there;

"substance" includes any natural or artificial substance or other matter, whether it is in solid or liquid form or in the form of a gas or vapour;

"treatment", in relation to any food, includes subjecting it to heat or cold.

(2) The following Table shows provisions defining or otherwise explaining expressions used in this Act (other than provisions defining or explaining an expression used only in the same section)—

authorised officer of a food authority	section 5(6)
Authorised officer of an enforcement authority	section 6(6)
business	section 1(3)
commercial operation	section 1(3) and (4)
contact material	section 1(3)
emergency control order	section 13(1)
emergency prohibition notice	section 12(1)
emergency prohibition order	section 12(2)
enforcement authority	section 6(1)
examination and examine	section 28(2)
food	section 1(1)
food authority	section 5
food business	section 1(3)

food premises	section 1(3)
food safety requirements	section 8
food source	section 1(3)
improvement notice	section 10(1)
premises	section 1(3)
prohibition order	section 11(5)
public analyst	section 27(1)
Regulation (EC) No 178/2002	section 1(2)
sale and related expressions	section 2
unfit for human consumption	section 8(4)

(3) Any reference in this Act to regulations or orders made under it shall be construed as a reference to regulations or orders made under this Act by the Secretary of State.

(4) For the purposes of this Act, any class or description may be framed by reference to any matters or circumstances whatever, including in particular, in the case of a description of food, the brand name under which it is commonly sold.

(5) Where, apart from this subsection, any period of less than seven days which is specified in this Act would include any day which is—

(*a*) a Saturday, a Sunday, Christmas Day or Good Friday; or

(*b*) a day which is a bank holiday under the Banking and Financial Dealings Act 1971 in the part of Great Britain concerned,

that day shall be excluded from that period.

[Food Safety Act 1990, s 53 as amended by the Food Standards Act 1999, Schs 5 and 6 and SI 2004/2990.]

---

1. A person other than the owner may be the "proprietor". A person "carrying on" a business need not be the owner, be involved in the business on a day to day basis or even have been to the premises (*Ahmed v Leicester City Council* (2000) Times, 29 March, DC). A parent company of a wholly owned subsidiary company can be a "proprietor" of a business owned by the latter; the court is entitled to make a realistic assessment of the actual role of the defendant in the group and to bear in mind that there may be much involved in carrying on a food business that falls outside the purely physical processes listed in reg 2 of the Food Safety (General Food Hygiene) Regulations 1995; it is not necessary for the "proprietor" to carry out any, let alone all, of the functions that appear in the definition of "food business" in reg 2 (*Greene King plc v Harlow District Council* [2003] EWHC Admin 2852, (2004) 168 JP 70).

8–12288 54. Application to Crown. (1) Subject to the provisions of this section, the provisions of this Act and of regulations and orders made under it shall bind the Crown.

(2) No contravention by the Crown of any provision of this Act or of any regulations or order made under it shall make the Crown criminally liable; but the High Court or, in Scotland, the Court of Session may, on the application of an enforcement authority, declare unlawful any act or omission of the Crown which constitutes such a contravention.

(3) Notwithstanding anything in subsection (2) above, the provisions of this Act and of regulations and orders made under it shall apply to persons in the public service of the Crown as they apply to other persons.

(4) If the Secretary of State certifies that it appears to him requisite or expedient in the interests of national security that the powers of entry conferred by section 32 above should not be exercisable in relation to any Crown premises specified in the certificate, those powers shall not be exercisable in relation to those premises; and in this subsection "Crown premises" means premises held or used by or on behalf of the Crown.*

(5) Nothing in this section shall be taken as in any way affecting Her Majesty in her private capacity; and this subsection shall be construed as if section 38(3) of the Crown Proceedings Act 1947 (interpretation of references in that Act to Her Majesty in her private capacity) were contained in this Act.

[Food Safety Act 1990, s 54.]

8–12289 55. Water supply: England and Wales. (1) Nothing in Part 2 of this Act or any regulations or order made under that Part shall apply in relation to the supply of water to any premises, whether—

(*a*) by a water undertaker;

(*b*) by a licensed water supplier (within the meaning of the Water Industry Act 1991); or

(*c*) by means of a private supply (within the meaning of Part 3 of that Act).

[Food Safety Act 1990, s 55 as substituted by SI 2005/2035.]

8–12290 56. *Water supply; Scotland.*

8–12291 57. Scilly Isles and Channel Islands. (1) *Repealed.*

(2) Her Majesty may by Order in Council direct that any of the provisions of this Act shall extend to any of the Channel Islands with such exceptions and modifications (if any) as may be specified in the Order.

[Food Safety Act 1990, s 57, as amended by the Food Standards Act 1999, Sch 6.]

8-12292 58. Territorial waters and the continental shelf. (1) For the purposes of this Act the territorial waters of the United Kingdom adjacent to any part of Great Britain shall be treated as situated in that part.

(2) An Order in Council under section 11 of the Petroleum Act 1998 (application of civil law) may make provision for treating for the purposes of food safety legislation—

(a) any installation which is in waters to which that section applies; and

(b) any safety zone around any such installation,

as if they were situated in a specified part of the United Kingdom and for modifying such legislation in its application to such installations and safety zones.

(3) Such an Order in Council may also confer on persons of a specified description the right to require, for the purpose of facilitating the exercise of specified powers under food safety legislation—

(a) conveyance to and from any installation, including conveyance of any equipment required by them; and

(b) the provision of reasonable accommodation and means of subsistence while they are on any installation.

(4) In this section—

"food safety legislation" means this Act and any regulations and orders made under it and any corresponding provisions in Northern Ireland;

"installation" means an installation to which subsection (3) of the said section 11 applies;

"safety zone" means an area which is a safety zone by virtue of Part III of the Petroleum Act 1987; and

"specified" means specified in the Order in Council.

[Food Safety Act 1990, s 58 as amended by the Petroleum Act 1998, Sch 4 and SI 1999/161.]

8-12293 59. Amendments, transitional provisions, savings and repeals. (1) The enactments mentioned in Schedule 3 to this Act shall have effect subject to the amendments there specified (being minor amendments and amendments consequential on the preceding provisions of this Act).

(2) The Secretary of State may by order make such modifications of local Acts, and of subordinate legislation[1] (within the meaning of the Interpretation Act 1978), as appear to them to be necessary or expedient in consequence of the provisions of this Act.

(3) The transitional provisions and savings contained in Schedule 4 to this Act shall have effect; but nothing in this subsection shall be taken as prejudicing the operation of sections 16 and 17 of the said Act of 1978 (which relate to the effect of repeals).

(4) The enactments mentioned in Schedule 5 to this Act (which include some that are spent or no longer of practical utility) are hereby repealed to the extent specified in the third column of that Schedule.

[Food Safety Act 1990, s 59 as amended by the Food Standards Act 1999, Sch 5.]

---

1. The Food Safety Act 1990 (Consequential Modifications) (England and Wales) Order 1990, SI 1990/2486 and the Food Safety Act 1990 (Consequential Modifications) (No 2) (Great Britain) Order 1990, SI 1990/2487 have been made.

8-12294 60. *Short title, commencement and extent.*

SCHEDULES

Section 16(3)   SCHEDULE 1
PROVISIONS OF REGULATIONS UNDER SECTION 16(1)
(*As amended by the Food Standards Act 1999, Sch 5*).

Composition of food

8-12295 1. Provision for prohibiting or regulating—

(a) the sale, possession for sale, or offer, exposure or advertisement for sale, of any specified substance, or of any substance of any specified class, with a view to its use in the preparation of food; or

(b) the possession of any such substance for use in the preparation of food.

Fitness etc of food

2. (1) Provision for prohibiting—

(a) the sale for human consumption; or

(b) the use in the manufacture of products for sale for such consumption,

of food derived from a food source which is suffering or has suffered from, or which is liable to be suffering or to have suffered from, any disease specified in the regulations.

(2) Provision for prohibiting or regulating, or for enabling enforcement authorities to prohibit or regulate—

(a) the sale for human consumption; or

(b) the offer, exposure or distribution for sale for such consumption,

of shellfish taken from beds or other layings for the time being designated by or under the regulations.

3. (1) Provision for regulating generally the treatment and disposal of any food—

(a) which is unfit for human consumption; or
(b) which, though not unfit for human consumption, is not intended for, or is prohibited from being sold for, such consumption.

(2) Provision for the following, namely—

(a) for the registration by enforcement authorities of premises used or proposed to be used for the purpose of sterilising meat to which sub-paragraph (1) above applies, and for prohibiting the use for that purpose of any premises which are not registered in accordance with the regulations; or
(b) for the issue by such authorities of licences in respect of the use of premises for the purpose of sterilising such meat, and for prohibiting the use for that purpose of any premises except in accordance with a licence issued under the regulations.

Processing and treatment of food

4. Provision for the following, namely—

(a) for the giving by persons possessing such qualifications as may be prescribed by the regulations of written opinions with respect to the use of any process or treatment in the preparation of food, and for prohibiting the use for any such purpose of any process or treatment except in accordance with an opinion given under the regulations; or
(b) for the issue by enforcement authorities of licences in respect of the use of any process or treatment in the preparation of food, and for prohibiting the use for any such purpose of any process or treatment except in accordance with a licence issued under the regulations.

Food hygiene

5. (1) Provision for imposing requirements as to—

(a) the construction, maintenance, cleanliness and use of food premises, including any parts of such premises in which equipment and utensils are cleaned, or in which refuse is disposed of or stored;
(b) the provision, maintenance and cleanliness of sanitary and washing facilities in connection with such premises; and
(c) the disposal of refuse from such premises.

(2) Provision for imposing requirements as to—

(a) the maintenance and cleanliness of equipment or utensils used for the purposes of a food business; and
(b) the use, for the cleaning of equipment used for milking, of cleaning agents approved by or under the regulations.

(3) Provision for requiring persons who are or intend to become involved in food businesses, whether as proprietors or employees or otherwise, to undergo such food hygiene training as may be specified in the regulations.

6. (1) Provision for imposing responsibility for compliance with any requirements imposed by virtue of paragraph 5(1) above in respect of any premises—

(a) on the occupier of the premises; and
(b) in the case of requirements of a structural character, on any owner of the premises who either—

 (i) lets them for use for a purpose to which the regulations apply; or
 (ii) permits them to be so used after notice from the authority charged with the enforcement of the regulations.

(2) Provision for conferring in relation to particular premises, subject to such limitations and safeguards as may be specified, exemptions from the operation of specified provisions which—

(a) are contained in the regulations; and
(b) are made by virtue of paragraph 5(1) above,

while there is in force a certificate of the enforcement authority to the effect that compliance with those provisions cannot reasonably be required with respect to the premises or any activities carried on in them.

Production of food sources

6A. Provision for prohibiting or regulating—

(a) the possession, sale or offer, exposure or advertisement for sale of any specified substance, or any substance of any specified class, with a view to its use in connection with the production of any food source;
(b) the use of any specified substance, or any substance of any specified class, in connection with the production of any food source;
(c) the carrying out of any other activity in connection with, or in a manner likely to affect, the production of any food source.

Inspection etc of food sources

7. (1) Provision for securing the inspection of food sources by authorised officers of enforcement authorities for the purpose of ascertaining whether they—

(a) fail to comply with the requirements of the regulations; or
(b) are such that any food derived from them is likely to fail to comply with those requirements.

(2) Provision for enabling such an officer, if it appears to him on such an inspection that any food source falls (or is likely to fall) within sub-paragraph (1)(a) or (b) above, to give notice to the person in charge of the food source that, until a time specified in the notice or until the notice is withdrawn—

(a) no commercial operations are to be carried out with respect to the food source; and

(b) the food source either is not to be removed or is not to be removed except to some place so specified.

(3) Provision for enabling such an officer, if on further investigation it appears to him, in the case of any such food source which is a live animal or bird, that there is present in the animal or bird any substance whose presence is prohibited by the regulations, to cause the animal or bird to be slaughtered.

Section 59(3)

SCHEDULE 4
TRANSITIONAL PROVISIONS AND SAVINGS

(*As amended by the Food Standards Act 1999, Sch 6*).

Ships and aircraft

8–12298 **1.** In relation to any time before the commencement of the first order under section 1(3) of this Act—

(a) any ship which is home-going ship within the meaning of section 132 of the 1984 Act or section 58 of the 1956 Act (interpretation) shall be regarded as premises for the purposes of this Act; and

(b) the powers of entry conferred by section 32 of this Act shall include the right to enter any ship or aircraft for the purpose of ascertaining whether there is in the ship or aircraft any food imported as part of the cargo in contravention of the provisions of regulations made under Part II of this Act;

and in this Act as it applies by virtue of this paragraph "occupier", in relation to any ship or aircraft, means the master, commander or other person in charge of the ship or aircraft.

Regulations under the 1984 Act

2. (1) In so far as any existing regulations made, or having effect as if made, under any provision of the 1984 Act specified in the first column of Table A below have effect in relation to England and Wales, they shall have effect, after the commencement of the relevant repeal, as if made under the provisions of this Act specified in relation to that provision in the second column of that Table, or such of those provisions as are applicable.

(2) In this paragraph and paragraphs 3 and 4 below "existing regulations" means—

(a) any regulations made, or having effect as if made, under a provision repealed by this Act; and

(b) any orders having effect as if made under such regulations,

which are in force immediately before the coming into force of that repeal; and references to the commencement of the relevant repeal shall be construed accordingly.

TABLE A

Provision of the 1984 Act	Provision of this Act
section 4 (composition etc of food)	sections 16(1)(a), (c) and (f) and (3) and 17(1)
section 7 (describing food)	section 16(1)(e)
section 13 (food hygiene)	section 16(1)(b), (c), (d) and (f), (2) and (3)
section 33 (milk and dairies)	section 16(1)(b), (c), (d) and (f), (2) and (3)
section 34 (registration), so far as relating to dairies or dairy farms	section 19
section 38 (milk: special designations)	section 18(2)
section 73(2) (qualification of officers)	section 5(6)
section 76(2) (public analysts)	section 27(2)
section 79(5) (form of certificate)	section 49(2)
section 119 (Community provisions)	section 17(2)

Regulations under the 1956 Act

3. Any existing regulations made, or having effect as if made, under any provision of the 1956 Act specified in the first column of Table B below shall have effect, after the commencement of the relevant repeal, as if made under the provisions of this Act specified in relation to that provision in the second column of that Table, or such of those provisions as are applicable.

TABLE B

Provision of the 1956 Act	Provision of this Act
section 4 (composition etc of food)	sections 16(1)(a), (c) and (f) and (3) and 17(1)
section 7 (describing food)	section 16(1)(e)
section 13 (food hygiene)	sections 5(6) and 16(1)(b), (c), (d) and (f), (2) and (3)
section 16(2) (regulations as to milk)	section 18(2)
section 27(2) (public analysts)	section 18(2)
section 29(3) (form of certificate)	section 49(2)
section 56A (Community provisions)	section 17(2)

Other regulations

4. In so far as any existing regulations made under section 1 of the Importation of Milk Act 1983 have effect in relation to Great Britain, they shall have effect, after the commencement of the relevant repeal, as if made under section 18(1)(c) of this Act.

5. *Orders with respect to milk in Scotland.*

Disqualification orders

6. The repeal by this Act of section 14 of the 1984 Act (court's power to disqualify caterers) shall not have effect as respects any order made, or having effect as if made, under that section which is in force immediately before the commencement of that repeal.

Food hygiene byelaws

7. *Repealed.*

Closure orders

8. The repeal by this Act of section 21 of the 1984 Act or section 1 of the Control of Food Premises (Scotland) Act 1977 (closure orders) shall not have effect as respects any order made, or having effect as if made, under that section which is in force immediately before the commencement of that repeal.

Food Standards Act 1999[1]
(1999 c 28)

The Food Standards Agency

8–12299   1. The Food Standards Agency.   (1) There shall be a body to be called the Food Standards Agency or, in Welsh, yr Asiantaeth Safonau Bwyd (referred to in this Act as "the Agency") for the purpose of carrying out the functions conferred on it by or under this Act.

(2) The main objective of the Agency in carrying out its functions is to protect public health from risks which may arise in connection with the consumption of food (including risks caused by the way in which it is produced or supplied) and otherwise to protect the interests of consumers in relation to food.

(3) The functions of the Agency are performed on behalf of the Crown.
[Food Standards Act 1999, s 1.]

---

1. the Food Standards Act 1999 establishes the Food Standards Agency and makes provision as to its functions; amends the law relating to food safety and other interests of consumers in relation to food; enables provision to be made in relation to the notification of tests for food-borne diseases and enables provision to be made in relation to animal feedingstuffs. The Act was brought fully into force on 1 April 2000 (SI 2000/1066).

8–12300   2. *Appointment of members etc*

8–12301   3. *Appointment of chief executive and directors*

8–12302   4. *Annual and other reports*

8–12303   5. *Advisory committees*

General functions in relation to food

8–12304   6. Development of food policy and provision of advice, etc to public authorities. (1) The Agency has the function of—

(a) developing policies (or assisting in the development by any public authority of policies) relating to matters connected with food safety or other interests of consumers in relation to food; and

(b) providing advice, information or assistance in respect of such matters to any public authority.

(2) A Minister of the Crown or government department, the National Assembly for Wales, the Scottish Ministers or a Northern Ireland Department may request the Agency to exercise its powers under this section in relation to any matter.

(3) It is the duty of the Agency, so far as is reasonably practicable, to comply with any such request.
[Food Standards Act 1999, s 6.]

8–12305   7. Provision of advice, information and assistance to other persons.   (1) The Agency has the function of—

(a) providing advice and information to the general public (or any section of the public) in respect of matters connected with food safety or other interests of consumers in relation to food;

(b) providing advice, information or assistance in respect of such matters to any person who is not a public authority.

(2) The function under subsection (1)(a) shall be carried out (without prejudice to any other relevant objectives) with a view to ensuring that members of the public are kept adequately informed

about and advised in respect of matters which the Agency considers significantly affect their capacity to make informed decisions about food.
[Food Standards Act 1999, s 7.]

8–12306   8. Acquisition and review of information.   (1) The Agency has the function of obtaining, compiling and keeping under review information about matters connected with food safety and other interests of consumers in relation to food.

(2) That function includes (among other things)—

(*a*)   monitoring developments in science, technology and other fields of knowledge relating to the matters mentioned in subsection (1);

(*b*)   carrying out, commissioning or co-ordinating research on those matters.

(3) That function shall (without prejudice to any other relevant objectives) be carried out with a view to ensuring that the Agency has sufficient information to enable it to take informed decisions and to carry out its other functions effectively.
[Food Standards Act 1999, s 8.]

General functions in relation to animal feedingstuffs

8–12307   9. General functions in relation to animal feedingstuffs.   (1) The Agency has the same general functions in relation to matters connected with the safety of animal feedingstuffs and other interests of users of animal feedingstuffs as it has under sections 6(1), 7(1) and 8 in relation to matters connected with food safety and other interests of consumers in relation to food.

(2) Section 6(2) and (3) apply in relation to the Agency's powers under this section corresponding to those under section 6(1).

(3) Section 7(2), in its application to the Agency's function under this section corresponding to that under section 7(1)(*a*), applies with the substitution, for the words "members of the public" and "food", of the words "users of animal feedingstuffs" and "animal feedingstuffs".

(4) In this section "safety of animal feedingstuffs" means the safety of animal feedingstuffs in relation to risks to animal health which may arise in connection with their consumption.
[Food Standards Act 1999, s 9.]

Observations with a view to acquiring information

8–12308   10. Power to carry out observations.   (1) The Agency may, for the purpose of carrying out its function, under section 8 or its corresponding function under section 9, carry out observations (or arrange with other persons for observations to be carried out on its behalf) with a view to obtaining information about—

(*a*)   any aspect of the production or supply of food or food sources; or

(*b*)   any aspect of the production, supply or use of animal feedingstuffs.

(2) Without prejudice to the generality of subsection (1), the information that may be sought through such observations includes information about—

(*a*)   food premises, food businesses or commercial operations being carried out with respect to food, food sources or contact materials;

(*b*)   agricultural premises, agricultural businesses or agricultural activities;

(*c*)   premises, businesses or operations involved in fish farming; or

(*d*)   premises, businesses or operations involved in the production, supply or use of animal feedingstuffs.

(3) In this section—

"agricultural activity" has the same meaning as in the Agriculture Act 1947 or, in Northern Ireland, the Agriculture Act (Northern Ireland) 1949;

"agricultural business" has the same meaning as in section 1 of the Farm Land and Rural Development Act 1988 or, in Northern Ireland, Article 3 of the Farm Business (Northern Ireland) Order 1988;

"agricultural premises" means any premises used for the purposes of an agricultural business; and

"fish farming" means the breeding, rearing or keeping of fish or shellfish (which includes any kind of crustacean or mollusc).
[Food Standards Act 1999, s 10.]

8–12309   11. Power of entry for persons carrying out observations.   (1) The Agency may authorise any individual (whether a member of its staff or otherwise) to exercise the powers specified in subsection (4) for the purpose of carrying out any observations under section 10 specified in the authorisation.

(2) No authorisation under this section shall be issued except in pursuance of a decision taken by the Agency itself or by a committee, sub-committee or member of the Agency acting on behalf of the Agency.

(3) An authorisation under this section shall be in writing and may be given subject to any

limitations or conditions specified in the authorisation (including conditions relating to hygiene precautions to be taken while exercising powers in pursuance of the authorisation).

(4) An authorised person may, if it appears to him necessary to do so for the purpose of carrying out the observations specified in his authorisation—

(a) enter any premises at any reasonable hour;

(b) take samples of any articles or substances found on any premises;

(c) take samples from any food source found on any premises;

(d) inspect and copy any records found on any premises which relate to a business which is the subject of the observations (and, if they are kept in computerised form, require them to be made available in a legible form);

(e) require any person carrying on such a business to provide him with such facilities, such records or information and such other assistance as he may reasonably request;

but in this subsection "premises" does not include a private dwelling-house.

(5) An authorised person shall on request—

(a) produce his authorisation before exercising any powers under subsection (4); and

(b) provide a document identifying any sample taken, or documents copied, under those powers.

(6) The references in subsection (4)(d) and (e) to records include any records which—

(a) relate to the health of any person who is or has been employed in the business concerned; and

(b) were created for the purpose of assessing, or are kept for the purpose of recording, matters affecting his suitability for working in the production or supply of food or food sources (including any risks to public health which may arise if he comes into contact with any food or food source).

(7) If an authorised person who enters any premises by virtue of this section discloses to any person any information obtained on the premises with regard to any trade secret he is, unless the disclosure is made in the performance of his duty, guilty of an offence and liable on summary conviction to a fine not exceeding **level 5** on the standard scale.

(8) A person who—

(a) intentionally obstructs a person exercising powers under subsection (4)(a), (b), (c) or (d);

(b) fails without reasonable excuse to comply with any requirement imposed under subsection (4)(e); or

(c) in purported compliance with such a requirement furnishes information which he knows to be false or misleading in any material particular or recklessly furnishes information which is false or misleading in any material particular;

is guilty of an offence and liable on summary conviction to a fine not exceeding **level 5** on the standard scale.

(9) In this section "authorised person" means a person authorised under this section.

[Food Standards Act 1999, s 11.]

Monitoring of enforcement action

8–12310   12. Monitoring of enforcement action.   (1) The Agency has the function of monitoring the performance of enforcement authorities in enforcing relevant legislation.

(2) That function includes, in particular, setting standards of performance (whether for enforcement authorities generally or for particular authorities) in relation to the enforcement of any relevant legislation.

(3) Each annual report of the Agency shall contain a report on its activities during the year in enforcing any relevant legislation for which it is the enforcement authority and its performance in respect of—

(a) any standards under subsection (2) that apply to those activities; and

(b) any objectives relating to those activities that are specified in the statement of objectives and practices under section 22.

(4) The Agency may make a report to any other enforcement authority on their performance in enforcing any relevant legislation; and such a report may include guidance as to action which the Agency considers would improve that performance.

(5) The Agency may direct an authority to which such a report has been made—

(a) to arrange for the publication in such manner as may be specified in the direction of, or of specified information relating to, the report; and

(b) within such period as may be so specified to notify the Agency of what action they have taken or propose to take in response to the report.

[Food Standards Act 1999, s 12.]

8–12311   13. Power to request information relating to enforcement action.   (1) For the purpose of carrying out its function under section 12 in relation to any enforcement authority the Agency may require a person mentioned in subsection (2)—

(a) to provide the Agency with any information which it has reasonable cause to believe that person is able to give, or

(b) to make available to the Agency for inspection any records which it has reasonable cause to believe are held by that person or otherwise within his control (and, if they are kept in computerised form, to make them available in a legible form).

(2) A requirement under subsection (1) may be imposed on—

(a) the enforcement authority or any member, officer or employee of the authority, or

(b) a person subject to any duty under relevant legislation (being a duty enforceable by an enforcement authority) or any officer or employee of such a person.

(3) The Agency may copy any records made available to it in pursuance of a requirement under subsection (1)(b).

[Food Standards Act 1999, s 13.]

8–12312   14. Power of entry for persons monitoring enforcement action.   (1) The Agency may authorise any individual (whether a member of its staff or otherwise) to exercise the powers specified in subsection (4) for the purpose of carrying out its function under section 12 in relation to any enforcement authority.

(2) No authorisation under this section shall be issued except in pursuance of a decision taken by the Agency itself or by a committee, sub-committee or member of the Agency acting on behalf of the Agency.

(3) An authorisation under this section shall be in writing and may be given subject to any limitations or conditions specified in the authorisation (including conditions relating to hygiene precautions to be taken while exercising powers in pursuance of the authorisation).

(4) An authorised person may—

(a) enter any premises mentioned in subsection (5) at any reasonable hour in order to inspect the premises or anything which may be found on them;

(b) take samples of any articles or substances found on such premises;

(c) inspect and copy any records found on such premises (and, if they are kept in computerised form, require them to be made available in a legible form);

(d) require any person present on such premises to provide him with such facilities, such records or information and such other assistance as he may reasonably request.

(5) The premises which may be entered by an authorised person are—

(a) any premises occupied by the enforcement authority;

(b) any laboratory or similar premises at which work related to the enforcement of any relevant legislation has been carried out for the enforcement authority; and

(c) any other premises (not being a private dwelling-house) which the authorised person has reasonable cause to believe are premises in respect of which the enforcement powers of the enforcement authority are (or have been) exercisable.

(6) The power to enter premises conferred on an authorised person includes power to take with him any other person he may consider appropriate.

(7) An authorised person shall on request—

(a) produce his authorisation before exercising any powers under subsection (4); and

(b) provide a document identifying any sample taken, or documents copied, under those powers.

(8) If a person who enters any premises by virtue of this section discloses to any person any information obtained on the premises with regard to any trade secret he is, unless the disclosure is made in the performance of his duty, guilty of an offence and liable on summary conviction to a fine not exceeding **level 5** on the standard scale.

(9) Where—

(a) the enforcement authority in relation to any provisions of the Food Safety Act 1990 (in this Act referred to as "the 1990 Act") or orders or regulations made under it is (by virtue of section 6(3) or (4) of that Act) a Minister of the Crown, the National Assembly for Wales, the Scottish Ministers or the Agency, or

(b) the enforcement authority in relation to any provisions of the Food Safety (Northern Ireland) Order 1991 (in this Act referred to as "the 1991 Order") or orders or regulations made under it is (by virtue of Article 26(1A), (1B), (2), (3) or (3A) of that Order) a Northern Ireland Department or the Agency,

this section applies to that authority (in relation to its performance in enforcing those provisions) with the omission of subsection (5)(a).

(10) In this section "authorised person" means a person authorised under this section.

[Food Standards Act 1999, s 14.]

8–12313   15. Meaning of "enforcement authority" and related expressions.   (1) In sections 12 to 14 "relevant legislation" means—

(a) the provisions of the 1990 Act and regulations or orders made under it;[1, 2]
(b) the provisions of the 1991 Order and regulations or orders made under it; and
(c) the provisions of Part IV of the Agriculture Act 1970 and regulations made under that Part of that Act, so far as relating to matters connected with animal feedingstuffs.

(2) In those sections "enforcement authority" means—

(a) in the case of provisions of the 1990 Act or regulations or orders made under it, the authority by whom they are to be enforced (including a Minister of the Crown, the National Assembly for Wales, the Scottish Ministers or the Agency itself if, by virtue of section 6(3) or (4) of the 1990 Act, that authority is the enforcement authority in relation to those provisions);
(b) in the case of provisions of the 1991 Order and regulations or orders made under it, the authority by whom they are to be enforced (including a Northern Ireland Department or the Agency itself if, by virtue of the Order, it is the enforcement authority in relation to those provisions); and
(c) in the case of provisions of Part IV of the Agriculture Act 1970 (or regulations made under it), an authority mentioned in section 67 of that Act;

and "enforcement", in relation to relevant legislation, includes the execution of any provisions of that legislation.

(3) Any reference in those sections (however expressed) to the performance of an enforcement authority in enforcing any relevant legislation includes a reference to the capacity of that authority to enforce it.

[Food Standards Act 1999, s 15.]

---

1. References to the provisions of regulations or orders made under the 1990 Act in sub-s (1)(a) above modified to include references to provisions (so far as they relate to England and Wales) of specific Regulations made under the European Communities Act 1972, s2(2), by SI 2000/656 and SSI 2000/62.

2. Includes provisions of the following Regulations made under s 2(2) of the European Communities Act 1972:
The Materials and Articles in Contact with Food Regulations 1987, SI 1987/1527; amended by SI 1994/979: All the provisions;
The Olive Oil (Marketing Standards) Regulations 1987, SI 1987/1783; amended by SI 1990/2487, 1992/2590, 1998/2410: All the provisions;
The Organic Products Regulations 1992, SI 1992/2111; amended by SI 1993/405, 1994/2286 and 1997/166: All the provisions;
The General Product Safety Regulations 1994, SI 1994/2328; amended by SI 1994/3142 and 3144, SI 1996/2756 and SI 1999/1820: Regulation 11;
The Infant Formula and Follow-on Formula Regulations 1995, SI 1995/77; amended by SI 1997/45: Regulation 21;
The Fresh Meat (Import Conditions) Regulations 1996, SI 1996/3 125: All the provisions;
The Products of Animal Origin (Import and Export) Regulations 1996, SI 1996/3124; amended by SI 1997/3023, 1998/994 and 1999/683: All the provisions;
The Olive Oil (Designations of Origin) Regulations 1999, SI 1999/1513: All the provisions;
The Animal Feeding Stuffs From Belgium (Control) (England and Wales) Regulations 2000, SI 2000/588: All the provisions.

8–12314   **16. Offences relating to sections 13 and 14.**   (1) A person who—

(a) intentionally obstructs a person exercising powers under section 14(4)(a), (b) or (c);
(b) fails without reasonable excuse to comply with any requirement imposed under section 13(1) or section 14(4)(d); or
(c) in purported compliance with such a requirement furnishes information which he knows to be false or misleading in any material particular or recklessly furnishes information which is false or misleading in any material particular;

is guilty of an offence.

(2) A person guilty of an offence under this section is liable on summary conviction to a fine not exceeding **level 5** on the standard scale.

[Food Standards Act 1999, s 16.]

Other functions of the Agency

8–12315   **17. Delegation of powers to make emergency orders.**   (1) Arrangements may be made between the Secretary of State and the Agency authorising the Agency to exercise on behalf of the Secretary of State the power to make orders under—

(a) section 1(1) of the Food and Environment Protection Act 1985 (emergency orders); and
(b) section 13(1) of the 1990 Act (emergency control orders).

(2) The authority given by any such arrangements is subject to any limitations and conditions provided for in the arrangements.

(3) Where by virtue of any such arrangements the Agency is authorised to exercise a power, anything done or omitted to be done by the Agency in the exercise or purported exercise of the power shall be treated as done or omitted by the Secretary of State.

(4) Nothing in any such arrangements prevents the Secretary of State exercising any power.

(5) This section applies with the necessary modifications—

(a) to any power mentioned in subsection (1) so far as it is exercisable by the National Assembly for Wales or the Scottish Ministers, and

(b) to the power of a Northern Ireland Department to make orders under section 1(1) of the Food and Environment Protection Act 1985 or Article 12(1) of the 1991 Order,

as it applies to a power exercisable by the Secretary of State.
[Food Standards Act 1999, s 17.]

8–12316　**18. Functions under other enactments.**　(1) Schedule 3 (which contains provisions conferring functions under certain enactments on the Agency) has effect.

(2) Any amendment made by Schedule 3 which extends to Scotland is to be taken as a pre-commencement enactment for the purposes of the Scotland Act 1998.
[Food Standards Act 1999, s 18.]

8–12317　**19. Publication etc by the Agency of advice and information.**　(1) The Agency may, subject to the following provisions of this section, publish in such manner as it thinks fit—

(a) any advice given under section 6, 7 or 9 (including advice given in pursuance of a request under section 6(2));

(b) any information obtained through observations under section 10 or monitoring under section 12; and

(c) any other information in its possession (whatever its source).

(2) The exercise of that power is subject to the requirements of the Data Protection Act 1998.

(3) That power may not be exercised if the publication by the Agency of the advice or information in question—

(a) is prohibited by an enactment;

(b) is incompatible with any Community obligation; or

(c) would constitute or be punishable as a contempt of court.

(4) Before deciding to exercise that power, the Agency must consider whether the public interest in the publication of the advice or information in question is outweighed by any considerations of confidentiality attaching to it.

(5) Where the advice or information relates to the performance of enforcement authorities, or particular enforcement authorities, in enforcing relevant legislation, subsection (4) applies only so far as the advice or information relates to a person other than—

(a) an enforcement authority, or

(b) a member, officer or employee of an enforcement authority acting in his capacity as such.

(6) Expressions used in subsection (5) and defined in section 15 have the same meaning as in that section.

(7) Except as mentioned above, the power under subsection (1) is exercisable free from any prohibition on publication that would apply apart from this section.

(8) In this section "enactment" means an enactment contained in, or in subordinate legislation made under, any Act, Act of the Scottish Parliament or Northern Ireland legislation.

(9) The Agency may also disclose to another public authority any advice or information mentioned in subsection (1); and the other provisions of this section apply in relation to disclosure under this subsection as they apply in relation to publication under that subsection.
[Food Standards Act 1999, s 19.]

8–12318　**20. Power to issue guidance on control of food-borne diseases.**　(1) The Agency may issue general guidance to local authorities or other public authorities on matters connected with the management of outbreaks or suspected outbreaks of food-borne disease.

(2) Guidance issued under this section must identify the authority or authorities to which it is addressed.

(3) The Agency shall publish any guidance issued under this section in such manner as it thinks fit.

(4) Any authority to whom guidance under this section is issued shall have regard to the guidance in carrying out any functions to which the guidance relates.

(5) In this section "food-borne disease" means a disease of humans which is capable of being caused by the consumption of infected or otherwise contaminated food.

(6) This section has effect without prejudice to any other powers of the Agency.
[Food Standards Act 1999, s 20.]

8–12319　**21. Supplementary powers.**　(1) The Agency has power to do anything which is calculated to facilitate, or is conducive or incidental to, the exercise of its functions.

(2) Without prejudice to the generality of subsection (1), that power includes power—

(a) to carry on educational or training activities;

(b) to give financial or other support to activities carried on by others;

(c) to acquire or dispose of any property or rights;

(*d*) to institute criminal proceedings in England and Wales and in Northern Ireland.

(3) The Agency may make charges for facilities or services provided by it at the request of any person.
[Food Standards Act 1999, s 21.]

General provisions relating to the functions of the Agency

8–12320 **22.** *Statement of general objectives and practices*

8–12321 **23.** *Consideration of objectives, risks, costs and benefits, etc*

8–12322 **24.** *Directions relating to breach of duty or to international obligations*

8–12323 **25. Power to modify enactments about disclosure of information.** (1) If it appears to the Secretary of State that an enactment prohibits the disclosure of any information and is capable of having either of the effects mentioned in subsection (5) he may by order make provision for the purpose of removing or relaxing the prohibition so far as it is capable of having that effect.

(2) If it appears to the Scottish Ministers that an enactment prohibits the disclosure of any information and is capable of having either of the effects mentioned in subsection (5) the Scottish Ministers may by order make provision for the purpose of removing or relaxing the prohibition so far as it is capable of having that effect.

(3) The power under subsection (2) may not be exercised to make provision which would not be within the legislative competence of the Scottish Parliament.

(4) If it appears to the First Minister and deputy First Minister acting jointly that any enactment dealing with transferred matters (within the meaning of section 4(1) of the Northern Ireland Act 1998) prohibits the disclosure of any information and is capable of having either of the effects mentioned in subsection (5) they may by order make provision for the purpose of removing or relaxing the prohibition so far as it is capable of having that effect.

(5) The effects mentioned in subsections (1), (2) and (4) are that the enactment in question—

(*a*) prevents the disclosure to the Agency of information that would facilitate the carrying out of the Agency's functions; or

(*b*) prevents the publication by the Agency of information in circumstances where the power under section 19 would otherwise be exercisable.

(6) An order under this section may—

(*a*) make provision as to circumstances in which information which is subject to the prohibition in question may, or may not, be disclosed to the Agency or, as the case may be, published by the Agency; and

(*b*) if it makes provision enabling the disclosure of information to the Agency, make provision restricting the purposes for which such information may be used (including restrictions on the subsequent disclosure of the information by the Agency).

(7) This section applies in relation to a rule of law as it applies in relation to an enactment, but with the omission of—

(*a*) subsection (5)(*b*) and any reference to the effect mentioned in subsection (5)(*b*); and
(*b*) in subsection (6)(*a*), the words from "or, as" to the end.

(8) In this section "enactment" means an enactment contained in any Act (other than this Act) or Northern Ireland legislation passed or made before or in the same Session as this Act.
[Food Standards Act 1999, s 25.]

Miscellaneous provisions

8–12324 **26. Statutory functions ceasing to be exercisable by Minister of Agriculture, Fisheries and Food and Department of Agriculture for Northern Ireland.** (1) The functions of the Minister of Agriculture, Fisheries and Food under—

(*a*) Part I of the Food and Environment Protection Act 1985;
(*b*) the 1990 Act; and
(*c*) the Radioactive Substances Act 1993,

shall cease to be exercisable by that Minister.

(2) *Northern Ireland*,

shall cease to be exercisable by that Department.

(3) Subsections (1) and (2) do not affect enforcement functions under directions or subordinate legislation under the enactments mentioned in those subsections (or any power under those enactments to confer such functions in directions or subordinate legislation).
[Food Standards Act 1999, s 26.]

8–12325   27. Notification of tests for food-borne disease. (1) Regulations may make provision for requiring the notification of information about tests on samples taken from individuals (whether living or dead) for the presence of—

(a) organisms of a description specified in the regulations; or

(b) any substances produced by or in response to the presence of organisms of a description so specified.

(2) A description of organisms may be specified in the regulations only if it appears to the authority making the regulations that those organisms or any substances produced by them—

(a) are capable of causing disease in humans; and

(b) are commonly transmitted to humans through the consumption of food.

(3) The power to make the regulations is exercisable for the purpose of facilitating the carrying out of functions of the Agency or any other public authority which relate to the protection of public health.

(4) The regulations shall, as respects each specified description of organisms—

(a) specify the information to be notified about them and the form and manner in which it is to be notified;

(b) make provision for identifying the person by whom that information is to be notified; and

(c) specify the person to whom that information is to be notified;

but the regulations may not require a person to notify information which is not in his possession, or otherwise available to him, by virtue of his position.

(5) The regulations may—

(a) make provision as to the tests about which information is to be notified;

(b) require or permit the person specified under subsection (4)(c) to disclose any information to any other person or to publish it;

(c) restrict the purposes for which any information may be used (whether by the person so specified or by any other person);

(d) make provision with a view to ensuring that patient confidentiality is preserved;

(e) create exceptions from any provision of the regulations;

(f) create summary offences, subject to the limitation that no such offence shall be punishable with imprisonment or a fine exceeding **level 5** on the standard scale.

(6) Before making regulations under this section the authority making them shall consult the Agency and such organisations as appear to the authority to be representative of interests likely to be substantially affected by the regulations.

(7) Any consultation undertaken before the commencement of subsection (6) shall be as effective, for the purposes of that subsection, as if undertaken after that commencement.

(8) The power to make regulations under this section is exercisable—

(a) as respects tests carried out in England, by the Secretary of State;

(b) as respects tests carried out in Wales, by the National Assembly for Wales;

(c) as respects tests carried out in Scotland, by the Scottish Ministers; and

(d) as respects tests carried out in Northern Ireland, by the Department of Health and Social Services for Northern Ireland.

[Food Standards Act 1999, s 27.]

8–12326   28. *Arrangements for sharing information about food-borne zoonoses*

8–12327   29. *Consultation on veterinary products*

8–12328   30. Animal feedingstuffs: Great Britain. (1) The Ministers may, for the purpose of regulating any animal feedingstuff or anything done to or in relation to, or with a view to the production of, any animal feedingstuff, make an order under this section.

(2) An order under this section is one which applies, or makes provision corresponding to, any provisions of the 1990 Act (including any power to make subordinate legislation or to give directions), with or without modifications.

(3) Such an order may be made by reference to the 1990 Act as it stands immediately before this Act is passed or as it stands following any amendment or repeal made by this Act.

(4) Such an order under this section may make provision with a view to protecting animal health, protecting human health or for any other purpose which appears to the Ministers to be appropriate.

(5) The provision which may be made in an order under this section by virtue of section 37(1)(a) includes provision amending or repealing any enactment or subordinate legislation.

(6) Before making such an order, the Ministers shall—

(a) consult such organisations as appear to them to be representative of interests likely to be substantially affected by the order; and

(b) have regard to any advice given by the Agency.

(7) Any consultation undertaken before the commencement of subsection (6) shall be as effective,

for the purposes of that subsection, as if undertaken after that commencement; and any consultation undertaken by the Agency may be treated by the Ministers as being as effective for those purposes as if it had been undertaken by them.

(8) In this section "the Ministers" means—

(*a*)　in the case of an order extending to England and Wales, the Secretary of State;

(*b*)　in the case of an order extending to Scotland, the Scottish Ministers.

(9) Subsection (6)(*a*) shall not apply in any case in which consultation is required by Article 9 of Regulation (EC) No 178/2002 of the European Parliament and of the Council laying down the general principles and requirements of food law, establishing the European Food Safety Authority and laying down procedures in matters of food safety.

[Food Standards Act 1999, s 30, as amended by SI 2002/794 and SI 2004/3254.]

8–12330　32. Modification of certain provisions of this Act.　(1) Her Majesty may by Order in Council make such provision as She considers appropriate for modifying—

(*a*)　the functions exercisable under this Act by any of the appropriate authorities (including functions exercisable jointly by two or more of them);

(*b*)　the powers under this Act of either House of Parliament, the Scottish Parliament or the Northern Ireland Assembly; or

(*c*)　the constitution of the Agency.

(2) Without prejudice to the generality of subsection (1), provision made under paragraph (*a*) or (*b*) of that subsection may—

(*a*)　confer on any one or more of the appropriate authorities functions (including powers to make subordinate legislation) which relate to anything connected with the Agency or its activities;

(*b*)　confer powers on either House of Parliament, the Scottish Parliament or the Northern Ireland Assembly.

(3) Where provision is made under subsection (1)(*a*) or (*b*), the provision which may be made in the Order by virtue of section 37(1)(*a*) includes provision modifying functions of, or conferring functions on, the Agency or any other person in connection with any one or more of the appropriate authorities or with any body mentioned in subsection (1)(*b*).

(4) For the purposes of subsection (1)(*c*) the reference to the constitution of the Agency is a reference to the subject-matter of sections 2 to 5 and 39(7) (together with Schedules 1, 2 and 4).

(5) The provision which may be made by an Order under this section does not include provision modifying this section or section 33 (except that where provision is made under subsection (1)(*c*) the Order may make consequential amendments to subsection (4)).

(6) No recommendation shall be made to Her Majesty in Council to make an Order under this section unless the Agency has been consulted.

[Food Standards Act 1999, s 32.]

8–12331　33. Consequences of Agency losing certain functions.　(1) This section applies if—

(*a*)　the Scottish Parliament passes an Act providing for any functions of the Agency to be no longer exercisable in or as regards Scotland; or

(*b*)　the Northern Ireland Assembly passes an Act providing for any functions of the Agency to be no longer exercisable in or as regards Northern Ireland.

(2) Her Majesty may by Order in Council make provision—

(*a*)　modifying this or any other Act as She considers necessary or expedient in consequence of the functions concerned being no longer exercisable by the Agency in or as regards Scotland or Northern Ireland;

(*b*)　for the transfer of any property, rights and interests of the Agency falling within subsection (3);

(*c*)　for any person to have such rights or interests in relation to any property, rights or interests falling within subsection (3) as She considers appropriate (whether in connection with a transfer or otherwise); or

(*d*)　for the transfer of any liabilities of the Agency falling within subsection (4).

(3) Property, rights and interests fall within this subsection if they belong to the Agency and appear to Her Majesty—

(*a*)　to be held or used wholly or partly for or in connection with the exercise of any of the functions concerned, or

(*b*)　not to be within paragraph (*a*) but, when last held or used for or in connection with the exercise of any function, to have been so held or used for or in connection with the exercise of any of the functions concerned.

(4) Liabilities of the Agency fall within this subsection if they appear to Her Majesty to have been incurred wholly or partly for or in connection with the exercise of any of the functions concerned.

(5) An Order under this section may make provision for the delegation of powers to determine

anything required to be determined for the purposes of provision made under subsection (2)(*b*), (*c*) or (*d*).

(6) No recommendation shall be made to Her Majesty in Council to make an Order under this section unless the Agency has been consulted.

[Food Standards Act 1999, s 33.]

8–12332 34. Duty to take account of functions of the Food Safety Promotion Board.
(1) The Agency must—

(*a*) take account of the activities of the Food Safety Promotion Board in determining what action to take for the purpose of Food Safety carrying out its functions; and

(*b*) consult that Board from time to time with a view to ensuring so far as is practicable that the activities of the Agency do not unnecessarily duplicate the activities of the Board.

(2) Nothing in this Act affects the functions of the Food Safety Promotion Board.

[Food Standards Act 1999, s 34.]

8–12333 35. *Devolution in Scotland and Northern Ireland*

Final provisions

8–12334 36. Interpretation. (1) In this Act—

"Agency" means the Food Standards Agency;

"animal feedingstuff" means feedingstuff for any description of animals, including any nutritional supplement or other similar substance which is not administered through oral feeding;

"appropriate authorities" means the Secretary of State, the National Assembly for Wales, the Scottish Ministers and the Department of Health and Social Services for Northern Ireland;

"Food Safety Promotion Board" means the body of that name established by the agreement establishing implementation bodies done at Dublin on 8th March 1999 between the Government of the United Kingdom and the Government of Ireland;

"the 1990 Act" means the Food Safety Act 1990; and

"the 1991 Order" means the Food Safety (Northern Ireland) Order 1991.

(2) Any reference in this Act to "the appropriate authority", in relation to Wales, Scotland or Northern Ireland, is a reference to the National Assembly for Wales, the Scottish Ministers or the Department of Health and Social Services for Northern Ireland (as the case may be).

(3) In this Act the expression "interests of consumers in relation to food" includes (without prejudice to the generality of that expression) interests in relation to the labelling, marking, presenting or advertising of food, and the descriptions which may be applied to food.

(4) Expressions used—

(*a*) as regards England and Wales and Scotland, in this Act and in the 1990 Act, or

(*b*) as regards Northern Ireland, in this Act and the 1991 Order,

have, unless the context otherwise requires, the same meaning in this Act as in that Act or that Order (except that in this Act "animal" includes any bird or fish).

(5) The purposes which may be specified in an order under section 1(3) of the 1990 Act (meaning of the term "premises" to include, for specified purposes, ships or aircraft of a description specified by order), or under the corresponding provision of Article 2(2) of the 1991 Order, include purposes relating to provisions of this Act.

[Food Standards Act 1999, s 36.]

8–12335 37. Subordinate legislation. (1) Subordinate legislation under section 25, 27, 30, 31, 32 and 33—

(*a*) may contain such supplementary, incidental, consequential, transitional or saving provision as the person making it considers necessary or expedient;

(*b*) may make different provision for different purposes.

(2) Any power under this Act to make an order or regulations is exercisable—

(*a*) in the case of an order or regulations made by the First Minister and deputy First Minister or a Northern Ireland Department, by statutory rule for the purposes of the Statutory Rules (Northern Ireland) Order 1979; and

(*b*) in any other case, by statutory instrument.

(3) No order under section 25, 30 or 31 shall be made unless a draft of it has been laid before and approved by resolution of—

(*a*) each House of Parliament, if it is made by the Secretary of State or the Minister of Agriculture, Fisheries and Food;

(*b*) the Scottish Parliament, if it is made by the Scottish Ministers;

(*c*) the Northern Ireland Assembly, if it is made by the First Minister and deputy First Minister or by a Northern Ireland Department.

(4) A statutory instrument made under section 27 or 42 is subject to annulment in pursuance of a resolution of—

(*a*) either House of Parliament, if it is made by the Secretary of State;
(*b*) the Scottish Parliament, if it is made by the Scottish Ministers;

and a statutory rule made under that section is subject to negative resolution within the meaning of section 41(6) of the Interpretation Act (Northern Ireland) 1954.

(5) No recommendation shall be made to Her Majesty to make an Order in Council under section 32 or 33 unless a draft of the Order has been laid before and approved by resolution of each House of Parliament, the National Assembly for Wales, the Scottish Parliament and the Northern Ireland Assembly.
[Food Standards Act 1999, s 37.]

8-12336 38. Crown application. (1) This Act binds the Crown (but does not affect Her Majesty in her private capacity).
(2) Subsection (1)—

(*a*) does not require subordinate legislation made under this Act to bind the Crown; and
(*b*) is to be interpreted as if section 38(3) of the Crown Proceedings Act 1947 (references to Her Majesty in her private capacity) were contained in this Act.

(3) If the Secretary of State certifies that it appears to him requisite or expedient in the interests of national security that the powers of entry conferred by sections 11 and 14 should not be exercisable in relation to any premises specified in the certificate, being premises held or used by or on behalf of the Crown, those powers shall not be exercisable in relation to those premises.
[Food Standards Act 1999, s 38.]

8-12337 39. *Financial provisions*

8-12338 40. Minor and consequential amendments and repeals. (1) Schedule 5 (minor and consequential amendments) has effect.
(2) Any amendment made by Schedule 5 which extends to Scotland is to be taken as a pre-commencement enactment for the purposes of the Scotland Act 1998.
(3) The National Assembly for Wales (Transfer of Functions) Order 1999 shall have effect, in relation to any Act mentioned in Schedule 1 to the Order, as if any provision of this Act amending that Act was in force immediately before the Order came into force.
(4) The enactments mentioned in Schedule 6 are repealed to the extent specified.
(5) Her Majesty may by Order in Council direct that any amendment or repeal by this Act of any provision in the 1990 Act shall extend to any of the Channel Islands with such modifications (if any) as may be specified in the Order.
[Food Standards Act 1999, s 40.]

8-12339 41. *Transfer of property, rights and liabilities to the Agency*

8-12340 42. *Power to make transitional provision etc*[1]

---

1. The Food Standards Act 1999 (Transitional and Consequential Provisions and Savings) (England and Wales) Regulations 2000, SI 2000/656, make transitional and consequential provisions and savings in preparation for, in connection with or in consequence of ,the coming into force of provisions of the Food Standards Act 1999. The Regulations also transfer functions to the Food Standards Agency under legislation having effect in relation to food safety, consumer protection and animal feed.

8-12341 43. Short title, commencement and extent. (1) This Act may be cited as the Food Standards Act 1999.
(2) This Act (apart from this section and paragraph 6(2) and (5) of Schedule 5) shall come into force on such day as the Secretary of State may by order[1] appoint; and different days may be appointed for different purposes.
(3) The provisions of this Act shall be treated for the purposes of section 58 of the 1990 Act (territorial waters and the continental shelf) as if they were contained in that Act.
(4) Until the day appointed under section 3(1) of the Northern Ireland Act 1998, this Act has effect with the substitution—

(*a*) for references to the First Minister and deputy First Minister acting jointly, of references to a Northern Ireland Department;
(*b*) for references to an Act of the Northern Ireland Assembly, of references to a Measure of the Northern Ireland Assembly; and
(*c*) for references to transferred matters within the meaning of section 4(1) of the Northern Ireland Act 1998, of references to transferred matters within the meaning of section 43(2) of the Northern Ireland Constitution Act 1973;

(*d*) for references to paragraph 1(*a*) of Schedule 2 to the Northern Ireland Act 1998, of references to paragraph 1(*a*) of Schedule 2 to the Northern Ireland Constitution Act 1973.

(5) This Act extends to Scotland and Northern Ireland.

[Food Standards Act 1999, s 43.]

---

1. The Food Standards Act 1999 (Commencement No 1) Order 2000, SI 2000/92 and the Food Standards Act 1999 (Commencement No 2) Order 2000, SI 2000/1066, have been made. All provisions of the Act, not previously in force, were brought into force on 1 April 2000.

8–12342

Section 2(4)

SCHEDULE 1
CONSTITUTION ETC OF THE AGENCY

8–12343

Section 5(4)

SCHEDULE 2
ADVISORY COMMITTEES

Section 18

SCHEDULE 3
THE AGENCY'S FUNCTIONS UNDER OTHER ENACTMENTS

PART I
FUNCTIONS UNDER THE 1990 ACT

8–12344   **1.** This Part has effect for conferring functions under the 1990 Act on the Agency (and references to sections are to sections of the 1990 Act).

Section 6 (enforcement)

2. The Agency—

(*a*) may be directed to discharge duties of food authorities under section 6(3);

(*b*) may be specified as an enforcement authority for regulations or orders in pursuance of section 6(4); and

(*c*) may take over the conduct of proceedings mentioned in section 6(5) either with the consent of the person who instituted them or when directed to do so by the Secretary of State.

Section 13(3) (emergency control orders)

3. The Agency may grant consent under subsection (3), and give directions under subsection (5), of section 13.

Section 40 (codes of practice)

4. (1) The Agency may, after consulting the Secretary of State—

(*a*) give directions to food authorities under section 40(2)(*b*) as to steps to be taken in order to comply with codes of practice under section 40; and

(*b*) enforce any such directions.

(2) The Agency may undertake consultation with representative organisations regarding proposals for codes of practice under section 40.

Section 41 (information from food authorities)

5. The Agency may exercise the power to require returns or other information from food authorities under section 41.

Section 42 (default powers)

6. The Agency may be empowered by an order under section 42 to discharge any duty of a food authority.

Section 48 (regulations and orders)

7. The Agency may undertake consultation with representative organisations required by section 48 regarding proposals for regulations or orders under the 1990 Act.

PART II
FUNCTIONS UNDER THE 1991 ORDER

8–14. *Northern Ireland*

PART III
OTHER FUNCTIONS

Medicines Act 1968 (c 67)

15. *Amendment of the Medicines Act 1968*

Food and Environment Protection Act 1985 (c 48)

16. (1) The Agency shall have the following functions under the Food and Environment Protection Act 1985.

(2) The Agency may exercise the following powers under section 2 (powers when emergency order has been made)—

(a) the power to give consents under subsection (1);
(b) the power to give directions or do anything else under subsection (3);
(c) the power to recover expenses under subsection (5) or (6).

(3)–(6) *Amendment of the Food and Environment Protection Act 1990*

Environmental Protection Act 1990 (c 43)

17–18. *Amendment of the Environment Protection Act 1990*

19. *Genetically Modified Organisms (Northern Ireland) Order 1991 (SI 1991/1714 (NI 19))*

Radioactive Substances Act 1993 (c 12)

21. The Agency shall have the right to be consulted in the circumstances mentioned in subsection (4A) of section 16 or subsection (2A) of section 17 of the Radioactive Substances Act 1993 (proposals for granting or varying authorisations) about the matters mentioned in paragraphs (a) and (b) of that subsection.

8–12345

Section 39(7)

SCHEDULE 4
ACCOUNTS AND AUDIT

Control of Pesticides Regulations 1986[1]

(SI 1986/1510 amended by SI 1990/2487, SI 1994/3142, SI 1997/188 and SI 2001/880)

8–12820   1. *Citation and commencement.*

1. Made by the Minister of Agriculture, Fisheries and Food and the Secretary of State in exercise of powers conferred by sections 16(2) and 24(3) of the Food and Environment Protection Act 1985. Contraventions of the provisions of the regulations, conditions of approval or requirements imposed by virtue of the regulations is an offence under section 16(12) of the 1985 Act. By section 21(3) of the Act the maximum penalty is a fine not exceeding the **statutory maximum**: for procedure in respect of an offence triable either way, see the Magistrates' Courts Act 1980, ss 17A–21, in PART I: MAGISTRATES' COURTS, PROCEDURE, ante.

Interpretation

8–12821   2. (1) In these Regulations, unless the context otherwise requires—

"the 1985 Act" means the Food and Environment Protection Act 1985;
"active ingredient" means a component of a pesticide which fits it for use as a pesticide;
"aerial application" means the application of a pesticide from an aircraft in flight;
"agricultural" has the meaning assigned to it in section 24(1) of the 1985 Act;
"approval" means an approval given jointly by the Ministers under regulation 5 in relation to a pesticide and "approved" shall be construed accordingly;
"contravenes" includes "fails to comply with";
"creature" has the meaning assigned to it in section 24(1) of the 1985 Act;
"crops" has the meaning assigned to it in section 24(1) of the 1985 Act;
"full approval" has the meaning assigned to it in regulation 5(2)(c);
"ground water" means any waters contained in underground strata;
"organism" means any animal, plant, fungus or micro-organism capable of carrying on life processes;
"pesticide" has the meaning assigned to it in section 16(15) of the 1985 Act;
"plants" has the meaning assigned to it in section 24(1) of the 1985 Act;
"provisional approval" has the meaning assigned to it in regulation 5(2)(b);
"sell" includes offer or expose for sale or have in possession for the purpose of sale and "sale" shall be construed accordingly;
"substance" means any chemical element or compound which occurs naturally or by manufacture and includes any impurity which results from the manufacturing process;
"supply" includes offer to supply;
"surface water" means estuarial and coastal waters and any lake, loch, pond, reservoir, river, stream or watercourse including the bottom, channel or bed of any lake, loch, pond, reservoir, river, stream or, as the case may be, watercourse which is for the time being dry.

(2) Any reference in these regulations to a numbered regulation or schedule shall be construed as a reference to the regulation or schedule numbered in these regulations.

Scope

8–12822   3. (1) Subject to the following provisions of this regulation, these Regulations apply to—

(a) any pesticide; or
(b) any substance, preparation or organism prepared or used for any of the following purposes—
  (i) protecting plants or wood or other plant products from harmful organisms;

    (ii) regulating the growth of plants;

    (iii) giving protection against harmful creatures;

    (iv) rendering such creatures harmless;

    (v) controlling organisms with harmful or unwanted effects on water systems (including sewage treatment works), buildings or other structures, or on manufactured products;

    (vi) protecting animals against ectoparasites;

as if it were a pesticide.

  (2) These Regulations do not apply to—

  (a) organisms, other than bacteria, protozoa, fungi, viruses and mycoplasmas, used for destroying or controlling pests;

  (b) substances, preparations or organisms whose use or sale within the United Kingdom is controlled under any of the following enactments—

    (i)   the Medicines Act 1968;

    (ii) Part IV of the Agriculture Act 1970;

    (iii) the Food Safety Act 1990;

    (iv) the Cosmetic Products (Safety) Regulations 1984;

    (v) the Water Supply (Water Quality) Regulations 1989;

    (vi) the Water Supply (Water Quality) (Scotland) Regulations 1990, when those substances, preparations or organisms are used or sold for the purpose over which control under that enactment is exercised;

  (c) substances, preparations or organisms controlled by the Marketing Authorisations for Veterinary Medicinal Products Regulations 1994;

  (d) any plant protection product the placing on the market and use of which are subject to the prohibitions specified in regulation 3(1) and (2) of the Plant Protection Products Regulations 1995 or which is approved under regulation 9 of those Regulations;

  (e) substances, preparations or organisms prepared or used for the purpose of disinfecting, bleaching or sterilising any substance (including water), other than soils, compost or other growing medium;

  (f) substances, preparations or organisms used in laboratories for the purpose of the micropropagation of plants or substances, preparations or organisms used in the production of novel food;

  (g) substances, preparations or organisms designed and used for—

    (i)   the stimulation of the growth of plants, excluding materials which act as plant growth hormones, or which mimic the action of such materials;

    (ii) the modification of micro-biological processes in soil, excluding soil sterilants;

    (iii) assistance in the anaerobic fermentation of silage;

  (h) substances, preparations or organisms designed and used for destroying or controlling pests by purely physical means;

  (i) pesticides—

    (i)   used in adhesive pastes, decorative paper or textiles;

    (ii) intended solely for exportation from the United Kingdom;

    (iii) applied externally or by impregnation as part of a manufacturing process, other than—

       (aa) in the preservation of timber or timber products, the production of food or the treatment of seed, compost or any other growing medium, or

       (bb) for the purpose of preventing the fouling of the hulls of vessels or structures below the waterline, or

       (cc) for the treatment of nets, floats or other apparatus to be used in the cultivation of fish;

    (iv) used in preparations intended for topical application to human beings for the purpose of repelling insects;

    (v) used in metal working fluids;

    (vi) used in paint for the sole purpose of preserving the paint;

    (vii) used in water-based cooling or heating systems, humidifying systems or swimming pools;

  (j) any biocidal product—

    (i)   authorised or registered under the 2001 Regulations,

    (ii) placed on the market for use in an experiment or test in accordance with regulation 16 of the 2001 Regulations, or

    (iii) the placing on the market and use of which are subject to any of the prohibitions specified in regulation 8 of the 2001 Regulations,

    and in this sub-paragraph, "the 2001 Regulations" means the Biocidal Products Regulations 2001 and "biocidal product" shall have the meaning assigned to it in regulation 2(1) of the 2001 Regulations.

  (3) In this regulation—

"disinfecting" means destroying micro-organisms other than bacterial spores;

"metal working fluid" means any fluid used to facilitate the cutting, drilling, forming or machining of metal;

"micropropagation" means the growth of plantlets from tissue culture or small parts of a plant in culture solution and under conditions which are sterile apart from the presence of the plant;

"mycoplasma" means a genus of organisms which have a unit membrane without a rigid cell wall and are highly pleomorphic, having no independent form or spore stage in the life cycle;

"novel food" has the same meaning as in section 18(3) of the Food Safety Act 1990;

"paint" includes surface coatings;

"pest" has the meaning assigned to it in section 16(15) of the 1985 Act;

"placing on the market" and "plant protection product" have the same meanings as in the Plant Protection Products Regulations 1995;

"preparation" means a mixture or solution composed of two or more substances;

"soil sterilant" means a product used for sterilising soil or compost;

"sterilising" means destroying all micro-organisms including any bacterial spores.

Prohibitions

8–12823 **4.** (1) No person shall advertise a pesticide unless—

(a) the Ministers jointly have given a provisional or full approval under regulation 5 in relation to that pesticide and a consent under regulation 6(a);

(b) any conditions of the approval related to advertisement and the conditions of the consent have been complied with.

(2) No person shall sell a pesticide unless—

(a) the Ministers jointly have given a provisional or full approval under regulation 5 in relation to that pesticide and a consent under regulation 6(b);

(b) any conditions of the approved related to sale and the conditions of the consent have been complied with.

(3) No person shall supply a pesticide unless—

(a) the Ministers jointly have given an approval under regulation 5 in relation to that pesticide and a consent under regulation 6(b);

(b) any conditions of the approval related to supply and the conditions of the consent have been complied with.

(4) No person shall store a pesticide unless—

(a) the Ministers jointly have given an approval under regulation 5 in relation to that pesticide and a consent under regulation 6(b);

(b) any conditions of the approval related to storage and the conditions of the consent have been complied with.

(5) No person shall use a pesticide unless—

(a) the Ministers jointly have given an approval under regulation 5 in relation to that pesticide and a consent under regulation 6(c);

(b)

(i) the conditions of the approval related to use[1];

(ii) the conditions of the consent imposed under regulation 6(c=k)(i), and,

(iii) in the case of pesticides applied from an aircraft in flight, the additional conditions of the consent imposed under regulation 6(c)(ii)

have been complied with.

---

1. Regulation 4(5)(b)(i) does not come into force until 1 January 1987.

Approvals

8–12824 **5.** (1) Subject to the following provisions of this regulation, the Ministers may jointly give their approval in relation to a pesticide of any description.

(2) The Ministers' approval may be given in relation to a pesticide, in the form of—

(a) an experimental permit, to enable testing and development to be carried out with a view to providing the Ministers with safety and other data;

(b) a provisional approval, for a stipulated period; or

(c) a full approval, for an unstipulated period.

(3) Each approval may authorise the use, supply and storage of the pesticide to which it relates and a provisional approval or a full approval may in addition authorise the sale and advertisement of that pesticide.

(4) An approval may be given subject to conditions imposed when or after it is given.

(5) The Ministers may jointly, at any time—

(a) review, revoke or suspend an approval,

(b) amend the conditions of an approval.

Consents

8–12825   6. The Ministers may jointly give their consent to—

   (a)   the advertisement of pesticides, subject to the conditions specified in Schedule 1;
   (b)   the sale, supply and storage of pesticides subject to the conditions specified in Schedule 2;
   (c)   the use of pesticides, subject to—

      (i)   the conditions specified in Schedule 3, and
      (ii)   in the case of the use of pesticides by aerial application, the conditions specified in Schedule 4,

and where they have given a consent under this regulation the Ministers shall jointly publish, in such manner as they consider appropriate, a notice specifying the fact.

Seizure, disposal etc.

8–12826   7. (1) Where there has been a breach, in relation to any pesticide, of any of the specified prohibitions imposed by regulation 4, any condition of an approval or any condition of a consent given under regulation 6, either of the Ministers shall have the power—

   (a)   to seize or dispose of the pesticide or require the holder of the approval, or any other person appearing to the Minister to be the owner or the person in charge of that pesticide, to dispose of it;
   (b)   to seize or dispose of anything treated with the pesticide or require any person appearing to the Minister to be the owner or the person in charge of anything so treated to dispose of it;
   (c)   to require the holder of the approval, or any other person appearing to the Minister to be the owner or the person in charge of the pesticide, to take such remedial action as appears to that Minister to be necessary as a result of the contravention including, where it appears to be necessary as a result of the contravention, recovery of the pesticide from the market in Great Britain.

(2) If any pesticide has been imported into—

   (i)   Great Britain in contravention of any of the specified prohibitions imposed by regulation 4, any condition of an approval or any condition of a consent given under regulation 6; or
   (ii)   Northern Ireland in contravention of any of the specified prohibitions imposed by regulation 4 of the Control of Pesticides Regulations (Northern Ireland) 1987, any condition of an approval granted under regulation 5 of those Regulations or any condition of a consent given under regulation 6 of those Regulations,

either of the Ministers may, by notice in writing served on the person appearing to him to be the owner, the importer or the person in charge of the pesticide, require that it shall be exported from the United Kingdom within such period as that Minister reasonably may determine.

Release of information to the public

8–12827   8. (1) The Ministers may, at the request of any person, at such reasonable time and place as they may determine, make any evaluation held by them available to that person for inspection.

(2) The Ministers may, at the request of any person, supply that person with a copy of any evaluation held by them on payment of such fee (which may not exceed the cost reasonably attributable to the supply) as the Ministers, with the consent of the Treasury, may determine.

(3) The Ministers may, at the request of any person to whom an evaluation has been made available for inspection under paragraph (1) above or to whom a copy of an evaluation has been supplied under paragraph (2) above, make available at such reasonable time and place as they may determine for inspection by that person any study reports held by them to which the evaluation relates.

(4) No person to whom any information or document has been made available for inspection under paragraph (1) or (3), or to whom a copy of any information or document has been furnished under paragraph (2), shall make any commercial use of it nor, unless authorised in writing by the Ministers to do so, publish any part of it.

(5) In this regulation—

"commercial use", in relation to any information or document, includes the use of that information or document in any manner whatsoever in connection with the manufacture, distribution, importation, advertisement, sale, supply, storage, use or export of any pesticide but does not include the use of that information or document for the purpose of books, journals or other publications with the written authorisation of the Ministers;

"evaluation" means a written evaluation of study reports or other data examined in the course of an appraisal of the active ingredient of a pesticide leading to the giving of a full approval or provisional approval, the amendment of any conditions imposed in relation to any such approval, or the revocation of any such approval, in relation to that pesticide;

"study reports" means study reports and any other data relating to an application for a full approval or provisional approval or the continuance of any such approval including the amendment of the conditions imposed in relation to any such approval.

(6) This regulation is without prejudice to the provisions of the Environmental Information

Regulations 1992 and Article 14 of Council Directive 91/414/EEC concerning the placing of plant protection products on the market.

SCHEDULES

8–12828

Regulation 6(*a*)

SCHEDULE 1
CONDITIONS RELATING TO CONSENT TO THE ADVERTISEMENT OF PESTICIDES

1. (1) An advertisement of a pesticide shall relate only to such conditions as are permitted by the approval given in relation to that pesticide.

(2) No advertisement of a pesticide shall contain any claim for safety in relation to that pesticide which is not permitted by the approval given in relation to that pesticide to be on the label for the pesticide.

2. (1) Any advertisement of a pesticide, other than a notice at the point of sale which is intended to draw attention solely to product name and price, shall include—

(*a*) a statement of each active ingredient of each pesticide mentioned in the advertisement, such statement being the name by which each active ingredient is identified in the approval given in relation to the pesticide in which it is contained;

(*b*) a general warning as follows:

"Always read the label. Use pesticides safely"; and

(*c*) where required by a condition of the approval given in relation to a pesticide mentioned in the advertisement, a statement of any special degree of risk to human beings, creatures, plants or the environment.

(2) Notwithstanding sub-paragraph (1)(*a*) above—

(*a*) any price list consisting only of an indication of product availability and price need not state the active ingredient of each pesticide;

(*b*) any advertisement of a range of pesticides need only state the active ingredients of those individual products which are identified by name.

(3) Any statement or warning given under this paragraph shall be—

(*a*) in the case of a printed or pictorial advertisement, clearly presented separately from any other text; and

(*b*) in the case of an advertisement which is broadcast or recorded or is stored or transmitted by electronic means, clearly spoken or shown separately.

3. In this Schedule "advertisement" means any printed, pictorial, broadcast or recorded advertisement and includes any advertisement which is stored or transmitted by electronic means.

8–12829

Regulation 6(*b*)

SCHEDULE 2
CONDITIONS RELATING TO CONSENT TO THE SALE, SUPPLY AND STORAGE OF PESTICIDES

1. It shall be the duty of all employers to ensure that persons in their employment who may be required during the course of their employment to sell, supply or store pesticides are provided with such instruction, training and guidance as is necessary to enable those persons to comply with any requirements provided in and under these Regulations.

2. (1) Any person who sells, supplies or stores a pesticide shall—

(*a*) take all reasonable precautions, particularly with regard to storage and transport, to protect the health of human beings, creatures and plants, safeguard the environment and in particular avoid the pollution of water; and

(*b*) be competent for the duties which that person is called upon to perform.

(2) In this paragraph "water" means—

(*a*) any surface water;

(*b*) any ground water.

3. No person shall sell, supply or otherwise market to the end-user an approved pesticide other than in the container which has been supplied for that purpose by the holder of the approval of that pesticide and labelled in a manner consistent with the approval.

4. No person shall store for the purpose of sale or supply a pesticide approved for agricultural use in a quantity in excess of, at any one time, 200 kg or 200 litres, or a similar mixed quantity, unless that person—

(*a*) has obtained a certificate of competence recognised by the Ministers, or

(*b*) stores that pesticide under the direct supervision of a person who holds such a certificate.

5. No person shall sell, supply or otherwise market to the end-user a pesticide approved for agricultural use unless that person—

(*a*) has obtained a certificate of competence recognised by the Ministers, or

(*b*) sells or supplies that pesticide under the direct supervision of a person who holds such a certificate.

6. (1) In paragraphs 4 and 5 above "pesticide approved for agricultural use" means a pesticide (other than a pesticide with methyl bromide or chloropicrin as one of its active ingredients) approved for one or more of the following uses—

(*a*) agriculture and horticulture (including amenity horticulture);

(*b*) forestry;

(*c*) in or near water other than for amateur, public hygiene or anti-fouling uses;

(*d*) industrial herbicides, including weed-killers for use on land not intended for the production of any crop.

(2) In this paragraph "water" means any surface water.

Regulation 6(*c*)(i)   SCHEDULE 3
CONDITIONS RELATING TO CONSENT TO THE USE OF PESTICIDES

1. It shall be the duty of all employers to ensure that persons in their employment who may be required during the course of their employment to use pesticides are provided with such instruction, training and guidance as is necessary to enable those persons to comply with any requirements provided in and under these Regulations.

2. (1) Any person who uses a pesticide shall take all reasonable precautions to protect the health of human beings, creatures and plants, safeguard the environment and in particular avoid the pollution of water.

(2) In this paragraph "water" means—

(a) any surface water;
(b) any ground water.

3. No person in the course of a business or employment shall use a pesticide, or give an instruction to others on the use of a pesticide, unless that person—

(a) has received adequate instruction, training and guidance in the safe, efficient and humane use of pesticides, and
(b) is competent for the duties which that person is called upon to perform.

4. Any person who uses a pesticide shall confine the application of that pesticide to the land, crop, structure, material or other area intended to be treated.

5. (1) Subject to sub-paragraph (4) below, no person shall use a pesticide in conjunction with an adjuvant in any manner unless—

(a) that adjuvant has been specified, upon application by any person (in this paragraph 5 referred to as "the applicant") to the Ministers, in a list of adjuvants published by the Ministers from time to time (in this paragraph 5 referred to as "the list"); and
(b) the use of that pesticide with that adjuvant in that manner is in accordance with—

  (i) the conditions of the approval given in relation to that pesticide; and
  (ii) any requirements to which the use of that adjuvant with that pesticide is subject, as determined or amended under sub-paragraph (2)(*a*)(ii) or (iii) below.

(2) In the application of this paragraph—

(a) the Ministers may, in relation to any adjuvant specified in the list, at any time—

  (i) determine data requirements concerning human safety or environmental protection) to which the specification of that adjuvant in the list shall be subject;
  (ii) determine requirements to which the use of that adjuvant with approved pesticides shall be subject;
  (iii) for reasons of human safety or environmental protection, or with the consent of the applicant, amend any requirement which has been determined under sub-paragraph (ii) above;

(b) the Ministers shall, in relation to any adjuvant specified in the list, also specify in that list any requirements which they have determined or amended under paragraph (*a*)(ii) or (iii) above.

(3) In the application of this paragraph—

(a) the Ministers may, in relation to any adjuvant specified in the list, remove that adjuvant from the list—

  (i) if it appears to them that the applicant has failed to comply with any data requirement which has been determined in relation to that adjuvant under sub-paragraph (2)(*a*)(i) above;
  (ii) if it appears to them that any relevant literature relating to the adjuvant is not in accordance with any requirement to which the use of that adjuvant is subject, as determined or amended under sub-paragraph (2)(*a*)(ii) or (iii) above;
  (iii) if it appears to them that—

    (*aa*)any relevant literature relating to the adjuvant refers to a pesticide, and
    (*bb*)the use of that adjuvant with that pesticide is not in accordance with the conditions of the approval given in relation to that pesticide;

  (iv) for reasons of human safety or environmental protection;
  (v) at the request of the applicant;

(b) the Ministers shall, upon a decision to remove an adjuvant from the list specify in the list—

  (i) that decision, and
  (ii) the date on which, and any conditions in accordance with which, the removal is to take effect;

(c) "relevant literature", in relation to any adjuvant, means—

  (i) the labelling of the packaging in which the adjuvant is contained;
  (ii) any leaflet accompanying that package;
  (iii) any other literature produced by, or on behalf of, the applicant describing the adjuvant.

(4) This paragraph shall not apply where the use of an adjuvant with an approved pesticide is for the purpose of research or development and is carried out under the direct control of the person intending to place the adjuvant on the market.

(5) In this paragraph "adjuvant" means a substance other than water, without significant pesticidal properties, which enhances or is intended to enhance the effectiveness of a pesticide when it has been added to that pesticide.

6. (1) No person shall combine or mix for use two or more pesticides which are anticholinesterase compounds unless such a mixture is expressly permitted by the conditions of the approval given in relation to at least one of those pesticides or by the labelling of the container in which at least one of those pesticides has been sold, supplied or otherwise marketed to that person.

(2) No person shall combine or mix for use two or more pesticides unless—

(a) all of the conditions of approval given in relation to each of those pesticides, and
(b) the labelling of the container in which each of those pesticides has been sold, supplied or otherwise marketed to that person.

can be complied with.

7. (1) No person in the course of a commercial service shall use a pesticide approved for agricultural use unless that person—

(a) has obtained a certificate of competence recognised by the Ministers; or
(b) uses that pesticide under the direct and personal supervision of a person who holds such a certificate; or
(c) uses it in accordance with an approval, if any, for one or more of the following uses—

    (i) home garden (amateur gardening);
    (ii) animal husbandry;
    (iii) food storage practice;
    (iv) vertebrate control (including rodenticides and repellents);
    (v) domestic use;
    (vi) wood preservation;
    (vii) as a surface biocide;
    (viii) public hygiene or prevention of public nuisance;
    (ix) other industrial biocides;
    (x) as an anti-fouling product;
    (xi) "other" (as may be defined by the Ministers).

(2) In this paragraph "commercial service" means the application of a pesticide by a person—

(a) to crops, land, produce, materials, buildings or the contents of buildings not in the ownership or occupation of that person or that person's employer;
(b) to seed other than seed intended solely for use by that person or that person's employer.

8. No person who was born later than 31 December 1964 shall use a pesticide approved for agricultural use unless that person—

(a) has obtained a certificate of competence recognised by the Ministers; or
(b) uses that pesticide under the direct and personal supervision of a person who holds such a certificate; or
(c) uses it in accordance with an approval, if any, for one of the uses specified in paragraph 7(1)(c) above.

9. (1) In paragraphs 7 and 8 above "pesticide approved for agricultural use" means a pesticide (other than a pesticide with methyl bromide or chloropicrin as one of its active ingredients) approved for one or more of the following uses—

(a) agriculture and horticulture (including amenity horticulture);
(b) forestry;
(c) in or near water, other than for amateur, public hygiene or anti-fouling uses;
(d) industrial herbicides, including weed-killers for use on land not intended for the production of any crop.

(2) In this paragraph "water" means any surface water.

8–12831

Regulation 6(c)(ii)

SCHEDULE 4

CONDITIONS RELATING TO CONSENT TO THE USE OF PESTICIDES BY AERIAL APPLICATION

1. No person shall undertake an aerial application of a pesticide unless—

(a) an aerial application certificate granted under article 42(2) of the Air Navigation Order 1985 is held by that person, that person's employer or the main contractor undertaking the aerial application, and
(b) the pesticide to be used has been approved for the intended aerial application.

2. (1) No person shall undertake an aerial application of a pesticide unless that person, or a person specifically designated in writing on that person's behalf, has—

(a) not less than 72 hours before the commencement of the aerial application consulted the relevant authority if any part of land which is a Local Nature Reserve, a Marine Nature Reserve, National Nature Reserve or Site of Special Scientific Interest lies within 1500 metres of any part of the land to which that pesticide is to be applied;
(b) not less than 72 hours before the commencement of the aerial application consulted the appropriate area office of the Environment Agency (if the area in which the intended aerial application is to take place is in England and Wales) or the appropriate area office of the Scottish Environment Protection Agency (if such area is in Scotland) if the land to which that pesticide is to be applied is adjacent to, or within 250 metres of, water;
(c) obtained the consent of such office if that pesticide is to be applied for the purpose of controlling aquatic weeds or weeds on the banks of watercourses or lakes;
(d) not less than 24 hours and (so far as is practicable) not more than 48 hours before the commencement of the aerial application, given notice of the intended aerial application to the Chief Environmental Health Officer for the district in which the intended aerial application is to take place;
(e) not less than 24 hours and (so far as is reasonably practicable) not more than 48 hours before the commencement of the aerial application given notice of the intended aerial application to the occupants or their agents of all property within 25 metres of the boundary of the land to which that pesticide is to be applied;
(f) not less than 24 hours and (so far as is practicable) not more than 48 hours before the commencement of the aerial application, given notice of the intended aerial application to the person in charge of any hospital, school or other institution any part of the curtilage of which lies within 150 metres of any flight path intended to be used for the aerial application; and
(g) not less than 48 hours before the commencement of the aerial application, given notice of the intended aerial application to the appropriate reporting point of the local beekeepers' spray warning scheme operating within the district in which the intended aerial application is to take place.

(2) A notice of an intended aerial application given under paragraph (e) or (f) of sub-paragraph (1) above shall be in writing and include details of—

(a) the name and address, and telephone number (if any), of the person intending to carry out the aerial application;

(b) the name of the pesticide to be applied and its active ingredient and approval registration number;

(c) the intended time and date of application; and

(d) an indication that the same details have been served on the Chief Environmental Health Officer for the district in which the intended aerial application is to take place.

3. No person shall undertake an aerial application of a pesticide unless—

(a) the wind velocity at the height of application at the place of intended aerial application does not exceed 10 knots, except where the approval given in relation to that pesticide permits aerial application when such wind velocity exceeds 10 knots;

(b) not less than 24 hours before the aerial application, that person has provided and put in place within 60 metres of the land to which that pesticide is to be applied signs, of adequate robustness and legibility, to warn pedestrians and drivers of vehicles of the time and place of the intended aerial application; and

(c) before the aerial application that person has provided ground markers in all circumstances where a ground marker will assist the pilot to comply with the provisions of paragraph 5 below.

4. Any person who undertakes the aerial application of a pesticide shall—

(a) keep and retain for not less than 3 years after each application records of—

(i)   the nature, place and date of that application;
(ii) the registration number of the aircraft used;
(iii) the name and permanent address of the pilot of that aircraft;
(iv) the name and quantity of the pesticide applied;
(v)   the dilution and volume of application of the pesticide applied;
(vi) the type and specification of application system (which may include nozzle type and size);
(vii) the method of application;
(viii)the flight times of the aerial application;
(ix) the speed and direction of the wind during the application; and
(x)   any unusual occurrences which affected the application;

(b) provide the Ministers with summaries of the records required by sub-paragraph (a) above, in any manner which they may require under section 16(1) of the 1985 Act, within 30 days after the end of the calendar month to which those records relate.

5. The pilot of an aircraft engaged in an aerial application shall—

(a) maintain the aircraft at a height of not less than 200 feet from ground level when flying over an occupied building or its curtilage;

(b) maintain the aircraft at a horizontal distance from any occupied building and its curtilage, children's playground, sports ground or building containing livestock of—

(i) not less than 30 metres, if the pilot has the written consent of the occupier; and
(ii) not less than 60 metres, in any case;

(c) maintain the aircraft at a height of not less than 250 feet from ground level over any motorway, or of not less than 100 feet from ground level over any other public highway, unless that motorway or public highway has been closed to traffic during the course of the application.

6. For the purposes of this Schedule—

"appropriate nature conservation agency" means English Nature, Scottish Natural Heritage and the Countryside Council for Wales;

"curtilage", in relation to any building, means the land attached to, and forming one enclosure with, that building;

"ground marker" includes a person who is instructed by a person intending to carry out an aerial application to be present on or near to the land to which the pesticide is to be applied so that that person is able to communicate with the pilot of the aircraft engaged in the aerial application for the purpose of ensuring the safe application of that pesticide;

"local beekeepers' spray warning scheme" means any scheme for the advance notification of the application of pesticides, organised by local beekeepers and notified to the Minister of Agriculture, Fisheries and Food, the Secretary of State for Scotland or the Secretary of State for Wales (being the Secretaries of State respectively concerned with agriculture in Scotland and Wales);

"Local Nature Reserve" means a nature reserve established by a local authority under section 21 of the National Parks and Access to the Countryside Act 1949 and "the relevant authority" in regard to such a reserve shall be the local authority which is providing or securing the provision of the reserve;

"Marine Nature Reserve" means an area designated as such by the Secretary of State under section 36 of the Wildlife and Countryside Act 1981 and the "relevant authority" in regard to such an area shall be the appropriate nature conservation agency;

"National Nature Reserve" means any land declared as such by the appropriate nature conservation agency under section 19 of the National Parks and Access to the Countryside Act 1949, or under section 35 of the Wildlife and Countryside Act 1981, and "the relevant authority" in regard to such land shall be the appropriate nature conservation agency;

"Site of Special Scientific Interest" means any area designated as such by the appropriate nature conservation agency under section 28 of the Wildlife and Countryside Act 1981, or in respect of which the Secretary of State has made an Order under section 29 of the Wildlife and Countryside Act 1981, and "the relevant authority" in regard to such an area shall be the appropriate nature conservation agency;

"water" means any surface water.

Food Labelling Regulations 1996[1]

(SI 1996/1499 as amended by SI 1998/141, 1998/1398 and 1998/2424, SI 1999/747, 1999/ 1136, 1999/1483 and 1999/1540, SI 2000/768, 2254 and 3290, SI 2001/60, 1232 and 1787 and 1440 (Wales), SI 2002/330 (Wales) and 379 (England), SI 2003/461, 474, 666 (E), 832 (W), 1182 (E), 1563 (E), 1564 (E), 1596 (E), 1659 (E), 2075 (E), 2243 (E), 2647 (E), 3037 (W), 3044 (W), 3047 (W), 3053 (W) and 3122 (E) and SI 2004/249 (W), 553 (W), 1396 (W), 1512 (E), 2145 (E), 2558 (W), 2731 (W), 2824 (E) and 3022 (W), SI 2005/899, 1309 (W), 2057 (E), 2626 (E), 2835 (W) (amended by 3236 (W)) and 2969 and SI 2006/14 and 31 (W))

PART I
PRELIMINARY

8–13000   **1.** *Title and commencement*

---

1. Made by the Minister of Agriculture, Fisheries and Food, the Secretary of State for Health and the Secretary of State for Wales in exercise of the powers conferred on them by ss 6(4), 16(1)(*e*) and (*f*), 17 (1), 26 (1) and (3) and 48(1) of the Food Safety Act 1990.

8–13001   **2. Interpretation.**   (1) In these Regulations, unless the context otherwise requires—

"the Act" means the Food Safety Act 1990;

"additive" means any substance not normally consumed as a food in itself and not normally used as a characteristic ingredient of food, whether or not it has nutritive value, the intentional addition of which to a food for a technological purpose in the manufacture, processing, preparation, treatment, packaging, transport or storage of such food results, or may be reasonably expected to result, in it or its by-products becoming directly or indirectly a component of such foods;

"the additives regulations" means the Flavourings in Food Regulations 1992, the Food Additives Labelling Regulations 1992, the Sweeteners in Food Regulations 1995, the Colours in Food Regulations 1995 and the Miscellaneous Food Additives Regulations 1995;

"advertisement" includes any notice, circular, invoice or other document, and any public announcement made orally or by any means of producing or transmitting light or sound, but does not include any form of labelling, and "advertise" shall be construed accordingly;

"allergenic ingredient" means an ingredient referred to in Schedule AA1;

"appropriate durability indication" means—

(*a*) in the case of a food other than one specified in sub-paragraph (*b*) of this definition, an indication of minimum durability, and

(*b*) in the case of a food which, from the microbiological point of view, is highly perishable and in consequence likely after a short period to constitute an immediate danger to human health, a "use by" date;

"aromatised wine" has the meaning assigned to it by Article 2 of Council Regulation (EEC) No 1601/91[1];

"biscuits" includes wafers, rusks, oatcakes and matzos;

"the Bread and Flour Regulations" means the Bread and Flour Regulations 1998;

"carbohydrate" means any carbohydrate which is metabolised in man and includes polyols;

"catering establishment" means a restaurant, canteen, club, public house, school, hospital or similar establishment (including a vehicle or a fixed or mobile stall) where, in the course of a business, food is prepared for delivery to the ultimate consumer and is ready for consumption without further preparation;

"cheese" means the fresh or matured product intended for sale for human consumption, which is obtained as follows—

(*a*) in the case of any cheese other than whey cheese, by the combining, by coagulation or by any technique involving coagulation, of any of the following substances, namely milk, cream, skimmed milk, partly skimmed milk, concentrated skimmed milk, reconstituted dried milk, butter milk, materials obtained from milk, other ingredients necessary for the manufacture of cheese provided that those are not used for replacing, in whole or in part, any milk constituent, with or without partially draining the whey resulting from coagulation;

(*b*) in the case of whey cheese—

(i) by concentrating whey with or without the addition of milk and milk fat, and moulding such concentrated whey, or

(ii) by coagulating whey with or without the addition of milk and milk fat;

"chocolate product" has the meaning assigned to it by the Cocoa and Chocolate Products Regulations 1976;

"clotted cream" means cream which has been produced and separated by the scalding, cooling and skimming of milk or cream;

"cream" means that part of cows' milk rich in fat which has been separated by skimming or otherwise and which is intended for sale for human consumption;

"cocoa product" has the meaning assigned to it by the Cocoa and Chocolate Products Regulations 1976;

"Community controlled wine" means wine, grape must, sparkling wine, aerated sparkling wine, liqueur wine, semi-sparkling wine and aerated semi-sparkling wine;

"confectionery product" means any item of chocolate confectionery or sugar confectionery;

"Directive 79/112" means Council Directive 79/112/EEC on the approximation of the laws of the Member States relating to the labelling, presentation and advertising of foodstuffs, as read in accordance with Schedule A1 and Commission Directive 1999/10/EC providing for derogations from the provisions of Article 7 of Council Directive 79/112/EEC as regards the labelling of foodstuffs;

"Directive 87/250" means Commission Directive 87/250/EEC on the indication of alcoholic strength by volume in the labelling of alcoholic beverages for sale to the ultimate consumer;

"Directive 89/398" means Council Directive 89/398/EEC on the approximation of the laws of the Member States relating to foodstuffs intended for particular nutritional uses;

"Directive 90/496" means Council Directive 90/496/EEC on nutrition labelling for foodstuffs, as amended by Commission Directive 2003/120/EC;*

"Directive 94/54" means Commission Directive 94/54/EC concerning the compulsory indication on the labelling of certain foodstuffs of particulars other than those provided for in Directive 2003/120/EC, as amended by Council Directive 96/21/EC and Commission Directive 2004/77/EC;

"Directive 99/2" means European Parliament and Council Directive 1999/2/EC on the approximation of the laws of the member States concerning foods and food ingredients treated with ionising radiation;

"Directive 2000/13" means Directive 2000/13/EC of the European Parliament and of the Council on the approximation of the laws of the Member States relating to the labelling, presentation and advertising of foodstuffs, as corrected by a corrigendum published on 25th May 2000, and as amended by Commission Directive 2001/101/EC, which was itself amended by Commission Directive 2002/86/EC, the Act concerning the conditions of accession of the Czech Republic, the Republic of Estonia, the Republic of Cyprus, the Republic of Latvia, the Republic of Lithuania, the Republic of Hungary, the Republic of Malta, the Republic of Poland, the Republic of Slovenia and the Slovak Republic and the adjustments to the Treaties on which the European Union is founded and Directive 2003/89/EC of the European Parliament and of the Council, and as read with Commission Directive 99/10/EC providing for derogations from the provisions of Article 7 of Directive 2000/13/EC, Commission Directive 2002/67/EC on the labelling of foodstuffs containing quinine, and of foodstuffs containing caffeine and Commission Directive 2005/26/EC establishing a list of food ingredients or substances provisionally excluded from Annex IIIa of Directive 2000/13/EC which was itself amended by Commission Directive 2005/63/EC;

"disease" includes any injury, ailment or adverse condition, whether of body or mind;

"edible ice" includes ice-cream, water ice and fruit ice, whether alone or in combination, and any similar food;

"EEA Agreement" means the Agreement on the European Economic Area[2] signed at Oporto on 2nd May 1992 as adjusted by the Protocol[3] signed at Brussels on 17th March 1993;

"EEA State" means a state which is a Contracting Party to the EEA Agreement;

"fancy confectionery product" means any confectionery product in the form of a figure, animal, cigarette or egg or in any other fancy form;

"fat", in the context of nutrition labelling, means total lipids, and includes phospholipids;

the noun "flavouring" means an additive consisting of material used or intended for use in or on food to impart odour, taste or both, provided that such material does not consist entirely of—

    (a) any edible substance (including herbs and spices) or product, intended for human consumption as such, with or without reconstitution, or

    (b) any substance which has exclusively a sweet, sour or salt taste,

and the components of which include at least one of the following—

    (i) a flavouring substance,
    (ii) a flavouring preparation,
    (iii) a process flavouring,
    (iv) a smoke flavouring;

"flavouring preparation" means a product (other than a flavouring substance), whether concentrated or not, with flavouring properties, which is obtained by physical, enzymatic or microbiological processes from appropriate material of vegetable or animal origin;

"flavouring substance" means a chemical substance with flavouring properties the chemical structure of which has been established by methods normally used among scientists and which is—

    (a) obtained by physical, enzymatic or microbiological processes from appropriate material of vegetable or animal origin,

(b) either obtained by chemical synthesis or isolated by chemical processes and which is chemically identical to a substance naturally present in appropriate material of vegetable or animal origin, or

(c) obtained by chemical synthesis but not included under sub-paragraph (b) of this definition,

and for the purposes of this definition and the definition of "flavouring preparation"—

(i) distillation and solvent extraction shall be regarded as included among types of physical process;

(ii) material of vegetable or animal origin is appropriate material of vegetable or animal origin if it either is raw or has been subjected to a process normally used in preparing food for human consumption and to no process other than one normally so used; and

(iii) drying, torrefaction and fermentation shall be treated as included among the types of process normally so used to which sub-paragraph (ii) above refers.

"flour confectionery" means any cooked food which is ready for consumption without further preparation (other than reheating), of which a characterising ingredient is ground cereal, including shortbread, sponges, crumpets, muffins, macaroons, ratafias, pastry and pastry cases, and also includes meringues, petits fours and uncooked pastry and pastry cases, but does not include bread, pizzas, biscuits, crispbread, extruded flat bread or any food containing a filling which has as an ingredient any cheese, meat, offal, fish, shellfish, vegetable protein material or microbial protein material;

"follow-on formula" has the meaning assigned to it by the Infant Formula and Follow-on Formula Regulations 1995;

"food for a particular nutritional use" means a food intended for human consumption which—

(a) owing to its special composition or process of manufacture, is clearly distinguishable from food intended for normal human consumption,

(b) is suitable for its claimed particular nutritional purpose, and

(c) is sold in such a way as to indicate that suitability;

"grape must" has the meaning assigned to it by Annex I to Council Regulation (EEC) No 822/87[4] on the common organisation of the market in wine;

"infants" means children under the age of twelve months;

"infant formula" has the meaning assigned to it by the Infant Formula and Follow-on Formula Regulations 1995;

"ingredient" means any substance, including any additive and any constituent of a compound ingredient, which is used in the preparation of a food and which is still present in the finished product, even if in altered form, and a "compound ingredient" shall be composed of two or more such substances;

"intense sweetener" means an additive with a sweetness many times that of sucrose, which is virtually non-calorific and used solely for its sweetening properties;

"ionising radiation" means any gamma rays, x-rays or corpuscular radiations which are capable of producing ions either directly or indirectly other than those rays or radiations—

(a) which are emitted by measuring or inspection devices,

(b) which are emitted at an energy level no higher than the appropriate maximum level, and

(c) the dose of energy imparted by which does not exceed 0.01 Gy in the case of inspection devices which utilise neutrons and 0.1 Gy in the case of inspection devices which utilise neutrons and 0.5 GY otherwise,

and for the purposes of this definition the appropriate maximum level is 10 MeV in the case of x-rays, 14 MeV in the case of neutrons and 5 MeV otherwise;

"irradiated" means subjected to treatment by ionising radiation;

"labelling", in relation to a food, includes any words, particulars, trade mark, brand name, pictorial matter or symbol relating to the food and appearing on the packaging of the food or on any document, notice, label, ring or collar accompanying the food;

"liqueur wine"—

(a) in relation to a drink produced in the European Community, has the meaning assigned to it by Annex I to Council Regulation (EEC) No 822/87, and

(b) in relation to a drink originating from elsewhere, has the meaning assigned to it by Article 2 of Council Regulation (EEC) No 2391/89[5];

"meat product" has the meaning assigned to it by the Meat Products (England) Regulations 2003;*

"milk" means the milk intended for sale, or sold, for human consumption of—

(a) one or more cows, and includes skimmed milk, semi-skimmed milk and whole milk, or

(b) one or more ewes, goats or buffaloes;

"mono-unsaturates" means fatty acids with one cis double bond;

"natural mineral water" has the meaning assigned to it by the Natural Mineral Water, Spring Water and Bottled Drinking Water Regulations 1999[6];

"nutrient", in the context of nutrition labelling, means any of the following: protein, carbohydrate, fat, fibre, sodium, any vitamin or mineral listed in Table A or B in Schedule 6 and present in any food in a significant amount as described in the Note to those Tables;

"nutrition claim" means any statement, suggestion or implication in any labelling, presentation or advertising of a food that that food has particular nutrition properties, but does not include a reference to any quality or quantity of any nutrient where such reference is required by law;

"nutrition labelling", in relation to a food (other than a natural mineral water or other water intended for human consumption or any food supplement) means any information appearing on labelling (other than where such appears solely as part of a list of ingredients) and relating to energy value or any nutrient or to energy value and any nutrient, including any information relating to any substance which belongs to, or is a component of, a nutrient;

"nutrition properties" means either or both of—

(a) the provision (including provision at a reduced or increased rate), or the lack of provision, of energy,

(b) the content (including content in a reduced or increased proportion), or the lack of content, of any nutrient (including any substance which belongs to, or is a component of, a nutrient);

"particular nutritional purpose" means the fulfilment of the particular nutritional requirements of—

(a) a person whose digestive processes are, or whose metabolism is, disturbed, or

(b) a person whose physiological condition renders him able to obtain a special benefit from the controlled consumption of any substance in food, or

(c) infants or young children in good health;

"polyunsaturates" means fatty acids with cis, cis-methylene interrupted double bonds;

"prepacked", in relation to a food, means put into packaging before being offered for sale in such a way that the food, whether wholly or only partly enclosed, cannot be altered without opening or changing the packaging and is ready for sale to the ultimate consumer or to a catering establishment, and includes a food which is wholly enclosed in packaging before being offered for sale and which is intended to be cooked without opening the packaging and which is ready for sale to the ultimate consumer or to a catering establishment, but does not include individually wrapped sweets or chocolates which are not enclosed in any further packaging and which are not intended for sale as individual items;

"prepacked for direct sale", means—

(a) in relation to a food other than flour confectionery, bread, edible ices and cows' milk, prepacked by a retailer for sale by him on the premises where the food is packed or from a vehicle or stall used by him,

(b) in relation to flour confectionery, bread and edible ices, prepacked by a retailer for sale as in sub-paragraph (a) of this definition, or prepacked by the producer of the food for sale by him either on the premises where the food is produced or on other premises from which he conducts business under the same name as the business conducted on the premises where the food is produced, and

(c) in relation to cows' milk, put into containers on the premises where the milk is produced by the person owning or having control of the herd from which the milk is produced for sale by him on those premises or from a vehicle or stall used by him;

"preparation", in relation to food, includes manufacture and any form of processing or treatment, and "prepared" shall be construed accordingly;

"prescribed nutrition labelling" means nutrition labelling given in accordance with Schedule 7;

"processing aid" means any substance not consumed as a food by itself, intentionally used in the processing of raw materials, foods or their ingredients, to fulfil a certain technological purpose during treatment or processing, and which may result in the unintentional but technically unavoidable presence of residues of the substance or its derivatives in the final product, provided that these residues do not present any health risk and do not have any technological effect on the finished product;

"process flavouring" means a product which is obtained according to good manufacturing practices by heating to a temperature not exceeding 180 degrees C for a continuous period not exceeding 15 minutes a mixture of ingredients (whether or not with flavouring properties) of which at least one contains nitrogen (amino) and another is a reducing sugar;

"protein" means the protein content calculated using the formula: protein = total Kjeldahl nitrogen x 6.25;

"raw milk", in relation to cows' milk, has the meaning assigned to it by Article 3(1) of Council Regulation (EC) No 2597/97[7] laying down additional rules on the common organisation of the market in milk and milk products for drinking milk, and in relation to the milk of ewes, goats or buffaloes means milk which has neither been heat-treated beyond 40 degrees C nor undergone any treatment having the same effect;

"recommended daily allowance", in relation to a vitamin or mineral, means the recommended daily allowance specified for that vitamin or mineral in column 2 of Table A or B in Schedule 6;

"saturates" means fatty acids without double bond;

"seasonal selection pack" means a pack consisting of two or more different items of food which are wholly or partly enclosed in outer packaging decorated with seasonal designs;

"sell" includes offer or expose for sale and have in possession for sale, and "sale" and "sold" shall be construed accordingly;

"semi-skimmed milk", in relation to cows' milk, has the meaning assigned to it by Article 3(1) of Council Regulation (EC) No 2597/97;

"skimmed milk", in relation to cows' milk, has the meaning assigned to it by Article 3(1) of Council Regulation (EC) No 2597/97;

"smoke flavouring" means an extract from smoke of a type normally used in food smoking processes;

"sparkling wine", "aerated sparkling wine", "semi-sparkling wine" and "aerated semi-sparkling wine"—

(a) in relation to drinks produced in the European Community, have the meanings respectively assigned to them by Annex I to Council Regulation (EEC) No 822/87, and

(b) in relation to drinks produced elsewhere, have the meanings respectively assigned to them by Article 2 of Council Regulation (EEC) No 2391/89;

"sterilised cream" means cream which has been subjected to a process of sterilisation by heat treatment in the container in which it is to be supplied to the consumer;

"sugars", in the context of nutrition labelling, means all monosaccharides and disaccharides present in food, but excludes polyols;

"treating", in relation to disease, includes doing or providing anything for alleviating the effects of the disease, whether it is done or provided by way of cure or not;

"ultimate consumer" means any person who buys otherwise than—

(a) for the purpose of resale,

(b) for the purposes of a catering establishment, or

(c) for the purposes of a manufacturing business;

"whole milk", in relation to cows' milk, has the meaning assigned to it by Article 3(1) of Council Regulation (EC) No 2597/97;

"wine" has the meaning assigned to it by Annex I to Council Regulation (EEC) No 822/87;

"young children" means children aged between one and three years.

(2) Unless the context otherwise requires, all proportions mentioned in these Regulations are proportions calculated by weight.

(3) Any reference in these Regulations to a numbered regulation or Schedule shall, unless the context otherwise requires, be construed as a reference to the regulation or Schedule so numbered in these Regulations.

(4) Where any Schedule to these Regulations contains any note or notes, the provisions of that Schedule shall be interpreted and applied in accordance with such note or notes.

---

*In relation to Wales the reference is to the Meat Products (Wales) Regulations 2004.

1. OJ No L149, 14.6.91, p 1; there is an amendment to the Council Regulation which is not relevant to these Regulations.

2. OJ No L1, 3.1.94, p 1.

3. OJ No L1, 3.1.94, p 571.

4. OJ No L84, 27.3.87, p 1, to which there are amendments not relevant to these Regulations.

5. OJ No L232, 9.8.89, p 10.

6. SI 1999/1540.

7. OJ No I351, 23.12.97, p 13.

8–13002 **3. Exemptions.** (1) Subject to paragraph (1A) of this regulation, these Regulations shall not apply in respect of—

(a) any food to which the provisions of the EEA Agreement apply brought into Great Britain from an EEA State in which it was lawfully produced and sold;

(b) any food lawfully produced in another member State brought into Great Britain from a member State in which it was lawfully sold; or

(c) any food lawfully produced outside the European Community brought into Great Britain from a member State in which it was in free circulation and lawfully sold,

if—

(i) the requirements of Article 2 of Directive 2003/13 are met in respect of that food;

(ii) that food is marked or labelled, in a language easily understood by the consumer, with the particulars provided for in Articles 3 and 4(2) of that Directive;

(iii) the name of the food and any other descriptive information accompanying it is in accordance with Article 5(1) of that Directive; and

(iv) where applicable, the requirements of Directive 87/250, Directive 89/398, Directive 90/496, Directive 94/54 and Directive 99/2 are met in respect of that food.

(1A) Nothing in paragraph (1) of this regulation shall prevent the enforcement of—

(a) regulation 44(1)(a) in relation to a contravention of regulation 31; or

(aa) regulation 44(1)(a) in relation to a contravention of regulation 34B concerning any prepacked food either contained in an indelibly marked glass bottle intended for re-use and having no label, ring or collar, or the largest surface of whose packaging has an area of less than ten square centimetres; or

   (b) regulation 44(1)(*c*), (*d*) or (*e*).

(2) For the purposes of paragraph (1) of this regulation "free circulation" has the same meaning as in Article 9.2 of the Treaty establishing the European Community.

(3) These Regulations, except in so far as they relate to advertising, shall not apply to any food which is—

   (a) not intended for sale for human consumption, or
   (b) supplied under Government contracts for consumption by Her Majesty's forces or supplied for consumption by a visiting force within the meaning of any of the provisions of Part I of the Visiting Forces Act 1952, and was prepared and labelled for sale before 16th November 1992.

(4) Subject to paragraph (5) of this regulation, regulation 29 and Part III of these Regulations shall not apply to natural mineral water (other than such water which has been artificially carbonated).

   (5) Regulations 40 and 41 shall apply to natural mineral water in so far as they relate to item 1 in Part II of Schedule 6, and regulation 42(1) shall apply to such water in so far as it relates to the descriptions "dietary" and "dietetic" in Schedule 8.

PART II

FOOD TO BE DELIVERED AS SUCH TO THE ULTIMATE CONSUMER OR TO CATERERS

Scope and general labelling requirement

8–13003   4. Scope of Part II.   (1) Subject to paragraphs (2) and (3) of this regulation, this Part of these Regulations applies to food which is ready for delivery to the ultimate consumer or to a catering establishment.

(2) Except for regulations 33 and 34 and, insofar as they relate to regulations 33 and 34, regulations 35 and 38, this Part of these Regulations does not apply to—

   (a) *revoked*
   (b) *revoked*
   (c) *revoked*
   (d) *revoked*
   (e) *revoked*
   (f) hen eggs, in so far as their labelling is regulated by Council Regulation (EEC) No 1907/90[1] on certain marketing standards for eggs, as amended[2], Commission Regulation (EEC) No 1274/91[3] introducing detailed rules for implementing Regulation (EEC) No 1907/90, as amended[4], and Council Decision 94/371/EC[5] laying down specific public health conditions for the putting on the market of certain types of eggs;
   (g) spreadable fats, in so far as their labelling is regulated by Council Regulation (EC) No 2991/94[6] laying down standards for spreadable fats;
   (h) wines or grape musts, in so far as their labelling is regulated by Council Regulation (EEC) No 2392/89[7] laying down general rules for the description and presentation of wines and grape musts, as amended[8];
   (i) sparkling wines and aerated sparkling wines, in so far as their labelling is regulated by Council Regulation (EEC) No 2333/92[9] laying down general rules for the description and presentation of sparkling wines and aerated sparkling wines;
   (j) liqueur wines, semi-sparkling wines and aerated semi-sparkling wines, in so far as their labelling is regulated by Council Regulation (EEC) No 3895/91[10] laying down rules for the description and presentation of special wines, and Commission Regulation (EEC) No 3901/91[11] laying down certain detailed rules on the description and presentation of special wines;
   (k) any spirit drinks, in so far as their labelling is regulated by Council Regulation (EEC) No 1576/89[12] laying down general rules on the definition, description and presentation of spirit drinks, Commission Regulation (EEC) No 3773/89[13] laying down transitional measures relating to spirituous beverages, as amended[14], and Commission Regulation (EEC) No 1014/90[15] laying down detailed implementing rules on the definition, description and presentation of spirit drinks, as amended[16];
   (l) fresh fruit and vegetables, in so far as their labelling is regulated by Council Regulation (EC) No 2200/96[17] on the common organisation of the market in fruit and vegetables;
   (m) preserved sardines, in so far as their labelling is regulated by Council Regulation (EEC) No 2136/89[18] laying down common marketing standards for preserved sardines;
   (n) preserved tuna and bonito, in so far as their labelling is regulated by Council Regulation (EEC) No 1536/92[19] laying down common marketing standards for preserved tuna and bonito;
   (o) any additive sold as such which is required to be labelled in accordance with regulation 4(3) of the Extraction Solvents in Food Regulations 1993, or the appropriate provisions of any of the additives regulations.

(3) This Part of these Regulations does not apply to—

   (a) any drink bottled before 1st January 1983 which has an alcoholic strength by volume of more than 1.2 per cent and which is labelled in accordance with the legislation in force at the time of bottling;

(*b*) any food prepared on domestic premises for sale for the benefit of the person preparing it by a society registered under the Industrial and Provident Societies Act 1965;

(*c*) any food prepared otherwise than in the course of a business carried on by the person preparing it.

---

1. OJ No L173, 6.7.90, p 5 as read with Corrigendum at OJ No L195, 26.7. 90, p 40.

2. Council Regulation (EEC) No 2617/93 (OJ No L240, 25.9.93, p 1) and Council Regulation (EC) No 3117/94 (OJ No L330, 12.12.94, p 4).

3. OJ No L121, 16.5.91, p 11.

4. Commission Regulation (EEC) No 3540/91 (OJ No L335, 6.12.91, p 12), Commission Regulation (EEC) No 2221/92 (OJ No L218, 1.8.92, p 81, as read with Corrigendum at OJ No L292, 8.10.92, p 34), Commission Regulation (EC) No 3300/93 (OJ No L296, 1.12.93, p 52), Commission Regulation (EC) No 1259/94 (OJ No L137, 1.6.94, p 54), Commission Regulation (EC) No 3239/94 (OJ No L338, 28.12.94, p 48), Commission Regulation (EC) No 786/95 (OJ L79, 7.4.95, p 12) and Commission Regulation (EC) No 2401/95 (OJ No L246, 13.10.95, p 6).

5. OJ No L168, 2.7.94, p 34.

6. OJ No L316, 9.12.94, p 2.

7. OJ No L232, 9.8.89, p 3.

8. Council Regulation (EEC) No 3886/89 (OJ No L378, 27.12. 89, p 12) and Council Regulation (EEC) No 3897/91 (OJ No L386, 3.12.91, p 5).

9. OJ No L231, 13.8. 92, p 9.

10. OJ No L368, 31.12.91, p 1.

11. OJ No L368, 31.12.91, p 15.

12. OJ No L160, 12.6.89, p 1.

13. OJ No L365, 15.12.89, p 48.

14. Commission Regulation (EEC) No 1759/90 (OJ No L162, 28.6.90, p 23), Commission Regulation (EEC) No 3207/90 (OJ No L307, 7.11.90, p 11), and Commission Regulation (EEC) No 3750/90 (OJ No L360, 22.12.90, p 40).

15. OJ No L105, 25.4.90, p 9.

16. Commission Regulation (EEC) No 1180/91 (OJ No L115, 8.5.91, p 5), Commission Regulation (EEC) No 1785/91 (OJ No L160, 25.6.91, p 5), and Commission Regulation (EEC) No 3458/92 (OJ No L350, 1.12.92, p 59).

17. OJ No L297, 2.11.96, p 1.

18. OJ No L212, 22.7.89, p 79.

19. OJ No L163, 17.6.92, p 1.

8–13004 5. General labelling requirement. Subject to the following provisions of this Part of these Regulations, all food to which this Part of these Regulations applies shall be marked or labelled with—

(*a*) the name of the food;

(*b*) a list of ingredients;

(*bA*)the quantity of certain ingredients or categories of ingredients;

(*c*) the appropriate durability indication;

(*d*) any special storage conditions or conditions of use;

(*e*) the name or business name and an address or registered office of either or both of—

(i) the manufacturer or packer, or

(ii) a seller established within the European Community;

(*f*) particulars of the place of origin or provenance of the food if failure to give such particulars might mislead a purchaser to a material degree as to the true origin or provenance of the food; and

(*g*) instructions for use if it would be difficult to make appropriate use of the food in the absence of such instructions.

8–13005

Name of the food

6. Name prescribed by law. (1) If there is a name prescribed by law for a food, that is to say if a particular name is required to be used for the food, that name shall be used as the name of the food.

(2) The name used for food specified in Schedule 1 shall be the name required by that Schedule.

(3) A name that is required to be used for a food by paragraph (1) or (2) of this regulation may be qualified by other words which make it more precise, unless such qualification is prohibited.

(4) In paragraph (1) of this regulation and in regulations 7 and 8(*a*) and Schedule 1, "prescribed by law" means prescribed by European Community law or, in the absence of such law, by law in Great Britain.

8–13006 7. Customary name. If there is no name prescribed by law for a food, a customary name, that is to say a name which is customary in the area where the food is sold, may be used for the food.

8–13007 8. Indication of true nature of food. If—

(*a*) there is no name prescribed by law for a food, and

(*b*) there is no customary name or the customary name is not used,

the name used for the food shall be sufficiently precise[1] to inform a purchaser of the true nature of the food and to enable the food to be distinguished from products with which it could be confused and, if necessary, shall include a description of its use.

---

1. Since regulation 10, post, provides that a trade mark or brand name shall not be substituted for the name of a food, it was held that the names "Coca Cola" and "Sprite" on cans, on which the rest of the words on the labels were in Dutch, were not sufficiently precise to inform a purchaser of the true nature of the food and to enable the food to be distinguished from products with which it could be confused (*Hackney London Borough v Cedar Trading Ltd* (1999) 163 JP 749).

8–13008   9. Form of name.   The name of a food may consist of a name or description or of a name and description and it may contain more than one word.

8–13009   10. Trade marks, brand names and fancy names.   A trade mark, brand name or fancy name shall not be substituted for the name of a food.

8–13010   11. Indication of physical condition or treatment.   (1) Where a purchaser could be misled by the omission of an indication—

   (a)   that a food is powdered or is in any other physical condition, or
   (b)   that a food has been dried, freeze-dried, frozen, concentrated or smoked, or has been subjected to any other treatment,

the name of the food shall include or be accompanied by such an indication.

(2) Without prejudice to the generality of paragraph (1) of this regulation, the name used for a food specified in Schedule 2 shall include or be accompanied by such indication as is required by that Schedule.

List of ingredients

8–13011   12. Heading of list of ingredients.   The list of ingredients must be headed or preceded by an appropriate heading which consists of or includes the word "ingredients".

8–13012   13. Order of list of ingredients.   (1) Subject to the following paragraphs of this regulation, when a food is marked or labelled with a list of ingredients, the ingredients shall be listed in descending order of weight determined as at the time of their use in the preparation of the food.

(2) Subject to regulation 16, water and volatile products which are added as ingredients of a food shall be listed in order of their weight in the finished product, the weight being calculated in the case of water by deducting from the total weight of the finished product the total weight of the other ingredients used.

(3) In the case of an ingredient which is used in a food in concentrated or dehydrated form and which is reconstituted during preparation of the food, the weight used in determining the order of the list of ingredients may be the weight of the ingredient before concentration or dehydration.

(4) Without prejudice to regulation 12, where a food is in concentrated or dehydrated form and is intended to be reconstituted by the addition of water, its ingredients may be listed in descending order of their weight in the food when reconstituted as directed if the heading of the list of ingredients includes or is accompanied by the words "ingredients of the reconstituted product" or "ingredients of the ready to use product" or by some other indication to similar effect.

(5) Where a food consists of, or contains, mixed fruit, vegetables or mushrooms which are used in proportions that are likely to vary and no particular fruit, vegetable or mushroom predominates significantly by weight, those ingredients may be grouped together in the list of ingredients under the designation "fruit", "vegetables" or "mushrooms" followed by the phrase "in varying proportions", followed by a list of the fruit, vegetables or mushrooms present; and in such a case the total weight of the fruit, vegetables or mushrooms shall determine the order in which this entry appears in the list of ingredients.

(6) Where a food consists of, or contains, mixed spices or herbs and no particular spice or herb predominates significantly by weight, those ingredients may be listed otherwise than in descending order of weight if—

   (a)   in the case of a food which consists entirely of such a mixture, the heading of the list of ingredients includes or is accompanied by the words "in variable proportion" or other words indicating the nature of the order in which the ingredients are listed; and
   (b)   in the case of a food which contains such a mixture, that part of the list where the names of those ingredients appear is accompanied by the words "in variable proportion" or other words indicating the nature of the order in which those ingredients are listed.

(7) Ingredients constituting less than 2 per cent of the finished product may be listed in a different order after the other ingredients.

(8) In the case of ingredients which—

   (a)   are similar or mutually substitutable;
   (b)   are likely to be used in the preparation of a food without altering its composition, its nature or its perceived value;
   (c)   are not additives or allergenic ingredients or ingredients originating from an allergenic ingredient referred to in paragraphs 1 to 11 in Schedule AA1 other than, until 25th

November 2007, ingredients which originate from an allergenic ingredient and are listed in column 2 of Schedule 2A in relation to that allergenic ingredient; and

(d) constitute less than 2 per cent of the finished product,

such ingredients may be referred to in the list of ingredients by the phrase "contains. . . .and/or. . ..", where at least one of no more than two such ingredients is present in the finished product.

8–13013 14. Names of ingredients. (1) Subject to the following paragraphs of this regulation, the name used for any ingredient in a list of ingredients shall be a name which, if the ingredient in question were itself being sold as a food, could be used as the name of the food.

(2) The name used in any list of ingredients for any food which has been irradiated shall include or be accompanied by the word "irradiated" or the words "treated with ionising radiation".

(3) Where in any case other than one to which paragraph (2) of this regulation applies a purchaser could be misled by the omission from the name used for an ingredient of any indication which, if the ingredient were itself being sold as a food, would be required to be included in or to accompany the name of the food, the name used for the ingredient in a list of ingredients shall include or be accompanied by that indication unless the provision requiring the indication provides to the contrary.

(4) Subject to regulation 34B a generic name which is listed in or referred to in column 1 of Part I of Schedule 3 may be used for an ingredient which is specified in the corresponding entry in column 2 of that Part of Schedule 3 in accordance with any conditions that are laid down in the corresponding entry in column 3 of that Part of Schedule 3.

(5) Subject to paragraph (5A) of this regulation and regulation 34B where an ingredient being a flavouring is added to or used in a food it shall be identified by either—

(a) the word "flavouring" or, where more than one such ingredient is used, "flavourings", or

(b) a more specific name or description of the flavouring (or flavourings).

(5A) In the case of quinine or caffeine added to or used in a food as a flavouring, quinine or caffeine (as appropriate) shall be identified by name immediately after the word "flavouring".

(6) The word "natural", or any other word having substantially the same meaning, may be used for an ingredient being a flavouring only where the flavouring component (or components) of such an ingredient consists (or consist) exclusively of—

(a) a flavouring substance (or flavouring substances) which is (or are) obtained, by physical, enzymatic or microbiological processes, from material of vegetable or animal origin which material is either raw or has been subjected to a process normally used in preparing food for human consumption and to no process other than one normally so used,

(b) a flavouring preparation (or flavouring preparations), or

(c) both (a) and (b) above.

(7) If the name of an ingredient being a flavouring refers to the vegetable or animal nature or origin of the material which it incorporates, the word "natural", or any other word having substantially the same meaning, may not be used for that ingredient unless, in addition to satisfying the requirements of paragraph (6) of this regulation, the flavouring component (or components) of that ingredient has (or have) been isolated by physical, enzymatic or microbiological processes, or by a process normally used in preparing food for human consumption, solely or almost solely from that vegetable or animal source.

(8) In paragraphs (6) and (7) of this regulation—

(a) distillation and solvent extraction shall be regarded as included among types of physical process, and

(b) drying, torrefaction and fermentation shall be treated as included among the types of process normally used in preparing food for human consumption.

(9) Subject to reguation 34B an additive which is added to or used in a food to serve the function of one of the categories of additives listed in Schedule 4 shall be identified by the name of that category followed by the additive's specific name or serial number (if any). An additive which is added to or used in a food to serve more than one such function shall be identified by the name of the category that represents the principal function served by the additive in that food followed by the additive's specific name or serial number (if any).

(10) An additive which is required to be named in the list of ingredients of a food and which is neither a flavouring nor serves the function of one of the categories of additives listed in Schedule 4 shall be identified by its specific name.

(11) In this regulation "serial number" means the number specified for an additive in any of the additive regulations.

8–13014 15. Compound ingredients. (1) Subject to paragraphs (3) and (4) of this regulation, where a compound ingredient is used in the preparation of a food, the names of the ingredients of the compound ingredient shall be given in the list of ingredients of the food either instead of or in addition to the name of the compound ingredient itself.

(2) If the name of a compound ingredient is given, it shall be immediately followed by the names of its ingredients in such a way as to make it clear that they are ingredients of that compound ingredient.

(3) Subject to regulation 34B, the names of the ingredients of a compound ingredient need not

be given in a case where the compound ingredient would not be required to be marked or labelled with a list of ingredients if it were itself being sold prepacked as a food.

(4) Subject to regulation 34B, the names of the ingredients of a compound ingredient need not be given in a case where—

(a) the compound ingredient is identified in the list of ingredients by a generic name in accordance with regulation 14(4), or

(b) subject to paragraphs (5) and (6), the composition of the compound ingredient is defined in Community legislation and the compound ingredient constitutes less than 2 per cent of the finished product; or

(c) subject to paragraphs (5) and (6), the compound ingredient consists of a mixture of spices or herbs or both and constitutes less than 2 per cent of the finished product.

(5) Subject to regulation 17, any additive which is an ingredient of such a compound ingredient as is mentioned in paragraph (4)(b) or (c) shall be named in the list of ingredients in accordance with paragraph (2).

(6) Where an ingredient of such a compound ingredient as is mentioned in paragraph (4)(b) or (c) has been irradiated, the name of the ingredient and the words required by paragraph 2 of Schedule 2 shall be given, except in the case of food which is prepared for patients requiring sterile diets under medical supervision.

8–13015 16. Added water. (1) Water which is added as an ingredient of a food shall be declared in the list of ingredients of the food unless—

(a) it is used in the preparation of the food solely for the reconstitution or partial reconstitution of an ingredient used in concentrated or dehydrated form; or

(b) it is used as, or as part of, a medium which is not normally consumed; or

(c) it does not exceed 5 per cent of the finished product.

(2) Water which is added to any frozen or quick-frozen chicken carcase to which Commission Regulation (EEC) No 1538/91[1] applies, as amended by Commission Regulation (EEC) No 2891/93[2], introducing detailed rules for implementing Council Regulation (EEC) No 1906/90 on certain marketing standards for poultry, need not be declared in the list of ingredients of the food.

---

1. OJ No L143, 7.6.91, p 11.
2. OJ No L263, 22.10.93, p 12.

8–13016 17. Ingredients which need not be named. Subject to regulation 34B the following ingredients of a food need not be named in its list of ingredients:

(a) constituents of an ingredient which have become temporarily separated during the manufacturing process and are later re-introduced in their original proportions;

(b) any additive whose presence in the food is due solely to the fact that it was contained in an ingredient of the food, if it serves no significant technological function in the finished product;

(c) any additive which is used solely as a processing aid;

(d) any substance other than water which is used as a solvent or carrier for an additive and is used in an amount that is no more than that which is strictly necessary for that purpose;

(e) any substance which is not an additive but which is used in the same way and for the same purpose as a processing aid.

8–13017 18. Foods which need not bear a list of ingredients. (1) Subject to regulation 34B the following foods need not be marked or labelled with a list of ingredients:

(a) fresh fruit and vegetables, including potatoes, which have not been peeled or cut into pieces;

(b) carbonated water, to which no ingredient other than carbon dioxide has been added, and whose name indicates that it has been carbonated;

(c) vinegar which is derived by fermentation exclusively from a single basic product and to which no other ingredient has been added;

(d) cheese, butter, fermented milk and fermented cream, to which no ingredient has been added other than lactic products, enzymes and micro-organism cultures essential to manufacture or, in the case of cheese other than fresh curd cheese and processed cheese, such amount of salt as is needed for its manufacture;

(e) flour to which no substances have been added other than those which are required to be present in the flour by regulation 4 of the Bread and Flour Regulations;

(f) any drink with an alcoholic strength by volume of more than 1.2 per cent;

(g) any food consisting of a single ingredient, where—

(i) the name of the food is identical with the name of the ingredient; or

(ii) the name of the food enables the nature of the ingredient to be clearly identified.

(2) Without prejudice to regulation 12, in the case of—

(a) any vinegar which is derived by fermentation exclusively from a single basic product and to which any other ingredient has been added, or (*b*) any cheese, butter, fermented milk or fermented cream, to which any ingredient, other than one which is mentioned in paragraph (1)(*d*) of this regulation, has been added,

only those other added ingredients need be named in the list of ingredients, if the heading of the list includes or is accompanied by the words "added ingredients" or other words indicating that the list is not a complete list of ingredients.

(3) The labelling of any food that is not required to bear a list of ingredients shall not include a list of ingredients unless the food is marked or labelled with a complete list of ingredients in accordance with regulations 12 to 17 and 34B as if it were required to be so marked or labelled.

Quantities of certain ingredients or categories of ingredients

8–13018   **19. Indication of quantities of certain ingredients or categories of ingredients.** (1) Subject to paragraph (2) and (2A) of this regulation, the quantity of an ingredient or category of ingredients used in the preparation of a food shall be indicated where—

(*a*) that ingredient or category of ingredients appears in the name of the food or is usually associated with that name by the consumer;

(*b*) that ingredient or category of ingredients is emphasised on the labelling in words, pictures or graphics; or

(*c*) that ingredient or category of ingredients is essential to characterise a food and to distinguish it from products with which it might be confused because of its name or appearance.

(2) Paragraph (1) of this regulation shall not apply—

(*a*) in respect of an ingredient or category of ingredients—

  (i) the drained net weight of which is indicated in accordance with Article 8(4) of Directive 2000/13;

  (ii) the quantities of which are already required to be given on the labelling under European Community provisions;

  (iii) which is used in small quantities for the purposes of flavouring; or

  (iv) which, though it appears in the name of the food, is not such as to govern the choice of the consumer because the variation in quantity is not essential to characterise the food or does not distinguish it from similar foods;

(*b*) where specific European Community provisions stipulate precisely the quantity of an ingredient or category of ingredients without providing for the indication thereof on the labelling; or

(*c*) in the cases referred to in regulation 13(5).

(2A) Sub-paragraphs (*a*) and (*b*) of paragraph (1) of this regulation shall not apply in the case of—

(*a*) any ingredient or category of ingredients covered by the indication "with sweetener(s)" or "with sugar(s) and sweetener(s)" if that indication accompanies the name of the food pursuant to regulation 34; or

(*b*) any added vitamin or mineral if that substance is the subject of nutrition labelling relating to the food in question.

(3) The indication of quantity of an ingredient or category of ingredients required by paragraph (1) of this regulation shall—

(*a*) subject to paragraph 4 of this regulation, be expressed as a percentage, which shall be determined as at the time of use of the ingredient or category of ingredients in the preparation of the food; and

(*b*) appear—

  (i) in or next to the name of the food, or

  (ii) in the list of ingredients in connection with the ingredient or category of ingredients in question.

(4) Notwithstanding sub-paragraph (*a*) of paragraph (3) of this regulation—

(*a*) where the food has lost moisture as a result of treatment, the indication of quantity of the ingredient or category of ingredients used shall be expressed as a percentage which shall be determined by reference to the finished product unless that quantity, or the total quantity of the ingredients or categories of ingredients indicated, would exceed 100%, in which case the indication of quantity shall be on the basis of the weight of the ingredient or category of ingredients used to prepare 100g of the finished product;

(*b*) the indication of quantity of a volatile ingredient or category of volatile ingredients used shall be on the basis of its proportion by weight in the finished product;

(*c*) the indication of quantity of an ingredient or category of ingredients which has been used in concentrated or dehydrated form and which is reconstituted during preparation of the food may be on the basis of its proportion by weight before concentration or dehydration;

(*d*) where the food is in concentrated or dehydrated form and is intended to be reconstituted by the addition of water as directed in the labelling of the food, the indication of quantity of the ingredient or category of ingredients may be on the basis of its proportion by weight in the food when reconstituted as so directed.

Appropriate durability indication

8–13019   **20. Form of indication of minimum durability.**   (1) Subject to the following paragraphs of this regulation, the minimum durability of a food shall be indicated by the words "best before" followed by—

     (a)   the date up to and including which the food can reasonably be expected to retain its specific properties if properly stored, and

     (b)   any storage conditions which need to be observed if the food is to retain its specific properties until that date.

     (2) The date in the indication of minimum durability shall be expressed in terms of a day, month and year (in that order), except that—

     (a)   in the case of a food which can reasonably be expected to retain its specific properties for three months or less, it may be expressed in terms of a day and month only;

     (b)   in the case of a food which can reasonably be expected to retain its specific properties for more than three months but not more than 18 months it may be expressed in terms of a month and year only, if the words "best before" are replaced by the words "best before end", and

     (c)   in the case of a food which can reasonably be expected to retain its specific properties for more than 18 months it may be expressed either in terms of a month and year only or in terms of a year only, if (in either case) the words "best before" are replaced by the words "best before end".

     (3) Either—

     (a)   the date up to and including which a food can reasonably be expected to retain its specific properties if properly stored, or

     (b)   that date and any storage conditions which need to be observed if the food is to retain its specific properties until that date,

may appear on the labelling of a food separately from the words "best before" or "best before end", as the case may be, provided that those words are followed by a reference to the place where the date (or the date and the storage conditions) appears (or appear).

8–13020   **21. Form of indication of "use by" date.**   (1) Where a "use by" date is required in respect of a food it shall be indicated by the words "use by" followed by—

     (a)   the date up to and including which the food, if properly stored, is recommended for use, and

     (b)   any storage conditions which need to be observed.

     (2) The "use by" date shall be expressed in terms either of a day and month (in that order) or of a day, a month and a year (in that order).

     (3) Either—

     (a)   the date up to and including which a food required to bear a "use by" date is recommended for use, or

     (b)   that date and any storage conditions which need to be observed,

may appear separately from the words "use by", provided that those words are followed by a reference to the place where the date (or the date and the storage conditions) appears (or appear).

8–13021   **22. Foods which need not bear an appropriate durability indication.**   The following foods need not be marked or labelled with an appropriate durability indication:

     (a)   fresh fruit and vegetables (including potatoes but not including sprouting seeds, legume sprouts and similar products) which have not been peeled or cut into pieces;

     (b)   wine, liqueur wine, sparkling wine, aromatised wine and any similar drink obtained from fruit other than grapes;

     (c)   any drink made from grapes or grape musts and coming within codes 2206 00 39, 2206 00 59 and 2206 00 89 of the Combined Nomenclature given in Council Regulation (EEC) No 2658/87[1] on the tariff and statistical nomenclature and on the Common Customs Tariff, as amended[2];

     (d)   any drink with an alcoholic strength by volume of 10 per cent or more;

     (e)   any soft drink, fruit juice or fruit nectar or alcoholic drink, sold in a container containing more than 5 litres and intended for supply to catering establishments;

     (f)   any flour confectionery and bread which, given the nature of its content, is normally consumed within 24 hours of its preparation;

     (g)   vinegar;

     (h)   cooking and table salt;

     (i)   solid sugar and products consisting almost solely of flavoured or coloured sugars;

     (j)   chewing gums and similar products;

     (k)   edible ices in individual portions.

---

1.   OJ No L256, 7.9.87, p 1
2.   Relevant amendment is Commission Regulation (EEC) No 2551/93, OJ No L241, 27.9.93, p 1)

Omission of certain particulars

8–13022   23. Food which is not prepacked and similar food, and fancy confectionery products.
(1) This regulation applies to—

(a) food which is—

    (i)   not prepacked, or

    (ii)   prepacked for direct sale,

other than any such food to which regulation 27 applies;

(b) any flour confectionery which is packed in a crimp case only or in wholly transparent packaging which is either unmarked or marked only with an indication of the price of the food and any lot marking indication given in accordance with the Food (Lot Marking) Regulations 1992, if there is not attached to the flour confectionery or its packaging any document, notice, label, ring or collar (other than a label (or labels) on which only the price of the food and any lot marking indication are marked); and

(c) individually wrapped fancy confectionery products which are not enclosed in any further packaging and which are intended for sale as single items.

(2) Subject to paragraph (3) of this regulation, food to which this regulation applies need not be marked or labelled with any of the particulars specified in regulation 5 except—

(a) the name of the food;

(b) in the case of milk, the particulars required by regulation 5(f) (where the appropriate circumstances described in that regulation apply) and, if such milk is raw milk, the particulars required by regulation 5(e)(i), and

(c) in the case of a meat product other than one listed in Schedule 4A, the particulars required by regulation 5(bA) in respect of those of its ingredients being meat, within the meaning assigned to it by Directive 2000/13/EC of the European Parliament and the Council on the approximation of the laws of the Member States relating to the labelling, presentation and advertising of foodstuffs, as amended by Commission Directive 2001/101/EC,

nor, where but for this regulation they would otherwise be required, with any of the particulars specified in regulations 32, 33 and 34.

(2A) Food falling within paragraph (1)(a) or (c) need not be marked or labelled with any of the particulars specified in regulation 34B or regulation 34C.

(3) Food to which this regulation applies which has not been irradiated and which is—

(a) not exposed for sale, or

(b) white bread or flour confectionery, or

(c) carcasses and parts of carcasses which are not intended for sale in one piece,

need not be marked or labelled with any of the particulars specified in regulation 5.

8–13023   24. Indication of additives.   (1) Subject to the following paragraphs of this regulation, any food which—

(a) by virtue of regulation 23 alone is not marked or labelled with a list of ingredients, and

(b) contains any additive which—

    (i)   but for regulation 23, would be required to be named in the list of ingredients of the food, and

    (ii)   was added to or used in the food or an ingredient of the food to serve the function of an antioxidant, colour, flavouring, flavour enhancer, preservative, or sweetener,

shall be marked or labelled with an indication of every such category of additive that is contained in the food.

(2) Any edible ice or flour confectionery which, but for this paragraph, would be required to be marked or labelled in accordance with paragraph (1) of this regulation need not be so marked or labelled if there is displayed in a prominent position near the edible ice or flour confectionery a notice stating, subject to paragraph (3) of this regulation, that edible ices or flour confectionery, as the case may be, sold at the establishment where the notice is displayed may contain such categories of additives.

(3) Where, in the circumstances described in paragraph (1) or (2) of this regulation, an additive serves more than one of the functions specified in the said paragraph (1), it shall only be necessary to indicate that category which represents the principal function served by the additive in the food or ingredient to which it was added or in which it was used.

(4) This regulation does not apply to food which is not exposed for sale

8–13024   25. Indication of irradiated ingredients.   (1) Subject to paragraph (2) of this regulation, any food which—

(a) by virtue of regulation 23 alone is exempted from the requirement to be marked or labelled with a list of ingredients, and

(b) contains any ingredient which has been irradiated (and which comprises a particular with which, had that food not been subject to that exemption, the food would have been required by these Regulations to be marked or labelled),

shall be marked or labelled with an indication that it contains that ingredient, and in such a case the reference within that indication to that ingredient shall include or be accompanied by the word "irradiated" or the words "treated with ionising radiation".

(2) This regulation does not apply to food which is not exposed for sale.

8–13025 26. Small packages and certain indelibly marked bottles. (1) Subject to the following paragraphs of this regulation, any prepacked food, either contained in an indelibly marked glass bottle intended for re-use and having no label, ring or collar, or the largest surface of whose packaging has an area of less than ten square centimetres, need not—

(a) by virtue of these Regulations be marked or labelled with—

  (i) any of the particulars specified in regulation 5 except the name of the food and, unless the food is not required to be marked or labelled with such an indication, the appropriate durability indication, or

  (ii) any of the particulars specified in regulations 33, 34 and 34C, where but for this regulation they would otherwise be required.

(2) Any bottle referred to in paragraph (1) of this regulation which contains milk shall also be marked or labelled with the particulars required by regulation 5(f) (where the appropriate circumstances described in that regulation apply) and, if such milk is raw milk, with the particulars required by regulation 5(e)(i).

(3) Subject to paragraphs (4) and (5) of this regulation, any prepacked food which—

(a) is sold or supplied as an individual portion, and

(b) is intended as a minor accompaniment to either—

  (i) another food, or

  (ii) another service,

need not be marked or labelled with any of the particulars specified in regulation 5 except the name of the food nor, where but for this regulation they would otherwise be required, with any of the other particulars mentioned in paragraph (3A) of this regulation. Such prepacked food shall include butter and other fat spreads, milk, cream and cheeses, jams and marmalades, mustards, sauces, tea, coffee and sugar, and such other service shall include the provision of sleeping accommodation at an hotel or other establishment at which such accommodation is provided by way of trade or business.

(3A) The other particulars for the purposes of paragraph (3) of this regulation are those specified in regulation 32 and, in the case of any food to which paragraph (1) of this regulation applies, the particulars specified in regulations 33, 34 and 34C.

(4) This regulation does not apply to any food to which regulation 23 or 27 applies.

(4A) Any food which—

(a) by virtue of paragraph (1) or (3) of this regulation alone is exempted from the requirement to be marked or labelled with a list of ingredients;

(b) contains any ingredient which has been irradiated; and

(c) is not prepared for patients requiring sterile diets under medical supervision,

shall be marked or labelled with an indication that it contains that ingredient, and in such a case the reference within that indication to that ingredient shall include or be accompanied by the word "irradiated" or the words "treated with ionising radiation".

(5) Any bottle referred to in paragraph (1) of this regulation need not—

(a) where it contains milk, or

(b) where it contains any other food, in which case until 1st January 1997,

be marked or labelled with an appropriate durability indication.

8–13026 27. Certain food sold at catering establishments. (1) Subject to the following paragraphs of this regulation, any food which is sold at a catering establishment and is either—

(a) not prepacked, or

(b) prepacked for direct sale,

need not be marked or labelled with any of the particulars specified in regulation 5 nor, where but for this regulation they would otherwise be required, with any of the particulars specified in regulations 32, 33, 34, 34B and 34C.

(2) In the case of any such food being milk which is prepacked for direct sale it shall be marked or labelled with the particulars required by regulations 5(f) (where the appropriate circumstances described in that regulation apply) and, if such milk is raw milk, the particulars required by regulation 5(e)(i).

(3) In the case of any such food which has been irradiated that food shall be marked or labelled with an indication of such treatment, which indication shall include or be accompanied by the word "irradiated" or the words "treated with ionising radiation".

(4) In the case of any such food which contains an ingredient which has been irradiated (and which comprises a particular with which, had that food been prepacked, the food would have been required by these Regulations to be marked or labelled), that food shall (subject to regulation 36(3) and (4)) be marked or labelled with an indication that it contains that ingredient and the reference within that indication to that ingredient shall include or be accompanied by the word "irradiated" or the words "treated with ionising radiation".

8–13027 28. Seasonal selection packs. The outer packaging of a seasonal selection pack need not be marked or labelled with any of the particulars specified by these Regulations, provided that each item contained in the pack is individually prepacked and is marked or labelled in accordance with the provisions of these Regulations or any other Regulations applying to such item.

Additional labelling requirements for certain categories of food

8–13028 29. Food sold from vending machines. (1) Subject to paragraph (2) of this regulation, where any food is sold from a vending machine, without prejudice to any other labelling requirements imposed by these Regulations, there shall appear on the front of the machine a notice indicating the name of the food (unless that name appears on the labelling of the food in such a manner as to be easily visible and clearly legible to an intending purchaser through the outside of the machine), together with—

(a) in the event that such food is not prepacked, and there is made in respect of it (whether on the machine or elsewhere) a claim of a type described in Part II of Schedule 6, a notice giving the prescribed nutrition labelling described in paragraph 2 of Part II of Schedule 7;

(b) in the event that such food is one which should properly be reheated before it is eaten, but suitable instructions for such reheating are not given on the packaging (if any) of the food, a notice giving such instructions.

(2) A notice required under sub-paragraph (a) or (b) of paragraph (1) of this regulation shall appear either—

(a) on the front of the vending machine, or

(b) in close proximity to the machine and in such a way as to be readily discernible by an intending purchaser.

8–13029 30. Prepacked alcoholic drinks other than Community controlled wine. (1) In the case of prepacked alcoholic drinks other than Community controlled wine, every drink with an alcoholic strength by volume of more than 1.2 per cent shall be marked or labelled with an indication of its alcoholic strength by volume in the form of a figure to not more than one decimal place (which may be preceded by the word "alcohol" or by the abbreviation "alc") followed by the symbol "% vol".

(2) Positive and negative tolerances shall be permitted in respect of the indication of alcoholic strength by volume and shall be those specified in Schedule 5, expressed in absolute values.

(3) For the purposes of this regulation, the alcoholic strength of any drink shall be determined at 20 degrees C.

8–13030 31. Raw milk. (1) Subject to paragraph (3) of this regulation, and except* in cases to which paragraph (2) of this regulation applies, the container in which any raw milk is sold shall be marked or labelled with the words "This milk has not been heat-treated and may therefore contain organisms harmful to health".

(2) Subject to paragraph (3) of this regulation, in* the case of any raw milk which is not prepacked and is sold at a catering establishment there shall appear—

(a) on a label attached to the container in which that milk is sold, or

(b) on a ticket or notice that is readily discernible by an intending purchaser at the place where he chooses that milk,

the words "Milk supplied in this establishment has not been heat-treated and may therefore contain organisms harmful to health".

(3) The provisions of paragraphs (1) and (2) of this regulation shall not apply to raw milk from buffaloes.*

---

*Words underlined revoked and "Except" and "In" substituted in paras (1) and (2) respectively and para (3) revoked in relation to Wales, by SI 2006/31.

8–13031 32. Products consisting of skimmed milk together with non-milk fat. The container in which any product—

(a) consisting of skimmed milk together with non-milk fat,

(b) which is capable of being used as a substitute for milk, and

(c) which is neither—

(i) an infant formula or a follow-on formula, nor

(ii) a product specially formulated for infants or young children for medical purposes,

is sold shall be prominently marked or labelled with a warning that the product is unfit, or not to be used, as food for babies.

8–13032 33. Foods packaged in certain gases. A food the durability of which has been extended by means of its being packaged in any packaging gas authorised pursuant to Council Directive 89/107/EEC[1], concerning food additives for use in foodstuffs intended for human consumption, shall be marked or labelled with the indication "packaged in a protective atmosphere".

1. OJ No L40, 11.2.89, p 27.

8–13033   34.   Foods containing sweeteners, added sugar and sweeteners, aspartame or polyols.
(1) A food containing a sweetener or sweeteners authorised pursuant to the Sweeteners in Food Regulations 1995 shall be marked or labelled with the indication "with sweetener(s)".
(2) A food containing both an added sugar or sugars and a sweetener or sweeteners authorised pursuant to those Regulations shall be marked or labelled with the indication "with sugar(s) and sweetener(s)".
(3) A food containing aspartame shall be marked or labelled with the indication "contains a source of phenylalanine".
(4) A food containing more than 10% added polyols shall be marked or labelled with the indication "excessive consumption may produce laxative effects".
(5) The indications required by paragraphs (1) and (2) above shall accompany the name of the food.

8–13033A   34A.   Drinks with high caffeine content.   (1) Subject to paragraph (2) of this regulation, in the case of a drink which—

(*a*) is intended for consumption without modification and contains caffeine, from whatever source, in a proportion in excess of 150 milligrams per litre, or
(*b*) is in concentrated or dried form and after reconstitution contains caffeine, from whatever source, in a proportion in excess of 150 milligrams per litre,

that drink shall be marked or labelled with the words "High caffeine content" in the same field of vision as the name of the drink, and those words shall be followed by a reference in brackets to the caffeine content expressed in milligrams per 100 millilitres.
(2) Paragraph (1) of this regulation shall not apply to any drink based on coffee, tea or coffee or tea extract where the name of the food includes the term "coffee" or "tea".

8–13033B   34B.   Foods containing allergenic ingredients or ingredients originating from allergenic ingredients.   (1) Subject to paragraphs (2) and (3), where any food containing any allergenic ingredient, or any ingredient originating from an ingredient referred to in paragraphs 1 to 11 of Schedule AA1, does not specify the allergenic ingredient in the name of the food, that food shall be marked or labelled with a clear reference to the name of the allergenic ingredient concerned.
(2) In the case of any drink which has an alcoholic strength by volume of more than 1.2 per cent—

(*a*) the presence of any allergenic ingredient shall be indicated by marking or labelling the drink with the word "contains" followed by the name of the allergenic ingredient; and
(*b*) subject to paragraph (3) of this regulation, the presence of any ingredient originating from an allergenic ingredient referred to in paragraphs 1 to 11 of schedule AA1 shall be indicated by marking or labelling the drink with the word "contains" followed by the name of the ingredient including a reference to the allergenic ingredient from which it originates,

unless the name of the allergenic ingredient is specified in the name of the drink or in the list of ingredients, if any.
(3) Paragraphs (1) and (2)(*b*) of this regulation shall not apply before 25th November 2007 as respects any ingredient which originates from an allergenic ingredient and is listed in column 2 of Schedule 2A in relation to that allergenic ingredient.

8–13033C   34C.   Confectionery and drinks containing glycyrrhizinic acid or its ammonium salt.
(1) This regulation applies to any confectionery or drink which contains glycyrrhizinic acid or its ammonium salt as a result of the addition of that acid or salt as such or of the liquorice plant *Glycyrrhiza glabra*, and references in this regulation to "relevant concentration" are to the concentration of that acid or salt in the food—

(*a*) manufactured as ready for consumption or,
(*b*) if it is not so manufactured, as reconstituted according to its manufacturer's instructions.

(2) In the case of—

(*a*) any confectionery which contains a relevant concentration of at least 100mg/kg but less than 4 g/kg,
(*b*) any drink which contains more than 1.2 per cent by volume of alcohol and a relevant concentration of at least 10 mg/l but less than 300 mg/l, and
(*c*) any drink which does not contain more than 1.2 per cent by volume of alcohol and which contains a relevant concentration of at least 10 mg/l but less than 50 mg/l,

that food shall be marked or labelled with the indication "contains liquorice", unless the term "liquorice" appears in the list of ingredients or in the name of the food.
(3) In the case of—

(*a*) any confectionery which contains a relevant concentration of at least 4g/kg,
(*b*) any drink which contains more than 1.2 per cent by volume of alcohol and a relevant concentration of at least 300 mg/l, and

(c) any drink which does not contain more than 1.2 per cent by volume of alcohol and which contains a relevant concentration of at least 50 mg/l,

that food shall be marked or labelled with the indication "contains liquorice – people suffering from hypertension should avoid excessive consumption".

(4) The indications required by paragraphs (2) and (3) of this regulation shall appear immediately after the list of ingredients or, in the absence of such a list, near the name of the food.

Manner of marking or labelling

8–13034 35. General requirement.   (1) When any food other than food to which regulation 23, 27 or 31 applies is sold, the particulars with which it is required to be marked or labelled by these Regulations shall appear—

  (a) on the packaging, or
  (b) on a label attached to the packaging, or
  (c) on a label that is clearly visible through the packaging,

save that where the sale is otherwise than to the ultimate consumer such particulars may, except as provided in paragraph (2) of this regulation, alternatively, appear only on the commercial documents relating to the food where it can be guaranteed that such documents, containing all such particulars, either accompany the food to which they relate or were sent before, or at the same time as, delivery of the food, and provided always that the particulars required by regulation 5(a), (c) and (e) shall also be marked or labelled on the outermost packaging in which that food is sold.

(2) In the case of food to which paragraph (1) of this regulation applies which has been irradiated, other than food which is prepared for patients requiring sterile diets under medical supervision, the alternative provided for in the full-out words to that paragraph shall not apply as regards the particulars specified in regulations 14(2) and 26(4A) and paragraph 2 of Schedule 2, and the word "irradiated" or the words "treated with ionising radiation" shall in all cases appear on the commercial documents relating to such food.

8–13035 36. Food to which regulation 23 or 27 applies.   (1) When any food to which regulation 23 or 27 applies is sold to the ultimate consumer, the particulars with which it is required to be marked or labelled by these Regulations shall, except in a case to which paragraph (2) of this regulation applies, appear—

  (a) on a label attached to the food, or
  (b) on a menu, notice, ticket or label that is readily discernible by an intending purchaser at the place where he chooses that food.

(1A) Paragraphs (2) to (4) of this regulation shall apply only to food which is prepared for patients requiring sterile diets under medical supervision.

(2) In any case where food to which paragraph (1)(b) of this regulation applies has been or contains an ingredient which has been irradiated and that food is sold and delivered to the ultimate consumer in a catering establishment, use of alternative labelling relating to irradiation shall not alone be treated as a contravention of these Regulations and for this purpose alternative labelling is used where, instead of the particulars referred to in that paragraph appearing in the manner specified therein, alternative particulars are displayed in accordance with paragraph (3), with paragraph (4) or with paragraphs (3) and (4) of this regulation.

(3) Alternative particulars are displayed in accordance with this paragraph in relation to any ingredient which has been irradiated if there appears, in the manner specified in paragraph (1)(b) of this regulation, an indication that the food of which that irradiated ingredient forms part may contain that irradiated ingredient and if the reference within that indication to that ingredient includes or is accompanied by the word "irradiated" or the words "treated with ionising radiation".

(4) Alternative particulars are displayed in accordance with this paragraph if the irradiated ingredients to which they relate are dried substances normally used for seasoning, if there appears, in the manner specified in paragraph (1)(b) of this regulation, an indication to the effect that food sold in the catering establishment contains (or may contain) those irradiated ingredients and if the reference within that indication to those ingredients includes or is accompanied by the word "irradiated" or the words "treated with ionising radiation".

(5) When any food to which regulation 23 applies is sold otherwise than to the ultimate consumer, the particulars with which it is required to be marked or labelled by these Regulations shall appear—

  (a) on a label attached to the food, or
  (b) on a ticket or notice that is readily discernible by the intending purchaser at the place where he chooses the food, or
  (c) (except as provided in paragraph (6) of this regulation) in commercial documents relating to the food where it can be guaranteed that such documents either accompany the food to which they relate or were sent before, or at the same time as, delivery of the food.

(6) Notwithstanding the foregoing paragraphs of the regulation (but subject to paragraph (7)

of the same), in the case of the sale of any food to which regulation 23 or 27 applies which has been irradiated—

(a)　the word "irradiated" or the words "treated with ionising radiation" shall in call cases appear on the commercial documents relating to such food; and

(b)　sub-paragraph (c) of paragraph (5) of this regulation shall not apply as regards the particulars specified in regulations 14(2), 25(1) and 27(3) and (4) and paragraph 2 of Schedule 2.

(7)　Paragraph (6) of this regulation shall not apply in relation to food which is prepared for patients requiring sterile diets under medical supervision.

8–13036　37. Milk.　(1) Subject to paragraph (2) of this regulation, in the case of milk that is contained in a bottle, any particulars which are required to be given under these Regulations may be given on the bottle cap.

(2)　In the case of raw milk contained in a bottle, the particulars specified in regulation 31(1) shall be given elsewhere than on the bottle cap.

8–13037　38. Intelligibility.　(1) The particulars with which a food is required to be marked or labelled by these Regulations, or which appear on a menu, notice, ticket or label pursuant to these Regulations, shall be easy to understand, clearly legible and indelible and, when a food is sold to the ultimate consumer, the said particulars shall be marked in a conspicuous place in such a way as to be easily visible.

(2)　Such particulars shall not in any way be hidden, obscured or interrupted by any other written or pictorial matter.

(3)　Paragraph (1) of this regulation shall not be taken to preclude the giving of such particulars at a catering establishment, in respect of foods the variety and type of which are changed regularly, by means of temporary media (including the use of chalk on a blackboard).

8–13038　39. Field of vision.　(1) Where a food is required to be marked or labelled with more than one of the following indications, such indications shall appear in the labelling of the food in the same field of vision—

(a)　the name of the food,

(b)　an appropriate durability indication,

(c)　an indication of alcoholic strength by volume,

(d)　the cautionary words in respect of raw milk,

(e)　the warning required on certain products by regulation 32, and

(f)　an indication of the net quantity as required by the Weights and Measures Act 1985 or by any Order or Regulations made thereunder.

(2)　Paragraph (1)(b), (c) and (f) of this regulation shall not apply to any food sold in a bottle or packaging where such bottle or packaging is the subject of regulation 26.

PART III
CLAIMS, NUTRITION LABELLING AND MISLEADING DESCRIPTIONS

8–13039　40. Claims.　(1) A claim of the type described in Part I of Schedule 6 shall not be made, either expressly or by implication, in the labelling or advertising of a food.

(2)　A claim of a type described in Part II of Schedule 6 shall not be made, either expressly or by implication, in the labelling or advertising of a food, except in accordance with the appropriate conditions set out in that Part of that Schedule.

(3)　Where a claim is a claim of two or more of the types described in Part II of Schedule 6, the conditions appropriate to each of the relevant types of claim shall be observed.

8–13040　41. Supplementary provisions relating to claims.　(1) Nothing in regulation 40 or Schedule 6 shall be taken to prevent the dissemination of useful information or recommendations intended exclusively for persons having qualifications in dentistry, medicine, nutrition, dietetics or pharmacy.

(2)　A reference to a substance in a list of ingredients or in any nutrition labelling shall not of itself constitute a claim of a type described in Schedule 6.

(3)　In Schedule 6 any condition that a food in respect of which a claim is made shall be marked or labelled with the prescribed nutrition labelling shall not apply in the case of—

(a)　a food (other than a food sold from a vending machine) which is not prepacked and which is sold to the ultimate consumer at a catering establishment, or

(b)　a claim contained within generic advertising,

but in respect of a food described in sub-paragraph (a) there may be given such of the elements of the prescribed nutrition labelling which, but for this paragraph, would have been required or permitted to be given, as it is wished to include, and where all or any such elements are given this shall be in accordance with Part I of Schedule 7, except that in applying paragraph 4 of that Part, in place of paragraphs (a)(i) and (ii) to that paragraph there shall be read references to—

(i)　an unquantified serving of the food, and

(ii)　any one portion of the food.

(4) Where nutrition labelling not being prescribed nutrition labelling is given it shall be given in all respects as if it were prescribed nutrition labelling except that in applying in this context the requirements for prescribed nutrition labelling described in Schedule 7, Part II of that Schedule shall be read as if paragraph 1(*d*), and the proviso to paragraph 1(*a*), were omitted.

8–13041 42. Misleading descriptions. (1) The words and descriptions specified in column 1 of Part I of Schedule 8 shall not be used in the labelling or advertising of a food, except in accordance with the appropriate conditions set out in column 2 of that Part of that Schedule.

(2) The name specified in column 1 of Part II of Schedule 8 shall not be used in the labelling or advertising of any cheese as the name of the cheese, whether or not qualified by other words, unless—

(*a*) the amount of water in the cheese expressed as a percentage of the total weight of the cheese does not exceed the percentage stated in column 2 of Part II of Schedule 8 opposite that name, and

(*b*) the amount of milk fat in the cheese expressed as a percentage of the dry matter of the cheese is not less than 48 per cent.

(3) The name specified in column 1 of Part III of Schedule 8 shall not be used in the labelling or advertising of any cream as the name of the cream, whether or not qualified by other words, unless the cream complies with the requirements specified in column 2 of that Part of that Schedule opposite that name; except that the relevant requirement as to milk fat content need not be complied with if the name contains qualifying words which indicate that the milk fat content of the cream is greater or less than that specified in column 2, as the case may be.

(4) In calculating the percentage of milk fat in any cream for the purposes of paragraph (3) of this regulation and Part III of Schedule 8, any ingredient added to the cream shall be disregarded.

8–13042 43. The word "wine". (1) Subject to the following provisions of this regulation, the word "wine" may be used in a composite name in the labelling or advertising of food for a drink which is not wine as defined in Annex I to Council Regulation (EEC) No 822/87.

(2) The word "wine" shall not be used pursuant to paragraph (1) of this regulation as part of a composite name which is likely to cause confusion with wine or table wine as defined in Annex I to Council Regulation (EEC) No 822/87.

(3) Each word that forms part of a composite name used pursuant to paragraph (1) of this regulation must appear in lettering of the same type and colour and of such a height that the composite name is clearly distinguishable from other particulars.

(4) The composite name "non-alcoholic wine" shall not be used pursuant to paragraph (1) of this regulation, except for a drink derived from unfermented grape juice which is intended exclusively for communion or sacramental use and which is described clearly in its labelling or advertising, as the case may be, as being exclusively for such use.

(5) When the word "wine" is used in a composite name for a drink which is derived from fruit other than grapes, that drink shall be obtained by an alcoholic fermentation of that fruit.

PART IV

OFFENCES AND LEGAL PROCEEDINGS

8–13043 44. Offences and penalties. (1) If any person—

(*a*) sells any food which is not marked or labelled in accordance with the provisions of Part II of these Regulations, or

(*b*) sells or advertises for sale any food in respect of which a claim is made, nutrition labelling is given or a description or a name is used in contravention of the provisions of Part III of these Regulations, or

(*c*) sells any food from a vending machine in contravention of regulation 29, or

(*d*) sells any food after the date shown in a "use by" date relating to it, or

(*e*) being a person other than whichever of—

(i) the manufacturer,

(ii) the packer, or

(iii) the seller established within the European Community,

was originally responsible for so marking the food, removes or alters the appropriate durability indication relating to that food,

he shall be guilty of an offence and shall be liable on summary conviction to a fine not exceeding **level 5** on the standard scale.

(2) Where an offence under these Regulations is committed in Scotland by a Scottish partnership and is proved to have been committed with the consent or connivance of, or to be attributable to any neglect on the part of, a partner, he as well as the partnership shall be guilty of the offence and be liable to be proceeded against and punished accordingly.

8–13044 45. Enforcement. (1) Subject to paragraph (2) of this regulation, each food authority shall enforce and execute these Regulations in its area.

(2) Each port health authority shall enforce and execute these Regulations in its district in relation to imported food.

(3) In this regulation "food authority" does not include—

(a) the council of a district in a non-metropolitan county in England except—

   (i) where the county functions have been transferred to that council pursuant to a structural change; or

   (ii) in relation to regulations 44(1)(*d*) and 44(1)(*e*);

(b) the appropriate Treasurer referred to in section 5(1)(*c*) of the Act (which deals with the Inner Temple and the Middle Temple).

8–13045 46. Defence in case of alteration of appropriate durability indication. In any proceedings for an offence under regulation 44(1)(*e*) it shall be a defence for the person charged to prove that each removal or alteration in respect of which the offence is alleged was effected under the written authorisation of a person capable of effecting that removal or alteration without contravention of that provision.

8–13046 47. Defence in relation to exports. *Revoked.*

8–13047 48. Application of various provisions of the Act. (1) The following provisions of the Act shall apply for the purposes of these Regulations and, unless the context otherwise requires, any reference in those provisions to the Act or Part thereof shall be construed for the purposes of these Regulations as a reference to these Regulations—

section 2 (extended meaning of "sale" etc);
section 3 (presumption that food is intended for human consumption);
section 20 (offences due to fault of another person);
section 21 (defence of due diligence) as it applies for the purposes of section 8, 14 or 15;
section 22 (defence of publication in the course of a business);
section 30(8) (which relates to documentary evidence);
section 33 (obstruction etc of officers);
section 36 (offences by bodies corporate);
section 44 (protection of officers acting in good faith).

(2) (*Revoked*)

(3) The penalty provisions in section 35(1) of the Act (punishment of offences) shall apply in relation to an offence under section 33(1) of the Act as applied by these Regulations, and the penalty provisions in section 35(2) and (3) of the Act shall apply in relation to an offence under 33(2) of the Act as applied by these Regulations.

PART V
REVOCATIONS, AMENDMENTS AND TRANSITIONAL PROVISION

8–13048 49. *Revocations and amendments*

8–13049 50. Transitional provision. (1) Subject to the following paragraphs of this regulation, in any proceedings for an offence under these Regulations it shall be a defence to prove that—

(a)

   (i) the act was committed before 1st July 1997, or

   (ii) the act was committed in relation to food prepacked before 1st July 1997; and

(b) the matters constituting the offence would not have constituted an offence under the Food Labelling Regulations 1984, the Food Labelling (Scotland) Regulations 1984, or the Milk Labelling (Scotland) Regulations 1983 or the Cheese and Cream Regulations 1995 if those Regulations had been in operation when the act was committed or the food was prepacked.

(2) In any proceedings for an offence under regulation 44(1)(*a*), as read with—

(a) regulation 14(4) and Schedule 3, or

(b) regulation 14(9) and Schedule 4,

paragraph (1) of this regulation shall be read as if for the date "1st July 1997" there were substituted, in both places where it occurs, the date "1st July 1996".

(3) In any proceedings for an offence under regulation 44(1)(*a*) as read with regulation 33, paragraph (1) of this regulation shall be read as if for the date "1st July 1997" there were substituted the date "1st January 1997".

(4) In any proceedings for an offence under regulation 44(1)(*a*), it shall be a defence to prove that—

(a) the food concerned was prepacked before 14th February 2000, and

(b) the matters constituting the offence would not have constituted an offence under these Regulations if the amendments made by the following provisions of the Food Labelling (Amendment) Regulations 1998, namely—

   (i) regulations 3 and 14 and the Schedule (in so far as they include in the definition of "Directive 79/112" a reference to European Parliament and Council Directive 97/4/EC),

   (ii) regulation 4 (in so far as it substitutes a new regulation 3(1)(iii)), and

   (iii) regulations 6 to 9, 15 and 16,

had not been made when the food was prepacked.

(5)–(7) *Revoked.*

(8) In any proceedings for an offence under regulation 44(1)(*a*) as read with regulation 14(9) and (11), it shall be a defence to prove that the food concerned was prepacked before 4th November 2000 and the matter constituting the offence would not have constituted an offence under these Regulations if the amendment made by regulation 14(3)(*a*) of the Miscellaneous Food Additives (Amendment) Regulations 1999 had not been made when the food was prepacked.

(9) In any proceedings for an offence under regulation 44(1)(*a*), it shall be a defence to prove that—

(*a*) the food concerned was prepacked before 14th February 2000, and

(*b*) the matters constituting the offence would not have constituted an offence under these Regulations if the amendments made by regulations 3, 5(*c*) and (*d*) and 6 of the Food Labelling (Amendment) (No 2) Regulations 1999 had not been made when the food was prepacked.

(10) *Scotland.*

(11) In any proceedings for an offence under regulation 44(1)(*a*), it shall be a defence to prove that—

(*a*) the food concerned was marked or labelled before 1st July 2004; and

(*b*) the matters constituting the offence would not have constituted an offence under these Regulations if the amendments made by regulations 5 and 6 of the Food (Provisions relating to Labelling) (England) Regulations 2003 had not been in operation when the food was sold.

(12) In any proceedings for an offence under regulation 44(1)(*a*), it shall be a defence to prove that—

(*a*) the food concerned was marked or labelled before 25th November 2005; and

(*b*) the matters constituting the alleged offence would not have constituted an offence under these Regulations if the amendments made by the following provisions of the Food Labelling (Amendment) (England) (No 2) Regulations 2004, namely—

(i) regulation 3(*b*),

(ii) regulation 5 in so far as it substitutes a new regulation 13(5), and

(iii) regulations 6, 7, 8(*a*), 9, 12 (as read with regulation 5 of the Food Labelling (Amendment) (England)[1] (No 2) Regulations 2005) and 15,

had not been in operation when the food was sold.

(13) In any proceedings for an offence under regulation 44(1)(*a*), it shall be a defence to prove that—

(*a*) the food concerned was marked or labelled before 20th May 2006; and

(*b*) the matters constituting the alleged offence would not have constituted an offence under these Regulations if the amendment made by regulation 7 of the Food Labelling (Amendment) (England)[1] Regulations 2005 had not been in operation when the food was sold.

---

[1] This reference is to "(Wales)" in relation to Wales.

8–13049AA

Regulations 2(1), 13(8)(c) and 34B

SCHEDULE AA1
ALLERGENIC INGREDIENTS

1. The following cereals containing gluten: wheat, rye, barley, oats, spelt, kamut and their hybridised strains
2. Crustaceans
3. Eggs
4. Fish
5. Peanuts
6. Soybeans
7. Milk
8. The following nuts: Almond (*Amygdalus communis* L), Hazelnut (*Corylus avellana*), Walnut (*Juglans regia*), Cashew (*Anacardium occidentale*), Pecan nut (*Carya illinoiesis (Wangenh) K Koch*), Brazil nut (*Bertholletia excelsa*), Pistachio nut (*Pistacia vera*), Macadamia nut and Queensland nut (*Macadamia ternifolia*)
9. Celery
10. Mustard
11. Sesame seeds
12. Sulphur dioxide and sulphites at concentrations of more than 10 mg/kg or 10 mg/litre expressed as SO2.

8–13049A

Regulation 2(1)

SCHEDULE A1
AMENDMENTS TO DIRECTIVE 79/112

Directive 79/112 has been amended by, and must be read subject to—

Act of Accession (Hellenic Republic) (OJ No L291, 19.11.79, p 17);
Act of Accession (Kingdom of Spain and Portuguese Republic) (OJ No L302, 15.11.85, p 218);
Council Directive 85/7/EEC (OJ No L2, 3.1.85, p 22);
Council Directive 86/197/EEC (OJ No L144, 29.5.86, p 38);
Council Directive 89/395/EEC (OJ No L186, 30.6.89 p 17);

Commission Directive 91/72/EEC (OJ No L42, 15.2.91, p 27);
EEA Agreement;
Commission Directive 93/102/EEC (OJ No L291, 25.11.93, p 14), as amended by Commission Directive 95/42/
EC (OJ No L182, 2.8.95, p 20);

and, except in relation to an EEA State which is not a member State,—

Act of Accession (Austria, Finland and Sweden) (OJ No LI, 1.1.95, p 1);
European Parliament and Council Directive 97/4/EC (OJ No L43, 14.2.97, p 21).

8–13050

Regulation 6(2)   SCHEDULE 1
                                        NAMES PRESCRIBED BY LAW
   1. Fish. (*Revoked*).

8–13050A

2. Melons. The name used for melons sold as such shall include or be accompanied by an indication
of their variety.

3. Potatoes. The name used for potatoes sold as such shall include or be accompanied by an indication of
their variety.

4. Vitamins. (1) The name used for a vitamin specified in Table A in Schedule 6 shall be the name specified
for that vitamin in column 1 of that Table, except that in respect of folacin the name "folic acid" may also be
used.
   (2) The name for vitamin K shall be "vitamin K".

8–13051

Regulation 11(2)   SCHEDULE 2
                                         INDICATIONS OF TREATMENT
   1. Tenderised meat. The name used for any meat which has been treated with proteolytic enzymes shall
include or be accompanied by the word "tenderised".

2. Irradiated food. The name used for a food which has been irradiated shall include or be accompanied by
the word "irradiated" or the words "treated with ionising radiation".

8–13051A

                                             SCHEDULE 2A
LIST OF INGREDIENTS WHICH ORIGINATE FROM ALLERGENIC INGREDIENTS AND IN RESPECT OF WHICH THE ALLERGEN LABELLING
                                  REQUIREMENTS DO NOT APPLY

Column 1	Column 2
Allergenic ingredient	Exempt ingredients originating from allergenic ingredient
Cereals containing gluten	Wheat based glucose syrups including dextrose.[1]
	Wheat based maltodextrins[1].
	Glucose syrups based on barley.
	Cereals used in distillates for spirits.
Eggs	Lysozym (produced from egg) used in wine.
	Albumin (produced from egg) used as fining agent in wine and cider.
Fish	Fish gelatine used as a carrier for vitamin or carotenoid preparations and flavours.
	Fish gelatine or Isinglass used as fining agent in beer, cider and wine.
Soybean	Fully refined soybean oil and fat[1].
	Natural mixed tocopherols (E306), natural D-alpha tocopherol, natural D-alpha tocopherol acetate, natural D-alpha tocopherol succinate from soybean sources.
	Phytosterols and phytosterol esters derived from vegetable oils obtained from soybean sources.
	Plant stanol ester produced from vegetable oil sterols from soybean sources.
Milk	Whey used in distillates for spirits.
	Lactitol.
	Milk (casein) products used as fining agents in cider and wines.
Nuts	Nuts used in distillates for spirits.
	Almonds and walnuts used as flavour in spirits.
Celery	Celery leaf and seed oil.
	Celery seed oleoresin.
Mustard	Mustard oil.
	Mustard seed oil.
	Mustard seed oleoresin.

[1]   And their products, in so far as the process that they have undergone is not likely to increase the level of
allergenicity assessed by the European Food Safety Authority for the relevant product from which they
originated.

SCHEDULE 3
GENERIC NAMES IN LIST OF INGREDIENTS

PART I
GENERAL

Regulation 14(4)

Column 1 Generic name	Column 2 Ingredients	Column 3 Conditions of use of generic name
Cheese	Any type of cheese or mixture of cheese	The labelling of the food of which the cheese is an ingredient must not refer to a specific type of cheese
Cocoa butter	Press, expeller or refined cocoa butter	
Crumbs *or* rusks, *as is appropriate*	Any type of crumbled, baked cereal product	
Dextrose	Anhydrous dextrose or dextrose monohydrate	
Fat	Any refined fat	The generic name must be accompanied by either– (a) the description "animal" or "vegetable", as is appropriate, or (b) an indication of the specific animal origin or the specific vegetable origin of the fat, as is appropriate. In the case of an hydrogenated fat, the generic name must also be accompanied by the description "hydrogenated".
Fish	Any species of fish	The labelling of the food of which the fish is an ingredient must not refer to a specific species of fish
Flour	Any mixture of flour derived from two or more cereal species	The generic name shall be followed by a list of the cereals from which the flour is derived in descending order of weight
Glucose syrup	Glucose syrup or anhydrous glucose syrup	The generic name may not be used where the glucose syrup contains fructose in a proportion of greater than 5% on a dry matter basis
Gum base	Any type of gum preparation used in the preparation of chewing gum	
Herb, herbs or mixed herbs	Any herb or parts of a herb or combination of two or more herbs or parts of herbs	The proportion of herb or herbs in the food of which it or they are an ingredient must not exceed 2 per cent by weight of the food
"Meat" and the name of the animal species from which it comes, or a word which describes the meat by reference to the animal species from which it comes	Any skeletal muscle, including the diaphragm and the masseters, of a mammalian or bird species recognised as fit for human consumption with any naturally included or adherent tissue, but excluding the heart, the tongue, the muscles of the head (other than the masseters), the muscles of the carpus, the tarsus, the tail and (g) the product obtained by removing the meat from flesh-bearing bones after boning or from carcases of farmed birds (including birds that are not considered as domestic but which are farmed as domestic animals, but not including ratites) using mechanical means resulting in the loss or modification of the muscle fibre structure.	The total fat and connective tissue content must not exceed the limits specified in Part II of this Schedule and the meat must constitute an ingredient of another food. If such a limit is exceeded, but the ingredient falls within the description in column 2 of this entry, any reference to the meat content must be adjusted downwards accordingly and the list of ingredients must also mention the presence of fat or connective tissue
Milk proteins	Any caseins, caseinates or whey proteins, or any mixture of these	
Oil	Any refined oil, other than olive oil	The generic name must be accompanied by either– (a) the description "animal" or "vegetable", as is appropriate, or

Column 1 Generic name	Column 2 Ingredients	Column 3 Conditions of use of generic name
		(b) an indication of the specific animal origin or the specific vegetable origin of the oil, as is appropriate. In the case of an hydrogenated oil, the generic name must also be accompanied by the description "hydrogenated".
Spice, spices or mixed spices	Any spice or any combination of two or more spices	The proportion of spice or spices in the food of which it or they are an ingredient must not exceed 2 per cent by weight of the food
Starch	Any unmodified starch or any starch which has been modified either by physical means or by enzymes	In the case of a starch which may contain gluten, the generic name must be accompanied by an indication of the specific vegetable origin of the starch.
Sugar	Any type of sucrose	
Wine	Any type of wine defined in Council Regulation (EEC) No 822/87	

Part II

Maximum Fat and Connective Tissue Contents for Ingredients for which the Generic Name Meat or Equivalent as Referred to in Part I of this Schedule is Used

Species	Fat (5)	Connective tissue (%)[1]
Mammals (other than rabbits and porcines) and mixtures of species with mammals predominating	25	25
Porcines	30	25
Birds and rabbits	15	10

Note

1..   The connective tissue content is calculated on the basis of the ratio between collagen content and meat protein content. The collagen content means the hydroxyproline content multiplied by a factor of 8.

8–13053

Regulation 14(9)   SCHEDULE 4

Categories of Additives which must be Identified in a List of Ingredients by their Category Name

Acid[1]
Acidity regulator
Anti-caking agent
Anti-foaming agent
Antioxidant
Bulking agent
Colour
Emulsifier
Emulsifying Salts
Firming agent
Flavour enhancer

Flour treatment agent
Gelling agent
Glazing agent
Humectant
Modified starch[2]
Preservative
Propellant gas
Raising agent
Stabiliser
Sweetener
Thickener

Notes

1 In the case of an additive which is added to or used in food to serve the function of an acid and whose specific name includes the word "acid", it shall not be necessary to use the category name.

2 Neither the specific name nor the serial number need be indicated. In the case of a modified starch which may contain gluten, the category name must be accompanied by an indication of the specific vegetable origin of the starch.

8–13053A

Regulation 23(2)(c)   SCHEDULE 4A[1]

Meat Products Not Required to Bear an Indication of the Quantity of an Ingredient or Category of Ingredients when Sold Not Prepacked or Prepacked for Direct Sale

1. Sandwiches, filled rolls and similar products, which are ready for consumption without further processing, other than products containing meat which are sold under a name, whether or not qualified by other words, included in the items "burger", "economy burger" or "hamburger" in Schedule 2 (reserved descriptions) to the Meat Products (England) Regulations 2003.

2. Pizzas and similar topped products.

3. Any food for which the name is "broth", "gravy" or "soup", whether or not qualified by other words.

4. A food consisting of an assemblage of two or more ingredients, which has not been subjected to any processing or treatment once it has been assembled, and which is sold to the ultimate consumer as an individual portion intended to be consumed without further processing or treatment.

1. Inserted in relation to England by SI 2003/2075 and in relation to Wales by SI 2004/1396.

8–13054
Regulation 30

SCHEDULE 5

POSITIVE AND NEGATIVE TOLERANCES PERMITTED IN THE INDICATION OF THE ALCOHOLIC STRENGTH BY VOLUME OF ALCOHOLIC DRINKS OTHER THAN COMMUNITY CONTROLLED WINE

Description of alcoholic drink	Positive or negative tolerance
1 (a) Beers having an alcoholic strength not exceeding 5.5% volume;	0.5% vol
(b) alcoholic drinks made from grapes and falling within subheading No 2206—0093 and No 2206—0099 of the combined nomenclature (1988).	0.5% vol
2 (a) Beers having an alcoholic strength exceeding 5.5% volume;	1% vol
(b) alcoholic drinks made from grapes and falling within subheading No 2206—0091 of the combined nomenclature (1988);	1% vol
(c) ciders, perries, fruit wines and other wines obtained from fruits other than grapes whether or not semi-sparkling or sparkling;	1% vol
(d) alcoholic drinks based on fermented honey.	1% vol
3 Alcoholic drinks containing macerated fruit or part of plants.	1.5% vol
4 Any other alcoholic drink.	0.3% vol

Note

The above tolerances shall apply without prejudice to the tolerances deriving from the method of analysis used for determining the alcoholic strength.

8–13055
Regulations 40, 41

SCHEDULE 6

CLAIMS

PART I

PROHIBITED CLAIMS

1. A claim that a food has tonic properties.

Note

The use of the word "tonic" in the description "Indian tonic water" or "quinine tonic water" shall not of itself constitute a claim of a type described in this item.

2. A claim that a food has the property of preventing, treating or curing a human disease or any reference to such a property.

Note

A claim of a type described in item 1 of Part II of this Schedule shall not of itself be regarded as a claim of a type described in this item.

PART II

RESTRICTED CLAIMS

Column 1 Types of Claim	Column 2 Conditions
Claims relating to foods for particular nutritional uses 1 A claim that a food is suitable, or has been specially made, for a particular nutritional purpose.	1 The food must be capable of fulfilling the claim. 2 The food must be marked or labelled with an indication of the particular aspects of its composition or manufacturing process that give the food its particular nutritional characteristics. 3 The food– (*a*) must be marked or labelled with the prescribed nutrition labelling and may be marked or labelled with further information in respect of either or both of– (i) any nutrient or component of a nutrient (whether or not a claim is made in respect of such nutrient or component), or (ii) any other component or characteristic which is essential to the food's suitability for its particular nutritional use, and (*b*) when sold to the ultimate consumer, must be prepacked and completely enclosed by its packaging.
Reduced or low energy value claims 2 A claim that a food has a reduced or low energy value.	1 If the claim is that the food has a reduced energy value, the energy value of a given weight of the food, or of a given volume in the case of a liquid food, must not be more than three quarters of that of the equivalent weight, or volume, of a similar food in relation to which no such claim is made, unless the food is–
Notes (a) The appearance, on the container of a soft drink, of the words "low calorie" given in accordance with the conditions specified in Schedule 8 in relation to that description for such drinks shall not of itself constitute a claim of a type described in this item.	(*a*) an intense sweetener, or
(b) Where a food is in concentrated or dehydrated form and is intended to be reconstituted by the addition of water or other substances, condition 2 shall apply to the food when reconstituted as directed.	(*b*) a product which consists of a mixture of an intense sweetener with other substances and which, when compared on a weight for weight basis, is significantly sweeter than sucrose.

Column 1
Types of Claim

Column 2
Conditions

2 If the claim is that the food has a low energy value–

(a) the energy value of the food must not be more than 167 kJ (40 kcal) per hundred grams or hundred millilitres, as is appropriate, unless the food is–

(i) an intense sweetener, or

(ii) a product which consists of a mixture of an intense sweetener with other substances and which, when compared on a weight for weight basis, is significantly sweeter than sucrose,

(b) the energy value of a normal serving of the food must not be more than 167 kJ (40 kcal), and

(c) in the case of an uncooked food which naturally has a low energy value, the claim must be in the form "a low energy food" or "a low calorie food" or "a low Joule food".

3 The food must be marked or labelled with the prescribed nutrition labelling.

Protein claims

3 A claim that a food, other than a food intended for babies or young children which satisfies the conditions of item 1 of this Part of this Schedule, is a source of protein.

1 The quantity of the food that can reasonably be expected to be consumed in one day must contribute at least 12g of protein.

2 (1) If the claim is that the food is a rich or excellent source of protein, at least 20 per cent of the energy value of the food must be provided by protein.

(2) In any other case, at least 12 per cent of the energy value of the food must be provided by protein.

3 The food must be marked or labelled with the prescribed nutrition labelling.

Vitamin claims

4 A claim that a food, other than a food intended for babies or young children which satisfies the conditions of item 1 of this Part of this Schedule, is a source of vitamins.
Note

1 (1) If the claim is not confined to named vitamins, every vitamin named in the claim must be a vitamin specified in column 1 of Table A below, and–

(a) where the claim is that the food is a rich or excellent source of vitamins, the quantity of the food that can reasonably be expected to be consumed in one day must contain at least one half of the recommended daily allowance of two or more of the vitamins specified in column 1 of Table A below, and

A reference to a vitamin in the name of a food shall not of itself constitute a claim of a type to which this item applies if the food consists solely of–

(b) in any other case, the quantity of the food that can reasonably be expected to be consumed in one day must contain at least one sixth of the recommended daily allowance of two or more of the vitamins specified in column 1 of Table A below.

(i) vitamins, or

(2) If the claim is confined to named vitamins, every vitamin named in the claim must be a vitamin specified in column 1 of Table A below, and–

(ii) a mixture of vitamins and minerals, or

(a) where the claim is that the food is a rich or excellent source of vitamins, the quantity of the food that can reasonably be expected to be consumed in one day must contain at least one half of the recommended daily allowance of every vitamin named in the claim, and

(iii) a mixture of vitamins, or of vitamins and minerals, and a carrying agent, or

(b) in any other case, the quantity of the food that can reasonably be expected to be consumed in one day must contain at least one sixth of the recommended daily allowance of every vitamin named in the claim.

2 The food must be marked or labelled–

(iv) a mixture of vitamins, or of vitamins and minerals, and other substances sold in tablet, capsule or elixir form.

(a) in the case of a food to which nutrition labelling relates–

(i) where the claim is in respect of unnamed vitamins (whether alone or together with named vitamins), then in respect of any of those unnamed vitamins which are listed in Table A, with the prescribed nutrition labelling and, in addition, with a statement of the percentages of the recommended daily allowance for such vitamins as are contained in either a quantified serving of the food or, provided that the total number of portions contained in the sales unit of the food is stated, in one such portion of the food, and

Column 1
Types of Claim

Column 2
Conditions

(ii) where the claim is in respect of a named vitamin or of named vitamins (whether alone or together with unnamed vitamins), then in respect of that named vitamin or those named vitamins, with the prescribed nutrition labelling and, in addition, with a statement of the percentages of the recommended daily allowance for such vitamins as are contained in either a quantified serving of the food or, provided that the total number of portions contained in the sales unit of the food is stated, in one such portion of the food; and

(b) in the case of food supplements or waters other than natural mineral waters, in respect of any vitamins, whether unnamed, named or both–

(i) with a statement of the percentage of the recommended daily allowance of those vitamins contained in either a quantified serving or (provided that the food is prepacked) a portion of the food, and

(ii) where the food is prepacked, of the number of portions contained in the package,

and the name used in such marking or labelling for any such vitamin shall be the name specified for that vitamin in column 1 of Table A below.

Mineral claims

5 A claim that a food, other than a food intended for babies or young children which satisfies the conditions of item 1 of this Part of this Schedule, is a source of minerals.

The conditions are the same as those set out in item 4 of this Part of this Schedule with the substitution of–

Notes

(a) A claim that a food has low or reduced levels of minerals shall not be regarded as a claim of a type described in this item.

(b) The note that applies to item 4 of this Part of this Schedule applies equally to this item with the substitution of–
(i) the word "mineral" for "vitamin",
(ii) the word "minerals" for "vitamins" wherever it occurs, and
(iii) the word "vitamins" for "minerals" wherever it occurs.

(a) the word "mineral" for "vitamin" wherever it occurs.
(b) the word "minerals" for "vitamins" wherever it occurs, and
(c) the expression "Table B" for "Table A" wherever it occurs.

Cholesterol claims

6 A claim relating to the presence or absence of cholesterol in a food.

1 Subject to condition 3 the food must contain no more than 0.005 per cent of cholesterol.

2 The claim must not be accompanied by a suggestion, whether express or implied, that the food is beneficial to human health because of its level of cholesterol.

3 If the claim relates to the removal of cholesterol from, or its reduction in, the food and condition I is not met, such claims shall only be made–
(a) as part of an indication of the true nature of the food,
(b) as part of an indication of the treatment of the food,
(c) within the list of ingredients, or
(d) as a footnote in respect of a prescribed nutrition labelling.

4 The food shall be marked or labelled with the prescribed nutrition labelling.

Nutrition claims

7 Any nutrition claim not dealt with under any other item in this Part of this Schedule.

1 The food must be capable of fulfilling the claim.

2 The food shall be marked or labelled with the prescribed nutrition labelling.

Claims which depend on another food

8 A claim that a food has a particular value or conveys a particular benefit.

The value or benefit must not be derived wholly or partly form another food that is intended to be consumed with the food in relation to which the claim is made.

TABLE A—Vitamins in respect of which claims may be made

Column 1 Vitamin	Column 2 Recommended daily allowance
Vitamin A	800 micro g
Vitamin D	5 micro g
Vitamin E	10 mg
Vitamin C	60 mg
Thiamin	1.4 mg

Column 1	Column 2
Riboflavin	0.16 mg
Niacin	18 mg
Vitamin B6	2 mg
Folacin	200 micro g
Vitamin B12	1 micro g
Biotin	0.15 mg
Pantothenic acid	6 mg

TABLE B—Minerals in respect of which claims may be made

Column I	Column 2
Vitamin	Recommended daily allowance
Calcium	800 mg
Phosphorus	800 mg
Iron	14 mg
Magnesium	300 mg
Zinc	15 mg
Iodine	150 micro g

Note

As a rule, a significant amount means 15% of the recommended daily allowance listed in respect of each vitamin and mineral specified in Table A and B above that is supplied by 100 g or 100 ml of a food, or per package of a food if the package contains only a single portion.

8–13056

Regulation 41(3), (4)   SCHEDULE 7

NUTRITION LABELLING

PART I

PRESENTATION OF PRESCRIBED NUTRITION LABELLING

1. Prescribed nutrition labelling shall consist of such of the following items as under Part II of this Schedule are either required or permitted to be given. Subject to paragraphs 2, 3, 4, 5 and 6 below, the items and, where applicable, their order and manner of listing, are—

energy	(x) kJ and (x) kcal
protein	(x) g
carbohydrate	(x) g
of which:	
–sugars	(x) g
–polyols	(x) g
–starch	(x) g
fat	(x) g
of which:	
–saturates	(x) g
–mono-unsaturates	(x) g
–polyunsaturates	(x) g
–cholesterol	(x) mg
fibre	(x) g
sodium	(x) g
(vitamins)	(x units)
(minerals)	(x units) .

2. In the event that there is also required to be given the name and amount of any substance which belongs to, or is a component of, one of the items already given such substance or component shall be listed immediately after the item to which it relates, and in the following manner—

(item)	(x) g or mg
of which	(x) g or mg.
–(substance or component)	

3

  (a) For (vitamins) and (minerals) there shall be substituted, as appropriate, the names of any vitamin or mineral listed in Table A or B in Schedule 6.

  (b) For (item) there shall be substituted the name of the relevant item from the list in paragraph 1 above.

  (c) For (substance or component) there shall be substituted the name of the substance or component.

  (d) For (x) there shall be substituted the appropriate amount in each case and, in respect of vitamins and minerals, such amounts—

    (i) shall be expressed in the units of measurement specified in relation to the respective vitamins and minerals given in Table A or B in Schedule 6, and

    (ii) shall also be expressed as a percentage of the recommended daily allowance specified for such vitamins and minerals in those Tables.

4. All amounts given—

  (a) are to be per hundred grams or hundred millilitres of the food, as is appropriate, and, where it is wished to do so, those in either—

    (i) a quantified serving of the food, or

    (ii) provided that the total number of portions contained in that sales unit of the food is stated, in one such portion of the food,

  (b) shall be such amounts as are contained in the food as sold to the ultimate consumer or to a catering establishment save that, where sufficiently detailed instructions are given for the preparation for consumption of the food, they may (if expressly said to be so) be such amounts as are contained in the food after the completion of such preparation in accordance with the said instructions, and

Column 1   Column 2

(c) shall be averages based, either alone or in any combination, on—

(i) the manufacturer's analysis of the food,
(ii) a calculation from the actual average values of the ingredients used in the preparation of the food,
(iii) a calculation from generally established and accepted data,

and "averages" for the purposes of this sub-paragraph means the figures which best represent the respective amounts of the nutrients which a given food contains, there having been taken into account seasonal variability, patterns of consumption and any other factor which may cause the actual amount to vary.

5. In the calculation of the energy value the following conversion factors shall be employed—

(a) 1 gram of carbohydrate (excluding polyols) shall be deemed to contribute 17 kJ (4 kcal);
(b) 1 gram of polyols shall be deemed to contribute 10 kJ (2.4 kcal);
(c) 1 gram of protein shall be deemed to contribute 17 kJ (4 kcal);
(d) 1 gram of fat shall be deemed to contribute 37 kJ (9 kcal);
(e) 1 gram of ethanol shall be deemed to contribute 29 kJ (7 kcal);
(f) 1 gram of organic acid shall be deemed to contribute 13 kJ (3 kcal);
(g) 1 gram of salatrims shall be deemed to contirbutre 25 Kj (6 kcal).

6. Any prescribed nutrition labelling shall be presented together in one conspicuous place—

(a) in tabular form with any numbers aligned, or
(b) if there is insufficient space to permit tabular listing, in linear form.

PART II
CONTENTS OF PRESCRIBED NUTRITION LABELLING

1. In respect of any food other than one to which paragraph 2 below applies, prescribed nutrition labelling shall be given as follows—

(a) it shall include either—

(i) energy and the amounts of protein, carbohydrate and fat, or
(ii) energy and the amounts of protein, carbohydrate, sugars, fat, saturates, fibre and sodium, provided that, where sugars, saturates, fibre or sodium is, or are, the subject of a nutrition claim, it shall be given in accordance with paragraph (ii);

(b) where such is the subject of a nutrition claim, it shall also include the amounts of any polyols, starch, mono-unsaturates, polyunsaturates, cholesterol, vitamins or minerals, and in the absence of such a claim it may include any of these, provided that in either case only those vitamins or minerals present in a significant amount as described in the Note to Tables A and B in Schedule 6 above shall, or may, be so included;

(c) where labelling is given in accordance with sub-paragraph (a)(i) above and, further to sub-paragraph (b) above the amount of any of mono-unsaturates, polyunsaturates or cholesterol has been included, it shall also include the amount of saturates, and

(d) where such is the subject of a nutrition claim, it shall also include the name and amount of any substance which belongs to, or is a component of, one of the nutrients already required or permitted to be included.

2. (1) In respect of any food which is not prepacked and which is sold—

(a) to the ultimate consumer other than at a catering establishment,
(b) to the ultimate consumer from a vending machine, whether or not such machine is located at a catering establishment, or
(c) to a catering establishment,

the prescribed nutrition labelling shall include such of energy and the amounts of any nutrient and the name and amount of any substance which belongs to, or is a component of, any nutrient, in respect of which a nutrition claim is made, and it may include any of the items listed in paragraph 1 of Part I of this Schedule in respect of which there is no such claim.

8–13057

Regulation 42   SCHEDULE 8
                                  MISLEADING DESCRIPTIONS

PART I
GENERAL

Column 1	Column 2
Words and descriptions	Conditions
The description "dietary" or "dietetic".	Shall not be applied to any food unless it is a food for a particular nutritional use (excluding such foods formulated for infants and young children in good health) which— (a) has been specially made for a class of persons whose digestive process or metabolism is disturbed or who, by reason of their special physiological condition, obtain special benefit from a controlled consumption of certain substances, and (b) is suitable for fulfilling the particular nutritional requirements of that class of persons.
Any description incorporating the name of a food in such a way as to imply that the food, or the part of a food, being described has the flavour of the food named in the description.	Shall not be applied to any food unless the flavour of the food being described is derived wholly or mainly from the food named in the description, except that any description incorporating the word "chocolate" which is such as to imply that the food being described has a chocolate flavour may be applied to a food which has a chocolate flavour derived wholly or mainly from non fat cocoa solids where the purchaser would not be misled by the description.

Column 1 Words and descriptions	Column 2 Conditions
	This shall not be taken to prevent the use of the word "flavour" preceded by the name of a food when the flavour of the food being described is not wholly or mainly from the food named in the description.
A pictorial representation of a food which is such as to imply that the food to which the representation is applied has the flavour of the food depicted in the representation.	Shall not be applied to any food unless the flavour of the food to which the representation is applied is derived wholly or mainly from the food depicted in the representation.
The description "ice cream".	Shall not be applied to any food other than the frozen product containing not less than 5 per cent fat and not less than 2.5 per cent milk protein, not necessarily in natural proportions, and which is obtained by subjecting an emulsion of fat, milk solids and sugar (including any sweetener permitted in ice cream by the Sweeteners in Food Regulations 1995), with or without the addition of other substances, to heat treatment and either to subsequent freezing or evaporation, addition of water and subsequent freezing.
The description "dairy ice cream"	Shall not be applied to any food other than one which fulfils the conditions relating to application of the description "ice cream" to a food (provided that the fat in respect of which a minimum of 5 per cent is specified shall here consist exclusively of milk fat) and which contains no fat other than milk fat or any fat present by reason of the use as an ingredient of such ice cream of any egg, any flavouring, or any emulsifier or stabiliser.
The word "milk" or any other word or description which implies that the food being described contains milk.	Shall not be used as part of the name of a food, which contains the milk of an animal other than a cow, unless– (a) (i) such milk has all the normal constituents in their natural proportions, and (ii) the word or description is accompanied by the name of that animal; or (b) (i) such milk has been subjected to a process or treatment, and (ii) the word or description is accompanied by the name of that animal and an indication of that process or treatment; or (c) the word or description is used in accordance with any regulations made, or having effect as if made, under the Act or any order having effect as if contained in regulations so made.
The word "milk".	Shall not be used as the name of an ingredient where the ingredient is the milk of an animal other than a cow unless– (a) the word is accompanied by the name of the animal, and (b) the use of the word as the name of the ingredient complies in all other respects with these Regulations.
The description "starch-reduced".	Shall not be applied to any food, unless– (a) less than 50 per cent of the food consists of anhydrous carbohydrate calculated by weight on the dry matter of the food, and (b) the starch content of a given quantity of the food is substantially less than that of the same quantity of similar foods to which the description is not applied.
The word "vitamin" or any other word or description which implies that the food to which the word or description relates is a vitamin.	Shall not be used in the labelling or advertising of any food, unless the food to which the word or description relates is– (a) one of the vitamins specified in column 1 of Table A in Schedule 6; or (b) vitamin K.
The description "alcohol-free".	Shall not be applied to any alcoholic drink from which the alcohol has been extracted, unless– (a) the drink has an alcoholic strength by volume of not more than 0.05 per cent, and (b) the drink is marked or labelled with an indication of its maximum alcoholic strength (in one of the forms specified in regulation 30(1) immediately preceded by the words "not more than") or, in an appropriate case, with an indication that it contains no alcohol.
The description "dealcoholised".	Shall not be applied to any drink, unless– (a) the drink, being an alcoholic drink from which the alcohol has been extracted, has an alcoholic strength by volume of not more than 0.5 per cent, and

Column 1 Words and descriptions	Column 2 Conditions
	(b) the drink is marked or labelled with an indication of its maximum alcoholic strength (in one of the forms specified in regulation 30(1) immediately preceded by the words "not more than") or, in an appropriate case, with an indication that it contains no alcohol.
The description "low alcohol" or any other word or description which implies that the drink being described is low in alcohol.	Shall not be applied to any alcoholic drink unless–
	(a) the drink has an alcoholic strength by volume of not more than 1.2 per cent, and (b) the drink is marked or labelled with an indication of its maximum alcoholic strength (in one of the forms specified in regulation 30(1) immediately preceded by the words "not more than").
The description "low calorie" or any other word or description which implies that the drink being described is low in calories.	Shall not be applied to any soft drink unless the soft drink (where applicable, after subsequent preparation (which may include dilution) in accordance with any accompanying instructions) contains not more than 10 kcal per 100 ml and 42 kJ per 100 ml of the drink.
The description "non-alcoholic".	Shall not be used in conjunction with a name commonly associated with an alcoholic drink, except in the composite name "non-alcoholic wine" when that composite name is used in accordance with regulation 43.
The name "liqueur".	Shall not be applied to any drink other than one so qualifying under the definition of liqueur contained in Article 1.4(r) of Council Regulation (EEC) No 1576/89.
The name "Indian tonic water" or "quinine tonic water".	Shall not be applied to any drink unless the drink contains not less than 57 mg of quinine (calculated as quinine sulphate BP) per litre of the drink.
The name "tonic wine".	Shall not be applied to any drink unless there appears in immediate proximity to the words "tonic wine" the clear statement: "the name 'tonic wine' does not imply health giving or medicinal properties". No recommendation as to consumption or dosage shall appear in the labelling or advertising of the drink.

PART II

CHEESE

Column 1 Variety of cheese	Column 2 Maximum percentage of water
Cheddar	39
Blue Stilton	42
Derby	42
Leicester	42
Cheshire	44
Dunlop	44
Gloucester	44
Double Gloucester	44
Caerphilly	46
Wensleydale	46
White Stilton	46
Lancashire	48

PART III

CREAM

Column 1	Column 2
Clotted cream	The cream is clotted and contains not less than 55 per cent milk fat.
Double cream	The cream contains not less than 48 per cent milk fat.
Whipping cream	The cream contains not less than 35 per cent milk fat.
Whipped cream	The cream contains not less than 35 per cent milk fat and has been whipped.
Sterilised cream	The cream is sterilised cream and contains not less than 23 per cent milk fat.
Cream or single cream	The cream is not sterilised cream and contains not less than 18 per cent milk fat.
Sterilised half cream	The cream is sterilised cream and contains not less than 12 per cent milk fat.
Half cream	The cream is not sterilised cream and contains not less than 12 per cent milk fat.

Regulation (EC) No 178/2002

of the European Parliament and of the Council of 28 January 2002 laying down the general principles and requirements of food law, establishing the European Food Safety Authority and laying down procedures in matters of food safety

SECTION 4
GENERAL REQUIREMENTS OF FOOD LAW

8–13057A   Article 14. Food safety requirements.   1. Food shall not be placed on the market if it is unsafe.

2. Food shall be deemed to be unsafe if it is considered to be:

(*a*) injurious to health;
(*b*) unfit for human consumption.

3. In determining whether any food is unsafe, regard shall be had:

(*a*) to the normal conditions of use of the food by the consumer and at each stage of production, processing and distribution, and
(*b*) to the information provided to the consumer, including information on the label, or other information generally available to the consumer concerning the avoidance of specific adverse health effects from a particular food or category of foods.

4. In determining whether any food is injurious to health, regard shall be had:

(*a*) not only to the probable immediate and/or short-term and/or long-term effects of that food on the health of a person consuming it, but also on subsequent generations;
(*b*) to the probable cumulative toxic effects;
(*c*) to the particular health sensitivities of a specific category of consumers where the food is intended for that category of consumers.

5. In determining whether any food is unfit for human consumption, regard shall be had to whether the food is unacceptable for human consumption according to its intended use, for reasons of contamination, whether by extraneous matter or otherwise, or through putrefaction, deterioration or decay.

6. Where any food which is unsafe is part of a batch, lot or consignment of food of the same class or description, it shall be presumed that all the food in that batch, lot or consignment is also unsafe, unless following a detailed assessment there is no evidence that the rest of the batch, lot or consignment is unsafe.

7. Food that complies with specific Community provisions governing food safety shall be deemed to be safe insofar as the aspects covered by the specific Community provisions are concerned.

8. Conformity of a food with specific provisions applicable to that food shall not bar the competent authorities from taking appropriate measures to impose restrictions on it being placed on the market or to require its withdrawal from the market where there are reasons to suspect that, despite such conformity, the food is unsafe.

9. Where there are no specific Community provisions, food shall be deemed to be safe when it conforms to the specific provisions of national food law of the Member State in whose territory the food is marketed, such provisions being drawn up and applied without prejudice to the Treaty, in particular Articles 28 and 30 thereof.

8–13057B   Article 15. Feed safety requirements.   1. Feed shall not be placed on the market or fed to any food-producing animal if it is unsafe.

2. Feed shall be deemed to be unsafe for its intended use if it is considered to:

— have an adverse effect on human or animal health;
— make the food derived from food-producing animals unsafe for human consumption.

3. Where a feed which has been identified as not satisfying the feed safety requirement is part of a batch, lot or consignment of feed of the same class or description, it shall be presumed that all of the feed in that batch, lot or consignment is so affected, unless following a detailed assessment there is no evidence that the rest of the batch, lot or consignment fails to satisfy the feed safety requirement.

4. Feed that complies with specific Community provisions governing feed safety shall be deemed to be safe insofar as the aspects covered by the specific Community provisions are concerned.

5. Conformity of a feed with specific provisions applicable to that feed shall not bar the competent authorities from taking appropriate measures to impose restrictions on it being placed on the market or to require its withdrawal from the market where there are reasons to suspect that, despite such conformity, the feed is unsafe.

6. Where there are no specific Community provisions, feed shall be deemed to be safe when it conforms to the specific provisions of national law governing feed safety of the Member State in

whose territory the feed is in circulation, such provisions being drawn up and applied without prejudice to the Treaty, in particular Articles 28 and 30 thereof.

8–13057C   Article 16. Presentation.   Without prejudice to more specific provisions of food law, the labelling, advertising and presentation of food or feed, including their shape, appearance or packaging, the packaging materials used, the manner in which they are arranged and the setting in which they are displayed, and the information which is made available about them through whatever medium, shall not mislead consumers.

8–13057D   Article 17. Responsibilities.   1. Food and feed business operators at all stages of production, processing and distribution within the businesses under their control shall ensure that foods or feeds satisfy the requirements of food law which are relevant to their activities and shall verify that such requirements are met.

2. Member States shall enforce food law, and monitor and verify that the relevant requirements of food law are fulfilled by food and feed business operators at all stages of production, processing and distribution.

For that purpose, they shall maintain a system of official controls and other activities as appropriate to the circumstances, including public communication on food and feed safety and risk, food and feed safety surveillance and other monitoring activities covering all stages of production, processing and distribution.

Member States shall also lay down the rules on measures and penalties applicable to infringements of food and feed law. The measures and penalties provided for shall be effective, proportionate and dissuasive.

8–13057E   Article 18. Traceability.   1. The traceability of food, feed, food-producing animals, and any other substance intended to be, or expected to be, incorporated into a food or feed shall be established at all stages of production, processing and distribution.

2. Food and feed business operators shall be able to identify any person from whom they have been supplied with a food, a feed, a food-producing animal, or any substance intended to be, or expected to be, incorporated into a food or feed. To this end, such operators shall have in place systems and procedures which allow for this information to be made available to the competent authorities on demand.

3. Food and feed business operators shall have in place systems and procedures to identify the other businesses to which their products have been supplied. This information shall be made available to the competent authorities on demand.

4. Food or feed which is placed on the market or is likely to be placed on the market in the Community shall be adequately labelled or identified to facilitate its traceability, through relevant documentation or information in accordance with the relevant requirements of more specific provisions.

5. Provisions for the purpose of applying the requirements of this Article in respect of specific sectors may be adopted in accordance with the procedure laid down in Article 58(2).

8–13057F   Article 19. Responsibilities for food:food business operators.   1. If a food business operator considers or has reason to believe that a food which it has imported, produced, processed, manufactured or distributed is not in compliance with the food safety requirements, it shall immediately initiate procedures to withdraw the food in question from the market where the food has left the immediate control of that initial food business operator and inform the competent authorities thereof. Where the product may have reached the consumer, the operator shall effectively and accurately inform the consumers of the reason for its withdrawal, and if necessary, recall from consumers products already supplied to them when other measures are not sufficient to achieve a high level of health protection.

2. A food business operator responsible for retail or distribution activities which do not affect the packaging, labelling, safety or integrity of the food shall, within the limits of its respective activities, initiate procedures to withdraw from the market products not in compliance with the food-safety requirements and shall participate in contributing to the safety of the food by passing on relevant information necessary to trace a food, cooperating in the action taken by producers, processors, manufacturers and/or the competent authorities.

3. A food business operator shall immediately inform the competent authorities if it considers or has reason to believe that a food which it has placed on the market may be injurious to human health. Operators shall inform the competent authorities of the action taken to prevent risks to the final consumer and shall not prevent or discourage any person from cooperating, in accordance with national law and legal practice, with the competent authorities, where this may prevent, reduce or eliminate a risk arising from a food.

4. Food business operators shall collaborate with the competent authorities on action taken to avoid or reduce risks posed by a food which they supply or have supplied.

8–13057G   Article 20. Responsibilities for feed: feed business operators.   1. If a feed business operator considers or has reason to believe that a feed which it has imported, produced, processed, manufactured or distributed does not satisfy the feed safety requirements, it shall immediately initiate procedures to withdraw the feed in question from the market and inform the competent authorities thereof. In these circumstances or, in the case of Article 15(3), where the batch, lot or consignment does not satisfy the feed safety requirement, that feed shall be destroyed, unless the competent authority is satisfied otherwise. The operator shall effectively and accurately inform users of the feed of the reason for its withdrawal, and if necessary, recall from them products already supplied when other measures are not sufficient to achieve a high level of health protection.

2. A feed business operator responsible for retail or distribution activities which do not affect the packaging, labelling, safety or integrity of the feed shall, within the limits of its respective activities, initiate procedures to withdraw from the market products not in compliance with the feed-safety requirements and shall participate in contributing to the safety of food by passing on relevant information necessary to trace a feed, cooperating in the action taken by producers, processors, manufacturers and/or the competent authorities.

3. A feed business operator shall immediately inform the competent authorities if it considers or has reason to believe that a feed which it placed on the market may not satisfy the feed safety requirements.It shall inform the competent authorities of the action taken to prevent risk arising from the use of that feed and shall not prevent or discourage any person from cooperating, in accordance with national law and legal practice, with the competent authorities, where this may prevent, reduce or eliminate a risk arising from a feed.

4. Feed business operators shall collaborate with the competent authorities on action taken in order to avoid risks posed by a feed which they supply or have supplied.

8–13057H   Article 21. Liability.   The provisions of this Chapter shall be without prejudice to Council Directive 85/374/EEC of 25 July 1985 on the approximation of the laws, regulations and administrative provisions of the Member States concerning liability for defective products.

General Food Regulations 2004[1]

(SI 2004/3279 as amended by SI 2005/2626)

8–13058   1. Title, extent and commencement.   These Regulations may be cited as the General Food Regulations 2004; they extend to Great Britain and come into force on 1st January 2005.

---

1. Made by the Secretary of State, in exercise of the powers conferred by ss 16(1), 17(2), 26(1) and (3) and 48(1) of the Food Safety Act 1990.

8–13059   2. Interpretation.   (1) In these Regulations—

"the Act" means the Food Safety Act 1990;
"the Agency" means the Food Standards Agency;
"port health authority" means—

(a) in relation to the London port health district (within the meaning given to that phrase for the purposes of the Public Health (Control of Disease) Act 1984 by section 7(1) of that Act), the Common Council of the City of London; and
(b) in relation to any port health district constituted by order under section 2(3) of the Public Health (Control of Disease) Act 1984, a port health authority for that district constituted by order under section 2(4) of that Act;

"Regulation (EC) No 178/2002" means Regulation (EC) No 178/2002 of the European Parliament and of the Council laying down the general principles and requirements of food law, establishing the European Food Safety Authority and laying down procedures in matters of food safety.

(2) Expressions used both in these Regulations and in Regulation (EC) No 178/2002 have the same meaning in these Regulations as they have in that Regulation.

8–13060   3. Competent authorities for the purposes of Regulation (EC) No 178/2002.   (1) The following bodies are designated as the competent authorities for the purposes of the provisions of Regulation (EC) No 178/2002 specified in paragraph (2)—

(a) the Agency,
(b) each port health authority in its district, and
(c) outside such districts, each food authority in its area.

(2) Those provisions of Regulation (EC) No 178/2002 are—

(a) Article 14(8) (power of competent authorities to take appropriate measures to impose restrictions on the placing of food on the market or to require its withdrawal from the market in certain circumstances);
(b) Article 18(2) and (3) (competent authorities to whom food business operators must make information available on demand as to the traceability of food);
(c) Article 19 (food business operators to inform and collaborate with competent authorities to avoid or reduce risks posed by a food).

8–13061 4. Requirements under Regulation (EC) No 178/2002[1]: offences[1]. Any person who contravenes or fails to comply with any of the following provisions of Regulation (EC) No 178/2002 shall be guilty of an offence—

(a) Article 12 (food and feed exported from the Community) in so far as it relates to food;
(b) Article 14(1) (food safety requirements);
(c) Article 16 (presentation) in so far as it relates to food;
(d) Article 18(2) or (3) (traceability) in so far as it relates to food business operators;
(e) Article 19 (responsibilities for food: food business operators).

1. In this title, ante.
2. Regulation reproduced as in force in England.

8–13062 5. Punishment of offences. (1) A person guilty of an offence under regulation 4 shall be liable—

(a) on conviction on indictment, to a fine or to imprisonment for a term not exceeding two years or to both;
(b) on summary conviction, to a fine not exceeding the relevant amount or to imprisonment for a term not exceeding six months or to both.

(2) In paragraph (1) "the relevant amount" means—

(a) in the case of an offence under regulation 4(b), £20,000;[1]
(b) in any other case, the statutory maximum.

1. Reproduced as in force in England.

8–13063 6. Enforcement. (1) Subject to paragraph (2), each food authority shall enforce and execute the following provisions of Regulation (EC) No 178/2002 and these Regulations in its area—

(a) Article 12 in so far as it relates to food;
(b) Article 14;
(c) Article 16 in so far as it relates to food;
(d) Article 18 in so far as it relates to food business operators; and
(e) Article 19.[1]

(2) Each port health authority shall enforce and execute those provisions of Regulation (EC) No 178/2002 and these Regulations in its district.

(3) The Agency shall also enforce and execute Articles 14 and 19 of Regulation (EC) No 178/2002 and these Regulations in so far as they relate to those Articles as regards relevant food.

(4) In paragraph (3) "relevant food" means food in respect of which the Agency is specified in regulations made pursuant to section 6(4) of the Act or made under the European Communities Act 1972 as being the enforcement authority.

1. Reproduced as in force in England.

8–13063A 6A. In any proceedings for an offence of contravening or failing to comply with food law it shall be a defence for the accused to prove—

(a) that the item in respect of which the offence is alleged to have been committed was intended for export to a country that is not a member State and that the item could lawfully be exported there under Article 12 of Regulation (EC) No 178/2002; or
(b) that the item in respect of which the offence is alleged to have been committed was intended for export to a member State and that—

(i) the legislation applicable to that item in that member State is compatible with the applicable provisions of food law (except in so far as it relates to feed produced for or fed to food producing animals) at Community level, and
(ii) the item complies with that legislation.[1]

1. Inserted in relation to England by SI 2005/2626.

8–13064 7. Application of various provisions of the Act. (1) The following provisions of the Act shall apply for the purposes of these Regulations with the modification that any reference in those provisions to the Act or Part thereof shall be construed as a reference to these Regulations—

(a) section 20 (offences due to fault of another person);
(b) section 21 (defence of due diligence) with the modifications that subsections (2) to (4) shall apply in relation to an offence under regulation 4(a) or (b) as they apply in relation to an offence under section 14 or 15, and in subsection (4) the references to "sale" shall be deemed to include references to "placing on the market";
(c) section 22 (defence of publication in the course of a business) with the modification that the words "for sale" shall be omitted;
(d) section 30(8) (which relates to documentary evidence);

(*e*) section 35(1) (punishment of offences) in so far as it relates to offences under section 33(1) as applied by paragraph (3) below;
(*f*) section 35(2) and (3) in so far as it relates to offences under section 33(2) as applied by paragraph (3) below;
(*g*) section 36 (offences by bodies corporate);
(*h*) section 36A (offences by Scottish partnerships).

(2) In the application of section 32 of the Act (powers of entry) for the purposes of these Regulations, the references in subsection (1) to the Act shall be construed as including references to Regulation (EC) No 178/2002.

(3) The following provisions of the Act shall apply for the purposes of these Regulations with the modification that any reference in those provisions to the Act shall be construed as including a reference to Regulation (EC) No 178/2002 and these Regulations—

(*a*) section 3 (presumptions that food is intended for human consumption) with the modifications that the references to "sold" and "sale" shall be deemed to include references to "placed on the market" and "placing on the market" respectively;
(*b*) section 33(1) (obstruction etc of officers);
(*c*) section 33(2), with the modification that the reference to "any such requirement as is mentioned in subsection (1)(b) above" shall be deemed to be a reference to any such requirement as is mentioned in that subsection as applied by sub–paragraph (b) above;
(*d*) section 44 (protection of officers acting in good faith).

(4) Section 34 of the Act (time limit for prosecutions) shall apply to offences under regulation 4 as it applies to offences punishable under section 35(2) of the Act.

8–15

8–13065 16. Consequential amendment of Regulations. (1) This regulation applies to any provision of any Regulations by virtue of which immediately before the coming into force of these Regulations section 8(3) of the Act applies where any requirements of those Regulations or any requirements referred to in those Regulations are contravened in respect of any food.

(2) Any provision to which paragraph (1) applies shall be construed as providing that where any requirements of those Regulations or any requirements referred to in those Regulations are contravened in respect of any food and that food is part of a batch, lot or consignment of food of the same class or description, it shall be presumed, until the contrary is proved, that all of the food in that batch, lot or consignment fails to comply with those requirements.

Materials and Articles in Contact with Food (England) Regulations 2005[1]

(2005/898 amended by SI 2005/2626)

PART 1
PRELIMINARY

8–13065A 1. Title, application and commencement. These Regulations may be cited as the Materials and Articles in Contact with Food (England) Regulations 2005, apply in relation to England only and come into force on 29th April 2005.

---

1. Made by the Secretary of State, in exercise of the powers conferred on him by sections 16(2), 17(1) and (2), 26(1)(a) and (3), 31 and 48(1) of the Food Safety Act 1990.

8–13065B 2. Interpretation. (1) In these Regulations—

"the Act" means the Food Safety Act 1990;
"Directive 93/10/EEC" means Commission Directive 93/10/EEC relating to materials and articles made of regenerated cellulose film intended to come into contact with food;
"import" means import in the course of a business from a place other than a Member State;
"plastics" means those materials and articles to which Commission Directive 2002/72/EC relating to plastic materials intended to come into contact with foodstuffs applies;
"preparation" in relation to food includes manufacture and any form of treatment or process;
"regenerated cellulose film" means a thin sheet material obtained from refined cellulose derived from unrecycled wood or cotton, with or without the addition of suitable substances, either in the mass or on one or both surfaces, but does not include synthetic casings of regenerated cellulose;
"the 1998 Regulations" means the Plastic Materials and Articles in Contact with Food Regulations 1998;
"Regulation 1935/2004" means Regulation (EC) No 1935/2004 of the European Parliament and of the Council on materials and articles intended to come into contact with food and repealing Directives 80/590/EEC and 89/109/EEC;
"sell" includes offer or expose for sale or have in possession for sale, and "sale" and "sold" shall be construed accordingly.

(2) Any reference in these Regulations to a numbered Article is a reference to the Article bearing that number in Regulation 1935/2004.

(3) Expressions used in these Regulations and in Regulation 1935/2004 have the same meaning in these Regulations as in that Regulation.

8–13065C   3. Scope.   The provisions of these Regulations do not apply to those materials and articles specified in sub-paragraphs (a), (b) and (c) of Article 1(3).

PART 2
GENERAL REQUIREMENTS FOR MATERIALS AND ARTICLES

8–13065D   4. Enforcement of Regulation 1935/2004.   Subject to the provisions of Article 27 (transitional arrangements), any person who contravenes any of the following provisions of Regulation 1935/2004 is guilty of an offence—

(a)   Article 3 (general requirements);
(b)   Article 4 (special requirements for active and intelligent materials and articles);
(c)   Article 11(4) and (5) (provisions relating to Community authorisation);
(d)   Article 15(1), (2), (3), (4), (7) and (8) (labelling);
(e)   Article 16(1) (declaration of compliance);
(f)   on or after 27th October 2006, Article 17(2) (traceability).

8–13065E   5. Competent authorities for the purposes of Regulation 1935/2004.   The following bodies are designated as the competent authorities for the purposes of the provisions of Regulation 1935/2004 as specified below—

(a)   in respect of Articles 9 and 13, the Agency;
(b)   in respect of Articles 16(1) and 17(2), the Agency and the authority having responsibility for enforcement pursuant to regulation 12(1).

PART 3
REQUIREMENTS FOR VINYL CHLORIDE

8–13065F   6. Limits and migration limits.   (1) Materials and articles which are manufactured with vinyl chloride polymers or copolymers—

(a)   must not contain vinyl chloride monomer in a quantity exceeding 1 milligram per kilogram of the material or article as measured by the method of analysis specified in regulation 7(1); and
(b)   must be manufactured in such a way that they do not transfer to foods with which they are in contact any quantity of vinyl chloride exceeding 0.01 milligrams of vinyl chloride per kilogram of food as measured by the method of analysis specified in regulation 7(2).

(2) No person may—

(a)   sell;
(b)   import; or
(c)   use in the course of a business in connection with the storage, preparation, packaging, selling or serving of food,

any such material or article that does not comply with this regulation.

8–13065G   7. Methods of Analysis.   (1) The method used in analysing any sample for the purpose of establishing the quantity of vinyl chloride monomer present in the material or article in order to determine whether it complies with regulation 6(1)(a) shall be the method specified in the Annex to Commission Directive No 80/766/EEC (which lays down the Community method of analysis for the official control of the vinyl chloride monomer level in materials and articles which are intended to come into contact with foodstuffs).

(2) The method used in analysing any food for the purpose of establishing the quantity of vinyl chloride present in the food in order to determine whether a material or article which is or has been in contact with the food complies with regulation 6(1)(b) shall be the method specified in the Annex to Commission Directive No 81/432/EEC (which lays down the Community method of analysis for the official control of vinyl chloride released by material and articles into foodstuffs).

PART 4
REQUIREMENTS FOR REGENERATED CELLULOSE FILM

8–13065H   8. Controls and limits.   (1) This Part applies to regenerated cellulose film which—

(a)   constitutes a finished product in itself; or
(b)   is part of a finished product containing other materials,

and is intended to come into contact with food, or by being used for that purpose does come into contact with food.

(2) Any reference in this regulation to Annex II is a reference to Annex II to Directive 93/10/EEC.

(3) Subject to paragraph (5), no person may manufacture any regenerated cellulose film

intended to come into contact with food using any substance or group of substances other than the substances named or described—

(a) in the first column (denominations) of Annex II in the case of—

    (i) uncoated film; or
    (ii) coated film where the coating is derived from cellulose;

(b) in the first column of the First Part of Annex II in the case of film to be coated, where the coating will consist of plastics;

and other than in accordance with the conditions and restrictions specified in the corresponding entry in the second column of the appropriate Part of Annex II, as read with the preamble to that Annex.

(4) No person may manufacture any coating to be applied to film referred to in paragraph (3)(b) using any substance or group of substances other than the substances listed in Schedules 1, 2 or 2A to the 1998 Regulations and other than in accordance with the appropriate requirements, restrictions and specifications contained in those Regulations and in the Schedules thereto.

(5) Substances other than those listed in Annex II may be used as colourants or adhesives in the manufacture of a film to which paragraph (3)(a) applies, provided that such film is manufactured in such a way that it does not transfer any colourant or adhesive to food in any detectable quantity.

(6) Subject to regulation 10 no person may—

(a) sell;
(b) import; or
(c) use in the course of a business in connection with the storage, preparation, packaging, selling or serving of food,

any regenerated cellulose film which has been manufactured in contravention of the requirements of paragraphs (3) or (4), or which fails to comply with paragraph (8).

(7) No person may use in the course of a business in connection with the storage, preparation, packaging, serving or selling of food—

(a) where the food contains water physically free at the surface, any regenerated cellulose film containing bis(2–hydroxyethyl) ether, ethanediol or both these substances;

(b) any regenerated cellulose film in such a way that any printed surface of that film comes into contact with the food.

(8) Any material or article made of regenerated cellulose film, unless by its nature clearly intended to come into contact with food, at a marketing stage other than the retail stage must be accompanied by a written declaration attesting that it complies with the legislation applicable to it.

8–13065I   9. Migration limits for regenerated cellulose film coated with plastics. (1) Subject to paragraph (2), no person shall manufacture or import any material or article made with regenerated cellulose film coated with plastics which—

(a) is intended to come into contact with food; and
(b) is capable of transferring its constituents to food in quantities exceeding an overall migration limit of 10 milligrams per square decimetre of the surface of the material or article in contact with food.

(2) In the case of any material or article made with regenerated cellulose film coated with plastics which—

(a) is or is comparable to a container or which can be filled with a capacity of not less than 500 millilitres and not more than 10 litres; or
(b) can be filled and for which it is impracticable to estimate the surface area in contact with food; or
(c) is a cap, gasket, stopper or similar device for sealing,

the overall migration limit shall be 60 milligrams of constituents transferred per kilogram of food.

(3) No person shall manufacture or import any material or article made with regenerated cellulose film coated with plastics manufactured with any substance listed in Part I of Schedule 1 to the 1998 Regulations (authorised monomers) which—

(a) is intended to come into contact with food; and
(b) is capable of transferring its constituents to food in quantities exceeding the specific migration limits set out in column 4 of that Part as read with Part II of that Schedule.

(4) Where the migration limit for a substance mentioned in paragraph (3) is expressed in milligrams per kilogram, in the case of regenerated cellulose film coated with plastics which—

(a) is or is comparable to a container or which can be filled with a capacity of less than 500 millilitres or more than 10 litres; or
(b) cannot be filled or for which it is impracticable to estimate the relationship between the surface area of the film and the quantity of food in contact with it,

the migration limit shall be divided by the conversion factor of 6 in order to express it in milligrams of constituents transferred per square decimetre of the material or article in contact with food.

(5) Subject to paragraph (6), the verification of compliance with migration limits shall be conducted in accordance with the provisions of Schedules 3 and 4 of the 1998 Regulations as read with regulation 6 of those Regulations and for the purposes of this paragraph any reference in those provisions to a plastic material or article shall be construed as a reference to regenerated cellulose film coated with plastic.

(6) Paragraph (5) shall not apply in any circumstances to which regulation 7(1) or (2) is applicable.

8–13065J   10. Saving and transitional provisions and defences.   (1) Notwithstanding the revocations in regulation 16, in relation to regenerated cellulose film manufactured before 29th April 1994 the defences in regulation 6A of the Materials and Articles in Contact with Food Regulations 1987 shall apply in relation to offences under these Regulations in like manner as they applied to offences under the equivalent provisions in those Regulations.

(2) In any proceedings for an offence under regulation 8(3), (4), (6) or (7), or regulation 9(1) or (3) it shall be a defence to prove that—

(a) the act constituting the offence was committed in relation to a material or article made with regenerated cellulose film which was manufactured or imported into the European Community before 29th January 2006; and

(b) the act constituting the offence would not have constituted an offence under the Materials and Articles in Contact with Food Regulations 1987 immediately before the coming into force of these Regulations.

(3) *Revoked.*

PART 5
GENERAL

8–13065K   11. Offences and penalties.   (1) Any person who contravenes the provisions of regulation 6(2), 8(3), (4), (6) or (7), or 9(1) or (3) is guilty of an offence.

(2) Any person guilty of an offence under paragraph (1) or under regulation 4 is liable—

(a) on conviction on indictment to a fine or to imprisonment for a term not exceeding two years or to both;

(b) on summary conviction to a fine not exceeding the statutory maximum or to a term of imprisonment not exceeding 6 months or to both.

8–13065L   12. Enforcement.   (1) Each food authority in its area and each port health authority in its district shall execute and enforce—

(a) the provisions of Regulation 1935/2004 mentioned in regulation 4, and

(b) these Regulations.

(2) The Agency shall also execute and enforce the provisions of Articles 16(1) and 17(2).

8–13065M   13. Analysis by Government Chemist.   (1) The court before which any proceedings are taken under these Regulations may, if it thinks fit for the purposes of the proceedings, cause—

(a) any material or article which is the subject of the proceedings and which, if it has already been tested is capable of being further tested, or

(b) any food which has been in contact with any such material or article,

to be sent to the Government Chemist who shall carry out such testing as is appropriate and transmit to the court a certificate of the result, and the costs of the testing shall be paid by the prosecutor or the person charged as the court may order.

(2) If in a case where an appeal is brought no action has been taken under paragraph (1), the provisions of that paragraph shall apply in relation to the court by which the appeal is heard.

(3) Any certificate of the results of testing transmitted by the Government Chemist under this regulation shall be signed by or on behalf of him, but the testing may be carried out by any person under the direction of the person who signs the certificate.

(4) Any certificate transmitted by the Government Chemist in accordance with paragraph (3) shall be taken as evidence of the facts stated therein unless any party to the proceedings requests that the person by whom the certificate is signed be called as a witness.

(5) In this regulation the term "testing" includes examination and analysis, and "tested" shall be construed accordingly.

8–13065N   14. Application of various provisions of the Act.   (1) The following provisions of the Act apply for the purposes of these Regulations with the modification that any reference in those provisions to the Act or Part thereof shall be construed as a reference to these Regulations—

(a) section 2 (extending meaning of "sale" etc);

(b) section 20 (offences due to fault of another person);

(c) section 21 (defence of due diligence) with the modification that in subsection (4) the references to "sale" shall be deemed to include references to "placing on the market";

(d) section 30(8) (which relates to documentary evidence);
(e) section 35(1) (punishment of offences) in so far as it relates to offences under section 33(1) as applied by paragraph (3) below;
(f) section 35(2) and (3) in so far as it relates to offences under section 33(2) as applied by paragraph (3) below;
(g) section 36 (offences by bodies corporate);
(h) section 36A (offences by Scottish partnerships).

(2) In the application of section 32 of the Act (powers of entry) for the purposes of these Regulations, the reference in subsection (1) to the Act shall be construed as including a reference to Regulation 1935/2004.
(3) The following provisions of the Act apply for the purposes of these Regulations with the modification that any reference in those provisions to the Act shall be construed as including a reference to Regulation 1935/2004 and these Regulations—

(a) section 3 (presumptions that food is intended for human consumption) with the modifications that the references to "sold" and "sale" shall be deemed to include references to "placed on the market" and "placing on the market" respectively;
(b) section 33(1) (obstruction etc of officers);
(c) section 33(2), with the modification that the reference to "any such requirement as is mentioned in subsection (1)(b) above" shall be deemed to be a reference to any such requirement as is mentioned in that subsection as applied by sub–paragraph (b);
(d) section 44 (protection of officers acting in good faith).

(4) Section 34 of the Act (time limit for prosecutions) applies to offences under these Regulations as it applies to offences punishable under section 35(2) of the Act.

8–13065O 15. Amendments to the 1998 Regulations. (1) The 1998 Regulations are amended in relation to England in accordance with paragraphs (2) to (6).
(2) In regulation 2 (interpretation)—

(a) omit the definition of "the 1987 Regulations";
(b) after the definition of "the 1992 Regulations" insert the following definition—

""the 2005 Regulations" means the Materials and Articles in Contact with Food (England) Regulations 2005;".

(3) In paragraph (1)(b) of regulation 6 (method of testing the capability of plastic materials or articles to transfer constituents and methods of analysis) for "regulation 14(2) of the 1987 Regulations" substitute "regulation 7(2) of the 2005 Regulations".
(4) In paragraph (1) of regulation 9 (enforcement) for "the 1987 Regulations" substitute "the 2005 Regulations".
(5) In regulation 11 (presumption as to food with which a plastic material or article, adhesive or material or article covered by a surface coating is to come into contact) for "the 1987 Regulations" substitute "Regulation (EC) No 1935/2004 of the European Parliament and of the Council".
(6) For regulation 12 (application of other provisions) substitute the following—

"**Application of other provisions 12.** (1) The following provisions of the Act shall apply for the purposes of these Regulations as they apply for the purposes of the Act—

(a) section 3 (presumption that food is intended for human consumption);
(b) section 30(8) (relating to documentary evidence);
(c) section 44 (protection of officers acting in good faith).

(2) Regulation 13 of the 2005 Regulations shall apply in relation to proceedings taken under these Regulations as it does to proceedings taken under those Regulations.".

8–13065P 16. Revocations. The following Regulations or parts thereof are revoked in so far as they apply in relation to England—

(a) The Materials and Articles in Contact with Food Regulations 1987;
(b) Regulation 3 of The Food Safety (Export) Regulations 1991;
(c) The Materials and Articles in Contact with Food (Amendment) Regulations 1994.

Food Hygiene (England) Regulations 2006[1]
(SI 2006/14)

PART 1
PRELIMINARY

PART 1
PRELIMINARY

8–13066 1. Title, commencement and application. These Regulations—

(a) may be cited as the Food Hygiene (England) Regulations 2006;

    (*b*)   come into force on 11th January 2006; and

    (*c*)   apply in relation to England only.

---

1. Made by the Secretary of State in exercise of the powers conferred on her by s 2(2) of the European Communities Act 1972.

8–13066A   **2. Interpretation.**   (1) In these Regulations—

"the Act" means the Food Safety Act 1990;

"the Agency" means the Food Standards Agency;

"authorised officer", in relation to an enforcement authority, means any person (whether or not an officer of the authority) who is authorised by them in writing, either generally or specially, to act in matters arising under the Hygiene Regulations;

"the Community Regulations" means Regulation 852/2004, Regulation 853/2004, Regulation 854/2004, Regulation 2073/2005 and Regulation 2075/2005;

"Directive 2004/41", "Regulation 178/2002", "Regulation 1642/2003", "Regulation 852/2004", "Regulation 853/2004", "Regulation 854/2004", "Regulation 882/2004", "Regulation 1688/2005", "Regulation 2073/2005", "Regulation 2074/2005", "Regulation 2075/2005" and "Regulation 2076/2005" have the meanings respectively given to them in Schedule 1;

"enforcement authority" means the authority which, by virtue of regulation 5, is responsible for executing and enforcing the Hygiene Regulations;

"food authority" has the meaning that it bears by virtue of section 5(1) of the Act, except that it does not include the appropriate Treasurer referred to in section 5(1)(*c*) of the Act (which deals with the Inner Temple and Middle Temple);

"the Hygiene Regulations" means these Regulations and the Community Regulations;

"premises" includes any establishment, any place, vehicle, stall or moveable structure and any ship or aircraft; and

"specified Community provision" means any provision of the Community Regulations that is specified in Column 1 of Schedule 2 and whose subject-matter is described in Column 2 of that Schedule.

(2) Subject to paragraph (3), any expression other than one defined in paragraph (1) that is used both in these Regulations and in the Act has the meaning it bears in the Act.

(3) Unless the context otherwise requires, any expression used both in these Regulations and in Regulation 178/2002 or the Community Regulations has the meaning that it bears in Regulation 178/2002 or the Community Regulations, as the case may be.

(4) Where any functions under the Act are assigned—

    (*a*)   by an order under section 2 or 7 of the Public Health (Control of Disease) Act 1984, to a port health authority;

    (*b*)   by an order under section 6 of the Public Health Act 1936, to a joint board for a united district; or

    (*c*)   by an order under paragraph 15(6) of Schedule 8 to the Local Government Act 1985, to a single authority for a metropolitan county,

any reference in these Regulations to a food authority shall be construed, so far as relating to those functions, as a reference to the authority to whom they are so assigned.

(5) Where, apart from this paragraph, any period of less than seven days which is specified in these Regulations would include any day which is—

    (*a*)   a Saturday, a Sunday, Christmas Day or Good Friday; or

    (*b*)   a day which is a bank holiday under the Banking and Financial Dealings Act 1971,

that day shall be excluded from the period.

8–13066B   **3. Presumptions that food is intended for human consumption.**   (1) The following paragraphs shall apply for the purposes of these Regulations.

(2) Any food commonly used for human consumption shall, if placed on the market or offered, exposed or kept for placing on the market, be presumed, until the contrary is proved, to have been placed on the market or, as the case may be, to have been or to be intended for placing on the market for human consumption.

(3) The following, namely—

    (*a*)   any food commonly used for human consumption which is found on premises used for the preparation, storage, or placing on the market of that food; and

    (*b*)   any article or substance commonly used in the manufacture of food for human consumption which is found on premises used for the preparation, storage or placing on the market of that food,

shall be presumed, until the contrary is proved, to be intended for placing on the market, or for manufacturing food for placing on the market, for human consumption.

(4) Any article or substance capable of being used in the composition or preparation of any food commonly used for human consumption which is found on premises on which that food is prepared shall, until the contrary is proved, be presumed to be intended for such use.

8–13066C **4. Competent authority.** The competent authority for the purposes of the Community Regulations shall be the Agency except where it has delegated competences as provided for in those Regulations.

8–13066D **5. Enforcement.** (1) In respect of any food business operator to whose operations Regulation 852/2004 applies but Regulation 853/2004 does not apply—

(a) the Agency or the food authority in whose area the food business operator carries out his operations shall execute and enforce the Hygiene Regulations in so far as the operator concerned is carrying out primary production and those associated operations listed in paragraph 1 of Part AI of Annex I to Regulation 852/2004 other than the associated operations described in sub–paragraphs (a) and (c) of that paragraph to the extent that they concern wild game; and

(b) the food authority in whose area the food business operator carries out his operations shall execute and enforce the Hygiene Regulations in so far as the operator concerned is carrying out operations which are not executed and enforced by the Agency or the food authority as provided for in sub–paragraph (a).

(2) In respect of any food business operator to whose operations both Regulation 852/2004 and Regulation 853/2004 apply—

(a) the Agency shall execute and enforce the Hygiene Regulations in so far as the operator concerned is carrying out operations in relation to—

(i) a slaughterhouse,

(ii) a game-handling establishment, or

(iii) a cutting plant; and

(b) the Agency or the food authority in whose area the food business operator carries out his operations shall execute and enforce the Hygiene Regulations in so far as the operator concerned is carrying out operations in relation to any establishment that is not specified in sub–paragraph (a).

(3) In respect of—

(a) collection centres and tanneries supplying raw material for the production of gelatine intended for human consumption pursuant to paragraph 5 of Chapter I of Section XIV of Annex III to Regulation 853/2004; and

(b) collection centres and tanneries supplying raw material for the production of collagen intended for human consumption pursuant to paragraph 5 of Chapter I of Section XV of Annex III to Regulation 853/2004,

the food authority in whose area the collection centre or tannery concerned is situated shall execute and enforce the Hygiene Regulations.

(4) Each food authority shall execute and enforce these Regulations in its area in relation to the matters regulated by—

(a) Schedules 3 to 5; and

(b) Schedule 6 in so far as it applies in relation to raw milk intended for direct human consumption other than raw cows' milk.

(5) The Agency shall execute and enforce these Regulations in relation to the matters regulated by Schedule 6 in so far as it applies in relation to raw cows' milk intended for direct human consumption.

(6) In this regulation—

"cutting plant" means an establishment which is used for boning and/or cutting up fresh meat for placing on the market and which—

(a) is approved or conditionally approved under Article 31(2) of Regulation 882/2004; or

(b) (although lacking the approval or conditional approval that it requires under Article 4(3) of Regulation 853/2004) was, on 31st December 2005, operating as licensed cutting premises under the Fresh Meat (Hygiene and Inspection) Regulations 1995 or the Poultry Meat, Farmed Game Bird Meat and Rabbit Meat (Hygiene and Inspection) Regulations 1995;

"game-handling establishment" means any establishment in which game and game meat obtained after hunting are prepared for placing on the market and which—

(a) is approved or conditionally approved under Article 31(2) of Regulation 882/2004; or

(b) (although lacking the approval or conditional approval that it requires under Article 4(3) of Regulation 853/2004) was, on 31st December 2005, operating as a licensed wild game processing facility under the Wild Game Meat (Hygiene and Inspection) Regulations 1995; and

"slaughterhouse" means an establishment used for slaughtering and dressing animals, the meat of which is intended for human consumption and which—

(a) is approved or conditionally approved under Article 31(2) of Regulation 882/2004; or

(b) (although lacking the approval or conditional approval that it requires under Article 4(3) of Regulation 853/2004) was, on 31st December 2005, operating as a licensed slaughterhouse under the Fresh Meat (Hygiene and Inspection) Regulations 1995 or the Poultry Meat, Farmed Game Bird Meat and Rabbit Meat (Hygiene and Inspection) Regulations 1995.

PART 2
MAIN PROVISIONS

8–13066E 6. Hygiene improvement notices.   (1) If an authorised officer of an enforcement authority has reasonable grounds for believing that a food business operator is failing to comply with the Hygiene Regulations, he may by a notice served on that person (in these Regulations referred to as a "hygiene improvement notice")—

- (a) state the officer's grounds for believing that the food business operator is failing to comply with the Hygiene Regulations;
- (b) specify the matters which constitute the food business operator's failure to comply;
- (c) specify the measures which, in the officer's opinion, the food business operator must take in order to secure compliance; and
- (d) require the food business operator to take those measures, or measures which are at least equivalent to them, within such period (not being less than 14 days) as may be specified in the notice.

(2) Any person who fails to comply with a hygiene improvement notice shall be guilty of an offence.

8–13066F 7. Hygiene prohibition orders.   (1) If—

- (a) a food business operator is convicted of an offence under these Regulations; and
- (b) the court by or before which he is so convicted is satisfied that the health risk condition is fulfilled with respect to the food business concerned,

the court shall by an order impose the appropriate prohibition.

(2) The health risk condition is fulfilled with respect to any food business if any of the following involves risk of injury to health (including any impairment, whether permanent or temporary), namely—

- (a) the use for the purposes of the business of any process or treatment;
- (b) the construction of any premises used for the purposes of the business, or the use for those purposes of any equipment; and
- (c) the state or condition of any premises or equipment used for the purposes of the business.

(3) The appropriate prohibition is—

- (a) in a case falling within sub–paragraph (a) of paragraph (2), a prohibition on the use of the process or treatment for the purposes of the business;
- (b) in a case falling within sub–paragraph (b) of that paragraph, a prohibition on the use of the premises or equipment for the purposes of the business or any other food business of the same class or description; and
- (c) in a case falling within sub–paragraph (c) of that paragraph, a prohibition on the use of the premises or equipment for the purposes of any food business.

(4) If—

- (a) a food business operator is convicted of an offence under these Regulations; and
- (b) the court by or before which he is so convicted thinks it proper to do so in all the circumstances of the case,

the court may, by an order, impose a prohibition on the food business operator participating in the management of any food business, or any food business of a class or description specified in the order.

(5) As soon as practicable after the making of an order under paragraph (1) or (4) (in these Regulations referred to as a "hygiene prohibition order"), the enforcement authority shall—

- (a) serve a copy of the order on the relevant food business operator; and
- (b) in the case of an order made under paragraph (1), affix a copy of the order in a conspicuous position on such premises used for the purposes of the food business as they consider appropriate,

and any person who knowingly contravenes such an order shall be guilty of an offence.

(6) A hygiene prohibition order shall cease to have effect—

- (a) in the case of an order made under paragraph (1), on the issue by the enforcement authority of a certificate to the effect that they are satisfied that the food business operator has taken sufficient measures to secure that the health risk condition is no longer fulfilled with respect to the food business; and
- (b) in the case of an order made under paragraph (4), on the giving by the court of a direction to that effect.

(7) The enforcement authority shall issue a certificate under sub–paragraph (a) of paragraph (6) within three days of their being satisfied as mentioned in that sub–paragraph; and on an application by the food business operator for such a certificate, the authority shall—

(a)   determine, as soon as is reasonably practicable and in any event within 14 days, whether or not they are so satisfied; and

(b)   if they determine that they are not so satisfied, give notice to the food business operator of the reasons for that determination.

(8) The court shall give a direction under sub–paragraph (b) of paragraph (6) if, on an application by the food business operator, the court thinks it proper to do so having regard to all the circumstances of the case, including in particular the conduct of the food business operator since the making of the order; but no such application shall be entertained if it is made—

(a)   within six months of the making of the hygiene prohibition order; or

(b)   within three months of the making by the food business operator of a previous application for such a direction.

(9) Where a magistrates' court makes an order under paragraph (2) of regulation 8 with respect to any food business, paragraph (1) shall apply as if the food business operator had been convicted by the court of an offence under these Regulations.

(10) Where the commission of an offence by a food business operator leads to the conviction of another person pursuant to regulation 10, paragraph (4) shall apply in relation to that other person as it applies in relation to the food business operator and any reference in paragraph (5) or (8) to the food business operator shall be construed accordingly.

8–13066G   8. Hygiene emergency prohibition notices and orders.   (1) If an authorised officer of an enforcement authority is satisfied that the health risk condition is fulfilled with respect to any food business he may by a notice served on the relevant food business operator (in these Regulations referred to as a "hygiene emergency prohibition notice") impose the appropriate prohibition.

(2) If a magistrates' court is satisfied, on the application of such an officer, that the health risk condition is fulfilled with respect to any food business, the court shall, by an order (in these Regulations referred to as a "hygiene emergency prohibition order"), impose the appropriate prohibition.

(3) Such an officer shall not apply for a hygiene emergency prohibition order unless, at least one day before the date of the application, he has served notice on the relevant food business operator of his intention to apply for the order.

(4) Paragraphs (2) and (3) of regulation 7 shall apply for the purposes of this regulation as they apply for the purposes of that regulation, but as if the reference in paragraph (2) to risk of injury to health were a reference to imminent risk of injury.

(5) As soon as practicable after the service of a hygiene emergency prohibition notice, an authorised officer of an enforcement authority shall affix a copy of the notice in a conspicuous position on such premises used for the purposes of the food business as he considers appropriate; and any person who knowingly contravenes such a notice shall be guilty of an offence.

(6) As soon as practicable after the making of a hygiene emergency prohibition order, an authorised officer of an enforcement authority shall—

(a)   serve a copy of the order on the relevant food business operator; and

(b)   affix a copy of the order in a conspicuous position on such premises used for the purposes of the food business as he considers appropriate,

and any person who knowingly contravenes such an order shall be guilty of an offence.

(7) A hygiene emergency prohibition notice shall cease to have effect—

(a)   if no application for a hygiene emergency prohibition order is made within the period of three days beginning with the service of the notice, at the end of that period; or

(b)   if such an application is so made, on the determination or abandonment of the application.

(8) A hygiene emergency prohibition notice or a hygiene emergency prohibition order shall cease to have effect on the issue by the enforcement authority of a certificate to the effect that they are satisfied that the food business operator has taken sufficient measures to secure that the health risk condition is no longer fulfilled with respect to the food business.

(9) The enforcement authority shall issue a certificate under paragraph (8) within three days of their being satisfied as mentioned in that paragraph; and on an application by the food business operator for such a certificate, the authority shall—

(a)   determine as soon as is reasonably practicable and in any event within 14 days whether or not they are so satisfied; and

(b)   if they determine that they are not so satisfied, give notice to the food business operator of the reasons for that determination.

(10) Where a hygiene emergency prohibition notice is served on a food business operator, the enforcement authority shall compensate him in respect of any loss suffered by reason of his complying with the notice unless—

(a)   an application for a hygiene emergency prohibition order is made within the period of three days beginning with the service of the notice; and

(b)   the court declares itself satisfied, on the hearing of the application, that the health risk condition was fulfilled with respect to the food business at the time when the notice was served, and any disputed question as to the right to or the amount of any compensation payable under this paragraph shall be determined by arbitration.

8–13066H 9. Remedial action notices and detention notices. (1) Where it appears to an authorised officer of an enforcement authority that in respect of an establishment subject to approval under Article 4(2) of Regulation 853/2004—

(a) any of the requirements of the Hygiene Regulations is being breached; or
(b) inspection under the Hygiene Regulations is being hampered,

he may, by a notice in writing (in these Regulations referred to as a "remedial action notice") served on the relevant food business operator or his duly authorised representative—

(c) prohibit the use of any equipment or any part of the establishment specified in the notice;
(d) impose conditions upon or prohibit the carrying out of any process; or
(e) require the rate of operation to be reduced to such extent as is specified in the notice, or to be stopped completely.

(2) A remedial action notice shall be served as soon as practicable and shall state why it is being served.

(3) If it is served under paragraph (1)(a), it shall specify the breach and the action needed to remedy it.

(4) An authorised officer of the enforcement authority whose authorised officer served the original remedial action notice shall, as soon as he is satisfied that such action has been taken, withdraw the notice by a further notice in writing served on the food business operator or his duly authorised representative.

(5) An authorised officer of an enforcement authority may, at an establishment subject to approval under Article 4(2) of Regulation 853/2004, by a notice in writing (in this regulation referred to as a "detention notice") served on the relevant food business operator or his duly authorised representative require the detention of any animal or food for the purpose of examination (including the taking of samples).

(6) An authorised officer of the enforcement authority whose officer served the original detention notice shall, as soon as he is satisfied that the animal or food need no longer be detained, withdraw the notice by a further notice in writing served on the food business operator or his duly authorised representative.

(7) Any person who fails to comply with a remedial action notice or a detention notice shall be guilty of an offence.

8–13066I 10. Offences due to fault of another person. Where the commission by any person of an offence under these Regulations is due to the act or default of some other person, that other person shall be guilty of the offence; and a person may be convicted of the offence by virtue of this regulation whether or not proceedings are taken against the first–mentioned person.

8–13066J 11. Defence of due diligence. (1) In any proceedings for an offence under these Regulations, it shall, subject to paragraph (2), be a defence for the accused to prove that he took all reasonable precautions and exercised all due diligence to avoid the commission of the offence by himself or by a person under his control.

(2) If in any case the defence provided by paragraph (1) involves the allegation that the commission of the offence was due to an act or default of another person, or to reliance on information supplied by another person, the accused shall not, without leave of the court, be entitled to rely on that defence unless—

(a) at least seven clear days before the hearing; and
(b) where he has previously appeared before a court in connection with the alleged offence, within one month of his first such appearance,

he has served on the prosecutor a notice in writing giving such information identifying or assisting in the identification of that other person as was then in his possession.

PART 3

ADMINISTRATION AND ENFORCEMENT

8–13066K 12. Procurement of samples. An authorised officer of an enforcement authority may—

(a) purchase a sample of any food, or any substance capable of being used in the preparation of food;
(b) take a sample of any food, or any such substance, which—

   (i) appears to him to be intended for placing on the market or to have been placed on the market, for human consumption, or
   (ii) is found by him on or in any premises which he is authorised to enter by or under regulation 14;

(c) take a sample from any food source, or a sample of any contact material, which is found by him on or in any such premises; and

(d) take a sample of any article or substance which is found by him on or in any such premises and which he has reason to believe may be required as evidence in proceedings under any of the provisions of these Regulations.

8–13066L   13. Analysis etc of samples. (1) An authorised officer of an enforcement authority who has procured a sample under regulation 12 shall—

(a) if he considers that the sample should be analysed, submit it to be analysed—

    (i) by the public analyst for the area in which the sample was procured, or

    (ii) by the public analyst for the area which consists of or includes the area of the authority; and

(b) if he considers that the sample should be examined, submit it to be examined by a food examiner.

(2) A person, other than such an officer, who has purchased any food, or any substance capable of being used in the preparation of food, may submit a sample of it—

(a) to be analysed by the public analyst for the area in which the purchase was made; or

(b) to be examined by a food examiner.

(3) If, in any case where a sample is proposed to be submitted for analysis under this regulation, the office of public analyst for the area in question is vacant, the sample shall be submitted to the public analyst for some other area.

(4) If, in any case where a sample is proposed to be or is submitted for analysis or examination under this regulation, the food analyst or examiner determines that he is for any reason unable to perform the analysis or examination, the sample shall be submitted or, as the case may be, sent by him to such other food analyst or examiner as he may determine.

(5) A food analyst or examiner shall analyse or examine as soon as practicable any sample submitted or sent to him under this regulation, but may, except where—

(a) he is the public analyst for the area in question; and

(b) the sample is submitted to him for analysis by an authorised officer of an enforcement authority,

demand in advance the payment of such reasonable fee as he may require.

(6) Any food analyst or examiner who has analysed or examined a sample shall give to the person by whom it was submitted a certificate specifying the result of the analysis or examination.

(7) Any certificate given by a food analyst or examiner under paragraph (6) shall be signed by him, but the analysis or examination may be made by any person acting under his direction.

(8) In any proceedings under these Regulations, the production by one of the parties—

(a) of a document purporting to be a certificate given by a food analyst or examiner under paragraph (6); or

(b) of a document supplied to him by the other party as being a copy of such a certificate,

shall be sufficient evidence of the facts stated in it unless, in a case falling within sub–paragraph (a), the other party requires that the food analyst or examiner shall be called as a witness.

(9) Where two or more public analysts are appointed for any area, any reference in this regulation to the public analyst for that area shall be construed as a reference to either or any of them.

(10) The Food Safety (Sampling and Qualifications) Regulations 1990 shall apply in relation to a sample procured by an authorised officer of a food authority under regulation 12 as if it were a sample procured by an authorised officer under section 29 of the Act.

(11) The certificate given by a food analyst or examiner under paragraph (6) shall be in the form set out in Schedule 3 to the Food Safety (Sampling and Qualifications) Regulations 1990.

8–13066M   14. Powers of entry. (1) An authorised officer of a food authority shall, on producing, if so required, some duly authenticated document showing his authority, have a right at all reasonable hours—

(a) to enter any premises within the authority's area for the purpose of ascertaining whether there is or has been on the premises any contravention of the provisions of the Hygiene Regulations;

(b) to enter any premises, whether within or outside the authority's area, for the purpose of ascertaining whether there is on the premises any evidence of any such contravention within that area; and

(c) to enter any premises for the purpose of the performance by the authority of their functions under the Hygiene Regulations,

but admission to any premises used only as a private dwelling–house shall not be demanded as of right unless 24 hours' notice of the intended entry has been given to the occupier.

(2) An authorised officer of the Agency shall, on producing if so required some duly authenticated document showing his authority, have a right at all reasonable hours to enter any premises for the purpose of—

(a) ascertaining whether there is or has been on the premises any contravention of the provisions of the Hygiene Regulations;

(b) ascertaining whether there is on the premises any evidence of any such contravention; and

(c) the performance by the Agency of its functions under the Hygiene Regulations,

but admission to any premises used only as a private dwelling–house shall not be demanded as of right unless 24 hours' notice of the intended entry has been given to the occupier.

(3) If a justice of the peace, on sworn information in writing, is satisfied that there is reasonable ground for entry onto any premises for any such purpose as is mentioned in paragraph (1) or (2) and either—

(a) that admission to the premises has been refused, or a refusal is apprehended, and that notice of the intention to apply for a warrant has been given to the occupier; or

(b) that an application for admission, or the giving of such a notice, would defeat the object of the entry, or that the case is one of urgency, or that the premises are unoccupied or the occupier is temporarily absent,

the justice may by warrant signed by him authorise the authorised officer to enter the premises, if need be by reasonable force.

(4) Every warrant granted under this regulation shall continue in force for a period of one month.

(5) An authorised officer entering any premises by virtue of this regulation, or of a warrant issued under it, may take with him such other persons as he considers necessary, and on leaving any unoccupied premises which he has entered by virtue of such a warrant shall leave them as effectively secured against unauthorised entry as he found them.

(6) An authorised officer entering premises by virtue of this regulation, or of a warrant issued under it, may inspect any records (in whatever form they are held) relating to a food business and, where any such records are stored in any electronic form—

(a) may have access to, and inspect and check the operation of, any computer and any associated apparatus or material which is or has been in use in connection with the records; and

(b) may require any person having charge of, or otherwise concerned with the operation of, the computer, apparatus or material to afford him such assistance as he may reasonably require.

(7) Any officer exercising any power conferred by paragraph (6) may—

(a) seize and detain any records which he has reason to believe may be required as evidence in proceedings under any of the provisions of these Regulations; and

(b) where the records are stored in any electronic form, require the records to be produced in a form in which they may be taken away.

(8) If any person who enters any premises by virtue of this regulation, or of a warrant issued under it, discloses to any person any information obtained by him on the premises with regard to any trade secret, he shall, unless the disclosure was made in the performance of his duty, be guilty of an offence.

(9) Nothing in this regulation authorises any person, except with the permission of the local authority under the Animal Health Act 1981, to enter any premises—

(a) on which an animal or bird affected with any disease to which that Act applies is kept; and

(b) which is situated in a place declared under that Act to be infected with such a disease.

8–13066N   15. Obstruction etc of officers.   (1) Any person who—

(a) intentionally obstructs any person acting in the execution of the Hygiene Regulations; or

(b) without reasonable cause, fails to give to any person acting in the execution of the Hygiene Regulations any assistance or information which that person may reasonably require of him for the performance of his functions under the Hygiene Regulations,

shall be guilty of an offence.

(2) Any person who, in purported compliance with any such requirement as is mentioned in sub–paragraph (b) of paragraph (1)—

(a) furnishes information which he knows to be false or misleading in a material particular; or

(b) recklessly furnishes information which is false or misleading in a material particular,

shall be guilty of an offence.

(3) Nothing in sub–paragraph (b) of paragraph (1) shall be construed as requiring any person to answer any question or give any information if to do so might incriminate him.

8–13066O   16. Time limit for prosecutions.   No prosecution for an offence under these Regulations which is punishable under paragraph (2) of regulation 17 shall be begun after the expiry of—

(a) three years from the commission of the offence; or

(b) one year from its discovery by the prosecutor,

whichever is the earlier.

8–13066P   17. Offences and penalties.   (1) Subject to paragraph (4), any person who contravenes or fails to comply with any of the specified Community provisions shall be guilty of an offence.

(2) Subject to paragraph (3), a person guilty of an offence under these Regulations shall be liable—

(a) on summary conviction to a fine not exceeding the statutory maximum; or
(b) on conviction on indictment to imprisonment for a term not exceeding two years, to a fine or to both.

(3) A person guilty of an offence under regulation 15 shall be liable on summary conviction to a fine not exceeding level 5 on the standard scale or to imprisonment for a term not exceeding three months or to both.

(4) A person shall be considered not to have contravened or failed to comply with Article 4(2) of Regulation 852/2004 as read with paragraph 4 of Chapter IV of Annex II to that Regulation (bulk foodstuffs in liquid, granulate or powder form to be transported in receptacles and/or containers/tankers reserved for the transport of foodstuffs) provided the requirements of Schedule 3 are complied with.

8–13066Q   18. Offences by bodies corporate.   (1) Where an offence under these Regulations which has been committed by a body corporate is proved to have been committed with the consent or connivance of, or to be attributable to any neglect on the part of—

(a) any director, manager, secretary or other similar officer of the body corporate; or
(b) any person who was purporting to act in any such capacity,

he as well as the body corporate shall be deemed to be guilty of that offence and shall be liable to be proceeded against and punished accordingly.

(2) In sub–paragraph (a) of paragraph (1) "director", in relation to any body corporate established by or under any enactment for the purpose of carrying on under national ownership any industry or part of an industry or undertaking, being a body corporate whose affairs are managed by its members, means a member of that body corporate.

8–13066R   19. Offences by Scottish partnerships.   Where an offence under these Regulations which has been committed by a Scottish partnership is proved to have been committed with the consent or connivance of, or to be attributable to any neglect on the part of, a partner, he, as well as the partnership shall be deemed to be guilty of that offence and liable to be proceeded against and punished accordingly.

8–13066S   20. Right of appeal.   (1) Any person who is aggrieved by—

(a) a decision of an authorised officer of an enforcement authority to serve a hygiene improvement notice;
(b) a decision of an enforcement authority to refuse to issue a certificate under paragraph (6) of regulation 7 or paragraph (8) of regulation 8; or
(c) a decision of an authorised officer of an enforcement authority to serve a remedial action notice,

may appeal to a magistrates' court.

(2) The procedure on an appeal to a magistrates' court under paragraph (1) shall be by way of complaint for an order, and the Magistrates' Courts Act 1980 shall apply to the proceedings.

(3) The period within which an appeal under paragraph (1) may be brought shall be—

(a) one month from the date on which notice of the decision was served on the person desiring to appeal; or
(b) in the case of an appeal against a decision to issue a hygiene improvement notice, the period specified in sub–paragraph (a) or, if it is shorter, the period specified in the notice pursuant to sub–paragraph (d) of paragraph (1) of regulation 6,

and the making of a complaint for an order shall be deemed for the purposes of this paragraph to be the bringing of the appeal.

8–13066T   21. Appeals to Crown Court.   A person who is aggrieved by—

(a) the dismissal by a magistrates' court of an appeal to it under paragraph (1) of regulation 20; or
(b) any decision of such a court to make a hygiene prohibition order or a hygiene emergency prohibition order,

may appeal to the Crown Court.

8–13066U   22. Appeals against hygiene improvement notices and remedial action notices.   (1) On an appeal against a hygiene improvement notice or a remedial action notice, the court may cancel or affirm the notice and, if it affirms it, may do so either in its original form or with such modifications as the court may in the circumstances think fit.

(2) Where any period specified in a hygiene improvement notice pursuant to sub–paragraph (d) of paragraph (1) of regulation 6 would otherwise include any day on which an appeal against that notice is pending, that day shall be excluded from that period.

(3) Any appeal shall be regarded as pending for the purposes of paragraph (2) until it is finally disposed of, is withdrawn or is struck out for want of prosecution.

8–13066V 23. Application of section 9 of the Food Safety Act 1990. Section 9 of the Act (inspection and seizure of suspected food) shall apply for the purposes of these Regulations with the modification that it shall apply in relation to an authorised officer of an enforcement authority as it applies in relation to an authorised officer of a food authority.

PART 4

MISCELLANEOUS AND SUPPLEMENTARY PROVISIONS

8–13066W 24. Power to issue codes of recommended practice. (1) For the guidance of food authorities, the Secretary of State may issue codes of recommended practice as regards the execution and enforcement of the Hygiene Regulations and any such code shall be laid before Parliament after being issued.

(2) The Agency may, after consulting the Secretary of State, give a food authority a direction requiring them to take any specified steps in order to comply with a code issued under this regulation.

(3) In exercise of the functions conferred on them by or under the Hygiene Regulations, every food authority —

(a) shall have regard to any relevant provision of any such code; and

(b) shall comply with any direction which is given under this regulation and requires them to take any specified steps in order to comply with such a code.

(4) Any direction under paragraph (2) shall, on the application of the Agency, be enforceable by mandatory order.

(5) The Agency shall consult the Secretary of State before making an application under paragraph (4).

(6) Before issuing any code under this regulation, the Secretary of State shall have regard to any relevant advice given by the Agency.

8–13066X 25. Protection of officers acting in good faith. (1) An officer of an enforcement authority is not personally liable in respect of any act done by him —

(a) in the execution or purported execution of the Hygiene Regulations; and

(b) within the scope of his employment,

if he did that act in the honest belief that his duty under the Hygiene Regulations required or entitled him to do it.

(2) Nothing in paragraph (1) shall be construed as relieving any enforcement authority of any liability in respect of the acts of their officers.

(3) Where an action has been brought against an officer of an enforcement authority in respect of an act done by him —

(a) in the execution or purported execution of the Hygiene Regulations; but

(b) outside the scope of his employment,

the authority may indemnify him against the whole or a part of any damages which he has been ordered to pay or any costs which he may have incurred if they are satisfied that he honestly believed that the act complained of was within the scope of his employment.

(4) A public analyst appointed by a food authority shall be treated for the purposes of this regulation as being an officer of the authority, whether or not his appointment is a whole–time one.

8–13066Y 26. Revocation and suspension of designations and appointments. (1) Subject to paragraphs (2) and (3), the Agency may at any time revoke or suspend —

(a) the appointment of an official veterinarian;

(b) the designation of an approved veterinarian; or

(c) the appointment of an official auxiliary,

if it appears to the Agency that the person in question is unfit to perform any of the functions of that post under the Hygiene Regulations.

(2) Where the Agency revokes or suspends a designation or appointment under paragraph (1), the Agency shall, as soon as practicable, give to the person whose designation or appointment has been revoked or suspended a notice in writing of the reasons for the revocation or suspension and shall afford him an opportunity of —

(a) making representations in writing to the Agency with regard to the revocation or suspension; or

(b) being heard by a person nominated by the Agency for the purpose pursuant to sub–paragraph (a) of paragraph (5).

(3) A notice given under paragraph (2) shall inform the person to whom it is given —

(a) of his right to make representations in writing;

(b) of the manner in which and the time (not being less than 21 days from the giving of the notice) within which such representations may be made;

(c) of his right to be heard; and

(d) of the manner in which and the time (not being less than 21 days from the giving of the notice) within which he may apply for an opportunity to be heard.

(4) In the event of the person whose designation or appointment has been revoked or suspended making any representations (whether orally or in writing) under paragraph (3) the Agency shall reconsider whether that person is unfit to perform any of the functions of the post held by him under the Hygiene Regulations and shall, as soon as practicable, reconsider its decision to revoke or suspend the designation or appointment under paragraph (1) in the light of those representations.

(5) Where a person requests the opportunity to be heard pursuant to sub–paragraph (b) of paragraph (2)—

(a) the Agency shall nominate a person to determine the matter from the list established under paragraph (6);

(b) the person so nominated shall serve a notice on the person requesting the opportunity to be heard and the Agency informing them of the time (not being less than 21 days from the giving of the notice) of the hearing; and

(c) the person so nominated shall, within 21 days of the hearing, notify the person requesting the opportunity to be heard, and the Agency of his decision.

(6) The Agency shall establish and maintain a list of people who may be nominated for the purposes of this regulation and shall consult those organisations appearing to it to represent official veterinarians, approved veterinarians and official auxiliaries before including any person on the list.

8–13066Z 27. Food which has not been produced, processed or distributed in accordance with the Hygiene Regulations. (1) On an inspection of any food, an authorised officer of an enforcement authority may certify that it has not been produced, processed or distributed in compliance with the Hygiene Regulations.

(2) Where any food is certified as mentioned in paragraph (1) it shall be treated for the purposes of section 9 of the Act as failing to comply with food safety requirements.

(3) Where any food certified as mentioned in paragraph (1) is part of a batch, lot or consignment of food of the same class or description, all the food in the batch, lot or consignment shall, until it is proved that it has been produced, processed or distributed in compliance with the Hygiene Regulations, be treated for the purposes of paragraph (2) as having been so certified.

8–13067 28. Service of documents. (1) Any document which is required or authorised under the Hygiene Regulations to be served on a food business operator may be served—

(a) by delivering it to that person;

(b) in the case of an incorporated company or body, by delivering it to their secretary at their registered or principal office, or by sending it in a prepaid letter addressed to him at that office; or

(c) in the case of any other food business operator, by leaving it or sending it in a prepaid letter addressed to him at his usual or last known residence.

(2) Where a document is to be served on a food business operator under the Hygiene Regulations and it is not reasonably practicable to ascertain the name and address of the person on whom it should be served, or the premises of the food business operator are unoccupied, the document may be served by addressing it to the food business operator concerned in the capacity of occupier of those premises (naming them), and—

(a) by delivering it to some other person at the premises; and

(b) if there is no other person at the premises to whom it can be delivered, by affixing it or a copy of it to some conspicuous part of the premises.

8–13067A 29. Bulk transport in sea-going vessels of liquid oils or fats and the bulk transport by sea of raw sugar. Schedule 3 (bulk transport in sea-going vessels of liquid oils or fats and the bulk transport by sea of raw sugar) shall have effect.

8–13067B 30. Temperature control requirements. Schedule 4 (temperature control requirements) shall have effect.

8–13067C 31. Direct supply by the producer of small quantities of meat from poultry or lagomorphs slaughtered on the farm. Schedule 5 (direct supply by the producer of small quantities of meat from poultry or lagomorphs slaughtered on the farm) shall have effect.

8–13067D 32. Restrictions on the sale of raw milk intended for direct human consumption. Schedule 6 (restrictions on the sale of raw milk intended for direct human consumption) shall have effect.

8–13067E 33. Consequential amendments. (1) In so far as they apply in relation to England, the instruments specified in Schedule 7 are amended to the extent specified there.

(2) For Note 3 to Schedule 1 to the Condensed Milk and Dried Milk (England) Regulations 2003 (partly or wholly dehydrated preserved milk products and their reserved descriptions) there is substituted the following Note—

"**3.** The preservation of the designated products shall be achieved—

(a) by heat treatment for the products referred to in paragraph 1(a) to (d) of column 1 of this Schedule;

(b) by the addition of sucrose for the products referred to in paragraph 1(e) to (g) of column 1 of this Schedule; and

(c) by dehydration for the products referred to in paragraph 2 of column 1 of this Schedule.''.

8–13067F 34. Revocation. The Food Hygiene (England) Regulations 2005 are revoked.

8–13067G

Regulation 2(1)

SCHEDULE 1

DEFINITIONS OF COMMUNITY LEGISLATION

"Directive 2004/41" means Directive 2004/41/EC of the European Parliament and of the Council repealing certain directives concerning food hygiene and health conditions for the production and placing on the market of certain products of animal origin intended for human consumption and amending Council Directives 89/662/EEC and 92/118/EEC and Council Decision 95/408/EC;

"Regulation 178/2002" means Regulation (EC) No 178/2002 of the European Parliament and of the Council laying down the general principles and requirements of food law, establishing the European Food Safety Authority and laying down procedures in matters of food safety as last amended by Regulation 1642/2003;

"Regulation 1642/2003" means Regulation (EC) No 1642/2003 of the European Parliament and of the Council amending Regulation (EC) No 178/2002 laying down the general principles and requirements of food law, establishing the European Food Safety Authority and laying down procedures in matters of food safety;

"Regulation 852/2004" means Regulation (EC) No 852/2004 of the European Parliament and of the Council on the hygiene of foodstuffs as read with Regulation 2073/2005;

"Regulation 853/2004" means Regulation (EC) No 853/2004 of the European Parliament and of the Council laying down specific hygiene rules for food of animal origin as amended by Regulation 2074/2005 and Regulation 2076/2005 and as read with Directive 2004/41, Regulation 1688/2005, Regulation 2074/2005 and Regulation 2076/2005;

"Regulation 854/2004" means Regulation (EC) No 854/2004 of the European Parliament and of the Council laying down specific rules for the organisation of official controls on products of animal origin intended for human consumption as amended by Regulation 882/2004, Regulation 2074/2005 and Regulation 2076/2005 and as read with Directive 2004/41, Regulation 2074/2005, Regulation 2075/2005 and Regulation 2076/2005;

"Regulation 882/2004" means Regulation (EC) No 882/2004 of the European Parliament and of the Council on official controls performed to ensure the verification of compliance with feed and food law, animal health and animal welfare rules as read with Regulation 2074/2005 and Regulation 2076/2005;

"Regulation 1688/2005" means Commission Regulation (EC) No 1688/2005 implementing Regulation (EC) No 853/2004 of the European Parliament and of the Council as regards special guarantees concerning salmonella for consignments to Finland and Sweden of certain meat and eggs;

"Regulation 2073/2005" means Commission Regulation (EC) No 2073/2005 on microbiological criteria for foodstuffs;

"Regulation 2074/2005" means Commission Regulation (EC) No 2074//2005 laying down implementing measures for certain products under Regulation (EC) No 853/2004 of the European Parliament and of the Council and for the organisation of official controls under Regulation (EC) No 854/2004 of the European Parliament and of the Council and Regulation (EC) No 882/2004 of the European Parliament and of the Council, derogating from Regulation (EC) No 852/2004 of the European Parliament and of the Council and amending Regulations (EC) No 853/2004 and (EC) No 854/2004;

"Regulation 2075/2005" means Commission Regulation (EC) No 2075/2005 laying down specific rules on official controls for *Trichinella* in meat; and

"Regulation 2076/2005" means Commission Regulation (EC) No 2076/2005 laying down transitional arrangements for the implementation of Regulations (EC) No 853/2004, (EC) No 854/2004 and (EC) No 882/2004 of the European Parliament and of the Council and amending Regulations (EC) No 853/2004 and (EC) No 854/2004.

8–13067H

Regulations 2(1) and 17

SCHEDULE 2

SPECIFIED COMMUNITY PROVISIONS

1 Provision of Community Regulations	*2 Subject-matter*
Article 3 of Regulation 852/2004	Requirement that food business operators ensure that all stages of production, processing and distribution of food under their control satisfy the relevant hygiene requirements laid down in Regulation 852/2004.
Article 4(1) of Regulation 852/2004	Requirement that food business operators carrying out primary production and specified associated operations comply with the general hygiene provisions laid down in Part A of Annex I to Regulation 852/2004 and any specific requirements provided for in Regulation 853/2004.
Article 4(2) of Regulation 852/2004	Requirement that food business operators carrying out any stage of production, processing and distribution of food after those stages to which Article 4(1) applies comply with the general hygiene requirements laid down in Annex II to Regulation 852/2004 and any specific requirements provided for in Regulation 853/2004.
Article 4(3) of Regulation 852/2004	Requirement that food business operators, as appropriate, adopt certain specific hygiene measures.
Article 5(1) of Regulation 852/2004	Requirement that food business operators put in place, implement and maintain a permanent procedure or procedures based on the HACCP principles.

1 Provision of Community Regulations	2 Subject-matter
Article 5(2) of Regulation 852/2004	Requirement that when any modification is made in the product, process, or any step, food business operators review the procedure referred to in Article 5(1) and make the necessary changes to it.
Article 5(4)(*a*) of Regulation 852/2004	Requirement that food business operators provide the competent authority with evidence of their compliance with Article 5(1).
Article 5(4)(*b*) of Regulation 852/2004	Requirement that food business operators ensure that any documents describing the procedures developed in accordance with Article 5 are up to date.
Article 5(4)(*c*) of Regulation 852/2004	Requirement that food business operators retain documents and records for an appropriate period.
Article 6(1) of Regulation 852/2004	Requirement that food business operators co–operate with the competent authorities in accordance with other applicable Community legislation or national law.
Article 6(2), first paragraph of Regulation 852/2004	Requirement that a food business operator notify the competent authority of each establishment under its control that carries out any of the stages of production, processing and distribution of food.
Article 6(2), second paragraph of Regulation 852/2004	Requirement that food business operators ensure that the competent authority has up to date information on establishments.
Article 6(3) of Regulation 852/2004	Requirement that food business operators ensure that establishments are approved by the competent authority when approval is required.
Article 3(1) of Regulation 853/2004	Requirement that food business operators comply with the relevant provisions of Annexes II and III to Regulation 853/2004.
Article 3(2) of Regulation 853/2004	Requirement that food business operators do not use any substance other than potable water or, when Regulation 852/2004 or Regulation 853/2004 permits its use, clean water, to remove surface contamination from products of animal origin unless use of the substance has been approved.
Article 4(1) of Regulation 853/2004	Requirement that food business operators place products of animal origin manufactured in the Community on the market only if they have been prepared and handled exclusively in establishments— (*a*) that meet the relevant requirements of Regulation 852/2004, those of Annexes II and III of Regulation 853/2004 and other relevant requirements of food law; and (*b*) that the competent authority has registered or, where required in accordance with Article 4(2), approved.
Article 4(2) of Regulation 853/2004	Requirement that establishments handling those products of animal origin for which Annex III to Regulation 853/2004 lays down requirements do not operate unless the competent authority has approved them in accordance with Article 4(3).
Article 4(3) of Regulation 853/2004	Requirement that establishments subject to approval in accordance with Article 4(2) do not operate unless the competent authority has, in accordance with Regulation 854/2004— (*a*) granted the establishment approval to operate following an on–site visit; or (*b*) provided the establishment with conditional approval.
Article 4(4) of Regulation 853/2004	Requirement that food business operators co–operate with the competent authorities in accordance with Regulation 854/2004 including ensuring that an establishment ceases to operate if it is no longer approved.
Article 5(1) of Regulation 853/2004	Requirement that food business operators do not place on the market a product of animal origin handled in an establishment subject to approval in accordance with Article 4(2) unless it has— (*a*) a health mark applied in accordance with Regulation 854/2004; or (*b*) when Regulation 854/2004 does not provide for the application of a health mark, an identification mark applied in accordance with Section 1 of Annex II to Regulation 853/2004.
Article 5(2) of Regulation 853/2004	Requirement that food business operators apply an identification mark to a product of animal origin only if the product has been manufactured in accordance with Regulation 853/2004 in establishments meeting the requirements of Article 4.
Article 5(3) of Regulation 853/2004	Requirement that food business operators do not remove a health mark applied in accordance with Regulation 854/2004 from meat unless they cut or process it or work upon it in another manner.
Article 6(1) and (2) of Regulation 853/2004	Requirement that food business operators ensure that importation of products of animal origin only takes place where certain conditions are met.
Article 6(3) of Regulation 853/2004	Requirement that food business operators importing products of animal origin shall ensure that— (*a*) products are made available for control upon importation in accordance with Council Directive 97/78/EC;

1 Provision of Community Regulations	2 Subject-matter
	(b) importation complies with the requirements of Council Directive 2002/99/EC; and
	(c) operations under their control that take place after importation are carried out in accordance with the requirements of Annex III to Regulation 853/2004.
Article 6(4) of Regulation 853/2004	Requirement that food business operators importing food containing both products of plant origin and processed products of animal origin ensure that the processed products of animal origin satisfy the requirements of paragraphs (1) to (3) of Article 6.
Article 7 of Regulation 853/2004	Requirement that food business operators ensure that certificates or other documents accompany consignments of products of animal origin when required in accordance with Annex II or III to Regulation 853/2004.
Article 8 of Regulation 853/2004	Requirement that food business operators intending to place specified foods of animal origin on the market in Sweden or Finland comply with the rules set out in Article 8(2).
Article 7(1) of Regulation 2073/2005	Requirement that food business operators take the measures laid down in paragraphs (2) to (4) of Article 7 when the results of testing against the criteria set out in Annex I to Regulation 2073/2005 (microbiological criteria for foodstuffs) are unsatisfactory.
Article 9 of Regulation 2075/2005	Requirement that food business operators of holdings recognised as free from *Trichinella* inform the competent authority of any requirement as laid down in Chapter I and II(b) of Annex IV to Regulation 2075/2005 (detailed conditions for *Trichinella-free* holdings and regions with a negligible *Trichinella* risk) that is no longer fulfilled or of any other change that might affect holdings' *Trichinella*-free status.

8–13067I

Regulation 29   SCHEDULE 3

BULK TRANSPORT IN SEA–GOING VESSELS OF LIQUID OILS OR FATS AND THE BULK TRANSPORT BY SEA OF RAW SUGAR

Offence

1. A person who contravenes or fails to comply with any of the requirements of this Schedule shall be guilty of an offence.

Liquid oils or fats

2. (1) The bulk transport in sea–going vessels of liquid oils or fats which are to be processed, and which are intended for or likely to be used for human consumption, is permitted in tanks that are not exclusively reserved for the transport of foodstuffs, subject to the following conditions—

(a) where the oil or fat is transported in a stainless steel tank, or tank lined with epoxy resin or technical equivalent, the immediately previous cargo transported in the tank shall have been a foodstuff or a cargo from the list of acceptable previous cargoes for liquid oils or fats; and

(b) where the oil or fat is transported in a tank of materials other than those specified in sub–paragraph (a), the three previous cargoes transported in the tanks shall have been foodstuffs or from the list of acceptable previous cargoes for liquid oils or fats.

(2) For the purposes of this paragraph, "list of acceptable previous cargoes for liquid oils or fats" means the list set out in the Annex to Commission Directive 96/3/EC

3. The bulk transport in sea–going vessels of liquid oils or fats which are not to be further processed, and which are intended for or are likely to be used for human consumption, is permitted in tanks that are not exclusively reserved for the transport of foodstuffs, subject to the following conditions—

(a) the tank shall be of stainless steel or lined with epoxy resin or technical equivalent; and

(b) the three previous cargoes transported in the tank shall have been foodstuffs.

4. The captain of a sea–going vessel transporting, in tanks, bulk liquid oils or fats intended for or likely to be used for human consumption shall keep accurate documentary evidence relating to the three previous cargoes carried in the tanks concerned, and the effectiveness of the cleaning process applied between those cargoes.

5. Where the cargo has been trans–shipped, in addition to the documentary evidence required by virtue of paragraph 4, the captain of the receiving vessel shall keep accurate documentary evidence that the transport of the bulk liquid oil or fat complied with the provisions of paragraph 2 or 3 during previous shipment and of the effectiveness of the cleaning process used between those cargoes on the vessel from which they were trans–shipped.

6. Upon request, the captain of the vessel shall provide the enforcement authority with the documentary evidence described in paragraphs 4 and 5.

Raw sugar

7. The bulk transport by sea of raw sugar which is not intended for use as food or as a food ingredient without a full and effective refining process is permitted in receptacles, containers or tankers that are not exclusively used for the transport of foodstuffs.

8. The receptacles, containers or tankers referred to in paragraph 7 shall be subject to the following conditions—

(a) prior to loading the raw sugar, the receptacle, container or tanker shall be effectively cleaned to remove residues of the previous cargo and other soiling and inspected to establish that such residues have been removed effectively; and

(b) the immediate previous cargo prior to the raw sugar shall not have been a bulk liquid.

9. A food business operator who is responsible for the transport of raw sugar by sea under paragraph 7 shall keep documentary evidence, accurately describing in detail the immediate previous cargo carried in the receptacle, container or tanker concerned, and the type and effectiveness of the cleaning process applied prior to the transport of the raw sugar.

10. The documentary evidence shall accompany the consignment of raw sugar during all stages of transport to the refinery and a copy shall be retained by the refinery. The documentary evidence shall be marked as follows in a clearly visible and indelible fashion, in one or more Community languages: "This product must be refined before being used for human consumption".

11. On request, a food business operator responsible for the transport of the raw sugar or the refining process shall provide the enforcement authority with the documentary evidence referred to in paragraphs 9 and 10.

12. Raw sugar which has been transported by sea in receptacles, containers or tankers which are not exclusively reserved for the transport of foodstuffs shall be subjected to a full and effective refining process before being considered suitable for use as food or as a food ingredient.

13. In fulfilling his obligations under Article 5(1) of Regulation 852/2004 (hazard analysis and critical control points) in relation to the bulk transport of raw sugar by sea under paragraph 7, a food business operator who is responsible for the transport or refining of raw sugar shall—

(a) consider the cleaning process undertaken prior to the loading of the sugar for transport by sea to be a critical control point as referred to in Article 5(2)(b) of Regulation 852/2004; and

(b) take into account the nature of the previous cargo which has been transported in any receptacle, container or tanker used for the transport of the sugar.

Interpretation
14. (1) For the purposes of this Schedule any words or expressions used both in this Schedule and in Commission Directive 96/3/EC or Commission Directive 98/28/EC granting a derogation from certain provisions of Directive 93/43/EEC on the hygiene of foodstuffs as regards the transport by sea of bulk raw sugar shall bear the same meanings as they respectively have in those Directives.

(2) In this Schedule, "Commission Directive 96/3/EC" means Commission Directive 96/3/EC granting a derogation from certain provisions of Council Directive 93/43/EEC on the hygiene of foodstuffs as regards the transport of bulk liquid oils and fats by sea as amended by Commission Directive 2004/4/EC amending Directive 96/3/EC granting a derogation from certain provisions of Council Directive 93/43/EEC on the hygiene of foodstuffs as regards the transport of bulk liquid oils and fats by sea.

8–13067J
Regulation 30   SCHEDULE 4
                              TEMPERATURE CONTROL REQUIREMENTS

Scope
1. This Schedule does not apply in relation to—

(a) any food business operation to which Regulation 853/2004 applies; or
(b) any food business operation carried out on a ship or aircraft.

Chill holding requirements
2. (1) Subject to sub–paragraph (2) and paragraph 3, any person who keeps any food—

(a) which is likely to support the growth of pathogenic micro–organisms or the formation of toxins; and
(b) with respect to which any commercial operation is being carried out,

at or in food premises at a temperature above 8˚C shall be guilty of an offence.

(2) Sub–paragraph (1) shall not apply in relation to any food which, as part of a mail order transaction, is being conveyed to the final consumer.

(3) Subject to paragraph 3, no person shall supply by mail order any food which—

(a) is likely to support the growth of pathogenic micro-organisms or the formation of toxins; and
(b) is being or has been conveyed by post or by a private or common carrier to the final consumer,

at a temperature which has given rise to or is likely to give rise to a risk to health.

General exemptions from the chill holding requirements
3. Sub–paragraphs (1) and (3) of paragraph 2 shall not apply in relation to—

(a) food which—
   (i) has been cooked or reheated,
   (ii) is for service or on display for sale, and
   (iii) needs to be kept at or above 63˚C in order to control the growth of pathogenic micro–organisms or the formation of toxins;

(b) food which, for the duration of its shelf life may be kept at ambient temperatures with no risk to health;
(c) food which is being or has been subjected to a process such as dehydration or canning intended to prevent the growth of pathogenic micro–organisms at ambient temperatures, but not where—
   (i) after or by virtue of that process the food was contained in a hermetically sealed container, and
   (ii) that container has been opened;

(d) food which must be ripened or matured at ambient temperatures, but not when the process of ripening or maturation is completed;
(e) raw food intended for further processing (including cooking) before human consumption, but only if that processing, if undertaken correctly, will render that food fit for human consumption;
(f) food to which Council Regulation 1906/90 applies; and
(g) food to which Council Regulation 1907/90 applies.

Upward variation of the 8˚C temperature by manufacturers etc
4. (1) In any proceedings for an offence consisting of a contravention of sub–paragraph (1) of paragraph 2, it shall be a defence for the accused to prove that—

(a) a food business responsible for manufacturing, preparing or processing the food, including, where relevant, the accused, has recommended that it is kept—
   (i) at or below a specified temperature between 8˚C and ambient temperatures, and
   (ii) for a period not exceeding a specified shelf life;

(b) that recommendation has, unless the accused is that food business, been communicated to the accused either by means of a label on the packaging of the food or by means of some other appropriate form of written instruction;

(c) the food was not kept by the accused at a temperature above the specified temperature; and

(d) at the time of the commission of the alleged offence, the specified shelf life had not been exceeded.

(2) A food business responsible for manufacturing, preparing or processing food shall not recommend that any food is kept—

(a) at or below a specified temperature between 8°C and ambient temperatures; and

(b) for a period not exceeding a specified shelf life,

unless that recommendation is supported by a well–founded scientific assessment of the safety of the food at the specified temperature.

Chill holding tolerance periods

5. (1) In any proceedings for an offence consisting of a contravention of sub–paragraph (1) of paragraph 2, it shall be a defence for the accused to prove that the food—

(a) was for service or on display for sale;

(b) had not previously been kept for service or on display for sale at a temperature above 8°C or, where a recommendation has been made pursuant to sub–paragraph (1) of paragraph 4, the recommended temperature; and

(c) had been kept for service or on display for sale for a period of less than four hours.

(2) In any proceedings for an offence consisting of a contravention of sub–paragraph (1) of paragraph 2, it shall be a defence for the accused to prove that the food—

(a) was being transferred—

  (i) from premises at which the food was going to be kept at or below 8°C or in appropriate circumstances the recommended temperature to a vehicle used for the purposes of a food business, or

  (ii) to such premises from such a vehicle; or

(b) was kept at a temperature above 8°C or, in appropriate circumstances, the recommended temperature for an unavoidable reason, such as—

  (i) to accommodate the practicalities of handling during and after processing or preparation,

  (ii) the defrosting of equipment, or

  (iii) temporary breakdown of equipment,

and was kept at a temperature above 8°C or, in appropriate circumstances, the recommended temperature for a limited period only and that period was consistent with food safety.

Hot holding requirements

6. Any person who in the course of the activities of a food business keeps at or in food premises at a temperature below 63°C any food which—

(a) has been cooked or reheated;

(b) is for service or on display for sale; and

(c) needs to be kept at or above 63°C in order to control the growth of pathogenic micro–organisms or the formation of toxins,

shall be guilty of an offence.

Hot holding defences

7. In any proceedings for an offence consisting of a contravention of paragraph 6, it shall be a defence for the accused to prove that—

(a) a well–founded scientific assessment of the safety of the food at temperatures below 63°C has concluded that there is no risk to health if, after cooking or re–heating, the food is held for service or on display for sale—

  (i) at a holding temperature which is below 63°C, and

  (ii) for a period not exceeding any period of time specified in that scientific assessment; and

(b) at the time of the commission of the alleged offence, the food was held in a manner which was justified in the light of that scientific assessment.

(2) In any proceedings for an offence consisting of a contravention of paragraph 6, it shall be a defence for the accused to prove that the food—

(a) had been kept for service or on display for sale for a period of less than two hours; and

(b) had not previously been kept for service or on display for sale by that person.

Interpretation

8. In this Schedule—

"Council Regulation 1906/90" means Council Regulation (EEC) No 1906/90 on certain marketing standards for poultry as last amended by Council Regulation (EC) No 1101/98 amending Regulation (EEC) No 1906/90 on certain marketing standards for poultry meat;

"Council Regulation 1907/90" means Council Regulation (EEC) No 1907/90 on certain marketing standards for eggs as last amended by Council Regulation (EC) No 2052/2003 amending Regulation (EEC) No 1907/90 on certain marketing standards for eggs;

"recommended temperature" means a specified temperature which has been recommended in accordance with sub–paragraph (1)(a)(i) of paragraph 4; and

"shelf life" means—

(a) in relation to food with respect to which an indication of minimum durability is required in accordance with regulation 20 of the Food Labelling Regulations 1996 (form of indication of minimum durability), the period up to and including the date required to be included in that indication;

(b) in relation to food with respect to which a "use by" date is assigned in the form required in accordance with regulation 21 of the Food Labelling Regulations 1996 (form of indication of "use by" date), the period up to and including that date; and

(c) in relation to food which is not required to bear an indication of minimum durability or a "use by" date, the period for which the food can be expected to remain fit for sale if it is kept in a manner which is consistent with food safety.

8–13067K

Regulation 31   SCHEDULE 5
DIRECT SUPPLY BY THE PRODUCER OF SMALL QUANTITIES OF MEAT FROM POULTRY OR LAGOMORPHS SLAUGHTERED ON THE
FARM

Scope
1. The requirements of this Schedule apply in relation to the direct supply by the producer of small quantities
of meat from poultry or lagomorphs that have been slaughtered on the farm to the final consumer or to local
retail establishments directly supplying such meat to the final consumer.

Requirements
2. (1) Where a producer supplies meat in the manner described in paragraph 1, he shall ensure that it bears
a label or other marking clearly indicating the name and address of the farm where the animal from which it is
derived was slaughtered.
(2) The producer shall—

(a) keep a record in adequate form to show the number of birds and the number of lagomorphs received
     into, and the amounts of fresh meat despatched from, his premises during each week;
(b) retain the record for a period of one year; and
(c) make the record available to an authorised officer on request.

Offence
3. A producer who fails to comply with any of the requirements of paragraph 2 shall be guilty of an offence.

8–13067L

Regulation 32   SCHEDULE 6
RESTRICTIONS ON THE SALE OF RAW MILK INTENDED FOR DIRECT HUMAN CONSUMPTION

1. Any person who sells raw milk intended for direct human consumption in contravention of paragraph 5
shall be guilty of an offence.
2. (1) If any person other than the occupier of a production holding or a distributor sells raw cows' milk
intended for direct human consumption he shall be guilty of an offence.
(2) If the occupier of a production holding sells raw cows' milk intended for direct human consumption in
contravention of paragraph 3 he shall be guilty of an offence.
(3) If a distributor sells raw cows' milk intended for direct human consumption in contravention of paragraph
4 he shall be guilty of an offence.
3. The occupier of a production holding may only sell raw cows' milk intended for direct human
consumption—

(a) at or from the farm premises where the animals from which the milk has been obtained are maintained;
     and
(b) to—

     (i)   the final consumer for consumption other than at those farm premises,
     (ii)   a temporary guest or visitor to those farm premises as or as part of a meal or refreshment, or
     (iii) a distributor.

4. A distributor may only sell raw cows' milk intended for direct human consumption—

(a) which he has bought pursuant to sub–paragraph (b)(iii) of paragraph 3;
(b) in the containers in which he receives the milk, with the fastenings of the containers unbroken;
(c) from a vehicle which is lawfully used as a shop premises; and
(d) direct to the final consumer.

5. The raw milk shall meet the following standards:

Plate count at 30˚C (cfu per ml)	£ 20,000
Coliforms (cfu per ml)	< 100

6. In the case where farm premises are being used for the sale of raw cows' milk intended for direct human
consumption pursuant to sub–paragraph (a) of paragraph 3, the Agency shall carry out such sampling, analysis
and examination of the milk as it considers necessary to ensure that it meets the standards specified in
paragraph 5.
7. In any case where the Agency carries out sampling, analysis and examination of raw cows' milk in
accordance with paragraph 6, there shall be due to the Agency from the occupier of the production holding
who is selling the milk a fee of £63, which is payable by the occupier to the Agency on demand.
8. In this Schedule—

"distributor" means a person who sells raw cows' milk that has been produced on a production holding of
     which he is not the occupier;
"farm premises" means a farm occupied by the occupier of a production holding as a single farm and
     includes the production holding and any other building situated on that farm and occupied by the same
     occupier;
"occupier" means any person carrying on the business of producing or handling raw cows' milk or his duly
     authorised representative;
"production holding" means premises at which milk-producing cows are kept; and
"shop premises" means premises from which any food is sold to the final consumer.

SCHEDULE 7
CONSEQUENTIAL AMENDMENTS

FORGERY AND COUNTERFEITING

8–13070   This title contains the following statutes—

    8–13089   FORGERY ACT 1861
    8–13110   LAW OF PROPERTY ACT 1925
    8–13140   FORGERY AND COUNTERFEITING ACT 1981
    8–13180   LAND REGISTRATION ACT 2002

and the following statutory instrument—

    8–13200   Protection of the Euro against Counterfeiting Regulations 2001

8–13080   **European Communities Act 1972: regulations.**   Within the scope of the title Forgery and Counterfeiting there falls the subject matter of the following regulations made under the very wide enabling power provided in section 2(2) of the European Communities Act 1972 and which create offences:

    Protection of the Euro against Counterfeiting Regulations 2001, SI 2001/3948.

Forgery Act 1861
(24 & 25 Vict c 98)

8–13089   **34. Acknowledging recognizance, bail, cognovit, etc, in the name of another.**
Whosoever, without lawful authority or excuse (the proof whereof shall lie on the party accused), shall in the name of any other person acknowledge any recognizance[1] or bail, or any cognovit actionem, or judgment, or any deed or other instrument, before any court, judge, or other person lawfully authorised in that behalf, shall be guilty of an offence, and being convicted thereof shall be liable to imprisonment for any term not exceeding **seven years**.
[Forgery Act 1861, s 34, as amended by the Statute Law Revision Act 1892, the Statute Law Revision (No 2) Act 1893, the Criminal Justice Act 1948, s 1, and the Criminal Law Act 1967, s 1.]

---

    1. This means a valid recognizance into which a person might lawfully be required to enter (*R v McKenzie* [1971] 1 All ER 729, 135 JP 26.)

8–13090   **36. Destroying, injuring, forging, or falsifying registers of births, baptisms, marriages, deaths, or burials, or certified copies.**   Whosoever shall unlawfully destroy, deface, or injure, or cause or permit to be destroyed, defaced, or injured, any register of births, baptisms, marriages, deaths, or burials which now is or hereafter shall be by law authorised or required to be kept in England or Ireland, or any part of any such register, or any certified copy of any such register, or any part thereof, or shall knowingly and unlawfully insert or cause or permit to be inserted in any such register, or in any certified copy thereof, any false entry of any matter relating to any birth, baptism, marriage, death, or burial, or shall knowing and unlawfully give any false certificate relating to any birth, baptism, marriage, death, or burial, or shall certify any writing to be a copy or extract from any such register, knowing such writing, or the part of such register whereof such copy or extract shall be so given, to be false in any material particular or shall offer, utter, dispose of, or put off any such register, entry, certified copy, certificate, knowing the same to be false, or shall offer, utter, dispose of, or put off any copy of any entry in any such register, knowing such entry to be false, shall be guilty of an offence, and being convicted thereof, shall be liable to imprisonment for **life**.
[Forgery Act 1861, s 36, as amended by the Statute Law Revision Act 1892, the Statute Law Revision (No 2) Act 1893, the Forgery Act 1913, s 20 and Sch, the Criminal Justice Act 1948, s 1, and the Criminal Law Act 1967, s 1.]

8–13091   **37. Making false entries in copies of registers of baptisms, marriages, or burials, directed to be sent to any registrar, or destroying or concealing copies of registers.**
Whosoever shall knowingly and wilfully insert or cause or permit to be inserted in any copy of any register directed or required by law to be transmitted to any registrar or other officer any false entry of any matter relating to any baptism, marriage, or burial, or shall knowingly and wilfully sign or verify any copy of any register so directed or required to be transmitted as aforesaid, which copy shall be false in any part thereof, knowing the same to be false, or shall unlawfully destroy, deface, or injure, or shall for any fraudulent purpose take from its place of deposit, or conceal, any such copy of any register, shall be guilty of an offence, and being convicted thereof shall be liable to imprisonment for **life**.
[Forgery Act 1861, s 37, as amended by the Statute Law Revision Act 1892, the Statute Law Revision (No 2) Act 1893, the Forgery Act 1913, s 20 and Sch, the Criminal Justice Act 1948, s 1, and the Criminal Law Act 1967, s 1.]
The Criminal Justice Act 1925 s 36, forgery of a passport, has been amended by the Forgery and Counterfeiting Act 1981, post, and now covers only the making of an untrue statement to procure a passport; the amended section is printed in PART I: MAGISTRATES' COURTS, PROCEDURE, *ante.*

Law of Property Act 1925

(15 & 16 Geo 5 c 20)

8–13110   183. Fraudulent concealment of documents and falsification of pedigrees by vendors or their agents.   (1) Any person disposing of property[1] or any interest therein for money or money's worth to a purchaser[2], or the solicitor or other agent of such person, who (*a*) conceals from the purchaser any instrument or incumbrance material to the title; or (*b*) falsifies any pedigree upon which the title may depend in order to induce the purchaser to accept the title offered or produced, with intent in any of such cases to defraud[3]—*Misdemeanour*[4].—PUN.—fine, **two years'** imprisonment, or both.
[Law of Property Act 1925, s 183.]

---

1. "Property" includes anything in action, and any interest in real or personal property (s 205(xx)).
2. Where the context so required "purchaser" includes an intending purchaser (s 205(xxi)).
3. An intent to defraud must be proved in any action brought under sub-s (2) (*District Bank Ltd v Luigi Grill Ltd* [1943] Ch 78, [1943] 1 All ER 136).
4. No prosecution for any offence under this section shall be commenced without the leave of the Attorney-General (s 183(4)), granted after notice to the defendant of the application (s 133(5)). See PART I: MAGISTRATES' COURTS, PROCEDURE, para **1–410 Criminal prosecutions**, ante.

Forgery and Counterfeiting Act 1981

(1981 c 45)

PART I[1]

FORGERY AND KINDRED OFFENCES

Offences

8–13140   1. The offence of forgery.   A person is guilty of forgery if he makes a false instrument[2], with the intention that he or another shall use it to induce somebody to accept it as genuine, and by reason of so accepting it to do or not to do some act to his own or any other person's prejudice[3].
[Forgery and Counterfeiting Act 1981, s 1.]

---

1. Part I contains ss 1–13. For defence to offences under Part I of this Act based on Article 31(1) of the Refugee Convention, see the Immigration and Asylum Act 1999, s 31, in title, IMMIGRATION, post.
2. Where a forged document is to be used to induce the victim to act to his own or another's prejudice, the offence of forgery is made out on the making of the original false document and it is not necessary to prove that when the document was actually received one or other of the forms of prejudice specified in s 1 has in fact resulted (*R v Ondhia* [1998] 2 Cr App Rep 150, [1998] Crim LR 339, CA).
3. "Prejudice" and "induce" are defined by s 10 post. The section does not cover an act to the forger's own prejudice, for example his prosecution (*R v Utting* [1987] 1 WLR 1375).

8–13141   2. The offence of copying a false instrument.   It is an offence for a person to make a copy of an instrument which is, and which he knows or believes to be, a false instrument, with the intention that he or another shall use it to induce somebody to accept it as a copy of a genuine instrument, and by reason of so accepting it to do or not to do some act to his own or any other person's prejudice.
[Forgery and Counterfeiting Act 1981, s 2.]

8–13142   3. The offence of using a false instrument.   It is an offence for a person to use an instrument which is, and which he knows or believes to be, false, with the intention of inducing somebody to accept it as genuine, and by reason of so accepting it to do or not to do some act to his own or any other person's prejudice[1].
[Forgery and Counterfeiting Act 1981, s 3.]

---

1. "Prejudice" and "induce" are defined by s 10, post. Where an accused has used a false instrument or furnished false information with a view to obtaining money or other property, the prosecution does not have to prove, either in relation to this offence or in relation to an offence under s 17 of the Theft Act 1968 (false accounting), that the accused had no legal entitlement to the money or property in question (*A-G's Reference (No 1 of 2002)* [2002] EWCA Crim 1768, [2002] 3 All ER 840, [2002] Crim LR 844).
The prosecution must prove a double intention; to induce someone to accept the instrument as genuine, and that the other person should act or omit to act to his own or someone else's prejudice (*R v Tobierre* [1986] 1 All ER 346, [1986] 1 WLR 125, CA). Where the instrument was a "clean" driving licence it is not a defence to say that the only convictions it should have shown were more than four years old, as the court is entitled to take these into consideration (*Chief Constable of West Mercia Police v Williams* [1987] RTR 188).

8–13143   4. The offence of using a copy of a false instrument.   It is an offence for a person to use a copy of an instrument which is, and which he knows or believes to be, a false instrument, with the intention of inducing somebody to accept it as a copy of a genuine instrument, and by reason of so accepting it to do or not to do some act to his own or any other person's prejudice.

[Forgery and Counterfeiting Act 1981, s 4.]

8–13144 5. Offences relating to money orders, share certificates, passports, etc. (1) It is an offence for a person to have in his custody or under his control an instrument to which this section applies which is, and which he knows or believes to be, false, with the intention that he or another shall use it to induce somebody to accept it as genuine, and by reason of so accepting it to do or not to do some act to his own or any other person's prejudice.

(2) It is an offence for a person to have in his custody or under his control, without lawful authority or excuse, an instrument to which this section applies which is, and which he knows or believes to be, false.

(3) It is an offence for a person to make or to have in his custody or under his control a machine or implement, or paper or any other material, which to his knowledge is or has been specially designed or adapted for the making of an instrument to which this section applies, with the intention that he or another shall make an instrument to which this section applies which is false and that he or another shall use the instrument to induce somebody to accept it as genuine, and by reason of so accepting it to do or not to do some act to his own or any other person's prejudice.

(4) It is an offence for a person to make or to have in his custody or under his control any such machine, implement, paper or material, without lawful authority or excuse.

(5) The instruments to which this section applies are—

(a)   money orders;

(b)   postal orders;

(c)   United Kingdom postage stamps;

(d)   Inland Revenue stamps;

(e)   share certificates;

(f)   passports and documents which can be used instead of passports;

(fa)   immigration documents;

(g)   cheques and other bills of exchange;

(h)   travellers' cheques;

(ha)   bankers' drafts;

(hb)   promissory notes;

(j)   cheque cards;

(ja)   debit cards;

(k)   credit cards;

(l)   credited copies relating to an entry in a register of births, adoptions, marriages, civil partnerships or deaths and issued by the Registrar General, the Registrar General for Northern Ireland, a registration officer or a person lawfully authorised to issue certified copies relating to such entries; and

(m)   certificates relating to entries in such registers.

(6) In subsection (5)(e) above "share certificate" means an instrument entitling or evidencing the title of a person to a share or interest—

(a)   in any public stock, annuity, fund or debt of any government or state, including a state which forms part of another state; or

(b)   in any stock, fund or debt of a body (whether corporate or unincorporated) established in the United Kingdom or elsewhere.

(7) An instrument is also an instrument to which this section applies if it is a monetary instrument specified for the purposes of this section by an order made by the Secretary of State.

(8) The power under subsection (7) above is exercisable by statutory instrument subject to annulment in pursuance of a resolution of either House of Parliament.

(9) In subsection (5)(fa) "immigration document" means a card, adhesive label or other instrument which satisfies subsection (10) or (11).

(10) A card, adhesive label or other instrument satisfies this subsection if it—

(a)   is designed to be given, in the exercise of a function under the Immigration Acts (within the meaning of section 44 of the Asylum and Immigration (Treatment of Claimants, etc) Act 2004), to a person who has been granted leave to enter or remain in the United Kingdom, and

(b)   carries information (whether or not wholly or partly electronically) about the leave granted.

(11) A card, adhesive label or other instrument satisfies this subsection if it is given to a person to confirm a right of his under the Community Treaties in respect of entry to or residence in the United Kingdom.

[Forgery and Counterfeiting Act 1981, s 5 as amended by the Crime (International Co-operation) Act 2003, s 88 and the Asylum and Immigration (Treatment of Claimants, etc) Act 2004, s 3, the Crime (International Co-operation) Act 2003, s 88 and the Civil Partnership Act 2004, Sch 27.]

Penalties, etc

8–13145 6. Penalties for offences under Part I. (1) A person guilty of an offence under this Part of this Act shall be liable[1] on summary conviction—

(a) to a fine not exceeding **the statutory maximum**; or
(b) to imprisonment for a term not exceeding **six months**; or
(c) to both.

(2) A person guilty of an offence to which this subsection applies shall be liable on conviction on indictment to imprisonment for a term not exceeding **ten years**.

(3) The offences to which subsection (2) above applies are offences under the following provisions of this Part of this Act—

(a) section 1;
(b) section 2;
(c) section 3;
(d) section 4;
(e) section 5(1); and
(f) section 5(3).

(4) A person guilty of an offence under section 5(2) or (4) above shall be liable on conviction on indictment to imprisonment for a term not exceeding **two years**.

(5) *Repealed.*

[Forgery and Counterfeiting Act 1981, s 6 amended by the Statute Law (Repeals) Act 1993, Sch 1.]

---

1. For procedure where, by virtue of s 6(2)–(4), an offence is triable either way, see the Magistrates' Courts Act 1980, ss 17A–21, in PART I: MAGISTRATES' COURTS, PROCEDURE, ante.

8–13146   7. Powers of search, forfeiture, etc.   (1) If it appears to a justice of the peace, from information given him on oath, that there is reasonable cause to believe that a person has in his custody or under his control—

(a) anything which he or another has used, whether before or after the coming into force of this Act, or intends to use, for the making of any false instrument or copy of a false instrument, in contravention of section 1 or 2 above; or
(b) any false instrument or copy of a false instrument which he or another has used, whether before or after the coming into force of this Act, or intends to use, in contravention of section 3 or 4 above; or
(c) any thing custody or control of which without lawful authority or excuse is an offence under section 5 above,

the justice may issue a warrant authorising a constable to search for and seize the object in question, and for that purpose to enter any premises specified in the warrant.

(2) A constable may at any time after the seizure of any object suspected of falling within paragraph (a), (b) and (c) of subsection (1) above (whether the seizure was effected by virtue of a warrant under that subsection or otherwise) apply to a magistrates' court for an order under this subsection with respect to the object; and the court, if it is satisfied both that the object in fact falls within any of those paragraphs and that it is conducive to the public interest to do so, may make such order as it thinks fit for the forfeiture of the object and its subsequent destruction or disposal.

(3) Subject to subsection (4) below, the court by or before which a person is convicted of an offence under this Part of this Act may order any object shown to the satisfaction of the court to relate to the offence to be forfeited and either destroyed or dealt with in such manner as the court may order.

(4) The court shall not order any object to be forfeited under subsection (2) or (3) above where a person claiming to be the owner of or otherwise interested in it applies to be heard by the court, unless an opportunity has been given to him to show cause why the order should not be made.

[Forgery and Counterfeiting Act 1981, s 7.]

Interpretation of Part I

8–13147   8. Meaning of "instrument".   (1) Subject to subsection (2) below, in this Part of this Act "instrument" means—

(a) any document, whether of a formal or informal character;
(b) any stamp issued or sold by the postal operator;
(c) any Inland Revenue stamp; and
(d) any disc[1], tape, sound track or other device[2] on or in which information is recorded or stored by mechanical, electronic or other means.

(2) A currency note within the meaning of Part II of this Act is not an instrument for the purposes of this Part of this Act.

(3) A mark denoting payment of postage which a postal operator authorises to be used instead of an adhesive stamp is to be treated for the purposes of this Part of this Act as if it were a stamp issued by the postal operator concerned.

(3A) In this section "postal operator" has the same meaning as in the Postal Services Act 2000.

(4) In this Part of this Act "Inland Revenue stamp" means a stamp defined in section 27 of the Stamp Duties Management Act 1891.
[Forgery and Counterfeiting Act 1981, s 8, as amended by SI 2001/1149.]

---

1. "Disc" embraces information stored as well as the medium on which it is stored and a computer disc is an "instrument" for the purposes of ss 1 and 8(1)(d) of the Act (*R v Governor of Brixton Prison, ex p Levin* [1997] QB 65, [1996] 4 All ER 350).
2. Electronic impulses keyed into a computer in the course of "hacking" are not a "device" of the type covered by s 8(1)(d), and cannot found a charge of forgery, because the customer identification number and password held momentarily in the control area of the computer for the purpose of allowing unauthorised access to its database is not "recorded or stored" information within the ambit of the definition (*R v Gold* [1988] AC 1063, [1988] 2 All ER 186, 152 JP 445, HL).

8–13148   9. Meaning of "false" and "making".   (1) An instrument is false for the purposes of this Part of this Act—

(a)   if it purports to have been made in the form in which it is made by a person who did not in fact make it in that form[1]; or

(b)   if it purports to have been made in the form in which it is made on the authority of a person who did not in fact authorise its making in that form; or

(c)   if it purports to have been made in the terms in which it is made by a person who did not in fact make it in those terms; or

(d)   if it purports to have been made in the terms in which it is made on the authority of a person who did not in fact authorise its making in those terms; or

(e)   if it purports to have been altered in any respect by a person who did not in fact alter it in that respect; or

(f)   if it purports to have been altered in any respect on the authority of a person who did not in fact authorise the alteration in that respect; or

(g)   if it purports to have been made or altered on a date on which, or at a place at which, or otherwise in circumstances[2] in which, it was not in fact made or altered; or

(h)   if it purports to have been made or altered by an existing person but he did not in fact exist[3].

(2) A person is to be treated for the purposes of this Part of this Act as making a false instrument if he alters an instrument so as to make it false in any respect (whether or not it is false in some other respect apart from that alteration).
[Forgery and Counterfeiting Act 1981, s 9.]

---

1. Section 9(1)(a) received consideration in *R v Lack* (1987) 84 Cr App Rep 342.
2. It was held in *R v Warneford and Gibbs* [1994] Crim LR 753, CA that any "lie in the document must relate to the actual circumstances of the making of the document (and) a lie about other facts, extraneous to the document, does not suffice". However, the Court of Appeal in *A-G's Reference (No 1 of 2000)* [2001] 1 Cr App Rep 218, [2001] Crim LR 127, CA, while agreeing with the above remarks in *R v Warneford and Gibbs*, regarded that case as coming to the wrong conclusion on the facts and held that a tachograph record sheet would be false for the purposes of s 9(1)(g) if it was a document which required, before it could be made or altered, that a set of circumstances should exist or should have existed and those circumstances did not or had not existed (the false circumstance was that the record was being made during a period when there wrongly purported to be a second driver who was driving). The Court also held that, in view of the decision in *Jeraj* [1994] Crim LR 595, CA, the case of *Donnelly* (1984) 79 Cr App Rep 76 was still binding on the Court of Appeal, though both *Jeraj* and *Donnelly* should be restricted to apply only where *circumstances* needed to exist before the document could properly be made or altered.
3. Where a defendant had stolen a cheque, opened a building society account in a name similar to that of the payee, paid the cheque into it and subsequently withdrew money from the account by completing a withdrawal form in the name in which he had opened the account, it was held that as the withdrawal form purported to be signed by the person who had opened the account, and had in that respect been accurate, it had not told a lie about itself and the defendant had not been guilty of forgery by making a false instrument under s 9(1)(h) (*R v More* [1987] 3 All ER 825, [1987] 1 WLR 1578).

8–13149   10. Meaning of "prejudice" and "induce".   (1) Subject to subsections (2) and (4) below, for the purposes of this Part of this Act an act or omission intended to be induced is to a person's prejudice if, and only if, it is one which, if it occurs—

(a)   will result—

(i)   in his temporary or permanent loss of property; or

(ii)   in his being deprived of an opportunity to earn remuneration or greater remuneration; or

(iii)   in his being deprived of an opportunity to gain a financial advantage otherwise than by way of remuneration; or

(b)   will result in somebody being given an opportunity—

(i)   to earn remuneration or greater remuneration from him; or

(ii)   to gain a financial advantage from him otherwise than by way of remuneration; or

(c)   will be the result of his having accepted a false instrument as genuine, or a copy of a false instrument as a copy of a genuine one, in connection with his performance of any duty.

(2) An act which a person has an enforceable[1] duty to do and an omission to do an act which a person is not entitled to do shall be disregarded for the purposes of this Part of this Act.

(3) In this Part of this Act references to inducing somebody to accept a false instrument as genuine, or a copy of a false instrument as a copy of a genuine one, include references to inducing a machine to respond to the instrument or copy as if it were a genuine instrument or, as the case may be, a copy of a genuine one.

(4) Where subsection (3) above applies, the act or omission intended to be induced by the machine responding to the instrument or copy shall be treated as an act or omission to a person's prejudice.

(5) In this section "loss" includes not getting what one might get as well as parting with what one has.

[Forgery and Counterfeiting Act 1981, s 10.]

---

1. Where the defendant had submitted forged documents in support of an application for housing benefit, although the contents of the documents were true, the local authority did not have an enforceable duty to pay the benefit as he was required to provide the evidence required by the Housing Benefit (General) Regulations 1987 (*R v Winston* [1998] 1 Cr App Rep 337, 162 JP 775, [1998] Crim LR 81, DC). In some cases, the demonstrated existence of a claim of right at the time when the false document was used may negative an intent to cause another to act to his prejudice; but where, in relation to the submission of a false expenses invoice by beneficiaries of a trust fund to the trustee, the evidence showed both an intention to induce the trustees to accept the false invoice as genuine, and an intention to cause them by reason of so accepting it to authorise and execute a cheque, which in the circumstances it was not their duty to do, both elements of the mens rea were present (*A-G's Reference (No 1 of 2002)* [2002] EWCA Crim 1768, [2002] 3 All ER 840, [2003] 1 Cr App Rep 131, [2002] Crim LR 844).

Miscellaneous

8–13150   13. Abolition of offence of forgery at common law.   The offence of forgery at common law is hereby abolished for all purposes not relating to offences committed before the commencement of this Act.

[Forgery and Counterfeiting Act 1981, s 13.]

PART II[1]
COUNTERFEITING AND KINDRED OFFENCES

Offences

8–13151   14. Offences of counterfeiting notes and coins.   (1) It is an offence for a person to make a counterfeit of a currency note or of a protected coin, intending that he or another shall pass or tender it as genuine.

(2) It is an offence for a person to make a counterfeit of a currency note or of a protected coin without lawful authority or excuse.

[Forgery and Counterfeiting Act 1981, s 14.]

---

1. Part II contains ss 14–28.

8–13152   15. Offences of passing etc counterfeit notes and coins.   (1) It is an offence for a person—

(a) to pass or tender as genuine any thing which is, and which he knows or believes to be, a counterfeit of a currency note or of a protected coin; or

(b) to deliver to another any thing which is, and which he knows or believes to be such a counterfeit, intending that the person to whom it is delivered or another shall pass or tender it as genuine.

(2) It is an offence for a person to deliver to another, without lawful authority or excuse, any thing which is, and which he knows or believes to be, a counterfeit of a currency note or of a protected coin.

[Forgery and Counterfeiting Act 1981, s 15.]

8–13153   16. Offences involving the custody or control of counterfeit notes and coins.   (1) It is an offence for a person to have in his custody or under his control any thing which is, and which he knows or believes to be, a counterfeit of a currency note or of a protected coin, intending either to pass or tender it as genuine or to deliver it to another with the intention that he or another shall pass or tender it as genuine.

(2) It is an offence for a person to have in his custody or under this control, without lawful authority or excuse[1], any thing which is, and which he knows or believes to be, a counterfeit of a currency note or of a protected coin.

(3) It is immaterial for the purposes of subsections (1) and (2) above that a coin or note is not in a fit state to be passed or tendered or that the making or counterfeiting of a coin or note has not been finished or perfected.

[Forgery and Counterfeiting Act 1981, s 16.]

---

1. Whilst an intent to hand in the counterfeit articles could amount to a lawful excuse (*R v Wuyts* (1969) 53 Cr App Rep 417) indecision as to what to do cannot (*R v Sunman* [1995] Crim LR 569).

8–13154   **17. Offences involving the making or custody or control of counterfeiting materials and implements.**   (1) It is an offence for a person to make, or to have in his custody or under his control, any thing[1] which he intends to use, or to permit any other person to use, for the purpose of making a counterfeit of a currency note or of a protected coin with the intention that it be passed or tendered as genuine.

(2) It is an offence for a person without lawful authority or excuse—

(*a*)   to make; or
(*b*)   to have in his custody or under his control.

any thing which, to his knowledge, is or has been specially designed or adapted for the making of a counterfeit of a currency note.

(3) Subject to subsection (4) below, it is an offence for a person to make, or to have in his custody or under his control, any implement which, to his knowledge, is capable of imparting to any thing a resemblance—

(*a*)   to the whole or part of either side of a protected coin; or
(*b*)   to the whole or part of the reverse of the image on either side of a protected coin.

(4) It shall be a defence for a person charged with an offence under subsection (3) above to show—

(*a*)   that he made the implement or as the case may be, had it in his custody or under his control, with the written consent of the Treasury; or
(*b*)   that he had lawful authority otherwise than by virtue of paragraph (*a*) above, or a lawful excuse, for making it or having it in his custody or under his control.

[Forgery and Counterfeiting Act 1981, s 17.]

---

1. This is wide enough to include printer's proofs used as a check in the making of counterfeit notes (*R v Maltman* [1995] 1 Cr App Rep 239, [1995] Crim LR 144, CA).

8–13155   **18. The offence of reproducing British currency notes.**   (1) It is an offence for any person, unless the relevant authority has previously consented in writing, to reproduce on any substance whatsoever, and whether or not on the correct scale, any British currency note or any part of a British currency note.

(2) In this section—

"British currency note" means any note which—

(*a*)   has been lawfully issued in England and Wales, Scotland or Northern Ireland; and
(*b*)   is or has been customarily used as money in the country where it was issued; and
(*c*)   is payable on demand; and

"the relevant authority", in relation to a British currency note of any particular description, means the authority empowered by law to issue notes of that description.

[Forgery and Counterfeiting Act 1981, s 18.]

8–13156   **19. Offences of making etc imitation British coins.**   (1) It is an offence for a person—

(*a*)   to make an imitation British coin in connection with a scheme intended to promote the sale of any product or the making of contracts for the supply of any service; or
(*b*)   to sell or distribute imitation British coins in connection with any such scheme, or to have imitation British coins in his custody or under his control with a view to such sale or distribution,

unless the treasury have previously consented in writing to the sale or distribution of such imitation British coins in connection with that scheme.

(2) In this section—

"British coin" means any coin which is legal tender in any part of the United Kingdom; and
"imitation British coin" means any thing which resembles a British coin in shape, size and the substance of which it is made.

[Forgery and Counterfeiting Act 1981, s 19.]

Prohibition of importation and exportation of counterfeits

8–13157   **20. Prohibition of importation of counterfeit notes and coins.**   The importation, landing or unloading of a counterfeit of a currency note or of a protected coin without the consent of the Treasury is hereby prohibited.

[Forgery and Counterfeiting Act 1981, s 20.]

8–13158   **21. Prohibition of exportation of counterfeit notes and coins.**   (1) The exportation of a counterfeit of a currency note or of a protected coin without the consent of the Treasury is hereby prohibited.

(2) A counterfeit of a currency note or of a protected coin which is removed to the Isle of Man from the United Kingdom shall be deemed to be exported from the United Kingdom—

(a) for the purposes of this section; and

(b) for the purposes of the customs and excise Acts, in their application to the prohibition imposed by this section.

(3) In section 9(1) of the Isle of Man Act 1979 (which relates to the removal of goods from the United Kingdom to the Isle of Man) after the word "below" there shall be inserted the words "and section 21(2) of the Forgery and Counterfeiting Act 1981".

[Forgery and Counterfeiting Act 1981, s 21.]

Penalties etc

8–13159 22. Penalties for offences under Part II.   (1) A person guilty of an offence to which this subsection applies shall be liable[1]—

(a) on summary conviction—

(i) to a fine not exceeding **the statutory maximum**; or

(ii) to imprisonment for a term not exceeding **six months**; or

(iii) to both; and

(b) on conviction on indictment—

(i) to a fine; or

(ii) to imprisonment for a term not exceeding **ten years**; or

(iii) to both.

(2) The offences to which subsection (1) above applies are offences under the following provisions of this Part of this Act—

(a) section 14(1);

(b) section 15(1);

(c) section 16(1); and

(d) section 17(1).

(3) A person guilty of an offence to which this subsection applies shall be liable[1]—

(a) on summary conviction—

(i) to a fine not exceeding **the statutory maximum**; or

(ii) to imprisonment for a term not exceeding **six months**; or

(iii) to both; and

(b) on conviction on indictment—

(i) to a fine; or

(ii) to imprisonment for a term not exceeding **two years**; or

(iii) to both.

(4) The offences to which subsection (3) above applies are offences under the following provisions of this Part of this Act—

(a) section 14(2);

(b) section 15(2);

(c) section 16(2);

(d) section 17(2); and

(e) section 17(3).

(5) A person guilty of an offence under section 18 or 19 above shall be liable[1]—

(a) on summary conviction, to a fine not exceeding **the statutory maximum**; and

(b) on conviction on indictment, to a fine.

(6) (*Repealed*).

[Forgery and Counterfeiting Act 1981, s 22 amended by the Statute Law (Repeals) Act 1993, Sch 1.]

---

1. For procedure in respect of this offence which is triable either way, see the Magistrates' Courts Act 1980, ss 17A–21, in PART I: MAGISTRATES' COURTS, PROCEDURE, ante.

8–13170 24. Powers of search, forfeiture, etc.   (1) If it appears to a justice of the peace, from information given him on oath, that there is reasonable cause to believe that a person has in his custody or under his control—

(a) any thing which is a counterfeit of a currency note or of a protected coin, or which is a reproduction made in contravention of section 18 or 19 above; or

(b) any thing which he or another has used, whether before or after the coming into force of this Act, or intends to use, for the making of any such counterfeit, or the making of any reproduction in contravention of section 18 or 19 above,

the justice may issue a warrant authorising a constable to search for and seize the object in question, and for that purpose to enter any premises specified in the warrant.

(2) A constable may at any time after the seizure of any object suspected of falling within

paragraph (*a*) or (*b*) of subsection (1) above (whether the seizure was effected by virtue of a warrant under that subsection or otherwise) apply to a magistrates' court for an order under this subsection with respect to the object; and the court, if it is satisfied both that the object in fact falls within one or other of those paragraphs and that it is conducive to the public interest to do so, may make such order as it thinks fit for the forfeiture of the object and its subsequent destruction or disposal.

(3) Subject to subsection (4) below, the court by or before which a person is convicted of an offence under this Part of this Act may order any thing shown to the satisfaction of the court to relate to the offence to be forfeited and either destroyed or dealt with in such other manner as the court may order.

(4) The court shall not order any thing to be forfeited under subsection (2) or (3) above where a person claiming to be the owner of or otherwise interested in it applies to be heard by the court, unless an opportunity has been given to him to show cause why the order should not be made.

(5) Without prejudice to the generality of subsections (2) and (3) above, the powers conferred on the court by those subsections include power to direct that any object shall be passed to an authority with power to issue notes or coins or to any person authorised by such an authority to receive the object.

(6) In the application of this section to Scotland—

(*a*) in subsection (1) for the words "justice of the peace" there shall be substituted the words "justice within the meaning of section 462 of the Criminal Procedure (Scotland) Act 1975"; and

(*b*) in subsection (2);

(i) for the words "A constable" there shall be substituted "The procurator fiscal"; and
(ii) for the words "a magistrates' court" there shall be substituted "the sheriff court".

[Forgery and Counterfeiting Act 1981, s 24.]

8–13171   25. Directors' etc liability.   (1) Where an offence under section 18 or 19 of this Act which has been committed by a body corporate is proved to have been committed with the consent or connivance of, or to be attributable to any neglect on the part of, a director, manager, secretary or other similar officer of the body corporate, or any person who was purporting to act in any such capacity, he, as well as the body corporate, shall be guilty of that offence and be liable to be proceeded against and punished accordingly.

(2) Where the affairs of a body corporate are managed by its members, subsection (1) above shall apply in relation to the acts and defaults of a member in connection with his functions of management as if he were a director of the body corporate.

[Forgery and Counterfeiting Act 1981, s 25.]

Interpretation of Part II

8–13172   27. Meaning of "currency note" and "protected coin".   (1) In this Part of this Act—
"currency note" means—

(*a*) any note which—

(i) has been lawfully issued in England and Wales, Scotland, Northern Ireland, any of the Channel Islands, the Isle of Man or the Republic of Ireland; and
(ii) is or has been customarily used as money in the country where it was issued; and
(iii) is payable on demand; or

(*b*) any note which—

(i) has been lawfully issued in some country other than those mentioned in paragraph (*a*) (i) above; and
(ii) is customarily used as money in that country; and

"protected coin" means any coin which—

(*a*) is customarily used as money in any country; or
(*b*) is specified in an order[1] made by the Treasury for the purposes of this Part of this Act

(2) The power to make an order conferred on the Treasury by subsection (1) above shall be exercisable by statutory instrument.

(3) A statutory instrument containing such an order shall be laid before Parliament after being made.

[Forgery and Counterfeiting Act 1981, s 27.]

---

1. See the Forgery and Counterfeiting (Protected Coins) Order 1981, SI 1981/1505 amended by SI 1999/2095. Protected coins include any coin which is customarily used as money in any country and also includes euro coins.

8–13173   28. Meaning of "counterfeit".   (1) For the purposes of this Part of this Act a thing is counterfeit of a currency note or of a protected coin—

(a)   if it is not a currency note or a protected coin but resembles a currency note or protected coin (whether on one side only or on both) to such an extent that it is reasonably capable of passing for a currency note or protected coin of that description; or

(b)   if it is a currency note or protected coin which has been so altered that it is reasonable capable of passing for a currency note or protected coin of some other description.

(2) For the purposes of this Part of this Act—

(a)   a thing consisting of one side only of a currency note, with or without the addition of other material, is a counterfeit of such a note;

(b)   a thing consisting—

    (i)   of parts of two or more currency notes; or

    (ii)   of parts of a currency note, or of parts of two or more currency notes, with the addition of other material,

is capable of being a counterfeit of a currency note.

(3) References in this Part of this Act to passing or tendering a counterfeit of a currency note or a protected coin are not to be construed as confined to passing or tendering it as legal tender.

[Forgery and Counterfeiting Act 1981, s 28.]

Land Registration Act 2002

(2002 c 9)

PART 12
MISCELLANEOUS AND GENERAL

Offences etc

8–13180   123. Suppression of information.   (1) A person commits an offence if in the course of proceedings relating to registration under this Act he suppresses information with the intention of—

(a)   concealing a person's right or claim, or

(b)   substantiating a false claim.

(2) A person guilty of an offence under this section is liable[1]—

(a)   on conviction on indictment, to imprisonment for a term not exceeding two years or to a fine;

(b)   on summary conviction, to imprisonment for a term not exceeding six months or to a fine not exceeding the statutory maximum, or to both.

[Land Registration Act 2002, s 123.]

---

1. For procedure in respect of this offence, which is triable either way, see the Magistrates' Courts Act 1980, ss 17A–21, in PART I: MAGISTRATES' COURTS, PROCEDURE, ante.

8–13181   124. Improper alteration of the registers.   (1) A person commits an offence if he dishonestly induces another—

(a)   to change the register of title or cautions register, or

(b)   to authorise the making of such a change.

(2) A person commits an offence if he intentionally or recklessly makes an unauthorised change in the register of title or cautions register.

(3) A person guilty of an offence under this section is liable[1]—

(a)   on conviction on indictment, to imprisonment for a term not exceeding 2 years or to a fine;

(b)   on summary conviction, to imprisonment for a term not exceeding six months or to a fine not exceeding the statutory maximum, or to both.

(4) In this section, references to changing the register of title include changing a document referred to in it.

[Land Registration Act 2002, s 124.]

---

1. For procedure in respect of this offence, which is triable either way, see the Magistrates' Courts Act 1980, ss 17A–21, in PART I: MAGISTRATES' COURTS, PROCEDURE, ante.

8–13182   125. Privilege against self-incrimination.   (1) The privilege against self-incrimination, so far as relating to offences under this Act, shall not entitle a person to refuse to answer any question or produce any document or thing in any legal proceedings other than criminal proceedings.

(2) No evidence obtained under subsection (1) shall be admissible in any criminal proceedings under this Act against the person from whom it was obtained or that person's spouse or civil partner.

[Land Registration Act 2002, s 125 as amended by the Civil Partnership Act 2004, Sch 27.]

Protection of the Euro against Counterfeiting Regulations 2001[1]
(SI 2001/3948)

8–13200   **1.** (1) These Regulations may be cited as the Protection of the Euro against Counterfeiting Regulations 2001 and shall come into force on 1st January 2002.

(2) In these Regulations—

(a) "the Community Regulation" means Council Regulation (EC) No 1338/2001 of 28th June 2001 laying down measures necessary for the protection of the euro against counterfeiting; and

(b) expressions used in the Community Regulation have the same meaning in these Regulations as they have in the Community Regulation.

---

1. Made in exercise of powers under s 2(2) of the European Communities Act 1972.

8–13201   **2.** A credit institution, or other institution or establishment within Article 6(1) of the Community Regulation, which fails to withdraw from circulation a euro note or euro coin received by it which it knows or has sufficient reason to believe to be counterfeit shall be guilty of an offence and liable—

(a) on summary conviction, to a fine not exceeding the statutory maximum or to three months' imprisonment, or to both; or

(b) on conviction on indictment, to a fine or to imprisonment for a term not exceeding two years, or to both.

8–13202   **3.** (1) A credit institution, or other institution or establishment within Article 6(1) of the Community Regulation, which fails immediately to hand over to the relevant body (or to a person with authority to act on behalf of the relevant body for the purposes of this regulation) a euro note or euro coin received by that institution or establishment which it knows or has sufficient reason to believe to be counterfeit shall be guilty of an offence and liable—

(a) on summary conviction, to a fine not exceeding the statutory maximum; or

(b) on conviction on indictment, to a fine.

(2) In paragraph (1), "the relevant body" means—

(a) in the case of euro notes, the Bank of England or the National Criminal Intelligence Service,

(b) in the case of euro coins, the Royal Mint or the National Criminal Intelligence Service.

8–13204   **4.** (1) If an offence under these Regulations committed by a body corporate is shown—

(a) to have been committed with the consent or connivance of any director, manager, secretary or other similar officer of the body corporate, or any person who was purporting to act in any such capacity, or

(b) to be attributable to any neglect on his part,

he as well as the body corporate shall be guilty of the offence and shall be liable to be proceeded against and punished accordingly.

(2) If the affairs of a body corporate are managed by its members, paragraph (1) applies in relation to the acts and defaults of a member in connection with his functions of management as if he were a director of the body.

(3) If an offence under these Regulations committed by a partnership is shown—

(a) to have been committed with the consent or connivance of any partner, or any person who was purporting to act as a partner, or

(b) to be attributable to any neglect on his part,

he as well as the partnership shall be guilty of the offence and shall be liable to be proceeded against and punished accordingly.

(4) If an offence under these Regulations committed by an unincorporated association (other than a partnership) is shown—

(a) to have been committed with the consent or connivance of an officer of the association or a member of its governing body, or any person who was purporting to act in any such capacity, or

(b) to be attributable to any neglect on his part,

he as well as the association shall be guilty of the offence and shall be liable to be proceeded against and punished accordingly.

FRIENDLY SOCIETIES

Note

8–13280   The legislation concerning friendly societies is not printed in this work. Friendly Societies are mutual insurance associations which, until 1992, were unincorporated and registered under the

Friendly Societies Act 1974. Registered friendly societies continue to be subject to certain provisions of the 1974 Act which create a number of offences (ss 98–100). The Act also contains general provisions concerning legal proceedings and the jurisdiction of magistrates' courts (ss 101–103).

The Friendly Societies Act 1992 provides for the cessation of registration under the 1974 Act and allows friendly societies to incorporate. Although the 1992 Act specifically regulates incorporated friendly societies (ss 7–26), many of its provisions also apply to registered friendly societies. The Act establishes a regulatory body, the Friendly Societies Commission (s 1), and prohibits (subject to exceptions) the conduct of business without the authorisation of the Commission (s 31). There are also provisions concerning the regulation of business (ss 44–67) and accounts and audit (ss 68–79). The Act creates a number of offences.

The Friendly Societies Acts 1974 and 1992 are amended by the Financial Services and Markets Act 2000, title **INDUSTRY AND COMMERCE**, below, when in force.

For the full text of these Acts, see *Halsbury's Statutes*, Fourth Edition, Vol 19 FRIENDLY SOCIETIES.

GAMBLING

8–13972T	Gaming Clubs (Hours and Charges) Regulations 1984
8–13973	Licensed Betting Offices Regulations 1986
8–13974	Gaming Clubs (Multiple Bingo) Regulations 1986
8–13974C	Lotteries Regulations 1993
8–13974Q	National Lottery Regulations 1994

Betting and gaming licensing

Betting and gaming committees

8–13300   Jurisdiction and composition.   The justices for each petty sessions area are required to appoint a betting and gaming licensing committee which is responsible in the area for—

(1)   the grant, renewal or cancellation of bookmaker's permits, betting agency permits and betting office licences[1],

(2)   the grant, renewal, cancellation and transfer of gaming licences[2], and

(3)   the registration, renewal and cancellation of registration of members' clubs or institutes under Parts II and III of the Gaming Act 1968[3].

The committee, which is appointed annually, must consist of between 5 and 15 justices[4].

Appointments to the betting licensing committee are made at the election meeting which the justices for each petty sessions area hold every year in October[4]. The method of appointment is not prescribed. Once appointed, membership lasts for one calendar year, starting on the following January 1[5]. Casual vacancies may be filled, but there is no obligation to do so and any justice appointed to fill a casual vacancy holds office for the remaining period of appointment, ending on 31 December of the same year[6]

The betting licensing committee is also the gaming licensing authority with responsibility for various applications under the Gaming Act 1968[7]. The committee is, therefore, referred to as the betting and gaming committee.

The committee has no jurisdiction over racecourses as these are regulated by the Horserace Totalisator Board[8]. Track licences and the registration of pools promoters are dealt with by the relevant local authority. In gaming matters, the Gaming Board of Great Britain acts in a supervisory capacity[9]. The committee receives advice from the Gaming Board[10] and its power to grant casino and bingo licences is subject to the Board's prior consent[11]. Some aspects of betting and gaming concerning premises for which there is a justices' on-licence for the sale of intoxicating liquor are dealt with by the licensing justices sitting as a divisional licensing committee (referred to hereafter as the "liquor" licensing justices[12]).

---

1. Betting, Gaming and Lotteries Act 1963, Sch 1, para 1, this PART, post.
2. Gaming Act 1968, Sch 2, para 1, this PART, post.
3. Gaming Act 1968, Sch 3, para 1 and Sch 7, para 1, this PART, post.
4. Betting (Licensing) Regulations 1960, reg 1(1), this PART, post. See also the Justices of the Peace (Size and Chairmanship of Bench) Rules 1995, in PART I: MAGISTRATES' COURTS, PROCEDURE, ante.
5. Betting (Licensing) Regulations 1960, reg 1(2), this PART, post.
6. Betting (Licensing) Regulations 1960, reg 2, this PART, post.
7. Gaming Act 1968, Sch 2, para 1(1), this PART, post.
8. Betting, Gaming and Lotteries Act 1963, ss 12–15, this PART, post.
9. Betting, Gaming and Lotteries Act 1968, s 10 and Sch 1, this PART, post.
10. Gaming Act 1968, Sch 2, para 19, this PART, post.
11. Gaming Act 1968, Sch 2, para 3, this PART, post.
12. Applications concerning the authorisation of the playing of games which constitute gaming in (liquor) licensed premises (Gaming Act 1968, s 6, this PART, post) and permits for amusements with prizes gaming machines in (liquor) licensed premises (Gaming Act 1968, s 34 and Sch 9, this PART, post) should be submitted to the licensing justices constituted under the Licensing Act 1964, this PART, post.

8–13301   Meetings.   The committee is required to meet at least four times a year in the months of January, April, July and October, although additional meetings may be held if necessary[1].

The committee may sit in two or more divisions to conduct its business and the quorum of any meeting or division is three[2]. There is power to adjourn the consideration of any application[3].

---

1. Betting, Gaming and Lotteries Act 1963, Sch 1, para 3; Gaming Act 1968 Sch 2, para 2A, this PART, post.
2. Betting, Gaming and Lotteries Act 1963, Sch 1, para 1, this PART, post.
3. Betting, Gaming and Lotteries Act 1963, Sch 1, para 13; Gaming Act 1968, Sch 2, para 16, this PART, post.

8–13302   Clerk to the committee.   The clerk to the justices for the petty sessions area covered by a betting and gaming committee is the clerk to that committee[1]. The justices' chief executive may take fees but only such as are prescribed[2].

The justices' chief executive is also responsible for commencing the procedures for renewal of bookmaker's permits and betting office licences[3].

---

1. Betting, Gaming and Lotteries Act 1963, Sch 1, para 2, this PART, post.
2. Betting, Gaming and Lotteries Act 1963, Sch 1, para 20, Gaming Act 1968, Sch 2, para 63, this PART, post.
3. Betting, Gaming and Lotteries Act 1963, Sch 1, para 8, this PART, post.

8–13303   Betting and gaming registers.   The clerk to the betting and gaming committee is required to keep registers containing details of betting and gaming applications and to provide specified external agencies with particulars of those applications.

In betting matters, the clerk to the committee is required to keep a register in the prescribed[1] form of prescribed[1] particulars concerning all bookmaker's permits, betting agency permits and betting office licences granted or renewed by the committee[2]. The register of betting permits and licences should be available for inspection by any constable or, upon payment of the prescribed fee[3], by any other person[2]. The clerk should also send details of every bookmaker's permit granted or renewed to the Horserace Betting Levy Board[4].

In gaming matters, the clerk to the committee is required to keep in the prescribed form registers containing particulars of applications under the Gaming Act 1968[5]. The register should be available for inspection by any constable or, upon payment of the prescribed fee[6], any other person[7]. The clerk is also required to send prescribed[8] particulars concerning gaming applications to the Gaming Board[9].

1. Betting (Licensing) Regulations 1960, para 8, this PART, post.
2. Betting, Gaming and Lotteries Act 1963, Sch 1, para 34, this PART, post.
3. Betting (Licensing) Regulations 1960, reg 9, this PART, post.
4. Betting, Gaming and Lotteries Act 1963, Sch 1, para 36; Betting Levy (Particulars of Bookmakers' Permits) Regulations 1961, this PART, post.
5. Gaming Act 1968, Sch 10, paras 1, 2, this PART, post.
6. Gaming Clubs (Licensing) Regulations 1969, reg 7(4), this PART, post.
7. Gaming Act 1968, Sch 10, para 3, this PART, post.
8. Gaming Clubs (Licensing) Regulations 1969, reg 8, this PART, post.
9. Gaming Act 1968, Sch 10, para 5, this PART, post.

Betting licensing applications

8–13305   Betting control.   Betting control is based on the underlying principle that betting in streets and other public places (except racecourses) is generally prohibited[1]. Contravention of this prohibition constitutes an offence[1]. Persons or premises involved in betting operations must be specifically authorised to conduct their business. As a result, a person may not receive or negotiate bets unless he does so under the authority of a *bookmaker's permit* and premises may not be used for betting transactions unless operating under a *betting office licence*.

Applications for bookmakers' permits and betting office licences are made to the betting licensing committee. Provision is also made for the betting licensing committee to grant a *betting agency permit* which authorises a person without a bookmaker's permit to hold a betting office licence[2]. Such applications are rare and, therefore, not considered in any detail.

A person who conducts betting operations, occasionally or regularly, is a "bookmaker"[3]. It is an offence to act as or on behalf of a bookmaker without the requisite authorisation[4]. Employees or those acting on behalf of bookmakers or the Totalisator Board are protected from prosecution if certain requirements are complied with[5]. Bookmakers are only permitted to operate either on a 'track'[3] or in premises which are licensed for betting[6].

1. Betting, Gaming and Lotteries Act 1963, s 8, this PART, post.
2. Betting, Gaming and Lotteries Act 1963, Sch 1, this PART, post.
3. Betting, Gaming and Lotteries Act 1963, s 55, this PART, post.
4. Betting, Gaming and Lotteries Act 1963, s 2, this PART, post.
5. Betting, Gaming and Lotteries Act 1963, s 3, this PART, post.
6. Betting, Gaming and Lotteries Act 1963, s 1, this PART, post.

8–13306   Bookmaker's permit.   A person is not authorised to act as a bookmaker[1] unless he is the holder of a bookmaker's permit[2]. An application for a bookmaker's permit must be made to the appropriate betting licensing committee. A fee is payable on grant or renewal to the clerk of the committee[3]. After compliance with various procedural requirements[4] the committee will fix a date for the hearing of the application. At the hearing[5], the committee may, and in certain circumstances must, hear any objections received. The committee's discretion to grant or refuse the application is strictly regulated by legislation. Once granted, a bookmaker's permit lasts until the end of the current licensing period, which can be up to three years. However, permits granted less than five months before the end of a licensing period last until the end of the next licensing period[6]. Since a bookmaker's permit cannot be transferred[6], an application for a new permit must be made[3]. Provision is also made for the renewal and cancellation of permits.

An application for a bookmaker's permit should be made to the betting licensing committee in whose area the applicant has his office, his principal office or his usual place or residence[7]. The application can be made at any time but must be in the prescribed form and supported by references as to the fitness of the applicant[8]. There are mandatory[9] and discretionary[10] grounds for refusal of the application. In considering the discretionary grounds for refusal the committee will have regard to whether the applicant or the person who will be conducting his business is a fit and proper person to hold a permit. If the committee refuses an application it must give the grounds for its refusal[11]. There is a right of appeal against refusal[12]. The grant of the permit is subject to the payment of the prescribed fee[11]. The holder of a bookmaker's permit must produce his permit for examination upon request by a constable and if he fails to do so, without reasonable cause, he commits an offence[13].

1. For definition, see Betting, Gaming and Lotteries Act 1963, s 55, this PART, post.
2. Betting, Gaming and Lotteries Act 1963, s 2, this PART, post.
3. Betting, Gaming and Lotteries Act 1963, Sch 1, para 20, this PART, post.
4. See para **8–13312**, post.
5. See para **8–13320**, post.
6. Betting, Gaming and Lotteries Act 1963, Sch 1, para 29, this PART, post.
7. Betting, Gaming and Lotteries Act 1963, Sch 1, para 2, this PART, post.
8. Betting, Gaming and Lotteries Act 1963, Sch 1, para 5; Betting (Licensing) Regulations 1960, reg 4, this PART, post.
9. Betting, Gaming and Lotteries Act 1963, Sch 1, para 15, this PART, post.
10. Betting, Gaming and Lotteries Act 1963, Sch 1, para 16, this PART, post.
11. Betting, Gaming and Lotteries Act 1963, Sch 1, para 20, this PART, post.
12. Betting, Gaming and Lotteries Act 1963, Sch 1, para 21, this PART, post.
13. Betting, Gaming and Lotteries Act 1963, s 2(3), this PART, post.

8–13307   Renewal.   In February, prior to the expiry of the bookmaker's permit, the justices' chief executive is required to notify each holder of a permit in the committee's area of the date, time and place in April when the committee will meet to consider any applications for renewal which must be submitted by a specified closing date[1]. The grounds for refusal to renew a permit (both mandatory and discretionary) are the same as for refusal to grant a permit, save for the additional ground that the application may be refused if the applicant has not previously discharged all liabilities for bookmaker's levy, general betting duty and pool betting duty[2].

1. Betting, Gaming and Lotteries Act 1963, Sch 1, para 8, this PART, post.
2. Betting, Gaming and Lotteries Act 1963, Sch 1, paras 15–17, this PART, post. See also the Horserace Betting Levy Act 1969, s 4, this PART, post, and the Finance Act 1966, Sch 3, in PART VII: CUSTOMS AND EXCISE, post.

8–13308   Cancellation.   A bookmaker's permit may be cancelled either by an order made as part of a sentence imposed for certain criminal offences[1] or alternatively, by an application for cancellation in the prescribed form made to the betting licensing committee[2].

1. Betting, Gaming and Lotteries Act 1963, s 11, this PART, post.
2. Betting, Gaming and Lotteries Act 1963, Sch 1, para 26, this PART, post.

8–13309   Betting office licence.   Premises cannot generally be used for betting transactions unless licensed as a betting office[1]. An application for a betting office licence must be made to the appropriate betting licensing committee. Only the holder of a bookmakers's permit (or his agent) or a betting agency permit or the Totalisator Board or its agent can apply[1]. A fee is payable on grant or renewal to clerk of the committee[2]. After compliance with various procedural requirements the committee will fix a date for the hearing of the application[3]. At the hearing[4] the committee may and, in certain circumstances must, hear any objections received. The committee's discretion to grant or refuse the application is strictly regulated by legislation. Once granted, the licence lasts until the end of the current licensing period, which can be up to three years. However, licences granted less than five months before the end of a licensing period last until the end of the next licensing period[5]. Since a betting office licence cannot be transferred[5], an application for a new licence must be made[2]. Provision for renewal and cancellation is also made. The conduct of licensed betting offices is strictly regulated and failure to comply with statutory requirements may constitute an offence[6].

An application for a betting office licence must be made to the betting licensing committee in whose area the premises are or will be situated[7]. The application can be made at any time but should be in the prescribed form and be supported by plans showing the location and layout of the premises[8]. There are mandatory[9] and discretionary[10] grounds for refusal. In considering the discretionary grounds for refusal the committee will have regard to the suitability of the premises and the local demand for betting offices. If the committee refuses the application it must give the grounds for its refusal[11]. There is a right of appeal against refusal[12].

The management of a licensed betting office is closely regulated by statute and by regulations. There are restrictions concerning hours of opening, the range of facilities available and written material that may be displayed on the premises[6]. It is an offence to allow any person under the age of 18 to enter or to remain on the premises[13].

Permitted hours.   Licensed betting offices may open between 7 a.m.–10 p.m. during April, May, June, July and August and between 7 a.m.–6 p.m. at any other time of the year[14].

Renewal.   In February, prior to the expiry of the licence, the justices' chief executive is required to notify each holder of a licence in the committee's area of the date, time and place in April when the committee will meet to consider any applications for renewal submitted by a specified closing date[15]. The grounds for refusal to renew a licence (both mandatory and discretionary) are the same as for refusal to grant a permit save for the additional ground that the application may be refused if the premises have not been conducted properly[16].

1. Betting, Gaming and Lotteries Act 1963, s 9, this PART, post.
2. Betting, Gaming and Lotteries Act 1963, Sch 1, para 20, this PART, post.
3. See **8–13312**, post.
4. See **8–13320**, post.
5. Betting, Gaming and Lotteries Act 1963, Sch 1, para 29, this PART, post.
6. Betting, Gaming and Lotteries Act 1963, s 10, Sch 4; Licensed Betting Office Regulations 1986, this PART, post.

7. Betting, Gaming and Lotteries Act 1963, Sch 1, para 2, this Part, post.
8. Betting, Gaming and Lotteries Act 1963, Sch 1, para 5; Betting (Licensing) Regulations 1960, reg 4, this Part, post.
9. Betting, Gaming and Lotteries Act 1963, Sch 1, para 19(*a*), this Part, post.
10. Betting, Gaming and Lotteries Act 1963, Sch 1, para 19(*b*), this Part, post.
11. Betting, Gaming and Lotteries Act 1963, Sch 1, para 20, this Part, post.
12. Betting, Gaming and Lotteries Act 1963, Sch 1, para 21, this Part, post.
13. Betting, Gaming and Lotteries Act 1963, s 10 and Sch 4, para 2, this Part, post.
14. Licensed Betting Office Regulations 1986, reg 6, this Part, post.
15. Betting, Gaming and Lotteries Act 1963, Sch 1, para 8, this Part, post.
16. Betting, Gaming and Lotteries Act 1963, Sch 1, para 19 (*b*)(iii), this Part, post.

8–13312   Procedure.   The requisite procedural steps to be taken upon an application for the grant or renewal of a bookmaker's permit or betting office licence are shown in the table which follows.

Grant of bookmaker's permit[1]		Grant of betting office licence[1]		Renewal of bookmaker's permit/betting office licence[2]	
Action	*Time limit*	*Action*	*Time limit*	*Action*	*Time limit*
Application in the prescribed form[3] made to the chief executive to the committee.	Application may be made at any time, but at least 28 days before any date fixed for hearing.	Application in the prescribed form[3] made to the chief executive to the committee.	Application may be made at any time, but at least 28 days before any date fixed for hearing.	Chief executive to the committee gives written notice to holders that renewal is required.	The chief executive's notice must be sent out in February giving details of the committee's meeting in April.
Applicant sends copy of application to the police and Customs and Excise.	Not later than 7 days after date application is made.	Applicant sends notice of application to the police, Customs and Excise and appropriate local authority.	Not later than 7 days after date application is made.	The notice must specify the day, time and place when the committee will meet to consider applications for renewal and a closing date for applications.	The closing date for applications for renewal should not e less than 14 days after the giving of notice.
Applicant advertises application in a newspaper stating date by which objections to be made.	Not later than 14 days after date of application. The closing date for objections should not be less than 14 days after publication.	Applicant advertises application in a newspaper stating date by which objections to be made.	Not later than 14 days after date of application. The closing date for objections should not be less than 14 days after application.	The chief executive advertises the committee's meeting to consider renewal applications in a newspaper stating the closing date for receipt of renewal.	The advertisement should be placed in February. The closing date for applications and objections should be not less than 14 days after publication.
Applicant sends copy of newspaper to chief executive.	Not later than 7 days after publication.	Applicant sends copy of newspaper to chief executive.	Not later than 7 days after publication.	Applicant sends copy of newspaper to chief executive.	Not later than 7 days after publication.
Chief executive (i) fixes hearing date and sends notice of date, time and place of hearing to applicant (enclosing any objections received), police, Customs and Excise and any objectors and (ii) displays public notice of hearing date.	Hearing to be fixed not less than 14 days after closing date for objections specified in newspaper. Notices to be sent/displayed after closing date for objections and not less than 7 days before the date fixed for hearing.	Applicant posts notice on premises. Chief executive (i) fixes hearing date and sends notice of date, time and place of hearing to applicant (enclosing any objections received), police, Customs and Excise and any objectors and (ii) displays public notice of hearing date.	Not less than 14 days before closing date for objections specified in newspaper. Hearing to be fixed not less than 14 days after closing date for objections specified in newspaper. Notices to be sent/displayed after closing date for objections and not less than 7 days before the date fixed for hearing.	Applicant makes application for renewal in the prescribed form. Chief executive sends objectors details of pending applications for renewal and applicants details of objections received.	By the closing date for applications specified in the chief executive's notice of renewal and newspaper advertisement. After the closing date for applications for renewal and not later than 7 days before the date fixed for hearing.

1. Betting, Gaming and Lotteries Act 1963, Sch 1, paras 3–7, this PART, post.
2. Betting, Gaming and Lotteries Act 1963, Sch 1, paras 8–10, this PART, post.
3. Betting (Licensing) Regulations 1960, reg 4, this PART, post.

Gaming licensing applications

8–13313   **Gaming control.**   Gaming control begins with the basic proposition that all gaming[1] in public places is prohibited[2]. Any failure to comply with various aspects of this prohibition may constitute an offence[3].

However, there are certain areas of gaming activity which are exempt from this control, namely:

(i)   gaming[4] and amusements with prizes[5] at 'entertainments not held for private gain'.

(ii)   playing dominoes or cribbage and other specifically authorised games on premises licensed for the sale of intoxicating liquor[6].

In addition, there are other forms of gaming which, although permitted, are strictly regulated by the requirements of the Gaming Act 1968, namely:

(i)   *gaming for money by games of chance* on premises licensed or registered under Part II of the Gaming Act 1968.

(ii)   *gaming by way of machines* in accordance with the registration requirements of Part III of the Gaming Act 1968.

The Gaming Act 1968 also established the Gaming Board for Great Britain, consisting of a chairman and other members appointed by the Secretary of State[7]. The Board acts in a supervisory capacity and is required to keep under review the extent, character and location of gaming facilities which come within the ambit of statutory control[7]. The Board issues an Annual Memorandum of Advice to Gaming Committees which contains a wide variety of general guidance on gaming issues. The Board may also advise gaming committees about individual applications for gaming licences.

Gaming for money by games of chance may be conducted legally in either.

(i)   a proprietary club with a *gaming licence*, or

(ii)   a bona fide members' club with a *registration certificate*.

1. For definition, see Gaming Act 1968, s 52(1), this PART, post.
2. Gaming Act 1968, s 5, this PART, post.
3. Gaming Act 1968, s 8, this PART, post.
4. Gaming Act 1968, s 41, this PART, post.
5. Lotteries and Amusements Act 1976, s 15, this PART, post.
6. Gaming Act 1968, s 6, this PART, post.
7. Gaming Act 1968, s 10, this PART, post.

8–13314   **Gaming licences.**   Gaming (otherwise than by way of machines) may take place in a proprietary club with a gaming licence. In this context, there are essentially two permissible types of gaming:

(i)   'hard gaming' involving casino-style banker's games such as roulette and blackjack, and

(ii)   'soft gaming' such as bingo and other forms of gaming.

A proprietary club can only be licensed for hard gaming by obtaining a casino licence if it is located in one of the 'permitted areas'[1]. The permitted areas tend to be located in large cities or seaside resorts. If a proprietary club is not within one of these permitted areas only a licence limited to bingo or other restricted forms of gaming may be granted[2]. A gaming licence lasts for a period of one year from the date it was granted and, as a result, must be renewed each year[3].

Before making an application to a gaming committee for a gaming licence under Part II of the Gaming Act 1968, the applicant must obtain a certificate of consent from the Gaming Board[4]. In deciding whether to grant such a certificate the Board is obliged to consider the character, reputation and financial standing of the applicant and any proposed method of management[5]. If granted, the certificate will specify a date by which an application for a licence must be made.

An application for a gaming licence should be made to the gaming committee for the petty sessions area in which the relevant premises are or are to be situated[6]. A fee is payable to the chief executive to the committee before a licence may be granted, renewed or transferred[7]. After compliance with various procedural requirements[8] a date is fixed for the hearing of the application. There are mandatory[9] and discretionary[10] grounds for refusal to grant a gaming licence. The discretionary grounds are concerned with the suitability of the premises, the suitability of the applicant and whether there is a local demand for the gaming facilities. Limited restrictions may be imposed on the licence[11]. An application for renewal of a gaming licence must be made not later than two months nor earlier than five months prior to the expiry date[12]. When considering an application for the renewal of a gaming licence, there are additional mandatory[9] and discretionary[13] grounds for refusing the application. A gaming licence may be transferred provided the applicant has obtained a certificate of consent from the Gaming Board[14]. A licence ceases to be of effect if the Gaming Board revokes the certificate of consent[15] or an application to the Committee for cancellation of the licence is successful[16].

1. See the Gaming Clubs (Permitted Areas) Regulations 1971, this PART, post.
2. Gaming Act 1968, Sch 2, para 25, this PART, post; Gaming Clubs (Licensing) Regulations 1969, reg 5, this PART, post.

3. Gaming Act 1968, Sch 2, para 52, this PART, post.
4. Gaming Act 1968, Sch 2, para 3, this PART, post.
5. Gaming Act 1968, Sch 2, para 4, this PART, post.
6. Gaming Act 1968, Sch 2, para 2, this PART, post.
7. Gaming Act 1968, s 48 and Sch 2, para 63, this PART, post.
8. See para **8–13318**, post.
9. Gaming Act 1968, Sch 2, para 22, this PART, post.
10. Gaming Act 1968, Sch 2, paras 18 and 20, this PART, post.
11. Gaming Act 1968, Sch 2, paras 24–26, this PART, post.
12. Gaming Act 1968, Sch 2, para 12, this PART, post. For the procedure on renewal see para **8–13318**, post.
13. Gaming Act 1968, Sch 2, para 21, this PART, post.
14. Gaming Act 1968, Sch 2, para 55, this PART, post.
15. Gaming Act 1968, Sch 2, para 35, this PART, post.
16. Gaming Act 1968, Sch 2, para 2, ss 36–48, this PART, post.

8–13315 Registration of members' clubs for gaming. A members' club or miners' welfare institute may be registered for gaming under Part II of the Gaming Act 1968. The types of gaming permitted by such a registration certificate are stipulated by the Act and regulations made under the Act[1]. The registration certificate lasts for a period of one year from the date it is granted[2] although it may be renewed thereafter for a period of up to ten years[3].

In order to be eligible for a registration certificate a members' club must be a bona fide members' club which is not of a merely temporary character and has 25 or more members[4]. The main object of the club must be for a purpose other than gaming although a club which is concerned exclusively with the playing of bridge and/or whist is permissible and may be registered[4]. A registration certificate permits members (with respect to whom at least twenty-four hours have elapsed since their application or nomination for membership) and their bona fide guests to participate in certain types of gaming[5].

Applications for the grant, renewal or cancellation of a registration certificate proceed in substantially the same way as comparative applications for a gaming licence[6]. An application for registration should be made to the gaming committee for the petty sessions area in which the premises are or will be situated[7]. A fee is payable[8]. There are mandatory[9] and discretionary[10] grounds for refusing to register. There are additional grounds for a refusal to renew registration[11]. Registration may be subject to such restrictions as a committee thinks fit[12].

1. Gaming Act 1968, Sch 2, para 25; Gaming Act (Registration under Part II) Regulations 1969; Gaming Clubs (Licensing) Regulations 1969; Gaming Clubs (Permitted Areas) Regulations 1971, this PART, post.
2. Gaming Act 1968, Sch 3, para 19, this PART, post.
3. Gaming Act 1968, Sch 3, para 20, this PART, post.
4. Gaming Act 1968, Sch 3, para 7, this PART, post.
5. Gaming Act 1968, s 12, this PART, post. For special provisions concerning bingo clubs see the Gaming Act 1968, s 20, this PART, post.
6. See para **8–13318**, post.
7. Gaming Act 1968, Sch 3, para 2, this PART, post.
8. Gaming Act 1968, s 48, and Sch 3, para 23, this PART, post.
9. Gaming Act 1968, Sch 3, para 7, this PART, post.
10. Gaming Act 1968, Sch 3, para 8, this PART, post.
11. Gaming Act 1968, Sch 3, paras 9 and 10, this PART, post.
12. Gaming Act 1968, Sch 3, para 11, this PART, post.

8–13316 Gaming by use of jackpot machines. Part III of the Gaming Act 1968 regulates the manufacture, supply, and use of gaming machines. For the purposes of the Act a gaming machine is defined as a slot machine for playing a game of chance[1] which offers a large jackpot to winners. A *jackpot machine* should not be confused with an *amusement with prizes macine*[2] which has a smaller payout and is frequently found in public houses and amusement arcades.

Gaming by use of jackpot machines is permitted—

(i)   on the premises where a gaming licence is in force[3],
(ii) at a club or miners' welfare institute which is registered for gaming under Part II of the Gaming Act 1968, and
(iii) at a club or miners' welfare institute which is registered for gaming by use of jackpot machines under Part III of the Gaming Act 1968.

The maximum number of jackpot machines which may be available for gaming varies according to the nature of the premises[4].

The use of jackpot gaming machines may also be permitted and non-commercial entertainments such as bazaars, fetes or sporting events[1].

An application for registration for gaming by use of jackpot machines under Part III of the Gaming Act 1968 should be made to the gaming committee for the petty sessions area in which the premises are situated[6]. A bona fide members' club or proprietary club may apply. A fee is payable[7]. There are mandatory[8] and discretionary grounds for refusal[9]. If granted, the registration certificate lasts for up to five years[10]. The registration will cease to be of effect if not renewed[9] or if an application for cancellation is granted[11]. A club or institute may at any time relinquish its registration under Part III of the 1968 Act by the chairman or secretary giving notice to the chief executive to the gaming licensing committee[12].

1. Gaming Act 1968, s 26, this PART, post.
2. Gaming Act 1968, s 34, this PART, post.

3. The holder of a gaming licence for premises such as a casino or bingo hall may apply to the Committee to have a specified number of amusement with prizes machines instead of the permitted maximum number of jackpot machines, see Gaming Act 1968, s 32, this Part, post.

4. The maximum numbers of machines permitted are as follows: (i) in a club or miners' welfare institute registered under Pt II or Pt III of the 1968 Act, three, (ii) in a bingo club, four, and (iii) on premises licensed for gaming, six (Gaming Act 1968, s 31, this Part, post.

5. Gaming Act 1968, s 33, this Part, post.

6. Gaming Act 1968, Sch 7, para 2, this Part, post.

7. Gaming Act 1968, s 48 and Sch 7, para 24, this Part, post.

8. Gaming Act 1968, Sch 7, para 7, this Part, post.

9. Gaming Act 1968, Sch 7, paras 8–10, this Part, post.

10. Gaming Act 1968, Sch 7, para 22, this Part, post.

11. Gaming Act 1968, Sch 7, paras 13–20, this Part, post.

12. Gaming Act 1968, Sch 7, para 25, this Part, post.

8–13317   Amusement with prizes machines.   An amusement with prizes machine is a slot machine designed for the playing of a game of chance where the payout is restricted to a small amount of money or money's worth[1]. An amusement with prizes machine may be used[1]—

(i)   on premises where a permit is in force,

(ii)   on premises with a gaming licence where a direction has been made permitting the use of a specified number of amusement with prizes machines instead of jackpot gaming machines[2], and

(iii)   at pleasure fairs.

An application for a permit should be made to the relevant local authority, unless the machines are to be used in a public house or other premises with a justices' on-licence[3] when the application should be made to the *liquor* licensing justices for the licensing district in which the premises are situated[3].

There is no prescribed procedure for an application for a permit. A fee is payable[4]. The liquor licensing justices or other appropriate licensing authority have a discretion as to whether the application is granted and it may be refused if they form the view that the use of such machines on the premises is undesirable[5]. The permit may be granted subject to a condition limiting the number of machines permitted[6]. A permit lasts for such period as the justices determine not being less than three years from the date of grant or renewal[7]. A permit is not transferable. If the liquor licensee leaves the premises any incoming licensee will have to apply for a new permit if the machines are to continue to be used[8]. There is a right of appeal from decisions of the committee to the Crown Court[9].

---

1. Gaming Act 1968, s 34, this Part, post.

2. Gaming Act 1968, s 32, this Part, post.

3. Premises with a restaurant and/or residential licence are excluded, see Gaming Act 1968, Sch 9, para 1, this Part, post.

4. Gaming Act 1968, s 48 and Sch 9, para 21, this Part, post.

5. Gaming Act 1968, Sch 9, paras 7, 8, this Part, post.

6. Gaming Act 1968, Sch 9, paras 9, 10, this Part, post.

7. Gaming Act 1968, Sch 9, para 18, this Part, post.

8. Gaming Act 1968, Sch 9, para 20, this Part, post.

9. Gaming Act 1968, Sch 9, paras 11–14, this Part, post.

8–13318   Procedure.   The requisite procedural steps to be taken upon an application for the grant, renewal or transfer of—

(i)   a gaming licence,

(ii)   a registration certificate under Part II of the Gaming Act 1968, and

(iii)   a registration certificate under Part III of the Gaming Act 1968 are shown in the table which follows.

Grant/Transfer of Gaming Licence[1]		Grant of Part II Registration[3]		Renewal of Gaming Licence[1]/ Part II Registration[3]	
Action	*Time limit*	*Action*	*Time limit*	*Action*	*Time limit*
Application made in prescribed form with copy of Gaming Board consent.	At any time	Application made in prescribed form	At any time	Application made in prescribed form.	Not earlier than five months or later than two months before the date of expiry.

Grant/Transfer of Gaming Licence[1]		Grant of Part II Registration[3]		Renewal of Gaming Licence[1]/ Part II Registration[3]	
Action	*Time limit*	*Action*	*Time limit*	*Action*	*Time limit*
Applicant sends copy application to the Gaming Board, the police the local authority, the fire authority[2] and the collector of duty.	Not later than 7 days after date application made.	Applicant sends copy application to the police, and the collector of duty.	Not later than 7 days after date application made.	(i) Application for renewal of gaming licence— applicant sends copy application to the Gaming Board, the police, the local authority, the fire authority and the collector of duty; (ii) Application for renewal of Part II registration— applicant sends copy application to police and collector of duty. Chief executive to committee places notice in newspaper specifying closing date for objections.	Not later than 7 days after date of application made.
Applicant places prescribed notice in newspaper specifying closing date for objections.	Notice to be placed not later than 14 days after date of application. Closing date for objections should be not earlier than 14 days after publication of notice.	Applicant places prescribed notice in newspaper specifying closing date for objections.	Notice to be placed not later than 14 days after date of application. Closing date for objections should be not earlier than 14 days after publication of notice.		Notice to be placed not later than 14 days after application. Closing date for objections should be at least 14 days after publication of notice.
Applicant sends copy newspaper to chief executive.	Not less than 7 days after publication.	Applicant sends copy newspaper to the chief executive.	Not less than 7 days after publication.		
Applicant displays notice outside premises.	Not later than 14 days before the closing date for objections.	Chief executive fixes date for hearing.	Hearing must be not less than 14 days after date specified in newspaper.	Chief executive sends notice of hearing to applicant (enclosing any objections received), the relevant authorities and any objectors.	On or after the closing date for objections but not less than 7 days before the hearing.
Chief executive fixes date for hearing.		Chief executive (i) sends notice of hearing to applicant (enclosing any objections received), relevant authoritiers, and any objectors and (ii) displays public notice of hearing date.	On or after the closing date for objections but not less than 7 days before the hearing.		
Chief executive (i) sends notice of hearing to applicant (enclosing any objections received), relevant authorities, and any objectors and (ii) displays public notice of hearing date.	Hearing must be not less than 14 days after date specified in newspaper. On or after the closing date for objections but not less than 7 days before the hearing.				

Grant of Part III Registration[4]		Renewal of Part III Registration[4]	
Action	*Time limit*	*Action*	*Time limit*
Application made in the prescribed form.	At any time	Application made in the prescribed form.	Not earlier than three months or later than six before date of expiry.
Applicant sends copy application to the police.	Not later than 7 days after date application made.	Applicant sends copy application to the police.	Not later than 7 days after date application made.

1. Gaming Act 1968, Sch 2, this PART, post.
2. Where the application is for the transfer of a gaming licence, the fire authority need not be notified, see Gaming Act 1968, Sch 2, para 58(2), this PART, post.
3. Gaming Act 1968, Sch 3, this PART, post.
4. Gaming Act 1968, Sch 7, this PART, post.

Proceedings before the betting and gaming committee

8–13320 The hearing. The committee has power to grant an application without hearing the applicant if no objection has been made or if any objection made has been withdrawn before the application is considered[1]. In other circumstances, those entitled to be heard or to make representations at the hearing are the applicant, any objectors who have made objections within the requisite time limits, the relevant statutory authorities and where appropriate, the Gaming Board and the Commissioners of Customs and Excise[1]. The committee may adjourn the proceedings[2], take evidence on oath[3] and make such orders as it thinks fit for the payment of costs[3].

When considering certain applications, the committee also has a discretion to entertain objections made out of time provided the objector has given, and the applicant has had time to consider, a brief statement in writing of the grounds of the objection[4].

1. Betting, Gaming and Lotteries Act 1963, Sch 1, para 11 (grant or renewal of bookmaker's permit or betting office licence); Gaming Act 1968, Sch 2, para 14 (grant or renewal of a gaming licence); Sch 3, para 6 (registration or renewal of registration under Pt II of the Act) and Sch 7, para 5 (registration or renewal of registration under Pt III of the Act).
2. Betting, Gaming and Lotteries Act 1963, Sch 1, para 13 (grant or renewal of bookmaker's permit or betting office licence); Gaming Act 1968, Sch 2, para 16 (grant or renewal of a gaming licence); Sch 3, para 6 (registration or renewal of registration under Pt II of the Act) and Sch 7, para 6 (registration or renewal of registration under Pt III of the Act).
3. Betting, Gaming and Lotteries Act 1963, Sch 1, para 14 (grant or renewal of bookmaker's permit or betting office licence); Gaming Act 1968, Sch 2, para 17 (grant or renewal of a gaming licence); Sch 3, para 6 (registration or renewal of registration under Pt II of the Act) and Sch 7, para 6 (registration or renewal of registration under Pt III of the Act).
4. Betting, Gaming and Lotteries Act 1963, Sch 1, para 12 (grant or renewal of bookmaker's permit or betting office licence); Gaming Act 1968, Sch 2, para 15 (grant or renewal of a gaming licence); Sch 3, para 6 (registration or renewal of registration under Pt II of the Act).

8–13321 Appeals. Where an application is refused or granted subject to restrictions, the applicant is entitled to notice of the committee's decision. The applicant may appeal to the Crown Court within 21 days of the service of that notice. The Crown Court may allow or dismiss the appeal or reverse or vary any part of the committee's decision and may deal with the application as if it had been made to the Crown Court in the first instance. The judgment of the Crown Court on the appeal is final[1].

Costs of Appeal. On appeals to the Crown Court in betting and gaming matters, the Crown Court may make such order for costs between the parties 'as it thinks fit'[2]. There is no rule of practice that costs do, or do not, follow the event. The appropriate order of costs will depend on what the Crown considers to be just on the facts of the particular case[3]. In certain circumstances a betting and gaming committee may be entitled to indemnification from all costs and charges by an order for costs out of central funds[4]. In some gaming matters there are additional provisions concerning costs on appeals by the Gaming Board[5].

1. Betting, Gaming and Lotteries Act 1963, Sch 1, para 21 (grant or renewal of bookmaker's permit or betting office licence); Gaming Act 1968, Sch 2, para 29 (grant or renewal of a gaming licence); Sch 3, para 12 (registration or renewal of registration under Pt II of the Act) and Sch 7, para 11 (registration or renewal of registration under Pt III of the Act).
2. See the Crown Court Rules 1982, r 12(2) in PART I: MAGISTRATES' COURTS, PROCEDURE, ante.
3. *R v Crown Court at Stafford, ex p Wilf Gilbert (Staffs) Ltd* [1999] 2 All ER 955.
4. Betting, Gaming and Lotteries Act 1963, Sch 1, para 23 (appeal against refusal to grant or renew betting office licence); Gaming Act 1968, Sch 2, para 30 (appeal by applicant against refusal to grant or renew a gaming licence) and para 61 (transfer of gaming licence); Sch 3, para 12 (appeal by applicant against refusal to register or renew registration under Part II of the 1968 Act) and Sch 7, para 12 (appeal by applicant to register or renew registration under Part III of the 1968 Act).
5. Gaming Act 1968, Sch 2, para 32 and Sch 3, para 13, in this PART, post.

Gaming Act 1845
(8 & 9 Vict c 109)

8–13301   17.   Cheating at play to be punished as obtaining money by false pretences.   That every person who shall, by any fraud or unlawful device or ill practice[1] in playing at or with cards, dice, tables or other game, or in bearing a part in the stakes, wagers[2] or adventures, or in betting on the sides or hands of them that do play, or in wagering[3] on the event of any game, sport, pastime or exercise, win[4] from any other person to himself, or any other or others, any sum of money or valuable thing, shall—

     (a)   on conviction on indictment be liable to imprisonment for a term not exceeding **two years;** or

     (b)   on summary conviction be liable to imprisonment for a term not exceeding **six months** or to a fine not exceeding **the statutory maximum** or to both.

[Gaming Act 1845, s 17, as amended by the Statute Law Revision Act 1891, the Theft Act 1968, ss 33 and 36, Sch 2, and the Criminal Law Act 1977, s 28.]

---

1. The cheating must be in the actual play itself, and not in any preliminary proceedings. The "three card trick" is a game of skill (*R v Governor of Brixton Prison, ex p Sjoland and Metzler* [1912] 3 KB 568, 77 JP 23). As to what frauds and games are within this section, see *R v Bailey* (1850) 4 Cox CC 390; *R v Hudson* (1860) Bell CC 263, 24 JP 325; *R v O'Connor and Brown* (1881) 46 JP 214. Whether a particular incident in the game is a "fraud", etc, within the section is a question of fact for the jury (*R v Moore* (1914) 10 Cr App Rep 54).

2. See cases collected at 40 JP 227, as to what is a wager. Gaming and wagering contracts are bets.

3. The real question in a case of bets is whether the accused was fraudulent throughout, which means that at the time he made the bets he intended to cheat and defraud the bookmaker (*R v Leon* [1945] KB 136, [1945] 1 All ER 14, 109 JP 58; applied *R v O'Rourke* [1959] 1 All ER 438, 123 JP 203).

4. If the money "won" is not paid and so not "obtained", the offence should be charged as an attempt (*R v Harris, R v Turner* [1963] 2 QB 44, [1963] 2 All ER 294, 127 JP 357).

Betting, Gaming and Lotteries Act 1963
(1963 c 2)

PART I
BETTING

General restrictions on betting[1]

8–13302   1.   Restriction on use of premises for betting transactions with person resorting thereto.   (1) Subject to subsections (4A) and (5) of this section and section 9(1)[2] of this Act, no person shall—

     (a)   save as permitted by section 4(1)*[3] of this Act, use any premises[4], or cause or knowingly permit any premises to be used as a place where persons resorting[5] thereto may effect pool betting[4] transactions; or

     (b)   use, or cause or knowingly[6] permit any other person to use, any premises for the purpose of the effecting of any other betting transactions[4] by that person or, as the case may be, that other person with person resorting to those premises;

and every person who contravenes any of the provisions of this subsection shall be guilty of an offence[8]:

Provided that paragraph (b) of this subsection shall not apply where both the person using the premises as mentioned in that paragraph and all the persons with whom the betting transactions so mentioned are effected—

     (i)   either reside or work on those premises or on premises of which those premises form part; or

     (ii)   are, or are acting on behalf of, holders of bookmakers' permits[4] which are for the time being in force.

(2) Any person who, for any purpose connected with the effecting of a betting transaction[4] resorts to any premises which are being used in contravention[9] of the foregoing subsection shall be liable on summary conviction to a fine not exceeding **level 3** on the standard scale.

(3) For the purposes of the last foregoing subsection, proof that any person was on any premises[9] while they were being used as mentioned in that subsection shall be evidence that he resorted to the premises for such a purpose as is so mentioned unless he proves that he was on the premises for bona fide purposes which were not connected with the effecting of a betting transaction.

(4) *Applies to Scotland.*

(4A) Subject to subsections (4B) and (4C) of this section, subsection (1)(a) of this section shall not apply to the use of premises as a place where persons may deliver—

     (a)   completed coupons or other entry forms for qualifying competitions promoted by a registered pool promoter in the course of his pool betting business; and

     (b)   the stake money in respect of such coupons or other entry forms;

for forwarding to the registered pool promoter.

(4B) Subsection (4A) of this section shall not affect the operation of subsection (1)(*a*) of this section in relation to any premises of a class or description for the time being prescribed for the purposes of this subsection.

(4C) In subsection (4A) of this section, the reference to coupons or other entry forms for qualifying competitions does not include any coupon or other entry form that can effect entry to a competition that is not a qualifying competition.

(4D) In subsections (4A) and (4C) of this section, "qualifying competition" means a competition—

(*a*)   that is a competition for prizes for making forecasts as to association football games, and

(*b*)   that requires each entry in the competition to consist of a forecast as to at least four such games.

(5) Subsection (1)(*b*) of this section shall not apply—

(*a*)   to anything done on an approval horse racecourse[9] on a day on which horse races but no other races* take place thereon;

(*b*)   subject to the next following subsection, to anything done on any track[9] on any day on which under sections 5, 6 and 20[10] of this Act bookmaking may lawfully be carried on on the track.

(6) Nothing in subsection (5)(*b*) of this section shall affect the operation of subsection (1)(*b*) of this section in relation to the use on a track which is not an approved horse racecourse by a bookmaker[9] for the purposes of his business—

(*a*)   of any permanent structure other than a structure used by him in common with members of the public resorting to the track; or

(*b*)   of any position specially appropriated for the use of that particular bookmaker by, or by any person purporting to act on behalf of, the occupier of the track.

(7) In the case of a track which is a dog racecourse, subsection (6) of this section shall not apply in relation to the use of a permanent structure by a bookmaker for the purposes of his business if—

(*a*)   the use takes place on a day on which the public are admitted to the track for the purpose of attending dog races; and

(*b*)   no betting transactions in connection with dog races run on the track are effected in the course of the use.

[Betting, Gaming and Lotteries Act 1963, s 1 as amended by the Criminal Justice Act 1982, ss 38 and 46, the National Lottery etc Act 1993, s 56, SI 1995/3231 and SI 1997/1073.]

---

*Words in sub-s (1) substituted and sub-s (5) repealed by the Horserace Betting and Olympic Lottery Act 2004, Sch 2 from a date to be appointed.

1.   For law concerning excise duties relating to betting, see title CUSTOMS AND EXCISE, in PART VIII, post.

2.   See this subsection, post: it authorises betting transactions in premises conducted as licensed betting offices.

3.   See this subsection, post: it imposes restriction on pool betting.

4.   For meaning of "betting transaction", "bookmaker's permit", "pool betting", "premises", see s 55(1), post.

5.   The "resorting" must be actual and physical: sending letters, telegrams, and telephone messages is not resorting to the premises to which they are sent (*R v Brown* [1895] 1 QB 119, 59 JP 485). There may be resorting if people go to premises without actually entering (*Taylor v Monk* [1914] 2 KB 817, 78 JP 194), or even if all the bets are handed over from just outside (*R v Worton* [1895] 1 QB 227).

6.   It has been held that a person acts "knowingly" when, intending what is happening, he deliberately looks the other way (*Ross v Moss* [1965] 2 QB 396, [1965] 3 All ER 145, 129 JP 537).

7.   For penalty, see s 52(1), post.

8.   For penalty, see s 52(1), post.

9.   For meaning of "contravention", "premises", "horse racecourse", "track", "bookmaker", see s 55(1), post.

10.   See these sections, post: they impose restrictions on betting on tracks, dog racecourses, and prohibition on betting on licensed tracks.

8–13303   2. Restriction of bookmaking except under bookmaker's permit.   (1) No person shall act as a bookmaker[1] on his own account unless he is the holder of a permit authorising him so to act (in this Act referred to as a "bookmaker's permit") which is for the time being in force; and if any person[2] acts as a bookmaker in contravention[1] of this subsection he shall be guilty of an offence[3]:

Provided that this subsection shall not apply to the receiving or negotiating by a registered pool promoter[4] of bets made by way of pool betting[4].

(2) Schedule 1[5] to this Act shall have effect for the purposes of bookmaker's permits[1].

(3) If the holder of a bookmaker's permit, on being required by a constable to produce his permit for examination, refuses or without reasonable cause fails so to do, he shall be liable on summary conviction to a fine not exceeding **level 1** on the standard scale.

[Betting, Gaming and Lotteries Act 1963, s 2 as amended by the Criminal Justice Act 1982, ss 38 and 46.]

---

1.   For meaning of "bookmaker's permit", "bookmaker", "contravention", see s 55(1), post.

2.   In the case of a partnership firm each partner who is actively engaged as a bookmaker requires a permit (*Dungate v Lee* [1969] 1 Ch 545, [1967] 1 All ER 241).

3.   For penalty, see s 52(1), post.

4.   For meaning of "registered pool promoter", "pool betting", see s 55(1), post.

5.   Post: this Schedule prescribes the constitution of a committee of justices as the authority responsible for granting bookmaker's permits, and the procedure in connection with applications and grants.

8–13304　3. Agent of bookmaker or Totalisator Board* to be authorised and registered.
(1) No person shall by way of business receive or negotiate bets as servant or agent to another bookmaker[1] or to the Totalisator Board*[1] unless—

(*a*)　he has attained the age of twenty-one years; and

(*b*)　he is authorised in that behalf in writing in the prescribed[2] form by that other bookmaker or, as the case may be, by the said Board*; and

(*c*)　in the case of a person acting as servant or agent to another bookmaker, that other bookmaker is the holder of a bookmaker's permit[1] or betting agency permit[1]:

Provided that this subsection shall not apply to any person who is the holder of such a permit as aforesaid, or who receives or negotiates bets as aforesaid on premises[1] occupied by the holder of such a permit or by the said Board*.

(2) If any bet is received or negotiated by any person as servant or agent to another bookmaker or to the said Board* in contravention of the foregoing subsection, both that person and that other bookmaker or, as the case may be, the Board* shall be guilty of an offence[3].

(3) The said Board and* every bookmaker who is the holder of a bookmaker's permit or betting agency permit shall keep a register in the prescribed[4] form showing every person who is for the time being authorised for the purposes of subsection (1) of this section by that Board or, as the case may be,* by that bookmaker, and shall not grant any such authorisation without making the appropriate entry in that register; and if any person contravenes any of the requirements of this subsection he shall, in respect of each contravention, be guilty of an offence[3].

(4) If any person who holds any authority in writing issued for the purposes of subsection (1) of this section or who is required by subsection (3) of this section to keep a register, on being required by a constable to produce that authority or, as the case may be, register for examination, refuses or without reasonable cause fails so to do, he shall be guilty of an offence[3].

(5) Any person guilty of an offence under this section shall be liable on summary conviction to a fine not exceeding **level 1** on the standard scale or, in the case of offences[5] under subsection (2) or subsection (3) of this section, on a second or any subsequent conviction under the same subsection, to a fine not exceeding **level 3** on the standard scale.

(6) Nothing in this section shall apply to the receiving or negotiating by any person as servant or agent to a registered pool promoter[6] of bets made by way of pool betting[6].
[Betting, Gaming and Lotteries Act 1963, s 3 as amended by the Criminal Justice Act 1982, ss 38 and 46.]

***Words in sub-ss (1)–(3) repealed by the Horserace Betting and Olympic Lottery Act 2004, Sch 2 from a date to be appointed.**
　1. For meaning of "bookmaker", "Totalisator Board", "bookmaker's permit", "betting agency permit" and "premises", see s 55(1), post.
　2. This form of agent's authority is prescribed in the Betting (Bookmakers' Agents) Regulations 1960, SI 1960/2333.
　3. For penalty, see sub-s (5), infra.
　4. This register is prescribed in the Betting (Licensing) Regulations 1960, SI 1960/1701.
　5. By virtue of s 35 of the Criminal Justice Act 1982 in Part III, ante, it would now appear that in the case of a first offence under subsection (2) or (3) a fine not exceeding **level 3** on the standard scale may be imposed.
　6. For meaning of "registered pool promoter", "pool betting", see s 55(1), post.

8–13305　4. Restriction of pool betting.　(1) No pool betting business[1] shall be carried on on any track[1] except—

(*a*)　on an approved horse racecourse[1] on a day on which horse races but no other races take place thereon, by the Totalisator Board[1] or, with the authority of that Board, by the persons having the management of that racecourse; or

(*b*)　on a dog racecourse which is a licensed track[1], by means of a totalisator[1] operated in accordance with the provisions of section 16[2] of this Act by, or by a person authorised in that behalf in writing by, the occupier of the track;

and every person who contravenes the provisions of this subsection shall be guilty of an offence[3]:
Provided that nothing in this subsection shall prohibit a person from receiving or negotiating bets on an approved horse racecourse with a view to those bets being made by way of sponsored pool betting or to the operation of a licensed inter-track betting scheme[1].

(2) No person shall carry on any pool betting business otherwise than on a track unless he is a registered pool promoter, that is to say, a person who is registered for the purpose and whose registration is for the time being in force; and any person who carries on any business in contravention[1] of this subsection shall be guilty of an offence[3]:
Provided that this subsection shall not apply to sponsored pool betting business.

(3) Schedule 2[4] to this Act shall have effect for the purposes of the registration of a person as, and the conduct of his pool betting business by, a registered pool promoter.*
[Betting, Gaming and Lotteries Act 1963, s 4, amended by SI 1995/3231.]

***Section substituted and new sub-ss 4A and 4B inserted by the Horserace Betting and Olympic Lottery Act 2004, s 10 from a date to be appointed.**
　1. For meaning of "pool betting business", "track", "approved horse racecourse", "licensed track", "sponsored pool

betting", "contravention", "totalisator", "Totalisator Board", "inter-track betting scheme", "licensed inter-track betting scheme", see s 55(1), post.

2. See this section, post: it sets out conditions in which totalisators may be set up on licensed tracks.

3. For penalty, see s 52(1), post.

4. Post.

8–13306 5. Restriction of betting on tracks. (1) Betting by way of bookmaking[1] or by means of a totalisator[1] shall not take place on any track[1]—

(a) *Repealed*; or

(b) on any Good Friday and Christmas Day;

(c) *Repealed*.

(1A) *Repealed*.

(2) If bookmaking is carried on, or a totalisator is operated, by any person on any track on a day on which betting on that track is prohibited by this section, that person, and, if that person is not the occupier of the track, that occupier also, shall be guilty of an offence[2]:

Provided that where the occupier of a track is charged with an offence by reason of a contravention[1] of this section on the part of another person, it shall be a defence for him to prove that the contravention occurred without his consent or connivance and that he exercised all due diligence[4] to prevent it.

(3) Where facilities for pool betting provided on an approved horse racecourse by the Totalisator Board[1] or, with the authority of that Board, by the persons, having the management of that racecourse★ are provided otherwise than by means of a totalisator, subsections (1) and (2) of this section shall have effect as if the provision of those facilities were the operation of a totalisator by that Board or, as the case may be, by those persons.★

[Betting, Gaming and Lotteries Act 1963, s 5, as amended by the Betting, Gaming and Lotteries (Amendment) Act 1971, s 1, the Betting, Gaming and Lotteries (Amendment) Act 1985, Sch and the Deregulation and Contracting Out Act 1994, s 20.]

★Words in sub-s (3) repealed by the Horserace Betting and Olympic Lottery Act 2004, Sch 2 from a date to be appointed.

1. For meaning of "track", "bookmaking", "contravention", "totalisator", "Totalisator Board", see s 55(1), post.

2. For penalty, see s 52(1), post.

4. This is a question of fact, not of law: there is no legal standard of diligence (*R C Hammett Ltd v Crabb, R C Hammett Ltd v Beldam* (1931) 95 JP 180).

8–13307 6. Restriction of bookmaking on tracks. (1) Except on an approved horse racecourse[1] on a day on which that racecourse is used only★ for the purpose of horse races, bookmaking[1] shall not be carried on on any track[1] unless the occupier of the track is the holder of a licence authorising the provision of betting facilities on that track granted and for the time being in force under Schedule 3[2] to this Act (in this Act referred to as a "track betting licence");

Provided that this subsection shall not apply in relation to anything done on any track on any day if—

(a) during the period of twelve months in which that day falls, being a period beginning with 1st July in any year, bookmaking has not been carried on on that track on more than seven previous days; and

(b) notice of the intention to permit bookmaking on that track on that day has been given by post not less than seven clear days beforehand by the occupier of the track to the chief officer of police for any police area in which the track or any part thereof is situated[3].

(2) *Repealed*.

(3) If bookmaking is carried on by any person on any track on any day in contravention of this section, that person and, if that person is not the occupier of the track, that occupier also, shall be guilty of an offence[4]:

Provided that where the occupier of a track is charged with an offence by reason of a contravention of this section on the part of another person, it shall be a defence for him to prove that the contravention occurred without his consent or connivance and that he exercised all due diligence[5] to prevent it.

[Betting, Gaming and Lotteries Act 1963, s 6, as amended by the Betting, Gaming and Lotteries (Amendment) Act 1971, s 1 and the Betting, Gaming and Lotteries (Amendment) Act 1985, Sch.]

★Word in sub-s (1) repealed by the Horserace Betting and Olympic Lottery Act 2004, Sch 2 from a date to be appointed.

1. For the meaning of "approved horse racecourse", "bookmaking", "track", see s 55(1), post.

2. This Schedule deals with the licensing of tracks for betting prescribes licensing authorities and procedure for applications and grants.

3. A local bye-law, which made no similar provisions authorising betting facilities, was held to be repugnant to the general law and invalid (*Powell v May* [1946] KB 330, [1946] 1 All ER 444, 110 JP 157).

4. For penalty, see s 52(1), post.

5. This is a question of fact, not of law: there is no legal standard of diligence (*R C Hammett Ltd v Crabb, R C Hammett Ltd v Beldam* (1931) 95 JP 180).

8–13308 7. *Repealed.*

8–13309 **8. Prohibition of betting in streets and public places.** (1) Any person[1] frequenting[2] or loitering in a street[3] or public place, on behalf either of himself or of any other person, for the purposes[4] of bookmaking, betting[5], agreeing[6] to bet, or paying, receiving[7] or settling bets shall be liable on summary conviction to imprisonment for a term not exceeding **three months**, or to a fine not exceeding **level 4** on the standard scale, or to both, and shall in any case be liable to forfeit[8] all books, cards, papers and other articles relating to betting which may be found in his possession:

Provided that this subsection shall not apply to anything done on any ground used, or adjacent to ground used, for the purpose of a racecourse[9] for racing with horses on a day on which horse races take place on that racecourse.

(2) Where a person is found committing an offence under this section, any constable may seize and detain any article liable to be forfeited under this section.

(3) Notwithstanding anything in section 52(3) of this Act, a conviction for an offence under the Street Betting Act 1906[10] shall be deemed to have been a conviction for an offence under this section only if the offence was committed after 1st December 1961.

(4) In this section—

(a) the expression "street" includes any bridge, road, lane, footway, subway, square, court, alley or passage, whether a thoroughfare or not, which is for the time being open to the public . . .[11]; and

(b) the doorways and entrances of premises abutting upon, and any ground adjoining and open to, a street shall be treated as forming part of the street.

[Betting, Gaming and Lotteries Act 1963, s 8 as amended by the Criminal Justice Act 1982, ss 35, 38 and 46 and the Police and Criminal Evidence Act 1984, Sch 6.]

---

1. This will include "backers" as well as "bookmakers".
2. For meaning of "loitering", see *Williamson v Wright* 1924 JC 57: "frequenting", see *R v Clark* (1884) 14 QBD 92, 49 JP 246. What amounts to frequenting depends on the circumstances of the particular case: being in a place sufficiently long to effect the object aimed at is frequenting (*Airton v Scott* (1909) 73 JP 148; *Clark v Taylor* (1948) 112 JP 439). There must be evidence either of a number of bets made on one day or a single bet on each of a number of days, or proof of a known itinerary at any point at which the defendant was willing to accept bets although in different streets (*Cook v Fretwell* (24 May 1928, unreported), DC).
3. "Street" is defined in sub-s (4)(a), infra.
4. The Scots court upheld a conviction in which the alternative charges were all included (*Stenhouse v Dykes* 1908 SC (J) 61).
5. Distribution in a public street of handbills containing offers by bookmakers to receive bets was held to be an offence, inasmuch as the defendant was doing a substantial part of the business of betting by indicating the terms and the means of betting (*Dunning v Swetman* [1909] 1 KB 774, 73 JP 191).
6. A person does not "receive" bets in circumstances that betting slips (without money), collected by his agent in a factory, are given to him in the street (*Bland v Cowan* [1963] 2 QB 735, [1963] 2 All ER 184, 127 JP 378): per curiam, the defendant might have been convicted of frequenting the street "for the purpose of bookmaking".
7. This offence will be complete though no actual ready-money betting or wagering takes place.
8. This will form the subject of an express order. These words do not include money (*Gordon v Metropolitan Police Chief Comr* [1910] 2 KB 1080, 74 JP 437). The forfeiture, if ordered, must be disposed of pursuant to the Magistrates' Courts Act 1980, s 140, ante.
9. A field, not permanently laid out and used as a racecourse for racing with horses, but used on occasion for athletic sports, part of the programme consisting of two horse races, was held not to be within the exemption (*Stead v Ackroyd* [1911] 1 KB 57, 74 JP 482).
10. Repealed by Betting, Gaming and Lotteries Act 1963, Sch 8.
11. Words omitted apply to Scotland.

Licensed betting offices

8–13310 **9. Betting office licences and betting agency permits.** (1) Where in the case of any premises[1] there is for the time being in force a licence authorising the holder of the licence to use those premises as a betting office (in this Act referred to as "a betting office licence"), section 1(1) of this Act shall not apply to the use of those premises for the effecting of betting transactions[1] with or through the holder of the licence or any servant or agent of his:

Provided that the licence shall not authorise the use of the premises for effecting any pool betting transaction made otherwise than by way of sponsored pool betting[1] except where the use consists of the use of the premises as a place where persons may collect amounts payable by way of winnings in respect of competitions of the kind mentioned in section 1(4A)(a) of this Act.★

(2) The following persons, and the following persons only, may apply for the grant or renewal of a betting office licence in respect of any premises, that is to say—

(a) a person who is for the time being the holder of, or an applicant for, a bookmaker's permit[1];
(b) the Totalisator Board[1];★
(c) a person who, not being the holder of, or an applicant for, a bookmaker's permit, is for the time being both—

(i) accredited by a bookmaker who is the holder of a bookmaker's permit or by the Totalisator Board★ as an agent for the purpose of receiving or negotiating bets by way of business

with a view to those bets being made with that bookmaker or, as the case may be, with or
through that Board*; and

(ii) the holder of, or an applicant for, a permit (in this Act referred to as "a betting agency
permit") authorising him to hold a betting office licence.

(3) An application for the grant of a betting office licence in respect of any premises may be made
notwithstanding that the premises have still to be constructed or are still in the course of construction.

(4) Subject to subsections (2) and (3) of this section, Schedule 1[2] to this Act shall have effect for
the purposes of betting office licences and betting agency permits.

(5) If the holder of a betting agency permit, on being required by a constable to produce his
permit for examination, refuses or without reasonable cause fails so to do, he shall be liable on
summary conviction to a fine not exceeding **level 1** on the standard scale.

[Betting, Gaming and Lotteries Act 1963, s 9 as amended by the Criminal Justice Act 1982, ss 38 and 46 and
SI 1996/1359.]

***Words in sub-ss (1) and (2) repealed by the Horserace Betting and Olympic Lottery Act 2004, Sch 2 from
a date to be appointed.**

1. For meaning of "betting transaction", "bookmaker's permit", "premises", "sponsored pool betting", "Totalisator
Board", see s 55(1), post.

2. Post: this Schedule prescribes the constitution of a committee of justices as the authority responsible for granting
betting office licences and betting agency permits.

8–13311   10. Conduct of licensed betting offices.   (1) A licensed betting office[1] shall be managed
in accordance with the rules set out in Schedule 4[2] to this Act, and in the case of any contravention of
any of those rules the licensee and any servant or agent of the licensee[3] by whom the contravention[3]
was committed shall be liable on summary conviction to a fine not exceeding **level 3** on the standard
scale:

Provided that, where any person is charged with an offence under this subsection by reason only
of his being the licensee, it shall be a defence to prove that the contravention took place without his
consent or connivance and that he exercised all due diligence[4] to prevent it.

(1A) The Secretary of State may, from time to time, by order made by statutory instrument
amend the provisions of Schedule 4 to this Act so as to make new provision with respect to the
facilities (other than those in respect of which a betting office licence is required) that may be
provided in a licensed betting office; and, without prejudice to the generality of the foregoing, such
an order may—

(a) require compliance with such restrictions as may be specified in the order in relation to—

     (i)   the use in a licensed betting office of any apparatus for making information or other
         material available in the form of sounds or visual images or both;

     (ii)   the use of a licensed betting office for any form of entertainment; and

     (iii)   the provision in a licensed betting office of any form of refreshment;

(b) provide that paragraphs 1 and 4 of that Schedule shall be construed, subject to those
restrictions, as not prohibiting such of the things referred to in sub-paragraphs (i) to (iii) of
paragraph (a) of this subsection, as may be specified in the order;

(c) repeal paragraph 5 of that Schedule.

(1B) Notwithstanding anything in an order under subsection (1A) of this section, Schedule 4 to
this Act shall continue to have the effect of prohibiting

(a) in a licensed betting office in England and Wales, the supply of alcohol (within the meaning
of section 14 of the Licensing Act 2003) in circumstances where that supply is a licensable
activity (within the meaning of that Act);

(b) in a licensed betting office in Scotland, the provision of any facility in respect of which a
licence is required under the Licensing (Scotland) Act 1976.

(1C) An order under subsection (1A) of this section shall not be made unless a draft of the order
has been laid before, and approved by a resolution of, each House of Parliament.

(2) Without prejudice[5] to any other right to refuse a person admission to premises or to expel a
person from premises, in the case of a licensed betting office the licensee or any servant or agent of
his may refuse to admit to, or may expel from, the licensed premises any person who is drunken,
violent, quarrelsome or disorderly, or whose presence on those premises would subject the licensee
or any servant of his to a penalty under subsection (1) of this section; and if any person liable to be
expelled[6] from the licensed premises under this subsection, when requested by the licensee, any
servant or agent of the licensee or any constable to leave those premises, fails to do so, he shall be
liable on summary conviction to a fine not exceeding **level 1** on the standard scale.

(3) Any constable[7] may, on the request of the licensee or any servant or agent of the licensee, help
to expel from a licensed betting office any person whom the constable has reasonable cause to believe
to be liable to be expelled therefrom under subsection (2) of this section; and the constable may use
such force as may be required for that purpose.

(4) Any constable may enter[8] any licensed betting office for the purpose of ascertaining whether

the provisions of subsection (1) of this section are being complied with, and any person who obstructs any constable in the exercise of his powers under this subsection shall be liable on summary conviction to a fine not exceeding **level 1** on the standard scale.

(5) If any advertisement[10], other than an advertisement published in a material form or an advertisement to which subsection (6) of this section applies, is published—

(a) indicating[11] that any particular premises are a licensed betting office; or

(b) indicating[11] where any such office may be found; or

(c) drawing attention to the availability of, or to the facilities afforded to persons resorting to, such offices,

then, in the case of an advertisement in connection with the office or offices of a particular licensee, that licensee, and in every case any person who published[12] the advertisement or caused or permitted it to be published shall be guilty of an offence[13]:

Provided that it shall be a defence for any person charged with an offence under this subsection to prove—

(i) that he did not know and had no reasonable cause to suspect that the advertisement was, and that he had taken all reasonable steps to ascertain that it was not, such an advertisement as aforesaid; or

(ii) if he is charged by reason only of being a licensee, that the advertisement was published without his consent or connivance and that he exercised all due diligence[4] to prevent the publishing of any such advertisement in connection with his office or offices.

(6) This subsection applies to an advertisement if it is published otherwise than in a material form and—

(a) it is published inside but not outside a licensed betting office; or

(b) it complies with such restrictions as may be prescribed[14] and is, in such manner as may be prescribed, published outside a licensed betting office—

(i) from a place inside such an office; or

(ii) in premises giving access to such an office;

(iii) *Repealed.*

[Betting, Gaming and Lotteries Act 1963, s 10 as amended by the Criminal Justice Act 1982, ss 38 and 46, the Betting, Gaming and Lotteries (Amendment) Act 1984, ss 1 and 2, SI 1997/1074 and the Licensing Act 2003, Sch 6.]

---

1. For meaning of "licensed betting office", see s 55(1), post.

2. Post: this Schedule sets out the rules for licensed betting offices. A contravention of these rules by a servant or agent of the licensee involves at least constructive knowledge of non-compliance: see *Mallon v Allon* [1964] 1 QB 385, [1963] 3 All ER 843, 128 JP 81.

3. For meaning of "licensee" and "contravention", see s 55(1), post.

4. This is a question of fact, not of law: there is no legal standard of diligence (*R C Hammett Ltd v Crabb, R C Hammett Ltd v Beldam* (1931) 95 JP 180).

5. The right of a licensee to keep his house free of objectionable customers is quite independent of this section: see *Sealey v Tandy* [1902] 1 KB 296, 66 JP 19: cf Licensing Act 1964, s 174, post.

6. A person who is not drunken, violent, quarrelsome or disorderly, or whose presence is not unlawful, is not a person liable to be expelled under this section; therefore he incurs no liability to penalty by refusing to leave: see *Dallimore v Sutton* (1898) 62 JP 423.

7. A constable has no power of arrest under this subsection.

8. Cf Licensing Act 1964, s 186, post, and notes thereto.

10. Whether or not material is an "advertisement" is a question of fact to be determined by the court (*Windsors (Sporting Investments) Ltd v Oldfield* [1981] 2 All ER 718, [1981] 1 WLR 1176).

11. This is to be construed strictly and a sign stating the registered name of a company, which included the words "Turf Accountants", was held not to contravene this subsection in *Maurice Binks (Turf Accountants) Ltd v Huss* [1971] 1 All ER 104, [1971] 1 WLR 52, 135 JP 148.

12. An advertisement, placed inside a betting office but visible to, and clearly aimed at, persons outside the office, was published outside the betting office, and accordingly contravened, s 10(5) *(Windsors (Sporting Investments) Ltd v Oldfield* [1981] 2 All ER 718, [1981] 1 WLR 1176).

13. For penalty, see s 52(2), post.

14. See the Licensed Betting Offices Regulations 1986, SI 1986/103, this PART, post.

8–13312 10A. Cancellation of betting office licence. (1) Where the holder of a betting office licence is convicted under section 10(1) of this Act of an offence in respect of the betting office to which the licence relates, the court by or before whom he is convicted may, if the court thinks fit, order that the licence shall be forfeited and cancelled.

(2) An order under subsection (1) of this section made by a court in England and Wales shall be deemed for the purposes of any appeal to be part of the sentence for the offence; and in the case of such an order, the licence to which the order relates shall not be forfeited or cancelled under it—

(a) until the end of the period within which notice of appeal against the conviction or sentence may be given; nor

(b) if notice of appeal against the conviction or sentence is duly given within that period, until the determination or abandonment of that appeal.

(3) Where an order under subsection (1) of this section is made by a court in Scotland, the holder

of the licence to which the order relates may, without prejudice to any other form of appeal under any rule of law, appeal against the order in the same manner as against a conviction; and the licence to which the order relates shall not be forfeited or cancelled under it—

(a) until the end of the period of 14 days commencing with the date on which the order was made; nor

(b) if an appeal against the order or the conviction which gave rise to it is made within that period, until the date when that appeal is determined or abandoned or deemed to have been abandoned.

(4) Where a licence is forfeited and cancelled in pursuance of an order under subsection (1) of this section, the proper officer of the court by whom the order was made shall, unless he is also proper officer of the authority who last either granted or renewed the licence, send a copy of the order to the proper officer of that authority.

(5) In subsection (4)—

"the proper officer of the authority" has the same meaning as in Schedule 1; and
"the proper officer of the court" means—

(a) in relation to a magistrates' court in England and Wales, the justices' chief executive for the court; and

(b) in relation to a court of summary jurisdiction in Scotland, the clerk of the court.

[Betting, Gaming and Lotteries Act 1963, s 10A as inserted by SI 1997/947 and amended by the Access to Justice Act 1999, Sch 13.]

Special provisions with respect to bookmaker's and betting agency permits

8–13313   11. Cancellation of and disqualification for bookmaker's or betting agency permit.
(1) If the holder of a bookmaker's permit[1] or of a betting agency permit[1] is convicted—

(a) of an offence under section 1(1), 4(1),* 5, 6, 8 or 21[2] of this Act; or

(b) of any offence[3] involving fraud or dishonesty,

or if the holder of a betting agency permit is convicted of an offence under section 2(1) of this Act, the court by or before whom he is convicted may, if the court thinks fit, order that his permit shall be forfeited and cancelled.

(2) An order under the foregoing subsection shall be deemed for the purposes of any appeal to be part of the sentence for the offence; and the permit shall not be forfeited or cancelled under that order—

(a) until the date of expiration of the period within which notice of appeal against the conviction or sentence may be given; nor

(b) if notice of appeal against the conviction or sentence is duly given within the period aforesaid, until the date of the determination or abandonment of the appeal.

(3) *Applies to Scotland.*

(4) A person whose bookmaker's permit or betting agency permit is forfeited and cancelled in pursuance of an order under subsection (1) of this section shall, by virtue of that order, be disqualified[4] for holding or obtaining a permit of either description for a period of five years beginning with the date of the conviction which gave rise to the order:

Provided that, in a case where it appears to the court making the order to be just in all the circumstances, that court may include[5] in the order a direction that the period of disqualification shall be such period shorter than five years as the court may specify.

(5) Where a bookmaker's permit or betting agency permit is forfeited and cancelled in pursuance of an order under subsection (1) of this section, the proper officer of the court by whom the order was made shall, unless he is also proper officer of the authority who last either granted or renewed the permit, send a copy of the order to the proper officer of that authority.

(5A) In subsection (5)—

"the proper officer of the authority" has the same meaning as in Schedule 1; and
"the proper officer of the court" means—

(a) in relation to a magistrates' court in England and Wales, the deisgnated officer for the court; and

(b) in relation to any other court, the clerk of the court.

(6) Any holder of a bookmaker's permit or betting agency permit who employs in his bookmaking business any person known to him to be for the time being disqualified under subsection (4) of this section shall be guilty of an offence[6].

[Betting, Gaming and Lotteries Act 1963, s 11 as amended by the Courts Act 2003, Sch 6.]

---

*Reference in sub-s (1) inserted by the Horserace Betting and Olympic Lottery Act 2004, Sch 2 from a date to be appointed.

1. For meaning of "betting agency permit", "bookmaker's permit", see s 55(1), post.
2. The offences mentioned are unlawful use of premises for betting (s 1(1)); unlawful pool betting (s 4(1)); unlawful betting or bookmaking on tracks (ss 5, 6); street betting (s 8); betting with young person (s 21).

3. Note that the discretionary power to order forfeiture and cancellation is here expressed in the widest terms, not restricting fraud or dishonesty to offence connected with betting, gaming or lotteries. For a second or subsequent conviction of an offence under the Betting and Gaming Duties Act 1981, Sch 1, para 13(1) or (3), in respect of the same premises the court must order forfeiture of the licence on application by the Comrs (ibid, Sch 1, para 15).

4. It is an offence to employ in a bookmaking business a person known to be disqualified: see sub-s (6), infra.

5. The direction must be included in the order at the time of making the order: the Act contains no power (such as is to be found, eg, in the Road Traffic Offenders Act 1988, s 42) to remove the disqualification before the date of expiry.

6. For penalty, see s 52(2), post.

8–13314   Sections 12, 13, 14, 15*.   The Horserace Totalisator Board (in this Act referred to as the "Totalisator Board") is constituted: it has a duty to approve horse racecourses, and has the exclusive power to carry on, and to authorise, pool betting business and the business of betting by way of totalisator (*summarised*). Certain amendments to these sections are made by the Horserace Totalisator and Betting Levy Boards Act 1972.

> ***Sections 12, 14 and 15 repealed and s 13 amended by the Horserace Betting and Olympic Lottery Act 2004, Sch 2 from a date to be appointed.**

Special provisions with respect to licensed tracks

8–13315   16. Totalisators on licensed tracks.   (1) Where in the case of any licensed track[1], by virtue of section 4(1)(b)* of this Act, the occupier of the track or any person authorised in that behalf in writing by the occupier of the track has set up a totalisator[1], that totalisator shall be operated only—

(a) Repealed;
(b) where the public are admitted to the track for the purpose of attending dog races and no other sporting events are taking place on the track; and
(c) for effecting with persons resorting to the track betting transactions on dog races run on that track or betting transactions under a licensed inter-track betting scheme,

and Schedule 5[2] to this Act shall have effect with respect to the totalisator.

(2) The occupier of a licensed track—

(a) shall not so long as a totalisator is being lawfully operated on the track exclude any person from the track[3] by reason only that he proposes to carry on bookmaking on the track; and
(b) shall take such steps as are necessary to secure that so long as a totalisator is being lawfully operated on the track there is available for bookmakers space on the track where they can conveniently carry on bookmaking in connection with dog races run on the track on that day;

and every person who contravenes any of the provisions of this subsection shall be guilty of an offence[4].
[Betting, Gaming and Lotteries Act 1963, s 16, as amended by the Betting, Gaming and Lotteries (Amendment) Act 1971, s 1, the Betting, Gaming and Lotteries (Amendment) Act 1985, s 2 and Sch 1 and SI 1995/3231.]

> ***Reference substituted by the Horserace Betting and Olympic Lottery Act 2004, Sch 2 from a date to be appointed.**
> 1. For meaning of "licensed track", "totalisator", see s 55(1), post.
> 2. Post: this Schedule relates to totalisators on dog racecourses.
> 3. But he may be excluded from a particular place on the track (*R v Greyhound Racing Association Ltd* (1955) 119 JP 501). The right of a bookmaker under sub-paragraph (a) not to be excluded from a licensed track is not absolute or unlimited. The occupier is entitled to make *bona fide* and reasonable decisions as to how many bookmakers should be admitted (*Poole Stadium Ltd v Squires* [1982] 1 All ER 404, [1982] 1 WLR 235).
> 4. For penalty, see s 52(1), post. The bookmaker has no right of action for damages (*Cutler v Wandsworth Stadium Ltd* [1948] 1 KB 291, [1947] 2 All ER 815, CA; affd [1949] AC 398, [1949] 1 All ER 544, HL).

8–13316   16A. Licensing of inter-track betting schemes.   Schedule 5ZA to this Act (which makes provision for and in connection with the licensing of inter-track betting schemes) shall have effect.
[Betting, Gaming and Lotteries Act 1963, s 16A, inserted by SI 1995/3231.]

8–13317   17. Special rights of occupier of licensed track where totalisator is operated.
(1) The provisions of this section shall apply in relation to any dog race on a licensed track in connection with which betting takes place by means of a totalisator on the track in accordance with section 16 of this Act.

(2) The occupier of the track shall have the exclusive right to authorise any person—

(a) to carry on pool betting business on any such race as aforesaid;
(b) by way of business to receive or negotiate bets on any such race on terms that the winnings or any part thereof shall be calculated or regulated directly or indirectly by reference to the amounts or rates of any payments or distributions in respect of winning bets on that race made by means of the totalisator,

and no persons shall have the right to carry on any form of pool betting business on any such race or by way of business to receive or negotiate bets on any such race on such terms as aforesaid except with the authority of the occupier; and in giving any authority under this subsection the occupier may do so on such terms, including terms as to payments to the occupier, as the occupier may think fit.

(3) Right of action by occupier for infringement of his rights (*summarised*).

[Betting, Gaming and Lotteries Act 1963, s 17.]

8–13318 18. Charges to bookmakers on licensed tracks. (1) The occupier of any licensed track[1] may make to a bookmaker[1] or to any assistant accompanying a bookmaker to the track for the purpose of his business any charge for admission to any particular part of the track not exceeding, in the case of the bookmaker, five times the amount[2]; or, in the case of an assistant, the amount, of the highest charge made to members of the public for admission to that part of the track:

Provided that there shall not be made to any bookmaker or bookmaker's assistant for admission to any particular part of the track any charge differing in amount from the charge made to any other bookmaker or bookmaker's assistant, as the case may be, for admission to that part of the track.

(2) If in the case of any licensed track any charge other than—

(a) a charge authorised by the foregoing subsection; or

(b) any amount payable by way of bookmakers' licence duty under section 4 of the Betting Duties Act 1963[3],

is made to a bookmaker or bookmaker's assistant, or any payment, valuable thing or favour, other than a charge so authorised or an amount so payable, is demanded or received by or for the benefit of the occupier of the track as a consideration for facilities[4] being given to a bookmaker for the carrying on of his business, the person immediately responsible, and, if that person is not the occupier of the track, that occupier also, shall be guilty of an offence[5]:

Provided that where the occupier of a track is charged with an offence under this section by reason of an act of another person, it shall be a defence for the occupier to prove that the act took place without his consent or connivance and that he exercised all due diligence[6] to prevent it.

(3) In the case of a track which is a dog racecourse, the reference in subsection (2) of this section to facilities shall be construed as a reference to facilities other than in relation to a permanent structure.

[Betting, Gaming and Lotteries Act 1963, s 18 amended by SI 1995/3231.]

---

1. For meaning of "bookmaker", "licensed track", see s 55(1), post.
2. This is the gross sum paid without reference to the manner in which that sum is made up (*Pearson v Wandsworth Stadium Ltd* [1939] 3 All ER 93, 103 JP 275).
3. Section 4 of the Betting Duties Act 1963 was repealed by the Finance Act 1966.
4. "Facilities" includes anything given, or any service rendered, by the occupier to the bookmaker which in fact facilitates the carrying on of the bookmaker's business (*Midland Greyhound Racing Co Ltd v Foley* [1973] 2 All ER 324, [1973] 1 WLR 324, 137 JP 457).
5. For penalty, see s 52(2), post.
6. This is a question of fact, not of law: there is no legal standard of diligence (*R C Hammett Ltd v Crabb, R C Hammett Ltd v Beldam* (1931) 95 JP 180).

8–13319 19. Occupiers of licensed tracks not to have an interest in bookmaking thereon. (1) It shall not be lawful for—

(a) the occupier of any licensed track[1] or any servant or agent of his; or

(b) any person having under a lease, agreement or licence granted by the occupier any interest in or right over or in respect of any party of the track,

to engage either directly or indirectly, and either on his own behalf or on behalf of another, in bookmaking[1] on that track; and if any persons contravenes[1] the provisions of this section, that person, and, if that person is not the occupier of the track, that occupier also, shall be guilty of an offence[2]:

Provided that where the occupier of a track is charged with an offence by reason of a contravention of this section on the part of another person it shall be a defence for the occupier to prove that the contravention occurred without his consent or connivance and that he exercised all due diligence[3] to prevent it.

(2) In the case of a track which is a dog racecourse, subsection (1) of this section shall only apply in relation to bookmaking in connection with races run on that track.

[Betting, Gaming and Lotteries Act 1963, s 19 amended by SI 1995/3231.]

---

1. For meaning of "bookmaking", "contravention", "licensed track", see s 55(1), post.
2. For penalty, see s 52(2), post.
3. This is a question of fact, not of law: there is no legal standard of diligence (*R C Hammett Ltd v Crabb, R C Hammett Ltd v Beldam* (1931) 95 JP 180).

8–13320 20. Saving for right of occupier of licensed track to prohibit betting. Nothing in this Act shall be construed as requiring the occupier of a licensed track to permit betting thereon at any time when no totalisator is being operated on that track.

[Betting, Gaming and Lotteries Act 1963, s 20.]

Special provisions with respect to young persons

8–13321 21. Betting with young persons. (1) If any person—

(a) has any betting transaction[1] with a young person; or

(b) employs a young person in the effecting of any betting transaction or in a licensed betting office[1], or

(c) receives or negotiates any bet through a young person,

he shall be guilty of an offence[2]:

Provided that a person shall not be guilty of an offence under this subsection by reason of—

(i) the employment of a young person in the effecting of betting transactions by post; or

(ii) the carriage by a young person of a communication relating to a betting transaction for the purposes of its conveyance by post.

(2) In this section, the expression "young person" means a person—

(a) who is under the age of eighteen years and whom the person committing an offence in relation to him under this section knows, or ought to know, to be under that age; or

(b) who is apparently under the said age:

Provided that in the case of any proceedings under this section for an offence in respect of a person apparently under the said age, it shall be a defence to prove that at the time of the alleged offence he had in fact attained that age.

(3) In any case concerning—

(a) a bet which is an entry in a qualifying competition (as defined in section 1(4D) of this Act), or

(b) a betting transaction relating to such a bet,

this section shall have effect with the substitution in subsection (2) of "sixteen" for "eighteen".

(4) Subsection (3) of this section does not apply in relation to the employment of a young person in a licensed betting office.

[Betting, Gaming and Lotteries Act 1963, s 21 amended by the National Lottery etc Act 1993, s 57.]

---

1. For meaning of "betting transaction", "licensed betting office", see s 55(1), post.

2. For penalty, see s 52(2), post.

8–13322 22. Betting circulars not to be sent to young persons. (1) If any person, for the purpose of earning commission, reward or other profit, sends or causes to be sent to a person whom he knows to be under the age of eighteen years any circular, notice, advertisement, letter, telegram or other document which invites or may reasonably be implied to invite the person receiving it to make any bet, or to enter into or take any share or interest in any betting transaction, or to apply to any person or at any place with a view to obtaining information or advice for the purpose of any bet or for information as to any race, fight, game, sport or other contingency upon which betting is generally carried on, he shall be guilty of an offence[1].

(2) If any such document as aforesaid names or refers to anyone as a person to whom any payment may be made, or from whom information may be obtained, for the purpose of or in relation to betting, the person so named or referred to shall be deemed to have sent that document or caused it to be sent unless he proves that he had not consented to be so named and that he was not in any way a party to, and was wholly ignorant of, the sending of the document.

(3) If any such document as aforesaid is sent to any person at any university[2], college, school or other place of education and that person is under the age of eighteen years, the person sending the document or causing it to be sent shall be deemed to have known that person to be under that age unless he proves that he had reasonable grounds for believing him to have attained that age.

(4) In any case concerning—

(a) a bet which is an entry in a qualifying competition (as defined in section 1(4D) of this Act),

(b) a betting transaction relating to such a bet, or

(c) information as to any game of association football upon which such betting is carried on,

this section shall have effect with the substitution in subsections (1) and (3) of "sixteen" for "eighteen".

[Betting, Gaming and Lotteries Act 1963, s 22, as amended by Sch 1 of the Family Law Reform Act 1969 and the National Lottery etc Act 1993, s 57.]

---

1. For penalty, see s 52(2), post.

2. For a case where a document was sent to an ambiguous address, eg, to an undergraduate living in lodgings licensed by the university, see *Milton v Studd* [1910] 2 KB 118, 74 JP 217.

Power of entry on tracks

8–13323 23. Power of entry on tracks. Any person authorised in writing in that behalf by the licensing authority under Schedule 3[1] to this Act for the area in which any track or the greater part of the superficial area thereof is situate, subject to the production on demand of his authority, and any

constable, may at all reasonable times enter upon that track for the purpose of ascertaining whether the provisions of this Part of this Act are being complied with; and every person who obstructs any constable or other person in the exercise of his powers under this section shall be liable on summary conviction to a fine not exceeding **level 1** on the standard scale.
[Betting, Gaming and Lotteries Act 1963, s 23 as amended by the Criminal Justice Act 1982, ss 38 and 46.]

---

1. Post: this Schedule relates to the licensing of tracks for betting.

Contributions for benefit of horseracing

8–13324 The Horseracing Betting Levy Board is constituted: it has powers to collect money contributions from bookmakers and the Totalisator Board in conjunction with a constituted Bookmakers' Committee. Money collected is to be applied to the improvement of breeds of horses and of horse racing and the advancement of veterinary science and education. Machinery is provided for assessing the amount to be paid by any bookmaker and for the setting up of Levy Appeal tribunals and for consequential matters.
[Betting, Gaming and Lotteries Act 1963, ss 24–31, as amended by the Horserace Betting Levy Act 1969—summarised.]

8–13325 **28. Restriction on disclosure of information.** (10) If, otherwise than with the consent in writing of the bookmaker concerned or—

(*a*) for the purposes of this section or section 2 of the Horserace Betting Levy Act 1969 or of a report of any proceedings before an appeal tribunal thereunder; or

(*b*) for the purposes of, or of a report of—

(i) proceedings for the recovery from that bookmaker of any amount due from him under this section by way of the levy; or

(ii) proceedings relating to that bookmaker before an appropriate authority within the meaning of Schedule 1 to this Act, or before any court on an appeal from any such authority; or

(iii) any criminal proceedings,

any person who is a member, officer or servant of the Levy Board, the Bookmakers' Committee or an appeal tribunal established in pursuance of section 29 of this Act, or who is consulted by the Bookmakers' Committee in pursuance of subsection (4) of this section, discloses to any other person in such a manner as to identify the bookmaker concerned any declaration by or assessment on any bookmaker for the purposes of the levy, or any other information concerning that bookmaker obtaining through the exercise of any functions under this section, or any ruling of the Bookmakers' Committee or an appeal tribunal as to the category into which any bookmaker falls, he shall be liable on summary conviction to a fine not exceeding **level 4** on the standard scale.
[Betting, Gaming and Lotteries Act 1963, s 28(10), as amended by the Horserace Betting Levy Act 1981, Sch, the Criminal Justice Act 1982, ss 39 and 46, and Sch 3 and the Horserace Betting Levy Act 1969, s 2.]

PART II
GAMING

The law as to gaming is now governed by the Gaming Act 1968, post.

8–13326 **40. References in other Acts to gaming or unlawful games.** In the following provisions, that is to say, section 44 of the Metropolitan Police Act 1839, section 28 of the City of London Police Act 1839, section 9 of the Late Night Refreshment Houses Act 1969 (which prohibit gaming in refreshment houses or on licensed premises), any reference to gaming or unlawful games shall be construed as a reference to the playing of any game in such circumstances that an offence under the Gaming Act 1968 is committed or a requirement or restriction for the time being in force under section 6[1] of that Act is contravened.
[Betting, Gaming and Lotteries Act 1963, s 40, as amended by Sch 11 of the Gaming Act 1968 and the Late Night Refreshment Houses Act 1969, Sch.]

---

1. Post: this section contains a saving for the playing of dominoes and cribbage on licensed premises.

PART III
LOTTERIES AND PRIZE COMPETITIONS

8–13327 **41–47.** *Repealed.*

PART IV
AMUSEMENTS WITH PRIZES

8–13328 **48–49.** *Repealed.*

PART V

GENERAL

8–13329   **51. Search warrants[1].**   (1) If a justice of the peace is satisfied on information on oath that there is reasonable ground for suspecting that an offence under this Act is being, has been or is about to be committed on any premises[2], he may issue[3] a warrant in writing authorising any constable to enter those premises, if necessary by force, and search them; and any constable who enters the premises under the authority of the warrant may—

     (*a*)   seize and remove any document, money[2] or valuable thing, instrument or other thing whatsoever found on the premises which he has reasonable cause to believe may be required as evidence for the purposes of proceedings in respect of any such offence; and

     (*b*)   search any person found on the premises whom he has reasonable cause to believe to be committing or to have committed any such offence.

   (2) *Application to Scotland.*

[Betting, Gaming and Lotteries Act 1963, s 51 as amended by the Police and Criminal Evidence Act 1984, Schs 6 and 7.]

---

   1. See also the Police and Criminal Evidence Act 1984, ss 15 and 16 (applications for, and execution of warrants) and ss 24 and 25 (arrest) in PART I: MAGISTRATES' COURTS, PROCEDURE.

   2. For meaning of "premises", "money", see s 55(1), post.

   3. See Precedent 19 in PART IX: PRECEDENTS AND FORMS, post.

8–13330   **52. Penalties and forfeitures.**   (1) A person guilty of an offence under any of the following provisions of this Act, that is to say, sections 1(1), 2(1), 4,* 5, 6, 16, 32(4), paragraph 29 of Schedule 2 and paragraph 17 of Schedule 5, shall be liable[1]—

     (*a*)   on summary conviction, to a fine not exceeding the prescribed sum or, in the case of a second or any subsequent conviction for an offence under the same provision, to imprisonment for a term not exceeding **three months** or to a fine not exceeding the prescribed sum or to both; or

     (*b*)   on conviction on indictment, to a fine or, in the case of a second or any subsequent conviction for an offence under the same provision, to imprisonment for a term not exceeding **one year** or to a fine or to both.

   (2) A person guilty of an offence under any provision of this Act not mentioned in the foregoing subsections, being a provision which does not specify any other penalty, shall be liable on summary conviction to a fine not exceeding **level 5** on the standard scale or to imprisonment for a term not exceeding **six months** or to both.

   (3) Subject to section 8(3) of this Act, for the purposes of any provision of this Act with respect to a second or subsequent conviction, a conviction for an offence under any provision repealed by this Act shall be deemed to have been a conviction for the like offence under the corresponding provision of this Act.

   (4) The court by or before whom a person is convicted of any offence under this act may order anything produced[2] to the court and shown to the satisfaction of the court to relate to the offence to be forfeited[3] and either destroyed or dealt with in such other manner as the court may order.

[Betting, Gaming and Lotteries Act 1963, s 52, as amended by the Criminal Law Act 1977, ss 28 and 32 and Sch 1, the Magistrates' Courts Act 1980, s 32 and the Criminal Justice Act 1982, s 46.]

---

   *New reference inserted by the Horserace Betting and Olympic Lottery Act 2004, Sch 2 from a date to be appointed.

   1. For procedure in respect of this offence triable either way, see Magistrates' Courts Act 1980, ss 18–21, in PART I, ante.

   2. "Produced" does not necessarily mean physically produced: enough if the machine or other thing is properly identified and is available for the court to look at, if the court so wishes (*R v Edmonton Justices, ex p Stannite Automatics Ltd* [1965] 2 All ER 750, 129 JP 411).

   3. Anything ordered to be forfeited will be dealt with as the court may order: if the court orders that a thing shall be dealt with as under the Magistrates' Courts Act 1980, pecuniary forfeitures fall within the definition of "fine" (see Magistrates' Courts Act 1980, s 150(1), ante; non-pecuniary forfeitures may be sold and the proceeds applied as if they were a fine (Magistrates' Courts Act 1980, s 140, ante).

8–13331   **53. Offences by bodies corporate.**   (1) Where an offence under this Act committed by a body corporate is proved to have been committed with the consent or connivance of, or to have been attributable to any neglect on the part of, any director, manager, secretary or other similar officer of the body corporate or any person who was purporting to act in any such capacity, he, as well as the body corporate, shall be guilty of that offence and be liable to be proceeded against and punished accordingly.

   (2) In the foregoing subsection, the expression "director", in relation to a body corporate established by or under any enactment for the purpose of carrying on under national ownership any industry or part of an industry or undertaking, being a body corporate whose affairs are managed by its members, means a member of that body corporate.

[Betting, Gaming and Lotteries Act 1963, s 53.]

8–13332   **54.** *Repealed by Lotteries and Amusements Act 1976.*

8–13333   **55. Interpretation, etc—general.**   (1) In this Act, except where the context otherwise requires, the following expressions have the following meaning respectively, that is to say—

"approved horse racecourse" means any ground in respect of which there is for the time being in force a certificate of approval of that ground as a horse racecourse issued by the Levy Board⋆ under section 13 of this Act;

"bet" does not include any bet made or stake hazard in the course of, or incidentally to, any gaming;

"betting agency permit" has the meaning assigned by section 9(2) of this Act;

"betting office licence" has the meaning assigned by section 9(1) of this Act;

"betting transaction" includes the collection or payment of winnings on a bet and any transaction in which one or more of the parties is acting as a bookmaker;

"bookmaker" means any person other than the Totalisator Board⋆ who—

(a) whether on his own account or as servant or agent to any other person, carries on, whether occasionally or regularly, the business of receiving or negotiating bets or conducting pool betting operations; or

(b) by way of business in any manner holds himself out, or permits himself to be held out, as a person who receives or negotiates bets or conducts such operations,

so, however, that a person shall not be deemed to be a bookmaker by reason only of the fact—

(i) that he carries on, or is employed in, sponsored pool betting business⋆; or

(ii) that he operates, or is employed in operating, a totalisator;

and the expression "bookmaking" shall be construed accordingly;

"Bookmakers' Committee" means the committee established in accordance with section 26 of this Act;⋆

"bookmaker's permit" has the meaning assigned by section 2(1) of this Act;

"contravention", in relation to any requirement, includes a failure to comply with that requirement, and cognate expressions shall be construed accordingly;

"dog race" means a race in which an object propelled by mechanical means is pursued by dogs, and "dog racecourse" shall be construed accordingly;

"game of chance" and "gaming" have the same meanings as in the Gaming Act 1968;⋆

"inter-track betting scheme" means a scheme for the pooling of bets made by means of totalisators on different licensed tracks, being bets on a dog race run on a track participating in the scheme or on a combination of dog races run on the same participating track;

"the Levy Board" means the Horserace Betting Levy Board established in accordance with section 24 of this Act;⋆

"levy period" has the meaning assigned by section 27(1) of this Act;⋆

"licensed betting office" means premises in respect of which a betting office licence is for the time being in force;

"licensed inter-track betting scheme" means an inter-track betting scheme in respect of which a licence under Schedule 5ZA to this Act is for the time being in force;

"licensed track" means a track in respect of which a track betting licence is for the time being in force;

"licensee" in relation to a licensed betting office, means the holder of the betting office licence for the time being in force in respect of that office;

"money" includes a cheque, banknote, postal order or money order;

"player", in relation to a game of chance, includes any person taking part in the game against whom other persons taking part in the game stake, play or bet;⋆

"pool betting" has the same meaning as for the purposes of the Betting and Gaming Duties Act 1981[1];

"pool betting business" means business involving the receiving or negotiating of bets made by way of pool betting;

"premises" includes any place and, in section 1 [32 and 33] of this Act, also includes any vessel;

"prescribed" means prescribed by regulations made by the Secretary of State by statutory instrument, which shall be subject to annulment in pursuance of a resolution of either House of Parliament, and any such regulations may make different provision for different circumstances;

"qualified accountant" means a person who is eligible for appointment as a company auditor under section 25 of the Companies Act 1989;

"recognised horse race" means a horse race run on an approved horse racecourse on a day when horse races and no other races take place on that racecourse;⋆

"registered pool promoter" has the meaning assigned by section 4(2)⋆ of this Act;

"sponsored pool betting" means pool betting by means of facilities provided by the Totalisator Board or provided on an approved horse racecourse with the authority of that Board by the persons having the management of that racecourse;⋆

"ticket", in relation to any lottery or proposed lottery, includes any document evidencing the claim of a person to participate in the chances of the lottery;

"totalisator" means the contrivance for betting known as the totalisator or pari mutuel, or any other machine or instrument of betting of a like nature, whether mechanically operated or not;

"the Totalisator Board" means the Horserace Totalisator Board established in accordance with section 12 of this Act;*

"track" means premises on which races of any description, athletic sports or other sporting events take place;

"track betting licence" has the meaning assigned by section 6 (1) of this Act;

"winnings" includes winnings of any kind and any reference to the amount or to the payment of winnings shall be construed accordingly.

(2) *Repealed by Lotteries and Amusements Act 1976.*

(3) *Repealed by Administration of Justice Act 1964.*

(4) *Applies to Scotland.*

(5) Save where the context otherwise requires, any reference in this Act to any enactment shall be construed as a reference to that enactment as amended by or under any other enactment.

[Betting, Gaming and Lotteries Act 1963, s 55, as amended by the Gaming Act 1968, Sch 11, the Betting and Gaming Duties Act 1981, Sch 5, the Companies Consolidation (Consequential Provisions) Act 1985, Sch 2 and SI 1991/1997.]

Definitions and words repealed and substituted, and new definitions inserted by the Horserace Betting and Olympic Lottery Act 2004, Sch 2 from a date to be appointed.

1. See the lengthy definition set out in the Betting and Gaming Duties Act 1981, s 10, in PART VIII, title CUSTOMS AND EXCISE, post; in short, a bet is by way of pool betting unless it is a bet at fixed odds.

8–13334   57. Repeals and savings.   (2) Where any provision contained in any local Act passed before the Betting and Gaming Act 1960 appears to the Secretary of State to have been superseded by, or to be inconsistent with, any enactment contained in this Act, being an enactment corresponding to any enactment in the said Act of 1960 which is repealed by this Act, the Secretary of State may by order[1] made by statutory instrument, a draft of which shall be laid before Parliament, specify that provision for the purposes of this subsection; and, without prejudice to the operation in the meantime of any rule of law relating to the effect on any such provision of any such enactment, any provision so specified is hereby repealed as from the date of the making of the order.

(3) Any regulation, licence, permit, register or other instrument or document whatsoever made, issued or kept, and any other thing done, under or by virtue of any of the enactments repealed by this Act shall be deemed for the purposes of this Act to have been made or issued, to be kept, or to have been done, as the case may be, under the corresponding provision of this Act; and anything begun under any of the said enactments may be continued under this Act as if begun under this Act.

(4) So much of any enactment or document as refers expressly or by implication to any enactment repealed by this Act shall, if and so far as the context permits, be construed as referring to this Act or the corresponding enactment therein.

(5) Nothing in this section shall be taken as affecting the general application of [section 16] of the Interpretation Act [1978] with regard to the effect of repeals.

[Betting, Gaming and Lotteries Act 1963, s 57, as amended by the Statute Law (Repeals) Act 1974.]

---

1. See Betting and Gaming (Repeal of Local Enactments) Order 1962, SI 1962/505.

SCHEDULES

SCHEDULE 1

BOOKMAKER'S PERMITS, BETTING AGENCY PERMITS AND BETTING OFFICE LICENCES

(*Amended by the Courts Act 1971, the Horserace Betting Levy Act 1981, Sch, the Criminal Justice Act 1982, ss 38 and 46, the Betting, Gaming and Lotteries (Amendment) Act 1984, s 3, SI 1991/2176, the National Lottery etc Act 1993, s 18, SI 1997/42 and 1997/947 and the Access to Justice Act, Sch 13.*)

Introductory

8–13335   1. The authority responsible for the grant or renewal of bookmakers' permits, betting agency permits and betting office licences shall be—

(*a*) in any petty sessions area in England, a committee constituted in the prescribed[1] manner of not less than five nor more than fifteen of the justices acting for that area, who may sit in two or more divisions, the quorum at any meeting of that committee or a division thereof being three;*

(*b*) *Applies to Scotland.*

2. In this Schedule, the following expressions have the following meanings respectively, that is to say—

"appropriate authority" means such a committee or board. . .[2] as is mentioned in paragraph 1 of this Schedule and, in relation to a bookmaker's permit or betting agency permit or in relation to an application for the grant, renewal or cancellation of a betting office licence, means, subject to paragraph 10 of this Schedule, the committee . . .[2] such as aforesaid for the petty sessions area . . .[2] in which the relevant premises are, or are to be, situated;*

"appropriate local authority" means—

    (a) in England, the local authority (being the council of a London borough or county district or the Common Council of the City of London) within whose area the relevant premises are, or are to be situated;

    (b) *Applies to Scotland;*

"appropriate officer of police" means the chief officer of police for the police area in which the relevant premises are, or are to be, situated;

"the proper officer of the appropriate authority" means—

    (a) in England, the chief executive to the justices comprising the committee referred to in paragraph 1 of this Schedule; and★

    (b) in Scotland, the clerk to the licensing court;

"relevant premises" means—

    (a) in relation to a bookmaker's permit or betting agency permit, the premises at which for the time being the applicant for or holder of the permit has his office or, if he has more than one office, his principal office or, if he is a company, his registered office or, if he has no office, his usual place of residence;

    (b) in relation to an application for the grant, renewal or cancellation of a betting office licence, the premises in respect of which the application is made.

---

1. This is the Betting Licensing Committee, to be appointed at the October meeting of the justices: see Betting (Licensing) Regulations 1960, SI 1960/1701, regs 1–3, this PART, post.
2. Words omitted relate to Scotland.

Applications for grant of permit or licence

8–13336 **3.** Each appropriate authority shall for each year fix a day in each of the months of—

    (a) January, April, July and October if the authority is in England; or

    (b) *Applies to Scotland,*

as a day on which, subject to paragraph 7 of this Schedule, they will hold a meeting for the purpose of considering any application for the grant of a bookmaker's permit, betting agency permit or betting office licence then awaiting consideration.

    4. In addition to any meeting on a day fixed in pursuance of the last foregoing paragraph, an appropriate authority may hold a meeting on any other day for the purpose of considering such applications as aforesaid.

    5. Any such application as aforesaid may be made at any time and shall be made to the proper officer of the appropriate authority in such form and manner, and shall contain such particulars, and, if the application is for a permit, give such references, as may be prescribed[1]; and, not later than seven days after the date when the application is made, the applicant shall send a copy of the application to the appropriate officer of police[2] and, in the case of an application for the grant of a betting office licence, to the appropriate local authority; and if the applicant knowingly makes any false statement in any such application or copy thereof he shall be liable on summary conviction to a fine not exceeding **level 3** on the standard scale.★

    6. Not later than fourteen days after the making of any such application as aforesaid to the appropriate authority, the applicant shall cause to be published by means of an advertisement in a newspaper[3] circulating in the authority's area a notice[4] of the making of the application which shall also state that any person who desires to object to the grant of the permit or licence should send to the proper officer of the authority, before such date not earlier than fourteen days after the publication of the advertisement as may be specified in the notice, two copies of a brief statement in writing of the grounds of his objection; and, in the case of an application for the grant of a betting office licence in respect of any premises, the applicant shall also cause a like notice to be posted up outside the entrance, or on the site of the proposed entrance, to the premises not later than fourteen days before the date specified as aforesaid and take such steps as he reasonably can to keep that notice so posted until that date.

    7. Not later than seven days after the publication of the newspaper containing the advertisement of any such application as aforesaid required by the last foregoing paragraph, the applicant shall send a copy of that newspaper to the proper officer of the appropriate authority, and the authority shall not consider the application earlier than fourteen days after the date specified in the advertisement; and, not earlier than the said date and not less than seven days before the date appointed for the consideration of the application, the proper officer of the authority shall send[5] notice in writing of the date, time and place of the meeting of the authority at which the application will be considered—

    (a) to the applicant;

    (b) to the appropriate officer of police[6]; and

    (c) if the proper officer has received from any person an objection in writing which has not been withdrawn and the address of that person is known to the proper officer, to that person,

and also cause notice of that meeting to be displayed at the place where the meeting is to be held in a position where the notice may conveniently be read by members of the public; and in sending such a notice to the applicant the proper officer shall include therewith a copy of any objection to the grant of the permit or licence which has been received by the proper officer from the appropriate officer of police, the appropriate local authority or any other person.

---

1. This is prescribed in the Betting (Licensing) Regulations 1960, SI 1960/1701, reg 4, this PART, post, and in Forms 1 (application for grant of bookmaker's permit), 2 (application for grant of betting agency permit) and 3 (application for grant of betting office licence) set out in the Schedule to the Regulations.
2. This includes a reference to the Collector of Customs and Excise for the area: see Finance Act 1966, Sch 3, para 6 in PART VIII: CUSTOMS AND EXCISE, post.
3. Not necessarily a local newspaper: in *R v Westminster Betting Licensing Committee, ex p Peabody Donation Fund (Governors)* [1963] 2 QB 750, [1963] 2 All ER 544, 127 JP 408, it was held that *The Sporting Life* qualified in the particular case.

4. There is no provision in this Act equivalent to that in para 6(4) of Sch 2 to the Gaming Act 1968 prohibiting the inclusion of material additional to that required by para 6 of this Schedule, so that the inclusion of such material in a notice under this Schedule will not invalidate the notice unless that addition should prevent the notice having its due force and effect (*R v Inner London (West Central Division) Betting Licensing Committee, ex p Pearcy* [1972] 1 All ER 932, 136 JP 273).

5. For manner of sending this notice, see para 35, post.

6. This includes a reference to the Collector of Customs and Excise for the area: Finance Act 1966, Sch 3, para 6 in PART VIII: CUSTOMS AND EXCISE, post.

Applications for renewal of permit or licence

8-13337 **8.** Each appropriate authority, in each year in which any application for the renewal of a bookmaker's permit, betting agency permit or betting office licence, other than an application to which paragraph 10(*b*) of this Schedule applies, falls to be made to the authority, shall in the month of February (if the authority is in England) . . .[1] give[2] in writing to the holder of that permit or licence, and cause to be published by means of an advertisement in a newspaper circulating in their area, notice of a day in April (if the authority is in England) . . .[1] on which they will hold a meeting for the purpose of considering such applications, and that notice shall include the time and place appointed for the meeting and shall state—

(*a*) in the case of the notice given to the holder of any permit or licence, that any such application must be received by the proper officer of the authority before a specified date, being a date not earlier than fourteen days after both the giving of the notice in writing and the publication of the advertisement aforesaid;

(*b*) in the case of the notice given by advertisement,

(i) that any person who desires to object to the renewal by the authority of any particular permit or licence should send to the proper officer of the authority before the same date two copies of a brief statement in writing of the grounds of his objection, and

(ii) where relevant, that there are circumstances in which an application for renewal may be dealt with under paragraph 20A of this Schedule by the proper officer of the authority instead of at the meeting.

9. Any application for the renewal of such a permit or licence as aforesaid, other than an application to which paragraph 10 (*b*) of this Schedule applies, shall be made to the proper officer of the appropriate authority before the date specified for the purpose in the notice given in pursuance of the last foregoing paragraph, and shall be in such form and contain such particulars as may be prescribed[3]; and, not earlier than that date nor later than seven days before the date in April . . .[4] appointed by the said notice for the consideration of such applications, the proper officer of the authority—

(*a*) If he has received from any person an objection in writing to the renewal of a particular permit or licence (being an objection which has not been withdrawn) and the address of that person is known to the proper officer, shall send[5] to that person in writing a notification as to whether or not an application for the renewal of that permit or licence has been made;

(*b*) shall send[5] to the person by whom any application for the renewal of a permit or licence has been duly made a copy of any objection to the renewal which he has received from the appropriate officer of police, the appropriate local authority or any other person and which has not been withdrawn.

10. Where in any year, by reason of a change in the office or usual place of residence of the holder of a bookmaker's permit or betting agency permit, an application for the renewal of that permit falls, or would but for this paragraph fall, to be made to an authority other than the authority by whom the permit was last either granted or renewed, then—

(*a*) unless the change takes place before 1st February . . .[6] in that year, any application for the renewal of the permit shall be made to and considered by the authority by whom the permit was last either granted or renewed;

(*b*) if the change takes place before the said 1st February . . .[6], paragraphs 5 to 7 of this Schedule shall apply to an application to the first-mentioned authority for the renewal of the permit as if it were an application for the grant thereof.

---

*Paragraphs 1 and 2 amended by the Courts Act 2003, Sch 8 from a date to be appointed.

1. Words omitted relate to Scotland.
2. For the manner of giving this notice, see para 35, post.
3. This is prescribed in the Betting (Licensing) Regulations 1960, SI 1960/1701, reg 5, this PART, post, and in Forms 5 (application for renewal of betting agency permit) and 6 (application for renewal of betting office licence) set out in the Schedule to the Regulations. The form of application for renewal of a bookmaker's permit is prescribed in the Betting (Licensing) Regulations 1963, SI 1963/859.
4. Words omitted relate to Scotland.
5. For manner of sending this notice, see para 35, post.
6. Words omitted relate to Scotland.

Proceedings before appropriate authority

8-13338 **11.** On any application for the grant or renewal of a bookmaker's permit, betting agency permit or betting office licence, the appropriate authority may grant or renew the permit or licence without hearing the applicant if no objection to the grant or renewal has been made by any person or if every such objection has been withdrawn before the beginning of the meeting of the authority at which the authority considers the application; but, save as aforesaid, at any such meeting any of the following persons, that is to say—

(*a*) the applicant;

(*b*) any person from whom an objection in writing which has not been withdrawn was received by the proper officer of the authority before the day on which he sent out the documents referred to in paragraph 7 or, as the case may be, paragraph 9 of this Schedule; and

(*c*) the person making any other objection which the authority have decided under paragraph 12 of this Schedule that they will hear, shall be entitled to be heard either in person or by counsel or a solicitor; and the authority shall also hear any representations made otherwise than by way of objection by, or by any person authorised in that behalf by, the appropriate officer of police[1].

12. Where in the case of an application for the grant or renewal of any such permit or licence as aforesaid an objection to the grant or renewal is received or made on or after the day referred to in paragraph 11(*b*) of this Schedule, the authority may refuse to entertain the objection and, unless the applicant requests otherwise, shall not hear it until the objector has given to the proper officer and to the applicant, and the applicant has had time to consider, a brief statement in writing of the grounds of his objection.

13. An appropriate authority may from time to time adjourn the consideration of any application for the grant or renewal of such a permit or licence as aforesaid, whether for the purposes of paragraph 12 of this Schedule or for any other purpose.

14. On the consideration of any application for the grant or renewal of any such permit or licence as aforesaid, the appropriate authority may take evidence on oath and may make such order as they think fit for the payment of costs . . .[2] by or to the applicant to or by any person who made an objection to the grant or renewal which was not withdrawn before the day referred to in paragraph 11(*b*) of this Schedule; and any costs ordered by an authority in England to be paid under this paragraph shall be recoverable summarily[3] as a civil debt.

1. This includes a reference to the Comrs of Customs and Excise: see Finance Act 1966, Sch 3, para 6 in PART VIII: CUSTOMS AND EXCISE, post.
2. Words omitted relate to Scotland.
3. See Magistrates' Courts Act 1980, s 58, ante, and notes thereto. Note that the costs are not prescribed to be "enforceable" as a civil debt, as are costs awarded under the Magistrates' Courts Act 1980, s 64 (see sub-s (3) thereof), ante: therefore the machinery to secure payment must begin with a complaint for an order.

Grounds for refusal to grant or renew bookmaker's or betting agency permit

8–13339 **15.** The appropriate authority shall refuse any application for the grant or renewal of a bookmaker's permit or betting agency permit if it appears that the applicant—

- (*a*) not being a body corporate, is under twenty-one years of age; or
- (*b*) is for the time being disqualified under section 11(4) of this Act; or
- (*c*) not being a body corporate, is not resident in Great Britain or was not so resident throughout the six months immediately preceding the date when the application was made; or
- (*d*) being a body corporate, is not incorporated in Great Britain; or
- (*e*) has within the immediately preceding twelve months been refused the grant or renewal—

  - (i) of a bookmaker's permit under paragraph 16(1) (*a*) or 18A of this Schedule; or
  - (ii) of a betting agency permit under paragraph 17 (*b*) or 18A of this Schedule[1]; or

- (*ee*) has within the immediately preceding twelve months been refused the renewal of a bookmaker's permit under section 4 of the Horserace Betting Levy Act 1969 and has not obtained the approval of the Levy Board to his application[2]; or
- (*f*) has been the holder of a bookmaker's permit which has been cancelled within the immediately preceding twelve months under paragraph 27 of this Schedule.

16. (1) In the case of an application for the grant or renewal of a bookmaker's permit, and subject to paragraph 18 of this Schedule, the appropriate authority may refuse the application if—

- (*a*) they are not satisfied that the applicant is, or satisfactory evidence is produced that the applicant is not, a fit and proper[3] person to be the holder of a bookmaker's permit; or
- (*b*) the authority are satisfied that, if the permit were to be granted or renewed, the business to which it relates would be managed by, or carried on for the benefit of, a person other than the applicant, being a person who would himself be refused the grant or renewal of such a permit either under paragraph 15 of this Schedule or under sub-paragraph (*a*) of this paragraph.

(2) In considering for the purposes of any application for the renewal of a bookmaker's permit whether any person is or is not a fit and proper person to be the holder of such a permit, the authority shall have regard to whether or not that person has discharged all his liabilities, if any, under assessments to the bookmakers' levy referred to in section 27[4] of this Act, and to the circumstances in which any failure to discharge any of those liabilities arose.

17. In the case of an application for the grant or renewal of a betting agency permit, the appropriate authority—

- (*a*) shall refuse the application unless the authority are satisfied that the applicant is for the time being accredited as mentioned in section 9(2)(*c*) of this Act;
- (*b*) subject to paragraph 18 of this Schedule, may refuse the application if they are not satisfied that the applicant is, or satisfactory evidence is produced that the applicant is not, a fit and proper person[3] to hold a betting office licence.

18. For the purposes of paragraph 16 or 17 of this Schedule, the appropriate authority shall disregard—

- (*a*) any conviction for an offence under the Betting Act 1853, or under section 393 or 407 of the Burgh Police (Scotland) Act 1892, section 51 of the Burgh Police (Scotland) Act 1903, or any corresponding provision of any local Act;
- (*b*) any conviction for an offence under the Street Betting Act 1906, unless the offence was committed after 1st December 1961[5]; and
- (*c*) any conviction for an offence under section 1(2) of the Betting and Gaming Act 1960, committed before the said 1st December[5],

and, without prejudice to their power under paragraph 13 of this Schedule to adjourn consideration of the application, shall also disregard—

- (i) any proceedings for such an offence as is mentioned in section 11(1) of this Act which have been commenced but not yet determined; and

(ii) any cancellation of a permit under the said section 11(1) or under paragraph 27 of this Schedule which has not yet taken effect.

---

1. Paragraph 15(*e*) is amended by the National Lottery etc Act 1993, s 18.
2. Added by s 4(4) of the Horserace Betting Levy Act 1969.
3. In considering whether an applicant is a fit and proper person regard shall be had to any failure by him to pay any amount due from him by way of the general betting duty or the pool betting duty: Finance Act 1966, Sch 3, para 6 in PART VIII: CUSTOMS AND EXCISE, post. Note that this expression must be construed in total disregard of previous convictions for betting offences as mentioned in para 18, infra. Regard must be had to s 13 of the Sex Discrimination Act 1975 (noted under s 3 of the Licensing Act 1964, post).
4. This is the contribution levied upon bookmakers by the Horserace Betting Levy Board for the benefit of horse racing. A statement that all liabilities have been discharged (or, if not, a note of the circumstances of the failure to discharge them) must be made in the application for renewal: see Betting (Licensing) Regulations 1963, SI 1963/859 and Home Office circular No 122/1963.
5. This is the date on which appropriate sections of the (repealed) Betting and Gaming Act 1960, were brought into operation: Betting and Gaming Act 1960 (Commencement No 2) Order 1961, SI 1961/2092.

8–13340 18A. (1) In the case of an application for the renewal of a bookmaker's permit or a betting agency permit, the appropriate authority shall refuse the application if they are satisfied that the applicant or an employee of his has, since the permit was granted, received or negotiated a bet on the outcome of any lottery forming part of the National Lottery for the purposes of Part I of the National Lottery etc Act 1993.

(2) For the purposes of sub-paragraph (1) above, the appropriate authority shall disregard any bet which ought properly to have been raised by way of objection on a previous occasion when the permit was renewed[1].

---

1. Paragraph 18A is inserted by the National Lottery Act 1993, s 18.

Grounds for refusal to grant or renew betting office licence

8–13341 19. In the case of an application for the grant or renewal of a betting office licence in respect of any premises, the appropriate authority—

(*a*) shall refuse the application if they are not satisfied—

(i) in the case of an applicant other than the Totalisator Board*, that on the date with effect from which the licence would come into force, or, as the case may be, would be continued in force, the applicant will be the holder either of a bookmaker's permit or of a betting agency permit; and

(ii) that the premises are or will be enclosed; and

(iii) that there are or will be means of access between the premises and a street otherwise than through other premises used for the effecting with persons resorting to those other premises of transactions other than betting transactions;

(*b*) may refuse the application on the ground—

(i) that, having regard to the lay-out, character, condition or location of the premises, they are not suitable for use as a licensed betting office[1]; or

(ii) that the grant or renewal would be inexpedient having regard to the demand[2] for the time being in the locality for the facilities afforded by licensed betting offices and to the number of such offices for the time being available to meet that demand; or**

(iii) that the premises have not been properly conducted under the licence.

---

*Words repealed by the Horserace Betting and Olympic Lottery Act 2004, Sch 2 from a date to be appointed.
**See amendments to this sub-paragraph made by the Horserace Totalisator and Betting Levy Boards Act 1972, when s 3 of that Act is brought into force.
1. A local authority has power under s 20 of the Local Government (Miscellaneous Provisions) Act 1976, post, to require the provision of sanitary appliances in a betting office.
2. On appeal the Crown Court will direct its own judgment of what constitutes sufficient evidence of demand (*R v Essex Quarter Sessions, ex p Thomas* [1966] 1 All ER 353, 130 JP 121).

Grant or renewal of permit or licence

8–13342 20. (1) Save as provided by paragraphs 15 to 19 of this Schedule, the appropriate authority shall not refuse any application[1] for the grant or renewal of a bookmaker's permit, betting agency permit or betting office licence made, so far as lies within the control of the applicant, in accordance with the provisions of this Act, but shall grant or renew the permit or licence on payment by the applicant to the proper officer of the authority of a fee[2] of—

(*a*) in the case of the grant of a bookmaker's permit, £160;
(*b*) in the case of the grant of a betting agency permit, £160;
(*c*) in the case of the grant of a betting office licence, £125;
(*d*) in the case of the renewal of a bookmaker's permit or betting agency permit, £20;
(*e*) in the case of the renewal of a betting office licence, £25;

and if the authority refuse any such application they shall state the grounds of their refusal.

(1A) The Secretary of State may by order made by statutory instrument amend sub-paragraph (1) above so as to vary any fee for the time being specified in that sub-paragraph; and a statutory instrument containing an order under this sub-paragraph shall be subject to annulment in pursuance of a resolution of either House of Parliament.

(2) *Applies to Scotland.*

1. There is no requirement for an applicant for a betting office licence to show that he has a legal interest in the property which is the subject of his application; where rival applications for a licence for the same premises are made it may be desirable for the justices to hear the evidence on both before coming to a decision in either (*R v Forest Betting Licensing Committee, ex p Noquet* (1988) Times, 21 June, (1988) Independent, 22 June).

2. The fees shown in paragraph 20(1)(*b*)–(*e*) are as substituted by the Betting, Gaming and Lotteries Act 1963 (Variation of Fees) Order 1997, SI 1997/42.

Unopposed applications for renewal

8–13343   **20A.** (1) Where—

(*a*)   an application for the renewal of a bookmaker's permit, betting agency permit or betting office licence (other than an application to which paragraph 10(*b*) of this Schedule applies) has been made in accordance with paragraph 9 of this Schedule, and

(*b*)   immediately before the meeting of the appropriate authority at which the application would, apart from this paragraph, fall to be considered—

     (i)   the proper officer of the authority has not received any objection to the renewal of the permit or licence, or

     (ii)   every such objection received by him has been withdrawn,

the clerk to the authority may act for the authority in relation to the determination of the application.

(2) Sub-paragraph (1) of this paragraph shall not have effect to enable the clerk to the appropriate authority to act for the authority in—

(*a*)   refusing the application, or

(*b*)   granting the application in circumstances where there is a discretion to refuse it.

(3) The clerk to the appropriate authority may not act under sub-paragraph (1) of this paragraph in any case where to do so would be contrary to the authority's directions.

(4) The functions of the clerk to the appropriate authority under sub-paragraph (1) of this paragraph shall also be exercisable by such other officer of the appropriate authority as the clerk may designate for the purposes of this paragraph.

(5) For the purposes of this paragraph, the clerk to the appropriate authority, where the authority is a committee of the justices acting for a petty sessions area, is the clerk to those justices or, if there are two or more clerks to those justices—

(*a*)   such one of those clerks as the magistrates' courts committee having power over the appointment of clerks to justices for that area may direct; or

(*b*)   in default of any such direction, any of those clerks.*

---

*Words repealed by the Courts Act 2003, Sch 8 from a date to be appointed.

Appeals against refusals in England

8–13344   **21.** (1) Where an appropriate authority in England refuse an application for the grant or renewal of a bookmaker's permit, betting agency permit or betting office licence, they shall forthwith notify[1] the applicant of the refusal, and within 21 days of being so notified the applicant may by notice to the proper officer of the authority appeal against the refusal to the Crown Court.

(2) As soon as practicable after receiving notice of appeal against the refusal, the proper officer of the authority shall send[1] the notice to the appropriate officer of the Crown Court together with a statement of the decision from which the appeal is brought and of the name and last known residence or place of business of the appellant and of any person who opposed the application before the authority.

(3) On receipt of the notice of appeal, the appropriate officer of the Crown Court shall enter the appeal and give[1] in writing not less than seven days' notice to the appellant, to the appropriate officer of police[2] and to any person who opposed the application before the authority and, if the appeal relates to a betting office licence, to the authority, of the date, time and place appointed for the hearing of the appeal.

(4) The Crown Court may by its order either—

(*a*)   confirm the refusal; or

(*b*)   on payment[3] by the appellant to the appropriate officer of the Crown Court for transmission to the proper officer of the appropriate authority of the appropriate fee under paragraph 20 of this Schedule, grant or renew the permit or licence in the same way as the appropriate authority could have done;

and the judgment of the Crown Court on the appeal shall be final.

(5) A justice shall not act in the hearing or determination of an appeal under this paragraph from any decision in which he took part.

(6) For the purposes of paragraphs 10, 33 and 34 of this Schedule, the grant or renewal of a permit or licence by the Crown Court under this paragraph shall be treated as if it were a grant or renewal by the appropriate authority who refused it.

23. (1) Where, in the case of an appeal under paragraph 21 of this Schedule with respect to a betting office licence, the Crown court

(*a*)   has allowed the appeal; or

(*b*)   has awarded the appropriate authority any costs under paragraph 22 of this Schedule and is satisfied that the appropriate authority cannot recover those costs,

the court shall order payment out of central funds of such sums as appear to the court sufficient to indemnify the appropriate authority from all costs and charges whatever to which they have been put in consequence of the appellant's having served notice of appeal.

24. *Relates to appeals against refusals in Scotland.*

1. For manner of sending this notice, see para 35, post.
2. This includes a reference to the Collector of Customs and Excise for the area: see Finance Act 1966, Sch 3, para 6 in Part VIII: Customs And Excise, post.
3. The order of the Crown Court should expressly state that the licence be granted on payment of "the appropriate fee"; see *R v Crown Court at Dudley, ex p Ladbroke Racing (West Midlands) Ltd* (1988) 152 JP 342.

Notification of change in directors during currency of bookmaker's permit

8–13345 25. If, where the holder of a bookmaker's permit is a body corporate, any change occurs in the persons who are directors thereof or in accordance with whose directions or instructions the directors thereof are accustomed to act, the holder of the permit shall as soon as reasonably practicable after the occurrence of the change give particulars thereof in writing to the proper officer of the appropriate authority and to the appropriate officer of police[1]; and if the holder of the permit fails to comply with this paragraph he shall be liable on summary conviction to a fine not exceeding **level 1** on the standard scale.

1. This includes a reference to the Collector of Customs and Excise for the area: see Finance Act 1966, Sch 3, para 6 in Part VIII: Customs And Excise, post.

Notification of change of relevant premises during currency of permit

8–13346 25A. If during the currency of a bookmaker's permit there is any change in the address of the relevant premises, the holder of the permit shall as soon as reasonably practicable after the change occurs give notice in writing of the change of address to the Levy Board; and if the holder of the permit fails to comply with this paragraph he shall be liable on summary conviction to a fine not exceeding **level 1** on the standard scale.★

★Paragraph repealed by the Horserace Betting and Olympic Lottery Act 2004, Sch 4 from a date to be appointed.

Cancellation of bookmaker's permit by appropriate authority

8–13347 26. If in the case of any bookmaker's permit an application is made at any time to the proper officer of the appropriate authority by any person in the prescribed[1] form and manner requesting that the permit be forfeited and cancelled and accompanied by two copies of a statement of the grounds on which the application is made, the proper officer of the authority shall submit the application to any one member of the authority who, after considering the statement accompanying the application—

(a) if he is of opinion—

   (i) that further consideration of the matters referred to in that statement is unnecessary or inexpedient before the renewal of the permit falls to be considered; or

   (ii) that the authority would be required by virtue of paragraph 27(3) of this Schedule to refuse the application,

shall cause notice in writing to be given[2] to the applicant that the application is refused without prejudice to the raising of the same matters by way of objection in accordance with the provisions of this Schedule to a renewal of the permit;

(b) unless he is of such opinion as aforesaid shall refer the application to the appropriate authority.

27. (1) Where an application for the cancellation of a permit is referred to the appropriate authority under the last foregoing paragraph, the proper officer of the authority shall, unless the application has been withdrawn, give[2] to the applicant, to the holder of the permit and to the appropriate officer of police[3] not less than twenty-one days' notice in writing of the date, time and place appointed for the consideration of the application by the authority, and shall send[2] to the holder of the permit together with that notice a copy of the applicants' statement of the grounds on which the application is made.

(2) Subject to the next following sub-paragraph, at any meeting of the appropriate authority to consider the application, the applicant and the holder of the permit shall be entitled to be heard either in person or by counsel or a solicitor; and where the applicant is a person other than the appropriate officer of police[4] the authority shall also hear any representations made by, or by any person authorised in that behalf by, that officer; and paragraphs 13 and 14 of this Schedule shall apply in relation to the application as they apply in relation to an application for the renewal of a permit, subject to the following modifications of the said paragraph 14, that is to say—

(a) as if the reference therein to the applicant for renewal were a reference to the holder of the permit; and

(b) as if the reference therein to any person who made an objection as mentioned in that paragraph were a reference to the person by whom the application under paragraph 26 of this Schedule was made.

(3) The appropriate authority shall refuse the application if they are satisfied that it is made on grounds which—

(a) have been or ought properly to have been raised previously by way of objection either when the permit was granted or on an occasion when it has been renewed; or

(b) are or have been the subject matter of proceedings for such an offence as is mentioned in section 11(1) of this Act.

(4) The appropriate authority shall not cancel the permit unless—

(a) satisfactory evidence is produced that the holder is no longer a fit and proper person[5] to hold such a permit; or

(b) the authority are satisfied that the business to which it relates is being managed by, or carried on for the benefit of, a person other than the holder, being a person who would himself be refused the grant of such a permit either under paragraph 15 or under paragraph 16(1) of this Schedule; or

(c)   the authority are satisfied that the holder of the permit or an employee of his has, since the permit was granted, received or negotiated a bet on the outcome of any lottery forming part of the National Lottery for the purposes of Part I of the National Lottery etc Act 1993[6].

Provided that for the purposes of this sub-paragraph the authority shall disregard any conviction such as is mentioned in paragraph 18 of this Schedule.

(5) If the appropriate authority decide not to cancel the permit, they shall cause notice in writing to be given[7] to the applicant that the application is refused without prejudice to the raising of the same matter by way of objection in accordance with provisions of this Schedule to a renewal of the permit.

(6) If the appropriate authority decide to forfeit and cancel the permit, the forfeiture and cancellation shall not take effect—

(a)   until the expiration of the time within which notice of an appeal under the next following paragraph may be given; or

(b)   if such notice is duly given, until the determination or abandonment of the appeal.

28. (1) Where the appropriate authority decide to forfeit and cancel a bookmaker's permit on an application under paragraph 26 of this Schedule, the holder of the permit may appeal against that decision to a court of a quarter sessions . . .[8] having jurisdiction in the authority's area, whose decision on the appeal shall be final.

(2) Paragraphs 21 (except sub-paragraphs (4) and (6) thereof), and paragraph 24 (1) of this Schedule shall apply for the purposes of an appeal under this paragraph against the forfeiture and cancellation of a bookmaker's permit as they apply for the purposes of an appeal against the refusal of an application for the renewal of such a permit subject to the following modifications, that is to say—

(a)   as if any reference therein to the applicant for renewal were a reference to the holder of the permit; and

(b)   as if any reference therein to a person who opposed the application before the appropriate authority were a reference to the person by whom the application under paragraph 26 of this Schedule was made.

---

1. See Betting (Licensing) Regulations 1960, SI 1960/1701, reg 7, this PART, post, and Form 9 (application for cancellation of bookmaker's permit) set out in the Schedule to the Regulations.
2. For manner of giving or sending this notice, see para 3.
3. This includes a reference to the Collector of Customs and Excise for the area: see Finance Act 1966, Sch 3, para 6 in PART VIII: CUSTOMS AND EXCISE, post.
4. This includes a reference to the Comrs of Customs and Excise: see Finance Act 1966, Sch 3, para 6 in PART VIII: CUSTOMS AND EXCISE, post.
5. In considering whether an applicant is a fit and proper person regard shall be had to any failure by him to pay any amount due from him by way of the general betting duty or the pool betting duty: Finance Act 1966, Sch 3, para 6 in PART VIII: CUSTOMS AND EXCISE, post.
6. Paragraph 27(4)(c) is inserted by the National Lottery Act etc Act 1993, s 18.
7. For manner of giving this notice, see para 35, post.

Cancellation of betting office licence by appropriate authority

8–13348   **28A.** (1) This paragraph applies where—

(a)   a person makes an application to the proper officer of the appropriate authority requesting that a betting office licence be forfeited and cancelled, and

(b)   the application is—

(i)   made in the prescribed form and manner, and

(ii)   accompanied by two copies of a statement of the grounds on which the application is made.

(2) The proper officer of the authority shall submit the application to any one member of the authority who shall consider whether it is necessary or expedient for the matters referred to in the statement to be given further consideration before the renewal of the licence falls to be considered.

(3) If the conclusion under sub-paragraph (2) of this paragraph is that further consideration of those matters before then is not necessary or expedient, the member shall cause the applicant to be given notice in writing that the application is refused without prejudice to the raising of the same matters by way of objection in accordance with the provisions of this Schedule to a renewal of the licence.

(4) If the conclusion under sub-paragraph (2) of this paragraph is that further consideration of those matters before then is necessary or expedient, the member shall refer the application to the appropriate authority.

8–13349   **28B.** (1) This paragraph applies where under paragraph 28A of this Schedule an application for the cancellation of a betting office licence is referred to the appropriate authority.

(2) Unless the application is withdrawn, the proper officer of the authority shall give not less than twenty-one days' notice in writing of the date, time and place appointed for the consideration of the application by the authority to—

(a)   the applicant,

(b)   the holder of the licence,

(c)   the appropriate officer of police, and

(d)   the Collector of Customs and Excise for the area in which the relevant premises are situated.

(3) The proper officer of the authority shall send with the notice under sub-paragraph (2)(b) of this paragraph a copy of the applicant's statement of the grounds on which the application is made.

(4) At any meeting of the authority to consider the application—

(a)   the applicant and the holder of the licence shall be entitled to be heard either in person or by counsel or a solicitor,

(b)   where the applicant is not the appropriate officer of police, the authority shall also hear any representation made by him, or a person authorised by him, and

(c)   where the applicant is not the Commissioners of Customs and Excise, the authority shall also hear any representation made by them, or a person authorised by them.

(5) The authority shall forfeit and cancel the licence if they are not satisfied—

(*a*) that the relevant premises are enclosed, and

(*b*) that there are means of access between the relevant premises and a street otherwise than through other premises used for the effecting with persons resorting to those other premises of transactions other than betting transactions,

but, apart from that, may only do so on the ground that the relevant premises fall within sub-paragraph (6) of this paragraph.

(6) The relevant premises fall within this sub-paragraph if—

(*a*) having regard to their layout, character or condition, they are not suitable for use as a licensed betting office,

(*b*) they have not been properly conducted under the licence, or

(*c*) they have not been used as a licensed betting office in the period of twelve months ending with the date on which the application is made and the licence has been in force for at least twelve months.

(7) The authority may from time to time adjourn consideration of the application.

(8) On consideration of the application, the authority make take evidence on oath and may make such order as they think fit for the payment of costs, or, in Scotland, expenses—

(*a*) by the applicant to the holder of the licence, or

(*b*) by the holder of the licence to the applicant.

(9) If the authority decide not to cancel the licence, they shall cause notice in writing to be given to the applicant that the application is refused without prejudice to the raising of the same matters by way of objection in accordance with the provisions of this Schedule to a renewal of the licence.

(10) If the authority decide to forfeit and cancel the licence, the forfeiture and cancellation shall not take effect—

(*a*) until the end of the time within which notice of an appeal under paragraph 28C or, as the case may be, 28D of this Schedule may be given, or

(*b*) if such notice is duly given, until the determination or abandonment of the appeal.

(11) Where an order for the payment of costs is made under sub-paragraph (8) of this paragraph by an authority in England and Wales, the costs shall be recoverable summarily as a civil debt.

8–13350 28C. (1) Where on an application under paragraph 28A of this Schedule an appropriate authority in England and Wales decide to forfeit and cancel a betting office licence, they shall forthwith notify the holder of the licence of the decision, and within twenty-one days of being so notified, he may by notice to the proper officer of the authority appeal against the refusal to the Crown Court.

(2) As soon as practicable after receiving notice of appeal under sub-paragraph (1) of this paragraph, the proper officer of the authority shall send the notice to the appropriate officer of the Crown Court together with a statement of—

(*a*) the decision from which the appeal is brought,

(*b*) the name and last known residence or place of business of the appellant, and

(*c*) the name and last known residence or place of business of the person whose application under paragraph 28A of this Schedule led to the decision appealed against.

(3) On receipt of notice of appeal under sub-paragraph (2) of this paragraph, the appropriate officer of the Crown Court shall enter the appeal and give not less than seven days notice in writing of the date, time and place appointed for the hearing of the appeal to—

(*a*) the appellant,

(*b*) the person mentioned in sub-paragraph (2)(*c*) of this paragraph,

(*c*) the authority whose decision is appealed against, and

(*d*) the appropriate officer of police.

(4) The decision of the Crown Court on an appeal under this paragraph shall be final.

28D. *Scotland.*

Duration of permit or licence

8–13351 29. (1) A bookmaker's permit, betting agency permit or betting office licence shall be in the prescribed form[1] and shall show the date with effect from which it is to be, or, as the case may be, to be continued, in force and, subject to paragraphs 30 to 33 of this Schedule, shall, unless renewed or, as the case may be, further renewed, cease to be in force at the end of the licensing period in which that date falls or, if that date falls in the last five months of that period, at the end of the next licensing period and shall not be transferable.

(2) In this paragraph "licensing period" means the period of three years beginning with 1st June 1997 and each successive period of three years.

30. Where application for the renewal of such a permit or licence as aforesaid has been made, so far as lies within the control of the applicant, in accordance with the provisions of this Act, the permit or licence shall not cease to be in force by virtue of paragraph 29 of this Schedule before the appropriate authority make their determination on the application.

31. Where the appropriate authority refuse to renew any such permit or licence as aforesaid, the permit or licence shall not cease to be in force by virtue of paragraph 29 of this Schedule before the expiration of the time within which notice of an appeal under paragraph 21 . . .[2] of this Schedule may be given nor, if such notice is duly given, before the determination or abandonment of the appeal.

32. A betting office licence held by the holder of a bookmaker's permit or betting agency permit shall cease to be in force upon that permit ceasing to be in force, whether by virtue of paragraph 29 of this Schedule or by virtue of its cancellation under section 11(1) of this Act or under paragraph 27 of this Schedule.

33. In the event of the death of the holder of such a permit or licence as aforesaid, then during the period of six months commencing with the death the permit or licence shall not cease to be in force by virtue of paragraph 29 of this Schedule and, except for the purposes of a renewal of that permit or licence, his legal personal representatives shall be deemed to be the holder thereof; and the authority by whom the permit or licence was last either granted or renewed may from time to time, on the application of those representatives, extend or further extend the said period of six months if the authority are satisfied that the extension is necessary for the purpose of winding up the deceased's estate and that no other circumstances make it undesirable.

---

1. See Betting (Licensing) Regulations 1960, SI 1960/1701, reg 6, this PART, post, and Forms 7 (grant of bookmaker's permit, betting agency permit, betting office licence), 8 (renewal of bookmaker's permit, betting agency permit, betting office licence) set out in the Schedule to the Regulations. By the Betting Levy (Particulars of Bookmakers' Permits) Regulations 1961, SI 1961/1547, this PART, post, the clerk to the betting licensing committee is required to give particulars of the grant and renewal of bookmakers' permits to the Horserace Betting Levy Board, but not until after the permit is actually issued: see Home Office Circular No 122/1963 and note to reg 6 this PART, post.
2. Words omitted relate to Scotland.

Registers of permits and licences

8–13352 34. The proper officer of to each appropriate authority shall keep registers in the prescribed[1] form and containing the prescribed[2] particulars of all bookmaker's permits, betting agency permits and betting office licences granted or renewed by that authority, and any such register shall be open during reasonable hours for inspection by any constable[3] or, on payment of the prescribed[4] fee, by any other person.

---

1. See Betting (Licensing) Regulations 1960, SI 1960/1701, reg 8, this PART, post, and Forms 10 (register of bookmakers' permits), 11 (register of betting agency permits) and 12 (register of betting office licences) set out in the Schedule to the Regulations.
2. These particulars are prescribed in the Betting (Licensing) Regulations 1960, SI 1960/1701, reg 8, this PART, post.
3. The reference to a constable includes a reference to any officer commissioned by the Comrs of Customs and Excise: see Finance Act 1966, Sch 3, para 6 in PART VIII: CUSTOMS AND EXCISE, post.
4. The prescribed fee is 5p (Betting (Licensing) Regulations 1960, SI 1960/1701, reg 9, this PART, post).

Service of documents

8–13353 35. Any provision of this Schedule requiring any notice or other document to be given or sent to any person shall be deemed to be satisfied if the document is either served personally on that person or sent to him by post at his usual or last-known residence or place of business in the United Kingdom or in the case of a company, at the company's registered office.

Provision of information

8–13354 36. The proper officer of each appropriate authority shall send to the Levy Board such particulars of any bookmaker's permit granted or renewed by, or by the court who determined any appeal from, that authority as the Secretary of State may by regulations made by statutory instrument direct.*

---

*Paragraph repealed by the Horserace Betting and Olympic Lottery Act 2004, Sch 2 from a date to be appointed.
37. (1). The proper officer of any appropriate authority shall furnish the Secretary of State with such statistical information at such times as the Secretary of State may from time to time require with respect to the performance by the authority of their functions under this Schedule; and the Secretary of State shall in respect of each relevant period lay before each House of Parliament, a report containing, in such form as may appear to him convenient, statistical information with respect to the grant, renewal, cancellation and expiry without renewal of bookmakers' permits, betting agency permits and betting office licences respectively in England . . .[1] during that period.
(2) In this paragraph "relevant period" means the period of three years beginning with 1st June 1997 and each successive period of three years.*

---

*New Schedule 1A inserted by the Horserace Betting and Olympic Lottery Act 2004, Sch 1 from a date to be appointed.
1. Words omitted apply to Scotland.

SCHEDULE 2
REGISTERED POOL PROMOTERS[1]

(Amended by the Courts Act 1971, the Local Government Act 1972, the Companies Act 1976, the Companies Consolidation (Consequential Provisions) Act 1985, Sch 2, the Companies Act 1989, Sch 10, SI 1991/2175 and the National Lottery etc Act 1993, ss 58 and 59.)

Registering authorities

8–13355 1[2]. (1) Subject to the provisions of this paragraph, each of the following councils shall be the registering authority for their area for the purposes of this Schedule, that is to say—

(a) In England, the council of any district or London borough and the Common Council of the City of London[3];
(b) . . .[4].

(2) *Applies to Scotland.*

---

1. For restrictions on carrying on a pool betting business otherwise than by a registered pool promoter, see s 4, ante.
2. These paragraphs shall have effect also in relation to the licensing of tracks for betting under s 6, ante: see Sch 3, para 1, post.

3. As amended by Local Government Act 1972, Sch 29.
4. Words omitted apply to Scotland.

Interpretation

8–13356   **4.** (1) In relation to any person who carries on or proposes to carry on a pool betting business, any reference in this Schedule to the registering authority shall be construed as a reference to the council or committee who, under paragraph 1 of this Schedule, are the registering authority for the area in which the place, or the principal place, at which that person carries on or proposes to carry on that business is situated.

(2) In this Schedule, the expression "the accountant" in relation to a registered pool promoter means the person appointed in the case of that promoter under paragraph 12 of this Schedule.

(3) References in this Schedule to stakes in, or in respect of entries in, any competition do not include references to stakes in respect of rejected entries.

(4) Any reference in this Schedule to the day on which the events on which a competition depends take place shall, where the events do not take place wholly on the same day, be construed as a reference to the last day on which any of those events takes place.

Registration of pool promoters

8–13357   **5.** (1) If any person makes an application to the registering authority for registration under this Schedule, the registering authority shall, on payment of the appropriate registration fee fixed under paragraph 11 of this Schedule, register him accordingly in a register to be kept by them for the purposes of this Schedule and shall notify him in writing that they have done so.

(2) Notwithstanding anything in the foregoing sub-paragraph, the registering authority may in the case of any person, after giving him an opportunity of being heard, refuse to register him or revoke his registration if that person or, where that person is a body corporate, any director or manager thereof, has been convicted of any offence under section 4(2) of this Act, under paragraph 29 of this Schedule or under the Pool Betting Act 1954, or of any offence involving fraud or dishonesty.

(3) If, after a person has been registered under this Schedule, the registering authority, after giving him an opportunity of being heard, are satisfied—

(a) that he does not intend to carry on a pool betting business; or
(b) that he has permanently ceased to carry on pool betting business; or
(c) that the place or principal place at which he carries on his pool betting business will not be, or has ceased to be, in their area,

they shall revoke his registration.

6. Where the registration of any person has been refused or revoked under the last foregoing paragraph by a registering authority in England, that authority shall forthwith notify that person of the refusal or revocation, and within twenty-one days of being so notified he may by notice to the appropriate officer of the Crown Court and to the registering authority appeal against the refusal of revocation to the Crown Court.

7. *Applies to Scotland.*

8. Where the registering authority revoke a registration under paragraph 5 of this Schedule, then, until the time within which notice of appeal under paragraph 6 or 7 thereof may be given has expired and, if such notice is duly given, until the determination or abandonment of the appeal, the registration shall be deemed to continue in force, and if the court of quarter sessions or, . . .[1] confirms the decision of the registering authority, the court . . .[1] may, if it thinks fit, order that the registration shall continue in force for a further period not exceeding two months from the date of that order.

9. If a registered pool promoter dies, his registration shall, for the period of three months beginning with the date of the death, endure for the benefit of his legal personal representatives.

---

1. Words omitted apply to Scotland.

Fees in respect of registration

8–13358   **10.** On 1st January in each year the appropriate continuation fee shall become payable to the registering authority by every person who is for the time being a registered pool promoter, and any such fee which remains unpaid after the date on which it becomes payable may be recovered by the registering authority as a debt.

11. For the purposes of paragraphs 5 and 10 of this Schedule the appropriate registration fee and the appropriate continuation fee shall be fees of such amounts respectively (not in either case exceeding £464) as may be fixed annually by the registering authority for the whole of their area; and different amounts may be so fixed by that authority in respect of businesses of different classes.

Appointment of accountant by registering authority

8–13359   **12.** (1) The registering authority shall, in the case of each registered pool promoter, appoint a person, being a qualified accountant and not being a person employed by the registered pool promoter in connection with his pool betting business, to exercise and perform, in relation to that registered pool promoter, the powers and duties conferred and imposed by the subsequent provisions of this Schedule on the accountant.

(2) The accountant shall hold office on such terms (including terms as to remuneration) as may be determined by the registering authority after consultation with the registered pool promoter.

(3) The remuneration of the accountant shall be payable by the registering authority, but any sum paid by them by way of such remuneration shall be recoverable by the registering authority as a debt due to them from the registered pool promoter.

(4) In this paragraph "remuneration" includes any sums paid or to be paid to the accountant in respect of his expenses.

Conduct of registered pool promoter's business

8–13360   **13.** Subject to paragraphs 14 to 19 of this Schedule, the pool betting business carried on by any registered pool promoter shall comply with the following requirements—

(a)   it shall take the form of the promotion of competitions for prizes for making forecasts as to sporting or other events[1], the bets being entries in the competitions and the winnings in respect of the bets being the prizes or shares in the prizes;

(b)   each bet shall be an entry in a particular competition;

(c)   the stakes and the winnings shall be wholly in money;

(d)   in each competition, the prizes shall be equally available for all the bets, and accordingly the question which bets qualify for, or for shares in, the prize of prizes and, save so far as it depends on the amounts staked, the amounts of the respective shares in prizes, shall be determined solely by the relative success of the forecasts embodied in the respective bets;

(e)   the total amount payable by way of winnings shall, in the case of each competition, be calculated in accordance with paragraph 13A of this schedule,

(f)   the rules applying to the competition shall be notified to the Comrs of Customs and Excise and[2] to the accountant before the first of the relevant sporting or other events takes place.

13A. (1) In any competition the total amount payable by way of winnings shall be the aggregate of—

(a)   the total amount of the stakes in respect of entries in the competition, less the relevant percentage of that total amount; and

(b)   any amount that has been duly carried over to the competition from a previous competition in accordance with any provision made under paragraph 14A of this Schedule;

less any amount that falls to be carried over from the competition in accordance with any such provision.

(2) In sub-paragraph (1) of this paragraph "relevant percentage" means such percentage as may be determined by the promoter, being—

(a)   the same percentage in respect of all his competitions which depend on the same events or on events taking place on the same day; and

(b)   a percentage which is determined and notified to the accountant before that day.

14. (1) Notwithstanding anything in paragraph 13 (d) or (e) or 13A of this Schedule, the rules applicable to any competition may provide—

(a)   that the winnings shall not, in the case of any bet, exceed a stated amount and that any resulting decrease in the total amount payable in the case of the winning bets qualifying for, or for shares in, a prize in the competition shall be applied in increasing the amount payable in the case of the winning bets qualifying for, or for shares in, another prize or other prizes in that competition;

(b)   that, in specified circumstances, one or more of the prizes shall not be paid and that the amount which would have been payable in the case of the winning bets qualifying for, or for shares in, that prize or those prizes shall be applied in increasing the amount payable in the case of the winning bets qualifying for, or for shares in, another prize or other prizes in that competition;

(c)   for the winnings of winning bets (being bets staking the minimum permissible under the rules of the competition) being increased or decreased (with a view to facilitating payment) by not more than 20 pence, and consequentially for the winnings of other winning bets (being bets staking more than the said minimum) being increased or decreased by not more than a proportionately greater sum than 20 pence,

and the total amount payable by way of winnings in the case of the competition may exceed or fall short of the amount specified in the said paragraph 13A to such extent as is reasonably necessary having regard to any such provision of the rules applicable thereto as is mentioned in paragraph (c) of this sub-paragraph.

(2) The Secretary of State may by order made by statutory instrument vary the sum for the time being specified in sub-paragraph (1)(c) of this paragraph; and an instrument containing such an order shall be subject to annulment in pursuance of a resolution of either House of Parliament.

14A. (1) Subject to any directions under paragraph 14B of this Schedule, the rules applicable to any competition may provide that if none of the bets in the competition qualifies for, or for a share in, the first prize—

(a)   the amount of that prize shall be carried over to the next relevant competition, or

(b)   part of that amount shall be carried over to the next relevant competition and the balance shall be applied as mentioned in paragraph 14(1)(b) of this Schedule.

(2) In sub-paragraph (1) of this paragraph—

(a)   "the first prize" means the highest prize that can be won, having regard to the outcome of the events on which the competition depends (and not any higher prize that could have been won had the outcome of those events been different),

(b)   "the next relevant competition" means the next competition to be held by the same registered pool promoter under the same rules within the fourteen days following the day on which the result of the competition is determined, and

(c)   the reference in paragraph (b) to part of the amount referred to in paragraph (a) is to such proportion of that amount as may be specified in the rules or as may be determined by the promoter in accordance with the rules.

14B. (1) The Secretary of State may direct that any provision made under paragraph 14A of this Schedule—

(a)   is not to have effect, or

(b)   is to have effect subject to such limitations as are specified in the direction.

(2) The limitations that may be specified under sub-paragraph (1)(b) of this paragraph include—

(a)   limitations as to the number of competitions from which amounts may be carried over, and

(b)   limitations as to the period within which any such competitions may be held.

(3) Any directions under this paragraph shall be given in writing and may be varied or revoked by subsequent directions.

15. Notwithstanding anything in paragraph 13 (*d*) or (*e*) or 13A of this Schedule, if it is found that a bet which ought to have been treated as a winning bet has been inadvertently overlooked, the promoter may pay to the person making that bet the sum paid by him to other persons making comparable bets, or, if there are no comparable bets, such sum as may be proper, and any sum paid under this paragraph shall be left out of account for the purposes of the said paragraph 13A.

16. Nothing in paragraph 13 (*b*) of this Schedule shall be construed as preventing—

(*a*) several bets being made by a person relating to the same competition; or

(*b*) several bets (whether relating to the same competition or to different competitions) being made by a person by means of the same coupon or other entry form; or

(*c*) the use of a formula for the purpose of making several bets and, in particular, the use for that purpose of any form of the device commonly known as a permutation.

17. Nothing in paragraph 13 (*f*) of this Schedule shall be construed as requiring, in the case of a series of competitions proposed to be held under the same rules, that those rules should be re-notified to the accountant on the occasion of each competition, and, if the rules are altered before the series is completed, it shall suffice if the alteration is notified to the accountant before any of the sporting or other events relevant to the first competition to which the alteration applies takes place.

18. Nothing in paragraphs 13 to 17 of this Schedule shall prevent the rules of any competition from providing that the competition may be declared void in specified circumstances.

19. Where two or more competitions of the same registered pool promoter are so conducted that entries in all of them can be affected by a person without completing more than a single coupon or other entry form, the promoter may arrive at the total amount of the stakes in respect of the entries in each competition by—

(*a*) ascertaining the aggregate total amount of the stakes in respect of the entries in all the competitions; and

(*b*) causing the said aggregate total amount to be apportioned among those competitions by reference to the results of an inspection of samples of the completed coupons or forms;

and if the sampling, inspection and apportionment is such (both as to the process adopted and as to the manner of carrying it out) that the amount apportioned to each competition is not likely to differ from the total amount actually staked therein by more than one per cent, the amount so apportioned to any such competition shall for all the purposes of this Schedule be deemed to be the total amount actually staked in that competition.

---

1. The natural meaning of these words connotes the exercise of some degree of skill. In a football competition in which the vast majority of participants made no forecast but relied on numbers that had been previously allotted to them and won prizes only if their numbers happened to be lucky, the House of Lords held that the competition had the character of a lottery and this character was not destroyed even though participants had the option to make a forecast if they so wished (*Singette Ltd v Martin* [1971] AC 407, [1970] 3 All ER 938, 135 JP 157).

2. Words added by Finance Act 1967, s 7.

Information to be given by promoters

8–13361 **20.** (1) As soon as may be after the events to which any of his competitions relates have taken place, and in any case not later than seven days after the announcement of the results of that competition, every registered pool promoter shall send to the accountant a statement showing—

(*a*) the total amount of the stakes in respect of entries in the competition;

(*b*) the total amount payable by way of winnings in that competition;

(*bb*) the amount (if any) carried over to the competition from a previous competition in accordance with any provision made under paragraph 14A of this Schedule;

(*bbb*)the amount (if any) carried over from the competition in accordance with any such provision;

(*c*) the total amount of the stakes in respect of winning bets in the competition and, if there are more prizes than one in the competition, the total amount of the stakes in respect of winning bets qualifying for, or for shares in, each of the prizes; and

(*d*) the amount payable in respect of each winning bet or, as the case may be, of each winning bet qualifying for, or for a share of, each of the prizes, bets staking more than the minimum which is permissible under the rules of the competition being treated for the purposes of this paragraph as if they were several separate bets each staking the said minimum.

(2) Where a payment is made in accordance with paragraph 15 of this Schedule after the sending of the statement to the accountant under the foregoing sub-paragraph, the registered pool promoter shall as soon as may be send particulars of that payment to the accountant.

21. (1) Every registered pool promoter shall, not more than twenty-one days after the events to which any of his competitions relate have taken place, send to every competitor in that competition a statement of the percentage (calculated to the nearest one-tenth of one per cent) which the first of the amounts hereinafter mentioned bears to the second of those amounts, that is to say—

(*a*) the aggregate total stakes in that competition and all other competitions of that promoter which depend on those events or on other events taking place on the same day, after making in respect of those competitions the deductions mentioned in sub-paragraph (1A) of this paragraph;

(*b*) the said aggregate total stakes, without any such deduction,

unless he has secured all such publicity as is reasonably necessary for the said statement by means of a newspaper announcement or newspaper announcements published within the said twenty-one days.

(1A) In relation to any competition, the deductions referred to are—

(*a*) a deduction of the aggregate of the total amount payable by way of winnings in the competition and any amount carried over from the competition in accordance with any provision made under paragraph 14A of this Schedule, less any amount carried over to the competition in accordance with any such provision, and

(*b*) a deduction of the amount of pool betting duty payable in respect of the competition.

(2) The statement aforesaid may take the following form, that is to say—

"Commission and expenses   per cent"

with the addition (if in the context this is necessary) or words identifying the competition or competitions to which the statement relates.

22. The statements and announcements referred to in paragraphs 20 and 21 of this Schedule may be expressed to be subject to some form of check or scrutiny, but where a statement expressed to be subject to a check or scrutiny is sent to the accountant under sub-paragraph (1) of the said paragraph 20, the registered pool promoter shall as soon as may be send to the accountant a further statement, stating that, as the result of the check or scrutiny, specified corrections or no corrections are necessary in the earlier statement or that the check or scrutiny has not been made and is not intended to be made.

23. (1) In August in each year every registered pool promoter shall send to the accountant and to the registering authority a statement showing, as respects his competitions depending on events which took place on any day during the period of twelve months ending with 31st July in that year—

(a) the aggregate total stakes in all the competitions;
(b) the said aggregate total stakes after making in respect of each of those competitions the deductions mentioned in paragraph 21(1A) of this schedule; and
(c) the amount of the promoter's commission or, at the option of the promoter, the percentage (calculated to the nearest one-tenth of one per cent) which the said commission bears to the said aggregate total stakes:

Provided that, if the percentage referred to in paragraph (c) of this sub-paragraph does not exceed three per cent, the statement required by that paragraph may, if the promoter so desires, be a statement that the said percentage does not exceed three per cent.

(2) In the foregoing sub-paragraph, the expression "the promoter's commission" means the amount by which the aggregate total stakes in all of the competitions referred to in that sub-paragraph exceeds the sum of—

(a) the aggregate prizes in those competitions; and
(b) the aggregate pool betting duty payable in respect of the competitions; and
(c) the expenses of the promoter actually incurred by him in the conduct of those competitions, excluding any expenses properly chargeable to capital and any interest on borrowed money, and, in particular, excluding any provision for depreciation of buildings or equipment, any emoluments payable to the promoter or, if the promoter is a partnership, to any of the partners, or, if the promoter is a body corporate, to any of the directors, and in any case, any emoluments payable to any person whose emoluments depend to any extent on the profits of the promoter.

(3) The registering authority shall preserve any statement sent to them under this paragraph for at least two years and shall deposit it at their office and permit any member of the public to inspect it during office hours free of charge.

24. (1) Where a registered pool promoter is a company to which section 241 of the Companies Act 1985 applies, then, whenever a copy of a profit and loss account of the company is laid before the company in general meeting in pursuance of that section, the company shall forthwith send a copy of that account and of the relevant auditor's report to the accountant.

(2) Every registered pool promoter to whom the foregoing sub-paragraph does not apply shall at least once in every calendar year send to the accountant a profit and loss account of his pool betting business, covering, in the case of the first account, a period beginning at the commencement of the business, and, in the case of subsequent accounts, a period beginning at the end of the period covered by the last account, together with a report thereon by an auditor, being a qualified accountant who neither is, nor is a partner of, nor is in the employment of any person who is, an officer or servant of the registered pool promoter; and sections 235(2) and 237(1) and (3) of the Companies Act 1985 (matters to be stated in auditors' report and responsibility of auditors in preparing their report) (which enumerates the matters which are to be expressly stated in auditors' reports) shall, with the necessary adaptations, apply in relation to every such report.

Duties and powers of the accountant

8–13362 25. The accountant shall—

(a) examine all statements submitted to him under paragraph 20, 22 or 23 of this Schedule with a view to determining whether there is cause to believe that any of the provisions of this Schedule are being contravened in relation to the competition in question; and
(b) retain all such statements for two years; and
(c) at any time during that period give facilities for their examination by any officer or servant of the registering authority authorised in that behalf by that authority.

26. The accountant and any servant of his authorised in that behalf by him in writing may at all reasonable times enter any premises on which a registered pool promoter is carrying on his business and enquire into the manner in which that business is being carried on, and may require the registered pool promoter or any servant of his to give to the accountant or his servant authorised as aforesaid all such information, and to produce all such accounts, books and other documents and carry out such checks or additional checks of coupons or other entry forms, as the accountant or his servant authorised as aforesaid may think necessary for the purpose of determining whether there is cause to believe that any of the provisions of this Schedule are being contravened; and it shall be the duty of the promoter to preserve, or, to such extent as he may prefer to do so, to preserve photographic copies of, all accounts, books or other documents (including coupons or other entry forms) which relate wholly or partly to any of his competitions for at least two months from the day on which the events take place on which that competition depends.

27. (1) If at any time the accountant has cause to believe that any of the provisions of this Schedule are being contravened in relation to any of the competitions of a registered pool promoter, he shall report the matter to the registering authority.

(2) Not later than the end of October in each year the accountant shall furnish to the registering authority a report stating, if such be the fact, that he—

(a) has examined all statements submitted to him by a registered pool promoter under paragraph 20, 22 or 23 of this Schedule in respect of the period of twelve months ending with 31st July in that year;

(b) has conducted such enquiries into the manner in which the business of that promoter is carried on and made such examination of that promoter's records as he considers necessary; and

(c) has no cause to believe that any of the provisions of this Schedule have been contravened in relation to any of the competitions of that promoter taking place during the said period except in relation to such matters (if any) as have been reported by the accountant in pursuance of the foregoing sub-paragraph.

28. Paragraphs 20 to 27 of this Schedule shall apply in relation to a competition declared void in pursuance of any such rule of the competition as is mentioned in paragraph 18 of this Schedule as they apply in relation to other competitions, except that—

(a) instead of the statements required by paragraphs 20 and 21 of this Schedule to be sent to the accountant in respect of the competition and to be included in announcements of the results of, or to be sent to competitors in, the competition, there shall be sent statements that the competition has been declared void and that sums paid as stakes therein will be repaid or credited to the payers thereof;

(b) the competition shall be left out of account in computing the percentage a statement of which is required by the said paragraph 21 to be included in announcements of the results of, or to be sent to competitors in, other competitions depending on the same events or other events taking place on the same day.

Enforcement

8–13363 **29.** (1) Any person who—

(a) obstructs the accountant or any servant of his in the execution of any powers or duties under this Schedule; or

(b) fails to comply with any requirement duly made of him by the accountant or any servant of his or, in response to such a requirement, knowingly gives any information which is false or misleading,

shall be guilty of an offence[1].

(2) If any registered pool promoter fails to comply with any duty imposed upon him by this Schedule or if any of the provisions of this Schedule, except so far as they impose duties on the accountant or the registering authority, are contravened in the case of the business of any registered pool promoter, the registered pool promoter shall be guilty of an offence.

(3) In England, the registering authority shall have power to take proceedings for offences under this paragraph or under section 4(2) of this Act.

---

1. For penalty, see s 52(1), ante. Where the offence consists of a failure to comply with the requirements of para 13(*f*) of this Schedule (rules relating to a betting competition to be notified to the Comrs of Customs and Excise and to the accountant) proceedings may not be taken by the registering authority, but the Customs and Excise Management Act 1979, s 145, post (institution of proceedings), and s 151, post (application of penalties), will apply (Finance Act 1967, s 7(8)).

SCHEDULE 3
LICENSING OF TRACKS FOR BETTING[1]

(Amended by the Courts Act 1971, the Local Government Act 1972, the Local Government Act 1985, Schs 8 and 17 and SI 1991/2175.)

Licensing authorities and interpretation

8–13364 **1.** Paragraphs 1, 2 and 3 of Schedule 2[2] to this Act shall have effect with respect to licensing authorities for the purposes of this Schedule as if—

(a) in sub-paragraph (1) of the said paragraph 1 for the words "the registering authority" there were substituted the words "the licensing authority"; and

(b) any reference in those paragraphs to the said Schedule 2 were a reference to this Schedule.

2. In this Schedule, except where the context otherwise requires—

(a) any reference to a track shall be construed as including a reference to the site of a proposed track;

(b) in relation to any particular track, any reference to the licensing authority shall be construed as a reference to the council or committee who, under paragraph 1 of this Schedule, are the licensing authority for the area in which that track or the greater part of the superficial area thereof is situated, and the expression "appropriate officer of police" means the chief officer of police for a police area which includes that track or any part thereof.

---

1. For restriction of bookmaking on tracks, see s 6, ante.
2. These paragraphs relate to registering authorities in respect of registered pool promoters: see Sch 2, ante.

Applications for licences

8–13365 **3.** An application for the grant of a track betting licence may be made to the licensing authority—

(a) in respect of an existing track, by the occupier thereof; or

(b) in respect of a track which it is proposed to construct, by any person who proposes to become the occupier of the track if the licence is granted.

4. Each licensing authority may from time to time fix dates on which they will entertain applications for the grant of track betting licences by them and shall cause information as to any dates so fixed to be given to any person who asks for it.

5. (1) No application for a track betting licence shall be entertained by the licensing authority unless, at least two months before the date on which the application is made, the applicant has given to the licensing authority and to each of the authorities specified in sub-paragraph (2) of this paragraph notice in writing—

(a) stating that it is intended to make the application on that date; and
(b) describing the situation of the track and the number and position of the exits provided or intended to be provided; and
(c) stating the number of spectators for whom accommodation is provided or is intended to be provided,

and has also published such a notice in at least two newspapers circulating in the locality in which the track is situated.

(2) The authorities referred to in the foregoing sub-paragraph are—

(a) if the track is situated in England—

(i) the council of any county in which the track or any part thereof is situated; and
(ii) the local planning authority within the meaning of the Town and Country Planning Act [1990] (not being the licensing authority) for any area which includes the track or any part thereof;

(b) *Applies to Scotland.*
(c) the appropriate officer or officers of police.

(3) Every notice given to the licensing authority under sub-paragraph (1) of this paragraph shall, until the hearing of the application to which the notice relates, be kept by the licensing authority at their offices so as to be available, at any time during office hours, for inspection by any member of the public free of charge.

6. (1) Upon the consideration by the licensing authority of an application for the grant of a track betting licence, the following persons in addition to the applicant shall be entitled to be heard in person or by a representative, that is to say—

(a) any appropriate officer of police;
(b) any person owning or occupying premises in the neighbourhood of the track;
(c) the governing body of any school or institution in the neighbourhood of the track;
(d) if the track is situated in England, any of the authorities specified in sub-paragraph (2) of this paragraph;
(e) *Applies to Scotland.*

Provided that no objector shall be heard unless he has given to the applicant and to the licensing authority at least seven days' notice in writing of the grounds on which he proposes to contend that the application ought to be refused.

(2) The authorities referred to in sub-paragraph (1) (d) of this paragraph are—

(a) the local planning authority within the meaning of the Town and Country Planning Act 1962 (not being the licensing authority) for any area which includes the track or any part thereof;
(b) the council of any county in which the track or any part thereof is situated;
(c) any other local authority whose area adjoins the area of the licensing authority:

Provided that no local authority shall be entitled to be heard as an objector if the licensing authority are a committee of that local authority or a joint committee including persons appointed by that local authority.

In this sub-paragraph, the expression "local authority" means any of the following councils, that is to say, the council of a county, London borough or county district and the Common Council of the City of London.

(3) *Applies to Scotland.*

Grant or refusal of licence

8–13366 **7.** (1) The provisions of this paragraph shall have effect with respect to any application to a licensing authority for the grant of a track betting licence in respect of any track.

(2) The licensing authority may refuse to grant the licence if they are satisfied that, in the event of the licence being granted, the existence or user of the track—

(a) would injuriously affect either the health or the comfort of persons residing in the neighbourhood of the track, or be detrimental to the interests of persons receiving instruction or residing in any school or institution in that neighbourhood; or
(b) would seriously impair the amenities of that neighbourhood; or
(c) would result in undue congestion of traffic or seriously prejudice the preservation of law and order.

(3) The licensing authority may also refuse to grant the licence if the applicant or, where the applicant is a body corporate, any director or the manager thereof has been convicted—

(a) of an offence under any of the following provisions of this Act, that is to say, sections 1(1) (a), 4(1), 5, 6, 7, 16, 18, 19, 21 and 23 and paragraphs 11 and 17 of Schedule 5;
(b) of any offence under Part I of, or Schedule 1 to, the Betting and Lotteries Act 1934 or under section 7 of the Betting and Gaming Act 1960; or
(c) of any offence involving fraud or dishonesty.

(4) If the licensing authority are not satisfied that any planning permission required under Part III of the Town and Country Planning Act 1962 . . .¹ for the establishment of the track, or for the continuance of the track during the period for which the licence would be in force, has been, or is deemed to be, granted, they shall either refuse to grant the licence or grant the licence but suspend its operation until the local planning authority within the meaning of the said Act of 1962 . . .¹ have notified the licensing authority that any such planning permission has been, or is deemed to be, granted.

(5) Save as is mentioned in sub-paragraph (2), (3) or (4) of this paragraph, the licensing authority shall not refuse the application; and if they do refuse it they shall send to the applicant by post a written statement of the grounds of their refusal.

1. Words omitted apply to Scotland.

Duration and transfer of licences

8–13367   **8.** A track betting licence shall, unless cancelled under paragraph 10 or revoked under paragraph 13 of this Schedule, be in force for seven years from the date on which it is expressed to take effect.

9. Where in the case of any track the licensing authority have granted a track betting licence to any person, they may at any time, if they think fit, on an application made to them after notice in writing to the appropriate officer or officers of police, direct that the licence shall be transferred to another person, and thereupon the transferee shall be deemed to be the holder of the licence, so, however, that, if the transferee is not the occupier of the track, the transfer shall not take effect until he becomes the occupier thereof.

10. The licensing authority by whom any track betting licence for the time being in force was granted shall, upon receiving from the holder of the licence a written request in that behalf accompanied by the licence, cancel the licence, which shall thereupon cease to be in force.

11. In the event of the death of the holder of a track betting licence, his legal personal representatives shall, during the period of three months from the date of the death, be deemed to be the holder of the licence, notwithstanding that it has not been transferred to them.

Fees in respect of licences

8–13368   **12.** (1) In respect of any application for a track betting licence, such fee not exceeding £46 as the licensing authority may from time to time fix for the whole of their area shall be payable by the applicant before the hearing of the application, but, if the licence is granted, the fee so paid shall be treated as a payment on account of the first annual payment to be made in respect of the licence under the next following sub-paragraph.

(2) In respect of every such licence, such annual fee not exceeding £46 as the licensing authority may fix annually for the whole of their area shall be payable during the currency of the licence by the person who is for the time being the holder thereof, and the first of those payments shall be made on the day on which the licence takes effect, and subsequent payments shall be made at intervals of twelve months thereafter.

(3) In respect of any transfer of such a licence, such fee not exceeding £46 as the licensing authority may from time to time fix for the whole of their area shall be payable by the person to whom the licence is transferred.

(4) Every fee which by virtue of this paragraph is payable by any person shall be recoverable from that person by the licensing authority as a debt due from him to them.

Revocation of licence and appeal therefrom

8–13369   **13.** (1) At any time while a track betting licence is in force in respect of any track, the licensing authority by whom it was granted may, after giving to the holder of the licence an opportunity of being heard, revoke the licence—

(*a*) if they are satisfied that the track has been conducted in a disorderly manner or so as to cause a nuisance; or

(*b*) if without their approval, to be given after such notice as they deem proper, the accommodation for spectators on the track as stated in the notice under paragraph 5(1) of this Schedule has been substantially increased, or the exits from the track as described in that notice have been materially altered, and the authority are satisfied that undue congestion of traffic, or serious prejudice to the preservation of law and order has resulted therefrom; or

(*c*) if on a report made to them by the accountant appointed under Schedule 5 to this Act, or upon a refusal of that accountant to give such a certificate as is mentioned in paragraph 15 of that Schedule, they are satisfied that any totalisator on the track has been maintained or operated otherwise than in accordance with the provisions of that Schedule; or

(*d*) if the holder of licence or, where the holder is a body corporate, any director or the manager thereof is convicted of any offence such as is mentioned in paragraph 7(3) (*a*) or (*c*) of this Schedule;

and if the authority revoke any such licence, they shall forthwith send notice of the revocation by post to the holder of the licence and to the appropriate officer or officers of police.

(2) The holder of a licence in respect of a track in England which has been revoked under the foregoing sub-paragraph may appeal to the Crown Court, and such appeal shall be commenced by giving notice to the appropriate officer of the Crown Court and to the licensing authority within twenty-one days of the holder's being notified of the revocation by the licensing authority.

(3) *Applies to Scotland.*

(4) Where a licensing authority revoke a licence under sub-paragraph (1) of this paragraph, then, until the time within which notice of appeal under sub-paragraph (2) or (3) of this paragraph may be given has expired and, if such notice is given, until the determination or abandonment of the appeal, the licence shall be deemed to continue in force, and if the court of quarter sessions . . .[1]confirms the decision of the licensing authority, the court . . .[1]may, if it thinks fit, order that the licence shall continue in force for a further period not exceeding two months from the date of the order.

1. Words omitted apply to Scotland.

SCHEDULE 4
RULES[1] FOR LICENSED BETTING OFFICES

(As amended by the Cable and Broadcasting Act 1984, Sch 5, SI 1986/11, the Deregulation and Contracting Out Act 1994, s 20, SI 1995/579, SI 1996/1359, SI 1997/1074 and SI 2002/1930.)

8–13370   **1.** The licensed premises shall be closed throughout Good Friday and Christmas Day, and at such other times, if any, as may be prescribed[2], subject to paragraphs 10A to 10C of this Schedule, and shall not be used for any purpose[3]other than the effecting of betting transactions[4].

2. No person who is apparently under the age of eighteen years, or who is known to any person connected with the licensee's business and present on the licensed premises[5] to be under that age, shall be admitted to or allowed to remain on those premises, so, however, that in any proceedings for a contravention of this rule in respect of a person apparently under the said age it shall be a defence to prove that at the time of the alleged contravention he had in fact attained that age.

3. The licensee—

(a) shall display his betting office licence on the licensed premises;

(b) shall exhibit on those premises such notices in such form and in such positions as may be prescribed[2]; and

(c) shall comply with any prescribed[2] restrictions with respect to the exhibiting of other written matter or of signs of any description on the licensed premises.

4. *Repealed.*

5. *Repealed.*

6. Except for the licensee and any servant or agent of his, no person resorting to the licensed premises shall be allowed to use any means of direct access between the licensed premises and other premises used for the effecting with persons resorting to those other premises of transactions other than betting transactions.

7. (1) Except as permitted by sub-paragraph (2) or (3) below, no apparatus for making information or other material available in the form of sounds or visual images or both shall be used on the licensed premises.

(2) Subject to paragraph 8 below, such apparatus may be used on the licensed premises provided that the matter seen or heard comprises only information about, and the coverage of, a sporting event including—

(a) information relating to any betting on such an event; and

(b) any other matter, including an advertisement, which is incidental to such an event or such coverage.

(3) Subject to paragraph 8 below, such apparatus may be used on the licensed premises provided that the matter seen or heard comprises only—

(a) information relating to betting on any event in connection with which betting transactions may be or have been effected on those premises; and

(b) the result of such an event.

8. (1) *Repealed.*

(2) No apparatus for showing visual images of a sporting event shall be used on the licensed premises if—

(a) the service by means of which such images appear is not intended to be received by the general public or other licensees generally; or

(b) in the case of images that appear by means of the use of video recordings, identical recordings of the same event are not available to other licensees generally.

In this sub-paragraph "video recording" has the same meaning as in section 1(3) of the Video Recordings Act 1984.

9. No music, dancing or other entertainment shall be provided or allowed on the licensed premises, except any entertainment which complies with the provisions of paragraph 7 above.

10. Refreshments may be provided on the licenced premises except—

(a) where those premises are in England and Wales, alcohol within the meaning of section 191 of the Licensing Act 2003; or

(b) where those premises are in Scotland, alcoholic liquor within the meaning of section 139(1) of the Licensing (Scotland) Act 1976.

10A. Machines to which Part III of the Gaming Act 1968 (gaming machines) applies may be used on the licensed premises, but only if—

(a) they are machines in respect of which the conditions mentioned in section 34(5A) of the Gaming Act 1968 are observed (cash prizes only), and

(b) they do not exceed two in number

10B. Publications may be sold on the licensed premises, but only if they are racing periodicals or specialist betting publications.

10C. The licensed premises may be used for—

(a) the sale of tickets in any lottery other than—

(i) a private lottery within the meaning of the Lotteries and Amusement Act 1976, or

(ii) a lottery the sale of tickets in which on the licensed premises is otherwise prohibited,

(b) the collection of amounts payable by way of winnings in any lottery for the sale of whose tickets the premises may be used,

(c) the delivery of entry forms and stakes relating to competitions in which success depends to a substantial degree on the exercise of skill, and

(d) the collection of amounts payable by way of winnings in any such competition as is mentioned in sub-paragraph (c) of this paragraph.

11. Paragraph 1 above shall be construed, subject to the restrictions in paragraphs 7 to 10 above, as not prohibiting the provision of the facilities permitted by paragraphs 7, 9 and 10 above.

---

1. Penalty upon licensee or his servant or agent for contravention of any rule set out in this Schedule, not exceeding **level 3** on the standard scale: see s 10(1), ante. A contravention of these rules by a servant or agent of the licensee involves at least constructive knowledge of non-compliance: see *Mallon v Allon* [1964] 1 QB 385, [1963] 3 All ER 843, 128 JP 81.

2. See the Licensed Betting Offices Regulations 1986, SI 1986/103, this PART, post.

3. The effect of this provision is to prohibit user for any purpose other than betting transactions even when the premises are closed (*Anderson v Gradidge* [1969] 2 All ER 206, 133 JP 368).

4. For meaning of "betting transaction", see s 55(1), ante. In *Seay v Eastwood* [1976] 3 All ER 153, 140 JP 589 (a case under the Betting and Lotteries Act (Northern Ireland) 1957) it was held that the operation, by insertion of a coin, of a

gaming machine on the licensed premises of a bookmaker was not a bet placed with the bookmaker, and was unlawful as it did not constitute the business of receiving bets.

5. Admitting to premises *and* allowing to remain thereon are separate offences: an information charging both is bad for duplicity (*Mallon v Allon* [1964] 1 QB 385, [1963] 3 All ER 843, 128 JP 81).

SCHEDULE 5
TOTALISATORS ON DOG RACECOURSES[1]

(*As amended by the Finance Act 1966, s 12, the Betting, Gaming and Lotteries (Amendment) Act 1971, s 1, the Criminal Justice Act 1982, ss 38 and 46, the Betting, Gaming and Lotteries (Amendment) Act 1985, s 2 and SI 1995/3231.*)

8–13371   1. The totalisator shall comply with the prescribed[2] conditions.

2. The person, whether the occupier of the track or a person authorised in that behalf in writing by that occupier, by whom the totalisator is operated (in this Schedule referred to as "the operator") shall take all such steps as are necessary to secure that, so long as the totalisator is in use, it is in proper working order and is properly operated.

3[3]. The operator shall, before receiving any bets in connection with any race, post in a conspicuous position on the track or, where bets may be made by means of the totalisator in more than one distinct area of the track, in each such area a notice showing the minimum stake (hereinafter referred to as "the betting unit") which will be accepted at the totalisator from persons betting on that race; and that notice shall also—

(a)   specify[4], prominently and in easily legible print the percentage, which will be deducted by the operator from amounts staked by means of the totalisator; and

(b)   if the terms on which the operator invites persons to bet include such a condition as is mentioned in paragraph 6 of this Schedule, specify the time referred to in that paragraph; and

(c)   specify such other particulars of the said terms as may be prescribed[2].

4. The operator shall, in the case of any bets made by means of the totalisator on any race or combination of races—

(a)   deduct from the aggregate amount staked—

(i)   any sums payable by the operator by way of the general betting duty in respect of those bets; and

(ii)   subject to paragraph 5 of this Schedule, the percentage specified in the notice posted in pursuance of paragraph 3 thereof; and

(b)   subject to paragraphs 4C to 6 of this Schedule, distribute the whole of the remainder of that amount among the persons making such of those bets as are winning bets.

4A. The terms on which the operator invites persons to bet on any race or combination of races on the track by means of the totalisator may include a condition that, in the event of there being no winning bets on that race or those races, the aggregate amount staked thereon by way of bets made by means of the totalisator (less any deductions made in pursuance of paragraph 4(a) of this Schedule) shall be carried over to a subsequent race or combination of races on the track by being added to the aggregate amount staked thereon by way of bets so made; and nothing in section 16(1) of this Act shall be construed as precluding the totalisator from being so operated as to allow any such amount to be carried over as aforesaid from one day to another.

4B. Where, in accordance with such a condition as is mentioned in paragraph 4A of this Schedule, any amount is to be added to the aggregate amount staked by way of bets made by means of the totalisator on any race or combination of races, that amount shall be disregarded for the purpose of making any deduction required by paragraph 4(a) of this Schedule.

4C. (1) This paragraph applies where the amount payable in respect of each betting unit staked by a person winning a bet is or includes a fraction of the betting unit where it is not one or more tenths of that unit.

(2) Where the fraction is less than a twentieth of the betting unit, the operator may retain it.

(3) Where the fraction is more than a tenth of the betting unit, but exceeds the next lower tenth of that unit by less than a twentieth of that unit, the operator may retain so much of it as exceeds that tenth of that unit.

(4) Otherwise, the amount payable in respect of each betting unit staked by a person winning a bet shall be deemed to be increased—

(a)   to the next higher tenth of the betting unit; or

(b)   where the fraction concerned exceeds nine tenths of the betting unit, to the next multiple of that unit.

5. Where the amount payable in respect of each betting unit staked by a person winning a bet, after any rounding under paragraph 4C of this Schedule, is or includes a fraction of a new penny, then—

(a)   if that fraction does not exceed one-half, it may be retained by the operator; but

(b)   if that fraction exceeds one-half, the amount payable in respect of each betting unit staked by the said person shall be deemed to be increased to the nearest multiple of a new penny[5].

6. The terms on which the operator invites persons to bet by means of the totalisator may include a condition entitling the operator to retain any sum payable to a person winning a bet unless the money won on the bet is claimed before such time, being a time not falling within the period of 7 days beginning with the day after that of the conclusion of the race, or as the case may be, of the last of the races, in connection with which the bet was made, as may have been specified in the notice posted in pursuance of paragraph 3 of this Schedule.

7. The licensing authority, that is to say, the authority by whom any track betting licence in respect of the track falls to be granted, shall appoint a qualified accountant (hereinafter in this Schedule referred to as "the accountant") who shall be charged with the duty of examining and certifying the accounts relating to the operation of the totalisator and, after consultation with the accountant, shall also appoint an experienced mechanician (hereinafter in this Schedule referred to as "the technical adviser") who shall act as technical adviser to the accountant and be charged with the duty of advising him as to the condition of the totalisator and all matters connected with the operation thereof.

8. The accountant and the technical adviser shall hold office on such terms (including terms as to remuneration) as may be determined by the licensing authority after consultation with the occupier of the track, and the remuneration of the accountant and the technical adviser shall be payable by the licensing authority; but so much of that remuneration as is paid to the accountant or the technical adviser in respect of the performance of his functions under this Schedule in relation to the totalisator and is attributable to any period during which a track betting licence was in force in respect of the track shall be recoverable by the licensing authority as a debt due to them from the holder of that licence.

9. The totalisator shall not be operated on any day unless the accountant has been given not less than 48 hours notice in writing that it is intended that betting should take place on that day by means of the totalisator.

10–10A. *Repealed.*

11. (1) The accountant, the technical adviser and their respective servants authorised in that behalf in writing may at all reasonable times enter the premises in which the totalisator is set up and examine any part of the mechanism and test and watch the working thereof, and may require the operator or any servant of his to give to them all such information, and to produce to them all such accounts, books and other documents, as they deem necessary for the purpose of ascertaining whether the provisions of this Schedule are being complied with.

(2) Every person who—

(a) obstructs any of the persons upon whom powers are conferred by the foregoing sub-paragraph in the exercise of any of those powers; or

(b) neglects or refuses to give to any of the said persons any such information, or to produce to him any such document, as may have been called for by him in pursuance of the said sub-paragraph; or

(c) knowingly gives to any of the said persons any information which is false or misleading, shall be liable on summary conviction to a fine not exceeding **level 3** on the standard scale.

12. (1) The operator shall, within seven days after the close of each month, submit to the accountant for examination by him a complete statement of account for that month.

(2) The statement required by sub-paragraph (1) of this paragraph shall—

(a) specify, in relation to any amount carried over from one race or combination of races to another in accordance with such a condition as is mentioned in paragraph 4A of this Schedule—

(i) the amount carried over; and
(ii) the date of the race or combination of races to which it is carried over; and

(b) give all such information as the accountant may require for the purpose of ascertaining whether the provisions of this Schedule have been complied with.

13. The accountant shall examine the statements of account submitted to him under the last foregoing paragraph and shall, so often as he thinks proper, consult with the technical adviser and carry out, or cause to be carried out, such inspections as either of them deem necessary for the purpose of ascertaining whether the provisions of this Schedule are being complied with, and shall forthwith make a report to the licensing authority if he has reason to believe that the totalisator no longer complies with the prescribed conditions, or is not being kept in proper working order, or is not being properly operated, or if in his opinion any of the provisions of this Schedule are not being complied with.

14. The accountant shall retain for a period of two years all statements of account submitted to him as aforesaid and shall at any time during that period give facilities for their examination by any person authorised in that behalf by the licensing authority.

15. Without prejudice to his duties under the foregoing paragraphs, the accountant shall, as soon as may be after the close of each calendar year, audit the accounts of the operator for the year and, if such be the fact, certify thereon that satisfactory statements of account have been submitted to him monthly in accordance with the provisions of paragraph 12 of this Schedule and have been examined by him, and that to the best of his information and belief, formed after consultation with the technical adviser, the accounts for the year are complete and accurate and the totalisator complies with the prescribed conditions and has throughout the year been maintained in proper working order and properly operated in accordance with the provisions of this Schedule; and the operator shall forthwith cause the accounts and certificate to be printed and, subject to paragraph 16 of this Schedule, shall transmit two copies thereof to the licensing authority, who shall cause one of those copies to be deposited at their offices for inspection at any time during office hours by any member of the public free of charge.

16. Where by virtue of paragraph 1 of Schedule 3 to this Act the licensing authority are a joint committee such as are mentioned in paragraph 1(4) of Schedule 2 to this Act, the operator shall transmit to the licensing authority such number of copies of the accounts and certificate referred to in paragraph 15 of this Schedule as is sufficient to enable the licensing authority to keep one copy at their offices for the purposes of record and to deposit for inspection as mentioned in that paragraph one copy at their offices and one copy at the offices of each council whose functions under Schedule 3 to this Act are delegated to that committee.

17. Without prejudice to paragraph 11(2) of this Schedule, if the operator contravenes any of the provisions of this Schedule other than the said paragraph 11 (2) he shall be guilty of an offence[6].

18. (1) In relation to the operation of the totalisator for effecting betting transactions under a licensed inter-track betting scheme, this Schedule shall have effect with the following modifications.

(2) Where the operation is in connection with racing on the track where the totalisator is situated, the references in paragraphs 4 and 4B to the totalisator shall be construed as references to any totalisator on a track participating in the inter-track betting scheme.

(3) Where the operation is in connection with racing on a track other than the track where the totalisator is situated—

(a) the references in paragraph 3(a) and (b) to the operator shall be construed as references to the operator of the totalisator on the track where the racing takes place; and

(b) paragraphs 4 and 4B to 6 shall be omitted.

(4) In paragraph 4A—

(a) references to a race or combination of races on the track shall be construed as references to a race or combination of races in relation to which betting takes place under the inter-track betting scheme; and

(b) references to bets made by means of the totalisator shall be construed as references to bets made under the inter-track betting scheme.

(5) In paragraph 13, the reference to the licensing authority shall be construed as including a reference to the authority by whom the inter-track betting scheme is licensed.

1. For provisions relating to totalisators on licensed tracks, see s 16, ante.
2. See the Dog Racecourse Totalisator Regulations 1995, SI 1995/3232.
3. This paragraph is printed as amended by the Betting, Gaming and Lotteries (Amendment) Act 1969.
4. A percentage of 29% is specified by the Dog Racecourse Totalisator (Percentage) Order 1991, SI 1991/2592.
5. As amended by the Decimal Currency Act 1969, Sch 2.
6. For penalty, see s 52(1), ante.

8–13372
SCHEDULE 5ZA
LICENSING OF INTER-TRACK BETTING SCHEMES[1]

1. Schedule 5ZA was inserted by SI 1995/3231 and makes provision for the licensing of inter-track betting schemes by way of application to a "licensing authority" which is the appropriate local authority. There is provision for appeals against the decisions of the licensing authority to be made to the Crown Court.

8–13373
SCHEDULE 5A
RIGHTS OF BETTING WORKERS AS RESPECTS SUNDAY WORKING[1]

1. Schedule 5A was inserted by the Deregulation and Contracting Out Act 1994, s 20 and Sch 8.

SCHEDULE 6
Repealed by Lotteries and Amusements Act 1976.

SCHEDULE 7
Repealed by Lotteries Act 1975.

Gaming Act 1968
(1968 c 65)
(*A memorandum explaining the purpose and nature of this Act was circulated with Home Office Circular* 25/1969.)

PART I
GAMING ELSEWHERE THAN ON PREMISES LICENSED OR REGISTERED UNDER PART II OF THIS ACT

8–13380 1. Gaming to which Part I applies. (1) Except as provided by the next following subsection, this Part of this Act applies to all gaming[1] which takes place elsewhere than on premises in respect or which either—

(a) a licence under this Act is for the time being in force, or
(b) a club or a miners' welfare institute is for the time being registered under Part II of this Act.

(2) This part of this Act does not apply to—

(a) gaming by means of any machine to which Part III of this Act applies, or
(b) gaming to which section 41 of this Act applies, or
(c) gaming which constitutes the provision of amusements with prizes as mentioned in section 15(1) or 16(1) of the Lotteries and Amusements Act 1976.

[Gaming Act 1968, s 1, as amended by the Lotteries and Amusements Act 1976, Schedule 4.]

1. Defined in s 52, post.

8–13381 2. Nature of game. (1) Subject to the following provisions of this section, no gaming to which this Part of this Act applies[1] shall take place where any one or more of the following conditions are fulfilled, that is to say—

(a) the game involves playing or staking against a bank, whether the bank is held by one of the players[2] or not;
(b) the nature of the game is such that the chances in the game are not equally favourable to all the players[2];
(c) the nature of the game is such that the chances in it lie between the player[2] and some other person, or (if there are two or more players) lie wholly or partly between the players and some other person, and those chances are not as favourable to the player or players as they are to that other person.

(2) The preceding subsection shall not have effect in relation to gaming which takes place on a domestic occasion in a private dwelling, and shall not have effect in relation to any gaming where the gaming takes place in a hostel, hall of residence or similar establishment which is not carried on by

way of a trade or business and the players consist exclusively or mainly of persons who are residents or inmates in that establishment.
[Gaming Act 1968, s 2.]

---

1. See s 1, ante.
2. Defined in Betting, Gaming and Lotteries Act 1963, s 55.

8–13382   3. No charge for taking part in gaming.   (1) Subject to the following provisions of this section, no gaming to which this Part of this Act applies[1] shall take place in circumstances where (apart from any stakes hazarded) a charge[2], in money or money's worth, is made in respect of that gaming.

(2) Subject to the next following subsection, any admission charge shall, unless the contrary is proved[3], be taken to be a charge made as mentioned in subsection (1) of this section.

(3) For the purpose of this section a payment which constitutes payment of, or of a quarterly or half-yearly instalment of, an annual subscription to a club, or which constitutes payment of an entrance subscription for membership of a club, shall not be taken to be a charge made as mentioned in subsection (1) of this section:

Provided that this subsection shall not apply to a club unless it is shown that the club is so constituted and conducted, in respect of membership and otherwise, as not to be of a temporary character, and, in relation to an entrance subscription, shall not apply unless it is shown that the payment is not made in respect of temporary membership of the club.

(4) The preceding provisions of this section shall have effect subject to section 40[2] of this Act.
[Gaming Act 1968, s 3.]

---

1. See s 1, ante.
2. By s 40 a small charge may be made by members' clubs and miners' welfare institutes. By virtue of the provisions of s 52(7), post, it is immaterial whether the charge or levy is compulsory, customary or voluntary; and by the Gaming Clubs (Prohibition of Gratuities) Regulations 1970, SI 1970/1644, the holder of a licence under Pt II of the Act and any member of staff may not accept from a member or guest any gratuity in respect of gaming to which Pt II of the Act applies.
3. The onus of proof will be on the defendant; but see *R v Carr-Briant* [1943] KB 607, [1943] 2 All ER 156, 107 JP 167, in which it was held that a defendant who availed himself of a statutory defence was not required to establish the defence "beyond a reasonable doubt", but according to probability.

8–13383   4. No levy on stakes or winnings.   Without prejudice to the generality of section 3 of this Act, no gaming to which this Part of this Act applies shall take place where a levy[1] is charged on any of the stakes or on the winnings[2] of any of the players, whether by way of direct payment or deduction, or by the exchange of tokens at a lower rate than the rate at which they were issued, or by any other means.
[Gaming Act 1968, s 4.]

---

1. By s 40 a small charge may be made by members' clubs and miners' welfare institutes. By virtue of the provisions of s 52(7), post, it is immaterial whether the charge or levy is compulsory, customary or voluntary; and by the Gaming Clubs (Prohibition of Gratuities) Regulations 1970, SI 1970/1644, the holder of a licence under Part II of the Act and any member of staff may not accept from a member or guest any gratuity in respect of gaming to which Part II of the Act applies.
2. Defined in s 52(1) post.

8–13384   5. Gaming in public places.   (1) No person shall take part in gaming[1] to which this Part of this Act applies—

(*a*) in any street, or
(*b*) (subject to the next following section) in any other place to which, whether on payment or otherwise, the public have access.

(2) *Repealed.*
(3) For the purpose of this section—

(*a*) "street" includes any bridge, road, lane, footway, subway, square, court, alley or passage, whether a thoroughfare or not, which is for the time being open to the public, and, in the application of this section to Scotland, includes also any common close or common stair; and
(*b*) the doorways and entrances of premises abutting upon, and any ground adjoining and open to, a street shall be treated as forming part of the street.
[Gaming Act 1968, s 5 as amended by the Police and Criminal Evidence Act 1984, Sch 7.]

---

1. Defined in s 52(1), post.
2. See s 1, ante.

8–13385   6. General provisions as to gaming on premises licensed for retail sale of liquor.
(1) The restriction imposed by section 5(1) of this Act does not apply—

(*a*) to the playing of dominoes or cribbage on any premises to which this section applies, or (*b*) in the case of any particular premises to which this section applies, to the playing of any other game which is authorised to be played on those premises by an order under subsection (3) of this section which is for the time being in force.

(2) This section applies to any premises in England and Wales in respect of which there is in force a premises licence authorising the supply of alcohol for consumption on the premises.

(2A) This section also applies to any premises in Scotland in respect of which a hotel licence or public house licence under the Licensing (Scotland) Act 1976 is in force.

(3) On the application—

(*a*) of the holder of the licence which has effect in respect of any premises to which this section applies,

(*b*) *Repealed*,

the relevant licensing authority, or, in Scotland, the licensing board for the licensing area in which the premises are situated, may by order[1] authorise the playing on those premises of a game specified in the order, other than dominoes and cribbage.

(4) In respect of any premises to which this section applies the relevant licensing authority, or, in Scotland, the licensing board for the licensing area in which the premises are situated, may by order[1] impose such requirements or restrictions with respect to gaming by the playing of dominoes or cribbage, or of any game authorised by virtue of subsection (3) of this section, in a part of those premises to which the public have access as the authority or board may consider necessary to secure that any such gaming in that part of the premises does not take place—

(*a*) for high stakes, or

(*b*) in such circumstances as to constitute an inducement to persons to resort to the premises primarily for the purpose of taking part in any such gaming.

(5) Where an order under subsection (3) or subsection (4) of this section has been made by a licensing authority or a licensing board, the authority or board may at any time revoke or vary the order by a subsequent order.

(6) On making any order under this section the relevant licensing authority or the licensing board shall give notice of the making of the order—

(*a*) to the holder of the licence,

(*b*) *Repealed*,

and shall send a copy of the notice to the chief officer of police . . . for each police area in which the premises are situated; and any such order shall come into force on the giving of the notice to the holder of the licence . . . and, subject to any subsequent order revoking or varying it, shall continue in force so long as the premises continue to be premises to which this section applies.

(7) Nothing in this section, or in any order made under this section, shall be construed as affecting the operation of sections 2 to 4 of this Act in relation to gaming on any premises to which this section applies.

(7A) A function conferred by this section on a licensing authority is, for the purposes of section 7 of the Licensing Act 2003 (exercise and delegation by licensing authority of licensing functions), to be treated as a licensing function within the meaning of that Act.

(8) In this section—

"licensing area" has the same meaning as in the Licensing (Scotland) Act 1976,

"licensing authority" and "premises licence" have the same meaning as in the Licensing Act 2003,

"relevant licensing authority", in relation to premises in respect of which a premises licence has effect, means the authority determined in relation to those premises in accordance with section 12 of that Act, and

"supply of alcohol" has the meaning given in section 14 of that Act.

[Gaming Act 1968, s 6, as amended by the Licensing (Scotland) Act 1976, Sch 7, the Statute Law (Repeals) Act 1986, Sch 1 and the Licensing Act 2003, Sch 6. Words omitted relate to Scotland.]

---

1. The first effect of this section is to release on-licensed premises from the general restriction on gaming (imposed by s 5) if the gaming is dominoes or cribbage. The second effect is to allow a licensee to apply to the (liquor) licensing justices for other games to be played. The third effect is to allow the justices to impose by order requirements or restrictions on any game played on the premises under the section; no procedure is prescribed leading to the making of an order, but it is suggested that no requirements or restrictions should be imposed until the licensee has been given an opportunity of being heard. It is intended that no gaming should be allowed under this section for high stakes *or* if it takes place so as to be an inducement to persons to resort to the premises. Therefore, the functions of the licensing justices under this section should not conflict with the functions of the "licensing authority" under the Act (the Betting Licensing Committee). Thus, the licensing justices will deal only with the limited gaming if any, desired by customers of the licensed premises, and not with gaming of a nature that it will attract people to the premises to participate in the gaming.

8–13386   7. Special provisions as to persons under 18.   (1) No person under eighteen shall take part in gaming to which this Part of this Act applies on any premises to which section 6 of this Act applies.

(2) Neither the holder of the licence which has effect in respect of premises to which section 6

applies, nor anybody employed by him, may knowingly allow a person under 18 to take part on those premises in gaming to which this Part applies.

(3), (4) *Repealed.*

[Gaming Act 1968, s 7 as amended by the Statute Law (Repeals) Act 1986, Sch 1 and the Licensing Act 2003, Sch 6.]

---

1. It has been held that a person acts "knowingly" when, intending what is happening, he deliberately looks the other way (*Ross v Moss* [1965] 2 QB 396, [1965] 3 All ER 145, 129 JP 537).

8-13387   8. Offences under Part I[1]**.** (1) If any gaming takes place in contravention[2] of any of the provisions of sections 2 to 4 of this Act, every person concerned in the organisation or management of the gaming shall be guilty of an offence.

(2) For the purposes of the preceding subsection any person who takes part in procuring the assembly of the players shall be taken to be concerned in the organisation of the gaming.

(3) Without prejudice to the preceding provisions of this section, where any gaming takes place on any premises, or in any vessel or vehicle, in contravention of any of the provisions of sections 2 to 4 of this Act, any person who, knowing or having reasonable cause to suspect that the premises, vessel or vehicle would be used for gaming in contravention of any of those provisions—

(*a*) allowed the premises, vessel or vehicle to be used for the purposes of gaming to which this Part of this Act applies, or

(*b*) let, or let on hire, the premises, vessel or vehicle, or otherwise made the premises, vessel or vehicle available, to any person by whom an offence under subsection (1) of this section is committed in connection with the gaming,

shall be guilty of an offence.

(4) Any person guilty of an offence under subsection (1) or subsection (3) of this section shall be liable—

(*a*) on summary conviction, to a fine not exceeding **the statutory maximum**;

(*b*) on conviction on indictment, to a fine or to imprisonment for a term not exceeding **two years** or to both.

(5) Any person who contravenes section 5(1) of this Act shall be guilty of an offence and liable on summary conviction to a fine not exceeding **level 4** on the standard scale.

(6) Any person who contravenes section 7(1) of this Act shall be guilty of an offence and liable on summary conviction to a fine not exceeding **level 1** on the standard scale.

(7) Any person who contravenes section 7(2) is guilty of an offence and—

(*a*) where the offence is committed in England and Wales, the person is liable on summary conviction to a fine not exceeding level 5 on the standard scale, and

(*b*) where the offence is committed in Scotland, the provisions of Schedule 5 to the Licensing (Scotland) Act 1976 are to have effect as they have effect in relation to a contravention of section 68(1) of that Act.

[Gaming Act 1968, s 8, as amended by the Criminal Law Act 1977, s 28 and Sch 6, the Criminal Justice Act 1982, ss 38 and 46, the Statute Law (Repeals) Act 1986, Sch 1 and the Licensing (Young Persons) Act 2000, s 2 and the Licensing Act 2003, Sch 6. Words omitted relate to Scotland.]

---

1. See s 43 for provision as to the personal liability of directors, etc, of bodies corporate; and s 44 for power of forfeiture.
2. "Contravention" is defined in s 55(1) of the Betting, Gaming and Lotteries Act 1963, and that definition is applied to this Act by s 50(8), post.
3. By virtue of this provision the penalty is that prescribed by s 169H and s 194(2): a fine not exceeding **Level 3** on the standard scale.

PART II

GAMING ON PREMISES LICENSED OR REGISTERED UNDER THIS PART OF THIS ACT

8-13388   9. Gaming to which Part II applies.   This Part of this Act applies to all gaming which takes place on premises in respect of which either—

(*a*) a licence under this Act is for the time being in force[1], or

(*b*) a club or a miners' welfare institute is for the time being registered under this Part of this Act,

and which is not gaming by means of any machine to which Part III of this Act applies.

[Gaming Act 1968, s 9.]

---

1. By reg 2 of the Gaming Clubs (Permitted Areas) Regulations 1971, this PART, post, a licence, other than one limited to bingo, bridge, or whist, or to bridge and whist, shall be refused if the premises are wholly or in part outside the areas specified in reg 3 of the Regulations.

8-13389   10. Gaming Board for Great Britain.   *Repealed.*

8-13390   11. Provisions as to licensing and registration.   (1) The provisions of Schedule 2 to this Act[1] shall have effect with respect to the licensing of premises under this Act.

(2) The provisions of Schedule 3[2] to this Act shall have effect with respect to the registration of clubs and miners' welfare institutes under this Part of this Act in England and Wales, and the provisions of Schedule 4 to this Act shall have effect with respect to the registration of clubs and miners' welfare institutes under this Part of this Act in Scotland.
[Gaming Act 1968, s 11.]

---

1. See also the Gaming Clubs (Licensing) Regulations 1969, and the Gaming Clubs (Permitted Areas) Regulations 1971, this PART, *post.*
2. See also the Gaming Act (Registration under Part II) Regulations 1969, this PART, *post.*

8–13391   12. Who may participate in gaming to which Part II applies[1]. (1) Where gaming to which this Part of this Act applies[2] takes place on any premises[3], then, subject to the following provisions of this section, no person shall participate in the gaming—

(*a*) if he is not present on the premises at the time when the gaming takes place there, or
(*b*) on behalf of another person who is not present on the premises at that time.

(2) Where gaming to which this Part of this Act applies[2] takes place on premises in respect of which a licence under this Act is for the time being in force, then, subject to the following provisions of this section, no person shall participate in the gaming unless either—

(*a*) he is a member of the club specified in the licence who, at the time when he begins to take part in the gaming, is eligible to take part in it, or
(*b*) he is a bona fide guest of a person who is a member of that club and who, at the time when the guest begins to take part in the gaming is eligible to take part in it,

and neither the holder of the licence nor any person acting on his behalf or employed on the premises in question shall participate in the gaming.

(3) For the purposes of subsection (2) of this section a member of the club specified in the licence is eligible to take part in the gaming at any particular time if[3]—

(*a*) he was admitted to membership of the club in pursuance of an application in writing—

  (i)   made by him in person on the premises, or
  (ii) sent by him to those premises,

  ; or

(*b*) since becoming a member, he has given notice in writing in person on the premises of his intention to take part in gaming on the premises—

  (i)   to the holder of the licence, or
  (ii) to a person acting on behalf of the holder of the licence,

  ; or

(*c*) since becoming a member, he has sent notice in writing of his intention to take part in gaming on those premises to the holder of the licence.

(4) Where gaming takes place on premises in respect of which a licence under this Act is for the time being in force, and consists of a game which involves playing or staking against a bank, nothing in subsection (1) or subsection (2) of this section shall prevent the holder of the licence or a person acting on his behalf from holding the bank or having a share or interest in it.

(5) For the purposes of subsection (2) of this section a person shall not be precluded from being a bona fide guest as mentioned in paragraph (*b*) of that subsection by reason only that he makes a payment which is lawfully required in accordance with section 14 of this Act.

(6) Where gaming to which this Part of this Act applies[4] takes place on premises in respect of which a club or miners' welfare institute is for the time being registered under this Part of this Act, no person shall participate in the gaming unless either—

(*a*) he is a member of the club or institute and there has been an interval of at least forty-eight hours between the time when he applied or was nominated for membership of the club or institute and the time when he begins to take part in the gaming, or
(*b*) he is a bona fide guest of a person who is a member of the club or institute and there has been an interval of at least forty-eight hours between the time when that person applied or was nominated for membership of the club or institute and the time when the guest begins to take part in the gaming;

and for the purposes of paragraph (*b*) of this subsection a person shall be taken not to be a bona fide guest if he himself makes any payment required for enabling him to obtain access to the premises, or to a part of them which is a part in which the gaming takes place, or if (apart from any stakes hazarded and the payment of any losses incurred by him in the gaming) he makes any payment in money or money's worth in respect of the gaming.

(7) For the purposes of this section a person participates in the gaming if—

(*a*) he takes part in the gaming as a player, or
(*b*) where the game involves playing or staking against a bank, he holds the bank or has a share or interest in it.

(8) The preceding provisions of this section shall have effect subject to section 20[5] of this Act.★
[Gaming Act 1968, s 12 amended by SI 1997/950, SI 1999/2136 and the Gambling Act 2005, Sch 16.]

★Repealed by the Gambling Act 2005, Sch 17 from a date to be appointed.
1. For modifications of s 12 in relation to a game of multiple bingo, see the Gaming (Bingo) Act 1985, s 2, post.
2. See s 9, ante.
3. See s 20, post, for special provisions as to bingo clubs.
4. See s 9, ante.
5. Section 20, post, contains special provisions as to bingo clubs.

8–13392   13. Restrictions on games to be played.   (1) Subject to the next following subsection, no gaming to which this Part of this Act applies[1] shall take place where any one or more of the conditions specified in section 2(1) of this Act are fulfilled[2].

(2) Regulations[3] made under this section may provide that the preceding subsection shall not have effect in relation to any gaming if the game played is of a kind specified in the regulations and is so played as to comply with such conditions (if any) as may be prescribed by the regulations in relation to that kind of game.
[Gaming Act 1968, s 13.]

---

1. See s 9 ante.
2. This Part of the Act applies to all gaming in clubs licensed or registered for gaming other than gaming by means of a machine. The effect of this section is to make all gaming unlawful unless (*a*) it is a game specified in Regulations made under s 13(2) and played under any conditions prescribed in those Regulations, or (*b*) it is gaming by means of a machine, or (*c*) it is gaming for prizes under s 21, post.
3. See the Gaming Act (Registration under Part II) Regulations 1969, this PART, post, for games which may be played in a club or institute registered under Pt II. In premises licensed under Pt II the games of roulette, dice, baccarat (whether it is baccarat banque, chemin de fer, punto banco or some other version), blackjack, casino stud poker, super pan 9, the big six, sic bo and three card poker may be played if played so as to comply with provisions specified in the Gaming Clubs (Banker's Games) Regulations 1994, SI 1994/2899 amended by SI 2000/597 and SI 2002/1130 and 1407. These Regulations do not affect any restriction contained in a licence under the Act as to the games which may be played on the premises.

8–13393   14. Charges for taking part in gaming.   (1) Subject to the following provisions of this section, section 3 of this Act shall have effect in relation to gaming to which this Part of this Act applies as it has effect in relation to gaming to which Part I of this Act applies[1].

(2) Regulations[2] made under this section may provide that charges which, apart from the regulations, would be prohibited by section 3 of this Act as applied by the preceding subsection may be made as follows, that is to say—

(*a*)   where the gaming takes place on premises in respect of which a licence under this Act is for the time being in force, such charges may, in such circumstances as may be prescribed by the regulations, be made if they comply with such conditions as are so prescribed;

(*b*)   where the gaming takes place on premises in respect of which a club or a miners' welfare institute is for the time being registered under this Part of this Act, such charges may, in such circumstances as may be prescribed by the regulations, be made at a rate not exceeding the rate so prescribed.

(3) Without prejudice to the application of section 51(3) of this Act, regulations made for the purposes of subsection (2) (*a*) of this section may enable different charges to be made in respect of different facilities (whether provided in different parts of the same premises or by way of different games or of the same game played at different tables or otherwise) or in respect of gaming facilities provided on any premises during different sessions of play.

(4) No charge shall be made in accordance with subsection (2) (*a*) of this section unless particulars of the charges and of the circumstances in which they are chargeable—

(*a*)   are displayed on the premises,

(*b*)   *repealed,*

and, if the regulations so provide, those particulars comprise such matters as the regulations prescribe and are displayed on the premises in a manner, and in positions, determined in accordance with the regulations.
[Gaming Act 1968, s 14, as amended by SI 2002/460.]

---

1. The effect of this section is that no charge may be made for gaming except (*a*) in clubs licensed for gaming, under conditions prescribed by Regulations, (*b*) in clubs registered for gaming, at a rate not exceeding that prescribed by Regulations, and (*c*) where the gaming is for prizes and complies with the conditions laid down in s 21, post. By the Gaming Clubs (Prohibition of Gratuities) Regulations 1970, SI 1970/1644, it is provided that where gaming to which Pt II of the Act applies takes place in premises licensed under that Part neither the holder of the licence nor any person employed on the premises shall accept any gratuity in respect of that gaming.
2. See the Gaming Act (Registration under Part II) Regulations 1969 and the Gaming Clubs (Hours and Charges) Regulations 1984, this PART, post.

8–13394   15. Levy on stakes or winnings.   (1) Subject to the next following subsection, section 4 of this Act shall have effect in relation to gaming to which this Part of this Act applies as it has effect in relation to gaming to which Part I of this Act applies[1].

(2) Regulations made under this section may provide that, where any gaming to which this Part of this Act applies takes place on premises in respect of which a licence under this Act is for the time being in force, a levy, of such amount or calculated in such manner as may be prescribed, may in prescribed circumstances be charged on the stakes or on the winnings of the players.
[Gaming Act 1968, s 15.]

1. The effect of this section is that no levy may be charged on stakes or winnings in a club registered for gaming and that such a levy may be charged in a club licensed for gaming only in the circumstances prescribed by Regulations. See also note 1 to s 4, *ante*.

8–13395   16. Provision of credit for gaming.   (1) Subject to subsections (2) to (2A) of this section, where gaming to which this Part of this Act applies takes place on premises in respect of which a licence under this Act is for the time being in force, neither the holder of the licence nor any person acting on his behalf or under any arrangement with him shall make any loan or otherwise provide or allow to any person any credit,[1] or release[2], or discharge on another person's behalf, the whole or part of any debt—

(a)   for enabling any person to take part in the gaming, or

(b)   in respect of any losses incurred by any person in the gaming.

(2) Neither the holder of the licence nor any person acting on his behalf or under any arrangement with him shall accept a cheque and give in exchange for it cash or tokens for enabling any person to take part in the gaming unless the following conditions are fulfilled, that is to say—

(a)   the cheque is not a post-dated cheque, and

(b)   it is exchanged for cash to an amount equal to the amount for which it is drawn[3], or is exchanged for tokens at the same rate as would apply if cash, to the amount for which the cheque is drawn, were given in exchange for them;

but, where those conditions are fulfilled, the giving of cash or tokens in exchange for a cheque shall not be taken to contravene subsection (1) of this section.

(2ZA) Neither the holder of the licence nor any person acting on his behalf or under any arrangement with him shall accept a debit card payment and give in exchange for it cash or tokens for enabling any person to take part in the gaming unless the following conditions are fulfilled, that is to say—

(a)   the payment is exchanged for cash to an amount equal to the amount of the payment, or is exchanged for tokens at the same rate as would apply if cash, to the amount of the payment, were given in exchange for them, and

(b)   the payment has been authorised by the holder of the card and by or on behalf of the issuer of the card;

but where those conditions are fulfilled, the giving of cash or tokens in exchange for a debit card payment shall not be taken to contravene subsection (1) above.

(2A) Neither the holder of a licence under this Act nor any person acting on his behalf or under any arrangement with him shall permit to be redeemed any cheque (not being a cheque which has been dishonoured) accepted in exchange for cash or tokens for enabling any person to take part in gaming to which this Part of this Act applies unless the following conditions are fulfilled, that is to say—

(a)   the cheque is redeemed by the person from whom it was accepted giving in exchange for it cash, or tokens, or a substitute cheque or a debit card payment, or any combination of these, to an amount equal to the amount of the redeemed cheque or (where two or more cheques are redeemed) the aggregate amount of the redeemed cheques;

(b)   it is redeemed during the playing session in which it was accepted, or within thirty minutes after the end of the session;

(c)   where a substitute cheque is given in whole or in part exchange for the redeemed cheque the substitute cheque is not a post-dated cheque;

(d)   where tokens are given in whole or in part exchange for the redeemed cheque, the value of each token is equal to the amount originally given in exchange for it or, if the token was won in the gaming, the value it represented when won; and

(e)   where a debit card payment is given in whole or in part exchange for the redeemed cheque, the payment has been authorised by the holder of the card and by or on behalf of the issuer of the card;

but, where those conditions are fulfilled, the return of a redeemed cheque in exchange for cash, or tokens, or a substitute cheque or a debit card payment, or any combination of these, shall not be taken to contravene subsection (1) of this section.

(3) Where the holder of a licence under this Act, or a person acting on behalf of or under any arrangement with the holder of such a licence, accepts a cheque in exchange for cash or tokens to be used by a player in gaming to which this Part of this Act applies or a substitute cheque, he shall not more than two banking days later cause the cheque to be delivered to a bank for payment or collection.

(3A) Subsection (3) of this section shall not apply to a redeemed cheque.

(3B) Where the holder of a licence under this Act, or a person acting on behalf of or under any arrangement with the holder of such a licence, accepts a debit card payment in exchange for cash or tokens to be used by a player in gaming to which this Part of this Act applies, or a substitute debit card payment, he shall not more than two banking days later do whatever is required under his arrangements with the issuer of the card to secure that he is credited with the amount of the payment.

(4) Nothing in the Gaming Act 1710, the Gaming Act 1835, the Gaming Act 1845, or the Gaming Act 1892, shall affect the validity of, or any remedy in respect of, any cheque or debit card payment which is accepted in exchange for cash or tokens to be used by a player in gaming to which this Part of this Act applies or any substitute cheque or substitute debit card payment.

(5) In this section "banking day" means a day which is a business day in accordance with section 92 of the Bills of Exchange Act 1882.

"debit card" means a card which may be used as a means of payment under arrangements which do not provide for the extension of credit to the cardholder, but provide for amounts paid by means of the card to be debited to a specified account in his name (or in his name jointly with one or more others);

"debit card payment" means a payment by means of a debit card;

"playing session" means a continuous period during one day, or two consecutive days, throughout which gaming is permitted by or under this Act to take place on premises in respect of which a licence under this Act is for the time being in force;

"redeemed cheque" means a cheque accepted in fulfilment of the conditions specified in subsection (2) of this section and returned to the person from whom it was accepted in fulfilment of the conditions specified in subsection (2A) of this section;

"substitute cheque" means a cheque accepted in accordance with subsection (2A) of this section by either the holder of a licence under this Act or a person acting on behalf of or under any arrangement with the holder of such a licence;

"substitute debit card payment" means a debit card payment accepted in accordance with subsection (2A) of this section by either the holder of a licence under this Act or a person acting on behalf of or under any arrangement with the holder of such a licence.

[Gaming Act 1968, s 16 as amended by the Gaming (Amendment) Act 1986, s 1 and SI 1997/1075.]

---

1. The repeated acceptance of cheques from persons whose previous cheques had been dishonoured, in circumstances in which the holder of the licence knew that those cheques would not be honoured on first presentation, has been held to amount to granting unlawful credit within s 16 (*R v Crown Court at Knightsbridge, ex p Marcrest Ltd* [1983] 1 All ER 1148, [1983] 1 WLR 300).

2. When a cheque is given by a customer to enable him to take part in gaming and is subsequently dishonoured, *prima facie* a debt has been incurred in respect of losses in the gaming and, unless that *prima facie* case can be destroyed, the acceptance of a sum less than the face value of the dishonoured cheque amounts to the release of part of a debt in respect of losses incurred in the gaming (*R v Crown Court at Knightsbridge, ex p Marcrest Ltd* [1983] 1 All ER 1148, [1983] 1 WLR 300).

3. See *Ladup Ltd v Shaikh* [1983] QB 225, [1982] 3 WLR 172.

8–13396 17. Exclusion of persons under 18. Except as provided by s 20 or s 21[1] of this Act, no person under eighteen shall be present in any room while gaming to which this Part of this Act applies takes place in that room.

[Gaming Act 1968, s 17.]

---

1. These sections contain special provisions as to bingo clubs and as to gaming for prizes; and provide that s 17 shall not prevent persons under 18 from being present while bingo is being played or where gaming for prizes takes place on bingo club premises, provided they do not take part in the gaming as players.

8–13397 18. Gaming on Sundays. (1) In England and Wales no gaming shall take place on any Sunday[1] between the hours of four in the morning and two in the afternoon on any premises in respect of which a licence under this Act is for the time being in force.

(2) *Relates to Scotland.*

(3) *Repealed.*

[Gaming Act 1968, s.18 as amended by the Gaming (Amendment) Act 1987, s 1.]

---

1. Hours of gaming generally may be controlled by Regulations made under s 22(4), post, and by the licensing authority through the imposition of restrictions on the hours of gaming in respect of particular premises under para 24 of Sch 2, post.

8–13398 19. Approval by Board of certain persons connected with gaming. (1) Where gaming to which this Part of this Act applies takes place on premises in respect of which a licence under this Act is for the time being in force, no person shall in pursuance of any service agreement perform any function to which this subsection applies unless a certificate has been issued by the Board, and is for the time being in force, certifying that he has been approved by the Board under this section in respect of the performance of that function on those premises[1].

(2) Subsection (1) of this section applies to any function which is performed on the premises in question and consists of[2]—

(*a*) taking part in the gaming as a player, or

(*b*) assisting the gaming by operating or handling any apparatus, cards, tokens or other articles used in the gaming, or

(*c*) issuing, receiving or recording cash or tokens used in the gaming or cheques given in respect of any such cash or tokens or in respect of sums won or lost in the gaming, or

(*d*) watching (otherwise than as manager, organiser or supervisor) the gaming or the performance by any person in pursuance of any service agreement of any function falling within paragraphs (*a*) to (*c*) of this subsection.

(3) In the case of any premises in respect of which a licence under this Act is for the time being in force, the Board may serve a notice under this subsection on any person (whether the holder of the licence or not) appearing to the Board to be acting in any capacity as manager, organiser or supervisor in relation to the gaming or in relation to persons who in pursuance of service agreements perform any functions to which subsection (1) of this section applies.

(4) A notice served under the last preceding subsection in the case of any premises shall require the person on whom it is served, before the end of such period (not being less than twenty-one days from the date of service of the notice) as may be specified in the notice, to obtain the approval of the Board to his acting in relation to those premises in any such capacity as is mentioned in the last preceding subsection; and, after the end of that period, the person on whom the notice is served shall not act in any such capacity in relation to those premises unless a certificate has been issued by the Board, and is for the time being in force, certifying that he has been approved by the Board under this section for acting in that capacity in relation to those premises.

(5) The provisions of Part I of Schedule 5 to this Act shall have effect with respect to applications to the Board for certificates of approval under this section and with respect to the issue and revocation of such certificates.

(6) An application made to the Board for the issue of a certificate of approval shall, in such circumstances and to such extent as is provided by Part II of Schedule 5 to this Act, have effect for the purposes of this section as if it were a certificate of approval issued by the Board, and for the time being in force, under this section.

(7) In this section "serving agreement" means any contract of service or of apprenticeship and any contract or arrangement for the rendering of services which is not a contract of service or of apprenticeship.

[Gaming Act 1968, s 19.]

---

1. One certificate may be issued in relation to a number of premises (Sch 5, para 4).

2. This does not apply to bingo clubs, as to which see s 20(7), post, and Regulations made thereunder.

8–13399   20. Special provisions as to bingo clubs.   (1) This section applies to any club specified in a licence under this Act where, by virtue of any restrictions which, on the grant or renewal of the licence, were imposed under paragraph 25 of Schedule 2 to this Act and are for the time being in force, gaming to which Part II of this Act applies is limited to the playing of bingo; and in this Part of the Act "bingo club premises" means premises in respect of which a licence under this Act is for the time being in force, where the club specified in the licence is one to which this section applies.

(2) Where a game of bingo is played simultaneously on different bingo club premises in circumstances where—

(*a*) all the players take part in the same game at the same time and all are present at that time on one or other of those premises, and

(*b*) the draw takes place on one or other of those premises while the game is being played, and

(*c*) any claim of one of the players to have won is indicated to all the other players before the next number is called,

then, if the conditions specified in the next following subsection are fulfilled, section 12(1) of this Act shall have effect in relation to that game as if those different premises were the same premises.

(3) The conditions referred to in subsection (2) of this section, in relation to a game of bingo played simultaneously on different premises, are that—

(*a*) the aggregate amount paid to players as winnings in respect of that game does not exceed the aggregate amount of the stakes hazarded by the players in playing that game, and

(*b*) the aggregate amount paid to players as winnings in respect of that game, together with the aggregate amount paid to players as winnings in respect of all games of bingo which, in the circumstances specified in that subsection, have previously been played in the same week and have been so played on premises consisting of, or including any of, those premises, does not exceed £500,000.

Provided that the Secretary of State may by order provide that this subsection shall have effect with the substitution, for the reference to £500,000, of a reference to such other sum as may be specified in the order.

(4) Where subsection (2) of this section has effect in relation to a game of bingo played simultaneously on different premises, then, for the purposes of the application of subsections (2) and

(3) of section 12 of this Act in relation to each of those premises, regard shall be had only to such of the players as are present on those particular premises.

(5) Section 12(3) shall not apply in relation to any club to which this section applies.

(6) In relation to gaming which takes place on bingo club premises section 17 of this Act shall not have effect so as to prevent persons under eighteen from being present in any room while a game of bingo is played there, if they do not take part in the game as players.

(7) In relation to any bingo club premises, section 19 of this Act shall have effect as if, in subsection (2) of that section, for the words from "and consists of" to the end of the subsection, there were substituted the words "and is a function of a kind prescribed by regulations made for the purposes of this subsection".

(8) Without prejudice to the operation (where applicable) of subsections (2) to (4) of this section, the aggregate amount paid to players as winnings in respect of all games of bingo[1] played in any one week on any particular bingo club premises shall not exceed the aggregate amount of the stakes hazarded by the players in playing those games by more than £20,000:

Provided that the Secretary of State may by order provide that this subsection shall have effect with the substitution, for the reference to £20,000, of a reference to such other sum as may be specified in the order.

(9) In this section "week" means a period of seven days beginning with Monday, any reference to an aggregate amount shall be construed as including a reference to an aggregate value in money's worth, and any reference to an aggregate amount paid shall be construed accordingly.*

[Gaming Act 1968, s 20, as amended by the Gaming (Amendment) Act 1980, s 1, the Deregulation (Casinos) Orders 1997, SI 1997/950 and 1999, SI 1999/2136, the Gaming Act (Variation of Monetary Limits) Order 2002, SI 2002/1904 and the Gambling Act 2005, Sch 16.]

 ***Repealed by the Gambling Act 2005, Sch 17 from a date to be appointed.**
 1. Except a game of bingo which constitutes gaming to which s 21 applies; see s 21(6), post. Section 20(8) does not apply to games of multiple bingo (Gaming (Bingo) Act 1985, s 2, post).

8–13400 21. Special provisions as to gaming for prizes. (1) This section applies to any gaming which (being gaming to which this Part of this Act applies) is gaming for prizes in respect of which the conditions specified in the next following subsection are fulfilled.

(2) Those conditions are that—

(*a*) the amount paid by any person for any one chance to win a prize does not exceed 50p[1];

(*b*) the aggregate amount taken by way of the sale of chances in any one determination of winners (if any) of prizes does not exceed £500.00, and the sale of those chances and the declaration of the result take place on the same day and on the premises on which, and at the time when, the game is played;

(*c*) no money prize exceeding £25 is distributed or offered;

(*d*) the winning of, or the purchase of a chance to win, a prize does not entitle any person (whether subject to a further payment by him or not) to any further opportunity to win money or money's worth by taking part in any other gaming or in any lottery; and

(*e*) the aggregate amount or value of the prizes on any one determination of winners does not exceed £500.00[1].

(3) Section 13 of this Act shall not have effect in relation to any gaming to which this section applies which takes place on premises in respect of which a licence under this Act is for the time being in force and, in relation to any such gaming, section 3 of this Act, as applied by section 14 of this Act, shall not be taken to be contravened by reason only that a person pays for a chance to win a prize.

(4) Where any gaming to which this section applies takes place on any bingo club premises, section 17 of this Act shall not have effect so as to prevent persons under eighteen from being present in any room on those premises while any such gaming takes place there, if they do not take part in the gaming as players.

(5) Where on the grant or renewal of a licence under this Act in respect of any premises the licensing authority impose restrictions under paragraph 25 of Schedule 2 to this Act whereby gaming on those premises is limited to a particular game or games, those restrictions, in so far as they so limit the gaming, shall not have effect in relation to any gaming to which this section applies.

(6) Where a game of bingo is played for prizes on any bingo club premises, and constitute gaming to which this section applies, the prizes won in that game shall be disregarded for the purposes of section 20(8) of this Act.

(7) No account shall be taken of subsection (5) of this section for the purpose of determining—

(*a*) whether a club is one to which section 20 of this Act applies, or

(*b*) whether any premises are bingo club premises, or

(*c*) whether, for the purposes of Schedule 2 to this Act, a licence under this Act is a bingo club licence.

(8) The Secretary of State may by order direct that any paragraph of subsection (2) of this section which is specified in the order and which specifies a sum shall have effect as if, for that sum, there were substituted such other sum as may be specified in the order.

[Gaming Act 1968, s 21, as amended by the Gaming Act (Variation of Monetary Limits) Order 2002, SI 2002/1904.]

8–13401   22. Further powers to regulate licensed club premises.   (1) The Secretary of State may make regulations[1] requiring the holder of a licence under this Act in respect of any premises—

(a)   to display, in such manner and in such position on those premises as may be prescribed by the regulations, the rules in accordance with which any game is to be played on the premises, either generally or in any particular circumstances;

(b)   to make, and to retain during such period as may be prescribed by the regulations, such records as may be so prescribed with respect to cheques and debit card payments (within the meaning of section 16 of this Act) given in exchange for cash or tokens to be used by players in gaming on those premises and with respect to redeemed cheques, substitute cheques and substitute debit card payments within the meaning of that section, and to provide such verification of those records as may be so prescribed.

(c)   during such period as may be so prescribed—

(i)   to keep those records or (if the regulations so provide) copies of them on the premises; or

(ii)   where those records are kept by means of a computer to secure that the records are accessible from the premises and that the information comprised in those records can readily be produced in a form in which it can be taken away and in which it is visible and legible.

(2)   The Secretary of State may make regulations imposing such prohibitions, restrictions or other requirements (in addition to those imposed by or under the preceding provisions of this Part of this Act) as may appear to the Secretary of State to be requisite—

(a)   for securing that gaming on any premises in respect of which a licence under this Act is for the time being in force is fairly and properly conducted, or

(b)   for preventing the use of any indirect means for doing anything which, if done directly, would be a contravention of this Part of this Act or of any regulations made thereunder.

(3)   The Secretary of State may by regulations[2] provide that a licensing authority—

(a)   shall refuse to grant or renew a licence under this Act in such circumstances as may be prescribed by the regulations, or

(b)   may refuse to grant or renew such a licence in such circumstances as may be so prescribed, without prejudice to any other grounds on which the grant or renewal could be refused apart from the regulations, or

(c)   shall, in such circumstances as may be so prescribed, impose such restrictions under paragraph 25 of Schedule 2 to this Act as the regulations may require.

(4)   Without prejudice to section 18 of this Act or to any powers exercisable by virtue of the preceding provisions of this section or by virtue of Schedule 2 to this Act, the Secretary of State may by regulations[3] impose restrictions with respect to the hours during which gaming will be permitted to take place on premises in respect of which a licence under this Act is for the time being in force.
[Gaming Act 1968, s 22 as amended by the Gaming (Amendment) Act 1986, s 2, the Gaming (Amendment) Act 1990, Sch and SI 1997/1075.]

---

1. The Gaming (Records of Cheques) Regulations 1997, SI 1997/1072, have been made.
2. The Gaming Clubs (Licensing) Regulations 1969, SI 1969/1110 amended by SI 2002/1910 have been made.
3. See the Gaming Clubs (Hours and Charges) Regulations 1984, this PART, post.

8–13402   23. Offences under Part II.   (1) Subject to the following provisions of this section, if any of the provisions of sections 12 to 20 of this Act, or of any regulations made under subsection (1), subsection (2) or subsection (4) of section 22 of this Act, are contravened[1] in relation to any premises—

(a)   the holder of the licence, if they are premises in respect of which a licence under this Act is for the time being in force, or

(b)   every officer of the club or institute, if they are premises in respect of which a club or a miners' welfare institute is for the time being registered under this Part of this Act,

shall be guilty of an offence[2].

(2)   Without prejudice to the preceding subsection, but subject to subsection (3) of this section, if any such provisions as are mentioned in the preceding subsection are contravened[1] in relation to any gaming (or, in the case of the provisions of section 16(3) of this Act, are contravened in relation to a cheque accepted in exchange for cash or tokens to be used by a player in any gaming), every person concerned in the organisation or management of the gaming shall be guilty of an offence[2].

(3)   Where a person is charged with an offence under either of the preceding subsections in respect of a contravention[1] of any such provisions as are mentioned in subsection (1) of this section, it shall be a defence for him to prove—

(a)   that the contravention occurred without his knowledge, and

(b) that he exercised all such care as was reasonable in the circumstances to secure that the provisions in question would not be contravened.

(4) Any person guilty of an offence under subsection (1) or subsection (2) of this section shall be liable—

(a) on summary conviction to a fine not exceeding **the statutory maximum**.

(b) on conviction on indictment, to a fine or to imprisonment for a term not exceeding **two years** or to both.

(5) Where, on the grant or renewal of a licence under this Act in respect of any premises, or on registering or renewing the registration of a club or a miners' welfare institute under this Part of this Act, the licensing authority or sheriff imposed any restrictions under paragraph 24 or paragraph 25 of Schedule 2, under paragraph 11 of Schedule 3 or under paragraph 13 of Schedule 4 to this Act, subsections (1) to (3) of this section shall have effect in relation to any contravention of those restrictions as they have effect in relation to any contravention of the provisions of sections 12 to 20 of this Act.

(6) If any person, for the purpose of obtaining, for himself or for any other person, a certificate of approval under section 19 of this Act, or the reinstatement of such a certificate after it has been revoked by the Board—

(a) makes a statement which he knows to be false in a material particular, or

(b) recklessly makes a statement which is false in a material particular,

he shall be guilty of an offence and liable on summary conviction to a fine not exceeding **level 4** on the standard scale.

[Gaming Act 1968, s 23, as amended by the Criminal Law Act 1977, s 28 and the Criminal Justice Act 1982, ss 38 and 46.]

---

1. See s 55(1) of the Betting, Gaming and Lotteries Act 1963, for definition of "contravention" and cognate expressions.
2. For penalty, see sub-s (4), infra, and for power to make disqualification order, see s 24, post. See also note 9 to s 2(1) of the Lotteries and Amusements Act 1976, post.

8–13403   24. Power of court to make disqualification order on conviction of certain offences.
(1) Where a person is convicted of an offence committed in respect of any premises under subsection (1) or subsection (2) of section 23 of this Act (including either of those subsections as applied by subsection (5) of that section), the court by which he is convicted may make a disqualification order[1] under this section prohibiting a licence under this Act from being held in respect of those premises during a period specified in the order.

(2) The period specified in a disqualification order under this section shall not exceed five years from the date on which the order comes into force.

(3) Where a disqualification order under this section is made, any licence within the prohibition obtained before the order is made or before it takes effect shall by virtue of the order be cancelled as from the time when the order takes effect, and any such licence obtained after the order takes effect shall be null and void.

[Gaming Act 1968, s 24.]

---

1. See Sch 2, para 35, for power of Gaming Board to revoke certificate of consent; and paras 36–47 for power of licensing authority to cancel licence. See also Sch 2, para 48, for power of court to cancel licence on conviction of an offence under the Finance Act 1966, Sch 3, in respect of a contravention of s 13 of that Act, or certain offences under the Betting and Gaming Duties Act 1981.

8–13404   25. Supplementary provisions as to disqualification orders.   (1) A disqualification order made under section 24 of this Act by a court in England or Wales—

(a) shall not take effect until the end of the period within which the person on whose conviction the order was made can appeal against the conviction or against the making of the order, and

(b) if he so appeals, shall not take effect until the appeal has been determined or abandoned.

(2) The person on whose conviction a disqualification order was made under section 24 of this Act by a court in Scotland may, without prejudice to any other form of appeal under any rule of law, appeal against the order as against the conviction; and the disqualification order—

(a) shall not take effect until the end of the period of fourteen days commencing with the date on which the order was made; and

(b) if an appeal against the order or the said conviction is taken within the said period, shall not take effect until the date when that appeal is determined or abandoned or deemed to have been abandoned.

(3) A court shall not make an order under that section prohibiting the holding of a licence in respect of premises specified in the order, unless an opportunity has been given to any person interested in the premises and applying to be heard by the court to show cause why the order should not be made.

(4) At any time while such a disqualification order is in force, the court by which the order was

made[1], on an application made by any person affected by the order, may revoke the order or vary it by reducing any period of prohibition specified in the order.

(5) Where on an application made under subsection (4) of this section the relief asked for is or includes the revocation or variation of a prohibition imposed by the order on the holding of a licence in respect of any premises, a copy of the application shall be served on the chief officer of police, or, in Scotland, the chief constable, for the police area in which the premises are situated.

(6) For the purposes of subsection (4) of this section, a disqualification order under section 24 of this Act made by a court of quarter sessions on appeal from the decision of a magistrates' court shall be treated as having been made by that magistrates' court.

[Gaming Act 1968, s 25.]

---

1. But note the effect of sub-s (6) in respect of an order made on appeal to the Crown Court.

PART III

GAMING BY MEANS OF MACHINES

Introductory

8–13405   **26. Scope of Part III.**   (1) This Part of this Act applies[1] to any machine which—

    (*a*)   is constructed or adapted for playing a game of chance by means of the machine, and

    (*b*)   has a slot or other aperture for the insertion of money or money's worth.

(2) In the preceding subsection the reference to playing a game of chance by means of a machine includes playing a game of chance partly by means of a machine and partly by other means if (but only if) the element of chance in the game is provided by means of the machine.

(3) In this Part of this Act "charge for play" means an amount paid in money or money's worth by or on behalf of a player in order to play one or more games by means of a machine to which this Part of this Act applies.

[Gaming Act 1968, s 26, as amended by SI 2003/3275.]

---

1. See s 35, post, where the general restrictions on gaming by machine is stated. The general scheme of Pt III is to bring the sale, supply and maintenance of all gaming machines under the control of the Gaming Board, and to impose statutory restrictions on the terms and conditions of the sale, supply or maintenance of such machines. The fundamentally different types of gaming machine are recognised: (i) the gaming machine which may only be used (*a*) on licensed or registered premises, and of which not more than 2 may be made available on any such premises (s 31), or (*b*) at other premises for non-commercial entertainments (s 33); (ii) the amusement with prizes machine, which offers prizes within specified limits and which may be made available (*a*) on premises for which a permit is in force, (*b*) on premises licensed for gaming where the licensing authority has directed that such machines may be made available instead of gaming machines (under s 32), and (*c*) at a travelling showmen's pleasure fair (s 34); and (iii) machines which offer no prize other than another opportunity to play or the return of an amount not exceeding the amount of the stake (s 52(5)).

Sale, supply and maintenance of machines

8–13406   **27. General restrictions.**   (1) Except as provided by subsections (2) to (4) of this section, no person shall, whether as principal or as a servant or agent, sell or supply[1] a machine to which this Part of this Act applies unless—

    (*a*)   he is the holder of a certificate issued for the purposes of this subsection by the Board which is for the time being in force, or of a permit in respect of that machine which has been granted for the purposes of this subsection by the Board and is for the time being in force, or

    (*b*)   where he sells or supplies the machine as the servant or agent of another person, that other person is the holder of such a certificate or permit.

(2) The preceding subsection does not apply—

    (*a*)   to the sale of machines of any description to a person who carries on a business which consists of or includes selling or supplying machines of that description;

    (*b*)   to the sale or supply of a machine to a person buying or agreeing or proposing to buy it under a credit-sale agreement, or to the supply of a machine to a person as being a person hiring or agreeing or proposing to hire it under a hire-purchase agreement, where (in any such case) the person who is or is to be the seller or owner in relation to the agreement has at no time had possession of the machine and became or becomes the owner of it only for the purpose of entering into the agreement;

    (*c*)   to the sale or supply of a machine as scrap; or

    (*d*)   to any transaction whereby the premises in which a machine to which this Part of this Act applies is installed are sold or let and the machine is sold or supplied to the purchaser or tenant as part of the fixtures and fittings of the premises.

(3) Subject to the next following subsection, subsection (1) of this section does not apply to the sale or supply of a machine for use exclusively at a travelling showmen's pleasure fair[2] or for use exclusively on premises used or to be used—

    (*a*)   wholly or mainly for the provision of amusements by means of machines to which this Part of this Act applies, or (*b*) wholly or mainly for the purposes of a pleasure fair consisting wholly or mainly of amusements, or

(*c*) as a pleasure pier.

(4) The Secretary of State may by order direct that subsection (3) of this section shall cease to have effect, or shall have effect subject to such exceptions as may be specified in the order.

(5) No person acting as principal shall—

(*a*) undertake for valuable consideration to maintain the mechanism of a machine to which this Part of this Act applies, or

(*b*) cause or permit another person to enter into such an undertaking on his behalf,

unless the person so acting as principal is the holder of a certificate issued for the purposes of this subsection by the Board which is for the time being in force, or of a permit in respect of that machine which has been granted for the purposes of this subsection by the Board and is for the time being in force.

(6) The provisions of Schedule 6 to this Act[3] shall have effect with respect to the issue of certificates, and the grant of permits, for the purposes of subsections (1) and (5) of this section.

(7) In this section "credit-sale agreement" means an agreement for the sale of goods under which the whole or part of the purchase price is payable by instalments, and "hire-purchase agreement" has the meaning assigned to it by section 1 of the Hire-Purchase Act 1965, or, in the application of this section to Scotland, by section 1 of the Hire-Purchase (Scotland) Act 1965.

[Gaming Act 1968, s 27.]

1. See s 29 for application of this provision to concessionaries.
2. Defined in s 52(1), post.
3. By Sch 6 the Gaming Board may grant a certificate for the function of (*a*) selling or supplying machines to which Pt III of the Act applies, (*b*) maintaining such machines, or (*c*) selling or supplying and maintaining such machines (para 1); the Board is to have regard only to whether the applicant is a fit and proper person (para 2); the certificate expires after 5 years but may be renewed for periods of 5 years (para 3); the certificate may be revoked by the Board (para 4). The Board may grant a permit to sell, supply or maintain a specified machine which will be effective for a specified period (paras 7 and 8).

8–13407 28. Restrictions as to terms and conditions. (1) The Secretary of State may by regulations impose such restrictions as he may consider necessary or expedient with respect to the terms and conditions on which machines to which this Part of this Act applies may be sold or supplied or undertaken to be maintained.

(2) Without prejudice to any restrictions imposed by regulations under the preceding subsection, but subject to subsection (3) of this section, no person shall sell or supply[1], or shall undertake to maintain, a machine to which this Part of this Act applies on terms and conditions which are in any way dependent upon, or provide for any calculation by reference to, the extent to which, or the manner in which, that machine, or any other machine or equipment (whether a machine to which this Part of this Act applies or not), is used.

(3) Subsection (2) of this section shall not have effect in relation to the sale or supply of a machine for use exclusively at a travelling showmen's pleasure fair or for use exclusively on premises used or to be used as mentioned in paragraph (*a*), paragraph (*b*) or paragraph (*c*) of section 27(3) of this Act, or in relation to an undertaking to maintain a machine at any such pleasure fair or on any such premises:

Provided that the Secretary of State may by order direct that this subsection shall cease to have effect, or shall have effect subject to such exceptions as may be specified in the order.

(4) In this section "terms and conditions" includes any terms and conditions as to price, rent or any other payment.

[Gaming Act 1968, s 28.]

1. See s 29 for application of this provision to concessionnaires.

8–13408 29. Application of ss 27 and 28 to concessionnaires. For the purposes of sections 27 and 28 of this Act a person (other than a travelling showman) who, in pursuance of any concession, licence or other right granted to him, places a machine, or causes a machine to be placed, on premises which are not in his occupation shall be treated as supplying the machine at the time when it is placed on those premises.

[Gaming Act 1968, s 29.]

Use of machines for gaming on premises licensed or registered under this Act

8–13409 30. Registration under Part III. The provisions of Schedule 7 to this Act[1] shall have effect with respect to the registration of clubs and miners' welfare institutes under this Part of this Act in England and Wales . . .

[Gaming Act 1968, s 30. Words omitted relate to Scotland.]

1. See also the Gaming Act (Registration under Part III) Regulations 1969, this PART, post.

8–13410 31. Use of machines by virtue of licence or registration. (1) Subject to any direction given under section 32 of this Act, the following provisions of this section shall have effect[1] where any machine to which this Part of this Act applies is used for gaming on any premises in respect of which—

(*a*) a licence under this Act is for the time being in force, or

(*b*) a club or a miners' welfare institute is for the time being registered under Part II or under this Part of this Act.

(2) The maximum number of machines to which this Part of this Act applies which may be made available for gaming shall be—

(*a*) in the case of premises in respect of which a club or a miners' welfare institute is for the time being registered under Part II or under this Part of this Act, three,

(*b*) in the case of bingo club premises (as defined by section 20 of this Act), four, and

(*c*) in the case of any other premises in respect of which a licence under this Act is for the time being in force, twenty.

(3) The charge for play for playing a game once by means of any such machine on the premises shall not exceed 50p or such other sum as may be specified in an order[2] made by the Secretary of State for the purposes of this subsection.

(3A) Where any such machine on the premises is able to accept payment of the charge for play in any form other than cash, any object capable of being inserted into the machine to pay for a game or games must be redeemable in accordance with subsection (3B) of this section.

(3B) Any such object is redeemable in accordance with this subsection if—

(*a*) it is redeemable on demand at the premises where the machine is used for gaming at any time when a machine to which this Part of this Act applies is available for use for gaming at those premises;

(*b*) a payment for redeeming it must be made in cash or by cheque (or partly in cash and partly by cheque);

(*c*) any such payment must be of the appropriate amount.

(3C) The appropriate amount is—

$(A + B) - C$

where—

A is the amount paid by or on behalf of the player for the use of the object;

B is the amount of any prize credited to the object in accordance with subsection (5B) of this section;

C is the amount charged for one or more services, where the object has been used to pay for the services.

(3D) Subsections (3E) to (3H) of this section apply if—

(*a*) a player inserts into any such machine on the premises something which is recognised by the machine as having a value exceeding the highest coin value;

(*b*) the machine immediately holds to the player's credit an amount in respect of the thing ("the initial amount") for the purpose of paying the charge for play for playing games by means of the machine.

(3E) The initial amount must not exceed the higher of—

(*a*) the highest coin value, or

(*b*) the charge for playing a game once by means of the machine.

(3F) The machine must not hold any further amount to the player's credit for the purpose of paying the charge for play for playing games by means of the machine unless the player takes action in respect of the machine to indicate that he wishes to play, or continue to play, games by means of the machine.

(3G) The further amount held to the player's credit by virtue of subsection (3F) of this section must not exceed the higher of—

(*a*) the highest coin value, or

(*b*) the charge for playing a game once by means of the machine.

(3H) The highest coin value is the value of the highest denomination coin which, when the games are played—

(*a*) is legal tender in the part of the United Kingdom in which the premises are situated, and

(*b*) is in general circulation in that part of the United Kingdom.

(4) In respect of any one game played by means of such a machine on the premises no player or person claiming under a player shall receive, or shall be entitled to receive, any article, benefit or advantage other than—

(*a*) a prize delivered in the form of cash, or

(*b*) a prize delivered in a form specified in subsection (4A) of this section.

(4A) The form referred to in subsection (4) of this section is one which enables the person entitled to it to obtain its value—

(a)   in the form of cash or a cheque drawn in his favour (or partly in the form of cash and partly in the form of a cheque drawn in his favour), and

(b)   on demand at the premises where the machine is used for gaming at any time when a machine to which this Part of this Act applies is available for use for gaming at those premises.

(5) If an amount is prescribed for the purposes of this subsection, the value of the prize in respect of any one game played by means of the machine shall not exceed the amount so prescribed[3].

(5A) Subsections (5B) and (5C) of this section apply where a player or person claiming under a player is entitled to receive a prize in respect of a game played by means of such a machine.

(5B) The prize may be delivered by crediting any object which is permitted to be inserted into the machine to pay for a game or games by subsection (3A) of this section.

(5C) Despite subsection (4) of this section, the person entitled to the prize may choose to use all or part of its value to pay for one or more services at the premises at which the machine is used for gaming.

(6) If a percentage is prescribed for the purposes of this subsection, then on any premises in respect of which a licence under this Act is for the time being in force there shall not be any such machine which, in accordance with the way in which the machine is constructed, adapted or for the time being regulated, is designed to pay out less than that percentage of the aggregate value of the charges for play inserted in the machine.

(7) There shall be displayed on any such machine on any such premises as are mentioned in subsection (1) of this section—

(a)   a statement specifying the value of the prize (or, if there are different prizes, the value of each prize) which can be won by playing a game once by means of the machine;

(b)   if there are any special circumstances in which that prize (or, as the case may be, those prizes) cannot be won, a statement of those circumstances; and

(c)   a statement of a percentage as being the percentage or minimum percentage of the aggregate value of the charges for play inserted in the machine which the machine is designed to pay out;

and, if the manner in which those statements are to be so displayed is prescribed, they shall be displayed in that manner.

(8) No such machine shall be used for gaming on the premises at any time when the public have access to the premises, whether on payment or otherwise.

(9) In this section "services" includes a game or games on a machine to which this Part of this Act applies.*

[Gaming Act 1968, s 31.]

---

*Repealed by the Gambling Act 2005, Sch 17 from a date to be appointed.

1. Under this section, the maximum number of gaming machines (as distinct from amusement machines under s 34, post) permitted differs according to whether the premises concerned are casinos, bingo clubs or registered members' clubs. The stake for playing a game is currently 50p, though this may be subsequently varied by order. The maximum prize is not specified in the section, but may be prescribed; further, in premises licensed for gaming, a percentage of the aggregate value of the charges for play may be required to be paid out by the machine.

2. The Gaming Act 1968 (Variation of Monetary Limits) Order 2005, SI 2005/2776 prescribes that the sum is 50 pence except (a) in the case of a casino jackpot gaming machine where the amount payable as a prize in respect of any one game played by means of the machine cannot exceed £500, the sum is £100 and (b) in the case of any other casino jackpot gaming machine, the sum is £2.

3. The Gaming Machines (Maximum Prizes) Regulations 2005, SI 2005 prescribe that the amount, in the case of a machine on any premises in respect of which a licence under this Act is for the time being in force other than bingo club premises (as defined in section 20 of this Act), is £4,000.

8–13411   32. Power for licensing authority to authorise more than two machines.   (1) In connection with any application for the grant or renewal of a licence under this Act the applicant may request[1] the licensing authority to give—

(a)   in the case of any premises, a direction under subsection (2);

(b)   in the case of bingo club premises (as defined by section 20), a direction under subsection (3).

(2) Where a request is made for a direction under this subsection, and the licensing authority grant or renew the licence, and, on doing so, give a direction[2] under this subsection specifying a maximum number of machines, then, in relation to any time when the number of machines to which this Part of this Act applies which are available for gaming on the premises does not exceed the number so specified,—

(a)   the provisions of subsections (2) to (7) of section 31 of this Act shall not have effect in relation to the premises to which the licence relates, but

(b)   the provisions of section 34(5E) of this Act shall have effect in relation to those premises.

(3) Where a request is made for a direction under this subsection, and the licensing authority grant or renew the licence, they may, on doing so, give a direction under this subsection specifying a maximum number of AWP machines.

(4) At any time when—

(*a*) a direction under subsection (3) is in force, and

(*b*) the number of AWP machines available for gaming on the premises does not exceed the number specified in the direction,

those machines shall be disregarded for the purposes of section 31.

(5) An "AWP" machine is a machine to which this Part of this Act applies and in respect of which either—

(*a*) the conditions specified in section 34(2) and (3), or

(*b*) the conditions specified in section 34(5B) and (5C),

are observed.

(6) In the case of a travelling showmen's pleasure fair, subsection (4) does not apply to a machine which is an AWP machine by virtue of subsection (5)(a) unless the condition specified in section 34(5) is observed.

[Gaming Act 1968, s 32, as amended by SI 1996/1359 and SI 2002/460.]

---

1. The effect of this section is to enable the applicant for the grant or renewal of a licence for gaming to seek a direction from the licensing authority that instead of two gaming machines being made available on the premises, a number (not exceeding the maximum specified by the licensing authority) of amusement machines (as described in s 34, post), may be made available. The section does not apply to clubs registered for gaming or registered for gaming machines.

2. See the Betting and Gaming Duties Act 1981, Sch 4, para 15 in PART VIII: title CUSTOMS AND EXCISE, post, requiring the clerk to keep a register of directions given under this section.

Use of machines for gaming by way of amusement with prizes

8–13412   33. Use of machines at non-commercial entertainments.   (1) This section applies to any entertainment which takes place elsewhere than on premises in respect of which—

(*a*) a licence under this Act is for the time being in force, or

(*b*) a club or a miners' welfare institute is for the time being registered under Part II or under this Part of this Act,

and which is an entertainment of any of the following kinds, that is to say, bazaars, sales of work, fêtes, dinners, dances, sporting or athletic events and other entertainments of a similar character, whether limited to one day or extending over two or more days.

(2) Where a machine to which this Part of this Act applies is used for gaming as an incident of any such entertainment[1], the whole proceeds of the entertainment, after deducting the expenses of the entertainment, shall be devoted to purposes other than private gain[2].

(2A) Where a machine to which this Part of this Act applies is used for gaming as an incident of an entertainment to which this section applies, the opportunity to win prizes by means of the machine, or that opportunity together with any other facilities for participating in lotteries or gaming shall not be the only, or the only substantial, inducement to persons to attend the entertainment.

(5) The Secretary of State may by regulations impose such restrictions (in addition to those specified in subsections (2) and (2A) of this section) as he may consider necessary or expedient with respect to the use of any machine to which this Part of this Act applies for gaming as an incident of an entertainment to which this section applies.

(6) Repealed by Lotteries and Amusements Act 1976.

[Gaming Act 1968, s 33, as amended by the Lotteries Act 1975, Sch 4.]

---

1. See also s 15 of the Lotteries and Amusements Act 1976, post, for similar provisions relating to amusements with prizes otherwise than by way of machine at exempt entertainments.

2. For construction of this section in respect of entertainment promoted on behalf of a society, see s 51A, post.

8–13413   34. Other uses of machines for amusement purposes.   (1) The conditions specified in subsections (2) to (3) and (5) of this section shall be observed where a machine to which this Part of this Act applies is used for gaming—

(*a*) on any amusement machine premises in respect of which there is for the time being in force a permit under this section which—

(i) is granted by the authority mentioned in paragraph 1(*b*) or, as the case may be, (*d*) of Schedule 9 to this Act, and

(ii) is expressed to be granted for the purposes of this subsection,

(*aa*) on any premises, other than amusement machine premises, in respect of which there is for the time being in force a permit under this section which is granted as mentioned in paragraph (*a*)(i) of this subsection,

(*b*) *Repealed*,

(*c*) on any premises used wholly or mainly for the purpose of a pleasure fair consisting wholly or mainly of amusements provided otherwise than by means of machines to which this Part of this Act applies, being premises in respect of which a permit granted under this section 16 of the Lotteries and Amusements Act 1976 is for the time being in force[1], or

(*d*) at a travelling showmen's pleasure fair[2].

(2) The charge for play for playing a game once by means of the machine shall be one or more coins or tokens inserted in the machine of an amount or value not exceeding (or, if more than one, not in the aggregate exceeding) 30p[3].

(3) Except as provided by subsections (4) and (9) of this section, in respect of any one game[4] played by means of the machine no player or person claiming under a player shall receive, or shall be entitled to receive, any article, benefit or advantage other than one (and only one) of the following, that is to say—

    (*a*) a money prize not exceeding £5·00[5] or a token which is, or two or more tokens which in the aggregate are, exchangeable only for such a money prize;

    (*b*) a non-monetary prize or prizes of a value or aggregate value not exceeding £8·00[5] or a token exchangeable only for such a non-monetary prize or such non-monetary prizes;

    (*c*) a money prize not exceeding £5·00[5] together with a non-monetary prize of a value which does not exceed £8·00[5] less the amount of the money prize, or a token exchangeable only for such a combination of a money prize and a non-monetary prize;

    (*d*) one or more tokens which can be used for playing one or more further games by means of the machine and, in so far as they are not so used, can be exchanged for a non-monetary prize or non-monetary prizes at the appropriate rate.

(4) The condition specified in subsection (3) of this section shall not be taken to be contravened by reason only that a player, after inserting in the machine an amount permitted in accordance with subsection (2) of this section and playing a game successfully, is afforded by the automatic action of the machine an opportunity to play one or more further games without inserting any further coin or token in the machine, if in respect of all those games—

    (*a*) he does not receive, and is not entitled to receive, any article other than a money prize or money prizes of an amount or aggregate amount not exceeding £5·00[5] and

    (*b*) he does not receive, and is not entitled to receive, any other benefit or advantage apart from the opportunity to play the further game or games.

(5) In the case of a travelling showmen's pleasure fair the opportunity to win prizes by means of amusements which constitute gaming (whether by the use of machines to which this Part of this Act applies or otherwise) shall not constitute the only, or the only substantial, inducement to persons to attend the fair.

(5A) The conditions specified in subsections (5B) to (5C) of this section shall be observed where a machine to which this Part of this Act applies is used for gaming on any premises in respect of which a betting office licence is for the time being in force.

(5B) The charge for play for playing a game once by means of the machine shall not exceed the amount specified in subsection (2) of this section.

(5BA) Payment of the charge for play shall be made in cash.

(5BB) Subsections (5BC) to (5BF) of this section apply if—

    (*a*) a player inserts into the machine something which is recognised by the machine as having a value exceeding the highest coin value;

    (*b*) the machine immediately holds to the player's credit an amount in respect of the thing ("the initial amount") for the purpose of paying the charge for play for playing games by means of the machine.

(5BC) The initial amount must not exceed the highest coin value.

(5BD) The machine must not hold any further amount to the player's credit for the purpose of paying the charge for play for playing games by means of the machine unless the player takes action in respect of the machine to indicate that he wishes to play, or continue to play, games by means of the machine.

(5BE) The further amount held to the player's credit by virtue of subsection (5BD) of this section must not exceed the highest coin value.

(5BF) The highest coin value is the value of the highest denomination coin which, when the games are played—

    (*a*) is legal tender in the part of the United Kingdom in which the premises are situated, and

    (*b*) is in general circulation in that part of the United Kingdom.

(5C) No player or person claiming under a player shall receive, or shall be entitled to receive, in respect of any one game played by means of the machine, any article, benefit or advantage other than a money prize not exceeding £25 delivered by the machine.

(5D) The condition specified in subsection (5C) of this section shall not be taken to be contravened by reason only that a player, after inserting in the machine an amount permitted in accordance with subsection (5B) of this section and playing a game successfully, is afforded by the automatic action of the machine an opportunity to play one or more further games without inserting any further payment in the machine, if in respect of all those games—

    (*a*) he does not receive, and is not entitled to receive, any article other than a money prize of an amount or aggregate amount not exceeding £25, and

    (*b*) he does not receive, and is not entitled to receive, any other benefit or advantage apart from the opportunity to play the further game or games.

(5E) Where a machine to which this Part of this Act applies is used for gaming—

(*a*) on any amusement machine premises in respect of which there is for the time being in force a permit under this section which—

(i)   is granted by the authority mentioned in paragraph 1(*b*) or, as the case may be, (*d*) of Schedule 9 to this Act, and

(ii) is expressed to be granted for the purposes of this subsection.

(*b*) on any premises in respect of which there is for the time being in force a permit under this section which is granted by the authority mentioned in paragraph 1(*a*) or, as the case may be, (*c*) of Schedule 9 to this Act, or

(*c*) on any premises in respect of which a licence under this Act and a direction given under section 32(2) of this Act are for the time being in force, where, by virtue of that direction, the provisions of this subsection have effect in relation to the premises,

either the conditions specified in subsections (2) to (3) and (5) of this section or the conditions specified in subsections (5B) to (5C) of this section shall be observed.

(6) The provisions of Schedule 9[6] of this Act shall have effect with respect to the grant and renewal of permits for the purposes of this section.

(7) No permit for the purposes of this section shall be granted in respect of any premises where a licence under this Act is for the time being in force in respect of them or where a club or a miners' welfare institute is for the time being registered in respect of them under Part II of this Act; and, where such a licence is granted or a club or a miners' welfare institute is so registered in respect of any premises, and a permit granted for the purposes of this section is then in force in respect of those premises, the permit shall thereupon cease to have effect.

(7A) In subsections (1) and (5E) of this section, references to amusement machine premises are to premises used wholly or mainly for the provision of amusements by means of machines to which this Part of this Act applies.

(8) In this section "non-monetary prize" means a prize which does not consist of or include any money and does not consist of or include any token which can be exchanged for money or money's worth or used for playing a game by means of the machine; and for the purposes of subsection (3) (*d*) of this section a token or tokens shall be taken to be exchanged for a non-monetary prize or prizes at the appropriate rate if either—

(*a*) the value or aggregate value of the prize or prizes does not exceed £8·00[5] and the token or tokens exchanged represent the maximum number of tokens which can be won by playing a game once by means of the machine, or

(*b*) in any other case, the value or aggregate value of the prize or prizes does not exceed £8·00[5] and bears to £8·00[5] a proportion not exceeding that which the number of tokens exchanged bears to the maximum number of tokens which can be won by playing a game once by means of the machine.

(9) The Secretary of State may by order direct that any provision of this section which is specified in the order and which specifies a sum shall have effect as if, for that sum, there were substituted such other sum as may be specified in that order.

[Gaming Act 1968, s 34, as amended by the Lotteries and Amusements Act 1976, Sch 4, the Gaming Act (Variation of Monetary Limits) Orders, SI 1996/1359, SI 2001/3971, SI 2002/460 and SI 2003/3275.]

---

1. The effect of paras (*a*) and (*c*) of sub-s (1), when read with s 16(1) of the Lotteries and Amusements Act 1976, is that the holder of a permit under s 34 and Sch 9 of the 1968 Act (to provide amusement machines) may also provide amusements with prizes (otherwise than by machine) under s 16 of the 1976 Act if the premises are used mainly for the purposes of amusements by means of machines, and *vice versa*.

2. Defined in s 52, post.

3. As substituted by the Gaming Act (Variation of Monetary Limits) (No 2) Order 1998, SI 1998/2152.

4. Section 34(3) does not prohibit the holder of a permit from offering to the player who wins a non-monetary prize or token in playing any one game, the right to accumulate his prizes from playing further games and to exchange them for a non-monetary prize of a value exceeding the limit within the section. Moreover, so long as the value of what can be obtained by trading up is limited to the aggregate of the value of the tokens given up in exchange, there is no additional benefit or advantage obtained by the player which can be said to be unlawful and contrary to s 34(3) (*R v Burt and Adams Ltd* [1998] 2 All ER 417, [1998] 2 WLR 725, HL).

5. As substituted by the Gaming Act (Variation of Monetary Limits) (No 2) Order 1998, SI 1998/2152.

6. See also the Betting and Gaming Duties Act 1981, Sch 4, para 15 in PART VIII: CUSTOMS AND EXCISE, post, requiring the clerk to keep a register of permits issued for the purposes of this section.

General restriction on other gaming by means of machines

8–13414 **35. Use of machines not falling within ss 31 to 34.** No machine to which this Part of this Act applies shall be used for gaming except—

(*a*) on premises in respect of which a licence under this Act is for the time being in force, or in respect of which a club or a miners' welfare institute is for the time being registered under Part II or under this Part of this Act, or

(*b*) as an incident of an entertainment to which section 33 of this Act applies, or

(*c*)   as mentioned in section 34(1)(*a*), (*aa*), (*c*) or (*d*), (5A) or (5E)(*a*), (*b*) or (*c*) of this Act.
[Gaming Act 1968, s 35, as amended by SI 1996/1359.]

Supplementary provisions

8–13415   36. Removal of money from machines.   (1) Where a machine to which this Part of this Act applies is installed on premises in respect of which—

(*a*)   a licence under this Act is for the time being in force, or
(*b*)   a club or a miners' welfare institute is for the time being registered under Part II or under this Part of this Act,

no person who is not an authorised person for the purposes of this section shall remove from the machine any money, other than any money delivered by the machine as, or as part of, a prize in respect of a game played by means of the machine.

(2) For the purposes of this section the following are authorised persons in relation to a machine according to the premises on which it is installed, that is to say—

(*a*)   in the case of premises in respect of which a licence under this Act is for the time being in force, the holder of the licence and any person employed by him in connection with the premises;
(*b*)   in the case of premises in respect of which a club is for the time being registered under Part II or under this Part of this Act, any officer or member of the club and any person employed by or on behalf of the members of the club in connection with the premises;
(*c*)   in the case of premises in respect of which a miners' welfare institute is for the time being so registered, any officer of the institute, any person for the time being enrolled as a member of the institute, and any person employed in connection with the premises by or on behalf of the persons so enrolled.

[Gaming Act 1968, s 36.]

8–13416   37. Regulations with respect to machines and records.   (1) The Secretary of State may by regulations—

(*a*)   prohibit, or impose such restrictions as he may consider necessary or expedient on, the sale, supply, maintenance or use of machines to which this Part of this Act applies which are of a description specified in the regulations;
(*b*)   prohibit, or impose such restrictions as he may consider necessary or expedient on, the sale or supply of tokens or other objects of a description so specified for use in machines to which this Part of this Act applies;
(*c*)   impose special requirements in respect of machines to which this Part of this Act applies which are installed, or are sold or supplied for the purpose of being installed, on any such premises as are mentioned in section 36 (1) of this Act.

(2) In respect of machines to which this Part of this Act applies which are installed on any such premises, regulations made by the Secretary of State may—

(*a*)   in the case of premises in respect of which a licence under this Act is for the time being in force, require the holder of the licence, or
(*b*)   in the case of premises in respect of which a club or a miners' welfare institute is for the time being registered under Part II or under this Part of this Act, require the officers of the club or institute,

to make, and to retain during a prescribed period, such records and accounts as may be prescribed with respect to matters to which this subsection applies, and to provide such verification of those records and accounts as may be prescribed; and the regulations may require the holder of the licence or the officers of the club or institute, as the case may be, to send to the Board and to the chief officer of police (or, in Scotland, the chief constable) for the police area in which the premises are situated an annual statement containing such particulars as may be prescribed with respect to matters to which this subsection applies.

(3) The matters to which subsection (2) of this section applies, in relation to a machine, are—

(*a*)   any payments made in respect of the machine, whether by way of rent, maintenance charges or otherwise;
(*b*)   any money or tokens inserted into the machine otherwise than as charges for play; and
(*c*)   any money or tokens removed from the machine, other than money or tokens delivered by the machine as prizes.

[Gaming Act 1968, s 37, as amended by SI 2003/3275.]

8–13417   38. Offences[1] under Part III.   (1) Any person who contravenes subsection (1) or subsection (5) of section 27 of this Act shall be guilty of an offence.

(2) Any person who sells, supplies or undertakes to maintain a machine in contravention of any regulations made under subsection (1) of section 28 of this Act, or who contravenes subsection (2) of that section, shall be guilty of an offence.

(3) Subject to subsection (11) of this section, where any of the provisions of section 31 of this Act, or of any regulations made in pursuance of section 37(1) of this Act in so far as they relate to the use of machines, or of any regulations made in pursuance of section 37(2) of this Act, is contravened in relation to any premises—

(a) the holder of the licence, if they are premises in respect of which a licence under this Act is for the time being in force, or

(b) every officer of the club or institute, if they are premises in respect of which a club or a miners' welfare institute is for the time being registered under Part II or under this Part of this Act,

shall be guilty of an offence; and where subsection (5E) of section 34 of this Act is contravened in relation to premises falling within paragraph (c) of that subsection, the holder of the licence in respect of the premises shall be guilty of an offence.

(4) Without prejudice to the last preceding subsection, but subject to subsection (11) of this section, where any such provisions as are mentioned in the last preceding subsection are contravened in relation to a machine on any premises, any person who allowed the machine to be on the premises shall be guilty of an offence.

(5) Where any of the provisions of section 33 of this Act or of any regulations made under that section is contravened in relation to an entertainment, every person concerned in the conduct of the entertainment shall be guilty of an offence unless he proves that the contravention occurred without his consent or connivance and that he exercised all due diligence to prevent it.

(6) Subject to subsection (11) of this section, where subsection (1) of section 34 of this Act is contravened, or where, in a case falling within paragraph (aa) of that subsection, a condition to which the permit is subject is contravened—

(a) the holder of the permit, in a case falling within paragraph (a) or (aa) or paragraph (c) of that subsection, or

(b) the person in charge of the machine, in a case falling within paragraph (d) of that subsection,

shall be guilty of an offence.

(6A) Subject to subsection (11) of this section, where subsection (5A) of section 34 of this Act is contravened, the holder of the betting office licence in respect of the premises shall be guilty of an offence.

(6B) Subject to subsection (11) of this section, where, in the case of any premises falling within paragraph (a) or (b) of subsection (5E) of section 34 of this Act—

(a) that subsection, or

(b) a condition to which the permit is subject,

is contravened, the holder of the permit shall be guilty of an offence.

(7) Where a machine to which this Part of this Act applies is used for gaming on any premises, or in any vessel or vehicle, in contravention of section 35 of this Act, any person who allowed the machine to be on the premises or in the vessel or vehicle shall be guilty of an offence unless he proves that the contravention occurred without his consent or connivance and that he exercised all due diligence to prevent it.

(8) Any person who contravenes section 36 of this Act shall be guilty of an offence.

(9) Any person who—

(a) sells, supplies or maintains a machine, or sells or supplies any token or other object for use in machines, in contravention of any regulations made under section 37(1) of this Act, or

(b) on any premises other than premises falling within paragraph (a) or paragraph (b) of subsection (3) of this section, causes or permits a machine to be used in contravention of any such regulations,

shall be guilty of an offence.

(10) Where any of the provisions of section 33, section 34 or section 35 of this Act is contravened in relation to a machine, then (without prejudice to any liability of any person under the preceding provisions of this section) any person who, knowing or having reasonable cause to suspect that the provisions in question would be contravened in relation to the machine, sold or supplied the machine shall—

(a) in the case of a contravention of section 33 or section 35 of this Act, be guilty of an offence under this paragraph, or

(b) in the case of a contravention of section 34 of this Act, be guilty of an offence under this paragraph.

(11) Where a person is charged with an offence under subsection (3), (4), (6), (6A) or (6B) of this section in respect of a contravention of any such provisions as are mentioned in any of those subsections, it shall be a defence for him to prove—

(a) that the contravention occurred without his knowledge, and

(b) that he exercised all such care as was reasonable in the circumstances to secure that the provisions in question would not be contravened.

(12) Section 29 of this Act shall have effect for the purpose of subsections (1) and (2) of this

section as it has effect for the purposes of sections 27 and 28 of this Act, and any reference in those subsections to contravening any provisions of those sections or any regulations made thereunder shall be construed accordingly.

[Gaming Act 1968, s 38, as amended by SI 1996/1359 and SI 2003/3275.]

---

1. For penalties, see s 39, post.

8–13418   **39. Penalties under Part III.**   (1) Any person guilty of an offence under section 38 of this Act shall be liable—

(a) on summary conviction, to a fine not exceeding **the statutory maximum**;

(b) on conviction on indictment, to a fine or to imprisonment for a term not exceeding **two years** or to both.

(2) Where a person is convicted of an offence under subsection (6) or (6B) of section 38 of this Act in respect of a contravention of a condition to which a permit under section 34 of this Act is subject, the court by which he is convicted may, if it thinks fit, make an order cancelling the permit.

(3) An order under subsection (2) of this section made by a court in England or Wales—

(a) shall not take effect until the end of the period within which the person on whose conviction the order was made can appeal against the conviction or against the making of the order, and

(b) if he so appeals, shall not take effect until the appeal has been determined or abandoned.

(4) The holder of a permit in respect of which an order under subsection (2) of this section is made by court in Scotland may, without prejudice to any other form of appeal under any rule of law, appeal against the order in the same manner as against a conviction, and a permit shall not be cancelled under an order so made—

(a) until the end of the period of fourteen days commencing with the date on which the order was made, nor

(b) if an appeal against the order or the conviction which gave rise thereto is taken within the said period, until the date when that appeal is determined or abandoned or deemed to have been abandoned.

[Gaming Act 1968, s 39, as amended by the Criminal Law Act 1977, s 28 and SI 1996/1359.]

PART IV

MISCELLANEOUS AND SUPPLEMENTARY PROVISIONS

8–13419   **40. Special charges for play at certain clubs and institutes.**   (1) This section applies to gaming which—

(a) is carried on as one of the activities of a club[1] or a miners' welfare institute, whether the club or institute is registered under Part II or Part III of this Act or not, and

(b) is gaming in respect of which none of the conditions specified in section 2(1) of this Act is fulfilled.

(2) Subject to the following provisions of this section, nothing in section 3 or section 14 of this Act shall have effect so as to prevent a charge from being made in respect of any person for the right to take part in gaming to which this section applies, if the charge or (if more than one) the aggregate amount of the charges made in respect of that person for the right to take part in such gaming on any one day does not exceed sixpence or such other sum as may be specified[2] in an order made by the Secretary of State for the purposes of this subsection.

The power of the Secretary of State under this subsection includes power to specify—

(a) in the case of gaming carried on as an activity of a members' club or a miners' welfare institute, a sum different from that applicable in the case of gaming carried on as an activity of any other club; and

(b) in the case of gaming which consists exclusively of playing bridge or whist, or bridge and whist, and takes place on a day on which the premises used therefor are not used for any other gaming, or for any other gaming except gaming by means of a machine to which Part III of this Act applies, a sum greater than that applicable in all other cases.

(3) Any such charge as is mentioned in subsection (2) of this section may be made in addition to—

(a) any stakes hazarded in the gaming, and

(b) in the case of a club or institute registered under Part II of this Act, any charge authorised by regulations under section 14(2) (b) of this Act.

(4) The preceding provisions of this section shall not have effect in relation to a club unless it is shown—

(a) *Repealed*;

(b) that it has not less than twenty-five members; and

(c) that it is so constituted and conducted, in respect of membership and otherwise, as not to be of a temporary character.

[Gaming Act 1968, s 40, as amended by the Gaming (Amendment) Act 1973, s 1.]

1. This section only covers gaming by a club or institute at the club or institute premises (*Lock v Rank Leisure Ltd* (1984) 148 JP 340—Bonanza Regional Final held at conference centre held illegal).

2. In the case of gaming which consists exclusively of playing bridge or whist, or bridge and whist, and takes place on a day on which the premises used therefor are not used for any other gaming, or for any other gaming except gaming by means of a machine to which Part III of the Act applies, the sum of £15 has been specified; in any other case the sum of 60p has been specified: see the Gaming (Small Charges) Order 2000, SI 2000/2802.

8–13420 41. Gaming at entertainments not held for private gain. (1) The provisions of this section[1] shall have effect in relation to gaming which—

  (a) consists of games played at an entertainment promoted otherwise than for purposes of private gain[2], and

  (b) is not gaming to which Part II of this Act applies or gaming by means of a machine[3] to which Part III of this Act applies, and

  (c) does not constitute the provision of amusements with prizes as mentioned in section 15(1) or 16(1) of the Lotteries and Amusements Act 1976;

and any reference in this Act to gaming to which this section applies is a reference to gaming in respect of which the conditions specified in paragraphs (a) to (c) of this subsection are fulfilled.

(2) Section 2 of this Act shall have effect in relation to gaming to which this section applies as it has effect in relation to gaming to which Part I of this Act applies.

(3) In respect of all games played at the entertainment which constitute gaming to which this section applies, not more than one payment (whether by way of entrance fee or stake or otherwise) shall be made by each player, and no such payment shall exceed £4.00[4].

(4) Subject to subsections (7) and (8) of this section, the total value of all prizes and awards distributed in respect of those games shall not exceed £400[4].

(5) The whole of the proceeds of such payments as are mentioned in subsection (3) of this section, after deducting sums lawfully appropriated on account of expenses or for the provision of prizes or awards in respect of the games, shall be applied for purposes other than private gain.

(6) The sum appropriated out of those proceeds in respect of expenses shall not exceed the reasonable cost of the facilities provided for the purposes of the games.

(7) Where two or more entertainments are promoted on the same premises by the same persons on the same day, subsections (3) to (6) of this section shall have effect in relation to those entertainments collectively as if they were a single entertainment.

(8) Where a series of entertainments is held otherwise than as mentioned in subsection (7) of this section—

  (a) subsections (3) to (6) of this section shall have effect separately in relation to each entertainment in the series, whether some or all of the persons taking part in any one of those entertainments are thereby qualified to take part in any other of them or not, and

  (b) if each of the persons taking part in the games played at the final entertainment of the series is qualified to do so by reason of having taken part in the games played at another entertainment of the series held on a previous day, subsection (4) of this section shall have effect in relation to that final entertainment as if for the words "£400"[4] there were substituted the words "£700"[4].

(9) The Secretary of State may by order provide that, in relation to entertainments held on or after the date on which the order comes into operation, this section shall have effect as if, for such one or more of the following sums as may be specified in the order, that is to say—

  (a) the sum of ten shillings specified in subsection (3) of this section;

  (b) the sum of fifty pounds specified in subsections (4) and (8) (b) of this section; and

  (c) the sum of one hundred pounds specified in subsection 8 (b) of this section,

there were substituted such larger sum as is specified in the order.

(10) Subsections (1) to (4) of section 8[5] of this Act shall have effect as if in those subsections any reference to sections 2 or 4 or to Part I of this Act included a reference to this section.

(11) *Repealed by Lotteries and Amusements Act 1976.*

[Gaming Act 1968, s 41, as amended by the Lotteries and Amusements Act 1976, Sch 4, the Gaming Act (Variation of Monetary Limits) Orders. and SI 2000/2803.]

---

1. This section applies only to entertainments not held for private gain. Further, it does not apply to (a) gaming in premises licensed or registered for gaming, or (b) gaming by machine under Pt III, or (c) amusements with prizes (otherwise than by way of machine) under s 15 or 16 of the Lotteries and Amusements Act 1976. The effect of sub-s (2) is that banker's games and unequal-chance games are excluded from the provisions of the section.

2. For construction of this section in respect of gaming promoted on behalf of a society, see s 51A, post.

3. For provisions for gaming by machine at an entertainment not held for private gain, see s 33, ante.

4. As substituted by SI 2000/2803.

5. Section 8 contains provisions as to offences under Pt I of this Act.

8–13421 42. Restrictions on advertisements relating to gaming. (1) Except as provided by this section, no person shall issue, or cause to be issued, any advertisement—

(*a*)   informing the public that any premises in Great Britain are premises on which gaming takes place or is to take place, or

(*b*)   inviting the public to take part as players in any gaming which takes place, or is to take place, on any such premises, or to apply for information about facilities for taking part as players in any gaming which takes place, or is to take place, in Great Britain, or

(*c*)   inviting the public to subscribe any money or money's worth to be used in gaming whether in Great Britain or elsewhere, or to apply for information about facilities for subscribing any money or money's worth to be so used,

(*d*)   *Repealed.*

(*e*)   *Repealed.*

(1A)   *Repealed.*

(2)   Subsection (1) of this section does not apply to any advertisement in so far as it relates to gaming which is, or is to be,—

(*a*)   gaming as an incident of an entertainment to which section 33¹ of this Act applies, or

(*b*)   gaming to which section 41² of this Act applies, or

(*c*)   gaming on any premises to which paragraph 4 of Schedule 9 to this Act applies and in respect of which a permit under section 34³ of this Act is for the time being in force, or

(*d*)   gaming on any premises to which paragraph 3 of Schedule 3 to the Lotteries and Amusements Act 1976 applies and in respect of which a permit under section 16³ of that Act is for the time being in force, or

(*e*)   gaming at any travelling showmen's pleasure fair⁴, or

(*f*)   gaming in the form of playing bingo.

(3)   Subsection (1) of this section does not apply to—

(*a*)   the display, on any premises in respect of which a licence under this Act is for the time being in force, of a sign or notice indicating that gaming takes place, or is to take place, on those premises, whether the sign or notice is displayed inside or outside the premises, or

(*b*)   the publication or display of a notice, where the notice is required to be published or displayed by any provision of Schedules 2 to 4 to this Act and the publication or display is so made as to comply with the requirements of that provision, or

(*c*)   the publication in any newspaper of a notice stating that a licence under this Act has been granted, if the notice is published not later than fourteen days from the date on which the licence was granted or from such later date as may be appointed by the licensing authority by whom the licence was granted, and the notice is in a form approved by the licensing authority;

(*d*)–(*g*)   *Repealed.*

(3A)–(3C)   *Repealed.*

(3D)   Subsection (1) of this section does not apply to the publication of an advertisement relating to premises, other than bingo club premises, in respect of which a licence under this Act is for the time being in force if—

(*a*)   the advertisement is contained in a publication which is not published wholly or mainly for the purpose of promoting premises on which gaming takes place or is to take place; and

(*b*)   the advertisement contains no more than—

     (i)   the name, logo, address, telephone and facsimile numbers of the premises; and

     (ii)   factual written information about the facilities provided on the premises, the ownership of the premises, the persons who may be admitted to the premises and the method by which such persons may become eligible to take part in gaming on the premises.

(4)   Subsection (1) of this section does not apply to the publication of an advertisement in a newspaper which circulates wholly or mainly outside Great Britain.

(5)   Where a person is charged with an offence under this section, it shall be a defence to prove that he is a person whose business it is to publish or arrange for the publication of advertisements and that he received the advertisement in question for publication in the ordinary course of business and did not know and had no reason to suspect that its publication would amount to an offence under this section.

(6)   For the purposes of this section an advertisement issued by displaying or exhibiting it shall be treated as issued on every day on which it is displayed or exhibited.

(7)   Subject to subsection (5) of this section, any person who contravenes subsection (1) of this section shall be guilty of an offence and liable—

(*a*)   on summary conviction, to a fine not exceeding **the statutory maximum;**

(*b*)   on conviction on indictment, to a fine or to imprisonment for a term not exceeding **two years** or to both.

(8)   In this section—

"advertisement" includes every form of advertising, whether in a publication or by the display of notices or by means of circulars or other documents or by an exhibition of photographs or a cinematograph film, or by way of sound broadcasting or television or by inclusion in a programme service (within the meaning of the Broadcasting Act 1990) that is not a sound or

television broadcasting service and references to the issue of an advertisement shall be construed
accordingly;

"bingo club premises" has the meaning given by section 20(1) of this Act;

"public" means the public in Great Britain, and includes any section of the public in Great Britain,
however selected.

[Gaming Act 1968, s 42, as amended by the Lotteries and Amusements Act 1976, Sch 4, the Criminal Law Act
1977, s 28, the Cable and Broadcasting Act 1984, Sch 5, the Broadcasting Act 1990, Sch 20, the Bingo Act 1992,
s 1, SI 1997/1074 and SI 1999/2136.]

---

1. Section 33 applies to non-commercial entertainments, eg bazaars, sales of work, etc, held otherwise than on premises
licensed or registered under the Act.

2. Section 41 applies to equal chance gaming at entertainments not held for private gain, not being (*a*) gaming to which
either Pt II (gaming on premises licensed or registered for gaming) or Pt III (gaming by machine) applies.

3. Permits under s 34 of this Act and s 16 of the 1976 Act are granted in respect of the use of machines for gaming in
the nature of amusements with prizes.

4. Gaming at a travelling showmen's pleasure fair is controlled by the conditions set out in s 34 of this Act and s 16 of
the 1976 Act.

8–13422   43. Provisions for inspectors and rights of entry and related rights.   (1) The Board
may appoint such number of persons as the Secretary of State may with the consent of the Treasury
determine to be inspectors for the purposes of this Act; and in this Act "inspector" means any person
so appointed.

(2) Any inspector or constable may at any reasonable time enter any premises in respect of which
a licence under this Act is for the time being in force, and, while on the premises, may

(*a*)   inspect the premises and any machine or other equipment on the premises, and any book or
document on those premises which he reasonably requires to inspect for the purpose of
ascertaining whether a contravention of this Act or of any regulations made under it is being
or has been committed;

(*b*)   take copies of any such book or document or of any entry in it; and

(*c*)   if any information reasonably required by him for that purpose is contained in a computer
and is accessible from the premises, require it to be produced in a form in which it can be
taken away and in which it is visible and legible.

(3) If any person, being the holder of a licence under this Act in respect of any premises or a
person acting on behalf of the holder of such a licence,—

(*a*)   fails without reasonable excuse to admit an inspector or constable who demands admission to
the premises in pursuance of subsection (2) of this section, or

(*b*)   on being required by an inspector or constable to do so, fails without reasonable excuse to
permit the inspector or constable to inspect the premises or any machine or other equipment
on the premises, or

(*c*)   on being required by an inspector or constable to produce any book or document in his
possession or under his control which relates to those premises and which the inspector or
constable reasonably requires to inspect for the purpose specified in subsection (2) of this
section, fails without reasonable excuse to produce it to the inspector or constable and to
permit the inspector or constable (if he so desires) to take copies of it or of any entry in it, or

(*ca*) fails without reasonable excuse to comply with a requirement imposed in relation to those
premises under subsection (2)(*c*) of this section, or

(*d*)   on being required by an inspector to furnish any information relating to the premises which is
reasonably required by the Board for the purposes of the performance of their functions, fails
without reasonable excuse to furnish that information to the inspector,

the holder of the licence shall be guilty of an offence.

(4) If, on information on oath with respect to any premises,—

(*a*)   a justice of the peace, if the premises are in England or Wales, or

(*b*)   the sheriff or a magistrate or justice of the peace having jurisdiction in the place where the
premises are situated, if they are situated in Scotland,

is satisfied that there are reasonable grounds for suspecting that an offence under this Act is being,
has been or is about to be committed on these premises, he may issue a warrant in writing[1] authorising
any constable, with or without one or more inspectors, to enter the premises, if necessary by force,
and to search the premises.

(5) Any constable who enters any premises under the authority of a warrant issued under
subsection (4) of this section may—

(*a*)   seize and remove any document, money or valuable thing, instrument or other thing
whatsoever found on the premises which he has reasonable cause to believe may be required
as evidence for the purposes of proceedings in respect of an offence under this Act,

(*aa*) if he has reasonable cause to believe that any information which is stored in any electronic
form and is accessible from the premises may be required for those purposes, require it to be

produced in a form in which it can be taken away and in which it is visible and legible, or from which it can readily be produced in a visible and legible form; and

(b) search any person found on the premises whom he has reasonable cause to believe to be committing or to have committed any such offence.

(5A) The holder of a licence under this Act in respect of any premises shall be guilty of an offence if he, or any person acting on his behalf, fails without reasonable excuse to comply with a requirement imposed in relation to those premises under subsection (5)(aa) of this section.

(6) Without prejudice to any power exercisable by virtue of the preceding provisions of this section, in the case of any premises in respect of which a licence under this Act is for the time being in force or a club or a miners' welfare institute is for the time being registered under Part II or Part III of this Act the Board may at any time serve on the holder of the licence or the chairman or secretary of the club or institute, as the case may be, a notice requiring him, in such manner and within such reasonable time as may be specified in the notice—

(a) to produce for inspection by or on behalf of the Board books or documents relating to those premises of any description specified in the notice which the Board reasonably require to inspect for the purpose specified in subsection (2) of this section, and

(b) to furnish to the Board information relating to those premises of any description specified in the notice which the Board reasonably require for that purpose.

(7) Any power exercisable by the Board by virtue of subsection (6) of this section in respect of any premises shall also be exercised by the chief officer of police (or, in Scotland, the chief constable) for the police area in which the premises are situated, as if in that subsection any reference to the Board included a reference to that chief officer or chief constable.

(8) If without reasonable excuse any requirement imposed in relation to any premises by a notice served by virtue of subsection (6) or subsection (7) of this section is not complied with,—

(a) the holder of the licence, if they are premises in respect of which a licence under this Act is for the time being in force, or

(b) every officer of the club or institute, if they are premises in respect of which a club or a miners' welfare institute is for the time being registered under Part II or Part III of this Act,

shall be guilty of an offence.

(9) In the case of any premises in respect of which a licence under this Act is for the time being in force, any person duly authorised in writing by the appropriate fire and rescue authority may at any reasonable time enter the premises for the purpose of ascertaining whether appropriate precautions against the danger of fire are being sufficiently observed; and, in relation to a person so authorised subsection (3) of this section (with the omission of paragraphs (c), (ca) and (d) shall have effect as if in that subsection—

(a) any reference to an inspector or constable were a reference to a person so authorised, and

(b) the reference in paragraph (a) to subsection (2) of this section were a reference to the preceding provisions of this subsection.[2]

(10) Any person guilty of an offence under this section shall be liable on summary conviction to a fine not exceeding **level 4** on the standard scale.

(11) In this section—

"document" means anything in which information of any description is recorded, and

"copy", in relation to a document, means anything onto which information recorded in the document has been copied, by whatever means and whether directly or indirectly.*

[Gaming Act 1968, s 43 as amended by the Criminal Justice Act 1982, ss 38 and 46, the Police and Criminal Evidence Act 1984, Sch 7, the Gaming (Amendment) Act 1990, Sch, the Civil Evidence Act 1995, Sch 1, the Criminal Justice and Police Act 2001, Sch 2 and the Fire and Rescue Services Act 2004, Sch 1 and SI 2005/1541.]

---

*Repealed by the Gambling Act 2005, Sch 17 from a date to be appointed.

1. See Part IX: Precedents and Forms, Betting and Gaming, post, may be adapted. The issue and execution of this warrant must conform to the Police and Criminal Evidence Act 1984, ss 15 and 16 in Part I: Magistrates' Courts, Procedure, ante.

2. Reproduced as in force in England and Wales.

8–13423   44. Local authority not to maintain or contribute to premises licensed under Part II.   (1) No local authority shall maintain, or contribute towards the maintenance of, any premises in respect of which a licence under this Act is for the time being in force.

(2) *Repealed.*

(3) In this section "local authority", in relation to England and Wales, means the council of a county, London borough or county district, and the Common Council of the City of London, and, in relation to Scotland, means a county council, town council or district council.

[Gaming Act 1968, s 44, as amended by the Local Government Act 1972, Sch 30, the Local Government Act 1985, Sch 17 and the Statute Law Repeals Act 2004.]

8–13424   45. Offences by bodies corporate.   (1) Where an offence under this Act committed by a body corporate is proved to have been committed with the consent or connivance of, or to be attributable to any neglect on the part of, any director, manager, secretary or other similar officer of the body corporate or any person who was purporting to act in any such capacity, he as well as the body corporate shall be guilty of that offence and shall be liable to be proceeded against and punished accordingly.

(2) In this section "director", in relation to a body corporate established by or under any enactment for the purpose of carrying on under national ownership any industry or part of an industry or undertaking, being a body corporate whose affairs are managed by its members, means a member of that body corporate.

[Gaming Act 1968, s 45.]

8–13425 **46. Forfeiture.**   (1) Subject to the next following subsection, the court by or before which a person is convicted of an offence under this Act may order anything produced to the court, and shown to the satisfaction of the court to relate to the offence, to be forfeited and either destroyed or dealt with in such other manner as the court may order.

(2) The court shall not order anything to be forfeited under this section, where a person claiming to be the owner of or otherwise interested in it applies to be heard by the court, unless an opportunity has been given to him to show cause why the order should not be made.

[Gaming Act 1968, s 46.]

8–13426 **47. Service of documents.**   Any notice or other document required or authorised by any provision of this Act to be served on any person, or to be given or sent to any person, except an application or notice under section 12(3) of this Act, may be served, given or sent—

(a) by delivering it to him; or

(b) by sending it by post[1] to him at his usual or last-known residence or place of business in the United Kingdom; or

(c) in the case of a body corporate, by delivering it to the secretary or clerk of the body corporate at its registered or principal office or sending it by post[1] to the secretary or clerk of that body corporate at that office.

[Gaming Act 1968, s 47 as amended by SI 1999/2136.]

---

1. See presumption of due delivery in s 7 of the Interpretation Act 1978, in PART II: EVIDENCE, ante.

8–13427 **48. Financial provisions.**   (1) All expenses incurred by the Secretary of State under this Act, together with—

(a) any expenses incurred by the Board under paragraph 6 of Schedule 1 to this Act, and

(b) to such amount as the Secretary of State with the consent of the Treasury may approve, any other expenses incurred by the Board,

shall be defrayed out of moneys provided by Parliament.

(2) There shall be paid out of moneys provided by Parliament any increase attributable to this Act in the sums payable out of moneys so provided under any other enactment.

(3) Except as provided by subsections (4) and (4A) of this section the following fees shall be charged under this Act, that is to say—

(a) in respect of the grant of a licence under this Act, a fee of £31,063;

(b) in respect of the renewal of such a licence, a fee of £8,541;

(c) in respect of the transfer of such a licence, a fee of £8,232;

(ca) in respect of an application for a certificate consenting to the making of an application for the grant of a licence under this Act, a fee of £8,594;

(cb) in respect of an application for a certificate consenting to the making of an application for the transfer of such a licence, a fee of £5,371;

(d) in respect of the registration of a club or a miners' welfare institute under Part II of this Act, a fee of £235, and, in respect of the renewal of any such registration, a fee of £120;

(e) in respect of the registration of a club or a miner's welfare institute under Part III of this Act, a fee of £115, and, in respect of the renewal of any such registration, a fee of £70;

(f) in respect of the issue of a certificate of approval under Part I of Schedule 5 to this Act, a fee of £210;

(g) in respect of the issue of a certificate under section 27 of this Act, a fee of £6,425, and, in respect of the renewal of any such certificate, a fee of £4,518;

(h) in respect of the grant or renewal of a permit under section 34 of this Act, other than one expressed to be granted for the purposes of subsection (5E) of that section, a fee of £32;

(i) in respect of the grant or renewal by a local authority (as defined by paragraph 3 of Schedule 9 to this Act) of a permit under section 34 of this Act which is expressed to be granted for the purposes of subsection (5E) of that section, such fee, as may be fixed annually by the authority for the whole of their area not exceeding

(i) £250, or

(ii) the rate mentioned in subsection (4B) of this section whichever is the less.

(4) Where on the grant or renewal of a licence under this Act in respect of any premises the licensing authority impose any restrictions under paragraph 25 of Schedule 2 to this Act limiting gaming to which Part II of this Act applies to the playing of bingo, the fee to be charged—

(a) under paragraph (a) of subsection (3) of this section, shall be £4,232 instead of £31,063; and

(b) under paragraph (b) of that subsection, shall be £1,616 instead of £8,150,

and, if the licence is transferred while those restrictions continue to be in force, the fee to be charged under paragraph (c) of that subsection shall be £1,724 instead of £8,232.

(4A) Where the licence to which the certificate relates is to be, or is, subject to the restrictions mentioned in subsection (4) above, the fee to be charged under paragraph (ca) or (cb) of subsection (3) of this section shall be £8,351 or £5,567 instead of £8,594 or £5,371.

(4B) The rate referred to in subsection (3)(i) of this section is such rate as the local authority reasonably consider necessary to balance their income and expenditure in connection with permits of the kind mentioned in that provision (including expenditure in connection with enforcement).

(5) The Secretary of State may by order direct that any provision of subsection (3), (4) or (4A) of this section which is specified in the order shall have effect as if, for any reference in that provision to a sum so specified, there were substituted a reference to such other sum as may be so specified.

(6) All fees charged in accordance with paragraph (ca), (cb), (f) or (g) of subsection (3) of this section, and all fees charged in Scotland in accordance with paragraph (d) or paragraph (e) of that subsection, shall be paid into the Exchequer.

[Gaming Act 1968, s 48, as amended by SI 1989/294, the Gaming (Amendment) Act 1990, Schedule, SI 1991/2177, SI 1995/321, SI 1996/1359, SI 1998/456, SI 2001/725, 726, 1212, SI 2002/460, 637, 642, SI 2003/508 and 509, SI 2004/531, SI 2005/566 and 567.]

8–13428   49. Provision of information by licensing authorities and sheriff clerks.   Schedule 10 to this Act shall have effect with respect to—

(a) the performance by or on behalf of licensing authorities of certain functions in connection with licences under this Act and in connection with registration in England and Wales under Part II or Part III of this Act, and

(b) *Relates to Scotland.*

[Gaming Act 1968, s 49.]

8–13429   50. Annual report of Board.   The Board shall, at such time in each year as the Secretary of State may direct, send to the Secretary of State a report with respect to the performance of their functions; and the Secretary of State shall lay before Parliament a copy of every such report.

[Gaming Act 1968, s 50.]

8–13430   51. Regulations and orders.   (1) Subject to the next following subsection, the Secretary of State may make regulations for any purpose for which regulations are authorised or required to be made under this Act.

(2) The Secretary of State shall not make any regulations under this Act except after consultation with the Board.

(3) Any power to make regulations or an order under this Act may be exercised so as to make different provision for different areas or in relation to different cases or different circumstances to which the power is applicable.

(4) Any power conferred by this Act to make an order shall include power to vary or revoke the order by a subsequent order¹.

(5) Any power to make regulations or orders under this Act shall be exercisable by statutory instrument; and any statutory instrument containing any such regulations or order shall be subject to annulment in pursuance of a resolution of either House of Parliament.*

[Gaming Act 1968, s 51, as amended by the Statute Law Repeals Act 2004 and the Gambling Act 2005, Sch 16.]

---

*Repealed by the Gambling Act 2005, Sch 17 from a date to be appointed.

8–13431   51A. Meaning of "private gain" in relation to non-commercial entertainments.

(1) In construing sections 33 and 41 of this Act, proceeds of any entertainment, lottery or gaming promoted on behalf of a society to which this subsection extends which are applied for any purpose calculated to benefit the society as a whole shall not be held to be applied for purposes of private gain by reason only that their application for that purpose results in benefit to any person as an individual.

(2) Subsection (1) above extends to any society which is established and conducted either—

(a) wholly for purposes other than purposes of any commercial undertaking; or

(b) wholly or mainly for the purposes of participation in or support of athletic sports or athletic games;

and in this section "society" includes any club, institution, organisation or association of persons, by whatever name called, and any separate branch or section of such a club, institution, organisation or association.

(3) For the purposes of sections 33 and 41 of this Act, where any payment falls to be made by

way of a hiring, maintenance or other charge in respect of a machine to which Part III of this Act applies or in respect of any equipment for holding a lottery or gaming at any entertainment, then if, but only if, the amount of that charge falls to be determined wholly or partly by reference to the extent to which that or some other machine or equipment is used for the purposes of lotteries or gaming, that payment shall be held to be an application of the proceeds of the entertainment for the purposes of private gain[1].

[Gaming Act 1968, s 51A, as inserted by the Lotteries and Amusements Act 1976, Sch 4.]

---

1. There would not be "private gain" if an indirect benefit accrued to an individual so that he was able to avoid a loss dependent upon the extent to which a machine was used (*Avais v Hartford Shankhouse and District Working Men's Social Club and Institute Ltd* [1969] 2 AC 1, [1969] 1 All ER 130, 133 JP 133, HL).

8–13432 52. Interpretation. (1) In this Act, except in so far as the context otherwise requires, the following expressions have the meanings hereby assigned to them respectively, that is to say;—

"the Act of 1963" means the Betting, Gaming and Lotteries Act 1963;

"the appropriate fire and rescue authority", in relation to premises, means—

    (a) where the Regulatory Reform (Fire Safety) Order 2005 applies to the premises, the enforcing authority within the meaning given by article 25 of that Order; and

    (b) in any other case, the fire and rescue authority under the Fire and Rescue Services Act 2004 for the area where the premises are (or are to be) situated;[1]

"the Board" means the Gaming Board for Great Britain established under this Act;

"game of chance" does not include any athletic game or sport, but, with that exception, and subject to subsection (6) of this section, includes a game of chance and skill combined and a pretended game of chance or of chance and skill combined;

"gaming"[2] (subject to subsections (3) to (5) of this section) means the playing of a game of chance for winnings in money or money's worth, whether any person playing the game is at risk of losing any money or money's worth or not[3];

"inspector" has the meaning assigned to it by section 43 of this Act;

"licensing authority" has the meaning assigned to it by paragraph 1 of Schedule 2 to this Act;

"machine" includes any apparatus;

"newspaper" includes any journal, magazine or other periodical publication;

"premises" includes any place;

"prescribed" means prescribed by regulations made under this Act;

"travelling showmen's pleasure fair" means a pleasure fair consisting wholly or mainly of amusements provided by travelling showmen which is held on any day of a year on premises not previously used in that year on more than twenty-seven days for the holding of such a pleasure fair;

"vehicle" includes a railway carriage and also includes an aircraft while it is on the ground and a hover vehicle (that is to say, a vehicle designed to be supported on a cushion of air) whether it is on the ground or not;

"vessel" includes any ship, boat, raft or other apparatus constructed or adapted for floating on water;

"winnings" includes any prize or other winnings of any kind and any reference to the amount or to the payment of winnings shall be construed accordingly.

(2) In this Act "miner's welfare institute" means an association organised for the social well-being and recreation of persons employed in or about coal mines (or of such persons in particular) where—

    (a) the institute is managed by a committee or board of which not less than two-thirds consists partly of persons appointed by or on the nomination of, or appointed or elected from among persons nominated by, a licensed operator or operators (within the meaning of the Coal Industry Act 1994) and partly of persons appointed by or on the nomination of, or appointed or elected from among persons nominated by, an organisation or organisations representing persons in or about coal mines;

    (aa) in the case of an institute in relation to which either—

        (i) the making of an appointment or nomination by a licensed operator, or

        (ii) the making of an appointment or nomination by such an organisation as is mentioned in paragraph (a) above,

    is not practicable or would not be appropriate, it is managed by a committee or board of which not less than two-thirds consists partly of persons employed or formerly employed in or about coal mines and partly of persons appointed by the Coal Industry Social Welfare Organisation or a body or person to which the functions of that Organisation have been transferred under section 12(3) of the Miners' Welfare Act 1952; or

    (b) the premises of the institute, if they are in England or Wales, are held on trusts to which section 2 of the Recreational Charities Act 1958, applies, or if they are in Scotland, are held on trust for charitable purposes ("charitable" being construed in the same way as if it were contained in the Income Tax Acts).

(3) Where apart from this subsection the playing of a game of chance would constitute gaming and also constitutes a lottery, then if—

(a) in so far as it is a lottery, it is a lottery promoted as mentioned in section 3 (small lotteries incidental to certain entertainments), 4 (private lotteries), 5 (societies' lotteries) or 6 (local lotteries) of the Lotteries and Amusements Act 1976 or a lottery forming part of the National Lottery for the purposes of Part 1 of the National Lottery etc Act 1993, and

(b) each winner of a prize is ascertained by reference to not more than three determining factors, each of those factors being either the result of a draw or other determination or the outcome of an event,

the playing of the game shall not constitute gaming for the purposes of this Act.

(4) In this Act "gaming" does not include the making of bets by way of pool betting.

(5) For the purposes of this Act a machine shall be taken not to be used for gaming if it is used in such a way that no game played by means of the machine can result in a player, or a person claiming under a player, receiving or being entitled to receive any article, benefit or advantage other than one (but not both) of the following that is to say—

(a) an opportunity afforded by the automatic action of the machine to play one or more further games without the insertion of any cash or token;

(b) the delivery by means of the machine of one or more coins or tokens as a prize in respect of a game where one or more coins or tokens of an equal or greater value or aggregate value were inserted into the machine by or on behalf of the player in order to play that game.

(6) In determining for the purposes of this Act whether a game, which is played otherwise than against one or more other players, is a game of chance and skill combined, the possibility of superlative skill eliminating the elements of chance shall be disregarded.

(7) For the purposes of any provision of this Act which relates to making a charge, or charging a levy, it is immaterial whether a charge or levy is compulsory, customary or voluntary, and any reference to making a charge or charging a levy shall be construed accordingly.

(8) Subject to subsections (1) to (7) of this section, expressions used in this Act to which a meaning is assigned by section 55(1) of the Act of 1963 have the same meanings in this Act as in that Act.

(9) Except in so far as the court otherwise requires, any reference in this Act to an enactment shall be construed as a reference to that enactment as amended or extended by or under any other enactment, including this Act.★

[Gaming Act 1968, s 52, as amended by the Lotteries and Amusement Act 1976, Schedule 4, the Coal Industry Act 1987, Sch 1, the National Lottery etc Act 1993, Sch 1, the Coal Industry Act 1994, Sch 2 and SI 2005/1541.]

★**Repealed by the Gambling Act 2005, Sch 17 from a date to be appointed.**

1. Definition inserted in relation to England and Wales by SI 2005/1541.

2. This involves some active participation in the game, not mere passive participation in a lottery (*DPP v Regional Pool Promotions Ltd* [1964] 2 QB 244, [1964] 1 All ER 65, 128 JP 150; *Armstrong v DPP* [1965] AC 1262, [1965] 2 All ER 745, 129 JP 493, HL). The playing of whist is gaming: so far as the holding of whist drives is concerned, note that s 41, ante, makes special provision for gaming at entertainments not held for private gain. Gaming in a private house on domestic occasions is lawful and not within the control of the Gaming Act 1968. As to the playing of whist and other games in liquor licensed premises, see s 6(3), ante.

3. This definition abrogates the decision of the House of Lords in *McCollom v Wrightson* [1968] AC 522, [1968] 1 All ER 514, 132 JP 261; based on the (now repealed) definition of "gaming" in the Betting, Gaming and Lotteries Act 1963.

8–13433 **53. Minor and consequential amendments, and repeals.** (1) Subject to the provisions of any order made under the following section—

(a) the Act of 1963 shall have effect subject to the amendments specified in Part I of Schedule 11 to this Act;

(b) the enactments specified in Part III of Schedule 11 to this Act shall have effect subject to the amendments specified in that Part of that Schedule; and

(c) the enactments specified in Schedule 12 to this Act are hereby repealed to the extent specified in the third column of that Schedule.

(2) The rules of law relating to common gaming houses are hereby abolished.

[Gaming Act 1968, s 53.]

8–13434

SCHEDULES

SCHEDULE 1

PROVISIONS AS TO GAMING BOARD FOR GREAT BRITAIN

Repealed by the Gambling Act 2005, Sch 17.

Section 11(1)　　　　　　　　　　SCHEDULE 2
GRANT, RENEWAL, CANCELLATION AND TRANSFER OF LICENCES*

(*As amended by Finance Acts 1969 and 1970, the Courts Act 1971, the Betting and Gaming Duties Act 1972, the Local Government Act 1972, the Betting and Gaming Duties Act 1981, Sch 5, the Gaming (Amendment) Act 1982, Sch 1, the Criminal Justice Act 1982, ss 38 and 46, the Gaming (Amendment) Act 1990, the Police and Magistrates' Courts Act 1994, Sch 8, the Finance Act 1997, Sch 2, the Fire and Rescue Services Act 2004, Sch 1 and SI 2005/1541.*)

Introductory

8–13435　**1.** (1) Subject to the provisions of this Schedule with respect to certificates of consent, the authority responsible for the grant, renewal, cancellation and transfer of licences under this Act—

(*a*)　in any petty sessions area in England or Wales, or

(*b*)　*Scotland*,

shall be the authority which under Schedule 1 to the Act of 1963 is responsible for the grant or renewal of book makers' permits, betting agency permits and betting office licences in that area and references to the proper officer of a licensing authority shall be construed accordingly.

(2) Any such authority is in this Act referred to as a "licensing authority".

2. (1) In this Schedule "the licensing authority", in relation to a licence under this Act or to an application relating to such a licence, means the licensing authority for the petty sessions area in England or Wales, or the licensing area in Scotland, in which the relevant premises are or are to be situated[1].

(2) In this Schedule—

"the appropriate collector of duty" means the Collector of Customs and Excise for the area in which the relevant premises are or are to be situated;

"the appropriate local authority"—

(*a*)　in England and Wales, means the local authority (being the council of a London borough or county district or the Common Council of the City of London) in whose area the relevant premises are or are to be situated, and

(*b*)　in Scotland, where the relevant premises are or are to be situated in a burgh, means the council of that burgh, and in any other case means the council of the county, and the council of the district, in which the relevant premises are or are to be situated;

"the appropriate officer of police" means the chief officer of police, or in Scotland, the chief constable, for the police area in which the relevant premises are or are to be situated;

"bingo club licence" means a licence under this Act granted in respect of any premises subject to restrictions under paragraph 25 of this Schedule whereby gaming to which Part II of this Act applies on those premises is limited to the playing of bingo;

"the relevant premises", in relation to a licence under this Act or to an application relating to such a licence, means the premises in respect of which the licence is for the time being in force or the premises to which the application relates, as the case may be.

2A. (1) Each licensing authority shall for each year fix a day in each of the months of—

(*a*)　January, April, July and October if the authority is in England or Wales; or

(*b*)　January, March, June and October if the authority is in Scotland,

as a day on which, subject to paragraphs 7 and 13 of this Schedule, they will hold a meeting for the purpose of considering any application for the grant or renewal of a licence under this Act then awaiting consideration.

(2) In addition to any meeting on a day fixed in pursuance of the preceding sub-paragraph, a licensing authority may hold a meeting on any other day for the purpose of considering such applications as are mentioned in that sub-paragraph.

---

*Repealed by the Gambling Act 2005, Sch 17 from a date to be appointed.
1. A gaming licensing committee may be required to hear an application for a licence even though the premises to which it relates have not yet been built. If in such circumstances a licence were granted, but the building was erected in non-conformity with the plan submitted to the justices, the building would not be licensed (*R v Gaming Licensing Committee, ex p Gala Leisure Ltd* (1996) Times, 5 April).

Certificate of consent for purposes of application for licence

8–13436　**3.** (1) An application for the grant of a licence under this Act in respect of any premises shall be of no effect unless—

(*a*)　the Board have issued to the applicant a certificate consenting to his applying for such a licence in respect of those premises, and that certificate is for the time being in force and the application is made within the period specified in the certificate, and

(*b*)　where the certificate is limited to a bingo club licence, the application is for the grant of a bingo club licence in respect of those premises.

(2) In the following provisions of this Schedule any reference to an application for the grant of a licence under this Act shall be construed as not including any application which by virtue of the preceding sub-paragraph is of no effect.

4.—(1) The provisions of this paragraph shall have effect with respect to any application for a certificate of consent (in this paragraph referred to as a "consent application") for the purposes of an application for the grant of a licence under this Act (in this paragraph referred to, in relation to a consent application, as "the relevant licence application").

(2) Any consent application shall be made to the Board by the person proposing to make the relevant licence application, and shall—

(a) specify the premises in respect of which the relevant licence application is proposed to be made, and

(b) state whether the relevant licence application will be for the grant of a bingo club licence or for a licence under this Act other than a bingo club licence.

(3) *Repealed.*

(4) The Board shall not issue a certificate on a consent application if it appears to the board that the applicant—

(a) not being a body corporate, is under twenty-one years of age, or

(b) not being a body corporate, is not resident in Great Britain or was not so resident throughout the period of six months immediately preceding the date on which the application was made, or

(c) being a body corporate, is not incorporated in Great Britain.

(5) Subject to sub-paragraph (4) of this paragraph, in determining whether to issue to an applicant a certificate consenting to his applying for the grant of a licence under this Act in respect of any premises, the Board shall have regard only to the question whether, in their opinion, the applicant is likely to be capable of, and diligent in, securing that the provisions of this Act and of any regulations made under it will be complied with, that gaming on those premises will be fairly and properly conducted, and that the premises will be conducted without disorder or disturbance.

(6) For the purposes of sub-paragraph (5) of this paragraph the Board shall in particular take into consideration the character, reputation and financial standing—

(a) of the applicant, and

(b) of any person (other than the applicant) by whom, if a licence were granted on the relevant licence application in respect of any club, that club would be managed, or for whose benefit, if a licence were so granted, that club would be carried on,

but may also take into consideration any other circumstances appearing to them to be relevant in determining whether the applicant is likely to be capable of, and diligent in, securing the matters mentioned in that sub-paragraph.

(7) If on a consent application made to the Board in respect of any premises the Board issue to the applicant a certificate consenting to his applying for the grant of a licence under this Act in respect of those premises, the certificate shall—

(a) specify the applicant and those premises;

(b) specify a period within the relevant licence application can be made; and

(c) state whether the consent is or is not limited to a bingo club licence.

Application for grant of licence (general provisions)[1]

5.—(1) An application for the grant of a licence under this Act may be made at any time.

(2) Any such application shall be made to the proper officer of the licensing authority in such form and manner as may be prescribed, and shall specify by name and description a club which either—

(a) is a club for whose purposes the relevant premises are used at the time when the application is made, or are intended, if the licence is granted, to be used, or

(b) is intended, if the licence is granted, to be formed as a club for whose purposes the relevant premises will be used,

and shall contain such other particulars as may be prescribed and shall be accompanied by a copy of the certificate of consent[2] issued by the Board for the purposes of that application.

(3) Not later than seven days after the date on which the application is made, the applicant shall send a copy of the application—

(a) to the Board;

(b) to the appropriate officer of police;

(c) to the appropriate local authority;

(d) to the appropriate fire and rescue authority, if that authority is not the same body as the appropriate local authority; and

(e) to the appropriate collector of duty.

6.—(1) Not later than fourteen days after the making of any such application to the licensing authority, the applicant shall cause notice of the making of the application to be published by means of an advertisement in a newspaper circulating in the licensing authority's area.

(2) A notice published in pursuance of this paragraph shall specify the name of the applicant, the name of the club and the location of the relevant premises, shall indicate whether the application is for a bingo club licence or for a licence under this Act other than a bingo club licence, and shall state that any person who desires to object to the grant of the licence should send to the proper officer of the licensing authority, before such date (not being

earlier than fourteen days after the publication of the advertisement) as may be specified in the notice, two copies of a brief statement in writing of the grounds of his objection.

(3) Not later than fourteen days before the date specified in the notice in accordance with the preceding sub-paragraph the applicant shall cause a like notice to be displayed outside³ the entrance to the relevant premises; and the applicant shall take such steps as he reasonably can to keep that notice so displayed until that date.

(4) A notice published or displayed under this paragraph shall not include any matter which is not required by the preceding provisions of this paragraph to be included in it.

7. (1) Not later than seven days after the publication of the newspaper containing the advertisement required by the last preceding paragraph, the applicant shall send a copy of that newspaper to the proper officer of the licensing authority; and the licensing authority shall not consider the application earlier than fourteen days after the date specified in the advertisement.

(2) On or after the date so specified, but not less than seven days before the date fixed by the licensing authority for the consideration of the application, the proper officer of the licensing authority shall send notice in writing of the date, time and place of the meeting of the authority at which the application will be considered—

(a) to the applicant;

(b) to all the persons and bodies specified in paragraph 5(3) of this Schedule; and

(c) if the proper officer has received from any other person an objection in writing which has not been withdrawn and the address of that person is known to the proper officer, to that person.

(3) The proper officer of the licensing authority shall also cause notice of that meeting to be displayed at the place where the meeting is to be held in a position where the notice may conveniently be read by members of the public.

(4) With the notice sent to the applicant in accordance with sub-paragraph (2) of this paragraph there shall be enclosed a copy of any objection to the grant of the licence which has been received by the proper officer of the licensing authority and which has not been withdrawn.

---

1. In a case decided upon the code set out in paras 8–11 of this Schedule, it was held that the provisions relating to the procedure on making an application were mandatory and, if not strictly complied with, invalidated the application (*R v Pontypool Gaming Licensing Committee, ex p Risca Cinemas Ltd* [1970] 3 All ER 241, 134 JP 648); and see *R v Leicester Gaming Licensing Committee, ex p Shine* [1971] 3 All ER 1082; cf *R v Dacorum Gaming Licensing Committee, ex p EMI Cinemas and Leisure Ltd* [1971] 3 All ER 666, 135 JP 610. However, purely formalistic objections to a notice under para (6) will not be upheld (*R v Brighton Gaming Licensing Committee, ex p Cotedale Ltd* [1978] 3 All ER 897, 143 JP 98).

2. An application for a licence is of no effect unless the Gaming Board has issued a certificate of consent: see para 3, ante.

3. "Displayed outside" means made visible outside so that those outside can read it, but the notice need not be affixed to the outside of the premises (*R v Newcastle upon Tyne Gaming Licensing Committee, ex p White Hart Enterprises Ltd* [1977] 3 All ER 961, [1977] 1 WLR 1135).

Application for grant of licence (initial period)

8–13437 **8–11.** *Repealed.*

Application for renewal of licence

8–13438 **12.** (1) Any application for the renewal of a licence under this Act shall (subject to sub-paragraph (2) of this paragraph) be made not earlier than five or later than two months before the date on which the licence is due to expire, and shall be made to the proper officer of to the licensing authority in such form and manner, and shall contain such particulars, as may be prescribed.

(2) The licensing authority may in any particular case entertain an application for the renewal of a licence under this Act which is made later than is required by the last preceding sub-paragraph if—

(a) they are satisfied that the failure to make the application in time was due to inadvertence, and

(b) the application is made before the end of such extended period as the licensing authority may in that case allow.

13. (1) Not later than seven days after the date on which an application for the renewal of a licence under this Act is made, the applicant shall send a copy of the application—

(a) to the Board;

(b) to the appropriate officer of police;

(c) to the appropriate local authority;

(d) to the appropriate fire and rescue authority, if that authority is not the same body as the appropriate local authority; and

(e) to the appropriate collector of duty.

(2) (Not later than fourteen days after the making of any such application, the proper officer of the licensing authority shall cause notice of the making of the application to be published by means of an advertisement in a newspaper circulating in the licensing authority's area.

(3) A notice published in pursuance of the preceding sub-paragraph shall state that any person who desires to object to the renewal by the licensing authority of the licence should send to the proper officer of the licensing authority, before such date (not being earlier than fourteen days after the publication of the advertisement) as may be specified in the notice, two copies of a brief statement in writing of the grounds of his objection.

(4) On or after the date so specified, but not less than seven days before the day appointed for the consideration

of the application, the proper officer of the licensing authority shall send notice in writing of the date, time and place of the meeting of the authority at which the application will be considered—

    (*a*)   to the applicant;

    (*b*)   to all the persons and bodies specified in sub-paragraph (1) of this paragraph; and

    (*c*)   if the proper officer has received from any other person an objection in writing which has not been withdrawn and the address of that person is known to the proper officer, to that person.

(5) With the notice sent to the applicant in accordance with the preceding sub-paragraph there shall be enclosed a copy of any objection to the renewal of the licence which has been received by the proper officer of the licensing authority and which has not been withdrawn.

Proceedings on application for grant or renewal

8–13439   **14.** (1) On any application for the grant or renewal of a licence under this Act, the licensing authority may grant or renew the licence without hearing the applicant if no objection to the grant or renewal has been made by any person or if every such objection has been withdrawn before the beginning of the meeting of the authority at which the authority considers the application.

(2) Except as provided by the preceding sub-paragraph, on any such application any of the following persons, that is to say—

    (*a*)   the applicant;

    (*b*)   any person from whom an objection in writing which has not been withdrawn was received by the proper officer of the licensing authority before the date on which he sent to the applicant the notice required by paragraph 7(2), or (as the case may be) the copy of that objection required to be sent to him by paragraph 13 (5), of this Schedule; and

    (*c*)   the person making any other objection which the authority have decided under paragraph 15 of this Schedule that they will hear,

shall be entitled to be heard either in person or by counsel or a solicitor; and the authority shall also hear any representations made by or on behalf of the Board, the appropriate officer of police, the appropriate local authority, the Comrs of Customs and Excise or the appropriate fire and rescue authority.

15. Where, in the case of an application for the grant or renewal of a licence under this Act, an objection to the grant or renewal is received by the proper officer of the licensing authority on or after the date referred to in paragraph 14(2) (*b*) of this Schedule, the authority—

    (*a*)   may refuse to entertain the objection, or

    (*b*)   may entertain it but, unless the applicant requests otherwise, shall not hear it until the objector has given to the proper officer and to the applicant, and the applicant has had time to consider, a brief statement in writing of the grounds of the objection.

16. A licensing authority may from time to time adjourn the consideration of any application for the grant or renewal of a licence under this Act, whether for the purposes of paragraph 15 of this Schedule or for any other purpose.

17. On the consideration of any application for the grant or renewal of a licence under this Act, a licensing authority may take evidence on oath and may make such order as they think fit for the payment of costs (or, in Scotland, expenses)—

    (*a*)   by the applicant to any person who made an objection to the grant or renewal which was not withdrawn before the date referred to in paragraph 14(2) (*b*) of this Schedule, or

    (*b*)   by any such person to the applicant.

Grounds for refusal to grant or renew licence

8–13440   **18.** (1) The licensing authority may refuse to grant a licence under this Act if it is not shown to their satisfaction that, in the area of the authority, a substantial demand already exists on the part of prospective players for gaming facilities of the kind proposed to be provided on the relevant premises[1].

(2) Where it is shown to the satisfaction of the licensing authority that such a demand already exists, the licensing authority may refuse to grant a licence if it is not shown to their satisfaction—

    (*a*)   that no gaming facilities of the kind in question are available in that area or in any locality outside that area which is reasonably accessible to the prospective players in question, or

    (*b*)   where such facilities are available, that they are insufficient to meet the demand.

19. (1) For the purposes of the last preceding paragraph, the Board may from time to time give advice[2] to any licensing authority as to the extent of the demand on the part of prospective players for gaming facilities of any particular kind, either generally in Great Britain or in any particular part of Great Britain, and as to the extent to which, and the places in which, gaming facilities of any particular kind are available.

(2) In determining whether, on an application for the grant of a licence under this Act, a licence should be refused on the grounds specified in the last preceding paragraph, the licensing authority shall take into account any advice given to them by the Board in pursuance of this paragraph, as well as any representations which, at the time when the application is being considered by the licensing authority, are made to the authority by or on behalf of the Board or any other person entitled to be heard on the consideration of the application.

20. (1) Without prejudice to paragraph 18 of this Schedule, the licensing authority may refuse to grant or renew a licence under this Act on any one or more of the following grounds, that is to say—

(a) that the relevant premises are unsuitable by reason of their lay-out, character, condition or location[3];*
(b) that the applicant is not a fit and proper person[4] to be the holder of a licence under this Act;
(c) that, if the licence were granted or renewed, the club specified in the application would be managed by, or carried on for the benefit of, a person (other than the applicant) who would himself be refused the grant or renewal of a licence under this Act on the grounds that he is not a fit and proper person to be the holder of such a licence;
(d) that the licensing authority, the Board, the appropriate officer of police, the appropriate local authority or the appropriate fire and rescue authority, or the authorised representatives of any of them, have been refused reasonable facilities to inspect the premises;
(e) that any duty payable in respect of the premises under section 13 of the Finance Act 1966 or section 2 of or Schedule 1 to the Finance Act 1970 or s 13 of or Schedule 2 to the Betting and Gaming Duties Act 1972, or section 14 of or Schedule 2 to the Betting and Gaming Duties Act 1981, remains unpaid;
(f) that any bingo duty payable in respect of bingo played on the premises remains unpaid;
(g) that any gaming duty charged on the premises remains unpaid.

(2) In determining for the purposes of this paragraph whether the relevant premises are unsuitable by reason of any matter mentioned in sub-paragraph (1) (a) of this paragraph, the licensing authority shall take into account any advice given to them by the Board with respect to that matter.*

(3) Where the licensing authority entertain an application for the grant or renewal of a licence under this Act in respect of any premises, and are satisfied that any bingo duty payable as mentioned in sub-paragraph (1) (f) of this paragraph remains unpaid, they shall refuse the application.

21. (1) The licensing authority may refuse to renew a licence under this Act on any one or more of the following grounds, in addition to those specified in paragraph 20 of this Schedule, that is to say—

(a) that it is not shown to their satisfaction that, in the area of the authority, a substantial demand exists on the part of players or prospective players for gaming facilities of the kind proposed to be provided on the relevant premises[5];
(b) that a person has been convicted of an offence under this Act in respect of a contravention, in connection with the relevant premises, of any of the provisions of this Act, or of any regulations made thereunder;
(c) that, while the licence has been in force, the relevant premises have not been so conducted as to prevent disturbance or disorder;
(d) that, while the licence has been in force, gaming on the relevant premises, has been dishonestly conducted;
(e) that, while the licence has been in force[6], the relevant premises have been used for an unlawful purpose or as a resort of criminals or prostitutes;
(f) that, while the licence has been in force, appropriate precautions against the danger of fire have not been observed, or have been insufficiently observed, in the use of the relevant premises.

(2) The licensing authority may also refuse to renew a licence under this Act on the grounds that, within the period of twelve months ending with the date on which the licensing authority consider the application for renewal of the licence, a notice under paragraph 7 of Schedule 5 to this Act has been served on a person stating that a relevant certificate issued in respect of him under section 19 of this Act is revoked as from the end of a period specified in that notice.

(3) For the purposes of sub-paragraph (2) of this paragraph a certificate issued in respect of a person under section 19 of this Act shall be taken to have been a relevant certificate if it was a certificate certifying that he had been approved by the Board under that section—

(a) in respect of the performance on the relevant premises of a function which, at the time when the notice referred to in that sub-paragraph was served, he was authorised or required to perform on those premises in pursuance of a service agreement which was then in force, or
(b) in respect of his acting in relation to those premises in a capacity in which, at the time when that notice was served, he was acting, or was authorised or required to act, in relation to those premises.

(4) Paragraph 19 of this Schedule shall have effect for the purposes of sub-paragraph (1) (a) of this paragraph as it has effect for the purposes of paragraph 18 of this Schedule.

(5) In this paragraph "service agreement" has the same meaning as in section 19 of this Act.

22. (1) The licensing authority shall refuse to grant or renew a licence under this Act if, by virtue of a disqualification order made under section 24 of this Act, such a licence is for the time being prohibited from being held in respect of the relevant premises.

(2) The licensing authority shall refuse to renew a licence under this Act if they are satisfied that, while the licence has been in force, the relevant premises have been habitually used for an unlawful purpose or as a resort of criminals or prostitutes.

23. Where for the purposes of paragraph 20(1) (a) of this Schedule it falls to be determined whether the relevant premises are unsuitable in respect of their location and those premises were used for the purpose of gaming during a period of not less than six months ending with 19th December 1967—

(a) the licensing authority shall consider what (if any) evidence there is that those premises appeared to be unsuitable for that purpose during that period, and
(b) if it appears to them that there is no evidence, or insufficient evidence, that they were unsuitable as mentioned in the preceding sub-paragraph, the licensing authority shall have regard in particular to that fact in determining that question.

1. The Committee has a discretion. It need not refuse an application just because a substantial existing demand is not proved; it may take into account more lavish facilities in proposed premises which may suit local people more than existing premises (*R v Crown Court at Manchester, ex p Cambros Enterprises Ltd* (1973) 117 Sol Jo 222, 137 JP Jo 266).

2. This "statutory" advice, which the licensing authority are required to take into account, is not defined in the Act, nor is any procedure for tendering or receiving it laid down. It is expected to fall into two categories: first, general advice as to the extent and character of gaming in the country or a particular area, and secondly, particular advice as to an application to the authority. By para 28 of Sch 2 the clerk of the licensing authority is required, on request, to furnish an applicant with a statement of any advice given by the Board which the authority propose to take into account in determining the application. It is anticipated that generally the Board will submit its advice in writing and, if it is concerned in a particular application, will be legally represented at the hearing. It seems clear that, although the advice is not in the nature of evidence, it will be a material and important factor in the determination of an application. As a result, it is submitted that, in so far as any advice is related to, or material to, any application, it should be known to the applicant so that he may deal with it if he wishes.

3. See reg 4 of the Gaming Clubs (Licensing) Regulations 1969, this PART, post, whereby a licence may be refused if a person might gain access to the premises from private premises not included in the licence.

4. Regard must be had to s 13 of the Sex Discrimination Act 1975 (noted under s 3 of the Licensing Act 1964, ante).

5. For the meaning of the term "relevant premises", see para 2(2), ante.

6. Unlawful conduct which occurred during the currency of an earlier licence cannot be relied upon for the purposes of this ground; see *R v Crown Court at Knightsbridge, ex p Marcrest Ltd* [1983] 1 All ER 1148, [1983] 1 WLR 300.

Restrictions attached to licence

8–13450   24. On granting or renewing a licence under this Act, the licensing authority may impose such restrictions (if any) on the hours during which gaming will be permitted to take place on the relevant premises as appear to the authority to be necessary for the purpose of preventing disturbance or annoyance to the occupiers of other premises in the vicinity.

25. (1) Without prejudice to the last preceding paragraph, on granting or renewing a licence under this Act the licensing authority, may impose restrictions of either or both of the following descriptions that is to say—

(*a*) restrictions limiting the gaming to a particular part or parts of the relevant premises, and

(*b*) restrictions limiting the gaming to a particular kind of game[1] or particular kinds of games.

(2) Subject to the following provisions of this paragraph, on granting or renewing a licence under this Act the licensing authority (whether they impose any restrictions under sub-paragraph (1) of this paragraph or not) may[2] impose restrictions limiting the purposes, other than gaming, for which, while the licence is in force, the relevant premises may be used, either generally or at such times as may be specified in the restrictions or at times when such conditions as may be so specified are fulfilled.

(3) Where an application for a licence under this Act is made in pursuance of a certificate of consent which states that the consent is limited to a bingo club licence, then—

(*a*) on granting a licence in pursuance of that consent, and

(*b*) if a licence has been so granted, on any renewal of that licence,

the licensing authority shall impose restrictions under sub-paragraph (1) of this paragraph in respect of the relevant premises limiting gaming to which Part II of this Act applies to the playing of bingo.

(4) No restrictions shall be imposed under sub-paragraph (2) of this paragraph where, whether in pursuance of sub-paragraph (3) of this paragraph or otherwise, the licensing authority on granting or renewing the licence, impose restrictions under sub-paragraph (1) of this paragraph in respect of the relevant premises limiting gaming to which Part II of this Act applies to the playing of bingo.

(5) Subject to sub-paragraphs (3) and (4) of this paragraph, in determining whether to impose any restrictions under this paragraph, the licensing authority shall take into account any advice given to them by the Board (whether given for the purposes of this paragraph or in pursuance of paragraph 19 of this Schedule), as well as any representations which, at the time when the application is being considered by the licensing authority, are made to the authority by or on behalf of the Board or any other person entitled to be heard on the consideration of the application.

26. Any restrictions imposed under paragraph 24 or paragraph 25 of this Schedule shall be imposed so as to have effect until the licence ceases to have effect or is next renewed (whichever first occurs), but without prejudice, where the licence is renewed, to any power or duty of the licensing authority under either of those paragraphs to impose the like or any other restrictions on renewing the licence.

1. A licence, other than one limited to bingo, bridge, or whist, or to bridge and whist, must include a restriction limiting the gaming to the playing of games other than bingo: reg 5 of the Gaming Clubs (Licensing) Regulations 1969, this PART, post. Restrictions imposed limiting the kind of game will not apply to games to which s 21 applies: see sub-s (5) of that section.

2. And *shall*, in the case of a licence other than one limited to bingo, bridge or whist, or bridge and whist, impose a restriction limiting the purposes for which the relevant premises may at any time be used to purposes *other than* dancing or the provision of music or entertainment by persons actually present and performing: reg 6 of the Gaming Clubs (Licensing) Regulations 1969, this PART, post.

Regulations under section 22(3)

8–13451   27. Notwithstanding anything in paragraphs 18 to 26 of this Schedule, the licensing authority, in dealing with any application for the grant or renewal of a licence under this Act, shall comply with any regulations under section 22(3) of this Act which are for the time being in force.

Notification of advice given by Board

8–13452   **28.** The proper officer of the licensing authority shall, at the request of any applicant for the grant or renewal of a licence under this Act, furnish him with a statement setting out any advice given to the licensing authority by the Board which the licensing authority propose to take into account in determining the application.

Appeal in England and Wales by applicant

8–13453   **29.** (1) Where on an application under this Schedule to a licensing authority in England or Wales the authority refuse to grant or renew a licence, or impose restrictions under paragraph 24 or paragraph 25 of this Schedule, the proper officer of the licensing authority shall forthwith give notice of the decision of the authority to the applicant; and, within 21 days from the date of service of that notice, the applicant may, by notice to the proper officer of the authority, appeal against the decision to the Crown Court.

(2) As soon as practicable after receiving notice of appeal against a decision of the licensing authority, the proper officer the authority shall send the notice to the appropriate officer of the Crown Court together with a statement of the decision against which the appeal is brought and of the name and last-known residence or place of business of the appellant and of any person who opposed the application before the authority.

(3) On receipt of the notice of appeal, the appropriate officer of the Crown Court shall enter the appeal and give in writing to the appellant, to the Board, to the appropriate officer of police, to the appropriate collector of duty, to any person who opposed the application before the authority and to the licensing authority not less than fourteen days' notice of the date, time and place appointed for the hearing of the appeal.

(4) The Crown Court may by its order allow or dismiss the appeal, or reverse or vary any part of the decision of the licensing authority, whether the appeal relates to that part of it or not, and may deal with the application as if it had been made to the Crown Court in the first instance; and the judgment of the Crown Court on the appeal shall be final.

(5) A justice shall not act in the hearing or determination of an appeal under this paragraph from any decision in which he took part.

   30. (2) Where the Crown Court—

    (*a*)   has allowed such an appeal, or
    (*b*)   has awarded the licensing authority any costs and is satisfied that the licensing authority cannot recover those costs,

the court shall order payment out of central funds of such sums as appear to the court sufficient to indemnify the licensing authority from all costs and charges whatever to which they have been put in consequence of the appellant's having served notice of appeal.

Appeal in England or Wales by Board

8–13454   **31.** (1) Where a licensing authority in England or Wales grant or renew a licence under this Act after hearing any objection or representations made by or on behalf of the Board or any other person, and the Board desire to contend—

    (*a*)   that the licence ought not to have been granted or renewed, or
    (*b*)   that, on granting or renewing the licence, the licensing authority ought to have imposed restrictions, or (where restrictions were imposed) ought to have imposed more stringent restrictions,

the Board may, by notice to the proper officer of the licensing authority, appeal against the decision of the licensing authority to the Crown Court.*

(2) As soon as practicable after receiving notice of appeal under this paragraph, the proper officer of the licensing authority shall send the notice to the clerk of the peace together with a statement of the decision against which the appeal is brought and the name and last-known residence or place of business of the applicant who applied for the grant or renewal and of any person (other than the Board) who opposed the application before the licensing authority.*

(3) On receipt of the notice of appeal, the appropriate officer of the Crown Court shall enter the appeal and give in writing to the Board, to the applicant, to the appropriate officer of police, to any person (other than the Board) who oppose the application before the licensing authority, and to the licensing authority, not less than seven days' notice of the date, time and place appointed for the hearing of the appeal.

(4) Sub-paragraphs (4) and (5) of paragraph 29 of this Schedule shall have effect in relation to appeals under this paragraph as they have effect in relation to appeals under that paragraph.

   32. (1) On determining any appeal under the last preceding paragraph, or on being satisfied that the Board, after giving notice of such an appeal, have failed to prosecute it, the Crown Court may make such order as it thinks fit for the payment of costs by or to—

    (*a*)   the applicant who applied for the grant or renewal to which the appeal relates;
    (*b*)   the Board;
    (*c*)   any person (other than the Board) who opposed the application before the licensing authority; or
    (*d*)   the licensing authority.

(2) Sub-paragraph (2) of paragraph 30 of this Schedule shall have effect for the purposes of this paragraph as they have effect for the purposes of that paragraph.

   33, 34. *Appeal in Scotland.*

Revocation by Board of certificate of consent

8–13455 35. (1) Where under the preceding provisions of this Schedule the Board have issued to a person a certificate of consent to his applying for a licence under this Act in respect of any premises, then, subject to the following provisions of this paragraph, the Board may at any time revoke that certificate, whether before that time—

(a) the holder of the certificate has applied for a licence under this Act in respect of those premises, or

(b) in pursuance of such an application, the licensing authority have granted him such a licence,

or not.

(2) Subject to the next following sub-paragraph, the Board shall not revoke a certificate of consent in respect of any premises at any time unless it appears to them—

(a) that, if the holder of the certificate were then applying for such a certificate under paragraph 4 of this Schedule, the Board would be precluded by sub-paragraph (4) of that paragraph from issuing such a certificate to him, or

(b) that any information which, in or in connection with the application on which the certificate was issued, was given to the Board by or on behalf of the applicant for the certificate was false in a material particular, or

(c) that, since the certificate was issued, a licence under this Act held by the holder of the certificate (whether in respect of the same or different premises) has been cancelled by virtue of a disqualification order made under section 24 of this Act or under this Schedule or in the exercise of the powers conferred on the licensing authority or the court by the following provisions of this Schedule.

(3) Where the holder of a certificate of consent in respect of any premises has in pursuance of the certificate applied for the grant of a licence under this Act in respect of those premises, and such a licence has been granted and is for the time being in force, the Board may revoke the certificate at any time if it appears to them—

(a) that, in relation to the conduct of the premises or the conduct of gaming on those premises, effective control is being exercised by a person other than the holder of the certificate, and

(b) that the other person in question, in view of his character and reputation, is not a person to whom, if he were then applying for a certificate of consent under the preceding provisions of this Schedule, the Board would issue such a certificate.

(4) Where the Board determine to revoke a certificate of consent by virtue of this paragraph they shall serve a notice on the holder of the certificate stating that the certificate is revoked as from the end of the period of eight weeks from the date of service of the notice; and the revocation shall take effect at the end of that period, unless before the end of that period the Board have served on the holder of the certificate a further notice stating that they have rescinded their decision to revoke the certificate.

(5) Where the Board serve any such notice as is mentioned in sub-paragraph (4) of this paragraph they shall send a copy of the notice to the proper officer of the licensing authority, to the appropriate officer of police and to the appropriate collector of duty.

(6) On the revocation by virtue of this paragraph of a certificate of consent in respect of any premises, any licence under this Act in respect of those premises which—

(a) specifies that certificate as being the certificate in pursuance of which the application for the licence was made, and

(b) is in force at the time when the revocation of the certificate takes effect,

shall thereupon cease to have effect.

Application for continuance of certificate following change of controller of body corporate

8–13456 35A. (1) Where the holder of a certificate of consent to his applying for the grant of a licence under this Act (other than a certificate limited to a bingo club licence) is a body corporate and at any time while the certificate is in force any person becomes a controller of the holder—

(a) the holder shall make an application to the Board for the continuance of the certificate in accordance with this paragraph; and

(b) on such an application the Board shall continue the certificate in force unless they determine to revoke it under the subsequent provisions of this paragraph.

(2) An application under this paragraph shall contain such particulars as the holder of the certificate can reasonably provide of the controller in question and of the nature and extent of his interest in the holder of the certificate and in any body corporate of which the holder is a subsidiary.

(3) An application under this paragraph shall be made within five weeks of the time when the person in question becomes a controller of the holder of the certificate but the Board may, in any particular case, entertain an application made later if—

(a) they are satisfied that the failure to make it before the end of that period was due to inadvertence; and

(b) the application is made before the end of such extended period as the Board may in that case allow.

(4) The Board may on an application under this paragraph revoke the certificate to which the application relates if it appears to them that, if the holder were then applying for such a certificate under paragraph 4 of this Schedule, they would in accordance with sub-paragraphs (5) and (6) of that paragraph determine not to issue it; and the Board may also revoke a certificate if the holder fails to make an application in respect of it in accordance with this paragraph in a case in which this paragraph requires him to do so.

(5) Where a licence (other than a bingo club licence) is transferred to a body corporate and—

(a) a person has become a controller of that body corporate at any time between the issuing of a certificate consenting to the application for the transfer and the transfer of the licence; or

(b) a person becomes a controller of that body corporate at any subsequent time.

sub-paragraphs (1) to (4) above shall apply to that body corporate as they apply to the holder of the certificate by virtue of which the application for the licence was originally made except that the period of five weeks mentioned in sub-paragraph (3) shall, in a case within paragraph (a) above, run from the date on which the licence was transferred.

(6) Where on an application under this paragraph the Board continue a certificate in force they shall serve on the applicant a notice stating that they have done so; and sub-paragraphs (4), (5) and (6) of paragraph 35 of this Schedule shall have effect in relation to the revocation of a certificate by virtue of this paragraph as they have effect in relation to the revocation of a certificate by virtue of that paragraph.

(7) In this paragraph "controller", in relation to a body corporate, means a person who, either alone or with any associate or associates, is entitled to exercise, or control the exercise of, 15 per cent or more of the voting power at any general meeting of the body corporate or of another body corporate of which it is subsidiary.

(8) In sub-paragraph (7) above "associate", in relation to a person entitled to exercise or control the exercise of voting power in relation to a body corporate means—

(a) the wife or husband or son or daughter of that person;

(b) any company of which that person is a director;

(c) any person who is an employee or partner of that person;

(d) if that person is a company—

(i) any director of that company;

(ii) any subsidiary of that company; and

(iii) any director or employee of any subsidiary; and

(e) if that person has with any other person an agreement or arrangement with respect to the acquisition, holding or disposal of shares or other interests in that body corporate or under which they undertake to act together in exercising their voting power in relation to it, that other person.

(9) In this paragraph "subsidiary" has the same meaning as in the Companies Act 1985.

Cancellation of licence by licensing authority or court

8–13457　36. (1) An application for the cancellation of a licence under this Act may be made by any person at any time to the proper officer of the licensing authority.

(2) Any such application shall be made in the prescribed form and manner and shall be accompanied by two copies of a statement of the grounds on which the application is made.

(3) On receipt of such an application, the proper officer of the licensing authority shall submit it to one member of the authority for consideration by him.

(4) If that member, after considering the application, is of the opinion that—

(a) further consideration of the matters referred to in the statement accompanying the application is unnecessary or inexpedient before the time when the renewal of the licence falls to be considered, or

(b) the licensing authority would be required by virtue of paragraph 41 of this Schedule to refuse the application,

he shall cause notice in writing to be given to the applicant that the application is refused, without prejudice to the raising of the same matters by way of objection to a renewal of the licence.

(5) In any other case, the member of the licensing authority to whom the application is submitted shall refer it to the licensing authority.

37. Where an application for the cancellation of a licence under this Act is referred to the licensing authority under the last preceding paragraph, and that application has not been withdrawn, the proper officer of the authority shall give to the applicant, to the holder of the licence, to the appropriate officer of police, to the Board and to the appropriate collector of duty not less than twenty-one days' notice in writing of the date, time and place appointed for the consideration of the application by the authority, and shall send to the holder of the licence together with that notice a copy of the applicant's statement of the grounds on which the application is made.

38. At any meeting of the licensing authority to consider such an application, the applicant and the holder of the licence shall be entitled to be heard either in person or by counsel or a solicitor; and, where the applicant is a person other than the appropriate officer of police, the licensing authority shall also hear any representations made by that officer or by any person authorised by him in that behalf.

39. A licensing authority may from time to time adjourn the consideration of any application for the cancellation of a licence under this Act.

40. On the consideration of any such application, a licensing authority may take evidence on oath and may make such order as they think fit for the payment of costs (or, in Scotland, expenses)—

(a) by the applicant to the holder of the licence, or

(b) by the holder of the licence to the applicant.

41. The licensing authority shall refuse any such application if they are satisfied that it is made on grounds which have been, or ought properly to have been, raised previously by way of objection either when the licence was granted or on an occasion when it has been renewed.

42. Subject to the last preceding paragraph, on any application for the cancellation of a licence under this Act

which is referred to them, the licensing authority may cancel the licence on any of the grounds[1] specified in paragraph 20 or paragraph 21 of this Schedule.

43. If on such an application the licensing authority decide not to cancel the licence, the authority shall cause notice in writing to be given to the applicant that the application is refused, without prejudice to the raising of the same matters by way of objection to a renewal of the licence.

44. If on such an application the licensing authority decide to cancel the licence, the cancellation—

(a) shall not take effect until the time within which the holder of the licence can appeal against that decision has expired, and

(b) if he so appeals, shall not take effect until the appeal has been determined or abandoned.

45. The provisions of paragraphs 29 and 30 of the Schedule (in England or Wales) or paragraph 33 of this Schedule (in Scotland) shall have effect in relation to the cancellation of a licence under this Act as they have effect in relation to a refusal to grant or renew such a licence, as if in those paragraphs—

(a) any reference to the applicant were a reference to the holder of the licence, and

(b) any reference to a person who opposed the application before the licensing authority were a reference to the person who made the application for the cancellation of the licence.

46. (1) Where a licensing authority in England or Wales refuse to cancel a licence under this Act, the Board may, by notice to the proper officer of the licensing authority, appeal against the decision of the licensing authority to the Crown Court.

(2) The provisions of paragraph 31(2) to (4) and paragraph 32 of this Schedule shall have effect in relation to any such appeal as they have effect in relation to an appeal by the Board against the grant or renewal of such licence, as if those provisions—

(a) any reference to any person (other than the Board) who opposed the application before the licensing authority were omitted, and

(b) any reference to the applicant who applied for the grant or renewal were a reference to the holder of the licence.

47. (1) Where a licensing authority in Scotland refuse to cancel a licence under this Act, the Board may, within such time, and in accordance with such rules, as may be prescribed by the Court of Session by Act of Sederunt, appeal against the decision of the licensing authority to the sheriff having jurisdiction in the authority's area.

(2) Sub-paragraphs (2) and (3) of paragraph 33 of this Schedule shall have effect in relation to appeals under this paragraph as they have effect in relation to appeals under that paragraph.

48. (1) Where the holder of a licence under this Act in respect of any premises is convicted of an offence under Schedule 3 to the Finance Act 1966, in respect of a contravention of section 13 of that Act, or of an offence under section 15 or 24 of the Betting and Gaming Duties Act 1981 or paragraph 7 of Schedule 2 or paragraph 16 of Schedule 4 to that Act (or under the corresponding provisions of the Betting and Gaming Duties Act 1972[2] or the corresponding provisions of the enactments consolidated by that Act or of an offence under paragraph 12 of Schedule 1 to the Finance Act 1997), and the Commissioners of Customs and Excise—

(a) certify to the court by or before which he is so convicted that the conviction is a second or subsequent conviction for such an offence committed (whether by the same or by some other person) in relation to gaming on those premises and while the same person has been the holder of a licence under this Act in respect of those premises, and

(b) apply to the court for effect to be given to this sub-paragraph,

that court shall order that the licence under this Act in respect of those premises shall be cancelled.

(2) An order made under this paragraph by a court in England or Wales—

(a) shall not have effect until the end of the period within which notice of appeal against the conviction which gave rise to the order may be given;

(b) if notice of appeal against that conviction is duly given, shall not have effect until the appeal has been determined or abandoned; and

(c) shall not have effect if, on such an appeal, the appeal is allowed.

(3) An order made under this paragraph by a court in Scotland—

(a) shall not have effect until the end of the period of fourteen days beginning with the date on which the order was made;

(b) if an appeal against the conviction which gave rise to the order is begun within that period, shall not have effect until the appeal has been determined or abandoned or deemed to have been abandoned; and

(c) shall not have effect if, on such an appeal, the appeal is allowed.

(4) Where a person is the holder of a licence under this Act, and the licence is cancelled by virtue of an order made under this paragraph, the proper officer of the court by which the order was made shall, unless he is also the proper officer of the licensing authority, send a copy of the order to the proper officer of the licensing authority; and (without prejudice to the renewal of any other licence under this Act held by the same person) the licensing authority shall, notwithstanding anything in the preceding provisions of this Schedule, refuse any application by that person for the grant of a licence under this Act in respect of the same or any other premises if it is made less than twelve months after the date of the order.

(5) In sub-paragraph (4) of this paragraph, "the proper officer of the court" means—

(*a*) in relation to a magistrates' court, the designated officer for the court, and

(*b*) in relation to any other court, the clerk of the court.

---

1. When considering whether a licence held by a limited company should be cancelled on the ground that the company is not a fit and proper person to hold a gaming licence, the licensing authority should take into account any restructuring of the company that has taken place since the conduct giving rise to the application occurred (*R v Crown Court at Knightsbridge, ex p International Sporting Club (London) Ltd* [1982] QB 304, [1981] 3 All ER 417).

2. See now the Betting and Gaming Duties Act 1981 in PART VIII: title CUSTOMS AND EXCISE, post.

Disqualification order on cancellation of licence

8–13458   **49.** (1) Where under paragraph 42 of this Schedule a licensing authority cancels a licence under this Act, the authority may make a disqualification order under this paragraph prohibiting such a licence from being held in respect of the relevant premises during a period specified in the order.

(2) The period specified in a disqualification order under this paragraph shall not exceed five years from the date on which the order comes into force.

(3) Subject to the next following paragraph, where a disqualification order under this paragraph is made, any licence within the prohibition, if previously obtained, shall by virtue of the order be cancelled, or, if subsequently obtained, shall be null and void.

50. Where a licensing authority decides to cancel a licence under this Act, and makes a disqualification order under the last preceding paragraph in respect of the relevant premises, paragraph 44, and the provisions applied by paragraph 45, of this Schedule shall have effect in relation to the disqualification order as they have effect in relation to the cancellation of the licence.

Form and duration of licence

8–13459   **51.** (1) A licence under this Act shall be in the prescribed form and shall—

(*a*) specify by name and description the club which was so specified in the application for the licence in accordance with paragraph 5(2) of this Schedule; and

(*b*) specify (in such manner as may be sufficient to identify it) the certificate of consent under this Schedule in pursuance of which that application was made.

(2) If any such licence as granted or renewed is subject to any restrictions imposed under paragraph 24 or paragraph 25 of this Schedule, the licence as granted or renewed shall include a statement of those restrictions.

52. (1) Subject to the following provisions of this Schedule, and without prejudice to the cancellation of any licence, whether in consequence of the revocation of a certificate of consent or by virtue of a disqualification order or otherwise, a licence under this Act—

(*a*) if not renewed, shall cease to be in force at the end of the period of one year beginning with the date on which it was granted, or

(*b*) if renewed, shall, unless further renewed, cease to be in force at the end of the period of one year from the date on which it would otherwise have expired.

(2) *Repealed.*

53. (1) Where an application for the renewal of a licence under this Act has been duly made, the licence shall not cease to be in force by virtue of the last preceding paragraph before the licensing authority have determined the application.

(2) Where, on such an application, the licensing authority refuse to renew the licence, it shall not cease to be in force by virtue of the last preceding paragraph before the time within which the applicant can appeal against the refusal has expired, and, if he so appeals, shall not cease to be in force by virtue of that paragraph until the appeal has been determined or abandoned.

54. If the holder of a licence under this Act dies while the licence is in force—

(*a*) the licence shall not cease to be in force by virtue of paragraph 52 of this Schedule before the end of the period of six months beginning with the date of his death, and

(*b*) except for the purposes of a renewal of the licence, his personal representative shall be deemed to be the holder of the licence;

and the licensing authority may from time to time, on the application of those personal representatives, extend or further extend the period for which the licence continues to be in force by virtue of this paragraph if satisfied that the extension is necessary for the purpose of winding up the estate of the deceased and that no other circumstances make it undesirable.

Certificate of consent for purposes of application for transfer of licence

8–13460   **55.** (1) An application for the transfer of a licence under this Act from one person to another shall be of no effect unless the Board have issued to the applicant a certificate consenting to his applying for a transfer of the licence to that other person, and that certificate is for the time being in force and the application is made within the period specified in the certificate.

(2) In the following provisions of this Schedule any reference to an application for the transfer of a licence under this Act shall be construed as not including any application which by virtue of the preceding sub-paragraph is of no effect.

56. (1) The provisions of this paragraph shall have effect in relation to any application to the Board for such a certificate of consent as is mentioned in the last preceding paragraph.

(2) The Board shall not issue a certificate on any such application if it appears to the Board that the person to whom the licence is proposed to be transferred (in this and the next following paragraph referred to as "the proposed transferee")—

(a) not being a body corporate, is under twenty-one years of age, or

(b) not being a body corporate, is not resident in Great Britain or was not so resident throughout the period of six months immediately preceding the date on which the application was made, or

(c) being a body corporate, is not incorporated in Great Britain.

(3) Subject to sub-paragraph (2) of this paragraph, in determining whether to issue such a certificate of consent the Board shall have regard only to the question whether, in their opinion, the proposed transferee is likely to be capable of, and diligent in, securing that the provisions of this Act and of any regulations made under it will be complied with, that gaming on the premises specified in the licence will be fairly and properly conducted, and that the premises will be conducted without disorder or disturbance.

(4) For the purposes of sub-paragraph (3) of this paragraph the Board shall in particular take into consideration the character, reputation and financial standing—

(a) of the proposed transferee, and

(b) of any person (other than the proposed transferee) by whom, if the licence in question were transferred to the proposed transferee, the club specified in the licence would be managed, or for whose benefit, if that licence were so transferred, the club would be carried on,

but may also take into consideration any other circumstances appearing to them to be relevant in determining whether the proposed transferee is likely to be capable of, and diligent in, securing the matters mentioned in that sub-paragraph.

(5) If on an application made under the last preceding paragraph the Board issue to the applicant a certificate consenting to his applying for the transfer of the licence to the proposed transferee, the certificate shall specify a period within which an application to the licensing authority for the transfer of the licence can be made.

57. (1) Where the Board have issued a certificate of consent in respect of the transfer of a licence under this Act, then, subject to the following provisions of this paragraph, the Board may revoke that certificate at any time before the licence has been transferred to the proposed transferee.

(2) The Board shall not revoke a certificate by virtue of this paragraph unless it appears to them either—

(a) that any information which, in or in connection with the application on which the certificate was issued, was given to the Board by or on behalf of the applicant for the certificate was false in a material particular, or

(b) that, since the certificate was issued, a licence under this Act held by the proposed transferee has been cancelled by virtue of a disqualification order made under section 24 of this Act or under this Schedule or in the exercise of the powers conferred on the licensing authority or the court by this Schedule.

(3) Where the Board determine to revoke a certificate by virtue of this paragraph they shall serve a notice on the holder of the certificate stating that the certificate is revoked; and the revocation shall take effect on the service of that notice.

(4) Where the Board serve a notice under sub-paragraph (3) of this paragraph they should send a notice to the proper officer of the licensing authority, to the appropriate officer of police and to the appropriate collector of duty.

Transfer of licence

8–13461 **58.** (1) An application for the transfer of a licence under this Act from one person to another may be made at any time, and shall be made to the proper officer of the licensing authority in such form and manner as may be prescribed and shall be accompanied by a copy of the certificate of consent[1] issued by the Board for the purposes of that application.

(2) Not later than seven days after the date on which the application is made the applicant shall send a copy of the application—

(a) to the Board;

(b) to the appropriate officer of police;

(c) to the appropriate local authority; and

(d) to the appropriate collector of duty.

59. Paragraphs 6 and 7 of this Schedule shall have effect in relation to any such application as they have effect in relation to an application for the grant of a licence under this Act.

60. On an application for the transfer of a licence under this Act the licensing authority shall not refuse to transfer the licence except on the grounds—

(a) that the person to whom the licence is proposed to be transferred is not a fit and proper person to be the holder of a licence under this Act;

(b) that, if the licence were transferred to that person, the club specified in the licence would be managed by, or carried on for the benefit of, a person (other than the proposed transferee) who would himself be refused the grant of a licence under this Act on the grounds that he is not a fit and proper person to be the holder of such a licence; or

(c) that any duty payable by the proposed transferee under section 13 of the Finance Act 1966 or section 2 of or Schedule 1 to the Finance Act 1970 or s 13 of or Schedule 2 to the Betting and Gaming Duties Act 1972, or section 14 of or Schedule 2 to the Betting and Gaming Duties Act 1981 or any bingo duty or gaming duty payable by him remains unpaid.

61. Paragraphs 29 to 34 of this Schedule (with the omission of paragraphs 31(1) (b) and 34(1) (b)) shall have effect in relation to the transfer of licences under this Act as they have in relation to the grant or renewal of such licences.

1. An application for a transfer of a licence shall be of no effect unless the Gaming Board have issued a certificate of consent: see para 55, ante.

Revocation of certificate after transfer of licence

8–13462   **62.** In relation to a licence under this Act which has been transferred, and in relation to the certificate of consent in pursuance of which the application for the grant of such a licence was made, the provisions of paragraph 35 of this Schedule shall have effect as if, in sub-paragraphs (2), (3)(a) and (4) of that paragraph, any reference to the holder of the certificate were a reference to the person who is for the time being the holder of the licence.

Payments of fees

8–13463   **63.** (1) Notwithstanding anything in the preceding provisions of this Schedule, no licence under this Act shall be granted, renewed or transferred except on payment by the applicant to the proper officer of the licensing authority of the fee chargeable in accordance with section 48 of this Act.

(2) *(Scotland.)*

8–13464   **63A.** No application for a certificate of consent under this Schedule shall be treated as duly made until the appropriate fee has been paid to the Board.

Notification of change in directors of body corporate holding licence

8–13465   **64.** (1) Where the holder of a licence under this Act is a body corporate, then if at any time a change occurs—

(a) in the persons who are directors of that body corporate, or
(b) in the persons in accordance with whose directions or instructions the directors of that body corporate are accustomed to act,

the body corporate shall as soon as reasonably practicable after that time serve on the proper officer of the licensing authority, the appropriate officer of police and the Board, a notice giving particulars of the change.

(2) A body corporate which fails to comply with the preceding sub-paragraph shall be guilty of an offence and shall be liable on summary conviction to a fine not exceeding **level 3** on the standard scale.

Notification of change in shareholding in public company

8–13466   **64A.** (1) Where the holder of a licence under this Act (other than a bingo club licence) is a public company, then, if at any time the company receives any notification under Part VI of the Companies Act 1985, the company shall send a copy of the notification to the Board as soon as reasonably practicable after that time.

(2) A company which fails to comply with sub-paragraph (1) of this paragraph shall be guilty of an offence and shall be liable on summary conviction to a fine not exceeding **level 3** on the standard scale.

(3) In this paragraph "public company" has the meaning given by section 1(3) of the said Act of 1985.

Relinquishment of licence

8–13467   **65.** (1) The holder of a licence under this Act may at any time relinquish the licence by notice to the proper officer of the licensing authority; and, where such a notice is given, the licence shall thereupon be treated as cancelled.

(2) Where the holder of a licence under this Act relinquishes the licence under this paragraph, the proper officer of the licensing authority shall give notice of that fact to—

(a) the Board;
(b) the appropriate officer of police;
(c) the appropriate local authority;
(d) the appropriate fire authority; if that authority is not the same body as the appropriate local authority; and
(e) the appropriate collector of duty.

8–13468

Section 11(2)   **SCHEDULE 3**
REGISTRATION OF MEMBERS' CLUBS UNDER PART II IN ENGLAND AND WALES

(*Amended by the Courts Act 1971, the Betting and Gaming Duties Act 1972, the Betting and Gaming Duties Act 1981, Sch 5, the Gaming (Amendment) Act 1982, Sch 1, the Gaming (Amendment) Act 1990, Sch, the Access to Justice Act 1999, Sch 13, the Fire and Rescue Services Act 2004, Sch 1, the Statute Law (Repeals) Act 2004 and the Courts Act 2003, Sch 8.)*

Introductory

1. (1) Each licensing authority in England or Wales shall, in respect of premises within the area of the authority as mentioned in paragraph 1 of Schedule 2 to this Act, be the authority responsible for the registration of clubs and institutes under Part II of this Act and for the renewal and cancellation of any such registration.

(2) In this Schedule "institute" means a miners' welfare institute.

2. Paragraphs 2 and 2A of Schedule 2 to this Act shall have effect for the purposes of this Schedule as if in those paragraphs references to a licence under this Act, to premises in respect of which such a licence is for the time being in force, and to an application relating to such a licence, were references respectively to registration under Part II of this Act, to premises in respect of which a club or institute is for the time being registered under Part II of this Act, and to an application relating to such registration.

Application for registration

8–13469 3. Paragraphs 5 to 7 of Schedule 2 to this Act shall have effect in relation to applications for registration under Part II of this Act as they have effect in relation to applications for licences under this Act, but as if—

    (*a*) in paragraph 5(2) of that Schedule the words from "and shall be accompanied by a copy of the certificate" onwards, and in paragraph 6(2) of that Schedule the words from "shall indicate" to "other than a bingo club licence" and

    (*aa*) the reference in paragraph 5(3) to the Board, and

    (*b*) paragraph 6(3) of that Schedule, and

    (*c*) any reference to the appropriate local authority or the appropriate fire and rescue authority,

were omitted.

Application for renewal of registration

8–13470 4. Paragraphs 12 and 13 of Schedule 2 to this Act shall have effect in relation to any application for renewal of the registration of a club or institute under Part II of this Act as they have effect in relation to applications for the renewal of licences under this Act, but as if in paragraph 13(1) of that Schedule the references to the Board, the appropriate local authority and the appropriate fire and rescue authority were omitted.

5. *Repealed.*

Proceedings on application for registration or renewal of registration

8–13471 6. Paragraphs 14 to 17 of Schedule 2 to this Act shall have effect in relation to any application for registration or renewal of registration of a club or institute under Part II of this Act as they have effect in relation to applications for the grant or renewal of licences under this Act, but as if in paragraph 14(2) of that Schedule the references to the appropriate local authority and the appropriate fire and rescue authority were omitted.

Grounds for refusal to register or to renew registration

8–13480 7. (1) The licensing authority shall refuse to register or to renew the registration of a club under Part II of this Act if it appears to the authority that the club—

    (*a*) is not a bona fide members' club, or

    (*b*) has less than twenty-five members, or

    (*c*) is of a merely temporary character.

(2) Without prejudice to the preceding sub-paragraph, the licensing authority shall refuse to register a club or to renew the registration of a club under Part II of this Act if it appears to the authority that the principal purpose for which the club is established or conducted is gaming, unless the authority are satisfied that the gaming in question consists exclusively of playing bridge or whist, or both bridge and whist.

8. The licensing authority may refuse to register a club or institute under Part II of this Act where the club or institute has previously been so registered and either—

    (*a*) its registration has been cancelled, or

    (*b*) an application for renewal of that registration has been refused.

9. The licensing authority may refuse to renew the registration of a club or institute under Part II of this Act on any one or more of the following grounds, in addition to those specified in paragraph 7 of this Schedule, that is to say—

    (*a*) that a person has been convicted of an offence under this Act in respect of a contravention, in connection with the relevant premises, of any of the provisions of this Act or of any regulations made thereunder;

    (*b*) that, while the club or institute has been registered under Part II of this Act, the relevant premises have not been so conducted as to prevent disturbance or disorder;

    (*c*) that while the club or institute has been so registered, gaming on the relevant premises has been dishonestly conducted;

    (*d*) that, while the club or institute has been so registered, the relevant premises have been used for an unlawful purpose or as a resort of criminals or prostitutes;

    (*e*) that any duty payable in respect of the premises under section 13 of the Finance Act 1966 or section 2 of or Schedule 1 to the Finance Act 1970 or s 13 of or Schedule 2 to the Betting and Gaming Duties Act 1972, or section 14 of or Schedule 2 to the Betting and Gaming Duties Act 1981, remains unpaid;

    (*f*) that any bingo duty payable in respect of bingo played on the premises remains unpaid;

and where the authority entertain an application for the renewal of registration and are satisfied that any bingo duty payable as mentioned in sub-paragraph (*f*) above remains unpaid, they shall refuse the application.

10. The licensing authority shall refuse to renew the registration of a club under Part II of this Act if they are satisfied that, while the club has been registered thereunder, the relevant premises have been habitually used for an unlawful purpose or as a resort of criminals or prostitutes.

Restrictions attached to registration

8–13481   **11.** (1) On registering or renewing the registration of a club or institute under Part II of this Act, the licensing authority may, if they think fit, impose restrictions limiting the gaming to a particular part or parts of the relevant premises.

(2) Any restrictions imposed under the preceding sub-paragraph shall be imposed so as to have effect until the registration of the club or institute under Part II of this Act ceases to have effect or is next renewed (whichever first occurs), but without prejudice, where the registration is renewed, to any power of the licensing authority under the preceding sub-paragraph to impose the like or any other restrictions on renewing the registration.

Appeal by applicant

8–13482   **12.** (1) Where on an application under this Schedule the licensing authority refuse to register or renew the registration of a club or institute under Part II of this Act, or impose restrictions under the last preceding paragraph, the designated officer for the licensing authority shall forthwith give notice of the decision of the authority to the applicant; and, within 21 days from the date of service of that notice, the applicant may, by notice to the designated officer for, appeal against the decision to the Crown Court.

(2) Sub-paragraphs (2) to (5) of paragraph 29 of Schedule 2 to this Act, and paragraph 30 of the Schedule, shall have effect in relation to appeals under this paragraph as they have effect in relation to appeals under paragraph 29 of that Schedule.

Appeal by Board

8–13483   **13.** (1) Where on an application under this Schedule the licensing authority register, or renew the registration of, a club or institute under Part II of this Act after hearing any objection or representations made by or on behalf of the Board or any other person, and the Board desire to contend that the registration or renewal ought to have been refused, the Board may, by notice to the designated officer for the licensing authority, appeal against the decision of the licensing authority to the Crown Court.

(2) On determining any appeal under this paragraph, or on being satisfied that the Board, after giving notice of such an appeal, have failed to prosecute it, the Crown Court may make such order as it thinks fit for the payment of costs by or to—

(*a*) the applicant who applied for the registration or renewal;
(*b*) the Board;
(*c*) any person (other than the Board) who opposed the application before the licensing authority; or
(*d*) the licensing authority.

(3) Sub-paragraphs (4) and (5) of paragraph 29, sub-paragraphs (2) of paragraph 30 and sub-paragraph (2) and (3) of paragraph 31 of Schedule 2 to this Act shall have effect in relation to appeals under this paragraph as they have effect in relation to appeals under paragraph 31 of that Schedule.

Cancellation of registration

8–13484   **14.** Paragraphs 36 to 44 of Schedule 2 to this Act shall have effect in relation to cancellation of the registration of a club or institute under Part II of this Act as they have effect in relation to cancellation of a licence under this Act, but as if—

(*a*) any reference to the holder of the licence were a reference to the chairman or secretary of the club or institute, and
(*b*) in paragraph 42 of that Schedule, the reference to the grounds specified in paragraphs 20 and 21 of that Schedule were a reference to the grounds specified in paragraph 9 of this Schedule.

15. (1) Where on an application made by virtue of paragraph 14 of this Schedule the licensing authority decide to cancel the registration of a club or institute under Part II of this Act, the designated officer for the licensing authority shall forthwith give notice of the decision of the authority to the chairman or secretary of the club or institute; and, within 21 days from the date of service of that notice the chairman or secretary may, by notice to the designated officer for the licensing authority, appeal against the decision to the Crown Court.

(2) The provisions of paragraph 29(2) to (5) of Schedule (2) to this Act, and of paragraph 30 of that Schedule, shall have effect in relation to appeals under this paragraph as they have effect in relation to appeals under paragraph 29 of that Schedule, but as if in those provisions any reference to a person who opposed the application before the licensing authority were a reference to the person who made the application for the registration to be cancelled.

16. (1) Where an application for cancellation of the registration of a club or institute under Part II of this Act is made by the Board, and the licensing authority refuse to cancel the registration, the Board may, by notice to the designated officer for the licensing authority, appeal against the decision of the licensing authority to the Crown Court.

(2) The provisions of paragraph 31(2) to (4) of Schedule 2 to this Act, and of paragraph 32 of that Schedule, shall have effect in relation to any such appeal as they have effect in relation to an appeal by the Board against the grant or renewal of a licence, but as if in those provisions—

(*a*) any reference to any person (other than the Board) who opposed the application before the licensing authority were omitted, and
(*b*) any reference to the applicant who applied for the grant or renewal were a reference to the chairman or secretary of the club or institute.

17. (1) Where a person is convicted of an offence under Schedule 3 to the Finance Act 1966, in respect of a contravention of section 13 of that Act or of an offence under section 24 of or paragraph 16 of Schedule 4 to the Betting and Gaming Duties Act 1981 (or under the corresponding provisions of the Betting and Gaming Duties Act 1972 or the corresponding provisions of the enactments consolidated by that Act) in relation to premises in respect of which a club or institute is for the time being registered under Part II of this Act, and the commissioners of Customs and Excise—

(a) certify to the court by or before which he is so convicted that the conviction is a second or subsequent conviction for such an offence committed (whether by the same or by some other person) in relation to gaming on those premises while that club or institute has been so registered, and

(b) apply to the court for effect to be given to this sub-paragraph, that court shall order that the registration of the club or institute under Part II of this Act shall be cancelled.

(2) An order made under this paragraph—

(a) shall not have effect until the end of the period within which notice of appeal against the conviction which gave rise to the order may be given;

(b) if notice of appeal against that conviction is duly given, shall not have effect until the appeal has been determined or abandoned; and

(c) shall not have effect if, on such an appeal, the appeal is allowed.

(3) Where the registration of a club or institute is cancelled by virtue of an order made under this paragraph, the proper officer of the court by which the order was made shall, unless he is also the designated officer for the licensing authority, send a copy of the order to the designated officer for the licensing authority; and the licensing authority shall, notwithstanding anything in the preceding provisions of this Schedule, refuse any application for the registration of that club or institute under Part II of this Act in respect of the same or any other premises if it is made less than twelve months after the date of the order.

(4) In sub-paragraph (3) of this paragraph the "proper officer of the court" means—

(a) in relation to a magistrates' court, the designated officer for the court, and

(b) in relation to the Crown Court, the appropriate officer of the court.

Issue and duration of registration certificates

8–13485 **18.** (1) Where on an application under this Schedule a club or institute is registered, or the registration of a club or institute is renewed, under Part II of this Act, the licensing authority shall issue to the applicant a certificate (in this Schedule referred to as a "registration certificate") which shall be in the prescribed form.

(2) If the registration or any renewal of the registration of a club or institute is subject to any restrictions imposed under paragraph 11 of this Schedule, the registration certificate shall include a statement of those restrictions.

19. (1) Subject to the following provisions of this Schedule, and without prejudice to the provisions of this Schedule as to cancellation the registration of a club or institute under Part II of this Act—

(a) if not renewed, shall cease to have effect at the end of the period of one year beginning with the date on which it was effected, or

(b) if renewed, shall, unless further renewed, cease to have effect at the end of the period for which it was renewed or last renewed, as the case may be.

(2) *Repealed.*

20. (1) An application for renewal of the registration of a club or institute under Part II of this Act may specify a number of years, not exceeding ten, for which the renewal is requested; and any renewal of the registration shall be for such number of years, not exceeding the number specified in the application, as the licensing authority think fit.

(2) Except as provided by the preceding sub-paragraph, any renewal of the registration shall be for a period of one year.

21. (1) Where the registration of a club or institute under Part II of this Act has been renewed for a period of two or more years, and is subject to any restriction imposed under paragraph 11 of this Schedule, then, with a view to the cancellation or variation of those restrictions, an application for renewal of the registration may be made in any of those years, notwithstanding that the registration is not due to expire in that year.

(2) On any application made by virtue of this paragraph the registration may be renewed as if it were due to expire on the day before the anniversary of the date on which it was renewed or last renewed.

22. (1) Where an application for renewal of the registration of a club or institute under Part II of this Act has been duly made, the registration shall not cease to have effect by virtue of paragraph 19 of this Schedule until the licensing authority have determined the application.

(2) Where, on such an application, the licensing authority refuse to renew the registration, it shall not cease to have effect by virtue of paragraph 19 of this Schedule before the time within which the applicant can appeal against the refusal has expired, and, if he so appeals, shall not cease to have effect by virtue of that paragraph until the appeal has been determined or abandoned.

Payment of fees

8–13486 **23.** Notwithstanding anything in the preceding provisions of this Schedule, a club or institute shall not be registered under Part II of this Act, and the registration of a club or institute thereunder shall not be renewed, except on payment by the applicant to the chief executive to the licensing authority of the fee chargeable in accordance with section 48 of this Act.

Relinquishment of registration

8–13487 **24.** (1) A club or institute registered under Part II of this Act may at any time relinquish its registration by notice given to the designated officer for the licensing authority by the chairman or secretary of the club or institute; and, where such a notice is given, the registration of the club or institute under Part II of this Act shall thereupon be treated as cancelled.

(2) Where the registration of a club or institute is relinquished under this paragraph, the designated officer for the licensing authority shall give notice of that fact to the Board, the appropriate officer of police and the appropriate collector of duty.

8–13488

SCHEDULE 4

REGISTRATION OF MEMBERS' CLUBS UNDER PART II IN SCOTLAND

8–13489

SCHEDULE 5

PROCEDURE FOR APPROVAL BY BOARD

8–13490

SCHEDULE 6

CERTIFICATES AND PERMITS UNDER SECTION 27

8–13491

Section 30

SCHEDULE 7

REGISTRATION UNDER PART III IN ENGLAND AND WALES

(*Amended by the Courts Act 1971 and the Access to Justice Act 1999, Sch 13.*)

Introductory

1. Each licensing authority in England or Wales shall, in respect of premises within the area of the authority as mentioned in paragraph 1 of Schedule 2 to this Act, be the authority responsible for the registration of clubs and institutes under Part III of this Act and for the renewal and cancellation of any such registration.

2. (1) Paragraph 2 of Schedule 2 to this Act shall have effect for the purposes of this Schedule as if in that paragraph references to a licence under this Act, to premises in respect of which such a licence is for the time being in force, and to an application relating to such a licence, were references respectively to registration under Part III of this Act, to premises in respect of which a club or institute is for the time being registered under Part III of this Act, and to an application relating to such registration.

(2) In this Schedule "institute" means a miners' welfare institute.

Application for registration

8–13492   **3.** (1) An application for the registration of a club or institute under Part III of this Act may be made at any time, and shall be made to the chief executive to the licensing authority in such form and manner as may be prescribed.

(2) Any such application shall specify the name, objects and address of the club or institute to which it relates and the premises in respect of which it is proposed that the club or institute should be registered, and shall contain such other particulars as may be prescribed.

(3) Not later than seven days after the date on which the application is made, the applicant shall send a copy of the application to the appropriate officer of police.

Application for renewal of registration

8–13493   **4.** (1) An application for renewal of the registration of a club or institute under Part III of this Act shall be made not earlier than three months and not later than six weeks before the date on which the registration is due to expire, and shall be made to the chief executive to the licensing authority in such form and manner as may be prescribed.

(2) The licensing authority may in any particular case entertain an application for renewal of registration under Part III of this Act made after the latest date on which the application could be made in accordance with sub-paragraph (1) of this paragraph if—

(a) they are satisfied that the failure to make the application before that date was due to inadvertence, and

(b) the application is made before the end of such extended period as the licensing authority may in that case allow.

(3) Not later than seven days after the date on which any such application is made, the applicant shall send a copy of the application to the appropriate officer of police.

Proceedings on application for registration or renewal of registration

8–13494   **5.** (1) On any application for the registration, or for renewal of the registration, of a club or institute under Part III of this Act, the licensing authority may register or renew the registration of the club or institute without hearing the applicant if no objection to the registration or renewal of registration has been made by or on behalf of the appropriate officer of police, or if any objection so made has been withdrawn.

(2) Except as provided by the preceding sub-paragraph, on any such application the applicant and the appropriate officer of police shall be entitled to be heard either in person or by counsel or a solicitor.

6. (1) A licensing authority may from time to time adjourn the consideration of any application for the registration or for renewal of the registration of a club or institute under Part III of this Act.

(2) On the consideration of any such application, a licensing authority may take evidence on oath, and, if the appropriate officer of police has made an objection which has not been withdrawn, may make such order as they think fit for the payment of costs—

(a) by the applicant to that officer, or

(b) by that officer to the applicant.

Grounds for refusal to register or to renew registration

8–13495   **7.** The licensing authority shall refuse to register, or to renew the registration of, a club or institute under Part III of this Act if it appears to them that the relevant premises are premises which (for whatever purposes) are frequented wholly or mainly by persons under eighteen.

8. The licensing authority may[1] refuse to register or to renew the registration of a club under Part III of this Act if it appears to the authority that the club—

(*a*) is not a bona fide members' club, or

(*b*) has less than twenty-five members, or

(*c*) is of a merely temporary character.

9. The licensing authority may refuse to renew the registration of a club or institute under Part III of this Act on the grounds that a person has been convicted of an offence under this Act in respect of a contravention, in connection with the relevant premises, of any of the provisions of Parts I to III of this Act or of any regulations made thereunder.

10. The licensing authority may refuse to register a club or institute under Part III of this Act where the club or institute has previously been so registered and either—

(*a*) its registration has been cancelled, or

(*b*) an application for renewal of that registration has been refused.

---

1. The licensing authority has a discretion and may register a proprietary club under this Schedule (*Tehrani v Roston* [1972] 1 QB 182, [1971] 3 All ER 790).

Appeal by applicant

8–13496 **11.** (1) Where on an application under this Schedule the licensing authority refuse to register or renew the registration of a club or institute under Part III of this Act, the chief executive to the licensing authority shall forthwith give notice of the decision of the authority to the applicant; and, within 21 days from the date of service of that notice, the applicant may, by notice to the chief executive to the authority, appeal against the decision to the Crown Court.

(2) As soon as practicable after receiving notice of appeal against such a decision of the licensing authority, the chief executive to the authority shall send the notice to the appropriate officer of the Crown Court together with a statement of the decision against which the appeal is brought and of the name and last-known residence or place of business of the appellant.*

(3) On receipt of the notice of appeal, the appropriate officer of the Crown Court shall enter the appeal and give in writing to the appellant, to the appropriate officer of police and to the licensing authority not less than seven days' notice of the date, time and place appointed for the hearing of the appeal.

(4) The Crown Court may by its order allow or dismiss the appeal and may deal with the application as if it had been made to the Crown Court in the first instance; and the judgment of the Crown Court on the appeal shall be final.

(5) A justice shall not act in the hearing or determination of an appeal under this paragraph from any decision in which he took part.

12. Paragraph 30 of Schedule 2 to this Act shall have effect in relation to appeals under the last preceding paragraph as it has effect in relation to appeals under paragraph 29 of that Schedule.

Cancellation of registration

8–13497 **13.** (1) Subject to the following provisions of this paragraph, an application for cancellation of the registration of a club or institute under Part III of this Act may be made at any time by the appropriate officer of police to the chief executive to the licensing authority.

(2) Any such application shall be made in the prescribed form and manner and shall be accompanied by two copies of a statement of the grounds on which the application is made.

14. Where such an application has been made and not withdrawn, the chief executive to the licensing authority shall give to the appropriate officer of police and to the chairman or secretary of the club or institute not less than twenty-one days' notice in writing of the date, time and place appointed for the consideration of the application by the authority, and shall send to the chairman or secretary of the club or institute together with that notice a copy of a statement by the appropriate officer of police of the grounds on which the application is made.

15. At any meeting of the licensing authority to consider such an application, the appropriate officer of police and the chairman or secretary of the club or institute shall be entitled to be heard either in person or by counsel or a solicitor.

16. A licensing authority may from time to time adjourn the consideration of any application for cancellation of the registration of a club or institute under Part III of this Act.

17. On the consideration of any such application, a licensing authority may take evidence on oath and may make such order as they think fit for the payment of costs—

(*a*) by the appropriate officer of police to the chairman or secretary of the club or institute, or

(*b*) by the chairman or secretary of the club or institute to the appropriate officer of police.

18. On any such application the licensing authority may cancel the registration of the club or institute under Part III of this Act if they are satisfied—

(*a*) that the relevant premises are frequented wholly or mainly by persons under eighteen, or

(*b*) that, in the case of a club, the club is not a bona fide members' club, or has less than twenty-five members, or is of a merely temporary character, or

(*c*) that a person has been convicted as mentioned in paragraph 9 of this Schedule,

and (if any such case) that in the circumstances the registration ought to be cancelled.

19. If on the consideration of any such application the licensing authority decide to cancel the registration, the cancellation—

(*a*) shall not take effect until the time within which the chairman or secretary of the club or institute can appeal against that decision has expired, and

(*b*) if he so appeals, shall not take effect until the appeal has been determined or abandoned.

20. (1) Where on any such application the licensing authority decide to cancel the registration, the chief executive to the licensing authority shall forthwith give notice of the decision to the chairman or secretary of the club or institute; and, within 21 days from the date of service of that notice, the chairman or secretary may, by notice to the chief executive to the licensing authority, appeal against the decision to the Crown Court.

(2) Sub-paragraphs (2) to (5) of paragraph 11 of this Schedule, and the provisions applied by paragraph 12 of this Schedule, shall have effect in relation to cancellation of the registration of a club or institute under Part III of this Act as they have effect in relation to refusal to register a club or institute.

Issue and duration of registration certificate

8–13498   21. Where on an application under this Schedule a club or institute is registered, or the registration of a club or institute is renewed, under Part III of this Act, the licensing authority shall issue to the applicant a certificate to that effect, which shall be in the prescribed form.

22. Subject to the following provisions of this Schedule, and without prejudice to the provisions of this Schedule as to cancellation, the registration of a club or institute under Part III of this Act—

(a) if not renewed, shall cease to have effect at the end of the period of five years beginning with the date of registration, or

(b) if renewed, shall, unless further renewed, cease to have effect at the end of the period of five years beginning with the date on which it was renewed or last renewed, as the case may be.

23. (1) Where an application for renewal of the registration of a club or institute under Part III of this Act has been duly made, the registration shall not cease to have effect by virtue of the last preceding paragraph until the licensing authority have determined the application.

(2) Where, on such an application, the licensing authority refuse to renew the registration, it shall not cease to have effect by virtue of the last preceding paragraph before the time within which the applicant can appeal against the refusal has expired, and, if he so appeals, shall not cease to have effect by virtue of that paragraph until the appeal has been determined or abandoned.

Payment of fees

8–13499   2. Notwithstanding anything in the preceding provisions of this Schedule, a club or institute shall not be registered under Part III of this Act, and the registration of a club or institute thereunder shall not be renewed, except on payment by the applicant to the chief executive to the licensing authority of the fee chargeable in accordance with section 48 of this Act.

Relinquishment of registration

8–13500   25. (1) A club or institute registered under Part III of this Act may at any time relinquish its registration by notice given to the chief executive to the licensing authority by the chairman or secretary of the club or institute; and, where such a notice is given, the registration of the club or institute under Part III of this Act shall thereupon be treated as cancelled.

(2) Where the registration of a club or institute is relinquished under this paragraph, the chief executive to the licensing authority shall give notice of that fact to the appropriate officer of police.

8–13501   SCHEDULE 8
                    REGISTRATION UNDER PART III IN SCOTLAND

                    SCHEDULE 9
                    PERMITS UNDER SECTION 34

(As amended by the Courts Act 1971, Sch 9, the Local Government Act 1972, the Licensing (Scotland) Act 1976, SI 1979/977, the Statute Law (Repeals) Act 1986, Sch 1, SI 1996/1359, the Access to Justice Act 1999, Sch 13, the Licensing Act 2003, Sch 6 and SI 2005/3027.)

Authority responsible for grant and renewal of permits

8–13502   1. In this Schedule "the appropriate authority"—

(a) in relation to any premises in England and Wales in respect of which there is in force a premises licence authorising the supply of alcohol for consumption on the premises, means the relevant licensing authority in relation to those premises;

(b) in relation to any other premises in England or Wales, means the council of the London borough or county district in which the premises are situated, or, where the premises are in the City of London, means the Common Council of the City;

(c) (Scotland.)

and "permit" means a permit under section 34 of this Act.

8–13502A   1A. A function conferred by this Schedule on a licensing authority is, for the purposes of section 7 of the Licensing Act 2003 (exercise and delegation by licensing authority of licensing functions), to be treated as a licensing function within the meaning of that Act.

Resolution by local authority as to grant or renewal of permits

8–13503   3. Any such council as is mentioned in sub-paragraph (b) or sub-paragraph (d) of paragraph 1 of this Schedule (in this Schedule referred to as a "local authority") may pass any of the following resolutions, that is to say—

(a) that (subject to paragraph 4 of this Schedule) the authority will not grant any permits in respect of premises of a class specified in the resolution;

(b) that (subject to paragraph 4 of this Schedule) the authority will neither grant nor renew any permit in respect of premises of a class specified in the resolution;

(*c*) that (subject to paragraph 4 of this Schedule) where the authority grant or renew a permit in respect of any premises, or in respect of premises of a class specified in the resolution, they will grant or renew it subject to a condition limiting the number of machines to which Part III of this Act applies which may be made available for gaming on the premises so as not to exceed such number as may be specified in the resolution.

4. (1) No resolution under paragraph 3 of this Schedule shall have effect in relation to the grant or renewal of permits in respect of premises to which this paragraph applies.

(2) This paragraph applies to any premises used or to be used wholly or mainly for the provision of amusements by means of machines to which Part III of this Act applies.

Application for grant or renewal of permit

8–13504   5. (1) An application for the grant of a permit in respect of any premises may be made as follows, that is to say—

(*a*) by the holder of the licence or certificate, in the case of any such premises as are mentioned in sub-paragraph (*a*) or sub-paragraph (*c*) of paragraph 1 of this Schedule, and

(*b*) in any other case, by the person who is, or by any person who proposes if the permit is granted to become, the occupier of the premises.

(1A) Where an application for the grant of a permit in respect of premises to which paragraph 4 of this Schedule applies is made to a local authority, the application shall be either—

(*a*) for the grant of a permit for the purposes of subsection (1) of section 34 of this Act, or

(*b*) for the grant of a permit for the purposes of subsection (5E) of that section.

(2) The holder of a permit may apply from time to time for the renewal of the permit.

6. The appropriate authority shall not refuse to grant or renew a permit without affording to the applicant or a person acting for him an opportunity of appearing before, and being heard by, the appropriate authority or (where that authority is a local authority) a committee of the local authority.

Grounds for refusal to grant or renew permit

8–13505   7. Where an application for the grant or renewal of a permit is made to a local authority, then if—

(*a*) there is for the time being in force a resolution passed by that authority as mentioned in sub-paragraph (*a*) or sub-paragraph (*b*) of paragraph 3 of this Schedule which is applicable to the premises to which the application relates, and

(*b*) the permit could not be granted or renewed without contravening that resolution,

it shall be the duty of the authority to refuse to grant or renew the permit.

8. (1) In the case of premises to which paragraph 4 of this Schedule applies—

(*a*) the grant of a permit shall be at the discretion of the appropriate authority; but

(*b*) the appropriate authority shall not refuse to renew a permit except

(i) on the grounds that, while the permit has been in force, they or their authorised representatives have been refused reasonable facilities to inspect the premises,

(ii) where the permit is expressed to be granted for the purposes of section 34(5E) of this Act, on the grounds that the condition specified in paragraph (*a*) of sub-paragraph (3) of paragraph 10B of this Schedule or, as the case may be, any of the conditions specified in paragraph (*b*) of that sub-paragraph has not been complied with to their satisfaction, or by reason of the conditions or manner in which machines to which Part III of this Act applies have been used on the premises, or

(iii) any other amusements have been provided or conducted on the premises, while the permit has been in force.

(1A) Where an application for the grant of a permit for the purposes of subsection (5E) of section 34 is made in respect of premises in respect of which the applicant holds a permit under that section which is expressed to be granted for the purposes of subsection (1) of that section, the appropriate authority may only refuse to grant the permit if they would have grounds for refusing an application to renew the existing permit.

(1B) Where an application for the grant of a permit for the purposes of subsection (1) of section 34 is made in respect of premises in respect of which the applicant holds a permit under that section which is expressed to be granted for the purposes of subsection (5E) of that section, the appropriate authority may only refuse to grant the permit if they would have grounds for refusing an application to renew the existing permit were it expressed to be granted for the purposes of subsection (1) of that section.

(2) In the case of premises other than premises to which paragraph 4 of this Schedule applies, the grant or renewal of a permit shall (subject to paragraph 7 of this Schedule) be at the discretion of the appropriate authority; and in particular, and without prejudice to the generality of that discretion, the appropriate authority may refuse[1] to grant or renew any such permit on the grounds that, by reason of the purposes for which, or the persons by whom, or any circumstances in which, the premises are or are to be used, it is undesirable that machines to which Part III of this Act applies should be used for providing amusements on those premises.

(3) The preceding provisions of this paragraph shall have effect subject to section 34(7) of this Act.

---

1. In a case decided on similar wording in the Betting, Gaming and Lotteries Act 1963 it was held that in general the opinion of the licensing authority that drinking and gambling do not mix was not a valid reason for refusing a permit (*Wolverhampton and Dudley Breweries Ltd v Warley County Borough Council* [1970] 1 All ER 158, [1970] 1 WLR 463, 134 JP 184).

Condition imposed on grant or renewal of permit

8–13506   9. Where an application for the grant or renewal of a permit is made to a local authority, and there is for the time being in force a resolution passed by that authority as mentioned in sub-paragraph (*c*) of paragraph 3 of this Schedule which is applicable to the premises to which the application relates, then, if the authority grant or renew the permit, it shall be their duty to do so subject to a condition limiting the number of machines to which Part III of this Act applies which may be made available for gaming on the premises to such number, not exceeding the number specified in the resolution, as the authority may determine.

10. Subject to paragraph 9 of this Schedule, on granting or renewing a permit in respect of any premises, other than premises to which paragraph 4 of this Schedule applies, the appropriate authority may grant or renew it subject to a condition limiting the number of machines to which Part III of this Act applies which may be made available for gaming on the premises to such number as the authority may determine.

Condition in case of premises with liquor licence

10A. (1) A permit in respect of any such premises as are mentioned in sub-paragraph (*a*) or sub-paragraph (*c*) of paragraph 1 of this Schedule shall be subject to the condition that any machine in respect of which the conditions mentioned in section 34(5A) of this Act are observed is located in a bar.

(2) In sub-paragraph (1), "bar"—

(*a*) in relation to any such premises as are mentioned in sub-paragraph (*a*) of paragraph 1 of this Schedule, means any place which, by virtue of a premises licence, may be used for the supply of alcohol and which is exclusively or mainly used for the supply and consumption of alcohol and

(*b*) in relation to any such premises as are mentioned in sub-paragraph (*c*) of that paragraph has the same meaning as in the Licensing (Scotland) Act 1976[2].

Grant by local authority of amusement machine premises permit

10B. (1) This paragraph applies where a local authority grant a permit in respect of premises to which paragraph 4 of this Schedule applies.

(2) The authority shall state in the permit whether it is granted for the purposes of subsection (1) or (5E) of section 34 of this Act.

(3) Where the permit is expressed to be granted for the purposes of section 34(5E) of this Act, it shall be subject to the following conditions, namely—

(*a*) in the case of premises where admission is restricted to persons aged 18 or over, that no person under 18 is admitted to the premises; and

(*b*) in the case of premises where admission is not restricted to persons aged 18 or over—

   (i) that any machine in respect of which the conditions mentioned in section 34(5A) of this Act are observed is located in an area of the premises which is separated from the remainder of the premises by a physical barrier which is effective to prevent access otherwise than by means of an entrance designed for the purpose;

   (ii) that only persons aged 18 or over are admitted to an area of the premises in which any such machine is located;

   (iii) that access to an area of the premises in which any such machine is located is supervised;

   (iv) that any area of the premises in which any such machine is located is so arranged as to permit all parts of it to be observed; and

   (v) that at the entrance to, and inside, any such area there are prominently displayed notices indicating that access to the area is prohibited to persons aged under 18.

Appeal in England or Wales against decision of appropriate authority

8–13507   11. (1) Where on an application under this Schedule in England or Wales the appropriate authority refuse to grant or renew a permit, or grant or renew it subject to a condition, the authority shall forthwith give to the applicant notice of that decision and of the grounds on which it is made.

(2) Where such a notice has been given, the applicant may, by notice to the clerk to the appropriate authority, appeal against the decision to the Crown Court having jurisdiction in the authority's area.

(3) As soon as practicable after receiving notice of appeal against a decision of the appropriate authority, the clerk to the authority shall send the notice to the appropriate officer of the Crown Court together with a statement of the decision against which the appeal is brought and of the name and last-known residence or place of business of the appellant.

(4) On receipt of the notice of appeal, the appropriate officer of the Crown Court shall enter the appeal and give to the appellant and to the appropriate authority not less than seven days' notice in writing of the date, time and place appointed for the hearing of the appeal.

(5) *Repealed.*

12. (1) Where the appeal is an appeal against a decision of a local authority refusing to grant or renew a permit, the Crown Court shall not allow the appeal if satisfied that, by virtue of paragraph 7 of this Schedule, it was the duty of the authority to refuse to grant or renew the permit.

(2) Where the appeal is against a decision of a local authority to grant or renew a permit subject to a condition, and the Crown Court is satisfied that, by virtue of paragraph 9 of this Schedule, it was the duty of the authority to grant or renew the permit subject to such a condition as is mentioned in that paragraph the court shall not reverse or vary the decision so as—

(*a*) to grant or renew the permit unconditionally, or

(*b*) to grant or renew the permit subject to a condition limiting the number of machines to which Part III of this Act applies which may be made available for gaming on the premises to a number exceeding the number specified in the resolution of the local authority.

13. Subject to paragraph 12 of this Schedule, on any appeal under paragraph 11 of this Schedule the Crown Court may by its order allow or dismiss the appeal, or reverse or vary any part of the decision of the appropriate authority, and may deal with the application as if it had been made to the Crown Court in the first instance; and the judgment of the Crown Court on the appeal shall be final[1].

14. *Repealed.*

15, 17. *Appeal in Scotland.*

Duration of permit

8–13508 **18.** Subject to the following provisions of this Schedule, and without prejudice to the cancellation of any permit under section 39 of this Act, a permit—

    (*a*) if not renewed, shall cease to have effect on such date, not being less than three years beginning with the date on which it was granted, as may be specified in the permit, or

    (*b*) if renewed, shall, unless further renewed, cease to have effect on such date, not being less than three years beginning with the date on which it was renewed or last renewed, as the case may be, as may be specified in the decision to renew it.

    19. (1) Where an application for the renewal of a permit is made not less than one month before the date on which it is due to expire, the permit shall not cease to have effect by virtue of the last preceding paragraph before the appropriate authority have determined the application or the application has been withdrawn.

    (2) Where, on such an application, the appropriate authority refuse to renew the permit, it shall not cease to have effect by virtue of the last preceding paragraph before the time within which the applicant can appeal against the refusal has expired, and, if he so appeals, shall not cease to have effect by virtue of that paragraph until the appeal has been determined or abandoned.

    20. (1) Subject to paragraph 20ZA, a permit shall not be transferable, and, subject to the following provisions of this paragraph, shall cease to have effect if—

    (*a*) in the case of premises falling within sub-paragraph (*a*) or sub-paragraph (*c*) of paragraph 1 of this Schedule, the holder of the permit ceases to be the holder of the licence or certificate in respect of the premises, or

    (*b*) in the case of any other premises, the holder of the permit ceases to be the occupier of the premises.

    (2) If the holder of a permit dies while the permit is in force—

    (*a*) the permit shall not cease to have effect by virtue of paragraph 18 of this Schedule or by virtue of the preceding sub-paragraph before the end of the period of six months beginning with the date of his death, and

    (*b*) except for the purposes of a renewal of the permit, his personal representatives shall be deemed to be the holder of the permit;

and the appropriate authority may from time to time, on the application of those personal representatives, extend or further extend the period for which the permit continues to have effect by virtue of this sub-paragraph if satisfied that the extension is necessary for the purpose of winding up the estate of the deceased and that no other circumstances make it undesirable.

    20ZA. (1) This paragraph applies where—

    (*a*) a premises licence authorising the supply of alcohol for consumption on particular premises has been granted under paragraph 4 of Schedule 8 to the Licensing Act 2003 (conversion of existing justices' licences to premises licences),

    (*b*) the application for the licence was made by virtue of paragraph 2(3)(b) of that Schedule (application made by a person with the consent of the existing licence holder), and

    (*c*) a permit granted by the licensing justices has effect in respect of the premises immediately before the premises licence takes effect.

    (2) This paragraph also applies where—

    (*a*) a premises licence authorising the supply of alcohol for consumption on particular premises has been granted under section 18 of the Licensing Act 2003 (determination of application for premises licence) before 24th November 2005,

    (*b*) a justices' licence granted under the Licensing Act 1964 has effect in respect of the premises immediately before that day ("the existing licence"),

    (*c*) the application for the premises licence was made by a person other than the holder of the existing licence, and

    (*d*) a permit granted by the licensing justices has effect in respect of the premises immediately before the premises licence takes effect.

    (3) The permit is transferred, at the time the premises licence takes effect, to the holder of that licence (and, accordingly, does not cease to have effect at that time under paragraph 20(1)(a)).

    (4) Subject to that, the permit continues to have effect in accordance with this Schedule.

    20A. (1) A permit expressed to be granted for the purposes of subsection (1) of section 34 of this Act shall cease to have effect on the grant in respect of the premises to which the permit relates of a permit expressed to be granted for the purposes of subsection (5E) of that section.

    (2) A permit expressed to be granted for the purposes of subsection (5E) of section 34 of this Act shall cease to have effect on the grant in respect of the premises to which the permit relates of a permit expressed to be granted for the purposes of subsection (1) of that section.

Payment of fees

8–13509 **21.** Notwithstanding anything in the preceding provisions of this Schedule no permit shall be granted or renewed except on payment by the applicant to the appropriate authority or their clerk of the fee chargeable in accordance with section 48 of this Act.

Supplementary provisions

8–13510 **22.** The grant or renewal of a permit shall not be invalidated by any failure to comply with any requirement of paragraph 7 or paragraph 9 of this Schedule; and any duty of a local authority to comply with such a requirement shall not be enforceable by any legal proceedings.

    23. In this Schedule—

'alcohol', 'licensing authority' and 'premises licence' have the same meaning as in the Licensing Act 2003;

'hotel licence' and 'public house licence' have the same meaning as in Schedule 1 to the Licensing (Scotland) Act 1976;

'relevant licensing authority', in relation to premises in respect of which a premises licence is in force, means the authority determined in relation to those premises in accordance with section 12 of the Licensing Act 2003; and

'supply of alcohol' is to be construed in accordance with section 14 of that Act.

24. *Repealed.*

Section 49   SCHEDULE 10

PROVISION OF INFORMATION BY LICENSING AUTHORITIES AND SHERIFF CLERKS

(As amended by the Finance Act 1970.)

8–13511   1. The clerk to each licensing authority shall keep in the prescribed form registers containing such particulars as may be prescribed with respect to the grant, renewal, cancellation and transfer by the licensing authority of licences under this Act.

2. The clerk to each licensing authority in England or Wales and each sheriff clerk in Scotland shall keep in the prescribed form registers containing such particulars as may be prescribed with respect to the registration by the authority or sheriff of clubs and miners' welfare institutes under Part II or Part III of this Act, and of the renewal and cancellation by the authority or sheriff of any such registration.

3. Each licensing authority shall permit any constable or officer of customs and excise, and any other person on payment of the prescribed fee[1], to inspect at any reasonable time any register kept by the authority under paragraph 1 or (in England or Wales) under paragraph 2 of this Schedule.

4. Any constable or officer of customs and excise, and any other person on payment of the prescribed fee, may inspect at any reasonable time any register kept by the sheriff clerk under paragraph 2 of this Schedule.

5. (1) The clerk to each licensing authority shall send to the Board such particulars as may be prescribed[2] with respect to matters in relation to which the authority are required to keep registers under paragraph 1, or in England or Wales under paragraphs 1 and 2, of this Schedule.

(2) Each sheriff clerk shall send to the Board such particulars as may be prescribed with respect to matters in relation to which he is required to keep registers under paragraph 2 of this Schedule.

6. The Board may request a licensing authority to send to the Board a statement setting out any particulars notified to the licensing authority under section 14(4) of this Act during a period specified in the request, and the licensing authority shall comply with any such request.

7. Without prejudice to the preceding provisions of this Schedule, the clerk to each licensing authority, and each sheriff clerk, on being requested by the Board to do so, shall compile from such information as is for the time being in his possession, and shall furnish the Board with, such statistics as the Board may from time to time require for the purpose of assisting the Board in the performance of their functions, and in particular their functions under section 10(3), of this Act.

---

1. The prescribed fee is 25p; reg 7(4) of the Gaming Clubs (Licensing) Regulations 1969, this PART, post.
2. See reg 8 of the Gaming Clubs (Licensing) Regulations 1969, this PART, post.

Horserace Betting Levy Act 1969

(1969 c 14)

8–13600   4. Non-renewal of bookmaker's permit in case of failure to pay levy.   (1) Subject to this section, where an application is made to the appropriate authority under Schedule 1 to the Act of 1963 for the renewal of a bookmaker's permit and the authority, at the time when they determine the application, are satisfied—

(*a*) that the applicant is in default in respect of bookmakers' levy and has been so for at least three months; and

(*b*) that on a previous occasion (not before the passing of this Act, nor before the period of five years ending with the date of the application), being an occasion on which the permit was renewed (whether by the same or another authority), he was so in default and had been so for at least three months,

the authority shall refuse the application.

(2) Subsection (1) of this section shall apply only where the Levy Board appear, by counsel or a solicitor, at the hearing of the application and maintain an objection duly made by them in accordance with Schedule 1 to the Act of 1963, being an objection to the renewal of the permit on the ground (either alone or among other grounds) that the applicant has failed to discharge his liabilities by way of the bookmakers' levy.

(3) For the purposes of subsection (1) of this section, a person is in default in respect of bookmakers' levy if—

(*a*) there has become due from him under section 28(7) of the Act of 1963 an amount assessed as payable by him by way of levy; and

(*b*) the whole or any part of that amount remains unpaid.

(4) . . .

(5) Nothing in this section shall be taken as prejudicing paragraph 16(2) of Schedule 1 to the Act

of 1963 (under which an authority dealing with an application for the renewal of a bookmaker's permit have a discretion to refuse the application on the ground of the character or conduct of the applicant, including his failure to pay levy).
[Horserace Betting Levy Act 1969, s 4.]

Lotteries and Amusements Act 1976
(1976 c 32)

PART I
LEGAL AND ILLEGAL LOTTERIES
General illegality of lotteries

8–13601   1. Illegality of lotteries.   All lotteries[1] which do not constitute gaming[2] are unlawful[3], except as provided by this Act and section 2(1) of the National Lottery etc Act 1993.
[Lotteries and Amusements Act 1976, s 14 amended by the National Lottery etc Act 1993, Sch 1.]

---

1. **Definition of lottery.**—In order to establish a lottery, three elements are required: a distribution of prizes, an element of pure chance, and a contribution by the participant towards his chance (*Reader's Digest Association Ltd v Williams* [1976] 3 All ER 737, 141 JP 52). It is not necessary to prove that money paid by the participants in return for obtaining a chance of winning is used to provide prizes or is paid into a fund out of which the prizes are provided. What is essential is that there is a distribution of prizes by lot or chance and that the chance of winning is secured by a payment, contribution or consideration by those taking part (*Imperial Tobacco Ltd v A-G* [1981] AC 718, [1980] 1 All ER 866, 144 JP 163).

A lottery is interpreted according to the obvious meaning of the term as applying only to distribution of prizes by chance, and nothing but chance, that is, by doing that which is equivalent to drawing lots (*Moore v Elphick* [1945] 2 All ER 155, 110 JP 66). If merit or skill plays a part in determining the distribution, it is not a lottery (*Scott v DPP* [1914] 2 KB 868, 78 JP 297), but there must be real skill which has some effect, such as where skill was exercised in connection with the selection of football pools conducted by a particular organisation (*Moore v Elphick*, supra). It is not an essential feature of a lottery that there should be an identifiable prize fund provided the scheme achieves the overall object of the distribution of money by chance (*Atkinson v Murrell* [1972] 2 All ER 1131). Where a scheme for a football pool gives a chance of winning any one of several prizes, on the occurrence of any one of several contingencies to only one of which a competitor has directed skill, the scheme is for a lottery (*Boucher v Rowsell* [1947] 1 All ER 870, 111 JP Jo 329). Where an article is conjoined with the chance, it is immaterial whether the scheme purports to sell only the article or the chance (*Taylor v Smetten* (1883) 11 QBD 207, 48 JP 36; *Williams and Moore v Varley* (1938) 102 JP Jo 68).

Held to be lotteries.—The sale of packets of tea with coupons attached, unknown to the purchaser, entitling him to a prize (*Taylor v Smetten*, supra); see also *Morris v Blackman* (1864) 2 H & C 912, 28 JP 199; *Minty v Sylvester* (1915) 79 JP 543; *Hunt v Williams* (1888) 52 JP 821; *Barratt v Burden* (1893) 57 JP Jo 772; *Whiteman v Z B Atkins (1940) Ltd* (1940) 109 LJ Ch 453 and *Imperial Tobacco Ltd v A-G* [1981] AC 718, [1980] 1 All ER 866, 144 JP 163.

A newspaper competition where the "missing word" was not necessarily the most appropriate (*Barclay v Pearson* [1893] 2 Ch 154), or where a real comparison of merits was impossible owing to the large number of competitors (*Blyth v Hulton & Co Ltd* (1908) 72 JP 401; *Smith's Advertising Agency v Leeds Laboratory Co* (1910) 26 TLR 335), or where the result depended on the previous choice of a third person (*Coles v Odhams Press Ltd* [1936] 1 KB 416, 100 JP 85), was held to be a lottery. On the other hand, where the actual facts as to the number of competitors had not been investigated, it was held that the alleged lottery had not been proved (*Scott v DPP* [1914] 2 KB 868, 78 JP 257). Where a scheme is severable, one part being a lottery the other requiring an element of skill or the doing of a service, the scheme is a lottery (*Kerslake v Knight* (1925) 89 JP 142; *DPP v Bradfute & Associates Ltd* [1967] 2 QB 29, [1967] 1 All ER 112, 131 JP 117.

An ordinary sweepstake is a lottery, and the organiser need not be a party to it (*Allport v Nutt* (1845) 1 CB 974; *R v Hobbs* [1898] 2 QB 647, 62 JP 551; *Hardwick v Lane* [1904] 1 KB 204, 68 JP 94). The contingency of the chain in a "snowball" scheme not being broken was held to be a matter of chance and to make the scheme a lottery (*Barnes v Strathern* 1929 JC 41). Where buyer and seller were not concerned with note-cases worth 1s 6d and sold at £1, but with the chance that the buyer might under a "snowball" scheme obtain a large sum of money from the acts of persons over whom he had no control, it was held to be a lottery (*DPP v Phillips* [1935] 1 KB 391, 98 JP 461). See also *Atkinson v Murrell* [1973] AC 289, [1972] 2 All ER 1131, [1972] 3 WLR 465, *Re Senator Hanseatische Verwaltungsgesellschaft mbH* [1996] 4 All ER 933, [1997] 1 WLR 515, CA (the "Titan Scheme") and *One Life Ltd (in liquidation) v Roy* [1996] 2 BCLC 608). The great uncertainty of the date of receipt was held to constitute a distribution to customers of cash bonuses by a tea merchant a lottery (*Howgate v Ralph* (1929) 93 JP 127); placing commodities in order of popularity as established by a general vote is pure chance and the giving of prizes to a successful competitor is therefore a lottery (*Hobbs v Ward* (1929) 93 JP 163; *Challis v Warrender* (1930) 95 JP 39). The sale of fastened-up coupons whereby the purchaser, if the football teams defined therein won, etc, received a prize, was the sale of a chance in a lottery, notwithstanding that the purchaser had the option of selecting other teams (*Challis v Newman* (1937) cited and affirmed in *Barker v Mumby* [1939] 1 All ER 611, 103 JP 125).

A postal bingo club's operations were held to constitute a lottery (and not gaming within the meaning of s 23(1), post) where participants were absent from the place where the draw was held and, in fact, had no active participation in the operation (*Armstrong v DPP* [1965] 1 All ER 1012, 129 JP 266; affd [1965] 2 All ER 745, 129 JP 493, HL; cf *DPP v Regional Pool Promotions Ltd* [1964] 2 QB 244, [1964] 1 All ER 65, 128 JP 150).

Held NOT to be lotteries.—A competition for forecasting the first four horses in a race is not a lottery (*Stoddart v Sagar* [1895] 2 QB 474, 59 JP 598), but one for forecasting all the horses in the correct order might be held to be otherwise. A postal offer of records gave each recipient six numbers, one of which might have drawn a prize. A purchaser returned an envelope marked "Yes", a non-purchaser an envelope marked "No". Prospects of winning a prize were the same either way; hence no lottery (*Reader's Digest Association Ltd v Williams* [1976] 3 All ER 737, 141 JP 52).

2. "Gaming" has the same meaning as in the Gaming Act 1968 (s 23(1), post); for that definition see the Gaming Act 1968, s 52, this title, ante.

3. This section does not create an offence (*Sales-Matic Ltd v Hinchliffe* [1959] 3 All ER 401, 123 JP 546).

4. For non-application of this section to amusements with prizes at certain entertainments, see ss 15(2), 16(2).

8–13601A   **2. General lottery offences[1].** (1) Subject to the provisions of this section, every person[2] who in connection with any lottery promoted or proposed to be promoted either in Great Britain or elsewhere—

- (a) prints[3] any tickets[4] for use in the lottery; or
- (b) sells or distributes[5], or offers or advertises for sale or distribution[6], or has in his possession for the purpose of sale or distribution, any tickets or chances in the lottery; or
- (c) prints, publishes[7] or distributes, or has in his possession for the purpose of publication or distribution—
  - (i) any advertisement of the lottery; or
  - (ii) any list, whether complete or not, of prize winners or winning tickets in the lottery; or
  - (iii) any such matter descriptive of the drawing or intended drawing of the lottery, or otherwise relating to the lottery, as is calculated to act as an inducement to persons to participate in that lottery or in other lotteries; or
- (d) brings, or invites any person to send, into Great Britain from a place outside the British Islands and the member States for the purpose of sale or distribution any ticket in, or advertisement of, the lottery[8]; or
- (e) sends or attempts to send out of Great Britain to a place outside the British Islands and the member States any money[9] or valuable thing received in respect of the sale or distribution, or any document recording the sale or distribution, or the identity of the holder, of any ticket or chance in the lottery; or
- (f) uses any premises, or causes or knowingly permits any premises to be used, for purposes connected with the promotion of conduct of the lottery; or
- (g) causes, procures or attempts to procure any person to do any of the above-mentioned acts,

shall be guilty of an offence[10].

(2) In any proceedings instituted under subsection (1) above, it shall be a defence to prove[11] either—

- (a) that the lottery to which the proceedings relate was a lottery declared not to be unlawful by section 3, 4 or 25(6) below, and that at the date of the alleged offence the person charged believed, and had reasonable ground for believing, that none of the conditions required by the relevant enactment to be observed in connection with the promotion and conduct of the lottery had been broken; or
- (b) that the lottery to which the proceedings relate was a society's lottery or a local lottery, and that at the date of the alleged offence the person charged believed, and had reasonable ground for believing, that it was being conducted in accordance with the requirements of this Act; or
- (c) that the lottery to which the proceedings relate was not promoted wholly or partly outside Great Britain and constituted gaming as well as a lottery; or
- (d) that the lottery to which the proceedings relate was a lottery forming part of the National Lottery for the purposes of Part I of the National Lottery etc Act 1993 or that at the date of the alleged offence the person charged believed, and had reasonable ground for believing, it to be such a lottery.

(2A) In any proceedings instituted under subsection (1) above in respect of the printing, sale or possession of any tickets, advertisements or other documents or in respect of anything done with a view to or in connection with the printing, sale or export from Great Britain of any tickets, advertisements or other documents, it shall be a defence to prove that at the date of the alleged offence the person charged believed, and had reasonable ground for believing—

- (a) that the lottery to which the proceedings relate was not being, and would not be, promoted or conducted wholly or partly in Great Britain; and
- (b) that the tickets, advertisements or other documents were not being, and would not be, used in Great Britain in or in connection with that or any other lottery.

(3) In England and Wales, proceedings under subsection (1) (c) (iii) above in respect of any matter published in a newspaper[12] shall not be instituted except by, or by direction of, the Director of Public Prosecutions.

[Lotteries and Amusements Act 1976, s 2 as amended by the Lotteries (Amendment) Act 1984, s 1 and the National Lottery etc Act 1993, s 46 and Sch 1.]

---

1. For the circumstances in which duty is payable see the provisions of PART I, Chapter II of the Finance Act 1993 in PART VIII, CUSTOMS AND EXCISE, post.

2. For statutory defence to a charge, see sub-s (2), infra.

3. "Printing" includes writing and other modes of reproducing words in a visible form (s 23(1), post). But tickets printed in anticipation of their being used in any lottery are outside the section (*McKay v Gillies* [1956] 3 All ER 583, 120 JP 587).

4. "Ticket", in relation to any lottery, includes any document evidencing the claim of a person to participate in the chances of the lottery (s 23(1), post).

5. "Distribute", in relation to documents or other matters, includes distribution to persons or places within or outside Great Britain, and "distribution" shall be construed accordingly (s 23(1), post).

6. This does not include a case where the possession is that of one member on behalf of all the members of a syndicate, no subsale being in contemplation (*Corfield v Dolby* (1936) 100 JP 75).

7. See *Coles v Odhams Press Ltd* [1936] 1 KB 416, 100 JP 85.

"Publish" only means making known, not necessarily publicly, the proposal to some person other than the originator, and may take place before the sale of any tickets, etc (*Dew v DPP* (1920) 85 JP 81; *Ranson v Burgess* (1927) 43 TLR 561, 91 JP 133; *A-G v Walkergate Press Ltd* (1930) 94 JP 90).

8. See *Moore v Elphick* [1945] 2 All ER 155, 110 JP 66.

9. "Money" includes a cheque, banknote, postal order or money order (s 23(1), post).

10. For penalty, see s 20(1), post. No offence is committed under this section if the lottery is not an unlawful lottery as provided by ss 3 or 4, notwithstanding that certain conditions laid down in these sections are broken (*Stacey v Wilkins* [1946] KB 271, [1946] 1 All ER 293, 110 JP 182).

11. The onus of proof will be on the defendant; but see *R v Carr-Briant* [1943] KB 607, [1943] 2 All ER 156, 107 JP 167, in which it was held that a defendant who availed himself of a statutory defence was not required to establish that defence "beyond reasonable doubt", but according to probability.

12. "Newspaper" includes any journal, magazine or other periodical publication (s 23(1), post).

Exceptions

8–13601B   **3. Small lotteries incidental to exempt entertainments.**   (1) In this Act "exempt entertainment[1]" means a bazaar, sale of work, fete, dinner, dance, sporting or athletic event or other entertainment of a similar character, whether limited to one day or extending over two or more days.

(2) Where a lottery is promoted as an incident of an exempt entertainment, that lottery is not unlawful, but the conditions set out in subsection (3) below shall be observed in connection with its promotion and conduct and, if any of those conditions is contravened, every person concerned in the promotion or conduct of the lottery shall be guilty of an offence[2] unless he proves[3] that the contravention[4] occurred without his consent or connivance and that he exercised all due diligence to prevent it.

(3) The conditions referred to in subsection (2) above are that—

   (*a*)   the whole proceeds of the entertainment (including the proceeds of the lottery) after deducting—

      (i)   the expenses of the entertainment, excluding expenses incurred in connection with the lottery; and

      (ii)   the expenses incurred in printing tickets in the lottery; and

      (iii)   such sum, if any, not exceeding £50[5] or such other sum as may be specified in an order made by the Secretary of State, as the promoters of the lottery think fit to appropriate on account of any expenses incurred by them in purchasing prizes in the lottery,

shall be devoted to purposes other than private gain[6];

   (*b*)   none of the prizes in the lottery shall be money prizes;

   (*c*)   tickets or chances in the lottery shall not be sold or issued, nor shall the result of the lottery be declared, except on the premises on which the entertainment takes place and during the progress of the entertainment; and

   (*d*)   the facilities for participating in lotteries under this section, or those facilities together with any other facilities for participating in lotteries or gaming, shall not be the only, or the only substantial, inducement to persons to attend the entertainment.

[Lotteries and Amusements Act 1976, s 3.]

---

1. For provision of amusements with prizes at exempt entertainment see s 15, post.

2. For penalty see s 20, post.

3. See note 11 in para **6–1081**, ante.

4. "Contravention", in relation to any requirement, includes a failure to comply with that requirement, and cognate expressions shall be construed accordingly (s 23 (1), post).

5. The sum of £250 has been specified by SI 1993/3222.

6. See *Payne v Bradley* [1962] AC 343, [1961] 2 All ER 882, 125 JP 514, HL; affg [1961] 2 QB 44, [1961] 2 All ER 36, 125 JP 352; *Cookson v Bowles* [1962] 2 All ER 760, 126 JP 392; but for the limited application of these decisions in relation to societies, see s 22, post.

8–13601C   **4. Private lotteries.**   (1) In this Act "private lottery" means a lottery in Great Britain which is promoted—

   (*a*)   for members of one society[1] established and conducted for purposes not connected with gaming, betting or lotteries;

   (*b*)   for persons all of whom work on the same premises; or

   (*c*)   for persons all of whom reside on the same premises,

and which satisfies the conditions in subsections (1A) and (1B) below.

(1A) The lottery must be promoted by persons each of whom—

   (*a*)   is one of the persons for whom the lottery is promoted; and

   (*b*)   in the case of a lottery promoted for the members of a society, is authorised in writing by the governing body of the society to promote the lottery.

(1B) The sale of tickets or chances in the lottery must be confined—

   (*a*)   to the persons for whom the lottery is promoted; and

(b) in the case of a lottery promoted for the members of a society, to any other persons on the society's premises.

(2) For the purposes of this section, each local or affiliated branch or section of a society shall be regarded as a separate and distinct society[2].

(3) A private lottery is not unlawful, but the following conditions shall be observed in connection with its promotion and conduct, that is to say—

(a) the whole proceeds, after deducting only expenses incurred for printing[3] and stationery, shall be devoted to the provision of prizes for purchasers of tickets or chances, or, in the case of a lottery promoted for the members of a society, shall be devoted either—

    (i) to the provision of prizes as aforesaid; or

    (ii) to purposes which are purposes of the society; or

    (iii) as to part to the provision of prizes as aforesaid and as to the remainder to such purposes as aforesaid;

(b) there shall not be exhibited, published or distributed any written notice or advertisement of the lottery other than—

    (i) a notice of it exhibited on the premises of the society for whose members it is promoted or, as the case may be, on the premises on which the persons for whom it is promoted work or reside; and

    (ii) such announcement or advertisement of it as is contained in the tickets, if any;

(c) the price of every ticket or chance shall be the same, and the price of any ticket shall be stated on the ticket;

(d) every ticket shall bear upon the face of it the name and address of each of the promoters and a statement of the persons to whom the sale of tickets or chances by the promoters is restricted, and a statement that no prize won in the lottery shall be paid or delivered by the promoters to any person other than the person to whom the winning ticket or chance was sold by them, and no prize shall be paid or delivered except in accordance with that statement;

(e) no ticket or chance shall be issued or allotted by the promoters except by way of sale and upon receipt of its full price, and no money or valuable thing so received by a promoter shall in any circumstances be returned; and

(f) no tickets in the lottery shall be sent through the post.

(4) Subject to subsection (5) below, if any of the conditions set out in subsection (3) above is contravened, each of the promoters of the lottery, and, where the person by whom the condition is broken is not one of the promoters, that person also, shall be guilty of an offence[4].

(5) It shall be a defence for a person charged with an offence under subsection (4) above only by reason of his being a promoter of the lottery to prove[5] that the contravention occurred without his consent or connivance and that he exercised all due diligence[6] to prevent it.

[Lotteries and Amusements Act 1976, s 4, amended by the National Lottery etc Act 1993, s 47.]

---

1. "Society" includes any club, institution, organisation or association of persons, by whatever name called, and any separate branch or section of such a club, institution, organisation or association (s 23(1), post).

2. A lottery promoted by a large society which is itself broken up into many branches, and where chances are sold among members of the branches is unlawful (*Keehan v Walters* [1948] 1 KB 19; *Hudson v Chamberlin* (1948) 113 JP 64). See, however, s 5, post.

3. "Printing" includes writing and other modes of reproducing words in a visible form (s 23(1), post).

4. For penalty, see s 20, post.

5. The onus of proof will be on the defendant; but see *R v Carr-Briant* [1943] KB 607, [1943] 2 All ER 156, 107 JP 167, in which it was held that a defendant who availed himself of a statutory defence was not required to establish that defence "beyond reasonable doubt", but according to probability.

6. This is a question of fact, not of law: there is no legal standard of diligence (*R C Hammett Ltd v Crabb, R C Hammett Ltd v Beldam* (1931) 95 JP 180).

8–13601D   5. Societies' lotteries.   (1) In this Act "society's lottery" means a lottery[1] promoted on behalf of a society[2] which is established and conducted wholly or mainly for one or more of the following purposes, that is to say—

(a) charitable purposes[3];

(b) participation in or support of athletic sports or games or cultural activities;

(c) purposes which are not described in paragraph (a) or (b) above but are neither purposes of private gain[4] nor purposes of any commercial undertaking.

(2) Any purpose for which a society is established and conducted and which is calculated to benefit the society as a whole shall not be held to be a purpose of private gain by reason only that action in its fulfilment would result in benefit to any person as an individual.

(3) Subject to the provisions of this Act, a society's lottery is not unlawful if—

(a) it is promoted in Great Britain; and

(b) the society is for the time being registered under the appropriate Schedule; and

(c) it is promoted in accordance with a scheme approved by the society;

(d) either—

  (i)   the total value of tickets or chances to be sold is £10,000 or less; or

  (ii) the scheme is registered with the Board[5] before any tickets or chances are sold.

(3A) The appropriate Schedule for the purposes of subsection (3)(*b*) above—

(*a*) is Schedule 1[6] to this Act if none of subsections (3B) to (3D) below applies to the lottery;

(*b*) is Schedule 1A[7] to this Act if any of those subsections applies to the lottery.

(3B) This subsection applies to a lottery if the total value of the tickets or chances sold or to be sold in the lottery is more than £20,000.

(3C) This subsection applies to a lottery if the total value of—

(*a*) the tickets or chances sold or to be sold in the lottery, and

(*b*) the tickets or chances sold or to be sold in all earlier lotteries held by the same society in the same year,

is more than £250,000.

(3D) This subsection applies to a lottery if subsection (3B) or (3C) above applied to any earlier lottery held by the same society in the same year or any of the three preceding years.

(3E) For the purposes of this section—

(*a*) a lottery is earlier than another lottery if any tickets or chances in it are sold, distributed or offered for sale before any tickets or chances in the other lottery are sold, distributed or offered for sale, and

(*b*) a lottery is held in the year in which the date of the lottery falls.

(3F) In this section "year" means a period of twelve months beginning with 1 January.

(4) The whole proceeds of a society's lottery, after deducting sums lawfully appropriated on account of expenses or for the provision of prizes, shall be applied to purposes of the society such as are described in subsection (1) above.

(5) Schedules 1 and 1A to this Act shall have effect.

[Lotteries and Amusements Act 1976, s 5 as amended by SI 1981/110 and the National Lottery etc Act 1993, s 48.]

---

1. For provisions relating to frequency of societies' lotteries and rules for such lotteries, see ss 10 and 11, post.
2. See note 1 to s 4, ante.
3. "Charitable purposes" is not defined (cf House to House Collections Act 1939, s 11(1), post).
4. For construction of the expression "purposes of private gain", see sub-s (2), infra.
5. "The Board" means the Gaming Board for Great Britain (s 23(1), post).
6. Schedule 1, post, provides for the registration of societies by local authorities.
7. Schedule 1A, post, provides for the registration of societies by the Gaming Board.

8–13601E   **6. Local lotteries.**   (1) In this Act "local lottery" means a lottery[1] promoted by a local authority[2].

(2) Subject to the provisions of this Act, a local lottery is not unlawful if—

(*a*) it is promoted in Great Britain; and

(*b*) it is promoted in accordance with a scheme approved by the local authority; and

(*c*) the scheme is registered with the Board[3] before any tickets or chances are sold.

(3) The functions of local authorities for the discharge of which arrangements may be made under section 101 of the Local Government Act 1972 or section 56 of the Local Government (Scotland) Act 1973 (arrangements for the discharge of a local authority's functions by a committee, a sub-committee or an officer of the authority, or by another local authority) do not include the approval of schemes for local lotteries.

(4) Schedule 2[4] to this Act shall have effect.

[Lotteries and Amusements Act 1976, s 6.]

---

1. For provisions relating to frequency of local lotteries and rules for such lotteries, see ss 10 and 11, post.
2. For meaning of "local authority", see s 23(1), post.
3. "The Board" means the Gaming Board for Great Britain (s 23(1), post).
4. Schedule 2 provides for the registration by the Gaming Board of any scheme approved by a local authority under s 6(2)(*b*) and of any scheme approved by a society under s 5(3)(*c*) where the total value of tickets or chances to be sold exceeds £5,000.

PART II

PROVISIONS RELATING TO SOCIETIES' LOTTERIES AND LOCAL LOTTERIES

Provisions relating to local lotteries

8–13601F   **7. Purposes of a local lottery.**   (1) A local authority[1] may promote a local lottery for any purpose for which they have power to incur expenditure under any enactment, including, without prejudice to the generality of this subsection, section 137 of the Local Government Act 1972 and section 83 of the Local Government (Scotland) Act 1973 (power of local authorities to incur expenditure for certain purposes not otherwise authorised).

(2) It shall be the duty of a local authority—

(a)   to give such publicity to the object of a local lottery as will be likely to bring it to the attention of persons purchasing tickets or chances; and

(b)   subject to the following provisions of this section, to apply money accruing from a local lottery only to the object of the lottery.

(3) In this section "object" means the particular purpose or purposes for which a local authority promote a local lottery.

(4) *Power of Secretary of State to consent to use of money from local lottery for purposes other than its object.*

(5) If the Secretary of State consents to the use of money accruing from a local lottery for a purpose other than its object, it shall be the duty of the local authority to use it only for the purpose for which the consent is given.

[Lotteries and Amusements Act 1976, s 7.]

---

1. For meaning of "local authority", see s 23(1), post.

8–13601G   **8. Proceeds of local lotteries.**   (1) A local authority[1] shall pay the whole proceeds of a local lottery, after deducting the expenses of promoting it and the sums required for prizes, into a fund (in this section referred to as a "lottery fund"), and any money in such a fund shall be invested by the local authority and any income arising from such investment shall be credited to the fund.

(2) It shall be the duty of a local authority to maintain a separate lottery fund for each local lottery which they promote.

(3) *Repealed.*

[Lotteries and Amusements Act 1976, s 8 amended by the Local Government, Planning and Land Act 1980, s 68 and the Local Government Finance Act 1987, Sch 5.]

---

1. For meaning of "local authority, see s 23(1), post.

Provisions relating to societies' lotteries and local lotteries

8–13601H   **9A. Lottery managers.**   (1) No person shall manage a society's lottery or a local lottery unless that person is—

(a)   a member of the society on whose behalf or of the local authority by whom the lottery is promoted, acting in his capacity as such,

(b)   an employee of that society or authority acting in the course of his employment,

(c)   in the case of a society's lottery, a company that is wholly owned by the society,

(d)   a person certified as a lottery manager under Schedule 2A to this Act, or

(e)   an employee of a person so certified acting in the course of his employment.

(2) In subsection (1) above "employee", in relation to an unincorporated body, includes an employee of a member of the body employed by him in his capacity as a member.

(3) For the purposes of subsection 1(c) above—

(a)   "company" means a company formed and registered under the Companies Act 1985 or a company to which the provisions of that Act apply as they apply to a company so formed and registered, and

(b)   a company is wholly owned by a society if the society is entitled (whether directly or through one or more nominees) to exercise, or control the exercise of, the whole of the voting power at any general meeting of the company.

(4) In subsection (1) above and Schedule 2A to this Act references to managing a lottery are to managing the promotion, or any part of the promotion, of a lottery.

(5) Schedule 2A to this Act shall have effect.

[Lotteries and Amusements Act 1976, s 9A inserted by the National Lottery etc Act 1993, s 50.]

8–13601I   **10. Frequency of lotteries.**   (1) The Secretary of State may by order prescribe—

(a)   the maximum number of lotteries that may be promoted under section 5 or 6 above in any period of twelve months on behalf of the same society or by the same local authority; and

(b)   the minimum number of days that must elapse between the dates[1] of any two lotteries promoted under section 5 or 6 above on behalf of the same society or by the same local authority.

(2) An order under subsection (1) above may make different provision for different cases or circumstances.

[Lotteries and Amusements Act 1976, s 10 as amended by SI 1989/1218 and substituted by the National Lottery etc Act 1993, s 51.]

---

1. "Date", in relation to a lottery, means the date on which the winners in that lottery are ascertained (s 23(1), post.)

8–13601J   **11. Rules for authorised lotteries.**   (1) In the case of a society's lottery—

(a) the promoter of the lottery shall be a member of the society authorised in writing by the governing body of the society[1] to act as the promoter; and

(b) every ticket distributed or sold shall specify the name of the society, the name and address of the promoter and the date of the lottery.

(2) No ticket or chance in a society's lottery or a local lottery shall be sold at a price exceeding £2.

(3) The price of every ticket distributed or sold or chance shall be the same, and the price of any ticket shall be stated on the ticket.

(4) No person shall be admitted to participate in a society's lottery or a local lottery in respect of a ticket or chance except after payment to the society or authority of the whole price of the ticket or chance; and no money received for or on account of a ticket or chance shall in any circumstances be returned.

(4A) No payment other than the price of a ticket or chance shall be required of a person as a condition of his admission to participate in a society's lottery or a local lottery.

(5) No prize in a society's lottery or a local lottery shall exceed in amount or value £25,000 or 10 per cent of the total value of the tickets or chances sold in the lottery (whichever is greater).

(6) The total value of the tickets or chances sold in any one such lottery shall not exceed £2,000,000.

(7) The total value of the tickets or chances sold in all such lotteries held in any one year and promoted on behalf of the same society or by the same local authority shall not exceed £10,000,000.

(8) For the purposes of subsection (7) above, a lottery is held in the year in which the date of the lottery falls.

(9) In this section "year" means a period of twelve months beginning with 1 January; but if subsection (7) above (as substituted by section 52 of the National Lottery etc Act 1993) comes into force on a date other than 1 January—

(a) the period beginning with that date and ending with the next 31 December shall be taken to be the first year for the purposes of that subsection, and

(b) in relation to that period, the reference to £5,000,000 in that subsection shall be read as a reference to a proportionately smaller amount.

(10) *Repealed.*

(11) The amount of the proceeds of a society's lottery or a local lottery appropriated for the provision of prizes shall not exceed 55 per cent of the whole proceeds of the lottery.

(12) The amount of the proceeds of a society's lottery or a local lottery appropriated on account of expenses (exclusive of prizes) shall not exceed whichever is the less of—

(a) the expenses actually incurred; and

(b) whichever of the amounts specified in subsection (13) below applies.

(13) The amounts referred to in subsection (12) (b) above are—

(a) where the whole proceeds of the lottery do not exceed £20,000, 35 per cent of those proceeds; or

(b) where the whole proceeds of the lottery exceed £20,000, 15 per cent of those proceeds or such larger percentage, not exceeding 35 per cent, as the Board may authorise in the case of a particular lottery.

(14) For the purposes of subsection (12) above, the amount of any expenses that are met—

(a) by the society on whose behalf, or the local authority by whom, the lottery is promoted, or

(b) by any beneficiary of the lottery,

shall be treated as having been appropriated on account of expenses from the proceeds of the lottery.

(15) In subsection (14) above "beneficiary of the lottery" means a person (other than the society on whose behalf, or the local authority by whom, the lottery is promoted) to whom or for whose benefit any of the proceeds of the lottery, other than amounts appropriated in respect of expenses or prizes, are lawfully paid or applied.

(16) The amount of the proceeds of a society's lottery or a local lottery appropriated for the provision of prizes and the amount of those proceeds appropriated on account of expenses (exclusive of prizes) shall not exceed in aggregate a prescribed percentage[2] of the whole proceeds of the lottery.
[Lotteries and Amusements Act 1976, s 11 as amended by SI 1989/1218, the National Lottery etc Act, 1993 s 52, SI 1997/43 and SI 2002/1410.]

---

1. For meaning of "society", see s 23(1), post.

2. The percentage prescribed for the purposes of this subsection is 80 per cent (Lotteries (Prizes and Expenses: Variation and Prescription of Percentage Limits) Order 1997, SI 1997/43).

8–13601K   **12.** *Power to make regulations*[1].

---

1. The Lotteries Regulations 1993, have been made, see this PART, post.

8–13601L 13. Offences relating to societies' lotteries and local lotteries. (1) If any requirement of this Act of any regulations[1] made under it or of any order made under section 10 above in respect of a society's lottery or a local lottery is contravened, the promoter of that lottery and any other person who is party to the contravention shall be guilty of an offence[2].

(2) It shall be a defence for a person charged with any such offence only by reason of his being the promoter to prove[3] that the contravention occurred without his consent or connivance and that he exercised all due diligence[4] to prevent it.

(2A) It shall be a defence for a person charged with an offence in respect of a contravention of section 11(5) above to prove—

(a) that the total value of the tickets or chances sold in the lottery fell short of the sum reasonably estimated; and

(b) that the amount or value of the prize in question would not have contravened section 11(5) above if the total value of the tickets or chances sold had amounted to the sum reasonably estimated; and

(c) that, if the amount or value of the prize had been any less, an unconditional undertaking as to prizes given in connection with the sale of tickets or chances would have been broken.

(3) It shall be a defence for any person charged with an offence in respect of an appropriation made in contravention of section 11(11) or (12) above to prove—

(a) that the proceeds of the lottery fell short of the sum reasonably estimated; and

(b) that the appropriation was made in order to fulfil an unconditional undertaking as to prizes given in connection with the sale of the relevant tickets or chances, or in respect of expenses actually incurred; and

(c) that the total amounts appropriated in respect of prizes or expenses did not exceed the amounts which could lawfully have been appropriated out of the proceeds of the lottery under the said subsections if the proceeds had amounted to the sum reasonably estimated.

(4) It shall be a defence for any person charged with an offence in respect of a contravention of an order made under section 10 above to prove that the date of a lottery was later than he had expected for reasons which he could not foresee.

[Lotteries and Amusements Act 1976, s 13 as amended by the National Lottery etc Act 1993, s 53.]

---

1. The Lotteries Regulations 1993, have been made, see this PART, post.
2. For penalty, see s 20, post.
3. See note 5 to s 4(5), ante.
4. See note 6 to s 4(5), ante.

PART III

COMPETITIONS AND AMUSEMENTS

Newspaper and other competitions

8–13601M 14. Prize competitions. (1) Subject to subsection (2) below, it shall be unlawful to conduct in or through any newspaper[1], or in connection with any trade or business[2] or the sale of any article to the public—

(a) any competition in which prizes[3] are offered for forecasts of the result either—

(i) of a future event[4]; or

(ii) of a past event the result of which is not yet ascertained, or not yet generally known;

(b) any other competition[5] in which success does not depend to a substantial degree on the exercise of skill[6].

(2) Nothing in subsection (1) above with respect to the conducting of competitions in connection with a trade or business shall apply in relation to sponsored pool betting or in relation to pool betting operations carried on by a person whose only trade or business is that of a bookmaker.

(3) Any person who contravenes this section shall, without prejudice to any liability to be proceeded against under section 2 above, be guilty of an offence[7].

(4) In this section "bookmaker", "pool betting" and "sponsored pool betting" have the meanings assigned to them by section 55 of the Betting, Gaming and Lotteries Act 1963.

[Lotteries and Amusements Act 1976, s 14.]

---

1. "Newspaper" includes any journal, magazine or other periodical publication, s 23(1), post.
2. There must be a nexus between the competition and the trade or business and not merely between the competition and the person carrying on the trade or business (*ITP (London) Ltd v Winstanley* [1947] KB 422, [1947] 1 All ER 177, 111 JP 68).
3. A scheme by which the total amounts invested in a football pool, less expenses, are distributed among those investors whose forecasts are correct, is a "competition in which prizes are offered", and constitutes an offence if advertised in a newspaper (*Bretherton v United Kingdom Totalisator Co Ltd* [1945] KB 555, [1945] 2 All ER 202, 110 JP 45; *Elderton v United Kingdom Totalisator Co Ltd* [1946] Ch 57, [1945] 2 All ER 624, 109 JP Jo 571).
4. A competition in which competitors were required to mark the most likely position of a football on a photograph and in which the winner was to be the person selecting the position closest to that selected at a later date by a panel of judges,

was held not to involve forecasts of the result of a future event (*News of the World Ltd v Friend* [1973] 1 All ER 422, 137 JP 249).

5. A competition requires participants in it actively to exercise some degree of effort or striving or dexterity (*Imperial Tobacco Ltd v A-G* [1981] AC 718, [1980] 1 All ER 866, 144 JP 163).

6. In *Witty v World Service Ltd* [1936] Ch 303, 100 JP 68, EVE, J, held that a prize picture puzzle competition did not infringe para (*b*). The words in para (*b*) cover the case where no skill is involved (*Whitbread & Co Ltd v Bell* [1970] 2 QB 547, [1970] 2 All ER 64, 134 JP 445).

7. For penalty, see s 20, post.

Amusements with prizes

8–13601N   15. Provision of amusements with prizes[1] at exempt entertainments. (1) This section applies to the provision at any exempt entertainment of any amusement with prizes which constitutes a lottery or gaming or both but does not constitute—

(*a*)   gaming to which Part II of the Gaming Act 1968[2] applies, or

(*b*)   gaming by means of a machine to which Part III of that Act[2] applies.

(2) Where any such amusement constitutes a lottery, nothing in section 1 or 2 above shall apply to it.

(3) In relation to any such amusement (whether it constitutes a lottery or not) the conditions set out in subsection (4) below shall be observed, and if either of those conditions is contravened every person concerned in the provision or conduct of that amusement shall be guilty of an offence[3] unless he proves[4] that the contravention occurred without his consent of connivance and that he exercised all due diligence to prevent it.

(4) The conditions referred to in subsection (3) above are—

(*a*)   that the whole proceeds of the entertainment, after deducting the expenses of the entertainment, shall be devoted to purposes other than private gain[5]; and

(*b*)   that the facilities for winning prizes at amusements to which this section applies, or those facilities together with any other facilities for participating in lotteries or gaming, shall not be the only, or the only substantial, inducement to persons to attend the entertainment.

(5) Where any payment falls to be made—

(*a*)   by way of a hiring, maintenance or other charge in respect of a machine to which Part III of the Gaming Act 1968 applies, or

(*b*)   in respect of any equipment for holding a lottery or gaming at any entertainment,

then if, but only if, the amount of that charge falls to be determined wholly or partly by reference to the extent to which that or some other such machine or equipment is used for the purposes of lotteries or gaming, that payment shall be held to be an application of the proceeds of the entertainment for the purposes of private gain[6].

(6) The reference to expenses in subsection (4) (*a*) above shall accordingly not include a reference to any charge mentioned in subsection (5) above and falling to be determined as there mentioned.

[Lotteries and Amusements Act 1976, s 15.]

1. "Amusements with Prizes" may well include activities which are described by the word "gaming" (*Fox v Adamson* [1968] 2 All ER 411, 132 JP 518).

2. Ante.

3. For penalty, see s 20, post.

4. See note 5 to s 4(5), ante.

5. See *Payne v Bradley* [1962] AC 343, [1961] 2 All ER 882, 125 JP 514, HL; affg [1961] 2 All ER 36, 125 JP 352; *Cookson v Bowles* [1962] 2 All ER 760, 126 JP 392; but for the limited application of these decisions in relation to societies, see s 22, post.

Note also the effect of sub-s (5).

6. There would not be "private gain" if an indirect benefit accrued to an individual so that he was able to avoid a loss dependent upon the extent to which a machine was used (*Avais v Hartford Shankhouse and District Working Men's Social Club and Institute Ltd* [1969] 2 AC 1, [1969] 1 All ER 130, 133 JP 133, HL).

8–13601O   16. Provision of amusements with prizes at certain commercial entertainments. (1) This section shall have effect for the purpose of permitting the provision of amusements with prizes where those amusements constitute a lottery or gaming or both but do not constitute gaming to which Part II of the Gaming Act 1968 applies or gaming by means of a machine to which Part III applies, and they are provided—

(*a*)   on any premises[1] in respect of which a permit under this section has been granted in accordance with Schedule 3[2] to this Act and is for the time being in force, or

(*b*)   on any premises used mainly for the purposes of amusements by means of machines to which Part III of the Gaming Act 1968 applies, being premises in respect of which a permit granted under section 34 of that Act is for the time being in force, or

(*c*)   at a pleasure fair consisting wholly or mainly of amusements provided by travelling showmen which is held on any day of the year on premises not previously used in that year on more than 27 days for the holding of such a pleasure fair.

(2) Nothing in section 1 or 2 above shall apply in relation to amusements falling within subsection

(1) above, but in relation to any such amusement the conditions set out in subsection (3) below shall be observed, and if any of those conditions is contravened every person concerned in the provision or conduct of that amusement shall be guilty of an offence[3] unless he proves[4] that the contravention occurred without his consent or connivance and that he exercised all due diligence[5] to prevent it.

(3) The conditions referred to in subsection (2) above are—

(a) that the amount paid by any person for any one chance to win a prize does not exceed 50p, and

(b) that the aggregate amount taken by way of the sale of chances in one determination of winners, if any, of prizes does not exceed £90, and that the sale of those chances and the declaration of the result take place on the same day and on the premises on which, and during the time when, the amusement is provided, and

(c) that no money prize is distributed or offered which exceeds £25, and

(d) that the winning of, or the purchase of a chance to win, a prize does not entitle any person, whether or not subject to a further payment by him, to any further opportunity[6] to win money[7] or money's worth by taking part in any amusement with prizes or in any gaming or lottery, and

(e) in the case of such a pleasure fair as is mentioned in subsection (1) (c) above, that the opportunity to win prizes at amusements to which this subsection applies is not the only, or the only substantial, inducement to persons to attend the fair.

(4) Schedule 3 to this Act shall have effect.

[Lotteries and Amusements Act 1976, s 16, as amended by the Amusements with Prizes (Variation of Monetary Limits) Orders, SI 1984/245 (as amended by SI 1988/1025), SI 1996/3208, SI 1997/2080, SI 1999/1259 and SI 2001/4034.]

---

1. "Premises" includes any place (s 23(1), post).

2. This Schedule, post, relates to the grant, etc, by the "appropriate authority" (which for certain purposes includes licensing justices) of permits under this section. Note the duty to keep a register of permits under the Betting and Gaming Duties Act 1981, Sch 4, para 15, in PART VIII: title CUSTOMS AND EXCISE, post.

3. For penalty, see s 20, post.

4. The onus of proof will be on the defendant; but see *R v Carr-Briant* [1943] KB 607, [1943] 2 All ER 156, 107 JP 167, in which it was held that a defendant who availed himself of a statutory defence was not required to establish that defence "beyond reasonable doubt", but according to probability.

5. This is a question of fact, not of law: there is no legal standards of diligence (*R C Hammett Ltd v Crabb, R C Hammett Ltd v Beldam* (1931) 95 JP 180).

6. The advantage of playing more games at rather better odds is not a "further opportunity" within the meaning of this paragraph (*Cronin v Grierson* [1968] AC 895, [1967] 3 All ER 153).

7. "Money" includes a cheque, banknote, postal order or money order (s 23(1), post).

8–13601P 17. Restriction on grant and provisions as to duration and forfeiture of permits.
(1) No permit under section 16 above shall be granted in respect of any premises where a licence under the Gaming Act 1968 is for the time being in force in respect of them or where a club or a miners' welfare institute is for the time being registered in respect of them under Part II of that Act; and, where such a licence is granted or a club or a miner's welfare institute is so registered in respect of any premises, and a permit under section 16 above is then in force in respect of those premises, the permit shall thereupon cease to have effect.

(2) The court by or before which the holder of a permit under section 16 above is convicted of an offence under that section in connection with the premises to which the permit relates may, if the court thinks fit, order that the permit shall be forfeited and cancelled.

(3) An order under subsection (2) above shall be deemed for the purposes of any appeal to be part of the sentence for the offence; and the permit shall not be forfeited or cancelled under that order—

(a) until the date of expiry of the period within which notice of appeal against the conviction or sentence may be given, nor

(b) if notice of appeal against the conviction or sentence is duly given within that period, until the date of the determination or abandonment of the appeal.

(4) *Scotland.*

[Lotteries and Amusements Act 1976, s 17.]

PART IV
SUPPLEMENTARY

8–13601Q 18. *Power to vary monetary limits, fees[1] etc.*

---

1. See the Lotteries (Gaming Board Fees) Order 2005, SI 2005/568.

8–13601R 19. Search warrants. If—

(a) in England or Wales, a justice of the peace, or

(b) Scotland,

is satisfied on information on oath that there is reasonable ground for suspecting that an offence under this Act is being, has been or is about to be committed on any premises[1], he may issue[2] a warrant[3] in writing authorising any constable to enter those premises, if necessary by force, and search them; and any constable who enters the premises under the authority of the warrant may—

    (*a*) seize and remove any document, money[4] or valuable thing, instrument or other thing whatsoever found on the premises which he has reasonable cause to believe may be required as evidence for the purposes of proceedings in respect of any such offence, and

    (*b*) search any person found on the premises whom he has reasonable cause to believe to be committing or to have committed any such offence.

[Lotteries and Amusements Act 1976, s 19, as amended by the Police and Criminal Evidence Act 1984, s 26 and Sch 7.]

---

  1. "Premises" includes any place (s 23(1), post).

  2. See PART IX: PRECEDENTS AND FORMS, BETTING AND GAMING, post.

  3. The issue and execution of this warrant must conform to the Police and Criminal Evidence Act 1984 ss 15 and 16 in PART I: MAGISTRATES' COURTS, PROCEDURE, ante. The Act removed a former express power of arrest under this section; see now s 25 of the 1984 Act.

  4. For meaning of "money" see s 23(1), post.

8–13601S **20. Penalties and forfeitures.** (1) A person guilty of an offence under this Act shall be liable[1]—

    (*a*) on summary conviction, to a fine not exceeding **the statutory maximum**; or

    (*b*) on conviction on indictment, to imprisonment for a term not exceeding **two years** or a **fine**, or **both**.

(2) The court by or before which a person is convicted of any offence under this Act may order anything produced[2] to the court and shown to the satisfaction of the court to relate to the offence to be forfeited[3] and either destroyed or dealt with in such other manner as the court may order.

[Lotteries and Amusements Act 1976, s 20, amended by the Criminal Law Act 1977, s 28.]

---

  1. For procedure in respect of this offence triable eithe r way, see Magistrates' Courts Act 1980, ss 18–21, in PART I, ante.

  2. "Produced" does not necessarily mean physically produced: enough if the machine or other thing is properly identified and is available for the court to look at, if the court so wishes (*R v Edmonton Justices, ex p Stannite Automatics Ltd* [1965] 2 All ER 750, 129 JP 411).

  3. Anything ordered to be forfeited will be dealt with as the court may order: if the court orders that a thing shall be dealt with as under the Magistrates' Courts Act 1980, pecuniary, forfeitures fall within the definition of "fine" (see Magistrates' Courts Act 1980, s 150, ante), non-pecuniary forfeitures may be sold and the proceeds applied as if they were a fine (Magistrates' Courts Act 1980, s 140, ante).

8–13601T **21. Offences by bodies corporate.** (1) Where an offence under this Act committed by a body corporate is proved to have been committed with the consent or connivance of, or to have been attributable to any neglect on the part of, any director, manager, secretary or other similar officer of the body corporate or any person who was purporting to act in any such capacity, he, as well as the body corporate, shall be guilty of that offence and be liable to be proceeded against and punished accordingly.

(2) In subsection (1) above, except as it applies for the purposes of section 13 above, "director", in relation to a body corporate established by or under any enactment for the purpose of carrying on under national ownership any industry or part of an industry or undertaking, being a body corporate whose affairs are managed by its members, means a member of that body corporate.

[Lotteries and Amusements Act 1976, s 21.]

8–13601U **22. Meaning of "private gain" in relation to proceeds of entertainments, lotteries and gaming promoted on behalf of certain societies[1].** (1) For the purposes of this Act proceeds of any entertainment, lottery or gaming promoted on behalf of a society to which this subsection extends which are applied for any purpose calculated to benefit the society as a whole shall not be held to be applied for purposes of private gain by reason only that their application for that purpose results in benefit to any person as an individual.

(2) Subsection (1) above extends to any society which is established and conducted either—

    (*a*) wholly for purposes other than purposes of any commercial undertaking; or

    (*b*) wholly or mainly for the purpose of participation in or support of athletic sports or athletic games.

[Lotteries and Amusements Act 1976, s 22.]

---

  1. This section re-enacts the (repealed) Lotteries and Gaming Act 1962, enacted to restrict the scope of the decision of the House of Lords in *Payne v Bradley* [1962] AC 343, [1961] 2 All ER 882, 125 JP 514.

8–13601V **23. Interpretation.** (1) In this Act, except where the context otherwise requires—

"the Board" means the Gaming Board for Great Britain;

"contravention", in relation to any requirement, includes a failure to comply with that requirement, and cognate expressions shall be construed accordingly;

"date", in relation to a lottery, means the date on which the winners in that lottery are ascertained;

"distribute", in relation to documents or other matters, includes distribution to persons or places within or outside Great Britain, and "distribution" shall be construed accordingly;

"employee" and "employment" have the same meanings as in the Employment Rights Act 1996;

"exempt entertainment" has the meaning assigned to it by section 3(1) above;

"gaming" has the same meaning as in the Gaming Act 1968;

"local authority" means—

    (a) in England, a county council, a district council, a London borough council, the Common Council of the City of London, the Council of the Isles of Scilly and a parish council;

    (b) in Wales, a county council, a county borough council and a community council; and

    (c) in Scotland, a regional council, an islands council and a district council;

"local lottery" has the meaning assigned to it by section 6(1) above;

"money" includes a cheque, banknote, postal order or money order;

"newspaper" includes any journal, magazine or other periodical publication;

"premises" includes any place;

"printing" includes writing and other modes of reproducing words in a visible form;

"private lottery" has the meaning assigned to it by section 4(1) above;

"registration authority" has the meaning given by paragraph 1 of Schedule 1 below.

"society" includes any club, institution, organisation or association of persons, by whatever name called, and any separate branch or section of such a club, institution, organisation or association;

"society's lottery" has the meaning assigned to it by section 5(1) above;

"ticket", in relation to any lottery, includes any document evidencing the claim of a person to participate in the chances of the lottery.

(2) In this Act, unless the context otherwise requires, a reference to the promotion of a society's lottery or a local lottery includes a reference to the conduct of that lottery, and "promote" shall be construed accordingly.

[Lotteries and Amusements Act 1976, s 23 as amended by the Local Government Act 1985, Sch 17, the National Lottery etc Act 1993, s 55, the Local Government (Wales) Act 1994, Sch 16 and the Employment Rights Act 1996, Sch 1.]

8–13601W **25.** (6) Nothing in this Act shall affect the operation of the Art Unions Act 1846[1], and a lottery promoted and conducted in accordance with that Act shall not be unlawful.

[Lotteries and Amusements Act 1976, s 25(6).]

---

1. 9 & 10 Vict c 48. Persons connected with art unions are protected from penalties.

Section 5   SCHEDULE 1

REGISTRATION OF SOCIETIES BY LOCAL AUTHORITIES

(*Amended by the Local Government (Wales) Act 1994, Sch 16.*)

PART I

Registration

PART II

RETURNS

8–13601X **11.** Subject to paragraph 12 below, the promoter of a society's lottery shall, not later than the end of the third month after the date of the lottery, send to the registration authority a return certified by two other members of the society being persons of full age appointed in writing by the governing body of the society, showing—

    (a) a copy of the scheme under which the lottery was promoted;

    (b) the whole proceeds of the lottery;

    (c) the sums appropriated out of those proceeds on account of expenses and on account of prizes respectively;

    (cc) whether any expenses were met otherwise than out of proceeds of the lottery and, if so, the amount and source of any sums used to meet them;

    (d) the particular purpose or purposes to which proceeds of the lottery were applied in pursuance of section 5(4) above, and the amount applied for that purpose, or for each of those purposes, as the case may be; and

    (e) the date of the lottery.

12. Paragraph 11 above shall not apply to a society's lottery if on the date of the lottery the society was registered with the Board under Schedule 1A below.

13. The registration authority shall preserve any return sent to them under paragraph 11 above for a period of at least 18 months, and during that period shall keep it deposited at their office and permit any member of the public to inspect it during office hours free of charge.

14. Any person who fails to send a return in accordance with the provisions of this Part of this Schedule, or who knowingly gives in any such return sent by him any information which is false in a material particular, or who certifies any such return knowing it to contain such information, shall be guilty of an offence[1].

15. (1) Where it appears to the registration authority that section 5(3c) above applies to a lottery in respect of which a return has been sent to them under paragraph 11 above, they shall notify the Board in writing of that fact.

(2) The notification shall have attached to it a copy of the return and of all other returns sent to the registration authority in respect of the earlier lotteries mentioned in section 5(3*c*)(*b*) above.

16. The registration authority may require a society that is registered under this Part of this Schedule—

(*a*) to allow the authority to inspect and take copies of any documents of the society, including any information kept by the society otherwise than in writing, relating to any lottery promoted on behalf of the society; and

(*b*) where such information is kept by means of a computer, to give the authority such assistance as they may require to enable them to inspect and take copies of the information in a visible and legible form and to inspect and check the operation of any computer, and any associated apparatus or material, that is or has been in use in connection with the keeping of the information.

---

1. For penalty, see s 20 ante.

SCHEDULE 1A

REGISTRATION OF SOCIETIES BY THE GAMING BOARD

PART I

Registration

PART II

INFORMATION

8–13601Y **7.** A society registered under this Schedule shall notify the Board in writing of any change in the address of the society's office or head office within the period of twenty-one days beginning with the day on which the change takes effect.

8. (1) A society registered under this Schedule shall notify the Board in writing of any modification of a scheme approved by the society under section 5(3)(*c*) above.

(2) A copy of the scheme as modified shall be attached to the notification.

(3) The notification shall be given to the Board at least four weeks before any tickets or chances in a lottery promoted in accordance with the scheme as modified are sold, distributed or offered for sale.

(4) In this paragraph references to the modification of a scheme include the substitution for that scheme of another scheme (and references to the scheme as modified are to be read accordingly).

9. (1) Where a society is registered under this Schedule on the date of a society's lottery promoted on its behalf, it shall, before the end of the period of three months beginning with that date, send a return in respect of the lottery to the Board.

(2) The return shall be in such form and contain such information as the Board may direct.

(3) A direction under sub-paragraph (2) above shall be given in writing and may be varied or revoked by a subsequent direction.

10. (1) The Board shall preserve any return sent to them under paragraph 9 above for a period of at least eighteen months, and during that period shall keep it deposited at their office and permit any member of the public to inspect it during office hours on payment of a prescribed fee.[1]

(2) Any fees received by the Board by virtue of this paragraph shall be paid into the Consolidated Fund.

11. (1) A society registered under this Schedule shall preserve all documents of the society, including all information kept by the society otherwise than in writing, relating to a lottery promoted on the society's behalf until the end of the period of two years beginning with the date of the lottery.

(2) The Board may direct that, subject to such conditions as may be specified in the direction, sub-paragraph (1) above shall not apply to documents or information specified, or of a description specified, in the direction.

(3) A direction under sub-paragraph (2) above shall be given in writing and may be varied or revoked by a subsequent direction.

12. The Board may require a society that is registered or has applied to be registered under this Schedule—

(*a*) to provide the Board with such information relating to any lottery promoted or to be promoted on behalf of the society as they may require;

(*b*) to allow the Board to inspect and take copies of any documents of the society, including any information kept by the society, including any information kept by the society otherwise than in writing, relating to such a lottery;

(*c*) where such information is kept by means of a computer, to give the Board such assistance as they may require to enable them to inspect and take copies of the information in a visible and legible form and to inspect and check the operation of any computer, and any associated apparatus or material, that is or has been in use in connection with the keeping of the information;

(*d*) to allow the Board to inspect any aspect of the management of such a lottery.

13. (1) Subject to sub-paragraph (10) below, where the total value of the tickets or chances sold in all lotteries held in any one year and promoted on behalf of the same society is more than £100,000 and any of those lotteries is a lottery to which section 5(3*b*), (3*c*) or (3*d*) above applies, the society shall send to the Board accounts in respect of those lotteries together with a report on the accounts prepared by a qualifying auditor.

(2) The accounts shall be sent to the Board within ten months of the end of the year in which the lotteries to which they relate were held.

(3) Accounts under this paragraph shall comply with any directions given by the Board as to the information to be contained in such accounts, the manner in which such information is to be presented or the methods or principles according to which such accounts are to be prepared.

(4) Any directions under sub-paragraph (3) above shall be given in writing and may be varied or revoked by subsequent directions.

(5) In sub-paragraph (1) above "qualifying auditor" means a person who—

(*a*) is eligible for appointment as a company auditor under section 25 of the Companies Act 1989; and

(*b*) is not disqualified by sub-paragraph (6) below.

(6) The following persons are disqualified—

(a) a member of the society;

(b) a partner, officer or employee of such a member;

(c) a partnership of which a person disqualified by paragraph (a) or (b) above is a member.

(7) The auditor's report on any accounts under this paragraph shall state whether in the auditor's opinion the accounts have been properly prepared in accordance with any directions given under sub-paragraph (3) above.

(8) The auditor shall, in preparing his report, carry out such investigations as will enable him to form an opinion as to—

(a) whether proper accounting records have been kept by the society; and

(b) whether the society's accounts are in agreement with the accounting records.

(9) If the auditor fails to obtain all the information and explanations that, to the best of his knowledge and belief, are necessary for the purposes of his audit, his report shall state that fact.

(10) Sub-paragraph (1) above does not apply to a society in relation to any year if the promotion of every lottery promoted on behalf of the society held in that year is managed by a person certified under Schedule 2A below as a lottery manager.

(11) For the purposes of this paragraph a lottery is held in the year in which the date of the lottery falls.

(12) In this paragraph "year" means a period of twelve months beginning with 1 January.

14. (1) Any person who, in pursuance of a requirement imposed by or under paragraph 7, 9, 12 or 13 above, knowingly or recklessly gives to the Board any information which is false in a material particular shall be guilty of an offence.

(2) Any person who knowingly or recklessly includes in a report under paragraph 13 above any information which is false in a material particular shall be guilty of an offence.

---

1. See the Lotteries (Gaming Board Fees) Order 2004, SI 2004/532.

Section 9   SCHEDULE 2
                        REGISTRATION OF SCHEMES

8–13601Z **6.** A local authority shall, before the end of the period of three months beginning with the date of any local lottery promoted by them, send a return in respect of the lottery to the Board.

(2) The return shall be in such form and contain such information as the Board may direct.

(3) A direction under sub-paragraph (2) above shall be given in writing and may be varied or revoked by a subsequent direction.

6A. (1) The Board shall preserve any return sent to them under paragraph 6 above for a period of at least eighteen months, and during that period shall keep it deposited at their office and permit any member of the public to inspect it during office hours on payment of a prescribed fee.[1]

(2) Any fees received by the Board by virtue of this paragraph shall be paid into the Consolidated Fund.

6B. (1) A local authority shall preserve all documents of theirs, including all information kept by them otherwise than in writing, relating to a local lottery promoted by them until the end of the period of two years beginning with the date of the lottery.

(2) The Board may direct that, subject to such conditions as may be specified in the direction, sub-paragraph (1) above shall not apply to documents or information specified, or of a description specified, in the direction.

(3) A direction under sub-paragraph (2) above shall be given in writing and may be varied or revoked by a subsequent direction.

6C. The Board may require a local authority—

(a) to provide the Board with such information as they may require relating to a local lottery promoted or to be promoted by the authority;

(b) to allow the Board to inspect and take copies of any documents of the authority, including any information kept by the authority otherwise than in writing, relating to such a lottery;

(c) where such information is kept by means of a computer, to give the Board such assistance as they may require to enable them to inspect and take copies of the information in a visible and legible form and to inspect and check the operation of any computer, and any associated apparatus or material, that is or has been in use in connection with the keeping of the information;

(d) to allow the Board to inspect any aspect of the management of such a lottery.

6D. (1) Subject to sub-paragraph (10) below, where the total value of the tickets or chances sold in all local lotteries held in any one financial year and promoted by the same local authority is more than £100,000, the authority shall send to the Board accounts for those lotteries together with a report on the accounts prepared by a qualifying auditor.

(2) The accounts shall be sent to the Board within ten months of the end of the financial year in which the lotteries to which they relate were held.

(3) Accounts under this paragraph shall comply with any directions given by the Board as to the information to be contained in such accounts, the manner in which such information is to be presented or the methods and principles according to which such accounts are to be prepared.

(4) Any directions under sub-paragraph (3) above shall be given in writing and may be varied or revoked by subsequent directions.

(5) In sub-paragraph (1) above "qualifying auditor" means a person who is—

(a) eligible for appointment as a company auditor under section 25 of the Companies Act 1989;

(b) a member of the Chartered Institute of Public Finance and Accountancy; or

(c) a firm each of the members of which is a member of that institute;

and who is not disqualified by sub-paragraph (6) below.

(6) The following persons are disqualified—

(a) a member, officer or employee of the local authority;

(b) a partner or employee of such a person;

(c) a partnership of which a person disqualified by paragraph (a) or (b) above is a member.

(7) The auditor's report on any accounts under this paragraph shall state whether in the auditor's opinion the accounts have been properly prepared in accordance with any directions given under sub-paragraph (3) above.

(8) The auditor shall, in preparing his report, carry out such investigations as will enable him to form an opinion as to—

(a) whether proper accounting records have been kept by the local authority; and
(b) whether the authority's accounts are in agreement with the accounting records.

(9) If the auditor fails to obtain all the information and explanations that, to the best of his knowledge and belief, are necessary for the purposes of his audit, his report shall state that fact.

(10) Sub-paragraph (1) above does not apply to a local authority in relation to any financial year if the promotion of every local lottery promoted by them held in that year is managed by a person certified under Schedule 2A below as a lottery manager.

(11) For the purposes of this paragraph a lottery is held in the financial year in which the date of the lottery falls.

(12) In this paragraph "financial year" means a period of twelve months beginning with 1 April.

7. (1) The following fees shall be payable by a local authority to the Board—

(a) a prescribed fee on an application for a scheme approved by the authority to be registered under this Schedule;
(b) a prescribed fee at such intervals whilst such a scheme is so registered as the Secretary of State may by order direct; and
(c) a prescribed fee for each lottery promoted under such a scheme.

(2) Any such fees received by the Board shall be paid into the Consolidated Fund.

8. Any person who, in pursuance of a requirement under paragraph 6, 6C or 6D above, knowingly or recklessly gives to the Board any information which is false in a material particular shall be guilty of an offence[1].

9. A person who knowingly or recklessly includes in a report under paragraph 6D any information which is false in a material particular shall be guilty of an offence[2].

---

1. See the Lotteries (Gaming Board Fees) Order 2002, SI 2002, SI 2002/638.
2. For penalty, see s 20, ante.

SCHEDULE 2A
LOTTERY MANAGERS

PART I

Certification

PART II
INFORMATION

8–13602 8. (1) A certificate holder shall preserve all documents of his, including all information kept by him otherwise than in writing, relating to the management of a society's lottery or a local lottery until the end of the period of two years beginning with the date of the lottery.

(2) The Board may direct that, subject to such conditions as may be specified in the direction, sub-paragraph (1) above shall not apply to documents or information specified, or of a description specified, in the direction.

(3) A direction under sub-paragraph (2) above shall be given in writing and may be varied or revoked by a subsequent direction.

9. The Board may require a certificate holder—

(a) to provide the Board with such information relating to the management of a society's lottery or a local lottery as they may require;
(b) to allow the Board to inspect and take copies of any documents of the certificate holder, including any information kept by him otherwise than in writing, relating to the management of such a lottery;
(c) where such information is kept by means of a computer, to give the Board such assistance as they may require to enable them to inspect and take copies of the information in a visible and legible form and to inspect and check the operation of any computer, and any associated apparatus or material, that is or has been in use in connection with the keeping of the information;
(d) to allow the Board to inspect any aspect of the management of such a lottery.

10. Where a certificate holder is a company to which section 241 of the Companies Act 1985 (directors' duty to lay and deliver accounts) applies, the company shall, immediately after copies of its accounts for a financial year have been laid before it under that section, send a copy of its profit and loss account for that year and the related auditors' report to the Board.

11. (1) A certificate holder to whom paragraph 10 above does not apply shall, in respect of each year in which he holds a certificate, send to the Board a profit and loss account of his business of managing lotteries under the certificate together with a report on the account prepared by a qualifying auditor.

(2) The account shall be sent to the Board within ten months of the end of the year to which it relates.

(3) An account under this paragraph shall comply with any directions given by the Board as to the information to be contained in such an account, the manner in which such information is to be presented or the methods and principles according to which such an account is to be prepared.

(4) Any directions under sub-paragraph (3) above shall be given in writing and may be varied or revoked by subsequent directions.

(5) In sub-paragraph (1) above "qualifying auditor" means a person who—

(a) is eligible for appointment as a company auditor under section 25 of the Companies Act 1989, and
(b) is not disqualified by sub-paragraph (6) below.

(6) The following persons are disqualified—

(a) the certificate holder;
(b) where the certificate holder is an unincorporated body of persons, any of those persons;
(c) a partner, officer or employee of the certificate holder or a person disqualified by paragraph (b) above;
(d) a partner or employee of a person disqualified by paragraph (c) above;
(e) a partnership of which any person disqualified by paragraph (a), (b) or (c) above is a member.

(7) The auditor's report on an account under this paragraph shall state whether in the auditor's opinion the account has been properly prepared in accordance with any directions given under sub-paragraph (3) above.

(8) The auditor shall, in preparing his report, carry out such investigations as will enable him to form an opinion as to—

(a) whether proper accounting records have been kept by the certificate holder, and
(b) whether the certificate holder's account is in agreement with the accounting records.

(9) If the auditor fails to obtain all the information and explanations that, to the best of his knowledge and belief, are necessary for the purposes of his audit, his report shall state that fact.

(10) In this paragraph "year" means a period of twelve months beginning with 1 January.

12. (1) A person who, in pursuance of a requirement imposed on him by or under paragraph 9, 10 or 11 above, knowingly or recklessly gives to the Board any information which is false in a material particular shall be guilty of an offence.

(2) A person who knowingly or recklessly includes in a report under paragraph 11 above any information which is false in a material particular shall be guilty of an offence.

Section 16

SCHEDULE 3
PERMITS FOR COMMERCIAL PROVISION OF AMUSEMENTS WITH PRIZES*

(Amended by SI 1991/2174 and the Access to Justice Act 1999, Sch 13, SI 2005/3028 and the Licensing Act 2003, Sch 6.)

Interpretation

---

*Repealed by the Gambling Act 2005, Sch 17 from a date to be appointed.

8–13602A   **1.** (1) In this Schedule "the appropriate authority" means—

(a) in relation to any premises in England and Wales in respect of which there is in force a premises licence authorising the supply of alcohol for consumption on the premises, the relevant licensing authority in relation to those premises;
(b) in relation to any other premises in England or Wales, the local authority within whose area the premises are situated;
(c), (d) *Scotland*.

(2) In this Schedule—

"alcohol", "licensing authority" and "premises licence" have the same meaning as in the Licensing Act 2003,
"hotel licence", "licensing area", "licensing board" and "public house licence" have the same meanings as in the Licensing (Scotland) Act 1976;
"local authority" means—

(a) in England, a district council, a London borough council and the Common Council of the City of London;
(b) in Wales, a district council; and
(c) *Scotland*; and

"permit" means a permit under section 16 above; and
"relevant licensing authority", in relation to premises in respect of which a premises licence is in force, means the licensing authority in relation to those premises determined in accordance with section 12 of the Licensing Act 2003;
"supply of alcohol" has the same meaning as in section 14 of the Licensing Act 2003.

(3) A function conferred by this Schedule on a licensing authority is, for the purposes of section 7 of the Licensing Act 2003 (exercise and delegation by licensing authority of licensing functions), to be treated as a licensing function within the meaning of that Act.

Resolution by local authority as to grant or renewal of permits

8–13602B   **2.** Any local authority may pass either of the following resolutions, that is to say—

(a) that (subject to paragraph 3 below) the authority will not grant any permits in respect of premises of a class specified in the resolution; or
(b) that (subject to paragraph 3 below) the authority will neither grant nor renew any permit in respect of premises of a class specified in the resolution.

3. (1) No resolution under paragraph 2 above shall have effect in relation to the grant or renewal of permits in respect of premises to which this paragraph applies.

(2) This paragraph applies to any premises used or to be used wholly or mainly for the purposes of a pleasure fair consisting wholly or mainly of amusements.

8–13602C   **4.** (1) An application to the appropriate authority for the grant of a permit in respect of any premises may be made—

(a) by the holder of the licence or certificate, in the case of premises such as are mentioned in paragraph 1(1)(a) or (c) above, and

(b) in any other case, by the person who is, or by any person who proposes if the permit is granted to become, the occupier of the premises.

(2) The holder of a permit may apply from time to time for the renewal of the permit.

5. The appropriate authority shall not refuse to grant or renew a permit without affording to the applicant or a person acting for him an opportunity of appearing before, and being heard by, the appropriate authority or (where that authority is a local authority) a committee of the local authority.

Grounds for refusal to grant or renew permit

8–13602D   **6.** (1) Where an application for the grant or renewal of a permit is made to a local authority, then if—

(a) there is for the time being in force a resolution passed by that authority in accordance with paragraph 2 above which is applicable to the premises to which the application relates, and

(b) the permit could not be granted or renewed without contravening that resolution.

it shall be the duty of the authority to refuse to grant or renew the permit.

(2) The grant or renewal of a permit shall not be invalidated by any failure to comply with this paragraph, and no duty of a local authority to comply with this paragraph shall be enforceable by legal proceedings.

7. (1) In the case of premises to which paragraph 3 above applies—

(a) the grant of a permit shall be at the discretion of the appropriate authority; but

(b) the appropriate authority shall not refuse to renew a permit except either on the grounds that they or their authorised representatives have been refused reasonable facilities to inspect the premises or by reason of the conditions in which amusements with prizes have been provided on the premises, or the manner in which any such amusements have been conducted, while the permit has been in force.

(2) In the case of premises other than premises to which paragraph 3 above applies, the grant or renewal of a permit shall (subject to paragraph 6 above) be at the discretion of the appropriate authority; and in particular, and without prejudice to the generality of that discretion, the appropriate authority may refuse to grant or renew any such permit on the grounds that, by reason of the purposes for which, or the persons by whom, or any circumstances in which, the premises are or are to be used, it is undesirable that amusements with prizes should be provided on those premises.

(3) The preceding provisions of this paragraph shall have effect subject to section 17(1) above.

(4) In this paragraph any reference to amusements with prizes includes any amusements provided by means of a machine to which Part III of the Gaming Act 1968 applies.

Appeal in England or Wales against decision of appropriate authority

8–13602E   **8.** (1) Where on an application under this Schedule in England or Wales the appropriate authority refuse to grant or renew a permit, or grant or renew it subject to a condition, the authority shall forthwith give to the applicant notice of their decision and of the grounds on which it is made.

(2) Where such a notice has been given, the applicant may, by notice to the clerk to the appropriate authority, appeal against the decision to the Crown Court.

(3) As soon as practicable after receiving notice of appeal against a decision of the appropriate authority, the clerk to the authority shall send the notice to the appropriate officer of the Crown Court together with a statement of the decision against which the appeal is brought and of the name and last-known residence or place of business of the appellant, and on receipt of the notice, that officer shall enter the appeal and give to the appellant and to the appropriate authority not less than seven days' notice in writing of the date, time and place appointed for the hearing of the appeal.

(4) *Repealed.*

9. The Court shall not allow an appeal under this Schedule if satisfied that, by virtue of paragraph 6 above, it was the duty of the appropriate authority to refuse to grant or renew the permit.

10. Subject to paragraph 9 above, on any such appeal the Court may by its order allow or dismiss the appeal, or reverse or vary any part of the decision of the appropriate authority, and may deal with the application as if it had been made to the Court in the first instance; and the judgment of the Court on the appeal shall be final.

11 *Repealed.*

12–14. *Appeal in Scotland.*

Duration of permit

8–13602F   **15.** Subject to the following provisions of this Schedule, and without prejudice to the cancellation of any permit under section 17(2) above, a permit—

(a) if not renewed, shall cease to have effect on such date, not being less than three years beginning with the date on which it was granted, as may be specified in the permit, or

(b) if renewed, shall, unless further renewed, cease to have effect on such date, not being less than three years beginning with the date on which it was renewed or last renewed, as the case may be, as may be specified in the decision to renew it.

16. (1) Where an application for the renewal of a permit is made not less than one month before the date on which it is due to expire, the permit shall not cease to have effect by virtue of paragraph 15 above before the appropriate authority have determined the application or the application has been withdrawn.

(2) Where, on such an application, the appropriate authority refuse to renew the permit, it shall not cease to have effect by virtue of paragraph 15 above before the time within which the applicant can appeal against the refusal has expired, and, if he so appeals, shall not cease to have effect by virtue of that paragraph until the appeal has been determined or abandoned.

17. (1) Subject to paragraph 17A, permit shall not be transferable, and, subject to the following provisions of this paragraph, shall cease to have effect if—

(a) in the case of premises falling within paragraph 1(1)(a) or (c) above, the holder of the permit ceases to be the holder of the licence or certificate in respect of the premises, or

(b) in the case of any other premises, the holder of the permit ceases to be the occupier of the premises.

(2) If the holder of a permit dies while the permit is in force—

(a) the permit shall not cease to have effect by virtue of paragraph 15 above or by virtue of the preceding sub-paragraph before the end of the period of six months beginning with the date of his death, and

(b) except for the purposes of a renewal of the permit, his personal representatives shall be deemed to be the holder of the permit;

and the appropriate authority may from time to time on the application of those personal representatives, extend or further extend the period for which the permit continues to have effect by virtue of this sub-paragraph if satisfied that the extension is necessary for the purpose of winding up the estate of the deceased and that no other circumstances make it undesirable.

17A. (1) This paragraph applies where—

(a) a premises licence authorising the supply of alcohol for consumption on particular premises has been granted under paragraph 4 of Schedule 8 to the Licensing Act 2003 (conversion of existing justices' licences to premises licences),

(b) the application for the licence was made by virtue of paragraph 2(3)(b) of that Schedule (application made by a person with the consent of the existing licence holder), and

(c) a permit granted by the licensing justices has effect in respect of the premises immediately before the premises licence takes effect.

(2) This paragraph also applies where—

(a) a premises licence authorising the supply of alcohol for consumption on particular premises has been granted under section 18 of the Licensing Act 2003 (determination of application for premises licence) before 24th November 2005,

(b) a justices' licence granted under the Licensing Act 1964 has effect in respect of the premises immediately before that day ("the existing licence"),

(c) the application for the premises licence was made by a person other than the holder of the existing licence, and

(d) a permit granted by the licensing justices has effect in respect of the premises immediately before the premises licence takes effect.

(3) The permit is transferred, at the time the premises licence takes effect, to the holder of that licence (and, accordingly, does not cease to have effect at that time under paragraph 17(1)(a)).

(4) Subject to that, the permit continues to have effect in accordance with this Schedule.

Payment of fees

8–13602G **18.** Notwithstanding anything in the preceding provisions of this Schedule, no permit shall be granted or renewed except on payment by the applicant to the appropriate authority or their clerk of a fee of £32[1].

---

1. As amended by SI 1991/2174.

Horserace Betting Levy Act 1981[1]

(1981 c 30)

8–13603 This Act makes provision with respect to the payment on account of the levy payable under s 27 of the Betting, Gaming and Lotteries Act 1963 by bookmakers to the Horserace Betting Levy Board.

8–13603A **4. Supplementary provisions.** (3) If, otherwise than with the consent in writing of the bookmaker concerned or—(a) for the purposes of this Act or a report of any proceedings before an appeal tribunal under s 2; or (b) for the purposes of, or a report of (i) proceedings for the recovery of any payment on account; (ii) proceedings relating to that bookmaker before a betting licensing committee or before any court on appeal from such a committee; or (iii) any criminal proceedings, any person discloses to any other person in such a manner as to identify the bookmaker concerned information concerning that bookmaker obtained through the exercise of any function under this Act, he shall be liable on summary conviction to a fine not exceeding level 4 on the standard scale.

(4) Subsection (3) above applies to any person who is a member, officer or servant of the Levy Board, Bookmakers' Committee or an appeal tribunal, or who is consulted by the members of the Levy Board in pursuance of this Act.

[Horserace Betting Levy Act 1981, s 4(3)–(4) as amended by the Criminal Justice Act 1982, s 46—summarised.]

Gaming (Bingo) Act 1985
(1985 c 35)

8–13604   1. "Multiple bingo".   (1) In this Act "a game of multiple bingo" means a game of bingo played jointly on different bingo club premises in circumstances where—

(*a*)   the draw is determined before the beginning of the game by the organiser of the game and announced on each of those premises while the game is being played there;

(*b*)   the game is played on each of those premises within a specified period which begins and ends at the same time for all of them; and

(*c*)   each player competes for a prize or prizes calculated by reference to the stakes hazarded at all those premises and also for either or both of the following—

(i)   a prize or prizes calculated by reference to the stakes hazarded at a group of those premises which includes the premises on which he is taking part in the game; and

(ii)   a prize or prizes calculated by reference to the stakes hazarded at the last-mentioned premises.

(2) In this Act "the organiser", in relation to a game of multiple bingo, means the person having the central management of the game on behalf of the persons holding licences under the principal Act in respect of the premises on which the game is played.

(3) In this Act "the principal Act" means the Gaming Act 1968, "bingo club premises" has the meaning given in section 20 of that Act, "the Board" means the Gaming Board for Great Britain and "premises" includes any place.

[Gaming (Bingo) Act 1985, s 1, as amended by SI 2002/460.]

8–13604A   2. Modifications of principal Act for multiple bingo.   (1) If the conditions specified in subsection (2) below are fulfilled in the case of a game of multiple bingo section 12 of the principal Act (restriction on persons who may participate in gaming under Part II of that Act) shall have effect in relation to the game with the following modifications—

(*a*)   for the purposes of subsection (1) a person shall be regarded as present on the premises where the game is being played and at the time when it is being played there if he is present on any of the premises where it is being played and at the time when it is being played on those premises; and

(*b*)   for the purposes of the application of subsections (2) and (3) in relation to each of those premises, regard shall be had only to such of the players as are present on those particular premises.

(2) The conditions referred to in subsection (1) above are that—

(*a*)   the aggregate amount paid to players as prizes in respect of the game does not exceed the aggregate amount of the stakes hazarded by the players in playing that game;

(*b*)   the amount of any such prize does not exceed £2,000,000 or such other sum as may be specified in an order made by the Secretary of State; and

(*c*)   the organiser of the game is a person holding a certificate of approval issued by the Board under the Schedule to this Act.

(3) Section 20(8) of the principal Act (maximum amount of winnings) shall not apply to games of multiple bingo.

(4) *Repealed.*

(5) The power to make an order under subsection (2)(*b*) above shall be exercisable by statutory instrument subject to annulment in pursuance of a resolution of either House of Parliament.

[Gaming (Bingo) Act 1985, s 2 as amended by the Bingo Act 1992, s 1 and SI 2002/1919.]

---

1. As substituted by the Gaming (Bingo) Act (Variation of Monetary Limit) Order 2002, SI 2002/1909.

8–13604B   3. Multiple bingo regulations.   (1) The Secretary of State may make regulations[1] with respect to the management and conduct of games of multiple bingo and in particular with respect to the following matters—

(a) the number of games that may be played on any bingo club premises in any period of twenty-four hours;

(b) the period for the playing of a game;

(c) the functions of the organiser of the game and of the persons conducting the game at any bingo club premises; and

(d) the maximum amount of the stakes and the method of calculating the amount of the prizes.

(2) The Secretary of State shall not make any regulations under this section except after consultation with the Board.

(3) The power to make regulations under this section shall be exercisable by statutory instrument subject to annulment in pursuance of a resolution of either House of Parliament.

[Gaming (Bingo) Act 1985, s 3.]

---

1. The Gaming Clubs (Multiple Bingo) Regulations 1986 have been made; see this PART, post.

8–13604C   4. Offences and enforcement.   (1) A person shall not act as the organiser of a game of multiple bingo unless he holds such a certificate as is mentioned in section 2(2)(c) above.

(2) The provisions of subsection (1) above and of any regulations made under section 3 above shall be included among the provisions a contravention of which is an offence under section 23 of the principal Act; and in subsection (6) of that section the reference to a certificate of approval under section 19 of that Act shall include a reference to any such certificate as is mentioned in section 2(2)(c) above.

(3) In section 43 of the principal Act (powers of entry)—

(a) references to premises in respect of which a licence under that Act is in force and to the holder of a licence in respect of any such premises shall include references to any premises used by the organiser of a game of multiple bingo for the management of such games and to the organiser using those premises for that purpose;

(b) the reference in subsection (2) to a contravention of that Act or of regulations made under it shall include a reference to a contravention of subsection (1) above or of regulations made under section 3 above; and

(c) the references in subsection (3) and (6) to books, documents or information relating to premises in respect of which a licence under that Act is in force shall, in relation to an organiser of games of multiple bingo, be construed as references to books, documents or information relating to his management of such games.

[Gaming (Bingo) Act 1985, s 4.]

8–13604D   5. *Short title, commencement and extent.*

Section 2(2)(c)

SCHEDULE
CERTIFICATES OF APPROVAL

Issue of certificate

8–13604E   1. (1) Any person may apply to the Board for the issue of a certificate of approval as an organiser of games of multiple bingo (in this Schedule referred to as "a certificate").

(2) Any application for a certificate shall specify the arrangements to be made by the applicant for the management of such games.

(3) If the applicant is a company the application shall specify the names and addresses of the directors of the company.

2. In determining whether to issue a certificate the Board shall have regard only to the question whether, in their opinion, the applicant is likely to be capable of, and diligent in, securing that the provisions of the principal Act and any regulations made under that Act or this Act will be complied with and that the games managed by him will be conducted fairly and properly.

3. A certificate shall continue in force unless and until it is revoked by the Board under paragraph 4 or terminated by virtue of an order under paragraph 5 below.

Revocation of certificate

4. (1) The Board may revoke a certificate—

(a) if they are no longer of the opinion that the holder of the certificate is likely to be capable of, or diligent in, securing the matters mentioned in paragraph 2 above; or

(b) if it appears to them that any information given to them by or on behalf of the applicant in or in connection with the application for the certificate was false in a material particular.

(2) Where the Board determine to revoke a certificate they shall serve a notice on the person to whom it relates stating that the certificate is revoked as from the end of the period of twenty-one days from the date of service of the notice; and the revocation shall take effect at the end of that period.

(3) Section 47 of the principal Act (service of documents) shall apply to any notice under this paragraph.

5. *Fees*[1].

---

1. See the Gaming (Bingo) Act (Fees) Order 1986, SI 1986/333, amended by SI 2005/570, which specifies the fees payable and provides that a certificate of approval issued under para 1 of the Schedule shall terminate if the fee for the continuing in force of the certificate is not paid.

National Lottery etc Act 1993[1]

(1993 c 39)

PART I[2]

AUTHORISATION AND REGULATION OF THE NATIONAL LOTTERY

8–13605   12.   Regulations as to the promotion of lotteries.   (1) The Secretary of State may by regulations[3] make such provision in relation to the promotion of lotteries that form part of the National Lottery as he considers necessary or expedient.

(2) Such regulations may in particular impose requirements or restrictions as to—

   (*a*)   the minimum age of persons to whom or by whom tickets or chances may be sold;
   (*b*)   the places, circumstances or manner in which tickets or chances may be sold or persons may be invited to buy them;
   (*c*)   the information that must appear in an advertisement for a lottery;
   (*d*)   the places, circumstances or manner in which signs relating to a lottery may be displayed.

(3) In subsection (2) "tickets" includes any document providing evidence of a person's claim to participate in the chances of a lottery.

(4) Regulations under this section may make different provision for different areas.
[National Lottery etc Act 1993, s 12.]

---

1. At the time of going to press the National Lottery etc Act 1993 (Commencement No 1 and Transitional Provisions) Orders 1993 and SI 1994/1055 have been made under s 65, and SI 1999/650 has been made under s 27: the following sections were in force: ss 1–55, ss 60–66, Schs 1–9, Sch 10 (partially).

2. Part I contains ss 1–20.

3. See the National Lottery Regulations 1994, SI 1994/189, in this PART, post. For the circumstances in which duty is payable, see the provisions of Pt I, Ch II of the Finance Act 1993 in PART VIII: CUSTOMS AND EXCISE, post.

8–13605A   13.   Contravention of regulations an offence.   (1) If any requirement or restriction imposed by regulations made under section 12 is contravened in relation to the promotion of a lottery that forms part of the National Lottery—

   (*a*)   the promoter of the lottery shall be guilty of an offence, except if the contravention occurred without the consent or connivance of the promoter and the promoter exercised all due diligence to prevent such a contravention,
   (*b*)   any director, manager, secretary or other similar officer of the promoter, or any person purporting to act in such a capacity, shall be guilty of an offence if he consented to or connived at the contravention or if the contravention was attributable to any neglect on his part, and
   (*c*)   any other person who was party to the contravention shall be guilty of an offence[1].

(2) A person guilty of an offence under this section shall be liable[2]—

   (*a*)   on summary conviction, to a fine not exceeding **the statutory maximum**;
   (*b*)   on conviction on indictment, to imprisonment for a term not exceeding **two years**, to a **fine** or to **both**.

(3), (4) (*Scotland*).
[National Lottery etc Act 1993, s 13.]

---

1. An offence of selling a National Lottery ticket to a person who has not attained the age of 16, contrary to reg 3 of the National Lottery Regulations 1994, is an offence of strict liability, *Harrow London Borough Council v Shah* [1999] 3 All ER 302, [2000] 1 WLR 83, [2000] Crim LR 692, 163 JP 525, DC.

2. For procedure in respect of offences triable either way, see Magistrates' Courts Act 1980, ss 17A–21, in PART I: MAGISTRATES' COURTS, PROCEDURE, ante.

8–13605B   16.   False representations as to the National Lottery.   (1) If a person advertising, or offering the opportunity to participate in, a lottery, competition or game of another description gives, by whatever means, a false indication that it is a lottery forming part of, or is otherwise connected with, the National Lottery, he shall be guilty of an offence.

(2) A person guilty of an offence under this section shall be liable[1]—

   (*a*)   on summary conviction, to a fine not exceeding **the statutory maximum**;
   (*b*)   on conviction on indictment, to imprisonment for a term not exceeding **two years**, to a **fine** or to **both**.

[National Lottery etc Act 1993, s 16.]

---

1. For procedure in respect of offences triable either way, see Magistrates' Courts Act 1980, ss 17A–21, in PART I: MAGISTRATES' COURTS, PROCEDURE, ante.

Horserace Betting and Olympic Lottery Act 2004[1]
(2004 c 25)

PART 1[2]
Sale of the Tote

Dissolution, and transfer of assets

8–13606   1. Dissolution of the Tote

2. Successor company: transfer

3. Sections 1 and 2: supplemental

4. Tax

1. This Act is concerned principally with: the dissolution of the Tote and the establishment of a successor company; the abolition of the horserace betting levy system; and the licensing of Olympic lotteries.

The Act is in 4 Parts and has 5 Schedules. It will be brought into force in accordance with commencement orders made under s 40. At the time of going to press the Horserace Betting and Olympic Lottery Act 2004 (Commencement No 1) Order 2004, SI 2004/3283 had been made: Horserace Betting and Olympic Lottery Act 2004 (Commencement No 1) Order 2004, SI 2004/3283; Horserace Betting and Olympic Lottery Act 2004 (Commencement No 2) Order 2005, SI 2005/1134; and Horserace Betting and Olympic Lottery Act 2004 (Commencement No 3) Order 2005, SI 2005/1831. Only those provisions of relevance to magistrates' courts are reproduced in this work.

2. Part 1 contains ss 1–14.

Operation of successor company

5. Pre-sale issue of shares, &c to government

6. Accounts

7. Shadow directors

Post-transfer control of horserace pool betting

8–13606A   8. Exclusive licence. (1) The Gaming Board shall, if the Secretary of State so requires, issue to the successor company a licence (referred to in this Part as "the exclusive licence") granting the successor company the right—

(a) to carry on pool betting business (in any form) in connection with horse races on approved horse racecourses,

(b) by way of business to receive or negotiate bets in connection with horse races on approved horse racecourses on terms that all or part of the winnings shall be calculated or regulated directly or indirectly by reference to the amounts or rates of payments or distributions in respect of winning bets made by way of pool betting, and

(c) to provide facilities in relation to a matter mentioned in paragraph (a) or (b).

(2) The exclusive licence shall, unless revoked under subsection (7), have effect for the period of seven years beginning with the date of issue.

(3) In requiring the issue of the exclusive licence the Secretary of State may specify terms or conditions of the licence.

(4) The Secretary of State—

(a) may require the issue of the exclusive licence before, on or after the appointed day,

(b) may require the issue of the exclusive licence after the successor company has ceased to be wholly owned by the Crown, and

(c) may not require the issue of the exclusive licence more than once.

(5) While the exclusive licence has effect—

(a) the successor company may authorise one or more other persons to do anything that the successor company is authorised to do by the exclusive licence, and

(b) a person other than the successor company may not do anything that the successor company is authorised to do by the exclusive licence, except in accordance with an authorisation under paragraph (a).

(6) An authorisation under subsection (5)(a) may be given on terms and conditions; which may, in particular, include provision—

(a) for payment to or by the successor company;

(b) for agency or commission;

(c) about facilities to be provided by the successor company under subsection (1)(c).

(7) The Gaming Board—

(a) may make an order revoking the exclusive licence if they think that a term or condition of the licence has been breached, and

(b) shall make an order revoking the exclusive licence if the Secretary of State so directs.

(8) A direction of the Secretary of State under subsection (7)(b) shall specify the reasons for the direction.

(9) An order revoking the exclusive licence—

(a) must specify the reasons for the revocation (or, in the case of revocation pursuant to a direction under subsection (7)(b), the reasons for the direction specified under subsection (8)), and

(b) shall take effect at such time as the order may specify.

(10) The Secretary of State may require revocation under subsection (7)(b) only while the successor company is wholly owned by the Crown.

(11) The exclusive licence may not be—

(a) renewed, or

(b) issued or revoked otherwise than in accordance with subsection (1) or (7).

[Horserace Betting and Olympic Lottery Act 2004, s 8.]

8–13606B   9. Section 8: supplemental.   (1) In considering whether to require the Gaming Board to issue or revoke the exclusive licence the Secretary of State shall consider whether the issue or revocation—

(a) would be in the best interests of members of the public who are in the habit of placing bets on horse races;

(b) would be in the best interests of the sport of horse racing;

(c) would promote the objectives of—

    (i) preventing betting from being a source of crime or disorder, being associated with crime or disorder or being used to support crime,

    (ii) ensuring that betting is conducted in a fair and open way, and

    (iii) protecting children and other vulnerable persons from being harmed or exploited by betting.

(2) While the exclusive licence has effect—

(a) sections 4(1) and 4A(1) of the Betting, Gaming and Lotteries Act 1963 (c 2) (restriction on pool betting) (as substituted by section 10 of this Act) shall not apply in relation to anything done—

    (i) by the successor company in pursuance of the exclusive licence, or

    (ii) in accordance with an authorisation under section 8(5)(a) above, and

(b) nothing in section 4 or 4A of that Act shall prejudice the generality of section 8(5)(b) above.

(3) While the exclusive licence has effect—

(a) the successor company or a person authorised under section 8(5)(a) above may apply under section 9(2) of that Act for the grant or renewal of a betting office licence authorising the use of premises for carrying on activity in accordance with the exclusive licence,

(b) a betting office licence under section 9(2) of that Act shall not authorise the use of premises for doing anything prohibited by section 8(5)(b), and

(c) section 9(1) of that Act disapplies section 1(1) of that Act only in relation to activity authorised by a betting office licence.

(4) While the exclusive licence has effect—

(a) the successor company shall not be treated as a bookmaker for the purposes of that Act by virtue of anything done in accordance with the exclusive licence, and

(b) a person authorised under section 8(5)(a) above shall not be treated as a bookmaker for the purposes of that Act by virtue of anything done in accordance with the authorisation.

(5) A person who acts in contravention of section 8(5)(b) above shall be treated as having committed an offence under—

(a) section 4(1) of that Act, in the case of anything done on a track, or

(b) section 4A(1) of that Act, in the case of anything done otherwise than on a track,

whether or not he otherwise would have committed the offence.

(6) If a person commits or threatens a breach of section 8(5)(b), the successor company may (whether or not criminal proceedings are instituted against him by virtue of subsection (5) above) proceed against him in the High Court or a county court for damages or such other relief as the court thinks appropriate.

(7) Subsection (6) is subject to—

(a) Civil Procedure Rules, and

(b)   section 1 of the Courts and Legal Services Act 1990 (c 41) (allocation of business between High Court and county courts).

[Horserace Betting and Olympic Lottery Act 2004, s 9.]

10. Control when no exclusive licence.   *Substitutes new provisions for s 4 of the Betting, Gaming and Lotteries Act 1963.*

General

8–13606C   11. Preparatory work by the Tote

12. Interpretation.   (1) In this Part "the Gaming Board" means the Gaming Board for Great Britain (established under section 10 of the Gaming Act 1968 (c 65)).

(2) For the purposes of this Part a company is wholly owned by the Crown if all its shares are held by the Crown.

(3) For the purposes of subsection (2) shares are held by the Crown if they are held—

(a)   by a Minister of the Crown,
(b)   by the nominee of a Minister of the Crown, or
(c)   by a company of which all the shares are held by the Crown.

(4) In this Part "securities" means shares (including stock), debentures, bonds and other securities, whether constituting a charge on the assets of a company or not.

(5) An expression used in this Part which is given a meaning by the Companies Act 1985 (c 6) for general purposes of that Act shall have the same meaning for the purposes of this Part.

(6) An expression used in this Part and in the Betting, Gaming and Lotteries Act 1963 (c 2) shall have the same meaning in this Part as in that Act.

[Horserace Betting and Olympic Lottery Act 2004, s 12.]

8–13606D

PART 2[1]
ABOLITION OF THE HORSERACE BETTING LEVY SYSTEM

1. This Part is concerned with the abolition of the horserace betting levy system and is not reproduced in this work.

PART 3[1]
NATIONAL LOTTERY: OLYMPIC LOTTERIES

1. This Part is concerned with the licensing of Olympic lotteries and is not reproduced in this work.

8–13606E

PART 4[1]
GENERAL

38. Repeals

39. Money

40. Commencement.   (1) The preceding provisions of this Act shall come into force in accordance with provision made by order of the Secretary of State.

(2) An order under subsection (1)—

(a)   may make provision that has effect generally or only for specified purposes,
(b)   may make different provision for different purposes,
(c)   may include incidental, consequential or transitional provision, and
(d)   shall be made by statutory instrument.

(3) Section 29 shall not be brought into force unless the Secretary of State has made an order under section 22(2).[2]

[Horserace Betting and Olympic Lottery Act 2004, s 40.]

1. Part 4 contains ss 38–42.
2. At the time of going to press the following commencement orders had been made: Horserace Betting and Olympic Lottery Act 2004 (Commencement No 1) Order 2004, SI 2004/3283; Horserace Betting and Olympic Lottery Act 2004 (Commencement No 2) Order 2005, SI 2005/1134; and Horserace Betting and Olympic Lottery Act 2004 (Commencement No 3) Order 2005, SI 2005/1831.

41. Extent

42. Short title

Section 10

SCHEDULE 1
New Schedule 1A to the Betting, Gaming and Lotteries Act 1963

"SCHEDULE 1A
Regulation of Horserace Pool Betting
Part 1
Introduction

1. Part 2 of this Schedule specifies the conditions to be complied with, for the purposes of sections 4(2)(d) and 4A(2)(b), in relation to pool betting business.

2. Part 3 of this Schedule makes provision for the supervision of pool betting business.

3. In this Schedule "pool betting business" means pool betting business in connection with horse racing.

Part 2
Conditions

4. Totalisator

Any totalisator being used must—

  (a)   be in proper working order, and
  (b)   be properly operated.

5. Publicity for arrangements

(1) A person receiving or negotiating bets in relation to a race or set of races must display in a conspicuous position a notice stating, prominently and in easily legible print—

  (a)   the minimum amount (if there is one) that he will accept as a stake,
  (b)   the amounts or percentage of the aggregate of the stakes that he will distribute by way of winnings,
  (c)   the principles that he will apply in calculating winnings (including any rules for rounding sums up or down),
  (d)   the arrangements that he will make for enabling persons to claim winnings,
  (e)   the arrangements that he will make in respect of winnings not claimed, and
  (f)   the arrangements that he will make if there is no winning bet.

(2) Where a person receives or negotiates bets by the use of remote communication of a kind that does not permit the display of a notice, sub-paragraph (1) shall not apply but the person must—

  (a)   have prepared a notice of the kind required by sub-paragraph (1),
  (b)   inform the person making the bet, or arrange for him to be informed, of a method by which he can see a copy of the notice, and
  (c)   if the person making the bet asks to be supplied with a copy of the notice, comply with the request.

(3) In sub-paragraph (2) "remote communication" means communication using—

  (a)   the internet,
  (b)   telephone,
  (c)   television,
  (d)   radio, or
  (e)   any other kind of electronic or other technology for facilitating communication.

(4) Nothing in sub-paragraph (1)—

  (a)   provides a defence to an offence under section 10, or
  (b)   excuses compliance with a provision of regulations under paragraph 3 of Schedule 4.

(5) The Secretary of State may by regulations—

  (a)   provide that a specified system or method of communication is or is not to be treated as a form of remote communication for the purposes of sub-paragraph (2) (and sub-paragraph (3) is subject to any regulations under this paragraph);
  (b)   provide that a specified system or method of communication is or is not to be treated for the purposes of sub-paragraph (2) as being of a kind that does not permit the display of a notice.

(6) Regulations under sub-paragraph (5)—

  (a)   may make different provision for different circumstances,
  (b)   shall be made by statutory instrument, and
  (c)   shall be subject to annulment in pursuance of a resolution of either House of Parliament.

6. (1) Where a person makes statements in accordance with paragraph 5 in respect of a race or set of races—

  (a)   he may not alter any of the statements in respect of that race or set of races, and
  (b)   he must act in accordance with the statements.

(2) But sub-paragraph (1) does not apply to a person before he has received or negotiated a bet in respect of the race or set of races to which the statements relate.

7. Where a person receives or negotiates bets in respect of a race or set of races, as soon as is reasonably practicable after the conclusion of the race or set he must make reasonable arrangements to announce or display details of the amounts payable by way of winnings.

8. Compliance with supervision

A person who receives or negotiates bets must—

(a) comply with any requirement imposed by or under Part 3 of this Schedule,

(b) co-operate with the supervising accountant appointed under that Part,

(c) co-operate with the technical adviser appointed under that Part, and

(d) co-operate with any person authorised by the supervising accountant or the technical adviser under paragraph 11(2)(e) or 13(2)(f).

9. Annual fee

(1) A person who carries on pool betting business in a calendar year must have paid the prescribed fee in respect of that year.

(2) In sub-paragraph (1) "prescribed" means prescribed by order of the Secretary of State.

(3) An order under sub-paragraph (2)—

(a) shall include provision about the timing and manner of payment,

(b) shall provide for fees to be paid (by the person who receives them in accordance with arrangements prescribed by virtue of paragraph (a)) into the Consolidated Fund,

(c) may make different provision for different circumstances,

(d) shall be made by statutory instrument, and

(e) shall be subject to annulment in pursuance of a resolution of either House of Parliament.

(4) In prescribing fees under this paragraph the Secretary of State shall aim, so far as is reasonably practicable, to ensure that the amount paid by way of fees in respect of a calendar year equals the expenditure incurred during that year in respect of—

(a) the performance of the functions of the supervising accountant and technical adviser under Part 3, and

(b) the activities of the Gaming Board in relation to pool betting business.

PART 3

SUPERVISION

10. Supervising accountant

(1) The Gaming Board shall appoint a person who is eligible for appointment as a company auditor (in accordance with section 25 of the Companies Act 1989 (c 40)) to carry out such activities as he thinks necessary or expedient for the purpose of determining whether the conditions in Part 2 of this Schedule are complied with by persons carrying on pool betting business.

(2) The person appointed under sub-paragraph (1) is referred to in this Part as the "supervising accountant".

11. (1) The supervising accountant may do anything that he thinks necessary or expedient for the purpose of determining whether the conditions in Part 2 of this Schedule have been complied with.

(2) In particular, the supervising accountant—

(a) may require access to premises on which pool betting business is being or has been carried on,

(b) may require any person to produce for examination any accounts or other document,

(c) may require any person to permit the supervising accountant to examine a record (whether held on computer or otherwise),

(d) may require any person to supply a copy of any accounts or other document,

(e) may authorise a person in writing to do anything that the supervising accountant could do by virtue of this paragraph, and

(f) may delegate a function under this Part.

12. Technical adviser

(1) The Gaming Board shall appoint a person to advise the supervising accountant on the working condition of totalisators ("the technical adviser").

(2) Before appointing an adviser under this paragraph the Gaming Board shall consult the supervising accountant.

13. (1) The technical adviser may do anything that he thinks necessary or expedient for the purpose of advising the supervising accountant whether the conditions in Part 2 of this Schedule have been complied with.

(2) In particular, the technical adviser—

(a) may require access to premises on which a totalisator is or has been in operation in relation to pool betting business,

(b) may carry out a process for the purposes of examining the operation of a totalisator,

(c) may require any person to produce a document for examination,

(d) may require any person to permit the technical adviser to examine a record (whether held on computer or otherwise),

(e) may require any person to supply a copy of a document,

(f) may authorise a person in writing to do anything that the technical adviser could do by virtue of this paragraph, and

(g) may delegate a function under this Part.

14. Submission of accounts

(1) A person who carries on pool betting business in any month shall send to the supervising accountant a statement of the person's accounts for pool betting business carried on by him in that month.

(2) A statement submitted under sub-paragraph (1) must, in particular—

(a) specify any amounts carried over from one race or set of races to another in accordance with arrangements of a kind described in paragraph 5(1)(f), and

(b) give such other information as the supervising accountant may require for the purpose of determining whether the conditions in Part 2 of this Schedule have been complied with.

(3) The requirement under sub-paragraph (1) must be complied with before the end of the period of 28 days beginning with the last day of the month to which the accounts relate.

(4) Where the supervising accountant imposes a requirement under sub-paragraph (2)(b)—

(a) he may impose the requirement in relation to accounts for any month, whether ending before or after the requirement is imposed and whether or not accounts for that month have been submitted, and

(b) if he imposes the requirement in relation to accounts for a month ending before the requirement is imposed—

    (i) a person who has already submitted accounts for that month must re-submit them, and

    (ii) in relation to a person obliged to re-submit accounts, sub-paragraph (3) shall have effect as if the period of 28 days began with the day on which the requirement came to his notice.

15. Where accounts are submitted to the supervising accountant under paragraph 14 he shall—

(a) examine them, and

(b) arrange for their retention for a period of at least two years.

16. Annual audit

(1) This paragraph applies to a person who submits accounts to the supervising accountant under paragraph 14 during a calendar year.

(2) As soon as is reasonably practicable after the end of the calendar year the supervising accountant shall, in relation to each person to whom this paragraph applies—

(a) audit the person's accounts for pool betting business in that year (as submitted under paragraph 14),

(b) certify whether, so far as he is reasonably able to ascertain—

    (i) the person has complied with paragraph 14,

    (ii) the accounts are complete and accurate, and

    (iii) the pool betting business carried on by the person during that year has been carried on in accordance with Part 2 of this Schedule.

(3) Having audited and certified a person's accounts under sub-paragraph (2) the supervising accountant shall as soon as is reasonably practicable send the audited accounts and the certificate to the person.

(4) As soon as is reasonably practicable after receiving audited accounts and a certificate under sub-paragraph (3) a person must send two copies of each to the Gaming Board.

(5) The Gaming Board shall make one copy of any accounts and certificate received under sub-paragraph (4) available for inspection by the public—

(a) at all reasonable times, and

(b) without charge.

17. Report to Gaming Board

If the supervising accountant suspects that pool betting business has been carried on otherwise than in accordance with Part 2 of this Schedule, he shall report the matter to the Gaming Board.

18. The supervising accountant and the technical adviser shall on request make available to the Gaming Board any accounts or other document supplied or provided under paragraph 11, 13 or 14.

19. Offences

A person commits an offence if he obstructs the supervising accountant or the technical adviser in the exercise of a function under this Part.

20. A person commits an offence if without reasonable excuse he fails to co-operate with the supervising accountant or the technical adviser in the exercise of a function under this Part.

21. A person commits an offence if he supplies to the supervising accountant or the technical adviser information which the person knows to be—

(a) false, or

(b) misleading.

22. In paragraphs 19 to 21 "person" does not mean only a person who carries on or has carried on pool betting business.

23. A person commits an offence if he fails to comply with paragraph 14(1) or 16(4).

24. (1) A person guilty of an offence under any of paragraphs 19 to 21 shall be liable on summary conviction to a fine not exceeding level 3 on the standard scale.

(2) A person guilty of an offence under paragraph 23 shall be liable on summary conviction to—

(a) imprisonment for a term not exceeding six months,

(b) a fine not exceeding level 5 on the standard scale, or

(c) both."

8–13606G

SCHEDULE 2[1]

SALE OF THE TOTE: CONSEQUENTIAL AMENDMENTS

---

1. Amendments of provisions that appear in this work will be shown when the amendments come into force.

SCHEDULE 3

HORSERACE BETTING LEVY BOARD: TRANSFER OF PROPERTY

SCHEDULE 4[1]

ABOLITION OF THE HORSERACE BETTING LEVY SYSTEM: CONSEQUENTIAL AMENDMENTS

---

1. Amendments of provisions that appear in this work will be shown when the amendments come into force.

SCHEDULE 5

THE OLYMPIC LOTTERY DISTRIBUTOR

SCHEDULE 6[1]

REPEALS

---

1. Where these concern provisions that appear in this work their effect will be noted when they come into force.

Gambling Act 2005[1]

(2005 c 19)

PART 1[1]

Interpretation of Key Concepts

Principal concepts

8–13607　　1. The licensing objectives.　In this Act a reference to the licensing objectives is a reference to the objectives of—

　(*a*)　preventing gambling from being a source of crime or disorder, being associated with crime or disorder or being used to support crime,

　(*b*)　ensuring that gambling is conducted in a fair and open way, and

　(*c*)　protecting children and other vulnerable persons from being harmed or exploited by gambling.

[Gambling Act 2005, s 1.]

　1.　The Gambling Act 2005 contains a new regulatory system to govern the provision of all forms of gambling in Great Britain, other than the National Lottery and spread betting (which remain regulated by the National Lottery Act 1993 and the Financial Services and Markets Act 2000, respectively).

　The Act repeals the Betting, Gaming and Lotteries Act 1963, the Gaming Act 1968 and the Lotteries and Amusements Act 1976.

　Gambling will be unlawful unless permitted by this Act. Two principal offences are established: (*a*) providing facilities for gambling; and (*b*) using facilities for gambling, in either case without the appropriate permission. Such permission may come from a licence, permit or registration granted under the Act or from an exception given by the Act.

　There are varying degrees of regulation under the Act, depending on the type of gambling, the means by which it is conducted, and the people by whom and to whom it is offered.

　The Act establishes a new unified regulator for gambling, namely the Gambling Commission. It also establishes a new licence regime for commercial gambling. The Act ends the jurisdiction of licensing justices and replaces it with shared responsibility between the Commission and licensing authorities.

　The Commission will take over from the Gaming Board the latter's current remit of regulating gaming and certain lotteries. The Commission will also assume responsibility for regulated betting. The Commission will be responsible for granting operating and personal licences for commercial gambling operators and personnel working in the industry. It will also regulate certain lottery managers and promoters.

　The Act sets out different types of operating licences, and makes provisions for the Commission to have powers of entry and inspection to regulate gambling, subject to safeguards.

　The Act establishes the Gambling Appeals Tribunal to hear appeals from decisions made by the Commission.

　Licensing authorities – in England and Wales local authorities – will have new powers to license gambling premises within their area. They will also undertake functions in relation to lower stake gaming machines and clubs and miners' welfare institutions.

　A new system of temporary use notices will authorise premises that are not generally licences to be used for certain types of gambling for limited periods.

　The Act prescribes three central licensing objectives: (*a*) protecting children and other vulnerable people from being harmed or exploited; (*b*) preventing gambling from being a source of, or being associated with, crime or disorder, or being used to support crime; and (*c*) ensuring the gambling is conducted in a fair way.

　Regulation will be achieved through secondary legislation, licence conditions, codes of practice and guidance.

　The Act regulates remote gambling, such as through the Internet. Operators based within Great Britain will require operators' licences before they can provide gambling through remote communication.

　The Act revises the law of gambling. Commercial bingo premises and casinos no longer have to operate as clubs with a 24-hour membership rule. The Act introduces a new class of betting intermediary operating licence, which will cater for betting exchanges. The Act repeals legislation that has prevented gambling contracts from being enforced through the courts.

　Three new categories of casino are introduced: regional, large and small. A casino's category determines the forms of gambling it can provide. The Act imposes an initial limit of 1 regional casino, 8 small and 8 large casinos to be licensed under its provisions. Casinos operating or able to operate lawfully immediately before the casino provisions come into effect will be able to continue operating. A licensing authority may pass a resolution not to license any new casino premises in its area.

　Gaming machines are re-defined, together with power to prescribe categories. Commercial operators will be entitled to use specified numbers and categories of machines in consequence of their licences. The Act also establishes permit procedures to authorise the use of lower stake gambling machines in specific locations.

　The Act's aim to protect children and other vulnerable persons is buttressed by a number of specific offences.

　The Act empowers the Commission to void bets that are unfair due, for example, to cheating.

　The Act contains a new regime in relation to lotteries. They will operate either as licensed lotteries or as exempt lotteries.

　The Act deals with advertising by creating new offences relating to advertising unlawful gambling and by providing powers for the Secretary of State to regulate the content of gambling advertisements.

　The Act also establishes a series of authorisations for private and non-commercial gambling, and it provides for gaming and lotteries at non-commercial events.

　The Act contains 18 Parts and 18 Schedules.

　　•　Part 1, and Schs 1 and 2 contain the fundamental concepts and definitions. Part 1 also deals with situations where activities may fall into more than one category of gambling

　　•　Part 2, and Schs 4 and 5 establish the Gaming Commissions and define its core powers and duties.

　　•　Part 3 sets out the general offences. It also prohibits chain gifting schemes, contains a revised offence of cheating and provisions on the manufacture of gambling software.

　　•　Part 4 establishes a number of specific offences relating to children and young people.

　　•　Part 5 and Sch 7 contain provisions relating to operators' licences.

　　•　Part 6 is concerned with personal licences issued by the Commission.

　　•　Part 7 and Sch 8 (not reproduced in this work) create the Gambling Appeals Tribunal and appeal procedures.

　　•　Part 8 concerns premises licences issued by licensing authorities. This part also contains provisions to limit the number of casino premises licences that may be granted.

- Part 9 contains provisions to authorise the temporary use of premises for gambling.
- Part 10 and Sch 10 provide a new framework of regulation for gaming machines.
- Part 11 and Sch 11 establish a new regime for lotteries.
- Part 12 and Sch 12 establish a new regime for gambling in clubs and miners' welfare institutes. There is a requirement for bingo operating licences to be obtained where the size of the games played exceeds a specified threshold. Part 12 and Sch 13 are concerned with gaming machines in premises licensed to supply alcohol. Part 12 also deals with gaming machines at travelling fairs.
- Part 13 and Sch 14 make provision for prize gaming.
- Part 14 and Sch 15 make provision for private and non-commercial gaming, which are authorised without any requirement for further permission.
- Part 15 deals with rights of inspection.
- Part 16 provides a new regime for advertising.
- Part 17 (not reproduced in this work) makes new provision for gambling contracts.
- Part 18 deals with interpretation and general matters.
- Schedules 16 and 17 deal with consequential amendments and repeals.

The Act extends generally to England and Wales (and nearly all of its provisions also apply to Scotland and Northern Ireland). Sections 359 and 360 are concerned with territorial extent in relation to vessels and aircraft.

The Act is to be brought into force in accordance with commencement orders made under s 358. At the time of going to press the Gambling Act 2005 (Commencement No 1) Order 2005, SI 2005/2425; and the Gambling Act 2005 (Commencement No 2 and Transitional Provisions) Order 2005, SI 2005/2455 had been made. However, most of the Act's provisions remain unimplemented. Notes to the title of Parts of the indicate state the provisions within those parts that are in force.

2. Part 1 contains s 1–19. Sections 1–6; 7(1)–(4), 8 and 9; 10(1) and (2); 11–14 and Schs 1 and 2; s 15(1)–(4); s 15(5) (for certain purposes only); and 16–19 are in force: see Gambling Act 2005 (Commencement No 2 and Transitional Provisions) Order 2005, SI 2005/2455.

8–13608 2. Licensing authorities.   (1) For the purposes of this Act the following are licensing authorities—

   (*a*) in relation to England—

    (i)   a district council,
    (ii) a county council for a county in which there are no district councils,
    (iii) a London borough council,
    (iv) the Common Council of the City of London, and
    (v)   the Council of the Isles of Scilly,

   (*b*) in relation to Wales—

    (i)   a county council, and
    (ii) a county borough council, and

   (*c*) in relation to Scotland, a licensing board constituted under section 1 of the Licensing (Scotland) Act 1976 (c 66).

   (2) For the purposes of Schedule 13, the Sub-Treasurer of the Inner Temple and the Under-Treasurer of the Middle Temple are licensing authorities.
[Gambling Act 2005, s 2.]

8–13609 3. Gambling.   In this Act "gambling" means—

   (*a*) gaming (within the meaning of section 6),
   (*b*) betting (within the meaning of section 9), and
   (*c*) participating in a lottery (within the meaning of section 14 and subject to section 15).
[Gambling Act 2005, s 3.]

8–13610 4. Remote gambling.   (1) In this Act "remote gambling" means gambling in which persons participate by the use of remote communication.
   (2) In this Act "remote communication" means communication using—

   (*a*) the internet,
   (*b*) telephone,
   (*c*) television,
   (*d*) radio, or
   (*e*) any other kind of electronic or other technology for facilitating communication.

   (3) The Secretary of State may by regulations provide that a specified system or method of communication is or is not to be treated as a form of remote communication for the purposes of this Act (and subsection (2) is subject to any regulations under this subsection).
[Gambling Act 2005, s 4.]

8–13611 5. Facilities for gambling.   (1) For the purposes of this Act a person provides facilities for gambling if he—

   (*a*) invites others to gamble in accordance with arrangements made by him,
   (*b*) provides, operates or administers arrangements for gambling by others, or
   (*c*) participates in the operation or administration of gambling by others.

(2) But a person does not provide facilities for gambling for the purposes of this Act by virtue only of—

(a) providing an article other than a gaming machine to a person who intends to use it, or may use it, in the course of any of the activities mentioned in subsection (1)(a) to (c),

(b) providing, otherwise than in the course of providing, operating or administering arrangements for gambling or participating in the operation or administration of gambling, an article to a person who intends to use it, or may use it, for gambling, or

(c) making facilities for remote communication available for use by—

(i) persons carrying on any of those activities, or
(ii) persons gambling in response to or in accordance with any of those activities.

(3) A person provides facilities for gambling (despite subsection (2)(c)) if—

(a) he makes facilities for remote communication available for use,

(b) the facilities are adapted or presented in such a way as to facilitate, or to draw attention to the possibility of, their use for gambling, and

(c) the nature, adaptation or presentation of the facilities is such that—

(i) they cannot reasonably be expected to be used for purposes other than gambling, or
(ii) they are intended to be used wholly or mainly for gambling.

(4) The Secretary of State may by order, for the purposes of subsection (3)(c)—

(a) provide that facilities of a specified nature, or adapted or presented in a specified way, cannot reasonably be expected to be used for purposes other than gambling;

(b) provide that facilities of a specified nature, or adapted or presented in a specified way, can reasonably be expected to be used for purposes other than gambling;

(c) specify criteria by which it is to be determined whether facilities can reasonably be expected to be used for purposes other than gambling;

(d) provide that facilities of a specified nature, or adapted or presented in a specified way, shall be taken as being intended to be used wholly or mainly for gambling;

(e) provide that facilities of a specified nature, or adapted or presented in a specified way, shall be taken as not being intended to be used wholly or mainly for gambling;

(f) specify criteria by which it is to be determined whether facilities are intended to be used wholly or mainly for gambling.

[Gambling Act 2005, s 5.]

Gaming

8–13612 6. Gaming & game of chance. (1) In this Act "gaming" means playing a game of chance for a prize.

(2) In this Act "game of chance"—

(a) includes—

(i) a game that involves both an element of chance and an element of skill,
(ii) a game that involves an element of chance that can be eliminated by superlative skill, and
(iii) a game that is presented as involving an element of chance, but

(b) does not include a sport.

(3) For the purposes of this Act a person plays a game of chance if he participates in a game of chance—

(a) whether or not there are other participants in the game, and

(b) whether or not a computer generates images or data taken to represent the actions of other participants in the game.

(4) For the purposes of this Act a person plays a game of chance for a prize—

(a) if he plays a game of chance and thereby acquires a chance of winning a prize, and

(b) whether or not he risks losing anything at the game.

(5) In this Act "prize" in relation to gaming (except in the context of a gaming machine)—

(a) means money or money's worth, and

(b) includes both a prize provided by a person organising gaming and winnings of money staked.

(6) The Secretary of State may by regulations provide that a specified activity, or an activity carried on in specified circumstances, is or is not to be treated for the purposes of this Act as—

(a) a game;

(b) a game of chance;

(c) a sport.

[Gambling Act 2005, s 6.]

8–13613 7. Casino. (1) For the purposes of this Act a casino is an arrangement whereby people are given an opportunity to participate in one or more casino games.

(2) In this Act "casino game" means a game of chance which is not equal chance gaming.

(3) But the Secretary of State may by regulations provide that a specified activity, or an activity carried on in specified circumstances, is to be or not to be treated as a casino game for the purposes of this Act (and subsection (2) is subject to regulations under this subsection).

(4) For the purposes of this section it is immaterial—

(a) whether an arrangement is provided on one set of premises or on more than one;

(b) whether an arrangement is provided wholly or partly by means of remote communication.

(5) The Secretary of State shall make regulations by reference to which any casino may be classified as—

(a) a regional casino,

(b) a large casino,

(c) a small casino, or

(d) below the minimum size for a licensed casino

(6), (7) *Concerned with the making of regulations.*

[Gambling Act 2005, s 7.]

8–13614   8. Equal chance gaming.   (1) For the purposes of this Act gaming is equal chance gaming if—

(a) it does not involve playing or staking against a bank, and

(b) the chances are equally favourable to all participants.

(2) For the purposes of subsection (1) it is immaterial—

(a) how a bank is described, and

(b) whether or not a bank is controlled or administered by a player.

[Gambling Act 2005, s 8.]

Betting

8–13615   9. Betting: general.   (1) In this Act "betting" means making or accepting a bet on—

(a) the outcome of a race, competition or other event or process,

(b) the likelihood of anything occurring or not occurring, or

(c) whether anything is or is not true.

(2) A transaction that relates to the outcome of a race, competition or other event or process may be a bet within the meaning of subsection (1) despite the facts that—

(a) the race, competition, event or process has already occurred or been completed, and

(b) one party to the transaction knows the outcome.

(3) A transaction that relates to the likelihood of anything occurring or not occurring may be a bet within the meaning of subsection (1) despite the facts that—

(a) the thing has already occurred or failed to occur, and

(b) one party to the transaction knows that the thing has already occurred or failed to occur.

[Gambling Act 2005, s 9.]

8–13616   10. Spread bets, &c.   (1) For the purposes of section 9(1) "bet" does not include a bet the making or accepting of which is a regulated activity within the meaning of section 22 of the Financial Services and Markets Act 2000 (c 8).

(2) An order under section 22 of that Act which has the effect that a class of bet becomes or ceases to be a regulated activity may, in particular, include transitional provision relating to the application of this Act to that class of bet.

(3) This section is subject to section 38(3).

[Gambling Act 2005, s 10.]

8–13617   11. Betting: prize competitions.   (1) For the purposes of section 9(1) a person makes a bet (despite the fact that he does not deposit a stake in the normal way of betting) if—

(a) he participates in an arrangement in the course of which participants are required to guess any of the matters specified in section 9(1)(a) to (c),

(b) he is required to pay to participate[1], and

(c) if his guess is accurate, or more accurate than other guesses, he is to—

(i) win a prize, or

(ii) enter a class among whom one or more prizes are to be allocated (whether or not wholly by chance).

(2) In subsection (1) a reference to guessing includes a reference to predicting using skill or judgment.

(3) Schedule 1 makes further provision about when a person is to be or not to be treated for the purposes of subsection (1)(b) as being required to pay to participate in an arrangement.

(4) In subsection (1)(c) "prize" includes any money, articles or services—

(a) whether or not described as a prize, and

(b) whether or not consisting wholly or partly of money paid, or articles or services provided, by the members of the class among whom the prizes are allocated.

[Gambling Act 2005, s 11.]

---

1. "Payment to enter" is defined in Sch 1.

8–13618 12. Pool betting. (1) For the purposes of this Act betting is pool betting if made on terms that all or part of winnings—

(a) shall be determined by reference to the aggregate of stakes paid or agreed to be paid by the persons betting,

(b) shall be divided among the winners, or

(c) shall or may be something other than money.

(2) For the purposes of this Act pool betting is horse-race pool betting if it relates to horse-racing in Great Britain.

[Gambling Act 2005, s 12.]

8–13619 13. Betting intermediary. (1) In this Act "betting intermediary" means a person who provides a service designed to facilitate the making or acceptance of bets between others.

(2) For the purposes of this Act acting as a betting intermediary is providing facilities for betting.

[Gambling Act 2005, s 13.]

Lottery

8–13620 14. Lottery. (1) For the purposes of this Act an arrangement is a lottery, irrespective of how it is described, if it satisfies one of the descriptions of lottery in subsections (2) and (3).

(2) An arrangement is a simple lottery if—

(a) persons are required to pay in order to participate in the arrangement[1],

(b) in the course of the arrangement one or more prizes are allocated to one or more members of a class, and

(c) the prizes are allocated by a process which relies wholly on chance.

(3) An arrangement is a complex lottery if—

(a) persons are required to pay in order to participate in the arrangement,

(b) in the course of the arrangement one or more prizes are allocated to one or more members of a class,

(c) the prizes are allocated by a series of processes, and

(d) the first of those processes relies wholly on chance.

(4) In this Act "prize" in relation to lotteries includes any money, articles or services—

(a) whether or not described as a prize, and

(b) whether or not consisting wholly or partly of money paid, or articles or services provided, by the members of the class among whom the prize is allocated.

(5) A process which requires persons to exercise skill or judgment or to display knowledge shall be treated for the purposes of this section as relying wholly on chance if—

(a) the requirement cannot reasonably be expected to prevent a significant proportion of persons who participate in the arrangement of which the process forms part from receiving a prize, and

(b) the requirement cannot reasonably be expected to prevent a significant proportion of persons who wish to participate in that arrangement from doing so.

(6) Schedule 2 makes further provision about when an arrangement is to be or not to be treated for the purposes of this section as requiring persons to pay.

(7) The Secretary of State may by regulations provide that an arrangement of a specified kind is to be or not to be treated as a lottery for the purposes of this Act; and—

(a) the power in this subsection is not constrained by subsections (1) to (6) or Schedule 2, and

(b) regulations under this subsection may amend other provisions of this section or Schedule 2.

[Gambling Act 2005, s 14.]

---

1. "Payment to enter lotteries" is defined in Sch 2.

8–13621 15. National Lottery. (1) Participating in a lottery which forms part of the National Lottery is not gambling for the purposes of this Act (despite section 3(c) but subject to subsections (2) and (3) below).

(2) Participating in a lottery which forms part of the National Lottery is gambling for the purposes of—

(a) section 42, and

(*b*)   section 335.

(3)   Where participating in a lottery which forms part of the National Lottery would also constitute gaming within the meaning of section 6, it shall be treated as gaming for the purposes of this Act if and only if a person participating in the lottery is required to participate in, or to be successful in, more than three processes before becoming entitled to a prize.

(4)   Participating in a lottery which forms part of the National Lottery shall not be treated as betting for the purposes of this Act where it would—

(*a*)   satisfy the definition of pool betting in section 12, or
(*b*)   satisfy the definition of betting in section 9 by virtue of section 11.

(5)   Schedule 3 shall have effect.
[Gambling Act 2005, s 15.]

Cross-category activities

8–13622   16. Betting and gaming.   (1)   This section applies to a transaction which satisfies—

(*a*)   the definition of betting in section 9, and
(*b*)   the definition of gaming in section 6.

(2)   A transaction to which this section applies which is pool betting (within the meaning of section 12) shall be treated for the purposes of this Act as betting (and not as gaming).

(3)   Any other transaction to which this section applies shall be treated for the purposes of this Act as gaming (and not as betting).

(4)   This section is subject to regulations under section 6(6).
[Gambling Act 2005, s 16.]

8–13623   17. Lotteries and gaming.   (1)   This section applies to an arrangement which satisfies—

(*a*)   the definition of a game of chance in section 6, and
(*b*)   the definition of a lottery in section 14.

(2)   An arrangement to which this section applies shall be treated for the purposes of this Act as a game of chance (and not as a lottery) if a person who pays in order to join the class amongst whose members prizes are allocated is required to participate in, or to be successful in, more than three processes before becoming entitled to a prize.

(3)   An arrangement to which this section applies shall, subject to subsection (2), be treated for the purposes of this Act as a lottery (and not as a game of chance) if—

(*a*)   it satisfies paragraph 1(1)(*a*) and (*b*) of Schedule 11,
(*b*)   it satisfies paragraph 10(1)(*a*) and (*b*) of Schedule 11,
(*c*)   it satisfies paragraph 11(1)(*a*) and (*b*) of Schedule 11,
(*d*)   it satisfies paragraph 12(1)(*a*) and (*b*) of Schedule 11,
(*e*)   it satisfies paragraph 20(1)(*a*) and (*b*) of Schedule 11,
(*f*)   it satisfies paragraph 30(1)(*a*) and (*b*) of Schedule 11, or
(*g*)   it is promoted in reliance on a lottery operating licence.

(4)   Any other arrangement to which this section applies shall be treated for the purposes of this Act as a game of chance (and not as a lottery).

(5)   This section is subject to regulations under section 6(6) or 14(7).
[Gambling Act 2005, s 17.]

8–13624   18. Lotteries and betting.   (1)   This section applies to a transaction which satisfies the definition of participating in a lottery in section 14 and also—

(*a*)   satisfies the definition of pool betting in section 12, or
(*b*)   satisfies the definition of betting in section 9 by virtue of section 11.

(2)   A transaction to which this section applies shall be treated for the purposes of this Act as participating in a lottery (and not as betting) if—

(*a*)   it satisfies paragraph 1(1)(*a*) and (*b*) of Schedule 11,
(*b*)   it satisfies paragraph 10(1)(*a*) and (*b*) of Schedule 11,
(*c*)   it satisfies paragraph 11(1)(*a*) and (*b*) of Schedule 11,
(*d*)   it satisfies paragraph 12(1)(*a*) and (*b*) of Schedule 11,
(*e*)   it satisfies paragraph 20(1)(*a*) and (*b*) of Schedule 11,
(*f*)   it satisfies paragraph 30(1)(*a*) and (*b*) of Schedule 11, or
(*g*)   it is promoted in reliance on a lottery operating licence.

(3)   Any other transaction to which this section applies shall be treated for the purposes of this Act as betting (and not as participating in a lottery).

(4)   This section is subject to regulations under section 14(7).
[Gambling Act 2005, s 18.]

Miscellaneous

8–13625　19. Non-commercial society.　(1) For the purposes of this Act a society is non-commercial if it is established and conducted—

(*a*)　for charitable purposes,

(*b*)　for the purpose of enabling participation in, or of supporting, sport, athletics or a cultural activity, or

(*c*)　for any other non-commercial purpose other than that of private gain.

(2) In subsection (1) "charitable purposes" means—

(*a*)　in relation to England and Wales, purposes which are exclusively charitable according to the law of England and Wales, and

(*b*)　in relation to Scotland, purposes which are charitable only (that expression having the same meaning as in the Income Tax Acts).

(3) The provision of a benefit to one or more individuals is not a provision for the purpose of private gain for the purposes of this Act if made in the course of the activities of a society that is a non-commercial society by virtue of subsection (1)(*a*) or (*b*).
[Gambling Act 2005, s 19.]

PART 2[1]

The Gambling Commission

8–13626　20. Establishment of the Commission.　(1) There shall be a body corporate to be known as the Gambling Commission.

(2) Schedule 4 (which makes provision about the constitution and proceedings of the Commission) shall have effect.
[Gambling Act 2005, s 20.]

1.　Part 2 contains ss 20–32. Section 20 and Sch 4; s 21 and Sch 5, ss 22 and 23; s 24(1) –(8), (10) and (11); ss 25 and 26; s 30 and Sch 6; and ss 21 and 32 are in force: see Gambling Act 2005 (Commencement No 2 and Transitional Provisions) Order 2005, SI 2005/2455.

8–13627　21. Gaming Board: transfer to Commission.　(1) Section 10 of and Schedule 1 to the Gaming Act 1968 (c 65) (Gaming Board for Great Britain) shall cease to have effect.

(2) The functions, rights and liabilities of the Gaming Board for Great Britain shall on commencement become functions, rights and liabilities of the Gambling Commission.

(3) The persons who immediately before commencement are the members of the Gaming Board for Great Britain shall be treated as if on commencement they were appointed as commissioners of the Gambling Commission under paragraph 1 of Schedule 4 to this Act.

(4) The person who immediately before commencement is the chairman of the Gaming Board for Great Britain shall be treated as if on commencement he were appointed as the chairman of the Gambling Commission under paragraph 1 of Schedule 4 to this Act.

(5) In this section "commencement" means the coming into force of this section.

(6) Schedule 5 (which makes supplementary provision in relation to the transfer of functions and property from the Gaming Board to the Gambling Commission) shall have effect.
[Gambling Act 2005, s 21.]

8–13628　22. Duty to promote the licensing objectives.　In exercising its functions under this Act the Commission shall aim—

(*a*)　to pursue, and wherever appropriate to have regard to, the licensing objectives, and

(*b*)　to permit gambling, in so far as the Commission thinks it reasonably consistent with pursuit of the licensing objectives.
[Gambling Act 2005, s 22.]

8–13629　23. Statement of principles for licensing and regulation.　(1) The Commission shall prepare a statement setting out the principles to be applied by it in exercising its functions under this Act.

(2) The statement under this section shall, in particular, explain how the principles to be applied are expected to assist the Commission in its pursuit of the licensing objectives.

(3) The Commission shall—

(*a*)　review the statement from time to time, and

(*b*)　revise the statement when the Commission thinks it appropriate.

(4) The Commission shall as soon as is reasonably practicable publish—

(*a*)　the statement, and

(*b*)　any revision.

(5) Before issuing or revising a statement under this section the Commission shall consult—

(*a*)　the Secretary of State,

(b) Her Majesty's Commissioners of Customs and Excise,

(c) one or more persons who appear to the Commission to represent local authorities (including, in Scotland, licensing boards),

(d) one or more persons who appear to the Commission to represent chief constables of police forces,

(e) one or more persons who appear to the Commission to represent the interests of persons carrying on gambling businesses,

(f) one or more persons who appear to the Commission to have knowledge about social problems relating to gambling, and

(g) to such extent and in such manner as the Commission thinks appropriate, members of the public.

[Gambling Act 2005, s 23.]

8–13630 24. Codes of practice. (1) The Commission shall issue one or more codes of practice about the manner in which facilities for gambling are provided (whether by the holder of a licence under this Act or by another person).

(2) In particular, a code shall describe arrangements that should be made by a person providing facilities for gambling for the purposes of—

(a) ensuring that gambling is conducted in a fair and open way,

(b) protecting children and other vulnerable persons from being harmed or exploited by gambling, and

(c) making assistance available to persons who are or may be affected by problems related to gambling.

(3) A code may include provision about how facilities for gambling are advertised or described.

(4) A code may be revised or revoked by the Commission.

(5) A code, and any revision, must state when it comes into force.

(6) The Commission shall publish a code and any revision in a manner which the Commission thinks likely to bring it to the attention of those whose activities it concerns.

(7) The Commission may make different provision under this section for different cases or circumstances (whether or not by way of separate codes of practice).

(8) A failure to comply with a provision of a code shall not of itself make a person liable to criminal or civil proceedings; but this subsection is subject to any provision of or by virtue of this Act making an exception to an offence dependent on compliance with a code.

(9) But a code—

(a) shall be admissible in evidence in criminal or civil proceedings,

(b) shall be taken into account by a court or tribunal in any case in which it appears to the court or tribunal to be relevant, and

(c) shall be taken into account by the Commission in the exercise of a function under this Act.

[Gambling Act 2005, s 24(1)–(9).]

8–13631 25. Guidance to local authorities. (1) The Commission shall from time to time issue guidance as to—

(a) the manner in which local authorities are to exercise their functions under this Act, and

(b) in particular, the principles to be applied by local authorities in exercising functions under this Act.

(2) A local authority shall have regard to guidance issued under subsection (1).

(6) In this section "local authority" means—

(a) in relation to England—

  (i) a district council,

  (ii) a county council for a county in which there are no district councils,

  (iii) a London borough council,

  (iv) the Common Council of the City of London,

  (v) the Sub-Treasurer of the Inner Temple and the Under-Treasurer of the Middle Temple, and

  (vi) the Council of the Isles of Scilly,

(b) in relation to Wales—

  (i) a county council, and

  (ii) a county borough council, and

(c) in relation to Scotland, a licensing board constituted under section 1 of the Licensing (Scotland) Act 1976 (c 66).

[Gambling Act 2005, s 25(1), (2) and (6).]

8–13632 27. Compliance. The Commission may undertake activities for the purpose of assessing—

(a) compliance with provision made by or by virtue of this Act;

(*b*) whether an offence is being committed under or by virtue of this Act.
[Gambling Act 2005, s 27.]

8–13633   28. Investigation and prosecution of offences. (1) The Commission—

(*a*) may investigate whether an offence has been committed under this Act, and
(*b*) may institute criminal proceedings in respect of an offence under this Act.

(2) The power in subsection (1)(*a*) may be exercised whether in response to information received by the Commission or otherwise.

(3) Subsection (1)(*b*) shall not apply in relation to the institution of proceedings in Scotland.
[Gambling Act 2005, s 28.]

8–13634   29. Licensing authority information. (1) The Commission may require a licensing authority to provide information that—

(*a*) forms part of a register maintained by the authority under this Act, or
(*b*) is in the possession of the authority in connection with a provision of this Act.

(2) A requirement under subsection (1) may include a requirement for information to be—

(*a*) compiled or collated in a specified manner;
(*b*) provided in a specified form.

(3) A licensing authority shall comply with a requirement under this section.
[Gambling Act 2005, s 29.]

8–13635   30. Other exchange of information. (1) The Commission may provide information received by it in the exercise of its functions to any of the persons or bodies listed in Schedule 6—

(*a*) for use in the exercise of the person's or body's functions, or
(*b*) for the purpose of a function of the Commission.

(2) Any of the persons or bodies listed in Part 1 or 2 of Schedule 6 may provide to the Commission, for use in the exercise of its functions, information received by the person or body in the exercise of his or its functions.

(3) The Commission may provide information received by it in the exercise of its functions to the Comptroller and Auditor General for use in the exercise of his functions under Part 2 of the National Audit Act 1983 (c 44).

(4) The Commission may provide information received by it in the exercise of its functions to a person if the provision is for the purpose of—

(*a*) a criminal investigation (whether in the United Kingdom or elsewhere), or
(*b*) criminal proceedings (whether in the United Kingdom or elsewhere).

(5) Note 2 to Schedule 6 shall not apply to the provision of information under subsection (3).

(6) Provision of information in reliance on this section may be subject to conditions (whether as to use, storage, disposal or otherwise).

(7) The Commission may charge a fee for the provision of information under subsection (1)(*a*).

(8) This section is subject to section 352.
[Gambling Act 2005, s 30.]

8–13636   31. Consultation with National Lottery Commission

8–13637   32. Consultation with Commissioners of Customs and Excise

PART 3[1]
GENERAL OFFENCES

Provision of facilities for gambling

8–13638   33. Provision of facilities for gambling. (1) A person commits an offence if he provides facilities[2] for gambling[3] unless—

(*a*) an exception provided for in subsection (2) or (3) applies, or
(*b*) an exception provided for by any of the following provisions applies—

(i)   sections 34 and 35,
(ii) sections 269 and 271 (clubs and miners' welfare institutes),
(iii) section 279 (premises with alcohol licence),
(iv) sections 289 to 292 (prize gaming),
(v)   section 296 (private gaming and betting), and
(vi) section 298 (non-commercial gaming).

(2) Subsection (1) does not apply to any activity by a person if—

(*a*) he holds an operating licence[4] authorising the activity, and
(*b*) the activity is carried on in accordance with the terms and conditions of the licence.

(3) Subsection (1) does not apply to any activity by a person if—

(*a*) he acts in the course of a business carried on by a person who holds an operating licence authorising the activity, and

(*b*) the activity is carried on in accordance with the terms and conditions of the licence.

(4) A person guilty of an offence under this section shall be liable on summary conviction to—

(*a*) imprisonment for a term not exceeding 51 weeks,

(*b*) a fine not exceeding level 5 on the standard scale, or

(*c*) both.

(5) In the application of subsection (4) to Scotland the reference to 51 weeks shall have effect as a reference to six months.

[Gambling Act 2005, s 33.]

---

1. Part 3 contains ss 33–44.
2. Defined in s 5, ante.
3. Defined in s 3, ante.
4. As to operators' licences, see Part 5, post.

8–13639   34. Exception: lotteries.   Section 33 shall not apply to the provision of facilities for a lottery.

[Gambling Act 2005, s 34.]

8–13640   35. Exception: gaming machines.   Section 33 shall not apply to making a gaming machine available for use.

[Gambling Act 2005, s 35.]

8–13641   36. Territorial application.   (1) For the purposes of section 33 it is immaterial whether facilities are provided—

(*a*) wholly or partly by means of remote communication;

(*b*) subject to subsections (2) and (3), inside the United Kingdom, outside the United Kingdom, or partly inside and partly outside.

(2) Section 33 applies to the provision of facilities for non-remote gambling only if anything done in the course of the provision of the facilities is done in Great Britain.

(3) Section 33 applies to the provision of facilities for remote gambling only if at least one piece of remote gambling equipment used in the provision of the facilities is situated in Great Britain (but whether or not the facilities are provided for use wholly or partly in the United Kingdom).

(4) In this Act "remote gambling equipment" means, subject to subsection (5), electronic or other equipment used by or on behalf of a person providing facilities for remote gambling—

(*a*) to store information relating to a person's participation in the gambling,

(*b*) to present, to persons who are participating or may participate in the gambling, a virtual game, virtual race or other virtual event or process by reference to which the gambling is conducted,

(*c*) to determine all or part of a result or of the effect of a result, or

(*d*) to store information relating to a result.

(5) In this Act "remote gambling equipment" does not include equipment which—

(*a*) is used by a person to take advantage of remote gambling facilities provided by another person, and

(*b*) is not provided by that other person.

[Gambling Act 2005, s 36.]

Use of premises

8–13642   37. Use of premises[1].   (1) A person commits an offence if he uses premises, or causes or permits premises to be used, to—

(*a*) operate a casino,

(*b*) provide facilities for the playing of bingo,

(*c*) make a gaming machine available for use,

(*d*) provide other facilities for gaming, or

(*e*) provide facilities for betting (whether by making or accepting bets, by acting as a betting intermediary or by providing other facilities for the making or accepting of bets).

(2) Subsection (1) does not apply in relation to the use of premises by a person if the use is authorised by a premises licence held by him.

(3) Subsection (1) does not apply in relation to the use of premises by a person if he acts in the course of a business carried on by another person who holds a premises licence authorising the use.

(4) Subsection (1) does not apply in relation to the use of a track by a person for accepting bets if the use is authorised by a premises licence (whether or not held by him).

(5) Subsection (1) does not apply in relation to the use of a casino for the provision of facilities for bingo or betting in accordance with an authorisation under section 174(3).

(6) Subsection (1) does not apply in relation to the use of premises to provide facilities which are to be used only by persons who—

(a) are acting in the course of a business, or
(b) are not on the premises.

(7) Other exceptions to subsection (1) are provided in—

(a) sections 39 and 40,
(b) section 214 (temporary use notice),
(c) sections 247, 248 and 249 (gaming machines),
(d) sections 269, 271 and 273 (clubs and miners' welfare institutes),
(e) sections 279, 282 and 283 (premises with alcohol licence),
(f) section 287 (travelling fairs),
(g) sections 289 to 292 (prize gaming),
(h) section 296 (private gaming and betting), and
(i) section 298 (non-commercial gaming).

(8) A person guilty of an offence under this section shall be liable on summary conviction to—

(a) imprisonment for a term not exceeding 51 weeks,
(b) a fine not exceeding level 5 on the standard scale, or
(c) both.

(9) In the application of subsection (8) to Scotland the reference to 51 weeks shall have effect as a reference to six months.
[Gambling Act 2005, s 37.]

---

1. For definitions of terms used in this section see s 353, post.

8–13643 38. Power to amend section 37. (1) The Secretary of State may by order amend section 37(1) so as to—

(a) add a gambling activity,
(b) remove a gambling activity, or
(c) vary the entry for a gambling activity.

(2) In subsection (1) "gambling activity" means an activity that is—

(a) a kind of gambling, or
(b) the provision of facilities for a kind of gambling.

(3) In particular, an order under subsection (1) may have the effect of applying section 37(1) to betting of the kind referred to in section 10(1) (subject to any specified exceptions).

(4) An order under subsection (1) may, in particular, make consequential amendment of—

(a) section 150;
(b) another provision of Part 8;
(c) any provision of this Act, or of another enactment, that relates to Part 8.
[Gambling Act 2005, s 38.]

8–13644 39. Exception: occasional use notice. (1) A person who accepts bets on a track, or who causes or permits premises to be used for the acceptance of bets, does not commit an offence under section 37 if—

(a) a notice has been given under this section in respect of the track, and
(b) the activity is carried on in accordance with the notice.

(2) A notice under this section (an "occasional use notice") in respect of a track may be given only by a person who is—

(a) responsible for the administration of events on the track, or
(b) an occupier of the track.

(3) An occasional use notice must—

(a) be given in writing to the licensing authority for any area in which the track is wholly or partly situated, and
(b) be copied to either—

(i) in England and Wales, the chief officer of police for any area in which the track is wholly or partly situated, or
(ii) in Scotland, the chief constable of the police force maintained for the police area comprising that area.

(4) An occasional use notice must specify a day on which it has effect.

(5) An occasional use notice may not be given in respect of a track for a day in a calendar year if eight occasional use notices have been given in respect of that track for days in that year.

(6) In this section—

(a) "chief officer of police" has the meaning given by section 101(1) of the Police Act 1996 (c 16), and

(b) a reference to a chief officer's area is a reference to the area in respect of which he has responsibility under that Act.

(7) The Secretary of State may by order amend subsection (5) so as to substitute a different maximum number of occasional use notices for a calendar year.

(8) An order under subsection (7) increasing the maximum number of occasional use notices for a calendar year may also make provision prohibiting the giving of a temporary use notice in a calendar year in respect of premises if a specified number of occasional use notices have been given in respect of the premises in that year.

[Gambling Act 2005, s 39.]

8–13645   40. Exception: football pools.   (1) A person does not commit an offence under section 37 if he uses premises to do anything in accordance with an authorisation under section 93(3).

(2) The Secretary of State may make regulations disapplying subsection (1) to specified classes of premises.

[Gambling Act 2005, s 40.]

Miscellaneous offences

8–13646   41. Gambling software.   (1) A person commits an offence if in the course of a business he manufactures, supplies, installs or adapts gambling software unless he acts in accordance with an operating licence.

(2) In this Act "gambling software"—

(a) means computer software for use in connection with remote gambling[1], but

(b) does not include anything for use solely in connection with a gaming machine[2].

(3) A person does not supply or install gambling software for the purposes of subsection (1) by reason only of the facts that—

(a) he makes facilities for remote communication or non-remote communication available to another person, and

(b) the facilities are used by the other person to supply or install gambling software.

(4) A person guilty of an offence under this section shall be liable on summary conviction to—

(a) imprisonment for a term not exceeding 51 weeks,

(b) a fine not exceeding level 5 on the standard scale, or

(c) both.

(5) In the application of subsection (4) to Scotland the reference to 51 weeks shall have effect as a reference to six months.

[Gambling Act 2005, s 41.]

---

1. Defined in s 4, ante.
2. Defined in s 235, post.

8–13647   42. Cheating.   (1) A person commits an offence if he—

(a) cheats at gambling, or

(b) does anything for the purpose of enabling or assisting another person to cheat at gambling.

(2) For the purposes of subsection (1) it is immaterial whether a person who cheats—

(a) improves his chances of winning anything, or

(b) wins anything.

(3) Without prejudice to the generality of subsection (1) cheating at gambling may, in particular, consist of actual or attempted deception or interference in connection with—

(a) the process by which gambling is conducted, or

(b) a real or virtual game, race or other event or process to which gambling relates.

(4) A person guilty of an offence under this section shall be liable—

(a) on conviction on indictment, to imprisonment for a term not exceeding two years, to a fine or to both, or

(b) on summary conviction, to imprisonment for a term not exceeding 51 weeks, to a fine not exceeding the statutory maximum or to both[1].

(5) In the application of subsection (4) to Scotland the reference to 51 weeks shall have effect as a reference to six months.

(6) Section 17 of the Gaming Act 1845 (c 109) (winning by cheating) shall cease to have effect.
[Gambling Act 2005, s 42.]

---

1. For procedure in respect of an offence triable either way, see the Magistrates' Courts Act 1980, ss 17A–21, in PART 1: MAGISTRATES' COURTS PROCEDURE, ante.

8–13648   **43. Chain-gift schemes.**   (1) A person commits an offence if he—

(*a*) invites another to join a chain-gift scheme, or
(*b*) knowingly participates in the promotion, administration or management of a chain-gift scheme.

(2) An arrangement is a "chain-gift" scheme if—

(*a*) in order to participate in the arrangement a person must make a payment to one or more other participants (a "joining fee"), and
(*b*) each person who participates in the arrangement—

     (i) is required or invited to invite others to participate, and
     (ii) is encouraged to believe that he will receive the joining fees, or part of the joining fees, of other participants, to an amount in excess of the joining fee paid by him.

(3) For the purposes of subsection (2)—

(*a*) "payment" means a payment of money or money's worth, but does not include the provision of goods or services, and
(*b*) it is immaterial whether a payment is made directly or through a person responsible for managing or administering the scheme.

(4) A person guilty of an offence under this section shall be liable on summary conviction to—

(*a*) imprisonment for a period not exceeding 51 weeks,
(*b*) a fine not exceeding level 5 on the standard scale, or
(*c*) both.

(5) In the application of subsection (4) to Scotland or Northern Ireland the reference to 51 weeks shall have effect as a reference to six months.
[Gambling Act 2005, s 43.]

8–13649   **44. Provision of unlawful facilities abroad.**   (1) A person commits an offence if he does anything in Great Britain, or uses remote gambling equipment situated in Great Britain, for the purpose of inviting or enabling a person in a prohibited territory to participate in remote gambling.

(2) In subsection (1) "prohibited territory" means a country or place designated for the purpose of this section by order made by the Secretary of State.

(3) An order under subsection (2) shall prescribe the mode of trial and maximum penalty for an offence under subsection (1).
[Gambling Act 2005, s 44.]

PART 4[1]
PROTECTION OF CHILDREN AND YOUNG PERSONS

Interpretation

8–13650   **45. Meaning of "child" and "young person".**   (1) In this Act "child" means an individual who is less than 16 years old.

(2) In this Act "young person" means an individual who is not a child but who is less than 18 years old.
[Gambling Act 2005, s 45.]

---

1. Part 4 contains ss 45–64.

Principal offences

8–13651   **46. Invitation to gamble[1].**   (1) A person commits an offence if he invites, causes or permits a child or young person to gamble.

(2) But subsection (1) does not apply in relation to—

(*a*) participation in private or non-commercial gaming,
(*b*) participation in private or non-commercial betting,
(*c*) participation in a lottery,
(*d*) participation in football pools,
(*e*) the use of a Category D gaming machine,
(*f*) participation in equal chance gaming in accordance with a prize gaming permit,
(*g*) participation in equal chance gaming at a licensed family entertainment centre,
(*h*) participation in prize gaming at a non-licensed family entertainment centre, or
(*i*) participation in prize gaming at a travelling fair in accordance with section 292.

(3) In subsection (1) a reference to inviting a child or young person to gamble includes, in particular, a reference to intentionally—

    (*a*)   sending to a child or young person any document which advertises gambling, or

    (*b*)   bringing to the attention of a child or young person information about gambling with a view to encouraging the child or young person to gamble.

(4) If a document which is sent to a child or young person and which advertises gambling gives the name or contact details of a person to whom payment may be made or from whom information may be obtained, that person shall be treated as having committed the offence under subsection (1) unless he proves that the document was sent—

    (*a*)   without his consent, and

    (*b*)   without his authority.

(5) If information about gambling is brought to the attention of a child or young person and includes the name or contact details of a person to whom payment may be made or from whom information may be obtained, that person ("the advertiser") shall be treated as having committed the offence under subsection (1) unless he proves that the information was brought to the attention of the child or young person—

    (*a*)   without the advertiser's consent or authority, or

    (*b*)   as an incident of the information being brought to the attention of adults and without a view to encouraging the child or young person to gamble.

(6) In subsections (4) and (5) "contact details" means—

    (*a*)   an address or other location,

    (*b*)   a telephone number,

    (*c*)   an internet site, or

    (*d*)   an email address.

[Gambling Act 2005, s 46.]

---

1. For definitions of terms used in this section see s 353, post.

8–13652   **47. Invitation to enter premises**[1].   (1) A person commits an offence if he invites or permits a child or young person to enter premises if—

    (*a*)   a casino premises licence has effect in respect of the premises, and

    (*b*)   the premises are being used in reliance on that licence when the child or young person is invited or permitted to enter.

(2) But subsection (1) does not apply where—

    (*a*)   a child or young person is permitted to enter a part of premises which are being used for a regional casino, and

    (*b*)   that part is not being used for the provision of facilities for gambling when the child or young person is permitted to enter.

(3) The Secretary of State may for the purposes of subsection (2) by regulations make provision for—

    (*a*)   distinguishing between one part of premises and another;

    (*b*)   determining when use is being made of a part of premises.

(4) A person commits an offence if he invites or permits a child or young person to enter premises other than a track if—

    (*a*)   a betting premises licence has effect in respect of the premises, and

    (*b*)   the premises are being used in reliance on that licence when the child or young person is invited or permitted to enter.

(5) A person commits an offence if he invites or permits a child or young person to enter premises if—

    (*a*)   an adult gaming centre premises licence has effect in respect of the premises, and

    (*b*)   the premises are being used in reliance on that licence when the child or young person is invited or permitted to enter.

(6) A person commits an offence if he invites or permits a child or young person to enter an area from which children and young persons are required to be excluded by virtue of section 182.

(7) A person commits an offence if he invites or permits a child or young person to enter part of premises if—

    (*a*)   the premises are a licensed family entertainment centre,

    (*b*)   a person entering that part of the premises has access to a Category C gaming machine, and

    (*c*)   at the time when the child or young person is permitted or invited to enter, a Category C gaming machine is being used or is available for use.

[Gambling Act 2005, s 47.]

1. For definitions of terms used in this section see s 353, post.

8–13653 48. Gambling[1]. (1) A young person commits an offence if he gambles.

(2) But subsection (1) does not apply to—

(a) participation in private or non-commercial gaming,

(b) participation in private or non-commercial betting,

(c) participation in a lottery,

(d) participation in football pools,

(e) the use of a Category D gaming machine,

(f) participation in equal chance gaming in accordance with a prize gaming permit,

(g) participation in equal chance gaming at a licensed family entertainment centre,

(h) participation in prize gaming at a non-licensed family entertainment centre, or

(i) participation in prize gaming at a travelling fair in accordance with section 292.

[Gambling Act 2005, s 48.]

1. For definitions of terms used in this section see s 353, post.

8–13654 49. Entering premises. A young person commits an offence if he enters premises in circumstances where a person would commit an offence under section 47 if he invited or permitted the young person to enter.

[Gambling Act 2005, s 49.]

8–13655 50. Provision of facilities for gambling[1]. (1) A young person commits an offence if he provides facilities for gambling.

(2) But subsection (1) does not apply to the provision of facilities in connection with—

(a) private or non-commercial gaming,

(b) private or non-commercial betting,

(c) a lottery,

(d) football pools, or

(e) prize gaming at a travelling fair in accordance with section 292.

[Gambling Act 2005, s 50.]

1. For definitions of terms used in this section see s 353, post.

Employment offences

8–13656 51. Employment to provide facilities for gambling[1]. (1) A person commits an offence if he employs a child or young person to provide facilities for gambling.

(2) But subsection (1) does not apply to the provision of facilities in connection with—

(a) private or non-commercial gaming,

(b) private or non-commercial betting,

(c) a lottery,

(d) football pools, or

(e) prize gaming at a travelling fair in accordance with section 292.

[Gambling Act 2005, s 51.]

1. For definitions of terms used in this section see s 353, post.

8–13657 52. Employment for lottery or football pools[1]. A person commits an offence if he employs a child to provide facilities for gambling in connection with—

(a) a lottery (other than a lottery which forms part of the National Lottery), or

(b) football pools.

[Gambling Act 2005, s 52.]

1. For definitions of terms used in this section see s 353, post.

8–13658 53. Employment on bingo and club premises[1]. A person commits an offence if he employs a child to perform any function on premises where, and at a time when—

(a) facilities are provided for the playing of bingo, or

(b) facilities for gambling are provided in accordance with a club gaming permit or a club machine permit.

[Gambling Act 2005, s 53.]

1. For definitions of terms used in this section see s 353, post.

8–13659   54. Employment on premises with gaming machines.   (1) A person commits an offence if—

 (a)   he employs a child or young person to perform any function on premises where a Category A, B, C or D gaming machine is situated, and

 (b)   the child or young person is or may be required in the course of his employment to perform a function in connection with the gaming machine.

 (2)   A young person commits an offence if he is employed in contravention of subsection (1).
[Gambling Act 2005, s 54.]

8–13660   55. Employment in casino, &c[1].   (1) A person commits an offence if he employs a child or young person to perform any function on premises in respect of which any of the following have effect—

 (a)   a casino premises licence,

 (b)   a betting premises licence, and

 (c)   an adult gaming centre premises licence.

 (2)   But subsection (1) does not apply—

 (a)   to employment at a time when no activity is being carried on in reliance on the premises licence, or

 (b)   to employment on a part of premises which are being used for a regional casino at a time when that part is not being used for the provision of facilities for gambling.

 (3)   The Secretary of State may for the purposes of subsection (2) by regulations make provision for—

 (a)   distinguishing between one part of premises and another;

 (b)   determining when use is being made of a part of premises.

 (4)   A young person commits an offence if he is employed in contravention of subsection (1).
[Gambling Act 2005, s 55.]

---

 1.   For definitions of terms used in this section see s 353, post.

Miscellaneous offences

8–13661   56. Invitation to participate in lottery[1].   (1) A person commits an offence if he invites, causes or permits a child to participate in a lottery other than—

 (a)   an incidental non-commercial lottery that is exempt for the purposes of section 258 by virtue of Part 1 of Schedule 11,

 (b)   a private lottery (whether a private society lottery, a work lottery or a residents' lottery) that is exempt for the purposes of section 258 by virtue of Part 2 of Schedule 11, or

 (c)   a lottery which forms part of the National Lottery.

 (2)   Subsections (3) to (6) of section 46 shall have effect in relation to subsection (1) of this section as they have effect in relation to subsection (1) of that section; and for that purpose—

 (a)   references to a child or young person shall be treated as references only to a child, and

 (b)   references to gambling shall be treated as references to participation in a lottery.
[Gambling Act 2005, s 56.]

---

 1.   For definitions of terms used in this section see s 353, post.

8–13662   57. Invitation to participate in football pools[1].   (1) A person commits an offence if he invites, causes or permits a child to participate in football pools.

 (2)   Subsections (3) to (6) of section 46 shall have effect in relation to subsection (1) of this section as they have effect in relation to subsection (1) of that section; and for that purpose—

 (a)   references to a child or young person shall be treated as references only to a child, and

 (b)   references to gambling shall be treated as references to participation in football pools.
[Gambling Act 2005, s 57.]

---

 1.   For definitions of terms used in this section see s 353, post.

8–13663   58. Return of stake.   A person commits an offence if without reasonable excuse he fails to comply with a condition attached to an operating licence by virtue of section 83.
[Gambling Act 2005, s 58.]

8–13664   59. Age limit for Category D gaming machines.   (1) The Secretary of State may by order create an offence of inviting, causing or permitting a child or young person below a specified age to use a Category D gaming machine.

 (2)   An order under subsection (1) may, in particular—

(*a*) apply (with modifications) or include provision similar to section 46(3) to (6);

(*b*) make consequential amendments of this Act.

(3) *Requirement to consult.*

(4) An order under subsection (1) may apply to a class of Category D gaming machine determined by reference to—

(*a*) the nature of the facilities for gambling which are made available on the machine,

(*b*) the nature or value of a prize offered by the machine,

(*c*) the manner in which the machine operates, or

(*d*) any other matter.

[Gambling Act 2005, s 59.]

General

8–13665 60. Temporary use notice.   (1) For the purposes of this Part—

(*a*) a temporary use notice in respect of the use of premises to carry on an activity shall be treated as if it were a premises licence authorising that activity, and

(*b*) an occasional use notice in respect of premises shall be treated as if it were a betting premises licence.

(2) Sections 47(6) and 182 shall apply in relation to a notice treated as a premises licence by virtue of subsection (1) above.

[Gambling Act 2005, s 60.]

8–13666 61. Employment.   (1) In this Part a reference to employing a person includes a reference to—

(*a*) employing or engaging the person whether or not under a contract of employment, and

(*b*) causing or permitting the person to be employed or engaged.

(2) Where a person commits an offence under this Part by employing a person or by being employed, he shall be treated as committing the offence on each day during any part of which the employment continues.

[Gambling Act 2005, s 61.]

8–13667 62. Penalty.   (1) A person guilty of an offence under this Part shall be liable on summary conviction to—

(*a*) imprisonment for a term not exceeding 51 weeks,

(*b*) a fine not exceeding level 5 on the standard scale, or

(*c*) both.

(2) But in relation to an offence committed by a young person subsection (1) shall have effect as if—

(*a*) paragraphs (*a*) and (*c*) were omitted, and

(*b*) in paragraph (*b*) the reference to level 5 were a reference to level 3.

(3) In the application of subsection (1) to Scotland the reference to 51 weeks shall have effect as a reference to six months.

[Gambling Act 2005, s 62.]

8–13668 63. Reasonable belief about person's age.   (1) Where a person is charged with an offence under this Part of doing anything in relation to an individual who is a child it is a defence for the person charged to prove that—

(*a*) he took all reasonable steps to determine the individual's age, and

(*b*) he reasonably believed that the individual was not a child.

(2) Where a person is charged with an offence under this Part of doing anything in relation to an individual who is a young person it is a defence for the person charged to prove that—

(*a*) he took all reasonable steps to determine the individual's age, and

(*b*) he reasonably believed that the individual was not a young person.

[Gambling Act 2005, s 63.]

8–13669 64. Use of children in enforcement operations.   (1) Nothing in this Part renders unlawful—

(*a*) anything done, in the performance of his functions, by a constable, an enforcement officer or an authorised person, or

(*b*) anything done by a child or young person at the request of a constable, enforcement officer or authorised person acting in the performance of his functions.

(2) Subsection (1) applies to an order under section 59 as to the provisions of this Part.

[Gambling Act 2005, s 64.]

PART 5[1]
OPERATING LICENCES

Introductory

8–13670   65. Nature of licence.   (1) The Commission may issue operating licences in accordance with the provisions of this Part.

(2) An operating licence is a licence which states that it authorises the licensee—

(*a*)   to operate a casino (a "casino operating licence"),

(*b*)   to provide facilities for playing bingo (a "bingo operating licence"),

(*c*)   to provide facilities for betting other than pool betting (a "general betting operating licence"),

(*d*)   to provide facilities for pool betting (a "pool betting operating licence"),

(*e*)   to act as a betting intermediary (a "betting intermediary operating licence"),

(*f*)   to make gaming machines available for use in an adult gaming centre (a "gaming machine general operating licence" for an adult gaming centre),

(*g*)   to make gaming machines available for use in a family entertainment centre (a "gaming machine general operating licence" for a family entertainment centre),

(*h*)   to manufacture, supply, install, adapt, maintain or repair a gaming machine, or a part of a gaming machine (a "gaming machine technical operating licence"),

(*i*)   to manufacture, supply, install or adapt gambling software (a "gambling software operating licence"), or

(*j*)   to promote a lottery (a "lottery operating licence").

(3) The issue of an operating licence does not affect the application of section 37.

(4) The Secretary of State may by order amend subsection (2) so as to—

(*a*)   add a kind of operating licence,

(*b*)   remove a kind of operating licence, or

(*c*)   vary a kind of operating licence.

(5) An order under subsection (4) may, in particular, make consequential amendment of this Part (or a provision of this Act or another enactment that relates to this Part).
[Gambling Act 2005, s 65.]

---

1. Part 5 contains ss 65–126. Sections 65(2); 75(1) and (2); 76(1)–(3); and 79 and 80 (partly) are in force: see Gambling Act 2005 (Commencement No 2 and Transitional Provisions) Order 2005, SI 2005/2455.

8–13671   66. Form of licence.   (1) An operating licence must specify—

(*a*)   the person to whom it is issued,

(*b*)   the period during which it is to have effect, and

(*c*)   any condition attached by the Commission under section 75 or 77.

(2) The Secretary of State may by regulations require the Commission to ensure that an operating licence—

(*a*)   is issued in such form as the regulations may specify, and

(*b*)   contains, in addition to the matters specified in subsection (1), such information as the regulations may specify (which may, in particular, include information about conditions attached to the licence by virtue of section 78).
[Gambling Act 2005, s 66.]

8–13672   67. Remote gambling.   (1) An operating licence is a "remote operating licence" if it authorises activity to be carried on—

(*a*)   in respect of remote gambling, or

(*b*)   by means of remote communication.

(2) A remote operating licence may not also authorise activity which is neither—

(*a*)   in respect of remote gambling, nor

(*b*)   carried on by means of remote communication.

(3) An operating licence must state whether it is a remote operating licence or not.
[Gambling Act 2005, s 67.]

8–13673   68. Combined licence.   (1) An operating licence may be a licence of more than one of the kinds described in section 65(2).

(2) Subsection (1) is subject to the following provisions of this section.

(3) A casino operating licence authorises the holder, by virtue of this subsection, to provide facilities—

(*a*)   for betting on the outcome of a virtual game, race, competition or other event or process, subject to any exclusion or restriction provided for by way of condition under section 75 or 77;

(b) for any game of chance other than bingo (and this paragraph does not prevent the combination of a casino operating licence and a bingo operating licence in reliance on subsection (1)).

(4) A general betting operating licence authorises the holder, by virtue of this subsection, to provide facilities for betting on the outcome of a virtual race, competition or other event or process other than a game of chance, subject to any exclusion or restriction provided for by way of condition under section 75 or 77.

(5) The following kinds of operating licence authorise the holder, by virtue of this subsection, to make one or more gaming machines within Categories A to D available for use (in addition to authorising the activities specified in accordance with section 65(2))—

(a) a non-remote casino operating licence,

(b) a non-remote bingo operating licence,

(c) a non-remote general betting operating licence, and

(d) a non-remote pool betting operating licence.

(6) No other kind of operating licence (other than a gaming machine general operating licence) may authorise the holder to make a gaming machine available for use.
[Gambling Act 2005, s 68.]

8–13674 74. Determination of application.   (1) On considering an application under section 69 the Commission shall—

(a) grant it,

(b) reject it, or

(c) grant it in respect of one or more of the activities specified in accordance with section 69(2)(a) and reject it in respect of the others.

(2) Where the Commission grants an application in whole or in part it shall as soon as is reasonably practicable—

(a) notify the applicant of the grant, and

(b) issue an operating licence to the applicant.

(3) Where the Commission rejects an application in whole or in part it shall as soon as is reasonably practicable notify the applicant of—

(a) the rejection, and

(b) the reasons for it.
[Gambling Act 2005, s 74.]

Conditions

8–13675 75. General conditions imposed by Commission.   (1) The Commission may specify conditions to be attached to—

(a) each operating licence, or

(b) each operating licence falling within a specified class.

(2) For the purposes of subsection (1)(b) a class may be defined wholly or partly by reference to—

(a) the nature of the licensed activities;

(b) the circumstances in which the licensed activities are carried on;

(c) the nature or circumstances of the licensee or of another person involved or likely to be involved in the conduct of the licensed activities.

(3) Where the Commission issues an operating licence it shall attach to the licence any condition specified under subsection (1) as a condition to be attached to operating licences of a class within which the licence falls.
[Gambling Act 2005, s 75.]

8–13676 77. Individual condition imposed by Commission.   Where the Commission issues an operating licence it may attach a condition to the licence.
[Gambling Act 2005, s 77.]

8–13677 78. Condition imposed by Secretary of State.   (1) The Secretary of State may by regulations provide for a specified condition to be attached to operating licences falling within a specified description.

(2) Transitional provision of regulations under this section (made by virtue of section 355(1)(c)) may, in particular, apply a condition (with or without modification) to licences issued before the regulations are made (or come into force).
[Gambling Act 2005, s 78.]

8–13678 84. Premises.   (1) An operating licence—

(a) may not include a condition (whether attached by virtue of section 75, 77 or 78)—

(i) requiring that the licensed activities be carried on at a specified place or class of place,

(ii) preventing the licensed activities from being carried on at a specified place or class of place, or

(iii) specifying premises on which the licensed activities may be carried on, but

(b) may include a condition about—

(i) the number of sets of premises on which the licensed activities may be carried on;

(ii) the number of persons for whom facilities may be provided on any premises where the licensed activities are carried on.

(2) An operating licence of any kind may authorise activities carried on in more than one place.
[Gambling Act 2005, s 84.]

8–13679 85. Equipment. (1) A condition attached to an operating licence by virtue of section 75, 77 or 78 may make provision about equipment used in connection with the licensed activities.

(2) In particular, a condition attached by virtue of this section may—

(a) make provision about the number of pieces of equipment, other than equipment for playing bingo, that may be used to provide facilities for gambling;

(b) make provision about the specification of equipment used to provide facilities for gambling.

(3) For the purposes of this section "equipment" includes—

(a) a computer,

(b) a device for the playing of a casino game, and

(c) any other piece of equipment.

(4) But a gaming machine is not equipment for the purposes of this section.
[Gambling Act 2005, s 85.]

8–13680 86. Gaming machines. (1) An operating licence may not include a condition (whether attached by virtue of section 75, 77 or 78)—

(a) about the number or categories of gaming machine that may be made available for use in accordance with the licence,

(b) that contradicts a provision of regulations under section 236, 240 or 241, or

(c) of a kind prohibited by regulations under any of those sections.

(2) An operating licence may be subject to a condition (whether imposed by virtue of section 75, 77 or 78) that a specified gaming machine may not be made available for use in reliance on the licence if the Commission has notified the licensee in writing that the manufacture, supply, installation, adaptation, maintenance or repair of the machine—

(a) was not carried out in reliance on a gaming machine technical operating licence, or

(b) did not comply with standards established under or by virtue of section 96.
[Gambling Act 2005, s 86.]

8–13681 87. Membership. An operating licence may not be subject to a condition (whether by virtue of section 75, 77 or 78)—

(a) requiring facilities to be provided by, or used in the course of the activities of, a club or other body with membership, or

(b) restricting the provision or use of facilities wholly or partly by reference to membership of a club or other body.
[Gambling Act 2005, s 87.]

8–13682 88. Information. (1) A condition attached to an operating licence by virtue of section 75 or 78 may require the provision of information of a specified kind to—

(a) the Commission, or

(b) another specified person or class of person.

(2) A condition attached by virtue of this section may, in particular—

(a) relate to information about the use made of facilities provided in accordance with the operating licence;

(b) require a person to provide any information that he suspects may—

(i) relate to the commission of an offence under this Act,

(ii) relate to a breach of a rule applied by a sporting or other body, or

(iii) lead to the making of an order under section 336.
[Gambling Act 2005, s 88.]

Rules for particular kinds of licence

8–13683 89. Remote operating licence. (1) This section applies to a remote operating licence[1].

(2) A remote operating licence shall, by virtue of this subsection, be subject to the condition that

remote gambling equipment used by the licensee in connection with the licensed activities must be situated in Great Britain.

(3) Where the Commission issues a remote operating licence it may exclude, generally or to a specified extent or for specified purposes, the condition that would otherwise be attached by virtue of subsection (2), if the Commission is satisfied that the exclusion is reasonably consistent with pursuit of the licensing objectives.

(4) The Commission may establish, or provide for the establishment of, standards in respect of—

(a) a system used for the generation of results in a virtual game, virtual race or other virtual event or process used in the course of remote gambling;

(b) any other aspect of the process of remote gambling.

(5) In particular, the Commission may—

(a) provide for the enforcement of standards by the attachment of conditions under section 75 or 77;

(b) make arrangements with any person for the establishment of standards;

(c) make arrangements with any person for the administration of tests of compliance with standards;

(d) for the purpose of considering whether a condition under section section 75 or 77 has been complied with, require the licensee under a remote licence—

    (i) to submit to a test in accordance with arrangements made under paragraph (c) above, and

    (ii) to produce specified evidence of the result of the test;

(e) for the purpose of considering whether to grant an application under this Part, require a licensee under a remote licence or an applicant for a remote licence—

    (i) to submit to a test in accordance with arrangements made under paragraph (c) above, and

    (ii) to produce specified evidence of the result of the test.

(6) Standards established under subsection (5) may, in particular, be expressed—

(a) by reference to the opinion of a specified person or class of persons;

(b) by reference to a specified process or piece of equipment.

(7) This section is without prejudice to the generality of sections 75, 77 and 78.
[Gambling Act 2005, s 89.]

---

1. Defined in s 67, ante.

8–13684 90. Casino operating licence. (1) A casino[1] operating licence may be subject to a condition (whether imposed by virtue of section 75, 77 or 78) restricting the class of casino game that may be made available.

(2) A casino operating licence may be subject to a condition imposed by virtue of section 75 or 77 specifying rules for the playing of—

(a) a casino game;

(b) another game of chance.
[Gambling Act 2005, s 90.]

---

1. Defined in s 7, ante.

8–13685 91. Bingo operating licence. (1) Regulations under section 78 may provide for the attachment to a bingo operating licence of a condition—

(a) limiting amounts that may be staked;

(b) limiting the amount that may be charged by way of participation fee;

(c) limiting the amount or value of a prize or class of prize;

(d) requiring that at least a specified proportion of stakes be paid out by way of prizes;

(e) imposing requirements that are specific to games of bingo played on more than one set of premises (whether facilities for the game are provided in accordance with one bingo operating licence or more than one).

(2) But subject to subsection (1) a bingo operating licence may not be subject to a condition—

(a) limiting the amount that may be accepted or charged by way of stakes,

(b) limiting the amount that may be charged by way of participation fee,

(c) restricting the nature, amount or value of prizes,

(d) controlling the proportion of stakes paid out by way of prizes,

(e) preventing the provision of prizes funded other than out of stakes,

(f) preventing or limiting an arrangement whereby the fact that a prize is not won or claimed in one game of bingo increases the value of the prizes available in another game of bingo,

(g) requiring a game of bingo to be played entirely on one set of premises, or (*h*) imposing requirements that are specific to games of bingo played on more than one set of premises (whether facilities for the game are provided in accordance with one bingo operating licence or more than one).

(3) Regulations by virtue of subsection (1)(*b*) may, in particular, make different provision for different kinds of fee.

(4) Provision made by virtue of subsection (1)(*c*) may define a class of prize—

(*a*) by reference to a game or a number of games,

(*b*) by reference to a period of time, or

(*c*) in any other way.

[Gambling Act 2005, s 91.]

8–13686   92. General betting[1] operating licence.   (1) A general betting operating licence shall, by virtue of this section, be subject to the condition that bets may be accepted on behalf of the licensee only by—

(*a*) the licensee,

(*b*) a person employed by the licensee under a written contract of employment, or

(*c*) the holder of another general betting operating licence.

(2) A general betting operating licence shall, by virtue of this subsection, contain an implied term permitting the use of postal services for the making of bets.

(3) The effect of the term implied by subsection (2) may not be disapplied or restricted by a condition attached under section 75, 77 or 78.

[Gambling Act 2005, s 92.]

---

1. Betting has the meaning given to it by ss 9–11, 37 and 150: see s 353, post.

8–13687   93. Pool betting[1] operating licence.   (1) A pool betting operating licence shall, by virtue of this section, be subject to the condition that bets may be accepted on behalf of the licensee only—

(*a*) by the licensee,

(*b*) by a person employed by the licensee under a written contract of employment,

(*c*) by the holder of another pool betting operating licence, or

(*d*) in accordance with subsection (2) or (3).

(2) A bet is accepted by a person ("the agent") on behalf of a licensee in accordance with this subsection if—

(*a*) the agent is authorised by the licensee in writing to accept bets on behalf of the licensee,

(*b*) the agent is an adult,

(*c*) at the time of accepting the bet the agent is on a track,

(*d*) the bet is accepted in reliance on an occasional use notice, and

(*e*) the bet is in connection with a horse-race or a dog race.

(3) The holder of a pool betting operating licence that authorises (whether expressly or impliedly) the provision of facilities for football pools may in writing authorise an adult or young person—

(*a*) to make documents or other facilities available in connection with the licensed activities;

(*b*) to receive entries on behalf of the licensee;

(*c*) to receive payments on behalf of the licensee;

(*d*) to make payments of winnings on behalf of the licensee.

(4) An authorisation under subsection (3)—

(*a*) shall be treated for the purposes of section 33 as if it were a pool betting operating licence, but

(*b*) shall have no effect in relation to any activity, entry or payment that relates partly to a football pool and partly to another form of gambling.

(5) An authorisation under subsection (3) may be issued on terms and conditions which may, in particular, include—

(*a*) provision for payment by the person issuing the authorisation;

(*b*) provision for commission.

(6) A condition of a pool betting operating licence (whether attached by virtue of section 75, 77 or 78) may make provision regulating or restricting the activities of persons authorised under subsection (3).

(7) A pool betting operating licence shall, by virtue of this subsection, contain an implied term permitting the use of postal services for the making of bets.

(8) The effect of the term implied by subsection (7) may not be disapplied or restricted by a condition attached under section 75, 77 or 78.

(9) The Secretary of State may by order—

(*a*) amend or repeal subsection (2)(*e*);

(*b*) amend subsection (3) so as to permit authorisation in relation to betting of a specified kind that relates to a sport but is not a football pool.

[Gambling Act 2005, s 93.]

---

1. Defined in s 12, ante.

8–13688 94. Horse-race pool betting[1] operating licence. (1) This section applies to a pool betting operating licence which provides for this section to apply.

(2) The holder of a licence to which this section applies may in writing authorise a person to provide facilities for horse-race pool betting.

(3) An authorisation under subsection (2) shall be treated for the purposes of section 33 as if it were a pool betting operating licence authorising the provision of facilities for horse-race pool betting.

(4) An authorisation under subsection (2) may be issued on terms and conditions which may, in particular, include—

(*a*) provision for payment to or by the person issuing the authorisation;

(*b*) provision for agency or commission.

(5) A condition of a pool betting operating licence to which this section applies (whether attached by virtue of section 75, 77 or 78) may make provision regulating or restricting the activities of persons authorised under subsection (2).

(6) A pool betting operating licence to which this section applies shall, by virtue of this subsection, contain an implied term permitting the use of postal services for the making of bets.

(7) The effect of the term implied by subsection (6) may not be disapplied or restricted by a condition attached under section 75, 77 or 78.

(8) The Secretary of State may by order repeal this section.

[Gambling Act 2005, s 94.]

---

1. Defined in s 12, ante.

8–13689 95. Betting on the National Lottery. (1) This section applies to—

(*a*) a general betting operating licence,

(*b*) a pool betting operating licence, and

(*c*) a betting intermediary operating licence.

(2) A licence to which this section applies shall, by virtue of this subsection, be subject to the condition that nothing may be done in reliance on the licence in relation to a bet on the outcome of a lottery which forms part of the National Lottery.

[Gambling Act 2005, s 95.]

8–13690 98. Lottery[1] operating licences. (1) A lottery operating licence may be issued only to—

(*a*) a non-commercial society,

(*b*) a local authority, or

(*c*) a person proposing to act as external lottery manager on behalf of a non-commercial society or a local authority.

(2) A lottery operating licence may authorise—

(*a*) promotion generally or only specified promoting activities;

(*b*) the promotion of lotteries generally or only the promotion of lotteries of a specified kind or in specified circumstances;

(*c*) action as an external lottery manager (in which case it is known as a "lottery manager's operating licence").

(3) In issuing a lottery operating licence to a society or authority the Commission—

(*a*) may attach a condition under section 75 or 77 requiring that the society or authority ensure that all the arrangements for the lottery are made by the holder of a lottery manager's operating licence, and

(*b*) may, if they attach a condition under paragraph (*a*), issue the lottery licence to the society or authority without consideration of the matters specified in section 70(1)(*b*).

(4) A lottery operating licence shall, by virtue of this subsection, permit the delivery of lottery tickets by post.

(5) The effect of the term implied by subsection (4) may not be disapplied or restricted by a condition attached under section 75, 77 or 78.

(6) In issuing a lottery operating licence the Commission may attach a condition under section 75 or 77 preventing, restricting or controlling the use of a rollover.

(7) In this section "local authority" means—

(*a*) in relation to England—

(i) a district council,

(ii)　a county council,
(iii)　a parish council,
(iv)　a London borough council,
(v)　the Common Council of the City of London, and
(vi)　the Council of the Isles of Scilly,

(b)　in relation to Wales—

(i)　a county council,
(ii)　a county borough council, and
(iii)　a community council, and

(c)　in relation to Scotland, a council constituted under section 2 of the Local Government etc (Scotland) Act 1994 (c 39).

[Gambling Act 2005, s 98.]

1.　Defined in s 14, ante.

8–13691　99. Mandatory conditions of lottery operating licence.　(1) In issuing a lottery operating licence to a non-commercial society or to a local authority the Commission shall attach conditions under section 75 or 77 for the purpose of achieving the requirements specified in this section.

(2)　The first requirement is that at least 20% of the proceeds of any lottery promoted in reliance on the licence are applied—

(a)　in the case of a licence issued to a non-commercial society, to a purpose for which the promoting society is conducted, and

(b)　in the case of a licence issued to a local authority, for a purpose for which the authority has power to incur expenditure.

(3)　The second requirement is that—

(a)　the proceeds of any lottery promoted in reliance on the licence may not exceed £2,000,000, and

(b)　the aggregate of the proceeds of lotteries promoted wholly or partly in a calendar year in reliance on the licence may not exceed £10,000,000.

(4)　The third requirement is that it must not be possible for the purchaser of a ticket in a lottery promoted in reliance on the licence to win by virtue of that ticket (whether in money, money's worth, or partly the one and partly the other) more than—

(a)　£25,000, or

(b)　if more, 10% of the proceeds of the lottery;

and any rollover must comply with this subsection.

(5)　The fourth requirement is that where a person purchases a lottery ticket in a lottery promoted by a non-commercial society in reliance on the licence he receives a document which—

(a)　identifies the promoting society,

(b)　states the name and address of a member of the society who is designated, by persons acting on behalf of the society, as having responsibility within the society for the promotion of the lottery, and

(c)　either—

(i)　states the date of the draw (or each draw) in the lottery, or

(ii)　enables the date of the draw (or each draw) in the lottery to be determined.

(6)　The fifth requirement is that the price payable for purchasing each ticket in a lottery promoted in reliance on the licence—

(a)　must be the same,

(b)　must be shown on the ticket or in a document received by the purchaser, and

(c)　must be paid to the promoter of the lottery before any person is given a ticket or any right in respect of membership of the class among whom prizes are to be allocated.

(7)　For the purpose of subsections (5) and (6) a reference to a person receiving a document includes, in particular, a reference to a message being sent or displayed to him electronically in a manner which enables him, without incurring significant expense or delay, to—

(a)　retain the message electronically, or

(b)　print it.

(8)　The sixth requirement is that membership of the class among whom prizes in any lottery promoted in reliance on the licence are allocated may not be dependent on making any payment (apart from payment of the price of a ticket).

(9)　Where—

(a)　conditions are attached to a lottery operating licence in accordance with this section, and

(b) the lottery operating licence is also subject to a condition under section 98(3)(a) requiring arrangements for the lottery to be made by the holder of a lottery manager's operating licence,

the conditions specified in paragraph (a) above shall, by virtue of this subsection, attach to the lottery manager's operating licence in so far as it is relied upon in pursuance of the condition specified in paragraph (b) above.

(10) Nothing in this section prevents the Commission from attaching a condition to a lottery operating licence of a kind similar to but more onerous than a requirement of this section.

(11) The Secretary of State may by order vary a monetary amount or a percentage in this section.
[Gambling Act 2005, s 99.]

Maintenance

8–13692   100. Annual fee.   (1) The holder of an operating licence—

(a) shall pay a first annual fee to the Commission within such period after the issue of the licence as may be prescribed, and

(b) shall pay an annual fee to the Commission before each anniversary of the issue of the licence.

(2) In this section—

"annual fee" means a fee of such amount as may be prescribed, and
"prescribed" means prescribed by the Secretary of State by regulations.

(3) Regulations under this section may, in particular, make different provision for—

(a) different kinds of operating licence, or
(b) different circumstances.

(4) Subsection (1)(b) does not apply in relation to an anniversary of the issue of a licence on or immediately before which the licence ceases to have effect by virtue of section 111.
[Gambling Act 2005, s 100.]

8–13693   101. Change of circumstance.   (1) The Secretary of State may make regulations requiring the holder of an operating licence—

(a) to notify the Commission of any change of circumstance of a prescribed kind in relation to him or to a licensed activity, and
(b) to give the Commission prescribed details of the change.

(2) If a change of circumstance notified under subsection (1) falsifies information contained in the operating licence in accordance with section 66 the notification must be accompanied by—

(a) the prescribed fee, and
(b) either—

(i) the licence, or
(ii) an application to the Commission for the issue of a copy of the licence under section 107.

(3) Where notification is accompanied by the licence, the Commission shall—

(a) make such alteration to the information contained in the licence as appears to it to be required by the change in circumstance, and
(b) return the licence to the licensee.

(4) Where the notification is accompanied by an application for a copy of the licence, the Commission shall, if it grants the application, issue the copy in a form which appears to the Commission to reflect the change in circumstance.

(5) In this section "prescribed" means prescribed by regulations under this section.

(6) The holder of an operating licence commits an offence if he fails without reasonable excuse to comply with regulations under this section.

(7) A person guilty of an offence under subsection (6) shall be liable on summary conviction to a fine not exceeding level 2 on the standard scale.

(8) This section does not prevent the imposition of a requirement to notify the Commission of a specified change of circumstance by way of the attachment of a condition to an operating licence.
[Gambling Act 2005, s 101.]

8–13694   102. Change of corporate control.   (1) This section applies where the holder of an operating licence is a company limited by shares ("the company").

(2) If a person becomes a controller of the company ("the new controller"), within the meaning of section 422 of the Financial Services and Markets Act 2000 (c 8), the company shall inform the Commission and either—

(a) surrender the operating licence under section 113, or
(b) apply to the Commission under this section for a determination that the operating licence shall continue to have effect.

(3) An application under subsection (2)(b) must be accompanied by such information as the Commission may direct about—

(*a*) the new controller,
(*b*) his interest in the company, and
(*c*) his interest in any company of which the company is a subsidiary (within the meaning of section 736 of the Companies Act 1985 (c 6)).

(4) On considering an application under section (2)(*b*) the Commission shall—

(*a*) make the determination sought, if satisfied that the Commission would have granted the operating licence to the licensee had the new controller been a controller of the company when the application for the operating licence was made, and
(*b*) otherwise, revoke the operating licence.

(5) If the Commission becomes aware that a company has failed to comply with the duty under subsection (2) within the period of five weeks beginning with the day on which the duty began to apply to the company, the Commission shall revoke the relevant operating licence.
(6) But the Commission may extend the period under subsection (5)—

(*a*) before it expires, or
(*b*) after it expires (if the relevant operating licence has not yet been revoked).
[Gambling Act 2005, s 102.]

8–13695 103. Section 102: supplemental. (1) The Secretary of State may by regulations provide for section 102 not to apply to the holder of a specified description of operating licence.
(2) An application under section 102(2)(*b*) must be accompanied by the prescribed fee.
(3) An application may be made under section 102(2)(*b*) in respect of a person who is expected to become a controller of a company.
(4) The Commission shall as soon as is reasonably practicable inform an applicant under section 102(2)(*b*) of—

(*a*) the Commission's decision, and
(*b*) the reasons for it.

(5) In giving a direction under section 102(3) the Commission shall have regard to normal commercial practices in relation to the confidentiality of information.
(6) Regulations under subsection (2) above may, in particular, provide for a reduction of fee where the application is a result of—

(*a*) the merger of more than one company, or
(*b*) the division of a company.

(7) Revocation of an operating licence under section 102 shall be treated for all purposes (including the application of section 119) as revocation under section 119.
[Gambling Act 2005, s 103.]

8–13696 104. Application to vary licence. (1) The holder of an operating licence may apply to the Commission to vary the licence by—

(*a*) adding, amending or removing a licensed activity,
(*b*) amending another detail of the licence, or
(*c*) adding, amending or removing a condition attached to the licence under section 77.

(2) A licence may not be varied under this section so as to authorise anyone other than the person to whom it was issued to provide facilities for gambling.
(3) The provisions of this Part shall apply in relation to an application for variation as they apply in relation to an application for a licence—

(*a*) subject to the provisions of this section, and
(*b*) with any other necessary modifications.

(4) Regulations under this Part which relate to an application for an operating licence may make—

(*a*) provision which applies only in the case of an application for variation;
(*b*) provision which does not apply in the case of an application for variation;
(*c*) different provision in relation to an application for variation from that made in relation to an application for an operating licence;
(*d*) different provision in relation to applications for variations of different kinds.

(5) An application for variation must (in addition to anything required by section 69) be accompanied by—

(*a*) a statement of the variation sought, and
(*b*) either—

　(i) the licence to be varied, or
　(ii) a statement explaining why it is not reasonably practicable to produce the licence.

(6) In granting an application for variation the Commission—

(*a*) shall specify a time when the variation shall begin to have effect, and

(*b*) may make transitional provision.
[Gambling Act 2005, s 104.]

8–13697   105. Amendment.   (1) The Commission may require the holder of an operating licence to submit it to the Commission for the purpose of amendment to reflect—

(*a*) a general variation of conditions under section 75,
(*b*) a change notified under section 101,
(*c*) the grant of an application for variation under section 104,
(*d*) the attachment of an additional condition, or the amendment of a condition, under section 117,
(*e*) the grant of an application for renewal under section 112, or
(*f*) anything done in relation to a personal licence under Part 6.

(2) A licensee shall comply with a requirement under subsection (1) within the period of 14 days beginning with the day on which he receives notice of the requirement.

(3) A person commits an offence if he fails without reasonable excuse to comply with a requirement imposed under subsection (1).

(4) A person guilty of an offence under subsection (3) shall be liable on summary conviction to a fine not exceeding level 2 on the standard scale.

(5) Subsection (1)(*a*) is without prejudice to section 76(4)(*c*).
[Gambling Act 2005, s 105.]

8–13698   106. Register of operating licences.   (1) The Commission shall—

(*a*) maintain a register of operating licences containing such details of and relating to each licence as the Commission thinks appropriate,
(*b*) make the register available for inspection by members of the public at all reasonable times, and
(*c*) make arrangements for the provision of a copy of an entry in the register to a member of the public on request.

(2) The Commission may refuse to provide access to the register or to provide a copy of an entry unless the person seeking access or a copy pays a fee specified by the Commission.

(3) The Commission may not specify a fee under subsection (2) which exceeds the reasonable cost of providing the service sought (but in calculating the cost of providing a service to a person the Commission may include a reasonable share of expenditure which is referable only indirectly to the provision of that service).
[Gambling Act 2005, s 106.]

8–13699   107. Copy of licence.   (1) The Commission may make arrangements to issue to a licensee on request a copy of an operating licence which has been lost, stolen or damaged.

(2) The arrangements may, in particular, include a requirement—

(*a*) for the payment of a fee not exceeding such sum as may be prescribed for the purposes of this subsection by the Secretary of State by regulations;
(*b*) in the case of a licence being lost or stolen, that the licensee has complied with specified arrangements for reporting the loss or theft to the police.

(3) A copy of a licence issued under this section shall be treated as if it were the licence.
[Gambling Act 2005, s 107.]

8–13700   108. Production of licence.   (1) A constable or enforcement officer may require the holder of an operating licence to produce it to the constable or enforcement officer within a specified period.

(2) A licensee commits an offence if he fails without reasonable excuse to comply with a requirement under subsection (1).

(3) A person guilty of an offence under subsection (2) shall be liable on summary conviction to a fine not exceeding level 2 on the standard scale.
[Gambling Act 2005, s 108.]

8–13701   109. Conviction.   (1) If the holder of an operating licence is convicted of an offence by or before a court in Great Britain he shall as soon as is reasonably practicable notify the Commission of—

(*a*) his conviction, and
(*b*) any sentence passed in respect of it.

(2) If the holder of an operating licence is convicted of a relevant offence by or before a court in Great Britain he shall immediately inform the court that he is the holder of an operating licence.

(3) If the holder of an operating licence is convicted of a relevant offence by or before a court outside Great Britain he shall as soon as is reasonably practicable notify the Commission of—

(*a*) his conviction, and
(*b*) any sentence passed in respect of it.

(4) A person commits an offence if he fails without reasonable excuse to comply with any of subsections (1) to (3).

(5) A person guilty of an offence under subsection (4) shall be liable on summary conviction to a fine not exceeding level 2 on the standard scale.
[Gambling Act 2005, s 109.]

Duration

8–13702 110. Indefinite duration. An operating licence shall continue to have effect unless and until it ceases to have effect in accordance with—

(*a*) a determination under section 111, or

(*b*) section 113, 114, 115, 118 or 119.
[Gambling Act 2005, s 110.]

8–13703 111. Power to limit duration. (1) The Commission may determine that operating licences, or a specified class of operating licence, shall cease to have effect at the end of a specified period (unless terminated earlier in accordance with section 113, 114, 115 or 119).

(2) The period specified under subsection (1)—

(*a*) in the case of an operating licence issued after the determination, must begin with the date on which the licence is issued, and

(*b*) in the case of an operating licence issued before the determination, must begin with the date of the determination.

(3) The Commission—

(*a*) may determine different periods under subsection (1) for operating licences authorising different classes of activity (but may not otherwise determine different periods for different licences),

(*b*) may alter a determination under subsection (1) (but an alteration shall have effect only in relation to licences issued after the alteration), and

(*c*) may revoke a determination under subsection (1) (in which case the determination shall cease to have effect in relation to licences already issued).

(4) The Commission shall publish any determination under subsection (1) as part of a statement (or revised statement) under section 23.
[Gambling Act 2005, s 111.]

8–13704 112. Renewal of licence. (1) Where an operating licence is subject to a determination under section 111, the licensee may apply to the Commission for renewal of the licence.

(2) The provisions of this Part shall apply in relation to an application for renewal as they apply in relation to an application for a licence—

(*a*) subject to the provisions of this section, and

(*b*) with any other necessary modifications.

(3) An application for renewal of an operating licence may be made only during the period which—

(*a*) begins three months before the date on which the licence would otherwise expire by virtue of section 111, and

(*b*) ends one month before the date on which the licence would otherwise expire by virtue of that section.

(4) Where an application for renewal of an operating licence is awaiting determination on the date when it would expire by virtue of section 111, the licence shall continue to have effect by virtue of this subsection until the application is determined (unless it ceases to have effect by virtue of section 113, 114, 115, 118 or 119).

(5) A direction or regulations under this Part which relate to an application for an operating licence may make—

(*a*) provision which applies only in the case of an application for renewal;

(*b*) provision which does not apply in the case of an application for renewal;

(*c*) different provision in relation to an application for renewal from that made in relation to an application for an operating licence.

(6) An application for renewal must (in addition to anything required by section 69) be accompanied by—

(*a*) the licence to be renewed, or

(*b*) a statement explaining why it is not reasonably practicable to submit the licence to be renewed.

(7) The Commission shall determine the period during which a renewed operating licence is to have effect (subject to sections 113, 114, 115, 118 and 119); and the Commission—

(*a*) may determine different periods for operating licences authorising different classes of activity (but may not otherwise determine different periods for different licences), (*b*) may alter a determination (but an alteration shall have effect only in relation to licences issued after the alteration), and

(*c*) shall publish any determination under this subsection as part of a statement (or revised statement) under section 23.

(8) The Secretary of State may by order amend subsection (3) so as to substitute a different time for a time specified.

[Gambling Act 2005, s 112.]

8–13705   113. Surrender.   An operating licence shall cease to have effect if the licensee—

(*a*) notifies the Commission of his intention to surrender the licence, and

(*b*) gives the Commission either—

    (i) the licence, or

    (ii) a written statement explaining why it is not reasonably practicable to produce the licence.

[Gambling Act 2005, s 113.]

8–13706   114. Lapse.   (1) In the case of an operating licence issued to an individual, the licence shall lapse if—

(*a*) the licensee dies,

(*b*) the licensee becomes, in the opinion of the Commission as notified to the licensee, incapable of carrying on the licensed activities by reason of mental or physical incapacity,

(*c*) the licensee becomes bankrupt (within the meaning of section 381 of the Insolvency Act 1986 (c 45)), or

(*d*) sequestration of the licensee's estate is awarded under section 12(1) of the Bankruptcy (Scotland) Act 1985 (c 66).

(2) In any other case an operating licence shall lapse if the licensee—

(*a*) ceases to exist, or

(*b*) goes into liquidation (within the meaning of section 247(2) of the Insolvency Act 1986).

[Gambling Act 2005, s 114.]

8–13707   115. Forfeiture.   (1) Where the holder of an operating licence is convicted of a relevant offence by or before a court in Great Britain the court may order forfeiture of the licence.

(2) Forfeiture under this section shall be on such terms (which may include terms as to suspension) as may be specified by—

(*a*) the court which orders forfeiture,

(*b*) a court to which an appeal against the conviction, or against any order made on the conviction, has been or could be made, or

(*c*) the High Court, if hearing proceedings relating to the conviction.

(3) Subject to any express provision made under subsection (2), an operating licence shall cease to have effect on the making of a forfeiture order under subsection (1).

(4) The terms on which a forfeiture order is made under this section shall, in particular, include a requirement that the licensee deliver to the Commission, within such time as the order may specify—

(*a*) the licence, or

(*b*) a statement explaining why it is not reasonably practicable to produce the licence.

(5) As soon as is reasonably practicable after making an order for forfeiture under this section the court shall notify the Commission.

[Gambling Act 2005, s 115.]

Regulation

8–13708   116. Review.   (1) The Commission may in relation to operating licences of a particular description review—

(*a*) the manner in which licensees carry on licensed activities, and

(*b*) in particular, arrangements made by licensees to ensure compliance with conditions attached under section 75, 77 or 78.

(2) The Commission may review any matter connected with the provision of facilities for gambling as authorised by an operating licence if the Commission—

(*a*) has reason to suspect that activities may have been carried on in purported reliance on the licence but not in accordance with a condition of the licence,

(*b*) believes that the licensee, or a person who exercises a function in connection with or is interested in the licensed activities, has acquired a conviction of a kind mentioned in section 71(1), or

(*c*) for any reason—

    (i) suspects that the licensee may be unsuitable to carry on the licensed activities, or

    (ii) thinks that a review would be appropriate.

(3) For the purposes of subsection (2)(*c*) a reason—

(*a*) may, in particular, relate to the receipt of a complaint about the licensee's activities;
(*b*) need not relate to any suspicion or belief about the licensee's activities.

(4) Before commencing a review of an operating licence under subsection (2) the Commission shall—

(*a*) notify the licensee, and
(*b*) inform him of the procedure to be followed in the conduct of the review.

(5) In conducting a review of an operating licence under subsection (2) the Commission—

(*a*) shall give the licensee an opportunity to make representations, and
(*b*) may give other persons an opportunity to make representations.

[Gambling Act 2005, s 116.]

8–13709   117. Regulatory powers.   (1) Following a review under section 116(1) or (2) the Commission may—

(*a*) give the holder of an operating licence a warning;
(*b*) attach an additional condition to a licence under section 77;
(*c*) remove or amend a condition attached to a licence under section 77;
(*d*) make, amend or remove an exclusion under section 89(3);
(*e*) exercise the power under section 118 to suspend a licence;
(*f*) exercise the power under section 119 to revoke a licence;
(*g*) exercise the power under section 121 to impose a penalty.

(2) Where the Commission determines to take action under subsection (1) in respect of a licence it shall as soon as is reasonably practicable notify the licensee of—

(*a*) the action, and
(*b*) the Commission's reasons.

(3) In determining what action to take under subsection (1) following a review the Commission may have regard to a warning under that subsection given to the licensee following an earlier review (whether or not of that licence).

[Gambling Act 2005, s 117.]

8–13710   118. Suspension.   (1) The Commission may suspend an operating licence if following a review under section 116(1) or (2) the Commission thinks that any of the conditions specified in section 120(1) applies.

(2) The Commission may suspend an operating licence if at the time of deciding to conduct a review under section 116(1) or (2), or at any time during the course of a review, the Commission suspects that any of the conditions specified in section 120(1) may apply.

(3) The Commission may suspend an operating licence if it thinks that any of the conditions specified in section 120(2) applies.

(4) Where the Commission suspends an operating licence it—

(*a*) shall specify the time when the suspension takes effect,
(*b*) shall specify either—

    (i) a period for which the suspension shall last (which is without prejudice to the re-exercise of the power under subsection (1) on or after the expiry of that period), or
    (ii) that the suspension shall last until some specified event occurs (which may be the giving of a notice by the Commission), and

(*c*) may make saving or transitional provision (which may, in particular, provide for a licence to continue to have effect in relation to a gaming machine supplied, or another thing done, before the time when the suspension takes effect for other purposes).

(5) An operating licence shall have no effect in respect of anything done while it is suspended under this section.

[Gambling Act 2005, s 118.]

8–13711   119. Revocation.   (1) The Commission may revoke an operating licence if following a review under section 116(1) or (2) the Commission thinks that any of the conditions specified in section 120(1) applies.

(2) The Commission may revoke an operating licence if it thinks that any of the conditions specified in section 120(2) applies.

(3) The Commission shall revoke an operating licence if the licensee fails to pay the annual fee in accordance with section 100; but the Commission may disapply this subsection if it thinks that a failure to pay is attributable to administrative error.

(4) Where the Commission revokes an operating licence it—

(*a*) shall specify the time when the revocation takes effect, and

(b)   may make saving or transitional provision (which may, in particular, provide for a licence to continue to have effect in relation to a gaming machine supplied, or another thing done, before the time when the revocation takes effect for other purposes).
[Gambling Act 2005, s 119.]

8–13712   120. Conditions for suspension or revocation.   (1) The conditions referred to in sections 118(1) and (2) and 119(1) are—

(a)   that a licensed activity is being or has been carried on in a manner which is inconsistent with the licensing objectives,
(b)   that a condition of the licence has been breached,
(c)   that the licensee has failed to cooperate with a review under section 116(1) or (2), or
(d)   that the licensee is unsuitable to carry on the licensed activities.

(2) The conditions referred to in sections 118(3) and 119(2) are—

(a)   that the licensee has failed to comply with a requirement of regulations under section 101, or
(b)   that the licensee has failed to submit the licence to the Commission for amendment in accordance with section 105.

(3) In considering a licensee's suitability for the purpose of subsection (1)(d) the Commission may, in particular, have regard to—

(a)   the integrity of the licensee or of any person who exercises a function in connection with or is interested in the licensed activities;
(b)   the competence of the licensee, or of any person who exercises a function in connection with the licensed activities, to carry on the licensed activities in a manner consistent with pursuit of the licensing objectives;
(c)   the financial and other circumstances of the licensee or of any person who exercises a function in connection with or is interested in the licensed activities (and, in particular, the resources available for the purpose of carrying on the licensed activities).
[Gambling Act 2005, s 120.]

8–13713   121. Financial penalty.   (1) The Commission may require the holder of an operating licence to pay a penalty if the Commission thinks that a condition of the licence has been breached.

(2) Before imposing a requirement on a licensee to pay a penalty under this section the Commission must notify him—

(a)   that the Commission proposes to require him to pay a penalty,
(b)   of the amount of the proposed penalty,
(c)   of the Commission's reasons, and
(d)   of a period within which he may make representations to the Commission.

(3) The Commission may not give a notice under subsection (2) in respect of the breach of a condition after the end of the period of two years beginning with—

(a)   the day on which the breach occurred or began to occur, or
(b)   if later, the day on which the breach came to the knowledge of the Commission.

(4) After the end of the period specified under subsection (2)(d) the Commission may give the licensee a notice requiring him to pay a penalty under this section.

(5) A penalty imposed by notice under subsection (4)—

(a)   shall be payable by the licensee to the Commission,
(b)   may be enforced as if it were a debt owed by the licensee to the Commission, and
(c)   on receipt by the Commission shall be paid into the Consolidated Fund after deduction of a sum which represents the direct costs to the Commission of, and a reasonable share of expenditure by the Commission which is indirectly referable to—

(i)   the investigation by the Commission of the matter in respect of which the penalty is imposed (whether by review under section 116 or otherwise), or
(ii) the imposition and enforcement of the penalty.

(6) The Commission shall—

(a)   prepare a statement setting out the principles to be applied by the Commission in exercising the powers under this section,
(b)   review the statement from time to time,
(c)   revise the statement when the Commission thinks it necessary,
(d)   as soon as is reasonably practicable—

(i)   send the statement and any revision to the Secretary of State, and
(ii) publish the statement and any revision, and

(e)   have regard to the statement when exercising a power under this section.

(7) The statement maintained under subsection (6) must, in particular, require the Commission

in considering the imposition of a penalty under this section or the amount of a penalty to have regard, in particular, to—

- (a) the seriousness of the breach of condition in respect of which the penalty is proposed,
- (b) whether or not the licensee knew or ought to have known of the breach, and
- (c) the nature of the licensee (including, in particular, his financial resources).

(8) Before preparing or revising a statement under subsection (6) the Commission shall consult—

- (a) the Secretary of State,
- (b) the Lord Chancellor, and
- (c) such other persons as the Commission thinks appropriate.

[Gambling Act 2005, s 121.]

8–13714 122. Information. (1) The holder of an operating licence shall comply with a request of the Commission to—

- (a) produce a written or electronic record relating to the licensed activities;
- (b) provide a copy of a written or electronic record relating to the licensed activities;
- (c) provide information about the licensed activities.

(2) A request under subsection (1) may specify—

- (a) the form and manner in which a record or information is to be produced or provided;
- (b) the period within which a record or information is to be produced or provided.

(3) The Commission may retain anything provided under subsection (1).

(4) The Commission may exercise a power under this section only for the purpose of—

- (a) determining whether activities have been carried on in purported reliance on the licence but not in accordance with a condition of the licence, or
- (b) determining the suitability of the licensee to carry on the licensed activities.

(5) A person commits an offence if he fails without reasonable excuse to comply with subsection (1).

(6) A person guilty of an offence under subsection (5) shall be liable on summary conviction to a fine not exceeding level 2 on the standard scale.

[Gambling Act 2005, s 122.]

General

8–13715 123. Levy. *Power to make regulations as to the payment of an annual levy by holders of operating licences.*

8–13716 124. Directions and requirements. Where the Commission has power under this Part to give a direction or impose a requirement it may give different directions or impose different requirements in relation to different cases or circumstances.

[Gambling Act 2005, s 124.]

8–13717 125. Relevant offence: disapplication of rehabilitation. Section 4 of the Rehabilitation of Offenders Act 1974 (c 53) (effect of rehabilitation) shall not apply for the purposes of or in connection with—

- (a) section 69(2)(d), or
- (b) section 71(1).

[Gambling Act 2005, s 125.]

8–13718 126. Interpretation. (1) In this Part—

"conviction"—

- (a) has the meaning given by section 1(4) of the Rehabilitation of Offenders Act 1974, and
- (b) includes, to the extent required by section 125, a spent conviction within the meaning of that Act,

"holder", in relation to an operating licence, means the person to whom the licence is issued,

"the licensed activities" in relation to an operating licence means the activities which it authorises, and

"licensee", in relation to an operating licence, means the person to whom the licence is issued.

(2) In this Act "relevant offence" means—

- (a) an offence listed in Schedule 7, and
- (b) an offence under the law of a country or territory outside the United Kingdom (a "foreign offence") which prohibits a kind of activity prohibited by an offence listed in that Schedule (a "domestic offence").

(3) For the purpose of subsection (2)(*b*) it is immaterial—

(*a*) whether or not the foreign offence prohibits all the kinds of activity prohibited by the domestic offence, and

(*b*) whether or not the foreign offence prohibits kinds of activity not prohibited by the domestic offence.

[Gambling Act 2005, s 126.]

PART 6[1]
PERSONAL LICENCES

8–13719　127. Nature of personal licence.　(1) For the purposes of this Act a "personal licence" is a licence which authorises an individual to perform the functions of a specified management office, or to perform a specified operational function, in connection with—

(*a*) the provision of facilities for gambling, or

(*b*) a person who provides facilities for gambling.

(2) In this section "management office" and "operational function" have the same meaning as in section 80.

[Gambling Act 2005, s 127.]

---

1. Part 6 contains ss 127–139. Section 128 is partly in force: see Gambling Act 2005 (Commencement No 2 and Transitional Provisions) Order 2005, SI 2005/2455.

8–13720　128. Application of provisions of Part 5.　(1) The provisions of Part 5 (other than section 65(2), (4) and (5)) shall apply to a personal licence as they apply to an operating licence, with—

(*a*) the modifications and exclusions specified in this Part,

(*b*) such modifications and exclusions as the Secretary of State may specify by regulations, and

(*c*) any other necessary modifications.

(2) Regulations under a provision of Part 5—

(*a*) may make different provision for purposes of this Part and for purposes of that Part, and

(*b*) in making provision for purposes of this Part, may make different provision in relation to personal licences authorising—

(i)　the performance of different kinds of function, or

(ii)　the performance of functions in different circumstances.

[Gambling Act 2005, s 128.]

8–13721　129. Exemption for small-scale operators.　(1) A condition may not be attached to an operating licence under section 75, 77 or 78 requiring possession of a personal licence if the licensee is a small-scale operator.

(2) In this section "small-scale operator" shall have such meaning as the Secretary of State may prescribe by regulations.

(3) Regulations under subsection (2) may, in particular, make provision by reference to—

(*a*) the size or value of business carried on, or expected to be carried on, in reliance on an operating licence;

(*b*) the number of persons employed, or expected to be employed, by the licensee.

(4) A constable or enforcement officer may under section 108(1) require a small-scale operator to produce his operating licence—

(*a*) within a specified period, or

(*b*) while the operator is carrying on a licensed activity, immediately.

[Gambling Act 2005, s 129.]

8–13722

PART 7[1]
OPERATING AND PERSONAL LICENCES: APPEALS

---

1. Part 7 contains ss 140–149.

PART 8[1]
PREMISES LICENCES

---

1. Part 8 contains ss 150–213.

The licence

8–13723 150. Nature of licence¹. (1) A premises licence is a licence which states that it authorises premises to be used for—

(a) the operation of a casino (a "casino premises licence"),

(b) the provision of facilities for the playing of bingo (a "bingo premises licence"),

(c) making Category B gaming machines available for use (an "adult gaming centre premises licence"),

(d) making Category C gaming machines available for use (a "family entertainment centre premises licence"), or

(e) the provision of facilities for betting, whether by making or accepting bets, by acting as a betting intermediary or by providing other facilities for the making or accepting of bets (a "betting premises licence").

(2) A casino premises licence is—

(a) a "regional casino premises licence" if it relates to a regional casino,

(b) a "large casino premises licence" if it relates to a large casino, and

(c) a "small casino premises licence" if it relates to a small casino

(3) Neither a premises licence nor any provision of this Part disapplies or provides a defence to the offence under section 33.

[Gambling Act 2005, s 150.]

---

1. For definitions of terms used in this section see s 353, post.

8–13724 151. Form of licence. (1) A premises licence must—

(a) specify the name of the person to whom it is issued,

(b) specify a home or business address of that person,

(c) specify the premises to which it relates,

(d) specify the activities for which it authorises the premises to be used,

(e) specify any condition attached by the licensing authority under section 169(1)(a),

(f) specify any exclusion of a default condition effected by the licensing authority under section 169(1)(b),

(g) include a plan of the premises, and

(h) if a period is prescribed under section 191 at the end of which the licence will expire (unless renewed or terminated earlier), specify the period.

(2) The Secretary of State may make regulations about—

(a) the form of a premises licence, and

(b) the content of a premises licence (which may, in particular, require the inclusion of information about mandatory conditions, default conditions or conditions attached to the licence by virtue of a provision of this Part).

(3) In relation to a premises licence issued in Scotland, subsection (2) shall have effect as if the reference to the Secretary of State were a reference to the Scottish Ministers.

[Gambling Act 2005, s 151.]

8–13725 152. Combined licence, &c. (1) A premises licence—

(a) may not authorise the use of premises for activities of more than one of the kinds specified in section 150(a) to (e) (subject to sections 172 to 174 and subsection (2) below), and

(b) may not be issued in respect of premises if a premises licence already has effect in relation to the premises (subject to subsection (3)).

(2) Subsection (1)(a) does not apply in the case of a track.

(3) More than one premises licence may have effect in relation to a track provided that—

(a) each licence relates to a specified area of the track, and

(b) not more than one premises licence has effect in relation to any area of the track.

(4) If a person applies for a premises licence in respect of an area of a track ("a subsidiary licence") and a premises licence already has effect in respect of the whole track or a part of the track that includes that area ("the main licence")—

(a) the application for the subsidiary licence must be accompanied by an application under section 187 to vary the main licence so that it does not have effect in relation to the area to which the subsidiary licence is to relate, and

(b) the application for the subsidiary licence may be granted only after, or together with, the grant of the application for variation.

[Gambling Act 2005, s 152.]

8–13726   **153. Principles to be applied**

8–13727   **154. Delegation of licensing authority functions: England and Wales**

8–13728   **155. Delegation of functions under Part 8: Scotland**

8–13729   **156. Register.**   (1) A licensing authority shall—

(a) maintain a register of premises licences issued by the authority together with such other information as may be prescribed,

(b) make the register and information available for inspection by members of the public at all reasonable times, and

(c) make arrangements for the provision of a copy of an entry in the register, or of information, to a member of the public on request.

(2) A licensing authority may refuse to provide a copy of an entry or of information unless the person seeking it pays a reasonable fee specified by the authority.

(3) The Secretary of State may make regulations about—

(a) the form of the register;

(b) the manner in which it is maintained.

(4) The Secretary of State may make regulations—

(a) requiring licensing authorities to give to the Commission specified information about premises licences issued by them,

(b) requiring the Commission to maintain a register of the information provided to it under paragraph (a),

(c) requiring the Commission to grant access to the register to members of the public (without charge),

(d) requiring the Commission to make copies of entries available on request, and on payment of a reasonable fee, to members of the public, and

(e) excusing licensing authorities, wholly or partly, from compliance with subsection (1).

[Gambling Act 2005, s 156.]

Other relevant persons

8–13730   **157. Responsible authorities.**   For the purposes of this Part the following are responsible authorities in relation to premises—

(a) a licensing authority in England and Wales in whose area the premises are wholly or partly situated,

(b) the Commission,

(c) either—

(i) in England and Wales, the chief officer of police for a police area in which the premises are wholly or partly situated, or

(ii) in Scotland, the chief constable of the police force maintained for a police area in which the premises are wholly or partly situated,

(d) the fire and rescue authority for an area in which the premises are wholly or partly situated,

(e) either—

(i) in England and Wales, the local planning authority, in accordance with Part I of the Town and Country Planning Act 1990 (c 8), for an area in which the premises are wholly or partly situated, or

(ii) in Scotland, the planning authority, in accordance with Part 1 of the Town and Country Planning (Scotland) Act 1997 (c 8), for an area in which the premises are wholly or partly situated,

(f) the council constituted under section 2 of the Local Government etc (Scotland) Act 1994 (c 39) for an area in which the premises are wholly or partly situated,

(g) an authority which has functions by virtue of an enactment in respect of minimising or preventing the risk of pollution of the environment or of harm to human health in an area in which the premises are wholly or partly situated,

(h) a body which is designated in writing for the purposes of this paragraph, by the licensing authority for an area in which the premises are wholly or partly situated, as competent to advise the authority about the protection of children from harm,

(i) Her Majesty's Commissioners of Customs and Excise, and

(j) any other person prescribed for the purposes of this section by regulations made by the Secretary of State.

[Gambling Act 2005, s 157.]

8–13731   **158. Interested party.**   For the purposes of this Part a person is an interested party in relation to a premises licence or in relation to an application for or in respect of a premises licence if, in the opinion of the licensing authority which issues the licence or to which the application is made, the person—

     (*a*)   lives sufficiently close to the premises to be likely to be affected by the authorised activities,

     (*b*)   has business interests that might be affected by the authorised activities, or

     (*c*)   represents persons who satisfy paragraph (*a*) or (*b*).

[Gambling Act 2005, s 158.]

Application for licence

8–13732   **159. Making of application.**   (1) A person may apply to a licensing authority for a premises licence to be issued to him authorising the use of premises to carry on an activity listed in section 37(1).

     (2) An application must be made to a licensing authority in whose area the premises are wholly or partly situated.

     (3) An application may be made only by a person who—

     (*a*)   holds an operating licence which authorises him to carry on the activity in respect of which the premises licence is sought, or

     (*b*)   has made an application, which has not yet been determined, for an operating licence which authorises him to carry on the activity in respect of which the premises licence is sought.

     (4) But subsection (3) does not apply to an application for a premises licence which authorises a track to be used for accepting bets (and which does not also, otherwise than by virtue of section 172, authorise it to be used for another purpose).

     (5) An application may be made only by a person who has a right to occupy the premises to which the application relates.

     (6) An application must—

     (*a*)   be made in the prescribed form and manner,

     (*b*)   contain or be accompanied by the prescribed information or documents, and

     (*c*)   be accompanied by the prescribed fee.

     (7) Regulations prescribing a matter for the purposes of this section may, in particular, make different provision for—

     (*a*)   applications in respect of different classes of activity, or

     (*b*)   different circumstances.

     (8) In this section "prescribed" means—

     (*a*)   in relation to applications to authorities in England and Wales, prescribed by regulations made by the Secretary of State, and

     (*b*)   in relation to applications to authorities in Scotland, prescribed by regulations made by the Scottish Ministers.

[Gambling Act 2005, s 159.]

8–13733   **160. Notice of application.**   (1) The Secretary of State may make regulations requiring an applicant for a premises licence—

     (*a*)   to publish notice of his application;

     (*b*)   to give notice of his application to the responsible authorities in relation to the premises;

     (*c*)   to give notice of his application to other persons.

     (2) Regulations under subsection (1) shall include provision—

     (*a*)   about the manner and form in which notice is to be published or given,

     (*b*)   about the period of time within which notice is to be published or given, and

     (*c*)   for the consequences of failure to comply with the regulations.

     (3) In so far as this section has effect in relation to applications to authorities in Scotland, the reference to the Secretary of State shall have effect as a reference to the Scottish Ministers.

[Gambling Act 2005, s 160.]

8–13734   **161. Representations.**   (1) Where an application is made to a licensing authority for a premises licence, an interested party or responsible authority in relation to the premises may make representations in writing to the licensing authority.

     (2) Representations under subsection (1) must be made within such period as the Secretary of State shall prescribe by regulations.

     (3) In so far as this section has effect in relation to applications to authorities in Scotland, the reference to the Secretary of State shall have effect as a reference to the Scottish Ministers.

[Gambling Act 2005, s 161.]

Determination of application

8–13735   162. Requirement for hearing.   (1) In determining an application for a premises licence a licensing authority must hold a hearing if—

   (*a*)   an interested party or responsible authority has made (and not withdrawn) representations about the application under section 161,

   (*b*)   the authority propose to attach a condition to the licence under section 169(1)(*a*), or

   (*c*)   the authority propose to exclude under section 169(1)(*b*) a condition that would otherwise be attached to the licence under section 168.

   (2) But a licensing authority may determine an application for a premises licence without a hearing despite subsection (1) with the consent of—

   (*a*)   the applicant, and

   (*b*)   any interested party or responsible authority who has made (and not withdrawn) representations about the application under section 161.

   (3) A licensing authority may also determine an application for a premises licence without a hearing despite subsection (1)(*a*) if the authority think that the representations made under section 161—

   (*a*)   are vexatious,

   (*b*)   are frivolous, or

   (*c*)   will certainly not influence the authority's determination of the application.

   (4) If a licensing authority propose to determine an application in reliance on subsection (3) they shall as soon as is reasonably practicable notify any person who made representations under section 161.

[Gambling Act 2005, s 162.]

8–13736   163. Determination of application.   (1) On considering an application for a premises licence (whether at a hearing or not) a licensing authority shall—

   (*a*)   grant it, or

   (*b*)   reject it.

   (2) A licensing authority shall not determine an application for a premises licence made in reliance on section 159(3)(*b*) until the relevant operating licence has been issued (in a form which authorises the applicant to carry on the activity in respect of which the premises licence is sought).

[Gambling Act 2005, s 163.]

8–13737   164. Grant of application.   (1) Where a licensing authority grant an application for a premises licence they shall as soon as is reasonably practicable—

   (*a*)   give notice of the grant to—

      (i)   the applicant,

      (ii)   the Commission,

      (iii) any person who made representations about the application under section 161,

      (iv) in England and Wales, the chief officer of police for any area in which the premises are wholly or partly situated,

      (v)   in Scotland, the chief constable of the police force maintained for a police area in which the premises are wholly or partly situated, and

      (vi) Her Majesty's Commissioners of Customs and Excise,

   (*b*)   issue a premises licence to the applicant, and

   (*c*)   give the applicant a summary of the terms and conditions of the licence in the prescribed form.

   (2) A notice under subsection (1)(*a*)—

   (*a*)   must be in the prescribed form,

   (*b*)   if the licensing authority have attached a condition to the licence under section 169(1)(*a*) or excluded under section 169(1)(*b*) a condition that would otherwise have attached by virtue of section 168, must give the authority's reasons, and

   (*c*)   if representations were made about the application under section 161, must give the authority's response to the representations.

   (3) In this section "prescribed" means—

   (*a*)   in relation to authorities in England and Wales, prescribed by regulations made by the Secretary of State, and

   (*b*)   in relation to authorities in Scotland, prescribed by regulations made by the Scottish Ministers.

[Gambling Act 2005, s 164.]

8–13738   165. Rejection of application.   (1) Where a licensing authority reject an application for a premises licence they shall as soon as is reasonably practicable give notice of the rejection to—

(*a*)   the applicant,

(*b*)   the Commission,

(*c*)   any person who made representations about the application under section 161,

(*d*)   either—

    (i)   in England and Wales, the chief officer of police for any area in which the premises are wholly or partly situated, or

    (ii)   in Scotland, the chief constable of the police force maintained for a police area in which the premises are wholly or partly situated, and

(*e*)   Her Majesty's Commissioners of Customs and Excise.

(2)   A notice under subsection (1)—

(*a*)   must be in the prescribed form, and

(*b*)   must give the authority's reasons for rejecting the application.

(3)   In this section "prescribed" means—

(*a*)   in relation to authorities in England and Wales, prescribed by regulations made by the Secretary of State, and

(*b*)   in relation to authorities in Scotland, prescribed by regulations made by the Scottish Ministers.

[Gambling Act 2005, s 165.]

8–13739   166. Resolution not to issue casino licences.   (1)   A licensing authority may resolve not to issue casino premises licences.

(2)   In passing a resolution under subsection (1) a licensing authority may have regard to any principle or matter.

(3)   A resolution under subsection (1)—

(*a*)   must apply to the issue of casino premises licences generally,

(*b*)   must specify the date on which it takes effect,

(*c*)   may be revoked by a further resolution, and

(*d*)   shall lapse at the end of the period of three years beginning with the date on which it takes effect (without prejudice to the ability to pass a new resolution).

(4)   A resolution under subsection (1)—

(*a*)   may be passed whether or not the licensing authority has already issued casino premises licences,

(*b*)   shall have no effect in relation to a casino premises licence issued before the resolution takes effect,

(*c*)   shall have no effect in relation to premises in respect of which a provisional statement relating to the operation of a casino is in force when the resolution takes effect,

(*d*)   shall have no effect in relation to anything converted into a casino premises licence by virtue of Schedule 18,

(*e*)   shall not affect the issuing of a casino premises licence in accordance with a requirement by virtue of Schedule 18, and

(*f*)   may not be taken into account in conducting a review of a casino premises licence under section 201.

(5)   A resolution under subsection (1) shall be published by being included in a statement or revision under section 349.

(6)   Section 153 is subject to this section.

(7)   The Secretary of State may by order require a licensing authority to consider whether or not to pass a resolution under subsection (1).

(8)   An order under subsection (7) may—

(*a*)   be directed to a particular licensing authority or to a class or description of licensing authority;

(*b*)   require the licensing authority to consult such persons or classes of persons as they think are likely to be affected by the resolution (having regard to any guidance given by the Secretary of State);

(*c*)   require the licensing authority to take other procedural steps;

(*d*)   specify a period within which the consideration must take place;

(*e*)   require consideration once or at specified intervals.

[Gambling Act 2005, s 166.]

Conditions

8–13740   167. Mandatory conditions.   (1)   The Secretary of State may by regulations provide for a specified condition to be attached to premises licences.

(2)   Regulations under this section may, in particular—

(*a*)   make provision which applies generally, only to premises licences in a specified class or only in specified circumstances;

(*b*)   make different provision for different classes of licence or for different circumstances.

(3) In relation to premises licences issued in Scotland subsection (1) shall have effect as if the reference to the Secretary of State were a reference to the Scottish Ministers.
[Gambling Act 2005, s 167.]

8–13741 168. Default conditions. (1) The Secretary of State may by regulations prescribe for a specified condition to be attached to any premises licence unless excluded by the authority who issue the licence.

(2) Regulations under this section may, in particular—

(a) make provision which applies generally, only to premises licences in a specified class or only in specified circumstances;

(b) make different provision for different classes of licence or for different circumstances.

(3) In relation to a premises licence issued by an authority in Scotland subsection (1) shall have effect as if the reference to the Secretary of State were a reference to the Scottish Ministers.
[Gambling Act 2005, s 168.]

8–13742 169. Conditions imposed or excluded by licensing authority. (1) Where a licensing authority issue a premises licence they may—

(a) attach a condition to the licence;

(b) exclude a condition that would otherwise be attached to the licence by virtue of section 168.

(2) A condition attached to the licence under subsection (1)(a) may, in particular, address a matter addressed by a condition excluded under subsection (1)(b).

(3) A condition attached to the licence under subsection (1)(a) may apply in relation to the premises generally or only in relation to a specified part of the premises.

(4) A licensing authority may not attach a condition to a premises licence which prevents compliance with a condition of the operating licence which authorises the holder to carry out the activity in respect of which the premises licence is granted.
[Gambling Act 2005, s 169.]

8–13743 170. Membership. A premises licence may not be subject to a condition (whether imposed by virtue of section 167, 168 or 169)—

(a) requiring all or part of the premises, or any activity taking place on the premises, to be operated or carried on as a club or other body with membership, or

(b) restricting use of any part of the premises wholly or partly by reference to membership of a club or other body.
[Gambling Act 2005, s 170.]

8–13744 171. Stakes, &c. (1) A premises licence may not be subject to a condition (whether imposed by virtue of section 167, 168 or 169) imposing limits on—

(a) stakes,

(b) fees,

(c) winnings, or

(d) prizes.

(2) The prohibition in subsection (1)(b) shall not prevent the imposition by virtue of section 167 of a condition about fees for admission to a track.
[Gambling Act 2005, s 171.]

Specific cases

8–13745 172. Gaming machines. (1) An adult gaming centre premises licence shall, by virtue of this section, authorise the holder—

(a) to make up to four Category B gaming machines available for use on the premises,

(b) to make any number of Category C gaming machines available for use on the premises, and

(c) to make any number of Category D gaming machines available for use on the premises.

(2) A family entertainment centre premises licence shall, by virtue of this section, authorise the holder—

(a) to make any number of Category C gaming machines available for use on the premises, and

(b) to make any number of Category D gaming machines available for use on the premises.

(3) A casino premises licence for a regional casino using at least 40 gaming tables shall by virtue of this section authorise the holder to make gaming machines available for use on the premises provided that—

(a) each gaming machine is of Category A, B, C or D, and

(b) the number of gaming machines—

(i) is not more than 25 times the number of gaming tables used in the casino, and

(ii) is not more than 1250.

(4) A casino premises licence for a large casino using at least one gaming table, or for a regional casino using fewer than 40 gaming tables, shall by virtue of this section authorise the holder to make gaming machines available for use on the premises provided that—

(a) each gaming machine is of Category B, C or D, and

(b) the number of gaming machines—

(i) is not more than 5 times the number of gaming tables used in the casino, and

(ii) is not more than 150.

(5) A casino premises licence for a small casino using at least one gaming table shall by virtue of this section authorise the holder to make gaming machines available for use on the premises provided that—

(a) each gaming machine is of Category B, C or D, and

(b) the number of gaming machines—

(i) is not more than twice the number of gaming tables used in the casino, and

(ii) is not more than 80.

(6) The Secretary of State may by regulations—

(a) define "gaming table" for the purposes of subsections (3) to (5);

(b) provide that a gaming table is to be treated as being used in a casino for the purposes of those subsections only if used—

(i) for a specified purpose,

(ii) in specified circumstances, and

(iii) to a specified extent;

(c) provide for a number of tables are to be treated as if they were a single gaming table in specified circumstances.

(7) A bingo premises licence shall, by virtue of this section, authorise the holder—

(a) to make up to four Category B gaming machines available for use on the premises,

(b) to make any number of Category C gaming machines available for use on the premises, and

(c) to make any number of Category D gaming machines available for use on the premises.

(8) A betting premises licence shall, by virtue of this section, authorise the holder to make up to four gaming machines, each of which must be of Category B, C or D, available for use.

(9) But subsection (8) applies to a betting premises licence in respect of a track only if the holder also holds a pool betting operating licence.

(10) A premises licence may not (whether by way of condition or otherwise)—

(a) make provision about the number or categories of gaming machine that may be made available for use that contradicts a provision of this section,

(b) make provision that contradicts a provision of regulations under section 236, 240 or 241, or

(c) make provision of a kind prohibited by regulations under any of those sections.

(11) The Secretary of State may by order amend a provision of this section so as to vary—

(a) the number of machines authorised by a specified kind of premises licence;

(b) the category of machines authorised by a specified kind of premises licence.

[Gambling Act 2005, s 172.]

8–13746 173. Virtual gaming. (1) The kinds of premises licence specified in subsection (2) shall by virtue of this section authorise the holder to make facilities available for betting on the outcome of a virtual game, race, competition or other event or process.

(2) Those kinds of licence are—

(a) a casino premises licence, and

(b) a betting premises licence.

[Gambling Act 2005, s 173.]

8–13747 174. Casino premises licence. (1) A casino premises licence may be issued only in respect of—

(a) a regional casino,

(b) a large casino, or

(c) a small casino.

(2) A casino premises licence shall, by virtue of this section and subject to subsections (3) and (4), authorise the holder to use the premises to make available any number of games of chance other than casino games.

(3) A casino premises licence shall, by virtue of this subsection and subject to subsection (4), authorise the holder, and any person authorised by him in writing, to use the premises for the provision of facilities for—

(a) bingo,

(*b*)   betting, or
(*c*)   both.

(4)   In respect of a small casino, subsection (3) shall not apply in so far as it authorises bingo.

(5)   The Secretary of State may by order repeal subsection (4) (and this subsection).

(6)   Regulations under section 167 shall, in particular, make provision in relation to casino premises licences imposing limits in respect of machines of a kind that would be gaming machines but for section 235(2)(i); and the limits may, in particular, operate by reference to—

(*a*)   the number of machines, or
(*b*)   the number of players that the machines are designed or adapted to accommodate.

(7)   Regulations under section 167 or 168 may, in particular, make provision in relation to casino premises licences, or in relation to a class of casino premises licence, for a condition requiring the provision of recreational or other facilities of a specified kind.

(8)   Subsection (7) is without prejudice to the generality of sections 167, 168 and 169.

[Gambling Act 2005, s 174.]

8–13748   175. Casino premises licence: overall limits.   (1)   No more than one casino premises licence may have effect at any time in respect of regional casinos.

(2)   No more than eight casino premises licences may have effect at any time in respect of large casinos.

(3)   No more than eight casino premises licences may have effect at any time in respect of small casinos.

(4)   The Secretary of State shall, having consulted the Scottish Ministers and the National Assembly for Wales, by order make provision for determining the geographical distribution of casino premises licences within the limits specified in subsections (1) to (3); for which purpose the order shall—

(*a*)   specify which licensing authorities may issue casino premises licences of a specified kind, and
(*b*)   in respect of each specified authority, specify the number of casino premises licences of each kind issued by the authority that may have effect at any time.

(5)   An application for a casino premises licence may not be made to a licensing authority if subsections (1) to (3) and the order under subsection (4) would prevent the authority from granting the application.

(6)   An application for a provisional statement may not be made to a licensing authority if it relates to a casino and is made at a time when subsections (1) to (3) and the order under subsection (4) would prevent the authority from granting a casino premises licence in response to an application made in reliance on the provisional statement.

(7)   Schedule 9 (which makes provision about the treatment of applications for casino premises licences and provisional statements) shall have effect.

(8)   The Secretary of State may by order—

(*a*)   amend any of subsections (1), (2) and (3) so as to substitute a new maximum number of casino premises licences;
(*b*)   repeal any of subsections (1), (2) and (3).

[Gambling Act 2005, s 175.]

8–13749   176. Casino premises licence: access by children.   (1)   The Commission shall issue one or more codes of practice under section 24 about access to casino premises for children and young persons.

(2)   The code or codes issued in accordance with subsection (1) shall, in particular—

(*a*)   require the holder of a casino premises licence to take specified steps to ensure that no child or young person enters premises or a part of premises which it would be an offence under section 47 to permit him to enter ("prohibited premises or areas"),
(*b*)   for that purpose, require the holder of a casino premises licence to ensure—

(i)   that each entrance to prohibited premises or to a prohibited area is supervised by one or more persons whose responsibilities include ensuring compliance with the code of practice ("the supervisor"), and
(ii)   that arrangements are made to require evidence of age to be produced by any person seeking admission to prohibited premises or to a prohibited area unless the supervisor, reasonably, is certain that the person seeking admission is an adult, and

(*c*)   make provision about the nature of evidence that may be used for the purpose of arrangements made in accordance with paragraph (*b*)(ii).

(3)   A casino premises licence shall by virtue of this section be subject to the condition that the licensee ensures compliance with any relevant code of practice issued in accordance with subsection (1).

[Gambling Act 2005, s 176.]

8–13750   **177. Credit.**   (1) This section applies to—

(*a*)   casino premises licences, and

(*b*)   bingo premises licences.

(2) A premises licence to which this section applies shall by virtue of this section be subject to the condition that the licensee does not—

(*a*)   give credit in connection with gambling authorised by the licence, or

(*b*)   participate in, arrange, permit or knowingly facilitate the giving of credit in connection with gambling authorised by the licence.

(3) But the condition in subsection (2) shall not prevent the licensee from permitting the installation and use on the premises of a machine enabling cash to be obtained on credit from a person (the "credit provider") provided that—

(*a*)   the licensee has no other commercial connection with the credit provider in relation to gambling,

(*b*)   the licensee neither makes nor receives any payment or reward (whether by way of commission, rent or otherwise) in connection with the machine, and

(*c*)   any conditions about the nature, location or use of the machine attached by virtue of section 167, 168 or 169 are complied with.

(4) In this section "credit" has the same meaning as in section 81.

[Gambling Act 2005, s 177.]

8–13751   **178. Door supervision.**   (1) Where a condition for door supervision is attached to a premises licence (whether by virtue of section 167, 168 or 169) subsection (3) shall apply in relation to the licence.

(2) In subsection (1) "condition for door supervision" means a condition requiring that one or more persons be responsible for guarding the premises against unauthorised access or occupation, against outbreaks of disorder or against damage.

(3) If the person carrying out the guarding mentioned in subsection (2) is required by the Private Security Industry Act 2001 (c 12) to hold a licence under that Act authorising the guarding, the requirement under that Act shall be treated for the purposes of this Act as if it were a condition of the premises licence attached by virtue of this section.

[Gambling Act 2005, s 178.]

8–13752   **179. Pool betting on track.**   (1) A betting premises licence in respect of a track may not authorise the acceptance of bets by way of pool betting except in a case to which subsection (2) applies.

(2) This subsection applies to the acceptance of bets, by way of pool betting on horse-racing or dog-racing—

(*a*)   by the holder of the betting premises licence, or

(*b*)   in accordance with arrangements made by him.

(3) The Secretary of State may by order amend this section so as to—

(*a*)   add an exception to subsection (1),

(*b*)   amend an exception to subsection (1), or

(*c*)   remove an exception to subsection (1).

[Gambling Act 2005, s 179.]

8–13753   **180. Pool betting on dog races.**   (1) A betting premises licence in respect of premises other than a dog track shall by virtue of this section be subject to the condition that pool bets may not be accepted in reliance on the licence in respect of dog-racing other than in accordance with arrangements made with the occupier of the dog track on which the racing takes place.

(2) The Secretary of State may by order repeal this section.

(3) A repeal by order under subsection (2) shall cause the condition attached by subsection (1) to premises licences in force on the date of the repeal to lapse in respect of anything done on or after the date of the repeal.

(4) This section shall cease to have effect at the end of 31st December 2012 (and the condition attached by subsection (1) to premises licences in force on that date shall lapse in respect of anything done after that date).

[Gambling Act 2005, s 180.]

8–13754   **181. Betting machines.**   (1) A condition of a betting premises licence may relate to—

(*a*)   the number of machines used on the premises for the purpose of making or accepting bets;

(*b*)   the nature of those machines;

(*c*)   the circumstances in which those machines are made available for use.

(2) A condition of a casino premises licence may relate to—

(*a*)   the number of machines used on the premises for the purpose of making or accepting bets;

(b)   the nature of those machines;

(c)   the circumstances in which those machines are made available for use.

(3)   In this section "condition" means a condition imposed by virtue of section section 167, 168 or 169.

[Gambling Act 2005, s 181.]

8–13755   182. Exclusion of children from track areas.   (1) A premises licence in respect of a track shall by virtue of this section be subject to the condition that the licensee shall ensure that children and young persons are excluded from—

(a)   any area where facilities for betting are provided, and

(b)   any area where a gaming machine, other than a Category D machine, is situated.

(2)   But subsection (1)(a)—

(a)   shall not apply to a dog track on a day on which dog-racing takes place, or is expected to take place, on the track, and

(b)   shall not apply to a horse-race course on a day on which horse-racing takes place, or is expected to take place, on the course.

(3)   For the purposes of this section a reference to the area where facilities are provided or where a machine is situated is a reference to any place in which it is possible to take advantage of the facilities or use the machine.

(4)   The Secretary of State may by order amend this section so as to—

(a)   provide an additional exception to subsection (1)(a),

(b)   remove an exception to subsection (1)(a), or

(c)   amend an exception to subsection (1)(a).

[Gambling Act 2005, s 182.]

8–13756   183. Christmas Day.   A premises licence shall, by virtue of this section, be subject to the condition that the premises shall not be used to provide facilities for gambling on Christmas Day.

[Gambling Act 2005, s 183.]

Maintenance

8–13757   184. Annual fee

8–13758   185. Availability of licence.   (1) The holder of a premises licence shall—

(a)   keep the licence on the premises, and

(b)   arrange for the licence to be made available on request to—

     (i)   a constable,

     (ii)   an enforcement officer, or

     (iii)   an authorised local authority officer.

(2)   A person commits an offence if he fails without reasonable excuse to comply with subsection (1).

(3)   A person guilty of an offence under subsection (2) shall be liable on summary conviction to a fine not exceeding level 2 on the standard scale.

[Gambling Act 2005, s 185.]

8–13759   186. Change of circumstance.   (1) If the holder of a premises licence ceases to reside or attend at the address specified in the licence under section 151(1)(b) he shall as soon as is reasonably practicable—

(a)   notify the licensing authority, and

(b)   inform the licensing authority of a home or business address at which he resides or attends.

(2)   The Secretary of State may make regulations requiring the holder of a premises licence—

(a)   to notify the licensing authority of any change of circumstance of a prescribed kind in relation to him or to an authorised activity, and

(b)   to give the licensing authority prescribed details of the change.

(3)   If a change of circumstance notified under or by virtue of this section falsifies information contained in the premises licence in accordance with section 151, the notification must be accompanied by—

(a)   the prescribed fee, and

(b)   either—

     (i)   the licence, or

     (ii)   an application under section 190 for a copy of the licence.

(4)   Where notification is accompanied by the licence, the licensing authority shall—

(a) make such alteration to the information contained in the licence as appears to them to be required by the change in circumstance, and

(b) return the licence to the licensee.

(5) Where the notification is accompanied by an application for a copy of the licence, the licensing authority shall, if they grant the application, issue the copy in a form which appears to them to reflect the change in circumstance.

(6) The holder of a premises licence commits an offence if he fails without reasonable excuse to comply with a provision of this section or of regulations made under this section.

(7) A person guilty of an offence under subsection (6) shall be liable on summary conviction to a fine not exceeding level 2 on the standard scale.

(8) This section does not prevent the imposition of a requirement to notify the licensing authority of a specified change of circumstance by way of the attachment of a condition to a premises licence.

(9) In subsection (3)(a) "prescribed" means—

(a) in relation to notification given to authorities in England and Wales, prescribed by regulations made by the Secretary of State, and

(b) in relation to notifications given to authorities in Scotland, prescribed by regulations made by the Scottish Ministers.

[Gambling Act 2005, s 186.]

8–13760 187. Application to vary licence. (1) The holder of a premises licence may apply to the licensing authority to vary the licence by—

(a) adding, amending or removing an authorised activity,

(b) amending another detail of the licence,

(c) excluding a condition attached by virtue of section 168, or

(d) adding, amending or removing a condition attached to the licence under section 169.

(2) A licence may not be varied under this section so as to relate to premises to which it did not previously relate.

(3) The provisions of this Part shall apply in relation to an application for variation as they apply in relation to an application for a premises licence—

(a) subject to the provisions of this section, and

(b) with any other necessary modifications.

(4) Regulations under this Part which relate to an application for a premises licence may make—

(a) provision which applies only in the case of an application for variation;

(b) provision which does not apply in the case of an application for variation;

(c) different provision in relation to an application for variation from that made in relation to an application for a premises licence;

(d) different provision in relation to applications for variations of different kinds.

(5) An application for variation must (in addition to anything required by section 159) be accompanied by a statement of the variation sought.

(6) An application for variation must (in addition to anything required by section 159) also be accompanied by—

(a) the licence to be varied, or

(b) both—

(i) a statement explaining why it is not reasonably practicable to produce the licence, and

(ii) an application under section 190 for the issue of a copy of the licence.

(7) In granting an application for variation a licensing authority—

(a) shall specify a time when the variation shall begin to have effect, and

(b) may make transitional provision.

[Gambling Act 2005, s 187.]

8–13761 188. Transfer. (1) A person may apply to a licensing authority for a premises licence to be transferred to him.

(2) The provisions of this Part shall apply in relation to an application for transfer as they apply in relation to an application for a premises licence—

(a) subject to the provisions of this section and section 189, and

(b) with any other necessary modifications.

(3) An application for transfer must (in addition to anything required by section 159)—

(a) specify the time when the transfer is to take effect, and

(b) be accompanied by a written statement by the licensee consenting to the transfer.

(4) A licensing authority shall grant an application for transfer unless they think it would be wrong to do so having regard to representations made under section 161 (as applied by subsection (2) above).

(5) On the grant of an application for the transfer of a premises licence the licensing authority—

(*a*) shall alter the licence so that the applicant for the transfer becomes the licensee,

(*b*) shall specify in the licence the time when the transfer takes effect (being either the time specified in the application under subsection (3) above or, if later, the time when the application is granted), and

(*c*) shall make such other alteration of the licence as appears to them to be required (which may, in particular, include an alteration to reflect a decision of the authority under section 169 as applied by subsection (2) above to make new or varied provision for the attachment or exclusion of conditions).

(6) A licence to which a condition is attached under section 169 for the purpose of giving effect to an agreement entered into under paragraph 5(3)(*b*) of Schedule 9 ("the original agreement") shall not be transferred unless—

(*a*) the transferee enters into an agreement ("the new agreement") which appears to the licensing authority to have substantially the same effect as the original agreement, and

(*b*) the condition is altered so as to give effect to the new agreement.

[Gambling Act 2005, s 188.]

8–13762   189. Transfer: supplemental.   (1) If an application for transfer under section 188 states that the applicant has failed to contact the licensee having taken all reasonable steps to do so, the licensing authority shall—

(*a*) disapply section 188(3)(*b*) and take all reasonable steps to notify the licensee, or

(*b*) determine not to disapply section 188(3)(*b*) and notify the applicant of their determination and the reasons for it.

(2) An application for transfer must (in addition to anything required by section 159) be accompanied by—

(*a*) the licence, or

(*b*) both—

  (i) a statement explaining why it is not reasonably practicable to produce the licence, and

  (ii) an application by the licensee under section 190 for the issue of a copy of the licence.

(3) In relation to an application for transfer to which subsection (1) applies, for the purposes of any application under section 190 required in accordance with subsection (2)(*b*)(ii) above—

(*a*) the application under that section shall be made by the applicant for transfer, and

(*b*) a reference to the licence being lost, stolen or damaged shall be treated as a reference to the licence being unavailable to the applicant for transfer.

(4) Regulations under section 160, as they have effect in relation to applications for transfer by virtue of section 188(2), may require notice to be given to specified responsible authorities (and not to all responsible authorities).

(5) Section 161 shall have effect in relation to an application for transfer with the omission of the reference to interested parties.

(6) If an application for the transfer of a premises licence includes a request that this subsection apply, the licence shall have effect as if the applicant for transfer were the licensee during the period—

(*a*) beginning with the receipt of the application for transfer by the licensing authority, and

(*b*) ending with the determination of the application by the licensing authority.

[Gambling Act 2005, s 189.]

8–13763   190. Copy of licence.   (1) Where a premises licence issued, or a summary given, under section 164 is lost, stolen or damaged, the licensee may apply to the licensing authority for a copy.

(2) An application under subsection (1) must be accompanied by the prescribed fee.

(3) A licensing authority shall consider an application under this section as soon as is reasonably practicable and shall grant it if satisfied—

(*a*) that the licence or summary to which the application relates has been lost, stolen or damaged, and

(*b*) where the licence or summary has been lost or stolen, that the loss or theft has been reported to the police.

(4) As soon as is reasonably practicable after granting an application under this section a licensing authority shall issue a copy of the licence or summary to the applicant—

(*a*) certified by the authority as a true copy, and

(*b*) in, or in relation to, the form in which the licence had effect before the loss, theft or damage.

(5) A copy of a licence or summary issued under this section shall be treated as if it were the licence or summary.

(6) In subsection (2) "prescribed" means—

(*a*) in relation to applications to authorities in England and Wales, prescribed by regulations made by the Secretary of State, and

(*b*) in relation to applications to authorities in Scotland, prescribed by regulations made by the Scottish Ministers.

[Gambling Act 2005, s 190.]

Duration

8–13764   191. Initial duration.   (1) The Secretary of State may by regulations prescribe a period at the end of which premises licences expire (unless they cease to have effect earlier in accordance with a provision of this Part).

(2) Regulations under this section may make provision about renewal (and may, in particular, apply or make provision similar to any provision of this Part about an application for a premises licence).

(3) Regulations under this section may make provision which applies to licences issued before the regulations are made.

(4) If the Secretary of State does not prescribe a period under this section in respect of a premises licence, it shall continue to have effect unless and until it ceases to have effect in accordance with a provision of this Part.

[Gambling Act 2005, s 191.]

8–13765   192. Surrender.   (1) A premises licence shall cease to have effect if the licensee—

(*a*) notifies the licensing authority of his intention to surrender the licence, and

(*b*) gives the licensing authority either—

    (i) the licence, or

    (ii) a written statement explaining why it is not reasonably practicable to produce the licence.

(2) As soon as is reasonably practicable after receipt of notification under subsection (1)(*a*) the licensing authority shall notify—

(*a*) the Commission,

(*b*) either—

    (i) in England and Wales, the chief officer of police for any area in which the premises are wholly or partly situated, or

    (ii) in Scotland, the chief constable of the police force maintained for a police area in which the premises are wholly or partly situated, and

(*c*) Her Majesty's Commissioners of Customs and Excise.

[Gambling Act 2005, s 192.]

8–13766   193. Revocation for failure to pay fee.   (1) Where the holder of a premises licence fails to pay the annual fee in accordance with regulations under section 184 the licensing authority shall revoke the licence.

(2) But the licensing authority may disapply subsection (1) if they think that a failure to pay is attributable to administrative error.

[Gambling Act 2005, s 193.]

8–13767   194. Lapse.   (1) In the case of a premises licence issued to an individual, the licence shall lapse if—

(*a*) the licensee dies,

(*b*) the licensee becomes, in the opinion of the licensing authority as notified to the licensee, incapable of carrying on the licensed activities by reason of mental or physical incapacity,

(*c*) the licensee becomes bankrupt (within the meaning of section 381 of the Insolvency Act 1986 (c 45)), or

(*d*) sequestration of the licensee's estate is awarded under section 12(1) of the Bankruptcy (Scotland) Act 1985 (c 66).

(2) In any other case a premises licence shall lapse if the licensee—

(*a*) ceases to exist, or

(*b*) goes into liquidation (within the meaning of section 247(2) of the Insolvency Act 1986).

(3) If a licensing authority become aware that a premises licence issued by them has lapsed, they shall as soon as is reasonably practicable notify—

(*a*) the Commission,

(*b*) either—

    (i) in England and Wales, the chief officer of police for any area in which the premises are wholly or partly situated, or

    (ii) in Scotland, the chief constable of the police force maintained for a police area in which the premises are wholly or partly situated, and

(*c*) Her Majesty's Commissioners of Customs and Excise.
[Gambling Act 2005, s 194.]

8–13768 195. Reinstatement. (1) This section applies where a premises licence lapses under section 194.

(2) During the period of six months beginning with the date of the lapse of the premises licence a person may apply to the licensing authority for the licence to be reinstated with the applicant as the licensee.

(3) The provisions of this Part shall apply in relation to an application for reinstatement as they apply in relation to an application for a premises licence—

(*a*) subject to the provisions of this section and section 196, and
(*b*) with any other necessary modifications.

(4) An application for reinstatement must (in addition to anything required by section 159) request that the reinstatement take effect upon the application being granted.

(5) A licensing authority shall grant an application for reinstatement unless they think it would be wrong to do so having regard to representations made under section 161 (as applied by subsection (3) above).

(6) On the grant of an application for the reinstatement of a premises licence the licensing authority—

(*a*) shall alter the licence so that the applicant for reinstatement becomes the licensee,
(*b*) shall specify in the licence that the reinstatement takes effect at the time when the application is granted, and
(*c*) shall make such other alteration of the licence as appears to them to be required (which may, in particular, include an alteration to reflect a decision of the authority under section 169 as applied by subsection (3) above to make new or varied provision for the attachment or exclusion of conditions).

[Gambling Act 2005, s 195.]

8–13769 196. Reinstatement: supplemental. (1) An application under section 195 for the reinstatement of a premises licence must (in addition to anything required by section 159) be accompanied by—

(*a*) the licence, or
(*b*) both—

    (i) a statement explaining why it is not reasonably practicable to produce the licence, and
    (ii) an application under section 190 for the issue of a copy of the licence.

(2) In the case of an application under section 190 made in accordance with subsection (1)(*b*)(ii) above—

(*a*) the application shall be made by the applicant for reinstatement, and
(*b*) a reference to the licence being lost, stolen or damaged shall be treated as a reference to the licence being unavailable to the applicant for reinstatement.

(3) Regulations under section 160, as they have effect in relation to applications for reinstatement by virtue of section 195(3), may require notice to be given to specified responsible authorities (and not to all responsible authorities).

(4) Section 161 shall have effect in relation to an application for reinstatement with the omission of the reference to interested parties.

(5) Where an application is made under section 195 for the reinstatement of a premises licence, the licence shall have effect as if the applicant for reinstatement were the licensee during the period—

(*a*) beginning with the receipt of the application for reinstatement by the licensing authority, and
(*b*) ending with the determination of the application by the licensing authority.

[Gambling Act 2005, s 196.]

Review

8–13770 197. Application for review. (1) A responsible authority or interested party may apply to the licensing authority for a review by the authority of a premises licence.

(2) An application must—

(*a*) be made in the prescribed form and manner,
(*b*) specify the grounds on which the review is sought, and
(*c*) contain or be accompanied by the prescribed information or documents.

(3) The Secretary of State may make regulations requiring an applicant—

(*a*) to give notice of his application to the licensee;
(*b*) to give notice of his application to the responsible authorities in relation to the premises.

(4) The Secretary of State may make regulations requiring the licensing authority to whom an application is made under this section to publish notice of the application.

(5) Regulations under subsection (2), (3) or (4) shall include provision—

(a) about the manner and form in which notice is to be published or given,

(b) about the period of time within which notice is to be published or given, and

(c) for the consequences of failure to comply with the regulations.

(6) Regulations by virtue of subsection (5)(a) shall, in particular, require a notice to specify a period of time during which representations about the application may be made to the licensing authority by—

(a) the licensee,

(b) a responsible authority, or

(c) an interested party.

(7) In relation to applications to authorities in Scotland, subsections (3) and (4) shall have effect as if the references to the Secretary of State were references to the Scottish Ministers.
[Gambling Act 2005, s 197.]

8–13771 198. Rejection of application. (1) A licensing authority may reject an application under section 197 for the review of a premises licence if they think that the grounds on which the review is sought—

(a) do not raise an issue relevant to the principles to be applied in accordance with section 153,

(b) are frivolous,

(c) are vexatious,

(d) will certainly not cause the authority to wish to take action of a kind specified in section 202(1),

(e) are substantially the same as the grounds specified in an earlier application under section 197 in respect of the premises licence, or

(f) are substantially the same as representations made under section 161 in relation to the application for the premises licence.

(2) In determining whether to exercise the power to reject an application under section 197 in accordance with subsection (1)(e) or (f), a licensing authority shall consider the length of time that has elapsed since the making of the earlier application or since the making of the representations under section 161.

(3) If a licensing authority consider that paragraphs (a) to (f) apply to some but not all of the grounds on which a review is sought, they may reject the application in so far as it relies on grounds to which those paragraphs apply.

(4) In this section a reference to section 161 includes a reference to that section as applied by section 187(3).
[Gambling Act 2005, s 198.]

8–13772 199. Grant of application. (1) This section applies where an application for review has been made to a licensing authority under section 197.

(2) If, or in so far as, the licensing authority do not reject the application under section 198 they shall grant it.
[Gambling Act 2005, s 199.]

8–13773 200. Initiation of review by licensing authority. (1) A licensing authority may review in relation to premises licences of a particular class—

(a) the use made of premises, and

(b) in particular, arrangements made by licensees to ensure compliance with conditions attached under section 167, 168 or 169 or by a provision of this Part.

(2) A licensing authority may review any matter connected with the use of premises in reliance on a premises licence if the authority—

(a) have reason to suspect that the premises may have been used in purported reliance on a licence but not in accordance with a condition of the licence, or

(b) for any reason (which may relate to the receipt of a complaint about the use of the premises) think that a review would be appropriate.

(3) Before reviewing a premises licence under subsection (2) the licensing authority shall—

(a) give notice of their intention to hold the review to the licensee, and

(b) publish notice of their intention to hold the review.

(4) The Secretary of State may make regulations about—

(a) the manner and form in which notice under subsection (3) is to be given or published, and

(b) the period of time within which notice is to be given or published.

(5) Regulations by virtue of subsection (4)(a) shall, in particular, require a notice to specify a period of time during which representations about the review may be made to the licensing authority by—

(a)　the licensee,

(b)　a responsible authority, or

(c)　an interested party.

(6)　In relation to notice given by a licensing authority in Scotland, subsection (4) shall have effect as if the reference to the Secretary of State were a reference to the Scottish Ministers.

[Gambling Act 2005, s 200.]

8–13774　　201. Review.　　(1)　This section applies where a licensing authority—

(a)　have granted an application for a review of a premises licence under section 199, or

(b)　have given notice under section 200 of their intention to hold a review of a premises licence.

(2)　As soon as is reasonably practicable after the expiry of any period for representations prescribed under section 197(6) or 200(5), the licensing authority shall review the premises licence.

(3)　The purpose of the review shall be to consider whether to take action of a kind specified in section 202(1) in relation to the licence.

(4)　In conducting a review of a premises licence a licensing authority shall hold a hearing unless—

(a)　the applicant for the review (if there is one), and each person who has made representations about the review under section 197(6) or 200(5), have consented to the conduct of the review without a hearing, or

(b)　the licensing authority think that each representation made about the review in accordance with section 197(6) or 200(5)—

　　　(i)　is frivolous,

　　　(ii)　is vexatious, or

　　　(iii)　will certainly not influence the review.

(5)　In considering whether to take action of a kind specified in section 202(1) the licensing authority shall have regard (in addition to the matters specified in section 153) to—

(a)　any representations made in accordance with section 197(6) or 200(5),

(b)　any representations made at the hearing of the review (if there is one), and

(c)　in the case of a review held in response to an application under section 197, the grounds specified in the application for the review (apart from any in relation to which the application was rejected under section 198(3)).

[Gambling Act 2005, s 201.]

8–13775　　202. Action following review.　　(1)　As a result of a review of a premises licence under section 201 a licensing authority may—

(a)　revoke the licence;

(b)　suspend the licence for a specified period not exceeding three months;

(c)　exclude a condition attached to the licence under section 168 or remove or amend an exclusion;

(d)　add, remove or amend a condition under section 169.

(2)　If the licensing authority decide to take action of a kind specified in subsection (1) they shall specify the time at which the action shall take effect.

(3)　A licensing authority may, in particular, take action under subsection (1) on the grounds that the licensee has not used the licence.

[Gambling Act 2005, s 202.]

8–13776　　203. Determination.　　(1)　As soon as possible after completion of a review of a premises licence under section 201 a licensing authority shall give notice of their decision on the review to—

(a)　the licensee,

(b)　the applicant for the review (if any),

(c)　the Commission,

(d)　any person who made representations in accordance with section 197 or 200,

(e)　either—

　　　(i)　in England and Wales, the chief officer of police for any area in which the premises are wholly or partly situated, or

　　　(ii)　in Scotland, the chief constable of the police force maintained for a police area in which the premises are wholly or partly situated, and

(f)　Her Majesty's Commissioners of Customs and Excise.

(2)　A notice under subsection (1)—

(a)　must be in the prescribed form, and

(b)　must give the authority's reasons for their decision.

[Gambling Act 2005, s 203.]

Provisional statement

8–13777 204. Application. (1) A person may make an application for a provisional statement in respect of premises—

(a) that he expects to be constructed,
(b) that he expects to be altered, or
(c) that he expects to acquire a right to occupy.

(2) The provisions of this Part shall apply in relation to an application for a provisional statement as they apply in relation to an application for a premises licence—

(a) subject to the provisions of this section and section 205, and
(b) with any other necessary modifications.

(3) An application for a provisional statement shall include such plans and other information in relation to the construction, alteration or acquisition as may be prescribed.

(4) Sections 152(1)(b) and 159(3) and (5) shall not apply in relation to an application for a provisional statement.
[Gambling Act 2005, s 20.4]

8–13778 205. Effect. (1) This section applies where—

(a) a licensing authority issue a provisional statement in respect of premises, and
(b) an application is made under section 159 for a premises licence in respect of the premises.

(2) The licensing authority shall disregard any representations made in relation to the application for the premises licence unless they think that the representations—

(a) address matters that could not have been addressed in representations in relation to the application for the provisional statement, or
(b) reflect a change in the applicant's circumstances.

(3) The licensing authority may refuse the application, or grant it on terms or conditions not included in the provisional statement, only by reference to matters which—

(a) the authority have considered in reliance on subsection (2)(a), or
(b) in the authority's opinion reflect a change in the applicant's circumstances.

(4) But subsections (2) and (3) do not apply in the case of a provisional statement issued in response to an application under section 204(1)(a) or (b) if the licensing authority think that the premises have been constructed or altered otherwise than in accordance with the plans and information included with the application for the provisional statement in accordance with section 204(3).
[Gambling Act 2005, s 205.]

Appeals

8–13779 206. Rights of appeal

8–13780 207. Process

8–13781 208. Stay pending appeal

8–13782 209. Further appeal

General

8–13783 210. Planning permission. (1) In making a decision in respect of an application under this Part a licensing authority shall not have regard to whether or not a proposal by the applicant is likely to be permitted in accordance with the law relating to planning or building.

(2) A decision by a licensing authority under this Part shall not constrain any later decision by the authority under the law relating to planning or building.
[Gambling Act 2005, s 210.]

8–13784 211. Vehicles and vessels. (1) A premises licence—

(a) may not be issued in relation to a vehicle (or part of a vehicle),
(b) may be issued in relation to all or part of a passenger vessel,
(c) may be issued in relation to all or part of a vessel (within the meaning of section 353(1)) situated at a fixed place in or on water, and
(d) may not be issued in relation to all or part of a vessel to which neither of paragraphs (b) and (c) applies.

(2) A premises licence in relation to a vessel may include a condition imposed by virtue of section 169 about the location of the vessel.

(3) In relation to a vessel, a reference in this Part to a place in which premises are wholly or partly situated shall be construed—

(a) in the case of a vessel (within the meaning of section 353(1)) situated at a fixed place in or on water, as a reference to that place,

(b) in the case of a vessel which is permanently moored at a place, as a reference to that place,

(c) in the case of a vessel which is habitually moored at one place more frequently or for longer periods than at any other place, as a reference to that place, and

(d) in any other case, as a reference to any place at which a vessel is moored or is likely to be moored, or to the place in the United Kingdom nearest to any place at which a vessel is or is likely to be, while activities are carried on in the vessel in reliance on a premises licence.

(4) In relation to a vessel, the following are responsible authorities for the purposes of this Part (in addition to the persons listed in section 157)—

(a) a navigation authority, within the meaning of section 221(1) of the Water Resources Act 1991 (c 57), which has functions in relation to any place where the vessel is or is likely to be while activities are carried on in the vessel in reliance on a premises licence,

(b) the Environment Agency,

(c) the British Waterways Board, and

(d) the Secretary of State.

[Gambling Act 2005, s 211.]

8–13785 212. Fees

8–13786 213. Interpretation. In this Part—

(a) "authorised activity", in relation to a premises licence, means an activity specified under section 151(1)(d),

(b) "chief officer of police" has the meaning given by section 101(1) of the Police Act 1996 (c 16),

(c) a reference to a chief officer's area is a reference to the area in respect of which he has responsibility under that Act,

(d) "holder", in relation to a premises licence, means the person to whom the licence is issued,

(e) "licensee", in relation to a premises licence, also means the person to whom the licence is issued,

(f) "the licensing authority", in relation to a premises licence, means the authority who issued the licence, and

(g) "prescribed" means (except where the contrary is provided) prescribed by regulations made by the Secretary of State.

[Gambling Act 2005, s 213.]

PART 9[1]

TEMPORARY USE OF PREMISES

Temporary use notice

8–13787 214. Exception to offence of using premises for gambling. (1) A person who uses premises to carry on an activity listed in section 37(1), or who causes or permits premises to be used to carry on an activity to which that section applies, does not commit an offence under that section if—

(a) a temporary use notice under this Part has effect in respect of the premises, and

(b) the activity is carried on in accordance with the terms of the notice.

[Gambling Act 2005, s 214.]

---

1. Part 9 contains ss 214–234

8–13788 215. Nature of notice. (1) A temporary use notice is a notice given in accordance with the provisions of this Part—

(a) by the holder of an operating licence, and

(b) stating his intention to carry on one or more specified prescribed activities.

(2) The Secretary of State may by regulations—

(a) prescribe activities which may be specified in a notice under subsection (1)(b);

(b) prescribe combinations of activity that may not be specified in a notice under subsection (1)(b);

(c) prescribe activities which may be specified under subsection (1)(b) only if no other prescribed activity is specified in the notice.

(3) A temporary use notice given by a person may specify an activity under subsection (1)(b) only if the person's operating licence authorises him to carry on the activity.

[Gambling Act 2005, s 215.]

8–13789 **216. Form of notice.** (1) A temporary use notice must—

   (*a*) be in the prescribed form,
   (*b*) specify the activity to be carried on in reliance on the notice,
   (*c*) specify the premises on which the activity is to be carried on,
   (*d*) specify the period of time during which the notice is to have effect,
   (*e*) specify the times of day during that period at which the activity is to be carried on,
   (*f*) specify any periods during the previous 12 months during which a temporary use notice has had effect in respect of the premises or any part of the premises,
   (*g*) specify the date on which the notice is given, and
   (*h*) contain any other prescribed information.

(2) In this section "prescribed" means prescribed by regulations made by the Secretary of State.
(3) In subsection (1)(*f*) "the previous 12 months" means the period of 12 months ending with the last day of the period specified under subsection (1)(*d*).
[Gambling Act 2005, s 216.]

8–13790 **217. Effect of notice.** A temporary use notice shall, subject to the provisions of this Part and provided that the requirements of this Part are complied with, have effect during the period specified in the notice in accordance with section 216(1)(*d*).
[Gambling Act 2005, s 217.]

8–13791 **218. Maximum permitted period.** (1) A set of premises may not be the subject of temporary use notification for more than 21 days in a period of 12 months.
(2) A set of premises may be the subject of more than one temporary use notice in a period of 12 months (provided that the aggregate of the periods for which the notices have effect does not exceed 21 days).
(3) If a temporary use notice is given to a licensing authority and subsection (1) would be contravened if the notice had effect for any part of the period specified in accordance with section 216(1)(*d*), the licensing authority shall give a counter-notice providing for the temporary use notice not to have effect.
(4) Subsections (5) and (6) apply where a temporary use notice is given to a licensing authority and—

   (*a*) subsection (1) would be contravened if the notice had effect for the whole of the period specified in accordance with section 216(1)(*d*) ("the specified period"), but
   (*b*) the notice could have effect for some part of the specified period without resulting in contravention of subsection (1).

(5) The licensing authority shall give a counter-notice providing that the temporary use notice—

   (*a*) shall not have effect during such part of the specified period as the licensing authority may specify in the counter-notice ("the excluded period"), and
   (*b*) shall be treated for the purposes of this Part as if it related only to the non-excluded period.

(6) Where there is a choice as to which part of the specified period to exclude under subsection (5), the licensing authority shall consult the person who gave the temporary use notice before giving a counter-notice by virtue of that subsection.
(7) A counter-notice under this section shall have effect; and subsections (4) and (6) of section 224 shall apply in relation to a counter-notice given under this section as they apply in relation to a counter-notice given under that section.
(8) For the purposes of this section a set of premises is the subject of temporary use notification (or of a notice) if any part of the premises is the subject of temporary use notification (or of a notice).
[Gambling Act 2005, s 218.]

Procedure

8–13792 **219. Giving notice.** (1) A temporary use notice must be given to the licensing authority for the area in which the premises specified under section 216(1)(*c*) are situated.
(2) A temporary use notice must be given before the period of three months ending with the day before the period specified under section 216(1)(*d*).
(3) A temporary use notice given under subsection (1) must be accompanied by—

   (*a*) a copy of the notice, and
   (*b*) such fee as may be prescribed by regulations made—

      (i) in relation to premises in England and Wales, by the Secretary of State, and
      (ii) in relation to premises in Scotland, by the Scottish Ministers.

(4) A person who gives a temporary use notice must give a copy of it to—

   (*a*) the Commission,

(b) either—

    (i) in England and Wales, the chief officer of police for any area in which the premises specified in the notice are wholly or partly situated, or

    (ii) in Scotland, the chief constable of the police force maintained for a police area in which the premises are wholly or partly situated, and

(c) Her Majesty's Commissioners of Customs and Excise.

(5) A person who gives a temporary use notice must ensure that it, and any copy required by this section to be given, are received within the period of 7 days beginning with the date specified under section 216(1)(g).

(6) In the case of premises situated partly in the area of one licensing authority and partly in the area of another, the person giving the notice—

(a) may give it to either authority, and

(b) shall give a copy of the notice to the other authority.

(7) In this Part—

(a) "chief officer of police" has the meaning given by section 101(1) of the Police Act 1996 (c 16), and

(b) a reference to a chief officer's area is a reference to the area in respect of which he has responsibility under that Act.

(8) Section 212 shall have effect in relation to fees under this section as it has effect in relation to fees under Part 8.

[Gambling Act 2005, s 219.]

8-13793   220. Acknowledgment of notice.   Where a licensing authority receive a temporary use notice in accordance with section 219(1) they shall as soon as is reasonably practicable send a written acknowledgment of the notice to the person who gave it.

[Gambling Act 2005, s 220.]

8-13794   221. Objections.   (1) This section applies where a person receives a temporary use notice, or a copy of a temporary use notice, in accordance with section 219.

(2) If the person thinks that having regard to the licensing objectives the temporary premises notice should not have effect, or should have effect only with modification, he may give a notice of objection to the person who gave the temporary use notice.

(3) A person who gives a notice of objection under subsection (2) must give a copy of the notice to the licensing authority to which the temporary use notice was given (unless it is that licensing authority which give the notice of objection).

(4) A notice of objection and any copy required by subsection (3) must be given within the period of 14 days beginning with the date on which the temporary use notice is given as specified under section 216(1)(g).

(5) A notice of objection must state—

(a) that the person giving the notice objects to the temporary use notice, and

(b) the person's reasons.

(6) If the person who gives a notice of objection later withdraws it by notice in writing to the persons mentioned in subsections (2) and (3), the notice of objection shall be disregarded.

[Gambling Act 2005, s 221.]

8-13795   222. Hearing of objections.   (1) This section applies where—

(a) a temporary use notice is given to a licensing authority in accordance with section 219, and

(b) a notice of objection is given in accordance with section 221.

(2) The licensing authority shall hold a hearing at which any of the following may make representations about the notice of objection—

(a) the person who gave the temporary use notice,

(b) the person who gave the notice of objection, and

(c) any other person who was entitled to receive a copy of the temporary use notice in accordance with section 219.

(3) But the licensing authority need not arrange a hearing if the authority and each person who would be entitled to make representations agree in writing that a hearing is unnecessary.

[Gambling Act 2005, s 222.]

8-13796   223. Modification by agreement.   (1) This section applies where—

(a) a person has given a temporary use notice to a licensing authority in accordance with section 219,

(b) a notice of objection has been given by a person ("the objector") in accordance with section 221, and

(c)   a hearing in accordance with section 222(2) has neither—

  (i)   taken place, nor
  (ii) been dispensed with in accordance with section 222(3).

(2) The objector may by notice in writing to the person who gave the temporary use notice propose a modification of that notice.

(3) If the person who gave the temporary use notice accepts the modification—

(a)   he shall give a new notice, incorporating the modification, in accordance with section 219, and

(b)   the objection shall be treated as withdrawn (but without prejudice to the right of any person other than the objector to give a notice of objection in relation to the new notice).

(4) The following provisions of section 219 shall not apply to a temporary use notice given under subsection (3)(a) above—

(a)   subsection (2), and
(b)   subsection (3)(b).

[Gambling Act 2005, s 223.]

8–13797   224. Counter-notice.   (1) This section applies where—

(a)   a person has given a temporary use notice to a licensing authority in accordance with section 219,

(b)   a notice of objection has been given in accordance with section 221, and

(c)   a hearing—

  (i)   has taken place in accordance with section 222(2), or
  (ii) has been dispensed with in accordance with section 222(3).

(2) If the licensing authority think that the temporary use notice should not have effect or should have effect only with modification, the authority may give a counter-notice under this subsection to the person who gave the temporary use notice.

(3) A counter-notice may provide for the temporary use notice—

(a)   not to have effect;
(b)   to have effect only in respect of a specified activity;
(c)   to have effect only in respect of activity carried on during a specified period of time or at specified times of day;
(d)   to have effect subject to compliance with a specified condition;

and provision made under this subsection shall have effect.

(4) A counter-notice must—

(a)   be in the prescribed form,
(b)   contain the prescribed information, and
(c)   be given as soon as is reasonably practicable.

(5) A counter-notice must state the licensing authority's reasons for giving it.

(6) Where a licensing authority give a counter-notice they shall as soon as is reasonably practicable give a copy to any person who was entitled to receive a copy of the temporary use notice.

(7) Section 153(1) shall apply to the exercise of a licensing authority's functions under this section as it applies to the exercise of a licensing authority's functions under Part 8.

(8) In this section "prescribed" means prescribed by regulations made by the Secretary of State.

[Gambling Act 2005, s 224.]

8–13798   225. Dismissal of objection.   (1) This section applies where—

(a)   a person has given a temporary use notice to a licensing authority in accordance with section 219,

(b)   a notice of objection has been given in accordance with section 221, and

(c)   the licensing authority has determined not to give a counter-notice.

(2) The licensing authority shall as soon as is reasonably practicable give notice of their determination to—

(a)   the person who gave the temporary use notice, and

(b)   each person who received a copy of the temporary use notice in accordance with section 219.

[Gambling Act 2005, s 225.]

8–13799   226. Appeal

8–13800   227. Endorsement of notice.   (1) This section applies where a temporary use notice has been given to a licensing authority under section 219.

(2) If no notice of objection is pending in relation to the temporary use notice when the 14 day period specified in section 221(4) expires, the licensing authority shall—

    (*a*)   endorse the copy submitted under section 219(3)(*a*) in such manner as may be prescribed by the Secretary of State by regulations, and

    (*b*)   return the endorsed copy, as soon as is reasonably practicable, to the person giving the notice.

  (3) If a notice of objection is pending in relation to a temporary use notice when the 14 day period specified in section 221(4) expires, then as soon as is reasonably practicable after the completion of proceedings on the temporary use notice the licensing authority shall, unless they give a counter-notice under section 224(3)(*a*)—

    (*a*)   endorse the copy submitted under section 219(3)(*a*) in such manner as may be prescribed by the Secretary of State by regulations, and

    (*b*)   return the endorsed copy, as soon as is reasonably practicable, to the person giving the temporary use notice.

  (4) For the purposes of this section a notice of objection is pending if it has been given in accordance with section 221 and—

    (*a*)   it has not been withdrawn, and

    (*b*)   it is not treated as withdrawn in accordance with section 223(3)(*b*).

  (5) For the purposes of this section proceedings on a temporary use notice are completed—

    (*a*)   if any notice of objection given in relation to the temporary use notice has been withdrawn, or

    (*b*)   if the licensing authority has given a counter-notice under section 224 or a notice under section 225.

  (6) A licensing authority shall make arrangements whereby if an endorsed copy of a temporary use notice is lost, stolen or damaged the person who gave the notice can obtain a new endorsed copy; and—

    (*a*)   the arrangements may include the charging of such fee as the Secretary of State may prescribe by regulations, and

    (*b*)   section 212 shall have effect in relation to fees under paragraph (*a*) above as it has effect in relation to fees under Part 8.

[Gambling Act 2005, s 227.]

8–13801   228. Consideration by licensing authority: timing.   (1) Where a licensing authority are given a temporary use notice in accordance with section 219 the authority shall complete proceedings on the notice before the end of the period of six weeks beginning with the date on which they receive the notice.

  (2) In subsection (1) the reference to proceedings on a temporary use notice is a reference to—

    (*a*)   considering whether to give a notice of objection under section 221,

    (*b*)   holding a hearing in relation to any notice of objection given under section 221 (whether or not by the licensing authority) or agreeing to dispense with a hearing in accordance with section 222(3), and

    (*c*)   giving a counter-notice under section 224 or a notice under section 225.

[Gambling Act 2005, s 228.]

Miscellaneous

8–13802   229. Availability of notice.   (1) A person who gives a temporary use notice in respect of premises shall—

    (*a*)   arrange for a copy of the notice to be displayed prominently on the premises at any time when an activity is being carried on in reliance on the notice, and

    (*b*)   arrange for the notice endorsed by the licensing authority in accordance with section 227 to be produced on request to—

        (i)   a constable,

        (ii)   an officer of customs and excise,

        (iii)   an enforcement officer, or

        (iv)   an authorised local authority officer.

  (2) A person commits an offence if he fails without reasonable excuse to comply with subsection (1).

  (3) A person guilty of an offence under subsection (2) shall be liable on summary conviction to a fine not exceeding level 2 on the standard scale.

[Gambling Act 2005, s 229.]

8–13803   230. Withdrawal of notice.   If a person who gives a temporary use notice to a licensing authority in accordance with section 219 notifies the licensing authority that the notice is withdrawn—

    (*a*)   the notice shall have no effect (or, if it has started to have effect, shall cease to have effect), and (*b*)   no further proceedings shall take place in respect of the notice (except in respect of a matter arising during or in relation to a time at which the notice had effect).

[Gambling Act 2005, s 230.]

8–13804   231. Vehicles and vessels.   (1) A temporary use notice—

(*a*)   may not be given in respect of a vehicle (or part of a vehicle),

(*b*)   may be given in respect of all or part of a passenger vessel,

(*c*)   may be given in respect of all or part of a vessel (within the meaning of section 353(1)) situated at a fixed place in or on water, and

(*d*)   may not be given in respect of all or part of a vessel to which neither of paragraphs (*b*) and (*c*) applies.

(2) In relation to a vessel, a reference in this Part to a place in which premises are wholly or partly situated shall be construed—

(*a*)   in the case of a vessel (within the meaning of section 353(1)) situated at a fixed place in or on water, as a reference to that place,

(*b*)   in the case of a vessel which is permanently moored at a place, as a reference to that place,

(*c*)   in the case of a vessel which is habitually moored at one place more frequently or for longer periods than at any other place, as a reference to that place, and

(*d*)   in any other case, as a reference to any place at which a vessel is moored or is likely to be moored, or to the place in the United Kingdom nearest to any place at which a vessel is or is likely to be, while activities are carried on in the vessel in reliance on a temporary use notice.

(3) In relation to a vessel, the following are responsible authorities for the purposes of this Part (in addition to the persons listed in section 157)—

(*a*)   a navigation authority, within the meaning of section 221(1) of the Water Resources Act 1991 (c 57), which has functions in relation to any place at which a vessel is moored or is likely to be moored, or to the place in the United Kingdom nearest to any place at which a vessel is or is likely to be, while activities are carried on in the vessel in reliance on a temporary use notice,

(*b*)   the Environment Agency,

(*c*)   the British Waterways Board, and

(*d*)   the Secretary of State.

[Gambling Act 2005, s 231.]

8–13805   232. Delegation of licensing authority functions: England and Wales.   (1) The functions under this Part of a licensing authority in England and Wales are by virtue of this subsection delegated to the licensing committee of the authority established under section 6 of the Licensing Act 2003 (c 17).

(2) The following provisions of the Licensing Act 2003 shall apply in relation to a function delegated to a licensing committee under this section as they apply in relation to a function delegated under that Act—

(*a*)   section 7(9) (referral back to licensing authority), and

(*b*)   section 10 (sub-delegation).

(3) In the application of section 10(4) of that Act (matters not to be delegated to officer) by virtue of subsection (2) above, for the list of functions there shall be substituted a reference to any function under section 224 of this Act.

(4) The provisions of section 9 of that Act and regulations under it apply to proceedings of licensing committees and their sub-committees in relation to the exercise of functions under this Part; and for that purpose regulations may, in particular, make provision which applies—

(*a*)   only in relation to functions under that Act,

(*b*)   only in relation to functions under this Part, or

(*c*)   differently in relation to functions under that Act and functions under this Part.

[Gambling Act 2005, s 232.]

8–13806   233. Delegation of functions under Part 9: Scotland

8–13807   234. Register.   (1) A licensing authority shall—

(*a*)   maintain a register of temporary use notices given to them together with such other information as may be prescribed,

(*b*)   make the register and information available for inspection by members of the public at all reasonable times, and

(*c*)   make arrangements for the provision of a copy of an entry in the register, or of information, to a member of the public on request.

(2) A licensing authority may refuse to provide a copy of an entry or of information unless the person seeking it pays a reasonable fee specified by the authority.

(3) The Secretary of State may make regulations about—

(*a*) the form of the register;

(*b*) the manner in which it is maintained.

(4) The Secretary of State may make regulations—

(*a*) requiring licensing authorities to give to the Commission specified information about temporary use notices given to them,

(*b*) requiring the Commission to maintain a register of the information provided to it under paragraph (*a*),

(*c*) requiring the Commission to grant access to the register to members of the public (without charge),

(*d*) requiring the Commission to make copies of entries available on request, and on payment of a reasonable fee, to members of the public, and

(*e*) excusing licensing authorities, wholly or partly, from compliance with subsection (1).

[Gambling Act 2005, s 234.]

PART 10[1]

GAMING MACHINES

Definitions

8–13808   235. Gaming machine[2]**.** (1) In this Act "gaming machine" means a machine which is designed or adapted for use by individuals to gamble (whether or not it can also be used for other purposes).

(2) But—

(*a*) a domestic or dual-use computer is not a gaming machine by reason only of the fact that it can be used to participate in remote gambling,

(*b*) a telephone or other machine for facilitating communication (other than a computer) is not a gaming machine by reason only of the fact that it can be used to participate in remote gambling,

(*c*) a machine is not a gaming machine by reason only of the fact that it is designed or adapted for use to bet on future real events,

(*d*) a machine is not a gaming machine by reason only of the fact that it dispenses lottery tickets or otherwise enables a person to enter a lottery provided that the results of the lottery—

(i) are not determined by the machine, and

(ii) are not announced by being displayed or communicated by the machine without there being an interval, between each entry to the lottery and the announcement, of at least such duration as the Secretary of State shall prescribe by order,

(*e*) a machine is not a gaming machine if—

(i) it is designed or adapted for the playing of bingo, and

(ii) it is used in accordance with a condition attached to a bingo operating licence under section 75 or 77 by virtue of section 85(2)(*b*),

(*f*) a machine is not a gaming machine if—

(i) it is designed or adapted for the playing of bingo by way of prize gaming, and

(ii) it is used in accordance with a condition attached to a gaming machine general operating licence under section 75 or 77 by virtue of section 85(2)(*b*),

(*g*) a machine is not a gaming machine if—

(i) it is designed or adapted for the playing of bingo by way of prize gaming,

(ii) it is made available for use in reliance on a family entertainment centre gaming machine permit or a prize gaming permit, and

(iii) any requirements prescribed for the purposes of this paragraph in a code of practice under section 24, as to the specification of the machine or the circumstances in which it is made available for use, are complied with,

(*h*) a machine is not a gaming machine by reason only of the fact that it is designed or adapted to be—

(i) controlled or operated by an individual employed or concerned in arranging for others to play a real game of chance, or

(ii) used in connection with a real game of chance the arrangements for which are controlled or operated by an individual, and

(*i*) a machine is not a gaming machine by reason only of the fact that it is designed or adapted to enable individuals to play a real game of chance, if—

(i) its design or adaptation is such that it does not require to be controlled or operated by a person employed or concerned in arranging for others to play the game,

(ii) it is not designed or adapted for use in connection with a game the arrangements for which are controlled or operated by an individual, and

(iii) it is used in accordance with a condition attached to a casino operating licence under section 75 or 77 by virtue of section 85(2)(*b*).

(3) In this Act—

(*a*) a reference to a machine is a reference to any apparatus which uses or applies mechanical power, electrical power or both,

(*b*) a reference to a machine being designed or adapted for a purpose includes—

(i) a reference to a computer being able to be used for that purpose (subject to subsection (2)), and

(ii) a reference to any other machine to which anything has been done as a result of which it can reasonably be expected to be used for that purpose (subject to subsection (2)),

(*c*) a reference to a part of a gaming machine—

(i) includes a reference to any computer software designed or adapted for use in a gaming machine, but

(ii) does not include a reference to a component of a gaming machine which does not influence the outcome of a game,

(*d*) a reference to installing a part of a gaming machine includes a reference to installing computer software for the purpose of altering the operation of a gaming machine,

(*e*) a reference to adapting a gaming machine includes a reference to adapting a machine so that it becomes a gaming machine, and

(*f*) "domestic computer" and "dual-use computer" shall have the meanings assigned by the Secretary of State by regulations.

(4) Regulations under subsection (3)(*f*) may, in particular, make provision by reference to—

(*a*) the location of a computer,

(*b*) the purposes for which a computer is used,

(*c*) the circumstances in which a computer is used,

(*d*) the software installed on a computer, or

(*e*) any other matter.

(5) The Secretary of State may make regulations providing for circumstances in which a single piece of apparatus is to be treated as more than one gaming machine for the purpose of provision made by or by virtue of this Act; and the regulations may, in particular, make provision by reference to the number of persons able to operate the apparatus at the same time.
[Gambling Act 2005, s 235.]

---

1. Part 10 contains ss 235–251.
2. For definitions of terms used within this section see s 353, post.

8–13809 236. Gaming machines: Categories A to D.   (1) The Secretary of State shall make regulations defining four classes of gaming machine for the purposes of this Act (to be known as Categories A, B, C, and D).

(2) Regulations under subsection (1) shall—

(*a*) divide Category B into sub-categories, and

(*b*) make provision for determining to which sub-category (or sub-categories) of Category B a reference in this Act to Category B shall be treated as referring.

(3) Regulations under subsection (1) shall operate by reference to the nature of the facilities for gambling provided by the machine.

(4) Regulations under subsection (1) may, in particular, make provision by reference to—

(*a*) amounts paid in respect of the use of a machine;

(*b*) the value of prizes;

(*c*) the nature of prizes;

(*d*) the nature of the gambling for which the machine can be used;

(*e*) the premises where a machine is used.

(5) Regulations under subsection (1) may identify matters (whether or not addressed by other provisions of the regulations) as to which a condition may not be attached to an operating licence or to a premises licence.

(6) In accordance with regulations under subsection (1) a machine may change category as a result of a change of the mechanism, or the loading or removal of software, which alters the nature of the facilities for gambling provided by the machine.
[Gambling Act 2005, s 236.]

8–13810 237. Adult gaming centre.   In this Act "adult gaming centre" means premises in respect of which an adult gaming centre premises licence has effect.
[Gambling Act 2005, s 237.]

8–13811   238. Family entertainment centre.   In this Act—

"family entertainment centre" means premises (other than an adult gaming centre) wholly or mainly used for making gaming machines available for use, and
"licensed family entertainment centre" means premises in respect of which a family entertainment centre premises licence has effect.
[Gambling Act 2005, s 238.]

8–13812   239. Prize.   In this Act "prize" in relation to a gaming machine—

(*a*) includes any money, article, right or service won, whether or not described as a prize, but
(*b*) does not include an opportunity to play the machine again.
[Gambling Act 2005, s 239.]

Regulations

8–13813   240. Use of machine.   (1) The Secretary of State may make regulations controlling the circumstances in which a gaming machine is made available for use.

(2) Regulations under subsection (1) may, in particular, make provision by reference to—

(*a*) the method by which stakes may be deposited or payments made for the use of a machine;
(*b*) the nature of, or arrangements in respect of receiving or claiming, prizes;
(*c*) rollover of stakes or prizes;
(*d*) the proportion of amounts staked or paid that is returned by way of prizes;
(*e*) the display of information;
(*f*) any other matter relating to the manner in which a machine operates.

(3) Regulations under subsection (1) may identify matters (whether or not addressed by other provisions of the regulations) as to which a condition may not be attached to an operating licence or to a premises licence.
[Gambling Act 2005, s 240.]

8–13814   241. Supply, &c.   (1) The Secretary of State may make regulations about the supply, installation, adaptation, maintenance or repair of a gaming machine or part of a gaming machine.

(2) Regulations under subsection (1) may identify matters (whether or not addressed by other provisions of the regulations) as to which a condition may not be attached to an operating licence or to a premises licence.
[Gambling Act 2005, s 241.]

Offences

8–13815   242. Making machine available for use.   (1) A person commits an offence if he makes a gaming machine available for use by another unless—

(*a*) he makes the machine available for use in accordance with an operating licence, or
(*b*) an exception in section 247, 248, 249, 271, 273, 282, 283 or 287 applies.

(2) A person commits an offence if he makes a gaming machine available for use in contravention of regulations under section 240.
[Gambling Act 2005, s 242.]

8–13816   243. Manufacture, supply, &c.   (1) A person commits an offence if he manufactures, supplies, installs, adapts, maintains or repairs a gaming machine or part of a gaming machine unless—

(*a*) he acts in accordance with an operating licence, or
(*b*) an exception in or under section 248 or 250 applies.

(2) A person commits an offence if he—

(*a*) supplies, installs, adapts, maintains or repairs a gaming machine or part of a gaming machine, and
(*b*) fails to comply with a provision of regulations under section 241.

(3) Subsections (1) and (2) do not apply to the supply of a gaming machine, or part of a gaming machine—

(*a*) as scrap (without any element of salvage), or
(*b*) incidental to the sale or letting of property on which the machine has previously been used in reliance on a provision of this Act.
[Gambling Act 2005, s 243.]

8–13817   244. Linked machines.   (1) A person commits an offence if—

(*a*) he makes a gaming machine ("the first gaming machine") available for use by another, and
(*b*) the amount or value of a prize available through use of the first gaming machine is or may be wholly or partly determined by reference to use made of another gaming machine ("the linked gaming machine").

(2) But subsection (1) does not apply where—

(*a*) the person who makes the first gaming machine available for use is the holder of a casino premises licence, and

(*b*) the first gaming machine and the linked gaming machine are situated on the same premises.

(3) The Secretary of State may by order amend, or modify the effect of, subsection (2) so that subsection (1) is disapplied to the linking of machines in casinos whether or not the machines are situated on the same premises—

(*a*) to such extent as the order may specify,

(*b*) in such circumstances as the order may specify, and

(*c*) subject to such conditions as the order may specify.

[Gambling Act 2005, s 244.]

8–13818 245. Credit.   (1) A person commits an offence if he supplies, installs or makes available for use a gaming machine which is designed or adapted to permit money to be paid by means of a credit card.

(2) In this section "credit card" means a card which is a credit-token within the meaning of section 14 of the Consumer Credit Act 1974 (c 39).

[Gambling Act 2005, s 245.]

8–13819 246. Penalty.   (1) A person guilty of an offence under this Part shall be liable on summary conviction to—

(*a*) imprisonment for a term not exceeding 51 weeks,

(*b*) a fine not exceeding level 5 on the standard scale, or

(*c*) both.

(2) In the application of subsection (1) to Scotland the reference to 51 weeks shall have effect as a reference to six months.

[Gambling Act 2005, s 246.]

Exceptions

8–13820 247. Family entertainment centre gaming machine permit.   (1) A person does not commit an offence under section 37 or 242 if he makes a Category D gaming machine available for use in accordance with a family entertainment centre gaming machine permit.

(2) A family entertainment centre gaming machine permit is a permit issued by a licensing authority authorising a person to make Category D gaming machines available for use in a specified family entertainment centre.

(3) Schedule 10 makes further provision about family entertainment centre gaming machine permits.

[Gambling Act 2005, s 247.]

8–13821 248. No prize.   (1) A person does not commit an offence under section 37 or 242 if—

(*a*) he makes a gaming machine available for use by an individual, and

(*b*) the individual does not, by using the machine, acquire an opportunity to win a prize.

(2) The Secretary of State may make regulations creating exceptions from the offence under section 243 in connection with machines which, by virtue of their nature or any other specified matter, are not designed or expected to be used to provide an opportunity to win a prize.

[Gambling Act 2005, s 248.]

8–13822 249. Limited prize.   (1) A person does not commit an offence under section 37 or 242 if—

(*a*) he makes a gaming machine available for use by an individual, and

(*b*) the individual does not, by using the machine, acquire an opportunity to win a prize of a value in excess of the amount that he pays for or in connection with his use of the machine.

(2) For the purpose of subsection (1)(*b*)—

(*a*) the reference to paying includes a reference to—

(i)   paying money by way of an entrance charge,

(ii) using a coin to activate a gaming machine where the coin will not or may not be returned,

(iii) transferring money's worth, and

(iv) paying for goods or services at a price or rate which reflects the opportunity to use a gaming machine, and

(*b*) it is immaterial—

(i)   to whom payment is made, and

(ii) who receives benefit from the payment.

[Gambling Act 2005, s 249.]

8–13823 250. Single-machine supply and maintenance permits. (1) A person does not commit an offence under section 33 or 243(1) by reason only of the fact that he supplies, repairs, installs or maintains a gaming machine or part of a gaming machine in accordance with a permit under this section.

(2) A person may apply to the Commission for a permit authorising him to supply, repair, install or maintain a gaming machine or part of a gaming machine.

(3) An application under this section must—

(*a*) be made in writing,
(*b*) specify the gaming machine or part in relation to which the permit is sought,
(*c*) give such details of the activity in relation to which the permit is sought as the Commission may direct,
(*d*) be in such form, and contain such other information, as the Commission may direct, and
(*e*) be accompanied by the prescribed fee.

(4) On consideration of an application under this section the Commission may—

(*a*) grant the application and issue a permit to the applicant, or
(*b*) refuse the application.

(5) The Commission may grant an application under this section only if satisfied that the licensing objectives are irrelevant to the activity for which the permit is sought.

(6) A permit under this section must specify—

(*a*) a period, not exceeding one year, during which it has effect,
(*b*) the machine or part to which it relates, and
(*c*) the activities which it authorises.

(7) A permit under this section may be subject to a condition attached by the Commission.

(8) In subsection (3)(*e*) "prescribed" means prescribed by regulations made by the Secretary of State.
[Gambling Act 2005, s 250.]

General

8–13824 251. Territorial application. This Part applies—

(*a*) to anything done in relation to a gaming machine which (or any part of which) is situated in Great Britain, and
(*b*) to anything done in Great Britain in relation to a gaming machine (irrespective of where it is situated).
[Gambling Act 2005, s 251.]

PART 11[1]
LOTTERIES[2]

Interpretation

8–13825 252. Promoting a lottery. (1) For the purposes of this Act a person promotes a lottery if he makes or participates in making the arrangements for a lottery.

(2) In particular, a person promotes a lottery if he—

(*a*) makes arrangements for the printing of lottery tickets,
(*b*) makes arrangements for the printing of promotional material,
(*c*) arranges for the distribution or publication of promotional material,
(*d*) possesses promotional material with a view to its distribution or publication,
(*e*) makes other arrangements to advertise a lottery,
(*f*) invites a person to participate in a lottery,
(*g*) sells or supplies a lottery ticket,
(*h*) offers to sell or supply a lottery ticket,
(*i*) possesses a lottery ticket with a view to its sale or supply,
(*j*) does or offers to do anything by virtue of which a person becomes a member of a class among whom prizes in a lottery are to be allocated, or
(*k*) uses premises for the purpose of allocating prizes or for any other purpose connected with the administration of a lottery.

(3) In subsection (2) "promotional material" means a document which—

(*a*) advertises a specified lottery,
(*b*) invites participation in a specified lottery,
(*c*) contains information about how to participate in a specified lottery, or
(*d*) lists winners in a specified lottery.

(4) Where arrangements for a lottery are made by an external lottery manager on behalf of a

society or authority, for the purposes of this Act both the external lottery manager and the society or authority promote the lottery.
[Gambling Act 2005, s 252.]

---

1. Part 11 contains ss 251–265.
2. "Lottery" has the meaning given to it by s 14 (and s 256).

8–13826   **253. Lottery ticket.**   (1) For the purposes of this Act a document or article is a lottery ticket if it confers, or can be used to prove, membership of a class for the purpose of the allocation of prizes in a lottery.

(2) A reference in this Act to the sale or supply of a lottery ticket by a person includes a reference to a person doing anything as a result of which another person becomes a member of the class among whom prizes in a lottery are to be allocated.

(3) A reference in this Act to purchase of a lottery ticket includes a reference to any action by a person as a result of which he becomes a member of the class among whom prizes in a lottery are to be allocated.
[Gambling Act 2005, s 253.]

8–13827   **254. Proceeds and profits.**   (1) In this Act a reference to the proceeds of a lottery is a reference to the aggregate of amounts paid in respect of the purchase of lottery tickets.

(2) In this Act a reference to the profits of a lottery is a reference to—

(a) the proceeds of the lottery, minus
(b) amounts deducted by the promoters of the lottery in respect of—

     (i) the provision of prizes,
     (ii) sums to be made available for allocation in another lottery in accordance with a rollover, or
     (iii) other costs reasonably incurred in organising the lottery.
[Gambling Act 2005, s 254.]

8–13828   **255. Draw.**   In this Act "draw", in relation to a lottery, includes any process by which a prize in the lottery is allocated.
[Gambling Act 2005, s 255.]

8–13829   **256. Rollover.**   (1) In this Act "rollover" in relation to a lottery means an arrangement whereby the fact that a prize is not allocated or claimed in one lottery increases the value of the prizes available for allocation in another lottery.

(2) For the purposes of this Act where prizes are allocated by means of more than one draw—

(a) the draws together constitute a single lottery if the class of persons among whom prizes are allocated is (and, by virtue of arrangements for the sale or supply of tickets, must be) the same in the case of each draw, and
(b) otherwise, the arrangements for each draw constitute a separate lottery.
[Gambling Act 2005, s 256.]

8–13830   **257. External lottery manager.**   A person acts as an external lottery manager for the purposes of this Act if he makes arrangements for a lottery on behalf of a society or authority of which he is not—

(a) a member,
(b) an officer, or
(c) an employee under a contract of employment.
[Gambling Act 2005, s 257.]

Offences

8–13831   **258. Promotion of lottery.**   (1) A person commits an offence if he promotes a lottery unless—

(a) the exception in subsection (2) or (3) applies, or
(b) the lottery is an exempt lottery.

(2) This section does not apply to activity by a person if—

(a) he holds an operating licence authorising the activity, and
(b) he acts in accordance with the terms and conditions of the licence.

(3) This section does not apply to activity by a person if—

(a) he acts, otherwise than as an external lottery manager, on behalf of a person who holds an operating licence authorising the activity, and
(b) the activity is carried on in accordance with the terms and conditions of the licence.

(4) It is a defence for a person charged with an offence under this section to show that he reasonably believed that—

(a) he was not committing the offence by reason of subsection (1)(*b*), (2) or (3),
(b) that the arrangement to which the charge relates was not a lottery, or
(c) that the arrangement to which the charge relates was a lottery forming part of the National Lottery.

(5) In this Act "exempt lottery" means a lottery which is exempt by virtue of a provision of Schedule 11.
[Gambling Act 2005, s 258.]

8–13832 259. Facilitating a lottery. (1) A person commits an offence if he facilitates a lottery unless—

(a) the exception in subsection (3) applies, or
(b) the lottery is an exempt lottery.

(2) For the purposes of this section a person facilitates a lottery if (and only if) he—

(a) prints lottery tickets for a specified lottery,
(b) prints promotional material for a specified lottery, or
(c) advertises a specified lottery.

(3) This section does not apply to activity by a person if he acts in accordance with the terms and conditions of an operating licence.
(4) It is a defence for a person charged with an offence under this section to show that he reasonably believed—

(a) that he was not committing the offence by reason of subsection (1)(*b*) or (3), or
(b) that the arrangement to which the charge relates was not a lottery, or
(c) that the arrangement to which the charge relates was a lottery forming part of the National Lottery.

(5) In subsection (2)(*b*) "promotional material" means a document which—

(a) advertises a specified lottery,
(b) invites participation in a specified lottery,
(c) contains information about how to participate in a specified lottery, or
(d) lists winners in a specified lottery.
[Gambling Act 2005, s 259.]

8–13833 260. Misusing profits of lottery. (1) This section applies to a lottery in respect of which the promoter has stated (in whatever terms) a fund-raising purpose for the promotion of the lottery.
(2) A person commits an offence if he uses any part of the profits of a lottery to which this section applies for a purpose other than that stated.
(3) The reference in subsection (2) to using profits includes a reference to permitting profits to be used.
(4) In subsection (1) the reference to a statement of a purpose for the promotion of a lottery is a reference to a statement appearing—

(a) on lottery tickets, or
(b) in an advertisement for the lottery.

(5) In subsection (4)(*b*) "advertisement" in relation to a lottery includes any written notice announcing that a lottery will take place or inviting people to participate in a lottery (in either case whether or not it also gives other information).
[Gambling Act 2005, s 260.]

8–13834 261. Misusing profits of exempt lottery. (1) This section applies to the following kinds of lottery—

(a) an incidental non-commercial lottery (within the meaning of Part 1 of Schedule 11),
(b) a private society lottery (within the meaning of Part 2 of that Schedule), and
(c) a small society lottery (within the meaning of Part 4 of that Schedule).

(2) A person commits an offence if he uses any part of the profits of a lottery to which this section applies for a purpose other than one for which the lottery is permitted to be promoted in accordance with Schedule 11.
(3) Subsection (3) of section 260 shall have effect for the purpose of this section as it has effect for the purpose of that section.
[Gambling Act 2005, s 261.]

8–13835 262. Small society lottery: breach of condition. A non-commercial society commits an offence if—

    (*a*) a lottery, purporting to be an exempt lottery under Part 4 of Schedule 11, is promoted on the society's behalf wholly or partly at a time when the society is not registered with a local authority in accordance with Part 5 of that Schedule,

    (*b*) the society fails to comply with the requirements of paragraph 39 of that Schedule, or

    (*c*) the society provides false or misleading information for the purposes of paragraph 39 of that Schedule.

[Gambling Act 2005, s 262.]

8–13836 263. Penalty. (1) A person guilty of an offence under this Part shall be liable on summary conviction to—

    (*a*) imprisonment for a term not exceeding 51 weeks,

    (*b*) a fine not exceeding level 5 on the standard scale, or

    (*c*) both.

(2) In the application of subsection (1) to Scotland the reference to 51 weeks shall have effect as a reference to six months.

[Gambling Act 2005, s 263.]

Miscellaneous

8–13837 264. Exclusion of the National Lottery. The preceding provisions of this Part do not apply to the National Lottery.

[Gambling Act 2005, s 264.]

General

8–13838 265. Territorial application. (1) This Part applies to anything done in relation to a lottery—

    (*a*) in Great Britain, or

    (*b*) by the provision of, or by means of, remote gambling equipment situated in Great Britain.

(2) But this Part does not apply in relation to a lottery if—

    (*a*) no person in Great Britain does anything by virtue of which he becomes a participant in the lottery, and

    (*b*) no person in Great Britain possesses tickets for the lottery with a view to selling or supplying them to a person in Great Britain who thereby becomes a participant in the lottery.

(3) It is a defence for a person charged with an offence under section 258 or 259 to show that he reasonably believed that this Part did not and would not apply to the lottery, by reason of subsection (2) above.

[Gambling Act 2005, s 265.]

PART 12[1]
CLUBS, PUBS, FAIRS, &C

Clubs

8–13839 266. Members' club. (1) In this Act members' club means a club—

    (*a*) which is established and conducted wholly or mainly for purposes other than the provision of facilities for gaming (subject to subsection (2)),

    (*b*) which is established and conducted for the benefit of its members (and which is not otherwise established or conducted as a commercial enterprise),

    (*c*) which is not established with the purpose of functioning only for a limited period of time, and

    (*d*) which has at least 25 individual members.

(2) A club is a members' club for the purposes of this Act despite subsection (1)(*a*) if—

    (*a*) it is established or conducted wholly or mainly for the purpose of the provision of facilities for gaming of a prescribed kind, and

    (*b*) facilities are not provided for any other kind of gaming in the course of the club's activities.

[Gambling Act 2005, s 266.]

---

1. Part 12 contains 266–287.

8–13840 267. Commercial club. (1) In this Act commercial club means a club—

    (*a*) which is established and conducted wholly or mainly for purposes other than the provision of facilities for gaming (subject to subsection (2)),

    (*b*) which is not established with the purpose of functioning only for a limited period of time, and

    (*c*) which has at least 25 individual members.

(2) A club is a commercial club for the purposes of this Act despite subsection (1)(*a*) if—

    (*a*) it is established or conducted wholly or mainly for the purpose of the provision of facilities for gaming of a prescribed kind, and

    (*b*) facilities are not provided for any other kind of gaming in the course of the club's activities.

[Gambling Act 2005, s 267.]

8–13841 268. Miners' welfare institute.   (1) In this Act miners' welfare institute means an association—

    (*a*) which is established and conducted for social and recreational purposes, and

    (*b*) which satisfies subsection (2) or (4).

(2) An association satisfies this subsection if its affairs are managed by a group of individuals of whom at least two thirds are miners' representatives.

(3) In subsection (2) "miners' representative" means a person who—

    (*a*) is nominated or appointed by a person who employs or has employed individuals in the course of a coal mining business,

    (*b*) is nominated or appointed by the charitable trust known as the Coal Industry Social Welfare Organisation,

    (*c*) is nominated or appointed by an organisation representing persons who are or were employed in connection with coal mining, or

    (*d*) is or was employed in connection with coal mining;

and the group mentioned in subsection (2) must contain both one or more persons of a kind specified in paragraph (*a*) or (*b*) and one or more persons of a kind specified in paragraph (*c*) or (*d*).

(4) An association satisfies this subsection if—

    (*a*) it operates on premises the use of which is regulated in accordance with a charitable trust, and

    (*b*) the trust has received money from—

        (i) the Miners' Welfare Fund established by section 20 of the Mining Industry Act 1920 (c 50),

        (ii) the former body corporate which was known as the Coal Industry Social Welfare Organisation and incorporated under the Companies Act 1948 (c 38), or

        (iii) the charitable trust known as the Coal Industry Social Welfare Organisation.

[Gambling Act 2005, s 268.]

8–13842 269. Exempt gaming.   (1) Sections 33 and 37 shall not apply to the provision of facilities for equal chance gaming which satisfies the conditions of this section by—

    (*a*) a members' club,

    (*b*) a commercial club,

    (*c*) a club that would be a members' club but for section 266(1)(*a*),

    (*d*) a club that would be a commercial club but for section 267(1)(*a*), or

    (*e*) a miners' welfare institute.

(2) The first condition of gaming for the purposes of subsection (1) is that the arrangements for the gaming satisfy the prescribed requirements (if any) in relation to—

    (*a*) amounts that may be staked, or

    (*b*) the amount or value of a prize.

(3) The second condition of gaming for the purposes of subsection (1) is that no amount is deducted or levied from sums staked or won.

(4) The third condition of gaming for the purposes of subsection (1) is that any participation fee does not exceed such maximum as may be prescribed.

(5) The fourth condition of gaming for the purposes of subsection (1) is that a game played on one set of premises is not linked with a game played on another set of premises.

(6) The fifth condition of gaming for the purposes of subsection (1), which does not apply to a club of a kind mentioned in subsection (1)(*b*) or (*d*), is that each person who participates—

    (*a*) is a member of the club or institute who applied for membership, was nominated for membership or became a member, at least 48 hours before he participates, or

    (*b*) is a guest of a member of the club or institute who would be entitled to participate by virtue of paragraph (*a*).

[Gambling Act 2005, s 269.]

8–13843 270. Section 269: supplementary.   (1) In section 269(1) a reference to the provision of facilities by a club or institute includes a reference to any provision of facilities made—

    (*a*) on behalf of or by arrangement with the club or institute, and

    (*b*) in the course of its activities.

(2) Regulations prescribing requirements in relation to stakes or prizes for the purposes of section 269(2) may, in particular—

(a) make different provision for different classes of club or institute;
(b) make different provision for different classes or descriptions of game.

(3) In section 269(3) the reference to a deduction or levy in respect of gaming provided by, on behalf of or by arrangement with a club or institute is to a deduction or levy made by or on behalf of—

(a) the club or institute, or
(b) a person providing facilities for gaming on behalf of, or by arrangement with, the club or institute.

(4) Regulations prescribing a maximum charge for the purposes of section 269(4) may, in particular—

(a) make different provision for different classes of club or institute;
(b) make provision depending on whether a club or institute holds a club gaming permit;
(c) make different provision for different classes or descriptions of game;
(d) make different provision for different classes or descriptions of fee.

(5) For the purposes of section 269(5) two games are linked if—

(a) the result of one game is or may be wholly or partly determined by reference to the result of the other game, or
(b) the amount of winnings available in one game is or may be wholly or partly determined by reference to the amount of participation in the other game;

and if a single game is played partly on one set of premises and partly on another it shall be treated as two linked games.

(6) For the purposes of section 269(6) a person shall not be treated as the guest of a member if the member extends an invitation—

(a) having had no previous acquaintance with the person, and
(b) for the purpose only of enabling the person to take advantage of facilities for gaming provided by or for the club or institute.

[Gambling Act 2005, s 270.]

8–13844 **271. Club gaming permit.** (1) Sections 33, 37 and 242 shall not apply to the provision of facilities for gaming in accordance with a club gaming permit.

(2) A club gaming permit is a permit issued by a licensing authority authorising the provision of facilities for gaming—

(a) on premises on which a members' club or a miners' welfare institute operates, and
(b) in the course of the activities of the club or institute.

(3) A club gaming permit shall, by virtue of this section, authorise—

(a) making up to three gaming machines available for use, each of which must be of Category B, C or D,
(b) the provision of facilities for gaming which satisfies the conditions in section 269 except for the first condition, and
(c) the provision of facilities for games of chance, of such class or description as may be prescribed, in accordance with the conditions specified in subsection (4).

(4) Those conditions are—

(a) that no participation fee is charged otherwise than in accordance with regulations (which may make provision about the circumstances in which a fee may be charged and about the amount of a fee),
(b) that no amount is deducted or levied from sums staked or won otherwise than in accordance with regulations (which may make provision about the circumstances in which an amount may be deducted or levied, about the amount of the deduction or levy and about the method by which the amount is determined),
(c) that the public is excluded from any area of the club's or institute's premises where gaming is taking place, and
(d) that children and young persons are excluded from any area of the club's or institute's premises where gaming is taking place.

(5) Regulations under subsection (4)(a) or (b) may—

(a) make different provision for different classes of club or institute;
(b) make different provision for different classes or descriptions of game;
(c) make different provision for different classes or descriptions of fee, deduction or levy.

(6) A club gaming permit shall, by virtue of this subsection, be subject to the condition that each person who participates in gaming in reliance on the permit—

(a) is a member of the club or institute who applied for membership, was nominated for membership or became a member, at least 48 hours before he participates, or
(b) is a guest of a member of the club or institute who would be entitled to participate by virtue of paragraph (a).

(7) A club gaming permit shall, by virtue of this subsection, be subject to the conditions—

(a) that no child or young person use a Category B or C gaming machine on the club's or institute's premises, and

(b) that the holder comply with any relevant provision of a code of practice under section 24 about the location and operation of a gaming machine.

[Gambling Act 2005, s 271.]

8–13845   272. Section 271: supplementary.   (1) For the purposes of section 271(4)(*b*) the reference to a deduction or levy in respect of gaming provided by, on behalf of or by arrangement with a club or institute is to a deduction or levy made by or on behalf of—

(a) the club or institute, or

(b) a person providing facilities for gaming on behalf of, or by arrangement with, the club or institute.

(2) In section 271(4)(*c*) "the public" means persons other than—

(a) members of the club or institute,

(b) guests of members of the club or institute,

(c) staff of the club or institute, and

(d) persons providing services to or for the club or institute.

(3) For the purposes of section 271(4)(*c*) and (*d*) a reference to an area where gaming is taking place is a reference to any place in which it is possible to participate in the gaming.

(4) For the purposes of section 271(6) and subsection (2) above a person shall not be treated as the guest of a member if the member extends an invitation—

(a) having had no previous acquaintance with the person, and

(b) for the purpose only of enabling the person to take advantage of facilities for gaming.

[Gambling Act 2005, s 272.]

8–13846   273. Club machine permit.   (1) Sections 37 and 242 shall not apply to making a gaming machine available for use in accordance with a club machine permit.

(2) A club machine permit is a permit issued by a licensing authority authorising up to three gaming machines, each of which must be of Category B, C or D, to be made available for use—

(a) on premises on which a members' club, a commercial club or a miners' welfare institute operates, and

(b) in the course of the activities of the club or institute.

(3) A club machine permit held by a members' club or a miners' welfare institute shall, by virtue of this subsection, be subject to the condition that each person to whom a machine is made available for use in reliance on the permit—

(a) is a member of the club or institute who applied for membership, was nominated for membership or became a member, at least 48 hours before he uses the machine, or

(b) is a guest of a member of the club or institute who would be entitled to use the machine by virtue of paragraph (*a*).

(4) A club machine permit shall, by virtue of this subsection, be subject to the conditions—

(a) that no child or young person use a Category B or C gaming machine on the club's or institute's premises, and

(b) that the holder comply with any relevant provision of a code of practice under section 24 about the location and operation of a gaming machine.

(5) For the purposes of subsection (3)(*b*) a person shall not be treated as the guest of a member if the member extends an invitation—

(a) having had no previous acquaintance with the person, and

(b) for the purpose only of enabling the person to take advantage of facilities for gaming.

[Gambling Act 2005, s 273.]

8–13847   274. Procedure, &c.   (1) Schedule 12 makes further provision about club gaming permits and club machine permits.

(2) Subsection (1) does not apply in relation to Scotland if the applicant for or holder of the permit in question is the holder of a certificate of registration under section 105 of the Licensing (Scotland) Act 1976 (c 66) (certificate of registration in respect of a club) or a relevant Scottish licence or if he falls within such other description as may be specified in regulations under section 285(1).

[Gambling Act 2005, s 274.]

8–13848   275. Bingo.   (1) The disapplication of section 33 by section 269 or 271 shall not apply to high turnover bingo played during a high turnover period.

(2) Bingo played in the course of the activities of a club or institute in any period of seven days is high turnover bingo if—

(a) the aggregate of stakes at bingo played during the period in the course of the activities of the club or institute exceeds £2,000, or

(b) the aggregate of prizes at bingo played during the period in the course of the activities of the club or institute exceeds £2,000.

(3) A high turnover period begins in relation to a club or institute at the end of a period of seven days during which—

(a) the aggregate of stakes at bingo played in the course of the activities of the club or institute exceeds £2,000, or

(b) the aggregate of prizes at bingo played in the course of the activities of the club or institute exceeds £2,000.

(4) A high turnover period expires at the end of the year beginning with the first day of the period of seven days which caused the high turnover period to begin.

(5) A period of seven days any of which is in a high turnover period does not cause a new high turnover period to begin.

(6) A club or institute in relation to which a high turnover period begins shall, unless the club or institute holds a bingo operating licence, inform the Commission as soon as is reasonably practicable.

(7) A club or institute commits an offence if it fails without reasonable excuse to comply with subsection (6).

(8) A club or institute guilty of an offence under subsection (7) shall be liable on summary conviction to a fine not exceeding level 3 on the standard scale.

(9) The Secretary of State may by order vary a monetary amount specified in this section.
[Gambling Act 2005, s 275.]

8–13849   276. Interpretation.   In sections 266 to 275—

"prescribed" means prescribed by regulations, and

"regulations" means regulations made by the Secretary of State.
[Gambling Act 2005, s 276.]

Pubs, &c

8–13850   277. Alcohol licence.   In this Act—

(a) "alcohol licence" means a premises licence under Part 3 of the Licensing Act 2003 (c 17),

(b) "on-premises alcohol licence" means a premises licence under that Part which authorises the supply of alcohol for consumption on the licensed premises, and

(c) "relevant Scottish licence" means any licence granted under section 9(1) of the Licensing (Scotland) Act 1976 (c 66) (licence for sale by retail or supply of alcoholic liquor) provided it is not an off-sale licence.
[Gambling Act 2005, s 277.]

8–13851   278. Application of sections 279 to 284.   (1) Sections 279 to 284 apply to premises (other than a vehicle)—

(a) in respect of which an on-premises alcohol licence or relevant Scottish licence has effect,

(b) which contain a bar at which alcohol is served for consumption on the premises (without a requirement that alcohol is served only with food), and

(c) at a time when alcohol may be supplied in reliance on the alcohol licence or sold for consumption on the premises in reliance on the relevant Scottish licence.

(2) In those sections a reference to a licensing authority includes a reference to the Sub-Treasurer of the Inner Temple and the Under-Treasurer of the Middle Temple.
[Gambling Act 2005, s 278.]

8–13852   279. Exempt gaming.   (1) Sections 33 and 37 shall not apply to the provision of facilities for equal chance gaming which—

(a) takes place on premises to which this section applies, and

(b) satisfies the conditions of this section.

(2) The first condition of gaming for the purposes of subsection (1) is that the arrangements for the gaming satisfy the prescribed requirements in relation to—

(a) limiting amounts that may be staked, or

(b) limiting the amount or value of a prize.

(3) The second condition of gaming for the purposes of subsection (1) is that no amount is deducted or levied from sums staked or won.

(4) The third condition of gaming for the purposes of subsection (1) is that no participation fee is charged.

(5) The fourth condition of gaming for the purposes of subsection (1) is that a game played on one set of premises is not linked with a game played on another set of premises.

(6) The fifth condition of gaming for the purposes of subsection (1) is that children and young persons are excluded from participation.

[Gambling Act 2005, s 279.]

8–13853   280. Section 279: supplementary.   (1) In section 279(2) "prescribed" means prescribed by regulations made by the Secretary of State; and regulations may, in particular, make different provision for different classes or descriptions of game.

(2) For the purposes of section 279(5) two games are linked if—

   (a) the result of one game is or may be wholly or partly determined by reference to the result of the other game, or

   (b) the amount or value of a prize available in one game is or may be wholly or partly determined by reference to the extent of participation in the other game;

and if a single game is played partly on one set of premises and partly on another it shall be treated as two linked games.

[Gambling Act 2005, s 280.]

8–13854   281. Bingo.   (1) The disapplication of section 33 by section 279 shall not apply to high turnover bingo played during a high turnover period.

(2) Bingo played on premises in any period of seven days is high turnover bingo if—

   (a) the aggregate of stakes at bingo played on the premises during the period exceeds £2,000, or

   (b) the aggregate of prizes at bingo played on the premises during the period exceeds £2,000.

(3) A high turnover period begins in relation to premises at the end of a period of seven days during which—

   (a) the aggregate of stakes at bingo played on the premises exceeds £2,000, or

   (b) the aggregate of prizes at bingo played on the premises exceeds £2,000.

(4) A high turnover period expires at the end of the year beginning with the first day of the period of seven days which caused the high turnover period to begin.

(5) A period of seven days any of which is in a high turnover period does not cause a new high turnover period to begin.

(6) The holder of an on-premises alcohol licence or relevant Scottish licence for premises in relation to which a high turnover period begins shall, unless he holds a bingo operating licence, inform the Commission as soon as is reasonably practicable.

(7) A person commits an offence if he fails without reasonable excuse to comply with subsection (6).

(8) A person guilty of an offence under subsection (7) shall be liable on summary conviction to a fine not exceeding level 3 on the standard scale.

(9) The Secretary of State may by order vary a monetary amount specified in this section.

[Gambling Act 2005, s 281.]

8–13855   282. Gaming machines: automatic entitlement.   (1) Sections 37 and 242 shall not apply to making one or two gaming machines, each of which is of Category C or D, available for use on premises to which this section applies, provided that the conditions in subsections (2) and (3) are satisfied.

(2) The first condition is that the person who holds the on-premises alcohol licence or the relevant Scottish licence sends the licensing authority—

   (a) written notice of his intention to make gaming machines available for use in reliance on subsection (1), and

   (b) the prescribed fee.

(3) The second condition is that any relevant provision of a code of practice under section 24 about the location and operation of a gaming machine is complied with.

(4) Subsection (1) does not disapply section 37 or 242 in respect of premises at a time when gaming machines are made available for use on those premises in reliance on a club gaming permit or a club machine permit.

(5) In this section "prescribed" means—

   (a) in the case of premises in respect of which an on-premises alcohol licence has effect, prescribed by regulations made by the Secretary of State, and

   (b) in the case of premises in respect of which a relevant Scottish licence has effect, prescribed by regulations made by the Scottish Ministers.

[Gambling Act 2005, s 282.]

8–13856   283. Licensed premises gaming machine permits.   (1) A person does not commit an offence under section 37 or 242 if he makes a gaming machine of Category C or D available in accordance with a licensed premises gaming machine permit.

(2) A licensed premises gaming machine permit is a permit issued by a licensing authority authorising a person to make gaming machines of Category C or D (or both) available for use on premises to which this section applies.

(3) A licensed premises gaming machine permit shall, by virtue of this subsection, be subject to the condition that the holder comply with any relevant provision of a code of practice under section 24 about the location and operation of a gaming machine.

(4) Subsection (1) does not disapply section 37 or 242 in respect of premises at a time when gaming machines are made available for use on those premises in reliance on a club gaming permit or a club machine permit.

(5) Schedule 13, which makes further provision about licensed premises gaming machine permits, shall have effect except in relation to Scotland.
[Gambling Act 2005, s 283.]

8–13857 **284. Removal of exemption.** (1) A licensing authority may make an order disapplying section 279 or section 282(1) to specified premises.

(2) A licensing authority may make an order disapplying a section under subsection (1) only if they think that—

(a) the application of the section is not reasonably consistent with pursuit of the licensing objectives,

(b) gaming has taken place on the premises in purported reliance on the section but in breach of a condition of that section,

(c) the premises are mainly used or to be used for gaming, or

(d) an offence under this Act has been committed on the premises.

(3) Before making an order under subsection (1) a licensing authority shall—

(a) give the holder of the on-premises alcohol licence or of the relevant Scottish licence ("the licensee") at least 21 days' notice of the authority's intention to consider making an order,

(b) consider any representations made by the licensee,

(c) hold a hearing if the licensee requests one, and

(d) comply with any prescribed requirements for the procedure to be followed in considering whether to make an order.

(4) If a licensing authority make an order under subsection (1), they shall as soon as is reasonably practicable give the licensee—

(a) a copy of the order, and

(b) written reasons for the decision to make the order.

(5) A licensee may appeal against the making of an order under subsection (1).

(6) An appeal under subsection (5) must be instituted—

(a) in the magistrates' court for a local justice area in which the premises to which the appeal relates are wholly or partly situated,

(b) by notice of appeal given to the designated officer, and

(c) within the period of 21 days beginning with the day on which the appellant receives a copy of the order against which the appeal is brought.

(7) On an appeal the magistrates' court may—

(a) dismiss the appeal;

(b) allow the appeal and quash the order made by the licensing authority;

(c) make an order about costs.

(8) In relation to premises in Scotland—

(a) subsection (6)(a) shall have effect as if it referred to a sheriff within whose sheriffdom the premises are wholly or partly situated,

(b) subsection (6)(b) shall not have effect,

(c) the reference in subsection (7) to the magistrates' court shall have effect as a reference to the sheriff, and

(d) the reference in subsection (7)(c) to costs shall have effect as a reference to expenses.

(9) In this section, "prescribed" means prescribed by regulations made by the Secretary of State.
[Gambling Act 2005, s 284.]

Clubs, pubs &c: special provision for Scotland

8–13858 **285. Permits**

Fairs

8–13859 **286. Interpretation: travelling fair.** For the purposes of this Act—

(a) "fair" means a fair consisting wholly or principally of the provision of amusements, and

(b) a fair held on a day in a calendar year is a "travelling fair" if provided—

(i) wholly or principally by persons who travel from place to place for the purpose of providing fairs, and

(ii) at a place no part of which has been used for the provision of a fair on more than 27 days in that calendar year.

[Gambling Act 2005, s 286.]

8–13860   287. Gaming machines.   A person does not commit an offence under section 37 or 242 if—

(a) he makes one or more Category D gaming machines available for use at a travelling fair, and

(b) facilities for gambling (whether by way of gaming machine or otherwise) amount together to no more than an ancillary amusement at the fair.

[Gambling Act 2005, s 287.]

PART 13[1]
PRIZE GAMING

8–13861   288. Meaning of "prize gaming".   Gaming is prize gaming for the purposes of this Act if neither the nature nor the size of a prize played for is determined by reference to—

(a) the number of persons playing, or

(b) the amount paid for or raised by the gaming.

[Gambling Act 2005, s 288.]

---

1. Part 13 contains 288–294.

8–13862   289. Prize gaming permits.   (1) A person does not commit an offence under section 33 or 37 by providing facilities for prize gaming if—

(a) the gaming satisfies the conditions specified in section 293, and

(b) the facilities are provided in accordance with a prize gaming permit.

(2) A prize gaming permit is a permit issued by a licensing authority authorising a person to provide facilities for gaming with prizes on specified premises.

(3) Schedule 14 makes further provision about prize gaming permits.

[Gambling Act 2005, s 289.]

8–13863   290. Gaming and entertainment centres.   (1) A person does not commit an offence under section 33 or 37 by providing facilities for prize gaming if—

(a) the gaming satisfies the conditions specified in section 293, and

(b) the facilities are provided in—

(i) an adult gaming centre, or

(ii) a licensed family entertainment centre.

(2) A person does not commit an offence under section 33 or 37 by providing facilities for equal chance prize gaming if—

(a) the gaming satisfies the conditions specified in section 293, and

(b) the facilities are provided on premises in respect of which a family entertainment centre gaming machine permit has effect.

[Gambling Act 2005, s 290.]

8–13864   291. Bingo halls.   (1) A person does not commit an offence under section 33 or 37 by providing facilities for prize gaming in premises in respect of which a bingo premises licence has effect.

(2) A condition may be attached under section 75 or 78 to an operating licence so as—

(a) to prevent facilities for a specified description of game from being provided in reliance on subsection (1), or

(b) to provide for subsection (1) to apply, whether generally or only in connection with a specified description of game, subject to specified conditions or only in specified circumstances.

(3) A condition attached under section 78 by virtue of subsection (2) above may, in particular, relate to a matter listed in section 91(1).

(4) Subsection (1) may not be disapplied or modified—

(a) by way of a condition attached to an operating licence under section 77, or

(b) by way of a condition attached to a premises licence under section 167, 168 or 169.

[Gambling Act 2005, s 291.]

8–13865   292. Fairs.   A person does not commit an offence under section 33 or 37 by providing facilities for equal chance prize gaming if—

(a) the gaming satisfies the conditions specified in section 293,

(b) the facilities are provided at a travelling fair, and

(c) facilities for gambling (in whatever form) amount together to no more than an ancillary amusement at the fair.

[Gambling Act 2005, s 292.]

8–13866   293. Conditions for prize gaming. (1) This section specifies the conditions mentioned in sections 289(1), 290(1) and (2) and 292 for prize gaming.

(2) The first condition is compliance with such limits as may be prescribed in respect of participation fees (and those limits may, in particular, relate to players, games or a combination; and different limits may be prescribed in respect of different classes or descriptions of fee).

(3) The second condition is that—

(a) all the chances to participate in a particular game must be acquired or allocated on one day and in the place where the game is played,

(b) the game must be played entirely on that day, and

(c) the result of the game must be made public—

(i) in the place where the game is played, and

(ii) as soon as is reasonably practicable after the game ends, and in any event on the day on which it is played.

(4) The third condition is that a prize for which a game is played, or the aggregate of the prizes for which a game is played—

(a) where all the prizes are money, must not exceed the prescribed amount, and

(b) in any other case, must not exceed the prescribed value.

(5) The fourth condition is that participation in the game by a person does not entitle him or another person to participate in any other gambling (whether or not he or the other person would also have to pay in order to participate in the other gambling).

(6) In this section "prescribed" means prescribed by regulations made by the Secretary of State.

[Gambling Act 2005, s 293.]

8–13867   294. Power to restrict exemptions. The Secretary of State may by order provide for sections 289, 290 and 292 not to have effect in relation to prize gaming of a specified description.

[Gambling Act 2005, s 294.]

PART 14[1]

PRIVATE AND NON-COMMERCIAL GAMING AND BETTING

Private gaming and betting

8–13868   295. Interpretation. Schedule 15 (which defines private gaming and betting) shall have effect.

[Gambling Act 2005, s 295.]

---

1. Part 14 contains ss 295–302.

8–13869   296. Exceptions to offences. (1) A person does not commit an offence under section 33 by providing facilities for—

(a) private gaming, or

(b) private betting.

(2) Section 37 shall not apply to or in respect of the use of premises to carry on—

(a) private gaming, or

(b) private betting.

(3) A person does not commit an offence under section 33 or 37 by making or accepting a bet, or by offering to make or accept a bet, if he acts otherwise than in the course of a business.

[Gambling Act 2005, s 296.]

Non-commercial gaming and betting

8–13870   297. Interpretation. (1) For the purposes of this Act gaming is non-commercial if it takes place at a non-commercial event (whether as an incidental activity or as the principal or only activity).

(2) An event is non-commercial if the arrangements for the event are such that no part of the proceeds is to be appropriated for the purpose of private gain[1].

(3) For the purposes of subsection (2) the proceeds of an event are—

(a) the sums raised by the organisers (whether by way of fees for entrance or for participation, by way of sponsorship, by way of commission from traders or otherwise), minus

(b) amounts deducted by the organisers in respect of costs reasonably incurred in organising the event.
[Gambling Act 2005, s 297.]

---

1. Section 19(3) excludes from "private gain" benefits provided to one or more individuals by non commercial societies in the course of their activities.

8–13871 298. Exceptions to offences. (1) A person does not commit an offence under section 33 by providing facilities for—

(a) non-commercial prize gaming which complies with the conditions in section 299, or
(b) non-commercial equal chance gaming which complies with the conditions in section 300.

(2) Section 37 shall not apply to or in respect of the use of premises to carry on—

(a) non-commercial prize gaming which complies with the conditions in section 299, or
(b) non-commercial equal chance gaming which complies with the conditions in section 300.
[Gambling Act 2005, s 298.]

8–13872 299. Conditions for non-commercial prize gaming. (1) This section specifies the conditions for non-commercial prize gaming mentioned in section 298.

(2) The first condition is that players are informed that the purpose of the gaming is to raise money for a specified purpose other than that of private gain.

(3) The second condition is that the arrangements for the gaming are such that the profits will be applied for a purpose other than that of private gain.

(4) The third condition is that the non-commercial event of which the gaming is part does not take place—

(a) on premises, other than a track, in respect of which a premises licence has effect,
(b) on a track at a time when activities are being carried on in reliance on a premises licence, or
(c) on premises at a time when activities are being carried on in reliance on a temporary use notice.

(5) The fourth condition is that the gaming is not remote.

(6) In this section "profits" in relation to gaming means—

(a) the aggregate of amounts—

(i) paid by way of stakes, or
(ii) otherwise accruing to the person organising the gaming directly in connection with it, minus

(b) amounts deducted by the person organising the gaming in respect of—

(i) the provision of prizes, or
(ii) other costs reasonably incurred in organising or providing facilities for the gaming.
[Gambling Act 2005, s 299.]

8–13873 300. Conditions for non-commercial equal-chance gaming. (1) This section specifies the conditions for non-commercial equal-chance gaming mentioned in section 298.

(2) The first condition is that persons participating in the gaming are informed that the purpose of the gaming is to raise money for a specified purpose other than that of private gain.

(3) The second condition is that the arrangements for the gaming are such that the profits will be applied for a purpose other than that of private gain.

(4) The third condition is that the arrangements for the gaming ensure compliance with regulations of the Secretary of State—

(a) limiting amounts staked;
(b) limiting participation fees;
(c) limiting other amounts paid by a person in connection with the gaming;
(d) limiting a combination of matters specified in paragraphs (a) to (c);
(e) limiting the amount or value of a prize;
(f) limiting the aggregate amount or value of prizes.

(5) Regulations under subsection (4) may, in particular—

(a) make provision by reference to whether or not a game is part of a series;
(b) make provision by reference to whether or not the non-commercial event of which the gaming is part is associated, as defined by the regulations, with another event;
(c) limit stakes in relation to a participant in more than one game;
(d) make different provision for different kinds of game or for games played in different circumstances.

(6) The fourth condition is that the non-commercial event of which the gaming is part does not take place—

(a) on premises, other than a track, in respect of which a premises licence has effect,

(b) on a track at a time when activities are being carried on in reliance on a premises licence, or

(c) on premises at a time when activities are being carried on in reliance on a temporary use notice.

(7) The fifth condition is that the gaming is non-remote.

(8) In this section "profits" in relation to gaming means—

(a) the aggregate of amounts—

(i) paid by way of stakes, or

(ii) otherwise accruing to the person organising the gaming directly in connection with it, minus

(b) amounts deducted by the person organising the gaming in respect of—

(i) the provision of prizes, or

(ii) other costs reasonably incurred in organising or providing facilities for the gaming.

[Gambling Act 2005, s 300.]

8–13874 301. Misusing profits of non-commercial prize gaming. (1) This section applies to—

(a) non-commercial prize gaming in respect of which a fund-raising purpose has been specified as mentioned in section 299(2), and

(b) non-commercial equal-chance gaming in respect of which a fund-raising purpose has been specified as mentioned in section 300(2).

(2) A person commits an offence if he uses any part of the profits of gaming to which this section applies for a purpose other than that specified.

(3) The reference in subsection (2) to the use of profits includes a reference to permitting profits to be used.

(4) A person guilty of an offence under this section shall be liable on summary conviction to—

(a) imprisonment for a term not exceeding 51 weeks,

(b) a fine not exceeding level 5 on the standard scale, or

(c) both.

(5) In the application of subsection (4) to Scotland the reference to 51 weeks shall have effect as a reference to six months.

(6) In this section "profits" has the same meaning as in sections 299 and 300.

[Gambling Act 2005, s 301.]

8–13875 302. Non-commercial betting. For the purposes of this Act a betting transaction is non-commercial betting if no party to the transaction—

(a) enters it in the course of a business, or

(b) holds himself out as being in business in relation to the acceptance of bets.

[Gambling Act 2005, s 302.]

PART 15[1]
INSPECTION

Inspectors

8–13876 303. Enforcement officers. (1) The Commission—

(a) may designate employees of the Commission as enforcement officers for the purposes of this Act, and

(b) may appoint persons other than employees of the Commission as enforcement officers for the purposes of this Act.

(2) The Commission may pay to or in respect of an enforcement officer who is not an employee of the Commission sums by way of or in respect of—

(a) remuneration;

(b) allowances;

(c) expenses;

(d) pension;

(e) gratuity.

[Gambling Act 2005, s 303.]

---

1. Part 15 contains ss 303–326.

8–13877 304. Authorised persons. (1) In this Act—

(a) "authorised person" has the meaning given by this section, and

(b) a reference to an authorised local authority officer is a reference to a person who is an authorised person by virtue of subsection (2).

(2) An officer of a licensing authority is an authorised person for a purpose relating to premises if—

(a) the premises are wholly or partly situated in the authority's area, and
(b) the officer is designated by the authority as an authorised person for the purposes of this section.

(3) An officer of an authority other than a licensing authority is an authorised person for a purpose relating to premises if—

(a) the authority has statutory functions, for an area in which the premises are wholly or partly situated, in relation to minimising or preventing the risk of pollution of the environment or of harm to human health, and
(b) the officer is authorised by the authority for the purpose of exercising any of those statutory functions.

(4) The following are authorised persons for purposes relating to any premises—

(a) an inspector appointed under section 18 of the Fire Precautions Act 1971 (c 40) (enforcement),
(b) an inspector appointed under section 19 of the Health and Safety at Work etc Act 1974 (c 37) (inspectors),
(c) an inspector or surveyor of ships appointed under section 256 of the Merchant Shipping Act 1995 (c 21) (enforcement),
(d) a person who is within a class prescribed by the Secretary of State by regulations.
[Gambling Act 2005, s 304.]

Kinds of inspection

8–13878   305. Compliance. A constable, enforcement officer or authorised person may undertake activities for the purpose of assessing—

(a) compliance with provision made by or by virtue of this Act;
(b) whether an offence is being committed under or by virtue of this Act.
[Gambling Act 2005, s 305.]

8–13879   306. Suspected offence. (1) A constable or enforcement officer may enter premises if he reasonably suspects that an offence under this Act may be—

(a) being committed on the premises, or
(b) about to be committed on the premises.

(2) A justice of the peace may on the application of a constable or enforcement officer issue a warrant authorising a constable or enforcement officer to enter premises if the justice of the peace is satisfied—

(a) that there are reasonable grounds for suspecting that an offence under this Act has been committed on the premises,
(b) that there are reasonable grounds for suspecting that evidence of the commission of the offence may be found on the premises, and
(c) that at least one of the conditions in subsection (3) is satisfied.

(3) Those conditions are—

(a) that admission to the premises has been refused,
(b) that admission to the premises is likely to be refused unless a warrant is produced,
(c) that the purpose of entry may be frustrated or seriously prejudiced unless a constable or enforcement officer arriving at the premises can secure immediate entry, and
(d) that there is likely to be nobody at the premises capable of granting admission.

(4) A warrant may be granted in reliance on subsection (3)(a) or (b) only if the justice of the peace is satisfied—

(a) that notice has been given to a person occupying the premises, or having responsibility for their management, of intent to apply for a warrant, or
(b) that the purpose of entry may be frustrated or seriously prejudiced by the giving of notice under paragraph (a).

(5) A warrant under subsection (2) shall cease to have effect at the end of the period of 28 days beginning with the day of issue.
(6) In the application of this section to Scotland, any reference to a justice of the peace is to be construed as a reference to the sheriff or a justice of the peace.
[Gambling Act 2005, s 306.]

8–13880   307. Inspection of gambling. (1) A constable, enforcement officer or authorised person may enter premises to which this section applies for a purpose specified in subsection (3).
(2) This section applies to premises if a constable, enforcement officer or authorised person reasonably suspects that facilities for gambling other than private and non-commercial gaming or betting may be being provided, may be about to be provided or have been provided, on the premises.
(3) The purposes mentioned in subsection (1) are—

(a) to discover whether facilities for gambling other than private and non-commercial gaming or betting are being provided, are about to be provided or have been provided on the premises,

(b) to determine whether an operating licence or premises licence is held in respect of the provision of facilities for gambling on the premises, and

(c) to determine whether facilities are being, will be or have been provided in accordance with the terms and conditions of an operating licence or premises licence.

[Gambling Act 2005, s 307.]

8–13881 308. Operating licence holders. (1) A constable or enforcement officer may enter premises to which this section applies for the purpose specified in subsection (3).

(2) This section applies to premises which a constable or enforcement officer reasonably believes to be used by the holder of an operating licence wholly or partly for purposes connected with the licensed activities.

(3) The purpose mentioned in subsection (1) is to determine whether the licensed activities are being carried on in accordance with the terms and conditions of the operating licence.

[Gambling Act 2005, s 308.]

8–13882 309. Family entertainment centres. (1) A constable, enforcement officer or authorised local authority officer may enter premises in respect of which an application has been made for a family entertainment centre gaming machine permit for a purpose connected with the consideration of the application.

(2) A constable, enforcement officer or authorised local authority officer may enter premises in respect of which a family entertainment centre gaming machine permit has effect for the purpose of determining whether the gaming machines used on the premises, and the arrangements for their use, comply with the requirements of this Act and regulations under it.

[Gambling Act 2005, s 309.]

8–13883 310. Premises licensed for alcohol. (1) An enforcement officer or an authorised local authority officer may enter premises in respect of which an application has been made under Schedule 13 for a purpose connected with the consideration of the application.

(2) A constable, enforcement officer or authorised local authority officer may enter premises in respect of which an on-premises alcohol licence has effect for the purpose of—

(a) determining whether gaming carried on satisfies the conditions in section 279;

(b) in the case of bingo played on the premises, determining—

(i) whether the terms and conditions of any relevant operating licence are being complied with;

(ii) whether section 281 applies;

(c) ascertaining the number and category of gaming machines being made available for use on the premises.

[Gambling Act 2005, s 310.]

8–13884 311. Prize gaming permit. (1) A constable, enforcement officer or authorised local authority officer may enter premises in respect of which an application has been made for a prize gaming permit for a purpose connected with the consideration of the application.

(2) A constable, enforcement officer or authorised local authority officer may enter premises in respect of which a prize gaming permit has effect for the purposes of determining whether prize gaming on the premises complies with the requirements of this Act and regulations under it.

[Gambling Act 2005, s 311.]

8–13885 312. Clubs. (1) A constable or enforcement officer may enter premises to which this section applies for a purpose specified in subsection (3).

(2) This section applies to premises which a constable or enforcement officer reasonably believes to be used by a members' club, a commercial club or a miners' welfare institute.

(3) The purposes mentioned in subsection (1) are—

(a) to determine whether gaming is taking place on the premises or is about to take place on the premises,

(b) to determine whether any gaming that is taking place or is about to take place on the premises is in accordance with—

(i) section 269,

(ii) a club gaming permit, or

(iii) a club machine permit.

(4) An authorised local authority officer may enter premises in respect of which an application has been made for a club gaming permit or a club machine permit for a purpose connected with the consideration of the application.

[Gambling Act 2005, s 312.]

8–13886   313. Licensed premises.   (1) A constable, enforcement officer or authorised person may enter premises in respect of which an application for a premises licence has been made to assess, having regard to the licensing objectives, the likely effects of activity carried on in reliance on the premises licence.

(2) A constable, enforcement officer or authorised person may enter premises in respect of which a premises licence has effect for a purpose connected with a review under section 201.
[Gambling Act 2005, s 313.]

8–13887   314. Lotteries: registered societies.   Where a society is registered with a local authority in accordance with Part 5 of Schedule 11, an enforcement officer or an authorised local authority officer may enter premises owned or used by the society for the purpose of making inquiries in connection with a lottery promoted on behalf of the society.
[Gambling Act 2005, s 314.]

8–13888   315. Temporary use notice.   (1) A constable, enforcement officer or authorised person may enter premises in respect of which a temporary use notice has been given to assess, having regard to the licensing objectives, the likely effects of activity carried on in reliance on the temporary use notice.

(2) A constable, enforcement officer or authorised person may enter premises in respect of which a temporary use notice has effect to determine whether an activity of a kind listed in section 37(1) is being carried on otherwise than in accordance with the temporary use notice.
[Gambling Act 2005, s 315.]

8–13889   316. Authorisations: production on demand.   (1) A constable or enforcement officer may require the holder of an operating licence to produce to the constable or enforcement officer within a specified period a copy of any authorisation given by the holder of the licence under section 93(2) or (3) or 94(2).

(2) While a person is holding himself out as willing to accept bets on behalf of the holder of an operating licence in accordance with section 93(2) or (3) or 94(2), a constable or enforcement officer may require the person to produce a copy of his authorisation under that section—

(a) within a specified period, or
(b) immediately.

(3) A constable or enforcement officer may require the holder of a casino premises licence to produce to the constable or enforcement officer within a specified period a copy of any authorisation given by the holder of the licence under section 174(3).

(4) While a person is carrying on an activity in reliance on an authorisation under section 174(3), a constable or enforcement officer may require the person to produce a copy of his authorisation under that section—

(a) within a specified period, or
(b) immediately.

(5) A person commits an offence if he fails without reasonable excuse to comply with a requirement imposed under this section.

(6) A person guilty of an offence under subsection (5) shall be liable on summary conviction to a fine not exceeding level 2 on the standard scale.
[Gambling Act 2005, s 316.]

Powers and procedure

8–13890   317. Powers.   (1) A constable, enforcement officer or authorised person exercising a power under or by virtue of this Part to enter premises may—

(a) inspect any part of the premises and any machine or other thing on the premises;
(b) question any person on the premises;
(c) require access to any written or electronic record which is kept on the premises;
(d) require to be supplied with a copy, in such form as he directs, of an entry in a written or electronic record which is kept on the premises;
(e) remove and retain anything if he reasonably believes that it constitutes or contains evidence of—

(i)   the commission of an offence under this Act, or
(ii) the breach of a term or condition of a licence issued under this Act;

(f) remove and retain anything if he reasonably believes that it is being used or has been used in the commission of an offence under this Act.

(2) The Secretary of State may by regulations make provision about the treatment of—

(a) copies supplied under subsection (1)(d), and
(b) things removed under subsection (1)(e) or (f).

(3) Regulations under subsection (2) may, in particular, make provision—

(a) about the retention, use, return, disposal or destruction of anything supplied or removed;

(b) conferring a right of appeal.

(4) The Secretary of State may by regulations make provision about the procedure to be followed in the exercise of a power under this section.

(5) Nothing in this Part authorises action to be taken in England and Wales in respect of anything of a kind specified in section 9(2) of the Police and Criminal Evidence Act 1984 (c 60) (legally privileged material, &c).

(6) A person exercising a power under or by virtue of this Part shall have regard to any relevant provision of a code of practice under that Act (and guidance under section 25 may refer to a provision of a code).

(7) Subsection (6) does not apply as respects the exercise of a power in relation to Scotland.
[Gambling Act 2005, s 317.]

8–13891   318. Dwellings.   (1) A power under this Part to enter premises without a warrant does not apply in relation to a dwelling.

(2) A justice of the peace may on the application of a constable, enforcement officer or authorised person issue a warrant authorising a constable, enforcement officer or authorised person to enter premises if the justice of the peace is satisfied—

(a) that, but for subsection (1), a constable, enforcement officer or authorised person would be able to enter the premises without a warrant in reliance on a provision of this Part, and

(b) that at least one of the conditions in subsection (3) is satisfied.

(3) Those conditions are—

(a) that admission to the premises has been refused,

(b) that admission to the premises is likely to be refused unless a warrant is produced,

(c) that the purpose of entry may be frustrated or seriously prejudiced unless a constable, enforcement officer or authorised person arriving at the premises can secure immediate entry, and

(d) that there is likely to be nobody at the premises capable of granting admission.

(4) A warrant may be granted in reliance on subsection (3)(a) or (b) only if the justice of the peace is satisfied—

(a) that notice has been given to a person occupying the premises, or having responsibility for their management, of intent to apply for a warrant, or

(b) that the purpose of entry may be frustrated or seriously prejudiced by the giving of notice under paragraph (a).

(5) A warrant under subsection (2) shall cease to have effect at the end of the period of 28 days beginning with the day of issue.

(6) In the application of this section or section 319 to Scotland, any reference to a justice of the peace is to be construed as a reference to the sheriff or a justice of the peace.
[Gambling Act 2005, s 318.]

8–13892   319. Records.   (1) A constable, enforcement officer or authorised person exercising a power of entry under or by virtue of this Part may exercise a power under section 317(1)(c) to (e) in relation to records (whether written or electronic) only if the records relate entirely to the matters to which the power of entry relates.

(2) A justice of the peace may on the application of a constable, enforcement officer or authorised person issue a warrant disapplying subsection (1) to a specified extent if the justice of the peace is satisfied that the disapplication is necessary.

(3) A warrant may be granted under subsection (2) only if the justice of the peace is satisfied—

(a) that notice has been given to a person in control of the records of intent to apply for a warrant, or

(b) that the purpose of exercising the power of entry may be frustrated or seriously prejudiced by the giving of notice under paragraph (a).

(4) A warrant under subsection (2) shall cease to have effect at the end of the period of 28 days beginning with the day of issue.
[Gambling Act 2005, s 319.]

8–13893   320. Timing.   A power under or by virtue of this Part may be exercised only at a reasonable time.
[Gambling Act 2005, s 320.]

8–13894   321. Evidence of authorisation.   An enforcement officer or authorised person seeking to exercise a power under or by virtue of this Part must produce evidence of his identity and authority to a person (if there is one) who appears to the enforcement officer or authorised person to be occupying the relevant premises or to have responsibility for their management.
[Gambling Act 2005, s 321.]

8–13895 **322. Information.**   (1) The Secretary of State shall make regulations requiring a person who exercises a power under or by virtue of this Part to provide information about the power and its exercise.

(2) Regulations under subsection (1) shall, in particular, make provision about—

(*a*) the information to be provided (which may include ancillary information about a provision of this Act or another enactment or about a rule of law);

(*b*) the form and manner in which the information is to be provided;

(*c*) the person to whom, or the place at which, the information is to be provided (which may, in particular, include provision for the supply of a copy if requested by a person within a specified class);

(*d*) timing.

(3) A constable, enforcement officer or authorised person exercising a power under or by virtue of this Part shall comply with any relevant provision of regulations under this section.
[Gambling Act 2005, s 322.]

8–13896 **323. Use of force.**   (1) A constable may use reasonable force for the purpose of entering premises in pursuance of a power under or by virtue of this Part.

(2) An enforcement officer may use reasonable force for the purpose of entering premises in pursuance of a power under or by virtue of section 306 or 307.

(3) An authorised person may use reasonable force for the purpose of entering premises in pursuance of a power under section 307.
[Gambling Act 2005, s 323.]

8–13897 **324. Person accompanying inspector, &c.**   A constable, enforcement officer or authorised person exercising a power under or by virtue of this Part to enter premises may take one or more persons with him.
[Gambling Act 2005, s 324.]

8–13898 **325. Securing premises after entry.**   A person who enters premises in reliance on a power under or by virtue of this Part shall take reasonable steps to ensure that when he leaves the premises they are as secure as they were before he entered.
[Gambling Act 2005, s 325.]

8–13899 **326. Obstruction.**   (1) A person commits an offence if without reasonable excuse he obstructs, or fails to cooperate with, a constable, enforcement officer or authorised person who is exercising or seeking to exercise a power under or by virtue of this Part.

(2) A person guilty of an offence under this section shall be liable on summary conviction to a fine not exceeding level 3 on the standard scale.
[Gambling Act 2005, s 326.]

PART 16[1]
ADVERTISING

8–13900 **327. Meaning of "advertising".**   (1) For the purposes of this Act a person advertises gambling if—

(*a*) he does anything to encourage one or more persons to take advantage (whether directly or through an agent) of facilities for gambling,

(*b*) with a view to increasing the use of facilities for gambling, he brings them or information about them to the attention of one or more persons, or

(*c*) he participates in or facilitates an activity knowing or believing that it is designed to—

(i)   encourage one or more persons to take advantage (whether directly or through an agent) of facilities for gambling, or

(ii) increase the use of facilities for gambling by bringing them or information about them to the attention of one or more persons.

(2) For the purposes of subsection (1) a person shall be treated as bringing facilities for gambling to the attention of one or more persons with a view to increasing the use of the facilities if—

(*a*) he enters into arrangements (whether by way of sponsorship, brand-sharing or otherwise) under which a name is displayed in connection with an event or product, and

(*b*) either—

(i)   the provision of facilities for gambling is the sole or main activity undertaken under that name, or

(ii) the manner or context in which the name is displayed is designed to draw attention to the fact that facilities for gambling are provided under that name.
[Gambling Act 2005, s 327.]

---

1. Part 16 contains ss 327–333.

8–13901 328. Regulations.   (1) The Secretary of State may make regulations controlling the advertising of gambling.

(2) The regulations may, in particular, make provision about—

(*a*) the form of advertisements;
(*b*) the content of advertisements;
(*c*) timing;
(*d*) location.

(3) Regulations by virtue of subsection (2)(*b*) may, in particular, require specified words to be included in advertisements.

(4) In making regulations under this section the Secretary of State shall, in particular, have regard to the need to protect children and other vulnerable persons from being harmed or exploited by gambling.

(5) A person commits an offence if he contravenes a requirement of regulations under this section.

(6) Regulations under this section may provide defences (whether similar to those provided by section 330 or otherwise).

(7) A person guilty of an offence under subsection (5) shall be liable on summary conviction to—

(*a*) imprisonment for a term not exceeding 51 weeks,
(*b*) a fine not exceeding level 5 on the standard scale, or
(*c*) both.

(8) Where a person commits an offence under this section by causing an advertisement to be displayed or made accessible, he shall be treated as committing the offence on each day during any part of which the advertisement is displayed or made accessible.

(9) Regulations under this section may, in particular, make provision generally or by reference to—

(*a*) specified classes of gambling,
(*b*) specified classes of advertisement, or
(*c*) activity undertaken in or in connection with specified places.

(10) In the application of subsection (7) to Scotland the reference to 51 weeks shall have effect as a reference to six months.
[Gambling Act 2005, s 328.]

8–13902 329. Broadcasting.   (1) Regulations under section 328 may not make provision about advertising by way of television or radio services to which section 319 of the Communications Act 2003 (c 21) applies.

(2) The Office of Communications shall under that section set, review and revise standards in respect of advertisements for gambling.

(3) In complying with subsection (2) the Office of Communications—

(*a*) shall consult the Gambling Commission, and
(*b*) shall ensure that the standards reflect the provisions of regulations under section 328.

(4) Regulations under section 328 may not make provision about advertising by way of a service which—

(*a*) is provided by the British Broadcasting Corporation, and
(*b*) would be licensable under Part 1 or 3 of the Broadcasting Act 1990 (c 42) or under Part 1 or 2 of the Broadcasting Act 1996 (c 55) were it provided by a person subject to licensing under that Part.
[Gambling Act 2005, s 329.]

8–13903 330. Unlawful gambling.   (1) A person commits an offence if he advertises unlawful gambling.

(2) For the purposes of this section advertised gambling is unlawful if—

(*a*) in order for the gambling to take place as advertised without the commission of an offence under this Act it would or might be necessary to rely on a licence, notice, permit or registration under this Act or an an exception to an offence under this Act, and
(*b*) at the time of advertising—

(i) arrangements for a licence, notice, permit or registration, sufficient to prevent the commission of an offence under this Act if the gambling takes place as advertised, have not been completed, and
(ii) the arrangements for the gambling as advertised are not such as to ensure that an exception to the offence will apply.

(3) Subsection (1) does not apply to anything done by way of promoting a lottery.

(4) It is a defence for a person charged with an offence under subsection (1) by reference to action of a kind described in section 327(1)(*a*) or (*b*) to show that he reasonably believed that the advertised gambling was lawful.

(5) Where a person acts in a way described in section 327(1)(*c*) he commits the offence under subsection (1) above only if he knows or should know that the advertised gambling is unlawful.

(6) A person does not commit an offence under subsection (1) by reason only of delivering, transmitting or broadcasting a communication or making data available if—

(*a*) he acts in the course of a business of delivering, transmitting or broadcasting communications (in whatever form or by whatever means) or making data available, and

(*b*) the nature of the business is such that persons undertaking it have no control over the nature or content of the communications or data.

(7) A person guilty of an offence under this section shall be liable on summary conviction to—

(*a*) imprisonment for a term not exceeding 51 weeks,

(*b*) a fine not exceeding level 5 on the standard scale, or

(*c*) both.

(8) Where a person commits an offence under this section by causing an advertisement to be displayed or made accessible, he shall be treated as committing the offence on each day during any part of which the advertisement is displayed or made accessible.

(9) In the application of subsection (7) to Scotland the reference to 51 weeks shall have effect as a reference to six months.
[Gambling Act 2005, s 330.]

8–13904 331. Foreign gambling. (1) A person commits an offence if he advertises foreign gambling other than a lottery.

(2) In this section "foreign gambling" means—

(*a*) non-remote gambling which is to take place in a non-EEA State, and

(*b*) remote gambling none of the arrangements for which are subject to the law about gambling of an EEA State (whether by being regulated, exempted, prohibited or otherwise).

(3) Subsection (2) shall apply to Gibraltar as it applies to EEA States.

(4) The Secretary of State may by regulations provide that a specified country or place is to be treated for the purposes of subsection (2) as if it were an EEA State.

(5) A person guilty of an offence under subsection (1) shall be liable on summary conviction to—

(*a*) imprisonment for a term not exceeding 51 weeks,

(*b*) a fine not exceeding level 5 on the standard scale, or

(*c*) both.

(6) In the application of subsection (5) to Scotland or Northern Ireland the reference to 51 weeks shall have effect as a reference to six months.
[Gambling Act 2005, s 331.]

8–13905 332. Territorial application: non-remote advertising. (1) Regulations under section 328 shall apply to anything in the way of advertising which is done—

(*a*) wholly or partly in Great Britain, and

(*b*) otherwise than by way of remote communication.

(2) The prohibition in section 330(1) applies to anything in the way of advertising which is done—

(*a*) wholly or partly in Great Britain, and

(*b*) otherwise than by way of remote communication.

(3) The prohibition in section 331(1) applies to anything in the way of advertising which is done—

(*a*) wholly or partly in the United Kingdom, and

(*b*) otherwise than by way of remote communication.

(4) For the purposes of this section the following are immaterial—

(*a*) the nature of gambling to which advertising relates (whether remote or non-remote), and

(*b*) the location of the gambling to which advertising relates.
[Gambling Act 2005, s 332.]

8–13906 333. Territorial application: remote advertising. (1) Regulations under section 328 shall have effect in relation to advertising by way of remote communication only if—

(*a*) the advertising satisfies the test in subsection (4),

(*b*) the advertising satisfies the additional test in subsection (5) or (6), if relevant, and

(*c*) the gambling to which the advertising relates satisfies the test in subsection (9).

(2) The prohibition in section 330(1) applies to advertising by way of remote communication only if—

(*a*) the advertising satisfies the test in subsection (4),

(*b*) the advertising satisfies the additional test in subsection (5) or (6), if relevant, and

(*c*) the gambling to which the advertising relates satisfies the test in subsection (9).

(3) The prohibition in section 331(1) applies to advertising by way of remote communication only if the advertising satisfies the test in subsection (4); for which purpose a reference to Great Britain shall be taken as a reference to the United Kingdom.

(4) The test referred to in subsections (1)(*a*), (2)(*a*) and (3) is that the advertising involves—

(*a*) providing information, by whatever means (and whether or not using remote communication), intended to come to the attention of one or more persons in Great Britain,

(*b*) sending a communication intended to come to the attention of one or more persons in Great Britain,

(*c*) making data available with a view to its being accessed by one or more persons in Great Britain, or

(*d*) making data available in circumstances such that it is likely to be accessed by one or more persons in Great Britain.

(5) In the case of a broadcast by television, the additional test is that the broadcaster—

(*a*) is under the jurisdiction of the United Kingdom for the purposes of Directive 89/552/EEC on the coordination of provisions concerning television broadcasting, or

(*b*) is not under the jurisdiction of an EEA State for the purposes of that Directive.

(6) In the case of the dissemination of information by way of an information society service within the meaning of Directive 2000/31/EC on electronic commerce, the additional test is that the service provider—

(*a*) is established in the United Kingdom for the purposes of that Directive,

(*b*) is established in a non-EEA State for the purposes of that Directive, or

(*c*) has been notified that the conditions for derogation specified in Article 3(4) of that Directive are satisfied in relation to the application to the service provider of regulations under section 328 and of section 330.

(7) The reference to notification in subsection (6)(*c*) is a reference to written notice which—

(*a*) has been given by the Commission,

(*b*) has neither expired nor been withdrawn, and

(*c*) states whether the Commission's opinion as to satisfaction of the conditions for derogation relates—

(i) to the conditions specified in Article 3(4)(*a*) and (*b*), or

(ii) by virtue of Article 3(5), only to the conditions specified in Article 3(4)(*a*).

(8) In a case to which subsection (7)(*c*)(ii) applies, the Commission shall perform the duties of notification imposed on the United Kingdom by Article 3(5).

(9) The test referred to in subsections (1)(*c*) and (2)(*c*) is—

(*a*) in the case of non-remote gambling, that it is to take place in Great Britain, or

(*b*) in the case of remote gambling, that at least one piece of remote gambling equipment to be used in providing facilities for the gambling is or will be situated in Great Britain.

[Gambling Act 2005, s 333.]

8–13907

PART 17[1]
LEGALITY AND ENFORCEABILITY OF GAMBLING CONTRACTS

---

1. Part 17 contains ss 334–338.

PART 18[1]
MISCELLANEOUS AND GENERAL
Miscellaneous

8–13908 339. Prize competitions. Participating in a competition or other arrangement under which a person may win a prize is not gambling for the purposes of this Act unless it is—

(*a*) gaming within the meaning of section 6,

(*b*) participating in a lottery within the meaning of section 14, or

(*c*) betting within the meaning of sections 9 to 11.

[Gambling Act 2005, s 339.]

---

1. Part 18 contains ss 339–362. Section 356(1), (2), (4) and (5) are in force so far as they relate to certain provisions of Schs 16 and 17; and s 373 in force: see Gambling Act 2005 (Commencement No 2 and Transitional Provisions) Order 2005, SI 2005/2455.

8–13909 340. Foreign betting. Sections 9 to 9B of the Betting and Gaming Duties Act 1981 (c 63) (prohibitions, for protection of the revenue, in relation to foreign betting) shall cease to have effect.

[Gambling Act 2005, s 340.]

8–13910 **341. Offence committed by body.** (1) Subsection (2) applies where an offence under this Act is committed by a body of persons corporate or unincorporate (other than a partnership) and it is proved that the offence was committed—

    (*a*) with the consent or connivance of an officer of the body, or

    (*b*) as a result of the negligence of an officer of the body.

    (2) The officer, as well as the body, shall be guilty of the offence.

    (3) In subsection (1) a reference to an officer of a body includes a reference to—

    (*a*) a director, manager or secretary,

    (*b*) a person purporting to act as a director, manager or secretary, and

    (*c*) if the affairs of the body are arranged by its members, a member.

    (4) Where an offence under this Act is committed by a partnership (other than a limited partnership) each partner shall be guilty of the offence.

    (5) Where an offence under this Act is committed by a limited partnership, subsections (1) and (2) shall have effect, but as if a reference to an officer of the body were a reference to a partner.

    (6) In relation to the prosecution of a body of persons unincorporate for an offence under this Act, the body shall be treated for all procedural purposes as if it were a body corporate.

    (7) The Secretary of State may by regulations make provision for the modification of a provision of this section in its application to a body of persons formed under, or in so far as the body is recognised by, law having effect outside the United Kingdom.
[Gambling Act 2005, s 341.]

8–13911 **342. False information.** (1) A person commits an offence if without reasonable excuse he gives to the Commission or a licensing authority for a purpose connected with a provision of this Act (whether or not in relation to an application under this Act) information which is—

    (*a*) false, or

    (*b*) misleading.

    (2) A person guilty of an offence under this section shall be liable on summary conviction to—

    (*a*) imprisonment for a term not exceeding 51 weeks,

    (*b*) a fine not exceeding level 5 on the standard scale, or

    (*c*) both.

    (3) In the application of subsection (2) to Scotland the reference to 51 weeks shall have effect as a reference to six months.

    (4) Where it appears to the Commission or a licensing authority that a decision under this Act was taken by them in reliance upon false or misleading information, they may do anything that they think expedient for the purpose of cancelling, terminating or varying an effect of the decision (but action under this subsection shall not make unlawful anything done before the action is taken).
[Gambling Act 2005, s 342.]

8–13912 **343. Value of prize.** (1) Regulations prescribing a maximum value of prizes for a purpose of this Act may include provision for determining the value of a prize.

    (2) Regulations by virtue of subsection (1) may, in particular—

    (*a*) apply (with or without modification) or make provision similar to a provision of section 20 of the Betting and Gaming Duties Act 1981 (c 63) (expenditure on bingo winnings);

    (*b*) confer a discretion on the Secretary of State, on the Gambling Commission or on another person;

    (*c*) provide for an appeal;

    (*d*) confer jurisdiction on a court or tribunal.

    (3) The imposition by or by virtue of this Act of a maximum on the value of a prize does not prevent an arrangement between a person who has won one or more prizes and a person who provides facilities for gambling whereby the prize or prizes are exchanged (whether for money or for one or more articles); provided that—

    (*a*) the amount of money or the value of the articles for which the prize or prizes are exchanged does not exceed the maximum amount or value of the prize, or the aggregate maximum amount or value of the prizes, that the person could lawfully have won, and

    (*b*) the nature of the substituted prize or prizes complies with any requirements of or by virtue of this Act as to the nature of the prize or prizes that the person could lawfully have won.
[Gambling Act 2005, s 343.]

8–13913 **344. Participation fees.** (1) In this Act "participation fee" means an amount paid in respect of entitlement to participate in gambling; and for that purpose—

    (*a*) it is immaterial—

        (i) how a fee is described,

        (ii) whether a fee is payable in money or in money's worth,

      (iii) when and how a fee is payable,

      (iv) to whom a fee is payable,

  (*b*) a charge for admission to premises where gambling takes place shall be treated as a participation fee,

  (*c*) a membership subscription is not a participation fee (subject to subsections (2) and (3)), and

  (*d*) a stake is not a participation fee.

(2) The Secretary of State may by regulations provide for a membership subscription to be treated as a participation fee in specified circumstances.

(3) For the purposes of section 279, a membership subscription is a participation fee.

(4) The Secretary of State may make regulations providing, in connection with the operation of a provision made by or by virtue of this Act in relation to a participation fee, for the apportionment of an amount which is payable partly in respect of entitlement to participate in gambling and partly in respect of another matter; and that provision may, in particular—

  (*a*) provide for apportionment by a specified person;

  (*b*) provide for apportionment in accordance with a specified formula or principle;

  (*c*) refer to the concept of reasonableness.

[Gambling Act 2005, s 344.]

8–13914 345. Forfeiture. (1) A court by or before which a person is convicted of an offence under this Act may make an order for the forfeiture of an article that appears to the court to relate to the offence.

(2) A forfeiture order—

  (*a*) may include such provision about the treatment of the article forfeited as the court thinks appropriate, and

  (*b*) subject to any provision made under paragraph (*a*), shall be treated as requiring any person in possession of the article to surrender it to a constable as soon as is reasonably practicable.

(3) Where—

  (*a*) a court proposes to make a forfeiture order in respect of an article, and

  (*b*) a person notifies the court that he has an interest in the article,

the court may not make the order without first giving the person an opportunity to make representations.

(4) The court which made a forfeiture order may order that the forfeited article be given up to a person who claims to have an interest in it.

(5) A person commits an offence if he fails to—

  (*a*) comply with a forfeiture order, or

  (*b*) co-operate with a step taken for the purpose of giving effect to a forfeiture order.

(6) A person guilty of an offence under subsection (5) shall be liable on summary conviction to—

  (*a*) imprisonment for a term not exceeding 51 weeks,

  (*b*) a fine not exceeding level 5 on the standard scale, or

  (*c*) both.

(7) In the application of subsection (6) to Scotland the reference to 51 weeks shall have effect as a reference to six months.

[Gambling Act 2005, s 345.]

8–13915 346. Prosecution by licensing authority. (1) A licensing authority may institute criminal proceedings in respect of an offence under any of the following provisions of this Act—

  (*a*) section 37,

  (*b*) section 185,

  (*c*) section 186,

  (*d*) section 229,

  (*e*) section 242,

  (*f*) section 258,

  (*g*) section 259,

  (*h*) section 260,

  (*i*) section 261,

  (*j*) section 262,

  (*k*) section 326,

  (*l*) section 342,

  (*m*) paragraph 20 of Schedule 10,

  (*n*) paragraph 10 of Schedule 13, and

  (*o*) paragraph 20 of Schedule 14.

(2) This section is without prejudice to section 222 of the Local Government Act 1972 (c 70) (power of local authorities to prosecute or defend legal proceedings).

(3) This section shall not apply to an authority in Scotland.
[Gambling Act 2005, s 346.]

8–13916 347. Prosecution: time limit. (1) A magistrates' court may try an information for an offence under this Act provided that the information was laid within the period of twelve months beginning with the date (or last date) on which the offence is alleged to have been committed.

(2) Section 127(1) of the Magistrates' Courts Act 1980 (c 43) shall not apply to an offence under this Act.
[Gambling Act 2005, s 347.]

8–13917 348. Excluded premises. (1) This Act shall have no effect in relation to anything done on, or in relation to any use of, premises of a kind specified for the purposes of this subsection by order of the Secretary of State.

(2) This Act shall have no effect in relation to anything done on, or in relation to any use of, premises certified for the purposes of this subsection, on grounds relating to national security, by the Secretary of State or the Attorney General.
[Gambling Act 2005, s 348.]

8–13918 349. Three-year licensing policy

General

8–13919 353. Interpretation. (1) In this Act, except where the context otherwise requires—

"adult" means an individual who is not a child or young person,
"adult gaming centre" has the meaning given by section 237,
"alcohol licence" has the meaning given by section 277,
"authorised local authority officer" has the meaning given by section 304,
"authorised person" has the meaning given by that section,
"betting" has the meaning given by sections 9 to 11, 37 and 150,
"betting intermediary" has the meaning given by section 13,
"bingo" means any version of that game, irrespective of by what name it is described,
"casino" has the meaning given by section 7,
"casino game" has the meaning given by that section,
"Category A gaming machine" (or B, C or D) means a gaming machine falling within Category A (or B, C or D) as prescribed under section 236,
"chief constables of police forces" has the same meaning in relation to England and Wales as in the Police Act 1996 (c 16),
"child" has the meaning given by section 45,
"club gaming permit" has the meaning given by section 271,
"club machine permit" has the meaning given by section 273,
"commercial club" has the meaning given by section 267,
"the Commission" means the Gambling Commission,
"director"—

    (*a*) has the meaning given by section 741 of the Companies Act 1985 (c 6), and
    (*b*) includes a shadow director within the meaning of that section,

"dog track" means premises which are designed, used or adapted for use for dog-racing,
"draw", in relation to a lottery, has the meaning given by section 255,
"EEA State" means a State which is a contracting party to the Agreement on the European Economic Area signed at Oporto on 2nd May 1992 (as it has effect from time to time),
"enactment" includes an enactment comprised in, or in an instrument made under, an Act of the Scottish Parliament,
"enforcement officer" means a person designated or appointed as an enforcement officer under section 303,
"equal chance gaming" has the meaning given by section 8,
"exempt lottery" has the meaning given by section 258,
"external lottery manager" has the meaning given by section 257,
"fair" has the meaning given by section 286,
"family entertainment centre" has the meaning given by section 238,
"family entertainment centre gaming machine permit" has the meaning given by section 247,
"football pools" means an arrangement whereby—

    (*a*) people compete for prizes by forecasting the results of association football games, and
    (*b*) each entry to the competition must forecast the results of at least four games,

"gambling" has the meaning given by section 3,
"gambling software" has the meaning given by section 41,
"game of chance" has the meaning given by section 6,
"gaming" has the meaning given by that section,

"gaming machine" has the meaning given by section 235,

"horse-race course" means premises which are designed, used or adapted for use for horse-racing,

"horse-race pool betting" has the meaning given by section 12,

"large casino" has the meaning given by regulations under section 7(5),

"licensed family entertainment centre" has the meaning given by section 238,

"licensed premises gaming machine permit" has the meaning given by section 283,

"the licensing objectives" has the meaning given by section 1,

"licensing authority" has the meaning given by section 2,

"lottery" has the meaning given by section 14 (and section 256),

"lottery manager's operating licence" has the meaning given by section 98,

"lottery ticket" has the meaning given by section 253,

"machine" has the meaning given by section 235(3)(*a*),

"members' club" has the meaning given by section 266,

"miners' welfare institute" has the meaning given by section 268,

"the National Lottery" has the meaning given by section 1 of the National Lottery etc Act 1993 (c 39)),

"non-commercial betting" has the meaning given by section 302,

"non-commercial gaming" has the meaning given by section 297,

"non-commercial society" has the meaning given by section 19,

"occasional use notice" means a notice given under section 39,

"operating licence" means a licence issued under Part 5,

"on-premises alcohol licence" has the meaning given by section 277,

"participant", in relation to a game of chance, includes a person who discharges an administrative or other function in relation to the game,

"participation fee" has the meaning given by section 344,

"passenger vessel" means a vessel which is carrying or expected to carry at least one passenger,

"personal licence" means a licence issued under Part 6,

"pool betting" has the meaning given by section 12,

"premises" includes any place and, in particular—

    (*a*)   a vessel, and

    (*b*)   a vehicle,

"premises licence" means a licence issued under Part 8,

"private betting" has the meaning given by section 295 and Part 2 of Schedule 15,

"private gaming" has the meaning given by section 295 and Part 1 of Schedule 15,

"private gain" is to be construed in accordance with section 19(3),

"prize" in relation to gaming (except in the context of a gaming machine) has the meaning given by section 6,

"prize" in relation to a gaming machine has the meaning given by section 239,

"prize" in relation to a lottery has the meaning given by section 14,

"prize gaming" has the meaning given by section 288,

"prize gaming permit" has the meaning given by section 289,

"proceeds", in relation to a lottery, has the meaning given by section 254,

"profits", in relation to a lottery, has the meaning given by that section,

"profits", in relation to non-commercial prize gaming, has the meaning given by section 299,

"racecourse" means premises on any part of which a race takes place or is intended to take place,

"real", in relation to a game, event or process means non-virtual,

"relevant offence" has the meaning given by section 126 and Schedule 7,

"remote communication" has the meaning given by section 4,

"remote gambling" has the meaning given by that section,

"remote gambling equipment" has the meaning given by section 36,

"remote operating licence" has the meaning given by section 67,

"rollover", in relation to a lottery, has the meaning given by section 256,

"small casino" has the meaning given by regulations under section 7(5),

"society" includes a branch or section of a society,

"stake" means an amount paid or risked in connection with gambling and which either—

    (*a*)   is used in calculating the amount of the winnings or the value of the prize that the person making the stake receives if successful, or

    (*b*)   is used in calculating the total amount of winnings or value of prizes in respect of the gambling in which the person making the stake participates,

"supply" includes—

    (*a*)   sale,

    (*b*)   lease, and

    (*c*)   placing on premises with permission or in accordance with a contract or other arrangement,

"temporary use notice" has the meaning given by section 215, "track" means a horse-race course, dog track or other premises on any part of which a race or other sporting event takes place or is intended to take place,

"travelling fair" has the meaning given by section 286,

"vehicle" includes—

(a) a train,
(b) an aircraft,
(c) a seaplane, and
(d) an amphibious vehicle (other than a hovercraft within the meaning of the Hovercraft Act 1968 (c 59)),

"vessel" includes—

(a) anything, other than a seaplane or an amphibious vehicle, designed or adapted for navigation or other use in, on or over water,
(b) a hovercraft (within the meaning of the Hovercraft Act 1968), and,
(c) anything, or any part of any place, situated in or on water,

"virtual" has the meaning given by subsection (3) below,

"winnings", in relation to a bet, means anything won, whether in money or in money's worth, and

"young person" has the meaning given by section 45.

(2) In this Act, except where the context otherwise requires—

(a) a reference to accepting a bet includes a reference to negotiating a bet,
(b) a reference to advertising is to be construed in accordance with section 327,
(c) a reference to participating in a lottery is to be construed in accordance with section 14,
(d) a reference to installing computer software includes a reference to downloading computer software,
(e) a reference to paying winnings in relation to a bet includes a reference to providing a prize in money's worth,
(f) a reference to postal services does not include a reference to facsimile transmission,
(g) a reference to premises includes a reference to part of premises,
(h) a reference to promoting a lottery is to be construed in accordance with section 252,
(i) a reference to providing facilities for gambling is to be construed in accordance with section 5,
(j) a reference to publication includes a reference to display, and
(k) a reference to the sale, supply or purchase of a lottery ticket is to be construed in accordance with section 253.

(3) For the purposes of this Act a reference to a virtual game, race or other event or process is a reference to—

(a) images generated by computer so as to resemble all or part of a game, race or other event or process of a kind that is played by or involves actual people, animals or things,
(b) images generated by computer so as to represent an imaginary game, race or other event or process, or
(c) any game, race or other event or process the result of which is determined by computer.

(4) A requirement under this Act to give a notice (or to notify) is a requirement to give notice in writing; and for that purpose—

(a) a message sent by facsimile transmission or electronic mail shall be treated as a notice given in writing, and
(b) a notice sent to a licensee at the address specified for that purpose in the licence shall, unless the contrary is proved, be treated as reaching him within a period within which it could reasonably be expected to reach him in the ordinary course of events.

(5) A reference in this Act to an act which is authorised by a licence or other document does not include a reference to an act which would be authorised by the licence or document but for failure to comply with a term or condition.

[Gambling Act 2005, s 353.]

8–13920　354. Crown application.　(1) This Act binds the Crown.

(2) But this Act shall have no effect in relation to anything done on, or in relation to any use of, premises occupied (temporarily or permanently) by Her Majesty's naval forces, military forces or air forces (within the meaning given by section 225(1) of the Army Act 1955 (c 18)).

(3) Section 40(3) of the Fire Precautions Act 1971 (c 40) (conversion of reference to fire and rescue authority into reference to Her Majesty's Fire Inspectorate in relation to Crown premises) shall apply to a provision of this Act as it applies to provisions of that Act (but with the substitution for the reference to section 40(1) of a reference to subsection (1) above).

[Gambling Act 2005, s 354.]

8–13921 **355. Regulations, orders and rules.** (1) Regulations or rules under this Act, or an order of the Secretary of State under this Act—

(a) may make provision which applies generally or only for specified purposes or in specified cases or circumstances,

(b) may make different provision for different purposes, cases or circumstances, and

(c) may include incidental, consequential or transitional provision.

(2) A provision of this Act which permits regulations, rules or an order to make provision of a specified kind is without prejudice to the generality of subsection (1).

(3) Regulations or rules under this Act, or an order of the Secretary of State under this Act, shall be made by statutory instrument.

(4) Regulations under any of the following provisions shall not be made by the Secretary of State unless a draft has been laid before and approved by resolution of each House of Parliament—

(a) section 4,

(b) section 6,

(c) section 7,

(d) section 14,

(e) section 78,

(f) section 123,

(g) section 167,

(h) section 168,

(i) section 236, and

(j) section 328.

(5) Regulations or rules made by a Minister of the Crown under any other provision of this Act shall be subject to annulment in pursuance of a resolution of either House of Parliament.

(6) An order of the Secretary of State under this Act shall not be made unless a draft has been laid before and approved by resolution of each House of Parliament (subject to subsections (7) and (8)).

(7) Subsection (6) shall not apply to an order under section 349(6), to an order under section 351 other than an order adding an entry to the list in Part 2 or 3 of Schedule 6 or to an order under Part 2 of Schedule 7 or Part 2 of Schedule 18, which shall instead be subject to annulment in pursuance of a resolution of either House of Parliament.

(8) Subsection (6) shall not apply to an order under section 358; but—

(a) an order under section 358(1) which includes provision made by virtue of section 358(4) or by virtue of Part 1 of Schedule 18 shall be subject to annulment in pursuance of a resolution of either House of Parliament, and

(b) an order under section 358(5) or (6) shall not be made unless a draft has been laid before and approved by resolution of each House of Parliament.

(9) Regulations under a provision specified in subsection (4) or under section 285 shall not be made by the Scottish Ministers unless a draft has been laid before and approved by resolution of the Scottish Parliament.

(10) Regulations made by the Scottish Ministers under any other provision of this Act shall be subject to annulment in pursuance of a resolution of the Scottish Parliament.

[Gambling Act 2005, s 355.]

8–13922 **356. Amendments and repeals.** (1) Schedule 16 (minor and consequential amendments) shall have effect.

(2) An amendment in that Schedule shall have the same extent as the enactment amended (or as the relevant portion of the enactment amended).

(3) The following shall cease to have effect—

(a) the Gaming Act 1710 (c 19),

(b) the Gaming Act 1738 (c 28),

(c) the Gaming Act 1835 (c 41),

(d) the Gaming Act 1845 (c 109),

(e) the Gaming Act 1892 (c 9),

(f) the Betting, Gaming and Lotteries Act 1963 (c 2),

(g) the Gaming Act 1968 (c 65),

(h) the Lotteries Act 1975 (c 58), and

(i) the Lotteries and Amusements Act 1976 (c 32).

(4) The enactments listed in Schedule 17 are hereby repealed to the extent specified.

(5) A repeal in that Schedule shall have the same extent as the provision repealed (subject to the Note to that Schedule).

[Gambling Act 2005, s 356.]

8–13923 **357. Money.** (1) Expenditure of a Minister of the Crown in connection with this Act shall be paid out of money provided by Parliament.

(2) A sum received by a Minister of the Crown in connection with this Act shall be paid into the Consolidated Fund.
[Gambling Act 2005, s 357.]

8–13924 358. Commencement. (1) The preceding provisions of this Act shall come into force in accordance with provision made by the Secretary of State by order [1].

(2) An order under subsection (1) may (without prejudice to the generality of section 355(1))—

(a) bring only specified provisions into force;
(b) bring different provisions into force at different times;
(c) bring a provision into force for a specified purpose only;
(d) bring a provision into force at different times for different purposes;
(e) in particular, bring Part 2 into force only for specified preliminary purposes relating to the establishment of the Commission (which may include the assumption of functions of the Gaming Board for Great Britain pending the commencement of repeals made by this Act);
(f) in particular, bring a provision of this Act into force for the purpose of enabling an advance application for a licence or permit to be made, considered and determined;
(g) in particular, bring an offence or other provision of this Act into force only in relation to gambling of a specified class or in specified circumstances;
(h) include transitional provision modifying the application of a provision of this Act pending the commencement of, or pending the doing of anything under, a provision of another enactment.

(3) Schedule 18 (transitional) shall have effect.

(4) Without prejudice to the generality of section 355(1)(c) or of Schedule 18, an order under this section may—

(a) make savings (with or without modification) or transitional provision in connection with Part 1 or 2 of the Horserace Betting and Olympic Lottery Act 2004 (c 25) (sale of the Horserace Totalisator Board ("the Tote") and abolition of the horserace betting levy system);
(b) modify a provision of this Act in its application in relation to a matter addressed by Part 1 or 2 of that Act or so as to reflect a provision of Part 1 or 2 of that Act;
(c) modify a provision of Part 1 or 2 of that Act (including a provision which amends another enactment) so as to reflect a provision of this Act.

(5) If the Secretary of State brings into force a repeal effected by this Act at a time when the appointed day for the purposes of Part 1 of that Act has not been appointed or has not arrived, he may by order—

(a) save, with or without modification, a provision repealed by this Act in so far as it relates to the Tote;
(b) make provision in connection with the Tote of a kind similar to provision made by a provision repealed by this Act;
(c) modify a provision of this Act for a purpose connected with the Tote;
(d) modify a provision of Part 1 of that Act (including a provision which amends another enactment) so as to reflect a provision of this Act.

(6) If the Secretary of State wholly or partly brings into force the repeal by this Act of the Betting, Gaming and Lotteries Act 1963 (c 2) at a time when the provisions listed in section 15(1)(a) to (c) of the Horserace Betting and Olympic Lottery Act 2004 (horserace betting levy system) have not been entirely repealed by order under that section, he may by order—

(a) save any of those provisions, with or without modification;
(b) make provision of a kind similar to any of those provisions;
(c) modify a provision of this Act for a purpose connected with a matter addressed by any of those provisions or by Part 2 of that Act;
(d) modify a provision of Part 2 of that Act (including a provision which amends another enactment) so as to reflect a provision of this Act.
[Gambling Act 2005, s 358.]

---

1. At the time of going to press the Gambling Act 2005 (Commencement No 1) Order 2005, SI 2005/2425; and the Gambling Act 2005 (Commencement No 2 and Transitional Provisions) Order 2005, SI 2005/2455 had been made. However, most of the Act's provisions remain unimplemented. Notes to the titles of Parts of the indicate state the provisions within those parts that are in force.

8–13925 359. Vessels: territorial limitations. (1) A person does not commit an offence under Part 3, 4, 10 or 11 of this Act if—

(a) the conduct which would otherwise constitute the offence takes place on board a vessel (within the meaning of section 353(1)), and
(b) the vessel is on a journey which has taken it or is intended to take it into international waters.

(2) Subject to subsection (1) a provision of this Act which applies in relation to a thing done in Great Britain applies to that thing if done on or in the territorial sea adjacent to Great Britain.

(3) In this section—

"international waters" means waters outside the territorial sea adjacent to Great Britain, and "the territorial sea" has the meaning given by section 1 of the Territorial Sea Act 1987 (c 49).
[Gambling Act 2005, s 359.]

8–13926   360. Aircraft: territorial limitations.   (1) A person does not commit an offence under Part 3, 4, 10 or 11 of this Act if the conduct which would otherwise constitute the offence takes place—

(*a*)   on board an aircraft, and
(*b*)   at a time when the aircraft is in international airspace.

(2)   In this section "international airspace" means airspace other than airspace above Great Britain or above the territorial sea adjacent to Great Britain (within the meaning given by section 1 of the Territorial Sea Act 1987).
[Gambling Act 2005, s 360.]

8–13927   361. Extent.   (1) The following provisions of this Act extend to England and Wales, Scotland and Northern Ireland—

(*a*)   section 43,
(*b*)   section 331, and
(*c*)   section 340 (and the related entry in Schedule 17).

(2)   The other provisions of this Act shall extend only to—

(*a*)   England and Wales, and
(*b*)   Scotland.

(3)   This section is subject to section 356.
[Gambling Act 2005, s 361.]

8–13928   362. Short title.   This Act may be cited as the Gambling Act 2005.

8–13929

Section 11

SCHEDULE 1
BETTING: PRIZE COMPETITIONS: DEFINITION OF PAYMENT TO ENTER

Introduction

1. This Schedule makes provision about the circumstances in which a person is to be or not to be treated for the purposes of section 11(1)(*b*) as being required to pay to participate in an arrangement.

Meaning of payment

2. For the purposes of section 11 and this Schedule a reference to paying includes a reference to—

(*a*)   paying money,
(*b*)   transferring money's worth, and
(*c*)   paying for goods or services at a price or rate which reflects the opportunity to participate in an arrangement under which a participant may win a prize.

3. It is immaterial for the purposes of section 11 and this Schedule—

(*a*)   to whom a payment is made, and
(*b*)   who receives benefit from a payment.

4. It is also immaterial for the purposes of section 11 and this Schedule whether a person knows when he makes a payment that he thereby participates in an arrangement as a result of which he may win a prize.

Stamps, telephone calls, &c

5. (1) For the purposes of section 11 and this Schedule a reference to paying does not include a reference to incurring the expense, at a normal rate, of—

(*a*)   sending a letter by ordinary post,
(*b*)   making a telephone call, or
(*c*)   using any other method of communication.

(2)   For the purpose of sub-paragraph (1)—

(*a*)   a "normal rate" is a rate which does not reflect the opportunity to participate in an arrangement under which a person may win a prize, and
(*b*)   ordinary post means ordinary first-class or second-class post (without special arrangements for delivery).

Payment to discover whether prize won

6. For the purposes of section 11 and this Schedule a requirement to pay in order to discover whether a prize has been won under an arrangement shall be treated as a requirement to pay to participate in the arrangement.

Payment to claim prize

7. For the purposes of section 11 and this Schedule a requirement to pay in order to take possession of a prize which a person has or may have won under an arrangement shall be treated as a requirement to pay to participate in the arrangement.

Choice of free entry

8. (1) For the purposes of section 11 and this Schedule an arrangement shall not be treated as requiring a person to pay to participate if under the arrangement—

(*a*) each person who is eligible to participate has a choice whether to participate by paying or by sending a communication,

(*b*) the communication mentioned in paragraph (*a*) may be—

　(i) a letter sent by ordinary post, or

　(ii) another method of communication which is neither more expensive nor less convenient than participating by paying,

(*c*) the choice is publicised in such a way as to be likely to come to the attention of each person who proposes to participate, and

(*d*) the system for allocating prizes does not differentiate between those who participate by paying and those who participate by sending a communication.

(2) In this paragraph "ordinary post" has the meaning given by paragraph 5(2)(*b*).

Power to make regulations

9. The Secretary of State may make regulations providing that an activity of a specified kind or performed in specified circumstances is to be or not to be treated for the purposes of section 11 as paying to participate in an arrangement.

8–13930

Section 15

SCHEDULE 3
Amendment of National Lottery etc Act 1993 (c 39)

Annual levy

1. After section 10B of the National Lottery etc Act 1993 (financial penalties: appeal) insert—

"10C. Annual levy.　(1) The Secretary of State may make regulations requiring holders of licences under section 5 or 6 to pay an annual levy to the Gambling Commission.

(2) The regulations shall, in particular, make provision for—

(*a*) timing of payment of the levy, and

(*b*) the amount of the levy.

(3) The regulations may, in particular, make provision—

(*a*) determining the amount of the levy by reference to a percentage of specified receipts of the holder of a licence under section 5 or 6,

(*b*) determining the amount of the levy by reference to a percentage of specified profits of the holder of a licence under section 5 or 6,

(*c*) providing for the determination of the amount of the levy according to a specified formula, or

(*d*) providing for the determination of the amount of the levy in some other way.

(4) Any sum due by way of levy by virtue of this section shall be treated for the purposes of this Act as if its payment were a condition of the licence under section 5 or 6.

(5) The Gambling Commission shall, with the consent of the Treasury and of the Secretary of State, expend money received by way of levy for purposes related to, or by providing financial assistance for projects related to—

(*a*) addiction to gambling,

(*b*) other forms of harm or exploitation associated with gambling, or

(*c*) any of the licensing objectives for the purposes of the Gambling Act 2005.

(6) In subsection (5) the reference to financial assistance is a reference to grants, loans and any other form of financial assistance, which may be made or given on terms or conditions (which may include terms and conditions as to repayment with or without interest).

(7) The Secretary of State may make regulations under this section only if—

(*a*) he has made regulations under the Gambling Act 2005 requiring holders of operating licences to pay an annual levy to the Gambling Commission, and

(*b*) he has consulted the National Lottery Commission.

(8) The Gambling Commission shall consult the National Lottery Commission before incurring expenditure under subsection (5)."

Consultation with Gambling Commission

2. After section 4 of the National Lottery etc Act 1993 (c 39) (overriding duties) insert—

"4A. Consultation with Gambling Commission.　(1) If in the course of the exercise of its functions the National Lottery Commission becomes aware of a matter about which the Gambling Commission is likely to have an opinion, the National Lottery Commission shall consult the Gambling Commission.

(2) The National Lottery Commission shall comply with any direction of the Secretary of State (which may be general or specific) to consult the Gambling Commission."

Definition of "lottery"

3. In section 20 of the National Lottery etc Act 1993 (interpretation) after the definition of "contravention" insert—

""lottery" has the same meaning as in the Gambling Act 2005;".

8–13931

Sections 30 and 350　　　　　　　　　　　SCHEDULE 6
　　　　　　　　EXCHANGE OF INFORMATION: PERSONS AND BODIES
　　　　　　　　　　　　　　　PART 1
　　　　　　　PERSONS AND BODIES WITH FUNCTIONS UNDER THIS ACT

A constable or police force
An enforcement officer
A licensing authority
Her Majesty's Commissioners of Customs and Excise
The Gambling Appeal Tribunal
The National Lottery Commission
The Secretary of State
The Scottish Ministers

　　　　　　　　　　　　　　　PART 2
　　　　　　　ENFORCEMENT AND REGULATORY BODIES

The Director and staff of the Assets Recovery Agency
The Charity Commission
The Financial Services Authority
The Director General and staff of the National Crime Squad
The Director General and staff of the National Criminal Intelligence Service
The Occupational Pensions Regulatory Authority
The Office of Fair Trading
The Serious Fraud Office

　　　　　　　　　　　　　　　PART 3
　　　　　　　　SPORT GOVERNING BODIES

The England and Wales Cricket Board Limited
The Football Association Limited
The Football Association of Wales Limited
The Horseracing Regulatory Authority
The Lawn Tennis Association
The Irish Football Association Limited
The Jockey Club
The National Greyhound Racing Club Limited
The Professional Golfers' Association Limited
The Rugby Football League
The Rugby Football Union
The Scottish Rugby Union
The Scottish Football Association Limited
UK Athletics Limited
The Welsh Rugby Union Limited

　　　　　　　　　　　　　　　PART 4
　　　　　　　　　　　　　　　NOTES

1. Where a person or body listed in this Schedule is by virtue of an enactment restricted in the use that may be made of information provided to him or it by another person or body, nothing in section 30 or 350 overrides that restriction—

(*a*) in relation to information provided to the person or body by the Commission, or
(*b*) so as to permit the person or body to disclose to the Commission information provided to the person or body by another.

2. Where by virtue of an enactment the use that may be made of information supplied by a person or body listed in this Schedule is restricted, or where the information may be further disclosed only with the consent of the person or body which provided the information, the prohibition or restriction on further disclosure shall apply to—

(*a*) the supply of information by virtue of this Act, and
(*b*) the supply of information to the Gambling Commission (whether or not by virtue of this Act).

3. Information provided to a person or body by Her Majesty's Commissioners of Customs and Excise in reliance on a provision of this Act may not be provided by that person or body to any other person or body without the consent of the Commissioners.

8–13932

Section 126

SCHEDULE 7
RELEVANT OFFENCES

PART 1
THE OFFENCES

Gambling offences

1. An offence under—

(*a*) this Act,
(*b*) the Betting, Gaming and Lotteries Act 1963 (c 2),
(*c*) the Gaming Act 1968 (c 65),
(*d*) the Lotteries and Amusements Act 1976 (c 32),
(*e*) the National Lottery etc Act 1993 (c 39), or
(*f*) the National Lottery Act 1998 (c 22).

Theft, &c

2. An offence under any of the following provisions of the Theft Act 1968 (c 60)—

(*a*) section 1 (theft),
(*b*) section 8 (robbery),
(*c*) section 9 (burglary),
(*d*) section 10 (aggravated burglary),
(*e*) section 11 (theft from exhibition, &c),
(*f*) section 12A (aggravated vehicle-taking),
(*g*) section 13 (abstracting electricity),
(*h*) section 15 (obtaining property by deception),
(*i*) section 15A (obtaining money transfer by deception),
(*j*) section 16 (obtaining pecuniary advantage by deception),
(*k*) section 17 (false accounting),
(*l*) section 19 (false statement by director, &c),
(*m*) section 20 (suppression of document, &c),
(*n*) section 21 (blackmail),
(*o*) section 22 (handling stolen goods),
(*p*) section 24A (retaining wrong credit), and
(*q*) section 25 (going equipped for stealing, &c).

3. An offence under section 1 or 2 of the Theft Act 1978 (c 31) (obtaining services, or evading liability, by deception).

4. An offence under section 170 or 170B of the Customs and Excise Management Act 1979 (c 2) (evasion of duty).

5. An offence under section 58(1) of the Civic Government (Scotland) Act 1982 (c 45) (convicted thief in possession).

6. Both in England and Wales and in Scotland, the offence at common law of conspiracy to defraud.

7. In Scotland the offences at common law of—

(*a*) theft,
(*b*) robbery,
(*c*) theft by housebreaking,
(*d*) fraud,
(*e*) extortion, and
(*f*) reset.

Miscellaneous

8. A sexual offence within the meaning of section 161(2) of the Powers of Criminal Courts (Sentencing) Act 2000 (c 6).

9. A violent offence within the meaning of section 161(3) of that Act.

10. An offence under—

(*a*) the Firearms Act 1968 (c 27), or
(*b*) the Firearms (Amendment) Act 1988 (c 45).

11. An offence under any of the following provisions of the Misuse of Drugs Act 1971 (c 38)—

(*a*) section 4(2) (production),
(*b*) section 4(3) (supply),
(*c*) section 5(3) (possession with intent to supply), and
(*d*) section 8 (permitting activity on premises).

12. An offence under the Forgery and Counterfeiting Act 1981 (c 45), except for sections 18 and 19 (reproduction and imitation notes and coins).

13. An offence under section 3 of the Private Security Industry Act 2001 (c 12) (unlicensed activity).

14. An offence under section 70 of the Army Act 1955 (c 18) in so far as it relates to an offence listed elsewhere in this Schedule.

15. An offence under section 70 of the Air Force Act 1955 (c 19) in so far as it relates to an offence listed elsewhere in this Schedule.

16. An offence under section 42 of the Naval Discipline Act 1957 (c 53) in so far as it relates to an offence listed elsewhere in this Schedule.

17. An offence under section 52 or 52A of the Civic Government (Scotland) Act 1982 (offences relating to indecent photographs of children).

18. An offence under any of the following provisions of the Criminal Law (Consolidation) (Scotland) Act 1995 (c 39)—

(a)   section 1 (incest),
(b)   section 2 (intercourse with a stepchild),
(c)   section 3 (intercourse with child under 16 by person in position of trust),
(d)   section 5 (unlawful intercourse with a girl under 16),
(e)   section 6 (indecent behaviour towards girl between 12 and 16),
(f)   section 8 (detention of woman in brothel or other premises),
(g)   section 10 (person having parental responsibilities causing or encouraging sexual activity in relation to a girl under 16), and
(h)   section 13(5) (homosexual offences).

19. In Scotland, the offences at common law of—

(a)   rape,
(b)   clandestine injury to women,
(c)   abduction of a woman or girl with intent to rape or ravish,
(d)   assault with intent to rape or ravish,
(e)   indecent assault,
(f)   lewd, indecent or libidinous behaviour or practices,
(g)   shameless indecency,
(h)   sodomy,
(i)   murder,
(j)   culpable homicide, and
(k)   assault.

20. In Scotland, the offence at common law of uttering and fraud.
21. An inchoate offence relating to an offence listed elsewhere in this Schedule.
22. A reference in this Part of this Schedule to an offence under an Act or a provision of an Act includes a reference to an offence under subordinate legislation made under that Act or provision.

PART 2
POWER TO AMEND PART 1

23. The Secretary of State may by order amend Part 1 of this Schedule so as to—

(a)   add an entry,
(b)   vary an entry, or
(c)   remove an entry.

8–13933

Section 175   SCHEDULE 9
APPLICATIONS FOR CASINO PREMISES LICENCES

Introduction

1. (1) This Schedule applies to an application for a casino premises licence of a kind in respect of which a limit under section 175 has effect.
   (2) An application for the variation or transfer of a premises licence is not to be treated for the purposes of this Schedule as an application for a premises licence (despite sections 187(3) and 188(2)).

Competition for licences

2. (1) Before considering an application to which this Schedule applies a licensing authority shall comply with regulations of the Secretary of State about inviting competing applications.
   (2) The regulations shall, in particular, make provision—

(a)   about the publication of invitations (including provision as to the manner and timing of publication and the matters to be published), and
(b)   about the timing of responses.

Two-stage consideration

3. Paragraph 4 applies where (whether or not as a result of the competition provided for by paragraph 2)—

(a)   a number of applications for a casino premises licence are made to a licensing authority ("the competing applications"), and
(b)   as a result of section 175 and the order under it the authority are able to grant one or more, but not all, of the competing applications.

4. (1) The licensing authority shall first consider in respect of each application whether they would grant it under section 163 if section 175 did not apply.
   (2) For that purpose—

(a)   the authority shall not have regard to whether any of the other competing applications is more deserving of being granted,

(b) subject to paragraph (a), each competing applicant is an interested party in relation to each of the other competing applications, and

(c) Part 8 shall apply, but with the substitution for a reference to the grant of an application in sections 163(1)(a) and 206(2) of a reference to a provisional decision to grant an application subject to the provisions of paragraph 5 below.

5. (1) This paragraph applies if a licensing authority determine under paragraph 4 that they would grant a number of competing applications greater than the number which they can grant as a result of section 175 and the order under it.

(2) The authority shall then determine which of those applications to grant under section 163(1)(a).

(3) For that purpose the authority—

(a) shall determine which of the competing applications would, in the authority's opinion, be likely if granted to result in the greatest benefit to the authority's area,

(b) may enter into a written agreement with an applicant, whether as to the provision of services in respect of the authority's area or otherwise,

(c) may determine to attach conditions under section 169 to any licence issued so as to give effect to an agreement entered into under paragraph (b), and

(d) may have regard to the effect of an agreement entered into under paragraph (b) in making the determination specified in paragraph (a).

(4) Having determined to grant one or more applications under sub-paragraph (2) the authority shall—

(a) grant that application or those applications under section 163(1)(a), and

(b) reject the other competing applications under section 163(1)(b).

(5) The list in section 164(1)(a) shall be treated as including any competing applicant whose application the authority decided provisionally to grant under paragraph 4.

6. (1) The Secretary of State may issue a code of practice about—

(a) the procedure to be followed in making the determinations required by paragraphs 4 and 5, and

(b) matters to which a licensing authority should have regard in making those determinations.

(2) A licensing authority shall comply with a code of practice under sub-paragraph (1).

7. (1) Where a licensing authority issue a casino premises licence following a determination to grant an application in accordance with paragraph 5, a condition attached to the licence under section 169 may, in particular, give effect to any agreement entered into under paragraph 5(3)(b) above.

(2) In that case—

(a) the condition shall refer to the agreement,

(b) a copy of the agreement shall be attached to the licence, and

(c) a variation of the agreement shall have effect only if accompanied by variation of the condition under section 187.

8. (1) An appeal may be brought under section 206(1) or (2) in respect of a decision under paragraph 4.

(2) While an appeal under section 206 could be brought by virtue of sub-paragraph (1), or has been brought by virtue of that sub-paragraph and has not yet been either finally determined or abandoned, the licensing authority shall take no action under paragraph 5(2).

(3) Sub-paragraph (2) has effect in place of section 208 in respect of an appeal by virtue of sub-paragraph (1).

(4) No appeal may be brought under section 206 in respect of a decision under paragraph 5.

Provisional statements

9. A reference in this Schedule to an application for a casino premises licence includes a reference to an application for a provisional statement where this Schedule would apply to an application for a premises licence made in reliance on the provisional statement.

10. (1) This paragraph applies where the process described in paragraphs 3 to 5 results in the issue of a provisional statement.

(2) Paragraphs 2 to 5 shall not apply by reason only of the fact that an application for a casino premises licence is made—

(a) in reliance on the provisional statement, and

(b) while it has effect.

(3) The licensing authority may provide in the provisional statement for it to cease to have effect at the end of a specified period.

(4) A licensing authority may extend a period specified under sub-paragraph (3) on the application of the person to whom the provisional statement is issued; and—

(a) the Secretary of State may by regulations provide for the procedure to be followed in relation to an application under this subsection, and

(b) sections 206 to 209 shall apply but—

(i) with the omission of section 206(2)(a),

(ii) as if section 208(1) referred not to a determination or other action under this Part but to a provision included in a provisional statement under sub-paragraph (3) above, and

(iii) with any other necessary modifications.

Section 247   SCHEDULE 10

FAMILY ENTERTAINMENT CENTRE GAMING MACHINE PERMITS

Interpretation

1. In this Schedule—

"holder", in relation to a permit, means the person to whom the permit is issued,
"the licensing authority"—

     (*a*) in relation to an application, means the licensing authority to whom the application is made, and
     (*b*) in relation to a permit, means the licensing authority who issue it,

"permit" means a family entertainment centre gaming machine permit,
"the premises", in relation to an application or permit, means the premises in respect of which the permit is sought or issued, and
"prescribed" means prescribed by regulations made by the Secretary of State except that in paragraphs 5(*d*) and 21(2) it means, where the application is made to a licensing authority in Scotland, prescribed by regulations made by the Scottish Ministers.

Making of application

2. (1) An application for a permit may be made only by a person who—

     (*a*) occupies or proposes to occupy the premises, and
     (*b*) proposes to use the premises as an unlicensed family entertainment centre.

(2) If the applicant for a permit is an individual, he must be an adult.
3. An application for a permit may not be made if a premises licence has effect in respect of the premises.
4. An application for a permit must be made to a licensing authority in whose area the premises are wholly or partly situated.
5. An application for a permit must—

     (*a*) be made in such form and manner as the licensing authority may direct,
     (*b*) specify the premises in respect of which the permit is sought,
     (*c*) contain or be accompanied by such other information or documents as the licensing authority may direct, and
     (*d*) be accompanied by the prescribed fee.

Consideration of application

6. Sections 154 and 155 shall have effect in relation to the functions of a licensing authority under this Schedule as they have effect in relation to functions of a licensing authority under Part 8.
7. (1) A licensing authority may prepare a statement of principles that they propose to apply in exercising their functions under this Schedule.

(2) A statement under sub-paragraph (1) may, in particular, specify matters that the licensing authority proposes to consider in determining the suitability of an applicant for a permit.
(3) In exercising their functions under this Schedule a licensing authority—

     (*a*) need not (but may) have regard to the licensing objectives, and
     (*b*) shall have regard to any relevant guidance issued by the Commission under section 25.

Determination of application

8. (1) On considering an application for a permit a licensing authority may—

     (*a*) grant it, or
     (*b*) refuse it.

(2) A licensing authority may not attach conditions to a permit.
(3) As soon as is reasonably practicable after granting an application a licensing authority shall issue a permit to the applicant.
(4) As soon as is reasonably practicable after refusing an application a licensing authority shall notify the applicant of—

     (*a*) the refusal, and
     (*b*) the reasons for it.

9. A licensing authority may grant an application for a permit only if they—

     (*a*) are satisfied that the applicant intends to use the premises as an unlicensed family entertainment centre, and
     (*b*) have consulted the chief officer of police for a police area in which the premises are wholly or partly situated.

10. (1) A licensing authority may not refuse an application unless they have—

     (*a*) notified the applicant of their intention to refuse the application and of their reasons, and
     (*b*) given the applicant an opportunity to make representations.

(2) A licensing authority may satisfy sub-paragraph (1)(*b*) by giving the applicant an opportunity to make—

     (*a*) oral representations,
     (*b*) written representations, or
     (*c*) both.

Form of permit

11. (1) A permit must be in the prescribed form and must specify—

(*a*) the person to whom it is issued,
(*b*) the premises, and
(*c*) the date on which it takes effect.

(2) If the person to whom a permit is issued changes his name or wishes to be known by another name—

(*a*) he may send the permit to the licensing authority with—

(i)   the prescribed fee, and
(ii) a request that a new name be substituted for the old name, and

(*b*) the licensing authority shall comply with the request and return the permit to the holder.

Duration

12. A permit shall cease to have effect at the end of the period of ten years beginning with the date specified under paragraph 11(1)(*c*) unless—

(*a*) it ceases to have effect before that time in accordance with a provision of this Schedule, or
(*b*) it is renewed in accordance with paragraph 18.

13. (1) A permit shall lapse if the holder ceases to occupy the premises specified under paragraph 11(1)(*b*).

(2) A permit shall not take effect if on the date specified under paragraph 11(1)(*c*) the person to whom the permit is issued is not an occupier of the premises specified under paragraph 11(1)(*b*).

14. A permit shall lapse if the licensing authority notify the holder that the premises are not being used as a family entertainment centre.

15. (1) A permit held by an individual shall lapse if—

(*a*) he dies,
(*b*) he becomes, in the opinion of the licensing authority as notified to him, incapable of carrying on the activities authorised by the permit by reason of mental or physical incapacity,
(*c*) he becomes bankrupt (within the meaning of section 381 of the Insolvency Act 1986 (c 45)), or
(*d*) sequestration of his estate is awarded under section 12(1) of the Bankruptcy (Scotland) Act 1985 (c 66).

(2) In any other case a permit shall lapse if the holder—

(*a*) ceases to exist, or
(*b*) goes into liquidation (within the meaning of section 247(2) of the Insolvency Act 1986).

(3) During the period of six months beginning with the date on which a permit lapses under this paragraph the following may rely on it as if it had effect and were issued to them—

(*a*) the personal representatives of the holder (in the case of an individual holder who dies),
(*b*) the trustee of the bankrupt's estate (in the case of an individual holder who becomes bankrupt), and
(*c*) the liquidator of the company (in the case of a company holder that goes into liquidation).

16. A permit shall cease to have effect if the holder gives to the licensing authority—

(*a*) notice of surrender, and
(*b*) either—

(i)   the permit, or
(ii) a statement explaining why it is not reasonably practicable to produce the permit.

17. (1) Where the holder of a permit is convicted of a relevant offence the court by or before which he is convicted may order forfeiture of the permit.

(2) Forfeiture under this paragraph shall be on such terms (which may include terms as to suspension) as may be specified by—

(*a*) the court which orders forfeiture,
(*b*) a court to which an appeal against the conviction, or against any order made on the conviction, has been or could be made, or
(*c*) the High Court, if hearing proceedings relating to the conviction.

(3) Subject to any express provision made under sub-paragraph (2), a permit shall cease to have effect on the making of a forfeiture order under this paragraph.

(4) The terms on which forfeiture is ordered under this paragraph shall, in particular, include a requirement that the holder of the permit deliver to the licensing authority within such time as the order may specify—

(*a*) the permit, or
(*b*) a statement explaining why it is not reasonably practicable to produce the permit.

(5) As soon as is reasonably practicable after making or suspending an order for forfeiture under this paragraph a court shall notify the licensing authority.

Renewal

18. (1) The holder of a permit may apply to the licensing authority for renewal of the permit.

(2) An application for renewal may not be made—

(*a*) before the period of six months ending with the date on which the permit would otherwise expire in accordance with paragraph 12, or
(*b*) after the beginning of the period of two months ending with that date.

(3) The provisions of this Schedule shall have effect (with any necessary modifications) in relation to an application for renewal as they have effect in relation to an application for a permit.

(4) A licensing authority may refuse an application for renewal of a permit only on the grounds—

(a) that an authorised local authority officer has been refused access to the premises without reasonable excuse, or

(b) that renewal would not be reasonably consistent with pursuit of the licensing objectives.

(5) Paragraph 12 shall have effect in relation to a renewed permit as if the date of renewal were the date specified under paragraph 11(1)(c).

(6) A permit shall not cease to have effect by virtue only of paragraph 12 while—

(a) an application for renewal of the permit is pending, or

(b) an appeal against a decision on an application for renewal of the permit is pending.

Maintenance

19. The holder of a permit shall keep it on the premises.

20. (1) An occupier of premises in respect of which a permit has effect commits an offence if without reasonable excuse he fails to produce the permit on request for inspection by—

(a) a constable,

(b) an enforcement officer, or

(c) an authorised local authority officer.

(2) A person guilty of an offence under this paragraph shall be liable on summary conviction to a fine not exceeding level 2 on the standard scale.

21. (1) Where a permit is lost, stolen or damaged, the holder may apply to the licensing authority for a copy.

(2) An application under sub-paragraph (1) must be accompanied by the prescribed fee.

(3) A licensing authority shall consider an application under this paragraph and shall grant it if satisfied—

(a) that the permit has been lost, stolen or damaged, and

(b) where the permit has been lost or stolen, that the loss or theft has been reported to the police.

(4) As soon as is reasonably practicable after granting an application under this paragraph a licensing authority shall issue a copy of the permit certified by the authority as a true copy.

(5) A copy of a permit issued under this paragraph shall be treated as if it were the permit.

Appeal

22. (1) The applicant for or holder of a permit may appeal if the licensing authority—

(a) reject an application for the issue or renewal of a permit,

(b) give a notice under paragraph 14, or

(c) give a notice under paragraph 15(1)(b).

(2) An appeal under this paragraph must be instituted—

(a) in the magistrates' court for a local justice area in which the premises to which the appeal relates are wholly or partly situated,

(b) by notice of appeal given to the designated officer, and

(c) within the period of 21 days beginning with the day on which the appellant or holder receives notice of the decision against which the appeal is brought.

(3) On an appeal the magistrates' court may—

(a) dismiss the appeal;

(b) substitute for the decision appealed against any decision that the licensing authority could have made (with effect from such date and on such transitional or other terms as the court may specify);

(c) restore a permit (with effect from such date and on such transitional or other terms as the court may specify);

(d) remit the case to the licensing authority to decide in accordance with a direction of the court;

(e) make an order about costs.

(4) Sub-paragraph (1) applies to a decision of a licensing authority following remittal under sub-paragraph (3)(d).

(5) In relation to premises in Scotland—

(a) sub-paragraph (2)(a) shall have effect as if it referred to a sheriff within whose sheriffdom the premises are wholly or partly situated,

(b) sub-paragraph (2)(b) shall not have effect,

(c) the reference in sub-paragraph (3) to the magistrates' court shall have effect as a reference to the sheriff, and

(d) the reference in sub-paragraph (3) to costs shall have effect as a reference to expenses.

Register

23. (1) A licensing authority shall—

(a) maintain a register of permits issued by the authority together with such other information as may be prescribed,

(b) make the register and information available for inspection by members of the public at all reasonable times, and

(c) make arrangements for the provision of a copy of an entry in the register, or of information, to a member of the public on request.

(2) A licensing authority may refuse to provide a copy of an entry or of information unless the person seeking it pays a reasonable fee specified by the authority.

(3) The Secretary of State may make regulations about—

(a) the form of the register;
(b) the manner in which it is maintained.

(4) The Secretary of State may make regulations—

(a) requiring licensing authorities to give to the Commission specified information about permits issued by them;
(b) requiring the Commission to maintain a register of the information provided to it under paragraph (a);
(c) requiring the Commission to grant access to the register to members of the public (without charge);
(d) requiring the Commission to make copies of entries available on request, and on payment of a reasonable fee, to members of the public;
(e) excusing licensing authorities, wholly or partly, from compliance with sub-paragraph (1).

Vehicles and vessels

24. A permit may not be issued in respect of a vehicle or vessel (or part of a vehicle or vessel).

8–13935

Section 258

SCHEDULE 11
EXEMPT LOTTERIES

PART 1
INCIDENTAL NON-COMMERCIAL LOTTERIES

The exemption

1. (1) A lottery is exempt if—

(a) it is incidental to a non-commercial event within the meaning of paragraph 2 ("the connected event"), and
(b) the conditions specified in this Part are satisfied.

(2) A lottery to which sub-paragraph (1) applies is referred to in this Part as an incidental non-commercial lottery.

2. An event is non-commercial if no sum raised by the organisers of the event (whether by way of fees for entrance or for participation, by way of sponsorship, by way of commission from traders or otherwise) is appropriated for the purpose of private gain.

Deductions from proceeds

3. The promoters of an incidental non-commercial lottery may not deduct from the proceeds of the lottery more than the prescribed sum in respect of the cost of the prizes (irrespective of their actual cost).

4. The promoters of an incidental non-commercial lottery may not deduct from the proceeds of the lottery more than the prescribed sum in respect of costs incurred in organising the lottery (irrespective of the amount of the costs incurred).

Purpose of lottery

5. An incidental non-commercial lottery must be promoted wholly for a purpose other than that of private gain.

No rollover

6. The arrangements for an incidental non-commercial lottery must not include a rollover.

Connection between lottery and event

7. (1) No lottery ticket for an incidental non-commercial lottery may be sold or supplied otherwise than—

(a) on the premises on which the connected event takes place, and
(b) while the connected event is taking place.

(2) The results of the lottery must be made public while the connected event is taking place.

Interpretation: "prescribed"

8. In this Part "prescribed" means prescribed by the Secretary of State by regulations.

PART 2
PRIVATE LOTTERIES

The exemption

9. (1) A lottery is exempt if—

(a) it is a private society lottery, a work lottery or a residents' lottery within the meaning of paragraphs 10 to 12, and
(b) the other conditions specified in this Part are satisfied.

(2) In this Part a reference to a private lottery is a reference to a private society lottery, a work lottery or a residents' lottery.

Private society lottery

10. (1) A lottery is a private society lottery if—

(*a*) it is promoted only by authorised members of a society, and
(*b*) each person to whom a ticket is sold is either a member of the society or on premises wholly or mainly used for the administration of the society or the conduct of its affairs ("society premises").

(2) In this Part "society" means any group or society established and conducted for purposes not connected with gambling.

(3) In sub-paragraph (1)(*a*) "authorised" means authorised in writing by the society or, if it has one, its governing body.

(4) In relation to a society which has branches or sections, the reference to a society in sub-paragraph (1)(*a*) is a reference to a single branch or section.

Work lottery

11. (1) A lottery is a work lottery if—

(*a*) the promoters work on a single set of premises ("the work premises"), and
(*b*) each person to whom a ticket is sold or supplied also works on the work premises.

(2) For the purposes of this paragraph a person works on premises if he—

(*a*) is employed under a contract of employment to work at or from the premises,
(*b*) undertakes to work at or from the premises (whether or not for remuneration), or
(*c*) conducts a business at or from the premises.

Residents' lottery

12. (1) A lottery is a residents' lottery if—

(*a*) the promoters live in a single set of premises ("the residential premises"), and
(*b*) each person to whom a ticket is sold or supplied also lives in the residential premises.

(2) For the purposes of this paragraph a person lives in premises if he habitually resides in any part of the premises (whether or not there are other premises in which he also habitually resides).

Purpose of lottery

13. (1) A private society lottery may be promoted for any of the purposes for which the society is conducted.

(2) A work lottery or residents' lottery must be organised in such a way as to ensure that no profits are made.

Advertising

14. (1) No advertisement for a private society lottery may be—

(*a*) displayed or distributed except on the society premises, or
(*b*) sent to any other premises.

(2) No advertisement for a work lottery may be—

(*a*) displayed or distributed except on the work premises, or
(*b*) sent to any other premises.

(3) No advertisement for a residents' lottery may be—

(*a*) displayed or distributed except on the residential premises, or
(*b*) sent to any other premises.

Lottery tickets

15. Each ticket in a private lottery must be a document (without prejudice to section 253).

16. (1) A ticket in a private lottery may be sold or supplied only by or on behalf of the promoters.

(2) The rights conferred by the sale or supply of a ticket in a private lottery shall not be transferable (and any purported transfer shall be treated by the promoters of the lottery as being ineffective).

17. Each ticket in a private lottery—

(*a*) must state the name and an address of each of the promoters of the lottery,
(*b*) must specify the class of persons to whom the promoters are willing to sell or supply tickets, and
(*c*) must explain the condition in paragraph 16(2).

Price

18. The price payable for each ticket in a private lottery—

(*a*) must be the same,
(*b*) must be shown on the ticket, and
(*c*) must be paid to the promoters of the lottery before any person is given the ticket or any right in respect of membership of the class among whom prizes are to be allocated.

No rollover

19. The arrangements for a private lottery must not include a rollover.

PART 3
CUSTOMER LOTTERY

The exemption

20. (1) A lottery is exempt if—

(a) it is promoted by a person ("the promoter") who occupies premises in Great Britain in the course of a business ("the business premises"),

(b) no ticket in the lottery is sold or supplied to a person except at a time when he is on the business premises as a customer of the promoter, and

(c) the other conditions of a customer lottery specified in this Part are satisfied.

(2) A lottery to which sub-paragraph (1) applies is referred to in this Part as a customer lottery.

(3) For the purposes of sub-paragraph (1)(a)—

(a) it is immaterial whether persons other than the person who occupies the business premises also perform activities which amount to promotion of the lottery in accordance with section 252, but

(b) a reference in this Part to the promoter does not include a reference to any of those other persons.

No profits

21. A customer lottery must be organised in such a way as to ensure that no profits are made.

Advertising

22. No advertisement for a customer lottery may be—

(a) displayed or distributed except on the business premises, or

(b) sent to any other premises.

Lottery tickets

23. Each ticket in a customer lottery must be a document (without prejudice to section 253).

24. (1) A ticket in a customer lottery may be sold or supplied only by or on behalf of the promoter.

(2) The rights conferred by the sale or supply of a ticket in a customer lottery shall not be transferable (and any purported transfer shall be treated by the promoter of the lottery as being ineffective).

25. Each ticket in a customer lottery—

(a) must state the name and an address of the promoter of the lottery,

(b) must specify the class of persons to whom the promoter is willing to sell or supply tickets, and

(c) must explain the condition in paragraph 24(2).

Price

26. The price payable for each ticket in a customer lottery—

(a) must be the same,

(b) must be shown on the ticket, and

(c) must be paid to the promoter of the lottery before any person is given the ticket or any right in respect of membership of the class among whom prizes are to be allocated.

Maximum prize

27. It must not be possible for the purchaser of a ticket in a customer lottery to win by virtue of that ticket more than £50 (whether in money, money's worth, or partly the one and partly the other).

No rollover

28. The arrangements for a customer lottery must not include a rollover.

Frequency

29. A draw in a customer lottery must not take place during a period of seven days beginning with a previous draw in—

(a) that customer lottery, or

(b) another customer lottery promoted on the business premises.

PART 4
SMALL SOCIETY LOTTERIES

The exemption

30. (1) A lottery is exempt if—

(a) it is promoted wholly on behalf of a non-commercial society ("the promoting society"),

(b) it is a small lottery (within the meaning of paragraph 31), and

(c) the other conditions of a small society lottery specified in this Part are satisfied.

(2) A lottery promoted wholly on behalf of a non-commercial society is referred to in this Part as a small society lottery.

31. (1) For the purposes of this Part a society lottery is a small lottery unless it is a large lottery by virtue of any of sub-paragraphs (2) to (5).

(2) A society lottery is a large lottery if the arrangements for it are such that its proceeds may exceed £20,000.

(3) A society lottery is a large lottery if it is promoted wholly or partly at a time in a calendar year at which the

aggregate of the promoting society's proceeds from society lotteries promoted wholly or partly during that year exceeds £250,000.

(4) A society lottery is a large lottery if the arrangements for it are such that (disregarding any other society lottery the sale of tickets for which is not concluded) it may during its promotion become a large lottery by virtue of sub-paragraph (3).

(5) If a society promotes a lottery that is a large society lottery by virtue of sub-paragraph (2), (3) or (4) ("the first lottery"), any other society lottery promoted by that society is a large lottery if it is wholly or partly promoted—

(*a*) after the beginning of the promotion of the first lottery and in a calendar year during which the first lottery is wholly or partly promoted, or

(*b*) in any of the three calendar years successively following the last calendar year during which the first lottery was wholly or partly promoted.

Purpose of lottery

32. A small society lottery may be promoted for any of the purposes for which the promoting society is conducted.

Minimum distribution for fund-raising purpose

33. The arrangements for a small society lottery must ensure that at least 20% of the proceeds of the lottery are applied to a purpose for which the society is conducted.

Maximum prize

34. It must not be possible for the purchaser of a ticket in a small society lottery to win by virtue of that ticket (whether in money, money's worth, or partly the one and partly the other) more than £25,000.

Rollover

35. (1) The arrangements for a small society lottery may include a rollover only if each other lottery which may be affected by the rollover is a small society lottery promoted by or on behalf of the same society.

(2) This paragraph is subject to paragraph 34.

Tickets

36. (1) Where a person purchases a lottery ticket in a small society lottery he must receive a document which—

(*a*) identifies the promoting society,
(*b*) states the price of the ticket,
(*c*) states the name and an address of—

    (i) a member of the society who is designated, by persons acting on behalf of the society, as having responsibility within the society for the promotion of the lottery, or
    (ii) if there is one, the external lottery manager, and

(*d*) either—

    (i) states the date of the draw (or each draw) in the lottery, or
    (ii) enables the date of the draw (or each draw) in the lottery to be determined.

(2) For the purpose of sub-paragraph (1) a reference to a person receiving a document includes, in particular, a reference to a message being sent or displayed to him electronically in a manner which enables him to—

(*a*) retain the message electronically, or
(*b*) print it.

Price

37. (1) The price payable for each ticket in a small society lottery—

(*a*) must be the same, and
(*b*) must be paid to the promoter of the lottery before any person is given the ticket or any right in respect of membership of the class among whom prizes are to be allocated.

(2) Membership of the class among whom prizes in a small society lottery are allocated may not be dependent on making any payment (apart from payment of the price of a ticket).

Registration

38. The promoting society of a small society lottery must, throughout the period during which the lottery is promoted, be registered with a local authority in accordance with Part 5 of this Schedule.

Filing of records

39. (1) The promoting society of a small society lottery must send to the local authority with which the society is registered under Part 5 of this Schedule a statement of the matters specified in sub-paragraph (2).

(2) Those matters are—

(*a*) the arrangements for the lottery (including the dates on which tickets were available for sale or supply, the dates of any draw and the arrangements for prizes (including any rollover),
(*b*) the proceeds of the lottery,
(*c*) the amounts deducted by the promoters of the lottery in respect of the provision of prizes (including the provision of prizes in accordance with any rollover),

(*d*) the amounts deducted by the promoters of the lottery in respect of other costs incurred in organising the lottery,

(*e*) any amount applied to a purpose for which the promoting society is conducted, and

(*f*) whether any expenses in connection with the lottery were defrayed otherwise than by deduction from proceeds, and, if they were—

    (i) the amount of the expenses, and
    (ii) the sources from which they were defrayed.

(3) The statement must be sent to the local authority during the period of three months beginning with the day on which the draw (or the last draw) in the lottery takes place.

(4) The statement must be—

(*a*) signed by two members of the society who are appointed for the purpose in writing by the society or, if it has one, its governing body, and

(*b*) accompanied by a copy of the appointment under paragraph (*a*).

(5) A member signing a statement in accordance with sub-paragraph (4) must be an adult.

40. (1) If after receiving a statement under paragraph 39 a local authority think that the lottery to which the statement relates was a large lottery, they shall notify the Commission in writing.

(2) A notice under sub-paragraph (1) shall be accompanied by a copy of—

(*a*) the statement relating to the lottery, and

(*b*) the statement relating to any other lottery as a result of which the lottery mentioned in paragraph (*a*) is a large lottery.

PART 5
REGISTRATION WITH LOCAL AUTHORITY

Local authority

41. In this Part "local authority" means—

(*a*) in relation to England—

    (i) a district council,
    (ii) a county council for a county in which there are no district councils,
    (iii) a London borough council,
    (iv) the Common Council of the City of London, and
    (v) the Council of the Isles of Scilly,

(*b*) in relation to Wales,

    (i) a county council, and
    (ii) a county borough council, and

(*c*) in relation to Scotland, a licensing board constituted under section 1 of the Licensing (Scotland) Act 1976 (c 66).

Application

42. (1) A society may apply to the relevant local authority for registration under this Part.

(2) An application under this paragraph—

(*a*) must be in the prescribed form,

(*b*) must specify the purposes for which the society is conducted,

(*c*) must contain such other information, and be accompanied by such documents, as may be prescribed, and

(*d*) must be accompanied by the prescribed fee.

43. In relation to the registration of a society, the relevant local authority is the local authority for the area in which the principal premises of the society are situated.

Registration

44. As soon as is reasonably practicable after receipt of an application under paragraph 42 a local authority shall, subject to paragraphs 47 and 48—

(*a*) enter the applicant, together with such information as may be prescribed, in a register kept by the authority for the purposes of this Part,

(*b*) notify the applicant of his registration, and

(*c*) notify the Commission of the registration.

Gambling Commission

45. As soon as is reasonably practicable after receipt of notice of a registration under paragraph 44(*c*) the Commission shall record the registration.

46. (1) A notice under paragraph 44(*c*) must be accompanied by such part of the application fee as may be prescribed.

(2) In sub-paragraph (1) "application fee" means the fee accompanying an application under paragraph 42.

Refusal of registration

47. A local authority shall refuse an application for registration if in the period of five years ending with the date of the application—

(*a*) an operating licence held by the applicant for registration has been revoked under section 119(1), or
(*b*) an application for an operating licence made by the applicant for registration has been refused.

48. A local authority may refuse an application for registration if they think that—

(*a*) the applicant is not a non-commercial society,
(*b*) a person who will or may be connected with the promotion of the lottery has been convicted of a relevant offence, or
(*c*) information provided in or with the application for registration is false or misleading.

49. A local authority may not refuse an application for registration unless they have given the applicant an opportunity to make representations.

Revocation

50. (1) A local authority may revoke a registration under this Part if they think that they would be obliged or permitted to refuse an application for the registration were it being made anew.

(2) Where a local authority revoke a registration under this Part they shall specify that the revocation takes effect—

(*a*) immediately, or
(*b*) at the end of such period, beginning with the day of the revocation and not exceeding two months, as they may specify.

(3) A local authority may not revoke a registration under this Part unless they have given the registered society an opportunity to make representations.

Appeal

51. (1) If a local authority refuse or revoke registration under this Part—

(*a*) the authority shall notify the applicant society or the formerly registered society as soon as is reasonably practicable, and
(*b*) the society may appeal to a magistrates' court.

(2) An appeal under this paragraph must be instituted—

(*a*) in a magistrates' court for a local justice area which is wholly or partly within the area of the local authority against whose decision the appeal is brought,
(*b*) by notice of appeal given to the designated officer, and
(*c*) in the period of 21 days beginning with the day on which the society is notified of the refusal or revocation of registration, and

(3) On an appeal under this paragraph a magistrates' court may—

(*a*) affirm the local authority's decision;
(*b*) reverse the local authority's decision;
(*c*) make any other order (which may include transitional provision).

(4) In relation to registration in Scotland—

(*a*) sub-paragraph (1)(*b*) shall have effect as if the reference to a magistrate's court were a reference to a sheriff whose sheriffdom is wholly or partly within the area of the local authority against whose decision the appeal is brought,
(*b*) sub-paragraph (2)(*a*) and (*b*) shall not have effect, and
(*c*) sub-paragraph (3) shall have effect as if the reference to a magistrate's court were a reference to the sheriff.

Cancellation

52. A registered society may apply in writing to the registering authority for the registration to be cancelled.
53. As soon as is reasonably practicable after receipt of an application under paragraph 52 a local authority shall—

(*a*) cancel the registration,
(*b*) notify the formerly registered society of the cancellation, and
(*c*) notify the Commission of the cancellation.

Annual fee

54. (1) A registered society shall pay an annual fee to the registering local authority.
(2) An annual fee—

(*a*) shall be paid within such period before each anniversary of the registration as may be prescribed, and
(*b*) shall be of the prescribed amount.

(3) If a registered society fails to comply with this paragraph the registering authority may cancel the society's registration.
(4) If a local authority cancel a registration under sub-paragraph (3) the authority shall as soon as is reasonably practicable notify—

(*a*) the formerly registered society, and
(*b*) the Commission.

Retention of records

55. (1) Where a statement is sent to a local authority under paragraph 39 the authority shall—

(*a*) retain it for at least 18 months,
(*b*) make it available for inspection by members of the public at all reasonable times, and
(*c*) make arrangements for the provision of a copy of it or part of it to any member of the public on request.

(2) But a local authority may refuse to provide access or a copy unless the person seeking access or a copy pays a fee specified by the authority.

(3) A local authority may not specify a fee under sub-paragraph (2) which exceeds the reasonable cost of providing the service sought (but in calculating the cost of providing a service to a person the authority may include a reasonable share of expenditure which is referable only indirectly to the provision of that service).

Interpretation: "prescribed"

56. In this Part "prescribed" means prescribed by the Secretary of State by regulations except that, in the following provisions, it means prescribed by the Scottish Ministers by regulations—

(*a*) in paragraph 42(2)(*d*), where the application is made to a local authority in Scotland,
(*b*) in paragraph 46(1), where the local authority giving notice is in Scotland, and
(*c*) in paragraph 54(2)(*b*), where the registering local authority is in Scotland.

PART 6
POWERS TO IMPOSE ADDITIONAL RESTRICTIONS, &c

Distributing lottery tickets by post

57. (1) The Secretary of State may by regulations impose a condition in relation to exempt lotteries requiring that tickets purchased be delivered to the purchaser by hand at the time of purchase and not by post.

(2) Regulations under this paragraph may apply generally, only in relation to a specified class of lottery or only in specified circumstances.

Rollover

58. (1) The Secretary of State may by regulations impose in relation to exempt lotteries conditions or limitations in respect of the use of a rollover (in addition to any conditions or limitations set out in this Schedule).

(2) Regulations under this paragraph may apply generally, only in relation to a specified class of lottery or only in specified circumstances.

Other additional provision

59. (1) The Secretary of State may by order impose in relation to a class of lottery a condition (in addition to any specified in this Schedule) with which a lottery must comply if it is to be an exempt lottery within the meaning of this Schedule.

(2) A condition imposed under this paragraph may, in particular, relate to—

(*a*) the persons who may sell or supply lottery tickets;
(*b*) the persons who may buy lottery tickets;
(*c*) the circumstances in which lottery tickets are sold or supplied;
(*d*) the nature of lottery tickets and information appearing on them;
(*e*) arrangements for advertising the lottery;
(*f*) the deductions which promoters may make from the proceeds of a lottery.

(3) The Secretary of State may by order restrict the extent to which a person may carry on activities in reliance on an exemption under this Schedule.

(4) An order under sub-paragraph (3) may, in particular, make provision—

(*a*) restricting the number of lotteries that may be promoted on behalf of a person wholly or partly within a specified period;
(*b*) prescribing a minimum interval between activity in connection with one lottery promoted on behalf of a person and activity in connection with another lottery promoted on behalf of that person.

(5) Before making an order under this paragraph the Secretary of State must consult the Commission.

Variation of monetary limits and percentages

60. The Secretary of State may by order vary a monetary amount or a percentage in this Schedule.

PART 7
GENERAL

Interpretation: advertisement

61. For the purposes of this Schedule—

(*a*) "advertisement", in relation to a lottery, includes any document, or electronic communication, announcing that a lottery will take place or inviting people to participate in a lottery (in either case whether or not it also gives other information), (*b*) a reference to displaying an advertisement includes a reference to publishing a notice, and

(*c*) in the case of an advertisement in the form of an electronic communication, the communication is to be treated as being—

    (i) distributed to any place at which a person can access it, and

    (ii) sent to any premises at which a person can access it.

Interpretation: business

62. In this Schedule "business" includes trade and profession.

Vessels

63. Nothing in Part 2 or 3 of this Schedule applies to anything done on a vessel.

8–13936

Section 274

SCHEDULE 12
CLUB GAMING PERMITS AND CLUB MACHINE PERMITS

Application

1. (1) A members' club or miners' welfare institute may apply to a licensing authority for a club gaming permit.

(2) A members club, commercial club or miners' welfare institute may apply to a licensing authority for a club machine permit.

2. An application must—

(*a*) be made to a licensing authority in whose area the premises are wholly or partly situated,

(*b*) specify the premises in relation to which the permit is sought,

(*c*) be made in the prescribed form and manner,

(*d*) contain or be accompanied by the prescribed information and documents, and

(*e*) be accompanied by the prescribed fee.

3. (1) A club or institute making an application for a permit must within the prescribed time send a copy of the application and of any accompanying documents to—

(*a*) the Commission, and

(*b*) the chief officer of police for any police area in which the premises are wholly or partly situated.

(2) If a club or institute fails to comply with sub-paragraph (1) the application, and any permit issued in response to it, shall have no effect.

Consideration of application

4. A person who receives a copy of an application for a permit in accordance with paragraph 3 may object to the application within the prescribed period of time and in the prescribed manner.

5. The licensing authority to whom an application for a permit is made shall consider the application and—

(*a*) grant it, or

(*b*) refuse it.

6. (1) A licensing authority may refuse an application for a permit only on one or more of the following grounds (having regard to the matters mentioned in paragraph 27)—

(*a*) that the applicant is not—

    (i) in the case of an application for a club gaming permit, a members' club or a miners' welfare institute, or

    (ii) in the case of an application for a club machine permit, a members' club, a commercial club or a miners' welfare institute,

(*b*) that the premises on which the applicant conducts its activities are used wholly or mainly by children, by young persons or by both,

(*c*) that an offence, or a breach of a condition of a permit, has been committed in the course of gaming activities carried on by the applicant,

(*d*) that a permit held by the applicant has been cancelled during the period of ten years ending with the date of the application, or

(*e*) that an objection to the application has been made under paragraph 4.

(2) If a licensing authority are satisfied in relation to an application for a permit of the matters specified in sub-paragraph (1)(*a*) or (*b*), they shall refuse the application.

7. (1) Before refusing an application for a permit a licensing authority must hold a hearing to consider the application and any objection made under paragraph 4.

(2) But a licensing authority may dispense with the requirement for a hearing with the consent of—

(*a*) the applicant, and

(*b*) any person who has made (and not withdrawn) an objection under paragraph 4.

8. (1) Where a licensing authority grant an application for a permit they shall as soon as is reasonably practicable—

(*a*) give notice of their decision and, where an objection was made under paragraph 4, of the reasons for it to—

    (i) the applicant,

    (ii) the Commission, and

    (iii) the chief officer of police for any area in which the premises specified in the application are wholly or partly situated, and

(b)   issue the permit to the applicant.

(2)   A licensing authority may not attach conditions to a permit.

9.   Where a licensing authority reject an application for a permit they shall as soon as is reasonably practicable give notice of their decision and the reasons for it to—

(a)   the applicant,

(b)   the Commission, and

(c)   the chief officer of police for any area in which the premises specified in the application are wholly or partly situated.

Fast-track procedure for holder of club premises certificate

10.   (1)   This paragraph applies to an application if—

(a)   the applicant for a permit is the holder of a club premises certificate under section 72 of the Licensing Act 2003 (c 17), and

(b)   the application asserts that paragraph (a) is satisfied and is accompanied by the certificate.

(2)   In the case of an application to which this paragraph applies—

(a)   paragraphs 3 to 6 shall not apply, and

(b)   paragraphs 7 and 8 shall apply with the omission of any reference to objections.

(3)   The authority to whom an application to which this paragraph applies is made shall grant it unless they think—

(a)   that the applicant is established or conducted wholly or mainly for the purposes of the provision of facilities for gaming, other than gaming of a prescribed kind,

(b)   that the applicant is established or conducted wholly or mainly for the purposes of the provision of facilities for gaming of a prescribed kind and also provides facilities for gaming of another kind, or

(c)   that a club gaming permit or club machine permit issued to the applicant has been cancelled during the period of ten years ending with the date of the application.

(4)   Regulations prescribing anything for the purposes of this Act may, in particular, make provision that differs in effect according to whether or not a permit is granted in pursuance of an application to which this paragraph applies.

(5)   This paragraph does not apply to Scotland.

Form of permit

11.   (1)   A permit must be in the prescribed form and must specify—

(a)   the name of the club or institute in respect of which it is issued,

(b)   the premises to which it relates,

(c)   whether it is a club gaming permit or a club machine permit,

(d)   the date on which it takes effect, and

(e)   such other information as may be prescribed.

(2)   If the application for the permit was made in accordance with paragraph 10, the permit must also identify the club premises certificate under section 72 of the Licensing Act 2003 (c 17).

Maintenance

12.   The holder of a permit shall keep it on the premises to which it relates.

13.   (1)   An occupier of premises to which a permit relates commits an offence if without reasonable excuse he fails to produce the permit on request for inspection by—

(a)   a constable, or

(b)   an enforcement officer.

(2)   A person guilty of an offence under sub-paragraph (1) shall be liable on summary conviction to a fine not exceeding level 2 on the standard scale.

14.   (1)   The holder of a permit—

(a)   shall pay a first annual fee to the issuing licensing authority within such period after the issue of the permit as may be prescribed, and

(b)   shall pay an annual fee to the issuing licensing authority before each anniversary of the issue of the permit.

(2)   In this paragraph "annual fee" means a fee of such amount as may be prescribed.

(3)   Sub-paragraph (1)(b) does not apply in relation to an anniversary of the issue of a permit immediately before which the permit expires in accordance with paragraph 17.

15.   (1)   If information contained in a permit ceases to be accurate the holder of the permit shall as soon as is reasonably practicable apply to the issuing licensing authority to have the permit varied.

(2)   An application under sub-paragraph (1) must be accompanied by—

(a)   the prescribed fee, and

(b)   either—

(i)   the permit, or

(ii)   a statement explaining why it is not reasonably practicable to produce the permit.

(3)   The licensing authority to whom an application is made under sub-paragraph (1) shall issue a copy of the permit varied in accordance with the application (and the copy shall be treated as if it were the original permit).

(4)   But if the authority think that they would refuse an application for the permit were it made anew, they may—

(*a*)   refuse the application for variation, and
(*b*)   cancel the permit.

(5) Paragraphs 7, 9 and 25 apply in relation to a decision under sub-paragraph (4) as they apply in relation to a decision to refuse an application for a permit (and paragraph 21 shall not apply).

(6) The holder of a permit commits an offence if without reasonable excuse he fails to comply with sub-paragraph (1).

(7) A person guilty of an offence under sub-paragraph (6) shall be liable on summary conviction to a fine not exceeding level 2 on the standard scale.

16. (1) Where a permit is lost, stolen or damaged, the holder may apply to the issuing licensing authority for a copy.

(2) An application under sub-paragraph (1) must be accompanied by the prescribed fee.

(3) A licensing authority shall grant an application under sub-paragraph (1) if satisfied—

(*a*)   that the permit has been lost, stolen or damaged, and
(*b*)   where the permit has been lost or stolen, that the loss or theft has been reported to the police.

(4) As soon as is reasonably practicable after granting an application under sub-paragraph (1) a licensing authority shall issue a copy of the permit certified by the authority as a true copy (and the copy shall be treated as if it were the original permit).

Duration

17. (1) A permit shall cease to have effect at the end of the period of ten years beginning with the date on which it is issued unless—

(*a*)   it ceases to have effect before that time in accordance with a provision of this Schedule, or
(*b*)   it is renewed in accordance with paragraph 24.

(2) But a permit issued in pursuance of an application to which paragraph 10 applies—

(*a*)   shall not cease to have effect by virtue of sub-paragraph (1),
(*b*)   may cease to have effect in accordance with paragraph 19, 21, 22 or 23, and
(*c*)   shall lapse if the club premises certificate on which the application relied ceases to have effect.

18. (1) If the holder of a permit ceases to be a members' club (whether or not it becomes a commercial club), a commercial club or a miners' welfare institute, the permit shall lapse.

(2) But this paragraph does not apply to a permit issued in pursuance of an application to which paragraph 10 applies.

19. (1) A permit shall cease to have effect upon being surrendered by notice given by the holder of the permit to the issuing licensing authority.

(2) A notice under sub-paragraph (1) must be accompanied by—

(*a*)   the permit, or
(*b*)   a statement explaining why it is not reasonably practicable to produce the permit.

20. (1) The licensing authority which issues a permit shall as soon as is reasonably practicable inform the persons specified in sub-paragraph (2) if the authority—

(*a*)   believe that the permit has lapsed under paragraph 17(2)(*c*) or 18, or
(*b*)   receive notice of surrender under paragraph 19.

(2) The persons mentioned in sub-paragraph (1) are—

(*a*)   the Commission, and
(*b*)   the chief officer of police for any area in which the premises to which the permit relates are wholly or partly situated.

Cancellation and forfeiture

21. (1) The licensing authority which issued a permit may cancel it if the authority think—

(*a*)   that the premises on which the holder of the permit conducts its activities are used wholly or mainly by children, by young persons or by both, or
(*b*)   that an offence, or a breach of a condition of a permit, has been committed in the course of gaming activities carried on by the holder of the permit.

(2) Before cancelling a permit under this paragraph a licensing authority shall—

(*a*)   give the holder of the permit at least 21 days' notice of the authority's intention to consider cancelling the permit,
(*b*)   consider any representations made by the holder,
(*c*)   hold a hearing if the holder requests one, and
(*d*)   comply with any prescribed requirements for the procedure to be followed in considering whether to cancel a permit.

(3) If a licensing authority cancel a permit they shall as soon as is reasonably practicable give notice of the cancellation and the reasons for it to—

(*a*)   the holder,
(*b*)   the Commission, and
(*c*)   the chief officer of police for any area in which the premises to which the permit relates are wholly or partly situated.

(4) The cancellation of a permit shall not take effect until—

(a)   the period specified in paragraph 25(5)(c) has expired without an appeal being brought, or

(b)   any appeal brought has been determined.

22. (1) The licensing authority which issued a permit shall cancel it if the holder fails to pay the annual fee in accordance with paragraph 14.

(2) But a licensing authority may disapply sub-paragraph (1) if they think that a failure to pay is attributable to administrative error.

23. (1) Where the holder of a permit, or an officer of the holder of a permit, is convicted of an offence under this Act by or before a court in Great Britain, the court may order forfeiture of the permit.

(2) Forfeiture under this paragraph shall be on such terms (which may include terms as to suspension) as may be specified by—

(a)   the court which orders forfeiture,

(b)   a court to which an appeal against the conviction, or against any order made on the conviction, has been or could be made, or

(c)   the High Court, if hearing proceedings relating to the conviction.

(3) Subject to any express provision made under sub-paragraph (2), a permit shall cease to have effect on the making of a forfeiture order under sub-paragraph (1).

(4) The terms on which a forfeiture order is made under this paragraph shall, in particular, include a requirement that the holder deliver to the licensing authority who issued the permit, within such time as the order may specify—

(a)   the permit, or

(b)   a statement explaining why it is not reasonably practicable to produce the permit.

(5) As soon as is reasonably practicable after making an order for forfeiture under this paragraph the court shall notify the licensing authority who issued the permit.

Renewal

24. (1) The holder of a permit may apply to the issuing authority for its renewal.

(2) An application for the renewal of a permit may not be made—

(a)   before the period of three months ending with the date on which the permit would otherwise expire, or

(b)   after the beginning of the period of six weeks ending with that date.

(3) The provisions of this Schedule shall have effect (with any necessary modifications) in relation to an application for renewal as they have effect in relation to an application for a permit.

(4) Paragraph 17 shall have effect in relation to a renewed permit with the substitution of the date of renewal for the date of issue.

(5) A permit shall not cease to have effect by virtue only of paragraph 17 while—

(a)   an application for renewal of the permit is pending, or

(b)   an appeal against a decision on an application for renewal of the permit is pending.

Appeal

25. (1) Where a licensing authority reject an application for the issue or renewal of a permit the applicant may appeal.

(2) Where a licensing authority grant an application for the issue or renewal of a permit in relation to which an objection was made under paragraph 4, the person who made the objection may appeal.

(3) Where a licensing authority cancel a permit the holder may appeal.

(4) Where a licensing authority determine not to cancel a permit, any person who in accordance with regulations under paragraph 21(2)(d) made representations to the authority in connection with their consideration whether to cancel the permit may appeal.

(5) An appeal under this paragraph must be instituted—

(a)   in the magistrates' court for a local justice area in which the premises to which the appeal relates are wholly or partly situated,

(b)   by notice of appeal given to the designated officer, and

(c)   within the period of 21 days beginning with the day on which the appellant receives notice of the decision against which the appeal is brought.

(6) On an appeal a magistrates' court may—

(a)   dismiss the appeal;

(b)   substitute for the decision appealed against any decision that the licensing authority could have made;

(c)   restore a permit (with effect from such date and on such transitional or other terms as the court may specify);

(d)   remit the case to the licensing authority to decide in accordance with a direction of the court;

(e)   make an order about costs.

(7) In relation to premises in Scotland—

(a)   sub-paragraph (5)(a) shall have effect as if it referred to a sheriff within whose sheriffdom the premises are wholly or partly situated,

(b)   sub-paragraph (5)(b) shall not have effect,

(c)   the reference in sub-paragraph (6) to the magistrates' court shall have effect as a reference to the sheriff, and

(d)   the reference in sub-paragraph (6)(e) to costs shall have effect as a reference to expenses.

(8) Sub-paragraphs (1) to (4) apply to a decision of a licensing authority following remittal under sub-paragraph (6)(d) above.

Register

26. (1) A licensing authority shall—

(*a*) maintain a register of permits issued by the authority together with such other information as may be prescribed,

(*b*) make the register and information available for inspection by members of the public at all reasonable times, and

(*c*) make arrangements for the provision of a copy of an entry in the register, or of information, to a member of the public on request.

(2) A licensing authority may refuse to provide a copy of an entry or of information unless the person seeking it pays a reasonable fee specified by the authority.

(3) The Secretary of State may make regulations about—

(*a*) the form of the register;

(*b*) the manner in which it is maintained.

(4) The Secretary of State may make regulations—

(*a*) requiring licensing authorities to give to the Commission specified information about permits issued by them;

(*b*) requiring the Commission to maintain a register of the information provided to it under paragraph (*a*);

(*c*) requiring the Commission to grant access to the register to members of the public (without charge);

(*d*) requiring the Commission to make copies of entries available on request, and on payment of a reasonable fee, to members of the public;

(*e*) excusing licensing authorities, wholly or partly, from compliance with sub-paragraph (1).

Exercise of functions by licensing authority: general

27. In exercising a function under this Schedule a licensing authority shall have regard to—

(*a*) any relevant guidance under section 25, and

(*b*) subject to paragraph (*a*), the licensing objectives.

28. (1) Sections 154 and 155 shall have effect in relation to the functions of a licensing authority under this Schedule as they have effect in relation to functions of a licensing authority under Part 8.

(2) In the application of section 154 to this Schedule the following shall be substituted for the list of functions in subsection (4) (which itself substitutes a list of functions for that in section 10(4) of the Licensing Act 2003)—

(*a*) determination of an application for a permit in respect of which an objection has been made under this Schedule (and not withdrawn), and

(*b*) cancellation of a permit under paragraph 21.

Vehicles and vessels

29. A club gaming permit or club machine permit may not be issued in respect of a vehicle or vessel (or part of a vehicle or vessel).

Interpretation

30. In this Schedule "prescribed" means prescribed by the Secretary of State by regulations except that in paragraphs 2(*e*), 15(2)(*a*) and 16(2) it means, where the application in question is made to a licensing authority in Scotland, prescribed by the Scottish Ministers by regulations.

31. This Schedule shall, in its application to Scotland, have effect as if references to a chief officer of police were references to a chief constable.

8–13937

Section 283   SCHEDULE 13
LICENSED PREMISES GAMING MACHINE PERMITS

Making of application

1. (1) A person who applies to a licensing authority (in its capacity as a licensing authority under the Licensing Act 2003 (c 17)) for an on-premises alcohol licence or who holds an on-premises alcohol licence issued by a licensing authority (in that capacity) may apply to that licensing authority (in its capacity as a licensing authority under this Act) for a licensed premises gaming machine permit.

(2) An application may not be made under this Schedule if a licence under Part 8 has effect in relation to the premises.

2. An application for a permit must—

(*a*) be made in such form and manner as the licensing authority may direct,

(*b*) specify the premises in respect of which the permit is sought,

(*c*) specify the number and category of gaming machines in respect of which the permit is sought,

(*d*) contain or be accompanied by such other information or documents as the licensing authority may direct, and

(*e*) be accompanied by the prescribed fee.

3. Sections 154 and 155 shall have effect in relation to the functions of a licensing authority under this Schedule as they have effect in relation to functions of a licensing authority under Part 8.

4. (1) A licensing authority to whom an application is made under this Schedule shall consider it having regard to the licensing objectives, any relevant guidance issued by the Commission under section 25 and such other matters as they think relevant.

(2) On considering an application for a permit a licensing authority shall—

(a) grant the application,
(b) refuse the application, or
(c) grant it in respect of—

    (i) a smaller number of machines than that specified in the application,
    (ii) a different category of machines from that specified in the application, or
    (iii) both.

5. (1) A licensing authority may not attach conditions to a permit.

(2) As soon as is reasonably practicable after granting an application, a licensing authority shall issue a permit to the applicant.

(3) As soon as is reasonably practicable after refusing an application a licensing authority shall notify the applicant of—

(a) the refusal, and
(b) the reasons for it.

6. (1) A licensing authority may grant an application under this Schedule only if the applicant holds an on-premises alcohol licence.

(2) A licensing authority may not refuse an application, or grant an application in respect of a different category or smaller number of gaming machines than that specified in the application, unless they have—

(a) notified the applicant of their intention to refuse the application, or grant the application in respect of—

    (i) a smaller number of machines than that specified in the application,
    (ii) a different category of machines from that specified in the application, or
    (iii) both, and

(b) given the applicant an opportunity to make representations.

(3) A licensing authority may satisfy sub-paragraph (2)(b) by giving the applicant an opportunity to make—

(a) oral representations,
(b) written representations, or
(c) both.

(4) Sub-paragraph (2)(b) shall not apply in respect of a refusal if the refusal was by virtue of sub-paragraph (1).

Form of permit

7. (1) A permit must be in the prescribed form and must specify—

(a) the person to whom it is issued,
(b) the premises,
(c) the number and category of gaming machines which it authorises, and
(d) the date on which it takes effect.

(2) If the person to whom a permit is issued changes his name or wishes to be known by another name—

(a) he may send the permit to the licensing authority with—

    (i) the prescribed fee, and
    (ii) a request that a new name be substituted for the old name, and

(b) the licensing authority shall comply with the request and return the permit to the holder.

Maintenance

8. The holder of a permit shall keep it on the premises to which it relates.

9. (1) The holder of a permit—

(a) shall pay a first annual fee to the issuing licensing authority within such period after the issue of the permit as may be prescribed, and
(b) shall pay an annual fee to the issuing licensing authority before each anniversary of the issue of the permit.

(2) In this paragraph "annual fee" means a fee of such amount as may be prescribed.

10. (1) An occupier of premises in respect of which a permit has effect commits an offence if without reasonable excuse he fails to produce the permit on request for inspection by—

(a) a constable,
(b) an enforcement officer, or
(c) an authorised local authority officer.

(2) A person guilty of an offence under this paragraph shall be liable on summary conviction to a fine not exceeding level 2 on the standard scale.

11. (1) Where a permit is lost, stolen or damaged, the holder may apply to the licensing authority for a copy.

(2) An application under sub-paragraph (1) must be accompanied by the prescribed fee.

(3) A licensing authority shall consider an application under this paragraph and shall grant it if satisfied—

(a) that the permit has been lost, stolen or damaged, and
(b) where the permit has been lost or stolen, that the loss or theft has been reported to the police.

(4) As soon as is reasonably practicable after granting an application under this paragraph a licensing authority shall issue a copy of the permit certified by the authority as a true copy.

(5) A copy of a permit issued under this paragraph shall be treated as if it were the permit.

12. A permit shall continue to have effect unless and until it ceases to have effect in accordance with a provision of this Schedule.

13. A permit shall cease to have effect if—

(a) an on-premises alcohol licence ceases to have effect with respect to the premises to which it relates, or

(b) the permit holder ceases to be the holder of an on-premises alcohol licence.

14. A permit shall cease to have effect if the permit holder gives to the licensing authority—

(a) notice of surrender, and

(b) either—

  (i) the permit, or

  (ii) a statement explaining why it is not reasonably practicable to produce the permit.

Variation

15. (1) The holder of a permit may apply to the licensing authority to vary the number or category (or both) of gaming machines authorised by the permit.

(2) Paragraphs 1 to 7 and 21 shall have effect (with any necessary modifications) in relation to an application for variation under this paragraph as they have effect in relation to an application for the issue of a permit.

Cancellation and forfeiture

16. (1) The licensing authority which issued a permit may cancel it, or may vary the number or category (or both) of gaming machines authorised by it, if they think that—

(a) it would not be reasonably consistent with pursuit of the licensing objectives for the permit to continue to have effect,

(b) gaming has taken place on the premises in purported reliance on the permit but otherwise than in accordance with the permit or a condition of the permit,

(c) the premises are mainly used or to be used for making gaming machines available, or

(d) an offence under this Act has been committed on the premises.

(2) Before cancelling or varying a permit under this paragraph a licensing authority shall—

(a) give the permit holder at least 21 days' notice of the authority's intention to consider cancelling or varying the permit,

(b) consider any representations made by the holder,

(c) hold a hearing if the holder requests one, and

(d) comply with any prescribed requirements for the procedure to be followed in considering whether to cancel or vary a permit.

(3) If a licensing authority cancel or vary a permit under this paragraph they shall as soon as is reasonably practicable give notice of the cancellation or variation and the reasons for it to—

(a) the permit holder, and

(b) the Commission.

(4) The cancellation or variation of a permit shall not take effect until—

(a) the period specified in paragraph 21(2)(c) has expired without an appeal being brought, or

(b) any appeal brought has been determined.

17. (1) The licensing authority which issued a permit shall cancel it if the holder fails to pay the annual fee in accordance with paragraph 9.

(2) But a licensing authority may disapply sub-paragraph (1) if they think that a failure to pay is attributable to administrative error.

18. (1) Where a permit holder, or the officer of a permit holder, is convicted of a relevant offence the court by or before which he is convicted may order forfeiture of the permit.

(2) Forfeiture under this paragraph shall be on such terms (which may include terms as to suspension) as may be specified by—

(a) the court which orders forfeiture,

(b) a court to which an appeal against the conviction, or against any order made on the conviction, has been or could be made, or

(c) the High Court, if hearing proceedings relating to the conviction.

(3) Subject to any express provision made under sub-paragraph (2), a permit shall cease to have effect on the making of a forfeiture order under this paragraph.

(4) The terms on which forfeiture is ordered under this paragraph shall, in particular, include a requirement that the permit holder deliver to the licensing authority within such time as the order may specify—

(a) the permit, or

(b) a statement explaining why it is not reasonably practicable to produce the permit.

(5) As soon as is reasonably practicable after making or suspending an order for forfeiture under this paragraph a court shall notify the licensing authority.

Transfer of permit

19. (1) A person may apply for the transfer of a permit to him if—

(a) he is applying for the transfer of an on-premises alcohol licence to him in accordance with—

  (i) section 42 of the Licensing Act 2003 (c 17) (application for transfer), or

  (ii) section 50 of that Act (transfer following death of holder), and

(b) a permit has effect in respect of the same premises.

(2) The provisions of this Schedule shall have effect (with any necessary modifications) in relation to an application for the transfer of a permit as they have effect in relation to an application for the issue of a permit.

(3) A person applying for the transfer of a permit to him must supply with his application—

(a) the permit, or

(b) a statement explaining why it is not reasonably practicable to produce the permit.

(4) A licensing authority may not approve an application for the transfer of a permit under this paragraph unless the transfer of the on-premises alcohol licence is approved under section 45 of the Licensing Act 2003 (determination of application).

(5) Where a licensing authority refuse an application for the transfer of a permit under this paragraph by virtue of sub-paragraph (4), the provisions of paragraph 6(2)(b) shall not apply to the refusal.

20. (1) This paragraph applies where—

(a) the transfer of an on-premises alcohol licence is to be given immediate effect under section 43 of the Licensing Act 2003 (interim effect of transfer application), and

(b) the applicant has also made an application under paragraph 19.

(2) A permit in respect of those premises shall have effect during the application period as if the applicant for the transfer were the permit holder.

(3) In this paragraph "application period" has the same meaning as in section 43 of the Licensing Act 2003.

Appeal

21. (1) The applicant for or holder of a permit may appeal if the licensing authority—

(a) reject an application for a permit,

(b) grant an application for a permit in respect of a smaller number of machines than that specified in the application or a different category of machines from that specified in the application (or both), or

(c) give a notice under paragraph 16.

(2) An appeal under this paragraph must be instituted—

(a) in the magistrates' court for a local justice area in which the premises to which the appeal relates are wholly or partly situated,

(b) by notice of appeal given to the designated officer, and

(c) within the period of 21 days beginning with the day on which the appellant or holder receives notice of the decision against which the appeal is brought.

(3) On an appeal the magistrates' court may—

(a) dismiss the appeal;

(b) substitute for the decision appealed against any decision that the licensing authority could have made (with effect from such date and on such transitional or other terms as the court may specify);

(c) restore a permit (with effect from such date and on such transitional or other terms as the court may specify);

(d) remit the case to the licensing authority to decide in accordance with a direction of the court;

(e) make an order about costs.

(4) Sub-paragraph (1) applies to a decision of a licensing authority following remittal under sub-paragraph (3)(d).

Register

22. (1) A licensing authority shall—

(a) maintain a register of permits issued by the authority together with such other information as may be prescribed,

(b) make the register and information available for inspection by members of the public at all reasonable times, and

(c) make arrangements for the provision of a copy of an entry in the register, or of information, to a member of the public on request.

(2) A licensing authority may refuse to provide a copy of an entry or of information unless the person seeking it pays a reasonable fee specified by the authority.

(3) The Secretary of State may make regulations about—

(a) the form of the register;

(b) the manner in which it is maintained.

(4) The Secretary of State may make regulations—

(a) requiring licensing authorities to give to the Commission specified information about permits issued by them;

(b) requiring the Commission to maintain a register of the information provided to it under paragraph (a);

(c) requiring the Commission to grant access to the register to members of the public (without charge);

(d) requiring the Commission to make copies of entries available on request, and on payment of a reasonable fee, to members of the public;

(e) excusing licensing authorities, wholly or partly, from compliance with sub-paragraph (1).

Interpretation

23. In this Schedule—

"permit" means a licensed premises gaming machine permit, and

"prescribed" means prescribed by regulations made by the Secretary of State.

SCHEDULE 14
PRIZE GAMING PERMITS

Interpretation

1. In this Schedule—

"holder", in relation to a permit, means the person to whom the permit is issued,
"the licensing authority"—

(a) in relation to an application, means the licensing authority to whom the application is made, and
(b) in relation to a permit, means the licensing authority who issue it,

"permit" means a prize gaming permit,
"the premises", in relation to an application or permit, means the premises in respect of which the permit is
    sought or issued, and
"prescribed" means prescribed by regulations made by the Secretary of State except that in paragraphs 6(e) and
    21(2) it means, where the application in question is made to a licensing authority in Scotland, prescribed by
    regulations made by the Scottish Ministers.

2. This Schedule shall, in its application to Scotland, have effect as if references to a chief officer of police were
references to a chief constable.

Making of application

3. (1) An application for a permit may be made only by a person who occupies or proposes to occupy the
premises.
    (2) If the applicant for a permit is an individual, he must be an adult.
4. An application for a permit may not be made if—

(a) a premises licence has effect in respect of the premises, or
(b) a club gaming permit has effect in respect of the premises.

5. An application for a permit must be made to a licensing authority in whose area the premises are wholly or
partly situated.
6. An application for a permit must—

(a) be made in such form and manner as the licensing authority may direct,
(b) specify the premises,
(c) specify the nature of the gaming in respect of which the permit is sought,
(d) contain or be accompanied by such other information or documents as the licensing authority may direct,
    and
(e) be accompanied by the prescribed fee.

Consideration of application

7. Sections 154 and 155 shall have effect in relation to functions of a licensing authority under this Schedule as
they have effect in relation to the functions of a licensing authority under Part 8.
8. (1) A licensing authority may prepare a statement of principles that they propose to apply in exercising their
functions under this Schedule.
    (2) A statement under sub-paragraph (1) may, in particular, specify matters that the licensing authority propose
to consider in determining the suitability of an applicant for a permit.
    (3) In exercising their functions under this Schedule a licensing authority—

(a) need not (but may) have regard to the licensing objectives, and
(b) shall have regard to any relevant guidance issued by the Commission under section 25.

Determination of application

9. (1) On considering an application for a permit a licensing authority may—

(a) grant it, or
(b) refuse it.

    (2) A licensing authority may not attach conditions to a permit.
    (3) As soon as is reasonably practicable after granting an application a licensing authority shall issue a permit to
the applicant.
    (4) As soon as is reasonably practicable after refusing an application a licensing authority shall notify the
applicant of—

(a) the refusal, and
(b) the reasons for it.

10. A licensing authority may grant an application for a permit only if they have consulted the chief officer of
police for a police area in which the premises are wholly or partly situated.
11. (1) A licensing authority may not refuse an application unless they have—

(a) notified the applicant of their intention to refuse the application and of their reasons, and
(b) given the applicant an opportunity to make representations.

    (2) A licensing authority may satisfy sub-paragraph (1)(b) by giving the applicant an opportunity to make—

(*a*) oral representations,
(*b*) written representations, or
(*c*) both.

Form of permit

12. (1) A permit must be in the prescribed form and must specify—

(*a*) the person to whom it is issued,
(*b*) the nature of the gaming in respect of which it has effect,
(*c*) the premises, and
(*d*) the date on which it takes effect.

(2) If the person to whom a permit is issued changes his name or wishes to be known by another name—

(*a*) he may send the permit to the licensing authority with—

(i) the prescribed fee, and
(ii) a request that a new name be substituted for the old name, and

(*b*) the licensing authority shall comply with the request and return the permit to the holder.

Duration

13. A permit shall cease to have effect at the end of the period of ten years beginning with the date specified under paragraph 12(1)(*d*) unless—

(*a*) it ceases to have effect before that time in accordance with a provision of this Schedule, or
(*b*) it is renewed in accordance with paragraph 18.

14. (1) A permit shall lapse if the holder ceases to occupy the premises specified under paragraph 12(1)(*c*).
(2) A permit shall not take effect if on the date specified under paragraph 12(1)(*d*) the person to whom the permit is issued is not an occupier of the premises specified under paragraph 12(1)(*c*).

15. (1) A permit held by an individual shall lapse if—

(*a*) he dies,
(*b*) he becomes, in the opinion of the licensing authority as notified to the individual, incapable of carrying on the activities authorised by the permit by reason of mental or physical incapacity,
(*c*) he becomes bankrupt (within the meaning of section 381 of the Insolvency Act 1986 (c 45)), or
(*d*) sequestration of his estate is awarded under section 12(1) of the Bankruptcy (Scotland) Act 1985 (c 66).

(2) In any other case a permit shall lapse if the holder—

(*a*) ceases to exist, or
(*b*) goes into liquidation (within the meaning of section 247(2) of that Act).

(3) During the period of six months beginning with the date on which a permit lapses under this paragraph the following may rely on it as if it had effect and were issued to them—

(*a*) the personal representatives of the holder (in the case of an individual holder who dies),
(*b*) the trustee of the bankrupt's estate (in the case of an individual holder who becomes bankrupt),
(*c*) the holder's interim or permanent trustee (in the case of an individual holder whose estate is sequestrated), and
(*d*) the liquidator of the company (in the case of a company holder that goes into liquidation).

(4) In relation to premises in Scotland—

(*a*) sub-paragraph (2)(*a*) shall have effect as if it referred to a sheriff within whose sheriffdom the premises are wholly or partly situated,
(*b*) sub-paragraph (2)(*b*) shall not have effect,
(*c*) the reference in sub-paragraph (3) to a magistrate's court shall have effect as a reference to the sheriff, and
(*d*) the reference in sub-paragraph (3)(*d*) to costs shall have effect as a reference to expenses.

16. A permit shall cease to have effect if the holder gives to the licensing authority—

(*a*) notice of surrender, and
(*b*) either—

(i) the permit, or
(ii) a statement explaining why it is not reasonably practicable to produce the permit.

17. (1) Where the holder of a permit is convicted of a relevant offence the court by or before which he is convicted may order forfeiture of the permit.
(2) Forfeiture under this paragraph shall be on such terms (which may include terms as to suspension) as may be specified by—

(*a*) the court which orders forfeiture,
(*b*) a court to which an appeal against the conviction, or against any order made on the conviction, has been or could be made, or
(*c*) the High Court, if hearing proceedings relating to the conviction.

(3) Subject to any express provision made under sub-paragraph (2), a permit shall cease to have effect on the making of a forfeiture order under this paragraph.
(4) The terms on which forfeiture is ordered under this paragraph shall, in particular, include a requirement that the holder of the permit deliver to the licensing authority within such time as the order may specify—

(*a*) the permit, or

(*b*) a statement explaining why it is not reasonably practicable to produce the permit.

(5) As soon as is reasonably practicable after making or suspending an order for forfeiture under this paragraph a court shall notify the licensing authority.

Renewal

18. (1) The holder of a permit may apply to the licensing authority for renewal of the permit.

(2) An application for renewal may not be made—

(*a*) before the period of six months ending with the date on which the permit would otherwise expire in accordance with paragraph 13, or

(*b*) after the beginning of the period of two months ending with that date.

(3) The provisions of this Schedule shall have effect (with any necessary modifications) in relation to an application for renewal as they have effect in relation to an application for a permit.

(4) Paragraph 13 shall have effect in relation to a renewed permit as if the date of renewal were the date specified under paragraph 12(1)(*d*).

(5) A permit shall not cease to have effect by virtue only of paragraph 13 while—

(*a*) an application for renewal of the permit is pending, or

(*b*) an appeal against a decision on an application for renewal of the permit is pending.

Maintenance

19. The holder of a permit shall keep it on the premises.

20. (1) An occupier of premises in respect of which a permit has effect commits an offence if without reasonable excuse he fails to produce the permit on request for inspection by—

(*a*) a constable, or

(*b*) an enforcement officer,

(*c*) an authorised local authority officer.

(2) A person guilty of an offence under this paragraph shall be liable on summary conviction to a fine not exceeding level 2 on the standard scale.

21. (1) Where a permit is lost, stolen or damaged, the holder may apply to the licensing authority for a copy.

(2) An application under sub-paragraph (1) must be accompanied by the prescribed fee.

(3) A licensing authority shall consider an application under this paragraph and shall grant it if satisfied—

(*a*) that the permit has been lost, stolen or damaged, and

(*b*) where the permit has been lost or stolen, that the loss or theft has been reported to the police.

(4) As soon as is reasonably practicable after granting an application under this paragraph a licensing authority shall issue a copy of the permit certified by the authority as a true copy.

(5) A copy of a permit issued under this paragraph shall be treated as if it were the permit.

Appeal

22. (1) Where a licensing authority reject an application for the issue or renewal of a permit the applicant may appeal.

(2) An appeal under this paragraph must be instituted—

(*a*) in the magistrates' court for a local justice area in which the premises to which the appeal relates are wholly or partly situated,

(*b*) by notice of appeal given to the designated officer, and

(*c*) within the period of 21 days beginning with the day on which the appellant receives notice of the decision against which the appeal is brought.

(3) On an appeal a magistrates' court may—

(*a*) dismiss the appeal;

(*b*) substitute for the decision appealed against any decision that the licensing authority could have made;

(*c*) remit the case to the licensing authority to decide in accordance with a direction of the court;

(*d*) make an order about costs.

(4) Sub-paragraph (1) applies to a decision of a licensing authority following remittal under sub-paragraph (3)(*c*) above.

Register

23. (1) A licensing authority shall—

(*a*) maintain a register of permits issued by the authority together with such other information as may be prescribed,

(*b*) make the register and information available for inspection by members of the public at all reasonable times, and

(*c*) make arrangements for the provision of a copy of an entry in the register, or of information, to a member of the public on request.

(2) A licensing authority may refuse to provide a copy of an entry or of information unless the person seeking it pays a reasonable fee specified by the authority.

(3) The Secretary of State may make regulations about—

(*a*) the form of the register;
(*b*) the manner in which it is maintained.

(4) The Secretary of State may make regulations—

(*a*) requiring licensing authorities to give to the Commission specified information about permits issued by them;
(*b*) requiring the Commission to maintain a register of the information provided to it under paragraph (*a*);
(*c*) requiring the Commission to grant access to the register to members of the public (without charge);
(*d*) requiring the Commission to make copies of entries available on request, and on payment of a reasonable fee, to members of the public;
(*e*) excusing licensing authorities, wholly or partly, from compliance with sub-paragraph (1).

Vehicles and vessels

24. A permit may not be issued in respect of a vehicle or vessel (or part of a vehicle or vessel).

8–13939

Section 295

SCHEDULE 15
PRIVATE GAMING AND BETTING
PART 1
GAMING

Introduction

1. Gaming is private if it satisfies the conditions specified in this Part of this Schedule.
2. (1) For the purposes of this Part of this Schedule gaming is domestic if it takes place—

(*a*) in a private dwelling, and
(*b*) on a domestic occasion.

(2) For the purposes of this Part of this Schedule gaming is residential if—

(*a*) it takes place in a hostel, hall of residence or similar establishment which is not administered in the course of a trade or business, and
(*b*) more than half of the participants are residents of the hostel, hall or establishment.

No charge for participation

3. (1) It is a condition of private gaming that no charge is made for participation.
(2) For the purposes of this paragraph—

(*a*) it is immaterial how a charge is described,
(*b*) it is immaterial whether a charge is in money or money's worth,
(*c*) an amount deducted or levied, by a person providing facilities for gaming, from sums staked or won in the course of gaming is a charge for participation in the gaming,
(*d*) a charge for admission to premises where gaming takes place shall be treated as a charge for participation in the gaming, and
(*e*) a stake is not a charge for participation.

Equal chance gaming

4. (1) It is a condition of private gaming that it is equal chance gaming.
(2) But this condition does not apply in relation to domestic or residential gaming.

Privacy

5. It is a condition of private gaming that it does not occur in a place to which the public have access (whether or not on payment).

PART 2
BETTING

Introduction

6. Betting is private betting if it is—

(*a*) domestic betting, or
(*b*) workers' betting.

Domestic betting

7. (1) A betting transaction is domestic betting if made on premises in which each party to the transaction lives.
(2) For the purposes of this paragraph a person lives in premises if he habitually resides in any part of the premises (whether or not there are other premises in which he also habitually resides).

Workers' betting

8. A betting transaction is workers' betting if made between persons each of whom is employed under a contract of employment with the same employer.

Section 356

SCHEDULE 16
Minor and Consequential Amendments

Part 1
Minor Amendments

Metropolitan Police Act 1839 (c 47)

1. In section 44 of the Metropolitan Police Act 1839 (refreshment houses)—

(*a*) omit ", or knowingly suffer any unlawful games or any gaming whatsoever therein,", and
(*b*) in the heading, omit ", or gaming".

Libraries Offences Act 1898 (c 53)

2. Section 2(3) of the Libraries Offences Act 1898 (offence of annoying library users) shall cease to have effect.

Gaming Act 1968 (c 65)

3. (1) The Gaming Act 1968 shall be amended as follows.
(2) For section 6(2) (premises licensed for the sale of alcohol) substitute—

"(2) This section applies to any premises in England and Wales—

(*a*) in respect of which a premises licence under Part 3 of the Licensing Act 2003 (c 17) has effect,
(*b*) which contain a bar at which alcohol is served for consumption on the premises (without a requirement that alcohol is served only with food), and
(*c*) at a time when alcohol may be supplied in reliance on the premises licence under Part 3 of the Licensing Act 2003."

(3) In section 12(3)—

(*a*) in paragraph (*a*) the words from "and at that time" to the end of the paragraph shall cease to have effect,
(*b*) in paragraph (*b*) the words from "and at that time" to the end of the paragraph shall cease to have effect, and
(*c*) in paragraph (*c*) the words from "and at that time" to the end of the paragraph shall cease to have effect.

(4) For section 20(5) substitute—

"(5) Section 12(3) shall not apply in relation to any club to which this section applies."
(5) In section 31—

(*a*) in subsection (2)(*c*) for "ten" substitute "twenty",
(*b*) for subsection (3E) substitute—

"(3E) The initial amount must not exceed the higher of—

(*a*) the highest coin value, or
(*b*) the charge for playing a game once by means of the machine." , and
(*c*) in subsection (3G) for "the highest coin value" substitute

"the higher of—

(*a*) the highest coin value, or
(*b*) the charge for playing a game once by means of the machine."

(6) In section 51(3) after "regulations" insert "or an order".
(7) In paragraph 10A(1) of Schedule 9, leave out "sub-paragraph (*a*) or".
(8) After paragraph 10A of Schedule 9 insert—

"**10AA.** A permit in respect of premises to which sub-paragraph (*a*) of paragraph 1 of this Schedule applies shall be subject to the conditions that a machine must—

(*a*) be located on premises which contain a bar at which alcohol is served for consumption on the premises (without a requirement that alcohol is served only with food), and
(*b*) be made available for use only at a time when alcohol may be supplied in reliance on the premises licence under Part 3 of the Licensing Act 2003."

Chronically Sick and Disabled Persons Act 1970 (c 44)

4. Section 8B(2)(*c*) of the Chronically Sick and Disabled Persons Act 1970 (report by Secretary of State on access to betting offices) shall cease to have effect.

Part 2
Consequential Amendments

Parliamentary Commissioner Act 1967 (c 13)

5. In Schedule 2 to the Parliamentary Commissioner Act 1967 (bodies subject to investigation) for "Gaming Board for Great Britain." substitute "Gambling Commission."

Superannuation Act 1972 (c 11)

6. In Schedule 1 to the Superannuation Act 1972 (employment to which superannuation schemes may extend) for "Gaming Board for Great Britain." substitute "Gambling Commission."

House of Commons Disqualification Act 1975 (c 24)

7. In Part II of Schedule 1 to the House of Commons Disqualification Act 1975 (c 24) (disqualifying offices) for "The Gaming Board for Great Britain." substitute "The Gambling Commission."

Local Government (Miscellaneous Provisions) Act 1976 (c 57)

8. In section 20(9) of the Local Government (Miscellaneous Provisions) Act 1976 (sanitation) for the definition of "betting office" substitute—

""betting office" means premises, other than a track within the meaning of the Gambling Act 2005, in respect of which a betting premises licence under Part 8 of that Act has effect;".

Race Relations Act 1976 (c 74)

9. In Schedule 1A to the Race Relations Act 1976 (bodies subject to general statutory duty) for "Gaming Board for Great Britain" substitute "Gambling Commission".

London Local Authorities Act 1995 (c x)

10. In section 14 of the London Local Authorities Act 1995 (interpretation of licensing provisions) for the provision excluding premises licensed under Part II of the Gaming Act 1968 substitute: "does not include premises in respect of which a casino premises licence, bingo premises licence, adult gaming centre premises licence, family entertainment centre premises licence or betting premises licence under Part 8, or a family entertainment centre gaming permit under section 247, of the Gambling Act 2005 has effect;".

Employment Rights Act 1996 (c 18)

11. For section 233 of the Employment Rights Act 1996 (betting workers) substitute—

"233. Betting workers.   (1) In this Act "betting worker" means an employee who under his contract of employment is or may be required to do betting work.
    (2) In this Act "betting work" means—

   (a)   work which consists of or includes dealing with betting transactions at a track in England or Wales and which is carried out for a person who holds a general betting operating licence, a pool betting operating licence or a horse-race pool betting operating licence, and
   (b)   work on premises in respect of which a betting premises licence has effect at a time when the premises are used for betting transactions.

    (3) In subsection (2) "betting transactions" includes the collection or payment of winnings.
    (4) Expressions used in this section and in the Gambling Act 2005 have the same meaning in this section as in that Act.
    (5) In this Act—

"notice period", in relation to an opted-out betting worker, has the meaning given by section 41(3),
"opted-out", in relation to a betting worker, shall be construed in accordance with section 41(1) and (2),
"opting-in notice", in relation to a betting worker, has the meaning given by section 36(6),
"opting-out notice", in relation to a betting worker, has the meaning given by section 40(2), and
"protected", in relation to a betting worker, shall be construed in accordance with section 36(1) to (5)."

Police Act 1997 (c 50)

12. In section 115 of the Police Act 1997 (enhanced criminal record certificates) for subsection (5)(a) to (c) substitute—

"(a) a process under the Gambling Act 2005".

Terrorism Act 2000 (c 11)

13. In paragraph 4 of Schedule 3A to the Terrorism Act 2000 (regulated sector and supervisory authorities) for "Gaming Board for Great Britain" substitute "Gambling Commission".

Regulation of Investigatory Powers Act 2000 (c 23)

14. In paragraph 20A of Schedule 1 to the Regulation of Investigatory Powers Act 2000 (relevant public authorities) for "Gaming Board for Great Britain" substitute "Gambling Commission".

Postal Services Act 2000 (c 26)

15. In section 7 of the Postal Services Act 2000 (exceptions to the restrictions on provision of postal services) for the definition of "authorised promoter" substitute—

""authorised promoter" means—

   (a)   the holder of a pool betting operating licence under Part 5 of the Gambling Act 2005,
   (b)   a person authorised under section 93(3) of that Act to do anything on behalf of the holder of a pool betting operating licence, and
   (c)   an associate, within the meaning of section 184 of the Consumer Credit Act 1974 (c 39), of a person within paragraph (a) or (b),".

Freedom of Information Act 2000 (c 36)

16. In Part 6 of Schedule 1 to the Freedom of Information Act 2000 (public authorities to which the Act applies) for "Gaming Board of Great Britain" substitute "Gambling Commission.

Private Security Industry Act 2001 (c 12)

17. For paragraph 8(3)(*e*) of Schedule 2 to the Private Security Industry Act 2001 (exceptions for certain premises) substitute—

"(*e*) in relation to any occasion on which a casino premises licence or a bingo premises licence is in force in respect of the premises under the Gambling Act 2005 and the premises are being used in reliance on that licence; or".

Criminal Justice and Police Act 2001 (c 16)

18. (1) In Schedule 1 of the Criminal Justice and Police Act 2001 (seizure powers to which extending provision of section 50 applies)—

(*a*) paragraphs 6, 11 and 20 cease to have effect,
(*b*) at the end of Part 1 (renumbering the entry for the Licensing Act 2003 as paragraph 73E) add—

"Gambling Act 2005

73F. The powers conferred by section 317 of the Gambling Act 2005 (inspection powers).",

(*c*) paragraphs 89, 93 and 97 cease to have effect, and
(*d*) at the end of Part 3 (renumbering the entry for the Licensing Act 2003 as paragraph 111) add—

"Gambling Act 2005

112. The powers conferred by section 317 of the Gambling Act 2005 (inspection powers)."

(2) For the purposes of the amendments made by this paragraph, the powers in section 317(1)(*d*), (*e*) and (*f*) are powers of seizure.

Proceeds of Crime Act 2002 (c 29)

19. In Part 2 of Schedule 9 to the Proceeds of Crime Act 2002 (supervisory authorities) in paragraph 4(*g*) for "Gaming Board for Great Britain" substitute "Gambling Commission".

Licensing Act 2003 (c 17)

20. (1) The Licensing Act 2003 shall be amended as follows.
(2) For section 175 (exemption for raffle, tombola, &c.) substitute—

"175. Exemption for incidental non-commercial lottery.   (1) The promotion of a lottery to which this section applies shall not constitute a licensable activity by reason only of one or more of the prizes in the lottery consisting of or including alcohol, provided that the alcohol is in a sealed container.
(2) This section applies to an incidental non-commercial lottery (within the meaning of Part 1 of Schedule 11 to the Gambling Act 2005)."
(3) In paragraph 10(3) of Schedule 1 (provision of regulated entertainment) for "section 22 of the Lotteries and Amusements Act 1976 (c 32)" substitute "section 19(3) of the Gambling Act 2005".
(4) In Schedule 4 (relevant offences) after paragraph 20 insert—

"21. An offence under section 46 of the Gambling Act 2005 if the child or young person was invited, caused or permitted to gamble on premises in respect of which a premises licence under this Act had effect."

Note

21. The amendments made by this Schedule are without prejudice to the generality of paragraph 4 of Schedule 5.

8–13941

Section 356   SCHEDULE 17
                                     REPEALS

Enactment	Repeal
Gaming Act 1710 (c 19)	The whole Act.
Gaming Act 1738 (c 28)	The whole Act.
Gaming Act 1835 (c 41)	The whole Act.
Metropolitan Police Act 1839 (c 47)	The words ", or knowingly suffer any unlawful games or any gaming whatsoever therein,".
Gaming Act 1845 (c 109)	The whole Act.
Gaming Act 1892 (c 9)	The whole Act.
Libraries Offences Act 1898 (c 53)	Section 2(3).
Betting, Gaming and Lotteries Act 1963 (c 2)	The whole Act.
Police Act 1964 (c 48)	In Schedule 9, the entry for the Betting, Gaming and Lotteries Act 1963.
Local Government Act 1966 (c 42)	In Schedule 3, paragraph 23.

Enactment	Repeal
Theft Act 1968 (c 60)	In Schedule 2, the entry for the Gaming Act 1845.
Gaming Act 1968 (c 65)	The whole Act.
Decimal Currency Act 1969 (c 19)	In Schedule 2, paragraph 17.
Family Law Reform Act 1969 (c 46)	In Schedule 1, the entry for the Betting, Gaming and Lotteries Act 1963.
Chronically Sick and Disabled Persons Act 1970 (c 44)	Section 8B(2)(*c*).
Courts Act 1971 (c 23)	In Schedule 6, paragraph 6. In Schedule 9 (*a*) the entry for the Betting, Gaming and Lotteries Act 1963, and (*b*) the entry for the Gaming Act 1968.
Local Government Act 1972 (c 70)	In Schedule 29, paragraph 13.
Gaming (Amendment) Act 1973 (c 12)	The whole Act.
Lotteries Act 1975 (c 58)	The whole Act.
Lotteries and Amusements Act 1976 (c 32)	The whole Act.
Licensing (Scotland) Act 1976 (c 66)	Section 133.
Criminal Law Act 1977 (c 45)	In Schedule 1, paragraph 17. In Schedule 6, the entry for the Gaming Act 1968. In Schedule 12, the entry for the Gaming Act 1968.
Gaming (Amendment) Act 1980 (c 8)	The whole Act.
Local Government, Planning and Land Act 1980 (c 65)	In Schedule 8, the entry for the Lotteries and Amusements Act 1976.
Supreme Court Act 1981 (c 54)	In section 28(2)(*b*), the references to the Betting, Gaming and Lotteries Act 1963 and the Gaming Act 1968.
Betting and Gaming Duties Act 1981 (c 63)	Sections 9 to 9B.
Gaming (Amendment) Act 1982 (c 22)	The whole Act.
Criminal Justice Act 1982 (c 48)	In Schedule 3, the entry for the Betting, Gaming and Lotteries Act 1963.
Lotteries (Amendment) Act 1984 (c 9)	The whole Act.
Betting, Gaming and Lotteries (Amendment) Act 1984 (c 25)	The whole Act.
Police and Criminal Evidence Act 1984 (c 60)	In Schedule 6, paragraph 12.
Companies Consolidation (Consequential Provisions) Act 1985 (c 9)	In Schedule 2, the entry for the Betting, Gaming and Lotteries Act 1963.
Betting, Gaming and Lotteries (Amendment) Act 1985 (c 18)	The whole Act.
Gaming (Bingo) Act 1985 (c 35)	The whole Act.
Local Government Act 1985 (c 51)	In Schedule 8, paragraph 6.
Social Security Act 1985 (c 53)	Section 25.
Gaming (Amendment) Act 1986 (c 11)	The whole Act.
Gaming (Amendment) Act 1987 (c 11)	The whole Act.
Companies Act 1989 (c 40)	In Schedule 10, paragraph 25.
Gaming (Amendment) Act 1990 (c 26)	The whole Act.
Bingo Act 1992 (c 10)	The whole Act.
National Lottery etc Act 1993 (c 39)	Section 2. Section 18(1) to (4). Section 45. Section 46(3). Sections 47 to 59. In Schedule 1, paragraphs 1 and 2. Schedules 7 to 9.
Local Government (Wales) Act 1994 (c 19)	In Schedule 16, paragraph 50.
Coal Industry Act 1994 (c 21)	Section 68(2)(*d*)(iv). In Schedule 9, paragraph 12.
Deregulation and Contracting Out Act 1994 (c 40)	Section 20.
Civil Evidence Act 1995 (c 38)	In Schedule 1, paragraph 4.
Employment Rights Act 1996 (c 18)	In Schedule 1, paragraph 9.
Access to Justice Act 1999 (c 22)	In Schedule 13, paragraphs 32 to 35.
Financial Services and Markets Act 2000 (c 8)	In section 412(1) (*a*) in paragraph (*a*), the words "section 18 of the Gaming Act 1845, section 1 of the Gaming Act 1892 or", and (*b*) paragraph (*b*).
Criminal Justice and Police Act 2001 (c 16)	Section 63(2)(*d*). In Schedule 1, paragraphs 6, 11, 20, 89, 93 and 97.
Licensing Act 2003 (c 17)	In Schedule 6, paragraphs 29 to 31, 48 to 52 and 62 to 66.
Courts Act 2003 (c 39)	In Schedule 8, paragraphs 113 to 115 and 132.
Criminal Justice Act 2003 (c 44)	In Schedule 25, paragraph 54.

The repeal of section 2 of the National Lottery etc Act 1993 shall not extend to Northern Ireland.

8–13942

Section 358   SCHEDULE 18
TRANSITIONAL

PART 1
TRANSITIONAL CONTINUATION OF OLD LICENCES, &c

Introduction

1. (1) In this Part a reference to a commencement order is a reference to an order under section 358(1).

(2) This Part is without prejudice to the generality of section 355(1)(*c*).

Transitional continuation of licences, &c

2. A commencement order may—

(*a*) provide for a licence or other document issued under an enactment repealed by this Act to have such effect as the order may specify after the commencement of the repeal until a time specified by or determined in accordance with the order;

(*b*) provide for the application of this Act, with any specified modifications, in relation to a licence or document to which paragraph (*a*) applies;

(*c*) disapply, or modify the application of, a provision of this Act in relation to specified things done in reliance on a licence or document to which paragraph (*a*) applies.

Transitional protection for casinos below minimum licensable size

3. A commencement order may—

(*a*) disapply section 174(1) in respect of premises that are in use, or could lawfully be used, for the operation of a casino (within the meaning of section 7(1) to (3)) when Part 8 of this Act comes into force;

(*b*) provide for the application of this Act, with any specified modifications, in relation to premises of that kind;

(*c*) disapply, or modify the application of, a provision of this Act in relation to specified things done on or in relation to premises of that kind.

References to procedures under this Act

4. A commencement order may include provision for a reference in this Act or in another enactment to anything done under or by virtue of this Act to be taken, for such transitional purposes as may be specified, as including a reference to a thing done under or by virtue of an enactment repealed by this Act.

PART 2
ADVANCE AND INTERIM APPLICATIONS, AND CONVERSION

Advance applications

5. In this Schedule a reference to an advance application for a licence or permit is a reference to an application made in advance of the commencement of the offence or other provision of this Act in connection with which the licence or permit is required.

6. The Secretary of State may by order—

(*a*) make provision about the making, consideration or determination of an advance application for a licence or permit;

(*b*) make provision about the effect of a licence or permit issued in response to an advance application;

(*c*) require the person to whom an advance application for a licence or permit under this Act is made to determine the application within a specified period;

(*d*) make provision for an advance application for a licence or permit under this Act to be treated as granted (for such purposes, with such effect and for such period as the order may specify) if not determined in accordance with a requirement imposed under paragraph (*c*).

7. An order under paragraph 6—

(*a*) may make provision about advance applications generally or only if made before a specified date or during a specified period, and

(*b*) may make different provision in relation to different classes of advance application or different classes of activity.

Interim applications

8. The Secretary of State may by order make provision for or about the grant or renewal of a licence or other document, or a registration, under an enactment to be repealed by this Act during a specified period between the passing of this Act and the commencement of the repeal.

Conversion of existing licences, &c

9. The Secretary of State may by order—

(*a*) make provision for the conversion of a licence or other document under an enactment to be repealed by this Act into a licence or permit under this Act (which may, in particular, include provision requiring a person to whom an advance application is made to grant it in specified circumstances or to a specified extent);

(b) make provision for the conversion of registration under an enactment to be repealed by this Act into registration under this Act or into possession of a licence or permit under this Act (which may, in particular, include provision requiring a person to whom an advance application is made to grant it in specified circumstances or to a specified extent).

10. An order under paragraph 9 may provide for conversion of licences, other documents or registrations generally or by reference to—

(a) the use made of a licence, document or registration,

(b) the age or duration of a licence, document or registration, or

(c) any other matter.

Orders: general

11. An order under this Part—

(a) may include provision modifying the effect of a provision of this Act or the effect of a provision to be repealed by this Act, and

(b) may apply or replicate a provision of this Act with or without modification (including a provision conferring a discretion or providing for the payment of a fee).

Betting (Licensing) Regulations 1960[1]
(SI 1960/1701)

PART I
BETTING LICENSING COMMITTEE

Annual appointments

8–13971 **1.** (1) The justices for each petty sessions area, at their annual meeting held in accordance with Rules made under section thirteen of the Justices of the Peace Act, 1949[2], for the purpose of electing a chairman of the justices, shall appoint a Betting Licensing Committee consisting of not less than five nor more than fifteen of their number, as they think fit, responsible under the First Schedule to the Act for the grant or renewal of bookmaker's permits, betting agency permits and betting office licences[3] in that area.

(2) A member of a Betting Licensing Committee appointed under this Regulation shall serve thereon from the first day of January next following his appointment for a period of one year.

---

1. Made in pursuance of the Betting and Gaming Act, 1960, and continued in force by virtue of the Betting, Gaming and Lotteries Act, 1963, s 57(3).

2. Now s 24 of the Justices of the Peace Act 1997. See also the Justices of the Peace (Size and Chairmanship of Bench) Rules 1995, in PART I: MAGISTRATES' COURTS, PROCEDURE, *ante*.

3. Granted in pursuance of the Betting, Gaming and Lotteries Act 1963, Pt I, this PART, *ante*.

Casual appointments

8–13971A **2.** (1) If a vacancy occurs in the membership of a Betting Licensing Committee for a petty sessions area, whether through death, resignation or otherwise, the justices for that area shall, as soon as practicable, unless they consider that it is not necessary, appoint one of their number to fill the vacancy.

(2) A member of a Betting Licensing Committee appointed under this Regulation shall serve thereon for the period for which the member he replaces would have served had the vacancy not occurred.

Re-appointments

8–13971B **3.** Nothing in this Part of these Regulations shall prevent a justice who is or has been a member of a Betting Licensing Committee from being re-appointed to that Committee.

PART II
PERMITS AND LICENCES

Application for grant of permits and licences

8–13971C **4.** An application made in accordance with paragraph 5 of the First Schedule to the Act for the grant of a bookmaker's permit, a betting agency permit or betting office licence, shall be made in writing in the form numbered 1, 2 or 3, as the case may be, in the Schedule to these Regulations and shall contain such particulars and, if the application is for a permit, give such references as are required thereby.

Application for renewal of permits and licences

8–13971D **5.** An application made in accordance with paragraph [9] of the First Schedule to the Act for the renewal of a bookmaker's permit, betting agency permit or betting office licence, shall be made in writing in the form numbered 4[1], 5 or 6, as the case may be, in the Schedule to these Regulations, and shall contain such particulars as are required thereby.

1. A new form is published by the Betting (Licensing) Regulations 1963, SI 1963/859.

Form of permits and licences

8–13971E 6. A bookmaker's permit, a betting agency permit or a betting office licence shall be granted in the form numbered 7, and renewed in the form numbered 8 in the Schedule to these Regulations[1]:

Provided that such a permit or licence, sealed or stamped with an official seal or stamp affixed or impressed under the authority of the Betting Licensing Committee, may be signed by the clerk to that Committee instead of by a member thereof.

1. The clerk to the betting licensing committee shall send to the Horserace Betting Levy Board particulars of every bookmaker's permit granted or renewed. This may be done by sending a carbon copy of each permit granted or renewed: see Home Office Circular No 122/1963. The particulars are prescribed by the Betting Levy (Particulars of Bookmaker's Permits) Regulations 1961, post. See Home Office Circular 138/1961, 16 August 1961.

Application for cancellation of bookmaker's permit

8–13971F 7. An application made in accordance with paragraph [26] of the First Schedule to the Act for the forfeiture and cancellation of a bookmaker's permit shall be made in writing in the form numbered 9 in the Schedule to these Regulations.

Register of permits and licences

8–13971G 8. The clerk to the Betting Licensing Committee shall, in accordance with paragraph [34] of the First Schedule to the Act, keep registers of bookmaker's permits, betting agency permits and betting office licences granted or renewed by the Committee in, and containing the particulars required by, the form numbered 10, 11 and 12 respectively in the Schedule to these Regulations and there shall be included in the appropriate register—

(*a*) in the case of a bookmaker's permit or betting agency permit renewed by a committee other than the appropriate authority by which it was last either granted or renewed, a copy of the entries relating to the permit in the register kept by the clerk to that appropriate authority;

(*b*) in the case of a bookmaker's permit or betting agency permit which is cancelled under section eight of the Act, or of a bookmaker's permit which is cancelled under paragraph [27] of the First Schedule to the Act, particulars of the cancellation;

(*c*) in the case of a betting office licence which, by virtue of paragraph [32] of the First Schedule to the Act, ceases to be in force, particulars of the circumstances in which it ceases to be in force; and

(*d*) in the case of a bookmaker's permit, betting agency permit or betting office licence which, by virtue of paragraph [33] of the First Schedule to the Act, is deemed to be held by the personal representatives of the person to whom it was granted, particulars of the period for which it is deemed to be so held and any extension thereof.

Fee for inspection of registers

8–13971H 9. A register of bookmaker's permits, of betting agency permits or of betting office licences shall, in accordance with paragraph [34] of the First Schedule to the Act, be open during reasonable hours for inspection on payment by persons other than constables of a fee of [5p].

PART III
GENERAL

Interpretation and application

8–13971I 10. (1) In these Regulations any reference to the British Licensing Committee is a reference to the Committee constituted in accordance with Part I of these Regulations, and responsible for the matters referred to in Regulation 1 of these Regulations, and any reference to the "appropriate authority" is a reference to the said Committee or, in Scotland, the licensing court.

(2) In these Regulations any reference to the Act is a reference to the Betting and Gaming Act, 1960[1].

(3) In Part II of these Regulations any reference to a form in the Schedule to these Regulations shall include a reference to a form to the like effect with such variations as the circumstances may require.

(4) Without prejudice to the generality of paragraph (3) of this Regulation, in relation to—

(*a*) an application for the grant or renewal of a betting agency permit or of a betting office licence by a person accredited by the Racecourse Betting Control Board for the purpose of receiving or negotiating bets by way of business with a view to those bets being made with the said Board; or

(*b*) an application for the grant or renewal of a betting office licence by the Racecourse Betting Control Board,

the form numbered 2, 3, 5 or 6, as the case may be, in the Schedule to these Regulations shall apply subject to the necessary adaptations.

---

1. Repealed and re-enacted in the Betting, Gaming and Lotteries Act 1963, by reference to which paragraph references to the First Schedule to the Act have been re-numbered here.

8–13971J   11. *Regulations not to extend to Scotland.*

8–13971K   12. *Citation and commencement.*

(Schedule of Forms)

Betting Levy (Particulars of Bookmakers' Permits) Regulations 1961[1]
(SI 1961/1547)

8–13972   1. The particulars of a bookmaker's permit granted or renewed under the Betting, Gaming and Lotteries Act, 1963, by a Betting Licensing Committee constituted for the purposes of the First Schedule to that Act, or by a court which determined any appeal from such a committee, which the clerk to that committee is required under s 5 of the Betting Levy Act, 1961, to send to the Levy Board, shall be as follows, that is to say—

(*a*) the name of the petty sessions area for which the committee acts;
(*b*) the name and address of the holder of the bookmaker's permit;
(*c*) the date from which the bookmaker's permit is in force, or, as the case may be, is continued in force;
(*d*) the date on which, subject to paragraphs 30 to 33 of the First Schedule to the Betting, Gaming and Lotteries Act, 1963, the permit will cease to be in force;
(*e*) in the case of a permit which is cancelled under s 11 of the said Act of 1963 or under paragraph 27 of the First Schedule thereto, the date from which the cancellation takes effect; and
(*f*) in the case of a permit which, by virtue of paragraph 33 of the First Schedule to the said Act of 1963, is deemed to be held by the personal representatives of the person to whom it was granted, the period for which it is deemed to be so held and any extension thereof.

---

1. Made under s 5(1) of the Betting Levy Act 1961 and having force by virtue of s 57(3) of the Betting, Gaming and Lotteries Act 1963. In this text, the statutory references have been amended to accord with the later Act.

8–13972A   2. *Citation and operation.*

Gaming Act (Registration Under Part II) Regulations 1969[1]
(SI 1969/550 amended by SI 1973/355 and SI 1976/1902)

8–13972B   1. (1) *Citation.*
(2) The Interpretation Act [1978] applies for the interpretation of these Regulations as it applies for the interpretation of an Act of Parliament.
(3) In these Regulations, "the Act" means the Gaming Act 1968.
(4) Nothing in these Regulations shall have effect in relation to any premises, or any part of any premises, in respect of which a licence under the Act is for the time being in force.

---

1. Made under ss 13(2), 14(2) and 51 of the Gaming Act 1968.

8–13972C   2. (1) Section 13(1) of the Act (which prohibits bankers' games) shall not have effect in relation to the games of pontoon and *chemin de fer* when played on premises in respect of which a club or miners' welfare institute is for the time being registered under Part II of the Act.
(2) The reference in this Regulation to the game of pontoon does not include a reference to the game of blackjack, or to any other form of the game of pontoon whose rules do not provide for the right to hold the bank to pass amongst the players in certain events arising in the course of play.

8–13972D   3. (1) Where, on any day, gaming takes place on premises in respect of which a club or miners' welfare institute is for the time being registered under Part II of the Act, one or more charges (which, apart from this Regulation, would be prohibited by section 3 as applied by section 14(1) of the Act) may be made in respect of a person taking part in the gaming on that day, if the amount of the charge, or (in the case of more than one charge being made) of the charges in aggregate, does not exceed £2·00 (exclusive of value added tax) in respect of that person for that day.

(2) In this Regulation, the reference to a day is a reference to the period between midday on one day and midday on the next.

8–13972E 4. (1) An application for registration, renewal of registration or cancellation of registration under Part II of the Act shall be made in writing, in the appropriate form set out in Schedule 1 to these Regulations, by lodging the application with the clerk to the licensing authority for the petty sessions area in which the relevant premises are situated.

(2) A certificate of registration or renewal of registration under Part II of the Act shall be in the appropriate form set out in Schedule 2 to these Regulations.

(3) The register to be kept under paragraph 2 of Schedule 10 to the Act for the purposes of registration under Part II of the Act shall be in the form set out in Schedule 3 to these Regulations.

(4) Any reference in this Regulation to a form includes a reference to a form to the like effect with any variations which the circumstances may require.

Gaming Act (Registration Under Part III) Regulations 1969[1]
(SI 1969/1109)

8–13972F 1. (1) *Citation.*

(2) The Interpretation Act [1978] applies for the interpretation of these Regulations as it applies for the interpretation of an Act of Parliament.

(3) In these Regulations, "the Act" means the Gaming Act 1968.

---

1. Made under s 51 of the Gaming Act 1968.

8–13972G 2. (1) An application for registration, renewal of registration or cancellation of registration under Part III of the Act shall be made in writing, in the appropriate form set out in Schedule 1 to these Regulations, by lodging the application with the clerk to the licensing authority for the petty sessions area in which the relevant premises are situated.

(2) A certificate of registration or renewal of registration under Part III of the Act shall be in the appropriate form set out in Schedule 2 to these Regulations.

(3) The register to be kept under paragraph 2 of Schedule 10 to the Act for the purposes of registration under Part III of the Act shall be in the form set out in Schedule 3 to these Regulations.

(4) Any reference in this Regulation to a form includes a reference to a form to the like effect with any variations which the circumstances may require.

Gaming Clubs (Licensing) Regulations 1969[1]
(SI 1969/1110 amended by SI 1971/1538, SI 2002/1910, SI 2004/3168 and SI 2005/2929 (W))

8–13972H 1. (1) *Citation.*

(2) The Interpretation Act [1978] applies for the interpretation of these Regulations as it applies for the interpretation of an Act of Parliament.

(3) In these Regulations, "the Act" means the Gaming Act 1968.

(4) These Regulations shall not extend to Scotland.

---

1. Made under ss 22(3) and 51 of the Gaming Act 1968.

PART II

Grounds of refusal of licence additional to those in Schedule 2 to the Act

8–13972I 2. This Part of these Regulations does not apply to licences to be granted or renewed subject to restrictions imposed under paragraph 25(1) of Schedule 2 to the Act limiting gaming (to which Part II of the Act applies) to bingo, bridge or whist or to both bridge and whist but, subject to that, it applies to all licences under the Act proposed to be granted or renewed.

8–13972J 3. *Revoked.*

8–13972K 4. (1) A licensing authority may refuse to grant or renew a licence to which this Part of these Regulations applies where the licence is to be in respect of premises to which a person might, otherwise than in an emergency, gain access directly from private premises not to be included in the licence.

(2) In this Regulation, a reference to premises includes a reference to any part of any premises, and in particular to any courtyard, lobby, passage or stairway; and the reference to private premises includes a reference to any premises to which the public have access (whether on payment or otherwise) only by permission of the owner, lessee or occupier.

Restrictions to be imposed in licences

8–13972L 5. A licensing authority shall, in the case of a licence to which this Part of these Regulations applies, impose a restriction under paragraph 25(1) of Schedule 2 to the Act limiting gaming (to which Part II of the Act applies) to the playing of games other than bingo.

8–13972M 6. *Revoked.*

PART III
Forms and other administrative matters

8–13972N 7. (1) An application for the grant, renewal, transfer or cancellation of a licence under the Act shall be made in writing, in the appropriate form set out in Schedule 2 to these Regulations, by lodging the application with the clerk to the licensing authority for the petty sessions area in which the relevant premises are situated.

(2) A licence under the Act, as granted or renewed, shall be in the appropriate form set out in Schedule 3 to these Regulations.

(3) The register to be kept under paragraph 1 of Schedule 10 to the Act shall be in the form set out in Schedule 4 to these Regulations.

(4) The prescribed fee for the purposes of paragraph 3 of Schedule 10 to the Act shall be [25p].

(5) A reference in this Regulation to a form includes a reference to a form to the like effect with any variation which the circumstances may require.

8–13972O 8. The particulars to be sent to the Board by the clerk to a licensing authority under paragraph 5(1) of Schedule 10 to the Act in relation to the grant, renewal, transfer or cancellation of a licence under the Act shall be as follows—

(*a*) the name of the club;

(*b*) the address of the relevant premises;

(*c*) the name of the licensee or, in the case of a transfer, of the old and new licensees;

(*d*) a statement or indication of any restriction under paragraph 25 of Schedule 2 to the Act as to the kinds of games which may be played;

(*e*) in the case of cancellation, a brief statement of the grounds or, in the case of cancellation on relinquishment under paragraph 65 of Schedule 2 to the Act, an indication of that fact.

Gaming Clubs (Permitted Areas) Regulations 1971[1]
(SI 1971/1538 amended by SI 1974/595)

8–13972P 2. (1) This Regulation does not apply to licences to be granted or renewed subject to restrictions imposed under paragraph 25(1) of Schedule 2 to the Act limiting gaming (to which Part II of the Act applies) to bingo, bridge or whist or to both bridge and whist but, subject to that, it applies to all licences under the Act proposed to be granted or renewed.

(2) A licensing authority shall refuse to grant or renew a licence to which this Regulation applies where the licence is to be in respect of premises situated, wholly or in part, outside the areas specified in Regulation 3 of these Regulations.

---

1. Made under ss 22(3) and 51 of the Gaming Act 1968.

8–13972Q 3. The areas referred to in Regulation 2 of these Regulations are—

(*a*) the area of every county borough which is shown as having an estimated population of 125,000 or more in any of the annual estimates made by the Registrar General for England and Wales and published between 1st December 1970 and 1st October 1973; and

(*b*) every area specified in the Schedule to these Regulations (being the areas, not qualifying under paragraph (*a*) above, which qualified under provisions revoked by Regulation 4 of these Regulations).

8–13972R 4. *Revocation.*

8–13972S

Regulation 3   SCHEDULE[1]

County boroughs

Great Yarmouth
Southport
Torbay

Non-county boroughs

Hove
Lytham St Annes
Margate
Ramsgate
Ryde
Scarborough

Urban districts

Sandown
Shanklin

London boroughs

Royal Borough of Kensington and Chelsea
City of Westminster
That part of the London borough of Camden which is within the area specified in the Licensing (Metropolitan Special Hours Area) Order 1961.

---

1. The Schedule is not affected by the abolition of areas affected by s 1(10) of the Local Government Act 1972: see r 4(9)(*b*) of SI 1974/595.

Gaming Clubs (Hours and Charges) Regulations 1984[1]

(SI 1984/248 amended by SI 1995/927, SI 1996/1109, SI 1998/961 and SI 1999/1258, SI 2000/899 and 1879 and SI 2002/1902)

8–13972T   **1.** *Citation, commencement and extent.*

---

1. Made by the Secretary of State in pursuance of ss 14(2) and (3), 22(4) and 51 of the Gaming Act 1968.

Interpretation

8–13972U   **2.** (1) In these Regulations—

"the Act" means the Gaming Act 1968;

"bingo club premises" has the meaning assigned to it by section 20(1) of the Act; and

"gaming" does not include gaming by means of any machine to which Part III of the Act applies.

(2) A reference in these Regulations to a charge in respect of gaming does not include an amount paid for a chance of winning a prize in gaming to which section 21 of the Act applies.

(3) Nothing in these Regulations precludes the making of different charges thereunder in respect of different facilities (whether provided in different parts of the same premises or by way of different games or of the same game played at different tables or otherwise) or in respect of gaming facilities provided on the premises during different sessions of play.

Bingo hours

8–13972V   **3.** (1) Subject to paragraphs (2) and (3) below, no gaming shall take place on bingo club premises except—

(*a*) between the hours of ten in the morning and midnight on a Saturday;
(*b*) between the hours of two in the afternoon and eleven in the evening on a Sunday; and
(*c*) between the hours of ten in the morning and eleven in the evening on any other day.

(2) Paragraph (1) above shall not have effect in respect of New Year's Eve and on that day no gaming shall take place on bingo club premises except—

(*a*) if that day is a Sunday, between the hours of two in the afternoon and midnight; and
(*b*) if it is any other day, between the hours of ten in the morning and midnight.

(3) This Regulation is without prejudice to section 18 of the Act (which prohibits gaming between certain hours on Sunday) and any restrictions imposed in exercise of the powers in Schedule 2 to the Act (powers of licensing authority).

General gaming hours

8–13972W   **4.** (1) No gaming shall take place on any premises (not being bingo club premises) in respect of which a licence under the Act is for the time being in force on any weekday between the hours of four in the morning and two in the afternoon.

(2) This Regulation is without prejudice to any restrictions imposed in exercise of the powers in Schedule 2 to the Act (powers of licensing authority).

Bingo charges

8–13972X   **5.** (1) Any charge which, apart from this regulation, would be prohibited by section 3 of the Act, as applied by section 14(1) of the Act, may be made in respect of gaming on bingo club premises, subject to the following conditions, namely—

    (*a*)   the charge shall be in respect of an individual person and shall be for his admission to premises in respect of which gaming in the form of playing bingo takes place or otherwise in respect of his participation in a game of bingo on those premises;

    (*b*)   in the case of his admission, the charge shall not exceed £20 per day; and

    (*c*)   in the case of his participation in a game of bingo, the charge shall not exceed £10 for each chance in playing the game.

(2) In the case of a charge for admission, a notice of that charge shall be displayed on the premises at or near the principal entrance.

(3) In the case of any other charge in respect of gaming, a notice in the name of the bingo club concerned containing the particulars of the charges specified in paragraph (4) below shall be displayed at the point (or, if more than one, the main point) where payment for the charge is to be made.

(4) The particulars to be contained in the notice are:

    (*a*)   the date from which the notice applies;

    (*b*)   the name of each ticket or game (or set of tickets or games) to be played during the currency of the notice;

    (*c*)   the cost (in money) of each ticket or game (or set of tickets or games);

    (*d*)   the charge in respect of each ticket or game (or set of tickets or games); and

    (*e*)   a statement to the effect that all or part of the charge may be waived at the discretion of the person making it.

(5) The notice may be displayed in electronic form.

General gaming charges

8–13972Y   **6.** (1) Any charge which, apart from this Regulation would be prohibited by section 3 of the Act, as applied by section 14(1) of the Act, may be made in respect of gaming on any premises (not being bingo club premises) in respect of which a licence under the Act is for the time being in force, if the charge satisfies the following requirements, which are that—

    (*a*)   the charge shall be of a fixed amount of money and shall be in respect of one or more facilities accorded to one person; and

    (*b*)   subject to paragraph (2) below, where the charge is of such a nature that it can be incurred more than once by one person (otherwise than by leaving and being readmitted to the premises, or any particular part of the premises or any particular table), the charge shall not be capable of being incurred again by the same person within one hour of the time when it was last incurred by him.

(2) A charge may be made for permission to take part in a series of games of *chemin de fer* (including a series which has already begun), notwithstanding that the charge may recur within one hour, if—

    (*a*)   the games comprised in the series consist of all the games which can be played with a shoe of not fewer than six packs of playing cards of fifty-two cards each; and

    (*b*)   neither the holder of the licence nor any person acting on his behalf holds the bank, or has a share or interest in it, in any of the games in the series.

Revocations and amendment

8–13972Z   **7.** *Revocations.*

Licensed Betting Offices Regulations 1986[1]

(SI 1986/103 amended by SI 1993/51, SI 1995/578 and SI 1997/1071)

PART I
GENERAL

8–13973   **1.** (1), (2) *Citation and commencement.*

    (3) *Scotland.*

---

1. Made by the Secretary of State in pursuance of the Betting, Gaming and Lotteries Act 1963, s 10(6) and Sch 4, paras 1 and 3.

8–13973A   **2.** In these Regulations "the 1963 Act" means the Betting, Gaming and Lotteries Act 1963.

8–13973B   **3.** *Revocation.*

Part II
Restrictions on Advertisements to which Section 10(6)(*b*) of the 1963 Act Applies

8–13973C **4.** (1) Except as provided by Regulation 5 below, no advertisement—

(*a*) which includes any of the matters set out in paragraphs (*a*), (*b*) and (*c*) of section 10(5) of the 1963 Act, and

(*b*) which is published outside a licensed betting office otherwise than in a material form in any of the ways set out in sub-paragraphs (i) and (ii) of section 10(6)(*b*) of that Act, and

(*c*) which consists of, or includes, text,

is permitted.

(2) For the purposes of this Regulation and Regulation 5 below, the expression "text" includes figures without words, as well as words, and words and figures.

8–13973D **5.** (1) To the extent that any of the matters set out in paragraph (2) below would otherwise contravene the provisions of section 10(5) of the 1963 Act, text in respect of all or any of them may nevertheless be included in an advertisement to which sub-paragraphs (*a*) and (*b*) of Regulation 4(1) above apply.

(2) The matters referred to in paragraph (1) above are—

(*a*) subject to paragraph (3) below, text indicating that the premises are, or give access to, a licensed betting office whether—

  (i) the expression "licensed betting office" or some other expression such as "bookmaker" or "turf accountant" is used, and

  (ii) the expression is included in the name of the licensee or otherwise;

(*b*) in the case of premises giving access to a licensed betting office, text indicating where any such office may be found;

(*c*) text indicating the hours during which a licensed betting office is open;

(*d*) text indicating the facilities afforded to persons resorting to the licensed betting office concerned;

(*e*) text indicating the range of bets available in the licensed betting office concerned; and

(*f*) text providing information relating to any event in connection with which betting transactions may be or have been effected in the licensed betting office concerned, including information as to the odds available on any particular event.

(3) Text in respect of the matter referred to in paragraph 2(*a*) above is not permitted if it exceeds three words in length.

Part III
Opening Hours of, and Notices in, Licensed Betting Offices

8–13973E **6.** The times at which a licensed betting office shall be closed shall, in any one day, include the periods between midnight and 7 am and—

(*a*) between 10.00 pm and midnight during April, May, June, July and August; and

(*b*) between 6.30 pm and midnight at any other time of the year.

8–13973F **7.** (1) The licensee shall exhibit in a conspicuous manner and in some conspicuous place or places inside the licensed premises—

(*a*) including a place near to the entrance of those premises, and

(*b*) where practicable, in a window of those premises so that it can be read from outside those premises,

a notice or notices stating that persons under the age of 18 years are not admitted thereto.

(2) The licensee shall exhibit in some conspicuous place or places inside the licensed premises, but not in such a place that the notice exhibited can be read from outside those premises, a notice or notices setting out the terms on which he invites persons to bet on those premises including—

(*a*) the amount of the various deductions that may be, or will be, made from winning bets,

(*b*) any maximum limit on the amount of winnings, and

(*c*) the procedure for the resolution of disputed bets.

Gaming Clubs (Multiple Bingo) Regulations 1986[1]
(SI 1986/834 amended by SI 1998/2151 and SI 2002/1901)

8–13974 **1.** *Citation and commencement.*

---

1. Made under s 3(1) of the Gaming (Bingo) Act 1985.

8–13974A **2.** The number of games of multiple bingo that may be played on any bingo club premises in any period of twenty fours hours beginning at midnight shall be five.

8–13974B 3. The period allowed for the playing of any game of multiple bingo shall be thirty minutes.

Lotteries Regulations 1993[1]

(SI 1993/3223 amended by SI 1996/1306)

8–13974C 1. *Citation commencement and revocation.*

---

1. Made under s 12 of the Lotteries and Amusements Act 1976. Contravention of these regulations is an offence (see s 13 of the Lotteries and Amusements Act 1976, in this Part ante. Offences are all triable either way, see s 20, ibid).

8–13974D 2. (1) A scheme approved by a society or local authority for the promotion of a lottery or any modification of such a scheme shall comply with the provisions of Schedule 2 to these Regulations.

(2) This regulation does not prevent the inclusion in a scheme of provisions not required by that Schedule.

8–13974E 3. No ticket or chance in a society's lottery or local lottery shall be sold by or to a person who has not attained the age of sixteen years.

8–13974F 4. (1) Subject to paragraph (2) below, no ticket or chance in a society's lottery or local lottery shall be sold to a person in any street.

(2) Paragraph (1) above shall not have effect in relation to the sale of a ticket or chance by a person present in a kiosk or shop premises having no space for the accommodation of customers.

(3) In this regulation, "street" includes any bridge, road, lane, footway, subway, court, alley or passage, whether a thoroughfare or not, which is for the time being open to the public without payment.

8–13974G 5. No ticket or chance in a society's lottery or local lottery shall be sold by means of a machine.

8–13974H 6. *Revoked.*

8–13974I 7. Every ticket distributed or sold in a society's lottery shall either specify the name of the registration authority with which the society is registered under Schedule 1 to the Lotteries and Amusements Act 1976 or, as the case may be, specify that the society is registered under Schedule 1A to that Act with the Gaming Board for Great Britain.

8–13974J 8. Every ticket distributed or sold in a local lottery shall specify the name of the local authority promoting the lottery, the date of the lottery and that the authority have registered a scheme with the Gaming Board for Great Britain under Schedule 2 to the Lotteries and Amusements Act 1976.

8–13974K 9. Where two or more lotteries are promoted by a society or local authority on the same date, the tickets to be sold in each such lottery shall indicate in which lottery they are sold by means of a serial number.

8–13974L 10. Where the information appearing on a ticket in a society's lottery or local lottery includes any reference in writing to a person who, for reward, is acting or assisting, or has acted or assisted, in the promotion of the lottery—

(a) the size of the lettering used in such reference shall not exceed the size of the smallest lettering used in the same ticket to specify the name of the society on whose behalf the lottery is promoted or, as the case may be, the name of the local authority promoting the lottery, and

(b) that reference shall be afforded no greater prominence than is afforded to that name in the same ticket.

8–13974M 11. (1) No request or requirement shall be made to any person supplying lottery tickets to which this regulation applies for use in a society's lottery or local lottery to the effect that those tickets shall be supplied in such a manner, or so marked, as to enable a ticket to be identified, before it is sold in the lottery, as a winning ticket.

(2) This regulation applies to lottery tickets manufactured or designed so as to conceal such information appearing in or on each ticket by way of words, figures, signs, symbols or other features as would, if revealed, indicate that the ticket is a winning ticket or is not.

(3) In this regulation, "winning ticket" means a ticket which, when sold in a lottery, entitles the holder of the ticket to claim a prize in the lottery.

8–13974N   **12.** (1) Subject to paragraph (2) below, no prize in a society's lottery or local lottery shall be offered on such terms that the winning of the prize depends upon the purchase of more than one ticket or chance in the lottery.

(2) The winning of a prize in a society's lottery or local lottery may depend upon the purchase of more than one chance provided that the price of the number of chances required to win a prize does not exceed the amount for the time being specified for the purposes of section 11(2) of the Lotteries and Amusements Act 1976.

8–13974O   **13.** (1) No person shall be invited to purchase any group of tickets or chances in a set of lotteries in which the determination of the winners in the lotteries is designed to secure that a person holding a group of winning tickets or chances is a winner of a prize in each lottery in the set of lotteries to which that group of tickets or chances relates.

(2) in paragraph (1) above, a reference to a set of lotteries is a reference to two or more lotteries in a set consisting of society's lotteries or local lotteries or both.

Regulation 2

SCHEDULE 2
LOTTERY SCHEMES

8–13974P   **1.** The scheme shall specify the name and address of the society or local authority by which the scheme was approved.

2. (1) Sub-paragraph (2) below applies where—

(a) a scheme is approved by a society; and
(b) the society is registered under Schedule 1 to the Lotteries and Amusements Act 1976.

(2) The scheme shall specify the following matters relating to the registration of the society for the purposes of section 5(3) of that Act (power of certain societies to promote lotteries), that is to say:—

(a) the name and address of the registration authority:
(b) the date of registration; and
(c) the reference number (if any) of the registration.

3. Where a scheme is modified by a society or local authority, the scheme shall specify the date on which the modifications shall come into effect.

4. A scheme approved by a society or local authority shall specify the maximum number of lotteries which are intended to be promoted under it in any period of 12 months and the scheme shall require that the number so specified shall not be exceeded.

5. (1) The scheme shall specify a proportion (not exceeding one half) as being the proportion of the whole proceeds of any lottery under the scheme which may be appropriated for the provision of prizes in that lottery; and shall require that the proportion so specified shall not be exceeded except in the special circumstances mentioned in sub-paragraph (2) below.

(2) The special circumstances referred to above are that—

(a) the proceeds of the lottery fall short of the sum reasonably estimated; and
(b) the appropriation is made in order to fulfil an unconditional undertaking as to prizes given in connection with the sale of the relevant tickets or chances; and
(c) the total amount appropriated in respect of prizes does not exceed the amount which could have been appropriated out of the proceeds of the lottery if the proceeds had amounted to the sum reasonably estimated.

6. In the case of a scheme approved by a local authority, the scheme shall make provision as to whether all or any class of—

(a) members of the authority; and
(b) officers of the authority,

are to be precluded from buying tickets or chances in any lottery under the scheme, or not.

National Lottery Regulations 1994[1]
(SI 1994/189)

8–13974Q   **1.** *Citation, commencement and extent.*

---

1. Made by the Secretary of State for National Heritage under s 12 of the National Lottery etc Act 1993.

Interpretation

8–13974R   **2.** In these Regulations—

"the Act" means the National Lottery etc. Act 1993; and
"National Lottery ticket" means a ticket or chance in a lottery that forms part of the National Lottery.

Age restriction on sales of National Lottery tickets

8–13974S   **3.** No National Lottery ticket shall be sold by or to a person who has not attained the age of 16 years[1].

---

1. This is an offence of strict liability. The prosecution is only required to prove the sale of a National Lottery ticket to a particular person and that, at the time of sale, he was under 16; the prosecution does not have to

prove that the defendant or his agent was aware of the buyer's age or was reckless as to his age, *Harrow London Borough Council v Shah* [1999] 3 All ER 302, 163 JP 525, DC.

Prohibition on sales of or invitations to purchase National Lottery tickets in a street

8–13974T **4.** (1) Subject to paragraph (2) below, no National Lottery ticket shall be sold to a person, nor shall a person be invited to purchase a National Lottery ticket, in any street.

(2) Paragraph (1) above shall not have effect in relation to the sale of or invitation to purchase a National Lottery ticket by a person present in a kiosk or shop premises having no space for the accommodation of customers.

(3) In this regulation, "street" includes any bridge, road, lane, footway, subway, court, alley or passage, whether a thoroughfare or not, which is for the time being open to the public without payment.

Prohibition of sales of or invitations to purchase National Lottery tickets on certain premises

8–13974U **5.** (1) No National Lottery ticket shall be sold to a person, nor shall a person be invited to purchase a National Lottery ticket—

(a) in any licensed betting office within the meaning of the 1963 Act or licensed office within the meaning of the 1985 Order;

(b) on any approved racecourse within the meaning of the 1963 Act on a day on which horse races take place thereon;

(c) on any licensed track within the meaning of the 1963 Act on any day on which under sections 5, 6 and 20 of that Act bookmaking may lawfully be carried out on the track or on any licensed track within the meaning of the 1985 Order on any day on which under articles 36, 47 and 48 of that Order betting may lawfully be carried out on the track;

(d) in any premises used wholly or mainly for providing amusements in the form of amusements with prizes or of amusements by means of slot machines or both; or

(e) in any bingo or other gaming club, that is to say, in any premises in respect of which a licence under the Gaming Act 1968 is for the time being in force or in any bingo club premises within the meaning of the 1985 Order.

(2) In paragraph (1) above—

(a) "the 1963 Act" means the Betting, Gaming and Lotteries Act 1963; and

(b) "the 1985 Order" means the Betting, Gaming, Lotteries and Amusements (Northern Ireland) Order 1985.

Restriction on sales of National Lottery tickets by vending machines

8–13974V **6.** (1) No National Lottery ticket shall be sold by means of a vending machine unless such machine is, at all times when tickets can be sold by means of it, attended by a person authorised by either—

(a) the holder of the licence under section 5 of the Act; or

(b) the holder of a licence under section 6 of the Act which authorises the promotion of the lottery, the tickets or chances of which are being sold by means of the vending machine.

(2) A vending machine shall not be treated as attended for the purposes of this regulation unless the person attending the vending machine is in a position where he can control the operation of the machine and in particular take action to prevent the purchase of tickets by any person whom he believes has not attained the age of 16 years.

Restriction on sales of or invitations to purchase National Lottery tickets at a person's home

8–13974W **7.** No National Lottery ticket shall be sold, nor shall a person be invited to purchase a National Lottery ticket, by a person when visiting any other person at his home in the discharge of any official, professional or commercial function (including the function of selling National Lottery tickets).

GAME

8–13604 This title contains the following statutes—

8–13910   Ground Game (Amendment) Act 1906
8–13930   Game Laws (Amendment) Act 1960
8–13950   Deer Act 1991

General Observations

8–13605 Owners and occupiers. The tenant has a right of sporting if this is not expressly reserved to the landlord. The right of killing game is *prima facie* in him unless there is something to take it away from him[1]. Where the landlord or any person other than the occupier is entitled to the exclusion of the occupier, the occupier is liable to a penalty for killing game or permitting any other person to do so[2]; except hares and rabbits as limited by the Ground Game Act 1880. A *bona fide* claim of right will oust the jurisdiction of the justices[3]; see "Claim of Right", infra. The exclusive right cannot be conveyed to a third party except by deed[4]. An agreement not under seal does not convey the right and must be revoked[5]. But if the tenancy is parol the reservation of game may be parol also[6]. An agreement which entitles one party to it to shoot over land and to take away a share of the game is more than a mere revocable licence to use the land, as it conveys an interest in the land coupled with a participation in the profits, and so is within s 3 of the Statute of Frauds (now the Law of Property Act 1925, s 53), and must be in writing[7].

The actual occupier or the owner of enclosed lands having a right to kill game thereon may kill hares without a game certificate, or authorise any one person to do so in manner prescribed by this Act (Hares Act 1848, 11 & 12 Vict c 29). Each occupier may, it would seem, authorise a separate person. See also the exemption of occupiers in the Ground Game Act 1880, post. Game started and killed wrongfully by one person on the land of another becomes the absolute property of the owner of the land when the game is reserved to him, and not of the captor, though it be killed and carried away in one continuous act[8]. Taking a wild creature will not amount to theft provided that it is not tamed nor ordinarily kept in captivity and has not been reduced into possession by or on behalf of another person. See s 4(4) of the Theft Act 1968, post. When a trespasser starts and kills game on the soil of another, the game becomes the absolute property of that other; but if the trespasser starts the game on the soil of another, and chases it into the soil of a third party, and there kills it, then it seems that it is the property of the trespasser[9]. As to the right of an owner or occupier of adjoining land to allure or frighten game, see *Ibottson v Peat* (1865) 3 H & C 644, 29 JP 344. Lords of manor have only right of free warren over wastes as incident to the ownership of the soil[10]. For provisions relating to a tenant's right to, and measure of compensation for damage done by game, and indemnity to landlord, see Agricultural Holdings Act 1986, s 20.

A gamekeeper may be appointed by writing under hand and seal to preserve or kill game for the use of the lord or steward of the manor, with authority to seize and take, for the use of the lord or steward, all such dogs, nets, and other engines or[11] instruments for the killing or taking of game, as shall be used within such manor by any person not authorised to kill game for want of a game certificate (Game Act 1831, s 13). The lord may also grant a deputation to any person to kill game for his own use, or for the use of any other person or persons specified in the appointment (Game Act 1831, s 14). A gamekeeper's licence to kill game can be taken out. (Game Licences Act 1860, s 7).

1. *Coleman v Bathurst* (1871) LR 6 QB 366, 35 JP 630.
2. *Barker v Davis* (1865) 29 JP 501, Game Act 1831, s 12.
3. *Adams v Masters* (1871) 35 JP 644.
4. *Barker v Davis* (1865) 29 JP 501.
5. *Brigstocke v Raynor* (1875) 40 JP 245.
6. *Jones v Williams and Roberts* (1877) 41 JP 614.
7. *Webber v Lee* (1882) 9 QBD 315, 47 JP 4.
8. See *Blades v Higgs* (1865) 11 HL Cas 621, 29 JP 390, as to rabbits, and *Rigg v Earl Lonsdale* (1857) 1 H & N 923, 21 JP 228, as to grouse.
9. *Blades v Higgs* (1865) 11 HL Cas 621, 29 JP 390.
10. *Sowerby v Smith* (1874) LR 9 CP 524; affg (1873) LR 8 CP 514.
11. This section does not authorise a gamekeeper to seize a gun (*Daddle v Hickton* (1868) 32 JP 119).

8–13606 Claim of right. The jurisdiction of the justices is ousted when a question of right is *bona fide* raised between the complainant and defendant, and on this justices must decide[1]. The claim must be made upon reasonable ground[2]; and justices have jurisdiction to decide upon the reasonableness and the sufficiency of the evidence to support it; a *bona fide* claim under a lease to land which, after several years' user, was found not to be included in the land demised, through an alleged mistake in a plan, was not sufficient to oust jurisdiction[3].

Production of a draft lease from a lord of the manor of the shooting over glebe land, without evidence of the right to include the glebe in the lease, was also held not to be sufficient[4]; and a mere *bona fide* belief in a right founded on payment for the game, upon an invalid agreement, is not enough to stop conviction[5]; but when doubtful questions are *bona fide* raised, such as a right to take rabbits from a common adjoining a forest, and the right might legally exist, the jurisdiction must be declined, and the parties left to their remedy at common law[6]. A tenant farmer, who had occupied a farm about twenty years and always shot rabbits on it without leave from any one, authorised his son to shoot rabbits on a day when he was challenged by the gamekeeper of a person to whom the right of taking game over the manor had been granted. The son set up his father's authority, and there was no evidence that the right to shoot rabbits was a manorial right. The Queen's Bench Division held a *bona fide* question of title was raised and quashed the conviction[7].

Whether or not the game is preserved is a question of fact for the justices, and their jurisdiction is not ousted when there is evidence *pro* and *con*, and they consider the defence is not *bona fide*. A trespasser in search of game set up as a defence the leave and licence of the occupier under a parol lease. The occupier denied that the game was reserved to the landlord, but evidence was given to show that it was; and it was held upon the evidence that the defence was not *bona fide*, and therefore the jurisdiction was not ousted[8]. But (*per* LUSH J) if there is any evidence of a legal right which a judge might leave to a jury, the justices should hold their hands[9]. A man, with a dog and gun, went along a public footpath in a field adjoining his own coverts and parallel with his own hedge, and sent his servant into his own field to drive the game out across the hedge. He set up a claim of right, and said he was only intending to shoot his own game; it was held that there was no merit in this defence, as no title to property was involved. GRANTHAM J, said that the defendant had a right of way over the footpath, but he was not there for the purpose of walking over it, he was there for the purpose of sporting. Costs were given against the defendant[10].

The defendant must make a *bona fide* claim of title in himself or in those under whom he claims. It is not necessary to support a conviction that the defendant should have intended to commit, or have been conscious that he was committing, a trespass. So trespassing by the permission of a person who held no right to give such licence, but who assumed to have such right, was no defence (KEATING J, *dub*)[11]. But on an information, under section 2 of the Poaching Prevention Act 1862, for obtaining game by unlawfully going on land in search or pursuit of game it is a good defence to prove that the defendant had a *bona fide* belief that he had permission to go on the land together with reasonable ground for that belief[12].

---

1. *Legg v Pardoe* (1860) 9 CBNS 289, 25 JP 39; *Adams v Masters* (1871) 35 JP 644; *Lovesy v Stallard* (1874) 38 JP 391.
2. *Watkins v Major* (1875) LR 10 CP 662, 39 JP 808; *Mann v Nurse* (1901) 17 TLR 569.
3. *Watkins v Smith* (1878) 42 JP 468.
4. *Birnie v Marshall* (1876) 41 JP 22.
5. *Brigstocke v Rayner* (1875) 40 JP 245.
6. *Newcombe v Fewins* (1876) 41 JP 581.
7. *Penwarden v Palmer* (1894) 10 TLR 362.
8. *R v Critchlow* (1878) 26 WR 681.
9. *Watkins v Smith* (1878) 42 JP 468.
   See also *Leatt v Vine* (1861) 25 JP 791; *Kiddle v Kayley* (1864) 28 JP 805, and *Birnie v Marshall* (1876) 41 JP 22 (sufficiency of assertion of right to oust jurisdiction). See also *Cornwell v Sanders* (1862) 3 B & S 206, 27 JP 148 (disputing the title of the person alleged in the information to be in the occupation of the land not sufficient).
10. *Philpot v Bugler* (1890) 54 JP 646.
11. *Morden v Porter* (1860) 7 CBNS 641, 25 JP 263, Treat 306.
12. *Dickinson v Ead* (1914) 78 JP 326.

8–13607   What is a trespass?.   It was held by Lord ELLENBOROUGH that a man who, from the outside of a close, discharged a gun into it, so that the shot must have struck the soil, was guilty of entering[1]; and a dog jumping into a close with the consent or by the incitement of the master was held to be a trespass on the part of the master for which an action would lie[2]. It has, however, been decided, that the words "entering or being" in the Game Act 1831, s 30, mean a personal and not constructive entry, but that a defendant was liable to conviction although he merely fired from the highway into the field, the highway being treated for the purpose of this Act as land in the occupation of the adjoining owner[3]. In *Pratt's Case* the defendant, by raising his hand to a dog, sent the dog into a cover on one side of the highway, and immediately afterwards a pheasant flew across the highway, at which Pratt fired. In *Wardley's Case* there was the firing of a gun, and the finding of a partridge recently killed. Lord CAMPBELL said, in *Pratt's Case*: "I think the mere sending a dog into the cover would not be sufficient to support the conviction, for the offence contemplated by the legislature was that the offender should be personally on the land on which the trespass is alleged to have been committed. The words are 'by entering or being', and by that must be meant a personal entering or being upon the land.[4]. Upon this construction there was evidence upon which the justices were warranted in finding the defendant did commit the trespass. The public have a right to use a highway for all purposes of a highway, but subject to the public easement, the land must be considered in the possession and occupation of the adjoining owner and occupier. No doubt the appellant was a trespasser when he went upon the highway, as he did, for the purpose of searching for game, and for that purpose only, and I think he must be considered as being in search of game *there*."

Land on both sides of a highway belonged to the Duke of Rutland. One day when the Duke and his friends were shooting over the moors, a man went on to the highway for the express purpose of preventing birds that were being driven towards the butts from crossing the highway. The Duke's keepers asked him to desist, and upon his refusal held him on the ground until the drive was over. The Court of Appeal (following *R v Pratt*) held, in an action against the Duke and his keepers, that as the soil of the road was vested in the Duke as owner of the adjoining land, and that the man was using the highway for a purpose other than that of passing and repassing, he was a trespasser, and the assault was justified. Judgment was given for defendants on a counter-claim for nominal damages, and an injunction would have been granted if it had been applied for[5]. The Queen's Bench would not interfere where defendant's intention of going upon a marsh with dogs was doubtful[6]. The remedy is by civil action.

A person who on his own land shoots a pheasant which was from the first on the land of another, and goes on such land to pick up the game, commits a trespass *in pursuit* under this clause, the pursuit commencing with the shot, and terminating with the picking up, and thus forming one transaction[7]. But when a man was shooting on his own land, and a pheasant rose and flew across the fence which divided his land from that of his neighbour, and after it had crossed the boundary the man fired at and killed the bird, which fell on the adjoining land, the fact that the man went over the fence whilst the pheasant lay dead and brought it away was held to be a mere act of entering the land for the purpose of picking up the game, which was then dead, and was not a trespass *in search* of game within the statute, distinguishing this case from *Osbond v Meadows*[8]. A gamekeeper who, two days after a shooting party had been over his master's land, went into an adjoining wood with dog and gun on full cock to pick up pheasants that had been seen to drop dead or wounded, and which he believed to be then dead, was not a trespasser within this section, there being no evidence that he was in pursuit of game, ie live game[9]. A man, standing on his own land, fired a shot over a wall into the land of another person, and killed a grouse there. He did not then enter upon the land to pick up the bird, but some hours afterwards he went upon the land in search of what he had killed, which had then been removed by a gamekeeper. The QB Division held that the two acts were sufficiently connected to form one transaction, and that the man had committed the offence of trespassing in search or pursuit of game[10]. In these cases it is necessary to distinguish between criminal and civil liability. To go upon the land of another, without permission, to pick up dead game (though legitimately shot), is a trespass for which a civil remedy lies. Such game, however, is not the property of the person on whose land it is found, and an action for conversion would be maintainable against him if he refused to give it up. When three persons were in a field, and another stood on the outside, and gave the alarm, it was held that all were equally guilty of the offence[11].

1. *Pickering v Rudd* (1815) 4 Camp 219.
2. *Brown v Giles* (1823) 1 C & P 118.
3. *R v Pratt* (1855) 4 E & B 860, 19 JP 578; *Mayhew v Wardley* (1863) 14 CBNS 550.
4. Followed in *Pratt v Martin* [1911] 2 KB 90, 75 JP 328.
5. *Harrison v Duke of Rutland* [1893] 1 QB 142, 57 JP 278. See also *Hickman v Maisey* [1900] 1 QB 752; cf *Hadwell v Righton* [1907] 2 KB 345, 71 JP 499.
6. *Dyer v Park* (1874) 38 JP 294.
7. *Osbond v Meadows* (1862) 12 CBNS 10, 26 JP 439.
8. *Kenyon v Hart* (1865) 6 B & S 249, 29 JP 260.
9. *Tanton v Jervis* (1879) 43 JP 784. See also *Nicholl v Strachan* 1913 SC(J) 18.
10. *Horn v Raine* (1898) 67 LJQB 533, 62 JP 420.
11. *R v Passey* (1836) 7 C & P 282. See also the Magistrates' Courts Act 1980, s 44, in PART I: MAGISTRATES' COURTS, PROCEDURE, ante, and *R v Littlechild* (1871) LR 6 QB 293, 35 JP 661.

Night Poaching Act 1828
(9 Geo 4 c 69)

8–13620   1. Persons taking or destroying game or rabbits by night, or entering any land for that purpose. If any person shall by night[1], unlawfully take or destroy any game[2] or rabbits in any land, whether open or[3] enclosed[4], or shall by night unlawfully enter[5] or be in any land, whether open or enclosed, with any[6] gun, net, engine, or other instrument, for the purpose of taking or destroying[7] game, he shall be liable on summary conviction to a fine not exceeding **level 3** on the standard scale[8]. [Night Poaching Act 1828, s 1, as amended by the Statute Law Revision (No 2) Act 1888, the Criminal Law Act 1977, Sch 1 and the Criminal Justice Act 1982, s 46.]

1. See the Ground Game Act 1880, s 6, post, as to penalty on persons having the right of killing ground game using firearms for the purpose at night.
2. "Game" is defined for the purposes of this Act in s 13, post.
3. On either side of land was a hedge, and a metalled road ran through the land between the hedges: the land was waste, varying in extent: this was not either open or enclosed within the meaning of this section (*Veysey v Hoskins* (1865) 34 LJMC 145).
4. Extended by the Night Poaching Act 1844, post, to apply to persons by night destroying game or rabbits on any public road, path, etc.
5. This is not the same offence as unlawfully taking or destroying game (*R v Disney* [1933] 2 KB 138, 97 JP 103; *Jones v Evans* [1978] Crim LR 230). The words "entering or being" mean a personal entry in Game Act 1831, s 30, and not a constructive entry (*R v Pratt* (1855) 4 E & B 860, 19 JP 578, and *Pratt v Martin* [1911] 2 KB 90, 75 JP 328). The same construction must be put on this statute. As to the right to convict a tenant, or person acting under his permission, where the game is reserved to the landlord, see *Pryce v Davies* (1872) 36 JP 214.
6. There is no mention of a dog, therefore a person unlawfully being by night on land in pursuit of game does not commit the offence unless he has a gun, net, engine, or other instrument of the same description in his possession. See Game Act 1831, s 30, post. Trespassing by *day* is not so limited.

7. The second part of this section does not extend to rabbits. The conviction must show that the party entered the land by night for the purpose of destroying game "there" or "therein" and for the purpose of taking game "by night" (*Fletcher v Calthrop* (1845) 6 QB 880, 9 JP 230; but see *R v Western* (1868) LR 1 CCR 122, 22 JP 390).

8. A police constable who has reasonable grounds for suspecting that an offence under this section is being committed may enter on the land for the purposes of arresting him in accordance with s 25 of the Police and Criminal Evidence Act 1984 (Game Laws (Amendment) Act 1960, s 2(1) post). For powers of search and seizure of game etc, and for powers of forfeiture on conviction, see the Game Laws (Amendment) Act 1960, s 4, post.

8–13621   2. Owners or occupiers of land, lords of manors, or their servants, may apprehend offenders[1]. Where any person shall be found upon any land committing any such offence as is herein-before mentioned it shall be lawful for the owner or occupier of such land, or for the lord of the manor or reputed manor wherein such land may be situate, and also for any gamekeeper[2] or servant of any of the persons herein mentioned, or any person assisting such gamekeeper or servant, to seize and apprehend such offender upon such land, or, in case of pursuit being made, in any other place to which he may have escaped therefrom, and to deliver him as soon as may be into the custody of a peace officer, in order to his being conveyed before two justices of the peace; and in case such offender shall assault[3] or offer any violence with any gun, crossbow, fire arms, bludgeon, stick, club, or any other offensive weapon whatsoever towards any person hereby authorised to seize and apprehend him, he shall be liable on summary conviction to imprisonment for a term not exceeding **six months** or to a fine not exceeding **level 4** on the standard scale, or to both.
[Night Poaching Act 1828, s 2, as amended by the Statute Law Revision (No 2) Act 1888, the Wild Creatures and Forest Laws Act 1971, Sch, the Criminal Law Act 1977, ss 15(4) and 30(3) and the Criminal Justice Act 1982, s 46.]

1. For powers of search and seizure of game, etc and for powers of forfeiture on conviction, see Game Laws (Amendment) Act 1960, s 4, post.
2. A gamekeeper appointed by the owner's agent, and having acted as such for a period, is within the statute (*R v King* (1884) 48 JP 149).
3. To convict a co-defendant who did not take any part in the assault, the evidence must show that the defendants went with a common purpose not merely to poach, but to resist apprehension at all costs, even by violence, if necessary (*R v Pearce* (1929) 21 Cr App Rep 79).

8–13622   9. If persons to the number of three, being armed, enter any land for the purpose of taking or destroying game or rabbits, they shall be deemed guilty of a misdemeanour. If any persons, to the number of three or more together, shall by night unlawfully enter[1] or be in any land whether open or enclosed, for the purpose of taking or destroying game or rabbits, any of such persons being armed with any gun, crossbow, fire arms, bludgeon, or any other offensive weapon, each and every of such persons shall be shall be liable on summary conviction to imprisonment for a term not exceeding **six months** or to a fine not exceeding **level 4** on the standard scale, or to both[2].
[Night Poaching Act 1828, s 9, as amended by the Statute Law Revision (No 2) Act 1888, the Criminal Law Act 1977, ss 15(4) and 30(3) and the Criminal Justice Act 1982, s 46.]

1. All the persons need not actually enter, if all are associated together for one common purpose, and some enter while others remain near enough to assist (*R v Whittaker, Holmes, Mawe, Williams, Wilson, and Getting* (1848) 1 Den 310, 12 JP 612) and the land entered may consist of two closes held by different occupiers, and one may be enclosed and the other open (*R v Uezzell, Eaton, and Parkins* (1851) 2 Den 274, 15 JP 324). It is not necessary to give direct evidence that the prisoners were on the land without the permission of the occupier (*R v Wood* (1856) Dears & B 1, 20 JP 310). If any one of the persons be armed, all are armed within the meaning of the statute (*R v Goodfellow* (1845) 1 Den 81, overruling *R v Davis* (1839) 8 C & P 759). Persons provided with things which might have been brought out to serve both harmless and offensive purposes are armed, and such things may be offensive weapons (*R v Sutton* (1877) 13 Cox CC 648, *Treat* 42 JP 241).
2. A police constable who has reasonable grounds for suspecting that an offence under this section is being committed may enter on the land for the purpose of arresting him in accordance with s 25 of the Police and Criminal Evidence Act 1984 (Game Laws (Amendment) Act 1960, s 2(1), post). For powers of search and seizure of game etc, and for powers of forfeiture on conviction, see the Game Law (Amendment) Act 1960, s 4, post.

8–13623   12. What time shall be considered night. Provided always that for the purposes of this Act the night shall be considered and is hereby declared to commence at the expiration of the first hour of sunset[1], and to conclude at the beginning of the last hour before sunrise.
[Night Poaching Act 1828, s 12, as amended by the Statute Law Revision (No 2) Act 1888.]

1. See note to s 3 of the Deer Act 1991, post.

8–13624   13. What shall be deemed game. For the purposes of this Act the word "game" shall be deemed to include hares, pheasants, partridges, grouse, heath or moor game, black game, and bustards.
[Night Poaching Act 1828, s 13, as amended by the Statute Law Revision (No 2) Act 1888.]

Game Act 1831
(1 & 2 Will 4 c 32)

8–13640   2. Definition of "game" under this Act. "Lord of Manor," etc, to include lady.
The word "game" shall for all the purposes of this Act be deemed to include hares, pheasants, partridges, grouse, heath or moor game, black game; and the words "lord of a manor, lordship, or royalty, or reputed manor, lordship, or royalty," shall throughout this Act be deemed to include a lady of the same respectively.
[Game Act 1831, s 2, as amended by the Statute Law Revision (No 2) Act 1888 and the Protection of Birds Act 1954, s 15(2) and Sch 6.]

8–13641   3. Penalty for killing or taking game on certain days and during certain seasons—Penalty for laying poison to kill game. If any person whatsoever shall kill or take any game[1], or use any dog, gun, net, or other engine[2] or instrument for the purpose of killing or taking any game, on a Sunday[3] or Christmas Day, such person shall, on conviction thereof before two justices of the peace, forfeit and pay for every such offence such sum of money, not exceeding **level 1** on the standard scale, as to the said justices shall seem meet; and if any person whatsoever shall kill or take[4] any partridge between the first day of February and the first day of September in any year, or any pheasant between the first day of February and the first day of October in any year, or any black game (except in the county of Somerset or Devon, or in the New Forest in the county of Southampton) between the tenth day of December in any year and the twentieth day of August in the succeeding year, or in the county of Somerset or Devon, or in the New Forest aforesaid, between the tenth day of December in any year and the first day of September in the succeeding year, or any grouse commonly called red game between the tenth day of December in any year and the twelfth day of August in the succeeding year, or any bustard between the first day of March and the first day of September in any year, every such person shall, on conviction of any such offence before two justices of the peace, forfeit and pay, for every head of game so killed or taken, such sum of money, not exceeding **level 1** on the standard scale, as to the said justices shall seem meet, together with the costs of the conviction[5]; and if any person, with intent to destroy or injure any game, shall at any time put or cause to be put any poison or poisonous ingredient on any ground, whether open or inclosed, where game usually resort, or in any highway, every such person shall, on conviction thereof before two justices of the peace, forfeit and pay such sum of money, not exceeding **level 1** on the standard scale, as to the said justices shall seem meet together with the costs of the conviction.
[Game Act 1831, s 3, as amended by the Statute Law Revision (No 2) Act 1888, the Game Act 1970, s 1, the Criminal Law Act 1977, s 31, the Criminal Justice Act 1982, ss 38 and 46 and the Statute Law (Repeals) Act 1989, Sch 1.]

---

   1. Conies are not game under this Act. They are game under the Poaching Prevention Act 1862, post. Hares, although protected on Sundays and Christmas Day, have no close season under this Act (but see the Hares Preservation Act 1892, s 2, post, and the Ground Game Act 1880, s 1(3), post).
   2. A snare is an engine *ejusdem generis* (*Allen v Thompson* (1870) LR 5 QB 336, 35 JP 117). The offence of using a gun may be committed by several persons who may be included in the same information, but each is liable to a penalty, and to be separately convicted. It is in the discretion of the justices to allow the cases to be heard together or separately (*R v Littlechild* (1871) LR 6 QB 293, 35 JP 661; *R v Heslop* (1871) LR 6 QB 293, 35 JP 661).
   3. A person may be convicted of using snares found on land on a Sunday although they were set on the previous Friday or Saturday, and there is no evidence of the defendant having been on the ground on Sunday (*Allen v Thompson* (1870) LR 5 QB 336, 35 JP 117).
   4. Taking away with the intention of keeping a live pheasant accidentally caught in a rabbit wire set on occupier's own land is within this section; but not if the occupier did not mean to appropriate the bird (*Watkins v Price* (1877) 42 JP 21).
   5. The Minister of Agriculture and Fisheries may issue a pest control notice for the killing and destruction of animals and birds, and the notice must be complied with even if it relates to game within the meaning of this section and to a time of the year when the killing or destruction of such game would otherwise be prohibited by this section (Agriculture Act 1947, s 98, title AGRICULTURE, ante).

8–13642   4. Penalty on dealers in game buying or selling birds of game after 10 days after expiration of season for killing, and on other persons buying or selling birds after 10 days, or . . . . If any person licensed to deal in game by virtue of this Act as herein-after mentioned[1] shall buy or sell, any bird[2] of game (except live birds for rearing or exhibition purposes or for sale alive) after the expiration of ten days (one inclusive and the other exclusive) from the respective days in each year on which it shall become unlawful to kill or take such birds of game respectively as aforesaid; or if any person, not being licensed to deal in game by virtue of this Act as hereinafter mentioned, shall buy or sell any bird of game (except live birds for rearing or exhibition purposes or for sale alive) after the expiration of ten days (one inclusive and the other exclusive) from the respective days in each year on which it shall become unlawful to kill or take such birds of game respectively as aforesaid; every such person shall, on conviction of any such offence before two justices of the peace, forfeit and pay for every head of game so bought or sold, such sum of money, not exceeding **level 1** on the standard scale, as to the convicting justices shall seem meet.
[Game Act 1831, s 4, as amended by the Statute Law Revision (No 2) Act 1888, the Game Act 1970, s 1 and the Criminal Justice Act 1982, ss 38 and 46 and the Statute Law (Repeals) Act 1989, Sch 1.]

1. For licences to deal in game, see the Game Licences Act 1860, *post.*
2. Alive or dead, tame or wild (*Loome v Baily* (1860) 3 E & E 444, 25 JP 55; *Harnett v Miles* (1884) 48 JP 455; *Cook v Trevener* [1911] 1 KB 9, 74 JP 469). Section 4 does not apply to game birds killed abroad (*Guyer v R* (1889) 23 QBD 100, 53 JP 436). But see Customs and Inland Revenue Act 1893, s 2 as to licence being required for dealing in imported game.

8–13643   5.   *Saving as to existing laws requiring game certificates.*

8–13644   6.   Every person holding a certificate may kill and take game, subject to proceedings for trespass—Certificate of gamekeeper shall not avail beyond the limits of his appointment.   Every person who shall have obtained an annual game certificate[1] shall be authorised to kill and take game, subject always to an action, or to such other proceedings as are hereinafter mentioned, for any trespass by him committed in search or pursuit of game: Provided always, that no game certificate on which a less duty than £3 is chargeable under the Acts relating to game certificates shall authorise any gamekeeper to kill or take any game, or to use any dog, gun, net, or other engine or instrument for the purpose of killing or taking game, except within the limits included in his appointment as gamekeeper; but that in any case where such gamekeeper shall kill or take any game, or use any dog, gun, net, or other engine or instrument for the purpose of killing or taking game, beyond such limits as aforesaid, he may be proceeded against under this Act, or otherwise, in the same manner to all intents and purposes as if he had no game certificate whatsoever.
[Game Act 1831, s 6, as amended by the Game Licences Act 1860, s 6 and the Statute Law Revision (No 2) Act 1888.]

1. The expression "game certificate" is, for the purposes of this Act, to be construed as a licence to kill game under the provisions of the Game Licences Act 1860; see s 6 of that Act, *post*. For penalties imposed on persons killing and taking game without a certificate, see s 4, Game Licences Act 1860, *post*, and for non-production of licence or refusal to give name etc, see s 10, Game Licences Act 1860, *post*.

8–13645   8–10.   *Right of landlord under existing leases to game; forest rights of the Crown and rights of lords of manors preserved.*

8–13646   11.   Landlords who have reserved the game may authorise others to kill it.   Where the lessor or landlord shall have reserved to himself the right of killing the game upon any land, it shall be lawful for him to authorise any other person or persons who shall have obtained an annual game certificate[1] to enter upon such land for the purpose of pursuing and killing game thereon.
[Game Act 1831, s 11, as amended by the Statute Law Revision (No 2) Act 1888.]

1. See note 1 to s 6, *ante.*

8–13647   12.   Where the landlord, etc, has the right to the game, in exclusion of the occupier, the occupier shall be liable to a penalty for killing or taking it.   Where the right of killing the game upon any land is by this Act given to any lessor or landlord, in exclusion of the right of the occupier of such land, or where such exclusive right hath been or shall be specially reserved by or granted to, or doth or shall belong to, the lessor, landlord, or any person whatsoever other than the occupier of such land, then and in every such case, if the occupier of such land shall pursue, kill, or take any game upon such land, or shall give permission to any other person so to do, without the authority of the lessor, landlord, or other person having the right of killing the game upon such land, such occupier shall, on conviction thereof before two justices of the peace, forfeit and pay for such pursuit such sum of money not exceeding **level 1** on the standard scale, and for every head of game so killed or taken such sum of money not exceeding one pound, as to the convicting justices shall seem meet.
[Game Act 1831, s 12, as amended by the Statute Law Revision (No 2) Act 1888, the Criminal Law Act 1977, s 31, the Criminal Justice Act 1982, s 46 and the Statute Law (Repeals) Act 1989, Sch 1.]

8–13648   13–16.   *Appointment of gamekeepers.*

8–13649   17.   Persons holding certificates may sell game to licensed dealers—Gamekeepers not to sell except on account and with authority of master.   Every person who shall have obtained an annual game certificate shall have power to sell game to any person licensed to deal in game, according to the provisions herein-after mentioned: Provided always, that no game certificate on which a less duty than £3 is chargeable under the Acts relating to game certificates shall authorise any gamekeeper to sell any game, except on the account and with the written authority of the master whose gamekeeper he is; but that any such gamekeeper selling any game not on the account and with the written authority of such master may be proceeded against under this Act in the same manner, to all intents and purposes, as if he had no game certificate whatsoever.
[Game Act 1831, s 17, as amended by the Game Licences Act 1860, s 6 and the Statute Law Revision (No 2) Act 1888.]

8–13650   18.   *Justices[1] to hold a special session yearly for granting licences to persons to deal in game—Dealers in game to put up a board*

1. The local licence with which this section deals is now granted by the council of the appropriate district council; see the Local Government Act 1894, ss 21, 27 and 32. In addition, an excise licence must be obtained from the appropriate council under the Game Licences Act 1860, s 14, post.

8–13651   21. Proviso as to licences in case of partnership.   Provided always, that persons being in partnership, and carrying on their business at one house, shop, or stall only, shall not be obliged by virtue of this Act to take out more than one licence in any one year to authorise them to deal in game at such house, shop, or stall.
[Game Act 1831, s 21, as amended by the Statute Law Revision (No 2) Act, 1888.]

8–13652   22. Licences to become void on any conviction under this Act.   If any person licensed by virtue of this Act to deal in game shall during the period of such licence be convicted of any offence whatever against this Act, such licence shall thereupon become null and void.
[Game Act 1831, s 22, as amended by the Statute Law Revision (No 2) Act, 1888.]

8–13653   23. Penalty for killing or taking game without a certificate[1]—Penalty to be cumulative.   If any person[2] shall kill or take any game, or use[3] any dog, gun[4], net, or other engine or instrument for the purpose of searching for or killing or taking[5] game, such person not being authorised[6] so to do for want of a game certificate[7], he shall, on conviction thereof before two justices of the peace, forfeit and pay for every such offence such sum of money, not exceeding **level 1** on the standard scale, as to the said justices shall seem meet: Provided always, that no person so convicted shall by reason thereof be exempted from any penalty or liability under any statute or statutes relating to game certificates, but that the penalty imposed by this Act shall be deemed to be a cumulative penalty.
[Game Act 1831, s 23, as amended by the Statute Law Revision (No 2) Act 1888, the Criminal Law Act 1977, s 31, the Criminal Justice Act 1982, s 46 and the Statute Law (Repeals) Act 1989, Sch 1.]

1. The words "game certificate" throughout this Act and the Hares Act 1848, shall be construed to mean a licence to kill game under the provisions of the Games Licences Act 1860 (Game Licences Act 1860, s 6). As from a date to be fixed by an Order in Council and until declared at an end by Her Majesty in Council, a game certificate taken out in Northern Ireland shall be available in Great Britain, provided the difference in the rate of duty, if the British rate is higher, has been paid (Finance Act 1924, s 17, as amended by the Statute Law (Repeals) Act 1976, Sch 1).
2. An uncertificated person accompanying a certificated person who uses his dogs in coursing does not incur the penalty imposed for using a dog for coursing game without licence. If the uncertificated person had his own dog with him the case would be different (*Lewis v Taylor* (1812) 16 East 49).
3. Walking about with a gun with intent to kill game is evidence of using it for that purpose (see *Hebden v Hentey* (1819) 1 Chit 607, citing *R v King* (1715) 1 Sess Cas KB 88). Where a gun was heard to go off, and seen to be fired by the defendant, on ground where there was game, and the defendant was walking about the ground, apparently in search of game, this was held sufficient (*R v Davis* (1795) 6 Term Rep 177). Where two persons who had used nets together were convicted in separate penalties on separate informations, but the two cases were heard as one, the court held such hearing to be irregular, but not an excess of jurisdiction, and refused a *certiorari* (*R v Staffordshire Justices* (1858) 23 JP 486; and *R v Littlechild* (1871) LR 6 QB 293, 35 JP 661).
4. A person who is charged with keeping and using a dog and gun on the same day may properly be convicted in one penalty (*R v Lovet* (1797) 7 Term Rep 152). As to using a gun without a licence, see title FIREARMS, ante.
5. A person using a trap for taking game without a certificate during the prohibited season would be liable to penalties under s 23 and under s 3; the penalties are cumulative (*Saunders v Baldy* (1865) LR 1 QB 87, 30 JP 148).
6. Taking out a licence later in the day after detection will not relieve from the penalty (*Campbell v Strangeways* (1877) 3 CPD 105, 42 JP 39).
7. An information for taking, killing, and pursuing, is not bad for charging three offences: one offence only is charged by these words (*Laxton v Jeffries* (1893) 58 JP 318). The information must be laid within three months of the commission of the offence (s 41, post).

8–13654   24. Penalty for taking or destroying the eggs of game, wild fowl, etc, or having eggs so taken in possession.   If any person not having the right of killing the game upon any land, nor having permission from the person having such right, shall wilfully take out of the nest or destroy in the nest upon such land the eggs of any bird of game, or of any swan, wild duck, teal, or widgeon, or shall knowingly have in his house, shop, possession, or control, any such eggs so taken, every such person shall, on conviction thereof before two justices of the peace, forfeit and pay for every egg[1] so taken or destroyed, or so found in his house, shop, possession, or control, such sum of money, not exceeding **level 1** on the standard scale, as to the said justices shall seem meet.
[Game Act 1831, s 24, as amended by the Statute Law Revision (No 2) Act 1888, the Criminal Law Act 1977, s 31, the Criminal Justice Act 1982, s 46 and the Statute Law (Repeals) Act 1989, Sch 1.]

1. As to seizure of eggs by a constable, this would be authorised by the Wildlife and Countryside Act 1981, s 19 in relation to a suspected offence under Pt I of that Act (see ante, this PART: CONSERVATION) or the Police and Criminal Evidence Act 1984, s 19, general power of seizure by constable lawfully on premises (see PART I: MAGISTRATES' COURTS, PROCEDURE).

8–13655   25. Penalty on persons not having game certificates selling game, and on persons having certificates selling to persons not licensed to deal in game.   If any person, not having obtained a game certificate, (except such person be licensed to deal in game according to this Act,) shall sell[1] or offer for sale any game to any person whatsoever, or if any person authorised to sell game under this Act by virtue of a game certificate shall sell or offer for sale any game to any person whatsoever, except a person licensed to deal in game according to this Act, every such offender shall, on conviction of any such offence before two justices of the peace, forfeit and pay for every head of game so sold or offered for sale such sum of money, not exceeding **level 1** on the standard scale, as to the said justices shall seem meet.

[Game Act 1831, s 25, as amended by the Statute Law Revision (No 2) Act 1888, the Criminal Law Act 1977, s 31, the Criminal Justice Act 1982, s 46 and the Statute Law (Repeals) Act 1989, Sch 1.]

---

1. There is a saving for an innkeeper or a tavernkeeper selling without licence for consumption in his own house, he having procured the game from a person licensed (s 26, post).

8–13656   26. Saving as to innkeepers.   Provided always, that it shall be lawful for any innkeeper or tavernkeeper, without any such licence for dealing in game as aforesaid, to sell game for consumption in his own house, such game having been procured from some person licensed to deal in game by virtue of this Act, and not otherwise.

[Game Act 1831, s 26, as amended by the Statute Law Revision (No 2) Act 1888.]

8–13657   27. Penalty on unlicensed persons buying game except from licensed dealers.   If any person, not being licensed to deal in game according to this Act, shall buy any game from any person whatsoever, except from a person licensed to deal in game according to this Act, or bona fide from a person affixing to the outside of the front of his house, shop, or stall a board purporting to be the board of a person licensed to deal in game, every such offender shall, on conviction thereof before two justices of the peace, forfeit and pay for every head of game so bought such sum of money, not exceeding **level 1** on the standard scale, as to the said justices shall seem meet.

[Game Act 1831, s 27, as amended by the Statute Law Revision (No 2) Act 1888, the Criminal Law Act 1977, s 31, the Criminal Justice Act 1982, s 46 and the Statute Law (Repeals) Act 1989, Sch 1.]

8–13658   28. Penalty on licensed dealers buying game from persons not authorised to sell, or otherwise offending; and on unlicensed persons feigning to be licensed.   If any person, being licensed to deal in game according to this Act, shall buy or obtain any game from any person not authorised to sell game for want of a game certificate, or for want of a licence to deal in game; or if any person, being licensed to deal in game according to this Act, shall sell or offer for sale any game at his house, shop, or stall, without such board as[1] aforesaid being affixed to some part of the outside of the front of such house, shop, or stall at the time of such selling or offering for sale, or shall affix or cause to be affixed such board to more than one house, shop, or stall, or shall sell any game at any place other than his house, shop, or stall where such board shall have been affixed; or if any person, not being licensed to deal in game according to this Act, shall assume or pretend, by affixing such board as aforesaid, or by exhibiting any certificate, or by any other device or pretence, to be a person licensed to deal in game; every such offender[2], being convicted thereof before two justices of the peace, shall forfeit and pay such sum of money, not exceeding **level 1** on the standard scale, as to the said justices shall seem meet.

[Game Act 1831, s 28, as amended by the Statute Law Revision (No 2) Act 1888, the Criminal Law Act 1977, s 31, the Criminal Justice Act 1982, s 46 and the Statute Law (Repeals) Act 1989, Sch 1.]

---

1. The obligation on a licensed dealer in game to affix to the outside of his premises a board showing his name and the fact that he is a licensed dealer in game is contained in Game Act 1831, s 18.

2. The servant of a licensed dealer may buy and sell game: one licensed dealer may sell on account of another, see s 29, post.

8–13659   29. Servants of licensed dealer may buy and sell game—One licensed dealer may sell on account of another.   Provided always, that the buying and selling of game by any person or persons employed on the behalf of any licensed dealer in game, and acting in the usual course of his employment, and upon the premises where such dealing is carried on, shall be deemed to be a lawful buying and selling in every case, where the same would have been lawful if transacted by such licensed dealer himself: Provided also, that nothing herein contained shall prevent any licensed dealer in game from selling any game which shall have been sent to him to be sold on account of any other licensed dealer in game.

[Game Act 1831, s 29, as amended by the Statute Law Revision (No 2) Act 1888.]

8–13670   30. Penalty on persons trespassing in the daytime upon lands in search of game, or woodcocks, etc—Leave of occupier not to be a defence where game is reserved to landlord, etc—Landlords and lords of manors, etc, to be deemed legal occupiers.   If any person whatsoever shall commit any trespass[1] by entering or being in the daytime upon any land in search[2] or pursuit of game, or woodcocks, snipes, or conies, such person shall, on conviction thereof before a justice of the peace[3], forfeit and pay such sum of money, not exceeding **level 3** on the standard scale, as to the justice shall seem meet[4]; and if any persons to the number of five or more together shall commit any trespass, by entering or being in the daytime upon any land in search or pursuit of game, or woodcocks, snipes, or conies, each of such persons shall, on conviction thereof before a justice of the peace, forfeit and pay such sum of money, not exceeding **level 4** on the standard scale, as to the said justice shall seem meet[4]: Provided always, that any person charged with any such trespass shall be at liberty to prove, by way of defence, any matter which would have been a defence to an action at law for such trespass[5]; save and except that the leave and licence of the occupier of the land so trespassed upon shall not be a sufficient defence in any case where the landlord, lessor, or other person shall have the right of killing the game upon such land, by virtue of any reservation or otherwise, as herein-before mentioned; but such landlord, lessor, or other person shall, for the purpose of prosecuting for each of the two offences herein last before mentioned, be deemed to be the legal occupier of such land, whenever the actual occupier thereof shall have given such leave or licence; and that the lord or steward of the crown of any manor, lordship, or royalty, or reputed manor, lordship, or royalty, shall be deemed to be the legal occupier of the land of the wastes or commons within such manor, lordship, or royalty, or reputed manor, lordship, or royalty[6].

[Game Act 1831, s 30, as amended by the Statute Law Revision (No 2) Act 1888, the Protection of Birds Act 1954, s 15 and Sch 6, the Game Laws (Amendment) Act 1960, s 5(1), the Criminal Justice Act 1982, ss 38 and 46, the Statute Law (Repeals) Act 1989, Sch 1 and the Criminal Justice and Public Order Act 1994, Sch 9.]

---

1. Immediately after the report of a gun was heard from a wood a man ran out of the wood with his gun and three dogs: he admitted that he had shot at a pigeon, but there was no direct evidence that he had been in pursuit of game. The Queen's Bench Division held that there was admissible evidence that the offence had been committed (*Burrows v Gillingham* (1893) 57 JP 423). For the offence of aiding and abetting the trespass, see *Stacey v Whitehurst* (1865) 18 CBNS 344, 29 JP 136. The offence only arises where there is a pursuit of live game.

2. If justices doubt defendant's intention to search for game they should dismiss the case (*Dyer v Park* (1874) 38 JP Jo 294). The dismissal is not a bar to a charge under s 23 for sporting without a certificate if further evidence be obtained (*Bollard v Spring* (1887) 51 JP 501). In order to support a conviction it is not necessary to prove that the "searching" and "pursuing" was with intention to kill at the time, or reduce the game into possession (*Stiff v Billington* (1901) 65 JP 424). Under the corresponding section of the Game (Scotland) Act 1832, the Court of Justiciary held that the section creates only one offence (trespass) which may be committed in several ways, and that a summons was not bad for duplicity which charged a trespass in pursuit of "game or rabbits" (*Morrison v Anderson* 1913 SC (J) 114).

3. Where the case is heard by one justice, the *penalty* may not exceed £1. (Magistrates' Courts Act 1980, s 121, in PART I: MAGISTRATES' COURTS, PROCEDURE, *ante*.

4. A conviction under this section renders a licence to kill game void (Game Licences Act 1860, s 11, *post*).

5. Where the right to shoot and to the game is reserved to the landlord, the tenant cannot give permission to a person to *sport* on the land (*Pryce v Davies* (1872) 36 JP 214); but this is subject to the provisions of the Ground Game Act 1880, *post*. Where the accused fails to prove the leave of the occupier, it is not necessary for the shooting tenant to prove strictly or by producing the deed that the shooting rights are vested in him (*Taylor v Jackson* (1898) 62 JP 424). Justices may infer want of authority where defendant's act is illegal, as, for instance, shooting game in the close season (*Gleeson v Hurley* [1961] 2 IR 180). A person *bona fide* employed by the tenant to kill rabbits for him cannot be convicted of an offence against this section (see *Spicer v Barnard* (1859) 1 E & E 874, 23 JP 311; and *Padwick v King* (1859) 7 CBNS 88, 23 JP 776). Parol permission of the landlord or person entitled to the game is sufficient to prevent a conviction: such permission is justification for a fresh pursuit of game upon an adjoining field within the meaning of s 35 (*Jones v Williams and Roberts* (1877) 41 JP 614). There may be a valid reservation of shooting and sporting rights otherwise than in writing (*Liversedge v Whiteoak* (1893) 57 JP 692).

6. A police constable who has reasonable cause for suspecting that an offence is being committed may enter upon land (Game Laws (Amendment) Act 1960, s 2, *post*).

8–13671 **31. Trespassers in daytime in search of game, etc, may be required to quit the land and to tell their names and abodes, and in case of refusal may be arrested—Persons arrested must be discharged unless brought before a justice within 12 hours.** Where any person shall be found on any land, in the daytime, in search or pursuit of game, or woodcocks, snipes, or conies, it shall be lawful for any person[1] having the right of killing the game upon such land, by virtue of any reservation or otherwise, as herein-before mentioned, or for the occupier of the land (whether there shall or shall not be any such right by reservation or otherwise), or for any gamekeeper or servant of either of them, or for any person authorised by either of them, to require the person so found forthwith to quit the land whereon he shall be so found, and also to tell his christian name, surname, and place of abode[2]; and in case such person shall, after being so required, offend by refusing to tell his real name or place of abode, or by giving such a general description of his place of abode as shall be illusory for the purpose of discovery, or by wilfully continuing or returning upon the land, it shall be lawful for the party so requiring as aforesaid, and also for any person acting by his order and in his aid, to apprehend[3] such offender, and to convey him or cause him to be conveyed as soon as conveniently may be before a justice of the peace; and such offender (whether so apprehended or not), upon being convicted of any such offence before a justice of the peace[4], shall forfeit and pay such sum of money, not exceeding **level 1** on the standard scale, as to the convicting justice shall seem meet[5]: Provided always, that no person so apprehended shall, on any pretence whatsoever, be detained for a longer period than twelve hours from the time of his apprehension until he shall be brought before some justice of the peace, and that if he cannot, on account of the absence or distance of the residence of any such justice of the peace, or owing to any other reasonable cause, be brought before a justice of the peace within such twelve hours as aforesaid, then the person so apprehended shall be discharged, but may nevertheless be proceeded against for his offence by summons or warrant, according to the provisions herein-after mentioned, as if no such apprehension had taken place.

[Game Act 1831, s 31, as amended by the Statute Law Revision (No 2) Act 1888, the Protection of Birds Act 1954, s 15 and Sch 6, the Game Laws (Amendment) Act 1960, s 1(2), the Wild Creatures and Forest Laws Act

1971, s 1 and Sch, the Criminal Law Act 1977, s 31, the Criminal Justice Act 1982, s 46, the Police and Criminal Evidence Act 1984, Sch 7 and the Statute Law (Repeals) Act 1989, Sch 1.]

1. A penalty not exceeding **level 2** on the standard scale (recoverable as an excise penalty) is imposed by the Game Licences Act 1860, s 10, post, on any person discovered doing any act which requires a game licence, and who shall refuse, on demand, to produce his licence, or shall give a false name, etc, to the owner, landlord, lessee, or occupier of the land, or to any person who shall have taken out a game licence. See note 1, in para **8–13821**, post.

2. Section 31A of this Act, post, added by the Police and Criminal Evidence Act 1984, Sch 6 enables the powers contained in this section to be exercised by a police constable.

3. It would not seem to be necessary that a trespasser should be asked both to quit the land and to give his name and place of abode before he can be apprehended (see *R v Prestney* (1849) 3 Cox CC 505); although in the earlier case of *R v Long* (1836) 7 C & P 314, it was held that to justify apprehension both requirements must have been made.

4. Where the case is heard by one justice, the *penalty* may not exceed £1. (Magistrates' Courts Act 1980, s 121, ante).

5. For powers of search and seizure of game, etc and for powers of forfeiture on conviction, see Game Laws (Amendment) Act 1960, s 4, post.

8–13672   31A. Powers of constables in relation to trespassers.   The powers conferred by section
31 above to require a person found on land as mentioned in that section to quit the land and to tell his christian name, surname, and place of abode shall also be exercisable by a police constable.
[Game Act 1831, s 31A, as inserted by the Police and Criminal Evidence Act 1984, Sch 6.]

8–13673   32. Penalty in case of five or more persons found armed in daytime in search of game, etc, and using violence, etc.   Where any persons, to the number of five or more together,
shall be found on any land, in the daytime, in search or pursuit of game, or woodcocks, snipes, or conies, any of such persons being then and there armed with a gun, and such persons or any of them shall then and there, by violence, intimidation, or menace, prevent or endeavour to prevent any person authorised as herein-before mentioned from approaching such persons so found, or any of them, for the purpose of requiring them or any of them to quit the land whereon they shall be so found, or to tell their or his christian name, surname, or place of abode respectively, as herein-before mentioned, every person so offending by such violence, intimidation, or menace as aforesaid, and every person then and there aiding or abetting such offender, shall, upon being convicted thereof before two justices of the peace, forfeit and pay for every such offence such penalty, not exceeding **level 5** on the standard scale, as to the convicting justices shall seem meet; which said penalty shall be in addition to and independent of any other penalty to which any such person may be liable for any other offence against this Act.
[Game Act 1831, s 32, as amended by the Statute Law Revision (No 2) Act 1888, the Protection of Birds Act 1954, s 15 and Sch 6, the Wild Creatures and Forest Laws Act 1971, s 1, the Criminal Law Act 1977, s 31, the Criminal Justice Act 1982, s 46, the Criminal Justice Act 1988, s 64, the Statute Law (Repeals) Act 1989, Sch 1, and the Criminal Justice and Public Order Act 1994, Sch 9.]

8–13674   34. What to be deemed daytime.   For the purposes of this Act the daytime shall be
deemed to commence at the beginning of the last hour before sunrise, and to conclude at the expiration of the first hour after sunset.
[Game Act 1831, s 34, as amended by the Statute Law Revision (No 2) Act 1888.]

8–13675   35. Provisions as to trespassers not to apply to persons hunting, etc.   Provided
always, that the aforesaid provisions against trespassers and persons found on any land shall not extend to any lord or any steward of the crown of any manor, lordship, or royalty, or reputed manor, lordship or royalty, nor to any gamekeeper lawfully appointed by such lord or steward within the limits of such manor, lordship, or royalty, or reputed manor, lordship, or royalty.
[Game Act 1831, s 35, as amended by the Statute Law Revision (No 2) Act 1888 and the Hunting Act 2004, Sch 2.]

8–13676   36. Game may be demanded from trespassers and seized if not delivered up when
demanded.   When any person shall be found by day or by night upon any land, in search or pursuit of game, and shall then and there have in his possession any game which shall appear to have been recently killed, it shall be lawful for any person having the right of killing the game upon such land, by virtue of any reservation or otherwise, as herein-before mentioned, or for the occupier of such land (whether there shall or shall not be any such right by reservation or otherwise), or for any gamekeeper or servant or either of them, or for any person[1] acting by the order and in aid of any of the said several persons, to demand from the person so found such game in his possession, and, in case such person shall not immediately deliver up such game, to seize and take the same from him, for the use of the person entitled to the game upon such land.
[Game Act 1831, s 36, as the amended by the Statute Law Revision (No 2) Act 1888 and the Wild Creatures and Forest Laws Act 1971, s 1 and Sch.]

1. See *Cooke v Woodward* (1843) 2 Burn's Justice 30th edn 777.

8–13677   41. Prosecutions to be commenced within three months. The prosecution for every offence punishable upon summary conviction by virtue of this Act shall be commenced within three calendar months after the commission of the offence[1].

[Game Act 1831, s 41, as amended by the Statute Law Revision (No 2) Act 1888 and the Statute Law Revision Act 1891.]

---

1. Any person may inform, and the information need not be by the owner or occupier of the land (*Midelton v Gale* (1838) 8 Ad & El 155, 2 JP 328; *Morden v Porter* (1860) 7 CBNS 641, 25 JP 263).

8–13678   42. *Repealed.*

8–13679   46. *Act not to preclude actions for trespass but double proceedings not to be taken for the same trespass.*

8–13680   48. *Extent of Act.*

Night Poaching Act 1844[1]
(7 & 8 Vict c 29)

8–13790   [1]. Punishments and forfeitures imposed by the recited Act on persons by night destroying game or rabbits in any open or inclosed land to apply to persons by night destroying game or rabbits on any public road, path, etc. All the pains, punishments, and forfeitures imposed by the said Act upon persons by night unlawfully taking or destroying any game or rabbits in any land, open or enclosed, as therein set forth, shall be applicable to and imposed upon any person by night unlawfully taking or destroying any game or rabbits on any public road, highway, or path, or the sides thereof, or at the openings, outlets, or gates from any such land into any such public road, highway, or path, in the like manner as upon any such land, open or inclosed; and it shall be lawful for the owner or occupier of any land adjoining either side of that part of such road, highway, or path where the offender shall be, and the gamekeeper or servant of such owner or occupier, and any person assisting such gamekeeper or servant, and for all the persons authorised by the said Act to apprehend any offender against the provisions thereof, to seize and apprehend any person offending against the said Act or this Act; and the said Act, and all the powers, provisions, authorities, and jurisdictions therein or thereby contained or given, shall be as applicable for carrying this Act into execution as if the same had been herein specially set forth.

[Night Poaching Act 1844, s 1, as amended by the Statute Law Revision Act 1891.]

---

1. This Act extends the provisions of the Night Poaching Act 1828, ante, to include poaching offences committed on the public highway, or on the sides thereof, or at the entrance to land from such highway. Any references in the Game Laws (Amendment) Act 1960, post, to the Night Poaching Act 1828 are references to the Act of 1828 as extended by the Night Poaching Act 1844 (Game Laws (Amendment) Act 1960, s 6(2), post).

Hares Act 1848
(11 & 12 Vict c 29)

8–13800   1 Owners, occupiers and persons authorised by them, may kill hares without a game certificate. It shall be lawful for any person, being in the actual occupation of any inclosed lands, or for any owner thereof who has the right of killing game thereon, by himself or by any person directed or authorised by him in writing, according to the form in the schedule to this Act annexed, or to the like effect, so to do, to take, kill[1], or destroy any hare then being in or upon any such inclosed lands without the obtaining of an annual game certificate.

[Hares Act 1848, s 1, as amended by the Statute Law Revision Act 1875 and the Statute Law Revision Act 1891.]

---

1. The right to kill hares without obtaining a game certificate is also vested in the occupier of land, and persons duly authorised by him, by the Ground Game Act 1880, s 4, post. The word "actual" in this section restricts the authority given by the Act to the person who is in fact living on the land, whereas the exemption conferred by s 4 of the 1880 Act is not so restricted.

8–13801   2. *Limitations of authority*[1].

---

1. This section limits the grant of authorisation under s 1, ante. In practice s 2 of this Act is now obsolete in view of the provisions of the Ground Game Act 1880, post, which are not so restrictive.

8–13802   5. Provision as to laying of poison and use of fire-arms by night.   Provided also, that nothing herein contained shall extend or be taken or construed to extend to the making it lawful for any person, with intent to destroy or injure any hares or other game, to put or cause to be put any poison or poisonous ingredient on any ground, whether open or inclosed, where game usually resort, or in any highway, or for any person to use any fire-arms or gun of any description by night, for the purpose of killing any game or hares.
[Hares Act 1848, s 5, as amended by the Statute Law Revision Act 1891.]

8–13803   6–8. *Savings, Interpretation and Extent.*

Game Licences Act 1860

(23 & 24 Vict c 90)

8–13820   2. *Duties herein mentioned to be granted.*

8–13821   3. Duties granted to be Excise duties under the Commissioners of Inland Revenue.
The duties by this Act granted shall be Excise duties[1].
[Game Licences Act 1860, s 3, as amended by the Customs and Excise Act 1952, s 320(1) and Sch 12.]

---

1. The power to levy duties in respect of licences to deal in game is transferred to district councils (Finance Act 1908, s 6; Order in Council, dated 19 October 1908 (SR & O 1908/844); Customs and Excise Management Act 1979, s 176, in title CUSTOMS AND EXCISE, *ante*. By the Transferred Excise Duties (Application of Enactments) Order 1952 (SI 1952/2205), in title CUSTOMS AND EXCISE, *ante*, relevant sections of the Customs and Excise Management Act 1979 are applied to the recovery of duties transferred to local authorities. For police prosecutions for offences relating to transferred duties, see s 176 of the 1979 Act (note to s 145 of the 1979 Act, in title CUSTOMS AND EXCISE, *ante*).

8–13822   4. Licence to be taken out for taking or killing game in Great Britain—Penalty for neglect.   Every person, before he shall in Great Britain take[1], kill, or pursue, or aid or assist in any manner in the taking, killing, or pursuing by any means whatever, or use any dog, gun, net, or other engine for the purpose of taking, killing, or pursuing any game, or any woodcock, snipe, or any coney, or any deer, shall take out a proper licence[2] to kill game under this Act, and pay the duty hereby made payable thereon; and if any person shall do any such act as herein-before mentioned in Great Britain without having duly taken out and having in force such licence as aforesaid, he shall forfeit the sum of **level 2** on the standard scale.
[Game Licences Act 1860, s 4, as amended by the Protection of Birds Act 1954, s 15(2) and Sch 6, the Criminal Law Act 1977, s 31 and the Criminal Justice Act 1982, s 46.]

---

1. To take or kill game without a licence is an offence not only under this section but also under the Game Act 1831, s 23 *ante*. Taking, killing and pursuing are one offence only (*Laxton v Jeffries* (1893) 58 JP 318). To walk with dog or gun on land where there is game or to point a gun at game is evidence of the commission of an offence (*R v Davis* (1795) 6 Term Rep 177). Where one licensed and several unlicensed persons together fire at the same bird all are offenders although the person who killed it cannot be identified (*Hunter v Clark* (1902) 66 JP 247, 18 TLR 366). If a person walks about with a gun with intent to kill game he will be guilty of an offence (*Hebden v Hentey* (1819) 1 Chit 607).
2. As to the availability of game certificates taken out in Northern Ireland, see note 1 to s 23 of the Game Act 1831, in para **8–13653**, *ante*.

8–13823   5. Exceptions and exemptions.   The following exceptions and exemptions from the duties and provisions of this Act are hereby made and granted; (that is to say,)

Exceptions

1. The taking of woodcocks and snipes with nets or springes in Great Britain.
2. The taking or destroying of conies in Great Britain by the proprietor of any warren or of any inclosed ground whatever, or by the tenant of lands, either by himself or by his direction or permission.
3. *Repealed.*
4. *Repealed.*
5. The taking and killing of deer in any enclosed lands[1] by the owner or occupier of such lands, or by his direction or permission.

Exemptions

1. Any of the Royal Family.
2. Any person appointed a gamekeeper on behalf of Her Majesty by the Commissioners of Woods under the authority of any Act of Parliament relating to the land revenues of the Crown.
3. Any person aiding or assisting in the taking or killing of any game, or any woodcock, snipe, or coney, or any deer, in the company or presence and for the use of another person who shall have duly obtained, according to the directions of this Act, and in his own right, a licence to kill game, and who shall by virtue of such licence then and there use his own dog, gun, net or other engine for the taking

or killing of such game, woodcock, snipe, coney, or deer, and who shall not act therein by virtue of any deputation or appointment.

4. And, as regards the killing of hares only, all persons who, under the provisions of the two several Acts, 11th and 12th Victoria, chapter 29[2], and chapter 30, respectively, are authorised to kill hares in England and Scotland respectively, without obtaining an annual game certificate.
[Game Licences Act 1860, s 5, as amended by the Statute Law Revision Act 1875, the Protection of Birds Act 1954, s 15(2) and Sch 6 and the Hunting Act 2004, s 15.]

---

1. This means enclosed lands such as lands used for farming and enclosed by normal agricultural hedges as contrasted with moorland (*Jemmison v Priddle* [1972] 1 QB 489, [1972] 1 All ER 539, 136 JP 230).
2. Hares Act 1848; see ante.

8–13824   6. Saving as to Hares Act[1]—Meaning of "game certificate".   Provided always, that nothing herein contained shall extend to repeal, alter, or affect any of the provisions of the said two several Acts of the eleventh and twelfth years of Her Majesty, chapter twenty-nine[1] and chapter thirty, further than that the term "game certificate" in the said Acts respectively used shall be construed to mean a licence to kill game under the provisions of this Act and shall be so read accordingly; and that the term "game certificate" used in the Game Act 1831[2] shall be construed and read in like manner; and that wherever in the said last-mentioned Act the duty of three pounds [67^1/$_2$p] on a game certificate is mentioned the duty of three pounds on a licence to kill game shall be read in lieu.
  [Game Licences Act 1860, s 6, as amended by the Decimal Currency Act 1969, s 10(1).]

---

1. Hares Act 1848; see ante.
2. See this title, ante.

8–13825   7. Licences may be taken out on behalf of assessed servants acting as gamekeepers, etc.   Any person having the right to kill game on any lands in England or Scotland employing any male servant as a gamekeeper[1] whether deputed or appointed or not, and any person granting a deputation or appointment in Great Britain to the male servant of any other person with power and authority to take or kill any game, shall respectively be at liberty to take out a licence to kill game on behalf of any such servant on payment of the duty of four pounds for the year ending on the fifth day of April[2]; and such licence shall exempt the servant named therein during his continuance in the same capacity and service, and on his quitting such service shall also exempt any servant who shall succeed him in the same service and capacity, or who shall succeed to the deputation of the same manor or royalty or lands within the year for which the licence is granted, during the remainder of such year; and no such servant on whose behalf a licence shall have been duly obtained as aforesaid shall be required to obtain a licence for himself, or be liable to any penalty by reason of not obtaining a licence in his own name.
[Game Licences Act 1860, s 7, as amended by the Finance Act 1937, s 5, and Sch 2 and SI 1968/120.]

---

1. Special provisions as to the appointment of gamekeepers are contained in ss 13–16 of the Game Act 1831.
2. Now 31 July; see the Customs and Inland Revenue Act 1883, s 4.

8–13826   8.   *On change of gamekeeper, etc, licence may be continued to successor.*

8–13827   9. Such licences not available for acts done on land whereon master has not a right to kill game.   Provided always, that no such licence taken out for or on behalf of any person, being such servant or acting under a deputation or appointment as aforesaid, shall be available for such person in any suit or prosecution where proof shall be given of his doing or having done any act for which a licence is required under this Act on land on which his master had not a right to kill game.
[Game Licences Act 1860, s 9.]

8–13828   10. Persons doing any act requiring a licence to kill game, to produce the same, on demand, or declare their names, places of residence, etc.—Penalty for refusal[1].   If any person shall be discovered doing any act whether in Great Britain in respect whereof a licence to kill game is required under this Act, by any officer of Inland Revenue, or by any lord or gamekeeper of the manor, royalty, or lands wherein such person shall then be, or by any person having duly taken out a proper licence to kill game under this Act, or by the owner, landlord, lessee, or occupier of the land on which such person shall then be, it shall be lawful for such officer or other person aforesaid to demand and require from the person so acting the production of a licence to kill game issued to him; and the person so acting is hereby required to produce such licence to the person so demanding the production thereof, and to permit him to read the same, and (if he shall think fit) to take a copy thereof or of any part thereof; or in case no such licence shall be produced to the person demanding the same as aforesaid, then it shall be lawful for the person having made such demand to require the person so acting forthwith to declare to him his christian and surname and place of residence, and the place at which he shall have taken out such licence; and if such person shall, after such demand made, wilfully refuse to produce and show the licence to kill game issued to him, or in default thereof as aforesaid to give to the person so demanding the same his christian and surname and place of

residence, and the place at which he shall have taken out such licence, or if he shall produce any false or fictitious licence, or give any false or fictitious name or place, or if he shall refuse to permit any licence which he may produce to be read, or a copy thereof or of any part thereof to be taken, he shall forfeit the sum of **level 2** on the standard scale.
[Game Licences Act 1860, s 10, as amended by the Criminal Law Act 1977, s 31 and the Criminal Justice Act 1982, s 46.]

----

1. For offence of refusal by trespassers in daytime in search of game to quit land and to tell their name and place of abode, see Game Act 1831, s 31, ante.

8–13829   **11. Licence void on conviction of offence under 1 & 2 Will 4 c 32, s 30, or 2 & 3 Will 4 c 68.**   If any person, having obtained a licence to kill game under this Act, shall be convicted of any offence under section thirty of the Game Act 1831[1] or under the Game (Scotland) Act 1832, the said licence shall thenceforth be null and void.
[Game Licences Act 1860, s 11.]

----

1. See this title ante.

8–13830   **12.** *Commissioners of Inland Revenue to publish lists of persons licensed to kill game.*

8–13831   **13.** *Provisions of the Game Act 1831 relating to licences to deal in game, etc, to be in force throughout the United Kingdom.*

8–13832   **14. Persons licensed by the justices[1] to deal in game, to pay for and obtain a licence under this Act—Penalty for dealing in game without such licence.**   Every person who shall have obtained any licence to deal in game[2], under the provisions of the said two several Acts in the preceding clause mentioned, shall annually, and during the continuance of such licence, and before he shall be empowered to deal in game under such licence, obtain a further licence[3] to deal in game under this Act, on payment of the duty[4] hereby charged thereon; and if any person shall purchase or sell or otherwise deal in game before he shall obtain a licence to deal in game under the provisions of this Act, he shall forfeit the sum of **level 2** on the standard scale[5].
[Game Licences Act 1860, s 14, as amended by the Statute Law Revision Act 1875, the Criminal Law Act 1977, s 31, the Criminal Justice Act 1982, s 46 and the Local Government (Wales) Act 1994, Sch 16.]

----

1. The licensing powers of justices in relation to licences to deal in game under s 18 of the Game Act 1831, ante, were transferred (except as to London) to councils of county boroughs and county districts by the Local Government Act 1894, ss 21, 27 and 32. By virtue of the Local Government Act 1972, s 179, the licensing powers were transferred to district councils (or in Wales, principal councils: Local Government (Wales) Act 1994, s 17). In London, the licensing authorities are the Common Council of the City of London and the London borough councils; see the London Government (Public General Acts) Order 1965, SI 1965/602, art 3.
2. No licence is required to deal in woodcock, snipe, quail, landrail, coney or deer.
3. The provisions of this Act relating to excise licences to deal in game and the dealing in and selling of game without an excise licence shall extend and apply to the dealing in and selling of hares, pheasants, partridges, grouse, heath or moor game, black game, and bustards, imported from foreign parts into Great Britain or Ireland (Customs and Inland Revenue Act 1893, s 2).
4. As to power to levy duties, see note 1 to s 3, ante.
5. The limitation of time for proceedings to be taken was six months, as prescribed by the Excise Act 1848, s 3, and not three months, as prescribed by the Game Act 1831, s 41, ante (*M'Lean v Johnston* 1913 SC (J) 1). The Excise Act 1848 was repealed and replaced by the Customs and Excise Act 1952, s 283(1) (now s 147 of the Customs and Excise Management Act 1979), which extends the time limit to three years. As s 283 does not extend to proceedings by a local authority, it appears that the time limit is six months (Magistrates' Courts Act 1980, s 127, ante): alternatively, it might now be held that s 41 of the Game Act 1831 applies as s 13 of the 1860 Act provides, in effect, that the two Acts shall be read as one.

8–13833   **15, 16, 16A.** *Grant of licences under this Act; form and duration of licences, provision as to foreign game.*

Poaching Prevention Act 1862
(25 & 26 Vict c 114)

8–13850   **1. Interpretation of terms.**   The word "game"[1] in this Act shall for all the purposes of this Act be deemed to include any one or more hares, pheasants, partridges, eggs of pheasants and partridges, woodcocks, snipes, rabbits, grouse, black or moor game, and eggs of grouse, black or moor game; and the words "justice" and "justices" in this Act shall, unless otherwise provided for, mean respectively a justice and justices of the peace respectively of or for the county, riding, division, liberty, city, borough, or place in which any game, gun, part of gun, or other article to which section two[2] of this Act applies shall be found★.
[Poaching Prevention Act 1862, s 1, as amended by the Game Laws (Amendment) Act 1960, s 3.]

*Repealed by the Courts Act 2003, Sch 8, from a date to be appointed.

1. This definition of "game" differs from that in the Night Poaching Act 1828, s 13, ante, in that it omits bustards, and the definition differs further from that Act and the Game Act 1831, s 2, ante, in that it includes rabbits, woodcock and snipe, and the eggs of certain game birds.

2. Section 2, post, must be read in conjunction with the extension of that section by the Game Laws (Amendment) Act 1960, s 3; see note 6 in para **8–13851**.

8–13851   **2. Power to constables to search persons, etc, in certain cases—Proceedings in case of game, etc, being found**[1]. It shall be lawful for any constable or peace officer in any county, borough, or place in Great Britain and Ireland, in any highway, street, or public place[2], to search any person[3] whom he may have good cause to suspect[4] of coming from[5] any land where he shall have been unlawfully in search or pursuit of game, or any person aiding or abetting such person, and having in his possession any game unlawfully obtained, or any gun, part of gun[6], and also to stop and search any cart or other conveyance in or upon which such constable or peace officer shall have good cause to suspect that any such game or any such article or thing is being carried by any such person, and should there be found[7] any game or any such article or thing as aforesaid upon such person, cart, or other conveyance, to seize and detain such game, article, or thing; and such constable or peace officer shall in such case apply to some justice of the peace for a summons[8] citing such person to appear before two justices of the peace assembled in petty sessions, as provided in the eighteenth and nineteenth of Her present Majesty, chapter one hundred and twenty-six, section nine, as far as regards England and Ireland, and before a sheriff in Scotland; and if such person shall have obtained such game by unlawfully going on any land[9] in search[10] or pursuit of game, or shall have used any such article or thing as aforesaid for unlawfully killing or taking game, or shall have been accessory thereto, such person shall, on being convicted thereof, forfeit and pay any sum not exceeding **level 3** on the standard scale[11].*

[Poaching Prevention Act 1862, s 2, as amended by the Statute Law Revision Act 1893, the Game Laws (Amendment) Act 1960, ss 3 and 5, and the Criminal Justice Act 1982, ss 38 and 46.]

*Amended by the Courts Act 2003, Sch 8, from a date to be appointed.

1. This section falls into three parts: (i) matters introductory (power to search and seize), (ii) matters consequential (issue of summons), and (iii) the substance of the offences; eg having obtained such game, etc, or having used such gun, etc, or being an accessory; it is essential to refer to one of the substantive offences in the information; see *Lundy v Botham* (1877) 41 JP 774; *Garman v Plaice* [1969] 1 All ER 62, [1969] 1 WLR 19, 133 JP 114.

2. Whether a railway platform is a "public place" has not been decided under the present statute. The question arose under the Vagrancy Act (*Re Freestone* (1856) 1 H & N 93, 20 JP 376), when POLLOCK CB, intimated his opinion that a railway is a public place, and it has been so held by the Scottish Court of Justiciary under a repealed statute relating to gaming (*Woods v Lindsay* 1910 SC (J) 88). But see *Case v Storey* (1869) LR 4 Exch 319, 33 JP 470. We think that a public-house to which poachers have been followed is not such a public place (see 43 JP 695).

3. The constable will be justified in making this search if he had good cause of suspicion, although it may turn out that his suspicion was unfounded, and no offence under the Act can be proved. Where a constable saw a man with a gun in his hand on a public footway in the act of picking up a rabbit, which another person threw to him out of the adjoining enclosed land, from the spot where a gun had just been fired, and the man ran away and escaped for the time, it was held that actual search was not necessary to lay a foundation for the right to apply for a summons, and proceed to conviction (*Hall v Knox* (1863) 4 B & S 515, 28 JP 22). It is not necessary that the defendant should have succeeded in catching game; it is sufficient if there is evidence that the net, etc, has been used with intent of unlawfully taking game (*Jenkin v King* (1872) LR 7 QB 478, 37 JP 53; and *Treat* 36 JP 322).

4. Justices dismissed an information under the Prevention of Crimes Act 1871, s 12, for assault on a constable on the ground that as the constable actually saw a man poaching he could not have suspected him of poaching, and, therefore, the constable was not acting in the execution of his duty in seizing his gun: *Held*, justices were wrong (*Hall v Robinson* (1889) 53 JP 310).

5. These words do not meet the case of a poacher suspected of *going to* and in search of game.

6. This section also applies:

    "(*a*) in relation to cartridges and other ammunition, and

    (*b*) in relation to nets, traps, snares and other devices of a kind used for the killing or taking of game,

as it applies in relation to any gun or part of a gun" (Game Laws (Amendment) Act 1960, s 3(2)).

7. It is not necessary that the game, etc, should be literally found in the clothing or hands of the person. It is sufficient if something is found in his immediate possession and control at the material time (*Ralph and Ralph v Smith* (16 October 1941, unreported).

8. The person searched must not be arrested even if a gun or game is found upon him. For power of arrest generally where it appears to a constable that service of a summons is impracticable or inappropriate because any of the general arrest conditions are satisfied, see s 25 of the Police and Criminal Evidence Act 1984, in PART I: MAGISTRATES' COURTS, PROCEDURE, ante.

9. It is not necessary to prove by direct evidence either the specific land on which, or the unlawful means by which, the game came into the possession of the accused. The justices must, however, require the prosecutor to satisfy them by direct evidence, or by reasonable and legitimate deduction from facts proved, and not by mere suspicion or conjecture, either that the defendant obtained the game by unlawfully going upon land, or that he used the gun, net, etc, for unlawfully killing or taking game, or with that intent, or that he was accessory thereto. It will be for the justices to decide how far the evidence in each case is sufficient to warrant the inference that an offence has been committed, bearing in mind that the *onus probandi* lies on the prosecutor.

In *Brown v Turner* (1863) 13 CBNS 485, 27 JP 103, it was held by the Court of Common Pleas that it was not essential to a conviction that the persons charged should have been actually seen upon or coming out of land where they were in pursuit of game, but that the justices might infer from the circumstances that they had been unlawfully on land in pursuit of game, without offering any evidence as to the specific land. In *Evans v Botterill* (1863) 3 B & S 787, 28 JP 21, and in *Fuller v Newland* (1863) 27 JP 406, the Court of Queen's Bench considered *Brown v Turner* a conclusive authority, and held that it was not necessary to prove specifically that the defendant was seen upon any particular land, and it is for the justices to draw the inference from the facts before them whether he obtained the game by going unlawfully on some land, and if there is some evidence to justify that conclusion the superior courts will not interfere. In the above case of *Evans v Botterill* it was held that proof that the defendants were found together on a highway at 6 am, with bags containing one hare and several rabbits, and with nets and stakes, was evidence upon which justices might convict the defendants of having obtained the game by having been unlawfully on land in pursuit of game, or having used the nets for the purpose of taking game, without direct proof that any of the defendants had been upon any land or had used any of the nets. Where rabbits were found in a carrier's cart at 3 am (which was the usual time for the carrier passing the place where he was stopped), and he gave a possible mode of becoming possessed of them, the refusal of the justices to convict was approved (*Shuttleworth v Grange* (1867) 31 JP 280); and in *Jones v Dicker* (1870) 34 JP 677, it was held that it was not sufficient to prove that game was found in a carrier's cart after he had denied having any game in his possession, or that the game was newly killed and the carrier's boots were muddy, there being no evidence that he had taken any part in obtaining the game unlawfully, or that he was coming from land where he had been poaching; so also in *Lawley v Merricks*, a carrier's cart on the way to market was stopped at 7.30 am on the highway, and searched by a constable; the carrier, who was a general game dealer, accounted for some rabbits she carried except two couples, which she said she bought of a man she did not know, and when the constable said "If you buy rabbits of a poacher you must expect to be summoned," she replied, "I won't have any more of them," the QB Division held that there was not sufficient evidence that the appellant had been accessory to the fact that the rabbits which had been found had been taken by poachers (*Lawley v Merricks* (1887) 51 JP 502).

But in *Ex p Whiteley* (1875) 39 JP 70, where a greengrocer was stopped with 129 rabbits in his cart, which he said he had been hired by a person he did not know, in a market where rabbits were disposed of in large quantities, to take to a railway station, the Court of Queen's Bench refused to order justices to state a case applied for on the ground that there was no evidence to justify his conviction, and QUAIN J and LUSH J, held the magistrates were justified in drawing conclusions against the defendant as an accessory; and in *R v Cheshire Justices* (1876) 40 JP 148, where a licensed game dealer, who had been stopped by a constable with rabbits in his conveyance, upon being charged with "aiding and abetting", called two poachers, who swore they sold the rabbits to him, but refused to say where they obtained them, the court discharged the rule *nisi* obtained to quash the conviction with costs, notwithstanding one of the poachers had a licence to kill game, and mentioned two or three farms where he had liberty to take rabbits. See *Stowe v Marjoram* (1909) 73 JP 498.

10. The search is limited to the highway, street, or public place, but an actual search is not necessary if the constable sees the game or gun, etc, actually upon the person (*Hall v Knox* (1863) 4 B & S 515, 28 JP 22). There must also be a seizure of the gun, net, game, etc, by the constable—"seizure (*per* SMITH J) being a necessary condition in order to give the constable a right to apply for a summons". It was not necessary in this case to decide whether the seizure must be on a highway; but Brett J, observed, "If the game is not seized on the highway the same constable has no power to go off the highway for that purpose". In *Clarke v Crowder* (1869) LR 4 CP 638, the conditions necessary to constitute an offence under this statute were fully discussed. It was held that there must be an actual finding of game, or guns, etc, on the accused person, or in his cart, by a constable on a "highway, street, or public place": that it was not sufficient that the accused should be seen on a highway and followed, and game found on him elsewhere; that a constable may not follow an accused person who leaves the highway, and upon overtaking him in fresh pursuit, search, seize, and detain him where he is caught, if that place is not a highway, street, or public place; and the constable who seizes the game, etc, can alone apply for the summons. In *Turner v Morgan* (1875) LR 10 CP 587, 39 JP 695, the subject was again fully considered; the cases cited above were reviewed, and it was held that to sustain a conviction it is a condition precedent that game, etc, should have been "seized" on the highway. But seizure in hot pursuit may be in another place. On seeing a constable, appellant, who was carrying rabbits on the highway, leaped over a fence and being pursued, threw down the rabbits in a field at a distance from the highway. The constable never lost sight of the appellant and the rabbits from the first, and the conviction was upheld (*Lloyd v Lloyd* (1885) 14 QBD 725, 49 JP 630). *Clarke v Crowder* and *Turner v Morgan*, supra, were distinguished by MATHEW J, from this case, inasmuch as in both cases the seizure did not take place at the time of the search, and in the first case something had been seen, but the prisoner was not searched, and in the second case no search had taken place; the Act therefore had not been complied with (see *Treat*, 49 JP 67, 83). See note 7, supra.

11. For further provisions as to seizure and forfeiture on conviction of an offence under this section, see the Game Laws (Amendment) Act 1960, s 3, post.

8–13852   3. Recovery of penalties.   Any penalty under this Act shall be recovered and enforced in England in the same manner as penalties under the Game Act 1831 and* in Scotland under the Game (Scotland) Act 1832 and in Ireland under the Petty Sessions, Ireland, Act 1851 when not otherwise directed in this Act.
[Poaching Prevention Act 1862, s 3.]

---

*Words repealed by the Courts Act 2003, Sch 8, from a date to be appointed.

8–13853   4. *Provisions of the Summary Jurisdiction Act 1848[1] extended to this Act.*

---

1. This Act was repealed by the Magistrates' Courts Act 1952, s 132 and Sch 6. Summary jurisdiction and procedure are now mainly governed by the Magistrates' Courts Act 1980 in PART I: MAGISTRATES' COURTS, PROCEDURE, ante.

Ground Game Act 1880
(43 & 44 Vict c 47)

8–13870   1. Occupier to have a right inseparable from his occupation to kill ground game concurrently with any other person entitled to kill the same on land in his occupation. Every occupier[1] of land shall have, as incident to and inseparable from his occupation of the land, the right to kill and take ground game[2] thereon, concurrently with any other person who may be entitled to kill and take ground game on the same land:

Provided that the right conferred on the occupier by this section shall be subject to the following limitations:

(1) The occupier shall kill and take ground game only by himself or by persons duly authorised by him in writing:

   (a) The occupier himself and one other person[3] authorised in writing by such occupier shall be the only persons entitled under this Act to kill ground game with firearms;

   (b) No person[4] shall be authorised by the occupier to kill or take ground game, except members of his household[5] resident on the land in his occupation, persons in his ordinary service on such land, and any one other person bona fide employed by him for reward[6] in the taking and destruction of ground game;

   (c) Every person so authorised by the occupier, on demand by any person having a concurrent right to take and kill the ground game on the land or any person authorised by him in writing to make such demand, shall produce to the person so demanding the document by which he is authorised, and in default he shall not be deemed to be an authorised person.

(2) A person shall not be deemed to be an occupier of land for the purposes of this Act by reason of his having a right of common over such lands; or by reason of an occupation for the purpose of grazing or pasturage of sheep, cattle, or horses for not more than nine months.

(3)[7] In the case of moorlands, and uninclosed lands (not being arable lands), the occupier and the persons authorised by him shall exercise the rights conferred by this section only from the eleventh day of December in one year until the thirty-first day of March in the next year, both inclusive; but this provision shall not apply to detached portions of moorlands or uninclosed lands adjoining arable lands, where such detached portions of moorlands or uninclosed lands are less than twenty-five acres in extent.
[Ground Game Act 1880, s 1.]

---

1. The word is not limited to the actual occupier as in the Hares Act 1848; where a farm is carried on by trustees or executors by means of a bailiff it seems that each of the trustees or executors would be an "occupier", although the bailiff resides at the farmhouse; occupying does not necessarily mean living upon the farm.
2. For the meaning of "ground game", see s 8, post.
3. If the occupier has full power to kill rabbits (which he could have unless he has entered into an agreement to the contrary) he can invite any number of people to shoot the animals without the necessity of giving written permission; but if he has only the concurrent right which the Ground Game Act renders compulsory when the tenant has not the full right, then he can authorise but one person to shoot, and the authority must be in writing, while the individual to whom he gives authority must be a member of his household or person *bona fide* employed. Whether a visitor temporarily staying at the farmhouse would be a member of the household or merely a person acting under a colourable pretence must be a question for the decision of the magistrate (*Stuart v Murray* (1884) Court of Judiciary, noted in *Field*, November 22nd).
4. The Act does not prevent an occupier from inviting as many persons as he pleases as spectators of coursing, or to see himself kill ground game.
5. The Court of Justiciary of Scotland held that a person *bona fide* invited by the occupier to stay with him for a week was a member of the household resident on the land (*Stuart v Murray*, supra). We doubt whether a friend invited for a day's sport would be so resident.
6. The Court of Justiciary of Scotland held that the right to take away the game killed by a person employed to kill the game and no other reward, was a *bona fide* employment for reward (*Bruce v Prosser* (1898) 62 JP 466).
7. The occupier of land to which this subsection applies shall, without prejudice to his existing rights under this Act, be entitled, between 1 September and 10 December, inclusive, in any year, to exercise the right of killing and taking ground game under this Act otherwise than by the use of firearms; see the Ground Game (Amendment) Act 1906, s 2, post.

8–13871   2. Occupier entitled to kill game on land in his occupation not to divest himself wholly of such right.

Where the occupier of land is entitled otherwise than in pursuance of this Act to kill and take ground game thereon, if he shall give to any other person a title to kill and take such ground game, he shall nevertheless retain and have, as incident to and inseparable from such occupation, the same right to kill and take ground game as is declared by section one of this Act. Save as aforesaid, but subject as in section six hereafter mentioned, the occupier may exercise any other or more extensive right which he may possess in respect of ground game or other game, in the same manner and to the same extent as if this Act had not passed.
[Ground Game Act 1880, s 2.]

8–13872   3. All agreements in contravention of right of occupier to destroy ground game void[1].

Every agreement, condition, or arrangement which purports to divest or alienate the right of the occupier as declared, given, and reserved to him by this Act, or which gives to such occupier any advantage in consideration of his forbearing to exercise such right, or imposes upon him any disadvantage in consequence of his exercising such right, shall be void[2].
[Ground Game Act 1880, s 3.]

---

1. This section shall not apply to prevent the occupier of lands to which s 1(3), ante, applies, and the owner of such lands or other persons having a right to take and kill game thereon, from making and enforcing agreements for the joint exercise of the right to kill and take ground game between 1st September and 10th December, inclusive, in any year; see the Ground Game (Amendment) Act 1906, s 3, post.
2. Only the clauses of the agreement in contravention of the Act are void; the other parts of the agreement may be good (*Beardmore v Meakin* (1884) 20 LJNC 8). In a later case the owner of a farm promised the tenant if he allowed the ground game to go unshot for benefit of defendant, the owner, who ultimately shot over the farm, defendant would compensate him for loss of damage to his crop. It was held that the agreement was absolutely void (*Sherrard v Gascoigne* [1900] 2 QB 279). See 64 JP 417, where the accuracy of the judgment is questioned. This section applies only to an agreement made between the tenant and his landlord, entered into to defeat the object of the Act. Where an occupier of land is entitled to

kill and take ground game otherwise than in pursuance of the Act (or where there is no reservation of the game or sporting rights), he may assign his sporting rights to a third person (*Morgan v Jackson* [1895] 1 QB 885, 59 JP 327). But it is otherwise where he is entitled to the ground game merely by reason of the Act; and where (having the sporting rights) he assigns them to a third person, he must still retain a concurrent right to the ground game.

8–13873　4. Exemption from game licences.　　The occupier and the persons duly authorised by him as aforesaid shall not be required to obtain a licence[1] to kill game for the purpose of killing and taking ground game on land in the occupation of such occupier, and the occupier shall have the same power of selling any ground game so killed by him, or the persons authorised by him, as if he had a licence to kill game.
[Ground Game Act 1880, s 4, as amended by the Local Government Act 1966, s 43 and Sch 6.]

　　1. As to licences to kill game, see the Game Licences Act 1860, *ante*.

8–13874　5. Saving clause.　　Where at the date of the passing of this Act the right to kill and take ground game on any land is vested by lease, contract of tenancy, or other contract bona fide made for valuable consideration in some person other than the occupier, the occupier shall not be entitled under this Act, until the determination[1] of that contract, to kill and take ground game on such land . .

　　Nothing in this Act shall affect any special right of killing or taking ground game to which any person other than the landlord, lessor, or occupier may have become entitled before the passing of this Act by virtue of any franchise, charter, or Act of Parliament.
[Ground Game Act 1880, s 5, as amended by Statute Law Revision Act 1894.]

　　1. A farm was demised for a term of years and thenceforth from year to year until determined by notice in writing to be given by either party six calendar months previous to the expiration of the current year. The game was reserved to the lessor. It was contended that the lease did not create a tenancy from year to year, but a term of two years certain, and afterwards from year to year, and reliance was placed upon *Wilkinson v Calvert* (1878) 3 CPD 360, 42 JP 776, where a similar point arose under the Agricultural Holdings Act. The lessee had exercised the right to shooting since the passing of the Ground Game Act. WILLS J, ordered a motion for injunction against the tenant to stand over until trial of the action, and observed that his mind was rather inclined towards defendant (*Kinnaird v Denney* (1898) 28 Sol Jo 761). A tenant held land from year to year upon the terms of an expired lease, which reserved to the lessor "the exclusive right of the lessor and his friends to enter upon the farm for sporting or otherwise". The QB Division held that the reservation was severable, and was void only as to ground game under s 3, and that a person who was shooting partridges by permission of the tenant was liable to be convicted (*Stanton v Brown* [1900] 1 QB 671, 64 JP 326).

8–13875　6. Prohibition of night shooting, spring traps[1] above ground or poison.　　No person[2] having a right of killing ground game under this Act or otherwise shall use any firearms for the purpose of killing ground game between the expiration of the first hour after sunset and the commencement of the last hour before sunrise; *and no such person shall, for the purpose of killing ground game employ poison*[3], and any person acting in contravention of this section shall, on summary conviction, be liable to a penalty not exceeding **level 1** on the standard scale.
[Ground Game Act 1880, s 6, as amended by the Pests Act 1954, s 15 and Sch, the Criminal Law Act 1977, s 31, and the Criminal Justice Act 1982, s 46.]

　　1. This section no longer makes it an offence to employ spring traps; for later law dealing with the open trapping of hares and rabbits and for restriction on the type of trap, see the Pests Act 1954, ss 8 and 9, title AGRICULTURE, *ante*.
　　2. Notwithstanding the provisions of s 6 of the Ground Game Act 1880 it shall not be unlawful for the occupier of any land himself, or one other person authorised by him under s 1 of that Act, to use firearms for the purpose of killing ground game thereon between the expiration of the first hour after sunset and the commencement of the last hour before sunrise if (except where he has the exclusive right) the occupier has the written authority of the other person or one of the other persons entitled to kill and take the ground game on the land; "ground game" means hares and rabbits (Wildlife and Countryside Act 1981, Sch 7).
　　3. These words in italics were repealed, except as to Greater London, by the Prevention of Damage by Rabbits Act 1939, ss 5(2), 6(3).

8–13876　7. As to non-occupier having right of killing game.　　Where a person who is not in occupation of land has the sole right of killing game thereon (with the exception of such right of killing and taking ground game as is by this Act conferred on the occupier as incident to and inseparable from his occupation), such person shall, for the purpose of any Act authorising the institution of legal proceedings by the owner of an exclusive right to game, have the same authority to institute such proceedings as if he were such exclusive owner, without prejudice nevertheless to the right of the occupier conferred by this Act.
[Ground Game Act 1880, s 7.]

8–13877　8. Interpretation clause.　　For the purposes of this Act—

　　The words "ground game" mean hares and rabbits.
[Ground Game Act 1880, s 8.]

8–13878   9. Exemption from penalties.   A person acting in accordance with this Act shall not thereby be subject to any proceedings or penalties in pursuance of any law or statute.
[Ground Game Act 1880, s 9.]

8–13879   10. Saving of existing prohibitions.   Nothing in this Act shall authorise the killing or taking of ground game on any days or seasons[1], or by any methods, prohibited by any Act of Parliament in force at the time of the passing of this Act.
[Ground Game Act 1880,s 10.]

---

1. The close days for killing hares (not rabbits) are Sunday and Christmas Day; see the Game Act 1831, s 3, ante. We are not aware of any close season for hares or rabbits, except the qualified close season in respect of moorlands, etc, under s 1(3), ante, as extended by the Ground Game (Amendment) Act 1906, s 2, post, and except for the sale of hares under the Hares Preservation Act 1892, post.

8–13880   11.   *Short title.*

Hares Preservation Act 1892
(55 & 56 Vict c 8)

8–13890   1. Short title.   This Act may be cited as the Hares Preservation Act 1892.
[Hares Preservation Act 1892, s 1.]

8–13891   2. Close time.   It shall not be lawful during the months of March, April, May, June, or July to sell or expose for sale in any part of Great Britain any hare or leveret, and any person who during the months aforesaid shall so sell or expose for sale any hare or leveret shall be liable to a penalty not exceeding **level 1** on the standard scale, including costs of conviction.
[Hares Preservation Act 1892, s 2, as amended by the Criminal Law Act 1977, s 31, and the Criminal Justice Act 1982, s 46.]

8–13892   3. Saving as to foreign hares.   This Act shall not apply to foreign hares imported into Great Britain, and there sold or exposed for sale.
[Hares Preservation Act 1892, s 3.]

8–13893   4. Prosecution of offences.   Every offence under this Act may be prosecuted in a summary manner, and every penalty imposed under this Act shall be applied in the manner directed by the Summary Jurisdiction Acts[1], and any Act amending the same.
[Hares Preservation Act 1892, s 4.]

---

1. See now the Magistrates' Courts Act 1980, in PART I: MAGISTRATES' COURTS, PROCEDURE, ante.

Ground Game (Amendment) Act 1906
(6 Edw 7 c 21)

8–13910   1. Short title and interpretation.   This Act may be cited as the Ground Game (Amendment) Act 1906; and the expressions "occupier"[1] and "ground game"[1] as used in this Act shall have the same meaning as they have in the Ground Game Act 1880.
[Ground Game (Amendment) Act 1906, s 1.]

---

1. As to "occupier", see s 1(2) of the Ground Game Act 1880, ante, and for the definition of "ground game", see s 8 of that Act, ante.

8–13911   2. Extension of right of occupiers of moorlands, etc, to kill ground game. Notwithstanding anything in section one, subsection (3), of the Ground Game Act 1880 contained, the occupier of lands to which that subsection applies shall, without prejudice to his existing rights under that Act, be entitled, between the first day of September and the tenth day of December, both inclusive, in any and every year, to exercise the right of killing and taking ground game by the said Act conferred otherwise than by the use of firearms.
[Ground Game (Amendment) Act 1906, s 2.]

8–13912   3. Agreements between occupiers and owners of moorlands, etc.   Section three of the Ground Game Act 1880 shall not apply to prevent the occupier of lands to which section one, subsection (3), of that Act applies, and the owner of such lands or other persons having a right to take and kill game thereon from making and enforcing agreements for the joint exercise, or the exercise for their joint benefit, of the right to kill and take ground game between the first day of September and the tenth day of December, both inclusive, in any or every year.
[Ground Game (Amendment) Act 1906, s 3.]

Game Laws (Amendment) Act 1960
(8 & 9 Eliz 2 c 36)

8–13930   1. *(Repealed).*

8–13931   2. Power of police to enter on land. (1) Subject to the provisions of subsection (3) of this section, a police constable who has reasonable grounds for suspecting that a person is committing an offence on any land under section one or section nine of the Night Poaching Act 1828, or under section thirty of the Game Act 1831 (which relate to persons trespassing in pursuit of game in the daytime), may enter on the land for the purpose—

    (*a*) of exercising in relation to him the powers under section 31 of the Game Act 1831 which section 31A of that Act confers on police constables; or

    (*b*) of arresting him in accordance with section 25 of the Police and Criminal Evidence Act 1984.

(2) In this section, as well as in the foregoing section, the word "land" includes land belonging to Her Majesty in right of the Crown or of the Duchy of Lancaster or in Her private capacity, and land belonging to the Duchy of Cornwall, and land belonging to a Government department or held in trust for Her Majesty for the purposes of a Government department, and, subject to subsection (3) of this section, this section shall be binding on the Crown.

(3) The power of entry conferred by subsection (1) of this section shall not be exercisable in relation to land occupied by or under the management of—

    (*a*) the Admiralty, the Secretary of State for War, or the Secretary of State for Air, or

    (*b*) the Minister of Aviation, or

    (*c*) the United Kingdom Atomic Energy Authority, or

    (*d*) the service authorities of a visiting force within the meaning of any of the provisions of Part I of the Visiting Forces Act 1952; or

    (*e*) any headquarters or organisation designated for the purposes of the International Headquarters and Defence Organisations Act 1964.

[Game Laws (Amendment) Act 1960, s 2, as amended by SI 1965/1536, the Wild Creatures and Forest Laws Act 1971, s 1, Sch, and the Police and Criminal Evidence Act 1984, Sch 6.]

8–13932   3. Amendment of Poaching Prevention Act 1862. (1)–(2) *Amendment of the Poaching Prevention Act 1862.*

(3) Where a person is convicted under the said section two the court convicting him may, if it thinks fit, direct that any game, gun or other article duly seized under that section which was in his possession or which was being carried by him in any cart or other conveyance shall (whether or not the offence of which he was convicted concerned that game, gun or other article) be forfeited; and in the said section the words from "and shall forfeit such game" to the end of the section shall cease to have effect.

(4) A person who, by the written direction of a justice of the peace, sells any game seized under the said section two shall not be liable to any penalty for the sale; and if no conviction takes place under that section, the game or other thing seized, or the value thereof, shall be restored to the person from whom it was seized.

(5) In this section the word "game" has the same meaning as in the Poaching Prevention Act 1862.

[Game Laws (Amendment) Act 1960, s 3.]

---

1. See this title, ante.

8–13933   4. Further provisions as to seizure and forfeiture. (1) Where a person is apprehended, in accordance with section 25 of the Police and Criminal Evidence Act 1984[1], for an offence under section one or section nine of the Night Poaching Act 1828[2], or under section thirty of the Game Act 1831[2], a police constable by or in whose presence he was apprehended may search him and may seize and detain any game or rabbits, or any gun, part of a gun or cartridges or other ammunition, or any nets, traps, snares or other devices of a kind used for the killing or taking of game or rabbits, which are found in his possession.

(2) Where the person so apprehended is convicted of an offence under either of the said Acts the court by or before whom he is convicted may, if it thinks fit, direct that any game or rabbit, or any gun or other article, duly seized under this section which was in his possession shall (whether or not the offence of which he was convicted concerned that game, rabbit, gun or other article) be forfeited[3].

(3) The provisions of this section shall be without prejudice to any other power which a police constable has to search a person whom he has arrested, and to detain things found in his possession, and shall also be without prejudice to the provisions of section thirty-six of the Game Act 1831[2] (which authorises gamekeepers and others to take game found in the possession of trespassers).

(4) Subsection (4) of the last foregoing section shall apply in relation to things seized under this section.

(5) For the purposes of this section the word "game" shall be deemed to include hares, pheasants, partridges, grouse, heath or moor game, black game, bustards, woodcocks and snipes.
[Game Laws (Amendment) Act 1960, s 4 as amended by the Police and Criminal Evidence Act 1984, Sch 6.]

---

1. See PART I: MAGISTRATES' COURTS, PROCEDURE, *ante.*
2. See this title, *ante.*
3. For disposal of things forfeited, see the Magistrates' Courts Act 1980, s 140, in PART I: MAGISTRATES' COURTS, PROCEDURE, *ante.*

8–13933A   4A. Forfeiture of vehicles.   (1) Where a person is convicted of an offence under section thirty of the Game Act 1831 as one of five or more persons liable under that section and the court is satisfied that any vehicle belonging to him or in his possession or under his control at the relevant time has been used for the purpose of committing or facilitating the commission of the offence, the court may make an order for forfeiture under this subsection in respect of that vehicle.

(2) The court may make an order under subsection (1) above whether or not it also deals with the offender in respect of the offence in any other way and without regard to any restriction on forfeiture in any enactment.

(3) Facilitating the commission of the offence shall be taken for the purposes of subsection (1) above to include the taking of any steps after it had been committed for the purpose of—

(*a*) avoiding apprehension or detection; or

(*b*) removing from the land any person or property connected with the offence.

(4) An order under subsection (1) above shall operate to deprive the offender of his rights, if any, in the vehicle to which it relates, and the vehicle shall (if not already in their possession) be taken into the possession of the police.

(5) Where any vehicle has been forfeited under subsection (1) above, a magistrates' court may, on application by a claimant of the vehicle, other than the offender from whom it was forfeited under subsection (1) above, make an order for delivery of the vehicle to the applicant if it appears to the court that he is the owner of the vehicle.

(6) No application shall be made under subsection (5) above by any claimant of the vehicle after the expiration of six months from the date on which an order in respect of the vehicle was made under subsection (1) above.

(7) No such application shall succeed unless the claimant satisfies the court either that he had not consented to the offender having possession of the vehicle or that he did not know, and had no reason to suspect, that the vehicle was likely to be used for a purpose mentioned in subsection (1) above.

(8) An order under subsection (5) above shall not affect the right of any person to take, within the period of six months from the date of an order under subsection (5) above, proceedings for the recovery of the vehicle from the person in possession of it in pursuance of the order, but on the expiration of that period the right shall cease.

(9) The Secretary of State may make regulations for the disposal of vehicles, and for the application of the proceeds of sale of vehicles, forfeited under subsection (1) above where no application by a claimant of the property under subsection (5) above has been made within the period specified in subsection (6) above or no such application has succeeded.

(10) The regulations may also provide for the investment of money and the audit of accounts.

(11) The power to make regulations under subsection (9) above shall be exercisable by statutory instrument which shall be subject to annulment in pursuance of a resolution of either House of Parliament.

(12) In this section, "relevant time", in relation to a person convicted of an offence such as is mentioned in subsection (1) above, means the time when the vehicle was used for the purpose of committing or facilitating the commission of the offence, or the time of the issue of a summons in respect of the offence.
[Game Laws (Amendment) Act 1960, s 4A, as inserted by the Criminal Justice and Public Order Act 1994, Sch 9.]

8–13934   6. Short title, interpretation, extent and commencement.   (1) This Act may be cited as the Game Laws (Amendment) Act 1960.

(2) References in this Act to the Night Poaching Act 1828 are to that Act as extended by the Night Poaching Act 1844 (which concerns poaching on public rights of way).

(3)–(4) *Extent; commencement.*
[Game Laws (Amendment) Act 1960, s 6.]

Deer Act 1991[1]

(1991 c 54)

Offences relating to deer

8–13950   1. Poaching of deer.   (1) Subject to subsection (3) below, if any person enters any land without the consent of the owner or occupier or other lawful authority in search or pursuit of any deer with the intention of taking, killing or injuring it, he shall be guilty of an offence[2].

(2) Subject to subsection (3) below, if any person while on any land—

(a) intentionally takes, kills or injures, or attempts to take, kill or injure, any deer,

(b) searches for or pursues any deer with the intention of taking, killing or injuring it, or

(c) removes the carcase of any deer,

without the consent of the owner or occupier of the land or other lawful authority, he shall be guilty of an offence[2].

(3) A person shall not be guilty of an offence under subsection (1) or subsection (2) above by reason of anything done in the belief that—

(a) he would have the consent of the owner or occupier of the land if the owner or occupier knew of his doing it and the circumstances of it; or

(b) he has other lawful authority to do it.

(4) If any authorised person suspects with reasonable cause that any person is committing or has committed an offence under subsection (1) or subsection (2) above on any land, he may require that person—

(a) to give his full name and address; and

(b) to quit that land forthwith;

and any person who fails to comply with a requirement under this subsection shall be guilty of an offence[2].

(5) In subsection (4) above "authorised person", in relation to any land, means the owner or occupier of the land or any person authorised by the owner or occupier, and includes any person having the right to take or kill deer on the land.

[Deer Act 1991, s 1.]

---

1. This Act consolidates enactments relating to deer and, in particular, has repealed the Deer Acts 1963, 1980 and 1987. The Act came into force on 25 October 1991.

2. For penalty, see s 9, post, and for powers of forfeiture and disqualification, see s 13, post.

8–13951   **2. Taking or killing of certain deer in close season.**   (1) Subject to sections 6 to 8 below and to subsection (3) below, if any person takes or intentionally kills any deer of a species and description mentioned in Schedule 1 to this Act during the prescribed close season, he shall be guilty of an offence[1].

(2) The prescribed close season, in relation to a particular deer, is the close season prescribed by Schedule 1 to this Act in relation to deer of that species and description.

(3) Where—

(a) any person, by way of business, keeps deer on land enclosed by a deer-proof barrier for the production of meat or other foodstuffs or skins or other by-products, or as breeding stock, and

(b) those deer are conspicuously marked in such a way as to identify them as deer kept by that person as mentioned in the preceding paragraph,

the killing of any of those deer by that person, or by any servant or agent of that person authorised by him for the purpose, shall not constitute an offence under this section.

(4) The Secretary of State[2] may by order amend Schedule 1 to this Act by the addition of any species not mentioned in that Schedule and of a close season for any description of deer of that species, or by varying or deleting any such addition.

(5) Before making any order under subsection (4) above the Secretary of State shall consult any organisations that appear to him to represent persons likely to be interested in or affected by the order.

[Deer Act 1991, s 2.]

---

1. For penalty, see s 9, post, and for forfeiture, see s 13, post.

2. Functions of the Minister, so far as exercisable in relation to Wales, have been transferred to the National Assembly for Wales, by the National Assembly for Wales (Transfer of Functions) Order 1999, SI 1999/672, art 2, Sch 1.

8–13952   **3. Taking or killing of deer at night.**   Subject to sections 6 and 8 below, if any person takes or intentionally kills any deer between the expiry of the first hour after sunset[1] and the beginning of the last hour before sunrise, he shall be guilty of an offence[2].

[Deer Act 1991, s 3.]

---

1. "Sunset" and "sunrise" are not expressions mentioned in what is now the Summer Time Act 1972, but a reference to a particular fact in the locality in which the offence is alleged to have been committed (*Gordon v Cann* (1899) 63 JP 324). The court should require evidence of the hours of sunset and sunrise where the time is in question: see 62 JP Jo 484, 80 JP Jo 110. But it would appear that a court can take judicial notice of such times by perusal of an almanac (cf *Walker v Stretton* (1896) 60 JP 313), although in borderline cases the inference which can be drawn from such perusal may be insufficient to satisfy the court. See commentary to *R v Crush* [1978] Crim LR 357.

2. For penalty, see s 9, post, and for powers of forfeiture, see s 13, post.

8–13953   **4. Use of prohibited weapons and other articles.**   (1) Subject to sections 6 and 8 below, if any person—

(*a*)   sets in position any article which is a trap, snare, or poisoned or stupefying bait and is of such a nature and so placed as to be calculated to cause bodily injury to any deer coming in contact with it, or

(*b*)   uses for the purpose of taking or killing any deer any trap, snare or poisoned or stupefying bait, or any net,

he shall be guilty of an offence[1].

(2) Subject to sections 6 to 8 below, if any person uses for the purpose of taking or killing or injuring any deer—

(*a*)   any firearm or ammunition mentioned in Schedule 2 to this Act,

(*b*)   any arrow, spear or similar missile, or

(*c*)   any missile, whether discharged from a firearm or otherwise, carrying or containing any poison, stupefying drug or muscle-relaxing agent,

he shall be guilty of an offence[1].

(3) The Secretary of State may by order amend Schedule 2 to this Act by adding any firearm or ammunition or by altering the description of, or deleting, any firearm or ammunition for the time being mentioned in that Schedule.

(4) Subject to subsection (5) below, if any person—

(*a*)   discharges any firearm, or projects any missile, from any mechanically propelled vehicle at any deer, or

(*b*)   uses any mechanically propelled vehicle for the purpose of driving deer,

he shall be guilty of an offence[1].

(5) An act which, apart from this subsection, would constitute an offence under subsection (4) above shall not constitute such an offence if it is done—

(*a*)   by, or with the written authority of, the occupier of any enclosed land where deer are usually kept; and

(*b*)   in relation to any deer on that land.

[Deer Act 1991, s 4.]

---

1. For penalty, se s 9, post, and for powers of forfeiture, see s 13, post.

8–13954   **5. Attempts to commit certain offences, etc.**   (1) Any person who attempts[1] to commit an offence under any of sections 2 to 4 above shall be guilty of an offence[2].

(2) If any person, for the purpose of committing an offence under any of sections 2 to 4 above, has in his possession—

(*a*)   any article the use of which is prohibited by section 4(1)(*b*), section 4(2)(*b*) or section 4(2)(*c*) above, or

(*b*)   any firearm or ammunition,

he shall be guilty of an offence[2].

[Deer Act 1991, s 5.]

---

1. See para **1–303 Criminal Responsibility—Attempts**, and see also the Criminal Attempts Act 1981, in Part I: Magistrates' Courts, Procedure, ante.

2. For penalty, see s 9, post, and for powers of forfeiture, see s 13, post.

8–13955   **6. General exceptions to certain provisions of this Act.**   (1) Nothing in section 2 or section 3 above shall make unlawful anything done in pursuance of a requirement by the Minister of Agriculture, Fisheries and Food under section 98 of the Agriculture Act 1947.

(2) A person shall not be guilty of an offence under section 2 or section 3 above by reason of any act done for the purpose of preventing the suffering of an injured or diseased deer.

(3) A person shall not be guilty of an offence under section 4(1)(*a*) or section 4(1)(*b*) above by reason of setting in position, or using, any trap or net for the purpose of preventing the suffering of an injured or diseased deer.

(4) A person shall not be guilty of an offence under section 4(2)(*a*) above by reason of the use of any smooth-bore gun for the purpose of killing any deer if he shows that the deer had been so seriously injured otherwise than by his unlawful act, or was in such a condition, that to kill it was an act of mercy.

(5) A person shall not be guilty of an offence under section 4(2)(*a*) above by reason of the use as a slaughtering instrument, for the purpose of killing any deer, of a smooth-bore gun which—

(*a*) is of not less gauge than 12 bore;
(*b*) has a barrel less than 24 inches (609.6 millimetres) in length; and
(*c*) is loaded with a cartridge purporting to contain shot none of which is less than .203 inches (5.16 millimetres) in diameter (that is to say, size AAA or any larger size).

[Deer Act 1991, s 6.]

8–13956 7. Exceptions for occupiers etc of land where deer are. (1) Subject to subsection (3) below, a person to whom this section applies shall not be guilty of an offence under section 2 above by reason of—

(*a*) the taking or killing of any deer by means of shooting, or
(*b*) the injuring of any deer by means of shooting in an attempt to take or kill it,

on any cultivated land, pasture or enclosed woodland.

(2) Subject to subsection (3) below, a person to whom this section applies shall not be guilty of an offence under section 4(2)(*a*) above by reason of the use, for the purpose of taking or killing any deer on any land, of any smooth-bore gun of not less gauge than 12 bore which is loaded with—

(*a*) a cartridge containing a single non-spherical projectile weighing not less than 22.68 grammes (350 grains); or
(*b*) a cartridge purporting to contain shot each of which is .203 inches (5.16 millimetres) in diameter (that is to say, size AAA).

(3) A person to whom this section applies shall not be entitled to rely on the defence provided by subsection (1) or subsection (2) above as respects anything done in relation to any deer on any land unless he shows that—

(*a*) he had reasonable grounds for believing that deer of the same species were causing, or had caused, damage to crops, vegetables, fruit, growing timber or any other form of property on the land;
(*b*) it was likely that further damage would be so caused and any such damage was likely to be serious; and
(*c*) his action was necessary for the purpose of preventing any such damage.

(4) The persons to whom this section applies are—

(*a*) the occupier of the land on which the action is taken;
(*b*) any member of the occupier's household normally resident on the occupier's land, acting with the written authority of the occupier;
(*c*) any person in the ordinary service of the occupier on the occupier's land, acting with the written authority of the occupier; and
(*d*) any person having the right to take or kill deer on the land on which the action is taken or any person acting with the written authority of a person having that right.

(5) The Secretary of State and the agriculture Minister acting jointly may by order, either generally or in relation to any area or any species and description of deer specified in the order—

(*a*) repeal subsection (2) above or amend it by adding any firearm or ammunition or by altering the description of, or deleting, any firearm or ammunition for the time being mentioned in it;
(*b*) amend subsection (3) above by adding any further conditions which must be satisfied or by varying or deleting any conditions so added.

(6) Before making any order under subsection (5) above the Secretary of State[1] and the agriculture Minister shall consult organisations that appear to them to represent persons likely to be interested in or affected by the order.

(7) In this section "agriculture Minister" means—

(*a*) in relation to England, the Secretary of State; and
(*b*) in relation to Wales, the Secretary of State.

[Deer Act 1991, s 7, as amended by SI 2002/794.]

---

1. Functions of the Minister, so far as exercisable in relation to Wales, have been transferred to the National Assembly for Wales, by the National Assembly for Wales (Transfer of Functions) Order 1999, SI 1999/672, art 2, Sch 1.

8–13957 8. Exceptions for persons licensed by the Nature Conservancy Council for England or the Countryside Council for Wales. (1) A licence may be granted to any person by the English Nature exempting that person, and any persons acting with his written authority, from sections 2 to 4 above in respect of any of the acts specified in subsection (3) below which are done in England for the purpose of removing deer from one area to another or of taking deer alive for scientific or educational purposes.

(2) A licence may be granted to any person by the Countryside Council for Wales exempting that person, and any persons acting with his written authority, from sections 2 to 4 above in respect of any of the acts specified in subsection (3) below which are done in Wales for the purpose of removing deer from one area to another or of taking deer alive for scientific or educational purposes.

(3) The acts referred to in subsections (1) and (2) above are—

(a) using any net, trap, stupefying drug or muscle-relaxing agent of a type authorised by the licence;

(b) using any missile carrying or containing such stupefying drug or muscle-relaxing agent and discharging any such missile by any means authorised by the licence.

(4) A licence granted under subsection (1) above may be revoked at any time by the English Nature and a licence granted under subsection (2) above may be revoked at any time by the Countryside Council for Wales; and a licence granted under either of those subsections may be granted subject to conditions.

(5) Without prejudice to any other liability to a penalty which he may have incurred under this or any other Act, any person who contravenes or fails to comply with any condition imposed on the grant of a licence under subsection (1) or subsection (2) above shall be guilty of an offence[1].

[Deer Act 1991, s 8, as amended by the Countryside and Rights of Way Act 2000, Sch 8.]

---

1. For penalty, see s 9, post.

8–13958 9. Penalties for offences relating to deer. (1) Subject to subsection (2) below, a person guilty of an offence under any of the preceding provisions of this Act shall be liable on summary conviction to a fine not exceeding **level 4** on the standard scale or to imprisonment for a term not exceeding **three months*** or to both.

(2) Where an offence under any of the preceding provisions of this Act was committed in respect of more than one deer the maximum fine which may be imposed under subsection (1) above shall be determined as if the person convicted had been convicted of a separate offence in respect of each deer.

[Deer Act 1991, s 9.]

***"51 weeks"** substituted by the Criminal Justice Act 2003, Sch 26, from a date to be appointed.

Offences relating to venison etc

8–13959 10. Offences relating to sale and purchase etc of venison. (1) If any person who is not a licensed game dealer—

(a) at any time during the prohibited period sells or offers or exposes for sale, or has in his possession for sale, any venison to which this paragraph applies, or

(b) at any time sells or offers or exposes for sale any venison otherwise than to a licensed game dealer,

he shall be guilty of an offence[1] and liable on summary conviction to a fine not exceeding **level 3** on the standard scale.

(2) Paragraph (a) of subsection (1) above applies to any venison which comes from a deer of a species and description in relation to which a close season is prescribed by Schedule 1 to this Act; and the prohibited period, in relation to any such venison, is the period beginning with the expiry of the tenth day, and ending with the expiry of the last day, of that close season.

(3) If any person—

(a) sells or offers or exposes for sale, or has in his possession for sale, or

(b) purchases or offers to purchase or receives,

any venison which comes from a deer to which this subsection applies, he shall be guilty of an offence[1] and liable on summary conviction to a fine not exceeding **level 4** on the standard scale or to imprisonment for a term not exceeding **three months** or to both.

(4) Subsection (3) above applies to any deer—

(a) which has been taken or killed in circumstances which constitute an offence under any of the preceding provisions of this Act; and

(b) which the person concerned knows or has reason to believe has been so taken or killed.

(5) In this section—

"licensed game dealer" means a person licensed to deal in game under the Game Act 1831 and the Game Licences Act 1860, and includes a servant of such a person; and

"sale" includes barter and exchange, and "sell" and "purchase" shall be construed accordingly.

[Deer Act 1991, s 10.]

---

1. For powers of forfeiture and disqualification, see s 13, post.

8–13960   11. Licensed game dealers to keep records.   (1) Every licensed game dealer who sells or offers or exposes for sale, or has in his possession for sale, any venison shall—

(a)   in accordance with the provisions of this section keep or cause to be kept a book containing records (in this section referred to as a "record book"); and

(b)   subject to subsection (3) below, enter or cause to be entered in his record book forthwith full particulars of all his purchases and receipts of venison;

and, subject to subsection (2) below, those records shall be in the form set out in Schedule 3[1] to this Act or a form substantially to the same effect.

(2) The Secretary of State may by order vary the form in which records are required to be kept under this section.

(3) Where a licensed game dealer has purchased or received venison from another licensed game dealer, or from a venison dealer licensed under section 33 of the Deer (Scotland) Act 1996, he need record in his record book only—

(a)   that the venison was so purchased or received;

(b)   the name and address of the other licensed game dealer or the venison dealer so licensed;

(c)   the date when the venison was so purchased or received; and

(d)   the total weight of the venison.

(4) Any authorised officer, on producing, if so required, his written authority, and any constable, may inspect—

(a)   the record book of a licensed game dealer,

(b)   any venison in the licensed game dealer's possession or under his control, or on premises or in vehicles under his control, and

(c)   any invoices, consignment notes, receipts and other documents which relate to entries in the record book (including, where the originals are not available, copies),

and may take copies of, or extracts from, the record book and any such documents.

(5) A record book shall be kept until the end of the period of three years beginning with the day on which the last entry was made in the book, and any such documents as are mentioned in subsection (4)(c) above shall be kept until the end of the period of three years beginning with the date of the entry to which they relate.

(6) Any licensed game dealer who, without reasonable excuse, fails to comply with the provisions of this section shall be guilty of an offence[2].

(7) If any person—

(a)   intentionally obstructs any authorised officer or constable making an inspection under this section, or

(b)   knowingly or recklessly makes or causes to be made in a record book any entry which is false or misleading in a material particular,

he shall be guilty of an offence[2].

(8) A person guilty of an offence[2] under this section shall be liable on summary conviction to a fine not exceeding **level 2** on the standard scale.

(9) In this section—

"authorised officer" means any officer of the council of a Welsh county or county borough, of a district or London borough, or of the Common Council of the City of London, who is authorised by them in writing to exercise the powers conferred by this section;

"licensed game dealer" has the same meaning as in section 10 above; and

"sale" has the same meaning as in that section, and "sell" and "purchase" shall be construed accordingly.

[Deer Act 1991, s 11 amended by the Local Government (Wales) Act 1994, Sch 16 and the Deer (Scotland) Act 1996, Sch 4.]

---

1. The Form set out in Sch 3 to the Act is not printed in this work.
2. For powers of forfeiture and disqualification, see s 13, post.

Enforcement etc

8–13961   12. Power of search, arrest and seizure.   (1) If a constable suspects with reasonable cause that any person is committing or has committed an offence under this Act, the constable may without warrant—

(a)   stop and search that person if the constable suspects with reasonable cause that evidence of the commission of the offence is to be found on that person;

(b)   search or examine any vehicle, animal, weapon or other thing which that person may then be using if the constable suspects with reasonable cause that evidence of the commission of the offence is to be found on that vehicle, animal, weapon or other thing;

(c)   seize and detain for the purposes of proceedings under this Act anything which is evidence of the commission of the offence and any deer, venison, vehicle, animal, weapon or other thing which is liable to be forfeited under section 13 below.

(2) For the purposes of—

(a) exercising the powers conferred by subsection (1) above, or

(b) arresting a person, in accordance with section 25 of the Police and Criminal Evidence Act 1984 (general arrest conditions), for an offence under this Act,

a constable may enter any land other than a dwelling-house.

(3) A constable may sell any deer or venison seized under this section and the net proceeds of the sale shall be liable to be detained and forfeited in the same manner as the deer or venison sold; but he shall not be subject to any liability on account of his neglect or failure to exercise the powers conferred on him by this subsection.

[Deer Act 1991, s 12.]

8–13962 13. Forfeitures and disqualifications. (1) The court by which a person is convicted of any offence under this Act may order the forfeiture of—

(a) any deer or venison in respect of which the offence was committed or which was found in that person's possession;

(b) any vehicle, animal, weapon or other thing which was used to commit the offence or which was capable of being used to take, kill or injure deer and was found in his possession.

(2) Where the offence of which the person is convicted is an offence under any of sections 1, 10 and 11 above or under subsection (3)(c) below, the court (without prejudice to its powers under subsection (1) above)—

(a) may disqualify that person for holding or obtaining a licence to deal in game for such period as the court thinks fit; and

(b) may cancel any firearm or shotgun certificate held by him.

(3) Where the court cancels a firearm or shotgun certificate under subsection (2)(b) above—

(a) the court shall cause notice in writing of that fact to be sent to the chief officer of police by whom the certificate was granted; and

(b) the chief officer of police shall by notice in writing require the holder of the certificate to surrender it; and

(c) if the holder fails to surrender the certificate within twenty-one days from the date of that requirement, he shall be guilty of an offence and liable on summary conviction to a fine not exceeding **level 2** on the standard scale.

[Deer Act 1991, s 13.]

8–13963 14. Offences by bodies corporate. (1) Where an offence under any of sections 1, 10 and 11 above which has been committed by a body corporate is proved to have been committed with the consent or connivance of, or to be attributable to any neglect on the part of, any director, manager, secretary or other similar officer of the body corporate or any person who was purporting to act in any such capacity, he as well as the body corporate shall be guilty of that offence and be liable to be proceeded against and punished accordingly.

(2) Where the affairs of a body corporate are managed by its members, subsection (1) above shall apply in relation to the acts and defaults of a member in connection with his functions of management as if he were a director of the body corporate.

[Deer Act 1991, s 14.]

Supplementary

8–13964 15. Orders. (1) Any power to make orders under this Act shall be exercisable by statutory instrument.

(2) A statutory instrument containing an order made under any of sections 2(4), 4(3) and 11(2) above shall be subject to annulment in pursuance of a resolution of either House of Parliament.

(3) No order shall be made under section 7(5) above unless a draft of the order has been laid before and approved by a resolution of each House of Parliament.

[Deer Act 1991, s 15.]

8–13965 16. Interpretation. In this Act, unless the context otherwise requires—

"ammunition" and "firearm" have the same meaning as in the Firearms Act 1968[1];

"deer" means deer of any species and includes the carcase of any deer or any part thereof;

"vehicle" includes an aircraft, hovercraft or boat; and

"venison" includes imported venison and means—

(a) any carcase of a deer, or

(b) any edible part of the carcase of a deer,

which has not been cooked or canned.

[Deer Act 1991, s 16.]

---

1. See title Firearms, ante.

8–13966   17. Transitional provisions, consequential amendment and repeals. (1) Anything done under any provision of the Deer Act 1963 or the Deer Act 1980 shall have effect as if it had been done under the corresponding provision of this Act.

(2) Without prejudice to the generality of subsection (1) above, a licence granted by the Nature Conservancy Council under section 11 of the Deer Act 1963 which, by virtue of paragraph 8 of Schedule 11 to the Environmental Protection Act 1990, has effect as if granted by the Nature Conservancy Council for England or the Countryside Council for Wales, shall be treated as if it had been granted under subsection (1) or, as the case may be, subsection (2) of section 8 above.

(3) Where a licence granted under section 11 of the Deer Act 1963 contains a reference to an enactment repealed by this Act, the licence shall be construed as referring, or, as the context requires, as including a reference to, the corresponding provision of this Act.

(4) Where a period of time specified in an enactment repealed by this Act is current at the commencement of this Act, this Act shall have effect as if the corresponding provision thereof had been in force when that period began to run.

(5) (*Repealed*).

(6) *Repeals.*

[Deer Act 1991, s 17 amended by the Deer (Scotland) Act 1996, Sch 5.]

8–13967   18. Short title, extent and commencement. (1) This Act may be cited as the Deer Act 1991.

(2) With the exception of section 17(5) above, which extends to Scotland only, this Act extends to England and Wales only.

(3) This Act shall come into force[1] at the end of the period of three months beginning with the day on which it is passed.

[Deer Act 1991, s 18.]

---

1. This Act came into force on 25th October 1991.

8–13968

SCHEDULES

Section 2

SCHEDULE 1
CLOSE SEASONS

RED DEER [Cervus elaphus]

Stags	1st May to 31st July inclusive
Hinds	1st March to 31st October inclusive

FALLOW DEER [Dama dama]

Buck	1st May to 31st July inclusive
Doe	1st March to 31st October inclusive

ROE DEER [Capreolus capreolus]

Buck	1st November to 31st March inclusive
Doe	1st March to 31st October inclusive

SIKA DEER [Cervus nippon]

Stags	1st May to 31st July inclusive
Hinds	1st March to 31st October inclusive.

8–13969

Section 4

SCHEDULE 2
PROHIBITED FIREARMS AND AMMUNITION

Firearms

1. Any smooth-bore gun.

2. Any rifle having a calibre of less than .240 inches or a muzzle energy of less than 2,305 joules (1,700 foot pounds).

3. Any air gun, air rifle or air pistol.

Ammunition

4. Any cartridge for use in a smooth-bore gun.

5. Any bullet for use in a rifle other than a soft-nosed or hollow-nosed bullet.

8–13970

Section 11

SCHEDULE 3
FORM OF RECORD TO BE KEPT BY LICENSED GAME DEALERS

HEALTH AND SAFETY

8–13980 This title contains the following statutes—

The following statutory instruments are also included—

8–13981 European Communities Act 1972: regulations. Within the scope of the title Health and Safety would logically fall the subject matter of a number of regulations made under the very wide enabling power provided in section 2(2) of the European Communities Act 1972. Where such regulations create offences they are noted below in chronological order. See also regulations noted to section 15 of the Health and Safety at Work etc Act 1974.

Falling Object Protective Structures for Construction Plant (EEC Requirements) Regulations 1988, SI 1988/362;

Roll-over Protective Structures for Construction Plant (EEC Requirements) Regulations 1988, SI 1988/363;

Self-Propelled Industrial Trucks (EEC Requirements) Regulations 1988, SI 1988/1736 amended by SI 1989/1035;

Electrical Equipment for Explosive Atmospheres (Certification) Regulations 1990, SI 1990/13 amended by SI 1990/2377, SI 1991/2826, SI 1995/1186, (until 1 July 2003) SI 1998, 1998/1469 and SI 1999/2550;

Simple Pressure Vessels (Safety) Regulations 1991, SI 1991/2749 amended by SI 2003/1400;

Electrically, Hydraulically and Oil Electrically Operated Lifts (Components) (EEC Requirements) Regulations 1991, SI 1991/2748;

Placing on the Market and Supervision of Transfers of Explosives Regulations 1993, SI 1993/2714;

Batteries and Accumulators (Containing Dangerous Substances) Regulations 1994, SI 1994/232 amended by SI 2000/3097 and SI 2001/2551;

Equipment and Protective Systems Intended for Use in Potentially Explosive Atmospheres Regulations 1996, SI 1996/192 amended by SI 2001/3766 and SI 2005/830;
Lifts Regulations 1997, SI 1997/831 amended by SI 2004/693 and SI 2005/831;
Working Time Regulations 1998, SI 1998/1833 amended by SI 1999/3242;
Pressure Equipment Regulations 1999, SI 1999/2001 amended by SI 2002/1267 and SI 2004/693;
Good Laboratory Practice Regulations 1999, SI 1999/3106 amended by SI 2004/994 and SI 2005/2114;
Ionising Radiations Regulations 1999, SI 1999/3232 amended by SI 2001/2975 and SI 2002/2099;
Biocidal Products Regulations 2001, SI 2001/880 amended by SI 2003/429 and SI 2005/2451 and 2759;
Personal Protective Equipment Regulations 2002, SI 2002/1144 amended by SI 2004/693;
Export and Import of Dangerous Chemicals Regulations 2005, SI 2005/928.

Explosives Act 1875[1]

(38 & 39 Vict c 17)

Preliminary

8–14000   1. Short title.   This Act may be cited as "The Explosives Act 1875."[2]
[Explosives Act 1875, s 1.]

1. The following Orders in Council and Orders of the Secretary of State have been made under this Act—

(A) ORDERS IN COUNCIL

No 13	Exemption of small arm nitro-compounds from the restrictions imposed in O in C Nos 6A and 12 (24 September 1886).
No 26	Picric acid, picrates and mixtures of picric acid with other substances, when deemed explosives (28 June 1926, SR & O 1926/823; amended by SI 1984/510).
No 30	Prohibiting the manufacture, importation, keeping, conveyance or sale of acetylene when an explosive as defined by the Order (2 February 1937, SR & O 1937/54, as amended by SR & O 1947/805, SI 1974/1885, SI 1978/1723, SI 1984/510, SI 2001/1426 and SI 2005/1082).

(B) ORDERS OF THE SECRETARY OF STATE

No 5	Exempting acetylene in admixture with oil-gas (28 March 1898, SR & O 1898/248; amended by SI 1984/510).
No 5A	Exempting acetylene generated by special process (29 September 1905, SR & O 1905/1128; amended by SI 1984/510).
No 9	Exempting compressed acetylene contained in a porous substance (23 June 1919, SR & O 1919/809; amended by SI 1984/510 and SI 2005/1732).

Conveyance in Harbours of Military Explosives Regulations 1977, SI 1977/890 as amended by SI 1983/1140.
Conveyance by Rail of Military Explosives Regulations 1977, SI 1977/889, as amended by SI 1983/1140.
2. The Explosives Act 1875 (Exemptions) Regulations 1979, SI 1979/1378, provide for the Health and Safety Executive to grant exemptions from any requirement or prohibition imposed by any provision of Pt I (except ss 30–32) or Pt II of this Act, or by any Regulation, Order in Council or Order made under such provisions or under s 83 of the Act.

8–14001   3. Substances to which this Act applies.   This Act shall apply to gunpowder and other explosives as defined by this section.
The term "explosive" in this Act—

(1) Means gunpowder, nitro-glycerine, dynamite, gun-cotton, blasting powders, fulminate of mercury or of other metals, coloured fires, and every other substance[1], whether similar to those above mentioned or not, used or manufactured with a view to produce a practical effect by explosion or a pyrotechnic effect; and

(2) Includes fog-signals, fireworks, fuzes, rockets, percussion caps, detonators, cartridges, ammunition of all descriptions, and every adaptation of preparation of an explosive as above defined.
[Explosives Act 1875, s 3.]

1. This may include a petrol bomb; see *R v Bouch* [1983] QB 246, [1982] 3 All ER 918, 76 Cr App Rep 11, CA.

PART I[1]
LAW RELATING TO GUNPOWDER

General Law as to Manufacture and Keeping of Gunpowder

8–14002
4–22   *Repealed.*

Supplemental Provisions

8–14016   23. Precautions against fire or explosion to be taken by occupier.   The occupier of every factory, magazine, store, and registered premises for gunpowder, and every person employed in or about the same, shall take all due precaution for the prevention of accidents by fire or explosion in the same, and for preventing unauthorised persons having access to the factory, magazine, or store, or to the gunpowder therein or in the registered premises, and shall abstain from any act whatever which tends to cause fire or explosion and is not reasonably necessary for the purpose of the work in such factory, magazine store, or premises.

Any breach (by any act or default) of this section in any factory, magazine, store, or registered premises shall be deemed to be a breach of the general rules applying thereto[1].
[Explosives Act 1875, s 23.]

---

1. For penalty, see the Health and Safety at Work etc Act 1974, s 33, this title, post.

8–14017   28. *Repealed.*

Sale of Gunpowder

8–14018   30. Restriction on sale of gunpowder in highways, etc.   Gunpowder shall not be hawked[1], sold, or exposed[2] for sale upon any highway, street, public thoroughfare, or public place.
If any gunpowder is hawked, sold, or exposed for sale in contravention of this section—

   (1)   The person hawking, selling, or exposing for sale the same, shall be liable[3] to a penalty not exceeding **the statutory maximum**; and
   (2)   All or any part of the gunpowder which is so hawked or exposed for sale, or is found in the possession of any person convicted under this section, may be forfeited.★

[Explosives Act 1875, s 30, as amended by the Criminal Law Act 1977, s 28.]

★Repealed by the Fireworks Act 2003, Schedule, from a date to be appointed.
1. As to the meaning of the term "hawk", see *Philpott v Allright* (1906) 70 JP 287.
2. Cf *Keating v Horwood* (1926) 90 JP 141.
3. This offence is triable either way by operation of s 91, post. For procedure, see the Magistrates' Courts Act 1980, ss 17A–21, in PART I: MAGISTRATES' COURTS, PROCEDURE, ante.

8–14019   31. Penalty for sale of gunpowder to children.   Gunpowder shall not be sold to any person apparently under the age of sixteen years; and any person selling gunpowder in contravention of this section shall be guilty of an offence and liable on summary conviction to a fine not exceeding **level 5** on the standard scale.★
[Explosives Act 1875, s 31, as amended by the Explosives (Age of Purchase, etc) Act 1976, s 1 and the Consumer Protection Act 1987, Sch 4.]

★Repealed by the Fireworks Act 2003, Schedule, from a date to be appointed.

8–14030   32. Sale of gunpowder to be in closed packages labelled[1].   All gunpowder exceeding 500 grams in weight, when publicly exposed for sale or sold, shall be in a substantial case, bag, canister, or other receptacle made and closed so as to prevent the gunpowder from escaping, and (except when the same is sold to any person employed by or on the property occupied by the vendor for immediate use in the service of the vendor or on such property,) the outermost receptacle containing such gunpowder shall have affixed the word "gunpowder" in conspicuous characters by means of a brand or securely attached label, or other mark.

If any gunpowder is sold or exposed for sale in contravention of this section—

1.   The person selling or exposing for sale the same shall be liable[2] on summary conviction to a penalty not exceeding **the statutory maximum**; and
2.   All or any part of the gunpowder so exposed for sale may be forfeited.★

[Explosives Act 1875, s 32, as amended by the Criminal Law Act 1977, s 28, and SI 1984/510.]

★Repealed by the Fireworks Act 2003, Schedule, from a date to be appointed.
1. These provisions apply also to the sale of those explosives (see note 1 to s 21, ante), for the keeping of which a person is not required to take out a licence or to register his premises, subject to qualification with respect to s 32, that for the words "exceeding one pound in weight" must be substituted the words "containing more than five pounds of gunpowder or any other explosive", and in the case of percussion caps and safety fuses it is not necessary to affix the word "explosive" on the outermost receptacle containing the same (Order in Council, No 9). See also s 39, applying the provisions as to gunpowder to every other explosive. By s 104 and the Orders in Council made thereunder, the word "explosive" includes fireworks, and therefore by s 39 the provisions of Pt I (including this section) apply to fireworks.
2. This offence is triable either way by operation of s 91, post. For procedure, see the Magistrates' Courts Act 1980, ss 17A–21, in PART I: MAGISTRATES' COURTS, PROCEDURE, ante.

Conveyance of Gunpowder

8–14031   33. General rules as to packing of gunpowder for conveyance.   *Repealed.*

PART II[1]
LAW RELATING TO OTHER EXPLOSIVES

Application of Part I to other Explosives

8–14033   39. Part I relating to gunpowder applied to other explosives.   Subject to the provisions hereafter in this Part of this Act contained; Part One of this Act relating to gunpowder shall apply to every other description of explosive, in like manner as if those provisions were herein re-enacted with the substitution of that description of explosive for gunpowder.
[Explosives Act 1875, s 39.]

---

1. Part II contains ss 39–51.

8–14035   41. Exemption of safety cartridges for private use.   *Repealed.*

Specially dangerous Explosives

8–14036   43. Power to prohibit manufacture, importation, storage, and carriage of specially dangerous explosives.   Notwithstanding anything in this Act, Her Majesty from time to time, by Order in Council, may prohibit, either absolutely, or except in pursuance of a license of the Health and Safety Executive under this Act, or may subject to conditions or restrictions the manufacture, keeping, importation from any place out of the United Kingdom, conveyance, and sale, or any of them, of any explosive which is of so dangerous a character that, in the judgment of Her Majesty, it is expedient for the public safety to make such order.

Provided that such order shall not absolutely prohibit anything which may be lawfully done in pursuance of any continuing certificate under this Act.

Any explosive manufactured or kept in contravention of any such order shall be deemed to be manufactured or kept, as the case may be, in an unauthorised place.

Any explosive conveyed in contravention of any such order shall be deemed to be conveyed in contravention of a byelaw made under this Act with respect to the conveyance of explosives.

If any explosive is imported or sold in contravention of any such Order, the owner or master of the ship in which it was imported, the person to whom it was delivered and the person selling the same shall each be guilty of an offence and liable to the penalties specified in s 33(3) of the Health and Safety at Work etc Act 1974[1].

The Commissioners of Customs and their officers shall have the same power with respect to any such explosive, and the ship containing the same, as they have for the time being with respect to any article prohibited to be imported by the law relating to customs or excise, and the ship containing the same, and the enactments for the time being in force relating to customs or excise and any such article or ship shall apply accordingly.
[Explosives Act 1875, s 43, as amended by SI 1974/1885 and the Customs and Excise Management Act 1979, Sch 4.]

---

1. See this title, post.

Provisions in favour of certain Manufacturers and Dealers

8–14037   44–50.   *Repealed.*

PART III[1]
ADMINISTRATION OF LAW

Government Supervision Inspection

8–14040   60. License and certified special rules to be evidence.   A copy of any license confirmed by the Secretary of State or the Health and Safety Executive under this Act, and of any special rules under this Act, certified by an inspector appointed by the Health and Safety Executive under s 19 of the 1974 Act, shall be evidence of such license and special rules respectively, and of the fact of such license having been duly granted and confirmed and such special rules duly established under this Act.
[Explosives Act 1875, s 60, as amended by SI 1974/1885.]

---

1. Part III contains ss 53–76.

Local Supervision

Definition and Powers of Local Authority

8–14041   67. Definition of local authority.   The local authority for the purposes of this Act, shall be—

(1) In the city of London except as hereafter in this section mentioned, the court of the Lord Mayor and aldermen of the said city; and

(2) *Repealed.*

(3) Outside Greater London and a metropolitan county, the council of a county or county borough; and

(3A) In a metropolitan county, the fire and rescue authority; and

(4) In any harbour within the jurisdiction of a harbour authority, whether situate or not within the jurisdiction of any local authority before in this section mentioned, the harbour authority, to the exclusion of any other local authority; and

(5) *Repealed.*

[Explosives Act 1875, s 67, as amended by the London Government Act 1963, Sch 18, Part II, the Local Government Act 1972, Schs 29 and 30, the Local Government Act 1985, Sch 11, the Local Government (Wales) Act 1994, Sch 16 and the Fire and Rescue Services Act 2004, Sch 1.]

General Power of Search

8–14042   **73. Search for explosive when in place in contravention of this Act, or offence being committed with respect to it**[1]. Where any of the following officers,—namely, any Government inspector, or any constable, or any officer of the local authority, if such constable or officer is specially authorised either (*a*) by a warrant of a justice (which warrant such justice may grant upon reasonable ground being assigned on oath), or (*b*) (where it appears to a superintendent or other officer of police of equal or superior rank or to a Government inspector, that the case is one of emergency and that the delay in obtaining a warrant would be likely to endanger life), by a written order[2] from such superintendent, officer, or inspector—has reasonable cause to believe that any offence has been or is being committed with respect to an explosive in any place (whether a building or not, or a carriage, boat, or ship), or that any explosive is in any such place in contravention of this Act, or that the provisions of this Act are not duly observed in any such place, such officer may, on producing, if demanded, in the case of a Government inspector a copy of his appointment, and in the case of any other officer his authority, enter at any time, and if needs be by force, and as well on Sunday as on other days, the said place, and every part thereof, and examine the same, and search for explosives therein, and take samples of any explosive and ingredient of an explosive therein, and any substance reasonably supposed to be an explosive, or such ingredient which may be found therein.

Any person who, by himself or by others, fails to admit into any place occupied by or under the control of such person any officer demanding to enter in pursuance of this section, or in any way obstructs such officer in the execution of his duty under this section, shall be liable[3] on summary conviction to a penalty not exceeding **the statutory maximum**, and shall also be liable to forfeit all explosives, and ingredients thereof, which are at the time of the offence in his possession or under his control at the said place.

Where a constable or officer of the local authority specially authorised by written authority other than a warrant of a justice of the peace, enters and searches as above provided, a special report in writing of every act done by such constable or officer in pursuance of that authority, and of the grounds on which it is done, shall be forthwith sent by the person by whom or under whose authority it was done to the Secretary of State.

[Explosives Act 1875, s 73, as amended by the Criminal Law Act 1977, s 28.]

---

1. This section is repealed except in so far as it relates to the powers of a constable: SI 1974/1885, as amended by SI 1974/2166.

2. The officer must produce his authority if demanded. A special report of every act done and of the ground on which it is done must be sent forthwith to the Secretary of State, see this section, post.

3. This offence is triable either way by operation of s 91, post. For procedure, see the Magistrates' Courts Act 1980, ss 17A–21, in PART I: MAGISTRATES' COURTS, PROCEDURE, ante.

8–14043   **74. Seizure and detention of explosives liable to forfeiture.** Where any of the following officers, namely, an inspector appointed by the Health and Safety Executive under s 19 of the 1974 Act or, or any constable, or any officer of the local authority, has reasonable cause to believe that any explosive or ingredient of an explosive or substance found by him is liable to be forfeited under this Act, he may seize and detain the same until some court of summary jurisdiction has determined whether the same is or is not so liable to be forfeited, and with respect thereto the following provisions shall have effect:

(1) The officer seizing may either require the occupier of the place in which it was seized (whether a building or not, or a carriage, boat, or ship) to detain the same in such place or in any place under the control of such occupier, or may remove it in such manner and to such place as will in his opinion least endanger the public safety, and there detain it, and may, where the matter appears to him to be urgent and fraught with serious public danger, and he is an inspector appointed by the Health and Safety Executive under s 19 of the 1974 Act, or is authorised by an order from an inspector appointed by the Health and Safety Executive under s 19 of the 1974 Act or a justice of the peace, or from a superintendent or other officer of police of equal or superior rank, cause the same to be destroyed or otherwise rendered harmless; but before destroying or rendering harmless the same he shall take and keep a sample thereof, and shall, if required, give a portion of the sample to the person owning the explosive, or having the

same under his control at the time of the seizure; and any such occupier who, by himself or by others, fails to keep the same when he is required in pursuance of this section to detain it, and any such occupier or other person who, except with the authority of the officer seizing the same, or of an inspector appointed by the Health and Safety Executive under s 19 of the 1974 Act, or in case of emergency for the purpose of preventing explosion or fire, removes, alters, or in any way tampers or deals with the same while so detained, shall be liable[1] to a fine and shall also be liable to forfeit all explosives, and ingredients thereof which are at the time of the offence in his possession or under his control at the said place:

(2) The proceedings before a court of summary jurisdiction for determining whether the same is or is not liable to forfeiture shall be commenced as soon as practicable after the seizure; and

(3) The receptacles containing the same may be seized, detained, and removed in like manner as the contents thereof; and

(4) The officer seizing the same may use for the purposes of the removal and detention thereof any ship, boat, or carriage in which the same was seized, and any tug, tender, engine, tackle, beasts, and accoutrements belonging to or drawing or provided for drawing such ship, boat, or carriage, and shall pay to the owner a reasonable compensation for such use, to be determined, in case of dispute, by a court of summary jurisdiction, and to be recovered in like manner as penalties under this Act; and

(5) The same shall, so far as practicable, be kept and conveyed in accordance with this Act, and with all due precaution to prevent accident, but the person seizing, removing, detaining, keeping, or conveying the same shall not be liable to any penalty, punishment, or forfeiture under this or any other Act, or to any damages, for keeping or conveying the same, so that he use all such due precautions as aforesaid; and

(6) The officer seizing the same, or dealing with the same in pursuance of this section, shall not be liable to damages or otherwise in respect of such seizure or dealing, or any act incidental to or consequential thereon, unless it is proved that he made such seizure without reasonable cause, or that he caused damage to the article seized by some wilful neglect or default.

[Explosives Act 1875, s 74, as amended by SI 1974/1885 and the Criminal Law Act 1977, s 32.]

1. This offence is triable only on indictment because s 91, post, has been repealed with respect to s 74. Section 33(3) of the Health and Safety at Work etc Act 1974, this title, post, has no application because until the passing of s 32 of the Criminal Law Act 1977, s 74 prescribed a penalty not exceeding £50 for such offence.

8–14044 75. Inspection of wharf, carriage, boat, etc, with explosives in transit[1]. (1) Any of the following officers, namely, any Government inspector under this Act any chief officer of police, and any superior officer appointed for the purposes of this Act *where the justices in petty sessions are the local authority, by the court of quarter sessions to which such justices belong, and in the case of any other local authority[2] by the local authority itself,* may, for the purpose of ascertaining whether the provisions of this Act with respect to the conveyance, loading, unloading, and importation of an explosive are complied with, enter, inspect, and examine at any time, and as well on Sundays as on other days, the wharf, carriage, ship, or boat of any carrier or other person who conveys goods for hire, or of the occupier of any factory, magazine, or store, or of the importer of any explosive, on or in which wharf, carriage, ship, or boat he has reasonable cause to suppose an explosive to be for the purpose of or in course of conveyance, but so as not to unnecessarily obstruct the work or business of any such carrier, person, occupier, or importer.

Any such officer, if he find any offence being committed under this Act in any such wharf, carriage, ship, or boat, or on any public wharf, may seize and detain or remove the said carriage, ship, or boat, or the explosive, in such manner and with such precautions as appear to him to be necessary to remove any danger to the public, and may seize and detain the said explosive, as if it were liable to forfeiture.

Any officer above mentioned in this section, and any officer of police, or officer of the local authority who has reasonable cause to suppose that any offence against this Act is being committed in respect of any carriage (not being on a railway) or any boat conveying, loading, or unloading any explosive, and that the case is one of emergency, and that the delay in obtaining a warrant will be likely to endanger life, may stop, and enter, inspect, and examine, such carriage or boat, and by detention or removal thereof or otherwise take such precautions as may be reasonably necessary for removing such danger, in like manner as if such explosive were liable to forfeiture.

Every officer shall for the purpose of this section have the same powers and be in the same position as if he were authorised by a search warrant granted under this Act, and any person failing to admit or obstructing such officer shall be liable[3] to the same penalty.★

(2) In subsection (1)—

(a) "officer of police" includes any member of the National Criminal Intelligence Service appointed under section 9(1)(b) of the Police Act 1997 (police members) and any member of the National Crime Squad appointed under section 55(1)(b) of that Act (police members), and

(b) "chief officer of police" includes the Director General of that Service and the Director General of that Squad.★

[Explosives Act 1975, s 75 as amended by the Police Act 1997, Sch 9.]

*Sub-section(1) amended and sub-s(2) substituted by the Serious Organised Crime and Police Act 2005, Sch 4 from a date to be appointed.

   1. This section is repealed except in so far as it relates to the powers of officers of police (SI 1974/1885, as amended by SI 1974/2166).

   2. The words in italics are obsolete since justices now have no administrative functions under the Act.

   3. This offence is triable either way by operation of s 91, post. For penalty, see s 73, ante.

PART IV[1]

SUPPLEMENTAL PROVISIONS, LEGAL PROCEEDINGS, EXEMPTIONS, AND DEFINITIONS

Supplemental Provisions

8–14045   **77, 78.** *Repealed.*

8–14047   **80. Penalty for throwing fireworks in thoroughfare.**   If any person throw, cast, or fire any fireworks in or into any highway, street, thoroughfare, or public place, he shall be guilty of an offence and liable on summary conviction to a fine not exceeding **level 5** on the standard scale.*
[Explosives Act 1875, s 80, as amended by the Criminal Justice Act 1967, Sch 3, the Explosives (Age of Purchase etc) Act 1976, s 1 and the Consumer Protection Act 1987, Sch 4.]

*Repealed by the Fireworks Act 2003, Schedule, from a date to be appointed.

8–14048   **82. Punishment for defacing notices.** *Repealed.*

8–14049   **83.** *Provisions as to Orders in Council and orders of the Secretary of State[1].*

   1. A list of Orders in Council and Orders of the Secretary of State made under this Act is given in note 1 to the title of this Act, ante.

8–14060   **89. Supplemental provisions as to forfeiture of explosive[1].**   Where a court before whom a person is convicted of an offence against this Act has power to forfeit any explosive owned by or found in the possession or under the control of such person, the court may, if it think it just and expedient, in lieu of forfeiting such explosive, impose upon such person, in addition to any other penalty or punishment, a penalty not exceeding such sum as appears to the court to be the value of the explosive so liable to be forfeited.

   Where any explosive, or ingredient of an explosive, is alleged to be liable under this Act to be forfeited, any indictment, information, or complaint may be laid against the owner of such explosive or ingredient, for the purpose only of enforcing such forfeiture; and where the owner is unknown, or cannot be found, a court may cause a notice to be advertised, stating that unless cause is shown to the contrary at the time and place named in the notice, such explosive will be forfeited, and at such time and place the court after hearing the owner or any person on his behalf (who may be present), may order all or any part of such explosive or ingredient to be forfeited.
[Explosives Act 1875, s 89.]

   1. Section 89 has been repealed except for the purposes of ss 30, 32 and 73 of this Act (SI 1974/1885 as amended by SI 1974/2166).

8–14061   **90. Jurisdiction in tidal waters or on boundaries.**   For all the purposes of this Act—

  (1) Any harbour, tidal water, or inland water which runs between or abuts on or forms the boundary of the jurisdiction of two or more courts shall be deemed to be wholly within the jurisdiction of each of such courts; and

  (2) Any tidal water not included in the foregoing descriptions and within the territorial jurisdiction of Her Majesty, and adjacent to or surrounding any part of the shore of the United Kingdom, and any pier, jetty, mole, or work extending into the same, shall be deemed to form part of the shore to which such water or part of the sea is adjacent, or which it surrounds.
[Explosives Act 1875, s 90.]

8–14062   **91. Prosecution of offences either summarily or on indictment[1].**   Every offence under this Act may be prosecuted[2] and every penalty under this Act may be recovered, and all explosives and ingredients liable to be forfeited under this Act may be forfeited either on indictment or before a court of summary jurisdiction, in manner directed by the Summary Jurisdiction Acts.

   Provided that the penalty imposed by a court of summary jurisdiction shall not exceed the statutory maximum, exclusive of costs, and exclusive of any forfeiture or penalty in lieu of forfeiture, and the term of imprisonment imposed by any such court shall not exceed **one month**[3].

   All costs and money directed to be recovered as penalties may be recovered before a court of summary jurisdiction in manner directed by the Summary Jurisdiction Acts.

   A court of summary jurisdiction may by order prohibit a person from doing any act for doing

which such person has twice been convicted under this Act, and may order any person disobeying such summary order to be imprisoned for any period not exceeding six months.
[Explosives Act 1875, s 91, as amended by the Criminal Law Act 1977, s 28.]

1. This section is repealed except for the purposes of ss 30, 32 and 73 of this Act (SI 1974/1885 as amended by SI 1974/2166). Only offences contrary to these sections are, therefore, made triable either way by virtue of s 91.

2. For procedure in respect of this offence which is triable either way, see the Magistrates' Courts Act 1980, ss 17A–21, in PART I: MAGISTRATES' COURTS, PROCEDURE, ante.

3. The meaning of this provision is too doubtful for justices to imprison for a longer period on non-payment of penalty. The imprisonment will be further regulated by the Magistrates' Courts Act 1980, Sch 4, in PART I: MAGISTRATES' COURTS, PROCEDURE, ante.

8–14063　　93, 94. *Repealed.*

8–14065　　95. Distress of ship.　Where the owner or master of a ship or boat is adjudged to pay a penalty for an offence committed with or in relation to such ship or boat, the court may, in addition to any other power they may have for the purpose of compelling payment of such penalty, direct the same to be levied by distress or arrestment and sale of the said ship or boat and her tackle.
[Explosives Act 1875, s 95.]

8–14066　　96. Application of penalties and disposal of forfeitures.　Any explosive or ingredient forfeited in pursuance of this Act may be sold, destroyed, or otherwise disposed of in such manner as the court declaring the forfeiture, or the Secretary of State, may direct, and the proceeds of any such sale or disposal shall be paid, applied, and accounted for in like manner as penalties under this Act.

The receptacle containing any such explosive or ingredient may be forfeited, sold, destroyed, or otherwise disposed of, in like manner as the contents thereof.

The provisions of Part Three of this Act with respect to an explosive, or ingredient of an explosive, seized in pursuance of this Act, and to the officer seizing, removing, detaining, keeping, or conveying, or otherwise dealing with the same, shall apply to any explosive and ingredient declared by any court to be forfeited, and to the officer removing, detaining, keeping, conveying, selling, destroying, or otherwise disposing of the same.

The court declaring the forfeiture, or the Secretary of State directing the sale or other disposal of any forfeited explosive or ingredient, and the receptacles thereof, may require the owner of such explosive or ingredient to permit the use of any ship, boat, or carriage containing such explosive or ingredient for the purpose of such sale or disposal upon payment of a reasonable compensation for the same, to be determined in case of dispute by a court of summary jurisdiction; and where the explosive or ingredient is directed to be destroyed, the owner and the person having possession of such explosive or ingredient, and the owner and master of the ship, boat, or carriage containing the same, or some, or one of them, shall destroy the same accordingly, and if the court or Secretary of State so order, the ship, boat, or carriage may be detained until the same is so destroyed; and if the Secretary of State is satisfied that default has been made in complying with any such direction by him or by a court, and that the detention of the ship, boat, or carriage will not secure the safety of the public, and that it is impracticable, having regard to the safety of the public or of the persons employed in such destruction, to effect the same without using such ship, boat, or carriage, or otherwise dealing with such ship, boat, or carriage, in like manner as if it were a receptacle for an explosive forfeited under this Act, the Secretary of State may direct such ship, boat, and carriage, or any of them, to be, and the same may accordingly be, so used or dealt with.
[Explosives Act 1875, s 96, as amended by SI 1974/1885.]

Exemptions and Savings

8–14067　　97. *Exemption of Government factories, etc, from the Act*[1]

1. Extended by Visiting Forces and International Headquarters (Application of Law) Order 1965, SI 1965/1536, art 12 Sch 3). Extended to ships, etc of a visiting force (Visiting Forces and International Headquarters (Application of Law) Order, supra, art 11, Sch 3), and to premises etc, of the United Kingdom Atomic Energy Authority (Atomic Energy Authority Act 1954, Sch 3). See also s 18 of the Road Traffic Act 1974 (in force from 1 January 1975: SI 1974/2075) authorising the use of pyrotechnic flares by the police for traffic purposes.

8–14068　　98–101. *Repealed.*

Definitions

8–14071　　104. Extension of definition of explosive to other explosive substances.　Her Majesty may, by Order in Council[1], declare that any substance which appears to Her Majesty to be specially dangerous to life or property by reason either of its explosive properties, or of any process in the manufacture thereof being liable to explosion, shall be deemed to be an explosive within the meaning of this Act and the provisions of this Act (subject to such exceptions, limitations, and restrictions as

may be specified in the order) shall accordingly extend to such substance in like manner as if it were included in the term explosive in this Act.
[Explosives Act 1875, s 104.]

---

1. See Orders in Council No 26 (picric acid, etc) and No 30 (acetylene and mixed acetylene), as amended by SR & O 1947/805 and SI 1978/1723.

8–14072   105. Persons carrying on certain processes to be deemed manufacturers.   Any person who carries on any of the following processes, namely, the process of dividing into its component parts or otherwise breaking up or unmaking any explosive, or making fit for use any damaged explosive, or the process of remaking, altering, or repairing any explosive, shall be subject to the provisions of this Act as if he manufactured an explosive, and the expression "manufacture" shall in this Act be construed accordingly.
[Explosives Act 1875, s 105.]

8–14073   106. *Definition and classification of explosives by Order in Council*[1].

---

1. See Orders in Council No 1 Classification of Explosives (5 August 1875; as amended by No 1A, 12 December 1891, and modified by No 1B, SR & O 1913/481).

8–14074   108. General definitions.   In this Act, unless the context otherwise requires—

The expression "this Act" includes any license, certificate, byelaw, regulation, rule, and order granted or made in pursuance of this Act:

The expression "existing" means existing at the passing of this Act:

The expression "person" includes a body corporate:

The expression "occupier" includes any number of persons and a body corporate; and in the case of any manufacture or trade, includes any person carrying on such manufacture or trade:

The expression "master" includes every person (except a pilot) having command or charge of a ship, and in reference to any boat belonging to a ship, means the master of the ship; and when used in reference to any other boat, includes every person having command or charge of such boat:

The expression "magazine" includes any ship or other vessel used for the purpose of keeping any explosive:

The expression "factory magazine" means a building for keeping the finished explosive made in the factory, and includes, if such explosive is not gunpowder, any building for keeping the partly manufactured explosive or the ingredients of such explosive which is mentioned in that behalf in the license:

The expression "store" means an existing gunpowder store as defined by this Act, or a place for keeping an explosive licensed by a license granted by a local authority under this Act:

The expression "warehouseman" includes all persons owning or managing any warehouse, store, wharf, or other premises in which goods are deposited:

The expression "carrier" includes all persons carrying goods or passengers for hire by land or water:

The expression "harbour authority" means any person or body of persons, corporate or unincorporate, being or claiming to be proprietor or proprietors of or intrusted with the duty or invested with the power of improving, managing, maintaining, or regulating any harbour properly so called, whether natural or artificial, and any port, haven, and estuary, or intrusted with the duty of conserving, maintaining, or improving the navigation of any tidal water, and any such harbour, port, haven estuary, tidal water, and any wharf, dock, pier, jetty, and work, and other area, whether land or water, over which the harbour authority as above defined have control or exercise powers, are in the other portions of this Act included in the expression "harbour":

The expression "canal company" means any person or body of persons, corporate or unincorporate, being owner or lessee or owners or lessees of, or working, or entitled to charge tolls for the use of any canal in the United Kingdom, constructed or carried on under the powers of any Act of Parliament, or intrusted with the duty of conserving, maintaining, or improving the navigation of any inland water, and every such canal and inland water under the control of a canal company as above defined, and any wharf, dock, pier, jetty, and work in or at which barges do or can ship or unship goods or passengers, and other area, whether land or water, which belong to or are under the control of such canal company, are in the other portions of this act included in the expression "canal":

The expression "tidal water" means any part of the sea or of a river within the ebb and flow of the tides at ordinary spring tides:

The expression "inland water" means any canal, river, navigation, lake, or water which is not tidal water:

The expression "railway company" means any person or body of persons, corporate or unincorporate, being the owner or lessee or owners or lessees of or working any railway worked by steam or otherwise than by animal power in the United Kingdom, constructed or carried on under the powers of any Act of Parliament and used for public traffic, and every building, station, wharf, dock, and place which belong to or are under the control of a railway company, are in the other portions of this Act included in the expression "railway":

The expression "wharf" includes any quay, landing-place, siding, or other place at which goods are landed, loaded, or unloaded:

The expression "carriage" includes any carriage, waggon, cart, truck, vehicle, or other means of conveying goods or passengers by land, in whatever manner the same may be propelled:

The expression "ship" includes every description of vessel used in sea navigation, whether propelled by oars or otherwise:

The expression "boat" means every vessel not a ship as above defined which is used in navigation in any inland water or any harbour, whether propelled by oars or otherwise:

The expression "prescribed" means prescribed by Order in Council:

The expression "safety cartridges" means cartridges for small arms of which the case can be extracted from the small arm after firing, and which are so closed as to prevent any explosion in one cartridge being communicated to other cartridges:

The expression "Gunpowder Act 1860," means the Act of the session of the twenty-third and twenty-fourth years of the reign of Her present Majesty, chapter one hundred and thirty-nine, intituled "An Act to amend the law concerning the making, keeping, and carriage of gunpowder and compositions of an exclusive nature, and concerning the manufacture, sale, and use of fireworks," and the Acts amending the same:

[Explosives Act 1875, s 108, as amended by the SLR (No 2) Act 1893, the Local Government Act 1972, Sch 30 and the Statute Law (Repeals) Act 1993, Sch 1.]

Explosive Substances Act 1883

(46 & 47 Vict c 3)

8–14180　1. Short title.　This Act may be cited as the Explosive Substances Act, 1883.
[Explosive Substances Act 1883, s 1.]

8–14181　2. Causing explosion likely to endanger life or property[1].　A person who in the United Kingdom or (being a citizen of the United Kingdom and Colonies) in the Republic of Ireland unlawfully and maliciously causes by any explosive substance an explosion of a nature likely to endanger life or to cause serious injury to property shall, whether any injury to person or property has been actually caused or not, be guilty of an offence and on conviction on indictment shall be liable to imprisonment for **life**.
[Explosive Substances Act 1883, s 2, as substituted by the Criminal Jurisdiction Act 1975, s 7.]

---

1. Sections 2 and 3 are extended to include any act committed outside the United Kingdom which would be an offence if committed in the United Kingdom; see the Suppression of Terrorism Act 1978, ss 1, 4, and Sch 1, in title EXTRADITION, FUGITIVE OFFENDERS AND BACKING OF WARRANTS, ante.

8–14182　3. Attempt to cause explosion, or making or keeping explosive with intent to endanger life or property[1].　(1) A person who in the United Kingdom or a dependency or (being a citizen of the United Kingdom and colonies) elsewhere unlawfully and maliciously—

(*a*)　does any act with intent to cause, or conspires to cause, by an explosive substance an explosion of a nature likely to endanger life, or cause serious injury to property, whether in the United Kingdom or the Republic of Ireland, or

(*b*)　makes or has in his possession or under his control an explosive substance with intent by means thereof to endanger life, or cause serious injury to property, whether in the United Kingdom or the Republic of Ireland, or to enable any other person so to do,

shall, whether any explosion does or does not take place, and whether any injury to person or property is actually caused or not, be guilty of an offence and on conviction on indictment shall be liable to imprisonment for **life**, and the explosive substance shall be forfeited.

(2) In this section "dependency" means the Channel Islands, the Isle of Man and any colony, other than a colony for whose external relations a country other than the United Kingdom is responsible.

(2) In the Schedule to the Irish Free State (Consequential Adaptation of Enactments) Order 1923 the entry for the Explosive Substances Act 1883, which is superseded by this section, shall cease to have effect.

(3) This section extends to all parts of the United Kingdom.

[Explosive Substances Act 1883, s 3, as substituted by the Criminal Jurisdiction Act 1975, s 7, and amended by the Criminal Law Act 1977, Sch 12.]

---

1. Sections 2 and 3 are extended to include any act committed outside the United Kingdom which would be an offence if committed in the United Kingdom; see the Suppression of Terrorism Act 1978, ss 1, 4, and Sch 1, in title EXTRADITION, FUGITIVE OFFENDERS AND BACKING OF WARRANTS, ante.

8–14183 4. Making or possession of explosive under suspicious circumstances. (1) Any person who makes or knowingly[1] has in his possession or under his control any explosive substance[2], under such circumstances as to give rise to a reasonable suspicion that he is not making it or does not have it in his possession or under his control for a lawful object[3], shall, unless he can show that he made it or had it in his possession or under his control for a lawful object, be guilty of felony[4], and on conviction, shall be liable to imprisonment for a term not exceeding **fourteen years**, and the explosive substance shall be forfeited.

(2) *Repealed.*

[Explosive Substances Act 1883, s 4, as amended by the Criminal Justice Act 1948, s 1 and the Police and Criminal Evidence Act 1984, Sch 7.]

---

1. The prosecution must prove (1) that the accused was knowingly in possession of a substance which he knew to be an explosive substance as defined by s 9; and (2) that the possession was under such circumstances as to give rise to a reasonable suspicion that he did not have it in his possession for a lawful object. It then lies on the accused to show that he did have it in his possession for a lawful object. Knowledge of the accused that the substance was of an explosive nature may be inferred from the facts of the case (*R v Hallam* [1957] 1 QB 569, [1957] 1 All ER 665, 121 JP 254. See also *R v Berry (No 3)* [1994] 2 All ER 913, 99 Cr App Rep 88). The word "knowingly" should be included in the particulars of the offence in an indictment (*R v McVitie* [1960] 2 QB 483, [1960] 2 All ER 498, 124 JP 404). The circumstances under which a person may be guilty of aiding and abetting this offence were explained in *R v McCarthy* [1964] 1 All ER 95, 128 JP 191.

2. The definition of "explosive" in s 3 of the Explosives Act 1875, ante, may be adopted and applied (*R v Wheatley* [1979] 1 All ER 954, 143 JP 376).

3. The defence of lawful object is available to a defendant if he can satisfy the jury on the balance of probabilities that his object was to protect himself or his family or his property against imminent apprehended attack, and to do so by means which he believed were no more than reasonably necessary to meet the force used by the attackers (*A-G's Reference (No 2 of 1983)* [1984] QB 456, [1984] 1 All ER 988, 149 JP 104). Evidence is admissible to show the nature of the conspiracy and the reasonableness of the suspicion that the object of the possession was unlawful (*R v Sidhu* [1993] Crim LR 773).

The "lawful object" is not confined to a purpose which takes place in the UK and the lawfulness of which is to be defined by English law (*R v Berry* [1985] AC 246, [1984] 3 All ER 1008, 149 JP 276, HL).

4. The distinctions between felony and misdemeanour were abolished, and the law and practice applying in relation to misdemeanour were in general made applicable to all offences, by the Criminal Law Act 1967, s 1, in PART I: MAGISTRATES' COURTS, PROCEDURE, ante.

8–14184 5. Punishment of accessories. Any person who within or (being a subject of Her Majesty) without Her Majesty's dominions by the supply of or solicitation for money, the providing of premises, the supply of materials, or in any manner whatsoever, procures, counsels, aids, abets, or is accessory to, the commission of any crime under this Act, shall be guilty of felony[1] and shall be liable to be tried and punished for that crime, as if he had been guilty as a principal.

[Explosive Substances Act 1883, s 5.]

---

1. See note 4 to s 4, ante.

8–14185 6. Inquiry by Attorney-General, and apprehension of absconding witnesses.
(1) Where the Attorney-General has reasonable ground to believe that any crime under this Act has been committed, he may order an inquiry under this section, and thereupon any justice for the county, borough, or place in which the crime was committed or is suspected to have been committed, who is authorised in that behalf by the Attorney-General may, although no person may be charged before him with the commission of such crime, sit at a petty sessional or occasional court-house, or police station in the said county, borough, or place, and examine on oath concerning such crime any witness appearing before him, and may take the deposition of such witness, and, if he see cause, may bind such witness by recognizance to appear and give evidence at the next petty sessions, or when called upon within three months from the date of such recognizance; and the law relating to the compelling of the attendance of a witness before a justice, and to a witness attending before a justice and required to give evidence concerning the matter of an information or complaint, shall apply to compelling the attendance of a witness for examination and to a witness attending under this section.★

(2) A witness examined under this section shall not be excused from answering any question on the ground that the answer thereto may criminate, or tend to criminate, that witness or the spouse or civil partner of that witness; but any statement made by any person in answer to any question put to him or her on any examination under this section shall not, except in the case of an indictment or other criminal proceeding for perjury, be admissible in evidence against that person or the spouse or civil partner of that person in any proceeding, civil or criminal.

(3) A justice who conducts the examination under this section of a person concerning any crime shall not take part in the committing for trial of such person for such crime.★★

(4) Whenever any person is bound by recognizance to give evidence before justices, or any criminal court, in respect of any crime under this Act, any justice, if he sees fit, upon information being made in writing and on oath, that such person is about to abscond, or has absconded, may issue his warrant for the arrest of such person, and if such person is arrested any justice, upon being satisfied that the ends of justice would otherwise be defeated, may commit such person to prison until the time at which he is bound by such recognizance to give evidence, unless in the meantime he produces sufficient sureties: Provided that any person so arrested shall be entitled on demand to receive a copy of the information upon which the warrant for his arrest was issued.

[Explosive Substances Act 1883, s 6, as amended by the Civil Evidence Act 1968, s 17 and Schedule and the Access to Justice Act 1999, Sch 15 and the Civil Partnership Act 2004, Sch 27.]

---

*Subsection (1) amended by the Courts Act 2003, Sch 8, from a date to be appointed.
**Subsection (3) repealed by the Criminal Justice Act 2003, Sch 3, from a date to be appointed.

8–14186   7. No prosecution except by leave of Attorney-General—Procedure and saving.
(1) Proceedings[1] for a crime under this Act shall not be instituted excepted by or with the consent[2] of the Attorney-General.

(2)–(4)   *Repealed.*

[Explosive Substances Act 1883, s 7, as amended by the Indictments Act 1915, s 9 and Sch 2, the Criminal Law Act 1967, s 10 and Sch 3, Part III, the Administration of Justice Act 1982, s 63 and the Statute Law (Repeals) Act 1989, Sch 1.]

---

1. "Proceedings" means the time when a person goes to court to answer a charge (*R v Elliott* (1984) 81 Cr App Rep 115, [1985] Crim LR 310, CA). See also the Prosecution of Offences Act 1985, s 25, in PART I: MAGISTRATES' COURTS, PROCEDURE, *ante*.

2. The absence of such consent invalidates the proceedings (*R v Bates* [1911] 1 KB 964, 75 JP 271). The consent may be in general terms, leaving the prosecutor free to pursue any charge under the Act justified by the evidence; see *R v Cain and Schollick* [1976] QB 496, [1975] 2 All ER 900, 139 JP 598.

8–14187   8. Search for and seizure of explosive substances.   (1) Sections seventy-three, seventy-four, seventy-five, eighty-nine, and ninety-six of the Explosives Act, 1875[1] (which sections relate to the search for, seizure and detention of explosive substances, and the forfeiture thereof, and the disposal of explosive substances seized or forfeited), shall apply in like manner as if a crime or forfeiture under this Act were an offence or forfeiture under the Explosives Act, 1875.

(2) Where the master or owner of any vessel has reasonable cause to suspect that any dangerous goods or goods of a dangerous nature which, if found, he would be entitled to throw overboard in pursuance of the safety regulations under section 85 of the Merchant Shipping Act 1995, are concealed on board his vessel, he may search any part of such vessel for such goods, and for the purpose of such search may, if necessary, break open any box, package, parcel, or receptacle on board the vessel, and such master or owner, if he finds any such dangerous goods or goods of a dangerous nature, shall be entitled to deal with the same in manner provided by the said Act, and if he do not find the same, he shall not be subject to any liability, civil or criminal, if it appears to the tribunal before which the question of his liability is raised that he had reasonable cause to suspect that such goods were so concealed as aforesaid.

[Explosive Substances Act 1883, s 8 as amended by the Merchant Shipping Act 1995, Sch 13.]

---

1. For ss 73, 74, 75, 89 and 96 of the Explosives Act 1875, see this title, *ante*.

8–14188   9. Definitions and application to Scotland.   (1) In this Act, unless the context otherwise requires—

The expression "explosive substance"[1] shall be deemed to include any materials for making any explosive substance; also any apparatus, machine, implement, or materials used, or intended to be used, or adapted for causing, or aiding in causing, any explosion in or with any explosive substance; also any part of any such apparatus, machine, or implement.

The expression "Attorney-General" means Her Majesty's Attorney-General for England or Ireland, as the case may be.

(2)   *Scotland.*

[Explosive Substances Act 1883, s 9 as amended by the Law Officers Act 1997, Sch.]

---

1. Any part of a vessel which, when filled with an explosive substance, is adapted for causing an explosion, ie for causing it to explode so as to be dangerous to life, limb or property, is an explosive substance within the Act (*R v Charles* (1892) 17 Cox CC 499). It also includes a shotgun; see *R v Downey* [1971] NI 224.

Employment of Women, Young Persons, and Children Act 1920[1]
(10 & 11 Geo 5 c 65)

8–14200   1. Restrictions on the employment of women, young persons, and children in industrial undertakings.   (1) No[2] child shall be employed in any[3] industrial undertaking.

(2)   *Repealed.*

(3)   *Repealed.*

(4) Where persons under the age of sixteen years are employed in any industrial undertaking, a register of all persons under that age who are so employed, and of the dates of their birth, shall be kept and shall at all times be open to inspection.

(5)   *Repealed.*

(6)   [4] This section, so far as it relates to employment in mines and quarries within the meaning of

the Mines and Quarries Act 1954 and in factories, shall have effect as if it formed part of the Mines and Quarries Act 1954 and the Factories Act 1961 respectively; and the provisions of those Acts relating to registers to be kept thereunder shall apply to the registers required to be kept under this Act.

In the case of employment in any place other than the places aforesaid—

(a) The following provisions, namely—

    (i) sections 21(1) and (2) and 28(1) and (3) of the Children and Young Persons Act 1933.

    (ii) sections 31(1) and (2) and 36(1) and (3) of the Children and Young Persons (Scotland) Act 1937, or

    (iii) sections 39(1) and (3) to (5) and 45(1), (3) and (4) of the Children and Young Persons Act (Northern Ireland) 1968,

shall have effect in relation to the employment of a child in an industrial undertaking in contravention of this Act as they have effect in relation to the employment of a child in contravention of Part II of that Act of 1933, of Part III of that Act of 1937 or of Part III of that Act of 1968, as the case may be; and

(b) *Repealed.*

(c) If any person being the employer of a person under the age of sixteen years fails to keep such a register so required to be kept by him as aforesaid, or refuses or neglects when required to produce it for inspection by an officer of a local authority under the said Act, he shall be liable on summary conviction to a fine not exceeding **level 2** on the standard scale.

(d) *Repealed.*

[Employment of Women, Young Persons, and Children Act 1920, s 1, as amended by, the Merchant Shipping Act 1970, Sch 5, the Criminal Law Act 1977, s 31, the Statute Law (Repeals) Act 1978, the Criminal Justice Act 1982, ss 35 and 46 and the Employment Act 1989, s 10, Schs 3, 6 and 7.]

---

1. This Act carries out certain conventions adopted at general conferences of the Industrial Labour Organisation of the League of Nations, and makes further provisions as to the conditions under which women and young persons may be employed in factories and workshops. The requirements of the Children and Young Persons Act 1933, are additional (s 29(4), in PART V: YOUTH COURTS, *ante*). See also the Education Act 1996, ss 558–560, in this PART: EDUCATION, *ante*.

2. For definition of "child", see the Education Act 1996, s 558, in this PART: EDUCATION, *ante*.

3. For definition of "industrial undertaking", see s 4, *post*.

4. This subsection is printed as it is required to be construed by the Mines and Quarries Act 1954, Sch 4, and the Factories Act 1961, s 184(1).

8–14201   2. Employment of women and young persons in shifts.   *These provisions are now contained in the Factories Act 1961, ss. 96, 97.*

[Employment of Women, Young Persons and Children Act 1920, s 2.]

8–14202   3. Savings.   (1) The provisions of this Act shall be in addition to and not in derogation of any of the provisions of any other Act restricting the employment of children.

(2) Nothing in this Act shall apply to an industrial undertaking or ship in which only members of the same family are employed.

(3) *Repealed.*

[Employment of Women, Young Persons and Children Act 1920, s 3, as amended by the Statute Law Revision Act 1927, the Statute Law (Repeals) Act 1978, Sch 2 and the Employment Act 1989, Sch 7.]

8–14203   4. Interpretation.   In this Act[1]—

The expression "young person" means a person who has ceased to be a child and who is under the age of eighteen years;

The expression "industrial undertaking" has the meaning assigned to it by Part I of the Schedule to this Act;

The expression "ship" means any sea-going ship or boat of any description which is registered in the United Kingdom as a British ship and includes any British fishing boat entered in the fishing boat register.

[Employment of Women, Young Persons, and Children Act 1920, s 4, as amended by the Statute Law (Repeals) Act 1978 and the Employment Act 1989, Sch 6.]

---

1. For definition of "child" see s 558 of the Education Act 1996, in this PART: EDUCATION, *ante*.

SCHEDULE

(As amended by the Statute Law (Repeals) Act 1978 and the Employment Act 1989, Schedules 3 and 7.)

PART I
CONVENTION FIXING MINIMUM AGE FOR ADMISSION OF CHILDREN TO INDUSTRIAL EMPLOYMENT

8–14204   Article 1.   For the purpose of this Convention, the term "industrial undertaking" includes particularly:

(a) Mines, quarries and other works for the extraction of minerals from the earth.

(b) Industries in which articles are manufactured, altered, cleaned, repaired, ornamented, finished, adapted for sale, broken up, or demolished, or in which materials are transformed; including shipbuilding, and the generation, transformation, and transmission of electricity and motive power of any kind.

(c) Construction, reconstruction, maintenance, repair, alteration, or demolition of any building, railway, tramway, harbour, dock, pier, canal, inland waterway, road, tunnel, bridge, viaduct, sewer, drain, well, telegraphic or telephone installation, electrical undertaking, gaswork, waterwork, or other work of construction, as well as the preparation for or laying the foundations of any such work or structure.

(d) Transport of passengers or goods by road or rail or inland waterway, including the handling of goods at docks, quays, wharves, and warehouses, but excluding transport by hand.

The competent authority in each country shall define the line of division which separates industry from commerce and agriculture.

8–14205   Article 2.   Children under the age of fourteen years shall not be employed or work in any public or private industrial undertaking, or in any branch thereof, other than an undertaking in which only members of the same family are employed.

8–14206   Article 3.   The provisions of Article 2 shall not apply to work done by children in technical schools, provided that such work is approved and supervised by public authority.

8–14207   Article 4.   In order to facilitate the enforcement of the provisions of this Convention, every employer in an industrial undertaking shall be required to keep a register of all persons under the age of sixteen years employed by him, and of the dates of their births.

PART II

(Repealed)

PART III

(Repealed)

PART IV

CONVENTION FIXING THE MINIMUM AGE FOR ADMISSION OF CHILDREN TO EMPLOYMENT AT SEA

(Repealed)

Petroleum (Consolidation) Act 1928[1]

(18 & 19 Geo 5 c 32)

8–14230   1. Petroleum spirit not to be kept without a licence.   (1) Subject to the provisions[2] of this Act, petroleum spirit[3] shall not be kept[4] unless a petroleum spirit licence is in force under this Act authorising the keeping thereof and the petroleum spirit is kept in accordance with such conditions, if any, as may be attached to the licence:

Provided that the foregoing provision shall not apply to any petroleum spirit kept either for private use or for sale, as long as

(a) it is kept in separate glass, earthenware, or metal vessels, securely stopped and containing not more than 570 millilitres each; and

(b) the aggregate amount kept would not, if the whole contents of the vessels were in bulk, exceed 15 litres[5].

(2) The occupier of any premises[6] in which petroleum spirit is kept in contravention of this section, shall be guilty of an offence[7].

(3) If any person to whom a petroleum spirit licence[8] is granted, contravenes any condition of the licence, he shall be guilty of an offence[6].

[Petroleum (Consolidation) Act 1928, s 1, as amended by SI 1974/1942 and SI 1992/1811.]

---

1. By the Petroleum (Consolidation) Act 1928 (Enforcement) Regulations 1979, SI 1979/427 amended by SI 1982/630, SI 1984/1244, SI 1986/1951 and SI 2002/2776, an authority empowered to grant petroleum spirit licences under the 1928 Act (but not the Health and Safety Executive) shall be the enforcing authority within its area for any provision of the 1928 Act (except s 13), including any such provision as applied by the Petroleum (Mixtures) Order 1929, SR & O 1929/993 and the Petroleum (Liquid Methane) Order 1957, SI 1957/859 amended by SI 2002/2776 as well as instruments made or having effect as if made under the 1928 Act. This does not apply to byelaws having provision for their own enforcement.

2. See also Regulations made under s 10, post.

3. "Petroleum spirit" means such petroleum as when tested in the manner set forth in Part II of Sch 2 gives off an inflammable vapour at a temperature of less than 73 degrees Fahrenheit (s 23). A substance which gave off an inflammable vapour under the test prescribed, contained about thirty-three per cent of petroleum, and about an equal quantity of oil mixed with pigments into the form of a composition, was held to require a licence (*LCC v Holzapfels Compositions Co* (1899) 63 JP 615). While any Order in Council is in force applying this Act to other substances, such substance will be included in this definition, subject to modification, if any (s 19(2)). See note 1 to s 19, post.

4. In *Grandi v Milburn* [1966] 2 QB 263, [1968] 2 All ER 816, the Divisional Court, without seeking to define the word "kept", held that an offence was committed where a heavily-laden petrol tanker remained stationary for four hours on a forecourt of a garage for the purpose of serving customers with petrol.

5. For provisions substituted for para (b) in the case of some Petroleum Mixtures, see Petroleum (Mixtures) Order 1929 (SR & O 1929/993), art 2.

6. In this context, "premises" bears its normal meaning of land or buildings on land (*Grandi v Milburn*, note 4, supra).

7. For penalty, see Health and Safety at Work etc Act 1974, s 33, in this title, post.

8. "Petroleum spirit licence" means a licence authorising the keeping of petroleum spirit granted by a local authority empowered under this Act to grant such a licence, or by the Secretary of State (s 23). As to the fees payable, see s 4.

8–14231   2. Provisions as to licences.   (1) The local authority empowered to grant such licences shall be

(*a*)   in Greater London, or a metropolitan county, the fire and rescue authority;

(*b*)   . . . ;

(*c*)   elsewhere, the county council or county borough council.

(2) Licences may be granted for a period.

(3) A local authority may attach to the licence such conditions[1] as they think expedient as to the mode of storage, the nature and situation of the premises in which, and the nature of the goods with which petroleum spirit is to be stored, the facilities for the testing of petroleum spirit from time to time, and generally as to the safe-keeping of petroleum spirit.

(4) *Repealed.*

[Petroleum (Consolidation) Act 1928, s 2, as amended by London Government Act 1963, s 50(2), Criminal Damage Act 1971, Sch, Local Government Act 1972, Sch 29; SI 1974/1942, the Local Government Act 1985, Sch 11, the Local Government (Wales) Act 1994, Sch 9, SI 1995/2923, SI 2002/2776 and the Fire and Rescue Services Act 2004, Sch 1.]

---

1. Seemingly a local authority cannot impose different conditions from those imposed by the Secretary of State (*Godfrey v Napier* (1901) 18 TLR 31).

8–14232   3. Appeals from refusals by local authorities to grant licences or conditions. Appeal lies to the Secretary of State.

[Petroleum (Consolidation) Act 1928, s 3, as substituted by SI 1974/1942.]

8–14233   5. Labelling of vessels containing petroleum spirit[1].   (1) Subject as hereinafter provided, where any petroleum spirit

(*a*)   is kept in any place; or

(*b*)   is sent or conveyed between any two places in Great Britain; or

(*c*)   is sold or exposed or offered for sale; there shall be attached to, or, where that is impracticable, displayed near, the vessel containing the petroleum spirit, a label showing, in conspicuous characters, the words "petroleum spirit" and the words "highly inflammable", and

    (i)   in the case of petroleum spirit kept, the name and address of the consignee or owner;

    (ii)   in the case of petroleum spirit sent or conveyed, the name and address of the sender;

    (iii)   in the case of petroleum spirit sold or exposed or offered for sale, the name and address of the vendor:

Provided that, for the purposes of the foregoing provisions

(*a*)   petroleum spirit shall not be deemed to be kept during the seven days next after it has been imported; and

(*b*)   petroleum spirit carried on any motor vehicle[2], ship[3], or aircraft, but intended to be used only for the purposes thereof, shall not be deemed to be conveyed.

(2) Any person who keeps, sends, conveys, sells, or exposes or offers for sale any petroleum spirit in contravention of this section, shall be guilty of an offence[4].

[Petroleum (Consolidation) Act 1928, s 5, as amended by SI 1974/1942.]

---

1. This section has ceased to have effect in relation to the conveyance by road of petroleum spirit in a road tanker or tank container, see now the Carriage of Dangerous Goods by Road Regulations 1996, SI 1996/2095 listed in the nte to the Health and Safety Act 1974, s 15, in this title, post.

The requirements of this section, including this section as applied to any dangerous substance by an Order in Council made under s 19 of the Act, are deemed to be satisfied where the package shows particulars in accordance with the Chemicals (Hazard Information and Packaging for Supply) Regulations 1994, SI 1994/3247 (reg 19) and the Carriage of Dangerous Goods (Classification, Packaging and Labelling) and Use of Transportable Pressure Receptacles Regulations 1996, SI 1996/2092; see note to the Health and Safety at Work etc Act 1974, s 15 in this title, post.

2. "Motor vehicles" includes all mechanically propelled vehicles intended or adapted for use on roads (s 23).

3. "Ship" includes every description of vessel used in navigation, whether propelled by oars or otherwise (s 23).

4. For penalty, see Health and Safety at Work etc Act 1974, s 33, in this title, post.

8–14234   6. *Regulations as to transport of petroleum spirit by road*[1].

---

1. See note 1 to s 10, post (repeal, but saving for existing regulations; penalty provisions) applies also to s 6.

8–14235   7. Bye-laws as to ships and carrying petroleum spirit in harbour.   (*Repealed*)

8–14236   8. Notice of ships carrying petroleum spirit to be given on entering harbour. (*Repealed*)

8–14237   9. Bye-laws as to loading, conveyance and landing of petroleum spirit in and upon canals.   (*Repealed*)

8–14238   10. *Regulations[1] as to the keeping and use of petroleum spirit for purposes of motor vehicles, motor boats, aircraft and engines.*

---

1. Sections 6, 10, 12, 14–16 and 19 are superseded by the Health and Safety at Work etc Act 1974 and were repealed by SI 1974/1942, but regulations made under the repealed sections are preserved. For penalties, see now the 1974 Act, s 33, in this title, post. The following regulations have been made under this section: the Petroleum-Spirit (Motor Vehicles etc) Regulations 1929, SR & O 1929/952 as amended by SI 1992/1811 and SI 1999/743 in this title, post.

8–14239   12. *Regulations as to classes of petroleum spirit likely to be dangerous or injurious to health[1].*

---

1. See note 1 to s 10, ante.

8–14240   14. *Inquiry into accidents connected with petroleum spirit[1].*

---

1. See note 1 to s 10, ante.

8–14241   16. *Powers of government inspectors[1].*

---

1. See note 1 to s 10, ante.

8–14242   17. Powers of officers of local authorities as to testing petroleum spirit.   *Repealed.*

8–14243   18. Warrants to search for and seize petroleum spirit[1].   (1) If a court of summary jurisdiction[2] is satisfied by information on oath that there is reasonable ground for suspecting that any petroleum spirit is being kept, sent, conveyed, or exposed or offered for sale within the jurisdiction of the court, in contravention of this Act, the court shall grant a search warrant authorising any person named therein to enter and examine any place, ship or vehicle named in the warrant, and to search for and take samples of petroleum therein, and to seize and remove any petroleum spirit that he may find therein kept, sent, conveyed or exposed or offered for sale in contravention of this Act, and the vessel containing any such petroleum spirit, and to detain such petroleum spirit and vessel until a court of summary jurisdiction has determined whether or not they are to be forfeited.

(2) Where any petroleum spirit or vessel is seized by virtue of a warrant granted under this section—

(a) proceedings shall be commenced *forthwith* for determining whether or not it is to be forfeited; and

(b) the person seizing it shall not be liable to any proceedings for detaining it or for any loss or damage incurred in respect thereof, except where the loss or damage is due to any wilful act or neglect while the petroleum spirit or vessel is so detained; and

(c) in the case of any petroleum spirit or vessel seized in any ship or vehicle, the person seizing it, may for the purposes of the removal thereof use, during twenty-four hours after the seizure, the ship or vehicle in which it was seized, with the tackle, beasts and accoutrements belonging thereto, but if he do so, shall pay to the owner of the ship or vessel, reasonable compensation for the use thereof; the amount of such compensation shall, in default of agreement, be assessed by the court of summary jurisdiction before which proceedings are taken for determining whether or not the petroleum spirit is to be forfeited, and may be recovered in like manner as fines[3] under this Act may be recovered.

(3) If any person by himself or by any one in his employ or acting by his direction or with his consent, refuses or fails to admit into any place, ship or vehicle occupied by him or under his control, any person authorised by a warrant granted under this section to enter that place, ship, or vehicle, or obstructs or prevents any person from making any search, examination or seizure or taking any samples which he is authorised by such a warrant to make or take, that person shall be guilty of an offence[4].

(4) This section does not apply to—

(a) a workplace within the meaning of the Dangerous Substances and Explosive Atmospheres Regulations 2002 used, or intended for use, for the dispensing of petroleum-spirit, or

(b) carriage by road to which the Carriage of Dangerous Goods and Use of Transportable Pressure Equipment Regulations 2004 apply.

[Petroleum (Consolidation) Act 1928, s 18, as amended by SI 1974/1942, SI 2002/2776 and SI 2004/568.]

---

1. This section has ceased to have effect in relation to the conveyance by road of petroleum spirit in a road tanker or tank container (Dangerous Substances (Conveyance by Road in Road Tankers and Tank Containers) Regulations 1992, SI 1992/743 as amended, see note to the Health and Safety at Work Act 1974, s 15 in this title post).

2. Note that the warrant must be issued by a court of summary jurisdiction; this, we think, may be a single justice sitting as a magistrates' court (see Magistrates' Courts Act 1980, ss 125, 148, ante).

3. Seemingly as a penalty.
4. For penalty see the Health and Safety at Work etc Act 1974, s 33 in this title, post.

8–14244   **19.** *Power to apply Act to other substances*[1].

1. See note 3 to "petroleum spirit" in s 1, ante, and note to the repealed s 10, ante. The following orders have been made: Petroleum (Mixtures) Order 1929, SR & O 1929/993 amended by SI 1992/1811, SI 1993/1746 and SI 1994/3247; Petroleum (Compressed Gases) Order 1930, SR & O 1930/34; Petroleum (Liquid Methane) Order 1957, SI 1957/859 amended by SI 2002/2776.

8–14245   **25. Savings.**   (1) The powers conferred by this Act shall be in addition to and not in derogation of any other powers conferred on any local authority, harbour authority or canal company by any Act (not being an enactment repealed by this Act), or by law or custom.

(2) Nothing in this Act shall be deemed to exempt any person from any penalty to which he would otherwise be subject in respect of a nuisance.

8–14245A   **25A.** (1) The provisions of this Act shall not apply in respect of—

(*a*) any establishment to which the Control of Major Accident Hazards Regulations 1999 [SI 1999/743] apply by virtue of regulation 3 of those Regulations; and

(*b*) any site in respect of which notification of an activity is required pursuant to regulation 3 of the Notification of Installations Handling Hazardous Substances Regulations 1982 [SI 1982/1357] or

(*c*) any workplace within the meaning of the Dangerous Substances and Explosive Atmospheres Regulations 2002, apart from a workplace used, or intended for use, for dispensing petroleum-spirit.

(2) For the purposes of subsection (1)(*c*), any part of a workplace where petroleum-spirit is kept other than for dispensing is not to be regarded as used, or intended for use, for dispensing petroleum-spirit.

[Petroleum (Consolidation) Act 1928, s 25, s 25A amended by SI 1999/743 and SI 2002/2776]

Fireworks Act 1951
(14 & 15 Geo 6 c 58)

8–14410   **1. Destruction of dangerous fireworks.**   (1) Where an inspector appointed by the Health and Safety Executive under s 19 of the Health and Safety at Work etc Act 1974 finds in a factory[1], magazine[1] or store fireworks which he has reason for thinking may be dangerous when in the possession of the public[2], he may take a number of them as a sample and require the occupier of the factory, magazine or store to keep the remainder of such fireworks in the factory, magazine or store for a period of three weeks, or such shorter period as the inspector may specify, and to take such steps as the inspector may specify to secure that they are not moved or tampered with during that period.

(2) If the Secretary of State is satisfied as a result of examination and testing that the fireworks removed by the inspector would be dangerous when in the possession of the public[2] and is satisfied that the sample is a fair one, the Secretary of State may require the occupier to deliver at the factory, magazine or store the fireworks kept there in pursuance of the inspector's requirement to a person authorised by the Secretary of State to receive them; and the Secretary of State shall cause the fireworks so delivered to be destroyed or otherwise rendered harmless and disposed of as he directs.

(3) Where the Secretary of State does not act under subsection (2) of this section, he shall return to the occupier any fireworks forming part of the sample unless their value after examination and testing is so small that it appears to him unreasonable so to do.

(4) If the occupier fails to comply with any requirement made under this section, he shall be liable on summary conviction to a fine not exceeding **level 3** on the standard scale.

(5) References in this section to fireworks include references to partly finished fireworks but in considering whether they would be dangerous it shall be assumed that they are finished before they come into the possession of the public.

[Fireworks Act 1951, s 1, as amended by SI 1974/1885 and the Criminal Justice Act 1982, ss 38 and 46.]

1. "Factory" means a factory licensed under the principal Act, "magazine" means a magazine licensed under the principal Act, other expressions have the same meanings as in the principal Act (s 9).
2. The standard to be applied is prescribed by s 3, post.

8–14411   **2. Determination or amendment of licences for factory where dangerous fireworks made.**   (1) If the Secretary of State is of opinion that in any factory there are being manufactured fireworks which would be dangerous when in the possession of the public[1], and considers that a notice should be served on the occupier of the factory under the following provisions of this section, he shall give to the occupier a statement setting out his opinion and the facts on which his opinion is based and shall afford to him a reasonable opportunity of making representations as to the accuracy of those facts.

(2) If the Secretary of State, having considered any representations made to him under the foregoing subsection, remains of the same opinion, he may at any time more than fourteen days after the giving of the statement serve a notice on the occupier of the factory—

(*a*) stating that on the expiration of a period of seven days beginning with the date of service of the notice any licence under the principal Act[2] relating to the factory shall be determined; and

(*b*) requiring the occupier within the said period to deliver any such licence as aforesaid to the Secretary of State for cancellation.

(3) Upon the expiration of the said period of seven days any licence under the principal Act relating to the factory shall (whether duly delivered up or not) be determined for all the purposes of the principal Act, but without prejudice to the granting of a new licence under that Act:

Provided that notwithstanding that on the determination of the licence the factory becomes an unauthorised place, no proceedings shall be taken under s 5 of the principal Act[3] in respect of the keeping of fireworks in the factory in pursuance of a requirement of an inspector under the foregoing section.

(4) Where a licence under the principal Act permits in the factory the manufacture of explosives other than fireworks, the notice may, if the Secretary of State thinks fit, instead of stating that on the expiration of the said period of seven days any licence shall be determined, state that on the expiration of the said period of seven days it shall be a term of any licence that no fireworks are manufactured and shall then refer to the amendment instead of the cancellation of any licence; and then on the expiration of the said period of seven days the last foregoing subsection shall not apply but for all the purposes of the principal Act it shall be a term of the licence for the factory (whether duly delivered up or not) that no fireworks shall be manufactured in the factory.

Any term imposed under this subsection shall be included among the terms which may be amended under the principal Act.

(5) If the occupier of a factory fails to deliver up a licence as required by this section, he shall be liable on summary conviction to a fine not exceeding **level 1** on the standard scale.

(6) Where the factory is a lawfully existing factory within the meaning of the principal Act (that is to say a factory already in use when that Act was passed) any reference in the foregoing provisions of this section to a licence (other than the reference to a new licence) shall be taken as a reference to a continuing certificate.

[Fireworks Act 1951, s 2, as amended by SI 1974/1885 and the Criminal Justice Act 1982, ss 38 and 46.]

---

1. The standard to be applied is prescribed by s 3, post.
2. See ss 6–8, and s 49 (*as amended*) of the Explosives Act 1875. A licence may be determined or amended by the Secretary of State when there is negligent manufacture (Fireworks Act 1951, s 4).
3. See 1875 Act, ante.

8–14412   3. Standard by which fireworks to be judged dangerous.   In deciding under either of the foregoing sections whether any fireworks would be dangerous when in the possession of the public it shall be assumed that a reasonable standard of care is maintained in handling and using the fireworks.

[Fireworks Act 1951, s 3.]

8–14413   5. Marking of fireworks[1].   (1) Subject to the provisions of this section, no fireworks shall be consigned from the factory in which they were made unless each firework bears conspicuously the name of the occupier of the factory and the address of the factory.

(2) The foregoing subsection shall not apply to—

(*a*) fireworks weighing less than one-eighth of an ounce each;

(*b*) fireworks of the kinds set out in the Schedule to this Act[2];

(*c*) fireworks of such other kinds as the Secretary of State may by regulations contained in a statutory instrument prescribe,

but no fireworks of the kinds set out in the foregoing paragraphs shall be consigned from the factory in which they were made unless every container in which they are consigned, including both containers in which they are to be sold to the public and containers for consignment in bulk, bears conspicuously the name of the occupier of the factory and the address of the factory.

(3) Nothing in either of the foregoing subsections shall apply to fireworks consigned from a factory under a contract for the supply of those fireworks to the Crown[3].

(4) If the foregoing provisions of this section are contravened in respect of any fireworks, the occupier of the factory shall on summary conviction be liable to a penalty not exceeding—

(*a*) **level 1** on the standard scale; or

(*b*) an amount equal to **level 1** on the standard scale for every pound weight of fireworks in respect of which he is convicted,

whichever is the greater:

Provided that the maximum fine in respect of fireworks consigned on any one day shall be **level 3** on the standard scale.

(6)[4] A person against whom proceedings are brought under this section shall, upon information duly laid by him and on giving to the prosecution not less than three clear days' notice of his intention, be entitled to have any person, to whose act or default he alleges that the contravention of the provisions in question was due, brought before the court in the proceedings, and, if after the contravention has been proved the original defendant proves that the contravention was due to the act or default of that other person, that other person may be convicted of the offence, and, if the original defendant further proves that he has used all due diligence to secure that the provisions in question were complied with, he shall be acquitted of the offence.

(7)[4] Where a defendant seeks to avail himself of the provisions of the last foregoing subsection—

(a) the prosecution, as well as the person whom the defendant charges with the offence, shall have the right to cross-examine him, if he gives evidence, and any witness called by him in support of his pleas, and to call rebutting evidence;

(b) the court may make such order as it thinks fit for the payment of costs by any party to the proceedings to any other party thereto.

(8) Where it appears to a government inspector for the purpose of the principal Act that an offence has been committed in respect of which proceedings might be taken under this section against the occupier of a factory and the inspector is reasonably satisfied that the offence of which complaint is made was due to an act or default of some other person and that the said occupier could establish a defence under subsection (6) of this section, he may cause proceedings to be taken against that other person without first causing proceedings to be taken against the said occupier.

In any such proceedings the defendant may be charged with and, on proof that the contravention was due to his act or default, be convicted of, the offence with which the said occupier might have been charged.

[Fireworks Act 1951, s 5, as amended by the Criminal Justice Act 1982, ss 38 and 46— summarised.]

---

1. Nothing in s 5(1) or (2) shall apply to fireworks consigned from a factory for transmission to a place outside the United Kingdom, the Channel Islands and the Isle of Man (Fireworks Act 1964).

2. Aluminium or magnesium torches ("Sparklers"), jumping crackers, and "Throw-downs" (Schedule).

3. This includes a reference to the service authorities of a visiting force, or the headquarters of an international organisation (Visiting Forces and International Headquarters (Application of Law) Order 1965, SI 1965/1536, art 12, Sch 3).

8–14414 **6. Penalty for defacement of marks.** If any person in the course of a trade or business sells, or offers or exposes for sale, any fireworks and a name or address put on them in pursuance of s 5 of this Act has been removed, obliterated or altered, he shall on summary conviction be liable to a fine not exceeding **level 2** on the standard scale:

Provided that it shall be a defence—

(a) to prove that the removal, obliteration or alteration was such as the defendant could not have reasonably been expected to observe; or

(b) in the case of fireworks which at the time of the alleged offence were in a container, to prove that the container had not been opened since it came into the possession of the defendant; or

(c) to prove that the removal, obliteration or alteration was not carried out for the purpose of concealing the identity of the maker, or, as the case may be, of the importer, of the fireworks.

[Fireworks Act 1951, s 6 as amended by the Criminal Justice Act 1982, ss 38 and 46.]

Mines and Quarries Act 1954

(2 & 3 Eliz 2 c 70)

8–14430 This Act consolidates and revises the law relating to the management and control of mines and quarries and is concerned with the safety and health of persons employed there.

The Act contains 195 sections to which are appended five schedules.

In this work it is practicable to include only those provisions which are likely to be of particular concern to magistrates' courts, and they are printed as amended by the Mines and Quarries (Tips) Act 1969 and as further amended by the Mines and Quarries Acts 1954 to 1971 (Repeals and Modifications) Regulations 1974, SI 1974/2013 and the Mines and Quarries (Metrication) Regulations 1976, SI 1976/2063 and SI 1993/208 and 1897.

In relation to mines, the Act has largely been superseded by the Management and Administration of Safety and Health at Mines Regulations 1993 and in relation to quarries by the Quarries Regulations 1999 both listed in the note to s 15 of the Health and Safety at Work Act 1974, post.

PART I
GENERAL DUTIES OF QUARRY OWNERS[1]

8–14431 **1.** *Repealed.*[2]

[Mines and Quarries Act 1954, s 1, amended by SI 1974/2013—summarised.]

1. For the duty on a mine owner see the Management and Administration of Safety and Health at Mines Regulations 1999, SI 1999/1897.

2. For the duties of employers etc in quarries see the Quarries Regulations 1999, SI 1999/2024 amended by SI 1999/3242.

PART II
MANAGEMENT AND CONTROL (MINES)

8–14432 This part (ss 2–20) except s 19 is repealed by the Management and Administration of Safety and Health at Mines Regulations 1993, SI 1993/1897 in this title, post. These provide for the appointment of a suitably qualified and competent manager and prescribe his authority and duties including the establishment of a suitable management structure of competent persons and an inspection system to ensure relevant health and safety requirements are complied with. Section 19 is amended by SI 1974/2013.

PART III
SAFETY, HEALTH AND WELFARE (MINES)

8–14433 Part III (ss 22–97) contains detailed provisions designed to ensure safe working conditions and adequate ventilation. (These provisions are affected by repeals and modifications set out in SI 1974/2013 and SI 1985/2023, and by amendments contained in SI 1976/2063 and SI 1993/302.) Sections 48–54 are repealed by the Mines (Control of Grand Movement) Regulations 1999, SI 1999/2463. Section 60 is repealed in full and ss 80 and 88 are repealed except for the purposes of s 115 by SI 1993/1897. Section 53 is modified by SI 1993/1897.

Ss 61–67 relate to lighting, lamps and contraband. In a "safety-lamp mine" or "safety-lamp part of a mine" (defined in s 182(1)) only "permitted lights" may lawfully be used. "Permitted lights" means locked safety lamps and other means of lighting authorised by regulations (see s 182(1)).

8–14434 65. Offences relating to safety-lamps. (1) A person who damages, destroys or loses or suffers to be damaged, destroyed or lost a safety-lamp given out to him at a mine shall be guilty of an offence[1].

Provided that, in any proceedings taken against a person in respect of an offence under this section with respect to a safety-lamp, it shall be a defence for him to prove that he took reasonable steps for the care and preservation of the lamp and that, immediately after the occurrence of the damage, destruction or loss, as the case may be, he notified an official of the mine of its occurrence.

(2) A person who tampers with a safety-lamp given out to him at a mine shall be guilty of an offence[1].

[Mines and Quarries Act 1954, s 65.]

1. For penalty, see Health and Safety at Work etc Act 1974, s 33.

8–14435 66. Prohibition of possession of smoking materials in certain mines and parts of mines. (1) A person who takes or has in his possession below ground in a safety-lamp mine or takes into, or has in his possession in, a safety-lamp part of a mine, any cigar or cigarette, any pipe or other contrivance for smoking or any match or mechanical lighter, shall be guilty of an offence[1].

(2) It shall be the duty of the manager of every safety-lamp mine and of every mine containing a safety-lamp part—

(*a*) to make, and to ensure the efficient carrying out of, arrangements whereby all persons employed below ground in the mine or, as the case may be, employed in the safety-lamp part thereof or such of those persons as may be selected in accordance with a system approved by an inspector by notice served on the manager of the mine, and any articles which they have with them, and all other persons and any articles which they have with them, will, for the purpose of ascertaining whether any of them, has in his possession any such article as is mentioned in subsection (1) of this section, be searched in the authorised manner immediately before, or (if that is impracticable) immediately after, they go below ground in the mine on any occasion or, as the case may be, enter the safety-lamp part thereof on any occasion; and

(*b*) to secure that, at any time when the said arrangements are not in operation, no person goes below ground in the mine or, as the case may be, enters the safety-lamp part thereof;

and the manager of every safety-lamp mine and of every mine containing a safety-lamp part may, at any time when a person is below ground in the mine or is in the safety-lamp part thereof, as the case may be, cause him and any article which he has with him to be searched in the authorised manner for the purpose of ascertaining whether he has in his possession any such article as is mentioned in subsection (1) of this section.

(3) Where, upon a search made in pursuance of this section, a person who is about to go below ground in a safety-lamp mine or to enter a safety-lamp part of a mine is found to have in his possession any such article as is mentioned in subsection (1) of this section, he shall be guilty of an offence[2].

(4) Without prejudice to the institution of proceedings against a person for an offence under this

section, any such article as is mentioned in subsection (1) of this section which is found upon any search made at a mine in pursuance of this section may be seized by the person making the search and dealt with in such manner as may be directed by the manager of the mine.

(5) No person shall, in pursuance of this section, search any other person on any occasion unless he has previously given on that occasion an opportunity to some two other persons to search himself and, if searched by them, has not been found to have in his possession any such article as is mentioned in subsection (1) of this section.

(6) A person who on any occasion refuses to allow himself or an article which he has with him to be searched in pursuance of this section shall be guilty of an offence[2] and, without prejudice to the institution of proceedings against him in respect of the offence, if the refusal occurs before he goes below ground in a mine shall not be allowed to go below ground in it on that occasion and, if the refusal occurs when he is in a mine, shall not be allowed to remain in it on that occasion.

(7) It shall be the duty of the manager of every safety-lamp mine and of every mine containing a safety-lamp part to secure that, at or near every place where searches are carried out under arrangements made in pursuance of paragraph (*a*) of subsection (2) of this section, notices warning persons of their liability under subsection (1) thereof are kept posted in such characters and in such positions as to be easily seen and read by persons liable to be searched.

(8) In this section the expression "mechanical lighter" means a mechanical, chemical or electrical contrivance designed or adapted primarily for the purpose of igniting tobacco and the expression "authorised manner" means such manner as may be specified in an order made by the Minister.
[Mines and Quarries Act 1954, s 66.]

---

1. It is not a condition precedent to a conviction that a search should have been made in accordance with sub-s (3), post (*Jones v Lewis* [1917] 2 KB 117, 31 JP 131). For penalty, see s 155, post.
2. For penalty, see Health and Safety at Work etc Act 1974, s 33.

8–14436   67. Prohibition of taking into certain mines and parts of mines of articles producing flames or sparks.   (1) Subject to the provisions of this section, no article designed or adapted to produce an unprotected flame or an unprotected spark shall be taken or used below ground in a safety-lamp mine or taken into, or used in, a safety-lamp part of a mine[1].

(2) Nothing in the foregoing subsection shall be construed as prohibiting—

(*a*)   the taking into, or use in, a mine or part of a mine of any article in accordance with this Act or regulations[2];

(*b*)   the taking into, or use in, a mine of any class or part of a mine of any class of an article of a description authorised by order or the Minister to be used in a mine of that class;

(*c*)   the taking into, or use in, a mine or part of a mine of an article of a description authorised in writing by an inspector to be used in that mine or, as the case may be, that part of that mine.
[Mines and Quarries Act 1954, s 67.]

The Factories Act 1961, does not apply to premises forming part of a mine or quarry unless specifically applied by an order of the Ministers of Power and Labour (s 184). Consequently, this Part of the Act contains the following corresponding sections relating to machinery, apparatus and buildings, contravention whereof attracts the operation of ss 152 and 155, post.

---

1. See s 152, post, for offences in event of contravention of a provision of this Act.
2. The Coal and Other Safety-Lamp Mines (Explosive) Regulations 1993, SI 1993/208 impose a series of requirements and prohibitions in relation to the use of explosives and associated material and equipment in safety-lamp mines. The Health and Safety Executive are enabled to grant exemptions from any requirements and prohibitions imposed by the regulations. The regulations provide that in certain cases of criminal proceedings it shall be a defence for the accused to prove that he took all reasonable steps and exercised all due diligence to avoid the commission of the offence. Section 157 of the Act (below) is disapplied in relation to any legal proceedings based on an allegation of a contravention of a requirement or prohibition imposed by or under the regulations.

Machinery and Apparatus

8–14437   81. Construction, maintenance, etc, of machinery and apparatus.   (1) All parts and working gear, whether fixed or movable, including the anchoring and fixing appliances, of all machinery and apparatus used as, or forming, part of the equipment of a mine, and all foundations in or to which any such appliances are anchored or fixed shall be of good construction, suitable material, adequate strength and free from patent defect, and shall be properly maintained[1].
[Mines and Quarries Act 1954, s 81, as amended by SI 1974/2013.]

---

1. This subsection imposes an absolute obligation (*Hamilton v National Coal Board* [1960] AC 633, [1960] 1 All ER 76, 124 JP 141; *Sanderson v National Coal Board* [1961] 2 QB 244, [1961] 2 All ER 796. For penalty for contravention see ss 152, 155, post.

8–14438   82. Fencing of exposed parts of machinery.   *Repealed.*

8–14439   83. Restrictions on use below ground of certain engines, etc.   No internal combustion engine, steam boiler or locomotive shall be used below ground in a mine otherwise than in accordance with the provisions of regulations in that behalf or with the consent of an inspector[1].
[Mines and Quarries Act 1954, s 83, as amended by SI 1974/2013.]

1. This subsection imposes an absolute obligation (*Hamilton v National Coal Board* [1960] AC 633, [1960] 1 All ER 76, 124 JP 141; *Sanderson v National Coal Board* [1961] 2 QB 244, [1961] 2 All ER 796. For penalty for contravention see ss 152, 155, post.

8–14440   84. Air, gas and steam containers.   (1) All apparatus used as, or forming part of the equipment of a mine, being apparatus which contains or produces air, gas or steam at a pressure greater than atmospheric pressure shall be so constructed, installed, maintained and used as to obviate any risk from fire, bursting, explosion or collapse or the production of noxious gases[1].

    (3) *Minister's powers of inspection.*

[Mines and Quarries Act 1954, s 84, as amended by SI 1974/2013.]

1. This subsection imposes an absolute obligation (*Hamilton v National Coal Board* [1960] AC 633, [1960] 1 All ER 76, 124 JP 141; *Sanderson v National Coal Board* [1961] 2 QB 244, [1961] 2 All ER 796. For penalty for contravention see ss 152, 155, post.

8–14441   85. Loading of cranes, etc.   (1) There shall be plainly marked on every crane, crab and winch used as, or forming, part of the equipment of a mine the safe working load or loads thereof, except that, in the case of a jib crane so constructed that the safe working load may be varied by the raising or lowering of the jib, there shall be attached thereto either an automatic indicator of safe working loads or a table indicating the safe working loads at corresponding inclinations of the jib or corresponding radii of the load.

    (2) No person shall, except for the purpose of a test, load any such crane, crab or winch as aforesaid beyond the safe working load marked or indicated thereon in pursuance of the foregoing subsection.

    (3) This section shall not apply to winding apparatus with which a mine shaft or staple-pit is provided or to any rope haulage apparatus, and regulations may provide that this section shall not apply to any other apparatus of a prescribed class.

[Mines and Quarries Act 1954, s 851.]

1. See s 152, post, for offences in event of contravention of a provision of this Act.

Buildings, Structures, Means of Access, etc

8–14442   86. Buildings and structures to be kept safe.   All buildings and structures on the surface of a mine shall be kept in safe condition.

[Mines and Quarries Act 1954, s 861.]

1. See s 152, post, for offences in event of contravention of a provision of this Act.

8–14443   87. Safe means of access and safe means of employment.   (1) There shall be provided and maintained safe means of access to every place in or on a building or structure on the surface of a mine, being a place at which any person has at any time to work.

    (2) Where a person is to work at any such place as aforesaid from which he will be liable to fall a distance of more than two metres, then, unless the place is one which affords secure foothold and, where necessary, secure hand-hold, means shall be provided by fencing or otherwise for ensuring his safety[1].

[Mines and Quarries Act 1954, s 87, as amended by the Mines and Quarries Act 1954, s 87, as amended by SI 1976/2063.]

1. See s 152, post, for offences in event of contravention of a provision of this Act.

8–14444   89.   *Repealed.*

8–14445   90.   *Repealed.*

8–14446   94. Sanitary conveniences.   (1) It shall be the duty of the manager of every mine to secure the provision thereat (as well below as above ground) of sufficient and suitable sanitary conveniences for the use of persons employed thereat being, in a case where persons of both sexes are, or are intended to be, so employed, conveniences affording proper separate accommodation for persons of each sex.

    (2) All sanitary conveniences provided in pursuance of the foregoing subsection shall be kept clean and properly maintained and reasonable provision shall be made for lighting them[1].

[Mines and Quarries Act 1954, s 94.]

1. See s 152, post, for offences in event of contravention of a provision of this Act.

8–14447   95. Measures against vermin and insects.   (1) It shall be the duty of the owner of every mine to take such steps as are necessary to secure that all parts of the mine below ground are kept free from rats and mice[1].

(2) Nothing in this section shall be construed as excluding the application to parts of mines below ground of any of the provisions of the Prevention of Damage by Pests Act 1949.
[Mines and Quarries Act 1954, s 95 as amended by SI 1974/2013.]

---

1. See s 152, post, for offences in event of contravention of a provision of this Act.

8–14448 **97. Supply of drinking water.** There shall be provided and maintained on the surface of every mine, at suitable points conveniently accessible to all persons employed in the mine, an adequate supply of wholesome drinking water[1].
[Mines and Quarries Act 1954, s 97.]

---

1. For penalty for contravention, see ss 152, 155, post.

PART IV
MANAGEMENT AND CONTROL (QUARRIES)[1]

8–14449

---

1. This Part has been repealed. See now the Quarries Regulations 1999, SI 1999/2024 amended by SI 1999/3242.

PART V
SAFETY, HEALTH AND WELFARE (QUARRIES)[1]

8–14460

---

1. This Part has been repealed. See now the Quarries Regulations 1999, SI 1999/2024 amended by SI 1999/3242.

PART VII
WORKMEN'S INSPECTIONS

8–14461 Section 123 permits appointed workmen to inspect a mine on behalf of those employed there; it is modified by SI 1985/2023 and SI 1999/2024 and 3242.

PART XII
GRANT, CANCELLATION AND SUSPENSION OF CERTIFICATES

8–14471 This Part (s 150 and Sch 3) concerns the qualifying certificates of managers and under-managers of mines.

8–14472 **150. Cancellation or suspension of certificates.** (1) On conviction of an offence under the relevant statutory provisions the holder of a certificate granted by the Health and Safety Executive under or by virtue of this Act or of a certificate of qualification issued under reg 18 of the Management of Safety and Health at Mines Regulations 1993 (SI 1993/1897) (whether issued by the Health and Safety Executive or some other body) the court by which he is convicted may, on an application for that purpose made on behalf of the Health and Safety Executive, cancel or suspend the certificate in addition to or instead of imposing any other penalty to which the person convicted may be liable if, having regard to the nature of the offence and the circumstances in which it was committed, the court is of opinion that that person is unfit to continue to hold the certificate:

(a) notice of intention to make an application thereunder has been served on the person convicted at the same time as the service or execution of the summons or warrant issued in pursuance of the information charging him with the offence of which he is convicted; and

(b) the said person has, on pleading to the charge, been given an opportunity to elect, but has not elected, to have the question of the cancellation or suspension of his certificate inquired into under subsection (3) of this section.

(2) Where, under the foregoing subsection, a court cancels or suspends a certificate held by a person, he shall have the same right of appeal as if the cancellation or suspension were a sentence passed by the court on his conviction.

(3) The Health and Safety Executive may, in the case of a person who is the holder of any such certificate as aforesaid with respect to whom a representation is made to the Minister by an inspector or otherwise that that person is, by reason of incompetence or gross negligence or misconduct in the performance of duties of his with respect to a mine, unfit to continue to hold the certificate, and shall, in the case of a person who is the holder of such a certificate and has made an election under paragraph (b) of the proviso to subsection (1) of this section, cause inquiry to be made into the question whether or not he is fit to continue to hold the certificate by a tribunal which shall have power to cancel or suspend the certificate if it finds that by reason aforesaid or, as the case may be, that having regard to the offence and the circumstances in which it is committed, he is unfit to continue to hold the certificate.

(4) The provisions of Part I of the Third Schedule to this Act shall have effect with respect to the

constitution and procedure of the tribunal holding an inquiry under the last foregoing subsection and with respect to the holding of the inquiry.

(5) Where, under subsection (1) of this section, an application is made to a court for the cancellation or suspension of a certificate and the holder does not elect under paragraph (*b*) of the proviso to that subsection to have the question of the cancellation or suspension inquired into under subsection (3) of this section, no inquiry into his conduct shall be held by a tribunal under this section on the same grounds as those considered by the court; and where an inquiry is held by a tribunal under this section into the conduct of the holder of a certificate, no application to a court for the cancellation or suspension of the certificate shall be made under subsection (1) of this section on the same grounds as those considered at the inquiry.

(6) The Health and Safety Executive may at any time, if it is shown to him to be just so to do, restore a certificate cancelled under this section or shorten the period for which a certificate is suspended thereunder.

(7) A certificate suspended under this section shall, during the period of suspension, be of no effect.

(8) The provisions of Part II of the Third Schedule to this Act shall have effect with respect to the delivery up of a certificate to a court or tribunal and with respect to the subsequent proceedings with respect to a certificate so delivered up, and the provisions of Part III of that Schedule shall have effect for the purposes of the application to Scotland of Parts I and II thereof.

(9) *Relates to Scotland.*

[Mines and Quarries Act 1954, s 150, as amended by SI 1974/2013, SI 1993/1897 and SI 1999/2024.]

PART XIII
FENCING OF ABANDONED AND DISUSED MINES AND OF QUARRIES

8–14474   151. Fencing of abandoned and disused mines and of quarries.   (1) It shall be the duty of the owner of every abandoned mine and of every mine which, notwithstanding that it has not been abandoned, has not been worked for a period of twelve months to secure that the surface entrance to every shaft or outlet thereof is provided with an efficient enclosure, barrier, plug or other device so designed and constructed as to prevent any person from accidentally falling down the shaft or from accidentally entering the outlet and that every device so provided is properly maintained[1]:

Provided that this subsection shall not apply to mines which have not been worked for the purpose of getting minerals or products thereof since the ninth day of August, eighteen hundred and seventy-two, being mines other than of coal, stratified ironstone, shale or fireclay.

(2) For the purposes of Part III of the Environmental Protection Act 1990[2], each of the following shall be deemed to be a statutory nuisance that is to say:

(*a*) a shaft or outlet of an abandoned mine (other than a mine to which the proviso to the foregoing subsection applies) or of a mine (other than as aforesaid) which, notwithstanding that it has not been abandoned, has not been worked for a period of twelve months, being a shaft or outlet the surface entrance to which is not provided with a properly maintained device such as is mentioned in that subsection;

(*b*) a shaft or outlet of a mine to which the proviso to the foregoing subsection applies, being a shaft or outlet with respect to which the following conditions are satisfied, namely—

(i) that its surface entrance is not provided with a properly maintained device such as is mentioned in that subsection; and

(ii) that, by reason of its accessibility from a highway or a place of public resort, it constitutes a danger to members of the public; and

(*c*) a quarry (whether in course of being worked or not) which—

(i) is not provided with an efficient and properly maintained barrier so designed and constructed as to prevent any person from accidentally falling into the quarry; and

(ii) by reason of its accessibility from a highway or a place of public resort constitutes a danger to members of the public.

(3) Any expenses incurred, by reason of the operation of Part III of the Environmental Protection Act 1990, by a person other than the owner (as defined for the purposes of this Act) of a mine or quarry for the purpose of abating, or preventing the recurrence of, a nuisance under the last foregoing subsection or in reimbursing a local authority in respect of the abatement, or prevention of the recurrence, of such a nuisance shall, subject to any agreement to the contrary, be recoverable by that person from the owner (as so defined) of the mine or quarry.

(4) *Repealed.*

(5) *Relates to Scotland.*

[Mines and Quarries Act 1954, s 151 as amended by the Environmental Protection Act 1990, Sch 15.]

---

1. Contravention of a provision of this Act is an offence, see s 152, post; for penalty for a contravention of s 151(1) see s 155, post.

2. See title PUBLIC HEALTH, post.

PART XIV

OFFENCES, PENALTIES AND LEGAL PROCEEDINGS

8–14475   **152. Offences[1].**   (1) In the event of a contravention, in relation to a mine[2], of—

(*a*)   a provision of this Act, or an order made thereunder or of regulations[3], not being a provision which expressly provides that a person is to be guilty of an offence; or

(*b*)   a direction, prohibition, restriction or requirement given or imposed by a notice served under or by virtue of this Act by an inspector; or

(*c*)   a condition attached to an exemption, consent, approval or authority granted or given under or by virtue of this Act by the Health and Safety Executive or an inspector; or

(*d*)   a requirement or prohibition imposed by or under health and safety regulations which expressly apply to all mines, any class of mine to which the mine belongs or the mine;

each of the following persons shall, subject to the following provisions of this Act, be guilty of an offence, namely, the owner of the mine, any person to whom written instructions have been given by the owner in pursuance of section one of this Act specifying as, or including amongst, the matters with respect to which that person is charged with securing the fulfilment in relation to the mine of statutory responsibilities of the owner, matters of the class to which the provision, direction, prohibition, restriction, requirement or condition relates, the manager of the mine, any person who is for the time being treated for the purposes of that Act as the manager, every under-manager of the mine and any person who is for the time being treated for the purposes of this Act as an under-manager thereof[4].

(2) *Repealed.*

(3) In the event of a contravention, in relation to a mine[2], by a person other than one mentioned in subsection (1) of this section, of such a provision as is mentioned in paragraph (*a*) of that subsection, or such a requirement or prohibition as is mentioned in paragraph (*d*) of that subsection, whereby there is expressly imposed on that person or on persons of a class to which he belongs a duty or requirement or he or persons of a class to which he belongs are expressly prohibited from doing a specified act, the person who contravened that provision, as well as the persons mentioned in the said subsection (1), shall be guilty of an offence,

(4) Neither the manager of a mine[2] as such, nor a person who is for the time being treated for the purposes of this Act as the manager of a mine, nor an under-manager of a mine, nor a person who is for the time being treated for the purposes of this Act as such an under-manager shall, by virtue of subsection (1) of this section, be guilty of an offence by reason of a contravention by the owner of the mine of—

(*a*)   any provision of this Act, of an order made thereunder or of regulations, being a provision which expressly imposes on the owner of the mine a duty or requirement or a prohibition;

(*b*)   any prohibition, restriction or requirement which, by virtue of a notice served under or by virtue of this Act by an inspector, is expressly imposed on the owner of the mine; or

(*c*)   any requirement or prohibition expressly imposed by or under such health and safety regulations as are mentioned in paragraph (*d*) of subsection (1) of this section on the owner of the mine;

[Mines and Quarries Act 1954, s 152 as amended by SI 1974/2013 and SI 1999/2024.]

---

1. For penalties see Health and Safety at Work etc Act 1974, s 33.

2. A "closed tip" is to be deemed to form part of the mine with which it is associated. (Mines and Quarries (Tips) Act 1969, Sch 3, para 7.)

3. Regulations may be made by the Minister (s 141) and previous regulations may be re-enacted (s 190). The Coal and Other Mines (General Duties and Conduct) Order 1956 (SI 1956/1761 amended by SI 1993/1897) is of particular concern to proceedings in magistrates' courts.

4. In other words, the legislature has said: "We shall not permit one to blame the other, but will hold all to account" Lord HEWART, CJ (*Charlton v Jacob* (1925) 89 JP 174).

8–14476   **153. Accessories.**   Without prejudice to the operation—

(*a*)   as respects England and Wales, of s 8 of the Accessories and Abettors Act 1861, and s 44 of the Magistrates' Courts Act 1980; and

(*b*)   *Relates to Scotland*;

any person who induces or procures, or consents to or connives at, the commission of an offence under this Act, shall be guilty of an offence.

[Mines and Quarries Act 1954, s 153, amended by the Magistrates' Courts Act 1980, Sch 7.]

8–14477   **154. Supplementary provisions as to offences.**   (1) If any persons are employed at a mine[1] otherwise than in accordance with the provisions of this Act, orders made thereunder and regulations, there shall be deemed to be a separate contravention in respect of each person so employed.

(2) If a person acts as manager of a mine in contravention of the provisions of subsection (1) of s 5 of this Act, of any condition attached to an approval granted under that subsection or of a

direction given by a notice served under subsection (2) of that section, there shall be deemed to be a separate contravention in relation to each mine as manager of which he acts.
[Mines and Quarries Act 1954, s 154, amended by SI 1999/2024.]

---

1. See note 2 to s 152 in para **8–14475**, ante.

8–14478   155. Penalty for offences for which no express penalty is provided[1]. (1) A person guilty of an offence under this Act for which no express penalty is provided shall be liable—

(a) if he is the owner of a mine or quarry, a person to whom instructions have been given by the owner of a mine or quarry in pursuance of s 1 of this Act, the manager of a mine or a manager of a quarry, a person who is for the time being treated for the purposes of this Act as the manager of a mine or a manager of a quarry, an under-manager of a mine, a person who is for the time being treated for the purposes of this Act as such an under-manager or the surveyor for a mine, to a fine not exceeding **level 4** on the standard scale[2]; and

(b) if not, to a fine not exceeding **level 1** on the standard scale;

and, if the contravention in respect of which he was convicted is continued after the conviction, he shall be guilty of a further offence and liable, in respect thereof, to a fine not exceeding £5 for each day on which the contravention is so continued.

(2) Where the court by which a person is convicted of any such offence as aforesaid is satisfied that the contravention in respect of which he is convicted—

(a) was likely to cause the death of, or serious bodily injury to, a person employed at the mine or quarry in relation to which the contravention occurred or a dangerous accident; or

(b) was likely to endanger the safety of any such person;

the court may impose upon the person convicted (either in addition to, or in substitution for, a fine) imprisonment for a term not exceeding **three months**.
[Mines and Quarries Act 1954, s 155 as amended by the Criminal Justice Act 1982, ss 38 and 46.]

---

1. This section is repealed except in respect of a contravention of s 151(1), ante.
2. For restriction upon prosecution, see s 164, post.

8–14479   156. Defence available to person charged with offence not committed personally.
In any proceedings under this Act which, by virtue of subsection (1) of s 152 of this Act, are taken against a person in respect of the contravention by a person other than himself of—

(a) a provision of the Act, of an order made thereunder or of regulations, being a provision which expressly imposes on that other person or on persons of a class to which, at the time of the contravention, he belonged, a duty or requirement or expressly prohibits him or persons of such class or all persons from doing a specified act; or

(b) a prohibition, restriction or requirement which by virtue of a notice served under or by virtue of this Act by an inspector is expressly imposed on that other person; or

(c) a requirement or prohibition imposed by or under health and safety regulations which expressly apply to all mines, any class of mine or a particular mine being a requirement expressly imposed on that person or on persons of a class to which, at the time of the contravention, he belonged, or a prohibition expressly imposed on him or on persons of such class or on all persons from doing a specified act;

it shall be a defence for the person charged to prove that he used all due diligence[1] to secure compliance with the provision, prohibition, restriction or requirement, as the case may be.
[Mines and Quarries Act 1954, s 156, as amended by SI 1974/2013 and SI 1999/2024.]

---

1. With regard to "due diligence", reference may usefully be made to decisions under the Food Safety Act 1990, s 21, title FOOD, ante.

8–14490   157. Persons not to be under liability for contraventions which it was impracticable to avoid or prevent. It shall be a defence[1] in any legal proceedings to recover damages and in any prosecution, in so far as the proceedings or prosecution are or is based on an allegation of a contravention, in relation to a mine of—

(a) a provision of this Act, of an order made thereunder or of regulations (not being a provision which expressly provides that a person is to be guilty of an offence); or

(b) a direction, prohibition, restriction, or requirement given or imposed by a notice served under or by virtue of this Act by an inspector; or

(c) a condition attached to an exemption, consent, approval or authority granted or given by or by virtue of this Act by the Health and Safety Executive or an inspector; or

(d) a requirement or prohibition imposed by or under such health and safety regulations as are mentioned in subsection (1)(d) or (2)(d) of section 152 of this Act;

to prove that it was impracticable to avoid or prevent the contravention[2].
[Mines and Quarries Act 1954, s 157, as amended by SI 1974/2013.]

1. Section 157 is disapplied to legal proceedings based on a contravention of the Coal and Other Safety-Lamp Mines (Explosives) Regulations 1993, SI 1993/208 amended by SI 1993/1987 and 3012: see note to s 67 above and the Management and Administration of Safety and Health at Mines Regulations 1993 (reg 42) in this PART post.

2. Such as where the repair of dangerous machinery cannot be tested without running it when the guard has not been replaced (*Coltness Iron Co Ltd v Sharp* [1938] AC 90, [1937] 3 All ER 593), but not where the machinery of a conveyor belt had not been stopped in order to substitute under the belt empty for full truck, and no signal was employed which gave the deceased cleaner time to stop cleaning and close the fence (*Caswell v Powell Duffryn Associated Collieries Ltd* [1939] 3 All ER 722). A company can only act by its servants and agents, and can only carry out the duties imposed on the owner of a coal-mine by this Act by its servants or agents. Where the breach of the Act is committed by a servant specially delegated to carry out the regulations, it cannot be said by the owner that "it was not reasonably practicable to avoid or prevent the breach" (*Yelland v Powell Duffryn Associated Collieries Ltd* [1941] 1 KB 154, [1941] 1 All ER 278).

8–14492 160. Liability of parents for unlawful employment of young persons. If a young person is employed at a mine in contravention of the provisions of this Act, the parent[1] of the young person shall be guilty of an offence and liable, on summary conviction, to a fine not exceeding **level 1** on the standard scale, unless it appears to the court that the contravention occurred without the consent, connivance or wilful default of the parent.
[Mines and Quarries Act 1954, s 160 as amended by the Criminal Justice Act 1982, ss 38 and 46 and SI 1999/2024]

1. "Parent" means a parent of a young person or any person who is not a parent of his but who has parental responsibility for him (within the meaning of the Children Act 1989), or who has parental responsibilities in relation to him (within the meaning of s 1(3) of the Children (Scotland) Act 1995, and includes, in relation to any young person, a person having direct benefit from his wages (Mines and Quarries Act 1954, s 182(1), as amended by the Children Act 1989, Sch 13 and the Children (Scotland) Act 1995, Sch 4).

8–14493 162. Removal or defacement of notices, etc. *Repealed.*

8–14494 163. Prosecution of offences. (1)[1] Any offence under this Act with respect to the trial of which no express provision is made by this Act may be tried either summarily or upon indictment[2].
[Mines and Quarries Act 1954, s 163 as amended by SI 1974/2013.]

1. This subsection is repealed except in respect of a contravention of a provision of s 151(1).
2. For procedure in respect of offences triable either way, see the Magistrates' Courts Act 1980, ss 17A–21, in PART I: MAGISTRATES' COURTS, PROCEDURE, ante.

8–14495 164. Restriction on institution of certain proceedings[1]. No proceedings for an offence under this Act shall, in England and Wales, be instituted against any such person as is mentioned in paragraph (*a*) of subsection (1) of s 155 of this Act except by an inspector or by or with the consent of the Minister[2] or the Attorney-General.
[Mines and Quarries Act 1954, s 164.]

1. This section is repealed except in respect of a contravention of a provision of s 151(1).
2. The Minister of Power (s 182 and SI 1957/48).

8–14496 166. Liability of parents for unlawful employment of children. For the purposes of any proceedings under this Act in respect of the employment of children in contravention of section 17 of the Education (Scotland) Act 1918, or section 1 of the Employment of Women, Young Persons and Children Act 1920 (being enactments which prohibit the employment of children in factories and mines and, so far as they relate to mines, are incorporated with this Act), the references in section 160 of this Act to a young person shall be construed as including references to a child within the meaning of the said section 17 or the said section 1, as the case may be.
[Mines and Quarries Act 1954, s 166, as amended by the Education Act 1973, Sch 2 and SI 1999/2024.]

PART XV
MISCELLANEOUS AND GENERAL

8–14497 *This Part contains ss 169–195 and refers to the 4th and 5th Schedules which provide for the amendment and repeal of the former Acts. Despite these provisions, the Minister has power to provide for the continuance of certain regulations and enactments (s 190).*
    Sections 180–183 prescribe detailed interpretation provisions, many of which are of a technical nature. The following are of general concern.

8–14498 180. Meaning of "mine" and "quarry". (1) In this Act the expression "mine" means an excavation or system of excavations, including all such excavations to which a common system of ventilation is provided, made for the purpose of, or in connection with, the getting, wholly or substantially by means involving the employment of persons below ground, of minerals (whether in their natural state or in solution or suspension) or products of minerals.
    (2) *Repealed.*
    (3) For the purposes of this Act—

(a) there shall be deemed to form part of a mine so much of the surface (including buildings, structures and works thereon) surrounding or adjacent to the shafts or outlets of the mine as is occupied together with the mine for the purpose of, or in connection with, the working of the mine, the treatment, preparation for sale, consumption or use, storage or removal from the mine of the minerals or products thereof gotten from the mine or the removal from the mine of the refuse thereof; and

(b) *Repealed.*

Provided that there shall not, for the said purposes, be deemed to form part of a mine premises in which a manufacturing process is carried on otherwise than for the purpose of the working of the mine or the preparation for sale of minerals gotten therefrom.

(4) For the purposes of this Act premises for the time being used for depositing refuse from a single mine, being premises exclusively occupied by the owner of that mine, shall be deemed to form part of that mine, and premises for the time being used for depositing refuse from two or more mines, being premises occupied by the owner of one of those mines (either exclusively or jointly with the owner of the other or any of the others) shall be deemed to form part of such one of those mines as the Health and Safety Executive may direct.

(5) For the purposes of this Act a railway line serving a single mine (not being a railway line falling within subsection (3) of this section or a railway line belonging to a railway company) shall be deemed to form part of that mine and a railway line jointly serving two or more mines (not being a railway line falling within subsection (3) of this section or a railway line belonging to a railway company) shall be deemed to form part of such one of them as the Health and Safety Executive may direct.

(6) For the purposes of this Act a conveyor or aerial ropeway provided for the removal from a mine of minerals gotten therefrom or refuse therefrom shall be deemed to form part of the mine.

[Mines and Quarries Act 1954, s 180, as amended by SI 1974/2013, SI 1993/1897 and SI 1999/2024.]

8-14499   181. Meaning of "owner". (1) Subject to the provisions of this section, in this Act the expression "owner" means, in relation to a mine, the person for the time being entitled to work it.

(2) *Repealed.*

(3) *Repealed.*

(4) Where the business of a person who, by virtue of the foregoing provisions of this section is, for the purposes of this Act, to be taken to be owner of a mine is carried on by a liquidator, receiver or manager, or by some other person authorised to carry it on by an order of a court of competent jurisdiction, the liquidator, receiver, manager or other person shall be taken for the purposes of this Act to be an additional owner of the mine.

(5) *Scotland.*

[Mines and Quarries Act 1954, s 181 as amended by SI 1999/2024.]

THIRD SCHEDULE

PART II

DELIVERY UP AND CUSTODY OF CERTIFICATES IN CONNECTION WITH PROSECUTIONS AND INQUIRIES

8-14500   11. The holder of any such certificate as is mentioned in section one hundred and fifty of this Act may, after notice of intention to make an application under subsection (1) of the said s 150 has been duly served on him, be required by the court dealing with an information or trying an indictment for an offence alleged to have been committed by him, or may be required by a tribunal making inquiry under the said s 150, to deliver up his certificate to the court or, as the case may be, the tribunal at the hearing.

12. A certificate so delivered up may be retained by the court or tribunal until the conclusion of the proceedings: Provided that a certificate delivered up to the court shall be returned to the holder thereof on his making an election under paragraph (b) of the proviso to subsection (1) of the said s 150.

13. Where the court or tribunal cancels or suspends a certificate it shall, at the conclusion of the proceedings, send the Minister notice thereof and shall also send him the certificate for retention by him.

14. Where on an appeal (whether by way of case stated or otherwise) the conviction of the holder of the certificate is quashed or the cancellation or suspension thereof is quashed or varied, the court by which the conviction is quashed or the appeal is allowed shall send notice thereof to the Minister:

Provided that where on an appeal by way of case stated the High Court remits the matter to a magistrates' court or a court of quarter sessions, notice of the order of the court or on remission shall be sent to the Minister by the magistrates' court or court of quarter sessions, as the case may be.

15. Where a certificate has been sent to the Minister under paragraph 13 of this Schedule, he shall—

(a) on receipt of a notice that the conviction of the holder thereof, or the cancellation or suspension thereof, has been quashed; or

(b) on the expiration of any period for which the certificate stands suspended (whether after conviction or appeal);

return the certificate to the holder.

16. For the purposes of this Part of this Schedule, the bringing of proceedings before the High Court to quash a conviction by order of certiorari shall be deemed to be an appeal.

Factories Act 1961

(9 & 10 Eliz 2 c 34)

8-14610   This Act consolidates the Factories Acts 1937–1959, and certain other enactments relating to the safety, health and welfare of employed persons.

There are included here those portions of the Act which are most usually of concern to magistrates' courts.

The 1961 Act came into force on 1st April 1962. Decisions prior to that date, noted to the text, are based upon the earlier legislation, but will remain applicable to the consolidation Act.

The Act confers various powers on the Minister of Labour (now the Secretary of State for Employment and Productivity), who is described throughout as "the Minister" (s 176(1)).

As a consequence of the enactment of the Health and Safety at Work etc Act 1974, the Act is amended by the Factories Act 1961 etc (Repeals and Modifications) Regulations 1974, SI 1974/1941. Reg 6 of those Regulations provides as follows—

References in any provision of an enactment, instrument or other document to any of the following, that is to say:

(*a*) an inspector appointed under the 1961 Act;
(*b*) the inspector for the district, the superintending inspector for the division or the chief inspector;
(*c*) an employment medical adviser appointed under the 1972 Act and
(*d*) the chief employment medical adviser or a deputy chief employment medical adviser,

shall, except where the context otherwise requires or where the reference is otherwise expressly amended, be construed as references respectively to—

(*a*) an inspector appointed by the Health and Safety Executive under section 19 of the 1974 Act;
(*b*) an inspector so appointed who is authorised to act for the purposes of the provision in question;
(*c*) an employment medical adviser appointed under section 56 of the 1974 Act; and
(*d*) an employment medical adviser so appointed who is authorised to act for the purpose of the provision in question.

The following regulations made under the Factories Act 1961, or made before the commencement of the Act but having effect under it, have been continued in force by SI 1974/1941:

SR & O 1906/679 amended by SI 1989/1327, SI 1989/2169, SI 1992/1811 and SI 1997/135 and 533	Use of Locomotives and Waggons on Lines and Sidings in or used in connection with Premises under the Factory and Workshops Act 1901;
SI 1950/65 amended by SI 1973/36, SI 1980/1248, SI 1982/877, SI 1988/1657, SI 1989/2311, SI 1990/305, SI 1992/3004, SI 1995/2923 and SI 1998/543	Pottery (Health and Welfare);
SI 1961/1580 amended by SI 1966/94, SI 1974/1681, SI 1981/1414, SI 1988/1657, SI 1989/635 and 682, SI 1992/2793, SI 1994/3140, SI 1995/2923 and SI 1996/1592	Construction (General Provision);
SI 1962/1667 amended by SI 1974/1681, SI 1981/1332, SI 1988/1657, SI 1992/2966 and 3004 and SI 1995/2923	Non-ferrous Metals (Melting and Founding)

PART II
SAFETY (GENERAL PROVISIONS)

8–14615 12. Prime movers. (1) Every flywheel directly connected to any prime mover[1] and every moving part of any prime mover, except such prime movers as are mentioned in subsection (3) of this section, shall be securely fenced[2], whether the flywheel or prime mover is situated in an engine-house or not.

(2) The head and tail race of every water wheel and of every water turbine shall be securely fenced.

(3) Every part of electric generators, motors and rotary converters, and every flywheel directly connected thereto, shall be securely fenced unless it is in such a position or of such construction as to be as safe[3] to every person employed or working on the premises as it would be if securely fenced.
[Factories Act 1961, s 12.]

---

1. See note to s 175, post.

2. The test whether machinery is "securely fenced" is whether it is so fenced as to give security from such dangers as might reasonably be expected (*Burns v Joseph Terry & Sons Ltd* [1951] 1 KB 454, [1950] 2 All ER 987, 114 JP 613). Apart from the exemption contained in s 15, post, the obligation is to fence securely, and the secure fencing must be fool-proof. Thus if a machine can be worked upwards or downwards (or reverse way), it must be securely fenced for each manner of working (*Pursell v Clement Talbot Ltd* (1914) 79 JP 1), or if the dangerous parts cannot be reached by the workman's hands, unless he operates the bimanual control in some other way than by his hands (*Sowter v Steel Barrel Co Ltd* (1935) 99 JP 379; approved in *Vowles v Armstrong-Siddeley Motors Ltd* [1938] 4 All ER 796, CA). The defence cannot insert after the words "securely fenced" the words "where an inspector so requires". It is therefore immaterial that the machinery has been often inspected by the inspectors, none of whom has made any suggestions or given any instructions by letter or otherwise (*Menzies v Wheeler* (18 July 1929, unreported); *Younger v Melyn Tinplate Co Ltd* (12 and 13 December 1929, unreported); *Rees v Jones* (17 December 1926, unreported)). It is equally immaterial that an accident was not anticipated (*Chandler v Caisby & Son* (30 July 1930, unreported), or that the machinery was 13 feet from the ground (*Atkinson v London and North Eastern Rly Co* [1926] 1 KB 313, 90 JP 17). If the defendant desires to cast the blame on the actual

offender, he should have recourse to s 161, post (*Thomas v Thomas Bolton & Sons Ltd* (1928) 92 JP 147; cf *Ward v W H Smith & Son* [1913] 3 KB 154, 77 JP 370; see also *Murray v Schwachman Ltd* [1938] 1 KB 130, [1937] 2 All ER 68).

3. See s 15, post.

8–14616 13. Transmission machinery. (1) Every part of the transmission machinery[1] shall be securely fenced[2] unless it is in such a position or of such construction as to be as safe to every person employed or working on[3] the premises as it would be if securely fenced.

(2) Efficient devices or appliances shall be provided and maintained in every room or place where work is carried on by which the power can promptly be cut off from the transmission machinery in that room or place.

(3) No driving-belt[4] when not in use shall be allowed to rest or ride upon a revolving shaft which forms part of the transmission machinery.

(4) Suitable striking gear or other efficient mechanical appliances shall be provided and maintained and used to move driving belts to and from fast and loose pulleys which form part of the transmission machinery, and any such gear or appliances shall be so constructed, placed and maintained as to prevent the driving belt from creeping back on to the fast pulley.

(5)[5] Where the Minister is satisfied that owing to special circumstances the fulfilment of any of the requirements of subsections (2) to (4) of this section is unnecessary or impracticable, he may by order direct that that requirement shall not apply in those circumstances.
[Factories Act 1961, s 13.]

1. "Transmission machinery" means every shaft, wheel, drum, pulley, system of fast and loose pulleys, coupling, clutch, driving-belt or other device by which the motion of a prime mover is transmitted to or received by any machine or appliance. "Driving-belt" includes any driving strap or rope (s 176(1)). See *Deane v Edwards & Co Ltd* [1941] 2 All ER 274, as to machinery used to operate a lift being held to be "transmission machinery". Transmission machinery ceases to be such when no power is being transmitted to it from the prime mover: the section does not prohibit the removal of a fence for the purpose of repairing the machinery (*Richard Thomas and Baldwins Ltd v Cummings* [1955] AC 321, [1955] 1 All ER 285).

2. See note 2 in para **8–14615**, supra. The commercial impracticability or mechanical impossibility is irrelevant (*Davies v Thomas Owen & Co* [1919] 2 KB 39, 83 JP 193; *Fowler v Yorkshire Electric Power Co Ltd* [1939] 1 All ER 407; *Dennistoun v Charles E Greenhill Ltd* infra), unless the Minister makes an order under sub-s (5). For exemptions, see s 15, post. See the observations of Viscount SIMON, LC, in *Lewis v Denye* [1940] AC 921, [1940] 3 All ER 299, as to the correctness of view in *Davies v Thomas Owen & Co*, supra, respecting the commercial impracticability, etc, of fenced machinery, and *Proctor v Johnson and Phillips Ltd* [1943] 1 KB 553, [1943] 1 All ER 565. In *Miller v William Boothman & Sons Ltd* [1944] KB 337, [1944] 1 All ER 333, it was the opinion that *Davies v Thomas Owen & Co*, supra, was rightly decided as a general proposition and in the absence of special regulations. See also *Dennistoun v Charles E Greenhill Ltd* [1944] 2 All ER 434 and *Pugh v Manchester Dry Docks Co Ltd* [1954] 1 All ER 600.

3. See note to s 12, ante. This person need not be employed by the occupier of the factory. He may not be under his control but merely working therein for a contractor (*Butler v Glacier Metal Co Ltd* (23 October 1924, unreported).

4. "Transmission machinery" means every shaft, wheel, drum, pulley, system of fast and loose pulleys, coupling, clutch, driving-belt or other device by which the motion of a prime mover is transmitted to or received by any machine or appliance. "Driving-belt" includes any driving strap or rope (s 176(1)). See *Deane v Edwards & Co Ltd* [1941] 2 All ER 274, as to machinery used to operate a lift being held to be "transmission machinery". Transmission machinery ceases to be such when no power is being transmitted to it from the prime mover: the section does not prohibit the removal of a fence for the purpose of repairing the machinery (*Richard Thomas and Baldwins Ltd v Cummings* [1955] AC 321, [1955] 1 All ER 285).

5. This subsection is repealed except in so far as it enables orders to be made otherwise than by statutory instrument: SI 1974/1941.

8–14617 14. Other machinery. (1) Every dangerous part[1] of any machinery[2], other than prime movers[3] and transmission machinery[4], shall be securely fenced[5], unless it is in such a position or of such construction as to be safe to every person employed or working[6] on the premises as it would be if securely fenced[7].

(2) In so far as the safety of a dangerous part of any machinery cannot by reason of the nature of the operation be secured by means of a fixed guard, the requirements of subsection (1) of this section shall be deemed to have been complied with if a device is provided which automatically prevents the operator from coming into contact with that part.

(5) Any part of a stock-bar[8] which projects beyond the headstock[8] of a lathe shall be securely fenced unless it is in such a position as to be as safe to every person employed or working on the premises as it would be if securely fenced.

The Minister may, as respects any machine or any process in which a machine is used, make regulations requiring the fencing of materials or articles which are dangerous while in motion in the machine.
[Factories Act 1961, s 14, as amended by SI 1974/1941.]

1. This subsection imposes an absolute duty to fence securely every dangerous part of machinery. It would be irrelevant that the machine was securely fenced in the best known method for which it was used (*Dennistoun v Charles E Greenhill Ltd* [1944] 2 All ER 434; *Davies v Thomas Owen & Co* [1919] 2 KB 39, 83 JP 193, followed); or that to provide fencing would render the machine commercially unusable (*Pugh v Manchester Dry Docks Co Ltd* [1954] 1 All ER 600; *Frost v John Summers & Sons Ltd* [1954] 2 QB 21, [1954] 1 All ER 901, CA; affd sub nom *John Summers & Sons Ltd v Frost* [1955] AC 740, [1955] 1 All ER 870, HL). But the fact that a machine is capable of causing injury and that injury had happened to an operator is not conclusive proof that the machine is dangerous within the meaning of the section (*Carr v Mercantile Produce Co Ltd* [1949] 2 KB 601, [1949] 2 All ER 531, 113 JP 488). Machinery is dangerous if in the ordinary course of

human affairs, danger can be reasonably anticipated from the use of it without protection (*Hindle v Birtwistle* [1897] 1 QB 192, 61 JP 70; *Kinder v Camberwell Metropolitan Borough Council* [1944] 2 All ER 315, 109 JP 81), even if the workman has disobeyed instructions or the accident was due to his haste, hurry, carelessness or indolence (*Sutherland v James Mills Ltd, Executors* [1938] 1 All ER 283; *Dunn v Bird's Eye Foods Ltd* [1959] 2 All ER 403). The decision in *Hindle v Birtwistle*, supra, must be read with reference to the subject matter of that case, and it turned upon an accident that had been caused by a flying shuttle doing something which it was never expected to do (*Sutherland v James Mills Ltd, Executors*, supra. See also the observations of DU PARCQ LJ, in *Stimpson v Standard Telephones and Cables Ltd* [1940] 1 KB 342, [1939] 4 All ER 225). It is otherwise with a shaft, the function of which is to revolve (*Peacock v Gyproc Products Ltd* (1935) 79 Sol Jo 904). Where it is proved that the machine is dangerous to a person who is employed to use it and actually causes injury to that person when he is so using it, it is a dangerous machine. The fact that it has been in use for 30 years without an accident and without objection by inspecting factory inspectors does not show that it was not dangerous (*Sutherland v James Mills Ltd, Executors*, supra). But it is a point that ought to be taken into account (*per* Lord GODDARD CJ, in *Carr v Mercantile Produce Co Ltd* [1949] 1 KB 601, [1949] 2 All ER 531, 113 JP 488). If the machinery is in fact dangerous, it is no defence that it was unlikely or improper that any workman should approach it (*Bourne v Mendip Concrete Co Ltd* (1941) 85 Sol Jo 248). If there is no reasonably foreseeable danger from the use of a machine, it is not dangerous machinery and no obligation to fence arises (*Close v Steel Co of Wales Ltd* [1962] AC 367, [1961] 2 All ER 953, HL).

The Factories Act is there not merely to protect the careful, the vigilant and the conscientious workman, but, human nature being what it is, also the careless, the indolent, the inadvertent, the weary, and even, perhaps, in some cases, the disobedient (*per* STABLE J, in *Carr v Mercantile Produce Co Ltd*, supra).

2. "Machinery" includes any driving-belt. "Driving-belt" includes any driving strap or rope (s 176(1)). "Any machinery" does not include machines which are products of the manufacturing processes of a factory (*Parvin v Morton Machine Co Ltd* [1952] AC 515, [1952] 1 All ER 670, 116 JP 211), but it does include machinery which has been installed in a factory with a view to modification and which will be used for productive purposes if the modification is successful (*TBA Industrial Products Ltd v Laine* [1987] ICR 75, 150 JP 556). A mobile crane is not excluded from the operation of s 14 by reason of its mobility or by reason of the fact that later sections of the Act make specific provision regarding such equipment (*British Railways Board v Liptrot* [1969] 1 AC 136, [1967] 2 All ER 1072, HL).

3. For definition of "prime mover", see note to s 175, post.

4. See note 1 in para **8–14616**, supra.

5. This means securely fenced for the purpose of preventing the body of the operator from coming into contact with machinery: not against potential dangers which might arise if the machinery breaks, or if part of it, or fragments of the material on which the machine is working, were to fly out (*Close v Steel Co of Wales Ltd* [1962] AC 367, [1961] 2 All ER 953, HL, in which earlier authorities were reviewed). The machine must be securely fenced even if the effect of such fencing is to render the machine commercially unusable (*Frost v John Summers & Sons Ltd* [1954] 2 QB 21, [1954] 1 All ER 901, affd sub nom *John Summers & Sons Ltd v Frost* [1955] AC 740, [1955] 1 All ER 870, HL). The "matter" of the information arises when the machinery is discovered in an unfenced condition, not when it was first installed and operated: thus the date when infringement of the law began does not affect the limitation prescribed by the Magistrates' Courts Act 1980, s 127, ante (*Rowley v T A Everton & Sons Ltd* [1941] 1 KB 86, [1940] 4 All ER 435, 104 JP 461). Regulations made under s 76, post, may modify this obligation (*Miller v William Boothman & Sons Ltd* [1944] KB 337, [1944] 1 All ER 333; *Whitten v Army and Navy Stores Ltd* [1943] KB 580, [1943] 2 All ER 244, 107 JP 179, overruled). Compliance with the requirements of Regulations does not absolve an occupier from taking proper steps to fence some other part of the machine for which no provision had been made in the Regulations (*Automatic Woodturning Co Ltd v Stringer* [1957] AC 544, [1957] 1 All ER 90, HL) explaining *Benn v Kamm & Co Ltd* [1952] 2 QB 127, [1952] 1 All ER 833.

6. See note 3 at para **8–14616**, ante.

7. See note 2 at para **8–14615**, ante.

8. A "head-stock" is that part of the lathe, consisting of a revolving spindle to which can be attached a chuck to hold in position the object to be turned, and a "stock-bar" is the object to be turned, from which, when revolving, parts can be cut off as and when required.

8–14618 **15. Provisions as to unfenced machinery.** (1) In determining for the purposes of the foregoing provisions[1] of this Part of this Act, whether any part of machinery[2] is in such a position or of such construction as to be as safe to every person employed[3] or working[4] on the premises as it would be if securely fenced the following paragraphs shall apply in a case where this section applies, that is to say—

(a) no account shall be taken of any person carrying out, while the machinery is in motion, an examination thereof or any lubrication or adjustment shown by the examination to be immediately necessary, if the examination, lubrication, or adjustment can only be carried out while the part of machinery is in motion; and

(b) in the case of any part of transmission machinery used in any such process as may be specified in regulations made by the Minister, being a process where owing to the continuous nature thereof the stopping of that part would seriously interfere with the carrying on of the process, no account shall be taken of any person carrying out, by such methods and in such circumstances as may be specified in the regulations, any lubrication or any mounting or shipping of belts.

(2) This section only applies where the examination, lubrication or other operation is carried out by such persons, who have attained the age[5] of eighteen, as may be specified in regulations made by the Minister, and all such other conditions as may be so specified are complied with.

[Factories Act 1961, s 15, as amended by the Sex Discrimination Act 1975, Sch 5.]

1. Ie ss 12 to 14 of Pt II
2. See note 2 at para **8–14617**, supra.
3. See note to s 12, ante.
4. Cf *Coltness Iron Co v Sharp* [1938] AC 90, [1937] 3 All ER 593, and *Atkinson v Baldwins Ltd* (1938) 102 JP 158.
5. As to when this age is attained, see *Re Shurey, Savory v Shurey* [1918] 1 Ch 263. A certificate of birth is admissible in evidence by the Evidence Act 1851, s 14, para **2–813**, ante, but proof of identity must be given (*R v Rogers* (1914) 79 JP 16). See also the Births and Deaths Registration Act 1953, s 34, title BIRTHS AND DEATHS, ante. A birth certificate can be obtained on payment of the appropriate fee (s 178). As to other evidence of age, see *R v Cox* [1898] 1 QB 179.

8–14619   16. Construction and maintenance of fencing.   All fencing or other safeguards provided in pursuance of the foregoing provisions[1] of this Part of this Act shall be of substantial construction, and constantly maintained[2] and kept in position while the parts required to be fenced or safeguarded are in motion or in use, except when any such parts are necessarily exposed for examination and for any lubrication or adjustment shown by the examination to be immediately necessary, and all such conditions as may be specified in regulations made by the Minister are complied with.
[Factories Act 1961, s 16.]

1. Ie, ss 12 to 15 of Pt II. Section 16 does not create an offence but defines the extent of an obligation (*Massey v S and P Lingwood Ltd* (1945) 89 Sol Jo 316; *Smith v Morris Motors Ltd and Harris* [1950] 1 KB 194, [1949] 2 All ER 715, 113 JP 521).
2. "Maintained" means maintained in an efficient state in efficient working order and in good repair (s 176(1)).

8–14620   17. Construction and sale of machinery.   (1) In the case of any machine in a factory[1] which is a machine intended to be driven by mechanical power—

> (*a*) every set-screw, bolt or key on any revolving shaft, spindle, wheel or pinion shall be so sunk, encased or otherwise effectively guarded as to prevent danger; and
> (*b*) all spur and other toothed or friction gearing, which does not require frequent adjustment while in motion, shall be completely encased unless it is so situated as to be as safe as it would be if completely encased.

(2) Any person who sells or lets on hire, or as agent of the seller or hirer causes or procures to be sold or let on hire, for use in a factory in the United Kingdom any machine intended to be driven by mechanical power which does not comply with the requirements of this section shall be guilty of an offence.

(3)–(5) *Repealed.*
(6) Nothing in this section applies to any machine constructed[2] before July 30th, 1937[3], and regulations under subsection (3) of this section shall not apply to any machinery or plant constructed before the making of the regulations.
[Factories Act 1961, s 17, as amended by SI 1974/1941.]

1. See s 175, ante.
2. For the purposes of this Act, machinery or plant shall be deemed to have been constructed or reconstructed, and a factory or building shall be deemed to have been constructed, reconstructed, extended, added to, or converted for use as a factory, before any date, if the construction, reconstruction, extension, addition, or conversion was begun before that date (s 176(2)).
3. The date of the passing of the Factories Act 1937.

8–14622   19. Self-acting machines.   (1) In any factory or part of a factory to which this subsection applies no traversing part of any self-acting machine and no material carried thereon shall if the space over which it runs is a space over which any person is liable to pass, whether in the course of his employment or otherwise, be allowed[1] on its outward or inward traverse to run within a distance of 500 millimetres from any fixed structure which is not part of the machine: but nothing in this subsection shall prevent any portion of the traversing carriage of any self-acting spinning mule being allowed to run to a point 310 millimetres distant from any part of the head stock of another such machine.

(2) The foregoing subsection applies—

> (*a*) to any factory erected after the 31st day of December 1895; and
> (*b*) to any factory or part of a factory reconstructed after the 30th day of July, 1937[2]; and
> (*c*) to any extension of or addition to a factory made after the said 30th day of July.

(3) All practicable steps shall be taken by instructions to the person in charge of the machine and otherwise to ensure that no person employed shall be in the space between any traversing part of a self-acting spinning mule and any fixed part of the machine towards which the traversing part moves on the inward run, except when the machine is stopped with the traversing part on the outward run.
[Factories Act 1961, s 19 as amended by SI 1983/978.]

1. If the person in charge of the machine *bona fide* believes that the person in question is clear of the machine, he does not so allow him (*Crabtree v Fern Spinning Co Ltd* (1901) 66 JP 181).
2. The date of the passing of the Factories Act 1937.

8–14623   20. *Repealed.*

8–14624   21. *Repealed.*

8–14625   22. Hoists and lifts—general.   (1) Every hoist or lift shall be of good mechanical construction, sound material and adequate strength, and shall be properly maintained.

(2) Every hoist or lift shall be thoroughly examined by a competent person at least once in every period of six months, and a report of the result of every such examination in the prescribed form and

containing the prescribed particulars shall within twenty-eight days be entered in or attached to the general register[1].

(3) Where the examination shows that the hoist or lift cannot continue to be used with safety unless certain repairs are carried out immediately or within a specified time, the person making the report shall within twenty-eight days of the completion of the examination send a copy of the report to the inspector for the district.

(4) Every hoistway or liftway shall be efficiently protected by a substantial enclosure fitted with gates, and the enclosure shall be such as to prevent, when the gates are shut, any person falling down the way or coming into contact with any moving part of the hoist or lift.

(5) Any such gate shall, subject to subsection (6) of this section and to section 25 of this Act, be fitted with efficient interlocking or other devices to secure that the gate cannot be opened except when the cage or platform is at the landing and that the cage or platform cannot be moved away from the landing until the gate is closed.

(6) If in the case of a hoist or lift constructed or reconstructed before the 30th July, 1937(1), it is not reasonably practicable to fit it with such devices as are mentioned in subsection (5) of this section, it shall be sufficient if the gate—

(*a*) is provided with such arrangements as will secure the objects of that subsection so far as is reasonably practicable, and

(*b*) is kept closed and fastened except when the cage or platform is at rest at the landing.

(7) Every hoist or lift and every such enclosure as is mentioned in subsection (4) of this section shall be so constructed as to prevent any part of any person or any goods carried in the hoist or lift from being trapped between any part of the hoist or lift and any fixed structure or between the counterbalance weight and any other moving part of the hoist or lift.

(8) There shall be marked conspicuously on every hoist or lift the maximum working load which it can safely carry, and no load greater than that load shall be carried on any hoist or lift.
[Factories Act 1961, s 22.]

---

1. A register kept in each factory in accordance with s 140 of the Act.

8–14626 23. Hoists and lifts used for carrying persons. (1) The following additional requirements shall apply to hoists and lifts used for carrying persons, whether together with goods or otherwise:

(*a*) efficient automatic devices shall be provided and maintained to prevent the cage or platform overrunning;

(*b*) every cage shall on each side from which access is afforded to a landing be fitted with a gate, and in connection with every such gate efficient devices shall be provided to secure that, when persons or goods are in the cage, the cage cannot be raised or lowered unless the gate is closed, and will come to rest when the gate is opened.

(2) In the case of a hoist or lift constructed or reconstructed before the 30th July, 1937[1], in connection with which it is not reasonably practicable to provide such devices as are mentioned in paragraph (*b*) of subsection (1) of this section it shall be sufficient if—

(*a*) such arrangements are provided as will secure the objects of that paragraph so far as is reasonably practicable; and

(*b*) the gate is kept closed and fastened except when the cage is at rest or empty.

(3) In the case of a hoist or lift used as mentioned in subsection (1) of this section which was constructed or reconstructed after the 29th July, 1937[2], where the platform or cage is suspended by rope or chain, there shall be at least two ropes or chains separately connected with the platform or cage, each rope or chain and its attachments being capable of carrying the whole weight of the platform or cage and its maximum working load, and efficient devices shall be provided and maintained which will support the platform or cage with its maximum working load in the event of a breakage of the ropes or chains or any of their attachments.
[Factories Act 1961, s 23.]

---

1. The date of the passing of the Factories Act 1937.
2. Ie, after the passing of the Factories Act 1937.

8–14628 25. Exceptions and provisions supplementary to sections 22–24. (1) For the purposes of sections 22 and 23 of this Act, no lifting machine or appliance shall be deemed to be a hoist or lift unless it has a platform or cage the direction of movement of which is restricted by a guide or guides.

(2) Subsections (3) to (8) of section 22 and section 23 of this Act shall not apply in the case of a continuous hoist or lift, and in such a case subsection (2) of the said section 22 shall have effect as if for the reference to six months there were substituted a reference to twelve months.

(3) Subsections (5) and (6) of the said section 22 and the said section 23 shall not apply in the case of a hoist or lift not connected with mechanical power; and in such a case—

(a) subsection (2) of the said section 22 shall have effect as if for the reference to six months there were substituted a reference to twelve months; and

(b) any gates to be fitted under subsection (4) of the said section 22 shall be kept closed and fastened except when the cage or platform is at rest at the landing.

[Factories Act 1961, s 25, as amended by SI 1974/1941.]

8–14629   26. Chains, ropes and lifting tackle.   (1) The following provisions shall be complied with as respects every chain, rope or lifting tackle used for the purpose of raising or lowering persons, goods or materials:

(a) no chain, rope or lifting tackle shall be used unless it is of good construction, sound material, adequate strength and free from patent defect[1];

(b) subject to subsection (2) of this section, a table showing the safe working loads of every kind and size of chain, rope or lifting tackle in use, and, in the case of a multiple sling, the safe working load at different angles of the legs, shall be posted in the store in which the chains, ropes or lifting tackle are kept, and in prominent positions on the premises, and no chain, rope or lifting tackle not shown in the table shall be used;

(c) no chain, rope or lifting tackle shall be used for any load exceeding its safe working load as shown by the table mentioned in paragraph (b) of this subsection or marked as mentioned in subsection (2) of this section;

(d) all chains, ropes and lifting tackle in use shall be thoroughly examined by a competent person at least once in every period of six months or at such greater intervals as the Minister may prescribe;

(e) no chain, rope or lifting tackle, except a fibre rope or fibre rope sling, shall be taken into use in any factory for the first time in that factory unless it has been tested and thoroughly examined by a competent person and a certificate of the test and examination specifying the safe working load and signed by the person making the test and examination has been obtained and is kept available for inspection;

(f) every chain and lifting tackle except a rope sling shall, unless of a class or description exempted by certificate of the chief inspector upon the ground that it is made of such material or so constructed that it cannot be subjected to heat treatment without risk of damage or that it has been subjected to some form of heat treatment (other than annealing) approved by him, be annealed at least once in every fourteen months or, in the case of chains or slings of 13 millimetres bar or smaller, or chains used in connection with molten metal or molten slag, in every six months, except that chains and lifting tackle not in regular use need be annealed only when necessary;

(g) a register containing the prescribed particulars shall be kept in respect of all such chains, ropes or lifting tackle, except fibre rope slings.

(2) Paragraph (b) of subsection (1) of this section shall not apply in relation to any lifting tackle if its safe working load or, in the case of a multiple sling, the safe working load at different angles of the legs is plainly marked upon it.

(3) In this section "lifting tackle" means chain slings, rope slings, rings, hooks, shackles and swivels.

[Factories Act 1961, s 26 as amended by SI 1983/978.]

---

1. See *Dawson v Murex Ltd* [1941] 2 All ER 483, as to a breach of this paragraph by the use of a defective sling.

8–14640   27. Cranes and other lifting machines.   (1) All parts and working gear, whether fixed or movable, including the anchoring and fixing appliances, of every lifting machine shall be of good construction, sound material, adequate strength and free from patent defect, and shall be properly maintained.

(2) All such parts and gear shall be thoroughly examined by a competent person at least once in every period of fourteen months and a register shall be kept containing the prescribed particulars of every such examination; and where the examination shows that the lifting machine cannot continue to be used with safety unless certain repairs are carried out immediately or within a specified time, the person making the report of the examination shall within twenty-eight days of the completion of the examination send a copy of the report to the inspector for the district.

(3) All rails on which a travelling crane moves and every track on which the carriage of a transporter or runway moves shall be of proper size and adequate strength and have an even running surface; and any such rails or track shall be properly laid, adequately supported or suspended and properly maintained.

(4) There shall be plainly marked on every lifting machine its safe working load or loads, except that in the case of a jib crane so constructed that the safe working load may be varied by the raising or lowering of the jib, there shall be attached thereto either an automatic indicator of safe working loads or a table indicating the safe working loads at corresponding inclinations of the job or corresponding radii of the load.

(5) No lifting machine shall, except for the purpose of a test, be loaded beyond the safe working load as marked or indicated under subsection (4) of this section.

(6) No lifting machine shall be taken into use in any factory for the first time in that factory unless it has been tested and all such parts and working gear of the machine as are specified in subsection (1) of this section have been thoroughly examined by a competent person and a certificate of the test and examination specifying the safe working load or loads of the machine and signed by the person making the test and examination has been obtained and is kept available for inspection.

(7) If any person is employed or working on or near the wheel-track of an overhead travelling crane in any place where he would be liable to be struck by the crane, effective measures shall[1] be taken by warning the driver of the crane or otherwise to ensure that the crane does not approach within 6 metres of that place.

(8) If any person is employed or working otherwise than mentioned in subsection (7) of this section but in a place above floor level where he would be liable to be struck by an overhead travelling crane, or by any load carried by such a crane, effective measures shall be taken to warn him of the approach of the crane, unless his work is so connected with or dependent on the movements of the crane as to make a warning unnecessary.

(9) In this section "lifting machine" means a crane, crab, winch, teagle, pulley block, gin wheel, transporter or runway.

[Factories Act 1961, s 27 as amended by SI 1983/978.]

---

1. This is an absolute duty on an employer that effective measures are taken to ensure that a crane does not approach within 20 feet of where a person is working or employed (*Lotinga v North Eastern Marine Engineering Co* [1941] 2 KB 399, [1941] 3 All ER 1, 106 JP 1; *Holmes v Hadfields Ltd* [1944] 1 KB 275, [1944] 1 All ER 235).

8–14644 31. Precautions with respect to explosive or inflammable dust, gas, vapour or substance. *Repealed.*

PART IV
HEALTH, SAFETY AND WELFARE (SPECIAL PROVISIONS AND REGULATIONS)

8–14652 65. Protection of eyes in certain processes. In the case of any such process as may be specified by regulations of the Minister, being a process which involves a special risk of injury to the eyes from particles or fragments thrown off in the course of the process, suitable goggles or effective screens shall, in accordance with any directions given by the regulations, be provided to protect the eyes of the persons employed in the process.

[Factories Act 1961, s 65.]

8–14655 69. Underground rooms. (1) The inspector for the district may certify any underground room as unsuitable for work other than work involved in the use of the room for the purpose of storage or such other purpose as the Health and Safety Executive may by order specify, and where such a certificate is in force with respect to any room no work for which it is certified as unsuitable shall be carried on in it.

(2) Where the inspector certifies as unsuitable any room which is in actual use, he shall suspend the operation of the certificate for such period as he considers reasonable with a view to enabling the occupier to render the room suitable or to obtain other premises.

(3) Except in the case of a room which on the 1st July, 1938 was part of a factory (within the meaning of the Factories Act 1937, as originally enacted) and was used for work for which it may be certified as unsuitable under this section, the occupier of an underground room—

(a) shall, before the room is used for work for which it may be certified as unsuitable under this section, give notice in the prescribed form and containing the prescribed[1] particulars to the inspector for the district; and

(b) shall not use the room for any such process as may be prescribed, being a process of a hot, wet or dusty nature or which is liable to give off any fume, without the consent in writing of the inspector for the district.

(4) If the occupier is aggrieved by any decision of an inspector under this section, he may, within twenty-one days of the date of issue of the certificate or the refusal of the consent, as the case may be, appeal to a magistrates' court, and, pending the final determination of an appeal against a decision under subsection (1) of this section in the case of a room in actual use, no offence shall be deemed to be committed under that subsection in respect of the room to which the appeal relates.

(5) In this section—

"underground room" means any room which, or any part of which, is so situate that at least half its height, measured from the floor to the ceiling, is below the surface of the footway of the adjoining street or of the ground adjoining or nearest to the room; and

"unsuitable" means unsuitable as regards construction, height, light or ventilation, or on any hygienic ground, or on the ground that adequate means of escape in case of fire are not provided.

(6) Any certificate issued under this section may be withdrawn by the inspector for the district if such alterations are made as in his opinion to render the room suitable.

[Factories Act 1961, s 69, as amended by SI 1974/1941.]

PART VI
EMPLOYMENT OF YOUNG PERSONS (*SUMMARISED*)

8–14658   117–119. Exemptions from provisions regulating hours of employment; power of inspector to require certificate of fitness for work.

PART X
NOTICES, RETURNS, RECORDS, ETC (*SUMMARISED*)

8–14671   137–141[1]. *Notice of occupation of factory and use of mechanical power* [s 137]. *Preservation of registers and records* [ss 140–141].

---

1. Sections 138 and 139 were repealed by SI 1995/2923.

PART XI
ADMINISTRATION

8–14673   154. Prohibition of disclosure of information.   If any person who, in pursuance of powers conferred by s 148 or s 153[1] of this Act, is admitted into any factory or place discloses to any person any information obtained by him in the factory or place with regard to any manufacturing process or trade secret, he shall, unless the disclosure was made in the performance of his duty, be guilty of an offence[2].
[Factories Act 1961, s 154, as amended by SI 1974/1941.]

---

1. These sections relate to the powers of entry to a factory conferred upon officers of fire authorities, fire brigades and county and district councils.
2. For penalty see Health and Safety at Work etc Act 1974, s 33.

8–14673A   154A. Exception to the prohibition: public authorities.   Section 154 does not apply if—

(*a*)   the person making the disclosure referred to in that section is, or is acting on behalf of a person who is, a public authority for the purposes of the Freedom of Information Act 2000, and

(*b*)   the information is not held by the authority on behalf of another person.
[Factories Act 1961, s 154A, as inserted by SI 2004/3363.]

PART XII
OFFENCES, PENALTIES AND LEGAL PROCEEDINGS

8–14674   155. Offences.   (1)[1] In the event of any contravention[2] in or in connection with or in relation to a factory of the provisions of this Act, or of any regulation or order made thereunder, the occupier[3], or (if the contravention is one in respect of which the owner is by or under this Act made responsible) the owner[4], of the factory shall, subject to the following provisions of this Part of this Act, be guilty of an offence[5].

(2)[1] In the event of a contravention by any person of any regulation or order made under this Act which expressly imposes any duty upon him, that person shall be guilty of an offence and the occupier or owner, as the case may be, shall not be guilty of an offence by reason only of the contravention of the provision imposing the said duty, as the case may be, unless it is proved that he failed to take all reasonable steps[6] to prevent the contravention; but this subsection shall not be taken as affecting any liability of the occupier or owner in respect of the same matters by virtue of some provision other than the provisions or provision aforesaid.

(3) If the occupier of a factory avails himself of any exception allowed by or under this Act and fails to comply with any of the conditions attached to the exception, he shall be deemed to have contravened the provisions of this Act.

(4) If any persons are employed in a factory otherwise than in accordance with the provisions of this Act or of any regulation or order made thereunder, there shall be deemed to be a separate contravention in respect of each person so employed.

(5) *Repealed.*
[Factories Act 1961, s 155, as amended by SI 1974/1941 and SI 1975/1012.]

---

1. In *Davies v Camerons Industrial Services Ltd* [1980] 2 All ER 680, it was stated that where there is a clear and absolute liability cast on an employer in his capacity as an employer of workmen under reg 3(1) of the Construction (Working Places) Regulations 1966, SI 1966/94, amended by SI 1984/1593, as well as a liability which may rest on him as a notional occupier under s 127(4), the information should be laid under s 155(2) instead of s 155(1). Note that s 155(2) refers only to contraventions of any regulation or order, thus it would appear that the defence will not be available in the case of a contravention of the provisions of the Act itself.
2. "Contravention" includes, in relation to any provision, a failure to comply with that provision, and the expression "contravene" shall be construed accordingly (s 176(1)).
3. "Occupier" in relation to a shipbuilding yard means, for the purpose of the Shipbuilding Regulations 1931, Parts 1 to 8, the occupier of the yard as a whole (*Smith v Cammell Laird & Co Ltd* [1940] AC 242, [1939] 4 All ER 381, 104 JP 51, HL; *Wilkinson v Rea Ltd* [1941] 1 KB 688, [1941] 2 All ER 50). The person repairing a ship in a public dry dock is a

notional occupier for the purpose of such regulations (*Rippon v Port of London Authority and J Russell & Co* [1940] 1 KB 858, [1940] 1 All ER 637, 104 JP 136).

4. See note to s 175, post.

5. For penalty in relation to other offences under this Act, see Health and Safety at Work etc Act 1974, s 33(3), this TITLE, post.

6. The occupier or owner may take advantage of this defence without bringing the workman alleged to be the actual offender before the court under s 137 (*Carr v Decca Gramophone Co Ltd* [1947] KB 728, [1947] 2 All ER 20, 111 JP 352). Where s 155(2) of the Act applies, the onus is upon the prosecution to prove that the occupier or owner has failed to take all reasonable steps to prevent the contravention (*Wright v Ford Motor Co Ltd* [1967] 1 QB 230, [1966] 2 All ER 518).

8–14676   158. Fine for offence by parent.   If a young person is employed in any factory in contravention of the provisions of this Act, the parent[1] of the young person shall be guilty of an offence and liable on summary conviction to a fine not exceeding **level 1** on the standard scale, unless it appears to the court that the contravention occurred without the consent, connivance, or wilful default of the parent.

[Factories Act 1961, s 158, as amended by SI 1974/1941 and the Criminal Justice Act 1982, ss 38 and 46.]

1. For the meaning of "young person" and "parent", see s 176, post.

8–14677   162. Proceedings against persons not primarily liable.   Where, under this Act, any person is substituted for another with respect to any provisions of this Act, any order, summons, notice or proceedings which for the purpose of any of those provisions is by or under this Act required or authorised to be served on or taken in relation to that other person, is hereby required or authorised (as the case may be) to be served on or taken in relation to the first-mentioned person.

[Factories Act 1961, s 162.]

8–14678   163. Owner of machine liable in certain cases instead of occupier.   Where in a factory the owner[1] or hirer of a machine or implement moved by mechanical power is some person other than the occupier of the factory, the owner or hirer shall, so far as respects any offence under this Act committed in relation to a person who is employed in or about or in connection with that machine or implement, and is in the employment or pay of the owner or hirer, be deemed to be the occupier of the factory.

[Factories Act 1961, s 163.]

1. See note to s 175, post.

8–14679   166. Special provisions as to evidence.   (1) If a person is found in a factory at any time at which work is going on or the machinery is in motion, except during the intervals for meals or rest, he shall until the contrary is proved, be deemed for the purposes of this Act, to have been then employed[1] in the factory, unless the factory is one in which the only persons employed are members of the same family dwelling there.

(2) Where in any proceedings under this Act with respect to a young person it appears to the court that that young person is apparently of or below the age alleged by the informant, or, in Scotland, by the prosecutor, it shall lie on the accused to prove that the young person is not of or below that age.

(3) *Repealed.*

[Factories Act 1961, s 166, amended by SI 1974/1941.]

1. For the purposes of this Act an apprentice shall be deemed to be a person employed (s 176(7)).

8–14680   167. Proceedings for offences in respect of the employment of children.   For the purposes of any proceedings under this Act in respect of the employment of children in contravention of s 1 of the Employment of Women, Young Persons, and Children Act 1920, or any other enactment prohibiting the employment of children which is incorporated with this Act, references in this Part of this Act to young persons shall be construed as including references to children within the meaning of any such enactment.

[Factories Act 1961, s 167, as amended by the Education Act 1973, Sch 2.]

PART XIII
APPLICATION OF ACT

8–14681   172. General application of Act.   Save as in this Act otherwise expressly provided, the provisions of this Act shall apply only to factories as defined by this Act, but shall, except where the contrary intention appears, apply to all such factories.

[Factories Act 1961, s 172.]

8–14682   173. *Application to factories belonging to the Crown* [s 173; as amended by SI 1974/1941].

8–14683   175. Interpretation of expression "factory".   (1) Subject to the provisions of this section, the expression "factory"[1] means any premises[2] in which, or within the close or curtilage or precincts[3] of which, persons are employed in manual labour[4] in any process[5] for or incidental to any of the following purposes, namely:

(*a*)   the making of any article or of part of any article; or

(*b*)   the altering, repairing, ornamenting, finishing, cleaning, or washing[6] or the breaking up or demolition of any article; or

(*c*)   the adapting for sale[7] of any article;

(*d*)   the slaughtering of cattle, sheep, swine, goats, horses, asses or mules; or

(*e*)   the confinement of such animals as aforesaid while awaiting slaughter at other premises, in a case where the place of confinement is available in connection with those other premises, is not maintained primarily for agricultural purposes[8] within the meaning of the Agriculture Act 1947 or, as the case may be, the Agriculture (Scotland) Act 1948, and does not form part of premises used for the holding of a market in respect of such animals;

being premises in which, or within the close or curtilage or precincts of which, the work is carried on by way of trade or for purposes of gain[9] and to or over which the employer of the persons employed therein has the right of access or control.

(2) The expression "factory" also includes the following premises in which persons are employed in manual labour (whether or not they are factories by virtue of subsection (1) of this section), that is to say—

(*a*)   any yard[10] or dry dock[11] (including the precincts thereof) in which ships or vessels[12] are constructed, reconstructed, repaired, refitted, finished or broken up;

(*b*)   any premises in which the business[13] of sorting[14] any articles is carried on as a preliminary to the work carried on in any factory or incidentally to the purposes of any factory;

(*c*)   any premises in which the business of washing or filling bottles or containers or packing articles is carried on incidentally to the purposes of any factory;

(*d*)   any premises in which the business of hooking, plaiting, lapping, making-up or packing of yarn or cloth is carried on;

(*e*)   any laundry carried on as ancillary to another business, or incidentally to the purposes of any public institution[15];

(*f*)   except as provided in subsection (10) of this section, any premises in which the construction, reconstruction or repair[16] of locomotives, vehicles or other plant for use for transport purposes is carried on as ancillary to a transport undertaking or other industrial[17] or commercial undertaking;

(*g*)   any premises in which printing by letterpress, lithography, photogravure, or other similar process, or bookbinding is carried on by way of trade or for purpose of gain or incidentally to another business so carried on;

(*h*)   any premises in which the making, adaptation or repair of dresses, scenery or properties is carried on incidentally to the production, exhibition or presentation by way of trade or for purposes of gain of cinematograph films or theatrical performances, not being a stage or dressing-room of a theatre in which only occasional adaptations or repairs are made;

(*j*)   any premises in which the business of making or mending nets is carried on incidentally to the fishing industry;

(*k*)   any premises in which mechanical power is used in connection with the making or repair of articles of metal or wood incidentally to any business carried on by way of trade or for purposes of gain;

(*l*)   any premises in which the production[18] of cinematograph films is carried on by way of trade or for purposes of gain, so, however, that the employment at any such premises of theatrical performers within the meaning of the Theatrical Employers Registration Act 1925, and of attendants on such theatrical performers shall not be deemed to be employment in a factory;

(*m*)   any premises in which articles are made or prepared incidentally to the carrying on of building operations[19] or works of engineering construction not being premises in which such operations or works are being carried on;

(*n*)   any premises used for the storage of gas in a gasholder[20] having a storage capacity of not less than 140 cubic metres.

(3) Any line or siding (not being part of a railway[21] or tramway[22]) which is used in connection with and for the purposes of a factory, shall be deemed to be part of the factory; and if any such line or siding is used in connection with more than one factory belonging to different occupiers, the line or siding shall be deemed to be a separate factory.

(4) A part of a factory may, with the approval in writing of the chief inspector[23], be taken to be a separate factory and two or more factories may, with the like approval, be taken to be a single factory.

(5) Any workplace in which, with the permission of or under agreement with the owner[24] or occupier[25], two or more persons carry on any work which would constitute the workplace[26] a factory if the persons working therein were in the employment of the owner or occupier, shall be deemed to be a factory for the purposes of this Act, and, in the case of any such workplace not being a tenement factory[27] or part of a tenement factory, the provisions of this Act shall apply as if the owner or occupier of the workplace were the occupier of the factory and the persons working therein were persons employed in the factory.

(6)[28] Where a place situate within the close, curtilage, or precincts forming a factory[29] is solely used for some purpose other than the processes carried on in the factory, that place shall not be deemed to form part of the factory for the purposes of this Act, but shall, if otherwise it would be a factory, be deemed to be a separate factory.

(7) Premises shall not be excluded from the definition of a factory by reason only that they are open air premises.

(8) Where the Minister by regulations[30] so directs as respects all or any purposes of this Act, different branches or departments of work carried on in the same factory shall be deemed to be different factories.

(9) Any premises belonging to or in the occupation of the Crown[31] or any municipal or other public authority[32] shall not be deemed not to be a factory, and building operations[19] or works of engineering construction undertaken by or on behalf of the Crown or any such authority shall not be excluded from the operation of this Act, by reason only that the work carried on thereat is not carried on by way of trade or for purposes of gain.

(10) Premises used for the purpose of housing locomotives or vehicles where only cleaning, washing, running repairs or minor adjustments are carried out shall not be deemed to be a factory by reason only of paragraph (*f*) of subsection (2) of this section[33], unless they are premises used for the purposes of a railway undertaking where running repairs to locomotives are carried out.
[Factories Act 1961, s 175 as amended by SI 1983/978.]

1. The provisions of this Act do not apply to any premises forming part of a mine or quarry (Mines and Quarries Act 1954, s 184(1)). A hospital workshop used for repair of hospital equipment is a factory (*Bromwich v National Ear, Nose and Throat Hospital* [1980] 2 All ER 663).

2. As to lines and sidings, see sub-s (3); as to parts of factories or different branches or departments constituting separate or different factories, see sub-ss (4) and (8); and as to workplaces, see sub-s (5), post. A technical institute is not a factory (*Weston v LCC* [1941] 1 KB 608, [1941] 1 All ER 555, 105 JP 213). The word "premises" does not necessarily mean the whole of the building, even though occupied by a single firm or undertaking, where parts of the building are used for purpose other than that of a factory (sub-s (6), post).

3. In the case of factories, the walls or fences built round the factory generally fix the boundaries and determine the area (*Back v Dick Kerr & Co Ltd* [1906] AC 325).

4. See *Grainger v Aynsley* (1880) 6 QBD 182, 45 JP 142; *Bromley v Tams* (1880) 6 QBD 182, 45 JP 142; *Jackson v Hill* (1884) 18 QBD 618; *Morgan v London General Omnibus Co* (1883) 12 QBD 201; affd (1884) 18 QBD 832, 48 JP 503; *Cook v North Metropolitan Tramways Co* (1887) 18 QBD 683, 51 JP 630; *Smith v Associated Omnibus Co* [1907] 1 KB 916, 71 JP 239; *Hunt v Great Northern Rly Co* [1891] 1 QB 601, 55 JP 470; and *Bound v Lawrence* [1892] 1 QB 226, 56 JP 118; *Squire v Midland Lace Co* [1905] 2 KB 448, 69 JP 257; *Joyce v Boots Cash Chemists (Southern)* [1950] 2 All ER 719, and *J & F Stone Lighting and Radio Ltd v Haygarth* [1968] AC 157, [1966] 3 All ER 539, HL.

5. "Process" in this Act and the (now revoked) Asbestos Regulations 1969 has been held to include any operation or series of operations involving some degree of continuity and repetition of a series of acts and being an activity of more than minimal duration; this could include the demolition of brick driers even though the firm's trade was the manufacture of crucibles (*Nurse v Morganite Crucible Ltd* [1989] AC 692, [1989] 1 All ER 113, HL).

6. As to the kitchen in a restaurant not being a factory, see *Wood v LCC* [1941] 2 KB 232, [1941] 2 All ER 230, 105 JP 299. The mincing of meat in a mincing machine is an "altering" of an article.

7. A building used for the manufacture of waste cotton into "half-stuff", which was afterwards conveyed to a distant factory to be converted into paper, was held to be a factory (*Coles v Dickinson* (1864) 16 CBNS 604). The following processes have been held to be an adapting for sale: Packing sweetmeats in boxes and tying them up (*Fullers Ltd v Squire* [1901] 2 KB 209, 65 JP 660). Bottling beer from casks and mixing it with carbonic acid gas (*Hoare v Truman, Hanbury, Buxton & Co* (1902) 66 JP 342). Making up wreaths, crosses, etc (*Hoare v Robert Green Ltd* [1907] 2 KB 315, 71 JP 341). Separating the saleable part of town refuse from the unsaleable parts (*Henderson v Glasgow Corpn* 1900 2 F 1127). Compressing waste paper into bales (*Kinder v Camberwell Metropolitan Borough Council* [1944] 2 All ER 315, 109 JP 81). Producing photographic prints (*Popper (Paul) Ltd v Grimsey* [1963] 1 QB 44, [1962] 1 All ER 864).

8. For meaning of "agricultural purposes", see s 109 of Agriculture Act 1947.

9. As to premises belonging to the Crown and municipal or other public authorities, see sub-s (9), post. Grinding meal on a farm for the purpose only of feeding farm stock, was held not to be carried on for trade or purposes of gain (*Nash v Hollinshead* [1901] 1 KB 700, 65 JP 357). The gain referred to must be direct gain (*Nash v Hollinshead*, supra, considered in *Stoke-on-Trent Revenue Officer v Stoke-on-Trent Assessment Committee* (1930) 94 JP 177; on appeal (1931) 95 JP 64; *Jones v Crosville Motor Services Ltd* [1956] 3 All ER 417).

10. See *Smith v Cammell Laird & Co Ltd* [1940] AC 242, [1939] 4 All ER 381, 104 JP 51.

11. As to the limited application of the Act to ships in a harbour or wet dock, see s 126. As to docks, see s 125. See *Rippon v Port of London Authority and Russell & Co* [1940] 1 KB 858, [1940] 1 All ER 637, 104 JP 186.

12. "Ship", "vessel" and "harbour" have the same meaning as in the Merchant Shipping Act 1894 (s 176(1)). See Merchant Shipping Act 1894, s 742.

13. Business does not necessarily involve the purpose of making a profit (*Rolls v Miller* (1884) 27 Ch D 71, CA).

14. Owing to this paragraph, it is doubtful whether *Paterson v Hunt* (1909) 73 JP 496, now applies.

15. An institution maintained by subscriptions and donations for which appeals were made to the public, is a public institution *Seal v British Orphan Asylum Trustees* (1911) 75 JP 152). Also an institution chiefly maintained by Freemasons entirely for the benefit of the children of those who belong to their own body *Royal Masonic Institution for Boys (Trustees) v Parkes* [1912] 3 KB 212, 76 JP 218). As to charitable and reformatory institutions generally, see s 124.

16. A repair shop at a tramcar depot in which damaged tramcars are repaired and broken parts replaced is a factory (*Griffin v London Transport Executive* [1950] 1 All ER 716, 114 JP 230).

17. "Industrial undertaking" is not defined in this Act.

18. As to storage of these films, see Celluloid and Cinematograph Film Act 1922, s 2, title THEATRE, CINEMATOGRAPH AND VIDEO. post.

19. "Building operation" means the construction, structural alteration, repair or maintenance of a building (including re-pointing, re-decoration and external cleaning of the structure), the demolition of a building, and the preparation for, and laying the foundation of, an intended building, but does not include any operation which is a work of engineering construction within the meaning of this Act (s 176 (1)).

20. As to gasholders, see s 39.

21. "Railway" means any railway used for the purposes of public traffic whether passenger, goods or other traffic and includes any works of the railway company connected with the railway (s 176(1)). ("Railway company" includes the Railway Boards created by the Transport Act 1962).

22. "Tramway" means a tramway authorised by or under any Act of Parliament and used for the purpose of public traffic (s 176(1)).

23. "Chief inspector" means the chief inspector appointed under this Act and includes a deputy chief inspector (s 176(1)).

24. "Owner" means the person for the time being receiving the rackrent of the premises in connection with which the word is used, whether on his own account or as agent or trustee for another person, or who would so receive the rackrent if the premises were let at a rackrent (s 176(1)).

25. A limited company may be an occupier (*R v Gainsford Justices* (1913) 29 TLR 359). See also *Turner v Courtaulds Ltd* [1937] 1 All ER 467. The occupier is the person who runs the factory and regulates and controls the work (*Ramsey v Mackie* 1904 7 F 106). A receiver and manager of a company appointed by a debenture holder is the occupier if he manages and carries on the business (*Meigh v Wickenden* [1942] 2 KB 160, [1942] 2 All ER 68, 106 JP 207).

26. "Workplace" does not include a factory or workshop, but save as aforesaid includes any place in which persons are employed otherwise than in domestic service, see the Public Health Act 1936, s 343(1), post.

27. "Tenement factory" means any premises where mechanical power from any prime mover within the close or curtilage of the premises is distributed for use in manufacturing process to different parts of the same premises occupied by different persons in such manner that those parts constitute in law separate factories (s 176 (1)). "Prime mover", means every engine, motor or other applicance which provides mechanical energy derived from steam, water, wind, electricity, the combustion of fuel or other source (s 176(1)).

28. The application of this subsection was considered in *Longhurst v Guildford, Goldalming and District Water Board* [1963] AC 265, [1961] 3 All ER 545 and *Newton v John Stanning & Son Ltd* [1962] 1 All ER 78.

29. A piece of land within the close, etc, of a factory, but used solely for crushing mortar for building purposes which was not the manufacturing process or handicraft carried on by the respondents in their factory, was held not to constitute a factory (*Lewis v Gilbertson & Co* (1904) 68 JP 323). An administrative block, having a separate entrance but within the perimeter of a factory, used for designing engines, etc to be manufactured in the factory, has been held to be part of the factory (*Powley v Bristol Siddeley Engines Ltd* [1965] 3 All ER 612). Cf *Cardiff Revenue Officer v Cardiff Assessment Committee* [1931] 1 KB 47, 94 JP 146; *London Co-operative Society Ltd v Southern Essex Assessment Committee* [1942] 1 KB 53, [1941] 2 All ER 252, 105 JP 399; *Simmonds Aerocessories (Western) Ltd v Pontypridd Area Assessment Committee* [1944] 1 All ER 264, [1944] KB 231, 108 JP 66; *Street v British Electricity Authority* [1952] 2 QB 399, [1952] 1 All ER 679; *Walsh v Allweather Mechanical Grouting Co Ltd* [1959] 2 QB 300, [1959] 2 All ER 588.

30. The power to make regulations is contained in s 180. Certain regulations are described in the Act as "special regulations", the procedure for making which is prescribed in Sch 4. Printed copies of "special regulations" or a prescribed abstract thereof must be kept posted in the factory and a copy shall be given to any person affected thereby (s 139).

31. Premises belonging, etc, to the United Kingdom Atomic Energy Authority shall be deemed to be premises belonging, etc, to the Crown (Atomic Energy Authority Act 1954, Sch 3). References to the Crown have effect as if they included references to the service authorities of visiting forces or to a headquarters of an international organisation (Visiting Forces and International Headquarters (Application of Law) Order 1965, SI 1965/1536, art 16).

32. A technical institute is not a factory (*Weston v LCC* [1941] 1 KB 608, [1941] 1 All ER 555, 105 JP 213); nor is a kitchen in an institution (*Wood v LCC* [1941] 2 KB 232, [1941] 2 All ER 230, 105 JP 299).

33. This accords with the earlier decision in *Jones v Crosville Motor Services Ltd* [1956] 3 All ER 417.

8–14684   176. General interpretation.   (1) In this Act, unless the context otherwise requires, the following expressions have the meanings hereby assigned to them respectively, that is to say—

"bakehouse" means any place in which bread, biscuits or confectionery is or are baked by way of trade or for purposes of gain;

"bodily injury" includes injury to health;

"building operation" and "work of engineering construction" mean "construction work" within the meaning assigned to that phrase by regulation 2(1) of the Construction (Design and Management) Regulations 1994 (SI 1994/3140);

"calendar year" means the period of twelve months beginning with the first day of January in any year;

"child" means any person who is not over—

(*a*) compulsory school age (construed in accordance with section 8 of the Education Act 1996); or

(*b*) school age (construed in accordance with section 31 of the Education (Scotland) Act 1980);

"class or description", in relation to factories, includes a group of factories described by reference to locality;

"contravention" includes, in relation to any provision, a failure to comply with that provision, and the expression "contravene" shall be construed accordingly;

"cotton cloth factory" means any room, shed or workshop, or part thereof, in which the weaving of cotton cloth is carried on;

"district council" means, as respects England and Wales, the council of a . . . district, and, as respects Scotland, an islands or a district council;

"driving-belt" includes any driving strap or rope;

"fume" includes gas or vapour;

"general register" means the register kept in accordance with the requirements of section one hundred and forty of this Act;

"humid factory" means a factory in which atmospheric humidity is artificially produced by steaming or other means in connection with any textile process;

"inspector" means an inspector appointed by the Health and Safety Executive under section 19 of the Health and Safety at Work etc Act 1974 and references in any provisions of this Act to the inspector for the district, the superintending inspector for the division or the chief inspector are references to an inspector so appointed for the purposes of that provision;

"machinery" includes any driving-belt;

"maintained" means maintained in an efficient state, in efficient working order, and in good repair;

"the Minister" means the Minister of Labour;

"owner"—

> (a) as respects England and Wales, means the person for the time being receiving the rackrent of the premises in connection with which the word is used, whether on his own account or as agent or trustee for another person, or who would so receive the rackrent if the premises were let at a rackrent; and
>
> (b) (*Scotland*);

"parent" means a parent of a child or young person or any person who is not a parent of his but who has parental responsibility for him (within the meaning of the Children Act 1989), or who has parental responsibilities in relation to him (within the meaning of section 1(3) of the Children (Scotland) Act 1995), and includes, in relation to any child or young person, any person having direct benefit from his wages;

"period of employment" means the period (inclusive of the time allowed for meals and rest) within which persons may be employed on any day;

"prescribed" means prescribed by order of the Minister;

"prime mover" means every engine, motor or other appliance which provides mechanical energy derived from steam, water, wind, electricity, the combustion of fuel or other source;

"process" includes the use of any locomotive;

"railway" means any railway used for the purposes of public traffic whether passenger, goods, or other traffic and includes any works of the railway company connected with the railway;

"railway company" includes . . . a company or person working a railway under lease or otherwise;

"sanitary conveniences" includes urinals, water-closets, earthclosets, privies, ashpits, and any similar convenience;

"ship" and "vessel" have the same meanings as "ship" in the Merchant Shipping Act 1995, and "harbour" has the same meaning as in the Merchant Shipping Act 1995;

"tenement factory" means any premises where mechanical power from any prime mover within the close or curtilage of the premises is distributed for use in manufacturing processes to different parts of the same premises occupied by different persons in such manner that those parts constitute in law separate factories;

"tramway" means a tramway authorised by or under any Act of Parliament and used for the purpose of public traffic;

"transmission machinery" means every shaft, wheel, drum, pulley, system of fast and loose pulleys, coupling, clutch, driving-belt or other device by which the motion of a prime mover is transmitted to or received by any machine or appliance;

"week" means the period between midnight on Saturday night and midnight on the succeeding Saturday night;

"woman" means a woman who has attained the age of eighteen;

"young person" means a person who has ceased to be a child but has not attained the age of eighteen.

(2) For the purposes of this Act, machinery or plant shall be deemed to have been constructed or reconstructed, and a factory or building to have been constructed, reconstructed, extended, added to, or converted for use as a factory, before any date, if the construction, reconstruction, extension, addition, or conversion was begun before that date.

(3) For the purposes of this Act, a factory shall not be deemed to be a factory in which mechanical power is used by reason only that mechanical power is used for the purpose of heating, ventilating or lighting the workrooms or other parts of the factory.

(4) A woman, young person, or child who works in a factory, whether for wages or not, either in a process or in cleaning any part of the factory used for any process, or in cleaning or oiling any part of the machinery or plant, or in any other kind of work whatsoever incidental to or connected with the process, or connected with the article made or otherwise the subject of the process therein, shall, save as is otherwise provided by this Act, be deemed to be employed therein for the purposes of this Act or of any proceedings thereunder.

(5) A young person who works in a factory, whether for wages or not, in collecting, carrying or delivering goods, carrying messages or running errands shall be deemed to be employed in the factory for the purposes of this Act or of any proceedings thereunder, but the provisions of Part VI of this Act shall not apply, except as expressly provided, to any such young person who is employed mainly outside the factory.

(6) For the purposes of this Act, employment shall be deemed to be continuous unless interrupted by an interval of at least half an hour.

(7) For the purposes of this Act, an apprentice shall be deemed to be a person employed.

(8) This Act shall in its application to London have effect as if for references to district councils there were substituted, as respects the City of London references to the common council . . .

(8A) In the application of this Act in relation to Wales—

(*a*) any reference to a district council shall be construed as a reference to a county council or (as the case may be) county borough council; and

(*b*) any reference to the district of a district council shall be construed as a reference to a county or county borough.

(9) References in this Act to any enactment shall be construed as references to that enactment as amended by any subsequent enactment, including this Act.†
[Factories Act 1961, s 176, as amended by the Transport Act 1962, s 95 and Sch 12, the London Government Act 1963, s 93 and Sch 18, the Banking and Financial Dealings Act 1971, s 4 and Sch 2, SI 1974/1941, the Local Government Act 1972, s 272 and Sch 30, the Local Government (Scotland) Act 1973, s 155, the Magistrates' Courts Act 1980, s 154 and Sch 7, SI 1983/978, the Employment Act 1989, Sch 7, the Children Act 1989, Sch 13, the Statute Law (Repeals) Act 1993, Sch 1, the Local Government (Wales) Act 1994, Sch 16, SI 1996/1592, the Merchant Shipping Act 1995, Sch 13, the Children (Scotland) Act 1995, Sch 4 and the Education Act 1996, Sch 37.]

Pipe-lines Act 1962[1]
(10 & 11 Eliz 2 c 58)

8–14790   NOTE.—Goods imported or exported by means of a pipe-line attract the application of Customs and Excise Acts by virtue of s 3 of the Customs and Excise Management Act 1979.

---

1. The Environment Agency, every water undertaker and every sewerage undertaker is deemed to be a statutory undertaker for the purposes of this Act (Water Act 1989, Sch 25, para 1). The holder of a licence under s 6(1) of the Electricity Act 1989 shall be deemed to be a statutory undertaker and his undertaking a statutory undertaking for the purposes of this Act (Electricity Act 1989, Sch 16, para 1(1)).

8–14791   1. Cross-country pipe-lines not to be constructed without the Minister's authority.
Cross-country[1] pipe-lines[2] may not be constructed otherwise than in accordance with an authorisation granted by the Minister. A person executing works in contravention of this provision is liable on summary conviction to a fine not exceeding **level 3** on the standard scale.
[Pipe-lines Act 1962, s 1 as amended by the Criminal Justice Act 1982, ss 38 and 46 and SI 1999/742—summarised.]

---

1. A "cross-country pipe-line" means a pipe-line whose length exceeds, or is intended to exceed, 10 miles (s 66(1)).
2. A "pipe-line" is defined to mean a pipe or system of pipes (with the associated apparatus and works) for the conveyance of anything other than air, water, water vapour or steam, but it does not include (i) a drain or sewer; (ii) a pipe for domestic heating or cooling; (iii) a pipe on a building site; (iv) a pipe on agricultural land and designed for use for agricultural purposes; (v) a pipe in premises used for education or research; or (vi) a pneumatic dispatch-tube (s 65, *summarised*).
Specified pipe-lines constructed by public bodies are excluded from the Act, while pipe-lines in factories, Mines, quarries, petroleum depots, docks, wharves or quays are also excluded, being the subject of other legislative provisions (ss 58–61, *summarised*).

8–14792   2. Local pipe-lines not to be constructed without notice to the Minister. (*Repealed*)

8–14793   Avoidance of construction of superfluous pipe-lines.   The Minister may by notice require the owner of a cross-country[1] pipe-line to be constructed to a certain capacity (s 9), require an additional pipe-line to be so constructed as to reduce necessity for construction of other pipe-lines (s 9A) and may require that such a pipe-line that is not fully used shall be shared with another person (s 10). A person failing to comply with the requirements of such a notice is liable on summary conviction to a fine not exceeding **level 5** on the standard scale; and, if failure continues after conviction to a fine not exceeding £25 for each day on which the failure continues. Diversion of pipe-lines subject to such requirements (s 10A).
[Pipe-lines Act 1962, ss 9–10F as amended by the Criminal Justice Act 1982, ss 38 and 46, SI 1999/742, SI 2000/1937 and Energy Act 2004, ss 151 and 197—summarised.]

---

1. A "cross-country pipe-line" means a pipe-line whose length exceeds, or is intended to exceed, 10 miles (s 66(1)).

8–14794   Compulsory acquisition of land for construction of pipe-lines.   The Minister may, by order, authorise the compulsory acquisition of required land, *etc* (ss 11, 12). Conditions may be attached to such an order (s 13). Breach of these conditions is an offence punishable[1] on summary conviction by a fine not exceeding **the statutory maximum** or imprisonment for not exceeding **3 months, or both**; or, on indictment, by a fine or imprisonment for not exceeding two years, or both.
[Pipe-lines Act 1962, ss 11–13, as amended by the Criminal Law Act 1977, s 28) and SI 1999/742—summarised.]

---

1. For procedure in respect of this offence which is triable either way, see the Magistrates' Courts Act 1980, ss 17A–21 in PART I: MAGISTRATES' COURTS, PROCEDURE, ante.

8–14796   Information.   A person executing works for the construction of a pipe-line must send to each local authority affected a map of the route thereof (s 35). Notice of abandonment, etc, must be given to the Minister (s 36), and notice of change of ownership to the Minister and to the owners, lessees, and occupiers of land through which the pipe-line runs (s 38). Notice must be given to the fire and rescue authority, police and specified authorities of any accidental escape or ignition of any thing in the pipe-line (s 37). Breach of any of these provisions is an offence punishable on summary conviction by a fine not exceeding **level 3** on the standard scale.

[Pipe-lines Act 1962, ss 35–38 as amended by the Criminal Justice Act 1982, ss 38 and 46, the Water Act 1989, Sch 25, the Local Government (Wales) Act 1994, Sch 16), SI 1999/742 and the Fire and Rescue Services Act 2004, Sch 1—summarised.]

8–14798   46. Penalties for uttering false documents and giving false information.   A person who—

(*a*)   sends to the Secretary of State an application for the grant of a pipe-line construction authorisation or the making of a compulsory purchase or rights order, being an application which he knows to be false in a material particular, or recklessly sends to the Secretary of State such an application which is so false; or

(*b*)   in purported compliance with section thirty-six or thirty-eight of this Act gives a notice which he knows to be false in a material particular or recklessly gives notice which is so false; or

(*c*)   in purported compliance with subsection (1) of section thirty-five of this Act or subsection (2) of section thirty-seven thereof, sends, deposits or furnishes a document which he knows to be false in a material particular or gives any information which he knows to be so false or recklessly sends, deposits or furnishes a document which is so false or recklessly gives any information which is so false;

shall be guilty of an offence and shall be liable[1]—

(i)   on summary conviction, to a fine not exceeding the prescribed sum or to imprisonment for a term not exceeding **three months**, or to **both** such fine and such imprisonment;

(ii)   on conviction on indictment, to a fine or to imprisonment for a term not exceeding **2 years** or to **both** a fine and such imprisonment.

[Pipe-lines Act 1962, s 46, amended by SI 1974/1986 and SI 1999/742 and Criminal Law Act 1977, s 28.]

---

1.   For procedure in respect of this offence which is triable either way, see the Magistrates' Courts Act 1980, ss 17A–21 in PART I: MAGISTRATES' COURTS, PROCEDURE, ante.

8–14799   54. Offences by corporations.   (1)   Where a body corporate is guilty of an offence under any of the provisions of this Act and that offence is proved to have been committed with the consent or connivance of, or to be attributable to any neglect on the part of, any director, manager, secretary or other similar officer of the body corporate or any person who was purporting to act in any such capacity, he, as well as the body corporate, shall be guilty of that offence and shall be liable to be proceeded against and punished accordingly.

(2)   In this section, the expression "director", in relation to a body corporate established by or under any enactment for the purpose of carrying on under national ownership any industry or part of an industry or undertaking, being a body corporate whose affairs are managed by its members, means a member of that body corporate.

[Pipe-lines Act 1962, s 54.]

Offices, Shops and Railway Premises Act 1963[1]

(1963 c 41)

Scope of Act

8–14810   1. Premises to which this Act applies.   (1)   The premises[2] to which this Act applies are office premises, shop premises and railway premises, being (in each case) premises in the case of which persons are employed to work therein.

(2)   In this Act—

(*a*)   "office premises" means a building or part of a building, being a building or part the sole or principal use of which is as an office or for office purposes;

(*b*)   "office purposes" includes the purposes of administration, clerical work, handling money and telephone and telegraph operating; and

(*c*)   "clerical work" includes writing, book-keeping, sorting papers, filing, typing, duplicating, machine calculating, drawing and the editorial preparation of matter for publication;

and for the purposes of this Act premises occupied together with office premises for the purposes of the activities there carried on shall be treated as forming part of the office premises.

(3)   In this Act—

(*a*)   "shop premises" means—

(i)   a shop[3];

    (ii) a building or part of a building, being a building or part which is not a shop but of which the sole or principal use is the carrying on there of retail trade or business;

    (iii) a building occupied by a wholesale dealer or merchant where goods are kept for sale wholesale or a part of a building so occupied where goods are so kept, but not including a warehouse belonging to the owners, trustees or conservators of a dock, wharf or quay;

    (iv) a building to which members of the public are invited to resort for the purpose of delivering there goods for repair or other treatment or of themselves there carrying out repairs to, or other treatment of, goods, or a part of a building to which members of the public are invited to resort for that purpose;

    (v) any premises (in this Act referred to as "fuel storage premises") occupied for the purpose of a trade or business which consists of, or includes, the sale of solid fuel, being premises used for the storage of such fuel intended to be sold in the course of that trade or business, but not including dock storage premises or colliery storage premises;

  (*b*) "retail trade or business" includes the sale to members of the public of food or drink for immediate consumption, retail sales by auction and the business of lending books or periodicals for the purpose of gain;

  (*c*) "solid fuel" means coal, coke and any solid fuel derived from coal or of which coal or coke is a constituent;

  (*d*) "dock storage premises" means fuel storage premises which constitute or are comprised in premises to which certain provisions of the Factories Act 1961, apply by virtue of s 125(1) (docks, etc) of that Act; and

  (*e*) "colliery storage premises" means fuel storage premises which form part of premises which, for the purposes of the Mines and Quarries Act 1954, form part of a mine or quarry, other than premises where persons are regularly employed to work by a person other than the owner (as defined by that Act) of the mine or quarry;

and for the purposes of this Act premises occupied together with a shop or with a building or part of a building falling within sub-paragraph (ii), (iii) or (iv) of paragraph (*a*) above for the purposes of the trade or business carried on in the shop or, as the case may be, the building or part of a building, shall be treated as forming part of the shop or, as the case may be, of the building or part of the building, and premises occupied together with fuel storage premises for the purposes of the activities there carried on (not being office premises) shall be treated as forming part of the fuel storage premises, but for the purposes of this Act office premises comprised in fuel storage premises shall be deemed not to form part of the last-mentioned premises.

(4) In this Act "railway premises" means a building[4] occupied by railway undertakers for the purposes of the railway undertaking carried on by them and situate in the immediate vicinity of the permanent way or a part (so occupied) of a building so situate, but does not include—

  (*a*) office or shop premises;

  (*b*) premises used for the provision of living accommodation for persons employed in the undertaking, or hotels; or

  (*c*) premises wherein are carried on such processes or operations as are mentioned in s 123(1) (electrical stations) of the Factories Act 1961, and for such supply as is therein mentioned.

(5) For the purposes of this Act premises maintained in conjunction with office, shop or railway premises for the purpose of the sale or supply for immediate consumption of food or drink wholly or mainly to persons employed to work in the premises in conjunction with which they are maintained shall, if they neither form part of those premises nor are required by the foregoing provisions of this section to be treated as forming part of them, be treated for the purposes of this Act as premises of the class within which fall the premises in conjunction with which they are maintained.
[Offices, Shops and Railway Premises Act 1963, s 1.]

    1. By SI 1974/1943 regulation SI 1968/1849, amended by SI 1974/1943 and SI 1983/1573 (Hoists and Lifts), has been continued in force despite repeal of the enabling provision of this Act.
    2. "Premises" is not defined by the Act. The word has been varyingly interpreted. It would appear that in the context of this statute it may be given a wide construction: cf. *Gardiner v Sevenoaks RDC* [1950] 2 All ER 84, 114 JP 352.
    "Office premises", "shop premises" and "railway premises" are respectively defined by sub-ss (2), (3) and (4), infra.
    3. "Shop" is not defined. Since it is used in this Act as part of the expression "shop premises", the wide construction on the word "shop" that has been applied in connection with the Shops Act 1950 may have no application.
    4. For the purposes of this sub-s , "building" does not include a mere structure (s 90 (1), post). Generally, this Act does not apply to factory premises (s 85).

8–14811   **2. Exception for premises in which only employer's relative or outworkers work.**
(1) This Act shall not apply to any premises to which it would, apart from this subsection, apply, if none of the persons employed to work in the premises is other than the husband, wife, civil partner, parent, grandparent, son, daughter, grandchild, brother or sister of the person by whom they are so employed.

(2) A dwelling shall not, for the purposes of this Act, be taken to constitute or comprise premises to which this Act applies by reason only that a person dwelling there who is employed by a person who does not so dwell does there the work that he is employed to do in compliance with a term of his contract of service that he shall do it there.
[Offices, Shops and Railway Premises Act 1963, s 2 as amended by the Civil Partnership Act 2004, Sch 27.]

8–14812　3. Exception for premises where only 21 man-hours weekly normally worked.
(1) This Act shall not apply to any premises to which it would, apart from this subsection, apply, if the period of time worked there during each week does not normally exceed twenty-one hours.

(2) For the purposes of this section the period of time worked in any premises shall be deemed to be—

(*a*)　as regards a week in which one person only is employed to work in premises, the period of time worked by him there;

(*b*)　as regards a week in which two persons or more are so employed, the sum of the periods of time for which respectively those persons work there.

[Offices, Shops and Railway Premises Act 1963, s 3, as amended by SI 1974/1943.]

Health, Safety and Welfare of Employees

(General Provisions)

8–14813　4. Cleanliness.　(1) All premises to which this Act applies, and all furniture, furnishings and fittings in such premises shall be kept in a clean state[1].

(2) No dirt or refuse shall be allowed to accumulate in any part of premises to which this Act applies in which work, or through which pass, any of the persons employed to work in the premises; and the floors of, and any steps comprised in, any such part as aforesaid shall be cleaned not less than once a week by washing or, if it is effective and suitable, by sweeping or other method[1].

(4) Neither subsection (2) of this section nor anything in regulations under the last foregoing subsection shall be construed as being in derogation of the general obligation imposed by subsection (1) of this section.

(5) Nothing in this section or in regulations thereunder shall apply to fuel storage premises[2] which are wholly in the open, and, in the case of such premises which are partly in the open, so much of them as is in the open shall, for the purposes of this section and of such regulations, be treated as not forming part of the premises.*

[Offices, Shops and Railway Premises Act 1963, s 4, as amended by SI 1974/1943.]

---

*.　**Sections 4–16 were repealed by the Workplace (Health, Safety and Welfare) Regulations 1992, in this PART, post, excepting the operation of any provision of the Offices, Shops and Railway Premises Act 1963 as that provision has effect by virtue of s 90(4) of that Act, post.**

1.　Contravention of this provision is an offence (s 63, post). For penalty see Health and Safety at Work etc Act 1974, s 33.

2.　Defined in s 1(3)(*a*)(v), ante.

8–14814　5. Overcrowding.　(1) No room comprised in, or constituting, premises to which this Act applies shall, while work is going on therein, be so overcrowded as to cause risk of injury to the health of persons working therein; and in determining, for the purposes of this subsection, whether any such room is so overcrowded as aforesaid, regard shall be had (amongst other things) not only to the number of persons who may be expected to be working in the room at any time but also to the space in the room occupied by furniture, furnishings, fittings, machinery, plant, equipment, appliances and other things (whether similar to any of those aforesaid or not)[1].

(2) The number of persons habitually employed at a time to work in such a room as aforesaid shall not be such that the quotient derived by dividing by that number the number which expresses in square metres the area of the surface of the floor of the room is less than 3·7 or the quotient derived by dividing by the first-mentioned number the number which expresses in cubic metres the capacity of the room is less than 11[1].

(3) Subsection (2) of this section—

(*a*)　shall not prejudice the general obligation imposed by subsection (1) thereof;

(*b*)　shall not apply to a room to which members of the public are invited to resort; and

(*c*)　shall not, in the case of a room comprised in, or constituting, premises of any class (being a room which at the passing of this Act is comprised in, or constitutes, premises to which this Act applies), have effect until the expiration of the period of three years[2] beginning with the day on which the said subsection (1) comes into force as respects premises of that class.*

[Offices, Shops and Railway Premises Act 1963, s 5 as amended by SI 1982/827.]

---

*.　**See note to s 4, ante.**

1.　Contravention is an offence under s 63, post.

2.　The Act was passed on 31 July 1963. Sub-s 1 came into force on 1 August 1964. Enforcing authorities may grant exemptions in accordance with s 46, post.

8–14815　6. Temperature.　(1) Effective provision shall be made for securing and maintaining a reasonable temperature in every room comprised in, or constituting, premises to which this Act applies, being a room in which persons are employed to work otherwise than for short periods, but no method shall be used which results in the escape into the air of any such room of any fume of such a character and to such extent as to be likely to be injurious or offensive to persons working therein[1].

(2) Where a substantial proportion of the work done in a room to which the foregoing subsection

applies does not involve severe physical effort, a temperature of less than 16 degrees Celsius shall not be deemed, after the first hour, to be a reasonable temperature while work is going on.

(3) The foregoing subsections shall not apply—

(a) to a room which comprises, or is comprised in or constitutes, office premises, being a room to which members of the public are invited to resort, and in which the maintenance of a reasonable temperature is not reasonably practicable; or

(b) to a room which comprises, or is comprised in or constitutes, shop or railway premises, being a room in which the maintenance of a reasonable temperature is not reasonably practicable or would cause deterioration of goods;

but there shall be provided for persons who are employed to work in a room to which, but for the foregoing provisions of this subsection, subsection (1) of this section would apply, conveniently accessible and effective means of enabling them to warm themselves[2].

(4) In premises to which this Act applies there shall, on each floor on which there is a room to which subsection (1) of this section applies, be provided in a conspicuous place and in such a position as to be easily seen by the persons employed to work in the premises on that floor a thermometer of a kind suitable for enabling the temperature in any such room on that floor to be readily determined; and a thermometer provided in pursuance of this subsection shall be kept available for use by those persons for that purpose[2].

(6) It shall be the duty of the employer of persons for whom means of enabling them to warm themselves are provided in pursuance of subsection (3) of this section to afford them reasonable opportunities for using those means, and if he fails so to do he shall be guilty of an offence[3].

(7) In this section "fume" includes gas or vapour.★

[Offices, Shops and Railway Premises Act 1963, s 6, as amended by SI 1974/1943 and SI 1982/827.]

★. **See note to s 4, ante.**
1. Contravention is an offence under s 63, post.
2. Contravention is an offence under s 63, post. Enforcing authorities may grant exemptions in accordance with s 46, post.
3. For penalty see Health and Safety at Work etc Act 1974, s 33.

8–14816 7. Ventilation.   (1) Effective and suitable provision shall be made for securing and maintaining, by the circulation of adequate supplies of fresh or artificially purified air, the ventilation of every room comprised in, or constituting, premises to which this Act applies, being a room in which persons are employed to work[1].★

[Offices, Shops and Railway Premises Act 1963, s 7, as amended by SI 1974/1943.]

★. **See note to s 4, ante.**
1. Contravention is an offence under s 63, post.

8–14817 8. Lighting.   (1) Effective provision shall be made for securing and maintaining, in every part of premises to which this Act applies in which persons are working or passing, sufficient and suitable lighting, whether natural or artificial[1].

(3) All glazed windows and skylights used for the lighting of any part of premises to which this Act applies in which work, or through which pass, any of the persons employed to work in the premises shall, so far as reasonably practicable, be kept clean on both the inner and outer surfaces and free from obstruction; but this subsection shall not affect the white-washing or shading of windows or skylights for the purpose of mitigating heat or glare[1].

(4) All apparatus installed at premises to which this Act applies for producing artificial lighting threat in parts in which the securing of lighting is required by this section to be provided for shall be properly maintained[1].★

[Offices, Shops and Railway Premises Act 1963, s 8, as amended by SI 1974/1943.]

★. **See note to s 4, ante.**
1. Contravention is an offence under s 63, post.

8–14818 9. Sanitary conveniences.   (1) There shall, in the case of premises to which this Act applies, be provided, at places conveniently accessible to the persons employed to work in the premises, suitable and sufficient sanitary conveniences for their use[1].

(2) Conveniences provided in pursuance of the foregoing subsection shall be kept clean and properly maintained and effective provision shall be made for lighting and ventilating them[1].

(5) Subsection (1) of this section shall be deemed to be complied with in relation to any premises as regards any period during which there are in operation arrangements for enabling the persons employed to work in the premises to have the use of sanitary conveniences provided for the use of others, being conveniences whose provision would have constituted compliance with that subsection had they been provided in pursuance thereof for the first-mentioned persons and with respect to which the requirements of subsection (2) of this section are satisfied.

(6) Neither section 45 of the Public Health Act 1936[2], nor s 29 of the Public Health (Scotland)

Act 1897 (which relate to the provision and repair of sanitary conveniences for factories, &c) shall apply to premises to which this Act applies.*

[Offices, Shops and Railway Premises Act 1963, s 9, as amended by SI 1974/1943 and the Building Act 1984, Sch 6.]

---

*. **See note to s 4, ante.**

1. Contravention is an offence under s 63, post. For provisions in respect of a building in single ownership, a part of which is premises to which the Act applies, see s 42(6), post. As to such a building owned by different persons, see s 43(4), post. See s 44, post, in respect of contiguous fuel storage premises, separately let, but in the same ownership.

Enforcing authorities may grant exemptions—in accordance with s 46, post.

2. See title PUBLIC HEALTH, post.

8–14819   10. Washing facilities. (1) There shall, in the case of premises to which this Act applies, be provided, at places conveniently accessible to the persons employed to work in the premises, suitable and sufficient washing facilities, including a supply of clean, running hot and cold or warm water and, in addition, soap and clean towels or other suitable means of cleaning or drying[1].

(2) Every place where facilities are provided in pursuance of this section shall be provided with effective means of lighting it and be kept clean and in orderly condition, and all apparatus therein for the purpose of washing or drying shall be kept clean and be properly maintained[1].

(5) Subsection (1) of this section shall be deemed to be complied with in relation to any premises as regards any period during which there are in operation arrangements for enabling the persons employed to work in the premises to have the use of washing facilities provided for the use of others, being facilities whose provision would have constituted compliance with that subsection had they been provided in pursuance thereof for the first-mentioned persons and which are provided at a place with respect to which the requirements of subsection (2) of this section are satisfied.*

[Offices, Shops and Railway Premises Act 1963, s 10, as amended by SI 1974/1943.]

---

*. **See note to s 4, ante.**

1. Contravention is an offence under s 63, post. For provisions in respect of a building in single ownership, a part of which is premises to which the Act applies, see s 42(7), post. As to such a building owned by different persons, see s 43(5), post. See s 44, post, in respect of contiguous fuel storage premises, separately let, but in the same ownership.

Enforcing authorities may grant exemptions in accordance with s 46, post.

8–14820   11. Supply of drinking water. (*1*) There shall, in the case of premises to which this Act applies, be provided and maintained, at suitable places conveniently accessible to the persons employed to work in the premises, an adequate supply of wholesome drinking water[1].

(2) Where a supply of water provided at a place in pursuance of the foregoing subsection is not piped, it must be contained in suitable vessels and must be renewed at least daily; and all practicable steps must be taken to preserve it and the vessels in which it is contained from contamination[1].

(3) Where water a supply of which is provided in pursuance of this section is delivered otherwise than in a jet from which persons can conveniently drink, there shall either—

(*a*) be provided, and be renewed so often as occasion requires, a supply of drinking vessels of a kind designed to be discarded after use; or

(*b*) be provided a sufficient number of drinking vessels of a kind other than as aforesaid, together with facilities for rinsing them in clean water[1].

(4) Subsection (1) of this section shall be deemed to be complied with in relation to any premises as regards any period during which there are in operation arrangements for enabling the persons employed to work in the premises to avail themselves of a supply of drinking water provided and maintained for the use of others, being a supply whose provision and maintenance would have constituted compliance with that subsection had it been provided and maintained for the use of the first-mentioned person, and—

(*a*) where the supply provided is not piped, the requirements of subsection (2) of this section are satisfied as respects it and the vessels in which it is contained; and

(*b*) where the water supplied is delivered as mentioned in subsection (3) of this section, the requirements of that subsection are satisfied.*

[Offices, Shops and Railway Premises Act 1963, s 11.]

---

*. **See note to s 4, ante.**

1. Contravention is an offence under s 63, post.

8–14821   12. Accommodation for clothing. (1) There shall, in the case of premises to which this Act applies—

(*a*) be made, at suitable places, suitable and sufficient provision for enabling such of the clothing of the persons employed to work in the premises as is not worn by them during working hours to be hung up or otherwise accommodated; and

(*b*) be made, for drying that clothing, such arrangements as are reasonably practicable or, if a standard of arrangements for drying that clothing is prescribed, such arrangements as conform to that standard[1].

(2) Where persons are employed to do such work in premises to which this Act applies as necessitates the wearing of special clothing, and they do not take that clothing home, there shall, in the case of those premises—

    (*a*) be made, at suitable places, suitable and sufficient provision for enabling that clothing to be hung up or otherwise accommodated; and*

    (*b*) be made, for drying that clothing, such arrangements as are reasonably practicable or, if a standard of arrangements for drying that clothing is prescribed, such arrangements as conform to that standard[1].*

[Offices, Shops and Railway Premises Act 1963, s 12, as amended by SI 1974/1943.]

---

  *. **See note to s 4, ante.**
  1. Contravention is an offence under s 63, post.

8-14822   13. Sitting facilities.   (1) Where persons who are employed to work in office, shop or railway premises have, in the course of their work, reasonable opportunities for sitting without detriment to it, there shall be provided for their use, at suitable places conveniently accessible to them, suitable facilities for sitting sufficient to enable them to take advantage of those opportunities[1].

(2) Where persons are employed to work in a room which comprises, or is comprised in or constitutes, shop premises, being a room whereto customers are invited to resort, and have in the course of their work, reasonable opportunities for sitting without detriment to it, facilities provided for their use in pursuance of subsection (1) of this section shall be deemed not to be sufficient if the number of seats provided and the number of the persons employed are in less ratio than 1 to 3.

(3) It shall be the duty of the employer of persons for whose use facilities are provided in pursuance of the foregoing provisions of this section to permit them to use them whenever the use thereof does not interfere with their work, and if he fails so to do he shall be guilty of an offence[2].*

[Offices, Shops and Railway Premises Act 1963, s 13.]

---

  *. **See note to s 4, ante.**
  1. Contravention is an offence under s 63, post.
  2. For penalty see Health and Safety at Work etc Act 1974, s 33, post.

8-14823   14. Seats for sedentary work.   (1) Without prejudice to the general obligation imposed by the last foregoing section, where any work done in any premises to which this Act applies is of such a kind that if (or a substantial part of it) can, or must, be done sitting, there shall be provided for each person employed to do it there a seat of a design, construction and dimensions suitable for him and it, together with a foot-rest on which he can readily and comfortably support his feet if he cannot do so without one[1].

(2) A seat provided in pursuance of the foregoing subsection, and a foot-rest so provided that does not form part of a seat, must be adequately and properly supported while in use for the purpose for which it is provided.

(3) For the purpose of subsection (1) of this section, the dimensions of an adjustable seat shall be taken to be its dimensions as for the time being adjusted.*

[Offices, Shops and Railway Premises Act 1963, s 14.]

---

  *. **See note to s 4, ante.**
  1. Contravention is an offence under s 63, post.

8-14824   15. Eating facilities.   Where persons employed to work in shop premises eat meals there, suitable and sufficient facilities for eating them shall be provided[1].*

[Offices, Shops and Railway Premises Act 1963, s 15.]

---

  *See note to s 4, ante.
  1. Contravention is an offence under s 63, post.

8-14825   16. Floors, passages and stairs.   (1) All floors, stairs, steps, passages and gangways comprised in premises to which this Act applies shall be of sound construction and properly maintained and shall, so far as is reasonably practicable, be kept free from obstruction and from any substance likely to cause persons to slip[1].

(2) For every staircase comprised in such premises as aforesaid, a substantial hand-rail or hand-hold shall be provided and maintained, which, if the staircase has an open side, shall be on that side; and in the case of a staircase having two open sides or of a staircase which, owing to the nature of its construction or the condition of the surface of the steps or other special circumstances, is specially liable to cause accidents, such a handrail or hand-hold shall be provided and maintained on both sides[2].

(3) Any open side of a staircase to which the last foregoing subsection applies, shall also be guarded by the provision and maintenance of efficient means of preventing any person from accidentally falling through the space between the handrail or hand-hold and the steps of the staircase[2].

(4) All openings in floors comprised in premises to which this Act applies shall be securely fenced, except in so far as the nature of the work renders such fencing impracticable[2].

(5) The foregoing provisions of this section shall not apply to any such part of any fuel storage premises as is in the open, but in relation to any such part the following provisions shall have effect, namely—

    (*a*)   the surface of the ground shall be kept in good repair;

    (*b*)   all steps and platforms shall be of sound construction and properly maintained;

    (*c*)   all openings in platforms shall be securely fenced, except in so far as the nature of the work renders such fencing impracticable★.

[Offices, Shops and Railway Premises Act 1963, s 16.]

★. **See note to s 4, ante.**

   1. Contravention is an offence under s 63, post. This section is comparable to s 28 of the Factories Act 1961 in this title, ante, and decisions upon that section may be applied. For provisions in respect of a building in single ownership, a part of which is premises to which the Act applies, see s 42(4), (5), post. As to such a building owned by different persons, see s 43(3), post.

   2. Contravention is an offence under s 63, post.

8–14826   17. Fencing of exposed parts of machinery.

(1) Every dangerous part of any machinery used as, or forming, part of the equipment of premises to which this Act applies shall be securely fenced unless it is in such a position or of such construction as to be safe to every person working in the premises as it would be if securely fenced[1].

(2) In so far as the safety of a dangerous part of any machinery cannot, by reason of the nature of the operation effected by means of the machinery, be secured by means of a fixed guard, the requirements of the foregoing subsection shall be deemed to be complied with if a device is provided that automatically prevents the operator from coming into contact with that part[1].

(3) *Repealed.*

(4) Fencing provided in pursuance of the foregoing provisions of this section shall be of substantial construction, be properly maintained and be kept in position while the parts required to be fenced are in motion or use.

(5) *Repealed.*

[Offices, Shops and Railway Premises Act 1963, s 17 as amended by the Employment Act 1989, s 9 and Sch 7.]

---

   1. Contravention is an offence under s 63, post. This section is comparable to ss 14–16 of the Factories Act 1961, in this title, ante, and decisions upon those sections may be applied.

8–14827   18. *Repealed.*

8–14828   19. Training and supervision of persons working at dangerous machines.

(1) No person employed to work in premises to which this Act applies shall work there at any machine to which this section applies unless he has been fully instructed as to the dangers arising in connection with it and the precautions to be observed, and—

    (*a*)   has received a sufficient training in work at the machine; or

    (*b*)   is under adequate supervision by a person who has a thorough knowledge and experience of the machine[1].

(2) This section applies to such machines as may be prescribed by order of the Minister, being machines which in his opinion are of such a dangerous character that persons ought not to work at them unless the foregoing requirements are complied with.

[Offices, Shops and Railway Premises Act 1963, s 19.]

---

   1. Contravention is an offence under s 63, post. This section is comparable to s 21 of the Factories Act 1961, in this title, ante.

8–14829   23. Prohibition of heavy work.

(1) No person shall, in the course of his work in premises to which this Act applies, be required to lift, carry or move a load so heavy as to be likely to cause injury to him[1].

[Offices, Shops and Railway Premises Act 1963, s 23, as amended by SI 1974/1943.]

---

   1. Contravention is an offence under s 63, post. Section 23 is repealed by the Manual Handling Operations Regulations 1992, this PART, post except in so far as the prohibition in this section applies to any person specified in s 90(4), post.

8–14840   27. Penalisation of dangerous acts and interference with equipment, &c.

(1) A person who, in premises to which this Act applies, wilfully and without reasonable cause does anything likely to endanger the health or safety of persons employed to work therein shall be guilty of an offence[1].

(2) A person who, in premises to which this Act applies, wilfully interferes with, wilfully misuses

or without reasonable excuse removes any equipment, appliance, facilities or other thing provided there in pursuance of this Act or regulations thereunder shall be guilty of an offence[1].
[Offices, Shops and Railway Premises Act 1963, s 27, as amended by SI 1974/1943.]

---

1. For penalty see Health and Safety at Work etc Act 1974, s 33, post.

Special Provisions with respect to Buildings whereof Parts are Office, &c, Premises and with respect to certain contiguous Fuel Storage Premises

8-14841 42. Provisions with respect to buildings in single ownership.   (1) A building to which this section applies is one all parts of which are in the same ownership and a part of which consists of premises to which this Act applies, being premises held under a lease or an agreement for a lease or under a licence; and in this section a reference to a common part of a building to which this section applies shall be taken to refer to a part of the building that is used for the purpose of, but is not comprised in, a part of the building that consists of premises to which this Act applies.

(2) The following provisions shall have effect for securing the cleanliness of common parts of buildings to which this section applies, that is to say:

(*a*) every common part of a building to which this section applies, and all furniture, furnishings and fittings in such a part, shall be kept in a clean state;

(*b*) *Repealed.*

(3) The following provisions shall have effect for securing the illumination of common parts of buildings to which this section applies, that is to say:

(*a*) effective provision shall be made for securing and maintaining, in every such part of a common part of a building to which this section applies as the following, namely, a part in which persons are working or passing, suitable and sufficient lighting whether natural or artificial;

(*b*) *Repealed*;

(*c*) all glazed windows and skylights used for the lighting of a part of a common part of a building to which this section applies in which the securing of lighting is required by this subsection to be provided for shall, so far as reasonably practicable, be kept clean on both the inner and outer surfaces and free from obstruction;

(*d*) all apparatus installed in a common part of a building to which this section applies for producing artificial lighting in a part of that part in which the securing of lighting is required by this subsection to be provided for shall be properly maintained;

but paragraph (*c*) above shall not affect the whitewashing or shading of windows or skylights for the purposes of mitigating heat or glare.

(4) Section 16(1) of this Act shall apply to floors, stairs, steps, passages and gangways comprised in, or constituting, a common part of a building to which this section applies as it applies to floors, stairs, steps, passages and gangways in premises to which this Act applies, s 16(2) of this Act shall apply to a staircase comprised in, or constituting, a common part of such a building as it applies to such a staircase as is mentioned in that subsection, and s 16(3) of this Act shall apply to an open side of such a staircase as is first mentioned in this subsection as it applies to an open side of such a staircase as is mentioned in the said subsection (2).

(5) In the event of a contravention, in relation to a common part of a building to which this section applies, of subsection (2) or (3) of this section or of regulations under either of those subsections, and in the event of a contravention, in relation to any thing constituting, or comprised in, any such common part, of s 16 of this Act as applied by the last foregoing subsection, the owner of the building shall be guilty of an offence[1].

(6) For a contravention, in relation to premises comprised in a building to which this section applies, of s 9 of this Act (other than a contravention consisting in a failure to keep clean conveniences provided in pursuance of that section, not being conveniences provided for use jointly by the persons employed to work in the premises and by other persons), the owner of the building shall be responsible instead of the occupier of the premises.

(7) For a contravention, in relation to premises comprised in a building to which this section applies, of s 10 of this Act (other than a contravention consisting in a failure to provide means of cleaning or drying or a failure to keep clean and in orderly condition the place where facilities are provided in pursuance of that section, not being facilities provided for use jointly by the persons employed to work in the premises and by other persons) the owner of the building shall be responsible instead of the occupier of the premises.
[Offices, Shops and Railway Premises Act 1963, s 42, as amended by SI 1974/1943 and SI 1976/2005.]

---

1. For penalty see Health and Safety at Work etc Act 1974, s 33, post.

8-14842 43. Provisions with respect to buildings plurally owned.   (1) A building to which this section applies is one of which different parts are owned by different persons and of which a part consists of premises to which this Act applies; and in this section a reference to a common part of a building to which this section applies shall be taken to refer to a part of the building that is used for the purposes of, but is not comprised in, a part of the building that consists of premises to which this Act applies.

(2) Subsections (2) and (3) of the last foregoing section shall, with the substitution, for references to buildings to which that section applies and to common parts thereof, of references respectively to buildings to which this section applies and to common parts thereof, have effect for securing the cleanliness and illumination of common parts of buildings to which this section applies as they have effect for securing the cleanliness and illumination of common parts of buildings to which that section applies; and in the event of a contravention, in relation to a common part of a building to which this section applies, of either of those subsections or of regulations under either of them, the owner of the part (or, if there are more owners than one of the part, each of them) shall be guilty of an offence.

(3) Section 16(1) of this Act shall apply to floors, stairs, steps, passages and gangways comprised in, or constituting, a common part of a building to which this section applies as it applies to floors, stairs, steps, passages and gangways in premises to which this Act applies, s 16(2) of this Act shall apply to a staircase comprised in, or constituting, a common part of such a building as it applies to such a staircase as is mentioned in that subsection, and s 16(3) of this Act shall apply to an open side of such a staircase as is first-mentioned in this subsection as it applies to an open side of such a staircase as is mentioned in the said subsection (2); and in the event of a contravention, in relation to any thing constituting, or comprised in, any such common part, of s 16 of this Act as applied by this subsection, the owner of the part (or if there are more owners than one of the part, each of them) shall be guilty of an offence.

(4) For a contravention, in relation to premises consisting of part of any such part of a building to which this section applies as is owned by one of the persons who own between them own the building (being premises held under a lease or an agreement for a lease or under a licence), of s 9 of this Act (other than a contravention consisting in a failure to keep clean conveniences provided in pursuance of that section, not being conveniences provided for use jointly by the persons employed to work in the premises and by other persons), the first-mentioned person shall be responsible instead of the occupier of the premises.

(5) For a contravention, in relation to premises consisting of part of any such part of a building to which this section applies as is owned by one of the persons who between them own the building (being premises held under a lease or an agreement for a lease or under a licence), of s 10 of this Act (other than a contravention consisting in a failure to provide means of cleaning or drying or a failure to keep clean and in orderly condition the place where facilities are provided in pursuance of that section, not being facilities provided for use jointly by the persons employed to work in the premises and by other persons) the first-mentioned person shall be responsible instead of the occupier of the premises.

[Office, Shops and Railway Premises Act 1963, s 43, as amended by SI 1974/1943 and SI 1976/2005].

8–14843 44. Provisions with respect to contiguous fuel storage premises in single ownership.
Where two sets or more of fuel storage premises any of which is held under a lease or an agreement for a lease or under a licence are established on a parcel of land all parts of which are in the same ownership then—

(a) for a contravention, in relation to any of those sets of premises, of s 9 of this Act (other than a contravention consisting in a failure to keep clean conveniences provided in pursuance of that section, not being conveniences provided for use jointly by the persons employed to work in that set of premises and by other persons); and

(b) for contravention, in relation to any of those sets of premises, of s 10 of this Act (other than a contravention consisting in a failure to provide means of cleaning and drying or a failure to keep clean and in orderly condition the place where facilities are provided in pursuance of that section, not being facilities provided for use jointly by the persons employed to work in that set of premises and by other persons);

the owner of that set of premises shall be responsible instead of the occupier thereof.

[Offices, Shops and Railway Premises Act 1963, s 44.]

8–14844 46. Power of authorities who enforce Act to grant exemptions from certain requirements thereof. (1) The authority having power to enforce, with respect to any premises, the following provisions of this Act, namely, section 5(2) and sections 6 and 9, may—

(a) exempt the premises or any room therein from all or any of the requirements imposed by the said sections 5(2) and 6;

(b) exempt the premises from all or any of the requirements imposed by the said section 9;

if satisfied that, in the circumstances affecting the subject of the exemption, compliance with the requirements or requirement from which exemption is granted is not reasonably practicable.

(2) The authority having power to enforce section 10(1) of this Act with respect to any premises may, if satisfied that it is not reasonably practicable for running water to be supplied there or for running water so supplied to be heated, exempt the premises from so much of that subsection as requires the water supplied to be running water.

(3) An exemption under subsection (1) of this section of, or of a room in, any premises from a

requirement of a provision of this Act may be granted for a period not exceeding two years, but may from time to time be extended for a further such period beyond the expiration of the period at the expiration of which it would otherwise expire if the authority having power to enforce that provision with respect to the premises are satisfied as mentioned in subsection (1) of this section and are further satisfied that the person who, if the exemption were not in force, would be responsible for a contravention in relation to the premises of that provision (being a contravention consisting in a failure to comply with that requirement) has not failed to do anything the doing of which might have rendered compliance with that requirement reasonably practicable.

(4) An exemption under subsection (2) of this section may be granted without limit of time or for a specified period; but the grant of such an exemption for a specified period shall not preclude the grant of the like exemption for further periods.

(5) An exemption of, or of a room in, any premises from a requirement imposed by a provision of this Act shall not be granted or extended under this section—

(a) except upon application made to the authority having power to enforce with respect to the premises the provisions imposing the requirement, in such form as may be prescribed by order made by the Minister—

　(i) in a case where the grant of an exemption is sought, by the person who would be responsible for a contravention in relation to the premises of that provision (being a contravention consisting in a failure to comply with that requirement);

　(ii) in a case where the extension of an exemption is sought, by the person who, if the exemption were not in force, would be responsible as aforesaid;

(b) unless the application is accompanied by a certificate in such form as may be so prescribed, that the obligation to which the applicant is subject by virtue of subsection (6)(a) below has been complied with; and

(c) until the expiration of the period of fourteen days beginning with the day next following that on which the application is made.

(6) In relation to an application for the grant or extension of an exemption under this section of, or of a room in, any premises, compliance by the applicant with the following requirements shall be requisite, namely—

(a) he must, immediately before the application is made, post in the premises, in such a position, and in such characters, as to be easily seen and read by the persons employed to work in the premises, a notice—

　(i) stating that such an application is being made;

　(ii) specifying the requirement from which exemption or, as the case may be, further exemption, is being sought;

　(iii) specifying the period for which the grant or, as the case may be, the extension, is being sought (or if, where a grant of exemption is being sought under subsection (2) of this section, it be the case that the grant thereof without limit of time is being sought, specifying that fact);

　(iv) specifying the name and address of the authority to whom the application is being made and notifying the persons aforesaid that written representations with respect to the application may be made by any of them to that authority before the expiration of the period of fourteen days beginning with the day next following that on which the notice is posted in compliance with this paragraph;

(b) he must keep the said notice posted as aforesaid throughout the last-mentioned period;

and a person making an application under this section who fails to comply with an obligation to which he is, in relation to the application, subject by virtue of this subsection shall be guilty of an offence and liable on summary conviction, to a fine not exceeding **level 1** on the standard scale[1].

(7) An exemption under this section of, or of a room in, any premises from a requirement imposed by a provision of this Act may, if the authority having power to enforce that provision with respect to the premises cease to be satisfied with respect to the matters with respect to which they were satisfied when the exemption was granted or, if the exemption has been extended under subsection (3) of this section, when it was extended, be withdrawn by that authority provided that three months' notice of intention to withdraw it has been given to the person who, if the exemption were not in force would be responsible for a contravention in relation to the premises of that provision (being a contravention consisting in a failure to comply with that requirement).

(8) Where an exemption of, or of a room in, any premises from a requirement imposed by a provision of this Act or an extension of such an exemption is granted under this section by an authority, a certificate of the grant or extension shall be sent by the authority to the person who, if the exemption were not in force, would be responsible for a contravention in relation to the premises of that provision (being a contravention consisting in a failure to comply with that requirement).

(9) *Repealed.*

(10) Notice of the refusal by an authority to grant or extend an exemption under this section shall be given by them to the applicant for the grant or extension and also (if it be the case that representations with respect to the application were duly made by the persons employed to work in

the premises to which the application related or any of those persons), either individually to such of those persons as duly made representations or to a person appearing to the authority to be representative of such of those persons as duly made representations or to each of a number of persons who appear to the authority to be representative between them of such of these persons as duly made representations.

(11) A person who is aggrieved—

(a) by the refusal of an authority to grant or extend an exemption under this section of, or of a room in, any premises; or

(b) by a notice of intention to withdraw such an exemption;

may, within twenty-one days of the refusal or, as the case may be, service of the notice, appeal, if the premises are situate in England or Wales, to a magistrates' court[2] acting for the petty sessions area in which they are situate, or, (*applies to Scotland*), and on any such appeal—

(i) in a case falling within paragraph (a) above, the court, if satisfied with respect to the matters with respect to which the authority would have to have been satisfied as a condition of their granting or extending the exemption, may order the authority to grant or extend it, in the case of an exemption under subsection (1) of this section, for such period not exceeding two years as may be specified in the order, and, in the case of an exemption under subsection (2) of this section, either without limit of time or for such period as may be so specified;

(ii) in a case falling within paragraph (b) above, the court, if satisfied with respect to the matters with respect to which the authority were satisfied when the exemption was granted or, if it has been extended, when it was extended, may order the authority to cancel the notice of intention to withdraw the exemption.

(13) In relation to an application made under this section with respect to, or to a room in, premises which form part of a building to which section 42 or 43 of this Act applies, subsection (6) above shall have effect with the substitution, for the words in paragraph (a) "post in the premises", of the words "post in the premises or in a part of the building which for the purposes of the said section 42 or the said section 43 (as the case may be) is referred to as a common part of the building".

[Offices, Shops and Railway Premises Act 1963, s 46, as amended by SI 1974/1943 and the Criminal Justice Act 1982, ss 38 and 46 and SI 1995/2923.]

---

1. Sections 65–67 and 70 (post), will apply.
2. Appeal will be by way of complaint. See Magistrates' Courts Rules 1981, r 34, in PART I: MAGISTRATES' COURTS PROCEDURE, ante.

Prohibition of Levying of Charges on Employees for Things done in Compliance with Act

8–14845 47. Prohibition of levying of charges on employees for things done in compliance with Act. If the owner or the occupier of premises to which this Act applies or a person who employs persons to work therein levies, or suffers to be levied, upon a person so employed, any charge in respect of anything done or provided in pursuance of this Act or regulations thereunder, he shall be guilty of an offence[1].

[Offices, Shops and Railway Premises Act 1963, s 47.]

---

1. For penalty see Health and Safety at Work etc Act 1974, s 33, post.

Information

8–14846 49. Notification of fact of employment of persons. (1) Before a person first begins, after the coming into operation of this subsection with respect to any office, shop or railway premises, to employ persons to work therein, he shall serve on the appropriate authority two copies of a notice stating that persons will be employed by him so to work and containing such other (if any) information as may be prescribed by order of the Minister, being a notice in such form and of such size as may be so prescribed.

(3) A person who fails to comply with an obligation to which he is subject by virtue of the foregoing subsection shall be guilty of an offence and liable on summary conviction to a fine not exceeding **level 1** on the standard scale[1].

(4) Proceedings for an offence under this section may be commenced at any time within twelve months from the time when the offence was committed.

(5) In this section "appropriate authority" has the same meaning as in the last foregoing section.

[Offices, Shops and Railway Premises Act 1963, s. 49, as amended by SI 1974/1943 and the Criminal Justice Act 1982, ss. 38 and 46.]

---

1. See ss 65–67 and 70, post. Sub-section (4) extends the normal time limit for prosecution under s 49.

Enforcement

8–14847 52. Authorities who are to enforce Act. (1)–(4) *Repealed*.

(5) It shall be the duty of each London borough council and the Common Council of the City of

London, as regards office or shop premises forming part of a place of public entertainment within the borough or the City, as the case may be, other than such a place occupied by them, to enforce the foregoing provisions of this Act and regulations thereunder.

(6)–(7) *Repealed.*

[Offices, Shops and Railway Premises Act 1963, s 52, as amended by the London Government Act 1963, s 51, the Administration of Justice Act 1964, s 39 and Sch 3, the Criminal Justice Act 1967, s 95, SI 1974/1943, SI 1976/2005 and the Local Government Act 1985, Sch 8.]

8–14848   59. Restriction of disclosure of information.   If a person discloses (otherwise than in the performance of his duty or for the purposes of any legal proceedings, including arbitrations, or for the purposes of a report of any such proceedings as aforesaid) any information obtained by him in any premises entered by him in exercise of powers conferred by or by virtue of this Act, he shall be guilty of an offence[1].

[Offices, Shops and Railway Premises Act 1963, s 59, as amended by SI 1974/1943.]

---

1. For penalty see Health and Safety at Work etc Act 1974, s 33.

8–14848A   59A. Exception to restriction: public authorities.   Section 59 does not apply if—

   (*a*)   the person making the disclosure referred to in that section is, or is acting on behalf of a person who is, a public authority for the purposes of the Freedom of Information Act 2000, and

   (*b*)   the information is not held by the authority on behalf of another person.

[Offices, Shops and Railway Premises Act 1963, s 59A, as inserted by SI 2004/3363.]

Offences, Penalties and legal Proceedings

8–14849   63. Offences.   (1) In the event of a contravention, in relation to any premises to which this Act applies, of any such provisions of this Act as are mentioned in subsection (2) of this section or of regulations made under any such provisions, then—

   (*a*)   except in a case falling within either of the two following paragraphs, the occupier of the premises shall be guilty of an offence;

   (*b*)   in a case where the contravention is one for which, by or by virtue of this Act, some other person or persons is or are made responsible as well as the occupier of the premises, that other person or those other persons and the occupier shall each be guilty of an offence;

   (*c*)   in a case where the contravention is one for which, by or by virtue of this Act, some other person or persons is or are made responsible instead of the occupier of the premises, that other person or each of those other persons shall be guilty of an offence.

(2) The provisions of this Act referred to in the foregoing subsection are sections 4, 5, 6(1) to (5), 7 to 12, 13(1), 14 to 19, 23, 24, 46(9) and 48(1) and (2)[1].

(3) A person who contravenes a provision of regulations under s 20 or 50 of this Act shall be guilty of an offence[2].

[Offices, Shops and Railway Premises Act 1963, s 63, as amended by SI 1974/1943 and SI 1976/2005.]

---

1. Section 63 has been noted to the provisions specified in sub-s (2).
2. For penalty see Health and Safety at Work etc Act 1974, s 33. Note that although ss 20 and 50 were repealed by SI 1974/1943, regulations made under those sections prior to 1 January 1975 continue in force: see reg 4(3) of SI 1974/1943.

8–14850   67. Defence available to persons charged with offences.   It shall be a defence for a person charged with a contravention of a provision of this Act or of regulations thereunder to prove that he used all due diligence to secure compliance with that provision.

[Offices, Shops and Railway Premises Act 1963, s 67.]

8–14851   69. Removal or defacement of documents posted in pursuance of Act or regulations under it.   If, without reasonable excuse, a person removes a notice or other document which is for the time being posted or displayed in any premises in pursuance of a provision of this Act or of regulations thereunder, he shall be guilty of an offence[1] and liable on summary conviction to a fine not exceeding **level 1** on the standard scale.

[Offices, Shops and Railway Premises Act 1963, s 69, as amended by the Criminal Damage Act 1971, Schedule and SI 1974/1943 and the Criminal Justice Act 1982, ss 38 and 46.]

---

1. Punishable on summary conviction (s 70, post).

8–14852   72. Appeal from orders made on complaint.   A person aggrieved by an order[1] made by a magistrates' court on determining a complaint under this Act may appeal therefrom to the Crown Court.

[Offices, Shops and Railway Premises Act 1963, s 72, as amended by the Courts Act 1971, Sch 9.]

1. A dismissal of a complaint is an "order" under this section (*R v Recorder of Oxford, ex p Brasenose College* [1970] 1 QB 109, [1969] 3 All ER 428, 133 JP 671).

8–14853   **78.** *Provision for securing exercise of local Act powers in conformity with this Act.*

8–14854   **83.** *Application to the Crown.*

8–14855   **84.** *Exclusion of application to visiting forces and international organisations.*

8–14856   **85.** *Exclusion of application to factories, to certain fish salerooms and to parts below ground of mines.*

8–14857   **86. Exclusion of application to premises occupied for transitory purposes.** (1) It shall be a defence in any legal proceedings to recover damages and in any prosecution, in so far as the proceedings or prosecution are or is based on an allegation of a contravention, in relation to any premises, of a provision of this Act or regulations thereunder, to prove that at the time of the alleged contravention the premises were occupied for a purpose that was accomplished before the expiration of a period beginning with the day on which they were occupied for that purpose and of such of the following lengths as is applicable to the circumstances of the case, that is to say, six months if the premises consist of a movable structure, and six weeks if not.

(2) The foregoing subsection shall not apply to a prosecution for an offence consisting in a failure to comply with an obligation imposed under s. 49 (1) of this Act to notify the appropriate authority that persons would be employed to work in any premises; but in any such prosecution it shall be a defence to prove that the persons in question were employed to work in the premises while they were occupied as mentioned in the foregoing subsection.

[Offices, Shops and Railway Premises Act 1963, s 86.]

Interpretation

8–14858   **90. Interpretation.** (1) In this Act unless the context otherwise requires, the following expressions have the meanings hereby assigned to them respectively, that is to say—

except in section 1(4) of this Act "building" includes structure;

"contravention" includes in relation to a provision of this Act or of regulations thereunder a failure to comply with the provision, and the expression "contravene" shall be construed accordingly;

"employed" means employed under a contract of service or apprenticeship (whether oral or in writing, express or implied);

"fish" includes molluscs and crustaceans;

"fuel storage premises" has the meaning assigned to it by section 1(3)(*a*)(v) of this Act;

"the Minister" means the Secretary of State for Employment[1];

"notice" means a notice in writing;

"office premises" has the meaning assigned to it by section 1(2) of this Act;

"owner"—

     (*a*) as respects England and Wales, means the person for the time being receiving the rackrent of the premises, building or part of a building in connection with which the word is used, whether on his own account or as agent or trustee for another person, or who would so receive the rackrent if the premises, building or part were let as a rackrent, and

     (*b*) Scotland.

and "owned" and "ownership" shall be construed accordingly;

"railway premises" has the meaning assigned to it by section 1(4) of this Act;

"railway undertakers" means any persons authorised by an enactment or a provision of an order or scheme made under or confirmed by an Act to construct, work or carry on a railway;

"shop premises" has the meaning assigned to it by section 1(3) of this Act;

"week" means the period between midnight on Saturday night and midnight on the succeeding Saturday night.

(2) *Repealed.*

(3) For the purposes of this Act—

     (*a*) persons employed by railway undertakers to do work the general control of the doing of which is exercised at railway premises, or at office premises occupied by the undertakers for the purposes of the railway undertaking carried on by them and situate in the immediate vicinity of the permanent way, shall be deemed to be employed to work in the premises at which the general control of the doing of their work is exercised notwithstanding that their work is in fact done elsewhere;

     (*b*) neither railway premises nor such office premises as aforesaid shall be taken to be premises in the case of which persons are employed to work therein by reason only of the fact that persons employed by the undertakers who occupy the premises resort to the premises for the purpose only of discharging duties whose discharge is incidental to the work that they are primarily employed to do.

(4) For the purposes of this Act, any such person as follows shall be taken to be employed, namely—

(*a*) a person appointed under section 6 or 7 of the Registration Service Act 1953, who exercises and performs his powers and duties in premises provided and maintained by the council within whose area his district or sub-district is situate;

(*b*) *Repealed*;

(*c*) a member of a police force maintained by a police authority.

(*d*) a member of the National Crime Intelligence Service within section 9(1)(*a*) or (*b*) of the Police Act 1997 or a member of the National Crime Squad within section 55(1)(*a*) or (*b*) of that Act (police members).*

(5) The definition of a class of premises, rooms or persons for the purposes of any regulations or order under this Act may be framed by reference to any circumstances whatever.

(6) Any reference in this Act to any other enactment shall, unless the context otherwise requires, be construed as a reference to that enactment as amended or extended by or under any subsequent enactment.

[Offices, Shops and Railway Premises Act 1963, s 90, as amended by the London Government Act 1963, s 51, the Registration of Births, Deaths and Marriages (Scotland) Act 1965, s 58, SI 1974/1943, SI 1976/2005, SI 1977/746, the Cinemas Act 1985, Sch 2, the Electricity Act 1989, Sch 18, the Statute Law (Repeals) Act 1993, Sch 1, the Police Act 1997, Sch 9 and the Licensing Act 2003, Sch 6.]

---

*Substituted by the Serious Organised Crime and Police Act 2005, Sch 4 from a date to be appointed.
1. See the Secretary of State for Employment and Productivity Order 1968, SI 1968/729.

Continental Shelf Act 1964
(1964 c 29)

8–14870　1. Exploration and exploitation of continental shelf.　(1) Any rights exercisable by the United Kingdom outside territorial waters with respect to the sea bed and subsoil and their natural resources, except so far as they are exercisable in relation to coal, are hereby vested in Her Majesty.

(2)–(5) *Repealed.*

(6) *Duties of Minister.*

(7) Her Majesty may from time to time by Order[1] in Council designate any area as an area within which the rights mentioned in subsection (1) of this section are exercisable, and any area so designated is in this Act referred to as a designated area; and the power to make Orders under this subsection shall include power to revoke Orders for the purpose of consolidating them.

(8) *Meaning of "coal".*

[Continental Shelf Act 1964, s 1, amended by the Oil and Gas (Enterprise) Act 1982, s 37 and Sch 3, the Petroleum Act 1987, Sch 3, the Coal Industry Act 1987, Sch 1, the Offshore Safety Act 1992, Sch 2, the Coal Industry Act 1994, Sch 11 and the Petroleum Act 1998, Sch 4.]

---

1. Areas to which the Act applies are designated by the Continental Shelf (Designation of Areas) (Consolidation) Order 2000, SI 2000/3062.

8–14871　4. Safety of navigation.　(1) Part II of the Coast Protection Act 1949[1] (which requires the consent of the Minister of Transport to the carrying out of certain works on the sea shore if obstruction or danger to navigation is likely to result) except section 34(1)(*b*) (which restricts the deposit of materials) shall apply in relation to any part of the sea bed in a designated area as it applies in relation to the sea shore; and section 46 of that Act (local inquiries) shall extend to any matter arising under this section.

(2) Any person guilty of an offence under the said Part II as applied by this section shall be liable[2], on summary conviction to a fine not exceeding **the statutory maximum**, and on conviction on indictment to a **fine**.

[Continental Shelf Act 1964, s 4, as amended by the Criminal Law Act 1977, ss 28 and 32.]

---

1. See title COAST PROTECTION, ante.
2. For procedure in respect of this offence which is triable either way, see the Magistrates' Courts Act 1980, ss 17A–21, in PART I: MAGISTRATES' COURTS, PROCEDURE, ante.

8–14872　6. Wireless Telegraphy.　*Repealed.*

8–14873　7. Radioactive substances.　An Order[1] in Council under section 11 of the Petroleum Act 1998 may make provision for treating for the purposes of the Radioactive Substances Act 1993[2] and any orders and regulations made thereunder any installation in an area or part with respect to which provision is made under that section and any waters within five hundred metres of such an installation

as if they were situated in such part of the United Kingdom as may be specified in the Order, and for modifying the provisions of that Act in their application to such an installation or waters.
[Continental Shelf Act 1964, s 7 as amended by the Oil and Gas (Enterprise) Act 1982, Sch 3, the Radioactive Substances Act 1993, Sch 4 and the Petroleum Act 1998, Sch 4.]

    1.　See the Continental Shelf (Jurisdiction) Order 1987, SI 1987/2197.
    2.　See title ENERGY (Atomic Energy and Radioactive Substances), ante.

8–14874　11. Prosecution of offences, etc.　(1)　Proceedings for any offence under another Act as applied by or under this Act may be taken, and the offence may for all incidental purposes be treated as having been committed in any place in the United Kingdom.

(2)　Where a body corporate is guilty of such an offence and the offence is proved to have been committed with the consent or connivance of, or to be attributable to any neglect on the part of, any director, manager, secretary or other similar officer of the body corporate or any person who was purporting to act in any such capacity he, as well as the body corporate, shall be guilty of the offence and shall be liable to be proceeded against and punished accordingly.

In this subsection, "director" in relation to a body corporate established for the purpose of carrying on under national ownership any industry or part of an industry or undertaking, being a body corporate whose affairs are managed by its members, means a member of that body corporate.

(3)　*Repealed.*
[Continental Shelf Act 1964, s 11 as amended by the Oil and Gas (Enterprise) Act 1982, Schs 3 and 4.]

8–14875　11A. Interpretation.　In this Act "installation" includes any floating structure or device maintained on a station by whatever means.
[Continental Shelf Act 1964, s 11A, as inserted by the Oil and Gas (Enterprise) Act 1982, s 37 and Sch 3.]

Mines and Quarries (Tips) Act 1969
(1969 c 10)

8–14890　This Act provides for measures to be taken, and for penalties in default, to prevent disused tips constituting a danger to members of the public. It has been amended by the Mines and Quarries Acts 1954 to 1971 (Repeals and Modifications) Regulations 1974, SI 1974/2013 consequent upon the enactment of the Health and Safety at Work etc Act 1974, and by SI 1988/1930.

PART I
SECURITY OF TIPS ASSOCIATED WITH MINES AND QUARRIES

8–14891　1. Security of certain tips and application of Mines and Quarries Act 1954.
(1)　Every tip[1] to which this Part of this Act applies shall be made and kept secure.

(2)　Power to make regulations—*repealed*[2].

(3)　This Part of this Act shall be construed as one with the Mines and Quarries Act 1954 (in this Part of this Act referred to as "the principal Act") and, without prejudice to the generality of this provision—

(*a*)　except where the context otherwise requires, any reference in the principal Act to that Act includes a reference to this Part of this Act and expressions used in that Act have the same meaning in this Part of this Act as in that Act; and

(*b*)　the principal Act shall have effect subject to the modifications in Schedule 1 to this Act[3].
[Mines and Quarries (Tips) Act 1969, s 1, as amended by SI 1974/2013.]

    1.　See s 2, infra.
    2.　The Mines and Quarries (Tips) Regulations 1971, SI 1971/1377 amended by SI 1999/2024 are continued in force by reg 7(3) of SI 1974/2013.
    3.　The text of the principal act (ante) has been amended where appropriate in accordance with Sch 1 to this Act.

8–14892　2. Tips to which Part I applies.　(1)　In this Act, except in this Part where the words "or quarry" shall be omitted, the expression "tip"[1] means an accumulation or deposit of refuse from a mine[2] or quarry[2] (whether in a solid state or in solution or suspension) other than an accumulation or deposit situated underground, and where any wall or other structure retains or confines a tip then, whether or not that wall or structure is itself composed of refuse, it shall be deemed to form part of the tip for the purposes of this Act.

(2)　Subject to subsections (3) and (4) below, a tip is one to which this Act applies if either—

(*a*)　the tip is on premises which are deemed to form part of a mine, or for the purposes of Part II of this Act, quarry for the purposes of the principal Act by virtue of section 180(4) of that Act (which relates to premises for the time being used for the deposit of refuse) as in force immediately before the coming into force of the Quarries Regulations 1999; or

(*b*)　the tip is not on such premises but the mine or for the purposes of Part II of this Act, quarry with which it is associated has not been abandoned and the premises on which the tip is situated continue to be occupied exclusively by the owner of that mine or for the purposes of Part II of this Act, quarry;

and for the purposes of this Part of this Act a tip is an "active tip" if it falls within paragraph (*a*) above and a "closed tip" if it falls within paragraph (*b*) above.

(3) If part, but not the whole, of any premises on which a tip is situated is occupied exclusively by the owner[3] of a mine and, by reason only that the whole of those premises is not occupied exclusively by the owner, the tip is not, apart from this subsection, one to which this Part of this Act applies (whether as an active tip or a closed tip) then—

    (*a*) subject to any direction under paragraph (*b*) below, the tip shall be deemed to be an active tip or a closed tip, as the case may be, and if an active tip, the premises on which it is situated shall be treated, for the purposes of the principal Act and this Part of this Act, as forming part of the mine with which it is associated; and

    (*b*) the Health and Safety Executive may direct that, as from such day as may be specified in the order, the whole or such part of the tip as may be so specified shall cease to be a tip to which this Part of this Act applies.

(4) If the whole or any part of a tip which, apart from this subsection, would be a tip to which this Part of this Act applies is appropriated to some use which, in the opinion of the Health and Safety Executive, is inconsistent with the resumption of tipping operations on the tip, or on a particular part of it, the Health and Safety Executive may direct that as from such day as may be specified in the order, the whole or such part of the tip as may be so specified shall cease to be a tip to which this Part of this Act applies.

(5) Notwithstanding anything in subsection (3)(*a*) above or in section 180(4) of the principal Act, where a direction is given under subsection (3)(*b*) or subsection (4) above in relation to a tip which, apart from the order, would be an active tip, then, for the purposes of the principal Act and this Part of this Act, the premises on which the tip, or the part thereof which is specified in the direction is situated shall cease to form part of mine as from the day specified in the direction; but where such a direction relates to part only of the tip, then (subject to any subsequent direction) the remainder of the tip shall, of itself, be treated as an active tip and accordingly the premises on which the remainder of the tip is situated shall continue to form part of the mine with which the tip is associated.

[Mines and Quarries (Tips) Act 1969, s 2 as amended by SI 1974/2013 and as modified by SI 1999/2024.]

---

    1. "A disused tip" is a tip which is neither an active nor a closed tip within the meaning of Pt I (s 11(2)).

    2. See definition in Mines and Quarries Act 1954, s 180, ante.

    3. "Owner" means the person for the time being entitled to work the mine, quarry or tip (Mines and Quarries Act 1954, s 181, ante.

8–14893 3–7. These sections contain provisions prescribing the duties of owners and managers and the powers of inspectors. Notice is to be given to the district inspector of the beginning and end of tipping operations. Managers and owners may be required to make rules regulating the conduct of tipping, and to keep plans and sections of the tip within the office of the mine together with a geological map of the district.

[Mines and Quarries (Tips) Act 1969, ss 3–7—summarised.]

8–14894 10. Interpretation of Part I. (1) In this Part of this Act (and in any provision of the principal Act where these expressions occur)—

    (*a*) "tip", "active tip" and "closed tip" shall be construed in accordance with section 2 above;

    (*b*) "tipping operations" means the depositing of refuse from a mine and the carrying out of any operations necessary for, or incidental to, the depositing of the refuse; and

    (*c*) "tipping rules" shall be construed in accordance with section 5(1) above.

(2) For the purposes of this Part of this Act and of the principal Act the mine with which a tip is associated shall be determined as follows—

    (*a*) in the case of a tip on premises which are deemed to form part of a mine for the purposes of the principal Act, the tip is associated with that mine;

    (*b*) in the case of a tip not falling within paragraph (*a*) above but on premises which, at any time after the commencement of the principal Act, were deemed to form part of a mine for the purposes of that Act, the tip is associated with that mine (or, as the case may be, the last such mine); and

    (*c*) in any other case, the tip is associated with the mine from which refuse was deposited on the tip, or, in the case of a tip which was used for the deposit of refuse from two or more mines, such one of those mines as the Health and Safety Executive may direct.

(3) Subject to subsection (4) any reference in this Part of this Act to any other enactment shall be taken as referring to that enactment as amended by or under any other enactment, including this Part of this Act.

(4) For the purposes of Part II of this Act, subsection (2) shall be read as applying to quarries as it does to mines and references to "the principal Act" in paragraphs (*a*) and (*b*) of that subsection shall

be read as references to that Act as in force immediately before the coming into force of the Quarries Regulations 1999.
[Mines and Quarries (Tips) Act 1969, s 10, as amended by SI 1974/2013 and as modified by SI 1999/2024.]

PART II
PREVENTION OF PUBLIC DANGER FROM DISUSED TIPS

8–14895   **11.**   Conferring of functions on to local authorities.
[Mines and Quarries (Tips) Act 1969, s 11—summarised.]

8–14896   **12. Information relating to disused tips.**   (1) For the purpose of enabling a local authority to assess whether a disused tip[1] which is situated wholly or partly within its area is stable and whether any instability of the tip is or is likely to constitute a danger to members of the public, the local authority may, by notice served[2] on the owner[3] of the tip or on any other person who the authority has reason to believe may be able to assist it, require him, within such time, not being less than fourteen days, as may be specified in the notice, to produce to the authority such documents in his possession or control (whether in the forms of maps, surveys, plans, records of work or otherwise, and whether relating to the tip itself or the land on which it is situated) as may be so specified.

(2) Any person who without reasonable excuse fails to comply with a notice under this section shall be liable on summary conviction to a fine not exceeding **level 3** on the standard scale, and any person who, in pursuance of such a notice—

(*a*)   with intent to deceive, produces any document or gives any information which is false in a material particular, or

(*b*)   knowingly or recklessly makes a statement which is false in a material particular,

shall be liable[4] on summary conviction to a fine not exceeding **the statutory maximum** or, on conviction on indictment, to imprisonment for a term not exceeding **two years** or to a fine or both[5].
[Mines and Quarries (Tips) Act 1969, s 12, as amended by the Criminal Law Act 1977, s. 28 and the Criminal Justice Act 1982, ss 38 and 46.]

---

     1. See s 2, ante, and note 1 thereto.
     2. For method of service see s 30, post.
     3. "Owner" in relation to a disused tip has the meaning defined in s 36(3), post.
     4. For procedure in respect of this offence which is triable either way, see the Magistrates' Courts Act 1980, ss 17A–21, in PART I: MAGISTRATES' COURTS, PROCEDURE, ante.
     5. Prosecutions for offences under this Part of the Act are restricted, see s 27, post.

8–14897   **13. Right of entry to carry out exploratory tests, etc.**   (1) Subject to the following provisions of this section, a person duly authorised in writing by a local authority may at any reasonable time enter upon the land on which a disused tip[1] is situated or upon any neighbouring land—

(*a*)   for the purpose of investigating whether any instability of the tip might constitute a danger to members of the public;

(*b*)   for the purpose of carrying out any operations (in this Part of this Act referred to as "exploratory tests") which, in the opinion of the local authority, are necessary to determine whether the tip is unstable; and

(*c*)   for the purpose of inspecting any operations which are being carried out on that land where those operations may affect the stability of the tip;

but, subject to the following provisions of this section, a person so authorised shall not demand admission as of right to any land which is occupied unless at least forty-eight hours' notice in writing of the intended entry has been given[2] to the occupier.

(2) If it is shown to the satisfaction of a justice of the peace on sworn information in writing—

(*a*)   that admission to any land which any person is entitled to enter under this section has been refused to that person, or that a refusal is apprehended, or that the occupier is temporarily absent, and

(*b*)   that there is reasonable ground for entry on to the land for the purpose for which entry is required,

the justice may by warrant under his hand authorise that person to enter the land, if need be by force; but such a warrant shall not be issued on the ground that entry has been refused or that a refusal of entry is apprehended unless the justice is satisfied that notice in writing of the intention to apply for a warrant has been given[2] to the occupier.

(3) Every warrant granted under this section shall continue in force until the purpose for which the entry is required has been satisfied.

(4) If a local authority has reasonable ground for believing that a disused tip is unstable and that possible danger to members of the public require an immediate entry on to any such land as is referred to in subsection (1) for one or more of the purposes, specified in that subsection, a person duly authorised in writing by the local authority may, at any time and without giving notice or obtaining a warrant under this section, enter upon the land for that purpose (or those purposes).

(5) A person duly authorised to enter on any land by virtue of this section shall, if so required, produce evidence of his authority before so entering and may take with him on to the land such other persons and such equipment as may be necessary.

(6) Any person who wilfully obstructs a person entitled to enter land by virtue of this section shall be liable[3] on summary conviction to a fine not exceeding **level 3** on the standard scale.

(7) *Applies to Scotland.*

[Mines and Quarries (Tips) Act 1969, s 13 as amended by the Criminal Justice Act 1982, ss 35, 38 and 46.]

---

1. See s 2, ante, and note 1 thereto.
2. The procedure for the giving of notices is contained in s 30, post.
3. For restrictions on the prosecution of offences under this Part of the Act, see s 27, post.

8–14898 14. Notice requiring owner of disused tip to carry out remedial operations. (1) If it appears to a local authority that a disused tip[1] situated wholly or partly within its area is unstable and, by reason of that instability, constitutes or is likely to constitute a danger to members of the public, the authority may by notice in the prescribed form served[2] on the owner[3] thereof require him to carry out, within such period as may be specified in the notice, being a period beginning not earlier than twenty-one days after the date of service of the notice, such remedial operations as may be so specified.

(2) In this Part of this Act "remedial operations", in relation to a disused tip, means operations which, in the opinion of the local authority concerned, are necessary to ensure the stability of the tip.

(3) A notice under this section may require the carrying out of remedial operations on the tip itself, on the land on which it is situated or on any neighbouring land which is in the occupation of the owner of the tip, or in which he has, otherwise than as a mortgagee, an estate or interest superior to that of the occupier.

(4) Where a local authority serves a notice under this section on the owner of a disused tip, then, within the period of seven days beginning with the day on which the notice was served, the authority shall serve[2] a copy of the notice on—

(a) any other person who is in occupation of the whole or part of the land on which any remedial operations specified in the notice are required to be carried out and any other person who, to the knowledge of the local authority, has an estate or interest, otherwise than as a mortgagee, in that land; and

(b) any other person who, to the knowledge of the local authority, either has an estate or interest, otherwise than as a mortgagee, in the land on which the tip is situated, or had such an estate or interest at any time within the period of twelve years immediately preceding the date of the service of the notice on the owner of the tip; and

(c) any other person who, to the knowledge of the local authority, has an interest in (including a right to acquire) all or any of the material comprised in the tip; and

(d) any other person who, to the knowledge of the local authority, has at any time within the period referred to in paragraph (b) above used the tip for the purpose of the deposit of refuse from a mine or quarry; and

(e) any other person who the local authority has reason to believe has, at any time within that period, caused or contributed to the instability of the tip by the carrying out of any operations on the tip, on the land on which it is situated, or on neighbouring land or by failing to take any steps which he might reasonably have taken to prevent the tip from becoming unstable.

(5) Where a local authority serves a notice under this section on the owner of a disused tip, then, within the period of twenty-one days beginning with the day on which the notice was served, the owner may serve[4] a counter-notice under this subsection, in the prescribed form requiring the local authority to exercise its powers under section 17; and where such a counter-notice is served—

(a) the local authority shall serve[4] a copy of the counter-notice on every person on whom, under subsection (4), it served a copy of the notice under this section;

(b) the notice under this section and any copy thereof served under subsection (4) shall be deemed for the purposes of the following provisions of this Part of this Act never to have been served; and

(c) the local authority shall, as soon as reasonably practicable, exercise its powers under section 17 in relation to the disused tip in question.

(6) Where the owner[3] of a disused tip[5] is required by a notice under this section to carry out remedial operations on any land which is not in his occupation but in which he has an estate or interest superior to that of the occupier, then, as against the occupier and any other person having an estate or interest in the land in question, the owner of the disused tip shall have the right to enter on to the land in order to carry out the remedial operations and any consequential works of reinstatement and to take with him on to the land such other persons and such equipment as may be necessary.

(7) Where, in the course of carrying out remedial operations specified in a notice under this section, material which is not the property of the owner of the disused tip is removed from the tip, the owner may sell the material but shall account to the owner thereof for the proceeds of sale; but nothing in this subsection shall prevent the owner of a disused tip from setting off the proceeds of

sale or any part thereof against any sum which he is entitled to recover from the owner of the material under the following provisions of this Part of this Act.

(8) If, without reasonable excuse, the owner[3] of a disused tip[5] on whom a notice is served under this section fails to carry out the remedial operations specified in the notice within the period specified therein or, if that period is extended on an application under subsection (3) or subsection (4) of section 15, within that period as so extended, he shall be liable on summary conviction to a fine not exceeding **level 5** on the standard scale[6].

[Mines and Quarries (Tips) Act 1969, s 14 as amended by the Criminal Justice Act 1982, ss 38 and 46.]

1. See s 2, ante, and note 1 thereto.
2. For method of service, see s 30, post.
3. "Owner" means the person for the time being entitled to work the mine, quarry or tip (Mines and Quarries Act 1954, s 181, ante).
4. For method of service see s 30, post.
5. See s 2, ante, and note 1 thereto.
6. See note 5 to s 12, ante.

8–14899 15–17. These sections contain provisions relating to appeals to the High Court against notices issued under s 14, ante, the power of a local authority to cancel such a notice, and the power of a local authority to carry out works of reinstatement instead of requiring the owner to do so.

[Mines and Quarries (Tips) Act 1969, ss 15–17—summarised.]

8–14900 18. Right of entry to carry out remedial operations and works of reinstatement.
(1) Where a local authority has served a notice under section 17(2) of its intention to carry out remedial operations in relation to a disused tip or where no such notice has been served but section 17(3) applies, a person duly authorised in writing by the local authority may at any reasonable time enter upon the land on which the disused tip is situated or upon any neighbouring land for any purpose connected with the carrying out of remedial operations or consequential works of reinstatement; but, subject to the following provisions of this section, a person so authorised shall not demand admission as of right to any land which is occupied unless twenty-four hours' notice in writing of the intended entry has been given[1] to the occupier.

(2) If it is shown to the satisfaction of a justice of the peace on sworn information in writing—

(a) that admission to any land which any person is entitled to enter under this section has been refused to that person, or that a refusal is apprehended, or that the occupier is temporarily absent, and

(b) that there is reasonable ground for entry on to the land for the purpose for which entry is required,

the justice may by warrant under his hand authorise that person to enter the land, if need be by force; but such a warrant shall not be issued on the ground that entry has been refused or that a refusal of entry is apprehended unless the justice is satisfied that notice in writing of the intention to apply for a warrant has been given[1] to the occupier.

(3) Every warrant granted under this section shall continue in force until the purpose for which the entry is required has been satisfied.

(4) Notwithstanding anything in subsection (1), in a case falling within section 17(3), a person duly authorised in writing by the local authority concerned may exercise the right of entry conferred by subsection (1) without giving notice or obtaining a warrant under this section.

(5) A person duly authorised to enter on any land by virtue of this section shall, if so required, produce evidence of this authority before so entering and may take with him on to the land such other persons and such equipment as may be necessary.

(6) Any person who wilfully obstructs a person entitled to enter land by virtue of this section shall be liable on summary conviction to a fine not exceeding **level 3** on the standard scale[2].

(7) *Applies to Scotland.*

[Mines and Quarries (Tips) Act 1969, s 18 as amended by the Criminal Justice Act 1982, ss 38 and 46.]

1. As to giving notices, see s 30, post.
2. See note 5 to s 12, ante.

8–14901 19–25. These sections contain provisions which enable the Court to order the payment of contributions towards the costs of remedial operations, a person interested in land damaged by remedial operations to obtain compensation, the recovery of expenses, appeals against claims for expenses, the right of a local authority to demand payment of certain expenses and appeals against those demands, and the Minister of Power to make grants to local authorities towards their costs of carrying out remedial work.

[Mines and Quarries (Tips) Act 1969, ss 19–25—summarised.]

8–14902 26. Penalty for obstructing remedial operations and damaging completed works.
(1) Any person who wilfully prevents or interferes with the carrying out of exploratory tests or

remedial operations shall be liable on summary conviction to a fine not exceeding **level 3** on the standard scale[1].

(2) Any person who wilfully damages or otherwise interferes with any works completed in the course of remedial operations for the purpose of ensuring the stability of a disused tip[2] shall be liable on summary conviction to a fine not exceeding **level 5** on the standard scale[1].

[Mines and Quarries (Tips) Act 1969, s 26 as amended by the Criminal Justice Act 1982, ss 38 and 46.]

---

1. For restrictions on prosecutions for offences under this part of the Act see s 27, infra.
2. See s 2, ante, and note 1 thereto.

8–14903　27. Offences under Part II. (1) Proceedings in respect of an offence under this Part of this Act shall not, in England and Wales, be instituted except by a local authority or by or with the consent of the Director of Public Prosecutions.

(2) Where an offence under this Part of this Act which has been committed by a body corporate is proved to have been committed with the consent or connivance of, or to be attributable to any neglect on the part of, a director, manager, secretary or other similar officer of the body corporate, or any person who was purporting to act in any such capacity, he, as well as the body corporate, shall be guilty of that offence and shall be liable to be proceeded against and punished accordingly.

(3) In this section "director", in relation to a body corporate established by or under any enactment for the purpose of carrying on under national ownership any industry or part of an industry or undertaking, being a body corporate whose affairs are managed by its members, means a member of that body corporate.

[Mines and Quarries (Tips) Act 1969, s 27.]

8–14904　28. In the application of this part to England and Wales, "the court" means the High Court or a County Court.

[Mines and Quarries (Tips) Act 1969, s 28 as substituted by SI 1991/724.]

8–14905　Section 29. *Regulations and Orders.*

8–14906　30. Service of documents. (1) Any document which is required or authorised under this Part of this Act to be given to or served on any person may be given to or served on him—

(*a*) by delivering it to him or by leaving it at his proper address[1]; or
(*b*) by sending it to him by post.

(2) Any document required or authorised under this Part of this Act to be given to or served on a body corporate shall be duly given or served if it is given to or served on the secretary or clerk of that body.

(3) For the purposes of this section and of section 26 of the Interpretation Act 1889[2] (service of documents by post) in its application to this section, the proper address of any person to or on whom any document is to be given or served shall, in the case of the secretary or clerk of a body corporate, be that of the registered or principal office of that body, and in any other case shall be the last known address of the person to be served:

Provided that, if the person to or on whom the document to be given or served has, in accordance with arrangements agreed, given an address in the United Kingdom for the giving or service of the document, his proper address for those purposes shall be that address.

(4) If the name or the address of any owner, lessee or occupier of land to or on whom any document is to be given or served under this Part of this Act cannot after reasonable inquiry[3] be ascertained by the local authority or person seeking to give or serve the document, but there is on that land a building occupied by some person, the document may be given or served by addressing it to the person to or on whom it is to be given or served by the description of "owner", "lessee" or "occupier" of the land (describing it) and either delivering it to some responsible person in the building or sending it by post to that building in a letter addressed to "the owner", "the lessee", or "the occupier", as the case may be.

(5) In relation to any document required or authorised under this Part of this Act to be given or served by a local authority, the preceding provisions of this section shall have effect in place of [section 287A of the Local Government Act 1933][4] or section 349 of the Local Government (Scotland) Act 1947 (service of notices by local authority), but nothing in this section shall affect the operation in relation to such a document of [section 287B of the said Act of 1933][4] or, as the case may be, section 247 of the said Act of 1947 (authentication of documents).

[Mines and Quarries (Tips) Act 1969, s 30.]

---

1. See s 30(3), infra.
2. Now s 7 of the Interpretation Act 1978.
3. Evidence should be given that proper enquiries have been made to find the owner (*R v Mead* [1898] 1 QB 110, 61 JP 759).
4. The 1933 Act was repealed by the Local Government Act 1972; ss 287A and 287B of the 1933 Act have been replaced by ss 233 and 234 of the 1972 Act.

8–14907 31. Special provisions relating to ecclesiastical property.
[Mines and Quarries (Tips) Act 1969, s 31—summarised.]

8–14908 36. Interpretation of Part II. (1) In this Part of this Act—

"appropriate Minister" shall be construed in accordance with subsection (4);
"contributory" has the meaning assigned to it by section 19(6);
"disused tip" has the meaning assigned to it by section 11(2);
"exploratory tests" has the meaning assigned to it by section 13(1)(*b*);
"local authority" shall be construed in accordance with subsections (3) and (4) of section 11;
"the Ministers" means the Minister of Housing and Local Government[1], the Secretary of State for Wales and the Secretary of State for Scotland acting jointly;
"operations" includes surveys and tests as well as tipping operations (within the meaning of Part I of this Act) and building, engineering, mining and other operations;
"prescribed" means prescribed by regulations made by the appropriate Minister;
"remedial operations" has the meaning assigned to it by section 14(2); and
"the specified percentage" has the meaning assigned to it by section 19(6).

(2) For the purposes of this Part of this Act, a disused tip shall be treated as unstable if and only if there is, or there is reasonable ground for believing that there is likely to be, such a movement of the refuse which makes up the tip as to cause a significant increase in the area of land covered by the tip.

(3) In this Part of this Act the expression "owner" in relation to a disused tip means—

(*a*) with respect to England and Wales, the person who has a legal estate in the land on which the tip is situated which—

   (i) is either the fee simple or a tenancy for a specific term which has not less than one year unexpired and is not a mortgage term; and

   (ii) is not in reversion expectant on the termination of such a tenancy; and

(*b*) (*Scotland*).

(4) Any reference in this Part of this Act to the appropriate Minister shall be construed—

(*a*) in the application of this Part of this Act to England, except Monmouthshire, as a reference to the Minister of Housing and Local Government;

(*b*) in its application to Wales and Monmouthshire, as a reference to the Secretary for Wales; and

(*c*) (*Scotland*).

(5) Any reference in this Part of this Act to a section or subsection which is not otherwise identified is a reference to that section of this Act or to that subsection of the section in which the reference occurs, as the case may be.

(6) Any reference in this Part of this Act to any other enactment shall be taken as referring to that enactment as amended by or under any other enactment.
[Mines and Quarries (Tips) Act 1969, s 36.]

---

1. Now Secretary of State for the Environment by virtue of SI 1970/1681.

Mineral Workings (Offshore Installations) Act 1971[1]
(1971 c 61)

8–15180

---

1. The regulation-making powers formerly contained in section 6 of this act have been repealed by SI 1993/1823 and replaced by those under the Health and Safety Act 1974, this title post. Existing regulations are preserved by SI 1993/1823 reg 6. The following regulations have been preserved:

   Offshore Installations (Logbooks and Registration of Death) Regulations 1972, SI 1972/1542, amended by SI 1991/679 and SI 1995/738;

   Offshore Installations (Inspectors and Casualties) Regulations 1973/1842 amended by SI 1991/679 and SI 1995/3163 and SI 1995/738.

8–15182 3. Construction and survey regulations for offshore installations. (1), (2), (3) *revoked*.

(4) It shall be the duty of the owner of the offshore installation to ensure that the provisions of regulations under this section are complied with, and if regulations under this section are contravened in any respect in relation to an offshore installation when it is within controlled waters the owner of the offshore installation shall be guilty of an offence under this section, and shall be liable—

(*a*) on summary conviction to a fine not exceeding **the statutory maximum**,

(*b*) on conviction on indictment to imprisonment for a term not exceeding two years, or to a fine, or both[1].

[Mineral Workings (Offshore Installations) Act 1971, s 3, as amended by the Criminal Law Act 1977, s 28, the Oil and Gas (Enterprise) Act 1982, Sch 3, SI 1993/1823 and SI 1995/738.]

1. For procedure in respect of this offence, which is triable either way, see the Magistrates' Courts Act 1980, ss 17A–21, in PART I: MAGISTRATES' COURTS, PROCEDURE, ante.

8–15186   7. Regulations: general provisions.   (3) The punishment for an offence created by regulations under this Act shall be[1]—

   (*a*)   on summary conviction a fine not exceeding **the statutory maximum**,
   (*b*)   on conviction on indictment imprisonment for a term not exceeding two years, or a fine, or both,

but without prejudice to any further restriction on the punishments which can be awarded contained in the regulations, and without prejudice to the exclusion of proceedings on indictment by the regulations.
[Mineral Workings (Offshore Installations) Act 1971, s 7(3), as amended by the Criminal Law Act 1977, s 28 and SI 1993/1823.]

1. For procedure in respect of this offence which is triable either way, see the Magistrates' Courts Act 1980, ss 17A–21, in PART I: MAGISTRATES' COURTS, PROCEDURE, ante.

8–15187   9. Offences: general provisions.   (1)   Where an offence under this Act which has been committed by a body corporate is proved to have been committed with the consent or connivance of, or to be attributable to any neglect on the part of, a director, manager, secretary or other similar officer of the body corporate, or any person who was purporting to act in any such capacity, he, as well as the body corporate, shall be guilty of that offence and shall be liable to be proceeded against and punished accordingly.

In this subsection "director", in relation to a body corporate established by or under any enactment for the purpose of carrying on under public ownership any industry or part of an industry or undertaking, being a body corporate whose affairs are managed by its members, means a member of that body corporate.

(2)   In proceedings for an offence under this Act an averment in any process of the fact that anything was done or situated within controlled waters shall, until the contrary is proved, be sufficient evidence of that fact as stated in the averment.

(3)   In proceedings for an offence under section 3 of this Act, it shall be a defence for the accused to prove—

   (*a*)   that he has used all due diligence to enforce the execution of this Act, and of any relevant regulation made under this Act, and
   (*b*)   that any relevant contravention was committed without his consent, connivance or wilful default.

(4)   Proceedings for any offence under this Act may be taken, and the offence may for all incidental purposes be treated as having been committed, in any place in the United Kingdom[1].

(5)   *Repealed.*
[Mineral Workings (Offshore Installations) Act 1971, s 9 as amended by the Oil and Gas (Enterprise) Act 1982, Schs 3 and 4 and SI 1995/738.]

1. Section 1 ante deals with the basic jurisdiction under this Act. Section 8 (not printed here) applies the existing law (eg s 3 of the Continental Shelf Act 1964) to offshore installations in territorial waters and designated areas, including those in transit.

8–15188   12. Interpretation.   (1)   In this Act, unless the context otherwise requires—

"the 1995 Regulations" means the Offshore Installations and Pipeline Works (Management and Administration) Regulations 1995,
"controlled waters" means—

   (*a*)   tidal waters and parts of these in or adjacent to Great Britain up to the seaward limits of territorial waters; and
   (*b*)   any area designated by order under section 1(7) of the Continental Shelf Act 1964,

"installation manager" has the meaning given by regulation 2(1) of the 1995 Regulations,
"offence under this Act" includes an offence under regulations made under this Act,
"offshore installation" has the same meaning as in regulation 3 of the 1995 Regulations,
"owner", in relation to an offshore installation, means the person who is, in relation to the installation, the duty holder as defined by regulation 2(1) of the 1995 Regulations in relation to that installation,
"prescribed" means prescribed by regulations under this Act,

(2) and (3)   *Repealed.*
(4)   It is hereby declared that, notwithstanding that this Act may affect individuals or bodies corporate outside the United Kingdom, it applies to any individual whether or not he is a British subject, and to any body corporate whether or not incorporated under the law of any part of the United Kingdom.

(5) Any reference in this Act to a contravention of a provision of this Act or of regulations made under this Act includes a reference to a failure to comply with such a provision.

(6) Any reference in this Act to any enactment or Act of Parliament includes a reference to an enactment or Act of the Parliament of Northern Ireland.

(7) Except where the context otherwise requires, any reference in this Act to any enactment shall be construed as a reference to that enactment as amended, extended or applied by or under any other enactment.

[Mineral Workings (Offshore Installations) Act 1971, s 12, as amended by the Petroleum and Submarine Pipelines Act 1975, s, 44(3), the Oil and Gas (Enterprise) Act 1982, Schs 3 and 4 and SI 1995/738.]

Health and Safety at Work etc Act 1974
(1974 c 37)

PART I[1]

HEALTH, SAFETY AND WELFARE IN CONNECTION WITH WORK AND CONTROL OF DANGEROUS SUBSTANCES AND CERTAIN EMISSIONS INTO THE ATMOSPHERE

Preliminary

8-15290   1. Preliminary.   (1) The provisions of this Part shall have effect with a view to—

(a) securing the health, safety and welfare of persons at work;

(b) protecting persons other than persons at work against risks to health or safety arising out of or in connection with the activities of persons at work;

(c) controlling the keeping and use of explosive or highly flammable or otherwise dangerous substances[2], and generally preventing the unlawful acquisition, possession and use of such substances;

(d) *(Repealed)*.

(2) The provisions of this Part relating to the making of health and safety regulations and the preparation and approval of codes of practice shall in particular have effect with a view to enabling the enactments specified in the third column of Schedule 1 and the regulations, orders and other instruments in force under those enactments to be progressively replaced by a system of regulations and approved codes of practice operating in combination with the other provisions of this Part and designed to maintain or improve the standards of health, safety and welfare established by or under those enactments.

(3) For the purposes of this Part risks arising out of or in connection with the activities of persons at work shall be treated as including risks attributable to the manner of conducting an undertaking, the plant or substances used for the purposes of an undertaking and the condition of premises so used or any part of them.

(4) References in this Part to the general purposes of this Part are references to the purposes mentioned in subsection (1) above.

[Health and Safety at Work etc Act 1974, s 1 as amended by the Employment Protection Act 1975, Sch 15 and the Environmental Protection Act 1990, Sch 16.]

---

1. The Secretary of State has power to repeal or revoke any existing statutory provision in Part I of this Act: Deregulation and Contracting Out Act 1994, s 37. Part I applies to persons on offshore installations or engaged on pipe-line works; see the Offshore Safety Act 1992, ss 1 and 2; and in respect of the safety of railways and other guided transport systems: see the Railways Act 1993, s 117; for the purposes for which Part I applies and for the listed statutory provisions within the meaning of Part I and specified in the third column of Sch 1, post.

2. This reference to "dangerous substances" is extended to include "environmentally hazardous substances" by the Health and Safety at Work etc Act 1974 (Application to Environmentally Hazardous Substances) Regulations 1996, SI 1996/2075 amended by SI 2004/463. As a result, regulations may be made under s 15 of the 1974 Act to implement EC Council Directives concerning the transport of dangerous goods by road and by rail and the control of volatile organic compound emissions resulting from the storage of petrol and its distribution from terminals to service stations.

General duties

8-15291   2. General duties of employers to their employees[1].   (1) It shall be the duty[2] of every employer[3] to ensure, so far as is reasonably practicable, the health, safety and welfare at work of all his employees[4].

(2) Without prejudice to the generality of an employer's duty under the preceding subsection, the matters to which that duty extends include in particular—

(a) the provision and maintenance of plant and systems of work that are, so far as is reasonably practicable, safe and without risks to health;

(b) arrangements for ensuring, so far as is reasonably practicable, safety and absence of risks to health in connection with the use, handling, storage and transport of articles and substances;

(c) the provision of such information, instruction, training and supervision as is necessary to ensure, so far as is reasonably practicable, the health and safety at work of his employees;

(*d*) so far as is reasonably practicable as regards any place of work under the employer's control, the maintenance of it in a condition that is safe and without risks to health and the provision and maintenance of means of access to and egress from it that are safe and without such risks;

(*e*) the provision and maintenance of a working environment for his employees that is, so far as is reasonably practicable, safe, without risks to health, and adequate as regards facilities and arrangements for their welfare at work.

(3) Except in such cases as may be[5] prescribed, it shall be the duty of every employer to prepare and as often as may be appropriate revise a written statement of his general policy with respect to the health and safety at work of his employees and the organisation and arrangements for the time being in force for carrying out that policy, and to bring the statement and any revision of it to the notice of all of his employees.[6]

(4) Regulations[7] made by the Secretary of State may provide for the appointment in prescribed cases by recognised trade unions (within the meaning of the regulations) of safety representatives from amongst the employees, and those representatives shall represent the employees in consultations with the employers under subsection (6) below and shall have such other functions as may be prescribed.

(6) It shall be the duty of every employer to consult any such representatives with a view to the making and maintenance of arrangements which will enable him and his employees to co-operate effectively in promoting and developing measures to ensure the health and safety at work of the employees, and in checking the effectiveness of such measures.

(7) In such cases as may be prescribed it shall be the duty of every employer, if requested to do so by the safety representatives mentioned in subsection (4) above, to establish, in accordance with regulations[7] made by the Secretary of State, a safety committee having the function of keeping under review the measures taken to ensure the health and safety at work of his employees and such other functions as may be prescribed.

[Health and Safety at Work etc Act 1974, s 2 as amended by the Employment Protection Act 1975, Sch 15.]

---

1. The employer's duties are not confined to employees engaged in work, the duty is to provide plant (or as the case may be) which is safe; provide means make available and the breach of duty could arise even if plant is not being used (*Bolton Metropolitan Borough Council v Malrod Insulation Ltd* [1993] ICR 358).

2. The duty under s 2(1) to ensure the health, safety and welfare at work of all his employees imposes liability on the employer whenever he fails in that duty, subject only to all reasonable precautions having been taken by the employer. The qualification places upon the defendant the onus of proving that all reasonable precautions were taken both by it and by its servants and agents on its behalf. Accordingly, the concept of the "directing mind" of the company has no application here (*R v Gateway Foodmarkets Ltd* [1997] 2 Cr App Rep 40). When sentencing a corporate defendant for a breach of the health and safety legislation, the court should have regard to the guidance contained in *R v F Howe and Son (Engineers) Ltd* [1999] 2 All ER 249, 163 JP 359, [1999] 2 Cr App Rep (S) 37, [1999] Crim LR 238; see para **3-206A** Fine: Imposition on a company in PART III: SENTENCING, ante.

3. In order to ensure his employees' health, safety and welfare, an employer may have to provide information and instruction as to potential dangers to people other than his own employees: see s 3, post and also *R v Swan Hunter Shipbuilders Ltd* [1982] 1 All ER 264, [1981] Crim L R 833.

4. The duty of an employer to ensure the safety of his employees is comprehensive. Therefore a charge should be founded on s 2(1) and it is not necessary to refer to the paragraphs of s 2(2) but even if the information refers to any of the paragraphs of s 2(2) or the subsection itself, it is not bad for duplicity (*Health and Safety Executive v Spindle Select Ltd* (1996) Times, 9 December, DC).

5. See the Employers' Health and Safety Policy Statements (Exception) Regulations 1975, SI 1975/1584; considered in *Osborne v Bill Taylor of Huyton Ltd* [1982] ICR 168.

6. Sub-sections (1)–(3) modified, in relation to an activity involving genetic modification, by SI 2000/2831.

7. The Safety Representatives and Safety Committees Regulations 1977, SI 1977/500 amended by SI 1999/2051, SI 1996/1513, SI 1997/1840 and SI 1999/860, have been made.

8–15292   3. General duties of employers and self-employed to persons other than their employees.   (1) It shall be the duty[1] of every employer to conduct his undertaking[2] in such a way as to ensure, so far as is reasonably practicable, that persons not in his employment who may be affected thereby[3] are not thereby exposed to risks[4] to their health or safety.

(2) It shall be the duty of every self-employed person to conduct his undertaking in such a way as to ensure, so far as is reasonably practicable, that he and other persons (not being his employees) who may be affected thereby are not thereby exposed to risks to their health or safety.[5]

(3) In such cases as may be prescribed, it shall be the duty of every employer and every self-employed person, in the prescribed circumstances and in the prescribed manner, to give to persons (not being his employees) who may be affected by the way in which he conducts his undertaking the prescribed information about such aspects of the way in which he conducts his undertaking as might affect their health or safety.

[Health and Safety at Work etc Act 1974, s 3.]

---

1. Subject to the defence of reasonable practicability s 3(1) creates an offence of absolute criminal liability, corporate liability is not avoided on the basis that the acts were not those of the "directing mind" of the company (*R v British Steel plc* [1995] 1 WLR 1356, [1995] Crim LR 654).

2. This section imposes a duty on an employer to conduct his undertaking in such a way that, subject to reasonable practicability, it does not create risks to people's health and safety. If the employer engages an independent contractor to do work which forms part of the conduct of his undertaking, he is required by s 3(1) to stipulate for whatever conditions are needed to avoid those risks and are reasonably practicable. In doing so he must take reasonably practical steps to avoid

risk to the contractor's employees arising not merely from the physical state of the premises but also from the inadequacy of the arrangements which the employer makes with the contractors for how they will do the work. The decisive question in determining culpability under s 3, therefore, is not whether the employer was vicariously liable or in a position to exercise control over work carried out by an independent contractor but simply whether the activity which has caused the risk amounts to part of the conduct by the employer of his undertaking, that being a question of fact in each case (*R v Associated Octel Ltd* [1996] 4 All ER 846, HL). Therefore if persons not in the employment of the employer are exposed to risks to their health and safety by the conduct of the employer's undertaking, the employer will be in breach of the duty under s 3(1) unless the employer can prove on the balance of probability that all that was reasonably practicable had been done by the employer or on the employer's behalf to ensure that such persons were not exposed to such risks. It is a question of fact in each case whether it was the conduct of the employer's business which exposed third persons to risks to their health and safety and the question of what was reasonably practicable is also a question of fact depending on the circumstances of each case. The fact that an employee carrying out the work has done so carelessly or has omitted to take a precaution he should have done does not itself preclude the employer from establishing that everything that was reasonably practicable in the conduct of the employer's undertaking to ensure that third persons affected by the employer's undertaking were not exposed to risks to their health and safety had been done (*R v Nelson Group Services (Maintenance) Ltd* [1998] 4 All ER 331, [1999] 1 WLR 1526, CA).

3. For example, employees of sub-contractors (*R v Swan Hunter Shipbuilders Ltd* [1982] 1 All ER 264, [1981] Crim L R 833). Employees, who, in accordance with an agreement, used cleaning machinery, which was defective, and had been left on their employer's premises by cleaning contractors, were held to be affected by the way in which the cleaning contractors conducted their undertaking (*R v Mara* [1987] 1 All ER 478, [1987] 1 WLR 87).

4. It is sufficient for the prosecution to prove that members of the public were exposed to a possibility of danger (*R v Board of Trustees of the Science Museum* [1993] 1 WLR 1171, 158 JP 39).

5. Sub-section (2) modified, in relation to an activity involving genetic modification by SI 2000/2831 and in relation to substances hazardous to health by SI 2002/2677.

8–15293   4.   General duties of persons concerned with premises to persons other than their employees.   (1) This section has effect for imposing on persons duties in relation to those who—

  (*a*) are not their employees; but
  (*b*) use non-domestic premises[1] made available to them as a place of work or as a place where they may use plant or substances provided for their use there,

and applies to premises so made available and other non-domestic premises used in connection with them.

(2) It shall be the duty of each person who has, to any extent, control of premises to which this section applies or of the means of access thereto or egress therefrom or of any plant or substance in such premises to take such measures as it is reasonable[2] for a person in his position to take to ensure, so far as is reasonably practicable, that the premises, all means of access thereto or egress therefrom available for use by persons using the premises, and any plant or substance in the premises or, as the case may be, provided for use there, is or are safe and without risks to health.

(3) Where a person has, by virtue of any contract or tenancy, an obligation of any extent in relation to—

  (*a*) the maintenance or repair of any premises to which this section applies or any means of access thereto or egress therefrom; or
  (*b*) the safety of or the absence of risks to health arising from plant or substances in any such premises;

that person shall be treated, for the purposes of subsection (2) above, as being a person who has control of the matters to which his obligation extends.

(4) Any reference in this section to a person having control of any premises or matter is a reference to a person having control of the premises or matter in connection with the carrying on by him of a trade, business or other undertaking (whether for profit or not).

[Health and Safety at Work etc Act 1974, s 4.]

---

1. The common parts of a block of flats are "non-domestic premises" and the Act protects persons who go there to repair and maintain lifts and electrical installations there; *Westminster City Council v Select Managements Ltd* [1985] 1 All ER 897, [1985] 1 WLR 576, CA. The duties imposed by s 4(1) also apply for the benefit and protection of children using a commercially operated play centre (*Moudem v Carlisle City Council* (1994) 158 JP 1110).

2. It is not reasonable to require measures to be taken against unknown and unexpected events. In a prosecution under s 4, the prosecutor must first prove that the premises are unsafe and constitute risks to health; if he so proves, he must then prove what persons have at that time any degree of control of those premises, and then that it would be reasonable for one or more of the persons having a degree of control to take measures which would ensure safety. If the prosecutor proves these three matters, the onus shifts to the accused to prove that it was not reasonably practicable to take the measures in question (*Mailer v Austin Rover Group plc* [1989] 2 All ER 1087, [1989] 3 WLR 520, HL).

8–15294   5.   *Repealed.*

8–15295   6.   General duties of manufacturers etc as regards articles and substances for use at work[1].   (1) It shall be the duty of any person who designs, manufactures, imports or supplies any article for use at work[2, 3] or any article of fairground equipment—

  (*a*) to ensure, so far as is reasonably practicable, that the article is so designed and constructed that it will be safe and without risks to health at all times when it is being set, used, cleaned or maintained by a person at work;

(b) to carry out or arrange for the carrying out of such testing and examination as may be necessary for the performance of the duty imposed on him by the preceding paragraph;

(c) to take such steps as are necessary to secure that persons supplied by that person with the article are provided with adequate information about the use for which the article is designed or has been tested and about any conditions necessary to ensure that it will be safe and without risks to health at all such times as are mentioned in paragraph (a) above and when it is being dismantled or disposed of; and

(d) to take such steps as are necessary to secure, so far as is reasonably practicable, that persons so supplied are provided with all such revision of information provided to them by virtue of the preceding paragraph as are necessary by reason of its becoming known that anything gives rise to a serious risk to health or safety.

(1A) It shall be the duty of any person who designs, manufactures, imports or supplies any article of fairground equipment—

(a) to ensure, so far as is reasonably practicable, that the article is so designed and constructed that it will be safe and without risks to health at all times when it is being used for or in connection with the entertainment of members of the public;

(b) to carry out or arrange for the carrying out of such testing and examination as may be necessary for the performance of the duty imposed on him by the preceding paragraph;

(c) to take such steps as are necessary to secure that persons supplied by that person with the article are provided with adequate information about the use for which the article is designed or has been tested and about any conditions necessary to ensure that it will be safe and without risks to health at all times when it is being used for or in connection with the entertainment of members of the public; and

(d) to take such steps as are necessary to secure, so far as is reasonably practicable, that persons so supplied are provided with all such revisions of information provided to them by virtue of the preceding paragraph as are necessary by reason of its becoming known that anything gives rise to a serious risk to health or safety.

(2) It shall be the duty of any person who undertakes the design or manufacture of any article for use at work or of any article of fairground equipment to carry out or arrange for the carrying out of any necessary research with a view to the discovery and, so far as is reasonably practicable, the elimination or minimisation of any risks to health or safety to which the design or article may give rise.

(3) It shall be the duty of any person who erects or installs any article for use at work in any premises where that article is to be used by persons at work or who erects or installs any article of fairground equipment to ensure, so far as is reasonably practicable, that nothing about the way in which the article is erected or installed makes it unsafe as a ride to health at any such time as is mentioned in paragraph (a) of subsection (1) or, as the case may be in paragraph (a) of subsection (1) or (1A) above.

(4) It shall be the duty of any person who manufactures, imports or supplies any substance—

(a) to ensure, so far as is reasonably practicable, that the substance will be safe and without risks to health at all times when it is being used, handled, processed, stored or transported by a person at work or in premises to which section 4 above applies;

(b) to carry out or arrange for the carrying out of such testing and examination as may be necessary for the performance of the duty imposed on him by the preceding paragraph;

(c) to take such steps as are necessary to secure that persons supplied by that person with the substance are provided with adequate information about any risks to health or safety to which the inherent properties of the substance may give rise, about the results of any relevant tests which have been carried out on or in connection with the substance and about any conditions necessary to ensure that the substance will be safe and without risks to health at all such times as are mentioned in paragraph (a) above and when the substance is being disposed of; and

(d) to take such steps as are necessary to secure, so far as is reasonably practicable, that persons so supplied are provided with all such revisions of information provided to them by virtue of the preceding paragraph as are necessary by reason of its becoming known that anything give rise to a serious risk to health or safety.

(5) It shall be the duty of any person who undertakes the manufacture of any substance to carry out or arrange for the carrying out of any necessary research with a view to the discovery and, so far as is reasonably practicable, the elimination or minimisation of any risks to health or safety to which the substance may give rise at all such times as are mentioned in paragraph (a) of subsection (4) above.

(6) Nothing in the preceding provisions of this section shall be taken to require a person to repeat any testing, examination or research which has been carried out otherwise than by him or at his instance, in so far as it is reasonable for him to rely on the results thereof for the purposes of those provisions.

(7) Any duty imposed on any person by any of the preceding provisions of this section shall extend only to things done in the course of a trade, business or other undertaking carried on by him (whether for profit or not) and to matters within his control.

(8) Where a person designs, manufactures, imports or supplies an article for use at work or an article of fairground equipment and does so for or to another on the basis of a written undertaking by that other to take specified steps sufficient to ensure, so far as is reasonably practicable, that the article will be safe and without risks to health at all such times as are mentioned in paragraph (*a*) of subsection (1) above or, as the case may be, in paragraph (*a*) of subsection (1) or (1A) above, the undertaking shall have the effect of relieving the first-mentioned person from the duty imposed by virtue of that paragraph to such extent as is reasonable having regard to the terms of the undertaking.

(8A) Nothing in subsection (7) or (8) above shall relieve any person who imports any article or substance from any duty in respect of anything which—

(*a*) in the case of an article designed outside the United Kingdom, was done by and in the course of any trade, profession or other undertaking carried on by, or was within the control of, the person who designed the article; or

(*b*) in the case of an article or substance manufactured outside the United Kingdom, was done by and in the course of any trade, profession or other undertaking carried on by, or was within the control of, the person who manufactured the article or substance.

(9) Where a person ("the ostensible supplier") supplies any article or substance to another ("the customer") under a hire-purchase agreement, conditional sale agreement or credit-sale agreement, and the ostensible supplier—

(*a*) carries on the business of financing the acquisition of goods by others by means of such agreements; and

(*b*) in the course of that business acquired his interest in the article or substance supplied to the customer as a means of financing its acquisition by the customer from a third person ("the effective supplier");

the effective supplier and not the ostensible supplier shall be treated for the purposes of this section as supplying the article or substance to the customer, and any duty imposed by the preceding provisions of this section on suppliers shall accordingly fall on the effective supplier and not on the ostensible supplier.

(10) For the purposes of this section an absence of safety or a risk to health shall be disregarded in so far as the case in or in relation to which it would arise is shown to be one the occurrence of which could not reasonably be foreseen; and in determining whether any duty imposed by virtue of paragraph (*a*) of subsection (1), (1A) or (4) above has been performed regard shall be had to any relevant information or advice which has been provided to any person by the person by whom the article has been designed, manufactured, imported or supplied or, as the case may be, by the person by whom the substance has been manufactured, imported or supplied.
[Health and Safety at Work etc Act 1974, s 6 as amended by the Consumer Protection Act 1987, Sch 3.]

---

1. The Supply of Machinery (Safety) Regulations 1992 have been made to implement Council Directive 98/37, which harmonised health and safety standards. Both s 6 and the Regulations impose criminal sanctions for behaviour alleged to have taken place which has rendered a piece of machinery unsafe, and for which the manufacturer is responsible, but they use different language and provide different penalties. However, it was held in *R (on the application of Junttan Oy) v Bristol Magistrates' Court* [2003] UKHL 55, [2004] 2 All ER 555 that nothing in the 1992 regulations prevented a prosecution under s 6 of the 1974 Act; it could hardly have been the purpose of the 1992 regulations that even the worst conceivable failure to ensure safety of machinery resulting in many deaths could only be prosecuted summarily, with penalties which would be derisory, rather than on indictment under the 1974 Act.

2. A prototype will not come within the meaning of "article for use at work" (*McKay v Unwin Pyrotechnics Ltd* [1991] Crim LR 547, DC).

3. Modified, in the case of articles for use at work where that work is work with ionising radiation, by SI 1999/3232.

8–15296 7. General duties of employees at work[1]. It shall be the duty of every employee while at work—

(*a*) to take reasonable care for the health and safety of himself and of other persons who may be affected by his acts or omissions at work[2]; and

(*b*) as regards any duty or requirements imposed on his employer or any other person by or under any of the relevant statutory provisions, to co-operate with him so far as is necessary to enable that duty or requirement to be performed or complied with.
[Health and Safety at Work etc Act 1974, s 7.]

---

1. Modified, in relation to an activity involving genetic modification, by SI 2000/2831.

2. This has been held not to include a collision between motorcars whilst a driver was driving his own car carelessly from a clocking-on point to work on a large work site containing 39 miles of public and private roads (*Coult v Szuba* [1982] RTR 376).

8–15297 8. Duty not to interfere with or misuse things provided pursuant to certain provisions.   No person shall intentionally or recklessly interfere with or misuse anything provided in the interests of health, safety or welfare in pursuance of any of the relevant statutory provisions.
[Health and Safety at Work etc Act 1974, s 8.]

8–15298 9. Duty not to charge employees for things done or provided pursuant to certain specific requirements. No employer shall levy or permit to be levied on any employee of his any charge in respect of anything done or provided in pursuance of any specific requirement of the relevant statutory provisions.
[Health and Safety at Work etc Act 1974, s 9.]

8–15299 14. *Power of Health and Safety Commission to direct inquiries; and power to make regulations governing such inquiries.*

8–15300 15. *Power to make "health and safety regulations"*[1].

1. Additional powers to make regulations under s 15 to implement certain EC Directives are provided by the Health and Safety at Work Act 1974 (Application to Environmentally Hazardous Substances) Regulations 2002, SI 2002/282 amended by SI 2005/1308:

Coal Mines (Respirable Dust) Regulations 1975, SI 1975/1433 amended by SI 1978/807 and SI 1996/2001;
Compressed Acetylene (Importation) Regulations 1978, SI 1978/1732 amended by SI 2004/568;
Mines (Precautions Against Inrushes) Regulations 1979, SI 1979/318;
Petroleum (Consolidation) Act 1928 (Enforcement) Regulations 1979, SI 1979/427 amended by SI 1982/630, SI 1984/1244, SI 1986/1951 and SI 2002/2776;
Notification of Accidents and Dangerous Occurrences Regulations 1980, in this PART, post;
Health and Safety (Leasing Arrangements) Regulations 1980, SI 1980/907;
Health and Safety (First-Aid) Regulations 1981, in this PART, post;
Petroleum Spirit (Plastic Containers) Regulations 1982, SI 1982/630 amended by SI 1999/743 and SI 2002/2776;
Notification of Installations Handling Hazardous Substances Regulations 1982, SI 1982/1357 amended by SI 2002/2979 and SI 2005/1082;
Classification and Labelling of Explosives Regulations 1983, SI 1983/1140 amended by SI 1999/303, SI 2004/994 and SI 2005/1082;
Asbestos (Licensing) Regulations 1983, SI 1983/1649 amended by SI 1998/3233;
Freight Containers (Safety Convention) Regulations 1984, SI 1984/1890 amended by SI 1987/605;
Dangerous Substances in Harbour Areas Regulations 1987, SI 1987/37 amended by SI 1990/2487, SI 1991/1914, SI 1992/743, SI 1993/1746, SI 1994/669 and 3247, SI 1996/2092 and 2095, SI 1997/2367, SI 1998/2885, SI 2002/2776, SI 2003/1431, SI 2004/568 and 3168 (E) and SI 2005/1082, 1541 and 2929 (W);
Docks Regulations 1988, SI 1988/1655 amended by SI 1992/195, SI 1997/1713 and SI 2005/735;
Loading and Unloading of Fishing Vessels Regulations 1988, SI 1988/1656 amended by SI 2005/735;
Control of Substances Hazardous to Health Regulations 1988, SI 1988/1657 amended by SI 1991/2431, SIs 1992/2382 and 2966 and SI 1993/745 and 1746;
Mines (Safety of Exits) Regulations 1988, SI 1988/1729 amended by SI 1995/3136;
Road Traffic (Carriage of Explosives) Regulations 1989, SI 1989/615 amended by SI 1992/744, SI 1993/1746 and SI 1994/669;
Electricity at Work Regulations 1989, SI 1989/635 amended by SI 1995/2005, SI 1997/1993 and SI 1999/2024;
Health and Safety Information for Employees Regulations 1989, SI 1989/682;
Genetic Manipulation Regulations 1989, SI 1989/1810;
Noise at Work Regulations 1989, in this PART, post;
Construction (Head Protection) Regulations 1989, SI 1989/2209 amended by SI 1992/2966 and SI 1997/2776;
Dangerous Substances (Notification and Marking of Sites) Regulations 1990, SI 1990/304 amended by SI 1993/1746, SI 1994/669, SI 1996/2092, SI 2004/568 and 3168 (E) and SI 2005/2929 (W);
Control of Asbestos in the Air Regulations 1990, SI 1990/556;
Dangerous Goods and Marine Pollutants Regulations 1990, SI 1990/2605;
Control of Explosives Regulations 1991, SI 1991/1531 amended by SI 1993/2714, SI 2004/568 and SI 2005/1082;
Lifting Plant and Equipment (Records of Test and Examination Etc) Regulations 1992, SI 1992/195;
Notification of Cooling Towers and Evaporative Condensers Regulations 1992, SI 1992/2225;
Display Screen Equipment Regulations 1992, in this PART, post;
Manual Handling Operations Regulations 1992, in this PART, post;
Personal Protective Equipment at Work Regulations 1992, SI 1992/2966 amended by SI 1993/3074, SI 1994/3246, SI 1999/860 and 3232 and SI 2002/2174;
Workplace (Health, Safety and Welfare) Regulations 1992, in this PART, post;
Asbestos (Prohibitions) Regulations 1992, SI 1992/3067 amended by SI 1999/2373 and 2977 and SI 2003/1889;
Supply of Machinery (Safety) Regulations 1992, SI 1992/3073 amended by SI 2004/693 and SI 2005/831;
Coal and Other Safety-Lamp Mines (Explosives) Regulations 1993, SI 1993/208 amended by SI 2004/568 and SI 2005/1082;
Management and Administration of Safety and Health at Mines Regulations 1993, SI 1993/1897 amended by SI 1995/2005 and SI 1996/1592;
Coal Mines (Owner's Operating Rules) Regulations 1993, SI 1993/2331;
Placing on the Market and Supervision of Transfers of Explosives Regulations 1993, SI 1993/2714 amended by SI 2005/1082;
Notification of New Substances Regulations 1993, SI 1993/3050 amended by SI 1994/3247, SI 1995/2646, SI 1997/654, SI 1999/3232, SI 2001/1055, SI 2002/2176, SI 2004/568 and 994 and SI 2005/928;
Railways (Safety Critical Work) Regulations 1994, SI 1994/299 amended by SI 1996/1592, SI 1999/2024 and SI 2000/2688;
Construction (Design and Management) Regulations 1994, SI 1994/3140 amended by SI 1996/1592, SI 1998/494, SI 1999/3242 and SI 2000/238;
Mines Miscellaneous Health and Safety Provisions Regulations 1995, SI 1995/2005 amended by SI 1999/2463;
Offshore Installations and Pipeline Works (Management and Administration) Regulations 1995, SI 1995/738 amended by SI 2002/2175 and SI 2005/3117;
Offshore Installations (Prevention of Fire and Explosion, and Emergency Response) Regulations 1995, SI 1995/743 amended by SI 2003/2175 and SI 2005/3117;
Borehole Sites and Operations Regulations 1995, SI 1995/2038, SI 1999/2463 and 3242;
Reporting of Injuries, Diseases and Dangerous Occurrences Regulations 1995, in this PART, post;
Health and Safety (Safety Signs and Signals) Regulations 1996, SI 1996/341 amended by SI 1996/2092, SI 1999/3242 and SI 2004/568;

Pipelines Safety Regulations 1996, SI 1996/825 amended by SI 2003/2563;

Marking of Plastic Explosives for Detection Regulations 1996, SI 1996/890;

Offshore Installations and Wells (Design and Construction, etc) Regulations 1996, SI 1996/913 amended by SI 2002/2175 and SI 2005/1093 and 3117;

Construction (Health, Safety and Welfare) Regulations 1996, SI 1996/1592 amended by SI 1999/3242 and SI 2005/735, 1541 and 2929 (W);

Work in Compressed Air Regulations 1996, SI 1996/1656, amended by SI 1997/2776;

Carriage of Dangerous Goods by Rail Regulations 1996, SI 1996/2089 amended by SI 1998/2885, SI 1999/303 and 2024, SI 2000/2688, SI 2001/1426, SI 2003/1431 and SI 2004/568;

Carriage of Dangerous Goods by Road Regulations 1996, SI 1996/2095 amended by SI 1998/2885, SI 2001/1426, SI 2002/2776, SI 2003/1431 and SI 2004/568;

Level Crossings Regulations 1997, SI 1997/487;

Railway Safety (Miscellaneous Provisions) Regulations 1997, SI 1997/553 amended by SI 1998/494 and SI 1999/2024;

Confined Spaces Regulations 1997, SI 1997/1713, amended by SI 1997/2776;

Diving at Work Regulations 1997, SI 1997/2776 amended by SI 2005/3117;

Health and Safety (Enforcing Authority) Regulations 1998, SI 1998/494 amended by SI 1999/2024 and 3232 and SI 2002/2675 and SI 2005/1082, 1541 and 2929 (W);

Provision and Use of Work Equipment Regulations 1998, SI 1998/2306 amended by SI 1999/860 and 2001, SI 2001/1701 and SI 2002/2174 and SI 2005/735, 830 and 1093;

Lifting Operations and Lifting Equipment Regulations 1998, SI 1998/2307 amended by SI 2002/2174 and SI 2005/831;

Gas Safety (Installation and Use) Regulations 1998, SI 1998/2451 amended by SI 1999/2024;

Prevention of Accidents to Children in Agriculture Regulations 1998, SI 1998/3262;

Control of Major Accident Hazards Regulations 1999, SI 1999/743 amended by SI 2002/2469 and SI 2005/1088;

Quarries Regulations 1999, SI 1999/2024 amended by SI 2005/1082;

Railway Safety Regulations 1999, SI 1999/2244 amended by SI 2000/2688 and SI 2001/3291 and SI 2002/2099 and 2174;

Management of Health and Safety at Work Regulations 1999, SI 1999/3242 amended by SI 2005/1541;

Pressure Systems Safety Regulations 2000, SI 2000/128 amended by SI 2001/1426, SI 2004/568 and SI 2005/2092;

Railways (Safety Case) Regulations 2000, SI 2000/2688 amended by SI 2001/3291, SI 2002/2099 and SI 2003/579; 1689 and SI 2004/568 and 3386

Genetically Modified Organisms (Contained Use) Regulations 2000, SI 2000/2831 amended by SI 2002/63 and 2443 and SI 2005/2466 and 2759;

Radiation (Emergency Preparedness and Public Information) Regulations 2001, SI 2001/2975 amended by SI 2002/2469 and 2099 and SI 2004/568;

Chemicals (Hazard Information and Packaging for Supply) Regulations 2002, SI 2002/1689 amended by SI 2004/568 and 3386, SI 2005/928, 984, 1806 (W), 1732, 2092 and 2571;

Control of Asbestos at Work Regulations 2002, SI 2002/2675 amended by SI 2004/568 and SI 2005/2929 (W);

Control of Lead at Work Regulations 2002, SI 2002/2676 amended by SI 2004/568 and 3386;

Control of Substances Hazardous to Health Regulations 2002**, SI 2002/2677 amended by SI 2003/978 and SI 2004/568 and 3386;

Dangerous Substances and Explosive Atmospheres Regulations 2002, SI 2002/2776 amended by SI 2004/568;

Nuclear Industries Security Regulations 2003, SI 2003/403;

Ammonium Nitrate Materials (High Nitrogen Content) Safety Regulations 2003, SI 2003/1082;

Carriage of Dangerous Goods and Use of Transportable Pressure Equipment Regulations 2004, SI 2004/568 amended by SI 2005/1082, 1732 and 2929 (W);

Justification of Practices Involving Ionising Radiation Regulations 2004, SI 2004/1769;

Control of Vibration at Work Regulations 2005, SI 2005/1093;

Manufacture and Storage of Explosives Regulations 2005, SI 2005/1082;

Control of Noise at Work Regulations 2005, SI 2005/1643, in this PART, post;

Offshore Installations (Safety Case) Regulations 2005, SI 2005/3117.

For penalty for contravening any of these regulations see s 33, post which also provides for a daily penalty for offences continuing after conviction. See introductory note to this title, ante, for regulations made under the European Communities Act 1972.

See also the following—Offshore Installations and Pipeline Works (First Aid) Regulations 1989, SI 1989/1671 amended by SI 2002/2175.

For regulations formerly made under the Mineral Workings (Offshore Installations) Act 1971, and the Petroleum and Submarine Pipe-lines Act 1975, and which whose effect is preserved by SI 1993/1823, reg 6, see the notes to those Acts in this title. The Secretary of State has power to repeal or revoke any provision of regulations under s 15: Deregulation and Contracting Out Act 1994, s 37.

*. For the criminal liability of employers under these regulations, see *R v Nelson Group Services (Maintenance) Ltd* [1998] 4 All ER 331, [1999] 1 WLR 1526, CA.

**. For the extent of the employer's absolute duty under reg 7(1) to ensure that exposure is prevented or adequately controlled, see *Dugmore v Swansea NHS Trust* [2002] EWCA Civ 1689, [2003] 1 All ER 333, [2003] ICR 574.

8–15301   16. Approval of codes of practice by the Commission.   (1) For the purpose of providing practical guidance with respect to the requirements of any provision of any of the enactments or instruments mentioned in subsection (1A) below, the Commission may, subject to the following subsection—

(*a*)   approve and issue such codes of practice (whether prepared by it or not) as in its opinion are suitable for that purpose;

(*b*)   approve such codes of practice issued or proposed to be issued otherwise than by the Commission as in its opinion are suitable for that purpose.*

(1A)   Those enactments and instruments are—

(*a*)   sections 2 to 7 above;

(*b*)   health and safety regulations, except so far as they make provision exclusively in relation to transport systems falling within paragraph 1(3) of Schedule 3 to the Railways Act 2005; and (c)　the existing statutory provisions that are not such provisions by virtue of section 117(4) of the Railways Act 1993.

(2)　The Commission shall not approve a code of practice under subsection (1) above without the consent of the Secretary of State, and shall, before seeking his consent, consult—

(a)　any government department or other body that appears to the Commission to be appropriate (and, in particular, in the case of a code relating to electro-magnetic radiations, the Health Protection Agency and

(b)　such government departments and other bodies, if any, as in relation to any matter dealt with in the code, the Commission is required to consult under this section by virtue of directions given to it by the Secretary of State.

(3)　Where a code of practice is approved by the Commission under subsection (1) above, the Commission shall issue a notice in writing—

(a)　identifying the code in question and stating the date on which its approval by the Commission is to take effect; and

(b)　specifying for which of the provisions mentioned in subsection (1) above the code is approved.

(4)　The commission may—

(a)　from time to time revise the whole or any part of any code of practice prepared by it in pursuance of this section;

(b)　approve any revision or proposed revision of the whole or any part of any code of practice for the time being approved under this section;

and the provisions of subsections (2) and (3) above shall, with the necessary modifications, apply in relation to the approval of any revision under this subsection as they apply in relation to the approval of a code of practice under subsection (1) above.

(5)　The commission may at any time with the consent of the Secretary of State withdraw its approval from any code of practice approved under this section, but before seeking his consent shall consult the same government departments and other bodies as it would be required to consult under subsection (2) above if it were proposing to approve the code.

(6)　Where under the preceding subsection the Commission withdraws its approval from a code of practice approved under this section, the Commission shall issue a notice in writing identifying the code in question and stating the date on which its approval of it is to cease to have effect.

(7)　References in this Part to an approved code of practice are references to that code as it has effect for the time being by virtue of any revision of the whole or any part of it approved under this section.

(8)　The power of the Commission under subsection (1)(b) above to approve a code of practice issued or proposed to be issued otherwise than by the Commission shall include power to approve a part of such a code of practice; and accordingly in this Part "code of practice" may be read as including a part of such a code of practice.

[Health and Safety at Work etc Act 1974, s 16 as amended by the Employment Protection Act 1975, Sch 15, the Health Protection Agency Act 2004, Sch 3 and the Railways Act 2005, Sch 3.]

8–15302　17. Use of approved codes of practice in criminal proceedings.

(1)　A failure on the part of any person to observe any provision of an approved code of practice shall not of itself render him liable to any civil or criminal proceedings; but where in any criminal proceedings a party is alleged to have committed an offence by reason of a contravention of any requirement or prohibition imposed by or under any such provision as is mentioned in section 16(1) being a provision for which there was an approved code of practice at the time of the alleged contravention, the following subsection shall have effect with respect to that code in relation to these proceedings.

(2)　Any provision of the code of practice which appears to the court to be relevant to the requirement or prohibition alleged to have been contravened shall be admissible in evidence in the proceedings; and if it is proved that there was at any material time a failure to observe any provision of the code which appears to the court to be relevant to any matter which it is necessary for the prosecution to prove in order to establish a contravention of that requirement or prohibition, that matter shall be taken as proved unless the court is satisfied that the requirement or prohibition was in respect of that matter complied with otherwise than by way of observance of the provision of the code.

(3)　In any criminal proceedings—

(a)　a document purporting to be a notice issued by the Commission under section 16 shall be taken to be such a notice unless the contrary is proved; and

(b)　a code of practice which appears to the court to be the subject of such a notice shall be taken to be the subject of that notice unless the contrary is proved.

[Health and Safety at Work etc Act 1974, s 17.]

8–15303　18. Authorities responsible for enforcement of the relevant statutory provisions.

(1)　*Duty of Health and Safety Executive to enforce except to extent that some other authority is made responsible.*

(2) *Power to make regulations making local authorities responsible for enforcement*[1].

(7) In this Part—

   (*a*) "enforcing authority" means the Executive or any other authority which is by any of the relevant statutory provisions or by regulations under subsection (2) above made responsible for the enforcement of any of those provisions to any extent; and

   (*b*) *(definition of field of responsibility of enforcing authority).*

[Health and Safety at Work etc Act 1974, s 18 as amended by the Railways Act 2005, Sch 13.]

---

   1. The Health and Safety (Enforcing Authority) Regulations 1998, SI 1998/494 amended by SI 1999/2024 and 3232, SI 2002/2675 and SI 2005/1082, 1541 and 2929 (W), have been made. Under these Regulations the identity of the enforcing authority changes when the defendant's main activity changes, but the transfer procedure under reg 5 is relevant only when it is found to be more convenient for either the Health and Safety Executive or the local authority to undertake the responsibility of enforcement (*Hadley v Hancox and Hancox* (1986) 151 JP 227). The Adventure Activities (Enforcing Authority) Regulations 2004, SI 2004/1359 have also been made.

   As to the enforcement and offence provisions of the Act being applied to agreements granting access or transit rights on certain railways; see the Railways Regulations 1992, SI 1992/3060.

8–15304   19. Appointment of inspectors.   (1) *Power of enforcing authority to appoint inspectors.*

(2) Every appointment of a person as an inspector under this section shall be made by an instrument in writing specifying which of the powers conferred on inspectors by the relevant statutory provisions are to be exercisable by the person appointed; and an inspector shall in right of his appointment under this section—

   (*a*) be entitled to exercise only such of those powers[1] as are so specified; and

   (*b*) be entitled to exercise the powers so specified only within the field of responsibility of the authority which appointed him.

(3) So much of an inspector's instrument of appointment as specifies the powers which he is entitled to exercise may be varied by the enforcing authority which appointed him.

(4) An inspector shall, if so required when exercising or seeking to exercise any power conferred on him by any of the relevant statutory provisions, produce his instrument of appointment or a duly authenticated copy thereof.

[Health and Safety at Work etc Act 1974, s 19.]

---

   1. Once evidence is given by an inspector that he is an inspector for the purposes of the Act, then he has authority by virtue of s 38, post, to institute proceedings even though this may not be stated specifically in his certificate: *Campbell v Wallsend Slipway and Engineering Co Ltd* (1977) 121 Sol Jo 334, [1977] Crim LR 351.

8–15305   20. Powers of inspectors.   (1) Subject to the provisions of section 19 and this section, an inspector may, for the purpose of carrying into effect any of the relevant statutory provisions within the field of responsibility of the enforcing authority which appointed him, exercise the powers set out in subsection (2) below.

(2) The powers of an inspector referred to in the preceding subsection are the following, namely—

   (*a*) at any reasonable time (or, in a situation which in his opinion is or may be dangerous, at any time) to enter any premises which he has reason to believe it is necessary for him to enter for the purposes mentioned in subsection (1) above;

   (*b*) to take with him a constable if he has reasonable cause to apprehend any serious obstruction in the execution of his duty;

   (*c*) without prejudice to the preceding paragraph, on entering any premises by virtue of paragraph (*a*) above to take with him—

      (i) any other person duly authorised by his (the inspector's) enforcing authority; and

      (ii) any equipment or materials required for any purpose for which the power of entry is being exercised;

   (*d*) to make such examination and investigation as may in any circumstances be necessary for the purposes mentioned in subsection (1) above;

   (*e*) as regards any premises which he has power to enter, to direct that those premises or any part of them, or anything therein, shall be left undisturbed (whether generally or in particular respects) for so long as is reasonably necessary for the purpose of any examination or investigation under paragraph (*d*) above;

   (*f*) to take such measurements and photographs and make such recordings as he considers necessary for the purpose of any examination or investigation under paragraph (*d*) above;

   (*g*) to take samples of any articles or substances found in any premises which he has power to enter, and of the atmosphere in or in the vicinity of any such premises;

   (*h*) in the case of any article or substance found in any premises which he has power to enter, being an article or substance which appears to him to have caused or to be likely to cause danger to health or safety, to cause it to be dismantled or subjected to any process or test (but not so as to damage or destroy it unless this is in the circumstances necessary for the purpose mentioned in subsection (1) above);

(*i*) in the case of any such article or substance as is mentioned in the preceding paragraph, to take possession of it and detain it for so long as is necessary for all or any of the following purposes, namely—

　(i) to examine it and do to it anything which he has power to do under that paragraph;

　(ii) to ensure that it is not tampered with before his examination of it is completed;

　(iii) to ensure that it is available for use as evidence in any proceedings for an offence under any of the relevant statutory provisions or any proceedings relating to a notice under section 21 or 22;

(*j*) to require any person whom he has reasonable cause to believe to be able to give any information relevant to any examination or investigation under paragraph (*d*) above to answer (in the absence of persons other than a person nominated by him to be present and any persons whom the inspector may allow to be present) such questions as the inspector thinks fit to ask and to sign a declaration of the truth of his answers;

(*k*) to require the production of, inspect, and take copies of or of any entry in—

　(i) any books or documents which by virtue of any of the relevant statutory provisions are required to be kept; and

　(ii) any other books or documents which it is necessary for him to see for the purposes of any examination or investigation under paragraph (*d*) above;

(*l*) to require any person to afford him such facilities and assistance with respect to any matters or things within that person's control or in relation to which that person has responsibilities as are necessary to enable the inspector to exercise any of the powers conferred on him by this section;

(*m*) any other power which is necessary for the purpose mentioned in subsection (1) above.

(3) The Secretary of State may by regulations make provision as to the procedure to be followed in connection with the taking of samples under subsection (2)(*g*) above (including provision as to the way in which samples that have been so taken are to be dealt with).

(4) Where an inspector proposes to exercise the power conferred by subsection (2)(*h*) above in the case of an article or substance found in any premises, he shall, if so requested by a person who at the time is present in and has responsibilities in relation to those premises, cause anything which is to be done by virtue of that power to be done in the presence of that person unless the inspector considers that its being done in that person's presence would be prejudicial to the safety of the State.

(5) Before exercising the power conferred by subsection (2)(*h*) above in the case of any article or substance, an inspector shall consult such persons as appear to him appropriate for the purpose of ascertaining what dangers, if any, there may be in doing anything which he proposes to do under that power.

(6) Where under the power conferred by subsection (2)(*i*) above an inspector takes possession of any article or substance found in any premises, he shall leave there, either with a responsible person or, if that is impracticable, fixed in a conspicuous position, a notice giving particulars of that article or substance sufficient to identify it and stating that he has taken possession of it under that power; and before taking possession of any such substance under that power an inspector shall, if it is practicable for him to do so, take a sample thereof and give to a responsible person at the premises a portion of the sample marked in a manner to identify it.

(7) No answer given by a person in pursuance of a requirement imposed under subsection 2(*j*) above shall be admissible in evidence against that person or the spouse or civil partner of that person in any proceedings.

(8) Nothing in this section shall be taken to compel the production by any person of a document of which he would on grounds of legal professional privilege be entitled to withhold production on an order for discovery in an action in the High Court or, as the case may be, on an order for the production of documents in an action in the Court of Session.

[Health and Safety at Work etc Act 1974, s 20 as amended by the Civil Partnership Act 2004, Sch 27.]

8–15306　21. Improvement notices. If an inspector is of the opinion that a person—

(*a*) is contravening one or more of the relevant statutory provisions; or

(*b*) has contravened one or more of those provisions in circumstances that make it likely that the contravention will continue or be repeated,

he may serve on him a notice (in this Part referred to as "an improvement notice") stating that he is of that opinion, specifying the provision or provisions as to which he is of that opinion, giving particulars of the reasons why he is of that opinion, and requiring that person to remedy the contravention or, as the case may be, the matters occasioning it within such period (ending not earlier than the period within which an appeal against the notice can be brought under section 24) as may be specified in the notice.

[Health and Safety at Work etc Act 1974, s 21.]

8–15307　22. Prohibition notices. (1) This section applies to any activities which are being or are likely to be carried on by or under the control of any person, being activities to or in relation to which any of the relevant statutory provisions apply or will, if the activities are so carried on, apply.

(2) If as regards any activities to which this section applies an inspector is of the opinion that, as carried on or likely to be carried on by or under the control of the person in question, the activities involve or, as the case may be, will involve a risk of serious personal injury, the inspector may serve on that person a notice (in this Part referred to as "a prohibition notice").

(3) A prohibition notice shall—

(*a*) state that the inspector is of the said opinion;

(*b*) specify the matters which in his opinion give or, as the case may be, will give rise to the said risk;

(*c*) where in his opinion, any of those matters involves or, as the case may be, will involve a contravention of any of the relevant statutory provisions, state that he is of that opinion, specify the provision or provisions as to which he is of that opinion, and give particulars of the reasons why he is of that opinion; and

(*d*) direct that the activities to which the notice relates shall not be carried on by or under the control of the person on whom the notice is served unless the matters specified in the notice in pursuance of paragraph (*b*) above and any associated contraventions of provisions so specified in pursuance of paragraph (*c*) above have been remedied.

(4) A direction contained in a prohibition notice in pursuance of subsection (3)(*d*) above shall take effect—

(*a*) at the end of the period specified in the notice; or

(*b*) if the notice so declares, immediately.

[Health and Safety at Work etc Act 1974, s 22 as amended by the Consumer Protection Act 1987, Sch 3.]

8–15308 23. Provisions supplementary to sections 21 and 22. (1) In this section "a notice" means an improvement notice or a prohibition notice.

(2) A notice may (but need not) include directions as to the measures to be taken to remedy any contravention or matter to which the notice relates; and any such directions—

(*a*) may be framed to any extent by reference to any approved code of practice; and

(*b*) may be framed so as to afford the person on whom the notice is served a choice between different ways of remedying the contravention or matter.

(3) Where any of the relevant statutory provisions applies to a building or any matter connected with a building and an inspector proposes to serve an improvement notice relating to a contravention of that provision in connection with that building or matter, the notice shall not direct any measures to be taken to remedy the contravention of that provision which are more onerous than those necessary to secure conformity with the requirements of any building regulations for the time being in force to which that building or matter would be required to conform if the relevant building were being newly erected unless the provision in question imposes specific requirements more onerous than the requirements of any such building regulations to which the building or matter would be required to conform as aforesaid.

In this subsection "the relevant building", in the case of a building, means that building, and, in the case of a matter connected with a building, means the building with which the matter is connected.

(4) Before an inspector serves in connection with any premises used or about to be used as a place of work a notice requiring or likely to lead to the taking of measures affecting the means of escape in case of fire with which the premises are or ought to be provided, he shall consult the fire and rescue authority.

In this subsection "fire and rescue authority", in relation to premises, means—

(*a*) where the Regulatory Reform (Fire Safety) Order 2005 applies to the premises, the enforcing authority within the meaning given by article 25 of that Order;

(*b*) in any other case, the fire and rescue authority under the Fire and Rescue Services Act 2004 for the area where the premises are (or are to be) situated.

(5) Where an improvement notice or prohibition notice which is not to take immediate effect has been served—

(*a*) the notice may be withdrawn by an inspector at any time before the end of the period specified therein in pursuance of section 21 or section 22(4) as the case may be; and

(*b*) the period so specified may be extended or further extended by an inspector at any time when an appeal against the notice is not pending.

(6) *Scotland.*

[Health and Safety at Work etc Act 1974, s 23 as amended by the Fire and Rescue Services Act 2004, Sch 1 and SI 2005/1541.]

8–15309 24. *Right of appeal to an industrial tribunal against an improvement notice or a prohibition notice.*

8–15320 25. Power to deal with cause of imminent danger. (1) Where, in the case of any article or substance found by him in any premises which he has power to enter, an inspector has reasonable cause to believe that, in the circumstances in which he finds it, the article or substance is a cause of imminent danger of serious personal injury, he may seize it and cause it to be rendered harmless (whether by destruction or otherwise).

(2) Before there is rendered harmless under this section—

(*a*)   any article that forms part of a batch of similar articles; or

(*b*)   any substance,

the inspector shall, if it is practicable for him to do so, take a sample thereof and give to a responsible person at the premises where the article or substance was found by him a portion of the sample marked in a manner sufficient to identify it.

(3) As soon as may be after any article or substance has been seized and rendered harmless under this section, the inspector shall prepare and sign a written report giving particulars of the circumstances in which the article or substance was seized and so dealt with by him, and shall—

(*a*)   give a signed copy of the report to a responsible person at the premises where the article or substance was found by him; and

(*b*)   unless that person is the owner of the article or substance, also serve a signed copy of the report on the owner;

and if, where paragraph (*b*) above applies, the inspector cannot after reasonable enquiry ascertain the name or address of the owner, the copy may be served on him by giving it to the person to whom a copy was given under the preceding paragraph.

[Health and Safety at Work etc Act 1974, s 25.]

8–15321   25A. Power of customs officer to detain articles and substances.   (1) A customs officer may, for the purpose of facilitating the exercise or performance by any enforcing authority or inspector of any of the powers or duties of the authority or inspector under any of the relevant statutory provisions, seize any imported article or imported substance and detain it for not more than two working days.

(2) Anything seized and detained under this section shall be dealt with during the period of its detention in such manner as the Commissioners of Customs and Excise may direct.

(3) In subsection (1) above the reference to two working days is a reference to a period of forty-eight hours calculated from the time when the goods in question are seized but disregarding so much of any period as falls on a Saturday or Sunday or on Christmas Day, Good Friday or a day which is a bank holiday under the Banking and Financial Dealings Act 1971 in the part of Great Britain where the goods are seized.

[Health and Safety at Work etc Act 1974, s 25A, as inserted by the Consumer Protection Act 1987, s 36 and Sch 3.]

8–15322   26. Power of enforcing authorities to indemnify their inspectors.   Where an action has been brought against an inspector in respect of an act done in the execution or purported execution of any of the relevant statutory provisions and the circumstances are such that he is not legally entitled to require the enforcing authority which appointed him to indemnify him, that authority may, nevertheless, indemnify him against the whole or part of any damages and costs or expenses, which he may have been ordered to pay or may have incurred, if the authority is satisfied that he honestly believed that the act complained of was within his powers and that his duty as an inspector required or entitled him to do it.

[Health and Safety at Work etc Act 1974, s 26.]

Obtaining and disclosure of information

8–15323   27. Obtaining of information by the Commission, the Executive, enforcing authorities, etc.   (1) For the purpose of obtaining—

(*a*)   any information which the Commission needs for the discharge of its functions; or

(*b*)   any information which an enforcing authority needs for the discharge of the authority's functions,

the Commission may, with the consent of the Secretary of State, serve on any person a notice requiring that person to furnish to the Commission or, as the case may be, to the enforcing authority in question such information about such matters as may be specified in the notice, and to do so in such form and manner and within such time as may be so specified.

In this subsection "consent" includes a general consent extending to cases of any stated description.

(2) Nothing in section 9 of the Statistics of Trade Act 1947 (which restricts the disclosure of information obtained under that Act) shall prevent or penalise—

(*a*)   the disclosure by a Minister of the Crown to the Commission or the Executive of information obtained under that Act about any undertaking within the meaning of that Act, being information consisting of the names and addresses of the persons carrying on the undertaking, the nature of the undertaking's activities, the numbers of persons of different descriptions who work in the undertaking, the addresses or places where activities of the undertaking are or were carried on, the nature of the activities carried on there, or the numbers of persons of different descriptions who work or worked in the undertaking there;

(b)   (*Repealed*).

(3) In the preceding subsection any reference to a Minister of the Crown, the Commission or the Executive includes respectively a reference to an officer of his or of that body and also, in the case of a reference to the Commission, includes a reference to—

(a)   a person performing any functions of the Commission or the Executive on its behalf by virtue of section 13(1)(*a*);

(b)   an officer of a body which is so performing any such functions; and

(c)   an adviser appointed in pursuance of section 13(1)(*d*).

(4) A person to whom information is disclosed in pursuance of subsection (2) above shall not use the information for a purpose other than a purpose of the Commission or, as the case may be, of the Executive.

[Health and Safety at Work etc Act 1974, s 27 as amended by the Employment Act 1988, Sch 3 and the Employment Act 1989, Schs 6 and 7.]

8–15324   27A. Information communicated by the Commissioners of Customs and Excise.

(1) If they think it appropriate to do so for the purpose of facilitating the exercise or performance by any person to whom subsection (2) below applies of any of that person's powers or duties under any of the relevant statutory provisions, the Commissioners of Customs and Excise may authorise the disclosure to that person of any information obtained for the purposes of the exercise by the Commissioners of their functions in relation to imports.

(2) This subsection applies to an enforcing authority and to an inspector.

(3) A disclosure of information made to any person under subsection (1) above shall be made in such manner as may be directed by the Commissioners of Customs and Excise and may be made through such persons acting on behalf of that person as may be do directed.

(4) Information may be disclosed to a person under subsection (1) above whether or not the disclosure of the information has been requested by or on behalf of that person.

[Health and Safety at Work etc Act 1974, s 27A, as inserted by the Consumer Protection Act 1987, s 36 and Sch 3.]

8–15325   28. Restrictions on disclosure of information.   (1) In this and the two following subsections—

(a)   "relevant information" means information obtained by a person under section 27(1) or furnished to any person under section 27A above, by virtue of section 43A(6) below or in pursuance of a requirement imposed by any of the relevant statutory provisions; and

(b)   "the recipient", in relation to any relevant information, means the person by whom that information was so obtained or to whom that information was so furnished, as the case may be.

(2) Subject to the following subsection, no relevant information shall be disclosed without the consent of the person by whom it was furnished.

(3) The preceding subsection shall not apply to—

(a)   disclosure of information to the Commission, the Executive, the Environment Agency, the Scottish Environment Protection Agency, a government department or any enforcing authority;

(b)   without prejudice to paragraph (*a*) above, disclosure by the recipient of information to any person for the purpose of any function conferred on the recipient by or under any of the relevant statutory provisions;

(c)   without prejudice to paragraph (*a*) above, disclosure by the recipient of information to—

(i)   an officer of a local authority who is authorised by that authority to receive it,

(ii)   an officer of a water undertaker, sewerage undertaker, water authority or water development board who is authorised by that undertaker or board to receive it,

(iii)   *Repealed*,

(iv)   a constable authorised by a chief officer of police to receive it;

(d)   disclosure by the recipient of information in a form calculated to prevent it from being identified as relating to a particular person or case;

(e)   disclosure of information for the purposes of any legal proceedings or any investigation or inquiry held by virtue of section 14(2), or for the purposes of a report of any such proceedings or inquiry or of a special report made by virtue of section 14(2);

(f)   any other disclosure of information by the recipient, if—

(i)   the recipient is, or is acting on behalf of a person who is, a public authority for the purposes of the Freedom of Information Act 2000, and

(ii)   the information is not held by the authority on behalf of another person.

(4) In the preceding subsection any reference to the Commission, the Executive, the Environment Agency, the Scottish Environment Protection Agency, a government department or an enforcing authority includes respectively a reference to an officer of that body or authority (including in the

case of an enforcing authority, any inspector appointed by it), and also, in the case of a reference to the Commission, includes a reference to—

(a) a person performing any functions of the Commission or the Executive on its behalf by virtue of section 13(1)(a);
(b) an officer of a body which is so performing any such functions; and
(c) an officer appointed in pursuance of section 13(1)(d).

(5) A person to whom information is disclosed in pursuance of any of paragraphs (a) to (e) of subsection (3) above shall not use the information for a purpose other than—

(a) in a case falling within paragraph (a) of that subsection, a purpose of the Commission or of the Executive or of the Environment Agency, the Scottish Environment Protection Agency or, of the government department in question, or the purposes of the enforcing authority in question in connection with the relevant statutory provisions, as the case may be;
(b) in the case of information given to an officer of a body which is a local authority, a water undertaker, a sewerage undertaker, a river purification board or a water development board, the purposes of the body in connection with the relevant statutory provisions or any enactment whatsoever relating to public health, public safety or the protection of the environment;
(c) in the case of information given to a constable, the purposes of the police in connection with the relevant statutory provisions or any enactment whatsoever relating to public health, public safety or the safety of the State.

(6) References in subsections (3) and (5) above, to a local authority include a joint authority established by Part IV of the Local Government Act 1985 and the London Fire and Emergency Planning Authority.

(7) A person shall not disclose any information obtained by him as a result of the exercise of any power conferred by section 14(4)(a) or 20 (including, in particular, any information with respect to any trade secret obtained by him in any premises entered by him by virtue of any such power) except—

(a) for the purposes of his functions; or
(b) for the purposes of any legal proceedings or any investigation or inquiry held by virtue of section 14(2) or for the purposes of a report of any such proceedings or inquiry or of a special report made by virtue of section 14(2); or
(c) with the relevant consent.

In this subsection "the relevant consent" means, in the case of information furnished in pursuance of a requirement imposed under section 20, the consent of the person who furnished it, and, in any other case, the consent of a person having responsibilities in relation to the premises where the information was obtained.

(8) Notwithstanding anything in the preceding subsection an inspector shall, in circumstances in which it is necessary to do so for the purpose of assisting in keeping persons (or the representatives of persons) employed at any premises adequately informed about matters affecting their health, safety and welfare, give to such persons or their representatives the following descriptions of information, that is to say—

(a) factual information obtained by him as mentioned in that subsection which relates to those premises or anything which was or is therein or was or is being done therein; and
(b) information with respect to any action which he has taken or proposes to take in or in connection with those premises in the performance of his functions;

and, where an inspector does as aforesaid, he shall give the like information to the employer of the first-mentioned persons.

(9) Notwithstanding anything in subsection (7) above, a person who has obtained such information as is referred to in that subsection may furnish to a person who appears to him to be likely to be a party to any civil proceedings arising out of any accident, occurrence, situation or other matter, a written statement of relevant facts observed by him in the course of exercising any of the powers referred to in that subsection.

(9A) Subsection (7) above does not apply if—

(a) the person who has obtained any such information as is referred to in that subsection is, or is acting on behalf of a person who is, a public authority for the purposes of the Freedom of Information Act 2000, and
(b) the information is not held by the authority on behalf of another person.(10)The Broads Authority and every National Park authority shall be deemed to be local authorities for the purposes of this section.

(10) The Broads Authority and every National Park authority shall be deemed to be local authorities for the purposes of this section.

[Health and Safety at Work etc Act 1974, s 28 as amended by the Employment Protection Act 1975, Sch 15, the Local Government Act 1985, Sch 14, the Consumer Protection Act 1987, Sch 3, the Norfolk and Suffolk Broads Act 1988, Sch 6, the Water Act 1989, Sch 25, the Education Reform Act 1988, Sch 13, the Environment Act

1995, Schs 10, 22 and 24, the Greater London Authority Act 1999, Sch 29 and the Railways and Transport Safety Act 2003, s 105 and SI 2004/3363.]

Provisions as to offences

8–15326   33. Offences.   (1) It is an offence[1] for a person—

   (a)   to fail to discharge a duty to which he is subject by virtue of sections 2 to 7[2];

   (b)   to contravene section 8 or 9;

   (c)   to contravene any health and safety regulations or any requirement or prohibition imposed under any such regulations (including any requirement or prohibition to which he is subject to by virtue of the terms of or any condition or restriction attached to any licence, approval, exemption or other authority issued, given or granted under the regulations);

   (d)   to contravene any requirement imposed by or under regulations under section 14 or intentionally to obstruct any person in the exercise of his powers under that subsection;

   (e)   to contravene any requirement imposed by an inspector under section 20 or 25;

   (f)   to prevent or attempt to prevent any other person from appearing before an inspector or from answering any question to which an inspector may by virtue of section 20(2) require an answer;

   (g)   to contravene any requirement or prohibition imposed by an improvement notice or a prohibition notice (including any such notice as modified on appeal)[3];

   (h)   intentionally to obstruct an inspector in the exercise or performance of his powers or duties or to obstruct a customs officer in the exercise of his powers under section 25A;

   (i)   to contravene any requirement imposed by a notice under section 27(1);

   (j)   to use or disclose any information in contravention of section 27(4) or 28;

   (k)   to make a statement which he knows to be false or recklessly to make a statement which is false where the statement is made—

      (i)   in purported compliance with a requirement to furnish any information imposed by or under any of the relevant statutory provisions; or

      (ii)   for the purpose of obtaining the issue of a document under any of the relevant statutory provisions to himself or another person;

   (l)   intentionally to make a false entry in any register, book, notice or other document required by or under any of the relevant statutory provisions to be kept, served or given or, with intent to deceive, to make use of any such entry which he knows to be false;

   (m)   with intent to deceive, to use a document issued or authorised to be issued under any of the relevant statutory provisions or required for any purpose thereunder or to make or have in his possession a document so closely resembling any such document as to be calculated to deceive;

   (n)   falsely to pretend to be an inspector;

   (o)   to fail to comply with an order made by a court under section 42.

(1A)   Subject to any provision made by virtue of section 15(6)(d), a person guilty of an offence under subsection (1)(a) above consisting of failing to discharge a duty to which he is subject by virtue of sections 2 to 6 shall be liable[4]—

   (a)   on summary conviction, to a fine not exceeding **£20,000**;

   (b)   on conviction on indictment, to a fine.

(2A)   A person guilty of an offence under subsection (1)(g) or (o) above shall be liable[4]—

   (a)   on summary conviction, to imprisonment for a term not exceeding six months, or a fine not exceeding **£20,000**, or both;

   (b)   on conviction on indictment, to imprisonment for a term not exceeding two years, or a fine, or both.

(2)   A person guilty of an offence under paragraph (d), (f), (h) or (n) of subsection (1) above, or of an offence under paragraph (e) of that subsection consisting of contravening a requirement imposed by an inspector under section 20, shall be liable on summary conviction to a fine not exceeding **level 5** on the standard scale.

(3)   Subject to any provision made by virtue of section 15(6)(d) or (e) or by virtue of paragraph 2(2) of Schedule 3, a person guilty of an offence under subsection (1) above not falling within subsection (1A), (2) or (2A) above or of an offence under any of the existing statutory provisions[5], being an offence for which no other penalty is specified, shall be liable[4]—

   (a)   on summary conviction, to a fine not exceeding **the statutory maximum**;

   (b)   on conviction on indictment—

      (i)   if the offence is one to which this sub-paragraph applies, to imprisonment for a term not exceeding two years, or a fine, or both;

      (ii)   if the offence is not one to which the preceding sub-paragraph applies, to a fine.

(4)   Subsection (3)(b)(i) above applies to the following offences—

(a) an offence consisting of contravening any of the relevant statutory provisions by doing otherwise than under the authority of a licence issued by the Executive something for the doing of which such a licence is necessary under the relevant statutory provisions;

(b) an offence consisting of contravening a term of or a condition or restriction attached to any such licence as is mentioned in the preceding paragraph;

(c) an offence consisting of acquiring or attempting to acquire, possessing or using an explosive article or substance (within the meaning of any of the relevant statutory provisions) in contravention of any of the relevant statutory provisions;

(d) *Repealed*;

(e) an offence under subsection (1)(j) above.

(5) *Repealed.*

(6) *Repealed.*

[Health and Safety at Work etc Act 1974, s 33, as amended by the Employment Protection Act 1975, Sch 15, the Criminal Law Act 1977, s 28 and Schs 1 and 6, the Forgery and Counterfeiting Act 1981, Sch, the Criminal Justice Act 1982, s 46, the Consumer Protection Act 1987, Sch 3 and the Offshore Safety Act 1992, s 4.]

1. Minimal risk to employees is not a mitigating factor (*R v Sanyo Electrical Manufacturing (UK) Ltd* (1992) 156 JP 863).

2. See Note 1 to s 6, ante. It is inappropriate and wrong for the Health and Safety Executive to prosecute for an offence under s 6 of the 1974 Act when there is a specific statutory offence under the Regulations covering exactly the same ground as in s 6 (*R (on the application of Junttan Oy (a company)) v Bristol Magistrates' Court* [2002] EWHC 566 (Admin), [2003] Crim LR 114. However, the above approach does not apply to s 3 of the 1974 Act, which creates an offence in relation to management or administrative default on behalf of the manufacturer, as opposed to a manufacturing default (s 6) (*R (on the application of Junttan Oy (a company)) v Bristol Magistrates' Court*, supra).

3. The provisions of s 40, post, have no application to an offence under s 33(1)(g) (*Deary v Mansion Hide Upholstery Ltd* [1983] ICR 610, 147 JP 311).

4. For procedure in respect of this offence which is triable either way, see the Magistrates' Courts Act 1980, ss 17A–21, in PART I: MAGISTRATES' COURTS, PROCEDURE, ante. When sentencing a corporate defendant for a breach of the health and safety legislation, the court should have regard to the guidance contained in *R v F Howe and Son (Engineers) Ltd* [1999] 2 All ER 249, 163 JP 359, [1999] 2 Cr App Rep (S) 37, [1999] Crim LR 238; see para **3–206A Fine: Imposition on a company** in PART III: SENTENCING, ante.

5. See Sch 1, post; this means, for example, that an offence under the Factories Act 1961 is punishable with the penalties set out in this section.

8–15327   34. Extension of time for bringing summary proceedings.   (1) Where—

(a) a special report on any matter to which subsection 14 of this Act applies is made by virtue of subsection (2)(a) of that section; or

(b) a report is made by the person holding an inquiry into any such matter by virtue of subsection (2)(b) of that section; or

(c) a coroner's inquest is held touching the death of any person whose death may have been caused by an accident which happened while he was at work or by a disease which he contracted or probably contracted at work or by any accident, act or omission which occurred in connection with the work of any person whatsoever; or

(d) a public inquiry into any death that may have been so caused is held under the Fatal Accidents Inquiry (Scotland) Act 1895 or the Fatal Accidents and Sudden Deaths Inquiry (Scotland) Act 1906,

and it appears from the report or, in a case falling within paragraph (c) or (d) above, from the proceedings at the inquest or inquiry, that any of the relevant statutory provisions was contravened at a time which is material in relation to the subject matter of the report, inquest or inquiry, summary proceedings against any person liable to be proceeded against in respect of the contravention may be commenced at any time within three months of the making of the report or, in a case falling within paragraph (c) or (d) above, within three months of the conclusion of the inquest or inquiry.

(2) Where an offence under any of the relevant statutory provisions is committed by reason of a failure to do something at or within the time fixed by or under any of those provisions, the offence shall be deemed to continue until that thing is done.

(3) Summary proceedings for an offence to which this subsection applies may be commenced at any time within six months from the date on which there comes to the knowledge of a responsible enforcing authority evidence sufficient in the opinion of that authority to justify a prosecution for that offence; and for the purposes of this subsection—

(a) a certificate of an enforcing authority stating that such evidence came to its knowledge on a specified date shall be conclusive evidence of that fact; and

(b) a document purporting to be such a certificate and to be signed by or on behalf of the enforcing authority in question shall be presumed to be such a certificate unless the contrary is proved.

(4) The preceding subsection applies to any offence under any of the relevant statutory provisions which a person commits by virtue of any provision or requirement to which he is subject as the designer, manufacturer, importer or supplier of any thing; and in that subsection "responsible enforcing authority" means an enforcing authority within whose field of responsibility the offence in question lies, whether by virtue of section 35 or otherwise.

(5)–(6) *Scotland.*
[Health and Safety at Work etc Act 1974, s 34 amended by the Gas Act 1986, Sch 7.]

8–15328 35. Venue. An offence under any of the relevant statutory provisions committed in connection with any plant or substance may, if necessary for the purpose of bringing the offence within the field of responsibility of any enforcing authority or conferring jurisdiction on any court to entertain proceedings for the offence, be treated as having been committed at the place where that plant or substance is for the time being.
[Health and Safety at Work etc Act 1974, s 35.]

8–15329 36. Offences due to fault of other person. (1) Where the commission by any person of an offence under any of the relevant statutory provisions is due to the act or default of some other person, that other person shall be guilty of the offence, and a person may be charged with and convicted of the offence by virtue of this subsection whether or not proceedings are taken against the first-mentioned person.

(2) Where there would be or have been the commission of an offence under section 33 by the Crown but for the circumstances that that section does not bind the Crown, and that fact is due to the act or default of a person other than the Crown, that person shall be guilty of the offence which, but for that circumstance, the Crown would be committing or would have committed, and may be charged with and convicted of that offence accordingly.

(3) The preceding provisions of this section are subject to any provision made by virtue of section 15(6).
[Health and Safety at Work etc Act 1974, s 36.]

8–15330 37. Offences by bodies corporate. (1) Where an offence under any of the relevant statutory provisions committed by a body corporate is proved to have been committed with the consent or connivance of, or to have been attributable to any neglect on the part of, any director, manager, secretary or other similar officer of the body corporate or a person who was purporting to act in any such capacity, he as well as the body corporate shall be guilty of that offence and shall be liable to be proceeded against and punished accordingly.

(2) Where the affairs of a body corporate are managed by its members, the preceding subsection shall apply in relation to the acts and defaults of a member in connection with his functions of management as if he were a director of the body corporate.
[Health and Safety at Work etc Act 1974, s 37.]

8–15331 38. Restriction on institution of proceedings in England and Wales. Proceedings for an offence under any of the relevant statutory provisions shall not, in England and Wales, be instituted[1] except by an inspector or the Environment Agency or by or with the consent of the Director of Public Prosecutions.
[Health and Safety at Work etc Act 1974, s 38 as amended by the Environment Act 1995, Sch 22.]

---

1. The power of an inspector to institute proceedings under this section cannot be delegated (*R v Croydon Justices, ex p W H Smith Ltd* (2000) Times, 22 November, DC).

8–15332 39. Prosecutions by inspectors. (1) An inspector, if authorised in that behalf by the enforcing authority which appointed him, may, although not of counsel or a solicitor, prosecute before a magistrates' court proceedings for an offence under any of the relevant statutory provisions.

(2) *Scotland.*
[Health and Safety at Work etc Act 1974, s 39.]

8–15333 40. Onus of proving limits of what is practicable etc. In any proceedings for an offence under any of the relevant statutory provisions consisting of a failure to comply with a duty or requirement to do something so far as is practicable or so far as is reasonably practicable, or to use the best practicable means to do something, it shall be for the accused to prove[1] (as the case may be) that it was not practicable or not reasonably practicable to do more than was in fact done to satisfy the duty or requirement, or that there was no better practicable means than was in fact used to satisfy the duty or requirement.
[Health and Safety at Work etc Act 1974, s 40.]

---

1. The language of s 40 clearly imposes a legal (ie persuasive) burden on the defendant; and interference with the presumption of innocence resulting from this burden is justified, necessary and proportionate (*R v Davies* [2002] EWCA Crim 2949, [2002] All ER (D) 275 (Dec), [2003] JPN 42).

8–15334 41. Evidence. (1) Where an entry is required by any of the relevant statutory provisions to be made in any register or other record, the entry, if made, shall, as against the person by or on whose behalf it was made, be admissible as evidence or in Scotland sufficient evidence of the facts stated therein.

(2) Where an entry which is so required to be so made with respect to the observance of any of

the relevant statutory provisions has not been made, that fact shall be admissible as evidence or in Scotland sufficient evidence that that provision has not been observed.

[Health and Safety at Work etc Act 1974, s 41.]

8–15335 42. Power of court to order cause of offence to be remedied or, in certain cases, forfeiture. (1) Where a person is convicted of an offence under any of the relevant statutory provisions in respect of any matters which appear to the court to be matters which it is in his power to remedy, the court may, in addition to or instead of imposing any punishment, order him, within such time as may be fixed by the order, to take such steps as may be specified in the order for remedying the said matters.

(2) The time fixed by an order under subsection (1) above may be extended or further extended by order of the court on an application made before the end of that time as originally fixed or as extended under this subsection, as the case may be.

(3) Where a person is ordered under subsection (1) above to remedy any matters, that person shall not be liable under any of the relevant statutory provisions in respect of those matters in so far as they continue during the time fixed by the order or any further time allowed under subsection (2) above.

(4) Subject to the following subsection, the court by or before which a person is convicted of an offence such as is mentioned in section 33(4)(*c*) in respect of any such explosive article or substance as is there mentioned may order the article or substance in question to be forfeited and either destroyed or dealt with in such other manner as the court may order.

(5) The court shall not order anything to be forfeited under the preceding subsection where a person claiming to be the owner of or otherwise interested in it applies to be heard by the court, unless an opportunity has been given to him to show cause why the order should not be made.

[Health and Safety at Work etc Act 1974, s 42.]

8–15336 46. Service of notices. (1) Any notice required or authorised by any of the relevant statutory provisions to be served on him or given to an inspector may be served or given by delivering it to him or by leaving it at, or sending it by post to, his office.

(2) Any such notice required or authorised to be served on or given to a person other than an inspector may be served or given by delivering it to him, or by leaving it at his proper address, or by sending it by post to him at that address.

(3) Any such notice may—

(*a*) in the case of a body corporate, be served on or given to the secretary or clerk of that body;

(*b*) in the case of a partnership, be served on or given to a partner or a person having the control or management of the partnership business or, in Scotland, the firm.

(4) For the purposes of this section and of section 26 of the Interpretation Act 1889[1] (service of documents by post) in its application to this section, the proper address of any person on or to whom any such notice is to be served or given shall be his last known address, except that—

(*a*) in the case of a body corporate or their secretary or clerk, it shall be the address of the registered or principal office of that body;

(*b*) in the case of a partnership or a person having the control or the management of the partnership business, it shall be the principal office of the partnership;

and for the purposes of this subsection the principal office of a company registered outside the United Kingdom or of a partnership carrying on business outside the United Kingdom shall be their principal office within the United Kingdom.

(5) If the person to be served with or given any such notice has specified an address within the United Kingdom other than his proper address within the meaning of subsection (4) above as the one at which he or someone on his behalf will accept notices of the same description as that notice, that address shall also be treated for the purposes of this section and section 26 of the Interpretation Act 1889 as his proper address.

(6) Without prejudice to any other provision of this section, any such notice required or authorised to be served on or given to the owner or occupier[2] of any premises (whether a body corporate or not) may be served or given by sending it by post to him at those premises, or by addressing it by name to the person on or to whom it is to be served or given and delivering it to some responsible person who is or appears to be resident or employed in the premises.

(7) If the name or the address of any owner or occupier of premises on or to whom any such notice as aforesaid is to be served or given cannot after reasonable inquiry be ascertained, the notice may be served or given by addressing it to the person on or to whom it is to be served or given by the description of "owner" or "occupier" of the premises (describing them) to which the notice relates, and by delivering it to some responsible person who is or appears to be resident or employed in the premises, or, if there is no such person to whom it can be delivered, by affixing it or a copy of it to some conspicuous part of the premises.

(8) The preceding provisions of this section shall apply to the sending or giving of a document as they apply to the giving of a notice.

[Health and Safety at Work etc Act 1974, s 46.]

1. Now s 7 of the Interpretation Act 1978, in Part II: Evidence, ante.

2. This provision does not authorise service of a notice on a person or company *as employer;* see *Health and Safety Executive v George Tancocks Garage (Exeter) Ltd* [1993] Crim LR 605.

8–15337 48. Application to Crown. (1) Subject to the provisions of this section, the provisions of this Part, except sections 21 to 25 and 33 to 42, and of regulations made under this Part of this Act shall bind the Crown.

(2) Although they do not bind the Crown, sections 33 to 42 shall apply to persons in the public service of the Crown as they apply to other persons.

(3) For the purposes of this Part and regulations made thereunder persons in the service of the Crown shall be treated as employees of the Crown whether or not they would be so treated apart from this subsection.

(4) Without prejudice to section 15(5), the Secretary of State may, to the extent that it appears to him requisite or expedient to do so in the interests of the safety of the State or the safe custody of persons lawfully detained, by order exempt the Crown either generally or in particular respects from all or any of the provisions of this Part which would, by virtue of subsection (1) above, bind the Crown.

(5) The power to make orders under this section shall be exercisable by statutory instrument, and any such order may be varied or revoked by a subsequent order.

(6) Nothing in this section shall authorise proceedings to be brought against Her Majesty in her private capacity, and this subsection shall be construed as if section 38(3) of the Crown Proceedings Act 1947 (interpretation of references in that Act to Her Majesty in her private capacity) were contained in this Act.

[Health and Safety at Work etc Act 1974, s 48.]

8–15338 51. Exclusion of application to domestic employment. Nothing in this Part shall apply in relation to a person by reason only that he employs another, or is himself employed as a domestic servant in a private household.

[Health and Safety at Work etc Act 1974, s 51.]

8–15338A 51A. Application of Part to police. (1) For the purposes of this Part, a person who, otherwise than under a contract of employment, holds the office of constable or an appointment as police cadet shall be treated as an employee of the relevant officer.

(2) In this section "the relevant officer"—

(a) in relation to a member of a police force or a special constable or police cadet appointed for a police area, means the chief officer of police,

(b) in relation to a member of a police force seconded to the Serious Organised Crime Agency to serve as a member of its staff, means that Agency, and

(c) in relation to any other person holding the office of constable or an appointment as police cadet, means the person who has the direction and control of the body of constables or cadets in question.*

(2A) For the purposes of this Part the relevant officer, as defined by subsection (2)(a) or (c) above, shall be treated as a corporation sole.

(2B) Where, in a case in which the relevant officer, as so defined, is guilty of an offence by virtue of this section, it is proved—

(a) that the officer-holder personally consented to the commission of the offence,

(b) that he personally connived in its commission, or

(c) that the commission of the offence was attributable to personal neglect on his part,

the office-holder (as well as the corporation sole) shall be guilty of the offence and shall be liable to be proceeded against and punished accordingly.

(2C) In subsection (2B) above "the office-holder", in relation to the relevant officer, means an individual who, at the time of the consent, connivance or neglect—

(a) held the office or other position mentioned in subsection (2) above as the office or position of that officer; or

(b) was for the time being responsible for exercising and performing the powers and duties of that office or position.

(2D) The provisions mentioned in subsection (2E) below (which impose the same liability for unlawful conduct of constables on persons having their direction or control as would arise if the constables were employees of those persons) do not apply to any liability by virtue of this Part.

(2E) Those provisions are—

(a) section 39 of the Police (Scotland) Act 1967;

(b) section 88(1) of the Police Act 1996;

(c) section 97(9) of that Act;

(d) paragraph 7(1) of Schedule 8 to the Police Act 1997;

(e) paragraph 14(1) of Schedule 3 to the Criminal Justice and Police Act 2001;

(*f*)   section 28 of the Serious Organised Crime and Police Act 2005.

(2F) In the application of this section to Scotland—

(*a*)   subsection (2A) shall have effect as if for the words "corporation sole" there were substituted "distinct juristic person (that is to say, as a juristic person distinct from the individual who for the time being is the office-holder)";

(*b*)   subsection (2B) shall have effect as if for the words "corporation sole" there were substituted "juristic person"; and

(*c*)   subsection (2C) shall have effect as if for the words "subsection (2B)" there were substituted "subsections (2A) and (2B)".

(3) For the purposes of regulations under section 2(4) above—

(*a*)   the Police Federation for England and Wales shall be treated as a recognised trade union recognised by each chief officer of police★ in England and Wales,

(*b*)   the Police Federation for Scotland shall be treated as a recognised trade union recognised by each chief officer of police★ in Scotland, and

(*c*)   any body recognised by the Secretary of State for the purposes of section 64 of the Police Act 1996 shall be treated as a recognised trade union recognised by each chief officer of police★ in England, Wales and Scotland.

(4) Regulations under section 2(4) above may provide, in relation to persons falling within subsection (2)(*b*) or (*c*)★ above, that a body specified in the regulations is to be treated as a recognised trade union recognised by such person as may be specified.
[Health and Safety at Work etc Act 1974, s 51A as inserted by the Police (Health and Safety) Act 1997, s 1 and amended by the Serious Organised Crime and Police Act 2005, s 158.]

★Sub-sections (1), (3) and (4), words underlined repealed and substituted by the Police Reform Act 2002, s 95, from a date to be appointed.

8–15339   52. Meaning of work and at work[1].   (1) For the purposes of this Part—

(*a*)   "work" means work as an employee or as a self-employed person;

(*b*)   an employee is at work throughout the time when he is in the course of his employment, but not otherwise;

(*bb*) a person holding the office of constable is at work throughout the time when he is on duty but not otherwise; and

(*c*)   a self-employed person is at work throughout such time as he devotes to work as a self-employed person;

and, subject to the following subsection, the expression "work" and "at work", in whatever context, shall be construed accordingly.

(2) Regulations made under this subsection may—

(*a*)   extend the meaning of "work" and "at work" for the purposes of this Part; and

(*b*)   in that connection provide for any of the relevant statutory provisions to have effect subject to such adaptations as may be specified in the regulations.

(3) The power to make regulations under subsection (2) above shall be exercisable by the Secretary of State.
[Health and Safety at Work etc Act 1974, s 52 as amended by the Employment Protection Act 1975, Sch 15, the Police (Health and Safety) Act 1997, s 2 and SI 2002/794.]

---

1. The meaning of "work" and "at work" has been extended by the Health and Safety (Training for Employment) Regulations 1990, SI 1990/1380 to include certain trainees.

8–15350   53. General interpretation of Part I.   (1) In this Part, unless the context otherwise requires—

"article for use at work" means—

(*a*)   any plant designed for use or operation (whether exclusively or not) by persons at work, and

(*b*)   any article designed for use as a component in any such plant;

"article of fairground equipment" means any fairground equipment or any article designed for use as a component in any such equipment;

"code of practice" (without prejudice to section 16(8)) includes a standard, a specification and any other documentary form of practical guidance;

"the Commission" has the meaning assigned by section 10(2);

"conditional sale agreement" means an agreement for the sale of goods under which the purchase price or part of it is payable by instalments, and the property in the goods is to remain in the seller (notwithstanding that the buyer is to be in possession of the goods) until such conditions as to the payment of instalments or otherwise as may be specified in the agreement are fulfilled;

"contract of employment" means a contract of employment or apprenticeship (whether express or implied and, if express, whether oral or in writing);

"credit-sale agreement" means an agreement for the sale of goods, under which the purchase price or part of it is payable by instalments, but which is not a conditional sale agreement;

"customs officer" means an officer within the meaning of the Customs and Excise Management Act 1979;

"domestic premises" means premises occupied as a private dwelling (including any garden, yard, garage, outhouse or other appurtenance of such premises which is not used in common by the occupants of more than one such dwelling), and "non-domestic premises" shall be construed accordingly;

"employee" means an individual who works under a contract of employment or is treated by section 51A as being an employee, and related expressions shall be construed accordingly;

"enforcing authority" has the meaning assigned by section 18(7);

"the Executive" has the meaning assigned by section 10(5);

"the existing statutory provisions" means the following provisions while and to the extent that they remain in force, namely the provisions of the Acts mentioned in Schedule 1 which are specified in the third column of that Schedule and of the regulations, orders or other instruments of a legislative character made or having effect under any provision so specified;

"fairground equipment" means any fairground ride, any similar plant which is designed to be in motion for entertainment purposes with members of the public on or inside it or any plant which is designed to be used by members of the public for entertainment purposes either as a slide or for bouncing upon, and in this definition the reference to plant which is designed to be in motion with members of the public on or inside it includes a reference to swings, dodgems and other plant which is designed to be in motion wholly or partly under the control of, or to be put in motion by, a member of the public;

"the general purposes of this Part" has the meaning assigned by section 1;

"health and safety regulations" has the meaning assigned by section 15 (1);

"hire-purchase agreement" means an agreement other than a conditional sale agreement, under which—

(a) goods are bailed or (in Scotland) hired in return for periodical payments by the person to whom they are bailed or hired; and

(b) the property in the goods will pass to that person if the terms of the agreement are complied with and one or more of the following occurs:

(i) the exercise of an option to purchase by that person;
(ii) the doing of any other specified act by any party to the agreement;
(iii) the happening of any other event;

and "hire-purchase" shall be construed accordingly;

"improvement notice" means a notice under section 21;

"inspector" means an inspector appointed under section 19;

"local authority" means—

(a) in relation to England, a county council, a district council, a London borough council, the Common Council of the City of London, the Sub-Treasurer of the Inner Temple or the Under-Treasurer of the Middle Temple,

(aa) in relation to Wales, a county council or a county borough council,

(b) in relation to Scotland, a regional, islands or district council except that before 16th May 1975 it means a town council or county council;

"micro-organism" includes any microscopic entity which is capable of replication;

"offshore installation" means any installation which is intended for underwater exploitation of mineral resources or exploration with a view to such exploitation;

"personal injury" includes any disease and any impairment of a person's physical or mental condition;

"plant" includes any machinery, equipment or appliance;

"premises" includes any place and, in particular, includes—

(a) any vehicle, vessel, aircraft or hovercraft,

(b) any installation on land (including the foreshore and other land intermittently covered by water), any offshore installation, and any other installation (whether floating, or resting on the seabed or the subsoil thereof, or resting on other land covered with water or the subsoil thereof), and

(c) any tent or movable structure;

"prescribed" means prescribed by regulations made by the Secretary of State;

"prohibition notice" means a notice under section 22;

"the relevant statutory provisions" means—

(a) the provisions of this Part and of any health and safety regulations; and

(b) the existing statutory provisions;

"self-employed person" means an individual who works for gain or reward otherwise than under a contract of employment, whether or not he himself employs others;

"substance" means any natural or artificial substance (including micro-organisms), whether in solid or liquid form or in the form of a gas or vapour;

"substance for use at work" means any substance intended for use (whether exclusively or not) by persons at work;

"supply", where the reference is to supplying articles or substances, means supplying them by way of sale, lease, hire or hire-purchase, whether as principal or agent for another.

[Health and Safety at Work etc Act 1974, s 53 as amended by the Employment Protection Act 1975, Sch 15, the Local Government Act 1985, Sch 17, the Consumer Protection Act 1987 Schs 3 and 5, the Local Government (Wales) Act 1994, Sch 9 and the Police (Health and Safety) Act 1997, s 6.]

PART III
BUILDING REGULATIONS

8–15351   82. General provisions as to interpretation and regulations. (1) In this Act—

(a) "Act" includes a provisional order confirmed by an Act;
(b) "contravention" includes failure to comply, and "contravene" has a corresponding meaning;
(c) "modifications" includes additions, omissions and amendments, and related expressions shall be construed accordingly;
(d) any reference to a Part, section or Schedule not otherwise identified is a reference to that Part or section of, or Schedule to, this Act.

(2) Except in so far as the context otherwise requires, any reference in this Act to an enactment is a reference to it as amended, and includes a reference to it as applied, by or under any other enactment, including this Act.

(3), (4) *Power to make regulations.*
[Health and Safety at Work etc Act 1974, s 82, as amended by the Railways and Transport Safety Act 2003, s 105.]

8–15352   84. *Extent, and application of Act*[1].

---

1. The Health and Safety at Work Etc Act 1974 (Application Outside Great Britain) Order 2001 deals with the application of the act to off-shore installations and pipe-lines and is contained in this title, post; see however the Offshore Safety Act 1992.

8–15353

Sections 1 and 53

SCHEDULE 1[1]
EXISTING ENACTMENTS WHICH ARE RELEVANT STATUTORY PROVISIONS

(*As amended by the Sex Discrimination Act 1987, s 7, the Atomic Energy Act 1989, s 6 and SI 2005/228.*)

Chapter	Short title	Provisions which are relevant statutory provisions
1875 c 17	The Explosives Act 1875	The whole Act except sections 30 to 32, 80 and* 116 to 121.
1882 c 22	The Boiler Explosions Act 1882	The whole Act.
1890 c 35	The Boiler Explosions Act 1890	The whole Act.
1906 c 14	The Alkali, &c Works Regulation Act 1906	The whole Act.
1909 c 43	The Revenue Act 1909	Section 11.
1920 c 65	The Employment of Women, Young Persons and Children Act 1920	The whole Act.
1922 c 35	The Celluloid and Cinematograph Film Act 1922	The whole Act.
1923 c 17	The Explosives Act 1923	The whole Act.
1926 c 43	The Public Health (Smoke Abatement) Act 1926	The whole Act.
1928 c 32	The Petroleum (Consolidation) Act 1928	The whole Act.
1936 c 22	The Hours of Employment (Conventions) Act 1936	The whole Act except section 5.
1936 c 27	The Petroleum (Transfer of Licences) Act 1936	The whole Act.
1937 c 45	The Hydrogen Cyanide (Fumigation) Act 1937	The whole Act.
1945 c 19	The Ministry of Fuel and Power Act 1945	Section 1(1) so far as it relates to maintaining and improving the safety, health and welfare of persons employed in or about mines and quarries in Great Britain.
1946 c 59	The Coal Industry Nationalisation Act 1946	Section 42(1) and (2).

Chapter	Short title	Provisions which are relevant statutory provisions
1948 c 37	The Radioactive Substances Act 1948	Section 5(1)(a).
1951 c 58	The Fireworks Act 1951	Sections 4 and 7.
1952 c 60	The Agriculture (Poisonous Substances) Act 1952	The whole Act.
1953 c 47	The Emergency Laws (Miscellaneous Provisions) Act 1953	Section 3.
1954 c 70	The Mines and Quarries Act 1954	The whole Act except section 151.
1956 c 49	The Agriculture (Safety, Health and Welfare Provisions) Act 1956	The whole Act.
1961 c 34	The Factories Act 1961	The whole Act except section 135.
1961 c 64	The Public Health Act 1961	Section 73.
1962 c 58	The Pipe-lines Act 1962	Sections 20 to 26, 33, 34 and 42, Schedule 5.
1963 c 41	The Offices, Shops and Railway Premises Act 1963	The whole Act.
1965 c 57	The Nuclear Installations Act 1965	Sections 1, 3 to 6, 22 and 24A, Schedule 2.
1969 c 10	The Mines and Quarries (Tips) Act 1969	Sections 1 to 10.
1971 c 20	The Mines Management Act 1971	The whole Act.
1972 c 28	The Employment Medical Advisory Service Act 1972	The whole Act except sections 1 and 6 and Schedule 1.

*Words repealed by the Fireworks Act 2003, Schedule, from a date to be appointed.

1. Further statutory provision is made for Part I of the Health and Safety at Work Act 1974 to apply for health and safety purposes relating to specified activities. The following provision has been made:

> Offshore Safety Act 1992, ss 1 and 2 (offshore installations, pipe-line works and the transmission or use of gas; Railways Act 1993, s 117 (proper construction and safe operation of certain transport systems and vehicles used on such systems, protection of railway employees and general public).
>
> Part I of the 1974 Act is to have effect as if the following enactments were specified in the third column of Sch 1 to the Act, and regulations made or having effect thereunder (or under s 2 of the European Communities Act 1972 for the purpose of implementing Directive 91/440/EEC as far as the regulations relate to safety purposes) were relevant statutory provisions.

Chapter	Short title	Provisions which are relevant statutory provisions
1875 c 45	Highway (Railway Crossings) Act 1839	The whole Act.
1842 c 55	Railway Regulation Act 1842	Sections 9 and 10
1868 c 119	Regulation of Railways Act 1868	Section 22
1871 c 78	Regulation of Railways Act 1871	The whole Act.
1889 c 57	Regulation of Railways Act 1889	Sections 1 and 4
1900 c 27	Railway Employment (Prevention of Accidents) Act 1900	The whole Act.
1933 c 53	Road and Rail Traffic Act 1933	Section 42.
1954 c lv	British Transport Commission Act 1954	Section 40
1975 c xxxiii	British Transport Commission Act 1954	Section 66
1962 c 58	Pipe-lines Act 1962	Sections 27 to 32 and 37
1968 c 73	Transport Act 1968	Sections 124 and 125
1971 c 61	Mineral Workings (Offshore Installations) Act 1971	The whole Act.
1975 c 74	Petroleum and Submarines Pipe-lines Act 1975	Sections 26, 27 and 32
1983 c 16	Level Crossings Act 1983	The whole Act.
1986 c 44	Gas Act 1986	Sections 16 (so far as relating to standards affecting safety) and 47(3) and (4) so far as relating to regulations under section 16 so far as so relating.
1987 c 12	Petroleum Act 1987	Sections 11(2) (a) (so far as relating to safety requirements) and 21 to 24.
1992 c 42	Transport and Works Act 1992	Sections 41 to 45

Safety of Sports Grounds Act 1975[1]

(1975 c 52)

8–15460   1. Safety certificates for large sports stadia.   (1) The Secretary of State may by order[2] designate as a sports ground requiring a certificate under this Act (in this Act referred to as a "safety certificate") any sports ground which in his opinion has accommodation for more than 10,000[3] spectators.

(1A) The Secretary of State may by order substitute for the number for the time being specified in subsection (1) above, such other number as he considers appropriate; but no order made under this subsection shall affect the validity of any designation previously made.

(1B) An order under subsection (1A) above may make different subsections for different classes of sports ground.

(2) The Secretary of State—

(*a*) may estimate, by any means which he considers appropriate, for how many spectators a sports ground has accommodation; and

(*b*) may require any person concerned with the organisation or management of a sports ground to furnish him within such reasonable time as he may specify with such information as he considers necessary for the purpose of making such an estimate.

(3) A safety certificate may be either—

(*a*) a certificate issued by the local authority for the area in which a sports ground situated in respect of the use of the sports ground for an activity or a number of activities specified in the certificate during an indefinite period commencing with a date so specified, or

(*b*) a certificate issued by that authority in respect of the use of the sports ground for an activity or a number of activities specified in the certificate on an occasion or series of occasions so specified.

(4) In this Act—

"designated sports ground" means a sports ground in respect of which a designation order is in operation;

"designation order" means an order under this section;

"general safety certificate" means such a safety certificate as is mentioned in subsection (3)(*a*) above; and

"special safety certificate" means such a safety certificate as is mentioned in subsection (3)(*b*) above.

[Safety of Sports Grounds Act 1975, s 1, as amended by the Fire Safety and Safety of Places of Sport Act 1987, ss 19 and 20 and Sch 2.]

---

1. The Fire Safety and Safety of Places of Sport Act 1987, Pt III, ss 26–41, this title, post, introduces a system of certification, similar to that which applies under this Act to designated sports grounds, for stands at undesignated grounds where there is covered accommodation for 500 or more spectators.

2. Numerous designation orders have been made.

3. The number 5,000 is substituted as the specified number of spectators for sports grounds at which association football matches are played and which are occupied by a club which is a member of the Football League Limited or the Football Association Premier League Limited. The number specified for all other classes of sports grounds remains 10,000: Safety of Sports Grounds (Accommodation of Spectators) Order 1996, SI 1996/499.

8–15461 2. Contents of safety certificates. (1) A safety certificate shall contain such terms and conditions as the local authority consider necessary or expedient to secure reasonable safety at the sports ground when it is in use for the specified activity or activities, and the terms and conditions may be such as to involve alterations or additions to the sports ground.

(2) In so far as an order under section 15A below so requires as respects any class of sports ground, a safety certificate shall include such terms and conditions as may be provided for in the order.

(2A) No condition of a safety certificate shall require the provision of the services at the ground of any members of a police force unless the extent of the provision of their services is reserved for the determination of the chief officer of police of the force.

(2B) No condition of a safety certificate shall require a person to contravene any provison of the Regulatory Reform (Fire Safety) Order 2005 or regulations made under it.[1]

(3) Without prejudice to subsection (1) above, a safety certificate may include a condition that the following records shall be kept—

(*a*) records of the attendance of spectators at the sports ground; and

(*b*) records relating to the maintenance of safety at the sports ground.

(4) A general safety certificate shall contain or have attached to it a plan of the sports ground, and the terms and conditions in the certificate, or in any special safety certificate issued for the sports ground, shall be framed, where appropriate, by reference to that plan.

(5) A safety certificate may include different terms and conditions in relation to different activities.

(6) Nothing in a safety certificate shall derogate from any requirements imposed by regulations under section 6(2) below.

[Safety of Sports Grounds Act 1975, s 2, as amended by the Fire Safety and Safety of Places of Sport Act 1987, ss 19 and 21 and Sch 2 and SI 2005/1541.]

---

1. Subsection (2B) in force in relation to England and Wales from 1 April 2006.

8–15462 3. Applications for certificates. (1) If a local authority receive an application for a safety certificate for a designated sports ground in their area, it shall be their duty to determine whether the applicant is a person likely to be in a position to prevent contravention of the terms and conditions of a certificate; and such a person is referred to in this Act as a "qualified person".

(2) If a local authority determine that an applicant is a qualified person—

    (a) where no general safety certificate for the sports ground is in operation, they shall issue such a certificate for it to him; and

    (b) where a general safety certificate for the sports ground is in operation, they may issue a special safety certificate for it to him.

(3) The local authority shall send a copy of an application for a safety certificate for a sports ground to—

    (a) the chief officer of police, and

    (b) if the local authority are not the fire and rescue authority, the fire and rescue authority, and

    (c) if the local authority are not the building authority, the building authority,

for the area in which the sports ground is situated, and shall consult them about the terms and conditions to be included in the certificate.

(4) The local authority may by notice in writing require an applicant for a safety certificate to furnish them within such reasonable time as they may specify in the notice with such information and such plans as they consider necessary to enable them to determine the terms and conditions which ought to be included in any certificate issued in response to his application.

(5) If an applicant for a safety certificate fails to comply with a requirement under subsection (4) above within the time specified by the local authority, or within such further time as they may allow, he shall be deemed to have withdrawn his application.

[Safety of Sports Grounds Act 1975, s 3, as amended by the Local Government Act 1985, s 16 and Sch 8, the Fire Safety and Safety of Places of Sport Act 1987, Sch 2, the Local Government (Wales) Act 1994, Sch 16 and the Fire and Rescue Services Act 2004, Sch 1 and the Fire and Rescue Services Act 2004, Sch 1.]

8–15463 4. Amendment etc of certificates. (1) The local authority may, in any case in which it appears appropriate to them to do so—

    (a) amend a safety certificate by notice in writing to its holder; or

    (b) replace a safety certificate

(1A) The local authority shall, if it appears to them that a safety certificate would require a person to contravene any provision of the Regulatory Reform (Fire Safety) Order 2005 or regulations made under it, amend the safety certificate by notice in writing to its holder; but nothing in this subsection shall be taken to require the local authority to take any action unless they are aware of any such inconsistency between a safety certificate and the Order.

(2) A safety certificate may be amended or replaced either on the application of the holder or without such an application.

(3) Section 2 above shall apply on the amendment or replacement of a safety certificate.

(4) A notice under subsection (1)(a) or (1A)[1] above amending a general safety certificate shall specify the date on which the amendment to which it relates is to come into operation, and the date so specified may be a date later than the date of issue of the notice.

(5) If the local authority receive an application for the transfer of a safety certificate from the holder to some other person, it shall be their duty to determine whether that person is a qualified person; and if they so determine, they may transfer the certificate to him.

(6) An application under subsection (5) above may be made either by the holder of a safety certificate or by a person to whom it is proposed that it should be transferred.

(7) The local authority shall send a copy of an application for the transfer of a safety certificate for a sports ground to—

    (a) the chief officer of police, and

    (b) if the local authority are not the fire and rescue authority, the fire and rescue authority, and

    (c) if the local authority are not the building authority, the building authority,

for the area in which the sports ground is situated.

(8) The local authority shall consult—

    (a) the chief officer of police, and

    (b) if the local authority are not the fire and rescue authority, the fire and rescue authority, and

    (c) if the local authority are not the building authority, the building authority,

about any proposal to amend, replace or transfer a safety certificate.

(9) The holder of a safety certificate may surrender it to the local authority, and it shall thereupon cease to have effect.

(10) The local authority may cancel a safety certificate if the holder dies or (if a body corporate) is dissolved.

[Safety of Sports Grounds Act 1975, s 4, as amended by the Local Government Act 1985, s 16 and Sch 8, the Fire Safety and Safety of Places of Sport Act 1987, Sch 2, the Local Government (Wales) Act 1994, Sch 16 and the Fire and Rescue Services Act 2004, Sch 1 ans SI 2005/1541.]

8–15463A 4A. Safety certificates: fire safety. A sfaety certificate has no effect to the extent that it would require a person to contravene any provision of the Regulatory Reform (Fire Safety) Order 2005 or regulations made under it.

[Safety of Sports Grounds Act 1975, s 4A, as inserted by SI 2005/1541.]

8–15464   5. Appeals.   (1) A local authority shall serve on a person whom they determine not be a qualified person notice in writing of their determination, and a person on whom such a notice is served may appeal against the determination to the court.

(2) An applicant for a special safety certificate may also appeal to the court against a refusal of his application on grounds other than a determination that he is not a qualified person.

(3) An interested party may appeal to the court against—

(*i*)   the inclusion of anything in, or the omission of anything from, a safety certificate; or
(*ii*)   the refusal of the local authority to amend or replace a safety certificate.*

(3A) An appeal to the court under this section in England and Wales shall be by way of complaint for an order, the making of the complaint shall be deemed to be the bringing of the appeal and the Magistrates' Courts Act 1980 shall apply to the proceedings.

(3B) *Scotland.*

(3C) In England and Wales any of the following persons may appeal to the Crown Court against an order under this section, namely—

(*a*)   the local authority; and
(*b*)   any interested party.

(3D) *Scotland.*

(4) *Repealed.*

(5) In this section "interested party" includes—

(*a*)   the holder of a safety certificate;
(*b*)   any other person who is or may be concerned in ensuring compliance with the terms and conditions of a safety certificate;
(*c*)   the chief officer of police; and
(*d*)   if the local authority are not the fire and rescue authority, the fire and rescue authority; and
(*e*)   if the local authority are not the building authority, the building authority.

(6)–(8) *Repealed.*

[Safety of Sports Grounds Act 1975, s 5, as amended by the Local Government Act 1985, s 16 and Sch 8, the Fire Safety and Safety of Places of Sport Act 1987, s 22 and Sch 4, the Local Government (Wales) Act 1994, Sch 16 and the Fire and Rescue Services Act 2004, Sch 1.]

---

*Amended by the Football Spectators Act 1989, s13(8), post, when in force.

8–15465   6. Regulations.   (1) The Secretary of State may by regulations[1]—

(*a*)   prescribe the procedure (subject to the provisions of this Act) for the issue, amendment, replacement, transfer and cancellation of safety certificates and the particulars to be given in applications for their issue, amendment, replacement or transfer;
(*b*)   authorise local authorities to determine, subject to such limits or in accordance with such provisions as may be prescribed by the regulations, the fees (if any) to be charged in respect of such applications; and
(*c*)   prescribe the time within which appeals under section 5 above are to be brought.

(2) The Secretary of State may by regulations make provision for securing safety at sports grounds.

(3) Regulations under subsection (2) above may provide, without prejudice to its generality, that the following records shall be kept—

(*a*)   records of the attendance of spectators at sports grounds; and
(*b*)   records relating to the maintenance of safety at sports grounds.

(4) Regulations under this section may contain such incidental and supplementary provisions as the Secretary of State thinks expedient.

[Safety of Sports Grounds Act 1975, s 6, as amended by the Fire Safety and Safety of Places of Sport Act 1987, s 22.]

---

1. See the Safety of Sports Grounds Regulations 1987, SI 1987/1941 amended by SI 2004/3168 (E) and SI 2005/2929 (W).

8–15466   7. Determinations and appeals—supplementary.   (1) Subject to subsection (2) below, if a local authority serve a notice under section 5(1) above on any applicant for a safety certificate, he shall be deemed to have withdrawn his application on the expiry of the period within which, by virtue of regulations under section 6 above an appeal against the authority's determination may be brought.

(2) Subsection (1) above shall not have effect if an appeal is brought before the expiry of the period there mentioned, but if the appeal is withdrawn or the court upholds the authority's determination, the appellant shall be deemed to have withdrawn his application on the date of the withdrawal of his appeal or of the court's determination.

(3) Where an appeal is brought against the inclusion of any term or condition in a safety certificate

(whether it was included in the certificate originally or only on its amendment or replacement), the operation of that term or condition shall be suspended until the court has determined the appeal.

(4)–(5) *Repealed.*

[Safety of Sports Grounds 1975, s 7, as amended by the Fire Safety and Safety of Places of Sport Act 1987, s 22 and Sch 4.]

8–15467 8. Alterations and extensions. (1) If while a general safety certificate is in operation with respect to a sports ground it is proposed to alter or extend that sports ground or any of its installations, and the alteration or extension is likely to affect the safety of persons at the sports ground, the holder of the certificate shall, before the carrying out of the proposals is begun, give notice of the proposals to the local authority.

(2) Subsection (1) above in particular requires notice when it is proposed to alter the entrances to or exits from a sports ground or any part of it (including any means of escape in case of fire or other emergency) or the means of access to any such entrances or exists.

[Safety of Sports Grounds Act 1975, s 8, as amended by the Fire Safety and Safety of Places of Sport Act 1987, Sch 2.]

8–15468 9. Exclusion of other statutory requirements. (1) While a general safety certificate is in force in relation to a sports ground, the following provisions shall not apply to it, that is to say—

(a) section 37(1) of the Public Health Acts Amendment Act 1890 (platform for public occasions);
(b) *applies to Scotland only*;
(c) section 24 of the Building Act 1984 (exits, entrances, etc in the case of certain public and other buildings);
(d) *repealed*
(e) any provision of a local Act in so far as it relates to any matter in relation to which requirements are imposed by the terms and conditions of the safety certificate.★

(2) Where any enactment provides for the licensing of premises of any class or description and the authority responsible for licences thereunder is required or authorised to impose terms, conditions or restrictions in connection with such licences, then, so long as there is in operation with respect to the premises a safety certificate covering the use of the premises by reason of which a licence under that enactment is required, any term, condition or restriction imposed with respect to those premises in connection with any licence under that enactment shall be of no effect in so far as it relates to any matter in relation to which requirements are imposed by the terms and conditions of that certificate.

(3) A person required by or under a local Act to do anything that would involve a contravention of the terms or conditions of a safety certificate shall not be treated as having contravened that Act if he fails to do it.

[Safety of Sports Grounds Act 1975, s 9, as amended by the Building Act 1984, s 133 and Sch 6, the Fire Safety and Safety of Places of Sports Act 1987, Sch 2 and SI 2055/1541.]

★Reproduced as in force in relation to England and Wales.

8–15469 10. Special procedure in case of serious risk: prohibition notices. (1) If the local authority are of the opinion that the admission of spectators to a sports ground or any part of a sports ground involves or will involve a risk to them so serious that, until steps have been taken to reduce it to a reasonable level, admission of spectators to the ground or that part of the ground ought to be prohibited or restricted, the authority may serve a notice (in this Act referred to as a "prohibition notice") on such persons as are specified in subsection (6) below.

(2) A prohibition notice shall—

(a) state that the local authority are of that opinion;
(b) specify the matters which in their opinion give or, as the case may be, will give rise to that risk; and
(c) direct that no, or no more than a specified number of, spectators shall be admitted to, or to a specified part of, the sports ground until the specified matters have been remedied.

(3) A prohibition notice may prohibit or restrict the admission of spectators generally or on a specified occasion.

(4) A prohibition notice may include directions as to the steps which will have to be taken to reduce the risk to a reasonable level and these may require alterations or additions to the ground or things to be done or omitted which would contravene the terms or conditions of a safety certificate for the ground or for any stand at the ground.

(5) No prohibition notice shall include directions compliance with which would require the provision of the services at the sports ground of any members of a police force unless the chief officer of police of the force has consented to their inclusion and the extent of the provision of their services is reserved for his determination.

(6) A prohibition notice shall be served on the persons specified in the following paragraphs in the circumstances specified in those paragraphs, that is to say—

(a) if a general safety certificate is in operation for the ground, on the holder of it;

(b) if the prohibition or restriction applies to an occasion in respect of which a special safety certificate for the ground is in operation, on the holder of it;

(c) if no safety certificate is in operation for the ground, on the person who appears to the local authority to be responsible for the management of the ground;

(d) if the prohibition or restriction applies to an occasion and no safety certificate is in operation for the ground, on each person who appears to the local authority to be responsible for organising an activity at the ground on that occasion;

(e) if a general safety certificate is in operation for a stand at the ground, on the holder of it;

(f) if the prohibition or restriction applies to an occasion in respect of which a special safety certificate for a stand at the ground is in operation, on the holder of it;

but the validity of a prohibition notice served on any person under any of the foregoing provisions shall not be affected by a failure to serve another person required to be served with such a notice under those provisions.

(7) A prohibition or restriction contained in a prohibition notice shall take effect immediately it is served if the authority are of the opinion, and so state in the notice, that the risk to spectators is or, as the case may be, will be imminent, and in any other case shall take effect at the end of a period specified in the notice.

(8) A copy of any prohibition notice shall be sent by the local authority to each of the following, namely—

(a) the chief officer of police; and

(b) if the local authority are not the fire and rescue authority, the fire and rescue authority; and

(c) if the local authority are not the building authority, the building authority.

(9) The local authority who have served a prohibition notice may, in any case where it appears appropriate to them to do so, amend the prohibition notice by notice served on the persons specified in subsection (6) above (subject to the saving in that subsection), and copies shall be sent to the officer and authorities specified in subsection (8) above.

(10) A notice under subsection (9) above amending a prohibition notice shall specify the date on which the amendment is to come into operation.

(11) Where a notice has been served under subsection (1) or (9) above the local authority may withdraw the notice at any time.

[Safety of Sports Grounds Act 1975, s 10, as substituted by the Fire Safety and Safety of Places of Sport Act 1987, s 23 and amended by the Local Government (Wales) Act 1994, Sch 16 and the Fire and Rescue Services Act 2004, Sch 1.]

8–15470 10A. Appeals against prohibition notices.   (1) Any person aggrieved by a prohibition notice may appeal to the court against the notice if he does so within such period as the Secretary of State may by regulations prescribe.

(2) Subsection (1) above applies to any amendment of a prohibition notice as it applies to the prohibition notice in its original form.

(3) An appeal to the court under this section in England and Wales shall be by way of complaint for an order, the making of the complaint shall be deemed to be the bringing of the appeal and the Magistrates' Courts Act 1980 shall apply to the proceedings.

(4) *Scotland.*

(5) On an appeal under subsection (1) above, the court may either cancel or affirm the notice or, in the case of an appeal against an amendment, annul or affirm the amendment and, if it affirms the notice or the notice as amended, as the case may be, may do so either in its original form or as amended, as the case may be, or with such modifications of the notice as the court may in the circumstances think fit.

(6) Where an appeal is brought under this section against a prohibition notice or an amendment of it, the bringing of the appeal shall not have the effect of suspending the operation of the notice or the notice as amended, as the case may be.

(7) In England and Wales any of the following persons may appeal to the Crown Court against an order under this section, namely—

(a) any person aggrieved by the notice;

(b) the local authority;

(c) the chief officer of police; and

(d) if the local authority are not the fire and rescue authority, the fire and rescue authority; and

(e) if the local authority are not the building authority, the building authority.

(8) *Scotland.*

(9) The persons who are, for the purposes of this section "aggrieved" by a prohibition notice are the persons on whom, in accordance with section 10(6) of this Act, the notice is required to be served.

[Safety of Sports Grounds Act 1975, s 10A, as inserted by the Fire Safety and Safety of Places of Sport Act 1987, s 24 and amended by the Local Government (Wales) Act 1994, Sch 16 and the Fire and Rescue Services Act 2004, Sch 1.]

8–15471 10B. Enforcement.   (1) It shall be the duty of every local authority to enforce within their area the provisions of this Act and of regulations made under it and for that purpose to arrange for the periodical inspection of designated sports grounds; but nothing in this subsection shall be taken to authorise a local authority in Scotland to institute proceedings for an offence.

(2) In performing the duty imposed by subsection (1) above so far as it requires designated sports grounds in their areas to be inspected, local authorities shall act in accordance with such guidance as the Secretary of State may give them.

(3) For the purposes of subsection (1) above, "periodical" means at least once in every twelve months.

[Safety of Sports Grounds Act 1975, s 10B, as inserted by the Fire Safety and Safety of Places of Sport Act 1987, s 25.]

8–15472 11. Powers of entry and inspection. A person authorised by—

(*a*) the local authority;

(*b*) the chief officer of police;

(*c*) if the local authority are not the fire and rescue authority, the fire and rescue authority;

(*ca*) if the local authority are not the building authority, the building authority; or

(*d*) the Secretary of State.

may, on production if so required of his authority, enter a sports ground at any reasonable time, and make such inspection of it and such inquiries relating to it as he considers necessary for the purposes of this Act, and in particular may examine records of attendance at the ground and records relating to the maintenance of safety at the ground, and take copies of such records.

[Safety of Sports Grounds Act 1975, s 11, as amended by the Local Government Act 1985, s 16 and Sch 8, the Local Government (Wales) Act 1994, Sch 16 and the Fire and Rescue Services Act 2004, Sch 1.]

8–15473 12. Offences. (1) Subject to subsection (4) below, if—

(*a*) spectators are admitted to a designated sports ground after the date on which the designation order relating to it comes into operation but at a time when no application for a general safety certificate in respect of it has been made or such an application has been made but has been withdrawn, or is deemed to have been withdrawn; or

(*b*) when a general safety certificate is in operation in respect of a sports ground spectators are admitted to the sports ground on an occasion when it is used for an activity to which neither the general safety certificate nor a special safety certificate relates; or

(*c*) spectators are admitted to a designated sports ground on an occasion when, following the surrender or cancellation of a safety certificate, no safety certificate is in operation in respect of that sports ground; or

(*d*) any term or condition of a safety certificate is contravened otherwise than in pursuance of a prohibition notice; or

(*e*) spectators are admitted to a sports ground in contravention of a prohibition notice under section 10 above,

any responsible person and, if a safety certificate is in operation, the holder of the certificate, shall be guilty of an offence.

(2) In subsection (1) above "responsible person" means a person who is concerned in the management of the sports ground in question or the organisation of any activity taking place at the time when an offence is alleged to have been committed.

(3) A person guilty of an offence[1] under subsection (1) above shall be liable—

(*a*) on summary conviction, to a fine of not more than **the statutory maximum**; or

(*b*) on conviction on indictment, to imprisonment for not more than two years or a fine or to both.

(4) Where any person is charged with an offence under subsection (1) above it shall be a defence to prove—

(*a*) that the spectators were admitted or the contravention of the certificate or prohibition notice in question took place without his consent; and

(*b*) that he took all reasonable precautions and exercised all due diligence to avoid the commission of such an offence by himself or any person under his control.

(5) Regulations under section 6(2) above may provide that a breach of the regulations shall be an offence punishable as provided by the regulations, but shall not provide that a person guilty of such an offence shall be liable to punishments greater than those specified in subsection (3) above.

(6) Any person who—

(*a*) without reasonable excuse, refuses, neglects or otherwise fails to comply with a requirement under section 1(2)(*b*) above[2] within the time specified by the Secretary of State; or

(*b*) in purporting to carry out such a requirement, or a requirement under section 3(4) above[3], or for the purpose of procuring a safety certificate or the amendment, replacement or transfer of a safety certificate, knowingly or recklessly makes a false statement or knowingly or recklessly produces, furnishes, signs or otherwise makes use of a document containing a false statement; or

(*c*) fails to give a notice required by section 8(1) above[4]; or (*d*) intentionally obstructs any person in the exercise of powers under section 11 above[5], or without reasonable excuse refuses, neglects or otherwise fails to answer any question asked by any person in the exercise of such powers,

shall be guilty of an offence and liable on summary conviction to a fine not exceeding **level 5** on the standard scale.

(7) Where an offence under this Act which has been committed by a body corporate is proved to have been committed with the consent or connivance of, or to be attributable to any neglect on the part of, a director, manager, secretary or other similar officer of the body corporate, or any person who was purporting to act in any such capacity, he, as well as the body corporate, shall be guilty of that offence and be liable to be proceeded against and punished accordingly.

(8) Where the affairs of a body corporate are managed by its members subsection (7) above shall apply in relation to the acts and defaults of a member in connection with his functions of management as if he were a director of the body corporate.

[Safety of Sports Grounds Act 1975, s 12, as amended by the Criminal Law Act 1977, s 28, the Criminal Justice Act 1982, ss 38 and 46 and the Fire Safety and Safety of Places of Sport Act 1987, ss 23 and 25, and Schs 2 and 4.]

---

1. For procedure in respect of this offence which is triable either way, see the Magistrates' Courts Act 1980, ss 17A–21, in PART I: MAGISTRATES' COURTS, PROCEDURE, ante.

2. A requirement under s 1(2)(*b*) is to furnish information necessary so that an estimate can be made of how many spectators a sports stadium can accommodate.

3. A requirement under s 3(4) is a written requirement by the local authority of necessary information and plans within a specified reasonable time, so appropriate terms and conditions can be determined for a certificate.

4. A notice under s 8(1) is required to the local authority of proposals to alter or extend a sports ground or any of its installations, where a general safety certificate is in operation, and where the alteration or extension is likely to affect the safety of persons at the sports ground. Notice is to be given before the carrying out of the proposals is begun.

5. Section 11 gives power of entry for a person authorised by the local authority, chief officer of police, building authority or Secretary of State. The authority must be produced on request, and permits entry to a sports ground at any reasonable time, inspection of the ground, examination and copying of attendance and safety records, and necessary inquiries.

8–15474   14. Service of documents.   (1) Any notice or other document required or authorised by or by virtue of this Act to be served on any person may be served on him either by delivering it to him or by leaving it at his proper address or by sending it by post.

(2) Any notice or other document so required or authorised to be served on a body corporate or a firm shall be duly served if it is served on the secretary or clerk of that body or a partner of that firm.

(3) For the purposes of this section, and of section 26 of the Interpretation Act 1889 in its application to this section, the proper address of a person, in the case of a secretary or clerk of a body corporate, shall be that of the registered or principal office of that body, in the case of a partner of a firm shall be that of the principal office of the firm, and in any other case shall be the last known address of the person to be served.

[Safety of Sports Grounds Act 1975, s 14.]

8–15475   15A. Power to modify Act for classes of grounds.   (1) The Secretary of State may, as respects any specified class of sports ground, by order modify the provisions of this Act (except section 1(1) above) in their application to sports grounds of that class.

(2) An order under this section May—

(*a*) make different modifications in relation to different activities at the same class of ground; and
(*b*) include such supplementary and transitional provision as the Secretary of State thinks expedient.

[Safety of Sports Grounds Act 1975, s 15A, as inserted by the Fire Safety and Safety of Places of Sport Act 1987, s 19.]

8–15476   16. Application to Crown.   (1) Sections 1 to 4 and 6(2) above bind the Crown, but shall have effect, in relation to premises occupied by the Crown, with the substitution of a reference to the Secretary of State for any reference to the local authority.

(2) Nothing in this Act shall be taken to authorise the entry of premises occupied by the Crown.

[Safety of Sports grounds Act 1975, s 16.]

8–15477   17. Interpretation.   (1) In this Act unless the context otherwise requires—

"building authority" means—

(*a*) in England outside Greater London and the metropolitan counties, the district council;
(*b*) (*applies to Scotland only*);

"the court" means, in relation to premises in England or Wales, a magistrates' court acting for the petty sessions area in which they are situated and, in relation to premises in Scotland, the sheriff within whose jurisdiction they are situated;

"designated sports ground" and "designation order" have the meanings assigned to them by section 1(4) above;

"general safety certificate" has the meaning assigned to it by section 1(4) above;
"local authority" means—

    (a) in Greater London, the London borough council or the Common Council of the City of London;

    (b) in England, the metropolitan counties, the district council;

    (c) in England outside Greater London and the metropolitan counties, the county council;

    (cc) in Wales, the county council or county borough council;

    (d) (*applies to Scotland only*);

"means of access" includes means of access from a highway;
"qualified person" has the meaning assigned to it by section 3(1) above;
"prohibition notice" has the meaning assigned to it by section 10(1);
"safety" does not include safety from danger inherent in participation in a sporting or competitive activity;
"safety certificate", except with reference to a stand at a sports ground, has the meaning assigned to it section 1(1) above and, where it refers to a stand, means a safety certificate (whether general or special) under Part III of the Fire Safety and Safety of Places of Sport Act 1987;
"special safety certificate" has the meaning assigned to it by section 1(4) above;
"spectator" means any person occupying accommodation provided for spectators at a sports ground;
"sports ground" means any place where sports or other competitive activities take place in the open air and where accommodation has been provided for spectators, consisting of artificial structures or of natural structures artificially modified for the purpose.

(2) Any reference in this Act to any enactment is a reference to it as amended, and includes a reference to it as applied by or under any other enactment, including this Act.
[Safety of Sports Act 1975, s 17, as amended by the Local Government Act 1985, s 16 and Sch 8, the Fire Safety of Places of Sport Act 1987, s 23, and Schs 2 and 4 and the Local Government (Wales) Act 1994, Sch 16.]

8–15478   **18.** *Orders and regulations.*

Criminal Law Act 1977
(1977 c 45)

8–15600   **51. Bomb hoaxes.**   (1) A person who—

    (a) places any article in any place whatever; or

    (b) dispatches any article by post, rail or any other means whatever of sending things from one place to another,

with the intention (in either case) of inducing in some other person a belief that it is likely to explode or ignite and thereby cause personal injury or damage to property is guilty of an offence.
In this subsection "article" includes substance.

(2) A person who communicates any information which he knows or believes to be false to another person with the intention of inducing in him or any other person a false belief that a bomb or other thing liable to explode or ignite is present in any place or location[1] whatever is guilty of an offence.

(3) For a person to be guilty of an offence under subsection (1) or (2) above it is not necessary for him to have any particular person in mind as the person in whom he intends to induce the belief mentioned in that subsection.

(4) A person guilty of an offence under this section shall be liable[2]—

    (a) on summary conviction, to imprisonment for a term not exceeding **six months** or to a fine not exceeding **the statutory maximum**, or both;

    (b) on conviction on indictment, to imprisonment for a term not exceeding **seven years.**

[Criminal Law Act 1977, s 51 as amended by the Criminal Justice Act 1991, s 26.]

---

1. This means "somewhere" and the section does not require a specific place or location. Therefore the statement "there is a bomb" necessarily implies there is a bomb somewhere and that is sufficient to comply with the terms of the subsection (*R v Webb* [1995] 27 LS Gaz R 31, CA).

2. For procedure in respect of this offence which is triable either way, see the Magistrates' Courts Act 1980, ss 17A–21, in PART I: MAGISTRATES' COURTS, PROCEDURE, ante.

Deep Sea Mining (Temporary Provisions) Act 1981
(1981 c 53)

8–15610   **1. Prohibition of unlicensed deep sea mining.**   (1) Subject to the following provisions of this Act, a person to whom this section applies shall not explore for the hard mineral resources of any part of the deep sea bed unless he holds an exploration licence granted under section 2 below in respect of that part of the deep sea bed or is the agent or employee of the holder of that licence (acting in his capacity as such).

(2) Subject to the following provisions of this Act, a person to whom this section applies shall not exploit the hard mineral resources of any part of the deep sea bed unless he holds an exploitation licence granted under section 2 below in respect of that part of the deep sea bed or is the agent or employee of the holder of that licence (acting in his capacity as such).

(3) Any person who contravenes subsection (1) or (2) above shall be guilty of an offence and liable[1]—

(a) on conviction on indictment, to a **fine**:

(b) on summary conviction, to a **fine** not exceeding **the statutory maximum**.

(4) This section applies to any person who—

(a) is a United Kingdom national, a Scottish firm or a body incorporated under the law of any part of the United Kingdom; and

(b) is resident in any part of the United Kingdom.

(5) Her Majesty may by Order in Council[2] extend the application of this section—

(a) to all United Kingdom nationals, Scottish firms and bodies incorporated under the law of any part of the United Kingdom who are resident outside the United Kingdom or to such nationals, firms and bodies who are resident in any country specified in the Order:

(b) to bodies incorporated under the law of any of the Channel Islands, the Isle of Man, any colony or an associated state.

(6) In this Act—

"deep sea bed" means that part of the bed of the high seas in respect of which sovereign rights in relation to the natural resources of the sea bed are neither exercisable by the United Kingdom nor recognised by Her Majesty's Government in the United Kingdom as being exercisable by another Sovereign Power or, in a case where disputed claims are made by more than one Sovereign Power, by one or other of those Sovereign Powers;

"hard mineral resources" means deposits of nodules containing (in quantities greater than trace) at least one of the following elements, that is to say, manganese, nickel, cobalt, copper, phosphorus and molybdenum;

"United Kingdom national" means—

(a) a British citizen, a British ocerseas territories citizen or a British Overseas citizen;

(b) a person who under the British Nationality Act 1981 is a British subject; or

(c) a British protected person (within the meaning of that Act).

(7) In any proceedings, a certificate issued by the Secretary of State certifying that sovereign rights are not exercisable in relation to any part of the sea bed by the United Kingdom or by any other Sovereign Power shall be conclusive as to that fact; and any document purporting to be such a certificate shall be received in evidence and shall, unless the contrary is proved, be deemed to be such a certificate.
[Deep Sea Mining (Temporary Provisions) Act 1981, s 1 as amended by the British Nationality Act 1981, Sch 7 and the British Overseas Territories Act 2002, s 2(3).]

---

1. For procedure in respect of this offence which is triable either way, see the Magistrates' Courts Act 1980, ss 17A–21, in PART I: MAGISTRATES' COURTS, PROCEDURE, ante.
2. The following Deep Sea Mining (Temporary Provisions) Act 1981 Orders have been made: Guernsey, SI 1997/2978; Jersey, SI 1997/2979; Isle of Man, SI 2000/1112.

8–15611   2. Exploration and exploitation licences.   (1) In this Act—

"exploration licence" means a licence authorising the licensee to explore for the hard mineral resources of such part of the deep sea bed as may be specified in the licence; and

"exploitation licence" means a licence authorising the licensee to exploit the hard mineral resources of such part of the deep sea bed as may be specified in the licence.

(2)–(6) *Power of Secretary of State to grant exploration and exploitation licences.*
[Deep Sea Mining (Temporary Provisions) Act 1981, s 2.]

8–15612   3. Licences granted by reciprocating countries.   (1) Where, in the opinion of Her Majesty, the law of any country contains provisions similar in their aims and effects to the provisions of this Act, Her Majesty may by Order[1] in Council designate that country as a reciprocating country for the purposes of this Act.

(2) Where a person holds a licence or other authorisation issued and for the time being in force under the law of a reciprocating country for the exploration or exploitation of the hard mineral resources of any area of the deep sea bed specified in that authorisation (the "authorised area")—

(a) the Secretary of State shall not grant an exploration or exploitation licence in respect of any part of the authorised area; and (*b*) if section 1 above applies to that person, he shall not be prohibited by that section from engaging in the exploration or, as the case may be, exploitation of the hard mineral resources of the authorised area.

(3) Any reference in this Act to a reciprocal authorisation is a reference to an authorisation within subsection (2) above; and references in subsection (2)(*b*) above to any person who holds a reciprocal authorisation include references to his agents or employees acting in their capacity as such.

(4) For the purposes of any proceedings, a reciprocal authorisation may be proved by the production of a copy of the authorisation certified to be a true copy by an official of the government or other body which issued the authorisation; and any document purporting to be such a copy shall be received in evidence and shall, unless the contrary is proved, be deemed to be such an authorisation.
[Deep Sea Mining (Temporary Provisions) Act 1981, s 3.]

---

1. The French Republic, the Federal Republic of Germany, Japan, the United States of America and Italy have been designated reciprocating countries by SI 1985/2000.

8–15613 4. Prevention of interference with licensed operations. (1) A person to whom section 1 above applies shall not intentionally interfere with any operations carried on in pursuance of an exploration or exploitation licence or a reciprocal authorisation.

(2) Any person who contravenes subsection (1) above shall be guilty of an offence and liable[1]—

(*a*) on conviction on indictment, to a **fine**;
(*b*) on summary conviction, to a **fine** not exceeding **the statutory maximum**.
[Deep Sea Mining (Temporary Provisions) Act 1981, s 4.]

---

1. For procedure in respect of this offence which is triable either way, see the Magistrates' Courts Act 1980, ss 17A–21, in PART I: MAGISTRATES' COURTS, PROCEDURE, ante.

8–15614 12. *Regulations[1] and orders.*

---

1. The Deep Sea Mining (Exploration Licences) (Applications) Regulations 1982, SI 1982/58, and the Deep Sea Mining (Exploration Licences) Regulations 1984, SI 1984/1230, have been made.

8–15615 13. Disclosure of information. (1) A person shall not disclose any information which he has received in pursuance of this Act and which relates to any other person except—

(*a*) with the written consent of that other person; or
(*b*) to the Treasury, the Comrs of Inland Revenue or the Secretary of State; or
(*c*) with a view to the institution of or otherwise for the purposes of any criminal proceedings under this Act or regulations made under this Act; or
(*d*) in accordance with regulations made under this Act; or
(*e*) to the government of a reciprocating country or an agency of such a government or to any international organisation designated for the purposes of section 10 above as the relevant international organisation.

(2) Any person who discloses any information in contravention of subsection (1) above shall be guilty of an offence and liable[1]—

(*a*) on conviction on indictment, to imprisonment for a term not exceeding **two years** or to a **fine** or to both;
(*b*) on summary conviction, to a **fine** not exceeding **the statutory maximum**.
[Deep Sea Mining (Temporary Provisions) Act 1981, s 13.]

---

1. The Deep Sea Mining (Exploration Licences) (Applications) Regulations 1982, SI 1982/58, and the Deep Sea Mining (Exploration Licences) Regulations 1984, SI 1984/1230, have been made.

8–15616 14. Supplementary provisions relating to offences. (1) Proceedings for an offence under this Act or under regulations made under this Act may be taken, and the offence may for incidental purposes be treated as having been committed, in any place in the United Kingdom.

(2) Proceedings for such an offence shall not be instituted in England and Wales or Northern Ireland except—

(*a*) in the case of proceedings in England and Wales, by or with the consent of the Director of Public Prosecutions; or
(*b*) in the case of proceedings in Northern Ireland, by or with the consent of the Director of Public Prosecutions for Northern Ireland; or
(*c*) in any case, by the Secretary of State or a person authorised by him in that behalf.

(3) A person may be guilty of an offence under regulations made under this Act whether or not he is a British citizen, a British overseas territories citizen or a British Overseas citizen or, in the case of a body corporate, it is incorporated under the law of any part of the United Kingdom.

(4) Where an offence has been committed by a body corporate and is proved to have been committed with the consent or connivance of, or to be attributable to any neglect on the part of, a director, manager, secretary or other similar officer of the body corporate or any person who was purporting to act in any such capacity, he as well as the body corporate shall be guilty of that offence and shall be liable to be proceeded against and punished accordingly.

In this subsection "director", in relation to a body corporate which—

(*a*) is established by or under any enactment for the purpose of carrying on under public ownership any industry or part of an industry or undertaking; and

(*b*) is a body whose affairs are managed by its members,

means a member of the body corporate.

(5) In any proceedings for an offence of failing to comply with any provision of this Act or of regulations made under this Act, it shall be a defence to prove that the accused used all due diligence to comply with that provision.

(6) (*Repealed*).

[Deep Sea Mining (Temporary Provisions) Act 1981, s 14 as amended by the British Nationality Act 1981, Sch 7, the Statute Law (Repeals) Act 1993, Sch 1 and the British Overseas Territories Act 2002, s 2(3).]

8–15617 16. Food and Environment protection Act 1985. Nothing in Part II of the Food and Environment Protection Act 1985 shall apply in relation to anything done in pursuance of an exploration or exploitation licence or a reciprocal authorisation.

[Deep Sea Mining (Temporary Provisions) Act 1981, s 16 as amended by the Food and Environment Protection Act 1985, s 15.]

8–15618 17. Interpretation. In this Act—

"ancillary operations", in relation to any licensed operations, means any activity carried on by or on behalf of the licensee which is ancillary to the licensed operations (including the processing and transportation of any substances recovered);

"deep sea bed" has the meaning given by section 1 above;

"deep sea bed mining operations" means any exploration or exploitation of the hard mineral resources of the deep-sea bed;

"exploitation" means commercial exploitation;

"exploitation licence" has the meaning given by section 2 above;

"exploration", in relation to the hard mineral resources of any part of the deep sea bed, means the investigation of that part of the deep sea bed for the purpose of ascertaining whether or not the hard mineral resources of that part of the deep sea bed can be commercially exploited;

"exploration licence" has the meaning given by section 2 above;

"hard mineral resources" has the meaning given by section 1 above;

"inspector" means a person appointed as inspector under section 11 above;

"licensed area" means any part of the deep sea bed in respect of which there is in force an exploration or exploitation licence;

"licensed operations" means any activities which the licensee may carry on by virtue of his licence;

"licensee" means the holder of an exploration or exploitation licence;

"prescribed" means prescribed by regulations under section 12 above;

"reciprocal authorisation" has the meaning given by section 3 above;

"reciprocating country" means a country designated as such by an Order under section 3 above; and

"ship" includes every description of vessel used in navigation.

[Deep Sea Mining (Temporary Provisions) Act 1981, s 17.]

8–15619 18. Short title, etc. (1) This Act may be cited as the Deep Sea Mining (Temporary Provisions) Act 1981.

(2) This Act shall come into force on such day as the Secretary of State may by order appoint; and different days may be appointed under this subsection for different purposes.

(3) If it appears to the Secretary of State that an international agreement on the law of the sea which has been adopted by a United Nations Conference on the Law of the Sea is to be given effect within the United Kingdom the Secretary of State may by order provide for the repeal of this Act.

(4) An order under subsection (3) above shall not be made unless a draft thereof has been approved by resolution of each House of Parliament.

(5) Such an order may contain such incidental, supplementary and transitional provisions as the Secretary of State thinks fit.

(6) Her Majesty may by Order in Council direct that any of the provisions of this Act shall extend, with such modifications (if any) as may be specified in the Order, to the Channel Islands, the Isle of Man or any colony.

(7) It is hereby declared that this Act extends to Northern Ireland.

[Deep Sea Mining (Temporary Provisions) Act 1981, s 18.]

Mineral Workings Act 1985[1]
(1985 c 12)

8–15790 **7. Power to enter former mining land etc.** (1) This section applies where a local authority have carried out, are carrying out or are considering whether to carry out works on any land under section 89(2) of the National Parks and Access to the Countryside Act 1949 (treatment of derelict land etc) for the purpose of reclaiming or improving land under which relevant operations have been, but are no longer being, carried out or of enabling it to be brought into use.

(2) In this section "relevant operations" has the same meaning as in section 89(2) (underground mining operations other than for coal).

(3) A person duly authorised in writing by the authority may at any reasonable time enter the land first-mentioned in subsection (1) above in order—

(a) to carry out works under section 89(2);

(b) to survey the land for the purpose of ascertaining the effect on it of works carried out under section 89(2);

(c) to survey the land for the purpose of ascertaining the location, extent and state of mine workings produced by relevant operations, the state of the land, the risk of collapse of its surface, the likely extent of collapse, and the nature and extent of any works which may be necessary to prevent collapse or to deal with a collapse which has occurred.

(4) The power conferred by this section to survey land includes power to search and bore for the purpose of ascertaining the nature of its subsoil.

(5) A person may not under this section demand admission as of right to any land unless at least 10 clear days' notice in writing of the intended entry has been given to every person who is an owner or occupier or the entry is authorised by a warrant granted under subsection (7) below.

(6) A notice under subsection (5) above shall specify the purpose for which entry is required and, in a case where entry is sought for the purpose of carrying out works, shall indicate so far as is practicable the nature of the intended works.

(7) If it is shown to the satisfaction of a justice of the peace on sworn information in writing—

(a) that a person entitled to enter land under this section is not or will not be able to gain admission to the land, or that any owner or occupier who has not been given notice under subsection (5) above is one who has, after reasonable inquiry by the authority, not been identified or (though identified) not been traced, and

(b) that there is reasonable ground for entering the land for the purpose for which entry is required,

the justice may by warrant under his hand authorise that person to enter the land, if need be by force; but such a warrant shall not be granted on the ground that a person is not or will not be able to gain admission to the land unless the justice is satisfied that the authority have taken reasonable steps to notify every person who is an owner or occupier of the intention to apply for a warrant.

(8) Every warrant granted under this section shall continue in force until the purpose for which entry is required has been satisfied.

(9) A person duly authorised under this section to enter any land shall, if so required, produce evidence of his authority before so entering and may take with him on to the land such other persons and such equipment as may be necessary.

(10) Any person who intentionally obstructs a person entitled under this section to enter land shall be guilty of an offence and liable on summary conviction to a fine not exceeding **level 3** on the standard scale.

(11)–(13) *Compensation for loss or damage arising from power to enter land.*

(14) In this section "owner", in relation to any land, means a person, other than a mortgagee not in possession, who is for the time being entitled to dispose of the fee simple of the land, whether in possession or in reversion, and includes also a person holding, or entitled to the rents and profits of, the land under a lease or agreement.

[Mineral Workings Act 1985, s 7 amended by the Statute Law (Repeals) Act 1993, Sch 1.]

---

1. This Act repeals certain provisions of the Mineral Workings Acts 1951 and 1971, transfers the assets of the Ironstone Restoration Fund to the British Steel Corporation, makes further provision about agricultural ironstone land and forestry on ironstone land and confers powers in connection with the reclamation, improvement or bringing into use of certain land. Only those provisions of the Act which are relevant to the work of magistrates' courts are printed in this Manual.

8–15791 **9. Interpretation.** In this Act—

"the 1951 Act" means the Mineral Workings Act 1951;

"the 1971 Act" means the Mineral Workings Act 1971;

"the fund" means the Ironstone Restoration Fund;

"the ironstone district" means the areas set out in Schedule 1[1] to this Act;

"the Minister" means the Secretary of State;

"restoration condition" means a condition requiring that, after operations for the winning and working of minerals have been completed, the site shall be restored by the use of any or all of the following, namely, subsoil, topsoil and soil-making material;

"worked ironstone land" means land which has been excavated in the course of winning and working ironstone by opencast operations, and includes land on which materials extracted in the course of such operations have been deposited.

[Mineral Workings Act 1985, s 9, as amended by SI 2002/794.]

---

1. Schedule 1 is not printed in this work.

Fire Safety and Safety of Places of Sport Act 1987[1]
(1987 c 27)

PART I[2]
FIRE SAFETY

Inspections of premises

8–15820   10. Inspections of premises.   Section 18 of the principal Act (enforcement) shall be amended—

   (a) by the insertion in subsection (1), after the word "inspectors", of the words "and cause premises to be inspected"; and

   (b) by the insertion, after subsection (2), of the following subsection—

   "(3) In performing the duty imposed by subsection (1) above so far as it requires premises in their areas to be inspected, fire authorities shall act in accordance with such guidance as the Secretary of State may give them."

[Fire Safety and Safety of Places of Sport Act 1987, s 10.]

---

1. This Act amends the Fire Precautions Act 1971, in this title ante, and other enactments relating to fire precautions, and also amends the Safety of Sports Grounds Act 1975, in this title, ante. The Act is to be brought into force in accordance with s 50 post. Most provisions of the Act have been brought into force by the Fire Safety and Safety of Places of Sport Act 1987 (Commencement Orders) (No 1) (SI 1987/1762), (No 2), (SI 1988/485), (No 4) (SI 1988/1806), (No 5) (SI 1989/75), (No 6) (SI 1990/1984), and (No 7) (SI 1993/1411). Consequential amendments which have been brought into force have been made to earlier enactments contained in this work. Of the provisions printed below, the following had not been brought into force at the date of going to press: s 10.
2. Part I contains ss 1–18.

PART II[1]
SAFETY OF SPORTS GROUNDS

Repealed.

8–15821

---

1. Part II contains ss 19–25.

PART III[1]
SAFETY OF STANDS AT SPORTS GROUNDS

8–15823   26. Safety certificates for stands at sports grounds.   (1) This Part applies in relation to a sports ground which—

   (a) provides covered accommodation in stands for spectators, and

   (b) is not a designated sports ground.

(2) A certificate under this Part (referred to as a "safety certificate") is required in respect of the use, at a sports ground in relation to which this Part applies, of each stand which provides covered accommodation for 500 or more spectators to view activities at the ground; but one certificate may be issued in respect of several such stands.

(3) The Secretary of State may by order amend subsection (2) above by substituting a smaller number for the number for the time being specified in it.

(4) The power to make an order under subsection (3) above is exercisable by statutory instrument which shall be subject to annulment in pursuance of a resolution of either House of Parliament.

(5) A stand in respect of the use of which a safety certificate under this Part is required is referred to in this Part as a "regulated stand".

(6) It shall be the function of the local authority to determine whether any, and if so, which of the stands at a sports ground in their area is a regulated stand, and to issue safety certificates.

(7) In determining whether any stand at a sports ground in their area is a regulated stand the local authority may apply any criteria which are appropriate for that purpose.

(8) In discharging their function of determination as respects the stands at sports grounds in their

areas, local authorities shall act in accordance with such guidance as the Secretary of State may give them.

(9) A final determination of a local authority that a stand at a sports ground is a regulated stand shall be conclusive of the question subject only to an appeal under section 30 below.

(10) A safety certificate in respect of the use of a regulated stand at a sports ground may be either—

(*a*) a certificate in respect of the use of the stand for viewing an activity or a number of activities specified in the certificate during an indefinite period commencing with a date so specified; or

(*b*) a certificate in respect of the use of the stand for viewing an activity or a number of activities specified in the certificate on an occasion or series of occasions so specified;

and any reference in this Part to a safety certificate's being "for" a stand is a reference to its covering the use of the stand for viewing an activity or activities during an indefinite period or, as the case may be, on an occasion or occasions.

(11) In this Part—

"final", in relation to a determination, is to be construed in accordance with section 28 below;

"general safety certificate" means such a safety certificate for a stand as is mentioned in subsection (10)(*a*) above;

"special safety certificate" means such a safety certificate for a stand as is mentioned in subsection (10)(*b*) above; and

"stand", in relation to a sports ground, means an artificial structure (not merely temporary) which provides accommodation for spectators and is wholly or partly covered by a roof, and, in relation to the number of spectators in a stand provided with covered accommodation, "covered" means covered by the roof or other part of the structure which constitutes the stand.

[Fire Safety and Safety of Places of Sport Act 1987, s 26.]

---

1. Part III contains ss 26–41.

8–15824   27. Contents of safety certificates for stands.   (1) A safety certificate for a regulated stand shall contain such terms and conditions as the local authority consider necessary or expedient to secure reasonable safety in the stand when it is in use for viewing the specified activity or activities at the ground, and the terms and conditions may be such as to involve alterations or additions to the stand or any installations in or serving the stand.

(2) In so far as an order under section 39 below so requires as respects any class of stand at sports grounds, a safety certificate shall include such terms and conditions as may be provided for in the order.

(3) No condition of a safety certificate shall require the provision of the services in or in the vicinity of the stand of any members of a police force unless the extent of the provision of their services is reserved for the determination of the chief officer of police of the force.

(4) Without prejudice to subsection (1) above, a safety certificate for a regulated stand may include a condition that the following records shall be kept—

(*a*) records of the number of spectators accommodated in covered accommodation in the stand; and

(*b*) records relating to the maintenance of safety in the stand.

(5) A general safety certificate shall contain or have attached to it a plan of the stand to which it applies and the area in the immediate vicinity of it, and the terms and conditions in the certificate or in any special safety certificate issued for the stand shall be framed, where appropriate, by reference to that plan.

(6) A safety certificate for a regulated stand at a sports ground may include different terms and conditions in relation to different activities taking place at the ground.

(7) Nothing in a safety certificate for a regulated stand at a sports ground shall derogate from any requirements imposed by regulations under section 6(2) of the Safety of Sports Grounds Act 1975.

[Fire Safety and Safety of Places of Sport Act 1987, s 27.]

8–15825   28. Issue of certificates.   (1) For the purposes of this Part, the following persons qualify for the issue of a safety certificate for a regulated stand at a sports ground, that is to say—

(*a*) the person who qualifies for the issue of a general safety certificate is the person who is responsible for the management of the ground; and

(*b*) the person who qualifies for the issue of a special safety certificate for viewing an activity from the stand on any occasion is the person who is responsible for organising that activity.

(2) The local authority for an area shall, in respect of any stand at a sports ground in their area which appears to them to be a regulated stand, make a preliminary determination whether or not that stand is a regulated stand and, if they determine that it is, they shall serve a notice on the person who appears to them to qualify for the issue of a general safety certificate stating their determination and the effects of it.

(3) Subject to subsection (4) below, a preliminary determination that a stand at a sports ground is

a regulated stand shall become final at the end of the period of two months beginning with the date of the notice of it.

(4) A local authority may revoke a determination of theirs that a stand at a sports ground is a regulated stand—

(a) at any time before it becomes final, or

(b) on considering an application for a general safety certificate for the stand, whether the determination has or has not become final.

(5) A local authority may, at any time before a determination of theirs that a stand at a sports ground is a regulated stand becomes final, withdraw the notice of it and serve a further notice under subsection (2) above on another person, but if they do so the period of two months at the end of which the determination becomes final shall be treated as beginning with the date of the further notice.

(6) If a local authority receive an application for a general safety certificate for a regulated stand at a sports ground in their area, it shall be their duty—

(a) if they have not already done so, to determine whether the stand is a regulated stand and, if they determine that it is, to determine whether the applicant is the person who qualifies for the issue of the general safety certificate for it;

(b) if they have made a determination that the stand is a regulated stand and do not decide to revoke it, to determine whether the applicant is the person who qualifies for the issue of the general safety certificate for it;

and a determination made under paragraph (a) above that a stand is a regulated stand is, when made, a final determination.

(7) If the local authority, on an application made under subsection (6) above in relation to a stand which they have determined or determine is a regulated stand, determine that the applicant is the person who qualifies for the issue of the general safety certificate they shall (if no such certificate is in operation) issue to him such a certificate.

(8) If a local authority receive an application for a special safety certificate for a regulated stand at a sports ground in their area as respects which stand a general safety certificate is in operation, it shall be their duty to determine whether the applicant qualifies for the issue of a special safety certificate for it and, if they determine that he does, they may issue to him a special safety certificate.

(9) The local authority shall, if they determine that an applicant for a safety certificate does not qualify for the issue of the certificate, serve on him a notice stating their determination.

(10) The local authority shall send a copy of an application for a safety certificate for a regulated stand at a sports ground to—

(a) the chief officer of police, and

(b) if the local authority are not the fire and rescue authority, the fire and rescue authority, and

(c) if the local authority are not the building authority, the building authority,

for the area in which the sports ground is situated, is situated, and shall consult them about the terms and conditions to be included in the certificate.

(11) The local authority may, by notice, require an applicant for a safety certificate to furnish them within such reasonable time as they may specify in the notice with such information and such plans of the ground as they consider necessary for the purpose of discharging their functions in respect of the issue of safety certificates for the regulated stands at the ground.

(12) If an applicant for a safety certificate fails to comply with a requirement under subsection (11) above within the time specified by the local authority, or within such further time as they may allow, he shall be deemed to have withdrawn his application.

[Fire Safety and Safety of Places of Sport Act 1987, s 28 as amended by the Local Government (Wales) Act 1994, Sch 16 and the Fire and Rescue Services Act 2004, Sch 1.]

8–15826   29. Amendment, cancellation etc of certificates.   (1) The local authority who have issued a safety certificate for a regulated stand at a sports ground—

(a) shall, if at any time it appears to them that the stand in respect of which it was issued is not or has ceased to be a regulated stand, revoke their previous determination and, by notice to its holder, cancel the certificate;

(b) may, in any case where it appears appropriate to them to do so, amend the certificate by notice to its holder; or

(c) may replace the certificate.

(2) A safety certificate may be cancelled, amended or replaced under subsection (1) above either on the application of the holder or without such an application.

(3) Section 27 above shall apply on the amendment or replacement of a safety certificate.

(4) A notice under subsection (1)(b) above amending a general safety certificate shall specify the date on which the amendment to which it relates is to come into operation, and the date so specified may be a date later than the date of issue of the notice.

(5) If the local authority receive an application for the transfer of a safety certificate for a regulated stand at a sports ground from the holder to some other person it shall be their duty to determine

whether that person would, if he made an application for the purpose, qualify for the issue of the certificate; and if they determine that he would, they may transfer the certificate to him and shall in any case notify him of their determination.

(6) An application under subsection (5) above may be made either by the holder of the safety certificate or by the person to whom it is proposed that it should be transferred.

(7) The local authority shall send a copy of an application for the transfer of a safety certificate for a regulated stand at a sports ground to—

(a) the chief officer of police, and
(b) if the local authority are not the fire and rescue authority, the fire and rescue authority, and
(c) if the local authority are not the building authority, the building authority,

for the area in which the sports ground is situated.

(8) The local authority shall consult—

(a) the chief officer of police, and
(b) if the local authority are not the fire and rescue authority, the fire and rescue authority, and
(c) if the local authority are not the building authority, the building authority,

about any proposal to amend, replace or transfer a safety certificate.

(9) The holder of a safety certificate may surrender it to the local authority, and it shall thereupon cease to have effect.

(10) The local authority may cancel a safety certificate if the holder dies or (if a body corporate) is dissolved.

[Fire Safety and Safety of Places of Sport Act 1987, s 29 as amended by the Local Government (Wales) Act 1994, Sch 16 and the Fire and Rescue Services Act 2004, Sch 1.]

8–15826A 29A. Safety certificates: fire safety. A safety certificate has no effect to the extent that it would require a person to contravene any provision of the Regulatory Reform (Fire Safety) Order 2005 or regulations made under it.

[Fire Safety and Safety of Places of Sport Act 1987, s 29A as inserted by SI 2005/1541.]

8–15827 30. Appeals. (1) A person who has been served with a notice of a determination, which is or has become a final determination, of a local authority that any stand at a sports ground is a regulated stand may appeal against the determination to the court.

(2) Any person who, on an application for the issue or transfer to him of a safety certificate for a regulated stand at a sports ground, has been served with a notice of the determination of a local authority that he does not or, in the case of an application for a transfer, would not qualify for the issue of the certificate may appeal against the determination to the court.

(3) An applicant for a special safety certificate for a regulated stand at a sports ground may also appeal to the court against a refusal of his application on grounds other than a determination that he does not qualify for the issue of the certificate.

(4) An interested party may appeal to the court against—

(a) the inclusion of anything in, or the omission of anything from, a safety certificate for a regulated stand at a sports ground; or
(b) the refusal of the local authority to amend or replace a safety certificate for a regulated stand at a sports ground.

(5) Any appeal under this section shall be brought within the period prescribed under section 31 below.

(6) An appeal to the court under this section in England and Wales shall be by way of complaint for an order, the making of the complaint shall be deemed to be the bringing of the appeal and the Magistrates' Courts Act 1980 shall apply to the proceedings.

(7) An appeal to the court under this section in Scotland shall be by summary application.

(8) In this section "interested party", in relation to a safety certificate, includes—

(a) the holder of the certificate;
(b) any other person who is or may be concerned in ensuring compliance with the terms and conditions of the certificate;
(c) the chief officer of police; and
(d) if the local authority are not the fire and rescue authority, the fire and rescue authority, and
(e) if the local authority are not the building authority, the building authority.

(9) Subject to subsection (10) below, if a local authority serve on any applicant for a safety certificate a notice of a determination of theirs that he does not qualify for the issue of the certificate, he shall be deemed to have withdrawn his application on the expiry of the period within which an appeal must, by virtue of subsection (5) above, be brought.

(10) Subsection (9) above shall not have effect if an appeal is brought before the expiry of the period referred to in that subsection, but if the appeal is withdrawn or the court upholds the authority's determination, the appellant shall be deemed to have withdrawn his application on the date of the withdrawal of his appeal or of the court's order on the appeal.

(11) Where an appeal is brought against the inclusion of any term or condition in a safety

certificate (whether it was included in the certificate originally or only on its amendment or replacement), the operation of that term or condition shall be suspended until the court has determined the appeal.

(12) In England and Wales any of the following persons may appeal to the Crown Court against an order under this section, namely—

(a)   the local authority; and

(b)   any interested party.

(13) In Scotland any of the following persons may appeal against an order under this section, namely—

(a)   the local authority; and

(b)   any interested party,

notwithstanding that that person was not party to the proceedings on the application.

[Fire Safety and Safety of Places of Sport Act 1987, s 30 as amended by the Local Government (Wales) Act 1994, Sch 16 and the Fire and Rescue Services Act 2004, Sch 1.]

8–15828   31. Regulations.   (1) The Secretary of State may by regulations[1]—

(a)   prescribe the procedure (subject to the provisions of this Part) for the issue, cancellation, amendment, replacement and transfer of safety certificates for regulated stands at sports grounds and the particulars to be given in applications for their issue, amendment, replacement or transfer;

(b)   authorise local authorities to determine, subject to such limits or in accordance with such provisions as may be prescribed by the regulations, the fees (if any) to be charged in respect of applications for the issue, amendment, replacement or transfer of safety certificates or in respect of applications for the cancellation of safety certificates for stands which have ceased to be regulated stands; and

(c)   prescribe the time within which appeals under section 30 above are to be brought.

(2)–(4) *Procedure for regulations.*

[Fire Safety and Safety of Places of Sport Act 1987, s 31.]

---

1. The Safety of Places of Sport Regulations 1988, SI 1988/1807 amended by SI 2004/3168 (E) and SI 2005/2929 (W) have been made.

8–15829   32. Alterations and extensions.   (1) If while a general safety certificate for a regulated stand at a sports ground is in operation it is proposed to alter or extend the stand or its installations, and the alteration or extension is likely to affect the safety of persons in the stand, the holder of the certificate shall, before the carrying out of the proposals is begun, give notice of the proposals to the local authority.

(2) Subsection (1) above in particular requires notice when it is proposed to alter the entrances to or exits from a regulated stand at a sports ground (including any means of escape in case of fire or other emergency) or the means of access to any such entrances or exits.

[Fire Safety and Safety of Places of Sport Act 1987, s 32.]

8–15830   33. Exclusion of other statutory requirements.   (1) While a general safety certificate is in force under this Part for a regulated stand at a sports ground, the following provisions shall not apply to the stand, that is to say—

(a)   section 37(1) of the Public Health Acts Amendment Act 1890 (platforms for public occasions);

(b)   any provision of the Fire Precautions Act 1971 or of a fire certificate issued under that Act in so far as it relates to any matter in relation to which requirements are imposed by the terms and conditions of the safety certificate;

(c)   (*Scotland*);

(d)   sections 24 and 71 of the Building Act 1984 (exits, entrances etc in the case of certain public and other buildings); and

(e)   any provision of a local Act in so far as it relates to any matter in relation to which requirements are imposed by the terms and conditions of the safety certificate.

(2) Where an enactment provides for the licensing of premises of any class or description and the authority responsible for licences thereunder is required or authorised to impose terms, conditions or restrictions in connection with such licences, then, so long as there is in operation with respect to the premises a safety certificate under this Part covering the use of the premises by reason of which a licence under that enactment is required, any term, condition or restriction imposed with respect to those premises in connection with any licence under that enactment shall be of no effect in so far as it relates to any matter in relation to which requirements are imposed by the terms and conditions of the certificate under this Part.*

(3) A person required by or under a local Act to do anything that would involve a contravention

of the terms or conditions of a safety certificate under this Part shall not be treated as having contravened that Act if he fails to do it.
[Fire Safety and Safety of Places of Sport Act 1987, s 33.]

---

*New sub-s (2A) inserted by the Licensing Act 2003, Sch 6, from a date to be appointed.

8–15831 34. Enforcement. (1) It shall be the duty of every local authority to enforce within their area the provisions of this Part and for that purpose to arrange for the periodical inspection of sports grounds at which there are regulated stands, but nothing in this subsection shall be taken to authorise a local authority in Scotland to institute proceedings for an offence.

(2) In performing the duty imposed by subsection (1) above so far as it requires sports grounds in their areas to be inspected, local authorities shall act in accordance with such guidance as the Secretary of State may give them.
[Fire Safety and Safety of Places of Sport Act 1987, s 34.]

8–15832 35. Powers of entry and inspection. A person authorised by—

(a) the local authority,
(b) the chief officer of police, or
(c) if the local authority are not the fire and rescue authority, the fire and rescue authority, or
(d) if the local authority are not the building authority, the building authority,

may, on production if so required of his authority, enter a sports ground at any reasonable time, and make such inspection of the stands and such inquiries relating to them as he considers necessary for the purposes of this Part, and in particular may examine records of the number of spectators accommodated, and the maintenance of safety, in the regulated stands at the ground, and take copies of such records.
[Fire Safety and Safety of Places of Sport Act 1987, s 35 as amended by the Local Government (Wales) Act 1994, Sch 16 and the Fire and Rescue Services Act 2004, Sch 1.]

8–15833 36. Offences. (1) Subject to subsections (2), (5) and (6) below, if—

(a) spectators are admitted to a regulated stand at a sports ground on an occasion when no safety certificate which covers their use of the stand is in operation for it, or
(b) any term or condition of a safety certificate for a regulated stand at a sports ground is contravened,

any responsible person and, if a safety certificate is in operation, the holder of the certificate, shall be guilty of an offence.

(2) No offence under subsection (1)(a) above is committed if—

(a) the determination that the stand is a regulated stand is not a final one, or
(b) an application has been made for a general safety certificate for the stand and has not been withdrawn or deemed to have been withdrawn.

(3) In subsection (1) above "responsible person" means the person who is concerned in the management of the sports ground or of the regulated stand in question or in the organisation of any activity taking place at the ground at the time when an offence is alleged to have been committed.

(4) A person guilty of an offence under subsection (1) above shall be liable—

(a) on summary conviction, to a fine not exceeding **the statutory maximum**; or
(b) on conviction on indictment, to a **fine** or to imprisonment for a term not exceeding **two years** or both.

(5) Where any person is charged with an offence under subsection (1) above it shall be a defence to prove—

(a) that the spectators were admitted or the contravention of the certificate in question took place without his consent; and
(b) that he took all reasonable precautions and exercised all due diligence to avoid the commission of such an offence by himself or any person under his control.

(6) Where any person is charged as a responsible person with an offence under subsection (1)(a) above it shall be a defence to prove that he did not know of the determination that the stand in relation to which the offence is alleged to have been committed is a regulated stand.

(7) Any person who—

(a) in purporting to carry out a requirement under section 28(11) above or for the purpose of procuring a safety certificate or the cancellation, amendment, replacement or transfer of a safety certificate, knowingly or recklessly makes a false statement or knowingly or recklessly produces, furnishes, signs or otherwise makes use of a document containing a false statement; or
(b) fails to give a notice required by section 32(1) above; or

(c) intentionally obstructs any person in the exercise of powers under section 35 above, or without reasonable excuse refuses, neglects or otherwise fails to answer any question asked by any person in the exercise of such powers,

shall be guilty of an offence and liable on summary conviction to a fine not exceeding level 5 on the standard scale.

(8) Where an offence under this Part which has been committed by a body corporate is proved to have been committed with the consent or connivance of, or to be attributable to any neglect on the part of, a director, manager, secretary or other similar officer of the body corporate, or any person who was purporting to act in that capacity, he, as well as the body corporate, shall be guilty of that offence and be liable to be proceeded against and punished accordingly.

(9) Where the affairs of a body corporate are managed by its members, subsection (8) above shall apply to the acts and defaults of a member in connection with his functions of management as if he were a director of the body corporate.

[Fire Safety and Safety of Places of Sport Act 1987, s 36.]

8–15834   37. Civil and other liability.   Except in so far as this Part otherwise expressly provides, and subject to section 18 of the Interpretation Act 1978 (offences under two or more laws), the provisions of this Part shall not be construed as—

(a) conferring a right of action in any civil proceedings (other than proceedings for the recovery of a fine) in respect of any contravention of this Part or of any of the terms or conditions of a safety certificate thereunder; or

(b) affecting any requirement or restriction imposed by or under any other enactment whether contained in a public general Act or in a local or private Act; or

(c) derogating from any right of action or other remedy (whether civil or criminal) in proceedings instituted otherwise than under this Part.

[Fire Safety and Safety of Places of Sport Act 1987, s 37.]

8–15835   38. Service of documents.   (1) Any notice or other document required or authorised by or by virtue of this Part to be served on any person may be served on him either by delivering it to him or by leaving it at his proper address or by sending it by post.

(2) Any notice or other document so required or authorised to be served on a body corporate or a firm shall be duly served if it is served on the secretary or clerk of that body or a partner of that firm.

(3) For the purposes of this section, and of section 7 of the Interpretation Act 1978 (service of documents) in its application to this section, the proper address of a person, in the case of a secretary or clerk of a body corporate shall be that of the registered or principal office of that body, in the case of a partner of a firm shall be that of the principal office of the firm, and in any other case shall be the last known address of the person to be served.

[Fire Safety and Safety of Places of Sport Act 1987, s 38.]

8–15836   39. Power to modify Part for classes of stand.   (1) The Secretary of State may, as respects any specified class of stand at sports grounds, by order modify the provisions of this Part in their application to stands of that class.

(2) An order under this section may—

(a) make different modifications in relation to different activities taking place at sports grounds; and

(b) include such supplementary and transitional provision as the Secretary of State thinks expedient.

(3) The power to make an order under this section is exercisable by statutory instrument which shall be subject to annulment in pursuance of a resolution of either House of Parliament.

(4) It shall be the duty of the Secretary of State, before making an order under this section, to consult with such persons or bodies of persons as appear to him requisite.

[Fire Safety and Safety of Places of Sport Act 1987, s 39.]

8–15837   40. Application to Crown.   (1) Sections 26 to 29 above bind the Crown, but shall have effect, in relation to premises occupied by the Crown, with the substitution of a reference to the Secretary of State for any reference to the local authority.

(2) Nothing in this Part shall be taken to authorise the entry of premises occupied by the Crown.

[Fire Safety and Safety of Places of Sport Act 1987, s 40.]

8–15838   41. Interpretation.   In this Part

"building authority" means—

(a) in England outside Greater London and the metropolitan counties, the district council

(b) *Scotland*;

"the court" means, in relation to a sports ground in England and Wales, a magistrates' court acting for the petty sessions area in which it is situated and, in relation to a sports ground in Scotland, the sheriff court within whose jurisdiction it is situated;

"general safety certificate" has the meaning assigned to it by section 26(11) above;

"local authority" means—

    (*a*) in Greater London, the London borough council or the Common Council of the City of London;

    (*b*) in England, in the metropolitan counties, the district council;

    (*c*) in England outside Greater London and the metropolitan counties, the county council;

    (*cc*) in Wales, the county council or county borough council;

    (*d*) in Scotland, the regional or islands council;

"means of access" includes means of access from a highway or, in Scotland, from a road;

"notice" means a notice in writing;

"safety" does not include safety from danger inherent in participation in a sporting or competitive activity;

"safety certificate" has the meaning assigned to it by section 26(2) above;

"special safety certificate" has the meaning assigned to it by section 26(11) above;

"spectator" means any person occupying accommodation provided in stands for spectators at a sports ground;

"sports ground" and "designated sports ground" has the same meaning as in the Safety of Sports Grounds Act 1975; and

"stand" has the meaning assigned to it by section 26(11) above; and "regulated stand" has the meaning assigned to it by section 26(5) above.

[Fire Safety and Safety of Places of Sport Act 1987, s 41 as amended by the Local Government (Wales) Act 1994, Sch 16 and the Building (Scotland) Act 2003, Sch 6.]

Part IV
Indoor Sports Licences

8–15839 *Repealed.*

Part V
Miscellaneous and General

Miscellaneous

General

8–15851 **49.** *Repeals transitional and saving provisions.*

8–15852 **50. Short title, commencement and extent.** (1) This Act may be cited as the Fire Safety and Safety of Places of Sport Act 1987.

(2) This Act shall come into force on such day as the Secretary of State may appoint by order[1] made by statutory instrument; and different days may be so appointed for different provisions or for different purposes.

(3) This Act does not extend to Northern Ireland and—

    (*a*) in Part IV, sections 42 and 43 extend to England and Wales only and section 44 extends to Scotland only; and

    (*b*) in Part V, sections 46 and 47 extend to England and Wales only and section 48 extends to Scotland only.

(4) Except as provided by an order under subsection (5) below, Parts II and III of this Act do not extend to the Isles of Scilly.

(5) The Secretary of State may by order direct that Parts II and III of this Act shall, subject to such exceptions, adaptations and modifications as may be specified in the order, extend to the Isles of Scilly.

(6) An order under subsection (5) above may contain such incidental and consequential provisions, including provisions conferring powers or imposing duties on the Council of the Isles of Scilly, as the Secretary of State thinks necessary.

(7) An order under subsection (5) above shall be subject to annulment in pursuance of a resolution of either House of Parliament.

[Fire Safety and Safety of Places of Sport Act 1987, s 50.]

---

1. For commencement orders, see note 1 to the short title, ante.

Employment Act 1989[1]
(1989 c 38)

Removal of restrictions and other requirements relating to employment

8–15960　11. Exemption of Sikhs from requirements as to wearing of safety helmets on construction sites.　(1) Any requirement to wear a safety helmet which (apart from this section) would, by virtue of any statutory provision or rule of law, be imposed on a Sikh who is on a construction site shall not apply to him at any time when he is wearing a turban.

(2) Accordingly, where—

(*a*)　a Sikh who is on a construction site is for the time being wearing a turban, and

(*b*)　(apart from this section) any associated requirement would, by virtue of any statutory provision or rule of law, be imposed—

(i)　on the Sikh, or

(ii)　on any other person,

in connection with the wearing by the Sikh of a safety helmet,

that requirement shall not apply to the Sikh or (as the case may be) to that other person.

(3) In subsection (2) "associated requirement" means any requirement (other than one falling within subsection (1)) which is related to or connected with the wearing, provision or maintenance of safety helmets.

(4)–(6) *Limitation on liability in tort arising from exemption by virtue of sub-s (1) or (2).*

(7) In this section—

"building operations" and "works of engineering construction" have the same meaning as in the Factories Act 1961;

"construction site" means any place where any building operations or works of engineering construction are being undertaken;

"injury" includes loss of life, any impairment of a person's physical or mental condition and any disease;

"safety helmet" means any form of protective headgear; and

"statutory provision" means a provision of an Act or of subordinate legislation.

(8) In this section—

(*a*)　any reference to a Sikh is a reference to a follower of the Sikh religion; and

(*b*)　any reference to a Sikh being on a construction site is a reference to his being there whether while at work or otherwise.

(9) This section shall have effect in relation to any relevant construction site within the territorial sea adjacent to Great Britain as it has effect in relation to any construction site within Great Britain.

(10) In subsection (9) "relevant construction site" means any construction site where there are being undertaken any building operations or works of engineering construction which are activities falling within Article 7(*a*) of the Health and Safety at Work etc Act 1974 (Application outside Great Britain) Order 1989.

[Employment Act 1989, s 11.]

Coal Industry Act 1994[1]
(1994 c 21)

PART II[2]
LICENSING OF COAL-MINING OPERATIONS
Coal-mining operations to be licensed

8–15961　25. Coal-mining operations to be licensed.　Subject to subsection (3), coal-mining operations to which this section applies shall not, at any time on or after the restructuring date, be carried on by any person except under and in accordance with a licence under this Part.

[Coal Industry Act 1994, s 25—summarised.]

1.　This Act is to be brought into force in accordance with s 68, post.

2.　Part II contains ss 25 to 36.

Enforcement

8–15962　31. Enforcement orders.　(1) Subject to subsections (2) and (5) and section 32 below, where the Authority is satisfied—

(*a*)　that any person is carrying on any coal-mining operations in contravention of section 25(1) above, or is likely so to carry on any coal-mining operations, or

(b) that any person is contravening, or is likely to contravene, any of the conditions of a licence under this Part,

the Authority may be a final enforcement order, make such provision in relation to that person as is requisite for the purpose of securing that there is no contravention of section 25(1) above or, as the case may be, that that condition is complied with.

[Coal Industry Act 1994, s 31(1).]

8–15963 34. Power to require information for the purposes of enforcement.   (1) Where it appears to the Authority—

(a) that there is or may have been a contravention of section 25(1) above, or

(b) that any person is contravening, or may have contravened, any condition of a licence under this Part,

the Authority may, for any purpose connected with such of its functions under section 31 above as are exercisable in relation to that matter, serve a notice under subsection (2) below on any person.

(2) A notice under this subsection is a notice which—

(a) requires the person on whom it is served to produce, at a time and place specified in the notice, to the Authority or to any person appointed by the Authority for the purpose, any documents which are specified or described in the notice and are in that person's possession or under his control; or

(b) requires that person, if he is carrying on a business, to furnish the Authority, at a time and place and in the form and manner specified in the notice, with such information as may be specified or described in the notice.

(3) No person shall be required under this section to produce any documents which he could not be compelled to produce in civil proceedings in the court or, in complying with any requirement for the furnishing of information, to disclose any information which he could not be compelled to give in evidence in any such proceedings.

(4) A person who without reasonable excuse fails to do anything required of him by a notice under subsection (2) above shall be guilty of an offence and liable, on summary conviction, to a fine not exceeding **level 5** on the standard scale.

(5) A person who intentionally alters, suppresses or destroys any document which he has been required by any notice under subsection (2) above to produce shall be guilty of an offence and liable[1]—

(a) on summary conviction, to a fine not exceeding **the statutory maximum**;

(b) on conviction on indictment, to a **fine**.

(6) If a person makes default in complying with a notice under subsection (2) above, the court may, on the application of the Authority, make such order as the court thinks fit for requiring the default to be made good; and any such order may provide that all the costs or expenses of and incidental to the application shall be borne by the person in default or by any officers of a company or other association who are responsible for its default.

(7) No proceedings shall be instituted in England and Wales in respect of an offence under this section except by or on behalf of the Authority or the Director of Public Prosecutions.

[Coal Industry Act 1994, s 34.]

---

1. For procedure in respect of this offence which is triable either way, see the Magistrates' Courts Act 1980, ss 17A–21, in PART I: MAGISTRATES' COURTS, PROCEDURE, ante.

Supplemental

8–15964 36. Insolvency of licensed operators etc.   *A liquidator who contravenes s 36(2) shall be guilty of an offence and liable on summary conviction to a fine not exceeding level 3 on the standard scale.*

PART III[1]
RIGHTS AND OBLIGATIONS IN CONNECTION WITH COAL MINING

Subsidence

8–15965 48. Offences with respect to subsidence information.   (1) A person shall be guilty of an offence under this section if he engages in any conduct falling within subsection (2) below for the purpose of—

(a) obtaining for himself or any other person any benefit under the 1991 Act; or

(b) facilitating the temporary or permanent avoidance, by himself or any other person, of the whole or any part of—

(i) any obligation under that Act;

(ii) any other requirement mentioned in section 47(9)(a) to (c) above; or

(iii) any liability for contravention of any such obligation or requirement.

(2) A person engages in conduct falling within this subsection if he—

(*a*) furnishes any other person whatever with any information which he knows to be false in a material particular;

(*b*) recklessly furnishes any other person whatever with any information which is false in a material particular; or

(*c*) with intent to deceive, withholds any information from any person whatever.

(3) A person who is or has been a licensed operator shall be guilty of an offence under this section if he—

(*a*) furnishes the Authority with any subsidence information which he knows to be false in a material particular;

(*b*) recklessly furnishes the Authority with any subsidence information which is false in a material particular; or

(*c*) with intent to deceive, withholds any subsidence information from the Authority.

(4) In subsection (3) above "subsidence information", in relation to a person who is or has been a licensed operator, means information relating to the extent of the existing or potential liabilities of that person in respect of subsidence damage.

(5) Any person who fails to give, in accordance with section 46 or 47 of the 1991 Act (notice to property owners etc. and local authorities), any notice that he is required to give under that section shall be guilty of an offence under this section.

(6) In any proceedings against a person for an offence by virtue of subsection (5) above it shall be a defence for that person to show that he took such steps as were reasonable to avoid the commission of the offence.

(7) A person guilty of an offence under this section shall be liable[2]—

(*a*) on summary conviction, to a fine not exceeding **the statutory maximum**;

(*b*) on conviction on indictment, to a **fine**.

[Coal Industry Act 1994, s 48.]

---

1. Part III contains ss 37–56.
2. For procedure in respect of this offence which is triable either way, see the Magistrates' Courts Act 1980, ss 17A–21, in PART I: MAGISTRATES' COURTS, PROCEDURE, *ante.*

Registration of rights

8–15966   56. Registration of rights.   (1) The Authority shall establish and maintain a register in which it shall enter particulars of—

(*a*) every notice under section 38 above a copy of which is sent to the Authority by the person giving it;

(*b*) every notice published under section 2 of the 1975 Act (notices conferring right for Corporation to withdraw support) a copy of which has been supplied to the Authority by the Corporation;

(*c*) every public notice under paragraph 6(2) of Schedule 2 to the Coal Act 1938 (withdrawal of support) a copy of which has been supplied to the Authority by the Corporation;

(*d*) every notice given by the Authority under section 41 above;

(*e*) every notice given for the purposes of section 49 above a copy of which is sent to the Authority by the person giving it;

(*f*) every notice published under section 3 of the 1975 Act (notices conferring right for the Corporation to work coal in copyhold land) a copy of which has been supplied to the Authority by the Corporation;

(*g*) every notice sent to the Authority under paragraph 9 of Schedule 7 to this Act and so much of any information known to the Authority as—

(i) relates to any compensation paid under section 3(4) of the 1975 Act or to any agreement for the purposes of paragraph 8 of Schedule 2 to the 1975 Act, and

(ii) is information which, in the case of any compensation or agreement under or for the purposes of Part I of Schedule 7 to this Act, would fall to be included in such a notice;

(*h*) the following, that is to say—

(i) every compulsory rights order under the Opencast Coal Act 1958,

(ii) every order under section 15 or 16 of that Act (rights of way, drainage and water supply), and

(iii) every designation under section 39 of that Act,

in so far as it is an order or designation made by the Authority or an order or designation of which a copy has been supplies to the Authority by the Corporation;

(*i*) every confirmation of an order mentioned in paragraph (*h*)(i) or (ii) above and every notice or other document for the purposes of that Act of 1958 which is, or a copy of which is, sent to the Authority under that Act or a copy of which has been supplied to the Authority by the Corporation; and

(j) every agreement entered into with a local planning authority (within the meaning of that Act of 1958) for the purposes of section 15(5) of that Act (agreements as to the restoration of a right of way).

(2) Where a copy of any notice under section 38 above is sent to the Authority more than fourteen days before the end of the period of three months mentioned in subsection (3)(a) of that section, the duty of the Authority, subject to subsection (3) below, to enter particulars of that notice in the register maintained under this section shall be discharged before the end of that period of three months.

(3) The Authority shall not enter in the register maintained under this section any particulars of—

(a) any notice under section 38 above, or

(b) any notice given for the purposes of section 49 above on or after the restructuring date,

unless it is satisfied that the notice has been properly given in accordance with the requirements of this Act and, in the case of a notice under section 38 above, that the requirements of section 39(4) above have been complied with in relation to that notice.

(4) It shall be the duty of the Authority to preserve a copy of every document particulars of which are, by virtue of subsection (1) above, for the time being entered in the register maintained under this section.

(5) If any person furnishes the Authority with any information for the purposes of this section which he knows to be false in a material particular or recklessly furnishes the Authority with any information for those purposes which is false in a material particular, he shall be guilty of an offence and liable—

(a) on summary conviction, to a fine not exceeding the statutory maximum;

(b) on conviction on indictment, to a fine.

(6) References in this section to the supply to the Authority by the Corporation of a copy of any document include references to the transfer in accordance with a restructuring scheme of possession of the document itself or of any copy of that document.
[Coal Industry Act 1994, s 56.]

PART IV[2]
GENERAL AND SUPPLEMENTAL

8–15967   64. Offences by bodies corporate etc.   (1) Where a body corporate is guilty of an offence under this Act and that offence is proved to have been committed with the consent or connivance of, or to be attributable to any neglect on the part of, any director, manager, secretary or other similar officer of the body corporate or any person who was purporting to act in any such capacity, then he, as well as the body corporate, shall be guilty of that offence and shall be liable to be proceeded against and punished accordingly.

(2) Where the affairs of a body corporate are managed by its members, subsection (1) above shall apply in relation to the acts and defaults of a member in connection with his functions of management as if he were a director of the body corporate.

(3) Where any partnership in Scotland or any unincorporated association in Scotland which is not a partnership is guilty of an offence under this Act and that offence is proved to have been committed with the consent or connivance of, or to be attributable to any neglect on the part of—

(a) any partner in the partnership or, as the case may be, any person concerned in the management or control of the association, or

(b) any person purporting to act in any such capacity,

then he, as well as the partnership or association, shall be guilty of that offence and shall be liable to be proceeded against and punished accordingly.
[Coal Industry Act 1994, s 64.]

---

1. Part IV contains ss 57 to 68.

8–15968   65. Interpretation.   (1) In this Act, except in so far as the context otherwise requires—

"the 1946 Act" means the Coal Industry Nationalisation Act 1946;

"the 1975 Act" means the Coal Industry Act 1975;

"the 1991 Act" means the Coal Mining Subsidence Act 1991;

"the Authority" means the Coal Authority;

"business" includes any trade or profession;

"coal" means bituminous coal, cannel coal and anthracite;

"coal mine" includes—

(a) any space excavated underground for the purposes of coal-mining operations and any shaft or adit made for those purposes,

(b) any space occupied by unworked coal, and

(c) a coal quarry and opencast workings of coal;

"coal-mining operations" includes—

(*a*) searching for coal and boring for it,

(*b*) winning, working and getting it (whether underground or in the course of opencast operations),

(*c*) bringing underground coal to the surface, treating coal and rendering it saleable,

(*d*) treating coal in the strata for the purpose of winning any product of coal and winning, working or getting any product of coal resulting from such treatment, and

(*e*) depositing spoil from any activities carried on in the course of any coal-mining operations and draining coal mines,

and an operation carried on in relation to minerals other than coal is a coal-mining operation in so far as it is carried on in relation to those mineral as part of, or is ancillary to, operations carried on in relation to coal;

"company" has the same meaning as in the Companies Act 1985;

"contravention" includes a failure to comply, and cognate expressions shall be construed accordingly;

"the Corporation" means the British Coal Corporation or, in relation to times before the commencement of section 1 of the Coal Industry Act 1987, the National Coal Board;

"debenture" includes debenture stock;

"the dissolution date" means the date appointed under section 23 above for the dissolution of the Corporation;

"financial year" means the twelve months ending with 31st March;

"holder", in relation to a licence under Part II of this Act, means the following person (whether or not the authorisation contained in the licence remains in force), that is to say—

(*a*) in a case where there has been no such transfer in relation to that licence as is mentioned in section 27(5) above, the person to whom the licence was granted, and

(*b*) in any other case, the person to whom the rights and obligations of the holder of that licence were last transferred;

"interest", in relation to land, includes estate;

"liability", in relation to the transfer of liabilities from one person to another or to the modification of any liability, does not include any criminal liability;

"licensed operator" means any person who is for the time being either—

(*a*) authorised by a licence under Part II of this Act to carry on coal-mining operations to which section 25 above applies, or

(*b*) authorised by virtue of subsection (3) of that section to carry on any such operations;

"modifications" includes additions, alterations and omissions, and cognate expressions shall be construed accordingly;

"the restructuring date" means the date appointed as that date under section 7(1) above;

"restructuring scheme" means a scheme under section 12 above;

"securities", in relation to a company, includes shares, debentures, bonds and other securities of the company, whether or not constituting a charge on the assets of the company;

"shares" includes stock;

"subordinate legislation" has the same meaning as in the Interpretation Act 1978;

"subsidence damage" has the same meaning as in the 1991 Act;

"subsidiary" and "wholly-owned subsidiary" have the meanings given by section 736 of the Companies Act 1985;

"successor company" means any company which, at a time when it is wholly owned by the Crown, becomes entitled or subject, in accordance with any restructuring scheme, to any property, rights or liabilities;

"undertaking", in relation to the Corporation, includes the undertakings of its wholly-owned subsidiaries.

(2) References in this Act to the treatment of coal in the strata shall be taken not to include references to any operations which—

(*a*) are carried on in relation to coal in or to which any oil or gas that exists in its natural condition in the strata is absorbed or adsorbed; and

(*b*) are so carried on wholly for the purpose of winning or getting that oil or gas;

and in this subsection "oil or gas" means oil or gas within the meaning of section 9 above.

(3) References in this Act to the creation, in favour of any person, of an interest in property include references to the vesting in that person of a freehold or leasehold interest in property.

(4) For the purposes of this Act a company shall be regarded as wholly owned by the Crown at any time if it is—

(*a*) a company limited by shares in which there are at that time no issued shares held otherwise than by, or by a nominee of, the Treasury, the Secretary of State or any other company wholly owned by the Crown; or

(*b*) a company limited by guarantee of which no person other than the Treasury or the Secretary of State, or a nominee of the Treasury or the Secretary of State, is a member.

[Coal Industry Act 1994, s 65.]

8–15969   68. Short title, commencement and extent.   (1) This Act may be cited as the Coal Industry Act 1994.

(2) The following provisions of this Act shall come into force on the restructuring date[1], that is to say—

(a)   sections 10, 11, 18 and 23;

(b)   sections 31 to 34 and section 36;

(c)   sections 38 to 44 and 48 to 53, section 55 and Schedules 6, 7 and 8;

(d)   Schedule 9, except (subject to the power to appoint the restructuring date under subsection (4) below) for so much of that Schedule as relates to—

   (i)   the Public Health Act 1961,

   (ii)   the Licensing Act 1964,

   (iii) *repealed*

   (iv)   the Gaming Act 1968,*

   (v)   *repealed*

   (vi)   the Overseas Development and Co-operation Act 1980,

   (vii) the National Audit Act 1983,

   (viii)the Road Traffic Regulation Act 1984,

   (ix)   sections 315(4)(b) and 317 of the Town and Country Planning Act 1990, and

   (x)   the Leasehold Reform, Housing and Urban Development Act 1993;

(e)   Part II of Schedule 11; and

(f)   subsections (1) and (8) of section 67 so far as they relate to provisions coming into force on that date by virtue of paragraphs (d) and (e) above.

(3) The following provisions of this Act shall come into force on the dissolution date, that is to say—

(a)   Schedule 9, so far as it relates to—

   (i)   the Public Health Act 1961,

   (ii)   the Overseas Development and Co-operation Act 1980,

   (iii)   the National Audit Act 1983,

   (iv)   the Road Traffic Regulation Act 1984, and

   (v)   the Leasehold Reform, Housing and Urban Development Act 1993;

(b)   Part IV of Schedule 11; and

(c)   subsections (1) and (8) of section 67 so far as they relate to provisions coming into force on that date by virtue of paragraphs (a) and (b) above.

(4) Apart from the provisions to which subsections (2) and (3) above apply and the provisions specified in subsection (6) below (which come into force on the passing of this Act), this Act shall come into force on such day as the Secretary of State may by order[2] made by statutory instrument appoint.

(5) An order under subsection (4) above may—

(a)   appoint different days for different provisions and for different purposes; and

(b)   make any such transitional provision (including provision modifying for transitional purposes any of the provisions of this Act or of any enactment amended or repealed by this Act) as the Secretary of State considers appropriate in connection with the bringing into force of any provision of this Act;

but, where an order under that subsection makes any such provision as is mentioned in paragraph (b) above, the statutory instrument containing the order shall be subject to annulment in pursuance of a resolution of either House of Parliament.

(6) The provisions of this Act mentioned in subsection (4) above are this section and—

(a)   sections 7 to 9;

(b)   sections 12 to 14 and 17 and Schedule 2;

(c)   section 54;

(d)   sections 62 to 66;

(e)   section 67(2) to (6); and

(f)   Part I of Schedule 11 to this Act and subsection (8) of section 67 so far as it relates to that Part of that Schedule.

(7) The following provisions of this Act do not extend to Scotland, that is to say—

(za) sections 4A to 4C and Schedules 1A and 1B; and

(a)   sections 49 and 50 and Schedule 7; and

(b)   so much of Schedules 9 and 11 as relates to enactments extending to England and Wales only.

(7) Sections 4D to 4F of, and Schedule 1C to, this Act extend to Scotland only.

(8) This Act, except for—

(a)   sections 7 to 9, 12 and 13 and Schedule 2,

(b)   sections 20 and 21 and Schedule 4,

(c) so much of Schedule 1 as amends the Parliamentary Commissioner Act 1967, the House of Commons Disqualification Act 1975 and the Northern Ireland Assembly Disqualification Act 1975,

(d) so much of Schedule 9 as amends any enactment that extends to Northern Ireland,

(e) the repeal, by virtue of their inclusion in Schedule 11, of—

(i) the entries relating to the Corporation in the Statutory Corporations (Financial Provisions) Act 1975, the House of Commons Disqualification Act 1975, the Northern Ireland Assembly Disqualification Act 1975 and the National Audit Act 1983,

(ii) the Coal Consumers' Councils (Northern Irish Interests) Act 1962,

(iii) section 2(4) and (5) of the Overseas Development and Co-operation Act 1980 and the entry relating to the Corporation in Schedule 1 to that Act,

(iv) section 1(2) of the Continental Shelf Act 1964 and section 2(3) of the Territorial Sea Act 1987,

(v) so much of the Coal Industry Act 1987 as extends to Northern Ireland, and

(vi) the British Coal and British Rail (Transfer Proposals) Act 1993, and

(f) so much of this Part as is required for the purpose of giving effect to the extension to Northern Ireland of the provisions mentioned in the preceding paragraphs, does not extend to Northern Ireland.

(9) This Act extends to the Isle of Man for the purpose of giving effect there to the repeal by this Act of subsection (3) of section 2 of the Territorial Sea Act 1987, to paragraph 10 of Schedule 10 and to so much of any restructuring scheme or any agreement under section 13 above as relates to rights mentioned in that paragraph; and, subject to that paragraph, that repeal shall accordingly include the repeal of that subsection as it extends to the Isle of Man by virtue of the Territorial Sea Act 1987 (Isle of Man) Order 1991.

[Coal Industry Act 1994, s 68 as amended by the Statute Law (Repeals) Act 1998, the Palnning (Consequential Provisions) (Scotland) Act 1997, Sch 1, the Water Act 2003, s 85 and the Water Services etc (Scotland) Act 2005, s 30.]

---

*Repealed by the Gambling Act 2005, Sch 17 from a date to be appointed.

1. The restructuring date was 31 October 1994 (SI 1994/2553).

2. At the date of going to press the following commencement orders had been made: (No 1) Order 1994, SI 1994/2189; (No 2 and Transitional Provision) Order 1994, SI 1994/2552; (No 3) Order 1994, SI 1994/3063, (No 4) Order 1995, SI 1995/159, (No 5) Order 1995, SI 1995/273, and (No 6) Order 1995, SI 1995/1507.

Activity Centres (Young Persons' Safety) Act 1995
(1995 c 15)

8–15970 1. Adventure activities: licensing. (1) The Secretary of State[1] shall by order[2] designate a person ("the licensing authority") to exercise such functions as may be prescribed by regulations relating to the licensing of persons providing facilities for adventure activities.

(2) The Secretary of State shall not make an order under subsection (1) designating a person other than one nominated by the Health and Safety Commission.

(3) In this section "facilities for adventure activities" means such facilities, for such sporting, recreational or outdoor activities, as may be prescribed by regulations[3]; but the expression does not include—

(a) facilities which are provided exclusively for persons who have attained the age of 18; or

(b) facilities which do not consist of, or include some element of, instruction or leadership.

(4) Regulations may make provision as to—

(a) the cases or circumstances in which persons providing facilities for adventure activities are, or are not, required to hold a licence;

(b) any requirements relating to safety (whether applying to facilities for adventure activities or to other facilities) which must be satisfied by an applicant for a licence;

(c) the conditions subject to which licences are granted (which may include conditions relating to inspection by the licensing authority and conditions imposing requirements of the kind referred to in paragraph (b));

(d) the variation of such conditions;

(e) the renewal, variation, transfer and revocation of licences by the licensing authority;

(f) the charging by the licensing authority of such fees in connection with licences as may be specified in the regulations;

(g) the making of payments by the licensing authority into the Consolidated Fund;

(h) the investigation by the licensing authority of complaints concerning licence-holders;

(i) the exercise of functions of the licensing authority by persons authorised by them;

(j) the keeping, and availability for inspection by the public, of a register of licences;

(k) the bringing of appeals to the Secretary of State against such decisions of the licensing authority as may be specified in the regulations; and (*l*)   the procedure to be followed on, and the orders which may be made on determination of, such appeals.

(5) In exercising their functions under regulations made under this section the licensing authority shall have regard to any guidance given to them from time to time by the Health and Safety Commission; and before giving guidance under this subsection the Commission shall consult such persons (if any) as they consider it appropriate to consult.
[Activity Centres (Young Persons' Safety) Act 1995, s 1.]

---

1. Functions of the Secretary of State, so far as exercisable in relation to Wales, have been transferred to the National Assembly for Wales, by the National Assembly for Wales (Transfer of Functions) Order 1999, SI 1999/672, art 2, Sch 1.
2. The Adventure Activities (Licensing) (Designation) Order 1996, SI 1996/771, has been made.
3. The Adventure Activities Licensing Regulations 1996, SI 1996/772, have been made.

8–15971   **2. Offences.**   (1) Regulations may provide for it to be an offence—

(*a*)   to do anything for which a licence is required under the regulations, otherwise than in accordance with a licence; or

(*b*)   for the purposes of obtaining or holding a licence—

     (i)   to make a statement to the licensing authority (or someone acting on their behalf) knowing it to be false in a material particular, or

     (ii)   recklessly to make a statement to the licensing authority (or someone acting on their behalf) which is false in a material particular.

(2) A person convicted of an offence under regulations made under subsection (1) shall be liable[1]—

(*a*)   on summary conviction, to a fine not exceeding **the statutory maximum**;

(*b*)   on conviction on indictment—

     (i)   for an offence under regulations made under subsection (1)(*a*), to imprisonment for a term not exceeding **two years**, or a **fine**, or **both**;

     (ii)   for an offence under regulations made under subsection (1)(*b*), to a fine.

(3) Regulations under subsection (1)—

(*a*)   may provide defences to be available in proceedings for an offence under the regulations either generally or in specified circumstances;

(*b*)   may make, in relation to provisions of the regulations, provision which applies (with or without modifications), or has a similar purpose to that of, any of the provisions of the Health and Safety at Work etc Act 1974 set out in subsection (4).

(4) The provisions mentioned in subsection (3)(*b*) are:

(*a*)   sections 15(7) and 35(venue);

(*b*)   sections 18 to 20 and 26 (enforcement authorities and inspectors);

(*c*)   sections 21 to 24 (improvement and prohibition notices);

(*d*)   section 25 (power to deal with cause of imminent danger);

(*e*)   sections 27 and 28 (obtaining and disclosure of information);

(*f*)   section 33(1)(*e*) to (*j*), (*n*) and (*o*), and (2) to (4) (ancillary offences);

(*g*)   section 34(2) to (6) (extension of time for bringing summary proceedings);

(*h*)   sections 36(1) and 37 (offences due to fault of other person and offences by bodies corporate);

(*i*)   sections 38 and 39 (prosecutions in England and Wales only by inspectors or by or with the consent of the Director of Public Prosecutions);

(*j*)   sections 40 and 41 (onus of proving limits of what is practicable, and evidence);

(*k*)   section 42 (power of court to order cause of offence to be remedied); and

(*l*)   section 46 (service of notices).
[Activity Centres (Young Persons' Safety) Act 1995, s 2.]

---

1. For procedure in respect of this offence which is triable either way, see the Magistrates' Court Act 1980, ss 17A–21, in PART I: MAGISTRATES' COURTS, PROCEDURE, ante.

8–15972   **3. Supplementary provisions.**   (1) An order under section 1(1) shall be made by statutory instrument; and an order revoking a previous order may include transitional or incidental provision (including provision for the transfer of property, rights and liabilities from the old licensing authority to the new).

(2) Regulations under section 1 or 2—

(*a*)   shall be made by the Secretary of State by statutory instrument;

(*b*)   may make different provision for different cases; and

(*c*)   may include transitional provisions.

(3) Before making regulations under section 1 or 2 the Secretary of State shall consult the Health and Safety Commission and such other persons (if any) as he considers it appropriate to consult.

(4) The Health and Safety Commission may from time to time submit to the Secretary of State such proposals as the Commission considers appropriate for the making of regulations under section

1 or 2; and where the Secretary of State proposes to make regulations in the form submitted under this subsection, the requirement under subsection (3) to consult the Commission shall not apply.

(5) Nothing in, or done by virtue of, this Act or regulations under it shall prejudice any of the relevant statutory provisions (whenever made) as defined in Part I of the Health and Safety at Work etc Act 1974 or anything done by virtue of any of those provisions.

(6) A statutory instrument containing an order or regulations under section 1 or 2 shall be subject to annulment in pursuance of a resolution of either House of Parliament.

(7) The Secretary of State may make grants to the licensing authority in respect of such of their expenses under this Act as are not met by fees; and grants under this subsection may be made subject to such conditions, including conditions as to repayment, as the Secretary of State may determine.

[Activity Centres (Young Persons' Safety) Act 1995, s 3.]

8–15973　4. *Expenses.*

8–15974　5. Commencement. This Act shall come into force[1] at the end of the period of two months beginning with the date on which it is passed.

[Activity Centres (Young Persons' Safety) Act 1995, s 5.]

---

1. This Act came into force on 28 August 1995.

8–15975　6. Short title and extent. (1) This Act may be cited as the Activity Centres (Young Persons' Safety) Act 1995.

(2) This Act shall not extend to Northern Ireland.

[Activity Centres (Young Persons' Safety) Act 1995, s 6.]

Petroleum Act 1998[1]
(1998 c 17)

PART I[2]
PETROLEUM

8–15976A　1. Meaning of "petroleum". In this Part of this Act "petroleum"—

  (a)　includes any mineral oil or relative hydrocarbon and natural gas existing in its natural condition in strata; but

  (b)　does not include coal or bituminous shales or other stratified deposits from which oil can be extracted by destructive distillation.

[Petroleum Act 1998, s 1.]

---

1. Sections 5(1)–(4) and (11) and 52 were brought into force on the passing of this Act (11 June 1998). The remaining provisions (except Sch 4 (part) and Sch 5 (part)) were brought into force on 15 February 1999 in accordance with the Petroleum Act 1998 (Commencement No 1) Order 1999, SI 1999/161.

2. Part I contains ss 1–9.

PART II[1]
OFFSHORE ACTIVITIES

8–15976B　10. Application of criminal law etc. (1) Her Majesty may by Order in Council provide that, in such cases and subject to such exceptions as may be prescribed by the Order, any act or omission which—

  (a)　takes place on, under or above an installation in waters to which this section applies or any waters within 500 metres of any such installation; and

  (b)　would, if taking place in any part of the United Kingdom, constitute an offence under the law in force in that part,

shall be treated for the purposes of that law as taking place in that part.

(2) Her Majesty may by Order in Council provide that, in such cases and subject to such exceptions as may be prescribed by the Order, a constable shall on, under or above any installation in waters to which this section applies or any waters within 500 metres of such an installation have all the powers, protection and privileges which he has in the area for which he acts as constable.

(3) Subsection (2) is without prejudice to any other enactment or rule of law affording any power, protection or privilege to constables.

(4) Where a body corporate is guilty of an offence by virtue of an Order in Council under this section and that offence is proved to have been committed with the consent or connivance of, or to be attributable to any neglect on the part of, any director, manager, secretary or other similar officer of the body corporate or any person who was purporting to act in any such capacity, he as well as the body corporate shall be guilty of that offence and shall be liable to be proceeded against and punished accordingly.

(5) Where the affairs of a body corporate are managed by its members, subsection (4) shall apply in relation to acts and defaults of a member in connection with his functions of management as if he were a director of the body corporate.

(6) Proceedings for anything that is an offence by virtue of an Order in Council under this section may be taken, and the offence may for all incidental purposes be treated as having been committed, in any place in the United Kingdom.

(7) The waters to which this section applies are—

(a) the territorial sea adjacent to the United Kingdom;
(b) waters in an area designated under section 1(7) of the Continental Shelf Act 1964; or
(c) waters in an area specified under subsection (8).

(8) Her Majesty may from time to time by Order in Council specify any area which—

(a) is in a foreign sector of the continental shelf; and
(b) comprises any part of a cross-boundary field,

as an area as respects which the powers conferred by this section and section 11 are exercisable.

(9) In this section—

"cross-boundary field" means a field that extends across the boundary between waters falling within paragraph (a) or (b) of subsection (7) and a foreign sector of the continental shelf;
"field" means a geological structure identified as such by Order in Council under subsection (8).

(10) This section applies to installations notwithstanding that they are for the time being in transit but it does not apply to an installation that is a renewable energy installation (within the meaning of Chapter 2 of Part 2 of the Energy Act 2004.

(11) A statutory instrument containing an Order in Council under this section shall be subject to annulment in pursuance of a resolution of either House of Parliament.

[Petroleum Act 1998, s 10 as amended by the Energy Act 2004, s 103.]

---

1. Part II contains ss 10–13.

8–15976C 12. Prosecutions. (1) Subject to subsection (2), this subsection applies to—

(a) any offence alleged to have been committed on, under or above an installation in waters to which section 10 applies or any waters within 500 metres of such an installation; and
(b) any offence committed on or as respects an aircraft which is not registered in the United Kingdom which is an offence created by virtue of paragraph 6(5) of Part III of Schedule 13 to the Civil Aviation Act 1982.

(2) Subsection (1) does not apply to any offence to which subsection (5) applies nor to any offence under, or under any provision which has effect under—

(a) the Customs and Excise Acts 1979, or any enactment to be construed as one with those Acts or any of them;
(b) except where it is created by virtue of paragraph 6(5) of Part III of Schedule 13 to the Civil Aviation Act 1982, that Act or any enactment to be construed as one with that Act;
(c) the Pilotage Act 1987;
(d) the Value Added Tax Act 1994 or any enactment to be construed as one with that Act;
(e) the Merchant Shipping Act 1995; or
(f) Part III or IV of this Act.

(3) No proceedings for an offence to which subsection (1) applies shall be instituted—

(a) in England and Wales, except by or with the consent of the Director of Public Prosecutions unless prosecution of the offence there requires the consent of the Attorney General;
(b) in Northern Ireland, except by or with the consent of the Director of Public Prosecutions for Northern Ireland unless prosecution of the offence there requires the consent of the Attorney General for Northern Ireland.

(4) Section 3 of the Territorial Waters Jurisdiction Act 1878 (restriction on prosecutions) shall not apply to any proceedings for an offence to which subsection (1) or (5) applies.

(5) This subsection applies to—

(a) any offence under section 23 of the Petroleum Act 1987 (safety zones); and
(b) any offence under any provision made under the Mineral Workings (Offshore Installations) Act 1971 which has effect by virtue of—

(i) paragraph (1) of regulation 6 (savings) of the Offshore Safety (Repeals and Modifications) Regulations 1993; or
(ii) paragraph (1) of regulation 6 (savings) of the Offshore Safety (Repeals and Modifications) Regulations (Northern Ireland) 1993.

[Petroleum Act 1998, s 12.]

8–15976D   13. Interpretation of Part II.   In this Part of this Act—

"foreign sector of the continental shelf" has the meaning given by section 48(1); and
"installation" includes any floating structure or device maintained on a station by whatever means.
[Petroleum Act 1998, s 13.]

PART III[1]
SUBMARINE PIPELINES

8–15976E   14. Construction and use of pipelines.   (1) No person shall—

(a)   execute in, under or over any controlled waters any works for the construction of a pipeline;
or

(b)   use a controlled pipeline of which the construction was begun on or after 1st January 1976,

except in accordance with an authorisation given in writing by the Secretary of State.
   (2) In this Part of this Act—

"controlled pipeline" means so much of any pipeline as is in, under or over controlled waters; and
"controlled waters" means the territorial sea adjacent to the United Kingdom and the sea in any
area designated under section 1(7) of the Continental Shelf Act 1964.
[Petroleum Act 1998, s 14.]

---

1. Part III contains ss 14–28.

8–15976F   16. Compulsory modifications of pipelines.   (1) If in the case of a controlled pipeline
it appears to the Secretary of State, on the application of a person other than the owner of the
pipeline—

(a)   that the capacity of the pipeline can and should be increased by modifying apparatus and
works associated with the pipeline; or

(b)   that the pipeline can and should be modified by installing in it a junction through which
another pipeline may be connected to the pipeline,

then, subject to section 17(8) or 17G(7), the Secretary of State may, after giving the owner of the
pipeline an opportunity of being heard about the matter, serve on the owner and the applicant a
notice in accordance with subsection (2).
   (2) A notice under subsection (1) shall—

(a)   specify the modifications which the Secretary of State considers should be made in
consequence of the application;

(b)   specify the sums or the method of determining the sums which the Secretary of State considers
should be paid to the owner by the applicant for the purpose of defraying the cost of the
modifications;

(c)   require the applicant to make, within the period specified for the purpose in the notice,
arrangements which the Secretary of State considers appropriate to secure that those sums
will be paid to the owner if he carries out the modifications or satisfies the Secretary of State
that he will carry them out;

(d)   require the owner, if the applicant makes those arrangements within that period, to carry out
the modifications within a period specified for the purpose in the notice; and

(e)   authorise the owner, if he satisfies the Secretary of State that he has carried out or will carry
out the modifications, to recover those sums from the applicant.

   (3) References in subsections (1) and (2) to modifications include, in the case of modifications of
any apparatus and works, references to changes in, substitutions for and additions to the apparatus
and works.
   (4) For the purposes of section 14(1) a notice under subsection (1) of this section requiring a
person to carry out modifications authorises him to carry out the modifications; but nothing in
Schedule 2 shall apply to such a notice.
[Petroleum Act 1998, s 16 as amended by SI 2000/1937.]

8–15976G   17. Acquisition of rights to use pipelines.   (1) Subsections (2) and (3) apply where
a person applies to the Secretary of State for a notice under this section securing to the applicant a
right to have conveyed, by a controlled pipeline of which he is not the owner, quantities specified in
the application of things which are of a kind so specified and which the pipeline is designed to convey.
   (1A) This section does not apply to controlled petroleum pipelines, and, in the case of a
downstream gas pipeline to which section 17B applies, is subject to that section.
   (2) The Secretary of State shall—

(a)   give notice to the owner of the pipeline and the applicant that he proposes to consider the
application; and

(b)   after the expiry of 21 days beginning with the date on which notice under paragraph (a) was
served, but before considering the application, give them an opportunity of being heard with
respect to the application.

(3) Where the Secretary of State is satisfied that, if he served a notice under this section the pipeline in question could be operated in accordance with the notice without prejudicing its efficient operation for the purpose of conveying, on behalf of its owner, the quantities of permitted substances which the owner requires or may reasonably be expected to require, the Secretary of State may serve such a notice on the owner and the applicant.

(4) In subsection (3), "permitted substances" means the things which may be conveyed by the pipeline in accordance with an authorisation (or, if no authorisation for the use of the pipeline is required by section 14(1), means the things which the pipeline is designed to convey).

(5) A notice under this section may contain such provisions as the Secretary of State considers appropriate for any of the following purposes—

    (a)   to secure to the applicant, without prejudicing the efficient operation of the pipeline for the purpose mentioned in subsection (3), the right to have conveyed by the pipeline the quantities specified in the application of the things so specified;

    (b)   to secure that the exercise of the right is not prevented or impeded;

    (c)   to regulate the charges which may be made for the conveyance of things by virtue of the right; and

    (d)   to secure to the applicant the right to have a pipeline of his connected to the pipeline by the applicant or owner.

(6) Such a notice may also authorise the owner to recover from the applicant payments by way of consideration for any right mentioned in subsection (5)(a) or (d) of amounts specified in the notice or determined in accordance with the notice.

(7) Before serving a notice under section 15(6) on a person other than the holder of the relevant authorisation, the Secretary of State shall give that person an opportunity to make an application under subsection (1) in respect of the proposed pipeline to which the authorisation relates; and subsections (1) to (6) shall have effect for this purpose as if references to a pipeline and the owner of it were references to the proposed pipeline and the proposed owner of it.

(8) Before serving a notice under section 16(1) on a person other than the owner of the relevant pipeline, the Secretary of State shall give that person particulars of the modifications which he proposes to specify in the notice and an opportunity to make an application under subsection (1) in respect of the pipeline; and subsections (1) to (6) shall have effect for this purpose as if references to a pipeline were references to the pipeline as it would be with those modifications.

(9) The use of a pipeline by any person in accordance with a right secured to him by virtue of this section is not a contravention of section 14(1); but a person to whom a right is so secured may not assign the right to any other person.

[Petroleum Act 1998, s 17 as amended by SI 2000/1937.]

8–15976H   **17A–17G.** *Downstream gas pipelines and offshore gas storage facilities; acquisition of rights to use controlled petroleum pipelines (summarised).*

8–15976I   **21. Enforcement.**   (1) Any person who—

    (a)   contravenes any provision of section 14(1); or

    (b)   contravenes any provision of a notice under section 16, 17 or 17F(9) served on him in his capacity as the owner of the pipeline to which the notice relates in a case where no authorisation for the use of the pipeline is required by section 14(1); or

    (c)   makes a statement which he knows is false in a material particular, or recklessly makes a statement which is false in a material particular, for the purpose of inducing the Secretary of State—

        (i)   to issue any authorisation; or

        (ii) to agree under section 18(1)(b) that an authorisation is to cease to be in force; or

        (iii) to specify a period under section 18(3)(b); or

        (iv) not to serve a notice under section 18(6),

shall be guilty of an offence and liable on summary conviction to a fine not exceeding the statutory maximum or on conviction on indictment to a fine.

(2) If a person executes any works in contravention of section 14(1) the Secretary of State may at any time serve on him a notice requiring him to remove such of the works as are specified in the notice as works to be removed.

(3) The recipient of a notice under subsection (2) shall comply with the notice within the period specified in the notice; and if he fails to do so the Secretary of State may comply with the notice on his behalf and recover from him any expenses reasonably incurred in doing so.

(4) If a person executes any works in contravention of section 14(1) and the Secretary of State considers that it is urgently necessary to do such things in relation to the works as he could have required that person to do by a notice under subsection (2), the Secretary of State may do those things and recover from that person any expenses reasonably incurred in doing so.

(5) The fact that any thing is done or omitted—

(*a*) by the recipient of a notice under subsection (2) for the purpose of complying with the notice; or

(*b*) by the Secretary of State under subsection (3) or (4),

shall not relieve him from liability for any damage which is attributable to the act or omission and for which he would have been liable had the act or omission not been authorised by this section; but the Secretary of State shall be entitled to recover from the person who executed the works in question the amount of any damages which, in consequence of the works, are paid by the Secretary of State by virtue of this subsection.

[Petroleum Act 1998, s 21 as amended by SI 2000/1937.]

8–15976J 22. Criminal proceedings. (1) Proceedings for an offence under section 21(1) or created by regulations made under this Part of this Act (a "relevant offence") may be taken, and the offence may for all incidental purposes be treated as having been committed, in any place in the United Kingdom.

(2) Proceedings for a relevant offence alleged to have been committed in, under or over controlled waters shall not be instituted in England and Wales except—

(*a*) by the Secretary of State or by a person authorised in that behalf by the Secretary of State; or
(*b*) by or with the consent of the Director of Public Prosecutions.

(3) Proceedings for a relevant offence alleged to have been committed in, under or over controlled waters shall not be instituted in Northern Ireland except—

(*a*) by the Secretary of State or by a person authorised in that behalf by the Secretary of State; or
(*b*) by or with the consent of the Director of Public Prosecutions for Northern Ireland.

(4) Subsections (2) and (3) do not apply to proceedings for an offence created by regulations made under section 20.

(5) In proceedings for a relevant offence an averment in the information, complaint or indictment that anything was done or situated in, under or over controlled waters shall, unless the contrary is proved, be sufficient evidence of the matter stated in the averment.

(6) Where a relevant offence committed by a body corporate is proved to have been committed with the consent or connivance of, or to be attributable to any neglect on the part of, any director, manager, secretary or other similar officer of the body corporate or any person who was purporting to act in any such capacity, he as well as the body corporate shall be guilty of that offence and shall be liable to be proceeded against and punished accordingly.

(7) In subsection (6), in relation to a body corporate which—

(*a*) is established by or under any enactment for the purpose of carrying on under public ownership any industry or part of an industry or undertaking; and
(*b*) is a body whose affairs are managed by its members,

"director" means a member of the body corporate.

(8) In any proceedings for—

(*a*) an offence under paragraph (*a*) of subsection (1) of section 21 of executing works or using a pipeline otherwise than in accordance with the terms of the relevant authorisation; or
(*b*) an offence under paragraph (*b*) of that subsection of contravening any provision of a notice,

it shall be a defence to prove that the accused used all due diligence to comply with those terms or, as the case may be, with that provision.

(9) Section 3 of the Territorial Waters Jurisdiction Act 1878 (restriction on prosecutions) shall not apply to any proceedings for a relevant offence.

[Petroleum Act 1998, s 22.]

8–15976K 26. Meaning of "pipeline". (1) Except where the context otherwise requires, in this Part of this Act "pipeline" means a pipe or system of pipes (excluding a drain or sewer) for the conveyance of any thing, together with any apparatus and works associated with such a pipe or system.

(2) For the purposes of this Part of this Act the apparatus and works associated with such a pipe or system are—

(*a*) any apparatus for inducing or facilitating the flow of any thing through, or through a part of, the pipe or system;
(*b*) any apparatus for treating or cooling any thing which is to flow through, or through part of, the pipe or system;
(*c*) valves, valve chambers and similar works which are annexed to, or incorporated in the course of, the pipe or system;
(*d*) apparatus for supplying energy for the operation of any apparatus or works mentioned in paragraphs (*a*) to (*c*);
(*e*) apparatus for the transmission of information for the operation of the pipe or system;
(*f*) apparatus for the cathodic protection of the pipe or system; and
(*g*) any structure used or to be used solely for the support of a part of the pipe or system.

(3) The Secretary of State may by order provide that a part of a pipeline specified in the order shall be treated for the purposes of this Part of this Act, except this subsection, as a pipeline.
[Petroleum Act 1998, s 26.]

8–15976L 27. Meaning of "owner". (1) For the purposes of this Part of this Act "owner" in relation to a pipeline, and "proposed owner" in relation to a proposed pipeline, mean the person for the time being designated as the owner of the pipeline, or as the case may be as the proposed owner of the proposed pipeline, by an order made by the Secretary of State.

(1A) For the purposes of this Part of this Act (other than section 16, section 17(1) and the first reference in section 17F(2)), in the case of downstream gas pipelines and controlled petroleum pipelines—

"owner" in relation to a pipeline includes a person in whom the pipeline is vested; and a person who has the right to use capacity in the pipeline, where such right has been acquired by that person on terms that—

(*a*) he is entitled to use the capacity for a period of one year or more; and
(*b*) the right is capable of being assigned or otherwise disposed of to another person; and

"proposed owner" in relation to a proposed pipeline includes a person in whom the pipeline is proposed to be vested.

(2) An order designating a person as the proposed owner of a proposed pipeline may also provide for him to be designated as the owner of the pipeline in question at a time determined by or under the order.

(3) Before designating a person under subsection (1) or (2), the Secretary of State shall give the person an opportunity of being heard with respect to the matter.

(4) Where a person for the time being designated under subsection (1) or (2) requests the Secretary of State in writing to cancel the designation, the Secretary of State shall—

(*a*) consider the request; and
(*b*) if he considers it appropriate to do so, give the person an opportunity of being heard in connection with the request.
[Petroleum Act 1998, s 27 as amended by SI 2000/1937.]

8–15976M 28. Interpretation of Part III. (1) Except where the context otherwise requires, in this Part of this Act the following expressions have the following meanings—

"authorisation" means an authorisation required by section 14;
"construction", in relation to a pipeline, includes placing, and cognate expressions shall be construed accordingly;
"controlled petroleum pipeline" means any controlled pipeline or one of a network of controlled pipelines operated or constructed as part of a petroleum production project or used to convey petroleum from the site of one or more such projects—

(*a*) directly to premises, in order for that petroleum to be used at those premises for power generation or for an industrial process;
(*b*) directly to a place outside Great Britain;
(*c*) directly to a terminal; or
(*d*) indirectly to a terminal by way of one or more other terminals, whether or not such intermediate terminals are of the same kind as the final terminal;

"controlled pipeline" and "controlled waters" have the meanings given to them by section 14;
"downstream gas pipeline" means a controlled pipeline, other than a controlled petroleum pipeline, which is used to convey gas to or from a place outside Great Britain;
"enactment" includes an enactment of the Parliament of Northern Ireland or of the Northern Ireland Assembly;
"gas" means any substance which consists wholly or mainly of—

(*a*) methane, ethane, propane, butane, hydrogen or carbon monoxide;
(*b*) a mixture of two or more of those gases; or
(*c*) a combustible mixture of one or more of those gases and air;

"gas processing facility" means any facility in Great Britain operated otherwise than by a public gas transporter which carries out gas processing operations;
"gas processing operation" means any of the following operations, namely—

(*a*) purifying, blending, odorising or compressing gas for the purpose of enabling it to be introduced into a pipeline system operated by a public gas transporter or to be conveyed to an electricity generating station, a gas storage facility or any place outside Great Britain;
(*b*) removing from gas for that purpose any of its constituent gases, or separating from gas for that purpose any oil or water; and
(*c*) determining the quantity or quality of gas which is or is to be so introduced, or so conveyed, whether generally or by or on behalf of a particular person;

"heard" means heard on behalf of the Secretary of State by a person appointed by him for the purpose;

"holder", in relation to an authorisation, means the person to whom the authorisation was issued;

"notice" means notice in writing;

"offshore gas storage facility" means the facility for the storage of gas known as the "Rough" facility, situated to the east of Hull in the Southern North Sea at grid reference 0° 27'E 53° 50'N;

"petroleum" has the same meaning as in Part I of this Act, and includes petroleum which has undergone any processing;

"petroleum production project" means a project carried out by virtue of a licence granted under section 3, or an equivalent project in a foreign sector of the continental shelf, and includes such a project which is used for the storage of gas;

"pipeline", in relation to an application for a works authorisation, means the proposed pipeline in respect of which the application is made;

"prescribed" means prescribed by regulations;

"public gas transporter" means a public gas transporter within the meaning of Part I of the Gas Act 1986;

"terminal" includes—

(a) onshore facilities in the United Kingdom for such initial blending and other treatment as may be required to produce stabilised crude oil and other hydrocarbon liquids to the point at which a seller could reasonably make a delivery to a purchaser of such oil and liquids;

(b) gas processing facilities; and

(c) a facility for the reception of gas prior to its conveyance to a place outside Great Britain; and

"works authorisation" means an authorisation—

(a) for works for the construction of a pipeline; or

(b) for such works and for the use of the pipeline.

(2) For the purposes of this Part of this Act, works at any place in, under or over controlled waters for the purpose of determining whether the place is suitable as part of the site of a proposed pipeline and the carrying out of surveying operations for the purpose of settling the route of a proposed pipeline are not works for the construction of a pipeline.

(3) Any reference in this Part of this Act to a contravention of a provision of this Part or regulations made or directions given under this Part includes a reference to a failure to comply with that provision.

(4) Subsections (1) to (3) of section 49 of the Pipe-lines Act 1962 (service of documents) have effect as if—

(a) references to that Act included references to this Part of this Act; and

(b) in subsection (3), after "arrangements agreed" there were inserted "or in accordance with regulations under Part III of the Petroleum Act 1998".

(5) In the application of subsection (4) to Northern Ireland, section 49(1) to (3) of the Pipe-lines Act 1962 shall have effect as if it extended to Northern Ireland.

(6) Except so far as this Part of this Act otherwise expressly provides, nothing in this Part of this Act—

(a) confers a right of action in any civil proceedings (other than proceedings for recovery of a fine) in respect of any contravention of this Part of this Act or an order or regulations made under it;

(b) affects any restriction imposed by or under any other enactment, whether public, local or private; or

(c) derogates from any right of action or other remedy (whether civil or criminal) in proceedings instituted otherwise than under this Act.

(7) Subsection (6) is subject to section 18 of the Interpretation Act 1978 (duplicated offences).
[Petroleum Act 1998, s 28 as amended by SI 2000/1937.]

PART IV[1]
ABANDONMENT OF OFFSHORE INSTALLATIONS

8–15976AN   40. Offences: penalties.   A person guilty of an offence under section 30, 33, 37 or 38 shall be liable—

(a) on summary conviction, to a fine not exceeding **the statutory maximum**;

(b) on conviction on indictment, to imprisonment for a term not exceeding **two years**, or to a **fine**, or to **both**.

---

1. Part IV contains ss 29–45.
[Petroleum Act 1998, s 40.]

8–15976O 41. Offences: general. (1) Proceedings for an offence under section 30, 33, 37 or 38 or under regulations made under section 39 shall not be instituted in England and Wales except—

(*a*) by the Secretary of State or by a person authorised in that behalf by the Secretary of State; or
(*b*) by or with the consent of the Director of Public Prosecutions.

(2) Proceedings for an offence under section 30, 33, 37 or 38 or under regulations made under section 39 shall not be instituted in Northern Ireland except—

(*a*) by the Secretary of State or by a person authorised in that behalf by the Secretary of State; or
(*b*) by or with the consent of the Director of Public Prosecutions for Northern Ireland.

(3) Where an offence committed by a body corporate under section 30, 33, 37 or 38 or under regulations made under section 39 is proved to have been committed with the consent or connivance of, or to be attributable to any neglect on the part of, any director, manager, secretary or other similar officer of the body corporate or any person who was purporting to act in any such capacity, he as well as the body corporate shall be guilty of that offence and shall be liable to be proceeded against and punished accordingly.

(4) Where the affairs of a body corporate are managed by its members, subsection (3) shall apply in relation to acts and defaults of a member in connection with his functions of management as if he were a director of the body corporate.

(5) If an offence under section 37 or under regulations made under section 39 is committed outside the United Kingdom, proceedings for the offence may be taken, and the offence may for all incidental purposes be treated as having been committed, in any place in the United Kingdom.

(6) Section 3 of the Territorial Waters Jurisdiction Act 1878 (restriction on prosecutions) shall not apply to proceedings for an offence to which subsection (1) of this section applies.
[Petroleum Act 1998, s 41.]

8–15976P 44. Meaning of "offshore installation". (1) In this Part of this Act, "offshore installation" means any installation which is or has been maintained, or is intended to be established, for the carrying on of any activity to which subsection (2) applies.

(2) This subsection applies to any activity mentioned in subsection (3) which is carried on from, by means of or on an installation which is maintained in the water, or on the foreshore or other land intermittently covered with water, and is not connected with dry land by a permanent structure providing access at all times and for all purposes.

(3) The activities referred to in subsection (2) are—

(*a*) the exploitation, or the exploration with a view to exploitation, of mineral resources in or under the shore or bed of relevant waters;
(*b*) the storage of gas in or under the shore or bed of relevant waters or the recovery of gas so stored;
(*c*) the conveyance of things by means of a pipe, or system of pipes, constructed or placed on, in or under the shore or bed of relevant waters; and
(*d*) the provision of accommodation for persons who work on or from an installation which is or has been maintained, or is intended to be established, for the carrying on of an activity falling within paragraph (*a*), (*b*) or (*c*) or this paragraph.

(4) In this Part of this Act, "relevant waters" means—

(*a*) tidal waters and parts of the sea in or adjacent to the United Kingdom up to the seaward limits of the territorial sea;
(*b*) waters in an area designated under section 1(7) of the Continental Shelf Act 1964; and
(*c*) such inland waters as may for the time being be specified for the purposes of this paragraph by Order in Council;

but Her Majesty may by Order in Council provide that, in such cases and subject to such exceptions and modifications as may be prescribed by the Order, this Part of this Act shall have effect as if—

(i) any reference in this Part of this Act to relevant waters included a reference to waters in any area specified under section 10(8); and
(ii) in relation to an installation which is or has been maintained, or is intended to be established, in relevant waters, any reference in subsection (3) to relevant waters included a reference to waters in a foreign sector of the continental shelf which are adjacent to such waters.

(5) For the purposes of this section—

"inland waters" means waters within the United Kingdom other than tidal waters and parts of the sea;
"installation" includes—

(*a*) any floating structure or device maintained on a station by whatever means; and
(*b*) in such cases and subject to such exceptions as may be prescribed by Order in Council, any apparatus or works which are by virtue of section 26 to be treated as associated with a pipe or system of pipes for the purposes of Part III of this Act,

but, subject to paragraph (*b*), does not include any part of a pipeline within the meaning of that section;

"modifications" includes additions, omissions and alterations.

(6) The fact that an installation has been maintained for the carrying on of an activity falling within subsection (3) shall be disregarded for the purposes of this section if, since it was so maintained, the installation—

(*a*) has been outside relevant waters or, where it was so maintained in a part of a foreign sector of the continental shelf adjacent to those waters, the area consisting of those waters and that part; or

(*b*) has been maintained for the carrying on of an activity not falling within that subsection.

(7) Any statutory instrument containing an Order under subsection (4) shall be subject to annulment in pursuance of a resolution of either House of Parliament.
[Petroleum Act 1998, s 44.]

8–15976Q   45. Interpretation of Part IV.   In this Part of this Act—

"abandonment programme" has the meaning given by section 29;
"foreign sector of the continental shelf" has the meaning given by section 48(1);
"offshore installation" has the meaning given by section 44;
"relevant waters" has the meaning given by section 44(4);
"submarine pipeline" means a pipeline within the meaning of section 26 which is in, under or over waters in—

(*a*) the territorial sea adjacent to the United Kingdom; or
(*b*) an area designated under section 1(7) of the Continental Shelf Act 1964.
[Petroleum Act 1998, s 45.]

PART V[1]
MISCELLANEOUS AND GENERAL

8–15976R   52. *Commencement*

_____

1. Part V contains ss 46–53.

8–15976S   53. *Short title and extent*

Care Standards Act 2000[1]
(2000 c 14)

PART I[2]
INTRODUCTORY

Preliminary

8–15977   1. Children's homes.   (1) Subsections (2) to (6) have effect for the purposes of this Act.

(2) An establishment is a children's home (subject to the following provisions of this section) if it provides care and accommodation wholly or mainly for children.

(3) An establishment is not a children's home merely because a child is cared for and accommodated there by a parent or relative of his or by a foster parent.

(4) An establishment is not a children's home if it is—

(*a*) a health service hospital;
(*b*) an independent hospital or an independent clinic; or
(*c*) a residential family centre,

or if it is of a description excepted by regulations[3].

(5) Subject to subsection (6), an establishment is not a children's home if it is a school.

(6) A school is a children's home at any time if at that time accommodation is provided for children at the school and either—

(*a*) in each year that fell within the period of two years ending at that time, accommodation was provided for children, either at the school or under arrangements made by the proprietor of the school, for more than 295 days; or
(*b*) it is intended to provide accommodation for children, either at the school or under arrangements made by the proprietor of the school, for more than 295 days in any year;

and in this subsection "year" means a period of twelve months.

But accommodation shall not for the purposes of paragraph (*a*) be regarded as provided to children for a number of days unless there is at least one child to whom it is provided for that number of days; and paragraph (*b*) shall be construed accordingly.

(7) For the purposes of this section a person is a foster parent in relation to a child if—

(*a*) he is a local authority foster parent in relation to the child;

(*b*) he is a foster parent with whom a child has been placed by a voluntary organisation under section 59(1)(*a*) of the 1989 Act; or

(*c*) he fosters the child privately.

[Care Standards Act 2000, s 1.]

1. This Act establishes a National Care Standards Commission; makes provision for the registration and regulation of children's homes, independent hospitals, independent clinics, care homes, residential family centres, independent medical agencies, domiciliary care agencies, fostering agencies, nurses agencies and voluntary adoption agencies. The Act also makes provision for the regulation and inspection of local authority fostering and adoption services; establishes a General Social Care Council and a Care Council for Wales and make provision for the registration, regulation and training of social care workers; to establish a Children's Commissioner for Wales; makes provision for the registration, regulation and training of those providing child minding or day care; makes provision for the protection of children and vulnerable adults; and amends the law about children looked after in schools and colleges. The provisions reproduced in this work are in force unless otherwise stated.

2. Part I comprises ss 1 to 10.

3. Under this provision the following regulations have been made: Children's Homes Regulations 2001, SI 2001/3967 amended by SI 2002/865 and 2469 and SI 2005/1541; Children's Homes (Wales) Regulations 2002, SI 2002/327 amended by SI 2002/2622 and SI 2004/1756 and 2414 and SI 2005/774, 1541 and 2929.

8–15978   2. Independent hospitals etc.   (1) Subsections (2) to (6) apply for the purposes of this Act.

(2) A hospital which is not a health service hospital is an independent hospital.

(3) "Hospital" (except in the expression health service hospital) means—

(*a*) an establishment—

   (i) the main purpose of which is to provide medical or psychiatric treatment for illness or mental disorder or palliative care; or

  (ii) in which (whether or not other services are also provided) any of the listed services are provided;

(*b*) any other establishment in which treatment or nursing (or both) are provided for persons liable to be detained under the Mental Health Act 1983.

(4) "Independent clinic" means an establishment of a prescribed[1] kind (not being a hospital) in which services are provided by medical practitioners (whether or not any services are also provided for the purposes of the establishment elsewhere).

But an establishment in which, or for the purposes of which, services are provided by medical practitioners in pursuance of the National Health Service Act 1977 is not an independent clinic.

(5) "Independent medical agency" means an undertaking (not being an independent clinic or an independent hospital) which consists of or includes the provision of services by medical practitioners.

But if any of the services are provided for the purposes of an independent clinic, or by medical practitioners in pursuance of the National Health Service Act 1977, it is not an independent medical agency.

(6) References to a person liable to be detained under the Mental Health Act 1983 do not include a person absent in pursuance of leave granted under section 17 of that Act.

(7) In this section "listed services" means—

(*a*) medical treatment under anaesthesia or sedation;

(*b*) dental treatment under general anaesthesia;

(*c*) obstetric services and, in connection with childbirth, medical services;

(*d*) termination of pregnancies;

(*e*) cosmetic surgery;

(*a*) other than—

   (i) ear and body piercing;

  (ii) tattooing;

 (iii) the subcutaneous injection of a substance or substances into the skin for cosmetic purposes; and

 (iv) the removal of hair roots or small blemishes on the skin by the application of heat using an electric current;

(*f*) treatment using prescribed techniques or prescribed[1] technology.

(8) Regulations[1] may—

(*a*) except any description of establishment from the definitions in subsections (2) to (4);

(*b*) except any description of undertaking from the definition in subsection (5);

(*c*) modify the definition in subsection (7).

[Care Standards Act 2000, s 2 as amended by the Health and Social Care (Community Health and Standards) Act 2003, s 106.]

1. Under this provision the following regulations have been made: Private and Voluntary Health Care (England) Regulations 2001, SI 2001/3968 amended by SI 2002/865, SI 2004/1771 and SI 2005/1541; Private and Voluntary Health Care (Wales) Regulations 2002, SI 2002/325 amended by SI 2002/2622 and SI 2004/1771 and 2414 and SI 2005/774, 1541, 2929 and 3302.

8–15979   3. Care homes.   (1) For the purposes of this Act, an establishment is a care home if it provides accommodation, together with nursing or personal care, for any of the following persons.
(2) They are—

(*a*) persons who are or have been ill;
(*b*) persons who have or have had a mental disorder;
(*c*) persons who are disabled or infirm;
(*d*) persons who are or have been dependent on alcohol or drugs.

(3) But an establishment is not a care home if it is—

(*a*) a hospital;
(*b*) an independent clinic; or
(*c*) a children's home,

or if it is of a description excepted by regulations[1].
[Care Standards Act 2000, s 3.]

1. Under this provision the following regulations have been made: Care Homes Regulations 2001, SI 2001/3965, amended by SI 2002/865, SI 2003/1534, 1703 and 1845, SI 2004/1770 and SI 2005/1541 and 2114; Care Homes (Wales) Regulations 2002, SI 2002/324 amended by SI 2002/2622 and 3295, SI 2003/947, 1004 and 1703, SI 2004/1314, 1756 and 2414 and SI 2005/1541, 2929 and 3302; Children Act 1989 and the Care Standards Act 2000 (Miscellaneous Regulations) (Amendment) (Wales) (No 2) Regulations 2002, SI 2002/2935; Care Homes (Adult Placements) (Amendment) Regulations 2003, SI 2003/1845; Adult Placement Schemes (Wales) Regulations 2004, SI 2004/1756 amended by SI 2005/3302.

8–15980   4. Other basic definitions.   (1) This section has effect for the purposes of this Act.
(2) "Residential family centre" means, subject to subsection (6), any establishment at which—

(*a*) accommodation is provided for children and their parents;
(*b*) the parents' capacity to respond to the children's needs and to safeguard their welfare is monitored or assessed; and
(*c*) the parents are given such advice, guidance or counselling as is considered necessary.

In this subsection "parent", in relation to a child, includes any person who is looking after him.
(3) "Domiciliary care agency" means, subject to subsection (6), an undertaking which consists of or includes arranging the provision of personal care in their own homes for persons who by reason of illness, infirmity or disability are unable to provide it for themselves without assistance.
(4) "Fostering agency" means, subject to subsection (6)—

(*a*) an undertaking which consists of or includes discharging functions of local authorities in connection with the placing of children with foster parents; or
(*b*) a voluntary organisation which places children with foster parents under section 59(1) of the 1989 Act.

(5) "Nurses agency" means, subject to subsection (6), an employment agency or employment business, being (in either case) a business which consists of or includes supplying, or providing services for the purpose of supplying, registered nurses or registered midwives.
(6) The definitions in subsections (2) to (5) do not include any description of establishment, undertaking or organisation excepted from those definitions by regulations[1].
(7) "Voluntary adoption agency" means an adoption society within the meaning of the Adoption and Children Act 2002 which is a voluntary organisation within the meaning of that Act.
(7A) "Adoption support agency" has the meaning given by section 8 of the Adoption and Children Act 2002.
(8) Below in this Act—

(*a*) any reference to a description of establishment is a reference to a children's home,*** an independent hospital, an independent hospital in which treatment or nursing (or both) are provided for persons liable to be detained under the Mental Health Act 1983, an independent clinic, a care home or a residential family centre;
(*b*) a reference to any establishment is a reference to an establishment of any of those descriptions.

(9) Below in this Act—

(*a*) any reference to a description of agency is a reference to an independent medical agency, a domiciliary care agency, a nurses agency, a fostering agency, a voluntary adoption agency or an adoption support agency;
(*b*) a reference to any agency is a reference to an agency of any of those descriptions.
[Care Standards Act 2000, s 4 as amended by the Adoption and Children Act 2002, Sch 3.]

***Words inserted by the Health and Social Care (Community Health and Standards) Act 2003, s 107, from a date to be appointed.**

1. Under this provision the following regulations have been made: Residential Family Centres Regulations 2002, SI 2002/3213 amended by SI 2005/1541; Nurses Agencies Regulations 2002, SI 2002/3212 amended by SI 2003/2323 and SI 2004/1269, 1770 and 1771; Domiciliary Care Agencies Regulations 2002, SI 2002/3214 amended by SI 2003/2323 and SI 2004/1770; the Residential Family Centres (Wales) Regulations 2003, SI 2003/781 amended by SI 2005/1541, 2929 (W) and 3302; the Nurses Agencies (Wales) Regulations 2003, SI 2003/2527 amended by SI 2003/3054 and SI 2004/1771 and 2414 and SI 2005/3302; Domiciliary Care Agencies (Wales) Regulations 2004, SI 2004/219 amended by SI 2004/1756 and 2414.

Registration authorities

8–15981 5. Registration authorities. (1) For the purposes of this Act—

(a) the registration authority in relation to England is

 (i) the CHAI, in the case of independent hospitals, independent clinics and independent medical agencies;

 (ii) the CSCI, in the case of children's homes, care homes, residential family centres, domiciliary care agencies, nurses agencies, fostering agencies, voluntary adoption agencies and adoption support agencies;

(b) the registration authority in relation to Wales is the National Assembly for Wales (referred to in this Act as "the Assembly").★

(2) This section is subject to section 36A.

[Care Standards Act 2000, s 5, as amended by the Adoption and Children Act 2002, Sch 3 and the Health and Social Care (Community Health and Standards) Act 2003, Sch 9.]

8–15981A 5A, 5B. *General duties of Commissions for Healthcare Audit and Inspection and Social Care Inspection*

8–15982 6. National Care Standards Commission. *Repealed.*

8–15983 7. General duties of the Commission. *Repealed.*

8–15984 8. General functions of the Assembly. (1) The Assembly shall have the general duty of encouraging improvement in the quality of Part II services provided in Wales.

(2) The Assembly shall make information about Part II services provided in Wales available to the public.

(3) In relation to Part II services provided in Wales, the Assembly shall have any additional function specified in regulations made by the Assembly; but the regulations may only specify a function corresponding to a function which, by virtue of section 5A or 5B is exercisable by the CHAI or the CSCI in relation to Part II services provided in England.

(4) The Assembly may charge a reasonable fee determined by it in connection with the exercise of any power conferred on it by or under this Act.

(5) The Assembly may provide training for the purpose of assisting persons to attain standards set out in any statements published by it under section 23.

(6) The Assembly must have particular regard to the need to safeguard and promote the rights ands welfare of children in the exercise of —

(a) its functions exercisable by virtue of section 5(b) and subsections (1) to (3) of this section; and

(b) any other functions exercisable by the Assembly corresponding to functions exercisable by the CSCI in relation to England.

(6) In this section, "Part II services" means services of the kind provided by persons registered under Part II, othere than the provision of —

(a) medical or psychiatric treatment, or

(b) listed services (as defined in section 2).

[Care Standards Act 2000, s 8, as amended by the Health and Social Care (Community Health and Standards) Act 2003, s 109 and Sch 9.]

8–15985 9. Co-operative working. *Repealed.*

8–15986 10. Inquiries. (1) *Repealed.*

(2) The appropriate Minister may cause an inquiry to be held into any matter connected with a service provided in or by an establishment or agency.

(3) Before an inquiry is begun, the person causing the inquiry to be held may direct that it shall be held in private.

(4) Where no direction has been given, the person holding the inquiry may if he thinks fit hold it, or any part of it, in private.

(5) Subsections (2) to (5) of section 250 of the Local Government Act 1972 (powers in relation

to local inquiries) shall apply in relation to an inquiry under this section as they apply in relation to a local inquiry under that section; and references in those provisions as so applied to a Minister shall be taken to include references to the Assembly.

(6) Subsections (3) and (4) apply in relation to an inquiry under section 35 of the Government of Wales Act 1998 into any matter relevant to the exercise of—

(a) any functions exercisable by the Assembly by virtue of section 5(b) or 8(3); or

(b) any other functions exercisable by the Assembly corresponding to functions by the CHAI or the CSCI under this Act in relation to England,

as they apply in relation to an inquiry under this section.

(7) The report of the person who held the inquiry shall, unless the Minister who caused the inquiry to be held considers that there are exceptional circumstances which make it inappropriate to publish it, be published in a manner which that Minister considers appropriate.

[Care Standards Act 2000, s 10 as amended by the Health and Social Care (Community Health and Standards) Act 2003, Sch 9.]

PART II[1]
ESTABLISHMENTS AND AGENCIES

Registration

8–15987   11. Requirement to register.   (1) Any person who carries on or manages an establishment or agency of any description without being registered under this Part in respect of it (as an establishment or, as the case may be, agency of that description) shall be guilty of an offence.

(2) Where the activities of an agency are carried on from two or more branches, each of those branches shall be treated as a separate agency for the purposes of this Part.

(3) The references in subsections (1) and (2) to an agency do not include a reference to a voluntary adoption agency.

(4) The Secretary of State may by regulations[2] make provision about the keeping of registers by the CHAI or the CSCI for the purposes of this Part.

(5) A person guilty of an offence under this section shall be liable on summary conviction—

(a) if subsection (6) does not apply, to a fine not exceeding **level 5** on the standard scale;

(b) if subsection (6) applies, to imprisonment for a term not exceeding **six months**, or to a fine not exceeding **level 5** on the standard scale, or to both.

(6) This subsection applies if—

(a) the person was registered in respect of the establishment or agency at a time before the commission of the offence but the registration was cancelled before the offence was committed; or

(b) the conviction is a second or subsequent conviction of the offence and the earlier conviction, or one of the earlier convictions, was of an offence in relation to an establishment or agency of the same description.

[Care Standards Act 2000, s 11, as amended by the Adoption and Children Act 2002, Sch 3 and the Health and Social Care (Community Health and Standards) Act 2003, Sch 14.]

---

1. Part II comprises ss 11 to 42.

2. The following regulations have been made: National Care Standards Commission (Registration) Regulations 2001, SI 2001/3969 amended by SI 2002/865 (E), SI 2003/369 and 2323, SI 2004/1031 and 1771 and SI 2005/2114 and 2720 (E); Adult Placement Schemes (England) Regulations 2004, SI 2004/2071 amended by SI 2005/2114; Adoption Support Agencies (England) and Adoption Agencies (Miscellaneous Amendments) Regulations 2005, SI 2005/2720.

8–15988   12. Applications for registration.   (1) A person seeking to be registered under this Part shall make an application to the registration authority.

(2) The application—

(a) must give the prescribed information about prescribed matters;

(b) must give any other information which the registration authority reasonably requires the applicant to give,

and must be accompanied by a fee of the amount determined under section 113A, where the registration authority is the CHAI or the CSCI, or of the prescribed amount, where the registration authority is the Assembly.

(3) A person who applies for registration as the manager of an establishment or agency must be an individual.

(4) A person who carries on or manages, or wishes to carry on or manage, more than one establishment or agency must make a separate application in respect of each of them.

[Care Standards Act 2000, s 12 as inserted by the Health and Social Care (Community Health and Standards) Act 2003, s 105.]

---

1. Under this provision the following regulations have been made: National Care Standards Commission (Registration) Regulations 2001, SI 2001/3969 amended by SI 2002/865 (E), SI 2003/369 and 2323, SI 2004/1031 and 1771 and

SI 2005/2114 and 2720 (E); National Care Standards Commission (Fees and Frequency of Inspections) Regulations 2001, SI 2001/3980 amended by SI 2002/1505 and 2070, SI 2003/368 and SI 2005/575; Registration of Social Care and Independent Health Care (Wales) Regulations 2002, SI 2002/919 amended by SI 2002/2622 and 2935, SI 2003/710 and 2527 and SI 2004/219 and 1756; National Care Standards Commission (Fees and Frequency of Inspections) (Adoption Agencies) Regulations 2003, SI 2003/368 amended by SI 2005/640 and 2720; Domiciliary Care Agencies (Wales) Regulations 2004, SI 2004/219 amended by SI 2004/1756 and 2414 and SI 2005/3302; Commission for Healthcare Audit and Inspection (Fees and Frequency of Inspections) Rules 2004, SI 2004/661 (E) amended by SI 2005/647; Adult Placement Schemes (England) Regulations 2004, SI 2004/2071 amended by SI 2005/2114; Adoption Support Agencies (England) and Adoption Agencies (Miscellaneous Amendments) Regulations 2005, SI 2005/2720.

8–15989   13. Grant or refusal of registration.   (1) Subsections (2) to (4) apply where an application under section 12 has been made with respect to an establishment or agency in accordance with the provisions of this Part.

(2) If the registration authority is satisfied that—

(*a*)   the requirements of regulations under section 22; and

(*b*)   the requirements of any other enactment which appears to the registration authority to be relevant,

are being and will continue to be complied with (so far as applicable) in relation to the establishment or agency, it shall grant the application; otherwise it shall refuse it.

(3) The application may be granted either unconditionally or subject to such conditions as the registration authority thinks fit.

(4) On granting the application, the registration authority shall issue a certificate of registration to the applicant.

(5) The registration authority may at any time—

(*a*)   vary or remove any condition for the time being in force in relation to a person's registration; or

(*b*)   impose an additional condition.

[Care Standards Act 2000, s 13.]

8–15990   14. Cancellation of registration.   (1) The registration authority may at any time cancel the registration of a person in respect of an establishment or agency—

(*a*)   on the ground that that person has been convicted of a relevant offence;

(*b*)   on the ground that any other person has been convicted of such an offence in relation to the establishment or agency;

(*c*)   on the ground that the establishment or agency is being, or has at any time been, carried on otherwise than in accordance with the relevant requirements;

(*d*)   on any ground specified by regulations[1].

(2) For the purposes of this section the following are relevant offences—

(*a*)   an offence under this Part or regulations made under it;

(*b*)   an offence under the Registered Homes Act 1984 or regulations made under it;

(*c*)   an offence under the 1989 Act or regulations made under it;

(*d*)   in relation to a voluntary adoption agency, an offence under regulations under section 9(2) of the Adoption Act 1976 or section 1(3) of the Adoption (Intercountry Aspects) Act 1999.

(3) In this section "relevant requirements" means—

(*a*)   any requirements or conditions imposed by or under this Part; and

(*b*)   the requirements of any other enactment which appear to the registration authority to be relevant.

[Care Standards Act 2000, s 14.]

---

1. Under this provision the following regulations have been made: National Care Standards Commission (Registration) Regulations 2001, SI 2001/3969 amended by SI 2002/865 (E), SI 2003/369 and 2323, SI 2004/1031 and 1771 and SI 2005/2114 and 2720 (E); Registration of Social Care and Independent Health Care (Wales) Regulations 2002, SI 2002/919 amended by SI 2002/2622 and 2935, SI 2003/710 and 2527, SI 2004/919 and 1756 and SI 2005/3302; Domiciliary Care Agencies (Wales) Regulations 2004, SI 2004/219 amended by SI 2004/1756 and 2414 and SI 2005/3302; Adult Placement Schemes (England) Regulations 2004, SI 2004/2071 amended by SI 2005/2114.

8–15991   15. Applications by registered persons.   (1) A person registered under this Part may apply to the registration authority—

(*a*)   for the variation or removal of any condition for the time being in force in relation to the registration; or

(*b*)   for the cancellation of the registration.

(2) But a person may not make an application under subsection (1)(*b*)—

(*a*)   if the registration authority has given him notice under section 17(4)(*a*) of a proposal to cancel the registration, unless the registration authority has decided not to take that step; or

(b) if the registration authority has given him notice under section 19(3) of its decision to cancel the registration and the time within which an appeal may be brought has not expired or, if an appeal has been brought, it has not been determined.

(3) An application under subsection (1) shall be made in such manner and state such particulars as may be prescribed and, if made under paragraph (a) of that subsection, shall be accompanied by a fee of such amount as may be prescribed[1].

(4) If the registration authority decides to grant an application under subsection (1)(a) it shall serve notice in writing of its decision on the applicant (stating, where applicable, the condition as varied) and issue a new certificate of registration.

(5) If different amounts are prescribed under subsection (3), the regulations may provide for the registration authority to determine which amount is payable in a particular case.
[Care Standards Act 2000, s 15 as amended by the Health and Social Care (Community Health and Standards) Act 2003, s 105.]

---

1. Under this provision the following regulations have been made: National Care Standards Commission (Registration) Regulations 2001, SI 2001/3969 amended by SI 2002/865 (E), SI 2003/369 and 2323, SI 2004/1031 and 1771 and SI 2005/2114 and 2720 (E); National Care Standards Commission (Fees and Frequency of Inspections) Regulations 2001, SI 2001/3980 amended by SI 2002/1505 and 2070, SI 2003/368 and SI 2005/575; Registration of Social Care and Independent Health Care (Wales) Regulations 2002, SI 2002/919 amended by SI 2002/2622 and 3295, SI 2003/710 and 2527, SI 2004/919 and 1756 and SI 2005/3302; National Care Standards Commission (Fees and Frequency of Inspections) (Adoption Agencies) Regulations 2003, SI 2003/368 amended by SI 2005/640 and 2720; Domiciliary Care Agencies (Wales) Regulations 2004, SI 2004/219 amended by SI 2004/1756 and 2414 and SI 2005/3302; Adult Placement Schemes (England) Regulations 2004, SI 2004/2071 amended by SI 2005/2114; Adoption Support Agencies (England) and Adoption Agencies (Miscellaneous Amendments) Regulations 2005, SI 2005/2720.

8–15992 16. Regulations about registration. (1) Regulations[1] may make provision about the registration of persons under this Part in respect of establishments or agencies, and in particular about—

(a) the making of applications for registration;
(b) the contents of certificates of registration.

(2) Regulations[2] may provide that no application for registration under this Part may be made in respect of a fostering agency, or a voluntary adoption agency, which is an unincorporated body.

(3) Persons registered under this Part must also pay to the registration authority, at such time as may be prescribed, an annual fee—

(a) of such amount as may be determined under section 113A, where the registration authority is the CHAI or the CSCI; and
(b) of such amount as may be prescribed, where the registration authority is the Assembly.

(4) A fee payable by virtue of this section may, without prejudice to any other method of recovery, be recovered summarily as a civil debt.
[Care Standards Act 2000, s 16 as amended by the Health and Social Care (Community Health and Standards) Act 2003, s 105.]

---

1. Under this provision the following regulations have been made: National Care Standards Commission (Registration) Regulations 2001, SI 2001/3969 amended by SI 2002/865 (E), SI 2003/369 and 2323, SI 2004/1031 and 1771 and SI 2005/2114 and 2720 (E); Registration of Social Care and Independent Health Care (Wales) Regulations 2002, SI 2002/919 amended by SI 2002/2622 and 3295, SI 2003/710 and 2527, SI 2004/919 and 1756 and SI 2005/3302; Residential Family Centres (Wales) Regulations 2003, SI 2003/781 amended by SI 2005/1541, 2929 (W) and 3302; Adult Placement Schemes (England) Regulations 2004, SI 2004/2071 amended by SI 2005/2114.
2. Under this provision the following regulations have been made: National Care Standards Commission (Fees and Frequency of Inspections) Regulations 2001, SI 2001/3980 amended by SI 2002/1505 and 2070, SI 2003/368 and SI 2005/575; National Care Standards Commission (Fees and Frequency of Inspections) (Adoption Agencies) Regulations 2003, SI 2003/368 amended by SI 2005/640 and 2720; Nurses Agencies (Wales) Regulations 2003, SI 2003/2527 amended by SI 2003/3054 and SI 2004/1771and 2414; Domiciliary Care Agencies (Wales) Regulations 2004, SI 2004/219 amended by SI 2004/1756 and 2414 and SI 2005/3302; Adoption Support Agencies (England) and Adoption Agencies (Miscellaneous Amendments) Regulations 2005, SI 2005/2720.

Registration procedure

8–15993 17. Notice of proposals. (1) Subsections (2) and (3) apply where a person applies for registration in respect of an establishment or agency.

(2) If the registration authority proposes to grant the application subject to any conditions which have not been agreed in writing between it and the applicant, it shall give the applicant written notice of its proposal and of the conditions subject to which it proposes to grant his application.

(3) The registration authority shall give the applicant notice of a proposal to refuse the application.

(4) Except where it makes an application under section 20, the registration authority shall give any person registered in respect of an establishment or agency notice of a proposal—

(a) to cancel the registration (otherwise than in accordance with an application under section 15(1)(b));
(b) to vary or remove (otherwise than in accordance with an application under section 15(1)(a)) any condition for the time being in force in relation to the registration; or

(c)   to impose any additional condition in relation to the registration.

(5)   The registration authority shall give the applicant notice of a proposal to refuse an application under section 15(1)(*a*).

(6)   A notice under this section shall give the registration authority's reasons for its proposal.
[Care Standards Act 2000, s 17.]

8–15994   **18. Right to make representations.**   (1) A notice under section 17 shall state that within 28 days of service of the notice any person on whom it is served may make written representations to the registration authority concerning any matter which that person wishes to dispute.

(2)   Where a notice has been served under section 17, the registration authority shall not determine any matter to which the notice relates until either—

(a)   any person on whom the notice was served has made written representations to it concerning the matter;

(b)   any such person has notified the registration authority in writing that he does not intend to make representations; or

(c)   the period during which any such person could have made representations has elapsed.
[Care Standards Act 2000, s 18.]

8–15995   **19. Notice of decisions.**   (1) If the registration authority decides to grant an application for registration in respect of an establishment or agency unconditionally, or subject only to conditions which have been agreed in writing between it and the applicant, it shall give the applicant written notice of its decision.

(2)   A notice under subsection (1) shall state the agreed conditions.

(3)   If the registration authority decides to adopt a proposal under section 17, it shall serve notice in writing of its decision on any person on whom it was required to serve notice of the proposal.

(4)   A notice under subsection (3) shall—

(a)   explain the right of appeal conferred by section 21;

(b)   in the case of a decision to adopt a proposal under section 17(2), state the conditions subject to which the application is granted; and

(c)   in the case of a decision to adopt a proposal under section 17(4)(*b*) or (*c*), state the condition as varied, the condition which is removed or (as the case may be) the additional condition imposed.

(5)   Subject to subsection (6), a decision of the registration authority to adopt a proposal under section 17(2) or (4) shall not take effect—

(a)   if no appeal is brought, until the expiration of the period of 28 days referred to in section 21(2); and

(b)   if an appeal is brought, until it is determined or abandoned.

(6)   Where, in the case of a decision to adopt a proposal under section 17(2), the applicant notifies the registration authority in writing before the expiration of the period mentioned in subsection (5)(*a*) that he does not intend to appeal, the decision shall take effect when the notice is served.
[Care Standards Act 2000, s 19.]

8–15996   **20. Urgent procedure for cancellation etc.**   (1) If—

(a)   the registration authority applies to a justice of the peace for an order—

     (i)   cancelling the registration of a person in respect of an establishment or agency;

     (ii)   varying or removing any condition for the time being in force by virtue of this Part; or

     (iii)   imposing an additional condition; and

(b)   it appears to the justice that, unless the order is made, there will be a serious risk to a person's life, health or well-being,

the justice may make the order, and the cancellation, variation, removal or imposition shall have effect from the time when the order is made.

(2)   An application under subsection (1) may, if the justice thinks fit, be made without notice.

(3)   As soon as practicable after the making of an application under this section, the registration authority shall notify the appropriate authorities of the making of the application.

(4)   An order under subsection (1) shall be in writing.

(5)   Where such an order is made, the registration authority shall, as soon as practicable after the making of the order, serve on the person registered in respect of the establishment or agency—

(a)   a copy of the order; and

(b)   notice of the right of appeal conferred by section 21.

(6)   For the purposes of this section the appropriate authorities are—

(a)   the local authority in whose area the establishment or agency is situated;

(b)   the Health Authority in whose area the establishment or agency is situated; and (*c*)   any statutory authority not falling within paragraph (*a*) or (*b*) whom the registration authority thinks it appropriate to notify.

(7)   In this section "statutory authority" means a body established by or under an Act of Parliament.
[Care Standards Act 2000, s 20.]

8–15997   21. Appeals to the Tribunal.   (1) An appeal against—

(*a*)   a decision of the registration authority under this Part; or
(*b*)   an order made by a justice of the peace under section 20,

shall lie to the Tribunal.

(2)   No appeal against a decision or order may be brought by a person more than 28 days after service on him of notice of the decision or order.

(3)   On an appeal against a decision of the registration authority the Tribunal may confirm the decision or direct that it shall not have effect.

(4)   On an appeal against an order made by a justice of the peace the Tribunal may confirm the order or direct that it shall cease to have effect.

(5)   The Tribunal shall also have power on an appeal against a decision or order—

(*a*)   to vary any condition for the time being in force in respect of the establishment or agency to which the appeal relates;
(*b*)   to direct that any such condition shall cease to have effect; or
(*c*)   to direct that any such condition as it thinks fit shall have effect in respect of the establishment or agency.
[Care Standards Act 2000, s 21.]

Regulations and standards

8–15998   22. Regulation of establishments and agencies.   (1) Regulations[1] may impose in relation to establishments and agencies any requirements which the appropriate Minister thinks fit for the purposes of this Part and may in particular make any provision such as is mentioned in subsection (2), (7) or (8).

(2)   Regulations may—

(*a*)   make provision as to the persons who are fit to carry on or manage an establishment or agency;
(*b*)   make provision as to the persons who are fit to work at an establishment or for the purposes of an agency;
(*c*)   make provision as to the fitness of premises to be used as an establishment or for the purposes of an agency;
(*d*)   make provision for securing the welfare of persons accommodated in an establishment or provided with services by an establishment, an independent medical agency or a domiciliary care agency;
(*e*)   make provision for securing the welfare of children placed, under section 23(2)(*a*) of the 1989 Act, by a fostering agency;
(*f*)   make provision as to the management and control of the operations of an establishment or agency;
(*g*)   make provision as to the numbers of persons, or persons of any particular type, working at an establishment or for the purposes of an agency;
(*h*)   make provision as to the management and training of such persons;
(*i*)   impose requirements as to the financial position of an establishment or agency;
(*j*)   make provision requiring the person carrying on an establishment or agency to appoint a manager in prescribed circumstances.

(3)   Regulations under subsection (2)(*a*) may, in particular, make provision for prohibiting persons from managing an establishment or agency unless they are registered in, or in a particular part of, one of the registers maintained under section 56(1).

(4)   Regulations under subsection (2)(*b*) may, in particular, make provision for prohibiting persons from working in such positions as may be prescribed at an establishment, or for the purposes of an agency, unless they are registered in, or in a particular part of, one of the registers maintained under section 56(1).

(5)   Regulations under paragraph (*d*) of subsection (2) may, in particular, make provision—

(*a*)   as to the promotion and protection of the health of persons such as are mentioned in that paragraph;
(*b*)   as to the control and restraint of adults accommodated in, or provided with services by, an establishment;
(*c*)   as to the control, restraint and discipline of children accommodated in, or provided with services by, an establishment.

(6)   Regulations under paragraph (*e*) of subsection (2) may, in particular, make provision—

(*a*)   as to the promotion and protection of the health of children such as are mentioned in that paragraph;

(b)   as to the control, restraint and discipline of such children.

(7) Regulations may make provision as to the conduct of establishments and agencies, and such regulations may in particular—

(a)   make provision as to the facilities and services to be provided in establishments and by agencies;

(b)   make provision as to the keeping of accounts;

(c)   make provision as to the keeping of documents and records;

(d)   make provision as to the notification of events occurring in establishments or in premises used for the purposes of agencies;

(e)   make provision as to the giving of notice by the person carrying on an establishment or agency of periods during which he or (if he does not manage it himself) the manager proposes to be absent from the establishment or agency, and specify the information to be supplied in such a notice;

(f)   provide for the making of adequate arrangements for the running of an establishment or agency during a period when the manager is absent from it;

(g)   make provision as to the giving of notice by a person registered in respect of an establishment or agency of any intended change in the identity of the manager or the person carrying it on;

(h)   make provision as to the giving of notice by a person registered in respect of an establishment or agency which is carried on by a body corporate of changes in the ownership of the body or the identity of its officers;

(i)   make provision requiring the payment of a fee of such amount as may be prescribed in respect of any notification required to be made by virtue of paragraph (h);

(j)   make provision requiring arrangements to be made by the person who carries on, or manages, an establishment or agency for dealing with complaints made by or on behalf of those seeking, or receiving, any of the services provided in the establishment or by the agency and requiring that person to take steps for publicising the arrangements;

(k)   make provision requiring arrangements to be made by the person who carries on, or manages, an independent hospital, independent clinic or independent medical agency for securing that any medical or psychiatric treatment, or listed services, provided in or for the purposes of the establishment or (as the case may be) for the purposes of the agency are of appropriate quality and meet appropriate standards;

(l)   make provision requiring arrangements to be made by the person who carries on, or manages, a care home for securing that any nursing provided by the home is of appropriate quality and meets appropriate standards.

(8) Regulations may make provision—

(a)   requiring the approval of the appropriate Minister for the provision and use of accommodation for the purpose of restricting the liberty of children in children's homes;

(b)   imposing other requirements (in addition to those imposed by section 25 of the 1989 Act (use of accommodation for restricting liberty)) as to the placing of a child in accommodation provided for the purpose mentioned in paragraph (a), including a requirement to obtain the permission of any local authority who are looking after the child;

(c)   as to the facilities which are to be provided for giving religious instruction to children in children's homes.

(9) Before making regulations under this section, except regulations which amend other regulations made under this section and do not, in the opinion of the appropriate Minister, effect any substantial change in the provision made by those regulations, the appropriate Minister shall consult any persons he considers appropriate.

(10) References in this section to agencies do not include references to voluntary adoption agencies.

(11) In subsection (7)(k), "listed services" has the same meaning as in section 2.

[Care Standards Act 2000, s 22.]

---

1. Under this provision the following regulations have been made: Care Homes Regulations 2001, SI 2001/3965 amended by SI 2002/865, SI 2003/1534, 1703 and 1845, SI 2004/1770 and SI 2005/1541 and 2114; Children's Homes Regulations 2001, SI 2001/3967 amended by SI 2002/865 and 2469; Fostering Services Regulations 2002, SI 2002/57 amended by SI 2002/865 and 2469 and SI 2005/1541; Care Homes (Wales) Regulations 2002, SI 2002/324 amended by SI 2002/2622 and 3295, SI 2003/947, 1004 and 1703, SI 2004/1314, 1756 and 2414 and SI 2005/1541, 2929 and 3302; Private and Voluntary Health Care (Wales) Regulations 2002, SI 2002/325 amended by SI 2004/1771 and 2414 and SI 2005/1541 and 2929; Children's Homes (Wales) Regulations 2002, SI 2002/327 amended by SI 2002/2622, SI 2004/1756 and 2414 and SI 2005/774, 1541, 2929 and 3302; Residential Family Centres Regulations 2002, SI 2002/3213 and SI 2005/1541; Nurses Agencies Regulations 2002, SI 2002/3212 amended by SI 2004/1269, 1770 and 1771; Domiciliary Care Agencies Regulations 2002, SI 2002/3214 amended by SI 2003/2323 and SI 2004/1770; Fostering Services (Wales) Regulations 2003, SI 2003/237 amended by SI 2003/896 and SI 2005/3302; Residential Family Centres (Wales) Regulations 2003, SI 2003/781 amended by SI 2005/1541, 2929 (W) and 3302; Nursing Agencies (Wales) Regulations 2003, SI 2003/2527 amended by SI 2003/3054 and SI 2004/1771 and 2414; Domiciliary Care Agencies (Wales) Regulations 2004, SI 2004/219 amended by SI 2004/1756 and 2414 and SI 2005/3302; Adult Placement Schemes (Wales) Regulations 2004, SI 2004/1756 amended by SI 2005/3302; Adult Placement Schemes (England) Regulations 2004, SI 2004/2071 amended by SI 2005/2114; Adoption Support Agencies (Wales) Regulations 2005, SI 2005/1514.

8–15999   23. National minimum standards.   (1) The appropriate Minister may prepare and publish statements of national minimum standards applicable to establishments or agencies.

(2) The appropriate Minister shall keep the standards set out in the statements under review and may publish amended statements whenever he considers it appropriate to do so.

(3) Before issuing a statement, or an amended statement which in the opinion of the appropriate Minister effects a substantial change in the standards, the appropriate Minister shall consult any persons he considers appropriate.

(4) The standards shall be taken into account—

(*a*) in the making of any decision by the registration authority under this Part;

(*b*) in any proceedings for the making of an order under section 20;

(*c*) in any proceedings on an appeal against such a decision or order; and

(*d*) in any proceedings for an offence under regulations under this Part or proceedings against a voluntary adoption agency for an offence under section 9(4) of the Adoption Act 1976 or against a voluntary adoption agency or adoption support agency for an offence under section 9 of the Adoption and Children Act 2002.★

[Care Standards Act 2000, s 23, as amended by the Adoption and Children Act 2002, Sch 3 and the Health and Social Care (Community Health and Standards) Act 2003, s 147, Sch 9.]

★Reproduced as in force in relation to England in so far as relating to the Adoption Act 1976 30 April 2003 (SI 2003/366, art 2(4)(c)); in relation to England for remaining purposes, and in relation to Wales, to be appointed (the Adoption and Children Act 2002, s 148(1), (2)).

Offences

8–16000   24. Failure to comply with conditions.   If a person registered in respect of an establishment or agency fails, without reasonable excuse, to comply with any condition for the time being in force by virtue of this Part in respect of the establishment or agency, he shall be guilty of an offence and liable on summary conviction to a fine not exceeding **level 5** on the standard scale.
[Care Standards Act 2000, s 24.]

8–16000ZR   25. Contravention of regulations.   (1) Regulations[1] under this Part may provide that a contravention of or failure to comply with any specified provision of the regulations shall be an offence.

(2) A person guilty of an offence under the regulations shall be liable on summary conviction to a fine not exceeding **level 4** on the standard scale.
[Care Standards Act 2000, s 25.]

---

1. Under this provision the following regulations have been made: Care Homes Regulations 2001, SI 2001/3965 amended by SI 2002/865, SI 2003/1534, 1703 and 1845, SI 2004/1770 and SI 2005/1541 and 2114; Children's Homes Regulations 2001, SI 2001/3967 amended by SI 2002/865 and 2469 and SI 2005/1541; Private and Voluntary Health Care (England) Regulations 2001, SI 2001/3968 amended by SI 2004/1031 and 1771 and SI 2005/1541 and 2114; National Care Standards Commission (Registration) Regulations 2001, SI 2001/3969 amended by SI 2002/865 (E), SI 2003/369 and 2323, SI 2004/1031 and 1771 and SI 2005/2114 and 2720 (E); Fostering Services Regulations 2002, SI 2002/57; Care Homes (Wales) Regulations 2002, SI 2002/324 amended by SI 2002/2622 and 3295, SI 2003/947, 1004 and 1703, SI 2004/1314, 1756 and 2414 and SI 2005/1541, 2929 and 3302; Private and Voluntary Health Care (Wales) Regulations 2002, SI 2002/325 amended by SI 2004/1771 and SI 2005/774, 1541, 2929 and 3302; Children's Homes (Wales) Regulations 2002, SI 2002/327 amended by SI 2002/2622, SI 2004/1756 and 2414 and SI 2005/774, 1541 and 2929; Care Standards Act 2000 (Establishments and Agencies) (Miscellaneous Amendments) Regulations 2002, SI 2002/865; Registration of Social Care and Independent Health Care (Wales) Regulations 2002, SI 2002/919 amended by SI 20022/2622 and 3295, SI 2003/710 and 2527 and SI 2004/219 and 1756 and SI 2005/3302; Nurses Agencies Regulations 2002, SI 2002/3212 amended by SI 2003/2323, SI 2004/1269, 1770 and 1771; Residential Family Centres Regulations 2002, SI 2002/3213 amended by SI 2005/1541; Domiciliary Care Agencies Regulations 2002, SI 2002/3214 amended by SI 2003/2323 and SI 2004/1770; Fostering Services (Wales) Regulations 2003, SI 2003/237 amended by SI 2003/896 and SI 2005/3302; Residential Family Centres (Wales) Regulations 2003, SI 2003/781 amended by SI 2005/1541, 2929 (W) and 3302; Nurses Agencies (Wales) Regulations 2003, SI 2003/2527 amended by SI 2004/1771 and 2414; Domiciliary Care Agencies (Wales) Regulations 2004, SI 2004/219 amended by SI 2004/1756 and 2414 and SI 2005/3302; Adult Placement Schemes (Wales) Regulations 2004, SI 2004/1756 amended by SI 2005/3302; Adult Placement Schemes (England) Regulations 2004, SI 2004/2071 amended by SI 2005/2114; Adoption Support Agencies (Wales) Regulations 2005, SI 2005/1514.

8–16000ZS   26. False descriptions of establishments and agencies.   (1) A person who, with intent to deceive any person—

(*a*) applies any name to premises in England or Wales; or

(*b*) in any way describes such premises or holds such premises out,

so as to indicate, or reasonably be understood to indicate, that the premises are an establishment, or an agency, of a particular description shall be liable on summary conviction to a fine not exceeding **level 5** on the standard scale unless registration has been effected under this Part in respect of the premises as an establishment or agency of that description.

(2) References to premises in subsection (1) shall be taken to include references to an undertaking or organisation.

(3) No person shall, with intent to deceive any person, in any way describe or hold out an

establishment or agency as able to provide any service or do any thing the provision or doing of which would contravene a condition for the time being in force by virtue of this Part in respect of the establishment or agency.

(4) A person who contravenes subsection (3) shall be liable on summary conviction to a fine not exceeding **level 5** on the standard scale.

[Care Standards Act 2000, s 26.]

8–16000ZT   27. False statements in applications.   (1) Any person who, in an application for registration under this Part or for the variation of any condition in force in relation to his registration, knowingly makes a statement which is false or misleading in a material respect shall be guilty of an offence.

(2) A person guilty of an offence under this section shall be liable on summary conviction to a fine not exceeding **level 4** on the standard scale.

[Care Standards Act 2000, s 27.]

8–16000ZU   28. Failure to display certificate of registration.   (1) A certificate of registration issued under this Part in respect of any establishment or agency shall be kept affixed in a conspicuous place in the establishment or at the agency.

(2) If default is made in complying with subsection (1), any person registered in respect of the establishment or agency shall be guilty of an offence and liable on summary conviction to a fine not exceeding **level 2** on the standard scale.

[Care Standards Act 2000, s 28.]

8–16000ZV   29. Proceedings for offences.   (1) Proceedings in respect of an offence under this Part or regulations made under it shall not, without the written consent of the Attorney General, be taken by any person other than—

(*a*)   the CHAI or the CSCI (as appropriate) or, in relation to any functions of either the CHAI or the CSCI which the Secretary of State is by virtue of section 113 for the time being discharging, the Secretary of State; or

(*b*)   the Assembly.

(2) Proceedings for an offence under this Part or regulations made under it may be brought within a period of six months from the date on which evidence sufficient in the opinion of the prosecutor to warrant the proceedings came to his knowledge; but no such proceedings shall be brought by virtue of this subsection more than three years after the commission of the offence.

[Care Standards Act 2000, s 29, as amended by the Health and Social Care (Community Health and Standards) Act 2003, Sch 9.]

8–16000ZW   30. Offences by bodies corporate.   (1) This section applies where any offence under this Part or regulations made under it is committed by a body corporate.

(2) If the offence is proved to have been committed with the consent or connivance of, or to be attributable to any neglect on the part of—

(*a*)   any director, manager, or secretary of the body corporate; or

(*b*)   any person who was purporting to act in any such capacity,

he (as well as the body corporate) shall be guilty of the offence and shall be liable to be proceeded against and punished accordingly.

(3) The reference in subsection (2) to a director, manager or secretary of a body corporate includes a reference—

(*a*)   to any other similar officer of the body; and

(*b*)   where the body is a local authority, to any officer or member of the authority.

[Care Standards Act 2000, s 30.]

Miscellaneous and supplemental

8–16000ZX   31. Inspections by persons authorised by registration authority.   (1) The registration authority may at any time require a person who carries on or manages an establishment or agency to provide it with any information relating to the establishment or agency which the registration authority considers it necessary or expedient to have for the purposes of its functions under this Part.

(1A)   The power under subsection (1) to require the provision of information includes—

(*a*)   power to require the provision of copies of any documents or records (including medical and other personal records); and

(*b*)   in relation to records kept by means of a computer, power to require the provision of the records in legible form.

(2) A person authorised by the registration authority may at any time enter and inspect premises which are used, or which he has reasonable cause to believe to be used, as an establishment or for the purposes of an agency.

(3) A person authorised by virtue of this section to enter and inspect premises may—

(a) make any examination into the state and management of the premises and treatment of patients or persons accommodated or cared for there which he thinks appropriate;

(b) inspect and take copies of any documents or records (including medical and other personal records) required to be kept in accordance with regulations under this Part, section 9 of the Adoption and Children Act 2002, section 23(2)(a) or 59(2) of the 1989 Act or section 1(3) of the Adoption (Intercountry Aspects) Act 1999;

(c) interview in private the manager or the person carrying on the establishment or agency;

(d) interview in private any person working there;

(e) interview in private any patient or person accommodated or cared for there who consents to be interviewed.

(4) The powers under subsection (3)(b) include—

(a) power to require the manager or the person carrying on the establishment or agency to produce any documents or records, wherever kept, for inspection on the premises; and

(b) in relation to records which are kept by means of a computer, power to require the records to be produced in a form in which they are legible and can be taken away.

(5) Subsection (6) applies where the premises in question are used as an establishment and the person so authorised—

(a) is a medical practitioner or registered nurse; and

(b) has reasonable cause to believe that a patient or person accommodated or cared for there is not receiving proper care.

(6) The person so authorised may, with the consent of the person mentioned in subsection (5)(b), examine him in private.

The power conferred by this subsection may be exercised in relation to a person who is incapable of giving consent without that person's consent.

(7) The Secretary of State may by regulations[1] require the CHAI or the CSCI to arrange for premises which are used as an establishment or for the purposes of an agency to be inspected on such occasions or at such intervals as may be prescribed.

(8) A person who proposes to exercise any power of entry or inspection conferred by this section shall if so required produce some duly authenticated document showing his authority to exercise the power.

(9) Any person who—

(a) intentionally obstructs the exercise of any power conferred by this section or section 32; or

(b) fails without a reasonable excuse to comply with any requirement under this section or that section,

shall be guilty of an offence and liable on summary conviction to a fine not exceeding **level 4** on the standard scale.

[Care Standards Act 2000, s 31, as amended by the Health and Social Care (Community Health and Standards) Act 2003, ss 108 and 147, Sch 9 and the Adoption and Children Act 2002, Sch 3.]

---

1. The following regulations have been made under this provision: National Care Standards Commission (Fees and Frequency of Inspections) Regulations 2001, SI 2001/3980 amended by SI 2002/1505, 2070 and 3211 and SI 2003/368; National Care Standards Commission (Fees and Frequency of Inspections) (Adoption Agencies) Regulations 2003, SI 2003/368 amended by SI 2005/640 and 2720; Commission for Healthcare Audit and Inspection (Fees and Frequency of Inspections) Regulations 2004, SI 2004/661; Commission for Social Care Inspection (Fees and Frequency of Inspections) Regulations 2004, SI 2004/662 amended by SI 2005/2720 (E); the Adult Placement Schemes (England) Regulations 2004, SI 2004/2071 amended by SI 2005/2114; Adoption Support Agencies (England) and Adoption Agencies (Miscellaneous Amendments) Regulations 2005, SI 2005/2720.

8–16000ZY **32. Inspections: supplementary.** (1) A person authorised by virtue of section 31 to enter and inspect any premises may seize and remove any document or other material or thing found there which he has reasonable grounds to believe may be evidence of a failure to comply with any condition or requirement imposed by or under this Part.

(2) A person so authorised—

(a) may require any person to afford him such facilities and assistance with respect to matters within the person's control as are necessary to enable him to exercise his powers under section 31 or this section;

(b) may take such measurements and photographs and make such recordings as he considers necessary to enable him to exercise those powers.

(3) A person authorised by virtue of section 31 to inspect any records shall be entitled to have access to, and to check the operation of, any computer and any associated apparatus which is or has been in use in connection with the records in question.

(4) The references in section 31 to the person carrying on the establishment or agency include, in the case of an establishment or agency which is carried on by a company, a reference to any director, manager, secretary or other similar officer of the company.

(5) Where any premises which are used as an establishment or for the purposes of an agency have been inspected under section 31, the registration authority—

(a) shall prepare a report on the matters inspected; and

(b) shall without delay send a copy of the report to each person who is registered in respect of the establishment or agency.

(6) The registration authority shall make copies of any report prepared under subsection (5) available for inspection at its offices by any person at any reasonable time; and may take any other steps for publicising a report which it considers appropriate.

(7) Any person who asks the registration authority for a copy of a report prepared under subsection (5) shall be entitled to have one on payment of a reasonable fee determined by the registration authority; but nothing in this subsection prevents the registration authority from providing a copy free of charge when it considers it appropriate to do so.

(8) *Repealed.*

[Care Standards Act 2000, s 32, as amended by the Health and Social Care (Community Health and Standards) Act 2003, s 196, Sch 14.]

8–16000ZZ   **33. Annual returns.**   (1) Regulations[1] may require the person carrying on an establishment or agency to make an annual return to the registration authority.

(2) Provision may be made by the regulations as to the contents of the return and the period in respect of which and date by which it is to be made.

[Care Standards Act 2000, s 33.]

---

1. The following regulations have been made: Care Homes (Wales) Regulations 2002, SI 2002/324 amended by SI 2002/2622 and 3295, SI 2003/947, 1004 and 1703, SI 2004/1314, 1756 and 2414 and SI 2005/1541, 2929 and 3302; Children's Homes (Wales) Regulations 2002, SI 2002/327 amended by SI 2002/2622, SI 2004/1756 and 2414 and SI 2005/774, 1541 and 2929 (W); Local Authority Adoption Service and Miscellaneous Amendments (Wales) Regulations 2003, SI 2003/710; Adult Placement Schemes (England) Regulations 2004, SI 2004/2071 amended by SI 2005/2114.

8–16000ZZA   **34. Liquidators etc.**   (1) Regulations[1] may—

(a) require any person to whom this section applies to give notice of his appointment to the registration authority;

(b) require any person to whom this section applies to appoint a person to manage the establishment or agency in question.

(2) This section applies to any person appointed as—

(a) a receiver or manager of the property of a relevant company;

(b) the liquidator or provisional liquidator of a relevant company; or

(c) the trustee in bankruptcy of a relevant individual.

(3) In this section—

"company" includes a partnership;

"relevant company" means a company which is registered under this Part in respect of an establishment or agency; and

"relevant individual" means an individual who is registered under this Part in respect of an establishment or agency.

[Care Standards Act 2000, s 34.]

---

1. Under this provision the following regulations have been made: Care Homes Regulations 2001, SI 2001/3965 amended by SI 2002/865, SI 2003/1534, 1703 and 1845, SI 2004/1770 and SI 2005/1541 and 2114; Children's Homes Regulations 2001, SI 2001/3967 amended by SI 2002/865 and 2469 and SI 2005/1541; Private and Voluntary Health Care (England) Regulations 2001, SI 2001/3968 amended by SI 2004/1031 and 1771 and SI 2005/1541 and 2114; Fostering Services Regulations 2002, SI 2002/57; Care Homes (Wales) Regulations 2002, SI 2002/324 amended by SI 2002/2622 and 3295, SI 2003/947, 1004 and 1703 and SI 2004/1314, 1756 and 2414 and SI 2005/1541, 2929 and 3302; Private and Voluntary Health Care (Wales) Regulations 2002, SI 2002/325 amended by SI 2004/1771and 2414; Children's Homes (Wales) Regulations 2002, SI 2002/327 amended by SI 2002/2622, SI 2004/1756 and 2414 and SI 2005/774, 1541, 2929 and 3302; Nurses Agencies Regulations 2002, SI 2002/3212 amended by SI 2003/2323, SI 2004/1269, 1770 and 1771; Residential Family Centres Regulations 2002, SI 2002/3213 amended by SI 2005/1541; Domiciliary Care Agencies Regulations 2002, SI 2002/3214 amended by SI 2003/2323 and SI 2004/1770; Fostering Services (Wales) Regulations 2003, SI 2003/237 amended by SI 2003/896 and SI 2005/3302; Voluntary Adoption Agencies and the Adoption Agencies (Miscellaneous Amendments) Regulations 2003, SI 2003/367 amended by SI 2005/3341; Local Authority Adoption Service and Miscellaneous Amendments (Wales) Regulations 2003, SI 2003/710; Residential Family Centres (Wales) Regulations 2003, SI 2003/781 amended by SI 2005/1541, 2929 (W) and 3302; Fostering Services (Wales) (Amendment) Regulations 2003, SI 2003/896; and Nurses Agencies (Wales) Regulations 2003, SI 2003/2527 amended by SI 2003/3054 and SI 2004/1771and 2414; Adult Placement Schemes (Wales) Regulations 2004, SI 2004/1756 amended by SI 2005/3302; Adult Placement Schemes (England) Regulations 2004, SI 2004/2071 amended by SI 2005/2114; Adoption Support Agencies (Wales) Regulations 2005, SI 2005/1514; Adoption Support Agencies (England) and Adoption Agencies (Miscellaneous Amendments) Regulations 2005, SI 2005/2720.

8–16000ZZB   35. Death of registered person.   (1) Regulations[1] may—

(a)   provide for the provisions of this Part to apply with prescribed modifications in cases where a person who was the only person registered under this Part in respect of an establishment or agency has died;

(b)   require the personal representatives of a deceased person who was registered in respect of an establishment or agency to notify the registration authority of his death.

(2) Regulations under subsection (1)(a) may in particular—

(a)   provide for the establishment or agency to be carried on for a prescribed period by a person who is not registered in respect of it; and

(b)   include provision for the prescribed period to be extended by such further period as the registration authority may allow.

[Care Standards Act 2000, s 35.]

---

1. Under this provision the following regulations have been made: Children's Homes Regulations 2001, SI 2001/3967 amended by SI 2002/865 and 2469 and SI 2005/1541; Children's Homes (Wales) Regulations 2002, SI 2002/327 amended by SI 2002/2622, SI 2004/1756 and 2414 and SI 2005/774, 1541 and 2929 (W); Registration of Social Care and Independent Health Care (Wales) Regulations 2002, SI 2002/919 amended by SI 2002/2622 and 2935, SI 2003/710 and 2527, SI 2004/1756, SI 2004/919 and 1756 and SI 2005/3302; Residential Family Centres Regulations 2002, SI 2002/3213 amended by SI 2005/1541; Nurses Agencies Regulations 2002, SI 2002/3212 amended by SI 2004/1771; Domiciliary Care Agencies Regulations 2002, SI 2002/3214; Fostering Services (Wales) Regulations 2003, SI 2003/237 amended by SI 2003/896 and SI 2005/3302; Nursing Agencies (Wales) Regulations 2003, SI 2003/2527 amended by SI 2003/3054 and SI 2004/1771 and 2414; Domiciliary Care Agencies (Wales) Regulations 2004, SI 2004/219 amended by SI 2004/2414 and SI 2005/3302; Adult Placement Schemes (England) Regulations 2004, SI 2004/2071 amended by SI 2005/1541; Adoption Support Agencies (Wales) Regulations 2005, SI 2005/1514; Adoption Support Agencies (England) and Adoption Agencies (Miscellaneous Amendments) Regulations 2005, SI 2005/2720.

8–16000ZZC   36. Provision of copies of registers.   (1) Subject to subsection (3), the registration authority shall secure that copies of any register kept for the purposes of this Part are available at its offices for inspection at all reasonable times by any person.

(2) Subject to subsections (3) and (4), any person who asks the registration authority for a copy of, or of an extract from, a register kept for the purposes of this Part shall be entitled to have one.

(3) Regulations[1] may provide that subsections (1) and (2) shall not apply—

(a)   in such circumstances as may be prescribed; or

(b)   to such parts of a register as may be prescribed.

(4) A fee determined by the registration authority shall be payable for the copy except—

(a)   in prescribed circumstances;

(b)   in any other case where the registration authority considers it appropriate to provide the copy free of charge.

[Care Standards Act 2000, s 36.]

---

1. The Care Standards Act 2000 (Establishments and Agencies) (Miscellaneous Amendments) Regulations 2002, SI 2002/865 have been made.

8–16000ZZCA   36A. Voluntary adoption agencies: distribution of functions.   (1) This section applies to functions relating to voluntary adoption agencies conferred on the registration authority by or under this Part or under Chapter 2 of Part 1 of the Adoption and Children Act 2002.

(2) Subject to the following provisions, functions to which this section applies are exercisable—

(a)   where the principal office of an agency is in England, by the CSCI,

(b)   where the principal office of an agency is in Wales, by the Assembly.

(3) So far as those functions relate to the imposition, variation or removal of conditions of registration, they may only be exercised after consultation with the Assembly or (as the case may be) the CSCI.

(4) But—

(a)   where such a function as is mentioned in subsection (3) is exercisable by the CSCI in relation to an agency which has a branch in Wales, it is exercisable only with the agreement of the Assembly,

(b)   where such a function as is mentioned in subsection (3) is exercisable by the Assembly in relation to an agency which has a branch in England, it is exercisable only with the agreement of the CSCI.

(5) The functions conferred on the registration authority by sections 31 and 32 of this Act in respect of any premises of a voluntary adoption agency are exercisable—

(a)   where the premises are in England, by the CSCI,

(b)   where the premises are in Wales, by the Assembly.

(6) In spite of subsections (2) to (5), regulations may provide for any function to which this section applies to be exercisable by the CSCI instead of the Assembly, or by the Assembly instead of

the CSCI, or by one concurrently with the other, or by both jointly or by either with the agreement of or after consultation with the other.

(7) In this section, "regulations" means regulations relating to England and Wales.

[Care Standards Act 2000, s 36A, as inserted by the Adoption and Children Act 2002, s 16, and amended by the Adoption and Children Act 2002, Schs 4 and 5 and the Health and Social Care (Community Health and Standards) Act 2003, s 147, Sch 9.]

8–16000ZZD 37. Service of documents. (1) Any notice or other document required under this Part to be served on a person carrying on or managing, or intending to carry on or manage, an establishment or agency may be served on him—

(a) by being delivered personally to him; or

(b) by being sent by post to him in a registered letter or by the recorded delivery service at his proper address.

(2) For the purposes of section 7 of the Interpretation Act 1978 (which defines "service by post") a letter addressed to a person carrying on or managing an establishment or agency enclosing a notice or other document under this Act shall be deemed to be properly addressed if it is addressed to him at the establishment or agency.

(3) Where a notice or other document is served as mentioned in subsection (1)(b), the service shall, unless the contrary is proved, be deemed to have been effected on the third day after the day on which it is sent.

(4) Any notice or other document required to be served on a body corporate or a firm shall be duly served if it is served on the secretary or clerk of that body or a partner of that firm.

(5) For the purposes of this section, and of section 7 of the Interpretation Act 1978 in its application to this section, without prejudice to subsection (2) above, the proper address of a person shall be—

(a) in the case of a secretary or clerk of a body corporate, that of the registered or principal office of that body;

(b) in the case of a partner of a firm, that of the principal office of the firm; and

(c) in any other case, the last known address of the person.

[Care Standards Act 2000, s 37.]

8–16000ZZE 38. Transfers of staff under Part II. (1) The appropriate Minister may by order make a scheme for the transfer to the new employer of any eligible employee.

(2) In this section—

"eligible employee" means a person who is employed under a contract of employment with an old employer on work which would have continued but for the provisions of this Part;

"new employer" means the registration authority;

"old employer" means a local authority or a Health Authority.

[Care Standards Act 2000, s 38.]

8–16000ZZF 39. Temporary extension of meaning of "nursing home". In section 21 of the Registered Homes Act 1984 (meaning of nursing home)—

(a) in subsection (1), after "(3)" there is inserted "and (3A)";

(b) in subsection (2), for "subsection (1) above" there is substituted "this section";

(c) in subsection (3)(e)(ii), "dental practitioner or" is omitted; and

(d) after subsection (3) there is inserted—

"(3A) The definition in subsection (1) above does not include any premises used, or intended to be used, wholly or mainly by a dental practitioner for the purpose of treating his patients unless subsection (3B) or (3C) below applies.

(3B) This subsection applies if—

(a) the premises are also used, or intended to be used, by that or another dental practitioner for the purpose of treating his patients under general anaesthesia; and

(b) the premises are not used, or intended to be used, by any dental practitioner for the purpose of treating his patients under general anaesthesia—

(i) in pursuance of the National Health Service Act 1977; or

(ii) under an agreement made in accordance with Part I of the National Health Service (Primary Care) Act 1997.

(3C) This subsection applies if the premises are used, or intended to be used, for the provision of treatment by specially controlled techniques and are not excepted by regulations under subsection (3)(g) above."

[Care Standards Act 2000, s 39.]

8–16000ZZG 40. Temporary extension of meaning of "children's home". In section 63(3)(a) of the 1989 Act (meaning of "children's home"), for "more than three children at any one time" there shall be substituted "children".

[Care Standards Act 2000, s 40.]

8–16000ZZH   41. Children's homes: temporary provision about cancellation of registration.
(1) In paragraph 1(4) of Schedule 5 to the 1989 Act (voluntary homes and voluntary organisations)—

(*a*)   in paragraph (*a*), after "is not" there shall be inserted ", or has not been,";
(*b*)   after "is" there shall be inserted ", or has been,".

(2) In paragraph 2 of that Schedule, after sub-paragraph (5) there shall be inserted—

"(6) In relation to a home which has ceased to exist, the reference in sub-paragraph (4) to any person carrying on the home shall be taken to be a reference to each of the persons who carried it on."

(3) In paragraph 3(3) of Schedule 6 to the 1989 Act (registered children's homes), after "is being" there shall be inserted "and has been".

(4) In paragraph 4 of that Schedule—

(*a*)   in sub-paragraph (3) after "is being" there shall be inserted ", or has been,";
(*b*)   after sub-paragraph (4) there shall be inserted—

"(5) In relation to a home which has ceased to exist, references in this paragraph and paragraph 5(4) to the person, or any person, carrying on the home include references to each of the persons who carried it on."

[Care Standards Act 2000, s 41.]

8–16000ZZI   42. Power to extend the application of Part II.   (1) Regulations[1] may provide for the provisions of this Part to apply, with such modifications as may be specified in the regulations, to prescribed persons to whom subsection (2) or (3) applies.

(2) This subsection applies to—

(*a*)   local authorities providing services in the exercise of their social services functions; and
(*b*)   persons who provide services which are similar to services which—

   (i)   may or must be so provided by local authorities; or
   (ii)   may or must be provided by Health Authorities, Special Health Authorities, NHS trusts, NHS foundation trusts or Primary Care Trusts.

(3) This subsection applies to persons who carry on or manage an undertaking (other than an establishment or agency) which consists of or includes supplying, or providing services for the purpose of supplying, individuals mentioned in subsection (4).

(4) The individuals referred to in subsection (3) are those who provide services for the purpose of any of the services mentioned in subsection (2).

(5) Regulations under subsection (1) made by the Secretary of State may in particular specify whether, for the purposes of the application of this Part to any person, the registration authority is to be the CHAI or the CSCI.

[Care Standards Act 2000, s 42, as amended by the Health and Social Care (Community Health and Standards) Act 2003, Schs 4 and 9.]

---

1. Under this provision the following regulations have been made: Care Standards Act 2000 (Extension of the Application of Part 2 to Adult Placement Schemes) (England) Regulations 2004, SI 2004/1972; Adult Placement Schemes (England) Regulations 2004, SI 2004/2071 amended by SI 2005/2114.

PART III[1]
LOCAL AUTHORITY SERVICES

8–16000ZZJ   43. Introductory.   (1) This section has effect for the purposes of this Part.

(2) "Relevant functions", in relation to a local authority, means relevant adoption functions and relevant fostering functions.

(3) In relation to a local authority—

(*a*)   "relevant adoption functions" means functions under the Adoption and Children Act 2002 of making or participating in arrangements for the adoption of children or the provision of adoption support services (as defined in section 2(6) of the Adoption and Children Act 2002; and
(*b*)   "relevant fostering functions" means functions under section 23(2)(*a*) of the 1989 Act or regulations under any of paragraphs (*a*), (*b*) or (*d*) to (*f*) of paragraph 12 of Schedule 2 to that Act.

[Care Standards Act 2000, s 43 as amended by the Adoption and Children Act 2003, Sch 3.]

---

1. Part III comprises ss 43 to 53.

8–16000ZZK   44. General powers of the Commission.   *Repealed.*

8–16000ZZL   45. Inspection by registration authority of adoption and fostering services.
(1)–(3) *Repealed.*
(4) The Secretary of State may by regulations[1] require the CSCI to arrange for premises which

are used by a local authority in its discharge of relevant functions to be inspected on such occasions or at such intervals as may be prescribed; and an inspection under this section shall be regarded for all purposes as undertaken under section 80 of the Health and Social Care (Community Health and Standards) Act 2003.

(5) *Repealed.*

[Care Standards Act 2000, s 45, as amended by the Health and Social Care (Community Health and Standards) Act 2003, Schs 9 and 14.]

---

1. The following regulations have been made: National Care Standards Commission (Fees and Frequency of Inspections) (Adoption Agencies) Regulations 2003, SI 2003/368 amended by SI 2005/640 and 2720; and Commission for Social Care Inspection (Fees and Frequency of Inspections) Regulations 2004, SI 2004/662 amended by SI 2005/2720 (E).

8–16000ZZM   **46. Inspections: supplementary.**   *Repealed.*

8–16000ZZN   **47.** *Action following inspection.*   *Repealed.*

8–16000ZZO   **48. Regulation of the exercise of relevant fostering functions.**   (1) Regulations[1] may make provision about the exercise by local authorities of relevant fostering functions, and may in particular make provision—

    (*a*)   as to the persons who are fit to work for local authorities in connection with the exercise of such functions;

    (*b*)   as to the fitness of premises to be used by local authorities in their exercise of such functions;

    (*c*)   as to the management and control of the operations of local authorities in their exercise of such functions;

    (*d*)   as to the numbers of persons, or persons of any particular type, working for local authorities in connection with the exercise of such functions;

    (*e*)   as to the management and training of such persons.

(2) Regulations under subsection (1)(*a*) may, in particular, make provision for prohibiting persons from working for local authorities in such positions as may be prescribed unless they are registered in, or in a particular part of, one of the registers maintained under section 56(1).

[Care Standards Act 2000, s 48.]

---

1. The following regulations have been made: Fostering Services Regulations 2002, SI 2002/57; Care Standards Act 2000 (Establishments and Agencies) (Miscellaneous Amendments) Regulations 2002, SI 2002/865; Fostering Services (Wales) Regulations 2003, SI 2003/237 amended by SI 2003/896 and SI 2005/3302.

8–16000ZZP   **49. National minimum standards.**   (1) Subsections (1), (2) and (3) of section 23 shall apply to local authorities in their exercise of relevant functions as they apply to establishments and agencies.

(2) *Repealed.*

[Care Standards Act 2000, s 49 as amended by the Health and Social Care (Community Health and Standards) Act 2003, Sch 14.]

8–16000ZZQ   **50. Annual returns.**   (1) Regulations may require a local authority to make to the registration authority an annual return containing such information with respect to the exercise by the local authority of relevant functions as may be prescribed.

(2) Provision may be made by the regulations as to the period in respect of which and date by which the return is to be made.

[Care Standards Act 2000, s 50.]

8–16000ZZR   **51. Annual fee.**   *Repealed.*

8–16000ZZS   **52. Contravention of regulations.**   (1) Regulations[1] under this Part may provide that a contravention of or failure to comply with any specified provision of the regulations shall be an offence.

(2) A person guilty of an offence under the regulations shall be liable on summary conviction to a fine not exceeding level 4 on the standard scale.

[Care Standards Act 2000, s 52.]

---

1. The Fostering Services Regulations 2002, SI 2002/57 and the Local Authority Adoption Service (Wales) Regulations 2005, SI 2005/3115 have been made.

8–16000ZZT   **53. Offences: general provisions.**   Sections 29 and 30 apply in relation to this Part as they apply in relation to Part II.

[Care Standards Act 2000, s 53.]

PART IV[1]
SOCIAL CARE WORKERS

Preliminary

8–16000ZZTA   54. Care Councils.   (1) There shall be—

(*a*) a body corporate to be known as the General Social Care Council[2] (referred to in this Act as "the English Council"); and

(*b*) a body corporate to be known as the Care Council for Wales or Cyngor Gofal Cymru (referred to in this Act as "the Welsh Council"),

which shall have the functions conferred on them by or under this Act or any other enactment.

(2) It shall be the duty of the English Council to promote in relation to England—

(*a*) high standards of conduct and practice among social care workers; and
(*b*) high standards in their training.

(3) It shall be the duty of the Welsh Council to promote in relation to Wales—

(*a*) high standards of conduct and practice among social care workers; and
(*b*) high standards in their training.

(4) Each Council shall, in the exercise of its functions, act—

(*a*) in accordance with any directions given to it by the appropriate Minister; and
(*b*) under the general guidance of the appropriate Minister.

(5) Directions under subsection (4) shall be given in writing.
(6) Schedule 1 shall have effect with respect to a Council.
(7) In this Act, references to a Council are—

(*a*) in relation to England, a reference to the General Social Care Council,
(*b*) in relation to Wales, a reference to the Care Council for Wales.

[Care Standards Act 2000, s 54.]

---

1. Part IV comprises ss 54 to 71.
2. The General Social Care Council (Appointments and Procedure) Regulations 2001, SI 2001/1744 amended by SI 2004/1771 have been made.

8–16000ZZU   55. Interpretation.   (1) This section has effect for the purposes of this Part.
(2) "Social care worker" means a person (other than a person excepted by regulations) who—

(*a*) engages in relevant social work (referred to in this Part as a "social worker");
(*b*) is employed at a children's home, care home or residential family centre or for the purposes of a domiciliary care agency, a fostering agency , a voluntary adoption agency or an adoption support agency;
(*c*) manages an establishment, or an agency, of a description mentioned in paragraph (*b*); or
(*d*) is supplied by a domiciliary care agency to provide personal care in their own homes for persons who by reason of illness, infirmity or disability are unable to provide it for themselves without assistance.

(3) Regulations[1] may provide that persons of any of the following descriptions shall be treated as social care workers—

(*a*) a person engaged in work for the purposes of a local authority's social services functions, or in the provision of services similar to services which may or must be provided by local authorities in the exercise of those functions;
(*b*) a person engaged in the provision of personal care for any person;
(*c*) a person who manages, or is employed in, an undertaking (other than an establishment or agency) which consists of or includes supplying, or providing services for the purpose of supplying, persons to provide personal care;
(*d*) a person employed in connection with the discharge of functions of the appropriate Minister under section 80 of the 1989 Act (inspection of children's homes etc);
(*e*) staff of the CSCI or the Assembly who—

(i) inspect premises under section 87 of the 1989 Act (welfare of children accommodated in independent schools and colleges) or section 31 of this Act or section 88 or 98 of the Health and Social Care (Community Health and Standards) Act 2003; or
(ii) are responsible for persons who do so;

and staff of the Assembly who inspect premises under section 79T of that Act (inspection of child minding and day care in Wales) or are responsible for persons who do so;

(*f*) a person employed in a day centre;
(*g*) a person participating in a course approved by a Council under section 63 for persons wishing to become social workers.

(4) "Relevant social work" means social work which is required in connection with any health, education or social services provided by any person.

(5) "Day centre" means a place where nursing or personal care (but not accommodation) is provided wholly or mainly for persons mentioned in section 3(2).

[Care Standards Act 2000, s 55 as amended by the Health and Social Care (Community Health and Standards) Act 2003, Sch 9 and the Adoption and Children Act 2002, Sch 3.]

---

1. For the purposes only of the function of the Care Council for Wales under s 54(3) of the Act persons of any of the descriptions in sub-paras (*a*) to (*g*) of para (3) of s 55 of the Act are to be treated as social care workers: Care Standards Act 2000 (Extension of Meaning of "Social Care Worker" (Wales) Regulations 2002, SI 2002/1176. A person participating in a course approved by the General Social Care Council (in Wales, the Care Council for Wales) under section 63 of the Act for persons wishing to become social care workers, is to be treated as a social care worker: General Social Care Council (Description of Persons to be Treated as Social Care Workers) Regulations 2004, SI 2004/561; Care Standards Act 2000 (Extension of Meaning of "Social Care Worker") (Wales) Regulations 2004, SI 2004/711.

Registration

8–16000ZZV   56. The register.   (1) Each Council shall maintain a register of—

     (*a*)   social workers; and

     (*b*)   social care workers of any other description specified by the appropriate Minister by order[1].

(2) There shall be a separate part of the register for social workers and for each description of social care workers so specified.

(3) The appropriate Minister may by order provide for a specified part of the register to be closed, as from a date specified by the order, so that on or after that date no further persons can become registered in that part.

(4) The appropriate Minister shall consult the Council before making, varying or revoking any order under this section.

[Care Standards Act 2000, s 57.]

---

1. In respect of England the General Social Care Council (Registration) (Description of Social Care Workers) Order 2004, SI 2004/562 specifies student social workers as being social care workers for the purposes of registration under this section. Equivalent provision for Wales is made by the Care Council for Wales (Specification of Student Social Workers) (Registration) Order 2004, SI 2002/709. In addition the Care Council for Wales (Specification of Social Care Worker) (Registration) Order 2004, SI 2004/2880 prescribes those (*a*) who fall within any of the descriptions in s 55(2)(*b*)–(*d*) of the Act; (*b*) who ordinarily perform some work in Wales or expect to do so; and (*c*) in respect of whom the Secretary of State may, by virtue of that work, issue a criminal record certificate under s 113(1) or 115(1) of the Police Act 1997.

8–16000ZZW   57. Applications for registration.   (1) An application for registration under this Part shall be made to the Council in accordance with rules made by it.

(2) An application under subsection (1) shall specify each part of the register in which registration is sought and such other matters as may be required by the rules.

[Care Standards Act 2000, s 57.]

8–16000ZZX   58. Grant or refusal of registration.   (1) If the Council is satisfied that the applicant—

     (*a*)   is of good character;

     (*b*)   is physically and mentally fit to perform the whole or part of the work of persons registered in any part of the register to which his application relates; and

     (*c*)   satisfies the following conditions,

it shall grant the application, either unconditionally or subject to such conditions as it thinks fit; and in any other case it shall refuse it.

(2) The first condition is that—

     (*a*)   in the case of an applicant for registration as a social worker—

         (i)   he has successfully completed a course approved by the Council under section 63 for persons wishing to become social workers;

         (ii)   he satisfies the requirements of section 64; or

         (iii)   he satisfies any requirements as to training which the Council may by rules impose in relation to social workers;

     (*b*)   in the case of an applicant for registration as a social care worker of any other description, he satisfies any requirements as to training which the Council may by rules impose in relation to social care workers of that description.

(3) The second condition is that the applicant satisfies any requirements as to conduct and competence which the Council may by rules impose.

[Care Standards Act 2000, s 58.]

8–16000ZZY   59. Removal etc from register.   (1) Each Council shall by rules determine circumstances in which, and the means by which—

(*a*) a person may be removed from a part of the register, whether or not for a specified period;

(*b*) a person who has been removed from a part of the register may be restored to that part;

(*c*) a person's registration in a part of the register may be suspended for a specified period;

(*d*) the suspension of a person's registration in a part of the register may be terminated;

(*e*) an entry in a part of the register may be removed, altered or restored.

(2) The rules shall make provision as to the procedure to be followed, and the rules of evidence to be observed, in proceedings brought for the purposes of the rules, whether before the Council or any committee of the Council.

(3) The rules shall provide for such proceedings to be in public except in such cases (if any) as the rules may specify.

(4) Where a person's registration in a part of the register is suspended under subsection (1)(*c*), he shall be treated as not being registered in that part notwithstanding that his name still appears in it.
[Care Standards Act 2000, s 59.]

8–16000ZZZ 60. *Rules about registration*

8–16000ZZZA 61. Use of title "social worker" etc[1]. (1) If a person who is not registered as a social worker in any relevant register with intent to deceive another—

(*a*) takes or uses the title of social worker;

(*b*) takes or uses any title or description implying that he is so registered, or in any way holds himself out as so registered,

he is guilty of an offence.

(2) For the purposes of subsection (1), a register is a relevant register if it is—

(*a*) maintained by a Council; or

(*b*) a prescribed[2] register maintained under a provision of the law of Scotland or Northern Ireland which appears to the appropriate Minister to correspond to the provisions of this Part.

(3) A person guilty of an offence under this section shall be liable on summary conviction to a fine not exceeding **level 5** on the standard scale.
[Care Standards Act 2000, s 61.]

---

1. In force in relation to England for the purpose only of the exercise of the power to make regulations: 1 March 2005: see SI 2005/375, art 2(1) (but fully in force in relation to Wales).

2. The Cares Standards Act 2000 (Relevant Registers of Social Workers) Regulations 2005, SI 2005/491 have been made.

Codes of practice

8–16000ZZZB 62. Codes of practice. (1) Each Council shall prepare and from time to time publish codes of practice laying down—

(*a*) standards of conduct and practice expected of social care workers; and

(*b*) standards of conduct and practice in relation to social care workers, being standards expected of persons employing or seeking to employ them.

(2) The Council shall—

(*a*) keep the codes under review; and

(*b*) vary their provisions whenever it considers it appropriate to do so.

(3) Before issuing or varying a code, a Council shall consult any persons it considers appropriate to consult.

(4) A code published by a Council shall be taken into account—

(*a*) by the Council in making a decision under this Part; and

(*b*) in any proceedings on an appeal against such a decision.

(5) Local authorities making any decision about the conduct of any social care workers employed by them shall, if directed to do so by the appropriate Minister, take into account any code published by the Council.

(6) Any person who asks a Council for a copy of a code shall be entitled to have one.
[Care Standards Act 2000, s 62.]

8–16000ZZZC 63–67. *Training*

8–16000ZZZD 68–71. *Miscellaneous and supplemental*

Part V[1]

The Children's Commissioner for Wales

8–16000ZZZE 72. Children's Commissioner for Wales. (1) There shall be an office of the Children's Commissioner for Wales or Comisiynydd Plant Cymru.

(2) Schedule 2² shall have effect with respect to the Children's Commissioner for Wales (referred to in this Act as "the Commissioner").
[Care Standards Act 2000, s 72.]

---

1. Part V contains ss 72 to 78.
2. Schedule 2 is not reproduced in this work.

8–16000ZZZEA   72A. Principal aim of the Commissioner.   The principal aim of the Commissioner in exercising his functions is to safeguard and promote the rights and welfare of children to whom this Part applies.
[Care Standards Act 2000, s 72A, as inserted by the Children's Commissioner for Wales Act 2001, s 2.]

8–16000ZZZEB   72B. Review of exercise of functions of Assembly and other persons.
(1) The Commissioner may review the effect on children to whom this Part applies of—

(a) the exercise or proposed exercise of any function of the Assembly, including the making or proposed making of any subordinate legislation; or
(b) the exercise or proposed exercise in relation to Wales of any function of any person mentioned in Schedule 2A.

(2) The Assembly may by order amend this section or Schedule 2A by—

(a) adding any person to that Schedule;
(b) omitting any person from that Schedule;
(c) altering the description of any person mentioned in that Schedule; or
(d) making provision specifying, in respect of a person mentioned in that Schedule and specified in the order, a function of the person which although exercisable in relation to Wales is not to be treated as such for the purposes of subsection (1)(b).

(3) An order under subsection (2) may add a person to Schedule 2A only if—

(a) some or all of the person's functions are in a field in which the Assembly has functions;
(b) the person is established under an enactment or by virtue of Her Majesty's prerogative or is established in any other way by a Minister of the Crown or government department or by the Assembly; and
(c) (unless consent is given by the Secretary of State under subsection (4)), at least half of the person's expenditure on the exercise of functions in relation to Wales (or, where the person's functions relate only to a part of Wales, in relation to the part of Wales to which they relate) is met directly from payments made by the Assembly.

(4) An order under subsection (2) may add to Schedule 2A a person who does not satisfy the condition in subsection (3)(c) if the Secretary of State gives consent.

(5) An order under subsection (2) must not add to Schedule 2A a person whose sole or main activity is—

(a) the investigation of complaints by members of the public about the actions of any person; or
(b) the supervision or review of, or of steps taken following, such an investigation.

(6) The Assembly may not make an order under subsection (2) if the result would be that the Commissioner could review the effect of the exercise or proposed exercise of a person's function in a field in which the Assembly does not have functions.

(7) In subsection (1)(a) "subordinate legislation" has the same meaning as in the Interpretation Act 1978 (c 30).
[Care Standards Act 2000, s 72B, as inserted by the Children's Commissioner for Wales Act 2001, s 3(1).]

8–16000ZZZF   73. Review and monitoring of arrangements.   (1) The Commissioner may review, and monitor the operation of, arrangements falling within subsection (2), (2A), (2B), (2C), (3) or (4) for the purpose of ascertaining whether, and to what extent, the arrangements are effective in safeguarding and promoting the rights and welfare of children—

(a) to or in respect of whom services are provided in Wales by, or on behalf of or under arrangements with, a person mentioned in Schedule 2B; or
(b) to or in respect of whom regulated children's services in Wales are provided.

(1A) The Commissioner may also assess the effect on such children of the failure of any person to make such arrangements.

(2) The arrangements falling within this subsection are the arrangements made by the providers of regulated children's services in Wales, or by the Assembly, for dealing with complaints or representations about such services made by or on behalf of children to whom such services are provided.

(2A) The arrangements falling within this subsection are the arrangements made by a person mentioned in Schedule 2B for dealing with complaints or representations made to the person by or on behalf of a child about services provided in Wales by the person to or in respect of the child.

(2B) The arrangements falling within this subsection are the arrangements made by a person providing services in Wales on behalf of, or under arrangements with, a person mentioned in Schedule 2B for dealing with complaints or representations made to the person by or on behalf of a child about a service which is so provided to or in respect of the child.

(2C) The arrangements falling within this subsection are the arrangements made by the Assembly for dealing with complaints or representations made by or on behalf of a child about a service which is provided in Wales to or in respect of the child by, or on behalf of or under arrangements with, a person mentioned in Schedule 2B (other than the Assembly).

(3) The arrangements falling within this subsection are arrangements made by the providers of regulated children's services in Wales, by the Assembly, or by another person mentioned in Schedule 2B or subsection (2B), for ensuring that proper action is taken in response to any disclosure of information which may tend to show—

(a)   that a criminal offence has been committed;
(b)   that a person has failed to comply with any legal obligation to which he is subject;
(c)   that the health and safety of any person has been endangered; or
(d)   that information tending to show that any matter falling within one of the preceding paragraphs has been deliberately concealed,

in the course of or in connection with the provision of [the services mentioned in subsection (3A).

(3A) The services are—

(a)   in the case of a person mentioned in Schedule 2B, services provided in Wales by the person to or in respect of a child;
(b)   in the case of a person mentioned in subsection (2B), services provided in Wales by the person to or in respect of a child on behalf of, or under arrangements with, a person mentioned in Schedule 2B;
(c)   in the case of a provider of regulated children's services in Wales, those services.

(4) The arrangements falling within this subsection are arrangements made (whether by providers of regulated children's services in Wales, by the Assembly or by any other person) for making persons available—

(a)   to represent the views and wishes of children —

(i)   to or in respect of whom services are provided in Wales by, or on behalf of or under arrangements with, a person mentioned in Schedule 2B; or
(ii)   to or in respect of whom regulated children's services in Wales are provided; or

(b)   to provide such children with advice and support of any prescribed[1] kind.

(5) Regulations[1] may confer power on the Commissioner to require prescribed persons to provide any information which the Commissioner considers it necessary or expedient to have for the purposes of his functions under this section.

(5A) The Assembly may by order amend this section or Schedule 2B by—

(a)   adding any person to that Schedule;
(b)   omitting any person from that Schedule;
(c)   altering the description of any person mentioned in that Schedule; or
(d)   making provision specifying, in respect of a person mentioned in that Schedule and specified in the order, services which although provided by the person in Wales are not to be treated as such for the purposes of the exercise of the Commissioner's functions.

(5B) An order under subsection (5A) may add a person to Schedule 2B only if—

(a)   the person provides services in Wales to or in respect of children;
(b)   some or all of the person's functions are in a field in which the Assembly has functions;
(c)   the person is established under an enactment or by virtue of Her Majesty's prerogative or is established in any other way by a Minister of the Crown or government department or by the Assembly; and
(d)   (unless consent is given by the Secretary of State under subsection (5C)), at least half of the person's expenditure on the exercise of functions in relation to Wales (or, where the person's functions relate only to a part of Wales, in relation to the part of Wales to which they relate) is met directly from payments made by the Assembly.

(5C) An order may add to Schedule 2B a person who does not satisfy the condition in subsection (5B)(d) if the Secretary of State gives consent.

(5D) An order under subsection (5A) must not add to Schedule 2B a person whose sole or main activity is—

(a)   the investigation of complaints by members of the public about the actions of any person; or
(b)   the supervision or review of, or of steps taken following, such an investigation.

(5E) The Assembly may not make an order under subsection (5A) if the result would be that the Commissioner could exercise functions in relation to a person's functions in a field in which the Assembly does not have functions.

[Care Standards Act 2000, s 73, as amended by the Children's Commissioner for Wales Act 2001, s 4(1).]

---

1. See the Children's Commissioner for Wales Regulations 2001, SI 2001/2787 amended by SI 2005/774.

8–16000ZZZG   74. Examination of cases.   (1) Regulations[1] may, in connection with the Commissioner's functions under this Part, make provision for the examination by the Commissioner of the cases of particular children to whom this Part applies.

(1A) The reference in subsection (1) to functions of the Commissioner does not include a reference to his power to consider and make representations by virtue of section 75A(1).

(2) The regulations may include provision about—

(*a*)   the types of case which may be examined;

(*b*)   the circumstances in which an examination may be made;

(*c*)   the procedure for conducting an examination, including provision about the representation of parties;

(*d*)   the publication of reports following an examination.

(3) The regulations may make provision for—

(*a*)   requiring persons to provide the Commissioner with information; or

(*b*)   requiring persons who hold or are accountable for information to provide the Commissioner with explanations or other assistance,

for the purposes of an examination or for the purposes of determining whether any recommendation made in a report following an examination has been complied with.

(4) For the purposes mentioned in subsection (3), the Commissioner shall have the same powers as the High Court in respect of—

(*a*)   the attendance and examination of witnesses (including the administration of oaths and affirmations and the examination of witnesses abroad); and

(*b*)   the provision of information.

(5) No person shall be compelled for the purposes mentioned in subsection (3) to give any evidence or provide any information which he could not be compelled to give or provide in civil proceedings before the High Court.

(6) The regulations may make provision for the payment by the Commissioner of sums in respect of expenses or allowances to persons who attend or provide information for the purposes mentioned in subsection (3).

[Care Standards Act 2000, s 74, as amended by the Children's Commissioner for Wales Act 2001, s 5(2).]

---

1. The Children's Commissioner for Wales Regulations 2001, SI 2001/2787 amended by SI 2005/774 have been made.

8–16000ZZZH   75. Obstruction etc.   (1) The Commissioner may certify an offence to the High Court where—

(*a*)   a person, without lawful excuse, obstructs him or any member of his staff in the exercise of any of his functions under regulations made by virtue of section 73(5) or 74; or

(*b*)   a person is guilty of any act or omission in relation to an examination under regulations made by virtue of section 74 which, if that examination were proceedings in the High Court, would constitute contempt of court.

(2) Where an offence is so certified the High Court may inquire into the matter; and after hearing—

(*a*)   any witnesses who may be produced against or on behalf of the person charged with the offence; and

(*b*)   any statement that may be offered in defence,

the High Court may deal with the person charged with the offence in any manner in which it could deal with him if he had committed the same offence in relation to the High Court.

[Care Standards Act 2000, s 75.]

8–16000ZZZHA   75A. Additional power of consideration and representation.   (1) The Commissioner may consider, and make representations to the Assembly about, any matter affecting the rights or welfare of children in Wales.

(2) The function of the Commissioner under subsection (1) is exercisable only where he does not have power to consider and make representations about the matter in question by virtue of any other provision of this Act or any other enactment.

[Care Standards Act 2000, s 75A, as inserted by the Children's Commissioner for Wales Act 2001, s 5(1).]

8–16000ZZZI   76. Further functions.   (1) Regulations[1] may confer power on the Commissioner to assist a child to whom this Part applies—

(*a*)   in making a complaint or representation to or in respect of a provider of regulated children's services in Wales; or

(*aa*) in making a complaint or representation to or in respect of a person mentioned in Schedule 2B or section 73(2B); or

(*b*)   in any prescribed proceedings,

and in this subsection "proceedings" includes a procedure of any kind and any prospective proceedings.

(1A) The proceedings which may be prescribed by virtue of subsection (1)(*b*) are proceedings relating to—

(*a*) the exercise or proposed exercise of a function as mentioned in section 72B(1);

(*b*) the provision of services as mentioned in section 78(1)(*b*) or (*c*).

(2) For the purposes of subsection (1), assistance includes—

(*a*) financial assistance; and

(*b*) arranging for representation, or the giving of advice or assistance, by any person,

and the regulations[1] may provide for assistance to be given on conditions, including (in the case of financial assistance) conditions requiring repayment in circumstances specified in the regulations.

(3) The Commissioner may, in connection with his functions under this Part, give advice and information to any person.

(4) Regulations[1] may, in connection with the Commissioner's functions under this Part, confer further functions on him.

(5) The regulations[1] may, in particular, include provision about the making of reports on any matter connected with any of his functions.

(5A) The references in subsections (4) and (5) to functions of the Commissioner do not include a reference to his power to consider and make representations by virtue of section 75A(1).

(6) Apart from identifying any person investigated, a report by the Commissioner shall not—

(*a*) mention the name of any person; or

(*b*) include any particulars which, in the opinion of the Commissioner, are likely to identify any person and can be omitted without impairing the effectiveness of the report,

unless, after taking account of the public interest (as well as the interests of any person who made a complaint and other persons), the Commissioner considers it necessary for the report to mention his name or include such particulars.

(7) For the purposes of the law of defamation, the publication of any matter by the Commissioner in a report is absolutely privileged.*

[Care Standards Act 2000, s 76, as amended by the Children's Commissioner for Wales Act 2001, s 6(a).]

---

*New sub-s (8) inserted by the **Children Act 2004, s 61** from a date to be appointed.

1. See the Children's Commissioner for Wales Regulations 2001, SI 2001/2787 amended by SI 2005/774.

8–16000ZZZJ 77. Restrictions.   (1) This Part does not authorise the Commissioner to enquire into or report on any matter so far as it is the subject of legal proceedings before, or has been determined by, a court or tribunal.

(2) This Part does not authorise the Commissioner to exercise any function which by virtue of an enactment is also exercisable by a prescribed person.

[Care Standards Act 2000, s 77.]

8–16000ZZZK 78. Interpretation.   (1) This Part applies to a child—

(*a*) who is ordinarily resident in Wales;

(*b*) to or in respect of whom services are provided in Wales by, or on behalf of or under arrangements with, a person mentioned in Schedule 2B; or

(*c*) to or in respect of whom regulated children's services in Wales are provided.

(1A) Regulations[1] may provide that, for the purposes of this Part of this Act, "child" includes a person aged 18 or over who falls within subsection (1B).

(1B) A person falls within this subsection if he is a person to or in respect of whom services are provided in Wales by, or on behalf of or under arrangements with, a county council or county borough council in Wales by virtue of—

(a) section 23C, 24, 24A or 24B of the Children Act 1989 (c 41) (which provide for the continuing duties of such councils towards young persons); or

(b) regulations made under section 23D of that Act (which may provide for the appointment of personal advisers for certain young persons).

(2) In this Part, "regulated children's services in Wales" means any of the following services for the time being provided in respect of children—

(*a*) services of a description provided by or in Part II undertakings, so far as provided in Wales;

(*b*) services provided by local authorities in Wales in the exercise of relevant adoption functions or relevant fostering functions;

(*c*) services of a description provided by persons registered under Part XA of the 1989 Act, so far as provided in Wales;

(*d*) accommodation provided by schools or by an institution within the further education sector (as defined in section 91 of the Further and Higher Education Act 1992), so far as provided in Wales.

(3) For the purposes of this Part—

(*a*) in the case of the services mentioned in subsection (2)(*a*), the person who carries on the Part II undertaking is to be treated as the provider of the services;

(*b*) in the case of the services mentioned in subsection (2)(*d*), the relevant person (as defined in section 87 of the 1989 Act) is to be treated as the provider of the services.

(4) For the purposes of this section, an establishment or agency, and an undertaking of any other description, is a Part II undertaking if the provider of the services in question is for the time being required to be registered under that Part.

(5) Where the activities of an undertaking are carried on from two or more branches, each of those branches shall be treated as a separate undertaking for the purposes of this Part.

(6) Regulations[1] may provide for the references to a child in subsection (1) to include references to a person (including a child) who was at any time (including a time before the commencement of this Part)—

(*a*) a child ordinarily resident in Wales;

(*b*) a child to or in respect of whom services were provided in Wales by, or on behalf of or under arrangements with, a person mentioned in Schedule 2B; or

(*c*) a child to or in respect of whom regulated children's services in Wales were provided.

(7) In this Part—

"information" includes information recorded in any form;

"regulations" means regulations made by the Assembly.

(8) In this section, "relevant adoption functions" and "relevant fostering functions" have the same meanings as in Part III.

[Care Standards Act 2000, s 78, as amended by the Children's Commissioner for Wales Act 2001, s 1(1).]

---

1. See the Children's Commissioner for Wales Regulations 2001, SI 2001/2787 amended by SI 2005/774.

PART VI[1]

CHILD MINDING AND DAY CARE

8–16000ZZZL   **79.** *Amendment of Children Act 1989*[2]

---

1. Part VI comprises s 79.
2. Section 79 inserts new Part XA in the Children Act 1989, in PART VI, FAMILY LAW, ante.

PART VII[1]

PROTECTION OF CHILDREN AND VULNERABLE ADULTS

Protection of vulnerable adults

8–16000ZZZM   **80. Basic definitions.**   (1) Subsections (2) to (7) apply for the purposes of this Part.

(2) "Care worker" means—

(*a*) an individual who is or has been employed in a position which is such as to enable him to have regular contact in the course of his duties with adults to whom accommodation is provided at a care home;

(*b*) an individual who is or has been employed in a position which is such as to enable him to have regular contact in the course of his duties with adults to whom prescribed services are provided by an independent hospital, an independent clinic, an independent medical agency or a National Health Service body;

(*c*) an individual who is or has been employed in a position which is concerned with the provision of personal care in their own homes for persons who by reason of illness, infirmity or disability are unable to provide it for themselves without assistance;

(*d*) an individual who has entered into an agreement with a person within subsection 7(*e*) and is employed to provide support, care or accommodation to an adult (not being a relative of the individual) who is in need of it.

(3) "Care position", in relation to an individual, means a position such as is mentioned in subsection (2)(*a*) to (*d*).

(4) "Employment" has the same meaning as in the Protection of Children Act 1999 (referred to in this Act as "the 1999 Act"); and references to an individual being employed shall be construed accordingly.

(4A) "Relative" in relation to an in individual mentioned in subsections (2)(*d*) and (6)(*d*) means—

(*a*) a spouse or civil partner;

(*b*) any parent, grandparent, child, grandchild, brother, sister, uncle, aunt, nephew or niece of the individual, or of his spouse or civil partner;

(*c*) the spouse or civil partner of any relative within subsection (*b*) of this definition, and for the purpose of determining any such relationship a person's step child shall be treated as his or her child, references to "spouse" include a former spouse and a person who is living with the person as if they were husband and wife and references to "civil partner" include a former civil partner and a person who is living with the person as if they were civil partners.

(5) "Supply worker"—

(a) in relation to an employment agency, means an individual supplied by the agency for employment in a care position or for whom the agency has found employment in a care position;

(b) in relation to an employment business, means an individual supplied by the business for employment in a care position.

(6) "Vulnerable adult" means—

(a) an adult to whom accommodation and nursing or personal care are provided in a care home;

(b) an adult to whom personal care is provided in their own home under arrangements made by a domiciliary care agency; or

(c) an adult to whom prescribed services are provided by an independent hospital, independent clinic, independent medical agency or National Health Service body; or

(d) an adult to whom support, care or accommodation is provided by an individual (not being a relative of that adult) under the terms of an agreement between that individual and a person within subsection (7)(e).

(7) The persons who provide care for vulnerable adults are—

(a) any person who carries on a care home;

(b) any person who carries on a domiciliary care agency;

(c) any person who carries on an independent hospital, an independent clinic or an independent medical agency, which provides prescribed services; and

(d) a National Health Service body which provides prescribed services; and

(e) any person who carries on a scheme under which an individual agrees with that person to provide support, care or accommodation to an adult who is in need of it.

(8) Regulations for the purposes of this section or section 91, 93 or 103 may only be made by the Secretary of State; and before making any regulations for the purposes of this section or section 93 or 103 the Secretary of State shall consult the Assembly.
[Care Standards Act 2000, s 80 as amended by SI 2004/2070 and SI 2005/3029.]

---

1. Part VII comprises ss 80 to 104.

8–16000ZZZN   **81. Duty of Secretary of State to keep list*.**   (1) The Secretary of State shall keep a list of individuals who are considered unsuitable to work with vulnerable adults.

(2) An individual shall not be included in the list except in accordance with this Part.

(3) The Secretary of State may at any time remove an individual from the list if he is satisfied that the individual should not have been included in it.
[Care Standards Act 2000, s 81.]

---

*At the date of going to press s 81 was not in force.

8–16000ZZZO   **82. Persons who provide care for vulnerable adults: duty to refer.**   (1) A person who provides care for vulnerable adults ("the provider") shall refer a care worker to the Secretary of State if there is fulfilled—

(a) any of the conditions mentioned in subsection (2); or

(b) the condition mentioned in subsection (3).

(2) The conditions referred to in subsection (1)(a) are—

(a) that the provider has dismissed the worker on the grounds of misconduct (whether or not in the course of his employment) which harmed or placed at risk of harm a vulnerable adult;

(b) that the worker has resigned, retired or been made redundant in circumstances such that the provider would have dismissed him, or would have considered dismissing him, on such grounds if he had not resigned, retired or been made redundant;

(c) that the provider has, on such grounds, transferred the worker to a position which is not a care position;

(d) that the provider has, on such grounds, suspended the worker or provisionally transferred him to a position which is not a care position but has not yet decided whether to dismiss him or to confirm the transfer.

(3) The condition referred to in subsection (1)(b) is that—

(a) in circumstances not falling within subsection (2), the provider has dismissed the worker, he has resigned or retired or the provider has transferred him to a position which is not a care position;

(b) information not available to the provider at the time of the dismissal, resignation, retirement or transfer has since become available; and

(c) the provider has formed the opinion that, if that information had been available at that time and if (where applicable) the worker had not resigned or retired, the provider would have dismissed him, or would have considered dismissing him, on such grounds as are mentioned in subsection (2)(a).

(4) If it appears from the information submitted with a reference under subsection (1) that it may be appropriate for the worker to be included in the list kept under section 81, the Secretary of State shall—

(a) determine the reference in accordance with subsections (5) to (7); and

(b) pending that determination, provisionally include the worker in the list.

(5) The Secretary of State shall—

(a) invite observations from the worker on the information submitted with the reference and, if he thinks fit, on any observations submitted under paragraph (b); and

(b) invite observations from the provider on any observations on the information submitted with the reference and, if he thinks fit, on any other observations under paragraph (a).

(6) Where—

(a) the Secretary of State has considered the information submitted with the reference, any observations submitted to him and any other information which he considers relevant; and

(b) in the case of a reference under subsection (2)(d), the provider has dismissed the worker or, as the case may be, has confirmed his transfer on such grounds as are there mentioned,

the Secretary of State shall confirm the worker's inclusion in the list if subsection (7) applies; otherwise he shall remove him from the list.

(7) This subsection applies if the Secretary of State is of the opinion—

(a) that the provider reasonably considered the worker to be guilty of misconduct (whether or not in the course of his employment) which harmed or placed at risk of harm a vulnerable adult; and

(b) that the worker is unsuitable to work with vulnerable adults.

(8) The reference in subsection (6)(b) to the provider dismissing the worker on such grounds as are mentioned in subsection (2)(d) includes—

(a) a reference to his resigning, retiring or being made redundant in circumstances such that the provider would have dismissed him, or would have considered dismissing him, on such grounds if he had not resigned, retired or been made redundant; and

(b) a reference to the provider transferring him, on such grounds, to a position which is not a care position.

(9) This section does not apply where—

(a) the provider carries on a domiciliary care agency, or an independent medical agency, which is or includes an employment agency or an employment business; and

(b) the worker in question is a supply worker in relation to him.

(10) Nothing in this section shall require a person who provides care for vulnerable adults to refer a worker to the Secretary of State in any case where the dismissal, resignation, retirement, transfer or suspension took place or, as the case may be, the opinion was formed before the commencement of this section.

[Care Standards Act 2000, s 82.]

8–16000ZZZP   83. Employment agencies and businesses: duty to refer. (1) A person who carries on an employment agency or an employment business ("the provider") shall refer a supply worker to the Secretary of State if there is fulfilled—

(a) in the case of an employment agency, any of the conditions mentioned in subsection (2); or

(b) in the case of an employment business, any of the conditions mentioned in subsection (3).

(2) The conditions referred to in subsection (1)(a) are—

(a) that the provider has decided not to do any further business with the worker on grounds of misconduct (whether or not in the course of his employment) which harmed or placed at risk of harm a vulnerable adult;

(b) that the provider has decided on such grounds not to find the worker further employment, or supply him for further employment, in a care position.

(3) The conditions mentioned in subsection (1)(b) are—

(a) that the provider has dismissed the worker on the grounds of misconduct (whether or not in the course of his employment) which harmed or placed at risk of harm a vulnerable adult;

(b) that the worker has resigned or retired in circumstances such that the provider would have dismissed him, or would have considered dismissing him, on such grounds if he had not resigned or retired;

(c) that the provider has, on such grounds, decided not to supply the worker for further employment in a care position.

(4) If it appears from the information submitted with a reference under subsection (1) that it may be appropriate for the worker to be included in the list kept under section 81, the Secretary of State shall—

(a) determine the reference in accordance with subsections (5) to (7); and

(b) pending that determination, provisionally include the worker in the list.

(5) The Secretary of State shall—

(a) invite observations from the worker on the information submitted with the reference and, if he thinks fit, on any observations submitted under paragraph (b); and

(b) invite observations from the provider on any observations on the information submitted with the reference and, if he thinks fit, on any other observations under paragraph (a).

(6) Where the Secretary of State has considered the information submitted with the reference, any observations submitted to him and any other information which he considers relevant, the Secretary of State shall confirm the worker's inclusion in the list if subsection (7) applies; otherwise he shall remove him from the list.

(7) This subsection applies if the Secretary of State is of the opinion—

(a) that the provider reasonably considered the worker to be guilty of misconduct (whether or not in the course of his employment) which harmed or placed at risk of harm a vulnerable adult; and

(b) that the worker is unsuitable to work with vulnerable adults.

(8) Nothing in this section shall require a person who provides care for vulnerable adults to refer a worker to the Secretary of State in any case where the dismissal, resignation or retirement took place or, as the case may be, the decision was made before the commencement of this section.
[Care Standards Act 2000, s 83.]

8–16000ZZZQ 84. Power of registration authority to refer. (1) The registration authority may refer a care worker to the Secretary of State if—

(a) on the basis of evidence obtained by it in the exercise of its functions under Part II of this Act, the authority considers that the worker has been guilty of misconduct (whether or not in the course of his employment) which harmed or placed at risk of harm a vulnerable adult; and

(b) the worker has not been referred to the Secretary of State under section 82 or 83 in respect of the misconduct.

(2) Section 82(4) to (7) shall apply in relation to a reference made by the registration authority under subsection (1) as it applies in relation to a reference made by a person under section 82(1).

(3) The reference in subsection (1) to misconduct is to misconduct which occurred after the commencement of this section.
[Care Standards Act 2000, s 84.]

8–16000ZZZR 85. Individuals named in the findings of certain inquiries. (1) Subsection (2) applies where—

(a) a relevant inquiry has been held;

(b) the report of the person who held the inquiry names an individual who is or has been employed in a care position; and

(c) it appears to the Secretary of State from the report—

(i) that the person who held the inquiry found that the individual was guilty of relevant misconduct; and

(ii) that the individual is unsuitable to work with vulnerable adults.

(2) The Secretary of State—

(a) may provisionally include the individual in the list kept under section 81; and

(b) if he does so, shall determine in accordance with subsections (3) to (5) whether the individual's inclusion in the list should be confirmed.

(3) The Secretary of State shall—

(a) invite observations from the individual on the report, so far as relating to him, and, if the Secretary of State thinks fit, on any observations submitted under paragraph (b); and

(b) invite observations from the relevant employer on any observations on the report and, if the Secretary of State thinks fit, on any other observations under paragraph (a).

(4) Where the Secretary of State has considered the report, any observations submitted to him

and any other information which he considers relevant, he shall confirm that individual's inclusion in the list if subsection (5) applies; otherwise he shall remove him from the list.

(5) This subsection applies if the Secretary of State is of the opinion—

(a) that the person who held the inquiry reasonably considered the individual to be guilty of relevant misconduct; and

(b) that the individual is unsuitable to work with vulnerable adults.

(6) In this section—

"relevant employer" means the person who, at the time mentioned in the definition of "relevant misconduct" below, employed the individual in a care position;

"relevant misconduct" means misconduct which harmed or placed at risk of harm a vulnerable adult and was committed (whether or not in the course of his employment) at a time when the individual was employed in a care position.

(7) In this section "relevant inquiry" means any of the following—

(a) an inquiry held under the Inquiries Act 2005 or

under—

(i) section 10;

(ii) section 35 of the Government of Wales Act 1998;

(iii) section 81 of the 1989 Act;

(iv) section 84 of the National Health Service Act 1977;

(v) section 7C of the Local Authority Social Services Act 1970;

(b) an inquiry to which the Tribunals of Inquiry (Evidence) Act 1921 applies;

(c) any other inquiry or hearing designated for the purposes of this section by an order made by the Secretary of State.

(8) Before making an order under subsection (7) the Secretary of State shall consult the Assembly.
[Care Standards Act 2000, s 85.]

8–16000ZZZS   86. Appeals against inclusion in list.   (1) An individual who is included (otherwise than provisionally) in the list kept by the Secretary of State under section 81 may appeal to the Tribunal against—

(a) the decision to include him in the list; or

(b) with the leave of the Tribunal, any decision of the Secretary of State not to remove him from the list under section 81(3).

(2) Subject to subsection (5), an individual who has been provisionally included for a period of more than nine months in the list kept by the Secretary of State under section 81 may, with the leave of the Tribunal, have the issue of his inclusion in the list determined by the Tribunal instead of by the Secretary of State.

(3) If on an appeal or determination under this section the Tribunal is not satisfied of either of the following, namely—

(a) that the individual was guilty of misconduct (whether or not in the course of his duties) which harmed or placed at risk of harm a vulnerable adult; and

(b) that the individual is unsuitable to work with vulnerable adults,

the Tribunal shall allow the appeal or determine the issue in the individual's favour and (in either case) direct his removal from the list; otherwise it shall dismiss the appeal or direct the individual's inclusion in the list.

(4) Where an individual has been convicted of an offence involving misconduct (whether or not in the course of his employment) which harmed or placed at risk of harm a vulnerable adult, no finding of fact on which the conviction must be taken to have been based shall be challenged on an appeal or determination under this section.

(5) Where the misconduct of which the individual is alleged to have been guilty is the subject of any civil or criminal proceedings, an application for leave under subsection (2) may not be made before the end of the period of six months immediately following the final determination of the proceedings.

(6) For the purposes of subsection (5), proceedings are finally determined when—

(a) the proceedings are terminated without a decision being made;

(b) a decision is made against which no appeal lies;

(c) in a case where an appeal lies with leave against a decision, the time limited for applications for leave expires without leave being granted; or

(d) in a case where leave to appeal against a decision is granted or is not required, the time limited for appeal expires without an appeal being brought.
[Care Standards Act 2000, s 86.]

8–16000ZZZT   87. Applications for removal from list.   (1) Subject to section 88, an individual who is included in the list kept by the Secretary of State under section 81 may make an application to the Tribunal under this section.

(2) On an application under this section the Tribunal shall determine whether or not the individual should continue to be included in the list.

(3) If the Tribunal is satisfied that the individual is no longer unsuitable to work with vulnerable adults it shall direct his removal from the list; otherwise it shall dismiss the application.
[Care Standards Act 2000, s 87.]

8–16000ZZZU   88. Conditions for application under section 87.   (1) An individual may only make an application under section 87 with the leave of the Tribunal.

(2) An application for leave under this section may not be made unless the appropriate conditions are satisfied in the individual's case.

(3) In the case of an individual who was a child when he was included (otherwise than provisionally) in the list, the appropriate conditions are satisfied if—

(a) he has been so included for a continuous period of at least five years; and
(b) in the period of five years ending with the time when he makes the application under this section, he has made no other such application.

(4) In the case of any other individual, the appropriate conditions are satisfied if—

(a) he has been included (otherwise than provisionally) in the list for a continuous period of at least ten years; and
(b) in the period of ten years ending with the time when he makes the application under this section, he has made no other such application.

(5) The Tribunal shall not grant an application under this section unless it considers—

(a) that the individual's circumstances have changed since he was included (otherwise than provisionally) in the list, or, as the case may be, since he last made an application under this section; and
(b) that the change is such that leave should be granted.
[Care Standards Act 2000, s 88.]

8–16000ZZZV   89. Effect of inclusion in list.   (1) Where a person who provides care to vulnerable adults proposes to offer an individual employment in a care position that person—

(a) shall ascertain whether the individual is included in the list kept under section 81; and
(b) if he is included in that list, shall not offer him employment in such a position.

(2) Where a person who provides care to vulnerable adults discovers that an individual employed by him in a care position is included in that list, he shall cease to employ him in a care position.
For the purposes of this subsection an individual is not employed in a care position if he has been suspended or provisionally transferred to a position which is not a care position.

(3) Where a person who provides care to vulnerable adults ("the provider") proposes to offer employment in a care position to an individual who has been supplied by a person who carries on an employment agency or employment business, there is a sufficient compliance with subsection (1) if the provider—

(a) satisfies himself that, on a date within the last 12 months, the other person ascertained whether the individual was included in the list kept under section 81;
(b) obtains written confirmation of the facts as ascertained by that person; and
(c) if the individual was included in the list on that date, does not offer him employment in a care position.

(4) It is immaterial for the purposes of subsection (1) or (3) whether the individual is already employed by the provider.*

(5) An individual who is included (otherwise than provisionally) in the list kept by the Secretary of State under section 81 shall be guilty of an offence if he knowingly applies for, offers to do, accepts or does any work in a care position.

(6) It shall be a defence for an individual charged with an offence under subsection (5) to prove that he did not know, and could not reasonably be expected to know, that he was so included in that list.

(7) An individual who is guilty of an offence under this section shall be liable[1]—

(a) on summary conviction, to imprisonment for a term not exceeding **six months**, or to a fine not exceeding **the statutory maximum**, or to both;
(b) on conviction on indictment, to imprisonment for a term not exceeding **five years**, or to a **fine**, or to both.
[Care Standards Act 2000, s 89.]

---

*New sub-ss (4A)–(4C) inserted by the Health and Social Care (Community Health and Standards) Act 2003, s 189, from a date to be appointed.

1. For procedure in respect of this offence which is triable either way, see the Magistrates' Courts Act 1980, ss 17A–21 in PART I: MAGISTRATES' COURTS, PROCEDURE, ante.

8–16000ZZZW   90. Searches of list under Part V of Police Act 1997. *Amendment of the Police Act 1997 (not yet in force).*

8–16000ZZZX   91. Access to list before commencement of section 90*.   (1) In relation to any time before the commencement of section 90, any person seeking to ascertain whether a relevant individual is included in the list kept under section 81 shall be entitled to that information on making application for the purpose to the Secretary of State.

(2) For the purposes of subsection (1) a relevant individual is—

(*a*)   an individual to whom the person proposes to offer employment in a care position;

(*b*)   an individual for whom the person proposes to find employment, or whom he proposes to supply for employment, in a care position; or

(*c*)   an individual of a prescribed description who does not fall within paragraph (*a*) or (*b*).

[Care Standards Act 2000, s 91.]

---

*At the date of going to press s 91 was not in force.

8–16000ZZZY   92. Persons referred for inclusion in list under Protection of Children Act 1999.   (1) Section 2(4) to (7) of the 1999 Act (referrals for inclusion in list of individuals who are considered unsuitable to work with children) shall, in the case of any reference under section 2, 2A or 2D of that Act, apply in relation to the list kept under section 81 as they apply in relation to the list kept under section 1 of that Act, but as if the reference in subsection (7)(*b*) to children were a reference to vulnerable adults.

(2) Section 2B of the 1999 Act shall apply in relation to the list kept under section 81 as it applies in relation to the list kept under section 1 of that Act, but as if the references in subsections (1)(c)(ii) and (5)(b) to children were references to vulnerable adults.

(3) But the Secretary of State may not by virtue of subsection (1) or (2) provisionally include an individual in the list kept under section 81, or confirm his inclusion in that list, unless he provisionally includes him in the list kept under section 1 of the 1999 Act or, as the case requires, confirms his inclusion in that list.

(4) Where an individual has by virtue of subsection (1) or (2) been included in the list kept under section 81, section 86 shall apply to him as if the references in subsections (3)(*a*) and (4) to a vulnerable adult were references to a child.

[Care Standards Act 2000, s 92.]

8–16000ZZZ   93. Power to extend Part VII.   (1) The Secretary of State may by regulations[1]—

(*a*)   add to the list in section 80(7) any prescribed persons to whom subsection (2) applies;

(*b*)   amend the definitions of "care worker", "care position" and "vulnerable adult" accordingly.

(2) This subsection applies to—

(*a*)   local authorities providing services to adults in the exercise of their social services functions;

(*b*)   persons who provide to adults services which are similar to services which—

(i)   may or must be so provided by local authorities; or

(ii)   may or must be provided by National Health Service bodies.

(3) In its application by virtue of subsection (1), this Part shall have effect—

(*a*)   if the regulations so provide, as if "may" were substituted for "shall" in sections 82(1) and 83(1), and section 89 were omitted;

(*b*)   with such other modifications as may be specified in the regulations.

[Care Standards Act 2000, s 93.]

---

1. The Care Standards Act 2000 (Extension of Protection of Vulnerable Adults Scheme) Regulations 2004, SI 2004/2070 have been made which make amendments to this Act.

8–16000ZZZZA   94–99. *Amendments to the 1999 Act*

8–16000ZZZZB   100–102. *Restrictions on working with children in independent schools*

General

8–16000ZZZZC   103. Temporary provision for access to lists.   (1) Any person seeking to ascertain whether a relevant individual is included in—

(*a*)   the list kept under section 1 of the 1999 Act;

(*b*)   the list kept for the purposes of regulations made under section 218(6) of the Education Reform Act 1988; or

(*c*)   any list kept by the Secretary of State or the Assembly of persons disqualified under section 470 or 471 of the Education Act 1996, shall be entitled to that information on making, before the relevant commencement, an application for the purpose to the Secretary of State.

(2) In this section "relevant individual" means—

(*a*) in relation to a person who carries on an employment agency, an individual with whom he proposes to do business or an individual of any other prescribed description;

(*b*) in relation to any other person, an individual to whom he proposes to offer, or whom he proposes to supply for employment in, a child care position or an individual of any other prescribed[1] description.

(3) The relevant commencement is—

(*a*) for applications relating to the list mentioned in subsection (1)(a) or (b), the commencement of section 8 of the 1999 Act; and

(*b*) for applications relating to the list mentioned in subsection (1)(c), the commencement of section 102.

(4) Paragraphs (*b*) and (*c*) of subsection (1) are without prejudice to any right conferred otherwise than by virtue of those provisions.
[Care Standards Act 2000, s 103.]

---

1. See the Protection of Children (Access to Lists) (Prescribed Individuals) Regulations 2000, SI 2000/2537 amended by SI 2001/744.

8–16000ZZZZD   104. *Amendment of the Police Act 1997*

Part VIII[1]
Miscellaneous

8–16000ZZZZE   105–109. *Boarding schools and colleges – Amendments to the Children Act 1989*

---

1. Part VIII comprises ss 105–112.

Fostering

8–16000ZZZZF   110. *Extension of Part IX to school children during holidays*

Employment agencies

8–16000ZZZZG   111. Nurses Agencies.   *Nurses Agencies Act 1957 shall cease to have effect*

Part IX[1]
General and Supplemental

Chapter I
General

8–16000ZZZZH   116. Minor and consequential amendments.   Schedule 4 (which makes minor amendments and amendments consequential on the provisions of this Act) shall have effect.
[Care Standards Act 2000, s 116.]

---

1. Part IX comprises ss 113 to 123.

8–16000ZZZZI   117. Transitional provisions, savings and repeals.   (1) Schedule 5 (which makes transitional and saving provision) shall have effect; but nothing in that Schedule shall be taken to prejudice the operation of sections 16 and 17 of the Interpretation Act 1978 (which relate to the effect of repeals).

(2) The enactments mentioned in Schedule 6 to this Act are repealed to the extent specified in that Schedule.
[Care Standards Act 2000, s 116.]

Chapter II
Supplemental

8–16000ZZZZJ   118. Orders and regulations.   (1) Any power conferred on the Secretary of State, the Assembly or the appropriate Minister to make regulations or an order under this Act except an order under section 38 or 79(3) shall be exercised by statutory instrument.

(2) An order making any provision by virtue of section 119(2) which adds to, replaces or omits any part of the text of an Act shall not be made by the Secretary of State unless a draft of the instrument has been laid before, and approved by resolution of, each House of Parliament.

(3) Subject to subsection (2), an instrument containing regulations or an order made by the

Secretary of State, except an instrument containing an order under section 122, shall be subject to annulment in pursuance of a resolution of either House of Parliament.

In subsection (2) and this subsection, references to the Secretary of State include the Secretary of State and the Assembly acting jointly.

(4) Subsections (5) to (7) apply to any power of the Secretary of State, the Assembly or the appropriate Minister to make regulations or an order under this Act; and subsections (5) and (6) apply to any power of Her Majesty to make an Order in Council under section 70.

(5) The power may be exercised either in relation to all cases to which the power extends, or in relation to all those cases subject to specified exceptions, or in relation to any specified cases or classes of case.

(6) The power may be exercised so as to make, as respects the cases in relation to which it is exercised—

(a) the same provision for all cases in relation to which the power is exercised, or different provision for different cases or different classes of case, or different provision as respects the same case or class of case for different purposes;

(b) any such provision either unconditionally or subject to any specified condition.

(7) The power may be exercised so as to make—

(a) any supplementary, incidental or consequential provision,

(b) any transitory, transitional or saving provision,

which the person exercising the power considers necessary or expedient.

(8) The provision which, by virtue of subsection (7), may be made by regulations or an order under the Part of this Act which relates to the Children's Commissioner for Wales includes provision amending or repealing any enactment or instrument.

[Care Standards Act 2000, s 118, as amended by the Children's Commissioner for Wales Act 2001, s 7.]

8–16000ZZZZK   119. Supplementary and consequential provision etc.   (1) The appropriate Minister may by order[1] make—

(a) any supplementary, incidental or consequential provision,

(b) any transitory, transitional or saving provision,

which he considers necessary or expedient for the purposes of, in consequence of or for giving full effect to any provision of this Act.

(2) The provision which may be made under subsection (1) includes provision amending or repealing any enactment or instrument.

[Care Standards Act 2000, s 119.]

---

1. The following regulations have been made: Children Act (Miscellaneous Amendments) (England) Regulations 2002, SI 2002/546; and Care Standards Act 2000 (Commencement No 8 (Wales) and Transitional, Savings and Consequential Provisions) Order 2002, SI 2002/920.

8–16000ZZZZL   120. Wales.   (1) Section 84(1) of the Government of Wales Act 1998 (payment of Assembly receipts into the Consolidated Fund) does not apply to any sums received by the Assembly by virtue of any provision of this Act.

(2) The reference to the 1989 Act in Schedule 1 to the National Assembly for Wales (Transfer of Functions) Order 1999 is to be treated as referring to that Act as amended by or under this Act.

(3) Subsection (2) does not affect the power to make further Orders varying or omitting that reference.

[Care Standards Act 2000, s 120.]

8–16000ZZZZM   121. General interpretation etc.   (1) In this Act—

"adult" means a person who is not a child;

"appropriate Minister" means—

(a) in relation to England, Scotland or Northern Ireland, the Secretary of State;

(b) in relation to Wales, the Assembly;

and in relation to England and Wales means the Secretary of State and the Assembly acting jointly;

"child" means a person under the age of 18;

"community home" has the same meaning as in the 1989 Act;

"employment agency" and "employment business" have the same meanings as in the Employment Agencies Act 1973; but no business which is an employment business shall be taken to be an employment agency;

"enactment" includes an enactment comprised in subordinate legislation (within the meaning of the Interpretation Act 1978);

"to foster a child privately" has the same meaning as in the 1989 Act;

"harm"—

    (*a*) in relation to an adult who is not mentally impaired, means ill-treatment or the impairment of health;

    (*b*) in relation to an adult who is mentally impaired, or a child, means ill-treatment or the impairment of health or development;

"health service hospital" has the same meaning as in the National Health Service Act 1977;

"illness" includes any injury;

"independent school" has the same meaning as in the Education Act 1996;

"local authority" has the same meaning as in the 1989 Act;

"local authority foster parent" has the same meaning as in the 1989 Act;

"medical" includes surgical;

"mental disorder" means mental illness, arrested or incomplete development of mind, psychopathic disorder, and any other disorder or disability of mind;

"National Health Service body" means a National Health Service trust, an NHS foundation trust, a Strategic Health Authority, a Health Authority, a Special Health Authority, a Primary Care Trust or a Local Health Board;

"parent", in relation to a child, includes any person who is not a parent of his but who has parental responsibility for him;

"parental responsibility" has the same meaning as in the 1989 Act;

"prescribed" means prescribed by regulations;

"proprietor", in relation to a school, has the same meaning as in the Education Act 1996;

"regulations" (except where provision is made for them to be made by the Secretary of State or the Assembly) means regulations made by the appropriate Minister;

"relative" has the same meaning as in the 1989 Act;

"school" has the same meaning as in the Education Act 1996;

"social services functions" means functions which are social services functions for the purposes of the Local Authority Social Services Act 1970;

"treatment" includes diagnosis;

"the Tribunal" means the tribunal established by section 9 of the 1999 Act;

"undertaking" includes any business or profession and—

    (*a*) in relation to a public or local authority, includes the exercise of any functions of that authority; and

    (*b*) in relation to any other body of persons, whether corporate or unincorporate, includes any of the activities of that body;

"voluntary organisation" has the same meaning as in the Adoption and Children Act 2002.

(2) For the purposes of this Act—

    (*a*) a person is disabled if—

        (i) his sight, hearing or speech is substantially impaired;

        (ii) he has a mental disorder; or

        (iii) he is physically substantially disabled by any illness, any impairment present since birth, or otherwise;

    (*b*) an adult is mentally impaired if he is in a state of arrested or incomplete development of mind (including a significant impairment of intelligence and social functioning).

(3) In this Act, the expression "personal care" does not include any prescribed activity.

(4) For the purposes of this Act, the person who carries on a fostering agency falling within section 4(4)(*b*), or a voluntary adoption agency, is the voluntary organisation itself.

(5) References in this Act to a person who carries on an establishment or agency include references to a person who carries it on otherwise than for profit.

(6) For the purposes of this Act, a community home which is provided by a voluntary organisation shall be taken to be carried on by—

    (*a*) the person who equips and maintains it; and

    (*b*) if the appropriate Minister determines that the body of managers for the home, or a specified member of that body, is also to be treated as carrying on the home, that body or member.

(7) Where a community home is provided by a voluntary organisation, the appropriate Minister may determine that for the purposes of this Act the home is to be taken to be managed solely by—

    (*a*) any specified member of the body of managers for the home; or

    (*b*) any other specified person on whom functions are conferred under the home's instrument of management.

(8) A determination under subsection (6) or (7) may be made either generally or in relation to a particular home or class of homes.

(9) An establishment is not a care home for the purposes of this Act unless the care which it provides includes assistance with bodily functions where such assistance is required.

(10) References in this Act to a child's being looked after by a local authority shall be construed in accordance with section 22 of the 1989 Act.

(11) For the purposes of this Act an individual is made redundant if—

(*a*) he is dismissed; and

(*b*) for the purposes of the Employment Rights Act 1996 the dismissal is by reason of redundancy.

(12) Any register kept for the purposes of this Act may be kept by means of a computer.

(13) In this Act, the expressions listed in the left-hand column have the meaning given by, or are to be interpreted in accordance with, the provisions listed in the right-hand column.

Expression	Provision of this Act
1989 Act	Children Act 1989
1999 Act	Protection of Children Act 1999★
Adoption support agency	Section 4
Assembly	Section 5
Care home	Section 3
CCETSW	Section 70
Children's home	Section 1
CHAI	Section 5A
CSCI	Section 5B
Commissioner	Section 72
Council, the English Council, the Welsh Council	Section 54
Domiciliary care agency	Section 4
Fostering agency	Section 4
Hospital and independent hospital	Section 2
Independent clinic and independent medical agency	Section 2
Registration authority	Section 5
Residential family centre	Section 4
Voluntary adoption agency	Section 4

[Care Standards Act 2000, s 121 as amended by SI 2002/2469, the National Health Service Reform and Health Care Professions Act 2002, s 6(2), Sch 5, the Health and Social Care (Community Health and Standards) Act 2003, ss 34, 147 and 196, and Schs 3, 9 and 13 and the Adoption and Children Act 2002, s 139(1), Sch 3.]

8–16000ZZZZN   122. Commencement. This Act, except section 70(2) to (5) and this Chapter, shall come into force on such day as the appropriate Minister may by order appoint, and different days may be appointed for different purposes.

[Care Standards Act 2000, s 122.]

---

1. At the time of going to press the following commencement orders had been made: Care Standards Act 2000 (Commencement No 1) Order 2000, SI 2000/2544; Care Standards Act 2000 (Commencement No 1 (England) and Transitional Provisions) Order 2000, SI 2000/2795; Care Standards Act 2000 (Commencement No 1) (Wales) Order 2000, SI 2000/2992; Care Standards Act 2000 (Commencement No 2 and Transitional Provisions) (Wales) Order 2001, SI 2001/1391; Care Standards Act 2000 (Commencement No 2 (England) and Transitional Provisions) Order 2001, SI 2001/2902; Care Standards Act 2000 (Commencement No 3) (England) Order 2001, SI 2001/731; Care Standards Act 2000 (Commencement No 4) (England) Order 2001, SI 2001/1193; Care Standards Act 2000 (Commencement No 5) (England) Order 2001, SI 2001/1210; Care Standards Act 2000 (Commencement No 6) (England) Order 2001, SI 2001/1536; Care Standards Act 2000 (Commencement No 7 and Transitional, Transitory and Savings (England)) Order 2001, SI 2001/20414; Care Standards Act 2000 (Commencement No 3) (Wales) Order 2001, SI 2001/2190; Care Standards Act 2000 (Commencement No 4) (Wales) Order 2001, SI 2001/2354; Care Standards Act 2000 (Commencement No 5 and Transitional Provisions) (Wales) Order 2001, SI 2001/25045; Care Standards Act 2000 (Commencement No 6) (Wales) Order 2001, SI 2001/2538; Care Standards Act 2000 (Commencement No 7) (Wales) Order 2001, SI 2001/2782; Care Standards Act 2000 (Commencement No 8) (England) Order 2001, SI 2001/3331; Care Standards Act 2000 (Commencement No 9) (England) and Transitional and Savings Provisions) Order 2001, SI 2001/38526; Care Standards Act 2000 (Commencement No 10 (England) and Transitional, Savings and Amendment

Provisions) Order 2001, SI 2001/415010; Care Standards Act 2000 (Commencement No 11) Order 2002, SI 2002/629; Care Standards Act 2000 (Commencement No 8 (Wales) and Transitional, Savings and Consequential Provisions) Order 2002, SI 2002/920; Care Standards Act 2000 (Commencement No 9) (Wales) Order 2002, SI 2002/1175; Care Standards Act 2000 (Commencement No 12) (England) Order 2002, SI 2002/1245; Care Standards Act 2000 (Commencement No 13) (England) Order 2002, SI 2002/839; Care Standards Act 2000 (Commencement No 14 (England) and Transitional, Savings and Amendment Provisions) Order 2002, SI 2002/149311; Care Standards Act 2000 (Commencement No 16) (England) Order 2002, SI 2002/2215; Care Standards Act 2000 (Commencement No 10) and Transitional Provisions (Wales) Order 2003, SI 2003/15215; Care Standards Act 2000 (Commencement No 17 (England) and Transitional and Savings Provisions) Order 2003, SI 2003/36516; Care Standards Act 2000 (Commencement No 11) (Wales) Order 2003, SI 2003/501; Care Standards Act 2000 (Commencement No 18) (England) Order 2003, SI 2003/933; Care Standards Act 2000 (Commencement No 12) (Wales) Order 2003, SI 2003/2528; Care Standards Act 2000 (Commencement No 19) (England) Order 2004, SI 2004/484; Care Standards Act 2000 (Commencement No 13) (Wales) Order 2004, SI 2004/1015; Care Standards Act 2000 (Commencement No 20) Order 2004, SI 2004/1757; Care Standards Act 2000 (Commencement No 21) Order 2005, SI 2005/375.

8–16000ZZZZO   123. Short title and extent.   (1) This Act may be cited as the Care Standards Act 2000.

(2) Subject to subsections (3) and (4), this Act extends to England and Wales only.

(3) Section 70 and, so far as relating to subsections (2) to (5) of that section, sections 114, 115 and 118 extend also to Scotland and Northern Ireland.

(4) The amendment or repeal by this Act of an enactment extending to Scotland or Northern Ireland extends also to Scotland or, as the case may be, Northern Ireland.

[Care Standards Act 2000, s 123.]

8–16000ZZZZP   SCHEDULE 1
                          THE COMMISSION AND THE COUNCILS

                                SCHEDULE 2
                     THE CHILDREN'S COMMISSIONER FOR WALES

                               SCHEDULE 2A
        PERSONS SUBJECT TO REVIEW BY THE THE COMMISSIONER UNDER SECTION 72B

Section 79   SCHEDULE 3
                  CHILD MINDING AND DAY CARE FOR YOUNG CHILDREN

               Insertion of a new Schedule 9A to the Children Act 1989

                                SCHEDULE 4
                     MINOR AND CONSEQUENTIAL AMENDMENTS

                                SCHEDULE 5
                      TRANSITIONAL PROVISIONS AND SAVINGS

                                SCHEDULE 6
                                  REPEALS

Fireworks Act 2003[1]

(2003 c 22)

Introductory

8–16001A   1. Introduction.   (1) In this Act "fireworks" means devices which—

(*a*)   are fireworks for the purposes of the British Standard Specification relating to fireworks published on 30th November 1988 (BS 7114) or any British Standard Specification replacing it, or

(*b*)   would be fireworks for those purposes if they were intended as a form of entertainment.

(2) The Secretary of State may by regulations substitute a new definition of "fireworks" for the definition in subsection (1).

(3) References in this Act to supplying fireworks include—

(*a*)   selling them,

(*b*)   exchanging them for any consideration other than money, and

(*c*)   giving them as a prize or otherwise making a gift of them,

but do not include supplying them otherwise than in the course of a business.

[Fireworks Act 2003, s 1.]

[1.] This Act establishes a new legal framework for fireworks. It will be brought into force in accordance with commencement orders made under s 18. At the time of going to press the following Commencement Orders had been made: Fireworks Act 2003 (Commencement No 1) Order 2003, SI 2003/3084; Fireworks Act 2003 (Commencement No 2) Order 2004, SI 2004/1831. Sections 10, 14, 15 and the Schedule are not in force. Sections 11–13 and 16 are in force only for the purposes of fireworks regulations made in the exercise of powers conferred by the provisions brought into force by the Commencement Orders referred to above.

Fireworks regulations

8–16001B 2–10. (*These provisions enable the Secretary of State to make regulations[1] concerning: the prevention of risk of harm to persons, animals or property; the prohibition from supply or offer to supply to persons below a certain age; the prohibition from supply, etc, during certain specified hours or in certain specified places or circumstances; the prohibition from supply, etc, to persons of certain specified descriptions; the prohibition from operating public fireworks displays unless certain conditions are met; the prohibition from supply by unlicensed persons; the provision of information in relation to fireworks; the prohibition from importing, etc., fireworks or certain specified fireworks; and the provision of training courses.*)

---

1. See the Fireworks Regulations 2004, SI 2004/1836, amended by SI 2004/3262, in this title.

Supplementary

8–16001C 11. Offences. (1) Any person who contravenes a prohibition imposed by fireworks regulations is guilty of an offence[1].

(2) Any person who fails to comply with a requirement imposed by or under fireworks regulations to give or not to give information is guilty of an offence[1].

(3) Where a requirement to give information is imposed by or under fireworks regulations, a person is guilty of an offence if, in giving the information, he—

(*a*) makes a statement which he knows is false in a material particular, or
(*b*) recklessly makes a statement which is false in a material particular.

(4) A person guilty of an offence under this section is liable on summary conviction to—

(*a*) imprisonment for a term not exceeding six months, or
(*b*) a fine not exceeding level 5 on the standard scale,

or to both.

(5) Fireworks regulations may not provide for any contravention of the regulations to be an offence.

(6) Paragraphs (*c*), (*e*) and (*f*) of section 11(3) of the Consumer Protection Act 1987 (c 43) (provision about offences which may be included in regulations) apply in relation to fireworks regulations as to regulations under section 11 of that Act, but as if references to an offence under section 12 of that Act were references to an offence under this section.

(7) Section 39 of that Act (defence of due diligence) applies to offences under subsections (1) and (2) of this section; and section 40(1) of that Act (liability of persons other than the principal offender) has effect accordingly.

(8) In proceedings against any person for an offence of contravening a prohibition imposed by fireworks regulations made by virtue of section 3(1) it is a defence for that person to show that he had no reason to suspect that the person to whom he supplied, offered to supply or agreed to supply the fireworks was below the age specified in the regulations.

(9) Section 40(2) and (3) of the Consumer Protection Act 1987 (c 43) (offences by bodies corporate) applies to an offence under this section as to an offence under that Act.
[Fireworks Act 2003, s 11.]

---

1. A magistrates' court may try an information in respect of an offence under s 11 of the 2003 Act arising from a contravention of a prohibition imposed by the Fireworks Regulations 2004 if the information is laid within 12 months from the time when the offence was committed: Fireworks Regulations 2004, reg 13, in this title, post.

8–16001D 12. Enforcement. (1) Section 27 of the Consumer Protection Act 1987 (enforcement authorities), apart from subsection (1)(*b*), applies in relation to fireworks regulations as to regulations under section 11 of that Act.

(2) The following provisions of that Act—

(*a*) section 28(1)(*a*) and (2) to (4) (test purchases), apart from the references to forfeiture and suspension notices,
(*b*) section 29(1) to (5), (6)(*a*) and (7) and section 30(1) to (9) (powers of search etc), apart from the references to forfeiture and suspension notices,
(*c*) section 32 (obstruction of officer),
(*d*) section 33 (appeals against detention), apart from subsections (2)(*a*)(ii) and (3)(*a*)(ii),
(*e*) section 34 (compensation for seizure and detention),
(*f*) section 35 (recovery of enforcement expenses), apart from subsections (1)(*b*) and (2)(*b*),
(*g*) section 37 (disclosure of information by Customs and Excise),
(*h*) section 41 (civil proceedings), and
(*i*) section 44 (service of documents),

apply in relation to fireworks regulations as to regulations under section 11 of that Act.

(3) In Schedules 14 and 15 to the Enterprise Act 2002 (c 40) (disclosure of information), insert at the appropriate place—

"Fireworks Act 2003.".
[Fireworks Act 2003, s 12.]

8–16001E   13. Savings for certain privileges.   Section 47 of the Consumer Protection Act 1987 (savings for privileges) applies in relation to this Act.
[Fireworks Act 2003, s 13.]

8–16001F   14. Prohibition of supply etc of other explosives.   (1) The power to make regulations under section 3 or 4(2) applies to explosives other than fireworks as to fireworks; and regulations made by virtue of this subsection are fireworks regulations for all the purposes of this Act.
(2) In subsection (1) "explosives" has the same meaning as in the Explosives Act 1875 (c 17).
(3) The Secretary of State may by regulations substitute a new definition of "explosives" for the definition in subsection (2).
[Fireworks Act 2003, s 14.]

8–16001G   15. Repeals and revocation.   The Schedule (repeals and revocation) has effect.
[Fireworks Act 2003, s 15.]

8–16001H   16. Parliamentary procedure for regulations.   (1) Any power to make regulations under this Act is exercisable by statutory instrument.
(2) Regulations under section 1(2) or 14(3) must not be made unless a draft of the statutory instrument containing them has been laid before Parliament and approved by a resolution of each House.
(3) A statutory instrument containing fireworks regulations is subject to annulment in pursuance of a resolution of either House of Parliament.
[Fireworks Act 2003, s 16.]

8–16001I   17. Financial provisions

8–16001J   18. Commencement.   (1) Sections 1 to 16 (and the Schedule) do not come into force until a day appointed by order made by the Secretary of State by statutory instrument; and different days may be appointed for different purposes.
(2) The Secretary of State may by order made by statutory instrument make such transitional provision in connection with the coming into force of any provision of this Act as the Secretary of State considers appropriate[1].
[Fireworks Act 2003, s 18.]

---

[1]. At the date of going to press the following Commencement Orders had been made: Fireworks Act 2003 (Commencement No 1) Order 2003, SI 2003/3084 and Fireworks Act 2003 (Commencement No 2) Order 2004, SI 2004/1831.

8–16001K   19. Short title and extent.   (1) This Act may be cited as the Fireworks Act 2003.
(2) This Act does not extend to Northern Ireland.
[Fireworks Act 2003, s 19.]

8–16001L   SCHEDULE
REPEALS AND REVOCATION

(*The schedule provides for various repeals. These repeals, so far as they effect statutory provisions reproduced in this work, will be shown in those statutes when they take effect.*)

Health and Social Care (Community Health and Standards) Act 2003[1]

(2003 c 43)

PART 1[2]
NHS FOUNDATION TRUSTS

Introductory

8–16001M   35. Conduct of elections.   (1) Regulations may make provision as to the conduct of elections for membership of the board of governors of an NHS foundation trust.
(2) The regulations may in particular provide for—
(*a*) nomination of candidates and obligations to declare their interests,
(*b*) systems and methods of voting, and the allocation of places on the board of governors, at contested elections,

(c) filling of vacancies,
(d) supervision of elections,
(e) election expenses and publicity,
(f) questioning of elections and the consequences of irregularities.

(3) Regulations under this section may create offences punishable on summary conviction with a maximum fine not exceeding level 4 on the standard scale.

(4) An NHS foundation trust must secure that its constitution is in accordance with regulations under this section.

(5) Pending the coming into force of regulations under this section, elections for membership of the board of governors of an NHS foundation trust, if contested, must be by secret ballot.
[Health and Social Care (Community Health and Standards) Act 2003, s 35.]

---

1. Part 1 of this Act establishes NHS foundation trusts. Such trusts are not subject to direction by the Secretary of State, but are instead monitored by an independent regulator. Each foundation trust has a Board of Governors responsible for representing the interests of the local community, staff and local partner organisations.

Part 2 of the Act establishes 2 new regulatory bodies: the Commission for Healthcare Audit and Inspection ("CHAI"); and the Commission of Social Care Inspection ("CSCI").

Part 3 of the Act deals with the recovery of NHS charges and provides for the NHS to recover hospital treatment and/or ambulance costs where people receive compensation for injuries. This extends the current scheme for traffic accident cases.

Part 4 of the Act is concerned with primary dental and primary medical services.

Part 5 of the Act provides for the replacement of the Welfare Food Scheme, and for the abolition of the Public Health Laboratory Service Board.

Part 6 of the Act contains financial, supplementary and consequential provisions.

Only the provisions of the Act that are directly relevant to magistrates' courts are reproduced in this work.

The Act will be brought into force in accordance with commencement orders made under s 199. At the date of going to press the following commencement orders had been made: Health and Social Care (Community Health and Standards) Act 2003 Commencement (No 1) Order 2003, SI 2003/3346; Health and Social Care (Community Health and Standards) Act 2003 Commencement (No 2) Order 2004, SI 2004/2881, as amended by SI 2004/866, SI 2004/1009; Health and Social Care (Community Health and Standards) Act 2003 (Commencement No 1) (Wales) Order 2004, SI 2004/4803, as amended by SI 2004/1019; Health and Social Care (Community Health and Standards) Act 2003 Commencement (No 3) Order 2004, SI 2004/759; Health and Social Care (Community Health and Standards) Act 2003 Commencement (No 2) (Wales) Order 2004, SI 2004/873; Health and Social Care (Community Health and Standards) Act 2003 Commencement (No 4) Order 2004, SI 2004/2626; Health and Social Care (Community Health and Standards) Act 2003 Commencement (No 5) Order 2005, SI 2005/38; Health and Social Care (Community Health and Standards) Act 2003 (Commencement) (No 6) Order 2005, SI 2005/457; Health and Social Care (Community Health and Standards) Act 2003 (Commencement) (No 7) Order 2005, SI 2005/2278 and Health and Social Care (Community Health and Standards) Act 2003 Commencement (No 8) Order 2005, SI 2005/2925. The provisions reproduced in this work are in force unless otherwise indicated.

2. Part 1 contains ss 1–40.

8–16001N   36. Offence.   (1) A person may not vote at an election for the board of governors of an NHS foundation trust unless, within the specified period, he has made a declaration in the specified form of the particulars of his qualification to vote as a member of the constituency, or class within a constituency, for which the election is being held.

(2) A person may not stand for election to the board unless, within the specified period, he has made a declaration in the specified form of the particulars of his qualification to vote as a member of the constituency, or class within a constituency, for which the election is being held and is not prevented from being a member of the board by paragraph 8 of Schedule 1.

(3) A person elected to the board may not vote at a meeting of the board unless, within the specified period, he has made a declaration in the specified form of the particulars of his qualification to vote as a member of the trust and is not prevented from being a member of the board by paragraph 8 of Schedule 1.

(4) This section does not apply to an election held for the staff constituency.

(5) Specified means specified for the purpose in the trust's constitution.

(6) A person is guilty of an offence if he—

(a) makes a declaration under this section which he knows to be false in a material particular, or
(b) recklessly makes such a declaration which is false in a material particular.

(7) A person guilty of an offence under this section is liable on summary conviction to a fine not exceeding level 4 on the standard scale.
[Health and Social Care (Community Health and Standards) Act 2003, s 36.]

PART 2[1]
STANDARDS

CHAPTER 1[2]
REGULATORY BODIES

8–16001O   41. The Commission for Healthcare Audit and Inspection.   (1) There is to be a body corporate known as the Commission for Healthcare Audit and Inspection (in this Part referred to as the CHAI).
[Health and Social Care (Community Health and Standards) Act 2003, s 41.]

1. Part 2 contains ss 41–149.
2. Chapter 1 contains ss 41–44.

8–16001P   42. The Commission for Social Care Inspection.   (1) There is to be a body corporate known as the Commission for Social Care Inspection (in this Part referred to as the CSCI).
[Health and Social Care (Community Health and Standards) Act 2003, s 42.]

8–16001Q   44. Abolition of former regulatory bodies.   (1) The Commission for Health Improvement is abolished.
   (2) The National Care Standards Commission is abolished.
[Health and Social Care (Community Health and Standards) Act 2003, s 44.]

CHAPTER 3[1]
NHS HEALTH CARE: FUNCTIONS OF CHAI

Supplementary

8–16001R   66. Right of entry.   (1) A person authorised to do so by the CHAI may, if the CHAI considers it necessary or expedient for the purposes of this Chapter, at any reasonable time enter and inspect—

   (*a*) any premises owned or controlled by an NHS body;
   (*b*) any other premises used, or proposed to be used, for any purpose connected with—

        (i)   the provision of health care by or for an NHS body, or
        (ii) the discharge of any of the functions of an NHS body.

   (2) A person who proposes to exercise any power of entry or inspection conferred by this section must if so required produce some duly authenticated document showing his authority to exercise the power.
[Health and Social Care (Community Health and Standards) Act 2003, s 66.]

1. Chapter 3 contains ss 48–69.

8–16001S   67. Right of entry: supplementary.   (1) A person authorised by virtue of section 66 to enter and inspect premises may, if he considers it necessary or expedient for the purposes of this Chapter—

   (*a*) inspect, take copies of and remove from the premises any documents or records (including personal records);
   (*b*) inspect any other item and remove it from the premises;
   (*c*) interview in private—

        (i)   any person working at the premises;
        (ii) any person receiving health care there who consents to be interviewed; and

   (*d*) make any other examination into the state and management of the premises and treatment of persons receiving health care there.

   (2) The power in subsection (1)(*a*) includes—

   (*a*) power to require any person holding or accountable for documents or records kept on the premises to produce them; and
   (*b*) in relation to records which are kept by means of a computer, power to require the records to be produced in a form in which they are legible and can be taken away.

   (3) A person authorised by virtue of subsection (1)(*a*) to inspect any records is entitled to have access to, and to check the operation of, any computer and any associated apparatus or material which is or has been in use in connection with the records in question.
   (4) A person authorised by virtue of section 66 to enter and inspect any premises may—

   (*a*) require any person to afford him such facilities and assistance with respect to matters within the person's control as are necessary to enable him to exercise his powers under section 66 or this section; and
   (*b*) take such measurements and photographs and make such recordings as he considers necessary to enable him to exercise those powers.

   (5) Any person who without reasonable excuse—

   (*a*) obstructs the exercise of any power conferred by section 66 or this section, or
   (*b*) fails to comply with any requirement of section 66 or this section,

is guilty of an offence and liable on summary conviction to a fine not exceeding level 4 on the standard scale.
[Health and Social Care (Community Health and Standards) Act 2003, s 67.]

8–16001T   68. Power to require documents and information etc.   (1) The CHAI may at any time require any person specified in subsection (2) to provide it with any information, documents, records (including personal records) or other items—

(a)   which relates or relate to—

(i)   the provision of health care by or for an NHS body, or
(ii)   the discharge of any of the functions of an NHS body; and

(b)   which the CHAI considers it necessary or expedient to have for the purposes of this Chapter.

(2)   The persons referred to in subsection (1) are—

(a)   the NHS body;
(b)   any person providing health care for, or exercising functions of, the NHS body;
(c)   a local authority.

(3)   The power in subsection (1) to require the provision of records includes, in relation to records kept by means of a computer, power to require the provision of the records in legible form.

(4)   Any person who without reasonable excuse fails to comply with any requirement imposed by virtue of this section is guilty of an offence and liable on summary conviction to a fine not exceeding level 4 on the standard scale.
[Health and Social Care (Community Health and Standards) Act 2003, s 68.]

8–16001U   69. Power to require explanation[1].   (1) The Secretary of State may by regulations make provision requiring prescribed persons to provide to the CHAI, or to persons authorised by it, an explanation of—

(a)   any documents, records or items inspected, copied or provided under sections 66 to 68,
(b)   any information provided under those sections, or
(c)   any matters which are the subject of the exercise of any functions of the CHAI under this Chapter,

in circumstances where the CHAI considers the explanation necessary or expedient for the purposes of this Chapter.

(2)   Regulations under subsection (1) may require explanations to be provided at such times and places as may be specified by the CHAI.

(3)   Any person who without reasonable excuse fails to comply with any requirement imposed by virtue of this section is guilty of an offence and liable on summary conviction to a fine not exceeding level 4 on the standard scale.★
[Health and Social Care (Community Health and Standards) Act 2003, s 69.]

---

1. At the time of going to press, s 69 was in force only in so far as conferring any power to make an order or regulations.

8–16001UA   69A. Provision of information by Auditor General for Wales.   The Auditor General for Wales must, on request, provide the CHAI with any information it may reasonably require for the purpose of making comparisons, in the exercise of its functions under sections 51, 52 and 57, between English NHS bodies and Welsh NHS bodies.
[Health and Social Care (Community Health and Standards) Act 2003, s 69A inserted by the Public Audit (Wales) Act 2004, Sch 2.]

CHAPTER 4[1]
NHS HEALTH CARE: FUNCTIONS OF NATIONAL ASSEMBLY FOR WALES

Ancillary powers

8–16001V   72. Right of entry.   (1) A person authorised to do so by the Assembly may, if the Assembly considers it necessary or expedient for the purposes of this Chapter, at any reasonable time enter and inspect—

(a)   any premises owned or controlled by a Welsh NHS body;
(b)   any other premises used, or proposed to be used, for any purpose connected with—

(i)   the provision of health care by or for a Welsh NHS body; or
(ii)   the discharge of any of the functions of a Welsh NHS body.

(2)   A person who proposes to exercise any power of entry or inspection conferred by this section must if so required produce some duly authenticated document showing his authority to exercise the power.
[Health and Social Care (Community Health and Standards) Act 2003, s 72.]

---

1. Chapter 4 contains ss 70–75.

8–16001W   73. Right of entry: supplementary.   (1) A person authorised by virtue of section 72 to enter and inspect premises may, if he considers it necessary or expedient for the purposes of this Chapter—

(a) inspect, take copies of and remove from the premises any documents or records (including personal records);

(b) inspect any other item and remove it from the premises;

(c) interview in private—

(i) any person working at the premises;

(ii) any person receiving health care there who consents to be interviewed; and

(d) make any other examination into the state and management of the premises and treatment of persons receiving health care there.

(2) The power in subsection (1)(a) includes—

(a) power to require any person holding or accountable for documents or records kept on the premises to produce them; and

(b) in relation to records which are kept by means of a computer, power to require the records to be produced in a form in which they are legible and can be taken away.

(3) A person authorised by virtue of subsection (1)(a) to inspect any records is entitled to have access to, and to check the operation of, any computer and any associated apparatus or material which is or has been in use in connection with the records in question.

(4) A person authorised by virtue of section 72 to enter and inspect any premises may—

(a) require any person to afford him such facilities and assistance with respect to matters within the person's control as are necessary to enable him to exercise his powers under section 72 or this section; and

(b) take such measurements and photographs and make such recordings as he considers necessary to enable him to exercise those powers.

(5) Any person who without reasonable excuse—

(a) obstructs the exercise of any power conferred by section 72 or this section, or

(b) fails to comply with any *requirement* of section 72 or this section,

is guilty of an offence and liable on summary conviction to a fine not exceeding level 4 on the standard scale.

[Health and Social Care (Community Health and Standards) Act 2003, s 73.]

8–16001X 74. Power to require documents and information. (1) The Assembly may at any time require any person specified in subsection (2) to provide it with any information, documents, records (including personal records) or other items—

(a) which relates or relate to—

(i) the provision of health care by or for a Welsh NHS body; or

(ii) the discharge of any of the functions of a Welsh NHS body; and

(b) which the Assembly considers it necessary or expedient to have for the purposes of this Chapter.

(2) The persons referred to in subsection (1) are—

(a) the Welsh NHS body;

(b) any person providing health care for, or exercising functions of, the Welsh NHS body;

(c) a local authority in Wales.

(3) The power in subsection (1) to require the provision of records includes, in relation to records kept by means of a computer, power to require the provision of the records in legible form.

(4) Any person who without reasonable excuse fails to comply with any requirement imposed by virtue of this section is guilty of an offence and liable on summary conviction to a fine not exceeding level 4 on the standard scale.

[Health and Social Care (Community Health and Standards) Act 2003, s 74.]

8–16001Y 75. Power to require explanation. (1) The Assembly may by regulations make provision requiring prescribed persons to provide to the Assembly, or to persons authorised by it, an explanation of—

(a) any documents, records or items inspected, copied or provided under sections 72 to 74,

(b) any information provided under those sections, or

(c) any matters which are the subject of the exercise of any function of the Assembly under section 70, and

in circumstances where the Assembly considers the explanation necessary or expedient for the purposes of this Chapter.

(2) Regulations under subsection (1) may require explanations to be provided at such times and places as may be specified by the Assembly.

(3) Any person who without reasonable excuse fails to comply with any requirement imposed by

virtue of this section is guilty of an offence and liable on summary conviction to a fine not exceeding level 4 on the standard scale.
[Health and Social Care (Community Health and Standards) Act 2003, s 75.]

CHAPTER 5[1]
SOCIAL SERVICES: FUNCTIONS OF CSCI

Supplementary

8–16001Z   88. Right of entry.   (1) A person authorised to do so by the CSCI may, if the CSCI considers it necessary or expedient for the purposes of this Chapter, at any reasonable time enter and inspect—

   (a) any premises owned or controlled by a local authority in England; or
   (b) any premises falling within subsection (2), other than premises used wholly or mainly as a private dwelling.

   (2) The premises referred to in subsection (1)(b) are premises—

   (a) which are used, or proposed to be used, by any person in connection with the provision of an English local authority social service; or
   (b) which the CSCI reasonably believes to be so used, or proposed to be so used.

   (3) A person who proposes to exercise any power of entry or inspection conferred by this section must if so required produce some duly authenticated document showing his authority to exercise the power.
[Health and Social Care (Community Health and Standards) Act 2003, s 88.]

---

¹· Chapter 5 contains ss 76–91.

8–16001ZA   89. Right of entry: supplementary.   (1) A person authorised by virtue of section 88 to enter and inspect premises may, if he considers it necessary or expedient for the purposes of this Chapter—

   (a) inspect, take copies of and remove from the premises any documents or records (including personal records) relating to the discharge by the local authority of its social services functions;
   (b) inspect any other item and remove it from the premises;
   (c) interview in private—

      (i) any person working at the premises; or
      (ii) any person accommodated or cared for there who consents to be interviewed; and

   (d) make any other examination into the state and management of the premises and treatment of persons accommodated or cared for there.

   (2) The power in subsection (1)(a) includes—

   (a) power to require any person holding or accountable for documents or records kept on the premises to produce them; and
   (b) in relation to records which are kept by means of a computer, power to require the records to be produced in a form in which they are legible and can be taken away.

   (3) A person authorised by virtue of subsection (1)(a) to inspect any records is entitled to have access to, and to check the operation of, any computer and any associated apparatus or material which is or has been in use in connection with the records in question.

   (4) A person authorised by virtue of section 88 to enter and inspect premises may—

   (a) require any person to afford him such facilities and assistance with respect to matters within the person's control as are necessary to enable him to exercise his powers under section 88 or this section; and
   (b) take such measurements and photographs and make such recordings as he considers necessary to enable him to exercise those powers.

   (5) Any person who without reasonable excuse—

   (a) obstructs the exercise of any power conferred by section 88 or this section, or
   (b) fails to comply with any requirement of section 88 or this section,

is guilty of an offence and liable on summary conviction to a fine not exceeding level 4 on the standard scale.
[Health and Social Care (Community Health and Standards) Act 2003, s 89.]

8–16001ZB   90. Power to require information etc.   (1) The CSCI may at any time require any person specified in subsection (2) to provide it with any information, documents, records (including personal records) or other items—

   (a) which relates or relate to the discharge by a local authority in England of its social services functions; and
   (b) which the CSCI considers it necessary or expedient to have for the purposes of this Chapter.

(2) The persons referred to in subsection (1) are—

(*a*) the local authority;

(*b*) a person providing an English local authority social service for the authority; or

(*c*) any NHS body.

(3) The power in subsection (1) to require the provision of information includes, in relation to records kept by means of a computer, power to require the provision of the records in legible form.

(4) Any person who without reasonable excuse fails to comply with any requirement imposed by virtue of this section is guilty of an offence and liable on summary conviction to a fine not exceeding level 4 on the standard scale.

[Health and Social Care (Community Health and Standards) Act 2003, s 90.]

8–16001ZC   91. Power to require explanation. (1) The Secretary of State may by regulations make provision requiring prescribed persons to provide to the CSCI, or to persons authorised by it, an explanation of—

(*a*) any documents, records or items inspected, copied or provided under sections 88 to 90,

(*b*) any information provided under those sections, or

(*c*) any matters which are the subject of the exercise of any functions of the CSCI under this Chapter,

in cases where the CSCI considers the explanation necessary or expedient for the purposes of this Chapter.

(2) Regulations under subsection (1) may require explanations to be provided at such times and places as may be specified by the CSCI.

(3) Any person who without reasonable excuse fails to comply with any requirement imposed by virtue of this section is guilty of an offence and liable on summary conviction to a fine not exceeding level 4 on the standard scale.

[Health and Social Care (Community Health and Standards) Act 2003, 91.]

CHAPTER 6[1]
SOCIAL SERVICES: FUNCTIONS OF NATIONAL ASSEMBLY FOR WALES
Ancillary powers

8–16001ZD   98. Right of entry. (1) A person authorised to do so by the Assembly may, if the Assembly considers it necessary or expedient for the purposes of this Chapter, at any reasonable time enter and inspect—

(*a*) any premises owned or controlled by a local authority in Wales;

(*b*) any premises falling within subsection (2), other than premises used wholly or mainly as a private dwelling.

(2) The premises referred to in subsection (1)(*b*) are premises—

(*a*) which are used, or proposed to be used, by any person in connection with the provision of a Welsh local authority social service; or

(*b*) which the Assembly reasonably believes to be so used, or proposed to be so used.

(3) A person who proposes to exercise any power of entry or inspection conferred by this section must if so required produce some duly authenticated document showing his authority to exercise the power.

[Health and Social Care (Community Health and Standards) Act 2003, s 98.]

---

1. Chapter 10 contains ss 92–101.

8–16001ZE   99. Right of entry: supplementary. (1) A person authorised by virtue of section 98 to enter and inspect premises may, if he considers it necessary or expedient for the purposes of this Chapter—

(*a*) inspect, take copies of and remove from the premises any documents or records (including personal records) relating to the discharge by the local authority of its social services functions;

(*b*) inspect any other item and remove it from the premises;

(*c*) interview in private—

(i) any person working at the premises; or

(ii) any person accommodated or cared for there who consents to be interviewed; and

(*d*) make any other examination into the state and management of the premises and treatment of persons accommodated or cared for there.

(2) The power in subsection (1)(*a*) includes—

(*a*) power to require any person holding or accountable for documents or records kept on the premises to produce them; and (*b*)　in relation to records which are kept by means of a computer, power to require the records to be produced in a form in which they are legible and can be taken away.

(3)　A person authorised by virtue of subsection (1)(*a*) to inspect any records is entitled to have access to, and to check the operation of, any computer and any associated apparatus or material which is or has been in use in connection with the records in question.

(4)　A person authorised by virtue of section 98 to enter and inspect premises may—

(*a*)　require any person to afford him such facilities and assistance with respect to matters within the person's control as are necessary to enable him to exercise his powers under section 98 or this section;

(*b*)　take such measurements and photographs and make such recordings as he considers necessary to enable him to exercise those powers.

(5)　Any person who without reasonable excuse—

(*a*)　obstructs the exercise of any power conferred by section 98 or this section, or

(*b*)　fails to comply with any requirement of section 98 or this section,

is guilty of an offence and liable on summary conviction to a fine not exceeding level 4 on the standard scale.

[Health and Social Care (Community Health and Standards) Act 2003, s 99.]

8–16001ZF　100. Power to require information.　(1)　The Assembly may at any time require any person specified in subsection (2) to provide it with any information, documents, records (including personal records) or other items—

(*a*)　which relates or relate to the discharge by a local authority in Wales of its social services functions; and

(*b*)　which the Assembly considers it necessary or expedient to have for the purpose of any of its functions under this Chapter.

(2)　The persons referred to in subsection (1) are—

(*a*)　the local authority;

(*b*)　a person providing a Welsh local authority social service for the authority; or

(*c*)　any NHS body.

(3)　The power in subsection (1) to require the provision of information includes, in relation to records kept by means of a computer, power to require the provision of the records in legible form.

(4)　Any person who without reasonable excuse fails to comply with any requirement imposed by virtue of this section is guilty of an offence and liable on summary conviction to a fine not exceeding level 4 on the standard scale.

[Health and Social Care (Community Health and Standards) Act 2003, s 100.]

8–16001ZG　101. Power to require explanation.　(1)　The Assembly may by regulations make provision requiring prescribed persons to provide to the Assembly, or to persons authorised by it, an explanation of—

(*a*)　any documents, records or items inspected, copied or produced under sections 98 to 100,

(*b*)　any information provided under those sections, or

(*c*)　any matters which are the subject of the exercise of any functions of the Assembly under this Chapter,

in cases where the Assembly considers the explanation necessary or expedient for the purposes of this Chapter.

(2)　Regulations under subsection (1) may require explanations to be provided at such times and places as may be specified by the Assembly.

(3)　Any person who without reasonable excuse fails to comply with any requirement imposed by virtue of this section is guilty of an offence and liable on summary conviction to a fine not exceeding level 4 on the standard scale.

[Health and Social Care (Community Health and Standards) Act 2003, s 101.]

CHAPTER 10[1]
SUPPLEMENTARY AND GENERAL

Information

8–16001ZH　136. Disclosure of information obtained by CHAI.　(1)　This section applies to information which—

(*a*)　has been obtained by the CHAI on terms or in circumstances requiring it to be held in confidence; and

(*b*)　relates to and identifies an individual.

(2)　Subject to section 137, a person is guilty of an offence if he knowingly or recklessly discloses information to which this section applies during the lifetime of the individual to which it relates.

(3) A person guilty of an offence under this section is liable—

(*a*) on summary conviction, to imprisonment for a term not exceeding 6 months or to a fine not exceeding the statutory maximum, or to both;

(*b*) on conviction on indictment, to imprisonment for a term not exceeding two years or to a fine or to both.

(4) For the purposes of subsection (1)(*b*), information obtained by the CHAI, or any person authorised by it, is to be regarded as identifying an individual if that individual can be identified—

(*a*) from that information, or

(*b*) from that information and from other information obtained by the CHAI or any person authorised by it.

[Health and Social Care (Community Health and Standards) Act 2003, s 136.]

---

1. Chapter 10 contains ss 120–149.

8–16001ZI 137. Section 136: defence. (1) It is a defence for a person charged with an offence under section 136 to prove that at the time of the alleged offence—

(*a*) any of the circumstances in subsection (2) applied in relation to the disclosure in question; or

(*b*) he reasonably believed that they applied.

(2) The circumstances referred to in subsection (1)(*a*) are that—

(*a*) the disclosure was made in a form in which the individual to whom it relates is not identified;

(*b*) the disclosure was made with the consent of the individual to whom the information relates;

(*c*) the information disclosed had previously been lawfully disclosed to the public;

(*d*) the disclosure was made under or pursuant to regulations under section 113 (complaints about health care);

(*e*) the disclosure was made in accordance with any enactment or court order;

(*f*) the disclosure was necessary or expedient for the purposes of protecting the welfare of any individual;

(*g*) the disclosure was made to any body or person in circumstances where it was necessary or expedient for the person or body to have the information for the purpose of exercising his or its functions under any enactment.

(3) It is also a defence for a person charged with an offence under section 136 to prove that the disclosure was made—

(*a*) for the purposes of facilitating the exercise of any functions of the CHAI (under any enactment);

(*b*) in connection with the investigation of a criminal offence (whether or not in the United Kingdom);

(*c*) for the purpose of criminal proceedings (whether or not in the United Kingdom).

(4) For the purposes of subsection (2)(*a*), information disclosed by a person is not to be regarded as being in a form in which an individual is not identified if the individual can be identified—

(*a*) from that information, or

(*b*) from that information and from other information disclosed by the CHAI, by any person authorised by it or by any of its members or employees.

[Health and Social Care (Community Health and Standards) Act 2003, s 137.]

8–16001ZJ 138. Information obtained by CHAI: supplementary. (1) The CHAI may, subject to section 136, use any information it obtains, or documents or records produced to it, in the course of exercising any of its functions for the purposes of any of its other functions.

(2) Where subsection (3) applies, the CHAI may disclose any information obtained by it notwithstanding any rule of common law which would otherwise prohibit or restrict the disclosure.

(3) This subsection applies where—

(*a*) in the case of information relating to an individual, the circumstances in paragraph (*a*) or (*b*) of subsection (2) of section 137 apply in relation to the disclosure;

(*b*) in any case, the circumstances in any of paragraphs (*c*) to (*g*) of that subsection apply in relation to the disclosure; or

(*c*) in any case, the disclosure is made as specified in paragraph (*a*), (*b*) or (*c*) of subsection (3) of that section.

(4) Subsection (4) of section 137 applies for the purposes of subsection (3)(*a*) above.

[Health and Social Care (Community Health and Standards) Act 2003, s 138.]

General

8–16001ZK 146. Offences by bodies corporate. (1) This section applies where any offence under this Part is committed by a body corporate.

(2) If the offence is proved to have been committed with the consent or connivance of, or to be attributable to any neglect on the part of—

    (*a*) any director, manager, or secretary of the body corporate, or

    (*b*) any person who was purporting to act in any such capacity,

he (as well as the body corporate) shall be guilty of the offence and shall be liable to be proceeded against and punished accordingly.

(3) The reference in subsection (2) to a director, manager or secretary of a body corporate includes a reference—

    (*a*) to any other similar officer of the body; and

    (*b*) where the body is a local authority or NHS body, to any officer or member of the authority or NHS body.

[Health and Social Care (Community Health and Standards) Act 2003, s 146.]

PART 6[1]

FINAL PROVISIONS

8–16001ZL 199. Commencement. (1) Subject to this section—

    (*a*) the provisions of Part 1 (except section 1 and Schedule 1) and Parts 2 to 5, and

    (*b*) section 196 and Schedule 14,

shall come into force on such day as the appropriate authority[2] may by order[3] appoint.
[Health and Social Care (Community Health and Standards) Act 2003, s 199.]

---

1. Chapter 6 contains ss 193–203.

2. As defined in s 199(2) (which is not reproduced in this work).

3. At the date of going to press the following commencement orders had been made: Health and Social Care (Community Health and Standards) Act 2003 Commencement (No 1) Order 2003, SI 2003/3346; Health and Social Care (Community Health and Standards) Act 2003 Commencement (No 2) Order 2004, SI 2004/2881, as amended by SI 2004/866, SI 2004/1009; Health and Social Care (Community Health and Standards) Act 2003 (Commencement No 1) (Wales) Order 2004, SI 2004/4803, as amended by SI 2004/1019; Health and Social Care (Community Health and Standards) Act 2003 Commencement (No 3) Order 2004, SI 2004/759; Health and Social Care (Community Health and Standards) Act 2003 Commencement (No 2) (Wales) Order 2004, SI 2004/873; Health and Social Care (Community Health and Standards) Act 2003 Commencement (No 4) Order 2004, SI 2004/2626; Health and Social Care (Community Health and Standards) Act 2005 Commencement (No 5) Order 2005, SI 2005/38; Health and Social Care (Community Health and Standards) Act 2003 (Commencement) (No 6) Order 2005, SI 2005/457; Health and Social Care (Community Health and Standards) Act 2003 (Commencement) (No 7) Order 2005, SI 2005/2278 and Health and Social Care (Community Health and Standards) Act 2003 Commencement (No 8) Order 2005, SI 2005/2925.

8–16001ZM 203. Short title. This Act may be cited as the Health and Social Care (Community Health and Standards) Act 2003.
[Health and Social Care (Community Health and Standards) Act 2003, s 203.]

Fire and Rescue Services Act 2004[1]

(2004 c 21)

PART 4[2]

EMPLOYMENT

Pensions etc

8–16001ZN 34. Pensions etc. (1) The Secretary of State may by order bring into operation one or more schemes making provision for the payment of pensions, allowances and gratuities to or in respect of—

    (*a*) persons who are or have been employed by a fire and rescue authority or by a Scottish fire authority;

    (*b*) persons who die or have died while so employed.

(2) A scheme brought into operation under this section may in particular—

    (*a*) provide for the classes of person in respect of whose service awards may be made;

    (*b*) provide for treating employment that is not employment by a fire and rescue authority or by a Scottish fire authority as if it were such employment for any purpose of the scheme, to the extent specified in the scheme and subject to any conditions specified in the scheme;

    (*c*) provide for the making of contributions by employers and by persons in respect of whose service awards may be made;

    (*d*) provide for the repayment of any such contributions or their application for the benefit of persons of a specified description;

    (*e*) provide for the making of payments by the Secretary of State, fire and rescue authorities and Scottish fire authorities into a fund to which contributions have been made under the scheme;

(f) provide for the making of payments to the Secretary of State out of a fund to which contributions have been made under the scheme;

(g) provide for substituting the Secretary of State for a fire and rescue authority or a Scottish fire authority, for any purpose of the scheme;

(h) provide for the making to a fire and rescue authority, a Scottish fire authority or the Secretary of State of payments in respect of a person's previous service, including provision for such payments to be made by the Secretary of State;

(i) provide for any such payments to be reimbursed out of a fund to which contributions have been made in respect of the previous service to which the payments related;

(j) provide for the payment and receipt by fire and rescue authorities or Scottish fire authorities of transfer values or of other lump sum payments made for the purpose of creating or restoring rights to pensions, allowances and gratuities;

(k) provide for conditions subject to which an award under the scheme may be made, for the manner in which questions arising under the scheme are to be determined and for appeals from determinations of such questions;

(l) provide for excluding or modifying rights to compensation or damages in respect of injuries, in cases where awards are made under the scheme in respect of the injuries;

(m) make incidental, supplemental, consequential and transitional provision.

(3) An order under this section may take effect from a date which is earlier than that on which the order is made.

(4) An order under this section may vary or revoke a scheme brought into operation by an order under this section.

(5) Before making, varying or revoking an order under this section the Secretary of State must consult any persons he considers appropriate.

(6) A person commits an offence if he does an act or makes an omission as a result of which he is injured or becomes ill, for the purpose of obtaining, for himself or another person—

(a) an award under a scheme brought into operation under this section, or

(b) a sum in respect of the repayment or application of contributions made under such a scheme.

(7) A person guilty of an offence under subsection (6) is liable—

(a) on summary conviction—

(i) in England and Wales, to imprisonment for a term not exceeding 12 months or a fine not exceeding the statutory maximum;

(ii) in Scotland, to imprisonment for a term not exceeding 3 months or a fine not exceeding the statutory maximum;

(b) on conviction on indictment, to imprisonment for a term not exceeding 2 years[3].

(8) A scheme brought into operation under this section may authorise the forfeiture of the whole or part of an award or sum obtained by a person who has been convicted of an offence under subsection (6).

(9) In relation to an offence under subsection (6) committed before the commencement of section 154(1) of the Criminal Justice Act 2003 (c 44), the reference in subsection (7)(a) to 12 months is to be read as a reference to 3 months.

(10) In this section and section 35 "Scottish fire authority" means—

(a) a fire authority which is a council constituted under section 2 of the Local Government etc (Scotland) Act 1994 (c 39), or

(b) a joint board constituted by virtue of section 36(4)(b) of the Fire Services Act 1947 (c 41) or section 147(4) of the Local Government (Scotland) Act 1973 (c 65).★

[Fire and Rescue Services Act 2004, 34.]

★Amended by the Fire (Scotland) Act 2005, Sch 3 from a date to be appointed.

1. This Act makes provision about fire and rescue services and their functions. It repeals the Fire Services Act 1947. All the provisions of the Act are in force.

2. Part 4 contains ss 32–27.

3. For procedure in respect of offences triable either way see the Magistrates' Courts Act 1980, ss 17A–21 in PART I: MAGISTRATES' COURTS' PROCEDURE, ante.

8–16001ZO 42. Fire hydrants. (1) A water undertaker must cause the location of every fire hydrant provided by it to be clearly indicated by a notice or distinguishing mark.

(2) A water undertaker may place such a notice or mark on a wall or fence adjoining a highway or public place.

(3) The expenses incurred by a water authority under subsection (1) in relation to a fire hydrant are to be borne by the fire and rescue authority in whose area the hydrant is located.

(4) The Secretary of State may make regulations providing for uniformity in fire hydrants provided by water undertakers and in the notices or marks indicating their location.

(5) An obligation of a water undertaker under subsection (1), or regulations under subsection (4),

is enforceable by the Secretary of State under section 18 of the Water Industry Act 1991 (c 56) (orders for securing compliance).

(6) A person commits an offence if he uses a fire hydrant otherwise than—

(a) for the purposes of fire-fighting or for any other purposes of a fire and rescue authority, or

(b) for any purpose authorised by the water undertaker or other person to whom the hydrant belongs.

(7) A person commits an offence if he damages or obstructs a fire hydrant, otherwise than in consequence of use for the purposes mentioned in subsection (6).

(8) A person guilty of an offence under subsection (6) or (7) is liable on summary conviction to a fine not exceeding level 2 on the standard scale.
[Fire and Rescue Services Act 2004, 42.]

8–16001ZP   43. Notice of works affecting water supply and fire hydrants.   (1) A person who proposes to carry out works for the purpose of supplying water to any part of the area of a fire and rescue authority must give at least 6 weeks' notice in writing to the authority.

(2) A person who proposes to carry out works affecting a fire hydrant must give at least 7 days' notice in writing to the fire and rescue authority in whose area the hydrant is situated.

(3) If it is not practicable for a person to give notice as required by subsection (1) or (2), he is to be regarded as having given the notice required by that subsection if he gives notice as soon as practicable.

(4) A person commits an offence if, without reasonable excuse, he fails to give notice as required by subsection (1) or (2).

(5) A person guilty of an offence under subsection (4) is liable on summary conviction to a fine not exceeding level 5 on the standard scale.
[Fire and Rescue Services Act 2004, 43.]

PART 6

SUPPLEMENTARY[1]

8–16001ZQ   44. Powers of fire-fighters etc in an emergency etc.   (1) An employee of a fire and rescue authority who is authorised in writing by the authority for the purposes of this section may do anything he reasonably believes to be necessary—

(a) if he reasonably believes a fire to have broken out or to be about to break out, for the purpose of extinguishing or preventing the fire or protecting life or property;

(b) if he reasonably believes a road traffic accident to have occurred, for the purpose of rescuing people or protecting them from serious harm;

(c) if he reasonably believes an emergency of another kind to have occurred, for the purpose of discharging any function conferred on the fire and rescue authority in relation to the emergency;

(d) for the purpose of preventing or limiting damage to property resulting from action taken as mentioned in paragraph (a), (b) or (c).

(2) In particular, an employee of a fire and rescue authority who is authorised as mentioned in subsection (1) may under that subsection—

(a) enter premises or a place, by force if necessary, without the consent of the owner or occupier of the premises or place;

(b) move or break into a vehicle without the consent of its owner;

(c) close a highway;

(d) stop and regulate traffic;

(e) restrict the access of persons to premises or a place.

(3) A person commits an offence if without reasonable excuse he obstructs or interferes with an employee of a fire and rescue authority taking action authorised under this section.

(4) A person guilty of an offence under subsection (3) is liable on summary conviction to a fine not exceeding level 3 on the standard scale.
[Fire and Rescue Services Act 2004, 44.]

---

1. Part 6 contains ss 44–54.

8–16001ZR   45. Obtaining information and investigating fires.   (1) An authorised officer may at any reasonable time enter premises—

(a) for the purpose of obtaining information needed for the discharge of a fire and rescue authority's functions under section 7, 8 or 9, or

(b) if there has been a fire in the premises, for the purpose of investigating what caused the fire or why it progressed as it did.

(2) In this section and section 46, "authorised officer" means an employee of a fire and rescue authority who is authorised in writing by the authority for the purposes of this section.

(3) An authorised officer may not under subsection (1)—

(*a*) enter premises by force, or

(*b*) demand admission as of right to premises occupied as a private dwelling unless 24 hours' notice in writing has first been given to the occupier of the dwelling.

(4) An authorised officer may not under subsection (1)(*b*) enter as of right premises in which there has been a fire if—

(*a*) the premises are unoccupied, and

(*b*) the premises were occupied as a private dwelling immediately before the fire,

unless 24 hours' notice in writing has first been given to the person who was the occupier of the dwelling immediately before the fire.

(5) An authorised officer may apply to a justice of the peace if—

(*a*) he considers it necessary to enter premises for the purposes of subsection (1), but

(*b*) he is unable to do so, or considers that he is likely to be unable to do so, otherwise than by force.

(6) If on an application under subsection (5) a justice is satisfied that—

(*a*) it is necessary for the officer to enter the premises for the purposes of subsection (1), and

(*b*) he is unable to do so, or is likely to be unable to do so, otherwise than by force,

he may issue a warrant authorising the officer to enter the premises by force at any reasonable time.

(7) An authorised officer may also apply to a justice of the peace if he considers it necessary to enter a dwelling for the purposes of subsection (1) without giving notice as required by subsection (3)(*b*) or (4).

(8) If on an application under subsection (7) a justice is satisfied that it is necessary for the authorised officer to enter the dwelling for the purposes of subsection (1) without giving notice as required by subsection (3)(*b*) or (4), the justice may issue a warrant authorising the officer to enter the premises at any time (by force if necessary).

(9) An authorised officer exercising a power of entry under this section must, if so required, produce evidence of his authorisation under subsection (2), and any warrant under subsection (6) or (8)—

(*a*) before entering the premises, or

(*b*) at any time before leaving the premises.

[Fire and Rescue Services Act 2004, 45.]

8–16001ZS 46. Supplementary powers. (1) If an authorised officer exercises a power of entry under section 45(1)(*a*), he may—

(*a*) take with him any other persons, and any equipment, that he considers necessary;

(*b*) require any person present on the premises to provide him with any facilities, information, documents or records, or other assistance, that he may reasonably request.

(2) If an authorised officer exercises a power of entry under section 45(1)(*b*) he may—

(*a*) take with him any other persons, and any equipment, that he considers necessary;

(*b*) inspect and copy any documents or records on the premises or remove them from the premises;

(*c*) carry out any inspections, measurements and tests in relation to the premises, or to an article or substance found on the premises, that he considers necessary;

(*d*) take samples of an article or substance found on the premises, but not so as to destroy it or damage it unless it is necessary to do so for the purpose of the investigation;

(*e*) dismantle an article found on the premises, but not so as to destroy it or damage it unless it is necessary to do so for the purpose of the investigation;

(*f*) take possession of an article or substance found on the premises and detain it for as long as is necessary for any of these purposes—

(i) to examine it and do anything he has power to do under paragraph (*c*) or (*e*);

(ii) to ensure that it is not tampered with before his examination of it is completed;

(iii) to ensure that it is available for use as evidence in proceedings for an offence relevant to the investigation;

(*g*) require a person present on the premises to provide him with any facilities, information, documents or records, or other assistance, that he may reasonably request.

(3) If an authorised officer exercises the power in subsection (2)(*d*) he must—

(*a*) leave a notice at the premises (either with a responsible person or if that is impracticable fixed in a prominent position) giving particulars of the article or substance and stating that he has taken a sample of it, and

(*b*) if it is practicable to do so, give to a responsible person at the premises a portion of the sample marked in a manner sufficient to identify it.

(4) If an authorised officer exercises the power in subsection (2)(*f*) he must leave a notice at the

premises (either with a responsible person or if that is impracticable fixed in a prominent position) giving particulars of the article or substance and stating that he has taken possession of it.

(5) If in the exercise of any power under section 45 or this section an authorised officer enters premises which are unoccupied, or from which the occupier is temporarily absent, he must on his departure leave the premises as effectively secured against unauthorised entry as he found them.

(6) A person commits an offence if without reasonable excuse—

(a) he obstructs the exercise of any power under section 45 or this section, or

(b) he fails to comply with any requirement under subsection (1)(b) or (2)(g).

(7) A person guilty of an offence under subsection (6) is liable on summary conviction to a fine not exceeding level 3 on the standard scale.
[Fire and Rescue Services Act 2004, 46.]

8–16001ZT 47. Notices: general. (1) The notice required by section 45(3)(b) may be given—

(a) by delivering it to the occupier of the dwelling,

(b) by leaving it for him at the dwelling, or

(c) by sending it by post to him at the dwelling.

(2) The notice required by section 45(4) may be given—

(a) by delivering it to the person who was the occupier of the dwelling immediately before the fire concerned,

(b) by leaving it for him at his proper address, or

(c) by sending it by post to him at that address.

(3) The proper address of a person for the purposes of subsection (2) and section 7 of the Interpretation Act 1978 (c 30) is—

(a) if he has specified an address in the United Kingdom as his address for the purposes of the notice required by section 45(4), that address;

(b) in any other case, his last known address.

(4) If the name or address of the person to whom notice under section 45(3)(b) or (4) is required to be given cannot be ascertained after reasonable inquiry, the notice may be given—

(a) by leaving it in the hands of a person who is or appears to be resident in the dwelling, or

(b) by leaving it affixed to a conspicuous part of the dwelling.
[Fire and Rescue Services Act 2004, 47.]

8–16001ZU 48. Notices given electronically. (1) This section applies if the notice required by section 45(3)(b) or (4) is transmitted to the person to whom it is required to be given ("the recipient")—

(a) by means of an electronic communications network (within the meaning given by section 32 of the Communications Act 2003 (c 21)), or

(b) by other means but in a form that nevertheless requires the use of apparatus by the recipient to render it intelligible.

(2) The transmission has effect as a delivery of the notice to the recipient only if he has indicated to the fire and rescue authority on whose behalf the transmission is made his willingness to receive a notice under section 45 transmitted in the form and manner used.

(3) An indication to a fire and rescue authority for the purposes of subsection (2)—

(a) must be given to the authority in any manner it requires;

(b) may be a general indication or one that is limited to notices of a particular description;

(c) must state the address to be used and must be accompanied by any other information which the authority requires for the making of the transmission;

(d) may be modified or withdrawn at any time by a notice given to the authority in any manner it requires.

(4) If the making of the transmission has been recorded in the computer system of the fire and rescue authority on whose behalf it is made, it must be presumed, unless the contrary is proved, that the transmission—

(a) was made to the person recorded in that system as receiving it;

(b) was made at the time recorded in that system as the time of delivery;

(c) contained the information recorded on that system in respect of it.
[Fire and Rescue Services Act 2004, 48.]

8–16001ZV 49. False alarms of fire. (1) A person commits an offence if he knowingly gives or causes to be given a false alarm of fire to a person acting on behalf of a fire and rescue authority.

(2) A person guilty of an offence under subsection (1) is liable on summary conviction—

(a) to a fine not exceeding level 4 on the standard scale,

(b) to imprisonment for a term not exceeding 51 weeks, or

(c) to both.

(3) In relation to an offence committed before the commencement of section 281(5) of the Criminal Justice Act 2003 (c 44), the reference in subsection (2)(*b*) to 51 weeks is to be read as a reference to 3 months.
[Fire and Rescue Services Act 2004, 49.]

Petroleum Spirit (Motor Vehicles, &c) Regulations 1929[1]

(S R & O 1929/952 amended by SI 1979/427, SI 1982/630, SI 1992/1811, SI 1999/743 and SI 2002/2776)

Exemption from Act and application of Regulations

8–16002 **1.** (1) Subject as hereinafter provided, the keeping and use of petroleum spirit by persons intending to use it for the purpose of any internal combustion engine and not either wholly or partly for the purposes of sale, shall be exempt from the operation of sections 1 to 9 inclusive of the Act[2], and petroleum spirit kept and used by persons intending to use it as aforesaid shall be kept and used in accordance with the regulations hereinafter contained;

(2) Provided that on the application of any person intending to use petroleum spirit as aforesaid, the local authority may grant a petroleum spirit licence authorising the keeping thereof, and the said exemption and regulations shall not apply in respect of any petroleum spirit so authorised to be kept.

---

1. Made under s 10 of the Petroleum (Consolidation) Act 1928. These Regulations were continued in force by reg 5(4) of the Petroleum (Regulation) Acts 1928) and 1936 (Repeals and Modifications) Regulations 1974, SI 1974/1942, and are to have effect as if any requirement or prohibition imposed by or under them was imposed by or under health and safety regulations (Petroleum (Consolidation) Act 1928 (Enforcement) Regulations 1979, SI 1979/427 amended by SI 1982/630, SI 1984/1244, SI 1986/1951 and SI 2002/2776; thus see Health and Safety at Work etc Act 1974, s 33, ante for penalties.
2. In these Regulations the Petroleum (Consolidation) Act 1928, is referred to as "the Act" (Introduction to Regulations).

Keeping of Petroleum-spirit[1]

8–16003 **2.** (1) Subject to paragraph (2), the petroleum-spirit shall not be kept otherwise than in metal vessels so constructed and maintained in such a condition as—

(*a*) to be reasonably secure against breakage; and
(*b*) to prevent the leakage of any liquid or vapour therefrom.

(2) Where the vessel in which the petroleum-spirit is to be kept is a fuel tank for an internal combustion engine, the requirement in paragraph (1) that the vessel be made of metal shall not apply.

---

1. But petroleum-spirit may be kept in plastic containers which comply with the Petroleum-Spirit (Plastic Containers) Regulations 1982, SI 1982/630 amended by SI 1999/743 and SI 2002/2776.

8–16004 **3.** No person shall repair or cause to be repaired any vessel in which, to his knowledge, any petroleum spirit is or has been kept until he has taken all reasonable precautions to ensure that the vessel has been rendered free from petroleum spirit and from any inflammable vapour occasioned thereby.

8–16005 **4.** Any vessel used for the purpose of keeping the petroleum spirit, not being the fuel tank of an internal combustion engine, shall bear in conspicuous characters, the words "petroleum spirit" and the words "highly inflammable" indelibly marked on the vessel, or, where that is impracticable, on a metal label attached thereto.

8–16006 **5.** The petroleum spirit shall not be kept in any storage place which does not comply with the following requirements, that is to say:

(*a*) the storage place shall, unless it is in the open air, be effectively ventilated to the open air;
(*b*) there shall, unless the storage place is in the open air, be an entrance thereto direct from the open air;
(*c*) in the storage place, or as near thereto as is reasonably practicable, there shall be kept fire extinguishing apparatus of a type capable of extinguishing fires occasioned by burning petroleum spirit, or a supply of sand or other effective means for extinguishing such fires;
(*d*) the storage place shall not form part of or be attached to any building used as a dwelling place or as a place where persons assemble for any purpose unless it is separated therefrom by a substantial floor[1] or partition which—

(i) is constructed of material not readily inflammable; and
(ii) has no opening therein, so, however, that in the case of a storage place in which the only petroleum spirit kept, in addition to that contained in the fuel tank of any internal combustion engine, is kept in not more than two vessels of capacity not exceeding 10 litres each, there may be an opening in any such partition (not being a floor) if the

opening is fitted with a self-closing door constructed of hard wood or other fire-resisting material;

(e) the storage place, if in any building, shall not be situated under any staircase or under any other means of exit likely to be required to be used for escape in case of fire unless it is separated therefrom by a substantial floor or partition conforming to the requirements contained in sub-paragraphs (i) and (ii) of the last foregoing paragraph.

---

1. It was an offence under the repealed regulations to use as a dwelling-house a loft below which petroleum spirit was contained in the tanks of motor cars housed in a garage situated below the loft, the intervening floor being of unsubstantial character (*Appleyard v Bangham* [1914] 1 KB 258, 77 JP 448).

8–16007   6. No more than 275 litres of petroleum spirit shall be kept at the same time in any one storage place, and in computing for the purposes of this regulation the amount of petroleum spirit kept in any one storage place—

(a) any petroleum-spirit contained in the fuel-tank of an internal combustion engine or otherwise for the time being within the storage place, shall be deemed to be kept in the storage place; and

(b) any two storage places not more than 6 metres apart, in the occupation of the same occupier, shall be deemed to be one storage place.

8–16008   7. (1) Subject to paragraph (3) below, the petroleum spirit shall not be kept in any vessel of capacity exceeding 10 litres, not being the fuel tank of an internal combustion engine, unless—

(a) it is kept in a storage place situated more than 6 metres from any building, highway or public footpath; and

(b) provision has been made by excavation or by the erection of retaining walls or otherwise to prevent the petroleum spirit from flowing out of the storage place in case of fire; and

(c) notice in writing that the petroleum spirit is proposed to be so kept has been given to the local authority in accordance with the provisions of this regulation.

(2) The said notice shall be given by the occupier of the storage place before keeping the petroleum spirit or permitting it to be kept in a vessel of capacity exceeding 10 litres, and thereafter annually in the month of January.

(3) The disapplication from the requirements of paragraph (1) above in respect of a fuel tank for an internal combustion engine shall only apply to a fuel tank which remains connected to the fuel system of the internal combustion engine it is serving in the way it would ordinarily be so connected when that engine is running.

8–16009   8. (1) The petroleum spirit shall not in any storage place situated within 6 metres of any building or of any stack of timber or other inflammable substance, be kept otherwise than—

(a) in the fuel tank of any internal combustion engine; and

(b) in not more than two other vessels of capacity not exceeding 10 litres each carried on any motor vehicle, motor boat, hovercraft or aircraft, unless notice in writing that petroleum spirit is proposed to be kept in the storage place otherwise than as aforesaid has been given to the local authority in accordance with the provisions of this regulation.

(2) The said notice shall be given by the occupier of the storage place before so keeping the petroleum spirit or permitting it to be so kept, and thereafter annually in the month of January.

8–16010   9. Any reasonable precautions shall be taken at every storage place to prevent any fire or artificial light liable to ignite inflammable vapour so near any vessel in which the petroleum spirit is kept as to be dangerous.

Use of petroleum-spirit

8–16011   10. No operation involving the exposure of petroleum spirit shall be carried on in the neighbourhood of any fire or artificial light liable to ignite inflammable vapour.

8–16012   11. Subject as hereinafter provided, no petroleum spirit shall be used in any storage place otherwise than as fuel for an internal combustion engine. Provided that petroleum spirit may be used therein—

(a) as fuel for any lamp or other apparatus used for the purpose of lighting or heating, so constructed and maintained in such condition as not to be liable to ignite inflammable vapour otherwise than as such fuel; and

(b) in quantities not exceeding at any one time 150 millilitres, for cleaning or as a solvent for repair purposes.

8–16013   12. No person shall wilfully or negligently empty, turn or permit to enter into any sewer[1] or any drain communicating with a sewer any petroleum spirit.

---

1. Where Pt III of the Public Health Act 1925, is in force, see also s 41 hereof.

Special Provisions as to Engines used in connection with the making or repair of Roads

8-16014　13. With respect to the keeping and use on any road of petroleum spirit for the purposes of any engine used in connection with the making or repair of roads, these regulations shall apply subject to the following modifications and additions:

(a) before any petroleum spirit is so kept the person intending to keep it shall give to the local authority notice in writing of his intention to do so;

(b) Regulation 6 (which limits the quantity of petroleum spirit that may be kept in a storage place) shall have effect as if for the words 275 litres there were therein substituted the words 140 litres

(c) Regulations 7 and 8 shall not apply;

(d) the petroleum spirit shall not be kept in any vessel of capacity exceeding two gallons, not being the fuel tank of the engine;

(e) not more than one such vessel shall be open at a time and no such vessel shall be open for any purpose other than that of fuelling the engine;

(f) all such vessels shall be kept in an iron locker;

(g) no such locker shall be situated within 15 metres of any means of exit from a theatre, music hall, cinema, or other place of public entertainment, or from a hospital, nor within 5 metres of any means of exit from any other place where persons assemble for any purpose, or from a dwelling-house;

(h) all reasonable precautions shall be taken to prevent any unauthorised person having access to any such locker and to prevent any fire or artificial light liable to ignite inflammable vapour being within twenty feet of any such locker.

Supplementary

8-16015　14. (1) The Interpretation Act [1978] applies for the purposes of the interpretation of these Regulations as it applies for the purposes of the interpretation of an Act of Parliament.

(2) In these Regulations the following expressions have the meanings hereby respectively assigned to them, that is to say—

"Local authority", in relation to any storage place or petroleum-spirit means the local authority empowered under the Act to grant petroleum-spirit licences in respect of the storage place or petroleum-spirit;

"Road" includes any highway and any street, bridge, lane, footway, square, court, mews, alley, or passage, whether a thoroughfare or not;

"Storage place" includes any room, building or place of any kind whatsoever, whether or not in the open air, used or proposed to be used for keeping therein petroleum-spirit for the purposes of any internal combustion engine.

8-16015A　15. *Revoking provision: revokes SR & Os 1907/614 and 1923/1359.*

8-16016　15A. Disapplication. The provisions of these Regulations shall not apply in respect of—

(a) any establishment to which the Control of Major Accident Hazards Regulations 1999 [SI 1999/743] apply by virtue of regulation 3 of those Regulations;

(b) any site in respect of which notification of an activity is required pursuant to regulation 3 of the Notification of Installations Handling Hazardous Substances Regulations 1982, SI 1982/1357; or

(c) any workplace within the meaning of the Dangerous Substances and Explosive Atmospheres Regulations 2002.

Health and Safety (First-Aid) Regulations 1981[1]

(SI 1981/917 amended by SI 1989/1671, SI 1997/2776, SI 1999/3242 and SI 2002/2174)

8-16230　1. *Citation and commencement.*

1. Made by the Secretary of State in exercise of the powers conferred on him by sections 15(1), (2), (3)(a), (4)(a), (5)(b) and (9) and 49(1) and (4) of, and paragraphs 10 and 14 of Sch 3 to, the Health and Safety at Work etc Act 1974. Contravention of the regulations would be an offence contrary to s 33(1) of the 1974 Act; such offences would be triable either way by virtue of s 33(3) of the Act.

Interpretation

8-16231　2. (1) In these Regulations, unless the context otherwise requires—
"first-aid" means—

(a) in cases where a person will need help from a medical practitioner or nurse, treatment for the purpose of preserving life and minimising the consequences of injury and illness until such help is obtained, and

(b) treatment of minor injuries which would otherwise receive no treatment or which do not need treatment by a medical practitioner or nurse;

"mine" means a mine within the meaning of section 180 of the Mines and Quarries Act 1954.

(2) In these Regulations, unless the context otherwise requires, any reference to—

(a) a numbered Regulation or Schedule is a reference to the Regulation of, or Schedule to, these Regulations bearing that number;

(b) a numbered paragraph is a reference to the paragraph bearing that number in the Regulation in which the reference appears.

Duty of employer to make provision for first-aid

8–16232 **3.** (1) An employer shall provide, or ensure that there are provided, such equipment and facilities as are adequate and appropriate in the circumstances for enabling first-aid to be rendered to his employees if they are injured or become ill at work.

(2) Subject to paragraphs (3) and (4), an employer shall provide, or ensure that there is provided, such number of suitable persons as is adequate and appropriate in the circumstances for rendering first-aid to his employees if they are injured or become ill at work; and for this purpose a person shall not be suitable unless he has undergone—

(a) such training and has such qualifications as the Health and Safety Executive may approve for the time being in respect of that case or class of case, and

(b) such additional training, if any, as may be appropriate in the circumstances of that case.

(3) Where a person provided under paragraph (2) is absent in temporary and exceptional circumstances it shall be sufficient compliance with that paragraph if the employer appoints a person, or ensures that a person is appointed, to take charge of—

(a) the situation relating to an injured or ill employee who will need help from a medical practitioner or nurse, and

(b) the equipment and facilities provided under paragraph (1)

throughout the period of any such absence.

(4) Where having regard to—

(a) the nature of the undertaking, and

(b) the number of employees at work, and

(c) the location of the establishment,

it would be adequate and appropriate if instead of a person for rendering first-aid there was a person appointed to take charge as in paragraph (3)(a) and (b), then instead of complying with paragraph (2) the employer may appoint such a person, or ensure that such a person is appointed.

(5) Any first-aid room provided pursuant to this regulation shall be easily accessible to stretchers and to any other equipment needed to convey patients to and from the room and be sign-posted, and such sign to comply with regulation 4 of the Health and Safety (Safety Signs and Signals) Regulations 1996 as if it were provided in accordance with that regulation.

Duty of employer to inform his employees of the arrangements made in connection with first-aid

8–16233 **4.** An employer shall inform his employees of the arrangements that have been made in connection with the provision of first-aid, including the location of equipment, facilities and personnel.

Duty of self-employed person to provide first-aid equipment

8–16234 **5.** A self-employed person shall provide, or ensure that there is provided, such equipment, if any, as is adequate and appropriate in the circumstances to enable him to render first-aid to himself while he is at work.

Power to grant exemptions

8–16235 **6.** . *Revoked.*

Cases where these Regulations do not apply

8–16236 **7.** These Regulations shall not apply—

(a) where the Diving at Work Regulations 1997 apply;

(b) where the Merchant Shipping (Medical Scales) (Fishing Vessels) Regulations 1974 apply;

(c) where the Merchant Shipping (Medical Stores) Regulations 1986 apply;

(d) on vessels which are registered outside the United Kingdom;

(e) to a mine of coal, stratified ironstone, shale or fireclay;

(f) in respect of the armed forces of the Crown and any force to which any provision of the Visiting Forces Act 1952 applies;

(g) where the Offshore Installations and Pipe-line Works (First-Aid) Regulations 1989 apply.

Application to miscellaneous mines

8–16237 **8.** In their application to mines not excluded from these Regulations by Regulation 7 (e), Regulations 3 and 4 shall have effect as if the manager for the time being of any such mine were an employer and as if the persons employed were his employees.

Application offshore

8–16238   9. Subject to Regulation 7, these Regulations shall apply to and in relation to any premises or activity to or in relation to which sections 1 to 59 of the Health and Safety at Work etc Act 1974 apply by virtue of Articles 6 and 7 (*a*), (*b*) and (*d*) of the Health and Safety at Work etc Act 1974 (Application outside Great Britain) Order [1989] (which relate respectively to mines extending beyond Great Britain and to certain activities concerning vessels and construction works in territorial waters).

Repeals, revocations and modification

8–16239   10. (1) The enactments mentioned in column (1) of Schedule 1 are hereby repealed to the extent specified opposite thereto in column (3) of that Schedule.

(2) The Orders and Regulations mentioned in column (1) of Schedule 2 are hereby revoked to the extent specified opposite thereto in column (3) of that Schedule.

(3) Section 91(1) of the Mines and Quarries Act 1954 shall be modified by after the words "every mine" inserting the words "of coal, stratified ironstone, shale or fireclay".

Criminal Jurisdiction (Offshore Activities) Order 1987[1]
(SI 1987/2198)

8–16265   1. (1) *Citation.*

(2) In this Order—

"the 1964 Act" means the Continental Shelf Act 1964;

"the 1982 Act" means the Oil and Gas (Enterprise) Act 1982;

"installation" includes an installation in transit.

---

1. Made by Her Majesty under s 22(1) and (2) of the Oil and Gas (Enterprise) Act 1982.

Waters to which Order applies

8–16266   2. The waters to which this Order applies are—

(*a*) territorial waters of the United Kingdom; and

(*b*) waters in any for the time being designated under section 1(7) of the 1964 Act.

Application of criminal law

8–16267   3. Any act or omission which—

(*a*) takes place on, under or above an installation in waters to which this Order applies or any waters, within five hundred metres of any such installation; and

(*b*) would, if taking place in any part of the United Kingdom, constitute an offence under the law in force in that part.

shall be treated for the purposes of that law as taking place in that part.

Application of police powers

8–16268   4. A constable shall on, under or above any installation in waters to which this Order applies or any waters within five hundred metres of such an installation have all the powers, protection and privileges which he has in the area for which he acts as constable.

Noise at Work Regulations 1989[1]*
(SI 1989/1790 as amended by SI 1997/1993 and SI 1999/2024)

8–16321   1. *Citation and commencement.*

---

*Regulations revoked by the Control of Noise at Work Regulations 2005, SI 2005/1643 (in this PART, POST), FROM 6 APRIL 2006 EXCEPT IN RELATION TO THE MUSIC AND ENTERTAINMENT SECTORS (IN FORCE 6 APRIL 2008) AND IN RELATION TO THE MASTER AND CREW OF A SEAGOING SHIP (IN FORCE 6 APRIL 2011).
1. Made by the Secretary of State, in exercise of the powers conferred on him by section 15(1), (2), (3)(*a*) and (*b*) and (5)(*b*) of, and paragraphs 1(1)(*a*) and (2), 6, 7, 8(1), 9, 11, 13(2) and (3), 15(1) and 16 of Schedule 3 to, the Health and Safety at Work etc Act 1974.

8–16322   2. (1) In these Regulations, unless the context otherwise requires—

"daily personal noise exposure" means the level of daily personal noise exposure of an employee ascertained in accordance with Part I of the Schedule to these Regulations, but taking no account of the effect of any personal ear protector used;

"exposed" means exposed whilst at work, and "exposure" shall be construed accordingly;

"the first action level" means a daily personal noise exposure of 85 dB(A);

"the peak action level" means a level of peak sound pressure of 200 pascals;

''the second action level'' means a daily personal noise exposure of 90 dB(A).

(2) In these Regulations, unless the context otherwise requires, any reference to—

(a) an employer includes a reference to a self-employed person and any duty imposed by these Regulations on an employer in respect of his employees shall extend to a self-employed person in respect of himself;

(b) an employee includes a reference to a self-employed person;

and where any duty is placed by these Regulations on an employer in respect of his employees, that employer shall, so far as is reasonably practicable, be under a like duty in respect of any other person at work who may be affected by the work carried on by him.

(3) Duties under these Regulations imposed upon an employer shall also be imposed upon—

(a) in a mine within the meaning of section 180 of the Mines and Quarries Act 1954, the manager; and

(b) in a quarry within the meaning of regulation 3 of the Quarries Regulations 1999, the operator,

in so far as those duties relate to the mine of which he is the manager or quarry of which he is the operator and to matters under his control.

(4) Unless the context otherwise requires, any reference in these Regulations to—

(a) a numbered regulation is a reference to the regulation in these Regulations so numbered; and

(b) a numbered paragraph is a reference to the paragraph so numbered in the regulation in which the reference appears.

Disapplication of duties

8–16323   **3.** (1) Subject to paragraph (2), these Regulations shall apply—

(a) in Great Britain; and

(b) outside Great Britain as sections 1 to 59 and 80 to 82 of the Health and Safety at Work etc Act 1974 apply by virtue of the provisions of the Health and Safety at Work etc Act 1974 (Application outside Great Britain) Order 1995.

(2) The duties imposed by these Regulations shall not extend to—

(a) the master or crew of a sea-going ship or to the employer of such persons, in relation to the normal ship-board activities of a ship's crew under the direction of the master; or

(b) the crew of any aircraft or hovercraft which is moving under its own power or any other person on board any such aircraft or hovercraft who is at work in connection with its operation.

Assessment of exposure

8–16324   **4.** (1) Every employer shall, when any of his employees is likely to be exposed to the first action level or above or to the peak action level or above, ensure that a competent person makes a noise assessment which is adequate for the purposes—

(a) of identifying which of his employees are so exposed; and

(b) of providing him with such information with regard to the noise to which those employees may be exposed as will facilitate compliance with his duties under regulations 7, 8, 9 and 11.

(2) The noise assessment required by paragraph (1) shall be reviewed when—

(a) there is reason to suspect that the assessment is no longer valid; or

(b) there has been a significant change in the work to which the assessment relates;

and, where as a result of the review changes in the assessment are required, those changes shall be made.

Assessment records

8–16325   **5.** Following any noise assessment made pursuant to regulation 4(1), the employer shall ensure that an adequate record of that assessment, and of any review thereof carried out pursuant to regulation 4(2), is kept until a further noise assessment is made pursuant to regulation 4(1).

Reduction of risk of hearing damage

8–16326   **6.** Every employer shall reduce the risk of damage to the hearing of his employees from exposure to noise to the lowest level reasonably practicable.

Reduction of noise exposure

8–16327   **7.** Every employer shall, when any of his employees is likely to be exposed to the second action level or above or to the peak action level or above, reduce, so far as is reasonably practicable (other than by the provision of personal ear protectors), the exposure to noise of that employee.

Ear protection

8–16328   **8.** (1) Every employer shall ensure, so far as is practicable, that when any of his employees is likely to be exposed to the first action level or above in circumstances where the daily personal noise exposure of that employee is likely to be less than 90 dB(A), that employee is provided, at his request, with suitable and efficient personal ear protectors.

(2) Every employer shall ensure, so far as is practicable, that when any of his employees is likely to be exposed to the second action level or above or to the peak action level or above, that employee is provided with suitable personal ear protectors which, when properly worn, can reasonably be expected to keep the risk of damage to that employee's hearing below that arising from exposure to the second action level or, as the case may be, to the peak action level.

(3) Any personal ear protectors provided by virtue of this regulation shall comply with any enactment (whether in an Act or instrument) which implements in Great Britain any provision on design or manufacture with respect to health or safety in any relevant Community directive listed in Schedule 1 to the Personal Protective Equipment at Work Regulations 1992 which is applicable to those ear protectors.

Ear protection zones

8–16329   **9.** (1) Every employer shall, in respect of any premises under his control, ensure, so far as is reasonably practicable, that—

(a)   each ear protection zone is demarcated and identified by means of the sign specified in paragraph A.3.3 of Appendix A to Part I of BS 5378, which sign shall include such text as indicates—

(i)   that it is an ear protection zone, and
(ii)   the need for his employees to wear personal ear protectors whilst in any such zone; and

(b)   none of his employees enters any such zone unless that employee is wearing personal ear protectors.

(2) In this regulation, "ear protection zone" means any part of the premises referred to in paragraph (1) where any employee is likely to be exposed to the second action level or above or to the peak action level or above, and "Part 1 of BS 5378" has the same meaning as in regulation 2(1) of the Safety Signs Regulations 1980.

Maintenance and use of equipment

8–16330   **10.** (1) Every employer shall—

(a)   ensure, so far as is practicable, that anything provided by him to or for the benefit of an employee in compliance with his duties under these Regulations (other than personal ear protectors provided pursuant to regulation 8(1)) is fully and properly used; and

(b)   ensure, so far as is practicable, that anything provided by him in compliance with his duties under these Regulations is maintained in an efficient state, in efficient working order and in good repair.

(2) Every employee shall, so far as is practicable, fully and properly use personal ear protectors when they are provided by his employer pursuant to regulation 8(2) and any other protective measures provided by his employer in compliance with his duties under these Regulations; and, if the employee discovers any defect therein, he shall report it forthwith to his employer.

Provision of information to employees

8–16331   **11.** Every employer shall, in respect of any premises under his control, provide each of his employees who is likely to be exposed to the first action level or above or to the peak action level or above with adequate information, instruction and training on—

(a)   the risk of damage to that employee's hearing that such exposure may cause;
(b)   what steps that employee can take to minimise that risk;
(c)   the steps that that employee must take in order to obtain the personal ear protectors referred to in regulation 8(1); and
(d)   that employee's obligations under these Regulations.

Modification of duties of manufacturers etc of articles for use at work and Articles of fairground equipment

8–16332   **12.** In the case of articles for use at work or articles of fairground equipment, section 6 of the Health and Safety at Work etc Act 1974 (which imposes general duties on manufacturers etc as regards articles for use at work, substances and articles of fairground equipment) shall be modified so that any duty imposed on any person by subsection (1) of that section shall include a duty to ensure that, where any such article as is referred to therein is likely to cause any employee to be exposed to the first action level or above or to the peak action level or above, adequate information is provided concerning the noise likely to be generated by that article.

Exemptions

8–16333   **13.** (1) Subject to paragraph (2), the Health and Safety Executive may, by a certificate in writing, exempt any employer from—

(a) the requirement in regulation 7, where the daily personal noise exposure of the relevant employee, averaged over a week and ascertained in accordance with Part II of the Schedule to these Regulations, is below 90 dB(A) and there are adequate arrangements for ensuring that that average will not be exceeded; or

(b) the requirement in regulation 8(2), where—

(i) the daily personal noise exposure of the relevant employee, averaged over a week and ascertained in accordance with Part II of the Schedule to these Regulations, is below 90 dB(A) and there are adequate arrangements for ensuring that that average will not be exceeded,

(ii) the full and proper use of the personal ear protectors referred to in that paragraph would be likely to cause risks to the health or safety of the user, or

(iii) (subject to the use of personal ear protectors affording the highest degree of personal protection which it is reasonably practicable to achieve in the circumstances) compliance with that requirement is not reasonably practicable;

and any such exemption may be granted subject to conditions and to a limit of time and may be revoked at any time by a certificate in writing.

(2) The Executive shall not grant any such exemption unless, having regard to the circumstances of the case and in particular to—

(a) the conditions, if any, which it proposes to attach to the exemption; and

(b) any other requirements imposed by or under any enactments which apply to the case,

it is satisfied that the health and safety of persons who are likely to be affected by the exemption will not be prejudiced in consequence of it.

Modifications relating to the Ministry of Defence etc

8–16334   **14.** (1) In this regulation, any reference to—

(a) "visiting forces" is a reference to visiting forces within the meaning of any provision of Part I of the Visiting Forces Act 1952; and

(b) "headquarters or organisation" is a reference to a headquarters or organisation designated for the purposes of the International Headquarters and Defence Organisations Act 1964.

(2) The Secretary of State for Defence may, in the interests of national security, by a certificate in writing exempt—

(a) Her Majesty's Forces;

(b) visiting forces; or

(c) any member of a visiting force working in or attached to any headquarters or organisation.

from any requirement imposed by these Regulations and any such exemption may be granted subject to conditions and to a limit of time and may be revoked at any time by a certificate in writing, except that, before any such exemption is granted, the Secretary of State for Defence must be satisfied that suitable arrangements have been made for the assessment of the health risks created by the work involving exposure to noise and for adequately controlling the exposure to noise of persons to whom the exemption relates.

8–16335   **15.** *Revocation.*

8–16336

SCHEDULE

PART I
DAILY PERSONAL NOISE EXPOSURE OF EMPLOYEES

PART II
WEEKLY AVERAGE OF DAILY PERSONAL NOISE EXPOSURE OF EMPLOYEES

Football Spectators (Corresponding Offences in Scotland) Order 1990[1]

(SI 1990/993 amended by SI 1992/1724)

8–16337   **1.** (1) *Citation and commencement.*
(2) In this Order "the 1989 Act" means the Football Spectator Act 1989.

---

1. Made under s 22(1) of the Football Spectators Act 1989.

8–16338   **2.** (1) The offences under the law of Scotland which are described in Schedule 1 to this Order are hereby specified as offences corresponding to the offences specified in Schedule 1 to the 1989 Act.

     (2) In Schedule 1 to this Order—

     (*a*) the expression "period relevant to" shall be construed in accordance with section 1(8) of the 1989 Act, and

     (*b*) "specified football match" means any association football match played in Scotland involving a team which represents—

         (i) a country or territory, or

         (ii) a club from England or Wales which is, at the time the match is played, a member (whether a full or associate member) of the Football League or the Football Association Premier League, or

         (iii) a club which is, at the time the match is played, a member of the Scottish Football League.

8–16339   **3.** The Crown Office, Edinburgh, is hereby specified as the authority in Scotland which is to certify the conviction of a person there of an offence specified in Schedule 1 to this Order, the nature and circumstances of the offence and whether or not the conviction is the subject of proceedings there questioning it.

8–16340   **4.** *Form of certificate.*

8–16341

Article 2   SCHEDULE 1

OFFENCES UNDER THE LAW OF SCOTLAND CORRESPONDING TO OFFENCES IN SCHEDULE 1 TO THE 1989 ACT

     1. Any offence under section 72 (possession of containers at sporting event), 73 (possession of alcohol at sporting event) or 74 (drunkenness at sporting event) of the Criminal Justice (Scotland) Act 1980 committed by the accused at any specified football match or while entering or trying to enter the ground.

     2. Any offence of breach of the peace or under any provision of Part III of the Public Order Act 1986 (racial hatred) committed during a period relevant to a specified football match at any premises while the accused was at, or was entering or leaving or trying to enter or leave, the premises.

     3. Any offence of assault committed during a period relevant to a specified football match at any premises while the accused was at, or was entering or leaving or trying to enter or leave, the premises.

     4. Any offence of malicious mischief or under section 78 of the Criminal Justice (Scotland) Act 1980 (vandalism) committed during a period relevant to a specified football match while the accused was at, or was entering or leaving or trying to enter or leave, the premises.

     5. Any offence under section 50(1) of the Civic Government (Scotland) Act 1982 (drunkenness) committed while the accused was on a journey to or from a specified football match, being an offence which related to football matches.

     6. Any offence under section 69 (alcohol on vehicle travelling to or from sporting event) or section 70A (alcohol on certain other vehicles) of the Criminal Justices (Scotland) Act 1980 committed while the accused was on a journey to or from a specified football match being an offence which related to football matches.

     7. Any offence of breach of the peace or under any provision of Part III of the Public Order Act 1986 committed while the accused was on a journey to or from a specified football match being an offence which related to football matches.

     8. Any offence under section 4 or 5 of the Road Traffic Act 1988 (driving etc. when under the influence of drink or drugs or with an alcohol concentration above the prescribed limit), committed while the accused was on a journey to or from a specified football match being an offence which related to football matches.

     9. Any offence of assault committed while the accused or the person assaulted was on a journey to or from a specified football match being an offence which related to football matches.

     10. Any offence of malicious mischief or under section 78 of the Criminal Justice (Scotland) Act 1980 (vandalism) committed while the accused was on a journey to or from a specified football match being an offence which related to football matches.

Health and Safety (Display Screen Equipment) Regulations 1992
(SI 1992/2792 amended by SI 2002/2174)

Citation, commencement, interpretation and application

8–16342   **1.** (1) These Regulations may be cited as the Health and Safety (Display Screen Equipment) Regulations 1992 and shall come into force on 1st January 1993.

     (2) In these Regulations—

     (*a*) "display screen equipment" means any alphanumeric or graphic display screen, regardless of the display process involved;

     (*b*) "operator" means a self-employed person who habitually uses display screen equipment as a significant part of his normal work;

     (*c*) "use" means use for in connection with work;

     (*d*) "user" means an employee who habitually uses display screen equipment as a significant part of his normal work; and

     (*e*) "workstation" means an assembly comprising—

   (i) display screen equipment (whether provided with software determining the interface between the equipment and its operator or user, a keyboard or any other input device),

  (ii) any optional accessories to the display screen equipment,

 (iii) any disk drive, telephone, modem, printer, document holder, work chair, work desk, work surface or other item peripheral to the display screen equipment, and

 (iv) the immediate work environment around the display screen equipment.

(3) Any reference in these Regulations to —

(a) a numbered regulation is a reference to the regulation in these Regulations so numbered; or

(b) a numbered paragraph is a reference to the paragraph so numbered in the regulation in which the reference appears.

(4) Nothing in these Regulations shall apply to or in relation to —

(a) drivers' cabs or control cabs for vehicles or machinery;

(b) display screen equipment on board a means of transport;

(c) display screen equipment mainly intended for public operation;

(d) portable systems not in prolonged use;

(e) calculators, cash registers or any equipment having a small data or measurement display required for direct use of the equipment; or

(f) window typewriters.

Analysis of workstations

8–16343 **2.** (1) Every employer shall perform a suitable and sufficient analysis of those workstations which —

(a) (regardless of who has provided them) are used for the purposes of his undertaking by users; or

(b) have been provided by him and are used for the purposes of his undertaking by operators,

for the purpose of assessing the health and safety risks to which those persons are exposed in consequence of that use.

(2) Any assessment made by an employer in pursuance of paragraph (1) shall be reviewed by him if —

(a) there is reason to suspect that it is no longer valid; or

(b) there has been a significant change in the matters to which it relates;

and where as a result of any such review changes to an assessment are required, the employer concerned shall make them.

(3) The employer shall reduce the risks identified in consequence of an assessment to the lowest extent reasonably practicable.

(4) The reference in paragraph (3) to "an assessment" is a reference to an assessment made by the employer concerned in pursuance of paragraph (1) and changed by him where necessary in pursuance of paragraph (2).

Requirements for workstations

8–16344 **3.** Every employer shall ensure that any workstation which may be used for the purposes of his undertaking meets the requirements laid down in the Schedule to these Regulations, to the extent specified in paragraph 1 thereof.

Daily work routine of users

8–16345 **4.** Every employer shall so plan the activities of users at work in his undertaking that their daily work on display screen equipment is periodically interrupted by such breaks or changes of activity as reduce their workload at that equipment.

Eyes and eyesight

8–16346 **5.** (1) Where a person —

(a) is a user in the undertaking in which he is employed; or

(b) is to become a user in the undertaking in which he is, or is to become, employed,

the employer who carries on the undertaking shall, if requested by that person, ensure that an appropriate eye and eyesight test is carried out on him by a competent person within the time specified in paragraph (2).

(2) The time referred to in paragraph (1) is —

(a) in the case of a person mentioned in paragraph (1)(a), as soon as practicable after the request; and

(b) in the case of a person mentioned in paragraph (1)(b), before he becomes a user.

(3) At regular intervals after an employee has been provided with an eye and eyesight test in accordance with paragraphs (1) and (2), his employer shall, subject to paragraph (6), ensure that he is provided with a further eye and eyesight test of an appropriate nature, any such test to be carried out by a competent person.

(4) Where a user experiences visual difficulties which may reasonably be considered to be caused by work on display screen equipment, his employer shall ensure that he is provided at his request with an appropriate eye and eyesight test, any such test to be carried out by a competent person as soon as practicable after being requested as aforesaid.

(5) Every employer shall ensure that each user employed by him is provided with special corrective appliances appropriate for the work being done by the user concerned where—

(a) normal corrective appliances cannot be used; and

(b) the result of any eye and eyesight test which the user has been given in accordance with this regulation shows such provision to be necessary.

(6) Nothing in paragraph (3) shall require an employer to provide any employee with an eye and eyesight test against that employee's will.

Provision of training

8-16347 6. (1) Where a person—

(a) is a user in the undertaking in which he is employed; or

(b) is to become a user in the undertaking in which he is, or is to become, employed,

the employer who carries on the undertaking shall ensure that he is provided with adequate health and safety training in the use of any workstation upon which he may be required to work.

(1A) In the case of a person mentioned in sub-paragraph (b) of paragraph (1) the training shall be provided before he becomes a user.

(2) Every employer shall ensure that each user at work in his undertaking is provided with adequate health and safety training whenever the organisation of any workstation in that undertaking upon which he may be required to work is substantially modified.

Provision of information

8-16348 7. (1) Every employer shall ensure that operators and users at work in his undertaking are provided with adequate information about—

(a) all aspects of health and safety relating to their workstations; and

(b) such measures taken by him in compliance with his duties under regulations 2 and 3 as relate to them and their work.

(2) Every employer shall ensure that users at work in his undertaking are provided with adequate information about such measures taken by him in compliance with his duties under regulations 4 and 6(2) as relate to them and their work.

(3) Every employer shall ensure that users employed by him are provided with adequate information about such measures taken by him in compliance with his duties under regulations 5 and 6(1) as relate to them and their work.

Exemption certificates

8-16349 8. (1) The Secretary of State for Defence may, in the interests of national security, exempt any of the home forces, any visiting force or any headquarters from any of the requirements imposed by these Regulations.

(2) Any exemption such as is specified in paragraph (1) may be granted subject to conditions and to a limit of time and may be revoked by the Secretary of State for Defence by a further certificate in writing at any time.

(3) In this regulation—

(a) "the home forces" has the same meaning as in section 12(1) of the Visiting Forces Act 1952;

(b) "headquarters" has the same meaning as in article 3(2) of the Visiting Forces and International Headquarters (Application of Law) Order 1965; and

(c) "visiting force" has the same meaning as it does for the purposes of any provision of Part I of the Visiting Forces Act 1952.

Extension outside Great Britain

8-16350 9. These Regulations shall, subject to regulation 1(4), apply to and in relation to the premises and activities outside Great Britain to which sections 1 to 59 and 80 to 82 of the Health and Safety at Work etc Act 1974 apply by virtue of the Health and Safety at Work etc Act 1974 (Application Outside Great Britain) Order 1989 as they apply within Great Britain.

8-16351

Regulation 3 THE SCHEDULE

(WHICH SETS OUT THE MINIMUM REQUIREMENTS FOR WORKSTATIONS WHICH ARE CONTAINED IN THE ANNEX TO COUNCIL DIRECTIVE 90/270/EEC ON THE MINIMUM SAFETY AND HEALTH REQUIREMENTS FOR WORK WITH DISPLAY SCREEN EQUIPMENT)

1. EXTENT TO WHICH EMPLOYERS MUST ENSURE THAT WORKSTATIONS MEET THE REQUIREMENTS LAID DOWN IN THIS SCHEDULE

An employer shall ensure that a workstation meets the requirements laid down in this Schedule to the extent that—

(a) those requirements relate to a component which is present in the workstation concerned;

(b) those requirements have effect with a view to securing the health, safety and welfare of persons at work; and

(c) the inherent characteristics of a given task make compliance with those requirements appropriate as respects the workstation concerned.

2. Equipment

(a) *General comment*

The use as such of the equipment must not be a source of risk for operators or users.

(b) *Display screen*

The characters on the screen shall be well-defined and clearly formed, of adequate size and with adequate spacing between the characters and lines.

The image on the screen should be stable, with no flickering or other forms of instability.

The brightness and the contrast between the characters and the background shall be easily adjustable by the operator or user, and also be easily adjustable to ambient conditions.

The screen must swivel and tilt easily and freely to suit the needs of the operator or user.

It shall be possible to use a separate base for the screen or an adjustable table.

The screen shall be free of reflective glare and reflections liable to cause discomfort to the operator or user.

(c) *Keyboard*

The keyboard shall be tiltable and separate from the screen so as to allow the operator or user to find a comfortable working position avoiding fatigue in the arms or hands.

The space in front of the keyboard shall be sufficient to provide support for the hands and arms of the operator or user.

The keyboard shall have a matt surface to avoid reflective glare.

The arrangement of the keyboard and the characteristics of the keys shall be such as to facilitate the use of the keyboard.

The symbols on the keys shall be adequately contrasted and legible from the design working position.

(d) *Work desk or work surface*

The work desk or work surface shall have a sufficiently large, low-reflectance surface and allow a flexible arrangement of the screen, keyboard, documents and related equipment.

The document holder shall be stable and adjustable and shall be positioned so as to minimise the need for uncomfortable head and eye movements.

There shall be adequate space for operators or users to find a comfortable position.

(e) *Work chair*

The work chair shall be stable and allow the operator or user easy freedom of movement and a comfortable position.

The seat shall be adjustable in height.

The seat back shall be adjustable in both height and tilt.

A footrest shall be made available to any operator or user who wishes one.

3. Environment

(a) *Space requirements*

The workstation shall be dimensioned and designed so as to provide sufficient space for the operator or user to change position and vary movements.

(b) *Lighting*

Any room lighting or task lighting provided shall ensure satisfactory lighting conditions and an appropriate contrast between the screen and the background environment, taking into account the type of work and the vision requirements of the operator or user.

Possible disturbing glare and reflections on the screen or other equipment shall be prevented by co-ordinating workplace and workstation layout with the positioning and technical characteristics of the artificial light sources.

(c) *Reflections and glare*

Workstations shall be so designed that sources of light, such as windows and other openings, transparent or translucid walls, and brightly coloured fixtures or walls cause no direct glare and no distracting reflections on the screen.

Windows shall be fitted with a suitable system of adjustable covering to attenuate the daylight that falls on the workstation.

(d) *Noise*

Noise emitted by equipment belonging to any workstation shall be taken into account when a workstation is being equipped, with a view in particular to ensuring that attention is not distracted and speech is not disturbed.

(e) *Heat*

Equipment belonging to any workstation shall not produce excess heat which could cause discomfort to operators or users.

(f) *Radiation*

All radiation with the exception of the visible part of the electromagnetic spectrum shall be reduced to negligible levels from the point of view of the protection of operators' or users' health and safety.

(g) *Humidity*

An adequate level of humidity shall be established and maintained.

4. Interface between computer and operator/user

In designing, selecting, commissioning and modifying software, and in designing tasks using display screen equipment, the employer shall take into account the following principles:

(a) software must be suitable for the task;

(b) software must be easy to use and, where appropriate, adaptable to the level of knowledge or experience of the operator or user; no quantitative or qualitative checking facility may be used without the knowledge of the operators or users;

(c) systems must provide feedback to operators or users on the performance of those systems;
(d) systems must display information in a format and at a pace which are adapted to operators or users;
(e) the principles of software ergonomics must be applied, in particular to human data processing.

Manual Handling Operations Regulations 1992
(SI 1992/2793 amended by SI 2002/2174)

Citation and commencement

8-16352　**1.** These Regulations may be cited as the Manual Handling Operations Regulations 1992 and shall come into force on 1st January 1993.

Interpretation

8-16353　**2.** (1) In these Regulations, unless the context otherwise requires—

"injury" does not include injury caused by any toxic or corrosive substance which—

(a) has leaked or spilled from a load;
(b) is present on the surface of a load but has not leaked or spilled from it; or
(c) is a constituent part of a load;

and "injured" shall be construed accordingly;
"load" includes any person and any animal;
"manual handling operations" means any transporting or supporting of a load (including the lifting, putting down, pushing, pulling, carrying or moving thereof) by hand or by bodily force.

(2) Any duty imposed by these Regulations on an employer in respect of his employees shall also be imposed on a self-employed person in respect of himself.

Disapplication of Regulations

8-16354　**3.** These Regulations shall not apply to or in relation to the master or crew of a sea-going ship or to the employer of such persons in respect of the normal ship-board activities of a ship's crew under the direction of the master.

Duties of employers

8-16355　**4.** (1) Each employer shall—

(a) so far as is reasonably practicable, avoid the need for his employees to undertake any manual handling operations at work which involve a risk of their being injured; or
(b) where it is not reasonably practicable to avoid the need for his employees to undertake any manual handling operations at work which involve a risk of their being injured—

　(i) make a suitable and sufficient assessment of all such manual handling operations to be undertaken by them, having regard to the factors which are specified in column 1 of Schedule 1 to these Regulations and considering the questions which are specified in the corresponding entry in column 2 of that Schedule,
　(ii) take appropriate steps to reduce the risk of injury to those employees arising out of their undertaking any such manual handling operations to the lowest level reasonably practicable, and
　(iii) take appropriate steps to provide any of those employees who are undertaking any such manual handling operations with general indications and, where it is reasonably practicable to do so, precise information on—

　　(aa)the weight of each load, and
　　(bb)the heaviest side of any load whose centre of gravity is not positioned centrally.

(2) Any assessment such as is referred to in paragraph (1)(b)(i) of this regulation shall be reviewed by the employer who made it if—

(a) there is reason to suspect that it is no longer valid; or
(b) there has been a significant change in the manual handling operations to which it relates;

and where as a result of any such review changes to an assessment are required, the relevant employer shall make them.

(3) In determining for the purposes of this regulation whether manual handling operations at work involve a risk of injury and in determining the appropriate steps to reduce that risk regard shall be had in particular to—

(a) the physical suitability of the employee to carry out the operations;
(b) the clothing, footwear or other personal effects he is wearing;
(c) his knowledge and training;
(d) the results of any relevant risk assessment carried out pursuant to regulation 3 of the Management of Health and Safety at Work Regulations 1999;
(e) whether the employee is within a group of employees identified by that assessment as being especially at risk; and

(*f*) the results of any health surveillance provided pursuant to regulation 6 of the Management of Health and Safety Regulations 1999.

Duty of employees

8–16356 5. Each employee while at work shall make full and proper use of any system of work provided for his use by his employer in compliance with regulation 4(1)(*b*)(ii) of these Regulations.

Exemption certificates

8–16357 6. (1) The Secretary of State for Defence may, in the interests of national security, by a certificate in writing exempt—

(*a*) any of the home forces, any visiting force or any headquarters from any requirement imposed by regulation 4 of these Regulations; or

(*b*) any member of the home forces, any member of a visiting force or any member of a headquarters from the requirement imposed by regulation 5 of these Regulations;

and any exemption such as is specified in sub-paragraph (*a*) or (*b*) of this paragraph may be granted subject to conditions and to a limit of time and may be revoked by the said Secretary of State by a further certificate in writing at any time.

(2) In this regulation—

(*a*) "the home forces" has the same meaning as in section 12(1) of the Visiting Forces Act 1952;

(*b*) "headquarters" has the same meaning as in article 3(2) of the Visiting Forces and International Headquarters (Application of Law) Order 1965;

(*c*) "member of a headquarters" has the same meaning as in paragraph 1(1) of the Schedule to the International Headquarters and Defence Organisations Act 1964; and

(*d*) "visiting force" has the same meaning as it does for the purposes of any provision of Part I of the Visiting Forces Act 1952.

Extension outside Great Britain

8–16358 7. These Regulations shall, subject to regulation 3 hereof, apply to and in relation to the premises and activities outside Great Britain to which sections 1 to 59 and 80 to 82 of the Health and Safety at Work etc Act 1974 apply by virtue of the Health and Safety at Work etc Act 1974 (Application Outside Great Britain) Order 1989 as they apply within Great Britain.

Repeals and revocations

8–16359 8. (1) The enactments mentioned in column 1 of Part I of Schedule 2 to these Regulations are repealed to the extent specified in the corresponding entry in column 3 of that part.

(2) The Regulations mentioned in column 1 of Part II of Schedule 2 to these Regulations are revoked to the extent specified in the corresponding entry in column 3 of that part.

8–16360

Regulation 4(1)(*b*)(i)   SCHEDULE 1

FACTORS TO WHICH THE EMPLOYER MUST HAVE REGARD AND QUESTIONS HE MUST CONSIDER WHEN MAKING AN ASSESSMENT OF MANUAL HANDLING OPERATIONS

Column 1 *Factors*	Column 2 *Questions*
1 The tasks	**Do they involve:** —holding or manipulating loads at distance from trunk? —unsatisfactory bodily movement or posture, especially: —twisting the trunk? —stooping? —reaching upwards? —excessive movement of loads, especially: —excessive lifting or lowering distances? —excessive carrying distances? —excessive pushing or pulling of loads? —risk of sudden movement of loads? —frequent or prolonged physical effort? —insufficient rest or recovery periods? —a rate of work imposed by a process?
2 The loads	**Are they:** —heavy? —bulky or unwieldy? —difficult to grasp? —unstable, or with contents likely to shift? —sharp, hot or otherwise potentially damaging?
3 The working environment	**Are there:** —space constraints preventing good posture? —uneven, slippery or unstable floors? —variations in level of floors or work surfaces?

Column 1 Factors	Column 2 Questions
	—extremes of temperature or humidity? —conditions causing ventilation problems or gusts of wind? —poor lighting conditions?
4 Individual capability	**Does the job:** —require unusual strength, height, etc? —create a hazard to those who might reasonably be considered to be pregnant or to have a health problem? —require special information or training for its safe performance?
5 Other factors	**Is movement or posture hindered by personal protective equipment or by clothing?**

8–16361

Regulation 8

SCHEDULE 2

REPEALS AND REVOCATIONS

PART I

REPEALS

Column 1 Short title of enactment	Column 2 Reference	Column 3 Extent of repeal
The Children and Young Persons Act 1933.	1933 c.12.	Section 18(1)(f) except insofar as that paragraph applies to such employment as is permitted under section 1(2) of the Employment of Women, Young Persons, and Children Act 1920 (1920 c.65).
The Children and Young Persons (Scotland) Act 1937.	1937 c.37.	Section 28(1)(f) except insofar as that paragraph applies to such employment as is permitted under section 1(2) of the Employment of Women, Young Persons, and Children Act 1920.
The Mines and Quarries Act 1954.	1954 c.70.	Section 93; in section 115 the word "ninety-three".
The Agriculture (Safety, Health and Welfare Provisions) Act 1956.	1956 c.49.	Section 2.
The Factories Act 1961.	1961 c.34.	Section 72.
The Offices, Shops and Railway Premises Act 1963.	1963 c.41.	Section 23 except insofar as the prohibition contained in that section applies to any person specified in section 90(4) of the same Act. In section 83(1) the number "23".

PART II

REVOCATIONS

Column 1 Short title of enactment	Column 2 Reference	Column 3 Extent of repeal
The Agriculture (Lifting of Heavy Weights) Regulations 1959.	S.I. 1959/2120.	The whole Regulations.
The Construction (General Provisions) Regulations 1961.	S.I. 1961/1580.	In regulation 3(1)(a) the phrase "and 55"; regulation 55.

Workplace (Health Safety and Welfare) Regulations 1992[1]

(SI 1992/3004 amended by SI 1995/2036, SI 1996/1592, SI 1999/2024, SI 2002/2174, 2776 and SI 2005/735)

Citation and commencement

8–16400 **1.** (1) *Citation.*

(2) Subject to paragraph (3), these Regulations shall come into force on 1st January 1993.

(3) Regulations 5 to 27 and the Schedules shall come into force on 1st January 1996 with respect to any workplace or part of a workplace which is not—

(a) a new workplace; or

(b) a modification, an extension or a conversion.

---

1. Made by the Secretary of State, in exercise of the powers conferred on her by ss 15(1), (2), (3)(a) and (5)(b), and 82(3)(a) of, and paras 1(2), 9 and 10 of Sch 3 to, the Health and Safety at Work etc Act 1974.

Interpretation

8–16401 **2.** (1) In these Regulations, unless the context otherwise requires—

"disabled person" has the meaning given by section 1 of the Disability Discrimination Act 1995.

"mine" means a mine within the meaning of the Mines and Quarries Act 1954;

"new workplace" means a workplace used for the first time as a workplace after 31st December 1992;

"public road" means (in England and Wales) a highway maintainable at public expense within the meaning of section 329 of the Highways Act 1980 and (in Scotland) a public road within the meaning assigned to that term by section 151 of the Roads (Scotland) Act 1984;

"quarry" means a quarry within the meaning of the Quarries Regulations 1999;

"traffic route" means a route for pedestrian traffic, vehicles or both and includes any stairs, staircase, fixed ladder, doorway, gateway, loading bay or ramp;

"workplace" means, subject to paragraph (2), any premises or part of premises which are not domestic premises and are made available to any person as a place of work, and includes—

(a) any place within the premises to which such person has access while at work; and

(b) any room, lobby, corridor, staircase, road or other place used as a means of access to or egress from that place of work or where facilities are provided for use in connection with the place of work other than a public road;

but shall not include a modification; an extension or a conversion of any of the above until such modification, extension or conversion is completed.

(2) Any reference in these Regulations, except in paragraph (1), to a modification, an extension or a conversion is a reference, as the case may be, to a modification, an extension or a conversion of a workplace started after 31st December 1992.

(3) Any requirement that anything done or provided in pursuance of these Regulations shall be suitable shall be construed to include a requirement that it is suitable for any person in respect of whom such thing is so done or provided.

(4) Any reference in these Regulations to—

(a) a numbered regulation or Schedule is a reference to the regulation in or Schedule to these Regulations so numbered; and

(b) a numbered paragraph is a reference to the paragraph so numbered in the regulation in which the reference appears.

Application of these Regulations

8–16402 3. (1) These Regulations apply to every workplace but shall not apply to—

(a) a workplace which is or is in or on a ship within the meaning assigned to that word by regulation 2(1) of the Docks Regulations 1988;

(b) a workplace where the only activity being undertaken is construction work within the meaning assigned to that phrase by regulation 2(1) of the Construction (Health, Safety and Welfare) Regulations 1996 (SI 1996/1592), except for any workplace from which the application of the said Regulations is excluded by regulation 3(2) of those Regulations;

(c) a workplace located below ground at a mine.

(2) In their application to temporary work sites, any requirement to ensure a workplace complies with any of regulations 20 to 25 shall have effect as a requirement to so ensure so far as is reasonably practicable.

(3) As respects any workplace which is or is in or on an aircraft, locomotive or rolling stock, trailer or semi-trailer used as a means of transport or a vehicle for which a licence is in force under the Vehicles (Excise) Act 1971 or a vehicle exempted from duty under that Act—

(a) regulations 5 to 12 and 14 to 25 shall not apply to any such workplace; and

(b) regulation 13 shall apply to any such workplace only when the aircraft, locomotive or rolling stock, trailer or semi-trailer or vehicle is stationary inside a workplace and, in the case of a vehicle for which a licence is in force under the Vehicles (Excise) Act 1971, is not on a public road.

(4) As respects any workplace which is in fields, woods or other land forming part of an agricultural or forestry undertaking but which is not inside a building and is situated away from the undertaking's main buildings—

(a) regulations 5 to 19 and 23 to 25 shall not apply to any such workplace; and

(b) any requirement to ensure that any such workplace complies with any of regulations 20 to 22 shall have effect as a requirement to so ensure so far as is reasonably practicable.

(5) As respects any workplace which is at a quarry or above ground at a mine regulation 12 shall only apply to a floor or traffic route which is located inside a building.

Requirements under these Regulations

8–16403 4. (1) Every employer shall ensure that every workplace, modification, extension or conversion which is under his control and where any of his employees works complies with any requirement of these Regulations which—

(a) applies to that workplace or, as the case may be, to the workplace which contains that modification, extension or conversion; and

(b) is in force in respect of the workplace, modification, extension or conversion.

(2) Subject to paragraph (4), every person who has, to any extent, control of a workplace,

modification, extension or conversion shall ensure that such workplace, modification, extension or conversion complies with any requirement of these Regulations which—

(a) applies to that workplace or, as the case may be, to the workplace which contains that modification, extension or conversion;

(b) is in force in respect of the workplace, modification, extension, or conversion; and

(c) relates to matters within that person's control.

(3) Any reference in this regulation to a person having control of any workplace, modification, extension or conversion is a reference to a person having control of the workplace, modification, extension or conversion in connection with the carrying on by him of a trade, business or other undertaking (whether for profit or not).

(4) Paragraph (2) shall not impose any requirement upon a self-employed person in respect of his own work or the work of any partner of his in the undertaking.

(5) Every person who is deemed to be the occupier of a factory by virtue of section 175(5) of the Factories Act 1961 shall ensure that the premises which are so deemed to be a factory comply with these Regulations.

8–16403A   4A. Where a workplace is in a building, the building shall have the stability and solidity appropriate to the nature of the use of the workplace.

Maintenance of workplace, and of equipment, devices and systems

8–16404   5. (1) The workplace and the equipment, devices and systems to which this regulation applies shall be maintained (including cleaned as appropriate) in an efficient state, in efficient working order and in good repair.

(2) Where appropriate, the equipment, devices and systems to which this regulation applies shall be subject to a suitable system of maintenance.

(3) The equipment, devices and systems to which this regulation applies are—

(a) equipment and devices a fault in which is liable to result in a failure to comply with any of these Regulations; and

(b) mechanical ventilation systems provided pursuant to regulation 6 (whether or not they include equipment or devices within sub-paragraph (a) of this paragraph); and

(c) equipment and devices intended to prevent or reduce hazards.

Ventilation

8–16405   6. (1) Effective and suitable provision shall be made to ensure that every enclosed workplace is ventilated by a sufficient quantity of fresh or purified air.

(2) Any plant used for the purpose of complying with paragraph (1) shall include an effective device to give visible or audible warning of any failure of the plant where necessary for reasons of health or safety.

(3) (*Revoked*).

Temperature in indoor workplaces

8–16406   7. (1) During working hours, the temperature in all workplaces inside buildings shall be reasonable.

(1A) Without prejudice to the generality of paragraph (1)—

(a) a workplace shall be adequately thermally insulated where it is necessary, having regard to the type of work carried out and the physical activity of the persons carrying out the work; and

(b) excessive effects of sunlight on temperature shall be avoided.

(2) A method of heating or cooling shall not be used which results in the escape into a workplace of fumes, gas or vapour of such character and to such extent that they are likely to be injurious or offensive to any person.

(3) A sufficient number of thermometers shall be provided to enable persons at work to determine the temperature in any workplace inside a building.

Lighting

8–16407   8. (1) Every workplace shall have suitable and sufficient lighting.

(2) The lighting mentioned in paragraph (1) shall, so far as is reasonably practicable, be by natural light.

(3) Without prejudice to the generality of paragraph (1), suitable and sufficient emergency lighting shall be provided in any room in circumstances in which persons at work are specially exposed to danger in the event of failure of artificial lighting.

Cleanliness and waste materials

8–16408   9. (1) Every workplace and the furniture, furnishings and fittings therein shall be kept sufficiently clean.

(2) The surfaces of the floors, walls and ceilings of all workplaces inside buildings shall be capable of being kept sufficiently clean.

(3) So far as is reasonably practicable, waste materials shall not be allowed to accumulate in a workplace except in suitable receptacles.

Room dimensions and space

8–16409   **10.** (1) Every room where persons work shall have sufficient floor area, height and unoccupied space for purposes of health, safety and welfare.

(2) It shall be sufficient compliance with this regulation in a workplace which is not a new workplace, a modification, an extension and which, immediately before this regulation came into force in respect of it, was subject to the provisions of the Factories Act 1961, if the workplace does not contravene the provisions of Part I of Schedule 1.

Workstations and seating

8–16410   **11.** (1) Every workstation shall be so arranged that it is suitable both for any person at work in the workplace who is likely to work at that workstation and for any work of the undertaking which is likely to be done there.

(2) Without prejudice to the generality of paragraph (1), every workstation outdoors shall be so arranged that—

(a) so far as is reasonably practicable, it provides protection from adverse weather;

(b) it enables any person at the workstation to leave it swiftly or, as appropriate, to be assisted in the event of an emergency; and

(c) it ensures that any person at the workstation is not likely to slip or fall.

(3) A suitable seat shall be provided for each person at work in the workplace whose work includes operations of a kind that the work (or a substantial part of it) can or must be done sitting.

(4) A seat shall not be suitable for the purpose of paragraph (3) unless—

(a) it is suitable for the person for whom it is provided as well as for the operations to be performed; and

(b) a suitable footrest is also provided where necessary.

Condition of floors and traffic routes

8–16411   **12.** (1) Every floor in a workplace and the surface of every traffic route in a workplace shall be of a construction such that the floor or surface of the traffic route is suitable for the purpose for which it is used.

(2) Without prejudice to the generality of paragraph (1), the requirements in that paragraph shall include requirements that—

(a) the floor, or surface of the traffic route, shall have no hole or slope, or be uneven or slippery so as, in each case, to expose any person to a risk to his health or safety; and

(b) every such floor shall have effective means of drainage where necessary.

(3) So far as is reasonably practicable, every floor in a workplace and the surface of every traffic route in a workplace shall be kept free from obstructions and from any article or substance which may cause a person to slip, trip or fall.

(4) In considering whether for the purposes of paragraph (2)(a) a hole or slope exposes any person to a risk to his health or safety—

(a) no account shall be taken of a hole where adequate measures have been taken to prevent a person falling; and

(b) account shall be taken of any handrail provided in connection with any slope.

(5) Suitable and sufficient handrails and, if appropriate, guards shall be provided on all traffic routes which are staircases except in circumstances in which a handrail can not be provided without obstructing the traffic route.

Falls or falling objects

8–16412   **13.** (1)—(4) *Revoked.*

(5) So far as is practicable, every tank, pit or structure where there is a risk of a person in the workplace falling into a dangerous substance in the tank, pit or structure, shall be securely covered or fenced.

(6) Every traffic route over, across or in an uncovered tank, pit or structure such as is mentioned in paragraph (5) shall be securely fenced.

(7) In this regulation, "dangerous substance" means—

(a) any substance likely to scald or burn;

(b) any poisonous substance;

(c) any corrosive substance;

(d) any fume, gas or vapour likely to overcome a person; or

(e) any granular or free-flowing solid substance, or any viscous substance which, in any case, is of a nature or quantity which is likely to cause danger to any person.

Windows, and transparent or translucent doors, gates and walls

8–16413   **14.** (1) Every window or other transparent or translucent surface in a wall or partition and every transparent or translucent surface in a door or gate shall, where necessary for reasons of health or safety—

   (a) be of safety material or be protected against breakage of the transparent or translucent material; and

   (b) be appropriately marked or incorporate features so as, in either case, to make it apparent.

Windows, skylights and ventilators

8–16414　**15.** (1) No window, skylight or ventilator which is capable of being opened shall be likely to be opened, closed or adjusted in a manner which exposes any person performing such operation to a risk to his health or safety.

(2) No window, skylight or ventilator shall be in a position when open which is likely to expose any person in the workplace to a risk to his health or safety.

Ability to clean windows etc safely

8–16415　**16.** (1) All windows and skylights in a workplace shall be of a design or be so constructed that they may be cleaned safely.

(2) In considering whether a window or skylight is of a design or so constructed as to comply with paragraph (1), account may be taken of equipment used in conjunction with the window or skylight or of devices fitted to the building.

Organisation etc of traffic routes

8–16416　**17.** (1) Every workplace shall be organised in such a way that pedestrians and vehicles can circulate in a safe manner.

(2) Traffic routes in a workplace shall be suitable for the persons or vehicles using them, sufficient in number, in suitable positions and of sufficient size.

(3) Without prejudice to the generality of paragraph (2), traffic routes shall not satisfy the requirements of that paragraph unless suitable measures are taken to ensure that—

   (a) pedestrians or, as the case may be, vehicles may use a traffic route without causing danger to the health or safety of persons at work near it;

   (b) there is sufficient separation of any traffic route for vehicles from doors or gates or from traffic routes for pedestrians which lead onto it; and

   (c) where vehicles and pedestrians use the same traffic route, there is sufficient separation between them.

(4) All traffic routes shall be suitably indicated where necessary for reasons of health or safety.

(5) Paragraph (2) shall apply so far as is reasonably practicable, to a workplace which is not a new workplace, a modification, an extension or a conversion.

Doors and gates

8–16417　**18.** (1) Doors and gates shall be suitably constructed (included being fitted with any necessary safety devices).

(2) Without prejudice to the generality of paragraph (1), doors and gates shall not comply with that paragraph unless—

   (a) any sliding door or gate has a device to prevent it coming off its track during use;

   (b) any upward opening door or gate has a device to prevent it falling back;

   (c) any powered door or gate has suitable and effective features to prevent it causing injury by trapping any person;

   (d) where necessary for reasons of health or safety, any powered door or gate can be operated manually unless it opens automatically if the power fails; and

   (e) any door or gate which is capable of opening by being pushed from either side is of such a construction as to provide, when closed, a clear view of the space close to both sides.

Escalators and moving walkways

8–16418　**19.** Escalators and moving walkways shall:—

   (a) function safely;

   (b) be equipped with any necessary safety devices;

   (c) be fitted with one or more emergency stop controls which are easily identifiable and readily accessible.

Sanitary conveniences

8–16419　**20.** (1) Suitable and sufficient sanitary conveniences shall be provided at readily accessible places.

(2) Without prejudice to the generality of paragraph (1), sanitary conveniences shall not be suitable unless—

   (a) the rooms containing them are adequately ventilated and lit;

   (b) they and the rooms containing them are kept in a clean and orderly condition; and

   (c) separate rooms containing conveniences are provided for men and women except where and so far as each convenience is in a separate room the door of which is capable of being secured from inside.

(3) It shall be sufficient compliance with the requirement in paragraph (1) to provide sufficient sanitary conveniences in a workplace which is not a new workplace, a modification, an extension or a conversion and which, immediately before this regulation came into force in respect of it, was subject to the provisions of the Factories Act 1961, if sanitary conveniences are provided in accordance with the provisions of Part II of Schedule 1.

Washing facilities

8–16420   21. (1) Suitable and sufficient washing facilities, including showers if required by the nature of the work or for health reasons, shall be provided at readily accessible places.

(2) Without prejudice to the generality of paragraph (1), washing facilities shall not be suitable unless —

(a) they are provided in the immediate vicinity of every sanitary convenience, whether or not provided elsewhere as well;

(b) they are provided in the vicinity of any changing rooms required by these Regulations, whether or not provided elsewhere as well;

(c) they include a supply of clean hot and cold, or warm, water (which shall be running water so far as is practicable);

(d) they include soap or other suitable means of cleaning;

(e) they include towels or other suitable means of drying;

(f) the rooms containing them are sufficiently ventilated and lit;

(g) they and the rooms containing them are kept in a clean and orderly condition; and

(h) separate facilities are provided for men and women, except where and so far as they are provided in a room the door of which is capable of being secured from inside and the facilities in each such room are intended to be used by only one person at a time.

(3) Paragraph (2)(h) shall not apply to facilities which are provided for washing hands, forearms and face only.

Drinking water

8–16421   22. (1) An adequate supply of wholesome drinking water shall be provided for all persons at work in the workplace.

(2) Every supply of drinking water required by paragraph (1) shall—

(a) be readily accessible at suitable places; and

(b) be conspicuously marked by an appropriate sign where necessary for reasons of health or safety.

(3) Where a supply of drinking water is required by paragraph (1), there shall also be provided a sufficient number of suitable cups or other drinking vessels unless the supply of drinking water is in a jet from which persons can drink easily.

Accommodation for clothing

8–16422   23. (1) Suitable and sufficient accommodation shall be provided—

(a) for the clothing of any person at work which is not worn during working hours; and

(b) for special clothing which is worn by any person at work but which is not taken home.

(2) Without prejudice to the generality of paragraph (1), the accommodation mentioned in that paragraph shall not be suitable unless—

(a) where facilities to change clothing are required by regulation 24, it provides suitable security for the clothing mentioned in paragraph (1)(a);

(b) where necessary to avoid risks to health or damage to the clothing, it includes separate accommodation for clothing worn at work and for other clothing;

(c) so far as is reasonably practicable, it allows or includes facilities for drying clothing; and

(d) it is in a suitable location.

Facilities for changing clothing

8–16423   24. (1) Suitable and sufficient facilities shall be provided for any person at work in the workplace to change clothing in all cases where—

(a) the person has to wear special clothing for the purpose of work; and

(b) the person can not, for reasons of health or propriety, be expected to change in another room.

(2) Without prejudice to the generality of paragraph (1), the facilities mentioned in that paragraph shall not be suitable unless they include separate facilities for, or separate use of facilities by, men and women where necessary for reasons of propriety and the facilities are easily accessible, of sufficient capacity and provided with seating.

Facilities for rest and to eat meals

8–16424   25. (1) Suitable and sufficient rest facilities shall be provided at readily accessible places.

(2) Rest facilities provided by virtue of paragraph (1) shall—

(*a*) where necessary for reasons of health or safety include, in the case of a new workplace, an extension or a conversion, rest facilities provided in one or more rest rooms, or, in other cases, in rest rooms or rest areas;

(*b*) include suitable facilities to eat meals where food eaten in the workplace would otherwise be likely to become contaminated.

(3) Rest rooms and rest areas shall—

(*a*) include suitable arrangements to protect non-smokers from discomfort caused by tobacco smoke; and

(*b*) be equipped with—

　(i) an adequate number of tables and adequate seating with backs for the number of persons at work likely to use them at one time; and

　(ii) seating which is adequate for the number of disabled persons at work and suitable for them.

(4) Suitable facilities shall be provided for any person at work who is a pregnant woman or nursing mother to rest.

(5) Suitable and sufficient facilities shall be provided for persons at work to eat meals where meals are regularly eaten in the workplace.

8–16424A　25A. Where necessary, those parts of the workplace (including in particular doors, passageways, stairs, showers, washbasins, lavatories and workstations) used or occupied directly by disabled persons at work shall be organised to take account of such persons.

Exemption certificates

8–16425　26. (1) The Secretary of State for Defence may, in the interests of national security, by a certificate in writing exempt any of the home forces, any visiting force or any headquarters from the requirements of these Regulations and any exemption may be granted subject to conditions and to a limit of time and may be revoked by the said Secretary of State by a further certificate in writing at any time.

(2) In this regulation—

(*a*) "the home forces" has the same meaning as in section 12(1) of the Visiting Forces Act 1952;

(*b*) "headquarters" has the same meaning as in article 3(2) of the Visiting Forces and International Headquarters (Application of Law) Order 1965

(*c*) "visiting force" has the same meaning as it does for the purposes of any provision of Part I of the Visiting Forces Act 1952.

Repeals, saving and revocations

8–16426　27. (1) The enactments mentioned in column 2 of Part I of Schedule 2 are repealed to the extent specified in column 3 of that Part.

(2) Nothing in this regulation shall affect the operation of any provision of the Offices, Shops and Railway Premises Act 1963 as that provision has effect by virtue of section 90(4) of that Act.

(3) The instruments mentioned in column 1 of Part II of Schedule 2 are revoked to the extent specified in column 3 of that Part.

Regulations 10 and 20　　　　　　　　SCHEDULE 1
PROVISIONS APPLICABLE TO FACTORIES WHICH ARE NOT NEW WORKPLACES, MODIFICATIONS, EXTENSIONS OR CONVERSIONS

PART I
SPACE

8–16427　1. No room in the workplace shall be so overcrowded as to cause risk to the health or safety of persons at work in it.

2. Without prejudice to the generality of paragraph 1, the number of persons employed at a time in any workroom shall not be such that the amount of cubic space allowed for each is less than 11 cubic metres.

3. In calculating for the purposes of this Part of this Schedule the amount of cubic space in any room no space more than 4·2 metres from the floor shall be taken into account and, where a room contains a gallery, the gallery shall be treated for the purposes of this Schedule as if it were partitioned off from the remainder of the room and formed a separate room.

PART II
NUMBER OF SANITARY CONVENIENCES

4. In workplaces where females work, there shall be at least one suitable water closet for use by females only for every 25 females.

5. In workplaces where males work, there shall be at least one suitable water closet for use by males only for every 25 males.

6. In calculating the number of males or females who work in any workplace for the purposes of this Part of this Schedule, any number not itself divisible by 25 without fraction or remainder shall be treated as the next number higher than it which is so divisible.

8–16428　　　　　　　　　　SCHEDULE 2
REPEALS AND REVOCATIONS

Reporting of Injuries, Diseases and Dangerous Occurrences Regulations 1995[1]

(SI 1995/3163 amended by SI 1996/2089 and 2092, SI 1997/2776, SI 1999/437, 2244 and 3232, SI 2001/2975, SI 2004/568 and SI 2005/1082 and 3117.)

8–16491   1. Citation and commencement. These Regulations may be cited as the Reporting of Injuries, Diseases and Dangerous Occurrences Regulations 1995 and shall come into force on 1 April 1996.

---

1. Made by the Secretary of State in exercise of powers conferred on him by ss 15 and 52 of and Sch 3 to the Health and Safety at Work Act 1974. Contravention of the regulations would be an offence contrary to s 33(1) of the 1974 Act; such offences would be triable either way by virtue of s 33(3) of the Act.

8–16492   2. Interpretation. (1) In these Regulations, unless the context otherwise requires—

"the 1995 Order" means the Health and Safety at Work etc. Act 1974 (Application outside Great Britain) Order 1995;
"accident" includes

  (a) an act of non-consensual physical violence done to a person at work; and
  (b) an act of suicide which occurs on, or in the course of the operation of, a relevant transport system;

"approved" means approved for the time being in writing for the purposes of these Regulations by the Executive and published in such form as the Executive considers appropriate;
"biological agent" has the meaning assigned to it by regulation 2(1) of the Control of Substances Hazardous to Health Regulations 1999;
"the Carriage Regulations" means the Carriage of Dangerous Goods and Use of Transportable Pressure Equipment Regulations 2004;
"construction site" means any place where there are carried out building operations or works of engineering construction such that those operations or works fall within section 127(1) of the Factories Act 1961;
"dangerous occurrence" means an occurrence which arises out of or in connection with work and is of a class specified in—

  (a) paragraphs 1–17 of Part I of Schedule 2;
  (b) paragraphs 18–21 of Part I of Schedule 2 and takes place elsewhere than at an offshore workplace;
  (c) paragraphs 22–40 of Part II of Schedule 2 and takes place at a mine;
  (d) paragraphs 41–48 of Part III of Schedule 2 and takes place at a quarry;
  (e) paragraphs 49–72 of Part IV of Schedule 2 and takes place where a relevant transport system is operated (other than at a factory, dock, construction site, mine or quarry); or
  (f) paragraphs 73–83 of Part V of Schedule 2 and takes place at an offshore workplace;

"disease" includes a medical condition;
"diving contractor" has the meaning assigned to it by the Diving at Work Regulations 1997;
"diving project" has the meaning assigned to it by the Diving at Work Regulations 1997;
"dock" means any place to which section 125(1) of the Factories Act 1961 applies;
"the Executive" means the Health and Safety Executive;
"factory" has the meaning assigned to it by section 175 of the Factories Act 1961;
"guided transport system" means a system using a mode of guided transport prescribed under regulation 3 of the Railways and Other Transport Systems (Approval of Works, Plant and Equipment) Regulations 1994;
"major injury" means an injury or condition specified in Schedule 1;
"mine" means a mine within the meaning of section 180 of the Mines and Quarries Act 1954 and for the purposes of these Regulations includes a closed tip within the meaning of section 2(2)(b) of the Mines and Quarries (Tips) Act 1969 which is associated with that mine;
"offshore installation" has the meaning assigned to it by article 4(2) of the 1995 Order but excluding the fixed structures specified in article 4(2)(a) of that Order;
"offshore workplace" means any place where activities are carried on or any premises such that prescribed provisions of the 1974 Act are applied to those activities or premises by virtue of articles 4, 5 or 6 of the 1995 Order, and for this purpose those articles shall be deemed to apply to activities or premises within Great Britain which are in tidal waters or on the foreshore or other land intermittently covered by such waters as they apply to activities and premises within territorial waters or a designated area;
"operator" in relation to a quarry has the meaning assigned to it by the Quarries Regulations 1999;
"operator", in relation to a vehicle to which paragraph 16 or 17 of Part I of Schedule 2 applies, means—

  (a) a person who holds an operator's licence (granted under Part V of the Transport Act 1968) for the use of that vehicle for the carriage of goods on a road; except that where by virtue of regulation 32(1) to (3) of the Goods Vehicles (Operators' Licences, Qualifications and Fees) Regulations 1984 the vehicle is included in a licence held by a holding company and that company is not operating the vehicle at the relevant time, the "operator" shall be the subsidiary company specified in the application made under the said regulation 32(1) or, if more than one subsidiary company is so specified, whichever one is operating the vehicle at the relevant time, and in this sub-paragraph "holding company" and "subsidiary company" have the same meanings as in the said Regulations of 1984; or

(b) where no such licence is held—

    (i) (in the case of a vehicle which is not registered in the United Kingdom) the driver of the vehicle, or

    (ii) (in the case of any other vehicle) the keeper of the vehicle; and for this purpose, where the vehicle is on hire or lease to any person, that person shall be treated as its keeper;

but where an employee who would otherwise be the operator of a vehicle in accordance with sub-paragraph (b)(i) above uses that vehicle for the carriage of any dangerous goods on behalf of his employer, that employer shall (notwithstanding that sub-paragraph) be regarded as the operator of the vehicle concerned;

"owner" means—

    (a) in relation to a mine or quarry, the person who is for the time being entitled to work it;

    (b) in relation to a pipeline, the person who is for the time being entitled to control the flow of anything through that pipeline or through that pipeline once it is commissioned;

"passenger train" means a train carrying passengers or made available for the carriage of passengers;

"pipeline" and "pipeline works" have the meaning assigned to them by article 6(2) of the 1995 Order;

"quarry" means a quarry within the meaning of regulation 3 of the Quarries Regulations 1999;

"railway" has the meaning assigned to it by section 67 of the Transport and Works Act 1992;

"relevant transport system" means a railway, tramway, trolley vehicle system or guided transport system;

"responsible person" means—

    (a) in the case of—

        (i) a mine, the manager of that mine;

        (ii) a quarry, the owner of that quarry;

        (iii) a closed tip, the owner of the mine or quarry with which that tip is associated;

        (iv) an offshore installation (otherwise than in the case of a disease reportable under regulation 5), the duty holder for the purposes of the Offshore Installations and Pipeline Works (Management and Administration) Regulations 1995 provided that for the purposes of this provision regulation 3(2)(c) of those Regulations shall be deemed not to apply;

        (v) a dangerous occurrence at a pipeline (being an incident to which paragraph 14(a)–(f) of Part I of Schedule 2 applies), the owner of that pipeline;

        (vi) a dangerous occurrence at a well, the person appointed by a licensee to execute the function of organising and supervising the drilling of, and all operations to be carried out by means of, that well or, where no such person has been appointed, the licensee (and, for this purpose, "licensee" means any person to whom a licence to search and bore for and get petroleum in respect of any area within relevant waters is granted pursuant to section 3 of the Petroleum Act 1998)

        (vii) a diving project (otherwise than in the case of a disease reportable under regulation 5), the diving contractor;

        (viii) a vehicle to which paragraph 16 or 17 of Part I of Schedule 2 applies, the operator of the vehicle;

    (b) (where sub-paragraph (a) above does not apply) in the case of the death of or other injury to an employee reportable under regulation 3 or of a disease suffered by an employee reportable under regulation 5, his employer, and

    (c) in any other case, the person for the time being having control of the premises in connection with the carrying on by him of any trade, business or other undertaking (whether for profit or not) at which, or in connection with the work at which, the accident or dangerous occurrence reportable under regulation 3, or case of disease reportable under regulation 5, happened;

"road" has the meaning assigned to it by section 192(1) of the Road Traffic Act 1988;

"road vehicle" means any vehicle, other than a train, on a road;

"running line" means any line which is not a siding and is ordinarily used for the passage of trains;

"train" includes a reference to a locomotive, tramcar or other power unit and to a vehicle used on a relevant transport system;

"tramway" has the meaning assigned to it by section 67 of the Transport and Works Act 1992;

"trolley vehicle system" has the meaning assigned to it by section 67 of the Transport and Works Act 1992;

"well" includes any structures and devices on top of a well;

(2) In these Regulations, unless the context otherwise requires, any reference to—

(a) a numbered regulation or Schedule is a reference to the regulation or Schedule in these Regulations so numbered;

(b) a numbered paragraph is a reference to the paragraph so numbered in the regulation or Schedule in which that reference appears; and

(c) an accident or a dangerous occurrence which arises out of or in connection with work shall include a reference to an accident, or as the case may be, a dangerous occurrence attributable to the manner of conducting an undertaking, the plant or substances used for the purposes of an undertaking and the condition of the premises so used or any part of them.

(3) For the purposes of these Regulations, a person who is at an offshore workplace shall be deemed to be at work at all times when he is at that workplace in connection with his work.

8–16493   3. Notification and reporting of injuries and dangerous occurrences.   (1) Subject to regulation 10, where—

(a) any person dies as a result of an accident arising out of or in connection with work[1];

(b) any person at work suffers a major injury as a result of an accident arising out of or in connection with work;

(c) any person not at work suffers an injury as a result of an accident arising out of or in connection with work and that person is taken from the site of the accident to a hospital for treatment in respect of that injury;

(d) any person not at work suffers a major injury as a result of an accident arising out of or in connection with work at a hospital; or

(e) there is a dangerous occurrence,

the responsible person shall—

(i) forthwith notify the relevant enforcing authority thereof by the quickest practicable means; and

(ii) within 10 days send a report thereof to the relevant enforcing authority on a form approved for the purposes of this sub-paragraph, unless within that period he makes a report thereof to the Executive by some other means so approved.

(2) Subject to regulation 10, where a person at work is incapacitated for work of a kind which he might reasonably be expected to do, either under his contract of employment, or, if there is no such contract, in the normal course of his work, for more than three consecutive days (excluding the day of the accident but including any days which would not have been working days) because of an injury resulting from an accident arising out of or in connection with work (other than one reportable under paragraph (1)), the responsible person shall as soon as practicable and, in any event, within 10 days of the accident send a report thereof to the relevant enforcing authority on a form approved for the purposes of this regulation, unless within that period he makes a report thereof to the Executive by some other means so approved.

---

1. The regulation is not limited to accidents or dangerous occurrences to employees, self-employed persons and persons undergoing training for employment but also extends to visitors, customers or other invitees on the premises (*Woking Borough Council v BHS plc* (1994) 159 JP 427).

8–16494   4. Reporting of the death of an employee.   Subject to regulation 10, where an employee, as a result of an accident at work, has suffered an injury reportable under regulation 3 which is a cause of his death within one year of the date of that accident, the employer shall inform the relevant enforcing authority in writing of the death as soon as it comes to his knowledge, whether or not the accident has been reported under regulation 3.

8–16495   5. Reporting of cases of disease.   (1) Subject to paragraphs (2) and (3) and to regulation 10, where—

(a) a person at work suffers from any of the occupational diseases specified in column 1 of Part I of Schedule 3 and his work involves one of the activities specified in the corresponding entry in column 2 of that Part; or

(b) a person at an offshore workplace suffers from any of the diseases specified in Part II of Schedule 3,

the responsible person shall forthwith send a report thereof to the relevant enforcing authority on a form approved for the purposes of this regulation, unless he forthwith makes a report thereof to the Executive by some other means so approved.

(2) Paragraph (1) shall apply only if—

(a) in the case of an employee, the responsible person has received a written statement prepared by a registered medical practitioner diagnosing the disease as one of those specified in Schedule 3; or

(b) in the case of a self-employed person, that person has been informed, by a registered medical practitioner, that he is suffering from a disease so specified.

(3) In the case of a self-employed person, it shall be a sufficient compliance with paragraph (1)

if that person makes arrangements for the report to be sent to the relevant enforcing authority by some other person.

8-16496   6. Reporting of gas incidents.   (1) Whenever a conveyor of flammable gas through a fixed pipe distribution system, or a filler, importer or supplier (other than by means of retail trade) of a refillable container containing liquefied petroleum gas receives notification of any death or any major injury which has arisen out of or in connection with the gas distributed, filled, imported or supplied, as the case may be, by that person, he shall forthwith notify the Executive of the incident, and shall within 14 days send a report of it to the Executive on a form approved for the purposes of this regulation.

(2) Whenever an employer or self-employed person who is a member of a class of persons approved by the Executive for the purposes of paragraph (3) of regulation 3 of the Gas Safety (Installation and Use) Regulations 1994 has in his possession sufficient information for it to be reasonable for him to decide that a gas fitting as defined in the said Regulations or any flue or ventilation used in connection with that fitting, by reason of its design, construction, manner of installation, modification or servicing, is or has been likely to cause death, or any major injury by reason of—

  (a)   accidental leakage of gas;
  (b)   inadequate combustion of gas; or
  (c)   inadequate removal of the products of combustion of gas.

he shall within 14 days send a report of it to the Executive on a form approved for the purposes of this regulation, unless he has previously reported such information.

(3) Nothing shall be reportable—

  (a)   under this regulation if it is notifiable or reportable elsewhere in these Regulations;
  (b)   under paragraph (2) in relation to any gas fitting, flue or ventilation undergoing testing or examination at a place set aside for that purpose.

(4) In this regulation "liquefied petroleum gas" means commercial butane (that is, a hydrocarbon mixture consisting predominantly of butane, butylene or any mixture thereof) or commercial propane (that is, a hydrocarbon mixture consisting predominantly of propane, propylene or any mixture thereof) or any mixture of commercial butane and commercial propane.

8-16497   7. Records.   (1) The responsible person shall keep a record of—

  (a)   any event which is required to be reported under regulation 3, which shall contain the particulars specified in Part I of Schedule 4;
  (b)   any case of disease required to be reported under regulation 5(1), which shall contain the particulars specified in Part II of Schedule 4; and
  (c)   such other particulars as may be approved by the Executive for the purpose of demonstrating that any approved means of reporting under regulations 3 or 5(1) has been complied with.

(2) Any record of deaths, injuries at work or disease which the responsible person keeps for any other purpose shall, if it covers the injuries recordable under these Regulations and includes the particulars specified in Schedule 4, be sufficient for the requirements of paragraph (1).

(3) The record referred to in paragraph (1) shall be kept either at the place where the work to which it relates is carried on or at the usual place of business of the responsible person and an entry in such a record shall be kept for at least three years from the date on which it was made.

(4) The responsible person shall send to the relevant enforcing authority such extracts from the record required to be kept under paragraph (1) as that enforcing authority may from time to time require.

8-16498   8. Additional provisions relating to mines and quarries.   The provisions of Schedule 5 (which contains additional provisions relating to mines and quarries) shall have effect.

8-16499   9. Additional provisions relating to offshore workplaces.   The provisions of Schedule 6 (which contains additional provisions relating to offshore workplaces) shall have effect.

8-16500   10. Restrictions on the application of regulations 3, 4 and 5.   (1) The requirements of regulation 3 relating to the death or injury of a person as a result of an accident shall not apply to an accident causing death or injury to a person arising out of the conduct of any operation on, or any examination or other medical treatment of, that person which is administered by, or conducted under the supervision of, a registered medical practitioner or a registered dentist (and for the purposes of this paragraph a registered dentist has the meaning assigned to it by section 53(1) of the Dentists Act 1984).

(2) The requirements of regulations 3 and 4 relating to the death or injury of a person as a result of an accident, shall apply to an accident arising out of or in connection with the movement of a vehicle on a road only if that person—

  (a)   was killed or suffered an injury as a result of exposure to a substance being conveyed by the vehicle; or

(b)   was either himself engaged in, or was killed or suffered an injury as a result of the activities of another person who was at the time of the accident engaged in, work connected with the loading or unloading of any article or substance onto or off the vehicle; or

(c)   was either himself engaged in, or was killed or suffered an injury as a result of the activities of another person who was at the time of the accident engaged in, work on or alongside a road, being work concerned with the construction, demolition, alteration, repair or maintenance of—

(i)   the road or the markings or equipment thereon;
(ii)   the verges, fences, hedges or other boundaries of the road;
(iii)   pipes or cables on, under, over or adjacent to the road; or
(iv)   buildings or structures adjacent to or over the road; or

(d)   was killed or suffered an injury as a result of an accident involving a train.

(3)   The requirements of regulations 3, 4 and 5 relating to any death, injury or case of disease shall not apply to a member of the armed forces of the Crown or of a visiting force who was on duty at the relevant time (and for the purposes of this paragraph a visiting force has the meaning assigned to it by section 12(1) of the Visiting Forces Act 1952).

(4)   Regulations 3, 4 and 5 shall not apply otherwise than in respect of offshore workplaces to anything which is required to be notified under any of the enactments or instruments specified in Schedule 7.

(5)   Regulation 3(1)(i) shall not apply to a self-employed person who is injured at premises of which he is the owner or occupier, but regulation 3(l)(ii) shall apply to such a self-employed person (other than in the case of death) and it shall be sufficient compliance with that sub-paragraph if that self-employed person makes arrangements for the report to be sent to the relevant enforcing authority by some other person.

8–16501   11. Defence in proceedings for an offence contravening these Regulations.   It shall be a defence in proceedings against any person for an offence under these Regulations for that person to prove that he was not aware of the event requiring him to notify or send a report to the relevant enforcing authority and that he had taken all reasonable steps to have all such events brought to his notice.

8–16502   12. Extension outside Great Britain.   These Regulations shall apply to and in relation to the premises and activities outside Great Britain to which sections 1 to 59 and 80 to 82 of the Health and Safety at Work etc. Act 1974 apply by virtue of the 1995 Order as they apply within Great Britain.

8–16503   13. Certificates of exemption.   (1) Subject to paragraph (2) and to any of the provisions imposed by the Communities in respect of the encouragement of improvements in the safety and health of workers at work, the Executive may, by a certificate in writing, exempt any person or class of persons from any requirement imposed by these Regulations and any such exemption may be granted subject to conditions and with or without limit of time and may be revoked by a certificate in writing at any time.

(2)   The Executive shall not grant any such exemption unless, having regard to the circumstances of the case and, in particular, to—

(a)   the conditions, if any, which it proposes to attach to the exemption; and
(b)   any other requirements imposed by or under any enactments which apply to the case,

it is satisfied that the health and safety of persons who are likely to be affected by the exemption will not be prejudiced in consequence of it.

8–16504   14. *Repeal and amendment of provisions in the Regulation of Railways Act 1871, the Railway Employment (Prevention of Accidents) Act 1900 and the Transport and Works Act 1992.*

8–16505   15. *Revocations, amendments and savings.*

8–16506

Regulation 2(1)   SCHEDULE 1
                               MAJOR INJURIES

1. Any fracture, other than to the fingers, thumbs or toes.
2. Any amputation.
3. Dislocation of the shoulder, hip, knee or spine.
4. Loss of sight (whether temporary or permanent).
5. A chemical or hot metal burn to the eye or any penetrating injury to the eye.
6. Any injury resulting from an electric shock or electrical burn (including any electrical burn caused by arcing or arcing products) leading to unconsciousness or requiring resuscitation or admittance to hospital for more than 24 hours.
7. Any other injury—

(a)   leading to hypothermia, heat-induced illness or to unconsciousness,
(b)   requiring resuscitation, or
(c)   requiring admittance to hospital for more than 24 hours.

8. Loss of consciousness caused by asphyxia or by exposure to a harmful substance or biological agent.

9. Either of the following conditions which result from the absorption of any substance by inhalation, ingestion or through the skin—

   (a)   acute illness requiring medical treatment; or
   (b)   loss of consciousness.

10. Acute illness which requires medical treatment where there is reason to believe that this resulted from exposure to a biological agent or its toxins or infected material.

Regulation 2(1)

SCHEDULE 2
DANGEROUS OCCURRENCES

PART I
GENERAL

8–16507   **1. Lifting machinery, etc.**   The collapse of, the overturning of, or the failure of any load-bearing part of any—

   (a)   lift or hoist;
   (b)   crane or derrick;
   (c)   mobile powered access platform;
   (d)   access cradle or window-cleaning cradle;
   (e)   excavator;
   (f)   pile-driving frame or rig having an overall height, when operating, of more than 7 metres; or
   (g)   fork lift truck.

8–16508   **2. Pressure systems.**   The failure of any closed vessel (including a boiler or boiler tube) or of any associated pipework, in which the internal pressure was above or below atmospheric pressure, where the failure has the potential to cause the death of any person.

8–16509   **3. Freight containers.**   (1) The failure of any freight container in any of its load-bearing parts while it is being raised, lowered or suspended.
   (2) In this paragraph, "freight container" means a container as defined in regulation 2(1) of the Freight Containers (Safety Convention) Regulations 1984.

8–16510   **4. Overhead electric lines.**   Any unintentional incident in which plant or equipment either—

   (a)   comes into contact with an uninsulated overhead electric line in which the voltage exceeds 200 volts; or
   (b)   causes an electrical discharge from such an electric line by coming into close proximity to it.

8–16511   **5. Electrical short circuit.**   Electrical short circuit or overload attended by fire or explosion which results in the stoppage of the plant involved for more than 24 hours or which has the potential to cause the death of any person.

8–16512   **6. Explosives.**   (1) Any of the following incidents involving explosives—

   (a)   any unintentional fire, explosion or ignition at a site—

      (i)   where explosives are manufactured by a person who holds a licence, or who does not hold a licence but is required to, in respect of that manufacture under the Manufacture and Storage of Explosives Regulations 2005; or
      (ii)   where explosives are stored by a person who holds a licence or is registered, or who is not licensed but is required to be in the absence of any registration, in respect of that storage under those Regulations;

   (aa)   the unintentional explosion or ignition of explosives at a place other than a site described in sub-paragraph (1)(a), not being one—

      (i)   caused by the unintentional discharge of a weapon where, apart from that unintentional discharge, the weapon and explosives functioned as they were designed to do; or
      (ii)   where a fail-safe device or safe system of work functioned so as to prevent any person from being injured in consequence of the explosion or ignition;

   (b)   a misfire (other than one at a mine or quarry or inside a well or one involving a weapon) except where a fail-safe device or safe system of work functioned so as to prevent any person from being endangered in consequence of the misfire;
   (c)   the failure of the shots in any demolition operation to cause the intended extent of collapse or direction of fall of a building or structure;
   (d)   the projection of material (other than at a quarry) beyond the boundary of the site on which the explosives are being used or beyond the danger zone in circumstances such that any person was or might have been injured thereby;
   (e)   any injury to a person (other than at a mine or quarry or one otherwise reportable under these Regulations) involving first-aid or medical treatment resulting from the explosion or discharge of any explosives or detonator or from any intentional fire or ignition.

   (2) In this paragraph—

"danger zone" means the area from which persons have been excluded or forbidden to enter to avoid being endangered by any explosion or ignition of explosives; and
"explosives" has the same meaning as in the Manufacture and Storage of Explosives Regulations 2005.

8–16513   **7. Biological agents.**   Any accident or incident which resulted or could have resulted in the release or escape of a biological agent likely to cause severe human infection or illness.

8–16514   8. Malfunction of radiation generators, etc. (1) Any incident in which—

(a) the malfunction of a radiation generator or its ancillary equipment used in fixed or mobile industrial radiography, the irradiation of food or the processing of products by irradiation, causes it to fail to de-energise at the end of the intended exposure period; or

(b) the malfunction of equipment used in fixed or mobile industrial radiography or gamma irradiation causes a radioactive source to fail to return to its safe position by the normal means at the end of the intended exposure period.

(2) In this paragraph, "radiation generator" means any electrical equipment emitting ionising radiation and containing components operating at a potential difference of more than 5 kV.

8–16515   9. Breathing apparatus. (1) Any incident in which breathing apparatus malfunctions—

(a) while in use, or

(b) during testing immediately prior to use in such a way that had the malfunction occurred while the apparatus was in use it would have posed a danger to the health or safety of the user.

(2) This paragraph shall not apply to breathing apparatus while it is being—

(a) used in a mine; or

(b) maintained or tested as part of a routine maintenance procedure.

8–16516   10. Diving projects. Any of the following incidents in relation to a diving project—

(a) the failure or the endangering of—

(i)   any lifting equipment associated with the diving project, or

(ii) life support equipment, including control panels, hoses and breathing apparatus, which puts a diver at risk;

(b) any damage to, or endangering of, the dive platform, or any failure of the dive platform to remain on station, which puts a diver at risk;

(c) the trapping of a diver;

(d) any explosion in the vicinity of a diver; or

(e) any uncontrolled ascent or any omitted decompression which puts a diver at risk.

8–16517   11. Collapse of scaffolding. The complete or partial collapse of—

(a) any scaffold which is—

(i)   more than 5 metres in height which results in a substantial part of the scaffold falling or overturning; or

(ii) erected over or adjacent to water in circumstances such that there would be a risk of drowning to a person falling from the scaffold into the water; or

(b) the suspension arrangements (including any outrigger) of any slung or suspended scaffold which causes a working platform or cradle to fall.

8–16518   12. Train collisions. Any unintended collision of a train with any other train or vehicle, other than one reportable under Part IV of this Schedule, which caused, or might have caused, the death of, or major injury to, any person.

8–16519   13. Wells. Any of the following incidents in relation to a well (other than a well sunk for the purpose of the abstraction of water)—

(a) a blow-out (that is to say an uncontrolled flow of well-fluids from a well);

(b) the coming into operation of a blow-out prevention or diversion system to control a flow from a well where normal control procedures fail;

(c) the detection of hydrogen sulphide in the course of operations at a well or in samples of well-fluids from a well where the presence of hydrogen sulphide in the reservoir being drawn on by the well was not anticipated by the responsible person before that detection;

(d) the taking of precautionary measures additional to any contained in the original drilling programme following failure to maintain a planned minimum separation distance between wells drilled from a particular installation; or

(e) the mechanical failure of any safety critical element of a well (and for this purpose the safety critical element of a well is any part of a well whose failure would cause or contribute to, or whose purpose is to prevent or limit the effect of, the unintentional release of fluids from a well or a reservoir being drawn on by a well).

8–16520   14. Pipelines or pipeline works. The following incidents in respect of a pipeline or pipeline works—

(a) the uncontrolled or accidental escape of anything from, or inrush of anything into, a pipeline which has the potential to cause the death of, major injury or damage to the health of any person or which results in the pipeline being shut down for more than 24 hours;

(b) the unintentional ignition of anything in a pipeline or of anything which, immediately before it was ignited, was in a pipeline;

(c) any damage to any part of a pipeline which has the potential to cause the death of, major injury or damage to the health of any person or which results in the pipeline being shut down for more than 24 hours;

(d) any substantial and unintentional change in the position of a pipeline requiring immediate attention to safeguard the integrity or safety of a pipeline;

(e) any unintentional change in the subsoil or seabed in the vicinity of a pipeline which has the potential to affect the integrity or safety of a pipeline;

(f) any failure of any pipeline isolation device, equipment or system which has the potential to cause the death of, major injury or damage to the health of any person or which results in the pipeline being shut down for more than 24 hours; or

(g) any failure of equipment involved with pipeline works which has the potential to cause the death of, major injury or damage to the health of any person.

8–16521   15. Fairground equipment. The following incidents on fairground equipment in use or under test—

(a) the failure of any load-bearing part;
(b) the failure of any part designed to support or restrain passengers; or
(c) the derailment or the unintended collision of cars or trains.

8–16522   16. Carriage of dangerous goods by road. (1) Any incident involving a road tanker or tank container used for the carriage of dangerous goods in which—

(a) the road tanker or vehicle carrying the tank container overturns (including turning onto its side);
(b) the tank carrying the dangerous goods is seriously damaged;
(c) there is an uncontrolled release or escape of the dangerous goods being carried; or
(d) there is a fire involving the dangerous goods being carried.

(2) *Revoked.*

8–16523   17. (1) Any incident involving a vehicle used for the carriage of dangerous goods, other than a vehicle to which paragraph 16 applies, where there is—

(a) an uncontrolled release or escape of the dangerous goods being carried in such a quantity as to have the potential to cause the death of, or major injury to, any person; or
(b) a fire which involves the dangerous goods being carried.

(2) *Revoked.*

8–16523A   17A. In paragraphs 16 and 17 above, "carriage" and "dangerous goods" have the same meaning as those terms in regulation 2(1) of the Carriage Regulations.

DANGEROUS OCCURRENCES WHICH ARE REPORTABLE EXCEPT IN RELATION TO OFFSHORE WORKPLACES

8–16524   18. Collapse of building or structure. Any unintended collapse or partial collapse of—

(a) any building or structure (whether above or below ground) under construction, reconstruction, alteration or demolition which involves a fall of more than 5 tonnes of material;
(b) any floor or wall of any building (whether above or below ground) used as a place of work; or
(c) any false-work.

8–16525   19. Explosion or fire. An explosion or fire occurring in any plant or premises which results in the stoppage of that plant or as the case may be the suspension of normal work in those premises for more than 24 hours, where the explosion or fire was due to the ignition of any material.

8–16526   20. Escape of flammable substances. (1) The sudden, uncontrolled release—

(a) inside a building—

(i) of 100 kilograms or more of a flammable liquid,
(ii) of 10 kilograms or more of a flammable liquid at a temperature above its normal boiling point,
(iii) of 10 kilograms or more of a flammable gas; or

(b) in the open air, of 500 kilograms or more of any of the substances referred to in sub-paragraph (a) above.

(2) In this paragraph, "flammable liquid" and "flammable gas" mean respectively a liquid and a gas so classified in accordance with regulation 5(2), (3) or (5) of the Chemicals (Hazard Information and Packaging for Supply) Regulations 1994.

8–16527   21. Escape of substances. The accidental release or escape of any substance in a quantity sufficient to cause the death, major injury or any other damage to the health of any person.

PART II
DANGEROUS OCCURRENCES WHICH ARE REPORTABLE IN RELATION TO MINES

8–16528   22. Fire or ignition of gas. The ignition, below ground, of any gas (other than gas in a safety lamp) or of any dust.
   23. The accidental ignition of any gas in part of a firedamp drainage system on the surface or in an exhauster house.
   24. The outbreak of any fire below ground.
   25. An incident where any person in consequence of any smoke or any other indication that a fire may have broken out below ground has been caused to leave any place pursuant to either Regulation 11(1) of the Coal and Other Mines (Fire and Rescue) Regulations 1956 or section 79 of the Mines and Quarries Act 1954.
   26. The outbreak of any fire on the surface which endangers the operation of any winding or haulage apparatus installed at a shaft or unwalkable outlet or of any mechanically operated apparatus for producing ventilation below ground.

8–16529   27. Escape of gas. Any violent outburst of gas together with coal or other solid matter into the mine workings except when such outburst is caused intentionally.

8–16530   28. Failure of plant or equipment. The breakage of any rope, chain, coupling, balance rope, guide rope, suspension gear or other gear used for or in connection with the carrying of persons through any shaft or staple shaft.

8–16531   29. The breakage or unintentional uncoupling of any rope, chain, coupling, rope tensioning system or other gear used for or in connection with the transport of persons below ground, or breakage of any belt, rope or other gear used for or in connection with a belt conveyor designated by the mine manager as a man-riding conveyor.

8–16532   30. An incident where any conveyance being used for the carriage of persons is overwound; or any conveyance not being so used is overwound and becomes detached from its winding rope; or any conveyance operated by means of the friction of a rope on a winding sheave is brought to rest by the apparatus provided in the headframe of the shaft or in the part of the shaft below the lowest landing for the time being in use, being apparatus provided for bringing the conveyance to rest in the event of its being overwound.

8–16533   31. The stoppage of any ventilating apparatus (other than an auxiliary fan) which causes a substantial reduction in ventilation of the mine lasting for a period exceeding 30 minutes, except when for the purpose of planned maintenance.
    32. The collapse of any headframe, winding engine house, fan house or storage bunker.

8–16534   33. Breathing apparatus. At any mine an incident where—
    (a) breathing apparatus or a smoke helmet or other apparatus serving the same purpose or a self-rescuer, while being used, fails to function safely or develops a defect likely to affect its safe working; or
    (b) immediately after using and arising out of the use of breathing apparatus or a smoke helmet or other apparatus serving the same purpose or a self-rescuer, any person receives first-aid or medical treatment by reason of his unfitness or suspected unfitness at the mine.

8–16535   34. Injury by explosion of blasting material etc. An incident in which any person suffers an injury (not being a major injury or one reportable under regulation 3(2)) which results from an explosion or discharge of any blasting material or device within the meaning of section 69(4) of the Mines and Quarries Act 1954 for which he receives first-aid or medical treatment at the mine.

8–16536   35. Use of emergency escape apparatus. An incident where any apparatus is used (other than for the purpose of training and practice) which has been provided at the mine in accordance with regulation 4 of the Mines (Safety of Exit) Regulations 1988 or where persons leave the mine when apparatus and equipment normally used by persons to leave the mine is unavailable.

8–16537   36. Inrush of gas or water. Any inrush of noxious or flammable gas from old workings.
    37. Any inrush of water or material which flows when wet from any source.

8–16538   38. Insecure tip. Any movement of material or any fire or any other event which indicates that a tip to which Part I of the Mines and Quarries (Tips) Act 1969 applies, is or is likely to become insecure.

8–16539   39. Locomotives. Any incident where an underground locomotive when not used for testing purposes is brought to rest by means other than its safety circuit protective devices or normal service brakes.

8–16540   40. Falls of ground. Any fall of ground, not being part of the normal operations at a mine, which results from a failure of an underground support system and prevents persons travelling through the area affected by the fall or which otherwise exposes them to danger.

PART III
DANGEROUS OCCURRENCES WHICH ARE REPORTABLE IN RELATION TO QUARRIES

8–16541   41. Collapse of storage bunkers. The collapse of any storage bunker.

8–16542   42. Sinking of craft. The sinking of any water-borne craft or hovercraft.

8–16543   43. Injuries. (1) An incident in which any person suffers an injury (not otherwise reportable under these Regulations) which results from an explosion or from the discharge of any explosives for which he receives first-aid or medical treatment at the quarry.
    (2) In this paragraph, "explosives" has the same meaning as in regulation 2(1) of the Quarries Regulations 1999.

8–16544   44. Projection of substances outside quarry. Any incident in which any substance is ascertained to have been projected beyond a quarry boundary as a result of blasting operations in circumstances in which any person was or might have been endangered.

8–16545   45. Misfires. Any misfire, as defined by regulation 2(1) of the Quarries Regulations 1999.

8–16546   46. Insecure tips. Any event (including any movement of material or any fire) which indicates that a tip, to which the Quarries Regulations 1999 apply, is or is likely to become insecure.

8–16547   47. Movement of slopes or faces. Any movement or failure of an excavated slope or face which—
    (a) has the potential to cause the death of any person; or
    (b) adversely affects any building, contiguous land, transport system, footpath, public utility or service, watercourse, reservoir or area of public access.

8–16548   48. Explosions or fires in vehicles or plant. (1) Any explosion or fire occurring in any large vehicle or mobile plant which results in the stoppage of that vehicle or plant for more than 24 hours and which affects—
    (a) any place where persons normally work; or
    (b) the route of egress from such a place.

(2) In this paragraph, "large vehicle or mobile plant" means—

(a) a dump truck having a load capacity of at least 50 tonnes; or
(b) an excavator having a bucket capacity of at least 5 cubic metres.

PART IV
DANGEROUS OCCURRENCES WHICH ARE REPORTABLE IN RESPECT OF RELEVANT TRANSPORT SYSTEMS

8–16549   49. Accidents to passenger trains.   Any collision in which a passenger train collides with another train.
  50. Any case where a passenger train or any part of such a train unintentionally leaves the rails.

8–16550   51. Accidents not involving passenger trains.   Any collision between trains, other than one between a passenger train and another train, on a running line where any train sustains damage as a result of the collision, and any such collision in a siding which results in a running line being obstructed.
  52. Any derailment, of a train other than a passenger train, on a running line, except a derailment which occurs during shunting operations and does not obstruct any other running line.
  53. Any derailment, of a train other than a passenger train, in a siding which results in a running line being obstructed.

8–16551   54. Accidents involving any kind of train.   Any case of a train striking a buffer stop, other than in a siding, where damage is caused to the train.
  55. Any case of a train striking any cattle or horse, whether or not damage is caused to the train, or striking any other animal if, in consequence, damage (including damage to the windows of the driver's cab but excluding other damage consisting solely in the breakage of glass) is caused to the train necessitating immediate temporary or permanent repair.
  56. Any case of a train on a running line striking or being struck by any object which causes damage (including damage to the windows of the driver's cab but excluding other damage consisting solely in the breakage of glass) necessitating immediate temporary or permanent repair or which might have been liable to derail the train.
  57. Any case of a train, other than one on a railway, striking or being struck by a road vehicle.
  58. Any case of a passenger train, or any other train not fitted with continuous self-applying brakes, becoming unintentionally divided.
  59. (1) Any of the following classes of accident which occurs or is discovered whilst the train is on a running line—

(a) the failure of an axle;
(b) the failure of a wheel or tyre, including a tyre loose on its wheel;
(c) the failure of a rope or the fastenings thereof or of the winding plant or equipment involved in working an incline;
(d) any fire, severe electrical arcing or fusing in or on any part of a passenger train or a train carrying dangerous goods;
(e) in the case of any train other than a passenger train, any severe electrical arcing or fusing, or any fire which was extinguished by a fire-fighting service; or
(f) any other failure of any part of a train which is likely to cause an accident to that or any other train or to kill or injure any person.

(2) In this paragraph "dangerous goods" has the meaning assigned to it in regulation 2(1) of the Carriage Regulations.

8–16552   60. Accidents and incidents at level crossings.   Any case of a train striking a road vehicle or gate at a level crossing.
  61. Any case of a train running onto a level crossing when not authorised to do so.
  62. A failure of the equipment at a level crossing which could endanger users of the road or path crossing the railway.

8–16553   63. Accidents involving the permanent way and other works on or connected with a relevant transport system.   The failure of a rail in a running line or of a rack rail, which results in—

(a) a complete fracture of the rail through its cross-section; or
(b) in a piece becoming detached from the rail which necessitates an immediate stoppage of traffic or the immediate imposition of a speed restriction lower than that currently in force.

  64. A buckle of a running line which necessitates an immediate stoppage of traffic or the immediate imposition of a speed restriction lower than that currently in force.
  65. Any case of an aircraft or a vehicle of any kind landing on, running onto or coming to rest foul of the line, or damaging the line, which causes damage which obstructs the line or which damages any railway equipment at a level crossing.
  66. The runaway of an escalator, lift or passenger conveyor.
  67. Any fire or severe arcing or fusing which seriously affects the functioning of signalling equipment.
  68. Any fire affecting the permanent way or works of a relevant transport system which necessitates the suspension of services over any line, or the closure of any part of a station or signal box or other premises, for a period—

(a) in the case of a fire affecting any part of a relevant transport system below ground, of more than 30 minutes, and
(b) in any other case, of more than 1 hour.

  69. *Any other fire which causes damage which has the potential to affect the running of a relevant transport system*

8–16554   70. Accidents involving failure of the works on or connected with a relevant transport system. (1) The following classes of accident where they are likely either to cause an accident to a train or to endanger any person—

(a) the failure of a tunnel, bridge, viaduct, culvert, station, or other structure or any part thereof including the fixed electrical equipment of an electrified relevant transport system;

(b) any failure in the signalling system which endangers or which has the potential to endanger the safe passage of trains other than a failure of a traffic light controlling the movement of vehicles on a road;

(c) a slip of a cutting or of an embankment;

(d) flooding of the permanent way;

(e) the striking of a bridge by a vessel or by a road vehicle or its load; or

(f) the failure of any other portion of the permanent way or works not specified above.

8–16555   71. Incidents of serious congestion. Any case where planned procedures or arrangements have been activated in order to control risks arising from an incident of undue passenger congestion at a station unless that congestion has been relieved within a period of time allowed for by those procedures or arrangements.

8–16556   72. Incidents of signals passed without authority. (1) Any case where a train, travelling on a running line or entering a running line from a siding, passes without authority a signal displaying a stop aspect unless—

(a) the stop aspect was not displayed in sufficient time for the driver to stop safely at the signal; or

(b) the line is equipped with automatic train protection equipment which is in operation.

(2) In this paragraph "automatic train protection equipment" means equipment which automatically controls the speed of a train, either by bringing it to a halt or reducing its speed, in the event that the train passes a signal without authority or exceeds a prescribed speed limit.

PART V
DANGEROUS OCCURRENCES WHICH ARE REPORTABLE IN RESPECT OF AN OFFSHORE WORKPLACE

8–16557   73. Release of petroleum hydrocarbon. Any unintentional release of petroleum hydrocarbon on or from an offshore installation which—

(a) results in—

(i) a fire or explosion; or

(ii) the taking of action to prevent or limit the consequences of a potential fire or explosion; or

(b) has the potential to cause death or major injury to any person.

8–16558   74. Fire or explosion. Any fire or explosion at an offshore installation, other than one to which paragraph 73 above applies, which results in the stoppage of plant or the suspension of normal work.

8–16559   75. Release or escape of dangerous substances. The uncontrolled or unintentional release or escape of any substance (other than petroleum hydrocarbon) on or from an offshore installation which has the potential to cause the death of, major injury to or damage to the health of any person.

8–16560   76. Collapses. Any unintended collapse of any offshore installation or any unintended collapse of any part thereof or any plant thereon which jeopardises the overall structural integrity of the installation.

8–16561   77. Dangerous occurrences. Any of the following occurrences having the potential to cause death or major injury—

(a) the failure of equipment required to maintain a floating offshore installation on station;

(b) the dropping of any object on an offshore installation or on an attendant vessel or into the water adjacent to an installation or vessel; or

(c) damage to or on an offshore installation caused by adverse weather conditions.

8–16562   78. Collisions. Any collision between a vessel or aircraft and an offshore installation which results in damage to the installation, the vessel or the aircraft.

79. Any occurrence with the potential for a collision between a vessel and an offshore installation where, had a collision occurred, it would have been liable to jeopardise the overall structural integrity of the offshore installation.

8–16563   80. Subsidence or collapse of seabed. Any subsidence or local collapse of the seabed likely to affect the foundations of an offshore installation or the overall structural integrity of an offshore installation.

8–16564   81. Loss of stability or buoyancy. Any incident involving loss of stability or buoyancy of a floating offshore installation.

8–16565   82. Evacuation. Any evacuation (other than one arising out of an incident reportable under any other provision of these Regulations) of an offshore installation, in whole or part, in the interests of safety.

8–16566   83. Falls into water. Any case of a person falling more than 2 metres into water (unless the fall results in death or injury required to be reported under sub-paragraphs (a)–(d) of regulation 3(1)).

Regulation 5(1) and (2)

SCHEDULE 3

REPORTABLE DISEASES

PART I

OCCUPATIONAL DISEASES

Column 1	Column 2
Diseases	**Activities**

Conditions due to physical agents and the physical demands of work

1 Inflammation, ulceration or malignant disease of the skin due to ionising radiation	
2 Malignant disease of the bones due to ionising radiation	Work with ionising radiation
3 Blood dyscrasia due to ionising radiation	
4 Cataract due to electromagnetic radiation	Work involving exposure to electromagnetic radiation (including radiant heat)
5 Decompression illness	
6 Barotrauma resulting in lung or other organ damage	Work involving breathing gases at increased pressure (including diving)
7 Dysbaric osteonecrosis	
8 Cramp of the hand or forearm due to repetitive movements	Work involving prolonged periods of handwriting, typing or other repetitive movements of the fingers, hand or arm
9 Subcutaneous cellulitis of the hand (*beat hand*)	Physically demanding work causing severe or prolonged friction or pressure on the hand
10 Bursitis or subcutaneous cellulitis arising at or about the knee due to severe or prolonged external friction or pressure at or about the knee (*beat knee*)	Physically demanding work causing severe or prolonged friction or pressure at or about the knee
11 Bursitis or subcutaneous cellulitis arising at or about the elbow due to severe or prolonged external friction or pressure at or about the elbow (*beat elbow*)	Physically demanding work causing severe or prolonged friction or pressure at or about the elbow
12 Traumatic inflammation of the tendons of the hand or forearm or of the associated tendon sheaths	Physically demanding work, frequent or repeated movements, constrained postures or extremes of extension or flexion of the hand or wrist
13 Carpal tunnel syndrome	Work involving the use of hand-held vibrating tools
14 Hand-arm vibration syndrome	Work involving:
	(a) the use of chain saws, brush cutters or hand-held or hand-fed circular saws in forestry or woodworking;
	(b) the use of hand-held rotary tools in grinding material or in sanding or polishing metal;
	(c) the holding of material being ground or metal being sanded or polished by rotary tools;
	(d) the use of hand-held percussive metal-working tools or the holding of metal being worked upon by percussive tools in connection with riveting, caulking, chipping, hammering, fettling or swaging;
	(e) the use of hand-held powered percussive drills or hand-held powered percussive hammers in mining, quarrying or demolition, or on roads or footpaths (including road construction); or
	(f) the holding of material being worked upon by pounding machines in shoe manufacture

Infections due to biological agents

15 Anthrax	(a) Work involving handling infected animals, their products or packaging containing infected material; or
	(b) work on infected sites
16 Brucellosis	Work involving contact with:
	(a) animals or their carcasses (including any parts thereof) infected by brucella or the untreated products of same; or
	(b) laboratory specimens or vaccines of or containing brucella
17 (a) Avian chlamydiosis	Work involving contact with birds infected with chlamydia psittaci, or the remains or untreated products of such birds

Column 1	Column 2
Diseases	**Activities**
(b) Ovine chlamydiosis	Work involving contact with sheep infected with chlamydia psittaci or the remains or untreated products of such sheep
18 Hepatitis	Work involving contact with: (a) human blood or human blood products; or (b) any source of viral hepatitis
19 Legionellosis	Work on or near cooling systems which are located in the workplace and use water; or work on hot water service systems located in the workplace which are likely to be a source of contamination
20 Leptospirosis	(a) Work in places which are or are liable to be infested by rats, fieldmice, voles or other small mammals; (b) work at dog kennels or involving the care or handling of dogs; or (c)work involving contact with bovine animals or their meat products or pigs or their meat products
21 Lyme disease	Work involving exposure to ticks (including in particular work by forestry workers, rangers, dairy farmers, game keepers and other persons engaged in countryside management)
22 Q fever	Work involving contact with animals, their remains or their untreated products
23 Rabies	Work involving handling or contact with infected animals
24 Streptococcus suis	Work involving contact with pigs infected with streptococcus suis, or with the carcasses, products or residues of pigs so affected
25 Tetanus	Work involving contact with soil likely to be contaminated by animals
26 Tuberculosis	Work with persons, animals, human or animal remains or any other material which might be a source of infection
27 Any infection reliably attributable to the performance of the work specified in the entry opposite hereto	Work with micro-organisms; work with live or dead human beings in the course of providing any treatment or service or in conducting any investigation involving exposure to blood or body fluids; work with animals or any potentially infected material derived from any of the above

Conditions due to substances

28 Poisonings by any of the following: (a) acrylamide monomer; (b) arsenic or one of its compounds; (c) benzene or a homologue of benzene; (d) beryllium or one of its compounds; (e) cadmium or one of its compounds; (f) carbon disulphide; (g) diethylene dioxide (dioxan); (h) ethylene oxide; (i) lead or one of its compounds; (j) manganese or one of its compounds; (k) mercury or one of its compounds; (l) methyl bromide; (m) nitrochlorobenzene, or a nitro- or amino- or chloro-derivative of benzene or of a homologue of benzene; (n) oxides of nitrogen; (o) phosphorus or one of its compounds	Any activity
29 Cancer of a bronchus or lung	(a) Work in or about a building where nickel is produced by decomposition of a gaseous nickel compound or where any industrial process which is ancillary or incidental to that process is carried on; or (b) work involving exposure to bis(chloromethyl) ether or any electrolytic chromium processes (excluding passivation) which involve hexavalent chromium compounds, chromate production or zinc chromate pigment manufacture
30 Primary carcinoma of the lung where there is accompanying evidence of silicosis	Any occupation in: (a) glass manufacture; (b) sandstone tunnelling or quarrying;

Column 1	Column 2
Diseases	**Activities**
	(c) the pottery industry;
	(d) metal ore mining;
	(e) slate quarrying or slate production;
	(f) clay mining;
	(g) the use of siliceous materials as abrasives;
	(h) foundry work;
	(i) granite tunnelling or quarrying; or
	(j) stone cutting or masonry
31 Cancer of the urinary tract	1 Work involving exposure to any of the following substances:
	(a) beta-naphthylamine or methylene-bis-orthochloroaniline;
	(b) diphenyl substituted by at least one nitro or primary amino group or by at least one nitro and primary amino group (including benzidine);
	(c) any of the substances mentioned in sub-paragraph (b) above if further ring substituted by halogeno, methyl or methoxy groups, but not by other groups; or
	(d) the salts of any of the substances mentioned in sub-paragraphs (a) to (c) above
	2 The manufacture of auramine or magenta
32 Bladder cancer	Work involving exposure to aluminium smelting using the Soderberg process
33 Angiosarcoma of the liver	(a) Work in or about machinery or apparatus used for the polymerisation of vinyl chloride monomer, a process which, for the purposes of this sub-paragraph, comprises all operations up to and including the drying of the slurry produced by the polymerisation and the packaging of the dried product; or
	(b) work in a building or structure in which any part of the process referred to in the foregoing sub-paragraph takes place
34 Peripheral neuropathy	Work involving the use or handling of or exposure to the fumes of or vapour containing n-hexane or methyl n-butyl ketone
35 Chrome ulceration of: (a) the nose or throat; or (b) the skin of the hands or forearm	Work involving exposure to chromic acid or to any other chromium compound
36 Folliculitis 37 Acne 38 Skin cancer	Work involving exposure to mineral oil, tar, pitch or arsenic
39 Pneumoconiosis (excluding asbestosis)	1 (a) The mining, quarrying or working of silica rock or the working of dried quartzose sand, any dry deposit or residue of silica or any dry admixture containing such materials (including any activity in which any of the aforesaid operations are carried out incidentally to the mining or quarrying of other minerals or to the manufacture of articles containing crushed or ground silica rock); or
	(b) the handling of any of the materials specified in the foregoing sub-paragraph in or incidentally to any of the operations mentioned therein or substantial exposure to the dust arising from such operations
	2 The breaking, crushing or grinding of flint, the working or handling of broken, crushed or ground flint or materials containing such flint or substantial exposure to the dust arising from any of such operations
	3 Sand blasting by means of compressed air with the use of quartzose sand or crushed silica rock or flint or substantial exposure to the dust arising from such sand blasting
	4 Work in a foundry or the performance of, or substantial exposure to the dust arising from, any of the following operations:
	(a) the freeing of steel castings from adherent siliceous substance; or

Column 1	Column 2
Diseases	**Activities**

	(b) the freeing of metal castings from adherent siliceous substance:
	    (i) by blasting with an abrasive propelled by compressed air, steam or a wheel, or
	    (ii) by the use of power-driven tools.
	5 The manufacture of china or earthenware (including sanitary earthenware, electrical earthenware and earthenware tiles) and any activity involving substantial exposure to the dust arising therefrom
	6 The grinding of mineral graphite or substantial exposure to the dust arising from such grinding
	7 The dressing of granite or any igneous rock by masons, the crushing of such materials or substantial exposure to the dust arising from such operations
	8 The use or preparation for use of an abrasive wheel or substantial exposure to the dust arising therefrom
	9 (a) Work underground in any mine in which one of the objects of the mining operations is the getting of any material;
	    (b) the working or handling above ground at any coal or tin mine of any materials extracted therefrom or any operation incidental thereto;
	    (c) the trimming of coal in any ship, barge, lighter, dock or harbour or at any wharf or quay; or
	    (d) the sawing, splitting or dressing of slate or any operation incidental thereto
	10 The manufacture or work incidental to the manufacture of carbon electrodes by an industrial undertaking for use in the electrolytic extraction of aluminium from aluminium oxide and any activity involving substantial exposure to the dust therefrom.
	11 Boiler scaling or substantial exposure to the dust arising therefrom

40 Byssinosis	The spinning or manipulation of raw or waste cotton or flax or the weaving of cotton or flax, carried out in each case in a room in a factory, together with any other work carried out in such a room
41 Mesothelioma	(a) The working or handling of asbestos or any admixture of asbestos;
42 Lung cancer	(b) the manufacture or repair of asbestos textiles or other articles containing or composed of asbestos;
43 Asbestosis	(c) the cleaning of any machinery or plant used in any of the foregoing operations and of any chambers, fixtures and appliances for the collection of asbestos dust; or (d) substantial exposure to the dust arising from any of the foregoing operations.

44 Cancer of the nasal cavity or associated air sinuses	1 (a) Work in or about a building where wooden furniture is manufactured;
	    (b) work in a building used for the manufacture of footwear or components of footwear made wholly or partly of leather or fibre board; or
	    (c) work at a place used wholly or mainly for the repair of footwear made wholly or partly of leather or fibre board
	2 Work in or about a factory building where nickel is produced by decomposition of a gaseous nickel compound or in any process which is ancillary or incidental thereto

45 Occupational dermatitis	Work involving exposure to any of the following agents: (a) epoxy resin systems; (b) formaldehyde and its resins; (c) metalworking fluids; (d) chromate (hexavalent and derived from trivalent chromium); (e) cement, plaster or concrete; (f) acrylates and methacrylates;

Column 1	Column 2
Diseases	**Activities**

	(g) colophony (rosin) and its modified products;
	(h) glutaraldehyde;
	(i) mercaptobenzothiazole, thiurams, substituted paraphenylene-diamines and related rubber processing chemicals;
	(j) biocides, anti-bacterials, preservatives or disinfectants;
	(k) organic solvents;
	(l) antibiotics and other pharmaceuticals and therapeutic agents;
	(m) strong acids, strong alkalis, strong solutions (eg brine) and oxidising agents including domestic bleach or reducing agents;
	(n) hairdressing products including in particular dyes, shampoos, bleaches and permanent waving solutions;
	(o) soaps and detergents;
	(p) plants and plant-derived material including in particular the daffodil, tulip and chrysanthemum families, the parsley family (carrots, parsnips, parsley and celery), garlic and onion, hardwoods and the pine family;
	(q) fish, shell-fish or meat;
	(r) sugar or flour; or
	(s) any other known irritant or sensitising agent including in particular any chemical bearing the warning "may cause sensitisation by skin contact" or "irritating to the skin"
46 Extrinsic alveolitis (including farmer's lung)	Exposure to moulds, fungal spores or heterologous proteins during work in:
	(a) agriculture, horticulture, forestry, cultivation of edible fungi or malt-working;
	(b) loading, unloading or handling mouldy vegetable matter or edible fungi whilst same is being stored;
	(c) caring for or handling birds; or
	(d) handling bagasse
47 Occupational asthma	Work involving exposure to any of the following agents:
	(a) isocyanates;
	(b) platinum salts;
	(c) fumes or dust arising from the manufacture, transport or use of hardening agents (including epoxy resin curing agents) based on phthalic anhydride, tetrachlorophthalic anhydride, trimellitic anhydride or triethylene-tetramine;
	(d) fumes arising from the use of rosin as a soldering flux;
	(e) proteolytic enzymes;
	(f) animals including insects and other arthropods used for the purposes of research or education or in laboratories;
	(g) dusts arising from the sowing, cultivation, harvesting, drying, handling, milling, transport or storage of barley, oats, rye, wheat or maize or the handling, milling, transport or storage of meal or flour made therefrom;
	(h) antibiotics;
	(i) cimetidine;
	(j) wood dust;
	(k) ispaghula;
	(l) castor bean dust;
	(m) ipecacuanha;
	(n) azodicarbonamide;
	(o) animals including insects and other arthropods (whether in their larval forms or not) used for the purposes of pest control or fruit cultivation or the larval forms of animals used for the purposes of research or education or in laboratories;
	(p) glutaraldehyde;
	(q) persulphate salts or henna;
	(r) crustaceans or fish or products arising from these in the food processing industry;

Column 1	Column 2
Diseases	**Activities**
	(s) reactive dyes;
	(t) soya bean;
	(u) tea dust;
	(v) green coffee bean dust;
	(w) fumes from stainless steel welding;
	(x) any other sensitising agent, including in particular any chemical bearing the warning "may cause sensitisation by inhalation"

8–16568

PART II
DISEASES ADDITIONALLY REPORTABLE IN RESPECT OF OFFSHORE WORKPLACES

48. Chickenpox.
49. Cholera.
50. Diphtheria.
51. Dysentery (amoebic or bacillary).
52. Acute encephalitis.
53. Erysipelas.
54. Food poisoning.
55. Legionellosis.
56. Malaria.
57. Measles.
58. Meningitis.
59. Meningococcal septicaemia (without meningitis).
60. Mumps.
61. Paratyphoid fever.
62. Plague.
63. Acute poliomyelitis.
64. Rabies.
65. Rubella.
66. Scarlet fever.
67. Tetanus.
68. Tuberculosis.
69. Typhoid fever.
70. Typhus.
71. Viral haemorrhagic fevers.
72. Viral hepatitis.

Regulation 7   SCHEDULE 4
                                        RECORDS

PART I
PARTICULARS TO BE KEPT IN RECORDS OF ANY EVENT WHICH IS REPORTABLE UNDER REGULATION 3

8–16569 1. Date and time of the accident or dangerous occurrence.
  2. In the event of an accident suffered by a person at work, the following particulars of that person—

  (a) full name;
  (b) occupation;
  (c) nature of injury.

  3. In the event of an accident suffered by a person not at work, the following particulars of that person (unless they are not known and it is not reasonably practicable to ascertain them)—

  (a) full name;
  (b) status (for example "passenger", "customer", "visitor" or "bystander");
  (c) nature of injury.

  4. Place where the accident or dangerous occurrence happened.
  5. A brief description of the circumstances in which the accident or dangerous occurrence happened.
  6. The date on which the event was first reported to the relevant enforcing authority.
  7. The method by which the event was reported.

PART II
PARTICULARS TO BE KEPT IN RECORDS OF INSTANCES OF ANY OF THE DISEASES SPECIFIED IN SCHEDULE 3 AND REPORTABLE
UNDER REGULATION 5

8–16570 1. Date of diagnosis of the disease.
  2. Name of the person affected.
  3. Occupation of the person affected.
  4. Name or nature of the disease.
  5. The date on which the disease was first reported to the relevant enforcing authority.
  6. The method by which the disease was reported.

Regulation 8 SCHEDULE 5
ADDITIONAL PROVISIONS RELATING TO MINES AND QUARRIES

8–16571 1. In this Schedule, unless the context otherwise requires—

"appropriate person" means—

(a) in the case of a coal mine, the responsible person or a person appointed in the management structure of that mine established pursuant to paragraph (1) of regulation 10 of the Management and Administration of Safety and Health at Mines Regulations 1993;

(b) in the case of any other mine, the responsible person;

(c) in the case of a quarry—

(i) the responsible person, or a person appointed in the management structure of that quarry established pursuant to paragraph (1) of regulation 8 of the Quarries Regulations 1999

"nominated person" means the person (if any) who is for the time being nominated—

(a) in a case where there is an association or body representative of a majority of the total number of persons employed at a mine or quarry, by that association or body;

(b) in any other case, jointly by associations or bodies which are together representative of such a majority,

to receive on behalf of the persons so employed notices under this Schedule.

2. Where at a mine or a quarry any person, as a result of an accident arising out of or in connection with work, dies or suffers any major injury, or where there is a dangerous occurrence, the responsible person shall—

(a) forthwith notify the nominated person thereof by the quickest practicable means; and

(b) within 7 days send a report thereof to the nominated person on a form approved for the purposes of regulation 3.

3. Where there is a non-fatal injury to any person at a mine or quarry which is reported in accordance with paragraph 2, after which that person dies and his death is as a result of the accident then as soon as it comes to his knowledge the responsible person shall give notice of the death to the nominated person.

4. (1) Where there is an accident or dangerous occurrence in relation to which paragraph 2 applies no person shall disturb the place where it happened or tamper with anything at that place before—

(a) the expiration of 3 clear days after the matter to which paragraph 2 applies has been notified in accordance with these Regulations; or

(b) the place has been visited by an inspector and by workmen's inspectors exercising the powers conferred on them by section 123 of the Mines and Quarries Act 1954 or, as the case may be, regulation 40 of the Quarries Regulations 1999;

whichever is the sooner.

(2) Nothing in sub-paragraph (1) of this paragraph shall prohibit the doing of anything by or with the consent of an inspector.

(3) The requirements of sub-paragraph (1) of this paragraph shall not apply to an accident or to a dangerous occurrence if an appropriate person—

(a) has taken adequate steps to ascertain that disturbing the site—

(i) is unlikely to prejudice any investigation by an inspector into the circumstances of the accident or dangerous occurrence, and

(ii) is necessary to secure the safety of any person at the mine or quarry or to avoid disrupting the normal working thereof; and

(b) (except in the case of a non-fatal accident or a dangerous occurrence, where the nominated person or any person designated by that nominated person pursuant to this sub-paragraph cannot be contacted within a reasonable time) has notified the nominated person, or any person designated in writing by the nominated person to receive any such notification, of the proposed disturbance, and gives such a person a reasonable opportunity to visit the site before it is disturbed; and

(c) has taken adequate steps to ensure that there is obtained such information as will enable a full and accurate plan to be prepared forthwith, which plan shall show the position of any equipment or other item relevant to the accident or dangerous occurrence immediately after it happened; and

(d) ensures that any equipment or other item relevant to the accident or dangerous occurrence is kept as it was immediately after the incident until an inspector agrees that it may be disposed of.

(4) The person who has taken the steps referred to in sub-paragraph (3)(c) of this paragraph shall ensure that the plan referred to in that sub-paragraph is signed by the person who prepared it and bears the date on which it was prepared, and that a copy of that plan is supplied on request to any inspector or to the nominated person.

(5) It shall be a defence in proceedings against any person for contravening sub-paragraph (1) of this paragraph in any case which consists of the doing of any act, for that person to prove that the doing of that act was necessary for securing the safety of the mine or quarry or of any person.

5. The record kept under regulation 7, excluding any health record of an identifiable individual, shall be available for inspection by—

(a) the nominated person; and

(b) workmen's inspectors exercising the powers conferred on them by section 123 of the Mines and Quarries Act 1954 or, as the case may be, regulation 40 of the Quarries Regulations 1999.

Regulation 9 SCHEDULE 6
ADDITIONAL PROVISIONS RELATING TO OFFSHORE WORKPLACES

8–16572 1. **Disturbance of site.** (1) In any case where any person, as a result of an accident arising out of or in connection with work at an offshore workplace, dies or suffers a major injury, no person shall disturb the place where it happened or tamper with anything at that place before—

(a) the expiration of 3 clear days after the matter has been notified in accordance with these Regulations; or
(b) the place has been visited by an inspector;

whichever is the sooner.

(2) Nothing in sub-paragraph (1) of this paragraph shall prohibit the doing of anything by or with the consent of an inspector or the doing of anything necessary to secure the safety of the workplace or of any person, plant or vessel.

8–16573

Regulation 10(4)   SCHEDULE 7
ENACTMENTS OR INSTRUMENTS REQUIRING THE NOTIFICATION OF EVENTS WHICH ARE NOT REQUIRED TO BE NOTIFIED OR REPORTED
UNDER THESE REGULATIONS

Regulation 15   SCHEDULE 8
8–16574

PART I
REVOCATIONS

Column 1	Column 2	Column 3
Title of Instrument	**Reference**	**Extent of Revocation**
The Reporting of Injuries, Diseases and Dangerous Occurrences Regulations 1985	SI 1985/2023	The whole Regulations
The Reporting of Injuries, Diseases and Dangerous Occurrences (Amendment) Regulations 1989	SI 1989/1457	The whole Regulations
The Offshore Installations (Inspectors and Casualties) Regulations 1973	SI 1973/1842	Part II and the Schedule; and the entry relating to "disease" in regulation 1(2)
The Submarine Pipe-lines (Inspectors etc) Regulations 1977	SI 1977/835	Regulations 5 and 6, the reference to regulations 5 and 6 in regulation 7(1)(a), and Schedule 2
The Railways (Notice of Accidents) Order 1986	SI 1986/2187	The whole Order
The Offshore Installations (Amendment) Regulations 1991	SI 1991/679	The whole Regulations

Health and Safety at Work etc Act 1974 (Application outside Great Britain) Order 2001[1]
(SI 2001/2127)

8–16600   1. Citation, commencement and revocation.   (1) This Order may be cited as the Health and Safety at Work etc Act 1974 (Application outside Great Britain) Order 2001 and shall come into force on 11th July 2001.

(2) The Health and Safety at Work etc Act 1974 (Application outside Great Britain) Order 1995 is hereby revoked.

---

1. Made under s 84 of the Health and Safety at Work Act 1974.

8–16601   2. Interpretation.   (1) In this Order, unless the context otherwise requires—

"the 1974 Act" means the Health and Safety at Work etc Act 1974;

"activity" includes a diving project;

"designated area" means any area designated by order under section 1(7) of the Continental Shelf Act 1964 and "within a designated area" includes over and under it;

"diving project" has the same meaning as it has in the Diving at Work Regulations 1997 save that it includes an activity in which a person takes part as a diver wearing an atmospheric pressure suit and without breathing in air or other gas at a pressure greater than atmospheric pressure;

"energy structure" means a fixed or floating structure, other than a vessel, for producing energy from wind or water;

"offshore installation" shall be construed in accordance with article 4(2) and (3) of this Order;

"the prescribed provisions of the 1974 Act" means sections 1 to 59 and 80 to 82 of the 1974 Act;

"supplementary unit" means a fixed or floating structure, other than a vessel, for providing energy, information or substances to an offshore installation;

"stand-by vessel" means a vessel which is ready to give assistance in the event of an emergency on or near an offshore installation;

"territorial sea" means the territorial sea adjacent to Great Britain and "within the territorial sea" includes on, over and under it;

"vessel" includes a hovercraft and any floating structure which is capable of being staffed.

(2) For the purposes of this Order, any structures and devices on top of a well shall be treated as forming part of the well.

8–16602   3. Application of the 1974 Act outside Great Britain. (1) The prescribed provisions of the 1974 Act shall, to the extent specified in the following articles of this Order, apply to and in relation to the premises and activities outside Great Britain which are so specified as those provisions apply within Great Britain.

(2) The reference in paragraph (1) of this article to premises and activities includes a reference to any person, article or substance on those premises or engaged in or, as the case may be, used or for use in connection with any such activity, but does not include a reference to an aircraft which is airborne.

8–16603   4. Offshore installations. (1) The prescribed provisions of the 1974 Act shall apply within the territorial sea or a designated area to and in relation to—

(a) any offshore installation and any activity on it;

(b) any activity in connection with an offshore installation, or any activity which is immediately preparatory thereto, whether carried on from the installation itself, in or from a vessel or in any other manner, other than—

(i) transporting, towing or navigating the installation; and

(ii) any activity in or from a vessel being used as a stand-by vessel;

(c) a diving project involving—

(i) the survey and preparation of the sea bed for an offshore installation;

(ii) the survey and restoration of the sea bed consequent on the removal of an offshore installation.

(2) In this Order "offshore installation" means—

(a) the fixed structures consisting of six towers referred to in the Schedule to this Order as NSR M-1, NSR R-1, NSR R-2, NSR R-3, NSR R-4 and NSR R-5 and settled on the sea bed at the locations specified in the Schedule and the related cables between each of those towers at sea bed level and the related cables which lie or extend outside the said locations; or

(b) subject to paragraph (3) of this article, a structure which is, or is to be, or has been, used while standing or stationed in water, or on the foreshore or other land intermittently covered with water—

(i) for the exploitation, or exploration with a view to exploitation, of mineral resources by means of a well;

(ii) for the storage of gas in or under the shore or bed of any water or the recovery of gas so stored;

(iii) for the conveyance of things by means of a pipe; or

(iv) mainly for the provision of accommodation for persons who work on or from a structure falling within any of the provisions of this sub-paragraph,

together with any supplementary unit which is ordinarily connected to it, and all the connections.

(3) Any reference in paragraph (2)(b) to a structure or unit does not include—

(a) a structure which is connected with dry land by a permanent structure providing access at all times and for all purposes;

(b) a well;

(c) a structure which has ceased to be used for any of the purposes specified in paragraph (2)(b) of this article and has since been used for a purpose not so specified;

(d) a mobile structure which has been taken out of use and is not yet being moved with a view to its being used for any of the purposes specified in paragraph (2)(b) of this article; and

(e) any part of a pipeline.

8–16604   5. Wells. (1) Subject to paragraph (2) of this article, the prescribed provisions of the 1974 Act shall apply within the territorial sea or a designated area to and in relation to—

(a) a well and any activity in connection with it; and

(b) an activity which is immediately preparatory to any activity in sub-paragraph (a) above.

(2) Paragraph (1) of this article includes keeping a vessel on station for the purpose of working on a well but otherwise does not include navigation or an activity connected with navigation.

8–16605   6. Pipelines. (1) The prescribed provisions of the 1974 Act shall apply within the territorial sea or a designated area to and in relation to—

(a) any pipeline;

(b) any pipeline works;

(c) the following activities in connection with pipeline works—

(i) the loading, unloading, fuelling or provisioning of a vessel;

(ii) the loading, unloading, fuelling, repair and maintenance of an aircraft in a vessel, being in either case a vessel which is engaged in pipeline works.

(2) In this article—

"pipeline" means a pipe or system of pipes for the conveyance of any thing, together with—

(a) any apparatus for inducing or facilitating the flow of any thing through, or through part of, the pipe or system;

(b) any apparatus for treating or cooling any thing which is to flow through, or through part of, the pipe or system;

(c) valves, valve chambers and similar works which are annexed to, or incorporated in the course of, the pipe or system;

(d) apparatus for supplying energy for the operation of any such apparatus or works as are mentioned in the preceding paragraphs;

(e) apparatus for the transmission of information for the operation of the pipe or system;

(f) apparatus for the cathodic protection of the pipe or system; and

(g) a structure used or to be used solely for the support of a part of the pipe or system;

but not including a pipeline of which no initial or terminal point is situated in the United Kingdom, within the territorial sea adjacent to the United Kingdom, or within a designated area;

"pipeline works" means—

(a) assembling or placing a pipeline or length of pipeline including the provision of internal or external protection for it;

(b) inspecting, testing, maintaining, adjusting, repairing, altering or renewing a pipeline or length of pipeline;

(c) changing the position of or dismantling or removing a pipeline or length of pipeline;

(d) opening the bed of the sea for the purposes of the works mentioned in sub-paragraphs (a) to (c) of this definition, and tunnelling or boring for those purposes;

(e) any activities incidental to the activities described in sub-paragraphs (a) to (d) of this definition;

(f) a diving project in connection with any of the works mentioned in sub-paragraphs (a) to (e) of this definition or for the purpose of determining whether a place is suitable as part of the site of a proposed pipeline and the carrying out of surveying operations for settling the route of a proposed pipeline.

8–16606   7. Mines.   (1) The prescribed provisions of the 1974 Act shall apply to and in relation to a mine within the territorial sea or extending beyond it, and any activity in connection with it, while it is being worked.

(2) In this article "mine" has the same meaning as in the Mines and Quarries Act 1954 ("the 1954 Act").

(3) For the purposes of this article a mine shall be treated as being worked when it is to be so treated for the purposes of the 1954 Act.

8–16607   8. Other activities within the territorial sea.   (1) Subject to paragraph (2), the prescribed provisions of the 1974 Act shall apply within the territorial sea to and in relation to—

(a) the construction, reconstruction, alteration, repair, maintenance, cleaning, use, operation, demolition and dismantling of any building, energy structure or other structure, not being in any case a vessel, or any preparation for any such activity;

(b) the transfer of people or goods between a vessel or aircraft and a structure (including a building) mentioned in sub-paragraph (a) of this paragraph;

(c) the loading, unloading, fuelling or provisioning of a vessel;

(d) a diving project;

(e) the construction, reconstruction, finishing, refitting, repair, maintenance, cleaning or breaking up of a vessel except when carried out by the master or any officer or member of the crew of that vessel;

(f) the maintaining on a station of a vessel which would be an offshore installation were it not a structure to which paragraph (3)(d) of article 4 of this Order applies;

(g) the operation of a cable for transmitting electricity from an energy structure to Great Britain;

(h) the transfer of people or goods between a vessel or aircraft and a structure mentioned in sub-paragraph (f) of this paragraph.

(2) This article shall not apply—

(a) to a case where article 4, 5, 6 or 7 of this Order applies; or

(b) to vessels which are registered outside the United Kingdom and are on passage through the territorial sea.

8–16608   9. Legal proceedings.   (1) Proceedings for any offence under section 33 of the 1974 Act, being an offence to which that section applies by virtue of this Order, may be taken, and the offence may for all incidental purposes be treated as having been committed, in any place in Great Britain.

(2) Section 3 of the Territorial Waters Jurisdiction Act 1878 (which requires certain consents for the institution of proceedings) shall not apply to proceedings for any offence to which paragraph (1) of this article relates.

8–16609　10. Miscellaneous provisions.　The prescribed provisions of the 1974 Act shall apply in accordance with this Order to individuals whether or not they are British subjects, and to bodies corporate whether or not they are incorporated under the law of any part of the United Kingdom.

8–16610　11.　Nothing in this Order except article 9(2) of this Order shall be taken to limit or prejudice the operation which any Act or legislative instrument may, apart from this Order, have in the territorial sea or elsewhere.

8–16611

Article 4(2)(*a*)

SCHEDULE
LOCATION OF TOWERS

Title		Degrees	Minutes	Seconds	
NSR M-1	Latitude	53	44	45	N
	Longitude	02	33	30	E
NSR R-1	Latitude	53	56	00	N
	Longitude	02	24	00	E
NSR R-2	Latitude	53	55	45	N
	Longitude	02	51	00	E
NSR R-3	Latitude	53	38	30	N
	Longitude	02	56	45	E
NSR R-4	Latitude	53	29	57	N
	Longitude	02	30	50	E
NSR R-5	Latitude	53	42	00	N
	Longitude	02	08	30	E

Fireworks Regulations 2004[1]

(SI 2004/1836 amended by SI 2004/3262)

8–16612　1. Citation, commencement and extent.　(1) These Regulations may be cited as the Fireworks Regulations 2004 and, except for regulations 9 and 11, shall come into force on 7th August 2004.

(2) Regulations 9 and 11 shall come into force on 1st January 2005.

(3) These Regulations shall not extend to Northern Ireland.

(4) Regulation 7 of these Regulations shall not extend to Scotland.

---

1. Made by the Secretary of State, in exercise of the powers conferred upon her by ss 2–5 and 7–9 of the Fireworks Act 2003 and by ss 11(3) and 27(2) of the Consumer Protection Act 1987.

8–16613　2. Revocation of the Fireworks Regulations 2003.　The Fireworks Regulations 2003 are revoked.

8–16614　3. Interpretation.　In these Regulations—

"adult firework" means—

(*a*) any firework which does not comply with the relevant requirements of Part 2 of BS 7114 when tested in accordance with the appropriate test method (if any) in Part 3 of BS 7114; or

(*b*) any firework (except for a cap, cracker snap, novelty match, party popper, serpent, sparkler or throwdown) which does comply with those requirements;

"amorce" means a firework which is a percussion cap designed for use in toys, which comprises a paper envelope containing a dot of impact-sensitive pyrotechnic composition and which forms part of a roll;

"assembly" means an assembly which includes any firework;

"BS 7114" means the British Standard Specification comprising the following parts—

(*a*) BS 7114: Part 1: 1988, the British Standard Specification for classification of fireworks published on 30th November 1988;

(*b*) BS 7114: Part 2: 1988, the British Standard Specification for fireworks published on 30th November 1988; and

(*c*) BS 7114: Part 3: 1988, the British Standard Specification for methods of test for fireworks published on 30th November 1988;

and references to Parts 1, 2 and 3 of BS 7114 shall be construed accordingly;

"BS EN 61672" means the British Standard Specification comprising the following parts—

(*a*) BS EN 61672–1:2003, "Electroacoustics. Sound Level Meters. Specifications", published on 25th March 2003; and

(*b*) BS EN 61672–2:2003, "Electroacoustics. Sound Level Meters. Pattern Evaluation Tests", published on 11th July 2003;

"cap" means a firework (including an amorce) designed for use in toys which comprises a non-metallic envelope or cup containing a dot of impact-sensitive pyrotechnic composition, and which produces a report when it is hit;

"category 3 firework" means a firework classified as category 3 under Part 1 of BS 7114;

"category 4 firework" means a firework classified as category 4 under Part 1 of BS 7114;

"cracker snap" means a firework—

(a) which comprises two overlapping strips of card or paper with a friction-sensitive explosive composition in sliding contact with an abrasive surface; and

(b) which produces a report when pulled apart;

"explosives" has the same meaning as in the Explosives Act 1875

"local licensing authority" means in relation to—

(a) the City of London, the Common Council for the City of London;

(b) an area in the rest of London, the London Borough Council for that area;

(c) an area where there is a fire and civil defence authority, that authority;

(d) the Isles of Scilly, the Council of the Isles of Scilly;

(e) an area in the rest of England, the county council for that area or where there is no county council for that area, the district council for that area;

(f) an area in Scotland, the council for the local government area; and

(g) an area in Wales, the county council or the county borough council for that area;

"novelty match" means a firework comprising a match with a dot of pyrotechnic composition which is designed to be held in the hand while functioning and whose functioning involves a report or the production of visual effects, or both;

"party popper" means a firework comprising a device—

(a) which is designed to be held in the hand while functioning;

(b) which is operated by a pull-string with an abrasive surface in sliding contact with a friction-sensitive pyrotechnic composition; and

(c) whose functioning involves a report with the ejection of streamers or confetti, or both;

"pyrotechnic composition" means a substance or a mixture of a substance designed to produce an effect by heat, light, sound, gas or smoke or a combination of these as the result of non-detonative self-sustaining exothermic chemical reactions;

"serpent" means a firework, comprising a pre-formed shape of pyrotechnic composition, with or without support, whose functioning involves the generation of expanded residue;

"sparkler" means a firework, other than a category 3 or category 4 firework, comprising a rigid wire partially coated with slow-burning pyrotechnic composition, whose functioning involves the emission of sparks without a report;

"the 1987 Act" means the Consumer Protection Act 1987;

"the 2003 Act" means the Fireworks Act 2003;

"the 1997 Regulations" means the Fireworks (Safety) Regulations 1997;

"the court" means—

(a) in relation to a decision by a local licensing authority located in England and Wales, a magistrates' court in whose jurisdiction the local licensing authority is situated; and

(b) in relation to a decision by a local licensing authority located in Scotland, the sheriff in whose jurisdiction the local licensing authority is situated;

"the importation enforcement duty" means the duty imposed by section 27(1) of the 1987 Act, insofar as that duty is, by virtue of section 12(1) of the 2003 Act, exercisable in relation to the enforcement of the prohibition imposed by regulation 11 below;

"the licensing enforcement duty" means the duty imposed by section 27(1) of the 1987 Act, insofar as that duty is, by virtue of section 12(1) of the 2003 Act, exercisable in relation to the enforcement of the prohibition imposed by regulation 9 below;

"the possession enforcement duty" means the duty imposed by section 27(1) of the 1987 Act, insofar as that duty is, by virtue of section 12(1) of the 2003 Act, exercisable in relation to the enforcement of the prohibitions imposed by regulations 4 and 5 below;

"the use enforcement duty" means the duty imposed by section 27(1) of the 1987 Act, insofar as that duty is, by virtue of section 12(1) of the 2003 Act, exercisable in relation to the enforcement of the prohibition imposed by regulation 7 below; and

"throwdown" means a firework comprising impact-sensitive explosive composition and grains of inert material wrapped in paper or foil and which functions to produce a report when thrown onto the ground.

8–16615   4. Prohibition of possession of fireworks by persons below the age of eighteen.
(1) Subject to regulation 6 below, no person under the age of eighteen years shall possess an adult firework in a public place[1].

(2) In paragraph (1) above "public place" includes any place to which at the material time the public have or are permitted access, whether on payment or otherwise.

---

1. Contravention of this provision is an offence by virtue of s 11 of the Fireworks Act 2003, in this title, ante. For time limit on prosecutions, see reg 13, post.

8–16616 5. Prohibition of possession of category 4 fireworks. Subject to regulation 6 below, no person shall possess a category 4 firework[1].

---

1. Contravention of this provision is an offence by virtue of s 11 of the Fireworks Act 2003, in this title, ante. For time limit on prosecutions, see reg 13, post.

8–16617 6. Exceptions to regulations 4 and 5. (1) Regulations 4 and 5 above shall not prohibit the possession of any firework by—

(a) any person who is employed by, or in business as, a professional organiser or operator of firework displays and who possesses the firework in question for the purposes of his employment or business;

(b) any person who is employed in, or whose trade or business (or part of whose trade or business) is, the manufacture of fireworks or assemblies and who possesses the firework in question for the purposes of his trade, employment or business;

(c) any person who is employed in, or whose trade or business (or part of whose trade or business) is, the supply of fireworks or assemblies, for the purpose of supplying them in accordance with the provisions of the 1997 Regulations;

(d) any person who is employed by a local authority and who, in the course of his employment, possesses the firework in question for any of the following purposes—

(i) the putting on of a firework display by that local authority; or

(ii) the use by that local authority of the firework in question at a national public celebration or a national commemorative event;

(e) any person for use, in the course of a trade or business of his or in the course of his employment, for special effects purposes in the theatre, on film or on television;

(f) any person employed by or otherwise acting on behalf of a local authority, enforcement authority or other body, where—

(i) the authority or body has enforcement powers, conferred by or under any enactment, applying to the firework in question; and

(ii) the person so employed possesses the firework in question for the purposes of the authority or body exercising those enforcement powers;

(g) any person who is employed by a department of the Government of the United Kingdom and who, in the course of his employment, possesses the firework in question for any of the following purposes—

(i) the putting on of a firework display by that department;

(ii) the use by that department of the firework in question at a national public celebration or a national commemorative event; or

(iii) the use by that department of the firework in question for research or investigations;

(h) any person who—

(i) is in business as or employed by a supplier of goods designed and intended for use in conjunction with fireworks or assemblies; and

(ii) possesses the firework in question solely for the purposes of testing those goods to ensure that, when used in conjunction with fireworks or assemblies of the same type, they will perform their intended function or comply with any provision made by or under any enactment and relating to the safety of those goods; or

(i) any person who is employed by an establishment of the naval, military or air forces of the Crown and who, in the course of his employment, possesses the firework in question for any of the following purposes—

(i) the putting on of a fireworks display by that establishment; or

(ii) the use by that establishment of the firework in question at a national public celebration or a national commemorative event.

(2) Regulation 5 above shall not prohibit the possession of any firework by any person who is employed in, or whose trade or business (or part of whose trade or business) is, the transport of fireworks and who possesses the firework in question for the purposes of his trade, employment or business.

8–16618 7. Prohibition of use of certain fireworks at night. (1) Subject to paragraph (2) below, no person shall use an adult firework during night hours[1].

(2) Paragraph (1) above shall not prohibit the use of a firework—

(a) during a permitted fireworks night; or

(b) by any person who is employed by a local authority and who uses the firework in question—

(i) for the purposes of putting on a firework display by that local authority; or

(ii) at a national public celebration or a national commemorative event.

(3) In this regulation, "night hours" means the period beginning at 11 pm and ending at 7 am the following day and a "permitted fireworks night" means a period—

(a) beginning at 11 pm on the first day of the Chinese New Year and ending at 1 am the following day;
(b) beginning at 11pm and ending at midnight on 5th November;
(c) beginning at 11 pm on the day of Diwali and ending at 1 am the following day; or
(d) beginning at 11 pm on 31st December and ending at 1 am the following day.

---

1. Contravention of this provision is an offence by virtue of s 11 of the Fireworks Act 2003, in this title, ante. For time limit on prosecutions, see reg 13, post.

8–16619 8. Prohibition of supply of excessively loud category 3 fireworks. (1) No person shall supply, or offer or agree to supply, any category 3 firework which, when used, produces a maximum A-weighted impulse sound pressure level exceeding 120 decibels when measured in accordance with paragraph (2) below[1].

(2) For the purposes of paragraph (1) above, the sound pressure level is to be measured—

(a) at a horizontal distance of fifteen metres from the testing point at a height of one metre above the ground; and
(b) using a sound measuring device which conforms to type 1 of BS EN 61672 with a free-field microphone.

---

1. Contravention of this provision is an offence by virtue of s 11 of the Fireworks Act 2003, in this title, ante. For time limit on prosecutions, see reg 13, post.

8–16620 9. Licensing of fireworks suppliers. (1) Subject to paragraphs (2) and (2A) below, no person shall supply or expose for supply any adult firework, save in accordance with either—

(a) a licence granted in respect of each premises under his control at which the fireworks are supplied or exposed for supply; or
(b) a licence granted to him, if the fireworks which he supplies or exposes for supply are kept at premises which are not under his control.

(2) Paragraph (1) above shall not prohibit the supply or exposing for supply, otherwise than in accordance with a licence, of adult fireworks—

(a) on the first day of the Chinese New Year and the three days immediately preceding it;
(b) on the day of Diwali and the three days immediately preceding it;
(c) during the period beginning on the 15th October and ending on the 10th November; or
(d) during the period beginning on the 26th December and ending on the 31st December.

(2A) Paragraph (1) above shall not prohibit the supply or exposing for supply, otherwise than in accordance with a licence, of adult fireworks—

(a) to a person who is employed in, or whose trade or business (or part of whose trade or business) is the supply of fireworks or assemblies, for the purpose of that person's supplying them in accordance with the provisions of the 1997 Regulations;
(b) to a person who is employed by, or in business as, a professional organiser or operator of firework displays for the purpose of that person's employment or business; or
(c) to a person who is employed in, or whose trade or business (or part of whose trade or business) is, the transport of fireworks, for the purpose of that person's trade, employment or business.

(3) An application for a licence under this regulation shall be made to the local licensing authority in whose area—

(a) the premises concerned are located in the case of a licence mentioned in paragraph (1)(a) above, or
(b) the principal business premises of the applicant are located in the case of a licence mentioned in paragraph (1)(b) above.

(4) A local licensing authority shall not grant a licence unless it is satisfied—

(a) in the case of an application under paragraph (3)(a) above, that the premises which are the subject of the application, are licensed or registered in accordance with the Explosives Act 1875; or
(b) in the case of an application under paragraph (3)(b) above, that the fireworks which will be supplied or exposed for supply by the applicant, will be kept at premises which are licensed or registered in accordance with that Act.

(5) A local licensing authority may refuse to grant a licence, or may revoke a licence which it has granted, if the applicant has committed—

(a) an offence under section 11 of the 2003 Act;
(b) an offence under section 12 of the 1987 Act arising from a contravention of the 1997 Regulations;
(c) an offence under sections 4, 5 or 32 of the Explosives Act 1875; or
(d) an offence in relation to the use, storage or keeping of fireworks under the Health and Safety at Work etc Act 1974.

(6) Where a local licensing authority refuses to grant a licence, or revokes a licence, it shall notify the applicant of its decision.

(7) A local licensing authority shall charge a fee of £500 a year in connection with the grant of a licence in accordance with this regulation.

(8) A person may appeal to the court against a decision of a local licensing authority to refuse to grant him a licence, or to revoke a licence, and any such appeal shall be made within 28 days of the decision in question being notified to that person.

---

1. Contravention of this provision is an offence by virtue of s 11 of the Fireworks Act 2003, in this title, ante. For time limit on prosecutions, see reg 13, post.

**8-16621	10. Information about fireworks.** (1) No person shall supply or expose for supply[1] any adult firework or sparkler unless—

(a) where adult fireworks or sparklers are supplied or exposed for supply in any premises, he displays in a prominent position in those premises a notice, which measures no less than 420 millimetres by 297 millimetres and whose letters are no less than 16 millimetres high, stating the required information, or

(b) where adult fireworks or sparklers are supplied or exposed for supply in circumstances not mentioned in sub-paragraph (a) above, he gives the required information to any person to whom the fireworks are supplied or exposed for supply.

(2) In paragraph (1) above, "the required information" means information that—

(a) it is illegal to sell adult fireworks or sparklers to anyone under the age of eighteen; and

(b) it is illegal for anyone under the age of eighteen to possess adult fireworks in a public place.

(3) No person shall supply[1] any adult firework unless he maintains for a period of three years, beginning with the date on which he supplies that firework, a record of the following information—

(a) the name and address of the person who supplied the firework to him;

(b) the name and address of the person to whom he is supplying the firework;

(c) the date when the firework was supplied to him;

(d) the date when he supplied the firework to another person; and

(e) the total amount of explosives contained in the firework supplied.

(3A) A person who supplies adult fireworks shall, if requested by a local licensing authority within the period mentioned in paragraph (3) above to provide any of the information mentioned in that paragraph, provide to that authority such information as is specified in the request.

(4) Paragraphs (3) and (3A) above shall not apply if, in a single transaction, the total amount of the explosives contained in the fireworks supplied is less than or equal to 50 kilograms.

---

1. Contravention of this provision is an offence by virtue of s 11 of the Fireworks Act 2003, in this title, ante. For time limit on prosecutions, see reg 13, post.

**8-16622	11. Importation of fireworks.** No person shall import any firework, unless he has given the following information to the Commissioners of Customs and Excise—

(a) his name and address;

(b) the name of the person who is to store the fireworks following their importation; and

(c) the address of the premises at which the fireworks are to be stored following their importation[1].

---

1. Contravention of this provision is an offence by virtue of s 11 of the Fireworks Act 2003, in this title, ante. For time limit on prosecutions, see reg 13, post.

**8-16623	12. Transfer of enforcement duties.** (1) The possession enforcement duty in England and Wales is hereby transferred to the chief officer of police of each police force and shall be the duty of every chief officer of police in relation to the police area for which the force in question is maintained.

(2) The possession enforcement duty in Scotland is hereby transferred to the chief constable of each police force and shall be the duty of every chief constable in relation to the police area for which the force in question is maintained.

(3) The use enforcement duty in England and Wales is hereby transferred to the chief officer of police of each police force and shall be the duty of every chief officer of police in relation to the police area for which the force in question is maintained.

(4) The importation enforcement duty is hereby transferred to the Commissioners of Customs and Excise and shall be the duty of the Commissioners of Customs and Excise.

(5) Every weights and measures authority of Great Britain is hereby relieved of the possession enforcement duty and the importation enforcement duty.

(6) Every weights and measures authority in England and Wales is hereby relieved of the use enforcement duty.

(7) In relation to every metropolitan county, the licensing enforcement duty is hereby transferred to the fire and rescue authority for that county and any weights and measures

authority for that county or any part of that county is hereby relieved of the licensing enforcement duty.

8–16623A 13. Proceedings. In England and Wales a magistrates' court may try an information in respect of an offence under section 11 of the 2003 Act arising from a contravention of a prohibition imposed by these Regulations if the information is laid within twelve months from the time when the offence was committed, and in Scotland summary proceedings for such an offence may be brought at any time within twelve months from the time when the offence was committed.

Regulatory Reform (Fire Safety) Order 2005[1]
(SI 2005/1541)

PART 1
GENERAL

8–16624 1. Citation, commencement and extent. (1) This Order may be cited as the Regulatory Reform (Fire Safety) Order 2005 and shall come into force in accordance with paragraphs (2) and (3).

(2) This article and article 52(1)(*a*) shall come into force on the day after the day on which this Order is made.

(3) The remaining provisions of this Order shall come into force on 1st April 2006.

(4) This Order extends to England and Wales only.

---

1. Made by the First Secretary of State, in exercise of the powers conferred by section 1 of the Regulatory Reform Act 2001.

8–16625 2. Interpretation. In this Order—

"alterations notice" has the meaning given by article 29;

"approved classification and labelling guide" means the Approved Guide to the Classification and Labelling of Dangerous Substances and Dangerous Preparations (5th edition) approved by the Health and Safety Commission on 16th April 2002;

"the CHIP Regulations" means the Chemicals (Hazard Information and Packaging for Supply) Regulations 2002;

"child" means a person who is not over compulsory school age, construed in accordance with section 8 of the Education Act 1996;

"dangerous substance" means—

(*a*) a substance or preparation which meets the criteria in the approved classification and labelling guide for classification as a substance or preparation which is explosive, oxidising, extremely flammable, highly flammable or flammable, whether or not that substance or preparation is classified under the CHIP Regulations;

(*b*) a substance or preparation which because of its physico-chemical or chemical properties and the way it is used or is present in or on premises creates a risk; and

(*c*) any dust, whether in the form of solid particles or fibrous materials or otherwise, which can form an explosive mixture with air or an explosive atmosphere;

"domestic premises" means premises occupied as a private dwelling (including any garden, yard, garage, outhouse, or other appurtenance of such premises which is not used in common by the occupants of more than one such dwelling);

"employee" means a person who is or is treated as an employee for the purposes of the Health and Safety at Work etc Act 1974 and related expressions are to be construed accordingly;

"enforcement notice" has the meaning given by article 30;

"enforcing authority" has the meaning given by article 25;

"explosive atmosphere" means a mixture, under atmospheric conditions, of air and one or more dangerous substances in the form of gases, vapours, mists or dusts in which, after ignition has occurred, combustion spreads to the entire unburned mixture;

"fire and rescue authority" means a fire and rescue authority under the Fire and Rescue Services Act 2004;

"fire inspector" means an inspector or assistant inspector appointed under section 28 of the Fire and Rescue Services Act 2004;

"general fire precautions" has the meaning given by article 4;

"hazard", in relation to a dangerous substance, means the physico-chemical or chemical property of that substance which has the potential to give rise to fire affecting the safety of a person, and references in this Order to "hazardous" are to be construed accordingly;

"inspector" means an inspector appointed under article 26 or a fire inspector;

"licensing authority" has the meaning given by article 42(3);

"normal ship-board activities" include the repair of a ship, save repair when carried out in dry dock;

"owner" means the person for the time being receiving the rackrent of the premises in connection with which the word is used, whether on his own account or as agent or trustee for another person, or who would so receive the rackrent if the premises were let at a rackrent;

"personal protective equipment" means all equipment which is intended to be worn or held by a person in or on premises and which protects that person against one or more risks to his safety, and any addition or accessory designed to meet that objective;

"place of safety" in relation to premises, means a safe area beyond the premises.

"premises" includes any place and, in particular, includes—

    (a) any workplace;

    (b) any vehicle, vessel, aircraft or hovercraft;

    (c) any installation on land (including the foreshore and other land intermittently covered by water), and any other installation (whether floating, or resting on the seabed or the subsoil thereof, or resting on other land covered with water or the subsoil thereof); and

    (d) any tent or movable structure;

"preparation" means a mixture or solution of two or more substances;

"preventive and protective measures" means the measures which have been identified by the responsible person in consequence of a risk assessment as the general fire precautions he needs to take to comply with the requirements and prohibitions imposed on him by or under this Order;

"prohibition notice" has the meaning given by article 31;

"public road" means a highway maintainable at public expense within the meaning of section 329 of the Highways Act 1980;

"rackrent" in relation to premises, means a rent that is not less than two-thirds of the rent at which the property might reasonably be expected to be let from year to year, free from all usual tenant's rates and taxes, and deducting from it the probable average cost of the repairs, insurance and other expenses (if any) necessary to maintain the property in a state to command such rent;

"the relevant local authority", in relation to premises, means—

    (a) if the premises are in Greater London but are not in the City of London, the London Borough in the area of which the premises are situated;

    (b) if the premises are in the City of London, the Common Council of the City of London;

    (c) if the premises are in England in a metropolitan county, the district council in the area of which the premises are situated;

    (d) if the premises are in England but are not in Greater London or a metropolitan county—

        (i) the county council in the area of which the premises are situated; or

        (ii) if there is no county council in the area of which the premises are situated, the district council in that area;

    (e) if the premises are in Wales, the county council or county borough council in the area of which the premises are situated;

"relevant persons" means—

    (a) any person (including the responsible person) who is or may be lawfully on the premises; and

    (b) any person in the immediate vicinity of the premises who is at risk from a fire on the premises,

but does not include a fire-fighter who is carrying out his duties in relation to a function of a fire and rescue authority under section 7, 8 or 9 of the Fire and Rescue Services Act 2004 (fire-fighting, road traffic accidents and other emergencies), other than in relation to a function under section 7(2)(d), 8(2)(d) or 9(3)(d) of that Act;

"responsible person" has the meaning given by article 3;

"risk" means the risk to the safety of persons from fire;

"risk assessment" means the assessment required by article 9(1);

"safety" means the safety of persons in respect of harm caused by fire; and "safe" shall be interpreted accordingly;

"safety data sheet" means a safety data sheet within the meaning of regulation 5 of the CHIP Regulations;

"ship" includes every description of vessel used in navigation;

"special, technical and organisational measures" include—

    (a) technical means of supervision;

    (b) connecting devices;

    (c) control and protection systems;

    (d) engineering controls and solutions;

    (e) equipment;

    (f) materials;

    (g) protective systems; and

    (h) warning and other communication systems;

"substance" means any natural or artificial substance whether in solid or liquid form or in the form of a gas or vapour;

"visiting force" means any such body, contingent, or detachment of the forces of any country as is a visiting force for the purposes of any of the provisions of the Visiting Forces Act 1952;
"workplace" means any premises or parts of premises, not being domestic premises, used for the purposes of an employer's undertaking and which are made available to an employee of the employer as a place of work and includes—

(a) any place within the premises to which such employee has access while at work; and
(b) any room, lobby, corridor, staircase, road, or other place—

(i) used as a means of access to or egress from that place of work; or
(ii) where facilities are provided for use in connection with that place of work,

other than a public road;

"young person" means any person who has not attained the age of 18.

8-16626 3. Meaning of "responsible person". In this Order "responsible person" means—

(a) in relation to a workplace, the employer, if the workplace is to any extent under his control;
(b) in relation to any premises not falling within paragraph (a)—

(i) the person who has control of the premises (as occupier or otherwise) in connection with the carrying on by him of a trade, business or other undertaking (for profit or not); or
(ii) the owner, where the person in control of the premises does not have control in connection with the carrying on by that person of a trade, business or other undertaking.

8-16627 4. Meaning of "general fire precautions". (1) In this Order "general fire precautions" in relation to premises means, subject to paragraph (2)—

(a) measures to reduce the risk of fire on the premises and the risk of the spread of fire on the premises;
(b) measures in relation to the means of escape from the premises;
(c) measures for securing that, at all material times, the means of escape can be safely and effectively used;
(d) measures in relation to the means for fighting fires on the premises;
(e) measures in relation to the means for detecting fire on the premises and giving warning in case of fire on the premises; and
(f) measures in relation to the arrangements for action to be taken in the event of fire on the premises, including—

(i) measures relating to the instruction and training of employees; and
(ii) measures to mitigate the effects of the fire.

(2) The precautions referred to in paragraph (1) do not include special, technical or organisational measures required to be taken or observed in any workplace in connection with the carrying on of any work process, where those measures—

(a) are designed to prevent or reduce the likelihood of fire arising from such a work process or reduce its intensity; and
(b) are required to be taken or observed to ensure compliance with any requirement of the relevant statutory provisions within the meaning given by section 53(1) of the Health and Safety at Work etc 1974.

(3) In paragraph (2) "work process" means all aspects of work involving, or in connection with—

(a) the use of plant or machinery; or
(b) the use or storage of any dangerous substance.

8-16628 5. Duties under this Order. (1) Where the premises are a workplace, the responsible person must ensure that any duty imposed by articles 8 to 22 or by regulations made under article 24 is complied with in respect of those premises.

(2) Where the premises are not a workplace, the responsible person must ensure that any duty imposed by articles 8 to 22 or by regulations made under article 24 is complied with in respect of those premises, so far as the requirements relate to matters within his control.

(3) Any duty imposed by articles 8 to 22 or by regulations made under article 24 on the responsible person in respect of premises shall also be imposed on every person, other than the responsible person referred to in paragraphs (1) and (2), who has, to any extent, control of those premises so far as the requirements relate to matters within his control.

(4) Where a person has, by virtue of any contract or tenancy, an obligation of any extent in relation to—

(a) the maintenance or repair of any premises, including anything in or on premises; or
(b) the safety of any premises,

that person is to be treated, for the purposes of paragraph (3), as being a person who has control of the premises to the extent that his obligation so extends.

(5) Articles 8 to 22 and any regulations made under article 24 only require the taking or observance of general fire precautions in respect of relevant persons.

8–16629 6. Application to premises. (1) This Order does not apply in relation to—
(a) domestic premises, except to the extent mentioned in article 31(10);
(b) an offshore installation within the meaning of regulation 3 of the Offshore Installation and Pipeline Works (Management and Administration) Regulations 1995;
(c) a ship, in respect of the normal ship-board activities of a ship's crew which are carried out solely by the crew under the direction of the master;
(d) fields, woods or other land forming part of an agricultural or forestry undertaking but which is not inside a building and is situated away from the undertaking's main buildings;
(e) an aircraft, locomotive or rolling stock, trailer or semi-trailer used as a means of transport or a vehicle for which a licence is in force under the Vehicle Excise and Registration Act 1994 or a vehicle exempted from duty under that Act;
(f) a mine within the meaning of section 180 of the Mines and Quarries Act 1954, other than any building on the surface at a mine;
(g) a borehole site to which the Borehole Sites and Operations Regulations 1995 apply.

(2) Subject to the preceding paragraph of this article, this Order applies in relation to any premises.

8–16630 7. Disapplication of certain provisions. (1) Articles 9(4) and (5) and 19(2) do not apply in relation to occasional work or short-term work involving work regulated as not being harmful, damaging, or dangerous to young people in a family undertaking.
(2) Articles 9(2), 12, 16, 19(3) and 22(2) do not apply in relation to the use of means of transport by land, water or air where the use of means of transport is regulated by international agreements and the European Community directives giving effect to them and in so far as the use of means of transport falls within the disapplication in article 1.2(e) of Council Directive 1999/92/EC on minimum requirements for improving the safety and health of workers potentially at risk from explosive atmospheres, except for any means of transport intended for use in a potentially explosive atmosphere.
(3) Articles 19 and 21 impose duties only on responsible persons who are employers.
(4) The requirements of articles 8 to 23, or of any regulations made under article 24, do not have effect to the extent that they would prevent any of the following from carrying out their duties—
(a) any member of the armed forces of the Crown or of any visiting force;
(b) any constable or any member of a police force not being a constable;
(c) any member of any emergency service.

(5) Without prejudice to paragraph (4), article 14(2)(f) does not apply to any premises constituting, or forming part of, a prison within the meaning of the Prison Act 1952 or constituting, or forming part of, a remand centre, detention centre or youth custody centre provided by the Secretary of State under section 43 of that Act or any part of any other premises used for keeping persons in lawful custody or detention.
(6) Where paragraph (4) or (5) applies, the safety of relevant persons must nevertheless be ensured so far as is possible.

PART 2
FIRE SAFETY DUTIES

8–16631 8. Duty to take general fire precautions. (1) The responsible person must—
(a) take such general fire precautions as will ensure, so far as is reasonably practicable, the safety of any of his employees; and
(b) in relation to relevant persons who are not his employees, take such general fire precautions as may reasonably be required in the circumstances of the case to ensure that the premises are safe.

8–16632 9. Risk assessment. (1) The responsible person must make a suitable and sufficient assessment of the risks to which relevant persons are exposed for the purpose of identifying the general fire precautions he needs to take to comply with the requirements and prohibitions imposed on him by or under this Order.
(2) Where a dangerous substance is or is liable to be present in or on the premises, the risk assessment must include consideration of the matters set out in Part 1 of Schedule 1.
(3) Any such assessment must be reviewed by the responsible person regularly so as to keep it up to date and particularly if—
(a) there is reason to suspect that it is no longer valid; or
(b) there has been a significant change in the matters to which it relates including when the premises, special, technical and organisational measures, or organisation of the work undergo significant changes, extensions, or conversions,
and where changes to an assessment are required as a result of any such review, the responsible person must make them.
(4) The responsible person must not employ a young person unless he has, in relation to risks to young persons, made or reviewed an assessment in accordance with paragraphs (1) and (5).
(5) In making or reviewing the assessment, the responsible person who employs or is to

employ a young person must take particular account of the matters set out in Part 2 of Schedule 1.

(6) As soon as practicable after the assessment is made or reviewed, the responsible person must record the information prescribed by paragraph (7) where—

  (*a*) he employs five or more employees;

  (*b*) a licence under an enactment is in force in relation to the premises; or

  (*c*) an alterations notice requiring this is in force in relation to the premises.

(7) The prescribed information is—

  (*a*) the significant findings of the assessment, including the measures which have been or will be taken by the responsible person pursuant to this Order; and

  (*b*) any group of persons identified by the assessment as being especially at risk.

(8) No new work activity involving a dangerous substance may commence unless—

  (*a*) the risk assessment has been made; and

  (*b*) the measures required by or under this Order have been implemented.

8–16633 10. Principles of prevention to be applied. Where the responsible person implements any preventive and protective measures he must do so on the basis of the principles specified in Part 3 of Schedule 1.

8–16634 11. Fire safety arrangements. (1) The responsible person must make and give effect to such arrangements as are appropriate, having regard to the size of his undertaking and the nature of its activities, for the effective planning, organisation, control, monitoring and review of the preventive and protective measures.

(2) The responsible person must record the arrangements referred to in paragraph (1) where—

  (*a*) he employs five or more employees;

  (*b*) a licence under an enactment is in force in relation to the premises; or

  (*c*) an alterations notice requiring a record to be made of those arrangements is in force in relation to the premises.

8–16635 12. Elimination or reduction of risks from dangerous substances. (1) Where a dangerous substance is present in or on the premises, the responsible person must ensure that risk to relevant persons related to the presence of the substance is either eliminated or reduced so far as is reasonably practicable.

(2) In complying with his duty under paragraph (1), the responsible person must, so far as is reasonably practicable, replace a dangerous substance, or the use of a dangerous substance, with a substance or process which either eliminates or reduces the risk to relevant persons.

(3) Where it is not reasonably practicable to eliminate risk pursuant to paragraphs (1) and (2), the responsible person must, so far as is reasonably practicable, apply measures consistent with the risk assessment and appropriate to the nature of the activity or operation, including the measures specified in Part 4 of Schedule 1 to this Order to—

  (*a*) control the risk, and

  (*b*) mitigate the detrimental effects of a fire.

(4) The responsible person must—

  (*a*) arrange for the safe handling, storage and transport of dangerous substances and waste containing dangerous substances; and

  (*b*) ensure that any conditions necessary pursuant to this Order for ensuring the elimination or reduction of risk are maintained.

8–16636 13. Fire-fighting and fire detection. (1) Where necessary (whether due to the features of the premises, the activity carried on there, any hazard present or any other relevant circumstances) in order to safeguard the safety of relevant persons, the responsible person must ensure that—

  (*a*) the premises are, to the extent that it is appropriate, equipped with appropriate fire-fighting equipment and with fire detectors and alarms; and

  (*b*) any non-automatic fire-fighting equipment so provided is easily accessible, simple to use and indicated by signs.

(2) For the purposes of paragraph (1) what is appropriate is to be determined having regard to the dimensions and use of the premises, the equipment contained on the premises, the physical and chemical properties of the substances likely to be present and the maximum number of persons who may be present at any one time.

(3) The responsible person must, where necessary—

  (*a*) take measures for fire-fighting in the premises, adapted to the nature of the activities carried on there and the size of the undertaking and of the premises concerned;

  (*b*) nominate competent persons to implement those measures and ensure that the number of such persons, their training and the equipment available to them are adequate, taking into account the size of, and the specific hazards involved in, the premises concerned; and

(c) arrange any necessary contacts with external emergency services, particularly as regards fire-fighting, rescue work, first-aid and emergency medical care.

(4) A person is to be regarded as competent for the purposes of paragraph (3)(*b*) where he has sufficient training and experience or knowledge and other qualities to enable him properly to implement the measures referred to in that paragraph.

8–16637 14. Emergency routes and exits. (1) Where necessary in order to safeguard the safety of relevant persons, the responsible person must ensure that routes to emergency exits from premises and the exits themselves are kept clear at all times.

(2) The following requirements must be complied with in respect of premises where necessary (whether due to the features of the premises, the activity carried on there, any hazard present or any other relevant circumstances) in order to safeguard the safety of relevant persons—

(a) emergency routes and exits must lead as directly as possible to a place of safety;

(b) in the event of danger, it must be possible for persons to evacuate the premises as quickly and as safely as possible;

(c) the number, distribution and dimensions of emergency routes and exits must be adequate having regard to the use, equipment and dimensions of the premises and the maximum number of persons who may be present there at any one time;

(d) emergency doors must open in the direction of escape;

(e) sliding or revolving doors must not be used for exits specifically intended as emergency exits;

(f) emergency doors must not be so locked or fastened that they cannot be easily and immediately opened by any person who may require to use them in an emergency;

(g) emergency routes and exits must be indicated by signs; and

(h) emergency routes and exits requiring illumination must be provided with emergency lighting of adequate intensity in the case of failure of their normal lighting.

8–16638 15. Procedures for serious and imminent danger and for danger areas. (1) The responsible person must—

(a) establish and, where necessary, give effect to appropriate procedures, including safety drills, to be followed in the event of serious and imminent danger to relevant persons;

(b) nominate a sufficient number of competent persons to implement those procedures in so far as they relate to the evacuation of relevant persons from the premises; and

(c) ensure that no relevant person has access to any area to which it is necessary to restrict access on grounds of safety, unless the person concerned has received adequate safety instruction.

(2) Without prejudice to the generality of paragraph (1)(*a*), the procedures referred to in that sub-paragraph must—

(a) so far as is practicable, require any relevant persons who are exposed to serious and imminent danger to be informed of the nature of the hazard and of the steps taken or to be taken to protect them from it;

(b) enable the persons concerned (if necessary by taking appropriate steps in the absence of guidance or instruction and in the light of their knowledge and the technical means at their disposal) to stop work and immediately proceed to a place of safety in the event of their being exposed to serious, imminent and unavoidable danger; and

(c) save in exceptional cases for reasons duly substantiated (which cases and reasons must be specified in those procedures), require the persons concerned to be prevented from resuming work in any situation where there is still a serious and imminent danger.

(3) A person is to be regarded as competent for the purposes of paragraph (1) where he has sufficient training and experience or knowledge and other qualities to enable him properly to implement the evacuation procedures referred to in that paragraph.

8–16639 16. Additional emergency measures in respect of dangerous substances. (1) Subject to paragraph (4), in order to safeguard the safety of relevant persons arising from an accident, incident or emergency related to the presence of a dangerous substance in or on the premises, the responsible person must ensure that—

(a) information on emergency arrangements is available, including—

(i) details of relevant work hazards and hazard identification arrangements; and

(ii) specific hazards likely to arise at the time of an accident, incident or emergency;

(b) suitable warning and other communication systems are established to enable an appropriate response, including remedial actions and rescue operations, to be made immediately when such an event occurs;

(c) where necessary, before any explosion conditions are reached, visual or audible warnings are given and relevant persons withdrawn; and

(d) where the risk assessment indicates it is necessary, escape facilities are provided and maintained to ensure that, in the event of danger, relevant persons can leave endangered places promptly and safely.

(2) Subject to paragraph (4), the responsible person must ensure that the information required by article 15(1)(*a*) and paragraph (1)(*a*) of this article, together with information on the matters referred to in paragraph (1)(*b*) and (*d*) is—

(*a*) made available to relevant accident and emergency services to enable those services, whether internal or external to the premises, to prepare their own response procedures and precautionary measures; and

(*b*) displayed at the premises, unless the results of the risk assessment make this unnecessary.

(3) Subject to paragraph (4), in the event of a fire arising from an accident, incident or emergency related to the presence of a dangerous substance in or on the premises, the responsible person must ensure that—

(*a*) immediate steps are taken to—

(i) mitigate the effects of the fire;

(ii) restore the situation to normal; and

(iii) inform those relevant persons who may be affected; and

(*b*) only those persons who are essential for the carrying out of repairs and other necessary work are permitted in the affected area and they are provided with—

(i) appropriate personal protective equipment and protective clothing; and

(ii) any necessary specialised safety equipment and plant,

which must be used until the situation is restored to normal.

(4) Paragraphs (1) to (3) do not apply where—

(*a*) the results of the risk assessment show that, because of the quantity of each dangerous substance in or on the premises, there is only a slight risk to relevant persons; and

(*b*) the measures taken by the responsible person to comply with his duty under article 12 are sufficient to control that risk.

8–16640 17. Maintenance.   (1) Where necessary in order to safeguard the safety of relevant persons the responsible person must ensure that the premises and any facilities, equipment and devices provided in respect of the premises under this Order or, subject to paragraph (6), under any other enactment, including any enactment repealed or revoked by this Order, are subject to a suitable system of maintenance and are maintained in an efficient state, in efficient working order and in good repair.

(2) Where the premises form part of a building, the responsible person may make arrangements with the occupier of any other premises forming part of the building for the purpose of ensuring that the requirements of paragraph (1) are met.

(3) Paragraph (2) applies even if the other premises are not premises to which this Order applies.

(4) The occupier of the other premises must co-operate with the responsible person for the purposes of paragraph (2).

(5) Where the occupier of the other premises is not also the owner of those premises, the references to the occupier in paragraphs (2) and (4) are to be taken to be references to both the occupier and the owner.

(6) Paragraph (1) only applies to facilities, equipment and devices provided under other enactments where they are provided in connection with general fire precautions.

8–16641 18. Safety assistance.   (1) The responsible person must, subject to paragraphs (6) and (7), appoint one or more competent persons to assist him in undertaking the preventive and protective measures.

(2) Where the responsible person appoints persons in accordance with paragraph (1), he must make arrangements for ensuring adequate co-operation between them.

(3) The responsible person must ensure that the number of persons appointed under paragraph (1), the time available for them to fulfil their functions and the means at their disposal are adequate having regard to the size of the premises, the risks to which relevant persons are exposed and the distribution of those risks throughout the premises.

(4) The responsible person must ensure that—

(*a*) any person appointed by him in accordance with paragraph (1) who is not in his employment—

(i) is informed of the factors known by him to affect, or suspected by him of affecting, the safety of any other person who may be affected by the conduct of his undertaking; and

(ii) has access to the information referred to in article 19(3); and

(*b*) any person appointed by him in accordance with paragraph (1) is given such information about any person working in his undertaking who is—

(i) employed by him under a fixed-term contract of employment, or

(ii) employed in an employment business,

as is necessary to enable that person properly to carry out the function specified in that paragraph.

(5) A person is to be regarded as competent for the purposes of this article where he has

sufficient training and experience or knowledge and other qualities to enable him properly to assist in undertaking the preventive and protective measures.

(6) Paragraph (1) does not apply to a self-employed employer who is not in partnership with any other person, where he has sufficient training and experience or knowledge and other qualities properly to assist in undertaking the preventive and protective measures.

(7) Paragraph (1) does not apply to individuals who are employers and who are together carrying on business in partnership, where at least one of the individuals concerned has sufficient training and experience or knowledge and other qualities—

(a) properly to undertake the preventive and protective measures; and
(b) properly to assist his fellow partners in undertaking those measures.

(8) Where there is a competent person in the responsible person's employment, that person must be appointed for the purposes of paragraph (1) in preference to a competent person not in his employment.

8–16642 **19. Provision of information to employees.** (1) The responsible person must provide his employees with comprehensible and relevant information on—

(a) the risks to them identified by the risk assessment;
(b) the preventive and protective measures;
(c) the procedures and the measures referred to in article 15(1)(a);
(d) the identities of those persons nominated by him in accordance with article 13(3)(b) or appointed in accordance with article 15(1)(b); and
(e) the risks notified to him in accordance with article 22(1)(c).

(2) The responsible person must, before employing a child, provide a parent of the child with comprehensible and relevant information on—

(a) the risks to that child identified by the risk assessment;
(b) the preventive and protective measures; and
(c) the risks notified to him in accordance with article 22(1)(c),

and for the purposes of this paragraph, "parent of the child" includes a person who has parental responsibility, within the meaning of section 3 of the Children Act 1989, for the child.

(3) Where a dangerous substance is present in or on the premises, the responsible person must, in addition to the information provided under paragraph (1) provide his employees with—

(a) the details of any such substance including—

(i) the name of the substance and the risk which it presents;
(ii) access to any relevant safety data sheet; and
(iii) legislative provisions (concerning the hazardous properties of any such substance) which apply to the substance; and

(b) the significant findings of the risk assessment.

(4) The information required by paragraph (3) must be—

(a) adapted to take account of significant changes in the activity carried out or methods or work used by the responsible person; and
(b) provided in a manner appropriate to the risk identified by the risk assessment.

8–16643 **20. Provision of information to employers and the self-employed from outside undertakings.** (1) The responsible person must ensure that the employer of any employees from an outside undertaking who are working in or on the premises is provided with comprehensible and relevant information on—

(a) the risks to those employees; and
(b) the preventive and protective measures taken by the responsible person.

(2) The responsible person must ensure that any person working in his undertaking who is not his employee is provided with appropriate instructions and comprehensible and relevant information regarding any risks to that person.

(3) The responsible person must—

(a) ensure that the employer of any employees from an outside undertaking who are working in or on the premises is provided with sufficient information to enable that employer to identify any person nominated by the responsible person in accordance with article 15 (1)(b) to implement evacuation procedures as far as those employees are concerned; and
(b) take all reasonable steps to ensure that any person from an outside undertaking who is working in or on the premises receives sufficient information to enable that person to identify any person nominated by the responsible person in accordance with article 15 (1)(b) to implement evacuation procedures as far as they are concerned.

8–16644 **21. Training.** (1) The responsible person must ensure that his employees are provided with adequate safety training—

(a) at the time when they are first employed; and
(b) on their being exposed to new or increased risks because of—

   (i)   their being transferred or given a change of responsibilities within the responsible person's undertaking;

   (ii)   the introduction of new work equipment into, or a change respecting work equipment already in use within, the responsible person's undertaking;

  (iii)   the introduction of new technology into the responsible person's undertaking; or

  (iv)   the introduction of a new system of work into, or a change respecting a system of work already in use within, the responsible person's undertaking.

(2) The training referred to in paragraph (1) must—

  (*a*)   include suitable and sufficient instruction and training on the appropriate precautions and actions to be taken by the employee in order to safeguard himself and other relevant persons on the premises;

  (*b*)   be repeated periodically where appropriate;

  (*c*)   be adapted to take account of any new or changed risks to the safety of the employees concerned;

  (*d*)   be provided in a manner appropriate to the risk identified by the risk assessment; and

  (*e*)   take place during working hours.

8–16645   22. Co-operation and co-ordination.   (1) Where two or more responsible persons share, or have duties in respect of, premises (whether on a temporary or a permanent basis) each such person must—

  (*a*)   co-operate with the other responsible person concerned so far as is necessary to enable them to comply with the requirements and prohibitions imposed on them by or under this Order;

  (*b*)   (taking into account the nature of his activities) take all reasonable steps to co-ordinate the measures he takes to comply with the requirements and prohibitions imposed on him by or under this Order with the measures the other responsible persons are taking to comply with the requirements and prohibitions imposed on them by or under this Order; and

  (*c*)   take all reasonable steps to inform the other responsible persons concerned of the risks to relevant persons arising out of or in connection with the conduct by him of his undertaking.

(2) Where two or more responsible persons share premises (whether on a temporary or a permanent basis) where an explosive atmosphere may occur, the responsible person who has overall responsibility for the premises must co-ordinate the implementation of all the measures required by this Part to be taken to protect relevant persons from any risk from the explosive atmosphere.

8–16646   23. General duties of employees at work.   (1) Every employee must, while at work—

  (*a*)   take reasonable care for the safety of himself and of other relevant persons who may be affected by his acts or omissions at work;

  (*b*)   as regards any duty or requirement imposed on his employer by or under any provision of this Order, co-operate with him so far as is necessary to enable that duty or requirement to be performed or complied with; and

  (*c*)   inform his employer or any other employee with specific responsibility for the safety of his fellow employees—

    (i)   of any work situation which a person with the first-mentioned employee's training and instruction would reasonably consider represented a serious and immediate danger to safety; and

    (ii)   of any matter which a person with the first-mentioned employee's training and instruction would reasonably consider represented a shortcoming in the employer's protection arrangements for safety,

in so far as that situation or matter either affects the safety of that first-mentioned employee or arises out of or in connection with his own activities at work, and has not previously been reported to his employer or to any other employee of that employer in accordance with this sub-paragraph.

8–16647   24. Power to make regulations about fire precautions.   (1) The Secretary of State may by regulations make provision as to the precautions which are to be taken or observed in relation to the risk to relevant persons as regards premises in relation to which this Order applies.

(2) Without prejudice to the generality of paragraph (1), regulations made by the Secretary of State may impose requirements—

  (*a*)   as to the provision, maintenance and keeping free from obstruction of any means of escape in case of fire;

  (*b*)   as to the provision and maintenance of means for securing that any means of escape can be safely and effectively used at all material times;

  (*c*)   as to the provision and maintenance of means for fighting fire and means for giving warning in case of fire;

  (*d*)   as to the internal construction of the premises and the materials used in that construction;

(e) for prohibiting altogether the presence or use in the premises of furniture or equipment of any specified description, or prohibiting its presence or use unless specified standards or conditions are complied with;

(f) for securing that persons employed to work in the premises receive appropriate instruction or training in what to do in case of fire;

(g) for securing that, in specified circumstances, specified numbers of attendants are stationed in specified parts of the premises; and

(h) as to the keeping of records of instruction or training given, or other things done, in pursuance of the regulations.

(3) Regulations under this article—

(a) may impose requirements on persons other than the responsible person; and

(b) may, as regards any of their provisions, make provision as to the person or persons who is or are to be responsible for any contravention of that provision.

(4) The Secretary of State must, before making any regulations under this article, consult with such persons or bodies of persons as appear to him to be appropriate.

(5) The power of the Secretary of State to make regulations under this article—

(a) is exercisable by statutory instrument, which is subject to annulment in pursuance of a resolution of either House of Parliament;

(b) includes power to make different provision in relation to different circumstances; and

(c) includes power to grant or provide for the granting of exemptions from any of the provisions of the regulations, either unconditionally or subject to conditions.

PART 3

ENFORCEMENT

8-16648 25. Enforcing authorities. For the purposes of this Order, "enforcing authority" means—

(a) the fire and rescue authority for the area in which premises are, or are to be, situated, in any case not falling within any of sub-paragraphs (b) to (e);

(b) the Health and Safety Executive in relation to—

(i) any premises for which a licence is required in accordance with section 1 of the Nuclear Installations Act 1965 or for which a permit is required in accordance with section 2 of that Act;

(ii) any premises which would, except for the fact that it is used by, or on behalf of, the Crown, be required to have a licence or permit in accordance with the provisions referred to in sub-paragraph (i);

(iii) a ship, including a ship belonging to Her Majesty which forms part of Her Majesty's Navy, which is in the course of construction, reconstruction or conversion or repair by persons who include persons other than the master and crew of the ship;

(iv) any workplace which is or is on a construction site within the meaning of regulation 2(1) of the Construction (Health, Safety and Welfare) Regulations 1996 and to which those Regulations apply, other than construction sites referred to in regulation 33 of those Regulations.

(c) the fire service maintained by the Secretary of State for Defence in relation to—

(i) premises, other than premises falling within paragraph (b)(iii), occupied solely for the purposes of the armed forces of the Crown;

(ii) premises occupied solely by any visiting force or an international headquarters or defence organisation designated for the purposes of the International Headquarters and Defence Organisations Act 1964;

(iii) premises, other than premises falling within paragraph (b)(iii), which are situated within premises occupied solely for the purposes of the armed forces of the Crown but which are not themselves so occupied;

(d) the relevant local authority in relation to premises which consist of—

(i) a sports ground designated as requiring a safety certificate under section 1 of the Safety of Sports Grounds Act 1975 (safety certificates for large sports stadia);

(ii) a regulated stand within the meaning of section 26(5) of the Fire Safety and Safety of Places of Sport Act 1987 (safety certificates for stands at sports grounds);

(e) a fire inspector, or any person authorised by the Secretary of State to act for the purposes of this Order, in relation to—

(i) premises owned or occupied by the Crown, other than premises falling within paragraph (b)(ii) and (c);

(ii) premises in relation to which the United Kingdom Atomic Energy Authority is the responsible person, other than premises falling within paragraph (b)(ii).

8-16649 26. Enforcement of Order. (1) Every enforcing authority must enforce the provisions of this Order and any regulations made under it in relation to premises for which it is the enforcing authority and for that purpose, except where a fire inspector or other person authorised by the Secretary of State is the enforcing authority, may appoint inspectors.

(2) In performing the duty imposed by paragraph (1), the enforcing authority must have regard to such guidance as the Secretary of State may give it.

(3) A fire and rescue authority has power to arrange with the Health and Safety Commission or the Office of Rail Regulation for such of the authority's functions under this Order as may be specified in the arrangements to be performed on its behalf by the Health and Safety Executive or the Office of Rail Regulation, as the case may be, (with or without payment) in relation to any particular workplace.

8–16650 27. Powers of inspectors. (1) Subject to the provisions of this article, an inspector may do anything necessary for the purpose of carrying out this Order and any regulations made under it into effect and in particular, so far as may be necessary for that purpose, shall have power to do at any reasonable time the following —

(a) to enter any premises which he has reason to believe it is necessary for him to enter for the purpose mentioned above and to inspect the whole or part of the premises and anything in them, where such entry and inspection may be effected without the use of force;

(b) to make such inquiry as may be necessary for any of the following purposes —

(i) to ascertain, as regards any premises, whether the provisions of this Order or any regulations made under it apply or have been complied with; and

(ii) to identify the responsible person in relation to the premises;

(c) to require the production of, or where the information is recorded in computerised form, the furnishing of extracts from, any records (including plans) —

(i) which are required to be kept by virtue of any provision of this Order or regulations made under it; or

(ii) which it is necessary for him to see for the purposes of an examination or inspection under this article,

and to inspect and take copies of, or of any entry in, the records;

(d) to require any person having responsibilities in relation to any premises (whether or not the responsible person) to give him such facilities and assistance with respect to any matters or things to which the responsibilities of that person extend as are necessary for the purpose of enabling the inspector to exercise any of the powers conferred on him by this article;

(e) to take samples of any articles or substances found in any premises which he has power to enter for the purpose of ascertaining their fire resistance or flammability; and

(f) in the case of any article or substance found in any premises which he has power to enter, being an article or substance which appears to him to have caused or to be likely to cause danger to the safety of relevant persons, to cause it to be dismantled or subjected to any process or test (but not so as to damage or destroy it unless this is, in the circumstances, necessary).

(2) An inspector must, if so required when visiting any premises in the exercise of powers conferred by this article, produce to the occupier of the premises evidence of his authority.

(3) Where an inspector proposes to exercise the power conferred by paragraph (1)(f) he must, if requested by a person who at the time is present in and has responsibilities in relation to those premises, cause anything which is to be done by virtue of that power to be done in the presence of that person.

(4) Before exercising the power conferred by paragraph (1)(f) an inspector must consult such persons as appear to him appropriate for the purpose of ascertaining what dangers, if any, there may be in doing anything which he proposes to do under that power.

8–16651 28. Exercise on behalf of fire inspectors etc of their powers by officers of fire brigades.
(1) The powers conferred by article 27 on a fire inspector, or any other person authorised by the Secretary of State under article 25(e), are also exercisable by an employee of the fire and rescue authority when authorised in writing by such an inspector for the purpose of reporting to him on any matter falling within his functions under this Order; and articles 27(2) and (3) and 32(2)(d) to (f), with the necessary modifications, apply accordingly.

(2) A fire inspector, or other person authorised by the Secretary of State, must not authorise an employee of a fire and rescue authority under this article except with the consent of the fire and rescue authority.

8–16652 29. Alterations notices. (1) The enforcing authority may serve on the responsible person a notice (in this Order referred to as "an alterations notice") if the authority is of the opinion that the premises —

(a) constitute a serious risk to relevant persons (whether due to the features of the premises, their use, any hazard present, or any other circumstances); or

(b) may constitute such a risk if a change is made to them or the use to which they are put.

(2) An alterations notice must —

(a) state that the enforcing authority is of the opinion referred to in paragraph (1); and (*b*) specify the matters which in their opinion, constitute a risk to relevant persons or may constitute such a risk if a change is made to the premises or the use to which they are put.

(3) Where an alterations notice has been served in respect of premises, the responsible person must, before making any of the changes specified in paragraph (4) which may result in a significant increase in risk, notify the enforcing authority of the proposed changes.

(4) The changes referred to in paragraph (3) are—

(*a*) a change to the premises;

(*b*) a change to the services, fittings or equipment in or on the premises;

(*c*) an increase in the quantities of dangerous substances which are present in or on the premises;

(*d*) a change to the use of the premises.

(5) An alterations notice may include a requirement that, in addition to the notification required by paragraph (3), the responsible person must—

(*a*) take all reasonable steps to notify the terms of the notice to any other person who has duties under article 5(3) in respect of the premises;

(*b*) record the information prescribed in article 9(7), in accordance with article 9(6);

(*c*) record the arrangements required by article 11(1), in accordance with article 11(2); and

(*d*) before making the changes referred to in paragraph (3), send the enforcing authority the following—

(i) a copy of the risk assessment; and

(ii) a summary of the changes he proposes to make to the existing general fire precautions.

(6) An alterations notice served under paragraph (1) may be withdrawn at any time and, for the purposes of this article, the notice is deemed to be in force until such time as it is withdrawn or cancelled by the court under article 35(2).

(7) Nothing in this article prevents an enforcing authority from serving an enforcement notice or a prohibition notice in respect of the premises.

8–16653 30. Enforcement notices. (1) If the enforcing authority is of the opinion that the responsible person or any other person mentioned in article 5(3) has failed to comply with any provision of this Order or of any regulations made under it, the authority may, subject to article 36, serve on that person a notice (in this Order referred to as "an enforcement notice").

(2) An enforcement notice must—

(*a*) state that the enforcing authority is of the opinion referred to in paragraph (1) and why;

(*b*) specify the provisions which have not been complied with; and

(*c*) require that person to take steps to remedy the failure within such period from the date of service of the notice (not being less than 28 days) as may be specified in the notice.

(3) An enforcement notice may, subject to article 36, include directions as to the measures which the enforcing authority consider are necessary to remedy the failure referred to in paragraph (1) and any such measures may be framed so as to afford the person on whom the notice is served a choice between different ways of remedying the contravention.

(4) Where the enforcing authority is of the opinion that a person's failure to comply with this Order also extends to a workplace, or employees who work in a workplace, to which this Order applies but for which they are not the enforcing authority, the notice served by them under paragraph (1) may include requirements concerning that workplace or those employees; but before including any such requirements the enforcing authority must consult the enforcing authority for that workplace.

(5) Before serving an enforcement notice which would oblige a person to make an alteration to premises, the enforcing authority must consult—

(*a*) in cases where the relevant local authority is not the enforcing authority, the relevant local authority;

(*b*) in the case of premises used as a workplace which are within the field of responsibility of one or more enforcing authorities within the meaning of Part 1 of the Health and Safety at Work etc Act 1974, that authority or those authorities; and section 18(7) of the Health and Safety at Work etc Act 1974 (meaning in Part I of that Act of "enforcing authority" and of such an authority's "field of responsibility") applies for the purposes of this article as it applies for the purposes of that Part;

(*c*) in the case of a building or structure in relation to all or any part of which an initial notice given under section 47 of the Building Act 1984 is in force, the approved inspector who gave that initial notice;

(*d*) in the case of premises which are, include, or form part of, a designated sports ground or a sports ground at which there is a regulated stand, the relevant local authority, where that authority is not the enforcing authority; and for the purposes of this sub-paragraph, "sports ground" and "designated sports ground" have the same meaning as in the Safety of Sports Grounds Act 1975 and "regulated stand" has the same meaning as in the Fire Safety and Safety of Places of Sport Act 1987;

(*e*) any other person whose consent to the alteration would be required by or under any enactment.

(6) Without prejudice to the power of the court to cancel or modify an enforcement notice

under article 35(2), no failure on the part of an enforcing authority to consult under paragraphs (4) or (5) makes an enforcement notice void.

(7) Where an enforcement notice has been served under paragraph (1)—

(a) the enforcing authority may withdraw the notice at any time before the end of the period specified in the notice; and

(b) if an appeal against the notice is not pending, the enforcing authority may extend or further extend the period specified in the notice.

8–16654   31. Prohibition notices.   (1) If the enforcing authority is of the opinion that use of premises involves or will involve a risk to relevant persons so serious that use of the premises ought to be prohibited or restricted, the authority may serve on the responsible person or any other person mentioned in article 5(3) a notice (in this Order referred to as "a prohibition notice").

(2) The matters relevant to the assessment by the enforcing authority, for the purposes of paragraph (1), of the risk to relevant persons include anything affecting their escape from the premises in the event of fire.

(3) A prohibition notice must—

(a) state that the enforcing authority is of the opinion referred to in paragraph (1);

(b) specify the matters which in their opinion give or, as the case may be, will give rise to that risk; and

(c) direct that the use to which the prohibition notice relates is prohibited or restricted to such extent as may be specified in the notice until the specified matters have been remedied.

(4) A prohibition notice may include directions as to the measures which will have to be taken to remedy the matters specified in the notice and any such measures may be framed so as to afford the person on whom the notice is served a choice between different ways of remedying the matters.

(5) A prohibition or restriction contained in a prohibition notice pursuant to paragraph (3)(c) takes effect immediately it is served if the enforcing authority is of the opinion, and so states in the notice, that the risk of serious personal injury is or, as the case may be, will be imminent, and in any other case takes effect at the end of the period specified in the prohibition notice.

(6) Before serving a prohibition notice in relation to a house in multiple occupation, the enforcing authority shall, where practicable, notify the local housing authority of their intention and the use which they intend to prohibit or restrict.

(7) For the purposes of paragraph (6)—

"house in multiple occupation" means a house in multiple occupation as defined by sections 254 to 259 of the Housing Act 2004, as they have effect for the purposes of Part 1 of that Act (that is, without the exclusions contained in Schedule 14 to that Act); and

"local housing authority" has the same meaning as in section 261(2) of the Housing Act 2004.

(8) Without prejudice to the power of the court to cancel or modify a prohibition notice under article 35(2), no failure on the part of an enforcing authority to notify under paragraph (6) makes a prohibition notice void.

(9) Where a prohibition notice has been served under paragraph (1) the enforcing authority may withdraw it at any time.

(10) In this article, "premises" includes domestic premises other than premises consisting of or comprised in a house which is occupied as a single private dwelling and article 27 (powers of inspectors) shall be construed accordingly.

PART 4

OFFENCES AND APPEALS

8–16655   32. Offences.   (1) It is an offence for any responsible person or any other person mentioned in article 5(3) to—

(a) fail to comply with any requirement or prohibition imposed by articles 8 to 22 and 38 (fire safety duties) where that failure places one or more relevant persons at risk of death or serious injury in case of fire;

(b) fail to comply with any requirement or prohibition imposed by regulations made, or having effect as if made, under article 24 where that failure places one or more relevant persons at risk of death or serious injury in case of fire;

(c) fail to comply with any requirement imposed by article 29(3) or (4) (alterations notices);

(d) fail to comply with any requirement imposed by an enforcement notice;

(e) fail, without reasonable excuse, in relation to apparatus to which article 37 applies (luminous tube signs)—

(i) to ensure that such apparatus which is installed in premises complies with article 37(3) and (4);

(ii) to give a notice required by article 37(6) or (8), unless he establishes that some other person duly gave the notice in question;

(iii) to comply with a notice served under article 37(9).

(2) It is an offence for any person to—

(a) fail to comply with article 23 (general duties of employees at work) where that failure places one or more relevant persons at risk of death or serious injury in case of fire;

(b) make in any register, book, notice or other document required to be kept, served or given by or under, this Order, an entry which he knows to be false in a material particular;

(c) give any information which he knows to be false in a material particular or recklessly give any information which is so false, in purported compliance with any obligation to give information to which he is subject under or by virtue of this Order, or in response to any inquiry made by virtue of article 27(1)(b);

(d) obstruct, intentionally, an inspector in the exercise or performance of his powers or duties under this Order;

(e) fail, without reasonable excuse, to comply with any requirements imposed by an inspector under article 27(1)(c) or (d);

(f) pretend, with intent to deceive, to be an inspector;

(g) fail to comply with the prohibition imposed by article 40 (duty not to charge employees);

(h) fail to comply with any prohibition or restriction imposed by a prohibition notice.

(3) Any person guilty of an offence under paragraph (1)(a) to (d) and (2)(h) is liable—

(a) on summary conviction to a fine not exceeding the statutory maximum; or

(b) on conviction on indictment, to a fine, or to imprisonment for a term not exceeding two years, or to both.

(4) Any person guilty of an offence under paragraph (1)(e)(i) to (iii) is liable on summary conviction to a fine not exceeding level 3 on the standard scale.

(5) Any person guilty of an offence under paragraph (2)(a) is liable—

(a) on summary conviction to a fine not exceeding the statutory maximum; or

(b) on conviction on indictment, to a fine.

(6) Any person guilty of an offence under paragraph (2)(b), (c), (d) or (g) is liable on summary conviction to a fine not exceeding level 5 on the standard scale.

(7) Any person guilty of an offence under paragraph (2)(e) or (f) is liable on summary conviction to a fine not exceeding level 3 on the standard scale.

(8) Where an offence under this Order committed by a body corporate is proved to have been committed with the consent or connivance of, or to be attributable to any neglect on the part of, any director, manager, secretary or other similar officer of the body corporate, or any person purporting to act in any such capacity, he as well as the body corporate is guilty of that offence, and is liable to be proceeded against and punished accordingly.

(9) Where the affairs of a body corporate are managed by its members, paragraph (8) applies in relation to the acts and defaults of a member in connection with his functions of management as if he were a director of the body corporate.

(10) Where the commission by any person of an offence under this Order, is due to the act or default of some other person, that other person is guilty of the offence, and a person may be charged with and convicted of the offence by virtue of this paragraph whether or not proceedings are taken against the first-mentioned person.

(11) Nothing in this Order operates so as to afford an employer a defence in any criminal proceedings for a contravention of those provisions by reason of any act or default of—

(a) an employee of his; or

(b) a person nominated under articles 13(3)(b) or 15(1)(b) or appointed under 18(1).

8–16656　**33. Defence.**　Subject to article 32(11), in any proceedings for an offence under this Order, except for a failure to comply with articles 8(1)(a) or 12, it is a defence for the person charged to prove that he took all reasonable precautions and exercised all due diligence to avoid the commission of such an offence.

8–16657　**34. Onus of proving limits of what is practicable or reasonably practicable.**　In any proceedings for an offence under this Order consisting of a failure to comply with a duty or requirement so far as is practicable or so far as is reasonably practicable, it is for the accused to prove that it was not practicable or reasonably practicable to do more than was in fact done to satisfy the duty or requirement.

8–16658　**35. Appeals.**　(1) A person on whom an alterations notice, an enforcement notice, a prohibition notice or a notice given by the fire and rescue authority under article 37 (fire-fighters' switches for luminous tube signs) is served may, within 21 days from the day on which the notice is served, appeal to the court.

(2) On an appeal under this article the court may either cancel or affirm the notice, and if it affirms it, may do so either in its original form or with such modifications as the court may in the circumstances think fit.

(3) Where an appeal is brought against an alterations notice or an enforcement notice, the bringing of the appeal has the effect of suspending the operation of the notice until the appeal is finally disposed of or, if the appeal is withdrawn, until the withdrawal of the appeal.

(4) Where an appeal is brought against a prohibition notice, the bringing of the appeal does not have the effect of suspending the operation of the notice, unless, on the application of the appellant, the court so directs (and then only from the giving of the direction).

(5) In this article "the court" means a magistrates' court.

(6) The procedure for an appeal under paragraph (1) is by way of complaint for an order, and—

(a) the Magistrates' Courts Act 1980 applies to the proceedings; and
(b) the making of the complaint is deemed to be the bringing of the appeal.

(7) A person aggrieved by an order made by a magistrates' court on determining a complaint under this Order may appeal to the Crown Court; and for the avoidance of doubt, an enforcing authority may be a person aggrieved for the purposes of this paragraph.

8–16659   36. Determination of disputes by Secretary of State.   (1) This article applies where—

(a) a responsible person or any other person mentioned in article 5(3) has failed to comply with any provision of this Order or of any regulations made under it; and
(b) the enforcing authority and that person cannot agree on the measures which are necessary to remedy the failure.

(2) Where this article applies, the enforcing authority and the person referred to in paragraph (1)(a) may agree to refer the question as to what measures are necessary to remedy the failure referred to in paragraph (1)(a) to the Secretary of State for his determination.

(3) The Secretary of State may, by notice in writing to both parties, require the provision of such further information, including plans, specified in the notice, within the period so specified, as the Secretary of State may require for the purpose of making a determination.

(4) If the information required under paragraph (3) is not provided within the period specified, the Secretary of State may refuse to proceed with the determination.

(5) Where the Secretary of State has made a determination under this article, the enforcing authority may not, subject to paragraph (6), take any enforcement action the effect of which would be to conflict with his determination; and in this article, "enforcement action" means the service of an enforcement notice or the inclusion of any directions in an enforcement notice.

(6) Paragraph (5) does not apply where, since the date of the determination by the Secretary of State, there has been a change to the premises or the use to which they are put such that the risk to relevant persons has significantly changed.

PART 5
MISCELLANEOUS

8–16660   37. Fire-fighters' switches for luminous tube signs etc.   (1) Subject to paragraph (11), this article applies to apparatus consisting of luminous tube signs designed to work at a voltage normally exceeding the prescribed voltage, or other equipment so designed, and references in this article to a cut-off switch are, in a case where a transformer is provided to raise the voltage to operate the apparatus, references to a cut-off switch on the low-voltage side of the transformer.

(2) In paragraph (1) the "prescribed voltage" means—

(a) 1000 volts AC or 1500 volts DC if measured between any two conductors; or
(b) 600 volts AC or 900 volts DC if measured between a conductor and earth.

(3) No apparatus to which this article applies is to be installed unless it is provided with a cut-off switch.

(4) Subject to paragraph (5), the cut-off switch must be so placed, and coloured or marked as to satisfy such reasonable requirements as the fire and rescue authority may impose to secure that it must be readily recognisable by and accessible to fire-fighters.

(5) If a cut-off switch complies in position, colour and marking with the current regulations of the Institution of Electrical Engineers for a fire-fighter's emergency switch, the fire and rescue authority may not impose any further requirements pursuant to paragraph (4).

(6) Not less than 42 days before work is begun to install apparatus to which this article applies, the responsible person must give notice to the fire and rescue authority showing where the cut-off switch is to be placed and how it is to be coloured or marked.

(7) Where notice has been given to the fire and rescue authority as required by paragraph (6), the proposed position, colouring or marking of the switch is deemed to satisfy the requirements of the fire authority unless, within 21 days from the date of the service of the notice, the fire and rescue authority has served on the responsible person a counter-notice stating that their requirements are not satisfied.

(8) Where apparatus to which this article applies has been installed in or on premises before the day on which this article comes into force, the responsible person must, not more than 21 days after that day, give notice to the fire and rescue authority stating whether the apparatus is already provided with a cut-off switch and, if so, where the switch is placed and how it is coloured or marked.

(9) Subject to paragraph (10), where apparatus to which this article applies has been installed in or on premises before the day on which this article comes into force, the fire and rescue authority may serve on the responsible person a notice—

(a) in the case of apparatus already provided with a cut-off switch, stating that they are not satisfied with the position, colouring or marking of the switch and requiring the responsible person, within such period as may be specified in the notice, to take such steps as will secure that the switch will be so placed or coloured or marked as to be readily recognisable by, and accessible to, fire-fighters in accordance with the reasonable requirements of the fire and rescue authority; or

(*b*) in the case of apparatus not already provided with a cut-off switch, requiring him, within such period as may be specified in the notice, to provide such a cut-off switch in such a position and so coloured or marked as to be readily recognisable by, and accessible to, fire-fighters in accordance with the reasonable requirements of the fire and rescue authority.

(10) If a cut-off switch complies in position, colour and marking with the current regulations of the Institution of Electrical Engineers for a fire-fighter's emergency switch, the fire and rescue authority may not serve a notice in respect of it under paragraph (9).

(11) This article does not apply to—

(*a*) apparatus installed or proposed to be installed in or on premises in respect of which a premises licence under the Licensing Act 2003 has effect authorising the use of premises for the exhibition of a film, within the meaning of paragraph 15 of Schedule 1 to that Act; or

(*b*) apparatus installed in or on premises before the day on which this article comes into force where, immediately before that date—

   (i) the apparatus complied with section 10(2) and (3) (requirement to provide cut-off switch) of the Local Government (Miscellaneous Provisions) Act 1982; and

   (ii) the owner or occupier of the premises, as the case may be, had complied with either subsection (5) or subsection (7) (notice of location and type of switch) of section 10 of that Act.

8–16661   38. Maintenance of measures provided for protection of fire-fighters.   (1) Where necessary in order to safeguard the safety of fire-fighters in the event of a fire, the responsible person must ensure that the premises and any facilities, equipment and devices provided in respect of the premises for the use by or protection of fire-fighters under this Order or under any other enactment, including any enactment repealed or revoked by this Order, are subject to a suitable system of maintenance and are maintained in an efficient state, in efficient working order and in good repair.

(2) Where the premises form part of a building, the responsible person may make arrangements with the occupier of any premises forming part of the building for the purpose of ensuring that the requirements of paragraph (1) are met.

(3) Paragraph (2) applies even if the other premises are not premises to which this Order applies.

(4) The occupier of the other premises must co-operate with the responsible person for the purposes of paragraph (2).

(5) Where the occupier of the other premises is not also the owner of those premises, the reference to the occupier in paragraphs (2) and (4) are to be taken to be references to both the occupier and the owner.

8–16662   39. Civil liability for breach of statutory duty.   (1) Subject to paragraph (2), nothing in this Order is to be construed as conferring a right of action in any civil proceedings (other than proceedings for recovery of a fine).

(2) Notwithstanding section 86 of the Fires Prevention (Metropolis) Act 1774, breach of a duty imposed on an employer by or under this Order, so far as it causes damage to an employee, confers a right of action on that employee in civil proceedings.

8–16663   40. Duty not to charge employees for things done or provided.   No employer may levy or permit to be levied on any employee of his any charge in respect of anything done or provided in pursuance of any requirement of this Order or of regulations made under it.

8–16664   41. Duty to consult employees.   (1) In regulation 4A of the Safety Representatives and Safety Committees Regulations 1977 (employer's duty to consult and provide facilities and assistance), in paragraph (1)(*b*), for "or regulation 4(2)(*b*) of the Fire Precautions (Workplace) Regulations 1997" substitute "or article 13(3)(*b*) of the Regulatory Reform (Fire Safety) Order 2005".

(2) In regulation 3 of the Health and Safety (Consultation with Employees) Regulations 1996 (duty of employer to consult), in paragraph (*b*), for "or regulation 4(2)(*b*) of the Fire Precautions (Workplace) Regulations 1997" substitute "or article 13(3)(*b*) of the Regulatory Reform (Fire Safety) Order 2005".

8–16665   42. Special provisions in respect of licensed etc premises.   (1) Subject to paragraph (2), where any enactment provides for the licensing of premises in relation to which this Order applies, or the licensing of persons in respect of any such premises—

(*a*) the licensing authority must ensure that the enforcing authority for the premises has the opportunity to make representations before issuing the licence; and

(b) the enforcing authority must notify the licensing authority of any action that the enforcing authority takes in relation to premises to which the licence relates; but no failure on the part of an enforcing authority to notify under this paragraph shall affect the validity of any such action taken.

(2) Paragraph (1) does not apply where the licensing authority is also the enforcing authority.

(3) In this article and article 43(1)(a) —

(a) "licensing authority" means the authority responsible for issuing the licence; and

(b) "licensing" includes certification and registration and "licence" is to be construed accordingly; and

(c) references to the issue of licences include references to their renewal, transfer or variation.

8–16666   43. Suspension of terms and conditions of licences dealing with same matters as this Order.   (1) Subject to paragraph (3), paragraph (2) applies if—

(a) an enactment provides for the licensing of premises in relation to which this Order applies, or the licensing of persons in respect of any such premises;

(b) a licence is issued in respect of the premises (whether before or after the coming into force of this Order); and

(c) the licensing authority is required or authorised to impose terms, conditions or restrictions in connection with the issue of the licences.

(2) At any time when this Order applies in relation to the premises, any term, condition or restriction imposed by the licensing authority has no effect in so far as it relates to any matter in relation to which requirements or prohibitions are or could be imposed by or under this Order.

(3) Paragraph (1) does not apply where the licensing authority is also the enforcing authority.

8–16667   44. Suspension of byelaws dealing with same matters as this Order.   Where any enactment provides for the making of byelaws in relation to premises to which this Order applies, then, so long as this Order continues to apply to the premises, any byelaw has no effect in so far as it relates to any matter in relation to which requirements or prohibitions are or could be imposed by or under this Order.

8–16668   45. Duty to consult enforcing authority before passing plans.   (1) Where it is proposed to erect a building, or to make any extension of or structural alteration to a building and, in connection with the proposals, plans are, in accordance with building regulations, deposited with a local authority, the local authority must, subject to paragraph (3), consult the enforcing authority before passing those plans.

(2) Where it is proposed to change the use to which a building or part of a building is put and, in connection with that proposal, plans are, in accordance with building regulations, deposited with a local authority, the authority must, subject to paragraph (3), consult with the enforcing authority before passing the plans.

(3) The duty to consult imposed by paragraphs (1) and (2)—

(a) only applies in relation to buildings or parts of buildings to which this Order applies, or would apply following the erection, extension, structural alteration or change of use;

(b) does not apply where the local authority is also the enforcing authority.

8–16669   46. Other consultation by authorities.   (1) Where a government department or other public authority intends to take any action in respect of premises which will or may result in changes to any of the measures required by or under this Order, that department or authority must consult the enforcing authority for the premises before taking that action.

(2) Without prejudice to any power of the court to cancel or modify a notice served by a government department or other authority, no failure on the part of the department or authority to consult under paragraph (1) invalidates the action taken.

(3) In paragraph (1), "public authority" includes an approved inspector within the meaning of section 49 of the Building Act 1984.

8–16670   47. Disapplication of the Health and Safety at Work etc Act 1974 in relation to general fire precautions.   (1) Subject to paragraph (2), the Health and Safety at Work etc Act 1974 and any regulations made under that Act shall not apply to premises to which this Order applies, in so far as that Act or any regulations made under it relate to any matter in relation to which requirements are or could be imposed by or under this Order.

(2) Paragraph (1) does not apply—

(a) where the enforcing authority is also the enforcing authority within the meaning of the Health and Safety at Work etc Act 1974;

(b) in relation to the Control of Major Accident Hazards Regulations 1999.

8–16671   48. Service of notices etc.   (1) Any notice required or authorised by or by virtue of this Order to be served on any person may be served on him either by delivering it to him, or by leaving it at his proper address, or by sending it by post to him at that address.

(2) Any such notice may—

(a) in the case of a body corporate, be served on or given to the secretary or clerk of that body; and

(b) in the case of a partnership, be served on or given to a partner or a person having control or management of the partnership business.

(3) For the purposes of this article, and of section 7 of the Interpretation Act 1978 (service of documents by post) in its application to this Order, the proper address of any person is his last known address, except that—

(a) in the case of a body corporate or their secretary or clerk, it is the address of the registered or principal office of that body;

(b) in the case of a partnership or person having control or the management of the partnership business, it is the principal office of the partnership,

and for the purposes of this paragraph the principal office of a company registered outside the United Kingdom or of a partnership carrying on business outside the United Kingdom is their principal office within the United Kingdom.

(4) If the person to be served with or given any such notice has specified an address in the United Kingdom other than his proper address as the one at which he or someone on his behalf will accept notices and other documents, that address is also to be treated for the purposes of this article and section 7 of the Interpretation Act 1978 as his proper address.

(5) Without prejudice to any other provision of this article, any such notice required or authorised to be served on or given to the responsible person in respect of any premises (whether a body corporate or not) may be served or given by sending it by post to him at those premises, or by addressing it by name to the person on or to whom it is to be served or given and delivering it to some responsible individual who is or appears to be resident or employed in the premises.

(6) If the name or the address of the responsible person on whom any such notice is to be served cannot after reasonable inquiry be ascertained by the person seeking to serve it, the document may be served by addressing it to the person on whom it is to be served by the description of "responsible person" for the premises (describing them) to which the notice relates, and by delivering it to some responsible individual resident or appearing to be resident on the premises or, if there is no such person to whom it can be delivered, by affixing it or a copy of it to some conspicuous part of the premises.

(7) Any notice required or authorised to be given to or served on the responsible person or enforcing authority may be transmitted to that person or authority—

(a) by means of an electronic communications network (within the meaning given by section 32 of the Communications Act 2003); or

(b) by other means but in a form that nevertheless requires the use of apparatus by the recipient to render it intelligible.

(8) Where the recipient of the transmission is the responsible person, the transmission has effect as a delivery of the notice to that person only if he has indicated to the enforcing authority on whose behalf the transmission is made his willingness to receive a notice transmitted in the form and manner used.

(9) An indication to an enforcing authority for the purposes of paragraph (8)—

(a) must be given to the authority in any manner it requires;

(b) may be a general indication or one that is limited to notices of a particular description;

(c) must state the address to be used and must be accompanied by any other information which the authority requires for the making of the transmission;

(d) may be modified or withdrawn at any time by a notice given to the authority in any manner it requires.

(10) Where the recipient of the transmission is the enforcing authority, the transmission has effect as a delivery of the notice only if the enforcing authority has indicated its willingness to receive a notice transmitted in the form and manner used.

(11) An indication for the purposes of paragraph (10)—

(a) may be given in any manner the enforcing authority thinks fit;

(b) may be a general indication or one that is limited to notices of a particular description;

(c) must state the address to be used and must be accompanied by any other information which the responsible person requires for the making of the transmission;

(d) may be modified or withdrawn at any time in any manner the enforcing authority thinks fit.

(12) If the making or receipt of the transmission has been recorded in the computer system of the enforcing authority, it must be presumed, unless the contrary is proved, that the transmission—

(a) was made to the person recorded in that system as receiving it;

(b) was made at the time recorded in that system as the time of delivery;

(c) contained the information recorded on that system in respect of it.

(13) For the purposes of this article—

"notice" includes any document or information; and

"transmission" means the transmission referred to in paragraph (7).

49. Application to the Crown and to the Houses of Parliament

50. Guidance

8–16672

SCHEDULE 1

PART 1
MATTERS TO BE CONSIDERED IN RISK ASSESSMENT IN RESPECT OF DANGEROUS SUBSTANCES

Article 9(2)

The matters are—

(a) the hazardous properties of the substance;
(b) information on safety provided by the supplier, including information contained in any relevant safety data sheet;
(c) the circumstances of the work including—

   (i) the special, technical and organisational measures and the substances used and their possible interactions;
   (ii) the amount of the substance involved;
   (iii) where the work will involve more than one dangerous substance, the risk presented by such substances in combination; and
   (iv) the arrangements for the safe handling, storage and transport of dangerous substances and of waste containing dangerous substances;

(d) activities, such as maintenance, where there is the potential for a high level of risk;
(e) the effect of measures which have been or will be taken pursuant to this Order;
(f) the likelihood that an explosive atmosphere will occur and its persistence;
(g) the likelihood that ignition sources, including electrostatic discharges, will be present and become active and effective;
(h) the scale of the anticipated effects;
(i) any places which are, or can be connected via openings to, places in which explosive atmospheres may occur; and
(j) such additional safety information as the responsible person may need in order to complete the assessment.

PART 2
MATTERS TO BE TAKEN INTO PARTICULAR ACCOUNT IN RISK ASSESSMENT IN RESPECT OF YOUNG PERSONS

Article 9(5)

The matters are—

(a) the inexperience, lack of awareness of risks and immaturity of young persons;
(b) the fitting-out and layout of the premises;
(c) the nature, degree and duration of exposure to physical and chemical agents;
(d) the form, range, and use of work equipment and the way in which it is handled;
(e) the organisation of processes and activities;
(f) the extent of the safety training provided or to be provided to young persons; and
(g) risks from agents, processes and work listed in the Annex to Council Directive 94/33/EC on the protection of young people at work.

PART 3
PRINCIPLES OF PREVENTION

Article 10

The principles are—

(a) avoiding risks;
(b) evaluating the risks which cannot be avoided;
(c) combating the risks at source;
(d) adapting to technical progress;
(e) replacing the dangerous by the non-dangerous or less dangerous;
(f) developing a coherent overall prevention policy which covers technology, organisation of work and the influence of factors relating to the working environment;
(g) giving collective protective measures priority over individual protective measures; and
(h) giving appropriate instructions to employees.

PART 4
MEASURES TO BE TAKEN IN RESPECT OF DANGEROUS SUBSTANCES

Article 12

1. In applying measures to control risks the responsible person must, in order of priority—

(a) reduce the quantity of dangerous substances to a minimum;
(b) avoid or minimise the release of a dangerous substance;
(c) control the release of a dangerous substance at source;
(d) prevent the formation of an explosive atmosphere, including the application of appropriate ventilation;
(e) ensure that any release of a dangerous substance which may give rise to risk is suitably collected, safely contained, removed to a safe place, or otherwise rendered safe, as appropriate;

(*f*) avoid—

(i)   ignition sources including electrostatic discharges; and
(ii) such other adverse conditions as could result in harmful physical effects from a dangerous substance; and

(*g*) segregate incompatible dangerous substances.

2. The responsible person must ensure that mitigation measures applied in accordance with article 12(3)(*b*) include—

(*a*) reducing to a minimum the number of persons exposed;
(*b*) measures to avoid the propagation of fires or explosions;
(*c*) providing explosion pressure relief arrangements;
(*d*) providing explosion suppression equipment;
(*e*) providing plant which is constructed so as to withstand the pressure likely to be produced by an explosion; and
(*f*) providing suitable personal protective equipment.

3. The responsible person must—

(*a*) ensure that the premises are designed, constructed and maintained so as to reduce risk;
(*b*) ensure that suitable special, technical and organisational measures are designed, constructed, assembled, installed, provided and used so as to reduce risk;
(*c*) ensure that special, technical and organisational measures are maintained in an efficient state, in efficient working order and in good repair;
(*d*) ensure that equipment and protective systems meet the following requirements—

(i)   where power failure can give rise to the spread of additional risk, equipment and protective systems must be able to be maintained in a safe state of operation independently of the rest of the plant in the event of power failure;
(ii) means for manual override must be possible, operated by employees competent to do so, for shutting down equipment and protective systems incorporated within automatic processes which deviate from the intended operating conditions, provided that the provision or use of such means does not compromise safety;
(iii) on operation of emergency shutdown, accumulated energy must be dissipated as quickly and as safely as possible or isolated so that it no longer constitutes a hazard; and
(iv) necessary measures must be taken to prevent confusion between connecting devices;

(*e*) where the work is carried out in hazardous places or involves hazardous activities, ensure that appropriate systems of work are applied including—

(i)   the issuing of written instructions for the carrying out of work; and
(ii) a system of permits to work, with such permits being issued by a person with responsibility for this function prior to the commencement of the work concerned.

Control of Noise at Work Regulations 2005[1]
(SI 2005/1643)

8-16673 1. Citation and commencement. These Regulations may be cited as the Control of Noise at Work Regulations 2005 and shall come into force on 6th April 2006, except that—

(*a*) for the music and entertainment sectors only they shall not come into force until 6th April 2008; and
(*b*) subject to regulation 3(4), regulation 6(4) shall not come into force in relation to the master and crew of a seagoing ship until 6th April 2011.

---

1. Made by the Secretary of State, in the exercise of the powers conferred on him by sections 15(1), (2) and (5), and 82(2) and (3) of, and paragraphs 1(1)(*a*) and (*c*), 8(1), 9, 11, 13(2) and (3), 14, 15(1), 16 and 20 of Schedule 3 to the Health and Safety at Work etc Act 1974 ("the 1974 Act") and of all other powers enabling him in that behalf.

8-16674 2. Interpretation.   (1) In these Regulations—

"daily personal noise exposure" means the level of daily personal noise exposure of an employee as ascertained in accordance with Schedule 1 Part 1, taking account of the level of noise and the duration of exposure and covering all noise;
"emergency services" include—

(*a*) police, fire, rescue and ambulance services;
(*b*) Her Majesty's Coastguard;

"enforcing authority" means the Executive or local authority, determined in accordance with the provisions of the Health and Safety (Enforcing Authority) Regulations 1998;
"the Executive" means the Health and Safety Executive;
"exposure limit value" means the level of daily or weekly personal noise exposure or of peak sound pressure set out in regulation 4 which must not be exceeded;
"health surveillance" means assessment of the state of health of an employee, as related to exposure to noise;
"lower exposure action value" means the lower of the two levels of daily or weekly personal noise exposure or of peak sound pressure set out in regulation 4 which, if reached or exceeded, require specified action to be taken to reduce risk;

"the music and entertainment sectors" mean all workplaces where—

- (a) live music is played; or
- (b) recorded music is played in a restaurant, bar, public house, discotheque or nightclub, or alongside live music or a live dramatic or dance performance;

- "noise" means any audible sound;

"peak sound pressure" means the maximum sound pressure to which an employee is exposed, ascertained in accordance with Schedule 2;

"risk assessment" means the assessment of risk required by regulation 5;

"upper exposure action value" means the higher of the two levels of daily or weekly personal noise exposure or of peak sound pressure set out in regulation 4 which, if reached or exceeded, require specified action to be taken to reduce risk;

"weekly personal noise exposure" means the level of weekly personal noise exposure as ascertained in accordance with Schedule 1 Part 2, taking account of the level of noise and the duration of exposure and covering all noise; and

"working day" means a daily working period, irrespective of the time of day when it begins or ends, and of whether it begins or ends on the same calendar day.

(2) In these Regulations, a reference to an employee being exposed to noise is a reference to the exposure of that employee to noise which arises while he is at work, or arises out of or in connection with his work.

8–16675 3. Application. (1) These Regulations shall have effect with a view to protecting persons against risk to their health and safety arising from exposure to noise at work.

(2) Where a duty is placed by these Regulations on an employer in respect of his employees, the employer shall, so far as is reasonably practicable, be under a like duty in respect of any other person at work who may be affected by the work carried out by the employer except that the duties of the employer—

- (a) under regulation 9 (health surveillance) shall not extend to persons who are not his employees; and
- (b) under regulation 10 (information, instruction and training) shall not extend to persons who are not his employees, unless those persons are present at the workplace where the work is being carried out.

(3) These Regulations shall apply to a self-employed person as they apply to an employer and an employee and as if that self-employed person were both an employer and an employee, except that regulation 9 shall not apply to a self-employed person.

(4) These Regulations shall not apply to the master or crew of a ship or to the employer of such persons in respect of the normal shipboard activities of a ship's crew which are carried out solely by the crew under the direction of the master, and for the purposes of this paragraph "ship" includes every description of vessel used in navigation, other than a ship forming part of Her Majesty's Navy.

8–16676 4. Exposure limit values and action values. (1) The lower exposure action values are—

- (a) a daily or weekly personal noise exposure of 80 dB (A-weighted); and
- (b) a peak sound pressure of 135 dB (C-weighted).

(2) The upper exposure action values are—

- (a) a daily or weekly personal noise exposure of 85 dB (A-weighted); and
- (b) a peak sound pressure of 137 dB (C-weighted).

(3) The exposure limit values are—

- (a) a daily or weekly personal noise exposure of 87 dB (A-weighted); and
- (b) a peak sound pressure of 140 dB (C-weighted).

(4) Where the exposure of an employee to noise varies markedly from day to day, an employer may use weekly personal noise exposure in place of daily personal noise exposure for the purpose of compliance with these Regulations.

(5) In applying the exposure limit values in paragraph (3), but not in applying the lower and upper exposure action values in paragraphs (1) and (2), account shall be taken of the protection given to the employee by any personal hearing protectors provided by the employer in accordance with regulation 7(2).

8–16677 5. Assessment of the risk to health and safety created by exposure to noise at the workplace. (1) An employer who carries out work which is liable to expose any employees to noise at or above a lower exposure action value shall make a suitable and sufficient assessment of the risk from that noise to the health and safety of those employees, and the risk assessment shall identify the measures which need to be taken to meet the requirements of these Regulations.

(2) In conducting the risk assessment, the employer shall assess the levels of noise to which workers are exposed by means of—

- (a) observation of specific working practices;
- (b) reference to relevant information on the probable levels of noise corresponding to any equipment used in the particular working conditions; and

   (*c*)   if necessary, measurement of the level of noise to which his employees are likely to be exposed,

and the employer shall assess whether any employees are likely to be exposed to noise at or above a lower exposure action value, an upper exposure action value, or an exposure limit value.
   (3) The risk assessment shall include consideration of—

   (*a*)   the level, type and duration of exposure, including any exposure to peak sound pressure;
   (*b*)   the effects of exposure to noise on employees or groups of employees whose health is at particular risk from such exposure;
   (*c*)   so far as is practicable, any effects on the health and safety of employees resulting from the interaction between noise and the use of ototoxic substances at work, or between noise and vibration;
   (*d*)   any indirect effects on the health and safety of employees resulting from the interaction between noise and audible warning signals or other sounds that need to be audible in order to reduce risk at work;
   (*e*)   any information provided by the manufacturers of work equipment;
   (*f*)   the availability of alternative equipment designed to reduce the emission of noise;
   (*g*)   any extension of exposure to noise at the workplace beyond normal working hours, including exposure in rest facilities supervised by the employer;
   (*h*)   appropriate information obtained following health surveillance, including, where possible, published information; and
   (*i*)   the availability of personal hearing protectors with adequate attenuation characteristics.

   (4) The risk assessment shall be reviewed regularly, and forthwith if—

   (*a*)   there is reason to suspect that the risk assessment is no longer valid; or
   (*b*)   there has been a significant change in the work to which the assessment relates,

and where, as a result of the review, changes to the risk assessment are required, those changes shall be made.
   (5) The employees concerned or their representatives shall be consulted on the assessment of risk under the provisions of this regulation.
   (6) The employer shall record—

   (*a*)   the significant findings of the risk assessment as soon as is practicable after the risk assessment is made or changed; and
   (*b*)   the measures which he has taken and which he intends to take to meet the requirements of regulations 6, 7 and 10.

8-16678   **6. Elimination or control of exposure to noise at the workplace.**   (1) The employer shall ensure that risk from the exposure of his employees to noise is either eliminated at source or, where this is not reasonably practicable, reduced to as low a level as is reasonably practicable.
   (2) If any employee is likely to be exposed to noise at or above an upper exposure action value, the employer shall reduce exposure to as low a level as is reasonably practicable by establishing and implementing a programme of organisational and technical measures, excluding the provision of personal hearing protectors, which is appropriate to the activity.
   (3) The actions taken by the employer in compliance with paragraphs (1) and (2) shall be based on the general principles of prevention set out in Schedule 1 to the Management of Health and Safety Regulations 1999 and shall include consideration of—

   (*a*)   other working methods which reduce exposure to noise;
   (*b*)   choice of appropriate work equipment emitting the least possible noise, taking account of the work to be done;
   (*c*)   the design and layout of workplaces, work stations and rest facilities;
   (*d*)   suitable and sufficient information and training for employees, such that work equipment may be used correctly, in order to minimise their exposure to noise;
   (*e*)   reduction of noise by technical means;
   (*f*)   appropriate maintenance programmes for work equipment, the workplace and workplace systems;
   (*g*)   limitation of the duration and intensity of exposure to noise; and
   (*h*)   appropriate work schedules with adequate rest periods.

   (4) The employer shall—

   (*a*)   ensure that his employees are not exposed to noise above an exposure limit value; or
   (*b*)   if an exposure limit value is exceeded forthwith—

     (i)   reduce exposure to noise to below the exposure limit value;
     (ii)   identify the reason for that exposure limit value being exceeded; and
     (iii) modify the organisational and technical measures taken in accordance with paragraphs (1) and (2) and regulations 7 and 8(1) to prevent it being exceeded again.

   (5) Where rest facilities are made available to employees, the employer shall ensure that exposure to noise in these facilities is reduced to a level suitable for their purpose and conditions of use.
   (6) The employer shall adapt any measure taken in compliance with the requirements of this

regulation to take account of any employee or group of employees whose health is likely to be particularly at risk from exposure to noise.

(7) The employees concerned or their representatives shall be consulted on the measures to be taken to meet the requirements of this regulation.

8–16679   7. Hearing Protection.   (1) Without prejudice to the provisions of regulation 6, an employer who carries out work which is likely to expose any employees to noise at or above a lower exposure action value shall make personal hearing protectors available upon request to any employee who is so exposed.

(2) Without prejudice to the provisions of regulation 6, if an employer is unable by other means to reduce the levels of noise to which an employee is likely to be exposed to below an upper exposure action value, he shall provide personal hearing protectors to any employee who is so exposed.

(3) If in any area of the workplace under the control of the employer an employee is likely to be exposed to noise at or above an upper exposure action value for any reason the employer shall ensure that—

(*a*)   the area is designated a Hearing Protection Zone;

(*b*)   the area is demarcated and identified by means of the sign specified for the purpose of indicating that ear protection must be worn in paragraph 3.3 of Part II of Schedule 1 to the Health and Safety (Safety Signs and Signals) Regulations 1996; and

(*c*)   access to the area is restricted where this is practicable and the risk from exposure justifies it,

and shall ensure so far as is reasonably practicable that no employee enters that area unless that employee is wearing personal hearing protectors.

(4) Any personal hearing protectors made available or provided under paragraphs (1) or (2) of this regulation shall be selected by the employer—

(*a*)   so as to eliminate the risk to hearing or to reduce the risk to as low a level as is reasonably practicable; and

(*b*)   after consultation with the employees concerned or their representatives

8–16680   8. Maintenance and use of equipment.   (1) The employer shall—

(*a*)   ensure so far as is practicable that anything provided by him in compliance with his duties under these Regulations to or for the benefit of an employee, other than personal hearing protectors provided under regulation 7(1), is fully and properly used; and

(*b*)   ensure that anything provided by him in compliance with his duties under these Regulations is maintained in an efficient state, in efficient working order and in good repair.

(2) Every employee shall—

(*a*)   make full and proper use of personal hearing protectors provided to him by his employer in compliance with regulation 7(2) and of any other control measures provided by his employer in compliance with his duties under these Regulations; and

(*b*)   if he discovers any defect in any personal hearing protectors or other control measures as specified in sub-paragraph (*a*) report it to his employer as soon as is practicable.

8–16681   9. Health Surveillance.   (1) If the risk assessment indicates that there is a risk to the health of his employees who are, or are liable to be, exposed to noise, the employer shall ensure that such employees are placed under suitable health surveillance, which shall include testing of their hearing.

(2) The employer shall ensure that a health record in respect of each of his employees who undergoes health surveillance in accordance with paragraph (1) is made and maintained and that the record or a copy thereof is kept available in a suitable form.

(3) The employer shall—

(*a*)   on reasonable notice being given, allow an employee access to his personal health record; and

(*b*)   provide the enforcing authority with copies of such health records as it may require.

(4) Where, as a result of health surveillance, an employee is found to have identifiable hearing damage the employer shall ensure that the employee is examined by a doctor and, if the doctor or any specialist to whom the doctor considers it necessary to refer the employee considers that the damage is likely to be the result of exposure to noise, the employer shall—

(*a*)   ensure that a suitably qualified person informs the employee accordingly;

(*b*)   review the risk assessment;

(*c*)   review any measure taken to comply with regulations 6, 7 and 8, taking into account any advice given by a doctor or occupational health professional, or by the enforcing authority;

(*d*)   consider assigning the employee to alternative work where there is no risk from further exposure to noise, taking into account any advice given by a doctor or occupational health professional; and

(*e*)   ensure continued health surveillance and provide for a review of the health of any other employee who has been similarly exposed.

(5) An employee to whom this regulation applies shall, when required by his employer and at the cost of his employer, present himself during his working hours for such health surveillance procedures as may be required for the purposes of paragraph (1).

8-16682   10. Information, instruction and training.   (1) Where his employees are exposed to noise which is likely to be at or above a lower exposure action value, the employer shall provide those employees and their representatives with suitable and sufficient information, instruction and training.

(2) Without prejudice to the generality of paragraph (1), the information, instruction and training provided under that paragraph shall include—

(a) the nature of risks from exposure to noise;
(b) the organisational and technical measures taken in order to comply with the requirements of regulation 6;
(c) the exposure limit values and upper and lower exposure action values set out in regulation 4;
(d) the significant findings of the risk assessment, including any measurements taken, with an explanation of those findings;
(e) the availability and provision of personal hearing protectors under regulation 7 and their correct use in accordance with regulation 8(2);
(f) why and how to detect and report signs of hearing damage;
(g) the entitlement to health surveillance under regulation 9 and its purposes;
(h) safe working practices to minimise exposure to noise; and
(i) the collective results of any health surveillance undertaken in accordance with regulation 9 in a form calculated to prevent those results from being identified as relating to a particular person.

(3) The information, instruction and training required by paragraph (1) shall be updated to take account of significant changes in the type of work carried out or the working methods used by the employer.

(4) The employer shall ensure that any person, whether or not his employee, who carries out work in connection with the employer's duties under these Regulations has suitable and sufficient information, instruction and training.

8-16683   11. Exemption certificates from hearing protection.   (1) Subject to paragraph (2), the Executive may, by a certificate in writing, exempt any person or class of persons from the provisions of regulation 6(4) and regulation 7(1) and (2) where because of the nature of the work the full and proper use of personal hearing protectors would be likely to cause greater risk to health or safety than not using such protectors, and any such exemption may be granted subject to conditions and to a limit of time and may be revoked by a certificate in writing at any time.

(2) The Executive shall not grant such an exemption unless—

(a) it consults the employers and the employees or their representatives concerned;
(b) it consults such other persons as it considers appropriate;
(c) the resulting risks are reduced to as low a level as is reasonably practicable; and
(d) the employees concerned are subject to increased health surveillance.

8-16684   12. Exemption certificates for emergency services.   (1) Subject to paragraph (2), the Executive may, by a certificate in writing, exempt any person or class of persons from the provisions of regulation 6(4) and regulation 7(1) to (3) in respect of activities carried out by emergency services which conflict with the requirements of any of those provisions, and any such exemption may be granted subject to conditions and to a limit of time and may be revoked by a certificate in writing at any time.

(2) The Executive shall not grant such an exemption unless it is satisfied that the health and safety of the employees concerned is ensured as far as possible in the light of the objectives of these Regulations.

8-16685   13. Exemptions relating to the Ministry of Defence.   (1) Subject to paragraph (2), the Secretary of State for Defence may, by a certificate in writing, exempt any person or class of persons from the provisions of regulation 6(4) and regulation 7(1) to (3) in respect of activities carried out in the interests of national security which conflict with the requirements of any of those provisions, and any such exemption may be granted subject to conditions and to a limit of time and may be revoked by a certificate in writing at any time.

(2) The Secretary of State shall not grant such an exemption unless he is satisfied that the health and safety of the employees concerned is ensured as far as possible in the light of the objectives of these Regulations.

8-16686   14. Extension outside Great Britain.   These Regulations shall apply to and in relation to any activity outside Great Britain to which sections 1 to 59 and 80 to 82 of the 1974 Act apply by virtue of the Health and Safety at Work etc Act 1974 (Application Outside Great Britain) Order 2001 as those provisions apply within Great Britain.

8–16687   **15. Revocations, amendments and savings.**   (1) In—

  (a)   regulation 3(3)(e) of the Personal Protective Equipment at Work Regulations 1992; and

  (b)   regulation 12(5)(d) of the Provision and Use of Work Equipment Regulations 1998,

for the reference in each case to the Noise at Work Regulations 1989 there shall be substituted a reference to these Regulations.

  (2) The revocations listed in Schedule 3 are made with effect from the coming into force of these Regulations.

  (3) In respect of the music and entertainment sectors only, the amendments and revocations in paragraphs (1) and (2) shall not come into force until 6th April 2008 and the provisions covered by those paragraphs shall continue in force, where applicable, until that date.

8–16688

SCHEDULE 1

PART 1
DAILY PERSONAL NOISE EXPOSURE LEVELS

PART 2
WEEKLY PERSONAL NOISE EXPOSURE LEVELS

SCHEDULE 2
PEAK SOUND PRESSURE LEVEL